ENCYCLOPÆDIA
BRITANNICA

MACROPÆDIA

The Encyclopædia Britannica
is published with the editorial advice
of the faculties of the University of Chicago;
a committee of persons holding
academic appointments at the universities
of Oxford, Cambridge, London, and Edinburgh;
a committee at the University of Toronto;
and committees drawn from members of the faculties
of the University of Tokyo
and the Australian National University.

THE UNIVERSITY OF CHICAGO

"Let knowledge grow from more to more
and thus be human life enriched."

The New
Encyclopædia
Britannica

in 30 Volumes

MACROPÆDIA
Volume 11

Knowledge in Depth

FOUNDED 1768
15TH EDITION

Encyclopædia Britannica, Inc.
William Benton, Publisher, 1943–1973
Helen Hemingway Benton, Publisher, 1973–1974
Chicago/London/Toronto/Geneva/Sydney/Tokyo/Manila/Seoul/Johannesburg

Livingstone, David

David Livingstone, through 30 years of heroic travel and Christian missionary work in southern, central, and eastern Africa—often in places where no white man had previously ventured—may have influenced Western attitudes toward Africa more than any other individual before him or since.

Early life. Born March 19, 1813, at Blantyre in Scotland, Livingstone grew up in a distinctively Scottish family environment of personal piety, poverty, hard work, zeal for education, and a sense of mission. His father's family was from the island of Ulva, off the west coast of Scotland; his mother, a Lowlander, was descended from a family of Covenanters, a group of militant Presbyterians. Both were poor; and Livingstone was reared as one of seven children in a single room at the top of a tenement building for the workers of a cotton factory on the banks of the Clyde. At the age of ten he had to help his family and was put to work in a cotton mill; and with part of his first week's wages he bought a Latin grammar. Brought up in the Calvinist faith of the established Scottish church, Livingstone, like his father, joined an independent Christian congregation of stricter discipline when he came to manhood. By this time he had acquired those characteristics of mind and body that were to fit him for his African career.

In 1834 an appeal by British and American churches for qualified medical missionaries in China made Livingstone determine to become a medical missionary. To prepare himself, while continuing to work part-time in the mill, he studied Greek, theology, and medicine for two years in Glasgow. In 1838 he was accepted by the London Missionary Society. The Opium War (1839–42) put an end to his dreams of going to China, but a meeting with Robert Moffat, the notable Scottish missionary in southern Africa, convinced him that Africa should be his sphere of service. On November 20, 1840 he was ordained as a missionary; he set sail for South Africa at the end of the year and arrived at Cape Town on March 14, 1841.

Initial explorations. For the next 15 years, Livingstone was constantly on the move into the African interior: strengthening his missionary determination; responding wholeheartedly to the delights of geographical discovery; clashing with the Boers and the Portuguese, whose treatment of the Africans he came to detest; and building for himself a remarkable reputation as a dedicated Christian, a courageous explorer, and a fervent antislavery advocate. Yet so impassioned was his commitment to Africa that his duties as husband and father were relegated to second place.

From Moffat's mission at Kuruman on the Cape frontier, which Livingstone reached on July 31, 1841, he soon pushed his search for converts northward into untried country where the population was reputed to be more numerous. This suited his purpose of spreading the Gospel through "native agents." By the summer of 1842, he had already gone further north than any other white man into the difficult Kalahari country and had familiarized himself with the local languages and cultures. His mettle was dramatically tested in 1844, when, during a journey to Mabotsa to establish a mission station, he was mauled by a lion. The resulting injury to his left arm was complicated by another accident, so that he could never again support the barrel of a gun steadily with his left hand and was obliged to fire from his left shoulder and to take aim with his left eye.

On January 2, 1845, Livingstone married Moffat's daughter, Mary, and she accompanied him on many of his journeys until her health and the family's needs for security and education forced him to send her and their four children back to Britain in 1852. Before this first parting with his family, Livingstone had already achieved a small measure of fame when, as surveyor and scientist of a small expedition, he had assisted in the discovery of Lake Ngami on August 1, 1849, and was awarded a gold medal and monetary prize by the British Royal Geographical Society. This was the beginning of his lifelong association with the society, which continued to encourage his ambitions as an explorer and to champion his interests in Britain.

Opening the interior. With his family safely in Scotland, Livingstone was ready to push Christianity, commerce, and civilization—the trinity that he believed was destined to open up Africa—northward beyond the frontiers of South Africa and into the heart of the continent. In a famous statement in 1853 he made his purpose clear: "I shall open up a path into the interior, or perish." On November 11, 1853, from Linyanti at the approaches to the Zambezi and in the midst of the Makololo peoples whom he considered eminently suitable for missionary work, Livingstone set out northwestward with little equipment and only a small party of Africans. His intention was to find a route to the Atlantic coast that would permit legitimate commerce to undercut the slave trade and that would also be more suitable for reaching the Makololo than the route leading through Boer territory. (In 1852 the Boers had destroyed his home at Kolobeng and attacked his African friends.) After an arduous journey that might have wrecked the constitution of a lesser man, Livingstone reached Luanda on the west coast on May 31, 1854. In order to take his Makololo followers back home and to carry out further explorations of the Zambezi, as soon as his health permitted he began the return journey September 20, 1854. He reached Linyanti nearly a year later on September 11, 1855. Continuing eastward on November 3, Livingstone explored the Zambezi regions and reached Quilimane in Mozambique on May 20, 1856. His most

Livingstone, oil painting by F. Havill (died 1884), after photographs. In the National Portrait Gallery, London.

Ordained as missionary

Discovery
of Victoria
Falls

spectacular visit on this last leg of his great journey was to the thundering, smokelike waters on the Zambezi at which he arrived on November 17, 1855, and with typical patriotism named Victoria Falls after his queen. Livingstone returned to England on December 9, 1856, as a national hero. News from and about him during the previous three years had stirred the imagination and pride of English-speaking peoples everywhere to an unprecedented degree.

Livingstone recorded his accomplishments modestly but effectively in his *Missionary Travels and Researches in South Africa* (1857), which quickly sold over 70,000 copies and took its place in publishing history as well as in that of exploration and missionary endeavour. Honours flowed in upon him. His increased income meant that he was now able to provide adequately for his family, which had lived in near poverty since their return to Britain. He was also able to make himself independent of the London Missionary Society. After the completion of his book, Livingstone spent six months speaking all over the British Isles. In his Senate House address at Cambridge on Dec. 4, 1857, he foresaw that he would be unable to complete his work in Africa, and he called on young university men to take up the task that he had begun. The publication of *Dr. Livingstone's Cambridge Lectures* (1858) roused almost as much interest as his book; and out of his Cambridge visit came the Universities' Mission to Central Africa in 1860, on which Livingstone set high hopes during his second expedition to Africa.

The Zambezi expedition. This time Livingstone was away from Britain from March 12, 1858 to July 23, 1864. He went out originally as British Consul at Quilimane "for the Eastern Coast and independent districts of the interior, and commander of an expedition for exploring eastern and central Africa, for the promotion of Commerce and Civilization with a view to the extinction of the slave-trade." This expedition was infinitely better organized than Livingstone's previous solitary journeys. It had a paddle steamer, impressive stores, ten Africans, and six Europeans (including his brother Charles and an Edinburgh doctor, John Kirk). That Livingstone's by then legendary leadership had its limitation was soon revealed. Quarrels broke out among the Europeans and some were dismissed. Disillusionment with Livingstone set in among members of both his own expedition and of the abortive Universities' Mission that followed it to central Africa. It proved impossible to navigate the Zambezi by ship; and Livingstone's two attempts to find a route along the Rovuma River bypassing Portuguese territory to districts around Lake Nyasa (Malawi) also proved impractical. Livingstone and his party had been the first Britons to reach (September 17, 1859) these districts that held out promise of colonization. To add to Livingstone's troubles, his wife, who had been determined to accompany him back to Africa, died at Shupanga on the Zambezi on April 27, 1862. His eldest son, Robert, who was to have joined his father in 1863, never reached him and went instead to the United States, where he died fighting for the North in the Civil War on December 5, 1864. The British government recalled the expedition in 1863, when it was clear that Livingstone's optimism about economic and political developments in the Zambezi regions was premature. Livingstone, however, showed something of his old fire when he took his little vessel, the "Lady Nyassa," with a small, untrained crew and little fuel, on a hazardous voyage of 2,500 miles across the Indian Ocean and left her for sale in Bombay. Furthermore, within the next three decades the Zambezi expedition proved to be anything but a disaster. It had amassed a valuable body of scientific knowledge; and the association of the Lake Nyasa regions with Livingstone's name and the prospects for colonization that he envisaged there were important factors for the creation in 1893 of the British Central Africa Protectorate, which in 1907 became Nyasaland, and in 1966 the republic of Malawi.

Recall
to England

Back in Britain in the summer of 1864, Livingstone, with his brother Charles, wrote his second book, *Narrative of an Expedition to the Zambesi and Its Tributaries* (1865). Livingstone was advised at this time to have a surgical

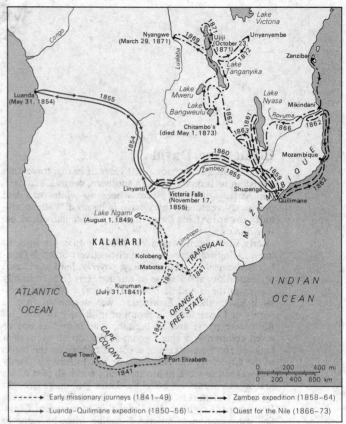

The expeditions of David Livingstone.

operation for the hemorrhoids that had troubled him since his first great African journey. He refused; and it is probable that severe bleeding hemorrhoids were the cause of his death at the end of his third and greatest African journey.

The quest for the Nile. Livingstone returned to Africa, after another short visit to Bombay, on January 28, 1866, with support from private and public bodies and the status of a British Consul at large. His aim, as usual, was the extension of the Gospel and the abolition of the slave trade on the East African coast; but a new object was the exploration of the central Africa watershed and the possibility of finding the ultimate sources of the Nile. This time Livingstone went without European subordinates and took only African and Asian followers. Trouble, however, once more broke out among his staff; and Livingstone, prematurely aged from the hardships of his previous expeditions, found it difficult to cope with. Striking out from Mikindani on the east coast, he was compelled by Ngoni raids to give up his original intention of avoiding Portuguese territory and reaching the country around Lake Tanganyika by passing north of Lake Nyasa. The expedition was forced south, and in September some of Livingstone's followers deserted him. To avoid punishment when they returned to Zanzibar, they concocted the story that Livingstone had been killed by the Ngoni. Although it was proved the following year that he was alive, a touch of drama was added to the reports circulating abroad about his expedition.

Drama mounted as Livingstone moved north again from the south end of Lake Nyasa. Early in 1867 a deserter carried off his medical chest, but Livingstone pressed on into central Africa. On November 8, 1867, he discovered Lake Mweru, and on July 18, 1868, Lake Bangweulu. Assisted by Arab traders, Livingstone reached Lake Tanganyika in February 1869. Despite illness, he went on, and arrived on March 29, 1871, at his ultimate northwesterly point, Nyangwe, on the Lualaba leading into the Congo River. This was farther west than any European had penetrated. Returning to Ujiji on the eastern shore of Lake Tanganyika on October 23, 1871, Livingstone was a sick and failing man, and the arrival of H.M. Stanley, a cor-

Rescue by Stanley

respondent of the *New York Herald*, provided him with desperately needed food and medicine. Livingstone felt strong enough to join Stanley in exploring the northern reaches of Lake Tanganyika and then accompanied him to Unyanyembe, 200 miles eastward. But he refused all of Stanley's pleas to leave Africa with him, and on March 14, 1872, Stanley departed for England to add, with journalistic fervour, to the saga of David Livingstone.

Replenished by Stanley's supplies, Livingstone moved south again, obsessed by his quest for the Nile sources and his desire for the destruction of the slave trade. But his illness overcame him. On May 1, 1873, at Chitambo's village in the Ilala district of what is now Zambia, Livingstone's African servants found him dead, kneeling by his bedside as if in prayer. In order to embalm Livingstone's body, they removed his heart and viscera and buried them in African soil. In a difficult journey of nine months, they carried his body to the coast. It was taken to England and, in a great Victorian funeral, was buried in Westminster Abbey on April 18, 1874. *The Last Journals of David Livingstone* were published in the same year.

Influence. In his time and since, the example of Livingstone has been one of the most powerful in stimulating the interest of the outside world in Africa. His discoveries—geographic, technical, medical, and social—provided a complex body of knowledge that is still being explored. In spite of his paternalism and Victorian prejudices, Livingstone believed wholeheartedly in the African's ability to advance into the modern world. He was, in this sense, a forerunner not only of European imperialism in Africa but also of African nationalism.

BIBLIOGRAPHY. The following books by DAVID LIVINGSTONE himself are fundamental: *Missionary Travels and Researches in South Africa* (1857); *Dr. Livingstone's Cambridge Lectures*, ed. by W. MONK (1858); *Narrative of an Expedition to the Zambesi and its Tributaries and of the Discovery of Lakes Shirwa and Nyassa, 1858–1867* (1865); *The Last Journals of David Livingstone in Central Africa, From 1865 to his Death*, 2 vol., ed. by H. WALLER (1874).

Although there is still no definitive biography of Livingstone, the most useful is GEORGE SEAVER, *David Livingstone: His Life and Letters* (1957). A much older work, which suffers from "bowdlerization" but is still useful for personal details, is W.G. BLAIKIE, *The Personal Life of David Livingstone* (1880). Various aspects of Livingstone's life and work are examined in: OWEN CHADWICK, *Mackenzie's Grave* (1959); REGINALD COUPLAND, *Kirk on the Zambesi* (1928) and *Livingstone's Last Journey* (1945); FRANK DEBENHAM, *The Way to Ilala* (1955), valuable for Livingstone as a geographer; MICHAEL GELFAND, *Livingstone the Doctor, His Life and Travels: A Study in Medical History* (1957); I. SCHAPERA (ed.), *David Livingstone: Family Letters, 1841–1856*, 2 vol. (1959), *Livingstone's Private Journals, 1851–1853* (1960), and *Livingstone's African Journal, 1853–1856*, 2 vol. (1963); GEORGE SHEPPERSON (ed.), *David Livingstone and the Rovuma* (1965); J.P.R. WALLIS (ed.), *The Zambezi Expedition of David Livingstone, 1858–1863* (1956); JAMES STEWART, *The Zambesi Journal, 1862–1863* (1952); and GEORGE MARTELLI, *Livingstone's River: A History of the Zambezi Expedition, 1858–1864* (1970). The following articles are also useful: R.C. BRIDGES, "The Sponsorship and Financing of Livingstone's Last Journey," *African Historical Studies*, 1:79–104 (1968); THOMAS PRICE, "Portuguese Relations with David Livingstone," *The Scottish Geographical Magazine*, 71:138–145 (1955); and GEORGE SHEPPERSON, "David Livingstone the Scot," *The Scottish Historical Review*, 39:113–121 (1960).

(G.A.S.)

Livy

With Sallust and Tacitus, Livy ranks as one of the three great Roman historians. His history of Rome from the foundation of the city (*Ab urbe condita*) established itself as a classic in his own lifetime and exercised a profound influence on the style and philosophy of historical writing down to the 18th century.

Early years and career. Livy (Titus Livius) was born at Patavium (Padua) in northern Italy in 59 BC (or possibly 64 BC). Little is known about his life and nothing about his family background. Patavium, a rich city, famous for its strict morals, suffered severely in the Civil Wars of the 40s. The wars and the unsettled condition of the Roman world after the death of Caesar in 44 BC

probably prevented Livy from studying in Greece, as most educated Romans did. Although widely read in Greek literature, he made mistakes of translation that would be unnatural if he had spent any length of time in Greece and had acquired the command of Greek normal among his contemporaries. His education was based on the study of rhetoric and philosophy, and he wrote some philosophical dialogues that do not survive. There is no evidence about his early career. His family apparently did not belong to the senatorial class, however distinguished it may have been in Patavium itself, and Livy does not seem to have embarked on a political or forensic profession. He is first heard of in Rome after Octavian (later known as the emperor Augustus) had restored stability and peace to the empire by his decisive naval victory at Actium in 31 BC. Internal evidence from the work itself shows that Livy had conceived the plan of writing the history of Rome in or shortly before 29 BC, and for this purpose he must have already moved to Rome, because only there were the records and information available. It is significant that another historian, the Greek Dionysius of Halicarnassus, who was to cover much the same ground as Livy, settled in Rome in 30 BC. A more secure age had dawned.

Most of his life must have been spent at Rome, and at an early stage he attracted the interest of Augustus and was even invited to supervise the literary activities of the young Claudius (the future emperor), presumably about AD 8. But he never became closely involved with the literary world of Rome—the poets Horace, Virgil, and Ovid, as well as the patron of the arts, Maecenas, and others. He is never referred to in connection with these men. He must have possessed sufficient private means not to be dependent on official patronage. Indeed, in one of the few recorded anecdotes about him, Augustus called him a "Pompeian," implying an outspoken and independent turn of mind. His lifework was the composition of his history.

Livy's history of Rome. Livy began by composing and publishing in units of five books, the length of which was determined by the size of the ancient papyrus roll. As his material became more complex, however, he abandoned this symmetrical pattern and wrote 142 books. So far as it can be reconstructed, the shape of the history is as follows (books 11–20 and 46–142 have been lost):

Plan of the history

1–5 From the foundation of the city until the sack of Rome by the Gauls (386 BC)
6–10 The Samnite wars
11–15 The conquest of Italy
16–20 The First Punic (Carthaginian) War
21–30 The Second Punic War (until 201 BC)
31–45 Events until the end of the war with Perseus (167 BC)
46–70 Events until the Social War (91 BC)
71–80 Civil wars until the death of Marius (86 BC)
81–90 Civil wars until the death of Sulla (78 BC)
91–103 Events until the triumph of Pompey in 62 BC
104–108 The last years of the Republic
109–116 The Civil War until the murder of Caesar (44 BC)
117–133 From the death of Caesar to the Battle of Actium
134–142 From 29 to 9 BC

Apart from fragments, quoted by grammarians and others, and a short section dealing with the death of the orator and politician Cicero from Book 120, the later books after Book 45 are known only from summaries. These were made from the 1st century AD onward, because the size of the complete work made it unmanageable. There were anthologies of the speeches and also concise summaries, two of which survive in part, a 3rd-century papyrus from Egypt (containing summaries of Books 37–40 and 48–55) and a 4th-century summary of contents (known as the *Periochae*) of the whole work. A note in the *Periocha* of Book 121 records that that book (and presumably those that followed) was published after Augustus' death in AD 14. The implication is that the last 20 books dealing with the events from the Battle of Actium until 9 BC were an afterthought to the original plan and were also too politically explosive to be published with impunity in Augustus' lifetime.

The sheer scope of the undertaking was formidable. It presupposed the composition of three books a year on average. Two stories reflect the magnitude of the task. In his letters the statesman Pliny the Younger records that Livy was tempted to abandon the enterprise but found that the task had become too fascinating to give it up; he also mentions a citizen of Cádiz who came all the way to Rome for the sole satisfaction of gazing at the great historian.

Livy's historical approach. The project of writing the history of Rome down to the present day was not a new one. Historical research and writing had flourished at Rome for 200 years, since the first Roman historian Quintus Fabius Pictor. There had been two main inspirations behind it—antiquarian interest and political motivation. Particularly after 100 BC, there developed a widespread interest in ancient ceremonies, family genealogies, religious customs, and the like. This interest found expression in a number of scholarly works: Titus Pomponius Atticus, Cicero's friend and correspondent, wrote on chronology and on Trojan families; others compiled lengthy volumes on Etruscan religion; Marcus Terentius Varro, the greatest scholar of his age, published the encyclopaedic work *Divine and Human Antiquities*. The standard of scholarship was not always high, and there could be political pressures, as in the attempt to derive the Julian family to which Julius Caesar belonged from the legendary Aeneas and the Trojans; but the Romans were very conscious and proud of their past, and an enthusiasm for antiquities was widespread.

Antiquarian interest of Roman historians

Previous historians had been public figures and men of affairs. Fabius Pictor had been a praetor, the elder Cato had been consul and censor, and Sallust had been a praetor. So, too, many prominent statesmen such as Sulla and Caesar occupied their leisure with writing history. For some it was an exercise in political self-justification (hence, Caesar's *Gallic War* and *Civil War*); for others it was a civilized pastime. But all shared a common outlook and background. History was a political study through which one might hope to explain or excuse the present.

Livy was unique among Roman historians in that he played no part in politics. This was a disadvantage in that his exclusion from the Senate and the magistracies meant that he had no personal experience of how the Roman government worked, and this ignorance shows itself from time to time in his work. It also deprived him of firsthand access to much material (minutes of Senate meetings, texts of treaties, laws, etc.) that was preserved in official quarters. So, too, if he had been a priest or an augur, he would have acquired inside information of great historical value and been able to consult the copious documents and records of the priestly colleges. But the chief effect is that Livy did not seek historical explanations in political terms. The novelty and impact of his history lay in the fact that he saw history in personal and moral terms. The purpose is clearly set out in his preface:

Interest in personal and moral aspects of history

I invite the reader's attention to the much more serious consideration of the kind of lives our ancestors lived, of who were the men and what the means, both in politics and war, by which Rome's power was first acquired and subsequently expanded, I would then have him trace the process of our moral decline, to watch first the sinking of the foundations of morality as the old teaching was allowed to lapse, then the final collapse of the whole edifice, and the dark dawning of our modern day when we can neither endure our vices nor face the remedies needed to cure them.

What chiefly makes the study of history wholesome and profitable is this, that in history you have a record of the infinite variety of human experience plainly set out for all to see, and in that record you can find for yourself and your country both examples and warnings.

Although Sallust and earlier historians had also adopted the outlook that morality was in steady decline and had argued that people do the sort of things they do because they are the sort of people they are, for Livy these beliefs were a matter of passionate concern. He saw history in terms of human personalities and representative individuals rather than of partisan politics. And his own experience, going back perhaps to his youth in Patavium, made him feel the moral evils of his time with peculiar intensity. He punctuates his history with revealing comments:

Fortunately in those days authority, both religious and secular, was still a guide to conduct and there was as yet no sign of our modern scepticism which interpets solemn compacts to suit its own convenience (3.20.5). Where would you find nowadays in a single individual that modesty, fairness and nobility of mind which in those days belonged to a whole people? (4.6.12).

In looking at history from a moral standpoint, Livy was at one with other thinking Romans of his day. Augustus attempted by legislation and propaganda to inculcate moral ideals. Horace and Virgil in their poetry stressed the same message—that it was moral qualities that had made and could keep Rome great.

The preoccupation with character and the desire to write history that would reveal the effects of character outweighed for Livy the need for scholarly accuracy. He showed little if any awareness of the antiquarian research of his own and earlier generations; nor did he seriously compare and criticize the different histories and their discrepancies that were available to him. For the most part he is content to take an earlier version (from Polybius or a similar author) and to reshape it so as to construct moral episodes that bring out the character of the leading figures. Livy's descriptions of the capture of Veii and the expulsion of the Gauls from Rome in the 4th century BC by Marcus Furius Camillus are designed to illustrate his piety; the crossing of the Alps shows up the resourceful intrepidity of Hannibal. Unfortunately, it is not known how Livy dealt with the much greater complexity of contemporary history, but the account of Cicero's death contains the same emphasis on character displayed by surviving books.

It would be misplaced criticism to draw attention to his technical shortcomings, his credulity, or his lack of antiquarian curiosity. He reshaped history for his generation so that it was alive and meaningful. It is recorded that the audiences who went to his recitations were impressed by his nobility of character and his eloquence. It is this eloquence that is Livy's second claim to distinction.

Together with Cicero and Tacitus, Livy set new standards of literary style. The earliest Roman historians had written in Greek, the language of culture. Their successors had felt that their own history should be written in Latin, but Latin possessed no ready-made style that could be used for the purpose: for Latin prose had to develop artificial styles to suit the different genres. Sallust had attempted to reproduce the Greek style of Thucydides in Latin by a tortured use of syntax and a vocabulary incorporating a number of archaic and unusual words, but the result, although effective, was harsh and unsuitable for a work of any size. Livy evolved a varied and flexible style that the ancient critic Quintilian characterized as a "milky richness." At one moment he will set the scene in long, periodic clauses; at another a few terse, abrupt sentences will mirror the rapidity of the action. Bare notices of archival fact will be reported in correspondingly dry and formal language, whereas a battle will evoke poetical and dramatic vocabulary, and a speech will be constructed either in the spirit of a contemporary orator such as Cicero or in dramatically realistic tones, designed to recapture the atmosphere of antiquity. "When I write of ancient deeds my mind somehow becomes antique," he wrote. Livy died at Patavium in AD 17.

His literary style

The work of a candid man and an individualistic thinker, Livy's history was deeply rooted in the Augustan revival and owed its success in large measure to its moral seriousness. But the detached attempt to understand the course of history through character (which was to influence later historians from Tacitus to Lord Clarendon) represents Livy's great achievement.

BIBLIOGRAPHY

Texts: Books 1-10, 21-35 have been edited and published in the "Oxford Classical Series"; the other books are in course of preparation. The complete text of surviving books and fragments has been published in the "Teubner Series".

Translations: Books 1–5 and 21–30 have been translated by A. DE SELINCOURT and published in the "Penguin Classics," with complete text and translation in the "Loeb Classical Library."

Commentaries: Books 1–5 by R.M. OGILVIE (1965), with bibliography. Individual books have been edited with commentaries in the "Macmillan Series." Complete commentary on the surviving books by w. WEISSENBORN, rev. by H.J. MULLER (1878–1910).

Studies: P.G. WALSH, *Livy: His Historical Aims and Methods* (1961), with bibliography; J. BRISCOE *et al.*, *Livy* (1971); R. SYME, "Livy and Augustus," *Harvard Studies in Classical Philology*, 64:27–87 (1959).

(R.M.Og.)

Llanos

The Llanos (Plains), a grassland, or savanna, that stretches across northern South America, occupy one-third of Venezuela and about one-fifth of Colombia. The Llanos are delimited by the Andes Mountains in the west and north, the Lower Orinoco River and the Guiana Highlands in the east, and the Río Guaviare and the Amazonian rain forest in the south. The region covers an area of some 220,000 square miles (570,000 square kilometres) and is comparable in size to France or Texas.

The savanna was named by the Spaniards in the 16th century and has been used as a vast cattle range since then. Until the mid-1900s, settlement was limited to widely scattered ranches known as *hatos* ("cow herds"), a few villages, and missionary stations along the lower courses of the region's rivers. Since the 1930s the region has experienced economic growth. (For a related physical feature, see ORINOCO RIVER.)

Physical features

Relief. Most of the Llanos lies within 1,000 feet above sea level. The High Plains (Llanos Altos) are most conspicuous near the Andes, where they form extensive platforms between rivers and are some 100 to 200 feet above the valley floors. Away from the mountains they are increasingly fragmented, as in the dissected tableland of the central and eastern Venezuelan Llanos (the Sabana de Mesas) and the hill country south of the Río Meta in Colombia (the Serranía).

The Low Plains (Llanos Bajos) are defined by the Río Apure in the north and the Río Meta in the south. The lowest portion of the Llanos, west of the Orinoco Valley, is annually converted into an inland lake by the flooding of the region's rivers.

Soils and drainage. The Llanos are drained by the Orinoco River and its left-bank tributaries, including the Guaviare, Meta, Apure, and Cojedes rivers. Seasonal changes between saturation and dehydration have led to advanced laterization of the soil, the process in which the base minerals have been leached away or incorporated into insoluble iron and aluminum silicates. Fine-grained soils form hardpans (cemented layers of soils), and in gravel regions, iron-cemented quartz conglomerates underlie the surface. Excessive acidity and the lack of nutrient bases, organic matter, and nitrogen make virtually all mature soils infertile.

Climate. The wet and dry seasons result from the annual migration of the Intertropical Convergence Zone, a low-pressure trough between the hemispheric easterlies, or trade winds. The zone remains south of the Equator from December to March, bringing the entire Llanos under the influence of the Northeast Trades, which cause the dry and hot summer weather. The zone enters the Llanos from the south in April, reaches its northernmost position along the north coast in July, and moves south again until December. The passage of the zone brings the rainy winter period.

Monthly precipitation is seldom less than ten inches in the Colombian Llanos between April and November. The rains peak about midyear in the Venezuelan north, with monthly totals of around ten inches. Annual precipitation is highest near the Andes, where Villavicencio receives 180 inches; and there is a pronounced decrease toward the central plains, where Puerto de Nutrias receives 45 inches.

Mean daily temperatures are above 75° F (24° C) throughout the year, and the annual range does not sur-

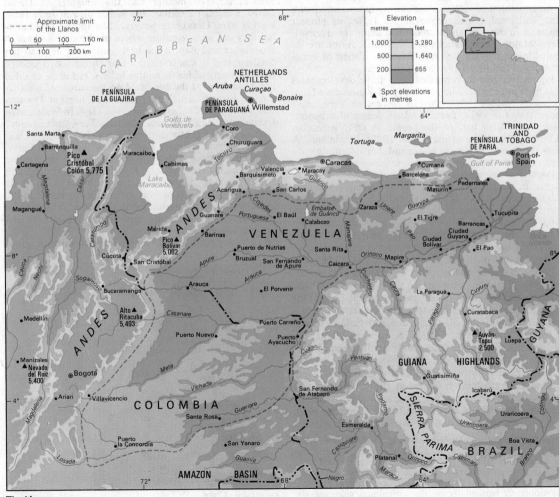

The Llanos.

pass 7° F (4° C). Daily maximum temperatures rise above 95° F (35° C) in the dry period; the dry winds and nocturnal cooling bring relief with normal minimum temperatures between 65° and 75° F (18° and 24° C).

Vegetation and animal life. Most of the Llanos is treeless savanna. In the low-lying areas, swamp grasses and sedges are to be found, as also is bunchgrass (*Trachypogon*). Long-stemmed grass dominates the dry savanna and is mixed with carpet grass (*Axonopus affinis*), the only natural grass to provide green forage during the dry season.

The most conspicuous trees occur in the gallery forests along the rivers and in the narrower files of trees known as *morichales*, after the dominant moriche palm that follow minor water courses. Broadleaved evergreens originally occupied the high-rainfall zone in the Andean piedmont. There is a handful of xerophytic trees (*i.e.*, those adapted to arid conditions), including the *chaparro* (scrub oak) and the dwarf palm scattered on the open savanna.

The Llanos have few animals. Most mammals nest in the gallery forests and feed on the grassland. The only true savanna dwellers are a few burrowing rodents and more than 20 species of birds (among them the white and scarlet ibis, the *morichal* oriole, and the burrowing owl). There are several species of deer and rabbit, the anteater and armadillo, the tapir, the jaguar, and the largest living rodent, the capybara. Crocodiles, caimans (a crocodile-like amphibian), and snakes, including the boa constrictor, inhabit the rivers, which also teem with little-known varieties of fish. Insects include butterflies, beetles, ants, and mound-building termites.

Population and resources. Cattle raising remains the mainstay of the economy, the base of which was widened by the discovery of petroleum in the 1930s. Oil strikes in the eastern and central Venezuelan Llanos at El Tigre (1937) and Barinas (1948) initiated industrial and urban development. Several of the "boom towns" of that period, such as El Tigre, have grown into sizable cities.

> The discovery of oil

An expansion of intensive agriculture has occurred with the settlement, which began in the 1950s, of pioneer farmers in the Andean piedmont and along the river valleys. Major concentrations of these small farms are located in the Barinas–Guanare–Acarigua district of Venezuela and the Ariari region in Colombia.

Population growth connected with these developments has been impressive. The population of Venezuela's Llanos states reached 1,800,000 (18 percent of Venezuela's population) in 1970. There is a high degree of urbanization; more than half of the people of the Venezuelan Llanos live in cities of more than 10,000 inhabitants. A few thousand Indians (of Carib and Arawak origin) are left on reservations in the Lower Orinoco area.

Population increase has been modest in the Colombian areas. In the Departmento del Meta, Colombia, the population expanded to 210,000 in 1970. Villavicencio, the department's capital, is the only city with more than 10,000 inhabitants (65,000 in 1970) in the Colombian Llanos. The rest of the area remains sparsely inhabited; the population of the Llanos Orientales numbers less than 2 percent of Colombia's total population of 22,000,000.

Prospects for the future. The Venezuelan Llanos benefit from Venezuela's continuing policy of exploiting the rich mineral and water-power resources of the Lower Orinoco and the Guiana Highlands. Flood-control schemes include the dams at Calabozo, San Carlos, and Guanare. Excellent trans-Andean roads, a highway along the Andes, and all-weather access routes to the Orinoco contribute to growing economic vitality.

Economic development in the Colombian Llanos is less promising. Agriculture is limited by the small proportion of cultivable land and by the low grazing capacity of the savanna. No mineral deposits had been found by 1970, but a road along the foot of the Andes has been planned.

BIBLIOGRAPHY. Published literature on the Llanos in English is scarce. No book deals with the region as a whole. General information on the geographic aspects of the Llanos and their importance to Venezuela and Colombia is found in P.E. JAMES, *Latin America* (1969). Problems of resource development, particularly on the agricultural side, are discussed in a report of the INTERNATIONAL BANK FOR RECONSTRUCTION AND DEVELOPMENT, *The Economic Development of Venezuela* (1961); and in the FOOD AND AGRICULTURAL ORGANIZATION, *Soil Survey of the Llanos Orientales, Colombia,* 4 vol. (1964–66). Ecological insights on the Llanos are given in J.S. BEARD, "Savanna Vegetation of Northern Tropical America," *Ecol. Monogr.,* 23:149–215 (1953); and in E.J. FITTKAU *et al.* (eds.), *Biogeography and Ecology in South America,* 2 vol. (1968–69). Accounts on the progress of colonization are given in R.E. CRIST, "Along the Llanos-Andes Border in Venezuela: Then and Now," *Geogrl. Rev.,* 46:187–208 (1956), and with ERNESTO GUHL, "Pioneer Settlement in Eastern Colombia," *An. Rep. Smithson. Inst.,* pp. 391–414 (1956). Still the most worthwhile reading is found in ALEXANDER VON HUMBOLDT's essays on the Llanos contained in his and A. BONPLAND's *Voyage de Humboldt et Bonpland,* pt. 1, *Voyage aux régions équinoxiales du nouveau continent,* 3 vol. (1814–34; Eng. trans., *Personal Narrative of Travels to the Equinoctial Regions of the New Continent During the Years 1799–1804,* 7 vol., 1814–29, reprinted 1966).

(Di.B.)

Lloyd George, David

For 16 years, from 1906 to 1922, English political life was dominated by the fiery personality of David Lloyd George. As leader of the radicals within the Liberal Party before World War I, he pushed through legislation that laid the foundation of the modern welfare state. A former pacifist, he headed a coalition government that guided Britain to victory in what then seemed the greatest of all wars. After 1922 he remained in the shadows of public life, but in the words of Winston Churchill, addressing the House of Commons after his death, "When the English history of the first quarter of the twentieth century is written it will be found that the greater part of our fortunes in peace and in war were shaped by this one man."

Lloyd George was born in Manchester on January 17, 1863. His father was a Welshman from Pembrokeshire and had become headmaster of an elementary school in Manchester. His mother was the daughter of David Lloyd, a Baptist minister. His father died in June 1864, leaving Mrs. George in poverty. She moved to Llanystumdwy in Carnarvonshire where her brother Richard, a shoemaker and Baptist minister, supported her and her children; and it was from him that David Lloyd George imbibed many of his formative beliefs. His uncle enabled him to embark at the age of 14 on the career of a solicitor; he became articled (1879) to a firm at Portmadoc, passing his final examination in 1884. In Wales, as in Ireland, an anglicized and Anglican Tory "ascendancy" class of landed gentry dominated a Celtic people of different race and religion. The cause of the Liberal Party, the Welsh nation, and Nonconformity were inseparable in the atmosphere in which Lloyd George was raised, and he first made his name by a successful battle in the courts to establish the right of Nonconformists to burial in the churchyard of their parish. Ironically, he who came to be the standard-bearer of the oppressed religious sects had lost his faith even as a boy.

As a young man, Lloyd George had the romantic, good

EB Inc.

Lloyd George, 1908.

looks that ensured success with women. After numerous love affairs, he was married in 1888 to Margaret Owen who bore him two sons and three daughters. It cannot be described as a happy marriage. Lloyd George was incapable of fidelity, and his affairs with other women were notorious. His wife stood by him on many occasions, but in the end his behaviour was too much for even her long-suffering tolerance.

Lloyd George entered Parliament in 1890, winning a by-election at Carnarvon Boroughs, the seat he retained for 55 years. He soon made a name for himself in the House of Commons by his audacity, charm, wit, and mastery of the art of debate. During the ten years of Liberal opposition that followed the election of 1895, he became a leading figure in the radical wing of the party. He bitterly and courageously opposed the South African War; and in 1901 was nearly lynched in Birmingham, the stronghold of Joseph Chamberlain and Conservative imperialism. With the arrival of peace, Lloyd George worked up a great agitation in Wales against tax-aided grants to church schools established by Balfour's Education Act (1902). This period saw him at the height of his reputation as the leader of Welsh nationalism. Cabinet office later somewhat reduced his fervour in this field, and with the passage of time his nationalism became cultural rather than political.

Arthur J. Balfour resigned in December 1905 and Sir Henry Campbell-Bannerman formed a Liberal administration, appointing Lloyd George to the Cabinet as president of the Board of Trade. In that office, he was responsible for important legislation: the Merchant Shipping Act (1906), improving seamen's living conditions, but also endangering their lives by raising the Plimsoll line on newly constructed ships; the Patents and Designs Act (1907), preventing foreign exploitation of British inventions; and the Port of London Act (1908), setting up the Port of London Authority. He also earned a high reputation by his patient work in settling strikes. He suffered a cruel bereavement in November 1907, when his daughter Mair died of appendicitis at the age of 17. Years afterward, the sight of her portrait could plunge him into tears.

CHANCELLOR OF THE EXCHEQUER

Campbell-Bannerman's health failed in 1908. He was succeeded as prime minister by the chancellor of the exchequer, Herbert Henry Asquith, who appointed Lloyd George to take his own place. This was a notable promotion and made him at least a very strong competitor for the premiership after Asquith. By this time, the Liberal Party's fortunes were beginning to languish. The House of Lords had blocked much of its social reform legislation, and the radical wing of the party was concerned that its thunder might be stolen by the nascent Labour Party unless the deadlock could be broken. At the same time, the demand for more battleships to match the German naval program threatened the finances available for social reform. It was to meet these difficulties that Lloyd George framed the famous "People's Budget" of 1909, calling for taxes upon unearned increment on the sale of land and on land values, higher death duties, and a supertax on incomes above £3,000. Moreover, it seemed for a time that the House of Lords' veto on progressive legislation would be bypassed, since the custom of the constitution forbade the upper house from interfering with the budget. In fact, however, the Conservative majority in the House of Lords, against the advice of some of its wiser members, decided to reject it. The consequences of this rejection were two general elections, a major constitutional crisis, and the ultimate passage of the Parliament Act of 1911, which severely curtailed the powers of the upper house. The principal burden of all this fell upon Asquith, but Lloyd George gave him vigorous support in a series of notable philippics against the aristocracy and the rich. The most famous of all was his speech at Limehouse, where he denounced the rapacity of the landlord class, especially the dukes, in unforgettable language.

In 1913 he faced one of the gravest personal crises in his career. In April 1912, along with Rufus Isaacs, the attorney general, he had purchased shares in the Marconi Wireless Telegraph Company of America at a rate well below that available to the general public. The American Marconi company was legally independent of the British concern, but the two companies were closely connected, and the latter's shares had recently boomed as a result of the government's decision to accept its proposal to construct a chain of radio stations throughout the empire, Lloyd George and Isaacs unluckily denied, in somewhat ambiguous language, any transactions in the shares of "the Marconi company," a denial that technically referred only to the British company but was generally assumed to cover the American as well. A select committee of the House of Commons revealed the facts and, although by a party majority it acquitted the ministers of blame, Lloyd George's reputation for integrity was damaged.

Social reform and the outbreak of war. Lloyd George's major achievement during the years immediately before the war was in the field of social insurance. Inspired by a visit to Germany (1908), where he studied the Bismarckian scheme of insurance benefits, Lloyd George decided to introduce health and unemployment insurance on a similar basis in Britain. This he did in the National Insurance Act of 1911. The measure inspired bitter opposition and was even unpopular with the working class who were not convinced by Lloyd George's slogan "ninepence for fourpence," the difference in these two figures being the employer's and the state's contribution. Lloyd George, undeterred, piloted his measure through Parliament with great skill and determination. He thus laid the foundations of the modern welfare state and, if he had done nothing else, would deserve fame for that achievement.

Though much of the government's time during these years was occupied by the Irish question, Lloyd George played little part in it and, on the whole, left foreign policy to his colleagues. It was, therefore, something of a surprise when, in July 1911, after careful consultation with Asquith and Sir Edward Grey, he issued a formidable warning to Germany over the Moroccan crisis. When the question of entry into the war convulsed the Cabinet in late July and early August 1914, he seemed at first to incline to the isolationist section. For a brief moment he contemplated retirement. But the tide of events swept him to the other side. As chancellor, he plunged into the financial problems posed by the war.

Minister of munitions and secretary of state for war. Throughout the remainder of 1914 and the early months of 1915, Lloyd George was a vigorous advocate of increased munitions production. Here he came into sharp conflict with Lord Kitchener in the War Office. The resignation of Admiral Fisher in 1915 forced Asquith to reconstruct the government on a coalition basis and admit the Conservatives. In the new administration, Lloyd George became minister of munitions. In this capacity, he made one of the most notable contributions to the victory of the Allies. His methods were unorthodox and shocked the civil service, but his energy was immense. He imported able assistants from big business and used his eloquence to induce the cooperation of organized labour. When, in the summer of 1916, the great Battle of the Somme began, supplies were forthcoming.

Lloyd George acquired definite views on war strategy at an early stage. He doubted the possibility of breaking through on the Western front and advocated instead a flank attack from the Near East. He was thus at loggerheads with the view of the official military hierarchy, cogently pressed by Sir Douglas Haig and Sir William Robertson, that the war could only be won in the West. On June 5, 1916, Kitchener was drowned on his way to Russia, when his ship struck a German mine. A last-minute accident—acute developments in the Irish situation—alone had prevented Lloyd George from travelling with him. After some hesitation, Asquith appointed him to the vacant position at the War Office.

Lloyd George held the post for five months, but Robertson as chief of the imperial general staff possessed nearly all the really important powers of the war minister. Lloyd George chafed under these restrictions, the more so because he profoundly disagreed with Robertson on vital

[margin notes:]
Pro-Boer sentiment

Promulgation of the "People's Budget"

Disagreement with military leaders

issues of strategy. Thus frustrated, he began to survey the whole direction of the war with increasing skepticism; and he did not conceal his doubts from his friends who, by the end of November, had become convinced that Asquith should delegate the day-to-day running of the war to a small committee whose chairman should be Lloyd George. There was undoubtedly widespread uneasiness at Asquith's conduct of affairs, particularly in the Conservative Party. Asquith was manoeuvred into resigning on December 5 and was replaced two days later by Lloyd George. He was supported by the leading Conservatives, Bonar Law becoming chancellor of the exchequer, leader of the house, and second in command of the government, and Balfour becoming foreign secretary. But the most prominent Liberal ministers resigned with Asquith, and, although about half the rank and file of the party supported the new government, Lloyd George was never forgiven by the old guard of his party for having jockeyed Asquith out of office.

PRIME MINISTER

Lloyd George was now 54 and at the height of his powers. His energy, eloquence, and ability had already made him the leading statesman of the day, and his accession to the premiership was highly popular in the country generally. A sense of renewed vigour, of "push and go," was given to the war effort. He immediately substituted a small War Cabinet of five, which was to be in constant session, for the unwieldy body of 23 that had hitherto conducted affairs. The result was a general speeding up of decisions and the disappearance of the procrastination that had marred the previous government.

War cabinet reorganized

One of Lloyd George's most notable efforts was in combatting the submarine menace which, in the early months of 1917, threatened to starve Britain into submission. He achieved this by forcing the adoption of the convoy system upon a reluctant admiralty. The food shortage resulting from the submarine war was acute. Drastic action had to be taken to step up agricultural production, and eventually a system of food rationing had to be introduced (1918). In these matters Lloyd George was at his best, contemptuous of red tape, determined to take action and to make his will prevail.

It was in the field of grand strategy that he was least successful. Lloyd George remained profoundly skeptical of the ability of the British high command to conduct even a "Western" strategy successfully. Without warning Haig or Robertson in advance, he confronted them at the Calais Conference of February 1917 with a plan to place the British Army under French command for Gen. Robert-Georges Nivelle's forthcoming offensive. Haig and Robertson deeply distrusted Lloyd George from that moment onward. The Nivelle offensive was a total failure, and Lloyd George was, as a result, on shaky ground when he endeavoured to resist Haig's proposals for a major British campaign in Flanders in the summer. After much hesitation, he gave way, and on July 31, 1917, the ill-fated Passchendaele offensive began. Although it may have forestalled a possible German attack on the French, Passchendaele, with enormous loss of life, achieved none of its main objectives. He was now convinced of the incompetence of the British high command.

He still dared not take action against them openly. Instead, he began what Sir Winston Churchill calls "a series of extremely laborious and mystifying maneuvers," with the object of creating a unified command under someone other than Haig. In February 1918, Robertson offered his resignation, which Lloyd George accepted, but Haig remained as commander in chief. Such was Lloyd George's distrust of Haig that, during the winter of 1917-18, he had deliberately kept him short of troops for fear that he might renew the attack. The result was that the Germans came near to launching a successful offensive. The emergency caused a unified command under Marshal Foch to be established (April), and by May the situation became stabilized. Out of these events arose the famous Maurice debate. Maj. Gen. Sir Frederick Maurice, who was in the War Office, published a letter claiming that Lloyd George had given incorrect figures in reply to a question about

manpower on the Western front. Lloyd George made a brilliant speech at the subsequent debate in Parliament, though later evidence shows that Maurice was undoubtedly right. The Asquithian Liberals pressed the matter to a division and were heavily beaten.

The Armistice of November 1918 faced Lloyd George with a dilemma. Should he allow a return to peacetime party politics or continue the coalition? There was little doubt of the answer. Bonar Law was willing to cooperate. A somewhat perfunctory offer to include Asquith was declined. The ensuing election in December gave the coalitionists an overwhelming victory. Many of those who followed Asquith at the Maurice debate were not granted the "coupon," the joint letter from Lloyd George and Bonar Law that certified the candidate as a coalitionist. Nearly all, Asquith included, lost their seats. The rift in the Liberal Party became wider, and Lloyd George was now largely dependent on Conservative support.

The "coupon election"

As one of the three great statesmen at Versailles, Lloyd George must bear a major responsibility for the peace settlement. He pursued a middle course between Georges Clemenceau and Woodrow Wilson. But, throughout, Lloyd George was under strong pressure at home to pursue the more draconian policy. It is to his credit that the final settlement was not far worse than it was. The treaty was well-received in Britain, and in August 1919 the king conferred on him the Order of Merit.

A major domestic problem was Ireland, where the Sinn Fein refused to recognize the British Parliament, and from 1919 to 1921 a civil war of massacre and reprisal raged. In the summer of 1921, Lloyd George, with full agreement of his Conservative colleagues, reversed the policy of repression in Ireland and initiated the negotiations that culminated in Irish independence in December 1921. The more rigid Tories never forgave this "surrender," as they deemed it. In 1922 Lloyd George ran into further trouble over the so-called honours scandal, when accusations against the coalition were made in both houses of Parliament that peerages and other honours were being regularly sold for large campaign contributions. Tory discontent was rife, when, from a wholly unexpected quarter, a crisis occurred that drove Lloyd George from power forever. This was the Çanak incident (see OTTOMAN EMPIRE AND TURKEY, HISTORY OF), when it seemed to critics that the reckless foreign policy of the government had led Britain to the verge of an unnecessary war with Turkey. When the Conservative leaders decided to appeal to the country on a coalition basis once again, a party revolt ensued. Bonar Law returned to the political scene; and on October 19 a two-to-one majority of Conservative members of Parliament endorsed his and Stanley Baldwin's plea to fight as an independent party. Lloyd George at once resigned.

Later years and assessment. The long twilight of Lloyd George's career was a melancholy anticlimax. The feud with the Asquithians was never healed, and from 1926 to 1931 he headed an ailing Liberal Party. He devoted himself thereafter to writing his *War Memoirs* (1933–36) and *The Truth About the Peace Treaties* (1938). Lengthy, yet supremely readable and interspersed with brilliant pen portraits, these volumes are an exercise in the forensic, rather than the historian's, art. He seldom admits error, and the endless diatribes against his opponents carry little conviction. In 1936 he visted Germany and met Hitler and was temporarily taken in by him; but in 1938 and 1939 he was a leading opponent of appeasement. In 1940 Churchill invited him to join his war cabinet, but Lloyd George declined, ostensibly on grounds of age and health. On January 1, 1945, he was elevated to the peerage as Earl Lloyd-George of Dwyfor. He died on March 26, 1945.

Publication of his memoirs

Lloyd George's personality is something of an enigma to the historian. It is easy to list his qualities: his eloquence; his extraordinary charm and persuasiveness; his sense of wit and fun; his capacity to see the heart of problems whose complexity baffled lesser men; his profound sympathy with oppressed classes and races; his genuine hatred of those who abused power, whether that power was based on wealth or caste or military might. But there was an obverse side to these virtues: his love of devious methods; his remarkable, albeit temporary, gullibility in the face of Hitler and the Nazis; his carelessness and want of discretion—some would use severer words—over appointments and honours; his defeatism in World War II, which contrasted so sadly with his earlier courage.

Lloyd George, for all his greatness, aroused in many persons a profound sense of mistrust, and it was in the upper-middle class, represented in politics by Stanley Baldwin and Neville Chamberlain, that he inspired the most acute misgivings. They were both determined to exclude him from office, and it would be wrong to ascribe his long years in the political wilderness solely to the declining fortunes of the Liberal Party. It is perhaps significant of his defects that Lloyd George, though possessing a host of acquaintances, never had a really intimate friend. There was in him a streak of ruthlessness that left little room for the cultivation of personal friendship. For these and other reasons, he was never able to recover the position he had lost in 1922. It was one of the tragedies of the interwar years that, in an era not notable for political talent, the one man of genius in politics should have had to remain an impotent spectator. But his earlier achievements make his place in history secure.

BIBLIOGRAPHY. Biographical studies include A.J. SYLVESTER, *The Real Lloyd George* (1947); THOMAS JONES, *Lloyd George* (1951); FRANK OWEN, *Tempestuous Journey* (1954); WILLIAM GEORGE, *My Brother and I* (1958); RICHARD LLOYD GEORGE, *Lloyd George* (1960); and MARTIN GILBERT (ed.), *Lloyd George* (1969), mainly selections from his speeches and writings, with an excellent bibliography. See also W.M. AITKEN (Lord Beaverbrook), *Politicians and the War, 1914–1916,* 2 vol. (1928–32, reprinted 1960) and *Men and Power, 1917–1918* (1956); ROBERT BLAKE, *The Unknown Prime Minister: The Life and Times of Andrew Bonar Law, 1858–1923* (1955); FRANCES STEVENSON, *Lloyd George, A Diary* (1971).

(B.)

Lobachevsky, Nikolay Ivanovich

Nikolay Ivanovich Lobachevsky, Russian mathematician, is, with his Hungarian contemporary János Bolyai, the founder of non-Euclidean geometry. This geometry is not based on Euclid's parallel postulate, according to which one and only one line can be drawn through a point in a plane parallel to a given line in the plane. First announced in 1826 and published in 1829, Lobachevsky developed it further in subsequent publications. By showing that a non-Euclidean geometry (*q.v.*) was logically possible, he and Bolyai (who published his theory in 1832) discovered the final solution of a problem— whether Euclid's parallel postulate could be deduced as a consequence of his other postulates—that had baffled mathematicians for 2,000 years. Their discovery that it could not would profoundly influence the mathematics, physics, and philosophy of the 20th century.

Novosti Press Agency

Lobachevsky, detail of a portrait by an unknown artist.

Lobachevsky was born on December 1 (November 20, old style), 1792, in Nizhny Novgorod (now Gorky), the son of an impecunious government official. His entire life centred around the University of Kazan, beginning at age 14, when he entered as a student. In 1811 he received the M.A. degree and then taught, from 1816 as extraordinary professor and from 1822 as ordinary professor.

His administrative talents were soon recognized; in 1820 he became dean of the faculty of mathematics and physics, in 1825 university librarian, and in 1827 rector of the university, a position he held, with repeated reelections, until 1846. In all of his duties, he exercised remarkable organizing and educational skill in rescuing the university from the chaotic conditions into which it had drifted. The previous administration had reflected the spirit of the later years of Tsar Alexander I, who was distrustful of modern science and philosophy, particularly that of the German philosopher Immanuel Kant, as evil products of the French Revolution and a menace to orthodox religion. The results at Kazan during the years 1819–26 were factionalism, decay of academic standards, dismissals, and departure of some of the best professors, including Johann Martin Christian Bartels, friend of the German mathematician Carl Friedrich Gauss, and Lobachevsky's teacher of mathematics.

Academic career

In 1826, a more tolerant period was inaugurated with the accession of Tsar Nicholas I, and Lobachevsky became the leading innovator at the university, restoring academic standards and faculty harmony. He was active in saving lives during the cholera epidemic of 1830, in rebuilding several university buildings after a devastating fire in 1842, and in popularizing science and modernizing primary and secondary education in the region of Kazan. Although burdened with this work, in addition to a heavy administrative teaching load, he still found time for extensive mathematical research.

Lobachevsky's ideas were rooted in his opposition to Kant's transcendental Idealism, which maintains that such ideas as space, time, and extension, are a priori, and that the mind imposes order on sense experience. For him space was an a posteriori concept, derived by the human mind from external experience.

Opposition to Kant

In addition to geometry, Lobachevsky also did distinguished work in the theory of infinite series, especially trigonometric series, integral calculus, and probability; in algebra he found, in 1834, a method for approximating the roots of algebraic equations, often called after the Swiss mathematician Carl Heinrich Gräeffe (1837).

His fame, like that of Bolyai, was posthumous. During his lifetime, few were impressed by his geometry, and the leading Russian mathematician of his day, Mikhail Vasilevich Ostrogradsky, who was well-known in western Europe, could not appreciate it. Moreover, Lobachevsky's first publications, in Russian—in 1829 in a local general periodical and in 1835–39 in the Kazan academic transactions—were little known abroad. But Lobachevsky, in contrast to Bolyai, refused to be discouraged. With characteristic perseverance he continued the publication of his ideas not only in Russian but also in French and German. In 1837 his "Géométrie imaginaire" ("Imaginary Geometry") appeared in *Crelle's Journal* (Berlin), and in 1840 his book *Geometrische Untersuchungen zur Theorie der Parallellinien* (*Geometrical Researches on the Theory of Parallels,* 1891) was published. There was no general recognition of his work, despite the praise bestowed on it by Gauss, the leading mathematician of Europe, who had reached, but never published, the same conclusions.

Toward the end of his life, nearly blind and grieved by domestic losses, Lobachevsky in 1855 once more presented his theory in French in the book *Pangéométrie,* also appearing in Russian.

He died in Kazan on February 24 (February 12, O.S.), 1856. Acceptance of non-Euclidean geometry had to wait until, under the influence of the German mathematician Bernhard Riemann's ideas on the principles underlying geometry in 1866, the Italian mathematician Eugenio Beltrami in 1868 and the German mathematician Felix Klein in 1871 demonstrated the consistency and general applicability of this geometry.

BIBLIOGRAPHY. The collected works of Lobachevsky were published in Russian, 5 vol. (1946–51). The *Geometrische Untersuchungen* of 1840 was translated by G.B. HALSTED as *Geometrical Researches on the Theory of Parallels*, new ed. (1914). It was republished in ROBERTO BONOLA, *Non-Euclidean Geometry* (1911, reprinted 1955), a good book for the study of this geometry, with biographical and bibliographical references. Halsted also published (1897) translations of Lobachevsky's early Russian papers from the German translation in F. ENGEL, *N.I. Lobatschewskij: Zwei geometrische Abhandlungen*, 2 vol. (1898–99)—vol. 2 contains an extensive biography. There is no modern biography in English, but much biographical and bibliographical information is presented in A. VUCINICH, "Nicolai Ivanovich Lobachevskii: The Man Behind The First Non-Euclidean Geometry," *Isis*, 53:465–481 (1962). SOPHIE PICCARD, *Lobatchevsky, grand mathématicien russe, sa vie, son oeuvre* (1957), is a short, popularly written account.

(D.J.S.)

Lock

A lock is a mechanical device for securing a door or receptacle so that it cannot be opened except by a key or by a series of manipulations that can be carried out only by a person knowing the secret or code.

EARLY HISTORY

The lock originated in the Near East; the oldest known example was found in the ruins of the palace of Khorsabad near Nineveh. Possibly 4,000 years old, it is of the type known as a pin-tumbler or, from its widespread use in Egypt, an Egyptian lock. It consists of a large wooden bolt, which secures the door, through which is pierced a slot with several holes in its upper surface. An assembly attached to the door contains several wooden pins positioned to drop into these holes and grip the bolt. The key is a large wooden bar, something like a toothbrush in shape; instead of bristles it has upright pegs that match the holes and the pins. Inserted in the large keyhole below the vertical pins it is simply lifted, raising the pins clear and allowing the bolt, with the key in it, to be slid back (Figure 1A). Locks of this type have been found in Japan, Norway, and the Faeroe Islands, and are still in use in Egypt, India, and Zanzibar. An Old Testament reference, in Isaiah, "And I will place on his shoulder the key of the house of David," shows how the keys were carried. The falling-pin principle, a basic feature of many locks, was developed to the full in the modern Yale lock (see below).

In a much more primitive device used by the Greeks, the bolt was moved by a sickle-shaped key of iron, often with an elaborately carved wooden handle. The key was passed through a hole in the door and turned, the point of the sickle engaging the bolt and drawing it back. Such a device could give but little security. The Romans introduced metal for locks, usually iron for the lock itself and often bronze for the key (with the result that keys are found more often today than locks). The Romans invent- **Use of** ed wards—*i.e.*, projections around the keyhole, inside the **wards** lock, which prevent the key from being rotated unless the flat face of the key (its bit) has slots cut in it in such a fashion that the projections pass through the slots. For centuries locks depended on the use of wards for security, and enormous ingenuity was employed in designing them and in cutting the keys so as to make the lock secure against any but the right key (Figure 1B). Such warded locks have always been comparatively easy to pick, since instruments can be made that clear the projections, no matter how complex. The Romans were the first to make small keys for locks—some so small that they could be worn on the fingers as rings. They also invented the padlock, which is found throughout the Near and Far East, where it was probably independently invented by the Chinese.

In the Middle Ages, great skill and a high degree of workmanship were employed in making metal locks, especially by the German metalworkers of Nürnberg. The moving parts of the locks were closely fitted and finished, and the exteriors were lavishly decorated. Even the keys were often virtual works of art. The security, however, was solely dependent on elaborate warding, the mechanism of the lock being developed hardly at all. One

refinement was to conceal the keyhole by secret shutters, another was to provide blind keyholes, which forced the lock picker to waste time and effort. The 18th-century French excelled in making beautiful and intricate locks.

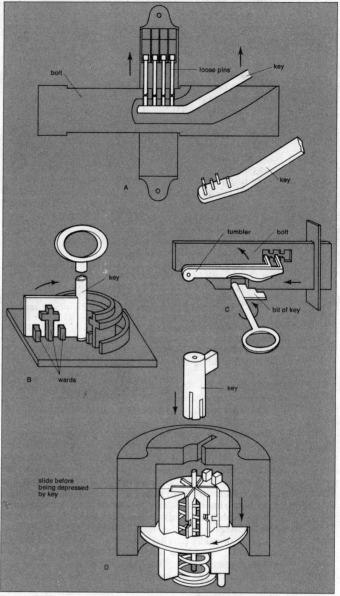

After F.P. Gillman

Figure 1: *Early lock types.*
(A) Ancient Egyptian lock. (B) Warded lock and key. (C) The Barron tumbler lock, 1778. (D) The Bramah lock, 1784.

DEVELOPMENT OF MODERN LOCK TYPES

The Barron lock. The first serious attempt to improve the security of the lock was made in 1778 when Robert Barron, in England, patented a double-acting tumbler lock. A tumbler is a lever, or pawl, that falls into a slot in the bolt and prevents it being moved until it is raised by the key to exactly the right height out of the slot; the key then slides the bolt. The Barron lock (see Figure 1C) had two tumblers and the key had to raise each tumbler by a different amount before the bolts could be shot. This enormous advance in lock design remains the basic principle of all lever locks.

The Chubb lock. But even the Barron lock offered little resistance to the determined lock picker, and in 1818 Jeremiah Chubb of Portsmouth, England, improved on the tumbler lock by incorporating a detector, a retaining spring that caught and held any tumbler which, in the course of picking, had been raised too high. This alone prevented the bolt from being withdrawn and also showed that the lock had been tampered with.

The Bramah lock. In 1784 (between Barron's lock and Chubb's improvements on it) a remarkable lock was patented in England by Joseph Bramah. Working on an entirely different principle, it used a very small light key, yet gave an unprecedented amount of security. Bramah's locks are very intricate (hence, expensive to make), and for their manufacture Bramah and his young assistant Henry Maudslay (later to become a famous engineer) constructed a series of machines to produce the parts mechanically. These were among the first machine tools designed for mass production. The Bramah key is a small metal tube that has narrow longitudinal slots cut in its end. When the key is pushed into the lock, it depresses a number of slides, each to the depth controlled by the slots. Only when all the slides are depressed to exactly the right distance can the key be turned and the bolt thrown (Figure 1D). So confident was Bramah of the security of his lock that he exhibited one in his London shop and offered a reward of £200 to the first person who could open it. For over 50 years it remained unpicked, until 1851 when a skilled American locksmith, A.C. Hobbs, succeeded and claimed the reward.

Lockmaking in the mid-19th century. The lock industry was in its heyday in the mid-19th century. With the rapidly expanding economy that followed the Industrial Revolution, the demand for locks grew tremendously.

The Newell lock. In this period lock patents came thick and fast. All incorporated ingenious variations on the lever or Bramah principles. The most interesting was Robert Newell's Parautoptic lock made by the firm of Day and Newell of New York. Its special feature was that not only did it have two sets of lever tumblers, the first working on the second, but it also incorporated a plate that revolved with the key and prevented the inspection of the interior, an important step in thwarting the lock picker. It also had a key with interchangeable bits so that the key could be readily altered. Newell displayed an example in London in the Great Exhibition of 1851. Despite many attempts, there is no record that it has ever been picked.

The Yale lock. In 1848 a far-reaching contribution was made by an American, Linus Yale, who patented a pin tumbler lock working on an adaptation of the ancient Egyptian principle. In the 1860s his son Linus Yale, Jr., evolved the Yale cylinder lock, with its small, flat key with serrated edge, now probably the most familiar lock and key in the world. Pins in the cylinder are raised to the proper heights by the serrations, making it possible to turn the cylinder. The number of combinations of heights of the pins (usually five), coupled with the warding effect of the crooked key and keyhole, give an almost unlimited number of variations (see Figure 2). It has come to be

After F.P. Gillman

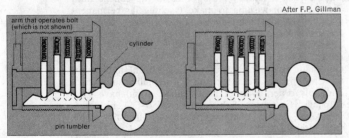

Figure 2: Contemporary version of the Yale lock, patented in the 1860s: (Left) Correct key lifts all pins to proper height and key can be turned. (Right) Wrong key lifts pins to incorrect height and lock will not open.

almost universally used for outside doors of buildings and automobile doors, although in the 1960s there was a trend toward supplementing it on house doors with the sturdy lever lock.

Time locks. In the 1870s a new criminal technique swept the United States: robbers seized bank cashiers and forced them to yield keys or combinations to safes and vaults. To combat this type of crime, James Sargent of Rochester, New York, in 1873 devised a lock based on a principle patented earlier in Scotland, incorporating a clock that permitted the safe to be opened only at a preset time.

Combination locks. The keyless combination lock derives from the "letter-lock," in use in England at the beginning of the 17th century. In it a number of rings (inscribed with letters or numbers) are threaded on a spindle; when the rings are turned so that a particular word or number is formed, the spindle can be drawn out because slots inside the rings all fall in line. Originally, these letter locks were used only for padlocks and trick boxes. In the last half of the 19th century, as developed for safes and strong-room doors, they proved to be the most secure form of closure. The number of possible combinations of letters or numbers is almost infinite and they have no keyholes into which an explosive charge can be placed. Furthermore, they are easy to manufacture.

A simple combination lock with four rings (tumblers, in the U.S.) and 100 numbers on the dial (*i.e.*, 100 positions for each ring) presents 100,000,000 possible combinations. Figure 3 shows how the single knob can set all the wheels; in this case the lock has three rings, or wheels, giving 1,000,000 possible combinations. If, for example,

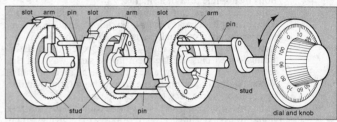

Figure 3: Combination safe lock. The lock cannot be opened until the slots of the three wheels are in line. The movement of the dial is transmitted to each wheel by a system of pins (in practice much shorter than shown), arms, and studs.

the combination is 48, 15, 90, the knob is turned counterclockwise until the 48 comes opposite the arrow for the fourth time, a process that ensures that there is no play between the other wheels. The slot on the first wheel (on the left in the diagram) is then in the correct position for opening and it will not move in subsequent operations. The knob is then turned clockwise until the 15 is opposite the arrow for the third time; this sets the slot of the middle wheel in line with the first. Finally, the knob is turned counterclockwise to bring the 90 for the second time to the arrow. All three slots are then in line and a handle can be turned to withdraw the bolts. The combination can easily be changed, for the serrations shown on each wheel enable the slot to be set to a different position relative to the stud for that wheel.

Master keys. It is frequently necessary, particularly in hotels and office buildings, for a manager or caretaker to have a master key that will open all the locks in the building. To design a set of single locks each of which can be opened by its own key, and also by the master key, requires a coordinated arrangement of the warding. The master key is so shaped as to avoid the wards of all the locks. Another method involves two keyholes, one for the normal key, the other for the master key, or two sets of tumblers or levers, or in the case of Yale locks, two concentric cylinders.

Electronic elements. In the 1960s an electronic cash dispenser for banks was introduced. This system allows a customer to withdraw money when the bank is closed. The customer has a personal card that is coded with magnetic and other markings. He inserts the card into the machine, located in the wall of the bank. The card is drawn inside and automatically checked for genuineness. The customer then sets up his personal account number (not marked on the card) by pressing a series of numbered buttons. This is also checked electronically and, if correct, a fixed amount of cash is ejected. The card remains within and is later returned to the customer by mail. The whole device constitutes a lock, but it is not a mechanical device, since all the information given by the card, which constitutes the key, is sorted by electronic circuits. Other electronic devices are being increasingly used in connection with security systems (see POLICE TECHNOLOGY).

Tube-like key of the Bramah lock

Possible combinations in multiple-ring locks

Basic
types
remaining
in use

Present status of locks and safes. Over the years, locks have been constructed with many specialized functions. Some have been designed to resist being blown open, others to shoot or stab intruders or seize their hands. Locks have been made that can be opened or closed by different keys but can be unlocked only by the key that closed them. So-called unpickable locks are usually devised to prevent a thief from exploring the positions of the lock parts from the keyhole or from sensing with his picking tool slight changes of resistance when pressure is applied to the bolt. The basic types, however, remain the Bramah, lever, Yale, and combination locks, though innumerable variations have been made, sometimes combining features of each. The Swiss Kaba lock, for example, employs the Yale principle but instead of having a serrated-edge key, the flat sides of the key are marked with deep depressions into which four complete sets of pin-tumblers are pressed. The Finnish Abloy lock is a compact combination lock, but the rings, instead of being turned separately by hand, are moved to the correct positions by a single turn of a small key.

Magnetic forces can be used in locks working on the Yale principle. The key has no serrations; instead, it contains a number of small magnets. When the key is inserted into the lock, these magnets repel magnetized spring-loaded pins, raising them in the same way that the serrations on a Yale-type key raise them mechanically. When these pins are raised the correct height, the cylinder of the lock is free to rotate in the barrel.

The importance of locks as a protection against professional thieves declined after World War II, during which the knowledge and use of explosives was widely disseminated. As most safe locks and strong-room locks became almost unpickable, criminals tended to ignore the locks and to use explosives to blow them off. An attempt to blow up the mechanism of a lock by detonating an explosive in the keyhole can be foiled by introducing a second series of bolts, not connected to the lock mechanism, but automatically inserted by springs when an explosion occurs; the safe then cannot be opened except by cutting through the armour.

Another method used by criminals is to burn away the plating or hinge of a safe by an electric arc or an oxyacetylene flame, an operation requiring many hours' work. To resist this type of entry, safe makers produced even more resistant materials and new methods of construction to carry away the heat of the cutting flame.

BIBLIOGRAPHY. G. PRICE, *A Treatise on Fire and Thief-Proof Depositories, and Locks and Keys* (1856); and C. TOMLINSON (ed.), *Rudimentary Treatise on the Construction of Locks* (1853, 1868), are the classic books on the history of locks and their mechanisms up to the mid-19th century (fully illustrated). For a great variety of types of locks, especially American locks, see A.A. HOPKINS, *The Lure of the Lock* (1928), a catalogue of the Mossman collection in New York that also includes historical notes and interesting, illustrated accounts of great robberies. V.J.M. ERAS, *Sloten en Sleutels door de eeuween Heen* (1941; Eng. trans., *Locks and Keys Throughout the Ages*, 1957), is an account of the Lips collection of locks at their factory in Dordrecht, The Netherlands. It also contains illustrations and descriptions of locks from many other collections throughout the world. J. PARKES AND SONS, LTD., *An Encyclopaedia of Locks and Builders' Hardware*, comp. by F.J. BUTTER (1958), is in the form of a lexicon and is an indispensable guide to the vocabulary and nomenclature of the locksmith's craft. For descriptions of the latest developments in locks and the announcement of new varieties, see the weekly London journals *The Engineer* and *Engineering*.

(G.B.L.W.)

Locke, John

John Locke was an English philosopher who was expert in many fields, more particularly in epistemology (theory of knowledge), politics, education, and medicine. His chief contributions were, first, a clear and emphatic formulation of the social and political principles that, in his opinion, emerged from the turbulence of 17th-century Britain and, second, an account of human knowledge, including his examination of the "new science" of his day—*i.e.*, of modern science.

Locke, oil painting by Sir Godfrey Kneller (1646/49–1723). In Christ Church, Oxford.
By courtesy of the Governing Body of Christ Church, Oxford

Early life. Locke was born in Wrington, Somerset, on August 29, 1632, and reared in Pensford, six miles south of Bristol. His family was Anglican with Puritan leanings. His father was a country attorney of modest means who fought on the Parliamentarian side in the Civil War —a fact that later helped him to find a place for his son in Westminster School, then controlled by a Parliamentarian committee (though its headmaster, Dr. Richard Busby, was a Royalist). The training there was thorough, but Locke later complained of the severity of its discipline. In 1652 Locke entered Christ Church, Oxford. Though the Puritans, led by the eminent John Owen, had introduced some reforms into Oxford life, they had made little change in the traditional curriculum of rhetoric, grammar, moral philosophy, geometry, and Greek, and Locke found the course insipid. Nonetheless, this link with traditional Scholastic methods was not wholly valueless. He graduated B.A. in 1656 and M.A. two years later.

Student
years

During his student years Locke had interested himself in studies not in the traditional curriculum; in particular, he had been drawn to experimental science (brilliantly taught at Oxford by John Wilkins) and to medicine. In 1660, the year of the restoration of the monarchy, Locke was appointed a tutor in Christ Church. He remained a student (*i.e.*, a fellow) with rooms in the college until 1684; but, not wishing to make teaching his permanent vocation, he taught undergraduates for four years only. He gained some experience in diplomacy as secretary to a diplomatic mission to Brandenburg in 1665, and on his return he was immediately offered, but refused, another diplomatic post. Nor did he feel called to the ministry of the Church, a fact that for him was definitive since entry into holy orders without being called would have been culpable. His papers of this period (1656–66), his correspondence, and his commonplace books all testify to his chief interests at the time, viz., natural science, on the one hand, and the study of the underlying principles of moral, social, and political life, on the other. In the latter connection, his "Essays on the Law of Nature," which he wrote in 1663–64 but never published, indicate how far this study had then proceeded. To remedy the narrowness of his education he read contemporary philosophy, particularly that of René Descartes, the father of modern philosophy. But more than all, experimental science engaged his interest. He collaborated with Robert Boyle, one of the founders of modern chemistry, who was a close friend, and, toward the end of the period, with another friend, Thomas Sydenham, an eminent medical scientist.

Association with Shaftesbury. It was as a physician that Locke first came to the notice of the statesman Lord Ashley (later to become the 1st earl of Shaftesbury), who at once recognized his worth and in 1667 invited him to become part of his household staff serving as physician. Locke accepted the invitation and very soon was Ashley's personal adviser not merely on medical matters but on his general affairs as well. Ashley was a forceful, aggressive politician who had many enemies (some of them men of letters—for instance, Locke's schoolfellow, the poet laureate John Dryden). It is doubtful, however—if only in view of Locke's respect for him—whether Ashley was as evil as his enemies sometimes made him out to be. It is known that he stood firmly for a constitutional monarchy, for a Protestant succession, for civil liberty, for toleration in religion, for the rule of Parliament, and for the economic expansion of Britain; and that he continued to make this stand when many influential men were working against these aims. Since these were already aims to which Locke had dedicated himself, there existed from the first a perfect understanding between the statesman and his adviser, one that meant much to both. Ashley entrusted Locke with the task of negotiating his son's marriage with the daughter of the Earl of Rutland; he also made him secretary of the group that he had formed to increase trade with America, particularly with the southern colonies.

Private studies and discussions

During the following decades, Locke persevered in his private studies, and many of his social meetings were in effect meetings with friends to discuss philosophical and scientific problems. As early as 1668 he had become a fellow of the newly formed (1663) Royal Society, which kept him in touch with scientific advances. It is known, too, that groups of friends met in his rooms (Lord Ashley; John Mapletoft; Thomas Sydenham; Sydenham's physician colleague, James Tyrrell, who was also a divine; and others), for one of its meetings is mentioned in the preface of his *Essay Concerning Human Understanding*, in which he reports that, because of the difficulties that beset the participants, they resolved to devote their next meeting to discussing the powers of the mind in order, as they said, "to examine our own abilities and see what objects our understandings were, or were not, fitted to deal with." Locke himself opened the discussion and, following the meeting, set out his view of human knowledge in two drafts (1671), still extant, which show the beginnings of the thinking that 19 years later would blossom into his famous *Essay*. In these London years, too, Locke encountered representatives of Cambridge Platonism, a school of Christian humanists, who, though sympathetic to empirical science, nonetheless opposed Materialism because it failed to account for the rational element in human life. They tended to be liberal both in politics and religion. Insofar as they taught a Platonism that rested on belief in innately known Ideas, Locke could not follow them; but their tolerance, their emphasis on practical conduct as a part of the religious life, and their rejection of Materialism were features that he found most attractive. This school was closely related in spirit to another school that influenced Locke at this time, viz., that of Latitudinarianism. For the latter school, if a man confessed Christ, that alone should be enough to entitle him to membership in the Christian Church; conformity in nonessentials should not be demanded. These movements prepared Locke for the anti-dogmatic, liberal school of theology that he would later encounter in Holland, a school in revolt against the narrowness of traditional Calvinism.

In 1672 Ashley was raised to the peerage as the 1st Lord Shaftesbury and at the end of that year was appointed lord high chancellor of England. Though he soon lost favour and was dismissed, he did, while in office, establish the Council of Trade and Plantations, of which Locke was secretary for two years. Locke, however, who suffered greatly from asthma, found the London air and his heavy duties unhealthful; and in 1675 he had to return to Oxford.

Intellectual contacts in France

Six months later he departed for France, where he stayed for four years (1675–79), spending most of his time at Paris and Montpellier. In France during the 1670s, Locke made contacts that deeply influenced his view of metaphysics (the nature of being) and epistemology, viz., with the Gassendist school, and particularly with

its leader, François Bernier. Pierre Gassendi, a philosopher and scientist, had rejected overspeculative elements in Descartes's philosophy and had advocated a return to Epicurean doctrines—*i.e.*, to empiricism (stressing sense experience), to hedonism (holding pleasure to be the good), and to corpuscular physics (with reality made of atomic particles). Knowledge of the external world, Gassendi held, depends upon the senses, though it is through reasoning that man may derive much further information from empirically gained evidence.

Upon Locke's return to England, he found the country torn by dissension. The heir to the throne, James (the brother of Charles II), was a Catholic, whom the Protestant majority led by Shaftesbury wished to exclude from the succession. For a year Shaftesbury had been imprisoned in the Tower, but by the time Locke returned he was back in favour once more as lord president of the Privy Council. When he failed, however, to reconcile the interests of the King and Parliament, he was dismissed; in 1681 he was arrested, tried, and finally acquitted by a London jury. A year later he fled to Holland, where, in 1683, he died.

Later life. No one of Shaftesbury's known friends was now safe in Britain; and Locke himself, who was being closely watched, crossed to Holland in September 1683.

Exile in Holland. Locke remained in Holland for over five years, until James II, who had become king in 1685, was overthrown. As an exile Locke's sojourn in Holland was happier than he had expected it to be: his health improved, he made many new friends, and he found the leisure that enabled him to bring his thoughts on many subjects to fruition. Locke spent his first winter in Amsterdam and soon became friendly with a distinguished Arminian theologian, Philip van Limborch, pastor of the Remonstrants' church there—a friendship that lasted till Locke's death. The companionship of Philip and other friends made it easier to bear bad news from home: at Charles II's express command, Locke (in 1684) was deprived of his studentship at Christ Church. The next year his name appeared on a list sent to The Hague that named 84 traitors wanted by the English government. Locke went into hiding for a while, but soon was able to move freely over Holland and became familiar with its different provinces.

Return to England and retirement to Oates. In the autumn of 1688, William left for England; and Locke himself in February 1689 crossed in the party that accompanied the Princess of Orange, now to be crowned Queen Mary II of England. The triumph was complete; Locke was home again, although not without a nostalgia for the Holland that he had come to love. He now took little part in public life. He refused ambassadorial posts but accepted a membership in the Commission of Appeals. (Much later, in 1696, he was appointed a commissioner in the resuscitated Board of Trade and Plantations, however, and for four years played a leading part in its deliberations.) But the London air again bothered him, and he was forced to leave the city for long visits to his friends in the country. In 1691 he retired to Oates in Essex, to the house of his friends Sir Francis and Lady Masham, and subsequently made only occasional visits to London. Nonetheless, he was not without influence in these last years of his life (1689–1704), for he was the intellectual leader of the Whigs. Their principal parliamentarians were frequently old friends of Locke, and the younger generation—particularly the ablest of them all, John Somers, who soon became lord chancellor—turned to him constantly for guidance. In "the glorious, bloodless revolution," the main aims for which Shaftesbury and Locke had fought were achieved—even though in William's reign strong Tory pressures limited the extent of the reform. First and foremost, England became a constitutional monarchy, controlled by Parliament. Second, real advances were made in securing the liberty of the subject in the law courts, in achieving a greater (though far from complete) measure of religious toleration, and in assuring freedom of thought and expression. Locke himself drafted the arguments that his friend Edward Clarke used in the House of Commons in arguing

Influence during retirement

for the repeal of the restrictive Act for the Regulation of Printing. The act was abolished in 1695 and the freedom of the press secured. These were major reforms.

Publication of his works. The main task of this last period of his life, however, was the publication of his works, which had been the product of long years of gestation. The *Epistola de Tolerantia* (Eng. trans., *A Letter Concerning Toleration,* 1689) was published anonymously at Gouda in 1689. Locke had been reflecting on this topic from his early days at Oxford. Though his correspondence and a paper that he wrote in 1667 show his support for toleration, in 1660–61 he wrote two tracts on this theme (published in 1967), which are surprisingly conservative. How he came to write them is rather mysterious. The 1667 paper is very much in line with the 1689 *Letter* in its demand for toleration of religion: (1) No man has such complete wisdom and knowledge, he held, that he can dictate the form of another man's religion; (2) each individual is a moral being, responsible before God, and this presupposes freedom; and (3) no compulsion that is contrary to the will of the individual can secure more than an outward conformity. *Two Treatises of Government* (1690) was also the fruit of years of reflection upon the true principles in politics, a reflection resting on Locke's own observations. Government, Locke held, is a trust; its purpose is the security of the citizen's person and property; and the subject has the right to withdraw his confidence in the ruler when the latter fails in his task. Government and political power are necessary, but so is the liberty of the citizen; and in a democratic, constitutional monarchy, a type of government is possible in which the people are still free.

In all of these social and political issues, Locke saw that the ultimate factor is man's nature. To understand man, however, it is not enough to observe his actions; one must also inquire about his capacities for knowledge. Locke had been conscious of this point in writing his paper on the *Law of Nature* as early as 1663. In 1671, as has been seen, he set out to write a book about human knowledge, the *Essay,* which was not published, however, until 1690—nor was it wholly completed even then, for Locke made changes, sometimes substantial ones, in three of the four following editions.

Development of his epistemology. Epistemology was a main concern in the last 30 years of his life. Human knowledge, he argued, rests (1) on the experience of the external world acquired through the senses, and (2) on that of the inner world of psychical happenings achieved through introspection (or, in Locke's terminology, "reflection"). The empirical knowledge derived from these sources is uncertain and never provides more than probability, whereas the ideal of knowledge is certainty. In Locke's opinion, this ideal is in fact attainable in some fields—for instance, in mathematics. Though knowledge originates in sensory and introspective experience, this is only the beginning; for many other factors are to be attended to as well—factors such as the reasoning that enables a person to derive, from empirically based propositions, more general conclusions about the world, both physical and mental. Such reasoning may be inductive (resting on the assumption that what usually happens always happens) or it may be deductive. Mathematical reasoning, for example, is deductive; and this kind of knowledge is only to be understood, Locke believed, in terms of an intellectual intuition of relations between ideas, which, though empirically derived, have the status of defined archetypes of such a nature that their empirical reference is irrelevant. In addition, the knower, by means of intuition, can discern the relations between statements that warrant the drawing of inferences. Through such intellectual intuitions, necessary and universal knowledge is possible. To facilitate his presentation of this theory, Locke considered the nature of (1) idea and (2) language. He concluded that, in the case of human beings, intuitive knowledge is limited in extent; for the most part, knowledge is only probable, and Locke examined the degrees of probability and the nature of evidence. He acknowledged that the natural sciences cannot give complete certainty: nonetheless, careful reasoning, with the application of mathematical reasoning wherever possible, will heighten the probability of attaining true knowledge in these fields. In the *Essay,* Locke set down the foundations of an epistemology of modern science.

Last years. Locke's last years were spent in the peaceful retreat of Oates. His hostess was a woman with whom he had been acquainted for many years, viz., Lady Masham, or Damaris, the daughter of Ralph Cudworth, one of the Cambridge Platonists, by whom Locke had been significantly influenced. He found friendship and comfort in this household, for which he never ceased to be thankful. Many of his friends visited him here: Sir Isaac Newton, who came to discuss the Epistles of Saint Paul, a subject of great interest to both; his nephew and heir Peter King, destined to become lord high chancellor of England; and Edward Clarke with his wife and children, Edward and Elizabeth, for whom Locke had great affection (as he had, too, for the children of the Oates household). Locke had written a series of letters to Edward Clarke from Holland, advising him on the best upbringing for his son. These letters formed the basis of his influential *Some Thoughts Concerning Education* (1693), setting forth new ideals in that field. He wrote and published pamphlets on matters of economic interest, on rates of interest, on the coinage of the realm, and more widely on trade (defending mercantilist views). In 1695 he published a dignified plea for a less dogmatic Christianity in *The Reasonableness of Christianity.* It is, finally, interesting to note that Locke never produced a book on morals, though this subject was possibly his greatest interest: for in this field he never succeeded in working out a coherent theory that would reconcile differences within his thinking.

John Locke died on October 28, 1704, and was buried in the parish church of High Laver. "His death," wrote Damaris Cudworth, "was like his life, truly pious, yet natural, easy and unaffected." This account of his character by one who knew him well seems singularly appropriate. There is adequate evidence of his piety, as there is of his natural simplicity, grace, and unaffectedness. He was orderly, careful about money, occasionally parsimonious, abstemious, and, though naturally emotional and hot-tempered, controlled and disciplined. He had a great love of children, and friendship was for him a necessity. Both in his books and in his life are found the marks of the prudence and wisdom for which he was famed.

MAJOR WORKS

PHILOSOPHY AND RELIGION: *Essays on the Law of Nature* (eight essays written *c.* 1662–64 in Latin with various Latin titles; first published, with Eng. trans., in 1954); *An Essay Concerning Human Understanding* (1690); *Epistola de Tolerantia* (1689; *A Letter Concerning Toleration,* 1689); *A Second Letter Concerning Toleration* (1690); *A Third Letter for Toleration* (1692); *The Reasonableness of Christianity* (1695); *Some Thoughts on the Conduct of the Understanding in the Search of Truth* (1762).

POLITICAL PHILOSOPHY AND ECONOMICS: *Two Treatises of Government* (1690); *Some Considerations of the Consequences of the Lowering of Interest, and Raising the Value of Money* (1692); *Short Observations on a Printed Paper, Intituled "For Encouraging the Coining of Silver Money in England"* (1695); *Further Considerations Concerning Raising the Value of Money* (1695).

EDUCATION: *Some Thoughts Concerning Education* (1693).

BIBLIOGRAPHY. HANS O. CHRISTOPHERSEN, *A Bibliographical Introduction to the Study of John Locke* (1930). At present, no modern standard edition of Locke's works exists, but the first volume of the Oxford edition is expected to appear soon.

Biography: PETER KING, *The Life of John Locke* (1829, fuller edition 1830), a poor biography, but King possessed and quoted from what is now known as the Lovelace Collection of Locke papers, and this gives the book great value; H.R. FOX BOURNE, *The Life of John Locke* (1876), an excellent study, still indispensable though not now definitive; MAURICE W. CRANSTON, *John Locke: A Biography* (1957), the best and most up-to-date biography, very readable and most illuminating.

On Locke's philosophy: RICHARD I. AARON, *John Locke,*

Later writings

Ideas of sense and of reflection

3rd ed. (1971), a general study, with bibliography; SAMUEL ALEXANDER, *Locke*, "Philosophies Ancient and Modern Series" (1908), brief, but a jewel; D.J. O'CONNOR, *John Locke* (1952), a concise, enlightening, and well-written introductory commentary; J. GIBSON, *Locke's Theory of Knowledge and Its Historical Relations* (1917), a thorough study of the topic; J.W. YOLTON, *John Locke and the Way of Ideas* (1956), much information on Locke's sources and early critics.

(R.Aa.)

Locomotion

Animals are, by definition, motile organisms. Large or small, their locomotor ability is expressed by their structural organization, from external shape to tissue and cell morphology. A fusiform (tapering) body, for example, suggests speed and a high level of activity, whether this shape is possessed by a protozoan (one-celled animal), molluskan (*e.g.*, squid), insect, or vertebrate. In contrast, a globular body enclosed in a protective shell, such as a clam, indicates slow or sedentary habits. Animals, however, are not machines; each individual is a precisely blended and balanced amalgamation of structures that enable it to perform the many functions necessary for its survival and reproduction. The fact that an animal's structure clearly reflects locomotor habits indicates the importance of mobility in all phases of its life.

GENERAL CONSIDERATIONS ABOUT LOCOMOTION

To locomote, all animals require both propulsive and control mechanisms. The diversity of animal propulsive mechanisms, all of which involve a contractile structure —muscle in most cases—to generate a propulsive force, are dealt with in the sections that follow. The quantity, quality, and position of contractions are initiated and coordinated by the nervous system: through this coordination, rhythmic movements of the appendages or body produce locomotion. Control of locomotion by the nervous system, locomotion as a learned behaviour, and physiological problems associated with locomotion, such as temperature control, metabolism, nutrition, and respiration, are described elsewhere in the articles NERVES AND NERVOUS SYSTEMS; BEHAVIOUR, ANIMAL; MUSCLE SYSTEMS; and MUSCLE CONTRACTION.

Physical restraints to movement. Animals successfully occupy a majority of the vast number of different physical environments (ecological niches) on earth; in a discussion of locomotion, however, these environments can be divided into four types: aerial (including arboreal), aquatic, fossorial (underground), and terrestrial. The physical restraints to movement—gravity and drag—are the same in each environment: they differ only in degree. Gravity is here considered as the weight and inertia (resistance to motion) of a body, drag as any force reducing movement. Although these are not the definitions of a physicist, they are adequate for a general understanding of the forces that impede animal locomotion.

Gravity. To counteract the force of gravity, which is particularly important in aerial, fossorial, and terrestrial locomotion, all animals that live in these three environments have evolved skeletal systems to support their body and to prevent the body from collapsing upon itself. The skeletal system may be internal or external, and it may act either as a rigid framework or as a flexible hydraulic (fluid) support.

To initiate movement, a sufficient amount of muscular work must be performed by aerial, fossorial, and terrestrial animals to overcome inertia. Aquatic animals

Buoyancy must also overcome inertia; the buoyancy of water, however, reduces the influence of gravity on movement. Actually, because many aquatic animals are weightless— *i.e.*, they possess neutral buoyancy by displacing a volume of water that is equal in weight to their dry weight —little muscular work is needed to overcome inertia. But not all aquatic animals are weightless. Those with negative buoyancy sink as a result of their weight; hence, the greater their weight, the more muscular energy they must expend to remain at a given level. Conversely, an animal with positive buoyancy floats to and rests on the surface, and must expend muscular energy to remain submerged.

Drag. In water, the primary force that retards or resists forward movement is drag, the amount of which depends upon the animal's shape and how that shape cleaves the water. Drag results mainly from the friction of the water as it flows over the surface of the animal and the adherence of the water to the animal's surface (*i.e.*, the viscosity of the water). Because of the water's viscosity, its flow tends to be lamellar; *i.e.*, different layers of the water flow at different speeds, with the slowest layer of flow being the one adjacent to the body surface. As the flow speed increases, the lamellar pattern is lost, and turbulence develops, thereby increasing the drag.

Another component of drag is the retardation of forward movement by the backward pull of the eddies of water behind the tail of the animal. As they flow off an animal, the layers of water from each side meet and blend. If the animal is streamlined (*e.g.*, has a fusiform shape), the turbulence is low; if, however, the water layers from the sides meet abruptly and with different speeds, the turbulence is high, causing a strong backward pull, or drag, on the animal.

Aerial locomotion also encounters resistance from drag, but, because the viscosity and density of air are much less than those of water, drag is also less. The lamellar flow of air across the wing surfaces is, however, extremely important. The upward force of flight, or lift, results from   Lift air flowing faster across the upper surface than across the   and drag lower surface of the wing. Because this differential in flow produces a lower air pressure on the upper surface, the animal rises. Lift is also produced by the flow of water across surfaces, but aquatic animals use the lift as a steering aid rather than as a source of propulsion.

Drag is generally considered a negligible influence in terrestrial locomotion; and, in fossorial locomotion, the friction and compactness (friability) of soils are the two major restraints. If the soil is extremely friable, as is sand, some animals can "swim" through it. Such fossorial locomotion, however, is quite rare; most fossorial animals must laboriously tunnel through the soil and thereafter depend upon the tunnels for active locomotion.

Axial and appendicular locomotion. Movement in animals is achieved by two types of locomotion, axial and appendicular. In axial locomotion, which includes the hydraulic ramjet method of ejecting water (*e.g.*, squid), production of a body wave (eel), or the contract–anchor–extend method (leech), the body shape is modified, and the interaction of the entire body with the surrounding environment provides the propulsive force. In appendicular locomotion, on the other hand, special body appendages interact with the environment to produce the propulsive force.

There are also many species of animals that depend upon their environment for transportation, a type of mobility that is called passive locomotion. Some jellyfish, for example, develop structures called floats that extend above the water's surface and act as sails. A few spiders have developed an elaborate means of kiting; when a strand of their web silk reaches a certain length after being extended into the air, the wind resistance of the strand is sufficient to lift and carry it away with the attached spider. In one fish, the remora, the dorsal (top) fin has moved to the top of the head and become modified into a sucker; by attaching itself to a larger fish, the remora is able to ride to its next meal.

AQUATIC LOCOMOTION

Micro-organisms. Most motile protozoans, which are strictly aquatic animals, move by locomotion involving one of three types of appendages: flagella, cilia, or pseudopodia. Cilia and flagella are indistinguishable in that both are flexible filamentous structures containing two central fibrils (very small fibres) surrounded by a ring of nine double fibrils. The peripheral fibrils seem to be the contractile units and the central ones, neuromotor (nervelike) units. Generally, cilia are short and flagella long, although the size ranges of each overlap.

Flagellar locomotion. Most flagellate protozoans possess either one or two flagella extending from the anterior (front) end of the body. Some protozoans, however,

Types of flagellar movement

have several flagella that may be scattered over the entire body; in such cases, the flagella usually are fused into distinctly separate clusters. Flagellar movement, or locomotion, occurs as either planar waves, oarlike beating, or three-dimensional waves. All three of these forms of flagellar locomotion consist of contraction waves that pass either from the base to the tip of the flagellum or in the reverse direction to produce forward or backward movement. The planar waves, which occur along a single plane and are similar to a sinusoid (S-shaped) wave form, tend to be asymmetrical; there is a gradual increase in amplitude (peak of the wave) as the wave passes to the tip of the flagellum. In planar locomotion the motion of the flagella is equivalent to that of the body of an eel as it swims. Although symmetrical planar waves have been observed, they apparently are abnormal, because the locomotion they produce is erratic. Planar waves cause the protozoan to rotate on its longitudinal axis, the path of movement tends to be helical (a spiral), and the direction of movement is opposite the propagation direction of the wave.

In oarlike flagellar movements, which are also planar, the waves tend to be highly asymmetrical, of greater side to side swing, and the protozoan usually rotates and moves with the flagellum at the forward end. In the three-dimensional wave form of flagellar movement, the motion of the flagella is similar to that of an airplane propeller; i.e., the flagella lash from side to side. The flagellum rotates in a conical configuration, the apex (tip) of which centres on the point at which the flagellum is attached to the body. Simultaneous with the conical rotation, asymmetrical sinusoidal waves pass from the base to the end of the flagellum. As a result of the flagellar rotation and its changing angle of contact, water is forced backward over the protozoan, which also tends to rotate, and the organism moves forward in the direction of the flagellum.

Ciliary locomotion. Cilia operate like flexible oars; they have a unilateral (one-sided) beat lying in a single plane. As a cilium moves backward, it is relatively rigid; upon recovery, however, the cilium becomes flexible, and its tip appears to be dragged forward along the body. Because the cilia either completely cover as in ciliate protozoans or are arranged in bands or clumps, the movement of each cilium must be closely coordinated with the movements of all other cilia. This coordination

Meta-chronal rhythm

is achieved by metachronal rhythm, in which a wave of simultaneously beating groups of cilia moves from the anterior to the posterior end of the organism. In addition to avoiding interference between adjacent cilia, the metachronal wave also produces continuous forward locomotion because there are always groups of cilia beating backward. Moreover, because the plane of the ciliary beat is diagonal to the longitudinal axis of the body, ciliate organisms rotate during locomotion.

Pseudopodial locomotion. Although ciliar and flagellar locomotion are clearly forms of appendicular locomotion, pseudopodial locomotion (Figure 1) can be classed as either axial or appendicular, depending upon the definition of the pseudopodium. Outwardly, pseudopodial locomotion appears to be the extension of a part of the body that anchors itself and then pulls the remainder of the body forward. Internally, however, the movement is quite different. The amoeba, a protozoan, may be taken as an example. Its cytoplasm (the living substance surrounding the nucleus) is divided into two parts: a peripheral layer, or ectoplasm, of gel (a semisolid, jellylike substance) enclosing an inner mass, or endoplasm, of sol (a fluid containing suspended particles; i.e., a colloid). As a pseudopodium, part of the ectoplasmic gel is converted to sol, whereupon endoplasm begins flowing toward this area, the cell wall expands, and the pseudopodium is extended forward. When the endoplasm, which continues to flow into the pseudopodium, reaches the tip, it extends laterally and is transformed to a gel. Basically, the movement is one of extending an appendage and then emptying the body into the appendage, thereby converting the latter into the former. Although the flow of the cytoplasm is produced by the same pro-

teins involved in the mechanism of muscle contraction, the actual molecular basis of the mechanism is not yet known. Even the mechanics of pseudopodial formation are not completely understood.

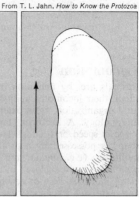

From T. L. Jahn, *How to Know the Protozoa*

ectoplasm — endoplasm

Figure 1: *Pseudopodial locomotion.*
Arrows indicate the direction of cytoplasmic flow (see text).

Undulating and gliding locomotion. Two other types of locomotion are observed occasionally in protozoans. Some protozoans, usually flagellates, have along their bodies a longitudinal membrane that undulates, thereby producing a slow forward locomotion. A gliding locomotion is commonly seen in some sporozoans (parasitic protozoans), in which the organism glides forward with no change in form and no apparent contractions of the body. Initially, the movement was thought to be produced by ejecting mucus, a slimy secretion; small contractile fibrils have been found that produce minute contraction waves that move the animal forward.

Invertebrates. As in the protozoans, aquatic locomotion in invertebrates (animals without backbones) consists of both swimming and bottom movements. When swimming, the propulsive force is derived entirely from the interaction between the organism and the water; in bottom movements, the bottom surface provides the interacting surface. Whereas some bottom movements are identical with terrestrial locomotor patterns, others can occur effectively only in the water, where buoyancy is necessary to reduce body weight.

Bottom locomotion. Small flatworms (Platyhelminthes) and some of the smaller molluskan species move along the bottom by ciliary activity. On their ventral (bottom) surface, a dense coat of cilia extends from head to tail. The direction of the ciliary beat is tailward, causing the animal to glide slowly forward. Generally, all animals that move by this type of ciliary activity secrete a copious stream of mucus over which the animal glides. The mucus not only attaches the animal to the surface but also raises its body so that the cilia can beat. Because ciliary forces are too weak for the movement of large flatworms, they must use muscular contraction for their propulsive force.

Aquatic invertebrates possess several other types of bottom locomotion. In species with well-developed legs, such as crabs and lobsters, bottom walking is common. Whereas the gaits in such cases are identical to those used on land, they tend to be slightly faster in water, because the buoyancy increases the animal's stability. (Walking gaits are described below; see *Terrestrial locomotion.*)

Another form of bottom locomotion is bottom creeping, which employs the contract–anchor–extend method of movement. Bottom creeping is best developed in leeches, which have two suckers, one at the anterior end and one at the posterior end. After the posterior sucker anchors the animal, it stretches its body forward and attaches the anterior one. It then releases the posterior sucker and contracts its body toward the anterior end. For effective contract–anchor–extend locomotion, the body musculature must consist of both circular and longitudinal muscles: the contraction of the circular muscles extends or elongates the body; the contraction of the longitudinal muscles flexes and shortens the body. Moreover, the skeleton should be hydrostatic; that is, a fluid skeleton that

Bottom creeping

changes shape but not volume, thereby providing a firm but flexible base.

In pedal locomotion, which is a slow, continuous gliding that is superficially indistinguishable from ciliary locomotion, propulsion along the bottom is generated by the passage of contraction waves through the ventral musculature, which is in contact with the bottom surface. The pedal contraction waves are either direct (in the same direction as the movement) or retrograde (in the direction opposite to the movement). The direct waves produce locomotion in a manner analogous to that in which a caterpillar walks. When a direct wave reaches a muscle, the muscle contracts and lifts a small part of the body; the body is carried forward and set down anterior to its original position as the wave passes. With direct waves, the surfaces of the body touching the bottom surface are not the ones that contract; with retrograde waves, however, these are the surfaces that do contract. As the retrograde wave approaches, the body area immediately adjacent to it is extended upward. The body surface within the contraction area then anchors itself to the bottom surface, after which the body is pulled forward.

Large flatworms use pedal locomotion instead of or in alternation with ciliary activity. In the gastropod and amphineuran molluscans (*e.g.*, snails and chitons, respectively), pedal locomotion is the primary locomotor mode and has become highly complex. The foot of these creeping animals is extremely muscular, penetrated by nerves, and capable of generating one, two, or four laterally adjacent contraction waves. If the foot generates a pair of waves, the lateral halves of the foot may alternate, thereby producing a shuffling movement, or they may be opposite. Generally, a foot can contain no more than one whole and two partial waves moving along a single axis.

Peristaltic locomotion is a common locomotor pattern in elongated, soft-bodied invertebrates, particularly in segmented worms, such as earthworms. It involves the alternation of circular- and longitudinal-muscle-contraction waves. Forward movement is produced by contraction of the circular muscles, which extends or elongates the body; contraction of the longitudinal muscles shortens and anchors the body. (This pattern is described more completely below; see *Fossorial locomotion*.)

Although peristaltic locomotion is frequently used by sea cucumbers, they and other echinoderms, such as sea urchins and starfishes, possess rows of tube feet that provide the main locomotor force. In starfishes, each arm bears hundreds of tube feet. Only one arm, however, becomes dominant in locomotion; while the tube feet on that arm move toward the tip of the arm, the tube feet of the other arms move in the same plane as those of the lead arm. Because there is no apparent metachronal wave of contraction within an arm, the movement of the tube feet is poorly coordinated, but small areas of the tube feet do move in synchrony. Each tube foot is a hollow elastic cylinder capped by a hollow muscular ampulla (a small, bladder-like enlargement). When the ampulla contracts, it forces fluid into the tube foot and extends it. Preferential contraction of muscles in the wall of the tube foot controls the direction of and the retraction of the tube foot. When the tube foot is fully contracted, fluid is withdrawn from it by relaxation of the ampulla, after which the muscles of the tube foot swing it forward in preparation for another step.

Swimming. Invertebrates have developed two distinct propulsive mechanisms for swimming: some use hydraulic propulsion; all others utilize undulations of all or parts of their bodies. The medusa (umbrella-shaped) body of coelenterates and ctenophores (*e.g.*, jellyfish and comb jelly, respectively) is a flexible hemisphere with tentacles and sense organs suspended from the edge; a manubrium (handle-shaped structure) bearing the digestive system hangs from the internal tip of the hemisphere. Enclosed in the outer margin of the medusa is a wide muscular band; when this band contracts, the opening of the medusa narrows. Simultaneously, water is ejected from the medusa through the narrow opening, and the animal is propelled upward. Because the contractions tend to be regular but slow, locomotion is somewhat jerky.

Scallops are the best swimmers among bivalve molluscans that can swim. Locomotion is produced by rapid clapping movements of the two shells, creating a water jet that propels the scallop. The muscular mantle (a membranous fold beneath the shell) acts as a valve and controls the direction of flow of the ejected water, thereby controlling the direction of movement. Normally, the flow is directed downward on each side of the hinge that joins the two shells, and the resulting water jet lifts the scallop and moves it in the direction of the shell's opening. If necessary, however, escape movement may occur in the opposite direction. The scallop is adapted to swim even though it is two or three times as dense as seawater. The hinge is elastic and opens the shell rapidly; this action, coupled with rapid and repeated contractions of the adductor muscle, which closes the shell, produces a powerful and nearly continuous water jet. Moreover, the body form of a closed scallop is an airfoil (like a wing, the curvature of its upper surface is greater than that of its lower surface); this shape, combined with the downward ejection of water, produces lift.

Cephalopods (*e.g.*, squids, octopuses) are another group of mollusks that use hydraulic propulsion. Unlike the scallops, they have lost most of their heavy shell and have developed fusiform bodies. The mantle of cephalopods encloses a cavity in which are contained the gills and other internal organs. It also includes, on its ventral surface, a narrow, funnel-shaped opening (siphon) through which water can be forcibly ejected when all the circular muscles surrounding the mantle cavity contract rapidly and simultaneously. This water jet shoots the cephalopod in a direction opposite to that in which the siphon is pointed.

Many invertebrates, particularly elongated ones such as open-sea-dwelling annelids and mollusks, swim by undulatory movements produced by contraction waves that alternate on each side of the body. Although the arrangement of the musculature differs between invertebrates and vertebrates, the mechanics of undulatory swimming are the same in both and are described in the following section.

Fish and fishlike vertebrates. Undulatory swimming is roughly analogous to using one oar at the stern of a boat. The side-to-side movements of the oar force the water backward and the boat forward. The undulatory movement of a fish acts similarly, although the motions involved are much more complex.

Anguilliform locomotion. When an elongated fish such as an eel swims, its entire body, which is flexible throughout its complete length, moves in a series of sinuous waves passing from head to tail. In this type of movement, which is called anguilliform (eel-like) locomotion, the waves cause each segment of the body to oscillate laterally across the axis of movement. Unlike the simple side-to-side movement of the oar, however, each oscillating segment describes a figure-eight loop, the centre of which is along the axis of locomotion. It is these oscillations and the associated orientation of each body segment that produce the propulsive thrust.

The undulatory body waves are created by metachronal contraction waves alternating between the right and left axial musculature. During steady swimming, several contraction waves simultaneously pass down the body axis from head to tail; the resultant undulatory waves move backward along the body faster than the body moves forward. As the undulatory wave passes backward, its amplitude and speed increase, thereby producing the greatest propulsive thrust in the tail (caudal) region. Propulsion, however, is not limited to the caudal region, for all undulating segments contribute to the thrust. Because the speed, amplitude, and inclination of each body segment differ, the thrust of each differs. In all segments, the greatest thrust is obtained as the segment crosses the locomotor axis, for here it is travelling at its greatest speed and inclination.

Carangiform and ostraciiform locomotion. All undulatory swimming movements generate forward thrust in the manner described above. Not all swimming animals, however, possess the elongated shape of an eel; only those

Tube feet

Undulatory swimming

with a similar body form, in which the surface area of the head end is the same as that of the tail end, have anguilliform locomotion. Fish with fusiform bodies exhibit carangiform locomotion, in which only the posterior half of the body flexes with the passage of contraction waves. This arrangement of body form and locomotion apparently is the most efficient one, for it occurs in the most active and fastest of fish. The advantage of carangiform locomotion appears to be related to the effectiveness of the posterior half of the body as a propulsive unit and the fact that the shape of the body and its small lateral displacement create little water turbulence. In contrast to ostraciiform locomotion, in which only the caudal fin oscillates from side to side in a manner similar to moving a boat with one oar, the length of the propulsive unit of carangiform fish enables the unit to obtain maximum oscillatory speed and inclination.

Whales also use undulatory body waves, but unlike any of the fishes, the waves pass dorsoventrally (from top to bottom) and not from side to side. In fact, many mammals that swim mainly by limb movements tend to flex their body in a dorsoventral plane. Whereas the body musculature of fish and tail musculature of amphibians and reptiles is highly segmental—that is, a muscle segment alternates with each vertebra—an arrangement that permits the smooth passage of undulatory waves along the body, mammals are unable to produce lateral undulations because they do not have this arrangement. Nor does the muscle arrangement of mammals permit true dorsoventral undulations; however, with an elongated caudal region, as in whales, they can attain a form of carangiform locomotion as effective as that of any fish.

Stabilization and steering. To stabilize and steer, most aquatic vertebrates have, in addition to the caudal fin, a large dorsal fin and a pair of large anterolateral fins. Although they may possess other fins, these are of less importance. The balance of a swimming animal may be maintained in several ways. Rolling, or rotation, along the longitudinal axis of the body is reduced or controlled by any fins that extend at right angles to the body. Pitching, or dorsoventral seesawing, movements are counteracted by the anterolateral fins, which are also the major steering organs of fish, whales, and seals. Yawing, or lateral seesawing, is prevented by the dorsal fin and, if present, a ventral fin; for these fins to be effective, however, most of their exposed surface area should be behind the fish's centre of gravity. Because fins of the above type are not common in most invertebrates that swim by undulation, their locomotion is less stable.

Tetrapodal vertebrates. Many of the various types of undulatory locomotion described above are also widely used by aquatic tetrapods (those with walking appendages). Larval frogs, crocodilians, aquatic salamanders, and lizards, for example, have long muscular tails that propel them by undulatory motion. Most aquatic tetrapods, however, move by appendicular locomotion, for which the major propulsive units are the hindlegs. The exceptions are sea turtles, auks, penguins, and fur seals; in these, the hindfeet are webbed and are used as rudders. For propulsion, these animals use their forelegs, which have become bladelike flippers in which the forearm and hand region are dorsoventrally compressed to form a single, inflexible unit. The movements of such flippers are analogous to the aerial flight of birds; by moving synchronously, they provide lift and thrust in the water. Unlike aerial flight, however, the upper arms do not produce lift or thrust; instead, they serve only as a pivotal or leverage point for driving the flippers.

Swimming movements in sea turtles, penguins, and auks are accomplished by the rotation of the flippers or wings through a figure-eight configuration. In the birds, however, the stroke is relatively faster than in sea turtles, because the entire cycle appears to be proportionally smaller in amplitude. Moreover, because the birds' bodies are more streamlined, they can attain greater speeds than the turtles. Penguins may attain speeds of 25 miles (40 kilometres) per hour in water and have sufficient speed and thrust to enable them to leap six or more feet above the water. The wings of penguins are so highly modified, however, that they have lost the ability to fly. The auks, on the other hand, are able to use their wings for both aerial and aquatic locomotion.

Some of the other aquatic birds, such as ducks and water ouzels, are said to propel themselves underwater through wing movements, but the evidence for such propulsion is incomplete and still open to question. The wing movements of ducks may be for steering and hydroplaning (skimming through the water) rather than for actual propulsion. The wings of the water ouzels, or dippers, were once thought to function as hydroplanes, but investigations have revealed that, although the wings are flapped underwater, the ability of dippers to bottom walk or fly underwater depends upon the velocity of the water flowing past the wings rather than the movement of the wings themselves.

Most aquatic birds are propelled by their webbed hindfeet, which tend to move alternately in surface swimming and in unison when the bird is submerged. Of all the swimming birds that use their hindfeet, the loons show the most extreme adaptations: the body, head, and neck are elongated and streamlined; the hindlegs are at the very posterior end of the body; the lower legs are compressed and bladelike; and the feet are strongly webbed. The webbing increases the surface area exposed to the water during limb retraction and also permits the folding of the foot, thereby reducing water resistance during protraction.

In frogs and freshwater turtles, the hindlegs are elongated and the feet enlarged and strongly webbed. But, whereas the hindlegs of frogs move synchronously, except occasionally in slow swimming, when they alternate, the limb movements always alternate in freshwater turtles. Some aquatic turtles, however, such as snapping, mud, and musk turtles, are very poor swimmers and will swim only under extreme conditions. These turtles are bottom walkers, and their limb movements in water are identical to those on land except that they can move faster in water than on land.

The swimming movements of many mammals are also identical with their terrestrial limb movements. Hippopotamuses spend much of their time in the water, yet they bottom walk rather than swim. Most of the aquatic mammals—e.g., otters, hair seals, aquatic marsupials, insectivores, and rodents—use their hindlegs and frequently their tails for swimming. The feet are webbed and usually move alternately; the tail tends to be flattened. Fur seals, polar bears, and platypuses swim mainly with forelimbs; only in the seals, however, are the movements of the forelimbs similar to those of sea turtles and penguins.

FOSSORIAL LOCOMOTION

The speed, manner, and ease with which animals move depends directly upon the compactness of the material and its cohesiveness. Many aquatic animals can swim through semisolid mud or muck suspensions, which lack compactness. Some lizards and snakes that live in an arid environment can swim through friable sand, which is compact but lacks strong cohesiveness. Although these swimming movements can be considered a form of fossorial locomotion, the following discussion considers only locomotor patterns in which most of the activity of the animals involved is confined to tunnels that they leave behind.

Fossorial invertebrates. Burrowing or boring invertebrates have evolved a number of different locomotor patterns to penetrate soil, wood, and stone, of which soil or mud is the easiest to penetrate. The soft-bodied invertebrates, such as worms and sea cucumbers, burrow either by peristaltic locomotion or by the contract–anchor–extend method. Their hydrostatic, or fluid, skeleton, combined with their circular and longitudinal musculature, permits controlled deformation of their shape, which allows them to squeeze into narrow spaces and then enlarge the spaces, thus creating a burrow or tunnel. Worms with a protrusible proboscis (a tubular extension of the oral region) generally burrow by the contract–anchor–extend method. Contraction of the circular muscles in the posterior half of the body drives the body

(margin: Locomotion of aquatic mammals)

(margin: Aquatic birds)

(margin: Burrowing)

fluids forward, causing the proboscis to evert (turn outward) and forcing it into the soil. When the proboscis is fully everted, the part of the body (collar) directly behind it dilates and anchors the proboscis in the soil. The entire body is then pulled forward by the longitudinal muscles and reanchored. This pattern produces the very jerky and slow forward progression typical of most fossorial locomotion.

Peristaltic locomotion (see Figure 2), which is generated by the alternation of longitudinal- and circular-muscle-contraction waves flowing from the head to the tail, is similar to the above pattern. Forward progression is

From J. Gray, *Animal Locomotion*; Weidenfeld & Nicolson Limited

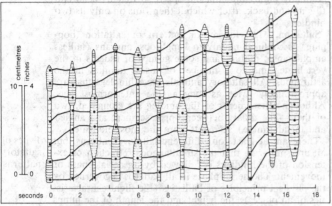

Figure 2: *Peristaltic locomotion in worms.*
Segments move forward except when they are longitudinally contracted (shown as wide areas with large dots). Individual points on the worm's body and their movements relative to each other are shown by the oblique lines.

more continuous, however, because of the contraction waves. The sites of longitudinal contraction are the anchor points; body extension is by circular contraction. The pattern of movement is initiated by anchoring the anterior end. As the longitudinal contraction wave moves posteriorly, it is slowly replaced by the circular contraction wave. The anterior end slowly and forcefully elongates, driving the tip farther into the surface as the circular contraction wave moves down the body. The tip then begins to dilate and anchor the anterior end as another longitudinal contraction wave develops. This sequence is repeated continuously, and the worm moves slowly forward. Reversing the direction of the contraction waves enables the worm to back up.

Burrowing bivalve mollusks, such as clams, use the contract–anchor–extend locomotor mode. Such bivalves have a large muscular foot that contains longitudinal and transverse muscles as well as a hemocoel (blood cavity). The digging cycle begins with the extension of the foot by contraction of the transverse muscles. The siphons (tubular-shaped organs that carry water to and from the gills) are closed, and the adductor muscle of the shell contracts, thereby forcing blood into the tip of the foot and causing it to dilate. With the tip acting as an anchor, the longitudinal muscles then contract, pulling the body down to the anchored foot. Frequently, the longitudinal muscles contract in short steps and alternate between the left and right sides; this causes the shell to wobble and penetrate deeper as it is pulled down.

Rock borers
Some invertebrates are able to bore through rock. Most of the rock borers are mollusks; they bore either mechanically by scraping or chemically by the secretion of acid. The piddock, or angel's wing, bivalves, for example, attach themselves to a rock with a sucker-like foot. The two valves, held against the rock, grind back and forth by the alternate contraction of two adductor muscles; the grinding slowly produces a tunnel.

Fossorial vertebrates. The fossorial vertebrates are found in three classes: amphibians, reptiles, and mammals. Although some fishes and birds dig or bore shallow burrows, they can hardly be considered truly fossorial, as are moles or earthworms. Locomotion of fossorial amphibians and reptiles tends to be axial; it is appendicular only in mammals. Fossorial mammals have strong fore-

legs with a tendency toward flattening; their hands and particularly the claws are enlarged. Forelegs show the greatest modification in such species as moles and gophers, whose entire lives are spent in burrows. These animals tend to dig with a breast stroke, either synchronously or alternately, by extending the foreleg straight forward in front of the snout and then retracting it in a lateral arc. The loosened soil is compacted against the side walls of the burrow. In those fossorial species that dig burrows as nests but forage above the ground—many rodents, such as prairie-dogs, ground squirrels, and groundhogs—the digging movements tend to be dorsoventral with alternating limb movement. The forelegs are extended forward and then retracted downward and backward; the loosened soil passes beneath the body and is frequently pushed to the surface.

Fossorial reptiles and amphibians are usually legless, or the legs are so reduced that they serve no locomotor function; in most species, the head is flattened dorsoventrally, and the snout extends beyond and somewhat over the mouth. Burrowing is accomplished by one of three patterns analogous to the contract–anchor–extend locomotion of invertebrates. In the most common of these, the snout is driven straight forward along the bottom of the tunnel, the head is then raised, and the soil is compacted to the roof. The head tends to be laterally compressed in animals that use the other two patterns. In one of these patterns, the snout is shoved forward and then swung from side to side; in the other, the snout is rotated as it swings from side to side and seems to shave the walls of the tunnel.

TERRESTRIAL LOCOMOTION

Walking and running. Only arthropods (*e.g.*, insects, spiders, and crustaceans) and vertebrates have developed a means of rapid surface locomotion. In both groups, the body is raised above the ground and moved forward by means of a series of jointed appendages, the legs. Because the legs provide support as well as propulsion, the sequences of their movements must be adjusted to maintain the body's centre of gravity within a zone of support; if the centre of gravity is outside this zone, the animal loses its balance and falls. It is the necessity to maintain stability that determines the functional sequences of limb movements, which are similar in vertebrates and arthropods. The apparent differences in the walking and in slow running gaits of these two groups are caused by differences in the tetrapodal (four-legged) sequences of vertebrates and in the hexapodal (six-legged) or more sequences of arthropods. Although many legs increase stability during locomotion, they also appear to reduce the maximum speed of locomotion. Whereas the fastest vertebrate gaits are asymmetrical, arthropods cannot have asymmetrical gaits, because the movements of the legs would interfere with each other.

Cycle of limb movements. The cycle of limb movements is the same in both arthropods and vertebrates. During the propulsive, or retractive, stage, which begins with footfall and ends with foot liftoff, the foot and leg remain stationary as the body pivots forward over the leg. During the recovery, or protractive, stage, which begins with foot liftoff and ends with footfall, the body remains stationary as the leg moves forward. The advance of one leg is a step; a stride is composed of as many steps as there are legs. During a stride, each leg passes through one complete cycle of retraction and protraction, and the distance the body travels is equal to the longest step in the stride. The speed of locomotion is the product of stride length and duration of stride. Stride duration is directly related to retraction: the longer the propulsive stage, the more time required to complete a stride and the slower the gait. A gait is the sequence of leg movements for a single stride. For walking and slow running, gaits are usually symmetrical—*i.e.*, the footfalls are regularly spaced in time. The gaits of fast-running vertebrates, however, tend to be asymmetrical—*i.e.*, the footfalls are irregularly spaced in time.

The different gaits of insects are based on the synchrony of leg movements on the left (*L*) and right (*R*) sides of the animal. The wave of limb movement for each side passes anteriorly; the posterior leg protracts first, then the middle leg, and finally the anterior leg, producing the sequence $R_3 R_2 R_1$ or $L_3 L_2 L_1$. There is no limb interference, because the legs of one side do not have footfalls along the same longitudinal axis. The slowest walking gait of insects is the sequence $R_3 R_2 R_1$ followed by the sequence $L_3 L_2 L_1$. As the rate of protraction increases, the protractive waves of the right and left sides begin to overlap. Eventually, the top speed is reached when the posterior and anterior legs of one side move synchronously. This gait occurs because the protraction times for all legs are constant, the intervals between posterior and middle legs and between middle and anterior legs are constant, and the interval between posterior and anterior legs decreases with faster movements. Other gaits are possible in addition to those indicated above by altering the synchrony between left and right sides.

Limb movements in millipedes and centipedes

The limb movements of centipedes and millipedes follow the same general rules as those of insects. The protraction waves usually pass from posterior to anterior. Because each leg is slightly ahead of its anteriorly adjacent leg during the locomotory cycle, one leg touches down or lifts off slightly before its anteriorly adjacent one. This coordination of limb movement produces metachronal waves, the frequency of which equals the duration of the complete protractive and retractive cycle. The length of the wave is directly proportional to the phase lag between adjacent legs.

Whereas the millipedes must synchronize leg movements to eliminate interference, the tetrapodal vertebrates must synchronize leg movements to obtain maximum stability. Four legs are the minimum requirement for symmetrical terrestrial gaits. Although bipedal (two-legged) gaits require extensive structural modifications of the body and legs, they still retain the leg-movement sequence of tetrapodal gaits (see Figure 3). The basic

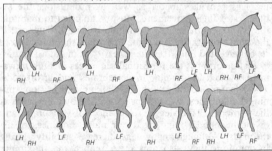

Figure 3: *Walking sequence of a five-gaited horse.*
LH and RH refer to left and right hindlegs; LF and RF refer to left and right forelegs.

walking pattern of all tetrapodal vertebrates is left hindleg (LH), left foreleg (LF), right hindleg (RH), right foreleg (RF), and then a cyclic repetition of this sequence, which is equivalent to the slow walking gait of insects but with the middle legs removed. Unlike the insects, however, vertebrates can begin to walk with any of the four legs and not just the posterior pair. The faster symmetrical gaits of vertebrates are obtained by overlapping the leg-movement sequences of the left and right sides in the same manner as insects; for example, an animal can convert a walk to a trot by moving diagonally contralateral legs (those on opposite sides) simultaneously, or to a pace by moving the ipselateral legs (those on the same side) simultaneously. Many other symmetrical gaits occur between the walk and the pace and the trot, which are extreme modifications of the walk.

Cursorial vertebrates. Cursorial (running) vertebrates are characterized by short, muscular upper legs and thin, elongated lower legs. This adaptation decreases the duration of the retractive–protractive cycle, thereby increasing the animal's speed. Because the leg's cycle is analogous to the swing of a pendulum, reduction of weight at the end of the leg increases its speed of oscillation. Cursorial mammals commonly use either the pace or the trot for steady, slow running. The highest running speeds,

such as the gallop, are obtained with asymmetrical gaits. When galloping, the animal is never supported by more than two legs and occasionally is supported by none. The fastest runners, such as cheetahs or greyhounds, have an additional no-contact phase following hindfoot contact.

In cursorial birds and lizards, both of which are bipedal, the feet are enlarged to increase support, and the body axis is held perpendicular to the ground, so that the centre of gravity falls between the feet or within the foot-support zone. The running gait is, of course, a simple alternation of left and right legs. In lizards, however, bipedal running must begin with quadrupedal (four-footed) locomotion. As the lizard runs on all four legs, it gradually builds up sufficient speed so that its head end tilts up and back, after which it then runs on only its two hindlegs.

Saltation. The locomotor pattern of saltation (hopping) is confined mainly to kangaroos, anurans (tailless amphibians), rabbits, and some groups of rodents in the vertebrates and to a number of insect families in the arthropods. All saltatory animals have hindlegs that are approximately twice as long as the anteriormost legs. Although all segments of the hindleg are elongated, two of them—the tibial (between upper segment and ankle) and tarsal (ankle) segments—are the most elongated.

There are at least four different saltatory patterns, but all are similar in that the simultaneous retraction or extension of the hindlegs is followed by an aerial phase of movement. The aerial phase in all patterns is governed by the physical principles of ballistics (the flight characteristics of an object): the height and the length of the jumps are functions of the takeoff velocity and angle. The longest jumps are attained when the takeoff angle is 45°.

Types of saltatory patterns

Before jumping, the femur (upper segment of the hindleg) of the flea is held perpendicular to the ground, the tibia extends obliquely posterior, and the remainder of the hindleg extends posteriorly along the ground. Just prior to the jump, the middle legs flex and tilt the body upward; then the femur of the hindlegs swings sharply backward simultaneously with the extension of the tibia. This retraction forces the animal upward and forward at an angle of 50°. As the flea approaches touchdown, the front legs are swung forward and downward, the middle legs are held perpendicular to the body axis, and the hindlegs project obliquely posterior. The anterior two pairs of legs thus act to absorb the landing shock.

The frog jump (Figure 4) is initiated with three simultaneous movements: the forelegs flex, and the back arches to tilt the entire body upward; the tarsus of the hindleg swings to a vertical position and locks; and the femur, extending anteriorly along the body, swings in a horizontal plane. When the femur is perpendicular to the body, the knee joint snaps open, and the frog jumps forward at a 30° to 45° angle. As the frog begins to land, the forelegs are protracted and held downward in front of the chest. The forefeet touch down first, the forelegs acting as shock absorbers. Simultaneously, the hindlegs are protracted so that they can be in jumping posture by the completion of landing.

The positions and movements of the hindlegs in rabbits and kangaroos are similar to those of the frog. The major difference is that rabbits, kangaroos, and all other mammals move their legs in a vertical plane instead of a

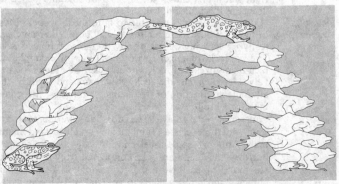

Figure 4: (Left) Jumping and (right) landing sequences of frogs.

horizontal plane, as do the frogs; because the femur and tibia move vertically, the tarsus need not be elevated to prevent the hindleg from hitting the ground. The saltatorial gait of rabbits is quadrupedal, whereas that of kangaroos is bipedal. A jumping rabbit stretches forward and lands on its forefeet; generally, both forefeet do not touch ground simultaneously, however. As the forefeet touch, the back flexes, and the hind end rotates forward and downward. The hindfeet touch down lateral to the forefeet, and, as the back extends, a new jump begins. In contrast, the kangaroo lands on its hindfeet, and the back is held fairly straight through all phases of the jump, although the body inclines forward at takeoff and posteriorly when landing.

Crawling. Invertebrates crawl either by peristaltic locomotion or by contract–anchor–extend locomotion, both of which have been described previously (see above *Fossorial locomotion*). Limbless vertebrates, however, crawl in one of four patterns: serpentine, rectilinear, concertina, and sidewinding. The most common pattern, serpentine locomotion, is used by snakes, legless lizards, amphisbaenids (worm lizards), and caecilians (wormlike amphibians). Rectilinear locomotion is used by the giant snakes and almost exclusively by fossorial vertebrates when burrowing. Concertina and sidewinding locomotion are largely confined to snakes.

Serpentine locomotion. In serpentine locomotion, in which the body is thrown into a series of sinuous curves, the movements appear identical to those of anguilliform swimming, but the similarity is more apparent than real. Unlike anguilliform swimming, when a snake starts to move, the entire body moves, and all parts follow the same path as the head. When the snake stops moving, the entire body stops simultaneously. Propulsion is not by contraction waves undulating the body but by a simultaneous lateral thrust in all segments of the body in contact with solid projections (raised surfaces). The muscular thrust against the projection is perpendicular to the axis of the pushing segment. To go forward, therefore, it is necessary for the strongest thrust to act against the side of the projection facing in the direction of movement. Because of this, thrust tends to occur at the anterior end of the concave (inward-curving) side of the loop of the snake's body.

Concertina locomotion. Concertina locomotion is used when there is not enough frictional resistance along the locomotor surface for serpentine locomotion. After the body is thrown into a series of tight, sinuous loops, forming a frictional anchor, the head slowly extends forward until the body is nearly straight or begins to slide. The anterior end forms a small series of loops and, with this anchor, pulls the posterior regions forward, after which the sequence of movements is repeated. This crawling pattern is analogous to the contract–anchor–extend locomotion of invertebrates, but, because snakes lack the body flexibility provided by a hydrostatic skeleton, they must depend upon the body loops.

Sidewinding. Sidewinding, which is also used when the locomotor surface fails to provide a rigid frictional base, is a specific adaptation for crawling over friable sandy soils. Like serpentine locomotion but unlike concertina locomotion, the entire body moves forward continuously in sidewinding locomotion (see Figure 5). Although the body moves through a series of sinuous curves, the track made by the snake is a set of parallel lines that are roughly perpendicular to the axis of movement. This is because only two parts of the body touch the ground at any instant; the remainder of the body is held off the ground. To begin sidewinding, the snake arches the anterior part of the body forward and forms an elevated loop with only the head and the middle of the body in contact with the ground. Because each part of the body touches the ground only briefly before it begins to arch forward again, the snake seems to roll forward like a short, coiled spring. In a continuously repeating cycle, as a segment arches forward, the posteriorly adjacent segment touches down.

Rectilinear locomotion. Unlike the three preceding patterns of movement, in which the body is thrown into a

(margin: Crawling patterns)

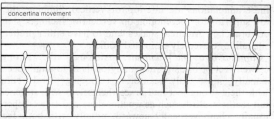
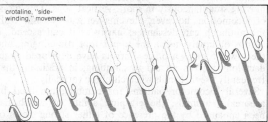

Figure 5: Two modes of locomotion in the snake.
From J. Gray, *Animal Locomotion*, Weidenfeld & Nicolson Ltd.

series of curves, in rectilinear locomotion in snakes the body is held relatively straight and glides forward in a manner analogous to the pedal locomotion of snails. The ventral (belly) surface of snakes is covered by scales elongated crosswise that overlap like roof shingles, with the opening of the overlap facing toward the posterior. Each ventral scale is moved by two pairs of muscles, both of which are attached to ribs but not to ribs of the same segment as the scale. One pair of muscles is inclined posterior at an angle (obliquely); the other is inclined anterior at an angle. As contraction waves move rearward from the head simultaneously on both sides, the anterior oblique muscles of a scale contract first and lift the scale upward and forward. When the posterior oblique muscles contract, the scale is pulled rearward, but its edge anchors it, and the body is pulled forward. This sequence is repeated by all segments as the contraction wave passes posteriorly, and, as a series of contraction waves follow one another, the body slowly inches forward.

ARBOREAL AND AERIAL LOCOMOTION

Climbing. The adaptation for climbing is unique for each group of arboreal animals. All climbers must have strong grasping abilities, and they must keep their centre of gravity as close as possible to the object being climbed. Because arthropods are generally small and, thus, not greatly affected by the pull of gravity, they show little specific structural adaptation for climbing. In contrast, the larger and heavier bodied vertebrates have many climbing specializations. In both arthropods and vertebrates, however, no leg is moved until the others are firmly anchored.

Arboreal amphibians and reptiles. Arboreal frogs are slender-bodied anurans with tapering legs and feet. The tips of the toes (digits) are expanded into large, circular disks that may function as suction cups, although such an action has not yet been definitely demonstrated. The disks, however, do increase the contact area, thereby improving grasping ability. The leg-movement sequence during climbing is that of a walking gait.

Arboreal lizards have the same type of climbing gait as arboreal frogs, and their climbing specializations are also similar to those of anurans. They have a different type of climbing foot, however, because of the presence of claws and scales on the digits. Moreover, the entire digits, rather than just their tips, may be expanded. On the bottom of each of these spatula-shaped expansions are one or two rows of transversely elongated scales. Although not visible to the naked eye, the surface of these scales is covered with fine projections that increase their ability to adhere to a surface. Because of this strong adherence, the toes roll off and on the surface on which the animal is walking. Unlike other arboreal lizards, chameleons possess a prehensile (grasping) tail and zygodactylous feet—i.e., the toes are fused into two opposable units. Although

(margin: Surface adherence)

these adaptations are inferior for vertical climbing, they are superior for locomotion on vertical or inclined, slender branches. Arboreal snakes tend to have either prehensile tails or extremely elongated bodies.

Climbing birds and mammals. Although the strong, clawed feet of birds permit many of them to climb occasionally, most truly scansorial (climbing) birds cling with their strong feet and brace themselves with stiffened tail feathers. Birds such as woodpeckers and tree creepers usually climb vertically upward, usually with both feet moving simultaneously in short, vertical hops. This mode of locomotion, however, prevents vertical descent. Only the nuthatch can descend as easily as it can ascend; it climbs obliquely, using the upper foot for clinging and the lower foot as a brace. Parrots have developed zygodactylous feet as an aid to climbing; in addition, they frequently use their bills when climbing vertically.

Use of prehensile fingers or claws Several locomotor patterns for climbing are used by arboreal mammals, the grasping ability of which has been enhanced by the presence of either strong claws or prehensile fingers. Many monkeys use a climbing gait similar to the leg sequence of walking. Occasionally, however, they use a leg sequence equivalent to that of a trot. Small-bodied climbers with sharp claws, such as squirrels, climb by the alternate use of forelegs and hindlegs; essentially, they hop up a tree. Prehensile-fingered climbers descend backward and generally with a walking type of leg sequence. Sharp-clawed species descend with a similar gait sequence but with the head downward.

Leaping. The mechanics of arboreal leaping do not differ from those of terrestrial saltation; the upward thrust in both is produced by the rapid, simultaneous extension of the hindlegs. Because of the narrowness of the arboreal landing site, however, landing behaviour does differ. Arboreal leaping also tends to be a discontinuous locomotor behaviour that is used only to cross wide gaps in the locomotor surface. Leaping from limb to limb, although occasionally employed by most climbers, appears to occur most frequently in animals with opposable or at least prehensile forefeet, particularly tree frogs and primates. Such forefeet enable the animal to grasp and hold onto the landing site.

Brachiation. True brachiation (using the arms to swing from one place to another) is confined to a few species of primates, such as gibbons and spider monkeys. Because the body is suspended from a branch by the arms, brachiation is strictly foreleg locomotion. When the animal moves, it relaxes the grip of one hand, and the body pivots on the shoulder of the opposite arm and swings forward; then the free arm reaches forward at the end of the body's swing and grabs a branch. The sequence is then repeated for the other arm. This locomotor pattern produces a relatively rapid and continuous forward movement but is restricted to areas with thick canopies of trees. Brachiators have arms that may be as long or longer than the body and a very motile shoulder joint.

Gliding. There are two functionally distinct forms of gliding, gravitational gliding and soaring: the former is used by gliding amphibians, reptiles, and mammals; the latter is restricted to birds. All gliders are able to increase the relative width of their bodies, thereby increasing the surface area exposed to wind resistance. The few gliding frogs flatten their bodies dorsoventrally and spread their limbs outward. Gliding snakes not only flatten their bodies but also draw in the ventral scales, thereby creating a trough. The best adapted gliding lizards have elongated ribs that open laterally like a fan.

Gliding mammals, such as the African flying squirrel and the colugo, usually have, on each side of the body, a fold of skin (the patagium) that extends from their wrist or forearm backward along the body to the shank of the hindleg or the ankle. When gliding, they assume a spread-eagle posture, and the patagia unfold.

Gravitational gliding. Gravitational gliding is equivalent to parachuting. Because the expanded lateral surface of the body increases the wind resistance against the body, the speed of falling is reduced. The directions of gliding can be controlled by adjusting the surface area—to curve to the right, the right patagium is relaxed. Glid-

ers can land on vertical surfaces by suddenly turning the anterior end of the body up as it reaches the surface. Mechanically, this stalls the flight—*i.e.*, the horizontal component of flight is eliminated.

Soaring. Gravitational gliding is one of the basic mechanisms of soaring, which is restricted to birds, although birds must obtain their initial elevation by means of flapping flight. The second basic mechanism of soaring involves wind or air currents. Soaring requires that air currents meet one of two conditions: either the air must have a vertical velocity exceeding the rate of descent in gravitational gliding, or it must have a horizontal velocity that is nonuniform in time and space. Whereas static soaring depends upon vertical air currents, dynamic soaring depends upon horizontal air currents. Both types of soaring are described below.

Static and dynamic soaring Vertical air currents for static soaring are produced when wind strikes an obstruction and is deflected upward. The sites of deflection are very local and discontinuous and seldom extend more than 100 feet above the obstruction. The height of deflection and the vertical velocity of the air are a function of the angle of deflection and the velocity of the wind. If the vertical velocity of the air equals the descent speed of the bird, the bird remains stationary in height relative to the ground. If, however, the vertical velocity is greater, the bird rises, and, if less, the bird falls at a speed equal to the gravitational descent speed minus the air's vertical ascent speed. The horizontal velocity of the air determines the bird's movements relative to the ground in the same manner as that of the vertical velocity.

The soaring flights of vultures and hawks depend upon vertical hot-air currents called thermals. Such currents are not continuous updrafts or downdrafts originating from a specific spot; instead, as a local region of the ground is heated, a vertical, hot-air updraft is created. At the top of the column, a thermal bubble is formed by the hot air curving outward, downward, and then around the bubble. It is then pinched off by cool air flowing into the column and floats upward. The free-floating thermal bubble is doughnut shaped, with the air rising in the centre and cycling outward and downward. Soaring birds spiral downward in the updraft; however, because the bubble rises faster than birds descend, soaring birds are carried upward, but at a speed less than that of the bubble. When a bird reaches the bottom of the bubble, it begins a straight gravitational glide until it reaches the next thermal bubble. Thus, static soaring in a thermal bubble can be recognized by its alternating flight pattern of circling and straight gliding.

Unlike static soaring, which is done at relatively high altitudes over land, dynamic soaring is done at low levels and is usually restricted to oceanic areas. Dynamic soaring depends upon a steady horizontal sea wind, which is laminated into layers of different velocities because of the frictional interaction between the water and the air; the lower layers have the lowest velocity. The flight path of a bird performing dynamic soaring tends to be a series of inclined loops that are perpendicular to the direction of the wind. A soaring albatross, for example, will begin its gravitational glide approximately 50 feet (15 metres) above the sea. Because it glides downwind, its velocity is increased both by descent and by the wind at its tail. As the bird nears the sea, it makes a turn into the wind, and the forward flight velocity derived from the downwind glide and the tailwind combine to lift the albatross slowly back to its initial gliding height, but with a loss of horizontal velocity. The bird therefore turns downwind again and begins to repeat the soaring cycle.

Because it depends upon the presence of a horizontal air current, the flight of flying fish is more akin to soaring than to true flying. As a flying fish approaches the water surface, its pectoral and pelvic fins, which are analogous to the forelimbs and hindlimbs of quadrupeds, are pressed along the side of the body. The greatly enlarged, winglike pectoral fins then spread out as the fish leaves the water. The wind against the fins provides lift to raise the body above the water, and the tail continues to undulate to provide additional thrust. When the entire body is out of the water, the enlarged pelvic fins extend, and the fish glides for a short distance until its forward velocity is lost. Occasionally, as a fish drops back into the water, it will undulate its tail to initiate another short flight.

True flight. Three animal groups have developed true flight: insects, birds, and mammals. All generate forward thrust by flapping lateral appendages, and all are free of any dependence on gravitational descent or air currents. It should be noted at the outset, however, that, although the aerodynamics of flight are identical in all three, the following cycles of wing movements described for the different animal groups are generalizations; each species in a group has a distinctive flight pattern and, therefore, a distinctive pattern of wing movement.

Wing move- ments

Flight is produced by the simultaneous rotation of the left and right wings in a circle or in a figure eight. This rotation produces the upward thrust, or lift, necessary to overcome gravity and the forward thrust required to overcome drag. As the downward and backward phase of rotation forces the air backward and the body forward, lift is produced by the unequal velocities of the air across the upper and lower wing surfaces.

Wings of insects. In flies with one pair of wings, the rotation of the tip inscribes a posterior inclined oval. At the top of the wing cycle, the tip lies above the junction of the thorax and abdomen. The wing then beats downward and forward so that the tip ends anterior and below the head. To insure maximum thrust, the broad surface of the wing lies parallel to the horizontal body plane during the downstroke. During the path of the upstroke, which is the reverse of the downstroke, the wing is feathered (turned) by inclining it perpendicular to the body plane. Although the rotational cycle of those insects with two pairs of wings follows a similar path, the upward and downward strokes of the anterior and posterior wings are not simultaneous; the anterior pair usually lags behind the posterior pair.

The wings of insects are rotated by pulsation of the thorax, not by a set of muscles. Basically, the thorax is a rigid box to which the wings are attached by a pair of longitudinal lateral hinges that enable the thorax to move dorsoventrally. Four sets of muscles control the major movements. Contraction of a perpendicular set, which extends from the centre of the floor of the thorax to its roof, depresses the thorax and, because of a reverse linkage between wing and thorax, raises the wing. Contraction of a diagonal set, which extends from the anterior roof of the thorax to its posterior floor, elevates the thorax and lowers the wing. Two diagonal sets of muscles extend laterally from the floor to the wall of the thorax and are responsible for maintaining a relatively constant width in the thorax.

Wings of birds and bats. Unlike insect wings, the wings of birds and bats are linked structures, the lateral extent and regional inclination of which are altered intrinsically by muscular and bony segments. The up-and-down strokes of a bird's wing are produced by large chest (pectoral) muscles that extend from the sternum (breastbone) to the lower surface of the humerus (a bone in the upper arm). When these muscles contract, the wing is lowered; it is raised by the contraction of a small anterior pectoral muscle that is attached to the upper surface of the humerus by a long tendon.

Hovering and propulsive flight

Birds exhibit two major flight patterns, hovering flight and propulsive flight. Hovering flight is of fairly restricted use and is observed most frequently in the hummingbirds. The path of the wings inscribes a horizontal figure eight whose centre is perpendicular to the shoulder joint. The downward stroke of the wings is actually a slightly inclined anterior stroke, and, because the longitudinal body axis is nearly perpendicular to the ground, the upward stroke is a horizontal posterior stroke. Both strokes are power strokes that produce lift: on the downstroke the dorsal wing surface is the top of the airfoil surface; on the upstroke the ventral surface is the top of the airfoil surface.

Most birds and bats, however, utilize propulsive flight. Because the body is not stationary, as it is in hovering flight, the wing always moves forward relative to the air,

and its tip generally inscribes an oval or figure-eight path. In a pigeon, for example, the downstroke begins with the wing fully extended and perpendicular to the back (Figure 6). As the wing moves downward and anterior, it

From J. Gray, *Animal Locomotion*; Weidenfeld & Nicolson, London

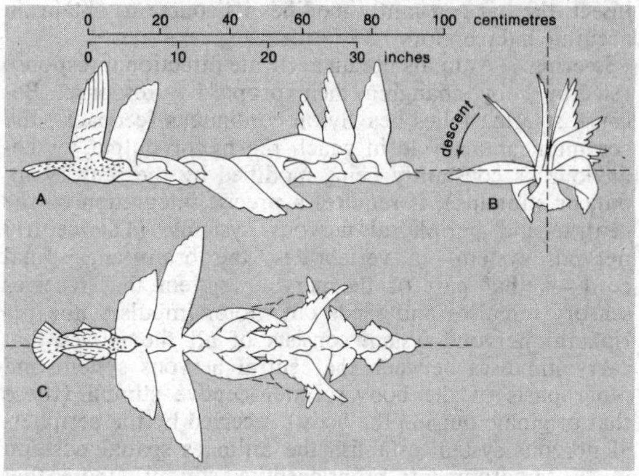

Figure 6: *Wing movements of a pigeon.*
(A) View from right side; (B) View from behind; (C) View from above.

draws level with the body, at which point the upper arm section stops while the distal part completes the downward path. At the bottom of the downstroke, the distal part turns outward and is elevated rapidly by the combined protraction of the humerus and the extension of the distal section.

DIRECTIONAL CONTROL

Although an animal's locomotor pattern may be controlled by its nervous system, directional control is impossible without sensory input. Two factors are involved in directional control: orientation, the ability of an animal to determine and to alter its position in the environment; and steering, the mechanical alteration of the locomotor pattern through which the animal adjusts its position.

Orientation. Orientation of locomotor behaviour is usually categorized as either kinesis or taxis. In kinesis, an animal's body is not oriented in relation to a sensory stimulus; rather, the stimulus causes an alteration in speed or direction of movement. In wood lice, for example, the kinetic response alters only the rate of movement. Because wood lice tend to aggregate in moist areas, their ambulatory activity increases or decreases as the relative humidity decreases or increases, respectively. In the planarian (an aquatic, ciliated flatworm), on the other hand, the kinetic response affects only the rate at which the planarian changes its direction. Because planaria tend to stay in or return to darker areas, an increase in light intensity causes an increase in their turning responses. Generally, however, animals tend to alter both direction and speed as a single kinetic response.

Kinesis and taxis

In taxis, an animal orients itself in a specific spatial relationship to a stimulus. The orientation may be simply an alteration of body position or it may be an alteration of locomotor direction so that the animal moves toward, away from, or at a fixed angle to the source of the stimulus. Sources that elicit a taxis response, which may cause a modification of speed, direction, or both, seem to encompass the entire range of environmental stimuli, such as gravity (geotaxis), temperature (thermotaxis), light (phototaxis), or chemicals (chemotaxis). If the response is negative, the animal moves away from the source; if it is positive, the animal moves toward the source.

The control of the response to a taxis is of two types. In open-system control, the initial response to a stimulus has no effect on subsequent responses to the same stimulus. A male firefly, for example, locates a female by the latter's brief flashes of light. When a male sees a female's flash, the male turns in the direction of the female, even though the source is no longer visible. If another female flashes, however, the male responds to the second flash in exactly the same manner as it did to the first. In close-system control, on the other hand, the response is progressively altered by feedback so that all subsequent responses are adjusted to the initial response. A bat chasing a flying insect will alter its flight path to intercept that of the insect. The bat's initial change in direction is only a general alteration of its course, but, as it approaches the insect, the bat constantly modifies its course to obtain an accurate interception.

Steering. Animals obtain accurate directional response (steering) by changing their propulsive response. Because steering relies heavily on continuous feedback (the communication cycle in which the motor output, or behaviour, is constantly being modified by the sensory input, or stimulus), it requires a precise integration of the central and peripheral nervous systems. (The central nervous system—in vertebrates, the brain and spinal cord—is that part of the nervous system that receives sensory impulses and sends out motor impulses; the peripheral nervous system consists of all the nerves that carry impulses between the central nervous system and other parts of the body.) Exteroceptive stimuli (those that originate outside the body) received by the peripheral nervous system establish the animal's spatial position in the environment; proprioceptive stimuli (those that originate inside the body), also received by the peripheral nervous system, establish the relative position of the body units to each other (see further SENSORY RECEPTION). Through integration of these two sets of stimuli, the central nervous system continuously adjusts the contraction of the motor units (*e.g.*, muscles) in order to obtain the desired orientation.

During locomotion, steering is a continual process. The direction of movements must be constantly adjusted to counteract environmentally produced deviations of direction. The apparently simple act of a bird flying from a tree to the ground illustrates the complexity of directional control. As the bird flies to the ground, it must be constantly aware of its height above the ground, the orientation of its body axis relative to the ground, deviations in flight direction resulting from air currents, and its speed of fall. All these parameters are determined primarily by exteroceptive stimuli received through the eyes and inner ears. The downward flight is constantly adjusted in response to these exteroceptive stimuli, and the fine control necessary for these adjustments is obtained by proprioceptive feedback.

BIBLIOGRAPHY. R.B. CLARK, *Dynamics in Metazoan Evolution* (1964), locomotor patterns of invertebrates with hydrostatic skeletons; J. GRAY, *Animal Locomotion* (1968), a synthesis of most aspects of invertebrate and vertebrate locomotion; H. HERTEL, *Struktur, Form Bewegung* (1963; *Structure, Form and Movement*, 1966), mechanics of flight and undulatory swimming; A.B. HOWELL, *Speed in Animals* (1944; reprinted facsimile 1965), anatomical modification of mammals for fast terrestrial gaits; E. MUYBRIDGE, *Animals in Motion* (1899, reprinted 1957), a classic work, the atlas of photographs of vertebrate terrestrial gaits is still useful; R.A.R. and B.J.K. TRICKER, *The Science of Movement* (1966), an introduction to the physics of locomotion; M. WILLIAMS and H.R. LISSNER, *Biomechanics of Human Motion* (1962).

(G.R.Z.)

Loess

True loess is a pale-yellow sedimentary deposit composed largely of silt-size grains that are loosely cemented by calcium carbonate. It is usually homogeneous, unstratified, highly porous, and is traversed by vertical capillaries that permit the sediment to fracture and form vertical bluffs. The word loess, with connotations of origin by eolian (wind-deposited) accumulation, is of German origin and means loose. It was first applied to Rhine Valley loess about 1821.

Thick loess blankets are composed of loess packets one to five metres thick, each of which contains intercalated strata of loessial and loess-like sediments, paleosols (ancient soils), sand layers, and similar material. The totality of these constitutes the loess complex. There are several regional variants of loess that, together with true loess, constitute a loess series, including loessial sand, sandy loess, loess loam, and clayey loess. The individual elements of the loess series are hard to distinguish, and the

several sediment types composing it are interpreted differently by workers in different regions or countries.

Most widespread in today's temperate zones and in the marginal semi-arid zones of the deserts, loess covers about 10 percent of the land surface of the earth. Loess usually exhibits a surficial cover of fertile soil that is conducive to intensive agriculture and consequently, has always had a concentrating influence on population. In densely populated loess regions, as in China, farming populations used to dig cellar-like dwellings in steep bluffs. In semi-arid regions people such as the Pueblo Indians made houses and fortress-like closed edifices from loess-based adobe. The present importance of loess for building construction, soil conservation and improvement, and soil engineering is enhanced by its erodibility, peculiar strength, and chemical properties.

This article is concerned with the physical and chemical properties of loess, its occurrence and distribution, and the several theories of loess formation. For further information on the transportation of silt by wind and water, see WIND ACTION and FLUVIAL PROCESSES, respectively. See also PLEISTOCENE EPOCH, for a discussion of the climatic significance of eolian deposits, and SEDIMENTARY ROCKS, for the relation of fine-grained rocks in general to others of sedimentary origin.

Physical and chemical properties. The dominant grain-size fraction of loess, called the loess fraction, ranges from 0.02 to 0.05 millimetre and includes grains of coarse and medium-grained dust. Grain-size analyses by various methods indicate that the abundance of this fraction is about 50 weight percent. Clay-size particles (less than 0.005 millimetre) make up another five to 10 percent. In some loess regions, the grain-size distribution shifts toward finer grains with increasing distance from the source of dust (*e.g.*, eastward from Sand Hills, Nebraska). The relative abundances of the dust, clay, and sand fractions may vary vertically, as well as horizontally, from one loess packet to another.

Loess typically exhibits a low moisture content of 10 to 15 percent that increases as porosity decreases. Its porosity is 50 to 55 percent, decreasing slightly downward to a depth of about 10 metres (33 feet). Below this depth, porosity varies as a function of the grain-size distribution. If the loess is enriched in clay, then the porosity may decrease to 34 to 45 percent. The porosity of sandy loess is about 60 percent. The bulk density of sandy loess is 1.5 grams per cubic centimetre and its specific gravity is 2.7 on the average.

With respect to mineralogical composition, loess contains 60 to 70 percent quartz with extremes of 40 and 80 percent. Feldspars and micas make up 10 to 20 percent and carbonates five to 35 percent. About two to five percent of the silt is composed of such heavy minerals as amphiboles, apatite, biotite, chlorite, disthene (cyanite), epidote, garnet, glauconite, pyroxenes, rutile, sillimanite, staurolite, tourmaline, and zircon. Grains are typically slightly weathered. In the finest grain-size fractions (below 0.002 millimetres), such clay minerals as montmorillonite, illite, and kaolinite predominate over the detrital (fragmental) constituents. Clay minerals may be formed by various colloidal and physicochemical processes during and after the accumulation of loess.

The mineralogical composition of loess is fairly uniform, but there are some local deviations due to differences in grain size and area of origin. The area of origin of the dust fraction is revealed by the heavy mineral assemblage and research has shown that the dust sources may be local, neighbouring, or distant.

The chemical composition of loess most often falls within the following percentage ranges: silica, SiO_2, 50 to 60; alumina, Al_2O_3, eight to 12; iron oxide as Fe_2O_3, two to four; iron oxide as FeO, 0.8 to 1.1; titanium dioxide, TiO_2, and manganese oxide, MnO, about 0.5; lime, CaO, four to 16; and magnesium oxide, MgO, two to six.

The characteristic carbonate content of loess depends on the nature of the dust source, on geochemical and biological processes that occur during and after deposition, and on precipitation and leaching by groundwater. Carbonates are present in loess in a variety of forms, primarily as

Grain-size distribution and mineralogy

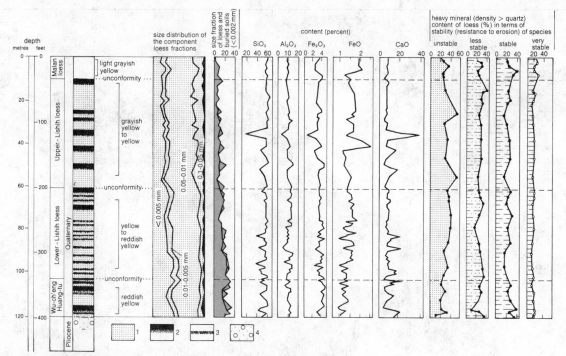

Figure 1: Chemical, mineralogical, and size analyses of loess profile from Wu-ch'eng, Shansi Province. Data show the variation of chemical and physical properties with depth.
From *Report of the VIth International Congress on Quaternary*, vol. 4, *Symposium on Loess* (1964); Panstwowe Wydawnictwo Naukowe Oddzial w Lodzi

incrustations on quartz grains and clay-particle aggregates and as small granules and shell fragments. Secondary concentrations include concretions of nodules (Loessdoll) and layers of lime accumulation (caliche). Lime forms frequent tubular incrustations along decayed plant roots, fissure fillings, and similar avenues.

Loess is a rather ill-consolidated sediment of low compressive strength ranging from 0.5 to 1.5 kilograms per square centimetre (7 to 21 pounds per square inch). It is stable, however, as long as it remains dry. Parting surfaces are vertical because capillary incrustations of lime, developed around the roots of a grassy plant cover, lend a vertical texture to loess. This is why the coefficient of permeability (a measure of ease of fluid penetration) is two to four times higher in the vertical than in the horizontal sense. This also is the cause of the cliff-forming ability of loess.

Soaked and loaded loess, however, is liable to collapse and slumping. Wetting decreases cohesion between grains by two-thirds, and the angle of internal friction also decreases (*e.g.*, from 32 to 20°). Groundwater flow in loess will carry away fine, insoluble mineral particles and this mechanical separation in loess can be accompanied by solution of mineral particles. This process gives rise to depressions, sinkholes, loess wells, and collapse ravines and is much accelerated by gully erosion.

Loess is generally pale yellow or buff in colour, but brownish-yellow and grayish-yellow varieties also occur. Variations in colour largely depend on the finely dispersed limonite (iron oxide) content, which is higher in the hotter, semi-arid regions than in the cooler areas of loess formation. Loess that is richer in limonite tends to be a darker yellow with a pink tint.

Distribution and classification. The world's largest loess-covered areas lie between latitude 55° and 24° N: in China on the banks of the Huang Ho; on the margins of the continental deserts of Inner Asia; in Central Asia in Kazakhstan, Uzbekistan, in the foreland of the Tien Shan, and east of the Caspian Sea; in Siberia along Lake Baikal and the Lena River, and in vast regions in the southern parts of the catchment areas of the Ob and Yenisey rivers. In Europe there is an extensive, uninterrupted loess cover in the South Russian Plain, large spots and belts in the Danube Basin, along the Rhine, along the margin of the former inland ice cap in the German-Polish

plain, and in the Paris Basin. In North America loess covers the plains of the Platte, Missouri, Mississippi, and Ohio rivers and the Columbia Plateau. In the Southern Hemisphere, between latitude 30° and 40° S, the most significant loess regions include the "pampas loesses" of Uruguay and Argentina and parts of New Zealand.

Loess blankets may cover a variety of relief forms; they occur most often in plains, on river valley slopes, flats, and rises, and on pediments in the forelands of mountains, and on alluvial fans. On mountain slopes and intermontane basins, loess occurs to a maximum elevation of 400 to 600 metres (1,300 to 2,000 feet) in Europe, 1,000 to 2,000 metres (3,300 to 6,600 feet) in Inner Asia, and up to 4,000 metres (13,000 feet) in China. Slope loesses tend to thicken downslope. The thickest loess blanket known occurs on mountain slopes in Shensi Province and the Canton area in China (up to 175 metres). The North China Plain is covered with 10 to 30 metres (30 to 100 feet) of redeposited loess and loam. In the southern zone of Asian loesses, the yellow loess is underlain by a thick complex of up to 100 metres (330 feet) of pink, so-called petrified loess. In the South Russian Plain, in the Danube Basin, and in Nebraska and Iowa loess attains thicknesses as great as 60 metres (200 feet). On floodplains, on alluvial fans, and on the margins of loess zones, however, typical thicknesses range from one to ten metres. Although adjacent loess and windblown sand covers often may represent the same deposit, they may also alternate in a vertical profile. In the marginal zone of the Pleistocene ice sheet, for example in Illinois, loess may overlie tills (glacial deposits) or may be interfingered with them.

The lithological classification of loess is based on physical and chemical properties, and the conditions of origin are partly or entirely neglected. In addition to typical loess, loessial deposits also are quite frequent in occurrence. The proportions of silt and other fractions and constituents (clay, sand, lime), as well as colour, porosity, strength, and plasticity of loessial deposits differ significantly from comparable properties of typical loess. This group of deposits includes sandy loess, loessial sand, loess loam, clayey loess, and loess that is altered pedogenically—*i.e.*, during soil-forming processes. Loess-like deposits, on the other hand, include sediments that resemble typical loess only in certain features (mineralogical composition, dominant dust fraction, colour, etc.). These de-

Structure and strength of loess

Lithological and environmental factors in classification

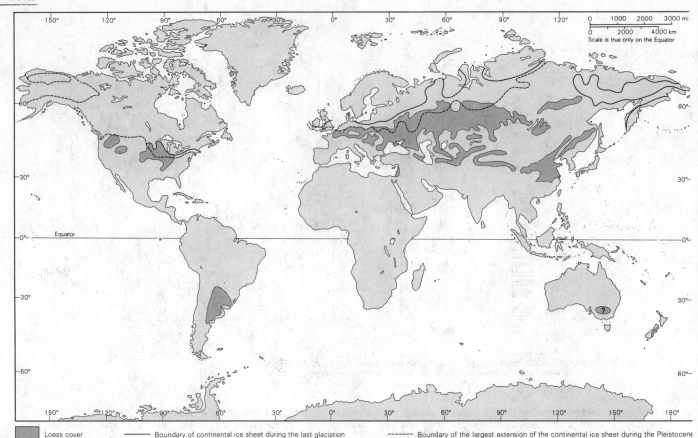

Loess cover   ——— Boundary of continental ice sheet during the last glaciation   ------- Boundary of the largest extension of the continental ice sheet during the Pleistocene

Figure 2: World distribution of loess and loess-like deposits.

posits also are terrestrial, occur within or on the margins of loess regions, and are most often mixed with other types of sediment. The group of loess-like deposits is not rigidly circumscribed; it usually is understood to include loess loam, loess mud, loess-containing rock debris, and stratified loess.

Genetic classifications of loess, in contrast to this lithological classification, are based on the origin of the silt and on the processes that have brought about its accumulation. This requires knowledge of the circumstances of loess formation, which involves many complications and, in all its ramifications, is termed the loess problem.

Environmental conditions in the areas of loess formation are revealed by bones, animal burrows, snail shells, pollen, bits of charcoal, and in many instances by the implements and habitats of Paleolithic man. The more frequent mammalian remains include mammoth, bison, musk ox, lemming, marmot, Siberian mouse, polar fox, cave bear, deer, elk, and reindeer. These lived in the Arctic tundra in cold, wooded steppes. Snail assemblages in loess indicate a cyclic alternation of species, reflecting both cold and humid climates and cold and dry climates; extremely dry conditions also may be indicated for restricted areas. The snails present in the loamy paleosols (ancient soils) that are intercalated between loess packets usually are indicative of a warmer climate. The cyclic alternation of forest and steppe snails shows that the climatic conditions during loess formation could not be exclusively cold and dry; such is the evidence of contained animal remains.

Pollen analysis reveals only the broad outlines of ancient plant ecology but pollen assemblages also indicate that cool grasslands, steppes, wooded steppes, and wooded tundras and tundras were among the preferred environments of loess deposition. These climatic zones lay south of the margins of the extensive Pleistocene ice sheets, significantly displaced from their normal (non-Ice Age) position, together with the zone of westerly winds. The dominant westerly winds were influenced and deflected by the high-pressure anticyclonic system that developed over the ice sheet and by high mountain chains.

The semi-arid zones on the margins of such continental deserts as those in Inner and Central Asia, however, were more humid during the period of Pleistocene loess formation than they are today. This is also indicated by the pollen spectra of Central Asian loesses.

Origin and age. For over a century a number of partly conflicting and partly complementary hypotheses have been put forward to explain the origin of the silt fraction of loess. The mineral constituents of loess, quartz and feldspar, for example, are reduced to minute particles by weathering (*q.v.*) action, principally in semi-arid and arid regions. But the source of dust may also be a silty, sandy unconsolidated sediment of Tertiary Age (from 65,000,000 to 2,500,000 years ago), as for instance, the Ogallala Group of the United States. The sand and silt may have been size sorted by the wind, which then transported and deposited the silt. Dust storms derived from such rock units are frequent even today in the continental deserts of Asia; the silt content of "continental loesses" is derived in this manner.

Another significant source of dust may have been the marginal zone of the Pleistocene ice sheet over Europe and North America. During the several ice advances, or glaciations, huge amounts of glacial till, rich in silt, could accumulate in the zone. The silt fraction, accumulating in the outwash plains, could then be carried away by the westerly winds and deposited on the lee side of some relief feature; this is sometimes called the theory of glacial loess.

Silt may also be removed from its site of origin of first deposition and be sorted by fluvial processes. Abundant silt is borne by rivers and deposited in times of flood in basins and on alluvial fans that border mountain regions. Some of the silt is then removed from broad floodplains by winds; this results in a double sorting, once by water and once by wind, and hence a more sharply defined typical grain size. In this case loess accumulation is not necessarily connected with a glaciation; indeed, most of the alluvial loesses do not date back to a glaciation.

The arguments made in support of wind transport as the origin of loess constitute the eolian theory and include

Origin of silt: the eolian and fluvial theories

the following points: (1) loess forms a blanket over a variety of relief forms; (2) the mean grain size of silt varies inversely with the distance from the dust source, and so does the thickness of loess; (3) the zones of loess and windblown sand are so arranged that they bear an obvious relation to the prevailing wind; (4) the mineralogical composition of loess is independent of the underlying rock formations; and (5) in some places there are interbedded layers of volcanic ash (a wind-derived deposit) between packets of loess.

The arguments supporting the fluvial theory, that the silt fraction of loess is transported and deposited by water, include these points: (1) detailed studies of mineral content in loess and in neighbouring rock formations have proved that the loess deposits covering vast areas of floodplains and alluvial fans are of flood-laid, alluvial origin; (2) rivers carry a great deal of suspended sediment in the silt-size range, particularly in semi-arid steppe and wooded steppe regions; (3) in stratified loessial or loess-like deposits, there are local significant enrichments of clay or sand; and (4) even existing divide areas could acquire fluvial silt deposits under appropriate circumstances of river damming.

Still another theory is invoked for loess deposits that occur on hillslopes because it would seem likely that the downhill movement of earth materials is involved. Loess and loess-like deposits on hillslopes often exhibit a rhythmic stratification parallel to the slope and the strata often alternate with rock debris and thin beds of reworked soils. The lithological character and field relations of such sediments indicate deposition from sheetwash or flash floods, but redeposition could occur because of soil movements over permafrost, downslope creep, or from similar processes.

The reason for conflicting opinions on loess formation is that the silt fraction may have been deposited or reworked by any of the various processes; and, depending on environment and other circumstances, the dominant process may change through time.

Processes in loess formation

There is a consensus that the accumulated dust fraction must have undergone diagenesis (physical and chemical changes after deposition) in order to turn into loess. Diagenesis includes the weathering of fine grains of lime, aluminum silicates, and other substances by hydration in arid climates. In near-surface silt the finest clay particles are cemented by migrating solutions of calcium carbonate and iron oxides and colloidal iron compounds; the quartz grains acquire crusts or coatings of lime or iron and adjacent grains are cemented together. As a result of these processes, some of the finer particles also attain loess fraction size of 0.01 to 0.05 millimetre. It has been proved that a grain size of about 0.05 millimetre is the most favourable for thriving grassy vegetation. Essentially, diagenesis turns sediment deposited in the form of dust into a loosely cemented siltstone.

The peculiar features of loess are thus developed during a process of loess genesis that is akin to that of soil formation. This circumstance served as a basis for the pedogenic (soil origin) theory of loess formation, which basically held that loess is a product of weathering and pedogenesis under semi-arid conditions in grasslands and wooded steppes. It would be difficult to explain the formation of a thick loess blanket subdivided by several horizons of paleosols in this way, however. More reasonable would be a polygenetic origin, in which dust can accumulate as the result of any process alternating in time and space, with loess formation resulting from pedogenetic processes acting under favourable climatic conditions.

These pedogenic processes may take place in three different ways. Epigenesis is an accumulation of a mineral mass without loess properties, perhaps with a high silt and lime content, which under weathering and soil formation acquires loess properties and is transformed into loess. In syngenesis, the accumulation of a mineral mass that is mainly of eolian origin and the acquisition of all loess properties occurs simultaneously, under the influence of soil formation. In protogenesis the accumulated mineral matter already has all the main loess proper-

Loess complex on the right bank of the Danube River in the Great Hungarian Plain, showing the vertical fracturing that is typical in loess deposits.
By courtesy of Marton Pecsi, Geographical Research Institute, Hungarian Academy of Sciences, Budapest

ties because transport occurred after weathering and soil formation.

The optimum conditions of loess formation are thought to have existed along the border of the continental ice sheet, including the cold steppes, wooded steppes, loess tundras, and in the steppes bordering the continental deserts. Under conditions other than optimum, the accumulated dust would likely turn into a loess-like deposit differing from typical loess, namely loess loam, limeless loess, brown earth, or reddish loam, or, alternatively, into a soil.

Loess chronology

The formation of loess packets is correlated with the cold, dry climatic phases of the Pleistocene glaciations in regions marginal to the ice. The climatic phases, and the occasions of loess formation, recurred three to five times as within the last glaciation. The sediment of a single loess packet can be subdivided; in the lower and upper third of each packet, finely stratified loesses tend to predominate, whereas the central third is composed largely of typical loess that is not stratified.

Within the loess series, the various paleosols, clay-rich sands, and water-laid sands, hiatuses (interruptions of the sedimentary record) due to erosion in Europe and North America usually represent warmer Pleistocene climatic stages—interglacial time intervals—or the more humid episodes of such climatic changes. The hiatuses in the accumulation of loess material in China and in Middle Asia are correlative with moist episodes. A more detailed subdivision must be restricted to the upper part of the loess series because in the lower portions the original texture of the loess layers underwent significant alteration.

A loess chronology can be based upon subdivision of the loess series, relating individual loess packets to geological formations or landforms such as river terraces, glacial moraines, etc., as well as to the paleontological and archaeological finds in the loess proper. Some of the younger loesses have been dated by the radiocarbon method. The loess chronology established in this way has revealed that upper Pleistocene "young loesses" are the most widespread in Eurasia and North America. These are subdivided by two to four paleosol horizons into three to five loess packets. The unconsolidated "young loess" developed in a full profile usually overlies a well-developed forest soil or a wooded-steppe-type soil complex of the last interglacial episode.

Loess tended to decay rather rapidly during periods of more abundant precipitation—e.g., during the interglacials. Consequently, the "older loesses" formed during the middle and lower Pleistocene, subdivided by closely spaced paleosols and lime concretion Loess-doll horizons, were preserved largely in the areas that are driest today: Columbia Plateau, Danube Basin, South Russian Plain, Central Asia and parts of China, and elsewhere. Although these older loess series tend to be incomplete, they may represent almost complete Pleistocene sequences in restricted areas. The deeper, older levels of the exposures usually consist of pink silt deposits alternating with red-earth paleosols.

BIBLIOGRAPHY. There are few if any books devoted entirely to loess. One of the best short summaries of the world distribution and inferred climatic significance of loess deposits is contained in R.F. FLINT, *Glacial and Quaternary Geology* (1971). Details of some deposits in eastern Europe, together with many references to the specialized literature, are given in M. PECSI, *Ten Years of Physico Geographic Research in Hungary* (Eng. trans., 1964); and by E. LITEANU, "Contributions to the Study of Loess-Like Deposits in the Wallach Depression, Rumania," *Spec. Pap. Geol. Soc. Am.*, no. 84 (1965). Also of interest is A.L. LUGN, *The Origin and Sources of Loess* (1962).

(Ma.P.)

Logic, Applied

The general discipline of logic embraces the principles by which concepts and propositions are related to one another and, consequently, the techniques of thought by which these relationships can be explored and valid inferences made about them. This discipline can be divided into pure and applied logic, a distinction that parallels that between pure and applied mathematics: pure logic develops a body of strictly abstract machinery—e.g., the syllogism—that displays only the skeletal form of the argument without regard to its content (example: "No *s* is *m*; some *p* are *m*; therefore, some *p* are not *s*."); in applied logic one adapts this machinery for deployment over concrete issues of a certain range of special subject matter—such as beliefs, commands, or duties. Such arguments often are not governed only by strictly formal issues (which alone are relevant in pure logic); they involve also certain subject-matter considerations of a particular area, generally called the material aspects. Applied logic, to be sure, has its formal aspects, as well, and so cannot be equated with material logic as such; nor can it be equated with practical logic (analysis of statements of the form "I choose . . . ."; "I prefer . . . ."; "I do . . . ."), which is only one of its branches.

Range of applications

The applications envisaged in applied logic cover a vast range, relating to reasoning in the sciences and in philosophy, as well as in everyday discourse. They include: (1) the various sorts of reasoning affecting the conduct of ordinary discourse as well as the theory of the logical relations that exist within special realms of discourse—between two commands, for example, or between one question and another; (2) special forms of logic designed for scientific applications, such as temporal logic (of what "was" or "will be" the case), or mereology (the logic of parts and wholes); and (3) special forms for concepts bearing upon philosophical issues, such as logics that deal with statements of the form "I know that . . . ."; "I believe that . . . ."; "It is permitted to . . . ."; "It is obligatory to . . . ."; or "It is prohibited to . . . ."

The critique of forms of reasoning

CORRECT AND DEFECTIVE ARGUMENT FORMS

An argument (in logic) is a body of discourse that presents evidence—or purported evidence—in support of some thesis. Correspondingly, an argument has two components: a conclusion, the thesis argued for; and certain premises, the considerations adduced on behalf of the conclusion. (The conclusion is said to be drawn, or inferred, from the premises.) An argument is deductively valid when its premises provide conclusive evidence for the conclusion—i.e., if the conclusion must be true whenever the premises are true. An argument that fails to be conclusively deduced is invalid; it is also said to be fallacious (unless reclassified as a nondeductive argument and reinstated by appeal to material or substantive considerations beyond its merely formal aspects).

An argument may be fallacious in three ways: in its material content, through a misstatement of the facts; in its wording, through an incorrect use of terms; or in its structure (or form), through the use of an improper process of inference. As shown in the diagram below, fallacies are correspondingly classified as (1) material, (2) verbal, and (3) formal. Groups (2) and (3) are called logical fallacies, or fallacies "in discourse," in contrast to the substantive, or material, fallacies of group (1), called fallacies "in matter"; and groups (1) and (2) are called informal fallacies, in contrast to group (3).

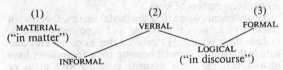

KINDS OF FALLACIES

Material fallacies. The material fallacies are also known as fallacies of presumption, because the premises "presume" too much—they either covertly assume the conclusion or avoid the issue in view.

The classification that is still widely used is that of Aristotle's *Sophistical Refutations*: (1) The fallacy of accident is committed by an argument that applies a general rule to a particular case in which some special circumstance ("accident") makes the rule inapplicable. The truth that "men are capable of seeing" is no basis for the conclusion that "blind men are capable of seeing." This is a special case of the fallacy of *secundum quid* (more fully: *a dicto simpliciter ad dictum secundum quid,* which means "from a saying [taken too] simply to a saying according to what [it really is]"; *i.e.*, according to its truth as holding only under special provisos). This fallacy is committed when a general proposition is used as the premise for an argument without attention to the (tacit) restrictions and qualifications that govern it and invalidate its application in the manner at issue. (2) The converse fallacy of accident argues improperly from a special case to a general rule. The fact that a certain drug is beneficial to some sick persons does not imply that it is beneficial to all men. (3) Thus, the fallacy of irrelevant conclusion is committed when the conclusion changes the point that is at issue in the premises. Special cases of irrelevant conclusion are presented by the so-called fallacies of relevance. These include: (*a*) the argument *ad hominem* (speaking "against the man" rather than to the issue), in which the premises may only make a personal attack on a person who holds some thesis, instead of offering grounds showing why what he says is false; (*b*) the argument *ad populum* (an appeal "to the people"), which, instead of offering logical reasons, appeals to such popular attitudes as the dislike of injustice; (*c*) the argument *ad misericordiam* (an appeal "to pity"), as when a trial lawyer, rather than arguing for his client's innocence, tries to move the jury to sympathy for him; (*d*) the argument *ad verecundiam* (an appeal "to awe"), which seeks to secure acceptance of the conclusion on the grounds of its endorsement by persons whose views are held in general respect; (*e*) the argument *ad ignorantiam* (an appeal "to ignorance"), which argues that something (*e.g.*, extrasensory perception) is so since no one has shown that it is not so; and (*f*) the argument *ad baculum* (an appeal "to force"), which rests on a threatened or implied use of force to induce acceptance of its conclusion. (4) The fallacy of circular argument, known as *petitio principii* ("begging the question"), occurs when the premises presume, openly or covertly, the very conclusion that is to be demonstrated (example: "Gregory always votes wisely." "But how do you know?" "Because he always votes Libertarian."). A special form of this fallacy, called a vicious circle, or *circulus in probando* ("arguing in a circle"), occurs in a course of reasoning typified by the complex argument in which a premise p_1 is used to prove p_2; p_2 is used to prove p_3; and so on, until p_{n-1} is used to prove p_n; then p_n is subsequently used in a proof of p_1, and the whole series $p_1, p_2, \ldots, p_n$ is taken as established. (Example: "McKinley College's baseball team is the best in the Association [$p_n = p_3$]; they are the best because of their strong batting potential [p_2]; they have this potential because of the ability

Accident, converse accident, irrelevant conclusion

Circular argument

of Jones, Crawford, and Randolph at the bat [p_1]." "But how do you know that Jones, Crawford, and Randolph are such good batters?" "Well, after all, these men are the backbone of the best team in the Association [p_3 again].") Strictly speaking, *petitio principii* is not a fallacy of reasoning but an ineptitude in argumentation: thus the argument from p as a premise to p as conclusion is not deductively invalid but lacks any power of conviction, since no one who questioned the conclusion could concede the premise. (5) The fallacy of false cause (*non causa pro causa*) mislocates the cause of one phenomenon in another that is only seemingly related. The most common version of this fallacy, called *post hoc ergo propter hoc* ("after which hence by which"), mistakes temporal sequence for causal connection—as when a misfortune is attributed to a "malign event," like the dropping of a mirror. Another, more sophisticated, and purely logical version of this fallacy occurs, however, in a complex form of the *reductio ad absurdum*—an argument that, in its simple form, declares that an assumption is false if a contradiction can be drawn from it. In the present case, a contradiction drawn jointly from several premises—say, p_1, p_2, p_3, and p_4—is taken to establish the falsity of one of them—say, p_2—when another—say, p_3—is really the source of the difficulty. Thus, the premises p_1 through p_4 may be those, for example, of the following two syllogisms:

p_1: "All statesmen are political figures who act in the public interest."
p_2: "Jones is a statesman."
C_1: Therefore, "Jones is a political figure who is acting in the public interest."

and

p_3: "Anyone who shamelessly campaigns for re-election is not acting in the public interest."
p_4: "Jones is shamelessly campaigning for re-election."
C_2: Therefore, "Jones is not acting in the public interest."

But conclusions C_1 and C_2 are contradictory. A critic might therefore argue that p_2 is false and that Jones is not a statesman. But he could be wrong, for the trouble could lie in p_3: far from acting at variance with the public interest, a man might campaign in the belief that he cannot accomplish his legislative program, which he believes to be in the public interest, unless he wins another term in office. His campaigning may, thus, be in the public interest; and he may be a statesman after all. (6) The fallacy of many questions (*plurimum interrogationum*) consists in demanding or giving a single answer to a question when this answer could either be divided (example: "Do you like the twins?" "Neither yes nor no; but Ann yes and Mary no.") or refused altogether, because a mistaken presupposition is involved (example: "Have you stopped beating your wife?"). (7) The fallacy of *non sequitur* ("it does not follow"), still more drastic than the preceding, occurs when there is not even a deceptively plausible appearance of valid reasoning, because there is a virtually complete lack of connection between the given premises and the conclusion drawn from them. Some authors, however, identify *non sequitur* with the fallacy of the consequent (see below *Formal fallacies*).

Verbal fallacies. These fallacies, called fallacies of ambiguity, arise when the conclusion is achieved through an improper use of words.

The principal instances are as follows: (1) Equivocation occurs when a word or phrase is used in one sense in one premise and another sense in some other needed premise or in the conclusion (example: "The loss made Jones mad [= angry]; mad [= insane] people should be institutionalized; so Jones should be institutionalized."). The figure-of-speech fallacy is the special case arising from confusion between the ordinary sense of a word and its metaphorical, figurative, or technical employment (example: "For the past week Joan has been living on the heights of ecstasy." "And what is her address there?"). (2) Amphiboly occurs when the grammar of a statement is such that several distinct meanings can obtain (example: "The king hopes you the enemy will slay. So he wishes you well."). (3) Accent is a counterpart of amphiboly arising when a statement can bear distinct meanings

depending upon which word is stressed (example: "Men are *considered* equal." "Men are considered *equal*."). (4) Composition occurs when the premise that the parts of a whole are of a certain nature is improperly used to infer that the whole itself must also be of this nature (example: a story made up of good paragraphs is thus said to be a good story). (5) Division—the reverse of composition—occurs when the premise that a collective whole has a certain nature is improperly used to infer that a part of this whole must also be of this nature (example: in a speech that is long winded it is presumed that every sentence is long). But this fallacy and its predecessor can be viewed as versions of *equivocation*, in which the distributive use of a term—*i.e.*, its application to the elements of an aggregate (example: "the crowd," viewed as individuals)—is equivocally confused with its collective use ("the crowd," as a unitary whole)—compare "The crowd were filing through the turnstile" with "The crowd was compressed into the space of a city block."

Formal fallacies. Strictly logical, or formal, fallacies arise not from the specific matter of the argument but from a structural pattern of reasoning that is generically incorrect.

A classic case is Aristotle's fallacy of the consequent, relating to reasoning from premises of the form: "If p_1, then p_2." The fallacy has two forms: (1) denial of the antecedent, in which one mistakenly argues from the premises "If p_1, then p_2" and "not-p_1" (symbolized $\sim p_1$), to the conclusion "not-p_2" (example: "If George is a man of good faith, he can be entrusted with this office; but George is not a man of good faith; therefore, George cannot be entrusted with this office"); and (2) affirmation of the consequent, in which one mistakenly argues from the premises "If p_1, then p_2" and "p_2," to the conclusion "p_1" (example: "If Amos was a prophet, then he had a social conscience; he had a social conscience; hence, Amos was a prophet"). Most of the traditionally considered formal fallacies, however, relate to the syllogism (see SYLLOGISTIC). One example may be cited, that of the fallacy of illicit major (or minor) premise, which violates the rules for "distribution." (A term is said to be distributed when reference is made to all members of the class. Example: in "Some crows are not friendly," reference is made to all friendly things, but not to all crows.) The fallacy arises when a major (or minor) term that is undistributed in the premise is distributed in the conclusion (example: "All tubers are high-starch foods [undistributed]; no squashes are tubers; therefore, no squashes are high-starch foods [distributed]").

Epistemic logic

Epistemic logic deals with the logical issues arising within the gamut of such epistemological concepts as knowledge, belief, assertion, doubt, question-and-answer, or the like. Instead of dealing with the essentially factual issues of alethic logic (Greek *alētheia*, "truth")—*i.e.*, with what is actually or must necessarily or can possibly be the case—it relates to what people know or believe or maintain or doubt to be the case.

THE LOGIC OF BELIEF

From the logical standpoint, a belief is generally analyzed as a relationship obtaining between the person who accepts some thesis on the one hand, and the thesis that he accepts, on the other. Correspondingly, given a person x, it is convenient to consider the set $\mathbf{B}_x$ of x's beliefs and represent the statement "x believes that p" as $p \in \mathbf{B}_x$. (The symbol $\in$ represents membership in a set, $\notin$ its denial.)

Alternative ways of construing belief. Before the formulation of any logical theory of belief can get under way, however, it is essential to specify the precise sense at issue when a person is said to believe something. It is necessary to choose between three alternative constructions of "x believes that p":

1. The disposition-to-explicit-assent construction, according to which "x believes that p" obtains if he overtly professes to do so (and is candid) or would overtly so profess (if candid) once the matter is duly explained to him. That is, x is

Other material fallacies

Equivocation, amphiboly, and others

simply asked if he believes p, and the matter is settled by his response, if there is no reason to suspect disingenuousness.

2. The commitment-to-assent construction, according to which "x believes that p" if he either (a) explicitly assents to p in the preceding manner or (b) is logically committed to giving assent, because p follows logically from propositions to which he does give assent.

3. The behavioristic construction, according to which "x believes that p" if x acts as though p were the case.

Shortcomings of the three constructions

The behavioristic construction has serious shortcomings insofar as it strays from the ordinary, presystematic concept at issue in ordinary discourse about beliefs. Fiji Islanders may well act as though Julius Caesar had never existed but cannot be said to have beliefs in the matter. The other two approaches also have shortcomings. The commitment-to-assent construction gives rise, for example, to the entailment principle (EP): "If p is one of the beliefs held by x, and if q follows deductively from p, then q is one of the beliefs held by x"; or, symbolically:

(EP)   If $p \in \mathbf{B}_x$ and $p \vdash q$, then $q \in \mathbf{B}_x$,

in which the symbol $\vdash$ signifies that the proposition on the right side follows as a deductively valid consequence from those on the left. Example: "That there are more people in Kōbe than the number of hairs that any human head can hold (p)" is a member of ($\in$) the set of Joe's beliefs ($\mathbf{B}_{\text{Joe}}$). It can be deduced from p, however, that "there are at least two people in Kōbe having the same number of hairs in their head (q)." The conclusion can be seen by supposing that one person is found (so far as possible) for each number of hairs, from a man with one hair to one with the maximum possible number. If these people are then seated in an amphitheatre in order by their number of hairs, there will still be people left unseated—each a contender for a seat already filled. Hence, Joe believes q, that "there are at least two people in Kōbe (viz., those pairs contending for seats) having the same number of hairs in their head," whether he realizes it or not. But while a person is certainly committed to accepting the consequences of his beliefs, it is implausible to say that he believes them; very possibly Joe may disavow that there are two such people in Kōbe. It is only in some strange and artificial sense of the term that one's belief in certain axioms can be held to entail belief in some extremely remote consequence thereof.

On the other hand, with the preparedness-for-explicit-assent construction, it seems impossible to build up any sort of logic whatsoever. On this construction, it may well be that:

1. "p is among the beliefs of x and not-p is among the beliefs of x"; i.e., $p \in \mathbf{B}_x$ and $\sim p \in \mathbf{B}_x$ (example: "x believes that he can jump the chasm"; "x believes that he cannot jump the chasm"); or that

2. A man may assent to (believe in) each of two statements, p and q, taken separately—i.e., both $p \in \mathbf{B}_x$ and $q \in \mathbf{B}_x$—but fail to assent to their conjunction—$(p \cdot q) \notin \mathbf{B}_x$ in which the centred dot means "and." For example, someone might assent to each of the statements "God is benevolent" and "There is evil in the world" but fail to assent to (or, perhaps, even deny) their conjunction; i.e., "God is benevolent but there is evil in the world."

Clearly, one may fail to develop a logic of belief when the beliefs at issue turn out to be highly illogical—as well they may.

Theory of belief.   To articulate a viable logic of belief, it is, at the very least, essential to postulate certain minimal conditions of rationality regarding the parties whose beliefs are at issue:

Conditions of rationality

1. Consistency: "If x believes that p, then x does not believe that not-p"; i.e.,

If $p \in \mathbf{B}_x$, then $\sim p \notin \mathbf{B}_x$.

"If not-p, then x does not believe that p"; i.e.,

If $\vdash \sim p$, then $p \notin \mathbf{B}_x$.

Example: If "Jesus was a Zealot" (p) is among ($\in$) the beliefs of Ralph ($\mathbf{B}_{\text{Ralph}}$), then "Jesus was not a Zealot" ($\sim p$) is not among ($\notin$) Ralph's beliefs. It is an accepted thesis ($\vdash$) that "Jesus was not a Zealot." Hence, "Jesus was a Zealot" is not among Ralph's beliefs. (Note that the symbol $\vdash$, in cases where it appears as an isolated prefix, represents

"thesis-hood"; i.e., a deductive consequence—as it were—from no premises.)

2. Conjunctive composition and division: "If x believes that p_1, and x believes that p_2, etc., to x believes that p_n, then x believes that p_1 and p_2, etc., and p_n"; i.e.,

If $(p_1 \in \mathbf{B}_x, p_2 \in \mathbf{B}_x, \ldots, p_n) \in \mathbf{B}_x$,
then $(p_1 \cdot p_2 \cdot \ldots \cdot p_n) \in \mathbf{B}_x$,

and conversely. Example: If "cats are affectionate" (p_1), "cats are clean" (p_2), etc., to "cats are furry" (p_n) are among ($\in$) Bob's beliefs ($\mathbf{B}_{\text{Bob}}$), then "cats are affectionate and clean, etc., and furry" ($p_1 \cdot p_2 \cdot \ldots \cdot p_n$) is also a belief of Bob's.

3. Minimal inferential capacity: "If x believes that p, and q is an obvious consequence of p, then x believes that q"; i.e.,

If $p \in \mathbf{B}_x$ and $p \models q$, then $q \in \mathbf{B}_x$.

Example: "If x believes that his cat is on the mat, and his cat's being on the mat has an obvious consequence that something is on the mat, then x believes that something is on the mat."

Here item 3 is a form of the entailment principle, but with $\models$ representing entailment of the simplest sort, designating obvious consequence—say, deducibility by fewer than two (or n) inferential steps, employing only those primitive rules of inference that have been classified as obvious. (In arguments about beliefs, however, all repetitions of the application of this version of the entailment principle must be avoided.) These principles endow the theory with such rules as:

1. "If x believes that not-p, then he does not believe that p"; i.e.,

If $\sim p \in \mathbf{B}_x$, then $p \notin \mathbf{B}_x$.

2. "If x believes that p, and x believes that q, then x believes that both p and q taken together"; i.e.,

If $p \in \mathbf{B}_x$ and $q \in \mathbf{B}_x$, then $p \cdot q \in \mathbf{B}_x$.

3. "If x believes that p, then x believes that either p or q"; i.e.,

If $p \in \mathbf{B}_x$, then $p \lor q \in \mathbf{B}_x$,

given "$p \vdash p \lor q$" as an "obvious" rule of inference (where $\lor$ means "either—or").

One key question of the logical theory of belief relates to the area of iterative beliefs (example: "Andrews believes that I believe that he believes me to be untrustworthy"). Clearly, one would not want to have such theses as:

Iterative beliefs

1. "If y believes that x believes that p, then x believes that p"; i.e.,

If $(p \in \mathbf{B}_x) \in \mathbf{B}_y$, then $p \in \mathbf{B}_x$ $(y \neq x)$

nor

2. "If y believes that x believes that p, then y believes that p"; i.e.,

If $(p \in \mathbf{B}_x) \in \mathbf{B}_y$, then $p \in \mathbf{B}_y$ $(y \neq x)$.

But when the iteration is subject-uniform rather than subject-diverse, it might be advantageous to postulate certain special theses, such as:

If $p \in \mathbf{B}_x$, then $(p \in \mathbf{B}_x) \in \mathbf{B}_x$,

which in effect limits the beliefs at issue to conscious beliefs. The plausibility of this thesis also implicates its converse; viz., whether there are circumstances under which someone's believing that he believes something would necessarily vouch for his believing of it—i.e., whether it is legitimate to argue that "If x believes that he believes that p, then he believes that p"; i.e.,

If $(p \in \mathbf{B}_x) \in \mathbf{B}_x$, then $p \in \mathbf{B}_x$.

According to this thesis, the belief set $\mathbf{B}_x$ is to have the feature of second-order—as opposed to direct—applicability. From $q \in \mathbf{B}_x$, it is not, in general, permissible to infer q, but one is entitled to do so when q takes the special form $p \in \mathbf{B}_x$; i.e., when the belief at issue is one about the subject's own beliefs.

A theory of belief along these lines is a halfway house between the commitment-to-assent conception of belief, which is too inclusive and the explicit-assent approach, which is too restrictive. The theory is predicated on the view that belief is subject to logical compulsion but that the range of this compulsion is limited since men are not logically omniscient. Belief here is like sight: man has a limited range of logical vision; he can see clearly in the immediate logical neighbourhood of his beliefs but only dimly afar.

THE LOGIC OF KNOWING

The propositional sense of knowing (*i.e.*, knowing that something or other is the case), rather than the operational sense of knowing (*i.e.*, knowing how something or other is done), is generally taken as the starting point for a logical theory of knowing. Accordingly, the logician may begin with a person x and consider a set of propositions $\mathbf{K}_x$ to represent his "body of knowledge." The aim of the theory then is to clarify and to characterize the relationship "x knows that p" or "p is among the items known to x," which is here represented as: $p \in \mathbf{K}_x$.

"Knowing as" and "being" true

There can be false knowledge only in the sense that "he *thought* he knew that p, but he was mistaken." When the falsity of purported knowledge becomes manifest, the claim to knowledge must be withdrawn. "I know that p, but it may be false that p" is a contradiction in terms. When something is asserted or admitted as known, it follows that this must be claimed to be true. But what sort of inferential step is at issue in the thesis that "x knows p" leads to "p is true"? Is the link deductive, inductive, presuppositional, or somehow "pragmatic"? Each view has its supporters: on the deductive approach, $p \in \mathbf{K}_x$ logically implies (deductively entails) p; on the inductive approach, $p \in \mathbf{K}_x$ renders p extremely probable, though not necessarily certain; on the presuppositional approach, $p \in \mathbf{K}_x$ is improper (nonsensical) whenever p is not true; and on the pragmatic approach, the assertion of $p \in \mathbf{K}_x$ carries with it a rational commitment to the assertion of p (in a manner, however, that does not amount to deductive entailment). From the standpoint of a logic of knowing, the most usual practice is to assume the deductive approach and to lay it down as a rule that if $p \in \mathbf{K}_x$, then p is true. This approach construes knowledge in a very strong sense.

According to a common formula, knowledge is "true, justified belief." This formulation, however, seems defective. Let the expression $\mathbf{J}xp$ be defined as meaning "x has justification for accepting p," then:

$$p \in \mathbf{K}_x = p \cdot \mathbf{J}xp \cdot p \in \mathbf{B}_x.$$

Example: The proposition "Jane knows that ($\mathbf{K}_{\text{Jane}}$) the gown is priceless (p)" means ($=$) "The gown is priceless, and Jane has justification for accepting that it is priceless ($\mathbf{J}_{\text{Jane}} \, p$) and Jane believes that it is priceless ($p \in \mathbf{B}_{\text{Jane}}$)." One cannot but assume that the conceptual nature of $\mathbf{J}$ is such as to underwrite the rule: "If x is justified in accepting p, then he is justified in accepting 'Either p or q' "; *i.e.*,

(J)   If $\mathbf{J}xp$, then $\mathbf{J}x\,(p \vee q)$,

in which q can be any other proposition whatsoever. The components p, q, and x may be such that all of the following obtain:

1. not-p
2. q
3. x believes that p; *i.e.*, $p \in \mathbf{B}_x$
4. x does not believe that q; *i.e.*, $q \notin \mathbf{B}_x$ and, indeed, x believes that not-q; *i.e.*, $\sim q \in \mathbf{B}_x$
5. x is justified in accepting q; *i.e.*, $\mathbf{J}xq$
6. x believes that either p or q; *i.e.*, $p \vee q \in \mathbf{B}_x$.

Clearly, on any reasonable interpretation of $\mathbf{B}$ and $\mathbf{J}$, this combination of six premises is possible. But the following consequences would then obtain:

7. $p \vee q$ by item 2 above
8. $\mathbf{J}x(p \vee q)$ by item 5 above and by $\mathbf{J}$
9. $(p \vee q) \in \mathbf{K}_x$ by items 6, 7, and 8.

However the conclusion 9 is wrong: x cannot properly be said to know that either p or q when $p \vee q$ is true solely because of the truth of q (which x rejects), but $p \vee q$ is believed by x solely because he accepts p (which is false). This example shows that the proposed definition of knowledge as "true, justified belief" cannot be made to

work; and the best plan, therefore, seems to be to treat the logic of knowing directly, rather than through the mediation of acceptance (belief) and justification.

Overt versus tacit knowledge

Since Aristotle's day, stress has been placed on the distinction between actual, overt knowledge that requires an explicit, consciously occurring awareness of what is known and potential, tacit knowledge that requires only implicit dispositional awareness. Unless $p \in \mathbf{K}_x$ is construed in the tacit sense, the following principles will not hold:

If $p \in \mathbf{K}_x$ and $p \vdash q$, then $q \in \mathbf{K}_x$.

If $p \in \mathbf{K}_x$ and $q \in \mathbf{K}_x$, then $(p \cdot q) \in \mathbf{K}_x$.

These two rules, if accepted, however, suffice to guarantee the principle:

If $p_1, p_2, \ldots, p_n \vdash q$, then $p_1 \in \mathbf{K}_x$, $p_2 \in \mathbf{K}_x$, $\ldots$, $p_n \in \mathbf{K}_x \vdash q \in \mathbf{K}_x$.

Similar considerations regarding the potential construction of knowledge govern the answer to the question of whether, when something is known, this fact itself is known: if $p \in \mathbf{K}_x$, then $(p \in \mathbf{K}_x) \in \mathbf{K}_x$. This principle is eminently plausible, provided that the membership of $\mathbf{K}_x$ is construed in the implicit (tacit) rather than in the explicit (overt) sense.

THE LOGIC OF QUESTIONS

Whether a given grouping of words is functioning as a question may hinge upon intonation, accentuation, or even upon context, rather than upon overt form: at bottom, questions represent a functional rather than a purely grammatical category. The very concept of a question is correlative with that of an answer; and every question correspondingly delimits a range of possible answers. One way of classifying questions is in terms of the surface characteristics of this range. On this basis, the logician can distinguish (among others):

1. Yes/no questions (example: "Is today Tuesday?");
2. Item-specification questions (example: "What is an instance of a prime number?");
3. Instruction-seeking questions (example: "How does one bake an apple pie?"); etc.

Propositional approach

From the logical standpoint, however, a more comprehensive policy and one leading to greater precision is to treat every answer as given in a complete proposition ("Today is not Tuesday"; "Three is an example of a prime number"; etc.). From this standpoint, questions can be classed in terms of the nature of the answers. There would then be factual questions (example: "What day is today?") and normative questions (example: "What ought to be done in these circumstances?").

The advantage of the propositional approach to answers is that it captures the intrinsically close relationship between question and answer. The possible answers to (1) "What is the population of A-ville?" and (2) "What is the population of B-burgh?" are seemingly the same; namely, numbers of the series 0, 1, 2, ... But once complete propositions are taken to be at issue, then an answer to (1), such as "The population of A-ville is 5,238," no longer counts as an answer to (2), since the latter must mention B-burgh. This approach has the disadvantage, on the other hand, of obscuring similarities in similar questions. One can now no longer say of two brothers that the questions "Who is Tom's father?" and "Who is John's father?" have the same answer.

With every question Q can be correlated the set of propositions $\mathbf{A}(Q)$ of possible answers to Q. Thus, "What day of the week is today?" has seven conceivable answers, of the form "The day of the week today is Monday," and the like. A possible answer to a question must be a possibly true statement. Accordingly, the question "What is an example of a prime number?" does not have "The Washington Monument is an example of a prime number" among its possible answers.

Truth-values in question theory

A question can be said to be true if it has a true answer; *i.e.*, if $(\exists p) \, [p \cdot p \in \mathbf{A}(Q)]$—which (taking the existential quantifier $\exists$ to mean "there exists . . .") can be read "There exists a proposition p such that p is true and p is among the answers of Q"; otherwise it is false; *i.e.*, when all of its answers are false. If he never came at all, the question "On what day of the week did he come?"

is a false question in the sense that it lacks any true answer.

A true question can be called contingent if it admits of possible answers that are false, as in "Where did Jones put his pen?" In logic and mathematics there are, presumably, no contingent questions.

Questions can have presuppositions, as in "Why does Smith dislike Jones?" Any possible answer here must take the form "Smith dislikes Jones because . . ." and so commits one to the claim that "Smith dislikes Jones." Every such question with a false presupposition must be a false question: all of its possible answers (if any) are false.

Besides falsity, questions can exhibit an even more drastic sort of "impropriety." They can be illegitimate in that they have no possible answers whatsoever. (Example: "What is an example of an even prime number different from two?") The logic of questions is correspondingly three valued: a question can be true (*i.e.*, have a true answer); illegitimate (*i.e.*, have no possible answer at all); or false (*i.e.*, have possible answers but no true ones).

One question, Q_1, will entail another, Q_2, if every possible answer to the first deductively yields a possible answer to the second, and every true answer to the first deductively yields a true answer to the second. In this sense the question "What are the dimensions of that box?" entails the question "What is the height of that box?"

Practical logic

The theory of reasoning with concepts of practice—of analyzing the logical relations obtaining among statements about actions and their accompaniments in choosing, planning, commanding, permitting, etc.—comprises the domain of practical logic.

THE LOGIC OF PREFERENCE

The logic of preference—also called the logic of choice, or prohairetic logic (Greek *proairesis*, "a choosing")—seeks to systematize the formal rules that govern the conception "*x* is preferred to *y*." A diversity of things can be at issue here: (1) Is *x* preferred to *y* by some individual (or group), or is *x* preferable to *y* in terms of some impersonal criterion? (2) Is on-balance preferability at issue or preferability in point of some particular factor (such as economy or safety or durability)? The resolution of these questions, though vital for interpretation, does not affect the formal structure of the preference relationships.

Symbolization and approach taken in prohairetic logic. The fundamental tools of the logic of preference are as follows: (1) (strong) preference: *x* is preferable to *y*, symbolically $x \gg y$; (2) indifference: *x* and *y* are indifferent, $x \cong y$, defined as "neither $x \gg y$ nor $y \gg x$"; (3) weak preference: *x* is no less preferred than *y*, $x \geqslant y$, defined as "either $x \gg y$ or $x \cong y$." Since preference comprises a relationship, its three types can be classed in terms of certain distinctions commonly drawn in the logic of relations: that of reflexivity (whether holding of itself: "John supports himself"), of symmetry (whether holding when its terms are interchanged: "Peter is the cousin of Paul"; "Paul is the cousin of Peter"), and of transitivity (whether transferable: "a > b"; "b > c"; therefore, "a > c"). Once it is established that the (strong) preference relation ($\gg$) is an ordering (*i.e.*, is irreflexive, asymmetric, and transitive), it then follows that weak preference ($\geqslant$) is reflexive, nonsymmetric, and transitive and that indifference ($\cong$) is an equivalence relation (*i.e.*, reflexive, symmetric, and transitive).

The "Measure of Merit" One common approach to establishing a preference relation is to begin with a "measure of merit" to evaluate the relative desirability of the items *x*, *y*, *z*, . . . , that are at issue. Thus for any item *x*, a real-number quantity is obtained, symbolized $\#(x)$. (Such a measure is called a utility measure, the units are called utiles, and the comparisons or computations involved comprise a preference calculus.) In terms of such a measure, a preference ordering is readily introduced by the definitions that: (1) *x* $\gg$ *y* is to be construed as $\#(x) > \#(y)$; (2) $x \geqslant y$ as

$\#(x) \geq \#(y)$; and (3) $x \cong y$ as $\#(x) = \#(y)$, in which $\geq$ means "is greater than or equal to." Given these definitions, the relationships enumerated above must all obtain. Thus, the step from a utility measure to a preference ordering is simple.

Construction of a logic of preference. In constructing a logic of preference, it is assumed that the items at issue are propositions *p*, *q*, *r*, . . . and that the logician is to introduce a preferential ordering among them, with $p \gg q$ to mean "*p*'s being the case is preferred to *q*'s being the case." The problem is to systematize the logical relationships among such statements in order to permit a determination of whether, for example, it is acceptable to argue that: If either *p* is preferable to *q* or *p* is preferable to *r*, then *p* is preferable to either *q* or *r*,

$$(p \gg q \vee p \gg r) \supset [p \gg (q \vee r)]$$

(in which $\supset$ means "implies" or "if . . . then"), or to argue similarly that

$$(p \gg q \cdot r \gg q) \supset [(p \cdot r) \gg q].$$

Example: "If eating pears (*p*) is preferable to eating quinces (*q*) and eating rhubarb (*r*) is preferable to eating quinces, then eating both pears and rhubarb is preferable to eating quinces." The task is one of erecting a foundation for the systematization of the formal rules governing such a propositional preference relation—a foundation that can be either axiomatic or linguistic (*i.e.*, in terms of a semantical criterion of acceptability).

Approach in terms of possible worlds One procedure—adapted from the ideas of the well-known contemporary Finnish philosopher, Georg Henrik von Wright (born 1916), a prolific contributor to applied logic—is as follows: beginning with a basic set of possible worlds (or states of affairs) $w_1, w_2, \ldots, w_n$, all of the propositions to be dealt with are first defined with respect to these by the usual logical connectives ($\vee$, $\cdot$, $\supset$, etc.). Given two elementary propositions *p* and *q*, there are just the following possibilities: both are true, *p* is true and *q* is false, *p* is false and *q* is true, or both are false. Corresponding to each of these possibilities is a possible world; thus,

$$w_1 = p \cdot q$$
$$w_2 = p \cdot \sim q$$
$$w_3 = \sim p \cdot q$$
$$w_4 = \sim p \cdot \sim q.$$

The truth of *p* then amounts to the statement that one of the worlds w_1, w_2 obtains, so that *p* is equivalent to $w_1 \vee w_2$. Moreover, a given basic preference/indifference ordering among the w_i is assumed. On this basis the following general characterization of propositional preference is stipulated: If delta (δ) is taken to represent any (and thus every) proposition independent of *p* and *q*, then *p* is preferable to *q*, $p \gg q$, if for every such δ it is the case that every possible world in which *p* and not-*q* and δ are the case, $p \cdot \sim q \cdot \delta$ is *w*-preferable to every possible world in which not-*p* and *q* and δ is the case, $\sim p \cdot q \cdot \delta$; *i.e.*, when $p \cdot \sim q$ is always preferable to $\sim p \cdot q$ provided that everything else is equal. It is readily shown that through this approach such general rules as the following are obtained:

1. If *p* is preferable to *q*, then *q* is not preferable to *p*; *i.e.*,

$$p \gg q \vdash \sim(q \gg p).$$

2. If *p* is preferable to *q*, and *q* is preferable to *r*, then *p* is preferable to *r*; *i.e.*,

$$(p \gg q \cdot q \gg r) \vdash (p \gg r).$$

3. If *p* is preferable to *q*, then not-*q* is preferable to not-*p*; *i.e.*,

$$p \gg q \vdash \sim q \gg \sim p.$$

4. If *p* is preferable to *q*, then having *p* and not-*q* is preferable to having not-*p* and *q*; *i.e.*,

$$p \gg q \vdash (p \cdot \sim q) \gg (\sim p \cdot q).$$

The preceding construction of preference requires only a preference ordering of the possible worlds. If, however, a measure for both probability and desirability (utility) of possible worlds is given, then one can define the corresponding #-value (see below) of an arbitrary proposition p as the probabilistically weighed utility value of all of the possible worlds in which the proposition obtains. As an example, p may be the statement, "The Franklin Club caters chiefly to business people" and q the statement, "The Franklin Club is sports oriented." It may then be supposed as given that the following values hold:

World	Probability	Desirability
$w_1 = p \cdot q$	1/6	-2
$w_2 = p \cdot \sim q$	2/6	$+1$
$w_3 = \sim p \cdot q$	3/6	-1
$w_4 = \sim p \cdot \sim q$	1/6	$+3.$

The #-value of a proposition is determined by first multiplying the probability times the desirability of each world in which the proposition is true, and then taking the sum of these. For example, the #-value of p is determined as follows: p is true in each of w_1 and w_2 (and only these); the probability times the desirability of w_1 is $\frac{1}{6} \times (-2)$ and of w_2 is $\frac{2}{6} \times (+1)$; thus #-(p) is $\frac{1}{6} \times (-2) + \frac{2}{6} \times (+1) = 0$. (The #-value corresponds to the decision theorists' notion of expected value.) By this procedure it can easily be determined that

$$\#(p) = 0 \qquad \#(\sim p) = \tfrac{1}{6}$$
$$\#(q) = -(\tfrac{1}{6}) \qquad \#(\sim q) = \tfrac{5}{6}.$$

Since both $\#(p) > \#(q)$ and $\#(\sim q) > \#(\sim p)$, one correspondingly obtains both $p \geqslant q$ and $\sim q \geqslant \sim p$ in the example at issue; *i.e.*, "That the Franklin Club should cater chiefly to business people is preferable to its being sports oriented" and "Its not being sports oriented is preferable to its not catering chiefly to business people." (The result is, of course, relative to the given desirability schedule specified for the various possible-world combinations in the above tabulation.)

A more complex mode of preference results, however, if —when some basic utility measure, $\#(x)$, is given—instead of having $p \geqslant q$ correspond to the condition that $\#(p) > \#(q)$, it is taken to correspond to $\#(p) - \#(\sim p) > \#(q) - \#(\sim q)$. This mode of preference will be governed by characteristic rules, specifically including all of those that were listed above.

THE LOGIC OF COMMANDS

Truth involvements

Some scholars have maintained that there cannot be a logic of commands (instructions, orders), inasmuch as there can be no logic in which validity of inference cannot be defined. Validity, however, requires that the concept of truth be applicable (an argument being valid when its conclusion must be true if its premises are true). But since commands—and, for that matter, also instructions, requests, etc.—are neither true nor false, it is argued that the concept of validity cannot be applied; so there can be no valid inference in this sphere. This line of thought, however, runs counter to clear intuitions that arise in specific cases, in which one unhesitatingly reasons from commands and sets of commands. If an examination has the instructions "Answer no fewer than three questions! Answer no more than four questions!" one would not hesitate to say that this implies the (tacitly contained) instruction, "Answer three or four questions!"

This seeming impasse can be broken, in effect, by importing truth into the sphere of commands through the back door: with any command one can associate its termination statement, which, with future-tense reference, asserts it as a fact that what the command orders will be done. Thus, the command "Shut all of the windows in the building!" has the termination statement "All of the windows in the building will be shut." In case of a pure command argument—*i.e.*, one that infers a command conclusion from premises that are all commands—validity can be assessed in the light of the validity of the purely assertoric syllogism composed of the corresponding termination statements. Thus the validity of the command argument given above is a derivative from the (orthodox) validity of the inference, from the premises "No fewer than three questions will be answered; no more than four questions will be answered" to the conclusion "Three or four questions will be answered."

Special cases

The logical issues of pure command inference can be handled in this manner. But what of the mixed cases in which some statement—premise or conclusion—is not a command?

Special case 1. One mixed case is that in which the premises nontrivially include noncommands, but the inferred conclusion is a command. Some writers have endorsed the rule that there is no validity unless the command conclusion is forthcoming from the command premises alone. This, however, invalidates such seemingly acceptable arguments as "Remove all cats from the area; the shed is in the area; so, remove all cats from the shed." It is more plausible, however, to stipulate the weaker condition that an inference to a command conclusion cannot count as valid unless there is at least one command premise that is essential to the argument. Subject to this restriction, a straightforward application of the above-stated characterization of validity can again be made. This approach validates the above-mentioned command inference via the validity of the assertion inference: "All cats will be removed from the area; the shed is in the area; so, all cats will be removed from the shed." (The rule under consideration suffices to block the unacceptable argument from the factual premise "All the doors will be shut" to the command conclusion "Shut all the doors.")

Special case 2. Another mixed case is that in which the premises nontrivially include commands, but the inferred conclusion is an ordinary statement of fact. Some authorities stipulate that no indicative conclusion can be validly drawn from a set of premises which cannot validly be drawn from the indicative among them alone. This rule would seem to be acceptable, though subject to certain significant provisos: (1) It must be restricted to categorical rather than conditional commands. "If you want to see the world's tallest building, look at the Empire State Building" conveys (*inter alia*) the information that "The Empire State Building is the world's tallest building." (2) Exception must be made for those commands that include in their formulation—explicitly or by way of tacit presupposition—reference to a factual datum. "John, give the book to Tom's brother Jim" yields the fact that Jim is Tom's brother; and "John, drive your car home" (= "John, you own a car: drive it home") yields "John owns a car." With suitable provisos, however, the rule can be maintained to resolve the issues of the special case in view.

DEONTIC LOGIC

The propositional modalities relating to normative (or valuational) classifications of actions and states of affairs, such as the permitted, the obligatory, the forbidden, or the meritorious, are characterized as deontic modalities (Greek *deontos*, "of that which is binding") and systematized in deontic logic. Though this subject was first treated as a technical discipline in 1926, its current active development dates from a paper published in 1951. As a highly abstracted branch of logical theory, it leaves to substantive disciplines—such as ethics and law —the concrete questions of what specific acts or states of affairs are to be forbidden, permitted, or the like (just as deductive logic does not meddle with what contingent issues are true but tells only what follows when certain facts or assumptions about the truth are given). It seeks to systematize the abstract, purely conceptual relations between propositions in this sphere, such as the following: if an act is obligatory, then its performance must be permitted and its omission forbidden. In given circumstances, any act is either permitted itself or its omission is permitted.

The systematization and relation to alethic modal logic. In the systematization of deontic logic, the symbols p, q, r, . . . may be taken to range over propositions dealing both with impersonal states of affairs and with the human acts involved in their realization. Certain special deontic operations can then be introduced: $\mathbf{P}(p)$ for "It is permitted that p be the case"; $\mathbf{F}(p)$ for "It is forbidden that p be the case"; and $\mathbf{O}(p)$ for "It is obligatory that p be the

Reduction to permissibility terms

case." In a systematization of deontic logic, it is only necessary to take one of these three operations as primitive (*i.e.*, as an irreducible given), because the others can then be introduced in terms of it. For example, when **P** alone is taken as primitive (as is done here), the following can be introduced by definition: "It is obligatory that *p*" means "It is not permitted that not-*p*"; and "It is forbidden that *p*" means "It is not permitted that *p*"; *i.e.*,

$$\mathbf{O}(p) = \sim\mathbf{P}(\sim p) \text{ and } \mathbf{F}(p) = \sim\mathbf{P}(p).$$

The logical grammar of **P** is presumably to be such that one wants to insist upon the rule:

Whenever $\vdash p \supset q$, then $\vdash \mathbf{P}(p) \supset \mathbf{P}(q)$.

Example: "Since one's helping Jones who has been robbed entails that one help someone who has been robbed, being permitted to help Jones (who has been robbed) entails that one be permitted to help someone who has been robbed." This yields such principles as: "If both *p* and *q* are permitted, then *p* is permitted and *q* is permitted"; and "If *p* is permitted, then either *p* or *q* is permitted"; *i.e.*,

$$\vdash \mathbf{P}(p \cdot q) \supset [\mathbf{P}(p) \cdot \mathbf{P}(q)] \text{ and } \vdash \mathbf{P}(p) \supset \mathbf{P}(p \vee q).$$

And, once it is postulated that "A *p* exists that is permitted"—*i.e.*, $\vdash (\exists p)\mathbf{P}(p)$—then the statement that "It is not permitted that both *p* and not-*p*"—*i.e.*, $\sim\mathbf{P}(p \cdot \sim p)$—is also yielded. Moreover, on any adequate theory of **P** it is necessary to have such principles as "Either *p* or not-*p* is permitted"; *i.e.*, $\vdash \mathbf{P}(p \vee \sim p)$.

On the other hand, certain principles must be rejected, such as that "If *p* is permitted and *q* is permitted, then both *p* and *q* taken together is permitted"; *i.e.*, $\dashv [\mathbf{P}(p) \cdot \mathbf{P}(q)] \supset \mathbf{P}(p \cdot q)$, in which $\dashv$ symbolizes the rejection of a thesis, and that "If either *p* or *q* is permitted, then *p* is permitted"; *i.e.*, $\dashv \mathbf{P}(p \vee q) \supset \mathbf{P}(p)$.

The first of these, accepted unqualifiedly, would lead to the untenable result that there can be no permission-indifferent acts; *i.e.*, no acts such that both they and their omission are permitted—since this would then lead to $\mathbf{P}(p \cdot \sim p)$. The second thesis would have the unacceptable result of asserting that, when at least one member of a pair of acts is permitted, then both members are permitted.

Analogy with possibility and necessity

In all of the respects that so far have been considered, deontic logic is wholly analogous to the already well developed field of alethic modal logic, which deals with statements of the form "It is possible that . . ." (symbolized $\diamond$), "It is necessary that . . ." (symbolized $\square$), etc. (see LOGIC, FORMAL: *IV. Other special systems of logic: Traditional logic and its developments: Modal logic*), with **P** in the role of possibility ($\diamond$) and **O** in that of necessity ($\square$). This parallel, however, does not extend throughout. In alethic logic, the principle that "necessity implies actuality" obviously holds (*i.e.*, $\vdash \square p \supset p$). But its deontic analogue, that "obligation implies actuality" (*i.e.*, $\vdash \mathbf{O}p \supset p$), must be rejected, or rather an analogous thesis holds only in the weakened form that "obligation implies permissibility" (*i.e.*, $\vdash \mathbf{O}p \supset \mathbf{P}p$). There is continuing controversy about the relation of deontic to alethic modal logic, principally in the context of Kant's thesis that "ought implies can" (*i.e.*, $\vdash \mathbf{O}p \supset \diamond p$), but also about the theses that "necessity implies permissibility" (*i.e.*, $\vdash \square p \supset \mathbf{P}p$) and *Ad impossibile nemo obligatur*—"no one is obliged to [do] the impossible" (*i.e.*, $\vdash \sim\diamond p \supset \sim\mathbf{O}p$). Although this thesis is generally accepted, some scholars want to strengthen the thesis to "necessity implies obligation" (*i.e.*, $\vdash \square p \supset \mathbf{O}p$), or, equivalently, to "permissibility implies possibility" (*i.e.*, $\vdash \sim\diamond p \supset \sim\mathbf{P}p$), with the result that only what is possible can count as permitted, so that the impossible is forbidden. Some would deny that it is wrong (*i.e.*, impermissible) to act to realize the impossible, rather than merely unwise or imprudent.

It has been proposed that deontic logic may perhaps be reduced to alethic modal logic. This approach is based on the idea of a normative code delimiting the range of the permissible. In this context, what signalizes an action as impermissible is that it involves a violation of the code:

the statement that the action has occurred entails that the code has been violated and so leads to a "sanction." This line of thought leads to the definition of a modal operator $\mathbf{F}p = \square(p \supset \sigma)$, "*p* necessarily implies a sanction," in which sigma (σ) is the sanction produced by code violation. Correspondingly, one then obtains: "For *p* to be permitted means that *p* does not imply by necessity a sanction"—*i.e.*, $\mathbf{P}p = \sim\square(p \supset \sigma)$—and "For *p* to be obligatory means that not doing *p* implies by necessity a sanction"—*i.e.*, $\mathbf{O}p = \square(\sim p \supset \sigma)$. Assuming a systematization of the alethic modal operator $\square$, these definitions immediately produce a corresponding system of deontic logic that—if $\square$ is a normal modality—has many of the features that are desirable in a modal operator. It also yields, however—through the "paradoxes of strict implication" (see LOGIC, FORMAL: *IV. Other special systems of logic: Traditional logic and its developments: Modal logic: Alternative systems of modal logic*)—the disputed principle that "The assumption that *p* is not possible implies that *p* is not permissible"; *i.e.*, $\vdash \sim\diamond p \supset \sim\mathbf{P}p$. This and other similar consequences of the foregoing effort to reduce deontic logic to modal logic have been transcended by other scholars, who have resorted to a mode of implication (symbolized as $\rightarrow$) that is stronger than strict implication (as necessary material implication is called) and then defining $\mathbf{F}p$ as $p \rightarrow \sigma$ instead of as above.

Alternative deontic systems. Each of the three principal deontic systems that have been studied to date is analogous to one of the alethic modal systems that were developed in the mid-20th century.

Analogies with "M," "S4," and "S5"

These foundational alethic systems differ by virtue of the different axioms and rules adopted for such modalities as necessity, possibility, and contingency. In the system designated **M**, for example, developed by the aforementioned Finnish logician G.H. von Wright, the adverb "possibly," symbolized M, is taken as the fundamental undefined modality in terms of which the other modalities are constructed. "Necessarily *p*," symbolized Lp, for example, is defined in the system **M** as "not possibly not-*p*"; *i.e.*, $Lp = \sim M\sim p$. Alternatively, in an equivalent system, **T**, "necessarily *p*" is taken as primitive, and "possibly *p*" is defined as "not necessarily not-*p*"; i.e., $Mp = \sim L\sim p$. Several nonequivalent systems have been developed by the conceptual Pragmatist C.I. Lewis (1883–1964), primary author of *Symbolic Logic* (1932), the foundational work in this field. Of these systems, that known as **S4** includes all of the system **M** but adds also the axiom that "'Necessarily *p*' implies 'It is necessary that necessarily *p*'"—*i.e.*, $Lp \supset LLp$—whereas, that known as **S5** adds still another axiom, that "'Possibly *p*' implies 'It is necessary that possibly *p*'"—*i.e.*, $Mp \supset LMp$ (see LOGIC, FORMAL: *IV. Other special systems of logic: Traditional logic and its developments: Modal logic: Alternative systems of modal logic*). The analogous deontic systems are then as follows:

1. **DM** (the deontic analogue of the system **M** of von Wright or of the system **T**). To a standard system of propositional logic the following rule is added: "Any proposition, if true, ought to be true"; *i.e.*, If $\vdash p$ then $\vdash \mathbf{O}p$. Example: Given that "To forgive is divine," (*p*) then "To forgive ought to be divine" (**O***p*). Axioms:
(A1): "If *p* is obligatory, then not-*p* is not obligatory"; *i.e.*, $\mathbf{O}p \supset \sim\mathbf{O}\sim p$.
(A2): "If *p* ought to imply *q*, then if *p* is obligatory *q* is obligatory"; *i.e.*, $\mathbf{O}(p \supset q) \supset (\mathbf{O}p \supset \mathbf{O}q)$.
2. **DS4** (the deontic analogue of Lewis's system **S4**). To **M** one adds the axiom:
(A3): "If *p* is obligatory, then *p* ought to be obligatory"; *i.e.*, $\mathbf{O}p \supset \mathbf{OO}p$. Example: "If John ought to pay his debts," (**O***p*) then it is obligatory that John ought to pay his debts" (**OO***p*).
3. **DS5** (the deontic analogue of Lewis's system **S5**). To **M** one adds the axiom:
(A4): "If *p* is not obligatory, then *p* ought to be nonobligatory"; *i.e.*, $\sim\mathbf{O}p \supset \mathbf{O}\sim\mathbf{O}p$.

Semantic systematization

A straightforward semantical systematization of systems of deontic logic can be provided as follows: given a domain of complex propositions built up from atomic propositions ($p, q, r, \ldots$) with the use of propositional connectives ($\sim, \cdot, \vee, \supset$) and **O**, a deontic model set Δ for this domain can be characterized as any set chosen from these propositions that meets the following conditions (in which "iff" means "if and only if"):

1. Not-p is in the set if and only if p is not in the set; i.e., $\sim p \in \Delta$ iff $p \notin \Delta$.

2. "Both p and q together" is in the set if and only if p is in the set and q is in the set; i.e., $(p \cdot q) \in \Delta$ iff $p \in \Delta$ and $q \in \Delta$.

3. "Either p or q" is in the set if and only if either p is in the set or q is in the set; i.e., $(p \vee q) \in \Delta$ iff $p \in \Delta$ or $q \in \Delta$.

4. "That p implies q" is in the set if and only if either p is not in the set or q is in the set; i.e., $(p \supset q) \in \Delta$ iff $p \notin \Delta$ or $q \in \Delta$.

5. "That p is obligatory" is in the set whenever p is posited; i.e., $\mathbf{O}p \in \Delta$ whenever $\vdash p$.

6. "That not-p is not obligatory" is in the set whenever "p is obligatory" is in the set; i.e., $\sim\mathbf{O} \sim p \in \Delta$ whenever $\mathbf{O}p \in \Delta$.

7. "That q is obligatory" is in the set whenever both "p is obligatory" is in the set and "That p implies q is obligatory" is in the set; i.e., $\mathbf{O}q \in \Delta$ whenever both $\mathbf{O}p \in \Delta$ and $\mathbf{O}(p \supset q) \in \Delta$.

A proposition can be characterized as a deontic thesis (D-thesis) if it can be shown that, in virtue of these rules, it must belong to every deontic model set. It can be demonstrated that the D-thesis in this sense will coincide exactly with the theorems of **DM**—No. 1 of the above three systems. Furthermore, if one adds one of the additional rules:

8′. "That p ought to be obligatory" is in the set whenever "p is obligatory" is in the set; i.e., $\mathbf{OO}p \in \Delta$ whenever $\mathbf{O}p \in \Delta$.

8″. "That p ought to be non-obligatory" is in the set whenever "p is not obligatory" is in the set; i.e., $\mathbf{O}\sim\mathbf{O}p \in \Delta$ whenever $\sim\mathbf{O}p \in \Delta$.

then the corresponding D′ or D″ theses will coincide exactly with the theorems of the deontic systems **DS4** and **DS5**, respectively—Nos. 2 and 3 above.

Logics of physical application

Certain systems of logic are built up specifically with particular physical applications in view. Within this range lie temporal logic; spatial, or topological, logic; mereology, or the logic of parts and wholes generally; as well as the logic of circuit analysis.

Since the field of topological logic is new and relatively undeveloped, the reader is referred to the bibliography for a recent source that provides some materials and references to the literature.

Of the physical applications of logic, the logic of circuit analysis is perhaps the most important and certainly the most extensively developed. Since the course of the analysis in this case, however, soon veers off from logical into mathematical considerations, this subject is not treated here.

TEMPORAL LOGIC

The object of temporal logic—variously called chronological logic or tense logic—is to systematize reasoning with time-related propositions. Such propositions generally do not involve the timeless "is" (or "are") of the mathematicians' "three is a prime," but rather envisage an explicitly temporal condition (examples: "Bob *is* sitting," "Robert *was* present," "Mary *will have been* informed"). In this area, statements are employed in which some essential reference to the before-after relationship or the past-present-future relationship is at issue; and the ideas of succession, change, and constancy enter in.

Classic historical treatments. Chronological logic originated with the Megarians of the 4th century BC, whose school (not far from Athens) reflected the influence of Socrates and of Eleaticism.

In the Megarian conception of modality, the *actual* is that which is realized *now*, the *possible* is that which is realized *at some time or other*, and the *necessary* is that which is realized *at all times*. These Megarian ideas can be found also in Aristotle, together with another temporalized sense of necessity according to which certain possibilities are *possible* prior to the event, *actual* then, and *necessary* thereafter, so that their modal status is not omnitemporal (as in the Megarian concept), but changes in time. The Stoic conception of temporal modality is

yet another cognate development, according to which the *possible* is that which is realized at *some* time in the present or future and the *necessary* that which is realized at *all* such times. The Diodorean concept of implication (named after the 4th-century BC Megarian logician Diodorus Cronus) holds, for example, that the conditional "If the sun has risen, it is daytime" is to be given the temporal construction "All times after the sun has risen are times when it is daytime." The Persian logician Avicenna (980–1037), the foremost philosopher of medieval Islām, treated this chronological conception of implication in the framework of a general theory of categorical propositions (such as "All A is B," etc.) of a temporalized type and considerably advanced and developed the Megarian-Stoic theory of temporal modalities.

Fundamental concepts and relations of temporal logic. The statements "It sometimes rains in London," "It always rains in London," and "It is raining in London on January 1, AD 3000, is a fact" are all termed chronologically definite in that their truth or falsity is independent of their time assertion. By contrast, the statements "It is now raining in London," "It rained in London yesterday," and "It will rain in London sometime next week" are all chronologically indefinite, in that their truth or falsity is not independent of their time of assertion. The notation $|t \vdash p$ is here introduced to mean that the proposition p, often in itself chronologically indefinite, is represented as being asserted at the time t. For example, if p_1 is the statement "It is raining in London today," and t_1 is January 1, 1900, then "$|t_1 \vdash p_1$" represents the assertion made on January 1, 1900, that it is raining today—an assertion that is true if and only if the statement "It is raining in London on January 1, 1900, is a fact" is true. If the statement p is chronologically definite, then (by definition) the assertions "$|t \vdash p$" and "$|t' \vdash p$" are materially equivalent (i.e., have the same truth value) for all values of t and t'. Otherwise p is chronologically indefinite. The time may be measured, for example, in units of days, so that the time variable is discretized. Then $(t + 1)$ will represent "the day after t-day," $(t - 1)$ will represent "the day before t-day," and the like. And, further, the statements p_1, q_1, and r_1, can then be as follows:

p_1: "It rains in London today."
q_1: "It will rain in London tomorrow."
r_1: "It rained in London yesterday."

The following assertions can now be made:

(P): $|t \vdash p_1$
(Q): $|t - 1 \vdash q_1$
(R): $|t + 1 \vdash r_1$.

Clearly, for any value of t whatsoever, the assertions (P), (Q), and (R) must (logically) be materially equivalent (i.e., have the same truth value). This illustration establishes the basic point—that the theory of chronological propositions must be prepared to exhibit the existence of logical relationships among such propositions of such a kind that the truth of the assertion of one statement at one time may be bound up essentially with the truth (or falsity) of the assertion of some very different statement at another time.

A (genuine) date is a time specification that is chronologically stable (such as "January 1, 3000," or "the day of Lincoln's assassination"); a pseudodate is a time specification that is chronologically unstable (such as "today" or "six weeks ago"). These lead to very different results depending upon the nature of the fundamental reference point—the "origin" in mathematical terms. If the origin is a pseudodate—say, "today"—the style of dating will be such that its chronological specifiers are pseudodates; e.g., tomorrow, day before yesterday, four days ago, etc. If, on the other hand, the origin is a genuine date, say that of the founding of Rome, or the accession of Alexander, the style of dating will be such that all of its dates are of the type: two hundred and fifty years *ab urbe condita* ("since the founding of the city"). Clearly, a chronology of genuine dates will then be chronologically definite, and one of pseudodates will be chronologically indefinite.

Megarian and Stoic logics

Definite versus indefinite reference

Dated versus pseudo-dated statements

Let p be some chronologically indefinite statement. Then, in general, another statement can be formed, asserting that p holds (obtains) at the time t. Correspondingly, let the statement-forming operation $\mathbf{R}_t$ be introduced. The statement $\mathbf{R}_t(p)$, which is to be read "p is realized at the time t," will then represent the statement stating explicitly that p holds (obtains) specifically at the time t. Thus, if t_1 is 3 PM Greenwich time on January 1, 2000, and p_1 is the (chronologically indefinite) statement "all men are (*i.e.*, are now) playing Chess," then "$\mathbf{R}_{t_1}(p_1)$" is the statement "It is the case at 3 PM Greenwich time on January 1, 2000, that all men are playing Chess."

If t is a proper date (not a pseudodate), then "$\mathbf{R}_t(p)$" is always temporally definite. For example, if p_1 is the temporally indefinite statement "It is raining in London today," and t_1 is as specified in the last paragraph, then '$\mathbf{R}_{t_1}(p_1)$" is the temporally definite statement "It is raining in London at 3 PM Greenwich time on January 1, 2000." On the other hand, if t is a pseudodate, "$\mathbf{R}_t(p)$" is temporally indefinite if p is indefinite. Thus, if t_2 is the pseudodate tomorrow, then "$\mathbf{R}_{t_2}(p_1)$" means "It is the case tomorrow that it is raining in London today." How is the **R**-operation to be construed in a chronology based on the indexical pseudodate "now" as origin? When two t's are involved, shall the second t be measured from the original now-point or from the now point newly established by the first t? That is, should "$\mathbf{R}_{t'}[\mathbf{R}_t(p)]$" be interpreted as:

1. It will be the case t' time units from now that it will be the case t time units from (the original) now that p—or, equivalently, simply as "$\mathbf{R}_{t'}(p)$"; or as
2. It will be the case t' time units from now that it will be the case t time units thence (*i.e.*, from the new now) that p—or, equivalently, as "$\mathbf{R}_{(t'\,+\,t)}(p)$"?

Since each of these represents a feasible alternative policy for the construction of **R**, it is necessary in fact to deal with the consequences of the adoption of either.

Systematization of temporal reasoning. On the basis of these ideas, the logical theory of chronological propositions can be developed in a systematic, formal way. It may be postulated that the operator **R** is to be governed by the following rules:

(T1) The negation of a statement p is realized at a given time if and only if it is not the case that the statement is realized at that time; *i.e.*, $\mathbf{R}_t(\sim p) \equiv \sim \mathbf{R}_t(p)$, in which $\equiv$ signifies equivalence and means "holds if and only if."

(T2) A conjunction of two statements is realized at a given time if and only if each of these two statements is realized at that time: $\mathbf{R}_t(p \cdot q) \equiv [\mathbf{R}_t(p) \cdot \mathbf{R}_t(q)]$. Example: "John and Jane will be at the railroad station at 10 AM—$\mathbf{R}_t(p \cdot q)$—if and only if John is at the station at 10 AM—$\mathbf{R}_t(p)$—and Jane is at the station at 10 AM—$\mathbf{R}_t(q)$."

If a statement is realized universally—*i.e.*, at any and every time whatsoever—it can then be expressed more simply as being true without any temporal qualifications; hence, the rule:

(T3) If for every time t the statement p is realized (**R**), then p obtains unqualifiedly; *i.e.*, $(\forall t)\mathbf{R}_t(p) \supset p$, in which $\forall$ is the universal quantifier (meaning "for all . . .").

If two times are involved, however (as in 1 and 2 above), then the left-hand term in rule T3 can be expressed within the second time frame as "It will be the case t' from now that, for every time t ($\forall t$), it will be the case t from the first now that p"; *i.e.*, $\mathbf{R}_{t'}[(\forall t)\mathbf{R}_t(p)]$. It is an algebraic rule, however, that an $\mathbf{R}_t$ operator can be moved to the right past an irrelevant quantifier; hence,

$$\mathbf{R}_{t'}[(\forall t)\mathbf{R}_t(p)] \equiv (\forall t)\{\mathbf{R}_{t'}[\mathbf{R}_t(p)]\};$$

and, correspondingly, with the existential quantifier $\exists$: "It will be the case τ from now that there exists a time t ($\exists t$) such that p will be realized at t" is equivalent to saying "There exists a time t such that it will be the case τ from now that p will be realized t from the first now" (in which τ is a second time); *i.e.*,

(T4) $\mathbf{R}_\tau[(\exists t)\mathbf{R}_t(p)] \equiv (\exists t)\{\mathbf{R}_\tau[\mathbf{R}_t(p)]\}$.

It is notable that the left-hand side of this equivalence is

itself equivalent with $(\exists t)\mathbf{R}_t(p)$ since what follows the initial $\mathbf{R}_\tau$ is a chronologically definite statement.

Finally, there are—as shown above—two distinct ways of construing iterations of the $\mathbf{R}_t$ operator, which provides a choice between the rules:

$$
\begin{array}{ll}
\text{(T5-I)} & \mathbf{R}_\tau[\mathbf{R}_t(p)] \equiv \mathbf{R}_t(p) \\
\text{(T5-II)} & \mathbf{R}_\tau[\mathbf{R}_t(p)] \equiv \mathbf{R}_{\tau\,+\,t}(p).
\end{array}
$$

Taking these rules as a starting point, two alternative axiomatic theories are generated for the logic of the operation of chronological realization.

Rules and modalities

Apart from strictly technical results establishing the formal relationships of the various systems of chronological logic to one another, the most interesting findings regarding the systems of tense logic relate to the theory of temporal modalities. The most striking finding here concerns the logical structure of the system of modalities, be it Megarian or Stoic:

Megarian	possibly p:	$(\exists t)\mathbf{R}_t(p)$
	necessarily p:	$(\forall t)\mathbf{R}_t(p)$
Stoic	possibly p:	$(\exists t)[\mathbf{F}(t) \cdot \mathbf{R}_t(p)]$
	necessarily p:	$(\forall t)[\mathbf{F}(t) \supset \mathbf{R}_t(p)]$

in which $\mathbf{F}(t)$ signifies "t is future." It has been shown that the forms, or structures, of both of these systems of temporal modalities are given by the aforementioned system **S5** of C.I. Lewis (see further LOGIC, FORMAL: *IV. Other special systems of logic: A. Traditional logic and its developments: 2. Modal logic: a. Alternative systems of modal logic*).

MEREOLOGY

Leśniewski's encounter with the paradoxes

The founder of mereology (Greek *meros*, "part") was a Polish logician, Stanisław Leśniewski (1886–1939), a dominant figure in the Warsaw school of logic and author of an original and elegant system of the philosophy of mathematics. Leśniewski was much exercised about Russell's paradox of the class of all classes not elements of themselves, so called after Bertrand Russell (1872–1970), an outstanding creative logician and polymath philosopher—if this class is a member of itself, then it is not; and if it is not, then it is. (Example: "This barber shaves everyone in town who does not shave himself." Does the barber then shave himself? If he does, he does not; if he does not, he does.)

Basic concepts and definitions. The paradox results, Leśniewski argued, from a failure to distinguish the distributive and the collective interpretations of class expressions. The statement "x is an element of the class of X's" is correspondingly equivocal. When its key terms (element of, class of) are used distributively, it means simply that x is an X. But if these terms are used collectively, it means that x is a part (proper or improper) of the whole consisting of the X's; *i.e.*, that x is a part of the object that meets the following two conditions: (1) that every x is a part of it; and (2) that every part of it has a common part with some x. On either construction of class membership, one of the inferences essential to the derivation of Russell's paradox is blocked.

Leśniewski presented his theory of the collective interpretation of class expressions in a paper published in 1916. Eschewing symbolization, he formulated his theorems and their proofs in ordinary language. Later he sought to formalize the theory by embedding it within a broader body of logical theory. This theory comprised two parts, viz., prototthetic (Greek *prōtos*, "first"; *tithēmi*, "I set up"), a logic of propositions (not analyzed into their parts); and ontology (Greek *on*, "being"), which contains counterparts to the predicational logic (of subjects and predicates), including the calculus of relations and the theory of identity. On his own approach, mereology was developed as an extension of ontology and prototthetic; but the practice of most later writers has been to develop as a counterpart to mereology a theory of parts and wholes that is simply an extension of the more familiar machinery of quantificational logic employing $\exists$ and $\forall$. This is the course adopted here.

An undefined relation **Pt** serves as the basis for an axiomatic theory of the part relation. This relation is operative with respect to the items of some domain **D**, over which the variables α, β, γ, . . . (alpha, beta, gamma, etc.) are assumed to range. Thus, $\alpha \mathbf{Pt}\beta$ is to be read "alpha is a part of beta"—with "part" taken in the wider sense in which the whole counts as part of itself. Two definitions are basic:

1. "α is disjoint from β"; i.e., $\alpha \mid \beta$ is defined as obtaining when "there exists no item γ such that γ is a part of α and γ is a part of β"; i.e., $\sim(\exists\gamma)(\gamma\mathbf{Pt}\alpha \cdot \gamma\mathbf{Pt}\beta)$. Example: "The transmission (α) is disjoint from the motor (β) if there exists no machine part (γ) such that it is a part of the transmission and also a part of the motor."

2. "S has the sum of (or sums to) α"; i.e., $S\Sigma\alpha$ is defined as obtaining when "for every γ, this γ is disjoint from α if and only if, for every β, to be a member of S is to be disjoint from γ"; i.e.,

$$(\forall\gamma)[\gamma|\alpha \equiv (\forall\beta)(\beta \in S \supset \beta|\gamma)].$$

$S\Sigma\alpha$ thus obtains whenever everything disjoint from α is disjoint from every S-element (β) as well, and conversely. Example: "A given group of buildings (S) comprises (Σ) Oxford University (α) when, for every room in the world (γ)—office, classroom, etc.—this room is disjoint from the university if and only if, in the case of each building (β), for it to be a member ($\in$) of the group that comprises the university (S) it must not have this room as a part ($\beta|\gamma$)."

Axiomatization of mereology. A comprehensive theory of parts and wholes can now be built up from three axioms:

The first axiom expresses the fact that "For every α and every β, if α is a part of β and β is a part of α, then α and β must be one and the same item"; i.e.,

$$(\forall\alpha)(\forall\beta)(\alpha\mathbf{Pt}\beta \cdot \beta\mathbf{Pt}\alpha \supset \alpha = \beta);$$

hence, the axiom:

(A1) Items that are parts of one another are identical. (This is analogous to the principle in number theory that given any pair of natural numbers n and m, if n is less than or equal to m and m is less than or equal to n, then n is equal to m.)

The second axiom expresses the fact that "For every α and every β, α is a part of β if and only if, for every γ, if this γ is disjoint from β it is then disjoint from α as well"; i.e.,

$$(\forall\alpha)(\forall\beta)[\alpha\mathbf{Pt}\beta \equiv (\forall\gamma)(\gamma|\beta \supset \gamma|\alpha)];$$

hence, the axiom:

(A2) One item is part of another only if every item disjoint from the second is also disjoint from the first. (Example: "This grain of sand (α) is a part of this pile of sand (β) just in case whatever is disjoint from the pile is disjoint from the grain.")

The third axiom expresses the fact that "If there exists an α that is a member of a nonempty set of items S, then there also exists a β that is the sum of this set"; i.e.,

$$(\exists\alpha)(\alpha \in S) \supset (\exists\beta)\,S\,\Sigma\,\beta;$$

hence, the axiom:

(A3) Every nonempty set has a sum. (If one considers the set of grains of sand in a given pile of sand, since such a set is nonempty, it will have a sum—namely, the pile of sand itself.)

Several theorems follow from these axioms:

The first states that "For every α, α is a part of α"; i.e.,

$$(\forall\alpha)\,\alpha\mathbf{Pt}\alpha;$$

hence, the theorem:

(T1) Every item is part of itself. (Example: "Not only are the pages parts of a book [α], but the book is a part of the book.")

The second theorem states that "For every α, for every β, and for every γ, if α is a part of β, and β is a part of γ, then α is a part of γ"; i.e.,

$$(\forall\alpha)(\forall\beta)(\forall\gamma)[(\alpha\mathbf{Pt}\beta \cdot \beta\mathbf{Pt}\gamma) \supset \alpha\mathbf{Pt}\gamma];$$

hence, the theorem:

(T2) The **Pt**-relation is transitive.

The third theorem states that "For every α, for every β, and for every γ, if γ is a part of α only when it is also a part of β then α is identical with β"; i.e.,

$$(\forall\alpha)(\forall\beta)(\forall\gamma)[(\gamma\mathbf{Pt}\alpha \equiv \gamma\mathbf{Pt}\beta) \supset \alpha = \beta];$$

hence, the theorem:

(T3) Any item is completely determined by its parts; items are identical when they have the same parts in common.

The fourth theorem states that "For every α and every β, there exists a γ that is the sum of α and β"; i.e.,

$$(\forall\alpha)(\forall\beta)(\exists\gamma)(\{\alpha, \beta\}\Sigma\gamma);$$

hence, the theorem:

(T4) Any two items whatsoever may be summed up.

In this form as a formal theory of the part relation, the history of mereology can be dated from some drafts and essays of the classic early modern Rationalist G.W. Liebniz prepared in the late 1690s.

Hypothetical reasoning and counterfactual conditionals

A simply conditional, or "if," statement asserts a strictly formal relationship between antecedent ("if" clause) and consequent ("then" clause) ("If p, then q"), without any reference to the status of the antecedent. The knowledge status of this antecedent, however, may be problematic (unknown), or known-to-be-true, or known-to-be-false. In these three cases, one obtains, respectively, the problematic conditional ("Should it be the case that p—which it may or may not be—then q"); the factual conditional ("Since p, then q"); and the counterfactual conditional ("If it were the case that p—which it is not—then q"). Counterfactual conditionals have a special importance in the area of thought experiments in history as well as elsewhere.

Material implication $p \supset q$, construed simply as the truth-functional "either not-p or q," is clearly not suited to represent counterfactual conditionals because any material implication with a false antecedent is true: when p is false, then $p \supset q$ and $p \supset \sim q$ are both true, regardless of what one may choose to put in place of q. But even when a stronger mode of implication is invoked, such as strict implication or its cognates, the problem of auxiliary hypotheses (soon to be explained) would still remain.

It seems most natural to view a counterfactual conditional in the light of an inference to be drawn from the contrary-to-fact thesis represented by its antecedent. Thus, "If this rubber band were made of copper, then it would conduct electricity" would be construed as an incomplete presentation of the argument resulting from its expansion into:

Assumption: "This rubber band is made of copper";

Known fact: "Everything made of copper conducts electricity";

Conclusion: "This rubber band conducts electricity."

On the analysis, the conclusion ($=$ the consequent of the counterfactual) appears as a deductive consequence of the assumption ($=$ the antecedent of the counterfactual). This truncated-argument analysis of counterfactuals is a contribution, in essence, of a Polish linguistic theorist, Henry Hiż (born 1917). On Hiż's analysis, counterfactual conditionals are properly to be understood as metalinguistic; i.e., as making statements about statements. Specifically, "If A were so, then B would be so" is to be construed in the context of a given system of statements S, saying that when A is adjoined as a supplemental premise to S, then B follows. This approach has been endorsed by Roderick Chisholm of Brown University, an important writer in applied logic, and has been put forward in one form or another by many recent writers, most of whom incline to take S, as above, to include all or part of the corpus of scientific laws.

The approach warrants a closer scrutiny. On fuller analysis, the following situation, with a considerably enlarged group of auxiliary hypotheses, comes into focus:

Known facts: 1. "This band is made of rubber";
2. "This band is not made of copper";
3. "This band does not conduct electricity";
4. "Things made of rubber do not conduct electricity";
5. "Things made of copper do conduct electricity."

Assumption: Not-(2); i.e., "This band is made of copper."

When this assumption is introduced within the framework of known facts, a contradiction obviously ensues. How can this situation be repaired? Clearly, the logician must begin by dropping items 1 and 2 and replacing them with their negations—the assumption itself so instructs him. But a contradiction still remains. The following alternatives are open:

Alternative 1:   Retain: 3, 4.
                   Reject: 1, 2, 5.
Alternative 2:   Retain: 4, 5.
                   Reject: 1, 2, 3.

That is, the analyst actually has a choice between rejecting 3 in favour of 5 or 5 in favour of 3, resulting in the following conditionals:

1. "If this rubber band were made of copper, then it would conduct electricity" (since copper conducts electricity), or
2. "If this rubber band were made of copper, then copper would not (always) conduct electricity" (since this band does not conduct electricity).

If the first conditional seems more natural than the second, this is owing to the fact that, in the face of the counterfactual hypothesis at issue, the first invites the sacrifice of a particular fact (viz., that the band does not conduct electricity) in favour of a general law (viz., that copper conducts electricity), whereas the second counterfactual would have sacrificed a law to a purely hypothetical fact. On this view, there is a fundamental epistemological difference between actual and hypothetical situations: in actual cases one makes laws give way to facts, but in hypothetical cases one makes the facts yield to laws.

In more complex cases, however the fact/law distinction may not help matters. For example, assume a group of three laws L_1, L_2, L_3, where $\sim L_1$ is inconsistent with the conjunction of L_2 and L_3. If asked to hypothesize the denial of L_1—so that the "fact" that one is opposing is itself a law—then what remains is a choice between laws; the distinction between facts and laws does not resolve the issue, and some more sophisticated mechanism for a preferential choice among laws is necessary.

BIBLIOGRAPHY

References on fallacies: ARISTOTLE, *De Sophisticis Elenchis* (Eng. trans., *Aristotle on Fallacies*, 1866); JEREMY BENTHAM, *The Book of Fallacies*, vol. 2 of his *Works*, ed. by J. BOWRING (1843); J.S. MILL, bk. 5 of *A System of Logic* (1843); R.H. THOULESS, *Straight and Crooked Thinking* (1930); C.L. HAMBLIN, *Fallacies* (1970), the only monographic study of the subject.

References for the logic of belief: K.J.J. HINTIKKA, *Knowledge and Belief* (1962), a technically sophisticated approach; N. RESCHER, *Topics in Philosophical Logic* (1968).

References for the logic of knowing: R.M. CHISHOLM, "The Logic of Knowing," *Journal of Philosophy*, 60:773–795 (1963), *The Theory of Knowledge* (1966), basic but authoritative; K.J.J. HINTIKKA, *Knowledge and Belief* (1962); N. RESCHER, *Topics in Philosophical Logic* (1968).

References for the logic of questions: N.D. BELNAP, JR., *An Analysis of Questions* (1963); D. HARRAH, *Communication: A Logical Model* (1963); L. AQVIST, *A New Approach to the Logical Theory of Interrogatives*, pt. 1 (1965).

References for the logic of preference: G.H. VON WRIGHT, *The Logic of Preference* (1963), the best introduction to the subject; S. HALLDEN, *On the Logic of "Better"* (1957); N. RESCHER, *Introduction to Value Theory* (1969).

References for the logic of commands: R.M. HARE, *The Language of Morals* (1952), a modern classic; N. RESCHER, *The Logic of Commands* (1966), with an extensive bibliography; G.H. VON WRIGHT, *Norm and Action* (1963); B.F. CHELLAS, *The Logical Form of Imperatives* (1969).

References for deontic logic: E. MALLY, *Grundgesetze des Sollens: Elemente der Logik des Willens* (1926); G.H. VON WRIGHT, "Deontic Logic," *Mind*, 60:1–15 (1951); A.R. ANDERSON, "The Formal Analysis of Normative Systems," in N. RESCHER (ed.), *The Logic of Decision and Action* (1966), comprehensive and monographic in scope; F.B. FITCH, "Natural Deduction Rules for Obligation," *American Philosophical Quarterly*, 3:27–38 (1966); N. RESCHER, *Topics in Philosophical Logic* (1969).

References for temporal logic: A.N. PRIOR, *Time and Modality* (1957), *Past, Present and Future* (1967); N. RESCHER and A. URQUHART, *Temporal Logic* (1970).

Reference for topological logic: N. RESCHER, *Topics in Philosophical Logic*, ch. 13 (1969).

References for mereology: A. TARSKI, "Appendix E to J.H. Woodger," *Axiomatic Method in Biology* (1937); E.C. LUSCHEI, *The Logical Systems of Leśniewski* (1962); E.S. LEONARD and N. GOODMAN, "The Calculus of Individuals and its Uses," *Journal of Symbolic Logic*, 5:45–55 (1940).

References for counterfactual conditionals: R.M. CHISHOLM, "The Contrary-to-Fact Conditional," *Mind*, 55:289–307 (1946); N. GOODMAN, "The Problem of Counterfactual Conditionals," *Journal of Philosophy*, 44:113–128 (1947); H. HIZ, "On the Inferential Sense of Contrary-to-Fact Conditionals," *ibid.*, 48:586–587 (1951); G.H. VON WRIGHT, *Logical Studies* (1957); N. RESCHER, *Hypothetical Reasoning* (1964), a comprehensive study with further references to the literature.

(N.R.)

Logic, Formal

The discipline known as formal logic takes as its main subject matter propositions (or statements, or assertively used sentences) and deductive arguments, and it abstracts from their content the structures or logical forms that they embody. The logician customarily uses a symbolic notation to express these structures clearly and unambiguously and to enable manipulations and tests of validity to be more easily applied. Although this article freely employs the technical notation of modern symbolic logic, its symbols are introduced gradually and with accompanying explanations so that the serious and attentive general reader should be able to follow the development of ideas.

Formal logic is an a priori, and not an empirical, study. In this respect it contrasts with the natural sciences and with all other disciplines that depend on observation for their data. Its nearest analogy is with pure mathematics; indeed, many logicians and pure mathematicians would regard their respective subjects as indistinguishable, or as merely two stages of the same unified discipline. Formal logic, therefore, is not to be confused with the empirical study of the processes of reasoning, which belongs to psychology. It must also be distinguished from the art of correct reasoning, which is the practical skill of applying logical principles to particular cases; and, even more sharply, it must be distinguished from the art of persuasion, in which invalid arguments are sometimes more effective than valid ones.

The main divisions of the article are as follows:

I. Introduction
II. The propositional calculus
    General features of PC
        Formation rules for PC
        Validity in PC
        Interdefinability of operators
        Axiomatization of PC
    Special systems of PC
        Partial systems of PC
        Nonstandard versions of PC
    Natural deduction method in PC
III. The predicate calculus
    The lower predicate calculus
        Validity in LPC
        Logical manipulations in LPC
        Classification of dyadic relations
        Axiomatization of LPC
        Special systems of LPC
    Higher-order predicate calculi
IV. Other special systems of logic
    Syllogistic logic
    Modal logic
        Alternative systems of modal logic
        Validity in modal logic
    Set theory
    Logical foundations of mathematics
        Axiomatization of arithmetic
        Scope and limitations of axiomatized arithmetic
        Applied logic
V. Varieties of notation in symbolic logic

For discussions of formal logic considered as a discipline, of its foundational philosophical issues, and of its relations to (and applications in) other disciplines, see LOGIC, PHILOSOPHY OF; and LOGIC, HISTORY OF.

I. Introduction

Probably the most natural approach to formal logic is through the idea of the soundness or validity of an argument of the kind known as deductive. A deductive argument can be roughly characterized as one in which the claim is made that some proposition (the *conclusion*) follows with strict necessity from some other proposition or propositions (the *premises*)—*i.e.*, that it would be inconsistent or self-contradictory to assert the premises but deny the conclusion. Not all arguments are of this type. Some involve only the weaker claim that the premises lend a certain degree of probability to the conclusion or that acceptance of the premises would make acceptance of the conclusion more reasonable than not. Such arguments, which are known as inductive, are dealt with in the articles SCIENCE, PHILOSOPHY OF; and PROBABILITY, THEORY OF, and will not be considered here.

Deductive validity If a deductive argument is to succeed in establishing the truth of its conclusion, two quite distinct conditions must be met: first, the conclusion must in fact follow from the premises—*i.e.*, the deduction of the conclusion from the premises must be logically sound; and, second, the premises themselves must be true. Of these two conditions, the logician as such is concerned only with the first; the second, the determination of the truth or falsity of the premises, is the task of some special discipline or of common observation, etc., appropriate to the subject matter of the argument. When the conclusion of an argument is correctly deducible from its premises, the *inference* from the premises to the conclusion is said to be (deductively) *valid*, irrespective of whether the premises are true or false. Other ways of expressing the fact that an inference is deductively valid are to say that the truth of the premises gives (or would give) an absolute guarantee of the truth of the conclusion or that it would involve a logical inconsistency (as distinct from a mere mistake of fact) to suppose that the premises were true but the conclusion false.

The deductive inferences with which formal logic is concerned are, as the name suggests, those for which validity depends not on any features of their subject matter but on their form or structure. Thus the two inferences

(A) "Every dog is a mammal"; "Some quadrupeds are dogs"; therefore, "Some quadrupeds are mammals"

and

(B) "Every anarchist is a believer in free love"; "Some members of the Government party are anarchists"; therefore, "Some members of the Government party are believers in free love"

differ in subject matter and hence require different procedures to check the truth or falsity of their premises. But their validity is ensured by what they have in common, viz., that the argument in each is of the form:

(C) "Every *X* is a *Y*"; "Some *Z*'s are *X*'s"; therefore "Some *Z*'s are *Y*'s."

Inference forms Line (C) above may be called an *inference form*, and (A) and (B) are then *instances* of that inference form. The letters—*X, Y,* and *Z*—in (C) mark the places into which expressions of a certain type may be inserted. Symbols used for this purpose are known as *variables;* their use is analogous to that of the *x* in algebra, which marks the place into which a numeral can be inserted. An instance of an inference form is produced by replacing all of the variables in it by appropriate expressions—*i.e.*, ones that make sense in the context—and by doing so uniformly—*i.e.*, by substituting the same (or some synonymous) expression wherever the same variable recurs. The feature of (C) that guarantees that every instance of it will be valid is its construction in such a manner that every uniform way of replacing its variables to make the premises true automatically makes the conclusion true, too; or in other words that no instance of it can have true premises but a false conclusion. In virtue of this feature, the form (C) is called a *valid* inference form. In contrast,

(D) "Every *X* is a *Y*"; "Some *Z*'s are *Y*'s"; therefore, "Some *Z*'s are *X*'s"

is not a valid inference form, for although instances of it can be produced in which premises and conclusion are all true, instances of it can also be produced in which the premises are true but the conclusion is false—*e.g.*,

(E) "Every dog is a mammal"; "Some winged creatures are mammals"; therefore, "Some winged creatures are dogs."

Formal logic as a study is concerned with inference forms rather than with particular instances of them; one of its tasks is to discriminate between valid and invalid inference forms and to explore and systematize the relations that hold among valid ones.

Valid proposition forms Closely related to the idea of a valid inference form is that of a valid proposition form. A proposition form is an expression of which the instances (produced as before by appropriate and uniform replacements for variables) are not inferences from several propositions to a conclusion but propositions taken individually; and a *valid* proposition form is one for which all of the instances are true propositions. A simple example is

(F) "Nothing is both an *X* and a non-*X*."

An invalid proposition form is one that has at least some false instances. Formal logic is concerned with proposition forms as well as with inference forms. The study of proposition forms can, in fact, be made to include that of inference forms in the following way: let the premises of any given inference form (taken together) be abbreviated by alpha (α) and its conclusion by beta (β). Then the condition stated above for the validity of the inference form "α, therefore β" amounts to saying that no instance of the proposition form "α and not-β" is true—*i.e.*, that every instance of the proposition form

(G) "Not both: α and not-β"

is true—or that line (G), fully spelled out, of course—is a valid proposition form. The study of proposition forms, however, cannot be similarly accommodated under the study of inference forms, and so for reasons of comprehensiveness it is usual to regard formal logic as the study of proposition forms. Because a logician's handling of proposition forms is in many ways analogous to a mathematician's handling of numerical formulas, the systems he constructs are often called *calculi*.

Much of the work of a logician proceeds at a more abstract level than that of the foregoing discussion. Even a formula such as (C) above, though not referring to any specific subject matter, contains expressions like "every" and "is a," which are thought of as having a definite meaning; and the variables are intended to mark the places for expressions of one particular kind (roughly, common nouns or class names). It is possible, however—and for some purposes it is essential—to study formulas without attaching even this degree of meaningfulness to them. The construction of a system of logic, in fact, involves two distinguishable processes: one consists in setting up a symbolic apparatus—a set of symbols, rules for stringing these together into formulas, and rules for manipulating these formulas; the second consists in attaching certain meanings to these symbols and formulas. If only the former is done, the system is said to be *uninterpreted*, or *purely formal;* if the latter is done as well, the system is said to be *interpreted*. This distinction is important because systems of logic turn out to have certain properties quite independently of any interpretations that may be placed upon them. An axiomatic system of logic can be taken as an example—*i.e.*, a system in which certain unproved formulas, known as axioms, are taken as starting points, and further formulas (theorems) are proved on the strength of these. As will appear later (II. *Axiomatization of PC*), the question whether a proof of a given theorem in an axiomatic system is a sound one or not depends solely on which formulas are taken as axioms and on what the rules are for deriving theorems from axioms, and not at all on what the theorems or axioms mean. Moreover, a given uninterpreted system is in general capable of being interpreted equally well in a number of different ways; hence in studying an uninterpreted system, one is studying the structure that is common to a variety of interpreted systems. Normally a logician who constructs a purely formal system does have a particular interpretation in mind, and his motive for constructing it is the belief that when this interpretation is given to it the formulas of the system will be able to express sound or true principles in some field of thought; but, for the above reasons among others, he will usually take care to describe the formulas and state the rules of the system without reference to interpretation and to indicate as a separate matter the interpretation that he has in mind.

Problems in the philosophy of logic

Many of the ideas used in the exposition of formal logic, including some that have already occurred above, raise problems that belong to philosophy rather than to logic itself (see the two articles PHILOSOPHY, HISTORY OF WESTERN; and LOGIC, PHILOSOPHY OF). Examples are: What is the correct analysis of the notion of truth? What is a proposition, and how is it related to the sentence in which it is expressed? Are there some kinds of sound reasoning that are neither deductive nor inductive? Fortunately, it is possible to learn to do formal logic without having satisfactory answers to such questions, just as it is possible to do mathematics without answering questions belonging to the philosophy of mathematics such as: Are numbers real objects or mental constructs?

II. The propositional calculus

GENERAL FEATURES OF PC

The simplest and most basic branch of logic is the propositional calculus, hereafter called PC, named from the fact that it deals only with complete, unanalyzed propositions and certain combinations into which they enter. Various notations for PC are used in the literature (see below, V. *Varieties of notation in symbolic logic*). In that

Funda- mental definitions

used here the symbols employed in PC comprise first, variables (for which the letters p, q, r, . . . are used, with or without numerical subscripts); second, operators (for which the symbols $\sim$, $\cdot$, $\vee$, $\supset$, $\equiv$ are employed); and third, brackets or parentheses. The rules for constructing formulas are deferred to II. *Formation rules for PC*; and the intended interpretations—*i.e.*, the meanings to be given to these symbols—are indicated here immediately: The variables are to be viewed as representing unspecified propositions, or as marking the places in formulas into which propositions, and only propositions, may be inserted. (This is sometimes expressed by saying that they *range over* propositions, or that they take propositions as their *values*.) Hence they are often called *propositional variables*. It is assumed that every proposition is either true or false and that no proposition is both true and false. Truth and falsity are said to be the *truth values* of propositions. The function of an operator is to form a new proposition from one or more given propositions, called the *arguments* of the operator. The operators $\sim$, $\cdot$, $\vee$, $\supset$, and $\equiv$ correspond respectively to the English expressions "not," "and," "or," "if . . . then" (or "implies"), and "is equivalent to," when these are used in the following senses:

(i) Given a proposition p, then $\sim p$ ("not p") is to count as false when p is true and true when p is false; $\sim$ (when thus interpreted) is known as the *negation sign* and $\sim p$ as the *negation* of p.

(ii) Given any two propositions, p and q, then $p \cdot q$ ("p and q") is to count as true when p and q are both true and as false in all other cases (viz., when p is true and q false, when p is false and q true, and when p and q are both false); $p \cdot q$ is said to be the *conjunction* of p and q; $\cdot$ is known as the *conjunction sign* and its arguments (p, q) as *conjuncts*.

(iii) $p \vee q$ ("p or q") is to count as false when p and q are both false and true in all other cases; thus it represents the assertion that at least one of p and q is true. $p \vee q$ is known as the *disjunction* of p and q; $\vee$ is the *disjunction sign* and its arguments (p, q) are known as *disjuncts*.

(iv) $p \supset q$ ("if p [then] q" or "p [materially] implies q") is to count as false when p is true and q is false, and as true in all other cases; hence it has the same meaning as "either not-p or q," or as "not both; p and not-q." The symbol $\supset$ is known as the (*material*) *implication sign*, the first argument as the *antecedent*, and the second as the *consequent*; $q \supset p$ is known as the *converse* of $p \supset q$.

(v) Finally, $p \equiv q$ ("p is [materially] equivalent to q" or "p if and only if q") is to count as true when p and q have the same truth value (*i.e.*, either when both are true or when both are false), and false when they have different truth values;

the arguments of $\equiv$ (the [*material*] *equivalence sign*) are called *equivalents*.

Brackets are used to indicate grouping; they make it possible to distinguish, for example, between $p \cdot (q \vee r)$ ("Both p and either-q-or-r") and $(p \cdot q) \vee r$ ("Either both-p-and-q or r"). Precise rules for bracketing are given below.

The above account is meant solely as an explanation of the meaning to be attached to the PC operators in logic; it is not intended as an explanation or theory of the meaning in everyday speech of the English expressions by which they have here been roughly translated. Reading $p \supset q$ as "If p, q," for example, is made convenient by the fact that "if" is often used in English in a "material-implication" sense (someone who asserted "If it isn't raining, it's snowing" would usually be held to have spoken truly *unless* the antecedent were true but the consequent false; *i.e.*, unless it was neither raining nor snowing); but no claim is thereby being made that this is the only standard use of "if." Other uses of "if" have in fact led to the construction of various other systems of logic (see below, IV. *Alternative systems of modal logic* and also *Applied logic*) and have also raised important questions in the philosophy of logic; but these are irrelevant to the understanding of the relation expressed by $\supset$ in PC, which is one of fundamental importance for logic.

All PC operators take propositions as their arguments, and the result of applying them is also in each case a proposition. For this reason they are sometimes called *proposition-forming operators on propositions*, or more briefly *propositional connectives*. An operator that, like $\sim$, requires only a single argument is known as a *monadic* operator; operators that, like all the others listed, require two arguments are known as *dyadic*.

All PC operators also have the following important characteristic: given the truth values of the arguments, the truth value of the proposition formed by them and the operator is determined in every case. An operator that has this characteristic is known as a *truth-functional* operator, and a proposition formed by such an operator is called a *truth function* of the operator's argument(s). The truth functionality of the PC operators is clearly brought out by summarizing the above account of them in Table 1. In

Truth function- ality

Table 1: Truth Table for Most Common Operators							
monadic operator		dyadic operators					
p	$\sim p$	p	q	$p \cdot q$	$p \vee q$	$p \supset q$	$p \equiv q$
1	0	1	1	1	1	1	1
0	1	1	0	0	1	0	0
		0	1	0	1	1	0
		0	0	0	0	1	1

it, "true" is abbreviated by "1" and "false" by "0," and to the left of the vertical line are tabulated all possible combinations of truth values of the operators' arguments. The columns of 1s and 0s under the various truth functions indicate their truth values for each of the cases; these columns are known as the *truth tables* of the relevant operators. It should be noted that any column of four 1s and/or 0s or both will specify a dyadic truth-functional operator. Because there are precisely 2^4 (*i.e.*, 16) ways of forming a string of four symbols each of which is to be either 1 or 0 (1111, 1110, 1101, . . . , 0000), there are 16 such operators in all; the four that are listed here are only the four most generally useful ones.

Formation rules for PC. In any system of logic it is necessary to specify which sequences of symbols are to count as acceptable formulas—or, as they are usually called, *well-formed formulas* (*wff*'s). Rules that specify this are called *formation rules*. From an intuitive point of view it is desirable that the *wff*'s of PC be just those sequences of PC symbols that, in terms of the interpretation given above, make sense and are unambiguous; and this can be ensured by stipulating that the *wff*'s of PC are to be all of those expressions constructed in accordance with the following PC formation rules, and only these:

Well- formed formulas (*wff*'s)

FR1. A variable standing alone is a *wff*

FR2. If α is a *wff*, so is $\sim \alpha$

FR3. If α and β are *wff*'s, $(\alpha \cdot \beta)$, $(\alpha \vee \beta)$, $(\alpha \supset \beta)$, and $(\alpha \equiv \beta)$ are *wff*'s.

(In these rules α and β are variables representing arbitrary formulas of PC. They are not themselves symbols of PC but are used in discoursing about PC. Such variables are known as *metalogical* variables. For further explanation, see METALOGIC.) It should be noted that the rules, though designed to ensure unambiguous sense for the *wff*'s of PC under the intended interpretation, are themselves stated without any reference to interpretation and in such a way that there is an effective procedure for determining, again without any reference to interpretation, whether any arbitrary string of symbols is a *wff* or not. (An *effective* procedure is one that is "mechanical" in nature and can always be relied on to give a definite result in a finite number of steps. The notion of effectiveness plays an important role in formal logic.)

Examples of *wff*'s are: p; $\sim q$; $\sim (p \cdot q)$, "not both p and q"; $[\sim p \vee (q \equiv p)]$, "Either not p or else q is equivalent to p."

For greater ease in writing or reading formulas the formation rules are often relaxed in various ways. The following relaxations are common:

(a) Brackets enclosing a complete formula may be omitted

(b) The typographical style of brackets may be varied within a formula, to make the pairing of brackets more evident to the eye

(c) Conjunctions and disjunctions may be allowed to have more than two arguments; *e.g.*, $p \cdot (q \supset r) \cdot \sim r$ may be written instead of $[p \cdot (q \supset r)] \cdot \sim r$. (The conjunction $p \cdot q \cdot r$ is then interpreted to mean that p, q, and r are all true, $p \vee q \vee r$ to mean that at least one of p, q, and r is true, and so forth.)

Validity in PC. Given the standard interpretation, a *wff* of PC becomes a proposition, true or false, when all of its variables are replaced by actual propositions. Such a *wff* is therefore a proposition form in the sense explained in the *Introduction* and hence is valid if and only if all its instances are true propositions. A *wff* of which all instances are false is said to be *unsatisfiable* or *inconsistent;* and one with some true and some false instances is said to be *contingent.*

Decision procedure with truth tables

An important problem for any logical system is the *decision problem* for the class of valid *wff*'s of that system (sometimes simply called the decision problem for the system). This is the problem of finding an effective procedure, in the sense explained in II. *Formation rules for PC,* for testing the validity of any *wff* whatsoever of the system. Such a procedure is called a *decision procedure.* For some systems a decision procedure can be found; the decision problem for that system is then said to be *solvable,* and the system is said to be a *decidable* one. For other systems it can be proved that no decision procedure is possible; the decision problem for that system is then said to be *unsolvable,* and the system is said to be an *undecidable* one.

PC is a decidable system. In fact, several decision procedures for it are known. Of these the simplest and most important theoretically (though not always the easiest to apply in practice) is the method of *truth tables,* which will now be explained briefly. Since all of the operators in a *wff* of PC are truth-functional, in order to discover the truth value of any instance of such a *wff*, it is unnecessary to consider anything but the truth values of the propositions replacing the variables. In other words, the assignment of a truth value to each of the variables in a *wff* uniquely determines a truth value for the whole *wff*. Since there are only two truth values and each *wff* contains only a finite number of variables, there are only a finite number of truth-value assignments to the variables to be considered (if there are n distinct variables in the *wff*, there are 2^n such assignments); these can easily be systematically tabulated. For each of these assignments the truth tables for the operators then enable one to calculate the resulting truth value of the whole *wff*; and if and only if this truth value is *truth* in each case,

is the *wff* valid. As an example, $[(p \supset q) \cdot r] \supset [(\sim r \vee p) \supset q]$ may be tested for validity. This formula states that "If one proposition implies a second one, and a certain third proposition is true, then if either that third proposition is false or the first is true, the second is true."

The calculation is shown in Table 2. As before, 1 repre-

Table 2: Test for Validity by Truth Table				
p	q	r	$[(p \supset q) \cdot r] \supset [(\sim r \vee p) \supset q]$	
1	1	1	1 1 1 0 1 1	
1	1	0	1 0 1 1 1 1	
1	0	1	0 0 1 0 1 0	
1	0	0	0 0 1 1 1 0	
0	1	1	1 1 1 0 0 1	
0	1	0	1 0 1 1 1 1	
0	0	1	1 1 1 0 0 1	
0	0	0	1 0 1 1 1 0	
			(1) (2) (6) (3) (4) (5)	

sents truth and 0 falsity. Since the *wff* contains three variables, there are 2^3 (*i.e.*, 8) different assignments to the variables to be considered, which therefore generate the eight lines of the table. These assignments are tabulated to the left of the vertical line. The numbers in parentheses at the foot indicate the order in which the steps (from 1 through 6) are to be taken in determining the truth values (1 or 0) to be entered in the table. Thus column (1), falling under the symbol $\supset$, sets down the values of $p \supset q$ for each assignment, obtained from the columns under p and q by the truth table for $\supset$; column (2), for $(p \supset q) \cdot r$, is then obtained by employing the values in column (1) together with those in the column under r by use of the truth table for $\cdot$; . . . until finally column (6), which gives the values for the whole *wff*, is obtained from columns (2) and (5). This column is called the truth table of the whole *wff*. Since it consists entirely of 1s, it shows that the *wff* is true for every assignment given to the variables and is therefore valid. A *wff* for which the truth table consists entirely of 0s is inconsistent, and a *wff* for which the truth table contains at least one 1 and at least one 0 is contingent. It follows from the formation rules and from the fact that an initial truth table has been specified for each operator that a truth table can be constructed for any given *wff* of PC.

Among the more important valid *wff*'s of PC are those of Table 3:

Table 3: Some Valid Formulas of Propositional Calculus	
law	formula
Law of Identity	$p \equiv p$
Law of Double Negation	$p \equiv \sim\sim p$
Law of Excluded Middle	$p \vee \sim p$
Law of Noncontradiction	$\sim(p \cdot \sim p)$
De Morgan Laws	$(p \cdot q) \equiv \sim(\sim p \vee \sim q)$
	$(p \vee q) \equiv \sim(\sim p \cdot \sim q)$
Commutative Laws	$(p \vee q) \equiv (q \vee p)$
	$(p \cdot q) \equiv (q \cdot p)$
Associative Laws	$[(p \vee q) \vee r] \equiv [p \vee (q \vee r)]$
	$[(p \cdot q) \cdot r] \equiv [p \cdot (q \cdot r)]$
Law of Transposition	$(p \supset q) \equiv (\sim q \supset \sim p)$
Distributive Laws	$[p \cdot (q \vee r)] \equiv [(p \cdot q) \vee (p \cdot r)]$
	$[p \vee (q \cdot r)] \equiv [(p \vee q) \cdot (p \vee r)]$
Law of Permutation	$[p \supset (q \supset r)] \equiv [q \supset (p \supset r)]$
Law of Syllogism	$(p \supset q) \supset [(q \supset r) \supset (p \supset r)]$
Law of Importation	$[p \supset (q \supset r)] \supset [(p \cdot q) \supset r]$
Law of Exportation	$[(p \cdot q) \supset r] \supset [p \supset (q \supset r)]$

Construction of valid *wff*'s

All of the above *wff*'s can be shown to be valid by a mechanical application of the truth-table method. They can also be seen to express intuitively sound general principles about propositions. For instance, because "not (. . . or—)" can be rephrased as "neither . . . nor—," the first De Morgan law can be read as: "Both p and q if and only if neither not-p nor not-q"; thus it expresses the principle that two propositions are jointly true if and only if neither of them is false.

Whenever, as is the case in most of the examples given, a *wff* of the form $\alpha \equiv \beta$ is valid, the corresponding *wff*'s

$\alpha \supset \beta$ and $\beta \supset \alpha$ are also valid. For instance, because $(p \cdot q) \equiv \sim(\sim p \vee \sim q)$ is valid, so are $(p \cdot q) \supset \sim(\sim p \vee \sim q)$ and $\sim(\sim p \vee \sim q) \supset (p \cdot q)$.

Moreover, although $p \supset q$ does not mean that q can be deduced from p, yet whenever a *wff* of the form $\alpha \supset \beta$ is *valid*, the inference form "α, therefore β" is likewise valid. This fact is easily seen from the fact that $\alpha \supset \beta$ means the same as "Not both: α and not-β"; for, as was noted in the *Introduction*, whenever the latter is a valid proposition form, "α, therefore β" is a valid inference form.

Let α be any *wff*. If any variable in it is now uniformly replaced by some *wff*, the resulting *wff* is called a *substitution-instance* of α. Thus $[p \supset (q \vee \sim r)] \equiv [\sim(q \vee \sim r) \supset \sim p]$ is a substitution-instance of $(p \supset q) \equiv (\sim q \supset \sim p)$, obtained from it by replacing q uniformly by $(q \vee \sim r)$. It is an important principle that whenever a *wff* is valid so is every substitution-instance of it (the *rule of* [uniform] *substitution*).

A further important principle is the *rule of substitution of equivalents*. Two *wff*'s, α and β, are said to be *equivalents* when $\alpha \equiv \beta$ is valid. (The *wff*'s α and β are equivalents if and only if they have identical truth tables.) The rule states that if any part of a *wff* is replaced by an equivalent of that part, the resulting *wff* and the original are also equivalents. Such replacements need not be uniform. The application of this rule is said to make an *equivalence transformation*.

Interdefinability of operators.   The rules that have just been stated would enable the first De Morgan law listed in Table 3 to transform any *wff* containing any number of occurrences of $\cdot$ into an equivalent *wff* in which $\cdot$ does not appear at all but in place of it certain complexes of $\sim$ and $\vee$ arise. Similarly, since $\sim p \vee q$ has the same truth table as $p \supset q$, $(p \supset q) \equiv (\sim p \vee q)$ is valid, and any *wff* containing $\supset$ can therefore be transformed into an equivalent *wff* containing $\sim$ and $\vee$ but not $\supset$. And since $(p \equiv q) \equiv [(p \supset q) \cdot (q \supset p)]$ is valid, any *wff* containing $\equiv$ can be transformed into an equivalent containing $\supset$ and $\cdot$ but not $\equiv$ —and thus in turn by the previous steps it can be further transformed into one containing $\sim$ and $\vee$ but neither $\equiv$ nor $\supset$ nor $\cdot$. Thus for every *wff* of PC there is an equivalent *wff*, expressing precisely the same truth function, in which the only operators are $\sim$ and $\vee$, though the meaning of this *wff* will usually be much less clear than that of the original.

Alternative primitives

An alternative way of presenting PC, therefore, is to begin with the operators $\sim$ and $\vee$ only and to define the others in terms of these. The operators $\sim$ and $\vee$ are then said to be *primitive*. If "$=_{\mathrm{Df}}$" is used to mean "is defined as," then the relevant definitions can be set down as follows:

$$(\alpha \cdot \beta) =_{\mathrm{Df}} \sim(\sim \alpha \vee \sim \beta)$$
$$(\alpha \supset \beta) =_{\mathrm{Df}} (\sim \alpha \vee \beta)$$
$$(\alpha \equiv \beta) =_{\mathrm{Df}} [(\alpha \supset \beta) \cdot (\beta \supset \alpha)]$$

in which α and β are any *wff*'s of PC. These definitions are not themselves *wff*'s of PC, nor is $=_{\mathrm{Df}}$ a symbol of PC; they are metalogical statements about PC, used to introduce the new symbols $\cdot$, $\supset$, and $\equiv$ into the system. If PC is regarded as a purely uninterpreted system, the expression on the left in a definition is simply a convenient abbreviation of the expression on the right. If, however, PC is thought of as having its standard interpretation, the meanings of $\sim$ and $\vee$ will first of all have been stipulated by truth tables, and then the definitions will lay it down that the expression on the left is to be understood as having the same meaning (*i.e.,* the same truth table) as the expression on the right. It is easy to check that the truth tables obtained in this way for $\cdot$, $\supset$, and $\equiv$ are precisely the ones that were originally stipulated for them.

An alternative to taking $\sim$ and $\vee$ as primitive is to take $\sim$ and $\cdot$ as primitive and to define $(\alpha \vee \beta)$ as $\sim(\sim \alpha \cdot \sim \beta)$, to define $(\alpha \supset \beta)$ as $\sim(\alpha \cdot \sim \beta)$, and to define $(\alpha \equiv \beta)$ as before. Yet another possibility is to take $\sim$ and $\supset$ as primitive and to define $(\alpha \vee \beta)$ as $(\sim \alpha \supset \beta)$, $(\alpha \cdot \beta)$ as $\sim(\alpha \supset \sim \beta)$, and $(\alpha \equiv \beta)$ as before. In each case, precisely the same *wff*'s that were valid in the original presentation of the system are still valid.

Axiomatization of PC.   The basic idea of constructing an *axiomatic system* is that of choosing certain *wff*'s (known as *axioms*) as starting points and giving rules for deriving further *wff*'s (known as *theorems*) from them. Such rules are called *transformation rules*. Sometimes the word "theorem" is used to cover axioms as well as theorems; the word "thesis" is also used for this purpose.

An *axiomatic basis* consists of:

(1) A list of primitive symbols, together with any definitions that may be thought convenient;
(2) A set of formation rules, specifying which sequences of symbols are to count as *wff*'s;
(3) A list of *wff*'s selected as axioms;
(4) A set of (one or more) transformation rules, which enable new *wff*'s (theorems) to be obtained by performing certain specified operations on axioms or previously obtained theorems.

Axiomatic basis and interpretation

Definitions, where they occur, can function as additional transformation rules, to the effect that, if in any theorem any expression of the form occurring on one side of a definition is replaced by the corresponding expression of the form occurring on the other side, the result is also to count as a theorem. A *proof* or *derivation* of a *wff* α in an axiomatic system S is a sequence of *wff*'s of which the last is α itself and each *wff* in the sequence is either an axiom of S or is derived from some axiom(s) or some already-derived theorem(s) or both by one of the transformation rules of S. A *wff* is a theorem of S if and only if there is a proof of it in S.

Care is usually taken, in setting out an axiomatic basis, to avoid all reference to interpretation. It must be possible to tell purely from the construction of a *wff* whether it is an axiom or not. Moreover, the transformation rules must be so formulated that there is an effective way of telling whether any purported application of them is a correct application or not and hence whether a purported proof of a theorem really is a proof or not. An axiomatic system will then be a purely formal structure, on which any one of a number of interpretations, or none at all, may be imposed without affecting the question of which *wff*'s are theorems. Normally, however, an axiomatic system is constructed with a certain interpretation in mind; the transformation rules are so formulated that under that interpretation they are *validity-preserving* (*i.e.,* the results of applying them to valid *wff*'s are always themselves valid *wff*'s); and the chosen axioms either are valid *wff*'s or are expressions of principles of which it is desired to explore the consequences.

Probably the best known axiomatic system for PC is the following one, which, since it is derived from *Principia Mathematica*, by Alfred North Whitehead and Bertrand Russell (published in 1910), is often called PM: *Primitive symbols:* $\sim$, $\vee$, (,), and an infinite set of variables, p, q, r, . . . (with or without numerical subscripts). *Definitions* of $\cdot$, $\supset$, $\equiv$ as above (II. *Interdefinability of operators*). *Formation rules* as above (II. *Formation rules for PC*), except that Rule 3 can be abbreviated to "If α and β are *wff*'s, $(\alpha \vee \beta)$ is a *wff*," since $\cdot$, $\supset$, and $\equiv$ are not primitive. *Axioms:*

Properties of an axiomatic system: PM

(1) $(p \vee p) \supset p$;   (3) $(p \vee q) \supset (q \vee p)$;
(2) $q \supset (p \vee q)$;   (4) $(q \supset r) \supset [(p \vee q) \supset (p \vee r)]$.

Axiom (4) can be read "If q implies r, then, if either p or q, either p or r." *Transformation rules:* (1) The result of uniformly replacing any variable in a theorem by any *wff* is a theorem (*rule of substitution*); and (2) if α and $(\alpha \supset \beta)$ are theorems, then β is a theorem (*rule of detachment*, or *modus ponens*).

Relative to a given criterion of validity, an axiomatic system is *sound* if every theorem is valid, and it is *complete* (or, more specifically, *weakly complete*) if every valid *wff* is a theorem. The axiomatic system PM can be shown to be both sound and complete relative to the criterion of validity given in II. *Validity in PC*.

An axiomatic system is *consistent* if, whenever a *wff* α is a theorem, $\sim \alpha$ is not a theorem. (In terms of the standard interpretation, this means that no pair of theorems can ever be derived one of which is the negation of the other.) It is *strongly complete* if the addition to it (as an extra axiom) of any *wff* whatever that is not already a theorem would make the system inconsistent. Finally, an axiom or transformation rule is *independent* (in a given axiomatic system) if it cannot be derived from the remainder of the basis (or—what comes to the same thing —if its omission from the basis would make the derivation of certain theorems impossible). It can, moreover, be shown that PM is consistent and strongly complete and that each of its axioms and transformation rules is independent.

A considerable number of other axiomatic bases for PC, each having all of the above properties, are known. The task of proving that they have these properties belongs to metalogic (*q.v.*).

Axiom schemata   In some standard expositions of formal logic, the place of axioms is taken by *axiom schemata*, which, instead of presenting some particular *wff* as an axiom, lay it down that any *wff* of a certain form is an axiom. For example, in place of Axiom (1) in PM one might have the axiom schema "Every *wff* of the form $(\alpha \lor \alpha) \supset \alpha$ is an axiom"; and analogous schemata can be substituted for the other axioms. The number of axioms would then become infinite; but, on the other hand, the *rule of substitution* would no longer be needed and *modus ponens* could be the only transformation rule. This method makes no difference to the theorems that can be derived; but in some branches of logic (though not in PC), it is simpler to work with axiom schemata rather than with particular axioms and substitution rules. Having an infinite number of axioms causes no trouble provided that there is an effective way of telling whether a *wff* is an axiom or not.

SPECIAL SYSTEMS OF PC

Partial systems of PC. Various propositional calculi have been devised to express a narrower range of truth functions than those of PC as expounded above. Of these, the one that has been most fully studied is the Pure Implicational Calculus (PIC), in which the only operator is $\supset$, and the *wff*'s are precisely those *wff*'s of PC that can be built up from variables, $\supset$, and brackets alone. Formation rules 2 and 3 of II. *Formation rules for PC* are therefore replaced by the rule that if α and β are *wff*'s, $(\alpha \supset \beta)$ is a *wff*. As in ordinary PC, $p \supset q$ is interpreted as "*p* materially implies *q*"; i.e., as true except when *p* is true but *q* false. The truth-table test of validity can then be straightforwardly applied to *wff*'s of PIC.

The task of axiomatizing PIC is that of finding a set of valid *wff*'s, preferably few in number and relatively simple in structure, from which all other valid *wff*'s of the system can be derived by straightforward transformation rules. The best-known basis, which was formulated in 1930, has the transformation rules of *substitution* and *modus ponens* (as in PM), and the axioms:

(1) $p \supset (q \supset p)$
(2) $[(p \supset q) \supset p] \supset p$
(3) $(p \supset q) \supset [(q \supset r) \supset (p \supset r)]$

Axioms (1) and (3) are closely related to axioms (2) and (4) of PM respectively (see above, II. *Axiomatization of PC*). It can be shown that the basis is complete and that each axiom is independent.

Under the standard interpretation the above axioms can be thought of as expressing the following principles: (1) "If a proposition *p* is true, then if some arbitrary proposition *q* is true, *p* is (still) true." (2) "If the fact that a certain proposition *p* implies some arbitrary proposition *q* implies that *p* itself is true, then *p* is (indeed) true." (3) "If one proposition (*p*) implies a second (*q*), then if that second proposition implies a third (*r*), the first implies the third." The completeness of the basis is, however, a formal matter, not dependent on these or any other readings of the formulas.

An even more economical complete basis for PIC contains the same transformation rules but the sole axiom

$$[(p \supset q) \supset r] \supset [(r \supset p) \supset (s \supset p)].$$

It has been proved that this is the shortest possible single axiom that will give a complete basis for PIC with these transformation rules.

Since PIC contains no negation sign, the previous account of consistency is not significantly applicable to it. Alternative accounts of consistency have, however, been proposed, according to which a system is consistent (a) if no *wff* consisting of a single variable is a theorem, or (b) if not every *wff* is a theorem. The bases stated are consistent in these senses.

Nonstandard versions of PC. Qualms have sometimes been expressed about the intuitive soundness of some formulas that are valid in "orthodox" PC, and these qualms have led some logicians to construct a number of propositional calculi that deviate in various ways from PC as expounded above.

The true-false dichotomy: its problems   Underlying ordinary PC is the intuitive idea that every proposition is either true or false, an idea that finds its formal expression in the stipulation that variables shall have two possible values only, viz., 1 and 0. (For this reason the system is often called the *two-valued* propositional calculus.) This idea has been challenged on various grounds. Following a suggestion made by Aristotle, some logicians have maintained that propositions about those events in the future that may or may not come to pass are neither true nor false but "neuter" in truth value. Aristotle's own example, which has been discussed frequently down to the present day, is "There will be a sea-battle tomorrow." It has also been maintained that for propositions with subjects that do not have anything actual corresponding to them—such as "The present King of France is wise" (assuming that France has no king) or "All John's children are asleep" (assuming that John has no children)—the question of truth or falsity "does not arise." Yet another view is that a third truth value (say "half-truth") ought to be recognized intermediate between truth and falsity; thus it has been held that certain familiar states of the weather make the proposition "It is raining" neither definitely true nor definitely false but something in between.

Three-valued logics. The issues raised by the above examples no doubt differ significantly; but they all suggest a threefold rather than a twofold division of propositions and hence the possibility of a logic in which the variables may take any of three values (say 1, ½, and 0), with a consequent revision of the standard PC account of validity. Several such three-valued logics have been constructed and investigated; a brief account will be given here of one of them, in which the most natural interpretation of the additional value (½) is as "half-true," with 1 and 0 representing truth and falsity as before. The formation rules are as they were for orthodox PC, but the meaning of the operators is extended to cover cases in which at least one argument has the value ½, by the following five entries in Table 4. (Adopting one of the

Table 4: Truth Values for Common Operators in a Three-Valued Logic															
		negation ($\sim p$)	conjunction ($p \cdot q$) *q*			disjunction ($p \lor q$) *q*			implication ($p \supset q$) *q*			equivalence ($p \equiv q$) *q*			
			1	½	0	1	½	0	1	½	0	1	½	0
	1	0	1	½	0	1	1	1	1	½	0	1	½	0
p	½	½	½	½	0	1	½	½	1	1	½	½	1	½
	0	1	0	0	0	1	½	0	1	1	1	0	½	1

three values of the first argument, *p*, given in the leftmost column [1, ½, or 0] and, for the dyadic operators, one of the three values of the second, *q*, in the top row— above the line—one then finds the value of the whole formula by reading across for *p* and down for *q*.) It will be seen that these tables, which are from Łukasiewicz, are the same as the ordinary two-valued ones when the arguments have the values 1 and 0. The other values are intended to be intuitively plausible extensions of the principles underlying the two-valued calculus to cover the cases involving half-true arguments. Clearly, these tables enable a person to calculate a determinate value (1, ½, or 0) for any *wff*, given the values assigned to the variables in it; and a *wff* is valid in this calculus if it has the value 1 for every assignment to

Validity
of *wff*'s
in
three-
valued
logic

its variables. Since the values of formulas when the variables are assigned only the values 1 and 0 are the same as in ordinary PC, every *wff* that is valid in the present calculus is also valid in PC. Some *wff*'s that are valid in PC are, however, now no longer valid. An example is $(p \lor \sim p)$, which, when p has the value ½, also has the value ½. This reflects the idea that if one admits the possibility of a proposition's being half-true, he can no longer hold of every proposition without restriction that either it or its negation is true.

Given the above tables for the operators, it is possible to take $\sim$ and $\supset$ as primitive and to define $(\alpha \lor \beta)$ as $[(\alpha \supset \beta) \supset \beta]$—though not as $(\sim\alpha \supset \beta)$ as in ordinary PC; $(\alpha \cdot \beta)$ as $\sim(\sim\alpha \lor \sim\beta)$; and $(\alpha \equiv \beta)$ as $[(\alpha \supset \beta) \cdot (\beta \supset \alpha)]$. With these definitions as given, all valid *wff*'s constructed from variables and $\sim$, $\cdot$, $\lor$, $\supset$, and $\equiv$ can be derived by *substitution* and *modus ponens* from the four axioms:

$$(1) \quad p \supset (q \supset p);$$
$$(2) \quad (p \supset q) \supset [(q \supset r) \supset (p \supset r)];$$
$$(3) \quad [(p \supset \sim p) \supset p] \supset p;$$
$$(4) \quad (\sim p \supset \sim q) \supset (q \supset p).$$

Other three-valued logics can easily be constructed. For example, the above tables might be modified so that $\sim$½, ½ $\supset$ 0, ½ $\equiv$ 0, and 0 $\equiv$ ½ all have the value 0 instead of ½ as before, leaving everything else unchanged. The same definitions are then still possible, but the list of valid formulas is different; *e.g.*, $\sim\sim p \supset p$, which was previously valid, now has the value ½ when p has the value ½. This system can also be successfully axiomatized. Other calculi with more than three values can also be constructed along analogous lines.

Intuitionistic calculus. Other nonstandard calculi have been constructed by beginning with an axiomatization instead of a definition of validity. Of these the best known is the *intuitionistic calculus*, devised by Arend Heyting, one of the chief representatives of the Intuitionist school of mathematicians, which denies the validity of certain types of proof used in classical mathematics. At least in certain contexts, members of this school regard the demonstration of the falsity of the negation of a proposition (a proof by *reductio ad absurdum*) as insufficient to establish the truth of the proposition in question. Thus they regard $\sim\sim p$ as an inadequate premise from which to deduce p and hence do not accept the validity of the *law of double negation* in the form $\sim\sim p \supset p$. They do, however, regard a demonstration that p is true as showing that the negation of p is false and hence accept $p \supset \sim\sim p$ as valid. For somewhat similar reasons, they also refuse to accept the validity of arguments based on the *law of excluded middle* ($p \lor \sim p$). The intuitionistic calculus aims at presenting in axiomatic form those and only those principles of propositional logic that are accepted as sound in intuitionist mathematics. In this calculus, $\sim$, $\cdot$, $\lor$, and $\supset$ are all primitive, the transformation rules as before are *substitution* and *modus ponens,* and the axioms are the following:

Dubious
logical
principles

$$(1) \quad p \supset (p \cdot p)$$
$$(2) \quad (p \cdot q) \supset (q \cdot p)$$
$$(3) \quad (p \supset q) \supset [(p \cdot r) \supset (q \cdot r)]$$
$$(4) \quad [(p \supset q) \cdot (q \supset r)] \supset (p \supset r)$$
$$(5) \quad p \supset (q \supset p)$$
$$(6) \quad [p \cdot (p \supset q)] \supset q$$
$$(7) \quad p \supset (p \lor q)$$
$$(8) \quad (p \lor q) \supset (q \lor p)$$
$$(9) \quad [(p \supset r) \cdot (q \supset r)] \supset [(p \lor q) \supset r]$$
$$(10) \quad \sim p \supset (p \supset q)$$
$$(11) \quad [(p \supset q) \cdot (p \supset \sim q)] \supset \sim p$$

From this basis neither $p \lor \sim p$ nor $\sim\sim p \supset p$ can be derived, though $p \supset \sim\sim p$ can. In this respect this calculus resembles the second of the three-valued logics described above. It is, however, not possible to give a truth table account of validity—no matter how many values are used—that will bring out as valid precisely those *wff*'s that are theorems of the intuitionistic calculus and no others (see also MATHEMATICS, FOUNDATIONS OF: *The crisis in foundations following 1900: Intuitionism*).

NATURAL DEDUCTION METHOD IN PC

PC is often presented by what is known as the method of *natural deduction.* Essentially this consists of a set of rules for drawing conclusions from hypotheses (assumptions, premises) represented by *wff*'s of PC and thus for constructing valid inference forms; but it also provides a method of deriving from these inference forms valid proposition forms, and in this way it is analogous to the derivation of theorems in an axiomatic system. One such set of rules is presented in Table 5 (and there are various other sets that yield the same results):

Table 5: Sample Set of Rules for the Natural Deduction Method in Propositional Calculus

rule	given	one may then conclude
1. Modus ponens	α and $\alpha \supset \beta$	β
2. Modus tollens	$\sim\beta$ and $\alpha \supset \beta$	$\sim\alpha$
3. Double negation	α	$\sim\sim\alpha$
	$\sim\sim\alpha$	α
4. Conjunction introduction	α and β	$\alpha \cdot \beta$
5. Conjunction elimination	$\alpha \cdot \beta$	α and also β
6. Disjunction introduction	either α or β separately	$\alpha \lor \beta$
7. Disjunction elimination	$\alpha \lor \beta$, a derivation of γ from α, and a derivation of γ from β	γ
8. Conditional proof	a derivation of β from the hypothesis α (perhaps with the help of other hypotheses)	$\alpha \supset \beta$ as a conclusion from these other hypotheses (if any)
9. Reductio ad absurdum	a derivation of $\beta \cdot \sim\beta$ from the hypothesis α (perhaps with the help of other hypotheses)	$\sim\alpha$ as a conclusion from these other hypotheses (if any)

A natural deduction proof is a sequence of *wff*'s beginning with one or more *wff*'s as hypotheses; fresh hypotheses may also be added at any point in the course of a proof. The rules may be applied to any *wff* or group of *wff*'s, as appropriate, that have already occurred in the sequence. In the case of rules 1–7, the conclusion is said to *depend on* all of those hypotheses that have been used in the series of applications of the rules that have led to this conclusion; *i.e.*, it is claimed simply that the conclusion follows from these hypotheses, not that it holds in its own right. An application of rule 8 or rule 9, however, reduces by one the number of hypotheses on which the conclusion depends; and a hypothesis so eliminated is said to be a *discharged* hypothesis. In this way a *wff* may be reached that depends on no hypotheses at all. Such a *wff* is a *theorem.* It can be shown that the theorems derivable by the rules stated above—together with the definition of $\alpha \equiv \beta$ as $(\alpha \supset \beta) \cdot (\beta \supset \alpha)$—are precisely the valid *wff*'s of PC. A set of natural deduction rules yielding as theorems all of the valid *wff*'s of a system is *complete* (with respect to that system) in a sense obviously analogous to that in which an axiomatic basis was said to be complete in II. *Axiomatization of PC.*

Rules of
inference
and
their
application

As an illustration, the formula $[(p \supset q) \cdot (p \supset r)] \supset [p \supset (q \cdot r)]$ will be derived as a theorem by the natural deduction method. (The sense of this formula is that, if a proposition [p] implies each of two other propositions [q,r], then it implies their conjunction.) Explanatory comments follow the proof.

Sample
proof of a
theorem

1	(1)	$(p \supset q) \cdot (p \supset r)$	hypothesis
2	(2)	p	hypothesis
1	(3)	$p \supset q$	1, conjunction elimination
1	(4)	$p \supset r$	1, conjunction elimination
1,2	(5)	q	2,3, *modus ponens*
1,2	(6)	r	2,4, *modus ponens*
1,2	(7)	$q \cdot r$	5,6, conjunction introduction
1	(8)	$p \supset (q \cdot r)$	2,7, conditional proof
	(9)	$[(p \supset q) \cdot (p \supset r)] \supset [p \supset (q \cdot r)]$	1,8, conditional proof

The figures in parentheses immediately preceding the *wff*'s are simply for reference. To the right is indicated either that the *wff* is a hypothesis or that it is derived from the *wff*'s indicated by the rules stated. On the left are noted the hypotheses on which the *wff* in question depends (either the first or the second line of the derivation, or both). Note that since (8) is derived by *conditional proof* from hypothesis (2) and from (7), which is itself derived from hypotheses (1) and (2), (8) depends only on hypothesis (1), and hypothesis (2) is discharged. Similarly (9) depends on no hypotheses and is therefore a theorem.

By varying the above rules it is possible to obtain natural deduction systems corresponding to other versions of PC. For example, if the second part of the *double negation* rule is omitted and the rule is added that, given $\alpha \cdot \sim \alpha$, one may then conclude: β, it can be shown that the theorems then derivable are precisely the theorems of the Intuitionistic Calculus. Natural deduction rules have also been formulated for some other branches of logic mentioned in this article—*e.g.*, for the lower predicate calculus (III.) and for various systems of modal logic (IV. *Alternative systems of modal logic*).

III. The predicate calculus

Funda-mental definitions

Propositions may also be built up, not out of other propositions but out of elements that are not themselves propositions. The simplest kind to be considered here are propositions in which a certain object or individual (in a wide sense) is said to possess a certain property or characteristic; examples are: "Socrates is wise" and "The number 7 is prime." Such a proposition contains two distinguishable parts: (1) an expression that names or designates an individual and (2) an expression, called a *predicate*, that stands for the property that the individual in question is said to possess. If x, y, z, . . . are used as individual variables (replaceable by names of individuals) and the symbols ϕ (phi), ψ (psi), χ (chi), . . . as predicate variables (replaceable by predicates), the formula ϕx is used to express the form of the propositions in question. Here x is said to be the *argument* of ϕ; a predicate (or predicate variable) with only a single argument is said to be a *monadic*, or *one-place*, predicate (variable). Predicates with two or more arguments stand not for properties of single individuals but for relations between individuals. Thus the proposition "Tom is a son of John" is analyzable into two names of individuals ("Tom" and "John") and a dyadic or two-place predicate ("is a son of"), of which they are the arguments; and the proposition is thus of the form ϕxy. Analogously, ". . . is between . . . and . . ." is a three-place predicate, requiring three arguments, and so on. In general, a predicate variable followed by any number of individual variables is a *wff* of the predicate calculus. Such a *wff* is known as an *atomic* formula, and the predicate variable in it is said to be of *degree n*, if n is the number of individual variables following it. The degree of a predicate variable is sometimes indicated by a superscript—*e.g.*, ϕxyz may be written as $\phi^3 xyz$; $\phi^3 xy$ would then be regarded as not well formed. This practice is theoretically more accurate, but the superscripts are commonly omitted for ease of reading when no confusion is likely to arise.

Atomic formulas may be combined with truth-functional operators to give formulas such as $\phi x \vee \psi y$ [Example: "Either the customer (x) is friendly (ϕ) or else John (y) is disappointed (ψ)"]; $\phi xy \supset \sim \psi x$ [Example: "If the road (x) is above (ϕ) the flood line (y), then the road is not wet ($\sim \psi$)"]; and so on. Formulas so formed, however, are valid when and only when they are substitution-instances of valid *wff*'s of PC and hence in a sense do not transcend PC. More interesting formulas are formed by the use, in addition, of *quantifiers*. There are two kinds of quantifiers: *universal* quantifiers, written as "($\forall$___)" —or often simply as "(___)"—where the blank is filled by a variable, which may be read "For all___"; and *existential* quantifiers, written as "($\exists$___)," which may be read "For some___," or "There is a ___ such that." ("Some" is to be understood as meaning "at least one.") Thus ($\forall x$)ϕx is to mean "For all x, x is ϕ," or more simply, "Everything is ϕ"; and ($\exists x$)ϕx is to mean "For some x, x is ϕ," or more simply, "Something is ϕ," or "There is a ϕ." Slightly more complex examples are: ($\forall x$)($\phi x \supset \psi x$) for "Whatever is ϕ is ψ"; ($\exists x$)($\phi x \cdot \psi x$)

Quantifiers $\forall$ and $\exists$

for "Something is both ϕ and ψ"; ($\forall x$)($\exists y$)ϕxy for "Everything bears the relation ϕ to at least one thing"; and ($\exists x$)($\forall y$)ϕxy for "There is something that bears the relation ϕ to everything." To take a concrete case, if ϕxy means "x loves y," and the values of x and y are taken to be human beings, then the last two formulas mean, respectively, "Everybody loves somebody" and "Somebody loves everybody."

Intuitively, the notions expressed by the words "some" and "every" are connected in the following way: to assert that something has a certain property amounts to denying that everything lacks that property (for example, to say that something is white is to say that not everything is nonwhite); and similarly, to assert that everything has a certain property amounts to denying that there is something that lacks it. These intuitive connections are reflected in the usual practice of taking one of the quantifiers as primitive and defining the other in terms of it. Thus $\forall$ may be taken as primitive, and $\exists$ introduced by the definition:

$$(\exists \mathbf{a})\alpha =_{\text{Df}} \sim (\forall \mathbf{a})\sim \alpha$$

in which **a** is any variable and α is any *wff;* or alternatively, $\exists$ may be taken as primitive, and $\forall$ introduced by definition:

$$(\forall \mathbf{a})\alpha =_{\text{Df}} \sim (\exists \mathbf{a})\sim \alpha$$

THE LOWER PREDICATE CALCULUS

A predicate calculus in which the only variables that occur in quantifiers are individual variables is known as a *lower* (or *first-order*) predicate calculus. Various lower predicate calculi have been constructed. In the most straightforward of these, to which the most attention will here be devoted and which will be referred to simply as LPC, the *wff*'s can be specified as follows: Let the primitive symbols be (a) x, y, . . . (individual variables); (b) ϕ, ψ, . . . , each of some specified degree (predicate variables); and (c) the symbols $\sim$, $\vee$, $\forall$, (, and). An infinite number of each type of variable can now be secured as before by the use of numerical subscripts. The symbols $\cdot$, $\supset$, and $\equiv$ are defined as in PC and $\exists$ as explained above. The formation rules are:

1. An expression consisting of a predicate variable of degree n followed by n individual variables is a *wff*.
2. If α is a *wff*, so is $\sim \alpha$.
3. If α and β are *wff*'s, so is ($\alpha \vee \beta$).
4. If α is a *wff* and **a** is an individual variable, then ($\forall$**a**) α is a *wff*. (In such a *wff*, α is said to be the *scope* of the quantifier.)

If **a** is any individual variable and α is any *wff*, every occurrence of **a** in α is said to be *bound* (by the quantifiers) when occurring in the *wff*'s ($\forall$**a**)α and ($\exists$**a**)α. Any occurrence of a variable that is not bound is said to be *free*. Thus in ($\forall x$) ($\phi x \vee \phi y$)—the x in ϕx is bound, since it occurs within the scope of a quantifier containing x, but y is free. In the *wff*'s of a lower predicate calculus, every occurrence of a predicate variable (ϕ, ψ, χ, . . .) is free. A *wff* containing no free individual variables is said to be a *closed wff* of LPC. If a *wff* of LPC is considered as a proposition form, instances of it are obtained by replacing all free variables in it by predicates or by names of individuals, as appropriate. A bound variable, on the other hand, indicates not a point in the *wff* where a replacement is needed but a point (so to speak) at which the relevant quantifier applies.

Bound and free variables

For example, in ϕx, in which both variables are free, each variable must be replaced appropriately if a proposition of the form in question (such as "Socrates is white") is to be obtained; but in ($\exists x$)ϕx, in which x is bound, it is necessary only to replace ϕ by a predicate in order to obtain a complete proposition (*e.g.*, replacing ϕ by "is white" yields the proposition "Something is white").

Validity in LPC. Intuitively, a *wff* of LPC is valid if and only if all of its instances are true—*i.e.*, if and only if every result of replacing each of its free variables appropriately and uniformly is a true proposition. A formal definition of validity in LPC to express this intuitive notion more precisely can be given as follows: for any *wff* of LPC any number of LPC *models* can be formed. An

Value
assign-
ments
in the
domain
of a model

LPC model has two elements: One is a set, *D*, of objects, known as a *domain*. *D* may contain as many or as few objects as one chooses, but it must contain at least one, and the objects may be of any kind. The other element, *V*, is a system of value assignments satisfying the following conditions. To each individual variable there is assigned some member of *D* (not necessarily a different one in each case). Assignments are next made to the predicate variables in the following way: if ϕ is monadic, there is assigned to it some subset of *D* (possibly the whole of *D*); intuitively this subset can be viewed as the set of all the objects in *D* that have the property ϕ. If ϕ is dyadic, there is assigned to it some set of ordered pairs (*i.e.*, pairs of objects of which one is marked out as the first and the other as the second) drawn from *D;* intuitively these can be viewed as all of the pairs of objects in *D* in which the relation ϕ holds between the first object in the pair and the second. In general, if ϕ is of degree *n*, there is assigned to it some set of ordered *n*-tuples (groups of *n* objects) of members of *D*. It is then stipulated that an atomic formula is to have the value 1 in the model if the members of *D* assigned to its individual variables form, in that order, one of the *n*-tuples assigned to the predicate variable in it; otherwise, it is to have the value 0. Thus in the simplest case, ϕx will have the value 1 if the object assigned to *x* is one of the set of objects that was assigned to ϕ; and if it is not, then ϕx will have the value 0. The values of truth functions are determined by the values of their arguments as in PC. Finally, the value of $(\forall x)\alpha$ is to be 1 if both (a) the value of α itself is 1 and (b) α would always still have the value 1 if a different assignment were made to *x* but all of the other assignments were left precisely as they were; otherwise $(\forall x)\alpha$ is to have the value 0. Since $\exists$ can be defined in terms of $\forall$, these rules cover all of the *wff*'s of LPC. A given *wff* may of course have the value 1 in some LPC models but the value 0 in others. But a valid *wff* of LPC may now be defined as one that has the value 1 in every LPC model. If 1 and 0 are viewed as representing truth and falsity, respectively, then validity is defined as truth in every model.

Although the above definition of validity in LPC is quite precise, it does not yield, as did the corresponding definition of PC validity in terms of truth tables, an effective decision procedure. It can, indeed, be shown that no generally applicable decision procedure for LPC is possible—*i.e.*, that LPC is not a decidable system. This does not mean that it is never possible to prove that a given *wff* of LPC is valid—the validity of an unlimited number of such *wff*'s can in fact be demonstrated—but it does mean that in the case of LPC, unlike that of PC, no advance assurance can be given that no matter what *wff* is produced it will always be possible to determine whether it is valid or not (see also METALOGIC: *Model theory*).

Logical manipulations in LPC. The intuitive connections between *some* and *every* noted at the end of the introduction to III. *The predicate calculus* are reflected in the fact that the following equivalences are valid:

$$(\exists x)\phi x \equiv \sim(\forall x)\sim\phi x$$
$$(\forall x)\phi x \equiv \sim(\exists x)\sim\phi x.$$

The former of these asserts that "Something is ϕ" is equivalent to "Not everything fails to be ϕ", and the latter that "Everything is ϕ" is equivalent to "Nothing fails to be ϕ" (literally, "It is not the case that there is something which is not ϕ"). These equivalences remain valid when ϕx is replaced by any *wff*, however complex; *i.e.*, for any *wff* α whatsoever,

$$(\exists x)\alpha \equiv \sim(\forall x)\sim\alpha$$
and
$$(\forall x)\alpha \equiv \sim(\exists x)\sim\alpha$$

are valid. Because the rule of substitution of equivalents can be shown to hold in LPC, it follows that $(\exists x)$ may be replaced anywhere in a *wff* by $\sim(\forall x)\sim$, or $(\forall x)$ by $\sim(\exists x)\sim$, and the resulting *wff* will be equivalent to the original. Similarly, because the law of double negation permits the deletion of a pair of consecutive negation signs, $\sim(\exists x)$ may be replaced by $(\forall x)\sim$, and $\sim(\forall x)$ by $(\exists x)\sim$.

These principles are easily extended to more complex cases. To say that there is a pair of objects satisfying a certain condition is equivalent to denying that every pair of objects fails to satisfy that condition; and to say that every pair of objects satisfies a certain condition is equivalent to denying that there is any pair of objects that fails to satisfy that condition. These equivalences are expressed formally by the validity, again for any *wff* α, of:

$$(\exists x)(\exists y)\alpha \equiv \sim(\forall x)(\forall y)\sim\alpha$$
and
$$(\forall x)(\forall y)\alpha \equiv \sim(\exists x)(\exists y)\sim\alpha$$

—and by the resulting replaceability anywhere in a *wff* of $(\exists x)(\exists y)$ by $\sim(\forall x)(\forall y)\sim$, or of $(\forall x)(\forall y)$ by $\sim(\exists x)(\exists y)\sim$.

Analogously, $(\exists x)(\forall y)$ can be replaced by $\sim(\forall x)(\exists y)\sim$ [*e.g.*, $(\exists x)(\forall y)$ (*x* loves *y*)—"There is someone who loves everyone"—is equivalent to $\sim(\forall x)(\exists y)\sim$ (*x* loves *y*)—"It is not true of everyone that there is someone whom he does not love"]; $(\forall x)(\exists y)$ can be replaced by $\sim(\exists x)(\forall y)\sim$; and in general the following rule, covering sequences of quantifiers of any length, holds:

(i) If a *wff* contains an unbroken sequence of quantifiers, then the *wff* that results from replacing $\forall$ by $\exists$ and vice versa throughout that sequence and inserting or deleting $\sim$ at each end of it is equivalent to the original *wff*.

This may be called the *rule of quantifier transformation*. It reflects, in a generalized form, the intuitive connections between *some* and *every* that were noted at the end of the introduction to III. *The predicate calculus.*

The following are also valid, again where α is any *wff*:

$$(\forall x)(\forall y)\alpha \equiv (\forall y)(\forall x)\alpha$$
$$(\exists x)(\exists y)\alpha \equiv (\exists y)(\exists x)\alpha$$

The extensions of these lead to the following rule:

(ii) If a *wff* contains an unbroken sequence either of universal or of existential quantifiers, these quantifiers may be rearranged in any order and the resulting *wff* will be equivalent to the original *wff*.

This may be called the *rule of quantifier rearrangement*.

Two other important rules concern implications, not equivalences:

(iii) If a *wff* β begins with an unbroken sequence of quantifiers, and β' is obtained from β by replacing $\forall$ by $\exists$ at one or more places in the sequence, then β is *stronger* than β'—in the sense that $(\beta \supset \beta')$ is valid but $(\beta' \supset \beta)$ is in general not valid.

(iv) If a *wff* β begins with an unbroken sequence of quantifiers in which some existential quantifier Q_1 precedes some universal quantifier Q_2, and if β' is obtained from β by moving Q_1 to the right of Q_2, then β is stronger than β'.

As illustrations of these rules, the following are valid for any *wff* α:

$(\forall x)(\forall y)\alpha \supset (\exists x)(\forall y)\alpha$	Rule (iii)
$(\exists x)(\forall y)(\forall z)\alpha \supset (\exists x)(\forall y)(\exists z)\alpha$	Rule (iii)
$(\exists x)(\forall y)\alpha \supset (\forall y)(\exists x)\alpha$	Rule (iv)
$(\exists x)(\exists y)(\forall z)\alpha \supset (\exists y)(\forall z)(\exists x)\alpha$	Rule (iv)

In each case the converses are not valid (though they may be valid in particular cases in which α is of some special form).

Some of the uses of the above rules can be illustrated by considering a *wff* α that contains precisely two free individual variables. By prefixing to α two appropriate quantifiers and possibly one or more negation signs, it is possible to form a closed *wff* (called a *closure* of α) that will express a determinate proposition when a meaning is assigned to the predicate variables. The above rules can be used to list exhaustively the nonequivalent closures of α and the implication relations between them. The simplest example is ϕxy, which for illustrative purposes can be taken to mean "*x* loves *y*." Application of Rules (i) and (ii) will show that every closure of ϕxy is equivalent to one or another of the following 12 *wff*'s (none of which is in fact equivalent to any of the others):

(a) $(\forall x)(\forall y)$ ϕxy ("Everybody loves everybody");

(b) $(\exists x)(\forall y)$ ϕxy ("Somebody loves everybody");

(c) $(\exists y)(\forall x)$ ϕxy ("There is someone whom everyone loves");

(d) $(\forall y)(\exists x)\,\phi xy$ ("Each person is loved by at least one person");

(e) $(\forall x)(\exists y)\,\phi xy$ ("Each person loves at least one person");

(f) $(\exists x)(\exists y)\,\phi xy$ ("Somebody loves somebody");

(g-1) The respective negations of each of the above.

Rules (iii) and (iv) show that the following implications among formulas (a)–(f) are valid:

$$(a) \supset (b); \quad (d) \supset (f); \quad (c) \supset (e);$$
$$(b) \supset (d); \quad (a) \supset (c); \quad (e) \supset (f).$$

The implications holding among the negations of (a)–(f) follow from these by the *law of transposition; e.g.,* since (a) $\supset$ (b) is valid, so is $\sim$(b) $\supset$ $\sim$(a). The quantification of *wff*'s containing three, four, etc., variables can be dealt with by the same rules.

Relettering of bound variables Intuitively, $(\forall x)\phi x$ and $(\forall y)\phi y$ both "say the same thing," viz., that everything is ϕ, and $(\exists x)\phi x$ and $(\exists y)\phi y$ both mean simply that something is ϕ. Clearly, so long as the same variable occurs both in the quantifier and as the argument of ϕ, it does not matter what letter is chosen for this purpose. The procedure of replacing some variable in a quantifier, together with every occurrence of that variable in its scope, by some other variable that does not occur elsewhere in its scope is known as *relettering a bound variable*. If β is the result of relettering a bound variable in a *wff* α, then α and β are said to be *bound alphabetical variants* of each other; and bound alphabetical variants are always equivalent. The reason for restricting the replacement variable to one not occurring elsewhere in the scope of the quantifier can be seen from an example: If ϕxy is taken as before to mean "x loves y," the *wff* $(\forall x)\phi xy$ expresses the proposition form "Everyone loves y," in which the identity of y is left unspecified, and so does its bound alphabetical variant $(\forall z)\phi zy$; but if x were replaced by y, the closed *wff* $(\forall y)\phi yy$ would be obtained, which expresses the proposition that everyone loves himself and is clearly not equivalent to the original.

Prenex normal form A *wff* in which all of the quantifiers occur in an unbroken sequence at the beginning, with the scope of each extending to the end of the *wff*, is said to be in *prenex normal form* (PNF—Latin: *pre*, "in front"; and *nectere*, "to bind"). *Wff*'s that are in PNF are often more convenient to work with than those that are not. For every *wff* of LPC, however, there is an equivalent *wff* in PNF (often simply called its PNF). One effective method for finding the PNF of any given *wff* is the following:

1. Reletter bound variables as far as is necessary to ensure (a) that each quantifier contains a distinct variable and (b) that no variable in the *wff* occurs both bound and free.

2. Use definitions or PC equivalences to eliminate all operators except $\sim$, $\cdot$, and $\vee$.

3. Use the *De Morgan laws* and the *rule of quantifier transformation* to eliminate all occurrences of $\sim$ immediately before parentheses or quantifiers.

4. Gather all of the quantifiers into a sequence at the beginning in the order in which they appear in the *wff* and take the whole of what remains as their scope.

Example: $(\forall x)\{[\phi x \cdot (\exists y)\psi xy] \supset (\exists y)\chi xy\} \supset$
$(\exists z)(\phi z \supset \psi zx).$

Step 1 can be achieved by relettering the third and fourth occurrences of y and every occurrence of x except the last (which is free); thus:

$(\forall w)\{[\phi w \cdot (\exists y)\psi wy] \supset (\exists u)\chi wu\} \supset (\exists z)(\phi z \supset$
$\psi zx)$

Step 2 now yields:

$\sim(\forall w)\{\sim[\phi w \cdot (\exists y)\psi wy] \vee (\exists u)\chi wu\} \vee (\exists z)$
$(\sim\phi z \vee \psi zx)$

By step 3 this becomes:

$(\exists w)\{[\phi w \cdot (\exists y)\psi wy] \cdot (\forall u)\sim\chi wu\} \vee (\exists z)(\sim\phi z$
$\vee \psi zx)$

Finally, step 4 yields:

$(\exists w)(\exists y)(\forall u)(\exists z)\{[(\phi w \cdot \psi wy) \cdot \sim\chi wu] \vee (\sim\phi z$
$\vee \psi zx)\}$

which is in PNF.

Classification of dyadic relations. Consider the closed *wff*,

$$(\forall x)(\forall y)(\phi xy \supset \phi yx)$$

which means that, whenever the relation ϕ holds between one object and a second, it also holds between that second object and the first. This expression is not valid, since it is true for some relations but false for others. A relation for which it is true is called a *symmetrical* relation. (*Example:* "is parallel to.") If the relation ϕ is such that whenever it holds between one object and a second it fails to hold between the second and the first; *i.e.,* if ϕ is such that

$$(\forall x)(\forall y)(\phi xy \supset \sim\phi yx)$$

then ϕ is said to be *asymmetrical.* (*Example:* "is greater than.") A relation that is neither symmetrical nor asymmetrical is said to be *nonsymmetrical.* Thus ϕ is nonsymmetrical if

$$(\exists x)\,(\exists y)\,(\phi xy \cdot \phi yx) \cdot (\exists x)\,(\exists y)\,(\phi xy \cdot \sim\phi yx)$$

(*Example:* "loves.")

Symmetry, transitivity, reflexivity

Dyadic relations can also be characterized in terms of another threefold division: A relation ϕ is said to be *transitive* if, whenever it holds between one object and a second and also between that second object and a third, it holds between the first and the third; *i.e.,* if

$$(\forall x)(\forall y)(\forall z)[(\phi xy \cdot \phi yz) \supset \phi xz]$$

(*Example:* "is greater than.") An *intransitive* relation is one that, whenever it holds between one object and a second and also between that second and a third, fails to hold between the first and the third; *i.e.,* ϕ is intransitive if

$$(\forall x)\,(\forall y)\,(\forall z)[(\phi xy \cdot \phi yz) \supset \sim\phi xz]$$

(*Example:* "is father of.") A relation that is neither transitive nor intransitive is said to be *nontransitive.* Thus ϕ is nontransitive if

$(\exists x)\,(\exists y)\,(\exists z)\,(\phi xy \cdot \phi yz \cdot \phi xz) \cdot$
$(\exists x)\,(\exists y)\,(\exists z)\,(\phi xy \cdot \phi yz \cdot \sim\phi xz)$

(*Example:* "is a first cousin of.")

A relation ϕ that always holds between any object and itself is said to be *reflexive; i.e.,* ϕ is reflexive if

$$(\forall x)\phi xx$$

(*Example:* "is identical with.") If ϕ never holds between any object and itself—*i.e.,* if

$$\sim(\exists x)\phi xx$$

—then ϕ is said to be irreflexive (*Example:* "is greater than.") If ϕ is neither reflexive nor irreflexive—*i.e.,* if

$$(\exists x)\phi xx \cdot (\exists x)\sim\phi xx$$

—then ϕ is said to be *nonreflexive* (*Example:* "admires.")

A relation such as "is of the same length as" is not strictly reflexive, since some objects do not have a length at all and therefore are not of the same length as anything, even as themselves. Nevertheless, this relation is reflexive in the weaker sense that whenever an object is of the same length as anything it is of the same length as itself. Such a relation is said to be *quasi-reflexive.* Thus ϕ is quasi-reflexive if

$$(\forall x)[(\exists y)\phi xy \supset \phi xx].$$

A reflexive relation is of course also quasi-reflexive.

For the most part, these three classifications are independent of each other; thus a symmetrical relation may be transitive (like "is equal to") or intransitive (like "is perpendicular to") or nontransitive (like "is one mile distant from"). There are, however, certain limiting principles, of which the most important are:

1. Every relation that is symmetrical and transitive is at least quasi-reflexive;

2. Every asymmetrical relation is irreflexive;

3. Every relation that is transitive and irreflexive is asymmetrical.

A relation that is reflexive, symmetrical, and transitive is called an *equivalence* relation.

Axiomatic
basis and
undecid-
ability of
theorems

Axiomatization of LPC. Rules of uniform substitution for predicate calculi, though formulable, are mostly very complicated; and, to avoid the necessity for these rules, axioms for these systems are therefore usually given by axiom schemata in the sense explained in II. *Axiomatization of PC.* Given the formation rules and definitions stated in the introductory paragraph of III. *The lower predicate calculus,* the following is presented as one standard axiomatic basis for LPC:

Axiom schemata:

1. Any LPC substitution-instance of any valid *wff* of PC is an axiom.

2. Any *wff* of the form $(\forall \mathbf{a})\alpha \supset \beta$ is an axiom, if β is either identical with α or differs from it only in that, wherever α has a free occurrence of $\mathbf{a}$, β has a free occurrence of some other individual variable $\mathbf{b}$.

3. Any *wff* of the form $(\forall \mathbf{a}) (\alpha \supset \beta) \supset [\alpha \supset (\forall \mathbf{a}) \beta]$ is an axiom, provided that α contains no free occurrence of $\mathbf{a}$.

Transformation rules:

1. *Modus ponens* (as given above, II. *Axiomatization of PC*).

2. If α is a theorem, so is $(\forall \mathbf{a})\alpha$, where $\mathbf{a}$ is any individual variable (*rule of universal generalization*).

The axiom schemata call for some explanation and comment. By an LPC substitution-instance of a *wff* of PC is meant any result of uniformly replacing every propositional variable in that *wff* by a *wff* of LPC. Thus one LPC substitution-instance of $(p \supset \sim q) \supset (q \supset \sim p)$ is $[\phi xy \supset \sim(\forall x)\psi x] \supset [(\forall x)\psi x \supset \sim \phi xy]$. Axiom schema 1 makes available in LPC all manipulations such as commutation, transposition, and distribution, which depend only on PC principles. Examples of *wff*'s that are axioms by axiom schema 2 are: $(\forall x)\phi x \supset \phi x$; $(\forall x)\phi x \supset \phi y$; $(\forall x) (\exists y)\phi xy \supset (\exists y)\phi zy$. To see why it is necessary for the variable that replaces $\mathbf{a}$ to be free in β, consider the last example: Here $\mathbf{a}$ is x, α is $(\exists y)\phi xy$, in which x is free, and β is $(\exists y)\phi zy$, in which z is free and replaces x. But had y, which would be bound by the quantifier $(\exists y)$, been chosen as a replacement, instead of z, the result would have been $(\forall x)(\exists y)\phi xy \supset (\exists y)\phi yy$, the invalidity of which can be seen intuitively by taking ϕxy to mean "x is a child of y": for then $(\forall x)(\exists y)\phi xy$ will mean that everyone is a child of someone, which is true; but $(\exists y)\phi yy$ will mean that someone is a child of himself, which is false. The need for the proviso in axiom schema 3 can also be seen from an example. Defiance of the proviso would give as an axiom $(\forall x)(\phi x \supset \psi x) \supset [\phi x \supset (\forall x)\psi x]$; and if ϕx were taken to mean "x is a Spaniard," ψx to mean "x is a European," and the free occurrence of x (the first occurrence in the consequent) to stand for General Franco, then the antecedent would mean that every Spaniard is a European, but the consequent would mean that, if General Franco is a Spaniard, then everyone is a European.

It can be proved—though the proof is not an elementary one—that the theorems derivable from the above basis are precisely the *wff*'s of LPC that are valid by the definition of validity given in III. *Validity in LPC.* Several other bases for LPC are known that also have this property. The axiom schemata and transformation rules here given are such that any purported proof of a theorem can be effectively checked to determine whether it really is a proof or not; nevertheless, theoremhood in LPC, like validity in LPC, is not effectively decidable, in that there is no effective method of telling with regard to any arbitrary *wff* whether it is a theorem or not. In this respect axiomatic bases for LPC contrast with those for PC.

Special systems of LPC. LPC as expounded above may be modified by either restricting or extending the range of *wff*'s in various ways.

a. Partial systems of LPC. Some of the more important systems produced by restriction are here outlined:

Monadic
LPC and
subsystem

1. It may be required that every predicate variable be monadic, while still allowing an infinite number of individual and predicate variables. The atomic *wff*'s are then simply those consisting of a predicate variable followed by a single individual variable. Otherwise, the formation rules remain as before, and the definition of validity is also as before, though simplified in obvious ways. This system is known as the monadic LPC; it provides a logic of properties but not of relations. One important characteristic of this system is that it is decidable. (The introduction of even a single dyadic predicate variable, however, would make the system undecidable; and in fact, even the system that contains only a single dyadic predicate variable and no other predicate variables at all has been shown to be undecidable.)

2. A still simpler system can be formed by requiring (a) that every predicate variable be monadic; (b) that only a single individual variable (*e.g.*, x) be used; (c) that every occurrence of this variable be bound; (d) that no quantifier occur within the scope of any other. Examples of *wff*'s of this system are: $(\forall x)[\phi x \supset (\psi x \cdot \chi x)]$ ("Whatever is ϕ is both ψ and χ"); $(\exists x) (\phi x \cdot \sim \psi x)$ ("There is something that is ϕ but not ψ"); $(\forall x)(\phi x \supset \psi x) \supset (\exists x)(\phi x \cdot \psi x)$ ("If whatever is ϕ is ψ, then something is both ϕ and ψ"). The notation for this system can be simplified by omitting x everywhere and writing $\exists \phi$ for "Something is ϕ," $\forall (\phi \supset \psi)$ for "Whatever is ϕ is ψ," and so on. Although this system is more rudimentary even than the monadic LPC (of which it is a fragment), the forms of a wide range of inferences can be represented in it. It is also a decidable system, and decision procedures of an elementary kind can be given for it.

b. Extensions of LPC. More elaborate systems, in which a wider range of propositions can be expressed, have been constructed, by adding to LPC new symbols of various types. The most straightforward of such additions are:

(a) One or more *individual constants* (say $a, b, \ldots$): these constants are interpreted as names of specific individuals; formally they are distinguished from individual variables by the fact that they cannot occur within quantifiers: *e.g.*, $(\forall x)$ is a quantifier but $(\forall a)$ is not.

(b) One or more *predicate constants* (say $\Phi, \Psi, \ldots$), each of some specified degree, thought of as designating specific properties or relations.

A further possible addition, which calls for somewhat fuller explanation, consists of symbols designed to stand for *functions.* The notion of a function may be sufficiently explained for present purposes as follows: There is said to be a certain function of n arguments (or, of degree n) when there is a rule that specifies a unique object (called the *value* of the function) whenever all of the arguments are specified. In the domain of human beings, for example, "the mother of—" is a monadic function (a function of one argument) since for every human being there is a unique individual who is his mother; and in the domain of the natural numbers (*i.e.*, 0, 1, 2, . . .), "the sum of — and —" is a function of two arguments since for any pair of natural numbers there is a natural number that is their sum. A function symbol can be thought of as forming a name out of other names (its arguments): thus whenever x and y name numbers, "the sum of x and y" also names a number, and similarly for other kinds of functions and arguments.

To enable functions to be expressed in LPC there may be added:

(c) One or more *function variables* (say $f, g, \ldots$) or one or more *function constants* (say, $F, G, \ldots$) or both, each of some specified degree. The former are interpreted as ranging over functions of the degrees specified, and the latter as designating specific functions of that degree.

When any or all of (a) – (c) are added to LPC, the formation rules listed in the first paragraph of III. *The lower predicate calculus* need to be modified to enable the new symbols to be incorporated into *wff*'s. This can be done as follows: A *term* is first defined as either (i) an individual variable or (ii) an individual constant or (iii) any expression formed by prefixing a function variable or function constant of degree n to any n terms (these terms—the arguments of the function symbol—are usually separated by commas and enclosed in parentheses). Formation rule 1 is then replaced by:

1'. An expression consisting of a predicate variable or predicate constant of degree n followed by n terms is a *wff*.

Defini-
tions:
"function,"
"degree,"
"term"

The axiomatic basis given in III. *Axiomatization of LPC* also requires the following modification: in axiom schema 2 any term is allowed to replace **a** when β is formed, provided that no variable that is free in the term becomes bound in β. The following examples will illustrate the use of the aforementioned additions to LPC: Let the values of the individual variables be the natural numbers; let the individual constants a and b stand for the numbers 2 and 3, respectively; let Φ mean "is prime"; and let F represent the dyadic function "the sum of." Then $\Phi F(a,b)$ expresses the proposition "The sum of 2 and 3 is prime" and $(\exists x)\Phi F(x,a)$ expresses the proposition "There exists a number such that the sum of it and 2 is prime."

The introduction of constants is normally accompanied by the addition, to the axiomatic basis, of special axioms containing those constants, designed to express principles that hold of the objects, properties, relations, or functions represented by them—though they do not hold of objects, properties, relations, or functions in general. It may be decided, for example, to use the constant Φ to represent the dyadic relation "is greater than" (so that Φxy is to mean "x is greater than y", etc.). This relation, unlike many others, is transitive; *i.e.*, if one object is greater than a second and that second is in turn greater than a third, then the first is greater than the third. Hence, the following special axiom schema might be added:
If t_1, t_2, and t_3 are any terms, then

$$(\Phi t_1 t_2 \cdot \Phi t_2 t_3) \supset \Phi t_1 t_3$$

is an axiom. By such means systems can be constructed to express the logical structures of various particular disciplines. The area in which most work of this kind has been done is that of natural-number arithmetic (see IV. *Axiomatization of arithmetic*).

PC and LPC are sometimes combined into a single system. This may be done most simply by adding propositional variables to the list of LPC primitives, adding a formation rule to the effect that a propositional variable standing alone is a *wff*, and deleting "LPC" in axiom schema 1. This yields as *wff*'s such expressions as: $(p \lor q) \supset (\forall x)\phi x$; $(\exists x)[p \supset (\forall y)\phi y]$.

c. LPC-with-identity. The word "is" is not always used in the same way. In a proposition such as (i) "Socrates is snub-nosed," the expression preceding the "is" names an individual and the expression following it stands for a property attributed to that individual. But in a proposition such as (ii) "Socrates is the Athenian philosopher who drank hemlock," the expressions preceding and following the "is" both name individuals, and the sense of the whole proposition is that the individual named by the first is the same individual as the individual named by the second. Thus in (ii) "is" can be expanded to "is the same individual as," whereas in (i) it cannot. As used in (ii), "is" stands for a dyadic relation, viz., identity, that the proposition asserts to hold between the two individuals. An identity proposition is to be understood in this context as asserting no more than this; in particular it is not to be taken as asserting that the two naming expressions have the same meaning. A much discussed example to illustrate this last point is "The morning star is the evening star." It is false that the expressions "the morning star" and "the evening star" mean the same, but true that the object referred to by the former is the same as that referred to by the latter.

To enable the forms of identity propositions to be expressed, a dyadic predicate constant is added to LPC, for which the most usual notation is $=$ (written between, rather than before, its arguments). The intended interpretation of $x = y$ is that x is the same individual as y, and the most convenient reading is "x is identical with y." Its negation $\sim(x = y)$ is commonly abbreviated to $x \neq y$. To the definition of an LPC model in III. *Validity in LPC*, there is now added the rule (which accords in an obvious way with the intended interpretation) that the value of $x = y$ is to be 1 if the same member of D is assigned to both x and y and that otherwise its value is to be 0; validity can then be defined as before. The following additions (or some equivalent ones) are made to the axiomatic basis for LPC: the axiom (I1) $x = x;$ and the axiom schema (I2) that where **a** and **b** are any individual

variables and α and β are *wff*'s that differ only in that, at one or more places where α has a free occurrence of **a**, β has a free occurrence of **b**, $(\mathbf{a} = \mathbf{b}) \supset (\alpha \supset \beta)$ is an axiom. Such a system is known as a *lower-predicate-calculus-with-identity;* it may of course be further augmented in the other ways referred to in III. *Extensions of LPC*, in which case any term may be an argument of $=$.

Identity is an equivalence relation; *i.e.*, it is reflexive, symmetrical, and transitive. Its reflexivity is directly expressed in Axiom I1, and theorems expressing its symmetry and transitivity can easily be derived from the basis given.

Certain *wff*'s of LPC-with-identity express propositions about the number of things that possess a given property. "At least one thing is ϕ" could, of course, already be expressed by $(\exists x)\phi x;$ "At least two distinct (non-identical) things are ϕ" can now be expressed by $(\exists x)(\exists y)(\phi x \cdot \phi y \cdot x \neq y);$ and the sequence can be continued in an obvious way. "At most one thing is ϕ" (*i.e.*, "No two distinct things are both ϕ") can be expressed by the negation of the last mentioned *wff* or by its equivalent, $(\forall x)(\forall y)$ $[(\phi x \cdot \phi y) \supset x = y];$ and the sequence can again be easily continued. A formula for "Exactly one thing is ϕ" may be obtained by conjoining the formulas for "At least one thing is ϕ" and "At most one thing is ϕ"; but a simpler *wff* equivalent to this conjunction is $(\exists x)[\phi x \cdot (\forall y)(\phi y \supset x = y)]$, which means "There is something that is ϕ, and anything that is ϕ *is* that thing." "Exactly two things are ϕ" can be represented by

$$(\exists x)(\exists y)\{\phi x \cdot \phi y \cdot x \neq y \cdot (\forall z)[\phi z \supset (z = x \lor z = y)]\};$$

i.e., "There are two non-identical things each of which is ϕ, and anything that is ϕ is one or the other of these." Clearly, this sequence can also be extended to give a formula for "Exactly n things are ϕ" for every natural number n. It is convenient to abbreviate the *wff* for "Exactly one thing is ϕ," however, to $(\exists^1 x)\phi x$, and in general to abbreviate the *wff* for "Exactly n things are ϕ" to $(\exists^n x)\phi x$, and in this way to obtain a sequence of *numerical* quantifiers each, however, definable in terms of the primitives of LPC-with-identity.

When a certain property ϕ belongs to one and only one object, it is convenient to have an expression that names that object. A common notation for this purpose is $(\imath x)\phi x$, which may be read as "the thing that is ϕ" or more briefly as "the ϕ." In general, where **a** is any individual variable and α is any *wff*, $(\imath \mathbf{a})\alpha$ then stands for the single value of **a** that makes α true. An expression of the form "the so-and-so" is called a *definite description;* and $(\imath x)$, known as a *description operator*, can be thought of as forming a name of an individual out of a proposition form. $(\imath x)$ is analogous to a quantifier in that, when prefixed to a *wff* α, it binds every free occurrence of x in α. Relettering of bound variables is also permissible: in the simplest case, $(\imath x)\phi x$ and $(\imath y)\phi y$ can each be read simply as "the ϕ."

As far as formation rules are concerned, definite descriptions can be incorporated into LPC by letting expressions of the form $(\imath \mathbf{a})\alpha$ count as terms; rule 1' of III. *Extensions of LPC* will then allow them to occur in atomic formulas (including identity formulas). "The ϕ is (*i.e.*, has the property) ψ" can then be expressed as $\psi(\imath x)\phi x;$ "y is (the same individual as) the ϕ" as $y = (\imath x)\phi x;$ "The ϕ is (the same individual as) the ψ" as $(\imath x)\phi x = (\imath y)\psi y;$ and so forth. The correct analysis of propositions containing definite descriptions has been the subject of considerable philosophical controversy. One widely accepted account, however—substantially that presented in *Principia Mathematica* and known as *Russell's theory of descriptions*, after Bertrand Russell, one of its co-authors—holds that "The ϕ is ψ" is to be understood as meaning that exactly one thing is ϕ and that thing is also ψ. In that case it can be expressed by a *wff* of LPC-with-identity that contains no description operators, viz.,

$$(1) \quad (\exists x)[\phi x \cdot (\forall y)(\phi y \supset x = y) \cdot \psi x].$$

Analogously "y is the ϕ" is analyzed as "y is ϕ and nothing else is ϕ," and hence as expressible by

$$(2) \quad \phi y \cdot (\forall x)(\phi x \supset x = y);$$

and "The ϕ is the ψ" is analyzed as "Exactly one thing is ϕ, exactly one thing is ψ, and whatever is ϕ is ψ," and hence as expressible by

$$(3)\,(\exists x)[\phi x \cdot (\forall y)(\phi y \supset x = y)]\cdot$$
$$(\exists x)[\psi x \cdot (\forall y)(\psi y \supset x = y)]\cdot(\forall x)(\phi x \supset \psi x)$$

or more briefly, using the abbreviations introduced earlier, by

$$(3')\ (\exists^1 x)\phi x \cdot (\exists^1 x)\psi x \cdot (\forall x)(\phi x \supset \psi x).$$

$\psi(\imath x)\phi x$, $y = (\imath x)\phi x$, and $(\imath x)\phi x = (\imath y)\psi y$ can then be regarded as abbreviations for (1), (2), and (3), respectively; and by generalizing to more complex cases, all *wff*'s that contain description operators can be regarded as abbreviations for longer *wff*'s that do not.

Negations with differing scopes

The analysis that leads to (1) as a formula for "The ϕ is ψ" leads to the following for "The ϕ is not ψ":

$$(4)\ (\exists x)[\phi x \cdot (\forall y)(\phi y \supset x = y) \cdot \sim\!\psi x].$$

It is important to note that (4) is not the negation of (1); this negation is, instead,

$$(5)\ \sim\!(\exists x)[\phi x \cdot (\forall y)(\phi y \supset x = y) \cdot \psi x].$$

The difference in meaning between (4) and (5) lies in the fact that (4) is true only when there is exactly one thing that is ϕ and that thing is not ψ, but (5) is true both in this case and also when nothing is ϕ at all and when more than one thing is ϕ. Neglect of the distinction between (4) and (5) can cause serious confusion of thought: in ordinary speech it is often unclear whether someone who denies that the ϕ is ψ is conceding that exactly one thing is ϕ but denying that it is ψ, or denying that exactly one thing is ϕ. Moreover, if (4) were mistakenly thought of as the negation of (1), the *law of excluded middle* would lead to the conclusion that at least one of them is true; and then, since each asserts *inter alia* that exactly one thing is ϕ and since, in addition, the argument would hold whatever property ϕ is taken to represent, the absurd result would be obtained that every property has exactly one instance.

The basic contention of Russell's theory of descriptions is that a proposition containing a definite description is not to be regarded as an assertion about an object of which that description is a name but rather as an existentially quantified assertion that a certain (rather complex) property has an instance. Formally, this is reflected in the rules for eliminating description operators that were outlined above. Some logicians, however, prefer instead to introduce $\imath$ as a new primitive symbol, accompanied by special axioms, and to treat expressions of the form $(\imath a)\alpha$ always as naming expressions, allowing them to replace individual variables in theorems (subject only to the restrictions about quantification mentioned in III. *Axiomatization of LPC*). The formula $(\forall x)\phi x \supset \phi(\imath y)\psi y$ —"If everything is ϕ, then the ψ is ϕ"—will then, for example, count as an axiom by axiom schema 2 and as a valid *wff*; whereas by Russell's theory of descriptions it will be invalid, since it is possible for everything to be ϕ without there being exactly one thing that is ψ. This approach gives rise to the problem of deciding, in constructing an *LPC* model, which member of D to assign to $(\imath x)\phi x$ in cases in which either nothing or more than one thing is ϕ. The solution usually adopted is to select some arbitrary member of D as the assignment in all such cases throughout the model. While this device may seem intuitively "unnatural," it proves to be technically satisfactory and convenient for many purposes.

HIGHER-ORDER PREDICATE CALCULI

A feature shared by LPC and all of its extensions so far mentioned is that the only variables that occur in quantifiers are individual variables. It is in virtue of this feature that they are called *lower* (or *first-order*) calculi. Various predicate calculi of higher order can be formed, however,

Binding of predicate variables

in which quantifiers may contain other variables as well, hence binding all free occurrences of these that lie within their scope. In particular, in the *second-order* predicate calculus quantification is permitted over both individual and predicate variables; hence *wff*'s such as $(\forall\phi)$ $(\exists x)\phi x$ can be formed. This last formula, since it contains no free variables of any kind, expresses a determinate proposition, viz., the proposition that every property has at least one instance. One important feature of this system is that in it identity need not be taken as primitive but can be introduced by defining $x = y$ as $(\forall\phi)(\phi x \equiv \phi y)$—i.e., "Every property possessed by x is also possessed by y and vice versa." Whether such a definition is acceptable as a general account of identity is a question that raises philosophical issues too complex to be discussed here; they are substantially those raised by the principle of the identity of indiscernibles, best known for its exposition in the 17th century by the German philosopher G.W. Leibniz.

IV. Other special systems of logic

SYLLOGISTIC LOGIC

Syllogistic logic was the earliest branch of formal logic to be developed—in its original form by Aristotle about 350 BC. Only a very brief account of the topic is given here; for a fuller treatment see SYLLOGISTIC. The system as outlined here combines elements contributed by Aristotle with others that are considerably later in origin; for the historical development of the subject see LOGIC, HISTORY OF.

Syllogistic logic deals with propositions of the four forms:

"Every . . . is (a)——";
"No . . . is (a)——";
"Some (*i.e.*, at least one) . . . is (a)——";
"Some . . . is not (a)——."
(*Examples:* "Every club member is a Bostonian"; "No club member is a Bostonian"; etc.)

Propositions of these forms are known as A, E, I, and O propositions, respectively. The expressions that fill the blanks are called *terms;* and in each case the first is the *subject*(*-term*) and the second the *predicate*(*-term*). (The use of the words "term" and "predicate" here should not be confused with their use in the account of LPC above.) As term variables, the letters S, P, and M are employed. "Every S is (a) P" is abbreviated to "SaP"; "No S is (a) P" to "SeP"; "Some S is (a) P" to "SiP"; and "Some S is not (a) P" to "SoP". A and E propositions are called *universal,* I and O propositions *particular;* A and I propositions are called *affirmative,* E and O propositions *negative.*

These propositional forms are to be so understood that the following are true for any terms S and P:

(1) Not both: SaP and SeP;
(2) If SaP, then SiP;
(3) If SeP, then SoP;
(4) Either SiP or SoP;
(5) SaP is equivalent to the negation of SoP;
(6) SeP is equivalent to the negation of SiP.

The *simple converse* of a proposition is formed by reversing the order of its terms. If, in addition, an A proposition is changed to an I, or an E to an O, the result is called the *limited converse* of the original. The logical relations holding between propositions and their converses are as follows: E and I propositions are equivalent to their simple converses; *i.e.,* SeP and SiP are equivalent to PeS and PiS, respectively. Moreover, an A proposition SaP though not equivalent to its simple converse PaS, implies, though it is not implied by, its limited converse PiS. SoP, however, neither implies nor is implied by PoS; this fact is often expressed by saying that an O proposition does not convert.

The syllogism

A (*categorical*) syllogism is an inference with two premises and one conclusion, in which (i) each of the three propositions is an A, E, I, or O proposition; (ii) the subject of the conclusion (called the *minor* term) also occurs in one of the premises (the *minor* premise); (iii) the predicate of the conclusion (called the *major* term) also occurs in the other premise (the *major* premise); and (iv) the two remaining term positions in the premises are filled by the same term (the *middle* term). A syllogistic *mood* is an inference form of which the instances are syllogisms (*e.g.,* MaP, SiM, $\therefore$ SiP). If S, P, and M are used for minor, major, and middle terms, respectively, and the convention of writing the major premise first is observed, the exhaustive list displayed in Table 6 is obtained

Table 6: The Four Figures of the Categorical Syllogism

I	II	III	IV
M — P	P — M	M — P	P — M
S — M	S — M	M — S	M — S
∴ S — P	∴ S — P	∴ S — P	∴ S — P

showing four arrangements of terms in a syllogistic mood.

These arrangements of terms are known as the first, second, third, and fourth *figures* of the syllogism, respectively. A mood can then be succinctly specified by mentioning its figure and indicating to which of the four forms each of the three propositions, in the conventional order, belongs. Thus "IIaeo" specifies the mood: PaM, SeM, ∴ SoP. The 24 moods shown in Table 7, and only these, are normally regarded as valid.

Table 7: The 24 Valid Moods of the Categorical Syllogism

Figure 1	aaa, aai, eae, eao, aii, eio
Figure 2	eae, eao, aee, aeo, eio, aoo
Figure 3	aai, iai, aii, eao, oao, eio
Figure 4	aai, aee, aeo, iai, eao, eio

Syllogistic logic is commonly extended by the introduction of *negative* terms. For any term S the corresponding negative term non-S applies to exactly those things to which S does not apply. A convenient notation for non-S is S̄. Negative terms enable additional proposition forms to be constructed, and the logical relations holding among them to be studied. Among the most important of these are:

1. The *obverse* of a proposition, which is formed by negating its predicate and changing the proposition from affirmative to negative or vice versa. (*Example:* "No mineral is phototropic"; obverse: "Every mineral is non-phototropic.") The obverses of SaP, SeP, SiP, and SoP are SeP̄, SaP̄, SoP̄, and SiP̄, respectively. Every proposition is equivalent to its obverse.

2. The *contrapositive* of a proposition, which is formed by reversing the order of its terms and negating each, though keeping the proposition affirmative or negative as the case may be. (*Example:* "Every Italian is a European"; contrapositive: "Every non-European is a non-Italian.") SaP and SoP are equivalent to their respective contrapositives P̄aS̄ and P̄oS̄. SeP is not equivalent to P̄eS̄; but it implies, though it is not implied by, its *limited* contrapositive P̄oS̄. S̄iP̄, however, neither implies nor is implied by P̄iS̄.

Axiomatic basis: affinities with LPC In the present century axiomatic bases have been devised for syllogistic logic. It has been shown that if a and i are taken as primitive and SeP is defined as ~(SiP) and SoP as ~(SaP), then all of the valid formulas in syllogistic logic that do not involve negative terms can be derived from PC together with the four axioms

(1) (MaP · SaM) ⊃ SaP; (3) SaS;
(2) (MaP · MiS) ⊃ SiP; (4) SiS

by the usual rules of *uniform substitution* and *modus ponens* and a rule of uniform substitution for term variables. A complete basis for deriving the valid formulas involving negative terms as well can be formed by replacing axioms (1) and (3) by

(1′) SeP̄ ⊃ SaP and (3′) SeS̄

and extending the last mentioned rule to allow a term variable to be replaced not only by another term variable but also by a term variable with one or more superimposed bars.

The formulas SaP, SeP, SiP, and SoP have obvious affinities with the LPC *wff*'s

$$(\forall x)(\phi x \supset \psi x), (\forall x)(\phi x \supset \sim\psi x), (\exists x)(\phi x \cdot \psi x),$$
$$\text{and } (\exists x)(\phi x \cdot \sim\psi x),$$

respectively. The analogy is not, however, complete; *e.g.*, SiP follows from SaP, but

$$(\forall x)(\phi x \supset \psi x) \supset (\exists x)(\phi x \cdot \psi x)$$

is not valid in LPC; and IIIaai is a valid mood, but its suggested analogue

$$[(\forall x)(\phi x \supset \psi x) \cdot (\forall x)(\phi x \supset \chi x)] \supset (\exists x)(\chi x \cdot \psi x)$$

is not valid. Nevertheless, one change in the definition of LPC validity given in III. *Validity in LPC* would make the proposed analogue of every valid syllogistic formula valid in (monadic) LPC; this change is that, in the construction of an LPC model when value assignments are made, *V* should be required to assign to each predicate variable not any subset of *D* that one cares to choose but, more restrictively, some nonempty proper subset of *D* (*i.e.*, some subset that has at least one member and is not coextensive with *D* itself). This suggests that one way of regarding syllogistic logic is as a logic of properties that have both instances and counterinstances.

MODAL LOGIC

True propositions can be divided into those—like "2 + 2 = 4"—that are true by logical necessity (*necessary* propositions), and those—like "France is a republic"—that are not (*contingently true* propositions). Similarly, false propositions can be divided into those—like "2 + 2 = 5"—that are false by logical necessity (*impossible* propositions), and those—like "France is a monarchy"—that are not (*contingently false* propositions). Contingently true and contingently false propositions are known collectively as *contingent* propositions. A proposition that is not impossible (*i.e.*, one that is either necessary or contingent) is said to be a *possible* proposition. Intuitively, the notions of necessity and possibility are connected in the following way: to say that a proposition is necessary is to say that it is not possible for it to be false; and to say that a proposition is possible is to say that it is not necessarily false.

If it is logically impossible for a certain proposition, *p*, to be true without a certain proposition, *q*, being also true (*i.e.*, if the conjunction of *p* and not-*q* is logically impossible), then it is said that *p strictly implies q*. An alternative, equivalent way of explaining the notion of strict implication is by saying that *p* strictly implies *q* if and only if it is necessary that *p* materially implies *q*. "John's tie is scarlet," for example, strictly implies "John's tie is red," because it is impossible for John's tie to be scarlet without being red (or: it is necessarily true that if John's tie is scarlet it is red); and in general, if *p* is the conjunction of the premises, and *q* is the conclusion, of a deductively valid inference, *p* will strictly imply *q*.

The notions just referred to—necessity, possibility, impossibility, contingency, strict implication—and certain other closely related ones are known as *modal* notions; and a logic designed to express principles involving them is called a *modal logic*.

The most straightforward way of constructing such a logic is to add to some standard nonmodal system a new primitive operator intended to represent one of the modal notions mentioned above, to define other modal operators in terms of it, and to add certain special axioms or transformation rules or both. A great many systems of modal logic have been constructed; but attention will be restricted here to a few closely related ones in which the underlying nonmodal system is ordinary PC.

Alternative systems of modal logic. All of the systems to be considered here have the same *wff*'s, but differ in their axioms. The *wff*'s can be specified by adding to the symbols of PC a primitive monadic operator *L*, and to the formation rules of PC the rule that if α is a *wff*, so is *L*α. *L* is intended to be interpreted as "It is necessary that," so that *Lp* will be true if and only if *p* is a necessary proposition. The monadic operator *M* and the dyadic operator ⥽ (to be interpreted as "It is possible that" and "strictly implies," respectively) can then be introduced by the following definitions, which reflect in an obvious way the informal accounts given above of the connections between necessity, possibility, and strict implication: if α is any *wff*, then $M\alpha$ is to be an abbreviation of $\sim L\sim\alpha$; and if α and β are any *wff*'s, then $\alpha \dashv \beta$ is to be an abbreviation of $L(\alpha \supset \beta)$ [or alternatively of $\sim M(\alpha \cdot \sim\beta)$].

The modal system known as T has as axioms some set of axioms adequate for PC (such as those of PM), and in addition

(1) $Lp \supset p$
(2) $L(p \supset q) \supset (Lp \supset Lq)$.

Axiom (1) expresses the principle that whatever is necessarily true is true and (2) the principle that, if q logically follows from p then, if p is a necessary truth, so is q (*i.e.*, that whatever follows from a necessary truth is itself a necessary truth). These two principles appear to have a high degree of intuitive plausibility, and almost all modal systems contain (1) and (2) as theorems. The transformation rules of T are *uniform substitution, modus ponens,* and a third rule to the effect that if α is a theorem so is $L\alpha$ (the *rule of necessitation*). The intuitive rationale of this last rule is that in a sound axiomatic system it is expected that every instance of a theorem α will be not merely true but necessarily true—and in that case every instance of $L\alpha$ will be true.

Among the simpler theorems of T are:

$p \supset Mp; L(p \cdot q) \equiv (Lp \cdot Lq); M(p \lor q) \equiv$
$(Mp \lor Mq); (Lp \lor Lq) \supset L(p \lor q)$

(but not its converse);
$M(p \cdot q) \supset (Mp \cdot Mq)$
(but not its converse);
$LMp \equiv \sim ML\sim p; (p\dashv q) \supset$
$(Mp \supset Mq); (\sim p\dashv p) \equiv Lp; L(p \lor q) \supset (Lp \lor Mq).$

There are many modal formulas that are not theorems of T but that have a certain claim to express truths about necessity and possibility. Among these are

$Lp \supset LLp; Mp \supset LMp;$ and $p \supset LMp.$

The first of these means that if a proposition is necessary, its being necessary is itself a necessary truth; the second means that if a proposition is possible, its being possible is a necessary truth; and the third means that if a proposition is true, then not merely is it possible but its being possible is a necessary truth. These are all various elements in the general thesis that a proposition's having the modal characteristics it has (such as necessity, possibility) is not a contingent matter but is determined by logical considerations. Though this thesis may be philosophically controversial, it is at least plausible, and its consequences are worth exploring; and one way of exploring them is to construct modal systems in which the formulas listed above are theorems. None of these formulas, as was said, is a theorem of T; but each could be consistently added to T as an extra axiom to produce a new and more extensive system.

The system obtained by adding $Lp \supset LLp$ to T is known as S4; that obtained by adding $Mp \supset LMp$ to T is known as S5; and the addition of $p \supset LMp$ to T gives the (less important) Brouwerian system, here called B for short.

The relations between these four systems are as follows: S4 is stronger than T; *i.e.*, it contains all of the theorems of T and others besides. B is also stronger than T. S5 is stronger than S4 and also stronger than B. S4 and B, however, are independent of each other in the sense that each contains some theorems that the other does not have. It is of particular importance that if $Mp \supset LMp$ is added to T then $Lp \supset LLp$ can be derived as a theorem, but that if one merely adds the latter to T the former cannot then be derived.

Examples of theorems of S4 that are not theorems of T are: $Mp \equiv MMp; MLMp \supset Mp; (p \dashv q) \supset (Lp\dashv Lq);$ and examples of theorems of S5 that are not theorems of S4 are:

$Lp \equiv MLp; L(p \lor Mq) \equiv (Lp \lor Mq); M(p \cdot Lq) \equiv$
$(Mp \cdot Lq); (Lp\dashv Lq) \lor (Lq\dashv Lp).$

One important feature of S5 but not of the other sys-

tems mentioned is that any *wff* that contains an unbroken sequence of monadic modal operators (L's and/or M's) is provably equivalent to the same *wff* with all of these operators deleted except the last.

Considerations of space preclude an account of the many other axiomatic systems of modal logic that have been investigated. Some of these are weaker than T: such systems normally contain the axioms of T either as axioms or as theorems but have only a restricted form of the *rule of necessitation*. Another group comprises systems that are stronger than S4 but weaker than S5; some of these have proved fruitful in developing a logic of temporal relations. Yet another group includes systems that are stronger than S4 but independent of S5 in the sense explained above.

Modal predicate logics can be formed also by making analogous additions to LPC instead of to PC.

Validity in modal logic. The task of defining validity for modal *wff*'s is complicated by the fact that, even if the truth values of all of the variables in a *wff* are given, it is not obvious how one should set about calculating the truth value of the whole *wff*. Nevertheless, a number of definitions of validity applicable to modal *wff*'s have been given, each of which turns out to match some axiomatic modal system in the sense that it brings out as valid those *wff*'s, and no others, that are theorems of that system. Most, if not all, of these accounts of validity can be thought of as variant ways of giving formal precision to the idea that necessity is truth in every "possible world" or "conceivable state of affairs." The simplest such definition is this: Let a *model* be constructed by first assuming a (finite or infinite) set W of "worlds." In each world, independently of all the others, let each propositional variable then be assigned either the value 1 or the value 0. In each world the values of truth functions are calculated in the usual way from the values of their arguments in that world. In each world, however, $L\alpha$ is to have the value 1 if α has the value 1, not only in that world but in every other world in W as well, and is otherwise to have the value 0; and in each world $M\alpha$ is to have the value 1 if α has the value 1 either in that world or in some other world in W, and is otherwise to have the value 0. These rules enable one to calculate a value (1 or 0) in any world in W for any given *wff*, once the values of the variables in each world in W are specified. A model is defined as consisting of a set of worlds together with a value assignment of the kind just described. A *wff* is *valid* if and only if it has the value 1 in every world in every model. It can be proved that the *wff*'s that are valid by this criterion are precisely the theorems of S5; for this reason models of the kind here described may be called S5-models, and validity as just defined may be called S5-validity.

A definition of T-validity (*i.e.*, one that can be proved to bring out as valid precisely the theorems of T) can be given as follows: a T-model consists of a set of worlds W and a value assignment to each variable in each world, as before; but in addition it includes a specification, for each world in W, of some subset of W as the worlds that are "accessible" to that world. Truth functions are evaluated as before; but in each world in the model, $L\alpha$ is to have the value 1 if α has the value 1 in that world and in every other world in W that is accessible to it, and is otherwise to have the value 0. And in each world, $M\alpha$ is to have the value 1 if α has the value 1 either in that world or in some other world accessible to it and is otherwise to have the value 0. (In other words, in computing the value of $L\alpha$ or $M\alpha$ in a given world, no account is taken of the value of α in any other world not accessible to it.) A *wff* is T-valid if and only if it has the value 1 in every world in every T-model.

An S4-model is defined as is a T-model except that it is required that the accessibility relation be transitive; *i.e.*, that where w_1, w_2, and w_3 are any worlds in W, if w_1 is accessible to w_2 and w_2 is accessible to w_3, then w_1 is accessible to w_3. A *wff* is S4-valid if and only if it has the value 1 in every world in every S4-model. The S4-valid *wff*'s can be shown to be precisely the theorems of S4.

Finally, a definition of validity is obtained that will match the system B by requiring that the accessibility relation be symmetrical but not that it be transitive.

Adaptations to other systems

For all four systems, effective decision procedures for validity can be given. Further modifications of the general method described have yielded validity definitions that match many other axiomatic modal systems; and the method can also be adapted to give a definition of validity for the Intuitionistic PC mentioned earlier. For a number of axiomatic modal systems, however, no satisfactory account of validity has yet been devised. Validity can also be defined for various modal predicate logics by combining the definition of LPC-validity given in III. *Validity in LPC* with the relevant accounts of validity for modal systems; but a modal logic based on LPC is, like LPC itself, an undecidable system.

SET THEORY

Only a sketchy account of set theory is given here; for further information see the article SET THEORY. Set theory is a logic of classes; *i.e.*, of collections (finite or infinite) or aggregations of objects of any kind, which are known as the *members* of the classes in question. Some logicians use the terms "class" and "set" interchangeably; others distinguish between them, defining a set (for example) as a class that is itself a member of some class and defining a proper class as one that is not a member of any class. It is usual to write "∈" for "is a member of" and to abbreviate $\sim (x \in y)$ to $x \notin y$. A particular class may be specified either by listing all of its members or by stating some condition of membership, in which (latter) case the class consists of all of those things and only those that satisfy that condition (it is used, for example, when one speaks of the class of inhabitants of London or the class of prime numbers). Clearly, the former method is available only for finite classes and may be highly inconvenient even then; the latter, however, is of more general applicability. Two classes that have precisely the same members are regarded as the same class or are said to be *identical* with each other, even if they are specified by different conditions; *i.e.*, identity of classes is identity of membership, not identity of specifying conditions. This principle is known as the *principle of extensionality*. A class with no members, such as the class of Chinese popes, is said to be *null*. Since the membership of all such classes is the same, there is only one null class, which is therefore usually called *the* null class (or sometimes the empty class); it is symbolized by Λ or ϕ. The notation $x = y$ is used for "x is identical with y" and $\sim (x = y)$ is usually abbreviated to $x \neq y$. The expression $x = \Lambda$ therefore means that the class x has no members, and $x \neq \Lambda$ means that x has at least one member.

Interrelations of classes

A member of a class may itself be a class. The class of dogs, for example, is a member of the class of species of animals. An individual dog, however, though a member of the former class is not a member of the latter—because an individual dog is not a species of animal (if the number of dogs increases, the number of species of animals does not thereby increase). Class membership is therefore not a transitive relation. The relation of class inclusion, however (to be carefully distinguished from class-membership), is transitive. A class x is said to be *included* in a class y (written: $x \subseteq y$) if and only if every member of x is also a member of y. (This is not meant to exclude the possibility that x and y may be identical.) If x is included in but is not identical with y—*i.e.*, if every member of x is a member of y but some members of y are not members of x—x is said to be *properly included* in y (written: $x \subset y$).

It is perhaps natural to assume that for every statable condition there is a class (null or otherwise) of objects that satisfy that condition. This assumption is known as the *principle of comprehension*. In the unrestricted form just mentioned, however, this principle has been found to lead to inconsistencies and hence cannot be accepted as it stands. One statable condition, for example, is *non-self-membership*, *i.e.*, the property possessed by a class if and only if it is not a member of itself. This in fact appears to be a condition that most classes do fulfill; the class of

dogs, for example, is not itself a dog and hence is not a member of the class of dogs.

Let it now be assumed that the class of all classes that are not members of themselves can be formed and let this class be y. Then any class x will be a member of y if and only if it is not a member of itself; *i.e.*, for any class x, $(x \in y) \equiv (x \notin x)$. The question can then be asked whether y is a member of itself or not, with the following awkward result: If it is a member of itself, then it fails to fulfill the condition of membership of y; and hence it is not a member of y; *i.e.*, not a member of itself. On the other hand, if y is not a member of itself, then it does fulfill the required condition; and therefore it *is* a member of y—*i.e.*, of itself. Hence the equivalence $(y \in y) \equiv (y \notin y)$ results, which is self-contradictory. This perplexing conclusion, which was pointed out by Bertrand Russell, is known as *Russell's paradox*. Russell's own solution to it and to other similar difficulties was to regard classes as forming a hierarchy of types and to posit that a class could only be regarded sensibly as a member, or a nonmember, of a class at the next higher level in the hierarchy. The effect of this theory is to make $x \in x$, and therefore $x \notin x$, ill-formed. Another kind of solution, however, is based upon the distinction made earlier between two kinds of classes, those that are sets and those that are not—a set being defined as a class that is itself a member of some class. The unrestricted *principle of comprehension* is then replaced by the weaker principle that for every condition there is a class the members of which are the individuals or *sets* that fulfill that condition. Other solutions have also been devised; but none has won universal acceptance, with the result that several different versions of set theory are found in the literature of the subject.

Russell's paradox: theory of types

Formally, set theory can be derived by the addition of various special axioms to a rather modest form of LPC that contains no predicate variables and only a single primitive dyadic predicate constant (∈) to represent membership. Sometimes LPC-with-identity is used and there are then two primitive dyadic predicate constants (∈ and =). In some versions the variables x, y, . . . are taken to range only over sets or classes; in other versions they range over individuals as well. The special axioms vary; but the basis normally includes the *principle of extensionality* and some restricted form of the *principle of comprehension*, or some elements from which these can be deduced.

A notation to express theorems about classes can be either defined in various ways (not detailed here) in terms of the primitives mentioned above, or else introduced independently. The main elements of one widely used notation are the following: if α is an expression containing some free occurrence of x, the expression $\{x : \alpha\}$ is used to stand for the class of objects fulfilling the condition expressed by α—*e.g.*, $\{x :$ "x is a prime number"$\}$ represents the class of prime numbers; $\{x\}$ represents the class the only member of which is x; $\{x, y\}$ the class the only members of which are x and y; and so on. $<x, y>$ represents the class the members of which are x and y *in that order* (thus $\{x, y\}$ and $\{y, x\}$ are identical; but $<x, y>$ and $<y, x>$ are in general not identical). Let x and y be any classes, as (for example) those of the dots on the two arms of a stippled cross. The *intersection* of x and y, symbolized as $x \cap y$, is the class the members of which are the objects common to x and y—in this case the dots within the area where the arms cross—*i.e.*, $\{z : z \in x \cdot z \in y\}$. Similarly, the *union* of x and y, symbolized as $x \cup y$, is the class the members of which are the members of x together with those of y—in this case all of the dots on the cross—*i.e.*, $\{z : z \in x \lor z \in y\}$; the *complement* of x, symbolized as $-x$, is the class the members of which are all those objects that are not members of x—*i.e.*, $\{y : y \notin x\}$; the complement of y in x, symbolized as $x - y$, is the class of all objects that are members of x but not of y—*i.e.*, $\{z : z \in x \cdot z \notin y\}$; the *universal* class, symbolized as Λ, is the class of which everything is a member, definable as the complement of the null class—*i.e.*, as $-\Lambda$. Λ itself is sometimes taken as a primitive

Notation, definitions, theorems

individual constant, sometimes defined as $\{x : x \neq x\}$—the class of objects that are not identical with themselves. Among the simpler theorems of set theory are:

$$(\forall x)(x \cap x = x); \; (\forall x)(\forall y)(x \cap y = y \cap x);$$

and corresponding theorems for $\cup$;

$$(\forall x)(\forall y)(\forall z)[x \cap (y \cap z) = (x \cap y) \cup (x \cap z)];$$
$$(\forall x)(\forall y)[-(x \cap y) = -x \cup -y];$$

and corresponding theorems with $\cap$ and $\cup$ interchanged;

$$(\forall x)(--x = x); \; (\forall x)(\forall y)(x - y = x \cap -y);$$
$$(\text{A}x)(\Lambda \subset x); \; (\forall x)(x \cap \Lambda = \Lambda); \; (\forall x)(x \cup \Lambda = x).$$

In these theorems the variables range over classes. In several cases, there are obvious analogies to valid *wff*'s of PC. For an account of further developments, more advanced axioms, etc., see SET THEORY.

Apart from its own intrinsic interest, set theory has an importance for the foundations of mathematics in that it is widely held that the natural numbers can be adequately defined in set-theoretic terms. Moreover, given suitable axioms, standard postulates for natural-number arithmetic can be derived as theorems within set theory.

LOGICAL FOUNDATIONS OF MATHEMATICS

It is possible to develop arithmetic in the form of a logical system without recourse to set theory.

Axiomatization of arithmetic. Axiomatic bases for the arithmetic of the natural numbers $(0, 1, 2, \ldots)$ can be constructed as extensions of LPC designed to have a direct numerical interpretation. One such basis, with the intended interpretation indicated, is the following: in addition to the usual operators and quantifiers, the symbols comprise (a) an infinite list of individual variables, the values of which are to be natural numbers; (b) one individual constant, 0, to represent zero; (c) one dyadic predicate constant, $=$, to represent equality; (d) three function constants: a monadic one, $'$, interpreted as "the successor of"; and two dyadic ones, $+$ and $\cdot$, interpreted as "the sum of" and "the product of," respectively. In view of their intended interpretations, it is convenient to write $'$ after its argument, and $=$, $+$, and $\cdot$ between their arguments. The numeral 1 may be defined as $0'$, the numeral 2 as $1'$ (or $0''$), and so on. Terms are defined as explained in III. *Extensions of LPC*; and since there are no predicate variables, an atomic *wff* will simply be any expression of the form $(t_1 = t_2)$, where t_1 and t_2 are terms. The following special axioms are added to the general axioms for LPC:

(1) $(x = y) \supset [(x = z) \supset (y = z)]$;
(2) $(x = y) \supset (x' = y')$;
(3) $0 \neq x'$;
(4) $(x' = y') \supset (x = y)$;
(5) $x + 0 = x$;
(6) $(x + y') = (x + y)'$;
(7) $x \cdot 0 = 0$;
(8) $x \cdot y' = (x \cdot y) + x$.

There is also the following special axiom schema:

(9) Let α be any *wff* and **a** any individual variable; let $\alpha(0)$ be α but with 0 replacing every free occurrence of **a**, and $\alpha(\mathbf{a}')$ be α but with free $\mathbf{a}'$ replacing every free occurrence of **a**: then

$$\alpha(0) \supset \{(\forall \mathbf{a}) \, [\alpha \supset \alpha(\mathbf{a}')] \supset (\forall \sim)\alpha\}$$

is an axiom.

The transformation rules are *modus ponens* and *universal generalization* as before. Axiom schema (9) expresses the principle of *mathematical induction*. It may be paraphrased by saying that if a property (i) belongs to 0 and (ii) belongs to the successor of any natural number to which it also belongs, then it belongs to every natural number whatsoever.

Propositions expressible in S

Scope and limitations of axiomatized arithmetic. In this system (which shall be called S), the axioms for identity given in III. *LPC-with-identity* are derivable as theorems. Since S contains no variables other than individual variables, every closed *wff*—i.e., every

Axiomatic basis and interpretations

wff containing no free individual variables—will (given the intended interpretation) express not a proposition form but a determinate proposition of natural-number arithmetic—possibly one containing no variables at all, such as $3 + 5 = 8$, or possibly one containing bound variables, such as

$$(\forall x)(\exists y)(4 + x = 3 + y) \text{ or}$$
$$(\forall x)(\forall y)(\forall z)[x \cdot (y + z) = (x \cdot y) + (x \cdot z)].$$

The range of arithmetical propositions expressible by *wff*'s of S is indeed much greater than might appear from the fact that its only primitive predicate is $=$ and its only primitive function symbols are $'$, $+$, and $\cdot$, inasmuch as many relations and properties not so far explicitly mentioned, such as "is less than," "is divisible (without remainder) by," and "is prime," can be defined in terms of the primitives of S; *e.g.*, $x < y$ can be defined as $(\exists z)$ $(x + z' = y)$. Moreover, even if a given numerical function is not directly definable in terms of the primitives of S, it may still be possible to express propositions involving that function as *wff*'s of S, in a way that can be sufficiently explained for present purposes as follows: A numerical function is one that always has a natural number as its value when its arguments are natural numbers. Now let $f(x)$ be such a function with one argument x. It may then be possible to find a *wff* of S, α, containing two free variables, x and y, such that (i) all values of x and y that make $f(x) = y$ true also turn α into a theorem of S, and (ii) whenever α' is formed from α by uniformly replacing x by a numeral, $(\exists^1 y)$ α' is a theorem of S. In that case every true proposition of natural-number arithmetic involving only that function will be expressible as a *wff*, appropriately constructed from α, that is a theorem of S; and α is then said to *represent* that function in S. For functions with more than one argument, the above account can be extended in a straightforward way and, provided that a true natural-number proposition involves only functions that are representable in S, the *wff* that expresses it will be a theorem of S.

A numerical function is said to be *effectively computable* if there is an effective (mechanical and finite) method of calculating the value of the function in all cases when its arguments are given (*e.g.*, the addition function $x + y$ is effectively computable since, given any two numbers, it is possible to calculate their sum mechanically in a finite number of steps). Various attempts have been made to give a precise mathematical analysis of the conditions for effective computability, and it is widely held that a satisfactory analysis of this kind is provided in the theory of recursive functions; *i.e.*, that the (intuitively defined) class of effectively computable functions coincides exactly with the (mathematically defined) class of recursive functions. An account of recursive functions will be found in the article MATHEMATICS, FOUNDATIONS OF: *The crisis in foundations following 1900: Logicism, formalism, and metamathematical method*, and is therefore omitted here. In the present context the essential point is that it can be proved that the numerical functions representable in S are precisely those that are recursive. And from this fact, given the assumption that effective computability and recursiveness do in fact coincide, it follows that every true proposition of natural-number arithmetic in which all of the functions are effectively computable can be expressed as a *wff* that is a *theorem* of S. In this sense, S is an adequate basis for natural-number arithmetic.

It would be natural to hope that S were also complete in the sense that every true arithmetical proposition whatever that can be expressed as a *wff* of S would be a theorem. It can be shown, however—at least if S is assumed to be consistent, which there seems no reason to doubt—that this hope is unfounded. That this is so is a direct consequence of the most important finding that has been made to date in this area, a finding that is known as *Gödel's incompleteness theorem*, after the mathematician and logician Kurt Gödel who formulated and proved it in 1931. An application of Gödel's argument to S shows how to construct a certain closed *wff* of S of

Effective computability and completeness

which it can be proved both that it expresses a true arithmetical proposition, and also that it is not a theorem of S, if S is a consistent system. Moreover, contrary to what one might expect, the incompleteness of S could not be overcome by adding extra axioms or rules to it; for, although it would be easy to strengthen the basis of S so as to obtain a system S′ in which the *wff* in question is indeed a theorem, Gödel's reasoning would then enable one to construct another closed *wff* which would stand to S′ exactly as the previous one does to S. The position in fact is that any consistent extension of S is bound also to be incomplete, and this fact is often expressed by saying that S is "essentially incomplete." Nor could one obtain a complete system for arithmetic by starting afresh with some other axioms and rules in place of those of S, for the upshot of Gödel's theorem is that any axiomatic system whatever that is sufficient for natural-number addition and multiplication is essentially incomplete; and as a result the otherwise natural ideal of giving a complete axiomatization of the whole, or even of some considerable part, of pure mathematics must be abandoned.

Summarizing distinctions

An important threefold distinction therefore exists among logical systems. There are those, like PC, that are both decidable and completely axiomatizable; there are those, like LPC, that are not decidable but are completely axiomatizable; and there are those, like natural-number arithmetic, that are neither decidable nor completely axiomatizable. The ability to draw this distinction with clarity and to demonstrate to which of the three groups a given system belongs is one of the most noteworthy achievements of contemporary logic.

Information about various theories of the nature of mathematical concepts and propositions and of the relation between logic and mathematics will be found in the articles MATHEMATICS, FOUNDATIONS OF; and METALOGIC.

APPLIED LOGIC

In a broad sense logic may be said to be applied when logical principles are used to test the validity of a particular inference or as a practical guide in discovering what conclusions one is or is not entitled to draw from a given set of premises. For this purpose lists of the forms of commonly encountered invalid inferences (logical fallacies) can be useful and are often given in textbooks, though the ways of going wrong, in reasoning as in other matters, are so multifarious that a fully systematic account of fallacies is perhaps a vain hope.

A logical system may, however, be an applied logic in the sense that it is meant to systematize the forms of sound reasoning, or to express a body of universal truths, in some relatively restricted field of thought or discourse. Typically such a system is constructed by setting up special constants (with specified interpretations) or new variables (with specified ranges of values) and extra axioms involving these and adding them to some "pure" logical system such as PC or LPC. (It has already been noted how this can be done in constructing extensions of LPC.) Some of the fields in which such applied logics have been constructed and investigated are noted briefly here. More detailed information will be found in the article LOGIC, APPLIED.

Various areas of application

1. Deontic logic is concerned with obligation, permissibility, and allied moral notions. Its simplest form involves adding two monadic operators, say O and P, to PC, with appropriate special axioms. Op is then understood to mean "It is obligatory that p" and Pp to mean "It is permissible that p." O may be defined as $\sim P\sim$ ("It is not permissible that not . . .") or P as $\sim O\sim$. More complex versions may involve the modal operators L and M (for necessity and possibility) as well, enabling formulas such as $Op \supset Mp$ ("Whatever is obligatory is possible") to be constructed; and versions based on LPC may contain formulas such as $O\phi xt$ to express "It is obligatory that x should ϕ at time t."

2. The logic of relative value can be somewhat analogously investigated. The dyadic operator B (for "is better than") could be thought of as having either propositions or names of individuals as its arguments; thus Bpq would

mean that it is better that p should be the case than that q should be the case, and Bxy would mean that object x is better than object y.

3. Epistemic logic is the logic of knowing and believing. Kxp can be used for "x knows that p" and Bxp for "x believes that p." K and B would be unlike other operators so far considered in that one of their arguments would be the name of an individual and the other a proposition. Plausible theorems would be $Kxp \supset p$ and $Kxp \supset Bxp$; a more contentious one would be $Bxp \supset \sim B x \sim p$—*i.e.*, "If x believes that p, then x does not believe that not-p."

4. In systems designed to express the logic of temporal relations, propositions have usually been conceived as capable of changing their truth value with the passage of time. Thus "It is raining in London" may be both true on Tuesday and false on Wednesday. The way is thus opened for a logic of tenses. The simple p is taken to mean "It is (now) the case that p," Fp to mean "It will be the case that p," and Pp to mean "It was the case that p." PFp will then mean "It was the case that it would be the case that p," and so forth. In this way a range of operators analogous to grammatical tenses can be built up and the logical relations between them systematized. Another development has been based on a reinterpretation of the modal necessity operator L so that Lp means "It is and always will be the case that p."

5. Attempts have also been made to give a formal logic of various classes of conditional propositions that seem to resist analysis in terms of the implication relations (such as material or strict implication) that are expressed in the standard logical systems. Causal propositions of the form "If p then as a causal consequence q" comprise one such class; counterfactual conditionals—*i.e.*, propositions of the form "If it were (had been) the case that p, then it would be (would have been) the case that q"—comprise another.

6. It should finally be mentioned that a certain amount of work—though not as yet a great deal—has been done toward constructing a formal logic of various non-propositional elements that play an important part in human discourse—elements such as questions, commands, exhortations, and expressions of intention.

V. Varieties of notation in symbolic logic

A wide variety of notations is found in works on formal logic. Sometimes in place of "literary" bracketing a system of dots is used, a larger group of dots having a wider scope than a smaller group; thus $(p \supset q) \supset [q \supset (r \supset p)]$ may be written as $p \supset q \cdot \supset : q \supset \cdot r \supset p$. Or a combination of dots and brackets may be used. Conventions are often laid down for reducing the number of brackets; *e.g.*, it may be stipulated that $p \supset q \supset r$ is to be understood as $(p \supset q) \supset r$, not as $p \supset (q \supset r)$. But these conventions vary considerably from author to author. The negation $\sim p$ is sometimes written as $-p$ or as $\bar{p}$; $p \cdot q$ as $p \wedge q$ or as $p \& q$ or simply as pq; $p \supset q$ as $p \to q$; $p \equiv q$ as $p \leftrightarrow q$ or as $p \sim q$. The symbol $\forall$ is frequently omitted and universal quantifiers written as (x), etc. $\exists$ is sometimes written as E. In modal logic, M is often replaced by $\Diamond$, and L by $\Box$ or less frequently by N. The choice of letters used as variables also varies considerably.

A more radically different symbolism is found in the so-called Polish notation, devised by Jan Łukasiewicz, in which all operators, dyadic as well as monadic, are written immediately before their arguments. In this notation $\sim p$ becomes Np, and $p \cdot q$, $p \vee q$, $p \supset q$, and $p \equiv q$ become respectively Kpq, Apq, Cpq, and Epq. In LPC, $(\forall x)$ is written as Πx, $(\exists x)$ as Σx, and $x = y$ as Ixy. In syllogistic logic, a, b, . . . are used as term variables and SaP, SeP, SiP and SoP are written as Aab, Eab, Iab and Oab, respectively. In modal logic, L and M are used as in this article, but $p \multimap q$ is written as $C'pq$ or as $\mathfrak{C}pq$. In this notation no brackets of any kind are required, the distinctions made in other notations by bracketing being marked instead by the order of the symbols. Thus $p \supset (q \vee r)$ is $CpAqr$ but $(p \supset q) \vee r$ is $ACpqr$.

BIBLIOGRAPHY. A great many books containing or consisting wholly of elementary introductions to modern formal logic are now available; thus the following list is bound to be rather arbitrary. ALFRED TARSKI, *Elementy logiki matematycznej*, 2nd ed. (1958; Eng. trans., *Introduction to Logic and to the Methodology of Deductive Sciences*, 3rd ed. rev., 1965); W.V.O. QUINE, *Elementary Logic*, rev. ed. (1965); ALICE AMBROSE and MORRIS LAZEROWITZ, *Fundamentals of Symbolic Logic* (1948); IRVING M. COPI, *Symbolic Logic*, 3rd ed. (1967); JOHN A. FARIS, *Truth-Functional Logic* (1962), propositional calculus only, and *Quantification Theory* (1964), lower predicate calculus only; E.J. LEMMON, *Beginning Logic* (1965); GEORGE E. HUGHES and D.G. LONDEY, *The Elements of Formal Logic* (1965). All of these, except where noted, contain introductions to both the propositional and lower predicate calculi. The natural deduction rules given in this article are derived from the book by Lemmon. Also introductory, but more advanced in character, are: W.V.O. QUINE, *Methods of Logic* (1950); ARTHUR N. PRIOR, *Formal Logic*, 2nd ed. (1962); RUDOLF CARNAP, *Introduction to Symbolic Logic and Its Applications* (1958); and PATRICK C. SUPPES, *Introduction to Logic* (1957). The most influential work in the field is ALFRED NORTH WHITEHEAD and BERTRAND RUSSELL, *Principia Mathematica*, 3 vol. (1910–13). In *Principia Mathematica to *56* (1962), those parts of the original that are of most concern to logicians as distinct from mathematicians are reprinted. Another important and influential work is DAVID HILBERT and W. ACKERMANN, *Grundzüge der theoretischen Logik*, 2nd ed. (1938; Eng. trans., *Principles of Mathematical Logic*, 1950). Probably the most definitive account of the propositional and lower predicate calculi is presented in ALONZO CHURCH, *Introduction to Mathematical Logic*, vol. 1 (1956). For Syllogistic Logic, see JOHN N. KEYNES, *Studies and Exercises in Formal Logic* (1906), for a comprehensive traditional account; and JAN LUKASIEWICZ, *Aristotle's Syllogistic from the Standpoint of Modern Formal Logic*, 2nd enl. ed. (1957); and OTTO A. BIRD, *Syllogistic and Its Extensions* (1964), for modern treatments. For Modal Logic, ROBERT FEYS, *Modal Logics* (1965), contains a comprehensive survey of axiomatic systems; GEORGE E. HUGHES and M.J. CRESSWELL, *An Introduction to Modal Logic* (1968), is a textbook and general survey. For brief introductions to set theory see P.R. HALMOS, *Naive Set Theory* (1960), and E.J. LEMMON, *Introduction to Axiomatic Set Theory* (1969); fuller accounts are given in PATRICK C. SUPPES, *Axiomatic Set Theory* (1960); and W.V.O. QUINE, *Set Theory and Its Logic* (1963). For an advanced treatment, see A.A. FRAENKEL, *Abstract Set Theory*, 3rd ed. (1965). For the logical foundations of mathematics (number theory and recursive functions), see ELLIOTT MENDELSON, *Introduction to Mathematical Logic* (1964); and J.W. ROBBIN, *Mathematical Logic: A First Course* (1969), though neither is easy reading. A standard advanced work in this field is S.C. KLEENE, *Introduction to Metamathematics* (1952). The most important journals in the field of formal logic are *The Journal of Symbolic Logic*, *Notre Dame Journal of Formal Logic*, *Logique et Analyse*, and *Zeitschrift für mathematische Logik und Grundlagen der Mathematik*.

(G.E.H.)

Logic, History of

A survey of the development of logic may appropriately begin by delineating the boundaries of the discipline. Traditionally, logicians have distinguished between deductive logic, whose principles are used in drawing new propositions out of premises in which they lie latent, and inductive logic, which ventures conclusions from particular facts that appear to serve as evidence for them. But this division is obsolete, because the problems earlier subsumed under induction are now apportioned to the methodology of the natural sciences. Thus, in the present account, logic is taken to mean deductive logic with all of its ramifications.

DEDUCTIVE LOGIC AS A DISCIPLINE

Divisions and nature of deductive logic. In its narrower sense deductive logic divides into (1) the logic of propositions (also called sentential logic) and (2) the logic of noun expressions. The logic of propositions or sentences is so named because, in it, propositions or sentences form the only basic semantic category (or part of speech). Some of them are simple and remain unanalyzed, others are compound and are analyzed into propositional connectives ("if . . . then," "and," "or," "it is not the case that," . . .) and their arguments, which themselves are propositions. In logical systems they are represented by p, q, r, ... In the logic of noun expressions simple propositions are broken down into their parts, which comprise

a second basic semantic category; namely, the category of names ("Socrates," "the father of Socrates") or the category of common nouns ("philosopher," "Athenian citizen"). In simple propositions names often occur as arguments in concatenation with predicates; that is to say, verbs ("moves," "lives") or verblike expressions ("is wise," "is a philosopher"). The theory whose vocabulary comprises propositional connectives, names (represented by a, b, c, . . . or x, y, z . . .), predicates (represented by F, G, H, . . .), and the quantifiers ("for all . . ." and "for some . . .") is known as the logic of predicates or lower functional calculus or logic of quantification. Verbs or verblike expressions that require one name to form a proposition are called one-place predicates. There are also two-place predicates, three-place predicates, etc.; *i.e.*, verbs or verblike expressions that require two or three or more names to form a proposition ("a is bigger than b," "a gives b to c"). It is the task of the logic of relations, another part of the logic of noun expressions, to exhibit the use of such predicates. Neither the logic of predicates nor the logic of relations accommodates common nouns as a semantic category in its own right. Both treat common nouns as integral parts of predicates. Common nouns, however, can be given the status of a basic semantic category, as was, in fact, done in Aristotle's syllogistic and in that part of the logic of noun expressions that is known as the logic of classes.

In a wider sense, logic comprises, in addition to the above, various theories of language—such as logical syntax, the study of the various relationships that hold between the meaningful expressions of a natural or an artificial language; and semantics, the study of the various relationships that hold between the expressions in a language and some objects outside the language. Systems of the logic of propositions as well as systems of the logic of noun expressions can become, in turn, objects of special studies that are part of what is now known as metalogic or the methodology of deductive systems, a logic of logics, as it were. Theories of modalities—*i.e.*, theories that are concerned with the notions of necessity, impossibility, possibility, and contingency—fall also within the scope of logic in its wider sense. Finally, in surveying the development of logic, the crucial role of logical fallacies and paradoxes cannot be overlooked.

As already mentioned, the principles or theses of the logic of propositions exhibit directly the use of such expressions as "if . . . then," "it is not the case that," "and," and "or," employed in concatenation with propositions, p, q, r. The principle of the hypothetical syllogism, which says that

For all p, q, r, if [(if p then q) and
(if q then r)] then (if p then r),

is an example of a thesis belonging to the logic of propositions. The theses of the logic of noun expressions exhibit the use of such constant terms as "is the same object as," "is," "every . . . is," "some . . . is," "no . . . is," and "some . . . is not," to mention only a few. In concatenation with noun expressions, a, b, c, these terms form propositions. Examples of statements belonging to the predicate logic are the law that asserts the symmetry of statements of identity:

For all a and b, if a is the same object
as b then b is the same object as a

and the Aristotelian syllogism (called *Darii*):

For all a, b, and c, if every b is c
and some a is b then some a is c.

It should be noted that, in the theses of the logic of noun expressions, a vocabulary belonging primarily to the logic of propositions is employed, which reflects the fact that the logic of propositions is logically prior to that of noun expressions.

Some logicians have wondered whether there are any logical theories that involve the use of three or more basic semantic categories; and the answer is "yes," though so far such theories have not been worked out in detail.

Alternative formats employed in presenting logical principles. The foregoing examples of logical theses have been formulated with the aid of propositional variables,

Deductive and inductive logic

Logic of propositions and logic of noun expressions

Direct method: theses and expressions

p, q, r, and with the aid of nominal variables, *a, b, c,* which stand for noun expressions. This formulation, first used by Aristotle, may be described as (1) the direct method of expressing logical principles. But Aristotle himself and many of his ancient and medieval followers often referred to logical principles also by means of (2) standard examples. For instance, the law of the hypothetical syllogism could be represented by the following example, adapted from a Greek commentator to Aristotle's *Analytica priora:*

Standard examples, metalogical terms, and schemata

If [(if a man exists then an animal exists) and (if an animal exists then a substance exists)] then (if a man exists then a substance exists).

Instead of expressing the law of the hypothetical syllogism directly or illustrating it with the aid of a standard example, it can be described in (3) metalogical terms:

For all *a, b,* and *c,* if (*a* implies *b* and *b* implies *c*) then *a* implies *c.* (Example: If [the universal affirmation (*a*) implies the corresponding particular affirmation (*b*), and the particular affirmation (*b*) implies the negation of the corresponding universal denial (*c*)], then the universal affirmation (*a*) implies the negation of the corresponding universal denial (*c*). For terminology see below *Theory of opposition.*)

Here the variables *a, b,* and *c* are nominal instead of propositional variables, and the term "implies"—which is not the same as the connective "if . . . then," because it requires noun expressions, and not propositions, as arguments—belongs to the vocabulary of metalogic. Many logical principles give rise to valid inferences, and some logicians have preferred using (4) schemata of valid inferences in presenting their systems of logic. The schema

If *p* then *q;* but if *q* then *r;* therefore if *p* then *r*

gives the form of inferences the validity of which is guaranteed by the law of the hypothetical syllogism. A less abstract way of referring to logical principles consists in making use of (5) standard inferences. Thus, the inference

If a man exists then an animal exists; but if an animal exists then a substance exists; therefore if a man exists then a substance exists

if used in the context of a logical discussion, can be understood as representing the law of the hypothetical syllogism. Note that standard examples that illustrate logical principles are propositions, whereas standard inferences are sets of propositions. In an inference one proposition, usually indicated by the preceding "therefore," is the conclusion; the remaining propositions are called premises. These five different ways of referring to logical principles must be kept in mind when tracing their gradual emergence in the course of the development of logic.

ANCIENT LOGIC

Precursors of ancient logic. Though in theory the logic of propositions is logically prior to the logic of noun expressions, it was the latter that historically preceded the former. The first system of the logic of noun expressions was worked out by Aristotle in the 4th century BC. Aristotle was right when he claimed that in creating syllogistic, which is a part of the logic of noun expressions that can be formulated in terms of categorical propositions, he was a pioneer—though preparatory work of considerable extent and significance had been done for him already by earlier Greek mathematicians, rhetoricians, and philosophers. The Greeks were, in fact, almost unique in their practice, cultivation, and enjoyment of argument and proof; and without interest in the art of argumentation one cannot have an intellectual climate conducive to the development of logical theories. The ability, however, to produce valid inferences in the course of an argument does not necessarily presuppose any knowledge of logic. Indeed, the preserved speeches of ancient Attic orators and the dialogues of Plato contain numerous valid inferences, but the logical laws that account for their validity were unknown at the time.

It was mentioned earlier that in its wider sense logic comprises theories of language. In this field, preparatory work had been done by the Sophists, a class of private tutors in ancient Greece who were the first to distinguish different types of sentences—affirmations, denials, questions, answers, and injunctions—and who were also interested in the study of synonyms. Further progress in theories of language was later made in the Academy, the school that Plato founded. In the *Sophist,* written in the 4th century BC, Plato remarked that neither a series of noun expressions alone nor a series of verbs alone can produce a proposition, a principle that is accepted even by logicians today, who have generalized it to read that no series of expressions belonging to one and the same semantic category can form a meaningful expression. More important for the development of logic, however, was Plato's conception of the axiomatic method, which lays down principles (usually self-evident) and deduces theorems from them, as an ideal means of systematizing knowledge. It was not until Aristotle and Euclid (*c.* 300 BC) that Plato's program was successfully turned into concrete achievement.

Theories of language of the Sophists and Plato

In discussing the prehistory of logic, mention should be made of fallacious arguments and paradoxes. These are arguments that, from premises that appear to be true, lead, by steps that appear to be valid, to a conclusion that appears to be false. The Sophists used to teach their pupils how to argue for and also against any propounded statement. This procedure, of course, gave occasion to fallacious arguments, which called for skillful refutation. In the 5th and 4th centuries BC, the interest in fallacious arguments was widespread, as is evidenced by Plato's *Euthydemus* and Aristotle's *De sophisticis elenchis.* The most famous of the early paradoxes was perhaps the "Achilles," invented by Zeno of Elea, an ancient Rationalist. Zeno argued that Achilles, reputed to be the fastest runner of all, could not overtake a tortoise in a race once the tortoise was allowed to get in front of him. For before overtaking the tortoise, Achilles would have to cover the distance that separated him from the tortoise at the time t_1. This he could accomplish at the time t_2; but at that time the tortoise would have moved away and Achilles would still be separated from it. The argument can then be repeated for the distance between them at the time t_2 and so on, pointing apparently to the conclusion that Achilles would never overtake the tortoise.

In a system of logic some of the theses are described as definitions. In introducing definitions, there are a number of conditions that must be carefully satisfied if they are to be used without endangering the consistency of the system. Though rules for thus introducing correct definitions into systems of logic are of recent origin, the credit for being the first to practice the art of definition should, according to Aristotle, be given to Socrates.

Aristotle and the logic of noun expressions. The collection of Aristotle's logical treatises is known as the *Organon,* a title invented probably by an ancient editor of his writings, which reflects the view that logic is a tool for sharpening thought. It consists of the *Categoriae,* the *De interpretatione,* the *Analytica priora* (two books), the *Analytica posteriora* (two books), the *Topica* (eight books), and the *De sophisticis elenchis.* The order of the treatises is supposed to be systematic; it does not seem to correspond to the chronological order, however. From the point of view of logic, the *De interpretatione* and the *Analytica priora* are by far the most important.

The Organon

Structure of language. In Aristotle, the discussion of the syntactical and semantical features of language constituted a preamble to his syllogistic. Following Plato, he distinguished between nouns and verbs and regarded them as essential parts of a proposition; but he seemed to concentrate his attention on nouns and, in particular, on referential common nouns with limited generality. He did so because he believed that nonreferential or empty noun expressions, like "goat-stag," singular nouns, and the nouns of ultimate generality, such as "thing" or "object," are of lesser importance for scientific inquiries. Noun expressions, which in Aristotle included adjectives, are used for the purpose of constructing simple affirmations and denials of the following four types:

1. Singular: *e.g.,* Socrates is white—Socrates is not white;
2. Universal: *e.g.,* Every man is white—No man is white;

3. Particular: *e.g.*, Some man is white—Some man is not white;

4. Indefinite: *e.g.*, Man is white—Man is not white.

In Aristotelian syllogistic, use is made of universal and particular propositions only. Called categorical propositions, these involve the following constant vocabulary: "Every . . . is," "No . . . is," "Some . . . is," and "Some . . . is not," which form propositions that were designated by medieval logicians as A, E, I, and O, respectively.

Theory of opposition. Syllogistic comprises (1) the theory of opposition, (2) the theory of conversion, and (3) the syllogistic proper. The theory of opposition, expounded in the *De interpretatione,* considers the logical relations that obtain between the four types of propositions formed by the affirmation and denial of universal and particular propositions. It stipulates that a universal affirmation, "Every *a* is *b*," and the corresponding particular denial, "Some *a* is not *b*," are contradictories; *i.e.*, that one of the pair must be true whereas the other must be false. A universal denial and the corresponding particular affirmation are also contradictories. A universal affirmation, "Every *a* is *b*," however, and the corresponding universal denial, "No *a* is *b*," form a pair of contrary propositions, which cannot both be true though they can both be false. A particular affirmation and the corresponding particular denial cannot both be false, though Aristotle did not state this fact. Finally, either of the two universal propositions implies the corresponding particular proposition (its "subaltern"), a fact that, judging from a passage in the *Topica,* was known to Aristotle. In the *De interpretatione,* the theory of opposition was stated in metalogical terms. Using the direct method, it is now possible to express the relevant logical principles as follows:

For all *a* and *b*, every *a* is *b* if and only if it is not the case that some *a* is not *b*.

For all *a* and *b*, no *a* is *b* if and only if it is not the case that some *a* is *b*.

For all *a* and *b*, if every *a* is *b*, then it is not the case that no *a* is *b*.

For all *a* and *b*, if it is not the case that some *a* is *b*, then some *a* is not *b*.

For all *a* and *b*, if every *a* is *b*, then some *a* is *b*.

For all *a* and *b*, if no *a* is *b*, then some *a* is not *b*.

Theory of conversion. Discussed in the *Analytica priora,* the theory of conversion considers the logical relationship that holds between a categorical proposition and its converse, obtained by reversing the order of the noun expressions *a* and *b*, and states in which cases such a converse can be inferred from the original proposition. The logical principles involved are not only described in metalogical terms and illustrated with the aid of standard examples but also are expressed directly. They are:

For all *a* and *b*, if every *a* is *b*, then some *b* is *a*.

For all *a* and *b*, if some *a* is *b*, then some *b* is *a*.

For all *a* and *b*, if no *a* is *b*, then no *b* is *a*.

For all *a* and *b*, if no *a* is *b*, then some *b* is not *a*.

This last principle, however, was not mentioned by Aristotle and has been disregarded by his successors.

Syllogistic proper. The *Analytica priora* contains also a systematic exposition of syllogistic proper. By a syllogism Aristotle understood a "propositional expression [*logos*] in which certain things having been laid down, something other than what has been laid down follows of necessity from their being so." This definition, however, is far too general; and it seems convenient for the present purposes to narrow it to apply to any inference for which the premises and conclusion are all categorical propositions—*i.e.*, simple propositions, rather than "if . . . then," "either . . . or," or "both . . . and" propositions—or to a logical principle that lends validity to such an inference. In Book I, chapters 4–7, Aristotle examined syllogisms with two premises. Such syllogisms, construed as logical principles, are all of the form

If *α* and *β*, then *γ*

in which the Greek letters alpha, beta, and gamma stand for categorical propositions with variable noun expressions called "terms." In syllogisms of this form, Aristotle distinguished: (1) the "major" term, which is the predicate in the conclusion and is assumed to occur in one of

the premises; (2) the "minor" term, which is the subject in the conclusion and is assumed to occur in the other premise; and (3) the "middle" term, which occurs in both premises but does not occur in the conclusion. Except for the definition of the middle term, which was employed by Aristotle, these definitions of the major and minor terms appear to have been introduced by John Philoponus, a 6th-century Christian theologian and Aristotelian commentator. In an Aristotelian syllogism the premises are also referred to as "the major" and "the minor," depending on which term (the major or the minor) they contain. Aristotle, in his exposition of syllogistic, was concerned to find out which pairs of categorical premises give rise to a valid syllogism. To systematize his search, he distinguished what he called the "three figures" of the syllogism, which he defined according to the placement of the middle term. First he examined those pairs of categorical propositions in which the middle term is the predicate in the minor premise and the subject in the major. Such combinations of premises are said to constitute the first syllogistic figure. Aristotle found that, in this figure, four different pairs of premises yield syllogistic principles. They are set out below together with their medieval names, the vowels of which indicate the kinds of propositions involved, whether A, E, I, or O (as earlier defined), and their sequence. The vowels of syllogism *Ferio*, for example, being EIO, indicate that the major (or first) premise is an E proposition ("No . . . is"), the minor (or second) premise is an I proposition ("Some . . . is"), and the conclusion is an O proposition ("Some . . . is not").

Barbara: For all *a*, *b*, and *c*, if every *b* is *c* and every *a* is *b*, then every *a* is *c*.

Celarent: For all *a*, *b*, and *c*, if no *b* is *c* and every *a* is *b*, then no *a* is *c*.

Darii: For all *a*, *b*, and *c*, if every *b* is *c* and some *a* is *b*, then some *a* is *c*.

Ferio: For all *a*, *b*, and *c*, if no *b* is *c* and some *a* is *b*, then some *a* is not *c*.

With the aid of appropriate counterexamples, Aristotle showed that the remaining combinations of premises in this figure do not yield valid syllogisms. The second figure is defined as the one in which the middle term occurs in the premises as the predicate. In this figure, too, four combinations of premises were found by Aristotle to give rise to syllogisms (*Cesare, Camestres, Festino, Baroco*). In the third figure, the middle term occurs in the premises as the subject. Here six combinations of premises prove to be syllogistic (*Darapti, Disamis, Datisi, Felapton, Bocardo, Ferison*). The syllogisms of the second and the third figures are not stated here explicitly since they can easily be reconstructed from their medieval names. As in the case of the first figure, the combinations of premises that, in the second and the third figures, do not produce valid syllogisms were shown by Aristotle to fail by means of counterexamples.

The most important features of Aristotle's presentation of syllogistic are the following: First, he gave his syllogisms the form of direct principles of logic and not the form of inferences or inference schemata. This he could do because, for the first time in the history of logic, he had thought of making use of variables, or letters that can stand for any noun expression. Second, he deduced his syllogisms of the second and the third figures from the syllogisms of the first figure, and by doing so he became the author of the first deductive system in the history of logic. In his deductions, Aristotle made explicit use of the theories of opposition and conversion. If his proofs were to be complete, however, he would have had to use a number of theses from the logic of propositions; but of this he was not aware.

In his syllogistic, Aristotle did not mention the combination of premises in which the major term is the subject and the minor is the predicate. Five such combinations yield valid syllogisms (*Bramantip, Camenes, Dimaris, Fesapo, Fresison*). They constitute a fourth figure, acknowledged by medieval logicians and the traditional logicians of modern times. To be sure, the syllogisms were known to Aristotle; but they were not included in his account of syllogistic. This fault was rectified by his pupil Theophrastus, who redefined the first figure as the one in which the middle term occurs as the subject in one premise and as the predicate in the other, thus making it possible for the five syllogisms in question to be incorporated into the system. A further expansion of syllogistic was apparently effected by Ariston of Alexandria (1st century BC), a Peripatetic (member of Aristotle's school), who is said to have included in the system the "subaltern" syllogisms; *i.e.,* the syllogisms that result from taking a syllogism of a form already recognized and replacing the universal conclusion by the corresponding particular conclusion (*Barbari, Celaront, Cesaro, Camestrop, Camenop*).

Modal logic. In addition to constructing the first system, however modest, of the logic of noun expressions, Aristotle initiated the development of modal logic, which deals with the notions of necessity, impossibility, possibility, and contingency. Not only did he study their application to syllogistic, but he also arrived at some more general principles. He seems to have abandoned his earlier view that a necessary proposition cannot be said to be possible in favour of the following principles:

1. A proposition is necessary if and only if its negation is not possible;
2. A proposition is possible if and only if its negation is not necessary;
3. A proposition is contingent if and only if it is neither necessary nor impossible.

Aristotle's modal syllogistic contains, however, a number of controversial ideas, which were widely discussed in his school, the Lyceum. Unfortunately, the treatise *On the Disagreement Concerning Mixed Moods Between Aristotle and his Friends* by the expositor of Aristotle, Alexander of Aphrodisias (AD 200), which could have thrown light on the controversy, has not survived. Even today modal logic is a subject of controversy, logicians being divided on the fundamental issue of the nature of modal principles. Some include them within the logic of propositions; others assign them a place in metalogic.

Aristotle was not aware that his syllogistic presupposes a more general logical theory, viz., the logic of propositions. To be sure, he mentioned "syllogisms from hypothesis," by which he may have meant some principles belonging to that logic; but he gave no details. As will be seen, there are firmer grounds for associating the origin of the logic of propositions with Theophrastus; with the Megarians, a 4th-century school of Socratic dialecticians and logicians; and with the Stoics.

Theophrastus and the logic of noun expressions. The writings of Theophrastus on logic are now lost; but evidence from secondary sources shows that he made creditable improvements in the systematization of syllogistic. He suggested, for instance, that the indefinite proposition, which asserts, for example, that "Man is white," should be treated as if it were particular (referring to "some men"), and he redefined the first figure and included in it five syllogisms originally omitted by Aristotle. Within the modal syllogistic he abandoned the notion of contingency. For the remaining modal notions, he introduced the principle of "the weaker premise," which regards a true proposition as weaker than a necessary one (since a proposition can be true, yet not necessary—but not vice versa) and a possible proposition as weaker than a true one, and demands that the conclusion in a valid syllogism should not be stronger, in respect of modality, than its weakest premise.

Theophrastus' theory of prosleptic syllogisms is perhaps his most interesting contribution to the logic of noun expressions. By prosleptic propositions he understood expressions of the form

For all x, if $F(x)$ then $G(x)$

in which both $F(x)$ and $G(x)$ stand for categorical propositions in each of which x occurs as one of the terms. (Example: "For all x, if every man is x, then every x is substance.") It should be noted that x is here a variable term bound by a universal quantifier, the expression "For all x." It was described by Theophrastus as indefinite and called the middle term. Depending on the position of the middle term, conceived in this way, prosleptic propo-

sitions can be divided into three figures. In combination with an appropriate categorical premise, a prosleptic premise yields a prosleptic syllogism, as exemplified in the following inference schema:

For all x, if every x is a, then no x is b;
but every c is a; therefore no c is b.

Some prosleptic propositions are equivalent to categorical propositions (Example: "For all x, if every x is a, then every x is b" is equivalent to "every a is b"), but this cannot be said about all of them, as Galen claimed that it could. For instance, no categorical proposition with a and b as arguments is equivalent to the prosleptic proposition which says that

For all x, if some a is not x, then every x is b.

It was Galen (died AD 199), however, one of the two greatest physicians of antiquity, who made the last major contribution to the logic of noun expressions in antiquity by developing a theory of compound syllogisms, occurring in four figures, in which two middle terms appear. Syllogisms of this sort can be illustrated by the following standard inference:

Every man is an animal; every man is rational; no irrational being is rational; therefore, some animal is not an irrational being.

Galen was of some importance as the transmitter of Greek logic to Arab scholars of the early Middle Ages. Their interest in Galen's writings on logic appears to have equalled that with which they read his medical works.

Founding of the logic of propositions. The earliest consideration of the logic of propositions occurred in the works of Theophrastus, of the Megarians, and of the Stoics. Theophrastus, according to Alexander of Aphrodisias, worked out a theory of totally hypothetical syllogisms, which, following the example of Aristotle, he neatly set out in three figures:

1st figure,   If p then q; if q then r; therefore if p then r.
   or   If p then q; if q then r; therefore if not-r then not-p.
2nd figure,   If p then q; if not-p then r; therefore if not-q then r.
   or   If p then q; if not-p then r; therefore if not-r then q.
3rd figure,   If p then r; if q then not-r; therefore if p then not-q.
   or   If p then r; if q then not-r; therefore if q then not-p.

In these inference schemata, the letters p, q, and r represent complete propositions; and for Theophrastus they probably represented categorical ones. But in fact, the nature of the propositions in this context is irrelevant to the validity of the inferences involved. By grouping the hypothetical syllogisms into three figures, Theophrastus tried to assimilate them to the Aristotelian categorical syllogisms of the predicate logic. He does not seem to have realized that hypothetical syllogisms belong to a different logical theory, to the logic of propositions and not to the logic of noun expressions. This fact, however, gradually became clear to the logicians in the Megarian school and in the Stoa (Stoic school).

The Megarian school was made famous by Eubulides (*c.* 4th century BC), a critic of Aristotle, by the dialectician Diodorus Cronus (died *c.* 307 BC), and by Philo of Megara, a pupil of Diodorus. To Eubulides logicians are indebted for certain paradoxes, including the celebrated "liar paradox" ("Does a man who says that he is now lying speak truly?"). Diodorus tried to connect modal notions, such as those of necessity and possibility, with the notions of past, present, and future; and Philo was the first to work out the truth-functional conception of implication; that is to say, of "if . . . then" propositions. (A compound proposition is said to be conceived truth-functionally if its truth or falsity is taken to depend exclusively on the truth or falsity of the propositions of which it is compounded.) Now, Philo argued, against Diodorus, that an implication is true if and only if its "if" proposition, known as the antecedent, is false or its "then" proposition, or consequent, is true; and that it is false if and only if its antecedent is true and its consequent is false.

Stoic logic. It is not known whether the truth-functional interpretation of the rest of the vocabulary of the logic of propositions is also attributable to Philo; but it is known that implication, conjunction ("and" propositions), exclusive disjunction ("either . . . or" propositions), and negation ("it-is-not-the-case-that" propositions) were all interpreted truth-functionally by Chrysippus of Soli (died *c.* 207 BC), the second founder of the Stoa. The truth-functional vocabulary was used by Chrysippus to formulate various logical principles. As a rule, these principles were represented by means of standard inferences or by inference schemata. The following schemata are said to have been set out by Chrysippus as indemonstrable:

1. If the first then the second; but the first; therefore the second;
2. If the first then the second; but not the second; therefore not the first;
3. Not both the first and the second; but the first; therefore not the second;
4. Either the first or the second; but the first; therefore not the second;
5. Either the first or the second; but not the second; therefore the first.

Various other inference schemata can be derived from these five in accordance with certain rules or directives. Two such rules, which can be reconstructed from preserved fragments, can be stated in terms of variables as follows:

A. For all *a*, *b*, *c*, and *d*, if *b* together with *c* implies *d* and *a* imply *b* then *c* together with *c* implies *d*.
B. For all *a*, *b*, and *c*, if *a* together with *b* implies *c*, then *a* together with the negation of *c* implies the negation of *b*.

By applying rule A—which, incidentally, was known to the Peripatetics and used by them for the purpose of constructing compound syllogisms—the Stoics could derive the following inference schemata:

6. If the first then if the first then the second; but the first; therefore the second;
7. If the first and the second then the third; however, not the third; but the first; therefore not the second.

It is clear from a moment's inspection that, in an appropriate context, schema 7 could replace rule B; and it is interesting to note that, according to Alexander of Aphrodisias, rule B results from dividing a rule that, in fact, was the same as rule A. From the modern point of view, rules A and B belong to a branch of metalogic.

In matters of logic there was little collaboration between the Lyceum and the Stoa. There was even some effort on the part of both schools to create quite artificial differences; they developed, for instance, two different logical terminologies. For the Stoics, logic was a part of philosophy, whereas for the Peripatetics it was a tool. Aristotle presented his syllogisms in the form of direct logical principles, whereas the Stoics preferred to make use of inference schemata. The Stoics knew, however, that inferences owe their validity to direct logical principles, and they had a simple method of converting schemata into principles. Aristotle and his followers used letters as variables; the Stoics used numerals. In their logical practice, the Peripatetics allowed for a considerable amount of linguistic flexibility, whereas the Stoics became notorious for the formalistic approach, which demanded that expressions should have the same form if they were to have the same meaning. The most important difference, however, between the logics of the two schools is that the Peripatetic syllogistic is part of the logic of noun expressions, whereas the schemata of the Stoics represent principles that belong to the logic of propositions. In the time of Galen both of these logics became part of the syllabus for general philosophical education.

Commentaries and compendiums. After Theophrastus and Chrysippus, little creative work in logic was done in ancient times. To be sure, Galen wrote critical commentaries on the logical writings of Aristotle, Theophrastus, and Chrysippus; but those commentaries have not survived. After Galen there were only certain compendiums of logic, on the one hand, and scholarly commentaries on Aristotle's logical treatises, on the other. Much of this literature has been lost, but the works of Alexander of Aphrodisias; of Porphyry (died *c.* 301), a pupil of Plotinus, the founder of Neoplatonism; of Ammonius Hermiae (5th century AD), a Neoplatonic mathematician and astronomer; and of the latter's pupil Simplicius have been preserved at least in part. Although these authors made, on occasion, improvements in the minutiae of the Aristotelian and Stoic logic, they can hardly be credited with any major contribution. Logicians are indebted to them, however, for salvaging numerous fragments from the lost writings of earlier logicians. The same can be said of certain Roman authors: of Cicero (died 43 BC); of Martianus Capella (5th century AD) and the senator Cassiodorus (died *c.* 582)—both of whom prepared compendiums of ancient learning; of the translator and commentator Boethius (died AD 524/5), whose influence dominated the early Middle Ages; and of others. These scholars worked out the Latin terminology for the field of logic and transmitted the achievements of the Greek logicians to the logicians of the Middle Ages.

MEDIEVAL LOGIC

Development of medieval logic. During the five centuries that followed the end of antiquity, little or nothing of any significance happened in the field of logic. As part of the basic curriculum (the trivium), logic was treated as a subsidiary subject providing useful training for students of law and theology. For the most part it was limited to discussing Porphyry's *Isagoge* and Aristotle's *Categoriae* and *De interpretatione* in a Latin translation by Boethius. Boethius' own logical writings were also read, along with some treatises by Gaius Marius Victorinus, a 4th-century African rhetorician, and the sections on logic to be found in the compendiums by Martianus Capella and Cassiodorus, and in the *Etymologiae* by the influential Spanish encyclopaedist Isidore of Seville (died *c.* 636). This sterility eventually began to change, however, because of the work of St. Anselm of Canterbury (died 1109), known for his ontological proof of the existence of God, and of Peter Abelard (died probably 1144), an eminent though controversial theologian and dialectician. During the 12th century, Latin translations of the remaining treatises of Aristotle's *Organon* were made, adding to the "old logic" a wealth of topics, then unfamiliar, that were given the name of the "new logic." In the 13th century logicians split: while some adhered to the Aristotelian orthodoxy and advocated the *logica antiqua*, others took a more liberal view and, in the faculties of arts of the newly established universities, propounded the *logica moderna*. The English logician William of Sherwood and his student Peter of Spain, later Pope John XXI, author of the most used textbook on logic for the next 300 years, seem to have been the most outstanding representatives of this new trend in logic. Among the logicians of the 14th century, mention should at least be made of the foremost philosopher of the century, William of Ockham; of Jean Buridan, also a scientist, who was the first to derive the laws of deduction deductively; and of his student and colleague Albert of Saxony. In the century that followed, Paul of Venice, an Augustinian theologian, produced a very comprehensive logic textbook under the descriptive title *Logica magna*. In the Greek world, the tradition of paraphrasing Aristotle's logical treatises and writing commentaries to them was continued by John Philoponus, by Stephanus of Alexandria, a 7th-century Neoplatonist, who transferred the tradition to Byzantium, and by others; and, in the 11th and 13th centuries, several logical compendiums were produced that deserve mention.

Logical studies were also cultivated by the Arabs. By the middle of the 9th century, Porphyry's *Isagoge* and Aristotle's *Categoriae*, *De interpretatione*, and *Analytica priora* had been translated first into Syriac and then into Arabic. The remaining parts of the *Organon* were similarly translated during the second half of the century. The works of Galen, too, attracted the attention of Arabic scholars, and it is through this channel that the logic of the Stoics percolated to Arab logicians. A more original work on the Aristotelian *Organon* was initiated in a school of

The inference schemata of Chrysippus

Comparison of the Lyceum and the Stoa

The logica antiqua *and the* logica moderna

Arabic logic

logicians that flourished at Baghdad in the 10th century, of which the most famous representatives were the Nestorian Abū Bishr Mattā ibn Yūnus; Abū Naṣr al-Fārābī, who acquainted the Arabs with Plato and Aristotle; and a pupil of both of the foregoing, the Jacobite Yaḥyā ibn ʿAdī. Unfortunately, their commentaries on Aristotle's logical writings and their own logical treatises, except for some commentaries by al-Fārābī, have been lost. In the view of the outstanding Persian philosopher Avicenna (died 1037), the school of Baghdad was too slavishly adherent to the Aristotelian tradition. He himself advocated a more independent line and gave expression to his concept of logic in his *Kitāb ash-shifaʾ* ("The Book of Healing"). The tradition of the school of Baghdad, which in Islām was regarded as Western, was revived in Muslim Spain during the 11th and 12th centuries. It reached its climax in the works of Ibn Rushd, known as Averroës, whose commentaries on the *Organon* played an important role in reviving the interest of Western scholars in Aristotle. In the 14th and 15th centuries, the logical studies by Arab scholars degenerated into the compiling of handbooks and the writing of explanatory notes to the handbooks bequeathed by earlier logicians.

The value of the Arabic contribution to the development of logic is not very great. Arab logicians kept interest in the *Organon* alive at a time when, in the West, only a small part of it was known to philosophers. They also preserved the Stoic tradition as transmitted by Galen; but so far, hardly any fresh light has been thrown on the logic of the Stoics from Arab sources. Of the three branches of medieval logic—the Byzantine, the Arabic, and the Scholastic—the latter appears to have been by far the most fruitful. Neither the Byzantine nor the Arab logicians seem to have achieved any lasting results. Even the hope that the writings of the Byzantine and Arab logicians might reveal important fragments of the logic of the ancient Greeks is not likely to be fulfilled.

Theories of language. As in antiquity, so also in the Middle Ages, the study of language played a significant part in the development of logic. Following Aristotle, the Scholastic logicians of the High Middle Ages distinguished between nouns and verbs; but this distinction was often replaced by the distinction between the subject and the predicate in a proposition. Expressions that could be used as subjects or as predicates were called *categoremata* (from Greek *katēgorein*, "to predicate") and distinguished from *syncategoremata* (from Greek *synkatēgorein*, "to predicate jointly"); *i.e.*, from such parts of propositions as "every," "all," "no," "some," "only," and the like. Both *categoremata* and *syncategoremata* were meaningful expressions; but whereas a categorematic expression designated something outside of the language (*i.e.*, had a referent), a syncategorematic expression was not capable of designation in the usual sense. By and large, syncategorematic expressions coincide with what is today described as logical vocabulary, and, indeed, some Scholastic texts implicitly suggested that logic should be construed as a theory of *syncategoremata*. According to Scholastic logicians, the function of a syncategorematic expression consists in changing or modifying the designation of categorematic expressions in a proposition—a problem connected with that of ambiguity in the use of *categoremata*. The Scholastics attempted to solve both of these problems with the aid of their theory of supposition, which is regarded as one of the original achievements of medieval logic. This theory appears to have originated in the 12th century; but it was Ockham and Albert of Saxony who gave it its traditional form. More than half a dozen different kinds of supposition can be distinguished. Supposition is a property of a term; *i.e.*, of a *categorema*, as used in a proposition. Thus, for instance, in the proposition "Man is mortal" the term man is supposed to have formal supposition; but the same term is said to have material supposition in the proposition "Man is a noun." The terminology could perhaps be more illuminating, but the distinction at issue clearly corresponds to the present distinction between use and mention. In the proposition "Every man is mortal," the term man designates several men; hence, its supposition is common. But in the proposition "This man is running," the term man designates exactly one man, and its supposition is described as discrete. This sort of distinction has special significance in the case of languages that, like Latin, have no articles. In such propositions as "Man is a species" and "Every animal apart from man is irrational," the term man has simple supposition. In application to the categorical propositions, the doctrine of supposition can be summarized, following Albert of Saxony, as follows: The subject in a singular proposition has discrete supposition, but in all indefinite or particular propositions it has determinate supposition. The supposition of the subject in a universal proposition is confused and distributive and so is the supposition of the predicate in a negative proposition. The supposition of the predicate in a particular affirmative proposition would be described, presumably, as determinate. The theory of supposition survives in traditional syllogistic as the theory of distributed terms, which asserts that in a given true proposition a term *a* is "distributed" if and only if, *a* having been replaced by a term *b* whose designata form a subclass of the designata of *a*, the proposition remains true.

Formal logic. Versions of the logics of noun expressions, of propositions, and of modal expressions can all be distinguished in the history of medieval logic.

Logic of noun expressions. In the Middle Ages the logic of noun expressions continued in the form of syllogistic. Medieval logicians abandoned the use of variables. Consequently, they had to illustrate logical principles with the aid of standard examples or describe them in metalogical terms; and they employed examples of inferences rather than of logical laws. One of the more important improvements in their syllogistic was the recognition of the fourth figure (in which the middle term is predicated of the major and the minor of the middle). To be sure, syllogisms constituting the fourth figure had been known to the Scholastics. But this figure was not recognized as such until the Averroistic Jewish philosopher Isaac Albalag did so in the 13th century. A great deal of ingenuity was devoted to the task of devising various mnemonics for the purpose of memorizing valid syllogisms and remembering the ways in which they can be "reduced" to syllogisms of the first figure (in which the middle term is predicated of the minor and the major of the middle).

Logic of propositions. The logic of propositions as developed by Theophrastus and the Stoics was transmitted to the Scholastics by Boethius. It seems not to have stimulated further development, however; it seems, instead, to have ossified in the early medieval compendiums; hence it had to be rediscovered. Its revival in the 13th century took the form of the theory of "consequences." At first its application was limited to syllogistic; but gradually it reached the level of abstraction at which the specific contents of the propositions involved lost their relevance, and the theory acquired the generality that it had possessed in the logic of the Stoics. The Scholastic consequences involved the use of conjunctions, inclusive disjunctions (*i.e.*, alternations), and implications. All of these kinds of compound propositions were interpreted by the Scholastics truth-functionally. According to Pseudo-Scotus, the author of *In universam logicam quaestiones* ("Questions on Universal Logic") formerly attributed to John Duns Scotus, a consequence is a hypothetical proposition composed of an antecedent and a consequent joined by means of a conditional connective ("if") or, more often, by one expressing a reason ("therefore," "hence") and thus forming an inference. These, however, can be divided into material and formal inferences. A consequence that is valid for any terms, provided that their arrangement is preserved, is formal; and a consequence that does not fulfill this condition is material. A material consequence is valid if by adjoining a true proposition as premise it can be reduced to a formal consequence. (Example: "Socrates is a man; therefore, Socrates is mortal" is a valid material consequence because "Every man is mortal; Socrates is a man; therefore, Socrates is mortal" is a formal consequence.) In the medieval logic of propositions, logical principles were either described in metalogical terms or il-

Categoremata and syncategoremata; theory of supposition

The fourth figure and reduction to the first figure

New
logical
principles
of the
Scholastics

lustrated with the aid of standard examples. Among the principles that were known to the Scholastics, but not known to the ancient logicians, the following can be mentioned:

1. An alternation follows from each of its parts; *i.e.*,
   For all *p* and *q*, if *p* then (*p* or *q*)
   and
   For all *p* and *q*, if *q* then (*p* or *q*).
2. From a conjunction of contradictories there follows any other proposition; *i.e.*,
   For all *p*, if *p* and not-*p* then *q*.
3. From a false proposition there follows any other proposition; *i.e.*,
   For all *p* and *q*, if not-*p* then (if *p* then *q*).
4. Every true proposition follows from any other proposition; *i.e.*,
   For all *p* and *q*, if *p* then (if *q* then *p*).
5. An alternation for which the parts are contradictories of the corresponding parts of a conjunction is itself a contradictory of the conjunction; *i.e.*,
   For all *p* and *q*, (*p* or *q*) if and only if it is not the case that (not-*p* and not-*q*)
   and
   For all *p* and *q*, (*p* and *q*) if and only if it is not the case that (not-*p* or not-*q*).
6. If the opposite of the consequent is consistent with the antecedent, the consequence is not valid; *i.e.*,
   For all *p* and *q*, if *p* and not-*q* then it is not the case that if *p* then *q*.
7. If the opposite of the consequent is not consistent with the antecedent, the consequence is valid; *i.e.*,
   For all *p* and *q*, if it is not the case that (*p* and not-*q*) then if *p* then *q*.

Logic of modal expressions. In the Middle Ages, modal logic continued to be applied to syllogistic, but there is also some evidence of a more general development. Thus, the notions of truth, falsity, knowledge, opinion, doubt, appearance, will, and preference were added to the list of the traditional modal notions, and a number of modal theses were set up by Pseudo-Scotus, Ockham, Albert of Saxony, and Walter Burley, a 14th-century English Scholastic. The following theses can serve as examples of their modal principles:

1. The contingent does not follow from the necessary.
2. The impossible does not follow from the possible.
3. Anything whatsoever follows from the impossible.
4. The necessary follows from anything whatsoever.
5. Actuality (truth) can be validly inferred from necessity.
6. Possibility can be validly inferred from actuality (truth).
7. The possibility of negation can be validly inferred from the negation of necessity, and conversely.
8. The necessity of negation can be validly inferred from the negation of possibility, and conversely.

Fallacies and paradoxes. Aristotle's work *De sophisticis elenchis* attracted a great deal of attention from medieval logicians after it became available in the 12th century. Some of them regarded the study of sophisms as an essential part of an education in logic. As an exercise in clarifying the ambiguities of ordinary language, the inventing and solving of linguistic puzzles was not entirely fruitless; but of greater significance for logic was the discussion of the *insolubilia.* According to the polymath Scholastic St. Albertus Magnus (died 1280), teacher of St. Thomas, insoluble propositions are such that, whichever side of the contradictory is granted, the opposite also follows. (Example: If someone swears that he swears falsely, then, if he swears falsely, what he swears is not true—*i.e.*, he does not swear falsely; but if he does not swear falsely, then what he swears is true—*i.e.*, he swears falsely.) This is one of the many different and sometimes quite complicated versions of the ancient paradox of the liar. Various solutions of this paradox were discussed by logicians of the 14th and 15th centuries; in fact, Paul of Venice gave a list of 15 different attempts at explaining it. But the most interesting suggestions are to be found in an anonymous manuscript dating from the beginning of the 14th century. According to one doctrine, whoever says "What I am saying now is false" is in fact saying nothing; his utterance is simply meaningless. Another way of dealing with the difficulty consists in pointing out that the word false occurring in that statement cannot refer to the proposi-

The liar
paradox

tion of which it is a part. Both solutions have found advocates among contemporary logicians and philosophers.

LOGIC IN THE EAST

Judging from the outline of the development of logic given so far, it would appear that logic has been an exclusive product of Western culture. Some historians of the subject, however, have found this view parochial and sought to identify traces of logic in Indian and Chinese thought. But research in these two fields is beset with tremendous difficulties: most of the texts remain unpublished or untranslated; some of the monographs are unreliable; and scholars well trained both in logic and philology are extremely rare. Thus, a fair evaluation is, as yet, impossible.

Indian logic. Indian logic, which arose in the last centuries BC, when certain grammarians and religious thinkers became interested in methods of philosophical discussion, involved the study of texts called *sūtras* and of numerous commentaries on them written over centuries. Around each of these texts a school developed, which cultivated and defended its doctrines, of which the Mīmāṃsā, Vaiśeṣika, Nyāya, and New Nyāya schools of Hindu logic are of particular interest. Although Pāṇini and Patañjali, Indian grammarians, were active as early as the 5th and 2nd centuries BC, the first millennium AD was the classical period in the development of Indian logic. Among the most important Hindu logicians of this period were Kumārila (7th–8th centuries) of the Mīmāṃsā school, Praśastapāda (5th–6th centuries) of the Vaiśeṣika school, and Vātsyāyana (5th–6th centuries) of the Nyāya school. Several Buddhist logicians also flourished during the classical period, most notably Dignāga (5th century), Dharmakīrti (7th century), and Dharmottara (8th–9th centuries). The second half of the second millennium AD consituted a new chapter in Indian logic, represented by the New Nyāya, among the followers of which were Raghunātha (16th century), and Mathurānātha, Jagadīśa, and Annam Bhaṭṭa (all 16th and 17th centuries).

Leading
Hindu
and
Buddhist
logicians

As the grammarians devised a special terminology for describing their language and formulating grammatical rules, they encountered problems similar to those of the modern distinction between language and metalanguage, as well as problems of definition, clarity, and economy in stating the rules of grammar.

In the *Vaiśeṣika-sūtra* (1st century AD), a doctrine was expounded that resembled Aristotle's theory of categories; *i.e.*, the theory of the kinds of entities that constitute the universe or of the generic terms that refer to them. The author distinguished (1) substances: earth, water, fire, air, ether, time, space, self, and mind; (2) attributes: colour, taste, smell, and touch, numbers, measures, separateness, conjunction and disjunction, priority and posteriority, understandings, pleasure and pain, desire and aversion, and volitions; and (3) actions: throwing upward, throwing downward, contraction, expansion, and motion. The remaining categories were (4) genus; (5) ultimate difference; and (6) inherence. To these, later texts added the category of (7) absence. It was no more clear, however, than it was in the case of Aristotle whether the list was meant to classify the meanings of words or the things denoted by words.

The *Nyāya-sūtra*, which was edited in the 2nd century AD, is regarded as the fundamental text of Indian logic. Its so-called five-member syllogism is usually illustrated by the following argument:

The
*Nyāya-
sūtra* and
the
five-
member
syllogism

Proposition:	There is fire on the mountain.
Reason:	Because there is smoke on the mountain.
Example:	As in a kitchen—not as in a lake.
Application:	It is so (*i.e.*, it is so in the present case).
Conclusion:	There is fire on the mountain.

The interpretation of the argument is not simple. In particular, the role of the example is obscure. If it is meant to remind one of instances in which smoke and fire are present and of instances in which they are absent, then the syllogism is an argument by analogy and has no validity in logic. On the other hand, the reason would imply the conclusion if the example could be interpreted as standing for a universal statement: "Where there is smoke there is fire." Development in this direction seems, in fact, to have taken place in Buddhist logic. Thus, according to Dignāga, the following three-membered rule holds: if (1) the presence of a definite mark in the subject has been stated, and if it is remembered that (2) the same mark is certainly in everything similar to the subject, but (3) absolutely absent in everything unlike it, then the result of the inference is certainly valid. Dharmakīrti, a commentator on Dignāga, used in fact a universal premise as the example. In the final form of the syllogism, as found in a textbook by Annam Bhaṭṭa of the New Nyāya school, the author distinguished between inference for oneself and inference for another. The inference for oneself consists of three steps such as:

1. Everywhere where there is smoke, there is fire.
2. There is smoke on this mountain.

From the combination there arises the knowledge:

3. There is fire on the mountain.

Inference for another involves five members and reads:

> The mountain is fiery—that is the proposition. Because smoky—that is the reason. All that is smoky is fiery—that is the example. So here—that is the application. Therefore it is so—that is the conclusion.

The member that is described as the application raises a problem. Although modern commentators seem to regard it as mere restatement of the reason, which is the second member, it is tempting to view it as the application of the universal statement—*i.e.*, the third member—to the particular instance under consideration. If this were correct, then the expressions "It is so" and "So here" could be interpreted as abbreviations standing for "If there is smoke in the mountain then there is fire in the mountain" or "If the mountain is smoky then the mountain is fiery." Be that as it may, the five-member syllogism bears a close resemblance to the prosleptic syllogism of Theophrastus (see above *Theophrastus and the logic of noun expressions*).

Nascent inference schemata

An argument reminiscent of the Stoic inference schemata has been found in a Buddhist work, the *Kathāvatthu*, which reads:

> If the soul be known in the sense of a real and ultimate fact, then indeed, good sir, you should also say, the soul is known in the same way as any other real and ultimate fact is known. (2) That which you say here is wrong, namely, that we ought to say, "The soul is known in the sense of a real and ultimate fact," but we ought not to say, the soul is known in the same way as any other real and ultimate fact is known. (3) If the latter statement cannot be admitted, then indeed the former statement should not be admitted. (4) In affirming the former statement, while denying the latter, you are wrong.

It is easy to say that this argument is an instance of the following schema:

	(1) If *p* then *q*;
therefore,	(2) Not (*p* and not-*q*);
therefore,	(3) If not-*q* then not-*p*;
therefore,	(4) Not-(*p* and not-*q*).

All of these inferences are valid; but although another argument of similar form, with "not *p*" instead of "*p*" and "not *q*" instead of "*q*," is found in the text, it would be too generous to credit the Buddhist logician with the discovery of the logic of propositions. In the *Kathāvatthu*, the arguments are not used as standard examples to represent any argument whatsoever of the same form. They occur in a discussion on the knowability of the soul and belong to psychology rather than to logic. Discussions of this kind do appear, however, to follow very strict rules based probably on practice and tradition.

The notion of negation seems to have been of particular interest to Indian logicians. Thus, the followers of the Mīmāṃsā explored the ways in which an injunction could be negated. They distinguished "He shall-not look," "He shall not-look," and "Not-he shall look" as possible negations of "He shall look." Mathurānātha, of the New Nyāya school, wrote, "Wherever one perceives a pot, there one does not perceive constant absence of a pot. . . . Accordingly, absence of constant absence of pot is essentially identical with pot." This statement looks like a double negation law expressed with the aid of a standard example. In the texts of the New Nyāya, the notion of negation often occurs in connection with abstract terms. Thus, instead of the simple proposition "The mountain is smoky," for instance, the cumbersome one "Not-mountain-ness qualifies the locus of not-being-smoky" is employed. This type of language invites comparison with the highly artificial Latin of the medieval logicians.

Evaluation of Indian logic

Compared with the logic of the ancient Greeks, Indian logic is not very impressive. It must be emphasized, however, that—unlike the logic of the Arabs—it developed independently of Greek thought. While it may be granted that the logic of propositions may have been anticipated by some Buddhist logicians, it does not seem that much progress was made. The logic of noun expressions asserted itself more firmly, as in the five-member syllogism and its variants, but it never reached the level of Aristotle's syllogistic. The development of Indian logic was severely handicapped by the failure of its logicians to make use of variables. As a result, no logical principles could be stated directly; they had to be illustrated by standard examples or described metalinguistically (*i.e.*, in talk about the language in which they might have been stated). Finally, in Indian thought, logical topics were not always separated from metaphysical and epistemological topics (on the nature of being and knowledge, respectively). It must be remembered, however, that present knowledge of the development of logic in India is incomplete and that it may have to be revised in the light of future research.

Chinese logic. For the most part, Chinese philosophy is concerned with practical and moral problems on the one hand and with mystical interpretations of life on the other. It has little room for the study of logic, which has remained neglected since the establishment of Neo-Confucianism in the 11th century AD. In the classical period of Chinese philosophy (5th to 3rd centuries BC), the controversies between the major philosophies of Confucianism, Taoism, and Moism gave rise to a kind of dialectic, which eventually was systematized to some extent by the Moists. They turned it into a weapon against the skepticism of the Taoists, who maintained that one point of view is as good as another because each is based upon different assumptions regarding the relations between names and objects. According to the Taoists, assumptions of this kind are entirely arbitrary. As dialecticians, the Moists were primarily interested in the study of names in relation to objects. They distinguished "unrestricted" names, which apply to every object; "private" names, which apply to one object each; and names like "horse," which apply to every object of a kind. (As noted earlier, a comparable classification of noun expressions had been worked out by Aristotle; see above *Aristotle and the logic of noun expressions: Structure of language*.) The Moists were also interested in defining the terms used in philosophical discussions and in listing various senses of ambiguous terms. Their definitions of "all" and "some" resemble the laws of obversion for the universal affirmative and particular affirmative propositions. They distinguished between absolute identity and relative identity (sameness in a specified respect). Gradually, the Moists developed an interest in the forms of propositions and in inferences from propositions of the same form; but, whereas Western logicians searched for the similarity of form in the structures of propositions with a view to establishing logical principles or schemata of valid inference, the Moists considered instances in which the similarity of form does not warrant any inference. "A white horse is a horse" implies "Riding white horses is riding horses"; but one may ask whether "A robber is a man" implies "Killing robbers is killing men." The Moists' answer was in the negative; and they supported it by pointing out that, although a robber is a man, abounding in robbers is not abounding in men, and disliking the abundance of robbers is not disliking the abundance of men. The purpose of this argument, however, does not seem to have been to elucidate any logical or linguistic

The Moist dialectic of names and objects

puzzle but to show that, contrary to the opponents of Moism, killing robbers was compatible with love for all men; it was not a point of logic that was at issue but a point of morals. Discussions of this sort could have led, in due course, to the investigation of logical problems, but as it happened, they did not do so. In developing logic, the Chinese thinkers did not advance beyond the stage of preliminaries, a stage that was reached in Greece by the Sophists in the 5th century BC.

MODERN LOGIC

Logic in the Renaissance and in Humanism. Returning to the West, the logical tradition of the Middle Ages survived for about three centuries after it had reached its maturity in the 14th century. The intellectual climate, however, that established itself in the West with the advent of the Renaissance and Humanism did not enhance logical studies. The Latin of the Roman writers Lucretius, Cicero, and Quintilian proved more attractive than the language of Boethius and the Scholastics; and rhetoric took precedence over logic. At the same time, the authority of Aristotle was gradually replaced by that of Plato and the Neoplatonist Plotinus. The rise of the natural sciences also contributed to the neglect of logic, which, as a deductive discipline, gave way to methodological investigations. These developments called for a new approach to logic; and in the mid-16th century such an approach was in fact taken by Petrus Ramus, an anti-Aristotelian logician and educational reformer. Ramus described logic as an "art of discussing" and distinguished it from grammar and rhetoric, which in his view were concerned with matters of style. Logic, according to Ramus, should treat of concepts, judgments, inferences, and proofs—in that order. Among inferences he counted syllogisms, both categorical and hypothetical. To the former he added syllogisms involving the use of singular propositions. In accordance with the spirit of the time, he used illustrations from classical literature. The divisions of logic suggested by Ramus were adopted by the authors of *La Logique: Ou l'art de penser* (1662; Eng. trans. in *The Port-Royal Logic*, 1851), which consisted of four parts. The discussion of concepts and judgments in parts I and II, respectively, seems to contain a few original observations, which belong, however, to epistemology rather than to logic. In part III, on reasoning, the validity of syllogisms is determined by giving rules for each of the figures and proving corollaries. Although some of these rules were known to the Scholastics, *The Port-Royal Logic* gives a systematic presentation of what later writers of textbooks developed into a metalogical theory of syllogistic. In part IV, on method, Euclid's *Elements* is recommended as a model of scientific method. Following René Descartes, the father of modern philosophy, they insisted that, in any scientific inquiry, obscure or equivocal terms should be defined; that only perfectly known terms should be used in definitions; that only self-evident truths should be used as axioms; and that all propositions that are not self-evident should be proved with the aid of axioms, definitions, and already proved propositions. Despite the competition of an entirely new conception of logic afforded by Gottfried Wilhelm Leibniz, a German Rationalist of widespread interests, the ideas expounded in *The Port-Royal Logic* continued to be popular to the mid-19th century.

Rise of mathematical logic during the Enlightenment. Modern logic began in the 17th century with Leibniz and developed in partnership with mathematics.

Leibniz' characteristica universalis. Leibniz influenced his contemporaries and successors through his ambitious program for logic, which for him had ceased to be "a scholar's diversion" and began to take the form of a "universal mathematics." His program envisaged a universal language based on an alphabet of thought, or *characteristica universalis*, a general calculus of reasoning, and a general methodology. In Leibniz' view, the universal language should be like algebra or like a version of the Chinese ideograms and consist of basic signs standing for simple unanalyzable notions. Complex notions would then be signified by appropriate constructions involving

the basic signs, which would thus reflect the structure of complex notions and, in the final analysis, that of reality. The use of numerals to represent unanalyzable notions would hopefully enable the truths of any science, when formulated in terms of the universal language, to be computed by arithmetical operations. Neither the idea of an artificial language nor that of reducing reasoning to computing was entirely new; it was owing to Leibniz' vision and confidence, however, that the two ideas came eventually to fruition—as witnessed by the arithmetization of logical languages by Kurt Gödel, a Moravian-U.S. mathematical logician, on the one hand, and by the emergence of contemporary computer science, on the other. Leibniz' more concrete contributions to the development of logic appear to be twofold: he successfully applied mathematical methods to the interpretation of the Aristotelian syllogistic, and in proposing a "calculus of real addition" he showed that parts of algebra are open to nonarithmetical interpretation.

In discussing Aristotle's syllogistic, Leibniz rightly insisted that each of the four categorical propositions has existential import (*i.e.*, its terms have instances), and that, consequently, there are six valid syllogisms in each of the four figures. He also correctly suggested that singular propositions could be treated as universal. But his most important finding consisted in a very ingenious arithmetical interpretation of syllogistic, which rests on the assumption that variables take ordered pairs of relatively prime numbers as their values. Leibniz showed how, on this assumption, the four categorical propositions should be interpreted, and he demonstrated that, when so interpreted, all valid syllogisms are verified and the rejected syllogisms falsified. Morever, his interpretation has proved to be adequate even in relation to a very intricate rule of rejection proposed for syllogistic in the 1940s by the Polish logician Jerzy Słupecki of the Warsaw school of logic, later professor at the University of Wrocław (formerly Breslau). The problem of defining the four propositions in terms of identity, difference, logical product of noun expressions, and logical complement long exercised Leibniz' mind. Anticipating the use of quantifiers, Leibniz suggested the following definitions (slightly streamlined): Arithmetical interpretation of syllogistic

1. For all *a* and *b*, every *a* is *b* if and only if for all *c*, if *c* is *a* then for some *d*, *d* is *b* and *c* is the same object as *d*.
2. For all *a* and *b*, some *a* is *b* if and only if for some *c*, *c* is *a* and for some *d*, *d* is *b* and *c* is the same object as *d*.
3. For all *a* and *b*, no *a* is *b* if and only if for all *c*, if *c* is *a* then for all *d*, if *d* is *b* then *c* is different from *d*.
4. For all *a* and *b*, some *a* is not *b* if and only if for some *c*, *c* is *a* and for all *d*, if *d* is *b* then *c* is different from *d*.

Leibniz claimed that, given these definitions, one can prove all of the valid syllogisms with the aid of two principles: one of them states that "For all *a*, *b*, and *c*, if *a* is the same object as *b* and *b* is the same object as *c*, then *a* is the same object as *c*"; and the other states that "For all *a*, *b*, and *c*, if *a* is the same object as *b* and *b* is different from *c*, then *a* is different from *c*." Actually, Leibniz was right, provided that one is entitled to assume that "For all *a* and *b*, *a* is different from *b* if and only if it is not the case that *a* is the same object as *b*," and that "For all *a*, for some *b*, *b* is *a*."

Leibniz' treatment of Aristotelian syllogistic reflects his interest in the notions of identity and difference. In one of his papers he stated that those terms are "the same" or "coincident" of which either can be substituted for the other wherever one pleases without loss of truth—*e.g.*, "triangular" and "trilateral." This informal definition expresses an idea that today would be expressed directly as the law of extensionality for noun expressions: "For all *a* and *b*, *a* = *b* if and only if [for all *F*, *F(a)* if and only if *F(b)*]," *F* standing for any predicate (verblike expression). Here "*a = b*" means that "*a*'s are the same as *b*'s." Leibniz expanded his calculus of identity through the notions of "complement" and "real addition": In his symbolism, the "real sum" of the terms *a* and *b* is expressed as "*a* $\oplus$ *b*," but the complement of *a* is simply expressed as "not-*a*." Leibniz' calculus of real addition has the form of a deductive system based on axioms and definitions. Calculus of identity

Period of neglect and the new approach of Ramus

The Port-Royal Logic

Given the theory of identity, the axiomatic foundations of this system can be condensed into the following simple proposition: "For all a, b, and c, $a = b \oplus c$ if and only if ($a = c \oplus b$ or it is not the case that $a = a \oplus a$)." If one wishes to incorporate the notion of complement, however, then the single axiom would have to be replaced by the following: "For all a, b, and c, $a = b \oplus c$ if and only if it is not the case that [$a = $ not-$(c \oplus b)$ and $a = a \oplus a$]." Leibniz' logical papers remained for the most part unknown until *La Logique de Leibniz* was published by Louis Couturat, a French philosopher of mathematics, in 1901. Had these papers been published during the lifetime of Leibniz, the revival of logic, which in fact occurred in the mid-19th century, would have happened much earlier.

Search for clarity and use of diagrams. The new approach to syllogistic and the search for an algebra capable of nonarithmetical interpretation characterized the development of logic after Leibniz. At the end of the 17th century and during the 18th century, these two lines of research were followed mainly by mathematicians. Girolamo Saccheri, an Italian Jesuit, influenced by the Cartesian methodology, proceeded to apply to logic the standards of clarity expected in geometrical proofs. He was dissatisfied with Aristotle's use of extra-logical counterexamples in rejecting invalid syllogisms. Consequently, he proposed a different method of rejection, suggested by a certain kind of proof found in Euclid. It was the method of *reductio ad absurdum*, but a *reductio* with a difference. Saccheri used, for example, the premises

1. Every syllogism of the first figure with a universal major and an affirmative minor premise is a valid syllogism;

and

2. No AEE-syllogism (*i.e.*, with A and E premises and an E conclusion) of the first figure is a syllogism with a universal major and an affirmative minor premise;

and concluded from them that

3. No AEE-syllogism of the first figure is a valid syllogism.

Actually, though the premises and the conclusion are true, the argument as it stands is not valid. A further premise, which Saccheri tacitly assumed, is needed, viz.,

4. If some AEE-syllogism of the first figure is a valid syllogism, then for all a, b, and c, if every b is c and no a is b then no a is c.

With this addition, given the syllogistic laws of contradiction, the premises (1), (2), and (4) now imply (3) as a conclusion and enable the usual *reductio* to be applied; for if, contrary to the conclusion, it is additionally assumed that "Some AEE-syllogism of the first figure is a valid syllogism," then it can be easily shown that, even on this assumption, the conclusion holds—which means that the assumption is redundant. No extra-logical vocabulary has here been used, provided that logic is understood to include metalogic, and in particular metasyllogistic.

The practice of illustrating categorical propositions by geometrical diagrams was already in evidence in the 16th century. Though it was later used by Leibniz, and by Johann Heinrich Lambert and Gottfried Ploucquet—authors of two early formulations of logical calculi—it has come to be associated with the name of Leonhard Euler, an 18th-century Swiss mathematician.

If one wants to go further than Euler and distinguish between singular, general, and nonreferential noun expressions, then properties and relations that belong to or hold between extensions of singular, general, and nonreferential noun expressions can be determined with reference to diagrams tabulated as shown in the figure. A small shaded circle represents the extension of a singular noun expression and an unshaded circle that of a general noun expression. No circle is used in the case of a nonreferential noun expression. The diagrams I.1, I.2, and I.3 illustrate the following propositions: "There exists exactly one a," "There exist more a's than one," and "There exist no a's." The spatial relations between the circles in diagrams II.1–II.16 correspond to the relations between the extensions of noun expressions represented by a and b. Some, but not all, of these relations are fairly familiar. Thus, for instance, diagrams II.1, II.2, and II.3 illustrate

Properties and relations belonging to or holding between extensions of singular, general, and nonreferential noun expressions (see text).
From *Ratio* (1958); Blackwell, Oxford

the following propositions: "a is the same object as b," "a is different from b," and "a is one of many b's." And the proposition "No a's are b's" is illustrated by diagram II.13.

In Euler's *Lettres à une princesse d'Allemagne* (3 vol., 1768–72), he used diagrams II.10 and II.13 to illustrate the universal affirmative and the universal negative propositions and used II.12 to illustrate the two particular propositions. If the interpretation suggested by his diagrams is adhered to rigorously, however, it is found to fail for the syllogistic laws of identity, contradiction, subalternation, and subcontrariety, as well as for the syllogisms that depend on these laws.

Development of mathematical logic in the 19th century. During the 19th century, and especially during its last half, the foundations were being laid for the most remarkable developments in the history of logic.

Expansions of syllogistic by Gergonne and Bentham. More than 100 years after Euler, his idea of geometrical diagrams was elaborated systematically by the Frenchman Joseph Diez Gergonne, a mathematician and editor of a mathematical journal. Following the Aristotelian tradition, Gergonne disregarded both singular and nonreferential noun expressions, but his treatment of general noun expressions can be regarded as complete. He needed only five diagrams to determine the five simple relations between the extensions of two general referential noun expressions, viz., $a \mid b$, $a \subset b$, $a \supset b$, $a \times b$, and $a \dashv b$ (in the foregoing table: II.9, II.10, II.11, II.12, and II.13). These simple relations can now be used to define the categorical propositions of syllogistic, as set out below:

For all a and b, every a is b if and only if $a \mid b$ or $a \subset b$;
For all a and b, no a is b if and only if $a \dashv b$;
For all a and b, some a is b if and only if $a \mid b$ or $a \subset b$ or $a \supset b$ or $a \times b$;
For all a and b, some a is not b if and only if $a \supset b$ or $a \times b$ or $a \dashv b$.

Gergonne's relations can be defined, conversely, in terms of the syllogistic constants. Thus, Gergonne's innovation

(margin labels) Saccheri's *reductio ad absurdum*

Diagrams for relations between kinds of noun expressions

Use of the diagrams by Euler and Gergonne

consisted, in fact, in expanding the vocabulary of syllogistic and proposing new kinds of inference based upon the expansion. He did not, however, axiomatize his system. This was done, instead, in the 20th century by John Acheson Faris, a Belfast logician.

From the point of view of logic, "every . . . is" (or "all . . . is") is treated as a single syntactically unanalyzable term, which in concatenation with two noun expressions forms a proposition. Traditionally, however, it had been held that "every" (or "all") modifies the way in which the subject should be construed. This suggested to logicians a similar modification of the predicate. The idea was not new, however; it had been discussed by Aristotle in the *De interpretatione*, only to be abandoned later. Some of Aristotle's ancient commentators determined that a modification of this sort would generate 16 different propositions. But the authority of Aristotle prevented them from enquiring more deeply into the problem. Because of the writings of Sir William Hamilton, an influential Scottish metaphysician, "the doctrine of the quantified predicate" became topical in the first half of the 19th century and led to a bitter controversy between him and Augustus De Morgan, an English mathematician and logician. Hamilton distinguished eight different forms of proposition that involved quantification of the predicate, but apparently he did not know that the same distinctions had already been made by George Bentham, an English botanist and systematist. Bentham was concerned with the relations of identity and exclusion (or outsideness) as holding between both total and partial extensions of two noun expressions. In his system of notation, "$tX = pY$" meant that the total extension of X is identical with a proper part of the extension of Y, and "$pX \parallel pY$" meant that a proper part of the extension of X is entirely outside a proper part of the extension of Y. Hamilton used a symbolism of his own to express his eight forms of proposition, but he also expressed them in ordinary language. The table shown below gives, on the left hand side, propositions distinguished by Bentham, and, on the right hand side, their Hamiltonian versions:

a. $tX = pY$ . . .   All X is some Y.
b. $tX \parallel pY$ . . .   Any X is not some Y.
c. $tX = tY$ . . .   All X is all Y.
d. $tX \parallel tY$ . . .   Any X is not any Y.
e. $pX = pY$ . . .   Some X is some Y.
f. $pX \parallel pY$ . . .   Some X is not some Y.
g. $pX = tY$ . . .   Some X is all Y.
h. $pX \parallel tY$ . . .   Some X is not any Y.

Obviously, Bentham arrived at his list of propositions by permuting his symbols, but he was not very clear about their interpretation. Thus, he claimed, for instance, that propositions (b) and (d) both represent the E proposition. He thought that proposition (d) was rather useless and that the remaining propositions could be reduced to the four standard types. Hamilton, too, was somewhat confused about the meanings of his eight propositions. He identified propositions (a), (d), (e), and (h) with the A, E, I, and O propositions, but, following Euler, he illustrated each of these propositions with the aid of one set of circles. This means, in fact, that each of these propositions exhibits the use of a Gergonne constant. For the purpose of such an interpretation, however, "some" had to be understood as meaning "some but not all." On these assumptions, propositions (a), (c), (d), (e), and (g) can be regarded as exemplifying the Gergonne constants C, I, H, X, and ⊃, respectively. Proposition (f) then turns out to be just another version of (e), whereas (b) and (h) can be taken to express compound relations between extensions: proposition (b) can be construed as equivalent to "All X is some Y or some X is some Y" and proposition (h) as equivalent to "Some X is all Y or some X is some Y." Alternatively, one can accept Hamilton's identification of propositions (a), (d), (e), and (h) with the four categorical propositions and treat propositions (b), (c), (f), and (g) as expanding the vocabulary of syllogistic. This, in fact, is how Hamilton viewed his contribution, though he also claimed, wrongly, that his scheme was an improvement on Aristotelian logic. Using the new vocabulary, Hamilton and his followers worked out a great number of additional syllogisms and tried to work out a simple criterion for testing their validity. At the root of the difficulties experienced by Hamilton was his pardonable failure to distinguish between "all" and "some" as integral parts, on the one hand, of the constants "all . . . are" and "some . . . are," and, as used, on the other hand, in "For all a, . . ." and "For some a, . . . ," which are quantifiers in the sense accepted today. When expressed in a more sophisticated logical idiom, the conceptions of Bentham and Hamilton reveal an affinity to the Leibnizian definitions involving identity and difference.

Expansion of syllogistic by De Morgan.   A more successful attempt at expanding syllogistic was made by Augustus De Morgan, who developed a logic of noun expressions in *Formal Logic* (1847), in his *Syllabus of a Proposed System of Logic* (1860), and also in a number of articles. Like Bentham and Hamilton, De Morgan was concerned with comparing the extensions of terms. In his symbolism, a parenthesis following the subject—as X)—or preceding the predicate—as (Y—indicates that the total extensions of X and Y are under consideration. If only part of the extension of a term is involved, the parenthesis is reversed—as $X($ or $)Y$. By placing the predicate after the subject together with the respective parentheses, a proposition is formed that states the identity of the extensions as specified by the parentheses. For instance, "X))Y" states that the total extension of X is identical with a part of the extension of Y—i.e., that "All X is Y"; and "X()Y" states that a part of the extension of X is identical with a part of the extension of Y—i.e., that "Some X is Y." To express exclusion between extensions instead of identity, a dot is placed between the parenthesis belonging to the subject and that belonging to the predicate. Thus, "X) . (Y" means that "No X is Y." De Morgan also made use of negated terms, introducing the notion of a logical complement. In his system negated terms are counted as primitive. They are symbolized by small letters; thus, "x" means the same as "non-X," "x" and "X" forming a pair of contradictory terms. Given the use of negative terms, De Morgan examined systematically all of the forms of affirmative categorical propositions. They are:

a. X))Y . . .   Every X is Y.
b. x))y . . .   Every non-X is non-Y.
c. X))y . . .   Every X is non-Y.
d. x))Y . . .   Every non-X is Y.
e. X()Y . . .   Some X is Y.
f. x()y . . .   Some non-X is non-Y.
g. X()y . . .   Some X is non-Y.
h. x()Y . . .   Some non-X is Y.

De Morgan formulated a simple rule for generating propositions equivalent to those above; viz., replace one of the terms by its contradictory, turn its bracket the other way, and put a dot between the brackets—or if there is a dot already present, remove it. Thus, from each of the eight propositions one derives three other equivalent propositions. One now finds that to each proposition involving a negated term there is an equivalent in which both terms are positive. Thus, the original list can now be replaced by the following:

a'. X))Y . . .   Every X is Y.
b'. X((Y . . .   Every Y is X.
c'. X).(Y . . .   No X is Y.
d'. X(.)Y . . .   Everything is either X or Y.
e'. X()Y . . .   Some X is Y.
f'. X)(Y . . .   Something is neither X nor Y.
g'. X(.(Y . . .   Some X is not Y.
h'. X).)Y . . .   Some Y is not X.

The meaning of (d') and that of its contradictory (f'), however, does not quite harmonize with the way in which the symbolism was to be interpreted originally. One would expect, for instance, that (f') should mean the same as "Only every X is Y," thus expressing an identity of the extension of X and that of Y. But this would not be compatible with the meaning of (f).

De Morgan achieved a further extension of his syllogistic vocabulary with the aid of definitions. This extension gave rise to new kinds of inference, both direct (involving

(margin note left) The work of Hamilton and Bentham

(margin note right) Relations between the extensions of terms

New kinds of inference and the theory of relations

one premise) and indirect (involving two premises). Through this symbolism he was able to work out purely structural rules for transforming a premise or a pair of premises into a valid conclusion.

Inferences that appeared to illustrate principles belonging to the logic of noun expressions, but which could not be accommodated in syllogistic, had been known to logicians before De Morgan. It is to him, however, that credit should be given for initiating and developing a theory of relations. He invented a symbolism in which such notions as the contradictory, the converse, and the transitivity of a relation could be expressed, as well as the union of two relations (by which he meant their relative product). He also stated some logical principles, among them:

Contradictories of converses are themselves converses;
Converses of contradictories are contradictories;
The contradictory of the converse is the converse of the contradictory;
If a first relation is contained in a second, then the converse of the first is contained in the converse of the second, and the contradictory of the second is contained in the contradictory of the first;
A transitive relation has a transitive converse;
The contradictory of a transitive relation is not necessarily transitive.

De Morgan also set out, in four figures, various inference schemata analogous, in a sense, to those of syllogistic.

Boole's algebra of logic. Leibniz' pioneering attempts at constructing an algebraical calculus capable of nonarithmetical interpretation were continued by Ploucquet, Lambert, Jean Castillon, an Italian-born mathematician, and others, but the results achieved by them were not of lasting value. Real progress was made by George Boole (died 1864), a self-taught English mathematician who presented his new ideas on logic in the *Mathematical Analysis of Logic* (1847) and in *An Investigation into the Laws of Thought, on Which are Founded the Mathematical Theories of Logic and Probabilities* (1854).

Notion of a "true calculus" and its laws of combination

In Boole's view, the notion of a "true calculus" rests on the employment of symbols in accordance with some general but well-determined laws of combination. Although the combining of symbols in this way should admit of a consistent interpretation, the interpretation should not prejudge the validity of what Boole called the process of analysis; *i.e.*, the process whereby interpretable combinations of symbols are obtained. Whereas Leibniz sought a calculus that admitted of a nonarithmetical interpretation, Boole was advocating a formal calculus that could accommodate a number of different interpretations —in particular, two: one relevant to relations among things, and the other to relations among facts as expressed by propositions. In other words, Boole appears to have been aware of the distinction between the logic of noun expressions and that of propositions, respectively. He did not, however, realize that the logic of noun expressions presupposes the logic of propositions.

Boole's calculus was not a deductive system but it is clear from the way in which it was developed that the following presuppositions were acceptable to him:

1. For all x and y, $xy = yx$.
2. For all x and y, $x + y = y + x$.
3. For all x, y, and z, $x(y + z) = xy + xz$.
4. For all x, y, and z, $x(y - z) = xy - xz$.
5. For all x, y, and z, if $x = y$ then $xz = yz$.
6. For all x, y, and z, if $x = y$ then $x + z = y + z$.
7. For all x, y, and z, if $x = y$ then $x - z = y - z$.
8. For all x, $x(1 - x) = 0$.

Except for the last formula, the system of these presuppositions lends itself to ordinary numerical interpretations. If the values of the variables are restricted to 0 and 1, then the eight presuppositions become interpretable in such a restricted algebra. "The laws, the axioms, and the processes of such an algebra," Boole claimed, "will be identical in their whole extent with the laws, the axioms, and the processes of an algebra of logic." Boole had in mind the interpretation relevant to relations among things; *i.e.*, the class interpretation within the logic of noun expressions. Thus, "$x = y$" means that the classes x

and y have the same members; "xy" represents the intersection of the classes x and y (*i.e.*, their common part); "$x + y$" represents the class consisting of the members of x and the members of y when they have no members in common; "$x - y$" represents the class of those members x that are not members of y; and finally, "1" represents the universal class, of which everything is a member, and "0" the null class, of which nothing is a member.

Boole's calculus can also be interpreted within the logic of propositions. In this interpretation, the variables x, y, and z become propositional variables, "xy" becomes a conjunction of two propositions (read "x and y"), "$x + y$" is exclusive disjunction "Either x or y but not both," and "$-x$" becomes "It is not the case that x." The symbols 1 and 0 are now construed as the standard true and the standard false propositions, respectively. The sign of identity "$=$" becomes that of equivalence "if and only if." Interpreted in this way, the calculus can be extended by adding to it

9. For all x, either $x = 1$ or $x = 0$,

which does not hold for the class interpretation.

Refinements by Jevons and Peirce

Refinements of the calculus. Boolean algebra was subsequently improved by various researchers. William Stanley Jevons, a British economist and logician, rightly urged that all intermediate formulas involved in the process of algebraic transformations should lend themselves to the same interpretation as the initial and final formulas. A further improvement was the replacement of the exclusive by the inclusive disjunction: thus, within the logic of noun expressions, "$x + y$" denoted all those objects each of which was either x but not y, or y but not x, or both x and y. Consequently, it was true to say that "For all x, $x + x = x$," and also that "For all x, $x + -x = 1$." Neither of these formulas obtains, however, in the arithmetical algebra.

For the purpose of computing the validity (or invalidity) of inferences, Jevons constructed a "logical piano," a forerunner of the modern computer.

Charles Sanders Peirce, a U.S. logician, engineer, and Pragmatist philosopher, also held that inclusive disjunction is more suitable for an algebra of logic than exclusive disjunction. In addition, he employed the notion of inclusion, for which he devised a special symbol: $-\!<$. Peirce interpreted "$a -\!< b$" as meaning "Whatever is a is b" or "If a then b." Thus believing, like Boole, that the logic of noun expressions and that of propositions are merely two different interpretations of one and the same algebra of logic, he assimilated propositions to terms expressing relations. Usually, such terms had been thought of as involving two arguments. According to Peirce, however, there is no reason for not subsuming under the notion of relations terms that require three or more arguments (a, b, c, . . .) as well as terms that require one argument (predicates), or no argument (propositions).

Peirce also set up, independently of Frege, an axiom system for the logic of propositions based on "if . . . then" and on the notion of a proposition that implies any proposition; and he systematically developed the truth-table method of defining constant terms within the algebra of logic. He calculated that, given two values T and F (obviously standing for "true" and "false"), there can be four different functors (or operators) for one argument, 16 for two arguments, and 256 for three. Apparently Peirce considered introducing more values than two and thus anticipated the 20th-century development of many-valued logics. Peirce introduced the notion of quantifiers, "For all a, . . ." and "For some a, . . . ," needed in elaborating his theory of relations. And finally, he was responsible for the idea of treating relations as classes of ordered pairs or, more generally, as classes of ordered n-tuples.

Refinements by Schröder

Boole's algebra of logic was given the form of a deductive system by Ernst Schröder, a German logician and mathematician, in his *Operationskreis des Logikkalkuls* (1877; "The Operational Sphere of the Logical Calculus") and, more systematically, in his *Vorlesungen über die Algebra der Logik* (1890–1905; "Lectures on the Algebra of Logic"), which includes the theories of identity and of relations. The system that he had constructed, like that of Peirce, made use of the notion of inclusion, the meaning of which can be determined by reference to diagrams II.1, II.3, II.8, II.9, II.10, II.15, and II.16 in the figure. If inclusion is symbolized thus: $\subset$, then its axioms are:

1. For all a, $a \subset a$.
2. For all a, b, and c, if $a \subset b$ and $b \subset c$ then $a \subset c$.
3. For all a, $0 \subset a$.
4. For all a, $a \subset 1$.
5. For all a, b, and c, $c \subset ab$ if and only if ($c \subset a$ and $c \subset b$).
6. For all a, b, and c, $a + b \subset c$ if and only if ($a \subset c$ and $b \subset c$).
7. For all a, b and c, $a(b + c) = ab + ac$.
8. For all a, $a - a \subset 0$.
9. For all a, $1 \subset a + -a$.

Schröder's interpretation of $+$ was in harmony with that of Jevons and Peirce. At the time of its publication, Schröder's *Vorlesungen* gave, and still gives, the fullest account of an algebra of logic and of its development.

One of the notions investigated by Schröder was that of being an individual, which he defined as follows:

10. For all a, a is an individual if and only if (it is not the case that $a \subset 0$ and for all x, $a \subset x$ or $a \subset -x$).

In addition, he characterized the new notion with the aid of an axiom that states that: "A nonempty class contains at least one individual," or more precisely

11. For all a, if it is not the case that $a \subset 0$, then for some x, $x \subset a$ and x is an individual.

Whereas Schröder's conception of an algebra of logic emphasized the logical aspect of the theory, the inquiries of Alfred North Whitehead, who later became a leading process metaphysician, as presented in *A Treatise on Universal Algebra* (1898), were aimed at integrating the algebra of logic with other branches of mathematics. Extensive studies of the axiomatic foundations of the algebra of logic were successfully undertaken by Edward Vermilye Huntington, a Harvard University mathematician, and by Alfred Tarski, the founder of semantics as part of metalogic.

Logic and the foundations of mathematics. As mentioned earlier, Boolean algebra has interpretations within both the logic of propositions and the logic of noun expressions. Neither Boole nor Schröder, however, was concerned with the relationship between the two interpretations or the two logics. But this was not true of Gottlob Frege, an outstanding German mathematician and an original philosopher. Frege set for himself a new problem, the elucidation of the notion of numbers. He felt that the notion of natural number could be reduced to logical notions and that, consequently, arithmetic could be shown to be a part of logic. Frege therefore devised a symbolic language that, in proving logical or arithmetical theses, dispensed with ordinary usage. By applying axiomatic methods, he hoped to determine the meaning of the vocabulary of the logic of propositions. Thus, for Frege, the problem was to develop a calculus or an algebra for a given interpretation. This he did for "if . . . then" and "it is not the case that" (or simply "not," construed as the negation of a proposition). In terms of ordinary usage, the axioms required for Frege's logic of propositions read as follows:

1. For all p and q, if p then if q then p.
2. For all p, q, and r, if (if p then if q then r) then if (if p then q) then (if p then r).
3. For all p and q, if (if p then q) then (if not-q then not-p).
4. For all p, if not-(not-p) then p.
5. For all p, if p then not-(not-p).

In his *Begriffsschrift: Eine der arithmetischen nachgebildete Formelsprache des reinen Denkens* (1879; "Concept-Script: A Formal Language of Pure Thought on the Pattern of Arithmetic"), the foregoing axiom system is supplemented by the following propositions:

6. For all a, b, and F, if a is the same object as b then if $F(a)$ then $F(b)$.
7. For all a, a is the same object as a.

8. For all a and F, if for all x, $F(x)$ then $F(a)$.

Axioms 6–8 constitute the foundations of a system of the logic of noun expressions or, more precisely, of the logic of predicates.

In *Die Grundlagen der Arithmetik* (1884; Eng. trans., *The Foundations of Arithmetic*, 2nd rev. ed., 1953), Frege discussed, thoroughly but not formally, the notion of number. He first introduced the notion of equality or equinumerosity between concepts by positing that "The concept F is equal to concept G if and only if for some R, R correlates one to one the objects falling under F with the objects falling under G." By the number that belongs to the concept F, Frege understands an extension of the concept "equal to the concept of F." Thus, the following definition of number is formulated: "For all n, n is a number if and only if for some F, n is the number that belongs to F."

A formal reduction of arithmetic to logic was given in Frege's *Grundgesetze der Arithmetik: Begriffsschriftlich abgeleitet* (1893 and 1903; "Basic Laws of Arithmetic: Conceptually Derived"). The axioms and rules of inference given in the *Grundgesetze* differ slightly from those laid down in the *Bergriffsschrift*, and he also added rules for determining the correctness of definitions. Frege also introduced the device of binding variables by the universal quantifier. Finally, Frege made important contributions to the theory of language. His analyses of the notions of sense and reference as well as of object, concept, and function have contributed greatly to the interest in semantics and in theories of meaning.

Another trend in the study of logic and the foundations of mathematics began with the establishment, by the German mathematician and philosopher Georg Cantor (died 1918), of the theory of manifolds or sets as a new mathematical discipline. By a set, Cantor understood "a collection into one whole of definite, distinct objects of our perception or our thought, which are called the elements of the set." Thus, the notion of set appears to have much in common with that of class. A set is uniquely defined by its elements. Sets with identical elements are themselves identical, and identical sets have identical elements. It would appear that set theory is just another version of the logic of noun expressions, similar to one of the interpretations of the algebra of logic. And indeed, a number of set-theoretical notions have their analogues in the algebra of logic and in systems such as that of Frege. Thus, whereas Frege talked about the number belonging to a concept, Cantor made use of the notion of the power or cardinal number of a set, a measure of its order of magnitude. He was especially interested in the cardinal numbers of nonfinite sets. His general theorem, to the effect that the cardinal number of a set is always smaller than that of the set of its subsets, gives rise to a series of transfinite numbers, each of which is the cardinal number of a nonfinite set. The smallest such number is the cardinal number of the set of natural numbers. Preoccupation with the notion of numerical infinity led Cantor to the idea of developing a general arithmetic of transfinite numbers within the framework of his theory of sets. Frege highly appreciated Cantor's *Grundlagen einer allgemeinen mannigfaltigkeitslehre* (1883; "Foundations of a Universal Theory of Manifolds"), which on many counts differed from his own system, mainly in terminology. But, whereas Frege's findings were presented as a deductive system based on axioms and developed in accordance with explicit rules, Cantor's theory of sets was still in a pre-axiomatic stage.

Cantor eventually discovered a paradox in the theory of sets. If one considers the set U that comprises all sets, then its subsets must be among its elements; hence, the cardinal number of U cannot be smaller than that of the set of the subsets of U; yet, in accordance with the general theorem mentioned above, the cardinal number of the set of the subsets of U should be greater than the cardinal number of U. The problem became acute when in 1902 Bertrand Russell, author (with A.N. Whitehead) of the monumental *Principia Mathematica*, discovered another paradox, this time in the system of Frege, involving the notion of the class C of all of those classes that are not

Marginal notes:

Frege's reduction of arithmetic to logic

Cantor's development of set theory

Discovery of fundamental paradoxes

elements of themselves. If the class C is an element of itself, then, like all of the elements of C, it is not an element of itself; but if C is not an element of itself, then it has the property that qualifies it for the membership of C; i.e., it is an element of itself—hence the contradiction. Frege could not find a fault in Russell's reasoning. In a postscript to volume II of his *Grundgesetze*, Frege tried to remedy the situation by altering one of his axioms. It is now known, however, that the corrected system remains contradictory, and Frege himself was not at all confident that he had found the right solution. Nonetheless, the collapse of Frege's system did not prevent Russell from holding, unreservedly, that arithmetic can be derived from logic.

TWENTIETH-CENTURY LOGIC

Logicism, intuitionism, and formalism. When, early in the 20th century, Bertrand Russell set out to show that arithmetic is an extension of logic, he had the benefit of the earlier research of Giuseppe Peano, an Italian mathematician and logician. Peano had not been convinced that the primitive notions of arithmetic—of 0, of number, and of the successor of a number—could be reduced to the vocabulary of logic. He thought it desirable, however, to base arithmetic on axiomatic foundations. A proposal to this effect was first published in his *Arithmetices Principia Nova Methodo Exposita* (1889). In his *Formulaire de mathématiques*, 5 vol. in 3 (1895–1908), Peano made use of the following axiom system for arithmetic:

1. 0 is a number.
2. The successor of any number is a number.
3. No two numbers have the same successor.
4. 0 is not the successor of any number.
5. Any property that belongs to 0, and also to the successor of every number that has the property, belongs to all numbers.

Supplemented with appropriate definitions, these axioms yield all of the characteristic laws of arithmetic; but they fail to single out the progression of natural numbers from other progressions. It is this defect that Russell was anxious to remove by deriving arithmetic from logic. He first approached the problem informally in *The Principles of Mathematics* (1903). Then, in collaboration with Whitehead, he produced the monumental *Principia Mathematica*, 3 vol. (1910–13), which has become a classic of logic. The *Principia* marked a climax of the researches in logic and the foundations of mathematics that had been flourishing since the time of Leibniz. At the same time, it provided a starting point for the development of logic in the 20th century.

In addition to Cantor's paradox in his theory of sets and Russell's proof that Frege's system is contradictory, several other paradoxes were discovered during the 15 years prior to the *Principia* that cast doubt upon men's logical intuitions. Among them were those known as Burali-Forti's paradox of the greatest ordinal number, Berry's paradox of the least integer not nameable in fewer than 19 syllables, Richard's paradox of the class of all decimal numbers definable in a finite number of words, and Grelling's paradox of autological and heterological adjectives. The liar paradox of Eubulides, already known among the ancient Megarian logicians, can also be included in this list. (See ANTINOMY in the *Ready Reference and Index*.)

In the *Principia*, where the paradoxes are discussed at considerable length, Russell argued that they result from a "vicious circle" that consists in assuming illegitimate totalities. A totality is illegitimate when it is supposed to involve *all* of a collection but is itself *one* of the same collection. In the *Principia*, such totalities cannot be generated because of Russell's adoption of the theory of logical types. The theory of logical types demands that a functor or an operator should be regarded as belonging to a higher logical type than any of its arguments, or that a class belongs to a higher logical type than that to which its elements belong. (Similarly, a predicate belongs to a higher logical type than the object of which it is predicated.) Consequently, to say that a class is an element of itself is neither true nor false but simply meaningless. Although the theory of logical types obviated the paradox of the class of all classes not

Russell's logicism and the theory of types

members of themselves, it raised certain problems of its own. It was by no means clear whether the theory was a kind of ontology that classified extra-linguistic entities or a kind of grammar that classified expressions of a logical language. Moreover, some critics charged that it was an ad hoc palliative against paradoxes, and that the ramifications of its hierarchy of types were unduly complicated. Far-reaching suggestions for simplifying the theory were offered by Leon Chwistek, a Polish logician, and the short-lived Cambridge philosopher Frank Ramsey. And, clearly, the paradoxes called for more individual treatment.

Another theory proffered by Russell, of particular interest to philosophers, was his theory of definite descriptions (see ANALYTIC AND LINGUISTIC PHILOSOPHY: *Diversifying and unifying aspects of analytic philosophy*). The *Principia* is a work of impressive scope that, in addition to purely logical topics such as the logic of propositions, and the theories of quantification, of classes, and of relations, includes cardinal arithmetic and the theories of ordinals and of relation-numbers in general, of series, and of measurement.

The view that mathematics is a continuation of logic, with no sharp demarcation between them, has been called "logicism." Opposed to it are intuitionism and formalism. "Intuitionism" is associated with the names of L.E.J. Brouwer, a Dutch mathematician, and his pupil Arend Heyting, according to whom mathematics presupposes mental constructions, which, in turn, presuppose the set of natural numbers. The progression of natural numbers is somehow derived from the intuition of time and the awareness of separable moments of human experience. Thus, intuitionistic mathematics is an activity of thought, and the statement of universal logical laws is not necessary. In particular, intuitionists reject "the thoughtless application of the logical theorem of tertium exclusum," which states that there can be no middle (third) between two contradictories; and by doing so, they believe that they are rejecting, in fact, the principle that every mathematical problem is soluble. They also reject the elimination of double negation, which, in their view, allows its proponents erroneously to infer the provability of a proposition from the unprovability of its negation. Existential statements of the form "There exists an x such that . . ." are prohibited unless they are implied by statements of the form "a is such that . . . ," a restriction that harmonizes with the intuitionistic insistence on constructivism, the view that mathematical proofs must be constrained by the possibilities of finitistic mental constructions. Finally, intuitionists reject the notion of complete or actual infinity; there are no infinite sets other than denumerable sets, such as the set of natural numbers, which exemplifies potential infinity.

Brouwer's intuitionism

Whereas Frege regarded the truth of the axioms of a theory as evidence that the theory is consistent, a Göttingen mathematician, David Hilbert, the founder of modern formalism, maintained that freedom from contradiction in an arbitrarily posited axiom system is the guarantor of the truth of the axioms. Although the problem of whether the fundamental notions of mathematics could be defined in terms of logical notions did not interest Hilbert, he would have answered the question in the negative. He conceived of mathematics as a stock of formulas, which constitute the subject matter of a new mathematics, a "metamathematics," the task of which is to examine and secure the foundations of the former. Hilbert, like Frege, thought very highly of axiomatic methods; but, unlike Frege, he was less concerned with the meaning of the axioms. Within mathematics proper, he advocated a complete formalization with purely formal inferences without any reference to a possible interpretation of the formulas involved. In metamathematics, however, inferences are to have regard to the subject matter. The principal problem of metamathematics is the search for mathematical theories that can be proved to be consistent and complete. As a result of the extensive studies undertaken by Gödel, however, it is known that most interesting mathematical theories are incomplete because every theory that includes the arithmetic of natural numbers is

Hilbert's formalism

incomplete; and in order to prove the consistency of such theories, the consistency of stronger theories must be assumed.

Logic of propositions. As logics became more specialized, it was the logic of propositions that, largely because of its simplicity, attracted the attention of those logicians who favoured specialization. Propositional connectives other than "if . . . then," "or," and "it is not the case that" were examined for their suitability as primitive (or basic) terms in systems of propositional calculus. The method of truth tables that display the T–F values of compound propositions for all combinations of the T–F values of the component propositions was developed by Peirce, by the Polish logician Jan Łukasiewicz, by the U.S. logician Emil Post, a specialist in recursive unsolvability, by the Austrian-English logician and philosopher Ludwig Wittgenstein, and by other logicians to determine the meanings of propositional connectives and to evaluate expressions consisting of connectives and variables. The problem of the interdefinability of the connectives was examined and solved by Henry M. Sheffer, a Harvard logician, who proved that the joint denial "neither . . . nor" and the alternative denial "either it is not the case that . . . or it is not the case that . . ." are each so fundamental that all of the remaining propositional connectives can be defined in terms of it—a finding that had been anticipated by Peirce. J.-G.-P. Nicod, a French logician, found that a system of the calculus of propositions equivalent to that of the *Principia* could be based on a single axiom with the alternative denial as the only primitive notion. On the problem of simplifying the axiomatic foundations of this logic, considerable work was done by Łukasiewicz (died 1956) and by his collaborators in Warsaw and later in Dublin. Efforts to develop systems of the logic of propositions that dispense with certain dubious principles have been made, as in Hilbert's positive calculus, in the minimal calculus of the mathematician Ingebright Johansson of the University of Oslo, and in Heyting's intuitionistic system. Here, too, belong Wilhelm Ackermann, one of Hilbert's collaborators, and his system of rigorous implication, and the system of entailment constructed by Alan Ross Anderson of the University of Pittsburgh, a philosopher of mathematics and science, and N.D. Belnap, his associate.

Leśniewski's prototothetic and Lewis' systems of strict implication

Another line of development consisted in strengthening systems of the logic of propositions by employing internal quantifiers to bind propositional variables. A system extended in this way was set up by Łukasiewicz and Tarski. A still stronger system was envisaged by Stanisław Leśniewski (died 1939), one of the founders of the Warsaw school, who called it a system of "prototothetic." It allowed for the use of functorial variables, such as those for which propositional connectives can be substituted. Axiomatic foundations can be obtained for prototothetic by subjoining to the axioms of a classical system the law of extensionality for propositions; *i.e.*, that "For all p and q (p if and only if q) if and only if for all f, $f(p)$ if and only if $f(q)$." In addition to employing the usual rules of inference, systems of prototothetic are equipped with rules of quantification, definition, and extensionality. The rule of extensionality enables laws of extensionality to be introduced for any semantic category that may be brought into the system by means of definitions. Systems of prototothetic are the richest as regards their vocabulary and syntactical variety, and the strongest as regards their deductive power.

In classical logic, a proposition of the form "If p then q" is considered to be true if and only if it is not the case that both p is true and q is false. This Philonian interpretation of "if . . . then," which was challenged in antiquity, was challenged again, soon after the publication of *Principia*, by Clarence Irving Lewis, a conceptual Pragmatist and author (with C.H. Langford) of *Symbolic Logic* (1932), a classic of modal logic. In this and an earlier work (1918), Lewis distinguished between the material implication of classical logic and strict implication, which he found preferable. Construed as an instance of strict impli-

cation, a proposition of the form "If p then q" is true if and only if it is not possible that p should be true and q false. Lewis's treatment of implication involves the modal notion of possibility and thus marks the beginning of new developments. Lewis suggested several different systems of strict implication (S_1–S_5), and many more have been constructed since. Among them, Gödel's system with necessity as a primitive notion deserves special mention, and so does the system with the notion of contingency, constructed by E.J. Lemmon, an Oxford logician. More recently, the logic of propositions has been enlarged to include deontic logic, the aim of which is to exhibit the use of such expressions as "it ought to be the case that," "it is permissible that," and "it is forbidden that" and to interrelate them with modal notions (see LOGIC, APPLIED: *Practical logic: Deontic logic*).

Łukasiewicz' multi-valued logic

A different approach to extending the logic of propositions was taken by Łukasiewicz. His analysis of the modal notions in Aristotle and his resolve to justify indeterminism suggested the idea of a three-valued logic and of many-valued logics in general (see LOGIC, FORMAL: *Special systems of PC: Nonstandard versions of PC*). In these systems, Łukasiewicz employed the notions of implication, alternation, conjunction, and negation, but the meanings of the corresponding constants— "if . . . then," "or," "and," and "it is not the case that"— differ from their meanings in two-valued logic. Łukasiewicz determined their new meanings with the aid of many-valued truth tables, which, in addition to truth and falsity, allow for intermediate truth-values—such as possibility, for instance. Although Łukasiewicz suggested axiomatic foundations for three-valued and infinitely-many-valued logics, his systems were not complete. Nor was it possible to define, within their framework, all of the constants for which the meaning could be determined with the aid of appropriate truth tables. Many-valued systems that have no such defects have been developed by Bolesław Sobociński, a Notre Dame logician, and by the Polish logician Jerzy Słupecki. Purely formal systems of many-valued logics have been constructed independently by Emil Post.

The most recent and, philosophically, by far the most exciting way of extending the logic of propositions consists in constructing systems of tense logic with a view to clarifying the conception of time (see LOGIC, APPLIED: *Logics of physical application: Temporal logic*). According to the British logician A.N. Prior, the characteristic constants of tense logic are "it has been the case that," "it is now the case that," and "it will be the case that." Several other constants can be introduced by means of appropriate definitions.

Modal logic, deontic logic, tense logic, and, of course, many-valued logics presuppose the abandonment of two-valued logic. In many cases, they also presuppose the rejection of the principle of extensionality. Some logicians, however, do not approve of these serious sacrifices and believe that alternative ways of solving these problems should be explored.

Logic of noun expressions. At the end of the 19th century, the logic of noun expressions had developed the following branches: Aristotle's syllogistic, Leibniz' theory of identity, Schröder's algebra of logic interpreted as a theory of classes and relations, Frege's theory of quantification, and Cantor's set theory. Although in the 20th century some of these branches have been growing on their own, the ideal of comprehensiveness, achieved by the authors of *Principia*, has not been abandoned altogether. As a result of Łukasiewicz' research, syllogistic has been given the form of a modern deductive theory. It has been axiomatized and proved to be consistent and decidable in the sense that every syllogistic or polysyllogistic expression can either be derived from the axioms or shown to be rejected. Other fragments of the logic of noun expressions have been distinguished by logicians and made objects of special studies—such as, for instance, the functional calculus of first order, functional calculi of higher orders, and the functional calculus of order omega (ω), often referred to as the simple theory of types.

The tendency toward comprehensiveness found expression in the system of the logic of noun expressions constructed by Leśniewski, whose interest was aroused by Russell's paradox of the class of all those classes not elements of themselves. Although Leśniewski accepted the need for a theory of logical types, he did not believe that the paradox resulted from confusing types (or "semantic categories" as he called them) but from the failure to realize that class expressions often are used ambiguously. In order to explain this ambiguity, he constructed two theories, called ontology and mereology. Ontology, which is a system of the logic of noun expressions, is obtained by subjoining some ontological axioms to the protothetic, adapting its rules to them, and setting up a rule of ontological definition and a rule of ontological extensionality. In standard systems of ontology, the copula "is" is the only primitive ontological term. Diagrams II.1 and II.3 determine its meaning. In Schröder's algebra, it can be defined as follows: "For all a and b, a is b if and only if both $a \subset b$ and a is an individual." In ontology, it is characterized by the following single axiom: "For all a and b, a is b if and only if (i) for some c, c is a, (ii) for all c and d, if c is a and d is a then c is d, and (iii) for all c, if c is a then c is b." As regards its contents, ontology comprises syllogistic, the theory of identity, a counterpart of the theory of classes, and counterparts of functional calculi of any orders. If required, ontology can be supplemented with the axioms of infinity and of choice. Whereas the logical language of the *Principia* presupposes the concept of proper name, that of ontology is based on common noun expressions, to which proper names are assimilated. The mere use of the language of ontology implies no existential assertions, which is not the case with the language of the *Principia*. Instead of a theory of logical types, Leśniewski had developed a theory of semantic categories, which was inspired by certain ideas of Edmund Husserl, the founder of Phenomenology, and was concerned with the grammar of logical language and not with any extralinguistic entities.

Mereology, which is the theory of part–whole relations, is obtained by subjoining mereological axioms to ontology and adapting the rules of ontology to them. Whereas ontology was meant to provide the foundations of arithmetic, mereology was to serve as the basis of geometry. Mereology, and *a fortiori* ontology, is consistent if prototothetic is consistent. Theories of part–whole relations have also been worked out independently of Leśniewski's mereology by J.H. Woodger, author of an axiomatized biology, by the U.S. logician Henry Leonard, and Nelson Goodman, a U.S. philosopher.

The development of Cantor's theory of sets was greatly affected by the discovery of paradoxes. For, it soon became clear that more solid foundations were required if paradoxes were to be eliminated. With this aim in view,

the German mathematician Ernst Zermelo axiomatized the theory and succeeded in avoiding the paradoxes without resort to the theory of types. The Israeli mathematician Abraham Fraenkel has informally set out Zermelo's axioms:

1. *Axiom of Extensionality:* Sets containing the same members are equal.
2. *Axiom of Pairing:* For any two different sets a and b, there exists a set c that contains just a and b.
3. *Axiom of Union:* For any set a that contains at least one member, there exists the set the members of which are just the members of the members of a.
4. *Axiom of Power-set:* For any set a there exists the set the members of which are just subsets of a.
5. *Axiom Schema of Singling-out:* For any set a and any monadic predicate P, there exists the set that contains just those members x of a that fulfill the condition $P(x)$.
6. *Axiom of Choice:* If a is a disjointed set that does not contain the null-set, the Cartesian product of the members of a is not empty (the Cartesian product of two sets is the set of all pairs having a member from each set).
7. *Axiom of Infinity:* There exists a set a such that the empty set is a member of a and for all b, if b is a member of a then the set of which the only member is b is also a member of a.

This axiom system is deductively strong enough to yield a substantial part of Cantor's theory, but it does not imply the existence of certain special sets presupposed by Cantor. To accommodate these sets, Fraenkel suggested

8. *Axiom of Replacement:* If the domain of a single-valued function is a set, its counter-domain is also a set.

And in order to eliminate certain extraordinary sets, the Hungarian-U.S. mathematician John von Neumann, a pioneer in computer mathematics, proposed:

9. *Axiom of Foundation:* Every non-empty set a contains a member b such that a and b have no members in common.

Von Neumann also distinguished between sets, which can be members of other sets, and classes, which have no such property. Both sets and classes can have members, but the notion of membership in the case of sets is not the same as membership in the cases of classes.

More recently, the Swiss logician and mathematician Paul Bernays, Hilbert's collaborator, has made important contributions to the study of the axiomatic foundations of set theory.

So far, the theory based on the above-listed axioms has proved to be free from contradictions, but the axioms have scarcely made the notion of a set any clearer. If the axioms describe some aspects of reality, it is not known what these aspects are. Thus, the theory is becoming detached from any interpretation.

According to Cantor's "continuum hypothesis," if the cardinal number of a denumerable set is denoted by $\aleph_0$ ("aleph-null") and that of the power-set (the set of all subsets) of a denumerable set by $2^{\aleph_0}$, then there is no cardinal number between $\aleph_0$ and $2^{\aleph_0}$—which means that $2^{\aleph_0} = \aleph_1$. In its generalized form, the hypothesis says that "For any α if α is the cardinal number of an infinite well-ordered set then there is no cardinal number between α and 2^{α}."

In the systems of the logic of noun expressions developed by W.V.O. Quine, a Harvard University logician, the theory of logical types is replaced by the much simpler theory of stratification. A propositional formula is said to be stratified if it is possible to put numerals for the variables in such a way that $\in$ occurs only in contexts of the form "$n \in (n + 1)$." Now, the rule of abstraction, which corresponds to the axiom schema of singling out, stipulates that the formula from which abstraction is made should be stratified. This sort of restriction enabled Quine to abandon the theory of types. His system, first published in 1937 and known as system **NF**, was subsequently developed into system **ML**, published in 1940 and revised in 1951.

Metalogical studies. Once systems of logic had been axiomatized, their development seemed to have slowed down. Instead of proving new theses within the framework of axiomatized systems, logicians began to examine the systems themselves and prove theses about them. This was the beginning of metalogic (*q.v.*), the development of which owes a great deal to Hilbert's conception of metamathematics and to his formalist philosophy of mathematics. The problems that are the concern of metalogic are many and various. In the first place, there are the problems of the consistency and completeness of deductive systems and their decidability (since for some systems one can construct intrinsically undecidable propositions) as well as the problem of the independence of the axioms and that of the definability of primitive terms within an axiom system.

For systems of the logic of propositions, methods have been developed for solving these problems. Thus, the consistency of the calculus of propositions was proved by Post and independently by Łukasiewicz. Methods of proving the completeness of the calculus were worked out by Łukasiewicz and others. Truth tables provided means of determining the decidability of systems and the mutual independence of their axioms. The Italian mathematician Alessandro Padoa (died 1938), a collaborator of Peano, found a method of proving the independence of primitive notions within an axiomatized theory.

Systems of the logic of noun expressions are more difficult objects for metalogical investigation, but here too there are several findings to be recorded. Because of Łukasiewicz' and Słupecki's researches, it is known that syllogistic, as axiomatized by Łukasiewicz, is consistent, decidable, and based upon independent axioms. The completeness of the first order functional calculus was proved by Gödel and its consistency by Hilbert. As Alonzo Church, an eminent U.S. logician, has shown, however, the decision problem for a pure functional calculus of first order is unsolvable, although there is a decision procedure for that part of the calculus that contains monadic functions only. The most interesting finding in this field of study was obtained by Gödel, who succeeded in proving that a system of logic that is deductively strong enough to yield the arithmetic of natural numbers, viz., the system of Russell's *Principia*, is not complete and cannot be made complete by extending its axiomatic foundations. Furthermore, Gödel proved that the consistency of systems that include the arithmetic of natural numbers can only be proved if one assumes the consistency of stronger systems. Other metalogical findings obtained by Gödel concern intuitionistic logic and the theory of sets. In the latter field, Gödel established the fact that the *axiom of choice* and the *generalized continuum hypothesis* are consistent with the remaining axioms provided that these axioms are consistent themselves. The independence of the *axiom of choice* and that of the *generalized continuum hypothesis* were proved, in 1963, by Paul J. Cohen, a Stanford University mathematician, thus opening a new chapter in the history of set theory. It has been proved that Quine's system **ML**, as revised, is consistent if system **NF** is consistent.

Another branch of metalogical studies is syntax, which is concerned with the language of logic and describes the purely formal aspects of that language. One of its tasks is to formulate the directives of a logical system; *i.e.*, the rules of inference, of extensionality, and of definition. Among logicians whose contributions to syntax have been of lasting value are the German-U.S. philosopher Rudolf Carnap, once a member of the Vienna Circle, who defined a number of fundamental syntactical concepts applicable to languages of any form; Leśniewski, who stated the directives of his systems, including the rule of definition, in purely syntactical terms; Kazimierz Ajdukiewicz, a Polish methodologist and philosopher of science, who developed a system of categorial indices to identify syntactical categories of a language; and Gödel, who devised a method of arithmetizing syntax—*i.e.*, of uniquely assigning a number to an expression of symbolic language.

Syntax must be distinguished from semantics, which is another metalogical discipline. Speaking generally, semantics studies the relationship between language and reality. Among semantical concepts are those of truth, denotation, satisfaction, and definition or rather determination. Semantics as a metalogical discipline was established by Tarski, whose paper "Der Wahrheitsbegriff in den formalisierten Sprachen" ("The Concept of Truth in the Formalized Languages"), in the *Studia Philosophica*, vol. I (1935), has become a classic. Tarski also laid the foundations for the theory of logical consequence, which provides a conceptual framework for the study of deductive systems in abstraction from the language in which they are formulated. Independently of Tarski's researches, a thorough study of the concept of logical deducibility was made by Karl Popper, an Austrian-British authority in scientific methodology.

An alternative to the method of expressing logical principles directly with the aid of variables consists in setting up schemata of valid inference. The method was developed by the German mathematician Gerhard Gentzen, who was for several years an assistant to Hilbert, and independently by Stanisław Jaśkowski, a logician of the Warsaw school. Both logicians tried to fashion their systems of logic to reflect the actual procedures of practicing mathematicians; they have therefore come to be known as systems of natural deduction. These systems are widely employed by logicians today.

ROLE OF LOGIC AS AN ELEMENT WITHIN A CULTURE

Both in the West and in the East, the origin of logic is associated with an interest in the grammar of language and in the methodology of argument and discussion, be it in the context of law, religion, or philosophy. More is needed, however, for the successful development of logic: it appears that logic can thrive only in a culture that upholds the conviction that controversies should be settled by the force of reason rather than by the orthodoxy of a dogma or the tradition of a prejudice. This is why logic has made much greater progress in the West than in the East.

It has been acknowledged since the time of Aristotle that logic has a part to play in general education. Before embarking on the study of any science, one should, as Aristotle thought, receive some training in logic. Today logic is taught at almost every university, and for many courses it is a compulsory subject; it is gradually taking over the role that the study of classical languages used to play in general instruction. Indeed, for better understanding the working of one's native language, the study of logic is as helpful as the study of Latin grammar.

According to Plato, the axiomatic method is the best method to use in presenting and codifying knowledge, and for centuries Euclid's *Elements* has served as the paradigm of deductive theory. In the 17th century, when, because of the work of René Descartes, the ideals of clarity and precision were vindicated, it became the ambition of many scholars to present their disciplines *more geometrico*; today, however, it is logic and not geometry that sets the example of precision.

Bertrand Russell once wrote that there are two ways of researching in mathematics: one aims at expansion, the other at exploring the foundations. And the same is true of any other discipline. But it is in exploring the foundations of a science that one again encounters logic; for every science that claims to describe some aspect of reality and allows for proof makes use of logical vocabulary. This means that logic lies at the head of a ramified hierarchy of sciences and can be conceived of as the most abstract and most general description of reality. Viewed in this way, logic has a part to play in philosophy and, more precisely, in metaphysics.

BIBLIOGRAPHY
General histories: CARL VON PRANTL, *Geschichte der Logik im Abendlande*, 4 vol. (1855–70, reprinted 1927 and 1955), notorious for misleading and outdated evaluations, but still useful as a vast collection of quotations; HEINRICH SCHOLZ, *Geschichte der Logik* (1931; Eng. trans., *The Concise History of Logic*, 1961); I.M. BOCHENSKI, *Formale Logik* (1956; rev. Eng. trans., *A History of Formal Logic*, 1961); WILLIAM and MARTHA KNEALE, *The Development of Logic* (1962). See also articles by various authors in *The Encyclopedia of Philosophy*, ed. by PAUL EDWARDS, 8 vol. (1967).

Special periods and cultures: (*Ancient*): I.M. BOCHENSKI, *Ancient Formal Logic* (1951); JAN LUKASIEWICZ, *Aristotle's Syllogistic from the Standpoint of Modern Formal Logic*, 2nd ed. enl. (1957); BENSON MATES, *Stoic Logic*, 2nd ed. (1961). (*Medieval*): PHILOTHEUS BOEHNER, *Medieval Logic* (1952); ERNEST A. MOODY, *Truth and Consequence in Medieval Logic* (1953); NICHOLAS RESCHER, *The Development of Arabic Logic* (1964). (*Modern*): CLARENCE I. LEWIS, *A Survey of Symbolic Logic* (1918; corrected reprint with the omission of ch. 5 and 6, 1960); GEOFFREY T. KNEEBONE, *Mathematical Logic and the Foundations of Mathematics* (1963); and PETER H. NIDDITCH, *The Development of Mathematical Logic* (1962).

Bibliographies: The Journal of Symbolic Logic (issued quarterly since 1936), gives complete bibliographies of logic and of its history from before Leibniz; Bochenski's *History of Formal Logic* (*op. cit.*), gives a full bibliography including bibliography to the Indian and Chinese logics.

(Cz.L.)

Logic, Philosophy of

The term logic comes from the Greek word *logos*. The variety of senses that *logos* possesses may suggest the difficulties to be encountered in characterizing the nature and scope of logic. Among the partial translations of *logos*, there are "sentence," "discourse," "reason," "rule," "ratio," "account" (especially the account of the meaning of an expression), "rational principle," and "definition." Not unlike this proliferation of meanings, the subject matter of logic has been said to be the "laws of thought," "the rules of right reasoning," "the principles of valid

Marginal notes:

Carnap's studies in philosophical syntax and Tarski's in semantics

Foundational function of logic in education

argumentation," "the use of certain words labelled 'logical constants'," "truths (true propositions) based solely on the meanings of the terms they contain," and so on.

LOGIC AS A DISCIPLINE

Nature and varieties of logic.   It is relatively easy to discern some order in the above embarrassment of explanations. Some of the characterizations are in fact closely related to each other. When logic is said, for instance, to be the study of the laws of thought, these laws cannot be the empirical (or observable) regularities of actual human thinking as studied in psychology; they must be laws of correct reasoning, which are independent of the psychological idiosyncrasies of the thinker. Moreover, there is a parallelism between correct thinking and valid argumentation: valid argumentation may be thought of as an expression of correct thinking, and the latter as an internalization of the former. In the sense of this parallelism, laws of correct thought will match those of correct argumentation. The characteristic mark of the latter is, in turn, that they do not depend on any particular matters of fact. Whenever an argument that takes a reasoner from p to q is valid, it must hold independently of what he happens to know or believe about the subject matter of p and q. The only other source of the certainty of the connection between p and q, however, is presumably constituted by the meanings of the terms that the propositions p and q contain. These very same meanings will then also make the sentence "If p, then q" true irrespective of all contingent matters of fact. More generally, one can validly argue from p to q if and only if the implication "If p, then q" is logically true—*i.e.*, true in virtue of the meanings of words occurring in p and q, independently of any matter of fact.

Logic may thus be characterized as the study of truths based completely on the meanings of the terms they contain.

In order to accommodate certain traditional ideas within the scope of this formulation, the meanings in question may have to be understood as embodying insights into the essences of the entities denoted by the terms, not merely codifications of customary linguistic usage.

The following proposition (from Aristotle), for instance, is a simple truth of logic: "If sight is perception, the objects of sight are objects of perception." Its truth can be grasped without holding any opinions as to what, in fact, the relationship of sight to perception is. What is needed is merely an understanding of what is meant by such terms as "if–then," "is," and "are," and an understanding that "object of" expresses some sort of relation.

The logical truth of Aristotle's sample proposition is reflected by the fact that "The objects of sight are objects of perception" can validly be inferred from "Sight is perception."

Many questions nevertheless remain unanswered by this characterization. The contrast between matters of fact and relations between meanings that was relied on in the characterization has been challenged, together with the very notion of meaning. Even if both are accepted, there remains a considerable tension between a wider and a narrower conception of logic. According to the wider interpretation, all truths depending only on meanings belong to logic. It is in this sense that the word logic is to be taken in such designations as "epistemic logic" (logic of knowledge), "doxastic logic" (logic of belief), "deontic logic" (logic of norms), "the logic of science," "inductive logic," and so on. According to the narrower conception, logical truths obtain (or hold) in virtue of certain specific terms, often called logical constants. Whether they can be given an intrinsic characterization or whether they can be specified only by enumeration is a moot point. It is generally agreed, however, that they include (1) such propositional connectives as "not," "and," "or," and "if–then" and (2) the so-called quantifiers "$(\exists x)$" (which may be read: "For at least one individual, call it x, it is true that") and "$(\forall x)$" ("For each individual, call it x, it is true that"). The dummy letter x is here called a bound (individual) variable. Its values are supposed to be members of some fixed class of entities, called individuals, a

Valid argument and matters of fact

The various branches of logic

class that is variously known as the universe of discourse, the universe presupposed in an interpretation, or the domain of individuals. Its members are said to be quantified over in "$(\exists x)$" or "$(\forall x)$." Furthermore, (3) the concept of identity (expressed by $=$) and (4) some notion of predication (an individual's having a property or a relation's holding between several individuals) belong to logic. The forms that the study of these logical constants take are described in greater detail in the articles LOGIC, FORMAL; SYLLOGISTIC; METALOGIC; and LOGIC, APPLIED—in which the different kinds of logical notation are also explained. Here, only a delineation of the field of logic is given.

When the terms in (1) alone are studied, the field is called propositional logic. When (1), (2), and (4) are considered, the field is the central area of logic that is variously known as first-order logic, quantification theory, lower predicate calculus, lower functional calculus, or elementary logic. If the absence of (3) is stressed, the epithet "without identity" is added, in contrast to first-order logic with identity, in which (3) is also included.

Borderline cases between logical and nonlogical constants are the following (among others): (1) Higher order quantification, which means quantification not over the individuals belonging to a given universe of discourse, as in first-order logic, but also over sets of individuals and sets of n-tuples of individuals. (Alternatively, the properties and relations that specify these sets may be quantified over.) This gives rise to second-order logic. The process can be repeated. Quantification over sets of such sets (or of n-tuples of such sets or over properties and relations of such sets) as are considered in second-order logic gives rise to third-order logic; and all logics of finite order form together the (simple) theory of (finite) types. (2) The membership relation, expressed by "ϵ," can be grafted on to first-order logic; it gives rise to set theory (*q.v.*). (3) The concepts of (logical) necessity and (logical) possibility can be added.

This narrower sense of logic is related to the influential idea of logical form. In any given sentence, all of the nonlogical terms may be replaced by variables of the appropriate type, keeping only the logical constants intact. The result is a formula exhibiting the logical form of the sentence. If the formula results in a true sentence for any substitution of interpreted terms (of the appropriate logical type) for the variables, the formula and the sentence are said to be logically true (in the narrower sense of the expression).

Features and problems of logic.   Three areas of general concern are the following.

Logical semantics.   For the purpose of clarifying logical truth and hence the concept of logic itself, a tool that has turned out to be more important than the idea of logical form is logical semantics, sometimes also known as model theory (see METALOGIC: *Model Theory*). By this is meant a study of the relationships of linguistic expressions to those structures in which they may be interpreted and of which they can then convey information. The crucial idea in this theory is that of truth (absolutely or with respect to an interpretation). It was first analyzed in logical semantics around 1930 by the Polish-American logician Alfred Tarski. In its different variants, logical semantics is the central area in the philosophy of logic. It enables the logician to characterize the notion of logical truth irrespective of the supply of nonlogical constants that happen to be available to be substituted for variables, although this supply had to be used in the characterization that turned on the idea of logical form. It also enables him to identify logically true sentences with those that are true in every interpretation (in "every possible world").

The ideas on which logical semantics is based are not unproblematic, however. For one thing, a semantical approach presupposes that the language in question can be viewed "from the outside"; *i.e.*, considered as a calculus that can be variously interpreted and not as the all-encompassing medium in which all communication takes place (logic as calculus versus logic as language).

Furthermore, in most of the usual logical semantics the

Truth as defined in model theory

very relations that connect language with reality are left unanalyzed and static. Ludwig Wittgenstein, an Austrian-born philosopher, discussed informally the "language-games"—or rule-governed activities connecting a language with the world—that are supposed to give the expressions of language their meanings; but these games have scarcely been related to any systematic logical theory. Only a few other attempts to study the dynamics of the representative relationships between language and reality have been made. The simplest of these suggestions is perhaps that the semantics of first-order logic should be considered in terms of certain games (in the precise sense of game theory) that are, roughly speaking, attempts to verify a given first-order sentence. The truth of the sentence would then mean the existence of a winning strategy in such a game.

Limitations of logic. Many philosophers are distinctly uneasy about the wider sense of logic. Some of their apprehensions, voiced with special eloquence by a contemporary Harvard University logician, Willard Van Quine, are based on the claim that relations of synonymy cannot be fully determined by empirical means. Other apprehensions have to do with the fact that most extensions of first-order logic do not admit of a complete axiomatization; *i.e.*, their truths cannot all be derived from any finite—or recursive (see below)—set of axioms. This fact was shown by the important "incompleteness" theorems proved in 1931 by Kurt Gödel, an Austrian (later, American) logician, and their various consequences and extensions. (Gödel showed that any consistent axiomatic theory that comprises a certain amount of elementary arithmetic is incapable of being completely axiomatized.) Higher-order logics are in this sense incomplete and so are all reasonably powerful systems of set theory. Although a semantical theory can be built for them, they can scarcely be characterized any longer as giving actual rules—in any case complete rules—for right reasoning or for valid argumentation. Because of this shortcoming, several traditional definitions of logic seem to be inapplicable to these parts of logical studies.

Incompleteness of higher-order logics

These apprehensions do not arise in the case of modal logic, which may be defined, in the narrow sense, as the study of logical necessity and possibility; for even quantified modal logic admits of a complete axiomatization. Other, related problems nevertheless arise in this area. It is tempting to try to interpret such a notion as logical necessity as a syntactical predicate; *i.e.*, as a predicate the applicability of which depends only on the form of the sentence claimed to be necessary—rather like the applicability of formal rules of proof. It has been shown, however, by Richard Montague, an American logician, that this cannot be done for the usual systems of modal logic.

Logic and computability. These findings of Gödel and Montague are closely related to the general study of computability, which is usually known as recursive function theory (see MATHEMATICS, FOUNDATIONS OF: *The crisis in foundations following 1900: Logicism, formalism, and the metamathematical method*) and which is one of the most important branches of contemporary logic. In this part of logic, functions—or laws governing numerical or other precise one-to-one or many-to-one relationships—are studied with regard to the possibility of their being computed; *i.e.*, of being effectively—or mechanically—calculable. Functions that can be so calculated are called recursive. Several different and historically independent attempts have been made to define the class of all recursive functions, and these have turned out to coincide with each other. The claim that recursive functions exhaust the class of all functions that are effectively calculable (in some intuitive informal sense) is known as Church's thesis (named after the American logician Alonzo Church).

One of the definitions of recursive functions is that they are computable by a kind of idealized automaton known as a Turing machine (named after Alan Mathison Turing, a British mathematician and logician). Recursive function theory may therefore be considered a theory of these idealized automata. The main idealization involved (as compared with actually realizable computers) is the availability of a potentially infinite tape.

The theory of computability prompts many philosophical questions, most of which have not so far been answered satisfactorily. It poses the question, for example, of the extent to which all thinking can be carried out mechanically. Since it quickly turns out that many functions employed in mathematics—including many in elementary number theory—are nonrecursive, one may wonder whether it follows that a mathematician's mind in thinking of such functions cannot be a mechanism and whether the possibly nonmechanical character of mathematical thinking may have consequences for the problems of determinism and free will. Further work is needed before definitive answers can be given to these important questions.

ISSUES AND DEVELOPMENTS IN THE PHILOSOPHY OF LOGIC

In addition to the problems and findings already discussed, the following topics may be mentioned.

Meaning and truth. Since 1950, the concept of analytical truth (logical truth in the wider sense) has been subjected to sharp criticism, especially by Quine. The main objections turned around the nonempirical character of analytical truth (arising from meanings only) and of the concepts in terms of which it could be defined—such as synonymy, meaning, and logical necessity. The critics usually do not contest the claim that logicians can capture synonymies and meanings by starting from first-order logic and adding suitable further assumptions, though definitory identities do not always suffice for this purpose. The crucial criticism is that the empirical meaning of such further "meaning postulates" is not clear.

Analytical truth

Logical semantics of modal concepts. In this respect, logicians' prospects have been enhanced by the development of a semantical theory of modal logic, both in the narrower sense of modal logic, which is restricted to logical necessity and logical possibility, and in the wider sense, in which all concepts that exhibit similar logical behaviour are included. This development, initiated between 1957 and 1959 largely by Stig Kanger of Sweden and Saul Kripke of the U.S., has opened the door to applications in the logical analysis of many philosophically central concepts, such as knowledge, belief, perception, and obligation. Attempts have been made to analyze from the viewpoint of logical semantics such philosophical topics as sense-datum theories, knowledge by acquaintance, the paradox of saying and disbelieving propounded by the British philosopher G.E. Moore, and the traditional distinction between statements *de dicto* ("from saying") and statements *de re* ("from the thing"). These developments also provide a framework in which many of those meaning relations can be codified that go beyond first-order logic, and may perhaps even afford suggestions as to what their empirical content might be.

Intensional logic. Especially in the hands of Montague, the logical semantics of modal notions has blossomed into a general theory of intensional logic; *i.e.*, a theory of such notions as proposition, individual concept, and in general of all entities usually thought of as serving as the meanings of linguistic expressions. (Propositions are the meanings of sentences, individual concepts are those of singular terms, and so on.) A crucial role is here played by the notion of a possible world, which may be thought of as a variant of the logicians' older notion of model, now conceived of realistically as a serious alternative to the actual course of events in the world. In this analysis, for instance, propositions are functions that correlate possible worlds with truth-values. This correlation may be thought of as spelling out the older idea that to know the meaning of a sentence is to know under what circumstances (in which possible worlds) it would be true.

Logic and information. Even though none of the problems listed seems to affect the interest of logical semantics, its applications are often handicapped by the nature of many of its basic concepts. One may consider, for instance, the analysis of a proposition as a function that correlates possible worlds with truth-values. An arbi-

Possible worlds and truth-values

trary function of this sort can be thought of (as can functions in general) as an infinite class of pairs of correlated values of an independent variable and of the function, like the coordinate pairs (x, y) of points on a graph. Although propositions are supposed to be meanings of sentences, no one can grasp such an infinite class directly when understanding a sentence; he can do so only by means of some particular algorithm, or recipe (as it were), for computing the function in question. Such particular algorithms come closer in some respects to what is actually needed in the theory of meaning than the meaning entities of the usual intensional logic.

This observation is connected with the fact that, in the usual logical semantics, no finer distinctions are utilized in semantical discussions than logical equivalence. Hence the transition from one sentence to another logically equivalent one is disregarded for the purposes of meaning concepts. This disregard would be justifiable if one of the most famous theses of Logical Positivists were true in a sufficiently strong sense, viz., that logical truths are really tautologies (such as "It is either raining or not raining") in every interesting objective sense of the word. Many philosophers have been dissatisfied with the stronger forms of this thesis, but only recently have attempts been made to spell out the precise sense in which logical and mathematical truths are informative and not tautologous.

Problems of ontology. Among the ontological problems—problems concerning existence and existential assumptions—arising in logic are those of individuation and existence.

Individuation. Not all interesting interpretational problems are solved by possible-world semantics, as the developments earlier registered are sometimes called. The systematic use of the idea of possible worlds has raised, however, the subject of cross identification; *i.e.*, of the principles according to which a member of one possible world is to be found identical or nonidentical with one of another. Since one can scarcely be said to have a concept of an individual if he cannot locate it in several possible situations, the problem of cross-identification is also one of the most important ingredients of the logical and philosophical problem of individuation. The criticisms that Quine has put forward concerning modal logic and analyticity (see above) can be deepened into questions concerning methods of cross identification. Although some such methods undoubtedly belong to everyone's normal unarticulated conceptual repertoire, it is not clear that they are defined or even definable widely enough to enable philosophers to make satisfactory sense of a quantified logic of logical necessity and logical possibility. The precise principles used in ordinary discourse —or even in the language of science—pose a subtle philosophical problem. The extent to which special "essential properties" are relied on in individuation and the role of spatio-temporal frameworks are moot points here. It has also been suggested that essentially different methods of cross identification are actually used together, some of them depending on impersonal descriptive principles and others on the perspective of a person.

Existence and ontology. Because one of the basic concepts of first-order logic is that of existence, as codified by the existential quantifier "$(\exists x)$," one might suppose that there is little room left for any separate philosophical problem of existence. Yet existence, in fact, does seem to pose a problem, as witnessed by the bulk of the relevant literature. Some issues are relatively easy to clarify. In the usual formulations of first-order logic, for instance, there are "existential presuppositions" present to the effect that none of the singular terms employed is without a bearer (as "Pegasus" is). It is a straightforward matter, however, to dispense with these presuppositions. Though this seems to involve the procedure, branded as inadmissible by many philosophers, of treating existence as a predicate, this can nonetheless be easily done on the formal level. Given certain assumptions, it may even be shown that this "predicate" will have to be "$(\exists x)\ (x = a)$" (for "a exists"—literally, "There exists an x such that x is a") or something equivalent. Furthermore, the

logical peculiarities of this predicate seem to explain amply philosophers' apparent denial of its reality.

The interest in the notion of existence is connected with the question of what entities a theory commits its holder to or what its "ontology" is. The "predicate of existence" just mentioned recalls Quine's criterion of ontological commitment: "To be is to be a value of a bound variable"—*i.e.*, of the x in $(\forall x)$ or in $(\exists x)$. According to Quine, a theory is committed to those and only those entities that in the last analysis serve as the values of its bound variables. Thus ordinary first-order theory commits one to an ontology only of individuals (particulars), whereas higher order logic commits one to the existence of sets—*i.e.*, of collections of definite and distinct entities (or, alternatively, of properties and relations). Likewise, if bound first-order variables are assumed to range over sets (as they do in set theory), a commitment to the existence of these sets is incurred.

Entities to which a theory is committed

The doctrine that an ontology of individuals is all that is needed is known as (the modern version of) nominalism. The opposite view is known as (logical) realism. Even those philosophers who profess sympathy with nominalism find it hard, however, to maintain that mathematics could be built on a consistently nominalistic foundation.

The precise import of Quine's criterion of ontological commitment, however, is not completely clear. Nor is it clear in what other sense one is perhaps committed by a theory to those entities that are named or otherwise referred to in it but not quantified over in it. Questions can also be raised concerning the very distinction between what in modern logic are usually called individuals ("particulars" would be a more traditional designation) and such universals as their properties and relations; and these questions can be combined with others concerning the "tie" that binds particulars and universals together in predication.

An interesting approach to these problems is the distinction made by Gottlob Frege, a pioneer of mathematical logic in the late 19th century, between individuals—he called them objects—and what he called functions (which in his view include concepts) and his doctrine of the unsaturated character of the latter, according to which a function (as it were) contains a gap, which can be filled by an object. Another approach is the "picture theory of language" of Wittgenstein's *Tractatus Logico-Philosophicus*, according to which a simple sentence presents a person with an isomorphic representation (a "picture") of reality as it would be if the sentence were true. According to this view (which was later given up by Wittgenstein), "a sentence [or proposition, *Satz*] is a model of reality such as we think of it as being."

Alternative logics. The natures of most of the so-called nonclassical logics can be understood against the background of what has here been said. Some of them are simply extensions of the "classical" first-order logic—*e.g.*, modal logics and many versions of intensional logic. The so-called free logics are simply first-order (or modal) logics without existential presuppositions.

One of the most important nonclassical logics is intuitionistic logic (see MATHEMATICS, FOUNDATION OF: *The crisis in foundations following 1900: Intuitionism*), first formalized by the Dutch mathematician Arend Heyting in 1930. It has been shown that this logic can be interpreted in terms of the same kind of modal logic serving as a system of epistemic logic. In the light of its purpose to consider only the known, this isomorphism is suggestive. The avowed purpose of the intuitionist is to consider only what can actually be established constructively in logic and in mathematics—*i.e.*, what can actually be *known*. Thus, he refuses to consider, for example, "Either A or not-A" as a logical truth, for it does not actually help one in knowing whether A or not-A is the case. This does not close, however, the philosophical problem about intuitionism. Special problems arise from intuitionists' rejection (in effect) of the nonepistemic aspects of logic, as illustrated by the fact that only a part of epistemic logic is needed in this translation of intuitionistic logic into epistemic logic.

Intuitionistic logic

Other new logics are obtained by modifying the rules of

those games that are involved in the game-theoretical interpretation of first-order logic mentioned above. The logician may reject, for instance, the assumption that he possesses perfect information, an assumption that characterizes classical first-order logic. One may also try to restrict the strategy sets of the players—to recursive strategies, for example.

Among the oldest kinds of alternative logics are many-valued logics. In them, more truth values than the usual true and false are assumed. The idea seems very natural when considered in abstraction from the actual use of logic. But a philosophically satisfactory interpretation of many-valued logics is not equally straightforward. The interest in finite-valued logics and the applicability of them are sometimes exaggerated. The idea, however, of using the elements of an arbitrary Boolean algebra—a generalized calculus of classes—as abstract truth-values has provided a powerful tool for systematic logical theory.

LOGIC AND OTHER DISCIPLINES

Technical disciplines. The relations of logic to mathematics, to computer technology, and to the empirical sciences are here considered.

Mathematics. It is usually said that all of mathematics can, in principle, be formulated in a sufficiently theorem-rich system of axiomatic set theory. What the axioms of a set theory that could accomplish this might be, however, and whether they are at all natural is not obvious in every case. (The recent development in abstract algebra known as category theory offers the most conspicuous examples of these problems.) The axioms of set theory may be presumed to hold in virtue of the meanings of the terms set, member of, and so on. Thus, in some loose sense all of pure mathematics falls within the scope of logic in the wider sense. This assertion is not very informative, however, as long as the logician has no ways of analyzing these meanings so as to be able to tell what assumptions (axioms of set theory) should be adopted. The definitions of basic mathematical concepts (such as "number") in logical terms proposed by Gottlob Frege (in 1884), by Bertrand Russell (in 1903), and by their successors do not help in this enterprise. It is not clear that more recent insights in logic help very much, either, in the search for strong set-theoretical assumptions. The relationship of mathematics to logic on this level therefore remains ambiguous.

Notwithstanding these deep problems, virtually all normal mathematical argumentation is carried out in logical terms—mostly in first-order terms, but with a generous sprinkling of second-order reasoning and various principles of set theory. Historically speaking, most specific early examples of nontrivial logical reasoning were taken from mathematics.

Often these examples were set in contrast to logical arguments understood in a narrow traditional sense—in a sense narrower still than the idea of logic as being exhausted by quantification theory. According to this traditional view, logic is equated with syllogistic (*q.v.*); *i.e.*, with a part of that part of first-order logic that deals with properties and not with relations. Much of what earlier philosophers said of mathematical reasoning must, thus, be understood as applying to relational (first-order) reasoning. The present-day philosophy of logic is therefore as much an heir to traditional philosophy of mathematics as to traditional philosophy of logic.

Specific logical results are applicable in several parts of mathematics, especially in algebra, and various concepts and techniques used by logicians have often been borrowed from mathematics. (Thus one can even speak of "the mathematics of metamathematics.")

Computers. It has already been indicated that recursive function theory is, in effect, the study of certain idealized automata (computers). It is, in fact, a matter of indifference whether this theory belongs to logic or to computer science. The idealized assumption of a potentially infinite computer tape, however, is not a trivial one: Turing machines typically need plenty of tape in their calculations. Hence the step from Turing machines to

finite automata (which are not assumed to have access to an infinite tape) is an important one.

This limitation does not dissociate computer science from logic, however, for other parts of logic are also relevant to computer science and are constantly employed there. Propositional logic may be thought of as the "logic" of certain simple types of switching circuits. There are also close connections between automata theory and the logical and algebraic study of formal languages. An interesting topic on the borderline of logic and computer science is mechanical theorem proving, which derives some of its interest from being a clear-cut instance of the problems of artificial intelligence, especially of the problems of realizing various heuristic modes of thinking on computers. In theoretical discussions in this area, it is nevertheless not always understood how much textbook logic is basically trivial and where the distinctively nontrivial truths of logic (including first-order logic) lie.

Methodology of the empirical sciences. The quest for theoretical self-awareness in the empirical sciences has led to interest in methodological and foundational problems as well as to attempts to axiomatize different empirical theories. Moreover, general methodological problems, such as the nature of scientific explanations, have been discussed intensively among philosophers of science. In all of these endeavours, logic plays an important role.

By and large, there are here three different lines of thought. (1) Often, only the simplest parts of logic—*e.g.*, propositional logic—are appealed to (over and above the mere use of logical notation). Sometimes, claims regarding the usefulness of logic in the methodology of the empirical sciences are, in effect, restricted to such rudimentary applications. This restriction is misleading, however, for most of the interesting and promising connections between methodology and logic lie on a higher level, especially in the area of model theory. In econometrics, for instance, a special case of the logicians' problems of definability plays an important role under the title "identification problem." On a more general level, logicians have been able to clarify the concept of a model as it is used in the empirical sciences.

In addition to those employing simple logic, two other contrasting types of theorists can be distinguished: (2) philosophers of science, who rely mostly on first-order formulations, and (3) methodologists (*e.g.*, Patrick Suppes, a U.S. philosopher and behavioral scientist), who want to use the full power of set theory and of the mathematics based on it. Both approaches have advantages. Usually realistic axiomatizations and other reconstructions of actual scientific theories are possible only in terms of set theoretical and other strong mathematical conceptualizations (theories conceived of as "set-theoretical predicates"). In spite of the oversimplification that first-order formulations often entail, however, they can yield theoretical insights because first-order logic (including its model theory) is mastered by logicians much more thoroughly than is set theory.

Many empirical sciences, especially the social sciences, use mathematical tools borrowed from probability theory and statistics, together with such outgrowths of these as decision theory, game theory, utility theory, and operations research. A modest but not uninteresting beginning in the study of their foundations has been made in modern inductive logic.

Human disciplines. The relations of logic to linguistics, psychology, law, and education are here considered.

Linguistics. The revival of interest in semantics among theoretical linguists in the late 1960s awakened their interest in the interrelations of logic and linguistic theory as well. It was also discovered that certain grammatical problems are closely related to logicians' concepts and theories. A near-identity of linguistics and "natural logic" has been claimed by the U.S. linguist George Lakoff. Among the many conflicting and controversial developments in this area, special mention may perhaps be made of attempts by Jerrold J. Katz, a U.S. grammarian-philosopher, and others to give a linguistic characterization of such fundamental logical notions as analyticity; the sketch by Montague of a "universal grammar" based on his intensional logic; and the suggestion (by several logicians and linguists) that what linguists call "deep structure" is to be identified with logical form. Of a much less controversial nature is the extensive and fruitful use of recursive function theory and related areas of logic in formal grammars and in the formal models of language users.

Psychology. Although the "laws of thought" studied in logic are not the empirical generalizations of a psychologist, they can serve as a conceptual framework for psychological theorizing. Probably the best known recent example of such theorizing is the large-scale attempt made in the mid-20th century by Jean Piaget, a Swiss psychologist, to characterize the developmental stages of a child's thought by reference to the logical structures that he can master.

Elsewhere in psychology, logic is employed mostly as an ingredient of various models using mathematical ideas or ideas drawn from such areas as automata or information theory. Large-scale direct uses are rare, however, partly because of the problems mentioned above in the section on logic and information.

Law. Of the great variety of kinds of argumentation used in the law, some are persuasive rather than strictly logical, and others exemplify different procedures in applied logic rather than the formulas of pure logic. Examinations of "Lawiers Logike"—as the subject was called in 1588—have also uncovered a variety of arguments belonging to the various departments of logic mentioned above. Such inquiries do not seem to catch the most characteristic kinds of legal conceptualization, however —with one exception, *viz.*, a theory developed by Wesley Newcomb Hohfeld, a pre-World War I U.S. legal scholar, of what he called the fundamental legal conceptions. Although originally presented in informal terms, this theory is closely related to recent deontic logic (in some cases in combination with suitable causal notions). Even some of the apparent difficulties are shared by the two approaches: the deontic logician's notion of permission, for example, which is often thought of as being unduly weak, is to all practical purposes a generalization of Hohfeld's concept of privilege.

Education. After having been one of the main ingredients of the general school curriculum for centuries, logic virtually disappeared from liberal education during the first half of the 20th century. It has made major inroads back into school curricula, however, as a part of the new mathematical curriculum that came into fairly general use in the 1960s, which normally includes the elements of propositional logic and of set theory. Logic is also easily adapted to being taught by computers and has been used in experiments with computer-based education.

Marginal note (left): Hohfeld's theory and deontic logic

BIBLIOGRAPHY. W.V. QUINE, *Philosophy of Logic* (1970), is the best compact introductory exposition. HILARY PUTNAM, *Philosophy of Logic* (1971), is useful as a complement to Quine. Much of the important recent literature, however, is in the form of brief papers rather than monographs. The most successful anthologies of such papers are perhaps L.W. SUMNER and JOHN WOODS (eds.), *Necessary Truth* (1969), on logical truth and analyticity; and LEONARD LINSKY (ed.), *Reference and Modality* (1971), on modal concepts and intensional logic. RAYMOND KLIBANSKY (ed.), *Contemporary Philosophy*, vol. 1 (1968), contains several survey articles covering thoroughly the whole field. Still central are the classical writings of the great modern philosophers of logic: PETER GEACH and MAX BLACK (eds.), *Translations from the Philosophical writings of Gottlob Frege*, 2nd ed. (1960); BERTRAND RUSSELL, *Logic and Knowledge* (1956); LUDWIG WITTGENSTEIN, *Tractatus logico-philosophicus* (Eng. trans., 1922) and *Philosophical Investigations* (Eng. trans., 1953); ALFRED TARSKI, *Logic, Semantics, and Metamathematics* (1956); and RUDOLF CARNAP, *Meaning and Necessity* (1947). The period 1879–1931 is also covered in a magnificent volume by JEAN VAN HEIJENOORT (ed.), *From Frege to Gödel: A Source Book in Mathematical Logic, 1879–1931* (1967), which contains valuable introductions to the different selections and comments on them. Of recent literature, especially noteworthy are the writings of Strawson and Quine: P.F. STRAWSON, *Logico-Linguistic Papers* (1971); W.V. QUINE, *From a Logical Point of View* (1953), *Word and Object* (1960), and *Ontological Relativity and Other Essays* (1969). Quine's ideas are discussed critically in DONALD DAVIDSON and JAAKKO HINTIKKA (eds.), *Words and Objections* (1969). A broad spectrum of new work on the borderline of philosophical logic and linguistics is represented in DONALD DAVIDSON and GILBERT HARMAN (eds.), *Semantics of Natural Language* (1972). Several problems mentioned above are discussed in JAAKKO HINTIKKA, *Logic, Language-Games, and Information* (1972); and in J.W. DAVIS, D.J. HOCKNEY, and W.K. WILSON (eds.), *Philosophical Logic* (1969).

(K.J.Hi.)

Logistics Systems, Military

The word logistics stems from the Greek word *logistikos*, "the science of computation, or calculating." "Logista" was the title of administrative officials in the Roman and Byzantine armies. A cognate French word, *loger*, means the billeting of soldiers, and in the late 17th century the French staff officer responsible for the quartering and movement of troops was the *maréchal des logis*, or quartermaster general. His staff was linked with a branch of the French military engineers, the *ingénieurs géographes*, whose task was to make maps and draw up memoranda of operational areas for use in planning the movement and maintenance of armies. Baron Jomini, an early 19th-century authority on Napoleonic warfare, in his book *Précis de l'art de la guerre* (1836), defined logistics as "the practical art of moving armies" in which he included reconnaissance, engineer, and staff work. The purpose was to produce a logistical approach to battle and so to achieve strategic and tactical mobility and surprise.

Jomini's logistic theories had little impact on military thought in Europe and the term itself fell into disuse. It was revived in 1882 by then U.S. Captain (later Admiral) Alfred Thayer Mahan, who defined logistics as the support of armed forces by the economic and industrial mobilization of a nation.

Marginal note (right): Mahan's definition of logistics

From 1918 the U.S. armed forces increasingly used logistics to describe the activities of the Ordnance Department and Quartermaster Corps, embracing a wide range of staff duties including supply, transportation, construction, and medical service. The term was seldom used elsewhere until World War II. In the Royal Army, administration covered all activities connected with the interior economy of units in peace, and their supply, movement, and maintenance in war. Neither logistics nor administration was used by European armies. The French *intendance*, "management of supply," led to the title of *intendant general* for the officer in continental armies responsible for supply.

Logistics is today an official term in the military terminology of NATO (North Atlantic Treaty Organization) countries, and with the complexity of modern war it has acquired a wider meaning. It is concerned not only with the movement and maintenance of forces and the evacuation and hospitalization of personnel but also with the design, development, acquisition, storage, and distribution of material—in other words, the procurement of weapons, their associated systems, and all other materials of war. The term administration is increasingly used to denote personnel management and the day-to-day handling of men in matters affecting pay, discipline and morale. The distinction between the two terms remains blurred. The British, for instance, have recently created a chief of personnel and logistics in the Ministry of Defense. Where administration ends and logistics begins is a matter of importance only to the military pedant and writer of official terms.

The complexity of modern war imposes many strains on the logistic planners who must recognize the speed and depth of operations, the vulnerability of lines of communication to air and ground attack, and the vast organization needed for the maintenance of modern forces.

Military logistics is an inexact science. Its data vary between the precise and the problematical. Though experience can minimize the uncertain factors, it will never eliminate the need for common sense, imagination, anticipation, and preparation. Logistic planning is the intelligent forecasting of the requirements of an operation.

The history and development of logistics systems

EARLY WARS

The armies of ancient history lived off the country or were self-contained; that is, the supplies they needed were brought with them in their invading ships. This was the pattern of maintenance when the Persian army invaded Greece in 490 and 481 BC. The larger Greek armies of Xenophon, Epaminondas, and Alexander the Great, in the 4th century BC, needed more support. Supply bases were established. Elephants and camels were used in Alexander's march of 4,000 miles from Egypt through Persia to India. The Roman wars of the 3rd and 2nd centuries BC saw supply depots established and stocked from local sources of food and forage. Hannibal's march from Spain across the Alps into Italy was a masterpiece of logistic planning. Large numbers of elephants brought from Africa were used to carry supplies over the Alps. The Roman legions stationed throughout the provinces of the Empire were supplied from fortified depots at regular intervals of 16 miles, or one day's march, along the routes of march. In an emergency a legion could carry up to 30 days' supply of food. The legions' ability to march fast and far owed much to the excellent roads built by the army. The engineers, artificers, and armourers brought repair shops with them.

Hannibal's march

After the fall of the Roman Empire, the army of the Byzantine Empire (AD 600) achieved a degree of administrative efficiency surpassing all previous efforts. Belisarius organized the provinces of the empire into military districts, each of which provided a field force of one cavalry division, maintained in peace by tax levied on the provinces and administered by their governors. Each field division of the standing army had its own engineers, supply trains, and medical services and was on a permanent war footing, always ready for operations outside the empire.

The Mongolian cavalry armies of Genghis Khan and Sabutai that invaded China and Europe had no supply problem. By nature they lived frugally and moved quickly. Each man had three spare horses. One was a mare from which he drew kumiss, the mare's milk, and the other two were his spare chargers, which in extremity he ate.

When the Mongol army drew near its objective it left the spare horses behind and, dividing into separate columns, converged on the enemy rapidly from several directions. Using this method in his invasion of Hungary (1241), Sabutai covered 180 miles in three days, outmanoeuvring Polish, German, and Bohemian armies before surprising and annihilating the Hungarian army on the Danube.

THE 17TH AND 18TH CENTURIES

The Thirty Years' War, 1618–48, devastated central Europe as essentially mercenary armies pillaged the countryside. Partly as a result, international laws on the conduct of war were introduced and pillage was prohibited. Armies became disciplined bodies of long-service professional soldiers restricted as to their conduct in peace and war. In 1650 the marquis de Louvois, war minister of Louis XIV of France, introduced a new system. The French Army was supplied by a regular commissariat service and a system of wagon trains based on magazines stocked from the home base or by purchase of local produce. This system contained the essential elements of a logistic organization and set the pattern for the supply and maintenance of armies for over a century. But the new system, instead of improving the mobility of armies, limited the speed and scope of military operations. Armies were restricted to the few roads, and even in the summer months movement was limited to seven marches from the nearest magazine and two from a field bakery. Defense or capture of the magazines, situated in fortresses or fortified towns, became the principal preoccupation of generalship. To force an enemy to consume his supplies was much; to compel him to supply his opponent was more; to take up winter quarters in his territory was victory. The supply and maintenance of armies had become the master of strategy instead of its servant.

The Duke of Marlborough broke away from these sterile theories in his march to the Danube and the victory of Blenheim, a masterpiece of logistic planning, in 1704. The commissary general ensured that provisions were ready at every halt of the 400-mile march down the Rhine. Credit for their payment was assured with German bankers. New boots were provided for the army of 40,000 men on its arrival in Bavaria. The good order of the men and the excellent condition of the horses was the result of Marlborough's genius in administrative planning and the meticulous detail of his preparations.

The French Revolutionary Wars (1792–99) brought about a change in the meaning of logistics. The *levée en masse* ("general conscription") placed France on a total war footing. Supplies, transport, and services were requisitioned from the civil authorities under penalty of imprisonment or fine. Payment was seldom made. Conscription was introduced; in the *levée en masse* young men were drafted into fighting units, older men into the forging of weapons and the transport of supplies, and women into tentmaking and hospital service.

Introduction of conscription

The Napoleonic Wars (1800–15) saw another change in the meaning of logistics. The French Army was reorganized into permanent corps and divisions, which Napoleon used to increase the scope of strategic manoeuvre and to accelerate tactical operations. Logistics and strategy became virtually synonymous. The duties of the quartermaster general became those of a chief of staff through whom the commander in chief issued his orders. Marshal Louis-Alexandre Berthier, formerly *maréchal des logis* ("quartermaster general") under the revolutionary regime, was Napoleon's chief of staff. Similarly Sir Archibald Murray, Wellington's quartermaster general in Spain, was chief of staff, with duties including intelligence, map making, and the issue of orders for all types of movement, both on the field of battle and in rear areas.

The commissary general and the ordnance department were responsible for the maintenance of the Royal Army in Spain. The commissaries were civilians who combined the responsibilities of treasury officials, paymasters, and purveyors. They bought, stored, transported, and issued rations for men and animals and issued cash for the pay of officers and soldiers.

The requisition system of Napoleon's armies had many advantages. Troops lived on the country they occupied and could move wherever local supplies were available, without administrative preplanning. Requisition, however, aroused resistance against French armies in Spain, Germany, and elsewhere, especially in the case of a prolonged occupation of the same district. The concentration of a large force in one place was difficult unless depots were maintained.

Despite these problems, Napoleon's campaigns in Italy and Germany were logistic triumphs; the movement of his army from Boulogne to Austerlitz in the 1805 campaign, for example, involved intricate planning and transport arrangements to overcome the advantages the Austrians and Russians enjoyed by their proximity to bases. In 1812, however, Napoleon made the mistake of taking a large army deep into enemy country without sufficient logistic preparation; the scarcity of supplies, especially forage, in Russia and the poor roads combined to create a logistic catastrophe.

THE 19TH CENTURY

The impact of the Industrial Revolution on logistics systems. The Industrial Revolution and the introduction of steam-driven machinery changed the nature of war. Logistics was affected by three major developments. First, by creating armaments of constantly increasing firepower, industry became the primary source of military power. Second, improved transport and communications permitted large increases in the size of armies. Third, medical science began the conquest of epidemic disease. Yet the production of new armaments lagged so far behind the pace of invention that in the Crimean War (1853–56) the British and French armies differed little from those of the Napoleonic Wars. In 1759 French inventor Nicolas Cugnot made the first steam-driven road vehicle, which he discussed in a paper "The Automobile in War," but the idea was to remain untested for over a hundred years. The Crimean War revived interest; a British-built machine fitted with revolving scythes was designed literally to mow down infantry, but was rejected by the government as unsuitable for civilized warfare. Steam-traction engines were, however, used in the Crimea to haul ammunition wagons from the magazines at Balaclava to the front. They were also used in the Franco-Prussian and Russo-Turkish wars a few years later. In 1899 the British War Office sent armoured steam-traction engines and wagons to the South African War, but they were not used forward of the bases.

Use of steam-traction engines

A similar technical lag occurred in 19th-century naval logistics. Because the British Admiralty opposed the introduction of steamships, sailing ships transported and maintained the Royal Army in the Crimea. A decade later steamships played a major part in the U.S. Civil War, both as gunboats and as supply ships.

The impact of railways.   The development of railways in the first half of the 19th century revolutionized military transportation by increasing the size of armies and speeding up deployment in the field. Prussia immediately recognized the importance of rail transportation. The ability to move troops rapidly from the centre of the country to its periphery was a greater advantage to it than to any other European power. In 1846 a Prussian Army Corps, 12,000 strong with horses and guns, made an experimental rail move. In the Austro-Prussian War of 1866 the Prussian general Moltke used the five available railways to deploy along a 250-mile front and to outmanoeuvre the Austrian army. In the Franco-Prussian War of 1870 the railways leading to the Rhine enabled him to encircle the French armies assembled in Alsace-Lorraine. In these and subsequent wars, armies depended on railways for their maintenance. Ease of supply encouraged commanders to swell their forces at the railheads. From these points men had to march, and supplies and ammunition had to be carried in animal-drawn transport. By the end of the 19th century the new magazine rifle and quick-firing artillery increased the demand for ammunition and expanded horse transport caused congestion on the roads, which were often unusable in winter. Railways thus were actually reducing mobility rather than increasing it. Although they gave strategy a speed of movement, they offered no logistic flexibility and were in addition vulnerable themselves to attack.

The U.S. Civil War was fought on and individual actions were fought for the new railways. Among the Confederacy's most effective military efforts throughout the war were raids on the railroads that maintained the large Union armies, especially in the western theatre. In 1864 the Confederacy was increasingly dependent on two railways that ran from the Mississippi to Richmond by way of Chattanooga and Atlanta. These railways carried grain and meat produced in the western states to the eastern seaboard. The capture of these two railway centres wrecked the Confederate supply system. These decisive operations foreshadowed the time when air and tank forces would sever supply lines.

In the South African War (1899–1902) the mounted Boer commandos repeatedly attacked the railways on which the Royal Army depended for its supply. Away from the railroads, a British division, with its 650 animal-drawn vehicles, including 200 heavy wagons each drawn by 16 oxen, moved less than two miles an hour. When Field Marshal Lord Roberts became commander in chief in 1900, he pooled the transport of the fighting units under the control of the Army Service Corps, sharply reduced baggage and tentage scales, and gave the Cavalry Division pack mules and carts. This reorganization

Relief of Kimberley and Ladysmith

of the army's transport contributed to the relief of the besieged towns of Kimberley and Ladysmith. The Boers then resorted to guerrilla warfare, forcing Major General Lord Kitchener, who became commander in chief in 1901, to build blockhouses a mile or so apart along the railways. Many infantry battalions were tied up in the static defense of railways instead of being available for offensive operations against the Boers.

THE 20TH CENTURY

Pre-World War I.   *The impact of the internal-combustion engine.* By the beginning of the 20th century a network of rails covered Europe, and the invention of the internal-combustion engine offered a solution to the problem of supplying troops from the railhead. Motor trucks could carry from three to four times as much as horse-drawn vehicles occupying a similar space on the road and travelled six times as fast. They brought supplies from railheads, delivered them to fighting formations, and returned rapidly. An illustration of this is the comparison between the forces used in the Franco-Prussian War of 1870 and those deployed at the start of World War I. In the Franco-Prussian War Germany placed armies of about 380,000 men in the field; France opposed them with 275,000 men. In August 1914 Germany deployed 1,500,000 men against France, and Belgium and France opposed with armies numbering 1,000,000. The initial military effort of the two countries had, thus, increased fourfold and it continued to develop until armies numbered millions. Transportation had ceased to be a limiting factor in the size of armies.

Medical science.   Before World War I epidemic diseases, chiefly enteric (typhoid) fever, typhus, and smallpox, were the scourge of armies. In the three years of the South African War 13,000 British soldiers died from enteric and nearly 64,000 cases were invalided home.

Deaths in Various Wars			
war	killed and died of wounds per thousand	died of disease per thousand	forces
Napoleonic Wars	35	270	French and British
Crimean	35	190	British and French
U.S. Civil War	20	71	Union and Confederate
South African	17	30	British

Deaths from enemy action were fewer than 8,000. Between 1902 and 1914 medical research and surgery advanced rapidly. Hygiene was improved, smallpox vaccination was introduced, and battle casualties were given aseptic surgical and hospital treatment. In World War I (1914–18) deaths from disease in the British and American armies fell to four per 1,000. Gangrene of wounds and trench fever were gradually controlled. Disease, instead of being a major, became a minor cause of loss, at least in western Europe where malaria was not endemic. In Macedonia and Salonika there were 126,000 malarial admissions to the hospital of whom 500 died. In this and other Middle East theatres of war dysentery became a problem but improved methods of hygiene kept it in check.

World War I (1914–18).   Many wars lasted longer than World War I, but it was unique in two respects: the size of the opposing armies and their permanent contact. From the logistic point of view it is best seen as a siege. After the first few weeks of mobile warfare, the armies lay static, facing each other in a continuous line of trenches that stretched from Switzerland to the North Sea. Siege warfare required massive supplies of munitions. By the beginning of 1915 the Germans had increased their production of ammunition to 250,000 rounds per day; the French were producing 100,000 rounds; British production lagged at only 22,000 rounds per day.

Munitions production

The problem of matériel.   Massive industrial mobilization took place in all the belligerent nations. As demands for war material continued to mount, shortages developed. Germany felt them in foodstuffs, textiles, metals, and oils. In Britain, too, shortages of food and raw materials became critical in the face of losses from U-boat sinkings. Food rationing was introduced in most warring countries. Transportation, too, was everywhere taken over by governments. Logistics thus became a universal concern, profoundly affecting all national life and introducing the concept of total war.

Logistics on the Western Front.   The logistic services of the warring armies stood the test of the mobile operations at the beginning of the war. Besides the roads and railways, the armies made use of canals in France and Belgium. Supplies arrived daily at railheads in packtrains loaded with the rations and ammunition of a division for the next 24 hours. Reserves were held at the base and only small balancing stocks were kept near the front line. The number and contents of ammunition trains arriving daily at railheads depended on expenditure, past or planned. The principle of ammunition resupply was based on the automatic replenishment of fighting units.

The Battle of Verdun in 1916 demonstrated the vulnerability of railways to shellfire, and the German offensive in the spring of 1918 aimed at disrupting the British lateral railway system. It stopped movement on the forward lateral rail line, and air attacks were bunched on the rear lateral. The danger was averted by the construction of new railways and bridges.

Motor transport. The French and British reorganized their motor transport in 1918, withdrawing trucks from units to form headquarters motor reserves. This pooling improved logistic mobility and flexibility. In the final Allied advances of 1918 military engineers concentrated on extending railways and roads behind the armies. Motor transport carried supplies forward from railheads. Yet it is worth noting that all the Western armies still used large amounts of horse-drawn transport throughout 1918.

Persistence of horse-drawn transport

The tendency in most armies in this war was to divide logistic responsibility into forward and rear areas. For example, for the French Army the forward zone, the "zone of advance," was controlled by a general staff officer, whereas the rear zone, or "zone of supply," was administered by the War Ministry in Paris. This system of supply and distribution was suitable for an army fighting in its own country. The U.S. Army had an assistant chief of staff at headquarters in control of logistic support for the fighting area and a general commanding the service of supply in the rear. Under the American system the heads of the various logistic corps were not at general headquarters but at their own headquarters.

Medical services. In World War I the adjutant general administered the British medical services. The French and American medical services were under the quartermaster general's branch of the staff. Collection, evacuation, and treatment of the wounded and sick were efficiently carried out in comparison with earlier wars. The test was severe. During the Somme battles British field ambulances collected 316,073 wounded between July 1 and November 30, 1916, including 26,675 in the first 24 hours; 305,285 were transferred to base hospitals, and on one day 10,112 arrived in hospital ships at Dover and Southampton.

The Eastern theatre. Railroads on the Eastern Front played a decisive logistic role, with horse-drawn transport almost universally used from the railheads. In the opening campaign of 1914 the limitations of the Russian railroad system in Poland and the effectiveness of the German system in East Prussia were largely responsible for a German victory at Tannenberg. But the difficulty the Germans experienced in turning their tactical successes of 1915 into meaningful strategic successes was also largely due to the shortcomings of the Russian railroad network.

The Middle East theatre. Allied amphibious landings at Gallipoli in 1915 were a triumph of naval improvisation with the army supplied over open beaches in the absence of a port facility. The campaign ended in failure, but not for logistic reasons.

The British campaign in Mesopotamia in 1916, on the other hand, suffered from poor logistic planning. Supplied aid administered from India, the army used the Tigris and Euphrates rivers for water and for lines of communication but did not bring along sufficient river transport. Land transport was similarly inadequate, and medical arrangements broke down, with hundreds of wounded dying from exhaustion and thirst in the desert sun. The object of the campaign, the relief of the garrison in Kūt al-Imāra, was not attained.

By way of contrast, the subsequent Palestine campaign (1916–18) was a masterpiece of careful logistic planning and execution. A 140-mile standard-gauge railway and a 12-inch water pipeline were built from the Suez Canal across the Sinai Desert. Filtering machinery, pumping stations, and reservoirs were included. This modern technology was supplemented with an ancient means of transport; the water was carried from the pipe head at Beersheba to the army by 35,000 camels. The campaign foreshadowed some of the extraordinary logistic achievements of World War II.

The interwar years. During the years of peace from 1919 to 1939, scientific and mechanical invention mapped the pattern of logistics in a future war. Motor vehicles were improved in design and given a cross-country performance capacity. This led to the mechanization of armies and the gradual disappearance of horse-drawn transport. Mobility was restored to the battlefield. Supply and maintenance in the field were changed to meet this new requirement. Motor transport was organized to maintain armies with supplies and ammunition 100 miles from railheads. Mechanical earth-moving equipment, the bulldozer, was invented, and bridging equipment of improved design increased mobility and simplified military engineering.

An area of neglect was the logistic potential of aircraft, although the Germans developed transport aircraft for airborne and parachute forces. The logistic problems of amphibious warfare and seaborne operations were also insufficiently considered.

Neglected areas of logistics

World War II. More than anything else, World War II (1939–45) was a war of logistics, this time on a global scale. Conventional and familiar logistics problems recurred on a much larger scale, as in the supply of the Soviet and German armies on the long Eastern Front through nearly four years of intensive war. This was essentially a railroad operation. The Russian rail network had been considerably improved since 1914–17. Movement of supplies from the railheads was chiefly by truck, though horse-drawn transport and tracked vehicles were both widely used.

The innovations in logistics in World War II grew largely out of the global commitments of the two major Western allies, particularly the United States. Even after the decision to give the defeat of Germany first priority, enormous questions remained in the realm of how to make the best use of available production, especially shipping. In the words of George C. Marshall, U.S. Army chief of staff, "the limitations in resources presented a most difficult and trying problem. Ocean tonnage, transport planes to fly supplies into China from India, an increase in the flow of troops into the United Kingdom for the invasion of Normandy, and landing craft for the Island campaigns in the southwest Pacific all had to be taken into consideration in the light of limitations in resources. Sacrifices would be required somewhere but if made at the wrong place would delay final victory." The extent to which these problems were overcome is the major part of the history of logistics in World War II.

Shipping. The largest single logistics problem on either side in the entire war was the Anglo-American shipping problem. Though other nations had shipping problems, the interior lines on which the Germans and Italians operated in the Mediterranean, and the Japanese in the western Pacific, made their problems small in comparison with those of the U.K. and U.S. planners. Throughout the war, cargo shipping and tanker shortages had a stranglehold effect, restricting the scope of Allied strategy and limiting the size of individual operations.

One aspect of the problem was submarine warfare in which twice as much Allied tonnage was sunk as was built in the first three months of 1943. The British merchant fleet was reduced from 17,000,000 tons to 13,500,000. The convoy system, tactically essential to defeat the U-boats, was logistically uneconomic. Convoys took time to assemble and had to sail at the speed of the slowest ship, thus reducing their rate of turnaround.

Disadvantages of convoy system

The loss of the Mediterranean and the unavailability of the Suez Canal aggravated the shipping shortage. Alternative routes from England to the Middle East, India, and beyond required going around South Africa. This was 9,000 miles longer, a voyage of two months instead of two weeks. A ship could make at most three round trips a year by the Cape as compared with ten through the Mediterranean.

To solve these difficulties, routes across Africa were developed. Those for stores and crated vehicles ran from the mouth of the Congo by river and rail to Egypt. Crated aircraft were shipped from America and the U.K. to Africa's Gold Coast, assembled at Takoradi (now Sekondi-Takoradi), and flown to the Middle East and India. The Congo route was designed to take 30,000 tons of stores and 800 crated vehicles a month. This was not fully operational when the Mediterranean was reopened to Allied shipping in the summer of 1943.

After the invasion of Russia by Germany in 1941, large tonnages of British and American munitions and supplies were shipped to Russia over one of two routes: south to the Persian Gulf and thence by rail and road through Iran to the Caspian; or north, around Norway to Murmansk. The northern route was open to German sea and air attack and involved nearly catastrophic losses; in June 1942, one convoy with a large naval escort lost 22 of its 33 merchant ships, and, as a result, the British Admiralty suspended northern convoys to Russia until the following winter, at the very moment the German Stalingrad offensive was developing.

Meantime, ship construction, though increasing in the U.S., was declining in the U.K. from the end of 1942. Desired Allied shipping requirements were never met, and less important requirements had to be cancelled. For example, 600,000 tons of British coastal shipping, much of it used to carry coal, were withdrawn for the invasion of Normandy in June 1944. In the following winter a nationwide fuel crisis threatened U.K. munitions production. The shortage of shipping was aggravated by other difficulties; the failure to capture enough ports in France made it necessary for 246 Allied ships to stand unable to dock; urgently required elsewhere, they became floating depots. The same problem occurred in the Pacific; during the attack on Okinawa in 1945, 100 ships lay helplessly off the island, some ultimately returning to Hawaii without unloading their cargoes.

Landing craft. Of all types of shipping, assault shipping was the most persistently in demand. Before the war, little attention had been given to this class of vessel. When the U.S. entered the war it was decided that British shipyards should concentrate on traditional naval craft, whereas American yards built landing craft and ships, including the landing ship tank, a large oceangoing assault ship carrying stores and heavy vehicles and capable of landing them directly on steep beaches. On flat beaches they discharged at low water or anchored offshore and unloaded into barges placed under the ramp.

This method of discharge was first used on a large scale in the Anglo-American invasion of Sicily in July 1943, a landmark in the history of amphibious warfare, which proved the practicability of prolonged maintenance over open beaches. In addition to 139 landing ship tanks, many smaller amphibious assault landing craft participated. The invasion of Normandy in 1944 required 236. Most of the landing ship tanks in the Mediterranean returned to the U.K., limiting the development of operations in Italy; the planned amphibious assault on Rangoon was cancelled, and allocations of new landing ship tanks for the Pacific were reduced.

Transport aircraft. Air transport was one of the most significant logistic developments of World War II. It sustained Resistance movements in Europe by dropping agents, arms, and demolition equipment by parachute. Transport aircraft, notably the American twin-engined C-47 (Dakota), resupplied the 1944–45 airborne assaults in Normandy, The Netherlands, and on the Rhine. Thousands of casualties were evacuated by air without loss, and hundreds of tons of stores a day were delivered. Air supply made possible the rapid advance of the Allied armies from the Rhine to the Baltic and the Danube. In April 1945, for example, U.S. Troop Carrier Command delivered 54,000 tons of stores and six field hospitals to American and French armies and flew out casualties, while British transport aircraft flew 8,000 tons of supplies

into north Germany and took out 6,000 casualties and 35,000 Allied former prisoners of war. The British Bomber Command also dropped food to the starving people of west Holland.

Air transport was essential for the development of Allied plans in Asia. Air supply solved the British logistic problem in Burma and was effectively used by the U.S. to sustain Chinese forces fighting the Japanese.

In 1943 it was decided to develop an air route over the Himalayan Mountains, to fly in 20,000 tons a month, from Assam, in northeast India, to Chung King, in central China. Twenty-four airfields were constructed in Assam for 600 U.S. cargo planes; the monthly capacity of the narrow-gauge railway from Calcutta to Assam was increased by about 250,000 tons, and 750 miles of gasoline pipeline were laid from Calcutta to the airfields. These remarkable logistic developments were completed by engineer and railway construction and operating units in less than 18 months.

Although air transport in World War II was an uneconomic method of movement compared with sea and land transport, it was of incalculable military value. As an air expert said, "Air transport was the best means to get supplies to many places, the only way to get supplies to some places and it proved to be the fastest way to get supplies to any place."

The growth of logistics systems. When the British expeditionary force crossed the English Channel in 1939 its passage and disembarkation were unopposed. Well-equipped French ports and railways handled the unloading and inland movement of 150,000 men, 25,000 vehicles and guns, and 140,000 tons of stores, in 24 days. In June 1944 the Allied expeditionary force that crossed the Channel assaulted a heavily defended coast, lacked a port of any significance, and had to be maintained over open beaches. During the first 24 days 900,000 men, 176,000 vehicles and guns, and 900,000 tons of stores were landed. The transformation in logistics thinking and capabilities was dramatically illustrated.

Before and after D day 1944, the Allies concentrated their air attack against the German supply system, the railways, and roads. After D day the Germans used the same policy in reverse. They attacked the Allied logistic buildup by destroying the ports. The repair and operation of the French ports and railways required large numbers of army engineers and transportation personnel and vast quantities of stores and bridging. Cherbourg was captured by July 1, 1944. The port and harbour were strewn with mines; deepwater quays were demolished and their cranes and elevators blown into the water. The port was reconditioned by Anglo-American naval and army units and two months later the port was handling 18,000 tons a day, double peacetime capacity.

Another area of growth in logistic requirements was the construction and maintenance of airfields, a major problem on all fronts. In northwest Europe alone British Army airfield construction units repaired over 100 forward airfields and built 50, each requiring 3,500 tons of material. Pierced steel track for runways was the largest item.

Large increases in motor transport in base areas and on the lines of communication were demanded by armies moving at rates in excess of 50 miles a day. Significantly, one of the largest categories of U.S. lend-lease aid to the U.S.S.R. was in trucks. In France a high-priority, high-speed truck transport system known as the Red Ball Express between Normandy and Reims used some 100 truck companies to operate fast convoys to General Patton's U.S. Third Army in the period August to October 1944. Results were excellent in spite of wastage from accident and breakdown. Such huge motor-transport and air-transport operations in support of mechanized warfare required extensive chains of ordnance depots, repair workshops, and maintenance facilities on airfields. Each aircraft had to be supported by a ground crew of about 35 officers and men. These increases in logistic systems are reflected in the organization of Allied forces, which show a large increase in logistic overhead in the rear echelons. For every combat division ashore (about 16,000 men),

Decline of British ship construction

Importance of the C-47 (Dakota)

Capture of Cherbourg

Motor and air transport systems

an additional 24,000 troops and 4,000 air force personnel were required in the theatre. This combined figure of 40,000 army personnel was known, for logistic planning purposes, as a divisional slice. Sometimes this slice was larger. It amounted to 68,000 in the Allied invasion of North Africa in 1942 and rose to 92,000 in Burma, owing to the long and difficult line of communications from Calcutta.

Daily maintenance tonnages and reserves also increased. The following figures show the daily quantities of gasoline and engineer stores required by a divisional slice in 1944:

Factor	Tons
Supplies (5.6 lb per man)	97
Ordnance	74
Gasoline (50 miles per vehicle)	194
Engineering stores	180
Ammunition (average expenditure)	130
	675

This excludes air force maintenance tonnages.

Two inventions alleviated the logistic burdens; an artificial harbour Mulberry and Pluto (pipeline under the ocean), the undersea gasoline pipelines that stretched from England to France. The plan for the invasion of Normandy included the early capture of the port of Cherbourg. But it was foreseen that demolitions might prevent its use for many weeks. The two Mulberry artificial harbours, each the size of Dover Harbour, were considered essential for the discharge of cargo over open beaches in the crucial early stages of the campaign. These harbours, it was hoped, would nullify the hazards of tide and weather. The gales that threatened the invasion of Europe with disaster continued to hamper the buildup, and culminated in a great storm. The British Mulberry with its breakwaters of concrete caissons and sunken ships protected the transport vessels and landing craft, and, though the American Mulberry broke up and had to be abandoned, the landing was secured. The Allied margin of maintenance was at times so perilously slight that the contribution of the Mulberries was a major one. Although heavy seas reduced the effectiveness of such things as so-called Rhino ferries (strings of pontoons towed by powered craft), small amphibious craft, and landing craft, the buildup went on. The millionth man stepped ashore 28 days after the invasion and 1,000,000 tons of stores and 300,000 vehicles had been landed by the 38th day.

The modification of supply systems. The German blitzkrieg of 1940 in France and Flanders demonstrated that the World War I system based on the daily arrival of supply and ammunition trains at railheads no longer worked. The system had to be altered to meet the needs of mechanized armies and fast-moving warfare. Demands for gasoline, ammunition, engineer, and ordnance stores varied frequently according to operations planned or in progress. The switching of a formation from one army or corps to another was normal operational practice. It became impossible to communicate orders for supplies with accuracy or in time for their movement up a long line of communication. The punctual arrival of road convoys was not predictable. The supply system had to be modified to give an army's staff closer control over the logistic services. Forward maintenance areas were formed to hold reserves against interruptions in the supply chain and to overcome inaccuracy in forward planning. Despite many improvements, formations outran their supplies in the rapid advance of the Allied armies from Normandy to the Rhine in 1944 and had to be halted for want of gasoline.

The supply of gasoline to the European continent was a major problem. A pipeline laid from Liverpool to the south coast of England and continued by undersea pipelines in the Channel saved shipping and also ensured against bad weather. Two types of submarine pipe were used. The first lines were submarine cable with the core removed, laid from the Isle of Wight to Cherbourg. The second were specially made and laid from Dungeness in Kent to Boulogne. In all, 16 lines delivered about 3,500 tons of gasoline (over 1,000,000 gallons) a day. Later in the campaign pipelines on the Continent were laid from Boulogne and Antwerp to east of the Rhine. The maintenance of the Allied forces in their final drive into Germany would have been impossible without these. By 1945 pipelines on the Continent were delivering 10,000 tons a day to forward maintenance areas.

The mechanization of armies. The mechanization of armies in World War II gave new emphasis to the importance of roads and bridges. For the Allied crossing of the Rhine in 1945, 16 floating bridges were built; and between the Rhine and the Elbe 508 bridges had to be built.

Medical services. New medical techniques were developed to meet the needs of mobile warfare. A major problem was to provide rapid surgical treatment for the wounded in fast-moving and wide-ranging battle in desert, jungle, and mountain terrain and in amphibious operations. Mobile field surgical and blood transfusion teams were attached to casualty-clearing stations behind the forward troops. These units and the quick evacuation of casualties by air, hospital carrier, or landing ship tank to base hospitals saved many lives.

In the Pacific, malaria was conquered by spraying mosquito-infested areas with DDT, by strict hygiene discipline, and by the daily use of paludrine and other suppressive drugs. At Okinawa, notoriously malarial, there were only two cases in one four-month period.

Lend-lease. One of the outstanding innovations of World War II, not itself in the realm of logistics, but with vast logistic consequences, was the U.S. lend-lease program. Lend-lease enabled America to act as "the arsenal of democracy" and permitted a degree of inter-Allied production planning. Thus, by ordering certain types of equipment from the U.S., such as jeeps and trucks, the Russians could concentrate on production of tanks. Cooperation between the U.S. and the U.K. was even more effective. A combined Munitions Board was set up in Washington and London.

In spite of the difficulties of coordination, the flow of supplies from the U.S. to British forces grew throughout 1943 and reached its peak before the invasion of Europe in June of 1944. In return, the British provided accommodations for 1,350,000 American troops, their rail movement, and their supplies within England all as part of the buildup of U.S. forces in the U.K.

Logistics problems of Germany. German munitions production stood the strain of war until the late summer of 1944. Three years of strategic bombing directed against its factories and cities were less crippling than Allied air attacks on the land and sea communications of its armed forces (Wehrmacht).

Gen. Alfred Jodl, chief of operations at Hitler's headquarters, recognized the Wehrmacht's dependence on supply and maintenance for its strategic and logistic flexibility. In December 1943 he pointed out the impossibility of defending the Atlantic coast along a front of over 3,000 kilometres, meanwhile maintaining large armies in the Soviet Union and the northern Mediterranean countries at the end of long and inadequate lines of communications. He advised reducing the defensive perimeter to provide a strong central reserve in Germany that could readily be moved to whatever area the Western powers chose to assault. Only thus could Germany continue to exploit the logistic advantage of fighting on interior lines and make full use of its excellent east-west railways and roads. Hitler, however, refused to give up a yard of ground.

Inside Germany there was no strategic reserve. Industrial statistics supported Hitler's belief that he could hold the fronts in the Soviet Union and Italy and repulse the cross-channel invasion. In spite of the Allied bombing of German war industries, the rate of munitions production, under the energetic direction of Albert Speer, was rising steadily.

Even this rise in munitions production was not enough to support long intensive operations on more than one front. From the summer of 1944 until the end of the war the Wehrmacht fought on three fronts with ever-decreasing air support. By June 1944 the Allies had virtual air supremacy. Rail traffic between Germany and Norman-

Undersea pipelines

dy was disrupted; the invasion area was sealed off from large-scale German reinforcement; and, later, as the front moved eastward, the railways and canals extending into Germany were attacked. Bombers flying from the airfields at Foggia in Italy attacked the Romanian oil fields at Ploesti and damaged war industry in southern Germany—up to then outside the range of air attack.

By October 1944 rail traffic in western Germany was paralyzed. This had a catastrophic effect on the distribution of coal from the Ruhr to munitions factories. The synthetic oil plants were also attacked. This dealt a serious blow to the production of aviation fuel, explosives, and synthetic rubber. If these targets had been attacked at an earlier stage in the war, the industrial capacity of Germany and the mobility of its armed forces might have been seriously weakened. As it turned out, the German Army retained a remarkable degree of tactical mobility and logistic flexibility until the final weeks of the war. This was a feat of high military competence in an adverse air situation.

Logistics problems of Japan. As was the case with Germany, the early victories of Japan spread its forces too far for logistic stability. They became dangerously dispersed and susceptible to defeat. But unlike Germany, Japan's economic and logistic position was unsound from the start. Its economic potential was only 10 percent of that of the United States, and its acreage of arable land not more than three percent; yet this land had to support a population over half as large as that of the U.S. The High Command failed to provide the army with the logistic support required for land and amphibious warfare against Western armies. The early tide of Japanese conquest extended from the Indo-Burmese border in the west to the Solomon and Midway islands in the Pacific. This over-dispersion resulted in defeats. Admiral Mitsumasa Yonai, navy minister, was alone in realizing that the destruction of the Japanese navy by the American Third and Seventh fleets in the Battle of Leyte Gulf, October 1944, sealed the fate of Japan. The merchant shipping on which Japan depended for the import of most of its raw materials and much of its food was now at the mercy of submarine attack. Such attacks accounted for some 55 percent of the 9,000,000 tons of Japanese merchant shipping sunk during the war.

By the end of 1944, if not before, Japan faced economic defeat. Its conquests in Southeast Asia were a liability; and it could no longer depend on essential imports of grain and minerals from Manchuria and Korea.

Logistics problems of the Soviet Union. Hitler's invasion of the U.S.S.R. tends to take its place in a historical niche beside Napoleon's, as a hopeless gamble doomed to failure from the start. No such conclusion emerges from a study of the campaign. The Soviet Union only survived by a narrow margin until its epic victory at Stalingrad in January 1943. The German offensives of 1941 and 1942 destroyed much of its army and air force. It was touch-and-go whether Stalin could scrape together new armies to halt Hilter and prevent the capture of the Caucasian oil fields and its resources up to the Volga.

In January 1943 the hinge of fate turned at Stalingrad, where Field Marshal von Paulus surrendered the remnants of his army. The German conquest had reached its high-water mark. A number of logistic factors enabled the Soviet Union to survive the German invasion, to turn to the offensive in the spring of 1943, and two years later to capture Berlin. As in Napoleon's defeat, the Soviet Union's reserves of manpower remained firm. Equally, the size of the country and the rigours of the winter were natural allies. In spite of Anglo-American supplies, the logistics of the Red Army were primitive, but the Soviet soldier was tough and could endure severe hardships. He was commanded by generals who combined the will to fight with a talent for logistic improvisation. Never perhaps in the history of war have fewer supplies been put to more effective use than by the Soviets during these years. Last, the Soviets excelled at making weapons the outstanding characteristics of which were their ruggedness of construction and ease of maintenance.

The Soviets concentrated on the mass production of one or two types of each weapon. Their crudeness was outweighed by the advantage of rapid output. Priority was given to the equipment of the tank arm. The mass-produced T-34 medium and Stalin heavy tanks were superior to comparable German types.

After Stalingrad the armoured divisions were the most efficient part of the Soviet army. Their mobility was improved by American trucks. The ordinary infantry divisions had to scrape along with a makeshift collection of transport—much of it horse drawn. Most of the 400,000 American trucks supplied under lend-lease were allotted to the armoured divisions and the rear logistic services.

The capacity of the Soviet soldier for logistic improvisation was illustrated by the fact that until late in the war the Soviet army lacked specialized river-crossing equipment, yet assaulted and crossed the broad rivers of the U.S.S.R. and Poland astonishingly quickly. The engineers felled trees near the riverbank and turned them into well-built wooden bridges. Some of these bridges were built under water to avoid detection by German aircraft.

The Soviet Union fought World War II with its own native skills. The Red Army's weapons and logistic support were rough and ready but proved remarkably effective in battle.

Logistics problems in the nuclear age

WEAPON DEVELOPMENT

Procurement. Modern logistics systems must meet the requirements of (1) limited war without the threat of nuclear attack, (2) limited war with a nuclear threat, and (3) nuclear war on a global scale.

The procurement of weapons for such a wide range of threats is complicated. The most vital and also the most difficult calculation involves the time factor between the development and testing of a new weapon and its actual production. This reflects difficulties in the methods by which defense policy is decided: the central control of programs, budgeting, and expenditure; the construction of a framework of strategic policy against which the requirements for new weapons can be assessed; and the machinery to control the competing demands of rival services for expensive weapon systems.

It takes from seven to ten years to develop a weapon system from drawing board to operational use. If the weapon's useful life is another ten or more years, then the defense planner has to assess values about 20 years ahead against the uncertain background of technical progress and economic, defense, and foreign policies. Critics argue that this time scale makes errors of judgment inevitable because the weapon can be outdated before it is operational. The best answer available is careful scrutiny of projects to ensure their operational need and cost effectiveness, but despite all precautions wrong decisions can be made. After the Korean War (1950–53), for example, the U.S. and U.K. planned weapon systems to maintain a global military presence and a nuclear delivery system, but the time and cost taken to develop these new weapons were underestimated. By 1961 research and development costs represented a third of a complex weapon system. The cost of military research and development in the U.K. was four-fifths of the nation's total research allocation. The arms race increased costs by making weapons obsolete even before they became operational. Changes in operational requirement and design led to delays in production and cancellation of major projects. The cancellation of the British Blue Streak nuclear missile and the costly argument between the U.S. Army and Air Force over two similar ballistic missile systems, Thor and Jupiter, show the difficulties.

By 1960 problems of cost dominated the whole field of weapon procurement. Smaller nations could not find the money to design and produce sophisticated weapon systems; yet they could not ignore the advance of technology, and affluent America could hardly afford to continue its mistakes of the past decade. Uncertainties in strategic planning aggravated the problem of allocation of resources. In the U.S. and the U.K. the defense departments assumed mandatory powers over all stages of weapon procurement.

Feasibility studies When the need for a new weapon has been established, the concerned service normally makes a "feasibility study" that gives a detailed description of the weapon, its required operational performance, and the anticipated cost in time, resources, and money. If this report is accepted, a "project study" normally follows to establish certain cost and development criteria. If the study shows that these conditions cannot be met the project can be abandoned without wasting more than 5 percent of the total estimated cost. Though such feasibility and project studies may take from 18 months to two years to complete, they are assumed to avoid much waste.

One U.S. secretary of defense in the 1960s encouraged U.S. universities and other institutions to study strategic threats and force requirements. These studies are called systems analysis. They seek to define, for example, whether in a nuclear war most lives would be saved by a full civil defense organization, an active missile defense, or a powerful nuclear delivery system with a counterforce capability. The techniques of cost effectiveness and quantitative analysis are applied to weapon systems—*i.e.*, to intercontinental ballistic missiles on the one hand, and airlift and air support requirements in limited war on the other.

In the Soviet Union the period from about 1953 to 1967 was marked by the evolution of military aircraft from the transonic to supersonic speed ranges and the replacement of centrifugal with axial turbojets. Since 1967 the emphasis has been on short takeoff and landing capabilities and the construction of such advanced, multipurpose aircraft as the MiG-23 high-altitude interceptor and strike aircraft.

All these aircraft were made from competitive prototypes designed and developed by civilian engineer teams —*i.e.*, MiG and Yak. These teams work apart from the aircraft industry, which is tooled for rapid mass production of completed aircraft. There is little indication that this costly method of procurement is more effective than Western methods. The information the Soviet designer learns at the competitive prototype stage emerges with greater certainty from the Western system of research and development.

The Soviet system probably reflects a comparative lack of wind tunnel and other technical aids to design. The development of new aircraft systems by competitive test flying is regarded as an essential step in technological progress.

The Soviet air force tends to base its procurement on proved advances in aerodynamic and engine technology, whereas in the West the emphasis is more on converting the theories of applied science to prototype design. Thus, as the Soviets think in terms of adequate aircraft, easy to maintain and operate in extreme cold, Western air forces and their designers think more in terms of technological perfection.

Research and development. A weapon is developed in four stages: technical development; operational research; the testing of prototypes; and trials of production models under operational conditions. Technical development is primarily concerned with applied research into the components of the weapon system. It does not consider cost or operational effectiveness.

Operational research Operational research (or operational analysis) seeks to suggest more effective ways of using weapons (see also OPERATIONS RESEARCH). It provides data on which the practical problems and cost of new weapons can be assessed. It was first developed by the British in World War II. A notable example of its use was in a study of depth-charge patterns by antisubmarine aircraft. Operational research is largely a matter for the individual services, their technical staffs, and scientific advisers. Production engineers and management experts are consulted. The study of nuclear, bacteriological, and chemical warfare requires experts in physics, chemistry, physiology, and other branches of medicine. Computers and data analysis machines are used to solve complicated development problems. The operational analysis of a new weapon system starts with a definition of the strategic and tactical background. This study must define the situation ten or more years in the future in terms of the strength, composition, deployment, strategy, and tactics of enemy and friendly forces. Some miscalculation is inevitable in assessing these due to uncertainty as to the comparative rates of technical development. The "scenario" is used to measure the operational effectiveness and cost of a weapon system with the technological possibilities. The task of a weapon must be precisely defined so that inherent weaknesses exploitable by the enemy may be discovered.

For example, a recent U.K. operational analysis of an airborne early warning system for fighter aircraft and surface-to-air missiles established that two surface-to-air missile weapon systems were required, one to meet attack by medium- and high-flying aircraft and the other to meet low-level attack by subsonic and supersonic aircraft.

The research, development, and manufacturing costs of producing a reliable high-performance weapon with low maintenance and repair costs are large. Reliability is the product of precision in manufacture and the prolonged testing of prototype and production models. Delays in large-scale delivery must be accepted.

It may be necessary to study the cost of inserting new weapons into existing combat forces. If, for example, the partial re-equipment of an air defense fighter force with surface-to-air missiles is planned, such study might relate reductions in total expenditure to the cost of each spare fighter aircraft. This is the "opportunity cost." These aircraft can be used in four ways: they can be sold at secondhand value; they can be given another role—for example, to reinforce an existing ground attack force; they may be used to reduce the procurement of new ground attack aircraft; finally, they may be placed in reserve and used to prolong the life of the fighter force, thus delaying expenditure on new fighter aircraft.

Operational analysis may also be used to study the ratio of increased cost of diminishing effectiveness—the law of diminishing returns. A study of targets for ballistic missiles, for example, may show that there are 100 potential targets, and operational analysis may prove that the theoretical chance of destroying any one target is, for example, not more than 50 percent. The first 100 missiles should therefore destroy 50 targets, and 200 missiles destroy a progressively smaller number of targets, the last 100 probably destroying three only.

Operational analysis is not a precise science. It can, however, identify problems and reduce the uncertainties of long-term weapons requirements. It provides the defense planner with an impartial investigation, based on a number of possible alternatives, from which he must draw his own common sense conclusions.

Programs and budgets. The final decision on the choice of weapon systems depends on political and economic factors. Research and development are therefore inseparable from programs and budgets. The object is to improve cost effectiveness. Defense costs are analyzed under functional heads and their requirements projected ten years ahead to allow for the time lag in weapon production. Estimates for the early years are firm; those for later years contain elements of guesswork. For this reason these forecasts are reviewed annually. Inevitably, difficulties occur: service programs require more money than governments are prepared to make available. Long-term functional cost assessments do not eliminate arbitrary decisions or do away with interservice disputes; but it can reduce them and provide a yardstick of information to settle misjudgments when they occur.

The problem of unification. The system of a single weapons procurement agency has been adopted in some countries. Areas of common use in modern weapon systems are growing; for example, the Royal Navy provides electronic components for all three services and the Army supplies all the guns, ammunition, and mechanical vehicles. Canada has adopted the pattern of one combat force.

The problem of reliability. A weapon must be easy to operate and maintain. Complete reliability can of course

Missile
reliability

never be attained. The larger the number of components the greater the chances of failure. A weapon system of 1,000 components, each with a failure rate of one in 1,000,000, has a failure rate of one in 1,000. A missile of 30,000 to 40,000 components, each with a failure rate of one in 100,000, has a theoretical misfire rate of one missile in three. These facts are unwelcome equally to the service staffs who decide operational requirements and to the scientists who encourage the staffs to press their requirements to the frontiers of technology. Design and development time and money for an advanced aircraft engine may amount to 500 times the production cost of one engine. Well-designed equipment stands up to long periods of overoperation and stress and to long periods without servicing. Less well-designed equipment can be kept serviceable only by frequent inspection, maintenance, and repair, during which it is nonoperational.

The prolonged testing of prototypes, followed by field and troop trials of early production models, plays an essential part in the search for reliability. Tests reveal defects in performance that can be rectified before large-scale production starts. Development does not end with these trials. The services and their design staffs strive to improve the breed of a weapon system. The original production model, a Mark I, is followed by further Marks and usually rather quickly by Mark II. Thereafter, the gap between sequential Marks tends to grow. The multiplication of minor modifications is often a sign that the weapon suffers from basic faults in design.

Maintenance and repair. Although advanced techniques in the design and production of weapon systems must be accepted, it is necessary to achieve simplicity in operation and easy diagnosis of failure, maintenance, and repair. Experience shows that some of the best ways of achieving these ends are by the standardization of equipment, the use of commercial components, and overhaul by the replacement of complete assemblies. The maintenance problems of the different services illustrate these points. The servicing and repair at sea of naval machinery is made more difficult by high steam pressures and speeds and confined machinery spaces. Complex automatic controls change the duties of the engine-room staff from operators to diagnosticians and maintainers. The upkeep of the electrical and mechanical equipment for the ship's armament and domestic purposes increases the maintenance load. A standard range of engines in a minimum number of sizes meeting a practical range of horsepowers has improved the reliability of naval machinery. Limitations on the exact speeds required for full power or cruising endurance are accepted. Every effort is made to use machinery with a wider market. Diesel generators and a large range of auxiliary machinery can be adapted for naval use.

Use of
multirole
aircraft

The gradual replacement of bomber and fighter aircraft by guided missiles concentrates development on fewer types of multirole combat aircraft for tactical strike, reconnaissance, and close support. The decision of the U.K., Italy, and West Germany to develop such aircraft is an example of European cooperation in defense procurement and standardization. The increasing use of helicopters and short takeoff and landing (STOL) and vertical takeoff and landing (VTOL) aircraft poses the problem of their servicing in forward fighting areas. There are four categories of military aircraft servicing. Scheduled and unscheduled servicing both follow civil aircraft practice and are based on flying hours and the immediate repair of minor faults. Flexible servicing is used when the aircraft is grounded for operational or weather reasons. A fourth, contingency servicing, is used only when operations require an exceptional rate of aircraft utilization. It is confined to the minimum necessary to success because of the difficulties of servicing in forward areas.

The mechanization of armies in World War II applied not only to wheeled transport vehicles but also to fighting vehicles, including artillery of many calibres and tracked vehicles of many types. The modern repair techniques that were largely developed then are based on the optimum compromise between military and technical engineering requirements. Repairs are carried out as far forward as possible in order to reduce both the time that equipment is out of action and the recovery and movement to field workshops of heavy equipment casualties such as tanks. The technical efficiency of army repair facilities in forward areas is limited. When operational conditions make forward repair essential, repair teams are sent up from workshops to repair vehicles on the spot. Repair is usually the fitting of a complete new or reconditioned assembly. Generally, a repair team can remove and replace a tank engine in six to eight hours.

Experience shows that in war a tank needs a major replacement assembly every 700–800 miles. It is not possible, however, to forecast with accuracy which of the six major assemblies in a tank will be needed. The engine alone weighs about 1½ tons. Producing the right assembly at the time and place is difficult and the extent to which forward repair will prove practicable in future war is subject to doubt. It is likely that the speed and dispersion of modern land fighting will result in greater scrapping of equipment damaged beyond the means of economic recovery and repair. Armies are now equipped with standard ranges of load carriers adapted from civil use; the all-purpose main battle tank has replaced the medium and heavy World War II tanks of many types. The complexity of modern equipment has, however, increased greatly; amphibious ability, sophisticated weapon guidance, night-fighting aids, additional radio and radar all increase the repair and maintenance load. To this must now be added guided weapon systems. A missile system consists of a large number of components that must be brought together, assembled, and tested before the system is operational. This presents little difficulty in the case of a small missile with solid propellant and a conventional warhead. A large missile with its ground handling, guidance, and other supporting equipment is a more difficult problem. A tactical missile system must be moved to its firing site and assembled and tested in time for its operational task. Nuclear warheads are stored and maintained by special units in guarded areas. Their movement by air or ground to missile firing sites requires special security and traffic-control arrangements.

The control of ordnance stores. Ordnance stores include all types of weapons, ammunition and vehicles, radar and other technical equipment, aircraft, and a vast range of spare parts. The latter may amount to 600,000 to 1,000,000 separate items, the demand for each of which is relatively small and predictable only in general terms. Normal practice is to stock a small range of common-user items in forward depots and to hold larger and less frequently required items in central depots in base and support areas. The efficient stocking and issue of stores requires (1) accurate requisitions, or orders, rapidly transmitted from the user to the depot; (2) quick identification and location of the item by the depot staff; (3) secure and protective storage and packing, particularly in tropical climates; (4) mechanical handling equipment; (5) quick delivery of stores to users; and (6) regular reviews of scales and stocks to ensure they meet changes in requirement. Improvements in these methods give greater economy in manpower and costs. Automatic data-processing machines have revolutionized the management of ordnance depots and similar establishments. Depots are linked, irrespective of their distances apart, by computers that store the data and give the requisite information, thus rationalizing the storage and flow of supplies and spare parts and eliminating paper work. Computers are invaluable in control of an establishment such as the U.S. early warning system of 150 stations and depots containing 400,000 items. Before the Six-day War of 1967 the Israeli army installed a computer to change their ordnance store holdings, in which there were critical shortages, from a peace to a war footing. It processed all requisitions and supply issues, ensuring sufficiency for operations. After the war it analyzed the cannibalization of captured equipment.

Use of
data-
processing
machines

LOGISTIC PROBLEMS IN LIMITED WAR OPERATIONS

It is impossible to predict how and where limited war situations will emerge or the form they will take. They may include military aid by large powers to warring factions, antisubversive and antiguerrilla operations, or local war between minor powers armed with conventional weapons. The essential requirement in meeting the problems posed by limited war situations of the 1950s and 1960s was a capacity to act swiftly. A small force on the spot quickly can achieve more than a large one later. The logistic plan for limited war must be capable of achieving a quick concentration of effort in the area of violence and of maintaining it there. Science and technology have made and continue to make significant contributions to the strategic and tactical mobility of air, land, and amphibious forces.

Logistics and mobility. The range and speed of aircraft, coupled with air refuelling, make most parts of the world accessible to land and air forces within a few days. There are few countries without civil airfields, but if air reinforcements are to provide more than a token force some prestocking of aircraft spare parts and fuel may be necessary. Political "air barriers" restricting the movement of military aircraft, as in the Middle East, can be circumvented. In the early 1970s new giant transport aircraft made possible lifting troops, with their heavy equipment, tanks, and guns, at a speed of 400 knots, for a distance of 5,800 miles from an 8,000-foot unpaved airstrip. In the future large aircraft may be propelled by nuclear power, providing unlimited flexibility. Short and vertical takeoff transport aircraft can supply combat troops in action. The extensive use of helicopters by the U.S. Army in Vietnam is one of the more notable logistic developments of recent years. Rear-door transport aircraft, parachutes, and cargo palettes of improved design simplify the airdrop of supplies, weapons, and equipment. Palettes can be skidded onto the ground from low-flying aircraft.

The sea endurance of naval forces has improved through nuclear power and techniques for replenishment of warships at sea. The mobility and logistic self-sufficiency of amphibious forces have also increased. Commando and assault ships, supported by fast logistic ships and improved landing ship tanks, achieve the rapid deployment of assault forces over long distances. Logistic ships are equipped with derricks of up to 120 tons capacity. Vehicles can also be carried in M.T. (motor transport) ships and roll-off-roll-through vehicle ferries. Dock landing ships (landing platform docks) can be beached or discharge their cargo from deep water by pontoons into powered lighters. The hovercraft provides mobility and support in otherwise impossible conditions—swamps, cataracts, and ice floes. Another development with logistic possibilities is the amphibious hydrofoil, a surface-skimming vehicle designed to carry cargo between ship and shore at a maximum speed of 35 knots. Although the threat of nuclear retaliation makes very large-scale amphibious operations most improbable, smaller seaborne landings and raids may well be practicable; certainly the logistic ability to mount them has improved greatly.

Nuclear-powered supertanker and bulk freight submarines for the commercial movement of crude oil and iron ore under the ice of Arctic waters are now a technical possibility. This invention has military application for the movement of supplies in war. A submarine freighter would open up new and shorter sea routes—*e.g.*, to the Pacific beneath the polar ice cap and through the Bering Strait—and a craft with a designed speed of 30 knots could reach Australia from Europe in two weeks.

To this concept of cargo submarines must be added the technical possibility of underwater bases anchored to the seabed. This is an adaptation of a floating bases project considered for the planned invasion of Japan in 1945. On land, armoured personnel carriers and large cargo vehicles cross rough country and sail across rivers and flooded areas. Better engines, improved suspensions, and lightweight armour provide protected vehicles for the movement of combat troops and their support on the battlefield. Cost, however, is a major factor in producing these new methods of transportation. Compared with an army truck carrying 1,500 pounds (680 kilograms), a helicopter with the same capacity costs 200 times as much; a

hovercraft with about eight times the lift costs 1,000 times as much. Thus, there seems little immediate prospect that older, cheaper methods of transport will be more than partially superseded by advanced vehicles.

Supply and maintenance in limited war. Limited war operations are most likely to occur in areas remote from strategic bases. The country may be undeveloped and with few communications. Airfields and ports could be poor and roads little more than tracks; communications may be by river or across waterless desert. There may be no military stockpiles in the country so that maintenance requirements must be met from overseas. On the other hand, local stocks of gasoline and basic engineer materials may be available, and buildings can be improvised for military use. Full use must be made of all local resources to achieve a rapid buildup of forces. These conditions pose peculiar logistic problems.

The initial entry in a future limited war will probably be by air using long-range transport aircraft. If lack of airfields makes the early landing of troops impracticable, a proportion of the force can be dropped by parachute or flown in by seaborne helicopters. The initial fly-in will include engineer and air force personnel with airfield construction equipment. The air-transported force may be followed by an amphibious force carried in commando, assault landing ships, or landing ship tanks supported by logistic ships loaded with heavy equipment. Logistic support within the area of operations will probably continue to be by air, except for bulk fuel supplies that must be moved by road. If the area of operations is large, a forward airhead maintenance area may be established for the use of medium- and short-range transport aircraft.

The coordination of sea, land, air, and civil agencies of supply and maintenance will involve joint plans and implementation. Items required by more than one service will be provided by the service best equipped to do so. The army may construct airstrips and landing pads for helicopters and light aircraft and the air force construct airfields for its tactical aircraft. The construction of larger airstrips for long- and medium-range transport aircraft may be a joint responsibility. The provision or repair of bulk gasoline storage and the distribution of gasoline by pipeline is the army's responsibility.

Troops may have to move rapidly from temperate to extreme climates and go into action on arrival. The best preparation is physical fitness. Experience shows that it compensates for the lack of a natural acclimatization period, about six weeks, provided there is a high standard of hygiene at unit level.

LOGISTICS AND THE NUCLEAR THREAT

In the circumstance imposed by nuclear war it is impossible to visualize land forces supported by conventional logistic systems with depots of supplies behind the shield of forward troops. The requirement is for a method of maintaining forces without the whole system collapsing if one part of it is destroyed. The efficient handling of logistic support will depend on conditions in rear areas that cannot be predicted with accuracy.

Dispersion is the main safeguard against the loss of installations and stores, though it is difficult to control and expensive in manpower, time, and stocks. Logistic dispersion is easier when fighting on interior or overland lines of communication. It is less practicable with exterior lines passing through ports, beaches, and airfields. These and their associated base complexes are vulnerable to nuclear attack. A partial solution may be to hold more reserve stocks in forward areas, thus making combat formations and units more self-reliant. Maximum use must be made of air maintenance. The extent to which it can be used depends on the air situation and weather. Neither may be entirely favourable. Air maintenance is therefore best superimposed on land links of supply.

These considerations suggest a reorganization of rear and forward maintenance areas. The proportion of stores held in the rear should be reduced while increasing those in the forward area. The proportions depend on a number of factors including the operational and air situations, terrain, distances, and the type of commodity.

Use of helicopters in Vietnam

Nuclear-powered ships and submarines

The significance of dispersion in a nuclear war

The number of forward maintenance areas will vary with the size of the force. Groups will be dispersed over wide areas, with medium-range transport aircraft delivering supplies, perhaps by airdrop. Short-range fixed-wing transport aircraft and helicopters can be used to supply combat formations. Large, high-speed helicopters may provide armoured forces with vital logistic support in fast-moving operations. Combat units will be dispersed over a far wider area than in the past, and will need to carry a large reserve of gasoline and ammunition.

No one knows, however, if such methods of supply and maintenance in the field would remain effective in the face of nuclear attack. There appears to be certain limita- *Uncer-* tions to which a solution is not immediately clear. The *tainties* most important are: (1) the extent to which continuous operations can be sustained by day and night; (2) the limited fuel carried by an armoured fighting vehicle and the difficulties of bulk resupply of gasoline to ensure full mobility; (3) the vulnerability of helicopters against a sophisticated enemy; (4) the problems of logistic command and control in large-scale dispersed and mobile operations. Such traditional logistic calculations as the daily movement of large tonnages would be out of the question. In fact it is difficult to think of logistic systems as a rational military term in large-scale nuclear war. Only sea, amphibious, air, and airborne forces would be capable of offensive action after the first shock.

THE PEACEFUL USES OF MILITARY LOGISTICS

War, with its potential for total destruction, can be averted, and the prevention of war may become the main purpose of armed forces. Within this concept the task of military logistics still remains the orderly deployment of armed force. The threshold of intervention must be lowered to avert and cure the discontents that produce violence.

The development of remote and less developed areas is now recognized as a major goal of the more affluent nations. The logistic services of an army are suited for these tasks.

The U.S. Army Corps of Engineers has a long and distinguished record of large-scale development at home and abroad. It has planned and constructed engineering schemes, including flood control of large rivers, irrigation of arid areas, canals, communications systems, and hydroelectric projects. The Australian army has been employed on similar projects in the development of the Snowy Mountains hydroelectric and irrigation project.

The logistic capacity of army engineer corps in terms of air and sea transportation, supply, repair, and medical facilities makes them more capable of quick deployment and self-maintenance in disaster areas than civilian rescue organizations. A good example is the mobilizing of Royal Army aid after the hurricane that struck Glasgow in 1968. Within 24 hours 600 army engineers were working on the roofs. Tarpaulins were flown in from army depots, and soldiers skilled as slaterers, bricklayers, and scaffolders were employed.

The notion There is a growing demand in some Western countries *of an* for an international rescue service. Such a service would, *inter-* it has been suggested, solve the problem of closing the *national* gap between willing donors and needful recipients. Aid *rescue* could be stockpiled in advance of emergencies. Anonymi- *service* ty would then protect both the donor and the eventual recipient. But world stockpiles of relief supplies would serve no useful purpose unless they could be moved quickly and distributed within disaster areas. In large disasters only the military logistic forces of nation-states have the means to do this. The alternative is for the United Nations to have its own logistic contingency planning staff and permanent rescue service. Under certain conditions this might also be a peace-keeping force. In future years this concept might provide the nucleus around which the peaceful uses of military logistic systems could be built.

A change in the nature of military logistics is slowly developing. The movement of the military away from the civil is gradually being reversed. There are many reasons for this. Business methods of management and adminis- tration are increasingly used to improve the efficiency of military establishments. The same techniques of planning and management are used by civil and military logisti- cians. The same equipment and machinery are used in civil and military engineering and construction projects. A civilian qualification, or at least skills of value in civil life, is the ideal for every serviceman. Technical skills acquired in the armed forces increasingly fit military personnel for employment in civilian life.

BIBLIOGRAPHY

Early history: J.W. HACKETT, *The Profession of Arms* (1962); H.M.D. PARKER, *The Roman Legions* (1928); M. ROBERTS, *The Military Revolution 1560–1660* (1956); A. VAGTS, *A History of Militarism* (1938); A.P. WAVELL, *The Good Soldier: Generals and Generalship* (1948).

The armies of the nation-states and particularly of Louis XIV of France (16th–17th century): WINSTON CHURCHILL, *Marlborough: His Life and Times,* vol. 2 (1933); J.W. HACKETT (cited above); A. BABEAU, *La vie militaire sous l'ancien Régime* (1889); E.M. EARLE, *Makers of Modern Strategy* (1944).

Napoleon and Wellington (18th–19th centuries): J.W. FORTECUE, *History of the British Army,* vol. 4, pt. 2 (1930), covers the development of supply and transport; A. FORBES, *History of the Ordnance Services,* 3 vol. (1929); J.F.C. FULLER, *The Conduct of War 1789–1961* (1961); A.H. DE JOMINI, *Précis de l'art de la guerre* (1836); B.H. LIDDELL-HART, *The Ghost of Napoleon* (1933); S.G.P. WARD, *Wellington's Headquarters* (1957).

The Industrial Revolution: J.W. FORTESCUE, *History of the British Army,* vol. 10 (1930); J.F.C. FULLER (cited above); B.H. LIDDELL-HART, *Strategy: The Indirect Approach,* 4th rev. ed. (1967); E.B. HAMLEY, *The Operations of War* (1922); D.P. JAMES, *Lord Roberts* (1954); F.B. MAURICE, *British Strategy* (1929); G.J. WOLSELEY, "The Standing Army of Great Britain," *Harper's Magazine,* 80:331–347 (1890).

World War I: J.E. EDMONDS, G.E. MacMUNN, and C.B. FALLS, *Official History of the War* (1923–47), a multivolume series covering the Western Front, Egypt, Palestine, and Macedonia; WINSTON CHURCHILL, *The World Crisis, 1911–18,* rev. ed. (1932); D.H. COLE, *Imperial Military Geography,* 10th ed. (1950); A. DUFF-COOPER, *Haig: A Biography* (1936); J.D.P. FRENCH, *Memoirs 1914–19* (1925); E.K.G. SIXSMITH, *British Generalship in the Twentieth Century* (1970).

World War II: L.F. ELLIS, *The War in France and Flanders 1939–1940* (1953), and *Victory in the West,* 2 vol. (1962–68); WINSTON CHURCHILL, *The Second World War,* 6 vol. (1948–54); H. ESSAME, *The Battle for Germany* (1969); J. EHRMAN and J.R.M. BUTLER, *Grand Strategy,* vol. 2–6 (1957–); M.M. POSTAN, *British War Production* (1952); W.S. SLIM, *Defeat into Victory* (1956, reprinted 1965).

Contemporary problems of procurement and supply: M. ARMACOST, *The Politics of Weapon Procurement* (1970); J. SCHLESINGER, *Defense Management* (1970); M. HOWARD, *The Central Organisation of Defence* (1970); H. HANNING, *The Peaceful Uses of Military Forces* (1968).

Technical books on military logistics: W.G. LINDSELL, *Military Organization and Administration,* 29th ed. rev. by J.R. EMERSON BAKER (1957).

(J.M.K.S.)

Loire River

France's longest and, perhaps, most beautiful river, the Loire flows some 630 miles (over 1,000 kilometres) from its source, near the uptilted southern edge of the Massif Central in the Cévennes near the Mediterranean coast, to the Atlantic Ocean, which it enters south of the Bretagne (Brittany) peninsula. For half its length it flows in a northerly direction and is oriented toward the centre of the Paris Basin, but then it swings in a great curve past Orléans and flows westward to the sea by its long estuary at Nantes. Its catchment basin covers more than 45,000 square miles (117,000 square kilometres), and the château-dotted scenery of its valley is among the nation's finest.

The course of the Loire. The river rises at about 4,500 feet above sea level, at the foot of the Gerbier de Jonc in the Cévennes. In its upper course it flows through a succession of downfaulted, flat-floored basins—Le Puy, Forez, and Roanne—inset in the crystalline highlands of the Massif Central, in crossing which its valley narrows to gorges. At Le Bec d'Allier, 560 feet above sea level, just downstream from Nevers, it receives on its left bank its major tributary, the Allier, which has pursued a roughly parallel course in draining the Monts d'Auvergne farther west. The greatly enlarged stream then traverses the limestone platform of Berry, and its valley is only a slight groove in low platforms of sedimentary rocks until in Anjou it finally breaks across the old rocks of the southern part of the Massif Armoricain in the lowest part of its course. Apart from the scarped hills of Sancerrois and La Puisaye, which its valley breaches below Cosne, the platforms that flank its middle course show few accidents of relief. They represent the bevelling of only slightly tilted sedimentary rocks that have been overspread in places with extensive sheets of unconsolidated sands and clays, brought down from the crystalline rocks of the Massif Central, and elsewhere with residual debris, the product of intense weathering under humid, tropical climatic conditions that have obtained in the past. This has resulted in the decalcification of impure limestones and chalk. Much of these extensive tracts of overburden, differing from the bedrock below, yield only poor, siliceous soils that are responsible, for example, for the *gâtines* (tracts of degraded woodland and heath) of Touraine and the ill-drained surface of Sologne within the great curve of the river south of Orléans. In Touraine the main stream is joined by further important left-bank tributaries, the Cher, Indre, and Vienne; and below the Val d'Anjou, where it finally engages in the crystalline rocks of the Bois d'Anjou, it is entered by its major right-bank tributary, the Maine, which is the product of the confluence a little to the north, near Angers, of the Loir, Sarthe, and Mayenne.

The upper course of the Loire in the Massif Central and as far as Cosne seems directed toward the centre of the Paris Basin, and its diversion west toward the Atlantic Ocean is the presumed result of geologically recent Earth movements that tilted the floor of the southwestern part of the Paris Basin and let in a gulf of the sea as far as Blois. The vigorous ancestor of the Lower Loire was thus able to extend its catchment at the expense of the Seine system, capturing the Upper Loire and diverting its drainage into the present generally westward course to the ocean.

The Loire Basin. The Loire Basin now experiences a temperate maritime climate, with no consistent dry season and with heavy precipitation, including winter snowfall, in the highlands that occupy its upper basin. The area of its headwaters is also subject to violent autumn storms from the Mediterranean. The river suffers from a somewhat irregular and notably capricious regime. At the end of summer its bed in the middle course is usually a long streak occupied mostly by pale sand rather than by water; in very dry years, such as 1949, the stream dwindles to such a degree that there was virtually no flow of water at Orléans. The river there is usually highest in late winter, but there is no reliable rule; and floods may occur in any month, except perhaps July and August. The worst recorded were in October 1846, May–June 1856, and September 1966, when the river rose 23 feet above normal at Tours.

The shallow but steep-sided groove occupied by the river in its middle course is successively called the Val de Loire, Val d'Orléans, Val de Blois, Val de Touraine, and Val d'Anjou. In this wide *val*, the river's position is usually eccentric. Its once-marshy floodplain is protected from flooding by *levées* ("embankments") built progressively from the 12th to the 19th centuries. Effective agricultural reclamation did not begin until the 14th century but was stimulated by the presence of the French court in the 15th and 16th centuries, when the Middle Loire Valley became a strip of intensive cultivation of money crops. In the 18th century, before the French Revolution, it reached the peak of its prosperity. The river was the great highway for movement of goods, and the cities on its banks were busy ports. River navigation by flat-bottomed vessels remained active until 1860, since when it has greatly declined with the coming of railways. During the period of developing river traffic in the 17th and 18th centuries, canal links were built connecting the Loire nav-

igation with the Seine system of navigable waterways by way of the Canal de Briare (1642) and the Canal d'Orléans (1692). These links allowed products such as wine to be carried to Paris. Later the Canal du Centre (1794) across the Loire–Saône watershed linked the Loire with the Rhône navigation and played an important part in the early development of the small coalfield it traverses. These connecting canals are too narrow for modern vessels, and the Loire navigation itself is a mere shadow of its former importance. The long estuary below Nantes is obstructed by islands and sandbanks; but a channel, dredged to a depth of 26 feet, is maintained as far as Nantes, which was once so important as a colonial port. The modern, deepwater outport at Saint-Nazaire has important shipbuilding and repair yards.

Left aside by modern developments, the Loire countryside today remains profoundly rural, Old World, and little affected by modern industry. With its numerous châteaus and parks, it abounds in monuments to its illustrious past, recalling the faded glory of the life and landscape of two centuries ago.

BIBLIOGRAPHY. ROGER DION, *Le Val de Loire: étude de géographie régionale* (1934), is one of the most important and typical works in the tradition of French geographical writing. It studies the physical and human aspects of the Loire Valley, from Decize to Nantes, and includes numerous references to the history of the area since the 15th century. JACQUES GRAS, *Le Bassin de Paris méridional: étude morphologique* (1963), is a recent and comprehensive work on the physical geography. Additional information, in English, may be found in HILDA ORMSBY, *France*, 2nd ed. rev. (1962).

(A.E.Sm.)

Lomonosov, Mikhail Vasilyevich

Mikhail Vasilyevich Lomonosov was a leading figure in Russian literature and science. His poetry brought new forms of expression to Russian poetic composition, and his *Ritorika* ("Rhetoric") and *Rossiyskaya grammatika* ("Russian Grammar") made him the foremost theoretician of his language. He made substantial contributions to the natural sciences, reorganized the St. Petersburg Imperial Academy of Sciences, established in Moscow the university that today bears his name, and created the first coloured glass mosaics in Russia.

Lomonosov was born on November 19 (November 8, old style), 1711, on an island in the Dvina River, near Kholmogory, and 50 miles (80 kilometres) from Arkhan-

Photo Larousse

Lomonosov, oil painting by an unknown artist. In the M. V. Lomonosov Museum of the Science Academy, Leningrad.

Diversion of the river by structural forces

Economic aspects

Early struggles and achievements

gelsk, where, at the age of ten, he began the life of a fisherman. When the few books he was able to obtain could no longer satisfy his growing thirst for knowledge, in December 1730, he left his native village, penniless and on foot, for Moscow. His ambition was to educate himself to join the learned men on whom the tsar Peter I the Great was calling to transform Russia into a modern nation.

The clergy and the nobility, attached to their privileges and fearing the spread of education and science, actively opposed the reforms of which Lomonosov was a lifelong champion. His bitter struggle began as soon as he arrived in Moscow. In order to be admitted to the Slavonic–Greek–Latin Academy he had to conceal his humble origin; the sons of nobles jeered at him, and he had scarcely enough money for food and clothes. But his robust health and exceptional intelligence enabled him in five years to assimilate the eight-year course of study; during this time he taught himself Greek and read the philosophical works of antiquity.

Noticed at last by his instructors, in January 1736 Lomonosov became a student at the St. Petersburg Academy. Seven months later he left for Germany to study at the University of Marburg, where he led the turbulent life of the German student. His work did not suffer, however, for within three years he had surveyed the main achievements of Western philosophy and science. His mind, freed from all preconception, rebelled at the narrowness of the empiricism in which the disciples of Isaac Newton had bound the natural sciences; in dissertations sent to St. Petersburg, he attacked the problem of the structure of matter.

In 1739, in Freiberg, Lomonosov studied firsthand the technologies of mining, metallurgy, and glassmaking. Also friendly with the poets of the time, he freely indulged the love of verse that had arisen during his childhood with the reading of Psalms. The "Ode," dedicated to the Empress, and the *Pismo o pravilakh rossiyskogo stikhotvorstva* ("Letter Concerning the Rules of Russian Versification") made a considerable impression at court.

Important publications

After breaking with one of his masters, the chemist Johann Henckel, and many other mishaps, among which his marriage at Marburg must be included, Lomonosov returned in July 1741 to St. Petersburg. The Academy, which was directed by foreigners and incompetent nobles, gave the young scholar no precise assignment, and the injustice aroused him. His violent temper and great strength sometimes led him to go beyond the rules of propriety, and in May 1743 he was placed under arrest. Two odes sent to the empress Elizabeth won him his liberation in January 1744, as well as a certain poetic prestige at the Academy.

While in prison he worked out the plan of work that he had already developed in Marburg. The *276 zametok po fizike i korpuskulyarnoy filosofi* ("276 Notes on Corpuscular Philosophy and Physics") set forth the dominant ideas of his scientific work. Appointed a professor by the Academy in 1745, he translated Christian Wolff's *Institutiones philosophiae experimentalis* ("Studies in experimental philosophy") into Russian and wrote, in Latin, important works on the *Meditationes de Caloris et Frigoris Causa* (1747; "Cause of Heat and Cold"); the *Tentamen Theoriae de vi Aëris Elastica* (1748; "Elastic Force of Air"); and the *Theoria Electricitatis* (1756; "Theory of Electricity"). His friend, the celebrated German mathematician Leonhard Euler, recognized the creative originality of his articles, which were, on Euler's advice, published by the Russian Academy in the *Novye kommentari*.

In 1748 the laboratory that Lomonosov had been requesting since 1745 was granted him; it then began a prodigious amount of activity. He passionately undertook many tasks and, courageously facing ill will and hostility, recorded in three years more than 4,000 experiments in his *Zhurnal laboratori*, the results of which enabled him to set up a coloured glass works and to make mosaics with these glasses. *Slovo o polze khimi* (1751; "Discourse on the Usefulness of Chemistry"), the *Pismo k I.I. Shuvalovu o polze stekla* (1752; "Letter to I.I. Shuva-

lov Concerning the Usefulness of Glass"), and the "Ode" to Elizabeth celebrated his fruitful union of abstract and applied science. Anxious to train students, he wrote in 1752 an introduction to the physical chemistry course that he was to set up in his laboratory. The theories on the unity of natural phenomena and the structure of matter that he set forth in the discussion on the *Slovo o proiskhozhdeni sveta* (1756; "Origin of Light and Colours") and in his theoretical works on electricity in 1753 and 1756 also matured in this laboratory.

Encouraged by the success of his experiments in 1760 Lomonosov inserted in the *Meditationes de Solido et Fluido* ("Reflections on the Solidity and Fluidity of bodies") the "universal law of nature"—that is, the law of conservation of matter and energy, which, with the corpuscular theory, constitutes the dominant thread in all his research.

To these achievements were added the composition of *Rossiyskaya grammatika* and of *Kratkoy rossiyskoy letopisets* ("Short Russian Chronicle"), ordered by the Empress, and all the work of reorganizing education, to which Lomonosov accorded much importance.

Development of Moscow University

From 1755 he followed very closely the development of Moscow University, for which he had drawn up the plans. Appointed a councillor by the Academy in 1757, he undertook reforms to make the university an intellectual centre closely linked with the life of the country. To that end, he wrote important works on the *Rassuzhdeniye o bolshey tochnosti morskogo puti* (1759; "Precision of the Maritime Route"); the *Rassuzhdeniye o proiskhozhdeni ledyanykh gor v severnykh moryakh* (1760; "Precision of the Formation of Icebergs in the Northern Seas"); the *Kratkoye opisaniye raznykh puteshestvy po severnym moryam* ("Northern Maritime Routes"); and the *O sloyakh zemnykh* ("Of the Layers of the Earth"), which constituted an important contribution both to science and to the development of commerce and the exploitation of mineral wealth.

Despite the honours that came to him, he continued to lead a laborious and simple life, surrounded by his family and a few friends. He left his house and the laboratory erected in his garden only to go to the Academy. His prestige was considerable in Russia, and his scientific works and his role in the Academy were known abroad. He was a member of the Royal Swedish Academy of Sciences and of that of Bologna. His theories concerning heat and the constitution of matter were opposed by the empiricist scientists of Germany, although they were analyzed with interest in European scientific journals, such as the *Journal encyclopédique* and the *Annales typographiques*.

The persecutions he suffered, particularly after the empress Elizabeth's death, exhausted him physically, and he died on April 15 (April 4, old style), 1765, in St. Petersburg. The empress Catherine II the Great had the patriotic scholar buried with great ceremony, but she confiscated all the notes in which were outlined the great humanitarian ideas he had developed. Publications of his works were purged of the material that constituted a menace to the system of serfdom, particularly that concerned with materialist and humanist ideas. Efforts were made to view him as a court poet and an upholder of monarchy and religion rather than as an enemy of superstition and champion of popular education. The authorities did not succeed in quenching the influence of his work, however. The complete publication of his *Polnoye Sobraniye sochineny* ("Works") in 1950–57 by Soviet scholars has revealed the full contributions of Lomonosov, who has long been misunderstood by historians of science.

BIBLIOGRAPHY. Lomonosov's complete works, Полное собрание сочинений, 10 vol., Latin and Russian texts with notes, have been published by the Russian Academy of Sciences (1950–59). BORIS N. MENSHUTKIN, *Russia's Lomonosov* (1952), is a translation of Menshutkin's 1937 biography. LUCE LANGEVIN, *Lomonossov* (1967), contains a biography and extracts from Lomonosov's works and summarizes recent evaluations by U.S.S.R. historians of science (in French). See also HENRY M. LEICESTER (trans.), *Mikhail Vasil'evich Lomonosov on the Corpuscular Theory* (1970).

(L.A.L.)

London

The
character
of the city

Capital city of the United Kingdom and the industrial, commercial, and political centre of a once vast empire, London lies astride the Thames in southeast England, 40 miles from the estuary on the North Sea. Its population of almost 7,400,000 persons places it among the six largest cities of the world: many would assert that it is the most hospitable of all. Urban tensions are moderated by a traditional sense of civic responsibility and by the relatively human proportions of a cityscape rich in greenery and open spaces. Although, like all of the other massive cities of the world, London has failed to come to terms with the late 20th century, it has at least managed to conserve many of the virtues of centuries past.

On a map, the outline of Greater London is a ragged oval that might be compared with a squashed tomato. Central London is an irregular blotch in the middle, about a sixth of the whole and containing 12 of the 32 boroughs and the historic core region (now associated with financial institutions) known as the City. An aerial view reveals surprisingly few skyscrapers and a preponderance of one-family houses. Despite the great density of population (almost 12,000 persons per square mile [4,600 per square kilometre]), there is considerable open space: hundreds of garden squares, hundreds of parks and playing fields (20,000 acres [8,000 hectares] in Greater London), scores of churchyards, and many former village commons. Of all London's parklands, the most celebrated are the six Royal Parks (5,900 acres), which sweep through the West End of Central London. The whole is surrounded by the Green Belt, established in 1935 and covering in 1972 about 967 square miles (2,505 square kilometres) with further extensions totaling 320 square miles planned for the early 1970s. The river itself, one of the largest continuous open spaces in the area, is characterized in a Greater London Council (GLC) report on the environment as "perhaps the greatest of London's assets." Seen from above, London is relatively unscarred by high-speed multilane highways and their ground-gobbling interchanges, but this condition is not likely to endure in the face of a Greater London Plan, offered in 1970, proposing a network of roads based on three concentric rings of motorway with connecting radials, to be completed by the late 1990s.

Although new major roads would alter the appearance of London and affect city living as drastically as did the introduction of rail lines in the 19th century, they are not the biggest changes in store. During the decade 1974–84, notable portions of Central London are expected to be radically altered.

This new cast to the face of London will express, as have the major changes of the past, a new phase in British history. The 25 years following World War II constituted the period of dissolution of empire and withdrawal from world power; the point of view and the sense of national mission that had been shaped over three centuries suddenly no longer pertained. Once the war damage had been repaired (a massive enterprise that included the erection of low-rent housing groups still models of their kind), there ensued a terrible sense of battle fatigue. The lights had gone on again, as had been promised in wartime song and speech, but the hopes of a bright new world were stupefyingly frustrated. The famous British "muddling through" was supposedly replaced by scientific planning, and "talented amateurism" was ostensibly supplanted by technocratic professionalism; nevertheless, error and fumbling persisted. The two decades of bewilderment, imitation, and vigorous half measures between 1950 and 1970 can be read in the stones of the city. By the 1970s, however, a new period had begun, one that saw a reaffirmation of London's ancient virtues of self-confidence, imagination, and courage. A growing humanism became manifest; the measure for governmental action seemed increasingly to be the living community rather than the statistical category.

The new
initiatives
of the
1970s

THE HISTORY OF LONDON

The city takes shape. The history of London begins effectively with the Roman period. Gracechurch Street,

Majestically dominating the London skyline are Big Ben, the Post Office Tower (left), and the Thorn Electric Building (right).
Fox Photos—Pictorial Parade

which leads from London Bridge up to Cornhill, led from the bridge in Roman times to the hub of Londinium, where the Romans built a basilica. Seventeen years after the Romans had installed themselves, Icenian tribesmen under Queen Boudicca revolted and sacked the city. From traces of the fires they set, it can be determined that the settlement had already begun to spread westward across Walbrook toward the hill where St. Paul's Cathedral would later be built. After the sack, a bigger basilica was built: an aisled hall 500 feet (150 metres) long. On the same spot today stands Leadenhall Market, an 1881 effusion of cast iron and glass. To protect the city, Cripplegate Fort was constructed at the northwestern edge, but walls were not built until the end of the 2nd century AD. Remains of the wall can still be seen at the edge of Barbican (the street is called London Wall) and in a small park on Tower Hill. In medieval times the walls were rebuilt and extended, necessitating construction of additional gates but retaining the Roman gates: Aldgate, Aldersgate, Bishopsgate, Cripplegate, Ludgate, and Newgate. The legions were recalled to Rome early in the 5th century, and what happened to the city in the next two centuries is a matter of conjecture, though the Roman street pattern was not obliterated. (Cheapside and Cannon Street were the medieval successors to Roman east–west roads.)

No records tell how or when London fell into Saxon hands, but it was still, or had once again become, a city of importance by AD 597, the year that Pope Gregory I the Great sent St. Augustine there from Rome. Aethelberht, king of Kent, founded St. Paul's Cathedral, and Mellitus was installed as bishop there in 604. In the following century the Venerable Bede described London as a mart of many people arriving by land and by sea. After that the city vanished from Anglo-Saxon chronicles for more than a century, until the time of Alfred the Great (died 899) and the wars with the Danes.

Medieval London. The city's future importance as a financial and military—and therefore political—power was made clear at the time of the Norman Conquest (1066). One of the first acts of William I the Conqueror was to accord a charter promising the citizens that they should enjoy the same laws as under King Edward I and that he would suffer no man to do them wrong. It was a further mark of respect for the city's latent puissance that he planted just outside its walls the intimidating Norman keep, the White Tower, central stronghold of the fortress–castle known as the Tower of London. A roughly square (118 by 107 feet) structure 90 feet high, it has towers at each corner of the walls, which are 15 feet thick at the base and 11 feet thick at the battlemented top. King Richard I returned from the Crusades with a new concept of fortification and began surrounding the keep with concentric systems of curtain walls with towers at intervals, a work completed by Henry III. Each reign since then has added its bit, and the Tower incorporates almost every period of English architecture. A royal residence until James I, it has also housed the Royal Mint, the Royal Menagerie, the public records, an observatory, and an arsenal. The history of its executions is long and tenebrous, and it has always served as a prison for state offenders. The first prisoner was the Bishop of Durham in 1101, and the last was the deputy party leader of Nazi Germany, Rudolph Hess, during World War II. The Crown Jewels are on display there, as is a superb collection of English arms and armour.

When Henry I died in 1135, Londoners, exercising their "right" to elect the king of England, chose Stephen, who was crowned three weeks later at Westminster Abbey. About 1136 a major fire destroyed many of the city's wooden houses and St. Paul's itself. In the rebuilding, houses of stone and tile began to appear, and streets were paved and at least partially cleansed by open sewers and conduits. By the end of the 12th century, the large colony of Danish merchants was outnumbered by the Germans, who had their own three-acre (1.2-hectare) trading enclave, the Steelyard on the riverfront, until 1598. Other important trading groups were the Gascons, the Flemish, and the northern Italians. When the last named were firmly established as bankers, the Jews (in 1290) were despoiled, imprisoned, and then banished, not to return for centuries.

By astute purchase from needy monarchs, the guilds—110 of them by 1400—were able to buy increasing freedom from royal intrusion in their affairs and further their self-government. The first mayor of London, Henry Fitz-ailwin, probably took office in 1192. The first evidence of a Common Council dates from 1332. Since disorder in the realm provoked unrest in the City, London usually supported strong, orderly government, especially in such crises as the deposition of Edward II (1327) and Richard II (1399), the English Peasants' Revolt in 1381, and the rebellion headed by Jack Cade (1450).

Elizabethan London. Toward the middle of the 16th century, London experienced a startling growth of trade and population. From 1530 to 1600 the number of Londoners trebled. The excess population at first found living space in the grounds of the religious institutions seized during the Reformation by Henry VIII. To fill the void left by the cessation of the religious charities, the city organized poor relief in 1547, providing grain in times of scarcity and instigating the foundation or reconstitution of the five royal hospitals: St. Bartholomew's, Christ's, Bethlehem (the madhouse known as Bedlam), St. Thomas's, and Bridewell. Many of the private charities founded at this time still function. Trade was further promoted by the establishment of monopolies such as those held by the Muscovy Company (1555), the Turkey (later Levant) Company (1581), and the East India Company (1600). By 1605 the City population had reached an incredible 75,000, and, despite laws that attempted to restrain its size, a further 150,000 lived outside the walls. Southwark, at the far end of the original London Bridge, became the City's 26th ward. New industries, including silk weaving and the production of glass and majolica pottery, were established, often outside the gates and thus outside the

restrictive regulations of the livery companies. The establishment of Henry VIII's naval dockyard at Deptford on the south bank was accompanied by a straggle of waterfront hovels on the north bank at Wapping.

When Henry VIII in 1529 began to convert Cardinal Wolsey's York Place into the royal palace of Whitehall and to build St. James's Palace across the fields, the City of Westminster began to take more definite shape around the court. Between Westminster and the City the great houses of nobles began to appear, with gardens down to the river and each with its own water gate. Along the Strand opposite these houses were distinguished lodgings for gentlemen who were in town during legal sittings. The name London was before long to embrace both the City of London and the City of Westminster and the built-up land between them.

The reign of Elizabeth I (1558–1603) marked the apogee of the City's domination of England. The Queen based her strength on its militia, its money, and its love. It provided one quarter of the men for service abroad in 1585 and 1589 and formed its armed "trainbands" to defend against the threatened Spanish invasion.

Caroline London. The trainbands remained a force to be reckoned with, and Charles I, who had damaged the City's trading interests and flouted its privileges as cavalierly as he had Parliament's, was deterred from attacking London in 1642 by their presence at Turnham Green. Hostility toward the King made the fortified City the core of parliamentary support, and Parliament's success in the Civil War was due in good part to City allegiance.

In 1664–65, the Plague, a frequent invader since the Black Death of 1348, killed 75,000 Londoners. The following year the Great Fire burned from September 2 to September 5 and consumed four-fifths of the City. From the unscorched corners in the northeast and extreme west, the rebuilding began. A rational street plan was rejected, but streets along the old traces were wider and a bit straighter. Between 1667 and 1671 most of the new houses (brick—no more half-timbering was allowed) were rebuilt. Many of the tiny parishes were combined, and a few churches had escaped the fire, so only 50 were rebuilt, in addition to a new St. Paul's. Sir Christopher Wren, mathematician, astronomer, physicist, and engineer (but not architect), was given the formidable task of designing them and supervising their construction.

There is a Wren inscription in St. Paul's Cathedral, *Lector, si monumentum requiris, circumspice* ("Reader, if you seek a memorial, look about you"). The whole City is in fact Wren's memorial. His churches, ranging from the homely Dutch to the Gothic but mostly in his own expression of the classical style, are all touched with the same felicity and springing vigour, a series of virtuoso variations on basic architectural concepts. St. Paul's dome is one of the most perfect in the world and, like the rest of the cathedral, is classical in theme with Baroque grace notes. The memorial column for the Great Fire was adapted from a Wren design and erected near Pudding Lane, where the fire had started in the house of the king's baker. Wren constructed four other churches outside the City, built the Royal Hospital located in Chelsea, parts of Kensington Palace, Greenwich Hospital, the Royal Observatory of Greenwich, and Hampton Court Palace.

Under Charles II royal abrogation of City rights was resumed, and although James II restored forfeited City charters before his flight in 1688, it was in Guildhall under protection of the trainbands that the lords spiritual and temporal met to declare allegiance to William, prince of Orange (henceforth known as William III of Great Britain).

To support the war against France in 1694, 40 City merchants formed the Bank of England, and thenceforth the City's money market became a prime factor in the affairs of state. Another aspect of the City's power in the nation was the centring of the national press in Fleet Street (*The Times*, founded in 1785 off Blackfriars Lane, has never budged).

19th- and 20th-century London. By 1820, when George IV succeeded to the throne, the whole character of Lon-

The importance of the Tower of London

Elizabethan charitable and trading foundations

The Great Fire and its effects

The foundation of the Bank of England

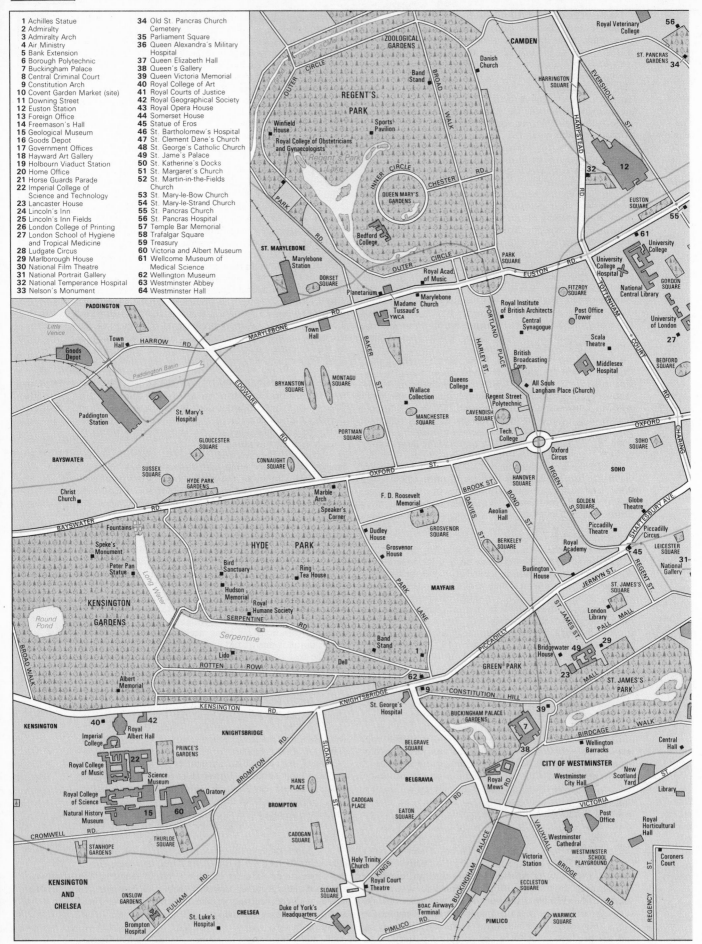

1 Achilles Statue
2 Admiralty
3 Admiralty Arch
4 Air Ministry
5 Bank Extension
6 Borough Polytechnic
7 Buckingham Palace
8 Central Criminal Court
9 Constitution Arch
10 Covent Garden Market (site)
11 Downing Street
12 Euston Station
13 Foreign Office
14 Freemason's Hall
15 Geological Museum
16 Goods Depot
17 Government Offices
18 Hayward Art Gallery
19 Holbourn Viaduct Station
20 Home Office
21 Horse Guards Parade
22 Imperial College of
Science and Technology
23 Lancaster House
24 Lincoln's Inn
25 Lincoln's Inn Fields
26 London College of Printing
27 London School of Hygiene
and Tropical Medicine
28 Ludgate Circus
29 Marlborough House
30 National Film Theatre
31 National Portrait Gallery
32 National Temperance Hospital
33 Nelson's Monument

34 Old St. Pancras Church
Cemetery
35 Parliament Square
36 Queen Alexandra's Military
Hospital
37 Queen Elizabeth Hall
38 Queen's Gallery
39 Queen Victoria Memorial
40 Royal College of Art
41 Royal Courts of Justice
42 Royal Geographical Society
43 Royal Opera House
44 Somerset House
45 Statue of Eros
46 St. Bartholomew's Hospital
47 St. Clement Dane's Church
48 St. George's Catholic Church
49 St. Jame's Palace
50 St. Katherine's Docks
51 St. Margaret's Church
52 St. Martin-in-the-Fields
Church
53 St. Mary-le-Bow Church
54 St. Mary-le-Strand Church
55 St. Pancras Church
56 St. Pancras Hospital
57 Temple Bar Memorial
58 Trafalgar Square
59 Treasury
60 Victoria and Albert Museum
61 Wellcome Museum of
Medical Science
62 Wellington Museum
63 Westminster Abbey
64 Westminster Hall

Central London and (inset) the Greater London metropolitan area.

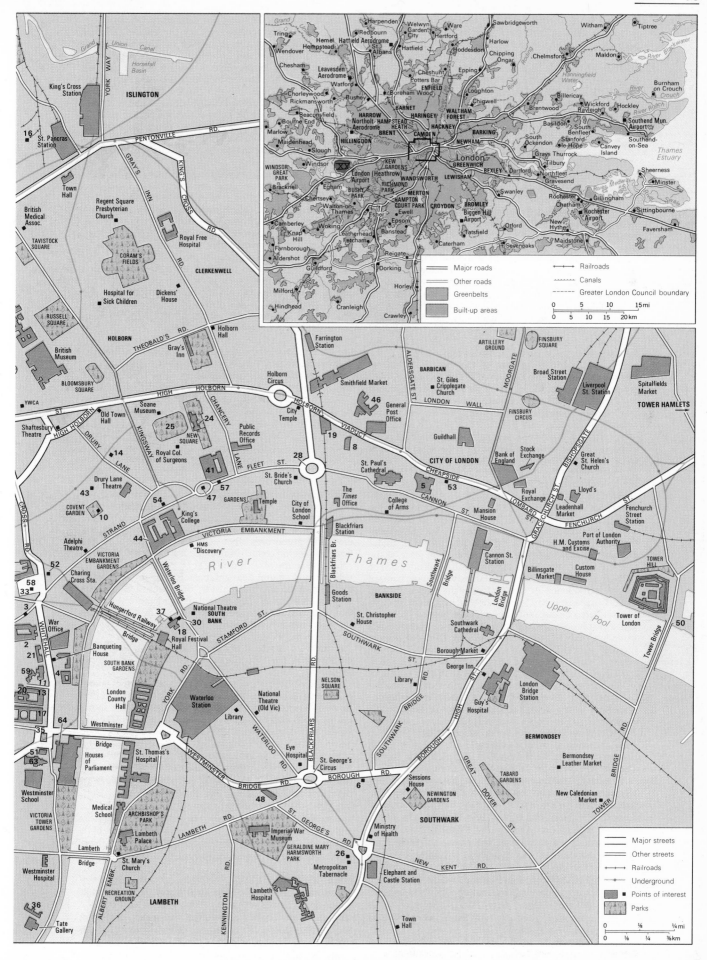

Major roads

Other roads

Greenbelts

Built-up areas

Railroads

Canals

Greater London Council boundary

0   5   10   15mi
0   5   10   15   20km

Major streets

Other streets

Railroads

Underground

■ Points of interest

Parks

0   ⅛   ¼mi
0   ⅛   ¼   ⅜km

don had changed. Its population had increased to more than 1,100,000. Villages and hamlets that in 1666 had been the objects of summer outings from the heart of the city had become part of the built-up area. Some of the building had been well-planned works of great landowners; some, however, the sorry work of the small and greedy. The Bedford, Portman, and Foundling estates produced streets and squares that embellished the town. On the other hand, to the east, parts of Stepney and Bethnal Green were constructed with ill-built cottage terraces. Agar Town, which lay near the modern King's Cross and St. Pancras railway stations, was a scandal.

The changes brought by the years 1689–1820 had followed no conscious plan. Inside the City its government was in full control and reasonably active. Beyond its boundaries, unchanged since the Middle Ages, government services and communications for the new areas came piecemeal. The important developers obtained local acts of Parliament enabling them to levy rates out of which to finance paving, lighting, cleansing, and the watch (a group of persons charged with protecting life and property). The popularity of the developers' streets depended in part on such services, and they were usually adequately administered. Lesser men left a legacy of slums and neglect for later generations to clear.

Socially, commercially, and financially, London was the hub of the kingdom. As a corollary to its great wealth, fed by the profits of the East and West Indies' trade and by trade with most of the known world, it reigned supreme in England in matters of the theatre, literature, and the arts. It was the London of David Garrick, Oliver Goldsmith, Samuel Johnson, and Sir Joshua Reynolds, of the great furniture makers and silversmiths, and of the world-famous foreign musicians. But its size brought increasing problems.

Organization, innovation, and reform. Although new dispensaries and new or enlarged hospitals were reducing mortality, the former riverside town required new forms of government, of communications, and of sanitation if it was to continue to grow. These were slowly and painfully evolved in the London of 1820–1914. Against a background of statistics that showed the population of the built-up area rising from 1,225,694 (1821) to 6,586,269 (1901), the innovations came piecemeal. In 1829 a centralized Metropolitan Police Force was provided, under the ultimate control of the home secretary, in place of the uncoordinated watchmen and parish constables. The lighting of streets by feeble oil lamps was revolutionized by the introduction of gas, and soon the Gas Light and Coke Company (1812) was followed by similar companies scattered throughout London. Omnibuses (1829) began a revolution in road transport, and carriage by rail came less than 10 years later. The year 1845 saw a great inquiry into public health, with the exposure of London's worst deficiencies, followed by legislation in 1852 ensuring a purer water supply. A statute in 1855 (the Metropolis Management Act) combined a number of the smaller units of local government and replaced the medley of franchises with a straightforward system of votes by all ratepayers. Major works, such as main drainage, were put in the hands of a Metropolitan Board of Works.

The momentum of these changes, established by such diverse reformers as Bishop C.J. Blomfield, Sir Robert Peel, Edwin (later Sir Edwin) Chadwick, and the Earl of Shaftesbury, continued throughout the century. New churches, new schools, better law and order, main drainage, and care for the outcasts were some of the reformers' legacy; Trafalgar Square, the Embankment, and roads, such as Shaftesbury Avenue and Charing Cross Road, driven through the worst of the slums are their most obvious monuments. The changes in government continued, if not so drastically. The London County Council superseded the Metropolitan Board of Works in 1888, the vestries were transformed into metropolitan boroughs by the London Government Act (1899), and the various water companies combined in 1902 into a publicly owned Metropolitan Water Board.

Public and private works continued to transform the face of London. The opening of the Metropolitan, a steam railway, in 1863 and the making of Holborn Viaduct in 1869 were accompanied by the building of new Thames bridges and the rebuilding of Battersea, Westminster, Blackfriars, and London bridges. After years of discussion and agitation, the road bridges outside the City passed into public ownership, and the tollgates disappeared. All the main railways carried their lines northward across the Thames into London, to the Victoria, Charing Cross, Blackfriars, and Cannon Street stations. It was an era in which an abundance of initiative and of capital was joined to abundant labour to make the widest use of new skills, cheap transport, and copious raw materials.

Technical progress continued gradually to alter the lives of Londoners and the face of the town. Cheap suburban trains enabled the skilled artisan to live farther and farther from his work. The London School Board, established under the Education Act of 1870, set about the task of providing elementary education for all. Trains or streetcars (horse-drawn), after an unsuccessful beginning in 1861, became important in the 1870s and a major factor in metropolitan transport as their electrification developed in the first years of the 20th century. By then electricity was being used as the motive power for traffic below ground, the Prince of Wales opening the world's first electric underground railway, from King William Street to Stockwell, on November 4, 1890. With the arrival, before 1914, of the gasoline-driven omnibus, the outline of transport in modern London was complete and the way opened for still faster development of suburbia.

Inevitably this was accompanied by rising land values in the central zone, by the construction of ever larger offices, factories, and warehouses in place of small houses, and by a continuous outlay of public and private funds on better housing and street improvements. World War I, in which air raids inflicted 2,632 casualties on London, brought only a temporary pause, and peace saw resumed development on a mounting scale. As a national and in some respects a world capital, London required institutions capable of meeting its needs. An era of amalgamation and expansion ensued. From banks to hospitals, and from telephone exchanges to power stations, almost all was expanded. Street congestion, well-known in the 1850s, was worse in the 1930s, despite the rationalization of traffic authorities. By 1939 the population of the Greater London conurbation exceeded 8,000,000.

Reconstruction after World War II. World War II, with evacuation and heavy damage by air raids, brought the greatest setback in the history of modern London. Air attacks killed more than 30,000, injured more than 50,000, damaged most public buildings, and, in such areas as the City and Stepney, obliterated whole sections of the street system. Westminster Abbey and the Houses of Parliament were damaged but saved, as were St. Paul's and Guildhall in the City. Ordinary houses and the docks suffered severely.

The end of hostilities brought a gradual return of many evacuees and a housing shortage made worse by the ravages of dry rot. Reconstruction, hampered by the shortage of most materials, began at once—and with the advantage of plans and surveys already put forward. The Town and Country Planning Act (1944), followed by acts of 1947, 1954, 1959, and 1968, gave unprecedented powers of purchase, direction, and control. The urgency of the Festival of Britain (1951) produced Lansbury (a redevelopment in Poplar) and the Royal Festival Hall, but the most significant postwar features have been the vast investment in new houses, the restoration of services and the Port of London, the general acceptance of a planned urban economy, and the sustained effort to divert industries to new or expanded towns outside London.

THE CONTEMPORARY CITY

Site and environment. The oval chalk basin through which the Thames meanders from west to east is filled with great thicknesses of younger sediments, including solid rock from the Eocene Epoch of the Tertiary Period, sands, clays, terraces of pebble gravels, and Thames alluvium. Central London has up to 20 feet of "made

margin notes:
The Victorian era

Innovations in transport in the 19th century

ground" accumulated in historic times. The earliest settlements were built on the well-watered gravel hills, and the clay produced bricks for building the city for many centuries.

The climate of the basin is typical of the eastern edge of the British Isles. St. James's Park, in the middle of Central London, receives 23.4 inches of rain a year, but, over the rest of the basin, the rainfall is irregular from year to year, with extremes of 70 to 130 percent of the average. Temperatures are mild (43°–64° F [5°–18° C] January–July mean) and vary little, although it is warmer in the city than in the suburbs. Since the passage of the Clean Air Act of 1956, there is as much sunshine in the city as in the nearby countryside: average visibility in winter has increased from one mile to four miles, and the amount of smoke in the air has been reduced to between 33 and 25 percent of that measured in 1964. Since the act went into effect, there has been no smog in London, and the celebrated pea-soup fogs have become much rarer.

Vegetation and animal life. London is of special interest to naturalists for the plants and animals that thrive there in close association with man.

In the centre, wild plants are found in the parks, squares, and private gardens, on building sites, railway banks, neglected gutters, and broken walls. Many of the most common ones have wind-borne fruits, so that they quickly colonize any soil available. Oxford ragwort, rosebay willow herb, bracken, the shrub *Buddleja davidii* (butterfly bush), and Canadian fleabane were the five most abundant plants growing on bombed sites during and after World War II, when 269 species were found in the "square mile" of the City.

In the suburbs the number of species is much greater. Wimbledon, Mitcham, and Barnes commons, Hampstead Heath, and Epping Forest have a good representation of wild plants. Within 20 miles of St. Paul's Cathedral, 1,835 species of flowering plants and ferns, 221 mosses, and 68 liverworts have been recorded since 1900.

Four kinds of birds have learned to live in great numbers in close association with man. Feral domestic pigeons have been a feature of London birdlife for at least 600 years and are familiar to visitors to Trafalgar Square, St. Paul's Cathedral, Victoria Station, and other places. House sparrows abound in Central London, and white-headed gulls have been regular winter visitors since 1895 and are seen in large numbers by the Thames and elsewhere. Immense numbers of starlings roost on buildings in Central London; the numbers are increased by immigrants from Europe in the winter. The mute swans on the Thames are the property of the crown and are marked by the Vintners and Dyers livery companies, which have a royalty. An ancient ceremony known as swan-upping takes place each July to mark the birds, and then congregations of 100 or more may sometimes be seen on the Thames in Central London. The ravens at the Tower of London are semidomesticated birds introduced from Wales.

In inner London 160 species of birds are recorded, and 37 of these species have bred. St. James's Park and Kew Gardens have good collections of waterfowl. Within 20 miles of St. Paul's 245 species have been recorded since 1900 in a wide range of habitats. Of these species, 100 are believed to nest annually.

The brown rat is a serious pest, and the black rat is found in the upper parts of buildings over a large area, including the West End. The house mouse is common, hedgehogs are frequent in the suburbs, and several species of bats occur.

Butterflies are often seen, and some species, such as the migrant red admiral, congregate around the flowers of buddleia and Michaelmas daisies. Many moths occur in Central London, where the lime hawk, eyed hawk, and poplar hawk (*Laothoë populi*) are among the larger species. The trend toward melanism is less general in moths in London than in other industrial cities but is shown in a few species.

Administration. As defined by the Registrar-General for England and Wales, Greater London covers 610 square miles, but there are, administratively speaking, a dozen different Londons. For electricity and gas supplies and hospital services, Greater London is only a portion of an administrative area for four electricity boards, three gas boards, and four metropolitan regional hospital boards. The City of London, which is independent of the Greater London Council, with its own police force and its own government headed by the lord mayor, is commonly thought to be one square mile in area (really larger, 677 acres [274 hectares]). The three great dock systems and 90 miles of river are controlled by the Port of London Authority. The London school area is only 117 square miles, the responsibility of the Inner London Education Authority; the 20 outer London boroughs have their individual school systems. The London postal area is 570 square miles. The Metropolitan Police district, which does not serve the City of London, covers 786 square miles. The area serviced by the London Transport Board is 900 square miles, and that serviced by the Metropolitan Water Board is 570 square miles. The area administered by the Greater London Council (GLC) is 610 square miles (1,580 square kilometres). Replacing the London County Council, which had taken over from the Metropolitan Board of Works as the city's government in 1889, the GLC came into being in 1964.

At the same time, the 90 separate local authorities were abolished, and 32 London borough councils (plus the City of London) were set up as the primary units of local government, little "cities" of 150,000 to 340,000 in population. The elected borough councils fix the annual rate payable on local property and have charge of such activities as housing, local parks, public libraries, refuse collection, street cleaning, and borough planning. The GLC is responsible for—among other things—overall planning, traffic control, roads, ambulance and fire brigades, education (in inner London), sewers, courts, historic buildings and public monuments, and disposal of the garbage collected by the boroughs.

Population. Within the Greater London conurbation a decline in population has occurred in the City of London since 1851, in inner London since 1901, and in outer London since 1951. Encircling the conurbation area is a broad fringe up to 30 miles wide of almost continuous population increase (more than 1,000,000 since 1951) that embraces satellite towns beyond the Green Belt areas and extends along every major road and rail route from London. The entire London and South East region had a population of more than 17,000,000 in the early 1970s, more than one-half of which was outside the Greater London conurbation.

Population of London				
	City of London	inner London*	outer London†	Greater London conurbation‡
1801	128,269	959,310	157,980	1,117,290
1851	127,869	2,363,341	321,707	2,685,048
1901	26,923	4,546,267	2,050,002	6,586,269
1951	5,324	3,347,956	5,000,041	8,348,023
1961	4,767	3,200,484	4,976,788	8,171,902
1971§	4,234	2,719,249	4,655,531	7,379,014

*Comprising the County of London after 1888 and the inner boroughs after 1965. †After 1965 the outer London boroughs. ‡Area reduced in 1965 when it became coterminous with that of the Greater London Council plus the City of London. §Preliminary 1971 census figures.

As hundreds of thousands of people move out annually, a smaller number of "new Londoners" move into those city neighbourhoods that had often lost their "village" character to bombs or urban renewal. New building, especially of hotels and offices, has gnawed into residential districts. Most enduring of all has been a change in the outlook of the mass of the population: the working class has been emancipated from belief in its own inferiority. Better housing, improved education, a complete scheme of health care, and social security have done much to terminate mute acceptance of the old social system.

The class system persists, the "old boy net" of former public (private) school students still aids its mem-

Margin notes:

The significance of the Clean Air Act

Administrative overlap and its effects

Erosion of the "working class mentality"

The River Thames flowing through Central London. On the north side of the river are government offices (centre left) and Westminster Abbey and the Houses of Parliament (lower right). Adjacent to Westminster Bridge on the south side are the London County Hall and Waterloo Station.
Aerofilms Ltd.

bers, but the society—if perhaps still only lacking the easy egalitarianism of Australian or North American cities—is more open, and the traditional "good family, good school, good regiment" endorsements are not essential to a career. Great tracts of Central London still belong to ducal families, and the most important corporations still decorate their boards of directors with the nobility. At the opposite end of the scale, inhabiting the last of the substandard houses and finding the least desirable employment, are the most recent bloc of unabsorbed immigrants, mostly non-whites from former colonies. Legislation now protects them against the worst effects of racial discrimination, and in the 1970s special efforts were being made to accelerate their integration into London life.

TRADITIONAL NEIGHBOURHOODS

The Thames and its environs. The central historical fact of London is the Thames. In the classic pattern, at the spot where a road crossed the stream, foreign invaders (the Claudian conquest of AD 43) displaced the natives and built a bridge and a city (Londinium). In those days the river was broader and shallower. Two small streams, the Walbrook and the Fleet, both of which still flow into the Thames but now through underground conduits, enabled the Romans to bring boats inside their fortified city. After the departure of the Romans, the foreign commerce they had established continued, even through the historically dim Anglo-Saxon period, and made the city rich and therefore powerful.

Two miles upstream at the Westminster river crossing, where there had been a small Roman settlement, a religious community in Saxon times, and a royal palace in the 11th century, the City of Westminster grew. Between the commercial city and the royal city the town houses of nobles and bishops were built, each with its own water

gate, and eventually a road (the Strand) ran from Charing Cross to Temple Bar, one of the City of London's 10 gates. Well into the 18th century it was the river rather than the road that served as the main highway.

All the bridges spanning the Thames from London to Southwark were wooden until, between 1176 and 1209, a single stone bridge was finally built. The tidal waters roared tumultuously through its 19 arches, and until 1831 "shooting the bridge" in a small boat was one of the thrills of London. A chapel was built on the bridge to St. Thomas à Becket, martyred in 1170. Soon after, shops lined both sides of the roadway between the fortified gates at either end, and then houses were built above the shops, 138 of them in 1350. In Queen Elizabeth I's time water mills were installed that added to the uproar. The houses were removed in 1760, the year the City gates were dismantled, but the bridge continued to serve for another 71 years, a total lifetime of 622 years. Its replacement was in its turn replaced piecemeal between 1969 and 1972. Tower Bridge, one-half mile downstream, built between 1886 and 1894 by Sir Horace Jones, who had previously designed Billingsgate, Smithfield, and Leadenhall markets, has twin Gothic towers and a central drawbridge and is a good deal more quaint and "Olde" English than London Bridge or the two other spans owned and maintained by the City, Blackfriars (originally constructed 1756–69) and Southwark (first built 1813–19).

After the Norman Conquest the port's foreign trade increased, and embankment of the river on the seaward side of London Bridge began in the 12th century and was completed in the 14th, reclaiming from the water 42½ square miles (110 square kilometres) of marshland at Rotherhithe and Deptford on the south bank and the Isle of Dogs on the north. Still boggy centuries later, this land was easily excavated for dock building.

The role of London Bridge

Thamesmead, a model city under development approximately nine miles east of Central London on the south bank of the River Thames.
Alan Hutchinson—Camera Press, London

Further embankment of the river was not achieved until the 19th century, when at last London stopped dumping its wastes into the Thames and constructed main sewers. From 1864 to 1870 the mains were laid along the north bank behind stone retaining walls and roadways laid over them from Blackfriars Bridge to Westminster. About 37½ acres (15 hectares) of mudbank were reclaimed and converted into parkland (Victoria Embankment Gardens between Waterloo Bridge and the Hungerford Railway Bridge). In 1874 Chelsea Embankment, also laid over new sewer mains, was completed. The embankment system, interrupted briefly at the Houses of Parliament, is four and a half miles (seven kilometres) long. On the riverside opposite Parliament, Albert Embankment was built in 1869 as a flood-control installation, extended—for pedestrian traffic only—in front of London's County Hall, downstream of Westminster Bridge, in 1910. The last of the embankments was made in 1951, when the South Bank cultural complex was started on a bombed site between London's County Hall (the headquarters of the GLC) and Waterloo Bridge.

Straightening the shoreline and jacketing the river with stone walls moved the tidal limit from London Bridge 19 miles (31 kilometres) upstream to Teddington Weir. The average high tide at London Bridge is rising at the rate of about three feet each century, as London sinks about one foot in the same period. High tide at London Bridge is four feet higher than it is downstream at Southend on the broad estuary 43 miles away. London's embankments were raised an additional one and a half feet in 1971 to guard against floods that might come when a wavelike surge mounts the river from the North Sea. This was provisional protection pending the construction of a movable barrier at Silvertown, in the Woolwich Reach section of the Thames, eight miles downstream from London Bridge, scheduled for completion by the late 1970s.

Development of the docks. During the reign of Queen Elizabeth I, "legal quays" were established on the north bank of the Thames between London Bridge and the Tower as the only place where ships could land dutiable goods legally. The traffic soon grew too great for the quays, and in 1663 Parliament allowed the establishment of alternative "sufferance wharves" on both banks. Port activity doubled between 1700 and 1770, and, by the end of that time, the Upper Pool (that part of the river that stretches a little less than a mile below London Bridge) held as many as 1,775 ships in a space allocated to 600. Unloaded into the 3,500 lighters that carried goods from ship to wharf, cargoes sometimes remained caught in the maritime traffic jam for weeks at a time, subject to pilfering and to raids by river pirates. To enable ships to discharge directly into guarded quays, where goods could be stored in secure warehouses, the West India Dock was opened in 1802 at the northern end of the Isle of Dogs, a marshy river peninsula opposite Greenwich Hospital. In 1805 the London Dock opened in Wapping, and downstream from the Isle of Dogs the East India Dock was inaugurated in 1806. In 1807 the existing Greenland Dock (where whale blubber was rendered) and Howland Wet Dock in Rotherhithe on the south bank were combined, later to be enlarged as the Surrey Commercial Docks, covering 410 acres, a tract bigger than Hyde Park. St. Katherine's Docks were built under the lee of the Tower in 1828. Except for the West India, all of these and the dock at the entrance to Regent's Canal are closed. The Port of London operates from three large dock systems: West India, Millwall (1868), and Poplar, on the Isle of Dogs; Royal Victoria (1855), Royal Albert (1880), and King George V (1921), six miles farther downstream; and Tilbury Docks (1886), 26 miles from London Bridge. In 1909 the Port of London Authority (PLA) was created to take over ownership of all existing docks and control of the river and the port.

Waterfront development. Having closed down the upstream docks in the 1960s, riverfront properties covering 850 acres, the PLA decided to sell, providing a historic opportunity to remake a rich portion of London. In 1969 the GLC bought the first parcel, St. Katherine's Docks (25 acres, 10 of them water), for £60,000 an acre; three years later, it was worth £250,000 an acre. Some of the original majestic warehouses were retained, and a theatre, hotel, cinema, yachting marina, restaurants, and pubs were built as part of a village for 2,000 residents occupying houses, flats, and studios with extraordinary river views at a wide variety of rents. At the same time, the GLC began construction of Thamesmead, 1,450 acres on the site of the 300-year-old Royal Arsenal of Woolwich. Designed to be a model town of social and architectural balance, it should have a population of 60,000 by 1986. Simultaneously, in the disused Royal Victorian Victualling Yards, Deptford, the GLC brilliantly converted the interiors of the 1795 rum warehouses into 65 flats, a sailing school, and yachting centre.

The originality and habitability of these projects generated a new enthusiasm for long-ignored areas. Private developers bought and restored 'forgotten' squares and terraces in waterfront neighbourhoods. The 12 miles of waterfront from Waterloo to Woolwich, formerly declining docks, factories, and decayed housing, became the subject for frantic bidding and fevered planning that ranged from the utopian to the crassly exploitative. The borough councils, the GLC, and those ministries that might be concerned pondered all the proposals that would eventually return a vast tract of the city to the living community.

The river about which all this excitement was concentrated was until recently foul-smelling and almost black with pollutants. Since the late 1960s it has become cleaner each year, thanks to strenuous antipollution policing; fish are returning in increasing numbers, and birds, not seen for many years, are nesting along the less clamorous portions of the river.

The City of London. One and five-eighths miles at its longest and seven-eighths of a mile at its widest, the City

The Tower of London and Tower Bridge.
The Times, London—Pictorial Parade

is a marvelous mélange of ancient elegance and modern efficiency, of outdated practices and newfangled irritations, a place where for 1,000 years tradition has been honoured and innovation has been essential. Thus, while the messengers ("waiters") of the Bank of England are dressed in top hats and pink tailcoats and a detachment of the Brigade of Guards has been reporting nightly to repel mobs ever since the Gordon Riots of 1780, the bank employs computers and other contemporary aids to expedite its labours.

The City is one of the world's great financial centres despite the deliberate dismantling of the sterling bloc. It also remains a pivotal point for world trade in commodities in spite of the fact that raw goods no longer originate in British possessions and that few of the commodities dealt with by the 14 exchanges are actually physically handled at the Port of London.

The City's institutions are as varied as they are ancient. Five "wise men" set the world price of bullion in the opulent Gold Room of N.M. Rothschild & Sons, St. Swithin's Lane, at 10:30 each morning, but, before these gentlemen are out of bed, the gentlemen from the Fishmongers Guild, their boots silvered with fish scales, are exercising their immemorial functions down by the river at Billingsgate, London's fish market. On the other side of the City, predawn buyers eye hook-hung carcasses at Smithfield, the world's largest dressed-meat market. Nearby, nurses begin to prepare patients for surgery at St. Bartholomew's ("Bart's"), London's first hospital (founded in 1123) and the place where, in the 17th century, William Harvey first demonstrated the circulation of the blood. Closer to St. Paul's Cathedral, the vans begin to deliver prisoners whose cases will be heard that day at Old Bailey, as the Central Criminal Court is known, where most of Britain's sensational murder trials have been held.

As the daylight broadens, the first of the 400,000 commuters begin their daily invasion, descending from five main railway stations, from buses, from the underground railway, and from the other side of the river across London Bridge in what seems to be a solid mass of pedestrians. The bankers, the insurance underwriters from Lloyd's, the Stock Exchange members, and the commodity exchange brokers arrive a little later than their employees, some by underground and others in their limousines.

The Barbican scheme.   Since 1973, there have been some City men who arrive at their desks after a short stroll from their homes in Barbican, a City redevelopment on 45 acres of World War II bomb craters around the 16th-century church of St. Giles Cripplegate. The modern buildings accord with the hues of the old church stones and bricks, and the whole is planned to bring inhabitants back to the City, where the nighttime population was just over 4,000 in 1971. Barbican will house 6,500 additional citizens in 2,113 flats and maisonettes. There are private patios and terraces, an artificial lake, a greenery, and subsurface service roads and parking for 2,500 cars. In addition to offices, shops, and restaurants, there is the new building for the old City of London School for Girls (boys resolutely some distance away at Blackfriars on the site of Henry VII's Baynard's Castle, which stood at the river edge from 1487 to the Great Fire). Also at Blackfriars are found an art gallery, cinema, library, exposition hall, new quarters for the famed City-run Guildhall School of Music and Drama, a theatre for the Royal Shakespeare Company, and a 2,000-seat concert hall for the new headquarters of the London Symphony Orchestra.

The hub of the City.   The central spot in the City is an open space from which eight streets radiate. On the south side is Mansion House, which was designed in the mid-18th century by George Dance as the lord mayor's residence, office, and court (he is first magistrate) and which is still so employed by each lord mayor during his one-year term. Clockwise from Mansion House is Lombard Street, the traditional banking street; on each of its establishments hang the fanciful signboards contrived in earlier centuries. Between Cornhill and Threadneedle Street sits the third restoration of Sir Thomas Gresham's 1567 Royal Exchange. Across the street, the original 18th-century ground-floor screen hides the four-acre Bank of England headquarters, which was built in the period 1921 to 1937 to replace Sir John Soane's 1782–1802 masterpiece, some believe the worst loss to the nation ever caused by the bank. Across a narrow lane east of the bank rises the 28-story Stock Exchange (1968), and a short distance to the northeast stands the twice-restored Guildhall, originally built in the period 1425–45, seat of the Corporation of London.

The Corporation of London operates without a charter of incorporation, the only one in the nation to do so. Some 14,000 voters of the 25 wards elect 159 common councilmen and 26 aldermen (one of whom is chosen as lord mayor by the aldermen from two candidates nominated annually by the 15,000 liverymen of the guilds). Voters are enfranchised by residence in the City or by tenancy or ownership of property of annual gross value of £10. Members of livery companies must be freemen of the City; freedom of the City, acquired through completion of guild apprenticeship, through inheritance or through purchase, was until the mid-19th century a pre-

The daily flood of commuters

The Corporation of London, the guilds and livery companies

requisite for trading or working at a craft in the City. Today 84 livery companies exist, successors of religious or social fraternities of the 11th century, and continue to multiply, the most recently granted livery being that of the Scientific Instrument Makers, 1964.

Some guilds—the Apothecaries, Goldsmiths, Fishmongers, Spectacle Makers, for example—still exercise a controlling influence in their trades, especially in the maintenance of high standards of quality. Livery companies conduct training schools or provide scholarships and grants for research and education in schools and universities.

The Inns of Court. The Temple, with an entrance off Fleet Street, represents another segment of the City's power machinery. Originally the British headquarters of the Knights Templar, after dissolution of the order it eventually became the first of the Inns of Court, where barristers had their chambers and where they trained (and still do train) the coming generation of trial lawyers. Middle Temple, Inner Temple, Lincoln's Inn, and Gray's Inn, the latter two just north of the borders of the City, are oases of calm, civility, and continuity. The Inns of Court were rebuilt almost entirely in the 18th century, but the Temple retains its much-rebuilt, round Norman church with a 13th-century addition. Near the entrance stood the most recently built of the City gates, Temple Bar.

Just across Fleet Street, Chancery Lane begins, with the Royal Courts of Justice on the west and the Public Record Office to the east. The Law Courts, as the Royal Courts of Justice are usually called, were designed by G.E. Street in the mid-19th century, a chill, gloomy Victorian Gothic mass. It is here that the Lord Mayor's Show comes to an end on the second Saturday of November, when the new lord mayor alights from his State Coach (a brewery lends the six horses) to pledge fealty to the monarch, represented by the lord chief justice. Until 1838 the show was waterborne, and the lord mayor went up river to Westminster in his State Barge.

The City of Westminster. Once the court stopped following the sovereign whenever he moved and settled itself in Westminster, executive departments such as the Chancery and Exchequer were able to develop. By the 16th century Parliament became institutionalized. Dukes of the realm and princes of the church found it expedient to maintain palaces close to the source of preferment.

The Strand

The Strand, link between the City of London and the City of Westminster, became more thickly built upon as time went on, but in Danish times there had already been a parish church outside the Roman wall, St. Clement Dane's. Its "twin" further west in the Strand, St. Mary-le-Strand, was first mentioned in 1147. Today both stand on tiny islands of land in the middle of the roadway, St. Clement's rebuilt around its 15th-century tower by Wren in 1680 and St. Mary's rebuilt (1714–17) by James Gibbs, in a handsome blend of Italian and English Baroque. St. Clement's was rebuilt again in 1958 after World War II bombing. Between the two churches, but back from the Strand, long stood the town houses of the ill-fated Earl of Essex and that of the Duke of Norfolk, who still owns the land.

On the south side of the Strand is Somerset House, constructed in 1776, possibly the first building in modern times specifically built for government offices. Designed by Sir William Chambers, it is most widely known for its archives of wills and birth and death records. Wings were added in the 19th century, and King's College (now part of London University) was installed in one in 1835. In 1970 two late-17th-century houses were removed from the Strand to permit construction of the college's architecturally flat-footed laboratories.

North and west of this part of the Strand, a parallelogram about three-quarters of a mile long and not quite half a mile wide would enclose 33 of London's 40 theatres and most of its first-run cinemas. Until almost the middle of the 19th century, the Strand was London's smartest theatre, hotel, and shopping street.

In 1972 construction of a new garden square—a hardy private venture—began just south of the Strand, only the second to be built in inner London since World War I. No amount of gracious building in this area can make good the loss of Robert and James Adam's magnificent 18th-century urban set piece, Adelphi. Red brick and Palladian, massive in total bulk but delicate in detail and proportion, it rose on arches above the riverbank in 1768 (completed 10 years later). In 1936 it was razed to clear space for more profitable development. In three narrow streets named for the brothers, nine of their houses survive, wistful reminders of a regrettably departed glory.

Today the City of Westminster, doubled in size (to 8.3 square miles) when the boroughs were reorganized under the 1963 local government act, is the wealthiest of any borough in the kingdom with a ratable value of £112,417,000. It stretches along the Thames from the Temple to Chelsea Bridge and north through the titillations of Soho and the consultations of Harley Street to the Grand Union Canal. It includes some of the most strenuously desired residential pockets in the kingdom and some of the least coveted slums. It owns more than 16,000 low-rent dwellings, and it plans new ones at an average of 750 a year, with an active renovation program for historically and aesthetically valuable old housing.

It contains Westminster Abbey (Anglican) and Westminster Cathedral (Roman Catholic), Buckingham, Westminster, and St. James's palaces, the principal government offices, the most important shopping districts of the country, New Scotland Yard, most of London's luxury hotels, Madame Tussaud's waxworks museum, and four museums of art, two of them of world rank. The National Gallery, Trafalgar Square, has a superb collection of masterpieces of Western painting. The Tate Gallery, on the river near Vauxhall Bridge, has a collection of 4,000 British paintings, more than 300 modern foreign works, and 360 pieces of sculpture. Named after donor Sir Henry Tate, it was built in the period 1893–97, and a new extension was to be completed in 1975.

Shopping districts and markets. The most important retail shopping concentration in the United Kingdom is Oxford Street, where its first palatial department store building was constructed in 1909 by Gordon Selfridge, a "retired" Chicago retail merchant. The heavy shopping activity flows southward along Regent Street to Piccadilly Circus, turns right along Piccadilly, with northward branches along Sackville Street and Savile Row, where eminent tailors still make some of the world's finest men's clothing. Just alongside the Royal Academy is one of retailing's most charming and luxurious shopping streets, the 600-foot-long Burlington Arcade. With 72 tiny shops under a glass-roofed promenade, it was built in 1815 at the same time that John Nash built his Royal Opera Arcade. Parallel and a little farther west, Bond Street is still a magnet for lavish spenders from around the world. South of Piccadilly, and parallel to it, Jermyn Street is studded with long-established makers of costly shirts, hats, and other male accoutrements.

Oxford Street, Regent Street, and the Burlington Arcade

Several streets east of Piccadilly Circus, an area along and around Charing Cross Road, is one of the world's great gleaning grounds for secondhand books, a treasure hunt for the collector and a university for the curious.

Kensington High Street and Knightsbridge are two other heavily patronized shopping districts that attract clients from all over. Kensington High Street is just south and west of Kensington Gardens, with several traditional department stores and a flurry of modish clothing and accessory shops that in the 1960s came to be called "boutiques."

About a mile to the west, the Knightsbridge shops cluster where Knightsbridge, Belgravia, and the stuffier parts of Chelsea convene haughtily south of Hyde Park. West along Brompton Road and then south down Sloane Street the shops progress toward King's Road in Chelsea. Traced from St. James's Palace to Hampton Court Palace across farmland and through several hamlets, the King's Road was, until Victoria's accession, reserved to court traffic. Aside from a few antique shops and a large department store in Sloane Square, it was a typical London "village high street" until the 1960s, when it was invaded by fashion shops, private dancing and drinking clubs, and

Royal Festival Hall on the South Bank of the Thames.
FPG

The character of Chelsea

coffee bars. From the mid-19th century Chelsea had been a heavily working class district with a few elegant old streets, the homes of some celebrated writers, the studios of noted painters, and a fringe of arty-crafty aspirants, but after World War II it became increasingly fashionable and expensive. The effect spread westward by the end of the 1960s, raising rents and the decibel count in neighbouring Fulham.

There are still at least 16 outdoor markets in Central London, most of them selling only fruit and vegetables but some offering a very general assortment of merchandise. Two of the best known general markets are on Petticoat Lane (really Middlesex Street), in the East End, and on Portobello Road, off Notting Hill Gate.

The East End.   Beyond the easternmost City gate down to the River Lea is London's East End. The neighbourhood names persist: Aldgate, Spitalfields, Whitechapel, Mile End, Bethnal Green, Wapping, Shadwell, Stepney, Limehouse, Poplar, and Isle of Dogs, but officially they comprise the borough of Tower Hamlets.

In the Middle Ages, the East End was part of vast Stepney Parish based on the Saxon church of St. Dunstan's, and, by the early 17th century, it was already a place to which the poor gravitated. With the development of the docks in the 19th century, offering casual employment, and the growth of the clothing and furniture industries, which battened on sweated labour, the increasing number of poor people competed for an intermittent pittance.

Among the overcrowded houses there was no drainage, and, despite the early foundation of hospitals and charities, the average age of death in Bethnal Green in 1840 was 16 years, 50 percent of all deaths among the labouring classes being children under five. Through the latter half of the century, there were continuing waves of immigrant groups, to whose poverty the onus of racial, religious, and anti-foreign prejudice was added. This was the London of Jack the Ripper, where life and gin were equally cheap.

The East End was the most savagely bombed and burned part of London in World War II. The rebuilding reflected far lower population densities, and many families accepted new homes and jobs in the New Towns started at this period; thus the population in 1960 was less than half that of 1901. Industry as well as population continued to drain away from Tower Hamlets, causing a decline in the borough tax revenues, from which local improvements are largely financed. The housing con-

struction program continues, with Spitalfields and Stepney–Poplar being two of the areas of concentration. Spitalfields, which has the borough's highest density of population, has been a receiving station for immigrants since the Huguenot silk weavers fled France at the end of the 17th century. The most recent immigrants have been Indian and Pakistani, mingling with an earlier wave of West Indians and little settlements left over from the turn-of-the-century Irish and east European Jewish arrivals, spreading down into Whitechapel. The whole district, after consultation with the residents, was to be remade in the 1970s. The Stepney–Poplar district, old Cockney territory, is to emerge as a "New Town" for 100,000 people. The new redevelopment of the dock areas has led to the private purchase and restoration of Georgian buildings by Londoners of a socio-economic category that last inhabited the district 200 years ago. The GLC has plans for a "green corridor" of open space from Victoria Park through Bethnal Green, Mile End, and Stepney down to the river at Limehouse and Shadwell. When the Fleet Line of the Underground is completed in 1976, it will attach more solidly to Central London the further reaches of the East End and accelerate the rehabilitation of the area.

South London.   The inner London boroughs of Greenwich, Lewisham, Southwark, Lambeth, and Wandsworth occupy the south bank of the Thames as far as six miles (10 kilometres) inland, but the term South Bank refers above all to the music and arts complex begun in 1951 for the Festival of Britain. It begins just downstream from London County Hall, GLC headquarters. The first permanent building on the South Bank site was the 3,000-seat Royal Festival Hall, which presents the world's great orchestras and ballet troupes in about 450 performances a year. The 1,000-seat Queen Elizabeth Hall (1967) and its chamber-music auditorium, the 370-seat Purcell Room, offer about 400 and 300 performances, respectively, each year. Many of the musical groups appearing in these halls receive grants from the GLC. The Hayward Art Gallery, opened in 1968, is leased for token rent by the GLC to the Arts Council of Great Britain, which stages major art exhibitions there. The National Film Theatre, tucked into a corner, shows classic films from all nations. The National Theatre, which was lodged for years at the Old Vic Theatre (built 1816), behind Waterloo Station, was to be moved into its new home just east of Waterloo Bridge on the South Bank in 1975. Next to it, on space originally designated for residential use, are the studios and offices

The South Bank Complex

of an independent television station. The riverside promenade for pedestrians that starts opposite the Houses of Parliament continues now all the way along the South Bank to Blackfriars Bridge, from which point waterfront redevelopment was planned to stretch more than 10 miles down to Woolwich.

Bankside, as the riverfront between Blackfriars and London bridges is called, is where Shakespeare's Globe Theatre and its rivals stood and where the palace of the bishop of Winchester neighboured the 13th-century Southwark Cathedral (largely rebuilt in the 19th century). Around this end of London Bridge, coaching inns, mentioned by Chaucer in the 14th century and by Shakespeare in the 17th, once clustered. One such inn, the George, rebuilt after the Southwark fire of 1667 and truncated by the railroad in 1889, continues to operate in an atmosphere of bustling bonhomie. The railway also displaced St. Thomas's Hospital, which had stood by the bridge since 1213. The hospital was removed to its present riverside site between Westminster and Lambeth bridges in 1871, and its medical school is just across the street from the much-restored 13th-century Lambeth Palace of the archbishop of Canterbury. Southwark still has a famed teaching hospital, Guy's, founded in 1721.

Southwark and Lambeth were both heavily bombed during World War II, and many popular proletarian resorts, Elephant & Castle and Lambeth Walk, for example, were later rebuilt out of all recognition. Lambeth, one of the most densely populated of the boroughs, has just over 300,000 persons jammed into little more than 6,700 acres. The Brixton district, where much of South London's shopping is still done, houses one of the city's principal West Indian concentrations. The borough programs called for demolition and replacement of 10 percent of its housing by 1977, but some of its old squares have been renovated rather than razed and have been brought back to life.

Upstream, the adjacent borough of Wandsworth shares its waterfront in part with the somewhat seedy Battersea Park, which contains a children's zoo and a fun fair that was erected for the Festival of Britain. The riverfront west of the Albert Bridge, an endearing iron suspension bridge of the cuckoo-clock school of design, is now taken up with factories, but a private development plan proposed a new neighbourhood of apartment housing in a park setting behind a public riverside walk.

London's squares and parks. Although almost nothing remains in London of the works of the architect Inigo Jones (1573–1652), his mark is stamped probably forever on the town. He came back from an Italian tour with a new architectural idol, Andrea Palladio. The two great examples of Jones's buildings, the Queen's House at Greenwich (designed 1616) and the Banqueting House of Whitehall Palace (1619–23), show that he did not swallow Palladio's classicism whole and spit it out again: he was no mere imitator but the personal interpreter of a concept and a style. His great contribution to London was not Palladian Venetian but Medician Tuscan: the city square. Derived from Cosimo I de Medici's Piazza d'Arme built in Livorno in 1571, which had already inspired Henry IV's Place des Vosges (1603) in Paris, the city square was to set the pattern of London city building for the next 200 years, sometimes fashioned into ellipses and crescents but always enhancing the variety and surprise of the urban composition.

Inigo Jones's contribution to the city layout

Jones's Covent Garden Piazza (1630) was surrounded on three sides by tall houses with an arcaded street floor, filled on the west by the low, solemn-porticoed St. Paul's Church. When it had stood there 50 years, Charles II gave permission for a vegetable market (Covent Garden Market) to operate in the square "forever," which turned out in fact to mean until 1974, when the Nine Elms market across the river was expected to replace it. The year before its departure, market traders in the 96 acres centring on the piazza handled £64,000,000 worth of fruit and vegetables and £11,000,000 worth of flowers.

Not long after the Jones square was completed, a cock-fighting hangar was opened in adjacent Drury Lane and was converted into a theatre in 1662. It was destroyed by fire several times, and the present building dates from 1812, with later external additions. For 115 years it was the only licensed theatre in London, until the opening of the Covent Garden theatre, where Handel's *Messiah* was first heard in 1742 and where all his succeeding oratorios were introduced. The present Royal Opera House, built by E.M. Barry in 1858, is the home of the Royal Ballet as well as the Royal Opera.

Some experts contend that Lindsey House on Lincoln's Inn Fields, the largest square in Central London, was built following a Jones design. With its rusticated lower floor and giant pilasters supporting the entablature, it was the prototype for a whole race of London town houses. Charles I gave a direct license in 1641 for the development of Lincoln's Inn Fields as a city square, but work was halted by an appeal to the House of Commons from the society of Lincoln's Inn (this Inn of Court, founded in the 14th century, still contains some 15th-century buildings), and so the square was not completed until 1656. Within the Inn's conclave is New Square, an elegant oblong of red-brick houses unchanged—except for the effects of German bombing in 1941—since it was built in 1685.

New Square, like Covent Garden and other West End squares, was built as a private speculation. Some of the loveliest portions of London—entire cherished neighbourhoods—were conceived for the benefit of (usually) noble and sometimes royal landlords. The Earl of Southampton in 1660 built Bloomsbury Square, the first to bear the word square in its name. The district was passed by marriage to the dukes of Bedford, who built a splendid series of garden squares, of which Bedford Square (1775) is one of London's handsomest and Russell Square (1800) one of the largest. The whole atmosphere of Bloomsbury, distinguished and intimate, was for long enhanced by the presence of teachers and scholars, painters, actors, and writers. In the area are the University of London and its University College and Birkbeck College, the London School of Hygiene and Tropical Medicine, the Royal Academy of Dramatic Art, the Slade School of Art, the Wellcome Museum of Medical Science, and the Courtauld Institute Galleries.

The atmosphere of Bloomsbury

The British Museum. The jewel in this cultural crown is the British Museum, founded here in 1753, its present building constructed in the period 1823–47. Its library, which is entitled to receive a copy of every book printed in the United Kingdom, has more than 6,000,000 volumes and has been cramped for space for 100 years. The Reading Room, in which Karl Marx wrote *Das Kapital*, was formed by roofing over the central courtyard. The museum's print room is justly famed, as is the manuscript collection, which ranges from Aristotle's *Constitution of Athens* to modern British classics. The museum collections are extraordinarily varied, especially in antiquities of Egypt, western Asia, the Orient, Greece, Rome, and Britain.

To the west of Bloomsbury, Cavendish Square was laid out in 1717 by the Duke of Newcastle, whose daughter married Edward Harley, 1st earl of Oxford, and whose granddaughter married the Duke of Portland. Oxford Street is named after the Earl, whose family name was given to one of the world's most celebrated concentrations of medical specialists, Harley Street.

The south side of Oxford Street belongs to the single largest private landowner in London, the Duke of Westminster (the Church of England, the crown, and the boroughs of London are the three biggest landlords). The lands stretch from Oxford Street through Mayfair, across Hyde Park Corner through Belgravia and Pimlico right down to the Thames. Originally Westminster Abbey property, by 1677 it was the dowry of Mary Davies when she wed Sir Thomas Grosvenor—Grosvenor being the family name of the dukes of Westminster. Grosvenor Square was built about 1700 (on the neighbouring estate to the east, Berkeley Square was built about the same time, Bond, Dover, and Stafford streets having been built up some 30 years earlier by Sir Thomas Bond and the earls of Dover and Stafford), and Mayfair became a fashionable district, as it remains today. The gardens

Tourist-filled Trafalgar Square, with Nelson's Monument and the National Gallery.
Pictorial Parade

around which Grosvenor Square was built were given to the nation in 1946 as a memorial to U.S. president Franklin D. Roosevelt by the 2nd Duke. Park Lane, where the town houses of the Grosvenors and other wealthy Londoners stood, has become a street of hotels and offices.

The last Grosvenor land to be developed, before the Grosvenors became the dukes of Westminster in 1847, included Belgravia and Pimlico. The original layout, made in 1815, was somewhat altered by the three builders, who took long leases on sections of the property and began construction in 1824. The owners wanted a mixed development—thus, the palatial mansions of Belgrave Square (now mostly embassies and institutions), the tall Parisian town houses of Eaton Square (still one of London's more chic addresses), the middle class residences in Chester and Wilton streets, and the more modest houses in Bourne Street, Graham Terrace, and Caroline Terrace. This imposing piece of town planning remains largely intact. Pimlico (by the Thames), until the 1970s ill-served by public transport, sloughed into slum by World War II, but those parts that survived the severe bombing were subsequently restored to something close to their original dignity.

Originally all the squares in all the developments, planted as gardens or parks on private property, were closed to all save house owners with keys to the gate. Leicester Square, a common grazing ground usurped by the Earl of Leicester to grace his town house, was surrounded by houses by 1680 but became public only in 1870, and Lincoln's Inn Fields remained private until 1894. The majority of the gardens are still fenced and available only to key holders from surrounding buildings. Among the buildings surrounding the garden in St. James's Square (built by Henry Jermyn, earl of St. Albans, 1664) are Chatham House (home of three British prime ministers, present headquarters of the Royal Institute for International Affairs), the London Library (a private subscription library with 600,000 volumes), several private clubs, and some discreet corporation headquarters. There are some modern intrusions, but most of the houses are 17th and 18th century. Fiscally, physically, and psychically, the square and its environs continue to constitute the conservatory of the "British Establishment," that astonishingly hardy perennial of island ecology.

Trafalgar Square. Possibly the most famous of all, Trafalgar Square, has always been public and has no garden. Seven major arteries pump automobiles around

the great paved space, in which stands a statue (17 feet, 4½ inches) of the hero of the Battle of Trafalgar (1805), Horatio Nelson, on a victory column (167 feet, 6½ inches). Two fountains, stone lions, live pigeons, and assorted memorial military statuary keep him company. The openness of the space attracts numbers of mass meetings every year and is a favourite resting place for tired sight-seeing visitors.

The name Trafalgar Square was bestowed on the site in 1832, after which hundreds of hovels were cleared from the area. Grading began 10 years later, and the column was erected in 1842. The National Gallery (into which architect William Wilkins in 1838 was obliged to incorporate the colonnade from the regent's razed palace, Carlton House) occupies most of the north side of the square, with the National Portrait Gallery next to it. To the east of the galleries is the church of St. Martin-in-the-Fields (1722–26) by James Gibbs, replacing a 1544 church on a site where a house of worship was first mentioned in 1222. The site shows off the church superbly. Just below, the Strand runs off to the City, one-half mile east, where it changes its name to Fleet Street.

South of Nelson's monument is a statue of Charles I, erected on the site of Charing Cross where the funeral cortege of Eleanor of Castile, wife of Edward I, rested in 1290. Several of the Cromwell supporters who voted the execution of Charles I were burned here after the Restoration, after which the rediscovered 1633 statue was erected. To the west is the 1910 Admiralty Arch, which frames the entrance to the pink-surfaced Mall, which leads to Buckingham Palace.

Whitehall. Directly south from Trafalgar Square–Charing Cross runs a street that was once the power centre of the world, Whitehall. Today it remains the seat of the government's executive branch. Interspersed among Victorian and post-World War II pachyderms are several graceful 18th-century buildings still in government service. On the east side is Inigo Jones's calm, lovely Palladian Banqueting House (1619–23), the only important part of Whitehall Palace to survive intact the fire of 1698. Across the street is the Horse Guards Parade, a 1760 replacement of an earlier headquarters. Every day the plumed troopers of the Household Cavalry ride in on black horses from their 35-story Knightsbridge Barracks (1970, Sir Basil Spence) to post guards at 11:00 AM.

Farther south is the Old Treasury, built around the remains of Henry VIII's tennis court after the fire, now

The seat of government

used as Cabinet offices, connected by a corridor to the Cabinet Room at 10 Downing Street. Sir George Downing built this very short street of houses as a speculation between 1663 and 1682, and behind the simple brick facades are 200 rooms reconstructed in the 1960s. The prime minister lives at No. 10, his chancellor of the exchequer at No. 11, and his party's chief whip at No. 12. Past the Foreign and Commonwealth offices, the Home Office, and the all-powerful Treasury is Parliament Square, which has a small central garden with benches and statues. It leads on to two of the most important buildings in Britain, the Houses of Parliament and Westminster Abbey.

Parliament. Parliament dates its beginnings from 1265, when Henry III had to accept the Parliament called by Simon de Montfort. Meetings on fixed dates began under Henry VIII, and in Tudor times the Commons evolved its basic rules of procedure. Early meetings were held in the Abbey's Chapter House, which was then, from 1547, in the deconsecrated chapel of St. Stephen of the Palace of Westminster. The House of Lords met in the palace Chamber of Requests in Old Palace Yard. Originally built for Edward the Confessor (reigned 1042–66), the palace served Parliament until destroyed by fire in 1834. The crypt of St. Stephen, a section of 1526 cloister, and the medieval Westminster Hall are all that remain today. The hall, completed in 1097, received its magnificent hammer-beam roof during 14th-century modifications. Damaged by incendiary bombs in May 1941, the roof was later restored.

After the 19th-century fire, a competition for a new Palace of Westminster was won by Charles Barry, who was knighted for his work, and Augustus Welby Northmore Pugin, an ardent medievalist, who died mad. Full of variety and movement that lighten its massiveness, the prize-winning design functioned well for the Parliament of its day and became almost instantly a symbol of that institution's power and solidity. The Clock Tower at the eastern end houses among its bells Big Ben, which sounds the hours and is marked "13 tons 3 cwts 3 qtrs 15 lbs."

Big Ben

Westminster Abbey. Built by Edward the Confessor, Westminster Abbey was consecrated in 1065. To honour Edward, Henry III undertook to build a more magnificent church in 1245, in Gothic, leaving of the original building only the Norman Undercroft, the Dark Cloister, and the Chapel of the Pyx, all of which still exist. After 25 years the work stopped, not to be resumed until more than a century later, but in perfect imitation of the style in which it had begun. The octagonal Chapter House is one of the identifiable portions built in the mid-13th century. Henry VIII completed the fan-vaulted and richly carved chapel begun in 1503 by his father at the eastern end of the abbey. The restorations and additions of the 18th and 19th centuries were drastic; the twin towers on the west front are from 1735–40, designed by Hawksmoor. The church is styled a Royal Peculiar, with Dean and Chapter (its officials) depending directly on the monarch, head of the Church of England. Nearly all British rulers since Harold II (who lost to William I the Conqueror in 1066) have been anointed and crowned here, and until 1760 they were buried here as well. National heroes of politics, literature, and war are interred here, although some of the most heroic (Shakespeare, Milton, Marlborough, Nelson, Churchill, for example) lie elsewhere.

The abbey, its boys' school (Westminster, one of the nation's most distinguished), and its neighbour, the medieval Gothic church of St. Margaret's (parish church of the Commons), form a placid precinct on the edge of Victoria Street, cut through slums in 1851 to Victoria Station. Much of the bold Victorian architecture along the street was replaced in the 1960s with indifferent contemporary buildings, including a 22-story glass box, the Westminster City Hall, and just off Victoria Street, in a building of the same mock-courageous cut, is the New Scotland Yard, 1964 headquarters of the Metropolitan Police. Scotland Yard, the 1891 Scottish baronial castle of convict-quarried granite, is half a mile east on Victoria Embankment.

St. James's Park. Behind Whitehall's ministries and Downing Street, westward toward Buckingham Palace, lies St. James's Park, the oldest and most romantic of the six central Royal Parks that give the West End of London a heritage of beauty, repose, and sense of continuity.

The swampy ground belonging to the Sisters of St. James-in-the-Field was taken in 1532 by Henry VIII, who built the red-brick toy-soldier castle toward the western end. To the court at this St. James's Palace the credentials of foreign diplomats are still addressed. The Stuarts admitted the public to the park, which Charles II had done up in the formal Versailles manner. The first Georges cut off one end of the ornamental water to form the Horse Guards Parade, where in early June the sovereign's official birthday is celebrated with the Trooping the Colour by the Brigade of Guards, to the music of the brigade's massed bands.

Horse Guards Parade

George IV had the park re-designed in its present seductive form by John Nash in 1828. The formal "canal" was changed into a long, irregular lake graced with a small bridge from which the Whitehall buildings, topped with pinnacles and pennants, form a rather "Arabian nights" silhouette. The weeping willows around the lake also lend an Oriental touch to what is an archetypal (and extremely artful) English landscape. The flower beds are the best in Central London. Among the many species of waterfowl to be seen are the pelicans originally introduced by Charles II. The northern border of the park is the half-mile-long, arrow-straight Mall, a splendid ceremonial way that terminates at the bulky Queen Victoria Memorial, around which are planted each spring 40,000 tulips, succeeded by 14,000 geraniums.

Buckingham Palace. The memorial stands before Buckingham Palace, built in 1703 by the Duke of Buckingham and bought by George III in 1762. When Nash reshaped the park, he enlarged and remodelled the palace and designed Marble Arch, which served as the entryway until 1851, when it was removed to the northeast corner of Hyde Park. The Mall facade of the palace was redesigned again in 1913. When the monarch is in residence, the flag flies from the roof and the guard is changed in the forecourt every morning. Victoria made Buckingham Palace the monarch's London residence, relegating St. James's to purely ceremonial use.

Green Park. Green Park, close by, is an unpretentious knoll of especially thick, rich grass and luxuriant stands of trees, the plainest of the Royal Parks. It is bordered on the east by the once-private homes that clustered around St. James's Palace: 19th-century Lancaster House, about which Queen Victoria remarked to the Duchess of Sutherland, "I have come from my house to your palace," now a government conference building; Bridgewater House, a 19th-century Florentine palazzo and one of the 280 buildings that are on the Grade I list of protected historic buildings; mid-18th-century Spencer House, which, like Bridgewater House, is now functioning as business offices.

Despite the increasing number of modern buildings, the district embraced by St. James's Street and Pall Mall still retains its great distinction. More than a dozen of the most illustrious gentlemen's clubs are located in this corner. There are also shops, some of which have been in St. James's for more than 200 years.

The part of Piccadilly that runs along the top of the park was from the 18th century the site of great town houses, some few of which survive today as clubs. No. 1 Piccadilly, once known simply as "No. 1, London," was the town house of the dukes of Wellington from 1815 until it was given to the nation in 1947 as the Wellington Museum. This mansion was built as Apsley House by Robert Adam in 1778, and the 1st Duke had the red brick clad in stone and added a big Corinthian portico. Constitution Arch, which stands at the highest point of Green Park opposite the house, was built as a memorial to Wellington.

Hyde Park and Kensington Gardens. Across the traffic of Hyde Park Corner is another work by the same architect, Decimus Burton, the triple-arched Ionic screen that was the original entrance to Hyde Park, for which he also designed the lodges at the other gates. From this corner a once-celebrated riding track, Rotten Row, starts westward under the arching boughs. Once the central part of Henry VIII's great forest hunting preserve watered by the West Bourne and Tyburn, Hyde Park and Kensington Gardens together have an area of 615 acres. The Tyburn Tree, a 12-foot-high triangular gibbet with room for eight malefactors on each arm, stood at the northeast corner of Hyde Park until 1783. Marble Arch, which gave its name to the adjacent crossroads, and Speakers' Corner, the traditional open-air, open-question forum, occupy this northeast corner of the park today. From there to the southwest corner of Kensington Gardens is a two-mile walk across meadows and through groves of fine old trees. Only in very rare spots is the public requested to keep off the grass, under which, on the violated eastern border of the park, is a 1963 parking garage for 11,000 cars.

From an Italianate water garden in Kensington Gardens flows the Long Water, which, once it enters Hyde Park, becomes the Serpentine, where there is boating and ice-skating and, at a strand called the Lido, swimming. William III nipped 26 acres off the western end of Hyde Park in 1689 to make a garden for Kensington Palace, enlarged by further acquisitions by succeeding reigns. Kensington Gardens was not opened to the general public until the mid-19th century and still retains some feeling of elevated separateness, one of the last repairs of nanny-tended prams, with expensive model boats being sailed in the Round Pond and hearty gentlemen fulfilling childhood dreams by flying magnificent kites. The traditions of Hyde Park have always been—aside from the vanished magnificence of Rotten Row—more popular, from public hanging to public swimming. The Great Exhibition of 1851 was held in the Crystal Palace, Paxton's remarkable iron-trussed glass building. The palace was erected in Hyde Park, almost, but not quite, in Kensington Gardens. It was destroyed by fire in 1936.

Unpretentious, domestic, red-brick Kensington Palace was the Earl of Nottingham's 1661 country house, enlarged by Wren for William III in 1689 and again by William Kent for George I. About 1700, Kensington Square to the south was built for those who wished to be near the court. When she succeeded to the throne (June 1837), the 18-year-old Victoria was living in Kensington Palace with her mother. It is still inhabited by members of the royal family, and its staterooms are open to the public.

In front of the palace runs a private road constructed in 1843 and lined with grandiose mansions of which a dozen are now embassies and some others are diplomatic residences. The southern end leads to lofty Kensington, and the northern end to sleazy Notting Hill, both parts of the Royal Borough of Kensington and Chelsea. Although the borough has the smallest percentage of public-housing tenants (about 5 percent) of any in London, it has one of the most troubled—and troubling—slum districts of the city.

Marble Arch and Speakers' Corner

Albert Memorial and Royal Albert Hall

Kensington Gardens accommodates one of London's more remarkable monuments, the Albert Memorial, 175 feet high, graced with 175 sculpted figures somewhat larger than life. This Victorian Gothic improbability was concocted in 1863–71 by Sir George Gilbert Scott, who, at the same time (1868–74), wrought even more fanciful gothic conceits at St. Pancras Station, fortunately preserved. Out of the park and across the street is the domed, elliptical, 7,000-seat Royal Albert Hall, part of an 80-acre cultural centre for which the ground was bought with profits from the 1851 exhibition. There are five colleges and four museums: the Royal College of Organists, the Royal College of Music, the Royal College of Science and the Imperial College of Science and Technology (the Royal College of Art was moved there from Exhibition Road in 1962); the Science Museum, the Geological Museum, the Natural History Museum, and the Victoria and Albert Museum.

Regent's Park. Regent's Park, with Primrose Hill abutting (472 acres in all), is about a quarter of an hour's walk north from Marble Arch. This parkland, too, was

part of Henry VIII's hunting preserve. The elongated lake was made by damming the Tyburn. It was opened to the public in 1815, the culminating point of John Nash's Triumphal Way, which started from St. James's Park. Starting in 1811 and working until 1830, he built Water-

J. Allan Cash

Regent's Park.

loo Place (the column to the Duke of York was erected later), then lower Regent Street to Piccadilly. From there he was unable to continue Regent Street on a straight line, but he did obtain a right-of-way in a quarter-mile curving arc. To join this curve to the straight, he contrived the city's first traffic roundabout—Piccadilly Circus. Along the curved section, known as the Quadrant, he swung twin lines of arcaded buildings. (The arcades were ripped out before Nash was dead a dozen years.) He thrust on until he came to the jog where his street would join Portland Place, already lined with buildings by Robert Adam (little of that work is left, either). There he constructed a church, All Souls Langham Place, with a circular portico, gently concealing the bad join between the two streets.

John Nash's Triumphal Way

The effect was ruined later in the century, when the curlicued Langham Hotel was erected, and the ruin was completed in 1931, when the British Broadcasting Company planted its Broadcasting House there.

Having already put Regent's Park in order, Nash massed around three sides of it one of London's most magnificent architectural showpieces, a series of terrace houses. The facades of the individual houses in each terrace, based on a continuous ground-floor arcade, were composed to form one grand entity with column-supported pediments and a unifying lattice of balcony across the front, so that each tenant seemed to occupy a portion of a palace. War damage and dry rot made the future of these terraces uncertain for years after 1945, but by 1970 they had been restored and put to educational, charitable, and residential uses.

The park is a series of romantic vales and has the amenities offered by most of the others, but two of its endowments are unique: the Zoological Gardens (very superior middle-sized city zoo; London's big zoo is at Whipsnade) and the Regent's (Grand Union) Canal. The GLC (Greater London Council) is clearing footpaths along the canal, and Westminster Council is encouraging home building on old factory and warehouse sites. The western end of the canal is a district of richly maintained large houses called Little Venice.

Nash's Piccadilly Circus was no longer circular after 1877, when Shaftesbury Avenue was started there and hacked through the rookeries (slums) of Soho and St. Giles, eventually becoming the principal theatrical street of the West End. The Soho district has been the special resort of foreign colonies since Frenchmen found refuge there from the 16th-century wars of religion, followed in turn by Greeks in 1677 and, in the 19th century, the Italians.

These three groups with their ethnically flavoured restaurants and grocery shops still thrive in Soho amid the grimy nightclubs and the remnants of between-wars Bohemia. They have been joined by a growing number of Chinese from Hong Kong. The old Chinatown in Limehouse in dockland was virtually deserted after World War II. A sizable Greek community flourishes in Bayswater near the Greek cathedral of Hagia Sophia.

Piccadilly Circus, a seedy traffic chute by day and a neon-loud gathering place by night, still attracts visitors from all over the world. The youth of all nations sprawl on the steps of its stone island, which is crowned by the 1893 aluminum statue of Eros (in reality, the Angel of Christian Charity, a memorial to the reformer, the 7th Earl of Shaftesbury).

The outer parks. Outside London and Westminster there are four other Royal Parks: Greenwich, Richmond, Hampton Court, and Bushy. Richmond Park, 2,358 acres, has changed little since it was first enclosed in 1637 for the grounds of the vanished Richmond Palace. The ponds abound in fish, and the centuries-old oaks shelter 600 deer. The Royal Ballet School occupies White Lodge in the middle of the park, which comes near to the Thames 15 miles upstream from Westminster Bridge. To the east are Wimbledon Common, Wimbledon Park, and Putney Heath, which together make an open space of 1,700 acres. On the edge of the park is Alton West Estate, Roehampton, a low-rent housing group built by the LCC (London County Council). In a garden setting, which includes some preserved 18th-century country houses, is a population of 9,600 served by its own schools, shops, and library.

Further upstream past the tidal head at Teddington are Hampton Court and Bushy parks. Hampton Court was built in 1514 by Cardinal Wolsey and was presented, along with its contents, to Henry VIII two years later in a futile effort to stave off disgrace. The house, an imposing red-brick building with white-stone accents and typically Tudor twisted chimneys, was enlarged for Henry and, in the 17th century, enlarged further for William and Mary by Sir Christopher Wren, who planted the avenue of flowering chestnut trees that grow today in Bushy Park, an 1,100-acre tract inhabited by deer, by horses belonging to the Royal Household, by the director of the National Physical Laboratory (in 18th-century Bushy House), and by the Admiralty Research Laboratory, in Charles II's Upper Lodge.

On the way back downstream is Kew Gardens, one mile below Richmond Park. Although it contains a former royal palace (1631), Kew is not a royal park. It is the site of the Royal Botanic Gardens, with four museums, a research and training centre, and gardens of trees and plants from all over the world.

The atmosphere of Soho

Hampton Court

Greenwich Park is 21 miles farther downstream, five miles below London Bridge. The 185-acre (81-hectare) park was first enclosed by Humphrey, duke of Gloucester, in 1433. He built a castle on the hill, which Henry VIII enlarged and which Charles II demolished in 1675, to make way for Wren's Royal Observatory, whence issued Greenwich Mean Time. The Duke also built a palace, Placentia, on the riverbank, where Henry VIII and his daughters Mary and Elizabeth were born. On the rise behind the palace, Charles I had Inigo Jones build for Henrietta Maria the Queen's House, now the National Maritime Museum. Charles II tore down Placentia and had John Webb start a new one. William and Mary made the building into a naval hospital and had Wren design further buildings. Nicholas Hawksmoor and Sir John Vanbrugh were architects for later additions. The English Baroque group, best seen from the river, is one of the best sited and finely balanced architectural compositions in London.

The park that rises behind them is graced with Spanish elms set out in the mid-17th century. Like the other Royal Parks, it is spacious, soothing, and deceptively "natural." Just to the south lies historic Blackheath (270.5 acres), where rebel armies gathered on several occasions down the centuries, where James I introduced the Scottish game of golf to England, and where highway robbers lurked in the 18th century.

Far to the opposite side of the city is another open space much prized by Londoners, the 800-acre Hampstead Heath. The residents of the wealthy and picturesque village of Hampstead, on the highest hill in London, organized into a protective society and fought in the courts from 1856 to 1872 to assure free access to an integrally preserved natural open space. The heath, the citizens' group, and a good many village aspects still prevail in Hampstead today.

Hampstead Heath

Highgate Wood, just north of the heath, belongs to the City of London, as do Queen's Wood and West Ham Park. Farther out, City-sustained greenery includes Epping Forest (6,000 acres) in Essex, Coulsdon Commons (423 acres) in Surrey, and Burnham Beeches in Buckinghamshire. Hainault Forest (1,108 acres), in Essex, belongs to the GLC, which maintains there and at Hersham and Stoke D'Abernon, in Surrey, tree banks (54,000 young, transplantable trees) to supply the streets and parks of London.

Most parks in and around Central London provide entertainment (band and symphony concerts, poetry readings, ballet, opera) and facilities for sports from bowling on the green to motor racing. Coaching is given in lawn tennis and skiing, and championships open to all Londoners are held every year in seven different sports. On Sunday mornings in the season, Hackney Marshe park offers the spectacle of 2,500 footballers at play.

BIBLIOGRAPHY

Topography and architecture: VICTOR S. PRITCHETT, *London Perceived* (1962), an evocative literary work on contemporary London; DAVID PIPER, *Companion Guide to London* (1965), a good introduction and guide; BLAKE EHRLICH, *London on the Thames* (1966), a popular account of the many "Londons" that make up the metropolis; STEEN E. RASMUSSEN, *London the Unique City*, 3rd ed. (1948, reprinted 1967), a Danish architect's study of the development of London into a metropolis unlike any other; NIKOLAUS PEVSNER, *The Buildings of England: London*, 2 vol. (1952–57), comprehensive, popular surveys of buildings and their architectural features; WILLIAM KENT (ed.), *An Encyclopaedia of London*, rev. ed. (1951), a useful source for a variety of information; ERIC DE MARE, *London's Riverside* (1958), a general account of the Thames and how London has developed along its banks; JOHN SUMMERSON, *Georgian London*, rev. ed. (1962), details of a distinguished architectural period, accompanied by maps and photographs with a list of Georgian buildings in each district; *Royal Commission on Ancient Monuments (Interim Reports),* no. 8–9, 11–13 (1924–30), a well-illustrated inventory of historical monuments in London; LONDON COUNTY COUNCIL, *Survey of London* (1900 *et seq.*), each volume deals in detail with a different area of London, describing the principal buildings and their situation, with maps, plans, photographs, and drawings; WALTER H. GODFREY, *A History of Architecture In and Around London*, new ed. (1962), finds examples to illustrate the history of architecture within a 40-mile radius of London.

Physical characteristics: s.w. WOOLDRIDGE and D.L. LINTON, *Structure, Surface and Drainage in South-East England* (1955), a comprehensive scientific treatment, with charts and maps; s.w. WOOLDRIDGE and G.E. HUTCHINGS, *London's Countryside: Geographical Field Work for Students and Teachers of Geography* (1957), on the geological build of the London region and aspects of its physiography and vegetation; ANGUS D. WEBSTER, *London Trees* (1920), an account of the trees that succeed in London; R.C. HOMES (ed.), *The Birds of the London Area Since 1900* (1957), by a committee of the London Natural History Society, on birds seen in their various habitats; T.J. CHANDLER, *The Climate of London* (1965), a thorough study of the climatic characteristics of the region with particular emphasis on the contrasts between the built-up area and the surrounding rural districts, including a chapter on atmospheric pollution; R. CLAYTON (ed.), *The Geography of Greater London: A Source Book for Teacher and Student* (1964); JOHN T. COPPOCK and HUGH PRINCE (eds.), *Greater London* (1964), a study by a group of geographers of contemporary London from the viewpoints of physical, social, and economic geography, with photographs, maps, and tables.

History: W.T. HILL, *Buried London* (1955), an early history of London in the light of the discoveries of the London Excavation Council, chiefly concerns the Roman period; GORDON C. HOME, *Roman London*, rev. ed. (1948), founded upon archaeological investigations; WILLIAM PAGE, *London: Its Origin and Early Development* (1929), a political history to the end of the 12th century; REGINALD R. SHARPE, *London and the Kingdom*, 3 vol. (1894–95), a well-documented history of the City in its relations with the monarchy and parliaments; GWYN A. WILLIAMS, *Medieval London, from Commune to Capital* (1963), an account of London during the rise of the merchants, based on City archives; JOHN STOW, *A Survey of London*, ed. by C.L. KINGSFORD (1908, 1956), reprinted from Stow's text of 1603 with additional notes tracing his source of information; N.G. BRETT-JAMES, *The Growth of Stuart London* (1935), a well-annotated work based principally on original sources; T.F. REDDAWAY, *The Rebuilding of London After the Great Fire* (1940), on the economic and social forces that shaped the rebuilding; M.D. GEORGE, *London Life in the XVIIIth Century*, 3rd ed. (1951), chiefly records the life and work of the poorer classes, using quotations to provide contemporary points of view; ROBERT CARRIER and O.L. DICK, *The Vanished City* (1957), a general account of the London of the 17th and 18th centuries that was obliterated by the changes of the 19th, with illustrations; HENRY WHEATLEY and P. CUNNINGHAM, *London, Past and Present*, 3 vol. (1891), a useful reference work describing various major buildings and localities.

Government: SIR IOAN G. GIBBON and R.W. BELL, *History of the London County Council, 1889–1939* (1939), a knowledgeable study of the development of the London County Council and its services; *Report of the Royal Commission on Local Government in Greater London*, 2 vol. (1960), a clearly-written study of the development of Greater London as influenced by social and economic factors—treats the nature and purpose of local government and planning; SYDNEY K. RUCK, *London Government and the Welfare Services* (1963), an account of the scope and variety of the services available, also includes a description of the reorganization of the services in the new London boroughs; P.G. HALL, *London 2000* (1963), on the town-planning problems of the London region, including a program for regional development and urban restructuring (thoroughly documented); SYDNEY K. RUCK and GERALD RHODES, *The Government of Greater London* (1970), an account of the workings of the new system of governing Greater London that went into effect on April 1, 1965, which traces the background of this modification and interprets its significance.

Commerce and industry: P.G. HALL, *The Industries of London Since 1861* (1961), a study of the locations of various industries in London and how these change, with an investigation of the new industries in the metropolis; JAMES BIRD, *The Geography of the Port of London* (1957), an analysis of the port, its docks and adjacent industrial development, and a study of the river traffic, markets, and trade; J.G. BROODBANK, *History of the Port of London*, 2 vol. (1921), based partly on Port of London Authority records; HENRY MAYHEW, *London Labour and the London Poor* (1851; 4 vol., 1861–62, reprinted 1969), a classic report; CHARLES BOOTH, *Life and Labour of the People of London*, 9 vol. (1892–97), a description of London life during a period of momentous changes—a pioneer work in the field of social investigation; LONDON SCHOOL OF ECONOMICS, *The New Survey of London Life and Labour*, 9 vol. (1930–39), a continuation along the lines of the Booth work, with the investigated region widened to take in all of Greater London; CENTRE FOR URBAN STUDIES, *London: Aspects of Change* (1964), views of historians and sociologists on the changing communities of the metropolis; DONALD L. FOLEY, *Controlling London's Growth* (1963), a study of planning for London since World War II and its results; MARY CATHCART BORER, *The City of London: Its History, Institutions, and Commercial Activities* (1962), on the commodity markets, Baltic Exchange, Stock Exchange, and other aspects of mercantile London.

Transport: IVAN MARGARY, *Roman Roads in Britain*, rev. ed. (1967), a study of these roads, most of them leading out of London; VERNON SOMMERFIELD, *London Transport* (1934), a record and a survey of the system, including a history of the events leading up to the creation of the London Passenger Transport Board that unified services and evolved into London Transport; and (ed.), *London's Buses* (1933), a brief but informative account of their 100-year history, with many illustrations; HOWARD LINECAR, *British Electric Trains*, 2nd ed. (1949), includes a study of the building of London's early tubes and the development of the London Transport lines; E.A. COURSE, *London Railways* (1962), a history of the development of the railways that provides insight into London's growth in the 19th century; H.P. WHITE, *A Regional History of the Railways of Great Britain*, vol. 3, *Greater London* (1963), investigates the reasons for placement of the railways and studies their relationship to the economic and social life of London.

(B.E.)

Lorenz, Konrad

Konrad Lorenz, an Austrian zoologist, is the founder of modern ethology, the study of animal and human behaviour by means of comparative zoological methods. His ideas contributed to an understanding of how behavioral patterns may be traced to an evolutionary past, and his later work on the roots of aggression reached a growing audience because of its possible application to understanding social violence in urban populations and, on a larger scale, to the prevention of war.

Hermann Kacher

Lorenz.

Lorenz was born in Vienna on November 7, 1903, the son of an orthopedic surgeon. He showed an interest in animals at an early age. Receiving considerable encouragement from his parents, he kept animals of various species—fish, birds, monkeys, dogs, cats, and rabbits—many of which he brought home from his boyhood excursions. While Lorenz was still young, he provided nursing care for sick animals from the nearby Schönbrunner Zoo. He also kept detailed records of bird behaviour in the form of diaries.

In 1922, after graduating from secondary school, he followed his father's wishes that he study medicine and spent two semesters at Columbia University, in New York City. He then returned to Vienna to study. In 1927 he married Margarethe Gebhardt, by whom he had two daughters and a son.

During his medical studies Lorenz continued to make

Medical studies

detailed observations of animal behaviour; a diary of a jackdaw that he kept was published in 1927 in the prestigious *Journal für Ornithologie*. He received the M.D. degree in Vienna in 1928. He then studied comparative anatomy and was awarded the Ph.D. degree in zoology in 1933. Encouraged by the positive response to his scientific work, Lorenz established colonies of birds, such as the jackdaw and greylag goose, published a series of research papers on what he observed, and soon gained an international reputation. In 1935 Lorenz described learning behaviour in young ducklings and goslings. At a certain critical stage soon after hatching, they learn to follow real or foster parents. The process, which is called imprinting, involves visual and auditory stimuli from the parent object; these elicit a following response in the young that affects their subsequent adult behaviour.

In 1936 the German Society for Animal Psychology was founded. The following year Lorenz became co-editor in chief of the new *Zeitschrift für Tierpsychologie* (a post he has held since then), which became a leading journal for ethology. Also in 1937, he was appointed lecturer in comparative anatomy and animal psychology at the University of Vienna. From 1940 to 1942 he was professor and head of the department of general psychology at the Albertus University at Königsberg.

Work at the Max Planck Institute

From 1942 to 1944 he served as a physician in the German Army and was captured as a prisoner of war in Russia. He was returned to Austria in 1948 and headed the Institute of Comparative Ethology at Altenberg from 1949 to 1951. In 1950 he established a comparative ethology department in the Max Planck Institute of Buldern, Westphalia, becoming co-director of the Institute in 1954. He has been at the Max Planck Institute for Behaviour Physiology, in Seewiesen, since 1958 and its director since 1961.

Lorenz' early contributions dealt with the nature of instinctive behavioral acts, particularly how such acts come about and the source of nervous energy for their performance. He has also investigated how behaviour may result from two or more basic drives that are activated simultaneously in an animal. Working with Niko Tinbergen of The Netherlands, Lorenz showed that different forms of behaviour are harmonized in a single action sequence.

His concepts have advanced the understanding of how behavioral patterns evolved in a species, particularly with respect to the role of ecological factors and the adaptive value of behaviour for species survival. He has proposed that animal species are genetically constructed to learn specific kinds of information that are important for the survival of the species. His ideas have also cast light on how behavioral patterns develop and mature in the life of an individual organism. In recent years, his ideas have been applied to the behaviour of humans as members of a social species, an application with controversial philosophical and sociological implications. In a popular book, *On Aggression* (1966), he argued that fighting and warlike behaviour in man have an inborn basis but can be environmentally modified by the proper understanding and provision for the basic instinctual needs of man. Fighting in lower animals has a positive survival function, he observed, such as the dispersion of competitors and the maintenance of territory. Warlike tendencies in man may likewise be ritualized into socially useful behaviour patterns.

Lorenz has received honorary degrees from Yale, Loyola, Leeds, Basel, and Oxford universities, as well as numerous prizes and honours.

BIBLIOGRAPHY

Works: Er redete mit dem Vieh, den Vögeln und den Fischen (1949; Eng. trans., *King Solomon's Ring*, 1952); and *So kam der Mensch auf den Hund* (1950; Eng. trans., *Man Meets Dog*, 1954), entertaining semipopular accounts of Lorenz's experiences with animals and his views on animal behaviour; "Phylogenetische Anpassung und adaptive Modifikation des Verhaltens," *Z. Tierpsychol.*, 18:139–187 (1961; Eng. trans., *Evolution and Modification of Behavior*, 1965), a scientific theoretical discussion on the dual sources of behaviour in evolution and individual experience; *Das sogenannte Böse* (1963; Eng. trans., *On Aggression*, 1966), a de-

scription of the phenomena of aggression in animal species, the ethological findings and interpretations of aggression, and the significance of these for the understanding of human behaviour; *Über Tierisches und Menschliches Verhalten* (1965; Eng. trans., *Studies in Animal and Human Behaviour*, 2 vol., 1970–71), contain several papers written by Lorenz during his career and document in detail his scientific methods in studying animal behaviour.

Lorenz's life and his general approach to the study of behaviour are well described in: O. KOEHLER, "Konrad Lorenz 60 Jahre," *Z. Tierpsychol.*, 20:385–401 (1963); and in J. ALSOP, "Profiles: A Condition of Enormous Improbability," *New Yorker*, 45:39–42 (1969).

(E.H.H.)

Los Angeles

A semitropical Southern California metropolis of palm trees and oil derricks, television studios and aerospace factories, Los Angeles is the third largest city in the United States, with a 1970 population in excess of 2,800,000. It has paid for its spectacular growth by acquiring such contemporary urban attributes as smog-filled skies, a polluted harbour, clogged freeways, explosive ghettos, overcrowded schools, and annual budgets teetering on the brink of bankruptcy. In the early 1970s, however, Los Angeles was still growing, whereas most major American cities, caught up in the same conditions, were shrinking. The essence of the city

The city sprawls across some 464 square miles (1,202 square kilometres) of a broad coastal plain agreeably situated between the San Gabriel Mountains and the Pacific Ocean. Its hallmark is a network of freeways that provide moving parking places for the county's 4,000,000 cars and trucks. Angelenos commute, shop, bank, and breed by automobile. The vehicle so dominates life in this uniquely mobile community that a visiting English architectural critic, taking his cue from intellectuals who study Italian in order to read Dante, is said to have learned to drive a car so he could "read Los Angeles in the original."

The city is the seat of Los Angeles County, which contains 76 other incorporated cities—including Beverly Hills, Pasadena, and Long Beach—within its 4,083.2 square miles. The county also encompasses two channel islands, Santa Catalina and San Clemente, a mountain peak—Mt. San Antonio, familiarly known as Old Baldy, 10,081 feet (3,073 metres) high—more than 900 square miles of desert, and 74 miles of seacoast. Only eight states in the U.S. exceed the county's population, more than 7,000,000 in 1970. Since city and county are so intertwined physically and spiritually, any consideration of Los Angeles must move back and forth between the two entities. (For information on related topics, see the article CALIFORNIA.)

THE GROWTH OF THE METROPOLIS

The Spanish–Mexican town and city. On August 2, 1769, the day after celebrating a jubilee mass for Our Lady of the Angels of Porciúncula, a Spanish expedition headed by Gaspar de Portolá, searching for mission sites, camped near a river they named the Porciúncula. The expedition leaders exchanged gifts with the peaceful, Shoshonean-speaking Indians of the nearby village of Yang-na and left on the following morning. Despite three earthquakes during his overnight stay, Father Juan Crespi noted in his diary that "this delightful place among the trees on the river" had "all the requisites for a large settlement."

Two years later the Mission San Gabriel Arcángel was established about nine miles northeast of the campsite. A decade went by before Gov. Felipe de Neve succeeded in colonizing the fertile river basin with 44 recruits from Mexico, half of them children and most of them of Indian and African blood. The illiterate settlers assembled on the west bank of what is now the Los Angeles River on September 4, 1781, to claim the land they had been promised. Little is known about the events of that momentous day, but mythmakers have cloaked the city's founding in a ceremonial splendour worthy of its destiny and its high-sounding name, El Pueblo de Nuestra Señora la The early settlers

Reina de Los Angeles (The Town of Our Lady the Queen of the Angels).

El Pueblo, as it was commonly called, remained so isolated from the United States during its formative years that Joseph Chapman, the first Yankee to become an Angeleno, was thought of as an Englishman ("El Inglés"). An engaging pirate from Boston, Chapman landed in 1818 with a black fellow privateer, Thomas Fisher. Both men took a liking to the place and stayed on. The first outsider to arrive by way of the arduous overland route was a fur trapper, Jedediah Smith, who turned up in 1826, four years after an independent Mexico had hoisted its flag above El Pueblo.

Los Angeles, with a population of nearly 1,250, had become a *ciudad* (city) in 1835 when the future writer Richard Henry Dana looked in on it. "In the hands of an enterprising people," he mused in *Two Years Before the Mast* (1840), "what a country this might be." By the time war broke out between the U.S. and Mexico in 1846, the California capital was so overrun with enterprising people that Gov. Pío Pico felt helpless against "the hordes of Yankee immigrants." When American forces under Capt. John C. Frémont and Commodore Robert F. Stockton entered the city on August 13, 1846, not a shot was fired. A revolt was put down the following January, and on July 4, 1847, Los Angeles celebrated its first Independence Day.

The American city. Los Angeles was incorporated on April 4, 1850, and designated the seat of Los Angeles County, which the state legislature had established as one of California's original 27 counties. According to the first United States census, the new county had a population of about 3,500, which included 13 physicians, six lawyers, 11 blacksmiths, 19 carpenters, one painter, 138 farmers, and two Angelenos listed merely as "Gentlemen." There were no schools, and 1,115 of the 1,734 adults were illiterate. The city comprised 28 square miles.

The lawless, adobe cow town—"gambling, drinking and whoring are the only occupations," grumbled a pioneer physician in 1849—prospered in the wake of the Gold Rush when hungry miners in San Francisco and Sacramento gorged on beef from Southern California. A catastrophic drought (1862–65) following several years of declining cattle prices brought an end to the era of the ranchos, with their hospitable adobe haciendas, dark-eyed señoritas, and hard-riding cowboys known as vaqueros. Vast Spanish and Mexican land grants, mortgaged and bankrupt, their owners ignorant of *Yanqui* laws and *Yanqui* interest rates, were broken up, fenced, and planted by a new breed of Angeleno. By 1860 the city had become so Americanized that it had banned bullfighting and formed a baseball club.

With the coming of the railroads (the Southern Pacific in 1876, the Santa Fe in 1885), Los Angeles began to ship its oranges back east and, by means of a massive advertising campaign, to lure immigrants westward to the New Eden. Aided by a railroad rate war, the boom of the 1880s more than quadrupled the city's population, from 11,183 in 1880 to 50,395 in 1890. Father Crespi's campsite was overrun by shrewd, aggressive Yankee boosters determined to build a city in their own image and requiring only two things denied them by a bountiful providence: a harbour and an adequate water supply.

Unlike San Francisco and San Diego, Los Angeles has no natural harbour. A narrow, artfully gerrymandered "shoestring strip" connects the inland city with its port, 23 miles south of City Hall. Los Angeles acquired its two harbour communities, San Pedro and Wilmington, by consolidation in 1909 following an epic struggle between the powerful Southern Pacific Railroad interests and the Free Harbour League. Work began on the harbour in 1899 and the first municipal wharf was ready in 1914.

Now one of the world's largest man-made harbours, the "cargo capital of the West" handles more tonnage than any other Pacific Coast harbour and accommodates the largest commercial fishing fleet and fish-canning enterprise in the U.S.

In 1904, casting about for new sources of water to sustain the city's relentless growth, William Mulholland, wa-

The search for a port and water

ter-bureau superintendent, explored the Owens Valley some 250 miles northeast of Los Angeles and returned with a bold plan for a long aqueduct to carry melted snow from the southern slopes of the Sierra Nevada to Los Angeles faucets. The plan outraged Owens Valley ranchers, enriched two syndicates of Los Angeles speculators, and gave rise to rumours of wrongdoing that historians have never quite managed to silence.

"There it is; take it," Mulholland told the thousands of Angelenos who assembled on November 5, 1913, to watch the Owens River water come cascading into a San Fernando Valley spillway at the rate of 26,000,000 gallons a day. The 233-mile-long aqueduct, with 142 separate tunnels totalling 52 miles in length, has been supplemented by a conduit. Together they supply 525,000,000 gallons a day, 80% of the city's present water needs. The remainder comes from local wells, the underground basin of the Los Angeles River, and the Colorado River (8%). Water from Northern California, carried south over a 450-mile-long aqueduct, is expected to meet the city's requirements for the foreseeable future.

The 20th-century city. In the first decade of the 20th century, while San Francisco tidied up the rubble of its 1906 earthquake, Los Angeles tripled its population, from about 100,000 to nearly 320,000. One local entrepreneur opened the first motion-picture theatre in the United States, in 1902, and another built the city's first garage to accommodate its growing number of automobiles, but the parasol-shaded girls from the red-plush brothels run by Pearl Morton and Cora Phillips still drove about in open carriages, much to the distress of the retired druggists, dentists, and wheat farmers from the Middle West who kept streaming into Los Angeles.

"Virtue has become virulent," reported Willard Huntington Wright, who later took to writing mystery stories under the pseudonym S.S. Van Dine. He depicted the city in 1913 as "an overgrown village" swarming with "spiritualists, mediums, astrologists, phrenologists, palmists and all other breeds of esoteric wind-jammers." Successive waves of migratory writers, taking much the same tack, have stereotyped the city as an open-air institution for the elderly and the insane, where, according to *The Saturday Evening Post* (1945), "you can drink in a drive-in saloon, eat in a café shaped like a toad, and when you die, they will bury you in a 'Happy Cemetery.'"

In recent years the city's more perceptive critics have echoed the note Wright sounded toward the end of his prescient article in *Smart Set* (March 1913): "Great problems are being worked out there. The city reeks with promise." Since then, the problems have magnified; the promise has become more difficult to redeem. Smog is no laughing matter in New York, London, or Tokyo and traffic congestion no source of amusement to motorists in Paris and Rome. Los Angeles has been called the "Prototype of Supercity" and the "Ultimate City."

More than half of the city's residents live in single-family homes, walled off from one another by their disparate life-styles. The surf-fishermen at Malibu, the Sunday sailors at Marina del Rey (described by county officials as "the world's largest man-made, shallow-draft, pleasure boat harbour"), the equestrian set in Calabasas, and the cliff dwellers in the Hollywood Hills all go their own way, surfing, yachting, riding, hiking, skiing, playing golf and tennis. Nowhere is the pursuit of happiness more unabashedly materialistic, and perhaps no city in modern times has been so universally envied, ridiculed, and, because of what it may portend, feared.

Emergence of the bizarre in the city

THE CONTEMPORARY CITY

Physical layout. The city is grotesquely shaped, like a charred scrap of paper, with independent municipalities such as Beverly Hills and Culver City as well as unincorporated county land lying within its 315-mile boundaries. Elevation averages about 275 feet, ranging from sea level to 5,082 feet at Elsie Peak. The Santa Monica Mountains, covering an area of 92 square miles and reaching heights of 3,000 feet, bisect the city, separating Hollywood, Beverly Hills, and Pacific Palisades from the southern boundary of the San Fernando Valley, a 219.6-square-mile area

The city of Los Angeles and vicinity.

1 Bradbury Building
2 California Museum of Science and Industry
3 California State University at Long Beach
4 California State University at Los Angeles
5 City Hall
6 Dodger Stadium
7 El Pueblo de Los Angeles State Historical Monument
8 Ft. McArthur
9 Greek Theatre
10 Hancock Park
11 Henry E. Huntington Library and Art Gallery
12 Hollywood Park
13 Hughes Airport (private)
14 Japanese Village
15 Long Beach Naval Station
16 Los Angeles County Museum of Art
17 Los Angeles International Airport
18 Marineland of the Pacific
19 Municipal Art Gallery
20 Museum of Natural History
21 Music Center of L.A. County
22 Pasadena Playhouse
23 Planetarium
24 Post Office
25 Santa Monica Municipal Airport
26 Torrance Municipal Airport
27 Union Passenger Terminal
28 Univ. of Southern California
29 Warner Brothers Studios

Hollywood and the "Sunset Strip"

in which nearly 1,000,000 Angelenos made their home in the early 1970s.

Hollywood, eight miles northwest of the central city, was laid out in 1887 by Horace Wilcox, a Prohibitionist, who intended his subdivision to be a sober, God-fearing community. It was gobbled up by Los Angeles in 1910 when its water supply ran low. The following year Blondeau Tavern at the corner of Sunset Boulevard and Gower Street was turned into Hollywood's first motion-picture studio—to be abandoned 60 years later when Columbia Pictures moved to Burbank. By then the stars had long since left Hollywood, many of them moving into secluded hillside mansions above Beverly Hills, the most famous of which is Pickfair, built by Douglas Fairbanks for Mary Pickford in 1919.

Sunset Boulevard meanders 21 miles west from the state park, which encompasses the city's birthplace, to the sea.

A one-mile section of the boulevard becomes the "Sunset Strip," or simply the "Strip," as it cuts through county land on the eastern border of Beverly Hills. It is one of the few places where Angelenos stroll and take the sun at sidewalk cafés. During the Prohibition era of the 1920s, the Strip served as an oasis for the thirsty film colony. Forty years later the promenade had been taken over by the marijuana-smoking subculture of the young, whose discothèques and psychedelic shops stood cheek by jowl with expensive boutiques and restaurants.

Natural phenomena. *Climate.* Nothing is predictable in this unpredictable land, least of all the weather, which is usually described as unusual. Coastal mountain ranges to the north and east act as buffers against extremes of summer heat and winter cold. Even in the hottest months the humidity tends to be mercifully low and the nights cool. "Night and morning low clouds" is the most common summer forecast, with the sun breaking through in the afternoon. Pronounced climatic differences occur in different sections of the city. The San Fernando Valley is generally several degrees cooler in winter and warmer in summer than communities on the opposite side of the Santa Monica Mountains. The city's mean temperature is about 64° F (18° C). The record high was 110° F (43° C) on September 1, 1955, the record low 27.9° F (−2.3° C) on January 4, 1949. The average annual rainfall is nearly 15 inches (380 millimetres) with nearly 85% of it falling in the winter months.

Smog. When Juan Cabrillo spotted a dark-brown pall hovering over the hunting grounds of Southern California Indians in 1542, he gave the name Bahia de los Fumos (Bay of Smokes) to what is now the city's harbour. Four centuries later, in September 1943, Angelenos got their first massive doses of air pollution. Their highly publicized sunshine literally was cooking the noxious vapours rising from the stacks of their wartime factories, from their oil refineries, and, most important, from their automobiles to produce photochemical smog.

By the early 1970s the county was discharging a daily average of 26,200,000 pounds of pollutants into the atmosphere, 1,100,000 more than in 1955. Although concentrations had not increased, carbon monoxide, which hastens the death of cardiac patients, had gone up from 17,500,000 pounds a day to 18,200,000. Oxides of nitrogen, which damage the lungs and cause constriction and irritation of the bronchial tubes, had shot up from 1,100,000 pounds a day to 2,100,000. The county's crop losses due to smog were estimated at $2,900,000 in 1970.

Earthquakes. The great San Andreas Fault is 33 miles from downtown Los Angeles at its closest point, but more than 40 known lesser faults crisscross the metropolitan area. No earthquakes of major intensity—*i.e.*, higher than 7 on the Richter scale of 10—have hit Southern California since the 1850s, but aside from the periodic minor jolts that Angelenos take for granted, destructive temblors have struck Santa Barbara (1925), Long Beach–Compton (1933), and the San Fernando Valley (1971).

Winds. The city is occasionally buffeted by a Santa Ana, a hot, dry wind named for the canyon through which it often blows. Santa Anas occur when air rushes down from the high inland plateaus and is heated by compression as much as 5.5° F (3° C) for every 1,000 feet of descent. The natives are noticeably restless during a Santa Ana, and the mystery-story writer Raymond Chandler once wrote, "Meek little wives feel the edge of the carving knife and study their husbands' necks."

Fires. Dry winds whipping through narrow canyons on hot days heighten the ever-present danger of fire in the city's brush-covered mountains. On November 6, 1961, during the driest season in Los Angeles history, a fire in the affluent Bel Air district was quickly spread by 50-mile-per-hour gusts of wind. No lives were lost, but 484 homes were destroyed. Property damage was estimated at $25,000,000, making it the fifth-costliest fire in the U.S. and the worst in California since the fire that followed the great San Francisco earthquake.

The Angelenos. *The making of the mix.* Around the turn of the 20th century, as might be expected in a country still predominantly rural and agrarian, most of the newcomers to Los Angeles from other states were from small farming communities. A generation later, the annual Iowa picnics were still drawing crowds of 100,000 persons. After World War II, as elderly Iowans died off, the city swarmed with young former soldiers who had passed through Los Angeles on their way to the South Pacific and had returned to make it their home. In 1950, while the veterans waged war on crabgrass in San Fernando Valley backyards, the Iowans mustered only 50,000 for their summer picnic; and by 1970 the *Los Angeles Times* no longer bothered to cover the event.

Angelenos have always been a mixed lot. In the 1850 census, 33 of the county's 3,500 residents had been born in England, 30 in Germany, 27 in Ireland, 18 in France, and one in the Sandwich Islands (Hawaii). In 1930, non-whites composed about 14% of its population, compared with about 6% in San Francisco and nearly 5% in New York. The county now has about 100,000 Japanese-Americans and a sizable number of Chinese, Filipinos, Cubans, and Puerto Ricans. According to 1970 census data, Angelenos are getting younger, and their impoverished black neighbourhoods tend to be considerably younger than their affluent white enclaves. While the city's overall median age dropped during the 1960s from 33.2 to 30.5 years, the median age in Watts (91% black) was about 17.18; in Bel Air (97% white) it was nearly 40.

The blacks. Although 26 of the city's 44 founders were of African ancestry and the granddaughter of a black tailor ended up owning the land now occupied by Beverly Hills, the city's blacks in 1930 numbered only 38,894, 3% of the total population. Forty years later, streams of black immigrants, mostly from the rural South, had swelled the figure to 503,606, nearly 18%. They live and go to school in the separate and unequal world of de facto segregation. Only about 6% of the city's 155,000 black public-school children were attending predominantly white schools at the start of the 1970–71 term, whereas in Mississippi the comparable figure was over 26%, in South Carolina, nearly 45%.

Watts, the 2.5-square-mile core of the city's south central black ghetto, exploded on the hot summer night of August 11, 1965. The flames of Charcoal Alley gave whites a glimpse of the misery and anger of rural blacks trapped in an urban slum. After six days of looting and burning, 34 persons were dead, 1,032 wounded, and 3,952 had been arrested. Property damage was estimated at $40,000,000. Six years later the black community's unemployment rate had increased to three times the national average, and, while the people of the San Fernando Valley (96% white) drove to work on multimillion-dollar freeways, Watts was still dependent on an overburdened, outmoded bus system in a city in which to be without a car is to be crippled.

The Mexican-Americans. In the simmering barrios (neighbourhoods) of East Los Angeles, young Mexican-American activists calling themselves Chicanos began to take to the streets in the early 1970s, protesting conditions that in some respects were worse than those in Watts. The Chicano not only was born to a world in which jobs were scarce, housing substandard, schools overcrowded, streets drug infested, and welfare checks inadequate, but also he had the handicap of speaking an alien tongue in the land of his forefathers. Chicanos were likely to drop out of school two years ahead of their black neighbours and roam the same dead-end streets.

Adding further injury, the more than 500,000 Mexican-Americans in East Los Angeles had been gerrymandered into political impotence. The barrios have not been represented on the city council since 1963, when their one councilman was elected to Congress. In the same election, blacks captured and have since held three of its 15 seats.

The Japanese-Americans. Before World War II, during which some 40,000 Southern Californians of Japanese ancestry were placed in isolated detention camps by the federal government, 85% had been farmers. Twenty years after their release in 1945, only 10% were farming. The first-generation, the Nisei, and their children, the Sansei, had gone into the professions. Whereas in 1950 only one out of 22 Japanese-Americans could be found in a professional field, in 1961 the figure was one out of six. By the end of the 1960s, young Sansei intellectuals were prepared to fight for the justice and equity their elders had meekly done without.

The city's economy. Once a land of vineyards, orange groves, and dairy farms, the Los Angeles area is now dominated by banks, savings and loan associations, insurance companies, steel plants, research and development facilities, oil refineries, and factories turning out everything from toy rockets and patio furniture to spacecraft and sportswear.

Agriculture. Los Angeles County, between 1950 and 1965, lost 31,000 acres of orange groves. While its population was shooting up nearly 50% in the 1950s, it sacrificed 3,000 acres a day to the bulldozer (freeways alone consume about 40 acres per mile), and it ceased to be the nation's wealthiest agricultural county, a position it had held since 1910. It remains the largest flower market and ranks second in the slaughtering of cattle.

Manufacturing. Before World War I, San Francisco was the state's manufacturing hub, but since the 1920s it has been far outstripped by Los Angeles. Manufacturing accounts for well over one-fourth of the county's more than 3,000,000 jobs. Major products include aerospace equipment, petroleum and refining, processed food, electronics, pharmaceuticals, glass, rubber, and cement.

Aviation. The first international air meet in the Western Hemisphere was held near Los Angeles in 1910. On opening day Glenn H. Curtiss achieved the Pacific Coast's first flight in a heavier-than-air craft. A dozen years later Donald W. Douglas was turning out an airplane a week in his Santa Monica plant. One-third of the nation's World War II military aircraft were built in the Los Angeles area. During the 1950s and 1960s, industrial emphasis shifted to aerospace, electronics, and such research and development "think tanks" as those operated by the Rand Corporation in Santa Monica, Hughes Aircraft on a hillside in Malibu, and the Aerospace Corporation just south of the city's International Airport.

Motion pictures. Weekly motion-picture attendance in the U.S. dropped from 85,000,000 in the mid-1940s to 17,300,000 in 1970. Faced with dwindling profits and soaring production costs, some studios began disposing of their valuable real estate holdings. The backlot of 20th Century-Fox Film Corporation was converted to Century City, a multimillion-dollar complex of office buildings, apartments, shops, and restaurants. Universal Pictures & Television made a tourist attraction of its film-making activities. Meanwhile, many producers had taken to shooting their pictures in foreign countries in which production facilities are available at lower cost. Despite this "runaway production," however, Los Angeles remains the nation's film capital and continues to play a leading role in the radio, television, and recording industries.

Oil. Los Angeles sits on one of its major resources, as Edward L. Doheny demonstrated in 1892 when he started selling local crude oil for industrial fuel. In 1921, after the automobile had created a ravenous appetite for petroleum products, the world's richest deposit in terms of barrels per acre turned up on Signal Hill. In its first half-century its 2,400 wells produced 859,000,000 barrels of oil.

Tourism. Nearly 8,500,000 vacationers visit Southern California in the course of a year and spend around $1,500,000,000. A 30-year campaign by the city's business interests to attract still more visitors culminated in 1971 with the dedication of a large, multimillion-dollar convention and exhibition centre.

The communications media. The city's first newspaper, the *Star*, began weekly publication in 1851. Thirty years later the *Los Angeles Times* published its first issue. Acquired the following year by Gen. Harrison Gray Otis, it became the bible for the city's boosters, conservative Republicans, and antilabour forces. Its plant was dynamited in the early morning hours of October 1, 1910, and 21 men were killed. When it passed into the hands of General Otis' grandson, Otis Chandler, in the 1960s, the paper took a more liberal editorial stance and enlarged its foreign coverage. A breakfast-table institution, its daily circulation passed the 1,000,000 mark in 1971. Evening newspapers, such as the *Daily News* and the *Mirror-News*, have faded into history, leaving only the *Herald-Examiner*. More than 70 radio stations slake the Angelenos' taste for news, sports events, music, and talk. They also have nine television stations, including one for the Spanish-speaking community.

Transportation. Half of California's 20,000,000 residents live in the four southern counties served by the state's Rapid Transit District, but fewer than one in ten ride its buses. Ironically, much of the city's astonishing growth in the early 1900s was due to the superb interurban transit service provided by the big red electric cars of railroad tycoon-art collector Henry E. Huntington. The system became a freeway casualty in the early 1940s, and Los Angeles found itself committed to a state master plan designed to put a freeway within four miles of

Demise of the urban transit system

every home in the metropolitan area. A generation later state, county, and city officials were generally agreed on the urgent need for a rapid transit system, but not on what form it should take or how it was to be financed.

During World War II as many as 5,000,000 travellers a year moved through the city's Union Passenger Terminal, but by the end of the 1960s it was virtually deserted. In that same decade, the number of passengers getting in and out of planes each year at Los Angeles International Airport rose from about 7,000,000 to nearly 21,000,000, and Ontario International Airport was handling more than 800,000 passengers by 1970. Projections for the main airport indicated 34,000,000 passengers by 1979, 7,000,000 for Ontario.

Administration. *Government.* The city's mayor and its 15 councilmen are elected to four-year terms, along with the city attorney, controller, and the seven-member board of education. The county, operating on an annual budget of more than $2,000,000,000, is run by a five-man board of supervisors serving four-year terms, each of them representing a constituency of more than 1,000,000 Angelenos. No ethnic minority has won a seat on the board, but in 1969 and 1971 the city council chose one of its three black members as president pro tempore.

Angelenos live in a jurisdictional jungle of overlapping city–county agencies. In downtown Los Angeles there are two crime laboratories, one run by the city, the other by the country; the city taxpayer supports both. He also supports two fire departments, and, in some border areas, his home may be the responsibility of a city engine company that is farther away than a fire station in county territory.

Overlapping government agencies

Some city departments—airports, harbour, water, and power (the last, the largest municipally owned electric utility in the U.S.)—are virtually autonomous, and all are under the control of five-member commissions appointed by the mayor with the approval of the council. Various studies of overlapping services and jurisdictions have produced reports recommending clearer lines of authority.

Politics. In the November 1968 election, registered Democrats outnumbered Republicans by wide margins in both the county and the city. Richard Nixon, a native son running for president on the Republican ticket, carried the county narrowly but lost the city by a large majority.

The city administration traditionally has been Democratic, but in the eyes of many observers it had become under Sam Yorty, mayor since 1961, more closely aligned with the conservative wing of the Republican Party. In his 1969 mayoralty campaign against black councilman Thomas Bradley, Yorty warned that a black mayor would form a racial coalition with left-wingers, and he strongly emphasized a "law and order" platform. He was re-elected.

Law enforcement. At the time of the Watts disorders in 1965, Police Chief William Parker had become something of a folk hero to white, middle class Angelenos. Technically, his department was considered to be one of the best in the world; blacks and Mexican-Americans conceded the point, but both communities complained that in its dealings with ethnic minorities it was bigoted and brutal. Parker's successors initiated corrective measures, including an improved recruitment program, but skeptical critics argued that emphasis was placed on public relations rather than community relations. Of the nation's six largest cities, however, none has so few policemen per 1,000 residents.

Education. At the start of the 1970s, nearly 650,000 young Angelenos were enrolled in the city's public schools; one-half of them white, one-quarter black, and about one-fifth with Spanish surnames. There are 20 junior colleges in the county and five state colleges with a combined enrollment of some 270,000. The area's two oldest institutions of higher learning are the University of Southern California (USC; 1880) and Occidental College (1887). USC is noted especially for its schools of law, medicine, dentistry, engineering, and performing arts. The state-supported University of California at Los Angeles (UCLA; 1919) is the largest, with around 27,000 students. It has a wide range of undergraduate and gradu-

Institutions of higher learning

Downtown Los Angeles. Water and Power Building is in the foreground adjacent to the Music Center of Los Angeles County. City Hall is at upper left.
H. Armstrong Roberts

ate offerings, with a particularly heavy commitment to the life and geophysical sciences and the arts. California Institute of Technology, founded in 1891 as Throop Polytechnic Institute, moved to its present location in Pasadena in 1910. Telemetric commands from its Jet Propulsion Laboratory controlled the movements of the first robot spacecraft to soft land on the moon, in 1966.

Recreational and cultural activity.   *Public and commercial parks.* When the Portolá–Crespi party broke camp on the Porciúncula River during their 1769 visit, they headed west toward the sea along what is now Wilshire Boulevard. They stopped to marvel at the black, bubbling lakes on their right, which excavations between 1906 and 1913 revealed to be a unique repository of fossilized skulls and bones of long-extinct mammals trapped in the seepage of *brea,* or "tar," that was scooped up by early-day Angelenos to waterproof their roofs. The 23-acre site of the Rancho La Brea pits was given to the county in 1916 by G. Allan Hancock, an oil tycoon for whom the park is named. It features life-size figures of such creatures as the imperial mammoth, the American mastodon, the sabre-toothed tiger, the ground sloth, and the short-faced bear.

Griffith Park is spread across 4,064 rugged mountainous acres, an area larger than Beverly Hills. Mule deer wander down from the park's hillsides to peer at some of the 3,000 more exotic creatures in the city's zoo. The ranches of humorist Will Rogers in Pacific Palisades and silent film cowboy-actor William S. Hart in Newhall have been preserved as public parks. Within easy reach of the city by freeway are such commercial ventures as Disneyland, Japanese Village and Deer Park, Knott's Berry Farm and Ghost Town, Marineland of the Pacific, and Magic Mountain.

Sports.   Intercollegiate athletics is highlighted by the intense USC–UCLA rivalry. The annual New Year's Day Rose Bowl football game is played in Pasadena. Angelenos also support professional major league teams in baseball, football, basketball, and ice hockey. There is horse racing at Santa Anita and Hollywood Park.

Historic landmarks.   Angelenos have held onto little of their Spanish–Mexican past, but through the efforts of Charles F. Lummis, a colourful turn of the century editor and writer, the missions of San Gabriel (1771) and San Fernando (1797) have been preserved. Olvera Street, a narrow, block-long string of Mexican shops, cafés, and

the Ávila family's adobe townhouse (*c.* 1818), has been a popular tourist attraction since its opening in 1930. It is now part of El Pueblo de Los Angeles State Historical Monument, a 40-acre area that includes the plaza where the city got its start and the first church its residents managed to build (dedicated in 1822, rebuilt in 1861–62).

The three Watts Towers (99, 97, and 55 feet high) in the Watts section were built of broken tiles, dishes, bottles, and seashells over a 33-year period by Simon Rodia, an unschooled Italian immigrant who later explained, "I had in mind to do something big, and I did." When his work was completed in 1954, he gave the property to a neighbour and left, never to return. The towers have been hailed by art critics around the world as a major achievement of 20th century American folk art. One of the astonishing delights of downtown Los Angeles is the Bradbury Building (1893). Sunlight warms and illuminates the five-story inner court with its delicate French ironwork, Belgian marble, and Mexican tile.

The living and preserved arts.   Los Angeles from time to time has sheltered such distinguished architects, composers, and writers as Frank Lloyd Wright, Igor Stravinsky, Arnold Schoenberg, Thomas Mann, F. Scott Fitzgerald, and Aldous Huxley. The city has been the subject of innumerable novels, the most durable of which appear to be those by Raymond Chandler, Fitzgerald's *Last Tycoon* (1941), Huxley's *After Many a Summer Dies the Swan* (1940), Evelyn Waugh's *Loved One* (1948), and Nathanael West's *Day of the Locust* (1939).

Los Angeles has developed a lively marketplace for works of art. Many of its leading galleries are scattered along La Cienega Boulevard, a popular promenade between Hollywood and Beverly Hills noted for its restaurants and its rare-book shops. The city draws primarily on New York City for its opera and on London, Copenhagen, and Moscow for its ballet, but it supports its own philharmonic orchestra, and chamber music is plentiful.

Other performing arts are magnificently housed in the Music Center of Los Angeles County, which includes a 3,250-seat pavilion for symphony and opera; a 2,100-seat theatre for plays, musical comedy, and light opera; and a 750-seat forum for experimental stage productions, chamber music, and intimate opera. The Hollywood Bowl, a natural amphitheatre in the Hollywood Hills, offered its first production, *Julius Caesar,* on May 19, 1916, and initiated its programs known as Symphonies Under

The performing arts

the Stars in 1922. The out-of-doors Greek Theatre (1930) in Griffith Park provides a wide range of summer entertainment, mostly musical. Small, innovative theatres continue to spring up around the city as such old standbys as the Pasadena Playhouse darken their stages.

Among other exhibits, the county's Museum of Natural History in Exposition Park displays artifacts of Hollywood's early days and skeletons of Hancock Park's prehistoric predators. The Southwest Museum in Highland Park contains a superb collection of American Indian materials. The observatory in Griffith Park has a planetarium and a twin refracting telescope available for public use. The Mount Wilson Observatory is north of Pasadena; it has the world's first 100-inch telescope, completed in 1917.

Museums, galleries, and libraries

The county's $12,000,000 Museum of Art (1965) seems to float in a black pool next door to the tar pits in Hancock Park. The Municipal Art Gallery in Barnsdall Park occupies Hollyhock House (1918–20), designed by Frank Lloyd Wright. The J. Paul Getty Museum, in Malibu, features Greek and Roman statuary and rare paintings and tapestries by Dutch and Italian masters. Tourists often overlook the charming sculpture garden on the UCLA campus, with works by Jacques Lipchitz, Henri Matisse, Henry Moore, and Auguste Rodin, but they have beaten a path to nearby San Marino to see Thomas Gainsborough's "The Blue Boy" and Sir Thomas Lawrence's "Pinkie" at the Henry E. Huntington Library and Art Gallery.

Other treasures at the Huntington, a centre for scholarly research, include a Gutenberg Bible, the Ellesmere Chaucer, and the original manuscript of Benjamin Franklin's autobiography. The city's central library (1926) was the last building designed by Bertram Goodhue. The county's law library is unequalled in the American West. One of the world's finest collections of the works of Leonardo da Vinci is at UCLA's research library, 13th in size among the nation's academic libraries. Its William Andrews Clark Memorial Library has major collections covering English cultural history between 1650 and 1750.

THE CHANGING FACE OF THE CITY

Building and rebuilding. The 28-story city hall (1928) dominated the Los Angeles skyline until 1957, when the municipal building code's 13-story (150 feet) height limit was lifted. Towering structures began to spring up in the central city and spread westward along Wilshire and Sunset boulevards. By 1970 there were 17 buildings in Los Angeles exceeding 300 feet in height.

Bunker Hill, a fashionable residential area at the turn of the century, had become a downtown slum in the 1940s when Raymond Chandler wrote of the pensioners holed up in its dilapidated Gothic mansions: "On the wide cool front porches, reaching their cracked shoes into the sun, and staring at nothing, sit the old men with faces like lost battles." Now brisk, successful lawyers, stockbrokers, and government officials live in skyscraper apartments on the levelled hill, within walking distance of the county courthouse, the local bourse, and a massive civic centre described as "the greatest concentration of government buildings outside of Washington, D.C."

Environmental ravages. Los Angeles had 130 professional planners on its payroll in the early 1970s, more than any other city in the U.S., but it still had no general plan. A prisoner of its past, the city remained a captive of the promoters, moneylenders, builders, and speculators who continued to shape its growth. With the blessing of a city council and city-planning officials generally sympathetic to what Angelenos have been reared to regard as "progress," the developers were busy mutilating the Santa Monica Mountains, flinging up high-rise buildings at random, and converting the softly rounded hills of the San Fernando Valley into a monotonous expanse of subdivisions and shopping centres.

Although their automobiles account for 80% of their smog, Angelenos refuse to press for a modern mass-rapid-transit system. Pollution follows them when they go deep-sea fishing. The city pours 340,000,000 gallons (1,000,000 cubic metres) of sewage into the ocean on an average day, two-thirds of which has received only primary treatment. In the course of a year Angelenos discard 145,000 tons of newspaper and cardboard, the equivalent of nearly 2,500,000 trees.

"We cannot continue as if growth can go on forever," the mayor's council on environmental management reported in 1971, shortly after the planning department had suggested that the city's population in the next 50 years might be held to 5,000,000 rather than swell to the projected 10,000,000, a figure that some officials viewed with equanimity, others with alarm. The environmental advisers called on city fathers to "accept the fact that there is a limit to how many people this basin can support." The city faces "the most crucial period in its history," the report warned, echoing a plea Aldous Huxley made to a magazine writer in 1962: "You must tell people they don't have much time."

BIBLIOGRAPHY. There is no single comprehensive book on Los Angeles. Three standard works, although dated, are still indispensable: J.M. GUINN, *A History of California and an Extended History of Los Angeles and Environs,* 3 vol. (1915); CAREY MCWILLIAMS, *Southern California Country: An Island on the Land* (1946); and FEDERAL WRITERS' PROGRAM, *Los Angeles: A Guide to the City and Its Environs,* 2nd ed. rev. (1951). The first 40 years as a city are covered in two classic studies: ROBERT GLASS CLELAND, *The Cattle on a Thousand Hills: Southern California, 1850–1880,* 2nd ed. (1951); and GLENN S. DUMKE, *The Boom of the Eighties in Southern California* (1944); and in two recent works: LEONARD PITT, *The Decline of the Californios: A Social History of the Spanish-Speaking Californians, 1846–1890* (1966); and ROBERT M. FOGELSON, *The Fragmented Metropolis: Los Angeles, 1850–1930* (1967).

Three early-day Angelenos have left invaluable recollections: HORACE BELL, whose *Reminiscences of a Ranger* (1881) should be read with caution; HARRIS NEWMARK, *Sixty Years in Southern California, 1853–1913,* 4th ed. rev. (1970); and BOYLE WORKMAN, *The City That Grew* (1936). One of the most useful and captivating records of pioneer days is to be found in J. ALBERT WILSON's compendium, *Reproduction of Thompson and West's History of Los Angeles County, California* (1880, reprinted 1959). Recent works include: RICHARD G. LILLARD, *Eden in Jeopardy; Man's Prodigal Meddling with His Environment: The Southern California Experience* (1966); REMI A. NADEAU, *Los Angeles: From Mission to Modern City* (1960); CHRISTOPHER RAND, *Los Angeles, the Ultimate City* (1967); W.W. ROBINSON, *Los Angeles: A Profile* (1968); WERNER Z. HIRSCH (ed.), *Los Angeles: Viability and Prospects for Metropolitan Leadership* (1971).

(J.D.W.)

Lottery

A lottery is a scheme or procedure for distributing something (usually money or prizes) among a group of people by lot or chance. The type of lottery that is the subject of this article is a form of gambling in which a usually large number of people purchase chances, called lottery tickets, and the winning tickets are drawn from a pool composed of all tickets sold (sweepstakes) or offered for sale. The value of the prizes is the amount remaining after expenses —including the profits for the promoter, the costs of promotion, and the taxes or other revenues—are deducted from the pool; in most large-scale lotteries a very large prize is offered along with many smaller ones. Lotteries have a very wide appeal as a means for raising money; they are simple to organize, easy to play, and, in general, popular but controversial.

History of lotteries. The practice of determining the distribution of property by lot is traceable to ancient times. Dozens of references can be found in the Bible to the practice. In one example from the Old Testament (Num. 26:55–56), the Lord instructed Moses to take a census of the people of Israel and to divide the land among them by lot. The Roman emperors Nero and Augustus used lotteries to give away property and slaves during Saturnalian feasts and other entertainments. (See also references to the casting of lots in the article GAMBLING.) Modern lotteries of a similar type include those used for military conscription, commercial promotions in which property is given away by a random procedure, and the selection of jury members from lists of registered voters. Under the strict definition of a gambling type of lottery, however, payment of a consideration (property, work, or money) must be made for a chance of receiving the prize.

Early Europe. The first European records of such lotteries are from 15th-century Burgundy and Belgium and reveal that towns attempted to raise money for such purposes as fortifying their defenses or aiding the poor. Francis I of France permitted the establishment of lotteries for private and public profit in several cities between 1520 and 1539. The first public lottery to have paid money as prizes is believed to be *La Lotto de Firenze* in Florence in 1530. This was such a successful enterprise that the practice quickly spread to other Italian cities. When the Italian nation was united, the first national lottery was created in 1863, with regular (weekly) drawings organized for the purpose of providing income for the state. *Lotto*, the Italian National Lottery, is regarded as the basis for such modern games as Policy, the Numbers Game, Lotto, Keno, and Bingo.

First public lotteries in Italy and England

Queen Elizabeth I chartered a general lottery in England in 1566 for the purposes of raising money for repairing harbours (of the Cinque Ports) and other public purposes. In 1612 the Virginia Company obtained permission from James I for a lottery to help in financing the settlement of Jamestown in the New World. While several lotteries organized by the company did not erase a desperate need for funds and although businessmen in some English towns complained of difficulties related to them, they were nevertheless thought to be the "first and most certaine" way to obtain funds. Lotteries accounted for almost half of the yearly income of the company by 1621 when, as a result of bitter dissension within the company itself, the company's lotteries were finally prohibited by the House of Commons. In 1627 a series of lotteries was licensed to raise money for the building of an aqueduct for London, and, in fact, except for a ban from 1699 to 1709, lotteries were held in England until 1826.

Problems and abuses. Some important problems developed in the manner of conducting lotteries in England in the 17th and 18th centuries. These were to affect public opinion and official attitudes in Britain and America to the present day. For most of that period lotteries were the only form of organized gambling available to the people; they were intensively advertised by such promotions as torchlight processions in the streets; contractors would often manage to purchase tickets at less than the standard prices for subsequent resale at excessive markups; and a type of side bet was popularized called insurance—a small wager that a ticket would or would not be drawn in the regular lottery. The state could not derive revenues from either of the latter two practices, but dishonest private operators could. Also, it was claimed that lotteries encouraged mass gambling and that drawings were fraudulent. Their abuses strengthened the arguments of those in opposition to lotteries and weakened their defenders, but before they were outlawed in 1826, the government and licensed promoters had used lotteries for all or portions of the financing of such projects as the building of the British Museum and the repair of bridges, plus many projects in the American colonies, such as supplying a battery of guns for the defense of Philadelphia, rebuilding Faneuil Hall in Boston, and, in a lottery managed by George Washington, the building of the road over the Cumberland Mountains.

Lotteries in America. It was natural for the Continental Congress in 1776 to vote to establish a lottery to try to raise funds for the American Revolution. The scheme was abandoned, but over the next 30 years the practice continued of holding smaller public lotteries, which were seen as mechanisms for obtaining "voluntary taxes" and helped build several American universities: Harvard, Dartmouth, Yale, King's College (now Columbia), William and Mary, Union, and Brown. Privately organized lotteries also were common in England and America as means for merchandisers to sell products or properties for more money than could be obtained from a regular sale. By 1832 lotteries had become very popular indeed;

the *Boston Mercantile Journal* reported that 420 had been held the previous year in eight states.

Abuses by private organizers continued, however, and once again voices of opposition began to dominate. In 1827 postmasters and their assistants were barred from selling lottery tickets. Most of the states began legislating antilottery laws. In 1868 Congress declared it unlawful to use the mail for letters or circulars concerning lotteries ". . . or other similar enterprises on any pretext whatever." This prohibition included a very strict definition of what could be allowed to travel through the mails, and the restriction was supported by an opinion of the Supreme Court in 1878 that held lotteries to have "a demoralizing influence upon the people."

The postal rules did not have an immediate effect in eliminating lotteries, for the most successful one in America was organized in Louisiana in 1869 and ran continuously for 25 years. Agents for the Louisiana Lottery were located in every city in the United States: the total sales per month were $2,000,000 at its peak; monthly drawings generated prizes up to $250,000, and twice-yearly prizes could go as high as $600,000. In 1890 Pres. Benjamin Harrison and Congress agreed in condemning lotteries as "swindling and demoralizing agencies" and prohibited the interstate transportation of lottery tickets. The Louisiana Lottery, the last state lottery in America until 1963 (New Hampshire), was killed, but not until it had acquired both enormous profits for its (private) promoters and a reputation for bribery and corruption.

The Louisiana lottery

France and Ireland. The history of lotteries in several European countries was roughly similar to those of England and America but not to that of Italy. In France, lotteries became increasingly popular after their introduction by Francis I in the 1500s. Their general appeal lasted until the 17th century, when Louis XIV and several members of his court managed to win the top prizes in a drawing—an event that seems to have generated some suspicion and resulted in the King's returning the money for redistribution. Perhaps this occasion was a turning point for French lotteries; in any event, they were abolished in 1836. Almost a century later (1933) a new *Loterie nationale* was established, closed just before World War II (probably because the state was receiving only 1.4 percent of the turnover), and later reopened. The state in the early 1970s was receiving 32 percent.

In the 1930s also, the Irish Hospitals' Sweepstake was established and a pattern set for the modern, highly organized lotteries of the 20th century. Yet the pattern of the sweepstakes was not very different from the state lotteries of Georgian England or 19th-century Europe.

Modern lottery operations. The basic elements of lotteries are usually quite simple. First, there must be some means of recording the identities of the bettors, the amounts staked by each, and the number or other symbol on which the money is bet. The bettor may write his name on a ticket that is deposited with the lottery organization for subsequent shuffling and possible selection in the drawing. Or the bettor may buy a numbered receipt, in the knowledge that this number will be entered into a pool of numbers, the bettor having the responsibility of determining later if his ticket was among the winners. Another procedure requires only that the bettor inform a representative of the lottery which number, usually up to three digits, he guesses will be drawn, and the representative is trusted to appear later with the prize, if any is won. This is the usual procedure in the Numbers Game, which has been popular for several decades in several large American cities.

Keeping records and drawing winners

The Numbers Game is defined in state laws as an illegal lottery. Hence for it to be carried on, other illegal practices, especially bribery of the police, must accompany it; it is often referred to as a racket.

A second element of all lotteries is the drawing, a procedure for determining winning numbers. This may take the form of a pool or collection of tickets or their counterfoils from which the winners are extracted. The tickets must first be thoroughly mixed by some mechanical means as shaking or tossing. This is a randomizing procedure designed to insure, in an honest lottery, that chance and only chance determines the selection of winners. Computers have come increasingly into use for this purpose, because of their capacity for storing information about large numbers of tickets and also for generating random numbers for identifying the winners. The Numbers Game follows special procedures for identifying winners that are both random and public. Under one method the amounts paid by winning horses in two or three races at a nearby racetrack are added together to produce the winning number. Under other methods, the "number" may be three digits from the total volume of stock-exchange transactions, from daily bank clearances, or from United States Treasury balances, or from other published figures.

Policy, similar to numbers, differs in that the winning numbers are determined by a drawing of pellets numbered 1 to 78 that have been whirled in a drum-shaped wheel (the "Policy Wheel"). Twelve of the pellets are drawn, and bets are made that three, four, or five particular numbers will be drawn. Bolita, a lottery similar to Policy, is played in Puerto Rico and, in the United States, among Cuban and Puerto Rican groups. The drawing is of one numbered ball from a sack of balls numbered 1 to 100.

Promoters of public, especially of large-scale, lotteries may exploit the opportunity to make the drawing and mixing process as colourful and dramatic as possible. Drawings such as those held by the Irish Sweepstakes may be combined with horse racing in which two drawings are held, one to identify winning numbers and another to associate those numbers with the names of horses entered in a major race; the success of the individual horses then determines the final order of the prizes.

Collecting and pooling stakes

A third element is the existence of a mechanism for collecting and pooling all the money placed as stakes. This is usually accomplished by a hierarchy of sales agents who pass money paid for the tickets up through the organization until it is "banked." A practice common in many national lotteries is to divide tickets into fractions, usually tenths. Each fraction if and when it is sold separately costs slightly more than its share of the total cost of an entire ticket. Many people then buy whole tickets, in effect at a premium or discounted price, for marketing in the streets where customers can place relatively small stakes on the fractions. In a large-scale lottery, the use of the regular mail system is desirable for communicating information and transporting tickets and stakes. In the United States and some other countries, however (see above), postal rules prohibit use of the mails. Postal prohibitions apply also to international mailings of lotteries. Though post-office authorities are diligent, it is clear that much smuggling and other violation of interstate and international regulations occurs.

Rules for payoffs

A fourth requirement is a set of rules determining the frequencies and sizes of the prizes. Costs of organizing and promoting the lotteries must be deducted from the pool, and a percentage normally goes as revenues and profits to the state or sponsor. Of the remainder available for the winners, a decision must be made on whether to pay few large prizes or many smaller ones. Potential bettors seem to be attracted to lotteries that offer very large prizes, but in some cultures they also demand a chance to win smaller ones (which, typically, are wagered again in the next round). Authorities on lotteries disagree about which of these choices is better for the welfare of the people and the economic success of the lottery. The amount of the pool returned to the bettors tends to be between 50 percent and 60 percent. The Numbers Game usually returns 54 percent to winners.

Distribution of modern lotteries. The list of countries that have state lotteries or license large-scale private ones is long and not limited by religious restrictions or geographical location. It includes many African and Near Eastern states, most European countries, all the Communist countries of eastern Europe and the Soviet Union itself, most Latin American countries, Japan, Australia, and several countries on the Asian mainland, but not the People's Republic of China and India (which permits "small" lotteries). It also includes three states of the United States—New Hampshire, New York, and New Jersey. Although religious traditions may have delayed the establishment of lotteries in many countries, it is clear they no longer suppress them entirely. Communist countries attempted for a few decades to reject public gambling institutions as decadent and anti-Marxist, but now only privately organized gambling appears to be in disfavour.

Australia, however, has been called the real home of the state lottery. There, all the states except South Australia conduct lotteries for financing public programs and projects. New South Wales, which had lotteries as early as 1849, has the largest, with sales of more than 1,000,000 tickets a week; it has financed, among other things, the spectacular Sydney Opera House (completed in the early 1970s). New South Wales also raffles houses, cars, and similar prizes on a scale unequalled anywhere in the world.

Australian state lotteries

Resistance to lotteries. In view of the worldwide adoption of lotteries, the resistance offered by England and most of the United States seems anachronistic. Both may be given a closer look.

England. Repeatedly in the recent past, Parliament and the London County Council have debated bills to institute national or county lotteries. These bills have always been rejected, but not easily. Perhaps of most relevance is the fact that many other gambling activities flourish in England. Indeed, so much gambling had been successfully promoted by 1967 that the Home Secretary complained that England had "become a gambler's paradise more wide open than any comparable country." Moreover, many forms of gambling played by Britishers are themselves either variations of ordinary lotteries or closely resemble them, including Bingo, which is extremely popular among a very large percentage of the British working class, and football (soccer) pools, which are ordinarily played in such a manner that they resemble lotteries in that they depend entirely on chance to identify several draws (tries) out of all the professional soccer games to be played on a given Saturday. A large percentage of Britain's adults play the pools weekly. The premium bonds also are in fact a special variety of national lottery. Purchasers of premium bonds do not collect regular interest, but, instead, raffles are held each month to distribute prizes—all of the interest that would ordinarily be evenly distributed—among a small percentage of the bond holders.

With all these forms of gambling activities, in addition to the fact that horse racing and many other forms of gambling have long been popular, it is not surprising that prolottery bills have failed to pass.

United States. American legislators have also feared that legalizing new forms of gambling would only increase the total amount rather than compete with less desirable forms. American public opinion has been sharply divided on the desirability of lotteries. The combination of America's Puritan heritage, its history of cheating and criminal involvement in gambling, and its distrust of foreign practices all appear to be important factors.

Readers are directed to the bibliography for analyses of arguments for and against lotteries.

BIBLIOGRAPHY. For general references, see the bibliography of GAMBLING.

Economics of lotteries: ALEX RUBNER, *The Economics of Gambling* (1966), a discussion of national and state lotteries.

Social and historical issues: JOHN S. EZELL, *Fortune's Merry Wheel: The Lottery in America* (1960), an historical survey; DONALD R. CRESSEY, *Theft of the Nation: The Structure and Operation of Organized Crime in America* (1969); JOSEPH L. ALBINI, *The American Mafia: Genesis of a Legend* (1971); ROBERT D. HERMAN (ed.), *Gambling* (1967), a survey of social and political issues in gambling.

(R.D.H.)

Louis I the Pious, Emperor

It was the destiny of Louis I, who inherited the undivided Frankish empire from his illustrious father, Charlemagne, to preside over the Frankish domains during a turbulent period that was decisive in the eventual breakup of the empire. Louis was born in 778 at Chasseneuil, near Poitiers, Aquitaine, the fifth child of Charlemagne's second wife, Hildegard the Swabian. From 781 until 814 Louis ruled Aquitaine with some success, though largely through counsellors. When Charlemagne died at Aachen in 814 and was succeeded by Louis, by then his only surviving legitimate son, Louis was well experienced in warfare; he was 36, married to Irmengard of Hesbaye, and was the father of three young sons, Lothair, Pepin, and Louis (later, Louis the German); he had inherited vast lands, which seemed to be under reasonable control; there was no other claimant to the throne; and on September 11, 813, shortly before his father's death, Louis had been crowned in Aachen as heir and co-emperor.

By courtesy of the Österreichische
Nationalbibliothek, Vienna

Louis I the Pious, portrait from *Hrabanus Maurus*, manuscript of the Fulda School, 831–840. In the Österreichische Nationalbibliothek, Vienna (Codex 652).

Louis' first task was to carry out the terms of Charlemagne's will. According to the Frankish chronicler Einhard, Louis did this with great scrupulousness, although other contemporary sources tell a different story.

Internal division of the empire

Louis next began to allocate parts of the empire to the various members of his family, and here began the difficulties and disasters that were to beset him for the remainder of his life. In August 814 he made Lothair and Pepin nominal kings of Bavaria and Aquitaine. He also confirmed Bernard, the son of his dead brother Pepin, as king of Italy, which position Charlemagne had allowed him to inherit in 813. But when Bernard revolted in 817, Louis had him blinded, and he died as a result of it. Louis sent his sisters and half sisters to nunneries and later put his three illegitimate half brothers—Drogo, Hugo, and Theodoric—into monasteries.

At the assembly of Aachen in July 817, he confirmed Pepin in the possession of Aquitaine and gave Bavaria to Louis the German; Lothair he made his co-emperor and heir. Charlemagne had been in his 70s and within a few months of death before naming his heir, and for Louis to give such premature expectations to a youth of 22 was to ask for trouble. Moreover, Louis did not anticipate that he would become father of another child: the empress Irmengard died in 818; and four months later Louis married Judith of Bavaria, who, in June 823, bore him a son, Charles (Charles the Bald), to whom the Emperor gave Alemannia in 829.

Backed by his two brothers, Lothair rose in revolt and deposed his father. The assembly of Nijmegen in October 830, however, restored Louis to the throne; and, the following February, at the Assembly of Aachen, in a second partition, Lothair was given Italy. In 832 Louis took Aquitaine away from Pepin and gave it to Charles. The three brothers revolted a second time, with the support of Pope Gregory IV, and at a meeting near Sigolsheim, in Alsace, once more deposed their father. In March 834 Louis was again restored to the throne and made peace with Pepin and with Louis the German. Later in 834,

Lothair rose again, but alone; Lothair retreated into Italy. Encouraged by his success, Louis made over more territories to his son Charles at the assemblies of Aachen and Nijmegen (837–838)—a move the three brothers accepted, but with bad grace. In 839 Louis the German revolted but was driven back into Bavaria.

Meanwhile, Pepin had died (December 838), and, at the assembly of Worms (May 30, 839), a fourth partition was made, the empire being divided between Lothair and Charles, with Bavaria left in the hands of Louis the German. Toward the end of 839 Louis the German marched his troops for the last time against his father, who once more drove him back. The Emperor called an assembly at Worms on July 1, 840. Before it could meet, however, Louis the Pious died at Petersaue, an island in the Rhine near Ingelheim (June 20, 840). He was 62 and had ruled for nearly 27 years. He was buried in the Church of St. Arnulf in Metz by Bishop Drogo, his half brother.

The empire he had inherited in peace, Louis left in disarray. He had engaged in no serious external conflict, although the Danes and others had continued to make inroads into the empire. From 829 his four sons had been a constant source of disruption; the quarrels among Lothair, Louis the German, and Charles the Bald were to continue for decades after his death. In many ways Louis seems to have been an estimable person. He was presumably given the epithet the Pious because of his devoutness, his liberality to the church, his interest in ecclesiastical affairs, and the good education he had received. Contemporary historians vary little in their judgment: the Astronomer of Limousin stresses his continued courage in the face of adversity; Thegan, bishop of Trier, gives a long and admiring description of his person, his talents, his Christian charity, his devoutness, and his skill as a hunter; and the poem of Ermoldus Nigellus is full of adulation.

Assessment of Louis' reign

Like his father Charlemagne, Louis the Pious is depicted in several of the chansons de geste of the 12th century, notably the *Chanson de Guillaume,* the *Couronnement de Louis,* and the *Charroi de Nîmes:* he appears as a kindly ruler, but a weak and vacillating one.

BIBLIOGRAPHY. An excellent study of Louis the Pious in English is that of RENE POUPARDIN in the *Cambridge Medieval History,* vol. 3, ch. 1 (1922), with bibliography.

(L.T.)

Louis IV, Emperor

Louis IV the Bavarian, Holy Roman emperor of the House of Wittelsbach from 1328, was duke of Bavaria for 46 years and king of Germany for 32. His rule marks the end of the rivalry between emperor and pope as universal authorities and heralds the change from universal domain to the power state.

Louis was born in 1283(?), probably in Munich. As the younger son of Louis II, count Palatine and duke in Upper Bavaria, Louis had no claim to the crown by birth. On his father's death in 1294, the 11-year-old boy was made a ward of his brother Rudolf, who was then 20, and of his mother, Mechthild, a Habsburg and a daughter of King Rudolf I. Louis immediately found himself involved in high politics; his brother took the side of King Adolf of Nassau and his mother that of her brother, Albert I of Austria, who was attempting to depose Adolf. Keeping her son out of Munich, she sent him to her brother's court in Vienna, where he was reared, together with his Habsburg cousins, Frederick and Leopold. This circumstance no doubt had a lasting effect on Louis, though he never let political decisions be influenced by family ties. Albert's victory over Adolf of Nassau at Göllheim (July 2, 1298) allowed Louis to assume the share in the government that was his by law but that his older brother had hitherto withheld from him. The rivalry between the brothers, which had flared up again after the assassination of King Albert (1308), ended in 1310 with a partition of territories, which Louis was able to impose on the strength of being the guardian of his Lower Bavarian cousins. But the traditionally anti-Austrian attitude of Lower Bavaria led to a quarrel with the Habsburgs. Having assured himself of his brother's goodwill by means of a compromise (June

Early life

21, 1313), Louis gained a decisive victory over the Habsburgs at Gammelsdorf (November 9), while the succession to the German crown, fallen vacant with the emperor Henry VII's unexpected death on August 24, was still the subject of negotiations.

The empire had become an elective monarchy, but counts no longer figured among the candidates. The houses of Habsburg and Luxembourg (Luxemburg), risen to the rank of major German powers as a result of acquiring Austria (1282) and Bohemia (1310), respectively, contended for the throne; had it not been divided into warring lines, the House of Wittelsbach might have been a third contender. On the strength of his victory, Louis, in 1314, became the candidate of the Luxembourgs, who had failed to gain the crown for John of Bohemia, the late emperor's son. The Habsburgs, however, would not acknowledge Louis, though he was grandson of King Rudolf; in the double election of October 19–20, 1314, Louis gained little advantage from the fact that his claims were rather more substantial than those of the anti-king, Frederick III of Austria, crowned on the same day, November 25. Military successes enabled Louis to wrest exclusive control over Upper Bavaria and the Rhenish Palatinate from his brother, who had voted against him; but a permanent settlement with the latter's descendants could be made only after the death of Rudolf, his widow Mathilde of Nassau, and his oldest son, Adolf. The dynastic Compact of Pavia (1329), dividing the House of Wittelsbach into a Bavarian and a Palatinate line, enabled Louis to gain the latter line's support in matters of imperial policy. He failed, however, to achieve a lasting understanding with his Lower Bavarian cousins; that conflict was not settled until this line became extinct in 1340.

Louis' struggle with the Habsburgs

Louis' most pressing problem was the struggle with the Habsburgs. The decisive battle was fought on September 28, 1322, at Mühldorf, where Louis gained victory, taking prisoner King Frederick with his brothers. By April 1323 he could risk investing his oldest son, Louis, still a minor, with the Margravate of Brandenburg, which had been in abeyance since 1319. Territorial aspirations motivated the conclusion of a hereditary alliance with the House of Wettin as well as Louis' second marriage, to Margaret of Holland (1324), which in 1345 led to the accession of Holland and its dependencies. These successes did not sit well with John of Bohemia, who refused to be pacified either by the donation of Upper Lusatia in 1320 or by the marriage of Duke Henry the Elder of Lower Bavaria with a Luxembourg the following year, or by the acquisition, by way of collateral, of the Egerland. Luxembourg finally allied itself with France, and this move, in turn, led to an increased hostility toward Louis on the part of the Pope, who was wholly under French influence.

Pope John XXII had taken advantage of the contest for the crown of Germany to appoint Robert of Naples imperial vicar in Italy *vacante imperio* (in the absence of a Holy Roman emperor) and to threaten the Italian Ghibellines with heresy proceedings. When Louis' own imperial vicar forced the Pope and Robert to raise the siege of Milan, the heresy proceedings were extended to Louis himself, who was excommunicated in March 1324. This interdiction, never lifted, exposed Louis' adherents to a conflict of conscience while providing his enemies with a convenient excuse for disobedience. In the eyes of the Curia and of his other enemies, he was thenceforth merely Ludovicus Bavarus, Louis the Bavarian, by which name he lives on in history.

Louis hit back with several proclamations of his own, notably, the so-called Sachsenhausen Appellation of May 22, 1324, in which the charge of heresy was turned against the Pope. The argumentation ill-advisedly dealt with constitutional problems touching on the empire as well as with doctrinal points. Louis quickly acknowledged this as a mistake and softened its effect, but at this time the Austrians also joined the alliance of France and Luxembourg (July 27, 1324). Louis broke up the hostile combination by agreeing to share the rule with his prisoner Frederick; even so, he overcame Duke Leopold's objections only by further agreeing (January 7,

1326) to abdicate altogether, provided that the Pope gave his approbation to Frederick's sole rule. There was little likelihood of that because the Curia was interested in perpetuating the rivalry for the German crown. Its reaction proved to Frederick that he had been callously used; he now became a loyal co-ruler with Louis.

When Duke Leopold died in February 1326, Louis boldly opposed the Pope in Italy itself. Supported by the Ghibellines, he accepted the iron crown of Lombardy in Milan (May 31, 1327) and the imperial crown in Rome (January 11, 1328), offered by the representatives of the Roman populace. This unusual move could be considered an emergency measure because the Pope had refused to crown the designated emperor, declaring him a heretic on purely political grounds.

Acceptance of the imperial crown

Louis let himself be persuaded to depose the Pope formally by a decree of April 18, 1328, and to countenance the appointment of an antipope whose incompetence furnished John XXII with an easy triumph. Moreover, Louis' forces were insufficient to subjugate Robert of Naples or to institute a stable order in Italy, for which he lacked the necessary prerequisite of a firm hold on Germany. Turning to the north again, he celebrated Christmas of 1329 in Trent, whence he had departed for Italy in February 1327.

King Frederick died on January 13, 1330. The problem of shared rule was thus solved. Yet Louis' German enemies had not been idle. John of Bohemia had arranged the marriage of his younger son, John Henry, with Margaret, the heiress of Carinthia-Tirol, in 1330. This caused Louis to enter into a secret covenant with the Habsburgs regarding the partition of this strategically important inheritance (May 31, 1331). He thus encircled John of Bohemia, forcing him to withdraw from Italy, where he had ensconced himself in the guise of an imperial vicar. In order to confuse his enemies, Louis issued a new decree of abdication, hedged with countless provisos, on November 19, 1333; this time he proposed to renounce the throne in favour of his Lower Bavarian cousin Henry. The death of Duke Henry of Carinthia-Tirol in 1335 compelled Louis to invest the Habsburgs with Carinthia, by way of carrying out his part of the secret compact; he also granted them southern Tirol in order to save at least the northern part for himself. But the Habsburgs, in their eagerness to secure Carinthia, concluded an agreement behind his back with Luxembourg, which thus acquired the whole of the Tirol. As a result, the influential Archbishop of Mayence came over to Louis' side (June 29, 1337), and Edward III of England made a treaty with him (August 26), thus proving that Louis was a desirable ally on the international plane.

The Germans, tired of the incessant quarrels over the crown, were disconcerted by the Pope's intransigence. Through their city magistrates and other representatives, they pressed for legitimization of Louis' rule and the rejection of papal interference. When Louis issued a statement of principle regarding the accession to the imperial throne before the Frankfurt Diet (*Fidem catholicam* of May 17, 1338), he had the support not only of the cities but also of the empire's ecclesiastical lords. He used this support in promulgating a basic electoral law (*Licet juris*) in Frankfurt (August 3) and again in Coblenz, where he met the King of England and bestowed on him an imperial vicarate on the Lower Rhine. The promulgation, however, remained an empty gesture because the electoral princes, while assembled at Rhens on July 16, had rejected the Pope's claims without declaring themselves in favour of Louis and withheld their approval. The conflict over the crown and the charge of heresy thus continued to smolder. By isolating John of Bohemia and issuing a formal waiver of his own claims to the Tirol, Louis managed nonetheless to force John to renounce all claims to Italy, to declare himself a vassal, and to acknowledge Louis emperor in 1339.

Seeing that the entire clergy of the empire, except for the border bishoprics of Liège and Cambrai, had submitted to his rule and that the English held out the prospect of subsidies, Louis had reason to hope that he could confront the French in battle and thereby make the Pope yield. When Edward III declared war on France on September 1, 1339, and had himself acknowledged as king of France in Ghent on January 27, 1340, Louis was in a position to arbitrate between England and France. But the Tirolean question spoiled everything. In November 1341 Margaret expelled her Luxembourg husband; whereupon Louis, declaring that the marriage had not been consummated and was therefore void, married her with ill-considered haste to his widowed son, Louis of Brandenburg, on February 10, 1342. This created an unfavourable impression throughout the empire. Worse, it led to the final rupture with Luxembourg and to Charles of Moravia declaring himself a candidate for the imperial crown now that the King of France, at war with England, was eliminated as a pretender. Louis vainly attempted to propitiate the Luxembourgs by the cession of Lower Lusatia and by the offer of one of his daughters in marriage. They negotiated with him but at the same time encouraged the new, intensely nationalistic French pope to renew the heresy proceedings against him and to demand a new election (August 1343). Once more Louis countered by offering to abdicate, this time in favour of his son, Louis of Brandenburg-Tirol (September 1343). The Luxembourgs maintained the negotiations until Charles of Moravia, who had granted excessive concessions to the Pope, gained all electoral votes except the two of the House of Wittelsbach and thus was elected king (July 1346). Preparing himself for the war that had become inevitable, Louis died of a heart attack while bear hunting near Munich on October 11, 1347.

The Tirolean question

Louis had wanted to raise his family to royal status, such as the houses of Habsburg and Luxembourg. But he failed to achieve the major prerequisite—the welding of his family into a uniform body motivated by a single political will. He strove for this unity with all the diplomatic and juridical means at his disposal, and the Upper Bavarian law code of 1346 (first formulated about 1335) remains a monument to these efforts. For, while Charles IV did what he could to erase Louis' memory within the empire, Charles' famous edict, the Golden Bull of 1356, represents only the final codification of fundamental imperial laws that had actually evolved under Louis. This codification enabled the empire to stand up to the juridically minded church of Avignon.

Louis possessed courage and tenacity without being rigid. He won men over by a jovial and chivalrous demeanour; and his suppleness, coupled with diplomatic skill, charmed them even as a certain mercurial quality made him appear unfathomable. He was a political man, whose guiding principle remained the *honor imperii*. Even in his darkest hours he brooked no interference with the imperial rights. It would be unfair to judge him solely by the yardstick of success. It was Louis' fate to come up repeatedly against adversaries who were talented and powerful.

BIBLIOGRAPHY. The documentary sources on Louis IV are extensive but have not yet been completely inventoried. Important summaries reflecting the current state of research are given by HERBERT GRUNDMANN, "Der Kampf um das Reichsrecht unter Ludwig dem Bayern," in BRUNO GEBHARDT, *Handbuch der deutschen Geschichte*, 9th ed., vol. 1, pp. 518–554 (1970); and on Louis IV as ruler, in articles by MAX SPINDLER and HEINZ ANGERMEIER in the *Handbuch der bayerischen Geschichte*, ed. by Spindler, vol. 2, pp. 104–137, 144–181 (1969), both with bibliographies. Important modern works include RUDOLF MOST, "Der Reichsgedanke des Ludwig d.B.," *Deutschen Archivs für Erforschung des Mittelalters*, vol. 4 (1941); CARL MUELLER, *Der Kampf Ludwigs des Baiern mit der römischen Curie*, 2 vol. (1879–80), fundamental for Louis' struggle with the Papal Curia, although partly out of date; H. LIEBERICH, "Kaiser Ludwig der Baier als Gesetzgeber," *Zeitschrift der Savigny-stiftung für Rechtsgeschichte, Germanistische*, 76: 173–245 (1959), on Louis as a legislator; and, in English, W.T. WAUGH, "Lewis the Bavarian," *Cambridge Medieval History*, vol. 7, ch. 4 (1932).

(H.Li.)

Louis IX of France

Louis IX, or St. Louis, king of France from 1226 to 1270, remains the most popular of the Capetian monarchs, his reign marking the high point of the ideal of kingship in the Middle Ages in Europe. His love of peace, his reputation for piety, and his concern for the poor made him one of the most celebrated figures of French history.

Giraudon

Saint Louis carrying the hand of justice, detail from the *Ordonnances de l'Hotel du Roi*, late 13th century. In the Archives Nationales, Paris.

Louis was born April 25, 1214, at Poissy in the modern *département* of Forêt des Yvelines. He was the fourth child of King Louis VIII and Queen Blanche of Castile, but, since the first three died at an early age, Louis, who was to have seven more brothers and sisters, became heir to the throne. He was raised with particular care by his parents, especially his mother.

Experienced horsemen taught him riding and the fine points of hunting. Tutors taught him biblical history, geography, and ancient literature. His mother instructed him in religion herself and educated him as a sincere, unbigoted Christian. Louis was a boisterous adolescent, occasionally seized by fits of temper, which he made efforts to control.

Education

When his father, who succeeded Philip II Augustus, ascended the throne in 1223, the long struggle between the Capetian dynasty and the Plantagenets of England (who still had vast holdings in France) was still not settled, but there was a temporary lull, since the English king, Henry III, was in no position to resume the war. In the south of France the Albigensian heretics, who were in revolt against both church and state, had not been brought under control. Finally, there was ferment and the threat of revolt among the great nobles, who had been kept in line by the firm hand of Philip Augustus.

Louis VIII managed to bring these external and internal conflicts to an end. In 1226 Louis VIII turned his attention to quelling the Albigensian revolt, but he unfortunately died at Montpensier, November 8, 1226, on returning from a victorious expedition. Louis IX, who was not yet 13, became king, under the regency of the redoubtable Blanche of Castile.

Accession to the throne. The Queen Mother's first concern was to take Louis to Reims to be crowned. Many of the most powerful nobles refrained from participating in the ceremony, but Blanche was not a woman to be discouraged by adversity. While continuing her son's education she vigorously attacked the rebellious barons, particularly Hugh of Lusignan and Peter of Dreux (Pierre Mauclerc), duke of Brittany. Without support from King Henry III of England the baronial coalition collapsed, and the Treaty of Vendôme gave Blanche a brief respite.

She took advantage of it to put an end to the Albigensian revolt. Louis's troops were sent into Languedoc, where they forced Raymond VII, count of Toulouse, to concede defeat. On April 11, 1229, the King imposed the

Treaty of Paris on Raymond, in accordance with the terms of which Raymond's daughter was to marry the King's brother Alphonse, and, after their deaths, all of Languedoc would revert to the royal domain. As a political debut it was a magnificent success. When the students at the University of Paris revolted for a trivial reason, Louis, on his mother's advice, closed the university and ordered the students and professors to disperse, thereby strengthening the royal authority.

The problem of the Plantagenet holdings in France remained. Supported by Peter of Dreux, Henry III attempted an expedition in the west of France and landed in Brittany. Louis IX, though only 15, personally commanded the troops. He ordered the château at Angers to be rebuilt and pushed toward Nantes, where Henry III was based. There was not even a battle, for, after a futile ride to Bordeaux, Henry withdrew. Truces were renewed, and Peter of Dreux submitted to Louis's authority.

When Blanche laid down the reins of government in 1234, the kingdom was temporarily at peace. Louis IX could now think about marriage. He was a splendid knight, tall and well-made, whose kindness and engaging manner made him popular. And he was a just king: although he exacted what was due him, he had no wish to wrong anyone, from the lowest peasant to the richest vassal. He often administered justice personally, either in the great hall of the Palais de la Cité, which he later endowed with a magnificent chapel, or in his Vincennes manor, where he assembled his subjects at the foot of an oak, a scene often recalled by his biographer Jean de Joinville, the good seneschal of Champagne. He was also a pious king, the protector of the church and friend of those in holy orders. In 1228 he founded the noted Abbey of Royaumont. Although respectful of the pope, he staunchly resisted unreasonable papal demands and protected his clergy.

Marriage Blanche of Castile had selected Margaret, daughter of Raymond Berenger IV, the count of Provence, as Louis's wife. The marriage was celebrated at Sens, May 29, 1234, and Louis showed himself to be an eager and ardent husband, which made Blanche intensely jealous of her daughter-in-law. Louis and Margaret had 11 children.

After subduing Thibaut of Champagne, Louis IX had to set out again on the road for Aquitaine. This time the rebel was Hugh of Lusignan, who had married John's widow, the mother of Henry III. Once again Henry descended on the Continent, this time at Royan, with a powerful force. The majority of the nobles in the west of France united with him. An almost bloodless encounter at the bridge of Taillebourg in 1242 resulted in defeat for the English, and Henry returned to London. With each truce slightly more progress was made toward gaining a peace that would put a permanent end to this first hundred-year war between France and England.

Leadership of the Sixth Crusade. After his victory over the English, Louis IX fell seriously ill with a form of malaria at Pontoise-lés-Noyon. It was then, in December 1244, that he decided to take up the cross and go to free the Holy Land, despite the lack of enthusiasm among his barons and his entourage. The situation in the Holy Land was critical; Jerusalem had fallen into infidel hands on August 23, 1244, and the armies of the Sultan of Egypt had seized Damascus. If aid from the West was not forthcoming, the Christian kingdom of the east would soon collapse. In Europe the times had never been more propitious for a Crusade. There was a respite in the great struggle between the Holy Roman Empire and the papacy; moreover, Louis IX's forceful attitude toward the Holy Roman emperor, Frederick II, had dampened the latter's enthusiasm for war. The kingdom of France was at peace, and the barons agreed to accompany their sovereign in the Sixth Crusade.

Objective of the Crusade The preparations were long and complex. After entrusting the regency to his mother, Louis IX finally embarked from Aigues-Mortes on August 25, 1248. He took his wife and children with him, since he preferred not to leave the mother and daughter-in-law alone together. His fleet was comprised of about 100 ships carrying 35,000 men. Louis' objective was simple: he intended to land in Egypt, seize the principal towns of the country, and use them as hostages to be exchanged for Syrian cities.

The beginning was promising. After wintering in Cyprus, the expedition landed near Damietta, Egypt, in June 1249. The King was one of the first to leap onto land, where he planted the oriflamme of St. Denis on Muslim territory. The town and port of Damietta were strongly fortified, but on June 6 Louis IX was able to enter the city. He then pushed on toward Cairo, but the rain-swollen waters of the Nile and its canals stopped him for several months. It was necessary to capture the citadel of al-Manṣūrah. After several attempts, a pontoon bridge was finally built, and the battle took place on February 8, 1250. The outcome of the struggle was for a long time undecided, and the King's brother Robert of Artois was killed. Louis finally gained control of the situation through his energy and self-possession.

Retreat and capture But the army was exhausted. The Nile carried thousands of corpses away from al-Manṣūrah, and plague struck the survivors. The King had to issue orders for the agonizing retreat toward Damietta. Louis IX, stricken in turn, dragged himself along in the rear guard of his disintegrating force. The Egyptians harassed the fleeing army and finally captured it on April 7, 1250.

After long negotiations, the King and his principal barons were freed for a high ransom, and Louis rejoined Margaret of Provence at Acre. The crusaders would have preferred to return to France, but the King decided instead to remain. In four years he was to transform a military defeat into a diplomatic success, conclude advantageous alliances, and fortify the Christian cities of Syria (see also CRUSADES). He returned to his kingdom only upon learning of his mother's death.

Achievement of peace and administrative reforms. The saintly Louis enjoyed immense prestige throughout western Christendom. He took advantage of this to open negotiations for a lasting peace with the English king, Henry III, who had become his brother-in-law. The discussions extended over several years, but the treaty was finally signed in Paris May 28, 1258. The terms of the treaty were generous with regard to the Plantagenets. Although Louis could have stripped Henry III of all his continental holdings, he left him Aquitaine and some neighbouring territories. In return, the King of England acknowledged himself to be Louis's vassal. In Louis's eyes this was the most important point, for in the 13th century the power of a sovereign was measured less by the extent of his possessions than by the number and importance of his vassals. A just and equitable ruler, Louis also wanted to create goodwill between his children and those of the Plantagenets. The King's reputation for impartiality was so great that he was often called upon to arbitrate disputes outside France, as he once did in a violent dispute between Henry III and his barons.

He took advantage of his authority to reorganize the administration of his kingdom. Some of his officials, profiting by his absence, had abused their power. Louis IX appointed royal investigators charged with correcting abuses on sight and with hearing complaints. Two well-known ordinances, in 1254 and 1256, carefully outlined the duties and responsibilities of officials in the royal domain, and Louis closely supervised their activities. Royal officials were forbidden to frequent taverns or to gamble; and business activities such as the purchase of land or the marriage of their daughters could be carried out only with the King's consent. Further ordinances forbade prostitution, judicial duels, and ordeal by battle. The King imposed strict penalties on counterfeiting, stabilized the currency, and compelled the circulation of royal coinage. In general, his measures strengthened royal justice and administration and provided a firm base for French commercial growth.

Louis should not, however, be portrayed as a stained-glass figure. Like all men he had faults. He was quick-tempered and sometimes violent, and he had to struggle against his gluttony. He made his decisions alone but knew how to choose wise counsellors, and his sincere piety did not prevent him from curbing the abuses of the clergy, sometimes brutally.

The King devoted attention to the arts and to literature. He directed the construction of several buildings in Paris, Vincennes, Saint-Germain, and Corbeil (to house relics of the "True Cross"). He encouraged Vincent of Beauvais, his chaplain, to write the first great encyclopaedia, *Speculum majus*. During his reign foreign students and scholars flocked to the University of Paris.

The King was very high-spirited. Nothing would be more inaccurate than to imagine him entirely steeped in piety. After meals he gladly descended into his gardens, surrounded by his intimates, and discussed diverse topics with them. There, each one indulged in quodlibet, or in talking about anything that pleased him.

Death and canonization. But throughout the latter part of his reign he was obsessed by the memory of the Holy Land, the territory of which was rapidly shrinking before the Muslim advance. In 1269 he decided once again to go to Africa. Perhaps encouraged by his brother Charles of Anjou, he chose Tunisia as the place from which to cut the Islāmic world in half. It was a serious mistake for which he must take responsibility, and he eventually had to bear the consequences of it. Ill and weak, he knew that he risked dying there.

The expedition landed near Tunis at the beginning of July 1270 and at first won a succession of easy victories. Carthage was taken. But once again plague struck the army, and Louis IX could not withstand it. After having entrusted the future of the kingdom of France to his son Philip, to whom he gave excellent instructions (*enseignements*), asking him especially to protect and assist the poor, who were the humblest of his subjects, he died in the afternoon of August 25, 1270.

The Crusade dissolved, and his body was brought back to France. All along the way, through Italy, the Alps, Lyons, and Cluny, crowds gathered and knelt as the procession passed. It reached Paris on the eve of Pentecost, 1271. The funeral rites were solemnly performed at Notre-Dame de Paris, and the coffin went to rest in the Abbey of Saint-Denis, the tomb of the kings of France.

Without awaiting the judgment of the Roman Catholic Church, the people considered Louis IX to be a saint and prayed at his tomb. Pope Boniface VIII canonized Louis IX, the only king of France to be numbered by the Roman Catholic Church among its saints, on August 11, 1297. His feast day is celebrated on August 25.

BIBLIOGRAPHY. Among contemporary sources are JEAN DE JOINVILLE, who lived close to the king for 25 years and wrote down his recollections between 1305 and 1309; and Queen Margaret of Provence's confessor, GUILLAUME DE SAINT-PATHUS, *Vie de Saint Louis*, written in 1302–03. All of the chroniclers have been published in the *Recueil des Historiens des Gaules et de la France*, new ed., vol. 20 (1894).

Modern works include HENRI WALLON, *Saint Louis et son temps*, 2 vol. (1875), old but still useful. JACQUES LEVRON, *Saint Louis; ou, l'apogée du Moyen Age* (1969), is a good recent study with an extensive bibliography. A number of books were published on the 700th anniversary of Louis IX's death. The most valuable of them, ed. by REGINE PERNOUD, is a collection of articles by about 30 French and foreign historians: *Le siècle de Saint Louis* (1970).

(J.Le.)

Louis XI of France

King of France from 1461 to 1483, Louis XI suppressed the rebellions of his semi-sovereign vassals, centralized the administration with the help of bourgeois officials, and continued the unending struggle with Burgundy, which he finally added to the domain of France.

Louis was born at Bourges on July 3, 1423, the son of Charles VII of France by his consort Mary of Anjou. When Louis was born, the English were ruling a large part of France, and he spent most of his childhood at the Loches in Touraine. Ugly and fat, Louis grew up in austere seclusion to become secretive, ruthless, and superstitious; yet, he was also devout, intelligent, and well-informed, a cunning diplomat and a bold warrior who was able to command loyalty. Known as the universal spider, he could still claim to personify the French national consciousness; as he was later to say to his rebellious vassals, "I am France."

Louis XI of France, limestone sculptured head from Toul, France. In the Art Institute of Chicago.
By courtesy of the Art Institute of Chicago

Louis was married to Margaret, daughter of James I of Scotland, in 1436—an unhappy union formed solely for political reasons. In 1439 the King sent him to superintend the defense of Languedoc against the English and then to act as royal lieutenant in Poitou. Louis, however, was impatient to reign and was induced by malcontent princes to put himself at their head in 1440 during the revolt known as the Praguerie, named after a contemporary disturbance in Bohemia. Charles VII pardoned his rebellion and installed him as ruler of the Dauphiné.

Louis took part in his father's campaigns of 1440–43 against the English, and in 1443 he forced the English to raise their siege of Dieppe. When the Anglo-French truce of 1444 left numbers of mercenary troops unemployed, he led a large body of them to attack Basel, in ostensible support of the German king Frederick V (later Holy Roman emperor as Frederick III) in his quarrel with the Swiss confederacy. Failing to take Basel, Louis attacked the Habsburg possessions in Alsace since Frederick would not grant him the promised winter quarters. Meanwhile, Charles VII had invaded Lorraine and was holding court at Nancy. When Louis rejoined him there, Charles was completely under the influence of Agnès Sorel and Pierre de Brézé. Father and son became wholly estranged after the death (1445) of the dauphine Margaret, to whom his father had been attached. Detected in a plot against Brézé, Louis was exiled to Dauphiné. He was never to see his father again.

Dauphin, rebel, and exile

In Dauphiné, Louis served his apprenticeship as a ruler. He set up a central chancellery, reconstituted the local administration, founded the University of Valence, instituted a parlement, reduced the nobles to obedience, and confirmed the privileges of the towns. He also started to exploit the country's mines and forests and to promote its trade. Exercising full sovereignty, he pursued a foreign policy sometimes at variance with his father's. After concluding a secret alliance with Savoy for a partition of the duchy of Milan, Louis, recently widowed, married Charlotte, daughter of Duke Louis of Savoy, despite Charles VII's prohibition (1451). Subsequently, however, Louis fell out with Savoy; and in 1456, when Charles approached Louis' frontiers with an army and summoned him to his presence, he fled to the Netherlands to the court of Philip the Good, duke of Burgundy.

Installed as Philip's guest, Louis could acquaint himself thoroughly with the working of the great Burgundian state, the ruin of which he was later to seek. (Charles VII remarked that Philip was feeding the fox that would eat his hens.) At the same time, Louis kept himself posted by spies with every detail of his father's illness, thus laying himself open to the unsubstantiated accusation that he had hastened his death by poison. At last, after five years of impatient exile, Louis became king of France when Charles died in 1461.

His first act was to strike at Charles VII's ministers.

Pierre de Brézé and Antoine de Chabannes were imprisoned, but they and some of their more serviceable colleagues were subsequently reinstated. Relying largely on men drawn from the lower nobility or from the middle class, Louis formed a circle of loyal advisers who helped him to impose his authority, to enlarge the royal domain, and to develop the wealth of the kingdom.

King of France

Louis XI's major preoccupation was with the princes and great vassals of the kingdom, who were ready to form alliances with each other or with England against him. Former officers of Charles VII stirred up hostility against the King's new men; Jean II, duc de Bourbon, and Francis II of Brittany emerged as the leaders of the malcontent nobility; Philip the Good's son and future successor, Charles the Bold of Burgundy, supported the King's enemies; and the King's own brother, Charles de France, at first duc de Berry, became a tool of the rebels.

In 1465 the malcontent princes formed the League of the Public Weal to make war against Louis. All France seemed on the verge of anarchy, but the lesser gentry refused to rise against the King and the bourgeoisie rallied to him. After some fighting, the league was brought to an end by treaties with the Burgundians and with Brittany, but Louis had to yield much: the Somme towns were given back to the Burgundians, and Normandy was granted, in exchange for Berry, to Charles de France, so that all northern France, from Brittany to Burgundian Artois, was linked in the hands of the former rebels. In 1466, however, the King reoccupied Normandy.

Charles the Bold, having become duke of Burgundy on Philip the Good's death (1467), allied himself with Francis of Brittany and with Edward IV of England; but in 1468 Louis invaded Brittany and detached Francis from the alliance. He then went to his disastrous interview with Charles the Bold at Péronne (October 1468). During the negotiations Charles learned of an insurrection in Liège, fomented by the French king's agents. Furious, he put Louis under house arrest, forced him to make far-reaching concessions, and finally took him to Liège to witness the suppression of the revolt.

After his humiliation at Péronne, Louis attempted to nullify the Anglo-Burgundian alliance by assisting the ousted House of Lancaster against Edward IV, but the final defeat of the Lancastrians (May 1471) put an end to his hope. Having already attacked Burgundy, Louis found himself facing a new host of enemies, comprising not only Charles the Bold, Edward IV, and Francis of Brittany but also, in the southwest, Charles de France, to whom Louis had granted the duchy of Guyenne in 1469, Jean V d'Armagnac, and John II of Aragon, who hoped to recover Roussillon. But, after Charles de France died in 1472, both Charles the Bold and Francis of Brittany signed truces; the royal army overran Armagnac, and France and Aragon agreed to suspend hostilities in Roussillon. Charles the Bold then began scheming for a partition of France between Burgundy, England, and other states, but Louis soon concluded truces with or bought off Charles's allies.

After 1475 it remained for Louis to destroy the power of Burgundy. He subsidized the Swiss confederates and René II of Lorraine in their war against Charles the Bold, and Charles was defeated and killed in battle at Nancy on January 5, 1477. Louis thereupon proceeded to dismember the Burgundian state, eager to reunite its French fiefs to the royal domain and to take as much else as he could. Charles's daughter Mary, however, married the Austrian archduke Maximilian, who defended her inheritance against Louis. Finally, by the Treaty of Arras (1482), Louis retained full sovereignty over the Duchy of Burgundy, Picardy, and Boulonnais and possession of Franche-Comté and Artois as the dowry of Margaret of Austria, daughter of Mary and Maximilian, fiancée of his infant son and heir, the future Charles VIII.

Louis regarded war as a precarious enterprise and made it only with reluctance, though he maintained the standing army that Charles VII had instituted. Diplomacy and inheritance were the means that he preferred for extending the royal domain. Even so, Louis pursued an active policy in Spain and in Italy. After Charles the Bold's death there was no one to prevent Louis from exercising a virtual protectorate over Savoy, where his sister Yolande was regent; and he made himself the arbiter of the affairs of northern Italy.

In France itself, having broken the resistance of the princes, Louis could impose his authority everywhere. Louis XI, in referring to the abstract concept of the crown, expressed a modern idea of the state. He reaffirmed tradition by making the feast of "Saint" Charlemagne a holiday and by founding the knightly Order of Saint Michael. Yet, in his time, the subordination of subject to sovereign definitely replaced the feudal ties of personal fidelity. Centralization developed. A section of the royal council administered the justice formerly "reserved" by a lord. The role of the administrative departments was expanded and the officers of the king, owning their offices, began to constitute an influential class. A network of messengers allowed Louis XI to be abreast of all developments, and he frequently travelled throughout his kingdom. A new concordat with the Pope, concluded in 1472, allowed him to control the appointment of bishops. He augmented the royal revenues by raising taxes on his own authority. The meetings of notables and the assemblies of the estates had only a consultative role. Nevertheless, Louis XI sought the support of the bourgeoisie, some of whom were among his most trusted advisers. Considering wealth to be an element of power, he encouraged the guilds and promulgated numerous ordinances for industry. He encouraged the exploitation of mines, introduced the silk industry to Lyons and Tours, established printing at the Sorbonne (1470), stimulated Rouen's commerce with England and the Hanseatic towns, and promoted the fairs of Lyons. He also planned to create a company for the spice trade in the Mediterranean.

Domestic achievements

Of delicate health, Louis XI was a tireless worker, and overwork may have precipitated the cerebral arteriosclerosis that finally affected him. For his last two or three years he lived in seclusion at Plessis-les-Tours, in Touraine, where he died on August 30, 1483.

BIBLIOGRAPHY. For general studies, see CHRISTOPHER HARE, *The Life of Louis XI* (1907); O.W. MOSHER, *Louis XI, King of France, As He Appears in History and in Literature* (1925); PIERRE CHAMPION, *Louis XI*, 2 vol. (1927; Eng. trans., 1929); JOSEPH CALMETTE, *Autour de Louis XI* (1947); and for an analysis of the character of the King, JEAN DUFOURNET, *La Destruction des mythes dans les mémoires de Ph. de Commynes* (1966). PAUL MURRAY KENDALL, *Louis XI, the Universal Spider* (1970), is a lively as well as scholarly biography, making use of new material from Italian diplomatic records.

(M.J.Mo.)

Louis XIV of France

The glory and prestige of Louis XIV earned him the name the Sun King. He ruled France in one of its most brilliant periods and remains the symbol of absolute monarchy and of the classic age. He inspired a style and way of living embraced by all of Europe after his death. The object of the extremes of adoration and hatred, his history is filled with great achievements and terrible mistakes, with victories won and defeats suffered. After dominating Europe, he left his country weakened and impoverished, but under his rule France acquired several provinces and became the model of civilization.

He was born September 5, 1638, the son of Louis XIII and his Spanish queen, Anne of Austria. He succeeded his father on May 14, 1643. At four years and eight months he was, according to the laws of the kingdom, not only the master but the owner of the bodies and property of 19,000,000 men. Though saluted as "a visible divinity," he was, nonetheless, a neglected child given over to the care of servants. He narrowly escaped drowning in a pond because no one was watching him. Anne of Austria, who was to blame for this negligence, inspired him with a lasting fear of "crimes committed against God."

Childhood

Louis was nine years old when the nobles and the Paris Parlement (a powerful law court), driven by hatred of the prime minister Cardinal Jules Mazarin, rose against

Louis XIV, portrait by H. Rigaud, 1701. In the Louvre, Paris.
Giraudon

the crown in 1648. This marked the beginning of the long civil war known as the Fronde, in the course of which Louis suffered poverty, misfortune, fear, humiliation, cold, and hunger. These trials shaped the future character, behaviour, and mode of thought of the young King. He would never forgive either Paris, the nobles, or the common people.

In 1653 Mazarin was victorious over the rebels and then proceeded to construct an extraordinary administrative apparatus with Louis as his pupil. The young King also acquired Mazarin's partiality for the arts, elegance, and display. Although he had been proclaimed of age, the King did not dream of disputing the Cardinal's absolute power.

The war begun in 1635 between France and Spain was then entering its last phase. The outcome of the war would transfer European hegemony from the Habsburgs to the Bourbons. A French king had to be a soldier, and so Louis served his apprenticeship on the battlefield.

In 1658 Louis faced the great conflict between love and duty, a familiar one for princes of that period. He struggled with himself for two years over his love for Maza-
Marriage rin's niece, Marie Mancini. He finally submitted to the exigencies of politics and in 1660 married Marie Thérèsa of Austria, daughter of the King of Spain, in order to ratify peace between their two countries.

The childhood of Louis XIV was at an end, but no one believed him capable of seizing the reins of power. No one suspected his thoughts. He wrote in his *Mémoires*:

In my heart I prefer fame above all else, even life itself . . . Love of glory has the same subtleties as the most tender passions . . . In exercising a totally divine function here on earth, we must appear incapable of turmoils which could debase it.

The young King. Mazarin died on March 9, 1661. The dramatic blow came on March 10. The King informed his astonished ministers that he intended to assume all responsibility for ruling the kingdom. This had not occurred since the reign of Henry IV. It cannot be overemphasized that Louis XIV's action was not in accordance with tradition; his concept of a dictatorship by divine right was his own. In genuine faith, Louis viewed himself as God's representative on earth and considered all disobedience and rebellion to be sinful. From this conviction he gained not only a dangerous feeling of infallibility but also considerable serenity and moderation.

He was backed up first by the great ministers Jean-Baptiste Colbert, the Marquis de Louvois, and Hugues de Lionne, among whom he fostered dissension, and later by

men of lesser capacity. For 54 years, Louis devoted himself to his task eight hours a day; not the smallest detail escaped his attention. He wanted to control everything from court etiquette to troop movements, from road building to theological disputes. He succeeded because he faithfully reflected the mood of a France overflowing with youth and vigour and enamoured of grandeur.

Despite the use of pensions and punishments, the monarchy had been unable to subdue the nobles, who had started 11 civil wars in 40 years. Louis lured them to his court, corrupted them with gambling, exhausted them with dissipation, and made their destinies dependent on their capacity to please him. Etiquette became a means of governing. From that time, the nobility ceased to be an important factor in French politics, which in some respects weakened the nation.

Louis's great fortune was in having among his subjects an extraordinary group of men in every area of activity. He knew well how to make use of them. He was the **Patron of** protector of writers, notably Molière and Jean Racine, **the arts** whom he ordered to sing his praises, and he imposed his own visions of beauty and nature on artists. France's appearance and way of life were changed; the great towns underwent a metamorphosis, the landscape was altered, and monuments arose everywhere. The King energetically devoted himself to building new residences. Little remains of his splendid palaces at Saint Germain and Marly, but Versailles—cursed as extravagant even as it was under construction and accused of having ruined the nation—still stands. Versailles was approximately the price of a modern airport; it was an object of universal admiration and enhanced French prestige. All the power of the government was brought to bear in the construction of Versailles. Louis XIV was not wrong, as some have claimed, to remove himself from unhealthy and tumultuous Paris, but he erred in breaking with the wandering tradition of his ancestors. The monarchy became increasingly isolated from the people and thus assumed a mythical quality.

While Louis watched his buildings going up, Colbert, who supervised the construction, obtained from him the means to carry out an economic revolution aimed at making France economically self-sufficient while maximizing exports. Manufacturers, the navy and merchant marine, a modern police organization, roads, ports, and canals all emerged at about the same time. Louis attended to every detail, while at the same time giving dazzling entertainment and carrying on a tumultuous love affair with Louise de La Vallière.

In 1967 he invaded the Spanish Netherlands, which he **Early wars** regarded as his wife's inheritance, thus beginning a series of wars that lasted for a good part of his reign. Louis himself on his deathbed said, "I have loved war too much," but his subjects, who often complained of his prudence and moderation, would not have understood had he not used force to strengthen the frontiers of France. After a brilliant campaign, the King had to retreat (1668) in the face of English and especially Dutch pressure. He never forgave the Dutch and swore to destroy their Protestant mercantile republic. To this end he allied himself with his cousin, Charles II of England, and invaded The Netherlands in 1672. The long war that ensued ended in 1678, in the first treaty of Nijmegen with Louis triumphant.

Zenith and decline. The Sun King was at his zenith. Almost alone he had defeated a formidable coalition (Spain and the Holy Roman Emperor had joined the Dutch against him) and dictated terms to the enemy. He had extended the frontier of France in the north by annexing part of Flanders and in the east by seizing Lorraine and the Franche-Comté. His fleet equalled those of England and Holland. Paris called him "the Great." In his court he was an object of adoration, and as he approached the age of 40 he could view himself as far surpassing all other men.

At the same time, great changes were occurring in his private life. In 1680 the Marquise de Montespan, who had replaced Madame de La Vallière as Louis's mistress in 1667, was implicated in the Affair of the Poisons, a scandal in which a number of prominent people were accused of sorcery and murder. Fearful for his reputation, the King dismissed Madame de Montespan and imposed piety on his entourage. The ostentation, gambling, and entertainments did not disappear, but the court, subjected to an outward display of propriety, became suffused with boredom. Hypocrisy became the rule.

The King had openly renounced pleasure, but the sacrifice was made easier for him by his new favourite, the very pious Madame de Maintenon. She was the widow of the satirist Paul Scarron and the former governess of the King's illegitimate children.

In 1682 the seat of government was transferred to Versailles. The following year marked a turning point in the life and reign of Louis XIV. The Queen died, and the King secretly married Madame de Maintenon, who imperceptibly gained in political influence. He remained devoted to her; even at the age of 70 she was being exhorted by her confessor to continue to fulfill her conjugal duties, according to letters still extant.

Colbert also died, leaving the way free for the bellicose Louvois. The repulse of a Turkish invasion of his Austrian domains left the Emperor free to oppose France in the West. In 1688–89 the fall of the Stuarts and William of Orange's accession to the throne of England further reversed the situation to the detriment of France.

Revocation of the Edict of Nantes

To his traditional enemies Louis now added the entire Protestant world. His mother had inculcated in him a narrow and simplistic religion, and he understood nothing of the Reformation. He viewed French Protestants as potential rebels. After having tried to convert them by force, he revoked the Edict of Nantes, which had guaranteed their freedom of worship, in 1685. The revocation, which was accompanied by a pitiless persecution, drove many artisans from France and caused endless misfortune.

Thus began the decline.

England, the Dutch, and the Emperor united in the Grand Alliance to resist Louis's expansionism. The resulting war lasted from 1688 to 1697. Despite many victories, Louis gave up part of his territorial acquisitions when he signed the Treaty of Rijswijk, for which the public judged him harshly. He reconciled himself to another painful sacrifice when he recognized William of Orange as William III of England, in violation of his belief in the divine right of the Stuart king James II to William's throne.

Three years later, in 1700, Charles II, the last Habsburg king of Spain, died, bequeathing his kingdoms to Louis's grandson, Philip of Anjou (Philip V). Louis, who desired nothing more than peace, hesitated but finally accepted the inheritance. He has been strongly criticized for his decision, but he had no alternative. With England against him, he had to try to prevent Spain from falling into the hands of the equally hostile Holy Roman Emperor Leopold I, who disputed Philip's claim.

In the War of the Spanish Succession (1701–14) the anti-French alliance was reactivated by William of Orange before his death. The disasters of the war were so great that, in 1709, France came close to losing all the advantages gained over the preceding century. Private griefs were added to Louis's public calamities. Almost

Final years

simultaneously he lost his son, the Grand Dauphin, two of his grandsons, the ducs de Bourgogne and Berry, his great grandson, the Duc de Bretagne, and the Duchesse de Bourgogne, who had been the consolation of his declining years.

An excess of flattery from within and an excess of malediction from without had created an artificial image of the King. He was viewed as an idol who would collapse under the blows of ill fortune, but the opposite occurred. Having first been the embodiment of a triumphant nation, Louis surpassed himself by bearing his own suffering and that of his people with unceasing resolution.

Finally, a palace revolution in London, bringing the pacific Tories to power, and a French victory over the imperial forces at the Battle of Denain combined to end the war. The treaties of Utrecht, Rastatt, and Baden, signed in 1713–14, cost France its hegemony but left it

territorially intact. It retained its recent conquests in Flanders and on the Rhine, which were so much in the order of things that neither later defeats nor revolutions would cause it to lose them.

Louis XIV died on September 1, 1715, at the age of 77. His body was borne, amid the jeers of the populace, to the Saint-Denis basilica.

His heir, the last son of the Duc de Bourgogne, was a five-year-old child who was not expected to live. Louis had distrusted his nephew, the Duc d'Orléans, and wanted to leave actual power in the hands of the Duc du Maine, his son by Madame de Montespan. In attempting to accomplish this, he had drawn up a will that was to help destroy the monarchy. The Parlement of Paris, convened to nullify the will after his death, rediscovered a political power that it used to prevent all reforms during the ensuing reigns, thus making the Revolution inevitable.

Evaluation.   During his lifetime, Louis was flattered ceaselessly by his subjects, while foreign journals compared him to a bloodthirsty tiger. Voltaire portrayed his grandeur in his *Age of Louis XIV*. The Duc de Saint-Simon, a member of his court whose *Mémoires* show equal proportions of literary genius and insincerity, dealt with him quite harshly, without denying his admiration for him. Later judgments of Louis varied according to the author's political views.

Louis XIV and the French monarchy

Louis XIV was the foremost example of the monarchy that brought France to its pinnacle. He has been accused of having dug the grave of that monarchy, particularly through his religious policy, his last will, and his isolation of the court from the people. These mistakes could have been corrected. His irremediable error was to have concentrated all the machinery of the state in his own person, thus making of the monarchy a burden beyond human strength.

His reign, compared by Voltaire to that of the Roman emperor Augustus, had both its strong and its weak points. Despite his victories and conquests, France lost her primacy under him. Yet the brilliance of his reign made up for his military policies. The aristocracy of Europe adopted the language and customs of the France where the Sun King had shone, although resentments lingered for a long time.

The King identified with his office to such an extent that it is difficult to find the individual. His harshness and courage, despotism and stoicism, prodigious pride and passion for order, megalomania and religion, intolerance and love of beauty can be understood only as a function of the exigencies of governing. He wanted France to be powerful, prosperous, and magnificent but was not overly concerned with the well-being of the French people. His armies committed atrocities, but the horrors of today have eclipsed them, and under his reign one did not see whole nations reduced to slavery, mass deportations, and genocide. When an Italian chemist offered him the first bacteriological weapon, he gave him a pension on condition that he never divulge his invention.

Louis was sometimes a tyrant, but in the words of Voltaire: "His name can never be pronounced without respect and without summoning the image of an eternally memorable age."

BIBLIOGRAPHY. LOUIS XIV, *Mémoires* (Eng. trans., *Memoirs of Lewis the Fourteenth, Written by Himself and Addressed to His Son*, 2 vol., 1806), is very important for an understanding of the psychology of Louis XIV. There are many French editions of this work. Contemporary accounts include: the DUCHESS D'ORLEANS (Madame Palatine), *Correspondance complète*, 2 vol. (1857); *Mémoires* of the DUC DE SAINT-SIMON; the *Journal* of DANGEAU; reports of the Venetian ambassadors and of the marquis de Saint Maurice, ambassador from Savoy; and EZECHIEL SPANHEIM, *Relation de la cour de France en 1690* (1704; Eng. trans., *Account of the Court of France*, 1900). VOLTAIRE, *La Siècle de Louis XIV*, 2 vol. (1751; Eng. trans., *The Age of Louis XIV*), an admirably written and well-documented study, remains an important source. JACQUES ROUJON, *Louis XIV* (1943), is a very objective and complete work. Two of the best books written on this period in the past century are PHILIPPE ERLANGER, *Louis XIV* (1965; Eng. trans., 1970); and JOHN B. WOLF, *Louis XIV* (1968).

(P.Er.)

Louis XVI of France

The last monarch in the line of French kings preceding the Revolution of 1789, Louis XVI (reigned 1774–92) was unfitted by temperament and education for the duties of kingship. Weak-willed and incapable of decision, he was unable to forestall by reform the French Revolution of 1789, and once the Revolution had begun, missed the opportunity to be its leader. He never responded to, because he never understood, the liberal and democratic forces of his age. He feebly attempted first to resist and then to betray the Revolution that might well have consolidated his royal authority.

Giraudon

Louis XVI, portrait by J.-S. Duplessis (1725–1802). In the Château de Versailles.

Louis was born at Versailles on August 23, 1754, the third son of the dauphin Louis and his consort Maria Josepha of Saxony. At first known as the duc de Berry, he became the heir to the throne on his father's death in 1765. His education was entrusted to the duc de La Vauguyon (Antoine de Quélen de Caussade), who made little effort to ensure that he should be properly trained for his responsibilities. Louis nevertheless possessed an excellent memory, acquired a sound knowledge of Latin and English, and took an interest in history and geography. In 1770 he married the Austrian archduchess Marie Antoinette, daughter of Maria Theresa and the Holy Roman emperor Francis I.

On the death of his grandfather Louis XV, Louis succeeded to the French throne on May 10, 1774. At that time he was still immature, lacking in self-confidence, austere in manner, and, because of a physical defect (later remedied by an operation), frigid in his relations with his young wife. Well-disposed toward his subjects and interested in the conduct of foreign policy, Louis had not sufficient strength of character or power of decision to combat the influence of court factions or to give the necessary support to reforming ministers, such as Anne-Robert-Jacques Turgot or Jacques Necker (*qq.v.*), in their efforts to give great stability to the tottering finances of the *ancien régime*. The prestige of the monarchy was also compromised early in his reign by the decision in August 1774 to restore the powers of the Parlements (judicial bodies supporting the interests of the aristocracy) whose political authority had been withdrawn in 1771. Louis XVI's reign before 1789 coincided with the increasing strength of the aristocratic reaction. It was aristocratic opposition to the fiscal, economic, and administrative reforms of the controller general of finance, Charles-Alexandre de Calonne, in 1787 that forced the King, in July 1788, to summon the Estates-General, the representatives of the clergy, nobility, and commoners, for the following year and thus set in motion the Revolution.

After 1789 Louis XVI's incapacity to rule, his irresolution, and his surrender to reactionary influences at court were partially responsible for the failure to establish in France the forms of a limited constitutional monarchy. Louis had at first rightly regarded the Revolution as the product of aristocratic intransigence and should, therefore, have grasped the opportunity of forming an alliance between the crown and the middle-class reformers. Instead he allowed himself, in the spring of 1789, to be dominated by the reactionary court faction surrounding his younger brother Charles, comte d'Artois (later King Charles X) and to be converted to the policy of defending the privileges of the clergy and nobility in the Estates-General. He continued to believe, even after the increasingly radical trend of popular movements in Paris and the provinces during the summer had demonstrated the futility of such hopes, that the Revolution would burn itself out.

By this time the fundamental weakness of the King's character had become evident: lethargic in temperament, lacking political insight and therefore incapable of appreciating the need to compromise, Louis continued to divert himself by hunting and with his personal hobbies of making locks and doing masonry. He dismissed Necker in early July 1789 and showed his reluctance to sanction the achievements of the National Assembly (as the Estates-General was now called) such as the Declaration of the Rights of Man and of the Citizen and the "destruction" of the feudal regime in August. His resistance to popular demands was one of the causes of the forcible transfer of the royal family from Versailles to the Tuileries Palace in Paris on October 6. Yet he made still more mistakes, refusing to follow the secret advice tendered to him after May 1790 by the royalist deputy, the comte de Mirabeau (*q.v.*), abdicating his responsibilities, and acquiescing in the disastrous attempt to escape from the capital to the eastern frontier on June 20, 1791. Caught at Varennes and brought back to Paris, he lost credibility as a constitutional monarch. Thenceforward he seems to have been completely dominated by the Queen, who must bear the chief blame for the court's subsequent political duplicity.

From the autumn of 1791 the King tied his hopes of political salvation to the dubious prospects of foreign intervention. At the same time he encouraged the Girondin faction in the Legislative Assembly in their policy of war with Austria, in the expectation that French military disaster would pave the way for the restoration of his authority. Prompted by Marie Antoinette, Louis rejected the advice of the moderate constitutionalists, led by Antoine Barnave, to implement faithfully the constitution of 1791, which he had sworn to maintain, and committed himself to a policy of subterfuge and deception. The outbreak of the war with Austria in April 1792, the suspected machinations of the Queen's "Austrian committee," and the publication of the manifesto by the Austrian commander, the duke of Brunswick, threatening the destruction of Paris if the safety of the royal family were again endangered, led to the capture of the Tuileries by the people of Paris and provincial militia on August 10, 1792. It also led to the temporary suspension of the King's powers by the Legislative Assembly and the proclamation of the first French republic on September 21. In November proof of Louis XVI's secret dealings with Mirabeau and of his counterrevolutionary intrigues with the foreigners was found in a secret cupboard in the Tuileries. On December 3 it was decided that Louis, who together with his family had been imprisoned since August, should be brought to trial for treason. He himself appeared twice before the Convention (December 11 and 23). Despite the last-minute efforts of the Girondins to save him, Citizen Capet, as he was then called, was found guilty by the Convention and condemned to death on January 18, 1793, by 387 votes (including 26 in favour of a debate on the

Louis's reaction to the Revolution

Attempt to flee the country

Condemned to death

possibility of postponing execution) against 334 (including 13 for a death sentence with the proviso that it should be suspended). When a final decision on the question of a respite was taken on January 19, Louis was condemned to death by 380 votes against 310. He was guillotined in the Place de la Révolution in Paris on January 21, 1793. Louis XVI's courage on June 20, 1792, when the royal palace was invaded by the Paris mob after his dismissal of the Girondin ministry, and his dignified bearing during his trial and at the moment of execution, did something to redeem, but did not re-establish, his reputation.

BIBLIOGRAPHY. S.K. PADOVER, *Life and Death of Louis XVI* (1939; new ed., 1963), is virtually the only serious biography available in English. J. DROZ, *Histoire du règne de Louis XVI*, 3 vol. (1858), though old-fashioned and written from an exclusively political angle, is still worth consultation on the attempts of the central government to reform the *ancien régime*. It has been superseded in that respect by D. DAKIN, *Turgot and the Ancien Régime in France* (1939); G. LEFEBVRE, *Quatre-vingt-neuf* (1939; Eng. trans., *The Coming of the French Revolution, 1789*, 1947); and J. EGRET, *La Pré-Révolution Française, 1787–1788* (1962). The most recent scholarly studies of royal policy after the flight to Varennes are: J. CHAUMIE, *La Réseau d'Antraigues et la Contre-Révolution, 1791–1793* (1965), which throws an entirely new light on the royal web of counterrevolutionary intrigue; A. SOBOUL, *Le Procès de Louis XVI* (1966), which gives a succinct analysis of the issues raised by the king's trial and execution, along with documentary material from the French archives; and M. REINHARD, *La Chute de la Royauté* (1969), which is likely to remain the definitive account of the final overthrow of the Bourbon monarchy.

(Al.G.)

Louisiana

With parts of its land lying farther south than any portion of the continental United States except for south Texas and the Florida peninsula, and with New Orleans, its largest city, lying on the same parallel as Cairo, Delhi, and Shanghai, Louisiana owes much of its complex personality to its geographical position.

The state commands a once strategically vital region where the waters of the great Mississippi–Missouri River System, draining the continental interior of North America, sweep out into the warm, northward-curving crescent of the Gulf of Mexico. It is not surprising that the flags of seven nations have flown over its territories since 1682, when the explorer La Salle placed a wooden cross in the ground and claimed the territory for France's Louis XIV. The consequent varieties of cultural heritage run like bright threads through many aspects—social, political, and artistic—of the state's life.

The subtropical climate of the state has provided the magnificent, brooding scenery of the coastal bayous, and the lush dank vegetation of its shores conceals a rich mineral wealth in the form of oil. The fertile soils covering much of its terrain made it the richest agricultural portion of the Union by 1860, with sugarcane and cotton plantations flourishing. A lumbering boom ushered in the 20th century, which was to see a rapid industrialization after World War II. Mineral output exceeded $3,000,000,000 annually by the 1970s, and the state ranked second only to Texas in petroleum production.

But progress has not been without its tragic and turbulent aspects: bitter territorial disputes, succeeded by violent internal struggles for political power, impeded the social and economic development of the state and crippled many of its political institutions. The wealth of the plantations was accumulated through the extensive use of slaves, whose descendants still comprise almost one-third of the population, and whose culture has contributed much to the social fabric of the state. Racism and racial conflict have marred the development of the state from the Civil War period, through Reconstruction and the ensuing reaction, marked by the activities of the Ku Klux Klan, down to the civil rights conflicts of the 1960s and beyond. Louisiana's Deep South heritage is a complex one.

The state is delineated from its neighbours by four natural and three man-made boundaries: Texas, Arkansas, and Mississippi. Over 3,000 square miles of its 48,523

square miles (125,675 square kilometres) consist of inland waters. (For further details see NEW ORLEANS; MISSISSIPPI RIVER; NORTH AMERICA; UNITED STATES; and UNITED STATES, HISTORY OF THE.)

THE HISTORY OF LOUISIANA

Early settlement. At least 16,000 years before European exploration, Indians were present in what was to become Louisiana. At least seven archaeological sites have been excavated, notably the so-called Poverty Point sites (dated at approximately 700 BC), and the Marksville site (dated AD 100 to 550). Most Louisiana Indians lived in hunting and gathering camps in the uplands and coastal prairies, though there were farming villages in the rich, low-lying areas known as bottoms. It is estimated that there were 15,000 Indians in the area when settlement by Europeans began in the 1700s. Only about one-fifth as many Indians can be identified as such today. Their heritage remains in the many place-names that lend colour to the state's map.

While the Spanish were first to discover the area, it was the French who colonized it. Serious colonization by France began in 1699, when Pierre Le Moyne, sieur d'Iberville, together with his brother Jean-Baptiste Le Moyne, sieur de Bienville, explored the area and struggled to found permanent colonies. The city of New Orleans was established by Bienville in 1718. Royal charters covering the area had been granted, first to Antoine Crozat, in 1712, and then, in 1717, to the Scottish businessman, John Law, whose Company of the West failed in 1720. When Louisiana became a French crown colony in 1731, its population had grown from less than 1,000 to nearly 8,000, including slaves. In addition to the Frenchmen, many thousand Germans arrived, settling on the river just above New Orleans on what became known as the German Coast. Colonization was significantly increased in the 1760s with the arrival of the French-speaking Acadians, who had been expelled from Nova Scotia by the British.

Initial colonization

In 1762, Louisiana and New Orleans were ceded to Spain by a secret treaty that was to establish nearly four decades of Spanish rule and influence. In 1779, the Spanish first wrested Baton Rouge from the British, and then took all West Florida, which then extended from the peninsula westwards across the Gulf Coast to the Mississippi. In 1800 the Spanish re-ceded Louisiana to France, and in 1803 the United States concluded the famous Louisiana Purchase.

The 19th century. Louisiana was subsequently divided into the Territory of Orleans, which consisted essentially of the present boundaries of the state, and the Territory of Louisiana, which included all the vast area drained by the Mississippi and Missouri rivers. In 1810 the Territory of Orleans consisted of 77,000 people, and statehood proposals were beginning to be heard. When, in 1812, the territory petitioned to enter the Union, the eastern region now called the Florida Parishes—where the people had rebelled against the Spanish and established the Republic of West Florida—was included.

An economic boom, generated by the slave labour from Africa now toiling on the flourishing sugarcane and cotton plantations, existed by the 1830s and sets of natural cleavages were asserting themselves in the political affairs of the state as first French–American, and later planter–farmer, interests clashed in the political process. While the yeoman farmer held the suffrage, representation rested in the hands of a plantation aristocracy that overcame one-man, one-vote principles by counting slaves in the determination of district units. Under this circumstance, and with the breakdown of the two-party system in the 1850s, sentiment in the state divided when the issue of secession from the union arose. The prosecession group prevailed in the convention of 1861, even though later research had made it appear that a majority of the state's citizens wanted to stay in the Union.

Separation was short lived in south Louisiana, for by May 1, 1862, New Orleans was occupied. Louisiana was readmitted into the Union in 1868 and the state experienced a most severe Reconstruction period. Political

The Civil War and its aftermath

conflict occurred between the federal Republicans located in New Orleans and the former Confederates in the rural parishes. After 1876, Democrat contested with Republican as the freed black man, whose vote represented the balance of power, became the pawn in the electoral struggle.

The plantation economy continued to prevail as the farmer class, white and black alike, was squeezed from farm ownership into sharecropping or tenancy. Subsequent agrarian protests that emerged in the 1880s and 1890s produced the Populist (People's) Party and what seemed at the time to be a chance to overthrow the planter–merchant–lawyer rule. Louisiana entered the 20th century, however, under a restrictive rule, as the elite was able to defeat the reform movement of the farmers in the gubernatorial election of 1896 and to enact the Constitution of 1898. As a result of this triumph of reaction nearly all blacks were legally denied the right to vote, while many whites lost the will to do so. The state was now firmly in the Deep South, with all the tragic historical connotations of that term.

The 20th century. Extensive lumbering operations attracted large corporations to Louisiana for three decades after 1890, and the discovery of oil and gas reserves in this period helped to increase industrial development. While these trends may have laid the foundations for the eventual development of the Louisiana economy, the early decades of the 20th century witnessed a political leadership that was not ready to take advantage of these developments in terms of increased tax revenues and services to the people. Louisiana remained a backward, segregated, and agrarian society.

Part of the rise of the demagogic and populist Huey P. Long to the governorship in the late 1920s may well be attributed to the seriously arrested socioeconomic development of the state. With the support of the rural areas and the emerging working class, Long substituted a realism for the romance perpetuated by the conservative leadership. Under his administration, welfare benefits and educational services were extended, and bridges and roads and hospitals were constructed, not on the old pay-as-you-go basis of the past but through the floating of bonded indebtedness. Since the rise of Longism, and its perpetuation under Huey's brother, Earl K. Long (governor in 1948 and 1956), no political administration has seen fit to turn back the series of public benefits financed by increased taxation.

During and after World War II, Louisiana underwent further economic development until, by 1960, industrial plants had begun to line the Mississippi between Baton Rouge and New Orleans. Such developments did not ordain more moderate politics, however, as, in the decade beginning in 1960, national policies began to take up where the state itself had lacked impetus, demanding school desegregation and the re-enfranchising of the black third of Louisiana's citizenry. Conflicts over race and religion broke the bridge the Longs had built between north and south Louisiana, and in the presidential election of 1968, the state, perhaps symbolically, gave its vote to Southern conservative segregationist George C. Wallace.

Civil rights in the 1960s

THE LANDSCAPE

The natural environment. *Physiography.* Louisiana shares the general physiographic characteristics common to the Gulf Coast states of the southern United States, with the vital exception of the Mississippi River, which flows through the state and extends its delta far into the Gulf of Mexico. The changing course of this great North American river has created the huge Atchafalaya Basin and has dumped tons of sediment along the coast. It has been estimated that the quite beachless coastline of Louisiana is eroding at a rate of about 16 square miles per year as the system of levees, or embankments, constructed by the federal government keeps the Mississippi in a central channel.

Three types of natural regions are found in Louisiana: lowlands, terraces, and hills. The lowlands consist of the coastal marshes and the Mississippi flood plain with its natural levees and moderate relief. Similarly, the Red River Valley has a low elevation relief but with many raft lakes, built up by impounding water from a number of log jams, and red soils in association with its alluvial plain. The terraces include much of the so-called Florida Parishes above and to the northeast of the Mississippi, as well as the prairies of southwest Louisiana. On either side of the Red River Valley and in the northern portion of the Florida Parishes are found upland hills; the state's highest elevation, in northwest Louisiana, is only 535 feet (160 metres) above sea level.

The soils of Louisiana have been one of the state's priceless resources; nearly one-third of the total land area is covered by the rich alluvium deposited by the overflowing of its rivers and bayous. Muck and peat soils are found within the coastal marshes, while the bottoms hold rich alluvial soils: the lighter and coarser bottom soils of the Mississippi and Red River valleys and older alluvium and loessial, or windblown soils. Finally, within the uplands, or hills, there are more mature soils that do not sustain such a high degree of fertility.

Climate. Louisiana's climate is subtropical, a natural result of its location on the Gulf of Mexico. As it also lies at the mouth of the vast Mississippi–Missouri River Valley, halfway between the Atlantic and the Pacific oceans, the state is also affected by continental weather patterns. Hot, humid summers, tempered by the frequent afternoon thunder showers maintained by high pressure areas located to the east, alternate with mild winters periodically affected by an influx of Arctic air as high pressure settles down across the midcontinent. Louisiana is subject to tropical storms and the hurricane season extends fully six months from June through November. Average annual temperatures range from 64° F (18° C) in the extreme north of the state, to 71° F (21° C) at the mouth of the Mississippi River. The highest monthly average is 83° F (28° C) in August, and the lowest is 46° F (8° C) in January. Summer averages do not extend above the low 80s Fahrenheit, and it is the humidity, rather than the heat, that is one of the more marked characteristics of the state's subtropical climate. The frost season begins between November 1 in northern Louisiana and December 14 in the extreme southeast. The average growing season ranges from 220 to 320 days and the average precipitation from just below 48 inches near Shreveport to over 64 inches between New Orleans and Baton Rouge.

Subtropical characteristics

Plant and animal life. Natural vegetation is found in three major divisions: the first consists of forest, upland pines and hardwoods, bottomland hardwoods, and bald cypress, the second of prairie or dry grassland, and the third of marshland or wet grassland. In the southern half of the state, along a zone running west from Baton Rouge, the live oak with its characteristic drapings of Spanish moss predominates, providing a memorable element in the state's landscape. The magnolia, whose blossom is the state flower, grows throughout the state.

Muskrats and other fur-bearing rodents, together with the alligator, have been trapped in the marshes of south Louisiana. There is a great variety of birds, native and migrant, but the once-frequent brown pelican (the state bird), the ivory-billed woodpecker, and the wild turkey are nearly extinct. The grey squirrel, deer, and dove are plentiful. Fish, shrimp, crayfish, crabs, and oysters are a source of food and of income in the coastal and swamp areas.

Natural regions. North Louisiana forms a natural region including the northeast Louisiana Delta, the Red River Valley, together with the north Louisiana hills. South Louisiana, which may be said to be composed of the parish of Avoyelles together with all the parishes that lie beneath the 31st parallel, has three major subregions: (1) the Florida Parishes, (2) southwest Louisiana—which contains many Anglo-Saxon Protestants but at the same time an important French minority—and (3) in between, a region variously known as the Cajun, or the river and bayou country, or the sugar bowl.

Settlement patterns. The earliest settlements in the river and bayou parishes were "line" villages, where farmsteads were built at the river front of a long and narrow lot, with the stream itself serving as a highway. This line village pattern contrasted with the irregular pattern stemming from the ancient land division system of metes and bounds used by the Anglo-Saxons of the Florida Parishes. Where the natural levee was wide enough, a further element, that of plantations, appeared. In north Louisiana, in the period before the Civil War, the uplands were peopled from the eastern states through the medium of isolated farmsteads amongst the pine woods. Southwest Louisiana was developed after 1880, and the prairies of this region given over to the cultivation of rice. The form of settlement here resembled the geometrical pattern—based on a grid system of land division—found throughout the interior of the United States.

Variety of land divisions (margin note)

THE LOUISIANIANS

Ethnic origins. If a diversity of landscapes and forms of settlement characterizes the state, its peoples and its cultures also make for many Louisianas. The earliest European settlers were French or Spanish, and only later were the Floridas region and the northern part of the state settled by *les Américains*. Each area of settlement managed to preserve a cultural heritage strongly marked by adherence to either the Catholic or Protestant faith. The Louisiana French, particularly the descendants of the Acadians, came to dominate much of south Louisiana: indeed many of those who have arrived to live among them have been assimilated to the Cajun way of life. The French language is still heard in many parishes, and throughout south Louisiana one may hear English spoken with a French accent. In addition, several cultural islands exist in both regions of the state. These are made up of Italian, Spanish (*Isleños*), Hungarians, Germans, and Dalmatian-Slavonian communities. There are, as well, several racially mixed settlements.

The peoples of Louisiana exhibit a greater variety than those in other Deep South states not only because of the patterns of historical settlement but also because of the migration to and through New Orleans from Europe and Latin America and, more recently, from Cuba. Of the state's nearly 124,000 foreign-born residents recorded in the 1960 census, slightly over half resided in New Orleans and adjacent Jefferson Parish and of these almost one-third were Italians. The vast majority of foreign-born residents are found within the most urbanized parishes of the state. The 1960 census showed, nevertheless, that over 80 percent of the total population was comprised of native-born Louisianians. The proportion of whites so born was 77 percent while the nonwhite ratio was even higher, at 90 percent.

From the earliest days of the state, blacks have played a significant role in it. By 1970, only two states had higher proportions of nonwhites than Louisiana, whose 30.2 percent nonwhite contrasted sharply with the 12.6 percent in the nation as a whole. Historically, the Negro population was concentrated in those areas containing the plantations sustained by their labour, initially under slavery. In the early decades of the 20th century a large out-of-state migration took place, supplemented, after World War II, by a black migration to the state's urban areas. Although Louisiana's black population has been denied many of the traditional avenues leading to social and economic power, the black experience has nevertheless contributed to the life and character of the state, and of New Orleans, its major city.

The black contribution (margin note)

Demographic trends. South Louisiana contains 70 percent of the state's population. The 1970 census figures reveal that about 34 percent of the people in both north and south Louisiana reside in their three most populated parishes. A predominantly urban population was achieved for the first time in 1950, and the proportion of the population residing in urban places had risen to 66.1 percent by 1970. New Orleans has always been the dominant urban settlement, and, since 1810, the population of the city has been about 20 percent of the total state population. The farm population, which constituted 36 percent of the total in 1940, had decreased to a proportion of barely 7 percent by the 1960s.

Louisiana has a young population. Fully 32 percent were under 15 years of age in 1970 while, on the other hand, only 8.4 percent were 65 years and over (the national figures were 28.5 percent and 9.9 percent, respectively). The parishes with greater than average numbers of young are found in south Louisiana, where the predominantly Catholic population sustains a higher birth rate and immigration is high. The heavier emigration of north Louisiana gives the area's population a higher average age.

The 1970 census showed a total Louisiana population of 3,641,306. The rate of growth between 1960 and 1970 was 11.9 percent, slightly below the national average, and resulted in a net gain of some 386,000 over the decade, mostly as a result of the excess of births over deaths. Death rates are slightly lower than the national average and the state's birth rate is slightly higher. The white population increased by 328,000 over the same period, while the black population increased by almost 50,000. This trend is expected to continue, with high rates of net in-migration in the urbanized areas and with net out-migration affecting the rural regions. Demographers expect south Louisiana, at least, to join the whole coastal region from South Carolina to south Texas as one of the fastest growing areas in the nation.

Migratory trends (margin note)

THE STATE'S ECONOMY

Louisiana has shared the general condition afflicting Southern states: economic underdevelopment. As late as 1940 nearly one-third of the labour force was employed in the primary, raw-material-oriented industries while only one-fifth worked in the secondary sector of mining, building, and manufacturing. Such an imbalance had the effect of depressing total personal income per capita, which, as late as 1929, was but slightly more than half of the national figure.

World War II hastened the industrial growth of Louisiana to the extent that the proportion of the labour force engaged in manufacturing alone increased from 13 percent to nearly 16 percent in the 20-year period ending 1960. The most important development was that of a chemical industry, based on the fortuitous local combination of oil, sulfur, salt, and water. An investment boom occurred from 1947 to 1957 when the first big move to offshore petroleum production was made. Though the trend subsequently fluctuated, the state may be expected to continue to experience industrial expansion as its program of offering inducement to industrial investment is maintained.

Resources. Petroleum resources are found in all areas of the state, but the main oil fields have been developed between Shreveport and Monroe, and throughout most of south Louisiana. In recent years, drilling has moved out into the open Gulf. Natural gas resources have also been utilized. Oil in Louisiana is often found in association with the more than 100 known salt domes, blister-like intrusions in the bedrock, and sulfur lies in the caprock overlying the salt. Conservation efforts have capitalized on the resources of soil and climate, and there is, as a result, extensive "tree farming." The natural gas resources of the state have been an important source of industrial power and the abundant mineral fuels which are available have been used to develop electrical power for the state. Louisiana also possesses a prime asset in its water resources.

Industry and agriculture. The total value added by manufacture in the state averaged over $2,000,000,000 annually by the late 1960s. Petroleum and chemical products, food processing, transportation equipment, and paper products were the leading items concerned. Cotton is no longer king in the agricultural domain: it was still first in cash farm receipts in 1960, but by 1969 beef cattle had become the leading agricultural product followed by rice, soybeans, dairying, sugarcane, with cotton reduced to sixth in importance. While the state has become much less dependent upon farming, it is estimated that the farm and farm-oriented business together constitute some 10 percent of the employment structure of the state. New Orleans remains the country's second-ranked port while

The decline of cotton (margin note)

Baton Rouge, at the head of deep channel navigation on the Mississippi, is important for shipping of petroleum and chemical products, including aluminum, and grain.

The growth in Louisiana's per capita personal income from 1960 to 1970 was 85 percent, although, with a figure of $3,065 (78.4 percent of the national average), the state still ranked only 41st among the U.S. states.

The public sector. In the public sector, state revenue is characterized by a high proportion—approaching 30 percent—of federal grants and a high degree of fiscal concentration on the level of state government. Louisiana's per capita state general revenue amounted to $280 in 1968, giving it sixth rank among the states, but this figure is somewhat misleading, as over one-third of all the state's revenues excluding federal funds came from taxes on oil and gas production, rather than from taxes paid directly by the people.

The state budget topped $1,000,000,000 for the first time in 1965: the bulk of tax revenues goes for expenditures for education, highways, and public welfare. Public welfare receives support above the national average, while education receives below average support. The state government has not been unwilling to initiate expenditures, although no major new source has been taxed since 1948, and the problem of balancing the budget has, in consequence, become increasingly difficult.

The tidelands controversy Many political leaders believe the state's current fiscal woes can be resolved if the "tidelands" oil controversy with the Federal government can be settled, as millions of dollars are now tied up in escrow awaiting the outcome. The major question involved remains that of the location of the seaward boundary of the state. State officials contest the federal government's claim to offshore leases beyond the three-mile limit until the question is settled as to what is the actual shoreline along the marshy, beachless edges of the state.

The labour movement has failed to gain a strong foothold in the state, though union leaders have become effective lobbyists in the state legislature. The percentage of nonagricultural employees who belonged to unions is, at some 18 percent, barely two-thirds of the corresponding national figure.

TRANSPORTATION

Louisiana waterways have never ceased to be an important means of transportation. By the 1970s, the state's 4,800–7,500 miles of navigable waterways included the intracoastal canal. This—Louisiana's only east–west waterway and canal system—runs some 400 miles from Mississippi Sound to the Sabine River and gives the important ports of Baton Rouge, New Orleans, and Lake Charles, access to the Mississippi River.

Railroads became common after the 1830s, initially as feeders to the steamboat traffic, with the Clinton and Port Hudson line being the state's first. Railroading reached its peak in the early 20th century in connection with a feverish lumbering boom and there are currently almost 4,000 miles of track in Louisiana. There are 53,000 miles of highway in the state. Louisiana has at least 65 airports and New Orleans International Airport, a leading continental link, is a major point of connection with Latin America.

Since the beginning of the 20th century, pipelines have existed to carry crude oil to refineries, or natural gas to provide energy for home or industry in state and distant markets. Many miles of electric power lines likewise crisscross the state.

ADMINISTRATION AND SOCIAL CONDITIONS

The constitutional framework. A constitution adopted in 1921 was the tenth in 108 years. It has managed to remain in force over the ensuing half-century, a period during which the state witnessed more fundamental change than had occurred in all the preceding 11 decades of experience with statehood.

The earliest document (1812) secured the political power of the planters and business classes and gave great appointive powers to the governor: the antebellum documents of 1845 and 1852 extended the suffrage and made every government office, including the judiciary, elective. Representation, based on total population, continued legislative domination by the planter masters. The Constitution of 1861, which substituted the phrase "Confederate States" for "United States," and its successors of 1864 and 1868, which extended the suffrage to all males, black as well as white, may be called the Civil War documents. The Constitution of 1879, marking the end of the Reconstruction period, sought to restrict the action of the legislature and granted executive powers rivalling those of 1812, while the Constitution of 1898 disenfranchised the black citizens of the state. The Constitutions of 1913 and 1921 were written by delegates of conventions called to grapple with the problems of the 20th century: in many respects, they failed, not least because of the shadows of the past that hung over them.

The governor remains the most powerful official, not only from the weight of tradition (and personal performance) but also because of the extent of his patronage among the more than 250 executive agencies in the state.

The parish system **Local government.** Local self-government in Louisiana followed the Virginia system of county government. The parish (county), together with municipality and special district, are the units of local government. There are 64 parishes with land areas and population varying from the 205 square miles and 593,471 people in Orleans to 1,441 square miles and 8,194 people in Cameron Parish. The name of the parish governing board, "the police jury," is unique.

The 265 incorporated municipalities in Louisiana are state units and exercise narrowly construed powers. The charter of incorporation detailed by law recognizes three classes of municipalities based upon population: city (5,000); town, (1,000–4,999); and village, (150–999).

Special districts established by the legislature provide for the administration of new or expanding functions of local government. There are about 630 units of local government of which just over 300 are special districts, nearly 70 of them being school districts.

Political life. The closed primary system is used in the nomination of congressmen, state legislators, and all other state, district, and parish officers. Usually a runoff is necessary, since nomination requires a majority of the votes cast. Democratic nomination has been tantamount to victory but, recently the Republicans have made the general election important again.

The State Central Committee, the governing body of both the Democratic and Republican parties, is presently entitled to 105 members elected every four years, although, since they are not organized in each parish, the Republicans actually have a smaller number. These committees determine the procedures for the selection of presidential electors.

The conduct of elections at the lowest level has been the responsibility of election commissioners. Since 1954, the use of voting machines has been mandatory in all elections.

While many whites continue to indicate a determination to maintain the ways of a segregated society, utilizing either their votes or more direct racist methods, the traditional barriers are nevertheless coming down. At polling booths, in schools, on public conveyances, in stores and plants, and even at some churches, desegregation of the races is taking place, although it must be admitted that this has come about not so much from voluntary choice on the part of the white power structure, as from the insistence of federal laws. A civil rights movement has been active in Louisiana, where the National Association for the Advancement of Colored People has, perhaps, been the most effective among various vehicles catering for the establishment of black rights and the organization of protests. From the 1950s on, communities have established varieties of biracial human relations councils. Their activities were supplemented in the 1960s by federal monies from the Office of Economic Opportunity, which sustained various organizations designed for community advancement. Through efforts beginning in New Orleans in the 1940s and extending to south Louisiana rural parishes and other urban areas in the 1950s, about 300,000 blacks, or about 60 percent of the potential total, have become registered voters.

The legal system. Louisiana's legal system is distinguished from that of the other 49 states in that it is based not on the common law but on civil law, which is code, or written, law. In this, the state draws upon her colonial inheritance, whereby she adopted a code based upon the Code Napoléon of France and further influenced by Spanish laws, each of which, in turn, had a common source in Roman law. The civil law consists of broad principles drafted by authorities in various fields of law. In Louisiana it is enacted in the constitution, which vests authority to make law in the legislature, whereas the functions of the courts are limited to the application of the law to given sets of facts, not bound by previous decisions. It governs all personal and property rights and has been extended to civil and criminal procedures.

Services. Close to 1,000,000 children are enrolled in the schools of Louisiana, approximately 15 percent of them in nonpublic parochial schools located primarily in south Louisiana. Public elementary and secondary education is administered by an elected state board of education and the state department of education, whose superintendent is also elected. The schools are locally administered by 64 parish school boards and three independent city school boards. The state board also administers nine colleges and universities, while the Louisiana State University system, with five campuses, two medical centres, and widespread agricultural activities, is administered by its own 15-member board of supervisors. Louisiana compares poorly with the national averages in educational attainment, with median school years completed by adults 25 years of age and over standing at 8.8 years, compared to 10.6 years for the nation. Part of this gap is the consequence of segregation practices. The comparable figures for whites was 10.5 years and for nonwhites 6.0 years.

Educational inadequacies

The Department of Highways is responsible for 53,000 miles of roads, 14,000 miles of which are state roads, 27,000 miles are parish, and 11,000 miles are city streets. It is administered by a board, which appoints a director to administer the department. Each parish governing board is responsible for its own road system.

The legislature has established programs to provide a system of economic security and social welfare for various categories of citizens including persons 65 years of age and over; aid and welfare to mothers and children; care and treatment of crippled children; and aid to the needy blind. Various state departments provide some aspects of welfare aid but by far the most important is the Department of Public Welfare.

The so-called Charity Hospital system supported and administered by the state is almost unique among the 50 states. The Charity Hospital of Louisiana in New Orleans has received some public support since 1811. Three kinds of charity hospitals were maintained in the early 1970s, ten general hospitals, three for the mentally ill, and three for the treatment of tuberculosis.

The Louisiana Department of Health provides health services to Louisiana citizens through a central office in New Orleans and local health units in 62 parishes.

Five penal and correctional institutions operated by the state are administered under the general authority of the Louisiana Board of Institutions. The penal system has suffered from an excess of political interference.

CULTURAL LIFE AND INSTITUTIONS

The extensive power of the Roman Catholic Church in south Louisiana and the domination of Baptists in north Louisiana and among the black population remain important influences on social and cultural life. New Orleans and many smaller communities have been able to support the arts and philanthropic institutions. The Creoles (descendants of French or Spanish settlers) developed a distinctive architecture, art, and cuisine centred on New Orleans. American planters emulated the Creoles, and to this day, the people of the alluvial parishes of north Louisiana are more cosmopolitan in outlook than the more sober-minded people of the uplands.

In any estimate of the state of the arts and of folk culture, it must be concluded that Louisiana more than holds her own. This is very much so in the realm of music, whether it be in Negro folk songs, including the celebrated rural blues; the Cajun bands at *fais-dodos*, country dances held in south Louisiana; the community hymn singings of north Louisiana; the jazz that New Orleans migrants took to Chicago and elsewhere; or the renaissance in dixieland music played by bands at New Orleans' Preservation Hall in the 1960s.

Musical traditions

New Orleans, with its opera, theatre, and painters, was one of the major "culture" centres in 19th-century America. Its French Quarter attracted such artists as John J. Audubon, the great wildlife painter, and George Catlin, noted for his portrayals of the American West, together with writers such as Walt Whitman, Sherwood Anderson, and William Faulkner. Since the 1930s other cities, notably Shreveport, Monroe, Baton Rouge, and Lafayette, have evolved their own museums and galleries, orchestras, choruses, and little theatres.

Tourism has developed as an important industry using the appeal, to some, of the antebellum past and the attraction of Creole cuisine, an exquisite blend of French, Spanish, Negro, and Indian dishes. A series of parades and balls culminating in the main celebration of Mardi Gras (Shrove Tuesday) has become a national attraction in New Orleans. Many parks and gardens are set aside for public use and display throughout the state. The state is advertised as a "sportsman's paradise" for hunting and fishing, and it is also football country, where junior and senior high school players prepare for big-time college and professional careers.

The literate Creole culture provided the state with a long press tradition with the first newspaper, *Le Moniteur de la Louisiane*, appearing in 1794. Eight others were published in New Orleans at the turn of the 19th century, and the rural parishes likewise published their own papers. In the 1970s the leading newspapers have been concentrated in the urban parishes. There are around two dozen dailies with a combined circulation of 764,000, ten Sunday papers and nearly 110 weeklies. The first radio stations appeared in New Orleans in 1922, and there are now 140 stations: of the 16 television stations, only one is an educational channel.

PROSPECTS

The Louisiana of the early 1970s has managed, as yet, to avoid much of the violence accompanying the contemporary national crisis in race relations. In part, this has been due to the leadership of the governor who, in 1965, established the Louisiana Commission on Human Relations, Rights and Responsibilities, a biracial body whose functions have been to advise the governor in all areas of human relations and to cooperate in efforts to avert and solve racial problems in the state. The state of Louisiana entered the 1970s with nearly all its school districts under court injunctions to integrate and with leadership on many levels trying to maintain a peaceful process of desegregation.

The quadrennial gubernatorial elections of 1971–72 brought many of the state's unresolved problems into focus. The credibility of state government remained unresolved. Most important, perhaps, are signs of a move to rewrite the state's outmoded constitution with its over 250,000 words and well over 500 amendments. In any event, Louisiana's long traditions, coupled with richer then average resources and a new social and political awakening, make the elusive promise of maturity a much more realistic challenge for the 1970s and beyond.

BIBLIOGRAPHY. T.R. BEARD (ed.), *The Louisiana Economy* (1969), a comprehensive review of recent economic processes in the state with prospects for the 1970s; J.R. BOBO and S.A. ETHERIDGE (comps.), *Statistical Abstract of Louisiana*, 2nd ed. (1967), a useful and comprehensive summary of the 1960 census and other materials, updated with estimates; H. CARTER (ed.), *The Past as Prelude: New Orleans 1718–1968* (1968), a wide canvas of the city's place in the state's history; E.A. DAVIS, *Louisiana: The Pelican State* (1959), a standard recent history of the state, and (ed.), *The Rivers and Bayous of Louisiana* (1968); N. GRAY, *A Short History of Louisiana* (1960, 1965), with attention given to the black community's role; R. HEBERLE, *The Labor Force in Louisiana* (1948), the only standard account of the topic, based on 1940 census data—provides a benchmark from which to study the state's industrial development; P.H. HOWARD, *Political Tendencies in Louisiana*, rev. ed. (1971), a comprehensive historical and sociological account of political structure and voting behaviour; F.B. KNIFFEN, *Louisiana: Its Land and People* (1968), exhaustive treatment from the standpoint of cultural geography; *Louisiana: A Guide to the State*, writer program of WPA (1941, reprinted 1959), an indispensable survey of life in Louisiana; *Louisiana Almanac* (1968), a useful general almanac; LOUISIANA LEGISLATIVE COUNCIL, *The History and Government of Louisiana* (1964), a brief narrative account of state history and extensive treatment of the organization and administration of state government; G. MCGINTY, *A History of Louisiana* (1949, 1951), the first of the modern historical summaries; R.W. SHUGG, *Origins of Class Struggle in Louisiana* (1968), a classic treatment of the political process from 1812 to 1880s; T.L. SMITH and H.L. HITT, *The People of Louisiana* (1952), the standard demographic analysis, unfortunately outdated.

(P.H.H.)

Louvois, François-Michel Le Tellier, Marquis de

François-Michel Le Tellier, Marquis de Louvois, French secretary of state for war under Louis XIV, was Louis's most influential minister in the period 1683–91.

Born in Paris and baptized on January 18, 1639, he was the son of one of the wealthiest and most powerful officials in France, Michel Le Tellier, secretary for war and a creature of Jules, cardinal Mazarin, Louis XIV's chief minister. Indeed, after the Cardinal's death many observers thought that Le Tellier would succeed his patron as first minister. Le Tellier, however, realizing that the King wanted no ambitious man to challenge his authority, subtly effaced himself while grooming his son as his replacement. His method was simple: he personally directed Louvois's education while planting the suggestion in the King's mind that the monarch deserved the credit for recognizing his son's administrative talents. The task was no easy one; Louvois was not a brilliant scholar, and he received no more than a superficial education at the Jesuit college of Clermont. He was, moreover, dissolute and seemed well on the road to becoming a wastrel in his father's eyes. If the secretaryship was to remain in the family—Louvois had acquired no more than the right of succession in 1655—he had to be reformed. Consequently, his father brought him into the war department and subjected him to an iron discipline that led the youth to the point of rebellion. Yet he emerged hardworking, supremely confident of his own ability, and with extensive experience in military administration.

As his knowledge increased, so did his position: in 1662 he obtained the right to exercise his father's functions in the latter's absence or incapacity. The same year he improved his social position by marrying Anne de Souvré,

Youth and instruction

Giraudon

Louvois, portrait by Pierre Mignard (1612–95). in the Musée des Beaux-Arts, Reims, France.

daughter of Marquis de Courtenvaux. In 1665 the King granted Louvois the right to handle all the duties of Le Tellier's office and to sign all papers, but only in his father's presence. His first important test came in the War of Devolution (1667–68) between France and Spain over Louis XIV's claim to the Spanish Netherlands, when Louvois accompanied the King into battle. Although this campaign revealed a disturbing lack of supplies, Louvois learned his lessons well, and his competence became unquestioned. Nevertheless Le Tellier continued to guide his son until 1677, when the father accepted the position of chancellor of France. Until this date, Louis XIV had in fact two secretaries of war, father and son, who cooperated closely. Indeed, the son consulted his father until the latter's death in 1685.

Louvois's successful career was tarnished by two acts: the dragonnades leading up to the revocation in 1685 of the Edict of Nantes, which had granted French Protestants certain liberties, and the destruction of the Palatinate. Historians have accused Louvois of originating the dragonnades, the quartering of troops in Protestant households with the intention of forcing conversion to Catholicism. Recent research, however, has demonstrated that Louvois was not responsible for this measure. Instead, the dragonnades were the result of ambitious subordinates, who saw that overstepping the letter of the law led to royal favour. Yet, although Louvois had no strong religious feelings himself, he was guilty of complicity. As an astute politician, he recognized Louis XIV's interest in religious unity and went along with the King's wishes. Personally, he disliked the methods of the dragonnades, for they encouraged a lack of discipline among the troops.

Louvois bore much more responsibility for the destruction of the Palatinate (1688), to which Louis XIV laid claim, thus leading to the War of the League of Augsburg. Louvois had never been afraid of using force in enemy territory, and now military necessity seemed to demand the destruction of the Rhineland to prevent it from being used as a base for the invasion of France. He encouraged the destruction of the major cities of the Palatinate: Worms, Speyer, Mannheim, and Heidelberg. Yet Louvois alone cannot bear the entire blame; the King also approved the measure.

Louvois's relationship with the King was often strained, particularly during the last years of the Minister's life. Louis XIV had always tried to play off his officials against each other, preventing any servant from becoming too powerful. With the death of Colbert in 1683, however, Louvois increasingly dominated affairs of state. War seemed to perpetuate itself, and every campaign made the War Minister indispensible, while Louis XIV's resentment grew as Louvois asserted himself. Finally, during the difficult years of the War of the League of Augsburg (1689–97), rumours circulated at court of Louvois's imminent disgrace, and, according to contemporaries, only the sudden death of Louvois at Versailles, on July 16, 1691, saved him from imprisonment in the Bastille. Most historians, however, reject this theory. Certainly, Louis XIV valued Louvois's military talents too highly to remove him in the middle of a war. Louvois, "this man who had served me well," was no more, and the King had reason to mourn his servant's loss, for Louvois's son and successor, the Marquis de Barbezieux, had little skill in military administration.

Most historians have allotted to Louvois all the glory for perfecting the French military machine. In reality, Le Tellier was the innovator; Louvois was only the brilliant administrator who brought his father's reforms to fruition. Memoir writers have pictured Louvois as a hard-working, aggressive, and exceedingly ruthless man: in his memoirs the Duc de Saint-Simon spoke of him as "brutal, inflated with his own authority"; Louis XIV's sister-in-law called him "horribly cruel and quite incapable of feeling any pity." Both, however, had personal reasons for disliking Louvois; one regarded him as an upstart who threatened the traditional aristocracy; the other disliked him for his role in the destruction of the Palatinate, her homeland. Louvois was, however, a loving

Louvois's involvement in the dragonnades and the destruction of the Palatinate

Assessment

son and a devoted friend. Some historians have mistakenly portrayed him as a war hawk and his rival Jean-Baptiste Colbert, Louis XIV's chief adviser after Mazarin's death, as a dove, but in reality both had surprisingly similar personalities. Each was harsh and egocentric with a sometimes violent temperament, bent on safeguarding his own interests and increasing his influence. Yet, beyond furthering his career, Louvois had done his work well. After his death the French army remained one of the most formidable in Europe.

BIBLIOGRAPHY. Standard works include CAMILLE ROUSSET, *Histoire de Louvois et de son administration politique et militaire*, 3rd ed., 4 vol. (1863–1865); and particularly LOUIS ANDRE, *Michel Le Tellier et Louvois* (1942). See also André's earlier work, *Michel Le Tellier et l'organisation de l'armée monarchique* (1906). JACQUES ROUJON, *Louvois et son maître* (1934), is a popular and less satisfactory study; while L.L. BERNARD's specialized article, "Foucault, Louvois, and the Revocation of the Edict of Nantes," *Church History*, 25:27–40 (1956), is a more recent scholarly effort.

(D.C.B.)

Lovell, Sir Bernard

The founder and director of England's Jodrell Bank Experimental Station (Nuffield Radio Astronomy Laboratories) and one of the foremost pioneers in this relatively new science, Alfred Charles Bernard Lovell has made significant contributions to man's knowledge of the universe and his exploration of space. Moreover, as a popularizer of science through his writings and lectures, Lovell shared with lay audiences his enthusiasm and concerns for space research while providing a better understanding of the importance of such efforts.

Born at Oldland Common, Gloucestershire, near Bristol, England, on August 31, 1913, Lovell attended grammar school in Bristol as well as the University of Bristol, from which he received the Ph.D. degree in 1936. After a year as an assistant lecturer in physics at the University of Manchester, he became a member of the cosmic-ray research team at that institution, working in this capacity until the outbreak of World War II in 1939. Meanwhile, in 1937 he married Mary Joyce Chesterman, who subsequently bore him five children. In 1939 he published his first book, *Science and Civilization*. During World War II, Lovell worked for the Air Ministry, doing valuable research in the use of radar for detection and navigation purposes for which he was awarded the Order of the British Empire in 1946.

On returning to the University of Manchester in 1945 as a lecturer in physics, Lovell acquired a surplus army radar set for use in his research on cosmic rays. Because interference from the surrounding city hampered his efforts, he moved the equipment, which included a searchlight base, to Jodrell Bank, an open field located about 20 miles south of Manchester. Shortly thereafter,

Camera Press—Pix from Publix

Lovell, 1964.

authorities at the university agreed to provide him with a permanent establishment at the site, which already belonged to the university's botany department, and to sponsor the construction of his first radio telescope, for which he used the searchlight base as a mounting.

Lovell's initial investigations with the instrument involved the study of meteors. About 15 years earlier, when radio waves had been bounced off meteors during certain meteor showers, some astronomers had noted that the number of meteors observed visually was much smaller than the number of radio echoes received, an indication that the showers actually consisted of more meteors than could be seen. To determine if the echoes were meteoric in origin, Lovell used his new radio telescope to observe a particularly intense meteor shower on the night of October 9–10, 1946. As the shower first increased and later decreased in intensity, radio signals from the instrument's transmitter were directed toward the shower. Throughout the evening, not only did the number of optical sightings coincide with the number of radio echoes being received, but the timing of the two rates was also as predicted, thereby conclusively proving that the echoes were caused by the meteors. Having established this fact, Lovell could now apply radio techniques to meteor showers previously unknown because they occurred during daylight hours. Further experiments with the radio telescope in 1947 and 1948 also determined that orbits of meteors are elliptical, thus confirming the belief that these bodies are members of the solar system and are not of interstellar origin.

In recognition of his work and growing reputation, Lovell was appointed by the University of Manchester to the position of senior lecturer in 1947 and reader in 1949; in 1951 he became the first professor of radio astronomy at the university. During this time, he had already begun planning and building a bigger and more sophisticated radio telescope, which, when it was completed in 1957, was the world's largest of its kind, with a diameter of 250 feet. The structure rotates horizontally at 20° per minute, and the reflector itself moves vertically at 24° per minute. Lovell described the instrument and the problems associated with its construction in *The Story of Jodrell Bank* (1968). While work on the telescope was in progress, Lovell also wrote three other books: *Radio Astronomy* (1952), *Meteor Astronomy* (1954), and *The Exploration of Space by Radio* (1957).

Lovell frankly admits that it was mainly the prospect of using the new radio telescope to track the first Sputnik, scheduled for launch by the Soviet Union on October 4, 1957, that spurred his efforts to complete the instrument by that time. By supplying a much-needed boost to the prestige of the project at a time when its financial viability was being seriously threatened by rapidly rising costs, this completely unforeseen application of the instrument guaranteed its success and Lovell's personal fame. Ever since, the giant radio telescope at Jodrell Bank has been a vital tool for pinpointing the exact locations of Earth satellites, space probes, and manned space flights, as well as for collecting data transmitted by instruments in some of these vehicles.

Because of the widespread publicity given to Jodrell Bank and its director, coupled with the latter's reputation as a popularizer of science, the British Broadcasting Corporation in 1958 invited Lovell to give a series of radio talks, known as the Reith Lectures, which were published in 1959 as *The Individual and the Universe*. When Lovell was knighted in 1961 for his pioneering work in radio astronomy, 20 investigations—mostly on radio emissions originating thousands of millions of light years away—were in progress at Jodrell Bank. Some of this work is discussed in his book *The Exploration of Outer Space* (1962). His research has since been concerned mainly with radio emissions from outer space, including those from pulsars (discovered in 1968), and measuring the angular diameters of distant quasars.

In addition to honorary degrees bestowed upon him by various academic institutions, Lovell was elected a fellow of the Royal Society in 1955, receiving its Royal Medal in 1960; he is also an honorary member of several foreign

Meteor studies

Tracking and monitoring space vehicles at Jodrell Bank

academies and professional organizations. Other honours include the Physical Society's Duddell Medal (1954), the Daniel and Florence Guggenheim International Astronautics Award (1961), the French Order of Merit (1962), and the Society of Engineers' Churchill Gold Medal (1964). From 1969 to 1971, he was president of the Royal Astronomical Society.

BIBLIOGRAPHY. The best summary of Lovell's scientific work is given in the biographical article in the 1966 edition of *McGraw-Hill Modern Men of Science*. The building of the Jodrell Bank telescope is described in full by Lovell himself in his *Story of Jodrell Bank* (1968).

(M.A.H.)

Low Countries, History of

A treatment of the medieval history of the Low Countries (the Netherlands) runs up against a considerable problem in that the area did not form a self-contained political unit; it was a part of a greater whole. Neither did it form a cultural or ethnic unit. A geographical limit to the area to be discussed must, therefore, be chosen somewhat arbitrarily. For the purposes of the present article, the term the Netherlands includes the area covered by the medieval duchy of Lower Lorraine, belonging to the Holy Roman Empire, and the county of Flanders, which was principally part of the Kingdom of France, but a small part of which also belonged to the Holy Roman Empire. It corresponds roughly to the area now covered by the states of The Netherlands, Belgium, and Luxembourg and by a small part of northern France (Artois). This article contains the following sections:

I. The Netherlands to *c.* 1600

ANCIENT AND EARLY MEDIEVAL TIMES (TO 925)

The Roman period. At the time of the Roman conquest (1st century BC), the Low Countries were inhabited by a number of Celtic tribes to the south and west of the Rhine and by a number of Germanic tribes to the north. Cultural and ethnic influences in both directions, however, make it difficult to draw the line between Celtic and Germanic peoples. On the coast of northern France and in Flanders lived the Morini; to the north of them, between the Scheldt and the sea, the Menapii; in Artois, the Nervii; between the Scheldt and the Rhine, the Eburones and the Aduatuci; and, in what is now Luxembourg, the Treveri. North of the Rhine, the Frisii (Frisians) were the principal inhabitants, although the arrival of the Romans brought about a number of movements: the Batavi came to the area of the lower reaches of the Rhine, the Canninefates to the western coastal area of the mouth of the Rhine, the Marsaci to the islands of Zeeland, the Toxandri to the Campine (Kempenland), the Cugerni to the Xanten district, and the Tungri to part of the area originally inhabited by the Eburones (who were wiped out by Julius Caesar).

The Roman conquest of Gaul, which was completed by Caesar in 59–52 BC, stopped short at the Rhine. The emperor Augustus' attempt to extend Roman military power over the Elbe failed, and the area occupied by the Frisians, north of the Rhine, was therefore never under Roman rule. In the Rhine delta and to the south and west of the Rhine, the Romans set up the same administrative organizations as those found in other parts of Gaul. The Low Countries formed part of the provinces of Belgica and Germania Inferior (later Belgica Secunda and Germania Secunda), which themselves were subdivided into *civitates:* in Belgica, those of the Morini, Menapii, Treveri, Tungri, and possibly the Toxandri; in Germania Inferior, those of the Batavi, Canninefates, and Cugerni. Because of the later adoption by the church of the division into *civitates*, a number of centres of the *civitates* have become the seats of bishoprics; among these are Thérouanne, Tournai, Tongres, and Trier (Trèves).

In the northern regions, fishing and cattle raising were the principal means of support, while to the south of the Rhine it was possible, with Roman protection, to engage in farming in the Gallo-Roman fashion, using villas as centres. There must also have been a certain amount of trading and other traffic, even if only to provision the Roman military and civil services.

In the mid-3rd century, Roman power in the Low Countries began to weaken, and the forts were abandoned. This was the result not only of a resurgence of the Germanic tribes but also probably of the encroachment of the sea, which probably brought about a drastic change in the area's economy. A temporary recovery began at the end of the 3rd century. In particular, Julian, caesar of Gaul, waged several wars in the Low Countries between 355 and 360 and was able to put new strength, for a time, into the Rhine border. A great invasion by Germanic tribes in 406–407, however, ended the Roman occupation of the Low Countries. The Romans had already tolerated the Germanic penetration of their territory and had given some tribes the task of protecting the borders of the empire. The Franks, who had settled in Toxandria, in Brabant, were given the job of defending the border areas, which they continued to do until the middle of the 5th century.

The Franks were probably influenced considerably by Roman culture, becoming familiar with the Roman world and way of life, although the expansion of their own race and their growing self-confidence were barriers to complete romanization. Around 450 they moved southward, founding a new Frankish kingdom centred on the region between the Somme and the Loire. The number of Franks in this Merovingian-Frankish kingdom has been vigorously debated: French and Belgian scholars believe that only a small number of ruling families made the move; German scholars claim a mass migration of the whole tribe. It is certain, however, that the Franks never achieved a majority in the population of the kingdom but probably settled in the conquered area as colonists and farmers. Their cultural influence was too slight to oust the Romance languages; thus, the linguistic frontier between the Romance and Germanic languages has re-

Decline of Roman power

mained the same as the limit of Roman culture in the north—crossing the Low Countries, in particular the later principalities of Flanders, Brabant, and Liège, in an east–west line.

Frankish rule. The first kings of the Merovingian Franks—Childeric (d. 481/482) and Clovis (ruled 481/482–511)—ruled the regions of Tournai and Cambrai before the great conquest of Gaul had even begun. Despite this, however, the Low Countries originally formed a border region in which the might of the Frankish state was hardly felt. The area occupied by the Frisians in the north was completely outside the Frankish sphere of influence, but the Rhine delta and even what is now Noord-Brabant also appear to have retained the virtually independent status they had possessed during the Roman era. It is possible, though not certain, that Nimwegen (Nijmegen) was a Merovingian outpost.

The area occupied by the Frisians was part of a North Sea culture that formed a distinct foil to Frankish power. The Frisians played an important role in trade, which sought routes along the Rhine and the Meuse and across the North Sea. Industrial products were imported from northern France, the Meuse plain, and the Rhineland, where Merovingian power was more firmly established and where centres of commerce (*e.g.*, Dinant, Namur, Huy, and Liège) developed. The more or less independent area on the North Sea coast, however, found itself threatened during the 7th century by the rise of the Frankish nobles. In particular, the family of the Pepins, who came from the centre of Austrasia (the Ardennes and upper Meuse), was able to secure land in Limburg. Moreover, encouraged by the Frankish king Dagobert (ruled 623–639), the Frankish church began an offensive that led to the foundation of the bishopric of Thérouanne (the *civitas* of the Morini) and of several monasteries.

This collaboration between church and nobles prepared the way for an expansion of political power to the north, which was carried out under the leadership of the Pepins, who as "mayors of the palace" in Austrasia had virtually taken over power from the weakened Merovingian kings. After defeating the mayor of the palace of Neustria (the western part of the Frankish Merovingian kingdom) at Tertry (687), Pepin II turned to the north, where he won a victory over the Frisian king Radbod near Dorestat (689). The Anglo-Saxon Willibrord was then ordained archbishop of the Frisians in Rome and, with Pepin's help, was given Utrecht as see of the bishopric and centre for his missionary activities. Even so, Frankish power expanded northward only gradually, making use of such bases as Utrecht and several former Roman forts. Charles Martel, a bastard son of Pepin II, who managed after several years' fighting (714–719) to grasp supreme power over the whole Frankish Empire, succeeded in 734 in forcing his way through to the northern centres of the Frisians and gaining a victory near the River Boorne. His victory was later consolidated by Pepin III (who in 751 became King Pepin I) and Charlemagne (ruled 768–814), his son. The whole area of the Low Countries thus effectively formed part of the Frankish Empire, which was then ruled by the Pepin, or Carolingian, dynasty.

Government. The administrative organization of the Low Countries during this period was basically the same as that of the rest of the Frankish Empire. Supreme authority was held by the king, who, aided by servants of the palace, toured the country incessantly. The Carolingian kings naturally made several visits to the Low Countries, where they had old palaces or built new ones (Herstal, Meerssen, Nijmegen, Aix-la-Chapelle) and where they also possessed extensive crown estates. Their authority (*bannus*) was delegated to counts who had control of counties, or *gauen* (*pagi*), some of which corresponded to Roman *civitates*. Among these counties in the Low Countries were the *pagus* Taruanensis (centred on Thérouanne), *pagus* Mempiscus, *pagus* Flandrensis (around Bruges), *pagus* Turnacensis (around Tournai), *pagus* Gandensis (Ghent), *pagus* Bracbatensis (between the Scheldt and the Dijle), *pagus* Toxandrie (modern Noord-Brabant), and, north of the great rivers, Marssum, Lake et Isla, Teisterbant, Circa oras Rheni, Kin-

nem, Westflinge, Texla, Salon, Hamaland, and Twente. In the north, however, it is frequently not possible to determine with certainty whether the word *gau* in fact denoted a region controlled by a count who exercised the king's authority or indicated simply a region of land without reference to its government. Smaller administrative units were the *centenae*, or hundreds, and districts called *ambachten*. These last were mainly in what are now the provinces of Vlaanderen, Zeeland, and Holland.

Religion. The conversion to Christianity of the southern Low Countries, which took place largely during the 7th century, led to the foundation of further bishoprics at Artois, Tournai, and Cambrai, which were part of the ecclesiastical province of Rheims (the former Roman province of Belgica Secunda). Germania Secunda contained the ecclesiastical province of Cologne, in which the *civitas* of Tongres seems to have had an uninterrupted existence as a bishopric since Roman times; the centre of this bishopric was moved for a time to Maastricht (6th and 7th centuries) until, in about 720, Liège became the seat of the bishopric. Christianity was brought to the north of the Low Countries mainly by Anglo-Saxon preachers, by Frisians influenced by them, and by Franks. This Anglo-Saxon Christianity was particularly important in the missionary bishopric of Utrecht, which at first, because of its missionary character, had no precisely defined borders. True, the city of Utrecht had been named as the see of the bishopric, but, as in England, the monasteries played an important part in the missionary work; among these was the monastery of Echternach in Luxembourg. The country between the Meuse and the Waal and the area around Nijmegen belonged to the bishopric of Cologne, while certain districts in the north and east were part of the bishopric of Münster (founded by Charlemagne). The bishoprics were subdivided into relatively large parishes, about the foundation of which only scanty information exists. With an increase in population during the 10th, 11th, and 12th centuries, the parishes were split into smaller ones, based on small chapels that at first had only limited rights. In the north and, above all, in Friesland, the initiative for founding parishes often came from the faithful themselves, who built a church and provided it with the necessary income in the form of estates (*dos*). The influence of laymen and, in particular, of the aristocracy was often extremely strong; and they usually collected the tithes and other revenues. On the other hand, this system of proprietary churches formed a distinct stimulus for the conversion of the country areas.

Justice. The administration of justice was the duty of the king and his appointed counts. They pronounced judgment principally in important cases (*causae majores*) or in cases involving prominent people: theirs was known as the higher court of justice. To fulfill this task, Charlemagne appointed groups of permanent judges, called *scabini* (French *échevins*), who under the direction of the count "found" the law and applied it as a verdict. At lower levels, it seems that justice must have been administered in the smaller legal units of hundreds and *ambachten*. Only to a small extent is the content of the law included in the codes of Germanic law, such as the Lex Salica, which consist largely of criminal law (robbery, theft, homicide, and rape) and property law (land and cattle). On Charlemagne's initiative, a large part of Frisian law was put down in writing as the Lex Frisionum, as well as the *ewa quae se ad Amorem habet,* "the law that exists on the Amor" (Amor being the name of an unidentified river, probably in the Waal and Meuse district). Charlemagne amplified the Lex Salica and Lex Saxonum in various of his *capitularia* (ordinances). The law was thus materially diverse, while formally the situation was complicated even further by the immunity that was frequently granted to churches or monasteries, which put their property beyond the reach of the legal and administrative powers of the count and his subordinates. The secular jurisdiction that in this way became the prerogative of bishops or abbots was the basis of later, more extensive secular powers, which in the Low Countries, more than anywhere else, were to play an important role in the foundation of the ecclesiastical territorial principalities.

Margin notes:

Resistance to the Franks

Life under the Franks

Social classes. The social structure of the Low Countries in the Frankish era included a number of classes. At the top was an elite that probably already operated on a hereditary system and of which the members were bound to the king as vassals and rewarded by fiefs (*beneficia*). Next were the freemen (*liberi, ingenui*), bound to the king by an oath of allegiance and traditionally under an obligation to serve in the army and in the law courts. A freeman's *Wergeld*—the sum that had to be paid to his family if he was killed—was in principle 200 shillings (*solidi*); but the *ingenui Franci*, or *homines Franci* (found in the region of the great rivers; probably descended from native nobles who had early placed themselves in the service of the Franks in their policy of conquest), had a much higher *Wergeld*. At the bottom of the ladder were the bondsmen, who were closely dependent on a lord (often an important landowner), in whose service they stood, in most cases working on his estates. It may be supposed that the position of the bondsmen was relatively favourable in the coastal areas of Holland and Friesland, where there were no large estates and, moreover, where the struggle against the sea required as much manpower as the community was able to offer.

Economy. Economically, the structure of the Low Countries in the Frankish period was principally agrarian. Particularly in the south and east, it was common practice to exploit the land from a central farmhouse (*villa* or *curtis*), using the services of dependent subjects (bondsmen), who were duty bound to work on the domain of the lord and to this end received small farms from him. The nature of the land in the west and north, however, probably to a large extent precluded this classical type of exploitation of the domains; there was scattered, even fragmentary, ownership of land, and the *curtis* was no more than a gathering place to which the bondsmen had to take a part of their produce. In Holland and Friesland, fishing and the raising and selling of cattle were of importance. This Frisian trade, of which Dorestat was a centre, was greatly stimulated by absorption into the Frankish Empire, and it reached its zenith under Charlemagne and Louis the Pious (ruled 814–840). Moreover, by virtue of its becoming part of the Frankish Empire, Friesland obtained an important hinterland in the southern regions of the Meuse and Rhine and was thus in a position to develop export and through trade to Denmark, Norway, and the Baltic countries. The importance of Frisian trade may be seen in the Carolingian coins found in Dorestat, where there was a toll and a royal mint. This trade was supplied by the southern Low Countries. Thus the cloths that were sold as Frisian cloths were produced in the area of the Scheldt (later called Flanders). Quentovic, at the mouth of the Canche, was another trading centre; it too had a toll and a mint. Smaller trade settlements (*portus*, or *vicus*) emerged at Tournai, Ghent, Bruges, Antwerp, Dinant, Namur, Huy, Liège, and Maastricht—a clear indication of the commercial importance of the Scheldt and the Meuse.

Decline of the Frankish Empire. The great Carolingian Empire passed into a decline as early as the reign of Louis the Pious, and the process was accelerated after his death, in 840. Repeated wars broke out under his sons,

leading eventually to the partition of the empire: by the Treaty of Verdun (843), the empire was divided into an eastern, western, and an extensive middle kingdom. The last of these, allotted to Louis's eldest son, Lothair, who also wore the imperial crown, was, after his death, further divided into three parts—the northern part, stretching from the Jura Mountains to the North Sea, falling to his son Lothair II, after whom it was named. After it had belonged alternately to the western and eastern Frankish kingdoms, Lorraine eventually (925) became part of the eastern kingdom, by then the German kingdom, because there were no longer any ruling Carolingians. The nobles of Lorraine had themselves taken an important part in this changing political game. Giselbert, a member of one of the most noble families, had turned the scales in favour of joining the German kingdom, for which service King Henry I presented him with what then became the duchy of Lorraine.

The dissolution of the Carolingian Empire had also been helped by Viking, Magyar, and Saracen attacks—the Viking attacks being of greatest import for the Low Countries. The attacks had begun immediately after the death of Charlemagne (814) in the form of plundering raids, the magnitude and danger of which soon increased. (Dorestat, for example, was destroyed four times between 834 and 837.) Churches and monasteries, with their rich treasures, were the principal targets for the Vikings, who soon took to spending the winter in the Low Countries. In order to ward off the danger, attempts were made to throw up walls around towns and monasteries or even to drive off the Vikings by fierce counterattacks—a procedure that enjoyed some success, so that the counts of Flanders, for example, were able to lay a firm foundation for their own power. Another method of defense was to admit the Vikings on the condition that they defend the areas given them against other Vikings. The danger diminished after 900, though it was not until about 920 that Bishop Balderic risked the journey from Deventer to Utrecht, whence his predecessor had fled.

LATE MEDIEVAL AND EARLY MODERN TIMES, 925–1579

The development of the territorial principalities and the rise of the towns (925–c. 1350). Politically speaking, the period between 925 and about 1350 is characterized by the emergence, growth, and eventual independence of secular and ecclesiastical territorial principalities. The rulers of these principalities—both secular and spiritual—had a feudal relationship with the German king (the Holy Roman emperor), with the exception of the count of Flanders, who held his land principally as the vassal of the French king, with only the northern part of his county, Imperial Flanders, being held in fealty to the German king. While the secular principalities came into being as a result of individual initiative on the part of local rulers and of their taking the law into their own hands, to the detriment of the king's authority, the development of the spiritual princes' authority was systematically furthered and supported from above by the king himself. The secular principalities that arose in the Low Countries and whose borders were more or less fixed at the end of the 13th century were the counties of Flanders and Hainaut, the duchies of Brabant and Limburg (after 1288 joined in personal union), the county of Namur, the county of Loon (which was, however, to a large degree dependent on the bishopric of Liège), the county of Holland and Zeeland, and the county (after 1339, duchy) of Guelders. The Frisian areas (approximately corresponding to the modern provinces of Friesland and Groningen, excluding, however, the city of Groningen itself) had no sovereign authority. The spiritual principalities were Liège and Utrecht. The secular authority of the bishop of Utrecht was exercised over two separate areas: the Nedersticht (what is now the province of Utrecht) and the Oversticht (what are now the provinces of Overijssel and Drenthe and the city of Groningen).

This article will sketch the emergence of these principalities, their relations with one another, their dissociation from the German king, and the increasing influence upon them of France and England. It must be noted that, although these principalities displayed common characteristics in their economies, social structures, and cultures, it was a pure coincidence—the intrusion of the Burgundian dynasty—that brought about a certain degree of political unity, which in turn furthered economic, social, and cultural unity and even led to the beginnings of a common national feeling (which was nevertheless too weak to prevent partition in 1579).

The secular principalities. The foundations upon which the secular princes built up their power were basically the following: In the first place, the count still exercised the rights that had for centuries been attached to the Carolingian office of count, denoted by the term *comitatus*. They included the administration of justice, various military powers, and the right to levy fines and tolls. To these rights fiefs were attached, which during the passage of time were expanded by the counts, who eventually owned such large estates that they were by far the greatest landowners in their territories. Soon the term *comitatus* covered not only the office, or duty, but also the whole area over which that office was exercised; thus it could be said that the count held his county in fief of the king. An important element of the count's authority was supervision over the county's religious foundations, especially the monasteries. In the 10th century, the counts sometimes even assumed the function of abbot (lay abbot); but they later contented themselves with the control of appointments to ecclesiastical offices, through which they often had great influence over the monasteries and profited from the income from monastic land. Thus, monasteries such as St. Vaast (near Arras), St. Amand (on the Scarpe), St. Bertin (near St. Omer), and St. Bavon and St. Pieter (in Ghent) became centres of the power and authority of the counts of Flanders; Nivelles and Gembloux, of the dukes of Brabant; and Egmond and Rijnsburg, of the counts of Holland.

Expansion of counts' power

At the end of the 9th and in the 10th centuries, during the Viking attacks and while connections with the empire were loosening, the local counts built up their power by joining a number of *pagi* together and building forts to ensure their safety. The counts of Flanders amalgamated the *pagi* Flandrensis, Rodanensis, Gandensis, Courtracensis, Iserae, and Mempiscus, the whole being thenceforth called Flanders; they fortified this area of their power with new or surviving Roman citadels. In the northern coastal regions, the Viking Gerulf was granted in about 885 the rights over a number of counties between the Meuse and the Vlie (Masalant, Kinnem, Texla, Westflinge, and a district known as Circa oras Rheni, which was, as the name implies, on both sides of the Rhine); his descendants consolidated their power there as counts of west Frisia and, after 1100, took the title of counts of Holland. In Brabant and Guelders, the amalgamation of fragmentary and dispersed estates took place later than in Flanders and Holland.

These secular princes were bound by a feudal relationship to the German or French kings, and they in turn used a similar relationship to bind the nobles to them. As supreme lords, they stood at the head of their vassals, who were duty bound to carry out services of *auxilium* and *consilium* (to serve in the army and at court). These services were rewarded with fiefs, and in most of the principalities a powerful feudal nobility emerged, to which the prince had to give the fullest consideration. At first, in the 10th and 11th centuries, the prince and his subjects had no direct link, and the princes had no specific duties to carry out, as bearers of authority, toward their subjects. On the contrary, the princes' activities during this period were almost exclusively motivated by greed for power and money.

During the 10th and 11th centuries, the German kings of the Saxon and Salian dynasties—particularly Otto I (ruled 936–973), Henry II (ruled 1002–24), Conrad II (ruled 1024–39), Henry III (ruled 1039–56), and Henry IV (ruled 1056–1106)—attempted to impose their authority on the increasingly powerful secular principalities by the appointment of dukes. In Lorraine, a duke was appointed to exercise imperial power over the local counts; but the plan failed, except for a short period (953–965) during the reign of Otto I, when the king's brother Bruno held the position (Bruno's success was largely due to the fact that he was also archbishop of Cologne). Taken all in all, the dukes of Lorraine had too little authority and no effective means to exercise their power to subdue the local counts. Lorraine was soon split into two dukedoms—Upper and Lower Lorraine. In Lower Lorraine, the title of duke was given to the counts of Louvain and the counts of Limburg—the former at first called themselves dukes of Lorraine but soon assumed the title of dukes of Brabant; the latter were known as the dukes of Limburg.

The spiritual principalities. That the German kings failed to integrate Lorraine into the Holy Roman Empire as a duchy ruled by a viceroy may be attributed to the fact that the kings soon developed another way to strengthen their power, not only in Lorraine but throughout the empire, by systematically investing bishops and abbots with secular powers and making them pillars of authority. This procedure, developed by Otto I and reaching its summit under Henry III, was carried out in phases and led eventually to the establishment of the Imperial Church (Reichskirche), in which the spiritual and secular principalities played an important part. The most important ecclesiastical principalities in the Low Countries were the bishoprics of Liège, Utrecht, and, to a lesser degree, Cambrai, which, though within the Holy Roman Empire, belonged to the French church province of Rheims. The secular powers enjoyed by these bishops were based on the right of immunity that their churches exercised over their properties and that meant that, within the areas of their properties, the counts and their subordinates had little or no opportunity to carry out their functions. This situation, which had existed during the Carolingian and Merovingian periods, enabled the bishops to exercise jurisdictional and military powers in these areas, helped by lay officials known as advocates (*advocati*), whom they themselves appointed. The German kings strengthened this immunity and put it to their own service by enlarging its jurisdictional powers, while at the same time investing the bishops' advocates with the *bannus* (public authority), so that they formed a link between the king and the immunities. Next, the kings gave certain bishops jurisdictional authority in areas outside their own property, such as in the towns where they resided; at the same time, the bishops' properties were extended by gifts of crown land, which were then also covered by the powers of immunity. Further, the kings transferred such regal powers (regalia) to the bishops as the right to found markets, raise tolls, and strike coins. Through the exercise of these regalia, the bishops became for the first time bearers of royal authority and, thus, of the public authority; and they also derived from these rights a considerable personal income. The last phase in the bishops' growth occurred when the kings decided to transfer to the bishops the powers of counts in certain areas that were not covered by immunity (the power thus acquired is referred to as ban-immunity). Certain bishops, such as those of Liège and Utrecht, were able to combine their rights of immunity, certain jurisdictional powers, regalia, and ban-immunities into a unified secular authority, thus forming a secular principality which was called a *Sticht* (as distinct from the diocese) or—where the power structure was very large and complex, as in the case of the bishop of Liège—a prince-bishopric. As princes, the bishops were vassals of the king, having to fulfill military and advisory duties in the same way as their secular colleagues. The advantage of this system to the kings lay in the fact that the bishops could not start a dynasty that might begin to work for its own ends, and its smooth running stood and fell with the authority of the kings to nominate their own bishops—an authority that they maintained firmly.

Rise of bishops and abbots

Thus the spiritual-territorial principalities of the bishops of Liège and Utrecht emerged—the prince-bishopric of Liège and the *Sticht* of Utrecht. In Liège this development was completed in 972–1008 under the guidance of Bishop Notker, appointed by Otto I. As early as 985 he was granted the rights of the count of Huy, and the German kings made use of the bishopric of Liège to try to strengthen their positions in Lorraine. Utrecht, which lay more on the periphery of the empire, developed somewhat later; although the foundations of this power had already been laid in the 10th century, it was principally the kings Henry II, Conrad II, and Henry III who strengthened the secular power of the bishops through privileges and gifts of land.

Struggle for independence. Thus, the Low Countries during the 10th and 11th centuries saw the development of the pattern of a number of more or less independent feudal states, both secular and ecclesiastical, each of which was struggling for more freedom from the king's authority, the enlargement of its sphere of influence, and the strengthening of its internal power. Flanders led the way. In the 10th and 11th centuries it needed to pay only scant attention to the weak French kings of the Capetian dynasty and was thus soon able to exercise its power farther south—in Artois—and was even able to play an important part in a political power struggle around the French crown. In 1066 the Count of Flanders lent his support to the expedition to England of his son-in-law, William, duke of Normandy. The counts of Flanders built up a strong administrative apparatus—the *curia comitis*, based on central officials and on local rulers called burgraves or castellans (*castellani*), who were in charge of districts known as castellanies, where they had extensive military and administrative powers. The reclamation of land from the sea and from marsh and wasteland in the coastal area, which began in the 11th century, enlarged the estates and the income of the counts and brought about the need for a rational administrative system. The nobles were a power to be reckoned with, but Count Robert I (ruled 1071–93) and his successors were able to find support and a balancing force in such developing towns as Bruges, Ghent, Ypres, Courtrai, and Cassel. The murder by a family of former bondsmen of the powerful and highly respected Count Charles the Good (ruled 1119–27), who was childless, plunged Flanders into a crisis that involved not only the nobles and the towns but also, for the first time, the French king.

Around 1100 such other territories as Brabant, Hainaut, Namur, and Holland began to expand and form principalities, helped by the weakening of the German crown during the Investiture Contest (a struggle between civil and church rulers over the right to invest bishops and abbots). The Concordat of Worms (1122) ruled that bishops were to be chosen by the chapter of canons of the cathedral; thus, the German king was obliged to transfer the secular powers to an *electus*, who was then usually ordained bishop by the metropolitan. Although the king still exercised some influence over the elections, the local counts were able to make their voices heard the loudest in the chapter, so that Utrecht, for example, soon had bishops from the families of the counts of Holland and Guelders. This was the end of the strong influence that German imperial power exercised through the bishops in the Low Countries. Thenceforth, the spiritual and secular princes stood together, although the death of a bishop still tended to plunge the principality into a crisis—a fact that did nothing to maintain the stability of government.

French and English influence. With the decline of the German kings, emperors could do little more than involve themselves almost incidentally in the affairs and many conflicts of the Low Countries. The German decline went hand in hand with the increasing influence of the French and English kings, particularly after 1200; this applied especially to French power in Flanders. A struggle for the throne that broke out in Germany at the death of Henry VI (1197) found the two powerful factions—the Ghibellines and Guelfs—on opposite sides; in the Low Countries, a game of political chance developed for the territorial princes, in which the Duke of Brabant (Henry I) played an important role, alternately supporting both parties. The French king Philip Augustus and his bitter opponent, King John of England, both interfered in the conflict, which polarized into an Anglo-Guelf and a Franco-Ghibelline coalition, each looking for allies in the Low Countries. A decisive victory won by the French king at the Battle of Bouvines, east of Lille (1214), put the Count of Flanders at his mercy.

Throughout the 13th century, the French kings increased their influence in Flanders, which was joined to Hainaut by personal union; by 1300, the annexation of Flanders was almost complete. Resistance by Count Guy, which was supported by the crafts in the towns, culminated in a resounding victory by the Flemish army (which consisted largely of citizens of the towns fighting on foot) over the French knights at Courtrai (the Battle of the Spurs, 1302) and prevented total annexation. French power in Flanders remained very strong, however, until the outbreak of the Hundred Years' War (1337). French political influence in Brabant was less powerful; an attempt at political infiltration was foiled by a coalition of the Duke of Brabant and the Count of Hainaut-Holland. English influence and money kept the balance of power in the Low Countries from passing into French hands; England had a strong commercial interest in relations in the Low Countries, particularly in the important ports and shipping of the coastal areas of Flanders, Zeeland, and Holland.

Social and economic structure. To obtain some insight into the social structure of the Low Countries between 900 and 1350, it is important to realize that, although the territorial princes wielded supreme power, the people were in fact directly dependent on an elite that, by virtue of owning land and possessing certain powers of jurisdiction and administration, had formed seigneuries, in which they held considerable effective power. These lords could control their dependents by demanding agricultural services, exercising certain rights over dependents' inheritances, levying monies in return for granting permission to marry, and forcing them to make use of the lords' mills, ovens, breweries, and stud animals. In the main, the owners of these seigneuries were treated as nobles and were often, though not always, bound to the territorial prince by feudal ties. A separated class was formed by the knights, who in the 12th century were usually *ministeriales* (servants who had originally been bondsmen) and were used by their lords for cavalry service or for higher administrative duties, for which they received a fief. It was not until the 13th century and, in many places, even later that the feudal nobility and ministerial knights became unified in a single aristocracy. Apart from these nobles, there were also freemen who owned their own land (*allodium*), but little is known about them; they were present, however, in large numbers in the cattle breeding regions of Flanders, Zeeland, Holland, and Friesland, where the numerous rivers and streams must have split up the land into many small farms. The descendants of noble families who were no longer able to live as richly as the nobles and who were known as *hommes de lignage* (in Brabant), *hommes de loi* (Namur), or *welgeborenen* (Holland), must have been very close in status to the freemen. In the agricultural areas of Hainaut, Brabant, Guelders, and the Oversticht were dependents whose legal status is difficult to determine, though they may be classed as bondsmen because of their being liable for various services and payments.

A factor of great, if not decisive, importance for social and economic relations, not only in the Low Countries but in all of western Europe, was the growth of the population, about which there is no direct statistical information but only a certain amount of indirect knowledge—after about 1050, it can be seen in the internal colonization (in the form of reclamation of such waste ground as woods and bogs), in the building of dikes and polders, in the expansion of agricultural land, and in the growth of the villages (new parishes) and towns.

The opening up of extensive areas of wood and heathland led to the foundation of new settlements (known in the French-speaking areas as *villes neuves*), to which colonists were attracted by offers of advantageous conditions—which were also intended to benefit the original estates. Many of these colonists were younger sons who had no share in the inheritance of their fathers' farms. The Cistercian and Premonstratensian monks, whose rules prescribed that they must work the land themselves, played an important part in this exploitation of new land. In the coastal regions of Flanders, Zeeland, and Friesland, they were very active in the struggle against the sea, building dikes both inland and on the coast itself. At first these dikes were purely defensive, but later they took on an offensive character and wrested considerable areas of land from the sea.

Especially important was the reclamation of marshland in the peat-bog areas of Holland and Utrecht and in the coastal regions of Flanders and Friesland. The Frisians had specialized in this work as early as the 11th century; Flemings and Hollanders soon adopted their methods, even applying them in the Elbe plain in Germany. The system, which consisted of digging drainage ditches, lowered the water table, leaving the ground dry enough for cattle grazing and later even for arable farming. The colonists, who were freemen, were given the right to cut drainage ditches as far back from the common water-

Decline of the German kings

Social classes

Expansion of the land

course as they wished. Certain restrictions were later imposed by the lords, however, who regarded themselves as the owners of these waste areas and demanded tribute money as compensation. Reclamation work was organized by a contractor (*locator*), who was responsible to the count and often carried out the function of local judge.

Thus, in the 12th and 13th centuries, a large area of land in the Holland–Utrecht peat-bog plain was made available for agriculture, facilitating the rise of nonagricultural communities (*i.e.*, the towns). In Flanders, Zeeland, Holland, and Utrecht, this struggle against the sea and the inland water was particularly noteworthy in that it led to the foundation of water boards, which in the 13th and 14th centuries were amalgamated to form higher water authorities (the *hoogheemraadschappen*). Mastery over the water had to be carried out on a large scale and in an organized fashion; the building of dikes required a higher authority and coordinated labour. Thus, various organizations emerged, acting independently in the field of canal and dike building and maintenance and responsible only to the government itself. These were *communitates*, with their own servants and their own managements (dike reeves and *heemraden*) and empowered to take necessary measures to maintain the waterworks, administer justice, and issue proclamations. The *hoogheemraadschappen* of Rijnland, Delfland, and Schieland were all in the county of Holland; the dike reeves at the head of these organizations were also the count's bailiffs and were delegated by the count the duties of supreme judge and administrator within their bailiwicks.

The increase in the population and the reclamation of land from the sea and marshes, as well as the fight to keep the sea out, all helped change the social and economic structures of the Low Countries. For centuries, the southern and eastern areas had been agricultural, often making use of the domain system. Fishing and cattle raising had also been important, especially in the water-rich areas of Flanders, Zeeland, Holland, and Friesland (Frisian trade, with Dorestat as its centre, had not been weakened by the Viking invasions). The increasing population and the growing importance of such regions as Flanders and Holland–Zeeland, together with increases in agricultural production, stimulated trade further, though new routes had to be found.

Dorestat itself fell into decay not so much as a result of Viking raids (it was rebuilt after each one) as of a change in the course of the river upon whose banks the town was situated. Dorestat's leading position in trade was then taken over by Tiel, Deventer, Zaltbommel, Heerewaarden, and the city of Utrecht. Wheat was imported from the Rhine plain, salt from Friesland, and iron ore from Saxony, and, before long, wine, textiles, and metal goods were brought along the Meuse and Rhine from the south. The IJssel in Guelders also began to carry trading traffic through Deventer, Zutphen, and Kampen and, on the coast of the Zuiderzee (now IJsselmeer), through Harderwijk, Elburg, and Stavoren.

In the south, Flanders became a second important trading and industrial area. For centuries, sheep farming had produced the wool needed in the cloth industry; but to meet an increased demand wool was imported from England, for which purpose merchants from various Flemish towns joined together in the Flemish Hanse in London. To a large extent, Flanders became economically dependent on England, a fact that must have had considerable political repercussions, particularly because it presented Flanders with the dilemma of having to choose which side to support in conflicts between France and England —on one hand, Flanders owed allegiance to its lord, the king of France, and, on the other, its economic interests were best served by taking the English side. These difficulties led to a reduction in Flemish commercial activity in England. Many Flemish craftsmen emigrated to England, while the English themselves took over the transport of wool. Nevertheless, Flemish cloth remained a high-quality product sold in large quantities at the fairs in the Champagne district and on the banks of the Rhine, to which it was transported by the people of Ghent.

On the whole, however, Flemish trade took on an ever more passive character. Although Flemish ships still sailed to Spain, Portugal, and Bordeaux to buy wine, the merchants of Bruges limited themselves to allowing colleagues from abroad to trade in the city. In this way, Bruges became the centre of trade with the Baltic countries, England, Spain, Portugal, the south of France, and —through the Champagne fairs—Italy. Grain, wood, tar, pitch, and furs were all brought from the east by the merchants of the German Hanse, who had formed a colony of their own in Bruges, where they bought Flemish cloth, wine from France and the Rhineland, and salt from France. Around 1300, the large Italian banking and trading houses set up branches in Bruges and began to send their fleets through the Strait of Gibraltar to Flanders; also, the English kings often sent their wool exports to Bruges, and the city became an international centre of trade and finance.

.For the cloth industry itself, Ghent and Ypres were the most important towns. In Ghent, the production process was run by drapers (*drapiers*), who bought the raw material, had it treated by spinners, weavers, fullers, and dyers, and eventually sold the final product. A drop in wool imports from England could therefore cause immediate social and political upheavals in the city, particularly from the large weavers' quarter.

The area of the Meuse also carried on considerable trade and industry; merchants from Liège, Huy, Namur, and Dinant are named in 11th-century toll tariffs from London and Coblenz. This trade was supplied mainly by the textile industry of Maastricht, Huy, and Nivelles and by the metal industry of Liège and Dinant. Trade in Brabant, actively supported by the dukes, used the road, or system of tracks (medieval road systems were not advanced), that ran from Cologne through Aix-la-Chapelle, Maastricht, Tongres, Louvain, and Brussels to Ghent and Bruges. The counts of Brabant wanted to control as much of this trade route as possible by expanding eastward, though there was also considerable north–south trade along the Dijle.

Since prehistoric times, fishing, particularly for herring, had been important in the coastal regions of Zeeland and Flanders. This fishing industry was given added stimulus by the shift of the herring shoals from the coast of Schonen (Sweden) to the North Sea. The ships, however, were increasingly placed at the disposal of general trade and, in particular, of the wool trade with England. The merchants of the German Hanse also turned their attention to Holland, where Dordrecht became the most important centre. Because of its central position in the rivers area, this town offered the counts the chance to raise tolls on all traffic in the neighbourhood; moreover, all cargoes had to be unloaded and offered for sale—wine, coal, millstones, metal products, fruit, spices, fish, salt, grain, and wood— an arrangment that led to further economic expansion of Dordrecht. Not until the 14th and 15th centuries did trade in other towns begin to catch up with that of Dordrecht. Among these were Delft, Rotterdam, and Amsterdam, while Leiden had been one of the first towns with a textile industry; none of them, however, outstripped Dordrecht itself.

The towns. The towns gave the Low Countries a special character of their own. Apart from some towns that had existed even in Roman times, such as Maastricht and Nimwegen, most towns arose in the 9th century; in the 11th and 12th centuries, they expanded and developed considerably. The emergence of the towns went hand in hand with the population increase and the extension of cultivable land, which made possible higher production. The population centres that emerged were not primarily agrarian but specialized in industry and trade.

The oldest towns were in the regions of the Scheldt and Meuse. Near existing counts' castles or walled monasteries, merchants formed settlements (*portus*, or *vicus*). These gradually merged with the original settlements to form units that both economically and in their constitutions took on their own characters with respect to the surrounding country, characters that were later manifested by defensive ramparts and walls. In this connection, mention must be made of Valenciennes, Bruges, Ghent, and Ypres (around the Scheldt) and of Dinant, Namur, Huy, Liège, Maastricht, Nivelles, and Gembloux (around the Meuse). A later group (though not much later) was formed by the northern towns of Deventer and Tiel, while Utrecht had long been a town in the sense of a commercial centre. Zutphen, Zwolle, Kampen, Harderwijk, Elburg, and Stavoren are other examples of early towns. Much younger (13th century) are the towns of Holland—Dordrecht, Leiden, Haarlem, Alkmaar, and Delft.

All the towns formed a new, nonfeudal element in the existing social structure, and from the beginning merchants played an important role. The merchants often organized into guilds, the origins of which may be traced back as far as the Carolingian era. From a manuscript dated about 1020, it appears that the merchants of Tiel met regularly for a drinking bout, had a common treasury, and could clear themselves of a charge by the simple expedient of swearing an oath of innocence (a privilege they claimed to have been granted by the emperor). Thus, there and elsewhere, the merchants constituted a horizontal community formed by an oath of cooperation and with the maintenance of law and order as its goal.

In contrast, therefore, to the vertical bonds in the feudal world and within the manors, horizontal bonds emerged between individuals who were naturally aiming at independence and autonomy. The extent to which autonomy was achieved varied greatly and depended on the power exercised by the territorial prince. Autonomy often developed spontaneously, and its evolution might have been accepted either tacitly or orally by the prince, so that no documentary evidence of it remains. Sometimes, however, certain freedoms were granted in writing, such as that granted by the Bishop of Liège to Huy as early as 1066. Such town charters often included the record of a ruling that had been the subject of demands or conflicts; they frequently dealt with a special form of criminal or contract law, the satisfactory regulation of which was of utmost importance to the town involved. Indeed, the first step a town took on the road to autonomy was to receive its own law and judicial system, dissociated from that of the surrounding countryside; a natural consequence of this was that the town then had its own governing authority and judiciary in the form of a board whose members were called *échevins*, headed by an *écoutète* (*scultetus, major, vilicus*). The *écoutète* was appointed by the territorial prince and had the prince's interests at heart. The *échevins* also had to take an oath before the prince, but they were always recruited from the inhabitants of the town itself and therefore more often favoured autonomy than did the *écoutète*. As the towns grew, the work of the board of *échevins* gained in importance, and functionaries appeared who had to look after the town's finances and its fortifications. They were often called burgomasters (*burgimagistri*).

The development of a town's autonomy sometimes advanced somewhat spasmodically as a result of violent conflicts with the prince. The citizens then united, forming *conjurationes* (sometimes called communes)—fighting groups bound together by an oath—as happened during a Flemish crisis in 1127–28 in Ghent and Bruges and in Utrecht in 1159. The counts of Flanders from the house of Alsace (Thierry, ruled 1128–68, and Philip, 1168–91) kept careful watch, supporting and aiding the towns in their economic development but otherwise keeping the process in check.

In their struggle for autonomy the towns had to fight for financial freedom, such as for the lessening or abolition of the taxes and tolls they had to pay to the prince but also and principally for the right to impose their own taxes, usually in the form of indirect taxation (*e.g.*, excise duties), in order to raise money for necessary public works. Especially important to them was the right to frame their own laws; this legislative right (the *keurrecht*) was in most towns originally restricted to the control of prices and standards in the markets and shops but was gradually extended to cover civil and criminal law. The extent of a man's obligation to serve in the prince's

armed forces was often fixed or limited or both (sometimes by the provision for payment in lieu, sometimes by a legal definition of the number of foot soldiers or manned ships to be made available).

Thus, the town in the Low Countries became a *communitas* (sometimes called *corporatio* or *universitas*)—a community that was legally a corporate body, could enter into alliances and ratify them with its own seal, could sometimes even make commercial or military contracts with other towns, and could negotiate directly with the prince. Land within the town's boundaries usually became its property, and the town's inhabitants were usually exempt from any dependent relationship with outsiders.

The size of the population naturally varied considerably from town to town, but, in general, a normal town in the northern Low Countries had a population of between 2,000 and 6,000; Dordrecht, with 10,000 inhabitants, was a very large town for the region, surpassed only by Utrecht. In comparison, the Flemish towns were exceptionally large: in the mid-14th century, the population of Ghent was about 56,000; that of Bruges, 35,000. On the other hand, Antwerp, which belonged to Brabant, had at that time only 5,000 inhabitants.

A town's population usually had a distinct social structure. The merchants, the oldest and leading group, soon emerged as a separate class (the patriciate); they generally managed to gain control of the offices of *échevin* and burgomaster and thus controlled the town's finances. Sometimes the *homines novi*, a new class of up-and-coming merchants, tried to become part of the patriciate, as in Dordrecht and Utrecht. Beneath the patriciate a lower class formed, called the *gemeen* ("common," in the strict sense of the word), which embraced the artisans and organized into crafts such as butchers, bakers, tailors, carpenters, masons, weavers, fullers, shearers, and coppersmiths. These crafts originally developed out of charitable organizations of people in the same profession and had to adhere to regulations laid down by the authorities. Gradually, however, they tried to obtain their independence, exercise influence in politics, cut themselves off from outsiders by means of compulsory membership, and introduce their own regulations regarding prices, working hours, quality of products, apprentices, journeymen, and masters. Early tension between crafts and patriciate developed in the Flemish towns and in Liège, Utrecht, and Dordrecht. In Ghent, Bruges, and other Flemish towns, the crafts were able, with the help of the count, to gain a victory over the French and their patriciate sympathizers.

In Flanders and in the bishopric of Liège, the towns rapidly attained such power that they constituted a threat to the territorial prince, which hindered stable development in these principalities and often resulted in violent conflicts. In contrast to this, relations between the prince and the towns of Brabant were extremely harmonious; the political interests of the prince and the economic interests of the towns usually coincided. In Holland, however, the towns did not really develop until as late as the 13th century, when they were deliberately helped by the counts William II (ruled 1234–56) and Florent V (ruled 1256–96), who granted them charters that included extensive rights.

During this period, foundations were laid for the dominant role the towns later played in the Low Countries in political, social, economic, and cultural fields. A decisive change also took place in the authority of the territorial prince. Originally he regarded his powers mainly as a means of increasing his income and of extending the area over which he could exercise power. He felt little duty toward his subjects or desire to further the welfare of the community as a whole. At best there were religious as well as material motives in his dealings with the churches and monasteries. There were no direct relations between the prince and all his subjects, for he was primarily lord of his vassals. The political, social, and economic developments discussed above, however, brought a change in this situation. In the first place, the prince's increasing independence meant that he himself began to

The struggle for autonomy

Size of towns

Relations between towns and territorial princes

behave like a king or sovereign lord. His authority was then referred to as *potestas publica* ("public authority"), and it was believed granted by God (*a Deo tradita*). The area over which he ruled was described as his *regnum* or *patria*. This implied not only the duty of a lord toward his vassals but also that of a prince (*princeps*) toward his subjects. This duty included as its first priority the maintenance of law and order (*defensio pacis*) by means of laws and their administration. He had further to protect the church (*defensio* or *advocatio ecclesiae*), while his involvement in land reclamation and in the building of dikes and with the development of the towns brought him into direct contact with the nonfeudal elements of the population, with whom his relations were no longer those of a lord toward his vassals but took on a more modern aspect—that of a sovereign toward his trusted subjects. He became, according to the 14th-century lawyer Philip of Leiden, the *procurator rei publicae* ("he who looks after the matters of the people"). Contact with his subjects was through the representatives of the *communitates* of the water boards and *heemraadschappen* and through the towns and nonurban communities, which were legally corporate bodies not only in dealings with outsiders but also with the prince. Sometimes the towns expressly placed themselves under the protection of the prince and declared themselves committed to loyalty to him. Such a town was Dordrecht, which, in a document dated 1266, expressed its loyalty and at the same time described the count of Holland as *dominus terrae* ("lord of the land"). These new notions of a sovereign lord and sovereign power point to a more modern conception of a state, to a growing awareness of territoriality, and to new possibilities of collaboration between prince and subjects.

Burgundian and Habsburg rule (1384–1579). Among the many territorial principalities of the Low Countries, Flanders, Brabant, Hainaut-Holland, and Guelders in the mid-14th century had a dominating military and diplomatic position. Flanders had already arrested the course of French domination, and its feeling of territoriality was strengthened by this and by many minor wars between the principalities. The feeling found expression when the prince's subjects increasingly set themselves up against him as organized estates—those of the clergy or *Organized* nobles and those of the towns. In the 14th century, this *estates* led almost everywhere to the formation of permanent organs that consisted of representatives of the estates. These organs represented the common interests of the estates against or, sometimes, in agreement with those of the territorial prince. At the same time, committees and law courts were set up to keep a watch on the prince's officials.

Constitutional developments. In Brabant, the close cooperation between duke and towns resulted in the harmonious growth of estates, though this was also due to the continuing lack of financial resources from which the dukes suffered and which gradually made them more and more dependent on the increasingly powerful and rich towns. The towns, therefore, set the pace, especially during periods of regency, when a ruler was below the age of majority. Between 1248 and 1356, the towns of Brabant developed cooperation between estates, culminating in the Joyeuse Entrée, in which this cooperation was defined and laid down in a constitution, the unity of Brabant and Limburg was declared indivisible, and the prince was obliged to choose his officials exclusively from among the people of Brabant and to win the approval of the towns and of his county before embarking on a war.

In Flanders, the power of the three towns of Ghent, Bruges, and Ypres was too great to enable smooth cooperation with the prince and the two other estates—those of the clergy and the nobles. The count succeeded only in making the Franc of Bruges—the countryside surrounding the town—a fourth estate, but there was no question of a constitution, written or otherwise.

Better results were obtained in Holland, although only after a political conflict between two political factions—Kabeljauwen ("codfish") and Hoeksen ("hooks")—in which the Kabeljauwen advocated cooperation between the estates and the prince but had too few noble families

among their supporters. Guelders, however, was late in its development, partly because the powerful Duke Willem (ruled 1379–1402) had his own financial resources as a result of his military activities in the service of the English and, later, French kings; under Willem's successors, however, the knights and the towns became more powerful and finally gained permanent representation as estates. In Utrecht, too, there was cooperation between the prince (the bishop) and the estates; and the clergy, particularly the collegiate churches of the town of Utrecht, played an important part: the Land Charter of Bishop Arnold in 1375 is comparable to the Joyeuse Entrée of Brabant. In the prince-bishopric of Liège, cooperation between prince and estates had to be won by violent conflicts between the towns and the bishop and, within the towns, between the patriciate and the crafts. It was mainly to these territorial estates that the princes had to turn for financial help, which was often voted to them only on limiting conditions.

The Burgundians. In the second half of the 14th century, the dukes of Burgundy (princes of the French royal house of Valois) began to penetrate these territorial principalities in the Low Countries, whose feelings of territoriality made them regard the dukes with suspicion. The marriage in 1369 of Philip of Burgundy (Philip the Bold) to the heiress of the Count of Flanders (Margaret) signified the beginning of this Burgundian infiltration, *Beginning* which was repeatedly furthered by such tricks of fate as *of* marriages and inheritances.   *Burgun-*

Through his marriage Philip gained possession, after the *dian* death of his father-in-law in 1384, of the counties of *infiltration* Flanders, Artois, and Rethel and also of the county of Nevers and the free county of Burgundy (Franche-Comté), the last of which was within the Holy Roman Empire. He thus not only gained a large and powerful part of the Low Countries but was also able to extend his Burgundian property. Though it seemed at first that French power might again become the dominant force in the Low Countries, it soon became clear that the Burgundian dukes, while happy to continue taking part in French politics, were extremely independent and more interested in forging a single powerful empire out of the Low Countries and Burgundy. Duke John the Fearless succeeded to all his father's lands in 1404, while his younger brother Anthony was given Brabant, where the childless Duchess Joanna had named him as her successor, which was accepted by the estates. Anthony's branch of the Burgundians died out as early as 1430, so that Brabant fell to the other branch under Philip the Good (ruled 1419–67), who also gained possession—through war, family relations, and purchase—of Hainaut-Holland, Namur, and Luxembourg. This Burgundian power structure was not a state but was founded on a personal union among the various principalities, each of which jealously guarded its own freedom and institutions. The Burgundian dukes did, however, attempt to set up central organizations to bridge the differences among the principalities and to keep the various regions under stricter control by appointing viceroys (stadholders); but this ambition ran aground on the forced and overly hasty centralization and expansion of power carried out by Charles the Bold (ruled 1467–77), who was able, nevertheless, to annex Guelders. Charles imposed increasingly high financial demands, which were put before the States General—an assembly that united the delegates from the various states at meetings called by the duke and held at regular intervals; he introduced a central law court (the Parliament of Malines) and a central exchequer and did all he could to gain the status and title of king. After his death, a movement for regional independence arose and won a series of privileges from his daughter Mary (ruled 1477–82) that virtually nullified the previous centralization. Moreover, the duchy of Burgundy itself was taken over by the French crown, so that the Burgundian union became a union without Burgundy. An important point was that both the States General and the territorial states demanded and were given the right to meet on their own initiative.

After Mary's position had become more firmly established by her marriage to Maximilian of Habsburg (the son and future successor to the Holy Roman emperor), the States General, because of its internal particularism, proved unable to provide a lasting administration. Gradually, a restoration took place, at first under the regency of Maximilian after Mary's death in 1482, but principally later, after their son Philip the Handsome took over the government. Philip resumed the centralization process by refounding the central law court (then known as the Great Council of Malines) and by setting up within the duke's council permanent commissions to discuss important political and financial questions.

The Habsburgs. The fate of the Low Countries was already closely bound up with that of Austria by virtue of the Habsburg marriage; in 1504, this situation was intensified when Philip and his wife, Joanna, inherited the Spanish crown. From then on, the Low Countries were merely a part of a greater whole, and their fate was principally decided by the struggle of this Spanish-Austrian empire for European hegemony. They repeatedly had to make sacrifices for the many wars waged against France, particularly under Emperor Charles V, who in 1519 had added the German imperial crown to his many possessions. The Emperor, who was almost always out of the country, placed the Low Countries under the rule of governesses—first his aunt Margaret and later his sister Mary, who retained control and worked toward further centralization even when he was in the country.

The States General could do little more than offer passive resistance, principally by providing financial obstructions to centralization. As a meeting place for the regional deputies, the States General did have a certain influence and, by its opposition, strengthened a sort of negative feeling of unity. That the Emperor himself also saw the Low Countries as a unit can be seen in his measures to separate them (but not entirely) from the empire as "Burgundian Kreis" (1548) and in the Pragmatic Sanction (1549), which stated that succession would be regulated in identical fashion in all the regions of the Low Countries that he had included in his empire (among these were Utrecht, Guelders, Groningen, and Friesland). The Low Countries were thus prevented from being split up.

In the meantime, the process of centralization had reached a decisive phase with the foundation of the collateral councils (1531), which were separate from the Great Council. They were the Council of Finance, which had in effect already existed for some time; the Council of State, in which members of the high nobility could advise the governess; and the Secret Council, in which permanent officials dealt with everyday administration and composed ordinances without having to wait for advice. All the government organs, except for the central law court in Malines, were in Brussels, which may thus be considered the capital of the Low Countries. The States General and territorial states were no longer allowed to sit whenever they wished; the territorial states were still a stumbling block in the acquisition of financial resources, so that Charles V was never able to provide himself with a standing army.

Under Charles's son Philip II, who in 1555–56 succeeded as king of Spain and prince of the Netherlands, the policy of centralization was continued. It culminated in the introduction of a new ecclesiastical hierarchy. The Low Countries (by then the Netherlands), which formerly had been, ecclesiastically speaking, merely an extension of the archbishoprics of Cologne and Rheims, became by virtue of a papal bull of 1559 a directly governed region of the church under three archbishops and 15 bishops. Resistance to this was fierce by the high nobles, who saw the high positions in the church slip from their grasp; by the abbots, who feared the incorporation of their monasteries; and by a number of territories, which were afraid of greater centralization activities under new bishops. The high nobles, who were often excluded from the activities of the Secret Council, led the resistance under the capable Prince William of Orange (1533–84) and the popular Count of Egmont. Resistance increased when the Burgundian Granvelle, who was bishop of Artois and

virtually Margaret of Parma's prime minister, was appointed cardinal and then archbishop of Malines and primate of the Netherlands. The government gave way, and Granvelle was forced to leave the country, yet the high nobles themselves hardly knew how to run affairs; the initiative was thus transferred to the low nobility, who in 1565 united by bond of oath in the Compromise and in 1566 presented to the Governess a petition requesting the relaxation of edicts and ordinances against the Calvinists and other Protestants. At the same time, they adopted the name Geuzen (*gueux*, "beggars"), originally a term of abuse.

The resistance grew stronger, the Calvinists became more confident, and fanatics started a violent campaign against churches—the "breaking of the images" (August 1566)—against which the governess took powerful measures and in the first few months of 1567 managed to restore peace. The King, however, whose information concerning these events was somewhat out of date because of slow communications and who was uneasy because of the "breaking of the images," decided to take stern measures. He sent his trusted general, the Duke of Alba, to the Netherlands. Alba's strict regime precipitated a revolt that eventually led to the partition of the Netherlands.

Economic structure. The economic structure of the country underwent far-reaching changes in the 14th–16th centuries. The growth in population, which in western Europe had begun in the 10th century, ceased with relative suddenness after 1300. Moreover, Europe in the mid-14th century was afflicted by wars, famines, and epidemics, which also affected the Low Countries. The Black Death of 1347–51 spared the Low Countries to a certain extent, but the cut in the population of the other European countries must have reduced the market for the Low Countries' trade and industry. The economy, relatively free in previous centuries, was now more limited and regulated, especially where the crafts had come to power, as in Flanders and Liège. The cloth industry of the large towns in Flanders and Brabant suffered a severe setback. Nevertheless, the economy during the 14th and, especially, during the 15th and 16th centuries sought and developed new areas for expansion. This led to a remarkable contrast between the apparent flourishing of trade and industry and the visible poverty of the mass of the people. The most noticeable development was the decline of trade in Bruges and its growth in Antwerp, which became the economic centre of the Netherlands in the late 15th century.

Antwerp, which as early as the 13th century had attained some importance, had attracted an increasingly large proportion of the English cloth imports during the 14th and 15th centuries. Conservative rule in Bruges and the insecurity created by the disturbances in Flanders caused many foreign merchants to move their business to Antwerp. The Portuguese, in particular, took their spices from the Indies to Antwerp, where they traded them for copper and silver brought by German merchants. Thus, Antwerp developed into an international port, where foreign merchants organized themselves into "nations" and where not only German but also Italian banking and trading houses had branches. New methods of trading and international finance developed in Antwerp, such as buying from samples and transferring money by means of bills of exchange. Even princes contracted loans in Antwerp.

A commercial capitalism was developing that stimulated the entire economy of the Netherlands. Although the cloth industry declined in the towns, it flourished in the villages and began to specialize in lighter cloths of coarser quality (principally in the country districts of Flanders, with Hondschoote as its centre).

The towns battled these rural industries in vain, though in 1531 Holland issued an edict to restrict them throughout the county, but it had little success. Moreover, Holland itself began to play an increasingly important economic role—Leiden boasted a growing textile industry, Delft and Haarlem had export breweries, and in the area of the River Zaan shipbuilding developed; nevertheless, fishing, shipping, and trade were its main means of

Centralization

Resistance to a new ecclesiastical hierarchy

Commercial capitalism

support apart from arable farming and cattle breeding. Dordrecht was rivalled by Rotterdam and Gorinchem and, by the 16th century, was even outstripped by Amsterdam, which cornered an increasing proportion of Baltic trade, as may be seen from the lists of the toll in the Sound (between Sweden and Denmark).

The regions along the Meuse and IJssel also maintained their commercial activity. In the bishopric of Liège there was even a metal industry with blast furnaces, paid for by capital raised by traders. Coal mining in the area between the Meuse and the Sambre was also organized according to modern capitalist methods.

The cultivation of commercially exploitable crops also developed in country areas—hemp for rope making, hops and barley for brewing, flax for the manufacture of linen. But all this was at the expense of wheat farming. Grain had to be imported in increasingly large quantities, and, whenever grain imports fell off, the people, particularly the lower classes, went hungry. The economic apparatus had become more versatile and brought greater prosperity, but at the same time, precisely because of this specialization, it had become more vulnerable. The distribution of prosperity was variable; the great mass of the people in the towns suffered the consequences and bore the main burden of the rise in prices occasioned by inflation. It is estimated that, of the total population of Brabant, Flanders, and Holland, between a third and a half lived in the towns, where the opportunities for earning a living were still greater than in the country and where charitable institutions concerned themselves with the lot of the poor.

Culture. The Netherlands played an important part in the artistic, scientific, and religious life of Europe. In the late Middle Ages, when prosperity was increasing and the princely houses, particularly that of the Burgundians, as well as the middle classes in the towns, were encouraging progress, the Netherlands began to make an independent contribution to cultural life. In the southern Netherlands, this was already the case with mysticism, which reached its zenith in the 13th and 14th centuries in the poems of Sister Hadewych and in the prose of the prior Joannes Ruusbroec (Jan van Ruysbroeck). Ruusbroec's writings were founded on a considerable knowledge of theology; it is not certain whether his work had a direct influence on the founding of the religious movement along the IJssel —the modern devotion (*devotio moderna*)—or whether mysticism merely created the intellectual climate in which the new school of thought could develop. The modern devotion was inspired by Geert Grote (Gerard Groote, 1340–84) of Deventer, who preached, as did many others, the ascetic and pious life and resistance to the secularization of the church. His message was well received, and many lay people found in themselves a desire to live in communities devoted to the service of God; these were the Brethren and Sisters of the Common Life, who later organized themselves into the Windesheim monasteries and convents, which followed Augustinian rules. Their communities were extremely important for both education and religion; they were industrious copyists and brought a simple piety to the lower classes. Their work, like that of the mendicant orders, was a typical product of life in the towns. The movement reached its peak in Thomas à Kempis, from Zwolle, whose *Imitatio Christi* (*The Imitation of Christ*) became quite widely read.

Within the modern devotion, where great importance was attached to good teaching, Dutch Humanism was able to develop freely. Of importance was the foundation in 1517 of the Collegium Trilingue in Louvain, where Latin, Greek, and Hebrew were taught. The greatest Dutch Humanist was Desiderius Erasmus (1469–1536), whose fame spread throughout the world and who had been taught in the schools of the Brethren of the Common Life. He drew his inspiration, as did many other Humanists, from antiquity and was famed for his pure Latin. He was in touch with the greatest minds of his time, visited England (Cambridge) and Italy, and worked for some years in Basel and in Freiburg. Erasmus' greatest achievement was to turn the science of theology, which had degenerated into meaningless Neoscho-

lastic disputes, back to the study of sources by philological criticism and by publishing a new edition of the Greek New Testament. Although he vociferously criticized the church and even the princes, he avoided out of conviction a break with the church and pleaded for a religious tolerance that can be seen under many rulers of the later republic.

The Humanists were principally intellectuals, however, expressing themselves in literary and scientific treatises and having little impact on the broad masses of the people. Many of them, like Erasmus, desired no break with the church and did not accept that break when it became a fact by the appearance of Martin Luther. Instead, they wanted reformation within the church. It was otherwise for the reforming movements that brought turmoil to the Netherlands in the first half of the 16th century. Even Lutheranism had few followers, despite its early appearance in the Netherlands (Luther's dogmas were condemned by the University of Louvain as early as 1520). There was a Lutheran community in Antwerp; but otherwise, support for Lutheranism was limited to individual priests and intellectuals. It was precisely over the question of the Eucharist that the Sacramentarians differed with Luther; they denied the consubstantiation of Christ in the Eucharist. Although the Sacramentarians enjoyed little support from the people, their questioning of the value of consubstantiation was of considerable significance and their teaching was propagated in heretical Bible translations and even in rhetoric competitions.

Uproar was caused by the Anabaptists (so called because they rejected the baptism of infants and therefore had themselves rebaptized as adults), who refused to swear the oath of allegiance to the prince or to serve in the armed forces or in government per se and who believed in a *lumen internum* ("inner light"). This baptist movement won great popularity in the Netherlands after 1530; from the very beginning there were two branches —the social revolutionaries and the "quiet baptists." The first of these was characterized by a lively enthusiasm and a willingness, once the external trappings of the church had been rejected, to organize itself into communities, which soon formed close ties with each other. Prophesies by the social-revolutionary branch of the imminent coming of Christ and of a New Jerusalem fascinated the masses, while their fanaticism and readiness to sacrifice themselves made a deep impression on a population suffering poverty and misery. In 1534 a section of the Anabaptists moved to Münster in Westphalia, where they supposed that the New Jerusalem would be built; and in 1535 an abortive attempt was made to take over the town hall in Amsterdam. After a long siege, the Bishop of Münster succeeded in reconquering his town, and the Anabaptists suffered terrible vengeance. Only the "quiet baptists" were able to continue, under the leadership of the Frisian pastor Menno Simons (these Mennonites are even today strongly represented in the provinces of Groningen, Friesland, and North Holland).

The future of the movement for reformation in the Netherlands was assured, however, not by the biblical Humanists nor by the Anabaptists but by a movement less intellectual than the first and more realistic than the second—Calvinism.

The theology of John Calvin (1509–64) was radical, strict, logical, and consistent. Its central theme was the absolute might and greatness of God, which made man a sinful creature of no significance who hoped merely to win God's grace by honouring him in daily hard work. Calvinism found its way to the Netherlands by way of France, though there may have been some direct influence from Geneva, Calvin's town. Calvinist writings were known in Antwerp as early as 1545, while the first translation into Dutch of his *Christianae religionis institutio* is dated 1560, which was also the year in which support for him spread in the Netherlands, largely because the Calvinists preached their creed in public and held open-air services.

Calvinist teaching appealed not only to the lower classes but also to the intellectual and middle classes because of its glorification of work, its discipline, its organization

Margin notes:

Artistic, scientific, and religious contributions

Reforming movements

Calvinism

into communities, and its communal singing of the psalms. The government saw the movement as a threat to its plans of unity and centralization, and it took stern measures against Calvinism. Calvinists forcibly removed their coreligionists from prisons and occasionally even attacked monasteries, and their rejection of icons, paintings, statues, and valuables in churches sometimes led them to remove them and hand them over to the town magistrates. But this idealism became corrupted, the leaders were unable to retain control of the movement, and it degenerated into the "breaking of the images" (1566), mentioned above. The nobility, and especially the lower nobility, which had been sympathetic to Calvinism, discarded the movement; the government besieged and captured the Calvinist centre, Valenciennes, by defeating a Calvinist army at Oosterweel, near Antwerp. The result was a great exodus of Calvinists. Nevertheless, Calvin's ideas had penetrated deeply, and his supporters, who had emigrated to England, East Friesland, and the Pfalz of Germany, were able to maintain their unity, which had been threatened by friction between the *rekkelijken* ("liberals") and the *preciezen* ("rigids"), and to support their coreligionists in the Netherlands. The Calvinists were to become the driving force behind the revolt against Spanish rule.

The revolt and the formation of the republic (1567–79). The forcible measures taken by the central government against the "breaking of the images" were followed by a brief period of peace. Ferdinand Álvarez de Toledo, duke of Alba (who became governor after the departure of Margaret of Parma on the last day of 1567), introduced stern measures at the express command of the King. These provoked a resistance to the government (often referred to as the "revolt") that triggered off the Eighty Years' War (1568–1648). The "breaking of the images" itself, which had raged across the country like a storm, had already shown a deep-rooted resistance that had many causes and was brought to a head by Alba's measures.

The revolt

It is impossible to label any of the causes of the revolt as the decisive factor. An important one, however, was a religious motive. Criticism of the structure of the church and the riches and worldly way of life of its prelates and the accompanying desire for reform had always been strong in the Netherlands; and Protestantism, through the teaching of Luther, the Sacramentarians, the Anabaptists, and, above all, the Calvinists, had gained a firm foothold. The measures taken against the resistance—harsh edicts, prison sentences, torture, and death sentences, carried out with great cruelty—fanned the flames all the more and among all classes. Social and economic causes, however, also lay behind the resistance, especially among the lower classes—the wars with France, the epidemics, poor harvests, hard winters, floods, and a frightening inflation and consequent rise in prices all combined to cause despair and misery among the masses and made them susceptible to radical ideas. At the same time, in the upper classes of the nobility and the urban patriciate, there was a sharply felt reaction against the absolutist centralization policy of the King, who lived far away in Spain and yet whose wish was law in the Netherlands. Towns felt their privileges being threatened, and the nobles found their independent status being undermined, by the ever-increasing activities of the secret council. The mercenaries, who were often stationed in a town as a garrison and acted as occupying forces, also aroused hostility. The fact that the resistance did not present a united front may be ascribed to the particularism among the territories—Holland, with its commercial interests, could hardly be expected to be enthusiastic on behalf of typically agrarian feudal provinces such as Hainaut or Artois.

It is clear, however, that the terror organized by Alba burst like a bombshell in this political, social, economic, and religious climate. The Prince of Orange, with sharp political insight, had decided not to wait for Alba's arrival; he had managed to escape in time to his birthplace in Nassau-Dillenburg, leaving behind all his possessions, which were promptly confiscated. His son, Philip William, was taken prisoner to Spain. Alba sent his troops to the principal towns and set up the Council of Troubles (or Council of Blood), which imposed severe penalties, often including the death sentence or confiscation of property, sparing nothing and nobody, not even the most powerful—the counts of Egmont and Hoorn were publicly beheaded in Brussels in June 1568.

Alba also rushed through installation of the new ecclesiastical hierarchy, which had not been completed. Furthermore, he attempted to make the central government independent of the provincial states by means of new taxes on property, on the sale of land or building, and on the sale of goods. This met with violent resistance because the taxes were to be general and permanent, so that the separate states would no longer have the means to make conditions for the furnishing of taxes (although they themselves already levied taxes on the sale of goods) and, more important, because a permanent tax system would make the king independent of his subjects, so that the taxes were the final link in the policy of absolutism and centralization, which would lead to a unified state controlled by a prince with unlimited power.

New taxes

The severity with which Alba ruled was not able to prevent the immediate appearance of resistance. The Geuzen conducted pillaging raids in the country and piracy at sea, for which they had "authority" in the form of letters of marque issued by William of Orange in his capacity as sovereign of the principality of Orange. Attacks took place as early as 1568. A small force led by Louis of Nassau, William's brother, enjoyed a modest victory over the Spaniards at Heiligerlee (in the province of Groningen), considered the beginning of the Eighty Years' War; but shortly afterward Louis was defeated near Jengum in East Friesland. A greater setback, however, was the complete failure, due to lack of funds, of a campaign led by William himself in the south of the country. During the sombre years of 1568–72 the "Wilhelmus" was written—a song of faith, hope, and trust that was to become the Dutch national anthem. Other songs written by the Geuzen kept up the spirits of the people during this period and in later years.

During these years, William negotiated for help from Germany, England, and, above all, the French Huguenots. A large-scale attack was planned for the summer of 1572. Before William could carry it out, the Geuzen seized the port of Briel (April 1, 1572), west of Rotterdam. This was a move of considerable strategic importance because the port controlled the mouth of both Meuse and Waal, and the Prince immediately supported the movement. The Geuzen then took Flushing, Veere, and Enkhuizen, so that William had useful bases in Holland and Zeeland. The help that the Geuzen received from the Calvinists in these towns was striking—the Calvinists, a radical minority, were again and again able to force the more conservative town magistrates either to cooperate or resign. Oudewater, Gouda, Dordrecht, Leiden, Hoorn, and Haarlem followed, only Amsterdam keeping the Geuzen out. The purposeful activities of the Calvinists also led to their gaining churches, often the principal church of a town, for their services; they closed monasteries, and Catholic services were soon forbidden.

The revolt was at first successful only in Holland because of its unique position. As a commercially oriented province, it had been more inclined to look after its own interests than to cooperate with other provinces. Trade had been seriously threatened by the Geuzen but was now free again. Moreover, the province lay in a strategically favourable position—difficult to reach from the central government in Brussels and almost inaccessible to the Spanish armies by virtue of its many rivers, lakes, drains, and bogs.

To give the revolt a legal basis, the fiction was invented that it had been a revolt not against the King but against his evil advisers, particularly the Governor. By their own authority, in July 1572 the states of Holland foregathered in Dordrecht, where William of Orange was proclaimed stadholder of Holland and Zeeland. The Prince himself went to Holland and, realizing that the Calvinists had been the driving force behind the revolt, became a mem-

Legal basis

ber of the Calvinist church. But he repeatedly expressly avowed his ideal of the United Netherlands, in which there would be room for Catholics and Calvinists alike.

Alba, disappointed by his failure to push through the tax reforms and about to return to Spain, learned of the fall of Briel and decided to stay and start a counteroffensive. The south was immediately brought under control with the occupation and plundering of Malines; then Zutphen and Naarden in the north were taken and likewise plundered. This provoked stronger resistance, and Haarlem was retaken only after a very long siege, which not only demoralized and decimated Alba's troops but also strengthened the other towns in their decision to offer resistance (1573). Thus, the Spaniards were unable to take Alkmaar, their fleet suffered a heavy defeat in the Zuiderzee, and a long siege of Leiden was relieved by flooding the surrounding country (1574). (As a reward, the town later was given a university, where Calvinistic theology was to be the principal subject for study.) Spanish troops were never again to force their way into Holland —a heavy blow for the most powerful monarchy in the world.

Alba left on December 18, 1573, and his successor, Don Luis de Requesens, was unable to prevent further secessions in the north. Even the south, which had been loyal to Spain until then, but where active Calvinist movements existed (especially in Ghent), became amenable to William's ambition for a united resistance to the Spanish regime. There were considerable problems involved, and one of the greatest points of difference was the question of religion—the more radical north demanded the total abolition of Catholicism in Holland and Zeeland and the acceptance of Calvinism by the southern provinces, though William was diplomatic enough not to make this demand. It was finally agreed that the States General would deal with the question later, and until such time the Calvinists would be masters only of their own house in Holland and Zeeland. A new governor (Requesens died in March 1576) was to be accepted only if he approved the pacification and sent away the foreign troops, who, because they had received no pay, were beginning to mutiny and plunder and were becoming an increasing nuisance. Another condition of his acceptance was that he govern with native officials and in close consultation with the states. On this basis, delegates from all the provinces came to an agreement, and on November 8, 1576, they signed the Pacification of Ghent. Their sense of unity was further strengthened by the news that on November 4 Antwerp had been invaded by mutinying Spanish troops, who had slaughtered 7,000 citizens in what came to be known as the "Spanish Fury."

The Pacification of Ghent

William's idealism, his desire for unity, and his tolerant ideas had apparently triumphed. Unity of thought, however, did not last long; and within three years signs of a split appeared between the northern and southern provinces (which later became a permanent split). It was immediately obvious that within the United Netherlands there were opposing powers of radicalism and reaction. For various reasons, they could not maintain equilibrium; the reactionaries tried to force their ideas on the country with the help of the new governor, Don Juan de Austria, a half-brother of the King, and the Calvinists continued their radical program to make theirs the official and only religion. Many factors caused these conflicts—deep-running religious differences between north and south, a deeply rooted particularism that hindered cooperation, structural and economic differences between Holland and Zeeland on the one hand (commerce and industry) and Hainaut and Artois on the other (agrarian economy and feudal possession of land). It is impossible to point to any one decisive factor. William did his utmost to save the Pacification, and he found support for his ideas of tolerance among the rich burghers; yet he was unable to bridge the differences between rich and poor, Catholics and Calvinists. Moreover, Don Juan died in 1578 and was succeeded by Alessandro Farnese (duke of Parma and son of the earlier governess Margaret), who was conspicuous for his military and diplomatic gifts, which made him a worthy opponent for William

and to which may be ascribed the bringing back of the southern provinces to loyalty to the king.

Notable, too, was the appearance in the north and south of movements in the direction of "limited unions," which within the whole of the United Netherlands were to bring about greater community of interests between certain provinces. On January 6, 1579, the Union of Arras (Artois) was formed in the south among Artois, Hainaut, and the town of Douay, based on the Pacification of Ghent but retaining the Catholic religion, loyalty to the king, and the privileges of the estates. Although William himself did not at first reject the idea of a northern union and expressly stated that it must be open to all provinces, matters subsequently developed in a direction not to his liking.

(C.v.d.K.)

II. The Netherlands since 1579
POLITICAL AND CONSTITUTIONAL DEVELOPMENTS, 1579–1609

The Union of Utrecht. On January 23, 1579, an agreement was concluded at Utrecht forming a "closer union" within the larger union of the Low Countries led by the States-General sitting in Brussels. Included in the Union were the provinces and cities committed to carrying on resistance to Spanish rule: Holland, Zeeland, Utrecht, Gelderland (Guelders), and Zutphen (a part of Overijssel) as the first signatories, followed in the next year by the whole of Overijssel and most of Friesland, and by Groningen, all in the north; and in the south, by the cities of Antwerp and Breda in Brabant, and Ghent, Bruges, and Ypres in Flanders. Designed to establish a league for conduct of the war of independence and ultimately to strengthen the central government in Brussels, the "Union of Utrecht" became in fact the foundation of a separate state and a distinct nation in the northern Netherlands. The new state was named the United Provinces of the Netherlands, or more briefly, the "Dutch Republic," and was known in the international community as the "States-General." The people of the northern Netherlands began to be distinguished from the inhabitants of the south (to whom the name of Flemings continued to cling) by the appellation Hollanders (French Hollandais, Italian Olandese, German Holländer, etc.), after their principal province. The English, however, came to apply exclusively to the Hollanders the name of Dutch, which previously they had applied to all German speakers (from German Deutsch, Dutch Duits). The name Netherlanders, which remained in use in the Low Countries for both the inhabitants of the United Provinces specifically and for all those, north or south, who spoke Dutch (Nederlands), passed out of currency in most foreign countries or came to be restricted to the northerners. The transformation had a price: the erosion of the bond of historical identity between northerners and southerners, Dutchmen and Belgians as they would be called in the 19th and 20th centuries.

The treaty that formed the basis of the new northern union established a military league to resist the Spaniards, but on a "perpetual" basis; and it provided for closer political arrangements among the provinces than those of "allies" in the ordinary sense. The provinces united, "for all time as if they were a single province"; each remained sovereign in its internal affairs, but all acted as a body in foreign policy. Decisions on war and peace and on taxation could be made only unanimously. The Union did not throw off the formal sovereignty of the king of Spain, but it confirmed the effective powers of the provincial stadholders (formally the "lieutenants," or governors, of the king) as their political leaders (there was no "stadholder of the United Provinces," as foreigners often assumed). The Union moved away from the religious settlement embodied in the Pacification of Ghent of two years before (see above) and toward a predominance of the Calvinists and their monopoly of public practice of religion in the key provinces of Holland and Zeeland.

The immediate political significance of the Union was that it dovetailed with the Union of Artois, concluded earlier in the month, which began the reconciliation of the southerners with Philip II. The two "unions," parallel but opposite, thus undermined William's policy of collaboration between Catholics and Calvinists throughout the Low Countries in resistance to the Spanish domination, which required mutual toleration among the religions. But it took some time before the "general union," with its base in the States-General at Brussels, fell apart irrevocably. For another half decade the Prince struggled to keep intact the broader union and at the same time to assure its military and political support from abroad. Although Archduke Matthias of Habsburg, named governor general by the States-General in 1577 after the deposition of Don Juan, remained the formal head of state until 1581, the Prince continued to exercise his leadership. That the Prince was the head and heart of the rebellion was recognized by Philip II in 1580 when he put him under the ban of outlawry. William's *Apology* in defense of his conduct was followed in 1581 by the Act of Abjuration (literally, "Act of Abandonment," *Akte van Verlating*) by which the States-General declared that Philip had forfeited his sovereignty over the provinces by his persistent tyranny. This was a declaration of independence for the whole of the Low Countries, but the military and political events of the next decade limited its permanent effect to the northern provinces, under the "closer union" of Utrecht.

Declaration of independence

Foreign intervention. Yet independence did not become William's objective even after the proclamation of the Act of Abjuration. Archduke Matthias returned home in 1581 after Orange turned to the Duc d'Anjou, who agreed to take over the "lordship" of the Low Countries in 1580. The Prince hoped for assistance from the Duc's brother, King Henry III of France, and considered the "lordship" of Anjou as only a kind of limited, constitutional "sovereignty" like that which the rebels had hoped to impose on Philip II at the beginning of their rising. Anjou, however, saw the lordship as a means to total dominion over the Netherlands. Irritated by restraints upon his authority, he even attempted the seizure of power by military force, resulting in the so-called French Fury of January 17, 1583, when his troops tried to capture Antwerp. The coup misfired, but Orange managed to keep Anjou (who returned to France) in his post despite the outraged feelings of the Netherlanders. Holland and Zeeland were on the verge of offering the title of count to William when he was assassinated on July 10, 1584, at Delft, by Balthasar Gerards, a fanatical young Catholic from Franche-Comté, spurred by the promises of the ban of Philip II. William's death did not end the rebellion, as Philip had hoped, but it did result in the almost unnoticed disappearance of the central government in Brussels. The States-General, which now met at The Hague in Holland, represented only the provinces in the Union of Utrecht. With the Spaniards steadily overrunning Flanders and Brabant, the Dutch in their plight did not immediately abandon William's policy of seeking foreign assistance. But after Henry III of France and Elizabeth of England both refused sovereignty over the country, the States-General in 1586 named as governor general Robert Dudley, earl of Leicester, whom Elizabeth had sent to command Dutch and English auxiliary forces against the Spaniards after the fall of Antwerp. Leicester, like Anjou before him, endeavoured to make himself absolute master of the country, relying on the support of popular Calvinism and of the outlying provinces that were jealous of Holland to create a strong centralized government under his authority. Holland thwarted Leicester's efforts, which culminated in an attempted invasion of Holland from Utrecht in 1587. With Leicester's departure, the United Provinces put aside all efforts to obtain a foreign protectorate and stood forth as an independent state.

Leicester as governor general

The formation of the new government. Although derived from historical institutions, the government of the United Provinces was in practice largely a new set of institutions, not created, but confirmed, by the Union of Utrecht. Their primary force lay in the provinces, seven in number (Holland, Zeeland, Utrecht, Gelderland, Overijssel, Friesland, and Groningen), which were ruled by assemblies of provincial States representing the towns and the landed nobility. Although the stadholders (who after a few years came to be drawn exclusively from the House of Orange) were elected by the States of the provinces, they at the same time possessed important prerogatives in the selection of members of the town governments from which the provincial assemblies ultimately derived their authority, and they were the acknowledged military leaders of the republic. Central government passed from the Council of State to the States-General, which was more explicitly subordinated to provincial authority. Although it conducted the military and diplomatic work of the republic, the States-General failed to obtain effective rights of direct taxation (except for import and export duties assigned to the admiralties), and its major decisions were taken under the rule of unanimity. In practice the province of Holland, by far the wealthiest province in the Union, and the contributor of more than half of the revenues of the central government, became the preponderant political force in the country, along with the stadholders of the House of Orange. The relationship between Holland and Orange governed the republic's politics for the two centuries of its existence. As collaborators, Holland and the princes of Orange could make the clumsy governmental system work with surprising effectiveness; as rivals, they imperilled its potency as a state, at least until one or the other emerged a temporary victor: but neither force was able to rule permanently without the other.

Dominance of Holland

The decades immediately after 1587 were marked by close collaboration between Johan van Oldenbarnevelt, "advocate" of Holland (the legal and executive secretary of the provincial States), and Maurice of Nassau, William the Silent's second son (the first, Philip William, became prince of Orange and remained loyal to Spain), who was named stadholder of Holland and Zeeland and became the commander of the republic's armies. The result was a series of military triumphs over the Spanish forces under Parma. Maurice recaptured the Dutch territories north of the great rivers and extended them southward into much of Brabant and enough of Flanders to cut off Antwerp from the sea. These victories are recorded in the historical memory of the Dutch as "the closing of the garden," the territory that became the republic of the United Provinces and then (with a few additions) the modern Kingdom of The Netherlands. These victories were accompanied by the emergence of the States-General diplomatically recognized by England and France as an independent state.

ASCENDANCY OF THE DUTCH ECONOMY

The military prowess of the fledgling republic rested upon the wealth of Holland—which managed in wartime to maintain and extend its trade to all of Europe and, after the turn of the century, even to the Far East. Amsterdam replaced Antwerp, the great port on the Scheldt River, as the principal warehouse and trading centre for all Europe, even while Holland maintained the leadership in shipping it had already garnered during the 16th century. The foundation of Dutch economic prosperity lay in the fishing and shipping industries. Even during the period of Antwerp's ascendancy, ships from Holland and Zeeland had carried a large portion of the goods that passed through the Scheldt, and now that Amsterdam had taken over from Antwerp, Dutch shipping only expanded its predominance. Dutch fishermen had harvested the North Sea for centuries, and the salted cargoes were sold widely through western and central Europe. Dutch trade benefitted, as had that of Flanders, from the location of the country at the nexuses of the great north–south and east–west trade routes of Europe. To these were added the route to the East Indies early in the 17th century. Amsterdam and the lesser ports of Holland and Zeeland became the principal European suppliers of grain and naval stores from the Baltic, to which they shipped manufactured goods and wines from the south. Germany's principal exports were now shipped down the Rhine, as Dutch ports replaced the Hanseatic towns of northern Germany. The bulk of French exports were carried in Dutch ships, and even Spain and Portugal depended on the Dutch for grain and naval stores (thereby enabling the

Amsterdam supplants Antwerp

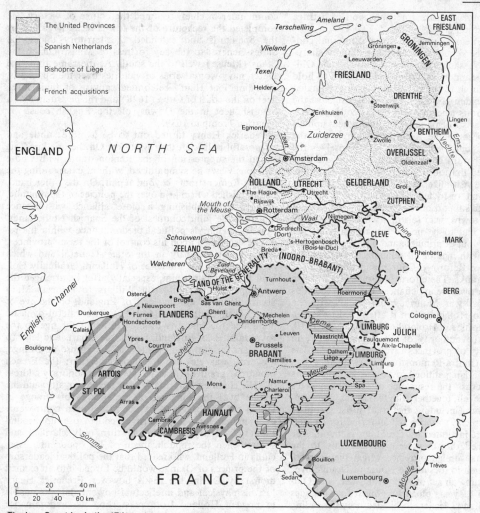

The Low Countries in the 17th century.
Adapted from R. Treharne and H. Fullard (eds.), *Muir's Historical Atlas: Medieval and Modern*, 9th ed. (1962); George Philip & Son Ltd., London

Dutch to finance their war of independence). During the 17th century the Dutch also assumed a major role in supplying grain and other northern commodities to the countries of the Mediterranean and also became the principal importer of spices and other luxury goods from the East. Even England relied to a great extent upon Dutch shipping. The Dutch advantages lay not only in their situation but also in the efficient design of their bulky flyboats (*fluiten*), manned by small crews at lesser cost than any of their competitors. Modern banking institutions developed to meet the needs of the vastly expanding trade. Amsterdam's "exchange bank" was instituted in 1609 to provide monetary exchange at established rates, but it soon became a deposit bank for the safe settling of accounts. Unlike the Bank of England, established almost a century later, it neither managed the national currency nor acted as a lending institution (except to the government in emergencies). Private bankers met the need for credit, as well as acting as brokers in financial transactions. The need for commercial exports, as well as a growing population at home, spurred industry in many towns. Although the shipbuilders on the Zaan, northwest of Amsterdam, and the sugar refiners in particular developed large-scale operations, sometimes including machinery, Dutch industry generally remained at the level of handicraft production. Dutch agriculture also responded to the new needs. Grain production was encouraged in the inland provinces, while the polderland of the delta islands and along the coast was drained and diked, providing pastureland for a flourishing dairy industry.

Banking (margin note)

POLITICAL DEVELOPMENTS, 1609–1713

The Twelve Years' Truce. The Twelve Years' Truce that began in 1609 arose out of political controversies

that were to dominate the republic for the next two centuries. The collaboration between the House of Orange and the leaders of the province of Holland, which had thwarted Spain in its reconquest of the Netherlands north of the great rivers, was replaced by an intermittent, but often fierce, rivalry between them, in which the other tensions of Dutch political life were reflected and incorporated: the jealousy among the lesser provinces of a Holland that they considered too wealthy, too mighty, and too arrogant, but which they knew they needed for their own defense; the misunderstanding between maritime and landward provinces; the annoyance of landed noblemen that they were dependent upon the goodwill of burghers in Holland (they preferred the prince of Orange, whom they saw as one of themselves); the resentment of the popular classes, men of small property and of none, toward the town regents, against whom they looked to the princes of Orange to protect them; and the antipathy of the Reformed clergy toward the regents, who obstructed their desire to make the state serve the church. The debate over whether or not to conclude a peace with Spain mingled these various interests with that of the House of Orange, partly because Maurice opposed peace, partly because it involved making some compromise with Spain, and partly because it would mean a reduction of his influence in the state; but the province of Holland in particular, under Oldenbarnevelt's leadership, felt that the independence and security of the United Provinces had been sufficiently assured to permit a reduction of the immense expenditures for the war. When Spain reduced its immediate proposal to a truce rather than permanent peace, agreed to treat the United Provinces as independent and sovereign, which was just short of outright recognition, and put aside efforts to win guarantees for

Dutch Catholics, the pressure for conclusion of a truce could not be withstood.

But the Twelve Years' Truce did not end internal controversy within the republic; if anything, it only sharpened Maurice of Nassau's opposition to Holland and Oldenbarnevelt. The staunch Calvinists endeavoured to hold the Reformed Church to the strict orthodoxy expounded by Gomarus, a Leiden professor of theology, against the broader, less rigorous tenets upheld by his colleague Arminius. The Gomarists demanded the government uphold their principles because the Reformed Church was the only true church, but they reserved for themselves the right to declare what the correct doctrines were; and they vigorously asserted that other religious groups, Catholic, Protestant, and Jewish alike, should be suppressed or at least penalized and restricted. On the other hand, the Arminians had the support of the leaders of Holland and a majority of its towns, who felt that what was in effect the state church had to be under the authority of the government. Both out of principle and out of a desire not to hamper trade with men of all religions, they favoured a broadly inclusive Reformed Church and toleration for those outside its ranks. The efforts of Gomarists to seize churches for their own use in defiance of town authorities led to incipient civil war. Maurice broke openly with the dominant party in Holland when it attempted to set up little provincial armies in Holland and Utrecht. In 1618, he acted under the authority of the States-General, in which the majority of provinces favoured the Gomarists (now called the Contra-Remonstrants because they had opposed an Arminian petition) over the Remonstrants (Arminians) to crush the resistance of Oldenbarnevelt's party. Oldenbarnevelt, together with two of his chief supporters in Holland (including the great jurist Grotius) and an ally in Utrecht, was arrested and tried for treason by a special court instituted by the States-General. The defendants affirmed that they were subject only to the authority of the sovereign province which they served. The sentence, which to foes of the House of Orange over the centuries became an act of judicial murder, sent Oldenbarnevelt, then 71 years old, with almost four decades of service as Holland's leader, to his death by beheading in May 1619. Grotius and another defendant (the third had committed suicide) were sentenced to life imprisonment, although Grotius escaped, sensationally, a few years later. During these fateful months, the Reformed Church held a national synod at Dordrecht. Dominated by the Contra-Remonstrants, the synod expelled the Remonstrants, reaffirmed the doctrines of the church along Gomarian lines, and ordered the preparation of a new translation of the Bible (the famous States Bible that consolidated the Dutch language much as the contemporary King James Version consolidated English). The triumph of Maurice and the Contra-Remonstrants meant that war with Spain would be a virtual certainty upon the expiration of the Twelve Years' Truce in 1621—all the more because the Spanish authorities in the southern Netherlands insisted upon including rights for Dutch Catholics in a permanent treaty and even sought an acknowledgment by the States-General of the nominal overlordship of the king of Spain. Maurice did not use his new uncontested power to reform the complicated incoherence of the Dutch constitution; the structure of government and the distribution of formal power remained the same. Maurice was not a politically minded ruler and was satisfied as long as he had his way in military matters. The United Provinces continued essentially republican in character.

War with Spain, 1621–48. The war resumed in 1621 under Maurice's leadership. But his touch of victory was gone, and the republic appeared in danger when the great fortress of Breda on the southern frontier fell to the Spaniards in 1625. Only a few weeks before, Maurice had died. The danger was all the greater because the Austrian Habsburgs, in alliance with their Spanish cousins, were waging a successful struggle against their Protestant foes in Germany, in the first stages of the Thirty Years' War (*q.v.*). But Maurice's half-brother, Frederick Henry, who succeeded him as prince of Orange, stadholder, and

commander in chief, resumed the course of victory. He completed the recapture of the towns recently gained by the Spaniards and extended the territory under the States-General to the key fortress of Maastricht on the Maas (Meuse) well to the south. At the same time, the Dutch navy won a series of victories over the Spaniards, including Piet Hein's celebrated capture of their silver fleet off the coast of Cuba (1628) and the destruction of a Spanish fleet in the Downs, off the English coast, by Maarten Tromp in 1639.

Frederick Henry turned out to be a more subtle and purposeful politician than Maurice. On the one hand, he ended the suppression of the Remonstrants, with whose religious views he sympathized, without exasperating the Contra-Remonstrants beyond repair. On the other hand, he established a firm grip over the policies of the republic, notably by establishing a close alliance with France aimed at the joint conquest of the Spanish Netherlands. Frederick Henry's political predominance within the republic was based upon his control of the lesser provinces, which had a majority in the States-General and which could outweigh the influence of Holland. Gradually Holland turned against him, especially after he arranged the marriage of his young son William to Princess Mary Stuart, daughter of Charles I of England, on the eve of the English Civil War (1642–51). This fateful dynastic bond tied the interests of the House of Orange to the royal families of England, first to the Stuarts and later to the Hanoverians. The position of the House of Orange, however, was elevated by the connection: the French monarchy granted Frederick Henry the honorary address of "His Highness," normally restricted to royalty; and the debate over the function of the princes of Orange in Dutch politics began to be conducted as a controversy over monarchy. A quasi-royal court rose up around Frederick Henry, and this in turn only clarified and strengthened the republicanism of his opponents, especially in Holland, who feared that the political leadership of the princes of Orange would be turned into an explicit monarchy. During the 1640s, however, Frederick Henry lost his physical and intellectual powers and was unable to prevent Holland from reasserting its predominance over the republic's policies. The States-General entered into peace negotiations with Spain at Münster in Westphalia. Frederick Henry died in 1647 before the conclusion of the talks, but his son, William II, could not prevent the signing and ratification of the treaty in January 1648. Spain now formally acknowledged the independence of the Dutch, and indeed even urged its friendship upon the United Provinces, warning of the threat to both the Dutch and the Spanish from the rising power of France.

Prince William was not ready to accept a permanent peace, and he negotiated secretly with the French for a resumption of the war, not only against Spain but also against republican England, which had executed his father-in-law, King Charles I, in January 1649. Needing a powerful army to meet the anticipated war, William bitterly fought the efforts of Holland to reduce the standing army and thereby to permit more rapid payment of the huge debt accumulated over the eighty years' struggle for independence. Efforts at compromise broke down during the spring of 1650, as the Hollanders and William each sought to compel the other to concede political inferiority. William decided to make use of his preponderance in the States-General, and he led a delegation from that body to the towns of Holland to seek a change of their vote in the States of Holland; such a delegation was a direct violation of what Holland saw as its provincial sovereignty. Rebuffed by a number of town governments, most importantly by those of Amsterdam and Dordrecht, William decided to cut through the resistance by force. At The Hague, on July 30, 1650, he arrested six of the States' deputies from the recalcitrant towns and sent them to the castle of Loevestein (where Grotius had been imprisoned) on charges of having resisted lawful orders of the States-General. At that same time he sent an army to seize Amsterdam but it was thwarted by delays on its march and by the determined resistance of the municipal

Gomarists versus Arminians

Execution of Oldenbarnevelt

Victories under Frederick Henry

Peace of Westphalia

Arrest of the deputies

authorities, supported by the common people. Amsterdam, however, faced a siege that might gravely imperil its trade, while the besiegers themselves ran the danger of being drowned should Amsterdam open the dikes. A compromise was soon worked out whereby William's opponents were released but were required to withdraw from government. William had cleared the way for his policies but at the price of arousing deep fears among the Dutch people—most of all in the powerful province of Holland—of military dictatorship, monarchical rule, and renewed involvement of the nation in war. But before he could carry out his plans, William II died of smallpox in early November. A posthumous son, William III, was born a week later.

The first stadholderless period. Fate thus intervened to give Holland's leaders, now intensely distrustful of Orangist influence, a chance to take over the country from the leaderless party of their antagonists. They governed the country for a little more than two decades, during what is known as the "first stadholderless period" (1650–72) because the five leading provinces did not appoint a successor to William II. (William II's cousin, William Frederick, of the junior branch of Orange-Nassau, continued to govern Friesland as well as Groningen, which also elected him as stadholder.) During the early months of 1651, a "Great Assembly" of the States-General, with expanded delegations from all the provinces, met at The Hague to consider the new situation. Holland was satisfied to consolidate the leadership it had so unexpectedly regained and conciliated the lesser provinces by leaving undisturbed the religious settlement of 1619 and by granting amnesty to those who had supported William II in 1650. But Holland's fears of the increased powers of the central government had been so stiffened that it depended upon its own preponderance, rather than upon constitutional reforms, to achieve effective government.

Anglo-Dutch war. Yet efficiency of rule, so difficult to obtain when the powers to make and apply policy were so widely scattered, became all the more necessary when the republic became embroiled in war with the English Commonwealth in 1652. That conflict arose out of a medley of causes: first, the English republicans, after their successes against the royalists, took up the cause of defending English commercial interests against the Dutch and passed the Navigation Act of 1651 forbidding Dutch shippers from acting as middlemen in English trade both in Europe and overseas; second, the English sought to bring the Dutch into a political union directed primarily against the Stuarts and their Orange cousins. But the Dutch, whatever resentment the Hollanders bore against the Orange dynasty, were unwilling either to court civil war or to abandon their dearly won independence in a union that would make them junior partners to the English. An accidental clash between the Dutch and English fleets led to full-scale war in which a greatly improved English navy won the upper hand. By 1654 the Dutch were compelled to accept peace on English terms, including a secret promise by Holland ("Act of Seclusion") to exclude forever the prince of Orange from the stadholderate or the supreme command.

The decision to accept a humiliating peace as the only way to terminate a disastrous war had been taken at the insistence of the young Johan de Witt, who had taken office in 1653 as councillor pensionary of Holland (the same office once held by Oldenbarnevelt). With the return of peace, de Witt became the brilliant leader of the republic's foreign and domestic policy. He rebuilt the Dutch navy, reduced indebtedness, improved the financial condition of both the States-General and the States of Holland, and restored the republic's prestige in Europe. Carefully averting any renewal of strife with England, he was able not only to compel France to back down in a naval dispute but also to send a powerful Dutch fleet to save Denmark from Swedish conquest in the first Northern War (1657–60). When the exiled English king Charles II was restored to his throne in 1660, de Witt continued his policy of staying on good terms with England no matter who ruled there; this policy, however, foundered on the same two issues—commercial rivalry and the status of

the House of Orange—that had brought about the war of 1652–54. Charles not only accepted the renewal of the Navigation Act of 1651 but intensified the rivalry with the Dutch by demanding forcefully that they acknowledge his sovereignty over the adjacent seas, pay tribute for the right to fish in the North Sea, and open the Dutch East Indies to English traders. When naval warfare resumed in 1664 off Africa, followed by war in Europe the next year, Charles took up the cause of the young Prince of Orange. By persuading the Orangists that his price for peace was restoration of William III to the offices of his forefathers, the English monarch built up a friendly party in the United Provinces that urged acceptance of his terms and even fostered a conspiracy to overthrow the government of de Witt and his friends. But de Witt managed to meet the new threat. When Charles had demanded too high a price for Dutch friendship in 1660–62, de Witt had negotiated an alliance with the French, who feared that the restoration of the Prince of Orange would create a hostile Anglo-Dutch coalition. Furthermore, the fighting at sea increasingly went to the newly rebuilt Dutch navy. In 1667 the Dutch fleet sailed up the Thames and the Medway to Chatham, destroying the English shipyards and burning the fleet at its moorings. An Orangist plot in Holland was uncovered and put down. In that same year, however, the French, under Louis XIV, who had only belatedly sent naval and land forces to aid the Dutch, began an invasion of the Spanish Netherlands in the War of Devolution. As French conquest of the southern Low Countries constituted a threat to both the Dutch Republic and Britain, the belligerents came to terms in the stand-off Peace of Breda (July 31, 1667), followed in January by an Anglo-Dutch alliance compelling France to make peace with Spain. This Triple Alliance (so-called because Sweden became a third partner) proved to be de Witt's undoing, although he had no effective diplomatic strategy to put in its place. Louis XIV, balked in his aim of conquest, considered that the Dutch had betrayed their alliance and turned to Charles II with proposals for a joint war against the United Provinces. Charles, bitterly resentful at his humiliating defeat, accepted the French offer of a richly subsidized alliance. Even as the threat from France emerged more clearly, the Orangists imagined that the Dutch could still win over Charles by the restoration of William III, but they were able to obtain only the Prince's appointment as commander in chief, early in 1672. Charles joined the French in open war in the spring of 1672, counting upon William to accept rule of a rump Dutch Republic after France and Britain had taken away important territories for themselves. But William, who was given full power, including the stadholdership, during a storm of riots and near rebellion that swept the country in June and July, after the French invasion penetrated to its heart, took over the leadership of the Dutch defense from de Witt, who was lynched by a mob in The Hague in August. With his support, the States-General rejected the Anglo-French terms.

William III. The tide of war now turned against the aggressors. The Dutch navy under Admiral de Ruyter repeatedly defeated the allied fleets off the coast of the republic, while the Dutch armies held on behind the flooded polders of the "water line." When other powers —Spain, at first as an auxiliary, then as a full participant, the Emperor, and Brandenburg—joined the Dutch side, the French armies withdrew from the republic. During six years of bitter war, William III was able to bring about the withdrawal of England (1674) and the defeat of all French war aims against the Dutch; yet his Grand Alliance was unable to bring Louis XIV to his knees, although Spain paid the price of a peace negotiated at Nijmegen in 1678. But during these years in which his political control of the republic, while strong, was not absolute, William was no more interested in constitutional reform than de Witt, his predecessor in the leadership of the country, had been. He was satisfied to expel adversaries from office and dominate the decisions taken by men who represented the same groups and the same social principles as those whom they replaced; but Holland,

English navigation acts

The Triple Alliance

whose wealth ultimately was the basis for all Dutch power, political and military, slipped from under his thumb and asserted its autonomy of judgment and decision. The transformation of the republic, which had been from its origins an aristocracy dominated by mercantile wealth, into an oligarchy of inherited power, continued unimpeded by William: he had used the violence of the urban citizenry during the crisis of 1672 to unseat his opponents, but he was no more sympathetic than they had been to the vague democratic aspirations that were expressed here and there. During the decade after the conclusion of the Peace of Nijmegen, the tension between William and Holland (particularly Amsterdam) worsened because the Prince was fixed upon a policy of renewed resistance to Louis XIV, while the Hollanders preferred peace at any reasonable price. But the upsurge of the threat from France in the late 1680s—the French incursions into western Germany and the threat of French domination of England under James II, a stalwart Catholic and a pensioner of Louis XIV—brought William and Holland into agreement upon the need to support the Prince's expedition to England in 1688, which resulted in his acceptance of the English throne, jointly with his wife Mary Stuart, early the next year. William, as king-stadholder, had to give primacy to English interests because England was the more powerful partner in the alliance. He therefore approved the arrangement whereby England concentrated her efforts against France on the sea, while the Dutch did so on land; the result was neglect of the Dutch navy. Ironically, the final triumph of the English over the Dutch in their commercial rivalry was a consequence of their alliance, not their enmity.

William accepts the English throne

The war begun in 1689 ended with a stalemate peace in 1697, followed by two treaties between the maritime powers and France for partition of the Spanish monarchy. In 1700, however, Louis XIV accepted the bequest of the Spanish throne for his grandson, Philippe d'Anjou, and war was resumed the next year.

William died, childless, in 1702. When Holland again took the initiative for government without a stadholder, it was followed by the other provinces with much greater alacrity than had been true in 1650–51. Resentment had built up against the harshness with which the Prince had governed the country for three decades, and the absence of an adult heir meant that there was no effective opposition to the new course. Leadership of the Dutch state for the next 45 years came from the councillor pensionaries of Holland, who were often able men but either unwilling or unable to do more than conduct current business, without attempting the delicate and explosive task of restructuring the government. On the contrary, constitutional rigidity became the credo not only of Dutch republicans but also of the Orangist party, with the only point in contention between them whether or not the Prince of Orange-Nassau, who was stadholder of Friesland, should be elected to the same office in the other provinces. William IV, who followed his father in Friesland in 1711, was chosen stadholder in Groningen in 1718 and in Gelderland (and the district of Drenthe) in 1722. Even without a stadholder in the principal provinces, Dutch subordination to English interests remained intact during the War of the Spanish Succession (1701–13) and the succeeding years of peace.

DUTCH CIVILIZATION IN THE GOLDEN AGE (1609–1713)

The century from the conclusion of the Twelve Years' Truce in 1609 until either the death of Prince William III in 1702 or the conclusion of the Peace of Utrecht in 1713 is known in Dutch history as the "Golden Age." It was a unique era of political, economic, and cultural greatness during which the little nation on the North Sea ranked among the most powerful and influential in Europe and the world.

The economy. It was a grandeur that rested upon the economic expansion that continued with scarcely an interruption until 1648, at the end of the Thirty Years' War. The half century that followed was marked by consolidation rather than continued expansion, under the impact of the revived competition from the other nations,

notably England and France, whose policies of mercantilism were in large degree directed against the near monopoly of the Dutch over the trade and shipping of Europe. Although the Dutch tenaciously resisted the new competition, the long-distance trading system of Europe was transformed from one largely conducted through the Netherlands, with the Dutch as universal buyer-seller and shipper, to one of multiple routes and fierce competitiveness. Nonetheless, the wealth earned during a long century of prosperity made the United Provinces a land of great riches, with more capital by far than could find outlet in investment. Yet the economic burden of repeated wars caused the Dutch to become one of the most heavily taxed people in Europe. Because the role of agriculture was secondary, taxes were to some extent imposed on the transit trade in and out of the country. But as mercantile competition became stiffer, the rate of such taxation could not be safely increased, and the burden therefore fell increasingly on the consumer. Excise and other indirect taxes made the Dutch cost of living one of the highest in Europe.

Increasing competition abroad

Dutch prosperity was built not only upon the "mother trades"—to the Baltic and to France and the Iberian lands—but also upon the overseas trades with Africa, Asia, and America. The attempt of the Spanish monarchs (who also ruled Portugal and its possessions from 1580 to 1640) to exclude Dutch merchants and shippers from the lucrative colonial commerce with the Far East led the Dutch to trade directly with the East Indies. Individual companies were organized for each venture, but the companies were united by command of the States-General in 1602 in order to reduce the costs and increase the security of such perilous and complex undertakings; the resulting United East India Company established bases throughout the Indian Ocean, notably Ceylon, mainland India, and the Indonesian archipelago. The Dutch East India Company, like its rival English counterpart, was a trading company granted quasi-sovereign powers in the lands under its dominion. Although the East India fleets that returned annually with cargoes of spices and other valuables provided huge profits for the shareholders, the East India trade of the 17th and 18th centuries never provided more than a modest fraction of Dutch earnings from European trade. The West India Company, established in 1621, was built upon shakier economic foundations; trade in commodities was less important than the trade in slaves, in which the Dutch were pre-eminent in the 17th century, and privateering, which operated primarily out of Zeeland ports and preyed upon Spanish (and other) shipping. The West India Company had to be reorganized several times during its precarious existence, while the East India Company survived until the end of the 18th century.

The Dutch East India Company

Society. The social structure that evolved with the economic transformation of Dutch life was complex and marked by the predominance of the business classes that later centuries called the bourgeoisie, although with some significant differences. It was an unabashedly "aristocratic" country, socially and politically. The social "betters" of Dutch aristocracy were only to a limited extent landed noblemen, most of whom lived in the economically less advanced inland provinces. Most of the Dutch elite were wealthy townsmen whose fortunes were made as merchants and financiers, but they frequently shifted their activities to government, becoming what the Dutch called regents, members of the ruling bodies of town and province, and drawing most of their incomes from these posts and from investments in government bonds and real estate. The common people comprised both a numerous class of artisans and small businessmen whose prosperity provided the base for the generally high Dutch standard of living and a very large class of sailors, shipbuilders, fishermen, and other workers. Dutch workers were in general well paid, but they were also burdened by unusually high taxes. The farmers, producing chiefly cash crops, prospered in a country that needed large amounts of food and raw materials for its urban (and seagoing) population. The quality of life was marked by less disparity between classes than prevailed elsewhere, although the

The regents

difference between a great merchant's home on the Herengracht in Amsterdam and a dock worker's hovel was too obvious to be remarked. What was striking was the comparative simplicity even of the wealthy classes and the sense of status and dignity among the ordinary people, although the exuberance that had earlier marked the society was toned down or even eliminated by the strict Calvinist morality preached and to some extent enforced by the official church. There was, too, a good deal of mingling between the burgher regents who possessed great wealth and political power and the landed gentry and lesser nobility who formed the traditional elite.

Religion.   One of the characteristic aspects of modern Dutch society began to evolve in this period—the vertical separation of society into "columns" identified with the different Dutch religions. Calvinist Protestantism became the officially recognized religion of the country, politically favoured and economically supported by government. But the Reformed preachers were thwarted in their efforts to oppress or drive out other religions, to which a far-reaching toleration was extended. Mass conversion to Calvinism had been confined mainly to the earlier decades of the Eighty Years' War, when Catholics still frequently bore the burden of their preference for the rule of the Catholic monarchs in the southern Netherlands. Sizable islands of Catholicism remained in most of the United Provinces except Zeeland, while Gelderland and the northern parts of Brabant and Flanders conquered by the States-General were overwhelmingly Catholic, as they remain today. Although public practice of Catholicism was forbidden, interference with private worship was rare, even if Catholics sometimes bought their security with bribes to local Protestant authorities. Catholics lost the traditional form of church government by bishops, whose place was taken by a papal vicar directly dependent upon Rome and supervising what was in effect a mission; the political authorities were generally tolerant of secular priests, but not of Jesuits, who were vigorous proselytizers and linked to Spanish interests. Protestants included, along with the predominant Calvinists of the Reformed Church, both Lutherans in small numbers and Mennonites (Anabaptists), who were politically passive but often prospered in business. In addition, the Remonstrants, who were driven out of the Reformed Church after the Synod of Dort (Dordrecht; 1618–19), continued as a small sect with considerable influence among the regents. There were also other sects emphasizing mystical experiences or rationalist theologies, notably the Collegiants among the latter. Jews settled in the Netherlands to escape persecution; the Sefardic Jews from Spain and Portugal were more influential in economic, social, and intellectual life, while the Ashkenazim from eastern Europe formed a stratum of impoverished workers, especially in Amsterdam. Despite unusually open contacts with the Christian society about them, Dutch Jews continued to live in their own communities under their own laws and rabbinic leadership. Successful though some Jews were in business, they were by no means the central force in the rise and expansion of Dutch capitalism, as has sometimes been maintained. Indeed, no clear pattern can be detected of religious affiliation affecting the growth of the Dutch business community; if anything, it was the official Dutch Reformed Church that fulminated most angrily against capitalist attitudes and practices, while the merely tolerated faiths often saw their adherents, to whom economic but not political careers were open, prospering and even amassing fortunes.

Culture.   The economic prosperity of the Dutch Republic in this "golden century" was matched by an extraordinary flowering of cultural achievement, which drew from the nation's prosperity not only the direct resources of financial nourishment but also a driving and sustaining sense of purpose and vigour. This was reflected in the first instance by a notable series of historical works: from the contemporary chronicles of the revolt by Pieter Bor and Emanuel van Meteren; through the highly polished account by Pieter Corneliszoon Hooft, a masterpiece of narration and judgment in the spirit of

Religious "columns" (margin)

The Jews (margin)

Tacitus; to the heavily factual chronicle of Lieuwe van Aitzema, with its interspersed commentary of skeptical wisdom, Abraham de Wicquefort's history of the republic (principally under the first stadholderless administration), and the histories and biographies by Geeraert Brandt. These were works in which a proud new nation took account of its birthpangs and its growth to greatness. Only in the latter part of the century did Dutch historians begin to express a sense that political grandeur may be transient. Political theorists shared the same concerns, although the effort to fit new experience and ideas into the traditional categories derived from Aristotle and Roman law created an air of unreality about their work, perhaps even more than was true of political thinkers elsewhere in Europe. Theorists such as the Gouda official Vrancken in the days of the foundation of the republic and Hugo Grotius in the early 17th century portrayed the republic as essentially unchanged since the early Middle Ages or even since antiquity—a country where sovereignty resided in provincial and town assemblies, which had partly lost their control to counts and kings before regaining it in the revolt against Philip II. The next surge of political debate came after midcentury, when for a little over two decades the country was governed without a prince of Orange as stadholder. The controversy over whether the young Prince William had any right by birth to the offices of his forefathers probed the fundamental character of the republic, for even a quasi-hereditary stadholdership created an incipient monarchy within the traditional structure of aristocratic republicanism. The debate involved the issue not so much of centralization versus provincialism as where the leadership of the republic properly lay, whether in the House of Orange or in the province of Holland and notably its greatest city, Amsterdam. Only the celebrated philosopher Benedict de Spinoza, an outsider by origin and character, elevated these political questions to the level of universality.

Two of the greatest philosophers of the 17th century resided in the Dutch Republic, but both were to some extent outsiders. The Frenchman René Descartes found there a freedom from intellectual inquisitions and personal involvements and lived in the Netherlands for two decades while engaged in the studies that helped transform modern thought. The second was Spinoza, a Jew by birth and upbringing but a key figure in the history of all modern Western philosophy. He was more than just Descartes' greatest exponent, for he was an independent thinker of the first order. Scientific activity in the United Provinces reached a high level. The physicist Christiaan Huygens approached Newton himself in power of mind and importance of scientific contribution. The engineer and mathematician Simon Stevin and the microscopists Antonie van Leeuwenhoek and Jan Swammerdam rank in the front of their fields.

Dutch literature, which knew great creativity during the "golden age," remained the possession of the relatively small number of those who spoke and read Dutch. Figures like the historian P.C. Hooft or the poets Constantijn Huygens and Joost van den Vondel, who was also a distinguished playwright, wrote with a power and a purity worthy of the best that France and England produced at that time. Music was hampered by the Calvinists' antipathy to what they saw as frivolity. Organ music was barred from services in Reformed Churches, although town authorities frequently continued its performance at other times. The great organist-composer J.P. Sweelinck was more influential in encouraging the creative wave in Germany than among his own countrymen. The art whose achievements rank at the very top was painting, which rested upon the broad patronage of a prosperous population. Group portraits of regents and other influential citizens adorned town halls and charitable establishments, while still lifes and anecdotal paintings of popular life hung in profusion in private homes. Some of the greatest work, from the brushes of such painters as Hals, Steen, and Vermeer, were painted for these markets, but the greatest of Dutch painters, Rembrandt van Rijn, broke through the boundaries of the group portrait to create works with his own extraordinary mood and inward

Political theory (margin)

Painting (margin)

meaning. The landscape painters, notably Ruysdael, captured the distinctive Dutch flat land, broad skies with massed clouds, and muted light. Architecture remained at a lesser level, merging with some success the native traditions of brick buildings and gable roofs and fashionable Renaissance styles. Sculpture remained a largely foreign art.

THE 18TH CENTURY

Economic and political stagnation. Once the Dutch fleet had declined, Dutch mercantile interests became heavily dependent upon English goodwill; yet the rulers of the country were more concerned to reduce the monumental debt that weighed heavily upon the country. During the 18th century Dutch trade and shipping were able to maintain the level of activity reached at the end of the 17th century, but they did not match the dramatic expansion of French and especially English competitors. The Dutch near monopoly was now only a memory. Holland remained rich in accumulated capital, although much of it could find no outlet for investment in business. Some went into the purchase of landed estates, but a great deal was used to buy bonds of foreign governments; the bankers of Amsterdam were among the most important in Europe, rivalling those of London and Geneva. Dutch culture failed to hold its eminence; a medical scientist like Hermann Boerhaave or a jurist like Cornelis van Bynkershoek was highly respected, but they were not the shapers and shakers of European thought. Dutch artists were no longer of the first order, and literature largely followed English or French models without matching their achievements. The quality of life changed: instead of the seething activity of the 17th century, the 18th century was one of calm and easeful pleasantness, at least for men of property. The middling classes in town and countryside also knew continuing prosperity; conditions for the labouring classes continued to be hard, although foreign visitors thought the workers lived better than elsewhere. The poor as such were not labourers but a residual class of unemployed who subsisted on the charity of town governments and private foundations. Religious life was more relaxed, particularly among Protestants. Catholics, still without political rights, but facing milder restrictions, fell into a quarrel between adherents of Jansenism, which denied free will, and supporters of Rome; the former split off to form the Old Catholic Church, a small denomination that still exists. The educated classes widely accepted the principles and attitudes of the Enlightenment, although without the sharp hostility to religion that characterized the French Philosophes.

During the second stadholderless period of Dutch government (1702–47), the republican system became an immobile oligarchy. The "liberty" defended by the regents as soundly republican was in practice the rule of hereditary patricians, responsible to neither the citizenry below nor a stadholder above. Although William IV yearned for restoration to the offices held by the princes of Orange before him in the provinces to the south, he accepted, with no less admiration and commitment than the regents, the perfection and immutability of the Dutch constitutional system, with the single difference that he envisioned it including the stadholderate for all the provinces. It was not until the War of the Austrian Succession (1740–48) that the power of the regents began to crumble. As in 1672, disaster on the battlefield proved the Achilles' heel of a regime that had not built up a broad popular political base. The regents had not been able to overcome the traditional commitment of the people to the House of Orange as their natural leader and saviour. French and Prussian armies swarmed over the Austrian (southern) Netherlands and were poised for invasion of the United Provinces, which were linked by alliance with England although they had remained formally neutral. When the French forces crossed into Dutch territory, rioting reminiscent of 1672, although less widespread and violent, led to the fall of the second purely republican government and the election of William IV as hereditary stadholder of all the provinces. Otherwise there was little change; some regents were compelled to step down from

War of the Austrian Succession

their posts, and leadership in the hands of the Prince of Orange was uncontested. William rebuffed the efforts of burghers in Amsterdam and other towns who had supported his restoration in order to achieve democratic reforms, in which participation in government would be extended to men of modest property who had been completely disfranchised (although not to wageworkers or to paupers).

The Patriotic movement. During the next decades, in the face of the rigid conservatism of the princes of Orange (William V succeeded his father in 1751 and assumed personal government in 1759) and under the influence of the French Enlightenment, an essentially new political force began to take shape. Known as the Patriot movement after an old party term used by both republicans and Orangists, it applied fundamental criticism to the established government. Although the Patriot movement was representative of the new democratic and Enlightenment ideals, it had strong roots in native Dutch traditions. From the beginning, the United Provinces had rejected specifically democratic institutions in favour of frankly aristocratic government (in the Aristotelian sense), but the notion that the regents had a duty to serve not their own private interests but those of the country and the people had persisted in theory and in mood. When the aristocracy ceased to recruit new members from below and thus became an enclosed caste, the discrepancy between its claim of service to the general welfare and the reality of its practice became evident. The Patriot movement took in a wide range of supporters: discontented noblemen like the Gelderland baron Joan Capellen tot den Pol; wealthy bankers and businessmen without a voice in government; artisans and shopkeepers, traditionally Orangist in sympathy, who were dismayed to find their claims to an effective role in the politics of their towns rebuffed by the princes; and intellectuals committed to the new Enlightenment rejection of arbitrary power. The Patriots included in their ranks many Protestant dissenters and Catholics, but the Jews continued to look to the prince of Orange as their protector. Some regents, holding firm to the republicanism of their ancestors and resenting the return of the stadholderate, found a new base for their ideas in the Patriot movement. Most regents, however, saw more peril in the new movement for broader popular government than in the stolid conservatism of the princes of Orange; a reconciliation between the camps of the patrician republicans and the Orangists began to take shape under the impact of a common threat from below.

Traditionalism of the Patriots

Again the events of war imperilled the established regime. Although the diplomacy of William V was firmly based upon the alliance with England, London became exasperated with the Dutch during the United States War of Independence (1775–83), when they attempted to continue and expand their profitable trade with the new American nation as well as with France. Dutch flirtations with the Russian-sponsored League of Armed Neutrality resisting British searches of neutral vessels and indications of Dutch negotiations for an alliance with the Americans only worsened relations. Finally open hostilities erupted in the fourth Anglo-Dutch War (1780–84). The Dutch navy, sorely neglected for more than a half century, was utterly unprepared to battle the powerful British fleet, and the Dutch fleet's attempts to convoy their merchantmen brought only disaster. The onus of defeat fell upon the Stadholder. He was unable to stand firm against the increased agitation of the Patriots, who forced their way into governments of town after town in Holland and other provinces. Holland began organizing its own army, distinct from that under the Prince's command, and civil war seemed in the offing. William V fled to Gelderland with his wife, Wilhelmina, the sister of the Prussian king Frederick II. Holland declared him deposed. It was the strong-willed Wilhelmina, rather than her hesitant and rather docile husband, who took the lead in the restoration of the stadholderate. Dutch politics had now become a concern of the great powers. France sided with the Patriots, not out of sympathy with their principles but because they opposed the

Stadholder, who had fallen back into dependence upon English and Prussian support. As long as Frederick II ruled in Prussia, Wilhelmina's pleas for armed intervention fell on deaf ears, but when the throne passed to his nephew Frederick William II in 1786, the way opened for action. The Patriots counted upon the support of the French, but the government at Versailles, then entering the final financial and political crisis of the monarchy that erupted in the Revolution of 1789, could give no more than verbal encouragement. Wilhelmina, working closely with the English ambassador, arranged to create a crisis by seeking to return to Holland; her detention at the provincial border was taken by Prussia as justification to send an army into the United Provinces. The Prussians quickly swept away the makeshift militias of Holland and Utrecht and restored the Stadholder to his offices. A period of repression of Patriots followed; many went into exile, first in the Austrian Netherlands and then in France. The outbreak of the French Revolution in 1789 gave new hope to the exiles and their friends at home.

Impact of the French Revolution

They looked now for more effective French assistance and at the same time found in the French Revolutionary experience practical ideas for the reorganization of the government at home, notably the principle of a single, indivisible republic. The Patriots' hopes rose when French Revolutionary armies swept over the Austrian Netherlands (which had had a brief interlude of independence in 1789–90) in 1792, but the French forces retreated the next year. It was not until 1794 that they returned to Belgium (as it now became customary to call the southern Netherlands), driving up to and then across the frontier of the United Provinces. The moment for which the Dutch Patriots had long been waiting was at hand: French power would more than overweigh the English and Prussian strength upon which the stadholder relied (Prussia made a separate peace with France in 1795), and a democratic revolution, thwarted in 1787, would be possible. The freezing of the great rivers during the winter permitted the French forces to cross into the Dutch heartland, but even before they arrived the Patriots seized the reins of state from helpless William V, who abandoned office and fled to England.

THE PERIOD OF FRENCH RULE, 1795–1813

The old republic was replaced by the Batavian Republic, and the political modernization of the Netherlands began —a process that would take more than half a century and pass through many vicissitudes; yet it was one marked by an extraordinary lack of violence. For all its flaws and inconsistencies, the old regime of the United Provinces had enjoyed many of the institutions and practices that other countries had to create in the fire of revolution: the sovereignty of parliamentary assemblies; wide-ranging political and religious toleration; equality of all citizens before the law; and an unusually broad distribution of the benefits of economic prosperity, however far the social system was from equality. Even the sense of nationhood had put down deep roots, although the awareness of differences of religion remained powerful. In a word, the Dutch had already achieved a large measure of the "liberty, equality and fraternity" that had become the slogan of the French Revolutionaries. The task that confronted the Batavian and the successor regimes was to adapt old institutions and create new ones that could meet the needs of a new era. But the Dutch statesmen had to operate within the confines of a small power shorn of most of its military and naval strength, and yet more dependent than most other countries upon its trading and shipping.

The Batavian Republic, 1795–1806. The Batavian Republic lasted 11 years, during which it proclaimed the sovereignty of the people but was in fact a protectorate of France. The organization of government had to be approved not only by the Dutch people but also by whatever government happened to be in control in France. The constitutions therefore reflected not only Dutch conditions and ideas but also the arrangements in effect in Paris; nonetheless, they did create a political system of the new type, a new regime, in the Netherlands. After

much debate, the ancient historic provinces—so unequal in wealth, population, and influence—were replaced by a unitary republic divided into departments and electoral constituencies that were roughly equal in population, if not in wealth. The representatives elected to the National Assembly (which replaced the historic States-General) were not delegates of provincial assemblies by whose decisions they were bound but deputies with full independence of judgment. The ancient system of government, with its medley of assemblies and boards with imperfectly differentiated functions, was replaced by a modern system of separate and explicitly defined legislative, executive, and judicial branches; functionally organized ministries directed the work of foreign affairs, internal affairs, war, and navy. The full legal equality of all citizens in all parts of the country was proclaimed; the residents of North Brabant, Zeeland-Flanders, Limburg, and Drenthe gained the same rights as all other citizens of the republic, just as their districts, once excluded from the States-General, now participated in the national government equally with all others. The Reformed Church lost its standing as the sole official, protected church, supported out of state revenues; equal status was accorded to all religious denominations, including Catholics and Jews. Yet full separation of church and state was not proclaimed, and their relationship was to continue as one of the central factors in Dutch politics for more than a century. The historic privileges of class and locality were abolished; the liberty of each and all under the law and before the courts replaced the diverse "liberties" of town and province, noble and regent. Where, before, town governments had co-opted their members, deputies to the National Assembly were now elected; but the franchise was limited to property holders, and these did not choose their representatives directly, but through electors named by primary assemblies. Most of these institutional changes were permanent, though the republican form of government was replaced by a kingdom in 1806 and never reestablished.

Reorganization of the provinces

Abolition of ancient privilege

While these momentous changes were being debated and adopted, the ordinary work of state and nation had to continue amid conditions of almost unprecedented difficulty. England reacted to the French occupation of the Netherlands and the flight and overthrow of the Stadholder by a declaration of war and a blockade. Dutch overseas trade and fishing, the country's most essential occupations, were brought to a near standstill, while most of the Dutch colonies were seized by the English on behalf of William V. The French, however, remained relentless in their own exploitation of the occupied "fraternal republic." The Dutch government, which took over the whole accumulated burden of national and provincial indebtedness, had also to bear the costs of the French occupying forces and to pay immense sums in tribute to the Paris government; indeed, the forced circulation of vastly inflated French assignats (paper currency) at face value was a scarcely disguised and very effective form of French taxation directly upon the Dutch people. Nor did the successive French governments—republican, consular, or imperial—grant the Dutch any greater freedom of trade with France or other countries under its control in compensation for the lost overseas business. As trade declined and industry languished, the Netherlands began to change in economic character toward a primarily agricultural country. The venturesome spirit for which Dutch businessmen had been so famed a century or two before seemed to be lost, replaced by what the Dutch themselves called a "jansalie" (stick-in-the-mud) attitude; once-bustling cities dwindled to mere market towns; even Amsterdam lost much of its population. As a result, it became difficult to consolidate the new government. A multiple executive modelled on the French Directory and lacking a firm base in established political institutions and practices reflected the intrigues of individuals rather than the programs of clearly delineated parties. The victors quarrelled among themselves and looked to Paris to decide among them, or at least passively accepted its dictum, given by coups d'état organized or approved by the French army command. In 1805, Napoleon gave quasi-dicta-

Shift toward agriculture

torial powers to R.J. Schimmelpenninck. Schimmelpenninck, called Councillor Pensionary after the fashion of the old provincial leaders, was actually an uncrowned and nearly absolute monarch (although, ultimately, power continued in Napoleon's hands); he nonetheless carried into practice many of the reforms that had been proposed but not adopted. But Napoleon decided the next year to incorporate the Dutch state directly into his "Grand Empire" of vassal states.

The Kingdom of Holland and the French Empire, 1806–13. Renamed the Kingdom of Holland, the Netherlands received as its monarch Napoleon's younger brother Louis. The four years of his kingship were one of the strangest episodes in Dutch history. Louis Bonaparte was a stranger in the land, yet he took its interests to heart, evading his brother's commands and winning the respect, if not quite the affection, of his subjects. The reconciliation of former Orangists, republicans, and Patriots began under his rule, for, in the face of the apparent permanence of the Napoleonic empire, they entered his government and worked together. Nonetheless the brute fact remained that, for Napoleon, Holland was the kingpin of the "continental system," which he hoped would bring England to its knees by cutting off its continental exports. French officials enforced the vigorous suppression of the smuggling of English and colonial goods to the Continent through Holland that had sprung up over the past decade with London's connivance. King Louis's resistance to his brother's efforts and his refusal to put French interests ahead of Dutch led to the Emperor's decision to oust his brother from his throne in 1810 and to incorporate Holland into the French Empire.

Kingship of Louis Bonaparte

Little changed, however; the same officials—some Dutch, some French—continued to do the work of government in the country, which remained outside the French tariff system. As long as the Napoleonic empire seemed firmly based and permanent, Dutchmen served the new sovereign as they had King Louis, all the more readily because the exiled Prince of Orange gave permission for such collaboration. Dutch soldiers continued to fight in Napoleon's campaigns, losing heavily in the Russian invasion of 1812. But as it became increasingly obvious, after the failure of the Russian and Spanish campaigns, that the Napoleonic empire was collapsing, influential Dutchmen began to prepare for the creation of a new and independent regime; it was taken for granted that its head would be the Prince of Orange—the son of William V, who had died in 1806—and that it was desirable that it be established by the Dutch people rather than imposed by the eventual allied victors. The movement for restoration was led by a remarkable figure, Gijsbert Karel van Hogendorp, a man of firm political principle who had refused to serve any of the governments that ruled in Holland after 1795, yet accepted the necessity for a re-established prince of Orange to govern the country as a limited constitutional sovereign.

Hogendorp's restoration

During the autumn of 1813, Hogendorp secretly planned a take-over of government from the French, which became possible without bloodshed during November, as French troops withdrew to their homeland. On November 30, the hereditary stadholder, at the invitation of Hogendorp's provisional authority, returned from England to proclaim his reign as hereditary prince. In 1814, he granted a charter establishing a constitutional monarchy, with restricted powers for a Parliament elected by a narrow property suffrage. At the insistence of the victorious powers meeting at the Congress of Vienna, he took the title of king of The Netherlands and was given sovereignty over the southern Netherlands, which included both Belgium and Luxembourg. During the campaign against Napoleon after his return from Elba in 1815, Dutch troops played a major role in his defeat at Waterloo.

THE KINGDOM OF THE NETHERLANDS (1814–1918)

King William I. The reign of King William I, as the restored Prince of Orange was now called, was one of the most critical periods in the history of The Netherlands. During this quarter-century the adaptation of the country to the conditions and requirements of modernity moved in a complex and even contradictory way, guided by a monarch who in his economic policy was far more forward-looking than most of his countrymen but who in politics resisted the expansion of Parliament and the introduction of liberal principles. He was a 19th-century version of the "enlightened despot," a man intent upon power, although not so much for its own sake as in order to serve the welfare of his country as he saw it. The role of the States-General—which continued to represent a general electorate of tax-paying citizenry—was strictly limited to the enactment of laws proposed by the government and to approval of a long-term budget; it was in no sense the representative of a sovereign people. The ministers of state were the agents of the king and responsible to him, not to the States-General. Yet the basic structure of modern government had been created in The Netherlands; constitutional debate would be concerned with redistributing powers and responsibilities among existing institutions.

William I was at his best in confronting the problem of reviving the economic life of the country after the shattering impact of the long French occupation. He put the support of both the government and his own private fortune behind encouragement of commerce and, to a lesser extent, of industry. He sponsored the formation of The Netherlands Trading Society, a nominally private firm which undertook the important but costly and risky enterprise of reorganizing Dutch long-distance trade and shipping, particularly to the Netherlands East Indies, that were returned to Dutch sovereignty by England as part of the peace settlement. With the reopening of trade between the European continent and the wider world, the advantages of the Dutch position at the mouth of the great rivers favoured the revival of the traditional branches of Dutch enterprise; but competition from the ports of other countries, notably from Hamburg and Bremen, as well as from Britain, remained strong. Only in the Netherlands East Indies did the Dutch have a clear advantage over their rivals, despite the abandonment of the monopoly formerly maintained under the East India Company.

Encouragement of trade

The most difficult problem faced by the new regime in The Netherlands was the relations between Holland (which now became the everyday name for all the northern Netherlands, in Dutch as well as foreign usage) and Belgium. The King was passionately devoted to the preservation of a single state encompassing all the Low Countries, a unity lost in the revolt against Spain more than two centuries before; but the sense of common nationhood, cultural and political, was quite weak among the people. The Belgians resented assuming a share of the burden of debt inherited by Holland; they were oriented toward industry, Hollanders toward trade; French was the language of the leading classes in the south, and the use of Dutch as the official language was bitterly opposed even by Flemings, who resented the Dutch version of the common Dutch-Flemish language. Most Flemings, as devout Catholics, were hostile to the predominantly Protestant Hollanders. William's efforts to assume the control that Napoleon had possessed over the Belgian Catholic Church met fierce resistance. At the same time the authoritarian character of William's government, particularly the sharp censorship of the press in Belgium, aroused the antipathy of liberals to the regime. The result was the outbreak of the Belgian Revolution of 1830 and the proclamation of Belgian independence. William, supported by a majority of Dutchmen, who were angered by what they saw as Belgian ingratitude, was able to defeat the hastily organized Belgian army; but the European powers intervened to secure Belgian independence, although it was not until 1839 that a final settlement was reached and the last Dutch troops withdrew from Belgian soil. William, deeply despondent, abdicated the next year, leaving to his son, King William II, the task of coming to terms with the new situation.

The Belgian Revolution of 1830

William II and William III. The new king was not a man of clear ideas or strong will, but he was able to do what his father dared not even envisage—to oversee the transformation of The Netherlands into a parliamentary, liberal state. When the crisis of the 1848 revolutions broke, first in France and then in central Europe, William II turned to the leading liberal thinker, J.R. Thorbecke, to guide the change. A new constitution was written, largely modelled on the British (and Belgian) pattern, which gave effective supremacy to the States-General and made the monarch a servant and not the master of government. The King died the next year, and the work of transformation continued under his son, William III (1849–90), who named Thorbecke prime minister. The constitutional monarchy was consolidated, even though Thorbecke stepped down in 1853 because of Protestant rioting against the re-establishment of a Roman Catholic archbishop at Utrecht. Gradually, over the next century,

Extension of the franchise the scope of Dutch democracy was extended to include ever broader sections of the Dutch population in the franchise; universal male suffrage was achieved during World War I, and suffrage was extended to women after World War II. During this period, political parties of the modern type took shape, organized along religious and ideological lines; to the original Liberal, Protestant, and Catholic parties were eventually added Socialist, Conservative-Protestant, Communist, and minor parties. As no single party was able to emerge with a majority, coalition politics became inevitable. The central issue of political controversy became the "school conflict" (*schoolstrijd*), which pitted the liberal (and later socialist) advocates of public schools against the combined Protestant and Catholic parties, which demanded that the state support private ("special") schools equally with the public schools. For several decades, the liberals remained generally in control and made few concessions on the school issue. But when the Protestant leader Abraham Kuyper formed a coalition with the Catholics in 1888, the religious parties were able to gain power and to favour the special over the public schools. Their policy was assailed by the secular parties, the traditional liberals, the progressives, and the socialists. The liberals, however, were at odds with the other anti-clerical parties on other issues, notably economic policies and the extension of the suffrage. The liberals tended to be the most conservative party on economic issues and favoured a restricted electorate; the progressives were vigorously democratic in outlook, as were the socialists, who also favoured universal suffrage, protection of the right to strike, labour legislation, and other welfare measures. The other major issue of the

The Dutch in the Indies latter half of the 19th century was the role of the Dutch East Indies. The income received by the Dutch treasury from Indonesian taxes helped balance the national budget; yet the revelations of harsh conditions in the distant archipelago made it impossible to maintain the "culture system," which had been introduced to force the production of certain crops for export, while the long Achin war drained the treasury.

Queen Wilhelmina and World War I. During the first half of the reign of Queen Wilhelmina (1890–1948), the political situation remained fundamentally unchanged. The major parties came to recognize that the school struggle interfered with the solution of other problems. An agreement in principle was reached on the eve of World War I, by which the secular parties accepted state support for religious schools on a basis of equal funds in exchange for enactment of universal male suffrage. When war broke out in 1914, Holland, which had declared its neutrality, put aside the proposed reforms in order to concentrate on the immediate problem of maintaining the country's livelihood in the face of blockades. The "Pacification," as the compromise was called, was adopted in 1917 and put into effect after the return of peace. The war years saw almost all political controversies set aside, while the government took unprecedented action in maintaining trade and guiding economic life. Although spared the horrors of combat, the Dutch had to maintain a large standing army, and mutinies broke out among the soldiers in 1918.

Economic transformation The century from the restoration of Dutch independence in 1813 until World War I saw fundamental transformations of Dutch life. The economic base was mod-

ernized; the role of agriculture fell off, with most Dutch farmers producing dairy and meat products for the market; trade and shipping were revived in the face of fiercely competitive conditions. But most important was the rise of industry—first textiles in the eastern provinces, then coal in the southeast in Limburg, and finally modern manufactures, notably the great Philips electrical products factories at Eindhoven. Rotterdam became one of the world's busiest ports and the centre of chemical and other industries. These changes were paralleled in society by the gradual extinction of pauperism, the domination of the middle class business and professional men, and the improvement of the conditions of working people and farmers, especially after the mid-19th century. Although religious freedom was generally as great as anywhere in Europe, Protestant conservatives faced major difficulties, especially during the first half of the century, when they protested the modernizing ideas of the Reformed (Hervormde) Church; their efforts to create independent religious communities met with sharp resistance from the government, which did not interfere in non-Protestant religions. Some of the Gereformeerden (the older name for "Reformed" used by the conservatives) emigrated, many of them to the United States; but by the latter half of the century, persecution ceased. The cultural life of Holland remained very largely confined within national boundaries; Dutch thinkers, writers, and artists responded strongly to influences from Germany, France, and England but themselves had little impact abroad. Dutch scientists maintained a respected position for their country; Hugo de Vries was one of the principal founders of the science of genetics, while physicist Hendrik Antoon Lorentz contributed greatly to Einstein's theories of relativity. Dutch artists were generally imitative, although the "Hague school" of Impressionists displayed great gifts; only Vincent van Gogh, who spent most of his active life in France, achieved world reputation. Dutch

19th-century literature literature ran parallel to main currents abroad; the Réveil early in the century was a movement of intensely religious romanticism with strongly conservative ideas, while Eduard Douwes Dekker (pseudonym Multatuli) in mid-century expressed the moods of social criticism with great power; the movement of "Men of the 'Eighties" (Tachtigers) brought to the fore a stress upon aesthetic values and spirituality; and early in the 20th century a literature of social protest re-emerged.

THE NETHERLANDS SINCE 1918

The movement of The Netherlands into modernity was accelerated after 1918. Although the country became a member of the League of Nations, it reaffirmed its neutrality, which seemed to have obtained the respect of the powers and which was symbolized by the presence of the International Court of Justice at The Hague. There was considerable harshness in relations with Belgium, which not only abandoned its neutrality for a close alliance with France but demanded territorial cessions from Holland. The Dutch government, although humiliated by a demand that it present its case before the peace conference at Versailles, successfully resisted any amputation of its territory. The Dutch, for their part, refrained from giving any official support to the Flemish nationalist movement in Belgium, although a "Great Netherlands" movement, principally among intellectuals, emphasized the underlying unity of Dutchmen and Flemings. Domestic politics continued in the same course, with the Protestant political parties continuing to provide leadership for generally conservative policies, especially after the onset of the world depression in the 1930s. Although their small country was particularly dependent for its livelihood upon intercourse with other nations, the Dutch were compelled to introduce tariff measures in order to counter the protectionist policies of other lands.

World War II. At the outbreak of World War II in 1939, the Dutch sedulously maintained their neutrality, although their sympathies lay overwhelmingly with the Western powers. Nonetheless, when Nazi Germany undertook the campaign against France in the spring of 1940, its forces struck not only against Belgium in order

to outflank the French defenses but also against Holland. The aerial destruction of the ancient heart of Rotterdam was the most dramatic episode of the brief campaign, in which the Dutch land armies were overwhelmed in less than a week. The government, accompanied by Queen Wilhelmina and the royal family, withdrew to England, where they formed a government in exile. The Netherlands suffered the next five years of war under German occupation. The work of public administration was continued by Dutch organs of state, which attempted to buffer German political repression, deportation of Jews, and forced employment of Dutch labour in Germany. A
The
resistance
movement
resistance movement sprang up, which, with the exception of a few Dutch Nazi collaborators, spanned all groups from the conservatives to the Communists. The Germans retaliated by executing Dutch hostages for such measures of resistance as the strike of Amsterdam dock workers against the seizure and deportation of Dutch Jews to extermination camps in Germany. Some Jews were able to "dive under" (go into hiding) with the assistance of friends, but the large majority were taken away to their deaths, almost eliminating from Dutch life a small but vigorous part of the population, who for more than three centuries had contributed colour, intelligence, and sensitivity to Dutch society. In the final phases of the war, particularly after the failure of Allied airborne attempts to capture bridgeheads across the great rivers at Nijmegen and Arnhem, the Dutch suffered from severe food shortages, and during the last months before liberation (May 1945) they were on the verge of famine.

The postwar period. After the war many aspects of Dutch life changed dramatically. Wilhelmina and her government returned from exile to re-establish a government more strongly democratic than ever, with both universal suffrage and proportional representation in elections. Anticipating the characteristic difficulties of postwar reconstruction, the government, industry, and labour agreed upon a plan for industrial and commercial expansion, with avoidance of the rapid expansion of prices or wages that would bring a threat of inflation. The plan worked effectively for more than two decades, so that the Dutch were able to avoid drastic inflation until the introduction of a new taxation system in the late 1960s. Dutch industrialization moved forward with speed and depth, expanding to include the large-scale production of steel, electronics, and petrochemicals. Holland,
Abandonment of neutrality
putting aside the policy of neutrality as a failure, entered vigorously into the postwar Western alliances, including the North Atlantic Treaty Organization (NATO), and the various organizations of European unity (the Common Market); but its influence was limited, even though it joined with Belgium and Luxembourg in a closer union ("Benelux"). Indonesia, where Dutch authority was re-established after wartime Japanese occupation, with the expectation that it would be a kind of self-governing dominion in a Dutch community of nations, soon became the scene of a nationalist revolution. After some hesitation and bitterness, the Dutch granted it full independence and later gave economic aid and technological assistance at the request of the Indonesian government. The Netherlands Antilles and Surinam remained part of the Dutch kingdom, although no longer under the authority of the government at The Hague. Dutch political alignments shifted somewhat under postwar conditions. The Socialist Party reorganized itself as the Party of Labour without the traditional Marxist commitments, while the Catholics, who had split politically in the interwar period, united into the Catholic People's Party. The first postwar governments were dominated by an alliance of the Labour and Catholic parties, which continued until the early '60s. When this coalition broke up, the Catholics—who, as the consistently largest single party at the polls, provided all the prime ministers from the late 1950s to the early 1970s—turned to the Protestants and the Liberals, renamed People's Party for Freedom and Democracy. The general policy of the government was not, however, greatly modified. During the '60s, the generally peaceful mood of Dutch public life was broken by rioting of youth and labour groups, especially in Amsterdam. The

most difficult crisis affected the royal family. The marriage (1966) of Princess Beatrix, the heiress to Queen Juliana (who had succeeded Wilhelmina on her abdication in 1948), to a German diplomat aroused bitter debate and imperilled the position of the House of Orange as a national symbol above partisanship. The marriage of Princess Irene to a Spanish Carlist prince had already come as a shock even to the Catholics but was less difficult politically because she lost her right of succession.

Dutch politics, like Dutch society in general, continued to practice what was called pillarization (*verzuiling*)—the organization not only of political parties but of labour unions, businessmen's organizations, social and sport clubs, and many professional groups on the basis of membership in a religious-ideological "pillar," either Catholic, Protestant, or Humanist (the latter including liberals and socialists). Pillarization had received official confirmation in the Pacification of 1917 and removed most of the tinder from Dutch politics; but it also kept ordinary Dutchmen separated from each other, by religion, to a greater degree than in any other Western country. Yet, because the leaders of the pillar organizations worked well with each other and the right of each pillar to exist and function was unquestioned, public life generally ran smoothly. A quarter-century after the end of World War II, there were signs of disquiet over the system, however, and efforts were being made to form new political parties on a comprehensive basis.   (H.Ro.)

Continued
pillari-
zation

III. The southern Netherlands, Belgium and Luxembourg (1579 to present)

THE PERIOD OF FOREIGN RULE

The Spanish regime. After 1579 Alessandro Farnese, supported by the Union of Arras, re-established Spanish authority in the predominantly Catholic southern Netherlands. This territory initially included what is now Belgium and Luxembourg, plus part of northern France and what later became the southernmost part of the United Provinces. In practice, its existence as a separate entity dates from Farnese's reconquest of Flanders in 1585, though Spain did not give up hope of resubjugating the north as well. With this end in view, Philip II granted the sovereignty of the Netherlands to his daughter Isabella and her husband, Archduke Albert, in 1598.

But the northern provinces were never recovered, and Spain allowed only a nominal independence to the south. In 1609 Albert was forced to make a 12-year truce with the United Provinces. He died in 1621, the same year the war was resumed, and Isabella was, from that time on, nothing more than a governor general. During the course of the war with the United Provinces, northern Brabant, as well as the region to the east of the Meuse,
Territorial
losses
and Zeeland, were lost (1621–48). In addition, France, which was allied to the United Provinces, seized Artois (1640). Philip IV agreed to the new northern boundary of the Spanish Netherlands in the Peace of Münster (January 30, 1648), which also confirmed the closing of the Scheldt River to foreign shipping, destroying the commercial importance of Antwerp. Hostilities between Spain and France continued during most of the latter part of the 17th century. The treaties that interrupted this conflict were marked, in almost every instance, by new losses of territory to the southern Netherlands. The Peace of the Pyrenees (1659) confirmed the loss of Artois and provided for a series of French fortifications to be built along the border of what is now Belgium. By the peace of Aix-la-Chapelle (1668), France occupied part of Flanders. In 1700 the Spanish Habsburg dynasty died out with Charles II, who had turned his holdings over to Philippe d' Anjou, grandson of Louis XIV of France. The Spanish Netherlands was thereafter under French rule until it was occupied by the British and Dutch in 1706. By the Treaty of Utrecht (1713), ending the War of the Spanish Succession, the territory comprising present day Belgium and Luxembourg passed under the sovereignty of the Holy Roman emperor Charles VI, head of the Austrian branch of the House of Habsburg.

Administration. The government of the Spanish Netherlands, though not independent, was characterized by a large degree of autonomy. The king was represented in Brussels by a governor general who was, more often than not, a prince of the Spanish royal family. The three councils that assisted the governor (the Council of State, the Privy Council, and the Council of Finances) were composed almost entirely of local leaders, though the Council of State did include a certain number of Spanish nominees. The president of the Privy Council became a sort of first minister. During the 17th century the principal presidents were Pieter Roose (1632–53) and Charles de Hovyne (1653–71). These men did not hesitate to show independence of Madrid in order to protect their interests, but they were essentially supporters of absolutism and regularly tried to assert the authority of the royal government at the expense of regional and local rights. After 1664 the Council of Finances, under its chief official, the treasurer general, began to act as a sort of ministry of economic affairs.

Internal autonomy

These councils gained considerable autonomy in internal affairs, but, with respect to foreign policy, they were controlled less by the governor general than by a Spanish official in Brussels called the secretary of state and war. In Madrid, there was a council of state for the Netherlands, the members of which were natives of the Belgian provinces. In this delicately balanced administration, divided between Brussels and Madrid, the Spanish element tended to predominate, especially in the field of foreign affairs.

There were representative bodies in the Spanish Netherlands. The most important were the provincial estates (assemblies) whose power lay in their authority to levy and collect taxes. This authority enabled them to see that a considerable portion of the revenue was spent within the country. A permanent deputation drawn from the estates supervised public works.

Before and during the revolt against Spain, the States-General, composed of delegates from all the provincial estates, had enjoyed great influence. When the country returned to Spanish rule, the role of the States-General was diminished; after 1632 it no longer met.

During the 16th century regionalism was deep-rooted in the provinces, but in the 17th century a wider feeling of unity developed. The nobles, angered by the government's centralizing policies, revolted in 1631–34; the aristocratic provincial governors involved in this revolt were forced to flee the country because the towns did not support them. Some were not replaced, and by 1700 only Hainaut, Luxembourg, Namur, Limburg, and south Gelderland, all of which had proved their loyalty, still had provincial governors.

In judicial matters, the supreme authority was still the Great Council of Malines, founded in 1504; but it had to defend its jurisdiction against the encroachments of the Privy Council. The provincial courts of justice were the councils of Flanders, Brabant, Namur, Luxembourg, south Gelderland, Hainaut, and (until 1659) Artois. The most important of these was the Council of Brabant, to which the king had originally granted autonomy in conformity with the provincial liberties of Brabant. Nevertheless, after 1603, he was represented in Brabant by financial officials under a procurer general. These magistrates, in accordance with a practice common at that time, had, in addition to their judicial duties, administrative functions that increased during the 17th century.

In the 17th century, the administration of the country was made difficult by constant warfare. Government finances, weakened by the loss of revenues from the northern provinces and the loans contracted during the 16th century, suffered further because of increased military expenses. Sale of public offices became a common practice.

Taxation

At the end of the 16th and the beginning of the 17th centuries, import and export duties provided a new source of revenue. Prior to this, the shipping of goods was taxed only as *tonlieu* (goods transported within the country). This tax remained but only supplied regional or local finances. Taxes on foreign trade originated from permits allowing trade with the rebellious northern provinces. At first these were sold to individuals, but they were later replaced with fixed duties which, by 1654, had become customs tariffs. After that, there were customs houses, not only at the frontiers but in Brabant and Flanders as well.

In the country's military organization, the fortresses of Antwerp, Ghent, Ostend, and Charleroi were manned by Spanish troops; other armed forces were raised locally.

The principality of Liège (in present eastern Belgium) was ruled as a separate territory by its bishops, as it had been since the Middle Ages. During the revolt against Spain, it maintained a strict neutrality and continued to do so during most of the 17th century. Its institutional development was, in the main, parallel to that of the Spanish Netherlands.

Economy. The economy of the country had, of course, suffered greatly during the struggle against Philip II, but recent research has shown that economic recovery was more rapid and more far-reaching than had previously been thought.

The fortunes of the important linen industry can be traced by studying tax fluctuations. In the region of Oudenaarde, excise taxes almost doubled between 1570 and 1579. The figure for 1579 represents the highest point of the century; the low point occurred in 1589. Slightly earlier, a similar pattern occurred in Courtrai. Thus the decade 1570–80 was a favourable one for the linen industry. A period of crisis followed, but after 1590 there was a marked recovery. In 1600, Oudenaarde again reached the standard of 1561, while Courtrai surpassed that of the preceding century. The 17th century, formerly thought to have been a time of unrelieved calamity, now appears to have known considerable prosperity. Between 1609 and 1610 production doubled in Courtrai; in 1642 it was eight times that of the best years of the 16th century.

A similar situation existed in other branches of the textile industry. In the sayette (serge) mills at Hondschoote, the ten years following 1570 were still a period of great prosperity; the crisis did not begin until about 1580. In this instance the lowest point also occurs between 1580 and 1590. Historians formerly believed that there was a massive emigration of Flemish weavers to the northern Low Countries during the period of turmoil. Recent research has shown that this emigration was on a much smaller scale than had previously been thought and that in 1588 Hondschoote, Bruges, and Ypres were again very active.

The economic crisis in Flanders, the most advanced region in the southern Netherlands, was so short-lived that its existence was not generally realized. It coincides with the reconquest of Alessandro Farnese, in 1585. When this is understood, evidences of prosperity in the 17th century become more comprehensible. After 1600, the war between Spain and the United Provinces and repeated invasions by the French did cause havoc, but the basis of the economy was not seriously threatened until the War of the League of Augsburg (1689–97) and the War of the Spanish Succession (1701–13). In the second half of the century, despite the fact that the Dutch were able to close Antwerp to sea traffic, commerce was kept alive by transporting goods overland from the ports of Holland and Zeeland. Other goods entered the country by the ports of Ostend, Nieuwpoort, and Dunkirk. The digging of new canals facilitated internal transport, and overland trade with France, Germany, and Italy remained active.

The populations of the important cities steadily increased during the 17th century and declined after 1700. In the small towns and the countryside, the rate of expansion continued into the 18th century. The development of the rural linen industry is significant in this connection. The increase in urban population during the 17th century can be explained by the prosperity of the export trade, mostly in the various branches of the textile industry. In Ghent, silks, velvets, and blended weaves of wool, flax, silk, and cotton were all produced in increasing quantities. In Bruges, serge and fustian (a cotton-linen weave) were manufactured; Ghent specialized in luxury fabrics, Bruges in cloth for everyday use. The products of these towns had an important place in the European and Spanish-American markets.

Linen dyers were especially numerous in Ghent. They processed large quantities of linen, which were shipped mainly to Spain and England. The majority of looms belonged to a restricted number of manufacturers. This concentration of the means of production in the hands of a few large entrepreneurs was increased by the mid-18th century to a point that presages the beginning of the Industrial Revolution. For a time Ghent rivalled Antwerp and Brussels as a centre of tapestry manufacture and trade, mainly because of the immigration of merchant entrepreneurs from Oudenaarde. In 1687 one manufacturer employed 200 labourers. In addition to simple floral designs, Ghent tapestries featured religious, mythological, and historic subjects, in the tradition of the great tapestry centres of Flanders. These goods were exported to France, Germany, Denmark, and the United Provinces.

Bruges in the mid-17th century had a population of about 35,000; some 1,500 adult labourers were employed there in the textile industry as weavers and in related jobs. If the wool combers and spinners living in the villages around Bruges are also counted, the total comes to more than 10,000.

The prosperity evident in the Flemish textile industry was not equalled in other areas of the economy, although metallurgy and mining in the principality of Liège were of considerable importance. Agricultural production was high enough to avert famine but increased too slowly to provide a base for much industrial expansion.

At Antwerp, the economic recovery that marked the end of Philip II's reign continued until at least the middle of the 17th century. The town had 42,000 inhabitants in 1589; 57,338 in 1644; and 65,711 in 1698. Although it lost much of its maritime commerce to other cities, Antwerp continued to prosper as an industrial centre. Goods made from Italian silk were exported to France, England, and Holland; ribbon and thread went to Spain and other parts of western Europe. English cloth continued to be distributed through Antwerp, thanks to a certain number of local entrepreneurs and to English merchants settled there. The city produced a great deal of lace for export; during the second half of the century a single lace manufacturer employed 300 persons. This lace was, for the most part, sent to Spain and Latin America. Antwerp was also a centre for the distribution of artworks throughout Europe and America. The paintings of Flemish artists were sent everywhere, and those of Italian masters were often distributed throughout western and central Europe via Antwerp. The same was true in printing and the book trade. Printers were important and numerous; the firm of Moretus was the largest industrial concern in Antwerp and one of the principal firms in Europe. The diamond industry and trade had an impressive development. Antwerp had 104 diamond cutters in 1608; by 1674 their number was 200. People came there from Frankfurt, Hamburg, London, and Paris to perfect their craft. The highly speculative diamond trade—the value of diamonds being contingent on their scarcity—was well suited to a city that dealt mainly in foreign commerce. Commercial firms of international importance were still centred in Antwerp. A recent estimate lists 46 of these in the period 1620–40, some Flemish and some foreign, a number of them controlling large amounts of capital. One of these firms, newly established and moderately prosperous, had commercial ties with Rouen, Calais, Lille, London, Dover, Canterbury, Amsterdam, Leiden, and Hamburg. It sold sugar and other colonial products, Spanish wool, and textiles. Within 30 years this company passed from ordinary trade to banking. It is clear, then, that the economic depression formerly attributed to the 17th century did not really begin until the latter part of that century and the beginning of the 18th.

The relative prosperity of the southern Netherlands, and particularly of Antwerp, no doubt partly explains its flourishing artistic life during this period. This was chiefly evident in the works of the Flemish School of 17th-century painters—among them Peter Paul Rubens, Anthony Van Dyck, and Jacob Jordaensz. Rubens (1577–1640),

court painter to Isabella and Archduke Albert, made Antwerp one of the cultural capitals of Europe. In the area of scholarship, the "Bollandists," a group of Antwerp Jesuits, made valuable contributions to historical methodology.

The Austrian regime (1713–95). Under the Austrian, as under the Spanish, Habsburgs, the southern Netherlands enjoyed political autonomy. But its prosperity had been ruined by the wars of the late 17th and early 18th centuries, and discontent was widespread. By 1719 there was opposition in Brussels to taxes levied by the new government. The emperor Charles VI attempted to relieve the economic distress of his new possession by founding the Ostend Company to trade with India (1722), but Britain and the United Provinces, wishing to avoid unwelcome competition, forced him to abandon the company in 1727.

At the death of Charles VI (October 20, 1740), the southern Netherlands passed to his daughter Maria Theresa without opposition. The War of the Austrian Succession, however, led to a new French occupation in 1744. Austrian rule was restored by the Treaty of Aix-la-Chapelle in 1748.

Maria Theresa's regime enjoyed popularity as the economic situation began to improve again toward the middle of the 18th century. As in contemporary England, an increase in agricultural productivity stimulated a population increase, especially in rural areas. This, in turn, spurred the development of various industries. The agricultural transformation occurred mainly on the small farms of Flanders; one of its main features was the spread of potato cultivation, which added an important element to the diet of the rural population. In addition, in the French-speaking part of the country, a number of landed proprietors invested in mining enterprises, notably in the area between the Sambre and the Meuse rivers, which belonged to the principality of Liège. In the southern Netherlands, urban merchants and manufacturers had more in common with the rural landowning class than was usual in continental European countries in the 18th century. As in the case of Britain, this created an atmosphere favourable to the development of industrial capitalism. During this period, Ghent, Antwerp, and Tournai had factories with more than 100 workers; wages, however, were poor. Verviers, in the principality of Liège, was an important center for woolen manufactures, Ghent for cotton goods.

Under the influence of the Enlightenment, the Austrian regime sponsored a number of reforms in the Netherlands. An academy was founded in 1772 and, when the Jesuits were suppressed in 1773, the government replaced their colleges with secular institutions. The government was not inclined to support the remnants of feudal privilege that caused so much discontent in 18th-century France.

Not all of its innovations were popular, however. The emperor Joseph II (reigned 1780–90) suppressed 163 religious houses, granted freedom of worship by his Edict of Toleration (1781), and closed the episcopal seminaries, replacing them with two state seminaries (1786). These measures alienated the Roman Catholic clergy. In 1787 the administration was modernized by replacing the traditional provinces with districts (cercles) governed by intendants. This caused dissatisfaction among the groups that controlled the provincial estates. The discontent of the privileged classes was increased by the suppression of the traditional councils and courts of justice, which, like the estates, were looked upon as safeguards of provincial autonomy.

Joseph's sister, Maria Christina, duchess of Saxony-Teschen, who was governor general, was reluctant to implement the unpopular edicts abolishing these traditional bodies. But other members of the administration, including Ferdinand von Trauttmansdorff, the Emperor's minister plenipotentiary, and Gen. Richard d'Alton, commander of the troops, insisted upon their enforcement. The estates of Hainaut and Brabant reacted by refusing to pay taxes (November 1788). In the following year, influenced by the outbreak of revolution in neighbour-

Marginal notes:

Ghent's textile industries

Foreign trade at Antwerp

Economic decline

The Brabant Revolution

ing France, conservatives led by Henri Van Der Noot and progressives led by Jean-François Vonck united in opposition to the Emperor. Raising a corps of volunteers, Vonck defeated an Austrian force at Turnhout (October 24–27, 1789). Nervous because of the situation in France, the Austrians retreated to Luxembourg, and Van Der Noot made a triumphant entry into Brussels, where he and his "Statists," were supported by the Estates of Brabant, this time not only against the Emperor but also in opposition to the progressive Vonck, who favoured the convening of a national assembly. They successfully incited the people of Brussels against Vonck, who had to take refuge in Lille.

This "Brabant Revolution" (so called because most of its leaders came from Brabant) had widespread support in the towns; but the peasants, having little in common with the middle class revolutionaries, generally supported the Austrians. This was particularly evident among that segment of the rural population that lived, at least in part, by domestic work for the new manufacturers in the towns. Thus, in Hainaut, the province where the estates had first rebelled, the peasants of the countryside of Chimay rose up in favour of the Emperor and against the Statists.

Thus, when Joseph II died, and his successor, Leopold II, decided to re-establish imperial authority, he encountered no opposition from the mass of people. On December 2, 1790, Brussels was reoccupied by Austrian troops. Nevertheless, in order not to provoke the Statists, the Emperor did not reintroduce his predecessor's reforms. The discontented now looked to revolutionary France for support. When the French general C.F. Dumouriez occupied the Austrian Netherlands after his victory at the Battle of Jemappes (November 6, 1792), he was very well received. Enthusiasm languished, however, when it became clear that France was not going to allow the Netherlands to be independent. Austrian rule was briefly restored in 1793–94; but France's victory at Fleurus, on June 26, 1794, was the prelude to French annexation. This proved more of a jolt for the Austrian Netherlands itself than for the principality of Liège, where a revolution against the prince-bishop had prepared the country for assimilation into the French Republic.

French and Dutch rule. On October 1, 1795, the French National Convention voted to annex Belgium and Luxembourg. Under French rule, there was no autonomy as there had been under the Spanish and Austrian regimes; the reforms of Joseph II were revived, although in a more radical form. The administration was centralized and the territory divided into departments. Aristocratic privileges were abolished and the church persecuted. Military conscription, introduced in September 1798, provoked a peasants' revolt in the same areas that had opposed the conservative Statists during the Revolution of 1789. Repression was extremely harsh.

Under the Napoleonic Consulate and Empire (1799–1814), the French civil code and the decimal metric system were introduced, and the position of the clergy was regulated by Napoleon's concordat with the papacy. A politically united Europe offered vast outlets for expanding Belgian industry.

The beginning of industrialization

The period of the Napoleonic Empire, recent research has revealed, may be considered the "take-off" stage of the Industrial Revolution in Belgium. The Belgian departments produced almost half the empire's coal; the department of Jemappes (the former county of Hainaut) alone accounted for 30 percent. The blast furnaces and forges of the Belgian departments provided 25 percent of the empire's iron production. In relation to its population, Belgium produced 450 kilograms (992 pounds) of coal per capita. At the same time the corresponding total in France was 40 kilograms (88 pounds). That this was the beginning of the Industrial Revolution may be seen by a comparison with contemporary England, where this revolution was in progress, and with France, where it had not begun. The 450 kilograms (992 pounds) of coal per capita are comparable to the English 500 (1,100 pounds), but not to French production, which was one-tenth that amount. Figures for iron production were similar: 11 kilograms (24 pounds) per capita in Belgium, 20 (44 pounds) in England, and 4 (9 pounds) in France. The Verviers textile industry was second in the empire. In Flanders, linen and cotton occupied an important place; the same was true for paper, leather, and glass. Thus, Belgium was the first country on the Continent to go through the process of industrialization. However, during the later years of French rule, it became evident in Belgium, as it had to all the people subjugated by Napoleon, that military domination had had its day. The allied occupation of Belgium in 1814 was welcomed.

The allied forces decided to unite the former United Provinces with Belgium to form a Kingdom of The Netherlands. The people were not consulted, but Prince William of Orange-Nassau ascended the throne on March 16, 1815, and the existence of the kingdom was confirmed by the Congress of Vienna the following June.

Thus the northern and southern Netherlands, which had been one country until the 16th century, were reunited. But in the two intervening centuries they had developed in markedly different ways. The north was commercial, the south increasingly industrial; the north Protestant, the south Catholic. Under the Dutch House of Orange, the north was to be predominant; the fundamental law of the new kingdom gave Belgium and Holland the same number of representatives in the States-General despite the fact that the population of Belgium was 3,500,000 and that of the former United Provinces 2,000,000. Belgian representatives rejected the constitution, but it was promulgated by the King over their objections.

In the beginning, the economic situation continued to be favourable. The textile industries of Ghent and Verviers continued their progress, while the coal mines and forges of Liège and Hainaut prospered. King William I created three state universities: Ghent and Liège, which were new, and Louvain, which he put under state control to remove it from Catholic influence. In secondary education, the secular *athénées* were established, and schools controlled by the Church were subject to state inspection. An attempt to interfere with the training of priests (1825) brought clerical dissatisfaction with the government to its height.

Dissatis-faction with Dutch rule

After 1820 the conflicting interests of north and south also created an economic split. The commercial north, with little industry, desired free trade; the south needed tariff protection to allow its industry to compete against British prices. This gave the middle classes a grievance against the government. Progressives and clericals joined forces in 1828; the programs were different, but the enemy was the same: the Dutch regime. Following the July Revolution in Paris (1830), rioting broke out among the workers in Brussels on August 25. The bourgeoisie armed themselves, and when the working class uprising was put down, they turned their arms against the Dutch troops. The Dutch, led by the Prince of Orange, were expelled from Brussels on September 3 and tried unsuccessfully to reoccupy it on September 23. Two days later a provisional Belgian government was established. This revolutionary government proclaimed the country's independence on October 4. Meanwhile, the Belgians occupied Antwerp; Dutch troops, besieged in the citadel, bombarded the city on October 27, further increasing ill-feeling among the Belgians.

A National Congress was elected and met on November 10. It reaffirmed Belgian independence on the 18th and on the 24th voted to exclude the House of Orange from the Belgian throne. William I prepared for war, but on December 20 the great powers intervened, imposing an armistice on both sides. On January 20, 1831, a conference in London recognized Belgium as an independent, neutral state; its neutrality to be guaranteed by the powers.

BELGIUM AND LUXEMBOURG (1831 TO PRESENT)

Independent Belgium. *The formation of the kingdom.* The National Congress had decided that Belgium should be a monarchy, but finding a king proved difficult. On February 3, 1831, the congress elected Louis, duc de Nemours, son of the new French king Louis-Philippe, but the British, fearing French expansionism, opposed this, and Louis declined. The next choice was Prince Leopold of Saxe-Coburg, who was related to the British royal family. Since Leopold married Louis-Philippe's daughter shortly afterward, he was acceptable to the French also. On July 21, 1831, he promised to support the constitution drawn up by the National Congress, which gave the greater part of the governing power to a Parliament elected by property owners. Some days later, the Dutch army invaded Belgium. The Belgians, who had no regular army, were defeated, but the London Conference agreed to intervention by the French army, which forced the Dutch to retire. The conference then decided (November 15, 1831) to divide the provinces of Limburg and Luxembourg, awarding part to Belgium and part to The Netherlands. William I, to the surprise of the powers, refused to accept this settlement, although he did conclude an armistice. The Belgians, therefore, continued to occupy Dutch Limburg and the future Grand Duchy of Luxembourg until William finally relented in 1838. He then became the first grand duke of Luxembourg. The western half of Luxembourg became a Belgian province. The new Belgian king Leopold I tried to increase his role in the government by asking Parliament for the right to appoint and dismiss the members of the provincial and local administrations. The Parliament, however, rejected this proposal in 1836.

The economy continued to develop. The first railroad, between Brussels and Malines, was inaugurated in 1836. Capital investments rose from 37 million francs in 1834 to 145 million in 1836. One of the most powerful corporations was the Société Générale, which now controlled a number of industries. At the same time, the traditional Flemish textile industry, which was slow to mechanize, was undergoing a severe crisis. But by 1848, the decisive leap to industrialization was made in this area also.

After Dutch recognition of Belgium in 1839, the coalition that had backed the independence movement showed signs of breaking up. Disputes arose between the liberals (middle class anticlericals) and the Catholics, and a separate Liberal Party was formed in 1846. Between 1847 and 1857, Catholics and Liberals alternated in office; the period 1857–1870 was one of Liberal rule.

Leopold I proved to be a prudent ruler, and when revolution spread across Europe in 1848, Belgium remained peaceful. But the downfall of Louis-Philippe and, to an even greater extent, the creation of the Second French Empire under Napoleon III (1852) eventually caused problems. French republicans sought refuge from political persecution in Belgium, where they spread propaganda against Napoleon. This caused the French government to adopt a hostile attitude toward Belgium; in 1853, Leopold asked that Parliament allow Antwerp to be fortified and the nation prepared to meet a possible invasion, which, however, failed to materialize.

Further economic progress In the economic sphere, industrial development allowed the gradual introduction of a free-trade policy beginning in 1849. A national bank having the right to issue currency was created in 1850. Municipal tolls on the entrance of foodstuffs into the cities were abolished in 1860. Finally, in 1863, the prosperity of the country permitted the redemption of The Netherlands' right to levy charges on shipping entering the Scheldt River. After more than two centuries, Antwerp was a free port again. Leopold I died on December 10, 1865, leaving Belgium a strong and united country.

The reign of Leopold II. Leopold II (reigned 1865–1909) found himself immediately faced with serious problems in foreign affairs. Prussia had become the dominant power in Germany, and Napoleon III wished to extend French control over Belgium and Luxembourg in compensation. A French rail company, with government support, attempted to acquire the railways of the province of Luxembourg in 1868; in 1869, the Belgian chamber reacted by forbidding the sale of railways. Only British support permitted the liberal ministry of Walther Frère-Orban to avoid hostilities with France.

When the Franco-German War broke out in 1870, Belgium remained neutral. Napoleon III's defeat momentar-

Conflict with The Netherlands

ily removed the French threat, but a unified Germany posed an equally serious problem on the eastern frontier. The subsequent rivalry between France and Germany in the period 1871–1914 constituted a continual danger to Belgium. In 1887 Leopold II asked Parliament for authority to erect two new fortifications, one to the east, at Liège, and the other to the south, at Namur.

Meanwhile, the process of industrialization continued. Coal and iron production increased; Belgium's population was the densest in Europe and, because there was no labour movement before 1870, labour was cheap. The Société Générale, one of the most powerful economic organizations in continental Europe, played an increasing role in financing industry.

The Belgian bourgeoisie increased both in number and wealth, and electoral property qualifications favoured their predominance. This class was the backbone of the Liberal Party. A Catholic reaction materialized in 1869, with the formation of a Catholic party opposed to the liberal Catholic deputies who, until then, had represented Catholic opinion in Parliament and in the government. The new party represented a militant and conservative position; in order to achieve its goals, it favoured eliminating property qualifications for voting, a measure also favoured by the more advanced Liberals. Socialism gained some adherents in Belgium after 1848, and the formation of the First Socialist (Marxist) International in 1867 increased its influence among industrial workers. Belgian socialism remained fragmented until the foundation of the Belgian Workers' Party (POB), the ancestor of the later Belgian Socialist Party (PSB), in 1885.

The opposition between Catholics and Liberals became acute in 1879, when the Liberal Frère-Orban ministry sponsored a law removing religion entirely from primary education. Controversy over this issue was extremely violent and even divided families. The church's opposition to the law led to a break in relations with the Vatican. In 1884 the Catholics won a majority in both chambers, and the Catholic party remained in power without interruption until 1914. Aside from the education controversy, the biggest factor in the Liberals' defeat was probably their advocacy of free trade, which was favoured by manufacturers but exposed farmers to ruinous foreign competition. In the early 1880s the Belgian market was flooded by American grain; the Catholic party became the champion of the rural classes by promising to protect agriculture. It also espoused the cause of the nascent "Flemish" movement that sought to expand opportunities for Dutch-speaking Belgians in a country until then dominated by a French-speaking upper bourgeoisie.

Church-state conflict

The working class did not have the right to vote because of the system of electoral property qualifications. The last years of the 19th century and the first of the 20th were years of violent social tension. In 1886 there was a disturbance among workers in Liège, followed by unrest in other industrial areas. The Catholic government of Auguste Beernaert suppressed this movement harshly, but beginning in 1889, a series of laws were passed regulating workers' housing, limiting labour by women and children, and providing workmen's compensation. The legislature revised the constitution in 1890, and, in 1893, universal suffrage was adopted for men 21 and over. Though this measure was modified by giving a plural vote to electors fulfilling certain conditions of income, age, and education and to heads of families, it resulted in the election of the first Socialist deputies to the legislature. Belgian industry, dominated by powerful financial groups, began to assume worldwide importance and was active in Asia and Latin America, as well as in Europe. In Africa, King Leopold II acquired the state of the Congo as a personal possession in 1885, but his subjects showed little interest in the area, leaving him to mismanage it until 1898, when the Matadi–Léopoldville railroad was completed, facilitating access to the interior of the Congo Basin. Then Belgian banks began to push for annexation, which eventually came in 1908. In 1909 the army recruitment system, which until then had favoured the wealthy by allowing them to hire substitutes for military service, was finally reformed.

Annexation of the Congo

Belgium since 1909. In 1909, Leopold II died, and was succeeded by his nephew Albert, who became king as Albert I (December 23). Social unrest, which had distinguished the last years of Leopold's reign, continued at the beginning of Albert's, but a general strike in 1913 caused no change in the parliamentary majority.

The international situation became increasingly tense at the end of July 1914, on the eve of World War I. The neutrality of Belgium and Luxembourg had been guaranteed by the great powers under the treaties of 1839. On July 30 the British government demanded assurance from France and Germany that Belgian neutrality would be respected in the event of the outbreak of war. Germany, after refusing to respond to the English request, invaded Luxembourg on August 2 and sent an ultimatum to Belgium demanding free passage of troops. Belgium refused and was invaded on the morning of August 4. Liège fell on August 16, Namur on August 23. The Germans occupied Brussels on August 20, but Antwerp, which was not attacked by the Germans advancing into France along the Marne, was not evacuated until October 6. The Belgian Army then retired behind the IJser in the west of Flanders and held this position until 1918.

During the war, the Belgian government sat at Le Havre, France, while the King, as commander-in-chief of the army, remained with his troops in unoccupied Belgium. After the invasion, the Catholic government named both a Liberal and a Socialist minister of state, and during the war, ministry offices were assigned to Liberals and Socialists.

Upon their return to Brussels, the King and Prime Minister announced the introduction of absolute universal suffrage (that is, the abandonment of plural votes). The elections of 1919 brought to power a government composed of Catholics, Liberals, and Socialists, which voted an eight-hour day, progressive taxes, and old-age insurance. The question of schools, which had divided Liberals and Catholics so strongly during Leopold II's reign, gave rise to a compromise whereby subsidies were granted to Catholic institutions.

The
Flemish
movement

Flemish nationalism had gained ground, and, in 1898, the Dutch language was finally recognized along with French as an official language of the country. Henceforth, the movement also took on an economic and social character, owing to the fact that in the coal-rich Walloon provinces, industrialization was very advanced. In contrast, economic development had been quite slow in the Flemish region after the Industrial Revolution. But, until 1914, the principal goal of the Flemish movement had been the creation of a university in which instruction would be given in Dutch. During World War I, Germany attempted to profit from Flemish–Walloon antagonism and supported the Activists—partisans of Flemish autonomy. Most Flemings, however, were resolutely hostile to collaboration with the enemy and refused to recognize either the Council of Flanders or the Flemish university, both founded during the occupation. Shortly after the liberation of the territory, the Belgian government made the University of Ghent, first partially, then completely, Flemish.

The Treaty of Versailles (1919) abolished Belgium's obligatory neutrality and returned the cantons of Eupen and Malmedy to its territory. In 1920 a treaty of military assistance was signed with France, and in 1921 an economic union was concluded with Luxembourg. The eastern frontier was guaranteed by the Pact of Locarno (1925). In Africa, Belgium received the mandates for Ruanda and Burundi, former German colonies that Belgian colonial forces had occupied during the conflict.

The decade following the Peace of Versailles was distinguished by a considerable increase in industrial and commercial wealth and by prosperity among the workers and peasants. The middle classes, caught between these two forces, lost much of their wealth and political influence.

Post-war
coalitions

The result was the retreat of the Liberal Party and the aggrandizement of the Catholic and Socialist parties. The three-party government born of the war did not survive the end of 1921; it was followed by a coalition of Catholics and Liberals that lasted until 1925, when the Social-ists allied themselves with the Christian Democrats, then becoming the most important wing of the Catholic party.

In 1930, when the effects of the Great Depression were beginning to be felt, Parliament voted a series of laws transforming Belgium into two linguistic areas with different administrations. Henceforth, the Flemish provinces were administered solely in Dutch, the Walloon solely in French. In the face of the Depression the Socialist Party advocated a program of economic planning in accordance with the ideas of the socialist theorist Hendrik de Man. At the same time there emerged two Belgian fascist parties: a strictly Flemish party that enjoyed little success and the broader-based Rexists under the leadership of Léon Degrelle. The latter party won 21 seats, more than 10 percent of the chamber, in the elections of 1936. Strikes broke out in the same year and led the tripartite government of Paul van Zeeland to establish paid holidays for workers and a 40-hour week for miners.

Meanwhile King Leopold III, who succeeded his father Albert I, in 1934, faced an increasingly tense international situation. Leopold advocated a policy of independent neutrality that aimed at keeping Belgium removed from the seemingly inevitable conflict. This policy was approved by Parliament, but Belgium reasserted its determination to resist all aggression. Consequently, a line of defense from Namur to Antwerp was constructed facing Hitler's Germany.

On May 10, 1940, Hitler invaded Belgium along with Holland and Luxembourg. Holland capitulated after six days, Belgium after 18. France, which along with Britain had sent troops to Belgium, had to lay down arms three weeks later. The British troops, covered by the Belgian army, retreated from Dunkirk in particularly dramatic circumstances.

The four years of ensuing Nazi occupation were distinguished by a growing resistance organization. When the Allied forces reached Belgium on September 3, 1944, the Belgian underground army was able to prevent the destruction of the port of Antwerp, which served as a provisioning point for Allied troops for the remainder of the war.

The
"royal
question"

While the economy recovered rapidly after the war, political stability deteriorated, notably over the "royal question." The King had been taken by the Germans and confined to his palace at Laeken; the government, on the other hand, had taken refuge in London. In 1944, at the time of the Allied offensive, the Germans transferred the King to Austria, where he was kept until 1945. The government, upon returning to Brussels, conferred the regency on the King's brother, Prince Charles. Opinion was divided between Leopold's opponents and supporters. Roughly, the Flemish were the King's partisans and the Walloons his opponents and the Catholics for, the Socialists and Liberals against, his return. In 1950 a referendum showed 57 percent of the voters to be in favour of the return of the sovereign, but the King's return signalled near civil war in the Walloon country. Leopold abdicated in favour of his eldest son, Baudouin I, who on August 11, 1950, took an oath of loyalty to the constitution. Because he was not yet of age, he took the title of prince royal until he became king on July 17, 1951. The composition of the government continued to fluctuate, although the Catholics achieved an absolute majority owing to the enfranchisement of women in 1949. The government was frequently composed of a leftist alliance of the Socialists and Liberals until the two most important parties, the Catholics and Socialists, formed a coalition that was frequently in power.

In 1947, Belgium joined with The Netherlands and Luxembourg in the economic union of Benelux, and in 1949 the country became one of 12 signatories of the North Atlantic Treaty Organization (NATO); on July 1, 1960, independence was given to the Congo, where unrest had earlier broken out.

In the '50s and '60s Belgian political parties underwent a marked change. The Catholic party became the Social Christian Party, supported by the middle classes and the peasants. Its Christian-Democratic wing was predominant. The Liberal Party became more conservative and is presently called the Party of Liberty and Progress (PLP). The Socialist Party has become moderate and has almost eliminated the Communist Party.

Belgium's main domestic difficulty is still the linguistic problem. As the numerical majority of Flemings has become increasingly apparent, it is not surprising that discontent has become manifest among the Walloons. Until World War II, heavy industry was concentrated in Walloon territory, but since then a displacement to the north of the country has begun. The Walloon syndicalist, André Renard, created, at the time of the strikes of December 1960–January 1961, the Walloon Popular Movement (MPW), which espouses protection for the Walloon economy and federalism. Reaction in the Flemish areas was at first negligible, but a struggle over the division of the University of Louvain into two universities, one Flemish and the other French, soon involved them. The Flemish Catholics demanded that the French university be established in the Walloon area and, thus, caused a split in the Demo-Christian party along linguistic lines. The Flemings have laid claim to Brussels, which is situated in Flemish territory but inhabited mainly by French-speakers, both native and immigrant. But the communal elections of October 11, 1970, indicated that Brussels wished to remain removed from the federalism that was shaping Belgium. That city, which is the seat of the European Common Market, appeared determined to preserve a position separate from the two linguistic regions of the country.

The Grand Duchy of Luxembourg. In 1839, by accepting the Treaty of 24 Articles, King William I of Holland also became grand duke of Luxembourg. The grand duchy, separated from Belgian Luxembourg, henceforth, was independent, but subject to personal union with the Low Countries. On October 7, 1840, the king-grand duke abdicated in favour of his son William II, under whose rule Luxembourg joined the German customs union (Zollverein). Under Grand Duke William III, who succeeded to the throne in 1849, the opposition of liberal industrialists favouring constitutional government gained support, and finally, in 1867, a constitution was promulgated. In the same year, Napoleon III wished to annex Luxembourg, but the Treaty of London (May 11, 1867) had made it a neutral state under the protection of the powers, as was also the case with Belgium. Prussian troops that occupied the citadel of Luxembourg in the name of the German Confederation withdrew as the Confederation was dissolved at the end of the 1866 war with Austria.

Shortly afterwards, Luxembourg experienced a powerful economic upsurge owing to the adoption of the Thomas and Gilchrist process for the dephosphorization of iron ore. The ore production increased from 1,000,000 tons in 1872 to 7,500,000 in 1907, the production of iron from 250,000 tons in 1875 to 2,500,000 in 1913.

The death of King-Grand Duke William III (1890) signified the end of the personal union with the Low Countries. Owing to a pact of succession concluded in 1783 between the Dutch and German branches of the House of Orange-Nassau, the throne reverted to Adolf of Nassau (1890–1905). His successor, William IV (reigned 1905–12), died without male issue and was succeeded by his eldest daughter, Maria Adelaide. The latter followed a reactionary policy and, after the German occupation of 1914–18, was forced to abdicate early in 1919. Under the government of her sister, Grand Duchess Charlotte (1919–64), Luxembourg concluded an economic union with Belgium in 1921 and joined the League of Nations. When it was invaded once again, on May 10, 1940, the grand-ducal family took refuge in England, but Nazi Germany annexed Luxembourg. Freed on September 10, 1944, by Allied troops, the grand duchy regained its independence; it joined the Benelux Union in 1947, abandoned its neutral stance in 1948, joined the North Atlantic Pact in 1949, and participated in the European Common Market. As of 1971, the country was governed by Grand Duke Jean, the son of Duchess Charlotte and Prince Félix of Bourbon. The ministry was composed of Christian-Socialists and Liberals.   (J.C.V.)

BIBLIOGRAPHY

General works: J.A. VAN HOUTTE et al. (eds.), *Algemene Geschiedenis der Nederlanden,* 12 vol. (1949–58), an extensive history of both the northern and southern Low Countries, with detailed bibliographies; G. EDMUNDSON, *History of Holland* (1922), still the best general history in English, although better for the republican than the modern period; P.J. BLOK, *Geschiedenis van het Nederlandsche Volk,* 4 vol. (1892–99; Eng. trans., *History of the People of the Netherlands,* 5 vol., 1898–1912), a classic history of the northern territories, now outdated, particularly so on the history of the Middle Ages; HENRI PIRENNE, *Histoire de Belgique,* 7 vol. (1900–32, with many revised editions), a brilliantly written history by the famous Belgian historian, covering for the period of the Middle Ages the southern as well as the northern parts of the Low Countries, although emphasis is on the south; I. SCHOFFER, *A Short History of the Netherlands* (Eng. trans. 1956), a brilliantly written and very useful survey of the history of the northern Netherlands up till the present time.

History of the Netherlands to 1579: S.J. DE LAET, *The Low Countries* (1958), a thorough survey of the Low Countries in prehistoric times; I.H. GOSSES and R.R. POST, *Handboek tot de staatkundige geschiedenis der Nederlanden,* vol. 1, *De Middeleeuwen* (1959), an accurate handbook of the political history, limited, however, to the Dutch-speaking territories; H.P.H. JANSEN, *Middeleeuwse geschiedenis der Nederlanden* (1965), a fairly thorough compendium of the medieval history of the Low Countries, with attention given to the political as well as to the social, economic, and cultural aspects; W. JAPPE ALBERTS and H.P.H. JANSEN, *Welvaart in wording: Sociaal-economische geschiedenis van Nederland van de vroegste tijden tot het einde van de Middeleeuwen* (1964), a social and economic history of the northern Netherlands during the Middle Ages, with emphasis on the economic aspects (the chapters on the Frisian trade and the trade of the 10th till the 13th century, written by J.F. NIERMEYER, belong to the best parts of the book); E. DE MOREAU, *Histoire de l'Église en Belgique,* 5 vol. with a suppl. vol. containing maps (1945–52), an extensive classic handbook of the church history of the southern Netherlands, containing exhaustive bibliographies; R.R. POST, *Kerkgeschiedenis van Nederland in de Middeleeuwen,* 2 vol. (1957), an extensive handbook of the church history of the northern Netherlands; D.P. BLOK, *De Franken (in Nederland), hun optreden in het licht der historie* (1968), a brilliant synthesis of the early history of the northern Netherlands; P.C.J.A. BOELES, *Friesland tot de elfde eeuw: Zijn vóór- en vroege geschiedenis,* 2nd ed. (1951; with an index by H.T. OBREEN, 1962), an authoritative work on the early Frisian history, with an English summary, pp. 559–598; D. JELLEMA, "Frisian Trade in the Dark Ages," *Speculum,* 30:15–36 (1955), a careful survey of Frisian trade and its background in the Merovingian period, drawing especially on archaeological and numismatic evidence; F.L. GANSHOF, *La Flandre sous les premiers comtes* (1948), a solid account of the history of the important principality of Flanders, tracing its origins and ending with the eventful crisis of 1127–28; H.S. LUCAS, *The Low Countries and the Hundred Years' War, 1326–1347* (1929), a very reliable and richly documented account of political events; R. VAUGHAN, *Philip the Bold: The Formation of the Burgundian State* (1962), *John the Fearless: The Growth of Burgundian Power* (1966), and *Philip the Good: The Apogee of Burgundy* (1970), well-documented studies of the Burgundian dukes and the growth of their political power; J. HUIZINGA, *Herfsttij der Middeleeuwen* (1921; Eng. trans., *The Waning of the Middle Ages: A Study in the Forms of Life, Thought and Art in France and the Netherlands in the 14th and 15th Centuries,* 1924), a classical work of cultural historical value; R.R. POST, *The Modern Devotion: Confrontation with Reformation and Humanism* (1968), the most recent and exhaustive work, based on old and new sources, with emphasis on the relationship between Modern Devotion and Humanism and the Reformation; G.N. CLARK, "The Birth of the Dutch Republic," in *Studies in History,* pp. 112–144 (1966), written with solid knowledge about the subject; *Geschiedkundige Atlas van Nederland,* 3 vol. of maps and 15 vol. of text (1911–38).

The Netherlands since 1579: H. DE BUCK, *Bibliografie der Geschiedenis van Nederland* (1968), the standard guide to the historical literature, primarily of the northern Low Countries; J.L. MOTLEY, *The Rise of the Dutch Republic,* 3 vol. (1856) and *History of the United Netherlands from the Death of William the Silent to The Twelve Years' Truce, 1609,* 4 vol. (1860–67), brilliantly written histories, rich with information, although highly partisan; P. GEYL, *Geschiedenis van de Nederlandsche Stam,* 2nd ed., 2 vol. (1948–49; rev. ed., 6 vol., 1961–62; Eng. trans., *The Revolt of the Netherlands Against Spain, 1555–1609,* 2nd ed., 1958; and *The Netherlands in the Seven-*

teenth Century, rev. ed., 2vol., 1961–64), partial English translations of Geyl's monumental work in which the linguistic-ethnic unity of the Dutch-speaking Low Countries is emphasized; and *History of the Low Countries: Episodes and Problems* (1964), a series of lectures carrying Geyl's analysis to the period after World War II; J. HUIZINGA, *Nederland's Beschaving in de Zeventiende Eeuw* (1941; Eng. trans., *Dutch Civilisation in the Seventeenth Century, and Other Essays*, 1941 and 1969), a masterpiece of condensation and illumination; C.R. BOXER, *The Dutch Sea-Borne Empire, 1600–1800* (1965), a vigorously written and well-informed account; C.H. WILSON, *The Dutch Republic and the Civilization of the Seventeenth Century* (1968) and *Profit and Power: A Study of England and the Dutch Wars* (1957), by the outstanding English historian of The Netherlands; A. COBBAN, *Ambassadors and Secret Agents: The Diplomacy of The First Earl of Malmesbury at the Hague* (1954), on the counterrevolution of 1787; A.J. BARNOUW, *Holland Under Queen Wilhelmina* (1923); A. LIJPHART, *The Politics of Accommodation: Pluralism and Democracy in the Netherlands* (1968), a sociological study of "pillarization," fundamental for the contemporary period.

Southern Netherlands, Belgium, and Luxembourg—1579 to the present: C. VERLINDEN, *En Flandre sous Philippe II: Durée de la crise économique* (1952); *Documents pour l'histoire des prix et des salaires en Flandre et en Brabant, XIVe–XIXe siècles*, 3 vol. (1959–65); H. VAN DER WEE, *The Growth of the Antwerp Market and the European Economy in the 14th and 16th Centuries*, 3 vol. (1963), until 1619; J. CRAEYBECKX, "Les industries d'exportation dans les villes flamandes au XVIIe siècle, particulièrement à Gand et à Bruges," in *Studi in onore di A. Fanfani*, vol. 4 (1962); H. COPPEJANS-DESMEDT, *Bijdrage tot de studie van de gegoede burgerij te Gent in de XVIIIe eeuw: De vorming van een nieuwe sociaal-economische stand ten tijde van Maria-Theresia* (1952), a study of the well-to-do middle class in Ghent during the 18th century and the formation of a new socio-economic class under Maria Theresa; P. LEBRUN, *L'industrie de la laine à Verviers pendant le XVIIIe et le début du XIXe siècle* (1948); P. HARSIN, *La révolution liégeoise de 1789* (1954). (French and Dutch rule): J. CRAEYBECKX, *Les Statistiques de la fin de l'Empire et le début de la révolution industrielle en Belgique* (1968). (Belgium and Luxembourg—1831 to the present): B.S. CHLEPNER, *Cent ans d'histoire sociale en Belgique* (1956); P. WEBER, *Histoire du Grand-Duché de Luxembourg* (1949); A.H. COOPER-PRICHARD, *History of the Grand Duchy of Luxembourg* (1947); FRANK E. HUGGETT, *Modern Belgium* (1969).

(C.v.d.K./H.Ro./J.C.V.)

Low-Temperature Phenomena

The term low-temperature phenomena refers to the behaviour of matter at temperatures below the boiling point of liquid nitrogen, about $-196°$ C ($-321°$ F). At temperatures close to absolute zero ($-273.2°$ C [$-459.7°$ F]) the thermal, electric, and magnetic properties of many substances undergo great change, and, indeed, the behaviour of matter may seem strange when compared to that at room temperature. Superconductivity and superfluidity can be cited as two such phenomena that occur below certain critical temperatures; in the former, many metals and alloys show no resistance whatsoever to the flow of electricity, and, in the latter, liquid helium can flow through tiny holes impervious to any other liquid.

Although the phenomena displayed by matter at low temperatures are many and diverse, they constitute a coherent body of study by virtue of the second law of thermodynamics (see THERMODYNAMICS, PRINCIPLES OF), which *Entropy* introduces the concept of entropy and provides a criterion for the direction of spontaneous change to a final equilibrium condition for any system at fixed absolute temperature, T. A system may be thought of as an isolated assemblage of a large number of particles; *i.e.*, a group of atoms, molecules, subatomic particles, or some combination of them. The macro (large scale) state of a system as a whole can be described by a few thermodynamic (*i.e.*, macro) variables such as pressure, volume, energy, entropy, and temperature. These few constraints can usually be satisfied by a tremendous number of arrangements (micro ways) of the modes of motion of the constituent particles in the system. Entropy is a measure of this number of detailed, different possible micro states open to the macro system, and it increases as this number increases.

The only changes a system can undergo at constant temperature to reach a final equilibrium macro state at that temperature are those for which the expression $\Delta U - T\Delta S$ is negative. The symbol ΔU means the magnitude of U after the change, less the magnitude of U before the change, and similarly for ΔS. $T\Delta S$ signifies temperature times change in entropy. The symbol U denotes the energy of the system or a closely related quantity, depending on what additional constraints beyond that of constant temperature (such as constant pressure or constant volume) are imposed on the system. The symbol S denotes the entropy of the system. As the temperature goes toward absolute zero ($T = 0$), the second term in the expression becomes of smaller and smaller magnitude, such that the only processes that can finally occur are those with ΔU negative, meaning only those processes that decrease the energy of the system. This significant unifying principle can be applied to all low-temperature phenomena.

Extremely tiny energy differences, the effects of which are not observable at ordinary temperatures, can be of great importance in arriving at a final observable low-temperature configuration—that is, physical arrangement —of the particles of a system. For physical science, the low-temperature region is an important field of study, because only within its confines can there be experimental elucidation of the nature of the interactions leading to the above-mentioned tiny energy differences. The effects manifested are often novel and unique, and in the case of superconductivity (see below *Superconductivity*) they are also of great technological importance.

Finally, there is a fundamental reason behind the fact that many phenomena not peculiar to the low-temperature region are best studied at low temperatures. The atomicity of the surroundings causes irregular fluctuations or noise in any measurable physical variable of a system such that the mean square fluctuation in any observable at equilibrium is directly proportional to the absolute temperature. Working at low temperatures thus means an enhanced sensitivity for all instruments in distinguishing real physical phenomena from background thermal noise.

GENERAL LOW-TEMPERATURE PHYSICAL PHENOMENA

The third law of thermodynamics. In addition to a deduction from the second law of thermodynamics, that a system will assume its lowest energy value as the temperature goes to zero, there is a deduction from the third law of thermodynamics, that in most cases the entropy change (ΔS) itself in the above expression goes to zero at the absolute zero. This rule in turn suggests that for all systems the entropies converge to the same constant value (conventionally zero) at the absolute zero irrespective of state, or phase, of aggregation (solid, liquid, or gas) or chemical nature of the substance. This rule further means that, for an entropy of zero, the minimum energy states reached must be ones of complete order; *i.e.*, that the constituent particles can be arranged in only one way, even from the point of view of microscopic modes of motion. The third law is best understood on the basis of the quantum-mechanical result that particles acquire or lose energy in quantized amounts and not in a continuous manner, as *Quantized* was assumed in classical, Newtonian mechanics, and that *energy* the number of particles having an energy, symbolized by *states* the Greek letter epsilon, ε, greater than the minimum energy is proportional to an exponential value of minus the energy difference divided by a universal constant of nature (k) times absolute temperature (T); *i.e.*, $e^{-\varepsilon/kT}$. Unless the product kT is numerically as large as ε, the number of particles in excited states (any state having more energy than the minimum) is small, and for zero temperature the number of particles is zero. Hence, at low temperature almost all particles will be in the configuration of lowest energy that can be arrived at only in one way, such that their entropy is zero. The third law as formulated above is not always observed to hold experimentally; this fact is believed to be not a failure of the principle but a result of the slow rates of transformation in the solid phase from higher to lower energy configurations, leaving the former unchanged for some substances. Because of the uncertainty principle of quantum physics

—*i.e.*, that it is fundamentally impossible to determine simultaneously both the location and momentum of a particle—even at absolute zero there is not a complete cessation of particle motion, as would be predicted from the classical view that temperature is directly proportional to the average kinetic energy of the particles. There remains an ineradicable zero-point vibratory motion of particles about the lattice sites in a solid (*i.e.*, positions that atoms would assume when at rest in a crystal structure) and a kinetic zero-point motion in a fluid. Indeed, the latter condition explains the fact that the two isotopes (atoms of the same element that have a difference in mass) of helium, helium-3 and helium-4, both remain liquid under their own vapour pressure when the temperature is reduced to absolute zero and can be solidified only by the application of an external mechanical pressure. The kinetic zero-point energy is inversely proportional to the particle mass and so is greatest for small masses. Although hydrogen molecules are lighter than helium atoms, hydrogen is solid for all pressures at absolute zero, because the attractive potential energy between two hydrogen molecules is much greater than the attraction between helium atoms, thus preventing the motion that characterizes liquids. The same argument shows that all other particles (atomic and subatomic) except electrons will also be in solid form at absolute zero. For electrons the Coulomb attractive force (the force between a negative and a positive charge) operative in their parent atoms or molecules serves to hold them localized in small regions of space except for metals, in which one or more electrons per atom are released into an electronic cloud that permeates the entire metallic volume. These metallic electrons are free to move at the lowest temperatures and can undergo an ordering process into the superconducting state if the electronic and lattice structure of the ions (charged molecules or atoms) is appropriate.

Heat capacity.   The loss of entropy in a substance as its temperature is reduced can be followed experimentally in detail by measuring its heat capacity under defined conditions as a function of temperature. Operationally, the heat capacity, C, is obtained by dividing a known heat-energy input to a system by its observed resulting tempera-

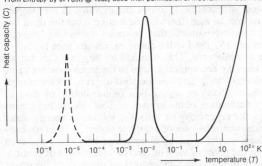

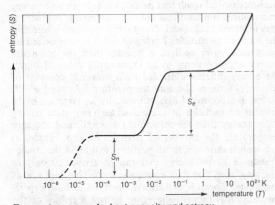

Temperature curves for heat capacity and entropy.
(Top) Heat capacity as a function of temperature. (Bottom) Entropy as a function of the temperature for a paramagnetic substance, the nuclei of which possess a magnetic moment. S_e is the maximum entropy of the electron spins, S_n that of the nuclear spins.

ture change. Theoretically, the heat capacity is equal to the temperature times the rate of change of entropy with temperature. Whenever there is a large entropy change in a small temperature interval, the change will show up as a peak in the heat-capacity, C, curve (see the Figure, top). In some cases these peaks may even represent an infinite heat-capacity value at one specific temperature, although this condition can never be strictly checked experimentally. It can be shown that the contribution to the heat capacity of masses vibrating about the lattice sites of a solid (the lattice contribution) can never give a peak in the heat-capacity curve. All such peaks are caused by the very or moderately sudden onset of an ordering process among other than the vibrational set of energy levels (energy states visualized as a series of levels) as the temperature is lowered. Some of the different physical systems exhibiting this behaviour may be described.

For solids with polyatomic molecules or ions on the lattice sites, there are, in addition to the vibration of the centre of mass, free rotational modes of motion of the group about the mass centre. These rotational modes have quantized energy states (expressed in finite increments) differing very slightly in energy; and, effectively, all such states will be equally occupied (*i.e.*, equally probable), giving rise to a relatively high entropy contribution. As the temperature drops and the fixed small energy differences become large compared to the product of the universal constant (k) and the absolute temperature (T), kT, only the lowest states will tend to be occupied, the entropy will drop, and the previously free rotation will turn into a hindered type scarcely different from a vibratory mode. The change from free to hindered rotation can be of avalanche proportions, resulting in a heat-capacity peak, because the behaviour at neighbouring lattice sites is correlated; this condition comes about because when one group quits its free rotation it is easier for adjoining groups to quit also. This is a typical cooperative phenomenon.

Magnetism and conductivity.   Every electron has the property of spin, or rotation about its own axis, which results in a mechanical property called angular momentum (a measure of momentum around an axis) and an associated magnetic dipole moment (a measure of the resistance to twisting in a magnetic field). For molecules and ions in solids at low temperatures, the coupling (combining effect) of the spin angular momenta determines the total magnetic moment of the groups as a whole. These magnetic moments at different sites can be aligned in an external magnetic field, giving rise to a magnetic property called paramagnetism (capacity to be weakly magnetized). Another magnetic property, ferromagnetism (capacity to be strongly magnetized), occurs when there is a spontaneous preferential parallel alignment of the magnetic moments in the absence of an external field; but ferromagnetism cannot be the result of a direct interaction of neighbouring magnetic moments; otherwise, contrary to experiment, all paramagnetic substances would become ferromagnetic at sufficiently low temperatures. The interaction responsible for ferromagnetism arises from the change in electronic spatial charge distribution between neighbours that, by the laws of quantum mechanics, inevitably accompanies the change of relative direction (*i.e.*, the axis of rotation) of neighbouring spins. Below a certain temperature at which there is a sharp peak in the heat capacity, called, for a 19th-century French physicist, Pierre Curie, the Curie temperature, the preferential parallel spin alignment can maintain itself against the randomizing influence of thermal motion. In some materials there can occur a preferentially ordered antiparallel arrangement of neighbouring spins below a certain temperature (Néel temperature, after a French physicist, Louis-Eugène-Félix Néel). This is the case of antiferromagnetism. Whereas most Curie temperatures are higher than the boiling point of nitrogen, many Néel temperatures occur in the low-temperature region as defined by this article.

The behaviour of mixtures as the temperature is lowered also exhibits several interesting methods of entropy reduction. In certain stoichiometric alloys (*i.e.*, alloys in

Vibrational and rotational energies

Order–
disorder
heat
capacity

which the relative number of various atoms is given by the ratio of small integers, 1:1, 1:2, etc.) below an ordering temperature, a single solid phase consisting of two interpenetrating lattices with only one species of atom on each lattice becomes favoured. This condition is manifested by a heat-capacity peak called order–disorder type. For nonstoichiometric alloys, several different ordered phases of different composition can result. In other cases below a critical point a first-order phase separation (see PHASE CHANGES AND EQUILIBRIA) may occur such that at the absolute zero two phases, possibly but not necessarily both pure, should exist physically separated from each other. This last behaviour is usually masked by the freezing in of nonequilibrium configurations. Helium-3–helium-4 mixtures, however, remain liquid to lowest temperatures, and these do separate into a pure helium-3 component and a mixture of the two isotopes.

In metals the released electrons can move coherently (in unison) under the influence of an external electric field, thus giving rise to the characteristic high conductivity of metals. The moving electrons are impeded by the vibrational motion of the lattice ions; and, because this motion is reduced as the temperature is lowered, the conductivity is greatly improved thereby. Defects in the lattice and impurities, or both, play a large role in the final low-temperature conductivity, and the study of these defects constitutes an important part of modern solid-state physics. On the other hand, the conductivity of semiconductors (substances the conductivity of which is increased at high temperatures) is greatly decreased as the temperature is lowered because the electrons in these substances are not free to move until they surmount a fixed energy barrier, and the lower the temperature, the fewer electrons there are with energy enough to break free.

SPECIAL PHYSICAL PHENOMENA
AT VERY LOW TEMPERATURES

The lack of spatial order for electrons in metals and for helium atoms in liquid helium, even at absolute zero, permits the most striking macroscopic effects of quantum mechanics known to science, because these systems lose their entropy by various means of momentum ordering. The momentum of a particle is its mass times velocity, and a momentum ordering in a system of like particles implies the possible generation of a stable, coherent, flowing mass of electrons or helium atoms.

Superconductivity. The existence of superconductivity (q.v.) exemplifies the above considerations in the case of electrons. All superconductors have the fundamental property of suddenly losing all their electrical resistance below a critical temperature, T_c, characteristic of each. Superconductors may be divided into Type I, mainly pure elements with T_c less than 10° K (and the majority with T_c less than 5° K), and Type II, usually alloys or compounds with T_c values generally higher than those of Type I, although none are yet known with T_c above 21° K (0° K equals about −273° C [−460° F]). The ordinary electrical resistance of Type I superconductors may be restored on application of a magnetic field, H_c, that depends on temperature, being zero at the critical temperatures and tending to a maximum field, H_o measured in oersteds, never much above 10^3 and often below 10^2) as the temperature goes to zero. In the superconducting state, Type I specimens are perfect diamagnetic materials; that is, they expel all magnetic flux (i.e., are devoid of a magnetic field) from their interior. Type II superconductors below the critical temperature may be driven into a mixed state along a lower critical-field curve, Hc_1. The mixed state can contain normal regions open to magnetic flux but remains superconducting below a much higher upper critical-field curve, Hc_2.

A generally successful microscopic theory of superconductivity (introduced in 1957 by United States physicists John Bardeen, John Cooper, and John Schrieffer and often referred to as the BCS theory) showed that, below the critical temperature, pairs of electrons with equal but opposite momenta and opposed spins (thus being diamagnetic entities) could maintain themselves against thermal excitation in a state of lower energy than that of

Type I
and Type II
super-
conductors

a randomly chosen pair with uncorrelated momenta. Their proposed mechanism leading to this attractive interaction was an indirect one involving an initial encounter of the first electron with a vibrating ion of the metallic lattice and a subsequent encounter of its partner with the same vibrating mode. The members of a pair are not spatially close to one another and may be separated by distances equal to several thousand times the distance between two adjacent lattice sites. The paired electrons, having a perfectly definite total momentum (zero if no net current is flowing or some common finite value if a current has been started), by the uncertainty principle of quantum mechanics cannot have their centre of mass localized in any particular region of the metallic volume. They can be said to move without momentum change (i.e., without meeting resistance) through the entire macroscopic specimen, just as on the microscopic level electrons in a single atom or molecule move coherently in their respective orbitals. It has become evident since the original theory was set forth that other mechanisms than the electron–vibrating-ion interaction do lead to bound electron pairs and thus to superconductivity. The elucidation of the nature of these interactions is a current field of active research.

Superfluidity. The superfluid properties of liquid helium-4 are heralded by a seemingly infinite lambda- (λ-) shaped heat-capacity peak at a temperature $T_\lambda = 2.2°$ K as the liquid is cooled under its own vapour pressure (see NOBLE GASES AND THEIR COMPOUNDS). Below the lambda temperature the liquid has a thermal conductivity some 3,000,000 times that of the liquid just above the lambda temperature, and it can flow or, at least, a part of it can flow without friction and without entropy transport through tiny capillaries and through leaks that just above T_λ are impassable not only to liquid but to gaseous helium-4. Many other strange phenomena have been investigated.

Early contributions to a theoretical understanding of liquid helium-4 behaviour by two physicists, Polish-born Fritz London and Lev Landau of the Soviet Union, were originally believed to exclude one another, but, with the later work of Richard Feynman and Chen Ning Yang, United States physicists, and a Norwegian chemist, Lars Onsager, their approaches have been seen to be complementary. Following London's interpretation, stress is put on the fact that helium-4 atoms are bosons; i.e., that they contain an even number of elementary particles (electrons, protons, neutrons) and as such any number of them can occupy the same quantum state of momentum. Fermions, on the other hand, of which helium-3 is an example, contain an odd number of elementary particles, and no more than a few (only two if they have minimum nuclear or electronic spin values) can occupy the same momentum quantum state. It is assumed that below the lambda temperature a finite fraction of the helium-4 atoms are condensed into the zero momentum state with zero entropy and that these constitute a superfluid component in the liquid. This component is not spatially condensed but distributed uniformly through the liquid in a way not unlike the paired electrons of superconductivity theory. In fact a pair of electrons is a boson.

Liquid helium-3 does not exhibit the superfluid properties of liquid helium-4, thus strengthening the belief that these properties are a result of a boson momentum ordering. Whether or not the helium-3 atoms as fermions will undergo a momentum ordering analogous to that of superconducting electrons is an open question, and no firm experimental evidence of it had been found by the early 1970s down to a temperature of $5 \times 10^{-3°}$ K.

Theory of
helium-4
behaviour

SPECIAL METHODS FOR OBTAINING LOW TEMPERATURES

Adiabatic cooling. When changes are made in a closed or isolated system without gain or loss of heat, the phenomenon is adiabatic. For example, an expanding gas that neither gains nor loses heat is expanding adiabatically. Primary gas thermometry depends on the variation in pressure of a gas with temperature and as such provides a temperature scale independent of the properties of any particular substance. The relation of this scale ($T°$ K) to the Celsius scale ($t°$ C) is $T = t + 273.15$, such that absolute zero is $-273.15°$ C. A convenient way of experimentally determining low temperature is to measure the vapour pressure of a sample of liquefied gas in thermal equilibrium with the sample the temperature of which is desired. This measurement requires use of tables of temperature as a function of the vapour pressure. To prepare these tables a few primary gas thermometric measurements must be made, which are supplemented at intermediate temperatures by simultaneously measuring the vapour pressure and one or more physical properties of an inserted probe that can be related to the temperature by means of empirical equations. These equations must express the probe property as a function of temperature and of a few constants the values of which are known by direct measurement of the probe property and the temperature at a few points. Use of the electrical resistance of certain pure metals or of carbon and the magnetic susceptibility of certain paramagnetic salts is common. Vapour-pressure thermometry with liquid helium-4 can be carried down to about 1° K and with liquid helium-3 to about 0.3° K.

By the third law of thermodynamics it is impossible to reduce the temperature of any sample precisely to zero, but in practice temperatures as low as $10^{-5}°$ K have been attained. Various liquefied gases boiling off under reduced pressure can serve admirably to cool samples down to about 1° K. To liquefy these gases they may be compressed to high pressure at a constant temperature (the heat generated by the compression being transferred via an exchange gas in an intermediate chamber to a liquid that can vaporize at constant temperature) and then isolated thermally (*i.e.*, heat is not allowed to flow in or out of the system) and allowed to expand to low pressure. In the expansion, work is done by the gas, and thus it cools. A series of such steps may be needed until the gas is cooled below its critical temperature and a portion of it liquefies. Alternatively, a process based on the Joule–Thomson phenomenon of adiabatic stationary flow can be made use of. In this process, when a gas flows through a porous plug or expansion valve from a constant high pressure to a constant low pressure, it undergoes a temperature change that depends in sign and magnitude on a balance between the cooling effect of increasing the separation of the molecules and the heating effect of work being done on the gas in pushing it through the valve. At low enough initial temperature and pressure, the effect is a cooling one. An initial expansion technique is quite often used to cool a gas until it is ready for a final Joule–Thomson liquefaction.

To cool a substance below $T_0 = 1°$ K there must exist one or more sets of energy levels with spacings still smaller than kT_0, the entropy of which can be manipulated by varying an external parameter (quantity). In practice there are two such sets of energy levels available: states of net electron-spin–magnetic-dipole orientations associated with paramagnetic atoms and states of nuclear-spin–magnetic-dipole orientations associated with some atomic nuclei. It was suggested in 1926–27, independently by the Dutch physicist Peter Debye and the American William Giauque, that, if electron spins could be isothermally (*i.e.*, without change in temperature) ordered at about 1° K in an external magnetic field, thus removing much of their entropy by evolving heat that could be conducted away, then a subsequent adiabatic demagnetization (being practically a constant entropy process in which energy is lost; *i.e.*, work is done by the spin system as the field is turned off) would result in a much lowered temperature for the spin system. This loss would then result in a lowered temperature for the paramagnetic salt, and any sample in contact with it, as these would have a negligible heat capacity compared with that of the spins. Temperatures as low as $10^{-2}°$ to $10^{-3}°$ K have been obtained with this widely used technique. The curves in the Figure (bottom) show the usual heat-capacity peaks corresponding to rapid entropy decreases, as first the electronic spins settle into their lowest orientational state determined by the interactions that exist in the crystal, even in the absence of an external

field, and then at still lower temperature as the nuclear spins are ordered. The energy exchanges leading to the final low temperature are controlled by the hump in the electronic heat capacity; the minimum reached will always be in the neighbourhood of the temperature of that peak for the paramagnetic salt used. To reach temperatures in the region of the peak of the nuclear-spin heat capacity, extremely high magnetic fields are needed to order the spins, even starting from temperatures of $10^{-2}°$ K attained by an initial salt demagnetization. Thus this method, first carried out in 1956 by a Hungarian physicist, Nicholas Kurti, when a temperature of about $10^{-5}°$ K was attained in the nuclear spin system but not in the sample as a whole, is seldom used.

Temperature measurement below 1° K is carried out by measurement of the magnetic susceptibility of a paramagnetic salt and then relating this property to the absolute-temperature scale. This last procedure must be done separately for each salt, by determining the susceptibility change for known heat inputs and for known entropy changes arising from demagnetization experiments from known liquid-helium temperatures. (For a general survey of low-temperature applications, see CRYOGENICS, APPLICATIONS OF.)

Adiabatic dilution. Another technique to obtain temperatures to about $10^{-2}°$ K, originally suggested by German physicist Heinz London in 1951 but only experimentally realized since 1965, is the adiabatic dilution of liquid helium-3 by liquid helium-4. It is difficult to explain without mathematical formulation, and only a brief reference to the principles can be made here. Below 0.1° K there is a small, nearly constant limiting solubility of helium-3 in concentrated helium-4 that persists to absolute zero. At the starting temperatures of about 0.5° K reached in ordinary liquid helium-3, helium-4 is entirely superfluid with zero entropy, providing a noninteracting inert background for the helium-3, which in concentrated solutions behaves like a pseudo-one-component liquid and in dilute solutions like a pseudo-one-component gas. The crucial step for cooling, which is a dilution of a concentrated helium-3 solution across the two-phase region to the dilute side, is thus analogous to an ordinary adiabatic evaporation of a liquid. Continuous-refrigeration devices based on this technique have been developed.

BIBLIOGRAPHY. F.E. SIMON *et al.*, *Low Temperature Physics: Four Lectures* (1952), classic nontechnical presentation; K. MENDELSSOHN, *The Quest for Absolute Zero: The Meaning of Low Temperature Physics* (1966), an excellent nontechnical summary; F. LONDON, *Superfluids*, vol. 1, *Macroscopic Theory of Superconductivity* (1950), vol. 2, *Macroscopic Theory of Superfluid Helium* (1954), the classic presentation of theory; G.K. WHITE, *Experimental Techniques in Low-Temperature Physics*, 2nd ed. (1968), detailed information on practical problems of experimentation in the low-temperature range; S. FLUGGE (ed.), *Handbuch der Physik*, vol. 14–15 (1956), technical articles in English with full bibliographies on all aspects of low-temperature phenomena, theoretical and experimental, up to 1955; C.J. GORTER (ed.), *Progress in Low Temperature Physics*, 6 vol. (1955–70), theoretical and experimental research reports and review articles, all with extensive bibliographies; K. MENDELSSOHN (ed.), *Progress in Cryogenics* (1959–70), complements the Gorter series, with more emphasis on applied problems and developments; H.M. ROSENBERG, *Low Temperature Solid State Physics* (1963), a fairly elementary treatment; C.G. KUPER, *An Introduction to the Theory of Superconductivity* (1968), and W.E. KELLER, *Helium-3 and Helium-4* (1969), modern advanced-level summaries of theory; A.C. ROSE-INNES and E.H. RHODERICK, *Introduction to Superconductivity* (1969), more emphasis on application; M. SITTIG, *Cryogenics: Research and Applications* (1963), a discussion of the applications of low-temperature phenomena. Articles on this subject appear regularly in *Cryogenics*, an international journal of low-temperature engineering and research, and in the *Journal of Low Temperature Physics* (both bimonthly).

(C.E.He.)

Lo-yang

Lo-yang (in Pin-yin romanization also Lo-yang; formerly Honan-fu and commonly called Honan), a city in northwest Honan Province, China, on the Lunghai Railway (joining Soochow with Sian), was important in Chinese history as the capital for several ruling dynasties and as a Buddhist centre. Lo-yang is a busy commercial hub and the site of a tractor plant important to the whole Chinese economy.

Lo-yang's position on the north bank of the Lo River, between the Ch'an and Chien rivers, is comparatively high and formerly was held to be so defensible that "one man could resist ten thousand." Lo-yang is divided into an east town and a west town, about one mile (two kilometres) apart. The smaller west town has an airfield and a military parade ground.

Historical beginnings

At the beginning of the Chou dynasty (late 12th century BC) the "royal city of Chou" was founded at Lo-i, thought to be near the present west town of Lo-yang, while the Chou capital remained at Hao Ching, near Ch'ang-an, in Shensi. In 771 BC King P'ing of Chou built a new capital on a site thought to be near Chien-hsi-ch'ih, just west of the present city of Lo-yang. The 11 succeeding Chou kings ruled there. King Ching (ruled 519–476 BC) moved the capital to a site about seven miles (11.5 kilometres) northeast of the present east town; it was named Lo-yang because it was north (*yang*) of the River Lo, and its ruins are now distinguished as the ancient city (*ku-ch'eng*) of Lo-yang.

The city of the Han period (206 BC–AD 220), west of the present town, was approximately on the site of the ancient Lo-i but was called Lo-yang. This name alternated with the name Honan-fu until modern times. Lo-yang did not become the Han capital until the 1st century AD, at the beginning of the Eastern Han period, though its economic importance had been recognized earlier. In AD 68 the Pai-ma-ssu, or "White Horse Temple," one of the earliest Buddhist foundations in China, was built about nine miles (14 kilometres) east of the modern east town. As capital of the Western Chin dynasty (AD 265–317), Lo-yang had walls measuring about 4.5 miles (7.5 kilometres) from east to west and about 3.6 miles from north to south and had a population of some scores of thousands.

During the 4th century Lo-yang changed hands several times between the rulers of Eastern Chin, Later Chao, and Yen, and it did not prosper again until 494. In that year the emperor Hsiao Wen of the Toba (Turkic) state of Northern Wei decided to move from near Ta-t'ung in Shansi to the more southerly Lo-yang, in order to take advantage of its strategic position to exercise his power over the whole of North China. Much of Lo-yang had been destroyed by war, and Hsiao Wen and his successors aimed at restoring the splendours of the Han metropolis.

Expansion of the city

The city was rapidly expanded to include 333 sections, craftsmen and traders were attracted, three markets were organized, and the residential quarter of merchants and artisans vied with the great houses of the nobles and officials. Lo-yang's population rose to 40,000. The city became noted for its money lenders, musicians, workers in precious metals, its pleasures and fine wine, and the elegance of its funeral furnishings. Its trade went forth in every direction.

At Lung-men (properly I-ch'üeh Lung-men, the "Dragon Gates of the I Peaks"), about nine miles (14 kilometres) south of Lo-yang, the Northern Wei emperors saw to the excavation of cave temples in limestone cliffs facing each other across the east–west I River. This inaugurated one of the greatest centres of Chinese Buddhism, the surviving sculptures of which are of prime importance to the history of Chinese art. The style in the Ku-yang cave, begun in 495, marks a decided shift from earlier styles toward a more characteristic Chinese manner. The sculpture style of the Pin-yang triple cave, begun in 505, takes a further step in adaptation to native taste. Both caves reflect the growing ascendancy of Chinese interpretations of Buddhist doctrine. Further caves were excavated before the end of Northern Wei rule in 535 (notably the Lien-hua and Wei-tzu caves); but thereafter work ceased until 570, when the Yao-fang cave was begun. The latest group of caves was begun, and all were mostly completed, in the reign of the T'ang emperor Kao Tsung (ruled 649–683).

In the T'ang period (618–907) Lo-yang was expanded to unprecedented size, and the part now constituting the east town was created, evidently to make Lo-yang the chief city in the national economy; Lo-yang was designated the eastern T'ang capital (Ch'ang-an in Shensi being the capital proper). Three markets that had been established in the Sui period (581–618) were reorganized, the streets were redivided into several hundred sections, and workers were separated according to their trades. But after a rebellion in the mid-8th century, Lo-yang fell into an economic decline, which lasted until recent times. From the later T'ang period economic primacy passed to the southern provinces around the lower Yangtze River.

The T'ang period

With a population approaching 500,000 in the 1970s, Lo-yang was one of the leading industrial towns of China's interior; it was an important trade centre and a processor of cotton, wheat, and other crops grown in the region. The Khaikov tractor works in Moscow trained 173 management personnel and technical cadres for the No. 1 Tractor Plant, which was established in Lo-yang in November 1959. Also built were a plant for mining machinery and a thermoelectric plant to take advantage of the deposits of hard coal in the vicinity.

Excavations recently carried out at Chung-chou-lu on the supposed site of Lo-i discovered tombs ranging in date from the 9th–8th centuries BC to the 2nd century AD. Tombs of the Han period were excavated on the edge of the modern city at Shao-kou.

BIBLIOGRAPHY. An important early account of the city is *Lo-yang chia-lan chi* by YANG HSUAN, a description of the the temples of Lo-yang, written in the early 6th century. For the role of Lo-yang in Buddhist art, see the standard work by L.C. SICKMAN and A. SOPER, *The Art and Architecture of China*, 3rd ed. (1968). References to Lo-yang are to be found in general histories, such as W. EBERHARD, *Chinas Geschichte* (1948; Eng. trans., *A History of China*, 1950); and C.P. FITZGERALD, *China: A Short Cultural History*, 3rd ed. rev. (1961). W.C. WHITE, *Tombs of Old Lo-yang* (1934), is the only specialized account in a Western language of archaeological finds made at the site of the ancient city. For the contemporary scene, see references in E. STUART KIRBY (ed.), *Contemporary China*, vol. 6 (1968); and J. WILSON LEWIS (ed.), *The City in Communist China* (1971).

(W.W.)

Loyola, Saint Ignatius of

St. Ignatius of Loyola, the founder of the Society of Jesus (Jesuits), was one of the most influential figures of the Catholic Reformation of the 16th century.

Early life. He was born in the ancestral castle of the Loyolas in the Basque province of Guipúzcoa, Spain, in 1491. The youngest son of a noble and wealthy family, Ignatius became, in 1506, a page in the service of a relative, Juan Velázquez de Cuéllar, treasurer of the kingdom of Castile. In 1517 Ignatius passed as a knight into the service of another relative, Antonio Manrique de Lara, duke of Nájera and viceroy of Navarre, who em-

Military career

By courtesy of the Archivum Romanum Societatis Iesu

St. Ignatius of Loyola, death mask.

ployed him in military undertakings and on a diplomatic mission. While defending the citadel of Pamplona against the French, Ignatius was hit by a cannonball on May 20, 1521, sustaining a bad fracture of his right leg and damage to his left. This event closed the first period of his life, during which he was, on his own admission, "a man given to the vanities of the world, whose chief delight consisted in martial exercises, with a great and vain desire to win renown" (*Autobiography*, 1). Although his morals were far from stainless, Ignatius was in his early years a proud rather than sensual man. He stood just under five feet two inches in height and had in his youth an abundance of hair of a reddish tint. He delighted in music, especially sacred hymns.

Period of reorientation. It is the second period of Ignatius' life, in which he turned toward a saintly life, that is the better known. After treatment at Pamplona, he was transported to Loyola in June 1521. There his condition became so serious that for a time it was thought he would die. When out of danger, he chose to undergo painful surgery to correct blunders made when the bone was first set. The result was a convalescence of many weeks, during which he read a life of Christ and a book on the lives of the saints, the only reading matter the castle afforded. He also passed time in recalling tales of martial valour and in thinking of a great lady whom he admired. In the early stages of this enforced reading, his attention was centred on the saints. The version of the lives of the saints he was reading contained prologues to the various lives by a Cistercian monk who conceived the service of God as a holy chivalry. This view of life profoundly moved and attracted Ignatius. After much reflection, he resolved to imitate the holy austerities of the saints in order to do penance for his sins.

In February 1522 Ignatius bade farewell to his family and went to Montserrat, a place of pilgrimage in northeastern Spain. He spent three days in confessing the sins of his whole life, hung his sword and dagger near the statue of the Virgin Mary as symbols of his abandoned ambitions, and, clothed in sackcloth, spent the night of March 24 in prayer. The next day he went to Manresa, a town 30 miles from Barcelona, to pass the decisive months of his career, from March 25, 1522, to mid-February 1523. He lived as a beggar, ate and drank sparingly, scourged himself, and for a time neither combed nor trimmed his hair and did not cut his nails. Daily he attended mass and spent seven hours in prayer, often in a cave outside Manresa.

The Spiritual Exercises

The sojourn at Manresa was marked by spiritual trials as well as by joy and interior light. While sitting one day on the banks of Cardoner River, "the eyes of his understanding began to open and, without seeing any vision, he understood and knew many things, as well spiritual things as things of the faith" (*Autobiography*, 30). At Manresa, he sketched the fundamentals of his little book *The Spiritual Exercises*. Until the close of his studies at Paris (1535), he continued to make some additions to it. Thereafter there were only minor changes until Pope Paul III approved it in 1548. *The Spiritual Exercises* is a manual of spiritual arms containing a vital and dynamic system of spirituality. During his lifetime, Ignatius used it to give spiritual retreats to others, especially to his followers. The booklet is indeed an adaptation of the Gospels for such retreats.

The remainder of the decisive period was devoted to a pilgrimage to Jerusalem. Ignatius left Barcelona in March 1523 and, travelling by way of Rome, Venice, and Cyprus, reached Jerusalem on September 4. He would have liked to have settled there permanently, but the Franciscan custodians of the shrines of the Latin church would not listen to this plan. After visiting Bethany, the Mount of Olives, Bethlehem, the Jordan, and Mount of Temptation, Ignatius left Palestine on October 3 and, passing through Cyprus and Venice, reached Barcelona in March 1524.

Period of study. "After the pilgrim had learned that it was God's will that he should not stay in Jerusalem, he pondered in his heart what he should do and finally decided to study for a time in order to be able to help souls"

(*Autobiography*, 50). So Ignatius, who in his *Autobiography* refers to himself as the "pilgrim," describes his decision to acquire as good an education as the circumstances permitted. He probably could have reached the priesthood in a few years. He chose to defer this goal for more than 12 years and to undergo the drudgery of the classroom at an age when most men have long since finished their training. Perhaps his military career had taught him the value of careful preparation. At any rate, he was convinced that a well-trained man would accomplish in a short time what one without training would never accomplish.

Ignatius studied at Barcelona for nearly two years. In 1526 he transferred to Alcalá. By this time he had acquired followers, and the little group had assumed a distinctive garb; but Ignatius soon fell under suspicion of heresy, was imprisoned and tried. Although found innocent, he left Alcalá for Salamanca. There not only was he imprisoned but his companions were also apprehended. Again he won acquittal but was forbidden to teach until he had finished his studies. This prohibition induced Ignatius to leave his disciples and Spain.

He arrived in Paris on Feb. 2, 1528, and remained there as a student until 1535. He lived on alms and in 1528 and 1529 he went to Flanders to beg from Spanish merchants. In 1530 he went to England for the same purpose. In Paris, Ignatius soon had another group of disciples whose manner of living caused such a stir that he had to explain himself to the religious authorities. This episode finally convinced him that he must abstain from public religious endeavour until he reached the priesthood.

During his long stay in the French capital, Ignatius won the coveted M.A. of the famous university. He also gathered the companions who were to be cofounders with him of the Society of Jesus, among them Francis Xavier, who became one of the order's greatest missionaries. On Aug. 15, 1534, he led the little band to nearby Montmartre, where they bound themselves by vows of poverty, chastity, and obedience, though as yet without the express purpose of founding a religious order.

Society of Jesus cofounders

Early in 1535, before the completion of his theological studies, Ignatius left Paris for reasons of health. He spent more than six months in Spain and then went to Bologna and Venice where he studied privately. On Jan. 8, 1537, his Parisian companions joined him in Venice. All were eager to make the pilgrimage to Jerusalem, but war between Venice and the Turkish Empire rendered this impossible. Ignatius and most of his companions were ordained on June 24, 1537. There followed 18 months during which they acquired experience in the ministry while also devoting much time to prayer. During these months, although he did not as yet say mass, Ignatius had one of the decisive experiences of his life. He related to his companions that on a certain day, while in prayer, he seemed to see Christ with the cross on his shoulder and beside him the Eternal Father, who said, "I wish you to take this man for your servant," and Jesus took him and said, "My will is that you should serve us." On Christmas Day 1538 Ignatius said his first mass at the Church of St. Mary Major in Rome. This ends the third period of his life, that of his studies, which were far from a formality. Diego Laínez, a cofounder of the Society of Jesus and an intelligent observer, judged that despite handicaps Ignatius had as great diligence as any of his fellow students. He certainly became in the difficult field of ascetic and mystical theology one of the surest of Catholic guides.

Founding of the Jesuit order. The final period of Loyola's life was spent in Rome or its vicinity. In 1539 the companions decided to form a permanent union, adding a vow of obedience to a superior elected by themselves to the vows of poverty, chastity, and obedience to the Roman pontiff that they had already taken. In 1540 Pope Paul III approved the plan of the new order. Loyola was the choice of his companions for the office of general.

The Society of Jesus developed rapidly under his hand. When he died there were about 1,000 Jesuits divided into 12 administrative units, called provinces. Three of these were in Italy, a like number in Spain, two in Germany one in France, one in Portugal and two overseas in India and

Brazil. Loyola was, in his last years, much occupied with Germany and India, to which he sent his famous followers Peter Canisius and Francis Xavier. He also dispatched missionaries to the Congo and to Ethiopia. In 1546 Loyola secretly received into the society Francis Borgia, duke of Gandía and viceroy of Catalonia. When knowledge of this became public four years later it created a sensation. Borgia organized the Spanish provinces of the order and became third general.

Emphasis on education

Loyola left his mark on Rome. He founded the Roman College, embryo of the Gregorian University, and the Germanicum, a seminary for German candidates for the priesthood. He also established a home for fallen women and one for converted Jews.

Although at first Loyola had been somewhat opposed to placing his companions in colleges as educators of youth, he came in the course of time to recognize the value of the educational apostolate and in his last years was busily engaged in laying the foundations of the system of schools that was to stamp his order as largely a teaching order.

Probably the most important work of his later years was the composition of the *Constitutions* of the Society of Jesus. In them he decreed that his followers were to abandon some of the traditional forms of the religious life, such as chanting the divine office, physical punishments, and penitential garb, in favour of greater adaptability and mobility; they also renounced chapter government by the members of the order in favour of a more authoritative regime; and their vows were generally of such a nature that separation from the order was easier than had been usual in similar Catholic groups. The Society of Jesus was to be above all an order of apostles "ready to live in any part of the world where there was hope of God's greater glory and the good of souls." Loyola insisted on long and thorough training of his followers. Convinced that women are better ruled by women than by men, after some hesitation he resolutely excluded a female branch of the order. The special vow of obedience to the pope was called by Loyola "the cause and principal foundation" of his society.

Vow of obedience to the pope

Loyola and his work were much admired during his lifetime. But he also met with opposition in the church and outside it. His innovations in the religious life were criticized and, while Protestant leaders early came to look on him as one of their principal opponents, some Catholics accused him and his followers of being secret Protestants.

While general of the order, Loyola was frequently sick. In January 1551 he became so ill that he begged his associates, though to no purpose, to accept his resignation as superior. Despite his condition he continued to direct the order until his death on July 31, 1556. Since his days at Manresa, Loyola had practiced a form of prayer that was later published in *The Spiritual Exercises* and appears to have rivalled that of the greatest mystics.

Canonization. Ignatius Loyola was beatified by Pope Paul V in 1609 and canonized by Pope Gregory XV in 1622; his feast day is July 31. In 1922 he was declared patron of all spiritual retreats by Pope Pius XI. His enemies no less than his friends agree that Ignatius Loyola was a maker of history. Scores of books could be cited in proof of this statement. The spirit of Loyola lives on in the Society of Jesus and in the Jesuit *Constitutions*, which still regulate the lives and aspirations of over 30,000 Jesuits, scattered through most countries of the world. *The Spiritual Exercises* molded 27 canonized saints, three of them, Francis Xavier, Peter Canisius, and Francis Borgia, intimates of Loyola. His achievements and those of his followers form a chapter in the history of the Roman Catholic Church that cannot be neglected by those who desire to understand that institution.

BIBLIOGRAPHY

Collected works: Collections of St. Ignatius' works may be found in the *Monumenta Ignatiana ex Autographis vel ex Antiquioribus Exemplis Collecta: Sancti Ignatii de Loyola . . . Epistolae et Instructiones*, 12 vol. (1903–11); *Exercitia spiritualia sancti Ignatii de Loyola et eorum directoria* (1919); *Sancti Ignatii de Loyola Constitutiones Societatis Iesu*, 4 vol. (1934–48); and *Scripta de Sancto Ignatio de Loyola*, 2 vol. (1904–18). There is a Spanish collection, *Obras completas*, ed. by I. IPARRAGUIRRE and C. DE DALMASES, 2nd ed. (1963). Selections include *Cartas espirituales de S. Ignasi de Loyola*, ed. by I. CASANOVAS, 2 vol. (1936); *Briefwechsel mit Frauen* (1956; Eng. trans., *Letters to Women*, ed. by H. RAHNER, 1960); and *Letters of St. Ignatius of Loyola*, selected and trans. by W.J. YOUNG (1959). English translations of Ignatius' two most important works are *The Spiritual Exercises of St. Ignatius*, trans. by L.J. PUHL (1951); and *The Constitutions of the Society of Jesus: Translated, with an Introduction and a Commentary*, by G.E. GANSS (1970).

Lives: The sources of the life of Ignatius have been published in more than 20 volumes in the *Monumenta Historica Societatis Iesu* (1894–1918, 1934–48). Loyola's *Autobiography* may be found in *Acta Patris Ignatii Scripta a P. Lud. González de Cámara, 1553/1555* (1943; Eng. trans., *St. Ignatius' Own Story As Told to Luis González de Cámara*, 1956). The most authoritative life in English is P. DUDON, *St. Ignace de Loyola* (1934; Eng. trans., 1949). Another excellent biography is A. GUILLERMOU, *St. Ignace de Loyola et la Compagnie de Jésus* (1965); while that of the poet FRANCIS THOMPSON, *St. Ignatius Loyola* (1909; rev. and ed. by J.H. POLLEN, 1962), is valuable as well as of literary interest. J. BRODRICK, *St. Ignatius of Loyola: The Pilgrim Years* (1956), is competent; while T. MAYNARD, *St. Ignatius and the Jesuits* (1956), is a much simpler work. L. VON MATT and H. RAHNER, *St. Ignatius of Loyola* (1956), is a pictorial biography.

Special aspects: H. RAHNER, *The Spirituality of St. Ignatius Loyola* (Eng. trans. 1953); G.E. GANSS, *St. Ignatius' Idea of a Jesuit University* (1956).

(E.A.R.)

Lübeck

Lübeck is a seaport of the *Land* (state) of Schleswig-Holstein, in the northern part of the Federal Republic of Germany (West Germany). In the Middle Ages, it was one of the main commercial centres of northern Europe and the chief city of the Hanseatic League (see below *History*).

The old city of Lübeck is built on a hill 52 feet (16 metres) above sea level, about nine miles (14 kilometres) from the Baltic Sea. It is bounded by the rivers Trave and Wakenitz. A modern highway connects it with Hamburg, and ferry traffic links Lübeck with 11 Scandinavian harbours. The border between West and East Germany lies just to the east of the city.

History. The original settlement on the site was Liubice, the seat of a Slavic principality consisting of a castle, settlement, harbour, and merchant colony, located at the mouth of the River Schwartau where it flows into the Trave River. Count Adolf II of Holstein founded the present German city about four miles (six kilometres) upstream in 1143. It grew rapidly, and Adolf's feudal lord, Henry the Lion, duke of Saxony, forced him to cede it in 1158. Henry the Lion rebuilt the city in 1159 after a destructive fire. This has traditionally been considered the date of the present city's foundation.

With the foundation of Lübeck, the type of settlement and law codes typical of German medieval cities began to appear on the coast of the Baltic Sea. The regular plan of the city, centred around the marketplace, was designed to serve the needs of its merchant inhabitants. The city's location was favourable: close to the Baltic and with inland access to Lower Saxony, Westphalia, and the lower Rhine regions. Hence, Lübeck was destined to become the focal point for trade between the raw-material-producing countries of northern and eastern Europe and the manufacturing centres in the west. Aided by privileges from their feudal overlords, the merchants of Lübeck were trading in all the important places along the Baltic coast as early as the end of the 12th century. After the overthrow of Henry the Lion (1180), the Holy Roman emperor Frederick I (Frederick Barbarossa) confirmed the special rights and the landholding privileges of the city (Barbarossa Privilege, 1188). For a short time (1201–26) Lübeck belonged to Denmark, but in 1226 the emperor Frederick II made it a free city, subject only to him. During this time Lübeck developed a form of self-government with its own laws and constitution. It also began to play an important role in the settling of Germans in the eastern Baltic area, supporting the colonizing efforts of the Teutonic Knights and promoting the efforts of already existing settlements to attain self-government

Lübeck, showing several of its famous church towers; left is the Marienkirche (c. 1250–1351); centre right is the Petrikirche (c. 1290–1350, tower completed 1427); right is the cathedral (1173–c. 1247). In the foreground are shops and warehouses, the oldest parts of which date from the Middle Ages.

By courtesy of the Museen fur Kunst und Kulturgeschichte, Lubeck, Germany

in cooperation with local Slavic and Baltic rulers. The "Laws of Lübeck" were granted to more than 100 cities in the Baltic area in the next decades, including Elbing, Kolberg, Reval, Memel, Danzig, and Wismar. Lübeck influenced the economic structure and even the appearance of these cities, and its language became the lingua franca.

The leading merchant dynasties of these various German Baltic cities found it expedient to form a political association in order to guard their common interests. This became the Hanseatic League, and the cities of the league elected Lübeck as their administrative headquarters in 1358. With the Peace of Stralsund (signed on May 24, 1370), by which King Valdemar IV of Denmark officially recognized all its commercial rights and trading licenses, the Lübeckian–Hanseatic League reached its high point. Earlier, in 1350, the city was greatly depopulated by the Black Death (bubonic plague). The period that followed was marked by uprisings of the artisans and craftsmen of the guilds (1380–84 and 1408–16) against the city council, which was controlled by the merchants. The uprisings, however, failed to have any lasting effect. The opening of the Stecknitz Canal in 1398 greatly facilitated the shipping of salt from Lüneburg.

Lübeck was, after Cologne, the largest city in northern Germany; it had approximately 22,000 inhabitants at the beginning of the 15th century. Sweeping changes came with the Protestant Reformation (1529–30). The city council was expelled, and the revolutionary Jürgen Wullenwever became burgomaster of Lübeck. Wullenwever waged an unsuccessful war against Denmark, Sweden, and the Netherlands, which caused Lübeck to lose its position as a great northern European power. The political weakness of the city and the slowly increasing disintegration of the Hanseatic League became obvious with the Peace Treaty of Hamburg in 1536. Wullenwever was forced to leave the city and was executed at Wolfenbüttel in 1537. Lübeck's success in a last war against Sweden (1563–70) had no lasting effects.

After the final breakup of the Hanseatic League (1630), Lübeck was still able to retain its position as the most important harbour on the Baltic Sea. It was able to remain neutral during the Thirty Years' War. The city maintained its position as middleman between Scandinavia and the continent of Europe; the recuperation of its economy continued through the 18th century, partly in consequence of the newly established shipping connections with the new Russian Baltic port of St. Petersburg (now Leningrad). But, during the French Revolutionary and Napoleonic Wars (1792–1815), the city's trade was completely ruined, for it was caught between economic pressures exerted by the rival powers. It was under French rule from 1811 to 1813. After 1815 the city was a member state of the German confederation, and it experienced a revival of prosperity.

From 1866 Lübeck belonged to the North German Confederation and from 1871 to the German Empire. A vast new trading territory in the interior was opened up for Lübeck with the construction of the Elbe–Lübeck Canal in 1900. The city's economic and social structure changed with the advancing industrialization after 1906. Its status as a separate, self-governing entity, dating from 1226, was finally ended in 1937, when the Nazi regime made the "Hanseatic city of Lübeck" part of the Prussian province of Schleswig-Holstein. An air attack by the British during World War II (March 28, 1942) destroyed a large part of the historic inner city, but it left the harbour and the industrial plants intact.

After the end of World War II, Lübeck's population was increased by 100,000 German refugees from the east. Postwar reconstruction restored the old inner city; new industrial plants and residential districts were built in the suburbs, and Lübeck's economy was enhanced.

The modern city. Among Lübeck's outstanding monuments are the Marienkirche (St. Mary's Church, a 13th- to 14th-century brick structure in the Gothic style), the Romanesque cathedral (begun in 1173 under Henry the Lion), the magnificent Rathaus (town hall) built in a combination Gothic and Renaissance style, and two towered gates, the Burgtor (1444) and the Holstentor (1477), remnants of the city's medieval fortifications.

The novelists Thomas Mann (1875–1955) and his brother Heinrich Mann (1871–1950) were both natives of Lübeck and belonged to one of its old patrician families. Thomas Mann created a vivid picture of life in 19th-century Lübeck in his novel *Buddenbrooks*.

The metropolitan area of Lübeck is divided into the inner city, four suburbs, and 23 urban municipalities; among the latter is the well-known Baltic sea resort Travemünde. Of Lübeck's population of about 244,000 in 1970, 38.4 percent was of eastern or central German origin; 87.1 percent of the people were Protestants; and 7.8 percent were Roman Catholic.

Lübeck is the largest Baltic harbour of the Federal Republic of Germany. It has two inland-harbour basins and nine sea-harbour basins on the lower course of the Trave River, which was enlarged to admit seagoing vessels.

Role in the Hanseatic League

End of its self-governing status

In 1970, 38 percent of the city's total work force made its living from the activities of the port, and Lübeck's merchant fleet numbered 116 seagoing vessels. Employing approximately one-third of the total work force, the industry centred mainly on shipyards, metal foundries, iron-construction works, ceramics, wood and lumber production, clothing manufacture, manufacture of instruments for medical use, and food processing.

BIBLIOGRAPHY. M. HOFFMANN, *Geschichte der freien und Hansestadt Lübeck* (1889-92), still the best history of Lübeck, although now in need of revision; W. KING, *Chronicles of Three Free Cities: Hamburg, Bremen, Lübeck*, pp. 303-434 (1914), a readable account, but also outdated, that includes descriptions of some of the artifacts since destroyed by bombs in 1942; F. ENDRES (ed.), *Geschichte der freien und Hansestadt Lübeck* (1926), an important collection of articles on the history of the city; A.B. ENNS, *Lübeck: A Guide to the Architecture and Art Treasures of the Hanseatic Town* (1970), an excellent presentation in the form of a tour through the city; W. NEUGEBAUER, "Lübeck," in *Schleswig Holstein: Handbuch der historischen Stätten Deutschlands*, 2nd ed., vol. 1 ed. by O. KLOSE (1964), a history of Lübeck from its beginnings to the present time.

(W.N.)

Lubrication

Although one of the main purposes of lubrication, derived from the Latin verb *lubricare*, meaning "to make slippery," is to reduce friction, any substance—liquid, solid, or gaseous—capable of controlling friction and wear between sliding surfaces can be classed as a lubricant.

In controlling friction and wear by lubrication, one type of friction frequently is substituted for another, such as the much lower friction of a fluid in an oil-film bearing for that of dry, sliding surfaces.

GENERAL CONSIDERATIONS

Primitive lubricants

Nature has been applying lubrication since the evolution of synovial fluid, which lubricates the joints and bursas. Prehistoric man used mud and reeds to lubricate sledges for dragging game or timbers and rocks for construction. Animal fat lubricated the axles of the first wagons and continued in wide use until the petroleum industry arose in the 19th century, after which petroleum became the chief source of lubricants. The natural lubricating capacity of crude petroleum has been steadily improved through the development of a wide variety of products designed for the specific lubricating needs of the automobile, the airplane, the diesel locomotive, the turbojet, and power machinery of every description. The improvements in petroleum lubricants have in turn made possible the increase in speed and capacity of industrial and other machinery. There are, however, other lubricant materials in use, as will be seen below.

Varieties of lubrication. *Unlubricated sliding.* Metals that have been carefully treated to remove all foreign materials seize and weld to one another when slid together. In the absence of such a high degree of cleanliness, adsorbed gases, water vapour, oxides, and contaminants reduce friction and the tendency to seize but usually result in severe wear; this is called "unlubricated" or dry sliding.

Fluid-film lubrication. Interposing a fluid film that completely separates the sliding surfaces results in fluid-film lubrication. The fluid may be introduced intentionally, as the oil in the main bearings of an automobile, or unintentionally, as in the case of water between a smooth rubber tire and a wet pavement. Although the fluid is usually a liquid such as oil, water, and a wide range of other materials, it may also be a gas. The gas most commonly employed is air.

Balancing the load on sliding surfaces

To keep the parts separated, it is necessary that the pressure within the lubricating film balance the load on the sliding surfaces. If the lubricating film's pressure is supplied by an external source, the system is said to be lubricated hydrostatically. If the pressure between the surfaces is generated as a result of the shape and motion of the surfaces themselves, however, the system is hydrodynamically lubricated. This second type of lubrication depends upon the viscous properties of the lubricant. Osborne Reynolds developed fluid-film lubrication theory in 1886, following Beauchamp Tower's discovery of hydrodynamic lubrication, when Tower studied railroad car journal bearings in England in 1885.

Boundary lubrication. A condition that lies between unlubricated sliding and fluid-film lubrication is referred to as boundary lubrication, also defined as that condition of lubrication in which the friction between surfaces is determined by the properties of the surfaces and properties of the lubricant other than viscosity. Boundary lubrication encompasses a significant portion of lubrication phenomena and commonly occurs during the starting and stopping of machines.

Solid lubrication. Solids such as graphite and molybdenum disulfide are widely used when normal lubricants do not possess sufficient resistance to load or temperature extremes. But lubricants need not take only such familiar forms as fats, powders, and gases; even some metals commonly serve as sliding surfaces in some sophisticated machines (see below *Solid lubricants*).

FUNCTIONS OF LUBRICANTS

Although a lubricant primarily controls friction and wear, it can and ordinarily does perform numerous other functions, which vary with the application and usually are interrelated.

Control functions. *Friction control.* The amount and character of the lubricant made available to sliding surfaces have a profound effect upon the friction that is encountered. For example, disregarding such related factors as heat and wear but considering friction alone between two oil-film lubricated surfaces, the friction can be 200 times less than that between the same surfaces with no lubricant. Under fluid-film conditions, friction is directly proportional to the viscosity of the fluid (see Table 1).

Table 1: Characteristics of Three Typical Lubricants			
lubricant	relative viscosity (air = 1)	typical minimum film thickness in bearing applications (in.)	typical unit load in bearing applications (pounds per sq in.)
Air	1	0.00005–0.0004	1–10
Water	33	0.0004–0.001	25–75
Oil	1,000	0.002–0.004	200–500

Range of viscosities

Some lubricants, such as petroleum derivatives, are available in a great range of viscosities and thus can satisfy a broad spectrum of functional requirements. Under boundary lubrication conditions, the effect of viscosity on friction becomes less significant than the chemical nature of the lubricant. For instance, delicate instruments must not be lubricated with fluids that would attack and corrode the finer metals.

Wear control. Wear occurs on lubricated surfaces by abrasion, corrosion, and solid-to-solid contact. Proper lubricants will help combat each type. They reduce abrasive and solid-to-solid contact wear by providing a film that increases the distance between the sliding surfaces, thereby lessening the damage by abrasive contaminants and surface asperities.

Corrosion wear is generally caused by the products of oxidation of petroleum lubricants. Use of oxidation inhibitors reduces deterioration of petroleum lubricants, and the addition of corrosion preventives protects metal surfaces from any oxidation products that do form.

Temperature control. Lubricants assist in controlling temperature by reducing friction and carrying off the heat that is generated. Effectiveness depends upon the amount of lubricant supplied, the ambient temperature, and the provision for external cooling. To a lesser extent, the type of lubricant also affects surface temperature.

Corrosion control. The role of a lubricant in controlling corrosion of the surfaces themselves is twofold. When machinery is idle, the lubricant acts as a preservative. When machinery is in use, the lubricant controls corrosion by coating lubricated parts with a protective film that may contain additives to neutralize corrosive materials. The ability of a lubricant to control corrosion is directly related to the thickness of the lubricant film remaining on the metal surfaces and the chemical composition of the lubricant. Additives that react with the sliding surfaces enhance the corrosion control of the lubricant.

Other functions. Lubricants are frequently used for purposes other than the reduction of friction. Some of these applications are described below.

Power transmission. Lubricants are widely employed as hydraulic fluids in fluid transmission devices.

Contaminant removal. Lubricants are used to remove contaminants in many systems. Flushing action is used to remove chips and solid contaminants in metalworking. Detergent-dispersant additives suspend sludges and remove them from the sliding surfaces of internal-combustion engines.

Insulation. In specialized applications such as transformers and switchgear, lubricants with high dielectric constants act as electrical insulators. For maximum insulating properties, a lubricant must be kept free of contaminants and water.

Shock dampening. Lubricants act as shock-dampening fluids in energy-transferring devices such as shock absorbers and around machine parts such as gears that are subjected to high intermittent loads.

Sealing. Lubricating grease frequently performs the special function of forming a seal to retain lubricants or to exclude contaminants.

TYPES OF LUBRICANTS

Liquid, oily lubricants. *Animal and vegetable lubricants.* Animal and vegetable products were certainly man's first lubricants and were used in large quantities. But, because they lack chemical inertness and because lubrication requirements have become more demanding, they have been largely superseded by petroleum products and by synthetic materials. Some organic substances such as lard oil and sperm oil are still in use as additives because of their special lubricating properties.

Petroleum lubricants. Petroleum lubricants are predominantly hydrocarbon products extracted from fluids that occur naturally within the Earth. They are used widely as lubricants because they possess a combination of the following desirable properties: (1) availability in suitable viscosities, (2) low volatility, (3) inertness (resistance to deterioration of the lubricant), (4) corrosion protection (resistance to deterioration of the sliding surfaces), and (5) low cost.

Petroleum lubricants formerly were referred to as paraffin-base, naphthene-base, or mixed-base, depending on whether the crude oil from which the lubricant was extracted was higher in paraffin or naphthene molecules. With improvements in refining methods that have made it possible to produce high-quality lubricants from a wide variety of crudes, the terms are no longer widely used.

Refining methods

Lubricants are refined from the crude petroleum by various processes: (1) vacuum distillation, (2) solvent extraction (extracting specific products with solvents), (3) solvent dewaxing (using solvents to remove wax), (4) hydrofining (treating with hydrogen in the presence of a catalyst).

Synthetic lubricants. Synthetic lubricants generally can be characterized as oily, neutral liquid materials not usually obtained directly from petroleum but having some properties similar to petroleum lubricants.

Interest in synthetics has increased greatly—more to meet some of the advanced demands of technology than because of any critical shortage of petroleum lubricants.

Among the improved properties offered by synthetics are low volatility, stability of viscosity with temperature changes, resistance to scuffing and oxidation, and fire resistance. Since the properties of synthetics vary considerably, each synthetic lubricant tends to find a special application. Some of the more common classes of synthetics and typical (but by no means exclusive) uses of each are shown in Table 2.

Lubricating greases. A lubricating grease is a solid or semisolid lubricant consisting of a thickening agent in a liquid lubricant. Soaps of aluminum, barium, calcium, lithium, sodium, and strontium are the major thickening

Table 2: Synthetic Lubricants and Typical Applications

synthetic lubricant	typical uses
Dibasic acid esters	instrument oil, jet turbine lubricant, hydraulic fluid
Phosphate esters	fire-resistant hydraulic fluid, low-temperature lubricant
Silicones	damping fluid, low-volatility grease base
Silicate esters	heat transfer fluid, high-temperature hydraulic fluid
Polyglycol ether compounds	synthetic engine oil, hydraulic fluids, forming and drawing compounds
Fluorol compounds	nonflammable fluid, extreme oxidation–resistant lubricant

agents. Nonsoap thickeners consist of such inorganic compounds as modified clays, fine silicas, or such organic materials as arylureas or phthalocyanine pigments. Solids, usually referred to as fillers, are sometimes added in concentrations up to several percent. Fillers are normally inorganic materials such as asbestos, graphite, metal oxides, metal powders, or metal sulfides. Additives are frequently incorporated to resist oxidation and corrosion and to improve film strength.

Lubrication by grease may prove more desirable than lubrication by oil under conditions when (1) less frequent lubricant application is necessary, (2) grease acts as a seal against loss of lubricant and ingress of contaminants, (3) less dripping or splattering of lubricant is called for, or (4) less sensitivity to inaccuracies in the mating parts is needed.

Conditions under which grease is preferable to oil

Solid lubricants. A solid lubricant is a film of solid material interposed between two rubbing surfaces to reduce friction and wear. The films may consist of inorganic or organic compounds or of metal.

Inorganic compounds. There are three general types of inorganic compounds that serve as solid lubricants:

1. Layer-lattice, or laminar, solids: materials such as graphite and molybdenum disulfide, commonly called molysulfide, have a crystal lattice structure arranged in layers. Strong bonds between atoms within a layer and relatively weak bonds between atoms of different layers allow the lamina to slide on one another. Other such materials are tungsten disulfide, mica, boron nitride, borax, silver sulfate, cadmium iodide, and lead iodide. Graphite's low friction is due largely to adsorbed films; in the absence of water vapour, graphite loses its lubricating properties and becomes abrasive. Both graphite and molysulfide are chemically inert and have high thermal stability.

2. Miscellaneous soft solids: a variety of organic solids such as white lead, lime, talc, bentonite, silver iodide, and lead monoxide are used as lubricants.

3. Chemical conversion coatings: a number of inorganic compounds can be formed on the surface of a metal by chemical reaction. The best known such lubricating coatings are sulfide, chloride, oxide, phosphate, and oxalate films.

Solid organic compounds. There are two general classes of solid organic lubricants:

1. Soaps, waxes, and fats: this class includes metallic soaps of aluminum, calcium, sodium, lithium; animal waxes such as beeswax and spermaceti wax; fatty acids such as stearic and palmitic acids; and fatty esters, such as lard and tallow.

2. Polymeric films: these are synthetic substances such as polytetrafluoroethylene and polychlorofluoroethylene. One major advantage of such film-type lubricants is their resistance to deterioration during exposure to the elements. Thus, one-half-inch-thick plates of polymeric film are used in modern prestressed concrete construction to permit thermal movement of beams resting atop columns. Such expansion and contraction of the structural members is facilitated by the long-lived polymeric film plate. Very thin films of such polymers also serve as protective coatings, as well as lubricants, for many types of industrial machinery subjected to great variations in temperature and humidity.

Lubricating structural concrete

Metal films. Thin films of soft metal on a hard substrate can act as effective lubricants, if the adhesion to the substrate is good. Such metals include lead, tin, and indium.

Bonded solid lubricant coatings. Since solid lubricants as a class lack adhesion, they are frequently applied using a mixture made from lubricant in powder form and an adhesive bonding agent. Organic binders include corn syrup and acrylic, phenolic, and epoxy resins; inorganic binders are sodium silicate, the phosphates of sodium, and powdered, low-melting metals.

Other types. *Gases.* Lubrication with a gas is analogous in many respects to lubrication with a liquid, since the same principles of fluid-film lubrication apply. Although both gases and liquids are viscous fluids, they differ in two important particulars. The viscosity of gases is much lower and the compressibility much greater than for liquids. Film thicknesses and load capacities therefore are much lower with a gas such as air (see Table 1). In equipment that handles gases of various kinds, it is frequently desirable to lubricate the sliding surfaces with gas in order to simplify the apparatus and reduce contamination to and from the lubricant. The list of gases used in this manner is extensive and includes air, steam, industrial gases, and liquid-metal vapours.

Special-purpose lubricants. In a sense, every lubricant application is special and could be benefitted by a lubricant specially formulated to meet its unique requirements. Since such an inventory of lubricants is impractical, compromises are usually made to reduce the number of lubricants needed. A few applications in which special characteristics are desirable are given in Table 3.

Table 3: Typical Special-Purpose Lubricants

lubricant application	lubricant properties of special interest
Aircraft jet engine	oxidation resistance, thermal stability, low-temperature properties, good temperature–viscosity characteristics, high film strength (for gears)
Hypoid gears	high film strength, oxidation resistance, corrosion resistance
Automatic transmission	low viscosity, good temperature–viscosity characteristics, oxidation resistance, corrosion resistance, high film strength
Steam turbine	high oxidation resistance, corrosion resistance, good water separation, low foaming
Vacuum pump	low vapour pressure, freedom from gas and moisture, oxidation resistance
Transformer	high dielectric strength, low viscosity, oxidation resistance, high resistivity
Refrigerator compressor	chemical stability in presence of refrigerant, freedom from moisture, chemical stability in presence of copper and iron
Fire-resistant hydraulic system	fire resistance, corrosion resistance, compatibility with seals and gaskets, low foaming

PROPERTIES OF LUBRICANTS

With so many types of materials capable of acting as lubricants under certain conditions, coverage of the properties of all of them is impractical. Mention will be made only of those properties usually considered characteristic of commercially significant fluid lubricants.

Viscosity. Of all the properties of fluid lubricants, viscosity is the most important since it determines the amount of friction that will be encountered between sliding surfaces and whether a thick enough film can be built up to avoid wear from solid-to-solid contact. Viscosity customarily is measured by a viscometer, which determines the flow rate of the lubricant under standard conditions; the higher the flow rate, the lower the viscosity. The rate is expressed in centipoises, reyns, or seconds Saybolt universal (SSU) depending, respectively, upon whether metric, English, or commercial units are used. In most liquids, viscosity drops appreciably as the temperature is raised. Since little change of viscosity with fluctuations in temperature is desirable to keep variations in friction at a minimum, fluids frequently are rated in terms of viscosity

Viscometer measurements [margin note]

index. The less the viscosity is changed by temperature, the higher the viscosity index.

Pour point. The pour point, or the temperature at which a lubricant ceases to flow, is of importance in appraising flow properties at low temperature. As such, the pour point can become the determining factor in selecting one lubricant from among a group with otherwise identical properties.

Flash point. The flash point, or the temperature at which a lubricant momentarily flashes in the pressure of a test flame, aids in evaluating fire-resistance properties. Like the pour point factor, the flash point may in some instances become the major consideration in selecting the proper lubricant, especially in lubricating machinery handling highly flammable material.

Oiliness. Oiliness generally connotes relative ability to operate under boundary lubrication conditions. The term relates to a lubricant's tendency to wet and adhere to a surface. There is no formal test for the measurement of oiliness; determination of this factor is chiefly through subjective judgment and experience. Animal and vegetable oils and fatty acids are considered to be high in oiliness. The most desirable lubricant for a specific use need not necessarily be the oiliest; *i.e.,* long-fibre grease, which is low in oiliness as compared with machine oils, is usually preferable for packing rolling bearings.

Neutralization number. The neutralization number is a measure of the acid or alkaline content of new oils and an indicator of the degree of oxidation degradation of used oils. This value is ascertained by titration, a standard analytical chemical technique, and is defined as the number of milligrams of potassium hydroxide required to neutralize one gram of the lubricant.

Penetration number. The penetration number, applied to grease, is a measure of the film characteristics of the grease. The test consists of dropping a standard cone into the sample of grease being tested. Gradations indicate the depth of penetration: the higher the number, the more fluid the grease.

Other properties. Measurements of other properties have been designed to determine chlorine content, dielectric constant, specific gravity, and interfacial tension as well as to evaluate corrosion, emulsion, foaming, oxidizing, carbonizing, and saponification characteristics.

Additives. Additives in lubricants (1) limit chemical change or deterioration of the lubricant, (2) protect a machine from harmful deposits or from failure of the lubricant to function properly, and (3) improve existing physical properties of the lubricant or impart new characteristics to it. There are two general classes of additives: those that affect physical properties such as the pour point and those that affect chemical characteristics such as detergency. Table 4 lists the more common additive materials and their principal functions.

Table 4: Common Lubricant Additives

additive purpose	typical material used
Oxidation inhibitor	zinc dithiophosphate
Corrosion inhibitor	zinc dithiophosphate
Antiwear improver	tricresyl phosphate
Detergent dispersant	soap of sulfonic acid
Rust inhibitor	metallic soaps
Pour depressant	polymers of methacrylic acid esters
Viscosity-index improver	acrylate polymers
Oiliness agent	fatty oils
Film-strength improver	chlorine compounds
Antifoam agent	silicone polymers
Emulsifier	soaps of fatty acids
Thickening agent	soaps, fine clay
Water repellent	organic silicone polymers
Colour stabilizer	aliphatic ammines
Odour-control agent	formaldehyde polymers
Antiseptic	phenol

METHODS OF APPLYING LUBRICANTS

To control friction and wear, a lubricant must reach the sliding surfaces when and as needed. It may be applied manually or automatically in association with machine operation. The main methods of application are shown below.

manual

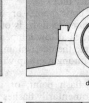
drop feed

splash

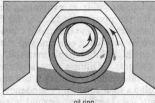
oil ring

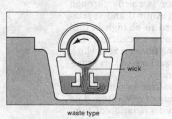
wick

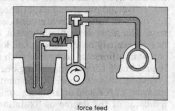
waste type

force feed

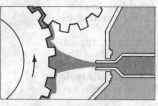
air–oil mist

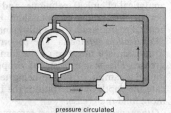
pressure circulated

centralized

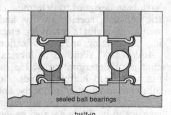
sealed ball bearings
built-in

Methods of applying lubrication.

From J.J. O'Connor and John Boyd (eds.), *Standard Handbook of Lubrication Engineering*, copyright 1968; used with permission of McGraw-Hill Book Company

In drop-feed lubrication, oil is supplied by gravity; in both splash and oil-ring lubrication, oil is picked up from a reservoir by contact with a moving surface. In waste-type lubrication, capillary action of oil in a fibrous material transfers oil from a reservoir to the sliding surfaces. Force-feed lubrication utilizes a pump to supply lubricant under pressure. If the pump furnishes oil to more than one point, the arrangement constitutes a centralized lubrication system; if the used lubricant is returned to the pump, it is classed as a pressure circulating system. In air-oil-mist lubrication, atomizing action of a liquid in a stream of air is used to pick up and transport the lubricant. In built-in lubrication, moving parts are lubricated in such a way that an external source of lubricant is not necessary. This can be done by supplying the sliding surfaces with a quantity of lubricant that is sealed against loss, as in sealed ball bearings, or by treating the parts with an adhesive coating containing solid lubricant. It also can be accomplished by making the sliding surfaces from porous materials impregnated with lubricant, as in "oilless" bearings, or by constructing the surfaces from self-lubricating materials.

The countries and regions that are the major world producers of lubricating oils are listed in Table 5.

Built-in lubrication

Table 5: World Production of Lubricating Oils
(in 000 metric tons)

major producers	1960	1970
Africa	...	180
South Africa	...	112
North America	9,750	11,460
United States	8,498	9,470
Netherlands Antilles	735	1,066
South America	380	820
Venezuela	200	546
Asia	660	2,730
Japan	578	2,103
Europe	3,810	7,020
United Kingdom	927	1,324
Germany, Federal Rep. of	566	1,200
Oceania	30	430
Australia	29	369

BIBLIOGRAPHY. J.J. O'CONNOR and J. BOYD (eds.), *Standard Handbook of Lubrication Engineering* (1968), on lubrication theory, lubricant properties, bearings, and applications to specific industries; A.E. NORTON, *Lubrication* (1942), basic text on lubrication and bearing theory; E.E. BISSON and W.J. ANDERSON, "Advanced Bearing Technology," NASA *Spec. Publs. 38* (1964), with special reference to aerospace application; V.B. GUTHRIE (ed.), *Petroleum Products Handbook* (1960), on the properties, characteristics, storage and handling, and utilization of petroleum products; AMERICAN PETROLEUM INSTITUTE, *Petroleum Facts and Figures* (1967).

(J.B.)

Lucian

The writings of Lucian, a Greek rhetorician, pamphleteer, and satirist of the 2nd century AD, are outstanding for their mordant and malicious wit, embodying a sophisticated and often embittered critique of the shams and follies of the literature, philosophy, and intellectual life of his day—which has been called the Golden Age of the Roman Empire. Lucian's sharply critical mind was, however, largely destructive and could suggest no new values to put in place of those that he attacked as outworn. Thus, ill at ease in a pretentious and superstitious world, he was condemned to a sterile pessimism. The only thing that had real value in his eyes and that provided him with a standard of judgment was classical Greek literature. In this turning toward a half-imaginary past Lucian was at one with his age. His own classicizing style served as a model for writers of the later Roman Empire and for the Byzantine period. He was the favourite Greek writer of the important 16th-century French comic and satirical writer François Rabelais and so has in turn influenced the development of European satire through such writers as Jonathan Swift, Henry Fielding, Cyrano de Bergerac, Voltaire, and Giacomo Leopardi. Today he interests the student of ideas as much as the student of literature.

One is entirely dependent on Lucian's writings for information about his life, but he says little about himself and not all that he says is to be taken seriously. Moreover, since the chronology of his works is very obscure, the events of his life can only be reconstructed in broad outline, and the order and dating of these events are matters of probability rather than certainty.

Lucian was born c. AD 120 in Samosata (the modern Samsat, in Turkey), formerly the capital of the kingdom of Commagene, which since AD 72 had been part of the Roman province of Syria. His mother's family had, for generations, been monumental sculptors, and his father's family were probably also artisans. Therefore, they would have been comfortably off, but not rich. They must have been strangers alike to political power in the city and to Greek culture, for the language of the people was Aramaic, though for centuries the upper classes had spoken Greek, the official tongue of the city. As a boy Lucian showed a talent for making clay models and was therefore apprenticed to his uncle, a sculptor. They quarrelled, and Lucian soon left home for western Asia Minor, in whose cities he acquired a Greek literary education.

So successfully did he master a new language and culture that he began a career as a public speaker, travelling from city to city giving model speeches to display his elo-

Career as a speaker

quence, public lectures (much as a modern musician gives concerts), and probably also pleading in court. After a tour of Greece he went on to Italy and Gaul (modern France), where there was at the time an eager, if not always discriminating, public for Greek oratory. To this period of his life belong many of his surviving declamations on mythological and other stock themes (*Phalaris, The Tyrannicide, Hippias, In Praise of the Fly*) and rhetorical prologues (including *Herodotus* and *The Scythian*). Lucian was evidently successful in a profession that conferred much prestige and often great influence on its leading practitioners. He won the friendship of distinguished Romans, senators, and provincial governors and became well-known in literary circles throughout the empire. Doubtless he earned a comfortable fortune, too. He never seems, however, to have reached the first rank in his profession. Philostratus, who wrote biographies of the leading rhetoricians of the age, never mentioned him.

It may have been disillusion with the emptiness of his career that led him to give up his wandering life and settle in Athens in the late 50s of the 2nd century. From there he attended the Olympic Games of 157, doubtless as a public speaker. In Athens, then a centre of higher studies, he was able to extend his knowledge of Greek literature and thought far beyond anything required of a rhetorician. As well as Attic comedy and classical and Hellenistic philosophy, he read the satirical pamphlets and lampoons of the 3rd-century-BC Cynic philosopher Menippus of Gadara (a fellow Syrian), which deeply impressed him. In this early Athenian period Lucian gave up public speaking and took to writing critical and satirical essays on the intellectual life of his time, either in the form of dialogues or, in imitation of Menippus, in a mixture of prose and verse. To this period probably belong such

Best known works works as *Nigrinus, Dialogues of the Gods* and *Dialogues of the Dead* (two of his best known works, the one making fun of aspects of Greek mythology and the other a grimly ironic revelation of the vanities of men while they are alive), *Dialogues of Courtesans, Prometheus, Charon, Zeus Confuted,* and *The Tragic Zeus*. Lucian's writings apparently sustained the reputation he had won as a public speaker. He attracted the attention of the emperor Verus, whose mistress Panthea he flattered in his *Imagines*. He probably accompanied Verus to Antioch in 162 when the Emperor went to take the field against the Parthians. At any rate, he spent some years in Antioch about this time. From there he made a return visit to his native Samosata, where, to an admiring audience of his fellow townsmen, he delivered a speech on his own career, *The Dream* (also known as *The Vision*). In view of the threatening military situation he decided to take his father back to Athens with him. They probably crossed Asia Minor and sailed westward from Amastris (Amasra). During this journey Lucian met the popular magician and wonder-worker Alexander of Abonouteichos (the modern Inebolu), a charlatan whom he depicted brilliantly in *Alexander; or The False Prophet*. Another whose acquaintance he made at this time was a convert from Christianity, the Cynic philosopher Peregrinus, his fellow passenger from the Troad (the district close by the city of Troy in Asia Minor) to Athens. Returning to Athens, Lucian visited the Olympic Games of 165, at which Peregrinus committed suicide by setting fire to himself. A few years later Lucian testified to the impression that the man and his macabre end had made upon him with his discerning, if somewhat malicious, *Death of Peregrinus*. He seems to have remained in Athens writing for some years and visited the Olympic Games again in 169. To this period probably belong such works as *Timon, The Assembly of the Gods, Twice Accused, The Auction of Lives,* and *How to Write History*, a penetrating and amusing critique provoked by the spate of panegyrical histories of Verus' Parthian campaign. He began, however, to grow dissatisfied with his life at Athens, where his biting wit no doubt made him many enemies. Thanks to the patronage of his Roman friends—perhaps in particular Gaius Calvisius Statianus, prefect of Egypt from 170 to 175—he obtained a post in Alexandria as *archistator*, a kind of chief court usher. The appointment

was one normally given to members of the equestrian order (next in rank below senators) who had held several military commands. It carried a substantial salary and could have been the prelude to a career in the higher ranks of the civil service, but Lucian was already too old to begin a new career and was temperamentally unfitted to be a functionary. For him it was an escape. During his years in Egypt he probably wrote his *Apology, On His Failure to Give Greetings,* and other works. After some years he returned to Athens and took up public speaking again. (It may be that he lost his post in the purge that followed the revolt of Avidius Cassius in 175.) Works written during this second Athenian period include *Lexiphanes, The Eunuch, The False Sophist,* and *Hercules*. He was married and had one son, born late in his life. Lucian died some time after 180.

The medieval manuscripts Lucian's works were doubtless published one by one. In late antiquity an unknown editor prepared a collected edition of such works as he could find, and this is the ancestor of the medieval Lucian manuscripts. The oldest of these was written down in 913, and several others also belong to the 10th century. They contain a corpus of 83 works, of which a few are spurious.

BIBLIOGRAPHY

Text: C. IACOBITZ, *Lucianus ex recensione*, 3 vol. (1852–53, reprinted 1913–21); new edition by N. NILEN (1906–23, incomplete).

Translations: A.M. HARMON, K. KILBURN, and M.D. MacLEOD, *Lucian*, 8 vol. (1913–67); B.P. REARDON, *Selected Works* (1965).

Biographical and critical studies: M. CROISET, *Essai sur la vie et les oeuvres de Lucien* (1882), a fundamental work, though somewhat out of date; F.G. ALLINSON, *Lucian, Satirist and Artist* (1926), a general survey of Lucian's works; B.P. MacCARTHY, "Lucian and Menippus," in *Yale Classical Studies*, vol. 4 (1934); F.W. HOUSEHOLDER, *Literary Quotation and Allusion in Lucian* (1941); J. BOMPAIRE, *Lucien écrivain* (1958), a study of Lucian's literary aims and his debt to earlier Greek literature; J. SCHWARTZ, *Biographie de Lucien de Samosate* (1965); B.P. REARDON, *Courants littéraires grecs des IIᵉ et IIIᵉ siècles après J.-C.* (1971), on Lucian's place in the literature of his age.

(R.B.)

Lucretius

Titus Lucretius Carus was a Latin poet and philosopher of the earlier half of the 1st century BC, whose single, long poem, *De rerum natura* (Eng. trans., *On the Nature of Things*, 1947), rendered in hexameters the atomic theory of Epicurus, the founder of a Greek school of moralists. Its declared purpose was to free mankind from religious fears by proving that the soul is material and is born and dies with the body and that, though gods exist, they cannot intervene to help or harm men.

Life and death. Apart from Lucretius' poem almost nothing is known about him. What little evidence there is, is quite inconclusive. Jerome, a leading Latin Church Father, in his chronicle for the year 94 BC (or possibly 96 or 93 BC), stated that Lucretius was born in that year and that years afterward a love potion drove him insane; and in lucid intervals having written some books, which Cicero afterward emended, he killed himself in his 44th year (51 or 50 BC). Aelius Donatus, a grammarian and teacher of rhetoric, in his "Life" of Virgil noticed that Virgil put on the *toga virilis* (the toga of an adult) in his 17th year, on his birthday (*i.e.*, 54 or 53 BC), and that Lucretius died that same day. But Donatus contradicted himself by stating that the consuls that year were the same as in the year of Virgil's birth (*i.e.*, Crassus and Pompey, in 55

Allusions to Lucretius by his contemporaries BC). This last date seems partly confirmed by a sentence in Cicero's reply to his brother in 54 BC (*Ad Quintum fratrem* 2, 9, 3), which suggests that Lucretius was already dead and also that Cicero may have been involved in the publication of his poem: "The poems of Lucretius are as you write in your letter—they have many highlights of genius, yet also much artistry." Excepting the single mention in Cicero, the only contemporary who named Lucretius was a Roman historian, Cornelius Nepos (*Atticus* 12, 4), in the phrase "after the death of Lucretius and Catullus," and the only contemporary whom Lucretius named was one Memmius, to whom he dedicated his poem, probably Gaius Memmius (son-in-law of Sulla, praetor of 58 BC, and patron of Catullus and Gaius Helvius Cinna), for whose friendship Lucretius "hopes."

Philosophical content of "De rerum natura." The title of Lucretius' work translates that of the chief work of Epicurus, *Peri physeōs* (*On Nature*), as also of the didactic epic of Empedocles, a pluralist philosopher of nature, of whom Lucretius spoke with admiration only less than that with which he praised his master Epicurus. The poem is the fullest extant statement of the physical theory of Epicurus, and it also alludes to his ethical and logical doctrines.

Structure of the poem. Lucretius distributed his argument into six books, beginning each with a highly polished introduction. Books I and II established the main principles of the atomic universe, refuted the rival theories of the pre-Socratic cosmic philosophers Heracleitus, Empedocles, and Anaxagoras, and covertly attacked the Stoics, a school of moralists rivalling that of Epicurus. Book III demonstrated the atomic structure and mortality of the soul and ended with a triumphant sermon on the theme "Death is nothing to us." Book IV described the mechanics of sense perception, thought, and certain bodily functions and condemned sexual passion. Book V described the creation and working of this world and the celestial bodies and the evolution of life and human society. Book VI explained remarkable phenomena of the Earth and sky, in particular, thunder and lightning. The poem ends with a description of the plague at Athens, a sombre picture of death contrasting with that of spring and birth in the invocation to Venus, with which it opened.

Argument of the poem. The argument in outline is as follows:

The nature of the universe

1. No thing is either created out of or reducible to nothing. The universe has an infinite extent of empty space (or void) and an infinite number of irreducible particles of matter (or atoms)—though their kinds are finite. Atoms differ only in shape, size, and weight and are impenetrably hard, changeless, everlasting, the limit of physical division. They are made up of inseparable minimal parts, or units. Larger atoms have more such parts; but even the larger are minute. All atoms would have moved everlastingly downward in infinite space and never have collided to form atomic systems had they not swerved at times to a minimal degree. To these indeterminate swerves is due the creation of an infinite plurality of worlds; they also interrupt the causal chain and so make room for free will. All things are ultimately systems of moving atoms, separated by greater or smaller intervals of void, which cohere more or less according to their shapes. All systems are divisible and therefore perishable (except the gods), and all change is explainable in terms of the addition, subtraction, or rearrangement of changeless atoms.

2. The soul is made of exceedingly fine atoms and has two connected parts: the *anima* distributed throughout the body, which is the cause of sensation, and the *animus* in the breast, the central consciousness. The soul is born and grows with the body, and at death it is dissipated like "smoke."

3. Though the gods exist, they neither made nor manipulate the world. As systems of exceedingly fine atoms, they live remote, unconcerned with human affairs, examples to men of the ideal life of perfect happiness (absence of mental fear, emotional turmoil, and bodily pain).

4. Men know by sense perception and argue by reason according to certain rules. Though the senses are infallible, reason can make false inferences. Objects can be seen because they discharge from their surface representative films, which strike the eye just as smells strike the nose. Separate atoms are in principle imperceptible, having no dischargeable parts. The senses perceive the properties and accidents of bodies; reason infers the atoms and the void, which exists to explain the perceived movement of bodies.

5. Men naturally seek pleasure and avoid pain. Their aim should be so to conduct their lives that they get, on balance, the maximum of pleasure and the minimum of pain. They will succeed in this only if they are able, through philosophy, to overcome the fear of death and of the gods.

Literary qualities of "De rerum natura." The linguistic style and spirit of the poem are notable. The problem of Lucretius was to render the bald and abstract Greek prose of Epicurus into Latin hexameters at a time when Latin had no philosophic vocabulary. He succeeded by applying common words to a technical use. Thus, he used *concilium* ("assembly of people") for a "system of atoms" and *primordia* ("first weavings") for the "atoms" that make up the texture of things. When necessary, he invented words. In poetic diction and style he was in debt to the older Latin poets, especially to Quintus Ennius, the father of Roman poetry. He freely used alliteration and assonance, solemn and often metrically convenient archaic forms, and old constructions. He formed expressive compound adjectives of a sort rejected by Augustan taste; *e.g.*, "the light-sleeping hearts of dogs," "forest-breaking winds." He imitated or echoed Homer; the dramatists Aeschylus and Euripides; Callimachus, a poet and critic; the historian Thucydides; and the physician Hippocrates. His hexameters stand halfway between those of Ennius, who introduced the metre into Latin, and Virgil, who perfected it. There is also some incoherence of rhythm, as well as harsh elisions and examples of unusual prosody.

His debt to early poets, dramatists, and historians

The influence of Lucretius on Virgil was pervasive, especially in Virgil's *Georgics*; and it is in clear allusion to Lucretius that Virgil wrote "Happy is the man who can read the causes of things" (*Georgics* II, 490).

Lucretius spoke in austere compassion for the ignorant, unhappy human race. His moral fervour expressed itself in gratitude to Epicurus and in hatred of the seers who inculcated religious fears by threats of eternal punishment after death, of the Etruscan soothsayers with their lore of thunder and lightning, of the false philosophers —Stoics with their belief in divine providence or Platonists and Pythagoreans who taught the transmigration of immortal souls. The first appearance of *religio* in the poem is as a monster that thrusts its fearful head from the regions of the sky. Epicurus, not intimidated by these spectres, had ranged beyond the "flaming ramparts of the world" through the infinite universe, broken into the citadel of nature, and brought back in triumph the knowledge of what can and what cannot be, of that "deep-set boundary stone" that divides the separate properties of things, the real from the not real. And "so religion is crushed beneath our feet and his [Epicurus'] victory lifts us to the skies."

BIBLIOGRAPHY. *De Rerum Natura*, ed., with prolegomena, critical apparatus, translation, and commentary by CYRIL BAILEY, 3 vol. (1947, reprinted 1963), the most authoritative text, translation, and commentary currently available; PIERRE BOYANCE, *Lucrèce et l'Épicurisme* (1963), a comprehensive and well-balanced account of the author, subject matter, and literary form of the *De rerum natura;* D.R. DUDLEY (ed.), *Lucretius* (1965), a collection of essays by eminent scholars on various aspects of the poem; RICHARD MINADEO, *The Lyre of Science: Form and Meaning in Lucretius' De Rerum Natura* (1969), a demonstration of how the formal design of the poem is derived from the cycle of creation and destruction; DAVID WEST, *The Imagery and Poetry of Lucretius* (1969), a perceptive study of the sources of Lucretius' images and their importance in the poem.

(A.F.We.)

Ludendorff, Erich

Among the great number of able chiefs of staff of the German Army during World War I, one man, Gen. Erich Ludendorff, distinguished himself through his exceptional gift of strategic planning. Always under the patronage of the elderly Field Marshal Paul von Hindenburg, he directed from 1914 to 1916 the campaign against Russia, and from 1916 to 1918, as "first quartermaster general," he determined the decisions of the supreme command.

His opponents—above all, the French generals—regarded him as the most effective strategist on the German

Ludendorff, *c.* 1930.
Archiv fur Kunst und Geschichte

Theory of "total war"

side. Consistently pursuing a purely military line of thought, Ludendorff developed, after the war, the theory of "total war," which in 1935 he published in a book bearing this title. In the first half of the 19th century, the great military theorist of the Prussian general staff, Carl von Clausewitz, had advanced the doctrine of war as an extension of politics with different means. Ludendorff advocated the diametrically opposite view that politics should serve the conduct of war, for which the entire physical and moral forces of the nation should be mobilized, because, according to him, peace was merely an interval between wars. He appears as an "anti-Clausewitz."

Ludendorff was born on April 9, 1865, in Kruszewnia, in Prussian Poland, the son of an impoverished landowner and cavalry captain. His mother was a member of an aristocratic military family. Ludendorff was educated in the cadet corps, became an infantry officer, and, because of his outstanding military qualities, was soon promoted to the general staff.

In 1908 he was put in charge of the 2nd (German) department in the army general staff, the institution generally known as the "great general staff," which was responsible for preparing contingency employment and mobilization plans. Under the chief of the general staff, Gen. Helmuth von Moltke, Ludendorff played a significant part in the revision of the Schlieffen Plan. This plan envisaged a gigantic outflanking movement involving the infringement of Belgian neutrality with the aim of crushing France with one blow. Moltke and Ludendorff decided to secure more firmly the extended southern flank between Switzerland and Lorraine. They also discarded the idea of forcing a way through southern Holland and instead made preparations for the surprise capture of Liège, the most important fortress in eastern Belgium, often characterized as "impregnable."

In Germany, supreme political and military power was traditionally wielded by the commander in chief and the emperor, and general staff officers were not expected to engage in politics. Ludendorff, however, violated this tradition by campaigning for a strengthening of the army, both in personnel and equipment, which the general staff considered essential in view of the general armaments race in Europe. His contact with extreme nationalist political circles favouring increased armament convinced him that, if policy was influenced by "strong men," a vigorous conduct of war was assured.

The excessively active departmental chief irritated the military authorities, and in 1913 Ludendorff was transferred to the infantry as regimental commander. When war broke out in 1914, he was appointed quartermaster in chief (supply and maintenance) of the 2nd Army in the west.

It was not until two Russian armies in August 1914 threatened to overrun the German 8th Army in East

Prussia that Ludendorff was appointed chief of staff of the 8th Army. Ludendorff, dynamic but occasionally harsh and in times of crisis often nervous, was assigned to the elderly Gen. Paul von Hindenburg, who was renowned for his iron nerves. Ludendorff regarded the problems with which he and his commander in chief were faced as difficult but never insoluble.

Military career during World War I

The spectacular victory of Hindenburg and Ludendorff over the Russians in August 1914 at Tannenberg, in East Prussia, a battle that brought Hindenburg worldwide fame, was followed by the German defeat on the Marne in the west that signalled the failure of Ludendorff's revised Schlieffen Plan. For two years Hindenburg and Ludendorff fought the Russians in the east. Ludendorff's plan of a general offensive against Russia by means of a temporary reduction of the German forces in the west was not approved by the supreme army command in the summer of 1915.

Only in August 1916, after the failure of the German offensive at Verdun and in view of the allied onslaught in both east and west, did the Emperor finally appoint the two generals to assume supreme military control. They attempted to conduct a sort of total war by mobilizing the entire forces of the home front, which was already suffering from the effects of the British blockade. Ludendorff staked everything on a single card, the stubborn pursuit of a "victorious peace" that was to secure German territorial gains in east and west. In 1917 he approved the unrestricted submarine warfare against the British that led to the entry of the United States into the war against Germany but not to England's collapse. After the Tsar had been deposed in March 1917, Ludendorff gave his blessing to the return of the Russian Bolshevik emigrants (including the as yet unknown Lenin), in the hope of persuading the Russians to conclude peace. Hindenburg and Ludendorff, who now exercised a sort of military semi-dictatorship, also brought about the dismissal of Chancellor Theobald von Bethmann Hollweg in the delusory hope that "a strong man" could be found to assume the leadership of the *Reich.*

On March 21, 1918, Ludendorff opened a general offensive on the Western Front with the object of smashing the Anglo-French armies and forcing a decision in Europe before the Americans landed. But he had overestimated the strength of the German armies; the offensive failed, and, when in the autumn of 1918 the collapse of the German allies—Austria-Hungary, Bulgaria, and Turkey—was imminent, Lundendorff demanded immediate negotiations for an armistice. For a while, the nerves of the hopelessly overworked general gave way, and a psychiatrist had to be summoned to supreme headquarters. When Ludendorff realized the severity of the armistice conditions, he insisted that the war be carried on. When he saw that the political leaders were not prepared to do this, he offered his resignation, which William II accepted on October 26, 1918. At the same time, the Emperor, much to Ludendorff's distaste, ordered Hindenburg to remain at his post. A titan of willpower and energy who had attempted the impossible was suddenly torn away from his sphere of activity; the shock was immense. Ludendorff met the revolution that broke out in November 1918 with complete resignation and went into exile in Sweden for several months.

Failure of the western offensive

While, according to Prussian custom, general staff officers were jointly responsible for all decisions, they had to preserve strict anonymity. Ludendorff, however, whose ambition was as immense as his strategic gifts, at the end of the lost war claimed to have been the sole real "commander" of World War I. He asserted that he had been deprived of victory by sinister forces operating behind the scene; he was, he claimed, like Siegfried in the heroic Germanic sagas, a victim of a stab in the back. By propagating the legend that the German Army, undefeated in the field, was sabotaged by the "home front," he did much to poison public life in the Weimar Republic.

During the next 20 years Ludendorff led a bizarre life. Adopting the role of the betrayed and misunderstood commander, he took part in the unsuccessful coups d'etat of Wolfgang Kapp in 1920 and of Hitler in 1923, and in

1925 he ran for president against his former commander in chief, Hindenburg, whom he now bitterly hated. From 1924 to 1928 he was a National Socialist member of parliament.

Ludendorff had always had a weakness for the female sex; his first wife, a striking beauty, divorced her husband in order to marry Ludendorff. In 1926, however, he insisted on dissolving this marriage and married the neurologist and popular philosopher Mathilde von Kemnitz. Ludendorff succumbed completely to this eccentric woman, who regarded him as the real "commander in chief" of the Germans and had developed a belief in the activities of "supernational powers"—Jewry, Christianity, Freemasonry. From then on he joined with his second wife in fighting against these imaginary foes who were supposed to have deprived him and Germany of victory. Both preached a German "divine faith." Over this faith he quarrelled both with the old officer corps and with Hitler and his National Socialists. Just as he had not permitted the Emperor to make him a count, he now forbade Hitler to promote him to field marshal. Apart from a group of fanatical followers, he was henceforth completely isolated. When, during the 1930s, he began to utter warnings against Hitler's tyranny, he found no echo. He died on December 20, 1937, in Tutzing. Many old soldiers mourned him, but most of them had long ceased to understand him.

BIBLIOGRAPHY. Among Ludendorff's memoirs and studies are *Meine Kriegserinnerungen, 1914–1918* (1919; Eng. trans., *My War Memoirs, 1914–1918*, 2 vol., 1919); *Mein militarischer Werdegang* (1933); *Kriegführung und Politik*, 2nd ed. (1922); and *Der Totale Krieg* (1935; Eng. trans., *The Nation at War*, 1936). JOHN W. WHEELER-BENNETT, "Ludendorff: The Soldier and the Politician," *Virginia Quarterly Review*, 14: 187–202 (1938); and D.J. GOODSPEED, *Ludendorff* (1966), contain some critical views. See also WALTER GOERLITZ, *Der deutsche Generalstab: Geschichte und Gestalt*, 2nd ed. (1953; Eng. trans., *History of the German General Staff, 1657–1945*, 1953).

(W.Go.)

Lugard, Lord

Frederick John Dealtry Lugard, later Lord Lugard, played a major part in Britain's colonial history between 1888 and 1945 in the opening up of Africa, in the administration of Nigeria, and, finally, as a national and international figure in colonial affairs.

Born in Madras, India, on January 22, 1858, of missionary parents, he was educated in England and after briefly attending the Royal Military Academy, Sandhurst, joined the Norfolk Regiment. Posted to India and swept into the British imperial advance of the 1880s, he served in the Afghan, Suakin (Sudan), and Burma campaigns. An officer with a promising career ahead of him in British India, he experienced a catastrophic love affair with a married woman. Highly strung and undermined by Bur-

By courtesy of the National Portrait Gallery, London

Lugard, painting by W.J. Carrow, 1936. In the National Portrait Gallery, London.

ma fever, he sought oblivion by following the explorer David Livingstone's lead in fighting Arab slave raiders in eastern Africa. In 1888 he was severely wounded while leading an attack upon a slaver's stockade near Lake Nyasa. But he had found his life's work in service for Africa and for Britain—work that he saw as having a mutually beneficial purpose.

His next enterprise was under the imperial British East Africa Company, one of the chartered companies that preceded imperial annexation in Africa. Leaving Mombasa in August 1890, he led a caravan for five months along an almost untrodden route of 800 miles (1,300 kilometres) to the advanced kingdom of Buganda. Here he found a complex struggle going on among pagans, Muslims, Protestants, and Roman Catholics—the latter two groups converted by British and French missionaries who had reached Buganda earlier by a southern route—and the nominal king, or *kabaka*. Within 18 months—not without a brief use of his one operative Maxim gun—Lugard imposed peace, carried out an immense march to the west, and won a treaty of allegiance from the Kabaka. Hearing that his company meant to abandon Uganda because of mounting expenses, he hurriedly returned to England to fight a successful two-pronged campaign to defend, first, the retention of Uganda plus imperial annexation, and, second, his own reputation against accusations of harshness and injustice.

In 1894–95 Lugard accepted another dangerous mission, this time for the Royal Niger Company, to race the French in a treaty-making exploration on the Middle Niger. He succeeded in that enterprise in spite of great hardships—including a poisoned arrow in his head. From the Niger he went, again at some risk to his life, to the semidesert of the Bechuanaland Protectorate for the private British West Charterland Company, which was prospecting for diamonds. There he was tracked down by a runner sent by the colonial secretary, Joseph Chamberlain, who was offering him his first official government appointment. He was to create a British-officered African regiment that he was to employ in a second attempt to fend off the French, who then were competing with the British right across Africa from the Niger to the Nile. This was to become the famous West African Frontier Force. Lugard's success in this difficult undertaking led to his appointment as high commissioner for Northern Nigeria.

Most of this vast region of 300,000 square miles (800,000 square kilometres) was still unoccupied and even unexplored by Europeans. In the south were pagan tribes and in the north, historic Muslim city-states with large walled cities whose emirs raided the tribal territories to the south for slaves. In three years, by diplomacy or the swift use of his small force, Lugard established British control, though in hastening to take the major states of Kano and Sokoto he forced the hands of his more cautious home government. Only two serious local revolts marred the widespread acceptance and cooperation that Lugard obtained. His policy was to support the native states and chieftainships, their laws and their courts, forbidding slave raiding and cruel punishments and exercising control centrally through the native rulers. This system, cooperative in spirit and economical in staff and expense, he elaborated in his detailed political memorandums. It greatly influenced British administration in Africa and beyond. Though sometimes misapplied or overprolonged, it helped to bridge the gap between tribal systems and the new movements toward democracy and unity. Lugard's main fault as an administrator was an unwillingness to delegate responsibility, but the variety of the conditions and the vast distances acted as a check on this fault. If some of his officers were critical, the majority greatly respected their chief, and a number of "Lugard's men" went on to govern other territories in Africa.

High
commis-
sioner
for
Northern
Nigeria

In 1902 Lugard married Flora Shaw, a beautiful and famous woman, herself a great traveller, an authority upon colonial policy, and a member of the staff of *The Times* of London. A very deep devotion and partnership grew up between them. As she could not stand the Nigerian climate, Lugard felt obliged to leave Africa and to accept the governorship of Hong Kong, which he held from 1907 to 1912. No greater contrast could be imagined than that between the vast untamed expanse of Northern Nigeria and the small island of Hong Kong with its highly civilized Chinese and sophisticated commercial British community. But the bushwhacker from Africa achieved a surprising degree of success and, on his own initiative, founded the University of Hong Kong.

Unification of Nigeria

He could not, however, resist the great opportunity offered to him in 1912 to unite the two parts of Nigeria into one vast state. The south and north showed wide contrasts in their original character and in their traditions of British rule. It was an immense task to unify their administration. Lugard did not attempt a complete fusion of their systems and retained a degree of dualism between south and north. He found the south, especially the sophisticated Africans of Lagos and the southeast, less easy to understand than the northerners; and in 1918 he had to deal with a serious outbreak in the important city-state of Abeokuta. Nor did he find it easy to extend the principles of indirect rule to the loosely organized societies of the Ibo and other southeastern tribes. His tenure of office also was made more difficult by World War I, with its interruption of communications, its resultant shortages of staff, and the war with the Germans in the Cameroons along his eastern frontier. Yet, in the main, Lugard carried through an immense task of unification, which was officially declared on January 1, 1914. Historians must judge the event by the decision of the Nigerians to obtain their independence in 1960 as a united state and to defend it against the attempted Ibo secession to set up an independent state, Biafra, in the late 1960s.

Years as an elder statesman

In 1919 he retired, but only to a life of unceasing activity in his role as the leading authority on colonial government. He wrote his classic *Dual Mandate in British Tropical Africa*, published in 1922. In 1928 he became Baron Lugard of Abinger and spoke with authority in the House of Lords on colonial subjects. He became British member of the Permanent Mandates Commission and of the International Committees on Slavery and Forced Labour and chairman of the International Institute of African Languages and Cultures. To the end of his life, deeply saddened by the death of his wife in 1929, he worked almost incessantly in his secluded house on a survey of matters affecting the interests of native races both inside and outside the British Empire.

Though to modern critics of colonialism there may seem much to criticize in his ideas and actions, there can be no questioning the great range and effectiveness of the three periods of his work: in the opening up of Africa, in its government at a most formative stage in its history; and as elder statesman working during his so-called retirement almost up to his death at Abinger, Surrey, on April 11, 1945.

BIBLIOGRAPHY. MARGERY PERHAM, *Lugard*, vol. 1, *The Years of Adventure, 1858–1898* (1956), vol. 2, *The Years of Authority, 1898–1945* (1960), is a major study, based upon Lugard's own voluminous papers, official sources, upon the writer's travels and researches in the African regions where Lugard operated, and upon a close association between the author and Lugard during the last 15 years of his life. While not uncritical in parts, it is, in the main, a favourable as well as an intimate and lively portrayal. The same author's *Native Administration in Nigeria* (1937, reprinted 1962), gives the longer background against which Lugard's work can be set; *Lugard: The Dual Mandate in British Tropical Africa*, 5th ed. (1965), the classic book on the subject for its period, sets Lugard's own experience against a wider background. See also *The Diaries of Lord Lugard*, ed. by MARGERY PERHAM and M. BULL, 3 vol. (1959). C.L. TEMPLE, *Native Races and Their Rulers*, 2nd. ed. (1968); and C.W.J. ORR, *The Making of Northern Nigeria* (1911), books by two of Lugard's senior officials, reflect contrasting views. D.J.M. MUFFETT, *Concerning Brave Captains* (1964); and I.F. NICHOLSON, *The Administration of Nigeria, 1900–1960* (1969), also by officials who served in Nigeria, represent a reaction against the almost universal approval of Lugard's achievements in Nigeria. They reflect the later, more critical attitude to colonialism. Other studies include A.H.M. KIRK-GREENE, *The Principles of Native Administration in Nigeria: Selected Documents, 1900–1947* (1965) and *Lugard and the Amalgamation of Nigeria* (1968).

(M.Pm.)

Luke, Saint

St. Luke, in Christian tradition, is the author of the third Gospel and the Acts of the Apostles, a companion of St. Paul, and the most literary of New Testament writers.

Luke is first mentioned in the letters of the Apostle Paul as the latter's "co-worker" and as the "beloved physician." The former designation is the more significant one, for it identifies him as one of a professional cadre of itinerant Christian "workers," many of whom were teachers and preachers. His medical skills, like Paul's tentmaking, may have contributed to his livelihood; but his principal occupation was the advancement of the Christian mission.

Details of Luke's life

By courtesy of the Kunsthistorisches Museum, Vienna

St. Luke drawing a picture of the Virgin, detail of a painting by Jan Gossaert, called Mabuse (d. *c.* 1533). In the Kunsthistorisches Museum, Vienna.

If Luke was the author of the third Gospel and the Acts of the Apostles, as is very probable, the course and nature of his ministry may be sketched in more detail. He excludes himself from those who were eyewitnesses of Christ's ministry. His participation in the Pauline mission, however, is indicated by the use of the first person in the so-called "we" sections of Acts. They reveal that Luke shared in instructing persons in the Christian message and possibly in performing miraculous healings.

The "we" sections are analogous to the style of travel reports found elsewhere in writings of the Greco-Roman period. They place the author with St. Paul during his initial mission into Greece; that is, as far as Philippi, in Macedonia (*c.* AD 51). At that place also Luke later rejoins Paul and accompanies him on his final journey to Jerusalem (*c.* AD 58). After Paul's arrest in that city and during his extended detention in nearby Caesarea, Luke may have spent considerable time in Palestine working with the Apostle as the occasion allowed and gathering materials for his future two-volume literary work, the Gospel and the Acts. In any case, two years later he appears with Paul on his prison voyage from Caesarea to Rome and again, according to II Tim. 4:11, at the time of the Apostle's martyrdom in the imperial city (*c.* AD 66). Further direct information about Luke is scanty in the New Testament, but certain inferences may be drawn. The literary style of his writings and the range of his vocabulary mark him as an educated man. The distinction drawn between Luke and other colleagues "of the circumcision" (Col. 4:11) has caused many scholars to conclude that he was a Gentile. If so, he would be the only New Testament writer clearly identifiable as a non-Jew. This conclusion, however, rests upon a doubtful equation of those "of the circumcision" with Jewish Christians. Actually, the phrase probably refers to a particular type of Jewish Christian, those who strictly observed the rituals of Judaism. It offers no support, therefore, to the view that Luke was a Gentile. His intimate knowledge of the Old Testament and the focus of interest in his writings favour, on balance, the view that he was a Jewish Christian who followed a Greek life-style and was comparatively lax in ritual observances.

Later traditions about Luke Writings from the latter half of the second century provide further information. A number of them—St. Irenaeus' *Against Heresies*, the Anti-Marcionite Prologue to the Gospel, and the *Muratorian Canon* listing the books received as sacred by the Christians—identify Luke as the author of the third Gospel and Acts. The Prologue begins:

> Luke is a man from Antioch, Syria, a physician by profession. He was a disciple of the apostles, and later he accompanied Paul until his martyrdom. Having neither wife nor child, he served the Lord without distraction. He fell asleep in Boeotia at the age of 84, full of the Holy Spirit. Moved by the Holy Spirit, Luke composed all of this Gospel in the districts around Achaia . . .

The assertion that St. Luke was "a man from Antioch, Syria" who wrote "moved by the Holy Spirit"—that is, as a prophet—receives a measure of support from the Lukan writings: the city of Antioch figures prominently in Acts, and there is a special interest in contemporary (Christian) prophets and prophecy. Whether Luke is to be identified, as some scholars believe, with the prophet Lucius mentioned in Acts 13:1 and with St. Paul's "fellow worker" (and kinsman) in Romans 16:21 is more questionable, although not impossible. Less than certain also is the comment of the prologue placing the writing of the Gospel and Luke's death in Greece; but, on the whole, it is more probable than the later traditions locating his literary work in Alexandria (or Rome) and his death in Bithynia. The identification of St. Luke as "a disciple of the Apostles," although true in a general sense, probably reflects the concern of the 2nd-century church to place all canonical Christian writings under an apostolic umbrella. Later notions that Luke was one of the 70 disciples appointed by the Lord, that he was the companion of Cleopas, and that he was an artist appear to be legendary. In liturgical tradition Luke's feast day is October 18.

Luke's writings Luke had a cultivated literary background and wrote in good idiomatic Greek. The Gospel bearing his name and the Acts of the Apostles were probably written during or shortly after the Jewish revolt (AD 66–73), although a somewhat later date is not to be excluded. Together they make up more than a fourth of the New Testament, and in them Luke is revealed to be not only Christianity's first historian but also a theologian of unusual perception. Some scholars have also associated Luke with the Pastoral Letters and the Letter to the Hebrews, either as author or as amanuensis, because of linguistic and other similarities with the Gospel and the Acts.

Some scholars, on the other hand, doubt that Luke is in fact the author of the two New Testament books traditionally ascribed to him. In some respects the issue is similar to that raised about the authorship of the works of Shakespeare or, in the classical field, of Plato's letters. But it is unlike the Shakespearean controversy in that no alternative author has been suggested and is unlike the problem of Plato's letters in that no larger Lukan corpus is available for comparison. Those questioning Luke's authorship point to the fact that the theological emphases of his Gospel and the Acts differ considerably from those of Paul's writings and that the description of the Council of Jerusalem (Acts 15) is divergent from the description of the conference in Galatians 2. These objections are based upon the assumption that Luke was the disciple of Paul (and would, therefore, reflect his theology) and upon the traditional identification of Acts 15 with the conference in Galatians 2. Both of these premises, however, are quite probably mistaken. A more serious objection is the difference between the portrait of Paul in Acts

and the impression one receives of him in his letters. But it has sometimes been exaggerated, and it does not in any case exceed the variation that might be expected between a sometime colleague's impressions of a man and the man's own letters. The Gospel and Acts were, in all likelihood, tagged with the name Luke when they were deposited in the library of the author's patron, Theophilus (Luke 1:3). Within a century there was a widespread and undisputed tradition identifying that Luke with an otherwise insignificant physician and colleague of Paul. The tradition is on the whole consistent with the literary and historical character of the documents, and one may be reasonably certain that it is correct.

Jesus' parting words, "It is not for you to know times [of the consummation of this age] . . . but you shall receive power . . . and you shall be my witnesses . . ." (Acts 1:7ff), provide a guideline for Luke's theology. Thus, he called the church back from overeager speculation about the precise time of the Lord's return and the end of the age to its proper task of faithful mission in the lengthening interim. By the selection and interpretation of his sources, he charted the path by which the church would understand both its own uniqueness in the world and also its continuing relationship to Judaism and to the world. His work was no small achievement, and through the centuries it has served the church well.

BIBLIOGRAPHY. C.K. BARRETT, *Luke the Historian in Recent Study* (1961), a brief and readable survey by a number of contemporary writers; "The Identity of the Editor of Luke and Acts", pp. 205–359, in F.J.F. JACKSON and K. LAKE (eds.), *The Beginnings of Christianity*, vol. 2, pt. 1, *The Acts of the Apostles* (1922), an extensive presentation and critical analysis of biblical and post-biblical traditions about St. Luke and their bearing on the question of the authorship of Luke-Acts; E.E. ELLIS (ed.), *The Gospel of Luke* (1967), a short summary of the background, life, and theology of the evangelist in the light of recent research; I.H. MARSHALL, *Luke: Historian and Theologian* (1970), Lukan writings treated from the viewpoint of a unifying theological theme; L.E. KECK and J.L. MARTYN (eds.), *Studies in Luke-Acts* (1966), a collection of historical and theological essays.

(E.E.E.)

Luminescence

Luminescence is the emission of light by certain materials when they are relatively cool. It is in contrast to light emitted from incandescent bodies, such as burning wood or coal, molten iron, and wire heated by an electric current. Luminescence may be seen in neon and fluorescent lamps; television, radar, and X-ray fluoroscope screens; organic substances such as luminol or the luciferins in fireflies and glowworms; certain pigments used in outdoor advertising; and also natural electrical phenomena such as lightning and the aurora borealis. In all these phenomena, light emission does not result from the material being above room temperature, and so luminescence is often called cold light. The practical value of luminescent materials lies in their capacity to transform invisible forms of energy into visible light.

Luminescence emission occurs after an appropriate material has absorbed energy from a source such as ultraviolet or X-ray radiation, electron beams, chemical reactions, and so on. The energy lifts the atoms of the material into an excited state, and then, because excited states are unstable, the material undergoes another transition, back to its unexcited ground state, and the absorbed energy is liberated in the form of either light or heat or both (all Luminescence a quantum process discrete energy states, including the ground state, of an atom are defined as quantum states). The excitation involves only the outermost electrons orbiting around the nuclei of the atoms. Luminescence efficiency depends on the degree of transformation of excitation energy into light, and there are relatively few materials that have sufficient luminescence efficiency to be of practical value.

Luminescence and incandescence. As mentioned above, luminescence is characterized by electrons undergoing transitions from excited quantum states. The excitation of the luminescent electrons is not connected with appreciable agitations of the atoms that the electrons belong to. When hot materials become luminous and radiate light, a process called incandescence, the atoms of the material are in a high state of agitation. Of course, the atoms of every material are vibrating at room temperature already, but this vibration is just sufficient to produce temperature radiation in the far infrared region of the spectrum. With increasing temperature this radiation shifts into the visible region. On the other hand, at very high temperatures, such as are generated in shock tubes, the collisions of atoms can be so violent that electrons dissociate from the atoms and recombine with them, emitting light: in this case luminescence and incandescence become indistinguishable.

Luminescent pigments and dyes. Nonluminescent pigments and dyes exhibit colours because they absorb white light and reflect that part of the spectrum that is complementary to the absorbed light. A small fraction of the absorbed light is transformed into heat, but no appreciable radiation is produced. If, however, an appropriate luminescent pigment absorbs daylight in a special region of its spectrum, it can emit light of a colour different from that of the reflected light. This is the result of electronic processes within the molecule of the dye or pigment by which even ultraviolet light can be transformed to visible—*e.g.*, blue—light. These pigments are used in such diverse ways as in outdoor advertising, blacklight displays, and laundering: in the latter case, a residue of the "brightener" is left in the cloth, not only to reflect white light but also to convert ultraviolet light into blue light, thus offsetting any yellowness and reinforcing the white appearance.

History of luminescence. Although lightning, the aurora borealis, and the dim light of glowworms and of fungi have always been known to mankind, the first investigations (1603) of luminescence began with a synthetic material, when Vincenzo Cascariolo, an alchemist and cobbler in Bologna, Italy, heated a mixture of barium sulfate (in the form of barite, heavy spar) and coal; the powder obtained after cooling exhibited a bluish glow at night, and Cascariolo observed that this glow could be restored by exposure of the powder to sunlight. The name *lapis solaris*, or "sunstone," was given to the material because alchemists at first hoped it would transform baser metals into gold, the symbol for gold being the sun. The pronounced afterglow aroused the interest of many learned men of that period, who gave the material other names, including phosphorus, meaning "light bearer," which thereafter was applied to any material that glowed in the dark.

First investigation

Today, the name phosphorus is used for the chemical element only, whereas certain microcrystalline luminescent materials are called phosphors. Cascariolo's phosphor evidently was a barium sulfide; the first commercially available phosphor (1870) was "Balmain's paint," a calcium sulfide preparation. In 1866 the first stable zinc sulfide phosphor was described. It is one of the most important phosphors in modern technology.

Bioluminescence and chemiluminescence. One of the first scientific investigations of the luminescence exhibited by rotting wood or flesh and by glowworms, known from antiquity, was performed in 1672 by Robert Boyle, an English scientist, who, although not aware of the biochemical origin of that light, nevertheless established some of the basic properties of bioluminescent systems: that the light is cold; that it can be inhibited by chemical agents such as alcohol, hydrochloric acid, and ammonia; and that the light emission is dependent on air (as later established, on oxygen).

Bioluminescence

In 1885–87 it was observed that crude extracts prepared from West Indian fireflies (*Pyrophorus*) and from the boring clam, *Pholas*, gave a light-emitting reaction when mixed together. One of the preparations was a cold-water extract containing a compound relatively unstable to heat, luciferase; the other was a hot-water extract containing a relatively heat-stable compound, luciferin. The luminescent reaction that occurred when solutions of luciferase and luciferin were mixed at room temperature suggested that all bioluminescent reactions are "luciferin–luciferase reactions." In view of the complex nature of bioluminescent reactions, it is not astonishing that this simple concept of bioluminescence has had to be modified. Only a small number of bioluminescent systems have been investigated for their respective luciferin and the corresponding luciferase, the best known being the bioluminescence of fireflies from the United States; a little crustacean living in the Japanese sea (*Cypridina hilgendorfii*); and decaying fish and flesh (bacterial bioluminescence). Although bioluminescent systems have not yet found practical applications, they are interesting because of their high luminescence efficiency.

The first efficient chemiluminescent materials were nonbiological synthetic compounds such as luminol (with the formula 5-amino-2,3-dihydro-1.4-phthalazinedione). The strong blue chemiluminescence resulting from oxidation of this compound was first reported in 1928.

Phosphorescence and fluorescence. The name luminescence has been accepted for all light phenomena not caused solely by a rise of temperature, but the distinction between the terms phosphorescence and fluorescence is still open to discussion. With respect to organic molecules, the term phosphorescence means light emission caused by electronic transitions between levels of different multiplicity (explained more fully below), whereas the term fluorescence is used for light emission connected with electronic transitions between levels of like multiplicity. The situation is far more complicated in the case of inorganic phosphors.

The term phosphorescence was first used to describe the persistent luminescence (afterglow) of phosphors. The mechanism described above for the phosphorescence of excited organic molecules fits this picture in that it is also responsible for light persistence up to several seconds. Fluorescence, on the other hand, is an almost instantaneous effect, ending within about 10^{-8} second after excitation. The term fluorescence was coined in 1852, when it was experimentally demonstrated that certain substances absorb light of a narrow spectral region (*e.g.*, blue light) and instantaneously emit light in another spectral region not present in the incident light (*e.g.*, yellow light) and that this emission ceases at once when the irradiation of the material comes to an end. The name fluorescence was derived from the mineral fluorspar, which exhibits a violet, short-duration luminescence on irradiation by ultraviolet light.

Luminescence excitation. *Chemiluminescence and bioluminescence.* Most of the energy liberated in chemical reactions, especially oxidation reactions, is in the form of heat. In some reactions, however, part of the energy is used to excite electrons to higher energy states, and, for fluorescent molecules, chemiluminescence results. Studies indicate that chemiluminescence is a universal phenomenon, although the light intensities observed are usually so small that sensitive detectors are necessary. There are, however, some compounds that exhibit brilliant chemiluminescence, the best known being luminol, which, when oxidized by hydrogen peroxide, can yield a strong blue or blue-greenish chemiluminescence. Other instances of strong chemiluminescences are lucigenin (an acridinium compound) and lophine (an imidazole derivative). In spite of the brilliance of their chemiluminescence, not all of these compounds are efficient in transforming chemical energy into light energy, because only about 1 percent or less of the reacting molecules emit light. During the 1960s, esters (organic compounds that are products of reactions between organic acids and alcohols) of oxalic acid were found that, when oxidized in nonaqueous solvents in the presence of highly fluorescent aromatic compounds, emit brilliant light with an efficiency up to 23 percent.

Bioluminescence is a special type of chemiluminescence catalyzed by enzymes. The light yield of such reactions can reach 100 percent, which means that almost without exception every molecule of the reacting luciferin is transformed into a radiating state. All of the bioluminescent reactions best known today are catalyzed oxidation reactions occurring in the presence of air.

Role of enzymes

Triboluminescence. When crystals of certain substances—*e.g.*, sugar—are crushed, luminescent sparkles are visible. Similar observations have been made with numerous organic and inorganic substances. Closely related are the faint blue luminescence observable when adhesive tapes are stripped from a roll, and the luminescence exhibited when strontium bromate and some other salts are crystallized from hot solutions. In all of these cases, positive and negative electric charges are produced by the mechanical separation of surfaces and during the crystallization process. Light emission then occurs by discharge, either directly, by molecule fragments, or via excitation of the atmosphere in the neighbourhood of the separated surface: the blue glow coming from adhesive tapes being unrolled is emitted from nitrogen molecules of the air that have been excited by the electric discharge.

Thermoluminescence. Thermoluminescence means not temperature radiation but enhancement of the light emission of materials already excited electronically by the application of heat. The phenomenon is observed with some minerals and, above all, with crystal phosphors after they have been excited by light.

Photoluminescence. Photoluminescence, which occurs by virtue of electromagnetic radiation falling on matter, may range from visible light through ultraviolet, X-ray, and gamma radiation. It has been shown that, in luminescence caused by light, the wavelength of emitted light generally is equal to or longer than that of the exciting light (*i.e.*, of equal or less energy). As explained below, this difference in wavelength is caused by a transformation of the exciting light, to a greater or lesser extent, to nonradiating vibration energy of atoms or ions. In rare instances—*e.g.*, when intense irradiation by laser beams is used or when sufficient thermal energy contributes to the electron excitation process—the emitted light can be of shorter wavelength than the exciting light (anti-Stokes radiation).

The fact that photoluminescence can also be excited by ultraviolet radiation was first observed by a German physicist, Johann Wilhelm Ritter (1801), who investigated the behaviour of phosphors in light of various colours. He found that phosphors luminesce brightly in the invisible region beyond violet and thus discovered ultraviolet radiation. The transformation of ultraviolet light to visible light has much practical importance.

Gamma rays and X-rays excite crystal phosphors and other materials to luminescence by the ionization process (*i.e.*, the detachment of electrons from atoms), followed by a recombination of electrons and ions to produce visible light. Advantage of this is taken in the fluoroscope used in X-ray diagnostics and in the scintillation counter that detects and measures gamma rays directed onto a phosphor disk that is in optical contact with the face of a photomultiplier tube (a device that amplifies light signals).

Electroluminescence. Like thermoluminescence, the term electroluminescence includes several distinct phenomena, a common feature of which is that light is emitted by an electrical discharge in gases, liquids, and solid materials. Benjamin Franklin, in the United States, for example, in 1752 identified the luminescence of lightning as caused by electric discharge through the atmosphere. An electric-discharge lamp was first demonstrated in 1860 to the Royal Society of London. It produced a brilliant white light by the discharge of high voltage through carbon dioxide at low pressure. Modern fluorescent lamps are based on a combination of electroluminescence and photoluminescence: mercury atoms in the lamp are excited by electric discharge, and the ultraviolet light emitted by the mercury atoms is transformed into visible light by a phosphor (see LIGHTING AND LIGHTING DEVICES).

The electroluminescence sometimes observed at the electrodes during electrolysis is caused by the recombination of ions (therefore, this is a sort of chemiluminescence). The application of an electric field to thin layers of luminescing zinc sulfide can produce light emission, which is also called electroluminescence.

A great number of materials luminesce under the impact of accelerated electrons (once called cathode rays); *e.g.*, diamond, ruby, crystal phosphors, and certain complex salts of platinum. The first practical application of catho-

doluminescence was in the viewing screen of an oscilloscope tube constructed in 1897; similar screens used in television, radar, oscilloscopes, and electron microscopes are made possible by the production of efficient and colour-selective crystal phosphors.

The impact of accelerated electrons on molecules can produce molecular ions, ions of molecule fragments, and atomic ions. In gas-discharge tubes these particles were first detected as "canal rays" or anode rays. They are able to excite phosphors but not as efficiently as electrons can.

Radioluminescence. Radioactive elements can emit alpha particles (helium nuclei), electrons, and gamma rays (high-energy electromagnetic radiation). The term radioluminescence, therefore, means that an appropriate material is excited to luminescence by a radioactive substance. When alpha particles bombard a crystal phosphor, tiny scintillations are visible to microscopic observation. This is the principle of the device used by an English physicist, Ernest Rutherford, to prove that an atom has a central nucleus. Self-luminous paints, such as are used for dial markings for watches and other instruments, owe their behaviour to radioluminescence. These paints consist of a phosphor and a radioactive substance, *e.g.*, tritium or radium. An impressive natural radioluminescence is the aurora borealis: by the radioactive processes of the sun, enormous masses of electrons and ions are emitted into space in the solar wind. When they approach the earth, they are concentrated by its geomagnetic field near the poles. Discharge processes of the particles in the upper atmosphere yield the famous luminance of the auroras.

Luminescent materials and phosphor chemistry. The first phosphor synthesized was probably an impure barium sulfide preparation with very low luminance efficiency and with the serious shortcoming that it was rather quickly decomposed in moist air, yielding hydrogen sulfide. A more stable sulfide-type phosphor was produced in 1866 by heating zinc oxide in a stream of hydrogen sulfide. In 1887 it became known that these sulfides do not luminesce in a chemically pure state but only when they contain small quantities of a so-called activator metal. Later, other materials, such as certain metal oxides, silicates, and phosphates, were found to luminesce if they were prepared by special procedures.

Sulfide-type phosphors, activators, fluxes. The sulfides of zinc and of cadmium are the most important basic materials of sulfide-type phosphors. An important condition of getting highly efficient phosphors is that these sulfides must first be prepared to the highest possible chemical purity before the necessary amount of activator can be added precisely. The emission of zinc sulfide can be shifted to longer wavelengths by increasing substitution of the zinc ions by cadmium ions. Zinc sulfide and cadmium sulfide phosphors are especially efficient in electroluminescence.

Sulfide-type phosphors are produced from pure zinc or cadmium sulfide or their mixtures by heating them together with small quantities (0.1–0.001 percent) of copper, silver, gallium, or other salts (activators) and with about 2 percent of sodium or another alkali chloride at about 1,000° C (1,832° F). The role of the alkali halides is to facilitate the melting process and, above all, to serve as coactivators (fluxes). Only small quantities of the alkali halide are integrated into the phosphor, but this small quantity is highly important for its luminescence efficiency. Copper-activated zinc and cadmium sulfides exhibit a rather long afterglow when their irradiation has ceased, and this is favourable for application in radar screens and self-luminous phosphors.

Oxide-type phosphors. Certain oxide-type minerals have been found to luminesce when irradiated. In some of them, activators must first be introduced into the crystal. Examples are ruby (aluminum oxide with chromium activator—bright-red emission) and willemite (zinc orthosilicate with manganese activator—green emission). On the other hand, scheelite (calcium tungstate) emits a blue luminescence without activator. All of these minerals have been made synthetically, with remarkably higher efficiencies than those that occur naturally. Silicates, bor-

Electric
discharge

Synthetic
phosphors

ates, and phosphates of the second group of the periodic table of elements, such as zinc silicate, zinc beryllium silicate, zinc and cadmium borates, and cadmium phosphates, become efficient phosphors when activated with manganese ions, emitting in the red to green region of the spectrum. They have been incorporated into colour television screens to emit the colours blue (silver-activated zinc sulfide), green (manganese-activated zinc orthosilicate), and red (europium-activated yttrium vanadate).

Centres, activators, coactivators, poisons. The study of phosphor chemistry has yielded a detailed picture of the role of the above-mentioned activators and fluxes. Philipp Anton Lenard, a physicist in Germany, was the first (1890) to describe activator ions as being distributed in zinc sulfide and other crystalline materials that serve as the host crystal. The activator ions are surrounded by host-crystal ions and form luminescing centres where the excitation–emission process of the phosphor takes place. These centres must not be too close together within the host crystal lest they inactivate each other. For high efficiency, only a trace of the activator may be inserted into the host crystal, and its distribution must be as regular as possible. In high concentration, activators act as "poisons" or "killers" and thus inhibit luminescence. The term killer is used especially for iron, cobalt, and nickel ions, whose presence, even in small quantities, can inhibit the emission of light from phosphors.

Phosphors, such as calcium tungstate or zinc sulfide, that need no activator appear to have their luminescing centres in special groups of atoms different from the symmetry of their own crystal lattice, such as the group WO_4 in the compound calcium tungstate, formula $CaWO_4$, or, similarly, the SiO_4 group in zinc orthosilicate, formula Zn_2SiO_4. That luminescing properties of a centre are strongly dependent on the symmetry of neighbouring ion groups with respect to the whole phosphor molecule is clearly proved by the spectral shifts of certain phosphors activated with lanthanide ions, which emit in narrow spectral regions. Because of this altering effect on the symmetry of luminescing centres, small quantities (about 0.2 percent) of titania incorporated in zinc orthosilicate give a remarkable increase in luminescence. Titania is called an intensifier activator because it increases the host-crystal luminescence, whereas a substance that produces luminescence not exhibited by the chemically pure host crystal is called an originative activator.

The fluxes (*e.g.*, sodium chloride) act as coactivators by facilitating the incorporation of activator ions. Copper ions, for instance, are used as activators of zinc chloride phosphors and are usually introduced in the copper(II), or cupric, form (the Roman numeral indicates the oxidation state; that is, I means that the element has one electron involved in a chemical bond and II that it has two electrons involved; the larger oxidation state is indicated by the *-ic* ending and the smaller by the *-ous* ending). If a copper(II) compound is incorporated into the zinc sulfide by heating, copper(I) sulfide (or cuprous sulfide, formula Cu_2S) will be produced with crystals that will not fit into the host-crystal zinc chloride because their form is so different, and only a relatively few luminescent centres will be possible. On the other hand, if a coactivator such as sodium chloride is introduced along with the copper(II) salt, the copper(II) ions are reduced to form copper(I) chloride (or cuprous chloride, formula CuCl) crystals with the same structure as the host crystal. Thus, many luminescent centres will be produced, and strong activation will result.

In describing a luminescent phosphor, the following information is pertinent: crystal class and chemical composition of the host crystal, activator (type and percentage), coactivator (intensifier activator), temperature and time of crystallization process, emission spectrum (or at least visual colour), and persistence. A few phosphors and their activators are listed in Table 1.

Organic luminescent materials. Although the inorganic phosphors are industrially produced in far higher quantities (several hundred tons per year) than the organic luminescent materials, some types of the latter are becoming more and more important in special fields of

Killers (margin note)

Table 1: Visual Properties of Some Luminescent Materials

phosphor (phosphor/activator; coactivator)	emission	
	colour*	persistence
rhombohedral Zn_2SiO_4/Mn 0.3 % (rhombohedral zinc orthosilicate/ manganese 0.3 %); 1,200° C 60 min, slow cooling	green (525 nm)	short (0.01 sec)
β-Zn_2SiO_4/Mn 0.3 % (beta zinc orthosilicate/manganese 0.3 %); 1,600° C 10 min, quench cooling	yellow (610 nm)	short (0.01 sec)
cubic ZnS/Cu 0.03 %; Cl (cubic zinc sulfide/copper 0.03 %; chloride); 950° C 10 min, slow cooling	green-blue (516 nm)	long (hours)
hexagonal ZnS/Cu 0.03 %; Cl (hexagonal zinc sulfide/ copper 0.03 %; chloride); 1,250° C 10 min, slow cooling	green (528 nm)	very long (up to 24 hours)

*The wavelengths of the respective emission maxima are given in parentheses. 1 nanometre (nm) = 10^{-9} metre = 1 millimicron = 10 angstroms.

practical application. Paints and dyes for outdoor advertising contain strongly fluorescing organic molecules such as fluorescein, eosin, rhodamine, and stilbene derivatives. Their main shortcoming is their relatively poor stability in light, because of which they are used mostly when durability is not required. Organic phosphors are used as optical brighteners for invisible markers of laundry, banknotes, identity cards, and stamps and for fluorescence microscopy of tissues in biology and medicine. Their "invisibility" is due to the fact that they absorb practically no visible light. The fluorescence is excited by invisible ultraviolet radiation (black light).

Photoradiation in gases, liquids, and crystals. When describing chemical principles associated with luminescence, it is useful, at first, to neglect interactions between the luminescing atoms, molecules, or centres with their environment. In the gas phase these interactions are smaller than they are in the condensed phase of a liquid or a solid material. The efficiency of luminescence in the gas phase will be far greater than in the condensed phases because in the latter the energy of the electrons excited by photons or by chemical-reaction energy can be dissipated as thermal, nonradiative energy by collision of the atoms or by the rotational and vibrational energy of the molecules. This effect has to be taken into account even more when the radiation of single atoms is compared with that of multi-atomic molecules. For molecules, radiative (electronic-excitation) energy is internally converted to vibrational energy; that is, there are radiationless transitions of electrons in atoms. This is the explanation for the fact that only a relatively small number of compounds are able to exhibit efficient luminescence. In crystals, on the other hand, the binding forces between the ions or atoms of the lattice are strong compared with the forces acting between the particles of a liquid, and electron-excitation energy, therefore, is not as easily transformed into vibrational energy, thus leading to a good efficiency for radiative processes.

Effect of binding force (margin note)

Luminescence physics. *Mechanism of luminescence.* The emission of visible light (that is, light of wavelengths between about 690 nanometres and 400 nanometres, corresponding to the region between deep red and deep violet) requires excitation energies the minimum of which is given by Einstein's law stating that the energy (E) is equal to Planck's constant (h) times the frequency of light (ν), or Planck's constant times the velocity of light (c) in a vacuum divided by its wavelength (λ); that is,

$$E = h\nu = \frac{hc}{\lambda}.$$

The energy required for excitation therefore ranges between 40 kilocalories (for red light), about 60 kilocalories (for yellow light), and about 80 kilocalories (for violet light) per mole of substance. Instead of expressing these energies in kilocalories, electron volt units (one electron volt = 1.6 x 10^{-12} erg; the erg is an extremely small unit of energy) may be used, and the photon energy thus required in the visible region ranges from 1.8 to 3.1 electron volts.

The excitation energy is transferred to the electrons responsible for luminescence, which jump from their ground-state energy level to a level of higher energy. The energy levels that electrons can assume are specified by quantum mechanical laws. The different excitation mechanisms considered below depend on whether or not the excitation of electrons occurs in single atoms, in single molecules, in combinations of molecules, or in a crystal. They are initiated by the means of excitation described above: impact of accelerated particles such as electrons, positive ions, or photons. Often, the excitation energies are considerably higher than those necessary to lift electrons to a radiative level; for example, the luminescence produced by the phosphor crystals in television screens is excited by cathode-ray electrons with average energies of 25,000 electron volts. Nevertheless, the colour of the luminescent light is nearly independent of the energy of the exciting particles, depending chiefly on the excited-state energy level of the crystal centres.

Electron excitation

Electrons taking part in the luminescence process are the outermost electrons of atoms or molecules. In fluorescent lamps, for example, a mercury atom is excited by the impact of an electron having an energy of 6.7 electron volts or more, raising one of the two outermost electrons of the mercury atom in the ground state to a higher level. Upon the electron's return to the ground state, an energy difference is emitted as ultraviolet light of a wavelength of 185 nanometres. A radiative transition between another excited state and the ground-state level of the mercury atom produces the important ultraviolet emission of 254-nanometre wavelength, which, in turn, can excite other phosphors to emit visible light. (One such phosphor frequently used is a calcium halophosphate incorporating a heavy-metal activator.)

This 254-nanometre mercury radiation is particularly intensive at low mercury vapour pressures (around 10^{-5} atmosphere) used in low-pressure discharge lamps. About 60 percent of the input electron energy may thus be transformed into near-monochromatic ultraviolet light; *i.e.*, ultraviolet light of practically one single wavelength.

Whereas at low pressure there are relatively few collisions of mercury atoms with each other, the collision frequency increases enormously if mercury gas is excited under high pressure (*e.g.*, eight atmospheres or more), Such excitation leads not only to collisional de-excitation of excited atoms but also to additional excitation of excited atoms. As a consequence, the spectrum of the emitted radiation no longer consists of practically one single, sharp spectral line at 254 nanometres, but the radiation energy is distributed over various broadened spectral lines corresponding to different electronic energy levels of the mercury atom, the strongest emissions lying at 303, 313, 334, 366, 405, 436, 546, and 578 nanometres. High-pressure mercury lamps can be used for illumination purposes because the emissions from 405 to 546 nanometres are visible light of bluish-green colour; by transforming a part of the mercury line emission to red light by means of a phosphor, white light is obtained.

When gaseous molecules are excited, their luminescence spectra show broad bands; not only are electrons lifted to levels of higher energy but vibrational and rotational motions of the atoms as a whole are excited simultaneously. This is because vibrational and rotational energies of molecules are only about 10^{-2} and 10^{-4}, respectively, those of the electronic transition energies, and these many energies can be added to the energy of a single electronic transition, which is represented by a multitude of slightly different wavelengths making up one band. In larger molecules, several overlapping bands, one for each kind of electronic transition, can be emitted. Emission from molecules in solution is predominantly bandlike caused by interactions of a relatively great number of excited molecules with molecules of the solvent. In molecules, as in atoms, the excited electrons generally are outermost electrons of the molecular orbitals.

The terms fluorescence and phosphorescence can be used here, on the basis not only of the persistence of luminescence but also of the way in which the luminescence is produced. When an electron is excited to what is called, in spectroscopy, an excited singlet state, the state will have a lifetime of about 10^{-8} second, from which the excited electron can easily return to its ground state (which normally is a singlet state, too), emitting its excitation energy as fluorescence. During this electronic transition the spin of the electron is not altered; the singlet ground state and the excited singlet state have like multiplicity (number of subdivisions into which a level can be split). An electron, however, may also be lifted, under reversal of its spin, to a higher energy level, called an excited triplet state. Singlet ground states and excited triplet states are levels of different multiplicity. For quantum mechanical reasons, transitions from triplet states to singlet states are "forbidden," and, therefore, the lifetime of triplet states is considerably longer than that of singlet states. This means that luminescence originating in triplet states has a far longer duration than that originating in singlet states: phosphorescence is observed.

Phospho-
rescence

The interactions of a large number of atoms, ions, or molecules are greater still in solution and in solids; to obtain a narrowing of the spectral band, subzero temperatures (down to that of liquid helium) are applied in order to reduce vibrational motions. The electronic energy levels of crystals such as zinc sulfide and other host crystals used in phosphors form bands: in the ground state practically all electrons are to be found on the valence band, whereas they reach the conduction band after sufficient excitation (see SEMICONDUCTORS AND INSULATORS, THEORY OF). The energy difference between the valence band and the conduction band corresponds to photons in the ultraviolet or still shorter wavelength region. Additional energy levels are introduced by activator ions or centres bridging the energy gap between valence band and conduction band, and, when an electron is transferred from the valence band to such an additional energy level by excitation energy, it can produce visible light on return to the ground state. A rather close analogy exists between the forbidden transitions of certain excited molecular electronic states (triplet–singlet, leading to phosphorescence) and the transition of an electron of an inorganic phosphor kept in a trap: traps (certain distortions in the crystal lattice) are places in the crystal lattice where the energy level is lower than that of the conduction band, and from which the direct return of an electron to the ground state is also forbidden.

When a solid is bombarded by photons or particles, the excitation of the centres can occur directly or by energy transfer. In the latter case, excited but nonluminescing states are produced at some distance from the centre, with the energy moving through the crystal in the form of excitons (ion–electron pairs) until it approaches a centre where the excitation process can occur. This energy transfer can also be realized by radiation in inorganic phosphors containing two activators, as well as in solutions of organic molecules.

Decay; stimulated emission. The radiative return of excited electrons to their ground state occurs spontaneously, and when there exists an assembly of excited electrons their individual spontaneous radiative transitions are independent of each other. Therefore, the luminescence light is incoherent (the emitted waves are not in phase with each other) in this case. Sometimes the emission of luminescence can be stimulated by irradiation with photons of the same frequency as that of the emitted light; such stimulated transitions are used in lasers, which produce very intensive beams of coherent monochromatic light.

The spontaneous luminescent emission follows an exponential law that expresses the rate of intensity decay and is similar to the equation for the decay of radioactivity and some chemical reactions. It states that the intensity of luminescent emission is equal to an exponential value of minus the time of decay divided by the decay time, or $L = L_0 \exp(-t/\tau)$, in which L is the intensity of emission at a time t after an initial intensity L_0, and τ is the decay time of the luminescence; that is, the time in which the

Exponential decay

assembly of the excited atoms would decrease in luminescence intensity to a value of 0.368 L_0.

When excited atoms of the centres are in contact with other atoms, as is the case in condensed phases (liquids, solids, in gases of not-too-low pressure), part of the excitation energy will be transformed into heat by collisional deactivation (thermal quenching). The decay time, therefore, has to be replaced by an effective excited-state lifetime, resulting in a more complicated exponential decay law that depends on the collision frequency, the energy imparted to the excited atoms of the centre that causes the transfer of excitation energy into heat (activation energy), a constant, and the temperature of the luminescent material. This law describes the actual luminescence decay of a great number of luminescent materials; *e.g.*, calcium tungstate.

Increase of activation energy for nonradiative deactivation of excited-centres luminescence decay can be achieved by changing the host crystal or by electron traps. The traps are imperfections in the crystal lattice where electrons are captured after they have been ejected from a luminescent centre by excitation energy. That the luminescent properties of phosphor centres are strongly dependent on the chemical nature of the host crystal may be seen in Table 2, showing that the same activator ions

Table 2: Influence of Host Crystal on the Lifetime and Emission Colour of the Excited Phosphors

host crystal	activator	time (second)	emission colour
Tetragonal zinc fluoride, ZnF_2	manganese(II)	0.1	orange
Rhombic cadmium sulfate, $CdSO_4$	manganese(II)	0.05	orange
Rhombic magnesium sulfate, $MgSO_4$	manganese(II)	0.03	red
Rhombic zinc phosphate, $Zn_3(PO_4)_2$	manganese(II)	0.02	red
Cadmium silicate, $CdSiO_3$	manganese(II)	0.019	orange
Zinc orthosilicate, Zn_2SiO_4	manganese(II)	0.018	yellow
Cadmium pyroborate, $Cd_2B_2O_5$	manganese(II)	0.015	red orange
Rhombohedral zinc orthosilicate, Zn_2SiO_4	manganese(II)	0.013	green
Rhombohedral zinc germanate, Zn_2GeO_4	manganese(II)	0.0105	green yellow
Cubic zinc aluminate, $ZnAl_2O_4$	manganese(II)	0.0055	blue green
Cubic zinc gallate, $ZnGa_2O_4$	manganese(II)	0.0043	green blue
Hexagonal zinc sulfide, ZnS	manganese(II)	0.0004	orange

(manganese ions with two positive charges, indicated as Mn^{2+}, or Mn[II]), in different host crystals yield remarkably different-coloured emissions and decay times (measured in fractions of a second).

Prolonging the emission time of phosphors up to days or even longer (production of phosphorescence of the phosphors) is possible by inserting traps into the host crystal. Trapped electrons cannot return directly to the centre. In order to be released from the traps they must first obtain additional thermal energy—in this case, thermal energy stimulates luminescence—after which they recombine with a centre and undergo radiative transition. Trapping in crystals has its analogy to forbidden transitions in molecules (triplet–singlet transitions) or in radiation processes from metastable atomic-energy levels.

An example of a practical application of stimulated emission of a phosphor with trapped electrons is cubic strontium sulfide/selenide activated with samarium and europium ions, the coactivators being strontium sulfate and calcium fluoride. This phosphor has been used in devices for viewing scenes at night by reflected infrared light emitted by infrared lamps. The traps in this phosphor have been identified as samarium ions, whereas europium ions are the active ions in the centres. The phosphor is first excited by photons of about three electron volts (blue light), which results in an ejection of an electron from a europium ion (Eu^{2+}) centre. This excited

electron is trapped by a triply charged samarium ion (Sm^{3+}), which is transferred to a doubly charged samarium ion (Sm^{2+}). Heat or irradiation by infrared photons releases one electron from the doubly charged samarium ion (Sm^{2+}). The electron is then recaptured from a triply charged europium ion (Eu^{3+}), yielding an excited doubly charged europium ion (Eu^{2+}), which returns to its ground state by emitting a photon of 2.2 electron volts energy (yellow light). The trap depth of this phosphor (*i.e.*, the energy required for release of an electron from it) is large compared to the thermal energy of the lattice of the host crystal, and, therefore, the lifetime of the traps at room temperature is many months long. Bombarding this phosphor with photons of energy higher than that of infrared photons but not sufficient for excitation can lead to photoquenching: the traps are emptied far more rapidly, and thermal deactivation of the centres is enhanced.

When iron, cobalt, or nickel ions are present in a phosphor, an excited electron can be captured by these ions. The excitation energy is then emitted as infrared photons, not as visible light, so that luminescence is quenched. These ions, therefore, are called killers—the killing process being opposite to stimulation.

In chemiluminescence, such as the oxidation of luminol, light emission depends not only on radiative and quenching or intramolecular deactivation processes but also on the efficiency of the chemical reaction leading to molecules in an electronically excited state.

In bioluminescence reactions, the production of electronically excited molecules, as well as their radiative transitions back to their ground state, is efficiently catalyzed by the enzymes acting here, and bioluminescence light output is therefore high.

The luminescence photons emitted by one kind of excited atom, molecule, or phosphor can excite another to emit its specific luminescence: this type of energy transfer is observed with inorganic as well as organic substances. Thus, excited benzene molecules can excite naphthalene molecules by radiative-energy transfer. The radiation produced by the luminol chemiluminescence can produce fluorescence when fluorescein is added to the reaction mixture. In most of these cases the acceptor molecules have luminescent electrons with energy levels lower than those of the primary excited molecules, and emitted secondary luminescence is therefore of longer wavelength than the primary. Practical application of this phenomenon, called cascading, is used in radar kinescopes, which have composite fluorescent screens consisting of a layer of blue-emitting zinc sulfide/silver (chloride) phosphor —the hexagonal crystal, ZnS/Ag(Cl) deposited on a layer of yellow-emitting zinc or cadmium sulfide/copper [chloride] phosphor [the hexagonal crystal, (Zn,Cd)S/Cu (Cl)].

The cathode-ray electrons excite the blue-emitting phosphor, whose photons, in turn, excite the yellow-emitting phosphor, which has traps with a decay time of about 10 seconds. Excitation of the blue-emitting phosphor alone would be unfavourable, as the sharply focussed cathode rays are absorbed by the blue phosphor to a small extent only, and its decay time is too short; also, direct excitation of the yellow-emitting phosphor alone would yield poor efficiency because the traps are emptied too rapidly by the heat produced by the relatively high-energetic electron impact.

Another energy-transfer mechanism is called sensitization: a calcium carbonate phosphor (rhombohedral $CaCO_3$/Mn), for example, emits orange light under cathode-ray irradiation but is not excited by the 254-nanometre emission of mercury atoms, whereas this emission produces the same orange light with calcium carbonate (rhombohedral $CaCO_3$) activated by manganese and lead ions. This is not cascade luminescence, because a mechanical mixture of a manganese and a lead-activated calcium carbonate exhibits no emission under ultraviolet radiation. In a phosphor containing both activators, the lead ions act as sensitizers in introducing an additional excitation band into the system from which the manganese ions get their excitation energy in a nonradiative

Cascading

energy transfer. Similar sensitization is observed in gases and in liquids.

Solid state energy-level diagrams; electroluminescence. The complicated problems concerning the energy states in solids of a luminescence centre are commonly visualized by adapting the energy-level diagram used in describing energy transitions in an isolated diatomic molecule (Figure 1).

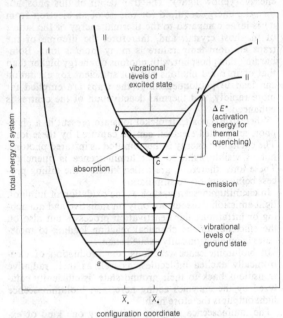

configuration coordinate
Figure 1: Energy levels of a luminescent centre (see text).

In this diagram, the potential energy of a centre is plotted as a function of the average distance $(\bar{x})$ between the atoms: $\bar{x}^*$ represents the ground state and $\bar{x}_o$ represents the lowest excited state of the centre. In a tetrahedral permanganate-ion centre (MnO_4), for example $\bar{x}$ would be the average distance between the central manganese ion and an oxygen ion in any of the corners of the tetrahedron.

At a temperature of absolute zero the ground-state energy level is near the bottom of curve I at the minimum amplitude of atomic vibration. At room temperature (300° K [81° F]) the ground state lies higher, at *a*, where the centre has considerable vibrational energy. When an electron of the centre is excited, it is lifted to the higher energy level at *b* in curve II. This electronic transition occurs far more rapidly than the readjustment of the atoms of the centre, which then occurs within a time of about 10^{-12} second to reach the minimum vibrational level at *c*. The energy difference $(b - c)$ is dissipated as heat in the host-crystal lattice. From the excited-state level *c*, the electron can return to the ground-state level *d* shown in Curve I, the liberated energy being emitted as a photon.

The last step is a readjustment of the centre to *a*, the energy difference $(d - a)$ again being dissipated as heat. Nonradiative transition of the excited electron back to its ground state occurs when the electron is excited to an energy level above the intersection point *f* of the ground-state and the excited-state energy curve. This is caused mainly by increasing the vibrations of the lattice by application of higher temperatures. The energy difference $(f - c)$ is equal to the activation energy already mentioned, and therefore most centres become increasingly nonradiative at higher temperatures. In trap-type phosphors the temperature must be sufficiently high, of course, to eject the electron from the traps.

In some phosphors—calcium tungstate ($CaWO_4$), for example—absorption and emission of the exciting energy appear to take place mainly in the same centre; the excited electron remains near the centre. Such phosphors do not exhibit photoconductivity because only a few excited electrons succeed in reaching the conduction band

where they are freely mobile. The luminescence decay is exponential.

Zinc sulfide phosphors, however, are photoconducting, which means that many excited electrons are lifted to the conduction band of the host crystal. The energy levels of different centres and of the host-crystal lattice have to be taken into account simultaneously.

The relative levels of the zinc sulfide valence band (ground state of the host-crystal lattice) and the conduction band (excited state of the host-crystal lattice), of activator levels and of trap levels are shown in Figure 2. Points 1, 2, 3, and 4 represent one situation in a host crystal, and points 5, 6, 7, 8, 9, and 10 represent another situation.

The activator ions introduce additional ground-state levels and excited-state levels of energies between those of the valence and the conduction band of the zinc sulfide. When the excitation energy is sufficiently high, an electron is raised to the conduction band ($1 \rightarrow 2$, $5 \rightarrow 6$, corresponding to the ionization continuum in a gas). It moves away from the centre ($2 \rightarrow 3$, $6 \rightarrow 8$) and may either be trapped by an imperfection of the lattice (8) or return to an ionized centre (activator), in which it first occupies an excited level ($3 \rightarrow 4$) and then drops to the ground state of the activator centre by emitting a photon. An activator centre that captures such an excited electron has already lost one of its own electrons to a positive hole (electron vacancy) in the host-crystal lattice.

The energetic level of the traps is about 0.25 electron volt beneath the conduction-band level. A trapped electron (8) must be raised to the conduction band by thermal energy before a recombination with an ionized activator centre can occur. The green emission (530 nanometres) of the zinc sulfide phosphor (ZnS/Cu) is explained by the recombination of an electron from the conduction band and a copper ion in an activator centre ($7 \rightarrow 9$); the blue emission (463 nanometres) is due to recombination of the excited electron and a copper ion in an interstitial place.

Direct excitation of the activator centres is also possible. When an electron recombines with a killer ion (10), no visible emission occurs.

In solid-state electroluminescence, the radiative processes occurring in a phosphor under irradiation are produced by applying external electric fields of several hundred volts, alternating at several thousand cycles per second. Special preparations of zinc sulfide (hexagonal ZnS), with an iodine coactivator and high concentrations of a copper activator, are embedded in a thin layer of about 0.01 centimetre (0.004 inch) of insulating organic material or glass which is mounted between the electrodes.

High luminescence efficiencies are obtained. Application of a direct-current field yields luminescence in crystals of gallium arsenide (GaAs), silicon carbide (SiC), cadmium sulfide (CdS), and zinc monocrystals of sulfide with copper activator (ZnS/Cu); the cathode injects electrons directly into the conduction band, whereas the anode creates holes by removing electrons.

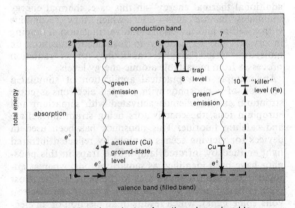

Figure 2: Transition of an electron from the valence band to the conduction band by light absorption (see text).

Efficiency of luminescence; luminance. The efficiency of luminescence emission must be regarded on an energy and a quantum basis. When every exciting photon yields an emitted photon of the same energy (which is the case for resonance excitation—*i.e.*, excitation of fluorescence by a monochromatic light of exactly the same wavelengths as the resulting fluorescence—and radiation of isolated atoms in very dilute gases), the luminescence efficiency is 100 percent with respect to input energy as well as to the number of quanta. When the number of secondary photons is equal to that of the primary, but their energy is less because some of the energy is dissipated as heat, the quantum efficiency is 100 percent, but the luminescence efficiency is less than 100 percent. The quantum efficiency of most luminescences is far lower than 100 percent, especially in the liquid and solid states; zinc sulfide phosphors have about 20 percent efficiency, and solid state electroluminescence is less than 10 percent efficient.

In chemiluminescence, the quantum efficiency of "brilliant" reactions, such as luminol, is about one percent and up to 23 percent in the oxalate chemiluminescence. Solid-state electroluminescence, or electroluminescence of gases excited by high-frequency electric fields, is usually less than 10 percent.

The light intensity of luminescent processes depends chiefly on the excitation intensity, the density, and the lifetime of the radiative atoms, molecules, or centres. For practical purposes this luminous intensity per unit area is called photometric brightness or luminance of a material and is measured in lambert or millilambert (0.001 lambert) units (one lambert is equal to one candle per square centimetre divided by π). The luminance of some luminescent light sources is listed in Table 3.

(Quantum efficiency)

Table 3: Luminance of Some Luminescent Light Sources

sources	lamberts
Fluorescent lamps	
20-watt T 12 standard warm white	1.67
40-watt T 12 standard warm white	2.1
96-watt T 12 standard warm white	2.052
Television screens	0.10
Fresh snow in full sunlight	10.
Sun (observed from Earth's surface at meridian)	519,000.
Lasers	exceeding that of Sun

BIBLIOGRAPHY

History: E.N. HARVEY, *A History of Luminescence: From the Earliest Times Until 1900* (1957), a classical work dealing rather extensively with the historical development of the different types of luminescence, especially bioluminescence and chemiluminescence.

General works: E.J. BOWEN (ed.), *Luminescence in Chemistry* (1968), a textbook for students and research workers, particularly in the biological and biochemical fields, that provides a good introduction to the whole field; C.A. PARKER, *Photoluminescence of Solutions* (1968), a detailed explanation of the basic principles of luminescence as applied to photoluminescence in solutions, kinetics, apparatus, and analytical applications; M. ZANDER, *Phosphorimetry* (1968), the first modern monograph dealing exclusively with phosphorescence of organic materials, with a complete bibliography; G.G. GUILBAULT (ed.), *Fluorescence: Theory, Instrumentation, and Practice* (1967), a fairly technical account written by outstanding specialists in their respective fields (good background knowledge is necessary); D.M. HERCULES (ed.), *Fluorescence and Phosphorescence Analysis* (1966), chapters of different grades of detail covering the luminescence field; G.F.J. GARLICK, "Luminescence," *Handbuch der Physik*, vol. 26, pp. 1–128 (1958), an extended text (written in English) systematically explaining the physical phenomena and theory of luminescence.

Chemiluminescence and bioluminescence: F. MCCAPRA, "The Chemiluminescence of Organic Compounds," *Q. Rev.*, 20:485–510 (1966), a review article on recent chemiluminescence investigations that attempts to find a general theory of transforming chemical energy into electronic excitation energy; W.D. MCELROY and B. GLASS (eds.), *A Symposium on Light and Life* (1961), a collection of papers useful as an introduction to modern luminescence physics and chemistry, mainly concerned with chemiluminescence and bioluminescence; F.H. JOHNSON and Y. HANEDA (eds.), *Bioluminescence in Progress* (1966), a collection of papers, a continuation of the above source, that may be used as an advanced-level textbook; H.H. SELIGER and W.D. MCELROY, *Light: Physical and Biological Action* (1965), a textbook useful as an introduction to luminescence and photochemistry.

Cathodoluminescence: L. MARTON and A.B. EL-KAREH (eds.), "Electron Beam and Laser Beam Technology," *Advances in Electronics and Electron Physics*, suppl. vol. 4 (1968), a handbook article useful for detailed information concerning cathodoluminescence; L. MARTON (ed.), "Photo-Electronic Image Devices," *ibid.*, vol. 22A (1966), an article on the most recent literature and developments in photoelectronic image devices.

Lasers and masers: A.E. SIEGMAN, *Microwave Solid-State Masers* (1964), a monograph giving a general introduction to the field.

Miscellaneous: R.D. CADLE and E.R. ALLEN, "Atmospheric Photochemistry," *Science*, 167:243–249 (1970), a condensed survey of new investigations of photochemistry of the lower atmosphere and production of excited molecules by radical reactions in the gas phase; R.P. GODWIN, "Synchrotron Radiation As a Light Source," in *Springer Tracts in Modern Physics*, vol. 51 (1969), an advanced discussion of the theory and applications of the "synchrotron light"; F. GUTMANN and L.E. LYONS, *Organic Semiconductors* (1967), a survey of solid-state physics, band models, and excited states of organic molecular crystals; B.J. O'BRIEN, "Auroral Phenomena," *Science*, 148:449–460 (1965), facts and theory of Aurora Polaris and related phenomena, including instructive illustrations and short bibliography.

(K.-D.G.)

Lumumba, Patrice

The first prime minister of the Democratic Republic of the Congo (now Zaire) after it achieved independence from Belgium, the radical nationalist leader Patrice Lumumba saw his regime disintegrate through a revolt of the army, the secession of the wealthiest province, and invasion by the country's former masters. He was evicted from office by the president less than three months after he assumed office and murdered by his political enemies four months later. But at the time of his death he was hailed throughout the continent as "the hero of Africa," and in his own country he has been officially proclaimed by successors who opposed him during his lifetime as "the national hero." He was thus the strange paradox of

Agence Dalmas—Pix

Lumumba.

the hero who failed, the hero whose memory evokes aspiration, not achievement.

Patrice Hemery Lumumba was born on July 2, 1925, in the village of Onalua in Kasai Province, Belgian Congo. He was a member of the small Batetela tribe, a fact that was to become significant in his later political life. His two principal rivals, Moise Tshombe, who led the breakaway of the Katanga Province, and Joseph Kasavubu, who later became the nation's president, both came from large, powerful tribes from which they derived their major support, giving their political movements a regional character. In contrast, Lumumba's movement emphasized its all-Congolese nature. Lumumba's parents were Catholics. At 13, however, he went to a Protestant mission school to receive training as a male nurse. He attended the school for two years but left before getting a diploma.

Education and early career

Lumumba then went to Kindu-Port-Empain, where he obtained employment and became active in the club of the *évolués* (educated Africans). He began to write essays and poems for Congolese journals. He applied for and received, not without difficulty, the *carte d'immatriculation*, the document that conferred full Belgian citizenship.

Lumumba moved to Léopoldville (now Kinshasa) to become a postal clerk and went on to become an accountant in the post office in Stanleyville (now Kisangani), the capital of Orientale Province. There he contributed his energy and intelligence to many organizations, and he continued to contribute to the Congolese press. In 1954 he applied to enter the opening class of the first Congolese university, Lovanium. He was refused admission because he was married and the university authorities insisted that all its students live on campus.

In 1955 Lumumba became president for Orientale Province of the APIC, a purely Congolese trade union of government employees which was not affiliated, as were other unions, to either of the two Belgian trade-union federations (Socialist and Catholic). He also became active in the Belgian Liberal Party in the Congo. Although conservative in many ways, the party was not linked to either of the trade-union federations, which were hostile to the APIC. In 1956 Lumumba was invited with others to make a study tour of Belgium under the auspices of the Minister of Colonies. On his return, as he disembarked from the airplane, he was arrested on a charge of embezzlement from the post office. He was convicted and condemned one year later, after various reductions of sentence, to 12 months imprisonment and a fine. Lumumba's friends collected money to pay his fine and support his family.

The year 1956 was a turning point in Congolese political life and the beginning of the expression of nationalist ideas. When Lumumba got out of prison, he obtained a position in a private firm, a beer concern, of which he became sales director in Léopoldville. He grew even more active in politics. In October 1958 he founded the Congolese National Movement (Mouvement National Congolais; MNC), the first nationwide Congolese political party. In December he attended the first All-African People's Conference in Accra, Ghana, where he met nationalists from all over the African continent and was made a member of the permanent organization set up by the conference. His outlook and terminology, inspired by pan-African goals, now took on the tenor of militant nationalism.

In 1959 the Belgian government announced a program intended to lead in five years to independence, starting with local elections in December 1959. The nationalists regarded this program as a scheme to install puppets before independence and announced a boycott of the elections. The Belgian authorities responded with repression. On October 30, there was a clash in Stanleyville that resulted in 30 deaths. Lumumba was imprisoned on a charge of inciting to riot.

The MNC now decided to shift tactics, entered the elections, and won a sweeping victory in Stanleyville (90 percent of the votes). In January 1960 the Belgian government convened a Round Table Conference in Brussels of all Congolese parties to discuss political change, but the MNC refused to participate without Lumumba. Lumumba was thereupon released from prison and flown to Brussels. The conference agreed on a date for independence, June 30, with national elections in May. Although there was a multiplicity of parties, the MNC came out far ahead in the elections; it was the only party to compete in all the provinces and gained 41 of 137 seats (the nearest other party having 13 seats). Lumumba emerged as the leading nationalist politician of the Congo. Manoeuvres to prevent his assumption of authority failed, and he was asked to form the first government, which he succeeded in doing on June 23, 1960.

Role in independence movement

A few days after independence, some units of the army rebelled, largely because their Belgian commander refused to acknowledge that independence should improve the Congolese soldiers' treatment, pay, and prospects of promotion. In the confusion, the mineral-rich province of Katanga proclaimed secession. Belgium sent in troops, ostensibly to protect Belgian nationals in the disorder. But the Belgian troops landed principally in Katanga where they sustained the secessionist regime of Moise Tshombe.

The Congo appealed to the United Nations to expel the Belgians and help them restore order. As prime minister, Lumumba did what he could to redress the situation, but it was not easy. His army was an uncertain instrument of power, his civilian administration untrained and untried, the United Nations forces (whose presence he had requested) condescending and assertive, and the political alliances underlying his regime very shaky. The Belgian troops did not evacuate and the Katanga secession continued.

Since the United Nations forces refused to aid him in ending the Katanga secession, Lumumba decided to use his army. He appealed to the Soviet Union for planes to assist in transporting his troops to Katanga. He asked the independent African states to meet in Léopoldville in August to unite their efforts behind him. His moves alarmed many inside and outside the country, particularly the Western powers and the supporters of President Kasavubu, a political rival of Lumumba's who pursued a moderate course in the coalition government and favoured some local autonomy in the provinces.

On September 5 President Kasavubu dismissed Lumumba. The legalities of the move were immediately contested by Lumumba. There were thus two groups now claiming to be the legal central government. The United Nations Secretariat was uncertain in its response but tended to favour Kasavubu. On September 14 power was seized by the Congolese army leader Col. Joseph Mobutu, (president of Zaire as Mobutu Sese Seko), who later reached a working agreement with Kasavubu. In October the General Assembly of the United Nations, by a divided vote, recognized the credentials of Kasavubu's government. The independent African states split sharply over the issue.

On November 27 Lumumba sought to travel from Léopoldville, where the United Nations had provided him with physical protection within the confines of his home, to Stanleyville, where his supporters had control. He was caught by the Kasavubu forces and arrested on December 2. On January 17, 1961, he was placed in an airplane and delivered to the Katanga secessionist regime, where he was murdered. Conflicting reports on the manner of his death were subsequently issued by Katanga, but even after a United Nations inquiry, the exact circumstances of the murder have not been established. His death caused a scandal throughout Africa, and later, retrospectively, his enemies proclaimed him a "national hero."

What was it about Lumumba that caused such intense emotion? His viewpoint was not exceptional. He was for a unitary Congo and against division of the country along tribal or regional lines. He supported pan-Africanism and the liberation of colonial territories. He proclaimed his regime one of "positive neutralism," which he defined as a return to African values and rejection of any imported ideology, including that of the Soviet Union. Many other African leaders have said the same.

Assessment

There were probably two things about Lumumba that aroused the wrath of his enemies. He was a man of strong character who intended to pursue his policies, regardless of the enemies he made within his country or abroad; and the country he headed was a key area in terms of the geopolitics of Africa. Its wealth, its size, and its contiguity to white-dominated southern Africa made his opponents fear the consequences of a radical or radicalized Congo regime. Moreover, in the context of the Cold War, the Soviet Union's support for Lumumba appeared as a threat to many in the West.

Lumumba developed in his own brief political life from an incipient nationalist member of an educated elite with grievances about the racial limitations of a colonial situation, to a radical nationalist tribune of the people who sought the liberation of the masses. It took a man of ambition, intelligence, energy, and courage to make this transition, although it led him to a confrontation with problems he was unable to master. Murdered for his virtues more than for his deeds, he has become a myth. As such, he has continued to play a role in emergent Africa.

BIBLIOGRAPHY. A good critical biography does not yet exist. PIERRE DE VOS, *Vie et mort de Lumumba* (1961), is a journalist's account. G. HEINZ and H. DONNAY, *Lumumba: Les cinquante derniers jours de sa vie* (1966; Eng. trans., *Lumumba: The Last Fifty Days*, 1970), is a detailed reconstruction of the last critical period of his life. The articles by JEAN VAN LIERDE and PIERRE CLEMENT in *Présence Africaine* (1961, 1962), both by Belgian friends of Lumumba, help create a portrait of the man. His own book *Le Congo* (1956; Eng. trans., *Congo: My Country*, 1962), is useful if taken in context. Far more important is the posthumous collection of essays edited by JEAN VAN LIERDE, *La Pensée politique de Patrice Lumumba* (1963).

(I.W.)

Luria, Isaac ben Solomon

Isaac ben Solomon Luria was the founder of an influential school of Kabbala (Jewish esoteric mysticism) named after him. In Kabbalistic literature after his time he was called ha-Ari (the Lion), an acronym of the Hebrew appellation ha-Elohi Rabbi Yitzḥaq (the Divine Rabbi Isaac) or possibly ha-Ashkenazi-Rabbi Yitzḥaq (the Ashkenazi Rabbi Isaac). His father was an Ashkenazi (that is, a German or Polish Jew), while his mother was a Sefardi (that is, of Iberian–North African Jewish stock). Luria was born in Jerusalem in 1534. Legend has it that the prophet Elijah appeared to his father and foretold the birth of the son, whose name was to be Isaac. As a child, Luria was described as a young genius, "a Torah scholar who could silence all opponents by the power of his arguments," and also as possessed of divine inspiration.

The main source for his life story is an anonymous biography, *Toledot ha-Ari* ("Life of the Ari"), written or perhaps edited some 20 years after his death, in which factual and legendary elements are indiscriminately mingled. According to the *Toledot*, Luria's father died while Isaac was a child, and his mother took him to Egypt to live with her well-to-do family. While there, he became versed in rabbinic studies, including Halakha (Jewish law), and even wrote glosses on a famous compendium of legal discussions, the *Sefer ha-Halakhot* of Isaac ben Jacob Alfasi. He also engaged in commerce during this period.

While still a youth, Luria began the study of mystical learning and lived for nearly seven years in seclusion at his uncle's home on an island in the Nile. His studies concentrated on the *Zohar* (late 13th–early 14th centuries), the central and revered work of the Kabbala, but he also studied the early Kabbalists (12th–13th centuries). The greatest Kabbalist of Luria's time was Moses ben Jacob Cordovero of Safed (modern Ẓefat), in Palestine, whose work Luria studied while still in Egypt. During this period he wrote a commentary on the *Sifra di-tzeni-'uta* ("Book of Concealment"), a section of the *Zohar*. The commentary still shows the influence of classical Kabbala and contains nothing of what would later be called Lurianic Kabbala.

Early in 1570 Luria journeyed to Safed, the mountain town in the Galilee that had become a centre of the Kabbalistic movement, and he studied there with Cordovero. At the same time, he began to teach Kabbala according to a new system and attracted many pupils. The greatest of these was Ḥayyim Vital, who later set Luria's teachings down in writing. Luria apparently expounded his teachings only in esoteric circles; not everyone was allowed to take part in these studies. While he devoted most of his time to the instruction of his pupils, he probably made his living in trade, which prospered at that time in Safed, situated as it was at the crossroads between Egypt and Damascus.

Years at Safed

At the time of Luria's arrival in Safed, the group of Kabbalists gathered there around Cordovero had already developed a unique style of living and observed special rituals, going out, for instance, into the fields to welcome the sabbath, personified as the Sabbath Queen. With Luria's arrival, new elements were added to these excursions, such as communion with the souls of the *tzaddiqim* (men of outstanding piety) by means of special *kawwanot* (ritual meditations) and *yiḥudim* ("unifications") that were in essence a kind of lesser redemption whereby the souls were lifted up from the *kelipot* ("shells"; *i.e.*, the impure, evil forms) into which they were banned until the coming of the messiah.

The strong influence of Luria's personality helped to bring about in Safed an atmosphere of spiritual intensity, messianic tension, and the fever of creation that accompanies the sense of a great revelation. Deep devoutness, asceticism, and withdrawal from the world marked the Kabbalists' way of life. Luria apparently looked upon himself as the messiah ben Joseph, the first of the two messiahs in Jewish tradition, who is fated to be killed in the wars (of Gog and Magog) that will precede the final redemption. In Safed there was an expectation (based on the *Zohar*) that the Messiah would appear in Galilee in the year 1575.

Even though he did not distinguish himself as a writer, as is evident from his own remarks about the difficulty of writing, Luria composed three hymns that became widely known and part of the cultural heritage of the Jewish people. These are hymns for the three sabbath meals, which became part of the Sefardic sabbath ritual and were printed in many prayer books. The three meals were linked by means of mystical "intention" or meditation (*kawwana*) to three *partzufim* (aspects of the Godhead). The hymns are known as "Azamer be-she-vaḥim" ("I Will Sing on the Praises"), "Asader se'udata" ("I Will Order the Festive Meal"), and "Bene hekh-ala de-khesi-fin" ("Sons of the Temple of Silver"). They are mystical, erotic songs about "the adornment (or fitting) of the bride"—*i.e.*, the sabbath, who was identified with the community of Israel—and on the other *partzufim*: *arikh anpin* (the long-suffering: the countenance of grace) and *ze'ir anpin* (the impatient: the countenance of judgment).

During his brief sojourn in Safed—a scant two years before his death—Luria managed to construct a many-faceted and fertile Kabbalistic system from which many new elements in Jewish mysticism drew their nourishment. He set down almost none of his doctrine in writing, with the exception of a short text that seems to be only a fragment: his commentary on the first chapter of the *Zohar*—"Be-resh hormanuta de-malka"—as well as commentaries on isolated passages of the *Zohar* that were collected by Ḥayyim Vital, who attests to their being in his teacher's own hand. Luria died, in an epidemic that struck Safed, on August 5, 1572.

What is called Lurianic Kabbala is a voluminous collection of Luria's Kabbalistic doctrines, recorded after his death by Ḥayyim Vital and appearing in two versions under different editorship. Because of this work Lurianic Kabbala became the new thought that influenced all Jewish mysticism after Luria, competing with the Kabbala of Cordovero. Vital laboured much to give Lurianic Kabbala its form as well as to win legitimization for it.

Lurianic Kabbala

Lurianic Kabbala propounds a theory of the creation and subsequent degeneration of the world and a practical method of restoring the original harmony. The theory is based on three concepts: *tzimtzum* ("contraction" or "withdrawal"), *shevirat ha-kelim* ("breaking of the vessels"), and *tiqqun* ("restoration"). God as the Infinite (En Sof) withdraws into himself in order to make room for the creation, which occurs by a beam of light from the Infinite into the newly provided space. Later the divine light is enclosed in finite "vessels," most of which break under the strain, and the catastrophe of the "breaking of the vessels" occurs, whereby disharmony and evil enter the world. Hence comes the struggle to rid the world of evil and accomplish the redemption of both the cosmos and history. This occurs in the stage of *tiqqun*, in which the divine realm itself is reconstructed, the divine sparks returned to their source, and *Adam Qadmon*, the symbolic "primordial man," who is the highest configuration of the divine light, is rebuilt. Man plays an important role in this process through various *kawwanot* used during prayer and through mystical intentions involving secret combinations of words, all of which is directed toward the restoration of the primordial harmony and the reunification of the divine name.

The influence of Luria's Kabbala was far-reaching. It played an important role in the movement of the false messiah Shabbetai Tzevi in the 17th century and in the popular Ḥasidic (mystical–pietistic) movement a century later. (For a more detailed presentation of Lurianic Kabbala see JEWISH MYSTICISM.) (R.S.-U.)

BIBLIOGRAPHY. A definitive biography of Isaac Luria does not exist. MEIR BENAYAHU, *Sefer Toledoth ha-Ari* (1967), an historical-literary analysis (in Hebrew) of the various medieval collections of legends about Luria, brings together much of the material necessary for a modern biography. Other useful studies include GERSHOM G. SCHOLEM, "Isaac Luria and His School," in his *Major Trends in Jewish Mysticism*, 3rd rev. ed., pp. 244–286 (1954), an epitome of the salient features of Lurianic *Kabbalah* by the leading modern historian of Jewish mysticism; and SOLOMON SCHECHTER, "Safed in the Sixteenth Century: A City of Legists and Mystics," in his *Studies in Judaism*, 2nd Series, pp. 202–285 (1908), a dated but vivid portrayal of the intellectualism and romanticism that permeated Safed during Luria's lifetime. Luria's teachings are known mostly from the writings of his disciples, most notably Ḥayyim Vital (1543–1620). SAMUEL A. HORODEZKY, *Torath ha-Kabbalah shel Rabbi Yiẓḥoq Ashkenazi* (1947), offers a representative anthology of Luriac teaching (in Hebrew), culled from the writings of Luria's disciples, and arranged topically. ISAIAH TISHBY, *Torath ha-Ra veha-Qelipah be-Kabbalath ha-Ari* (1942), analyzes the notions of evil and "breaking of the vessels" in Lurianic thought (in Hebrew).

(S.Z.L.)

Luther, Martin

The founder of the 16th-century Reformation and of Protestantism, Martin Luther is one of the pivotal figures of Western civilization, as well as of Christianity. By his actions and writings he precipitated a movement that was to yield not only one of the three major theological units of Christianity (along with Roman Catholicism and Eastern Orthodoxy) but was to be a seedbed for social, economic, and political thought.

LUTHER AS EDUCATOR AND MONK

Early life and education. Martin Luther was born on November 10, 1483, at Eisleben in Thuringian Saxony (Germany). His parents, Hans and Margarethe Luther, who had moved there from Möhra, soon moved on again to Mansfeld where Hans Luther worked in the copper mines, prospering enough to be able to rent several furnaces and to obtain a position among the councillors of the little town in 1491. Luther's few recollections of childhood that have survived reflect a sombre piety and strict discipline common in that age. His schooling seems to have been unremarkable: the Latin school at Mansfeld, a year at a school in Magdeburg (run by Brethren of the Common Life, a medieval lay group dedicated to Bible study and education) and at Eisenach in his 15th year, where he made valued older friends. In the spring of 1501 he matriculated in arts at the University of Erfurt, one of

the oldest and best attended universities in Germany. There he talked long and enough to be nicknamed "the Philosopher," and played the lute. He took the usual arts course and graduated with the B.A. degree in 1502. He took his M.A. in 1505, placing second among 17 candidates. In an age when few students got as far as the master of arts degree, he had fulfilled his parents' hopes. Like many other parents of his time, Hans Luther intended his son to become a lawyer, and he paid cheerfully enough for the expensive textbooks when Martin began legal studies. He was chagrined to learn that his son, without consulting his parents, had decided to enter religion and had sought admission to the house of Augustinian Hermits in Erfurt.

Luther, oil painting by Lucas Cranach, 1526. In the Nationalmuseum, Stockholm.

Brother Martin Luther. Evidence on the reason for his decision to enter the religious life is scanty. In his later, not always reliable, *Tischreden* ("Table Talk"), it is related that on July 2, 1505, he was returning from a visit to his parents when he was overtaken by a thunderstorm near the village of Stotternheim and cried out in terror, "Help, St. Anne, and I'll become a monk." In his *De votis monasticis* ("Concerning Monastic Vows," 1521) Luther says "not freely or desirously did I become a monk, but walled around with the terror and agony of sudden death, I vowed a constrained and necessary vow." He sold most of his books, keeping back his Virgil and Plautus, and on July 17, 1505, entered the monastery at Erfurt.

Augustinian Order at Erfurt. In joining the eremitical order of St. Augustine, Luther had joined an important mendicant order, which by the middle of the 15th century had over 2,000 chapters. As a result of reforms carried through in 1473, the house at Erfurt, to which Luther went, accepted the strict, observant interpretation of the rule. Under Johann von Staupitz, Luther's mentor and vicar general to the order, a revised constitution was made in 1504. Luther made his profession as a monk in September 1506 and was then prepared for ordination. He was ordained priest in April 1507 and his first mass took place at the beginning of May. He had studied a treatise on the canon of the mass by a famous Tübingen Nominalist Gabriel Biel (d. 1495), who, like other "modern" Nominalists, claimed that only named particulars exist and that universal concepts are formed through intuition, and he approached the ceremony with awe. To this occasion his father came with a group of friends, and Luther took this first opportunity to explain personally the imperious nature of his vocation. His father's disgruntled retort, "Did you not read in Scripture that one shall honour one's father and mother?" struck deep into his memory.

The thunderstorm experience

Wittenberg University. Luther was selected for advanced theological studies; some of his university teachers were Nominalists of the "modern" way of the English philosopher theologian William of Ockham, whose views tended to undercut the prevailing rationalism of Scholasticism, the theological school of thought founded in the 11th century that attempted to reconcile revelation with reason. In 1508 Luther went to the new University of Wittenberg (founded 1502), where, though Ockhamism had a foothold, the school of Realism that claimed that universals exist and can be known by reason was championed by scholars such as the Realist Martin Pollich. The little town was a contrast to Erfurt, but at least the university was young and forward-looking, and to its comparative remoteness Luther would one day owe his life. The Schlosskirche (called the Church of All Saints) was closely connected with the university, and the elector of Saxony, Frederick III the Wise (1463–1525), lavished generous patronage on both. In March 1509 Luther took the degree of *baccalaureus biblicus* at Wittenberg, returning to Erfurt for his next degree, of *sententiarius,* which involved expounding on the *Sententiae* (*Sentences*), a medieval theological textbook by Peter Lombard. He had begun his teaching with a course on Aristotle's *Nicomachean Ethics* and now began his career as a theologian with lectures on the *Sentences.* Some of his notes have survived, and if their theology is unexciting there is apparent an acid vehemence at the intrusion of philosophy and above all of Aristotle into the realm of theology.

Influence of Johann von Staupitz

Johann von Staupitz, vicar general of the German Augustinians, was very important in Luther's career as his teacher, friend, and patron. Staupitz seems to have been theologically trained as a Thomist (Realist) and was also influenced by the Augustinian tradition of his order, though his theology shows elements derived from the conflation in the late 15th century of the *devotio moderna* (modern devotion, a term used to describe the spirituality of the Brethren of the Common Life) with German mysticism. His attempt to revive stricter discipline and to unite the observant and conventual Augustinians in Germany led to dispute, and Luther was one of two monks chosen to go to Rome to present the appeal of some dissident houses. He made the journey, the longest of his life, probably late in 1510, and his earnestness was shocked by the levity of the Roman clergy and by the worldliness so evident in high places. The appeal failed, and Luther returned to become a loyal supporter of Staupitz.

Staupitz became interested in his gifted pupil and, perhaps alarmed by his introspectiveness, encouraged him to proceed to his doctorate and to a consequent public teaching career. Luther took his D.Th. on October 19, 1512. The degree was important for Luther, with its implications of public responsibility. He soon took on the duties of a professor in succeeding Staupitz in the chair of biblical theology. This was his lifelong calling, and the exposition of the Bible to his students was a task that called forth his best gifts and energies, one that he sustained until ill health and old age made him relinquish it at the end of his life. In between lectures, in a manner of speaking, he began the Protestant Reformation.

Religious and theological questions. Meanwhile, Luther's own religious and theological difficulties were becoming acute. He had entered into the search for evangelical perfection with characteristic and serious zeal, and sought exactly to fulfill the rule of his order. Nonetheless, he soon found himself in problems difficult for him to understand, struggling against uncertainties and doubts, unhappily bearing a crippling burden of guilt, which neither the sacramental consolations (*e.g.,* the Lord's Supper and penance) of the church nor the wise advice of skilled directors was able to assuage. This distress, which had its centre in his unquiet conscience, brought him into states of anxiety and despair. Nor were his difficulties lessened by the emphases of the Ockhamist theology, which encouraged an extroverted moralism, stressed the human will, and left aspects of uncertainty at the very points where Luther needed most to be reassured. "Temptation" (*Anfechtung*) was to become an important word for Luther's theology, a term that suggests the fight for faith, of

which Staupitz could say that such experiences were meat and drink to Martin Luther. These inward, spiritual difficulties were enhanced by theological problems.

Discovery of "the righteousness of God." At the entrance to the world of the thought of St. Paul, Luther was halted—the road blocked by a word that intensified his difficulties to an almost intolerable degree. This was the conception of the "righteousness of God." His sombre childhood piety had made him intensely aware of God's judgment, and as a lecturer in the arts faculty at Wittenberg he had had to expound the Hellenic conception of justice, as he found it in the *Nicomachean Ethics* of Aristotle. Encouraged by the use of *justitia* ("righteousness" or "justice") in the works of several Nominalists, he came to think of God's justice as being primarily the active, punishing severity of God against sinners—*i.e.,* in particular actions. It was for him a final aggravation of his trouble that in Rom. 1:17 it is asserted that the justice of God is revealed in the gospel. Thus, Luther concluded, the divine demand was shown as extending beyond outward obedience to the Law, revealed in the Commandments, to purity of heart, to inward motive and intention, so that grace itself became a demand and an exaction. Such a God could be feared but not loved, could be obeyed out of constraint but never with that happy spontaneity that Luther felt to be of the essence of Christian obedience.

Luther's sense of hypocrisy

Luther's inner conflict. To Luther's sense of failure to obey the Law was added the feeling of hypocrisy, which drove him to the edge of what moral theologians described as "open blasphemy." In 1545, in a celebrated autobiographical fragment that he prefaced to his complete works, he thus described his feelings:

> For however irreproachably I lived as a monk, I felt myself in the presence of God to be a sinner with a most unquiet conscience, nor could I believe that I pleased him with my satisfactions. I did not love, indeed I hated this just God, if not with open blasphemy, at least with huge murmuring, for I was indignant against him, saying "as if it were really not enough for God that miserable sinners should be eternally lost through original sin, and oppressed with all kind of calamities through the law of the ten commandments, but God must add sorrow on sorrow, and even by the gospel bring his wrath to bear." Thus I raged with a fierce and most agitated conscience, and yet I continued to knock away at Paul in this place, thirsting ardently to know what he really meant.

Thus, the dilemma. Illumination came at last, as in prayer and meditation he pondered the text, examining the connection of the words.

Justification by faith

> At last I began to understand the justice of God as that by which the just man lives by the gift of God, that is to say, by faith, and this sentence, "the justice of God is revealed in the Gospel," to be understood passively, that by which the merciful God justifies by faith, as it is written. "The just man shall live by faith." At this I felt myself to have been born again, and to have entered through open gates into paradise itself.

There has been great controversy about this inner conflict, but it seems certain that there was for Luther just such a crisis as he later described and that it was resolved in the manner he narrates. There has also been argument about the novelty of this discovery. There is in fact a profound difference between the Hellenic conception of distributive justice and the biblical doctrine of the righteousness of God as a divine, saving activity displayed in the field of history and of human experience, and Luther had penetrated deeply into the Pauline vocabulary at this point. The accuracy of Luther's memory about this and, indeed, his integrity have sometimes been impugned, but the verdict of a modern Catholic historian, Joseph Lortz, may stand: that if the discovery were not new, it was at any rate "new for Luther."

Salvation as grace. Had Luther not written this account, it would have been necessary to conjecture something like it to account for the new importance that he gave to justification by faith, a priority it retained in the new theological framework of Protestantism. This became for him the nerve of the gospel, that salvation is to be thought of primarily in terms of grace, and of a divine gift; that God's free, forgiving mercy is displayed in Jesus Christ; that the conscience, forgiven and cleansed, may be at peace, and that the soul, free from the burden of guilt, may serve God with a joyful, spontaneous, creative obedience. In his translation of the Bible Luther came to add "alone" after the word "faith" (*sola fide*) in the verse "For we hold that a man is justified by faith apart from works of law" (Rom. 3:28) because he felt it was demanded by the German language. The word alone or only was retained by the Reformers after him because it seemed to safeguard this important doctrine against such perversions as might seem to make salvation dependent on human achievement or a reward for human merit.

Evaluation of Luther's experience of justification. This experience ought not to be isolated, for Luther speaks of other problems of vocabulary (*e.g.*, the conception of "repentance," *poenitentia*), and it cannot be assumed that this was for him a catastrophic personal experience such as befell St. Augustine, who had a mystical experience of God in the garden at Milan, or the 18th-century founder of Methodism John Wesley, who had a conversion experience at Aldersgate Street, London. About the date of the occurrence there has been much controversy. The publication of Luther's early lectures led naturally to the examination of these firstfruits of the young professor. Though an early view that it must have occurred during the period of Luther's first lectures on the Psalms (1513–15) has been damagingly criticized, Luther's use of the many-sided allegorism of the Middle Ages, which often found three or four levels of meaning in a single text, his concentration on the one historical meaning, and the Christ-centred core of theology of justification have led some scholars to believe that the illumination must have come to him before his lectures on the Letter to the Romans (1515–16).

Something depends on how the discovery itself is assessed: if it was a discovery that justification is a gift, that it is to be taken passively rather than actively, then (as the reference to Augustine's *De spiritu et littera*—"Concerning the Spirit and the Letter"—suggests) Luther was hardly moving beyond the Augustinian framework and it is probably from an early period. If, on the other hand, it was the more mature discovery of the relation of saving faith to the Word of God, then it must be placed later, perhaps in 1518–19. Many scholars now tend in this later direction and they emphasize how Luther's thinking was stimulated and redirected by the urgent pressure of the church struggle that began in 1517.

The net gain of this chronological discussion has been to demonstrate how important is the whole period of Luther's development from 1509 to 1521, and that his technical vocabulary and the categories of his theology were in movement throughout the whole of this period. Certainly his great courses of lectures on the Psalms (1513–15), on Romans (1515–16), Galatians (1516–17), and Hebrews (1517–18) reveal the growing richness and maturity of his thought.

Luther's growth in theological thought

Luther as preacher and administrator. Meanwhile, his other duties had accumulated. From 1511 he had been preaching in his monastery and in 1514 he became preacher in the parish church. This pulpit became the centre of a long and fruitful preaching ministry wherein Luther expounded the Scriptures profoundly and intelligibly for the common people and related them to the practical context of their lives. Within his order, he had become prior, and, in April 1515, district vicar over 11 other houses. Thus he became involved in a world of practical administration and of pastoral care that gave him valuable experience, standing him in good stead in later years when a large part of his vast correspondence would be concerned with the care of the German churches and the cure of needy souls.

The new University of Wittenberg found it must take sides in an academic crisis that faced the European universities of that day, the tension between an old and a new academic program. Before Luther's advent Martin Pollich, a leading professor at Wittenberg, had shown himself hospitable to Humanist influences, despite his preference for the older Thomism. Now Luther took the lead in inaugurating a new program, involving the displacement of Aristotle and the Scholastic theologians by a biblical humanism that turned to the direct study of the Bible, using as tools the revival of Greek and Hebrew and a renovated Latin and as a dogmatic norm the "old Fathers" (the early Church Fathers, or teachers) and especially St. Augustine. Such a program Luther planned with the help of his senior colleague, Karlstadt, and his young friend Philipp Melanchthon. In February 1517 he penned a series of theses against the Scholastic theologians, which he offered to defend at other universities. Though this attempt to export the Wittenberg program met with no success he could write in May that the battle was won at least in Wittenberg—"our theology, and that of St. Augustine reign." But if his theses remained dormant, a very different fate awaited those that he wrote later in that same year. He could hardly have thought that these would fire a train that would explode the Western Christian world.

LUTHER AS REFORMER

The indulgence controversy. *The nature of indulgences.* The nature and scope of indulgences had been more and more defined during the later Middle Ages, but there was still an element of that dogmatic uncertainty that has been called a theological weakness of the age. Indulgences were the commutation for money of part of the temporal penalty due for sin, of the practical satisfaction that was a part of the sacrament of penance, which also required contrition on the part of the penitent and absolution from a priest. They were granted on papal authority and made available through accredited agents. At no time at all did they even imply that divine forgiveness could be bought or sold, or that they availed for those who were impenitent or unconfessed. But during the Middle Ages, as papal financial difficulties grew more complicated, they were resorted to so often that the financial house of Fugger of Augsburg had to superintend the sacred negotiations involved in them.

The way was open for further misunderstanding when in 1476 Pope Sixtus IV extended their authority to souls in purgatory. The appeal to cupidity and fear, the pomp and circumstance with which these indulgences were attended, the often outrageous statements of some indulgence sellers were a matter of complaint. Luther himself had frequently preached against these abuses, for his patron, the elector Frederick, had amassed a great collection of relics in the castle church at Wittenberg, to which indulgences were attached. But the immediate cause of Luther's public protest was an indulgence that Frederick had prohibited from his lands, though it was available in nearby territory. This was a jubilee indulgence, offering special privileges, the ostensible purpose of which was the rebuilding of St. Peter's basilica in Rome. By a secret arrangement, half of the German proceeds were to go to the young Albert, archbishop of Mainz, who was deeply in debt owing to his rapid promotion to and payment for a number of high ecclesiastical offices.

The immediate cause of the indulgence controversy

The Ninety-five Theses. Of this Luther knew nothing until some time afterward. For him, the provocation lay in the extravagant claims of an old, tried hand at this kind of thing, the Dominican salesman of indulgences Johann Tetzel. With these claims in mind, Luther drew up the Ninety-five Theses, "for the purpose of eliciting truth," and fastened them on the door of All Saints Church, Wittenberg, on October 31, 1517, the eve of All Saints' Day and of the great exposure of relics there. These were tentative opinions, about some of which Luther himself was not committed. They did not deny the papal prerogative in this matter, though by implication they criticized papal policy; still less did they attack such established teaching as the doctrine of purgatory. But they did stress the spiritual, inward character of the Christian religion, and the first thesis, which claimed that repentance involved the whole life of the Christian man, and the 62nd, that the true treasure of the church was the most holy gospel of the glory and the grace of God, showed the author's intention. The closing section attacked the false peace, that "security," which as a young lecturer Luther had so often attacked, of those who thought of divine grace as something cheaply acquired and who refused to recognize that to be a Christian involved embracing the cross and entering heaven through tribulation. Luther sent copies of the theses to the archbishop of Mainz and to his bishop. And here the invention of printing intervened. Copies were circulated far and wide, so that what might have been a mere local issue became a public controversy discussed in ever widening circles.

Reaction to the Ninety-five Theses. The archbishop of Mainz, alarmed and annoyed, forwarded the documents to Rome in December 1517, with the request that Luther be inhibited, at the same time reprimanding the indulgence sellers for their extravagance. At the time, it seemed to many that this was simply another squabble between the Dominicans and the Augustinians. Colour was given to this belief by the counter-theses prepared by a theologian, Konrad Wimpina, that Tetzel had defended before a Dominican audience at Frankfurt at the end of January 1518. When copies of these reached Wittenberg in March they were publicly burned by excited students. At Rome the pope merely instructed Gabriel della Volta, the vicar general of the Augustinians, to deal with the recalcitrant monk through the usual channels, in this case through Staupitz. Luther himself prepared a long Latin manuscript with explanations of his Ninety-five Theses, publication of which was held up until the autumn of 1518; it is a document of some theological importance, and shows how far from superficial Luther's original protest had been. Meanwhile, the chapter of the German Augustinians was held at Heidelberg, April 25, 1518. Luther was relieved of his extra duties as district vicar, in the circumstances a great relief and intended as such. He found great comfort in the support of his friends, and was himself in great form, winning over two young men, Martin Bucer, a Dominican, and Theodor Bibliander.

Counter-theses and student reaction

At this period Luther's theology was most especially a "theology of the cross"; *i.e.*, a theology that stressed the revelation of Christ on the cross. According to Luther, the "theology of the cross" seems foolishness to the wisdom of the world and is opposed to the natural theology of divine power and majesty, which he attacked as a Scholastic "theology of glory." Important for him at this time was the inward religion preached by the 14th-century German mystic Johann Tauler and a short 14th-century mystical tract, the *Theologia Germanica*, that he himself edited and published (1516–18). In these months, therefore, he lay great stress on the need for the Christian to share the cross of Christ, in suffering and in temptation. Though these stresses were to recede into the background of Luther's developing theology, they were to remain important for the radical Reformation, for which the *Theologia Germanica* would be an important and seminal document.

"Theology of the cross"

Involvement of Johann Eck. During Luther's absence, and perhaps catastrophically, his senior colleague, Karlstadt, had taken action that was greatly to widen the scope and publicity of the controversy. The scholar Johann Eck (1486–1543) of Ingolstadt, a man of some learning, and with a zest for disputation, with whom Luther was already in friendly contact through a common friend, became involved in the controversy. He had written some observations on the Ninety-five Theses for his friend, the bishop of Eichstädt, and these manuscript observations, the so-called Obelisks, reached Wittenberg shortly before Luther went off to his chapter at Heidelberg; Luther himself replied with a few "Asterisks," but Karlstadt, concerned to defend the Wittenberg program, sprang into the fray with 379 theses, adding another 26 before publication. In some of these Eck was impugned. The Dominicans continued to press for Luther's impeachment, and proceedings against him for heresy began to move slowly in Rome. Luther himself did not improve matters by publishing a bold sermon on the power of excommunication that made it clear that here was not a man who would accept unquestioned whatever might be decided by the pope in terms of some undefined plenitude of power.

The Augsburg interview, 1518. *Luther before Cajetan.* A papal citation summoning Luther to Rome was sent to the cardinal Cajetan (1468–1534), a renowned Thomist, at Augsburg. But at this perilous moment politics fatefully intervened, and the period during which the Luther affair might have been swiftly, drastically disposed of without wider disaster to the church was eroded by considerations of policy. The elector Frederick, as one of the seven prince electors of the Holy Roman Empire, was most important to the pope, in view of the imminent choice of a new emperor, and the pope could not afford to antagonize him. The result was that Luther was bidden to a personal interview with Cajetan at Augsburg. He arrived there on October 7 with an imperial safe-conduct. The discussion had moved from indulgences to the discussion of the relation between faith and sacramental grace (the unmerited gifts of God in such acts as Baptism and the Lord's Supper), when an argument developed between the two theologians about the meaning of the "treasure" of merits that the papal definition of Sixtus IV said that Christ had acquired, and the incensed cardinal dismissed Luther from his presence, telling him to stay away unless he would unconditionally recant.

Dispute over meaning of merits

Luther's flight from Augsburg. While Luther waited uneasily, the Saxon councillors reported rumours that he would be taken in chains to Rome. Eventually, bundled through a postern by his friends, he fled the city. Now he wrote an appeal from the pope to a general (or ecumenical) council and a full defense of his actions to his prince. Cajetan, meanwhile, lost no time in denouncing Luther to Frederick, who was in something of a dilemma, though it counted much for Luther that he had the admiring friendship of the elector's secretary, the Humanist Georg Spalatin. At this time, too, the Wittenberg theological faculty addressed the prince on Luther's behalf, pointing out that the fate of the university and its reputation would be involved in Luther's disgrace. At one moment, it seemed that Luther might have to depart, perhaps for France or Bohemia. There then appeared Karl von Miltitz, a papal diplomat, who applied "stick and carrot" tactics to the elector, dangling before him at one moment threats against Luther and at the next the signal compliment of the golden rose, symbol of high papal honour and recognition. The diplomat promised more than he could possibly perform, and after an interview with him at Altenburg, in January 1519, Luther sensed this and came to distrust him. A papal definition about indulgences, issued at Cajetan's request, seemed to show that Luther had indeed put his finger on some fatal ambiguities.

The Leipzig disputation, 1519. *Debate between Luther and Eck.* At Augsburg Luther had been in touch with Eck and arrangements were made for a public disputation at Leipzig in the summer. This was to be in the first place a debate between Eck and Karlstadt, though Luther was Eck's ultimate objective, but the hostility of George, duke of Saxony (the elector Frederick's first cousin), toward the Reformer raised difficulties about Luther's participation. Eventually it was arranged that Eck should debate with the two Wittenberg theologians in turn, in the castle of the Pleissenburg, Leipzig, at the end of July. There was a preliminary pamphlet skirmish. The issue between Eck and Karlstadt was the Augustinian doctrine of grace and free will, and Karlstadt wished to meddle neither with indulgences nor with papal authority. Among the preliminary matters, the origin of the papal power was raised and so Luther turned to a study of church history and Canon Law in the fateful weeks before the debate. A large contingent from Wittenberg attended, and in the presence of theologians from both universities, Duke George and notables of church and state, the debate began. Eck showed some skill in manoeuvring Luther into a position in which he cast doubt on the authority of the great General Council of Constance (1414–18), and also defended some of the propositions of Jan Hus, a Bohemian Reformer who had been declared a heretic at Constance and burned to death at the stake. Leipzig was a part of Germany with a strong feeling against Bohemia, and the admission was received as damaging, giving ground for Eck's loud boast that the disputation had been his personal triumph. Luther, who had earlier said of the debate that it had not begun in God's

Luther's relationship to Jan Hus

name and would not end in his name, left Leipzig somewhat shaken and disturbed by Eck's verbal manoeuvring.

Luther's questioning of authority. Eck was able to go off to Rome with new prestige to give sharpness to the process of Luther's official condemnation. Luther had now to examine the further implications of his actions to date, in relation to the authority of the church, of councils and of Scripture; his correspondence shows that he was reaching something like a crisis in his attitude to papal authority. There had been a small pamphlet war after the disputation that made it plain that there was strong support for Luther among the Humanists in Germany and Switzerland. Luther himself became involved in controversy with diverse theologians of Leipzig, and if he now wrote in the vernacular with increasing power and violence, his polemical writings reveal also his deep perceptions of the issues between himself and contemporary theology. Two Catholic universities, strongholds of tradition, Cologne and Louvain, next condemned Luther's teaching. But polemic was not Luther's main concern, and his *Sermon von den guten Werken* ("Sermon on Good Works"), issued in June 1520, is an important exposition of the ethical implications of justification by faith. As a tract it deserves to be associated with Luther's more famous tract on Christian liberty issued in the next months. On June 15, 1520, there appeared the papal bull (a decree issued under the papal seal) *Exsurge Domine* or "Lord, cast out," against 41 articles of Luther's teaching, followed by the burning of Luther's writings in Rome. Eck and the Humanist diplomat and cardinal Girolamo Aleandro (1480–1542) were entrusted with the task of taking the bull to the cities of Germany.

The Reformation treatises of 1520. Eck and Aleandro were alarmed to discover how swiftly German opinion had moved to Luther's side. In contrast to his treatment the year before, Eck had to seek refuge in Leipzig from physical violence. Aleandro did what he could in agitated correspondence to shock the Curia (papal administrative bureaucracy) into realizing the grave danger facing the church in Germany. Luther's friends, aware of how precarious his position was, sought to moderate his violence, but he now moved well beyond their horizon. In Luther's own opinion of himself, he was far too temperate in view of all the ecclesiastical hypocrisy and offenses. The result was the defiant tracts of the summer of 1520. The first, the real manifesto, was his *An den christlichen Adel deutscher Nation* ("Address to the Christian Nobility of the German Nation"), addressed to the rulers of Germany, princes, knights, cities, under the young emperor Charles V. It argued that in the crisis, when the spiritual arm had refused to take in hand the amendment of the church and the often expressed grievances of the German people against Rome (*i.e.*, the papacy), it was necessary for the secular arm to intervene and call a reforming council. The document was ill arranged and tailed off, but it found deep response among sections of the nation, and in the next months Luther was carried along with the tide of national resentment against Rome.

His second treatise, *De captivitate Babylonica ecclesiae praeludium* ("A Prelude Concerning the Babylonian Captivity of the Church"), intended for clergy and scholars, was an act of ecclesiastical revolution. It inevitably estranged many moderate Humanists, for it reduced to only three (Baptism, the Lord's Supper, and penance) the seven sacraments of the church, denied mass and attacked transubstantiation (the doctrine that the substance of the bread and wine is changed into the body and blood of Christ in the sacrament of the Lord's Supper), made vehement charges against papal authority, and asserted the supremacy of Holy Scripture and the rights of individual conscience. The third work, dedicated to the pope, was, as a still, small voice after the uproar, a minor classic of edification, *Von der Freiheit eines Christenmenschen* ("Of the Freedom of a Christian Man"), which made clear the ethical implications of justification by faith, and showed that his thought and his public actions were connected by a coherent theological core. On December 10, 1520, the students lit a bonfire before the Elster Gate in Wittenberg, and as they fed the works of

the canonists to the flames Luther added the papal bull (*Exsurge Domine*) against himself with suitable imprecation—"Because you have corrupted God's truth, may God destroy you in this fire."

In January 1521 the pope issued the bull of formal excommunication (*Decet Romanum pontificem*), though it was some months before the condemnation was received throughout Germany. Meanwhile, the imperial Diet was meeting at Worms, and there was a good deal of lobbying for and against Luther. In the end, Frederick the Wise obtained a promise from the emperor that Luther should not be condemned unheard and should be summoned to appear before the Diet. This enraged Aleandro, who asserted that the papal condemnation was sufficient and that the secular arm had only to carry out its orders. It also alarmed Luther's friends, who did what they could to dissuade him. Luther was firm in his determination to go, and began the journey in April 1521, undeterred by the news, on the way, that the emperor had ordered his books to be burned. What was meant to be the safe custody of a heretic turned out to be something like a triumphal procession, and when Luther entered Worms on April 16 he was attended by a cavalcade of German knights and the streets were so thronged as to enrage his enemies.

The Diet and Edict of Worms, 1521. *Luther's defiance of the Diet.* In the early evening of April 17, 1521, Luther appeared before the notables of church and state and faced the young emperor Charles V, whom he found cold and hostile. A pile of writings lay before him, but when he was formally asked whether he acknowledged them, his legal adviser insisted that the titles be read. In view of the gravity of recantation, Luther asked for time to think, a request that may have taken his enemies off guard. A day's respite was granted, and the following afternoon, in a larger hall, and before an even more crowded assembly, Luther reappeared. This time he could not be prevented from making a long speech. He distinguished between his writings: for the works of edification he need not and ought not to recant, for the violence of his polemic he would apologize, but for the rest he could not recant; and, as he went on to explain why, the demand was brusquely made for a plain, simple answer. This he now gave in words of unyielding defiance. He would recant if convinced of his error either by Scripture or by evident reason. Otherwise he could not go against his conscience, which was bound by the Word of God. Though evidence is now tilted against the authenticity of the famous conclusion, "Here I stand. I can do no other," it at least registers the authentic note of Luther's reply in a moment that captured the imagination of Europe. There was a moment of confusion with Eck and Luther shouting, and then the emperor cut short the proceedings. Luther strode through his thronging enemies to his friends, his arm raised in a gesture of relief and triumph.

There followed a diplomatic flurry. It was evident that Luther had powerful friends; there was some sabre rattling from the knights and the peasant emblem appeared in the streets. There is evidence to support Luther's boast that had he wished he could have started such a game that the emperor's life would not have been safe. The radical Reformer and social revolutionary, Thomas Müntzer, later asserted that had Luther recanted the angry knights would have killed him. At any rate, Luther was now given what he had long asked for in vain, something like a real hearing before reasonably impartial judges, while he was kindly handled by the archbishop of Trier. But he could not now make even minor concessions, and the discussions broke down on the fallibility of councils. He was formally dismissed and departed under his safe-conduct.

Despite his spectacular moral triumph, Luther's enemies, nonetheless, achieved something important at this point when a rump Diet passed the Edict of Worms. It declared Luther to be an outlaw whose writings were proscribed. The edict was to shadow him and fetter his movements all his days. It meant also that his prince must, for a time at least, walk delicately and could not publicly support his protégé. The result was the pretended

"Address to the Christian Nobility"

Excommunication

"Here I stand. I can do no other."

kidnapping of Luther who was lodged secretly in the romantic castle of the Wartburg, near Eisenach.

Luther at the Wartburg. In this aerie among the trees Luther remained until March 1522. Known as Junker Georg, or Knight George, he dressed as a layman, grew a beard, and put on weight. The lack of exercise and the unwontedly rich diet brought on physical distress, whereas his mind, flung back on itself after months of crisis, knew intense reaction in a period of acute depression of the kind that Luther ranked high among temptations. But he was far from idle. He finished a beautiful exposition of the Magnificat (the song of Mary, the mother of Christ, in the liturgy) and prepared an edition of sermons on the Epistles and Gospels at mass, which he thought was perhaps his best writing. Although away from books, he wrote his ablest controversial piece, *Rationis Latomianae pro Incendiariis Lovaniensis Scholae sophistis redditae Lutheriana confutatio* ("Refutation of the argument of Latomus"—who was a member of the theological faculty of the University of Louvain), containing a luminous exposition of justification. Most important of all, he began to translate the New Testament from the original Greek into German. He did not believe that such work should be left to one mind, and soon enlisted his colleagues, notably Melanchthon, in the enterprise. But Luther's was the controlling genius, and the resulting New Testament (published in September 1522), like the Old Testament, translated from the Hebrew, which followed later (1534), was a monumental work, which had deep and lasting influence on the language, life, and religion of the German people. He had now to deal with some of the practical implications of his revolt. Private masses, celibacy of clergy, religious vows were no theoretical questions, but were themselves entangled in a network of legal, financial, and liturgical affairs. He wrote about these things forthrightly, and Spalatin tried in vain to hold up their publication, for in Wittenberg there were growing difficulties, and the prince, the university, and the cathedral chapter were all, for various reasons, anxious to go slowly.

Commotion in Wittenberg, 1521–22. *Radical reform.* There was a lively section of the town and of the university, however, that was determined to force the pace, and there were violent scenes in the streets and churches early in October 1521. Yet Luther, on a secret visit to his friends early in December, was not alarmed, and it was his influence that led the Augustinians to decide, in the new year, that those of them who wished might return to the world. Two radical leaders now appeared, the incorrigible troublemaker Karlstadt and Gabriel Zwilling, an ebullient spellbinder from the Augustinians. When Karlstadt announced his betrothal to a girl of 16, and at Christmas administered Communion in both kinds (bread and wine) while dressed as a layman, attacked images in a violent tract and in innumerable theses denounced vows and masses, and demanded a vernacular liturgy, it was evident that here was a program that in timing and method differed from Luther's. Moreover, its appeal to Scripture was legalistic and made matters of necessity things that for Luther lay within the option of Christian liberty. In the new year, the town council issued a notable and pioneering ordinance regulating religion, public morals, and poor relief, a document that owes much to Luther's teaching and perhaps something to the initiative of Karlstadt. At the end of 1521 confusion was increased by the arrival of the so-called Zwickau prophets, radicals on the run from the town of Zwickau, who spoke impressively of revelations given them through dreams and visions, claiming that the end of the world was near and that all priests should be killed. A flustered and outmanoeuvred Melanchthon wrote urgently for advice to Luther, who sent wise and calm counsel.

Restoration of balanced reform. In the next months the situation worsened and in March 1522 Luther returned to Wittenberg, explaining the reason for his disobedience to instructions in a justly famous letter to his prince. Then, deliberately habited as an Augustinian monk once more, he took charge of his town pulpit and in a powerful series of sermons redressed the balance of reform. In these important utterances, the difference be-

tween Luther's conservatism and the radical pattern of reform is made plain. Luther deplored the use of violence, for the Word of God must be the agent of reform. He believed that revolt could not take place without destruction and the shedding of innocent blood; that the real idols are in the hearts of men and if their hearts are changed the images on church walls must fall into disuse. Moreover, the pace of reform must take into account the unconverted, weaker brethren. From this time onward Luther fought a war on two fronts, against the Catholics and against those whom he lumped together as *Schwärmer* ("fanatics"). One result of the Wittenberg crisis was to slow down the practical reforms, and though Luther introduced a reformed rite (*Formula Missae* or "Formula of the Mass," 1523) it was not until 1526 that he provided a vernacular liturgy (*Deutsche Messe*, or "German Mass"). Throughout Germany the evangelical movement continued to grow, and it was apparent that the Edict of Worms would not be everywhere enforced. A Diet at Nürnberg, 1522–23, refused to suppress the evangelical preachers and demanded a reforming, national council; though Catholic pressure was stronger in the following year, the Diet again pressed for a council and would consent only to the enforcement of the edict "as far as possible."

The Peasants' War. *Activities of the radical Reformers.* On his journeys to and from Worms Luther had been dismayed by the evident social and political unrest. In the next months he wrote open letters, warning the rulers of Saxony and the councils of such cities as Strassburg of the danger that the new radical teaching would provoke revolution. In 1523 he made his own views of secular government plain in an important treatise *Von weltlicher Obrigkeit* ("Of Earthly Government"), in which he firmly asserted the duty of a Christian prince and the place of secular government within God's ordinances for mankind; he distinguished between the two realms of spiritual and of temporal government, through which the one rule of God is administered, and stressed the duty of civil obedience and the sinfulness of rebellion against lawful authority.

In Saxony the radical teachers posed a problem for their untheological rulers. In Orlamünde, after having been rebuked at Wittenberg, Karlstadt had converted the community to his own brand of mystical quietism. Luther made a preaching tour of the area at the request of his prince, and was greeted with hostility and ridicule. Luther himself denounced such social evils as usury, but in Eisenach the fiery preacher Jakob Strauss conducted a violent campaign against usury and tithes. Most formidable of all, in the little town of Allstedt, Thomas Müntzer, an unruly genius, combined his own ingenious liturgical reforms with a program of holy war. Himself a former "Martinian" (or follower of Martin Luther), he not only shared Karlstadt's enthusiasm for the mystics but added an explosive element (perhaps influenced by Hussite teaching) that gave point to Luther's worst fears. Müntzer threatened revolution and claimed that God would rid the world of its shame. Luther's warnings and events themselves forced the rulers to take action, and in the summer of 1524 Müntzer fled and Karlstadt was exiled. Müntzer wrote in a pamphlet that Luther was nothing more than a shameless monk, "whoring and drinking," and called him Dr. Liar. Karlstadt also wrote a series of tracts against his former comrades, denouncing, among other things, the corporeal presence in the Eucharist. Luther replied in a devastating and profound treatise, *Wider die himmlischen Propheten, von den Bildern und Sakrament* ("Against the Heavenly Prophets in the Matter of Images and Sacraments"). He claimed that the radical Reformers sought glory and honour, not the salvation of men's souls.

Luther's response to the Peasants' War. In the summer of 1524 the Peasants' War had broken out in the Black Forest area. Their program was variously motivated. Their demands were for concrete medieval liberties connected with the game and forest laws or with tithes. Some of them drew on Catholic teaching, others on the theology of Zwingli and of Luther, who had set an example of

[margin left] Influence of Luther's translation of the Bible on the German language

[margin right] Luther's dislike for violence

[margin right] The two realms theory

successful defiance of authority, had been no respecter of dignities, and whose teachings about Christian liberty and a priesthood in which all believers shared were plainer than his subtle distinctions between two kingdoms. Thus, both where he was understood and where he was misunderstood, Luther's influence in the Peasants' War has to be taken into account. Some of the moderate peasants included Luther among possible arbitrators. He himself published in May 1525 the *Ermahnung zum Frieden* ("Exhortation for Freedom"), an analysis of the "12 articles" of the Swabian peasants, sympathizing with just grievances, criticizing the princes, but repudiating the notion of a so-called Christian rebellion: "My dear friends, Christians are not so numerous that they can get together in a mob." Luther also claimed that the worldly kingdom cannot exist without inequality of persons.

In the spring of 1525 the Thuringian peasants rose, with Thomas Müntzer among their leaders, and at first seemed likely to carry all before them. Faced with imminent political chaos, Luther wrote a brutal, virulent broadsheet, *Wider die räuberischen und mörderischen Rotten der andern Bauern* ("Against the Murdering and Thieving Hordes of Peasants"). The writing was less violent than Müntzer's hysterical manifestos, but it was bad enough. It appeared, however, as an appendix to his moderate tract about the "12 articles." Moreover, words written at the height of the peasant success read very differently after their collapse at the Battle of Frankenhausen, May 15, 1525, and in the bloody reprisal that followed. It was typical of Luther that he refused to climb down, to regain lost popularity, and neither thereafter nor at any time can he be accused of subservience to rulers. As he had once refused to become the tool of the knights, so he had never "taken up" the peasant cause. But he confirmed many peasants in their preference for the radical ideology, which was soon to find more peaceful coherence in the Anabaptist movement.

Watershed year, 1525. *Luther and Erasmus.* In other ways, too, 1525 was a watershed in Luther's career. At the height of the Peasants' War in June 1525, "to spite the devil" he had married Katherina von Bora, a former nun. He certainly needed looking after, and she proved an admirable wife and a good businesswoman. His home meant a great deal to him and was an emblem for him of Christian vocation, so that he included domestic life among the three hierarchies (or "orders of creation") of Christian existence in this world, the other two being political and church life. In the same year there came his open break with the great Humanist Erasmus. The differences between the two men had long been apparent, and Erasmus, who found in Luther the type of violent, dogmatic mendicant theologian he had always detested, liked what he saw of the Reformation less and less. Nonetheless, both men had a common band of admirers and friends and entered the arena with reluctance. Erasmus, in his *De libero arbitrio*, or "Concerning Free Will" (1524), attacked Luther's doctrine of the enslaved will and provoked a resounding reply in Luther's *De servo arbitrio*, or "Concerning the Bondage of the Will" (1525), a one-sided, violent treatise that, nevertheless, includes profundities still fruitfully debated. In that year, too, Frederick the Wise died. The two men had met only once, but Luther owed much to this prince. The new ruler, the elector John, and his successor John Frederick were Luther's devout supporters and with other princes, notably Philip, landgrave of Hesse, and Albert of Brandenburg, formed a coherent group in the imperial Diet.

The Diets of Speyer. The hostility of Charles V to the Reformers and his devotion to the Catholic faith never altered, but he had to take account of political exigencies, his quarrels with the Pope and with the king of France, and the need for support against the Turks. At the Diet of Speyer in 1526, the Edict of Worms was suspended, pending a national council; in the interval it was ruled that each prince must behave as he could answer to God and to the emperor. Luther stated that there was no fear or discipline any longer and that everyone did as he pleased. As a result, it was possible to plan the reorganization of

the Saxon Church, and a visitation was carried out by jurists and theologians (1527–28). Some scholars have seen a tension between Melanchthon's *Instruktion für die Visitatoren,* or "Instructions for the Visitation" (1528), and Luther's comments, which may reveal his distrust of secular intervention in spiritual affairs; and though he thoroughly approved of the development of the evangelical *Landeskirchen* ("territorial churches") there were to be aspects of Lutheranism that blurred rather than reflected Luther's theological distinctions. At the second Diet of Speyer in 1529, renewed Catholic pressure led to the reversal of earlier concessions, drawing from the evangelical princes, and from a number of cities, a protest that won them, for the first time, the name Protestant.

The eucharistic controversy. *Doctrinal differences among the Reformers.* Doctrinal differences about the Eucharist broke the common evangelical front. Though all the Reformers repudiated the sacrifice of the mass, they were deeply divided about the nature of the divine Presence. Luther, with simple biblicism, insisted that Christ's words "This is my body" must be literally interpreted, because allegory is not to be used in interpreting Scripture unless the context plainly requires it. Karlstadt's fanciful argument (that the word this referred not to bread and wine but the Lord's physical body) was soon dropped. Zwingli won many to his view that "is" must be taken as "means," and his learned friend, the Humanist John Oecolampadius, brought support from the early Church Fathers for a spiritual Presence and stressed the idea of the 2nd-century Tertullian that "body" meant "sign of the body." Thus, the initial debate was about interpretive principles, about the words of institution, though the scriptural argument moved to the relevance or irrelevance of the Gospel According to John (*e.g.,* "he who eats my flesh and drinks my blood has eternal life" [John 6:54]).

The debate turned to the intricate matter of Christology (*i.e.,* doctrine of Christ). Zwingli insisted on the distinction between the two natures of Christ and that because it is the property of a human body to be in one place, Christ's human body was not here but in heaven. Luther, on the other hand, stressed the indivisible unity of the one Person of Jesus Christ, the mediator. Without going into a metaphysical doctrine of "ubiquity," or Presence everywhere (which was developed by other Lutherans), he asserted that Christ is present wherever he wills to be and that we are not to think of him in heaven "like a stork in a nest." Martin Bucer and the Strassburg theologians echoed the more positive stresses of the Swiss, and Bucer used the Realist language of the early Church Fathers to support a true, spiritual Presence. Luther's treatise *Dass diese Worte Christi "Das ist mein Leib" noch fest stehen wider die Schwärmgeister* ("That these words of Christ 'This is my Body' still stand firm against the Fanatics," 1527) showed that in three years of controversy he had not budged. Zwingli's Latin tract *Amica exegesis* ("A Friendly Exegesis," 1527) was far less amicable than the title suggests and brought a great outburst from Luther, the impressive *Vom Abendmahl Christi, Bekenntnis* ("Confession of the Lord's Supper," 1528). This convinced Bucer that he had misunderstood Luther, who did not mean a local, confined Presence; and from then on he intensified his awkward, well-intended attempts to make peace.

The Marburg Colloquy and the Diet of Augsburg. The political advantages of a common front were obvious, not least to the vulnerable Zwingli and Philip, landgrave of Hesse, and the prince invited theologians of both sides to a private colloquy at Marburg in October 1529. Luther began by saying that in his opinion Zwingli did not know much about the gospel. When Zwingli asked if it was permissible for a Christian to ask how Christ could be present in the bread and wine of the Lord's Supper, Luther replied that if the Lord commanded him to eat crab apples and manure, he would do it because it was a command. After three days' debate, there was no agreement about the Eucharist, though the air had been cleared of many misunderstandings. But if the conference failed, there were agreements on other

Luther's view of rebellion

Luther's marriage

Luther and Zwingli

issues, and these might have been fruitful had not the coming imperial Diet caused the Wittenberg theologians to draw away from the Swiss. As an outlaw, Luther could not attend this fateful Diet of Augsburg and had to fidget in the castle of Coburg, leaving the care of the gospel to Melanchthon, who did very well and produced in the Augsburg Confession (1530), one of the great documents of the Reformation as well as a normative confession of Lutheranism.

The Augsburg Confession

Luther used his influence to stiffen the elector against compromise, though from this time onward he could not refuse his consent to political Protestantism as it took a more and more military shape in the Schmalkaldic League, which was established by Protestant princes in preparation for armed resistance to Catholic aggression. The political situation again changed swiftly, however, and, confronted with the Turkish invasion, the Emperor agreed to a truce with the Protestants in the Religious Peace of Nürnberg (1532). This was a valuable breathing space, and its effects are evident in Luther's writings in the next years. Now, more and more, Luther left matters to the action of Melanchthon. Opponents attempted to break up the friendship of the two. Luther said, regarding this matter, that if Melanchthon would allow himself to be won over by their opponents, "he could easily become a cardinal and keep wife and child."

Growth of Lutheranism, 1530–46. *Melanchthon's leadership.* Luther acquiesced in the eucharistic agreement —by which the south Germans reached agreement on the Lord's Supper—that the triumphant Bucer brought off with Melanchthon in 1536 (the Wittenberg Concord), though Bucer was unable to widen the agreement and bring in the Swiss. When an English embassy from Henry VIII arrived to discuss joining the Schmalkaldic League, it was Melanchthon who drew up the theological agenda (the Wittenberg Articles, 1535) with an ambiguous statement of justification of which Luther wrote "this agrees well with our teaching." But he would not follow Melanchthon when he thought he wrote too irenically about the papacy, and as the papal council loomed near he penned his own uncompromising Schmalkald Articles (1537).

Melanchthon's great work in the field of education was to earn him the name preceptor of Germany, but Luther too was important in this matter. His open letter to the councillors of Germany about the need for schools (1524), and his published sermon *Dass man Kinder zur Schulen halten solle* ("On Keeping Children at School," 1530) show how wise and forward looking was his concern for education. He himself composed two important catechetic documents, the lovely classic, *Kleiner Katechismus* ("Small Catechism"), and *Grosser Katechismus* ("Large Catechism," 1529), for teachers and pastors.

In Wittenberg Luther had a group of able colleagues: Justus Jonas, Johannes Bugenhagen, Feliks Krzyzak (Cruciger). In scores of cities his disciples and friends spread the evangelical teaching that formed the Lutheran pattern of church life. Luther, though not pre-eminent as a liturgist, provided orders of worship from which numerous other *Kirchenordnungen* ("church orders") were derived. The influence of Luther's writings was everywhere felt in the Western Christian world. It was in Scandinavia that the Lutheran Church struck its deepest roots and won its most complete ascendancy, but it also had deep influence in Austrian and Hungarian lands. Luther realized the importance of hymns and encouraged his friends to write them. He wrote a score of fine hymns, four of which appeared in his first Protestant hymnbook in 1524. The famous "Ein feste Burg ist unser Gott" ("A Safe Stronghold Our God is Still" or "A Mighty Fortress Is Our God") became almost an event in European history. During the last decade of his life, John Calvin (1509–64) was the rising portent in Switzerland, though Luther's personal contact with him was slight. He continued to attack bitterly the *Schwärmer* ("fanatics"), who then included besides the Anabaptists a number of radicals such as Kaspar Schwenckfeld, a Reformer who tried to mediate between various groups. Although he maintained to the end his view that error can be con-

Luther's hymns

quered only by the Word, Luther came to accept the punishment of the Anabaptists.

The affair of Philip of Hesse. In 1540 Bucer and Melanchthon took the initiative in conniving at the deplorable bigamy of Philip of Hesse, but Luther was involved and had he willed could have stopped it. It would have been easy for Philip to remedy his incorrigible incontinence by taking a mistress, but this he refused to do, though his guilty conscience kept him from the sacrament. The desperate device, as a lesser of evils, was to grant him a secret dispensation to take a second wife. When the affair became public Luther angrily threatened to expose the whole story. He himself was so far from lowering moral standards that in the next years he threatened to leave Wittenberg because public morals there were a shame on a city that had known the evangelical teaching so long. After a serious illness in 1537 he was an almost chronic invalid, prematurely aged, seldom free from discomfort, often in pain, and he brought his teaching career to an end with lectures on Genesis. In the last decade of his life he had to witness the recovery of the papacy, which he thought to have been mortally wounded, in the preparations for the Council of Trent (1545–63), and the growing menace of Catholic military might. His last outstanding controversial treatise was *Von den Conciliis und Kirchen* ("Of Councils and Churches," 1539). Among his last writings, *Against the Anabaptists*, *Against the Jews*, *Against the Papacy at Rome, Founded by the Devil*, the most violent is the last, coarse and angry but still defiant.

Luther's last activities. Early in 1546 Luther was asked to go to Eisleben to mediate in a quarrel between two arrogant young princes, Counts Albrecht and Gebhard of Mansfeld. He was old and ill, but they were his *Obrigkeiten* ("authorities") to whom he owed obedience, and he set off in the snowy winter, leaving his wife stiff with anxiety. His letters to her teased her, comforted her, and spoke at last of a mission successfully accomplished. But he had overtaxed his strength, and in a few hours the chill of death came upon him. He died in Eisleben, the town where he was born, on February 18, 1546, and his body was interred in the Church of All Saints, Wittenberg. The great funeral orations by Bugenhagen and Melanchthon, who knew him so well, are not to be dismissed as simply panegyric. They witness that his intimates regarded him as a really great man, standing within the historic succession of prophets and doctors of the church, through whose life and witness the Word of God had gone forth, conquering and to conquer.

Luther's death

LUTHER AS THEOLOGIAN

Luther was no systematizer, like Melanchthon or Calvin, though the dissensions among Lutheran theologians after his death, each appealing to one aspect of his thought, testify to the width, coherence, and delicate balance of Luther's own teaching. The basis of his theology was Holy Scripture; and though the differences between his own and Augustine's thought are important, Augustine must stand next to the Bible among the influences upon his mind. The doctrines of salvation were of prime importance for him, and here the two great, many-sided complex conceptions of the Word and of faith are important. His often subtle doctrine about civil obedience was not always understood by his later followers, and nontheological factors in German history perpetuated and even perverted this misunderstanding. His doctrine of Christian vocation in this world and the importance of human life in the world became part of the general Protestant and Puritan inheritance. In other matters—in the room allowed for Christian liberty, in his conception of the part played by law in Christian life, and in his insistence on the Real Presence in the Eucharist—his theology differs from the patterns that emerged in the Reformed (Presbyterian) churches, in Puritanism, and in the sects such as the Anabaptists.

MAJOR WORKS
In Latin

THEOLOGICAL WORKS: *Epistola Lutheriana ad Leonem decimum summum pontificem. Dissertatio de libertate Christiana per autorem recognita* (1519; "Concerning Christian Liberty"); *De votis monasticis* (1521); *De captivitate Babylonica ecclesiae praeludium* (1520; "A Prelude Concerning the Babylonian Captivity of the Church"); *De servo arbitrio* (1525; "Concerning the Bondage of the Will").

CONTROVERSIAL WRITINGS: *B. Martini Lutheri theses Tezelio, indulgentiarum institori oppositas* (1517; Ninety-five Theses); *Rationis Latomianae pro incendiariis Lovaniensis scholae sophistis redditae Lutheriana confutatio* (1521).

EXEGESIS: *Enarrationes epistolarum et evangeliorum, quas postillas vocant* (1521).

In German

THEOLOGICAL WORKS: *Von den guten Wercken* (1520; "Of Good Works"); *Von welltlicher Uberkeytt, wie weytt man yhr gehorsam schuldig sey* (1523; "Of Earthly Government"); *Das diese wort Christi (Das ist mein leib etc.) noch fest stehen widder die Schwermgeister* (1527; "That These Words of Christ 'This is My Body' Still Stand Firm Against the Fanatics"); *Vom Abendmal Christi, Bekentnis* (1528; "Confession of the Lord's Supper"); *Von den Conciliis und Kirchen* (1539; "Of Councils and Churches").

CONTROVERSIAL WRITINGS: *An den christlichen Adel deutscher Nation* (1520; "Address to the Christian Nobility of the German Nation"); *Widder die hymelischen Propheten von den Bildern und Sacrament* (1525; "Against the Heavenly Prophets in the Matter of Images and Sacraments"); *An die Radssherrn aller Stedte deutschs Lands: Das sie Christliche Schulen auffrichten und hallten sollen* (1524); *Ermanunge zum Fride auff die zwelff Artikel der Bawrschafft ynn Schwaben* (1525); *Wider die mordischen uñ reubischen Rotten der Bawren* (1525); *Wider Hans Worst* (1541); *Wider das Bapstum zu Rom vom Teuffel gestifft* (1545).

TRANSLATIONS AND EXEGESIS: *Das Newe Testament Deutzsch* (1522); *Biblia, das ist, die gantze Heilige Scrifft Deudsch* (1534); *Das Magnificat verteuschet und ausgelegt* (1521).

OTHER WORKS (LITURGICAL): *Deudsche Messe* (1526). (DIDACTIC): *Der kleine Catechismus* (1559; "Small Catechism"); *Deudsch Catechismus* (1529; "Large Catechism"). Among his hymns the most famous is probably "Ein feste Burg ist unser Gott" ("A Mighty Fortress Is Our God").

BIBLIOGRAPHY

Luther's writings: The *Works of Martin Luther*, 6 vol. (Philadelphia edition, 1915–32); *Luther's Works* (American edition), ed. by J. PELIKAN and P. LEHMANN, 56 vol. (1955–), henceforth an indispensable tool for English study. There is a single-volume anthology edited by J. DILLENBERGER, *Martin Luther: Selections from His Writings* (1961); and also E.G. RUPP and W.B. DREWERY, *Martin Luther* (1970). The following are important volumes in the "Library of Christian Classics": vol. 15, *Luther's Lectures on Romans*, ed. by W. PAUCK (1961); vol. 16, *Early Theological Writings*, ed. by J. ATKINSON (1962); vol. 17, *Luther and Erasmus*, ed. by E.G. RUPP and P.S. WATSON (1969); vol. 18, *Letters of Spiritual Counsel*, ed. by T.G. TAPPERT (1955). See also *A Commentary on St. Paul's Epistle to the Galatians*, ed. by P.S. WATSON (1953). In German the definitive edition is the Weimar edition by J.C.F. KNAAKE *et al.* (1883–).

Studies: Of biographical studies in English, the most readable are: R.H. BAINTON, *Here I Stand!* (1950); FRANZ LAU, *Luther* (1959; Eng. trans., 1963); and W.J. KOOIMAN, *Maarten Luther* (1946; Eng. trans., *By Faith Alone*, 1954). P. SMITH, *The Life and Letters of Martin Luther* (1911), is the best of the older studies. For a broad survey, see E. G. SCHWIEBERT, *Luther and His Times* (1950); on the young Luther: R.H. FIFE, *The Revolt of Martin Luther* (1957); for a brief account: E.G. RUPP, *Luther's Progress to the Diet of Worms, 1521* (1951); on Luther and his age: J. ATKINSON, *Martin Luther and the Birth of Protestantism* (1968); A.G. DICKENS, *Reformation and Society in Sixteenth Century Europe* (1966); J. LORTZ, *Die Reformation in Deutschland*, 5th ed., 2 vol. (1965; Eng. trans., *The Reformation in Germany*, 2 vol., 1968); and W. PAUCK, *Heritage of the Reformation*, rev. ed. (1961). (*On Luther's theology*): G. EBELING, *Luther* (1964; Eng. trans., *Luther: An Introduction to His Thought*, 1970); P.S. WATSON, *Let God be God* (1947); E.G. RUPP, *The Righteousness of God* (1953); H. BORNKAMM, *Luthers geistige Welt* (1953; Eng. trans., *Luther's World of Thought*, 1958); B.A. GERRISH, *Grace and Reason* (1962); R. PRENTOR, *Spiritus Creator* (1944; Eng. trans., 1953); D.K. SIGGINS, *Martin Luther's Doctrine of Christ* (1970). (*On the influence of Luther*): E.W. ZEEDEN, *Martin Luther und die Reformation*, 2 vol. (1950–52; Eng. trans., *The Legacy of Luther*, vol. 1, 1954); C.M. CARLSON, *The Reinterpretation of Luther* (1948), a survey of Scandinavian Luther studies. Important studies in languages other than English are: K. HOLL, *Gesammelte Aufsätze zur Kirchengeschichte*, 3 vol. (1928–32); E. HIRSCH, *Lutherstudien*, 2 vol. (1954); R. HERMANN, *Gesammelte Studien zur Theologie Luthers und der Reformation* (1960); E. WOLF, *Peregrinatio*, 2 vol. (1954); J. HECKEL, *Lex Charitatis* (1953); E. BIZER, *Fides ex auditu*, 3rd ed. (1966); O.H. PESCH, *Die Theologie der Rechtfertigung bei Martin Luther und Thomas von Aquin* (1967); R. SCHWARZ, *Fides, spes und Caritas beim Jungen Luther* (1962); B. LOHSE, *Mönchtum und Reformation* (1963).

Psychological studies: P.J.S. REITER, *Martin Luthers Umwelt, Charakter und Psychose*, 2 vol. (1937–41); E.H. ERIKSON, *Young Man Luther: A Study in Psychoanalysis and History* (1958).

(E.G.R.)

Lutheran Churches

Lutheran churches, numerically the largest (over 75,000,000) of the Protestant churches, have, since the 16th century, spread throughout much of the world. They are, along with Calvinist and Anglican churches, one of the three classical Protestant churches of the Reformation.

NATURE AND SIGNIFICANCE

The Reformation, which broke upon Western Christendom in the 16th century, was inspired and guided in its early stages chiefly by Martin Luther, whose thought has remained a continuing influence in Protestantism. The major effect of the Reformation on the external structure of the Christian Church was to dissolve the unity of Western Christendom and to create a Lutheran, a Calvinist, an Anglican, and a Spiritualist type of Protestant Church.

Lutheranism's existence as a distinct church dates to the presentation of the Augsburg Confession at the Diet of Augsburg in 1530. The name Lutheran, which was at first used derogatorily by Luther's opponents (such as Johann Eck at the Leipzig Debate in 1519), was avoided as a self-designation until the 17th century. The Lutheran confessions spoke of the "evangelical churches" or the "churches of the Augsburg Confession," and the theologians of the time used "apostolic catholic church" or "catholic evangelical church" as a designation.

Lutheranism has contributed to Christianity a distinct theology (Luther, P. Melanchthon, A. Ritschl, P. Tillich); a distinct mysticism (J. Böhme, J.G. Hamann, E. Swedenborg, J.G. Fichte); philosophical developments (G.W. Leibniz: mathematical theory, monadology; I. Kant and G.W.F. Hegel: critical and speculative Idealism; F.W.J. Schelling and S. Kierkegaard: Existentialism); philosophies of religion (Rudolf Otto, Lundensian school, Tillich); a method of biblical interpretation (Luther, R. Bultmann); historical-critical studies of the Scriptures (J.S. Semler, D.F. Strauss, F.C. Baur, J. Wellhausen, H. Gunkel); a linguistically oriented classical educational system (Melanchthon); a distinct theory of law (Werner Elert); ecumenical initiatives (Leibniz, N. Söderblom); choral and instrumental music (Paul Gerhardt, J.S. Bach).

Lutheranism's specific character has resulted from the mixture of theological, cultural, and personal factors that marked Luther's career and its effects—his religious struggle with the judgment of God upon man ("Where will I find a gracious God?"), the emergence of individuality in persons and of the sense of sound (rhetoric, music) in culture, and the convergence of ecclesiastical and national or territorial interests. Its inner development has been shaped by the tension and conflict between the conservative element (preservation of the ancient faith) and the revolutionary element (a radical trust in God who justifies man). This tension has affected both the understanding of the Bible (is it a sourcebook of unalterable teachings or a witness to the trustworthiness of God manifest in the grace of Christ?) and the understanding of Lutheranism's central article of justification (is it a formulation to be accepted and believed or the basis of a new relation to the world and man?).

Lutherans today number about 75,200,000 throughout the world. Seven countries have a Lutheran population of more than one million: Germany (37.6), the United States (8.9), Sweden (7.0), Finland (4.6), Denmark (4.5), Norway (3.5), and Indonesia (1.26). By continents, the distribution is 60,400,000 in Europe, 9,200,000 in North America,

The sources of its characteristics

1,800,000 in South America, 2,200,000 in Asia, 1,800,000 in Africa, and 500,000 in Australia.

The Reformation period. By attacking the indulgence traffic of the church (in the Ninety-five Theses of 1517), Luther ultimately struck at the foundation of the papal church. His Leipzig Debate with Johann Eck was a decisive turning point when Eck elicited from him the claim that church councils could err (Luther contended that the Council of Constance of 1415 had wrongly condemned some views of the Bohemian reformer Jan Hus) and the denial that the papal church was necessary for salvation. Thus labelled a heretic, Luther was first threatened with excommunication (in the papal bull of 1520, *Exsurge Domine*) and then excommunicated (Jan. 3, 1521, in the papal bull *Decet Romanum Pontificem*) after he had publicly burned the bull of 1520.

The impact of political ferment The religious conflict was soon intertwined with political developments. Emperor Charles V of the Holy Roman Empire summoned Luther to give account of his teaching at the Diet of Worms. The result was the Edict of Worms (signed May 26, 1521), placing Luther and his followers under imperial ban and decreeing the burning of his writings. But Luther's thought continued to spread. Since political circumstances in Europe were not favourable for a forceful suppression of the movement, Charles sought a negotiated settlement at the Diet of Augsburg in 1530. The Protestants presented the Augsburg Confession, composed by Luther's associate Philipp Melanchthon, as a statement of their teaching. It emphasized the continuity between what they taught and the faith of the whole catholic church ("the whole dissension is about a few small abuses"). Charles rejected both the Augsburg Confession and the Apology of the Augsburg Confession, which Melanchthon wrote in reply to the Catholics' rebuttal. The Protestants then left the Diet, and the remaining majority reinstated the Edict of Worms coupled with a promise to convoke a general church council within the year.

Religious wars In 1531 the Protestants formed the Schmalkaldic League for military protection against execution of the imperial edict. Aided by renewed threats of war from the Turks, the efforts of the league led to the armistice of Nürnberg (1532), in which the Protestants were granted tolerance until the promised general council. (That council was not held until 1545-63, the Council of Trent.) There were further threats of war (Catholic League of Nürnberg of 1538, Frankfurt armistice of 1539) and more negotiations (colloquies of Worms and Regensburg, 1540–41), followed by the defeat of the Schmalkaldic League and its subsequent recovery when Maurice of Saxony, a master diplomat, switched allegiance to the Protestant cause. The Treaty of Passau (1552) granted armistice to the Protestants. The Religious Peace of Augsburg (1555) officially acknowledged the churches of the Augsburg Confession and related churches, but it contained ambiguities that were not resolved until the Peace of Westphalia (1648) after the Thirty Years' War, in which King Gustavus II Adolphus of Sweden played a decisive role for the Lutheran forces.

A far-reaching consequence of these events for the Lutheran churches lay in the fact that the territorial princes had in the process become primates of the territorial churches. At first regarded as an emergency measure, this arrangement was justified by Lutheran theologians in the 17th century by the claim (today regarded as historically inaccurate) that the suspension of episcopal powers in Protestant lands at Passau and Augsburg had transmitted that power to the territorial princes. Luther's conception (in the 1520s) of the autonomy of the Christian congregation was not put into practice nor theoretically developed until later (*e.g.*, by N.F.S. Grundtvig in Denmark, C.F.W. Walther in the U.S.).

In some measure the Lutheran movement affected all European lands. It gained exclusive dominance in the Scandinavian countries (Sweden, after 1527; Denmark and Norway, 1536; Iceland, 1539), in Prussia (1525), and in the Baltic provinces (1523–39). It influenced Italy and Spain hardly at all and France very little. Among eastern European countries, Protestantism made the largest gain in Hungary (Lutheran until 1543, then Calvinist) and Transylvania (a Lutheran Church after 1545). The Lutheran Church of Sweden was unique in the extent to which it kept continuity with the pre-Reformation church (retention of vestments, titles of bishop and archbishop, apostolic succession, and such ceremonies as elevation of the host at mass).

The Post-Reformation in Germany. During the 16th century, Lutheranism was torn by the conflicts between the Philippists, centred in Wittenberg, who represented a Melanchthonian humanism, and the Gnesio-Lutherans (Genuine Lutherans), centred in Jena. A mediating settlement was adopted in the Formula of Concord of 1577 (published in the Book of Concord in 1580 on the 50th anniversary of the Augsburg Confession), but not all Lutheran churches accepted it.

Lutheran orthodoxy and pietism From 1580 to 1700 the dominant power was orthodoxy, characterized by an exactness in theological formulation and by large-scale doctrinal theologies in the form either of *loci* (main topics) or of systems. The standard work from this period is Johann Gerhard's *Loci theologici* (finished in 1622). Orthodox theology was school theology in the sense that it carefully defined Lutheran theology as against Catholic, Calvinist, Spiritualist, anti-Trinitarian, and other theologies. It was strictest at Wittenberg, least strict at Altdorf and Helmstedt, with Jena between. Toward the end of the 17th century it became sterile, though it had in the meantime contributed to studies in theological method, in logic, and patristics (writings of the early Church Fathers). In addition to orthodox there were also irenic theologians, notably George Calixtus of Helmstedt, who proposed a unity of churches on the basis of the teachings of the first five centuries (*consensus quinquesaecularis*); and the mysticism of Johann Arndt's *True Christianity* had a wide influence.

Orthodoxy was superseded by Pietism (1670–1760), characterized by its emphasis on the inwardness of religion, a consciousness of separateness from the world and its pleasures, and an inner estrangement from the state church. Its prime mover was Philipp Jakob Spener. It developed at three centres. At Halle (led by August Hermann Francke), it affected the nobility and promoted schools for the poor, orphanages, and missionary work. In Württemberg it affected all levels of society and did not become separated from the church leaders. Two of its representatives were the biblical scholar J.A. Bengel and the theosophist F.C. Oetinger. The Herrnhut Brethren, founded by Count von Zinzendorf, constituted a third type. Their theology was Lutheran in origin, but the different accent on the Person of Jesus and the cultic devotion to the blood and wounds of Jesus gave it a distinct character.

The Enlightenment Pietism was followed by the Enlightenment (1750–90), characterized by its intellectualism, its thrust for new knowledge, and its rejection of authoritarianism. In Germany its character was prepared by the philosophers G.W. Leibniz (*Theodicy, New Essays Concerning Human Understanding*), who sought to unite Christianity and the new mechanics, and Christian Wolff. It reached its high point under Frederick II of Prussia in such men as H.S. Reimarus, J.A. Ernesti, and J.G. Toellner. The "neology" of J.S. Semler, the critical philosophy of Immanuel Kant, and the literary work of G. Lessing, J.G. von Herder, and J.W. von Goethe represented, but also transcended, the Enlightenment.

The Enlightenment brought about a general split between Supernaturalists (*e.g.*, F.V. Reinhard) and Rationalists (*e.g.*, P.K. Henke and H.E.G. Paulus) in theology that has continued to the present day, although Rationalism began to wane after the 1830s (thoroughly attacked in K.A. von Hase's *Hutterus redivivus* of 1828). Supernaturalism maintains that faith is permanently dependent upon external authority (revelation), whereas Rationalism maintains that authoritative revelation serves only a pedagogical purpose for precritical reason.

In the 19th century Lutheranism was shaped by Idealism (1790–1835) and its aftermaths, by a new Confessionalism (1835–75), and also by neo-Idealism (1875–1915).

Idealism overcame the Rational–Supernatural split, though not in a form that could be appropriated by most churchgoers. It began as critical Idealism (in Kant), that is, the rational self-limitation of human reason; but it developed into romantic Idealism (*e.g.*, Herder, Goethe, F.D.E. Schleiermacher), in which reason is subordinated to feeling and the immediacy of living; and it culminated in speculative or absolute Idealism (*e.g.*, J.G. Fichte, F.W.J. Schelling, G.W.F. Hegel, the Hegelians Karl Daub, Philipp Konrad Marheineke, Richard Rothe, and D.F. Strauss), in which human reason is a retracing or recapitulation of the divine reason.

The reactions to Idealism (in the Existentialism of Kierkegaard and the later thought of Schelling and the pessimism of A. Schopenhauer) affected the educated laity and were in part the cause of increasing alienation from the institutional church.

Lutheran Confessionalism took a repristinating (restorative) direction in a few theologians (*e.g.*, A. Vilmar, F.A. Philippi), but it was chiefly an attempt to mediate between the Lutheran tradition and Idealism. Its chief seat was the Erlangen school (represented by A. von Harless, J.C.K. von Hofmann, and F.H.R. von Frank), but others took part (*e.g.*, Theodosius Harnack, C.E. Luthardt).

At the end of the century, Idealism re-emerged in the Neo-Kantianism of Albrecht Ritschl, Wilhelm Herrmann, Martin Kähler, and Adolf von Harnack as well as in a Neo-Hegelianism (Otto Pfleiderer).

The event most decisive for Lutheran churches in Germany and the Americas was the Prussian Union of 1817, bringing the Lutherans and Reformed into one church. At first it met with welcome, but it soon became entangled in Frederick William III's liturgical reform (introducing a new, somewhat archaic, liturgy) and new church order (Schleiermacher was a leading opponent). It had two important results. The territorial regent now served as chief bishop of the church, not in his capacity as head of the state but as the person who had highest status in the congregation; and a number of Lutherans refused to join the Union, some forming the "Old Lutheran" church and others emigrating to America and Australia.

In the 20th century several new factors appeared. A delayed appreciation of Kierkegaard and the "dialectical theology" of the 1920s (*e.g.*, F. Gogarten, Karl Barth) gave wide currency to the problems broached in 19th-century Idealism at the same time as they reinforced Supernatural tendencies in theology. Nihilism (*e.g.*, F. Nietzsche), atheistic Existentialism, and the implications of science and technology provided major problems for attention. The ecumenical movement altered the focus of traditional controversies.

The National Socialism of Hitler brought the church in Germany into a grave crisis. The fall of the government of William II and the princes in 1918 had ended the relation of church and state existing since the Reformation. In the next years the desperate economic and political conditions had complicated the situation and prepared the way for the nationalism fostered by Hitler. The struggle between the nationalist church, which Hitler tried to erect (*i.e.*, the German Christians under Bishop Müller), and the Confessing Church, which issued the Declaration of Barmen, 1934, was intense and protracted; some 7,000 pastors had been denounced or arrested by 1939 (Martin Niemöller was imprisoned, and Dietrich Bonhoeffer martyred). The Confessing Church, emerging as the clear victor in 1945, however, was a major force in rebuilding the country and in making reparations for the persecutions under Hitler.

Lutheran churches in Scandinavia.

In the Scandinavian countries the history of Lutheranism followed basically the same pattern as in the German lands. These countries used the works of orthodoxy and received the currents of Pietism (Erik Pontoppidan's catechism, widely used in Denmark and Norway, was a blend of orthodoxy and Pietism); they had their representatives of the Enlightenment (*e.g.*, Ludvig Holberg in Denmark–Norway, Christian Bastholm in Denmark, Johannes Gunnerus in Norway), their Rationalists (*e.g.*, Henrik Clausen), and

their Idealists (*e.g.*, Hans Martensen in Denmark, Henry Reuterdahl in Sweden).

Sweden (and Finland) remained somewhat apart, less affected by the new movements. Pietism was limited by the Conventicle Act of 1726 for a century; the Enlightenment made few inroads; Idealism was mixed with Supernaturalism; and Emanuel Swedenborg produced a distinct mystical Rationalism.

In Denmark the 19th century brought developments of international significance. Through N.F.S. Grundtvig the church received a folk character—based on the Apostles' Creed, the Lord's Prayer, and Baptism—that prevented the various tensions (*i.e.*, Pietism, Rationalism, Revivalism) from causing a split. The writings of Kierkegaard were to become a worldwide influence in the 20th century. In Norway, independent of Denmark, Lutheranism was shaped by the moralism of Hans Nielsen Hauge, whose disciple E. Eilsen came to America in 1839 and founded a Norwegian Lutheran church.

The Neo-Kantianism of the last third of the 19th century produced a distinctive type in the "Lundensian school" (G. Aulén, A. Nygren), that made special contributions to philosophy of religion and theology (motif-research). A prime mover for ecumenicism in the 20th century was Nathan Söderblom, archbishop of Uppsala.

Lutheran churches in America.

In the 17th century, the devastation of the Thirty Years' War led some Lutherans to emigrate to America (New York, Pennsylvania, the Carolinas), where they were served at first by pastors from European missionary societies. Henry Melchior Muhlenberg, the most prominent of the early Lutherans, came from the Francke Halle mission in 1742. He was instrumental in organizing the Lutherans in America, and his congregational constitution for St. Michael's Church in Philadelphia became a prototype for American Lutheran churches. During the 19th century some 5,000,000 German and 2,000,000 Scandinavian immigrants—reacting against the Prussian Union and the state churches as well as to the revolutions—greatly increased the numbers of Lutherans in America.

A turning point of Lutheran history in America came in the 1860s and 1870s when, spurred by the Ministerium of Pennsylvania, several synods united on the basis of the Unaltered Augsburg Confession (1860); the Synodical Conference was formed (1872) to unite the stricter Lutherans under the leadership of the Missouri Synod.

There was a continuous struggle with the question of language (*i.e.*, whether English could replace German, Swedish, or Danish in worship), the problem of adapting to the new environment without losing a Lutheran identity (*e.g.*, S. Schmucker, Frederick H. Quitman), and the doctrinal controversies concerning the church and ministry (are they essentially congregational or institutional?), and predestination.

The 20th century has brought new mergers (United Lutheran Church in America, constituted in 1918; American Lutheran Church, 1930) and councils (National Lutheran Council, 1918). By 1970 most Lutherans were included in the Lutheran Church in America (3,280,000 members), the American Lutheran Church (2,580,000), and the Lutheran Church—Missouri Synod (2,870,000). The Lutheran Council in the U.S.A. (LCUSA, 1966), formed by these three groups and the Synod of Evangelical Lutheran Churches, brought almost all Lutherans into one cooperative organization.

Lutheran missions.

Early Lutheranism was not oriented to missionary work. The first mission impulses came from the pietists and the 19th-century Awakening. By the 20th century, missions had been established in all parts of the world. The chief agencies for the missionary work were the German and Scandinavian mission societies (Dresden Mission, Leipzig Mission, Neuendettelsau Mission, and others in Germany; Danish Missionary Society; Norwegian Missionary Society; Finnish Missionary Society; plus the Board of Missions of the Church of Sweden) and later on the mission boards of the several Lutheran churches in America.

Present status.

In the last third of the 20th century the Lutheran churches face the same questions as the churches generally: urbanization, secularization, increasing technology, planetary concern, re-examination, and transformation of the traditions. Symptomatic of the last concern is the fact that the Fourth Assembly of the Lutheran World Federation in 1963 dealt with the meaning of Lutheranism's central article of justification in the present day. The extent to which Lutheran unity will be achieved is not yet clear, but the question is now interwoven with the more general question of the ecumenical movement, as well as with the meeting of the world religions and the fate of religious institutions generally in the future.

TEACHINGS

Lutheran Confessions. The official teaching of the Lutheran churches is that of the Book of Concord (1580), which contains the three ancient creeds (Apostles', Nicene, and Athanasian), the Augsburg Confession, the Apology of the Augsburg Confession, Luther's Schmalkald Articles, Luther's Small and Large Catechism, Melanchthon's "Treatise on the Power and Primacy of the Pope," and the Formula of Concord. Of these Lutheran symbols, only the Augsburg Confession and Luther's Small Catechism are accepted by all Lutheran churches. No general confessions of faith were adopted after 1580 by the Lutheran churches, although other doctrinal statements have served a confessional purpose for particular churches.

> **Book of Concord**

Partly because of the circumstances of its composition and partly because the Reformers understood their work to be a restoration of Christianity amidst contemporary corruptions, the Augsburg Confession emphasizes the continuity of the Lutheran teaching with the ancient Christian Church.

Justification. The teaching centres in the *Gospel*, or "justification": the doctrine that men "are justified freely on account of Christ through faith when they believe that they are received into grace and their sins forgiven on account of Christ, who by his death made satisfaction for our sins"; God "imputes [this faith] as righteousness in his sight" (Augsburg Confession, IV). Recent Lutheran theologians (*e.g.*, Ménégoz, Kähler, Bultmann, Tillich) have applied this doctrine to doubt as well as to guilt and have called attention to the change in the cultural and religious situation since the 16th century. Thus, Paul Tillich interprets justification through faith as a man's accepting his having been accepted in spite of his inacceptability.

This doctrine ("the article by which the church stands or falls") provides the key for understanding the Bible (Apology, IV. 3–5) as a book that has two kinds of content—law and promises. Law demands a perfect inward as well as outward obedience to the divine will, which reason can never achieve. As such it drives men to despair, but the despair is conquered by the promise that God justifies the unjust man. Theologically, the doctrine of justification gives a Christocentric (*i.e.*, what honours Christ) stress and a practical (*i.e.*, whether afflicted consciences are consoled) emphasis to the other articles of faith.

> **Law and Gospel**

Man. The doctrine of man, as shaped by the article of justification, defines man's natural state as one in which he does not fear or love God and is self-seeking. Man has freedom of will concerning the outward observance of laws (civic righteousness) but not before God (where he is inevitably unrighteous). He has a knowledge of God but not a true knowledge (he thinks, for example, that righteousness is what God has rather than what God gives).

Similarly, the meaning of predestination is to be sought not in the hidden counsel of God but in his revelation (Formula of Concord, Epitome XI). Lutheran teaching differs from the Calvinist double predestination by accepting the formal inconsistency of saying that believers are predestined to salvation without saying that unbelievers are predestined to damnation, for the purpose of the article on predestination is to console the troubled conscience. The mechanism of predestination has been the subject of controversy within Lutheranism (whether the decision of God is made "in view of faith"), but the basic position expressed in the symbols has been maintained.

Church, sacraments, and ministry. In opposition to the claim that the Roman Catholic Church was the only legit-

imate ecclesiastical organization, as well as to the biblicist demand to restructure the Christian Church according to the New Testament pattern, the Augsburg Confession (Art. VII) defines the church as the "congregation of saints [believers] in which the gospel is purely taught and the sacraments rightly administered." "Gospel" is interpreted to mean that God justifies believers on account of Christ, not on account of their merits (Augsburg Confession, V). Right administration includes the practice of communion under both kinds (bread and cup). For the unity of the church it is sufficient to agree concerning the gospel and administration of the sacraments.

> **The church**

Luther regarded the church as essentially hidden or invisible in the sense that it is as weak and sinful an institution as any other one, but one can believe that God works in and through it because it is founded on God's word.

This doctrine has undergone transformations since the 16th century. Orthodoxy and Pietism understood the invisibility of the church to mean that only God knows who among the assembled people are true believers (the invisible church as distinguished from the visible congregation). In the 19th century a sacramental-institutional conception was formulated by some Lutheran theologians (*e.g.*, T. Kliefoth, W. Löhe, F. Stahl), a congregational conception by others (*e.g.*, C.F.W. Walther), a national or folk conception by others (*e.g.*, N. Grundtvig), and a historical-evolutionary conception (*i.e.*, the church as the first actualization of the Kingdom of God to be progressively realized in history) by others. Though these differences worked divisively in the 19th century, particularly in America, they are today competitive conceptions within Lutheranism.

Of the three sacraments (Baptism, Lord's Supper, penitence-absolution) recognized by Luther and the Lutheran symbols in the Book of Concord, the Lutheran churches generally hold to two by combining absolution in part with Baptism (daily repentance is the repeated actualization of Baptism) and in part with the Lord's Supper (confession and absolution). The criterion used in determining the number of sacraments was that they were actions instituted by Christ and connected with God's promise (Apology XIII). The symbols do not define the relation between word and sacraments except to say that they come together, and both have the effect of creating and strengthening faith. This rejects the view that sacraments are effective *ex opere operato* (operative apart from faith) and that they are only memorial actions.

> **The sacraments**

The Formula of Concord's teaching on the Lord's Supper is that Christ is really bodily present "in, with, and under the bread and wine" (Solid Declaration, 35 ff., adopting Luther's terminology over Melanchthon's "with the bread and wine"). The Formula of Concord left undecided whether the presence is ubiquity (*i.e.*, the Swabian view that Christ is present because he is everywhere) or ubivolipresence (*i.e.*, the northern German view that Christ is present because he chooses to be).

In the 19th century some Lutherans (*e.g.*, G. Thomasius) distinguished word and sacrament by saying that the sacraments are intended for man's natural life as the word is for his conscious personal life. This view in some cases was carried so far (*e.g.*, in Martensen and Stahl) as to subordinate the word (as the presentation of salvation) to the sacrament (as the participation in salvation).

The ministry is conceived of as a service in word and sacrament but not a special status. Every baptized Christian is a priest by status (universal priesthood of believers), but the public preaching and administration of sacraments devolves upon "rightly called" ministers, who are priests by office.

Church and state. The Lutheran churches generally have understood the relation of church and state on the basis of God's two ways of ruling in the world (two kingdoms). Through the "laws, orders, and estates" of the world, God rules by compelling external obedience through fear and threat of punishment. Through preaching and sacrament he rules in apparent weakness by converting man's heart. This conception has provided Lutherans with a basis for understanding the constitutional separation of state and church in America.

The two domains of power and grace

The two domains of power and grace are interdependent because the word alone cannot preserve peace and justice —so the civil government must even protect the freedom of the church to proclaim the Gospel—and civil power alone cannot effect salvation.

Lutheranism has rejected the view that civil power is of itself evil and the view that civil obedience has merit for salvation in the sight of God.

To define a citizen's relation to government one may say that in ordinary circumstances a Christian obeys the powers that be (except in matters of faith) as the agent of God's rule. But if a law or government is unjust, a Christian has the right and duty to resist it, passively accepting the consequences of disobedience for himself but actively defending his fellow man against that law or government. If the government is tyrannical, a Christian not only resists but rebels. Those Christians who also are holders of civil power have an obligation to resist and oppose misuse of such power by other rulers (as the territorial princes opposed the emperor in Luther's time).

The view so described was apparently held by Luther (there is no complete agreement among scholars) as it is by recent theorists (e.g., E. Berggrav).

In the 19th century the romantic view of the national state as expressing the spirit of a people was widely influential, but later it became suspect because of the demonic character of nationalism in the 20th century.

Scripture and tradition. The Lutheran confessions, unlike the Reformed, have no article on Scripture, although the Formula of Concord does designate the Scriptures of the Old and New Testaments as the "sole and most certain rule" for judging teachings and teachers.

Toward tradition the attitude of Luther and the confessions was conservative; they retained whatever did not conflict with the Gospel of justification through faith. They viewed the written tradition of the fathers as useful for interpreting the Scriptures but not as a source or norm of teaching. Some Lutheran theologians in the 19th century (e.g., A. Vilmar and G. Thomasius) developed an organic view of the relation of the two (i.e., Scripture contains a truth that is unfolded in the course of history) not unlike that of the Catholics J. Möhler and John Henry Newman.

Ethics. Lutheran teaching on ethics is determined by the perspective of the two kingdoms—the domain of law is not to be confused with that of the Gospel—and by the relation of faith and love implicit in justification. Works of love are the result, rather than the condition, of faith. Man has freedom from his self-concern by the act of God and is enabled to direct his concern to his fellow men.

Man's works

The works a man is to do are specified in part by his status in the world (as father, as ruler, as subject, and other roles). Though early Lutherans thought of status in more natural terms (as "orders of creation"), recent Lutheran thought gives the concept a historical reference (e.g., a person's particular destiny or opportunities). A man's calling is to do well whatever his status requires.

A second factor defining the works a man is to do is the concrete need of his fellowman.

Controversies. Lutheran teaching has been shaped in part by the theological controversies in its history, almost all of which were at one time divisive. They had to do with such questions as the relation between divine and human agency (synergistic controversy, predestinarian controversy); whether works are indifferent, necessary, or dangerous for salvation (antinomian controversy, Majoristic controversy); whether in a state of confessional disagreement any questions are neutral (adiaphoristic controversy); what the nature of the sacramental presence is; whether the divine power resides in the Scriptures only when they are being used or also apart from their use (Rathmann controversy); what are sufficient grounds for church unity (syncretistic controversy); and whether God's election of believers is made "in view of faith" or not (predestinarian controversy).

WORSHIP AND ORGANIZATION

Liturgy and music. The worship service also was affected by the theology of the Reformers. Luther's "German Mass" of 1526 reflects changes that began about 1523. Apart from shifting the emphasis from sacrifice to thanksgiving, Luther's chief innovation here was to take the words of institution out of the framework of prayer and make of them a proclamation of the Gospel. This change has been preserved to the present day, although there is now a tendency to put the words again into a eucharistic prayer.

Because of the Reformers' emphasis upon the importance of the word, the sermon took an essential place in the service. Preaching is usually based upon a biblical text, a biblical story or doctrine, or a theological theme. Partly in reaction to the 19th century, there is an effort to keep preaching biblically oriented, though not necessarily tied to specified texts.

The term mass, at first retained, is not normally used except in the Church of Sweden (högmessa) as a name for the main service of worship. The other minor services disappeared from use during the 17th century, though some have been recovered in the liturgical reforms of the last century. Only Matins and Vespers are used with any regularity.

The service, sacraments, and rites

The basic order of service in most Lutheran churches is the same. It consists of two main portions (preaching and sacrament) in which the Kyrie, Introit, Gloria, Credo, and Agnus Dei are incorporated. Under the impact of the liturgical movement in this century, the didactic emphasis has given way to an emphasis on celebration in the service. Liturgical revisions (Swedish order of 1942, German of 1954, in the United States in 1941 and 1958) have brought an even greater uniformity in the basic order. They have also restored communion as a normal part of the regular Sunday service.

Lutherans observe two sacraments, Baptism and the Lord's Supper (communion, Eucharist). The common practice is to baptize children and adults who have not been baptized previously. The frequency of communion has increased in recent years, but there are still many congregations where it is celebrated only once a month or less often. Though the usual practice has been that only those who have been confirmed may participate in the Eucharist, in 1970 the Lutheran Church in America and the American Lutheran Church approved participation for ten-year-old baptized children, whether they have been confirmed or not.

The rites of the Lutheran churches are confirmation, ordination, marriage, and burial. In the rite of confirmation (usually between the ages of 10 and 15) a member makes public profession of the faith received in his Baptism. In the rite of marriage the church ceremony may replace the civil ceremony or it may serve as an invocation of blessing on the civil ceremony. Ordination of the clergy does not endow them with a special character or give them a special status, but it sets them apart for the particular office of preaching the word and administering the sacraments. This rite is interpreted either institutionally (i.e., preaching is an order instituted by Christ and transmitted from generation to generation [succession]) or congregationally (i.e., the congregations call certain of their members to assume the functions of preaching and administering the sacraments for them). In 1970 the Lutheran Church in America and the American Lutheran Church approved the ordination of women. There is no sacrament of extreme unction, but there is a burial service for the dead.

Hymnody

An important role was played in the Reformation by the hymns, which not only conveyed the evangelical teaching but also allowed for popular participation in the church services. The best known Lutheran hymns come from the 16th and 17th centuries (e.g., "A Mighty Fortress Is Our God" by Luther, "All Glory Be to God on High" by N. Decius, "O Sacred Head Now Wounded" by Paul Gerhardt, "Wake, Awake, for Night Is Flying" by P. Nicolai, "Now Thank We All Our God" by M. Rinkart). But each nation has made its contribution (e.g., Thomas Kingo in Denmark and Norway), and Lutheran hymnals today include hymns from all ages and countries.

Among composers of choral music (cantatas, motets, masses, settings of the Passion of Christ) Johann Sebastian Bach ranks highest (*e.g.*, *Mass in B Minor, St. Matthew Passion* and *St. John Passion*). But others of importance were Michael Praetorius, Heinrich Schütz, and Dietrich Buxtehude. To this music should be added the Scandinavian folk tunes (*e.g.*, L.M. Lindeman in Norway).

Education. Education of the laity and clergy was an early problem for the Reformers. The means developed to meet it have had a formative influence on Lutheranism to the present day.

The catechisms
To instruct the people in Christian teaching, Luther not only translated the Bible into the vernacular but wrote his Small and Large Catechisms (1528–29). The small one was to be used by heads of households to instruct those under their care. It includes not only the three parts that had been in use before (the Ten Commandments, the Creed, and the Lord's Prayer) but also three additional parts on Baptism, the Lord's Supper, and absolution. Each topic in the various parts is connected with an explanation in the form of an answer to the question, "What does this mean?", a device Luther used in order to avoid mechanical memorization.

The Small Catechism, with various expositions, has remained a basic instructional tool in the Lutheran churches, though it has been supplemented by other materials (*e.g.*, Bible courses, Sunday school literature, projects).

In the last century efforts have been made to connect the secular world and the Christian tradition by establishing institutions such as the academies for laymen in Europe (which provide opportunity for regular meetings of laity from specific vocations to discuss the relevance of Christianity to those vocations) and the church colleges in the United States.

Organization. The polity of the Lutheran churches varies from country to country. The Church of Sweden has maintained the episcopal succession unbroken, and congregations there are given great freedom to appoint their own pastors. The Danish church lost but later regained the episcopacy. In Norway there is a closer tie between church and state than in the other Scandinavian countries. Since 1869, by an arrangement with Russia, the Finnish Church is independent of state control but is supported by public funds.

Until the end of World War I the churches in Germany were under secular authority, administered by a commission of laymen and clergy, a system that grew out of the emergency situation of the Reformation. After the collapse of the government in 1918, the churches drew up new constitutions placing the congregations under a General Synod in some provinces and under a bishop in others; and the several provincial churches (*Landeskirchen*) were united in the German Evangelical Church Federation (1922). At the end of World War II, after the conflicts under Hitler, the Evangelical Church in Germany was organized under Bishop Wurm and Pastor Niemöller, adopting the Declaration of Barmen (1934) as a binding statement. The United Evangelical Lutheran Church of Germany, formed in 1948, became a unit within the Evangelical Church in Germany.

In America the Lutheran churches have the same denominational standing as other churches. The polity is congregational, and the local congregations are united in regional and national groups with elected officials. Elected heads are called presidents rather than bishops or superintendents. Recent efforts to restore episcopal titles and polity had not made much progress before 1970, when the American Lutheran Church adopted the title supervising bishop for its newly elected head. Other developments in that direction are possible.

Besides these larger Lutheran churches, there are a number of Lutheran free churches in Europe (*e.g.*, Evangelical Lutheran [Old Lutheran] Church, Germany) and America (*e.g.*, Church of the Lutheran Confession), which have complete congregational autonomy.

Lutheran World Federation
The Lutheran World Federation, established in 1947—the Fifth Assembly, which was to have met in Pôrto Alegre, Brazil, in 1970, was moved to France because of information regarding alleged political persecutions in Brazil—is a cooperative organization.

BIBLIOGRAPHY

General: C. BERGENDOFF, *The Church of the Lutheran Reformation* (1967), a survey of all aspects of Lutheranism, containing a wealth of basic information in a very readable narrative, with bibliography; E. HIRSCH, *Geschichte der neuern evangelischen Theologie*, 5 vol. (1949–54), the standard scholarly work on the history of Protestant theology since the Reformation; J. PELIKAN, *From Luther to Kierkegaard* (1950), a brief history of developments in Lutheran theology to the mid-19th century.

Reference works: J. BODENSIEK (ed.), *The Encyclopedia of the Lutheran Church*, 3 vol. (1965), the standard English reference on Lutheranism although articles vary from the scholarly to the propagandistic; *Lutheran Directory*, pt. 1, *Lutheran Churches of the World*, pt. 2, *The Lutheran World Federation* (1963–64), a sourcebook of statistical and other factual information on Lutheran churches.

On the nature of Lutheranism: W. ELERT, *Morphologie des Luthertums* (1958; Eng. trans., *The Structure of Lutheranism*, 2 vol, 1962), an influential interpretation of Lutheranism based on a distinction between law and Gospel.

On Orthodoxy and Pietism: R.P. SCHARLEMANN, *Thomas Aquinas and John Gerhard* (1964), a comparative study of the Scholastic theology of Lutheran orthodoxy and that of medieval Thomism; H. SCHMID, *Die Dogmatik der evangelisch-lutherischen Kirche* (1843; Eng. trans., *The Doctrinal Theology of the Evangelical Lutheran Church*, 1899), a collation of texts from theologians of the 16th and 17th centuries under specific doctrinal headings; a standard work, but not critical or historical in its treatment, now being replaced by C.H. RATSCHOW, *Lutherische Dogmatik zwischen Reformation und Aufklärung*, 3 vol. (1964–70).

On the 19th and 20th centuries: B.M.G. REARDON (ed.), *Religious Thought in the Nineteenth Century* (1966), a good selection of texts; H. STEPHAN, *Geschichte der deutschen evangelischen Theologie seit dem deutschen Idealismus*, ed. by M. SCHMIDT (1960), a compact and technical study of the last century and a half in Germany; PAUL TILLICH, *Perspectives on 19th and 20th Century Protestant Theology* (1967), an edited transcript of lectures by an influential theologian of this period; J.S. CONWAY, *The Nazi Persecution of the Churches 1933–1945* (1968), based on documents recently made available.

National developments: For the Scandinavian countries see the book by Bergendoff and the bibliography it contains. On Lutheranism in America, see S.E. AHLSTROM, "Theology in America," in *Religion in American Life*, vol. 1, pp. 232–321 (1961), a survey that sets Lutheran theology in the context of other developments in America; A.R. WENTZ, *A Basic History of Lutheranism in America*, rev. ed. (1964), a standard work on the major developments.

On the teachings: *The Book of Concord* (1959), official translation of the Lutheran confessions; E. SCHLINK, *Theologie der lutherischen Bekenntnisschriften* (1946; Eng. trans., *The Theology of the Lutheran Confessions*, 1961), a study of the theology from the point of view of a Lutheran dialectical theology; PAUL TILLICH, *Systematic Theology*, 3 vol. (1951–63), a systematics by the most original Lutheran theologian of the 20th century; L.D. REED, *The Lutheran Liturgy* (1947), a detailed examination of the origin and function of each of the sections of the Lutheran service of worship; K.F. MULLER and W. BLANKENBURG, *Leiturgia: Handbuch des evangelischen Gottesdienstes*, 5 vol. (1954), a historical and theological examination of the Lutheran service.

(R.P.S.)

Lutuli, Albert

A South African tribal chief, Albert Lutuli was the first African to be awarded the Nobel Prize (1960), in recognition of his long nonviolent struggle against racial discrimination. Teacher, Christian leader, and African patriot, he led the African National Congress (ANC) from 1952 until its proscription by the South African government in 1960.

Albert John Mvumbi (Zulu: "continuous rain") Lutuli was born in 1898 in Rhodesia, where his father, John Bunyan Lutuli, a missionary interpreter, had gone from Zululand. After his father's death, the ten-year-old Albert returned to South Africa and learned Zulu traditions and duties in the household of his uncle, the chief of Groutville, a community associated with an American Congregational mission in Natal's sugar lands. Educated through his mother's earnings as a washerwoman and by a scholarship, he graduated from the American Board Mission's teacher training college at Adams, near Durban, and be-

Lutuli, 1961.
PHOTOWORLD—FPG

came one of its first three African instructors. In 1927 Lutuli married Nokukhanya Bhengu, a teacher and granddaughter of a clan chief.

In 1936 Lutuli left teaching to become the elected chief of the community of 5,000 at Groutville. Though confronted by land hunger, poverty, and political voicelessness, he did not yet recognize the need for political action. In those early years he was, variously, secretary of the Natal African Teachers' Association and of the South African Football Association, founder of the Zulu Language and Cultural Society, and member of the Christian Council Executive, of the Joint Council of Europeans and Africans, and of the Institute of Race Relations in Durban.

Membership in African National Congress

Lutuli's first political step in joining the African National Congress in 1945 was motivated by friendship with its Natal leader; far more significant was his election to the Natives Representative Council (an advisory body of chiefs and intellectuals set up by government), at the very time in 1946 when troops and police were crushing a strike of African miners at the cost of eight lives and nearly a thousand injured. Lutuli immediately joined his people's protest against the council's futility. When he toured America in 1948 as a guest of the Congregational Board of Missions, he warned that Christianity faced its severest test in Africa because of racial discrimination. On return home he found that the Afrikaner Nationalists had newly come to power with their policy of apartheid.

At this crucial time, Lutuli was elected president of the Natal African National Congress. Since its founding in 1912, the ANC's efforts to achieve human rights by deputation, petition, or mass protests had met with increasing repression. In 1952, stimulated by young black intellectuals, the ANC joined the South African Indian Congress in a countrywide campaign to defy what were deemed unjust laws; 8,500 men and women went voluntarily to prison. As a result of Lutuli's leadership in Natal, the government demanded that he resign from the ANC or from chieftainship. He refused to do either, stating, "The road to freedom is via the cross." The government deposed him. Not only did he continue to be affectionately regarded as "chief," but his reputation spread. In that same year, 1952, the ANC elected him president general. Henceforth, between repeated bans (under the Suppression of Communism Act), he attended gatherings, visited towns, and toured the country to address mass meetings (despite a serious illness in 1954).

Trial for treason

In December 1956 he and 155 others were dramatically rounded up and charged with high treason. His long trial failed to prove treason, a Communist conspiracy, or vio-

lence; and in 1957 he was released. During this time Lutuli's quiet authority and his inspiration to others profoundly impressed distinguished foreign observers, leading to his nomination for the Nobel Prize. Nonwhite people responded in large numbers to his call for a stay-at-home strike in 1957; later whites also began attending his mass meetings. In 1959 the government confined him to his rural neighbourhood and banned him from gatherings—this time for five years—for "promoting feelings of hostility" between the races.

In 1960, when police shot down Africans demonstrating against the pass laws at Sharpeville, Lutuli called for national mourning, and he himself burned his pass. (Too ill to serve the resulting prison sentence, he paid a fine.) The government outlawed the ANC and its rival offshoot, the Pan-Africanist Congress.

In December 1961 Lutuli was allowed to leave Groutville briefly when, with his wife, he flew to Oslo to receive the Nobel Prize. His acceptance address paid tribute to his people's nonviolence and rejection of racialism despite adverse treatment, and he noted how far from freedom they remained despite their long struggle. A week later, throughout South Africa, a sabotage group called the Spear of the Nation attacked installations; the policy of nonviolence had at last been abandoned, and Lutuli, back in enforced isolation, was an honoured elder statesman, dictating his autobiography and receiving only those visitors permitted by the police.

On July 21, 1967, in Stanger, South Africa, as he made a habitual crossing of a railway bridge near his small farm, Chief Lutuli was struck by a train and died.

BIBLIOGRAPHY. ALBERT LUTULI, *Let My People Go* (1962), a comprehensive autobiography; MARY BENSON, *Chief Albert Lutuli of South Africa* (1963), a short biography, and *South Africa: Struggle for a Birthright*, rev. ed. (1969), Lutuli's life in the history of the African National Congress; COLIN and MARGARET LEGUM, *The Bitter Choice: Eight South Africans' Resistance to Tyranny* (1968), contains an essay on Lutuli.

(D.M.B.)

Luxembourg

The Grand Duchy of Luxembourg is a tiny sovereign state of only 998 square miles (2,586 square kilometres) surrounded by Belgium, France, and Germany. A natural and historical meeting point of, and crossroads for, these countries, Luxembourg has come under the control of many states and ruling houses in its long history, but it has been a separate, if not always autonomous, political unit since the 10th century. The ancient Saxon name of its capital city, Lucilinburhuc ("little fortress"), symbolized its strategic and long impregnable position as "the Gibraltar of the north," astride a major military route linking Germanic and Frankish territories.

Strategic location

The heterogeneous peoples of Luxembourg and their language, economic pursuits, and ways of life reflect the grand duchy's multiplicity of common interests with its neighbours as well as the close historical relations. The farming villages and agricultural landscapes that abound across the broad and high northern tableland and the lower plateaus of the south delight the tourists, but in the few urban centres the smokestacks of industry signal an economic diversity. Luxembourg was an original member of the Benelux customs union, established in 1944, that linked its economic life with that of The Netherlands and of Belgium (the acronym is derived from the initial letters of each nation) and that formed the core of the European Economic Community, a broader union created in 1958 that comprised France, Italy, and West Germany as well.

The land. The northern third of Luxembourg, known as the Oesling, comprises a corner of the Ardennes Mountains, which lie mainly in southern Belgium. A very level plateau 1,300 to 1,600 feet in altitude, it is a region of broad vistas and few forests. Its rocky valleys support the ruins of numerous castles, a major attraction for its tourists. The relatively thin mountain soil of the Oesling was much improved by the introduction in the 1890s of a basic slag fertilizer that is a by-product of the

Main regions

grand duchy's steel industry. The iron mines are located in the south near the French border.

In contrast, the heavily wooded south, known as the Gutland or Bon Pays (German and French: "good land"), has more fertile soil and rich pasturelands, and along the Moselle and lower Sûre valleys wine vineyards producing a good white wine. At an average altitude of 900 feet, the Gutland contains the capital, the city of Luxembourg, founded in 963, as well as Eschur-Alzette and other major industrial centres. In the east central section, near the German border, lies a great beech forest, the Muellertal (Müllerthal). Nearby is the small town of Echternach, to which a traditional dancing procession, with roots deep into the past, attracts many visitors.

From both the Oesling and the Gutland, the rivers flow into the Moselle, a tributary of the Rhine. Most farming is mixed, including both gardening and animal raising. The mean temperatures in Luxembourg City range from 37° F (3° C) in January to 67° F (19° C) in July, but in the Oesling both extremes are slightly lower. The Oesling generally has more precipitation than the Gutland, but the greatest amount, about 40 inches, and the least, about 27 inches, fall in the southwest and southeast, respectively.

Luxembourg, Area and Population				
	area		population	
	sq mi	sq km	1966 census	1970 census
Districts				
Diekirch				
Cantons				
Clervaux	116.73	302.34	10,000	10,000
Diekirch	92.42	239.37	19,000	20,000
Redange	103.28	267.49	11,000	10,000
Vianden	20.88	54.08	3,000	3,000
Wiltz	113.50	293.96	10,000	10,000
Grevenmacher				
Cantons				
Echternach	71.64	185.54	10,000	10,000
Grevenmacher	81.61	211.37	15,000	15,000
Remich	49.37	127.87	10,000	11,000
Luxembourg				
Cantons				
Capellen	76.91	199.21	20,000	21,000
Esch	93.73	242.77	115,000	115,000
Luxembourg-Campagne	72.20	187.00	22,000	25,000
Luxembourg-Ville	19.87	51.46	77,000	76,000
Mersch	86.45	223.90	13,000	14,000
Total Luxembourg	998.59	2,586.36	335,000	340,000

Source: Official government figures.

Ethnologists have identified an interesting array of types in human dwelling and in the physical organization of villages throughout Luxembourg. Many date from ancient Celtic and Roman times to the circular villages of the Germanic and Frankish settlements after about AD 400. In addition, many castle villages continue to thrive, centuries after the castles themselves fell to ruin.

The people. Luxembourg has been one of the historic crossroads of Europe, and myriad peoples have left their bloodlines as well as their cultural imprints on the grand duchy. The Celts, the Ligurians and Romans from Italy, the Belgic peoples known as the Treveri, and especially the Franks were most influential. The dialect spoken by all of Luxembourg's 340,000 inhabitants is Letzeburgesch, a member of the Germanic language group. Most Luxembourgers speak French and German as well, and all three are designated as official national languages. There is a strong sense of national identity among Luxembourgers despite the prevalence of these foreign influences, which can be seen in their country's past as well as present.

Luxembourg's people are over 94 percent Roman Catholic, with a small number of Protestants, mainly Lutherans, and Jews. The nearly 60,000 foreigners in the country include many workers in the mining and steel industries or in foreign firms and international organizations located in the capital. Over 67,000 persons are engaged in industry, nearly 16,000 in agriculture, and some 61,000 in various service occupations. There has been a continued trend away from the countryside to urban areas. This has led the government to locate some industries in rural areas, which in turn has altered somewhat the character of rural life, most noticeably in housing and modern amenities of living.

In 1970 births and deaths numbered 4,411 and 4,154, respectively, with marriages and divorces at 2,156 and 217.

The national economy. *Business and industry.* During the 1960s the economy of Luxembourg altered its directions somewhat. Although the steel and iron-producing industries continued to account for nearly a quarter of the national output, there was a definite trend toward the production of finished goods. U.S. companies pro-

National languages

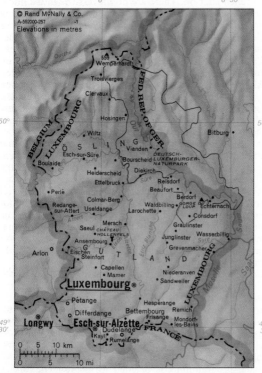

LUXEMBOURG

ducing tires, plastics, and synthetic fibres were among the industries that found the economic climate to be advantageous. There are also large food-processing and chemical plants, and tourism played an increasing role in the economic picture.

In 1929 the government began a policy of encouraging the formation in Luxembourg of holding companies, large corporations that each control a number of subsidiary companies but are heavily taxed in many areas of the world. The liberal tax climate produced by this policy led many financial corporations as well to maintain offices, often as the European headquarters, in Luxembourg City. The main offices of the European Investment Bank are there, as are the representatives of many banking institutions from around the world who keep in contact with the European Economic Community, or Common Market.

Agriculture. In the late 1960s, about three-quarters of the 55,000 acres under cultivation in Luxembourg were in farms of under 50 acres. Grains, root vegetables, and animal fodders are produced in about equal quantities. Mechanization had replaced animal and human labour in most areas, but the farmer still looked for further help from Common Market agreements. Cattle raising remained important, sheep raising less so than in former years.

Power and transportation. Luxembourg is without indigenous coal deposits, but much of the nation's electricity is supplied by the steel mills. In addition, three hydroelectric plants have been built, one of them in conjunction with the reservoir supplying water to most of the country.

Internal road systems are not extensive, but they are well maintained. More extensive highways linking Luxembourg with its neighbours are among the objectives of the European economic planners. During the 1960s the opening of a new harbour on the Moselle and of a canal connecting it with the system of Rhine waterways opened a new avenue for the international movement of goods.

The state has operated the railroads since World War II. They are electrified, mostly double decked, and modern. Most international transportation to and from Luxembourg is by train, and the country is connected with its neighbours by a large number of lines. Findel Airport outside Luxembourg has become a major European air terminal served by the lines of many countries. A national company, Luxair, is in the process of growth in the early 1970s.

Administration and social conditions. The grand duchy is a constitutional monarchy with hereditary succession. The constitution, which vests sovereign power in the people and provides guarantees of numerous liberties and freedoms, was revised in 1956 to anticipate the possible transfer of certain sovereign powers to future supranational organs linking several European nations.

Government. Executive power lies with the grand duke and is executed through a ministerial council, or cabinet. It is responsible to the Chamber of Deputies, comprising 56 members popularly elected. Voting by all adult citizens, begun in 1919, is compulsory. In addition, a 21-member council of state named by the grand duke functions essentially as a second legislative chamber. It is consulted on all draft legislation and can postpone the enactment of bills. Six official groups, representing agriculture, handicrafts, commerce, civil servants, private employees, and labour, are consulted before the passage of legislation affecting their particular segment of the national working force. Justice is in the hands of magistrates appointed by the grand duke, the final appeal lying with the Superior Court of Justice. In the criminal court of assizes, six magistrates sit as jury as well as judge. The army, under command of the grand duke, is voluntary. Its main functions are to recruit municipal and state police.

Public works, health, and education are among the responsibilities of the 126 communes throughout Luxembourg, which are governed by an elected council. The mayor and aldermen are appointed by the grand duke. These bodies also maintain liaison with the central government and act as its local agents.

Division of government responsibilities

Social conditions and services. After World War I, a broad system of social security and health services was introduced. Sickness benefits, in which patients pay only a small part of medical costs, as well as birth, family, and unemployment payments, are included in the plans. Existing facilities that require further development include nursing homes for the aged and mental institutions. Housing standards are generally above the European average. There has been some difficulty, however, in assimilating the many thousands of foreign workers and their families.

Education. Education is compulsory from ages 6 to 15. Primary and secondary education are run by state and local governments and by religious institutions. Great stress is laid on language studies. Instruction is generally given in German in the early years, with an increasing use of French later on. There are no universities in the grand duchy, leading many young Luxembourgers to study abroad, but the International University of Comparative Sciences in Luxembourg City offers, among other courses, postgraduate work in law and economics.

Cultural life and the future. The major cultural institution of Luxembourg is the Institut Grand-Ducal, which has sections devoted to history; natural sciences; medical sciences; languages, folklore, and toponymy, the study of place names; arts and letters; and moral and political sciences. It functions as an active promoter of the arts, humanities, and culture in general rather than as a conservator. The Museum for History and Fine Arts has a special section devoted to education in the fine arts. There is considerable public use of the National Library, the Public Archives, and the Conservatory of Music. Luxembourg maintains cultural agreements with several European and other nations that provide the grand duchy with the finest in the musical and theatrical arts. The orchestra of Radio Luxembourg is considered outstanding. There is an extensive market for works of painting and sculpture, both traditional and modern.

Communications. A small publishing industry exists, printing literary works in French, German, and Letzeburgesch. The grand duchy's seven newspapers express diverse political points of view—conservative, liberal, socialist, and communist. The government operates all postal and telegraph services and has some control in the private corporation running Radio Luxembourg, which is heard throughout Europe. Some of its multilingual programming is beamed to the resident foreign workers.

Prospects. Luxembourg is very much a pan-European country, as by accident of geography and history it has always been. Among its most famous sons was Robert Schuman, founder of the European Coal and Steel Community, a European federation that anticipated the growing European economic unity of the 1970s. Many of its hopes for the future are directed toward a realization of a broader European union, both economically and politically. "Rather friends than enemies" is the rule of conduct for its rising generations. Its supranational outlook is underscored by the number of foreign and international companies and bodies within its borders and the great increase during the late 1960s in the number of its students scattered abroad and studying the languages of the world. It is a small country looking hopefully beyond its borders for more understandings with the larger members of the community of nations.

BIBLIOGRAPHY

History and politics: ARTHUR HERCHEN, *Manuel d'histoire nationale*, 5th ed. enl. (1947; Eng. trans. by A.H. COOPER-PRICHARD, *History of the Grand Duchy of Luxemburg*, 1950), provides a wide-ranging account. JOSEPH PETIT, *Luxembourg, Yesterday and To-day*, 6th ed. (1966); AUGUSTE COLLART, *Am Wege zur Unabhängigkeit Luxemburgs* (1938); and ALBERT CALMES, *Au Fil de l'histoire*, 2nd ed. (1968), are also useful. PAUL MARGUE, *A Short History of Luxembourg* (Eng. trans. 1970), is a briefer account; CHRISTIAN CALMES, *1867. L'Affaire du Luxembourg* (1967), covers an important moment in Luxembourg's history. PIERRE MAJERUS, *L'État luxembourgeois*, 3rd ed. (1970; Eng. trans., *The Institutions of the Grand Duchy of Luxembourg*, 1970), explains the constitution.

Other writings include G.L. WEIL, *The Benelux Nations: The Politics of Small-Country Democracies* (1970); K.C. EDWARDS, *Luxembourg: The Survival of a Small Nation* (1967); and W.J. TAYLOR-WHITEHEAD, *Luxembourg: Land of Legends* (1951), interesting on national lore.

Topography: TUDOR EDWARDS, *Belgium and Luxemburg* (1966), has a useful section on the country, while BERYL MILES, *Attic in Luxembourg* (1956); and ROGER PILKINGTON, *Small Boat to Luxembourg* (1967), are personal accounts. JEAN ROUBIER and JOSEPH DELMELLE, *Benelux: Holland, Belgium, Luxembourg* (1958), is a picture book.

Economics: The ORGANIZATION FOR ECONOMIC CO-OPERATION AND DEVELOPMENT, *Belgium-Luxembourg Economic Union* (annual), provides a general guide to the economy, supplemented by J.R. YONGE and G. FRANKIS, *Transport in the Grand Duchy of Luxembourg* (1966).

(V.Bi./J.P.E.)

Luxemburg, Rosa

Polish-German revolutionary theoretician and agitator, Rosa Luxemburg was one of the recognized leaders of the radical left wing of the German Social Democratic Party. She played a key role in the founding of the Polish Social Democratic and German Communist parties and developed a humanitarian theory of Marxism that was at once internationalist, anti-revisionist, and dynamic, stressing democracy and revolutionary mass action to achieve Socialism.

Interfoto—Friedrich Rauch, Munich

Rosa Luxemburg.

Rosa Luxemburg was born on March 5, 1871, in Zamość, Russian Poland (now Poland), the youngest of five children of a lower middle class Jewish family. She became involved in underground activities while still in high school. Like many of her radical contemporaries from the Russian empire who were faced with prison, she emigrated to Zürich, Switzerland (1889), where she studied law and political economy, receiving a doctorate in 1898. In Zürich she became involved in the international Socialist movement and met Georgy Valentinovich Plekhanov, Pavel Axelrod, and other leading representatives of Russian Social Democracy with whom, however, she soon began to disagree. Together with a fellow student, Leo Jogiches, who was to become a lifelong friend and sometime lover, she challenged both the Russians and the established Polish Socialist Party because of their support of Polish independence. Consequently, she and her colleagues founded the rival Polish Social Democratic Party, which was to become the nucleus of the future Polish Communist Party. The national issue became one of Luxemburg's main themes. To her, nationalism and national independence were regressive concessions to the class enemy, the bourgeoisie. She consistently underrated nationalist aspirations and stressed Socialist internationalism. This became one of her major points of disagreement with Lenin and his theory of national self-determination.

In 1898, after marrying Gustav Lübeck to obtain German citizenship, she settled in Berlin to work with the largest and most powerful constituent party of the Second International, German Social Democracy. Almost at once, she jumped into the revisionist controversy that divided the party. In 1898 the German revisionist Eduard Bernstein had argued that Marx was essentially outdated and that Socialism in highly industrialized nations could best be achieved through a gradualist approach, with parliamentary and trade-union pressure on the establishment. This, Luxemburg denied categorically in *Sozialreform oder Revolution?* (1889, Eng. trans., *Reform or Revolution*, 1937), in which she defended orthodoxy and the necessity of revolution, arguing that parliament was nothing more than a bourgeois sham. Karl Kautsky, the leading theoretician of the Second International, agreed with her, and revisionism consequently became a Socialist heresy both in Germany and abroad, though it continued to make headway, especially in the labour movement.

The Russian Revolution of 1905 proved to be the central experience in Rosa Luxemburg's life. Until then, she had believed that Germany was the country in which world revolution was most likely to originate. She now believed it would catch fire in Russia. She went to Warsaw, participated in the struggle, and was imprisoned. From these experiences emerged her theory of revolutionary mass action, which she propounded in *Massenstreik, Partei und Gewerkschaften* (1906; Eng. trans., *The Mass Strike, the Political Party, and the Trade Unions*, 1925). Luxemburg represented the mass strike as the single most important tool of the proletariat, Western as well as Russian, in attaining a Socialist victory. The mass strike, the spontaneous result of "objective conditions," would radicalize the workers and drive the revolution forward. In contrast to Lenin, she deemphasized the need for a tight party structure, believing that organization would emerge naturally from the struggle. For this, she has been repeatedly chastized by orthodox Communist parties.

Released from her Warsaw prison, she taught at the Social Democratic Party school in Berlin (1907–14), where she wrote *Die Akkumulation des Kapitals* (1913; Eng. trans., *The Accumulation of Capital*, 1951). In this analysis, she described imperialism as the result of a dynamic capitalism's expansion into underdeveloped areas of the world. It was during this time also that she began to agitate for mass actions and broke completely with the established party leadership of August Bebel and Karl Kautsky, who disagreed with her incessant drive toward proletarian radicalization.

The Social Democratic Party backed the German government at the outbreak of World War I, but Rosa Luxemburg immediately went into opposition. In an alliance with Karl Liebknecht and other like-minded radicals, she formed the Spartakusbund, or Spartacus League, which was dedicated to end the war through revolution and the establishment of a proletarian government. The organization's theoretical basis was Luxemburg's pamphlet *Die Krise der Sozialdemokratie* (1916; Eng. trans., *The Crisis in the German Social Democracy*, 1919), written in prison under the pseudonym Junius. In this work she agreed with Lenin in advocating the overthrow of the existing regime and the formation of a new International strong enough to prevent a renewed outbreak of mass slaughter. The actual influence of the Spartacus group during the war, however, remained small.

Released from prison by the German revolution (November 1918), Luxemburg and Liebknecht immediately began agitation to force the new order to the left. They exercised considerable influence on the public and were a contributing factor in a number of armed clashes in Berlin. Like the Bolsheviks, Luxemburg and Liebknecht demanded political power for the workers' and soldiers' soviets but were frustrated by the conservative socialist establishment and the army. In late December 1918, they became founders of the German Communist Party, but Luxemburg attempted to limit Bolshevik influence in this new organization. In fact, her *Die russische Revolution* (1922; Eng. trans., *The Russian Revolution*, 1940) chastized Lenin's party on its agrarian and national self-determination stands and its dictatorial and terrorist methods.

Marginal notes:

Opposition to nationalism

Theory of the mass strike

Formation of the Spartacus League

Assassination

Luxemburg always remained a believer in democracy as opposed to Lenin's democratic centralism. She was never able, however, to exercise a decisive influence on the new party, for she and Liebknecht were assassinated in Berlin, on January 15, 1919, by reactionary troops.

Rosa Luxemburg's writings inspired a generation of radicals and challenged the whole of the international Social Democratic establishment for two decades. That she was unable to put her theories into practice was the result of that Socialist establishment's rejection of her theories, the conservatism of German society, and the Communist parties' process of Stalinization that took place after Lenin's death (1924). Rosa Luxemburg is still revered by Marxists, however, despite her unorthodox views, and interest in her has revived recently with the liberalization of the post-Stalin period.

BIBLIOGRAPHY. There is as yet no complete edition of Rosa Luxemburg's works; the most comprehensive survey of her writings, however, is OSSIP K. FLECHTHEIM (ed.), *Rosa Luxemburg. Politische Schriften*, 3 vol. (1966–68). In English, the most useful edition of her works is DICK HOWARD (ed.), *Selected Political Writings of Rosa Luxemburg* (1971). ROSA LUXEMBURG, *Die Akkumulation des Kapitals* (1921; Eng. trans., *The Accumulation of Capital*, 1951), is one of her most important theoretical pieces giving her views on imperialism. The best biography by far is PETER NETTL, *Rosa Luxemburg*, 2 vol. (1966; abridged one-volume paperback, 1969), the most objective and comprehensive study based on a wealth of primary sources, placing its subject in a historical perspective. PAUL FRÖLICH, *Rosa Luxemburg: Her Life and Work* (1940, reprinted 1969), is another good biography written by one of Luxemburg's contemporaries—Frölich is a Marxist, which is reflected in his writings, but with a strong anti-Stalinist bias. For the orthodox Stalinist view, FRED OELSSNER, *Rosa Luxemburg: Eine kritische biographische Skizze* (1951), is the standard work. For an excellent in-depth analysis of the struggle between the Social Democratic left and right wings during most of Rosa Luxemburg's active political life, CARL E. SCHORSKE, *German Social Democracy, 1905–1917* (1955), is invaluable.

(H.D.S.)

Lycopsida

The Lycopsida are generally considered to constitute a class of spore-bearing vascular plants comprising the club mosses and their allies, living and fossil. Present-day lycopsids are grouped into four genera and between 900 to 1,000 species of wide distribution, but especially numerous in the tropics: *Lycopodium*, the club mosses or "ground pines"; *Selaginella*, little club mosses or spike mosses; the unique tuberous plant *Phylloglossum*; and *Isoetes*, the quillworts. Representative extinct genera are *Lepidodendron* and *Sigillaria*, which are the tree lycopods, and *Protolepidodendron*, a herbaceous *Lycopodium*-like plant. Lycopsids are known from rocks of the Devonian Period (about 395,000,000 years ago) of the Paleozoic Era. The remains of *Lepidodendron* and other extinct lycopods form most of the great coal beds of the world.

General features. Many of the ancient lycopsids, such as *Lepidodendron*, were trees that often exceeded 30 metres (100 feet) in height. The living genera are all small plants, some erect and others low creepers. Regardless of their size or geological age, all share certain group features. Branching is fundamentally dichotomous; that is, the shoot tip forks repeatedly. The two branches that result may become either equal in length or of different lengths. The leaves (or sporophylls) are generally small, although they sometimes achieved a length of one metre (three feet) in the giant lycopod *Lepidodendron*. Generally each leaf (microphyll) is narrow and has an unbranched midvein in contrast to the megaphyll of the ferns and seed plants (Pteropsida), which generally has branched venation. The sporangia (spore cases) occur singly on the upper side facing the stem (adaxial side) of the leaf.

The lycopsids in general have conelike structures called strobili, which are aggregations of sporophylls telescoped down.

Life cycle. As with other vascular plants there is an alternation of generations between a small sex-cell producing phase (gametophyte) and the conspicuous spore-

producing phase (sporophyte). The lycopsids represented by the order Lycopodiales commonly have terrestrial or subterranean gametophytes that vary in size and shape depending on the species.

Although gametophytes are rarely found in nature, enough is known about them to recognize two types, based principally upon the mode of growth and nutrition. In some species, the gametophyte, which develops from a spore, becomes a small, green plant growing on the surface of the soil; the time interval between spore germination and sexual maturity of the gametophyte may be eight months to one year. In other species, including nearly all those of the north Temperate Zone, the gametophyte is subterranean, slower growing, and dependent upon an associated fungus for continued growth. The underground plant may become carrot-shaped or disk-shaped and one to two centimetres (less than an inch) in length or width. It is yellow to brown but, apparently, can develop chlorophyll and thus turn green if the plant is growing near the soil surface where light can reach it. Generally, a gametophyte of this type remains subterranean, and five or more years are required before it becomes sexually mature. Gametophytes are monoecious (bisexual)—*i.e.*, the sperm-producing antheridia and the egg-producing archegonia occur on the same plant. Fertilization occurs after a flagellated sperm swims to the archegonium. The embryo, or young sporophyte, consists of a shoot, root, and a food-absorbing outgrowth called a haustorial "foot." One gametophyte may support more than one sporophyte for a period of time, but ultimately the sporophyte becomes physiologically independent of the gametophyte, and the latter dies.

In the other two extant orders—Selaginellales and Isoetales—the gametophytes are microscopic and undergo most of their development while still within the spore wall (endosporic development).

Definite strobili are formed in *Selaginella*, and the sporophylls generally differ from the vegetative leaves, but not as much as in the species of *Lycopodium* that form definite strobili. There are two types of sporangia in *Selaginella*, called microsporangia and megasporangia, and the sporophylls associated with them are termed microsporophylls and megasporophylls. A mature microsporangium may be red, yellow, or brown, from the colour of the microspores within the sporangium. Megasporangia are usually a pale green or whitish. Numerous microspores are produced, and cell division within the microspore wall initiates male gametophyte development. These divisions may occur before the spores are shed from the microsporangium. Final development of the "male" gametophyte, or microgametophyte, usually occurs on the soil prior to the release of sperm. Usually only four large megaspores are produced in a megasporangium. Development of the "female" gametophyte, or megagametophyte, may also begin while the megaspore is still within the megasporangium: free nuclear divisions (without wall formation) occur for a time, but ultimately walls appear, and the megagametophyte ruptures the megaspore wall. These final stages in development usually occur on the soil after the megaspore with the enclosed female gametophyte is shed from the megasporangium. Fertilization occurs when a sperm swims to an archegonium. The young sporophyte remains in physical contact with the megaspore and the enclosed female gametophyte tissue for some time.

Selaginella is said to be heterosporous because it produces two types of spores that give rise to two different types of sexual gametophytes.

The general processes of sexual reproduction of *Isoetes*, or quillworts, are very similar to those in *Selaginella*, except that many more spores are formed per sporangium. In fact, the microsporangia of some species are the largest in vascular plants and produce immense numbers of spores.

Form and function. In growth habit the sporophytes of *Lycopodium* species may arise erect from a system of rhizomes (underground stems), or they may creep. Many are epiphytes; *i.e.*, they grow attached to tree branches or other supports. Branching is fundamentally dichotomous,

The underground plant

Contributors to the coal beds

Growth habit

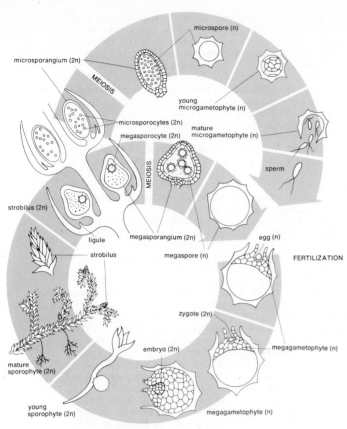

Life cycle of *Selaginella*.

but, in species with well-developed rhizomes, one branch of a dichotomy usually becomes much longer and larger than the other one and remains close to the surface. The shorter one may undergo several limited dichotomies, the ultimate upright branches terminating in strobili. The leaves may be spirally arranged or grouped in four vertical rows along the shoot. Each leaf has one unbranched midvein. Adventitious roots, initiated near the shoot tip, may grow within the stem cortex for some distance before emerging. The roots branch dichotomously, but no extensive root system is formed. In terrestrial species, the roots have root hairs that function for a long time.

The stem is protostelic (without a central pith), but there is great variety in the disposition of xylem and phloem in the central vascular cylinder. Either sporophylls may be aggregated into definite strobili, or there may be simply fertile and sterile regions along a stem, the sporophylls resembling vegetative leaves. Often the sporophylls of compact strobili differ from the vegetative leaves of the same plant. The kidney-shaped sporangia are yellow or orange and have short stalks.

The foliage leaves of *Selaginella*, only a few millimetres long, may be dark green or bluish and in some species are iridescent. As in *Lycopodium*, branching is fundamentally dichotomous. The sporophyte may consist of several upright branches from a rhizome; prostrate branches creeping along the surface of the soil; or large, flat, erect frondlike side branches from strong rhizome systems. The entire branch system is often considered to be just a leaf by the untrained observer. One distinctive feature of *Selaginella* is the rhizophore, a proplike structure that originates at points of branching and that forms roots after making contact with the soil or a hard surface. Rhizophores are most readily seen in clambering species. Morphologically the rhizophore is considered by some botanists to be a leafless stem that can give rise to leafy branches if the normally leafy branches of a dichotomy are cut off. The leaves are arranged as in *Lycopodium*, the occurrence of four vertical rows being common. Anisophylly (the occurrence of two sizes of leaves) is common in creeping and strongly rhizomatous species. As the rhizophore is a distinctive feature for *Selaginella*, so is the

presence of an unusual structure on the adaxial side (upper side facing the stem) of a leaf. This is the ligule, a peculiar tonguelike outgrowth from the leaf surface near the leaf base. Leaves of *Lycopodium* and *Selaginella* can be distinguished on this basis. The ligule, which appears very early in the development of a leaf, is a surprisingly complex structure at maturity. Its evolutionary origin is obscure. Functionally, the ligules are believed to be secretory organs that, by exuding water and possibly mucilage, serve to keep young leaves and sporangia moist. Short-lived structures, they become shrunken and inconspicuous in older leaves. The ligule was a characteristic feature of the extinct giant lycopods (*e.g.*, *Lepidodendron*).

The species of *Isoetes*, or quillworts, have a plant body that is relatively small, consisting of a short axis and tufts of leaves and roots. Many species are similar in appearance to certain aquatic grasses, which are seed plants. The majority of species occur in the cooler climates of the world and are often immersed continuously in water. Each leaf is actually a sporophyll, bearing either a microsporangium or a megasporangium at its base on the adaxial side. Each leaf also has a ligule, a morphological feature similar to *Selaginella*. *Isoetes* differs from both *Selaginella* and *Lycopodium* in the occurrence of secondary growth in the stem and the possession of a definite root-producing meristem that gives rise to sets of roots in a definite sequence. Annual top growth rises from a cormlike base that persists from one growing season to the next.

Evolution and classification. The lycopsids represent a wide range of extinct and living plants that have contributed important data on evolutionary trends in primitive vascular plants. The earliest lycopsids included *Baragwanathia* and *Protolepidodendron*, dating from the Devonian Period (beginning 395,000,000 years ago). Both were small herbaceous plants. During the Carboniferous Period (beginning 345,000,000 years ago), the treelike forms of the Lepidodendrales appeared.

Over the years, fossil parts of lepidodendronic plants have been discovered and assigned to so-called form genera, or organ genera: *Lepidophylloides*, for detached leaf fossils; *Lepidostrobus*, for fossil strobili. These form genera are now recognized as portions of one main fossil genus designated *Lepidodendron*. Other lycopsids coexisting with the tree lycopsids were small herbaceous plants that resemble the modern *Lycopodium* and *Selaginella* species.

Annotated classification. The class Lycopsida is often divided into five orders, as listed below. Some authorities recognize six orders. Groups with a dagger (†) are extinct and known only from fossils.

CLASS LYCOPSIDA
Primitive seedless vascular plants with true roots, stems, and leaves. Four extant genera, with 900 to 1,000 species, worldwide but concentrated in the tropics.

Order Lycopodiales
Living and extinct plants with primary growth only. Homosporous (producing spore of 1 type). Two living genera, *Lycopodium*, with 200 species, mostly tropical; *Phylloglossum*, with 1 species, restricted to Australia. Among the extinct members were *Lycopodites*, *Protolepidodendron*, and *Baragwanathia*.

Order Selaginellales
Living and extinct plants with primary growth only. Heterosporous (producing 2 types of spores). The sole living genus is *Selaginella*, with more than 700 species, widely distributed round the world. *Selaginelites* is an extinct genus.

† Order Lepidodendrales
Extinct tree lycopsids, and, therefore, capable of secondary growth. Heterosporous, with some strobili (cones) forming seedlike structures. Included are *Lepidodendron* and *Sigillaria* (and their form genera).

Order Isoetales
Living and extinct plants with secondary growth. Heterosporous, with endosporic gametophytes (*i.e.*, gametophytes that begin development within the spore wall). *Isoetes* includes more than 60 species in swampy, cooler parts of the world. *Isoetites* is an extinct genus.

† Pleuromeiales
Extinct unbranched plants, with subterranean rootlike rhizophores. Heterosporous. A single fossil genus, *Pleuromeia*.

The form genera

Critical appraisal. Paleobotanical consensus favours the recognition of this group as a class; however, some authorities would raise it to a subdivision or even to a higher category, a division, Lycophyta.

The five orders given above are occasionally expanded to six by separation of *Protolepidodendron* from the Lycopodiales as a separate order, the Protolepidodendrales.

Certain species of *Isoetes*-like plants are sometimes split off to form an additional genus, *Stylites.*

BIBLIOGRAPHY. F.O. BOWER, *Primitive Land Plants* (1935), dated but still useful; H.N. ANDREWS, *Studies in Paleobotany* (1961); and THEODORE DELEVORYAS, *Morphology and Evolution of Fossil Plants* (1962), textbooks of college-level difficulty on paleobotany with extensive bibliographies to specific works; H.P. BANKS, *Evolution and Plants of the Past* (1970), a short introduction to newer concepts of plant evolution as revealed by extinct (fossil) plants; A.S. FOSTER and E.M. GIFFORD, JR., *Comparative Morphology of Vascular Plants* (1959); and D.W. BIERHORST, *Morphology of Vascular Plants* (1971), both general textbooks of college level on vascular plant morphology to include living and extinct plants. Selected list of journals that publish articles on vascular plant morphology: *American Journal of Botany* (10/year), *Botanical Gazette* (quarterly), *Phytomorphology* (quarterly), *Annals of Botany* (5/year), *Paleontographica* (1–3 vol./year).

(E.M.G.)

Lyell, Sir Charles

Charles Lyell was a leading geologist of early- to mid-Victorian Britain whose great contribution was to insist upon and prove that all features of the Earth's surface, including even its mountains, are produced by natural processes operating, often imperceptibly, over very long periods of time. In doing this, he also proved that the rocks of the Earth's crust record a history of thousands of millions of years that could be interpreted objectively, without recourse to the biblical explanations or catastrophes customarily invoked in his century. These achievements laid the foundations for evolutionary biology as well as for an understanding of the Earth. Lyell's predecessor, James Hutton, who died the year of Lyell's birth, had clearly seen that the Earth was molded by agents still at work, such as rivers, ice, and volcanism, but his work had received little appreciation. Lyell raised Hutton's findings from obscurity, adding much that was new concerning the most recent rocks, faunas, floras, and movements of the Earth's crust.

Early life. Lyell was born November 14, 1797, at Kinnordy, the stately family home at the foot of the Grampian Mountains in eastern Scotland. His princi-

By courtesy of the National Portrait Gallery, London

Lyell, replica in oil by L. Dickinson, 1883. In the
National Portrait Gallery, London.

pal childhood associations, however, were with the New Forest near Southampton, England, where his parents moved before he was two years old. His father, a talented naturalist who later turned to more literary pursuits, kept the study well-stocked with books on every subject, including geology. The eldest of ten children, Charles attended a series of private schools, where he was not a particularly diligent student; he much preferred rambles in the New Forest and his father's instruction at home to those places, with their schoolboy pranks and pecking orders whose spirit he never really shared. His first scientific hobby was collecting butterflies and aquatic insects, an activity pursued intensively for some years, even though labelled unmanly by local residents. His observations went far beyond those of any ordinary boy, and later this instinct for collecting and comparing led to important discoveries.

At 19 Lyell entered Oxford University, where his interest in classics, mathematics, and geology was stimulated, the latter by the enthusiastic lectures of William Buckland, later famous for his attempt to prove Noah's Flood by studies of fossils from cave deposits. Lyell spent the long vacations between terms travelling and geologizing. Notes made in 1817 on the origin of the Yarmouth lowlands clearly foreshadow his later work. The penetrating geological and cultural observations Lyell made while on a continental tour with his family in 1818 were as remarkable as the number of miles he walked in a day. In December 1819 he earned a B.A. with honours and moved to London to study law.

Career. Lyell's eyes were weak and were so hurt by hard law study that he sought and found relief by spending much time on geological work outdoors. Among these holidays was an 1822 visit to see evidence of vertical movements of the Earth's crust in Sussex. In 1823, on a visit to Paris, he met the famous naturalists Alexander von Humboldt and Georges Cuvier and examined the Paris Basin with the French geologist Louis-Constant Prévost. In 1824 Lyell studied sediments forming in freshwater lakes near Kinnordy. When in London, Lyell participated in its vigorous intellectual life, meeting such literati as Sir Walter Scott and taking active part in several scientific societies.

New approach to geology. Prodded to finish his law studies, Lyell was admitted to the bar in 1825, but with his father's financial support he practised geology more than law, publishing his first scientific papers that year. Lyell was rapidly developing new principles of reasoning in geology and began to plan a book which would stress that there are natural (as opposed to supernatural) explanations for all geologic phenomena, that the ordinary natural processes of today and their products do not differ in kind or magnitude from those of the past, and that the Earth must therefore be very ancient because these everyday processes work so slowly. With the ambitious young geologist Roderick Murchison, he explored districts in France and Italy where proof of his principles could be sought. From northern Italy Lyell went south alone to Sicily. Poor roads and accommodations made travel difficult, but in the region around Mt. Etna he found striking confirmation of his belief in the adequacy of natural causes to explain the features of the Earth and in the great antiquity even of such a recent feature as Etna itself. *In France and Italy*

The results of this trip, which lasted from May 1828 until February 1829, far exceeded Lyell's expectations. Returning to London, he set to work immediately on his book, *Principles of Geology*, the first volume of which was published in July 1830. A reader today may wonder why this book filled with facts purports to deal with principles. Lyell had to teach his principles through masses of facts and examples because in 1830 his method of scientific inquiry was novel and even mildly heretical. A remark of Charles Darwin shows how brilliantly Lyell succeeded: "The very first place which I examined . . . showed me clearly the wonderful superiority of Lyell's manner of treating geology, compared with that of any other author, whose work I had with me or ever afterwards read."

During the summer of 1830 Lyell travelled through the geologically complex Pyrenees to Spain, where the closed, repressed society both fascinated and repelled him. Returning to France, he was astonished to find King Charles X dethroned, the tricolour everywhere, and geologists able to talk only of politics. Back in London he set to work again on the *Principles of Geology*, finishing Volume II in December 1831 and the third and final volume in April 1833. His steady work was relieved by occasional social or scientific gatherings and a trip to a volcanic district in Germany close to the home of his sweetheart, Mary Horner, in Bonn, whom he married in July 1832, taking a long honeymoon and geological excursion in Switzerland and Italy. Mary, whose father had geological leanings, shared Charles's interests. For 40 years she was his closest companion; the happiness of their marriage increased because of her ability to participate in his work.

During the next eight years the Lyells led a quiet, regular life. Winters were devoted to study, scientific and social activities, and revision of Lyell's *Principles of Geology*, which sold so well that new editions were frequently required. Data for the new editions were gathered during summer travels, including two visits to Scandinavia in 1834 and 1837. In 1832 and 1833 Lyell delivered well-received lectures at King's College, London, afterward resigning the professorship as too time-consuming.

Scientific eminence. Publication of the *Principles of Geology* placed him among the recognized leaders of his field, compelling him to devote more time to scientific affairs. During these years he gained the friendship of men like Darwin and the astronomer Sir John Herschel. In 1838 Lyell's *Elements of Geology* was published; it described European rocks and fossils from the most recent, Lyell's specialty, to the oldest then known. Like the *Principles of Geology*, this well-illustrated work was periodically enlarged and updated.

In 1841 Lyell accepted an invitation to lecture and travel for a year in North America, returning again for nine months in 1845–46 and for two short visits in the 1850s. During their travels, the Lyells visited nearly every part of the United States east of the Mississippi River and much of eastern Canada, seeing almost all of the important geological "monuments" along the way, including Niagara Falls. Lyell was amazed at the comparative ease of travel, although they saw many places newly claimed from the wilderness. A veteran of coach and sail days, Lyell often praised the speed and comfort of the new railroads and steamships. Lyell's lectures at the Lowell Institute in Boston attracted thousands of people of both sexes and every social station. Lyell wrote enthusiastic and informative books, in 1845 and 1849, about each of his two long visits to the New World.

Unlike the majority of well-off Victorians, Lyell was a vocal supporter of the Union cause in the American Civil War. Familiar with both North and South, he admired the bravery and military skill of the South but believed in the necessity and inevitability of a Northern victory.

In the 1840s, Lyell became more widely known outside the scientific community, socializing with Lord John Russell, a leading Whig; Sir Robert Peel, founder of Scotland Yard; and Thomas Macaulay, the historian of England. In 1848 Lyell was knighted for his scientific achievements, beginning a long and friendly acquaintance with the royal family. He studied the prevention of mine disasters with the English physicist Michael Faraday in 1844; served as a commissioner for the Crystal Palace Exposition in 1851–52; and in the same year helped to begin educational reform at Oxford University—he had long objected to church domination of British colleges. Lyell's professional reputation continued to grow; during his lifetime he received many awards and honorary degrees, including, in 1858, the Copley Medal, the highest award of the Royal Society of London; and he was many times president of various scientific societies or functions. Expanding reputation and responsibilities brought no letup in his geological

Expanding reputation

explorations. With Mary, he travelled in Europe or Britain practically every summer, visiting Madeira in the winter of 1854 to study the origin of the island itself and of its curious fauna and flora. Lyell especially liked to visit young geologists, from whom he felt "old stagers" had much to learn. After exhaustive restudy carried out on muleback in 1858, he proved conclusively that Mt. Etna had been built up by repeated small eruptions rather than by a cataclysmic upheaval as some geologists still insisted. He wrote Mary that "a good mule is like presenting an old geologist with a young pair of legs."

In 1859 publication of Darwin's *Origin of Species* gave new impetus to Lyell's work. Although Darwin drew heavily on Lyell's *Principles of Geology* both for style and content, Lyell had never shared his protégé's belief in evolution. But reading the *Origin of Species* triggered studies that culminated in publication of *The Geological Evidence of the Antiquity of Man* in 1863, in which Lyell tentatively accepted evolution by natural selection. Only during completion of a major revision of the *Principles of Geology* in 1865 did he fully adopt Darwin's conclusions, however, adding powerful arguments of his own that won new adherents to Darwin's theory. Why Lyell was hesitant in accepting Darwinism is best explained by Darwin himself: "Considering his age, his former views, and position in society, I think his action has been heroic."

After 1865 Lyell's activities became more restricted as his strength waned, although he never entirely gave up outdoor geology. His wife, 12 years his junior, died unexpectedly in 1873 after a short illness, leaving Lyell to write, "I endeavour by daily work at my favourite science, to forget as far as possible the dreadful change which this had made in my existence." He died February 22, 1875, in London, while revising his *Principles of Geology* for its 12th edition and was buried in Westminster Abbey.

Assessment. Lyell typified his times in beginning as an amateur geologist and becoming a professional by study and experience. Unlike most geologists then and now, however, he never considered observations and collections as ends in themselves but used them to build and test theories. The *Principles of Geology* opened up new vistas of time and change for the younger group of scientists around Darwin. Only after they were gone did Lyell's reputation begin to diminish, largely at the hands of critics who had not read the *Principles of Geology* as carefully as had Darwin and attributed to Darwin things he had learned from Lyell. Lyell is still underestimated by some geologists who fail to see that the methods and principles they use every day actually originated with Lyell and were revolutionary in his era. The lasting value of Lyell's work and its importance for the modern reader is clear in Darwin's assessment:

The great merit of the *Principles* was that it altered the whole tone of one's mind, and therefore that, when seeing a thing never seen by Lyell, one yet saw it partially through his eyes.

BIBLIOGRAPHY. KATHERINE M. LYELL (ed.), *Life, Letters, and Journals of Sir Charles Lyell, Bart.*, 2 vol. (1881), is the best source of Lyell's own observations. CHARLES LYELL, *Principles of Geology, Being an Attempt to Explain the Former Changes of the Earth's Surface by Reference to Causes Now in Operation*, 3 vol. (1830–33, reprinted 1969), and *Principles of Geology, or The Modern Changes of the Earth and Its Inhabitants*, 11th ed., 2 vol. (1872), are the two best editions to consult and compare. T.G. BONNEY, *Charles Lyell and Modern Geology* (1895), is a perceptive 19th-century view. J.M. DRACHMAN, *Studies in the Literature of Natural Science* (1931), is excellent on Lyell and Darwin. L.C. EISELEY, "Charles Lyell," *Scient. Am.*, 201:98–106 (1959), is concise, original, informative, and moving. See also M.J.S. RUDWICK, "Lyell on Etna, and the Antiquity of the Earth," in C.J. SCHNEER (ed.), *Toward a History of Geology* (1969), splendid on Lyell's formative experiences; and *Sir Charles Lyell's Scientific Journals on the Species Question* (1970), written by the leading student of Lyell's life and work, L.G. WILSON, who also provided the definitive biography *Charles Lyell. The Years to 1841: The Revolution in Geology* (1972).

(R.W.Ma.)

Lymphatic System, Human

The lymphatic system helps to maintain the proper fluid balance in the tissues and the blood, to conserve protein, and to remove bacteria and other particles from the tissues. It consists of a network of fluid-filled vessels that open into the blood-vessel system, together with masses of lymphoid tissue, the structure and activity of which will be discussed below. The lymphoid tissue is, in part, intimately associated with the network of vessels, as in the lymph nodes or glands, is less intimately associated with the vessels, as in the tonsils and thymus, or has no obvious connection with the vessel network, as in the spleen.

The fluid in the lymphatic vessels, called lymph, is as a rule clear or faintly opalescent, except the lymph called chyle, which comes from the intestines. Chyle at times may be white and milky in appearance because of the minute globules of fat that it contains. The thin-walled vessels through which chyle flows are referred to as lacteals because of their milky appearance. Modern knowledge of the lymphatic vessels may be said to date from the observations of Gaspare Aselli (Gaspar Asellius), who gave (1627) the first description of these vessels after observing the white lacteals in the mesentery (a fold of membrane such as that which attaches the small intestine to the dorsal wall of the abdomen) of a well-fed dog. Since these first observations of Asellius, it has become well established that the lymphatic vessels are constantly receiving fluid from the bloodstream, to which they ultimately return it. There is thus a continuous circulation of lymph.

First description of lymphatic vessels

The lymphocytes. Of the variety of cells in the lymph nodes, the most numerous are lymphocytes, which are also found in the lymph, in blood, and elsewhere. Lymphocytes vary in size, but the smallest are about the size of red blood cells and consist almost entirely of nucleus with very little cytoplasm—the cell substance outside the nucleus. The nuclear chromatin (the most readily stainable substance in the nucleus) is disposed in dense clumps. The cytoplasm has no distinctive granules, such as are to be found in most of the other white cells (leukocytes) of the blood. Lymphocytes are capable of active movement and can migrate through the walls of blood vessels and through the various tissues. Until a few years ago they were thought to be incapable of growth or differentiation. In the late 1950s it was shown that an extract of the red bean (*Phaseolus vulgaris*), which has since been termed phytohemagglutinin, is capable of stimulating the growth and subsequent division of small lymphocytes; these are now regarded as primitive cells capable of growth and proliferation if suitably stimulated. Since this discovery, a number of substances have been found capable of stimulating the growth of small lymphocytes. Consequently, the small lymphocyte is now regarded as the temporarily inactive phase of a cell, which on appropriate stimulation can enter upon a period of great activity. In the inactive phase the lymphocyte has been compared to a cellular spore form since it can remain inactive for a long time.

Locations of lymphocytes

Lymphocytes exist in a number of places in addition to the lymph nodes—namely, the spleen, the lymphoepithelial tissues, the thymus, and the bone marrow—and large numbers of the cells are scattered throughout the connective tissues of the body. The lymphoepithelial tissues are masses of lymphocytes in close relation to the epithelium (covering) of the alimentary canal. At the upper end, they form both the tonsils and the tissues at the back of the nose that when enlarged are called adenoids. The appendix is made up largely of lymphoepithelial tissue; and throughout the intestine there are lymphoid nodules, arranged either singly or in groups, known as the aggregated nodules, or Peyer's patches. The lymphoepithelial tissues are separated from the bacterial contents of the mouth or the intestine only by thin epithelial layers through which bacteria may pass; hence, the tonsils and the appendix are notoriously subject to infection. The thymus is a lymphoid organ that is particularly well developed at birth and during the growth period. After puberty it undergoes progressive atrophy. The bone marrow contains a large population of lymphocytes scattered among its other cells and not arranged in dense nodules. A considerable number of lymphocytes are to be found in the connective tissues all over the body. It is now known that these various lymphoid masses and scattered lymphocytes do not exist in watertight compartments but, on the contrary, are integrated by the continual migration of lymphocytes between them. These migrations are described as cellular migration streams.

The lymphatic vessels. The lymphatic vessels commence as a network of closed microscopic vessels—capillaries—whose walls consist essentially of a single layer of cells, the endothelium. This resembles the endothelium of the blood capillaries but is much more freely permeable to large molecules such as proteins and even to particles such as India ink. The classical method of demonstrating lymphatics, interstitial injection, has depended upon the great permeability of lymphatic endothelium. A solution of a dye or a suspension of particles is injected into the tissue spaces or interstices and immediately enters the lymphatic capillaries by passing through their endothelium. This can be demonstrated in man by injecting a dye into skin, the colour appearing as streamers in the lymph vessels leaving the site of injection. In general, with certain exceptions due to special local circulatory arrangements, wherever there are blood capillaries, lymphatic capillaries also are to be found.

The lymphatic capillaries join to form progressively larger vessels whose walls become somewhat thicker because of their small amounts of muscle and elastic tissue. These larger collecting vessels usually accompany the veins, and, like the veins, they possess valves, but in far greater numbers. The compression of valved lymphatic trunks by surrounding muscles is an important factor in the propulsion of lymph; in addition, lymphatic vessels themselves may possess a rhythmic contractility. At the points at which valves are attached, the walls of lymphatic trunks are thicker than elsewhere, and, consequently, distended lymph trunks usually have a beaded appearance.

Main trunks

The intermediate vessels join to form a series of main lymph trunks. The main lymph trunk draining the lower limbs enters the abdomen; after passing through lymph nodes in the lumbar region (the small of the back), it becomes known as the lumbar trunk and enters the cisterna chyli; the latter also receives the large common intestinal trunk, which conveys the lymph from the greater part of the intestine. The cisterna chyli is a dilated sac lying at the back of the abdomen opposite the first lumbar vertebra, and from its upper end the thoracic duct ascends through the chest, or thorax; it inclines slightly to the left and ends at the base of the neck by entering the left innominate vein formed by the junction of the great veins draining the left side of the head and neck and the left arm. The thoracic duct thus returns to the blood stream the lymph from both legs, the pelvis and abdomen, the left side of the thorax, the left arm, and the left side of the head and neck—in other words, the lymph from the greater part of the body. Lymph from the right side of the head and neck, the right arm, and the right side of the thorax returns to the blood through the right lymph duct, which opens into the great veins at the base of the neck on the right side. There are valves in both the thoracic duct and the right lymph duct, including a particularly well-developed valve close to their termination.

Lymph nodes. Lymph nodes are a relatively recent evolutionary development and in their characteristic form are present only in mammals, though a rudimentary type of lymph node is found in birds. Lymph nodes are found in both superficial and deep situations. There is a well-marked node—or nodes—at the back of the knee, while there are a number of both superficial and deep nodes in the region of the groin. There is a large collection of nodes in the armpit. There are numerous nodes in the thorax and abdomen, especially in the mesentery. It is distinctive of man and primates that lymph passes through chains of several small lymph nodes instead of through one or two large nodes, as in other mammals.

This is readily seen in the mesentery, where in man there are many scattered small nodes, while in the dog the nodes are all gathered together in a large mass at the root of the mesentery. Asellius thought that this was a small pancreas, and it is still sometimes known as the pancreas of Asellius.

The human lymph node is enclosed in a fibrous capsule; in the interior are masses of cells, mainly lymphocytes, which in the outer part of the node—the cortex—are in dense masses, whereas in the interior, the medulla, they form a series of branching cords of cells, the medullary cords; between the cords are clearer spaces, the lymph sinuses. In some animals, though not in man, there is a well-developed system of partitions (trabeculae) extending into the node from the capsule and partially subdividing the node into segments. Nodes tend to be more or less bean shaped; lymph vessels bring lymph to the outer convex surface of the node, where they pierce the capsule. Immediately under the capsule there is a lymph channel termed the subcapsular (or cortical) sinus; from this sinus other sinuses extend radially into the node to reach the network of medullary sinuses. The medullary sinuses converge to the concave side of the bean-shaped node and leave the node in the form of two or three lymphatic vessels that quickly join to form a single vessel. Vessels bringing lymph to the lymph node are termed afferent; vessels draining lymph away, efferent. Freshly formed lymph that has not passed through a node is called peripheral lymph. Lymph that has passed through only one node is called intermediate lymph. Lymph that has passed through all the nodes that it is going to traverse and is on its way to the blood without further interruption is termed central lymph.

Peripheral, intermediate, and central lymph   Peripheral lymph contains a small number of lymphocytes, around 500 to 1,000 per cubic millimetre, whereas intermediate and central lymph contain many more, up to 40,000 or more per cubic millimetre. For many years this difference in cell content between peripheral and intermediate lymph was taken to mean that large numbers of cells were constantly being formed in the node and entering the blood via the lymph stream. This view found further support because of the presence in the cortex of the node of lymphoid nodules with a clear central area called the germinal centre. Walter Flemming (1885), the German biologist who first described the germinal centre, observed that it contained numerous cells in the process of dividing. It was, in fact, one of the first animal tissues in which cell division was observed.

It is now known that the position is far from being as simple as was first thought. In addition to the new formation of cells, there is appreciable migration of lymphocytes through the node. A small number of these reaches the node through its afferent lymph, while a larger number reaches it via the bloodstream. Lymph nodes contain a special type of blood vessel, the postcapillary veins, through the walls of which lymphocytes pass from the blood into the lymph node substance; the cells then move out of the node either into the efferent lymph or through the walls of other blood vessels into the bloodstream again. In either case, there is extensive recirculation of lymphocytes in lymph nodes as well as new formation. Cells that leave the node thus may be newly formed, or they may have been derived from the afferent lymph or from the blood.

Cells that reach the blood via the lymph stream are termed indirect-entry lymphocytes, as opposed to the direct-entry cells that obtain access to the bloodstream directly by migrating through the walls of blood vessels in lymphoid tissue without first entering the lymph. Considerable numbers of lymphocytes are of the direct-entry variety. The few cells reaching the node via peripheral lymph are derived from the blood, passing first from the blood capillaries into connective tissue and thence into peripheral lymph. The steady drift of a small number of lymphocytes through the connective tissues of the body may possess much greater importance than the numbers suggest. Furthermore, under abnormal conditions the number of lymphocytes in peripheral lymph may be greatly increased.

The lymph sinuses are not, as a rule, clear channels but are broken up by a network (reticulum) of cells that are capable of engulfing bacteria and other foreign particles; i.e., they are phagocytic. Foreign particles, whether inert, such as carbon, or living, such as bacteria or fragments of cancerous growths, may all be held up for a time in the lymph node, where they are mechanically trapped by the cells of the sinus reticulum. This led Rudolf Virchow, in the middle of the last century, to ascribe a defensive, or barrier, function to lymph nodes; these observations on lymph nodes led to assignment of a defensive function to lymphoid tissue generally. It is now known that Virchow was to a large extent right, though for the wrong reasons. When bacteria reach a lymph node, they stimulate rapid proliferation of a small part of the total lymphocyte population of the node, and this proliferation is accompanied by a gradual change of the lymphocytes into another type of cell, the plasma cell, that forms antibodies to the bacteria. The plasma cells may be formed in large numbers and would quickly swamp the lymph node were it not that large numbers of young plasma cells leave in the efferent lymph to settle in various parts of the organism where they go on producing antibodies. In this way a relatively small amount of lymphoid tissue can give rise to a large number of plasma cells. At the same time, through the migration of plasma cells, the lymph node is cleared, as it were, for further action. _{Formation of plasma cells and antibodies}

Little is known, as yet, about the origin of the cells migrating to the lymph node either in peripheral lymph or through the bloodstream. Although it has been established that some lymphocytes are derived from the bone marrow and others from the thymus, it is not known what determines the extent of these cell migrations or their direction. Among the best established groups of cellular migration streams are those that originate in the bone marrow. Cells from the bone marrow seem ultimately to colonize the remainder of the lymphomyeloid complex—i.e., the rest of the lymphatic system and the bone marrow. In addition, it is highly probable that there are not only single but also serial migration streams from one part of the complex to another. It is possible, for example, that the thymus is an intermediate station to which cells migrate from the bone marrow and that the cells undergo some change there before continuing their migration to other parts of the complex such as the spleen and lymph nodes. The most extensive and rapid migration streams pass through the blood and consist to a large extent of direct-entry lymphocytes that have been formed in the bone marrow. The indirect-entry cells of the lymph contain a varying number of lymphocytes that have been conditioned to respond to an immunological stimulus. It is also clear that cells originating in the marrow can find their way into the connective tissues in considerable numbers. In most of these migrations the majority of the migrating cells are small lymphocytes. It seems that the small lymphocyte is the stage in the life history of the lymphocyte that is best adapted for speed of mobilization, ease of transport, and economy of storage in the minimum of space.

Other aggregates of lymphoid tissue.   One of the many problems that arise out of the diffuseness of distribution of the lymphoid tissues is that of determining how much there is in the body as a whole. In the smaller laboratory animals, such as the rat or rabbit, the more clearly defined members of the complex have all been dissected out and weighed. In practice this has meant thymus, spleen, most of the lymph nodes, the appendix, and Peyer's patches, but it does not take into account the large population of lymphocytes present in the bone marrow and the connective tissues nor the numerous solitary nodules found in the alimentary canal. It is also clear that usually not all the lymph nodes are identified in such procedures; in man, in whom there are many hundreds of nodes, the attempt to dissect them all out is fraught with even greater difficulty. On the basis of the animal data, in the young adult the lymphoid tissue of the body as a whole is somewhere between 1. and 1.5 percent of the body weight. If all the scattered elements could be collected into a single mass, they would form an organ of approximately the same weight as the liver, which in the normal man ranges from 1.2 to 1.6 kilograms. This lymphoid "organ" undergoes marked changes with age. The thymus, in particular, which is large in infancy, begins to shrink fairly rapidly after puberty. Tonsils and adenoids are also large and well developed until puberty. Before this was fully appreciated, perfectly normal tonsils were sometimes removed under the impression that their large size was due to disease.

Composition of lymph. Lymph contains all the protein fractions present in blood plasma (the blood except for its cells) but at a lower level. Thus, in one set of observations in man, the total protein was 7.08 percent in the blood plasma and 4.89 percent in the lymph of the thoracic duct. The difference between plasma and lymph was due mainly to the globulin fraction, which was 4.16 percent in plasma against 2.56 percent in lymph; the albumen was 2.86 percent in plasma compared with 2.34 percent in lymph. The protein content of lymph varies in different regions. Liver lymph contains the highest percentage of protein, whereas lymph from the skin and subcutaneous tissues usually contains the lowest. Antibodies are associated with serum globulins, and it is the globulin content of lymph that is relatively more reduced in relation to blood plasma than the albumin content; hence, as a rule, lymph contains less antibody than blood plasma, a fact that may on occasion affect the efficiency with which the body can deal with infections. Apart from proteins, lymph—and more especially intestinal lymph—contains appreciable amounts of fat after a fatty meal. The fat particles have a surface membrane that consists largely of protein enclosing the fatty core. This structure can be readily seen under the electron microscope. It should be noted that cholesterol is absorbed almost entirely by means of the lymph stream, whereas fats are absorbed only in part.

Electro-
lytes,
sugar,
and
urea

Electrolytes (*e.g.*, calcium, sodium, potassium, chloride) in lymph are found in virtually the same concentration as in blood plasma. The same is basically true of glucose and urea. After a carbohydrate meal or the injection of glucose into a vein, the blood sugar rises rapidly, and the sugar content of lymph lags behind for a short time until equilibrium is re-established. The levels of nonprotein nitrogen and of the nitrogen components urea, amino acid, and creatinine are approximately the same in plasma and lymph except in the kidney, where the level of urea is slightly higher in lymph than in plasma. Some hormones are absorbed in small amounts through the lymph stream—*e.g.*, testosterone and progesterone. Enzymes present in the blood plasma behave, in general, like the other plasma proteins and are therefore found in lymph also. They are usually in smaller amounts in the lymph, although there are exceptions to this—*e.g.*, serum alkaline phosphatase, which is derived to a considerable extent from the intestines and obtains access to the blood stream mainly through the lymphatics, is found in higher levels in the lymph.

Formation, pressure, and flow of lymph. Lymph is derived from the blood by a process that begins with filtration through the wall of the blood capillary. This primary filtrate then undergoes some modifications as it passes through the tissues that it finally leaves by entering the lymphatics. The amount of tissue fluid at any time represents an equilibrium between the amount of fluid leaving the blood capillary and the amount entering the lymphatic capillary. The normal functioning of the tissues depends to a large extent on the effective control of the tissue-fluid balance.

Small molecules, such as those of oxygen, carbon dioxide, or sodium chloride, diffuse rapidly through the blood capillary endothelium in both directions and have little effect on the fluid balance. The mechanical (hydrostatic) pressure of the blood inside the capillaries forces fluid out of the blood into the surrounding tissues. On the other hand, since the capillary lining (endothelium) functions almost as a semipermeable membrane, the osmotic pressure of the plasma proteins, mainly the albumin, exerts a force in the opposite direction and absorbs fluid from the tissue spaces into the capillaries. This essentially is the

basis of the hypothesis first put forward by the English physiologist Ernest H. Starling; if this were all that happened, lymphatics would be unnecessary, and fluid balance could be adequately maintained without them.

There is one complication in this apparently simple arrangement for maintaining the tissue-fluid balance: the endothelium of the blood capillaries functions almost as a semipermeable membrane, but not completely, since now and again the relatively high pressure of the blood inside the capillary forces out a few molecules of plasma protein. This protein cannot be reabsorbed, since the tissue pressure outside the capillaries is far too low to drive it back into the bloodstream. Consequently, this slight but steady leak of protein would lead to its gradual accumulation in the tissues if it were not for the presence of lymphatics with their much more permeable endothelium. The prime purpose of the lymphatics, therefore, is to return extravascular protein to the bloodstream. Though what is now usually known as the Starling hypothesis is fundamentally correct, its operation can be modified in a number of ways. It is now thought, for example, that the blood capillary is more permeable at its arterial than at its venous end. Furthermore, in some tissues the blood capillaries let little or no protein through.

In the central nervous system, only small amounts of protein escape from the blood vessels, and this protein is removed by the cerebrospinal fluid. In the thymus, similarly, little protein escapes from the blood. This so-called blood–thymus barrier is believed to be the reason that the thymus does not normally share in the reaction to foreign proteins. In the bone marrow the specialized blood capillaries known as sinusoids possess numerous small apertures that allow blood plasma to pass quite freely in either direction; thus, here too, the need for lymphatics is obviated.

Structures
lacking
lymphatics

The pressure of lymph is much lower than that of blood. It ranges from 1 to 25 millimetres of mercury, though under conditions of severe exercise the pressure of lymph in the limbs may rise on rare occasions to as much as 60 millimetres of mercury.

The flow of lymph is caused by a variety of factors. The lymph hearts found in lower vertebrates are absent in higher vertebrates, including man. In some parts of the body the flow of lymph may be aided by the concentration of the smooth muscle in the walls of the lymphatic vessels. Although such contraction occurs to a greater extent than had previously been realized, it is probably true that the propulsion of lymph is still, in the main, caused by forces from outside the vessels, such as muscular contraction and respiratory movement.

Conditions that increase the flow of lymph. Provided that the endothelium of the blood capillary remains healthy, the flow of lymph can be increased by altering the two major factors that control it. Either lowering the osmotic pressure of the blood or raising its hydrostatic pressure will upset the normal balance and will result in increased formation of lymph. Compared with the blood vascular system, the lymphatic vessels can transport relatively small amounts of fluid; hence, they can deal with only a moderate increase in lymph flow. Beyond this point lymph accumulates in the tissues, which become waterlogged, or are said to have developed edema. The commonest cause of lowering the plasma proteins is starvation, or a diet deficient in protein. The key protein from the point of view of osmotic pressure is serum albumin; if this falls beyond a certain point, nutritional edema develops.

Most commonly a rise in the venous pressure is reflected almost at once by a rise in the capillary pressure and a corresponding increase in lymph formation. This is one of the reasons that edema often develops in cases of heart disease, when the back pressure from the heart results in increased venous pressure, as shown clearly by the distended veins. Increased capillary pressure is most likely to occur in the legs when a person is upright, since, in addition to other factors, the force of gravity is exerted through a long column of blood extending downward from the heart. This effect will be maximal at the lower

Edema in
heart
disease

end of the venous column, so that even in normal individuals prolonged standing will not infrequently cause some edema with a resultant feeling that the shoes have become tight. In pregnancy, when the enlarged uterus presses in the abdomen on the veins draining blood from the lower limbs, the tendency toward edema is accentuated, and some degree of swelling of the feet and legs is not uncommon.

Even if the osmotic pressure of the blood plasma and the hydrostatic pressure of the blood in the capillaries are within the normal range, edema can still develop if the wall of the blood capillary is unduly permeable. This can result from injury, as from the ultraviolet rays of the sun in sunburn. The capillary endothelium is especially sensitive to oxygen deficiency, and in heart disease, when there is a combination of increased capillary pressure and oxygen deficiency, edema may be especially well marked.

Other causes of edema In some people the capillary endothelium is readily damaged by cold; such persons tend to develop chilblains, which are essentially local patches of edema. In others prolonged warmth, which causes enlargement of the blood vessels, may also bring about some edema. In sensitive persons the capillaries may be damaged by allergic stimuli; e.g., small amounts of foreign proteins absorbed in undigested form and giving rise to local "spots," which are small patches of edema. Many types of injury result when damaged cells form substances that increase the permeability of the neighbouring capillaries. In some persons firmly stroking the skin liberates these substances—either histamine or histamine-like compounds—so that a wheal develops.

The fluid balance also may be upset through varying degrees of lymphatic obstruction. In a few individuals whose lymphatic vessels do not reach full development, some degree of lymphatic obstruction may be said to exist almost from birth. The obstruction in these cases is never great, but its effects are continuous. If every day even two or three drops more of tissue fluid are formed than the lymph trunks can cope with, there is a slowly developing but progressive edema. This usually occurs in the leg; as the edema becomes greater and greater, elephantiasis is said to have developed. Other forms of lymphatic obstruction may be due to involvement of collecting trunks in scar tissue; e.g., the vessels in the armpit after extensive removal of the breast, in which case the edema involves the arm.

Functions of the system. *Return of protein and tissue fluid to blood.* The essential function of the lymph is to return to the blood the extravascular protein that is continually leaking out in small quantities. Though the rate of leakage is slow, it is continuous, so that in the course of 24 hours well over 50 percent of the total plasma proteins have left the bloodstream. Without the operation of the lymphatics and the steady return of protein to the blood, the delicate balance of the tissue fluids would be rapidly upset. Some of the protein that passes through the tissues en route from blood to lymph is actually made use of by the tissue cells. For tissues that manufacture proteins of various kinds, the lymphatics provide the main channel of entry of the proteins into the bloodstream.

Removal of bacteria and foreign particles. Foreign particles in the tissues are usually removed by the lymphatic vessels and then are held up in the sinus reticulum of the lymph nodes draining the region affected. If the particles are antigens—i.e., if they stimulate antibody formation—they may initially give rise to pain and tenderness in the nodes, which undergo considerable swelling while the antibody-forming cells are developing. The fate of bacteria when they reach the lymph node has been investigated by many observers in an effort to elucidate the basic mechanisms of immunity.

Transplantation antigens In the case of bacteria, the antigen can be readily identified. In recent years great interest has developed in "transplantation antigens" that are discharged from grafted foreign tissue and stimulate the development of immune reactions resulting in rejection of the graft. Although transplantation antigens cannot be identified with certainty, their existence must be postulated to explain the phenomena of graft acceptance and rejection. In some types of graft the immune mechanism operates through lymph nodes. Five or six days after a tissue or organ has been grafted, if lymphatic connections have been re-established, a stream of "sensitized" lymphocytes leaves the nodes, reaches the bloodstream, and then obtains access to the graft; there, together with nonsensitized cells, the lymphocytes bring about rejection of the graft. Lymphatics and lymph node connections do not seem essential for rejection, however, since apparently lymphocytes can become sensitized while circulating in the bloodstream, thereby coming into contact with the blood vessels of the graft. Lymphocytes sensitized to the foreign cells can destroy them by producing antibodies that circulate in the blood or are liberated only when the lymphocytes come into contact with their target cells, the cells of the foreign graft to which they have become sensitized. One of the great practical problems in organ and tissue grafting is how to suppress the capacity of the host to mount an immune response against the foreign tissue. In practice, this usually means destroying a sufficient number of lymphocytes. The danger of too successful a program of immunosuppression is that the body is not left with sufficient lymphocytes to help it overcome infections that it would normally take in its stride.

Though cancer cells are not foreign cells in quite the same way as a foreign graft, they have nevertheless somehow become foreign to the body in which they are growing. The available evidence indicates that the mechanisms by which the body deals with cancerous growths are similar to, if not identical with, those by which it deals with grafts of foreign organs. In each case the lymphocyte seems to play a leading role (see also LYMPHATIC SYSTEM DISEASES).

BIBLIOGRAPHY. J.M. YOFFEY and F.C. COURTICE, *Lymphatics, Lymph and the Lymphomyeloid* (1970), a comprehensive survey including an extensive bibliography; N.R. LING, *Lymphocyte Stimulation* (1969), an excellent, modern account of methods of making lymphocytes grow, and of their properties after stimulation; F.T. RAPAPORT and J. DAUSSET (eds.), *Human Transplantation* (1968), an admirable account of the progress thus far in the transplantation of tissues and organs, together with the broader biological background of the problems involved in the acceptance or rejection of grafts, and the practical aspects of testing for histocompatibility, of immunosuppression, and of organ preservation; H.S. MICKLEM and J.F. LOUTIT, *Tissue Grafting and Radiation* (1966), an excellent account of the effects of radiation and of some of the basic observations of the Harwell group on the use of chromosome markers.

(J.M.Y.)

Lymphatic System Diseases

The lymphatic system, made up of a network of vessels, the lymph channels, and of masses of tissue, including the lymph nodes, serves (1) to drain fluid and proteins from the tissues and return them to the blood circulatory system and (2) to resist invasion of the body by disease organisms and other foreign particles. The second of these functions—largely immunological in nature—and the disorders concerned with it are discussed in the article IMMUNITY.

Types of lymphatic system disease Diseases of the lymphatic system include a variety of unrelated conditions whose common feature is that they involve abnormalities of the lymphatic vessels or tissues. This group of diseases is conveniently subdivided into those in which it is the drainage function of lymphatic vessels that is impaired and those in which there is abnormality in the lymphatic tissues. Lymphedema, or swelling of tissue due to inadequate lymph drainage, is the commonest manifestation of the first group, although drainage of lymph by abnormal routes also falls into this category. The second group most often becomes evident as some unusual degree of enlargement of lymph nodes (sometimes still referred to as lymph "glands" though they are not generally thought to have any strictly glandular function) or of the spleen.

In each main group, disease may be either primary, involving the lymphatic system first or most obviously, or secondary, in which some process that has begun elsewhere comes to involve the lymphatic system.

This article outlines the conditions most commonly responsible for the main abnormalities of lymphatic system structure or function, and briefly characterizes currently available treatments.

It must be stressed that the identification of the cause of enlarged lymph nodes, while often straightforward, may on occasion present great difficulty and may require blood analysis, X-ray investigation, and even microscopic examination of the affected tissue, before it can be firmly established.

Disorders of lymphatic vessels. *Impairment of lymph drainage.* Impairment of lymph drainage from any tissue leads to swelling as tissue fluid accumulates in excessive amounts in the spaces between the cells. This variety of swelling is known as lymphedema and is characteristically harder and less easily dispersed than that seen in other forms of edema. Chronic inflammation and formation of scar tissue occur often in lymphedematous tissues.

Simple obstruction of a major lymphatic trunk such as that draining a limb rarely results in lymphedema because of the great capacity of other, smaller lymphatic vessels to grow and bypass the obstruction. The presence of lymphedema, therefore, implies a widespread involvement of lymphatic vessels in the disease process. Once the obstruction is established, it is unlikely to disappear spontaneously. Elephantiasis is the name often given to advanced lymphedema, from the increase in size and thickening of the affected part, often a limb.

Causes of lymphedema include inherited, infective, and malignant conditions. Milroy's disease, which often appears in childhood or early adult life and causes enlargement of one or both legs, has a familial incidence and is thought to result from some inherited abnormality of the lymphatics. Lymphatic cysts, seen in the neck as swellings under the skin, also appear early in life and probably represent disorders of development of lymphatic vessels.

Infective lymphedema most frequently results from filariasis, a tropical disease in which small worms, spread by mosquitoes, grow and proliferate in the lymphatics, causing mechanical obstruction and chronic inflammation. The result is lymphedema, which may be extremely severe, of the lower limbs and sometimes of the external genitalia. This is the condition of tropical elephantiasis.

Cancer may produce lymphedema either by the invasion and consequent obstruction of lymphatic vessels by the malignant process or by damage to the lymphatics resulting from surgery or radiation therapy. Removal of the breast and of local lymph nodes is not infrequently followed by lymphedema of the arm on the affected side. In this, and in other circumstances, malignant changes occasionally develop in the walls of the lymphatic vessels (lymphangiosarcoma) with consequent further obstruction.

Treatment of lymphedema, apart from attention to any causative condition, such as chemotherapy to eliminate the worms in filariasis, is in severe cases usually surgical, involving the bridging of the area of obstruction by a grafted strip of tissue with healthy lymphatics, to bypass the blockage.

Abnormal drainage of lymph. Abnormal drainage of lymph, or lymph fistula, is nearly always associated with some obstruction to lymph drainage, although it can also occur as a result of injury. The effects depend on the site involved and include the chronic discharge of lymph through a skin wound, or into the urinary tract (chyluria), the abdominal cavity (chylous ascites), or the thoracic cavity (chylothorax). If substantial lymphatics are involved, the volume of fluid lost may be considerable, leading to dehydration and collapse. If the lymph includes that draining from the intestinal tract, it has a characteristically milky appearance because of the fat absorbed by lymph in this area.

Treatment is essentially surgical and is directed to relieving any obstruction that may be present as well as to closing the fistula and restoring a route by which the lymph may find its way to its normal destination, the venous system.

Lymphangitis. Inflammation of lymphatics, or lymphangitis, is seen in certain inflammatory conditions of the skin, particularly in infections with streptococcus organisms. The striking picture of discrete red lines along the course of the subcutaneous lymphatic vessels that drain the area of the primary infection is usually accompanied by painful enlargement of the local lymph nodes. Treatment is directed to the primary infection, if it is still present.

Disorders of lymphoid tissue. Lymphoid, or lymphatic, tissue is found in the lymph nodes, spleen, and thymus, and also in the tonsils, adenoids, and the walls of the intestine. Enlargement or overgrowth of such tissue may be local or generalized, acute or chronic, and primary or secondary. To determine the cause of a particular person's lymphoid tissue enlargement it is necessary to take account of the history of the condition, associated local or general disorders, and the nature and distribution of the enlarged lymphatic tissue. If the cause is still not apparent it is necessary to investigate further with blood tests, X-ray examination, or even microscopic examination of a specimen of the affected tissue.

Generalized lymph node enlargement. In primary lymphoid tissue diseases the first or most prominent site of the disease process is in the lymphatic tissues, and there is no condition in some other tissue to account for the lymphatic tissue involvement. Many of the diseases in this category have features of malignant disease. This group includes the diseases known as the reticuloses and also lymphatic leukemia. (Leukemia is characterized by the presence of abnormally high numbers of white cells in the blood; in lymphatic leukemia the white cells in abnormal numbers are lymphocytes.) The cause of this group of diseases is unknown; although the diseases have many of the features associated with malignant disease, such as spread of the condition at and beyond the site of origin and a uniformly fatal outcome in the absence of treatment, there is a school of thought that holds that there may be an infective, possibly viral, basis for the conditions. These two views are not mutually exclusive, since several types of animal and human tumour are known to be virus induced.

Lymphatic leukemia is distinguished from the reticuloses by the presence in the circulating blood of numerous lymphocytes. These cells are characteristic cells of the lymphatic system and normally form some 20 to 30 percent of the white blood cells in adults (up to 60 percent in children), being present in concentrations of 1,000 to 3,000 per cubic millimetre. This figure may rise as high as 500,000 per cubic millimetre in lymphatic leukemia. Two forms of the disease occur: the acute, which is predominantly a disease of children, and the chronic, which affects mainly those over 45 years old and is more common in men than in women. Enlargement of lymph nodes and spleen is a feature of both types but is generally more marked in the chronic form.

In acute leukemia the onset is usually sudden, and the course rapidly progressive to a fatal conclusion, with severe anemia requiring blood transfusion, with spontaneous hemorrhages, and with uncontrollable infection among the clinical manifestations. The lymphatic form of acute leukemia is, however, somewhat amenable to treatment, and remissions of two years or more have been produced by corticosteroid (adrenal hormone) and cytotoxic (cell-poisoning) therapy. The greatest hope for improvement in therapeutic results in this as in certain other malignant conditions seems at present to lie in the technique of intensive cytotoxic chemotherapy combined with nursing in completely sterile conditions to protect the patient from the increased susceptibility to infections that results from the inevitable depression of the normal white blood cells.

Chronic lymphatic leukemia runs a much slower and more insidious course and may come to the affected person's notice as generalized enlargement of lymph nodes. The characteristic abnormalities in the blood and bone marrow enable this condition to be differentiated from other causes of generalized lymph node enlargement. Treatment is often confined to correcting the resulting anemia; the disease is often quite slow to progress, a course of five years being not uncommon. If the disease

Margin notes:

Causes of lymphedema

Lymph fistula

Lymphatic leukemia

enters a more acute phase, X-ray therapy, particularly to the spleen, and cytotoxic therapy may be employed.

The reticuloses have certain similarities to chronic lymphatic leukemia, but without the changes in the blood. Involvement of the lymph nodes may be generalized from the start—in which case the outlook is rather more serious—or localized to a single node or group of nodes. Diagnosis of reticulosis, and determination of the type, rests largely on microscopic examination of affected tissue; in the localized forms of these conditions the affected tissues may be surgically removed for this purpose, this operation being apparently curative in a certain small proportion of cases. Usually there is recurrence sooner or later, often in several sites distant from the site of onset. It is not known whether these conditions always spread from a single, sometimes unobtrusive, site of origin, or whether they genuinely originate at several different points. The clinical features of the other reticuloses—that is, lymphosarcoma and reticulum-cell sarcoma—are similar to those of lymphadenoma, the outlook being rather worse.

Hodgkin's disease

The commonest and least malignant of the reticuloses is lymphadenoma, often known as Hodgkin's disease. This typically starts in early adult life and occurs in both men and women. Apart from enlargement of accessible lymph nodes, which may cause the affected person to notice a lump in the neck, armpit, or groin, there may be symptoms from enlargement of deeper node groups, such as those in the chest or abdomen. Such enlargement commonly causes some obstruction of the alimentary or respiratory tracts, leading to vomiting, difficulty in swallowing, or cough. Some degree of anemia is often present, as is fever, which may point misleadingly to the possibility of a systemic infection as the cause of the enlarged nodes. Pain in the affected nodes following the taking of alcoholic drinks is a mysterious but not uncommon feature of Hodgkin's disease. Weight loss, as in many other malignant conditions, is often noted as the disease progresses. Treatment by irradiation or cytotoxic drugs may produce remissions of ten to 20 years or even apparent cures, particularly when the disease is diagnosed in its localized form. Untreated, the course varies greatly from case to case, being sometimes slow, sometimes rapidly progressive to a fatal end.

Syphilis and other infections

Syphilis in both primary and secondary stages involves lymph node enlargement. In the primary stage it is the inguinal (groin) glands that are most likely to be involved; generalized enlargement follows in the secondary stage and persists, if untreated, longer than any other feature of this stage.

Glandular fever, also called infectious mononucleosis, is a virus disease that is accompanied by general lymph node enlargement, often most marked in the neck region. The spleen, too, is often involved, as in many conditions in this category.

Rubella (German measles) can be distinguished from measles and some of the other childhood rashes by enlargement of the lymph nodes, especially those at the back of the neck.

Plague in some cases leads to marked lymph node enlargement, the masses of glands swollen to prominence in the inguinal region being the "buboes" that give their name to the bubonic form of this condition.

Primary amyloid disease and sarcoidosis are diseases, of unknown cause, in which generalized lymph node enlargement may occur. (In amyloidosis an abnormal protein substance, superficially like starch, accumulates in various bodily organs such as the heart, lungs, and skin. In sarcoidosis, small lumps, or tubercles, of epithelioid cells develop in any of a number of the bodily organs. Epithelioid cells are connective tissue cells that form layers like the coverings and linings of the body.)

If sufficiently widespread, infections of the skin with staphylococci or other organisms may result in generalized enlargement of lymph nodes.

Just as all the conditions mentioned may on occasion be confined for a time at least to an isolated group of nodes, or even to a single node, so most of the conditions in the next category will sometimes give rise to misleadingly widespread involvement.

Local lymph node enlargement. By far the commonest cause of local lymph node enlargement is infection in the area drained by the nodes concerned. So common is this that most normal people will be found on careful examination to have one or more nodes in the armpits or groins that are enlarged enough to be perceptible by touch. The primary infection responsible may be trivial or may have subsided some weeks previously and thus may have been forgotten. Before any serious significance is placed on the presence of such nodes, a thorough search must be made of the relevant skin areas and of the person's memory. Sometimes the affected nodes themselves become involved in the infective process to the point of pus and abscess formation. Staphylococcal skin infections are the usual cause of such lymph node involvement when nodes in the groin or the armpit are acutely involved in this way, the enlarged nodes being typically tender to the touch. When nodes in the neck are thus involved, the likely sites of primary infection include the throat and particularly the tonsil. Acutely enlarged tender nodes in this region, as frequently seen in childhood, are most often due to streptococcal throat infections. Dental infections also may involve lymph nodes.

Skin and other infections

Chronic infections also may give rise to local lymph node enlargement, the best known example of this being tuberculosis. When the tuberculosis organism gains entrance to the body by the respiratory tract, the pharynx, or the alimentary tract, it most often gives rise to a small lesion at the site of entry, and shortly afterward the lymph nodes to which the site drains become involved in the tuberculous process. Thus nodes at the root of a lung (near the point where bronchi, nerves, and blood vessels enter), in the neck, or in the abdomen may become infected. Frequently, in the case of the lung, the condition progresses no further than this stage, and the patient recovers, being left with a small scar and sometimes with a lymph node that is calcified. Calcification is a typical reaction of the body to healed tuberculosis in any site. If the condition is not arrested by the natural defenses of the body, or by chemotherapy, the affected nodes, like other tissues affected by tuberculous infection, may progress from overgrowth to caseation (the tissue dies and turns into a cheese-like substance) and to discharge of tuberculous pus. This picture is known as a cold abscess, as it lacks the acute inflammatory features of, for example, a staphylococcal abscess. Tuberculous lymph node enlargement is often the first abnormality noted when it occurs in the neck. In this situation it is almost always associated with the bovine form of the disease, acquired from drinking infected milk, and virtually eliminated in some countries by immunization and testing of dairy herds. There are still many people to be seen who bear on their necks the scars of the drainage or surgical removal of such nodes.

Tuberculosis

The other main category of lymph node enlargement confined to local areas is that of secondary malignant disease, the appearance of a cancerous growth at a distance from its original site. As with the infections, such involvement may on occasion be the first sign of the cancer to be seen, particularly when the primary tumour is deeply situated. Certain types of tumour are much more likely to spread by the lymphatic route than others. Carcinomas, or malignant tumours of skin, lining membranes, and glandular tissues, are much more susceptible to this type of spread than are sarcomas, malignant tumours of connective tissues, such as bone, cartilage, and muscle. The malignant cells find their way from the primary growth along lymphatics to the lymph nodes, where they tend to be held up and may grow to form a secondary cancer or metastasis. If the primary source is not apparent, inspection of a specimen of tissue from the secondary tumour may be able to settle the question, particularly when the tumour is a well-differentiated one. A knowledge of the lymphatic drainage pathways helps the physician to select likely sites to investigate for primary tumour. The typical malignant lymph node metastasis is hard and painless and is often fixed to surrounding tissues. Such metastases sometimes appear months or even years after the apparently successful removal of the primary tumour. Some surgical operations for cancer aim to remove not only the primary tumour but the local lymph nodes and the lymphatic vessels between. The operation of radical mastectomy (breast removal) for breast cancer is one such operation, in which the armpit is cleared of all visible nodes, even if apparently normal, in case there are present malignant cells that might persist if only the primary growth were removed.

Occasionally lymph node metastases appear at sites surprisingly distant from the primary tumour, as when an abdominal growth such as a stomach carcinoma gives rise to a solitary metastasis in the neck, having spread there by the thoracic lymph duct.

Significance of enlargement of accessible lymph nodes. The lymph nodes that are most likely to draw attention to themselves when enlarged are those in the easily accessible subcutaneous groups. Nodes in the neck, the armpit, and the groin fall into this group, also occasionally nodes behind the knee or near the elbow. Deeper groups of nodes, when they become enlarged, may take some time to draw attention to themselves; thus enlarged nodes in the chest may cause cough, shortness of breath, difficulty in swallowing, or congestion of the veins in the upper part of the body, but by the time such symptoms are present the enlargement is likely to be considerable. Similarly, abdominal nodes have to be much enlarged before they give rise to a mass that can be felt through the abdominal wall or that causes symptoms of alimentary tract obstruction. Establishing that such symptoms are due to an enlarged mass of lymph nodes and the elucidation of the cause of such enlargements require X-rays and other investigation, including exploratory surgery and securing of specimens of the tissue.

Below are summarized the possible causes of localized enlargements of subcutaneous nodes at various sites. It should be borne in mind, first, that any of the causes of generalized enlargements may initially become evident by localized involvement; second, that many people, particularly if their work or mode of life involves repeated minor trauma or chronic infection of their hands or feet, have permanently palpable nodes in the armpits or groin; and, third, that inflammatory causes are more common than cancer.

The undermentioned causes apply mainly when the stated group of nodes is the only group affected.

Cervical nodes. Enlargement of nodes in the neck (cervical nodes) may be due to tonsillitis and other acute inflammatory diseases of the throat or mouth and teeth; infections or infestations of the skin of the face or scalp; tuberculosis (see above); secondary carcinomas, the most likely site for the primary being the mucous membrane of the mouth, the skin of the face, the larynx (voice box), or the esophagus. Enlarged nodes low in the neck or just above the collar bone may contain secondary tumours from cancer in the chest or the abdomen. Posterior or occipital nodes are enlarged in scalp infections.

Axillary nodes. Nodes in the armpit, axillary nodes, are involved in infections of the arm. When malignant enlargement occurs in the armpit, a common primary source is carcinoma of the breast.

Inguinal nodes. Inguinal nodes (nodes in the groin) are enlarged in infection of the skin of the feet, legs, buttocks, abdomen, or external genitalia. Primary or secondary stages of syphilis, gonorrhea, and other venereal diseases may be responsible. Carcinoma of the external or internal genitalia or of the skin anywhere in the drainage area may result in secondary growths in these nodes.

In summary, enlargement of subcutaneous lymph nodes, unless associated with a recent infection in the drainage area of the nodes concerned, requires elucidation of the cause. If generalized, such enlargement is most often part of some generalized infection, such as glandular fever, but occasionally is due to leukemia or reticulosis. Localized enlargement in the absence of nearby infection raises the possibility of tuberculosis or secondary cancer from some deep-seated primary growth. Microscopic inspection of a specimen of the affected node may in some cases be the only way of firmly establishing the cause.

BIBLIOGRAPHY. I. RUSZNYAK *et al.*, *Lymphatics and Lymph Circulation*, 2nd ed. (1967), a comprehensive review of the physiology and pathology of lymphatic vessels, with an extensive bibliog.; *Cecil-Loeb Textbook of Medicine*, 12th ed. by P.G. BEESON and W. MCDERMOTT (1967), a standard and reliable medical text; H. BAILEY and R.J.M. LOVE, *Short Practice of Surgery*, 14th ed. rev. by A.J.H. RAINS and W.M. CAPPER (1968), a good, copiously illustrated text, including diagnosis and surgical management of disorders of both lymph vessels and glands; P. MANSON, *Tropical Diseases: A Manual of the Diseases of Warm Climates*, 16th ed. by P.H. MANSON-BAHR (1966), a standard text.

(L.J.F.Y.)

Lyon

By virtue of its population, the importance and variety of its economic and cultural activity, the extent of its commercial ties, and the often dramatic role it has played in French history, Lyon (Lyons) must be counted among the great cities of Europe. In terms of national importance, it is in many respects second only to Paris. Lyon may be said to owe its 2,000 years of vigorous development and a future of dramatic opportunities to its location. Situated in southeastern France, at the strategic junction of the Rhône and Saône rivers and at the termination of major routes across the Alps, it dominates that portion of the European continent that has historically served as a bridge between the ancient cultures of the Mediterranean and the societies that evolved in the lands bordering the North Sea. From its foundation, Lyon functioned both as a crossroads and as a warehouse: as far back as the 16th century, it was also a manufacturing centre and the French capital of the silk industry. For nearly 500 years, the silk industry distinguished Lyon from other similar cities and impressed its mark on the life of the inhabitants as well as on the physical appearance of the city.

Historical development. Before the spectacular development which it experienced in the mid-20th century, Lyons went through three remarkable periods—the Roman conquest, the Renaissance, and the industrialization of the 19th century—each, in its own way, worthy of the admirable geographic situation of the city. Together, they represented three major opportunities for the development of the city, as well as three stages in its physical formation and growth.

Foundation. At the time of Caesar, the settlement at Lyons was a village inhabited by fishermen and boatmen at a spot where the Saône narrowed, facilitating contact between what were to become the districts of Saint-Vincent and Saint-Paul. This early dwelling site bore the name of Condate. In 43 BC Lucius Munatius Plancus, a former lieutenant of Caesar, founded a military colony, Lugdunum, on the nearby hill of Fourvière, overlooking the Rhône-Saône confluence. The Roman emperor Augustus subsequently made Lyons the capital of the Gauls, while his son-in-law, Agrippa, created a network of roads converging on the city. Lyons reached the peak of its classical development in the 2nd century AD, when the youthful settlement was composed of three clusters: the Roman city around the forum (*forum vetus* ["old forum"]=Fourvière); the Gallic city on the slopes of the hill of Croix-Rousse, between the Rhône and the Saône, with the altar of Rome and Augustus and the amphitheatre; and finally the lower city, on the frequently flooded lands of the narrow peninsula at the river confluence, where the tradesmen and the boatsmen had their quarters. It was in this cosmopolitan environment—in which dealers from as far away as Asia were numerous—that the first Christian community of Gaul was established. In 177, under the reign of Marcus Aurelius, the community was persecuted, and in 197 the aristocracy of Lyons, which had sided with the Roman Albinus in his bid for imperial power, was decimated by his rival, Septimius Severus. The decline of the city began shortly after, the decisive blow being the destruction of the aqueducts that brought water to Lyons. The many vestiges of this period of the first flowering of Lyons have made the city of today one of the main centres of Gallo-Roman archaeology.

The Middle Ages. The turbulent Middle Ages coincided with a period of relative obscurity for Lyons, whose inhabitants deserted their hills to settle in a close com-

The rise and fall of the classical city

munity around the churches of Saint-Nizier and Saint-Jean on either side of the bridge across the Saône. The city came under the domination of the archbishop and the church lords of Lyons, whose influence was sufficient to cause important ecumenical councils to be held there in 1245 and again in 1274. Situated in a strife-torn border zone between the Holy Roman Empire and the emergent kingdom of France, Lyons was finally annexed to the latter in 1312, after a long struggle between rising mercantile elements—who had asked the king for aid—and ecclesiastical forces, who were forced, in 1320, to accept the creation of a secular town.

The Renaissance ushered in a period of economic prosperity and intellectual brilliance. The establishment, in 1464, of commercial fairs together with the arrival in the city of Italian merchant bankers, who were welcomed by the local merchants, enabled Lyons to participate in the great economic prosperity which spread across the whole of the contemporary Western world. For a century or more, the city was to be one of the major commercial and banking capitals of Europe. Merchants, notably from Italy and Germany, flocked to Lyons in large numbers, and the local exchange established relations with all the great banking centres of the Continent. Through the abundance of its credit, the city supported the adventures of the king of France in Italy. In 1536 Lyons became a centre for the manufacture of silks in its own right, having initially served as a market for Italian silks in France. Surviving the banking and commercial collapse at the end of the 16th century, the industry, by the 17th century, attained a high degree of perfection in the manufacture of the fine materials that were then captivating Europe. Nor did Lyons fail to shine in the intellectual realm. Printing was introduced as early as 1473, and Lyons soon became one of the most active printing centres in Europe. Poets and architects were among the leading cultural figures of the period during which the city was, in effect, the political, economic, and cultural centre of France.

The French Revolution and its aftermath. For Lyons, the French Revolution brought uneasy times. The collapse of the domestic market and the closing of foreign markets brought a slump in the silk industry, and the political crisis culminated in the tragedy of 1793, when the city—hitherto a supporter of royalist and moderate factions—was besieged by republican forces of the Montagnards and subjected to ruthless reprisals.

The First Empire, by contrast, witnessed another period of reconstruction. Until the end of the 19th century, the commercial prosperity of Lyons was to be based on the manufacture of silk. The city became famous as the home of the *soyeux* (merchants and manufacturers) and the *canuts* ("weavers"). Through the medium of the silk industry, the reputation of Lyons was carried all the way to China. At the same time, Lyons became the seat of workers' uprisings; riots that took place in November 1831 and April 1834 were the prototypes of the class struggles that were soon to characterize the modern industrial era. Furthermore, the silk industry, as a consequence of the large amounts of capital required at all stages of the production and distribution process, brought new prosperity to the banking system. The Credit Lyonnais, founded in 1863 by the financier Henri Germain, developed, through the volume of its transactions, from a purely regional institution into a national and international bank and, for a few years toward the end of the 19th century, the largest in the world in the amount of its deposits.

In the 1880s and 1890s Lyons's overall economic growth accelerated, bringing about a considerable expansion of the silk industry and creating chemical and metallurgical industries. It was the takeoff point for the fourth phase of urban development, one that did not really assert itself until the 1950s, after the periods of stagnation and depression between 1920 and the end of World War II. Only then did Lyon assume the distinctive urban character that continued to pattern its life during the 1970s.

The contemporary city. *Demography.* The vitality of the city has been reflected in its population growth. During the Renaissance, the population grew from approximately 20,000 to between 60,000 and 80,000, placing it among the largest European cities of the period. In the 18th century, the population reached 100,000. Subsequent regular census figures provide an index to the ensuing rate of growth.

Population Growth of Lyon (000)								
	census dates							
	1851	1876	1901	1911	1931	1946	1962	1968
Lyon	177	343	459	524	580	461	536	528
Greater Lyon*	—	—	412	655	702	883	943	1,075

*Includes the city proper and 31 neighbouring communities.

More than two-thirds of the total increase is due to immigration. From 1954 to 1962, for example, 180,000 people settled in Lyon: of these 68 percent were French, and 32 percent were of foreign extraction, of whom 34 percent were North Africans, 31.5 percent Italians, and 18.2 percent Spaniards.

Economic growth. Diversification has been the distinguishing feature of Lyon economic development to the early 1970s. In the mid-19th century, the textile industry, dominated by the manufacture of silk, represented 90 percent of the industrial output. By 1970 this figure had dropped to 20 percent; the production of synthetic fibres such as rayon ranked first. Lyon remains one of the great world centres for the production of high-quality silk, but the production of chemicals has become the key industry. Originally connected with the treatment of textiles, it was given fresh impetus by the manufacture of dyes, synthetic fibres, and—quite markedly in recent years—oil products. At Feyzin, an oil refinery—the largest French unit for steam cracking—is the key factor behind the local organic chemistry industry, which is the most advanced in the country. The important metallurgical industry includes a wide variety of processes, varying from foundries to the construction of mechanical, electrical, and electronic equipment. The Berliet works at Vénissieux, southeast of Lyon, are responsible for more than 50 percent of the national output of buses and trucks. The construction, food, and printing industries are prosperous.

Sources of émigrés

Bernard P. Wolff—Photo Researchers

Cathedral of Saint-Jean, Lyon, on the bank of the Saône, seen from the west front. Grouped around the cathedral are medieval and Renaissance buildings.

Early worker uprisings

City regions. Throughout its history, Lyon had expanded to meet the needs created by a succession of new activities. As the city gradually spread to the left bank of the Rhône, its centre of gravity moved steadily toward the east. In the 10th century, it was located on either side of the bridge crossing the Saône, shifting to the centre of the nearby peninsula in the 18th and 19th centuries. It then ran along an axis running from the Place des Terreaux and the town hall—a masterpiece of French civic architecture—to the north, and to Perrache, the main railroad station, to the south. This urban core consisted of several large parallel streets laid out during the Second Empire, a period marked for Lyon no less than for Paris by energetic town planning. By the early 1970s the centre of gravity seemed permanently established on the left bank of the Rhône, where an ambitious project was under construction at Part-Dieu.

The urban core

There is a zone of factory and residential suburbs encircling Lyon, a belt whose total population exceeds that of the city proper. On the right bank of the Saône, Vieux Lyon ("Old Lyon") remains as one of the finest surviving architectural complexes of the Renaissance era. The peninsula is now the heart of the business district, crowded with banks, offices, and hotels. The east bank of the Rhône is divided between a wealthy area, the Brotteaux, sited around a diverted portion of the river near the Parc de la Tête d'Or, and a district with factories and workers' houses extending east toward the fringing communities of Villeurbanne and Bron. To the south, along the Rhône, Feyzin and Saint-Fons constitute one of the largest oil-refining complexes in France. On the plateau between the Saône and the Rhône, the old district of La Croix-Rousse, once the home of the *canuts*, has now grown toward the north and has become a suburb characterized by factories and residential buildings.

Administration. This recent urban expansion has affected the administrative and political organization not so much in terms of overall structure but rather in the way that structure functions. The city is administered by a mayor assisted by a municipal council. One man, Édouard Herriot, a powerful local figure, held the position of mayor for half a century (1905–57). The Paris government is represented by a *préfet* ("prefect"), combining the powers of *préfet* of the Rhône *département* and *préfet* of the Rhône-Alps region, grouping eight *départements*. In an effort to meet new problems common to the city and to its rapidly growing suburbs, new institutions have been created. These are the *agglomération urbaine* ("urban agglomeration"), made up of 31 towns including Lyon; the *communauté urbaine* ("urban community"), established in 1969 and made up of 56 towns; and the *région métropolitaine* ("metropolitan area"), in which Lyon is associated with the urban and industrial centre of Saint-Étienne to the southwest.

Transportation. Caught in fierce competition with the other French metropolitan centres, which act as counterweights to Paris, the Lyon of the 1970s found its future closely linked with the availability and quality of transportation facilities. By train, Lyon is only four hours away from Paris and three from Marseille. Navigation on the Saône has benefitted from improvements that make it accessible to the type of heavy barges (up to 1,350 tons) that are used on the Rhine; likewise, considerable work has been done on the Rhône (*q.v.*), resulting in the development of irrigation and electric energy and opening the river to navigation. Crude oil is carried by pipeline from the Gulf of Berre on the Mediterranean coast to the oil refinery of Feyzin, while another pipeline brings natural gas from Lacq in the southwest of France. An expressway provides a strong road link between Paris, Lyon, and Marseille, while in the 1960s Lyon became an important centre for domestic air travel. The rapid growth of air traffic, coupled with the construction of a new airport at Satolas, seemed certain to make Lyon one of the major international travel centres.

Culture. First and foremost a business centre, Lyon is nevertheless a city with a remarkable cultural tradition. In the 16th century culture and wealth went hand in hand, but it was not until the 19th century that Lyon became a university town. In 1896 the schools of law, medicine and pharmacy, sciences, and liberal arts were merged into one university that 75 years later had over 43,000 students. A few prestigious schools helped give Lyon the reputation of being the most important educational centre outside Paris. Educational reforms in 1968 provided for the development of several interdisciplinary universities. Cultural life is reflected in the riches of the local museums, which include a textile collection, the archaeological museum at Fourvière, a museum of fine arts, and a museum of printing and banking. The collections of the municipal library are noted for their specimens of items from the first 50 years of printing and rare books. City theatres include the Opéra, the Célestins (a municipal theatre), and some avant-garde companies that have gained national recognition. Music and drama festivals, held every year in June in the Roman theatre at Fourvière, provide a reminder of the long history of the city.

BIBLIOGRAPHY. R. GASCON, *Grand Commerce et vie urbaine au XVIème siècle: Lyon et ses marchands* (1971), deals with economic history in the 16th century, and, together with A. AUDIN, *Lyon, miroir de Rome dans les Gaules* (1965), on ancient history; C.M. LEONARD, *Lyon Transformed: Public Works of the Second Empire, 1853–64* (1961); J. BOUVIER, *Le Crédit Lyonnais de 1863 à 1882: les années de formation d'une banque de dépôts*, 2 vol. (1961), an economic history; M. LAFERRERE, *Lyon, ville industrielle* (1960), an industrial-historical study; F. RUDE, *L'Insurrection lyonnaise de novembre 1831*, 2nd ed. (1969), a study of 19th-century riots; and A. KLEINCLAUSCZ, *Histoire de Lyon*, 3 vol. (1939–52), all offer pictures of Lyon's history at different times. C.G.E. BUNT, *The Silks of Lyons* (1960), deals with the city's longest established industry, while J. LABASSE, *Les Capitaux et la region* (1955), studies its economic supremacy. R. JULLIAN, *Lyon, ville d'art* (1960), describes Lyon and its monuments from an aesthetic standpoint.

(R.Ga.)

Lysenko, Trofim Denisovich

Trofim Denisovich Lysenko, a Soviet biologist and agronomist, became the virtual dictator of biology in the Communist world in the 1930s, during the regime of Josef Stalin. As such, Lysenko succeeded in having his own biological theories officially adopted throughout the Soviet Union, even though Lysenkoism was rejected by virtually all scientists elsewhere. After Stalin's death in 1953, he was supported by Nikita Khrushchev and was not removed from his administrative duties until 1965, after Khrushchev himself had lost his position of authority.

Sovfoto

Lysenko, 1938.

Lysenko was born in 1898 in Karlovka (now Poltava *oblast* [region]). He was graduated from the Uman School of Horticulture in 1921 and was stationed at the Belaya Tserkov Selection Station in the same year. After his 1925 graduation from the Kiev Agricultural Institute, with the degree of doctor of agricultural science, he was stationed at the Gandzha (now Kirovabad) Experimental Station until 1929. From 1929 to 1934 he held the office of senior specialist in the department of physiology of the Ukrainian All-Union Institute of Selection and Genetics in Odessa. Rising rapidly to the top of his profession, he became, in turn, the scientific director of the All-Union Selection and Genetics Institute at Odessa from 1935 to 1936 and its Director from 1936 to 1938. Ultimately, he became the Director of the Institute of Genetics of the U.S.S.R. Academy of Sciences from 1940 to 1965.

Advocacy of vernalization

Lysenko first rose to prominence through his advocacy of vernalization, a method of breaking the rest period of the seeds that are normally shed in autumn. The method involves immersing the seeds in water, which is then frozen. Lysenko was credited with the discovery of this technique, although it was an ancient practice and had been used elsewhere since the 19th century. It speeded the germination of winter wheat so that even seeds planted in the spring could mature before the killing frosts of autumn. Lysenko promised quick results without time-consuming field tests. He also tried vernalization of spring varieties. The practice had been abandoned in the United States after the development of new varieties of wheat. In 1929, however, the practice became official in the Soviet Union. Lysenko claimed that the changes induced by vernalization were inherited and that the practice need not be repeated year after year. A number of biologists outside of the U.S.S.R. promptly called attention to this revival of the doctrine of the inheritance of acquired characters (Lamarckism), which had long been scientifically discredited. Even though vernalization failed to increase farm production, Lysenko in 1935 obtained the public support of Stalin.

As his influence increased, Lysenko undertook to modify and redefine all biological theory. Some of his innovations were mere exercises in verbalism, such as his doctrine of the phasic development of plants. According to this concept, the plant develops in recessive phases, each of which has requirements that differ from those of the other phases; and each plant requirement manifests itself in its own way. Altering one stage in development by environmental means would cause successive stages to be changed, he claimed; such changes, presumably beneficial adaptations, would be inherited. He redefined heredity as the capacity of the living body to demand definite conditions for its life and development and to react in a definite way to any given set of conditions. Heredity, he stated, is the end result of environmental changes that have been assimilated during the course of the preceding generations. Ultimately, of course, this concept of heredity led Lysenko to attack Mendelian genetics, which was universally accepted by biologists elsewhere. Even though by the 1930s sound ideas concerning the biochemistry of the gene were being advanced in the West, and the process of natural selection was indeed explained by Mendelian genetics, Lysenko dismissed the chromosome theory of heredity as "idealistic" and anti-Darwinian. Lysenko was so successful with the attack that the topic could not be taught in the Soviet Union from 1948 to 1964.

Lysenko also claimed that he could produce new types of developmental cycles in plants by regulating the quality of their nutrients. To do this he first had to shatter the conservatism of the plant and thus render it more sensitive to environmental changes. He shattered this conservatism by using adverse environmental conditions, hybridization, and grafting. He was especially impressed with the consequences of grafting and held that the stock and the scion (or cutting) so influenced each other that they fused to form a true hybrid.

Lysenko was not alone in the Soviet Union in his advocacy of an aberrant biology, nor was genetics the only biological science that came under attack. By the early 1930s a powerful antiscientific cabal had developed; ultimately it succeeded in gaining complete control of all biological teaching and research in the U.S.S.R. Lysenko was the spearhead of the group, but he was ably seconded by the theoretician Isaak Israilovich Prezent and the agronomist Vasily Robertovich Vilyams. At first other Soviet biologists resisted, but the strength of the attackers was soon evident. Genetics had made such progress in the Soviet Union that under the leadership of N.I. Vavilov

the International Congress of Genetics scheduled its 1937 meeting to be held in Moscow. Vavilov was widely respected outside the Soviet Union because of his expeditions in many parts of the world to study the origin, diversity, and distribution of cultivated plants. In December 1936, however, the Soviets suddenly cancelled the meeting, an unmistakable indication of the political strength of the Lysenko group. In 1939 Lysenko gave his report as chairman of the Lenin All-Union Academy of Agricultural Science; in it he assailed Vavilov personally. The next year Vavilov was arrested and exiled in Siberia, where he died in 1942 or 1943. With the elimination of Vavilov, Lysenko and his group secured complete control of biology in the U.S.S.R.

Suppression of Mendelian genetics

Lysenko succeeded in extirpating Mendelian genetics when he presided at the 1948 meeting of the Lenin Academy of Agricultural Science. Five geneticists who had defended Mendel recanted, admitted their errors, and committed themselves to the biology that Lysenko advocated. The entire transactions of the meeting were published in the Soviet newspaper *Pravda*, and the official *Proceedings* was soon issued in both Russian and English. At this meeting, Lysenko reached the full height of his political power. Previous honours included election to the U.S.S.R. and Ukrainian academies of science, being proclaimed a Hero of Socialist Labour, a receipt of the Order of Lenin eight times and the Stalin Prize three times (in 1941, 1943, and 1949). He served as president of the Lenin Academy of Agricultural Science from 1938 to 1956 and from 1961 to 1962.

In 1948 Soviet authorities apparently were anticipating a worldwide revolution in biology, which did not occur. Wherever biologists were free to reject Lysenko's line, they did so. Even in the Soviet Union, he did not persuade scientists in other fields. By 1952 his interpretations were being assailed by men in his own field, and in 1954 his personal honesty was questioned. (A dissertation of one of Lysenko's students was rejected, and it took all of his political power and a vicious struggle later to have it accepted.) The rehabilitation of Vavilov's reputation was begun, and the struggle in biological theory was soon resumed. Lysenko was weakened because he had personally made it impossible for the collective farms to grow hybrid corn. His position against hybrid corn gave his opponents the opportunity to continue their own work, and only the support of Khrushchev kept Lysenko in a position of importance.

Following Khrushchev's fall in 1964, Lysenko was stripped of his political authority. He and his followers, however, retained their degrees, their titles, and their academic positions, and remained free to support their aberrant trend in biology.

BIBLIOGRAPHY. Lysenko's rise to power and the beginning of his fall are recorded in CONWAY ZIRKLE (ed.), *The Death of a Science in Russia* (1949), and in "L'Affaire Lysenko," *J. Hered.*, 47:46–54 (1956). DAVID JORAVSKY, *Soviet Marxism and Natural Science* (1961) and his *Lysenko Affair* (1970), contain excellent factual accounts of the entire imbroglio. ZHORES A. MEDVEDEV, *The Rise and Fall of T.D. Lysenko* (Eng. trans. 1969), gives a detailed inside view of the entire controversy. LYSENKO's own books, in translation, *Heredity and Its Variability* (1946), and *The Science of Biology Today* (1948), record his views.

(C.Z.)

MacArthur, Douglas

Brilliant and controversial throughout his long career, Gen. Douglas MacArthur was summoned from retirement in 1941 and achieved greatness as Allied commander of the Southwest Pacific Theater in World War II, of the postwar Japanese occupation, and finally of the United Nations forces in Korea, 1950–51. Earlier he had won fame in World War I as a heroic general and during the Great Depression as the United States Army's chief of staff.

Early life

MacArthur was born January 26, 1880, at Little Rock, Arkansas, the third son of Arthur MacArthur, later the army's senior ranking officer, and Mary Hardy MacArthur, an ambitious woman who strongly influenced Douglas. He graduated from West Point in 1903 with the highest honours in his class and served the next ten years as an aide and a junior engineering officer, following this with four years on the general staff. He spent several months with the U.S. troops that occupied Veracruz, Mexico, in 1914.

MacArthur, 1945.

On the 42nd Division's staff in 1917–19, MacArthur was variously chief of staff, brigade commander, and divisional commander during combat operations in France during World War I and in the Rhine occupation that followed. During the 1920s he initiated far-reaching reforms while superintendent at West Point, served on William ("Billy") Mitchell's court-martial, held two commands in the Philippines, commanded two U.S. corps areas, and headed the 1928 American Olympic Committee.

Having advanced in rank to brigadier general in 1918 and to major general seven years later, MacArthur was promoted to general when he was selected as army chief of staff in 1930. His efforts as military head for the next five years were largely directed toward preserving the army's meagre strength during the Depression. MacArthur was widely criticized in mid-1932 when he sent regular troops to oust the Bonus Army of veterans from Washington. In 1935–41 he served as Philippines military adviser (and field marshal), endeavouring, despite inadequate funds, to build a Filipino defense force. He retired from the U.S. Army in December 1937.

MacArthur married Mrs. Louise Cromwell Brooks in 1922, but the childless union ended in divorce seven years later. In 1937 he married Jean Faircloth; Arthur, their only child, was born in Manila the next year.

Duty in World War II

Recalled to active duty in July 1941, MacArthur conducted a valiant delaying action against the Japanese in the Philippines after war erupted in December. He was ordered to Australia in March 1942 to command Allied forces in the Southwest Pacific Theater. He soon launched an offensive in New Guinea that drove the Japanese out of Papua by January 1943. In a series of operations in 1943–44, MacArthur's troops seized strategic points in New Guinea from Lae to Sansapor, while capturing the Admiralties and western New Britain. The simultaneous northward movement of South Pacific forces in the Solomons, over whom MacArthur maintained strategic control, neutralized Rabaul and bypassed many Japanese units.

After winning a decision to invade the Philippines next rather than Formosa, MacArthur attacked Morotai, Leyte, and Mindoro in autumn 1944. Not until the Leyte operation did he have overwhelming logistical support; his earlier plans had been executed despite inadequacies of personnel and matériel and with little assistance from the Pacific Fleet. MacArthur seriously questioned his superiors' decision to give priority to the European war over the Pacific conflict and to the Central Pacific Theater over his Southwest Pacific area.

His largest, costliest operations occurred during the seven-month Luzon campaign in 1945. That spring he also undertook the reconquest of the southern Philippines and Borneo. Meanwhile, he left the difficult mopping-up operations in New Guinea and the Solomons to the Australian Army. He was promoted to general of the army in December 1944 and was appointed commander of all U.S. army forces in the Pacific four months later. He was in charge of the surrender ceremony in Tokyo Bay on September 2, 1945.

As Allied commander of the Japanese occupation, 1945–51, MacArthur effectively if autocratically directed the demobilization of Japanese military forces, the expurgation of militarists, the restoration of the economy, and the drafting of a liberal constitution. Significant reforms were inaugurated in land redistribution, education, labour, public health, and women's rights. While he was in Japan, MacArthur also headed the army's Far East command.

When the Korean War began in 1950, MacArthur was soon selected to command United Nations forces there. After stemming the North Korean advance near Pusan, he carried out a daring landing at Inch'ŏn in September and advanced into North Korea in October as the North Korean Army rapidly disintegrated. In November, however, massive Chinese forces attacked MacArthur's divided army above the 38th parallel and forced it to retreat to below Seoul. Two months later MacArthur's troops returned to the offensive, driving into North Korea again. On April 11, 1951, Pres. Harry S. Truman relieved MacArthur of his commands because of the general's insubordination and unwillingness to conduct a limited war. Returning to the United States for the first time since before World War II, MacArthur at first received widespread popular support; the excitement waned after a publicized Senate investigation of his dismissal.

UN command in Korean War

In 1944, 1948, and 1952, conservative Republican groups tried in vain to obtain MacArthur's nomination for the presidency. MacArthur accepted the board chairmanship of the Remington Rand Corporation in 1952; thereafter, except for these duties and rare public appearances, he lived in seclusion in New York City. He died in Washington, D.C., on April 5, 1964, and was buried at Norfolk, Virginia.

In personality MacArthur was enigmatic and contradictory. To many he seemed imperious, aloof, egotistical, and pretentious. To others, especially his headquarters staff, he appeared warm, courageous, unostentatious, and even humble. Most authorities agree that he possessed superior intelligence, rare command ability, and zealous dedication to duty, honour, and country.

BIBLIOGRAPHY. D. CLAYTON JAMES, *The Years of MacArthur*, vol. 1, *1880–1941* (1970), the first volume of a projected three-volume study by a United States historian; FRAZIER HUNT, *The Untold Story of Douglas MacArthur* (1954), by an admiring correspondent; GAVIN LONG, *MacArthur As Military Commander* (1969), a candid Australian view; DOUGLAS MACARTHUR, *Reminiscences* (1964), completed just before his death; CHARLES A. WILLOUGHBY and JOHN R. CHAMBERLAIN, *MacArthur, 1941–1951* (1954); CHARLES A. WILLOUGHBY (ed.), *Reports of General MacArthur*, 4 vol. (1966), by MacArthur's intelligence chief, covering the years 1941–48; COURTNEY WHITNEY, *MacArthur* (1956), by a general close to MacArthur.

(D.C.J.)

Macau

Macau, or Macao, is an overseas province of Portugal situated on the south China coast. It is located on the western side of the Chu Chiang (Pearl River) Estuary, at the head of which is the Chinese port of Kwang-chou (Canton), and it stands opposite the British crown colony of Hong Kong, on the eastern side of the estuary. It has a total area of six square miles (16 square kilometres) and a population in the early 1970s of about 250,000. Macau consists of a small and narrow peninsula projecting from the Chinese mainland province of Kwangtung, from which it is separated by the symbolically imposing Barrier Gate, and of two small offshore islands, Taipa and Coloane. The city of Macau stands on the peninsula, overlooking the Chinese island of La-pa Shan (Lappa), from which it is separated by Duck Channel. The name Macau is derived from the Chinese A-mangao, or Bay of the Goddess A-ma, the patroness of sailors.

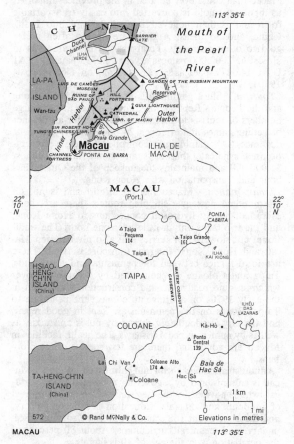

MACAU

A possession of Portugal for more than 400 years, Macau is now Portuguese by the terms of a treaty with China concluded in 1887. Despite a veneer of Portuguese architecture and custom, it has retained its Chinese character, and during the 20th century the province has been much affected by events in China. Macau's existence has always been closely related to trade activities, and trade has been restricted by the government of the People's Republic of China. Since about 1950 a large number of refugees from China have crossed the border into Macau. While the province's frontiers are not definitely agreed upon, a conciliatory policy by the Portuguese has met with a favourable response from the Peking government, so that peaceful relations based upon mutual advantage are maintained between the small province and its powerful neighbour. Apart from being a focus for trading with mainland China, Macau is renowned for its gambling and gold-smuggling activities. While Portugal continues to view Macau as an overseas province, the United Nations in 1960 declared it to be a Portuguese non-self-governing territory. (For articles on political units in the immediate vicinity, see HONG KONG; KWANGTUNG; see also CANTON; for associated physical features, see CHINA SEA; HSI CHIANG; for historical aspects see CHINA, HISTORY OF; PORTUGAL, HISTORY OF).

The natural landscape. *Relief.* The peninsula of Macau occupies a total area of about two square miles; the island of Taipa has an area of about 1.5 square miles, and the island of Coloane is some 2.5 square miles in area. No part of Macau is of any great height, though the peninsula is undulating enough to form an attractive urban site. The highest point, 571 feet, is on the island of Coloane. There are no permanent rivers, and water either is collected during rains or is imported from China.

Both the peninsula and the islands consist of small granite hills surrounded by limited areas of flatland formed by recent alluvial deposits from the Chu Chiang. Additional

Taipa and Coloane (margin note)

flatland has been created on the peninsula by reclamation, primarily on the eastern side. Between the western side of the peninsula and the Chinese mainland, at the mouth of Duck Channel, is a narrow stretch of sheltered water known as the Pôrto Interior (Inner Harbour). This formed a safe anchorage in the earliest days of the Portuguese presence and was subsequently developed with wharves and jetties. Today, it is the anchorage for Macau's fishing fleet and is also a berthing place for freighters and for the large river steamers that ply as ferries between Macau and Hong Kong, 40 miles to the east. The newer Pôrto Exterior (Outer Harbour) is protected by a breakwater on the eastern side of the peninsula. Over the years it has become heavily silted, but access is still possible by the hydrofoil service that runs between Macau and Hong Kong, operated by two companies that have interests in both places.

Climate. Macau lies just within the tropics. Four-fifths of its total annual rainfall of between 40 and 100 inches falls within the summer rainy season, when the southwest monsoon blows from April to September. Besides being rainy, the summer months are also hot, humid, and unpleasant. The hottest month of the year is July, when temperatures average 82° F (28° C). Relative humidities of over 80 percent are quite usual in the summer. Winters, on the other hand, can be delightful. Very little rain falls, and the relative humidity is low. November is the best month; bright and sunny weather can be expected almost without interruption. The coldest month is January; its average temperature is 59° F (15° C).

Vegetation and animal life. The natural vegetation is evergreen monsoonal forest, but the hills have long since been stripped of their timber for firewood and construction. For the most part, they are covered with short grasses and patches of scrub. Reforestation has been undertaken on Coloane. There is very little animal life apart from a few civet cats.

Settlement patterns. Only small, restricted patches of farmland exist on the islands, and the rural settlements are small. Rectangular wooden buildings roofed with sheets of corrugated metal are scattered among irrigated patches of farmland. The chief crops are vegetables, especially Chinese cabbage, onions, lettuce, and beans. Almost the entire peninsula is occupied by Macau city, which has a placid atmosphere. The tempo of life is nevertheless increasing, especially because of the growing volume of tourists. In the early 1970s there were still relatively few buildings of more than five stories in height, and the Portuguese imprint was clear in much of the architecture and in the wash colouring—pink, lime, and pale yellow—of many of the buildings, some of which remain from the early days of the occupation.

Macau city (margin note)

History. The history of Macau as a Portuguese possession spans more than four centuries. The first Portuguese ship anchored in the Chu Chiang Estuary in 1513, and further Portuguese visits followed regularly. Trade with China was placed on an official basis in 1553. Although Chinese records indicate that the Portuguese used Macau as early as 1535, the occupation of the colony is traditionally recognized as dating from 1557. The Roman Catholic diocese of Macau was created by the Holy See in 1575 and was initially given jurisdiction over the whole of the Far East. Trade flourished, and Macau became the principal entrepôt for international trade with China and Japan.

Toward the end of the 18th century, however, China's trade with the outside world was gradually centralized in Canton, where trading posts were opened for the use of foreign merchants. But since merchants were allowed into Canton only during the trading season—from November to May—the international merchant community established itself at Macau. A period of prosperity for Macau followed, but it soon ended because of disputes between the Chinese authorities and the European merchants over the opium trade, the consequent war between Great Britain and China, and the occupation of Hong Kong as a British colony in 1841. In 1849 the Portuguese abolished the Chinese customhouse in Macau and established Portuguese jurisdiction over the territory. But

Decline of trade (margin note)

Hong Kong quickly eclipsed Macau in trade, and within a few years the merchants had largely deserted the Portuguese possession, which never again became a major entrepôt. The Outer Harbour was built in 1926. In 1939, after the capture of Canton by the Japanese and the closure of the Hong Kong–Kowloon border, much of southern China's trade was briefly diverted to Macau.

The people. There have always been relatively few Portuguese in Macau, and many of the Portuguese residents have come from other Portuguese possessions, rather than from Portugal itself. The Chinese element in the population, until recent years, had been largely local in character. But, with the unsettled state of China since the 1920s, refugees have arrived even from relatively distant Chinese provinces. Between 1920 and 1927 the population showed a sudden increase, due to immigration, from about 80,000 to some 160,000, and by 1939 it had reached a total of 245,000. Many returned to China during the 1940s, when the war with Japan reached southern China, but refugee immigration increased immediately after World War II. By 1960 the population numbered 169,000. Census figures in 1970 showed an increase to about 1939 levels.

There were 7,460 Portuguese nationals living in Macau in 1970, 240,000 Chinese (97 percent of the total population), and about 1,170 foreigners. Most members of the civil service, the police, and the armed forces are Portuguese, 89 percent of whom were born in Macau. In contrast, more than half of the Chinese—53 percent—were born outside Macau. Although during the course of its history Macau achieved fame as an evangelical centre, the number of Roman Catholics in 1970 was only 23,000. There were also about 2,000 Protestants. Non-Christians, including Buddhists and Taoists, numbered 191,000, and those of no stated religion about 30,000.

(margin) The ethnic composition

Macau, Area and Population

Municipalities	area		population	
	sq mi	sq km	1960 census	1970 census
Ilhas*	3.90	10.09	8,000	7,000
Macau	2.09	5.42	161,000†	241,000
Total Macau	5.99	15.51	169,000	249,000‡

*Comprising the islands of Coloane and Taipa; administered from Macau. †Includes all population living on sampans and other vessels. ‡Figures do not add to total given because of rounding.
Source: Official government figures.

The economy. *Fishing, trade, and industry.* Except for fish in the nearby Chu Chiang Estuary, Macau has few natural resources. It is, however, a free port, and trade continues to be economically important. In recent years the fishing industry encountered difficulties because of China's insistence that the limits of its territorial waters be respected, with the result that nearby Chinese communes exact a proportion of each catch from Macau boats. The pattern of trade has also changed radically, because China has restricted the entry of goods from Macau. Yet China continues to be of major importance to Macau as a supplier of food and certain cheap consumer goods, such as textiles, clothing, toys, and cheap electrical goods; in fact, Macau ranks second only to Hong Kong in the importation of goods from China. Some industrialization has taken place in Macau during the 1950s and 1960s, largely in response to the availability of the settlement's relatively cheap labour. As a result, textiles now form by far the most important export, and footwear and enamelware industries are also developing. The free movement of industrial goods produced in Macau to the Portuguese overseas provinces has been permitted since 1957. This concession has greatly helped Macau's export industries.

In addition to the newer products, Macau has long manufactured firecrackers (largely for use in the United States), Chinese wines, incense sticks, and camphorwood chests. At present Hong Kong is Macau's biggest export market, followed by West Germany. Tourism is grow-

(margin) Manufactures for export

ing rapidly in importance, often in the form of day visits of hydrofoil parties of Japanese tourists, who come via Hong Kong. Macau has long had a reputation for gold smuggling. Certainly, far more gold is imported into Macau than could ever be used in the province. Imported as ingots, the gold is converted into easily transportable form and is then believed to find its way into India, China, and Southeast Asia, where people often prefer gold to other currency. Total visible trade amounts to almost 650,000,000 patacas a year (6.0533 patacas = $1 U.S.; 14.5279 patacas = £1 sterling, on December 1, 1970).

Tourism. Since gambling is prohibited in Hong Kong and the People's Republic of China, Macau attracts large numbers of tourists to its casinos, which offer all manner of betting games and are open 24 hours a day, and to its dog races. All gambling is controlled by a government-licensed syndicate that pays an annual tax of almost $1,000,000 and maintains the upkeep of the Outer Harbour and transportation with Hong Kong.

Transportation. Macau has no airport and is not on international passenger-shipping routes; there are, however, half-hourly hydrofoil connections to Hong Kong, and the trip takes only a little over one hour. The traditional but slower river ferries still also ply between Macau and Hong Kong. Internal transport is good. There are local ferries between the peninsula and the islands. Taipa and Coloane are connected by a causeway over which an auto road runs, and construction was begun in the early 1970s on a bridge to connect the peninsula to Taipa. Roads on the peninsula are kept in good repair, and the city is adequately served by buses and taxis, as well as by numerous pedal trishaws. The health facilities in Macau are good, and there are few serious crime problems.

Administration and social and cultural conditions. Macau is administered by a governor appointed from Portugal, who is advised by the Legislative Council, composed of residents and officials. Education is not compulsory, and there are about 168 schools, offering elementary, secondary, and technical curriculums. About 80 percent of the population over the age of 10 is literate.

Chinese culture is dominant in the province; it is manifest in Macau city's many pleasant gardens, in its statue of the Chinese Nationalist leader Sun Yat-sen, and in the local passion for the Chinese game of Mah-Jongg, a form of rummy played with painted tiles instead of cards. Portuguese influence can be seen in the frequent performances of traditional dancers and fado singers, who present plaintive Portuguese folk tunes at the leading hotels. The cuisine is a delicious blend of Chinese, Portuguese, and African cooking. Cultural institutions include the Biblioteca Nacional de Macau (National Library of Macau), Biblioteca Sir Robert Ho Tung (Sir Robert Ho Tung's Chinese Library), and the Museu Luis de Camões (Luis de Camões Museum), commemorating the 16th-century Portuguese poet. There is no television broadcasting, though programs can be received from Hong Kong. There are several Chinese newspapers, both Communist and non-Communist. English-language newspapers arrive from Hong Kong daily.

(margin) Chinese and Portuguese cultural influences

Prospects for the future. Macau was seriously affected by pro-Communist riots early in 1967, which led to, among other things, the withdrawal of the British consulate and a perhaps greater measure of concealed control over Macau from Peking than before. Yet, with the rapid development of tourism and the expansion of manufacturing that has characterized the period since the riots, the economic future of Macau in the mid-1970s seemed brighter than for many years, provided the modus vivendi that prevailed with Peking could be maintained.

BIBLIOGRAPHY. J.M. BRAGA, *Macau: A Short Handbook*, rev. ed. (1968), a readable general survey, strong on the historical side, but also dealing with contemporary Macau, especially its trade; PROVINCIA DE MACAU, *X Recenseamento Geral da População em Macau, Taipa e Coloane* (1960), the latest census report available; INSTITUTO NACIONAL DE ESTATISTICA, DELEGACAO DE MACAU, *Anuário Estatístico de Macau* (1969), a convenient handbook of official statistics covering climate, population, trade, cultural life, religious affiliation, public administration, and other matters; and *Comércio Externo* (annual), the official trade statistics.

(D.J.D.)

Macaulay, Thomas Babington

English politician, orator, administrator, essayist, and historian, Macaulay, after early years in political life, achieved celebrity with his *Critical and Historical Essays* and lasting fame with his *History of England*, which brought him contemporary acclaim and a secure, if diminished, place among English historians as the founder, with his contemporary Henry Hallam, of what is now known as the Whig interpretation of history. Fostered in the traditions of sturdy evangelical piety and liberal reform, he saw the origin and triumph of these values in the Revolution of 1688, which firmly established the supremacy of Parliament and restricted the monarchy to a constitutional status. He planned to write the history of England from 1688 to 1820 (the death of George III) but died before he had completed the reign of William III, who became king at the revolution and died in 1702. Macaulay's work is thus an account of that revolution, with a narration of the years preceding and following it. In stressing the unique importance for England of the revolution and, by implication, the superior virtues of those who brought it about, traditionally the Whig Party (though the Tories were also involved), Macaulay popularized a view of English history that was notably followed by his nephew Sir George Otto Trevelyan and his great-nephew George Macaulay Trevelyan and that affected the teaching of history as late as World War II. His essays helped to mold the outlook of a generation of Englishmen and to give to many their first vivid glimpse of the past, together with a conviction that their own institutions would serve the best interests of developing countries under their care. His style, clear, emphatic, and insensitive, with short sentences forming a self-contained paragraph, came to be for half a century the characteristic English style in higher journalism and exposition of all kinds. Macaulay's reputation, immense during the last decade of his life, fell steadily in the 50 years that followed. His undisguised political partisanship, his arrogant assumption that English bourgeois standards of culture and progress were to be forever the norm for less favoured nations, and the materialism of his judgments of value and taste all came under heavy fire from such near-contemporary critics as Thomas Carlyle, Matthew Arnold, and John Ruskin. Moreover, a revolution in the realm of historical studies, already accomplished in Germany during Macaulay's lifetime but never appreciated by him, soon affected English historiography. Wide as was Macaulay's reading, his approach was largely uncritical, as his enthusiasm often carried him away. By taste and training an orator, his writing was special pleading rather than impartial presentation. Yet, despite these severe limitations, his greatness is incontrovertible, and, regarded solely as a work of art, the status of his *History* remains unassailed. In the grasp and range of his knowledge, in his powers of vivid and sustained narrative, and in his marshalling of topics to serve a great design, his *History* is unsurpassed among the work of English historians, save, perhaps, by *The History of the Decline and Fall of the Roman Empire* of Edward Gibbon.

Early life and political career. Macaulay was born at Rothley Temple, the house of an uncle in Leicestershire, on October 25, 1800. His father, Zachary Macaulay, the son of a Presbyterian minister from the Hebrides, had been governor of Sierra Leone; an ardent philanthropist and an ally of William Wilberforce, who fought for the abolition of slavery, he was a man of severe evangelical piety. Macaulay's mother, a Quaker, was the daughter of a Bristol bookseller. Thomas was the eldest of their nine children and devoted to his family, his deepest affection being reserved for two of his sisters, Hannah and Margaret. When eight years old he had written a compendium of universal history and also "The Battle of Cheviot," a romantic narrative poem in the style of Sir Walter Scott. After attending a private school, in

Marginal note: Development of a new view of history

Macaulay, oil painting by J. Partridge, 1840. In the National Portrait Gallery, London.
By courtesy of the National Portrait Gallery, London

1818 he went to Trinity College, Cambridge, where he held a fellowship until 1831 and where he gained a reputation for inexhaustible talk and genial companionship in a circle of brilliant young men. In 1825 the first of his essays, that on Milton, published in *The Edinburgh Review*, brought him immediate fame and the chance to display his social gifts on a wider stage; he was courted and admired by the most distinguished personages of the day.

He studied law and was called to the bar in 1826, but never practiced seriously. When his father's commercial interests failed, he undertook the support of his whole family by writing and teaching, and obtained a minor government post. He aspired to a political career, and in 1830 he entered Parliament as member for Calne in Wiltshire.

Marginal note: Parliamentary career

During the debates that preceded the passage of the Reform Act (1832), he eloquently supported the cause of parliamentary reform and was regarded as a leading figure in an age of great orators. He became a member and later the secretary of the Board of Control, which supervised the administration of India by the East India Company. Working on Indian affairs by day and attending the House of Commons in the evenings, he nevertheless found time to write a ballad, "The Armada," as well as eight literary and historical essays for *The Edinburgh Review*.

In the first parliament elected after the act of 1832, Macaulay was one of the two members from the newly enfranchised borough of Leeds. He soon faced a problem of conscience when the question of slavery was debated. As a holder of government office he was expected to vote for an amendment proposed by the ministry but disapproved by the abolitionists. He offered his resignation and spoke against the government; but since the House of Commons supported the abolitionists and the government gave way, he remained in office.

Administration in India. In 1834 Macaulay accepted an invitation to serve on the recently created Supreme Council of India, foreseeing that he could save from his salary enough to give him a competence for life. He took his sister Hannah with him and reached India at a vital moment when effective government by the East India Company was being superseded by that of the British crown. In this he was able to play an important part, throwing his weight in favour of the liberty of the press and of the equality of Europeans and Indians before the law. He inaugurated a national system of education, Western in outlook, and as president of a commission on Indian jurisprudence he drafted a penal code that later became the basis of Indian criminal law. Meanwhile, he suffered two personal blows: his sister Margaret died in England, and in 1835 his sister Hannah left him to marry a promising young servant of the East India Company, Charles Trevelyan.

History of England

Later life and writings. Macaulay returned to England in 1838 and entered Parliament as a member for Edinburgh. He became secretary for war in 1839, with a seat in Lord Melbourne's cabinet, but the ministry fell in 1841, and he found the leisure to publish his *Lays of Ancient Rome* (1842) and a collection of *Critical and Historical Essays* (1843). He was made paymaster general when Lord John Russell became prime minister in 1846, but spoke only five times in the parliamentary session of 1846–47. In the latter year he lost his seat at Edinburgh, where he had neglected local interests. He had, in fact, lost much of his interest in politics, and retired into private life with a sense of relief, settling down to work on his *History of England*. His composition was slow, with endless corrections both of matter and style; he spared no pains to ascertain the facts, often visiting the scene of historical events. The first two volumes appeared in 1849 and achieved an unprecedented success, edition after edition selling well both in Britain and in the United States. When the Whigs returned to power in 1852 he refused a seat in the cabinet, but was returned to Parliament by Edinburgh, and took his seat. Soon afterward he developed a heart disease and thenceforth played little part in politics. The third and fourth volumes of his *History* were published in 1855 and at once attained a vast circulation. Within the generation of its first appearance more than 140,000 copies had been sold in the United Kingdom, and sales in the United States were correspondingly large. The work was translated into German, Polish, Dutch, Danish, Swedish, Hungarian, Russian, Bohemian, French, and Spanish.

In 1856 Macaulay left Albany in Piccadilly, where he had lived since 1840, and moved to Holly Lodge, Campden Hill, then a district of lawns and trees. In the following year he was raised to the peerage, with the title of Baron Macaulay of Rothley. His health was now visibly failing; he never spoke in the House of Lords, and he accepted that he would live scarcely long enough to complete the reign of William III in his *History*. He died at Campden Hill on December 28, 1859, and was buried in Westminster Abbey. The fifth volume of his *History*, edited by his sister Hannah, was published in 1861.

Character. Macaulay's exceptional gifts of mind were never, as they have been for many men of genius, a source of calamity or mental anguish. Had he wished, he could have risen to high political place, perhaps to the highest; instead, he chose to devote his powers to the portrayal of England's past. His command of literature was unrivalled. That of Greece and Rome, stored in his extraordinary memory, was familiar from college days, and to it he added the literature of his own country, of France, of Spain, and of Germany. He had limitations. In later life he never gave expression to any religious conviction, and he had no appreciation of spiritual, as distinct from ethical, excellence. All religious and philosophical speculation was alien to his mind, and he showed no interest in the discoveries of science as distinct from technology. Of art he confessed himself ignorant, and to music he was completely deaf. At games, sports, and physical skills—even those of shaving or tying a cravat—his incompetence was complete. In appearance he was short and stocky, with plain features that reflected a powerful mind and a frank and open character.

Macaulay never married. His great capacity for affection found its satisfaction in the attachment and close sympathy of his sisters, particularly of Hannah, later Lady Trevelyan, who remained in almost daily contact with him even after her marriage, and whose children were to him as his own. He had a keen relish for the good things of life and welcomed fortune as the means of obtaining them for himself and others, but there was nothing mercenary or selfish in his nature; when affluent, he gave away with an open hand, often rashly, and his last act was to dictate a letter to a poor curate and sign a check for £25.

BIBLIOGRAPHY. The standard edition of Macaulay's complete works is that originally edited by LADY TREVELYAN, in the Albany edition, 12 vol. (1898). JOHN CLIVE and THOMAS PINNEY, *Thomas Babington Macaulay: Selected Writings* (1972), include further material. For the *History*, see SIR CHARLES H. FIRTH, *A Commentary on Macaulay's History of England* (1938, reprinted 1964); and for his speeches, G.M. YOUNG, *Speeches by Lord Macaulay* (1935). There is no complete or critical edition of his *Essays*.

The Life and Letters of Macaulay, 2 vol. (1876; enlarged 1908, and with full index 1959), by his nephew, SIR GEORGE OTTO TREVELYAN, is acknowledged as one of the best biographies in the English language. Of shorter, derivative studies J.A.C. MORISON, *Macaulay* (1882); and SIR ARTHUR BRYANT, *Macaulay* (1932), deserve mention. JOHN CLIVE has used previously unpublished material for *Thomas Babington Macaulay: the Shaping of the Historian* (1973). Scholarly research on Macaulay, long dormant, has recently awakened, and a complete edition of his letters, now preserved at Trinity College, Cambridge, is being prepared by THOMAS PINNEY, while ROBERT ROBSON is editing Macaulay's unpublished *Journal* of 1838–59. There is no bibliography of Macaulay. The best lists are in *The New Cambridge Bibliography of English Literature*, vol. 2 (1969); and BRYANT (*op. cit.*).

(M.D.K.)

Maccabees

The Maccabees were a priestly family from the vicinity of Jerusalem who during the 2nd century BC led an armed rebellion against King Antiochus' suppression of Judaism and its law. The name Maccabee was a title of honour given to Judas, a son of Mattathias, the hero of the Jewish wars of independence, 168–164 BCE (Before the Common Era, or BC). Later, the name the Maccabees was given to his whole family, specifically to Mattathias, Judas' father, along with all Mattathias' other sons; that is, Judas' four brothers—John, Simon, Eleazar, and Jonathan. Its use was stretched to include even John Hyrcanus, Simon's son, who was next in succession once all the brothers were dead.

There is no unanimity about the meaning of the title Maccabee. The Hebrew may be read as (1) Hammer, (2) Hammerer, or (3) Extinguisher. Since Judas held the initiative in the long war against the Syrians, he was probably regarded in the same light as King Edward I of England, known as the "Hammer of the Scots."

Historical context of the Maccabees

Throughout the 2nd century BCE the city-state of Jerusalem–Judah lay between the two great powers of Egypt and of Syria. The Ptolemies ruled in Egypt and the Seleucids in Syria. These were residual states that had been left when Alexander the Great's empire had broken up about 20 years after his death. Antiochus IV ruled Syria from 175 to 164/163 BCE. He carried the substitute name of Epiphanes, a Greek word meaning "god manifest." A conqueror of overweening pride, as the Bible remembers him (Daniel), he set out to seize Judaea (or Judah), which till then had been a province of Egypt. He aimed incidentally to rid the world of the annoying (and to him peculiar) exclusive "nonconformist" religion of the Jewish people. In order to unify his vast and racially heterogeneous empire, which stretched as far as the Caspian Sea, he planned to create one religion for all.

In Antiochus' day the Syrians were devotees of the culture of Greece. Antiochus sought to continue what he regarded as the "civilizing" colonization process of Alexander. For him culture meant the pursuit of the "good." The restless, inquiring, creative spirit of Greece—what might today be called the scientific spirit—was based on the assumption that "man is the measure of all things." The Jewish view of life, on the other hand, was totally in opposition to that of the Hellenism that had spread throughout the Near East. It, too, was a total way of life, one lived in accordance with what the Jewish people believed was revelation. They regarded Hellenism as basically a form of nature worship. They saw it as the spiritual continuation of the religion of the Canaanites who had presented their views against Israel's for all the centuries since the days of Joshua. They were aghast that Antiochus encouraged the Semitic peoples of the Mediterranean coast to regard him as the ancient god Baal of the Canaanites. The Canaanite gods, they asserted, were merely the mythologizing of the anger, hate, lust, envy and greed of unregulated human hearts.

Israel, on the other hand, its prophets insisted, was the

chosen instrument of the transcendent God, whose name was Yahweh. Yahweh was utterly "other" than man, that is to say, he was "holy." It was God who had created man, not man the gods. And Israel was God's chosen instrument to be "a light to lighten the nations" (Isaiah). To make the meaning of its special relationship to Yahweh evident to the world was therefore Israel's reason for being. Its task was to put the revelation of God into purposeful use by producing an ordered human society that was ruled by God's justice and love and not by man's force and greed.

Antiochus' prohibition of Jewish religious practices

This conception of revealed religion and of loyalty to the Word of God, rather than to a human king, Antiochus could not appreciate, particularly since he himself delighted in the name "god manifest." In order to extirpate the faith of Israel, therefore, he attacked Israel's religious practices. He thus forbade the observance of the sabbath and of the traditional feasts, for these had been ordained by a "jealous" or intolerant God. All sacrifices were to come to an end. He forbade the reading of the Law of Moses and gave orders to search out and burn any copies that could be found. He forbade the practice of circumcision; for it was this that set the Jews off from other peoples as the one "people of God." In place of these practices Antiochus encouraged the development of cultural clubs called gymnasia, in which people gathered to study, to learn, and to enjoy each other's company. After competing in various forms of athletics, men and women used to soak themselves in hot baths. But because the pursuit of the "good" included a delight in the body beautiful, such activities were performed naked. A circumcised Jew taking part in the games in a gymnasium could not therefore hide where his loyalty lay. Finally, in 168 BCE, Antiochus invaded Jerusalem and desacralized the Holy of Holies in the Temple. This was the one place on earth about which Yahweh said "My name" (the expression of his Person) "shall be there" (I Kings).

A number of Jews, under their leader Jason the high priest, took the easy way of conformity with the new universal trends. But with Antiochus' impious act a strong general reaction set in. Thus, when, later in the same year, Antiochus again entered Jerusalem, this time plundering and burning and setting up his citadel, the Acra, on the hill overlooking the Temple courts, he went too far; for his final act of spite, on December 25, 167 BCE, was to rededicate the Temple in Jerusalem to the Olympian god Zeus.

Resistance to Antiochus

The home of Mattathias, a priest at Modein, 17 miles (27 kilometres) northwest of Jerusalem, quickly became the centre of resistance. With him were his five sons, John Gaddi, Simon Thassi, Judas Maccabeus, Eleazar Avaran, and Jonathan Apphus. Josephus, the Jewish historian, gives Mattathias' great-grandfather the surname Asamonaios. From this title comes the name Hasmonean that was applied to the dynasty that descended from the Maccabees in the following century. Mattathias sparked the resistance movement by striking a Jew who was preparing to offer sacrifice to the new gods and by killing the king's officer who was standing by. Then he and his family took to the hills. Many joined them there, especially the Hasideans, a pious and strict group deeply concerned for the Law of Moses. These at first refused to fight on the sabbath day and at once lost a thousand lives. Mattathias then insisted that all groups of resisters should fight if required on the holy sabbath. The guerrilla war that followed was as much a civil war as a war of national resistance. Mattathias treated all degrees of collaborators with the same bitterness as he did the Syrian enemy.

After the death of Mattathias (*c.* 166 BCE), Judas Maccabeus, the third son, became the leader of the resistance movement. In his first battle he seized the sword of Apollonius, governor of Samaria, the general leading the opposing army. But he was also a man of faith in the God of his fathers. He saw himself as a charismatic, divinely appointed leader, like Gideon of old. He would pause in his guerrilla tactics to assemble his men to "watch and pray" and to read the Torah (the divinely revealed Law of Moses) together. Judas saw his task as that of the successor of Moses and Joshua. "Remember how our fathers were saved at the Red Sea," he told his men, "When Pharaoh with his forces pursued them" (I Maccabees 4:9). Then they would blow their trumpets, as in the days of Joshua, and engage the enemy with a vigour that was not their own. Moreover, Judas could be as cruel as Joshua was. After the manner of his time and also of his enemies he was ready to exterminate all the males of a conquered city. Some of his activities are in accord with what today would be called the "Rules for holy war" as found scattered in sections of Deuteronomy and as developed in great detail in one of the scrolls from the Dead Sea, written within the century following Judas, and now entitled *The War of the Sons of Light Against the Sons of Darkness*.

In December 164 BCE, three years after Antiochus had defiled it, Judas recaptured Jerusalem, all except the Acra. Judas then had "blameless priests" cleanse the Holy Place and erect a new altar of unhewn stones. They then reconsecrated the sanctuary. The Hebrew word for this act, Ḥanukkah ("dedication"), is the name used till today for the Jewish eight-day Festival of Lights that commemorates the event. Beginning on Kislev 25 in the Jewish religious year, it occurs near or at the same time as the Christian celebration of Christmas.

Judas next continued the war elsewhere—in Galilee and even in Transjordan. His name was greatly honoured "in all Israel and among the Gentiles" (I Maccabees 5:63). The Syrians, in the war against him, fastened wooden towers on elephants' backs, and the beast then charged into battle with a thousand armoured warriors surrounding it. Eleazar, Judas' second youngest brother, lost his life in 163 BCE when he stabbed an elephant from underneath. In dying, the beast fell on top of him and crushed him.

When Antiochus Epiphanes died in 164 or 163 BCE, others administered the kingdom because his son, Antiochus Eupator, was still a minor. Lysias, the Syrian general, was now the real power. A peace of a sort was agreed between Judas and the Syrian general, who was having trouble elsewhere; and the Jews secured liberty of conscience and worship. The war, however, soon resumed. Judas sent a delegation to Rome at one point in the war to seek for help. This marked the first step toward the eventual take-over by Rome. Judas was killed in battle after more than five years of leadership.

Jonathan, his brother, succeeded him as general. Jonathan more than sustained the dignity of Judas. King Alexander Balas (also known as Alexander Epiphanes), now in control, made peace with Jonathan, calling him his "friend." In 153 or 152 BCE he elected Jonathan as high priest in Jerusalem. Thus was born the high priestly Hasmonean line. The strict upholders of the Law, however, were alienated, because the Law held that no man should be high priest who was not of priestly descent from Aaron. From now on this group formed a strong opposition party, later to be known as the most conservative section of the Pharisees (the religious group whose interpretations and applications of the law, written and oral, became accepted tradition in later Judaism).

The war continued. The Acra was still in enemy hands, and Jonathan sought to wall it off from the city. He died by treachery and was succeeded by his brother Simon, a man of character and prudence as well as a born leader who had quietly and loyally served under his other brothers. On his own initiative Simon brought peace and security to Jerusalem. He was the second Hasmonean high priest. In about 134 BCE he was assassinated.

Hyrcanus I

Thus it was that none of the five brothers died a natural death. The succession was maintained by Simon's son John, known later as Hyrcanus I. He remained as high priest in Jerusalem until his death in 104 BCE. His was a long and disturbed reign; but he consolidated and extended Jewish control, bringing Samaria into subjection, and even forcing the Idumaeans (the descendants of the ancient Edomites who lived southeast of the Dead Sea) into the fold of Judaism. That is how the Idumaean King Herod of Jesus' day was a Jew by religion.

John Hyrcanus' reign marked a turning point in the history of the Maccabees. The movement that had begun with intense conviction and deep patriotic zeal had so completely succeeded that all memory of its first wild enthusiasm had gone. John did not inherit the Pharisaic tendencies of his grandfather Mattathias. He had become a Sadducee in spirit. The Sadducees were an upper class conservative sect that accepted only the Written Law as divinely revealed and authoritative. In outlook he was worldly, agnostic, and urbane. The Revolution had become the Establishment.

BIBLIOGRAPHY. *The First Book of Maccabees*, found in any edition of the Bible that includes the Apocrypha, especially the *Oxford Annotated Apocrypha*, R.S.V. (1965), an anonymously written, sober account of events between 175 and 135 BC; *The Second Book of Maccabees*, also in the Apocrypha, popular, hero-worshipping, with miraculous tales—covering only 175–161 BC; *The Apocrypha and Pseudepigrapha of the Old Testament*, 2 vol., ed. by R.H. CHARLES (1913), a critical study of the text of the two above books; J.C. DANCY, *A Commentary on I Maccabees* (1954), a popular yet detailed guide; J.H.P. BEVAN, *Jerusalem and the High Priests* (1904); G.M. BICKERMAN, *The Maccabees* (1947); R.H. PFEIFFER, *History of New Testament Times*, with an "Introduction to the Apocrypha" (1949); M.I. ROSTOVTSEV, *The Social and Economic History of the Hellenistic World*, 3 vol. (1941); W.W. TARN and G.T. GRIFFITH, *Hellenistic Civilization*, 3rd ed. rev. (1952); A. EDERSHEIM, *The Life and Times of Jesus the Messiah*, 2 vol. (1883); E. SCHUERER, *A History of the Jewish People in the Time of Jesus Christ*, div. 1, vol. 1 (1890); D.S. RUSSELL, *Between the Testaments* (1960); JOSEPHUS, *Antiquities*, Loeb edition, vol. 12–13 (1943).

(G.A.F.K.)

McCormick, Cyrus Hall

United States industrialist and inventor, Cyrus Hall McCormick is generally regarded as the man who, in the early 19th century, gave the world its most formidable weapon in its battle against hunger: the mechanical reaper. In tribute to his achievement, the emperor Napoleon III himself affixed the cross of the Legion of Honour to McCormick's chest, and the French Academy of Sciences honoured him as "having done more for the cause of agriculture than any other living man." If the Legion of Honour was a tribute to McCormick the inventor, his competitors' hatred may well be considered a tribute to McCormick the tough, aggressive, innovative manufacturer and businessman who founded what was later to become the International Harvester Company.

Culver Pictures

McCormick.

McCormick's inventions

Cyrus Hall McCormick was born February 15, 1809, on Walnut Grove farm in Rockbridge County, Virginia, eldest son of Robert McCormick, a farmer, blacksmith, and inventor. McCormick's education, in local schools, was limited. Reserved, determined, and serious-minded, he spent all of his time in his father's workshop.

The elder McCormick had invented several practical farm implements but, like other inventors in the United States and England, had failed in his attempt to build a successful reaping machine. In 1831 Cyrus, aged 22, tried his hand at building a reaper. Resembling a two-wheeled, horse-drawn chariot, the machine consisted of a vibrating cutting blade, a reel to bring the grain within its reach, and a platform to receive the falling grain. The reaper embodied the principles essential to all subsequent grain-cutting machines.

For farmers in the early 19th century, harvesting required a large number of labourers, and, if they could be found, the cost of hiring them was high. When McCormick's reaper was tested on a neighbour's farm in 1831, it offered the hope that the yield of the farmer's fields would soon not be limited to the amount of labour available. The machine had defects, not the least of which was a clatter so loud that slaves were required to walk alongside to calm the frightened horses.

McCormick took out a patent in 1834, but his chief interest at that time was the family's iron foundry. When the foundry failed in the wake of the Bank Panic of 1837, leaving the family deeply in debt, McCormick turned to his still unexploited reaper and improved it. He sold two reapers in 1841, seven in 1842, 29 in 1843, and 50 the following year.

An 1844 visit to the prairie states in the Middle West convinced McCormick that the future of his reaper and of the world's wheat production lay in this vast fertile land rather than in the rocky, hilly East. In 1847, with further patented improvements, he opened a factory in the then small, swampy, lakeside town of Chicago in partnership with the mayor, William Ogden, who capitalized the venture with $50,000 of his own money. The first year, 800 machines were sold. More were sold the next year, and McCormick was able to buy out Ogden.

Career as a businessman

McCormick's main rival was Obed Hussey, whose machine proved to be inferior as a reaper but superior as a mower. When McCormick's basic patent expired in 1848, competing manufacturers—Hussey among them—tried to block renewal. The ensuing legal battle was but one of many in McCormick's career. He was involved in endless litigation not only with rival manufacturers and infringers but also with the New York Central Railroad, which he sued for $20,000 damages following an altercation over an $8.75 overcharge on his wife's baggage. He fought this particular case up to the Supreme Court three times—and won, even though it took 20 years. He did not win his 1848 patent renewal battle, however. Except for improvements on the reaper patented after 1831, the basic machine passed into the public domain. McCormick then set out to beat his manufacturing competitors another way: by outselling them.

Pockets stuffed with order blanks, McCormick rode over the plains selling his reaper to farmers and would-be farmers. To increase sales, he used innovations such as mass production, advertising, public demonstration, warranty of product, and extension of credit to his customers. Soon the factory expanded, and the company had a travelling sales force. By 1850 the McCormick reaper was known in every part of the United States, and at the Great Exhibition of 1851 in London it was introduced to European farmers. Although mocked by *The Times* of London as "a cross between an Astley Chariot, a wheelbarrow, and a flying machine," the reaper took the Grand Prize. In 1855 it won the Grand Medal of Honour at the Paris International Exposition. There followed a long series of prizes, honours, and awards that made the McCormick reaper known to farmers throughout the world.

By 1856 McCormick was selling more than 4,000 machines a year. In the 1858 account of his marriage at age 49 to Nancy (Nettie) Fowler, the *Chicago Daily Press* referred to him as the "massive Thor of industry." Business did not absorb all of his energy, however. He became active in the Democratic Party and in the Presbyterian Church, establishing McCormick Theological Seminary in Chicago.

In 1871 the Chicago fire gutted his factory. Then—over 60 years old, his fortune long since made—he rebuilt.

When he died on May 13, 1884, his business was still growing. In 1902 the McCormick Harvesting Company joined with other companies to form International Harvester Company, with McCormick's son, Cyrus, Jr., as its first president.

BIBLIOGRAPHY. R.G. THWAITES, *Cyrus Hall McCormick and the Reaper* (1909); H.N. CASSON, *Cyrus Hall McCormick: His Life and Work* (1909); L.J. MCCORMICK, *Family Record and Biography* (1896); CYRUS MCCORMICK, *The Century of the Reaper* (1931).

(M.Wi)

McGillivray, Alexander

In the ten years following the American Revolution, Alexander McGillivray (born c. 1759) was the principal chief of the Creek Indians. Though not a warrior, he held the loose association of Creek towns together, strengthened their posture with their Indian neighbours, and skillfully directed relations with the whites who encircled the Creek homeland, which comprised western Georgia and most of Alabama. He dealt successfully with the states of Georgia and South Carolina, the United States government, encroaching American settlers, British and American traders, and the revitalized Spanish regime in East and West Florida and Louisiana. Thanks largely to his exertions, the Creeks retained their tribal identity and the major part of their homeland for another generation.

McGillivray's parentage

In a letter to the Spanish commandant at Pensacola in 1783, McGillivray identified himself as "a Native of and a chief of the Creek Nation." The penmanship and the name made that statement seem improbable, but it was correct. McGillivray was, in fact, of mixed Indian and European blood. His father was Lachlan McGillivray, a Scottish trader. His mother was Sehoy Marchand, a half-breed French-Creek woman. By blood McGillivray was thus only one-quarter Indian. But the Creeks, with whom descent was matrilineal, had no difficulty in claiming Alexander as Creek. As was the custom, his early upbringing was primarily by his mother and, though bilingual, was in the ways of her people.

At 14 Alexander was sent to Charleston, South Carolina, for tutoring and served a short apprenticeship in a countinghouse in Savannah, Georgia. He might have stayed on, but the Revolution intervened. His father was proscribed as a loyalist, and his properties were confiscated. Father and son decided to go home, Lachlan to Scotland and Alexander to the Creek nation, where he was given status as a chief and where the British commissioned him colonel and Indian agent. During the War of Independence the Creeks were opportunists. Some of them fought alongside the patriots. McGillivray contributed toward keeping a larger number on the loyalist side.

By 1782 British military defeats made it clear that the Creeks would lose their British connection. Deeply distrusting American land speculators and encroaching settlers, McGillivray put out feelers for Spanish support and suggested a council at Pensacola, West Florida. There, on June 1, 1784, he and governors Estevan Miró and Arturo O'Neill signed a treaty headed "Articles of Agreement, Trade, and Peace." Spain would extend a protectorate over the Creeks within Spanish territorial limits and would supply an adequate trade. McGillivray's more remarkable success was in persuading the Spanish that the trade should be in English goods and that a contract for the purpose should go to a British merchant, William Panton.

Over the next several years, McGillivray staunchly resisted overtures from Georgia and the United States to concede lands and trading privileges. On occasion he sent raiding parties to clear the Indian hunting grounds. Then, in 1788, Miró gave notice that Spanish support would be reduced. McGillivray indicated that in the circumstances he could not refuse discussions with commissioners sent by Georgia and the American Congress.

In 1789 President Washington sent distinguished commissioners to negotiate with the Creeks. They proposed a boundary well into the Creek hunting lands and recognition of American sovereignty over the entire Creek area. Bolstered by reactivated Spanish support, McGillivray objected. Obtaining no concession, he and his companions decamped. Washington then sent another commissioner to invite McGillivray and a delegation of chiefs to come to New York City to make a treaty "as strong as the hills and as lasting as the rivers."

Negotiations with the U.S. government

With the commissioner, the delegation members travelled overland to New York City, where they were welcomed by the newly formed political Society of St. Tammany. Secretary of War Henry Knox and McGillivray worked out the terms of a treaty specifying American sovereignty over Creek lands within the limits of United States territory and setting a line near the Altamaha River separating Georgian and Creek lands. McGillivray accepted an American Army commission as a brigadier general and a salary of $100 a month, but he did not promise American trade except in the event of war between Britain and Spain, at the time a possibility.

In 1792 McGillivray went to New Orleans, Louisiana, to establish a better understanding with the Spanish. The new treaty specified that the Creeks would order Americans off their lands and that Spain would guarantee territorial integrity within Spanish limits and provide sufficient arms and ammunition. Although the Spanish urged that the Americans be driven back, McGillivray wisely pursued a much less aggressive course.

En route home, McGillivray contracted a violent fever that immobilized him for months. He had never been robust and was sickly, plagued by severe headaches and afflicted by gout, rheumatism, and the symptoms of venereal disease. On February 17, 1793, in his 34th year, he died at Pensacola. Panton, in whose garden he was buried, attributed his death to "gout of the stomach" and "perepneumonia." Neither Panton nor the Spaniards found a suitable replacement for him, nor did his tribesmen the Creeks, though the policies he had put into effect carried on and served the Creek nation well.

BIBLIOGRAPHY. J.W. CAUGHEY, *McGillivray of the Creeks* (1938), reproduces much McGillivray correspondence; A.P. WHITAKER, "Alexander McGillivray," *North Carolina Historical Review*, 5:181–203, 289–309 (1928), is a masterly summation of his post-Revolution work; R.S. COTTERILL, *The Southern Indians* (1954), devotes a chapter (pp. 57–99) to McGillivray.

(J.W.C.)

Machiavelli, Niccolò

The Italian statesman and writer Niccolò Machiavelli, a patriot and thinker of genius whose acute understanding of contemporary politics and profound insight into human nature produced masterpieces that have often been misjudged as immoral or cynical, was born in Florence on May 3, 1469. His family, from the 13th century onward, had been counted among the wealthy and prominent houses of the city, holding on occasion the most important offices. His father, a doctor of laws, was nevertheless among the poorest members of the family; he lived frugally, administering his little landed property near the city and supplementing his meagre income from it with small earnings from the restricted and almost clandestine exercise of his profession, since he was debarred from any public office as an insolvent debtor of the commune of Florence. Niccolò was to write later that he had "learnt to do without before he learnt to enjoy"; and this poverty may have been the reason why he did not have the education suited to his ability. In the years when young Florentines crowded to the lectures of Politian, then Italy's leading scholar of Greek and Latin, Machiavelli never embarked on the study of Greek. His father's memoirs show Niccolò working at Latin under obscure teachers: he learned more by himself in the books that were the only luxury of his home than he did at school. This kind of education saved him from the faults and excesses of humanist erudition and preserved the originality of his thought and the unequaled force of his style, which was elevated and popular at the same time.

Under the republic. In 1498, after the changes in the Florentine government following the execution of Savonarola—the ascetic monk who tried to impose extreme

Machiavelli, oil painting by Santi di Tito (1536–1603).
In the Palazzo Vecchio, Florence.
Alinari

Head of second chancery

political and religious reforms on the republic—and the triumph of the opposing faction, Niccolò Machiavelli was made head of the second chancery (*cancelleria*) at the early age of 29. He was then completely unknown; the tradition of his having an apprenticeship in the lower grades of the chancery from 1494 onward is not confirmed by documentary evidence, and his own statements tend to disprove it. The office to which he was appointed, though not comparable in power with that of first chancellor, was an important one. Originally it dealt only with internal affairs of the republic, but it was later merged with the secretariat of the Ten (*i Dieci*), the executive council. Machiavelli was, moreover, secretary to the magistracy, which, in the name of the Signoria, the governing council, and under its authority, directed foreign affairs and defense. The chancellors were often entrusted with diplomatic missions to Italian and foreign courts when it was not desirable to send ambassadors. Machiavelli's first important mission was to the French court in 1500. Five months spent beyond the Alps enriched his experience, introducing to his eager mind the people and customs of a strong nation united under the rule of a single prince.

On his return to Florence, Machiavelli found much to do, as the republic was on the verge of being ruined by the ambitions of Cesare Borgia, who was then in the midst of attempting to create a principality for himself in central Italy. Besides dictating letters in the chancery, Machiavelli undertook missions whenever the need arose; he was always ready to ride off and to face danger and hardship, being fonder of action than of words. His short work *Del modo di trattare i sudditi della Val di Chiana ribellati* (1503; "On the Way to Deal With the Rebel Subjects of the Valdichiana") belongs to this period. In it, the fundamental principle of a new doctrine is enunciated for the first time: "The world has always been inhabited by human beings who have always had the same passions." He was sent twice to Cesare Borgia; and he was a witness to the bloody vengeance taken by Cesare on his mutinous captains at the town of Sinigaglia (December 31, 1502), of which he wrote a famous account, *Descrizione del modo tenuto dal Duca Valentino nello ammazzare Vitellozzo . . .* ("On the Manner Adopted by the Duke Valentino to Kill Vitellozzo . . ."). That strong, sinister prince caught the imagination of the Florentine statesman with his natural bent for abstraction and theory. Implacable, resolute, ferocious, and cunning, Cesare Borgia had conquered a dominion for himself in a few months; and Machiavelli adapted Cesare's qualities and methods to his own ideal of a "new prince" who would provide a desperate remedy for the desperate ills of Italy.

It is clear that this was a case of idealization and that his admiration for the Prince did not go hand in hand with admiration for the man. When Pope Alexander VI, the father of Cesare Borgia, died in 1503 and his successor, Pius III, also died shortly afterward, Machiavelli was sent to Rome for the duration of the conclave that elected Julius II, an implacable enemy of the Borgias. There, with ever-increasing scorn, Machiavelli witnessed the inglorious decline of his hero and finally celebrated Cesare's imprisonment "which he deserved as a rebel against Christ."

In Florence, meanwhile, Piero Soderini had been elected gonfalonier (chief magistrate) for life, and Machiavelli was immediately able to win his favour and become his right-hand man. This remarkable influence over the head of state encouraged him to realize his military ideas. For centuries the states of Italy had used mercenary troops in their wars, and Machiavelli had seen in practice their lack of discipline, their faithlessness, and their unbearable arrogance. Inspired both by the military enterprises of ancient Rome and by his own observations in France (where he went on a second mission early in 1504) and in Romagna (where Cesare Borgia had replaced mercenaries with levies from his own territory), Machiavelli ardently pursued the idea of giving the Florentine state a militia of its own, recruited from the peoples under its control. Age-old prejudices had to be overcome, as well as the reluctance of suspicious townsmen, to arm men from the country districts around. Having set to work immediately after his return from the Roman legation, he succeeded in persuading the gonfalonier to risk an experiment and then to have a law passed in order to establish a militia (1505). His first "Decennale"—a short poem in terza rima (three lines in interlocking rhyme), somewhat prosaic, like the rest of his verses—ends with a call to arms. In 1506, as the importance of the new militia increased, the council of the Nine (*i Nove*) was created to control it, and Machiavelli was made secretary of this body also. To get the law on the militia passed, he had also written a *Discorso dell'ordinare lo stato di Firenze alle armi* ("Discourse on Arming the State of Florence"), a lucid and closely argued work. The territory of the republic was divided into districts, and Machiavelli himself went out to see to the levies and to carry out inspections, alternating these military tasks with those of the chancery and with a further mission (1506) to Julius II, whose armies, moving up to free the states of the Church from their various usurpers, entered Bologna in triumph.

Promotion of a Florentine militia

In December 1507 the Holy Roman emperor, Maximilian I, was preparing an invasion of Italy from Germany. Florence's gonfalonier, who did not trust his own ambassador at the imperial court, accordingly sent Machiavelli on another journey beyond the Alps. On the journey Machiavelli passed through Switzerland, and three days spent in that country were enough for him to produce some brief but acute observations on it. He did the same, at greater length, for Germany, composing on the day after his return to Florence (June 17, 1508) a *Rapporto delle cose della Magna* ("Report on the State of Germany"). In this work, compiled in the course of his official duties, and likewise in the literary version made four years later under the title *Ritratto delle cose della Magna* ("Portrait . . ."), he was able to pick out with great acumen the reasons both for the strength of the German nation and for its political weaknesses. Yet all his official reports, though marvelously intuitive, are marred by a tendency to theorize; they are bold syntheses, not complete and accurate sources of information.

On his return from Germany, as the Florentines were showing new strength in an effort to recapture the city of Pisa, which had temporarily freed itself from Florentine rule, Machiavelli was able to try out the militia that he had created. He went to command his troops at the front and put all his usual enthusiasm into the task: when the Ten begged him to remain at headquarters, he answered that they must let him be with his soldiers, since behind the lines he would die of melancholy. Such was the patriotism and passion of a man who has been represented as skeptical, cautious, and cynical. Pisa capitulated on June

8, 1509, and Machiavelli with his militia had no small share in this success for Florence.

After a mission to Mantua (Mantova) in connection with yet another invasion by Maximilian, Machiavelli had to go again to France, in July 1510, to persuade Florence's ally Louis XII to make peace with Pope Julius II or at least not to drag Florence into a war that would bring the republic to certain, swift, and needless ruin, emphasizing that a neutral Florence could be very useful to the French. The French, however, "who knew nothing about statecraft," were not influenced by what Machiavelli had to tell them. From this mission, which resulted in the *Ritratto di cose di Francia,* he returned in October 1510 convinced that there would be a major war between the French king and the pope and that the Florentines would be involved. All of his efforts now were to arm his country. As he carried out his military duties and those of the chancery, he was continually travelling about. At the end of the summer of 1511 he went once more to France to persuade Louis XII to remove the schismatic council that he was sponsoring in Pisa, since this had brought upon the Florentines the rage of Julius II. As soon as he was back from France, Machiavelli himself went to Pisa to remove this council and did so without much ceremony. For the free republic, however, the last hour had already come: the army of the pope's Holy League was already on its way to punish Florence. The gonfalonier Soderini was deposed, and in 1512 the Medici returned as masters of the city.

Under the Medici. Machiavelli lost his position and was forbidden to enter the Palazzo della Signoria. Also, when a conspiracy against the Medici was found early in 1513, Machiavelli, already an object of suspicion to the new government, was accused of complicity. Thrown into prison, he maintained his innocence even under tortures that often persuaded the innocent to declare themselves guilty. His name, however, was on a list taken from the conspirators (perhaps merely a list of persons attached to the old regime); and finally, though he was released from prison, restrictions were put on his freedom of residence. In the meantime, Julius II had died, and Giovanni de' Medici had become pope under the name of Leo X. Machiavelli composed for the celebrations on that occasion a pious "Canto degli spiriti beati" ("Song of the Blessed Spirits"). He sought in vain to get into the good graces of the Medici through the intercession of Francesco Vettori, his old colleague in the German legation and now Florentine ambassador to a Florentine pope; but his brilliant letters to Vettori were powerless to stir that selfish and opportunistic friend.

Reduced to poverty, Machiavelli sought refuge in the little property near Florence that he had inherited from his father. In a letter to Vettori, which is one of the most remarkable in any language, he describes his life in the country with its violent contrasts, its mixture of coarse living conditions and dreams of greatness. There he employed his leisure in writing, between spring and autumn 1513, his two most famous works, *Il principe* (*The Prince*) and a large part of the *Discorsi sopra la prima deca di Tito Livio* ("Discourses on the First Decade of Tito Livy").

Machiavelli's affections always lay with the republic, and all of his theories were intended for its betterment; but the corruption of the times, the weakness of the states of Italy, and the threat of foreign conquest made him long for that "new prince" who might give reality to his great dream of the redemption of Italy. This "redeemer," to whom he sought in vain to give a face and a name, would have had to overcome superhuman difficulties; nor could there be much choice of means in attaining such ends. Machiavelli, in a book that is not a moral treatise, attempted to indicate to the prince those means that were compatible with the conditions of the time and with human nature. Even religion—for which he had a deep feeling though he was not outwardly pious—was subordinated by him, in matters of state, to the state's iron necessity and made into an *instrumentum regni,* or tool of power. Indeed, Machiavelli is regarded as the inventor of the "reason of state" (*ragione di stato*), though that

expression appears for the first time 20 years after his death. *Il principe,* while its underlying ideas are the same as those of the *Discorsi,* won a greater reputation, thanks to its concision, its vigorous imagery, and the bluntness of some of its aphorisms, which were taken too literally by contemporaries and by posterity. He remarked of certain cynical precepts that he would not have proffered them if mankind had not been wicked. This bleak pessimism is certainly not refuted by the annals of his own time. Yet his longing was for a society of good and pure men; he sought it in ancient times and, in his own day, admired less civilized nations as being less corrupt. Machiavelli's great hope was that *Il principe,* dedicated to Lorenzo de' Medici, ruler of Florence from 1513, would obtain from the Medici an office to support his family and satisfy his love of action; but the hope was in vain. Full of bitterness, he then dedicated the *Discorsi* (of which he had been giving public readings in the Oricellari Gardens) not to a prince but to two private citizens.

From this time also dates the marvelous comedy first entitled *Commedia di Callimaco e di Lucrezia,* later *La Mandragola* (1518; "The Mandrake"). What has already been said about Machiavelli's hidden but strong and deep morality could be repeated in connection with *La Mandragola,* in which the wickedness and corruption of men, particularly of the clergy, are the subject of laughter—but of a bitter and painful laughter that is never an end in itself. It reminds the reader of what was written about the author by his friend and critic Francesco Guicciardini: "He laughs at the failings of men because he cannot cure them."

Machiavelli's hopes were raised when, on the death of Duke Lorenzo, the cardinal Giulio de' Medici came to govern Florence. He was presented to the cardinal by Lorenzo Strozzi, to whom in gratitude he dedicated the dialogue *Dell'arte della guerra* (1520; "On the Art of War"). In this, as in the *Discorsi* and in *Il principe,* his study of classical authors was combined with his experience of modern affairs; *i.e.,* his recent military adventures. The *Arte della guerra,* properly considered, is merely complementary to Machiavelli's two political treatises, but it is more closely linked with *Il principe* and its great dream of Italian unity than with the *Discorsi.* Like the *Discorsi,* it has the defect of taking the ancient Romans in everything as its model; and this fault appears greater in the *Arte* because too little attention is paid in it to technical advances, such as the use of artillery—which in those very years was beginning to make its weight felt decisively in battle. Even so, Machiavelli can be said to have laid the foundations of modern tactics.

The first employment given him by the cardinal was to go to Lucca on a matter of small importance. Presently, however, the cardinal agreed to have Machiavelli elected official historiographer of the republic, a post to which he was appointed by the Studio or University of Florence in November 1520 with a salary of 57 gold florins a year, later increased to 100. The university's terms allowed for Machiavelli's also being employed in other ways. In the meantime, he was to compose for the Medici pope Leo X a *Discorso* on the organization of the government of Florence after the death of Duke Lorenzo; in this he boldly advised the Pope to restore the city's ancient liberties. Shortly after, in May 1521, he was sent to the Franciscan chapter at Carpi. The commission was an insignificant one; but on this occasion he met Francesco Guicciardini, governor of nearby Modena, and the friendship, resulting in a lively and perceptive correspondence, was to have a great importance for Italian literature.

After Pope Leo X's death (December 1521), the cardinal Giulio de' Medici, who remained sole master of Florence, was more than ever inclined to reform its government. He sought the advice of Machiavelli, who simply refurbished the *Discorso* composed for Leo X. After the death of Pope Adrian VI in September 1523, Giulio de' Medici was himself elected pope, taking the name of Clement VII. Machiavelli now worked with more enthusiasm on the *Istorie fiorentine,* his official history of Flor-

Marginal notes:

Imprisonment and torture

The Prince and "Discourses"

"Mandrake"; "Art of War"; "History of Florence"

ence; in June 1525 he was able to present the pope with eight books, and he received in return 120 florins and encouragement to continue the work. The *Istorie fiorentine*, like his earlier writings, bears the impress of a powerful and original mind. In this work, written by fits and starts and unwillingly and wearily dragged on into his later years, Machiavelli enters on a new road, leaving behind him the traditions and methods of humanist historiography. His love of truth often in conflict with the necessity to avoid offending his powerful patrons, he writes history more as a politician than as a historian set on discovering the truth, often accepting sources uncritically and accommodating facts to his thesis. It is not narrative exactitude that is to be sought in the *Istorie* but the power of synthesis, the brilliant coordination and organization of facts. Early in the same year he had written the *Clizia*, a free imitation of the *Casina* of Plautus, which he produced within a few days for a festival. In this comedy he probably intended to satirize himself and his affair with Barbera, a singer with whom he was infatuated.

In April 1526 Machiavelli was elected secretary of the Cinque Provveditori Alle Mura, a five-man body lately constituted to superintend the fortifications. Next, the pope having formed the League of Cognac against the Holy Roman emperor Charles V, Machiavelli went with the army to join Francesco Guicciardini, the pope's lieutenant, with whom he remained almost continuously until the sack of Rome by the emperor's forces brought the war to an end in May 1527. Florence having regained its freedom by casting off the Medici, Machiavelli on his

Rebuff by restored republic

return hoped to be restored to his old post in the chancery; but the little favours that the Medici had so meagrely doled out to him caused the supporters of the free republic to forget the love that he had always had for his native city and for freedom. It was the last of his disappointments and the greatest. Machiavelli fell ill and died, with the comforts of religion, on June 21, 1527, at the age of 58.

Character and thought. Machiavelli was of medium height, thin, with a bony face, a high forehead, black hair, piercing eyes, and thin lips compressed in an enigmatic smile. He was an upright man, a good citizen, and a good father. He was not by any means a faithful husband but lived in affectionate harmony with his wife Marietta Corsini (whom he had married in the latter part of 1501) and had five children by her. As he said in a letter, he loved his native city "more than his own soul"; and even in his devotion to the state he must often have written "state" while thinking "native land."

Out of a desire to shock his contemporaries, Machiavelli liked to appear more wicked than he was. This, together with certain blunt maxims in his works, gave him a reputation for immorality. In fact, those maxims were purely theoretical abstractions of an art itself not always based on moral scruples, least of all in Machiavelli's time; but their bold, lapidary style made it easy to detach them from their context and to ignore the purpose that had inspired them and the needs that had conditioned them. The maxims thus became a target for attacks by the Catholic Counter-Reformation; and the word "Machiavellianism" was coined as a term of opprobrium by the French, out of hatred for all things Italian, during the rule of the Italian-born Catherine de Médicis. On the other hand, Machiavelli was an innovator and, as such, was inclined to give extreme form to his utterances. He himself, in the *Discorsi*, forecast the dangers that awaited him and all of those who have sought "new methods and new orders . . . undiscovered seas and lands." He "was a scapegoat because he was a great man and because he was unfortunate."

In judging Machiavelli one must likewise take account of his anguished despair of ever seeing virtue triumphant and of his tragic sense of evil. Again, on the basis of sentences taken out of context and of outward appearances, he was judged a cold and cynical man, a sneerer at religion and virtue; but, in fact, there is hardly a page of his writings and certainly no action of his life that does not show him to be passionate, generous, ardent, and

basically religious. Nothing conveys a better understanding of Machiavelli than the self-portrait that he drew in two lines of verse:

> *Io rido, e il rider mio non passa dentro:*
> *Io ardo, e l'arsion mia non par di fore*

("I laugh, and my laughter is not within me; I burn, and the burning is not seen outside.")

As a thinker and writer, Machiavelli displayed a very speculative mind. Unlike Guicciardini, who was empirical and pragmatic, he was irresistibly drawn to reduce human actions to scientific formulas and rules, to go beyond particular facts and to seize on universal motives. As one of the founders of the philosophy of history, he well knew (as he wrote in the preface to the *Discorsi*) that he was opening "a road as yet untrodden by man." As he had been the first to appreciate in histories "that flavour which they possess in themselves" beyond any merely literary or entertaining ends, so he was the first to propound the thesis of historical cycles and—starting from the principle that human nature does not change— the first to build a political science based on the study of man. Machiavelli's fallacy of always referring to the example of the Romans, without taking account of changed conditions, was criticized—even in his own day—by Guicciardini; but the latter was by nature inclined to concern himself rather with particular errors and inaccuracies than with his friend's universal theories.

Philosophy of history

Machiavelli was a great writer because he was a great thinker. He was also a poet; his poetry, however, is to be found not so much in his verse as in his prose, which has no equal in Italian literature. It is also noteworthy that his great gifts showed themselves in nearly all the genres that he attempted: in historical writings, in political treatises, in the short story and, particularly, in comedy.

BIBLIOGRAPHY. R. RIDOLFI, *Vita di Niccolò Machiavelli*, 4th enlarged ed., 2 vol. (1969; Eng. trans., 1964), is the best informed and most up-to-date biography. P. VILLARI, *Niccolò Machiavelli e i suoi tempi*, 3 vol. (1877–82; 3rd ed., 1912–14; Eng. trans., *Niccolò Machiavelli and His Times*, 2 vol., 1878), is still perceptive and fundamental, especially for the numerous documents in the appendix. O. TOMMASINI, *La vita e gli scritti di Niccolò Machiavelli*, 2 vol. (1883–1911), is a confused work, very weak in its judgments but an inexhaustible source of bibliographical and archival materials. G. SASSO, *Niccolò Machiavelli, storia del suo pensiero politico* (1958), is the most modern and complete study on this aspect of his thought. A. GERBER, *Niccolò Machiavelli: Die Handschriften, Ausgaben und Uebersetzungen seiner Werke*, 3 parts with a sheaf of facsimiles (1912–13), is important for its description of manuscripts and old editions of Machiavelli's works. A. NORSA, *Il principio della forza nel pensiero politico di Niccolò Machiavelli* (1936), is valuable chiefly for its appendix, which contains a bibliography citing 2,143 publications on Machiavelli. The basic translation of the *Discourses* is by LESLIE J. WALKER, 2 vol. (1950).

(Ro.Ri.)

Machines and Machine Components

The word machine has been given a wide variety of definitions, but for the purpose of this article it is a device, having a unique purpose, that augments or replaces human or animal effort for the accomplishment of physical tasks. Tools, which may be regarded as the simplest class of machines, are described in separate articles, chiefly HAND TOOLS and CARPENTRY.

GENERAL CONSIDERATIONS

The operation of a machine may involve the transformation of chemical, thermal, electrical, or nuclear energy into mechanical energy, or vice versa, or its function may simply be to modify and transmit forces and motions. All machines have an input, an output, and a transforming or modifying and transmitting device.

Machines that receive their input energy from a natural source, such as air currents, moving water, coal, petroleum, or uranium, and transform it into mechanical energy are known as prime movers. Windmills, waterwheels, turbines, steam engines, and internal-combustion engines are prime movers. In these machines the inputs vary; the outputs are usually rotating shafts capable of

Prime movers

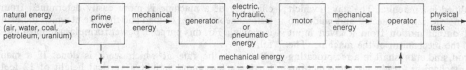

natural energy
(air, water, coal,
petroleum, uranium) → prime mover → mechanical energy → generator → electric, hydraulic, or pneumatic energy → motor → mechanical energy → operator → physical task

mechanical energy

Figure 1: Flow of energy in machines.

being used as inputs to other machines, such as electric generators, hydraulic pumps, or air compressors. All three of the latter devices may be classified as generators; their outputs of electrical, hydraulic, and pneumatic energy can be used as inputs to electric, hydraulic, or air motors. These motors can be used to drive machines with a variety of outputs, such as materials processing, packaging, or conveying machinery, or such appliances as sewing machines and washing machines. All machines of the latter type and all others that are neither prime movers, generators, nor motors may be classified as operators. This category also includes manually operated instruments of all kinds, such as calculating machines and typewriters.

If the operator is a washing machine driven by an electric motor, the flow of energy from the prime mover at the power plant through the generator and motor to the operator is as shown in Figure 1. The operator can also be driven directly by a small, direct-connected prime mover, such as a gasoline engine, as shown by the dotted line in Figure 1; for most power-driven operators, however, the flow of energy from the prime mover follows the solid lines.

In some cases, machines in all categories are combined in one unit. In a diesel-electric locomotive, for example, the diesel engine is the prime mover, which drives the electric generator, which, in turn, supplies electric current to the motors that drive the wheels.

As part of an introduction to machine components, some examples supplied by an automobile are of value.

Machine components in an automobile

In an automobile, the basic problem is harnessing the explosive effect of gasoline to provide power to rotate the rear wheels. The explosion of the gasoline in the cylinders pushes the pistons down, and the transmission and modification of this translatory (linear) motion to rotary motion of the crankshaft is effected by the connecting rods that join each piston to the cranks (Figure 21) that are part of the crankshaft. The piston, cylinder, crank, and connecting rod combination is known as a slider-crank mechanism; it is a commonly used method of converting translation to rotation (as in an engine) or rotation to translation (as in a pump).

To admit the gasoline–air mixture to the cylinders and exhaust the burned gases, valves are used; these are opened and closed by the wedging action of cams (projections) on a rotating camshaft that is driven from the crankshaft by gears or a chain.

In a four-stroke-cycle engine with eight cylinders, the crankshaft receives an impulse at some point along its length every quarter revolution. To smooth out the effect of these intermittent impulses on the speed of the crankshaft, a flywheel is used. This is a heavy wheel, attached to the crankshaft, that by its inertia opposes and moderates any speed fluctuations.

Since the torque (turning force) that it delivers depends on its speed, an internal-combustion engine cannot be started under load. To enable an automobile engine to be started in an unloaded state and then connected to the wheels without stalling, a clutch and a transmission are necessary. The former makes and breaks the connection between the crankshaft and the transmission, while the latter changes, in finite steps, the ratio between the input and output speeds and torques of the transmission. In low gear, the output speed is low and the output torque higher than the engine torque, so that the car can be started moving; in high gear, the car is moving at a substantial speed and the torques and speeds are equal.

The axles to which the wheels are attached are contained in the rear axle housing, which is clamped to the rear springs, and are driven from the transmission by the drive shaft. As the car moves and the springs flex in response to bumps in the road, the housing moves relative to the transmission; to permit this movement without interfering with the transmission of torque, a universal joint is attached to each end of the drive shaft.

The drive shaft is perpendicular to the rear axles. The right-angled connection is usually made with bevel gears having a ratio such that the axles rotate at from one-third to one-fourth the speed of the drive shaft. The rear axle housing also holds the differential gears that permit both rear wheels to be driven from the same source and to rotate at different speeds when turning a corner.

Like all moving mechanical devices, automobiles cannot escape from the effects of friction. In the engine, transmission, rear axle housing, and all bearings, friction is undesirable, since it increases the power required from the engine; lubrication reduces but does not eliminate this friction. On the other hand, friction between the tires and the road and in the brake shoes makes traction and braking possible. The belts that drive the fan, generator, and other accessories are friction-dependent devices. Friction is also useful in the operation of the clutch. Some of the devices cited above, and others that are described below, are found in machines of all categories, assembled in a multitude of ways to perform all kinds of physical tasks. Because of this diversity of function and the lack of common characteristics, this article will not be concerned with specific operators. Neither will it deal with the overall performance of prime movers, nor with the operation of hydraulic, pneumatic, or electrical devices. It will consider only the operation and structure of the basic mechanical devices that are the constituent parts of machines. The function of most of these devices is to transmit and modify force and motion. Other devices, such as springs, flywheels, shafts, and fasteners, perform supplementary functions.

For the purposes of this article a machine may be further defined as a device consisting of two or more resistant, relatively constrained parts that may serve to transmit and modify force and motion in order to do work. The requirement that the parts of a machine be resistant implies that they be capable of carrying imposed loads without failure or loss of function. Although most machine parts are solid metallic bodies of suitable proportions, nonmetallic materials, springs, fluid pressure organs, and tension organs such as belts are also employed.

Constrained motion

The most distinctive characteristic of a machine is that the parts are interconnected and guided in such a way that their motions relative to one another are constrained. Relative to the block, for example, the piston of a reciprocating engine is constrained by the cylinder to move on a straight path; points on the crankshaft are constrained by the main bearings to move on circular paths; no other forms of relative motion are possible.

On some machines the parts are only partially constrained. If the parts are interconnected by springs or friction members, the paths of the parts relative to one another may be fixed, but the motions of the parts may be affected by the stiffness of the springs, friction, and the masses of the parts.

If all the parts of a machine are comparatively rigid members whose deflections under load are negligible, then the constrainment may be considered complete and the relative motions of the parts can be studied without considering the forces that produce them. For a specified rotational speed of the crankshaft of a reciprocating engine, for example, the corresponding speeds of points on the connecting rod and the piston can be calculated. The determination of the displacements, velocities, and accelerations of the parts of a machine for a prescribed input motion is the subject matter of kinematics of machines. Such calculations can be made without considering the forces involved, because the motions are constrained.

According to the definition, both forces and motions are

Mechanism of a machine

transmitted and modified in a machine. The way in which the parts of a machine are interconnected and guided to produce a required output motion from a given input motion is known as the mechanism of the machine. The piston, connecting rod, and crankshaft in a reciprocating engine constitute a mechanism for changing the rectilinear motion of the piston into the rotary motion of the crankshaft.

Although both forces and motions are involved in the operation of machines, the primary function of a machine may be either the amplification of force or the modification of motion. A lever is essentially a force increaser, while a gearbox is most often used as a speed reducer. The motions and forces in a machine are inseparable, however, and are always in an inverse ratio. The output force on a lever is greater than the input force, but the output motion is less than the input motion. Similarly, the output speed of a gear reducer is less than the input speed, but the output torque is greater than the input torque. In the first case a gain in force is accompanied by a loss in motion, while in the second case a loss in motion is accompanied by a gain in torque.

Although the primary function of some machines can be identified, it would be difficult to classify all machines as either force or motion modifiers; some machines belong in both categories. All machines, however, must perform a motion-modifying function, since if the parts of a mechanical device do not move, it is a structure, not a machine. It is customary for machinery designers, when studying the motions of the parts, to speak of the mechanism of a machine.

While all machines have a mechanism, and consequently perform a motion-modifying function, some machines do not have a planned force-modifying purpose; the forces that exist are caused by friction and the inertia of the moving masses and do not appear as a useful output effort. This group would include measuring instruments and clocks.

The "work" referred to in the definition will be interpreted in its scientific sense. In the science of mechanics, work is something that forces do when they move in the direction in which they are acting, and it is equal to the product of the average force and the distance moved. If a man carries a weight along a horizontal path, he does no work according to this definition, since the force and the motion are at right angles to one another; that is, the force is vertical and the motion horizontal. If he carries the weight up a flight of stairs or a ladder, he does work, since he is moving in the same direction in which he is applying a force. Mathematically, if F equals force (in pounds or kilograms), and S equals distance (in feet or metres), work is then equal to the applied force F multiplied by the distance this force moves S; or WORK $= F \times S$.

When a force causes a body to rotate about a fixed axis, or pivot, the work done is obtained by multiplying the torque (T) by the angle of rotation.

Calculating efficiency

These concepts of work are fundamental in defining the mechanical work function of machines in terms of forces and motions, and they bring out the inseparability of forces and motions in machines. Because of friction, the work output from a machine is always less than the work input, and the efficiency, which is the ratio of the two, is always less than 100 percent.

The ratio of the output to input forces is the mechanical advantage (MA), and it defines the force-modifying function, while the ratio of the input to output motions is the velocity ratio (VR), and it defines the motion-modifying function. When the efficiency is high, these ratios are approximately equal; if the output force is ten times the input force, the input motion must be ten times the output motion; *i.e.*, what is gained in force is lost in motion. Friction affects the mechanical advantage but not the velocity ratio.

To calculate the efficiency from the ratio of output to input work, it would be necessary to know the work done by the output and input forces over a specified distance. Since this would entail the determination of average forces over the interval, it would be inconvenient. The efficiency of a machine is more easily determined from instantaneous values of load and the rate at which the load is moving. For this purpose, power formulas are most useful.

Power is the rate at which work is done. If a man carries a ten-pound weight a vertical height of 12 feet (*i.e.*, up a ladder or stairs) in half a minute, his power expenditure is 10×12 or 120 foot-pounds in half a minute; his rate of doing work is then 240 foot-pounds per minute.

The unit of power or rate of doing work in English-speaking countries is the horsepower (hp), which is equal to 33,000 foot-pounds per minute, so that 240 foot-pounds per minute equals $240/_{33,000} = 0.00727$ hp.

In dealing with simple force-amplifying machines such as the lever and the wheel and axle, it is convenient to call the input force the "effort" and the output force the "load." The mechanical advantage is then the ratio of the load to the effort, and the velocity ratio is the motion (displacement or velocity) of the effort divided by the corresponding motion of the load.

THE SIMPLE MACHINES

History. The origin of the five simple machines—the lever, wedge, wheel and axle, pulley, and screw—is largely conjectural. All early people used the lever in some form, for moving heavy stones or as digging sticks for land cultivation. The principle of the lever was used in the swape, or shadoof, a long lever pivoted near one end with a platform or water container hanging from the short arm and counterweights attached to the long arm. A man could lift several times his own weight by pulling down on the long arm. This device is said to have been used in Egypt and India for raising water and lifting soldiers over battlements as early as 1500 BC.

The Egyptian shadoof

Another interesting lever device, probably used in Egypt about 5000 BC, was a balance beam for weighing, consisting of a bar pivoted at its centre and weights that were hung on one end to balance the object being weighed on the other end.

The wedge was used in prehistoric times to split logs and rocks; for rocks, wooden wedges, caused to swell by wetting, were employed. The wheel and axle is believed to have been first employed around 3000 BC for bringing ore up mine shafts and for raising water buckets in wells. The pulley came later, probably in the 8th century BC.

Although the Pythagorean philosopher Archytas of Tarentum (5th century BC) is the alleged inventor of the screw, the exact date of its first appearance as a useful mechanical device is obscure. Though invention of the water screw is usually ascribed to Archimedes (3rd century BC), evidence exists of a similar device used for irrigation in Egypt at an earlier date.

The screw press, probably invented in Greece in the 1st or 2nd century BC, has been used since the days of the Roman Empire for pressing clothes. A drawing of a clothes press with right- and left-hand screws was found in the ruins of Pompeii, which was destroyed by the eruption of Vesuvius in AD 79. In the 1st century AD, wooden screws were used in wine and olive-oil presses, and cutters (taps) for cutting internal threads were in use.

In the notebooks of Leonardo da Vinci (1452–1519) there are sketches of a screw-operated printing press and a machine for cutting screws. James Watt (1736–1819) invented a screw press in which a letter, written in special ink, was squeezed against moist copy sheets to obtain duplicates.

The mathematical relationships between loads and displacements in the "simple" machines did not appear in permanent written form until many years after their estimated dates of origin; practice preceded theory. Archimedes, however, traditionally associated with the lever, did understand the mathematical theory of its operation. Since he is reported to have used compound pulleys (employing two or more wheels to obtain a mechanical advantage) to pull a ship onto dry land, and was primarily interested in theoretical relationships, he was doubtless well informed on the theory of all the simple machines.

To Hero of Alexandria (1st century AD), a Greek writer and inventor, the five simple machines were all devices for moving heavy weights whose main attribute was a high mechanical advantage. Hero was also aware of the reciprocal relation between mechanical advantage and velocity ratio, and is credited with recognizing the need for a precise technical definition of "work" in terms of force and distance.

It is believed that the wheel, as applied to transportation vehicles, evolved from the logs or rollers used to move heavy objects. Apart from its value in transportation, the wheel made controlled rotary motion a reality and was therefore of particular importance in machine design. The rotating treadmill operated by men or animals and the waterwheel activated by running water were among the first prime movers. Rotating machines performing repetitive operations, and driven by steam engines, were important elements in the Industrial Revolution of the 18th century. Rotary motion permits a continuity in magnitude and direction that is impossible with linear motion, which, in a machine, always involves reversals and changes in magnitude.

The crank   Next to the wheel, the crank is the most important motion-transmitting device, since, with the connecting rod, it provides means for converting linear to rotary motion, and vice versa. There are many conflicting claims concerning the origin of the crank, but it has been reasonably well established that the first recognizable crank appeared in China early in the 1st century AD.

The first cranks had two right-angle bends and were hand-operated. The carpenter's brace, invented about AD 1400 by a Flemish carpenter, may be considered the first complete crank, since it had four right-angle bends, with the arm and wrist of the operator forming the connecting rod. The first mechanical connecting rods were used, it is said, on a treadle-operated machine in AD 1430. About this time flywheels were added to the rotating members to carry the members over the "dead" positions when the rod and the crank arm are lined up with each other (collinear).

Until the invention of the steam engine, the waterwheel was the greatest source of power for driving machinery. The most important waterwheel, invented by the 1st-century-BC Roman engineer Vitruvius, was a vertical wheel with a horizontal axis driven by a stream of water flowing beneath it; *i.e.*, it was undershot. This wheel was the first notable achievement in the design of power-driven machinery and the most important contribution of the Romans to mechanical engineering.

In the Middle Ages, the waterwheel was applied to a variety of tasks, such as grinding corn, operating weaving machines, and hammering hot metal into a desired shape (forging). For centuries, wire was drawn through dies by manual labour, and the amount of reduction in cross-sectional area that could be obtained was limited by the strength of the drawer. About the middle of the 14th century AD, waterwheels were harnessed for wiredrawing in Germany; they were used for this purpose until the introduction of the steam engine.

Many machine components have little history. For those with substantial historical backgrounds it will be convenient to treat the history individually.

Operation.   Figure 2 shows three arrangements of a straight lever; in each case f is the fulcrum; P the effort, applied at b; and W the load, applied at c. When the lever is balanced or in equilibrium, the tendency of P to turn the lever about f in one direction must be balanced by the tendency of W to rotate the lever in the opposite direction. Neglecting friction at the fulcrum, this relation can be expressed mathematically as

$$P \times bf = W \times cf, \qquad (1)$$

which states that the applied effort multiplied by the distance to the fulcrum on one side is equal to the same product on the other side. From this can be derived a quantity known as the mechanical advantage, which is equal to the load divided by the effort:

$$\text{mechanical advantage} = \frac{W}{P} = \frac{bf}{cf}. \qquad (2)$$

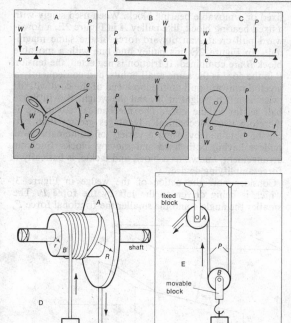

Figure 2: *Simple machines.*
(A–C) Straight lever arrangements. (D) Wheel and axle. (E) Pulley and blocks (see text).

In Figure 2A, if $bf/cf = 3$, it means that a load W of 30 pounds, for example, can be balanced by an effort P of 10 pounds. If P exceeds this value slightly, the bar will rotate about f with P moving farther and faster than W by the ratio of bf to cf, the velocity ratio, which again is the mechanical advantage, neglecting friction. Obviously, the shorter the distance between f and c the greater the force-amplifying ability of the lever, and the shorter the distance c will move for a given movement of b.

The arrangement in Figure 2A is found on pliers and scissors, while that in Figure 2B is found on wheelbarrows; f represents the wheel, W the load, and P the effort exerted on the handles by the operator. In Figure 2C the lever functions as a motion-multiplying device. It is used on foot treadles for driving small looms and manually operated grindstones and sewing machines. A small movement of the foot at b produces a larger movement at c.

The wheel and axle shown in Figure 2D operates basically on a leverage principle. The wheel A, of radius R, and the axle B, of radius r, are fastened to the shaft, which can rotate. The effort P is applied by means of a cord lying in a groove on the periphery of the wheel, and the load W is raised by a cord wrapped around the axle. When the axle is stationary, the tendencies of P and W to cause rotation are equal and opposite. Neglecting bearing friction, the product of the effort P and the wheel radius R is equal to the product of the load W and the axle radius r:

$$P \times R = W \times r.$$

The mechanical advantage is again equal to W/P, which is equal to the ratio of the radius of the wheel R to the radius of the axle r.

The situation is similar to that for the lever. A lever, however, can move a load for only short distances, while the wheel and axle can move the load for a distance limited only by the available lengths of the cords.

With the wheel A and cord replaced by a spoked wheel, the wheel and axle is well suited for raising buckets of water from a well. More importantly, however, the wheel-and-axle principle is perceptible in many tools and machines. On a screwdriver, for example, the force applied by the hand on a large radius is converted to a larger force on the screw at a smaller radius.

The pulley is one of the most useful of the basic simple machines. It consists essentially of a wheel with a grooved rim carrying a flexible cord and supported in either a

Wheel
and
axle

fixed or a movable bearing block. When used singly with a fixed bearing block, like pulley *A* in Figure 2E, a downward pull creates an upward force of the same magnitude. In Figure 2E this pulley and one with a movable block *B* are combined. If friction is neglected, the tension *P* in the cord is the same at all points, and consequently a given downward pull on the loose end of the cord will lift twice as much weight at *W*, and the weight *W* will move half as far as the cord. The mechanical advantage is therefore two. Mechanical advantages greater than two can be obtained by using a variety of combinations of pulleys having both fixed and moving blocks. Such an arrangement, known as a block and tackle, is basically a force-amplifying device.

Consider now the action of the wedge in Figure 3, which is being driven to the left by the force *P*. The smaller the angle *θ* and the smaller the frictional force *F*,

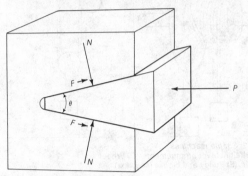

Figure 3: Wedge action (see text).

the greater the splitting force *N* in terms of *P*. For any surface smoothness of the wedge, and corresponding frictional resistance, if *θ* is greater than a given value the wedge will fall out of its own accord when *P* is removed; if *θ* is less than a given value, the wedge will stay in place or "stick" when *P* is removed.

Sticking tapers are used for holding cutting tools such as drills and reamers in machine tool spindles. Other mechanical devices that operate on the wedge principle are wood planes, chisels, knives, metal-cutting tools, and cams.

The screw

The screw may be thought of as a wedge wrapped around a cylinder. A screw is formed by cutting a continuous groove in a solid circular cylinder, successive turns of the groove being separated by the remaining solid material, called the thread. Both the thread and the groove are helical in form; *i.e.*, shaped like a corkscrew. The geometry of the helix was developed by the Greek mathematician Apollonius of Perga about 200 BC.

If the sheet of paper *ACC'A'* at the right in Figure 4, with the lines *AB'* and *BD* drawn on it, were wrapped around the cylinder of diameter *d* at the left, the lines

would form one and one-half turns of a helix. The distance *l*, which is the axial distance corresponding to one turn of the helix, is called the lead. The lead angle *λ* is a measure of the slope of the helix.

Some early screws were cut by a method that resembles the method used to develop the helix at the left in Figure 4. A thin sheet of pliable material in the form of a right triangle was wrapped around the cylindrical "blank" so that one arm of the right angle was parallel to the axis. The hypotenuse would then form a helix on the cylinder and serve as a guide for the tool when cutting the helical groove.

If a sliding member such as *F* in Figure 4 were constrained to move parallel to the axis of the cylinder, such as along the axis *OO'*, it could be actuated either by a rotation of the cylinder and helix or a translation of the straightened-out helix. In either case the wedging action is apparent. If the member *F* were part of a nut constrained against rotation but free to move axially, the screw–nut combination would constitute a mechanism for converting rotary to rectilinear motion.

As a force amplifier, the screw has few equals. In the form of a screw jack its capacity for lifting weights is limited only by the strength of the material from which it is made. On a screw jack the nut is fixed, the load is carried on the end of the screw, and the effort is applied as a turning moment or torque on the screw.

In Figure 4 (left) let *P* be the effort, applied to the screw at a radius *R*, and *W* the load, moving with *F*. In one revolution the effort moves a distance equal to the circumference of the circle of radius *R*, or $2\pi R$, while the load is raised a distance *l*. Thus the velocity (and the distance) ratio is $2\pi R/l$ and, if friction is neglected, this is also the mechanical advantage. Since the screw acts like a wedge, however, the force relationships are heavily dependent on friction. If a screw–nut combination is used for motion conversion, a high efficiency is desirable; if the efficiency is high enough (that is, if friction is reduced sufficiently) and *λ* is large enough, the nut can drive the screw. Such a high efficiency is undesirable on a screw jack since the load would descend by itself if the force *P* were removed; that is, a screw jack should be self-locking. Stated in other words, the screw taper must be less than the sticking taper. High efficiency and self-locking are incompatible.

In addition to its usefulness as a fastening device, a force amplifier, and a motion converter, the helix appears in many mechanical devices. Among these are a corkscrew, a helical gear, a meat grinder, a propeller, a carpenter's drill bit, a screw conveyor, and a twist drill for metal. In the latter, the helical groove provides the proper angle for the cutting point and a channel for the escape of chips.

Most of the simple machines have been shown to be essentially hand-operated devices for lifting heavy weights or creating large forces with smaller ones. Some writers claim that all machines, no matter how complicated, are combinations of these simple machines. This may have been true when human or animal muscle was the only source of power; it is certainly not true today.

The effectiveness of any of the simple machines is based on either the leverage principle or a wedging action. Insofar as these effects are built into many of the mechanical devices found in machinery, the simple machines do exert an influence on machine operation. The devices that have the greatest influence on machine performance, however, are the basic mechanisms. It is from combinations of these that most machines are created.

MECHANISMS

History. Linkages, cams, and gears are usually grouped together in books on the kinematics of mechanisms. The major portion of the history of mechanisms below deals with linkages, partly because few historical facts exist concerning cams and partly because the history of gears is covered later in this article.

In 1806 the first course in the study of mechanisms, separate from both general mechanics and the science of machines, was introduced at the École Polytechnique in Paris. For use in this course, a synoptic chart of elemen-

Origin of kinematics

Figure 4: Graphical construction of a helix (see text).

tary mechanisms was prepared that classified them by the means employed to effect transformations of motion; this chart was the prototype for several subsequent charts. The French physicist André-Marie Ampère gave the new science the name *cinématique* in 1834 and outlined its scope, which, according to him, was the study of the motions that occur in mechanisms without considering the forces that produce them. Thus, kinematics as a separate study was born in France; almost all the early kinematicians were French.

The next forward step in the analysis of mechanisms was made in England by Robert Willis, who published a book on the subject in 1841. Willis presented another synoptic table of elementary mechanisms, but his main contribution was in the analysis of relative motion. Though he had hoped to develop formulas that would enable a designer to determine all the possible ways in which a problem in motion conversion could be solved, he did not succeed.

A noteworthy contribution to applied kinematics was made in Germany by Franz Reuleaux in a book that presented a new way of looking at mechanisms. In older books on machinery, each machine was analyzed as a whole; Reuleaux recognized that all machines have common elements connected by joints that permit only certain kinds of relative motion. All joints have two co-acting surfaces that Reuleaux called pairs. A turning, or revolute, pair, for example, is a pin joint with axial restraints and permits relative rotation only; a prismatic pair is a sliding joint that permits relative translation (linear motion) only. A closed chain of links joined together by pairs forms a kinematic "chain," and when one of the links is fixed a mechanism is obtained. Reuleaux also showed that, depending on which link in the chain is fixed, mechanisms with different characteristics can be created; this is the principle of inversion, which has great analytical significance.

The analysis of mechanisms, particularly linkages, was greatly enhanced by the work of A.B.W. Kennedy (translator of Reuleaux's book in 1876) and R.H. Smith in England. In 1885 Smith presented methods for obtaining velocities and accelerations in linkages by means of graphical analysis. This was a real contribution to kinematic analysis; no simpler or more direct method has been devised. In certain cases, however, additional procedures may be necessary to effect a solution; in the 1950s two of these procedures were devised, so that practically any problem in velocity and acceleration analysis of a linkage can be solved by graphical constructions. Until recently, Germany was the leader in both quality and quantity in the field of kinematic analysis and synthesis, and most of the graphical procedures for the synthesis of linkages were worked out there. In recent years the Soviet Union has shown an increasing interest in kinematics, particularly in analytical procedures for the synthesis of linkages. In the United States, considerable interest in kinematics developed after World War II, and many computer programs for the analysis and design of linkages are available.

Basic types. The purpose of a mechanism is to transmit motion, either with or without modification, and although mechanisms are made in a wide variety of forms, there are only three general classes or types, as shown in Figure 5.

In each of the mechanisms in the figure, links 2 and 4 are pivotally connected at O and Q to the fixed link 1. The three ways of transmitting motion shown in Figure 5 are: (A) by a flexible wrapping connector such as a

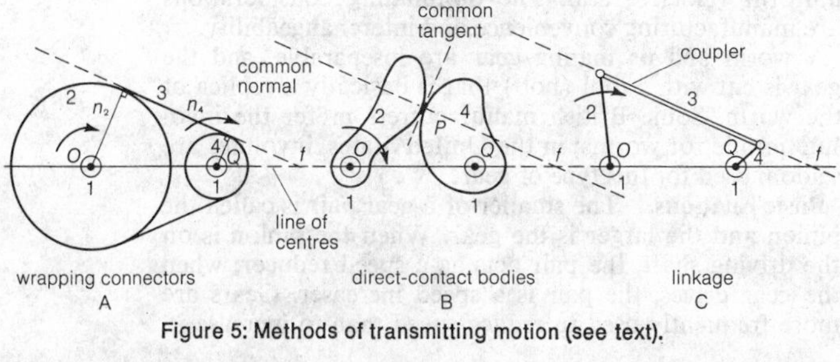

belt, rope, cable, or chain; (B) by direct contact, as in cams, gears, or friction wheels; and (C) by a rigid connecting link, or coupler. In each case, link 2 is the driver, rotating at n_2 revolutions per minute, while link 4 is the follower, rotating at n_4 revolutions per minute. For all three cases, the ratio of the rotary speed of link 4 to the rotary speed of link 2 is given by the ratio of the length Of to the length Qf. In Figure 5A, since point f remains fixed on the line of centres OQ, the speed ratio is constant; in Figures 5B and 5C, since f will move as the bodies rotate, the speed ratio will vary. Direct-contact bodies can be designed only to oscillate, like those in Figure 5B, or to rotate continuously. In all cases, point f lies at the intersection of the common normal and the line of centres.

Direct-contact mechanisms. In the most general case, the surfaces of bodies in direct contact slide on one another, and the more sliding that occurs, the greater will be the deterioration of the surfaces. Under certain conditions, pure rolling contact, which results in lower surface wear, can be effected; if other conditions are satisfied, the bodies will transmit motion with a uniform (constant) velocity ratio. These special cases are of interest in connection with gears and cams. The condition for pure rolling is that the point of contact lies on the line of centres.

There are three types of pure rolling contact. When the two bodies are circular cylinders, the common normal will lie on the line of centres, and the load that can be transmitted will depend on the friction between the surfaces. This is known as friction-dependent rolling. For a positive drive (one independent of friction) the common normal must not pass through the centre of either the driver or the follower. Since, neglecting friction, the force between two bodies in direct contact acts along the normal, the follower will be positively driven when the line of action of the force does not pass through the pivotal axis of the follower. The bodies in Figure 5B, making contact at point P, provide a positive drive.

Bodies can be designed so that continuous rolling takes place. A pair of identical ellipses pivoted at their foci will contact one another on the line of centres in all positions (see Figure 9B).

For any pair of direct-contact bodies the only variable in the formula for velocity ratio is the position of f in Figure 5B. Consequently, the condition for a uniform or constant velocity ratio is that the common normal cut the line of centres at a fixed point. The normal may rotate, but as long as it cuts the line of centres at the same point the velocity ratio will remain constant.

For almost any given body shape or profile, another profile can be constructed that will transmit motion with a uniform velocity ratio. This is called a conjugate profile. There are also mathematically describable curves inherently capable of conjugate action; two of them, the cycloid and the involute, are used for gear teeth. A cycloid is the path traced in space by a point on the rim of a rolling wheel. The profile of a gear tooth is obtained from the path traced by a point on the rim of a small circle rolling on the inside and outside of a larger circle. An involute is the path traced by a point on a string as it is unwound from a circular cylinder. The way in which the contacting surfaces of involute gear teeth co-act with one another can best be understood by studying a pair of involutes in contact. In Figure 6, two involutes generated from base circles 1 and 2 are shown in contact at three points, m, f, and n. Note that since base circle 2 is larger than base circle 1, the involutes have different shapes.

Since two contacting curves must have a common tangent and a common normal at the point of contact, the common normal for the involutes in all of the three positions shown in Figure 6 must be xy, the common tangent to the base circles. The intersection of this normal and the line of centres OQ is at f, which remains fixed, and, consequently, the bodies are conjugate. All involutes are conjugate to one another.

If the involutes in Figure 6 were generated on metal plates mounted on pivots at O and Q, and if 1 were the driver, rotating counterclockwise, then contact between the involutes would begin at r and end at s. During this

Pure rolling contact

The involute

Figure 5: Methods of transmitting motion (see text).

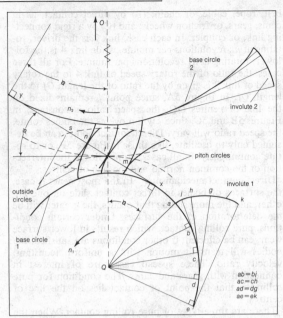

Figure 6: *Involute gear surfaces in contact.*
Involutes 1 and 2 are examples of involutes that may be
generated from the base circles (see text).

partial rotation the point of contact between the involutes
would move along the line *xy* from *r* to *f* to *s*. At *f*, since
the condition for pure rolling is satisfied, the involutes
would roll on one another; at all other points there would
be sliding contact.

The two circles of radii *Of* and *Qf* in Figure 6 are known
as the pitch circles, and *f* is the pitch point. The circles are
useful for reference purposes in analyzing gears, and
when the shafts are parallel they represent the pair of
friction disks that, by pure rolling contact, would transmit the motion at the same rate as the gears. The outside
circles are the circles represented by the outer periphery
of the gear teeth.

The two involutes in Figure 6 would remain in contact
for only part of a revolution. To obtain continuous rotation, as in gears, a number of equally spaced involutes
would be required on each base circle.

The possibility of obtaining pure rolling, a positive drive,
and a uniform velocity ratio simultaneously and continuously has long challenged inventors. It is easy to demonstrate that any two of the states can coexist continuously,
but not all three. The rolling ellipses in Figure 9B provide a positive drive, except in the end positions, but the
velocity ratio is not uniform. Rolling circular disks or
truncated cones provide a uniform velocity ratio, but the
drive is not positive. A positive drive is always a requirement of gear teeth and so also, in most cases, is a
uniform velocity ratio. When the teeth touch on the line
of centres they also have pure rolling contact, but only
for an instant.

GEARS

Gears are direct-contact bodies, operating in pairs, that
transmit motion and force from one rotating shaft to
another, or from a shaft to a slide (rack), by means of
successively engaging projections called teeth. The four
main types of gears (spur, helical, worm, and bevel) and
a rack and pinion are shown in Figure 7.

History. The earliest known gears were those in the
Chinese South-Pointing Chariot in the 27th century BC.
The gear teeth were wooden pins arranged in a complex
gear train that drove a statuette with outstretched arm
that always pointed in the same direction, regardless of
the direction in which the chariot was moving. The
earliest written descriptions of gears were made by Aristotle in the 4th century BC. Ctesibius (3rd century BC), a
Greek inventor, used spur and bevel gears in his water
clocks and organs, and Archimedes mentions worm
gears in his writings. Vitruvius, who invented the vertical
waterwheel, used a right-angle pin-gear drive from the

horizontal wheel shaft to the vertical shaft of the mill-
stone. The notebooks of Leonardo da Vinci contain
sketches of spur, bevel, and worm gears. It is probable
that none of these men paid much attention to the
problem of kinematically correct tooth profiles that
would provide a constant velocity ratio (conjugate
profiles).

Although the cycloid curve had been known for over
200 years, it was not until 1674 that its suitability for
gear-tooth profiles was demonstrated. For the next century and a half the respective merits of the cycloid and involute were debated; since the 1830s involutes have been
preferred for power drives; for clocks and watches, cy-
cloids have advantages.

The first spur and bevel gears were cut with form cutters shaped to correspond to the spaces between the teeth.
The oldest known rotating cutter of this type was handmade by a French mechanic, Jacques de Vaucanson, in
1782. This cutter was used on a milling machine; special
machines for cutting gears did not appear until about the
mid-19th century.

Tooth profiles. The contacting surfaces of gear teeth
must be aligned in such a way that the drive is positive;
i.e., the load transmitted must not depend on frictional
contact. As shown in the treatment of direct-contact
bodies, this requires that the common normal to the surfaces must not pass through the pivotal axis of either the
driver or the follower.

Most gears are also required to have tooth profiles of
such a shape that the velocity ratio of the gears remains
constant (unless otherwise noted, this article will deal
with such gears only). This requires that the common
normal must cut the line between the pivots at a fixed
point.

As shown in the section on direct-contact bodies, cycloidal and involute profiles provide both a positive
drive and a uniform velocity ratio; *i.e.*, conjugate action.

Some of the advantages of the involute as a gear-tooth Gear-
profile have already been enumerated. The factors to be tooth
considered in evaluating a gear-tooth profile include ease profiles
of manufacture, sensitivity to maladjustment, and load-
carrying capacity. On all of these counts the involute is
superior or equal to the cycloid. Involutes, however, are
unsuitable for the teeth of driven gears having as few as
six or seven teeth and capable of action through 60 degrees of rotation. This is a requirement for watch and
clock gears, and since they can supply it, cycloidal teeth
or ogival (circular arc) approximations thereto are used
on watches, clocks, and small instruments. Another type
of pinion (small gear) used in clockwork is the lantern
pinion, or pin gear. The teeth are short lengths of hard,
polished, steel wire held between two end plates, and the
teeth on the mating gear are conjugate epicycloids. By
using rollers in place of fixed pins, the friction is reduced.

Circular profiles have been proposed for gears, most
recently in the Soviet Union. Since contacting involutes
are both convex, the contact stresses are higher than in a
convex-concave pair such as can be obtained with circular
profiles. In spite of their higher surface load-carrying capacity, however, circular-profile gears are seldom used,
because they lack the profile interchangeability of involute
gears, are difficult to manufacture, and are sensitive to
centre-distance variations.

In spite of some deficiencies, the involute is still the most
commonly used gear-tooth profile. As far as the transmission of motion is concerned, it does not matter what
shape the teeth on a gear pair have as long as they are
conjugate to one another; *i.e.*, transmit the motion with a
uniform velocity ratio. The dominating considerations
are manufacturing convenience and interchangeability.

A worm and its mating gear are inseparable, and the
gear is cut with a tool (hob) that is basically a replica of
the worm. Some British manufacturers prefer the involute profile for worms; in the United States, involutes are
seldom used for this type of gear.

Basic relations. The smaller of a gear pair is called the
pinion and the larger is the gear. When the pinion is on
the driving shaft, the pair acts as a speed reducer; when
the gear drives, the pair is a speed increaser. Gears are
more frequently used to reduce speed than to increase it.

Figure 7: *Gears*.
(Left to right) Rack and pinion, spur gears, helical gears, worm and gear, bevel gears (see text).
By courtesy of Illinois Gear Division, Wallace-Murray Corporation

Gear ratio and speed ratio

If a gear having N teeth rotates at n revolutions per minute, the product Nn has the dimension "teeth per minute." This product must be the same for both members of a mating pair if each tooth is to acquire a partner from the mating gear as it passes through the region of tooth engagement.

For conjugate gears of all types, the gear ratio and the speed ratio are both given by the ratio of the number of teeth on the gear to the number of teeth on the pinion. If a gear has 100 teeth and a mating pinion 20, the ratio is $^{100}\!/_{20} = 5$. Thus the pinion rotates five times as fast as the gear, regardless of the speed of the gear.

If the shafts are parallel, the gear and pinion could be replaced by a pair of cylinders that would transmit the motion by pure rolling contact at the same speed ratio as the gears. On the gears, the circles that represent these imaginary cylinders are called the pitch circles; these are useful for reference purposes in the analysis of gears. Their point of tangency is called the pitch point, and since it lies on the line of centres, it is the only point at which the tooth profiles have pure rolling contact. Gears on nonparallel, non-intersecting shafts also have pitch circles, but the rolling-pitch-circle concept is not valid.

Gear types are determined largely by the disposition of the shafts; in addition, certain types are better suited than others for large speed changes. This means that if a specific disposition of the shafts is required, the type of gear is more or less fixed. On the other hand, if a required speed change demands a certain type, the shaft positions are fixed.

Spur and helical gears. A gear having tooth elements that are straight and parallel to its axis is known as a spur gear. A spur pair can be used to connect parallel shafts only. Parallel shafts, however, can also be connected by gears of another type, and a spur gear can be mated with a gear of a different type.

In Figure 6, if the involutes are on a single pair of teeth on mating involute spur gears, then, since contact begins at r and ends at s, to obtain continuous transmission of motion, a pair must come into contact at r before the preceding pair goes out of contact at s. Whether this does or does not occur depends on the tooth spacing and the length of the line rs, which depends on the amounts that the teeth project above and below the pitch circles. Satisfactory values of those dimensions have been standardized.

Since the pitch circles roll on one another, the spacing of the teeth on these circles on a mating pair must be equal. This spacing, which is known as the circular pitch p and is a measure of tooth size, is the distance between corresponding points on adjacent teeth, measured on the pitch circle.

To prevent jamming as a result of thermal expansion, to aid lubrication, and to compensate for unavoidable inaccuracies in manufacture, all power-transmitting gears must have backlash. This means that on the pitch circles of a mating pair, the space width on the pinion must be slightly greater than the tooth thickness on the gear, and vice versa. On instrument gears, backlash can be elimi-

nated by using a gear split down its middle, one half being rotatable relative to the other. A spring forces the split gear teeth to occupy the full width of the pinion space.

If an involute spur pinion were made of rubber and twisted uniformly so that the ends rotated about the axis relative to one another, the elements of the teeth, initially straight and parallel to the axis, would become helices. The pinion then in effect would become a helical gear.

Helical gears have certain advantages; for example, when connecting parallel shafts they have a higher load-carrying capacity than spur gears with the same tooth numbers and cut with the same cutter. Because of the overlapping action of the teeth, they are smoother in action and can operate at higher pitch-line velocities than spur gears. The pitch-line velocity is the velocity of the pitch circle. Since the teeth are inclined to the axis of rotation, helical gears create an axial thrust. If used singly, this thrust must be absorbed in the shaft bearings. The thrust problem can be overcome by cutting two sets of opposed helical teeth on the same blank. Depending on the method of manufacture, the gear may be of the continuous-tooth herringbone variety or a double-helical gear with a space between the two halves to permit the cutting tool to run out. Double-helical gears are well suited for the efficient transmission of power at high speeds. An important application of such gears is for geared-turbine ship drives. On the former British passenger liner "Queen Mary," of 80,000 tons displacement, there were four single-reduction, double-helical gearboxes transmitting a total of 160,000 horsepower from turbines rotating at 1,500 and 1,050 revolutions per minute to a propeller shaft rotating at 180 revolutions per minute. Each large driven gear was approximately 13.5 feet (4 metres) in diameter.

Ship propulsion gears

Helical gears can also be used to connect nonparallel, non-intersecting shafts at any angle to one another. Ninety degrees is the commonest angle at which such gears are used. When the shafts are parallel, the contact between the teeth on mating gears is "line contact" regardless of whether the teeth are straight or helical. When the shafts are inclined, the contact becomes "point contact." For this reason, crossed-axis helical gears do not have as much load-carrying capacity as parallel-shaft helicals. They are relatively insensitive to misalignment, however, and are frequently employed in instruments and positioning mechanisms where friction is the only force opposing their motion.

As stated above, the rolling-pitch-circle concept, which applies to gears on parallel shafts, does not apply to gears on nonparallel, non-intersecting shafts. This means that a large speed ratio on one pair of gears, 100 for example, is more easily obtained when the axes are crossed than when they are parallel. With parallel shafts, the pinion pitch diameter would have to be $^1\!/_{100}$ of the gear pitch diameter, an impractical proportion. With crossed axes, the pinion could have only one helical tooth—or thread—and be as large as necessary for adequate strength. The pinion would look like a screw, and the gear would have 100 teeth.

Worm and bevel gears.   In order to achieve line contact and improve the load-carrying capacity of the crossed-axis helical gears, the gear can be made to curve partially around the pinion, in somewhat the same way that a nut envelops a screw. The result would be a cylindrical worm and gear. Worms are also made in the shape of an hourglass, instead of cylindrical, so that they partially envelop the gear. This results in a further increase in load-carrying capacity.

Worm gears provide the simplest means of obtaining large ratios in a single pair. They are usually less efficient than parallel-shaft gears, however, because of an additional sliding movement along the teeth. Because of their similarity, the efficiency of a worm and gear depends on the same factors as the efficiency of a screw. Single-thread worms of large diameter have small lead angles and low efficiencies. Multiple-thread worms have larger lead angles and higher efficiencies. For lead angles of about 15 degrees and a coefficient of friction less than 0.15, the efficiency ranges from about 55 percent to 95 percent, and the gear can drive the worm. Such units make compact speed increasers; they have been used for driving superchargers on aircraft engines. In self-locking worms, the gear cannot drive the worm, and the efficiency is less than 50 percent.

For transmitting rotary motion and torque around corners, bevel gears are commonly used. The connected shafts, whose axes would intersect if extended, are usually but not necessarily at right angles to one another. The pitch surfaces of bevel gears are rolling, truncated cones, and the teeth, which must be tapered in both thickness and height, are either straight or curved. Although curved-tooth bevel gears are called spiral bevel gears, the curve of the teeth is usually a circular arc. The curvature of the teeth results in overlapping tooth action and a smoother transmission of power than with straight teeth. For high speeds and torques, spiral bevel gears are superior to straight bevel gears in much the same way that helical gears are superior to spur gears for connecting parallel shafts.

Hypoid gears

When adapted for shafts that do not intersect, spiral bevel gears are called hypoid gears. The pitch surfaces of these gears are not rolling cones, and the ratio of their mean diameters is not equal to the speed ratio. Consequently, the pinion may have few teeth and be made as large as necessary to carry the load. This permits higher speed ratios than with intersecting axes, just as crossed-axis helicals and worm gears can provide higher ratios than parallel helicals. The absence of the proportional rolling-pitch surface requirement is a benefit.

Hypoid gears are used on automobiles to connect the drive shaft to the rear axles. The axis of the pinion on the drive shaft is below the gear axis, which permits lowering of the engine and the centre of gravity of the vehicle. Since the shafts do not intersect, several gear shafts may be driven from pinions mounted on a single pinion shaft, as in tandem axles for trucks.

The profiles of the teeth on bevel gears are not involutes; they are of such a shape that the tools for cutting the teeth are easier to make and maintain than involute cutting tools. Since bevel gears come in pairs, as long as they are conjugate to one another they need not be conjugate to other gears with different tooth numbers.

Planetary and differential gears.   The external spur gears in Figure 7 rotate in opposite directions, and the centre distance is the sum of their pitch radii. A pinion and an internal or ring gear rotate in the same direction, and the centre distance is the difference of their pitch radii. The teeth on an internal gear, which may be straight or helical, are cut on the inside of a cup-shaped member.

A useful arrangement of external gears and an internal gear is shown in Figure 8 (left). The sun gear S on shaft 1 meshes with three planet gears P that are carried on bearings on a carrier A attached to shaft 2. The planet gears also mesh with the internal ring gear 3, whose supporting hub, not shown, is coaxial with shafts 1 and 2.

Since there are three rotatable coaxial shafts, any two of them must be inputs if the arrangement is to have con-

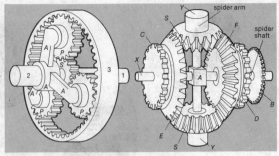

Figure 8: *Two types of gear assemblies* (see text). (Left) Planetary or epicyclic gear train. (Right) Bevel gear differential (see text).

strained motion and serve a useful purpose. Usually, one of the shafts is fixed, which corresponds to a zero input, and the other two shafts serve as either inputs or outputs. The three different speed ratios that can be obtained depend on which of the three shafts is fixed, and the ratio of the number of teeth on the ring gear to the number of teeth on the sun gear. If this ratio is three, for example, the following different speed ratios can be obtained. If the arm (shaft 2) is fixed, the sun gear and shaft 1 rotate three times as fast as the internal gear and shaft 3, and in the opposite direction. Since all gears rotate about fixed axes, this is an ordinary gear train.

If the internal ring gear 3 is locked, a planetary or epicyclic system results; shaft 1 rotates at four times the speed of shaft 2 and in the same direction. The planet gears have a planetary motion, moving around the sun gear in a circular orbit while rotating relative to the arm. When the sun gear (shaft 1) is fixed, for every three revolutions of shaft 2, shaft 3 makes four revolutions in the same direction. This is also a planetary system.

Planetary arrangements of the type described are used in the automatic transmissions of automobiles; in these, the fixing and interconnecting are done automatically with brakes and clutches.

Gears can be arranged to form planetary systems in a variety of ways. The planet gears may be compounded (*i.e.*, have more than one gear on the same shaft) and mesh with other sun and internal gears. None of the gears may be fixed; in this case any two (including the arm) may be attached to input shafts and the remainder to output shafts. Speed ratios of 10,000 and higher can be obtained.

Differential gears

Planetary arrangements with bevel gears are also available. The bevel gear differential in Figure 8 (right; invented in 1827 by a French mechanic for steam-powered road vehicles) is such an arrangement; it can perform many useful functions in the operation of machines. The strictly planetary action is confined to the two pairs of equal bevel gears (SS and EF), which are free to rotate on the arm and shaft of the cross-shaped "spider" A, which in turn can rotate about the fixed axis XX; the axis YY of the spider arm sweeps out a plane perpendicular to the spider shaft and carries the gears S with it. If gear E is fixed and gear F rotated about the spider shaft, the gears S will act like levers, with fulcrums at gear E, efforts at gear F, and loads perpendicular to the axis YY. Since YY is halfway between E and F, it (and shaft A) will rotate only half as much as gear F. Mathematically, with E fixed, $A = F/2$ in which A and F are either the angular displacements or angular velocities of the spider arm and the gear F, respectively. With F fixed, $A = E/2$, and, combining the two effects, the fundamental equation for the bevel gear differential is $A = \dfrac{E + F}{2}$. This means that the rotation of the spider shaft is half the sum of the rotations of the side gears.

Since there are three variables in this equation, any two must be known before the third can be calculated. This means that the bevel gear differential must have two inputs. Usually the inputs come from outside sources to the spur gears C and D, which are fixed to the side gears E and F, respectively; the output is delivered to another outside source through the spur gear B, which is fixed to the spider shaft A. If E makes 100 revolutions while F makes 80 revolutions in the same direction, then $A = 180/2 = 90$ revolutions. If E and F rotate in opposite directions at the same speed, then $E - F = 0$ and the spider shaft will stand still. This effect can be used to synchronize the speeds of two engines or to detect errors in automatic-control mechanisms. Differentials of the type shown in Figure 8 (right) are widely used in analogue computers and instrument systems.

In an automobile, the differential permits the driving wheels to rotate at different speeds (as when turning) while both are being driven from the same source. The spider shaft is the input or driving member, while the side gears are connected to the wheel axles. The road acts as a gear train that controls the ratio of the wheel speeds.

Since the tooth loads between gears S and E and between S and F in Figure 8 (right) are always equal, the torques on both rear axles in an automobile are always equal. If one wheel slips on the ice, it can develop little torque and neither can the other wheel. To correct this basic weakness of the automobile differential, "limited slip" differentials have been developed.

Gear trains and reducers. The maximum gear ratio obtainable with a single pair of gears varies with the type of gear and the application. The following are approximate maxima for the various types for average load conditions: spur, 8; parallel-shaft helical, 10; straight bevel, 6; spiral bevel, 8; hypoid, 12; and worm, 80. For lightly loaded, instrument, and positioning gears, these ratios can be exceeded. Ratios as high as 400 or higher can be obtained with gears that resemble tapered worms meshing with hypoid gears. For heavily loaded gears, the given ratios may be so high that a reasonable gear size precludes a satisfactory pinion.

Since the ratio in a single pair of gears is the quotient of the tooth numbers, and since there usually are limitations on both the minimum and maximum numbers of teeth on the available gears, it follows that the number of ratios obtainable in a single pair is limited. To enlarge the coverage it is necessary to use multiple pairs, or trains (Figure 9A). The overall speed ratio in a train is the product

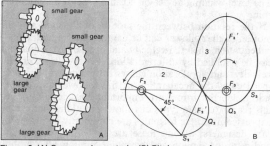

Figure 9: (A) Compound gear train. (B) Pitch curves of elliptical gears (see text).

of the ratios in each pair. In certain cases an exact ratio cannot be obtained with gears, but by using two or more pairs, the desired ratio can be approximated to any degree of precision.

As a convenience for machine builders and users, packaged speed reducers, following an industry-accepted pattern, are manufactured in a wide variety of types, configurations, speed ratios, and capacities; these consist of a box or housing containing bearings, shafts, gears, lubricant, and shaft oil seals. Speed increasers are usually custom built.

All speed reducers when operating continuously become hot because of friction in the teeth, in the lubricant, in the bearings, and in the oil seals. If the heat is generated at a faster rate than it can be dissipated to the atmosphere, the lubricant may deteriorate and the gears or bearings fail.

Materials and cutting methods. The first toothed wheels were made of wood, and wooden gears are still to be found in rural gristmills driven by waterpower. These "mortise" wheels consist of maple teeth set in a grooved rim. Many of the early metallic gears were cast to shape in sand molds. The hard skin on the surface of uncut as-

cast iron and steel has excellent wearing qualities, and gears with cast teeth are still used on low-speed agricultural machinery and on equipment that is exposed to the atmosphere.

Zinc, brass, aluminum, and magnesium gears of the smaller sizes are made in die-casting machines. These machines have permanent metallic cavities or dies into which molten metal is forced. Many small gears of nylon, Bakelite, and other thermoplastic materials are produced in large quantities in injection molding machines. Sintered gears are made by pouring a metallic powder into a mold, compressing the powder into a briquette with a punchlike tool, stripping the briquette from the mold with another tool, and then baking the briquette in an oven. Cold-drawn pinion stock, in the form of a long rod with continuous teeth, is also available. Pinions of any required length can be cut from the rod. Nylon gears

The machining of gears involves the cutting of grooves to form teeth on a previously machined blank; it always requires special tools and, in most cases, special machines. Practically all gear-cutting processes can be classified as either forming, in which the shape of the tool is reproduced on the blank, or generating, in which the shape produced depends on both the shape of the tool and the relative motion between the tool and the blank.

Spur gears can be form-cut, one space at a time, with a disk-type or an end-mill-type milling cutter (see also MACHINE TOOLS). They can also be cut with a broach, which forms all the tooth spaces simultaneously. These cutters resemble long internal gears, with teeth of continuously increasing depth and relieved to provide cutting edges. The broach is pushed over the gear blank, usually in a hydraulic press, and all the tooth spaces can be cut in one pass. Broaches for internal gears resemble long spur gears. Since the shape of an involute depends on the size of the base circle, a form cutter is accurate for only one number of teeth of a given pitch.

Because all involutes are conjugate to one another, any one of a set of involute spur gears (including a rack) of the same pitch but different numbers of teeth could be used to generate all other gears in the set if it were provided with cutting edges and reciprocated parallel to its axis as it rotated, as if in mesh with the blank. This is the principle of operation of a gear shaper, which can generate both external and internal spur and helical gears.

Worms are usually cut with disk-shaped milling cutters in thread-milling machines and finished with a grinding wheel. Worm gears are cut on hobbing machines with a hob (a replica of the worm with longitudinal gashes) and, as both rotate, it is fed to depth in a radial or tangential direction relative to the blank. If a hob has teeth with straight sides similar to a rack, and after being fed to depth radially is fed longitudinally parallel to the blank axis, it will generate a spur gear. One involute hob of a given pitch can generate all gears of that pitch, regardless of the number of teeth. Hobbing machines are used extensively for the rapid production of spur and helical gears of medium and small pitches. Hobbing gears

Bevel gears with straight teeth are roughed out with a form cutter and then generated on special generating machines. Spiral bevel gears are cut with a special cutter on a special machine that can be set up to cut with either a forming or a generating action.

For improving the surface finish and profile accuracy of cut gears, shaving and grinding machines are available. Shaving machines are used extensively in the automotive industry for spur and helical gears. Gear grinding wheels and machines operate on both the forming and generating principles.

A recent development (1969) gives promise of superseding traditional gear finishing methods. This new process is known as roll forming, or "chipless machining," and involves the squeezing of a prehobbed gear with finish-roll allowance between two diametrically opposed hardened master gears or dies. Tests on roll-formed gears indicate that the new method reduces manufacturing costs and improves the physical properties of the gears.

Non-circular gears. The rolling-pitch-circle concept applies only to gears connecting parallel shafts. Parallel shafts can also be connected by gears with non-circular pitch curves. These non-circular gears transmit the motion with a varying speed ratio and can be designed for almost any prescribed spectrum of speed ratios. Their speed-changing capabilities depend entirely on the shapes of their rolling pitch curves. As indicated in the section on direct-contact bodies, rolling contact between two bodies rotating about fixed pivots requires that the point of contact remain always on the line of pivot centres, and the speed ratio is the inverse ratio of the segments into which the distance between the pivots (the centre distance) is divided by the point of contact.

The pitch curves of non-circular gears may be open (like a circular arc) or closed (like a complete circle). Those with open curves can oscillate only through angles less than 360 degrees and are usually employed to generate mathematical functions in analogue computers; those with closed curves can make complete revolutions and are used to convert uniform to variable rotary motion.

Elliptical gears

Figure 9B shows two identical ellipses pivoted at their foci F_2 and F_3; the other foci are F_2' and F_3'. These ellipses will always touch on the line of centres $F_2 F_3$, and they could represent the pitch curves of a pair of non-circular gears. From symmetry, arc PQ_2S_2, which corresponds to 45 degrees on ellipse 2, will roll on arc PQ_3S_3, which corresponds to 180 degrees on ellipse 3. With the scale shown, ellipse 3 will make half a revolution while ellipse 2 makes only one-eighth of a revolution during one portion of a complete cycle; during another portion, ellipse 3 will make half a revolution while ellipse 2 makes seven-eighths of a revolution. If ellipse 2 were rotating at a constant speed, ellipse 3 would have a fluctuating speed. The cyclically repeating quick–slow rotations obtained with elliptical gears are useful on machines that operate intermittently and perform useful work during only a part of the revolution of a shaft or during only one stroke of a reciprocating member. On a printing press, for example, the motion of the platen should be rapid when the press is open but slow and powerful when the impression is being made.

CAMS

A cam is the driving or input member of a pair of bodies in direct contact, so shaped that its reciprocation, oscillation, or rotation, combined with a wedging action, imparts a prescribed motion of reciprocation or oscillation to a follower or output member. The shape of the cam is determined by the prescribed motion and the profile of the follower, which is usually flat or circular.

Cam–follower mechanisms can be designed to satisfy almost any input-output relationship within their scope. For some applications the capabilities of cams and linkage mechanisms overlap; in fact, German engineers use linkages to perform tasks American engineers do with cams. Cams are easier to design than linkage mechanisms for mutually appropriate applications, and they can do many things that a linkage cannot do. Linkages, on the other hand, are easier to make than cams.

Cams and linkages compared

Cam–follower mechanisms are particularly useful when a simple motion of one part of a machine is to be converted to a more complicated prescribed motion of another part that is accurately timed with respect to the simple motion and combined with periods of rest. The motion of the camshaft on an automobile engine, for example, is a simple rotation that is a fixed ratio of the crankshaft speed, while the valve motion produced by the cams is accurately timed relative to the crankshaft rotation and includes rest periods, or dwells, when the valves remain closed. Cams are essential elements in automatic machine tools, textile machinery, wire-drawing machines, shoe machinery, sewing machines, and printing machines.

On some machines the cam is a fixed disk with a suitably shaped periphery around which the follower, in its support, is rotated. In other cases, the roles of the cam and follower can be reversed; *i.e.*, the follower can drive the cam. These are known as inverse cam mechanisms and are not common. Because of their wedging action, cams make effective locking devices or force and torque amplifiers when rotatably mounted on fixed pivots.

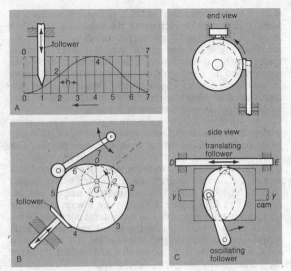

Figure 10: *Types of cams.*
(A) Translation cam. (B) Disk cam. (C) Cylindrical cam (see text).

The translation cam, Figure 10A, produces a vertical motion of the follower when the cam is moved horizontally. The disk cam, Figure 10B, is a flat, rotating plate with a curved contour. The disk cam can be conceived as having been formed by bending the translation cam around a disk of radius OG; the seven equal angular increments, such as θ, in Figure 10B, correspond with the seven equal linear increments, such as h, in Figure 10A. The cylindrical cam (Figure 10C) can be envisioned as having been formed by bending a rectangular plate such as 0077 of Figure 10A and a groove like the curved line into a circular cylinder. The groove would resemble the thread on a screw, but it would be endless and a follower fitting in the groove could be guided to move on the straight path DE parallel to the axis by a rotation of the drum about the yy axis. Oscillating arms with rollers fitting the groove in the drum are also used on these cams. The level-winding device on a fishing reel is a cylindrical cam.

If the relation between the motion of the cam and the motion of the follower can be expressed by a mathematical equation, then the velocity and acceleration equations can be obtained by differentiation, and the displacement, velocity, and acceleration curves can be drawn. On high-speed cams the acceleration of the follower and the resulting inertial forces are important considerations. For this reason, certain types of follower motions that can be expressed in simple formulas are commonly employed by cam designers; among these are uniformly accelerated and retarded motion and harmonic motion (the motion of a simple pendulum).

On the end that contacts the cam, reciprocating followers usually have either a roller or a flat face (Figure 10B). Oscillating followers are also made with flat faces. In all cases, the follower must be constrained to follow the cam either by a spring or by gravity.

In addition to disk and cylindrical cams there are many other types. Among these are the disk cam with dual rollers or an encircling yoke that keeps the follower and cam in contact at all times; the face cam with a follower groove cut in the face of a disk; the rolling cam, in which the cam and follower are in continuous pure rolling contact; and the three-dimensional cam. In the latter, the cam, which resembles a stack of infinitesimally thin disk cams of smoothly changing contour, rotates and translates so that the motion of the follower is a function of two variables. One application of three-dimensional cams is in the computation of the flight time of guided missiles.

LINKAGES

A linkage may be defined as an assemblage of solid bodies, or links, in which each link is connected to at least two others by pin connections (hinges) or sliding joints. To satisfy this definition, a linkage must form an endless, or closed, chain or a series of closed chains.

It is obvious that a chain with many links will behave differently from one with few. This raises the vitally important question regarding the suitability of a given linkage for the transmission of motion in a machine. This suitability depends on the number of links and the number of joints.

Degrees of freedom. A three-bar linkage (containing three bars linked together) is obviously a rigid frame; no relative motion between the links is possible. To describe the relative positions of the links in a four-bar linkage it is necessary only to know the angle between any two of the links. (Including the fixed link *OQ*, the mechanism in Figure 5C has four links and is thus a four-bar linkage.) This linkage is said to have one degree of freedom. Two angles are required to specify the relative positions of the links in a five-bar linkage; it has two degrees of freedom.

Con-
strained
motion Linkages with one degree of freedom have constrained motion; *i.e.*, all points on all of the links have paths on the other links that are fixed and determinate. The paths are most easily obtained or visualized by assuming that the link on which the paths are required is fixed, and then moving the other links in a manner compatible with the constraints.

Four-bar mechanisms. When one of the members of a constrained linkage is fixed, the linkage becomes a mechanism capable of performing a useful mechanical function in a machine. On pin-connected linkages the input (driver) and output (follower) links are usually pivotally connected to the fixed link; the connecting links (couplers) are usually neither inputs nor outputs. Since any of the links can be fixed, if the links are of different lengths, four mechanisms, each with a different input-output relationship, can be obtained with a four-bar linkage. These four mechanisms are said to be inversions of the basic linkage.

When the shortest link *a* in Figure 11 (top) is fixed, links *b* and *d* can make complete revolutions. This is known as a drag-link mechanism. If crank *b* rotates at a constant

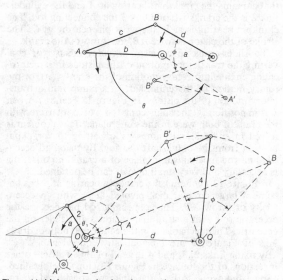

Figure 11: *Linkage mechanisms* (see text).
(Top) Drag-link mechanism. (Bottom) Crank-rocker mechanism.

speed, the crank *d* will rotate in the same direction at a varying speed. By itself, or in series with other mechanisms, the drag link can provide useful kinematic effects. In the figure, crank *b* is the driver, rotating counterclockwise at a uniform rate; crank *d* is the follower. Both cranks make a complete revolution in the same time, but while *b* sweeps out the angle θ, which is 150 degrees, the follower *d* sweeps out the angle ϕ which is only 50 degrees. This means that crank *d* will move more slowly than crank *b* when moving from *B* to *B'* and more quickly than *b* when moving from *B'* to *B*. If crank *d* were attached to a shaft in a packaging machine, for example, the slow part of its motion, which with some link proportions is almost a pause or a dwell, could be utilized for performing operations that must be done at a slow speed.

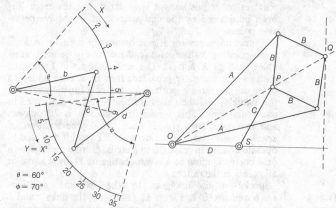

Figure 12: *Representative four-bar linkages and their applications.*
(Left) Function generator. (Right) Peaucellier straightline mechanism (see text).

The second inversion of the four-bar mechanism is obtained by using the shortest link *a* as the driver. As shown in Figure 11 (bottom), link *a* can make complete revolutions while the opposite link, which may be either *b*, *c*, or *d*, can only oscillate through the angle ϕ. This is called the crank-rocker mechanism; it is a useful device for producing oscillatory motion combined with a quick-return action that results from the fact that for counterclockwise rotation of *a*, the oscillation of *c* from *B* to *B'* corresponds with angle θ_1, while oscillation from *B'* to *B* corresponds with angle θ_2. Since crank *a* rotates at a constant speed and θ_1 is greater than θ_2, the rocker will take longer to swing from right to left than the other way. On machines that do useful work only when the active members are moving in one direction, quick-return devices return the members quickly to their initial position. Crank-
rocker
mecha-
nism

In the extreme positions, shown dotted in Figure 11 (bottom), the crank *a* and the coupler link *b* are lined up (collinear), and if the rocker *c* were the driver, means would have to be provided to carry the follower link *a* past these dead positions. On foot-operated grindstones the foot pedal is attached to link *c* and the grindstone shaft to link *a*. The angular momentum of the grindstone is utilized to carry the links past the dead positions.

On the third inversion of the four-bar mechanism, the shortest link *a* is the coupler, and the other moving links can only oscillate. This is called the double-rocker mechanism.

Linkage synthesis. Graphical and analytical methods can be readily employed for determining the displacement, velocity, and acceleration of the links in a linkage mechanism. The design, or synthesis, of linkages to satisfy specific requirements is much more difficult. There is no known method for designing a drag-link mechanism to satisfy a given spectrum of input-output relationships. The best that can be done is to survey the performance characteristics of a selected number of specific configurations and pick the optimum.

On the crank-rocker mechanism the designer can control the angle of oscillation of the rocker and, to a degree, the quick-return ratio. The crank and rocker displacements, velocities, and accelerations cannot be correlated.

If the cranks in a four-bar mechanism always rotate in the same or in opposite directions, and if their rotations are limited to considerably less than 180 degrees, it may be possible to correlate the crank rotations in three, four, five, or even a larger number of positions. Both analytic and graphic methods are available for making the correlations.

Figure 12 (left) shows a function generator that correlates the rotation of crank *b* over a 60-degree range with the rotation of crank *d* over a 70-degree range. The correlation is such as to satisfy the relationship $Y = X^2$, with *X* varying from 1 to 6 and *Y* from 1 to 36. The rotation of crank *b* is the mechanical analogue of *X*, while the rotation of crank *d* is the analogue of *Y*. The relation between *X* and *Y* is accurate at $X = 1.19$, 2.54, 4.46, and

5.81; at other positions it is in error, but the error has been minimized by the odd spacing of the above precision points.

A function generator is not ordinarily used to indicate corresponding values of two functionally related variables such as X and Y. The scales shown in Figure 12 (left) are not usually provided; they have been added to bring out the most important feature of a function generator, namely, that the scales are uniform; i.e., graduated in equal divisions. This means that, since ϕ is 70 degrees and the range of Y is 35, each two-degree rotation of crank d corresponds with one unit of Y, and if d is used to operate a valve in response to a signal from b, the rotation of d corresponding to a given change in Y is the same at all points in the range.

Toggle principle

Special-purpose linkages. In the extreme positions OAB and $A'OB'$ in Figure 11 (bottom), the links 2 and 3 are said to be in toggle and most effective for the transmission of torque from link 2 to link 4. The toggle principle is used extensively in machine construction for obtaining large force or torque amplification or as a self-locking clamp; the latter effect is obtained if the links are allowed to go slightly past the toggle position and held there by a stop.

There are a number of useful linkage devices that derive their characteristics from the properties of a parallelogram. Among these are the drafting machine and the pantograph. The links in Figure 11 (bottom) will form a parallelogram when $a=c$ and $b=d$; then the coupler link b will have motion of translation so that any line fixed on b will not change its inclination to d as the links move. If the link d' of another parallelogram linkage is fixed to b, then its coupler b' will also have translatory motion, and a straight edge adjustably fixed to b' will maintain its inclination to d in all positions of the links; this is how a drafting machine operates.

The linkage next to be described was invented in 1873 by Captain Charles-Nicolas Peaucellier of the French corps of engineers. It was the first linkage capable of describing a circle of any radius, including an infinite one (a straight line), in the manner of a pair of compasses. When he first operated a working model of the linkage, Lord Kelvin, the famous physicist, is reputed to have remarked that it was the most beautiful thing he had ever seen.

Peaucellier straight-line mechanism

The Peaucellier straight-line mechanism, shown in Figure 12 (right), consists of a parallelogram of equal links B connected with two equal links A pivoted to the frame at O. From symmetry, points O, P, and Q will always lie on the same straight line, and if P is guided on a circular path by link C pivoted at S, then Q will have a circular path concave to the right when D is greater than C; for D less than C the curve will be concave to the left; for $D=C$ (as in the figure) the radius of the path of Q is infinite and the curve is a straight line. The letters refer to the lengths of the links.

There are other linkage mechanisms that will produce exact straight-line motion, but in all of them either there are more than four pin-connected links or one of the links is a sliding block. No point on the coupler of a four-bar, pin-connected linkage can generate an exact, straight-line motion. There are techniques, however, for designing four-bar linkages to generate approximate straight-line motions; in practice these are usually satisfactory and are preferred because of their simplicity. One such linkage was designed by James Watt to guide the piston rod of his steam engine on a straight path. Another generates a D-shaped coupler-point curve that is used for the intermittent movement of the film in some motion-picture cameras.

An infinite variety of closed curves can be generated by points on the coupler of a four-bar linkage. An atlas is available that contains over 7,000 curves drawn to a large scale. By paging through the atlas a designer may find a shape suitable for a specific application.

Slider-crank inversions. When one of the pin connections in a four-bar linkage is replaced by a sliding joint, a number of useful mechanisms can be obtained from the resulting linkage. In Figure 13 (top) the connection between

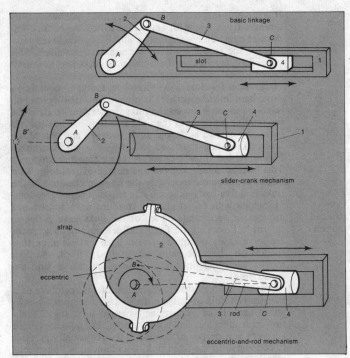

Figure 13: Types of linkages (see text).

links 1 and 4 is a sliding joint that permits block 4 to slide in the slot in link 1. It would make no difference, kinematically, if link 1 were sliding in a hole or slot in link 4.

If link 1 in Figure 13 (top) is fixed, the resulting slider-crank mechanism is shown in Figure 13 (centre). This is the mechanism of a reciprocating engine. The block 4 represents the piston; link 1, shown shaded, is the block that contains the crankshaft bearing at A and the cylinder; link 2 is the crankshaft and link 3 the connecting rod. The crankpin bearing is at B, the wrist pin bearing at C. The stroke of the piston is twice AB, the throw of the crank.

The slider-crank mechanism provides means for converting the translatory motion of the pistons in a reciprocating engine into rotary motion of the crankshaft, or the rotary motion of the crankshaft in a pump into a translatory motion of the pistons. In Figure 13 (centre), when B is in position B', the connecting rod would interfere with the crank if both were in the same plane. This problem is solved in engines and pumps by offsetting the crankpin bearing from the crankshaft bearing. By using an eccentric-and-rod mechanism in place of a crank, no offsetting is necessary and very small throws can be obtained.

In Figure 13 (bottom) the crankpin bearing at B has become a large circular disk pivoted at A with an eccentricity or throw AB. The connecting rod has become the eccentric rod with a strap that encircles and slides on the eccentric. The mechanisms in the centre and bottom drawings of Figure 13 are kinematically equivalent.

By fixing links 2, 3, and 4 instead of link 1, three other inversions of the linkage in Figure 13 (top) are obtained.

Space linkages. All of the linkages considered so far have been planar; i.e., their motions have been confined to a single plane or to parallel planes, and the shafts they connect have been parallel. Space linkages operate in three dimensions and are used to transmit motion between nonparallel shafts. Although some well-known linkage mechanisms in use for many years are special forms of space linkages, it was not until about the 1950s that kinematicians became seriously interested in developing procedures for describing, analyzing, and synthesizing these linkages. Though some advances in this field have been made, many problems remain unsolved.

Whereas a plane linkage can be described with a two-dimensional drawing and analyzed and synthesized with plane geometrical constructions, this is not possible with a space linkage. At least two views are required to define a link in three-dimensional space, and the additional dimension complicates the analysis of velocity and acceler-

Uses of the slider-crank mechanism

ation. Thus, analysis of space linkages involves the use of higher mathematics.

In plane linkages there are only two types of connectors or joints, namely, pin or hinge joints and sliding joints (crossheads). Since it takes two elements to make a joint, kinematicians call them kinematic "pairs." Thus a pin joint is a revolute, or turning, pair and a sliding joint is a prismatic pair. In space linkages there are additional pairs, namely, the cylindric pair, which permits both relative translation and rotation, the screw pair (screw and nut), and the spheric pair (ball and socket joint).

The space linkage in Figure 14 could be used to link the butterfly valve on the throttle of a carburetor (the output) to the shaft rotated by the foot pedal (the input).

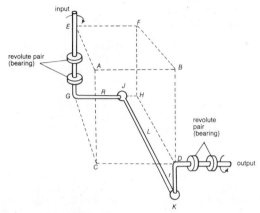

Figure 14: Space linkage (see text).

The L-shaped input shaft oscillates in bearings lying along the edge *GE* of the box *ABCDEFGH*, and the arm *R* swings about the mid-position shown and in the plane *CDGH*. The L-shaped output shaft oscillates in bearings lying along the edge *CD* of the box, and the arm *r* swings about the midposition shown and in the plane *BDFH*. The link *L* connects the shafts with spheric pairs (ball and socket joints) at *J* and *K*.

FLYWHEELS

A flywheel is a heavy wheel attached to a rotating shaft in a machine for the purpose of opposing and moderating any fluctuations in the speed of the machine caused by irregularities in the rate at which power is supplied to, or required by, the machine. Flywheels are also used for testing brakes and for storing energy that can be used in emergencies or, when dissipated quickly, can produce large forces.

Moment of inertia — The measure of the opposition of a rotating body to having its speed changed is its moment of inertia. This property depends on the disposition of the material of the body about the axis of rotation. It is proportional to the sum obtained by multiplying the weight of each particle of the body by the square of its distance from the axis of rotation. Moments of inertia of bodies of common geometric shapes are given in handbooks; for uncommon shapes they can be determined with integral calculus or by experiment. From the nature of the moment of inertia it follows that the material in a flywheel is most effective when it is concentrated as far from the axis of rotation as possible. Thus the best flywheel has a heavy rim connected to a central hub by spokes or a circular plate.

The behaviour of a flywheel depends entirely on the torque, or turning force, applied to it. If a clockwise torque is applied to a stationary flywheel for a period of time, the flywheel will acquire a clockwise angular velocity proportional to the product of the average torque multiplied by the time period, and inversely proportional to the moment of inertia of the wheel. If a rotating flywheel is subjected to a torque acting in the same direction in which it is rotating, its speed will increase; the converse is also true. The larger the moment of inertia of the flywheel the smaller the speed changes produced by a given torque. If no torque acts on a flywheel, its speed will not change.

On a reciprocating engine the torque applied to the crankshaft varies during each revolution. This variation is caused by the non-uniformity of the steam or gas pressure in the cylinders and the varying angle between the connecting rod (which converts the piston pressure to the crankshaft torque) and the crankshaft. When the crank and connecting rod are collinear, which happens twice during each revolution, no torque can be transmitted to the crankshaft. A subsidiary function of the flywheel on an engine is to carry the crankshaft past these "dead centre" positions.

All rotating machine members have moments of inertia and respond, like flywheels, to torque variations. The torques that are required to start, stop, or vary the speed of these members are known as inertia torques or loads. Inertia loads exist in all machines, and their presence is particularly noticeable when machines are being started.

Flywheels are especially useful on machines that deliver mechanical work intermittently. On a punch press, for example, the large forces required to punch or form sheet metal are exerted during a part of the downward stroke of the ram only. During the remainder of the downward stroke, throughout the upward stroke, and between strokes, the machine is idling, and the power required from the driving motor is low. It would be uneconomical to use a driving motor capable of delivering a torque large enough to create the large forces required for punching and forming. A flywheel acts as a reservoir of energy that is built up by a comparatively low-powered motor while the machine is idling and partially dissipated during the active portion of the downstroke.

A spinning flywheel was used as a power source for a propulsion system on a torpedo in 1884; it is reported that a speed of 24 knots (24 nautical miles per hour) was obtained for a distance of 500 yards (450 metres). A flywheel 10 inches (25 centimetres) in diameter, rotating at 52,000 revolutions per minute, has sufficient energy to raise and lower the landing gear on a B-70 aircraft. This flywheel energy-storing system weighs 200 pounds (90 kilograms) less than a hydraulic system for accomplishing the same function. A recent (1970) application to bus transportation is the proposal to use flywheels on the trolleybuses for San Francisco's Municipal Railway. New high-density steel wheels, of special design, weighing 700 pounds (300 kilograms) and rotating at 20,000 revolutions per minute, would permit the buses to leave the power lines to serve undeveloped adjacent areas for distances up to six miles (about ten kilometres). The key to obtaining a high energy-storing capacity in a flywheel is the magnitude of the centrifugal stresses, produced by rotation, that the material can take. With the same material, a plain disk can store about 50 percent more energy than a rim-type wheel, while a tapered, constant-stress disk can store about 100 percent more.

Flywheels as power sources

BELT AND CHAIN DRIVES

Quite probably, wrapping connectors in the form of ropes were among the earliest devices used by man for transmitting forces over long distances; for this purpose they are still unmatched. Commonly used connectors today also include bands, belts, and chains.

Belt drives. *Bands and flat belts.* Band, or tape, drives are useful substitutes for gears when the connected shafts do not make complete revolutions. The band drive in Figure 15 (left) provides a positive drive and the equivalent of pure rolling contact between the drums *A* and *B* that are pivoted on fixed axes. The ends of the thin, flexible, metallic bands 12 and 34 are clamped to the drums. If drum *A* or drum *B* drives counterclockwise, band 12 will be in tension, while for clockwise rotation of the drums, band 34 will be in tension. The bands lie side by side on the surface of the drums; there is no backlash as there would be in a gear drive; for the arrangement shown in Figure 15 (left), drum *A* can rotate about 145 degrees, while drum *B* can rotate about 240 degrees. Band drives can also operate with non-circular drums; they are used on the dial indicator mechanism of weighing machines.

When used to connect shafts that rotate continuously in one direction, the ends of ropes and belts cannot be

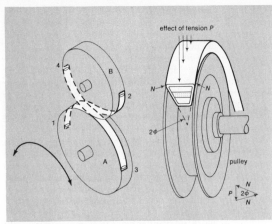

Figure 15: (Left) Band drive. (Right) V-belt drive (see text).

clamped to the drums; they must be wrapped around them so that the forces are transmitted by the frictional grip of the rope or belt on the drum. The force that can be carried without slip by a rope wrapped around a drum, such as a capstan, increases rapidly as the number of wraps is increased.

Flat belts can be used to connect any pair of shafts in space, but when the shafts are not parallel it is necessary to exercise greater care in locating the pulleys than when the shafts are parallel. The pulleys must be so arranged that the centre line of a belt as it approaches a pulley lies in the plane that bisects the pulley and is perpendicular to its axis; otherwise, the belt will run off. To satisfy this requirement it may be necessary to use additional (idler) pulleys to guide the belt.

Flat belts are most often used to connect parallel shafts. Figure 16 shows a pair of parallel shafts connected by an open flat belt on pulleys A and B and by a crossed flat belt on pulleys C and D. To prevent the belts from running off the pulleys, the surfaces of the pulleys are crowned (that is, the pulley diameter is greater at the midsection than at the edges) or the pulleys are provided with low flanges.

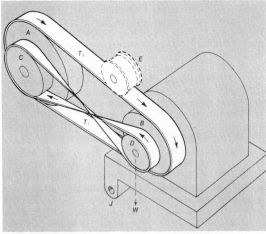

Figure 16: Flat-belt drives.

If there are no slip losses and belt thickness is neglected, the surface (peripheral) speeds of the pulleys must be equal; their angular velocities will be inversely proportional to their diameters. For pulleys A and B,

$$\frac{\text{speed of } A}{\text{speed of } B} = \frac{\text{diameter of } B}{\text{diameter of } A}.$$

An equation of similar kind can be written for pulleys C and D.

A phenomenon known as creep causes the driven pulley to rotate at a slower speed than that given by the formula. Creep is unavoidable on belts made of any material that stretches elastically under load and contracts when the load is reduced. The amount of creep in a given drive

depends on the belt material and the magnitude of the load; it seldom results in the surface speed of the driven pulley being more than 2 percent less than that of the driving pulley.

If the initial tension in a belt is inadequate, the frictional grip of the belt may be insufficient to carry the load without some forward slip of the driving pulley relative to the belt and some forward slip of the belt relative to the driven pulley. On a well-designed flat-belt drive the combined creep and slip seldom exceed 4 percent.

Although successful friction drives with steel belts have been reported, most flat belts are made of more flexible materials such as leather, rubber, fabric, rubberized fabric, or reinforced plastic. In the days when all machines in a shop were driven by overhead belts connected to countershafts or long lineshafts, leather was the most commonly used belt material; it may still be.

Leather belts develop an excellent frictional grip on pulleys, and if periodically lubricated with a suitable belt dressing such as neat's-foot oil and not overloaded they will last as long as or longer than any other belt material. Because of variations in humidity, however, leather belts stretch and shrink, and with time they always get longer. If the pulleys are a fixed distance apart and means are not provided for keeping the belts tight, they must be "taken up" (shortened) periodically by cutting the belt and joining the cut ends.

The strongest leather-belt joint is made by gluing together the scarfed (chamfered) and overlapped ends of the belt. This is known as a cemented lap joint, and belts joined in this way are classified as endless. As an everyday procedure for joining belts, cemented lap joints are impractical. There are several commercially available metallic belt-lacing devices. One of these involves the insertion of a row of steel loops in the ends of the belt by means of a special press, and hinging them together with a rawhide pin. This joint is easily made and separated.

Speed ratios as high as 16 to 1 have been obtained with flat leather belts. If the shaft centre distance is short, high ratios with an open belt will result in the angle of wrap on the smaller pulley being considerably less than 180 degrees. To increase the angle and keep the belt tight, an idler pulley can be used. The one shown at E in Figure 16 could be mounted on a weighted arm pivoted at the right and would normally occupy a position closer to pulley B.

Short-centre electric motor drives can be improved by using a pivoted mount for the motor. In Figure 16 the base of the motor is pivoted at J, and the clockwise turning moment about J of the motor weight W is balanced by the counterclockwise turning moment of the belt tensions T_1 and T_2. Belt tensions are controlled by the position of the motor on the base.

Flat-belt pulleys usually are made either of cast iron or of pressed steel, although some are wood, and others have cast-iron centres and paper rims. At all speeds the grip of a belt on a pulley is lessened by centrifugal action, and at approximately 6,000 feet (1,800 metres) per minute the power that a leather belt can transmit starts to drop off on account of this effect. When possible, pulley diameters for leather belts should be chosen so that the belt speed is between 4,500 and 6,000 feet (1,400 and 1,800 metres) per minute.

The driven pulley of an open-belt drive may be connected to the load shaft by a clutch, so that the load may be started and stopped while the belt pulleys rotate continuously. In place of a clutch, a loose (freely rotating) pulley may be installed next to the driven pulley. A belt shifter, consisting of two fingers that guide the belt between them, moves the belt from one pulley to another when actuated by a lever. A double-width driving pulley is required.

V belts. The frictional grip of a wrapping connector on a pulley can be greatly increased by using a belt with a V-shaped cross section fitting in a V-shaped groove in the pulley. In Figure 15 (right) the effect of tension in the V belt (called P) is to wedge the belt in the groove and create the normal forces N. The two normal forces and P must be in equilibrium as shown by the force triangle (lower right). On a flat pulley the angle 2ϕ is 180 degrees, and from the force triangle the sum of the normal forces N would be equal to P. Consequently, the V groove increases the normal forces created by a given belt tension. For standard commercial V belts the average angle 2ϕ is 35 degrees and the sum of the normal forces is $3.3\ P$, which, since the frictional grip equals the normal force times the coefficient of friction, represents a substantial gain in capacity over a flat belt. In actual practice, gains of this magnitude are seldom realized, since satisfactory results can be obtained without the high tensions necessary on flat belts.

For a V-belt drive a thick belt is strained more than a thin belt on the same pulley, and a small-diameter pulley creates more bending in a belt than a large-diameter pulley. The amount of strain that a material can tolerate without permanent damage is given by its strength:stiffness ratio. For mild steel the ratio is approximately 1:1,000, which means that a fibre of steel can be stretched or compressed one one-thousandth of its original length without permanently changing shape. For some types of rubber the corresponding value is one.

Although the cross-sectional shapes of available V belts are more or less standardized, the composition of the structural elements and their distribution throughout the cross section are not. Nevertheless, most V belts are constructed in such a way that the bending strains are carried by a flexible material, while the transmitted load is carried by a stronger and stiffer material located near the neutral plane, where there is no bending strain.

V belts are available in a variety of sizes, types, and lengths for transmitting almost any amount of power. They operate best at belt speeds between 1,600 and 6,000 feet (500 and 1,800 metres) per minute, with an optimum speed of about 4,200 feet (1,300 metres) per minute. The narrow, high-capacity belts used on automobile engines for driving the fan, water pump, and generator can operate at higher speeds. As with flat belts, the speed-limiting factor is centrifugal action. Though maximum speed ratio for satisfactory performance is approximately 7:1, higher ratios can be used.

V belts may be used singly or in multiples. For some belt sizes sheaves with from 1 to 14 grooves are available as standard manufactured parts. Because of the wedging action in the grooves, less initial tension is necessary than with a flat belt. This reduces the load on the shafts and bearings.

V belts are well suited for short-centre drives. When the speed ratio is greater than about 3:1, the advantages of a V-belt drive can be obtained without using a large and expensive grooved pulley on the low-speed shaft. This is known as a V-flat drive and consists of a small grooved sheave, a large flat-belt pulley, and a set of V belts. Because of the comparatively large speed ratio, the angle of wrap on the large pulley is so great that, even without grooves, its frictional grip on the belt may equal or exceed that of the small grooved sheave. V-flat drives are frequently used on punch presses, the grooved sheave being on the driving motor and the flywheel with an uncrowned cylindrical periphery serving as the driven pulley.

Grooved and timing belts. Two other types of flexible belts, both of comparatively recent origin, are used for the transmission of power: the V-ribbed, or grooved, belt and the toothed, or timing, belt. The grooved belt is basically a flat belt with sharp-pointed, V-shaped longitudinal ribs on the side next to the grooved pulley. Although it resembles a set of V belts glued together, there is no wedging action. The overall width is less than for a multiple V-belt drive, and the belt-length matching problem, which always exists when a number of V belts are running on the same pulleys, is eliminated.

The toothed, or timing, belt (also called a synchronous belt) is basically a flat belt with a series of evenly spaced transverse teeth that fit in a series of matching grooves on the periphery of the pulley. These belts provide a positive no-slip drive and can be used at speeds as high as 16,000 feet (5,000 metres) per minute. They are used on automobile camshaft drives, machine tools, pumps, textile machinery, and on such business machines as electric type-

No-slip drive with a belt

writers, card sorters, and electric calculating machines. Although the positive drive provided by these belts has many advantages, it lacks the overload and sudden-start protection provided by belts that slip.

Chain drives. For hoisting and moving materials, chains are reported to have been used in the Near East hundreds of years before the birth of Christ. A notebook of Leonardo da Vinci's contains a sketch of a chain like those used on modern bicycles, and there is evidence that chains of a similar type were actually in use in Europe in the 16th century. In 1879 the silent chain (see below) was invented by Hans Renold of Manchester, England.

The first chain-driven or "safety" bicycle appeared in 1874, and chains were used for driving the rear wheels on early automobiles. Today, as a result of modern design and production methods, chain drives that are much superior to their prototypes are available, and these have contributed greatly to the development of efficient agricultural machinery, well-drilling equipment, and mining and construction machinery. Since about 1930 chain drives have become increasingly popular, especially for washing machines, power lawnmowers, power saws, and motorcycles. They are also used on vending machines and escalators.

There are at least six types of power-transmission chain; three of these will be covered in this article, namely the roller chain, the inverted tooth, or silent, chain, and the bead chain. The essential elements in a roller-chain drive are a chain with side plates, pins, bushings (sleeves), and rollers, and two or more sprocket wheels with teeth that look like gear teeth. Roller chains are assembled from pin links and roller links. A pin link consists of two side plates connected by two pins inserted into holes in the side plates. The pins fit tightly into the holes, forming what is known as a press fit. A roller link consists of two side plates connected by two press-fitted bushings, on which two hardened steel rollers are free to rotate. When assembled, the pins are a free fit in the bushings and rotate slightly, relative to the bushings, when the chain goes on and leaves a sprocket.

Roller-chain drive

Standard roller chains are available in single strands or in multiple strands. In the latter type, two or more chains are joined by common pins that keep the rollers in the separate strands in proper alignment. The speed ratio for a single drive should be limited to about 10:1; the preferred shaft centre distance is from 30 to 50 times the distance between the rollers; and chain speeds greater than about 2,500 feet (800 metres) per minute are not recommended. Where several parallel shafts are to be driven without slip from a single shaft, roller chains are particularly well suited.

An inverted tooth, or silent, chain is essentially an assemblage of gear racks, each with two teeth, pivotally connected to form a closed chain with the teeth on the inside, and meshing with conjugate teeth on the sprocket wheels. The links are pin-connected flat steel plates usually having straight-sided teeth with an included angle of 60 degrees. As many links as are necessary to transmit the power are connected side by side. Compared with roller-chain drives, silent-chain drives are quieter, operate successfully at higher speeds, and can transmit more load for the same width. Some automobiles have silent-chain camshaft drives.

Bead chains provide an inexpensive and versatile means for connecting parallel or nonparallel shafts when the speed and power transmitted are low. The sprocket wheels contain hemispherical or conical recesses into which the beads fit. The chains look like key chains and are available in plain carbon and stainless steel and also in the form of solid plastic beads molded on a cord. Bead chains are used on computers, air conditioners, television tuners, and venetian blinds. The sprockets may be steel, die-cast zinc or aluminum, or molded nylon.

COUPLINGS

A coupling is a device for connecting the ends of adjacent bodies. In machine construction, couplings are used to effect a semipermanent connection between adjacent rotating shafts. The connection is permanent in the sense

Rigid
coupling

that it is not meant to be broken during the useful life of the machine, but it can be broken and restored in an emergency or when worn parts are replaced.

There are several types of shaft couplings; their characteristics depend on the purpose for which they are used. If an exceptionally long shaft is required for a line shaft in a manufacturing plant or a propeller shaft on a ship, it is made in sections that are coupled together with rigid couplings. A common type of rigid coupling consists of two mating radial flanges (disks) that are attached by key-driven hubs to the ends of adjacent shaft sections and bolted together through the flanges to form a rigid connection. Alignment of the connected shafts is usually effected by means of a rabbet joint on the face of the flanges; *i.e.*, a short cylindrical projection on the face of one flange fits snugly in a circular recess on the face of the other flange.

In connecting shafts belonging to separate devices (such as an electric motor and a gearbox), precise aligning of the shafts is difficult and a flexible coupling is used. This coupling connects the shafts in such a way as to minimize the harmful effects of shaft misalignment. Flexible couplings also permit the shafts to deflect under their separate systems of loads and to move freely (float) in the axial direction without interfering with one another. Flexible couplings can also serve to reduce the intensity of shock loads and vibrations transmitted from one shaft to another.

The flexibility provided by a coupling may be only spatial, or it may be both spatial and resilient (springy); in other words, the coupling may compensate for shaft misalignment but provide no resilience, or it may be resilient and provide also for a small amount of misalignment.

Universal joints. For connecting shafts whose axes intersect at angles up to about 40 degrees, the Hooke, or Cardan, joint can be used. Many commercial forms of the joint are available, but they all consist of two forked members that are connected to the shaft ends and a central connecting cross-shaped piece, or a block, on which the forks can turn (Figure 17A). This coupling is not

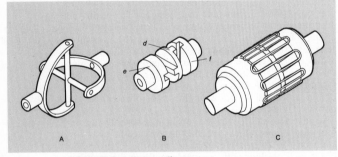

Figure 17: *Types of couplings.*
(A) Hooke joint. (B) Oldham coupling. (C) Falk Steelflex coupling (see text).

resilient, and if the driving (input) shaft rotates at a constant speed the driven (output) shaft will rotate at a varying speed if the shafts are not collinear. A constant velocity ratio can be obtained by using two Hooke joints and an intermediate shaft. The intermediate shaft forks must lie in the same plane, and the output and input shafts must make the same angle with the intermediate shaft.

On an automobile, the rear axle moves up and down relative to the transmission as the springs deflect. To permit this movement without restraint, the transmission and rear axle are connected to the propeller or drive shaft by means of Hooke joints. One of these must have a sliding joint to permit free axial movement, or float, to allow for the slight changes in distance between the transmission and the rear axle.

On some machines a varying angular speed can cancel out or modify unwanted speed variations in one member produced by a constant-speed driver. If a slider-crank mechanism, for example, is being used to convert the uniform rotary motion of an electric motor to a translatory motion on a slider, the velocity of the slider will

vary. By installing a Hooke joint between the motor and the crankshaft, the variation in the slider's velocity can be controlled by varying the angle of inclination of the joint. Still greater control of the slider's velocity can be obtained by using two Hooke joints and varying the relative positions of the forks on the intermediate shaft.

The Hooke joint is a member of a class of couplings known as universal joints, and in spite of its deficiencies it is a widely used machine component. Many other universal joints, embodying diverse means for connecting intersecting shafts, have been invented. At least three of these are constructed in such a way that they transmit rotary motion with a constant velocity ratio at shaft angles up to about 40 degrees.

Constant-
velocity
universal
joint

Commercially available constant-velocity joints are considerably more complex than the Hooke joint. They are used on vehicles with front-wheel drives, or independently sprung rear-wheel drives; for driving helicopter rotors; and on high-speed drives where the speed variations produced by a single Hooke joint would cause vibrations.

Flexible couplings. For connecting shafts that are parallel but are not lined up with each other (non-collinear) the Oldham coupling, shown in Figure 17B, is useful. The centre piece *d* has two projecting rectangular bars at right angles to one another that fit into grooves on the faces of the flanges on the hubs *e* and *f*, which are attached to the ends of the coupled shafts. When the shafts are out of line (offset) the centre piece slides in the grooves in the flanges as the shafts rotate, but it cannot rotate relative to either of the flanges. Consequently, this coupling transmits motion with a uniform velocity ratio. The Oldham coupling can operate with considerable amounts of parallel misalignment.

A variation of the Oldham coupling is obtained by widening the bars on the centre member until it becomes a square block that engages widened slots on the flanges. The bearing surfaces of the block can be provided with replaceable strips of bronze or nonmetallic material that are lubricated by grease stored in the hollow block. On instrument assemblies, where the motion of a driving shaft must be transmitted accurately to a driven shaft, the Oldham coupling is frequently employed.

Some types of machinery require a torsionally rigid coupling that can tolerate slight amounts of angular and parallel misalignment and permit axial float. For such applications, gear couplings are well adapted. These consist of two identical hubs with external gear teeth that are attached to the shafts and coupled together by means of a sleeve with internal gear teeth that mesh with the teeth on the hubs. The hubs and the sleeve have the same number of teeth, so that there is no relative rotary motion between the internal and external gear teeth. Gear couplings are used on all types of equipment and are particularly well suited for high speeds and loads.

Gear
couplings

There are many types of commercially available resilient couplings in which the resilience is obtained by either metallic or nonmetallic elements. The widely used Falk Steelflex coupling (Figure 17C) utilizes a flat steel spring forming a series of hairpin bends to obtain its resilience. This coupling consists of two flanged members with tapered slots, connected by a continuous steel spring laced through the slots. When the coupling is unloaded, the unsupported length of the spring elements is a maximum and the coupling has its minimum torsional stiffness. At full load the spring elements contact the tapered sides of the slots, thus reducing their unsupported length and increasing the stiffness of the coupling. The stiffening effect of load application is a useful characteristic for shafts subject to torsional vibration.

The simplest form of nonmetallic resilient coupling is a rubber or fabric hose fitting over and clamped to the ends of the coupled shafts. The rubber elements are usually reinforced with corded material, and no lubricant is required. These couplings are particularly effective in reducing the transmission of shock loads and vibrations.

Magnetic and hydraulic couplings. The transmission of rotary motion through the wall of a hermetically sealed chamber without mechanical contact can be accomplished by means of a magnetic coupling. If the wall is nonmagnetic and nonconductive, magnetic lines of force emanating from permanent magnets attached to the ends of the shafts will couple the shafts together. These couplings are particularly valuable for connecting pumps for corrosive fluids to their driving motors.

An overload release coupling is a torque-limiting device, and, as the name implies, it limits the torque that can be transmitted from one rotating member to another by either slipping or breaking the connection when the torque reaches a predetermined value. When the maximum torque of a magnetic coupling is exceeded, the driven member stops and cannot be restarted until the torque is removed and the driving member stopped and restarted. Other types of overload devices resemble mechanical friction clutches with spring-loaded friction members adjusted for prescribed torques. On some outboard motors the propeller is fixed to the shaft by means of a metal pin driven radially through the hub and the shaft. If the propeller is overloaded by striking an obstacle, the pin shears off and prevents further damage. This is probably the cheapest method of obtaining overload protection, but since a sheared pin must be replaced it is not the most convenient.

Hydraulic couplings have been used in passenger cars and buses since the 1920s. Functionally, they resemble automatic clutches and in many respects are unlike the other types of couplings that have been described. The driving and driven elements are housed in a circular container partially filled with a liquid (usually oil) and having coaxial input and output shafts. A fluid coupling provides a rotationally yielding connection and prevents the transmission of shock loads and torsional vibration; it does not provide for shaft misalignment.

Active elements of a hydraulic coupling

The two active elements of a hydraulic coupling resemble a pair of half-grapefruit sections with the pulp removed (the membranes remaining intact) and facing each other so that the dividing membranes become radial partitions. One of the elements acts like a pump and is known as the impeller, while the other element acts like a turbine and is known as the runner. In the impeller, which is attached to the input shaft, kinetic energy is imparted to the fluid; while in the runner, which is attached to the output shaft, the kinetic energy of the fluid is converted into mechanical torque. If no torque is applied to the output shaft, the impeller and the runner will rotate at the same speed, the fluid will not circulate from the impeller to the runner, and there will be no transfer of kinetic energy. When a torque is applied to the output shaft the runner will slow down, the fluid will circulate, and there will be a transfer of energy. The maximum torque is developed when the output shaft is stalled.

On an automobile, a fluid coupling permits a smooth pickup of speed and prevents the engine from stalling if the car is stopped with gears engaged. Under normal driving conditions the output speed is about 97 percent of the input speed; i.e., the slip is about 3 percent. The input and output torques are equal.

Hydraulic couplings are sometimes placed between an electric driving motor and a gearbox. Since the hydraulic torque varies as the square of the input speed, the couplings permit the motor to come up to speed before any appreciable load is applied to it. When high-inertia loads must be started, hydraulic couplings are particularly useful.

CLUTCHES

A clutch is a device for quickly and easily connecting or disconnecting a rotatable shaft and a rotating coaxial shaft. Clutches are usually placed between the input shaft to a machine and the output shaft from the driving motor, and provide a convenient means for starting and stopping the machine and permitting the driver motor or engine to be started in an unloaded state.

The rotor (rotating member) in an electric motor has rotational inertia, and a torque is required to bring it up to speed when the motor is started. If the motor shaft is rigidly connected to a load with a large rotational inertia, and the motor is started suddenly by closing a switch, the

motor may not have sufficient torque capacity to bring the motor shaft up to speed before the windings in the motor are burned out by the excessive current demands. A clutch between the motor and the load shafts will restrict the starting torque on the motor to that required to accelerate the rotor and parts of the clutch only.

On some machine tools it is convenient to let the driving motor run continuously and to start and stop the machine by operating a clutch. Other machine tools receive their power from belts driven by pulleys on intermediate shafts that are themselves driven by belts from long lineshafts that serve a group of machines. Two pulleys that can be connected to the intermediate shaft by clutches, and driven in opposite directions by open and crossed belts from the line shaft, can provide forward and reverse rotations for the machine.

Positive and friction clutches. A mechanical clutch may provide either a positive drive with no slip, or the torque transmitted may depend on friction. In the latter case, the rate at which a stationary shaft is brought up to the speed of the driving shaft can be controlled; for this reason friction clutches are more common than positive clutches.

Positive clutches are collars with square jaws that interlock. One member is rigidly attached to its shaft while the other member slides on its shaft and on a key fixed to its shaft. Positive clutches must be engaged at low relative speeds if high shock loads are to be avoided. They are used on hoisting, conveying, and farm machinery and on punch presses and shears.

Friction clutches have pairs of mating conical, disk, or ring-shaped surfaces and means for pressing the surfaces together. The pressure may be created by a spring or by a series of levers locked in position by the wedging action of a conical spool. On a spring-loaded clutch the operator, by controlling the rate at which the spring pressure is applied to the clutch, can regulate the speed of clutch engagement and the torque applied to the driven shaft. There is always some slippage, however, and the efficiency of a friction clutch can never exceed 50 percent; i.e., during a clutching operation at least one-half of the input energy is lost by friction in the clutch and produces heat.

The friction surfaces on clutches should have a high coefficient of friction and be able to conduct the heat away rapidly. These properties are difficult to obtain in a single material and for this reason, one of each pair of mating surfaces is usually metallic, while the other is either leather, cork, or an asbestos-based facing rivetted to a metal plate. Some friction clutches are run dry, while others operate in oil. Dry clutches have a higher coefficient of friction than wet clutches, but the oil helps to carry off the heat.

Cone clutches

Cone clutches, with male and female cones, were widely used on the first automobiles. On cones with a slight taper, a small axial force can produce a large pressure between the surfaces because of the wedge effect. Cone clutches require close alignment of the shafts, and the development of asbestos-based friction disks has rendered them almost obsolete, at least for automobiles.

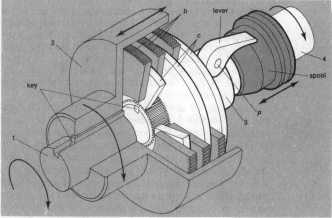

Figure 18: Multiple-plate disk clutch (see text).

Figure 18 shows a half-section of a multiple-plate disk clutch in which input member 2 is keyed to the driving shaft 1 and output member 3 is keyed to the driven shaft 4. The friction plates b have external gear teeth or splines that mate with teeth on the inside of member 2, while friction plates c have internal teeth that mate with external teeth on member 3. Plates b can slide axially in 2, while plates c can slide axially on 3. The clutch is engaged by moving the spool to the left, which, by a wedging action, rotates the lever about the pivot P and creates a force that squeezes the plates together.

Automatic and magnetic clutches. Automatic, smooth engagement is obtained with a centrifugal clutch. The friction shoes are segments of rings that are pivoted to or carried around by the driving member. As the driver's speed increases, the shoes gradually make firmer and firmer contact with the internal cylindrical surface of the driven member. Centrifugal clutches allow the driving motor to reach operating speed before being loaded. They are particularly useful on internal-combustion engines driving chain saws, and on helicopter rotor drives. They eliminate the need for a manually operated clutch, and the engine cannot stall when overloaded, since the clutch will slip when the speed drops below that necessary to create the torque required by the load.

An overrunning clutch transmits torque in one direction only and permits the driven shaft of a machine to "freewheel," or keep on rotating when the driver is stopped. Modern designs utilize the wedging action of rolls or sprags (struts). With rolls, a series of wedge-shaped pockets, with a roll in each, is formed between the periphery of one member and the inside of a ring on the other member. Rotation of either member in one direction causes the rolls to roll up the incline in the pocket and lock the members together. In sprag clutches a number of especially shaped rocking wedges are located in the annular space between concentric circular races, and are kept in contact with both races at all times by means of a spring.

On bicycles, freewheeling clutches permit the rider to coast without moving the pedals. They can also be used to prevent damage to machines by accidental reversal of the input rotation, and if one of the members is fixed they can function as brakes or "backstops" that prevent reverse rotation of a loaded output shaft when the driving effort is removed.

Magnetic-particle clutches have an annular (ring-shaped) gap between the driving and driven members that is filled with powdered iron and graphite. When a magnetic field is induced across the gap by a direct-current control coil, the iron particles form chains across the gap and transmit a torque that depends on the strength of the field. Controlled by varying the current, the load can be engaged smoothly and there is no slippage when the clutch is transmitting the torque for which it was designed.

BRAKES

Basically, brakes are devices for controlling the flow of motion in machines, and in this respect they resemble clutches; clutches start the flow while brakes arrest it. Before the engagement of a clutch or a brake, one of the two members in the device is moving while the other is stationary; after the engagement of a clutch both members are moving at the same speed, while after the application of a brake the moving member is either slowed down or stationary. In both cases the desired effects are produced by devices that are so alike, structurally, that they can sometimes serve in either capacity.

In arresting the motion of bodies, brakes must be capable of absorbing kinetic energy. Even when acting on translating bodies (like automobiles) most brakes are designed to act on rotating mechanical elements and to absorb energy either mechanically, hydraulically, or electrically. Mechanical brakes are the most common; they dissipate kinetic energy in the form of heat generated by mechanical friction between a rotating metallic element and a nonrotating friction element, when they are brought into contact by either mechanical, hydraulic,

pneumatic, or electrical means. The material in the friction element may be organic, metallic, or ceramic. Organic materials with an asbestos base are satisfactory for the majority of applications. When service requirements are severe, however, the heat generated may cause "fading" (a drop in braking effectiveness caused by a reduction in the coefficient of friction). In such cases sintered metallic linings are preferred because of their high thermal conductivity and freedom from fading. By adding ceramic particles to sintered metallic linings, extremely hard and fade-resistant linings can be produced.

The rotating element in a mechanical brake is either a drum, a disk, or a series of disks. The nonrotating friction element in a drum brake may be either a band or a pair of shoes (blocks) that contract around the outside of the drum or a pair of shoes that expand against the inside of the drum. A disk brake may be similar to a plate clutch, with alternate rotating metallic and nonrotating friction elements, or it may be of the caliper type, with a single rotating disk and two opposed friction pads that squeeze the disk between them in a pinching action.

Shoe brakes. Most of the early automobiles had band brakes with bands that almost completely encircled the drum. Since they were exposed to the elements and road debris, and the heat radiation was poor, they were superseded by other types. The shoe-type friction elements that are used on drum brakes in place of bands are usually arranged in diametrically opposite pairs that are pressed against the outside or the inside surface of the drum. In the external-shoe brake in Figure 19 (left) the

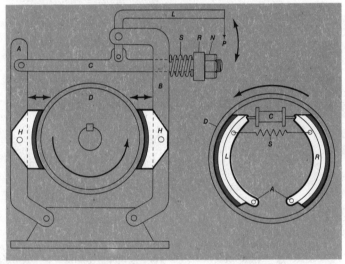

Figure 19: *Types of shoe brakes.*
(Left) External-shoe brake. (Right) Internal-shoe brake (see text).

shoes H are pivoted to the arms A and B and are pressed against the outside of the drum D by the spring S, which is compressed between the end of the arm B and the collar R. The position of R and the spring pressure can be adjusted by means of the nut N. The rod C passes freely through the arm B and is pivotally connected to both the arm A and the lever L. The brake is released by applying a downward force P, which rotates the lever L clockwise, forces the arms A and B apart, and compresses the spring.

Spring-set brakes of the type just described are used on electric elevators. When the starting switch for the hoisting motor is closed, the current actuates a device that applies the brake-releasing load P. This device may create a magnetic pull or it may be a hydraulic unit driven by an electric motor.

The braking of railroad cars is effected by cast-iron shoes that bear directly on the periphery of the wheels, as the shoes in Figure 19 (left) act on the drum. These brakes are usually activated by compressed air.

Figure 19 (right) shows an internal-shoe brake. The friction shoes L and R rotate on the fixed pivots A and are pressed against the inner cylindrical surface of the rotating drum D by means of oil pressure in the cylinder C, which contains two pistons that push outward on the upper ends of the shoes. The tension spring S retracts the shoes and releases the brake when the oil pressure is reduced. For counterclockwise rotation of the drum, the shoe L is self-energizing, since the frictional force tends to rotate it in the same direction as the piston in the cylinder C.

Because they provide better protection from water and dust and have superior mechanical characteristics, internal-shoe drum brakes are superior to band brakes, and they are still in widespread use on automobiles. The capacity of drum brakes to dissipate heat, however, is limited, and for heavy cars travelling at high rates of speed they are inferior to disk brakes.

Disk, hydrodynamic, and electric brakes. The simplest form of disk brake is the caliper brake, which consists of a rotating metal disk and two stationary circular pads or buttons fitted with friction linings that are pressed against opposite sides of the disk by hydraulic pressure. The buttons act on the disk as do the jaws of a pair of pliers. Because of the large area of the disk that is not covered by the pads, these brakes have a high heat-dissipating capacity. In addition, thermal expansion, since it acts principally to increase the thickness of the disk, has less effect on brake performance and there is less fading than on drum brakes. Disk brakes are used on airplanes, automobiles, and trains. Disk brakes are also made with multiple disks, and their action is similar to that of the multiple-disk friction clutch described above. The coaster brake found on bicycles and operated by reverse pressure on the pedals is an example of a multiple-disk brake.

A hydrodynamic brake has a rotor (rotating element) and a stator (stationary element) that resemble the impeller and runner in a hydraulic coupling. Resistance to rotation is created by fluid friction and the circulation of a liquid (usually water) from a series of pockets in the rotor to a series of complementary pockets in the stator. The magnitude of the resistance to rotation (torque) depends on the square of the angular velocity, so that a hydrodynamic brake is most effective at high speeds but cannot bring a rotating shaft to a dead stop. By circulating the liquid through a radiator, these brakes dissipate energy very effectively. They are used as supplemental brakes on oil-well drilling rigs for lowering drill pipe, tools, and casing into the well. They are also used as dynamometers for loading and measuring the output torque of machines and as auxiliary brakes on trucks to control their speed on long downgrades.

Electric brakes are commercially available in three types—eddy-current, hysteresis, and magnetic-particle. Eddy-current brakes have no braking capacity at zero speed, may require cooling fins or a liquid coolant, but are smooth in operation and do not wear. In hysteresis brakes the torque is independent of speed and can be controlled by varying the current. These brakes are sometimes used as dynamometers for testing small motors. Magnetic-particle brakes develop appreciable torque when stationary, but their thermal capacity is limited.

BEARINGS

A bearing is a connector that permits the connected members to either rotate or translate (move to and fro) relative to one another but prevents them from separating in the direction in which loads are applied. In many cases one of the members is fixed, and the bearing acts as a support for the moving member.

The relative motion in bearings is always opposed by friction, and the work done in overcoming friction is lost power in all machines. Consequently, much thought and effort have been devoted to the development of bearings with minimum friction. In all bearings there are two surfaces (one belonging to each of the connected parts) that move relative to one another. To minimize friction, the co-acting surfaces may be partially or completely separated by a film of liquid or gas; these are known as sliding-contact bearings. The surfaces may be separated also by an assemblage of rolling elements such as balls and rollers; these are known as rolling-contact bearings.

Sliding bearings are the simplest to construct and, con-

Fluid-film bearings

sidering the multitude of pin-jointed devices and structures in use, are probably the most commonly used. Nevertheless, man must have discovered thousands of years ago that it is easier to roll a log than to slide it and that heavy masses can be moved more easily when resting on rolling logs than on sliding skids. Recognition of the superiority of rolling over sliding motion resulted in most attention being devoted to the improvement of rolling rather than sliding bearings. This continued until the discovery in the 1880s that under certain conditions a film of oil sufficient to separate the surfaces could be built up in a sliding bearing, and that in this way the frictional resistance could be very substantially reduced.

Precise values of the frictional resistance between moving bodies are difficult to predict or measure, but rough comparisons between different types of friction can be made. To slide a 1,000-pound (450-kilogram) steel block on a dry cast-iron surface, for example, could require a force of 200 pounds (90 kilograms), while to roll a 1,000-pound dry cast-iron wheel on a dry steel surface might require only two pounds. If the block were separated from the cast-iron surface by an oil film, the required force could be only two pounds, and if the film were a gas, the needed force could be considerably less.

Rolling-contact bearings. *History.* The roller, in the form of a rolling log, was probably the predecessor of the wheel, which is reported to have been in use prior to 3000 BC. A Greek historian stated about 450 BC that rollers were used to transport ships on land, and about a hundred years later another Greek historian described a battering ram supported on rollers. Discoveries made in 1928 when Lake Nemi in Italy was drained revealed that primitive ball bearings were used by the Romans shortly before the birth of Christ.

Leonardo da Vinci made what was probably the first and most complete study of friction up to his time, and rolling bearings are shown on many of the sketches in his notebooks. Up to the middle of the 20th century many patents for ball and roller bearings were issued in France, Germany, Great Britain, and the United States. These patents cover a wide variety of methods of assembling and separating the rolling elements and the design of the races for the rollers or balls to roll on. Time and experience have shown, however, that although many of these designs were ingenious, they were complicated. Thus most have been superseded by simpler types that are easier to manufacture and more reliable.

The first patent for ball bearings for bicycles appears to have been issued in 1862, but the first successful applications took place in 1868, when ball-bearing bicycles appeared in both England and France. Further development resulted in a patent in 1879 for a bearing that closely resembles the present-day bicycle bearing. By this time the number of bicycles had increased to such an extent that the manufacture of steel balls had become a substantial industry. The success of ball bearings in bicycles had a significant influence on the growth of the ball-bearing industry. By 1898 many other uses for these bearings in machine construction had been found, and factories were turning out balls of assorted sizes by the millions every day.

Bicycle bearings

Ball bearings. Figure 20 (top) shows two views of one quarter of the most widely used type of modern ball bearing. It consists of four parts: an inner race b, an outer race c, the balls d, and a separator or retainer e, which is also called a cage. The inside surface of the inner race fits snugly on the outside surface of one of the connected members, which is usually a fixed or rotating shaft, while the outside surface of the outer race fits snugly in the inside surface of the other member, which could be the base or frame of a machine, a rotating member such as a gear, a wheel, or a pulley. The dotted arrows in the figure indicate the directions of the rotations of the races relative to one another and the resulting rotation of the balls about their own geometric axes, assuming that there is no slip between the balls and the races; the balls also rotate bodily about the geometric centre of the bearing, just like the planet gears in a planetary gearset.

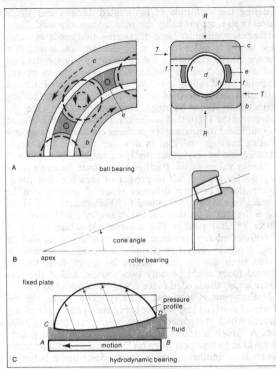

Figure 20: Types of bearings (see text).

The races in which the balls roll have grooves with radii of curvature slightly greater than the radius of a ball. Some bearings are assembled by moving the inner race radially, inserting the balls, centring the inner race, spacing the balls uniformly, and applying the retainer that holds the balls loosely in an equally spaced position. Other bearings have a notch in one of the races that permits more balls to be inserted. With more balls, the bearing can carry more radial load R (Figure 20 [top]) but less thrust load T on account of the notch.

Although the bearing in Figure 20 (top) is classified as a radial ball bearing, it has considerable thrust or axial-load capacity. The thrust capacity T can be increased by extending the races to sections ff so that the groove in the outer race is deeper on the left side and the groove in the inner race is deeper on the right side; some angular-contact bearings are made like this. If all of the load on a bearing is axial, an axial-thrust bearing can be used. This is simply two grooved washers with balls between them.

Ball bearings of the three basic types—radial, angular-contact, and thrust—are manufactured with either a single or a double row of balls. Radial bearings are also made with seals that retain the grease applied at the factory and exclude dirt and contaminants. Neither of the basic bearings has much tolerance for axial misalignment; in Figure 20 (top), for example, if the axes of the inner and outer races are not collinear within about plus or minus a quarter of a degree or less, then an additional load will be placed on the balls. Self-aligning bearings have especially designed outer races, and they permit axial misalignment up to about plus or minus two degrees or more without loading the balls.

Special types of ball bearings are made for specific industrial applications. A number of special ball bearings, for example, are made to satisfy the particular needs of the automobile manufacturers. Among these are bearings designed especially for front-wheel service, where the heavy radial and thrust loads imposed when turning corners may alternate or combine with the shock loads generated when driving over rough roads. These bearings are of the angular-contact type and are used in pairs, the larger of each pair being on the inside of the wheel hub. For ease of assembly and removal of the wheels, the outer races are press-fitted in the wheel hubs, while the inner races are separable, and easy push fits on the front axle. The correct running adjustment is obtained by means of a nut fitting a thread on the end of the axle that

Special types of ball bearings [margin note]

is screwed in against the smaller (outside) inner race until the balls and races are in firm angular contact.

Roller bearings. These bearings have rollers instead of balls between the races. The rollers may be cylindrical, tapered, or spherical. Cylindrical roller bearings have rollers with a length to diameter ratio of about one and run in cylindrical races, one of which may have retaining shoulders; they cannot carry a thrust load. Needle bearings have long, small-diameter rollers and may be installed with or without retainers and with or without races. When no races are used, the surfaces on which the needles roll must be hardened.

Needle bearings cannot carry thrust loads, but they have the highest radial load capacity, for a given radial space, of all roller bearings. Since unguided needles have a tendency to skew, needle bearings without retainers are particularly suitable for oscillating loads and where space is limited, such as for the wrist-pin bearings in automobile pistons, and in universal joints.

Tapered roller bearings (Figure 20 [centre]) have rollers and races that are truncated cones with elements that would intersect at a common apex if extended; this is the basic requirement for pure rolling contact between conical surfaces. These bearings have a high load capacity and when used in opposed pairs can carry thrust loads in either direction. The races are separable and are axially positioned during assembly to preload the bearing or to provide axial looseness to permit free thermal expansion.

Tapered roller bearings are available with different cone angles and with one, two, or four rows of rollers. They are widely used in rolling mills, transmissions, worm and spiral bevel gear speed reducers, and machine tool spindles. In tapered-roller thrust bearings the rollers are arranged like the spokes of a wheel between two flat washers with tapered grooves.

Spherical roller bearings have either convex or concave rollers in both single and double rows. Some of the rollers are basically cylindrical rollers with curved instead of straight elements, while some are tapered with curved elements. All these bearings have a self-aligning ability obtained by grinding either the outer or inner race spherical. The most commonly used type of spherical roller bearing is the double-row bearing with convex rollers.

Linear-motion rolling bearings. If the cage of a cylindrical roller bearing were cut and stretched out flat, it would form a self-contained pack (cartridge) of rollers that could be inserted between flat surfaces, or "ways," on adjacent machine parts to reduce the friction of relative linear motion; linear-motion rolling bearings of the ladder type are constructed in a similar way. Since the cartridge moves relative to both the fixed and moving ways —as can be demonstrated by rolling a pencil between the palm of one's hand and a table—the distance that the moving body can move is limited by the extent of the rolling surfaces on both ways and the length of the cartridge. This disadvantage can be overcome by using a "recirculating" ball or roller bearing, which, when attached to either the fixed or moving body, rolls on the ways attached to the other body and permits a movement limited only by the length of the ways.

Ball bearings that permit both rotary and linear motion are available. One such bearing is used on the spindle of a machine tool that oscillates as it reciprocates. The balls are held loosely in holes in a cage in the form of a brass sleeve that is thinner than the diameter of the balls; this permits the balls to protrude and contact the spindle on the inside of the cage and the housing or a special sleeve on the outside.

Service life. At ordinary ambient temperatures and under a nonvarying load that causes no permanent deformation, a machine component can be expected to carry the load for an unlimited period; a statically loaded machine component is assumed to have an infinite life.

When subjected to a dynamic (fluctuating) load the service life of a machine part depends on the nature and magnitude of the repetitive load; in such a case, life is the number of times that the load cycle can be repeated before the part fails (becomes unserviceable). For some materials and certain types of loads there is a limiting

Endurance limit

stress (load per unit area) known as the endurance limit or fatigue limit; if the maximum stress is less than the endurance limit, the life of the part is assumed to be infinite. Since there is a practical limit to the number of times a test specimen can be loaded, it is customary to assume that the maximum stress a test specimen can carry without failure for 10,000,000 repetitions is the endurance limit.

For some nonferrous materials and for parts subjected to certain types of loads, there is no endurance limit; the life of all parts is limited and depends on the magnitude of the maximum load imposed during the cycle. The higher the load the less the number of load repetitions that can be tolerated; rolling bearings are in this category.

Ball and roller bearings become unserviceable when the load-carrying surfaces develop pits. This pitting, or spalling, is initiated by subsurface cracks caused by the high surface-contact pressures between the rolling elements and the races. Under a repetitive load the cracks spread to the surface and eventually, aided by the lubricant that gets squeezed into the crack, a flake of metal is peeled off. The ultimate fatigue failure of a rolling bearing is unavoidable, but the life of the bearing or number of revolutions that the bearing can make before flaking begins depends on the load.

No material is more uniform in composition nor more carefully heat-treated and hardened than the steel used for rolling bearings. Few other machine components are manufactured to higher standards of accuracy and finish; in some bearings the difference between ball diameters is maintained at less than 0.00005 inch (0.0013 millimetre). In spite of this, rolling bearings that are apparently identical and operate under identical conditions may have substantially different lives. In this respect they have a mortality curve and a life expectancy like human beings.

Sliding-contact bearings. These bearings, also known as plain bearings to distinguish them from ball and roller bearings, can be designed to carry either radial or thrust loads on shafting and to control linear motion between adjacent machine parts. On journal, or sleeve, bearings the inner member, or shaft, is the journal, while the outer member, or sleeve, is the bearing; journal bearings can carry radial loads only and are the most commonly used type of sliding bearing.

When the load is light and the motion intermittent or slow, a journal bearing may be run without a lubricant; with some bearing materials no lubricant is necessary. In most cases, however, a solid or fluid lubricant is used. The type of lubrication that these lubricants provide may be a dry film, a fully developed fluid film that separates the sliding surfaces completely, or boundary lubrication with some contact between the sliding surfaces.

History. Although it has been known for centuries that oil or grease reduces the friction between sliding surfaces, the two ways in which a fully developed fluid film can be established in a bearing were not discovered until the latter part of the 19th century. One of the exhibits at the Paris exposition in 1878 was a large metallic block mounted on four legs having flat feet resting on a steel plate. Oil was pumped down each leg to the feet, and sufficient pressure was built up to raise the block on a film of oil. The friction between the feet and the plate was so low that the heavy block could be easily pushed around. This was probably the first recorded example of a hydrostatic or externally pressurized bearing, but its significance was not immediately appreciated by engineers.

One of the most spectacular hydrostatic bearings was installed in the late 1930s to support the 500-ton (450,000-kilogram) Hale telescope in the observatory on Palomar Mountain, in California. To rotate the telescope on these bearings at the speed necessary to follow the stars requires only a small clock motor.

Oil film without pumping

The discovery of the conditions under which a fully developed oil film can be established in a bearing without an external pumping system was more or less accidental. In the 1880s, while testing railroad journal bearings, it was discovered that with a copious supply of oil the friction was surprisingly low and that extraordinarily high maximum pressures were built up in the oil film.

These phenomena were later studied, and, by making some simplifying assumptions, it was mathematically proved that these results were explainable on the basis of hydrodynamic action in a wedge-shaped fluid film.

In Figure 20 (bottom) the plate AB is moving to the left under a fixed plate having the profile CD and separated from it by a tapered fluid film. Because of the taper, a pressure is developed in the fluid film that depends on the viscosity (internal friction) of the fluid, the velocity of the plate, and the geometry of the bearing. Bearings in which a fully developed oil film is created within the bearing in this way are known as hydrodynamic bearings. Film thicknesses are in the range of 0.0005–0.001 inch (0.013–0.025 millimetre).

At standstill the shaft in a journal bearing rests on the bottom of the bearing. When the shaft starts rotating it climbs the wall of the bearing, and if the speed is sufficiently high a tapered wedge of pressurized fluid will form and push the shaft to the other side of the bearing, where it will float on a hydrodynamic film.

In 1896 it was accidentally discovered in the United States that a journal bearing could be adequately lubricated with air. An experimental rotor was found to operate on a film of air at speeds above 250 revolutions per minute, with practically no friction. On the basis of these experiments, it was concluded that the hydrodynamic principle could be used on thrust bearings for heavy machinery, which at that time were very unsatisfactory, and in 1910 a United States patent was issued on a tilting-pad thrust bearing in which the stationary element was an assemblage of several flat pie-shaped segments, or shoes, arranged in a circle and contacting a ring-shaped rotating element. The shoes were supported on fixed pivots and could tilt automatically to provide the tapered oil film. Because of the oil film, the new thrust bearing had lower friction losses and could tolerate higher unit pressures than the existing thrust bearings in which both the rotating and stationary members were flat surfaces and the bearing operated in a state of boundary lubrication.

When a fully developed oil film exists in a sliding bearing there is no metal-to-metal contact, and the bearing material does not affect the performance of the bearing. Bearings do start and stop, however, and some may have to operate with boundary lubrication or no lubricant at all for short periods. Under such conditions the bearing material is important; in practice, the selection of a suitable material is a necessary step in the design of all sliding bearings. The greatest contribution to the development of improved bearing materials was made by Isaac Babbitt, who in 1839 obtained a United States patent for a railroad journal box lined with a special alloy that was largely tin with small amounts of antimony, copper, and lead. Babbitt, or "white," metal, as it is called, has served since its invention as a standard of excellence for all bearing materials.

Babbitt metal

There are two main types of babbitt metal in common use; one is largely tin, like the original, while the other is largely lead, and all babbitts have characteristics that make them particularly suitable for bearings. They deform readily in response to shaft and bearing deflections and without surface damage to either shaft or bearing. They have a favourable embeddability characteristic; *i.e.*, dirt particles that enter the bearing tend to become embedded in the soft babbitt and do not cut grooves in the shaft or the bearing. Babbitt metals operate satisfactorily with unhardened steel journals, while materials with lower deformability and embeddability characteristics require harder shafts; they also have less tendency than other materials to adhere or weld to the shaft in the absence of a lubricant. The latter characteristic, which is known as compatibility, is usually high for materials with a low coefficient of friction.

Journal bearings. There are five principal ways in which journal bearings differ from one another that can be used as bases for classification. Journal bearings differ in structure, in material, in the type of lubricant used, in the method of introducing the lubricant, and in the nature of the lubrication that exists. The only element common to all journal bearings is the journal, which is usually steel because steel is cheap, readily available, and stiffer than any other common material.

The simplest journal bearing is a block with a hole in it that provides a free fit for a pin or shaft. To facilitate replacement for wear, a separate bushing (sleeve) can be press-fitted in the block. Many standard sizes of sleeve bearings are commercially available.

Clearance adjustment and takeup for wear can also be obtained with a bearing that is split on a plane through the shaft axis and held together with bolts. Wear is taken up by removing shims (thin metallic sheets) or some of the metal between the two halves. In automobile crankshaft bearings, for example, split replaceable bushings are used. When the load on a bearing is always in the same direction, a partial bearing that envelops only about 120 degrees of the shaft can be used. Such bearings are used for supporting the axles on railroad cars.

The tilting or pivoted-pad principle can be applied to journal bearings as well as to thrust bearings. The bearing consists of a number of concave segments pivoted at their centres that tilt to form wedge-shaped oil films that tend to force the shaft toward the centre of the bearing. Freedom of the pads to tip both longitudinally and circumferentially produces a self-aligning effect.

As a rule, bodies in sliding contact wear least when they are of different materials. Bronze and steel wear well together, and for this reason the majority of commercially available sleeve bearing bushings are bronze, of many different compositions. Bronze can tolerate higher pressures than babbitt metal and it can be easily cast and machined.

Aluminum bearings have a high load-carrying capacity, good thermal conductivity, excellent corrosion resistance, and low cost. They are being used extensively in internal-combustion engines and aircraft accessory drives. The journals should be relatively hard and have a good surface finish.

Silver bearings, with an overlay of lead, were used on almost all of the aircraft engines developed during World War II. They can carry higher loads without seizure than can any other material.

Cast iron is one of the oldest and cheapest bearing materials, and it is still used where loads are light and speeds low. When factory machines are driven by belts from long lineshafts or countershafts, practically all of these shafts are supported on cast-iron bearings.

When bearings are inaccessible or periodic lubrication would be inconvenient, porous-metal, self-lubricating bearings can be used. The material in these bearings is usually bronze, but porous iron and aluminum bearings are also available. The manufacturing process creates voids or pores that take up from 10 to 35 percent of the total volume and are filled by submerging the bearings in oil. These bearings are simple in construction, cheap and easy to manufacture, and have proved their worth in home appliances, small motors, business machines, and farm machinery.

Self-lubrication can also be obtained with plastic bearings, which also provide freedom from corrosion, availability in easily molded shapes, and quiet operation. Among the many different compositions available, nylon is probably the most commonly used for the small, lightly loaded bushings used in office machines and instruments. Teflon, one of the most slippery materials known, is constantly extending its field of usefulness, particularly as a thin film deposited on hard metals.

Wooden bearings Wooden bearings are still used in a surprisingly large number of cases. For propeller-shaft bearings on ships, lignum vitae is exceptionally well suited. This wood is 33 percent heavier than water and has a high resin content, which makes it practically self-lubricating. It is also non-contaminating and can be used for the bearings of food-processing machinery. Rubber is another material that has found wide application in propeller-shaft and pump bearings in which water is used as a lubricant and also as a coolant.

Lubricants are used in a bearing to reduce friction and wear and to carry off heat; the three functions are not independent, since the greater the reduction in friction

the smaller the quantity of heat that must be removed and the lower the wear. Practically speaking, the prevention of wear and the extension of the life of the bearing are of prime importance (see also LUBRICATION).

Thrust bearings. When loads are light and speeds low, the simplest and cheapest type of thrust bearing consists of a collar on the shaft rubbing on a stationary washer that may have radial grooves to improve the distribution of the lubricant. Since a state of boundary lubrication is probable, the washer material is important and may be any of the materials used for journal bearings. For heavier loads multiple collars have been used, but exceptional manufacturing precision is necessary to ensure equal sharing of the load by each collar.

For carrying heavy thrust loads, either a hydrodynamic or a hydrostatic oil film is necessary in a bearing. As previously noted, a hydrodynamic film can be developed in a tilting-pad bearing. Because each pad adjusts to provide an optimum oil-film taper, these bearings can carry high loads over a wide speed range. A similar effect is obtained by supporting the pads on nests of coiled springs. Such bearings have been built with diameters of six feet (two metres) to support hydroelectric generators.

A hydrodynamic film can also be developed in a tapered-land thrust bearing and in a step thrust bearing. The tapered-land bearing is made by cutting radial grooves in a thick washer and machining tapered lands in the spaces between the grooves. The step bearing, which was first described in 1918, contains steps on the stationary member that produce a sudden reduction in the film thickness rather than a gradual one. The calculated load-carrying capacity of these bearings is slightly greater than that of a tilting-pad or tapered-land bearing.

An external pumping system is necessary to develop a hydrostatic oil film in a thrust bearing. These bearings are particularly useful in cases where reliability is important and a substantial oil film must be maintained at all speeds from zero up. On these bearings there are recesses or pockets of constant depth in either the rotating or the stationary member to which oil from a constant-displacement pump is delivered through orifices.

Gas bearings. Although feasibility of using air as a lubricant was suggested as early as 1854, and an air-lubricated journal bearing was constructed in 1896, engineers did not begin to show a serious interest in gas bearings until about 1949. This interest was stimulated by the shortcomings of oil-lubricated bearings for very-low-temperature (cryogenic) and high-temperature missile applications. In addition, since oil may disintegrate in a radioactive atmosphere while gases do not, gas bearings are well suited for applications in nuclear power plants. Although helium, hydrogen, and nitrogen have been used in gas bearings, air is the most commonly used lubricant.

Air bearings Like liquid-lubricated bearings, air bearings may operate on a self-induced aerodynamic film or on an aerostatic film generated by an external pump; they may be designed as journal bearings or thrust bearings. At low speeds the self-induced aerodynamic film in a journal bearing breaks down, while at high speeds the journal may become unstable and whirl around with a planetary motion in the bearing. In order to avoid metallic contact between the journal and the bearing in either case, "pressure-jacking" is used. This involves pumping high-pressure air into the bearing through holes in the bearing wall. If the jacking air is fed to the bearing continuously, the bearing is essentially an aerostatic bearing—a "hybrid" bearing—in which a substantial part of its load-carrying capacity is generated by aerodynamic action.

Because air has a much lower viscosity than oil, in order to develop a load-supporting film in an aerodynamic journal bearing, the clearance between the shaft and the bearing must usually be less than in an oil-lubricated bearing. Since air film thicknesses of 0.0005 inch (0.013 millimetre) are common, precise manufacturing and finishing techniques are required if such microscopic thicknesses are to be realized in practice. Although air bearings are usually tailor-made for the machine on which they are used, some air bearings are now available as standard, off-the-shelf components.

The friction in a properly functioning gas bearing is negligible; small hybrid bearings have been operated at speeds in excess of 500,000 revolutions per minute without overheating. If air is the gas, its ready availability is obviously an asset, and the possibility of contamination, which is always present when oil or grease is used, is eliminated. In addition to the applications previously mentioned, gas bearings are used in gyroscopes, instruments, high-speed drilling and grinding machines, dental drills, and refrigerators. Compared with oil-lubricated bearings the load-carrying capacity of aerodynamic bearings is low; it can be greatly increased by supplying high-pressure gas to the bearing.

Other types of bearings. Jewel bearings are used in instruments, clocks, watches, and other devices in which the only loads are friction and the weights of the moving parts. Usually the rotating element is a shaft with a flat end, spherical end, or conical end, while the fixed element or jewel may be in the form of a ring (a ringstone) that carries shafts in a hole, or a flat plate (an endstone) that carries end thrust from shafts with a spherical end, or a thick plate with a conical or V-shaped notch that is a receptacle for the conical end of a shaft.

Jewel bearings

The shafts or pivots in jewel bearings must be highly polished, free from surface scratches, and wear resistant, especially those with conical tips. Common materials are high-carbon steel, stainless steel, and Monel metal (a trademarked alloy consisting principally of nickel and copper). The commonest jewel materials are sapphire and borosilicate glass. When meters and instruments are subjected to vibration and shock, the jewels are mounted on shock-absorbing springs or silicone rubber cushions. Jewels are available with many special shapes and properties; in all cases minimum friction is the primary objective.

Bearings that rely on the forces created by magnetic, electrostatic, and electrodynamic fields to float the moving member in a bearing have many advantages; they eliminate friction and wear and the need for lubricants, and can operate in a vacuum and at extreme temperatures.

Liquid metals such as sodium and mercury are particularly useful as lubricants in high-temperature bearings. Their load-carrying capacity is usually poor, however, because of their relatively low viscosity. Recent developments indicate that by using superconducting magnets to create strong magnetic fields in electrically conducting fluids, the load-carrying capacity of liquid metal bearings can be greatly increased. These magnet-stiffened, liquid-metal bearings are known as magnetohydrodynamic (MHD) bearings.

Bearings in helicopters

A bearing that permits oscillations of up to 30 degrees without sliding or rolling contact has been developed for helicopter rotor hubs. It consists of alternate sleeves of steel and rubber bonded together to provide a cylindrical bearing that is extremely stiff in a radial direction but offers little resistance to being twisted within the 30-degree range. These bearings have operated successfully for long periods without lubrication or maintenance.

Improvements in the performance of aircraft jet engines are, to a large extent, attributable to the ability of rolling bearings to operate at higher and higher speeds. Research has shown that bearings with hollow balls can operate successfully at higher speeds and have longer useful lives than conventional bearings. Hollow balls, being lighter than solid balls, create lower centrifugal forces and stress on the outer race.

Another promising development is a hybrid arrangement with a ball bearing whose inner race forms a fluid-film bearing with the shaft. Because of the fluid film the inner race rotates at a slower speed than the shaft, reducing the relative speed in the ball bearing and increasing the fatigue life.

Comparison of bearings. All sliding and rolling bearings have their own particular advantages and disadvantages. The most important advantage of rolling bearings over sliding bearings is their availability as standardized off-the-shelf units covering a wide range of sizes and with known load-carrying capacities and life expectancies.

They require more radial space but less axial space than journal bearings, and the dimensions of the shaft and housing to which they are fitted must be kept within close limits. In addition, if properly sealed, there is practically no leakage of lubricant, and the starting friction is less than on hydrodynamic or aerodynamic bearings but greater than on externally pressurized bearings.

Rolling bearings are noisier than sliding bearings, particularly at high speeds, and they are usually more expensive than off-the-shelf sleeve bearings and bushings. All rolling bearings have a finite life, while the life of a full-film sliding bearing has no bounds.

In some applications, the superiority of one type of bearing over the other may be clearcut, but in other cases either type may be satisfactory, and the selection will depend on the designer's preferences.

Electric motors have bearings of both types; fractional horsepower motors usually have sleeve bearings made from a rolled strip in large quantities. From about 1 to 500 horsepower, ball and roller bearings are usually preferred, while above 500 horsepower, sleeve bearings are popular. Grease-lubricated ball bearings are preferred when motors must be started and stopped in cold weather.

In automotive engines sliding bearings are used for crankshafts, connecting rods, and wrist pins. These are low-cost, mass-produced sleeve bearings that have been improved from year to year and function successfully when well supplied with a lubricant. Ball and roller bearings are found in the front wheels, rear axle, and transmission. In the suspension systems of automobiles there are many joints in which the relative motion between the connected parts is small and can be easily taken care of with a flexible rubber connection. These bearings require no lubricant, since there is no relative sliding and nothing to wear.

As previously noted, the starting friction in a hydrodynamic bearing is higher than a rolling bearing. Since the gas turbine in a jet engine must start easily in low temperatures, rolling bearings are commonly used. These bearings are subjected to heavy thrust loads and also to high radial loads caused by gyroscopic effects during manoeuvring. Since they are replaced at regular intervals, the required life is comparatively short.

Jet engine bearings

SHAFTS

Solid shafts. As a machine component a shaft is commonly a cylindrical bar that supports and rotates with devices for receiving and delivering rotary motion and torque. The crankshaft of a reciprocating engine receives its rotary motion from each of the cranks, via the pistons and connecting rods (the slider-crank mechanisms), and delivers it by means of couplings, gears, chains, or belts to the transmission, camshaft, pumps, and other devices. The camshaft, driven by a gear or chain from the crankshaft, has only one receiver or input, but each cam on the shaft delivers rotary motion to the valve-actuating mechanisms.

An axle is usually defined as a stationary cylindrical member on which wheels and pulleys can rotate, but the rotating shafts that drive the rear wheels of an automobile are also called axles, no doubt a carryover from horse-and-buggy days. It is common practice to speak of short shafts on machines as spindles, especially tool-carrying or work-carrying shafts on machine tools.

In the days when all machines in a shop were driven by one large electric motor or a prime mover, it was necessary to have long lineshafts running the length of the shop and supplying power, by belts, to shorter counter-shafts, jackshafts, or headshafts. These lineshafts were assembled from separate lengths of shafting clamped together by rigid couplings. Although it is usually more convenient to drive each machine with a separate electric motor, and the present-day trend is in this direction, there are still some situations in which a group drive is more economical.

A single-throw crankshaft that could be used in a single-cylinder reciprocating engine or pump is shown in Figure 21. The journals A and B rotate in the main

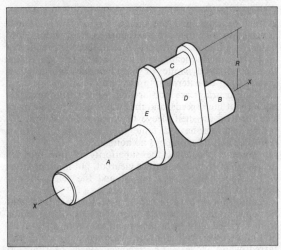

Figure 21: Single-throw crankshaft (see text).

bearings, C is the crankpin that fits in a bearing on the end of the connecting rod and moves on a circle of radius R about the main bearings, while D and E are the cheeks or webs. The throw R is one half the stroke of the piston, which is connected, by the wrist pin, to the other end of the connecting rod and guided so as to move on a straight path passing through the axis XX. On a multiple-cylinder engine the crankshaft has multiple throws—eight for a straight eight and four for a V-8—arranged in a suitable angular relationship.

Stresses and strains. In operation, shafts are subjected to a shearing stress, whose magnitude depends on the torque and the dimensions of the cross section. This stress is a measure of the resistance that the shaft material offers to the applied torque. All shafts that transmit a torque are subjected to torsional shearing stresses.

In addition to the shearing stresses, twisted shafts are also subjected to shearing distortions. The distorted state is usually defined by the angle of twist per unit length; *i.e.,* the rotation of one cross section of a shaft relative to another cross section at a unit distance from it.

Bending stresses

Shafts that carry gears and pulleys are bent as well as twisted, and the magnitude of the bending stresses, which are tensile on the convex side of the bend and compressive on the concave side, will depend on the load, the distance between the bearings, and the dimensions of the shaft cross section.

The combination of bending and twisting produces a state of stress in the shaft that is more complex than the state of pure shear produced by torsion alone or the state of tension-compression produced by bending alone.

To the designer of shafts it is important to know if the shaft is likely to fail because of an excessive normal stress or an excessive shearing stress. If a piece of chalk is twisted, it will invariably rupture on a plane at about 45 degrees to the axis, not on a plane perpendicular to the axis. This is because the maximum tensile stresses act on this plane, and chalk is weak in tension. Steel shafting is usually designed so that the maximum shearing stress produced by bending and torsion is less than a specified maximum.

Shafts with circular cross sections are easier to produce in the steel mill, easier to machine, and easier to support in bearings than shafts with other cross sections; there is seldom any need for using noncircular shapes. In addition, the strength and stiffness, both in bending and torsion, are more easily calculated for circular shafts. Lastly, for a given amount of material the circular shaft has the smallest maximum shearing stress for a given torque, and the highest torsional rigidity.

The shearing stress in a circular shaft is highest at the surface and drops off to zero at the axis. This means that most of the torque is carried by the material on and near the surface.

Critical speeds. In the same way that a violin string vibrates when stroked with a bow, a cylindrical shaft suspended between two bearings has a natural frequency of lateral vibration. If the speed of revolution of the shaft coincides with the natural frequency, the shaft will experience a whirling critical speed and become noisy. These speeds are more likely to occur with long, flexible shafts than with short, stiff ones. The natural frequency of a shaft can be raised by increasing its stiffness.

If a slender rod is fixed to the ceiling at one end and supports a heavy disk at the other end, the disk will oscillate back and forth around the rod axis like a torsion pendulum if given an initial twist and let go. The frequency of the oscillations will depend on the torsional stiffness of the rod and the weight of the disk; the stiffer the rod and the lighter the disk the higher the frequency. Similar torsional oscillations can occur in the crankshafts of reciprocating engines, particularly those with many crank throws and a heavy flywheel. Each crank throw and part of the associated connecting rod acts like a small flywheel, and for the crankshaft as a whole, there are a number of ways or modes in which these small flywheels can oscillate back and forth around the shaft axis in opposition to one another and to the main flywheel. For each of these modes there corresponds a natural frequency of oscillation.

When the engine is operating the torques delivered to the crankshaft by the connecting rods fluctuate, and if the crankshaft speed is such that these fluctuating impulses are delivered at a speed corresponding to one of the natural torsional frequencies of the shaft, torsional oscillations will be superimposed on the rotary motion of the shafts. Such speeds are known as torsional critical speeds, and they can cause shaft failures. A number of devices to control the oscillations of crankshafts have been invented.

Torsional critical speeds

Flexible shafts. A flexible shaft consists of a number of superimposed tightly wound right- and left-hand layers of helically wound wires wrapped about a single centre wire or mandrel. The shaft is connected to the source of power and the driven member by special fittings attached to the ends of the shaft. Flexible casings of metallic or nonmetallic materials, which guide and protect the shaft and retain the lubricant, are also available. Compared with solid shafts, flexible shafts can be bent to much smaller radii without being overstressed.

For transmitting power around corners and for considerable distances flexible shafts are usually cheaper and more convenient than belts, chains, or gears. Most speedometers on automobiles are driven by flexible shafts running from the transmission to the dashboard. When a valve, a switch, or other control device is in a hard-to-reach location, it can be operated by a flexible shaft from a more convenient position. For portable tools such as sanders, grinders, and drilling machines, flexible shafts are practically indispensable.

SHAFT ACCESSORIES

Keys, splines, and pins. When power is being transmitted from a machine member such as a coupling, a clutch, a gear, a flywheel, or a pulley to the shaft on which it is mounted, means must be provided for preventing relative motion between the shaft and the member. On helical and bevel gears, relative movement along the shaft caused by the thrust (axial) loads is prevented by a step in the shaft or by having the gear contact the bearing directly or through a tubular spacer. When axial loads are incidental and of small magnitude, the members are kept from sliding along the shaft by means of a set screw. The primary purpose of keys, splines, and pins is to prevent relative rotary movement.

A commonly used type of key has a square cross section (Figure 22A) and is sunk half in the shaft and half in the hub of the other member. If the key is made of steel (which is commonly the case) of the same strength as the shaft and has a width and depth equal to one fourth of the shaft diameter (this proportion is closely approximated in practice) then it will have the same torque capacity as the solid shaft if its length is 1.57 times that of the shaft diameter. Another common type of key has a rectangular cross section with a depth to width ratio of 0.75. Both of these keys may either be straight or tapered in depth. The

Square keys

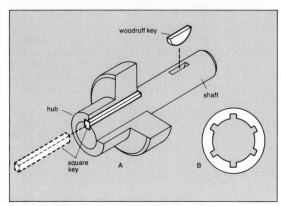

Figure 22: (A) Shaft keys. (B) Internal spline.

straight keys fit snugly on the sides of the keyways only, the tapered keys on all sides. Gib-head keys are tapered keys with a projection on one end to facilitate removal.

Woodruff keys (Figure 22A) are widely used on machine tools and motor vehicles. The key is a segment of a disk and fits in a keyway in the shaft that is cut with a special milling cutter. Though the extra depth of these keys weakens the shaft considerably, it prevents any tendency of the key to rotate or move axially. Woodruff keys are particularly suitable for tapering shaft ends.

Because they weaken the shaft less, keys with straight or tapered circular cross sections are sometimes used in place of square and rectangular keys, but the keyways, half in the shaft and half in the hub, must be cut with a drill after assembly, and interchangeability of parts is practically impossible. When a large gear blank is made by shrinking a high-strength rim on a cheaper cast centre, circular keys, snugly fitted, are frequently used to ensure a permanent connection.

Splines (Figure 22B) are permanent keys integral with the shaft, fitting in keyways cut in the hub. The dimensions of splined fittings are standardized for both permanent (press) fits and sliding fits. The teeth have either straight or involute profiles; the latter are stronger, more easily measured, and have a self-centring action when twisted.

Tapered circular pins can be used to restrain shaft-mounted members from both axial and rotary movement. The pin fits snugly in a reamed tapered hole that is perpendicular to the shaft axis and either radial or tangential to the shaft surface. A number of straight pins that grip by deforming elastically or plastically when driven into straight holes are commercially available.

All the keys and pins that have been described are standard driving devices. In some cases they are inadequate, and unorthodox means must be employed. For driving small gears in which there is no room between the bore and the roots of the teeth for a longitudinal keyway, a transverse radial slot on the end of the gear can be made to fit a radial protuberance on the shaft. For transmitting moderate loads, a cheap and effective connection can be made by forming a series of longitudinal serrations on the shaft with a knurling tool and pressing the shaft into the hole in the driven member. If the shaft is hard enough relative to the member, it will cut grooves in the hole and provide, in effect, a press-fitted splined connection. Press and shrink fits are also used, and they can provide surprisingly firm connections, but the dimensions of the connected members must be closely controlled.

Fluid seals. When a reciprocating or rotating shaft extends from a bearing or a housing (enclosure) containing a fluid, such as a pump, a gearbox, or a hydraulic transmission, the shaft must be free to move relative to the housing, and at the same time leakage of fluids and entry of contaminants at the shaft-housing interface must be restricted. The purpose of a seal is to restrict the leakage with the least possible restraint on the relative motion.

There are four basically different types of seals: shaft seals, face seals, labyrinth seals, and hydrodynamic seals. The sealing element in shaft seals acts directly on the surface of the shaft. One of the oldest shaft seals is the

The four types of seals

stuffing box and gland; it was used by James Watt on his steam engine and, with modern compression packings, is still used for sealing acids, ammonia, water, oil, gasoline, steam, gas, and air. The stuffing box, which is an annular (ringlike) space between the surface of the shaft and an enlarged opening in the housing, is filled with a ropelike packing. The gland has a tubular member with a cross section that fits the stuffing box and can be moved axially to reduce the length of the stuffing box and create a pressure on the packing. A common type of packing consists of twisted strands of asbestos or cotton lubricated with oil and graphite. A wide variety of fabric, metallic, and plastic packings is available.

Shaft and face seals. The radial lip seal is probably the most commonly used oil or shaft seal. Figure 23A shows a cross section of a bonded-type seal in which the elasto-

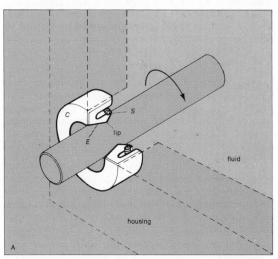

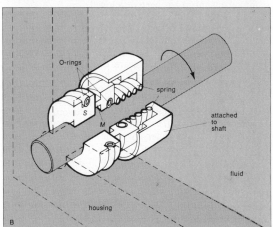

Figure 23: (A) Shaft (lip) seal; (B) face seal (see text).

mer sealing element E is bonded to the metallic case C, which is pressed into the housing. The initial interference pressure between the lip of the sealing element and the shaft is augmented by the helically wound garter spring S and pressure from the fluid in the housing.

When properly designed and installed, the lip rides on a film of lubricant about 0.0001 inch (0.0025 millimetre) thick. If the film gets too thick, fluid leaks, while if too thin the lip gets hot and the seal may fail. Although the finish on the shaft is important, some laboratory tests indicate that too smooth a finish may be undesirable, as it may retard development of an oil film. Leather, synthetic rubber, and silicones are among the materials used for lip seals.

In the face seal (Figure 23B) the sealing is done on the radial face where the rotating element M, attached to the shaft, contacts the stationary element S, attached to the housing. The element M, which may be carbon-graphite, and the element S, which may be steel, have precision-finished contacting surfaces and are spring-loaded against

O-ring
seals

one another. The O-rings are flexible rings with a circular cross section and provide static sealing. O-ring materials include neoprene, butyl, fluorinated silicones, and natural rubber; they are widely used for static seals and sometimes also for dynamic applications. Face seals are expensive, precision components and must be handled and installed with care. They have been used under pressures up to 3,000 pounds per square inch (200 kilograms per square centimetre) and at speeds up to 50,000 feet (15,-000 metres) per minute; their leakage rate is exceptionally low.

Labyrinth and hydrodynamic seals. The labyrinth seal provides a series of annular spaces between disks attached to the shaft and matching grooves in the stationary member; this arrangement merely limits leakage by restricting the annular clearance between the disks and the grooves. These seals are used in large steam and gas turbines, where the friction and wear of a contact seal is less tolerable than a small loss in efficiency caused by leakage. A labyrinth seal consisting of a row of tapered rings fixed in the housing and a plain shaft has proven effective for sealing gas. The rings are tapered to an edge thickness of about 0.010 inch (0.25 millimetre) at the shaft surface. When assembled there is some interference and the edges of the rings are worn off when the shaft rotates.

The hydrodynamic seal consists of a housing with a smooth bore and a helically grooved rotating shaft. If the radial clearance between the shaft and the bore is sufficiently small, a pumping action tending to move the oil along the shaft will be created. A similar pumping effect can be obtained with a plain shaft and a helix cut in the housing.

Hydrodynamic seals have some limitations; they do not seal when the shaft is stationary, they are usually restricted to unidirectional applications, and close radial clearance between the elements is required. By themselves, neither the lip nor the hydrodynamic seal is ideal, but by utilizing the best features of each, a more reliable sealing mechanism has been developed.

In the United States, the automotive industry is probably the largest user of seals. Dissatisfied with the performance of lip seals, one of the largest automobile manufacturers has developed a seal in which the lip and hydrodynamic methods of sealing are combined. This seal is basically a lip-type seal in which a circumferential static ridge and a series of helical grooves are molded in the elastomer element. Seals with right- and left-hand helices have been developed for bidirectional rotation.

Modern developments. Man's urge to travel faster, fly higher, and explore outer space has created a need for seals with capabilities of a high order. Since World War II, with the advent of nuclear power plants, space vehicles, and supersonic aircraft, the temperature levels at which seals must operate have risen from about 200° F (90° C) to about 900° F (500° C). In addition, operating speeds have increased and ambient pressures have dropped below atmospheric.

There has been considerable recent development in seal technology, and a variety of high-performance seals is available for applications involving gas, liquid metals, and all of the common fluids. One of these is a face seal with spiral grooves to produce a hydrodynamic effect; it has been used to seal liquid sodium.

With the introduction of automobile warranties, car manufacturers became increasingly concerned with oil seal performance. Car owners are seldom aware of oil seals until one leaks, and although the seals themselves may be inexpensive, labour costs for replacement are high. If seal leakage leads to engine, transmission, or rear axle failure—which can easily happen—the costs are much higher.

Successful application of seals requires that the seal be properly designed, carefully manufactured, and correctly applied. Unfortunately, there is no seal technology to which a designer can turn to learn the science and art of seal design. The importance of the problem has been recognized; in 1967 research in sealing was being carried out in over 100 laboratories throughout the world, and the volume of literature had increased tenfold since 1947.

Research
in sealing
methods

SCREWS

Screw fasteners. Screws have been used as fasteners for a long time. Medieval jewelers used screws to fasten bracelets, and taps and dies for cutting internal and external threads, respectively, were in use in the 14th century. A book written in the 16th century has a drawing of a tapered screw with a flat, slotted head that is apparently a wood screw.

As indicated in the section on simple machines, a screw acts with a wedging action and consists of a circular cylinder (or truncated cone) with a helical groove in it. When used for fastening, all screws are provided with means for applying a torque (twisting moment) to them; this may consist of a square or hexagonal head for a wrench, a head with a slot or a cross-shaped recess for a screwdriver, a cylindrical head with a recess fitting a special wrench, or a slot or recess on one end fitting a screwdriver or special wrench and no head.

Screws with screwdriver slots have heads of several shapes, such as flat, oval, round, and fillister (cylindrical with a round top). Wood screws are tapered, and self-tapping screws have tapered ends and a variety of special points. The latter are usually hardened and cut or form a mating internal thread when screwed into the proper size hole.

Screws with hexagonal heads are usually known as cap screws. Screws with other types of heads are also known as cap screws in the larger sizes and as machine screws in the smaller sizes. All of these screws are used to clamp machine parts together when one of the parts has an internal thread. If neither part is threaded a bolt must be used; this consists of a screw with a hexagonal head, a nut (hexagonal ring with an internal thread), and usually a washer (flat ring). A stud has threads on both ends and no means for turning. It is permanently screwed into one member and clamps by means of a nut on the other end. All of these fasteners stretch when tightened, and the tensile load created in this way clamps the members together.

Set screws differ in form and function from the other types of screws. They are hardened and have cup, cone, oval, flat, and dog (cylindrical) ends or points. They are usually headless and are frequently used as substitutes for keys or in conjunction with keys in shaft-mounted members. The set screw fits in a threaded radial hole in the hub, and the point is tightened down into a hole, a flat, or a dimple in the shaft or key. Set screws are stressed in compression, and in action they create a helical wedge between the connected parts.

Standard thread forms. Until 1841 there was no standard for the form and size of the helical groove in threaded fasteners; there was little likelihood that a screw made by one manufacturer would fit a nut or a tapped hole made by another manufacturer. Interchangeability of screw threads requires standardization of the form of the groove and the dimensions of the groove as a function of the diameter of the blank in which the groove is cut. Since 1841 several forms have been proposed and adopted; these forms are all referred to a longitudinal plane passing through the axis of the screw (an axial plane).

Over the years, but especially during the world wars, the non-interchangeability between British and United States screw threads was inconvenient. To remedy this, a Unified Screw Thread Standard was recommended by the International Organization for Standardization and accepted by Canada, the United Kingdom, and the United States in an accord signed at Washington, D.C., on November 18, 1948. The form of the Unified Screw Thread for an external thread is shown in Figure 24. Unified and United States threads have substantially the same thread form.

Unified
Screw
Thread

In Figure 24 the distance between the crests of adjacent threads is given by the pitch p, which in terms of the number of threads per inch N can be expressed as $p = 1/N$. This is a measure of the size of a thread, and to create a standard it is necessary to correlate the pitch p (or N) and the diameters of the various screws in a series. Of the 11 standard Unified Screw Thread series the coarse, fine, and extra fine series are the most commonly

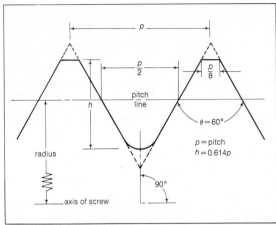

Figure 24: Unified external screw thread.

used; they are designated as UNC, UNF, and UNEF, respectively. A 1-inch (25-millimetre) diameter UNC bolt, for example, has eight threads per inch, while a 1-inch UNF bolt has 12, and a 1-inch UNEF bolt 20 threads per inch.

The coarse-thread series is used for quick and easy assembly, the fine-thread series for automotive and aircraft applications, and the extra-fine-thread series for thin-walled sections. In addition to the thread series, thread classes, distinguished from one another by the manufacturing tolerances, have been established.

Loads in bolts. Machine screws and set screws are usually installed without much concern for the loads they may be carrying, which in any event are usually light. For cap screws and bolts, however, the imposed loads must be given some consideration by the designer, especially if the load fluctuates. When a bolt is tightened, as on the head of a pressure cylinder, the bolt is stretched and the cylinder head and gasket are compressed. Subsequent applied loads on the head stretch the bolt further and reduce the compression of the head and gasket. If the applied load is large enough the joint will open up. If the applied load fluctuates, the optimum load and stress state for the bolt is obtained when the joint is just on the point of opening up under the maximum applied load.

Measuring
preload
in bolts There is a great deal of interest, especially in the aircraft and aerospace industries, in devices for measuring the initial tightening load (preload) in bolts. The torque wrench is one of the oldest methods, but its effectiveness depends on being able to establish a functional relationship between the torque applied to the wrench and the tensile load produced in the bolt. Tests have shown that the friction in the threads has considerable influence on this relationship; with a well-lubricated thread the tensile load for a given torque may be many times greater than the load with a similar dry thread.

Direct measurement of the stretch of the bolt is the most accurate method of measuring preload, and a number of devices, some of them surprisingly complex and involving auxiliary strain-measuring equipment, have been developed. Other methods utilize the turns of the nut, and some rely on the compression of calibrated plastic washers.

Unless means for maintaining the preload are provided, all screw fasteners tend to work loose, especially when the load fluctuates. For machine screws a variety of conical, wavy, and helical spring lock washers is available. For bolted connections additional locking effects can be obtained with locknuts. One of the most effective is a nut with slots that is kept from rotating by a cotter or split pin that passes through one of the slots and a hole in the bolt. A jam nut is a second nut that is tightened against the loaded nut. There are a number of nuts with special features that permit them to spin freely for a few turns; they then must be turned with a wrench to their final position. In one of these nuts the final resistance is produced by a nonmetallic collar that fits tightly around the bolt thread.

Power screws. A power screw is a mechanical force or motion modifier that is used to convert torque to thrust (or vice versa) or rotary motion to linear motion (or vice versa). Although at one time they were most often used as force amplifiers in presses, power screws are more commonly used for converting rotary to linear motion.

Thread forms and efficiency. Early power screws had square threads with a thread angle $\theta = 0°$ and thread height $h = p/2$ (see Figure 24). This thread is more efficient than the V-thread but more difficult to manufacture. The Acme thread, introduced in the 1890s, is a cross between the V and the square thread, with $\theta = 29°$ and $h = p/2$. The Acme thread and the Stub Acme, with $h = 0.3\ p$, are now used almost exclusively for power screws.

If the helix in Figure 4 were a narrow groove, there would be room on the cylinder for a number of similar grooves, equally spaced axially and starting at equally spaced points around the end of the cylinder such as 1, 2, 3, 4, and so on. Such an arrangement of helices is found on a "multiple-start" screw. The axial distance between the helices is the pitch and is the same as the pitch p on the screw thread in Figure 24. A screw with two "starts" one-half turn apart has a double thread and $l = 2\ p$; one with three "starts" has a triple thread, and so on. Multiple-thread screws are used to obtain a large axial movement per revolution of the screw without using a large pitch and the coexisting deep thread. A multiple-thread screw is also more efficient than a single-thread screw with the same pitch and diameter. This gain in efficiency results from the increase in the lead angle.

Efficiencies of 90 percent and higher are obtainable with a ball screw, which consists of a screw and nut with matching semicircular helical grooves and balls that roll in the grooves between the nut and the screw. The balls travel at half the relative speed of the grooves and leave the load zone at the trailing end of the nut, where a return tube conducts them to the leading end of the nut. Ball screws convert either torque to thrust or thrust to torque. They are most commonly used to convert torque to thrust either by rotating an axially fixed screw to drive a rotationally fixed nut along the screw or by rotating an axially fixed nut to drive a rotationally fixed screw through the nut. Ball screws

Applications. Machines that remove material from a workpiece by cutting usually require the workpiece or the tool, or both, to move on a straight path. Since most machines are driven by rotating motors, a screw is a convenient means for converting rotation to translation by mechanical means, especially if a slow and precisely controllable movement is required. On one precision boring machine the table on which the workpiece is clamped can be moved in increments of 0.0001 inch (0.00025 centimetre) by a screw with an error of only 0.0002 inch (0.0005 centimetre) in 16 inches (41 centimetres).

The micrometer caliper depends on an accurate screw for the precision of its measurements. On a one-inch micrometer the screw has 40 threads on a length of one inch, so that in one revolution the screw advances one-fortieth inch or 25 thousandths of an inch. The thimble attached to the screw has a circumference of 1.57 inches and is graduated in 25 divisions, each approximately 0.0625 inch apart. This means that a 0.001-inch axial movement of the screw corresponds with a rotary movement on the thimble of 0.0625 inch. Consequently, each one thousandth of an inch on the part being measured is magnified 62.5 times by the screw.

Screw thread production. There are five principal methods of producing screw threads, namely: (1) die cutting and tapping, (2) chasing, (3) milling and hobbing, (4) grinding, (5) rolling.

A hand-threading die is basically a hardened nut from which some material has been removed to provide cutting edges. A hand tap is a hardened screw with longitudinal grooves that provide cutting edges. Once a tap or a die has started to cut, its advance into the workpiece is self regulated. Hand taps and dies are usually hand operated but can be used with special attachments in drill presses and in lathes. Dies with adjustable cutters that open up after cutting and collapsible taps that retract after cutting are also available for use in production machines.

Thread chasings

In chasing, a tool is moved at a controlled rate parallel to the axis of the rotating workpiece and fed in radially at the end of each pass until the thread is the proper depth. On an engine lathe the tool has only one cutting point, and its longitudinal movement is controlled by the lead screw that is driven by gears from the spindle. Thread chasing can also be done with a multiple-point tool that looks like a comb.

Thread milling can be done with a single disk-type milling cutter shaped on its periphery to the profile of the thread to be cut and rotating about its own axis as it moves parallel to the axis of the workpiece under the control of a lead screw; it can also be done with a cutter that is essentially a stack of single cutters, or with a hob, which has cutting edges arranged on a helix. Thread milling is usually done on special machines. Thread grinding is done in much the same way as thread milling; the milling cutter is replaced by a disk-type grinding wheel that reproduces its peripheral shape on the workpiece.

Thread rolling is done with dies that are either flat plates or rolls with grooves in them to match the thread being formed. When flat dies are used, one die is fixed and the other reciprocates longitudinally at a fixed distance above it. The grooves on the opposed faces of the dies are straight and inclined to the long sides at an angle equal to the lead angle of the screw. The screw blank, which is fed in at the starting end as the moving die starts its forward stroke, rolls along the stationary die and, being wedged between the dies, is impressed with the thread form. When two roll dies are used, one is mounted on a fixed spindle and the other, connected to it by gears, is mounted on a movable slide. The workpiece rests on a stationary blade between the rolls and is impressed with the thread form when the movable roll is advanced. The rolling process improves the strength of the part on account of the cold deformation of the workpiece. Compared with cut threads, rolled threads can be up to 50 percent stronger under repetitive loads.

When large numbers are required, the threads on machine screws, and cap screws and bolts in the smaller sizes, are rolled. The production rate is higher and the cost lower than for any other method. It is probable that more screws are produced by rolling than by any other method. Although rolling is usually restricted to V-shaped threads, the successful rolling of Acme threads has been reported.

SPRINGS

A spring is a load-sensitive, energy-storing device the chief characteristics of which are an ability to tolerate large deflections without failure and to recover its initial size and shape when loads are removed. Although most springs are mechanical and derive their effectiveness from the flexibility inherent in metallic elements, hydraulic springs and air springs are also obtainable.

Uses of springs

Springs are used for a variety of purposes, such as supplying the motive power in clocks and watches, cushioning transport vehicles, measuring weights, restraining machine elements, making resilient connections, launching and retarding missiles and vehicles, mitigating the transmission of periodic disturbing forces from unbalanced rotating machines to the supporting structure, and providing shock protection for delicate instruments during shipment.

Mechanical springs. *Elasticity and Hooke's law.* If a solid body recovers its original size and shape after being deformed, it is said to be elastic. Most mechanical elements used in machine construction are practically elastic up to a limiting load that depends on the dimensions of the element and the material from which the element is made. In order to eliminate the dimensional effect and obtain a measure of elastic capability that depends only on the material, the stress concept is utilized. The elastic limit stress is the load at which a straight bar of the material with a circular cross section of one square inch would cease to be elastic when pulled in a tensile-testing machine. Thus, if a specimen with a cross-sectional area of 0.5 square inch becomes inelastic at a load of 15,000 pounds, the elastic limit would be $15,000/0.5 = 30,000$

pounds per square inch (2,100 kilograms per square centimetre). This is an average value for low-carbon steel.

If the deflection of an elastic body is proportional to the load, the body is said to be linearly elastic and to satisfy Hooke's law. This means that if the load is doubled the deflection is doubled. The relation between load and deflection for two linearly elastic bodies is shown in Figure 25A. Under the same load P, the deflection of body 1 is Δ_1, which is less than half the deflection of body 2; body 1 is obviously stiffer than body 2. The stiffness K of a linearly elastic body is the ratio of the load to the corresponding deflection and is commonly expressed in pounds per inch or kilograms per centimetre.

The stiffness of a body when loaded in a given manner depends on its dimensions and configuration, and on an important property of the material known as the modulus of elasticity. The modulus of elasticity in tension, designated by E, is very close to 30,000,000 pounds per square inch (2,100,000 kilograms per square centimetre) for all steels, and it represents the stress required to stretch a steel bar to twice its original length, if such a large elongation were possible. The modulus of elasticity in compression is usually assumed to be the same as in tension. Like the elastic limit, the modulus of elasticity is strictly a material property; it is a measure of the stiffness of a material and influences the stiffness or spring rate of all mechanical springs that are stressed in tension or compression.

Stiffness and energy. In order to deflect a linearly elastic spring, a gradually increasing force must be applied. By definition, work is average force times distance. In the case of a spring, the work done during a deflection is stored in the spring as elastic energy, which can be recovered when the load is relaxed. The energy stored in a spring can be used to cushion shocks or to actuate mechanisms. In Figure 25A the energy stored in body 1 is $P\Delta_1/2$, while the energy stored in body 2, $P\Delta_2/2$, is much greater because body 2 is more flexible. The stiffness K is a measure of the flexibility and is given by the slope of the line in the Figure.

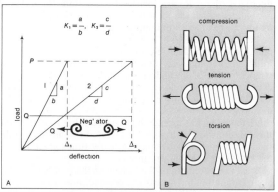

Figure 25: (A) Spring characteristics. (B) Helical springs (see text).

Under load, all mechanical springs have either tensile, compressive, or shear stresses, or combinations of these stresses. In most cases the stresses are produced by simple pull or push loads, bending, or torsion.

Common types. The helical spring (Figure 25B) is probably the most commonly used of all springs. It can be designed to carry pull or push loads or a torque. In the latter case, the torque produces a bending stress in the wire. Among the applications of springs of this type are hinges, engine starters, and handles. Helical tension and compression springs have innumerable uses, among which are measuring weights in spring balances, restoring moving machine elements to their initial positions, and closing valves on engines; they are also used for automobile suspension systems, for gun recoil mechanisms, and for shock-modifying mounts.

Helical springs

The torsion-bar spring is favoured by some automobile manufacturers for wheel suspensions. It consists of a long steel bar fixed at one end and supported but free to rotate at the other end. It is twisted by a load applied by a crank at the free end. The leaf spring is used mainly for vehicle suspension, and in its simplest form is a cantilever beam of uniform rectangular cross section loaded at the free end. Since the bending stress is proportional to the bending moment, which is equal to the product of the load and the distance to the cross section, the stress is a maximum at the fixed end and zero at the load. This means that the material is being inefficiently used in a beam of uniform width. To obtain a uniform stress along the beam it should be in the form of a triangular plate of uniform thickness with the apex at the free end. In practice, the triangular plate is replaced by a stack of narrow plates of uniform width and varying length. The leaf spring in Figure 26A can be treated as two cantilevers, each supporting half the load, or $P/2$.

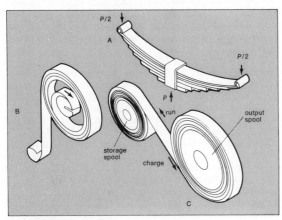

Figure 26: *Types of springs.*
(A) Leaf spring; (B) spiral spring; (C) Neg'ator motor.

The spiral spring (Figure 26B) is made from flat strip or wire; as a mainspring or hairspring it provides a compact source of energy in clocks and watches. It is also used on typewriters, parking meters, and wind-up toys.

The Neg'ator. A spring of unusual interest and usefulness and having characteristics totally unlike those of other springs was introduced in 1949. It is called the Neg'ator, or constant-force spring, and consists of a strip of flat spring material that has been given a curvature by continuous heavy forming so that in its relaxed or unstressed condition it is in the form of a tightly wound spiral. When mounted for free rotation the material resists withdrawal from the coil with a force (Q) that remains essentially constant regardless of the extension as shown in Figure 25A. In this form the Neg'ator is widely used as a long-deflection spring for retracting, constant-force tensioning, and counterbalancing.

Neg'ator
motors

Figure 26C shows a Neg'ator motor. The coil is mounted on, but not usually fixed to, the smaller storage spool, which can rotate freely. The other end of the coil is fixed to the larger output spool. To charge the motor, the output spool is rotated and the spring withdrawn from the storage spool. When fully charged, most of the spring is wound on the output spool. Because of the difference in the diameters of the spools, the spring will return to the storage spool when released and create a torque on the output spool that is essentially constant through 50 to 60 revolutions or more. Neg'ator spring motors are used extensively in movie cameras, clocks, phonographs, slide projectors, retracting steel tape rules, and in counterbalancing movable lighting fixtures and venetian blinds.

Recapitulation. Most mechanical springs are made from high-strength steel. Since the stiffness depends on the modulus of elasticity and this property is practically the same for all grades of steel, this stiffness of a steel spring cannot be increased by making it stronger or harder. Increasing the strength only increases the maximum load that the spring can carry. Since the modulus of elasticity of phosphor bronze wire is approximately half that of steel, a significant reduction in stiffness can be obtained by switching from steel to phosphor bronze.

Summarizing, the essential characteristics of mechanical springs are strength and flexibility, whereas in structures, strength and rigidity are the usual requirements. Control of these two properties in a spring or a structure to satisfy diverse requirements is possible only because of the fortunate circumstance that the stress and the deflection that a given load produces in an elastic body are not affected in the same degree by changes in the dimensions of the body. The strength of a torsion bar, for example, depends only on the area of the cross section, while the stiffness depends on both the area and the length. If the area is sufficient to carry the load, the stiffness can be adjusted by varying the length. The stress in a loaded helical spring depends on the wire diameter and the coil diameter; the stiffness can be altered by changing the number of coils, which has no effect on the stress.

Air and hydraulic springs. An air spring is basically a column of air confined within a rubber-and-fabric container that may take the form of a bellows. The spring action results from the compression and expansion of the air. Air springs provide means for control of load capacity, height, and spring rate; they are used in aircraft landing gear, shock and vibration isolators, seat suspensions, and for suspension systems for machines and vehicles. When used on buses, air springs can keep the vehicle at a constant standing height regardless of load. Hydraulic or liquid springs are comparatively small, thick-walled, hydraulic cylinders in which the spring effect is produced by applying a load to the fluid in the cylinder through a comparatively small piston entering at the centre of one end of the cylinder. The piston movement, which represents the spring deflection, results from the compression of the fluid and the deformation (bulging) of the cylinder. Some special oils, under a given pressure, have twice the percentage of volume reduction of water.

A helical spring and a hydraulic spring of the same energy capacity are approximately equal in weight; the hydraulic spring, however, is much smaller. Hydraulic springs are particularly suited for applications in which high load capacities and stiffnesses are required. They are widely used in punch and die assemblies in machine tools and as recoil springs and buffers in gun systems.

BIBLIOGRAPHY. HARRY WALTON, *The How and Why of Mechanical Movements* (1968), a profusely illustrated description of the working principles of a wide variety of mechanical devices; FRANZ REULEAUX, *Theoretische Kinematik* (1875; Eng. trans., *The Kinematics of Machinery*, 1876, reprinted 1963), a classic study of the geometric principles underlying machine motions; ALEXANDER COWIE, *Kinematics and Design of Mechanisms* (1961), a comprehensive treatment of motion transmission by linkage, gears, and cams with the most complete coverage in English of the kinematics of direct-contact bodies; H.E. MERRITT, *Gears*, 3rd ed. (1954), a leading British treatise on the geometry, design, and manufacture of gears; HAROLD A. ROTHBART, *Cams* (1956), an authoritative treatise on the kinematics, design, manufacture, and dynamic performance of cam–follower mechanisms; RICHARD S. HARTENBERG and JACQUES DENAVIT, *Kinematic Synthesis of Linkages* (1964), an up-to-date textbook containing original material on geometric and algebraic methods for the design of planar (two-dimensional) and spatial (three-dimensional) linkage mechanisms; PAUL H. BLACK and O. EUGENE ADAMS, JR., *Machine Design*, 3rd ed. (1968); RICHARD M. PHELAN, *Fundamentals of Mechanical Design*, 3rd ed. (1970); SAMUEL J. BERARD, EVERETT O. WATERS, and CHARLES W. PHELPS, *Principles of Machine Design* (1955), three textbooks containing information on all the machine components; DUDLEY D. FULLER, *Theory and Practice of Lubrication for Engineers* (1956), covers the analysis and design of sliding (fluid film) bearings and bearing materials.

(A.Co.)

Machine Tools

Machine tools are stationary power-driven machines for shaping or forming parts made of metal or other materials. The shaping is accomplished in four general ways: (1) by cutting excess material from the part in the form of chips; (2) by shearing the material; (3) by squeezing metallic parts to the desired shape; and (4) by application of electricity, ultrasound, or the corrosive action of chemicals. The fourth category covers recently developed machine tools and processes for machining ultrahard metals not machinable by older methods.

Machine tools that form parts by removal of metal chips include lathes, shapers and planers, drilling machines, milling machines, grinders, and power saws. Cold forming of metal parts such as cooking utensils, automobile bodies, and similar items is done on punch presses, while hot forming of white-hot blanks in appropriately shaped dies is done on forging presses.

Tolerances Modern machine tools cut or form parts to tolerances of plus or minus one ten-thousandth of an inch (0.0025 millimetre). In special applications parts are produced to within plus or minus two millionths of an inch (0.00005 millimetre) with precision lapping machines. Because of the precise dimensional requirements of the parts and the heavy cutting forces exerted on the cutting tool, machine tools combine weight and rigidity with delicate accuracy.

Machine tools process parts for all production machinery, service machinery, and consumer products and make other machine tools.

HISTORY

Before the Industrial Revolution of the 18th century, hand tools were used to cut and shape materials for the production of goods such as cooking utensils, wagons, ships, furniture, and other products. After the advent of the steam engine, material goods were produced by power-driven machines that could only be manufactured by machine tools. Machine tools capable of producing dimensionally accurate parts in large quantities and jigs and fixtures for holding the work and guiding the tool were indispensable in permitting mass production and the interchangeability of parts to become realities in the course of the 19th century.

The earliest steam engines suffered from inaccurate boring of their large cast cylinders by machines powered by water wheels and originally designed to bore cannon. During the following half century the basic machine tools, with all the fundamental features required for machining heavy metal parts, were designed and developed. Some of them were adaptations of earlier woodworking machines; thus the metal lathe derived from wood cutting lathes in use in France as early as the 16th century. In 1774 John Wilkinson of England built a precision machine for boring engine cylinders. In 1797 Henry Maudslay, also of England and one of the great inventive geniuses of his day, designed and built a screw-cutting engine lathe. The outstanding feature of Maudslay's lathe was a lead screw for driving the carriage, geared to the spindle of the lathe, which made it possible to advance the tool at a constant rate of speed, thus guaranteeing accurate screw threads. By 1800 Maudslay had equipped his lathe with 28 change gears for cutting threads of various pitches by controlling the ratio of the lead-screw speed and the spindle speed.

The shaper was invented by James Nasmyth, who had worked in Henry Maudslay's shop in London. In Nasmyth's machine a workpiece could be clamped horizontally to a table and worked on by a cutter with a reciprocating motion that could plane small surfaces, cut keyways, or machine other straight-line surfaces. A few years later (1839), Nasmyth invented the steam hammer for forging

Invention of the steamhammer heavy pieces. Another disciple of Maudslay, Joseph Whitworth, invented or improved a great number of machine tools and came to dominate the field; at the International Exhibition of 1862 his firm's exhibits took up a quarter of all the space devoted to machine tools.

Considerable efforts were made by Britain to keep its lead in machine-tool development by prohibiting exports, but the attempt was foredoomed by industrial development elsewhere. British tools were imported to continental Europe and to the U.S. despite the prohibition, and new tools developed outside Britain. Notable was the milling machine produced by Eli Whitney of the U.S. about 1818 and used by Simeon North to manufacture firearms. The first fully universal milling machine was built in 1862 by J.R. Brown of the U.S. and used to cut helical flutes in twist drills. The turret lathe, developed in the U.S. in the middle of the 19th century, was made fully automatic for some purposes, such as making screws, presaging momentous developments in the 20th century. Various gear-cut-

ting machines reached their developmental climax in a gear shaper designed in 1896 by F.W. Fellows, an American, that could turn out rapidly almost any type of gear.

The production of artificial abrasives in the late 19th century opened up a whole new field, that of grinding machines. C.H. Norton of Massachusetts dramatically illustrated the potential of the grinding machine by making one that could grind an automobile crankshaft in 15 minutes, a process that had previously required five hours of turning, filing, and hardening.

By the end of the 19th century a complete revolution had taken place in the working and shaping of metals, creating the basis for a mass-production, industrialized society. The 20th century has witnessed the introduction of numerous refinements, such as multiple-point cutters for milling machines, the development of automated operations governed by electronic and fluid-control systems, and "chipless" techniques, such as electrochemical and ultrasonic machining. Yet even in the 1970s the basic machine tools remain largely the legacy of the 19th century.

MACHINE-TOOL CHARACTERISTICS

All machine tools must provide work-holding and tool-holding devices and means for accurately controlling the depth of cut. Relative motion between the cutting edge of the tool and the work is called the cutting speed, while the feed motion brings uncut material into contact with the tool. Means must be provided for varying all of these.

Because an overheated tool may lose cutting ability, it is important to control temperature. The amount of heat developed depends on the shearing force and the cutting speed, but because shearing force varies with the material being cut and tool material varies in its tolerance for high temperatures, the optimum cutting speed depends both on Optimum the material being cut and the cutting-tool material. It is cutting also influenced by the rigidity of the machine, the shape of speed the workpiece, and the depth of cut.

CUTTING TOOLS

Metal-cutting tools are classified as single point or multiple point. A single-point cutting tool is shown in Figure 1 (left) performing a turning operation on a rotating cylindrical workpiece. Such tools are also used for increasing the size of holes, or boring. Turning and boring are performed on lathes and boring mills.

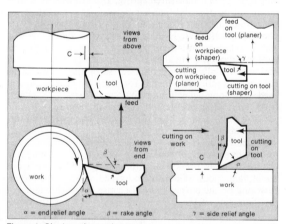

Figure 1: *Single-point cutting tools.*
(Left) Lathe tool; (right) planer and shaper tool. Depth of cut is indicated by C.

Figure 1 (right) represents two types of operation: either the tool moving on a straight path against the stationary work, as on a shaper, or the work moving against the stationary tool, as on a planer.

Multiple-point cutting tools have two or more cutting edges and include milling cutters, drills, and broaches (Figure 2). Relief or clearance angles must be provided to prevent the tool surface below the cutting edge from rubbing against the workpiece.

Rake angles are often provided on cutting tools to cause a wedging action in the formation of chips and to reduce friction and heat.

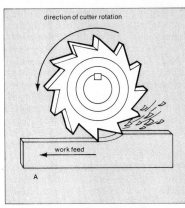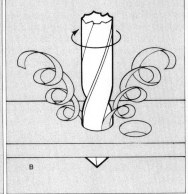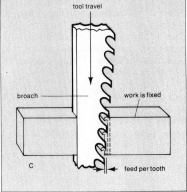

Figure 2: *Multiple-point cutting tools.*
(A) Milling with plain milling cutter. (B) Machining with twist drill. (C) Action of broaching tool.

Tool materials. In order to remove chips from a workpiece, a cutting tool must be harder than the workpiece and maintain a cutting edge at the temperature produced by the friction of the cutting action.

Carbon steel. Steel with a carbon content ranging from 1 to 1.2 percent was the earliest material used. Tools made of this carbon steel are comparatively inexpensive but tend to lose cutting ability at temperatures around 400° F (205° C).

High-speed steel. The introduction of high-speed steel about 1900 permitted operation of tools at twice or three times the speeds allowable with carbon steel, thus doubling or trebling the capacities of the world's machine shops. One of the commonest types of high-speed steel contains 18 percent tungsten, 4 percent chromium, 1 percent vanadium, and only 0.5 to 0.8 percent carbon.

Cast alloys. A number of cast-alloy cutting-tool materials have been developed; these nonferrous alloys contain cobalt, chromium, and tungsten and are particularly effective in penetrating the hard skin on cast iron and retaining their cutting ability even when red hot.

Cemented tungsten carbide. This material was first used for metal cutting in Germany in 1926. Its principal ingredient is finely divided tungsten carbide held in a binder of cobalt; its hardness approaches that of a diamond. Tungsten carbide tools can be operated at cutting speeds many times higher than those used for high-speed steel.

Oxides. Ceramic or oxide tool tips are the latest development in cutting-tool materials. They consist primarily of fine aluminum oxide grains, bonded together.

Diamonds. Diamonds have been used for many years for truing grinding wheels, for wire-drawing dies, and as cutting tools. For cutting applications they are used largely for taking light finishing cuts at high speed on hard or abrasive materials and for finish-boring bronze and babbitt-metal bearings.

Cutting fluids. On many machine-tool operations, cutting fluids or coolants are used to modify the harmful effects of friction and high temperatures. In general, the major functions of a coolant are to lubricate and cool. In cutting a screw thread, either on a lathe or with a tap, the lubricating function is most important; on production-grinding operations, the cooling function predominates. Water is an excellent cooling medium but corrodes ferrous materials. Lard oil has excellent lubricating qualities but tends to become rancid with time. Sulfurized mineral oil is one of the most popular coolants. The sulfur tends to prevent chips from the work from welding to the tip of the tool. For sawing and grinding operations, soluble oil, which is an oily emulsion freely miscible in water, is commonly used.

BASIC MACHINE TOOLS

Hundreds of varieties of metal machine tools, ranging in size from small machines mounted on workbenches to huge production machines weighing several hundred tons, are used in modern industry. They still retain the basic characteristics of their 19th- and early 20th-century ancestors and are still classed as one of the following: (1) turning machines (lathes and boring mills), (2) shapers and planers, (3) drilling machines, (4) milling machines, (5) grinding machines, (6) power saws, and (7) presses.

Turning machines. The engine lathe, as the horizontal metal-turning machine is commonly called, is the most important of all the machine tools (Figure 3). It is usually considered the father of all other machine tools. Many of the fundamental mechanical elements of the engine lathe are incorporated in the design of the other machine tools.

The engine lathe is a basic machine tool that can be used for a wide variety of turning, facing, and drilling operations. It utilizes a single-point cutting tool for turning and boring operations (Figure 4). Turning operations involve

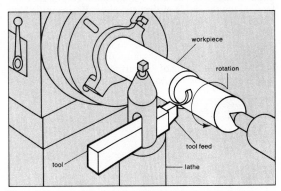

Figure 4: Turning of steel shaft mounted between centres.

cutting excess metal, in the form of chips, from the external diameter of a workpiece and include turning straight or tapered cylindrical shapes, grooves, shoulders, and

The engine lathe

Cutting at red heat

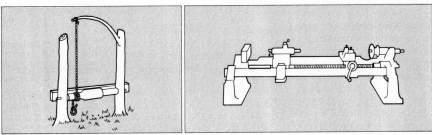

Figure 3: (Left) Primitive lathe. (Right) Maudslay's lathe of 1797.

screw threads and facing flat surfaces on the ends of cylindrical parts. Internal cylindrical operations performed on the engine lathe include most of the common hole-machining operations such as drilling, boring, reaming, counterboring, countersinking, and threading with a single-point tool or a tap (Figure 5).

Adapted from W.J. McCarthy and
R.E. Smith, *Machine Tool Technology*

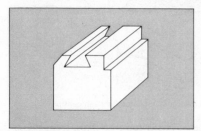

Figure 5: Common hole-machining operations.

Boring involves enlarging and finishing a hole that has been cored or drilled. Bored holes are more accurate in roundness, concentricity, and parallelism than drilled holes. A hole is bored with a single-point cutting tool that feeds along the inside of the workpiece. Boring mills have circular horizontal tables that rotate about a vertical axis, and they are designed for boring and turning operations on parts that are too large to be mounted on a lathe.

Shapers and planers. Shaping and planing operations involve the machining of flat surfaces, grooves, shoulders, T-slots, and angular surfaces (Figure 6) with single-point

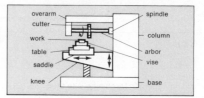

Figure 6: Surface shapes cut on shaper, planer, or milling machines.

tools. The largest shapers have a 36-inch cutting stroke and can machine parts up to 36 inches long. The cutting tool on the shaper reciprocates back and forth, cutting on the forward stroke, with the workpiece feeding automatically toward the tool during each return stroke.

Planing machines perform the same operations as shapers but can machine longer workpieces. Some planers have a capacity to machine parts up to 50 feet in length. The workpiece is mounted on a reciprocating table that moves the workpiece under a cutting tool. This tool, which remains stationary during the cutting stroke, feeds into the workpiece automatically after each cutting stroke.

Drilling machines. Drilling machines, also called drill presses, cut holes in metal with a twist drill (Figure 2). They also utilize a variety of other cutting tools for performing the following basic hole-machining operations: (1) reaming, (2) boring, (3) counterboring, (4) countersinking, and (5) tapping internal threads with the use of a tapping attachment (Figure 5).

Milling machines. A milling machine cuts metal as the workpiece is fed against a rotating cutting tool called a milling cutter (Figures 2 and 7). Cutters of many shapes

Figure 7: Horizontal knee-and-column milling machine.

and sizes are available for a wide variety of milling operations. Milling machines cut flat surfaces, grooves, shoulders, inclined surfaces, dovetails, and T-slots. Various form-tooth cutters are used for cutting concave forms, convex grooves, rounding corners, and for cutting gear teeth.

Milling machines are available in a variety of designs, which can be classified under the following general classifications: (1) standard knee-and-column machines, including the horizontal type (Figure 7) and the vertical type, (2) bed-type or manufacturing machines, and (3) special machines designed for special milling jobs.

Grinding machines. Grinding machines remove small chips from metal parts that are brought into contact with a rotating abrasive wheel called a grinding wheel (see also ABRASIVES), or an abrasive belt. Grinding is the most accurate of all of the basic machining processes. Modern grinding machines grind hard or soft parts to tolerances of plus or minus 0.0001 inch (0.0025 millimetre).

The common types of grinding machines include (1) plain cylindrical, (2) internal cylindrical, (3) centreless (Figure 8), (4) surface (Figure 8), (5) off-hand, (6) special, and (7) abrasive-belt.

Power saws. Metal-cutting power saws are of three basic types: (1) power hacksaws, (2) band saws, (3) circular disc saws. Vertical band saws are used for cutting shapes in metal plate, internal and external contours, and for angular cuts.

Presses. This large class of machines includes equipment used for forming metal parts through application of the following processes: shearing, blanking, forming, drawing, bending, forging, coining, upsetting, flanging, squeezing, and hammering. All of these processes require presses that are provided with a movable ram that is pressed against an anvil or base. Power to the movable ram may be furnished through gravity, mechanical linkages, or through hydraulic or pneumatic systems.

Appropriate die sets, with one part mounted on the movable ram and the matching part mounted on the fixed bed or platen, are an integral part of the machine. Punch presses punch out metal parts from sheet metal and form the parts to the desired shape. Dies with cavities having a variety of shapes are used on forging presses that form white-hot metal blanks to the desired shape. Power presses are also used for shearing, bending, flanging, and shaping sheet metal parts of all sizes. Power presses are made in various sizes, ranging from small presses mounted on a workbench to machines weighing more than 1,000,000 pounds (450,000 kilograms).

MODIFICATIONS OF BASIC MACHINES

Certain production machine tools have been designed to speed up production. These tools include features of the basic machine tools and perform the same operation, but they incorporate design modifications that make it possible to perform either complex or repetitive operational sequences more rapidly. Furthermore, after the production machine has been set up by a skilled worker

Tapping

Dies

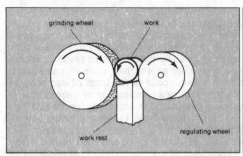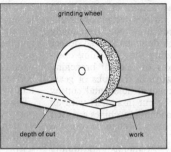

Figure 8: (Left) Centreless grinding operation. (Right) Surface grinding operation.

or machinist, a less skilled operator can produce parts accurately and rapidly. The following are examples of production machine tools that are modifications of basic machine tools: (1) turret lathes, including screw machines, (2) multiple-station machines, (3) gang drills, and (4) production milling machines.

Turret lathes. Horizontal turret lathes have two features that distinguish them from the engine lathe. The first is a multiple-sided main turret, which takes the place of the tailstock on the engine lathe (Figure 9). A variety of

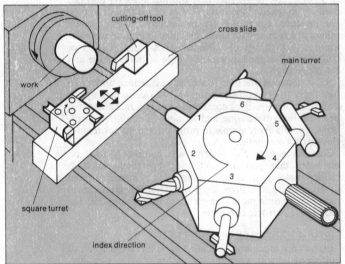

Figure 9: Horizontal turret lathe.

turning, drilling, boring, reaming, and thread-cutting tools can be fastened to the main turret, which can be rotated intermittently about its vertical axis with a hand wheel. Either a hand wheel or a power feed can be used to move the turret longitudinally against the workpiece mounted on the machine spindle.

The second distinguishing feature of the turret lathe is the square turret mounted on the cross slide. This turret also can be indexed about its vertical axis and permits the use of a variety of turning tools. A tool post or tool block can be clamped to the rear of the cross slide for mounting additional tools. The cross slide can be actuated either by hand or by power.

Turret lathes may be classified as either chucking machines or bar machines. Bar machines formerly were called screw machines, and they may be either hand controlled or automatic. A bar machine is designed for machining small threaded-type parts, bushings, and other small parts from bar stock fed through the machine spindle. Automatic bar machines produce parts automatically, including automatic replacement of bar stock into the machine spindle. A chucking machine is designed primarily for machining larger parts, such as castings, forgings, or blanks of stock that usually must be mounted in the chuck manually.

Multiple-station machines. Several types of multistation vertical lathes have recently been developed. These machines are essentially chucking-type turret lathes for machining threaded cylindrical parts. The machine has 12 spindles, each equipped with a chuck. Directly above

The chucking machine

each spindle, except one, tooling is mounted on a ram. Parts are mounted in each chuck and indexed for up to 11 machining operations. At the 12th station the finished part is removed and a rough part is inserted.

Gang drills. A gang-drilling machine consists of several individual columns, drilling heads, and spindles mounted on a single base and utilizing a common table. Various numbers of spindles may be used, but four or six are common. These machines are designed for machining parts requiring several hole-machining operations, such as drilling, countersinking, counterboring, or tapping. The workpiece is moved from one drilling spindle to the next for sequential machining operations by one or more operators.

Production millers. Milling machines used for repetitive-production milling operations generally are classified as bed-type milling machines because of their design. The sliding table is mounted directly on the massive bed of the machine, without provision for table elevation or transverse table movement. Table movement is longitudinal only. The spindle head may be adjusted vertically to establish the depths of cut. Some machines are equipped with automatic controls. Thus, a semiskilled operator can load parts in fixtures at each end of the table and start the machine. One part can be unloaded and replaced while the other is being machined.

SPECIAL-PURPOSE MACHINES

Special-purpose machine tools are designed to perform special machining operations, usually for production purposes. Examples include gear-cutting and gear-grinding machines, broaching machines, lapping and honing machines, and boring machines.

Gear-cutting machines. Three basic cutting methods are used for machining gears: (1) form cutting, (2) template cutting, and (3) generating. The form-cutting method involves the use of a cutting tool that has the same form as the space between two adjacent teeth on a gear. This method is used for cutting gear teeth on a milling machine. The template-cutting method makes use of a template for guiding the single-point cutter on large bevel-gear cutting machines.

Most cut gears produced in large lots are made on machines that utilize the gear-generating principle. This principle is based on the fact that two involute gears, or a gear and rack, with the same diametral pitch mesh together properly. Therefore, a cutting tool with the shape of a gear or rack but with proper grinding may be used to cut gear teeth in a gear or rack blank. This principle is applied in the design of a number of widely used gear-cutting machines of the generating type. Some gear-generating machines cut with reciprocating strokes and are called gear shapers.

Gear-hobbing machines use a rotating, multiple-tooth cutting tool called a hob for generating teeth on spur gears, worm gears, helical gears, splines, and sprockets. More gears are cut by hobbing than by other methods. The hobbing cutter cuts continuously and produces accurate gears at high production rates.

In gear-making machines gears can be (1) entirely cut, (2) entirely ground, or (3) produced by a combination of cutting and grinding operations. Gear-grinding machines of special design are used for grinding gear teeth.

Broaching machines. Broaching is classified in a general way as a planing or shaping art, because the action of

Hobbing

a broaching tool resembles the action of planer and shaper tools. Broaching tools of various designs are available (Figure 2). The teeth on broaching tools are equally spaced, with each successive tooth designed to feed deeper into the workpiece, thus completing the broaching operation in a single stroke. Examples of internal broaching applications include cutting keyways in the hubs of gears or pulleys, cutting square or hexagonal holes, and cutting gear teeth. External grooves can be cut in a shaft with an external broaching tool. Some broaching machines are used for pulling or pushing broaching tools through or over the workpiece.

Lapping and honing machines.   Lapping and honing operations are classified under the basic art of grinding. Lapping involves the use of abrasive pastes or compounds impregnated in a soft cloth and rubbed against the surface of a workpiece. Lapping is done to produce a high quality surface finish or to finish to very close size limits. Dimensional tolerances of two millionths of an inch (0.00005 mm) can be achieved by either hand or machine lapping precision parts such as gages or gage blocks.

Honing is a low-speed surface finishing process used for removing small amounts of metal, usually less than 0.0005 inch (0.0125 mm) from ground or machined surfaces for the purpose of removing scratches or machine marks. Honing is done with bonded abrasive sticks or stones that are mounted in a honing head. For a typical honing operation, such as honing automotive engine cylinder walls, a honing machine with one or more spindles is used. The honing head rotates slowly with an oscillating motion, holding the abrasive sticks against the work surface under controlled light pressure.

Abrasive sticks

Boring machines.   Boring can be done on any type of machine equipped to hold a boring tool and a workpiece and equipped to rotate either the tool or the workpiece in proper relationship (Figure 5). Special boring machines of various designs are used for boring workpieces that are too large to be mounted on a lathe, drill press, or milling machine. Boring and turning operations are also performed on large vertical turret lathes or on larger boring mills. Standard boring machines are able to bore or turn work up to 12 feet (3.6 m) in diameter.

AUTOMATIC CONTROL

To be truly automatic a machine tool must be capable of producing parts repetitively without operator assistance in loading parts, starting the machine, and unloading parts. In this sense, some bar-turning machines are automatic. In practice, however, some machine tools designated as automatic are actually semi-automatic, since they require an operator to load the workpiece into the machine, press the start button, and unload the part when completed.

The tooling for automatic machines is more complex than for hand-controlled machines and usually requires a skilled worker for making the setup. After the setup, a less skilled operator can operate one or more machines simultaneously. Tracer lathes and numerically controlled machine tools are examples of machines utilizing varying degrees of automatic and semi-automatic control.

Tracer techniques.   The tool slide on a tracer lathe is guided by a sensitive stylus, hydraulically actuated, that follows an accurate template. The template may be an accurate profile on a thin plate or a finish-turned part. Tracing mechanisms generally are accessory units that are attached to engine lathes, but some lathes are especially designed as automatic tracing lathes. Optional accessories for use on tracing lathes include automatic-indexing toolheads and one or more cross slides for operations such as facing, grooving, and chamfering.

Tracing lathes machine all common cylindrical shapes; straight, tapered shoulders; and irregular curves. Accessory tools permit facing, grooving, and chamfering operations. An unlimited combination of cutting speeds, feeds, and types of cuts may be used, including roughing cuts and finishing cuts. On machines equipped for automatic operation, changes in speed, feed, and cutting tools are automatic.

Numerical control.   Many types of machine tools and other industrial processes are equipped for numerical con-

trol, now commonly called NC. An NC system or device is one that controls the actions of a machine or process through direct insertion of numerical data at some point, and the system must automatically interpret at least some portion of these data. Perhaps the term symbolic control would have been more appropriate, since various kinds of NC systems use data coded in the form of numbers, letters, symbols, words, or a combination of these forms.

Symbolic control

The machining instructions necessary for machining a part by NC are derived from the part drawing and are written in coded form on a program manuscript. The following kinds of data may be included on the manuscript: (1) sequence of operations, (2) kind of operation, (3) depth of cut, (4) coordinate dimensions for the centre of the cutting tool, (5) feed rate, (6) spindle speed, (7) tool number, and (8) other miscellaneous operations.

The coded information is then punched into a ribbon of one-inch wide machine-control tape with a tape-punching machine similar to a typewriter. The tape, usually made of paper or plastic, is inserted into the NC system, which is connected to the machine tool. The NC system interprets the information on the tape, thus activating relays and electrical circuits that cause the machine's servomechanisms and other controls to perform a sequence of operations automatically. On some NC systems, the coded information is inserted into the machines on punched cards or magnetic tape instead of punched tape. The tape can be stored for future use on the same machine or on others like it at any location. NC machines produce parts accurately to limits of 0.001 or 0.0001 inch (0.025 or 0.0025 mm) depending on the design of the machine and the NC system.

NC systems on machine tools can be classified under two basic types: (1) point-to-point and (2) continuous-path. Point-to-point systems, commonly used on machines that perform hole-machining and straight-line milling operations, are relatively simple to program and do not require the aid of a computer.

Continuous-path NC systems are commonly used on machines that perform contouring operations, such as milling machines, lathes, flame-cutting machines, and drafting machines. Program preparation for continuous-path machines is more complex and usually requires the aid of an electronic computer.

CHIPLESS METHODS OF REMOVING METAL

Plasma arc machining.   Called PAM, this is a method of cutting metal with a plasma-arc, or tungsten inert-gas-arc, torch. The torch produces a high velocity jet of high-temperature ionized gas (plasma) that cuts by melting and displacing material from the workpiece. Temperatures obtainable in the plasma zone range from 20,000° to 50,000° F (11,000° to 28,000° C). The process may be used for cutting most metals, including those that cannot be cut efficiently with an oxyacetylene torch. With heavy-duty torches, aluminum alloys up to six-inch (15 cm) thicknesses and stainless steel up to four-inch (10 cm) thicknesses have been cut by the PAM process. The process also has been used on lathes for turning large, hardened steel rolls.

Laser-beam machining.   Known as LBM, this is a method of cutting metal or refractory materials by melting and vaporizing the material with an intense beam of light from a laser (see LASER AND MASER). The beam of light is used to produce small-diameter holes that can be spaced along a layout line to cut materials. Applications of LBM are limited to cutting or drilling thin metals and refractory materials that cannot be cut more economically by other methods.

Cutting holes with lasers

Electrical-discharge machining.   This technique, called EDM, involves the direction of high-frequency electrical spark discharges from a graphite or soft metal tool, which serves as an electrode, to disintegrate electrically conductive materials such as hardened steel or carbide. The electrode and workpiece are immersed in a dielectric liquid, and a feed mechanism maintains a spark gap of from 0.0005 to 0.020 inch (0.013 to 0.5 mm) between the electrode and the workpiece. As spark discharges melt or vaporize small particles of the workpiece, the particles are flushed away, and the electrode advances. The process is used for machining dies, molds, holes, slots, and cavities of almost any desired shape.

Electrochemical machining. In electrochemical machining (ECM) metal is dissolved from a workpiece at a controlled rate with direct current in an electrolytic cell. The workpiece serves as the anode and is separated by a gap of 0.001 to 0.030 inch (0.025 to 0.75 mm) from the tool, which serves as the cathode. The process is essentially a deplating process. The electrolyte, usually a saline solution, is pumped under pressure through the servocontrolled tool gap, thus flushing away dissolved waste removed from the workpiece. The process is used for machining odd-shaped parts and deep holes in hard metals.

Chemical machining. This nonelectrical process, called CHM, removes metal from selected or overall areas by controlled chemical action. Masking tape is used to protect areas not to be removed. The method is related to the process used for making metal-printing and engraving plates. Two types of chemical machining processes include: (1) chemical blanking, which is used for blanking thin metal parts and (2) chemical milling, which is used for removing metal from selective or overall areas of metal parts.

Ultrasonic machining. In USM, material is removed from a workpiece with particles of abrasive that vibrate at high frequency in a water slurry circulating through a narrow gap between a vibrating tool and a workpiece. The tool, shaped like the cavity to be produced, oscillates up and down about 0.0005 to 0.0025 inch (0.013 to 0.062 mm) at 19,000 to 25,000 hertz (cycles per second). The tool vibrates the abrasive grains against the surface of the workpiece, thus removing material. USM is used primarily for cutting hard, brittle materials that may be conductors of electricity or insulators. It also is used for machining hardened steels, carbide, and semiconductors.

Electron-beam machining. This technique, EBM, is used for cutting fine holes and slots in any material, enclosed in a vacuum, with the use of a focussed beam of high-velocity electrons. The kinetic energy of the electrons, upon striking the workpiece, changes to heat that vaporizes minute particles of the material. The vacuum prevents the electrons from scattering, due to collisions with gas molecules. EBM is used for cutting holes as small as 0.001 inch (0.025 mm) diameter or slots as narrow as 0.001 inch in materials up to 0.250-inch (6.25 mm) thickness. Welding also can be done on very fine wire or tiny parts with an electron beam by reducing its energy level.

BIBLIOGRAPHY. The best sources of general information on machine tools are w.j. mccarthy and r.e. smith, *Machine Tool Technology*, 3rd ed. (1968); and e.p. degarmo, *Materials and Processes in Manufacturing*, 3rd ed. (1969). The most authoritative, although highly technical, source for all phases of machine tools is the american society for metals, *Metals Handbook*, vol. 3, *Machining*, 8th ed. (1967). An excellent source on the history of machine tools is l.t.c. rolt, *A Short History of Machine Tools* (1965). o.a. ludwig and w.j. mccarthy, *Metalwork: Technology and Practice*, 5th ed. (1969), is a good secondary school text. A comprehensive source of technical data is e. oberg and f.d. jones, *Machinery's Handook: A Reference Book for the Mechanical Engineer, Draftsman, Toolmaker and Machinist*, 18th ed. (1968).

(W.J.McC.)

Mackenzie River

Size of the system

Draining an area that, at 711,000 square miles (1,841,-000 square kilometres), is almost as large as that of Mexico, the Mackenzie River is one of the major river systems in the drainage pattern of North America: its basin is the largest in Canada, and it is only exceeded on the continent by the Mississippi–Missouri system. From the headwaters of the Finlay River, which flows into the Peace River Reservoir west of the Rocky Mountains, the entire river system runs for 2,635 miles (4,240 kilometres) through the sparsely settled, lake-strewn Canadian north to empty into the cold waters of the Beaufort Sea in the Arctic Ocean. The Mackenzie itself is 1,060 miles (1,706 kilometres) long, according to the conventional measurement from Great Slave Lake. The river is

generally wide, mostly from one to two miles across, and in island-dotted sections, three or four miles wide. It has a strong flow. Its lake-covered triangular delta measures more than 120 miles from north to south and is about 50 miles wide along the Arctic shore.

The headwaters of the system include several large rivers, which themselves drain vast forested plains of northeastern British Columbia and northern Alberta. These drainage basins include the Liard River (107,000 square miles), the Peace River (125,250 square miles), and the Athabasca River (62,900 square miles). Much shorter rivers flow into the system from the east, draining the low rocky hills of the ancient structural mass known as the Canadian Shield. The system also includes the huge Great Slave Lake (10,980 square miles), Great Bear Lake (12,275 square miles), and the smaller Lake Athabasca (940 square miles).

The whole basin is sparsely populated, and its resources are few and less accessible than those of southern Canada. Yet the whole region is one of the few great unspoiled areas of the world, offering a rich wildlife and spectacular scenery, as well as a somewhat harsh climatic environment.

Exploration of the region. Explorers and fur traders pushed westward across Canada in the late 18th century to the headwaters of rivers that flowed into Hudson Bay, seeking to tap the fur resources in the lands beyond. In 1778 one of them, Peter Pond, found Portage La Loche (Methy Portage) connecting the headwaters of Churchill River with the Clearwater River, itself one of the eastbank tributaries of the Athabasca River. In 1789 Alexander Mackenzie made his historic journey northward from the trading post of Fort Chipewyan on Lake Athabasca, exploring with a crew of 12 persons in three canoes, the full length of the mighty river now bearing his name.

Other fur traders of the North West Company followed early in the 19th century, establishing posts at several sites along the river and on its headwater tributaries. From the mid-1820s, supplies were carried in by the distinctive York boats, shallow-draft vessels with a sharply angled stern and bow. In 1884 the first steamer began to operate northward from McMurray, at the junction of the Clearwater and Athabasca rivers, to Fitzgerald on the Slave River. At this point there are 16 miles of rapids in Slave River, the only break in 1,700 miles of shallow-draft river navigation from McMurray to the Arctic Ocean. In 1886 the first steamer began operating north of Fort Smith, on the present Northwest Territories–Alberta border, taking supplies to the Mackenzie River trading posts and bringing out bales of fur. During the 1920–40 period, flat-bottomed, stern paddle-wheeled vessels operated on the Mackenzie River, but they were replaced after 1945 by small diesel tugs that could push several barges.

The course of the river. *The role of ice.* The Mackenzie River itself begins at the western end of Great Slave Lake, at 513 feet (156 metres) above sea level. Deep (more than 1,000 feet in some places), clear water fills the lake's eastern arm, and shallow, murky water is found in the western part. Because of its large size and extent of winter ice cover, Great Slave Lake is the last part of the Mackenzie waterway to be free of ice in the spring, with some ice remaining until mid-June in the lake's centre.

Great Slave Lake

The ice on the Mackenzie River begins to break up in early to mid-May in its southern section, being preceded by breakup on the Liard River. Tributary rivers are free of ice before the Mackenzie itself, and high water and flooding are common during the breakup period, particularly when ice dams form. The ice across the lower Mackenzie River breaks up in late May; the channels in the Mackenzie River Delta are usually free of floating river ice by the end of May or early June, with the western channels being influenced by the earlier breakup of the Peel River. Sea ice usually remains offshore from the delta in the Beaufort Sea during June, particularly if prevailing winds are onshore.

The upper course. The head of the Mackenzie River is about six miles wide where the western end of the Great Slave Lake narrows and is filled by one large island and several small ones. The river narrows to less than a half mile in width near Fort Providence, and it is there that ice bridges are built across the river in early winter to carry truck traffic along the Mackenzie–Slave Lake Highway. Ferries are used for this crossing in summer, but all road traffic ceases during the breakup period in May. A branch road extends to Fort Simpson, and except for a winter trail that is used only occasionally, there are no through roads farther north along the Mackenzie Valley. Mills Lake is a shallow broadening of the Mackenzie River west of the village of Fort Providence. To the west the river again narrows to about a mile in width, and the current is fast at Green Island Rapids, about 12 miles east of Fort Simpson. There is, however, a seven- to ten-foot channel among the boulders in these rapids, sufficient for the flat-bottomed barges pushed by shallow-draft tugs that operate out of the southern terminal of Hay River and along the Mackenzie.

At Fort Simpson the 755-mile-long Liard joins the Mackenzie from the west from its source in the southeastern Yukon Territory. The contrast between the muddy, silt-laden water of the Liard and the clear water of the Mackenzie is very apparent in the river after the junction, as these "two rivers in one" remain separate in terms of certain physical properties for about 300 miles downstream. At Fort Simpson, as for much of its course, the Mackenzie flows between steep, gray gravel banks, 100 to 200 feet high, which obscure the adjacent lowlands from view.

The "two rivers in one"

The Mackenzie River Lowlands are about 250 miles wide near Fort Simpson. Although it is classed as forested, mainly with a few species of coniferous trees, such as black and white spruce, and some poplar, much of the lowland away from the tributary rivers is covered by swamps, muskegs (bogs), and lakes, as well as many open areas of grassy vegetation and low bushes. The Mackenzie Mountains rise steeply on the western side of the Mackenzie Valley to altitudes of 5,000 to 6,000 feet; since the tree line is at about 3,000 feet, the upper slopes are barren. The eastern edge of the Mackenzie Lowlands is formed by ancient hills of the Canadian Shield, which slope up to altitudes of about 1,000 feet.

The Mackenzie River Lowlands are underlain by flat-lying sedimentary rock of Cretaceous (100,000,000 years old) and Devonian (350,000,000 years old) geological ages. Little of this rock is exposed at the surface, however, because it is mantled with glacial and alluvial deposition of clays, sands, and gravels.

North of Fort Simpson the Mackenzie River is a little less than 400 feet above sea level, is a mile wide, and flows between steep banks. The mean discharge is measured at 228,000 cubic feet per second at Fort Simpson; the average flow at high water during June is above 400,000 cubic feet per second, and this seems to be equally obtained from the Liard and upper Mackenzie. The latter supplies a larger share of the river's volume during winter.

The lower course. North of the trading post at Wrigley, the Redstone and Keele rivers enter from the west; they have deep canyons where they break out of the Mackenzie Mountains but flow across the lowland as shallow, braided streams. These rivers and the others that drain from the Mackenzie Mountains have their peak flows in June after the snow melts in the mountains; they become shallow rivers in late summer. The Mackenzie River picks up relatively little volume within its valley lowland, as the average summer precipitation recorded at dispersed settlements is only about seven or eight inches (175 to 200 millimetres); total annual precipitation throughout the Mackenzie Valley is ten to 14 inches (250 to 350 millimetres).

Rainfall in the lowlands

At the village of Fort Norman the cold, clear water of Great Bear River enters from the east. This short river empties out of Great Bear Lake; it is navigable for shallow-draft vessels, except for a short portage around rapids about 30 miles east of its mouth. Once more, there is a distinct summer demarcation for 50 miles northward in the Mackenzie River between its silt-laden water and the clear water from the Great Bear River on the eastern bank. At Norman Wells the Mackenzie River broadens

to about four miles in width and is less than 175 feet above sea level. The mean annual discharge of the river there is 311,000 cubic feet per second but flows during June and July will usually exceed 500,000 cubic feet per second.

The Mackenzie Valley Lowland is only about 30 miles wide in this section, being broken by the treeless summits of the Franklin Mountains, which rise to a little more than 3,000 feet altitude on the east side of the river. Small lakes are not so common across the Mackenzie Valley in this area as they are on the lowland west of Great Slave Lake. Forest vegetation is scanty except in the river valleys and in areas of better drainage; most of the trees are stunted spruce.

Where Mountain River joins the Mackenzie from the west there is a fast water section known as Sans Sault Rapids; the river drops about 20 feet within a few miles. There is ample depth of water for the shallow-draft barges during July, but, despite deepening of the channel by rock blasting, shallow water is sometimes a navigation problem in late summer. South of the Indian village of Fort Good Hope, the Mackenzie narrows as it flows between 100- to 150-foot perpendicular limestone walls known as The Ramparts. North of Fort Good Hope, the Mackenzie crosses the Arctic Circle. It is slightly entrenched and meanders across its flat valley floor, its banks being two or three miles apart; low islands are numerous, and shifting sandbars are a problem for the riverboats. Where the Arctic Red River enters from the south, the Mackenzie again flows between steep rock walls, which rise about 100 to 200 feet directly from the water.

The delta region. At Point Separation the Mackenzie River Delta begins. From the south the 425-mile Peel River is the last major tributary to add water to the Mackenzie. The mean discharge of water into the Mackenzie Delta is estimated at 400,000 cubic feet per second, more than doubling at flood peaks. The delta covers about 4,700 square miles and is a maze of branching, intertwining channels, numerous cutoff lakes, and circular ponds. These lakes are an excellent habitat for muskrat, and the trapping of these animals became the main source of income for the Indian and Eskimo inhabitants of the delta from 1920 to 1950.

The perpetually frozen subsurface layer known as permafrost lies a few feet beneath the surface of the islands in the delta and exists in a discontinuous layer beneath the whole Mackenzie River Lowlands north of Great Slave Lake. Depending on the type of vegetation cover, the top few inches to several feet of ground above the permafrost melts during the summer months. Northern construction of airfields, roads, and pipelines has to be adapted to these permafrost conditions; houses and other buildings are usually placed on wooden piles that are sunk and frozen into the permafrost to give stability. One of the distinctive features of the town of Inuvik, built in the 1950s, is a utilidor, a linear boxlike metal container raised slightly above the surface of the ground, in which the separate sewer, water, and heating pipes are placed. Mackenzie River water-transport routes terminate at Tuktoyaktuk on the Arctic coast northeast of the delta, where cargo is transferred to other vessels of greater draft, which serve the small settlements and defensive radar stations along the western Arctic coast.

The permafrost region

Human exploitation. The Mackenzie River Basin is sparsely populated. Its natural resources are few, and they are less accessible than comparable resources in southern Canada. Fur-bearing animals were the resource attraction of the 19th century; although they are still trapped throughout the forests of the river basin, particularly by the Indian population, furs now constitute a minor element in the regional economy. Muskrat, marten, beaver, lynx, and fox are the main pelts sought. The forests in the southern part of the basin have been utilized for local lumber in the Peace River area and near other small settlements. The small trees may have future value as a source of pulpwood.

Agricultural land is developed only in the south, particularly in the Peace River area. Settlers moved into the Athabasca River, Lesser Slave Lake, and Peace River areas in large numbers after 1920, when the farmlands of the Canadian prairies were almost all occupied. When railroad connections were established southward to Edmonton, these farms were able to produce grain, livestock, and legume seed for external markets. A few farms and many gardens produced well along the Mackenzie River before 1940, but the improved transport of recent decades has permitted most food to be imported. With July mean temperatures averaging about 60° F (16° C), and daily temperatures that reach into the 70s and sometimes 80s, climate does not prevent the growth of certain crops.

The role of oil and minerals

Minerals are the economic basis of some of the larger settlements in the basin. The first oil field was discovered at Norman Wells in 1921, but production did not begin until the 1930s. These wells and the small refinery at Norman Wells still produce for the industries, transport, and homes of the central and northern parts of the Mackenzie Valley. Other oil fields were discovered in the early 1970s near the Mackenzie River Delta. The largest oil fields are in the southern parts of the river basin, in northwestern Alberta and northeastern British Columbia. This oil is carried southward by pipeline to Edmonton to be distributed to refineries in southern Canada and the northern United States. An enormous reserve of petroleum lies in the Tar Sands along the Athabasca River north of McMurray; production there has been limited by a quota system.

Metallic minerals were found along the eastern edges of the basin. Valuable radium and uranium ores were produced from 1933 to 1961 at Port Radium on the eastern shores of Great Bear Lake, despite very high transportation costs. Other uranium mines came into production after 1950 at Uranium City on the north side of Lake Athabasca. High-quality gold mines, discovered after 1935, brought into existence the city of Yellowknife, the present capital of the Northwest Territories, on the north arm of Great Slave Lake. Lead-zinc deposits were developed in the 1960s at Pine Point on the south side of Great Slave Lake. When the deposits proved to be large enough, the first railroad into the Northwest Territories was built from the Peace River area along the Mackenzie Highway to Hay River and Pine Point.

The water of the Mackenzie River system was too far away from large industrial and urban markets to be used for hydroelectric power until the late 1960s. At that time the Peace River was dammed as it broke out of the Rocky Mountains and a large storage lake formed westward in the Rocky Mountain Trench. This electric power is transmitted 600 miles to Vancouver, British Columbia. Otherwise, the only developed waterpower sites are on the Snare and Talston rivers, which drop westward out of the Canadian Shield to the Mackenzie Lowlands and supply power to the mines and residents at Yellowknife and Pine Point. There is no utilization of the water of the Mackenzie River itself, except for river transportation.

The large lakes of the Mackenzie Basin are a source of lake trout and whitefish. Lake Athabasca was first exploited during the 1930s, and then Great Slave Lake was opened to commercial fishing after 1945. In the latter lake, fish are caught in both summer and winter and transported south by truck or rail to urban markets in both Canada and the United States. The catch is controlled by seasonal quotas that prevent depletion of the species. The cold water of Great Bear Lake has some fish, but they grow too slowly to withstand commercial fishing except by sports fishermen. Fish of the Mackenzie River are netted by some local residents to supplement their imported food.

BIBLIOGRAPHY. LESLIE ROBERTS, *The Mackenzie* (1949), is a popular account of the history and use of the river.

(J.L.Ro.)

Mackinder, Sir Halford John

Sir Halford Mackinder introduced into political geography a view of the Earth as potentially ranged in two camps—the land power of Eurasia, the "heartland," which had, following the decline in the military importance of navies and the opening up of Siberia, gained

Mackinder, drawing by Sir William Rothenstein, 1933. In the collection of the London School of Economics and Political Science.
By courtesy of the London School of Economics and Political Science; photograph, J.R. Freeman & Co. Ltd.

ascendance over the sea power of the "maritime lands," including the other continents.

Mackinder was born on February 15, 1861, at Gainsborough, Lincolnshire, where his father, of Scottish descent, practiced as a doctor. He was early fascinated by the natural history of the countryside and was a voracious reader of the great Victorian travellers. In 1880 he entered Christ Church, Oxford, where he studied natural sciences with a preference for biology; he obtained first class honours in 1883 and, one year later, a second class in modern history. His political aspirations found expression in his election as president of the Oxford Union, the principal debating society at the university. After leaving Oxford he read for the bar at the Inner Temple, one of the law "colleges" in London, and qualified as a barrister in 1886. As a lecturer for the Oxford extension movement—formed to give educational opportunities to people unable to attend a university—he travelled widely through the country, particularly among the workingmen of the north of England, expounding what he called the "new geography." With this new, clear-cut concept of geography as a bridge between the natural sciences and the humanities, he soon won attention. Tall, of distinguished presence, and with a gift for generalization, he excelled in his ability to drive home the fundamental points of a theme. His *Britain and the British Seas* (1902, 2nd ed. 1930), written with assurance and style, is a recognized landmark in British geographical literature.

The "new geography"

At that time, a group of men at the Royal Geographical Society were making strong efforts to raise the status of geography as an academic discipline in Britain and to secure for it an adequate place in the educational system. Learning of Mackinder's success, the society invited him to address it on the new geography. He met the challenge boldly, delivering his paper on "The Scope and Methods of Geography" with great persuasiveness. In 1887 he had become reader in geography at Oxford, the first such appointment in a British university. When in 1899 the Royal Geographical Society and the university established the Oxford School of Geography, it was almost inevitable that Mackinder should be the first director. It was typical of the man that in the same year he organized and led an expedition to East Africa, where he made the first ascent of Mt. Kenya. As he commented, in the popular view, the geographer must also be "an explorer and adventurer."

Mackinder, working also at Reading and London, continued at Oxford until 1904, when he was appointed director of the recently founded London School of Economics and Political Science, a constituent body of the University of London. There, for four years, he devoted

Director of London School of Economics

his energies to its administration and to that of the university. He played a prominent part in ensuring that the university centre was established at Bloomsbury in the heart of London and not on the periphery of the metropolis. Though he continued as reader in economic geography for another 18 years, his resignation as director marked the beginning of the third phase of his career. He entered Parliament in 1910 as Unionist (Conservative) member for the Camlachie division of Glasgow. Holding strong imperialist views, his circle of friends included similarly minded men, among them the politician L.S. Amery and Lord Milner, the imperial administrator. In the House, Mackinder did not make a strong impact, perhaps because the Commons are not overfond of academics. He retained his seat at the general election of 1918, when he described his opponent as "boldly defensive of the Russian Bolsheviks," but was defeated in 1922.

"The Geographical Pivot of History"

Studying the prerequisites for a stable peace settlement during World War I, he developed a thesis in political geography that he had first outlined in a paper read to the Royal Geographical Society in 1904, "The Geographical Pivot of History." In it he argued that interior Asia and eastern Europe (the heartland) had become the strategic centre of the "World Island" as a result of the relative decline of sea power as against land power and of the economic and industrial development of southern Siberia. His extended views were set out in a short book, *Democratic Ideals and Reality*, published early in 1919 while the Paris Peace Conference was in session. The role of Britain and the United States, he considered, was to preserve a balance between the powers contending for control of the heartland. As a further stabilizing factor, he urged the creation of a tier of independent states to separate Germany and Russia, much along the lines finally imposed by the peace treaty. The book included, apart from the main theme, many farsighted observations; *e.g.*, his insistence on the "one world" concept, the need for regional organizations of minor powers, and the warning that chaos in a defeated Germany would inevitably lead to dictatorship. The book attracted little attention in Britain but rather more in America. There was an unexpected sequel, however, for the concept of the heartland was seized upon by the German geopolitician Karl Haushofer to support his grand design for control of the World Island. Thus, during World War II there were suggestions that Mackinder, through Haushofer, had inspired Hitler. More sober evaluation disposed of this absurd notion, and, though developments have affected some of the arguments, the thesis is recognized as an important view of world strategy. In 1924, mindful of the lessons of World War I, Mackinder published his prophetic theory of the Atlantic community that became reality after World War II and assumed military form in the North Atlantic Treaty Organization (NATO). In his hypothesis—which remained largely unnoticed—Mackinder argued that the power of the Eurasian heartland could be offset by western Europe and North America, which "constitute for many purposes a single community of nations."

In 1919 Mackinder went as British high commissioner to south Russia in an attempt to unify the White Russian forces and was knighted on his return. After the close of his academic career in 1923, he served as chairman of the Imperial Shipping Committee, 1920–45, and of the Imperial Economic Committee, 1926–31. He was made a privy councillor (an honorific office) in 1926; among the other honours he received were the Patron's Medal, Royal Geographical Society, 1946, and the Charles P. Daly Medal of the American Geographical Society, 1944. He died on March 6, 1947.

BIBLIOGRAPHY. E.W. GILBERT, *Sir Halford Mackinder, 1861–1947* (1961), the most detailed biographical sketch yet available; H.J. MACKINDER, *The Scope and Methods of Geography and the Geographical Pivot of History* (papers of the Royal Geographical Society, reprinted 1951), detailed discussion in the introduction by E.W. GILBERT of Mackinder's contribution to the advancement of geography and the "Heartland" thesis; "Round World and the Winning of the Peace," *Foreign Affairs*, 21:595–605 (1943), a classic restatement of Mackinder's thesis; H.W. WEIGERT, V. STEFANSSON and R.E. HARRISON (eds.), *New Compass of the World* (1949), includes a brief discussion of the geopolitics of the "Heartland" thesis; G.R. CRONE, *Modern Geographers*, rev. and enl. ed. (1970), sketch of the general background of Mackinder's work as a geographer.

(G.R.C.)

Madagascar

Madagascar, or the Malagasy Republic (République Malgache), is an island republic off the southeast coast of Africa. Madagascar is the fourth largest island in the world, after Greenland, New Guinea, and Borneo, with a surface area of 226,444 square miles (586,486 square kilometres). Located in the southwestern Indian Ocean, it is separated from the African coast by the 500-mile-wide Mozambique Channel. The population numbers about 7,000,000. The national capital is at Tananarive.

In spite of its proximity to the continent, Madagascar's population is not related to the African peoples but rather to those of Indonesia, over 3,000 miles to the east. The Malagasy peoples do not consider themselves as Africans and have virtually no relations with neighbouring East African countries. Instead, because of the continuing bond with France that resulted from former colonial rule, the island is specially linked with French-speaking countries of West Africa; French, as well as Malagasy, has official status as a language.

Madagascar remains a geographical and historical paradox, linked in practice to Africa but in feeling identified with Indonesia, which is so far away as to have hardly any awareness of Madagascar or to maintain any substantial contemporary ties of substance with it. The Malagasy government has sought a role as a hyphen joining Africa and Asia, but this has not been expressed in any institutional form. The animal life and vegetation is equally anomalous, differing greatly from that of nearby Africa and being, in many respects, unique.

Although the coastlands have been known to Europeans for over 400 years and for much longer to Arabs, recent development has been more intense and concentrated in the central plateau, which contains the capital city of Tananarive. The road network and communications are generally better on the plateau, and the majority of its inhabitants have received some school education and are professing Christians, whereas in the coastal areas the majority follow traditional religions and have not attended school. The coastal peoples are, however, well represented in the ruling party, which arose from a coalition of forces the main strength of which lay off the plateau.

Although many small deposits of minerals and semiprecious stones are found, none has led to profitable exploitation on any large scale. The country remains overwhelmingly agricultural in production and in its exports. (For an associated physical feature see INDIAN OCEAN; for historical aspects see MADAGASCAR, HISTORY OF.)

(Ai.S.)

THE LANDSCAPE

The natural landscape. *Relief features.* Madagascar consists of three large parallel longitudinal zones—the central plateau, the narrow coastal strip to the east, and the zone of low plateaus and vast plains in the west.

The plateau

Situated between 2,500 and 4,500 feet above sea level, the plateau has been folded and worn down several times and is tilted to the west, where the slope is less sheer than it is to the east. Three massifs (mountain masses) are over 6,500 feet high. The Massif de Tsaratanana in the north is separated from the rest of the plateau by the ridge of Androna, whose volcanic summit at 9,436 feet (2,876 metres) is the highest point on the island. The Ankaratra Mountains in the centre comprise an enormous volcanic mass whose summit, Tsiafajavona, is 8,671 feet (2,643 metres) high. They act as a watershed separating three main river basins. Farther south, the Andringitra Mountains are a vast granite massif between the southern Betsileo and Bara districts.

The plateau slopes more regularly toward the extreme southern plain, but its boundaries to the east and west are more abrupt. To the east it descends in a sharp fault, by steps of 1,000 to 2,000 feet. This cliff, called the Great Cliff or Cliff of Angavo, is often impassable and is itself bordered by the Betsimisaraka Escarpment, a second and lower cliff to the east, which overhangs the coastal plain.

Behind the scarp face are the remains of ancient lakes, including one called Alaotra. To the south the two steep gradients meet and form the Mahafaly and the Androy plateaus, which overhang the sea in precipitous cliffs. Toward the west the descent is made in a series of steps. In places, however, the central plateau is bordered by an impassable escarpment, such as the Cliff of Bongolava. To the extreme north, the plateau is separated by the low belt of the Montagne de Ambre, which includes a series of volcanic craters.

The coasts
The eastern coast has an average width of 30 miles. It is a narrow alluvial plain that terminates at the sea in a low coastline bordered with extensive lagoons linked together by the Canal des Pangalanes, which is 400 miles long. To the south of Farafangana, the coast becomes rocky, and in the southeast there are little bays. The deep Baie d'Antongil (Bay of Antongil) is located to the northeast.

The western zone is between 60 and 125 miles wide. Its sedimentary layers slope toward the Mozambique Channel and produce a succession of hills. The inland (eastern) side of these steep hills dominates the hollows formed in the soft sediments, while the other side descends to the sea in rocky slopes.

The coastline is straight, bordered by small dunes and fringed with mangroves. The currents in the Mozambique Channel have favoured the deposit of alluvium and the growth of river deltas. On the northwestern coast there are estuaries and bays. This coast is bordered by coral reefs and volcanic islands, such as Nosy Be, which protects the Baie d'Ampasindava. (Je.D.)

Soils. The central plateau and the eastern coast are mainly composed of gneiss (a granite-like rock formed under heat and pressure), granite, quartz, and other crystalline formations. The gneiss decomposes into red murrum (solid ironstone) and laterite (an infertile red soil with a high content of iron oxides and aluminum hydroxide) but also deeper and more fertile red earths, giving Madagascar its colloquial name of the Great Red Island. Fertile soils in the valleys support intensive cultivation. There are also northern, central, and southeastern volcanic intrusions that produce very fertile but easily erodible soils. Lac Alaotra (Lake Alaotra) is a sedimentary pocket in the central plateau, north of Imerina. The western third of the island consists entirely of sedimentary deposits that were raised up from under the sea or that underlay ancient lakes.

Drainage. The steep eastern face of the plateau is drained by numerous short, torrential rivers, which discharge either into the coastal lagoons or directly into the sea over waterfalls and rapids. They include the Mandrare, the Mananara, the Faraony, the Ivondro, and the Maningory. The more gently sloping western side of the plateau is crossed by longer and larger rivers, including the Onilahy, the Mangoky, the Tsiribihina–Mania, and the Betsiboka–Ikopa, which bring huge deposits of fertile sediments down into the vast plains and many-channelled estuaries; the river mouths, while not completely blocked by this sediment, are full of sandbanks.

The volcanic lakes
There are numerous lakes of volcanic origin, such as Lac Itasy. Alaotra is the last surviving lake of the eastern slope. Lac Tsimanampetsotsa, near the coast south of Tuléar, is a large body of saline water that has no outlet.

Climate. The hot, wet season extends from November to April and the cooler, drier season from May to October. The climate is governed by the combined effects of the southeast trade winds and the northwest monsoon (rain-bearing) winds as they blow across the central plateau. The trade winds, which blow throughout the year, are strongest from May to October. The east coast is to the windward and receives a high rate of annual precipitation, reaching about 146 inches (3,700 millimetres) at Maroantsetra on the Bay of Antongil. As the winds cross the plateau, they lose much of their humidity, causing drizzle and mists on the plateau and leaving the west dry.

The monsoon, bringing rain to the northwest coast and the plateau, is most noticeable during the hot, humid season. The wind blows obliquely onto the west coast, which receives a moderate rate of precipitation; the southwest, which is protected, remains arid. Annual rainfall drops from 92 inches (2,300 millimetres) on the northwestern island of Nosy Be to 30 inches (760 millimetres) at Maintirano and Morondava (both on the west coast) and to 13 inches (330 millimetres) at Tuléar in the southwest. The plateau receives moderate rains, with 53 inches falling annually at Tananarive and 48 inches at Fianarantsoa, about 200 miles further south.

July is the coolest month, with temperatures between about 54° and 77° F (12° and 25° C), and December the hottest month, with temperatures between 68° and 82° F (about 20° and 28° C). Temperatures are highest on the northwest coast and lowest on the plateau. The annual average temperature at Diégo-Suarez, on the extreme northern coast, is 80° F (27° C) and at Fort-Dauphin, on the extreme southeastern coast, 73° F (23° C). On the plateau, however, the annual average temperature is 64° F (18° C) at Tananarive and 65° F at Fianarantsoa.

Cyclones—turbulent windstorms that often bring torrential rain—are an important climatic feature. They form far out over the Indian Ocean, especially from December to March, and approach the eastern coast, bringing destructive floods.

Vegetation and animal life. Much of the island was once covered with evergreen and deciduous forest, but little now remains except on the eastern escarpment and in scattered pockets in the west. The plateau is particularly denuded and suffers seriously from erosion. The forest has been cut to clear rice fields, to obtain fuel and building materials, and to export valuable timber, such as ebony, rosewood, and sandalwood. About seven-eighths of the island is covered with prairie grasses and bamboo or small thin trees, including the travellers' tree, which holds water in its cellular trunk and produces the long banana-like leaves that are widely used for thatching. There are also screw pines, palms, and reeds on the coasts. In the arid south are thorn trees, giant cacti, dwarf baobab trees, and drought-resistant plants that are peculiar to the island.

The grassland vegetation

Because of the island's isolation, many zoologically primitive primates have survived and evolved into unique forms. Three-quarters of all known species of lemurs—nocturnal, arboreal mammals related to monkeys—are indigenous to Madagascar. Several unique hedgehog-like insectivores have evolved, and there are all sizes of chameleons. Birds are numerous and include guinea fowls, partridges, pigeons, herons, ibis, flamingoes, egrets, owls, and several kinds of birds of prey. There are about 800 species of butterfly, many moths, and a variety of spiders. The only large or dangerous animals are the crocodiles, which occupy the rivers. The snakes, including the *do,* which is 10 to 13 feet in length, are harmless.

There are few freshwater fish, but marine fish and crustaceans abound on the coasts and in the lagoons, as well as in the streams of the plateau. Certain species, such as the spiny globefish (a marine fish that inflates when disturbed) and the cofferfish, are peculiar to Madagascar.

The landscape under human settlement. *Rural settlement.* Despite the importance of intensive rice cultivation, the land is primarily used for pastoral purposes. Cattle are kept in all parts and are more numerous than the human population; they are fewer in the dense forest areas of the eastern escarpment. Elsewhere, pastoralism predominates, although the people also cultivate subsistence crops. On the plateau, the valley bottoms and irrigable slopes are mainly used for rice growing. The forest peoples traditionally grew hill rice, after cutting and burning the forest; this practice still continues, although it is discouraged by the government, which promotes the establishment of permanent irrigated rice fields.

The older villages of the Merina and Betsileo were often perched on hilltops and defended by huge ditches. Today, villages have been rebuilt on lower ground, and hamlets and homesteads are scattered over the landscape.

On the plateau, cattle enclosures are built of dry stone walls; the landscape is also dotted with funerary or com-

MAP INDEX

Political subdivisions
Diégo-Suarez....13·30s 49·10e
Fianarantsoa....22·00s 47·00e
Majunga.......17·00s 46·00e
Tamatave......18·00s 48·40e
Tananarive.....19·00s 47·00e
Tuléar.........24·00s 45·00e
The names of the political subdivisions do not appear on the map because they are the same as the names of their capital cities.

Cities and towns
Alakamisy.....21·19s 47·14e
Alarobia
  Vohiposa.....20·59s 47·09e
Ambahikily....21·36s 43·41e
Ambahita.....24·01s 45·16e
Ambakaka.....24·10s 46·17e
Ambalabe.....18·24s 49·10e
Ambalafany...22·32s 47·36e
Ambalanjana-
  komby......16·42s 47·05e
Ambalavao....21·50s 46·56e
Ambanja......13·41s 48·27e
Ambararata....15·03s 48·33e
Ambarijeby....14·56s 47·41e
Ambato.......13·24s 48·29e
Ambato Boeni...16·28s 46·43e
Ambatofinandra-
  hana.......20·33s 46·48e
Ambatolampy..19·23s 47·25e
Ambatomainty..17·41s 45·40e
Ambatomanoina.18·18s 47·37e
Ambatondrazaka.16·59s 48·25e
Ambatosoratra..17·34s 48·32e
Ambenja......15·17s 46·58e
Ambevongo....15·27s 47·27e
Ambilobe.....13·12s 49·04e
Ambinanyn-
  drano......20·20s 48·19e
Ambinanytelo..15·21s 49·35e
Ambinda.....16·25s 45·52e
Ambivy.......21·31s 44·02e
Amboahangy...24·15s 46·22e
Amboasary....18·26s 48·16e
Amboasary....25·02s 46·23e
Ambodifototra..16·59s 49·52e
Ambodilazana..18·06s 49·10e
Ambodiriana...17·55s 49·18e
Ambohibary...19·20s 46·17e
Ambohidratrimo.18·50s 47·26e
Ambohidray...18·36s 48·18e
Ambohimahama-
  sina........21·56s 47·11e
Ambohimahasoa.21·07s 47·13e
Ambohimanga
  du Sud......20·52s 47·36e
Ambohimitombo.20·43s 47·26e
Ambondro....25·13s 45·44e
Ambositra.....20·31s 47·15e
Ambovombe...25·11s 46·05e
Ampanavoana..15·41s 50·22e
Ampanihy.....24·42s 44·45e
Amparafaravola.17·35s 48·13e
Amparihy.....16·40s 49·49e
Amparihy.....23·57s 47·20e
Ampasibe.....22·56s 46·58e
Ampasinambo..20·31s 48·00e
Ampitsikinana..12·57s 49·49e
Ampombian-
  tambo......12·42s 48·57e
Ampotaka....25·03s 44·41e
Ampoza......22·20s 44·44e
Analalava....14·38s 47·45e
Analapetsa.....25·10s 46·42e
Analavoka.....22·33s 46·30e
Andaingo.....18·12s 48·17e
Andapa......14·39s 49·39e
Andevoranto...18·57s 49·06e
Andilamena....17·01s 48·35e
Andramasina...19·11s 47·35e
Andranopasy..21·17s 43·44e
Andranovory...23·08s 44·10e
Andriamena....17·26s 46·30e
Andriandampy..22·45s 45·41e
Andriba......17·36s 46·55e
Androka......25·02s 44·05e
Anivorano.....18·44s 48·58e
Anivorano Nord..12·44s 49·13e
Anjavimihavana.12·32s 49·16e
Anjiabe......12·07s 49·20e
Anjozorobe...18·24s 47·52e
Ankaramena...21·57s 46·39e
Ankarimbelo...18·56s 47·09e
Ankasakasa...16·21s 44·52e
Ankavandra...18·46s 45·18e
Ankazoabo....22·18s 44·31e
Ankazobe.....18·21s 47·07e
Ankazomiriotra..19·38s 46·32e
Ankiabe......13·13s 48·56e
Ankilimalinika..22·58s 43·45e
Ankilizato....20·25s 45·01e
Ankisabe.....19·17s 46·29e
Ankororoka....25·30s 45·11e
Anorotsangana.13·56s 47·55e
Anosibe.....19·26s 48·13e

Antalaha........14·53s 50·16e
Antambohobe...22·20s 46·47e
Antanambao
  Manampotsy...19·29s 48·34e
Antanambe.....16·26s 49·52e
Antanetibe.....18·27s 46·42e
Antanifotsy.....19·39s 47·19e
Antanimora.....24·49s 45·40e
Antetikireja.....14·42s 47·29e
Antevamena.....21·02s 44·08e
Antoetra.......20·46s 47·20e
Antonibe.......15·07s 47·24e
Antsakabary....15·03s 48·56e
Antsalova......18·40s 44·37e
Antsenavolo....21·24s 48·03e
Antsiafabositra..17·18s 47·02e
Antsirabe......14·00s 49·59e
Antsirabe......15·57s 48·58e
Antsirabe......19·51s 47·02e
Antsohihy......14·52s 47·59e
Arivonimamo...19·01s 47·15e
Bandabe.......15·31s 49·04e
Basibasy......22·10s 43·40e
Bealanana......14·33s 48·44e
Bebao.........17·22s 44·33e
Befandriana....15·16s 48·32e
Befandriana....22·06s 43·54e
Befasy.........20·33s 44·23e
Befotaka......13·15s 48·16e
Befotaka......14·32s 48·01e
Befotaka......21·29s 44·44e
Befotaka......23·49s 46·59e
Bekily.........24·13s 45·19e
Bekisopa......21·40s 45·54e
Bekitro........24·33s 45·18e
Bekodoka.....16·58s 45·07e
Bekopaka......19·09s 44·48e
Belavenona....24·50s 47·04e
Belo...........19·42s 44·33e
Beloha........25·10s 45·03e
Belo-sur-mer....20·44s 44·00e
Bemarivo......16·56s 44·21e
Bemarivo......21·45s 44·45e
Bemavo.......21·37s 45·24e
Bemolanga....17·44s 45·06e
Benenitra......23·27s 45·05e
Beraketa......23·07s 44·25e
Beraketa......24·11s 45·42e
Beravina......18·10s 45·14e
Berevo........17·14s 44·17e
Berevo........19·44s 44·58e
Beroroha......21·41s 45·10e
Besalampy.....16·45s 44·30e
Betafo........19·50s 46·51e
Betioky........22·27s 43·44e
Betioky........23·42s 44·22e
Betroka.......23·16s 46·06e
Betsioky......21·31s 44·28e
Bevoalavo....25·13s 45·26e
Bezaha........23·30s 44·31e
Brickaville.....18·49s 49·04e
Daraina......13·12s 49·40e
Didy..........18·07s 48·32e
Diégo-Suarez...12·16s 49·17e
Doany.........14·22s 49·31e
Ejeda.........24·20s 44·31e
Esira.........24·20s 46·42e
Etrotroka.....22·53s 47·36e
Fanambana....13·34s 50·00e
Fandriana.....20·14s 47·23e
Fanjakana.....21·10s 46·53e
Farafangana...22·49s 47·50e
Farahalana....14·26s 50·10e
Faratsiho.....19·24s 46·57e
Faux-Cap.....25·33s 45·32e
Fénérive.....17·22s 49·25e
Fenoarivo.....18·26s 46·34e
Fenoarivo.....20·52s 46·53e
Fenoarivo.....21·43s 46·24e
Fianarantsoa...21·26s 47·05e
Fiantsonana...19·09s 46·12e
Fierenana.....18·29s 48·24e
Fihaonana....18·36s 47·12e
Folakara......18·20s 45·02e
Fort-Carnot...21·53s 47·28e
Fort-Dauphin..25·02s 47·00e
Fotadrevo.....24·03s 45·01e
Foulpointe....17·41s 49·31e
Hell-Ville.....13·25s 48·16e
Iakora........23·06s 46·40e
Ianakaly.....23·21s 45·28e
Ifanadiana....21·19s 47·39e
Ihorombe.....23·00s 47·33e
Ihosy.........22·24s 46·08e
Ikalamavony..21·09s 46·35e
Ilaka.........19·33s 48·52e
Ilaka.........20·20s 47·09e
Imanombo....24·26s 45·49e
Imerimandroso..17·23s 48·38e
Isoanala......23·50s 45·44e
Itampolo......24·41s 43·57e
Itandrano.....21·45s 45·17e
Ivahona......23·27s 46·10e
Ivato.........20·37s 47·12e
Ivohibe.......22·29s 46·52e
Ivondro.......24·47s 46·52e
Jangany.......22·54s 45·41e
Janjina.......20·30s 45·50e
Kandreho.....17·29s 46·06e

Karianga.......22·22s 47·26e
Katsepe.......15·45s 46·15e
Kiangara......17·58s 47·02e
Kilimavony....23·48s 43·41e
Kiranomena....18·17s 46·03e
Lambomakondro.22·41s 44·44e
Lavanono......25·24s 44·55e
Lavaraty......23·16s 46·59e
Lazarivo......23·54s 44·59e
Loky..........12·47s 49·39e
Madirobe.....16·04s 46·15e
Madirovalo....16·26s 46·30e
Maevatanana..16·56s 46·49e
Mahabe.......17·05s 45·20e
Mahabo.......23·40s 46·08e
Mahabo.......20·23s 44·40e
Mahanoro.....19·54s 48·48e
Mahasoa......22·12s 46·06e
Mahasolo......19·07s 46·22e
Mahatsinjo....21·26s 45·51e
Maintirano....18·03s 44·01e
Majunga......15·43s 46·19e
Malaimbandy..20·20s 45·36e
Manakara.....22·08s 48·01e
Manambato....13·14s 49·54e
Manambato....13·43s 49·07e
Manambolosy..16·02s 49·40e
Manampatrana..21·40s 47·35e
Mananara.....16·10s 49·46e
Manandaza....19·19s 45·23e
Mananjary.....21·13s 48·20e
Manantenina...24·17s 47·19e
Manaravolo....23·59s 45·39e
Mandabe......20·55s 45·49e
Mandabe......21·03s 44·55e
Mandoto......19·34s 46·17e
Mandritsara...15·50s 48·49e
Mandronarivo..21·07s 45·38e
Manera........22·55s 44·20e
Mangaoka.....12·19s 49·07e
Mangindrano..14·17s 48·58e
Manja........21·26s 44·20e
Manjakandriana..18·55s 47·47e
Manombo.....22·52s 45·44e
Marerano......21·23s 44·52e
Mariarano.....15·29s 46·42e
Maroala.......15·23s 47·59e
Maroantsetra..15·26s 49·44e
Marofandilia...20·07s 44·34e
Marolambo.....20·02s 48·07e
Maromandia...14·13s 48·08e
Maroseranana..18·32s 48·51e
Marotandrano..16·10s 48·50e
Marotolana....14·01s 48·37e
Marovato......15·48s 48·05e
Marovato......16·28s 48·25e
Marovoay.....16·06s 46·39e
Marovoay Nord..16·57s 44·34e
Masoala......15·59s 50·10e
Masoarivo.....19·03s 44·19e
Masomeloka...20·17s 48·37e
Miandrivazo...19·31s 45·28e
Miarinarivo....16·38s 48·15e
Miarinarivo....18·57s 46·55e
Miarinavaratra..20·13s 47·31e
Midongy Nord..20·45s 46·13e
Midongy Sud...23·35s 47·01e
Milanoa......13·35s 49·47e
Mitsinjo......16·01s 45·52e
Morafenobe...17·49s 44·55e
Moramanga...18·56s 48·12e
Morombe.....21·45s 43·22e
Morondava....20·17s 44·17e
Nosy Varika...20·35s 48·32e
Port-Bergé....15·33s 47·40e
Poste Ramartina.19·38s 45·58e
Ranohira......22·29s 45·24e
Ranomafana..18·57s 48·50e
Ranomafana..24·36s 46·58e
Ranomena....23·25s 47·17e
Ranopiso.....25·03s 46·40e
Ranotsara Nord..22·48s 46·36e
Rantabe......15·42s 49·39e
Sahana
  Ambodipont....14·37s 50·11e
Sahasinaka....21·49s 47·49e
Saint-Augustin..23·33s 43·46e
Sakaraha......22·55s 44·32e
Sambava......14·16s 50·10e
Sitampiky.....16·41s 46·06e
Soahanina....18·42s 44·13e
Soalala.......16·06s 45·20e
Soalary......23·36s 43·44e
Soaloka......18·32s 45·15e
Soamanonga..23·52s 44·47e
Soanierana
  Ivongo......16·55s 49·35e
Soanindrariny..19·54s 47·14e
Soavina......20·23s 46·56e
Soavinandriana.19·09s 46·45e
Solila........21·25s 46·37e
Tamatave.....18·10s 49·23e
Tambohorano..17·30s 43·58e
Tananarive....18·55s 47·31e
Tangainony...22·42s 47·45e
Tolongoina...21·33s 47·31e
Tongobory....23·32s 44·20e
Trangahy.....19·07s 44·43e

Tranoroa......24·42s 45·04e
Tritriva........22·46s 46·07e
Tsarabaria....13·46s 49·58e
Tsaramandroso..16·22s 47·02e
Tsaratanana...16·47s 47·39e
Tsianaloka....18·08s 44·50e
Tsihombe.....25·18s 45·29e
Tsimilofo.....24·59s 45·10e
Tsinjoarivo...19·37s 47·40e
Tsinjomiton-
  draka.......15·36s 47·08e
Tsiroanoman-
  didy........18·46s 46·02e
Tsitondroina...21·19s 46·00e
Tsivory........24·04s 46·05e
Tuléar........23·21s 43·40e
Vangaindrano..23·21s 47·36e
Vatomandry...19·20s 48·59e
Vavatenina....17·28s 49·12e
Vohémar......13·21s 50·02e
Vohilava......21·04s 48·00e
Vohipeno.....22·22s 47·51e
Vohitsora.....23·54s 44·17e
Vondrozo.....22·49s 47·20e
Zazafotsy....22·13s 46·26e

**Physical features
and points of interest**
Alaotra, Lac, *lake*.17·30s 48·30e
Ambaro, Baie d',
  bay.........13·23s 48·38e
Ambre, Cap d',
  cape.......11·57s 49·17e
Ambre,
  Montagne d',
  mountain.....12·30s 49·10e
Ampasilava, Baie
  d', *bay*......21·16s 43·43e
Ampasindava,
  Baie d', *bay*..13·16s 48·43e
Analamaitso,
  Plateau d',
  upland......16·15s 48·15e
Anavelona,
  mountains...22·37s 44·10e
Andramaimba,
  Baie, *bay*.....12·15s 48·50e
Andringitra,
  mountains....22·20s 46·55e
Androna, *ridge*.15·15s 48·40e
Androy, *upland*.25·00s 45·30e
Angavo, *cliff*...19·40s 47·50e
Ankaratra,
  mountains....19·25s 47·12e
Ankaroaka,
  mountain....17·48s 48·32e
Antolana,
  mountain....17·04s 48·09e
Antongil, Baie d',
  bay.........15·45s 49·50e
Bambetoka,
  Baie de, *bay*...15·50s 46·17e
Barren, Îles,
  islands......18·25s 43·40e
Beampingaratra,
  mountains...24·30s 46·50e
Bellone, Cap,
  cape........16·14s 49·51e
Bemaraha,
  Plateau du....20·00s 45·15e
Bemarivo, *river*..14·09s 50·09e
Bemarivo, *river*..15·27s 47·40e
Betsiboka, *river*.16·03s 46·36e
Betsimisaraka,
  escarpment....18·00s 49·00e
Bezavona,
  mountain....15·02s 49·52e
Boby, Pic, *peak*..22·12s 46·55e
Bongolava, *cliff*..18·45s 46·00e
Chesterfield, Île,
  island.......16·20s 43·58e
Est, Cap, *cape*...15·16s 50·29e
Faraony, *river*....21·47s 48·10e
Fiherenana, *river*.23·19s 43·37e
Ihosy, *river*......21·58s 43·38e
Ihotry, Lac, *lake*.21·56s 43·41e
Ikahavo, Plateau
  de l'...........17·25s 45·50e
Ikepa, *river*......17·01s 46·45e
Imaloto, *river*...23·27s 45·13e
Imerina,
  physical region.18·30s 46·50e
Indian Ocean....22·00s 50·00e
Inkony, Lac, *lake*.16·08s 45·50e
Ionaivo, *river*....22·56s 46·54e
Isalo, Parc,
  National de l',
  national park...22·45s 45·15e
Itaperina, Pointe,
  point........24·59s 47·06e
Itasy, Lac,
  lake.........19·04s 46·17e
Ivakoany, Massif
  de l', *mountains*.23·50s 46·25e
Ivondro, *river*....18·15s 49·22e
Kinangaly,
  mountain.....19·12s 45·40e
Koraraika, Baie
  de, *bay*.......17·45s 43·57e

CAP D'AMBRE 274
Baie Andramaimba
Mangaoka • **Diégo-Suarez**
CAP SAINT-SÉBASTIEN Montagne d'Ambre
1475 • Anjavimihavana
Ampombiantambo
NOSY MITSIO Anivorano Nord • Loky
Ambilobe 679 • Ampitsikinana
Manambato Daraina
Ambato Vohémar
Manambato Milanoa Fanambana
Tsarabaria
MASSIF DU Mangindrano Antsirabe
TSARATANANA Maromokotro Sambava
2876 Doany Farahalana
LES RADAMA Marotolana Andapa Sahana Ambodipont
Baie Ramanetaka Maromandia Antalaha
PRESQU'ÎLE RADAMA Befotaka Bealanana Bezavona
NOSY LAVA Analalava 1484
Antetikireja Ambararata Antsakabary
Ambarijeby Manakalampona
Antonibe Maroala 1397 Ambinanytelo Maroantsetra
Baie de la Mahajamba Ambenja Bandabe Rantabe PRESQU'ÎLE
Mariarano Ambevongo Port-Bergé Marovato MASOALA
Majunga Tsinjomitondraka Antsirabe Masoala
Katsepe PLATEAU Mampikony Manambolosy CAP MASOALA
Mitsinjo D'ANALAMAITSO Marotandrano Manara
CAP SAINT-ANDRÉ Madirobe Marovato CAP BELLONE
ÎLE CHESTERFIELD Soalala Tsaramandroso Antanambe
Ankasakasa 1300 Miarinarivo ÎLE SAINTE-MARIE
Amparihy Madirovalo Tsaratanana Soanierana Ivongo Ambodifototra
Besalampy Sitampiky Ambato Antolana 1315 Fénérive
Bekodoka Boeni 1204 Andilamena Vavatenina
Bemarivo Marovoay Ambalanjanakomby Imerimandroso Foulpointe
Maevatanana Amparafaravola Lac Alaotra
Nord Andriamena Ambatosoratra
Mahabe Antsiafabositra Ankaratra Ambatondrazaka
Bebao PLATEAU DE L'IKAHAVO Kandreho Vatoloha 1445 Ambodiriana
720 Andriba 1565 Ambodilazana
Morafenobe Bemolanga Ambatomainty Kiangara Didy Amboasary Ambalabe
Maintirano Beravina Antanetibe Andaingo **Tamatave**
Tsianaloka 1303 Kiranomena Ambatomanoina Maroseranana
ÎLES BARREN Folakara Ankazobe Vazobe Anjozorobe Fierenana Anivorano
Soaloka Fihaonana 1778 Ambohidray Brickaville
Soahanina Antsalova 940 Ankavandra Tsiroanomandidy Ambohimirimo Andevoranto
Masoarivo Ambohidratrimo **Tananarive** Ranomafana
Trangahy Bekopaka Miarinarivo Arivonimamo Moramanga Vatomandry
Kinangaly Fiantsonana Mahasolo Manjakandriana
Miandrivazo 1319 Soavinandriana Andramasina Ilaka Antananambao Manampotsy
Belo Manandaza Tsiafajavona Faratsiho 2643 Anosibe
Poste Ambatolampy Mahanoro
Ramartina Mandoto Ambohibary
Ankazomiriotra Tsinjoarivo
Betafo Antanifotsy
Antsirabe Soanindrariny
509 2023 Marolambo
Marofandilia Fandriana Ambinanyndrano
Morondava Ilaka Miarinavaratra
Mahabo Malaimbandy Masomeloka
Ankilizato Janjina 1470 Spavina Ampasinambo
Befasy 1858 **MADAGASCAR**
Belo-sur-mer Ikalamavony Ambositra Nosy Varika
Antevamena Midongy Nord 1922 2053 Ivato Ambohimitombo
Mandabe 1034 Ambatofinandrahana Antoetra
Baie d'Ampasilava Mandronarivo Fenoarivo Alarobia Ambohimanga du Sud
Andranopasy Tsitondroina Vohiposa Vohilava
Marerano Fanjakana Atakamisy Itandiana
Manja Befotaka Solila 1464 Mananjary
Ambiky Betsioky Bemavo Bekisopa Tolongoina Antsenavolo
Morombe Bemarivo Itandrano Fenoarivo Manampatrana
Lac Ihotry 705 Ambalavao Sahasinaka
CAP SAINT-VINCENT Ankaramena Ambohimahasina
Befandriana Fort-Carnot
Basibasy Ankoazabe PARC Mahasoa Pic Boby Ankarimbelo Manakara
Betioky Ampoza NATIONAL 2658 Karianga Vohipeno
1320 DE L'ISALO Zazafotsy Antambohobe
Manombo Lambomakondro Ihosy Tangainony
Manera Ranohira Analavoka Vohibe Ambalafany
Ankilimalinika Sakaraha 1128 Andriandampy Ranotsara Vondrozo Farafangana
Beraketa Tritriva Nord Ampasibe Ihorombe
Andranovory Jangany Iakora
Ivahona Betroka Lavaraty Vangaindrano
Tuléar Tongobory Benenitra 1825 Ranomena
St-Augustin Bezaha Mahabo Midongy Sud Tropic of Capricorn
Soalary Betioky Isoanala Befotaka
Kilimavony Soamanonga 1636 Amparihy
Vohitsora Lazarivo Manaravolo MASSIF DE L'IVAKOANY
Fotadrevo Ambahita Tsivory
Ejeda Bekily Imanombo Ambakaka Manantenina
Tranoroa Beraketa Amboahangy
Ampanihy Bekitro Esira Ranomafana
Antanimora 1956 Ivondro
PLATEAU MAHAFALY Imanombo Belavenona
Lac Tsimanampetsotsa Androka Amboasary POINTE ITAPERINA
Itampolo Ampotaka Tsimilofo Ranopiso **Fort-Dauphin**
Androka Ambovombe
Bevoalavo ANDROY Ambondro Analapetsa
Beloha
Lavanono Tsihombe
Ankororoka
CAP SAINTE-MARIE Faux-Cap

COMORO ISLANDS
(France)
• Dzaoudzi
MAYOTTE

CHANNEL

MOZAMBIQUE

ÎLE JUAN DE NOVA
(Fr.)

Baie de Koraraika

Baie de Bombetoka

INDIAN

OCEAN

MADAGASCAR

Elevations in metres

© Rand McNally & Co.
A-582700-257

0   100   200   300 km
0   100   200 mi

Size of symbol indicates relative size of town • ○ ⊚ ▣

memorative monuments; in parts of the south and west, these take the form of wooden posts, beautifully carved.

Urban settlement. Madagascar, which has six main cities, has had an urban tradition since the 16th and 17th centuries. Tananarive, in the centre of the plateau, is the national capital and has a population of more than 380,-000; it is six and a half times larger than the port of Tamatave in the east, which has 59,000 inhabitants. Fianarantsoa in the south of the plateau and the ports of Majunga in the northwest, Diégo-Suarez on the northern tip of the island, and Tuléar in the southwest have less than 57,000 inhabitants each. The smaller urban centre of Antsirabe (population 28,000), south of Tananarive, is mainly important as a tourist centre.

Racial or economic separation is not noticeable in the older cities such as Tananarive and Fianarantsoa, but the newer towns are often divided into socio-economic sectors. On the plateau, the cities are almost entirely composed of a particular ethnic group, but the ports are ethnically mixed.

THE PEOPLE

Population groups. *Origin of the population.* Madagascar has been inhabited by man for the relatively short period of only about 2,000 years. Language and culture point unequivocally to Indonesian origins, but there is no empirical evidence of how, why, or by what route the first settlers came to the island. Studies of the winds and currents of the Indian Ocean indicate that the voyage from Indonesia could have been made. It is assumed that the original peopling of the island, however sparse, was accomplished by a single cultural group, probably as the result of a single voyage.

There is also widespread evidence from vocabulary, archaeology, and tradition of influence from Afro-Arab settlers on the coasts before AD 1000. There is slighter evidence of an Indian influence in vocabulary, but there is no trace of Hinduism in Malagasy culture and none of orthodox Islām except in later coastal settlements.

Language. The inhabitants of Madagascar speak Malagasy, which, written in the Latin alphabet, is a standardized version of the Merina language. Although there are numerous local dialects, they are all mutually intelligible.

French is widely spoken and is also officially recognized. It is used as a medium of instruction, as is Malagasy.

Ethnic groups. The population is divided into about 20 ethnic groups, the largest and most dominant of which is the Merina people, who are scattered throughout the island and number about 2,000,000. The name Merina (Imerina) is said to mean Elevated People, deriving from the fact that they lived on the plateau. There are almost 1,000,000 members of the Betsimisaraka (The Inseparable Multitude), who live generally in the east. The third most numerous people is the Betsileo (The Invincible Multitude), about 900,000 of whom inhabit the plateau around Fianarantsoa. Other important peoples are the Tsimihety (Those Who Do Not Cut Their Hair), 533,-000; the Sakalava (People of the Long Valley), 434,000; the Antandroy (People of the Thorn Bush), 384,000; the Tanala (People of the Forest), 250,000; the Antaimoro (People of the Banks), 248,000; and the Bara (a name of uncertain origin), 250,000. Smaller groups are the Antanosy (People of the Island), 165,000; the Antaifasy (People of the Sand), 88,000; the Sihanaka (People of the Lake), 143,000; the Antakarana (People of the Rocks), 44,000; the Betanimena (People of the Red Soil), who are now largely absorbed by the Merina; the Bezanozano (Those with Many Braided Hair), 56,000; and the Mahafaly (the Joyful People), 117,000.

Religious groups. About half of the population has been converted to Christianity, and the Christian community is about equally divided between Protestantism and Roman Catholicism. There is a sizable community of Muslims in the northwest.

The rest of the people continue to practice their traditional religion, which is based upon ancestor worship. The dead are buried in tombs and are believed to reward or punish the living. There is a supreme being called Zanahary (the Creator) or Andriamanitra (the Fragrant One). There is also a belief in local spirits; a complex system of taboos constrains Malagasy life.

Demography. The population exceeded 6,000,000 during the 1960s and has been expanding at a rate of about 150,000 to 200,000 a year. All but about 105,000 are Malagasy. The main foreign communities are the French, 42,000; the Comorians, 34,000; the Indians, 14,000; and the Chinese, 8,000.

Birth and mortality rates. Births greatly outnumber deaths, and in 1970, for example, the estimated rate of registered births was 39 per thousand, while registered deaths were 14 per thousand, representing an annual rate of increase of 25 per thousand. Registration of births and deaths is, however, incomplete.

Immigration and emigration. Emigration of the non-Malagasy population exceeded immigration during the post-independence years from 1961 to 1965. The French, Comorian, and Chinese groups fell, while the Indian community showed a slight increase. There is no significant emigration abroad.

Distribution of the population. The eastern part of the central plateau is the region of highest population density, averaging over 130 persons per square mile (50 persons per square kilometre). The eastern forest zone and the northeast coast have densities that vary from 25 to 50 persons per square mile, while the east coast plain has the second highest density, with over 50 persons per square mile. The whole of the western two-thirds of the country is sparsely inhabited, averaging less than 25 persons per square mile.

The eastern half of the island contains almost all the major cities and towns. Tananarive alone contains approximately 5 percent of the total population; perched on two precipitous mountain ridges, the old part of the city is dominated by the palace and has an extremely picturesque, almost medieval appearance.

Demographic trends. In the early 1970s it seemed probable that the prevailing rapid rate of growth would continue, if not increase, throughout the decade because government policy was opposed to any form of population control. While there are large tracts of empty land, they are not easy to exploit, and the more favoured areas may quickly reach the point of acute overcrowding.

Indonesian origins [margin note]

Population densities [margin note]

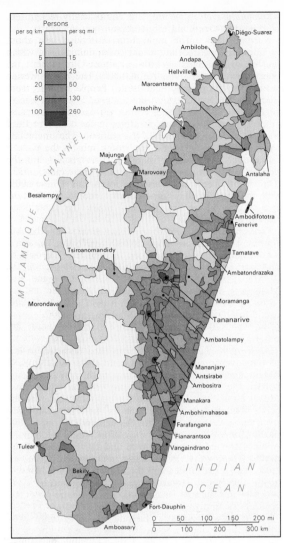

Population density of Madagascar.

There is every reason to expect continued population growth in Tananarive—a growth that is likely to outstrip employment opportunities.

Madagascar, Area and Population				
	area		population	
	sq mi	sq km	1966 census	1970 estimate*
Provinces				
Diégo-Suarez	16,496	42,725	550,000	615,000
Fianarantsoa	38,736	100,326	1,565,000	1,811,000
Majunga	58,751	152,165	665,000	888,000
Tamatave	27,495	71,212	1,025,000	1,184,000
Tananarive	22,307	57,775	1,580,000	1,799,000
Tulear (Tuléar)	62,658	162,283	815,000	1,127,000
Total Madagascar	226,444	586,486	6,200,000	7,424,000

*Official de jure estimate; may be as much as 500,000 or more persons too high. UN midyear 1970 estimate (reported as being of doubtful validity): 6,750,000. Source: Official government figures.

THE ECONOMY

The economic position of Madagascar has been defined by its colonial connection with France, which in the early 1970s still took nearly half of its exports and supplied more than half of its imports. Currency, banking, finance, loans, and economic planning are influenced not only by accords with France but by French personnel in government, commerce, and technical assistance. Madagascar is sheltered by this from certain risks and gains some material advantages, but the full exercise of political and economic responsibility is thereby delayed.

The regional position of Madagascar has been as anomalous as its geographical and cultural connections. It hardly belongs to Africa yet is remote from Asia. It has close connections with the Indian Ocean island of Réunion. Otherwise, economic links with Senegal have been closer than with any nearer part of Africa, although in the last few years increasing interest and investment from South Africa have been welcomed. Despite great efforts in development and increases in production, inflation and population growth had resulted in real income per head falling slightly in the decade of the 1960s.

The extent and distribution of resources. *Mineral resources.* The Great Red Island disappointed those who hoped to discover precious metals in large quantities. Considerable small-scale gold mining was conducted towards the end of the 19th century, both by French and Malagasy prospectors. There is a wide variety of semiprecious stones, but deposits are not of significant economic importance. Mineral deposits include chromite, which is found north of Tananarive and near Tamatave; ilmenite (a black mineral, iron titanate), found on the southeast coast and near Fenerive; low-grade iron, found in scattered deposits in the southern half of the island; low-grade coal near Antsirabe, north of Tuléar and inland from Besalampy; nickel near Fianarantsoa; and copper north of Ampanihy and near Ambilobe. There are also smaller deposits of zircon, monazite, bauxite, lead, graphite, quartzite, gold, uranothorianite, bentonite, kaolin, and alunite. The various gems include beryl and columbite.

Principal mineral deposits

Biological resources. The eastern evergreen forest and the remnants of the deciduous forest are valuable for their timber. Except for the fish and crustaceans of the rivers and coasts, the indigenous animal life is of little economic importance. Domestic animals include the zebu (an Asiatic ox), which has great importance in Madagascan life, the fat-tailed sheep, and dogs, poultry, and pigs.

Power resources. Although there are many magnificent waterfalls, especially on the eastern escarpment, only about six of them have been developed. Hydroelectric power stations serve the cities of Tananarive, Tamatave, Antsirabe, and Fianarantsoa and are supplemented by thermal stations, which burn coal. There are also thermal stations serving Majunga, Tuléar, Diégo-Suarez, Ambositra, Manakara, and Morondava.

Sources of national income. *Agriculture, forestry, and fishing.* By far the most important crop in Madagascar is rice. Various types of both dry and wet rice are raised by irrigation in the central plateau; dry rice is also produced in the eastern forests, and wet rice in the western estuaries. Annual production surpassed 1,500,000 tons after 1965, and rice occupied almost half the total acreage devoted to crops.

Slash-and-burn techniques (the temporary clearance of land for agriculture) are used in the escarpment forest and along the east coast. In the river valleys of the west, cultivation is permanent; irrigation and rainfall are used.

Sugarcane is grown on plantations in the northwest, around Majunga, and on the east coast near Tamatave. Estimated 1970 production was 1,300,000 metric tons of cane from only 54,000 acres (22,000 hectares). Manioc is grown all over the island, producing an estimated 940,000 metric tons from 640,000 acres, and the production of potatoes and yams is estimated at 280,000 metric tons, mainly in the highland region of Ankaratra. Bananas are produced commercially on the east coast, with production reaching about 180,000 metric tons annually. Corn (maize) is grown mainly in the central plateau, in the south, and in the west. Fruits include apples, grapefruits, avocado pears, plums, grapes, litchis (the fruit of a type of soapberry tree), pineapples, guavas, pawpaws, passion fruits, and bananas. Robusta coffee is grown on the east coast and arabica coffee on the plateau. Other significant crops are beans, peanuts, *pois du cap* (Lima beans), coconuts, cloves, pepper, vanilla, cocoa, sisal, raffia, tobacco, and castor beans.

Agricultural produce

The estimated 10,000,000 head of cattle are distributed throughout the island. The large numbers of pigs, sheep, goats, chickens, ducks, geese, and turkeys are found mainly on the plateau.

One-fourth of an estimated 40,000,000 acres of forest is degraded (*i.e.*, regenerated after repeated burnings, with many original species lost and smaller, fewer, less valuable species becoming dominant); the rest is wet or dry tropical forest. Major reforestation has taken place since 1960, with as many as 15,000,000 trees being planted annually, mainly eucalyptus, pine, and cypress.

Fisheries are poorly developed and depend mostly on the small traditional fishing communities of the west coast; production is badly adjusted to the island's needs and to the potential market. Only the inshore waters are fished, and the distant offshore waters are neglected; inland distribution of the fish caught is poor or nonexistent, except in main towns. The bulk of the catch is composed of fresh fish, shrimps, crabs, and crayfish; some fish are also dried. There is also considerable raising of fish in the irrigated rice fields, mainly for home consumption.

Mining and quarrying. Mining and quarrying is little developed. The most important products are graphite, mica, monazite, quartz, garnet, and amethyst. Less valuable amounts of gold, tourmaline, citrine (a black quartz that is changed into a yellow semiprecious stone by heating), beryl, ilmenite, columbite (a black mineral, grading into tantalite), chromite, zircon, and jasper are produced. Merina jewellers polish and set semiprecious stones at small workshops in most towns of the plateau.

Manufacturing. There are no large or heavy industries, and there were fewer than 200 small industrial establishments during the mid-1960s. More than half of the manufacturing is located in the province of Tananarive. Products include oils, soap, sugar, cigarettes and tobacco, sisal rope and mats, bricks, processed foods, and beverages. There is also a small printing industry.

Energy. The installed electric capacity in the mid-1960s reached almost 36,000 kilowatts of hydroelectric power and more than 67,000 kilowatts of thermal power. Most of the hydroelectric plants are located on the plateau and in the neighbouring eastern escarpment.

Financial services. The Malagasy franc is the monetary unit and is equivalent to the CFA (Communauté Financière Africaine) franc, which it replaced in 1963. The Institut d'Emission Malgache (Malagasy Issuing Institute) was formed in 1962 with a capital of 500,000,000 Malagasy francs that were equally subscribed by France and by Madagascar. There are five main commercial banks; all are of French derivation and have branches both in Tananarive and Tamatave. Other provincial capitals have three or four of these banks represented, but smaller towns usually have fewer banking offices.

Foreign trade. More than half the value of exports derives from vegetable products, of which coffee, vanilla, sisal, raffia, rice, and *pois du cap* are the most important. Other exports include processed foods, meat and fish, tobacco and cigarettes, minerals, hides and skins, and cloves. Export earnings rose during the 1960s as exports of rice, cloves, and coffee increased; there was, however, a decrease in the production of sisal and vanilla. The most important imports are processed foods and beverages, cement, gasoline, oils, paper, manufactured textiles, and metal products, including machinery and vehicles.

Foreign trade is overdependent upon France, which receives 36 percent of Madagascar's exports and supplies 52 percent of its imports. The remaining trade is carried out mainly with the United States, the European Economic Community, Senegal, and Japan. Exports are more varied than those of other African countries, but a number of them, such as coffee, cloves, vanilla, and sisal, are endangered by world overproduction or by the manufacture of synthetic substitutes. There is virtually no trade with the countries of eastern and southern Africa.

Management of the economy. *The private sector.* The economy is primarily one of free capitalist enterprise, with a slowly increasing governmental participation. Despite an increasing diversification of foreign interests, most of the important businesses are French. There are less than a dozen large firms engaged in the export–import trade, banking, mining, electricity, and water supply. An intricate network of diverse smaller operations and subsidiaries is connected with these large firms.

The public sector. Within the limits of its means, including the foreign aid received mainly from France, the government has put its main thrust into the development of improved transportation and communications systems and of an improved agricultural sector. Producers' and consumers' cooperatives, Animation Rurale (a rural development program), and state farms pioneer new methods and try to extend and increase the commercial production of rice, cattle, coffee, oil palm, cotton, and silk. The producers' cooperatives collect and process most of the rice crop, while the national consumers' cooperative has established retail stores in most towns.

Taxation. Taxation is mainly indirect and is largely derived from various customs, import, and export duties. The various excise taxes are also important. Direct taxes take the form of taxes on company income, registration fees, stamp duties, and personal taxes; the latter bear heavily on the peasants.

Trade unions and employer associations. The unions represent a total of about 20,000 employees, most of whom hold office jobs or work in industry. The largest and most extensive trade union is the Union des Syndicats de Madagascar, followed by the Union des Travailleurs Malgaches; there are also two smaller unions.

The main employers' association is the Union des Syndicats d'Intérêt Économique de Madagascar, which represents over 2,700 enterprises. There are also more than 20 other syndicates that represent 1,000 enterprises.

Contemporary economic policies. The declared policy of the government is one of gradual grass roots (rural) development of a mixed economy, with increasing state participation and with strong emphasis on cooperative organization. Private and foreign capital investment receive continued encouragement as well as guarantees from the government, despite the demands of opposition parties for a policy of nationalization. The predominant reliance for aid is upon France and the European Economic Community, while lesser amounts are received from the United States and the United Nations. Nationalist China, India, Israel, Italy, and Switzerland have all provided aid for smaller projects, and there are plans for South African investment in tourist facilities.

Problems and prospects. Despite improved crop production, the economy seems to have been caught in an impasse since the late 1960s. Urban unemployment was increasing in the early 1970s. The population and the civil service continue to grow rapidly; at the same time there is serious inflation and a mounting trade deficit. The First Five-Year Plan of 1964 to 1969 realized less than a 2 percent growth rate for internal production, instead of the projected 5 percent per annum. The first serious austerity budget was adopted in 1970. Hopeful prospects of finding oil deposits off the east coast provide one indication of a possible solution to current economic problems. There is also a good potential for tourism; there are many unused beaches.

Transportation. Transport facilities are primarily on the plateau and along the east coast. Service is rudimentary on the western half of the island, although the country's best natural harbours are located there.

Roads. The country has about 5,300 miles (8,500 kilometres) of roads, of which only 2,000 miles are paved. Roads down the eastern escarpment and across the western coastal strip, as well as minor roads everywhere, become impassable during the wet season.

The main paved road runs south from Tananarive to Ambalavao, after which it continues part of the way to Ihosy, where the main dirt road forks southwest to Tuléar and southeast to Fort-Dauphin. A paved road runs for a short distance east from Tananarive toward Tamatave and another part of the way west to Arivonimamo. Other road connections from Tananarive to the west coast, to the entire northern half of the island, and down the eastern escarpment are poor and rapidly become impassable after rain.

Railways. There are about 550 miles (880 kilometres) of railway track. Two railways connect the plateau with the east coast; they run from Tananarive to Tamatave and from Fianarantsoa to Manakara. A plateau route

Trading partners (margin note)

Foreign aid (margin note)

from Tananarive south to Antsirabe was being connected to Fianarantsoa in the early 1970s.

Port facilities and waterways. The main port is Tamatave, which has a fine deepwater harbour, equipped with quay berths and directly linked to Tananarive by rail as well as by road. Majunga is second in importance but is only accessible to small ships of shallow draft; it has considerable dhow traffic with the Comoro Islands. Diégo-Suarez has one of the finest natural harbours in the world but is as yet too remote from the main centres of economic activity; it contains the French naval base, arsenal, and dry dock and also has a small commercial port. Fort-Dauphin also has a small port, and there are small wharves and minor facilities at Tuléar, Manakara, Morondava, Analalava, and Vohemar. The coastal lagoons and swamps of the Canal des Pangalanes on the east coast, linked by artificial channels where necessary, provide a waterway 400 miles long.

Air transport. The island has about 50 airports. The main international airport is at Ivato, near Tananarive, and some international flights make secondary landings at Majunga. Madagascar is mainly served from abroad by Air France, but there are a few flights by South African Airways and Alitalia. Air Madagascar, the national airline, is technically assisted by Air France and mainly operates internal routes.

ADMINISTRATION AND SOCIAL CONDITIONS

The structure of government. *Constitutional framework.* Madagascar has been an autonomous republic within the French Community since 1958 and, as the Malagasy Republic, received its independence from France in 1960. The head of state is the president. Until 1972, the legislature was bicameral, and the National Assembly consisted of 107 members elected by universal suffrage for five years; the Senate had 54 members—one-third of whom were nominated by the president and council of ministers, and two-thirds of whom were elected by the representatives of provincial, municipal, and rural councils—serving six-year terms. In 1972, however, parliamentary rule was suspended and full executive powers given to the army chief of staff, which formed a cabinet composed of officers of the armed forces.

Regional, state, and local government. The country is divided into six provinces, each under a *chef de province* ("provincial head"), and is further subdivided into 18 prefectures, 91 subprefectures, and 692 cantons (small administrative divisions). The 36 urban and 735 rural communes are divided among the 692 cantons, with some cantons containing several communes. The cantons are further subdivided first into *quartiers* (districts) and then into villages. The *chefs de province*, prefects, and subprefects are transferable civil servants, while the *chefs de canton* ("canton heads") are administratively appointed but are usually local people. The district and village heads are locally chosen by informal elections. They are responsible for collecting taxes, maintaining order, and transmitting government instructions. The urban communes have their own budgets, and their elected councillors, in turn, elect mayors and deputy mayors. Each province also has an elected council, which exercises a degree of financial responsibility and autonomy.

The political process. The elections of district and village heads are conducted entirely on a local basis when circumstances require them to be held. Before 1972 municipal elections for the urban communes were nationally coordinated, as were the elections for the National Assembly and the presidency. Adult franchise is available to all mentally fit, noncriminal male and female citizens. Voting participation in the early 1970s was extremely high in and around Tananarive, where the opposition is strong; elsewhere, participation is low.

Political parties

The Parti Social Démocrate (Social Democratic Party or PSD) has held power since the attainment of independence in 1960. It has a national following but is regarded as particularly representative of the coastal districts. The main opposition party, Ankoton'ny Kongresi'ny Fahaleovantenan Madagasikara (AKFM) or Parti du Congrès de l'Indépendance de Madagascar (Congress Party of the Independence of Madagascar), is believed particularly to represent the plateau region and the Merina people. A third party is Monima (Mouvement National pour l'Indépendance de Madagascar). AFKM supports a more radical form of Socialism than does the PSD, while Monima favours the Chinese Communist position.

Much of the support for the PSD in the vast rural areas is attributed to strong administrative encouragement. Mass discontent has not been directly manifested at the ballot box but obliquely and anonymously in devastating reactions, such as the widespread burning of forests—a tactic that has harmed the previously successful reforestation program. In 1972 mass demonstrations by thousands of students and workers erupted in Tananarive and Tamatave. Pres. Philibert Tsiranana, who had led the country since independence, dissolved his government and handed power over to the army. Subsequent events seemed to presage a renewal of Merina influence in the central government and a corresponding increase in the power of Monima.

Justice. The former Merina state that ruled the island throughout the 19th century had an elaborate system of laws, courts, and justice. The present Malagasy legal system, however, is based upon French codes and practices, and most judges and magistrates have had French training. French citizens (both of French and Malagasy origin) have certain special rights in relation to France and the French Community. There is a supreme court, an appeal court, criminal tribunals, and tribunals of first instance; there is also a criminal code, a code of criminal procedure, and a code of civil procedure. The customary law of Imerina and other ethnic groups is taken into account by state magistrates when judging marriage, family, land, and inheritance cases.

The armed forces. The army, until 1972, had played no direct role in political life, although the regime in power was strengthened by the presence of French army contingents. The Malagasy Army consists of about 3,700 men, and there is an 8,000-man security force. Under a defense agreement the French also maintain armed forces in Tananarive and a naval base at Diégo-Suarez. The United States has a satellite tracking station near Tananarive. Officers of the Malagasy Army and security forces are trained in France.

The social sector. *Educational services.* About half of the school-age children attend classes. In the early 1970s there were over 1,000,000 students in over 6,000 primary schools, about 100,000 students in over 500 secondary schools, and more than 2,000 in teacher training colleges. The University of Madagascar had almost 4,000 students, of whom the overwhelming number were Malagasy. The level both of school attendance and of educational attainment is higher on the plateau than in the coastal areas. Protestant and Roman Catholic missions have been providing education since the 19th century, and the missions still educate a majority of the school children, although the government now maintains official schools at all levels. In the main towns there are also privately run schools, catering to those unable to enter either government or mission schools.

The role of mission schools

Health and welfare services. Malagasy doctors began to practice Western medicine in 1880; there is now a medical school in Tananarive. The health system includes principal and secondary hospitals, dispensaries, and medical centres. Medical personnel includes more than 600 doctors, as well as pharmacists, dentists, midwives, social assistants, visiting nurses, and health assistants.

Hospitals and specialists are mainly in the towns, apart from some rural hospitals run by Christian missions. Health insurance and other social benefits are mainly available to better paid and professional elements among the employed population.

Housing. Houses are typically rectangular and are usually crowned with steeply angled roofs. In the rural areas, most houses are made of either mud and wattle or woven matting supported by poles. In the eastern forest they are built of interlaced split bamboo and are thatched with palm, while in the south, overlapping wooden planks are used for the walls. In the urban areas, upper income housing consists of two- or three-story homes surrounded by wide balconies supported by brick columns and crowned with steep tiled roofs. Lower income housing is constructed of earth blocks and thatched roofing.

The French colonial government provided housing for the more senior civil servants, and the Malagasy government has continued the practice. The government-sponsored housing authority conducts research into design, materials, and methods of production and is endeavouring to promote inexpensive urban housing, but the problem of overcrowding is expected to increase with continued urban growth. The existence of a well-established craft of house construction, however, may successfully alleviate housing pressures without resorting to the use of imported materials or relying upon foreign enterprise.

The police. Detachments of police are stationed at the headquarters of each province, prefecture, and subprefecture, as well as in Tananarive. They have general responsibility for keeping the peace, enforcing laws, and apprehending criminals. The whole force is under unified command and falls within the responsibility of the ministry of the interior.

Wages and the cost of living. The size of the labour force employed for wages varies between 150,000 and 200,000; average monthly cash wages are higher in commerce and transportation than they are in industry and agriculture. While the average annual income dropped during the 1960s to about U.S. $95, the prices for such important commodities as rice, flour, charcoal, and meat rose sharply.

Health conditions. The extension of health services is largely credited for the steady population increase. Infant mortality remains high, but infant deaths from malaria, which is endemic all over the island, have been cut by half. Debilitating parasitic diseases, such as schistosomiasis, an infection of the bladder or intestines, remain serious and are hard to control since their breeding grounds are the irrigated rice fields and the streams that feed them. Venereal disease is also widespread, especially in its incipient form. Rural diet is often deficient in protein and some vitamins.

Prevalent diseases

Social and economic divisions. Traditionally, society was divided into three castes—the nobles, the freemen, and the former slaves and their descendants. These social distinctions are no longer strict and are manifest only on ceremonial occasions, such as weddings and funerals. They do, however, form the basis of other economic and social distinctions. During the 19th century, the Merina élite conquered the island, established themselves as rulers, and adopted Protestant Christianity; in the late 1800s, some also became Roman Catholics. Under French rule in the 20th century, the Merina retained their supremacy in education, business, and the professions, while the remainder of the population retained its sense of "difference" from the dominant peoples and adopted Roman Catholicism.

A further distinction is made between the peoples of the plateau and those of the coast, who are called *cotiers*. The coastal peoples feel deprived of the education, power, and wealth that is concentrated on the plateau. Since independence, the government has been composed of *cotiers*, and a conscious effort has been made to keep the Merina elite of the plateau from power.

CULTURAL LIFE AND INSTITUTIONS

The cultural milieu. The culture is basically Indonesian. Arabic and Islāmic contributions include an intricate system of divination, or *sikidy*, and calendrical features, such as the names of the days of the week, which are particularly significant in their application to markets. The coastal areas of the west, north, and south might be expected to show African cultural elements, but, apart from some Bantu words, these are often difficult to identify conclusively.

The state of the arts. The conquest of the plateau peoples by the French and their assimilation of Western values has deprived them of most of their traditional institutions. Western dance and musical instruments have been adapted to Malagasy rhythms. The tube zither, the

conch, and the cone drum are of Indonesian origin, while other types of drums and animal horns suggest African influence. Folk music has been retained, but much of the singing is of Western church hymns and chants adapted to the distinctive Malagasy musical style. Social and religious life centres upon the church congregation, and the cultural emphasis on ancestral tombs is now largely expressed in Christian terms. More time, money, and care is spent on building tombs than houses. The dead are always brought back to their ancestral tombs, however long or far away they have spent their lives. Tombs are opened every few years, the corpses taken out and carried in procession with much ceremony, then replaced rewrapped in new shrouds, which are still woven from locally produced silk, coloured with natural, herbal dyes.

The cult of the dead

The male peasants wear cloth trousers with tunics reaching to the knees. Women wear cloth dresses but wrap a silk cloth under one arm and over the other shoulder, even when wearing Western fashions.

Most of the coastal peoples have retained their traditional customs. Funeral practices are similar to those of the plateau, with local variations of detail. In the eastern forests men wear shorts rather than trousers, and many still wear the short tunic that is woven from raffia fibres. In the far south some older men wear a homespun silk cloth that is wrapped around the waist and between the legs, but most have adopted imported cotton clothes.

The Mahafaly have a remarkable wood-carving industry, and their tombs of coloured stones and carved wooden posts are the most beautiful on the island. The Betsileo also have a thriving wood-carving industry, making inlaid furniture of valuable hardwoods. They also produce ornamental cloths of very finely woven raffia and have become specialists in the production of coloured straw hats. Betsileo and Merina women have become experts in French-style embroidery, sewing, and dressmaking.

Handicrafts

The Malagasy language is very rich in proverbs, and there is now an extensive written literature including poetry, legend, history, and scholarly works, as well as contemporary themes. Literary production is aided by an excellent printing industry, for which the Merina have shown a flair since learning it from the London Missionary Society in the 1820s. The peoples of the southeast still preserve their manuscripts in Arabic script with great reverence; few can be more than 200 years old, although some may be copies of much earlier manuscripts.

Cultural institutions. Since 1960 a number of new seasonal festivals have been promoted, including the Festival of Rice, the Festival of the Trees, the Festival of the Party, and Independence Day. The ministries of cultural affairs and of traditional arts encourage the blending of old and new cultural expressions. Towns, churches, schools, and private groups hold concerts or dances, and in the cities there are cultural associations based on the members' home districts.

The main libraries and museums, located in Tananarive, include the Bibliothèque Nationale (which has a good general collection and extensive coverage of Madagascar), the library of the Académie Malgache (containing a valuable collection of works on Madagascar), the university library, and the university museum (containing especially interesting collections from recent archaeological and ethnographic expeditions). The Organisation pour la Recherche Scientifique et Technique d'Outre Mer (a French agency) houses the main museum collection of Malagasy culture and archaeology, as well as natural science collections and a zoo composed of lemurs and other animals specific to Madagascar.

The press and broadcasting. There are over 200 newspapers and magazines published in Malagasy and in French. The main press publications are the *Courrier de Madagascar*, a daily; the *Bulletin d'Information*, a daily; *La Lumière* and *l'Info-Madagascar*, both weeklies; *Le Lien*, a monthly bulletin of statistics; the *Bulletin de Madagascar*, a monthly economic review; and *Revue de Madagascar*, published three times monthly.

There are four radio services. The two major services broadcast in Malagasy, and the third most important station broadcasts in French. The fourth station is an international service that broadcasts programs in French and English to Africa, the Far East, and Latin America. The Tananarive area has daily television service in French, organized by the French Bureau of Radiophonic Cooperation.

PROSPECTS FOR THE FUTURE

Madagascar desperately needs to raise its productivity. Population growth is very rapid, but no official anxiety is expressed, on the grounds that large areas of the country are underpopulated—especially the west, south, and north. It is much more likely, however, that continued population growth will lead to a massive increase of unemployed and underemployed immigrants to Tananarive and other cities. The west can be developed for ranching, but this does not require a large labour force. The growers of irrigated rice on the plateau, although they could be assisted further by technological improvements adapted to local conditions, nevertheless have a very highly developed system of mixed farming, including the raising of cattle, pigs, poultry, and fish, combined with a very hard-working tradition. It would be disastrous to disrupt this pattern by ill-considered interference. Communications need considerable improvement, and much more could be done in processing and exporting the varied temperate- and tropical-fruit crop. Tourism and offshore oil exploitation offer the most promising future possibilities. There may be a temptation to exploit the rivalry between the Soviet Union, on the one hand, and the United States, the United Kingdom, France, and South Africa, on the other, for control of the Indian Ocean—especially since the Suez Canal has been closed or partially superseded by the use of giant tankers and merchant vessels plying directly around the Cape of Good Hope.   (Ai.S.)

BIBLIOGRAPHY

Official publications: MALAGASY REPUBLIC, INSTITUT NATIONAL DE LA STATISTIQUE ET DE LA RECHERCHE ECONOMIQUE, *Inventaire socio-économique de Madagascar, 1960–1965*, 2 vol. (1966), information on social and economic conditions; *Recensements urbains: Ambositra, Ambalavao, Mananjary, Manakara, Farafangana* (1966), special surveys carried out in the main cities in addition to the general census; *Recensement Industriel* (1967), a survey of industries; SERVICE DE STATISTIQUE ET DES ETUDES SOCIO-ECONOMIQUES, *Population de Madagascar au 1ᵉʳ janvier 1965* (1966), a detailed compendium of demographic information; *Enquête agricole* (1966), details of agricultural production by crops and regions; MADAGASCAR, SERVICE GEOGRAPHIQUE, *Madagascar et Archipel des Comores*, 1:500,000 (1947–48).
General references: The *Antananarivo Annual and Madagascar Magazine*, 24 vol. (1875–78, 1881–1900), a journal in English produced by members of the London Missionary Society in Madagascar, containing unique articles on history, custom, belief, fauna, and flora; *Bulletin de l'Académie Malgache* (1905–), the main scholarly journal of Madagascar; MAURICE BLOCH, *Placing the Dead: Tombs, Ancestral Villages and Kinship Organization in Madagascar* (1971), a detailed ethnographic account of the numerically and culturally dominant Merina people; ANDRE DANDOUAU, *Manuel de géographie de Madagascar*, 10th ed. (1960), a useful general geography; HUBERT J. DESCHAMPS, *Les Migrations intérieures passées et présentes à Madagascar* (1959), the only detailed study of internal population movements, and with SUZANNE VIANES, *Les Malgaches du Sud-Est* (1959), an ethnographic account of the southeastern peoples through whom Arabic scripts and elements of Islāmic belief and practice influenced Madagascar; GUILLAUME GRANDIDIER, *Bibliographie de Madagascar*, 3 vol. (1905–57), an authoritative, cumulative bibliography, and with ALFRED GRANDIDIER, *Histoire physique, naturelle et politique de Madagascar* and *Ethnographie de Madagascar* (1908–28), two works that represent the most monumental attempt to present a complete account of the natural history and culture of Madagascar and its peoples; NIGEL HESELTINE, *Madagascar* (1971), a recent general study of the land and people; *Madagascar* ("Les Guides Bleus," 1968), information on all towns and places of interest; AIDAN SOUTHALL (ed.), "Kinship, Descent, and Residence in Madagascar," *Am. Anthrop.*, 73:144–208 (1971), a comparative analysis of variations in Malagasy kinship and family structure; MARCELLE URBAIN-FAUBLEE, *L'Art Malgache* (1963), a publication devoted to Malagasy art.

(Ai.S./Je.D.)

Madagascar, History of

Although the Malagasy people are of mixed African and Indonesian ancestry, their language is basically Indonesian, with a few words of Bantu. The Indonesian element probably migrated to Madagascar in successive waves during the 1st millennium AD; one hypothesis is that they came by way of the African coast and reached the island after mingling with Africans. Archaeological evidence indicates that these people were living on the island in the 10th century.

Madagascar to 1810. After the 14th century, small groups of Muslims, coming perhaps from the eastern coast of Africa, set up trading colonies in the north; others, mingling with Africans, founded in the southeast the kingdoms of Zafi-Raminia and Antemoro. The settlement of the Indonesian Merina (or Hova) in the central-plateau region probably occurred at the same time.

Early European contacts. Madagascar is mentioned in the writings of Marco Polo, but the first European known to have visited the island is Diogo Dias, a Portuguese navigator, in 1500. It was called the Isle of St. Lawrence by the Portuguese, who frequently raided Madagascar during the 16th century, attempting to destroy the Muslim settlements. Other European nations also moved in; in 1643 the French established Fort-Dauphin in the southeast and maintained it until 1674. One of their governors, Étienne de Flacourt, wrote the first substantial description of the island. In the late 17th and early 18th centuries, Madagascar was frequented by European pirates (among them Capt. William Kidd) who preyed upon shipping in the Indian Ocean.

In the 18th century, the Mascareigne Islands to the east were colonized by the French with the help of Malagasy slaves. Two attempts at fortified settlements failed, one at Fort-Dauphin by the comte de Modave, the other at Antongil Bay by Baron Benyowski; however, French trading settlements prospered, notably at Tamatave.

The kingdoms. In Madagascar as on the African mainland, new states arose between 1500 and 1800, and many of them engaged in the traffic in slaves and firearms with the Europeans. The traditional clan organization of the Malagasy gave way to a number of autocratic kingdoms. In the 17th century, the southern Sakalava state spread northward into the sparsely populated plains of the far west. Antemoro chieftains founded kingdoms in the interior, among the Tanala and the Betsileo peoples. In the 18th century, the short-lived Betsimisaraka kingdom was founded on the east coast by Ratsimilaho, a half-English Malagasy.

The Merina kingdom was founded toward the end of the 16th century in the swampy Ikopa Valley in the centre of the island. Tananarive became its capital. In the 18th century, Merina was divided among four warring kings. One of them, Andrianampoinimerina, who reigned 1787–1810, reunited the kingdom about 1797. He gave it uniform laws and administration, and sold slaves to the French on the coast, using the guns he got in return to conquer his neighbours, the Betsileo. Under Andrianampoinimerina, Merina society was divided into a ruling noble class (*Andriana*), a class of freemen (*Hova*), and a slave group (*Andero*). The name Hova was sometimes used for all Merinas. At his death, he left to his son Radama a single political ambition: "The sea will be the boundary of my rice field" (*i.e.*, of his kingdom).

The kingdom of Madagascar. *Formation of the kingdom (1810–61).* Radama I (1810–28) allied himself with Sir Robert Farquhar, the British governor of the nearby island of Mauritius. In order to prevent reoccupation of the east coast by the French, Farquhar supported Radama's annexation of the area by supplying him with weapons and advisers and giving him the title "king of Madagascar." At the same time, Radama agreed to cooperate with Britain's new campaign to end the slave trade. In 1817 he took Tamatave. From then on, he launched yearly expeditions against the coastal populations. In this way, he conquered almost the entire east coast, the northern part of the island, and most of the two large Sakalava kingdoms. Only the south and a part of the west remained

Merina expansion

independent. The French retained no more than the small island of Sainte-Marie. In addition, Radama invited in European workmen; the London Missionary Society spread Christianity and influenced the adoption of a Latin alphabet for the Malagasy language. Radama died prematurely in 1828; he was succeeded by his wife, Ranavalona I, who reversed his policy of Europeanization. Under the influence of traditional beliefs, she expelled Christian missionaries and persecuted Malagasy converts. A very few Europeans, notably the Frenchman Jean Laborde, maintained external trade and local manufacture, but eventually they also were expelled. The British and French launched an expedition against Ranavalona, but were repulsed at Tamatave in 1845. By the end of her reign (1861), Madagascar was isolated from European influence. She made several unsuccessful attempts to subdue the island's independent areas.

Outside influences (1861–95). Ranavalona died in 1861. Her son, Radama II, readmitted the foreigners; English Protestants and French Roman Catholics vied for supremacy; businessmen obtained excessive concessions. This policy led to Radama's overthrow by the Merina oligarchy (1863). The head of the army, Rainilaiarivony, a Hova, became prime minister and remained in power by marrying three queens in succession: Rasoherina, Ranavalona II, and Ranavalona III. He embarked on a program of modernization; in 1869 he caused Protestantism to be adopted and suppressed the Malagasy religion. European-style ministries were created and governors set up in the provinces. Villages were supervised by former soldiers. Education was declared obligatory under the direction of the Christian missions. A code of laws was worked out that combined ancient customs with Western innovations, such as monogamy. After 1880, France revived its claims to Madagascar. The French had installations at Nosy Be, and began to extend their influence over the Sakalava. In 1883 the first "Franco-Merina" War broke out, terminating in 1885 with an ambiguous treaty: France was given the right to maintain a settlement at Diégo-Suarez, and a resident at Tananarive, but the prime minister temporarily managed to avoid the institution of a protectorate. The succeeding period was marked by disorder and internal strife. In 1890 the British recognized Madagascar as a French protectorate, removing the last barrier to France's control over the island. When Rainilaiarivony refused to submit, France decided to use force. In January 1895, French troops landed at Majunga. The opposing Merina forces were not well armed and were poorly organized. Moreover, the Merina were not supported by their subject peoples; some of the Sakalava even assisted in the French offensive. Once they had worked their way out of the swamps of the coastal areas, the invaders formed a mobile column which, on September 30, 1895, after the only significant battle of the war, occupied Tananarive. The prime minister was exiled. The queen signed a treaty recognizing the protectorate and was maintained on the throne as a figurehead.

The French period. *The colonial period (1896–1945).* The occupation soon extended to the entire part of the island conquered by the Merina. But in Imerina itself, armed bands (the Menalamba, or "red togas") resisted modernization and French rule. The French Parliament voted the annexation of the island on August 6, 1896, and sent Gen. J.S. Gallieni first as military commander, then as governor general. Slavery was abolished. Gallieni established military posts in Merina that gradually put down the insurrection; he subdued the oligarchy by putting two hostile ministers to death and sent the queen into exile on February 27, 1897. In 1898 the old Merina kingdom was pacified; Gallieni then undertook the difficult task of subjugating the independent peoples. Two insurrections, in the northwest (1898) and in the southeast (1904), were quickly put down. When he left the island in 1905, unification had been achieved and the organization of the government had a solid base. The Merina governors had been replaced by French administrators with leaders taken from local peoples. The teaching of French in the schools was made compulsory.

Customs duties favoured French products, though Malagasy enterprise was also encouraged. The Tamatave-Tananarive railroad was begun, roads were built, and a modern health service was inaugurated.

The economic development of the island continued under Gallieni's successors. The railroad and its branch lines were completed in 1913. A second line, the Fianarantsoa-Manakara, was finished in 1935. Automobile roads increased after 1920, airlines after 1936. The seaports were built up and equipped, as were the cities. Loans, contracted in France, supplemented the resources of the colony.

Exports were confined to agricultural products and raw material for industry. Rice, manioc, rubber, raffia, meat, and graphite predominated at first. Between World Wars I and II, coffee, vanilla, cloves, and tobacco, introduced by the Europeans and then taken up by native planters, became more important. Cultivation of these products was sustained by subsidies during the depression of the 1930s. Three-quarters of all trade was with France. From 1900 to 1940 the population rose from 2,500,000 to 4,000,000; internal migrations populated the far west. Material aspects of life became westernized, especially in the cities. Half the population became Christianized.

Political progress lagged, however. In 1915 a nationalist secret society, the vvs (Vy Vato Sakelika), was outlawed by the government. In 1920 a teacher, Jean Ralaimongo, launched a campaign in the press to give the Malagasy French citizenship (they were classed as "subjects") and to make Madagascar a French *département*. When France failed to respond to the demand for assimilation, the emancipation movement turned toward nationalism. Still weak, it suspended all activity during World War II. In 1940 Madagascar, though hesitant at first, rallied to the Vichy government. Then came a blockade, occupation by the British and South Africans (1942), and finally a return to Free France. But these events, added to the unfavourable economic situation, increased nationalist sentiment among the Malagasy.

The French Union (1946–1958). In the elections of 1945, two Malagasy nationalists were elected to the French parliament. The constitution of 1946, creating the French Union, made Madagascar an Overseas Territory of the French Republic, with representatives to the Paris assemblies and a local assembly at Tananarive. Six provincial assemblies were created later. The political struggle irrupted in violence on March 30, 1947, with an insurrection in eastern Madagascar. The leaders of the MDRM (Mouvement Démocratique de la Rénovation Malgache), including the three deputies, were outlawed. More than 11,000 lives were lost before the revolt was ended.

A period of political inactivity followed. In 1954, when the ministry of Pierre Mendès-France was in power in France, the nationalist movement was revived. After the "Overseas Territories Law" of 1956 gave Madagascar an executive elected by the local assembly, Vice Premier Philibert Tsiranana founded the PSD (Parti Social Démocrate), which, though most of its members were non-Merina from the coastal areas, offered to cooperate with the Merina in a spirit of unity.

In 1958 the government of French President Charles de Gaulle agreed to let the overseas territories decide their own fate. In a referendum on September 28, Madagascar voted for autonomy within the French Community 77 percent to 22 percent; the opposing votes were mainly Merina. On October 14, 1958, the autonomous Malagasy Republic was proclaimed; Tsiranana headed the provisional government.

The Malagasy Republic. The opposition regrouped under the name of AKFM (Ankoton'ny Kongresy ny-Fahaleovantena Malagasy), which included the Protestant Merina dissidents and Communists. Tananarive was this party's stronghold; it also had some support in the provinces but, owing to the electoral system established by the PSD, held only three seats in the legislature.

The PSD also settled the provincial question: local assemblies continued in existence but executive power in the provinces was vested in a minister delegated by the central government. Tsiranana was elected president of

The French invasion (margin note)

Malagasy nationalism (margin note)

the republic. He obtained independence for the republic on June 26, 1960, but maintained military, financial, and cultural ties with France. Madagascar was admitted to the United Nations, and on July 19 Tsiranana brought the three former MDRM deputies back from France, and two of them entered his government.

The PSD remained in power through the first decade of independence. Successive development plans, inspired, according to Tsiranana, by a "grass roots socialism," aimed at improving the lot of the peasantry. The increase in agricultural production through fertilizers has permitted a rise in population from 5,500,000 to 7,000,000 with no adverse effects on the economy.

In foreign policy, the bond with France remained strong, and close relations were established with the United States, West Germany, Taiwan, South Africa, and other anti-Communist powers. Measures were taken to halt an influx of immigrants from India. In the Organization of African Unity, Madagascar plays a conservative role. In 1971, the poor state of Tsiranana's health made him yield to pressure to modify the government, and a rebellion in the south was quashed without difficulty.

BIBLIOGRAPHY. General histories include: HUBERT DESCHAMPS, *Histoire de Madagascar*, 3rd ed. (1965); and GUILLAUME GRANDIDIER, *Bibliographie de Madagascar*, 4 vol. (1905–57). For the Traditional Period, see ALFRED GRANDIDIER (ed.), *Collection des ouvrages anciens concernant Madagascar*, 9 vol. (1903–20; see esp. vol. 8 and 9 for the works of Flacourt); GUILLAUME GRANDIDIER, *Histoire politique et coloniale de Madagascar*, 3 vol., the last in collaboration with RAYMOND DECARY (1947–58); and R.K. KENT, *Early Kingdoms in Madagascar, 1500–1700* (1970). Information on the 19th century may be found in WILLIAM ELLIS, *History of Madagascar*, 2 vol. (1838), *Three Visits to Madagascar* (1858), *Madagascar Revisited* (1867); and R.P. MALZAC, *Histoire du royaume Hova* (1912); on the 20th century, HUBERT DESCHAMPS and P. CHAUVET, *Gallieni pacificateur* (1949); and VIRGINIA THOMPSON and RICHARD ADLOFF, *The Malagasy Republic, Madagascar Today* (1965).

(H.J.D.)

Madhya Pradesh

Madhya Pradesh, with an area of 171,220 square miles (443,459 square kilometres), is the largest of the states of the Republic of India, but, with a population of about 41,651,000 at the time of the 1971 census, is only the sixth most populous. As its name implies—*madhya* means central and *pradesh* means region—it is situated in the heart of India. It has no coastline and no international frontier. The state capital is Bhopāl.

Boundary changes in 1947

When India became independent in 1947, the British Indian Central Provinces, together with Berār, were grouped together to form Madhya Pradesh. Boundary changes followed: the old Central Indian Agency (divided after independence into Madhya Bhārat and Vindhya Pradesh) was added to Madhya Pradesh, and eight Marathi-speaking districts were detached from it and joined to Bombay (later Mahārāshtra) state. The present boundaries of the state were defined in 1956. Madhya Pradesh is bordered by the states of Rājasthān to the northwest, Uttar Pradesh to the north, Bihār to the northeast, Orissa to the east, Andhra Pradesh and Mahārāshtra to the south, and Gujarāt to the west. (For historical background, see INDIAN SUBCONTINENT, HISTORY OF THE.)

History. The history of Madhya Pradesh extends to the remote past. Several remains of prehistoric cultures, including rock paintings and stone and metal implements, have been found in various parts of the state.

One of the earliest states that existed in the territory of the present Madhya Pradesh was Avanti, which had Ujjain as its capital. This was part of the Mauryan Empire (4th–3rd century BC); it was later known as Mālwa and was situated in the western part of the state.

Among the various dynasties that ruled part or the whole of Madhya Pradesh between the 2nd century BC and the 16th century AD were the Śuṅgas (185 to 73 BC), who ruled in eastern Mālwa; the Andhras (Sātavāhanas; 1st century BC–3rd century AD); the Kṣatrapas (2nd–4th century AD), and the Nāgas (2nd–4th century AD). The whole of Madhya Pradesh lying north of the Narmada

River formed part of the Gupta Empire (4th–5th century AD) and was the scene of a power struggle against the Huns (a nomadic, pastoral people) in this area. Yaśodharman was an important Mālwa 6th century king who wrested power from the Huns and established his rule. Mālwa was annexed by the emperor of northern India, Harṣa, during the first part of the 7th century.

The 10th century was a period of confusion: of the various dynasties, the Kalacuris ruled over the Narmada Valley and some other regions; their contemporaries were the Paramāras at Dhār in what is now the western region, the Kacchwāhās at Gwalior in the north, and the Candellas at Khajurāho, about 100 miles southeast of Jhānsi. Later the Tomaras ruled at Gwalior and the tribal Gonds ruled over several districts.

The period of sultanate rule

The Muslim invasion of the area took place in the 11th century, and Gwalior was conquered. The Hindu domains there were incorporated into the Delhi sultanate in 1231 by the sultan Iltutmish. Later the Khaljī sultans of Delhi overran Mālwa, which was subsequently annexed into the Mughal Empire by Akbar (1556 to 1605), the greatest of the Mughal emperors. Marāthā power extended into Mālwa at the beginning of the 18th century and a large part of what is now Madhya Pradesh had come under Marāthā rule by 1760. With the defeat of Peshwas (hereditary Marāthā prime ministers who centralized Marāthā rule) in 1761, the Sindhia (Marāthā) dynasty was established at Gwalior in the north and the Holkar dynasty (also Marāthā) at Indore in the southwest.

In 1817–18 the "Saugor-Nerbudda territories," as they were known, were ceded to the British; 43 years later this area and certain other districts were grouped into the Central Provinces, Berār being added in 1903. On the north and west, the Central India Agency was formed in 1854, with Mālwa, Bundelkhand, and Baghelkhand as the main units. Subsequent territorial changes were as described earlier in this article.

The landscape. *Relief.* Forested hills with steep slopes, extensive plateaus, and river valleys characterize the physiography of Madhya Pradesh. The state forms part of the Deccan Plateau and includes the Vindhya and Kaimur ranges in the west and north, which in places are 1,500 feet above sea level; the Sātpura-Mahādeo-Maikala ranges in the south have elevations of over 3,000 feet.

Northwest of the Vindhya Range is the Mālwa Plateau (1,500 to 2,000 feet). Other features are the Bundelkhand Plateau (north of the Vindhyas), the Madhya Bhārat Plateau in the extreme northwest, the Baghelkhand Plateau in the northeast, the Chhattīsgarh Basin in the east, and the Bastar Hills in the extreme southeast.

The rivers

Madhya Pradesh is the source region of some of the most important peninsular rivers: the Narmada, the Tāpti, the Mahānadi, and the Wainganga (a tributary of the Godāvari). Other rivers include the Chambal and other tributaries of the Yamuna and the Son (a tributary of the Ganges).

Soils. Fertile black soils are found in the Mālwa Plateau, in the Narmada Valley, and in parts of the Sātpuras. Eastern Madhya Pradesh has mainly red and yellow soils, which are sandy and less fertile than the black.

Climate. The climate is monsoonal (characterized by rain-bearing winds), with much of the rain falling from June to October. The season preceding the rains (March to May) is hot and dry, with temperatures everywhere higher than 85° F (29° C). The temperature falls during the rainy season. Winters are usually pleasant and largely dry. Generally speaking, rainfall decreases westward and northward, being 60 inches and above in the east and southeast, but less than 40 inches in the extreme west and less than 30 inches in the Chambal Valley.

Forests and wildlife. Some 33 percent of the state is under forest; about another 7 percent consists of permanent pasture or other grazing land. The main forested areas include the Vindhya-Kaimur ranges, the Sātpura-Maikala ranges, the Baghelkhand Plateau, and Bastar. Economically, the most important trees are teak, sal, bamboo, and salai (which yields a resin used for incense and as a medicine).

The forests abound in wild animals such as tigers, panthers, bison, chital (spotted deer), bears, wild buffalo, sambar (deer), and black bucks. Birds of many species are found. There are national parks at Kanha Kisli (famous for its swamp deer) and at Shivpuri; another park has been established at Bandhogarh (Rewa) and is known for its white tigers.

Population. A variety of tribes lives in Madhya Pradesh, including Bhīl, Baiga, Gond, Korku, Kol, Kamar, and Maria. At the 1961 census, 6,700,000—about 20 percent of the total population—were classified as members of scheduled tribes. In at least 12 districts, more than 25 percent of the total population was tribal. In Jhābua in the extreme west, the percentage was about 85. The average density of population in 1971 was 243 per square mile. The distribution of the rural population is very uneven, high densities being found in the Mahānadi Valley, the Upper Wainganga Valley, the Lower Chambal Valley, and in the Tīkamgarh, Rewa, Satna, and Jabalpur districts, as well as districts in scattered patches in western Madhya Pradesh. The provisional census figure for April 1, 1971, was almost 41,651,000, the growth rate being 2.5 percent per annum.

Hindi is the language most widely spoken. The state had in all 25,000,000 Hindi-speakers at the time of the 1961 census. Eastern Hindi, represented by the Awadhi, Bagheli, and Chhattisgarhi dialects, is spoken in Baghelkhand, Surguja, and Chhattīsgarh, and also in the Jabalpur and Mandla districts. Bundeli, a Western Hindi dialect, is spoken in the central districts of Madhya Pradesh and in Bundelkhand; Malvi, recognized by some as a Western Hindi dialect, is the speech of western Madhya Pradesh. The Bhīls speak Bhīli, and Gondi is spoken by nearly 1,000,000 people.

The second most important language is Marathi (1,260,000 speakers). Urdu, Oriya, Gujarati, and Punjabi are each spoken by over 100,000 persons. Also spoken are Telugu, Bengali, Tamil, and Malayalam.

Hindus in the state numbered 30,000,000 at the time of the 1961 census, representing 94 percent of the total population. There are, however, sizable minorities of Muslims, Jains, Christians, and Buddhists. There is also a small Sikh population.

At the time of the 1961 census, there were more than 70,000 inhabited villages in Madhya Pradesh. In the greater part of the state, the number of settlements within 100 square miles of rural area was 45 or less.

In 1971 there were 11 urban agglomerations, each with a population exceeding 100,000—Indore (572,600), Jabalpur (533,750), Gwalior (406,760), Bhopāl (392,100), Ujjain (209,100), Raipur (205,900), Durg-Bhilai (245,300), Sāgar (154,800), Bilāspur (130,800), Ratlām (118,600), and Burhānpur (105,350). These 11 cities, with a total population of more than 3,075,000, together had only 613,700 inhabitants at the beginning of the 20th century. Besides these cities, there were about 230 towns with populations of less than 100,000.

Administration. Executive power in the state is vested in the governor, and there is a council of ministers to aid and advise him in the exercise of his functions. The legislative assembly has 297 members.

The state has been divided into seven divisions and 43 districts. The divisions are Raipur (which in 1971 had a population of about 6,587,000); Bilāspur (about 5,041,000); Jabalpur (about 7,357,000); Rewa (about 5,405,000); Gwalior (about 4,350,000); Indore (about 7,752,000); and Bhopāl (about 5,159,000).

Since the State Panchayat (village council) Act of 1962, local administration has been entrusted to about 12,800 village *pañcāyat*s. In 1968 to 1969, there were more than 180 urban local authorities, including six municipal corporations.

Social conditions. *Health*. Malaria, which was formerly endemic throughout the state, has been largely eradicated. Diseases common in Madhya Pradesh are filariasis (a parasitic disease of the blood), tuberculosis, venereal diseases, leprosy, and dysentery. There were about 1,400 dispensaries and hospitals in the state in the early 1970s. There were also several eye hospitals, mental hospitals, tuberculosis hospitals, and sanatoriums as well as a number of clinics for the treatment of tuberculosis. There were antirabies inoculation centres in every district, and several venereal-disease clinics.

Education. About 22 percent of the state population was literate in 1971; but only about 5 percent had had any schooling in 1961. In 1967 to 1968 there were more than 44,000 schools, in which more than 4,000,000 students were receiving primary, middle, or high school education. There were universities at Sāgar, Jabalpur, Raipur, Ujjain, Gwalior, Indore, Rewa, Bhopāl, and Khairāgarh (music); these, together with some 400 colleges in the state, had nearly 136,000 students enrolled. Jabalpur also has an agricultural university.

Welfare. The government has undertaken several social-welfare schemes, including adult literacy classes, *yuvak* ("youth") and *mahila mandals* ("women's clubs"), and youth competitions. Grants-in-aid are given to social welfare and physical welfare institutions, while the Directorate of Panchayats and Social Welfare also runs rescue homes, beggars' homes, and leprosy clinics. Scholarships are granted to crippled children, and there is a scheme to give aid to old people needing care. The government also runs schools for the deaf and dumb. Welfare schemes for tribal groups include scholarships, free books, and hostel facilities.

Economy. *Agriculture*. Agriculture is the basis of Madhya Pradesh's economy, and 88 percent of the rural workers in the state were cultivators or agricultural labourers in 1971. At this time only 41 percent of the total area of the state was under cultivation, though the cultivated acreage had been increased during the 1950s and 1960s. The distribution of the sown area is very uneven, being governed by variations in topography, rainfall, and soils. The chief cultivated areas are found in the Chambal Valley, the Mālwa Plateau, the Rewa Plateau, and the Chhattīsgarh Plain. The Narmada Valley is another fertile area. Agriculture in Madhya Pradesh in the early 1970s was characterized by low productivity and the use of traditional methods of cultivation. Only about 7 percent of the sown area was irrigated. Irrigation was carried out chiefly by means of canals, tanks (village lakes or ponds), and wells; the main development in this respect had been through medium-sized or small projects executed during the various Indian five-year plans.

The most important crops are rice, wheat, *jowār* (sorghum), pulses (leguminous plants, such as peas, beans, or lentils), and peanuts (groundnuts). Rice is grown principally in the east, where rainfall is more than 50 inches; in western Madhya Pradesh wheat and *jowār* are more important. Other crops include linseed, sesame, and inferior millets which are grown in hilly areas.

Minerals and mining. Madhya Pradesh is rich in minerals, though these resources had not yet been fully exploited in the early 1970s. There are large reserves of coal and important deposits of iron ore, manganese ore, bauxite, limestone, dolomite, fireclay, and china clay. Diamond reserves at Panna were of particular interest.

Power resources. The state is well endowed with hydroelectric-power potentials. A pioneer hydroelectric scheme is the Chambal Valley project, which has been jointly developed with Rājasthān. There are also plans to harness the Narmada to produce hydroelectric power.

Industry. Before planned development took place, western Madhya Pradesh was the main industrial area—primarily producing consumer goods. The aim of the first three Indian five-year plans was to ensure balanced industrial development.

In the early 1970s there were more than 100 large- and medium-scale industries, important centres being Indore, Gwalior, Bhopāl, Ujjain, and Jabalpur. The only heavy industries were the iron and steel plant at Bhilai and the heavy electrical factory at Bhopāl, both government undertakings. Other government-owned factories include the newsprint factory at Nepa Nagar, the plant for the production of equipment for the Post and Telegraph Department at Jabalpur, and the ordnance factories at Katni and Jabalpur. As part of the planned development, industrial estates were established at Indore, Gwalior, Bhopāl,

Margin notes:
The tribal groups

Languages

Divisions and districts

The universities

Industrial centres

Raipur, Bhilai, and Jabalpur. In the private sector, there were cement works, paper mills, sugar mills, and textile mills (cotton, woollen, silk, and jute), besides flour, oil, and saw mills. There were also some general engineering industries.

There are more than 2,000 registered small-scale industrial units in the state. The handloom industry is flourishing, and various traditional crafts are practiced.

Transport and communications. In comparison with other Indian states, Madhya Pradesh is rather poorly served with transport and communications facilities. The main railroads that pass through the state were originally laid down to connect the ports of Madras, Bombay, and Calcutta with their hinterlands. Inadequate transport facilities have hindered the development of the state's rich resources.

There are both broad-gauge and narrow-gauge rail lines. The five main broad-gauge lines are Bombay–Delhi via Bhopāl, Bombay–Howrah (Calcutta) via Jabalpur, Bombay–Howrah (Calcutta) via Raipur, Madras–Delhi, and Bombay–Delhi via Ratlām.

The state is connected with Delhi and Bombay by air via Bhopāl and Indore.

The roads

In the early 1970s there were more than 23,000 miles of roads in the state, including about 1,600 miles of national highways. The latter connected Āgra with Bombay, Allāhābād with Nāgpur, Jhānsi with Lakhnādon, and Raipur with Vishākhapatnam. Many districts had fewer than ten miles of roads for every 100 square miles of territory. In the absence of a dense rail network, roads played an important part in the developing economy. The construction of bridges across the Narmada and other rivers has greatly helped the development of all-weather traffic routes.

Cultural life. There are a number of temples, fortresses, and cave works in Madhya Pradesh that have left fascinating evidence for historical studies, both on the early story of mankind in general and on local dynasties and kingdoms. One of the earliest monuments was the *stūpa* (Buddhist mound forming a memorial shrine) at Bhārhut (*c.* 175 BC), near Satna, the remains of which are now in the Indian Museum at Calcutta. Another such monument is the *stūpa* at Sānchi (six miles south of Vidisha), originally constructed by Aśoka, emperor of India from about 265 to 238 BC; additions to the *stūpa* were made by the Śuṅga kings. The Bāgh caves near Mhow, with their wonderful paintings on Buddhist topics, merit a special mention; the Udayagiri caves (Brahmanical and Jain monasteries) near Vidisha exhibit art and architecture in the rock-cut tradition. Among the temples known the world over for their erotic art are those at Khajurāho in the Chhatarpur district in the north of the state; dating from AD 1000, they were built by the Candella kings. The temples at Gwalior and in its vicinity should also be mentioned. The palaces at Mandu (near Dhār) and the Gwalior Fort, perhaps the most impressive of the residences of the former princes of Madhya Pradesh, represent other notable architectural achievements.

Tribal mythology and folklore

Many of the tribal traditions in Madhya Pradesh are still vital and strong, though they have been exposed in varying degrees to outside cultural influences. A great deal of tribal mythology and folklore is also preserved. The *pardhān* (bards of the Gond) still sing of the legendary deeds of Lingo-pen, the mythical originator of the Gond tribe. The *Pandwāni* is the Gond equivalent of the *Mahābhārata* (one of the two great epics of India), while the *Lachmanjati* legend is the Gond equivalent of the *Rāmāyaṇa,* the other great epic. Other epics are also popular. All tribes have myths and legends regarding their origin. There are songs for the ceremonies of birth and marriage, while various dance styles have songs to accompany them. Folktales, riddles, and proverbs are another feature of the cultural heritage.

BIBLIOGRAPHY. The *Census of India, 1961,* vol. 8, *Madhya Pradesh,* pt. 2 (1963), is a collection of general population tables; while the *Statistical Abstract of Madhya Pradesh* (annual) is a compendium of Madhya Pradesh statistics. See also the *Economic and Statistical Atlas of Madhya Pradesh* (1958). An account of the state's economy is found in the NATIONAL COUNCIL OF APPLIED ECONOMIC RESEARCH, *Techno-Economic Survey of Madhya Pradesh* (1960). O.H.K. SPATE and A.T.A. LEARMONTH, *India and Pakistan,* 3rd ed. rev. (1967), is a general economic and regional geography. D.R. PATIL, *The Cultural Heritage of Madhya Bharat* (1953), deals with the pre-1956 state of Madhya Bharat in its geographical and cultural setting.

(N.P.A.)

Madison, James

James Madison, fourth president of the United States, was one of the founding fathers of his country. He became known as the "father" of the Constitution because of his influence in planning and gaining ratification of the U.S. Constitution. He was secretary of state under Pres. Thomas Jefferson when Louisiana was purchased from France. The War of 1812 was fought during his presidency.

By courtesy of The New-York Historical Society

Madison, oil painting by A.B. Durand, 1833.

Early life and political activities

Madison was born March 16 (March 5, old style), 1751, at the home of his maternal grandmother, in what is now Port Conway, Virginia. The son and namesake of a leading Orange County landowner and squire, he lived for 85 years at Montpelier, in the shadow of the Blue Ridge Mountains. In 1769 he rode horseback to the College of New Jersey (Princeton University), selected for its hostility to episcopacy. He completed the four-year course in two years, finding time also to demonstrate against England and to lampoon members of a rival literary society in ribald verse. Overwork produced several years of epileptoid hysteria and premonitions of early death, which thwarted military training but did not prevent home study of public law, mixed with early advocacy of independence (1774) and furious denunciation of the imprisonment of nearby dissenters from the established Anglican Church. Madison never became a church member, but in maturity he expressed a preference for Unitarianism.

His health improved, and he was elected to Virginia's 1776 Revolutionary convention, where he drafted the state's guarantee of religious freedom. In the convention-turned-legislature he helped Thomas Jefferson disestablish the church but lost re-election by refusing to furnish the electors with free whisky. After two years on the governor's council, he was sent to the Continental Congress in March 1780. Five feet six inches tall, small boned, boyish in appearance, and weak of voice, he waited six months before taking the floor; but strong actions belied his mild manners. He rose quickly to leadership against the devotees of state sovereignty and enemies of Franco-U.S. collaboration in peace negotiations, contending also for the Mississippi as a western territorial boundary and the right to navigate that river through its Spanish-held delta. Defending Virginia's charter title to the vast Northwest against states that had no claim to western territories and whose major motive was to validate barrel-of-rum purchases from Indian tribes, Madison defeated the land speculators by persuading Virginia to cede the western lands to Congress as a national heritage.

Following the ratification of the Articles of Confederation in 1781, Madison undertook to strengthen the Union by asserting implied power in Congress to enforce financial requisitions upon the states by military coercion. This move failing, he worked unceasingly for an amendment conferring power to raise revenue and wrote an eloquent address adjuring the states to avert national disintegration by ratifying the submitted article. The chevalier de la Luzerne, French minister to the United States, wrote that Madison was "regarded as the man of the soundest judgment in Congress."

Re-entering the Virginia legislature in 1784, he defeated Patrick Henry's bill to give financial support to "teachers of the Christian religion." To avoid the political effect of his extreme nationalism, he persuaded the states-rights advocate John Tyler to sponsor the calling of the Annapolis Convention of 1786, which, aided by Madison's influence, produced the Constitutional Convention of 1787.

There his Virginia Plan, put forward through Gov. Edmund Randolph, furnished the basic framework and guiding principles of the Constitution. Delegate William Pierce, of Georgia, wrote that in the management of every great question, Madison "always comes forward the best informed Man of any point in debate." Pierce called him "a Gentleman of great modesty—with a remarkable sweet temper. He is easy and unreserved among his acquaintances, and has a most agreeable style of conversation." Besides earning the title of father of the Constitution, Madison took day-by-day notes of debates, which furnish the only comprehensive history of the convention proceedings. To promote ratification he collaborated with Alexander Hamilton and John Jay in newspaper publication of *The Federalist Papers* (Madison wrote 29 out of 85), which became the standard commentary on the Constitution. His influence produced ratification by Virginia and led John Marshall to say that, if eloquence included "persuasion by convincing, Mr. Madison was the most eloquent man I ever heard."

Elected to the new House of Representatives, Madison sponsored the first ten amendments to the Constitution, placing emphasis, in debate, on freedom of religion, speech, and press. His leadership in the House, which caused Massachusetts congressman Fisher Ames to call him "our first man," came to an end when he split with Treasury Secretary Hamilton over methods of funding the war debts. Hamilton's aim was to strengthen the national government by cementing men of wealth to it; Madison sought to protect the interests of Revolutionary veterans. Hamilton's victory turned Madison into a strict constructionist of the congressional power to appropriate for the general welfare. He denied the existence of implied power to establish a national bank to aid the Treasury. Later, as president, he asked for and obtained a bank as "almost [a] necessity" for that purpose, but he contended that it was constitutional only because Hamilton's bank had gone without constitutional challenge. Unwillingness to admit error was a lifelong characteristic. The break over funding turned Congress into Madisonian and Hamiltonian factions, with Fisher Ames now calling Madison a "desperate party leader" who enforced a discipline "as severe as the Prussian" (Madisonians turned into Jeffersonians after Jefferson, having returned from France, became secretary of state).

In 1794 Madison married Dolley Payne Todd, a handsome, buxom, vivacious Quaker 16 years his junior, who rejected church discipline and loved social activities.

Madison left Congress in 1797, disgusted by John Jay's treaty with England, which frustrated his program of commercial retaliation against wartime oppression of U.S. maritime commerce. The Alien and Sedition Acts of 1798 inspired him to draft the Virginia Resolutions of that year, denouncing those statutes as violations of the First Amendment of the Constitution and affirming

the right and duty of the states "to interpose for arresting the progress of the evil." Carefully worded to mean less legally than they seemed to threaten, they forced him to spend his octogenarian years combatting South Carolina's interpretation of them as a sanction of state power to nullify federal law.

During eight years as Jefferson's secretary of state (1801–09), Madison used the words "The President has decided" so regularly that his own role can be discovered only in foreign archives. British diplomats dealing with Madison encountered "asperity of temper and fluency of expression." Senators John Adair and Nicholas Gilman agreed in 1806 that he "governed the President," an opinion held also by French minister Louis-Marie Turreau.

Although he was accused of weakness in dealing with France and England, Madison won the presidency in 1808 by publishing his vigorous diplomatic dispatches. Faced with a senatorial cabal on taking office, he made a senator's lacklustre brother secretary of state, Robert Smith, and wrote all important diplomatic letters for two years before removing him. Although he had fully supported Jefferson's wartime shipping embargo, Madison reversed his predecessor's policy two weeks after assuming the presidency by secretly notifying both Great Britain and France, then at war, that, in his opinion, if the country addressed should stop molesting U.S. commerce and the other belligerent continued to do so, "Congress will, at the next ensuing session, authorize acts of hostility . . . against the other." An agreement with England providing for repeal of its Orders in Council, which limited trade by neutral nations with France, collapsed because the British minister violated his instructions; he concealed the requirements that the United States continue its trade embargo against France, renounce wartime trade with Britain's enemies, and authorize England to capture any American vessel attempting to trade with France. Madison expelled the minister's successor for charging, falsely, that the President had been aware of the violation. Believing that England was bent on permanent suppression of American commerce, Madison proclaimed nonintercourse with England on November 2, 1810, and notified France on the same day that this would "necessarily lead to war" unless England stopped its molestations. One week earlier, unknown to Congress (in recess) or the public, he had taken armed possession of the Spanish province of West Florida, claimed as part of the Louisiana Purchase. He was reelected in 1812, despite strong opposition.

With his actions buried in secrecy, Federalists and politicians pictured Madison as a timorous pacifist dragged into the War of 1812 (1812–15) by congressional war hawks. In fact, he sought peace but accepted war. As wartime commander in chief he was hampered by the refusal of Congress to heed pleas for naval and military development and made the initial error of entrusting army command to aging veterans of the Revolution. The small U.S. Navy sparkled, but on land defeat followed defeat. By 1814, however, Madison had lowered the average age of generals from 60 to 36 years; victories resulted, reversing British Cabinet policy and ending a war the principal cause of which had been removed by revocation of the Orders in Council the day before the conflict began. Contemporary public opinion in the United States, Canada, England, and continental Europe proclaimed the result a U.S. triumph. The Federalist Party was killed by its sedition in opposing the war, and the President was lifted to a pinnacle of popularity. Madison's greatest fault was delay in discharging incompetent subordinates, including Secretary of War John Armstrong, who had scoffed at the President's repeated warnings of a coming British attack on Washington and ignored presidential orders for its defense.

On leaving the presidency, Madison was eulogized at a Washington mass meeting for having won national power and glory "without infringing a political, civil, or religious right." Even in the face of sabotage of war operations by New England Federalists, he had lived up to the maxim he laid down in 1793 when he had said:

The father of the Constitution

Madison's presidency

"If we advert to the nature of republican government we shall find that the censorial power is in the people over the government, and not in the government over the people."

Later life Never leaving Virginia, for 19 years Madison managed his 5,000-acre (2,000-hectare) farm, cultivating it by methods regarded today as modern innovations; and, as president of the Albemarle Agricultural Society, he warned that human life might be wiped out by upsetting the balance of nature, including invisible organisms. He hated slavery, which held him in its economic chains, and worked to abolish it through government purchase of slaves and their resettlement in Liberia, financed by sale of public lands. When his personal valet ran away in 1792 and was recaptured—a situation that usually meant sale into the yellow-fever-infested West Indies—Madison set him free and hired him. Another slave managed one-third of the Montpelier farmlands during Madison's years in federal office. Madison participated in Jefferson's creation of the University of Virginia (1819) and later served as its rector. Excessive hospitality, chronic agricultural depression, the care of superannuated slaves, and the squandering of $40,000 by and on a wayward stepson made him land-poor in old age. His last years were spent in bed, barely able to bend his rheumatic fingers, which nevertheless turned out an endless succession of letters and articles combatting nullification and secession—the theme of his final "Advice to My Country." Henry Clay called him, after Washington, "our greatest statesman." Madison died at Montpelier, on June 28, 1836.

BIBLIOGRAPHY. Madison's life is most competently and exhaustively treated in IRVING BRANT, *James Madison*, 6 vol. (1941–61), which sets out to counter the hitherto prevailing misrepresentation of the Madison and Jefferson administrations and particularly the derogation of Madison relative to Jefferson; *The Fourth President* (1970) is a selective condensation of the former into a single volume, which, ignoring nothing of importance, aims at bringing Madison's life and career into sharper focus; in the first part of *James Madison and American Nationalism* (1968), Brant provides an account of Madison's role in the formation and development of U.S. institutions against the background of the popular attitude, and in the second provides corroboratory documentary readings. A good one-volume biography is RALPH KETCHAM, *James Madison* (1971). *The Papers of James Madison*, ed. by W.T. HUTCHISON and W.M.E. RACHAL (1962–), is the most extensive collection of Madison's writings, annotated and with background notes, the last volume so far in the series appearing in 1973. S.G. BROWN, *The First Republicans* (1954), is concerned with Madison, Monroe, and Jefferson, its main theme being the development in the 30 years after 1795 of the essential partisan ideas that bound together the republican faction. GAILLARD HUNT (ed.), *The Writings of James Madison*, 9 vol (1900–10), comprises Madison's public papers and private correspondence; he also edited *The Journal of the Debates in the Convention Which Framed the Constitution of the United States, May-September 1787, As Recorded by James Madison*, 2 vol. (1908), which is the only continuous and almost exhaustive record of that constitution. N.E. CUNNINGHAM, *The Jeffersonian Republicans* (1957), covering the period 1789–1801, traces the formation and operation of the party organization behind Jefferson's rise to the presidency, with ample treatment of Madison's role. C.E. HILL, *James Madison*, vol. 3 in S.F. BEMIS (ed.), *American Secretaries of State and Their Diplomacy* (1927–29), provides a survey of the chief political problems facing Madison as secretary of state from 1801. E. MCNALL BURNS, *James Madison, Philosopher of the Constitution* (1938), is concerned with the analysis of Madison's political philosophy and discusses its influence and significance. ADRIENNE KOCH, *Jefferson and Madison: The Great Collaboration* (1950), is a systematic study of the friendship of Jefferson and Madison in working out a comprehensive ideology of democracy and attempts to show how much Jeffersonian political philosophy owes to Madison; the same author's *Madison's "Advice to My Country"* (1966) consists of these essays on Madison's philosophy of moral and political discourse, arranged under the topics liberty, justice, and union. The first section of J.Q. ADAMS, *The Lives of James Madison and James Monroe, Fourth and Fifth Presidents of the United States* (1850), is devoted to an account and evaluation of Madison's political career and administrations; S.H. GAY, *James Madison* (1884), covers the period up to 1797; and W.C. RIVES, *History of the Life and Times of James Madison*, 3 vol. (1859–68), concentrates on the period from the American Revolution until 1797. S.K. PADOVER, *The Complete Madison* (1953), organizes Madison's speeches and writings under apposite titles, including constitutional problems, political principles, and foreign affairs.

(I.Bt.)

Madras

The fourth largest city in India, Madras is the capital of Tamil Nadu. Located on India's eastern coast, it covers an area of about 50 square miles (130 square kilometres). Though it does not have the commercial and industrial opulence of Calcutta or the planned beauty of New Delhi, the city presents a characteristic blend of the traditional and the modern. With a population of 2,470,000, most of Madras is less congested than other Indian cities; hence, the tenor of life is more peaceful.

Madras is the shortened name of the fishing village Madraspatnam, where the British East India Company built a factory in the 17th century. The Tamil-speaking Indians refer to the city as Chennai, an abbreviation of the name Chennapatnam, which was applied to the Indian section of the original British town.

HISTORY

Indian origins. In their contemporary records the moneylenders of Madras referred to the pre-British villages as towns. Several of them, such as Mylapore, Tiruvottiyūr, and Triplicane, were small temple towns, the legends and history of which dated back to the 3rd or 4th century AD. The home-based industries and farming of the pre-British villagers were sufficiently productive to support several large temples, with their elaborate paraphernalia. In fact, it was local skill and industry that provided the basis for the development of British commerce at Madras.

The British town. In 1639, Francis Day, an English agent of the East India Company, obtained permission to erect a fort and trading post at Madraspatnam. The site granted to the company was a stretch of sandy waste north of the Cooum River, which was occupied by a fishing settlement. Beyond the coastal ridge of sand were other small villages surrounded by rice fields. The weaving of cotton fabrics was a local cottage industry in the region, and the English merchants invited the weavers and native merchants to settle down in the neighbourhood of the proposed fort. By 1652 the new factory of Ft. St. George was recognized as a presidency (an administrative unit governed by a president). Between 1668 and 1749 the company acquired administrative control within a radius of five miles of Ft. St. George. At about 1801, by which time the last of the local rulers had been shorn of his powers, the English had become masters of southern India, and Madras had become their administrative and commercial capital.

During the earlier phases of the history of Madras, the English merchants lived in the fort—known as White Town. As their numbers increased and trade grew in volume, the merchants spread out into garden houses in Nungambakkam, Adyār, and Kilpauk. The Indian part of Madras—Black Town (now George Town)—also enlarged rapidly, as did the surrounding villages. In the course of three centuries, the rice fields, orchards, and swamps between the villages vanished and became residential areas. **White Town and Black Town**

THE CONTEMPORARY CITY

The city site. Madras is situated on a low-lying, level strip of land on the Coromandel Coast of the Bay of Bengal. Its north–south length along the coast is about 11 miles, and its east–west width is about six miles. The highest part of the city is only 23 feet above sea level. For purposes of general administration, the city is one of the 14 districts of Tamil Nadu. Until 1946 the city's area was only 27 square miles; in order to alleviate congestion, however, urbanized villages to the south and west were incorporated in that year. Tiruvottiyūr and Ennore on the north, Avadi and Ambattur on the northwest, Kodambakkam on the west, and Nandanbakkam and Guindy on the southwest are fast-developing industrial suburbs. Ribbon development was in progress in the early 1970s, particularly along the Southern Railway line and

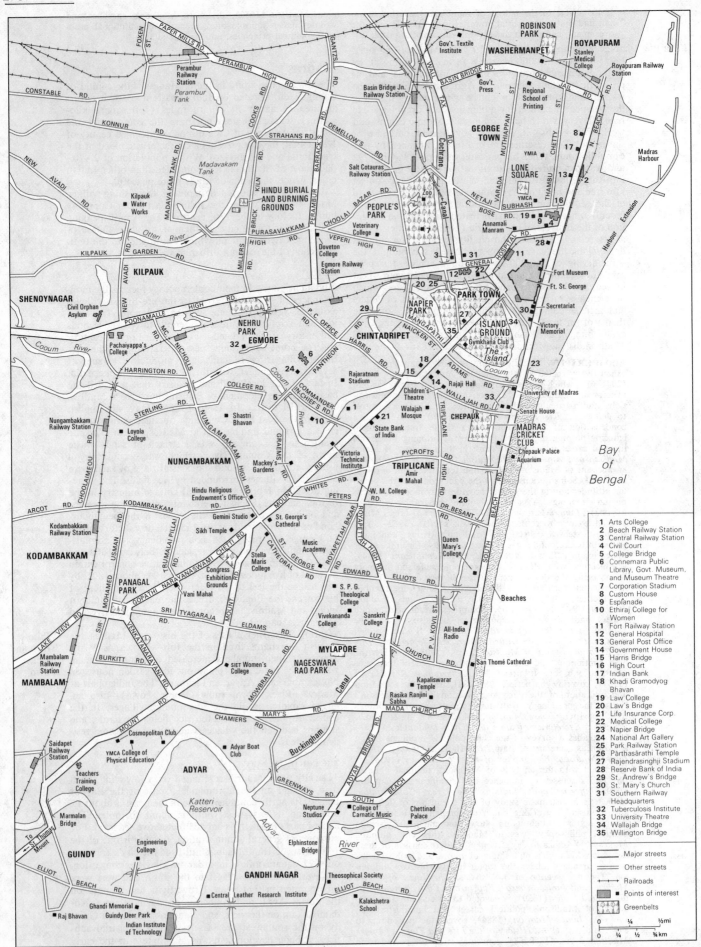

Madras.

Legend / Points of Interest:

1. Arts College
2. Beach Railway Station
3. Central Railway Station
4. Civil Court
5. College Bridge
6. Connemara Public Library, Govt. Museum, and Museum Theatre
7. Corporation Stadium
8. Custom House
9. Esplanade
10. Ethiraj College for Women
11. Fort Railway Station
12. General Hospital
13. General Post Office
14. Government House
15. Harris Bridge
16. High Court
17. Indian Bank
18. Khadi Gramodyog Bhavan
19. Law College
20. Law's Bridge
21. Life Insurance Corp.
22. Medical College
23. Napier Bridge
24. National Art Gallery
25. Park Railway Station
26. Pārthasārathi Temple
27. Rajendrasinghji Stadium
28. Reserve Bank of India
29. St. Andrew's Bridge
30. St. Mary's Church
31. Southern Railway Headquarters
32. Tuberculosis Institute
33. University Theatre
34. Wallajah Bridge
35. Willington Bridge

Major streets
Other streets
Railroads
Points of interest
Greenbelts

0   ¼   ½ mi
0   ¼   ½   ¾ km

trunk roads. Previously isolated residential and industrial areas were becoming interconnected.

The environment. *Climate.* The climate has been uncharitably described as "three months hot and nine months hotter." In fact, it does not have the extremely hot and humid summer of Calcutta, and sea breezes moderate the summer heat. May is the hottest month, with a mean temperature of 91° F (33° C); January is the coolest month, with a mean temperature of 75° F (24° C). Madras receives about 50 inches of rainfall a year, two-thirds of it between October and January and the rest between June and September. Several low-lying areas are subject to floods during the rainy season. It is a dusty city, but air pollution is not severe.

Vegetation and animal life. Trees in the area include coconut and palmyra palms, margosa, coral tree, pongam tree, pubescent bauhinia, and tamarind, as well as white mangrove, Indian fir, portia tree, and rain tree. The spreading banyan tree at Adyār is famous for its size.

Among the common snakes are the rat snake and the green snake. Birds include the magpie, robin, woodpecker, and kingfisher. The garden lizard, the toddy cat (palm civet), and the hedgehog are also common.

The city plan. Madras developed without a plan from its 17th-century core, formed by the fort and Black Town. The business areas of the city are the North Beach Road, facing the harbour; the Esplanade in George Town; and Mount Road. To the north and northwest are the industrial areas; the main residential areas are to the west and south, and the old villages are in the centre.

The main streets in George Town generally run from north to south. The new residential extensions—including Mambalam, Shenoynagar, and Gandhi Nagar—are well planned and have better roads and amenities. Of the total land area 68 percent is occupied by residences and streets; the remainder is used for commerce, the harbour and railways, administration, parks and playgrounds, and for other purposes.

Traditional neighbourhoods. In the past, castes and religious communities were concentrated in different districts. Mylapore and Triplicane were mainly Brahmin neighbourhoods, Chepauk was Muslim, Royapuram was Christian, and Chintadripet and Washermanpet were inhabited by weavers. This pattern was changing in the early 1970s; the new suburbs, inhabited by more affluent citizens, are cosmopolitan in character.

Transportation. The city has more than 440 miles of paved roads, and more than 14 miles of metre-gauged and 9 miles of broad-gauged railway. Its bus service is nationalized, and there is an air terminal at Meenambakkam. Vehicles include autos, horse-drawn, two-wheeled jutkas (passenger vehicles drawn by a single horse), bullock carts, and handcarts. With poor sidewalks and unplanned roads, traffic problems are acute in congested areas, particularly in George Town.

The population. The population was about 2,470,000 in 1971, representing an increase of more than 43 percent at the 1961 census. A little over 37 percent of the people had immigrated into the city since 1941. Population density was almost 50,000 per square mile.

Of the total population at the 1961 census, some 72 percent spoke Tamil, 14 percent spoke Telugu, and 3 percent Malayalam. Urdu is spoken by nearly 5 percent of the population, and English is used as a subsidiary language by 17 percent of the Tamil-speakers. Almost the entire population is Hindu, but there are communities of Muslims and Christians.

Housing and architecture. Housing is generally unsatisfactory for more than half of the citizens, who live either in one-room huts or in one- or two-room "portions" of crowded houses. In the early 1970s the Tamil Nadu Housing Board, the City Improvement Trust, several cooperative house-construction societies, and the Slum Clearance Board were building better houses for the middle- and low-income groups. As old slums are cleared, however, new ones spring up.

Domestic architecture has been extensively modernized because of changes in building materials, though older houses with tiled roofs can still be seen. The most distinctive buildings are the seven large city temples in the Dravidian style, situated in George Town, Mylapore, and Triplicane. Of the buildings of the British period, the Chepauk Palace and the University Senate House (both in the Deccan Muslim style) and the Victoria Technical Institute and the High Court buildings (both in the Indo-Saracenic style) are generally considered to be the most attractive. Modern skyscrapers, such as the Life Insurance Corporation building, had begun to appear in the early 1970s.

The economy. *Industry.* Industrial development in the Madras metropolitan area was rapid between about 1956 and the early 1970s. Industrial concerns include vehicle factories, an electrical engineering firm, rubber and fertilizer factories, and a refinery. There are two industrial estates, one for small-scale industries at Guindy and another at Ambattur for medium-scale industries. In 1961 there were about 870 factories, some 60 of which were owned by the government and about 800 of which were private concerns.

Trade. The principal commodities exported from Madras are leather, iron ore, mill-made and handloom cotton textiles, cotton yarn, peanuts (groundnuts), mica, onions, chillies, coffee, human hair, palm fibre for brushes, and sandalwood oil. The chief imports, which have three times the value of the exports, include wheat, machinery, iron and steel, ammonium sulfate, raw cotton, newsprint, urea (a nitrogenous compound used in fertilizers and in making plastics), soybean oil, drugs, petroleum products, and rock phosphate.

Commerce. Madras-based banks, such as the Indo-Commercial Bank and the Indian Bank, are now among India's large nationalized banks. The Tamil Nadu Industrial Investment Corporation and three other corporations and cooperative banking institutions aid large and small businessmen. The Madras Chamber of Commerce and Industry, the Andhra Chamber of Commerce, and the South India Film Chamber of Commerce play useful roles in the coordination of the city's business efforts. Import, export, and wholesale trade, as well as banking and industry, which were formerly in the hands of the British and later of north Indian Marwaris and Gujaratis, have come to be increasingly shared by Madras businessmen. A favourable investment climate has been created by the Tamil Nadu government, and the city has been able to attract capital from within the state and from abroad.

Administration and social conditions. *Political and governmental institutions.* The political parties are the Dravida Munnetra Kazhagam (DMK), the Indian National Congress, the Communist Party, the Swatantra Party, and the Muslim League. In the early 1970s the DMK, together with the Congress, commanded the most votes. The Communist movement was weak.

The state legislature, secretariat, and administrative departments are all located in the city. The state governor has his official residence in nearby Guindy, while government offices are scattered throughout the area. The several central government offices located in Madras include the Southern Railway headquarters in Park Town; the offices of the accountant general and of the postmaster general on Mount Road; the income-tax, passport, and other offices in Nungambakkam; and the headquarters of the southern command of the Indian Army at St. Thomas Mount.

Under the control of the state government, exercised through the Local Administration Department, the municipal administration is vested in the Corporation of Madras, established in 1687. It is composed of a mayor and 120 councillors who are elected by adult franchise.

Public utilities. The water supply, which is filtered, is obtained from Red Hills Lake, eight miles northwest of Madras, which is fed by channels from the Poondi and Tamarapakkam reservoirs on the Korttalaiyār River. When the monsoon rains fail—which happens frequently—Madras experiences acute water shortages. The Veeranam Project, expected to be completed by 1974, will bring water from the Cauvery River.

Because of the city's low altitude and high water table,

drainage and sewage disposal problems are encountered. Sewage is pumped to the surface at several points and, finally, dumped into the sea. Storm water is drained into the stagnant Cooum River and into Buckingham and Cochrane canals. Market and street sanitation is poor, and mosquito control and garbage disposal are inadequate.

Electricity is supplied to the city from the Basin Bridge and Ennore thermal stations.

Social conditions. Madras has a number of state and municipal hospitals; the largest and oldest hospital is the state-run Madras General Hospital. Health centres include 14 large medical establishments and about 200 child-welfare centres and dispensaries. The city health department runs an infectious disease hospital, ensures that food is not adulterated, and enforces sanitation in public places, such as hotels and restaurants.

The city fire and police services are departments of the state government. There are 12 fire stations; 60 police stations are responsible for law and order and for controlling traffic.

Municipal and state governments and Christian missions are the most important educational agencies. The city runs more than 340 primary and middle schools and almost 30 high schools. These are of poor standard compared to the schools managed by Christian agencies and by the Ramakrishna Mission. Higher education in the arts and sciences is provided by a dozen colleges, three of which are state owned and the remainder, privately run. Professional education can be obtained in three state medical colleges, four colleges of engineering and technology, the College of Carnatic Music, the Kalakshetra (school of dance), the College of Arts and Crafts, and four teacher-training colleges.

Educational institutions

The University of Madras has advanced centres of research in plant pathology, mathematical physics, biophysics, and Indian philosophy. The Indian Institute of Technology, the Central Leather Research Institute, and the Regional Laboratories of the Council of Scientific and Industrial Research are other noteworthy scientific institutions.

Harrison Forman

University of Madras.

Cultural life. *Cultural institutions.* The Madras Music Academy is an influential establishment devoted to the encouragement of Carnatic music (the music of the historic region between the southern Coromandel Coast of the Bay of Bengal and the Deccan Plateau). The Kalakshetra is a centre of dance and music, with an international reputation, and the Rasika Ranjini Sabha, in Mylapore, encourages the theatrical arts. The suburban town of Kodambakkam, with its numerous film stu-

dios, is described as the Hollywood of southern India. Three theatres—the Children's Theatre, the Annamali Manram, and the Museum Theatre—are popular. The Madras Government Museum has well-displayed collections illustrating the archaeology, history, vegetation, animal life, geology, and ethnology of Tamil Nadu. There is a small collection of East India Company antiquities in the Fort Museum and a collection of paintings in the National Art Gallery. The chief libraries are the Madras University Library and the Connemara Public Library.

The media. The press is influential and publishes in English, Tamil, and Telugu. Apart from the national daily, *The Hindu,* there are two other English dailies—*The Mail* and the *Indian Express.* Important Tamil dailies are the *Swadesamitran, Dinathanthi,* and *Dinamani;* the most popular Tamil weeklies are *Ananda Vikatan, Kalki,* and *Kumudam.*

The All-India Radio station at Madras broadcasts programs in Tamil, Telugu, Malayalam, and English.

Recreation. Madras is justly proud of its two-mile-long sandy beach and its promenade, the Marina, which on warm evenings is crowded by thousands of people. The city has a number of parks, the largest of which are the People's Park, Napier Park, Robinson Park, and the Island Ground. There is a zoo in the People's Park, a small aquarium on the Marina beach, and a deer park in Guindy, near the Gandhi Memorial.

Parks and recreational facilities

Cricket is popular and most colleges have cricket teams. Matches of importance are played at the Madras Cricket Club grounds in Chepauk. Next in popularity comes lawn tennis, followed by football (soccer), basketball, and hockey. Sports facilities are provided by the Cosmopolitan, Gymkhana and Presidency clubs, the YMCA, the YWCA, the YMCA College of Physical Education, the Adyār Boat Club, the Madras Flying Club, and the numerous clubs and associations of the various caste and linguistic groups. Apart from the playing fields attached to educational institutions, Madras has two stadia—the Corporation Stadium and the Police Stadium, in Egmore.

BIBLIOGRAPHY. P.K. NAMBIAR, *Census of India 1961*, vol. 9, *Madras*, parts 1–9 (1965–67), contains a good account of the city. See also R. BALAKRISHNA, *Report on the Economic Survey of Madras* (1961), a basic reference work; and the CORPORATION OF MADRAS, *Administration Report for 1968–69* (1969). RAMA REDDY VENKATA, *City of Madras: Official Handbook* (1950), although out of date, presents a sound view of the city.

(A.Ai.)

Madrid

Almost exactly in the centre of the Iberian Peninsula, on the sun-beaten central highland of New Castile, the city of Madrid, capital of Spain and of Madrid Province and a sprawling modern metropolis, entered the 1970s with a population slightly in excess of 3,000,000. At an altitude of 2,100 ft (635 metres) above sea level, on an undulating plateau of sand and clay known as the meseta (from the Spanish *mesa,* "table"), it is the highest capital city in Europe.

There is no compelling geographical, economic, or military reason for Madrid to be where it is. Not on a major river (it is watered by the subdued Manzanares), not on a major trade route (the important highways came to Madrid in the wake of the kings), not the site of a religious shrine, nor a key military position, it was, during the Middle Ages, merely the location of a small Moorish fort named Majrit on a bluff over the river, a part of the outlying defenses of Toledo, 40 miles to the southwest. Political sagacity indicated that a new 16th-century capital should be founded in the centre of the country, but there were other towns in the region that were prettier, better sheltered from the harsh seasons, and more easily defensible against attack. Madrid's great advantage as the capital for a then recently united Spain was its obscurity, which guaranteed its political innocence and its independence of all established power save that of the king of Spain. Taken from the Muslim occupiers in 1083 by Alfonso VI of León and Castile, it had long been the resi-

Foundation

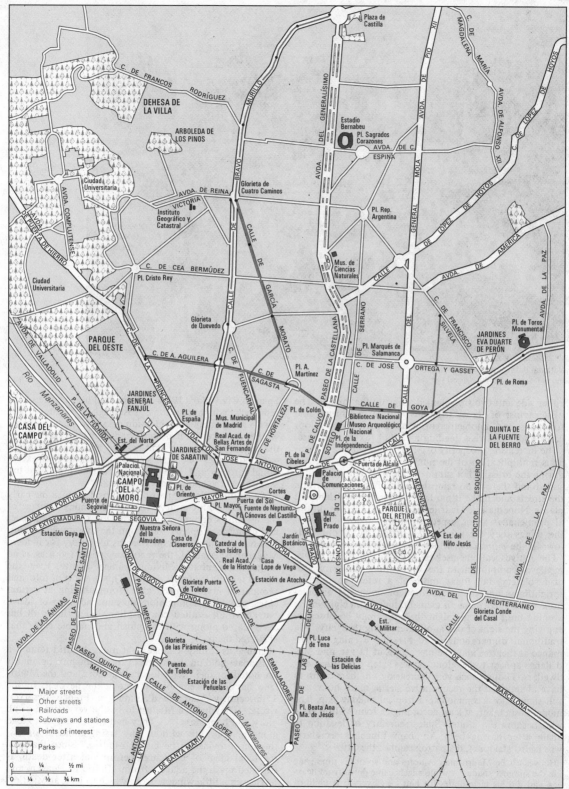

Central Madrid.

dence of kings, and parliament (the Cortes) was first summoned there in 1329.

In 1561 Philip II established his court at Madrid, on what was to prove to be a permanent basis. It remained for his successor, Philip III, to make the city the nation's official capital, in 1607. The city that subsequently developed was broadly Spanish, rather than narrowly Castilian, in character, and it is now one of the most ebullient capitals of the Continent. It lies on tableland, open to the trumpet blasts of crystalline light and mountain wind. It is, as observers have remarked, a city in which light is more important than colour, grace more than beauty.

CHARACTER AND SETTING

In the Madrid of the 1970s a few 30-story buildings, locally esteemed as skyscrapers, contend with older spires, and there is a moderate amount of office building in the contemporary idiom. The city's outskirts are sown with new housing—luxury or low-cost, depending on the neighbourhood—but central Madrid gives an impression of continuity and stability, a rich blend of royal antiquity and steam-age solidity. The north–south axis, which changes its name four times in the four miles between the Prado Museum and the Bernabeu football stadium, is a broad boulevard with trees fronting the buildings on

National Palace and Gardens, Madrid.
By courtesy of the Spanish National Tourist Office

either side and two tree-planted strips up the middle. The westernmost of these strips has mosaic pavements and fountains and kilometres of awning-sheltered outdoor cafes under the trees, lending an air of luxury and ease.

The increasing prosperity of Madrid has led to a vertiginous multiplication of the numbers of automobiles, and during the brassily hot summer months when the wind is stilled and there is no rain, the traffic fumes can curtain the streets and make it hard to see across the celebrated plazas. Nonetheless, Madrileños persist in their traditional promenades afoot, especially after sundown. One of the things they are said to find wonderful about their town is the *animación*, which they themselves supply.

The natives call themselves *gatos* (cats), originally a medieval compliment to the wall-scaling ability of Madrid soldiery, but today more of a reference to their sprightliness and to the tradition of nocturnal ambulation. When the weather is clement, then from eight in the evening until after midnight the *gatos* may be observed enjoying the sight of one another enjoying their city. The traditional dinner hour is 10 PM, the evening performance at theatres and cinemas begins at 11 PM, and Madrileños appear to get along on less sleep than other city dwellers. Though each year increasing numbers claim to have abandoned the recuperative siesta, office hours are still shaped to accommodate a tropical midday nap. The model siesta taker, at least according to John Milton Hay, who became the United States secretary of legation to Spain after having been Abraham Lincoln's secretary, was Isidro (Isidore), the patron saint of the city:

> He was a true Madrilenian in tastes and spent his time lying in the summer shade . . . while angels came down from heaven and did his farm duties for him. . . . Every true child of Madrid reveres the example and envies the success of the San Isidro method of doing business.

The pace of life in Madrid is accelerating with increasing commercial activity and modernization. The population is swelling (1,000,000 inhabitants added in the decade 1960–70), and road traffic becomes daily more dense. These growing 20th-century pressures have not yet diminished the grave good manners of the *gato*, nor his readiness to laugh. Native wit, once as noted as the pure air and the delicious drinking water, has, however, appreciably dimmed. In 1911, when the central post office was completed, grandiose and pinnacled, a veritable cathedral among post offices, Madrid dubbed it Nuestra Señora de las Comunicaciones. Then, 25 years later, during the

Spanish Civil War (1936–39), the building, centre of the republic's communications, sustained 155 direct hits. Like a good many Madrid landmarks it was later restored so that it looked as if nothing had ever happened. While the fighting lasted, the light-hearted and courtly citizens —on both sides—became killers and wreckers of exceptional ferocity and joke making was for some time unseemly and the habit of gaiety broken.

The cultural life of Madrid has subsided since the early days of the 20th century. The overwhelming heritage of the novelist Cervantes, author of *Don Quixote*, the poet and dramatist Lope de Vega, and the monumental paintings of Goya and Velázquez seems too heavy for modern Madrileños: Madrid, the repository of past glories, is no longer the capital of living Spanish culture. Even the famed *tertulia* is almost extinct. This is a sort of informal seminar, a nonorganized club, foregathering at certain cafes, providing companionship and exchange of ideas, but above all exalted conversation. These have all but disappeared along with the plush and marble cafes that sheltered them.

Change as it may, change as it must, Madrid retains a passionate hold on the hearts of its inhabitants. Spaniards are noted for their fierce local allegiances, and the Madrileño has long been notable among the devoted. In the 17th century Madame d'Aulnoy, a French observer, wrote, "They believe Madrid to be the very centre of all glory and happiness. . . . They had rather choose to lead a mean, poor life without any train, grandeur or distinction, provided it be but at Madrid." Since that era, the local ideal of existence, before and after death, is summed up in the adage, "From Madrid to Heaven, and in Heaven a little window from which to look at Madrid."

GROWTH AND TOPOGRAPHY

When resident in Madrid the Spanish monarchs lodged in the captured Moorish Alcazar. The castle was little changed through the centuries until an earthquake tumbled portions of it in 1466. Henry IV of Castile (1454–74) built a medieval palace on the site and died there. Charles I enlarged it and Philip II continued the embellishment, including the addition of a theatre to the 500 rooms. Philip III, who made Madrid the capital de jure as well as de facto, was born there.

Destruction of the palace by fire in 1734 gave Philip V the chance to create a personal monument to supplement those national monuments, the Real Academia Española,

Daily life of the gatos

Cultural values

The
National
Palace

the Biblioteca Nacional, and the Real Academia de la Historia. He died 20 years before a Turinese architect, Giovan Sacchetti, had finished the work, which was much smaller and less ornate than the palace of 1,700-foot-long facades and 23 inner courts that the king had envisaged. What did emerge was nevertheless vast and weighty, a great marble and limestone quadrangle in Neoclassical style with elaborately decorated salons, including a ceiling painted by Tiepolo for the throne room. The armoury contains one of the world's great collections of body armour, as well as the swords of the conquistadores Cortés and Pizarro, and a magnificent campaign tent of Francis I, taken when the French king was captured at the Battle of Pavia (1525). It was from this armoury that the citizens snatched swords and pikes in a vain and bloody one-night uprising against Napoleon's occupying forces, on May 2, 1808.

Napoleon's brother Joseph occupied the throne from 1808 until 1813. One of his nicknames among his subjects was "el Rey Plazuelas," because of his passion for making clearings in the urban thickets of old Madrid. He created at least a dozen plazas, mostly by levelling convents constructed by previous occupants of the palace. The Plaza de Oriente, facing the palace, was cleared of 56 houses, a library, a church, and several convents. The last king of Spain to inhabit the palace was Alfonso XIII, whose apartments are preserved just as he left them when he abandoned throne and country in 1931.

Adjoining the palace on the south is Madrid's first cathedral, Nuestra Señora de la Almudena, for which construction began in 1895 and is still under way. The temporary status of cathedral was conferred upon the 17th-century church of San Isidro el Real.

For centuries the town huddled close to the castle and then began a slow expansion eastward. Eventually, it opened out in all directions but did not manage to cross westward to the far bank of the Manzanares River until 1948. Madrid's growth was achieved, as the novelist Benito Pérez Galdós noted, in *brusquedades* ("stages of abrupt growth"). Starting in the early part of the 17th century, these outward thrusts have occurred about every hundred years. The 20th-century push has been the greatest of all: between 1948–51, for example, the city swallowed its suburbs and enlarged itself tenfold, to cover an area of 205 square miles (531 square kilometres).

For much of its history, the city was referred to as *los Madriles* ("the Madrids"), because each quarter had its own distinct character. Later there grew up the custom of considering the city as composed of three *barrios* (districts): upper (*altos*), middle (*centrales*), and lower (*bajos*), the extremes indicating an economic as well as a geodetic level. The *barrios bajos*, spilling downhill from the Plaza Mayor along the Calle de Toledo toward the river, are still the poor and picturesque parts of Madrid, but many of their former inhabitants have moved even further downhill onto reclaimed marshland on both sides of the river where stand the large low-rent housing developments. Just over the brow of the hill is the Rastro, for generations a flea market with as many rare bargains as fleas. Today there are no fleas and the accent is on market.

In medieval times the town inched eastward up both sides of the Calle Mayor and the Calle Segovia, centring on the Straw Market (now the Plaza del Marques de Comillas) with the Moors jammed into the southwest corner, still called the Moreria. The whole of the medieval core of Madrid was no more than 500 yards long and 900 yards wide. Some of the street pattern of Madrid before the 16th century remains, but few buildings. Among the rare medieval structures is the much-restored Casa de los Lujanez, in the tower of which Francis I of France is said to have been imprisoned. In the same small square, the Plaza de la Villa, is the astonishingly small Madrid Town Hall, designed in the early 17th century by Juan Gómez de Mora adapting and mellowing the style favoured by the late King Philip II (1556–98). The *estilo desornamento,* as it was known, best typified by Philip's fortress-palace-abbey at the Escorial, produced sturdy red blocks out of which pushed stubby towers topped by gay, slender

City
regions

slate steeples with flared skirts. The frivolity of the steeples relieved the austerity of the plain facades.

It was under the Habsburgs, starting with Philip II, that Madrid made its first brusque expansion. The Foreign Ministry (1634), originally the Court Prison, the Church of San Isidro, the Casa de Cisneros, and the Segovia Bridge over the Manzanares date from this time. The gem of "Austrian" Madrid, and perhaps the finest architectural creation of all Madrid, is the Plaza Mayor, one of Europe's most graceful and beguiling city squares. Built between 1617–19, it is an oblong 120 metres long and 100 metres wide surrounded by 68 balconied houses five stories high, struck with steeples in the royally approved style. Nine archways penetrate at oblique angles from surrounding streets, and today shops and restaurants occupy the street level beneath the continuous arcade. The plaza was dedicated with an eight-day fiesta celebrating the beatification of Isidro. In 1622 there were fireworks, bullfights (at that period still fought by noblemen on horseback), and a new Lope de Vega play to mark the canonization of Isidro and four other saints—Teresa of Avila, Ignatius of Loyola, Francis Xavier, and Philip Neri. Heretics condemned by the Inquisition went through their auto-da-fé (the execution of the judicial sentence) in the square but were led away for their immolation. Until 1765 common criminals were garroted publicly in the square. The Plaza Mayor's last bullfight was in celebration of Isabella II's royal wedding in 1846.

During the War of the Spanish Succession (1701–14) Madrid espoused the Bourbon cause against the Habsburgs, whose foreign troops succeeded in occupying the capital briefly. After the Bourbons were installed, there was a small flurry of building in the San Bernardo quarter, north of the Calle Mayor, employing a Baroque architecture, exemplified in the richly sculptured Toledo Bridge (1735). The Museo Municipal de Madrid in the Calle de Fuencarral has an ornate portal of this period.

The 16th-century university, after its removal from the town of Alcalá de Henares, was implanted in the San Bernardo neighbourhood in 1836 and removed again 90 years later to Ciudad Universitaria on the northwestern outskirts. In the front lines during the Civil War, Ciudad Universitaria was destroyed and has since been rebuilt and expanded. San Bernardo was bisected in 1910 by a broad new street driven through the tangled old neighbourhood from the Calle de Alcalá downhill to the Plaza de España, where the city's first tall 20th-century commercial buildings were erected. As its name—the Gran Vía—indicated, it was designed as the main street of the city, since crammed with cinemas, coffeehouses, shops and banks, and by the 14-story Telefónica, telephone exchange. Following the Civil War it was named Avenida José Antonio, after the martyr of the winning side, but Madrileños persist in calling it the Gran Vía.

The second Bourbon king, Charles III (1759–88), was called the mayor of Madrid, because of his devotion to the improvement and beautification of the town. In his ambition to make Madrid a noble, modern capital, he was aided by a trio of distinguished Neoclassical architects, Francisco Sabatini, Ventura Rodríguez, and Juan de Villanueva. He pushed the city still further eastward to the present Plaza de la Independencia, where stands the Alcalá city gate, a triumphal arch designed for the king in 1778. One of the many new buildings erected under Charles's reign was the central post office, in the wall of which is set Spain's zero-kilometre stone. In the Puerta del Sol, the structure was eventually occupied by the Ministry of Interior (Gobernación, which it is still popularly called), and since the Civil War by the headquarters of the national police. For local inhabitants this building's clock is one of the principal landmarks of the city. Those who crowd the Puerta del Sol to welcome the New Year carry little bags holding a dozen grapes, one to be swallowed at each stroke of midnight.

The name Puerta del Sol (Sun Gate) is thought to have originated because a sun was carved on the city gate, which stood there until 1510. For centuries the square was the physical and emotional centre of Madrid. Not only did the mail and passenger coaches from the rest of

Bourbon
influence

The
Puerta
del Sol

Spain converge here (the subway, built in 1919, still does) but this was the first spot to be blessed with the innovations of 19th-century technology, from the first gas lamps in 1830 through the first mule trams and first public urinal to the first electric street lights and electric streetcars. When reconstruction of the plaza was decreed in 1856, protesters rioted and the government fell. Eventually the Puerta del Sol was given its new shape, but there were other reasons for continuing social disorder, which accelerated in tempo and seriousness through the 19th century and into the 20th until the monarchy was deposed in 1931. Crises continued and five years later the city was convulsed by civil war. After two years of siege, which saw the sacking of church properties, artillery and aerial bombardment, and house-to-house combat, the Nationalist insurrectionists took the Republican capital. The victorious general, with a fine flourish of historical irony, entered the city with a guard of Moors.

From the Puerta del Sol, the new Madrid of Charles III marched down the Calle de Alcalá, still one of the principal arteries of the city, fraught with ministries and ponderously ornate banking establishments, down to the Puerta de Alcalá. Just to the west of the city gate was the Buen Retiro Palace of Philip III, destroyed in the Peninsular War, and of which a remnant serves as a war museum. In the gardens Charles set up a porcelain factory, hoping to rival the work of the French royal pottery at Sèvres. He set aside another portion of the parkland for a botanical garden (1774), part of which was a physic garden from which he ordered medicinal herbs to be given free every morning to anyone who asked, an order still in force. He commanded the building of a museum of natural history and sciences, adjacent to the botanical garden, but died before it was completed. It was only after Ferdinand VII returned to ascend the throne after Napoleon's defeat that the construction was completed, and into it in 1819 the new king moved 311 pictures from the royal collections. This was the start of one of the world's major picture galleries, the Prado. Devoted to works primarily from the 15th to the early 19th century, it has more than 3,000 paintings, half of them on exhibition, with pride of place given to the Spaniards, especially Goya and Velázquez, whose effigies, in bronze, stand before the entrances. Other fine paintings, including some superb Goyas, hang in the Real Academia de Bellas Artes de San Fernando, another Charles III structure in the Alcalá. A Goya masterwork is a fresco done in 1798 for the court chapel of Charles IV, the Ermita de San Antonio de la Florida. After Goya died in France in 1828, he was taken back to Madrid and buried in the little white church. The dome, on which he painted the people of Madrid crowded around a balustrade listening to St. Anthony of Padua preach, provides a fitting memorial. A twin church was built alongside in 1928, and the original became a Goya monument.

At the time the fresco was painted, the street fronting the church, the Paseo de la Florida, was the promenade of fashionable Madrid, but in the early 19th century favour switched to the street that Charles III had had laid out and landscaped in front of his museum and botanical garden quite on the opposite side of town. This was the Paseo del Prado, popularly known as the Salón del Prado. When the era of the palatial city hotel arrived, it was there, on opposite sides of the plaza bearing the Neptune fountain, that the Ritz and the Palace were established.

Off this huge plaza (Canovas del Castillo) is a far smaller one, where the Spanish parliament, the Cortes, is located. Built in the 19th century with a Neoclassic columned and porticoed entrance, it is one of the smallest parliament buildings in Europe. Further north, where the Prado crosses the Alcalá, there is another vast oval plaza, named Cibeles, for the central figure of its fountain. This grand crossroads also embraces an Apollo fountain and an obelisk commemorating the uprising of 1808. In 1830, the Paseo del Prado was continued northward by a new boulevard named the Paseo de los Recoletos (since renamed Calvo Sotelo, after another Nationalist martyr), which after a half mile or so becomes the Paseo de la Castellana, and much further on, the

Avenida del Generalissimo. The original road building was achieved by Joaquín Vizcaíno, mayor of Madrid (the mayor is traditionally a nobleman appointed by the national government), who also instituted street numbers for buildings (one to a plot rather than one to each building), street lighting, and municipal refuse collection.

Now the Paseo is the site of the newest tall office buildings, luxury hotels, apartment houses as well as embassies, the 2,200,000-volume Biblioteca Nacional, the Museo Arqueológico Nacional, and the Museo Español de Arte Contemporáneo, but for years it remained almost rural, bordered by imposing town houses set in great gardens. One of these mansions, now appropriately converted into a bank, belonged to the marqués de Salamanca, author of the true expansion of Madrid toward the north. On a plot parallel to the Paseo the banker-marquis in 1872 built 28 streets on a grid plan starting north from the Alcalá. This immediately became, and to a large extent remains, the chic quarter of Madrid. The main street of the Salamanca district is the Calle de Serrano, where small, exclusive, expensive shops serve a similarly qualified neighbourhood clientele. Salamanca razed the historic bullring on the Alcalá and replaced it with one built further east on the same road; this in turn was replaced in 1934 by another further east, though still on the Alcalá. Called El Monumental, it seats 23,000 spectators, is the largest bullring in Spain, and the only Moorish-styled edifice in town. Attached to it is a museum of bullfighting. To become a full-fledged matador, the Spanish *novillero* must take, or confirm his official test of mastery, the *alternativa*, in this ring. The season lasts from March through October.

The high point of the season is the festival of San Isidro, in mid-May, when there are 10 or 11 days of bullfighting. This is also the time of the soccer classic, Madrid versus Barcelona, and a plenitude of other sporting events, folk dancing displays, art shows, concerts, and plays. At this time of year begins the production of *zarzuelas*, open-air comic operettas, usually dating from the 19th century, singing the privilege and joy of living in Madrid.

Following the feast of the city's patron saint, each district in turn stages its own fiesta (*verbena*) for a week or two. As they succeed one another, sometimes overlapping, the summer is sung and danced away. Two of the *verbenas* spread into the large city parks at each end of the east–west axis, the Retiro behind the Prado and the Casa de Campo on the far side of the Manzanares. The garden of the long-vanished Buen Retiro Palace, opened to the public in 1869, has a rowing pond, a small zoo, a 1794 observatory, some rustic cafes, a few night club-restaurants, and trees with a special gift for giving a dense, grateful shade. The Casa de Campo was bought by Philip II in 1559 as a royal hunting preserve and still retains a good deal of its woodland. To its amenities, such as a boating lake and municipal swimming pool, a "park of attractions," with amusement park, theatre, night clubs, open-air dancing, and restaurants, was added in 1969, connected to central Madrid by aerial cable car.

Madrid has several other extensive parks, and many tree-shaded squares, some the location of the city's 30 museums. Among the varied collections are a railway museum, a reconstruction of Lope de Vega's house (in a street now named for Cervantes), and the still-functioning 16th-century convent of Las Descalzas Reales, an Order of Franciscan Poor Clares with a rich store of sculpture, painting, and tapestry. The city has more than 100 libraries, four of them noted for their source manuscripts and rare books: the Biblioteca Nacional, that of the Palacio Nacional, of the municipality, and that of the culturally once-powerful Ateneo (Atheneum).

For long, modern Madrid made its living from government, banking, insurance, and tourism and derived income as the transportation hub of the nation, with six principal stations serving Spain's converging rail lines. After World War II, however, Madrid became an important manufacturing city producing automobile and truck engines, electric and electronic equipment, plastics, rubber, aircraft, and optical goods.

Urban planning, under the jurisdiction of the Comisión

The Prado (margin)

Northern extensions (margin)

Bullfighting and fiestas (margin)

Economic life (margin)

de Planeamiento y Coordinación del Area Metropolitana, accounts for housing developments for both workers (as in the case of *barrios* La Concepción and La Quintana) and a middle class that is removing itself to such newly created suburbs as Puerto de Hierro and La Florida. Madrid is still the administrative centre of the nation, being the see of the bishopric; headquarters of the army corps and residence of the captain general of the first military region; and seat of the national supreme court and of all branches of central administration.

BIBLIOGRAPHY

General: NINA EPTON, *Madrid* (1964), on the various quarters of the city, its inhabitants, and a personal note on the author's early experiences there; ARCHIBALD LYALL, *Well Met in Madrid*, rev. ed. (1960), an informal guide to the city and its way of life; JUAN ANTONIO CABEZAS, *Madrid* (1954), a district by district account (in Spanish) of Madrid and an examination of its daily life and cultural institutions, accompanied by maps and copious illustrations; F.C. SAINZ DE ROBLES, *Madrid, Crónica y guía de una ciudad impar* (1962).

Social life and customs: M.A. KENNY, *A Spanish Tapestry* (1961), contrasts the life of the people in a parish in Madrid with those living in a rural Castilian parish.

Art: H.B. WEHLE, *Great Paintings from the Prado Museum* (1963), excellent reproductions and a sketch of the museum's history, with commentaries by the author, former curator of paintings at the Metropolitan Museum of Art; F.J. SANCHEZ CANTON, *The Prado*, new rev. ed. (1966), reproductions in colour and black and white, with a brief history of the museum and a gallery plan; MANUEL LORENTE, *The Prado, Madrid*, 2 vol. (1965), an introductory note on the museum's history and many reproductions in black and white and colour.

(B.E.)

Maecenas, Gaius

Rich and possessing an ancestry stretching back to Etruscan royalty, Maecenas was an outstanding diplomat and counsellor to the Roman emperor Augustus and the greatest patron of letters in all antiquity. His personal interest quite as much as his wealth made him the dedicatee of Virgil's *Georgics* and Horace's first three books of *Odes.* The same capacity for loyal friendship made Maecenas the most intimate associate of Augustus and permitted his important shaping of history. He was better as a lover of literature than as its practitioner. The tastelessly affected fragments of his extant work, parodied by Augustus and criticized by Seneca, reconcile one to the loss of the remainder. More important were his personal qualities: candour, simplicity, and warmth of affection. These won him the abiding friendship first of Virgil, then, through his mediation, of Horace (in 38 BC). Maecenas set out to interest Virgil, Horace, and Propertius in themes of public importance, hoping their genius would glorify Rome and the new regime. But he was no minister of propaganda, exploiting and misdirecting their talents. Virgil found the way to his own poetic fulfillment in the wider, noble themes of the *Aeneid,* while Horace and Propertius likewise went their own ways. Maecenas respected the poets' independence and artistic integrity.

Friendships with famous poets

Alinari

Gaius Maecenas, marble bust. In the Palazzo dei Conservatori, Rome.

His place and date of birth are unrecorded (he was born in about 70 BC), but his mother's family, the Cilnii, had lorded it centuries earlier in Arretium (modern Arezzo, about 90 miles north of Rome), and this was apparently also the hometown of his father's family. Tacitus once calls him Cilnius Maecenas (Etruscans used the mother's family name), but officially he was Gaius Maecenas. His great wealth may have been partly inherited, but he owed his position and influence to Octavian, later the emperor Augustus. Maecenas felt that, though a knight (slightly humbler than a senator but basically a nonpolitical member of the privileged class), his lineage and power overtopped any senator's, and he refused a career as one.

He was perhaps present at Philippi (the battle, in 42 BC, in which Antony, at first an ally of Octavian, defeated Caesar's assassins Cassius and Brutus), though if he were there it was hardly as a combatant. As a counsellor he negotiated two years later the short-lived marriage of Octavian and Scribonia, designed to conciliate her kinsman the formidable Sextus Pompeius, last of the great republican generals. Before the year's end he had secured greater advantages for his leader: a treaty had ended the dangerous armed confrontation with Antony at Brundisium (modern Brindisi, on the eastern side of Italy's heel), and Antony had married Octavia, Octavian's sister. In 38–37 he persuaded Antony to come to Tarentum (Taranto, on the northernmost part of Italy's instep) and lend the warships that Octavian needed to win complete control of the West. Maecenas administered Rome and Italy, while Octavian fought Pompeius, in 36, and Antony, in 31. Although holding no office or military command, he swiftly and secretly scotched a plot to kill Octavian on his return from the East. If not on this occasion, at least in general, Maecenas kept his hands unstained by bloodshed and, in an age of ruthless violence, won praise for his mildness and humanity.

During Octavian's continued absence from Rome, Maecenas shared with Agrippa (Octavian's executive lieutenant) the position of informal vicegerent. He could use Octavian's seal and even alter his dispatches at will and continued to be deeply involved with foreign and domestic affairs after Octavian, now Augustus, had established his principate (27). He was the most trusted of advisers, holding his own in competition with the Agrippa faction.

Role as Octavian's vicegerent

Maecenas shared Augustus' dynastic hopes and worked for the eventual succession of Marcellus, the Emperor's nephew. Meanwhile, Maecenas had recently married the beautiful, petulant Terentia. Her brother by adoption, Varro Murena, quarrelled with Augustus, was disgraced, and plotted his assassination. The conspiracy was detected and Murena executed, though Maecenas had earlier revealed the plot's discovery to Terentia, thus giving his kinsman a chance to escape. Augustus had to forgive the indiscretion, but from that point on Maecenas' influence waned. Agrippa had emerged from the crises of 23 as coregent, son-in-law, and Augustus' prospective successor. Maecenas had become a sick man, aging rapidly, though in 17 he was still sufficiently buoyant to mock Agrippa, the man without a pedigree, while Augustus pretended not to notice.

The domestic life of Maecenas was unhappy. Terentia tired of him and is said to have become Augustus' mistress. Maecenas, though hardly a model husband, was uxorious; his "daily divorce" of the morose Terentia provoked amused comment. He died childless in 8 BC and left all his wealth, including his palace and gardens on the Esquiline Hill (the eastern plateau of Rome), to Augustus, with whom he had never ceased to be on friendly terms.

Ancient writers dwelt on the contrast between the energy and abilities of Maecenas, the statesman, and the luxurious habits flaunted by Maecenas, the courtier. He was ever the Etruscan aristocrat, displaying hypercivilized, fastidious love of the good things of life, basically un-Roman but less reprehensible than moralizing satirists would have one believe. His severest critic, Seneca, disillusioned by his own failure to become Maecenas of a new Golden Age, denounced his undisciplined style of

Criticism by Seneca

writing as the reflection of a character undermined by good and bad fortune alike. He was "lolling Maecenas," with his tunic let down like a petticoat, hobnobbing with eunuchs or the notorious pantomimist Bathyllus. Maecenas certainly loved gracious living, jewelry, dainty food, wine, and women. He gave the Romans a taste for pantomime, heated swimming pools, and other harmless amenities. With his vast wealth he could be the most munificent of patrons, and every parasite in Rome knew it. It was in his circle of intimate friends that he revealed his discrimination and unerring judgment of men's character and quality.

BIBLIOGRAPHY. No trace of any formal biography of Maecenas survives from antiquity. His literary fragments are collected in R. AVALLONE (ed.), *Mecenate: I Frammenti* (1945). A recent biography is J.M. ANDRE, *Mécène, essai de biographie spirituelle* (1967). Two older works are R. SCHOMBERG, *The Life of Maecenas: With Critical, Historical and Geographical Notes*, 2nd ed. (1766), a brief life with very useful notes; and H. RICHER, *Vie de Mécénas, avec des notes historiques et critiques* (1746), also brief, with copious reference to contemporary sources.

(E.W.G.)

Magellan, Ferdinand

Often referred to as the first circumnavigator of the earth, Ferdinand Magellan, since he died before the completion of the first voyage round the world, is more correctly described as initiator and leader of the Magellan-Elcano expedition. The voyage was successfully terminated by the Basque navigator Juan Sebastián de Elcano (del Cano). Fernão de Magalhães, the son of Rui de Magalhães and Alda de Mesquita, belonged to the Portuguese nobility; his birthplace was most probably Porto, which he left to serve as a page to Queen Leonor in Lisbon.

Alinari

FERDINAN·MAGAGLIANE

Magellan, painting by an unknown artist. In the Uffizi Gallery, Florence, Italy.

Portuguese service. In early 1505 he enlisted in the fleet of Francisco de Almeida, first Portuguese viceroy in the East, whose expedition, sent by King Manuel to check Muslim sea power in Africa and India, left Lisbon on March 25; at a naval engagement at Cannanore on the Malabar Coast of India, Magellan is said by the chronicler Gaspar Correia to have been wounded. Though Correia states that during this early period of his Indian service he acquired considerable knowledge of navigation, little is known of Magellan's first years in the East until he appears among those sailing in November 1506 with Nuno Vaz Pereira to Sofala on the Mozambique coast, where the Portuguese established a fort. In 1508 he was back in India, taking part, on February 2–3, 1509, in the great Battle of Diu, which gave the Portuguese supremacy over most of the Indian Ocean. Reaching Cochin in the fleet of Diogo Lopes de Sequeira, he left as one of the men-at-arms for Malacca. Magellan is mentioned as being sent to warn the commander of impending attack by Malays, and during the subsequent fighting courageously

(margin: Indian expedition)

saved the life of a Portuguese explorer, Francisco Serrão, who later from the Moluccas (Maluku) sent him helpful information about those islands. At a council held at Cochin on October 10, to decide on plans for recapturing Goa, he advised against taking large ships at that season, but the new viceroy, Afonso de Albuquerque, did so, the city falling on November 24; Magellan's name does not appear among those who fought. There is no conclusive evidence for the theory that during his Indian service he attained the rank of captain.

The Portuguese victories off the eastern coast of Africa and the western coast of India had broken Muslim power in the Indian Ocean, and the purpose of Almeida's expedition—to wrest from the Arabs the key points of sea trade—was almost accomplished; but without control of Malacca their achievement was incomplete. At the end of June 1511, therefore, a fleet under Albuquerque left for Malacca, which fell after six weeks. This event, in which Magellan took part, was the crowning Portuguese victory in the Orient. Through Malacca passed the wealth of the East to the harbours of the West, and in the command of the Malacca Strait the Portuguese held the key to the seas and ports of Malaysia. It remained to explore the wealth-giving Moluccas, the islands of spice. Accordingly, early in December 1511 they sailed on a voyage of reconnaissance and after reaching Banda returned with spice in 1512. The claim made by some that Magellan went on this voyage rests on unproved statements by Giovanni Battista Ramusio and Leonardo de Argensola, and the want of evidence argues against its acceptance. Even if he did, in truth, reach the Moluccas, a further voyage—which he later commanded from Spain to the Philippines—was required to complete the circle of navigation.

In 1512 Magellan was back in Lisbon; the following year he joined the forces sent against the Moroccan stronghold of Azamor, and in a skirmish after its fall sustained a wound that caused him to limp for the rest of his life. Returning to Lisbon in November 1514 he asked King Manuel for a token increase in his pension, signifying a rise in rank. But unfounded reports of irregular conduct on his part after the siege of Azamor had reached the King, who, refusing his request, ordered him back to Morocco. Early in 1516 Magellan renewed his petition; the King, refusing once more, told him he might offer his services elsewhere.

Allegiance to Spain. Magellan therefore went to Spain, reaching Seville on Oct. 20, 1517. He was joined by the Portuguese cosmographer Rui Faleiro, and together they journeyed to the court at Valladolid. There, having renounced their nationality, the two men offered their services to King Charles I (later, Emperor Charles V). Magalhães henceforward became known by the Spanish version of his name—Fernando de Magallanes.

By decree of a papal bull, 1493, all new territories discovered or that should be discovered east of a line of demarcation (redrawn 1494) were assigned to Portugal, all that lay west to Spain. Magellan and Faleiro now proposed by sailing west to give practical proof of their claim that the wealth-giving Spice Islands lay west of the line of demarcation—that is, within the Spanish, not the Portuguese, hemisphere. On March 22, 1518, their proposal received royal assent; they were appointed joint captains general of an expedition directed to seek an all-Spanish route to the Moluccas. The government of any lands discovered was to be vested in them and their heirs, and they were to receive a one-twentieth share of the net profits from the venture; both were invested with the Order of Santiago. Magellan was convinced that he would lead his ships from the Atlantic to the "Sea of the South" by discovering a strait through Tierra Firme. This idea did not originate with him; others had sought a passage by which vessels sailing continuously westward would reach the East and thus avoid the route around the Cape of Good Hope, which was controlled by the Portuguese; in the royal agreement Magellan and Faleiro were directed to find "the" strait. The officials entrusted with East Indian affairs were instructed to furnish five ships for the expedition, prepared in Seville, where an unsuccessful attempt to wreck the project was made by Portuguese

(margin: Expedition of the Moluccas)

agents. Magellan's flagship, "Trinidad," had as consorts "San Antonio," "Concepción," "Victoria," "Santiago." An attack of insanity prevented Faleiro from sailing.

Magellan, who in 1517 married Beatriz Barbosa, daughter of an important official in Seville, said farewell to his wife and infant son Rodrigo before his ship left Sanlúcar de Barrameda on Sept. 20, 1519, carrying about 270 men, among whom nine countries were represented. The fleet reached Tenerife on September 26, sailing on October 3 for Brazil; becalmed off the Guinea coast, it met storms before reaching the line; on November 29 it was 27 leagues southwest of Cape St. Augustine. Rounding Cabo Frio, Magellan entered the Bay of Rio de Janeiro on December 13, then sailing south to the Río de la Plata vainly probed the estuary, seeking the strait. On March 31 he reached Port St. Julian in latitude 49°20′ S, where on Easter day at midnight Spanish captains led a serious mutiny against the Portuguese commander. Magellan with resolution, ruthlessness, and daring resourcefulness quelled it, executing one of the captains and leaving another to his fate ashore when, on Aug. 24, 1520, the fleet left St. Julian.

After reaching the mouth of the Santa Cruz, near which "Santiago," reconnoitring, had been wrecked earlier, Magellan started south again, on October 21 rounding the Cape of the Virgins (Cabo Vírgenes), and at approximately 52°50′ S entered the passage that proved to be the strait of his seeking, later to bear his name. "San Antonio" having deserted, only three of his ships reached the western end of the passage; at the news that the ocean had been sighted the iron-willed admiral broke down and cried with joy.

On November 28 "Trinidad," "Concepción," and "Victoria" entered the "Sea of the South," from their calm crossing later called the Pacific Ocean. Tortured by thirst, stricken by scurvy, feeding on rat-fouled biscuits, finally reduced to eating the leather off the yardarms, the crews, driven first by the Peru Current and throughout the voyage by the relentless determination of Magellan, made the

Crossing the Pacific

great crossing of the Pacific. Till December 18 they had sailed near the Chilean coast; then Magellan took a course northwestward; not till Jan. 24, 1521, was land sighted, probably Pukapuka in the Tuamotu Archipelago. Crossing the equinoctial line at approximately 158° W on February 13, the voyagers on March 6 made first landfall at Guam in the Marianas, where they obtained fresh food for the first time in 99 days. A *Memorial*, sent by Magellan to King Charles before leaving Spain, suggests that he knew (probably partly from Serrão's letters) the approximate position of the Moluccas; in sailing now from the Marianas to the Philippines instead of direct to the Spice Islands, he was doubtless dominated by the idea of early revictualing and the advantage of securing a base before visiting the Moluccas.

Leaving on March 9, Magellan's course west-southwestward next brought him to islands later called the Philippines, where at Massava he secured the first alliance in the Pacific for Spain, at Cebú the conversion to Christianity of the ruler and his chief men; but on Mactan Island, April 27, 1521, Magellan was killed in a fight with natives.

After his death only two of the ships, "Trinidad" and "Victoria," reached the Moluccas; only one, "Victoria" (85 tons), returned to Spain, under command of Elcano, originally master on "Concepción," and participator in the mutiny at Port St. Julian. For bringing home, on Sept. 8, 1522, the leaking but spice-laden ship, with only 17 other European survivors and 4 Indians, "weaker than men have ever been before," Elcano received from the emperor an augmentation to his coat of arms, a globe with the inscription "Primus circumdedisti me" ("You were the first to encircle me"). It had been left for Elcano, returning by the Cape route, to give practical proof that the earth was round.

Achievement. The supreme distinction of Magellan lies not in any feat of circumnavigation but in his bold conception and masterly direction of the enterprise that achieved that feat. The first navigator to cross the Pacific from East to West, he disproved the prevailing idea that a mere few days westward sailing from the New World would bring ships to the East Indies. Instead, after a crossing lasting more than three months, he brought a fleet within easy distance of them. Magellan, with a character so complex and of such extreme contradictions, will remain an enigma; psychologically he cannot have been at peace with himself. For his transference of allegiance many writers have denounced him, bearing in mind that in his time the loyalty of a Portuguese to his sovereign was second only to his loyalty to his God; others have pointed out that in offering his services to another ruler Magellan did what Columbus, Cabot, and Vespucci had done, and that limitations imposed by nationality are irreconcilable with the advancement of knowledge. But on one thing all Portuguese are agreed: "he is ours."

The fullest account of the voyage is that of Antonio Pigafetta, Knight of Rhodes, native of Vicenza, who sailed with Magellan and returned with Elcano. The true text of the Italian version, translated, edited, and annotated by J.A. Robertson, is in *Magellan's Voyage Around the World by Antonio Pigafetta*, 2 vol. (1906). *The First Voyage Round the World by Magellan*, Hakluyt Society, vol. lii (1874), includes, as well as Pigafetta's account, the following by other members of the expedition: "The Genoese Pilot's Account of Magellan's Voyage" (believed to be Leon Pancaldo of Savona); the "Narrative of a Portuguese Companion of Odoardo Barbosa" (probably Vasco Gomes Galego, of Bayona, Galicia); the "Log-Book of Francisco Alvo or Alvaro," commencing Nov. 29, 1519, and recording on the return voyage the discovery in Cape Verde Islands that by sailing continuously westward a day had been "lost." This volume also contains the account of a contemporary writer, the "Discourse of M. Giovanni Battista Ramusio," and Gaspar Correia's account of the voyage (taken from *Lendas da India*, vol. ii, ch. xiv).

BIBLIOGRAPHY. Important introductory works to the life of Magellan include F.H.H. GUILLEMARD, *The Life of Ferdinand Magellan and the First Circumnavigation of the Globe, 1480–1521* (1890, reprinted 1971); E.F. BENSON, *Ferdinand Magellan* (1929); and VISCOUNT DE LAGOA, *Fernão de Magalhäis: A sua Vida e a sua Viagem*, 2 vol. (1938). For chronicles of the voyage, see FRANCISCO LOPEZ DE GOMARA, *La Historia general de las Indias* (1554); and PIETRO MARTIRE D'ANGHIERA, *The Decades of the Newe Worlde* (1555). For a historic interpretation of the voyage, see OSCAR KOELLIKER, *Die Erste Umseglung der Erde durch Fernando de Magellanes und Juan Sebastian del Cano, 1519–1522* (1908). The life and achievements of Elcano are discussed in MAIRIN MITCHELL, *Elcano: The First Circumnavigator* (1958).

(M.Mi.)

Maghrib, Cultures of the

Arab writers gave the name Maghrib (Setting Sun, or the West) to the regions of North Africa conquered by the Muslims between the years 670 and 700. The word Maghrib denotes the whole of Morocco, Algeria, and Tunisia and the western part of Libya known as Tripolitania. It is bounded on the south by the Sahara.

The country of the Atlas, as the Greeks named it, is distinguished from the rest of the Islāmic world by its population and history. The native peoples have been able to resist successive invaders from the vastness of their mountain ranges. Yet Punic, Roman, and Christian influences left their successive marks. In the 7th and 8th centuries, the victorious Arabs, by imposing Islām and the language of the Qur'ān, absorbed the Maghrib into the Muslim civilization once and for all. Nevertheless, the North African societies have preserved their cultural identity throughout the centuries.

The country of the Atlas

The people of the Maghrib are ethnically Berbers and Arabs. The Berbers have lived in the Maghrib since ancient times, probably originating in a mingling of races in the Paleolithic and Neolithic periods. The Berber stock displays a wide variety of physical characteristics; their social and cultural characteristics are also quite diverse. Underlying all these differences, however, is a common ethnic substratum. A long succession of invasions, ranging from the Phoenicians to the Arabs and finally to the French, did not lead to much interbreeding. Some foreign minorities settled in the towns, but the rural Maghrib

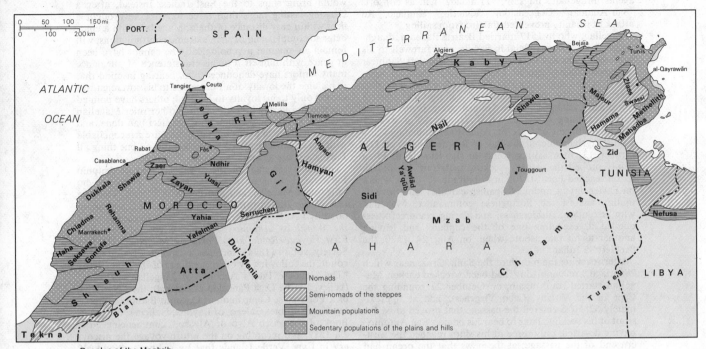

Peoples of the Maghrib.
Adapted from J. Despois, *L'Afrique du Nord;* Presses Universitaires de France

received little new blood. The second wave of Arab invasions in the 11th and 12th centuries consisted of Bedouins, a few tens of thousands of nomads from the Middle East.

The mixture of languages and ways of life makes a simple classification of the peoples of the Maghrib impossible. There are Arabized Berbers, where tribes of the latter have come under Arab cultural influence. It must also be remembered that nomadic tribes lived in the Maghrib long before the Muslim conquest. Although the area has been largely taken over by the Islāmic language and civilization, there still exist populations in the mountainous regions and in certain oases who have retained predominantly Berber idioms and traditions.

Between one-fifth and one-quarter of the population (about 6,000,000) still speak Berber. The proportion rises as one moves westward, reaching two-thirds in Morocco. Berber is a purely oral language, composed of hundreds of different dialects that can be classified in three groups: (1) Maṣmūdah (or Tachelhit), spoken by the Shleuhs of the Anti-Atlas and Haut Atlas mountain regions of Morocco, a people who are sedentary arboriculturists: (2) Ṣanhājah, the dialects of the sedentary Kabyle mountain people, the semi-nomadic sheep grazers of the Moyen Atlas, and the Tuareg pastoralists of the Sahara; (3) Zanātah, dialects originating in the eastern Maghrib (Tripolitania, Tunisia, and Constantine). The Shawia (Chaouïa) people of the Aurès area represent the most important Berber group in this region. But some Zanātah-speaking tribes moved westward, and their dialects are also found in the oases of Touggourt and Mzab and in Morocco.

By far the majority of the population of the Maghrib speak some form of Arabic. This is quite different from classical Arabic, known only by educated people. In the towns, in the Petite Kabylie regions and in the western Rif Mountains, pre-Hilālien dialects are spoken; elsewhere, the Bedouin forms of Arabic are heard.

TRADITIONAL PATTERNS OF CULTURE

Importance of religion and the family

All Maghrib societies were organized around two central institutions, Islām and the clan. Islām transcended the family, ordering all life, spiritual and secular, by a body of unbreakable rules. The social structures, from political organizations to the home, are built around the word of God as laid down in the Qur'ān and in Muslim tradition. Although many differences exist between urban society, where Muslim orthodoxy prevails, and the rural societies, where Berber beliefs and customs still exist, all the people of the Maghrib belong to the community of believers. Islām has sanctified the ancient values of the Maghrib's patriarchal societies. To seek the will of Allāh means above all that the believer must submit to the will of his parents. The pre-Islāmic cults are thus sublimated by the precepts of the Qur'ān; popular traditions are incorporated into religious ritual. As a religion of everyday life, Islām has a code of practical conduct governing the whole range of private and public behaviour, combining complex ritual with spiritual exercise, indissolubly linking the religious and the secular.

The politeness that dominates all social intercourse is not merely the refined courtesy of the bourgeois or the nomads' traditional hospitality; it is above all an expression of the state of being of the believer, in possession of his tradition and proclaiming his convictions. In the roughest country community, good manners are the rule: the *ḥashūmah,* a term that combines modesty, shame, and reserve, weaves a subtle etiquette of courtesy among men and women, old and young, members of the group and strangers. Whether at home or in the mosque, at the public baths or the market, with father or brother, wife or son, every inhabitant of the Maghrib knows what is proper to say or to do according to his age, sex, and status. This code of behaviour guarantees social cohesion and the priority of the group over the individual; it favours the survival of communities in regions that are inhospitable and insecure. In the same way, Berber groups, converted to Islām, found in the universal vocation of their religion the strength necessary to challenge the political supremacy of the Arabs.

Social organization. *Local and territorial organization.* For many sedentary groups as well as for nomads, the fundamental sociopolitical group has been the tribe. The founders of dynasties depended upon their tribe when creating their kingdoms or empires, which were often short-lived. Subject to historical vicissitudes and the hazards of the climate, the tribe could group together several hundred or several thousand households. A powerful tribe could organize other tribes into a strong confederacy, while a weak tribe would be absorbed by an allied or conquering tribe.

The members of a tribe call themselves *banī ʿamm,* or cousins (literally, "paternal uncle's sons"). They claim descent from a common ancestor, the founder and namesake of the tribe; *e.g.*, the Awlād Ya'qūb tribesmen are the children of Ya'qūb. In reality, these ancestors are rather legendary characters (relatives of the Prophet, holy men, famous warriors), worshipped as heroes and whose tombs are pilgrimage centres. This fictitious consanguinity is a system of allegiance to the protector of the group, who serves as its guide, its invisible defender, and its permanent mediator with the supernatural powers.

With the exception of some Berber districts in which the same population has lived since time immemorial, the tribe does not identify itself with an ancestral ground. Over the centuries, a tribe may move its location by 100 miles or more. These movements can be explained partly by pastoral necessity, partly by the fact that group solidarity prevails over individual attachment to inherited land. This solidarity reveals itself above all in such matters as war, the drawing of lots for plots of agricultural land, and the protection of common pastures. The tribe is composed of a number of rural communities and is governed by a *jamā'ah*, or assembly, composed of representatives of the important families. Normally, the Berber *jamā'ah* elects its chief, whereas the Arab tribes frequently have a hereditary system of chieftainship.

The tribe is composed of three to six segments (*firqahs*), which are patrilinear clans based on certain patterns—fictitious pedigrees, an ancestral name, or political or economic practices—that have been transposed into a tribal organization. Membership in a clan is not necessarily linked to vicinity; for example, in Kabylie, each village constitutes an autonomous *firqah*, whereas in the Aurès area a village can contain several different *firqahs*.

Family and kinship patterns. The biological kinship of a family differs from the mythical kinship of the clan or tribe. All descendants of the male offspring of a common ancestor belong to the same family. The consanguinity must be actual in order to be legitimate in the eyes of Muslim orthodoxy. Berber customs, on the other hand, allow legitimation or adoption. All the family members have certain rights concerning the family heritage and certain obligations, according to their level of kinship; they also share responsibility for every member's acts (*e.g.*, collective responsibility in the case of murder). In the Berber villages, the houses of a large family are often grouped together in the same district. Elsewhere, the "great family" disperses in many domestic units, living in autonomous farmsteads or in isolated camps. Kinship forms the basis of all social organization; the domestic unit, the extended family, the clan, and the tribe are concentric circles of kinship, each denoting a certain range of obligations. As an Arab proverb has it: "Myself against my brothers; my brothers and myself against my cousins; and my cousins, my brothers, and myself against the world." The nucleus of the domestic group consists of close relatives living under the firm authority of the head of the family—a grandfather, father, or elder brother. A married son continues to live with his father; a girl, if she does not marry a cousin on her father's side (preferential marriage), goes to live with her husband's family; if widowed, repudiated, or divorced, a woman returns to live with her parents. Sometimes three or four generations live together in a household comprising as many as 50 people.

To belong to a respected family, to be the bearer of an honourable name, is of great importance, since social status depends on that of one's family. The family imposes upon its members a discipline that dictates the position and tasks of each person. Fear of banishment (the supreme sanction) guarantees the submission of the individual to the interests of the collectivity. The fundamental unity, however, arises from mutual confidence and is not subjection to a tyrannical sovereign. The family head controls and administers everything, but he can do nothing without the implicit consent of the others. The balance of opposing forces amounts to a kind of authoritarian democracy.

Stratification. The dualities of town and country, sedentary and nomadic, were fundamental in the traditional Maghrib societies. In the cities, life was dominated by an ancient bourgeoisie often of Spanish or Turkish descent. There were separate Jewish and European quarters. The area near the town walls was inhabited by the humbler classes, newcomers, and seasonal workers. The black slaves were dispersed around their masters' homes. Closed in on itself, the town drew its prestige from its religious functions. In the absence of the clergy, the *qāḍi*, or judge, was the leading personality of the town, sharing his eminence with the '*ulamā*', or doctors of the law.

In the rural communities, the social group known as Sharīfs is highest in the class hierarchy. They are reputed to be descendants of the Prophet and to possess supernatural powers. The Sharīfs are venerated in the same way as the heads of religious brotherhoods and the saintly men known as *marabout*s. The next highest social position in these self-sufficient communities is accorded to families known more for the bravery and wisdom of their members than for the size of their herds or plantations.

The nomads constituted a permanent threat to the village societies. The nomads were herdsmen, while the villagers were tillers of the soil. In addition, the villagers were Berbers, while the nomads represented the Bedouin conquerors. Nevertheless, a modus vivendi was generally established. In exchange for their livestock and goods, the nomads were allowed to graze their flocks on the land of the sedentary communities, which, in turn, sold them their cereal products. In the oases, the inhabitants cultivated palm trees belonging to the nomads, who, in return, protected them against the raids of hostile tribes.

Socialization and education. The boy is removed from his mother's influence at an early age; after circumcision at six or seven, his education is taken over by male kinsmen. He learns to distrust the opinion of women; as a Maghrib proverb runs, "Angels and men work for unity; Satan and women work for division." Obedience and respect are taught at an early age. The spontaneous brotherly relationship is replaced at ten or 12 years of age by a more formalized, distant relationship: boys learn to address their older brothers with deference and avoid them in public places. To their parents, children owe total submission at the risk of being cursed if they disobey. At the same time, male and female cousins learn equalitarian relationships, which are as important in social life as the hierarchical ones. The family, as the guardian of tradition, hands on the many customs of daily life.

In the town but rarely in the country, the boys often attended the Qur'ānic school, where they learned the basics of reading and writing and got the Qur'ān by heart. In the mosques they received a complementary education in grammar and Muslim law. Only two towns in the Maghrib possessed Muslim universities: Tunis (az-Zaytūnah Mosque) and Fès (the Qarawīyīn Mosque). Here students received an education in law and religion, along with fundamentals of grammar, astronomy, and geography.

Economic systems. *Settlement patterns and housing.* The variety of dwellings reflects the different ways of life and the cultural diversity of the Maghrib. Broadly speaking, there are three types of shelter: the house, the hovel (*gourbi*), and the tent. The well-to-do family's house, constructed in the shade of the mosque, is a mixture of Spanish and Moorish architecture. The rooms open onto a central patio. There are no exterior windows, although roof terraces allow conversation among women of the neighbourhood. In the outlying parts of the town, sumptuous palaces surrounded by gardens and outbuildings stand next to apartment houses and poor tenements.

In the mountains the Berber villages perch cautiously on the slopes, like refuges. Their defensive aspect is often strengthened by fortified collective barns known as *agadir, guelâa,* or *gasr*. On certain Mediterranean mountainsides one sees houses with double-thatched roofs. Elsewhere, the houses are built with terraces and walls of stone, mud, or sun-dried brick. The Saharan Berbers have created a spectacular form of architecture using mud, examples of which are the *tighremt*, a rectangular fortress with a tower at each corner, and the *ksar*, a fortified

The agnatic family

The Sharīfs

Berber villages

village surrounded by towers and bastions; this form of building is also seen in Morocco.

In the plains, the sedentary groups generally live in hamlets of hovels (*gourbi*) and tents. These are people engaged in cereal farming and herding but always at the mercy of nomads or mountain tribes on the lookout for workable land. The *gourbi* is a hut made of branches or earth, covered with thatch, that can easily be erected wherever the group moves. An enclosure of thorny plants or prickly pears surrounds the cabin and serves as an animal fold during the night.

In the steppes live the true nomads. Their tents, similar to those of the Bedouins, are made of long strips (*flīj*) woven by the womenfolk from wool, camel's hair, or goat hair and sewn together. The four side walls are made of the same fabric. The dwelling is supported by wooden posts and held in place by ropes of wool or hair. Matting or carpets cover the ground inside. At night the tents are grouped in a circle, forming an enclosure for the herd.

Production and technology. The economy of the desert is predominantly pastoral, as is also that of the steppes and of certain coastal plains where the natural vegetation is conducive to the raising of sheep, goats, and dromedaries. The nomads follow their herds in the search for pasture, camping in the south in the winter and passing the summer in the Atlas Mountains of the north or in the maritime hills.

Agricultural practices The cultivation of corn and barley is done with rudimentary techniques. The ground is left fallow every other year but not fertilized. Plowing begins after the autumn rains, with a wooden plow drawn by two animals. Harvesting is done by sickle and threshing by letting the livestock trample the sheaves. Every family head who owns a plow and a team has the right to work the common land. In regions where there is privately owned land, there are small farmers (fellahs) and also men (*khammāsīn*) employed by others in return for one-fifth of the harvest. But the irregular rainfall, the political instability, the property laws, and above all the priority accorded to grazing do not encourage farmers to improve their soil.

In the oases and certain mountains, however, peasants have inherited proven agricultural techniques. Despite the poor quality of the land, an intensive mixed farming —cereals, vegetables, olives, dates, fruit orchards—supports a dense population.

There is little manufacturing. Except for milling, work in the villages is done by hand in small family workshops using archaic tools. The activities consist mainly of making clothes and tools and of building. Most of the clothes are coarse woollens, although sometimes a weaver may produce more delicate work for a wealthy customer. Tanneries exist everywhere to process the hides of cattle, sheep, and goats, which are dyed with such local pigments as saffron and cochineal. The leather industry employs many specialized craftsmen, such as shoemakers, saddlers, and morocco leather tanners. The urban construction industry employs artists, such as mosaicists, potters, and sculptors in plaster and in wood; they have helped to make Maghribian architecture famous.

Property and exchange. Houses, gardens, plantations, and livestock are private property and can be inherited. In principle, the family unit is predominant but each relative can demand that he be given his share of the property. In order to avoid breaking up the family heritage or to modify the order of succession, charitable foundations (*ḥabūs*) are often created. These are untransferable, but the donee can assign the life interest to the beneficiary of his choice.

As a rule, however, all land belongs to the Muslim community, including conquered territory whose tenants pay an annual rent or lands conceded to loyal tribes by the sultans and *bey*s. Tribes and clans that own their land distribute plots to each family, divide up the water supplies, and administer the pastureland.

Outside each town a weekly livestock market is held. Other weekly markets (*sūq*s) take place in country areas. Peddlers sell articles made in Europe or by town craftsmen. Trade between different regions is limited, and

goods are carried by camels and mules. The Maghrib as a whole exports agricultural products, such as cereals, wool, leather, and livestock, and imports cloth, sugar, coffee, and tea.

Belief and aesthetic systems. Religious beliefs in the Maghrib combine Islām with local traditions. Muslim theologians have denounced many a heresy, an ancient task in this land where St. Augustine used to flay the Donatists. While the main ritual obligations are observed by the whole population, only a minority of educated citizens conform to the orthodoxy of the Qur'ān. Even this orthodoxy admits the existence of "spirits," against which people must protect themselves. In the activities of daily life it is as important to protect oneself against hostile powers as it is to seek divine favour, and this is done through a variety of practices. A pregnant woman wears amulets and sometimes a talisman of black pearls in the form of a hand (the hand of Muḥammad's daughter Fāṭimah). Into the ear of the newborn child the father murmurs the Muslim profession of faith. On the seventh day after birth, the child is named, and a sheep is sacrificed. Religious syncretism

Animal sacrifices are typical features of Muslim feasts. The sacrifice of a sheep on the day of ʿĪd al-Aḍḥā (Īd al-Kabīr), the grandest festival of Islām, commemorates the offering of Abraham. A sacrifice, followed by a communal meal, also accompanies the pilgrimage to the saints' tombs, precedes the annual plowing, and is used in efforts to cure sickness or to overcome a woman's sterility. Sacrifice renews the pact of alliance between the living and the dead; the spilling of blood continues the contract with the ancestors, who protect the family and the clan in a world dominated by invisible forces. The cult of the dead conditions the agrarian rituals of the Berbers, since fecundity, namely life, depends on the goodwill of the spirits of the Earth. The symbolic representations of the crop-growing cycle are identical with those marking the stages of man's life. The rituals of possessing the ground and fertilizing it guarantee permanence of life. These moments of plowing and sowing are a period of rejoicing and marriage. Inversely, funeral rites accompany the harvest. The last sheaf of corn ends the cycle, and the dead return beneath the ground.

The agrarian rites that punctuate the solar year are accompanied by Muslim festivals that follow the lunar calendar. The religious year opens with the ʿĀshūrā, the festival of children and also of ancestors, whose tombs are visited. The Mūlūd, commemorating the birth of the Prophet, is a joyous ceremony; several religious brotherhoods choose this day to organize their great annual festival. The ʿĪd al-Fiṭr (ʿĪd as-Ṣaghīr) and the ʿĪd al-Aḍḥā are canonical celebrations held throughout the Muslim world. The first, known as the "little festival," marks the end of the Ramaḍān fast. There is much gaiety, and gifts are made to the poor. The second is the "great festival," marking the last rite of the pilgrimage to Mecca. These religious ceremonies are also family ceremonies, accompanied by feasting and visiting.

Islām provides the chief aesthetic inspiration for the craftsmen of the towns. Urban architecture and furniture show the influence of the Middle East and of Muslim Spain. Córdoba, Seville, and Granada were particular sources of inspiration for the Maghrib, and Andalusian exiles spread their refined techniques from Fès to Tunis. This Hispano-Moorish art had its strongest impact in Morocco. Tunisia was also strongly influenced by the artistic trends of Fāṭimid Egypt in the 10th and 11th centuries and later, like Algeria, by those of the Ottoman Empire. Arts and crafts

Religious architecture expresses the deep unity of Muslim art, showing in its forms the originality of the Maghrib. For example, the prayer room of the Great Mosque of Tlemcen is composed of 13 long naves, with wooden beams and covered in tiles. The middle nave has two domes. The minaret is a quadrangular tower, topped by a square edifice at the base of which is the platform from which the muezzin calls the believers to prayer. The decoration of Maghrib mosques consists of multiple variations of the lobed arch and the cornice, with linear elements on the walls, such as epigraphy, geometric designs, and flora, either sculpted or designed in mosaic.

Berber art objects have a rectilinear decoration, the richest motifs deriving from the chevron or lozenge and varying from one tribal group to another. The overall composition is simple, with alternating decorated and coloured strips, as in the woollen carpets of the Moyen Atlas region. Pottery is handmade, without a wheel, and glazed in an oven; it is very similar to Neolithic potteries, although the richest wares recall certain ancient Aegean ceramics.

RECENT TENDENCIES

The 19th century saw the beginning of a period of far-reaching political and economic change. The French conquest of North Africa, followed by the massive immigration of Europeans, introduced the French language and European culture. The political power of the tribes was destroyed. A strong centralized power dominated the whole country. This, in turn, was ultimately destroyed by nationalism and the desire for emancipation.

Social changes since independence

By July 1962 the entire Maghrib was independent. The new political regimes in Algeria, Morocco, and Tunisia have tried to rediscover their cultural identity and to develop their economies. There has been a rapid evolution of institutions, social structures, and collective values. New elites have emerged; the present-day civil servants and technicians form a middle class very different from the traditional petty bourgeoisie from which many of them come. Industrialization has created a class of factory workers. At the same time there has been a mass exodus of uprooted peasants to the cities, where they form a sub-proletariat living in shantytowns. Modern hygiene has lowered the death rate so that the natural population increase has become among the highest in the world; this has caused considerable migration into the prosperous agricultural regions and to the large coastal towns, as well as an outflow of workers to France. These movements have in turn contributed extensively to the breakdown of family groups and traditional communities. They have allowed an intensive mixing of the population, established new kinds of social relationships, and led to profound changes in attitudes and conduct.

Although there is a striking difference between town and country and between developed and undeveloped areas, the rural areas should not be regarded as lost in the past. Since the 1930s many of the rural societies of the Maghrib have begun to modernize. To plains that were previously underexploited, advanced agricultural techniques have brought vineyards, olive groves, and the intensive production of citrus fruits and vegetables. Road and railway networks carry foreign ideas and products to regions that were formerly isolated, while "villages of colonization" and rural towns have introduced urban ideas and products into the countryside. The colonial regime limited and distorted cultural contacts between Europeans and the people of the Maghrib, but it was also the vehicle of technical progress and a symbol of modernity. If foreign domination exploited the national resources, it also introduced a monetary economy and new ways of behaviour. The priority given by the post-colonial governments to economic development has intensified the process of change.

Like all societies in transition, the Maghrib displays a number of cultural contradictions. Along with an emphasis on Arab–Islāmic origins, there has been an increase of contacts with the industrialized countries. The Arabization of education has been accompanied by the teaching of French in the rapidly expanding school system. While Islām has assumed its former place in public life, political and administrative activity is determinedly secular.

Effects of modernization

Despite the growth of the towns, the majority of the population in the Maghrib remain rural. The old family values continue to have a strong influence on social life. While the extended family group is becoming rare, solidarity among male relatives is still an imperative. One is obligated to give help to distant cousins and to former allies of one's village or *douar* (district). Social relationships, even in the most modern enterprises, remain deeply personalized. Even in the civil service, the formal, hierarchical relationships are often paralleled by informal ones that provide the real chain of command.

Except for a small Europeanized minority, most of the population favour large families. Even though many people think that the very high birth rate of the old days is no longer desirable, families with three or four children are very common. Celibacy is frowned upon; children, particularly girls, are married as soon as possible. While the emancipation of young people, especially in the towns, has tended to reduce paternal influence, marriages are still commonly arranged by the family, preference being given to a paternal cousin, some other relative, or at least a member of one's *douar*.

The position of women has improved since independence. The development of education for young girls and the increase of female employees in business have tended to break down the strict separation of men and women in public life. More and more women are seen without veils, at least in the big towns, although few women appear in public places.

The evolution of customs and ideas has not spared religious life. Strict conformity is disappearing; there is more tolerance for those who do not strictly observe the fast of Ramaḍān or who drink alcoholic beverages. But the general fervour of religious observances shows the common fidelity of everyone to Islām.

There have been profound changes in the hierarchy of status and prestige. For everyone, the civil servant is the symbol of social success. Among country people, to become a salaried worker is an enviable promotion. Class consciousness has spread throughout society, although tensions between civil servants, workers, small-town clerks, and peasants are tempered by the traditional system of relationships. At the same time, the desire for material improvement, coupled with the impatience of the masses and their increasing interest in politics, tends to widen social antagonisms. The future of the Maghrib will depend largely on the choices of the younger generation, which, for the first time in the Maghrib's history, will be predominantly an educated one.

BIBLIOGRAPHY. An excellent handbook is NEVILL BARBOUR, *A Survey of North West Africa*, 2nd ed. (1962). A good geographical reference book is JEAN DESPOIS, *L'Afrique du Nord* (1964). There are many works devoted to Muslim civilization, including H.A.R. GIBB, *Mohammedanism: An Historical Survey* (1949); S.D. GOITEIN, *Studies in Islamic History and Institutions* (1966); D.T. RICE, *Islamic Art* (1965); and JOSEPH SCHACHT, *An Introduction to Islamic Law* (1964). The best history of the trans-Saharan trade is E.W. BOVILL, *The Golden Trade of the Moors* (1958). Works on the religious beliefs of the Maghrib include ERNEST GELLNER, *Saints of the Atlas* (1969); G.E. VON GRUNEBAUM, *Muhammadan Festivals* (1958); JEAN SERVIER, *Les Portes de l'année: rites et symboles: l'Algérie dans la tradition méditerranéenne* (1962); and EDWARD A. WESTERMARCK, *Ritual and Belief in Morocco* (1926). Among the most interesting anthropological studies are: JACQUES BERQUE, *Les Structures sociales du Haut-Atlas* (1955); LLOYD CABOT BRIGGS, *The Living Races of the Sahara Desert* (1955) and *Tribes of the Sahara* (1960); CARLETON S. COON, *Tribes of the Rif* (1931); JULIEN COULEAU, *La Paysannerie marocaine* (1968); ROBERT DESCLOITRES and LAID DEBZI, *Systèmes de parenté et structures familiales en Algérie* (1963); JEAN DUVIGNAUD, *Chebika, Mutations dans un village du Maghreb* (1968); and ROGER LE TOURNEAU, *Les Villes musulmanes de l'Afrique du Nord* (1957) and *Fez in the Age of the Marinides* (1961). Contemporary changes are discussed in ANDRE ADAM, *Casablanca: essai sur la transformation de la société marocaine au contact de l'Occident* (1968); JACQUES BERQUE, *Le Maghreb entre deux guerres* (1962); ROBERT and CLAUDINE DESCLOITRES and JEAN-CLAUDE REVERDY, *L'Algérie des bidonvilles: le Tiers-Monde dans la cité* (1961); and HORACE MINER and GEORGE DE VOS, *Oasis and Casbah: Algerian Culture and Personality in Change* (1960). For the politics of the new countries, see DOUGLAS E. ASHFORD, *National Development and Local Reform: Political Participation in Morocco, Tunisia and Pakistan* (1967); CHARLES F. GALLAGHER, *The United States and North Africa: Morocco, Algeria and Tunisia* (1963); CLEMENT HENRY MOORE, *Tunisia Since Independence* (1965); and IRA WILLIAM ZARTMANN, *Destiny of a Dynasty: The Search for Institutions in Morocco's Developing Society* (1964).

(R.De.)

Magic

Magic is a term used for a wide range of phenomena, from the elaborate ritual beliefs and practices that are at the core of many religious systems, to acts of conjuring and sleight of hand for entertainment. Used in the former sense magic is a social and cultural phenomenon found in all places and at all periods, with varying degrees of importance.

NATURE AND SIGNIFICANCE

Magic and religion

Magic essentially refers to a ritual performance or activity that is thought to lead to the influencing of human or natural events by an external and impersonal mystical force beyond the ordinary human sphere. The performance involves the use of objects or the recitation of spells or both by the magician. The nature of magic is frequently misunderstood because of uncertainty as to its definition, its relationship to other religious behaviour and institutions, and its social and psychological functions. This uncertainty is largely a consequence of 19th-century views on cultural and historical evolution that set magic apart from other religious phenomena as being especially prevalent in archaic and primitive societies and as merely a form of superstition without cultural or theological significance. This view has led to magic being considered as different and distinct from other religious rites and beliefs and the overlooking of its essential similarity and connection with them, since both magical and non-magical rites and beliefs are concerned with the effects on human existence of outside mystical forces. The frequently held view that magical acts lack the intrinsically spiritual nature of religious acts, comprising external manipulation rather than supplication or inner grace, and that they are therefore of a simpler and lower kind in theological terms, has compounded the misunderstanding. The definition given above recognizes a main point of distinction between magic and other religious phenomena, in that the latter are concerned with a direct relationship between men and spiritual forces, whereas magic is regarded as rather an impersonal or technical act in which the personal link is not so important or is absent, even though the ultimate force behind both religious and magical acts is believed to be the same. The distinction made by Émile Durkheim (1858–1917), a seminal French sociologist of religion (see below), that a religious practitioner has a congregation whereas a magician has a clientele, is also a meaningful one. The difficulty of definition of magic and its differentiation from religion is due largely to Western ethnocentric views. In Judeo-Christian belief it has been distinguished from other religious acts, but this distinction is not always found in other religious systems and in fact would appear to be unusual. Many writers have referred to "magico-religious" phenomena, a convenient blanket term.

Magic is often confused with witchcraft, especially in the history of European religions. Modern anthropologists, however, make the useful distinction between magic as the manipulation of an external power by mechanical or behavioral means to affect others, and witchcraft as an inherent personal quality to the same ends. In this classification, the word sorcery is used for magic that aims to harm other people; that is, sorcery is "black" magic, whereas magic used for beneficent ends is "white" magic. This distinction does not always hold for specific societies but is a useful one in analysis. Divination, the skill of understanding mystical agents that affect people and events, should be distinguished from magic in that its purpose is not to influence events but rather to understand them. The ultimate mystical power of diviners, however, may be thought to be the same as that behind the forces of magic. In some societies, magicians act as diviners, but the two skills should be distinguished. Magicians are often confused with priests, shamans, and prophets, mainly because many activities of the other personages include acts that are traditionally defined as "magical"; *i.e.*, while essentially they are regarded as intermediaries between men and gods or spirits, in the sense of acting in

a direct personal relationship, some of their acts are also impersonal or "magical." It is often, perhaps usually, impossible clearly to distinguish between priests and magicians; as stated above, the distinction is largely a Western ethnocentric one and lies in the kind of actions they perform in particular situations rather than in any true distinction between the kinds of practitioners themselves.

HISTORY AND DISTRIBUTION

Magic in one form or other appears to be a part of all known religious systems, at all levels of historical development, although the degree of importance given to it varies considerably. The term has been used loosely by many writers, especially when discussing European magic. Also the ethnographic accounts of small-scale preliterate societies vary in the degree to which they contain detailed descriptions even when magic is important in a particular culture. Thus the analyses of magic in its total cultural setting are remarkably few.

Knowledge of magic in prehistory is limited by lack of reliable data. Many cave paintings and engravings, from all parts of the world, have been claimed to represent figures practicing hunting magic and sorcery, but this can at present be no more than conjecture or interpretive reconstruction (see PREHISTORIC RELIGION). More certain information about magical phenomena is available for the ancient Near Eastern and Greco-Roman cultures, Christian Europe, and contemporary preliterate societies.

Magic in the ancient world. There are many recorded texts of what appear to be magic spells and formulae from ancient Mesopotamia and Egypt. Most accounts of these cultures class almost all records of ritual as forms of magic and as examples of magical or mythopoeic ways of thought. This is usually because the writers themselves assumed that these cultures were examples of "prelogical" modes of thought (as compared with the thought of civilized man), and so took any religious record as evidence of this. The pharaohs of Egypt, for example, were what are usually called "divine kings," and as such had powers believed to control nature and fertility. Many writers refer to their powers as magical, but the evidence is rather that they were representations of royal omnipotence, expressing the power and the permanence of the kingship, their believed magical powers being contingent on their divine status. Examples of true magical spells and formulae are recorded from both Mesopotamia and Egypt; *e.g.*, spells to ward off witches and sorcerers. Spells addressed to gods, to fire, to salt, and to grain are recorded from Mesopotamia and Egypt, as are spells said by sorcerers and including necromancy or invocation of the spirits of the dead, who were referred to as a last resort against evil magic. Excellent examples of spells are recorded from the earliest times, and especially in Greco-Egyptian papyruses of the 1st to the 4th centuries AD. They include both magical recipes involving animals and animal substances, and also instructions for the ritual preparations and purification necessary to ensure the efficacy of the spells.

Magic in Egypt and Mesopotamia

In ancient Roman culture much importance was given to sorcery and counter-sorcery, both forms of magic. These seem to have been associated with the development of new urban classes whose members had to rely on their own efforts both in material and magical terms to defeat their rivals and to rise in the new regimes, where individual merits and talents were rewarded. Spells are recorded to ensure victory in love as well as in business, games, and academic pursuits such as oratory. With these are counter-spells to defeat rival sorcerers.

Magic in Christian Europe. For the European Middle Ages and later periods there is a vast corpus of written records. As is known from recent anthropological and historical work on witchcraft, magic, and religious syncretism, magic is specially prevalent during periods of rapid social change and mobility, when new personal relations and conflicts assume greater importance than the more traditional kin and family relations more typical of times of social stability. This appears to have been true in Europe also, and particularly at the times when accusations of magic against its rivals were part of the struggle of the church to assert its spiritual and temporal hegemony. There are three main aspects to the history of European magic, much of which is ill-described and almost always without adequate accounts of the full cultural setting. One is that of magic and sorcery in petty everyday relationships at the village and community level from the end of the Classical world until recent years when beliefs in magic have in general become weakened. In most cases these beliefs were part of the culture of lowly rural people and records are scant. An exception was sorcery used by wealthier and urban people, especially in Italy and Spain from the 14th century onward, a concomitant of increased social mobility and growth of class hierarchies. A second aspect is the better known but frequently misunderstood belief in magic defined by the church as the heretical practice of making pacts with the devil and evil spirits. Saint Augustine and other early Christian writers had considered magic to be a relic of paganism and removable by conversion and education. After a papal bull in 1320, magic came to be defined as heresy, and the Inquisition's records begin to mention the Witches' Sabbath (midnight assembly in fealty to the devil) and the Black Mass (a travesty of the Christian mass) as forms of magic and witchcraft, the two being regarded as synonymous. They were defined as magic because of the supposed use of material objects, philtres, spells, and poisons. The spells included the perverted use of prayers and the use of sacred writings and objects for diabolical ends. This aspect of European magic has persisted into recent times in the activities of self-styled satanists.

Whereas these forms of magic were regarded as evil and symptomatic of heresy, the third aspect has usually been considered as good, or "white," in intent. This is the use of magic as part of the alchemical tradition. It is true that many reputed alchemists were considered as evil magicians, acquiring their knowledge by a pact with the devil (as in the Faust legends), probably because much of their knowledge came from Kabbalistic sources (esoteric Jewish mysticism). But most of them were considered to be essentially in the main and culturally acceptable Judaic and Christian traditions, their antisocial pretensions and activities not being central to the alchemical studies and being as much simple trickery as anything else (as in the activities of the 18th-century charlatan Alessandro Cagliòstro and others).

Magic in preliterate societies. Most knowledge of magic in its social setting is derived from anthropological accounts of people of the non-Western world who today believe in magic. The importance of first-hand anthropological accounts, even though many anthropologists tend to make use of the ethnocentric distinction between religion and magic, is that they show how the people themselves actually regard magic and what they actually do with it and against it, rather than relying on the records of inquisitors and missionaries whose duty it was to stamp out magic. Detailed descriptions of magic come mostly from accounts of societies in Oceania and Africa; information from other parts of the world is less adequate although it is clear that magic is equally widespread elsewhere. It is reported particularly from many Muslim societies where pre-Islāmic beliefs still exist, as in Malaya and Indonesia. A difficulty in this respect is that accounts only rarely distinguish magic from witchcraft and divination, both of which are found in virtually every known Oriental society.

STRUCTURE AND FUNCTIONS

Structure. A general point to be made is that the frequent tales of peoples living in fear of evil magicians and black magic are merely fanciful travellers' stories. Magic is normally regarded as an everyday aspect of religion used to explain certain kinds of events and to help bring about desired eventualities. Like most religious phenomena, magic may be regarded with some sense of awe and mystery, but this is more often a sign of the importance given to it than of fear or terror. Typically people perform magical acts themselves or they go to a magi-

cian, a person unusually knowledgeable in the art, who knows how to observe the necessary ritual precautions and taboos, and who may be a professional consulted for a fee. Depending upon the beliefs of the particular culture, the skill may be transmitted by inheritance or bought from other magicians, or may be invented by the magician for himself. Magicians may be consulted for nefarious purposes, to protect a client from the evil magic of others, or for purely benevolent reasons. It seems universal that magic is morally neutral, although the emphasis in any particular society may be on either good or evil magic.

In some religions, especially those of small-scale preliterate societies, magic may be considered as important and even central to religious belief; whereas in others, especially in the main world religions, it may be unimportant, and often regarded as a mere superstition that is not acceptable to official dogma. It has often been maintained that magic is important in societies that possess a particular world view or cosmology, in which a scientifically or empirically correct cause-effect relationship between human and natural phenomena is seen as a symbolic one. This view, which is associated particularly with the British anthropologist Sir James Frazer (1854–1941), is based on a misunderstanding of patterns of thought in pre-scientific cultures. It is true that they may lack the scientifically accurate knowledge of Western industrial societies, but the importance of this may be exaggerated. To some extent it is true: members of pre-industrial societies may use magical techniques (for example, rainmaking) whereas in an industrial society it is known that such techniques are instrumentally ineffective. But magic is also performed for expressive purposes, *i.e.*, stating and maintaining the formal culture and organization of the society, so that rainmaking magic has also the function of stressing the importance of rain and the farming activities associated with it.

It has been stated that magic includes the use of material objects, or the recitation of spells; *i.e.*, the use of words that are attributed an innate essence or power of their own. There are usually considered to be three main elements in magic: the spell, the rite itself, and the ritual condition of the performer. This was first stated by the anthropologist Bronisław Malinowski (1884–1942) in his study of the Trobriand Islanders of Melanesia. With the spell may be included the material objects or "medicines" used in many other societies.

The spell. The importance of the spell or incantation has been somewhat exaggerated by the influence of Malinowski's work. Among the Trobriand Islanders this aspect is extremely important: the immaculateness of the words is regarded as essential to the efficacy of the rite. Among the Maori of New Zealand this element is thought so important that a mistake in the recitation of a spell would lead to the magician's own death. Frequently spells have an archaic or esoteric vocabulary that adds to the respect in which the rite is held. But in many societies the spell is of minimal importance, the magician using his own words and regarding the content as being more significant.

Material objects or "medicines." Equally widespread —perhaps more so than the use of spells—is the use of material objects, often known in the literature as "medicines" (hence the popular use of the term medicine man for magician). The nature of the medicines varies greatly. Among many peoples the medicines are in fact poisons that may actually cause the desired effect (as among some African peoples who place magical poisons in rivers to stun and catch fish, but regard them as they do any other "medicines"—that are not in fact efficacious). More usually they do not empirically bring about the effect but in some way present it; for example, it is common practice for a magician to try to harm another person by destroying something from his body (*e.g.*, hair or nail-parings), or something that has been in contact with him (*e.g.*, a piece of clothing or other personal possession). From the beneficial aspect, this is similar to the old European belief that to touch the king's garment would cure scrofula (swelling or tuberculosis of the lymphatic

The magical view

glands). Another kind of symbolism is exemplified by the Trobriand use of light vegetable leaves in rites to ensure a canoe's speed, symbolizing the ease by which it will glide over the water; the Azande of the Sudan place a stone in a tree fork to postpone the setting of the sun; many Balkan peoples used to swallow gold to cure jaundice.

The rite. The significance of the magical rite itself is often overlooked by those who hold the view that magic is something apart from religion. But it seems universal that magic is practiced only in formal and carefully defined ritual situations. The rite itself may be symbolic, as with the sprinkling of water on the ground to make rain or the destruction of a waxen image to harm a victim.

Condition of the performer. The ritual nature of magical performances may also be seen in a third element, that of the condition of the performer. Even though regarded as an everyday and "natural" phenomenon, magic is none the less considered as potentially dangerous and polluting, as is any sacred or religious object or activity. Both the magician and the rite itself are typically surrounded by the observance of taboos, by the purification of the participants, and so on. The magician may observe restrictions on certain foods or on sexual activity, and he may be regarded as polluting to other people at these times. There are two obvious reasons: failure to observe such precautions nullify the magic, and they indicate to the participants and others the importance of the rite itself and the ends desired. They mark off the rite from ordinary and profane situations and invest it with sanctity and more than usual importance.

Functions. The functions of magic are several, but there are two main aspects, the instrumental and the expressive. A basic feature of magical rites and beliefs is that the practitioners believe that these are instrumental; *i.e.*, they are designed to achieve certain ends in nature or in the behaviour of other people. This is the aspect that is usually the most important for the people concerned and regarded as most important by past writers on the subject. The symbolic or expressive aspect is always present, however; it is precisely because of its symbolic content that magic may best be understood as a part of any system of religion.

Instrumental functions. Malinowski and his followers have distinguished three main instrumental functions: the productive, the protective, and the destructive. Productive magic is concerned to bring about a good harvest, to increase the food supply, to ensure a successful outcome to some creative or productive activity both in terms of human labour and of natural bounty. Malinowski showed clearly how it may foster confidence in situations in which technology is weak or uncertain; his famed example of the Trobriand Islanders making magic when fishing in the open sea but not doing so when fishing in the calm and protected lagoon makes the point clearly. In addition, productive magic may also assist the efficient organization of labour and give greater incentive to those who feel confident of success. Protective magic aims to prevent or remove danger, to cure sickness, and to protect an individual or community from the vagaries of nature and the evil acts of others. Again, it may give confidence for people to continue their normal ways of life and activities. Destructive magic is sorcery, directed specifically against other people to harm them or their activities. It has been pointed out that the fear of this form of magic may reduce individual initiative since a successful or wealthy person in an egalitarian society may fear the sorcery of those jealous of him. On the other hand, the use of counter-magic against it rids a community of its internal fears and tensions.

Expressive functions. The expressive functions of magic are symbolic, and usually latent in the sense that the performers may not themselves be immediately aware of them. They have largely to do with the effects of individual acts upon society at large. It is in regard to this point that the part played by magic in a total system of religion may be seen (see below *Magic, religion, and science*).

MAGIC, RELIGION, AND SCIENCE

Magic and religion. The relationship of magic to other religious phenomena depends on three main considerations. The first is the nature of the power toward which the rites are directed. The eminent British anthropologist Edward B. Tylor (1832–1917) and his successors distinguished a personal, conscious, and omnipotent spiritual being as the object of religious ritual; magical performances have no power in themselves but are usually thought by the people to be an expression of an external, impersonal force in nature, for which the Melanesian term *mana* has typically been used. A second consideration is that of the personnel involved: the magician and those who go to him. As noted above, Durkheim pointed out that a priest has a church or congregation whereas the magician has a clientele. A religious ritual has as its principal function (in sociological terms) the maintenance of a sense of cohesion among the members of the church, whereas the magical rite lacks this function, and is, indeed, often anti-religious in quality. This view has been influential in the past and has by now become part of general anthropological thinking, although some of its details have been ignored by recent researchers, as it is based mainly on Australian aboriginal data that are today more accurately known and are not directly relevant elsewhere.

The third consideration is that of the function of magic and of other religious phenomena. The magician may see the overt function of his action as instrumental, as geared to a specific end; the external observer may accept this but also see a latent function. Malinowski, for example, maintained that much of Trobriand magic was performed as an extension of human ability, as a power beyond the normal or understood. It had as its most important function the instillation of confidence in situations where human knowledge and competence cease. In addition, the rite helps to throw the importance of the activity and the cooperation needed for it into relief and thus to help maintain the high social value of cooperation in a small community beset by disruptive jealousies and competition over scarce and difficult resources. A.R. Radcliffe-Brown (1881–1955) pointed out in his work on the Andaman Islanders that their magical rites and precautions at childbirth and death may comfort those concerned, although they are also irksome, but that their main function is to highlight the social importance of birth and death and to bring to public notice the changes in patterns of local and kinship organization that follow them. Some of the hypotheses of Malinowski and Radcliffe-Brown are today regarded as questionable and are difficult of definitive proof, but they have been influential in later studies in that they were concerned not only with the individual's belief in magic but also with its function in the total social system.

In brief, it may be said that religious rites are ways of acting out beliefs about the relationships of man to God, man to man, and man to nature. Magic is rather a way of achieving certain ends beyond the knowledge and competence of everyday people, especially in technologically limited societies, and of expressing these desires in symbolic terms. There are certain functions that are common to both: the provision of explanation for the otherwise inexplicable; a means of coping with the unusual and mysterious; and the enhancing of the social values of certain activities and situations and of coordinating socially valuable activities.

Magic, technology, and science. The problem of the relationship of magic to technical and scientific knowledge has concerned most writers on the subject. Magical rites contain at least superficial similarities to nonmagical technical activities. In each the actor performs an action that he expects will have a certain consequence. The distinction between the two processes made by Tylor and Frazer (see below) was that the magician assumes a direct cause-effect relationship between the action and the later event, whereas in empirical fact the relationship is one of the association of ideas only. Many writers have pointed out that magic is used when technical knowledge is missing or uncertain. This view does not really state that

Margin notes:
Taboos, purifications, and precautions

Distinctive functions of magic and religion

magic is a substitute for technical knowledge but that its performance gives confidence to people aware of their technical limitations (as in the example of Trobriand fishing magic mentioned above). The magician does not regard his magic as being the same kind of activity as weeding a field or sharpening a knife; the magical rite is of a different order, dealing with external and mystical forces.

A problem that is relevant here is that of the scientific proof of the efficacy of magic. Why do people continue to believe in magic when it is clear (at least to outside observers) that there is empirically no cause-effect relationship between a magical rite and the desired and supposed consequence? The main purpose of magic is not so much to achieve a certain technical end as to perform an act that has symbolic or psychological value. It is thus pointless to test it, in the sense that a Christian does not test the efficacy of prayer as he might that of an internal combustion engine. The problem was discussed by Tylor (see below), who produced reasons why failure of magic was not easily apparent. The idiom of magic pervades all in contact with it and cannot be tested scientifically in its own terms, so that tests as to the magic's efficacy are not in fact tests at all but rational statements about common-sense experience.

THE MAIN THEORIES OF MAGIC

There is a voluminous literature on magic. The earliest studies were those of Judaic and Christian scholars concerned with the relationship of magic to their faiths, both as relics of paganism and as heresy. During the latter part of the 19th century, anthropologists entered the field, with the aim of analyzing magic by looking at cases as reported from peoples throughout the world and to see the place of magic in the evolution of all religions of mankind from prehistory to the contemporary world.

Anthropological. The first important figure was E.B. Tylor, who, in his *Primitive Culture* (1871), regarded magic as a "pseudo-science" in which the "savage" postulated a direct cause-effect relationship between the magical act and the desired event, whereas in reality the link is one of the association of ideas only. Although Tylor regarded magic as "one of the most pernicious delusions that ever vexed mankind," he studied it not as a superstition or heresy but as a phenomenon based on the "symbolic principle of magic," a logical scheme of thought founded on a quite rational process of analogy. He also faced the question of why the believer in magic did not realize its inefficacy. His reasons included the frequent association of magic with empirical behaviour, nature often performing what the magician tries to do; the attribution of failure to the breaking of taboos or to hostile magic forces; the plasticity of the notions of success and failure; and the weight of cultural belief and authority behind the magician. He also realized that magic and religion are parts of a total system of thought; they are not alternatives but complementary, and thus not stages in the evolutionary development of mankind—although he considered that magic and animistic beliefs decreased in the later stages of history.

Frazer's theory

In *The Golden Bough* (1890 and later editions) James G. Frazer refined Tylor's views on magical thought, discussed the relationship of magic to religion and science, and placed them all in a grandiose evolutionary scheme. He analyzed the principles of thought that lay behind the false cause-effect relationship between magical and natural events. They were that "like produces like, or that an effect resembles its cause" (the Law of Similarity) and that things once in physical contact with each other later continue to act on each other at a distance (the Law of Contact or Contagion). Magic based on the former he called homeopathic magic, that based on the latter he called contagious magic. He added the notion of taboo as negative magic, acting on the same principles of association. He accepted Tylor's linking of magical and scientific thought as both being based on the belief that a particular act necessarily or invariably results in a particular effect, magic thus being a "spurious system of natural law."

Frazer also developed an evolutionary scheme for mag-

ic and religion. He saw magic and religion as belonging to different stages in the development of human thought. Magic was prior because it seemed to him to be logically more simple, because he assumed (erroneously, as was shown later) that the Australian aborigines, examples of an archaic people, believed in magic but not in religion, and because magic forms a substratum of superstition even in advanced societies. Individuals in the earliest cultures must have come to realize the inefficacy of magic and the powerlessness of men to control nature; from this they postulated the existence of omnipotent spiritual beings who required supplication to direct nature as men wanted. Thus there came into existence religion. The final stage in this schema is when men begin to recognize the existence of empirical natural laws, aided by the discoveries of alchemy and then of science proper. With this final development religion joins magic as superstition.

These writers, and their followers such as Robert Ranulph Marett (1866–1943), regarded magic as essentially an individual and intellectual matter, one of the ways in which individuals think about the world. Another line of writers has widened the discussion by regarding the problem as essentially one of the social function of magic. The first such writers of note were the French sociologists Marcel Mauss (1872–1950) and Émile Durkheim. Durkheim, in *The Elementary Forms of the Religious Life* (Eng. trans., 1915), considered that magical rites comprised the manipulation of sacred objects by the magician on behalf of individual clients; the socially cohesive significance of religious rites proper, by the priests, was therefore largely lacking. His views were followed by A.R. Radcliffe-Brown (*The Andaman Islanders*, 1922) and to a lesser extent by Bronisław Malinowski (*Argonauts of the Western Pacific*, 1922, and various papers brought together as *Magic, Science and Religion*, 1925), the latter influenced more by Frazer and the early psychoanalysts. Radcliffe-Brown's main hypothesis has been mentioned above: the social function of magic was to express the social importance of the desired or protected event. Malinowski, on the other hand, regarded magic as being opposed to religion, and as directly and essentially concerned with the psychological needs of the individual. It acted to extend his normal knowledge and competence; to provide confidence in situations of technical uncertainty by "ritualizing optimism"; to express desires that are otherwise unrealizable in a small and technically limited community; and, as counter-magic, to explain failure. Malinowski's influence has been marked, due largely to the fact that his was the first detailed and first-hand account of the actual working of an ongoing system of magic. Other writers, notably R.R. Marret in England and Robert Lowie and Alexander Goldenweiser in the United States, differed from Tylor and Frazer in pointing out that the distinction between magic and religion is largely untenable, reflecting an ethnocentric distinction between the "natural" and the "supernatural" that is not made by most other religions.

Theories of Malinowski, Radcliffe-Brown, and E.E. Evans-Pritchard

In recent years there have been many reports of the working of systems of magic, especially from Africa and Oceania. On the whole they have followed Malinowski and Radcliffe-Brown and have been based on the single most important work on the topic that has appeared since them, E.E. Evans-Pritchard's (1902–   ) *Witchcraft, Oracles and Magic Among the Azande* (1937). He shows concisely how magic is an integral part of religion and culture, being used to explain events the normal understanding and control of which are beyond the technical competence of this southern Sudan people. The Azande accept magic as a normal part of nature and society, together with witchcraft and oracles. These various phenomena form a closed logical system, each part of which buttresses the other and provides a rational system of causation of both natural order and the social order as well as disorder or coincidence.

Psychological. These various anthropological approaches to magic have had the advantage of regarding it as a social phenomenon rather than one of individual psychology. The views of Tylor and Frazer, however, are eventually psychological in nature, since they are based on their notions of individual ways of thought. Their work was considerably based on that of Herbert Spencer and Wilhelm Wundt, thinkers of pronounced psychological interest, and was followed by anthropologists with psychological views on origins of magic and religion, such as Lowie, Paul Radin, and Goldenweiser, all of whom were concerned with the problem of the individual psychological status of believers. Much of Malinowski's work depends on providing psychological reasons for belief in magic. Sigmund Freud (*Totem and Taboo*, 1918) had at one time considerable influence in his view that magic, the earliest phase in the development of religious thought (following Frazer), was similar in its essential processes to the thought of children and neurotics. This view was based on his theory of the "Omnipotence of Thought," by which savages, children, and neurotics all assumed that wish or intention led automatically to the fulfillment of the desired end. This view has long been abandoned as a tenable hypothesis, due not so much to its inherent misunderstanding of the expressive nature of magical ritual as to the general recognition that the assumption of the similarity between primitive, infantile, and neurotic modes of thought is false; it arose largely from the ignorance of the nature of primitive culture before the development of modern anthropological field researches.

Conclusion.   The study of magic as a distinct cultural phenomenon has a long history in anthropological and historical studies. Although the distinction between it and other religious phenomena may often heuristically be useful, it cannot be studied in isolation as was once the fashion. It is essentially an aspect or reflection of the worldview held by a particular people at a particular stage of development in scientific and technical knowledge. It is thus a part, although to the people concerned often a very important part, of their total system of religion and cosmology.

BIBLIOGRAPHY.   The more important earlier anthropological writings on magic include: SIR EDWARD BURNETT TYLOR, *Primitive Culture: Researches into the Development of Mythology, Philosophy, Religion, Art, and Custom*, 2 vol. (1871, reprinted 1958); SIR JAMES GEORGE FRAZER, *The Golden Bough*, 3rd ed., 12 vol. (1911–15); HENRI HUBERT and MARCEL MAUSS, *Esquisse d'une théorie générale de la magie* (1904); EMILE DURKHEIM, *Les formes élémentaires de la vie religieuse* (1912; Eng. trans., *The Elementary Forms of the Religious Life*, 1915); and SIGMUND FREUD, *Totem und Tabu* (1913; Eng. trans., *Totem and Taboo*, 1918). The more important reports of magic in particular societies include: BRONISLAW MALINOWSKI, *Argonauts of the Western Pacific: An Account of Native Enterprise and Adventure in the Archipelagoes of Melanesian New Guinea* (1922, reprinted 1960); and "Magic, Science and Religion," in N.J.T. NEEDHAM (ed.), *Science, Religion and Reality* (1925, reprinted 1948); A.R. RADCLIFFE-BROWN, *The Andaman Islanders* (1922, reprinted 1964); and E.E. EVANS-PRITCHARD, *Witchcraft, Oracles and Magic among the Azande* (1937). More recent general and comparative studies are: HUTTON WEBSTER, *Magic: A Sociological Study* (1948); R.H. LOWIE, *Primitive Religion* (1948); W.J. GOODE, *Religion among the Primitives* (1951); FRANZ STEINER, *Taboo* (1956, reprinted 1967) M. DOUGLAS (ed.), *Witchcraft Confessions and Accusations* (1970); and M. and R. WAX, "The Notion of Magic," *Curr. Anthrop.*, 4: 495–518 (1963). There are also useful articles in the collections of essays, W.A. LESSA and E.Z. VOGT (eds.), *Reader in Comparative Religion: An Anthropological Approach*, 2nd ed. (1965); and JOHN MIDDLETON (ed.), *Magic, Witchcraft, and Curing* (1967). For European magic the most reliable works are E.M. BUTLER, *Ritual Magic* (1949); ELIPHAS LEVI, *Histoire de la Magie* (1860; Eng. trans., *The History of Magic*, 4th ed., 1948, reprinted 1963); H.C. LEA (comp.), *Materials toward a History of Witchcraft*, 3 vol. (1939); and K. THOMAS, *Religion and the Decline of Magic: Studies in Popular Beliefs in 16th and 17th Century England* (1971).

(J.F.M.)

Magnesium Products and Production

Magnesium is a silvery-white metallic element similar in appearance to aluminum but weighing approximately one-third less. It has a density of 0.0628 pound per cubic inch (1.738 grams per cubic centimetre). Like many other metals, magnesium in its pure form has few appli-

cations, but magnesium alloys are widely used, particularly where light weight and high strength are important, as in aerospace and automotive applications. The chemical compounds of magnesium have wide application in industry, medicine, and agriculture.

History.   The English chemist Sir Humphry Davy is said to have produced an amalgam of magnesium (an alloy with mercury) in 1808 by reduction of the oxide, using a mercury cathode. But the first free metallic magnesium was produced in 1828 by the French scientist A.-A.-B. Bussy. His work involved the reduction of fused magnesium chloride by metallic potassium.

First production of metallic magnesium

In 1833 the English scientist Michael Faraday was the first to produce magnesium by the electrolytic reduction (breaking down by an electric current) of magnesium chloride. Magnesium remained a laboratory curiosity until 1886, when I.G. Farbenindustrie of Germany undertook the manufacture of metallic magnesium on a production basis, using Faraday's electrolytic process.

Until 1915 Germany was the sole producer of magnesium, but during World War I this source was shut off from most of the world. Operations to produce magnesium were initiated in the United States by several organizations, most successfully by the Dow Chemical Company of Midland, Michigan. The Dow process, involving the electrolytic reduction of magnesium chloride, originally utilized deep brine wells at Midland as the raw material source, but these have been superseded by the use of seawater.

Raw material sources of magnesium.   A number of extractive methods are used in the recovery of metallic magnesium from its raw sources. These methods vary considerably depending upon the type of primary raw mineral, which may be found either in mineral deposits or in aqueous solutions.

Among the raw ore deposits, the most common minerals are the carbonates dolomite (a compound of magnesium and calcium carbonates, $MgCO_3 \cdot CaCO_3$) and magnesite, or magnesium carbonate ($MgCO_3$). The oxide mineral brucite, magnesium oxide associated with water ($MgO \cdot H_2O$), is less common, while the chloride mineral carnallite, a compound of magnesium and potassium chlorides and water ($MgCl_2 \cdot KCl \cdot 6H_2O$), is rarer still.

Magnesium is recoverable from aqueous solutions of brine wells, but by far the largest source of magnesium is the oceans of the world, where it appears in its chloride form. While seawater is only approximately 0.13 percent magnesium, this proportion remains quite constant and represents an almost inexhaustible source of supply—approximately 12,000,000,000 pounds (5,500,000,000 kilograms) of magnesium per cubic mile of seawater.

Magnesium in seawater

The uniformity of magnesium content in seawater facilitates standardization in process recovery and offers certain economic advantages, which can vary with geographic location of the producer.

Refining and recovery.   Magnesium is produced by two distinctly different methods. One is the direct reduction of the magnesium ores by strong reducing agents such as carbon, silicon, etc. The other is by electrolytic reduction of magnesium chloride. In the past, magnesium produced by direct reduction was of higher purity than that derived by electrolytic reduction, but because of process refinements, this is no longer the case. Where power costs are low, electrolytic reduction is the cheaper method; and, indeed, it accounts for much the greater part of world production.

Electrolytic reduction processes.   Both the early German process and the Dow process use magnesium chloride as the basic source, differing primarily in the characteristics of the electrolytic cell employed.

Magnesium chloride as raw material

The flow chart of the Dow process is shown in Figure 1 and represents the method used by the Dow plant near Freeport, Texas, where abundant natural gas is available for cheap power; nearby Galveston Bay provides an inexhaustible supply of lime in the form of oyster shells. In this process, seawater is mixed with calcium hydroxide in a processing unit called a flocculator. The calcium hydroxide is obtained by processing oyster shells. In the flocculator the calcium from the calcium hydroxide is

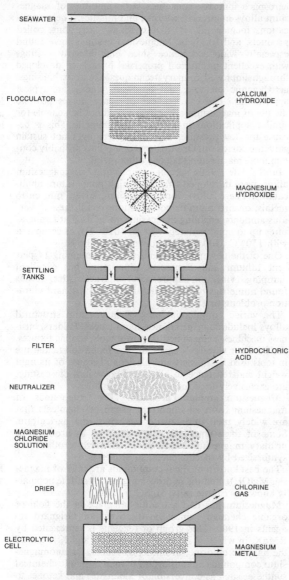

Figure 1: Stages in the Dow process for obtaining magnesium from seawater (see text).
Drawing by D. Meighan

The dolomite combines with the ferrosilicon to yield metallic magnesium and a combination of calcium and silicon oxides and iron.

Several hours are required for the reduction cycle. The magnesium yield may run from 30 to 500 pounds, depending upon retort size. For the process to compete economically with electrolytic reduction methods, plants must be located near sources of raw materials and power.

The metal and its alloys. Primary commercial magnesium metal is approximately 99.8 percent pure when produced by either of the methods. It is cast into small ingots or pigs, usually weighing from 20 to 50 pounds (9 to 23 kilograms). Higher purity can be attained by further processing in which the metal is remelted in a vacuum.

Many nonstructural uses of magnesium utilize the unalloyed metal, while specific alloy compositions are required for structural uses.

Nonstructural applications. The use of magnesium as an alloying element in aluminum-base alloys constitutes its greatest metallurgical application. In these aluminum alloys, magnesium is present in amounts ranging from less than 1 percent to approximately 10 percent. The use of the magnesium enhances the mechanical properties, as well as the corrosion resistance of such alloys. Similarly, pure aluminum is used as an alloying element in many magnesium-base alloys and has a similar beneficial effect upon structural properties.

Magnesium is frequently used to protect steel against corrosion by a method known as cathodic protection. When magnesium comes into electrical contact with steel in the presence of water, the magnesium corrodes sacrificially, leaving the steel intact. Ship hulls, water heaters, storage tanks, bridge structures, pipelines, and a variety of other steel products are protected in this manner.

Magnesium has been used in military pyrotechnics for many years and has found numerous uses in incendiary devices, flares, etc. Magnesium, in the form of finely divided particles, has been used as a fuel component, particularly in solid rocket propellants.

Drawing by D. Meighan

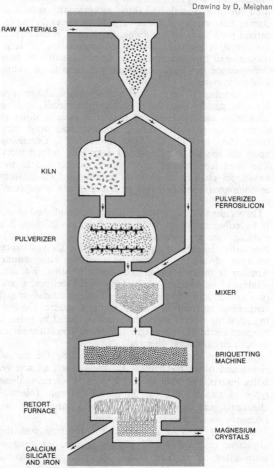

exchanged with the magnesium from the magnesium chloride in the seawater, forming the insoluble precipitate magnesium hydroxide. The seawater containing the magnesium hydroxide precipitate flows from the flocculator to large settling tanks. After the magnesium hydroxide has settled on the bottom, it is pumped out as a slurry, filtered, and converted to magnesium chloride by reaction with hydrochloric acid. After drying, the magnesium chloride is fed to electrolytic cells where it is broken down into magnesium metal and chlorine gas.

Direct reduction processes. Among the several direct reduction processes for the production of magnesium, by far the most important is the ferrosilicon process (sometimes referred to as the Pidgeon process for its originator, L.M. Pidgeon of Canada).

In the ferrosilicon process, dolomite is calcined (converted to lime by heating) and mixed with finely pulverized ferrosilicon Si–Fe. This mixture is briquetted and then placed in retorts at approximately 1,200° C (2,192° F). The direct reduction takes place within these retorts under very carefully controlled process conditions, the pressure and temperature being especially critical. A flow chart for the ferrosilicon direct-reduction process is shown in Figure 2.

The reaction taking place in the retorts is as follows:

$$2 \, MgO \cdot CaO + Si\text{–}Fe \rightarrow 2 \, Mg + (CaO)_2 \, SiO_2 \, (Fe).$$

Figure 2: Stages in the ferrosilicon magnesium process.

Magnesium metal is used as an alloying element in zinc die castings to promote dimensional stability and to improve mechanical properties. It is also used as an oxygen scavenger and desulfurizing agent in the manufacture of copper and nickel alloys and as a reducing agent in the manufacture of titanium and zirconium.

The use of magnesium in making nodular cast iron is well established and is based upon the nodular form imparted to the graphite present. This, in turn, gives cast iron vastly improved mechanical properties.

The magnesium dry cell

The magnesium dry cell has achieved some degree of prominence, particularly for specialized applications in which long storage life and light weight are desirable. Such dry cells usually consist of magnesium plus either silver chloride or cuprous chloride. When activated with water, these dry cells rapidly build up voltages of 1.3 to 1.8 volts per cell. Silver chloride–magnesium cells operate with constant potential in the range of $+94°$ to $-54°$ C ($200°$ to $-65°$ F). Cuprous chloride–magnesium cells exhibit similar output characteristics but with somewhat lower power output per unit of weight. Both cells use synthetic porous fibers for separation of the electrodes. The shelf life of both is almost indefinite, and the primary usage is in military applications.

The use of magnesium in photoengraving plates, a relatively new use of the metal, is based primarily upon its ease of etching by certain reagents.

Structural applications. Magnesium is useful as a structural metal when it is alloyed with small amounts of other metals. These alloying metals are aluminum, zinc, manganese, silver, zirconium, lithium, thorium, and the rare-earth metals. In most cases, the alloying elements form intermetallic compounds that permit heat treatment for enhanced mechanical properties as well as other benefits, such as corrosion resistance, size stabilization, and improved fabricability.

Structural forms of magnesium include sand, permanent mold, and die castings as well as extrusions, forgings, and rolled sheet and plate.

Magnesium alloys are fabricated by most of the methods used for other metals and show exceptionally good machining characteristics. While magnesium alloys do require careful processing in machining, fire hazard is minimal if the metal is properly handled. Accumulation of large quantities of magnesium chips or fines is usually the only circumstance in which magnesium will burn in an industrial environment.

Forming at elevated temperatures

The forming of magnesium into structural shapes follows the pattern used for most common metals, such as aluminum and steel, except that it is usually done at elevated temperatures. These temperatures may vary from $160°$ to $400°$ C ($320°$ to $750°$ F), depending upon the specific alloy and the degree of deformation. The need for elevated temperatures is ascribed to the hexagonal close-packed crystal structure of magnesium as compared with the cubic structure of the other common metals.

The welding of magnesium alloys is accomplished readily by either resistance welding or inert-gas-shielded arc welding (see also WELDING, BRAZING, AND SOLDERING). Normally the type of equipment used for the resistance welding of aluminum may be used for magnesium, whether it be spot welding or seam welding. For arc welding of magnesium, an inert gas shield (helium, argon, or a mixture) around the weld area prevents oxidation and contamination from the surrounding atmosphere. Depending upon the type of weld, the arc is produced by either a tungsten electrode or a magnesium wire. The latter serves as both electrode and filler rod.

Magnesium structures also are formed by the use of rivets and other mechanical fasteners, such as screws, bolts, inserts, and other special devices. When using these types of attachments, the danger of galvanic (electrochemical) corrosion is very real, particularly since the fasteners are not made of magnesium.

Because of the ease of fabrication, together with the attractive mechanical and physical properties, magnesium alloys have been widely accepted in structures where light weight and high strength are needed. The aerospace industry consumes large amounts of magnesium alloys in aircraft, rockets, and missiles. These applications include all types of castings, extrusions, rolled products, and forgings. Magnesium castings have found especially wide acceptance since high-integrity castings with excellent mechanical properties have been developed through improved foundry techniques. Gearbox housings, aerodynamic surfaces, and hardware chassis are typical applications. The environment of space makes possible the use of magnesium alloys that would not be suitable for similar applications in an earth environment. This is because the low-pressure, dry atmosphere does not sustain galvanic corrosion. Orbiting space satellites probably contain more magnesium than any other metal.

Magnesium alloys in outer space

In the late 1950s special compositions of magnesium alloys were developed for use in high temperature applications. These alloys contain thorium, silver, rare earth metals, or zirconium or combinations of all these in various amounts, enabling magnesium to be used at temperatures up to approximately $320°$ C ($610°$ F), as compared with $150°$ C ($300°$ F) for conventional alloys.

One of the newer magnesium alloys, containing 14 percent lithium and 1 percent aluminum, has excellent damping (vibration-suppression) characteristics. It has found numerous uses in structures where resonant vibration problems existed.

The varied commercial uses of magnesium structural alloys include luggage frames, hand trucks, ladders, business machines, camera bodies, power tools, tooling fixtures, and race-car wheels. Magnesium has found substantial use in tools used by masons and plasterers because of its light weight and resistance to alkalies. Magnesium die castings are extensively used, notably in automobiles.

Magnesium compound products. The compounds of magnesium form an important group of chemicals that are widely used in industry, medicine, and agriculture. Some of these chemicals are formed as by-products of primary magnesium metal production while others are synthesized by specific chemical processes.

Epsom salts

The best known medical compounds are milk of magnesia, $Mg(OH)_2$, and the hydrous magnesium sulfate popularly known as Epsom salts, $MgSO_4 \cdot 7H_2O$.

Magnesium has had a traditional place in the field of organic chemistry since the discovery of Grignard reagents in 1900. This group of reagents is represented by RMgX, in which R is an organic radical and X is one of the halides: chlorine, bromine, or iodine. Organomagnesium compounds are important in many organic chemical syntheses such as conversion of aldehydes and ketones to alcohols.

Magnesium carbonate, $MgCO_3$, is one of the most widely used magnesium compounds in industry. It is used in large quantities for refractory (high-temperature) bricks and linings of open-hearth furnaces used in steel manufacture. In this application, magnesite and dolomite ores are the principal sources of supply.

While basic magnesium carbonate serves primarily as a component of insulating compounds, the technical (high-purity) grade is widely used for fireproofing and as a filler for paper, plastics, paints, and varnishes. The principal pharmaceutical uses are as a bulking compound in powder formulations and as an antacid.

The most important use of magnesium chloride is in the recovery of magnesium metal, but it is also used in wall-plaster compositions and as a fireproofing agent for wood.

In addition to its medical applications, magnesium sulfate is used as a tanning agent, a conditioning agent for cotton, a mordant for dyeing wool, and as a component of fertilizers.

Economic importance. Although the greatest production of magnesium metal occurred during the war years of 1943 and 1944, expanded uses have required steadily increasing tonnages since that time. The U.S. Bureau of Mines estimated in 1970 that the total world production of primary magnesium was 243,250 short tons (220,673 metric tons). Three nations accounted for nearly 85 percent of this production: the U.S. (112,007 short tons), the U.S.S.R. (55,000 short tons), and Norway (39,000 short tons).

BIBLIOGRAPHY. *Encyclopedia of Chemical Technology,* 2nd ed., vol. 12 (1963), a comprehensive text detailing the production methods of primary magnesium metal; C.S. ROBERTS, *Magnesium and Its Alloys* (1960), a thorough review of the history of magnesium, production methods, alloys, and uses; W.H. GROSS, *The Story of Magnesium* (1949), historical data on magnesium presented in an interesting manner; AMERICAN SOCIETY FOR METALS, *Magnesium* (1946), semi-technical data on the progress of magnesium production and its uses at that time period, *Metals Handbook,* 8th ed., vol. 1 (1961), excellent illustrations on magnesium applications and property data on the material; M. CAMPBELL and H. HATTON, *Herbert H. Dow: Pioneer in Creative Chemistry* (1951), a classic story of the man who pioneered magnesium in the U.S.; J.H. RIZLEY, *Magnesium: A Material of the Space Age* (1960), a paper on the use of magnesium in space presented at the Magnesium International Conference of May 1960.

(J.H.R.)

Magnetic Resonance

Magnetic resonance is said to occur when atoms or atomic nuclei respond to the application of certain magnetic fields by absorbing or emitting electromagnetic radiation. The principles of magnetic resonance are applied in the laboratory to analyze the atomic and nuclear properties of matter.

In order to understand magnetic resonance, which may be either electron-spin resonance or nuclear magnetic resonance, it is necessary to understand magnetic moments and the effect of magnetic fields on them.

GENERAL CONSIDERATIONS AND HISTORY
OF RESONANCE INVESTIGATIONS

First principles. The classical model of the atom posits negatively charged electrons in orbit about a positively charged nucleus of protons and neutrons. An electron speeding in an orbit is like any other mass, such as a stone on the end of a string, moving in a circle: its speed can be characterized by a mechanical angular momentum, which also depends on its mass and orbital radius, and is represented by a vector that points at right angles to the plane of rotation. A moving electric charge produces a magnetic field; thus, the motion of an electron in its orbit gives rise to a magnetic field that is not unlike that of a tiny bar magnet in that it is a dipole, having a north and south pole. Specifically, it is said to have a magnetic dipole moment, or a magnetic moment, a term that expresses the amount of torque or turning force a dipole such as an orbiting electron or bar magnet will experience when it is placed in the given magnetic field. The magnetic moment, too, is represented by a vector pointing in a direction at right angles to the plane of rotation. Although the angular-momentum vector and magnetic-moment vector coincide, they may point in opposite directions, depending on the sign of the rotating charge and the direction of rotation.

Thus, because a moving charge produces a magnetic field, a subatomic particle having angular momentum and charge has a magnetic moment associated with it. Not only does an electron rotate about the nucleus in an orbit, but it spins on its own axis; hence, in addition to having an orbital angular momentum and orbital magnetic moment, it has a spin angular momentum and a consequent spin magnetic moment. Inside the atom, the nucleus also possesses an angular momentum due to the rotation of itself or its parts, and so it, too, has a magnetic moment, called its nuclear magnetic moment, or magnetic moment due to nuclear spin.

Orbital and spin electronic moments are expressed in Bohr magnetons; *i.e.,* a fundamental atomic unit equal to the product of the electron charge and Planck's universal constant (that associates a quantum of energy with frequency of vibration) divided by the product of four pi (π) times the electron mass and the velocity of light, or $\beta = eh/4\pi mc$, in which β represents a Bohr magneton, e is electronic charge, h is Planck's constant, m is the electron mass, and c is the velocity of light. There is also a nuclear magneton equal to the product of the electron charge and Planck's constant divided by the product of four pi (π) times the proton mass and the velocity of light, or $\beta_n = eh/4\pi Mc$, but it is 1,836 times smaller because

Magnetic moment (margin note)

Bohr magnetons (margin note)

this number is the ratio of the mass M of the proton to the mass m of the electron.

When a bar magnet is placed in a steady magnetic field, it experiences a torque because its north pole seeks the south pole of the field, and vice versa. When the magnet comes to rest, it is said to be in the parallel position; work would be required to change its orientation to a position other than parallel. This means that the system can store potential energy. The energy associated with the magnet depends, therefore, on its magnetic moment, the strength of the pervading magnetic field, and the angle of direction that the bar magnet makes with respect to the magnetic field.

Atoms and nuclei, because of their magnetic dipole moments, are also endowed with potential energy when subjected to a strong, external magnetic field. The magnetic energy (energy state) of the atomic or nuclear dipole is restricted because the angular momentum with which it is associated must conform to a quantum mechanics rule which states that angular momentum of the atom or nucleus must be a whole multiple (such as one, two, or three times) of a fundamental unit of angular momentum; thus the magnetic energy of the atom or nucleus is said to be quantized. A large number of atoms will have many energy states, each characterized by a different quantum of energy.

Such energy states can be shown schematically by a series of horizontal parallel lines, called an energy level diagram, in which each energy state is represented by a single line, or energy level. When a dipole is parallel to a magnetic field it has the least amount of potential energy and is in the ground state or lowest energy level; when antiparallel, it is in the highest energy level.

Quantized energies (margin note)

In magnetic-resonance experiments, when atoms are placed in a strong magnetic field, the electrons and nuclei of the atoms will seek various energy levels. If, in addition, an alternating magnetic field, relatively weak and oscillating at the proper synchronous or resonant frequency, called the resonant magnetic field, is applied in a plane at right angles to the strong magnetic field, many of the atoms and nuclei can, as will be explained later, be induced to shift to higher energy levels; *i.e.,* their moments will be flipped over—that is to say, from parallel to antiparallel. The consequence of the transition between two levels is that energy will be extracted from the resonant magnetic field and can be displayed on a magnetic-resonance spectrometer as part of a magnetic-resonance spectrum (Figure 1). The frequency of the resonance

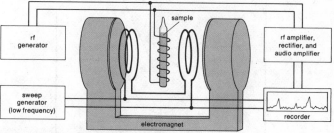

Figure 1: *Magnetic resonance device.*
Sample to be measured is placed between poles of a direct current (dc) electromagnet. A radio frequency (rf) magnetic field is generated by the coil surrounding the sample. The sweep generator coils augment the dc electromagnet so that its static field can be changed slightly until resonance occurs. At the moment of resonance, the magnetic moments of the sample absorb energy from the rf field, which is displayed as a peak in the recorder. By synchronizing the sweep generator and the recorder, many resonances can be scanned to give a spectrum.

magnetic field applied to the sample determines the transitions that take place, depending on which of the magnetic moments are to be affected: those arising from electrons, nuclei, or both. The resulting spectrum can, of course, be analyzed so that the scientist will know what energies and energy perturbations are involved. Resonance frequencies in the microwave region (in the neighbourhood of a centimetre in wavelength) are used for electron-spin resonance (ESR) and at radio frequency (high frequency–very high frequency [HF–VHF] band, 10–100 megacycles) for nuclear magnetic-resonance (NMR) studies. Both ESR and NMR are major, powerful investigative tools employed in most branches of science —in physics, in chemistry, in biology, and even in geology, and archaeology.

Early studies. The first observation of resonance due to electron spin, or electron-spin resonance (ESR), was made in 1944 by a Soviet physicist Y.K. Zavoysky using several concentrated salts of the iron group. Later, an increase in sensitivity made it possible to observe the resonance in dilute samples in which only a fraction of the atoms carry electron magnetic moments. The better resolution of resonance lines in dilute samples led to the important discovery that they were split into finer lines, called the electron-spin-resonance hyperfine structure. The ever-increasing sensitivity of electron-spin-resonance detecting equipment has permitted study of such phenomena as structural defects in crystals that give them their colour, free radicals (a type of molecular fragment, with unpaired electron spins) in liquid and solid samples, free or conduction electrons in metals, and metastable states (those energy states that are relatively long lived because transfer from them by radiation is prohibited) in molecular crystals.

First observations

The first observations of nuclear magnetic resonance (NMR) were made in the U.S. in 1946 by Felix Bloch, William W. Hansen, and Martin E. Packard with the protons of water and independently by Edward M. Purcell, Robert V. Pound, and Henry C. Torrey with the protons of paraffin. The number of nuclear species in which scientists observed NMR increased rapidly until it included practically all the stable nuclei with nuclear moments greater than zero, about one hundred nuclear species. New discoveries with NMR include electric quadrupole effects (an electric quadrupole consists of a charge distribution equivalent to a special arrangement of two electric dipoles), the observation of an important shift of NMR lines in metals, multiplet line splitting in liquids due to chemical structure and to the influence of one nuclear

spin on another and the presence of NMR in superconductors (conductors having negligible electrical resistance).

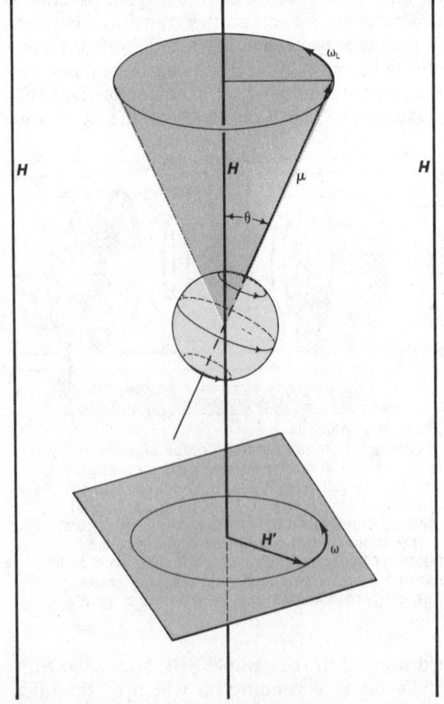

Besides pure ESR and NMR, double-resonance methods have been employed with both simultaneously, such as electron-nuclear-double resonance and dynamic nuclear polarization. It is difficult to discuss the complete theory of magnetic resonance without resorting to vector and tensor analysis. The theory underlying electron-spin resonance and nuclear magnetic resonance is common to both kinds of resonances and an elementary presentation is given below.

MAGNETIC RESONANCE IN BULK MATTER

General theory. Every magnetic dipole (spin system) can be represented by a vector μ that is determined by the magnitude and direction of its magnetic moment. In Figure 2, this vector is depicted as lying along the axis about which an atomic nucleus (as an example) is spinning. Any particle, such as an electron, proton, neutron, and many species of atoms and nuclei, that has both a magnetic moment and a mechanical angular momentum and that is surrounded by a magnetic field (symbolized by the vector H characterizing the strength and direction of the magnetic field) will experience a force such that the spin axis (and magnetic-moment vector) will precess around the magnetic field direction, describing a cone about it. The behaviour of the spinning nucleus will be analogous to the precession of a spinning top about a line in the direction of the Earth's gravitational pull. According to classical electrodynamics, the frequency (ω_L) of the Larmor precession (number of rotations per second of the magnetic-moment vector about the magnetic-field vector) should be independent of the orientation angle (θ), that is, the amount that the spin axis is tilted away from the field direction. But according to quantum mechanics, the orientation angle of a single nucleus can assume only certain limited values because the angular momenta of the nucleus are quantized, corresponding to an equal number of magnetic energy states. (In practice, the resultant magnetization of a large number of nuclei is observed, and so it can make any angle with the applied field.)

Larmor precession

In magnetic-resonance devices, a small oscillating field (H') is superimposed on a large constant field (H), as shown in Figure 2, and has an angular velocity (ω) in a plane perpendicular to the magnetic-field direction. For simplicity, one can imagine that a small precessing bar magnet is substituted for the nucleus and that the superimposed magnetic field (vector H') represents another bar magnet rotating about the large constant field (H) direction as an axis. When the rate of rotation (ω) of the superimposed field magnet is different from the Larmor frequency ω_L of the nuclear magnet, the two magnets will be out of phase, or not synchronized; the nuclear magnet will successively be attracted and repulsed (tilted) by the superimposed rotating magnet during complete revolutions, with the nuclear magnet wobbling only slightly. When they are synchronized, however, there will be a steady force acting on the nuclear magnet. Thus, in magnetic resonance, when the frequency of the superimposed magnetic field is equal to the Larmor frequency, the orientation angle will change suddenly and the nucleus will be raised or lowered to another energy state. This synchronism is the condition of resonance. When a spin system is raised to a higher state, energy is extracted from the superimposed field, and vice versa. The use of an oscillating field to produce resonance is sometimes referred to as "driving a resonance."

Analysis. Every experiment in magnetic resonance involves detecting the resonance; *i.e.*, ascertaining that the transition has actually taken place. Magnetic resonance (MR) makes use of electromagnetic detection, in which the energy liberated or absorbed in a transition is precisely that which is measured. The interpretation of MR in bulk matter is considerably complicated by the relationship of the spins with each other and with the other degrees of freedom of the sample. This complication, however, turns out to be an asset rather than a drawback for magnetic resonance, because it is the very existence of

Figure 2: *Precession of a magnetic dipole moment μ in the presence of a constant field H and a rotating field H'.*
The dipole precesses due to the Larmor effect with angular velocity ω_L about the field direction H, whereas the superimposed field H' rotates about the field direction with angular velocity ω. At resonance, the frequency of the superimposed field rotation and the Larmor precession are equal.

these interactions that makes MR such a remarkable tool for the study of bulk matter.

In many kinds of atoms all of the electrons are paired; that is, the spins are oppositely directed and therefore neutralized, and there is no net spin angular momentum or magnetic moment. In other species of atoms there are one or more electrons that give rise to a cooperative effect between their spins, or between their spins and orbital motions. It is therefore possible for any of these atoms to acquire or lose various quantum multiples of energy, and in a large assembly of identical spin systems, the energy states of the systems will be characterized by many different energy levels. What has been said of electron-spin systems may also be said of many species of nuclei, in that there can be a coupling effect between the spin of a nucleus and an external magnetic field, so that nuclei can lie in different energy states. Indeed, one odd-numbered nucleon can give rise to two different energy states because its spin is either $-\frac{1}{2}$ or $+\frac{1}{2}$ nuclear magnetons.

The structure of a crystal system is in the form of a lattice; it is composed of atoms arranged in layers in an orderly manner. Atoms are not fixed in position at the lattice sites but vibrate about the sites as centres. Each vibration implies a mechanical energy; because of the restrictions of quantum mechanics theory, these energies are quantized into what is known as phonons, having energies equal to Planck's constant times frequency. Phonons make up the thermal energy of a crystal. When the lattice sites are occupied by spin systems, electronic or nuclear, it is possible for the phonons and spin systems to interact; that is, to exchange energy in quantum multiples. Spin systems gaining phonon energy give rise to higher energy levels, and vice versa. If the exchange is such that there is thermal equilibrium—a constant energy exchange keeps the thermal energy in balance—the phenomenon is known as spin-lattice relaxation. Other types of motion of the atoms, such as free or restricted rotation of groups of atoms, random motion due to diffusion, etc., can also give rise to thermal spin-lattice relaxation.

During spin-lattice relaxation, successively higher energy levels will be occupied by fewer spin systems because the population of a given energy level is regulated according to the absolute temperature of the material. Should the material be placed in a radio-frequency field generator, as in magnetic resonance, and should the radio-frequency field be sufficiently strong, spin systems will be raised from one energy level to a higher one until all of the levels are populated equally, a situation known as saturation. Thus, the saturating effect of magnetic resonance is opposed by spin-lattice relaxation. The amount of electromagnetic energy absorbed gives a measure of the energy levels.

For magnetic fields of the order of a few kilogauss (gauss is a unit of magnetic intensity; the horizontal intensity of the Earth's magnetic field is roughly 0.2 gauss) currently used in laboratories, nuclear magnetic-resonance (NMR) frequencies fall into the radio-frequency or broadcasting range, whereas electron-spin-resonance (ESR) frequencies occur in the microwave or radar range. For instance, the proton NMR frequency in a field of 10 kilogauss is 42,577 megahertz (million cycles per second), and in the same field the ESR frequency of a free spin is 28,000 megahertz. With regard to sensitivity, the number of spins detectable by magnetic resonance varies widely with the applied field, the temperature, the nature of the sample, and for NMR the nuclear species; under the best conditions, it can be as low as 10^{18} spins for NMR and 10^{10} spins for ESR.

An important aspect of magnetic resonance in bulk matter is the finite width of resonance lines. Part of this width is caused by the spin-lattice relaxation that, by inducing relaxation transitions between spin levels, shortens the lifetimes of these levels and broadens them accordingly. This result follows from Heisenberg's uncertainty principle that the inaccuracy in measurement of energy, manifested as a widening of an energy level, increases as the lifetime of the state decreases.

Usually, a larger contribution to line width originates in spin-spin interactions. These are the typical interactions between two dipole moments in which, for example, local fields act on a spin, the fields being produced by its neighbouring spins. There is a wide variation in direction and magnitude of local fields by the many spins of the sample, which results in a width that is far greater in solids than that due to spin-lattice relaxation. In NMR, local fields have strengths of only a few gauss; in ESR it can be a few thousand gauss for similar concentrations of spins. These enormous contributions by local field interaction explain why samples must be dilute in order to give reduced line widths.

The values quoted above are those actually observed in solids; the lines observed in liquid samples are one hundred to one million times narrower, due to a phenomenon known as motion narrowing. Because the local field fluctuates in a random fashion and at a fast rate, each spin is acted on by only the average value of the local field taken over many fluctuations. Whereas in liquids the instantaneous value of the local field is of the same order of magnitude as in solids, the effective line width is reduced by as much as one-millionth in NMR and one-hundredth in ESR.

Another type of narrowing, specific to ESR in concentrated samples, is the so-called exchange narrowing. The exchange interaction that exists between two neighbouring electronic spins can be interpreted qualitatively as an interchange of their orientation within a finite time. By a mechanism similar to that of motion narrowing, this interaction results in a narrowing of ESR lines by a factor of one hundred or so. Exchange narrowing does not operate in dilute samples because of the short range over which exchange interactions take place.

NUCLEAR MAGNETIC RESONANCE

Nuclear magnetic resonance in solids. Most observations of nuclear magnetic resonance (NMR) in solids are made in diamagnetic substances (substances in which the electron spins are paired off in opposite directions to neutralize one another so that there is no residual magnetic field from electrons), and thus the shape of the NMR line is determined by the positions of the nuclear spins alone. In the absence of atomic motion in rigid lattices (crystals), it is possible to determine molecular structures not observable by other means.

In many solids, even at low temperatures, there exist internal movements of relatively large amplitude caused by atomic diffusion and free or restricted rotation of groups of atoms. These movements modulate the local field and have a drastic effect on the shape of the NMR line. A study of these effects as a function of temperature can supplement the other physical measurements.

In metals, the nuclei are influenced by an electronic field produced by the alignment of the spins of the conduction electrons (electrons not bound to atoms that move freely through the metal) by the applied field. This condition results in a relative shift of the resonant frequency that is characteristic of the metal for NMR, which has a different value for an insulator.

Metallic shifts, varying in size from a small fraction of a percent (0.025 percent for lithium) to a few percent (2.5 percent for mercury), provide important information on the magnetic susceptibility, the wave functions of quantum mechanics that describe energy states, and the density of states of conduction electrons in the metal. In superconductors, the shape of the NMR line provides detailed information on the penetration and distribution of the magnetic field inside the superconductor. In ferromagnets or antiferromagnets (crystals in which not all electrons are paired), the NMR is shifted by the internal magnetic fields produced by the array of ordered electronic spins. In ferromagnets the shift is a measure of the lattice magnetization; in an antiferromagnet there are at least two shifts that give the magnetization of each antiferromagnetic sublattice separately, a result unattainable by conventional magnetic measurements.

For nuclei with quantum spins greater than one-half, the NMR spectrum is modified by the existence of nuclear electric quadrupole moments (an electric quadrupole

Spin-lattice relaxation

Importance of line width

Motion narrowing

Magnetic resonance in metals

consists of a charge distribution equivalent to a special arrangement of two electric dipoles), which interact with the electric fields that exist at the nuclear sites. As the fields are electric rather than magnetic, these interactions remain unchanged when the direction of the nuclear spin is reversed. In their presence, the various transitions correspond to different frequencies and the NMR is split into several lines. The positions and the widths of these lines and their dependence on the orientation of the magnetic field with respect to the crystal axes provide information on the microscopic distribution of electric charge around the nucleus.

Nuclear magnetic resonance in liquids. The most important consequence of the extraordinary sharpness of nuclear magnetic resonance (NMR) lines in liquids, caused by motion narrowing, is the possibility of measuring the chemical shifts; that is, the separations between NMR lines from nuclear spins of the same species but in different molecular environments. The physical origin of chemical shifts is the following: an external magnetic field applied to a diamagnetic substance polarizes the closed electron shells of the atoms and produces a small magnetic field, proportional to the external field, which shifts the NMR line with respect to its position for the bare nucleus; *e.g.*, one which is devoid of electrons. The bare nucleus itself is never observed, but the atomic diamagnetic shifts that correspond to atoms located in different molecular sites are slightly different, and it is their differences that produce the chemical shifts. As an example, the proton NMR spectrum of a molecule of ethyl alcohol, with the formula $CH_3–CH_2–OH$, exhibits three peaks with relative weights or intensities of 3:2:1. In more complicated molecules such spectra contain much chemical information and can help in the determination of unknown molecular structures.

The multiplicity of lines is further increased by the interaction between nuclear spins. As already mentioned in connection with motion narrowing in liquids, the usual magnetic dipolar interactions are averaged out by molecular motion and do not split the NMR spectra. There exists, however, an indirect interaction between nuclear spins, caused by the electrons, that splits the resonance line of a specific nuclear spin into many components.

High-resolution nuclear magnetic resonance has become one of the most prized tools in the fields of organic chemistry and biochemistry. On the experimental side, the requirements to be met by the equipment are severe. In order to match natural line widths of a fraction of a cycle, the applied magnetic fields must have a relative stability and homogeneity throughout the sample better than one part in 10^8. Special magnets that give uniform fields and are stabilized, devices that twirl samples in order to smooth out the magnetic inhomogeneity, and sophisticated radio-frequency detection equipment are commercially available. The trend toward higher fields (over 100 kilogauss), resulting from superconducting solenoids, improves the resolution by increasing the chemical shift splittings and the signal-to-noise ratio.

Magnetic mapping. The measurement of the precession frequency of proton spins in a magnetic field can give the value of the field with high accuracy and is widely used for that purpose. In low fields, such as the Earth's magnetic field, the NMR signal is expected to be weak because the nuclear magnetization is small, but special devices can enhance the signal a hundred or thousand times. Incorporated in existing portable magnetometers, these devices make them capable of measuring fields to an absolute accuracy of about one part in one million and detecting field variations of about 10^{-8} gauss. Apart from the direct measurement of the magnetic field on Earth or in space, these magnetometers prove to be useful whenever a phenomenon is linked with variations of magnetic field in space or in time, such as anomalies arising from submarines, skiers buried under snow, archaeological remains, and mineral deposits.

ELECTRON-SPIN RESONANCE

Theory. In contrast to nuclear magnetic resonance, electron-spin resonance (ESR) is observed only in a restricted class of substances. These substances include transition elements—that is, elements with unfilled inner electronic shells—free radicals (molecular fragments), metals, and various paramagnetic defects and impurity centres. Another difference from NMR is a far greater sensitivity to environment; whereas the resonance frequencies in NMR in general are shifted from those of bare nuclei by very small amounts because of the influence of conduction electrons, chemical shifts, spin-spin couplings, and so on, the ESR frequencies in bulk matter may differ from those of free spins or free atoms by appreciable factors. This difference is due to the orbital magnetism originating in the orbital electronic currents circulating in unfilled subshells of the atom. The distortion of these shells by the interactions existing in bulk matter modifies considerably the orbital magnetic contribution to the observed ESR frequency.

A model that has been highly successful for the description of magnetism in bulk matter is based on ligand field theory concerned with the effect of the crystal lattice on the magnetic centre under study. As an explanation of the large amount of detailed and accurate experimental evidence accumulated in ESR work, the ligand field model, depending heavily on the mathematical apparatus of group theory, has risen to a high level of sophistication. Basically, the effect of the crystal field is to reduce (quench) the magnetism caused by orbital motion, the more so the lower the symmetry of the field. In quantum mechanics, the existence of orbital momentum is closely related to the rotational symmetry of the free atom. To some extent the orbital magnetism is preserved against ligand fields of low symmetry by the spin-orbit coupling of the electrons. Its effect is to associate closely the spin and orbital momentum of an atom to form a resultant angular momentum. The ligand field, being electric rather than magnetic, is powerless against spin moment, however, and if the orbital momentum is closely coupled to the spin, the orbital momentum partakes of a certain immunity from the reduction caused by the crystal field.

The total energy of the magnetic centre consists of two parts: (1) the energy of coupling between magnetic moments due to the electrons and the external magnetic field, and (2) the electrostatic energy between the electronic shells and the ligand field, which is independent of the applied magnetic field. The energy levels, found by standard quantum mechanical methods, give rise to a spectrum with many different resonance frequencies, the fine structure.

Another important feature of electron-spin resonance is the hyperfine structure—that is, the interaction of the electronic magnetization with the nuclear moment—which is quantized by the nuclear spin. The magnetic electron dipoles produce a magnetic field at the nucleus, and its interaction with the nuclear moment is an energy that can be added to the total energy of the interaction in the ligand field together with an energy for the nuclear interaction with the applied field. Each component of the fine-structure resonance spectrum thus is split further into many so-called hyperfine components.

If the electronic magnetization is spread over more than one atom it can interact with more than one nucleus; and in the expression for hyperfine levels, the hyperfine coupling of the electrons with a single nucleus must be replaced by the sum of the coupling with all the nuclei. When the magnetic electrons are strongly localized on a single atom, the main hyperfine coupling relative to its nucleus is much larger than the couplings with the neighbouring nuclei. Each main hyperfine line is then split further by the smaller couplings into what is known as superhyperfine structure.

The key problem in electron-spin resonance is, on one hand, to calculate from first principles the parameters (variables) of the total energy of the interaction in the ligand field plus the applied magnetic field and, on the other hand, to extract these same parameters from an analysis of the observed spectra. The confrontation of the two sets of parametric values permits a detailed quantitative test of the microscopic description of the structure of matter in the compounds studied by ESR.

Chemical shifts

High-resolution spectroscopy

Super-hyperfine structure

Electron-spin resonance in transition elements. The transition elements include the following groups of atoms: the iron group, the lanthanide or rare-earth group, the palladium group, the platinum group, and the actinide group; the lanthanide and iron groups are, by far, the most extensively studied. The resonance behaviour of the compounds containing these elements is conditioned by the relative strength of the ligand field and the spin-orbit coupling. In the lanthanides, for instance, the ligand field is weak and unable to uncouple the spin and orbital momentum, leaving the latter largely unreduced. On the other hand, in the iron group, the components of the ligand field are, as a rule, stronger than the spin-orbit coupling, and the orbital momentum is strongly reduced.

Although the transition-element compounds have been studied by such means as static magnetic measurements and specific-heat measurements, the advent of ESR has marked a new understanding of these substances. Thus, until the advent of ESR it was generally admitted that the structure of the paramagnetic centres in the iron group and the lanthanide group were purely ionic (ions of the crystal bound together solely by their electrostatic attraction), the magnetic electrons being completely localized on the transition ion. The discovery of superhyperfine structure, with the neighbouring nuclei, demonstrated conclusively that some covalent bonding to neighbouring ions exists.

Defects, impurity centres, and free radicals. With few exceptions, the magnetic moments of the numerous defects (imperfections such as vacancies at lattice sites) and impurity centres in crystals that give rise to an observable ESR have the characteristics of a free electronic spin. In the study of these centres, the role of hyperfine and superhyperfine structure is paramount: it provides a mapping of the electronic magnetization and establishes the correctness of the model chosen to describe the defect. As an example, one of the best known of crystal defects, the F-centre, a term for an electron captured in the vacancy of a negative ion in alkali halides, has an ESR line with no central hyperfine structure, but the electronic magnetization spills over the neighbouring ions and gives rise to an extensive superhyperfine structure.

As an example of ESR in impurity atoms, the most widely studied by resonance are the atoms of such elements as phosphorus, arsenic, and antimony, substituted in such semiconductors as silicon and germanium. Again, extensive theoretical and experimental studies of hyperfine and superhyperfine structure give detailed information on the theory of these impurities.

Free radicals, having unpaired electronic spins, are ideally suited for study by electron-spin resonance. They can be studied in a concentrated form in which the lines are considerably narrowed and the hyperfine structures washed out by exchange, or to the contrary, caused by the sensitivity of ESR, in very dilute solutions. This sensitivity is particularly important for the study of very short-lived species that have to be created inside the detecting cavity. The ESR of free radicals in solutions gives an extreme wealth of hyperfine lines because the magnetic electron is not localized on one nucleus but interacts with several nuclei of the radical (mainly protons, but also nitrogen-14 and phosphorus-31). A high-resolution ESR of free radicals, in many respects analogous to high-resolution NMR, has been developed.

An important development in the study of free radicals is the electron-spin resonance of excited triplet energy levels or states of organic molecules, such as naphthalene, in which two electronic spins, paired off to a total spin of zero in the ground or lowest state, combine to form a spin value of one in a higher, excited state. The excited state, which has a sufficient lifetime—a few seconds—to be observed by ESR, may be raised by ultraviolet excitation to an even higher state, with subsequent de-excitation.

Free radicals (margin note)

COMBINED ELECTRON-SPIN AND NUCLEAR MAGNETIC RESONANCES

When a spin system offers more than one resonance, it may be advantageous to study two or more of them simultaneously. In general, this study involves driving one resonance while detecting the other. Thus, an apparatus with two oscillating magnetic fields is employed, one for the driver and the other for the detector. Driving an NMR and detecting its effect on an ESR is known as ENDOR (electron-nuclear double resonance), whereas driving an ESR to increase a nuclear magnetization, observed by NMR, is DNP (dynamic nuclear polarization).

ENDOR and DNP (margin note)

The main purpose of electron-nuclear double resonance is to measure accurately hyperfine and superhyperfine splittings. In the ENDOR method, driving an NMR resonance changes the populations of at least one of the energy levels between which occurs an observed ESR transition, and thus the strong ESR signal is measurably modified. ENDOR thus combines the sensitivity of ESR with the resolution of NMR and is widely used for detailed mapping of electron-spin densities by resolving superhyperfine structures. In the dynamic nuclear polarization (DNP) method known as solid effect, a strong microwave field of a frequency that is the sum or difference of electronic and nuclear Larmor frequencies, can transfer to the nuclei of a diamagnetic sample a polarization equal or opposite to that of fixed paramagnetic impurities embedded in the sample, an enhancement of a hundred to a thousand. The solid effect is widely used for making polarized proton targets for nuclear and high energy physics.

BIBLIOGRAPHY. An introductory work on the subject nuclear magnetic resonance (NMR) is E.R. ANDREW, *Nuclear Magnetic Resonance* (1956); on electron-spin resonance (ESR), G.E. PAKE, *Paramagnetic Resonance* (1962). An intermediate work covering both NMR and ESR is C.P. SLICHTER, *Principles of Magnetic Resonance* (1963). More advanced and comprehensive works include: (on NMR), A. ABRAGAM, *The Principles of Nuclear Magnetism* (1961); and (on ESR), A. ABRAGAM and B. BLEANEY, *Electron Paramagnetic Resonance of Transition Ions* (1970).

(A.A./B.G.Sa.)

Magnetism

The phenomenon known as magnetism is most familiar through the compass, indicating the direction of the Earth's magnetic poles, and through small permanent magnets used in household fixtures and as children's toys. Permanent magnets are pieces of iron or certain metal alloys with strong attraction or repulsion for one another. Most of the important properties of magnetism, however, are connected with the relations between magnetism and current electricity, which may be summarized as follows:

1. An electric current flowing along a wire generates a magnetic field in the space around the wire. The strength of this field is proportional to the size of the current and diminishes as the distance from the wire increases. The field can be made strongest by winding the wire into a coil of many turns and can be concentrated in space by filling the volume inside the coil with iron, thus creating a device known as an electromagnet, in which the magnetic field can be controlled by adjusting the size of the current flowing in the coil.

2. When placed in a magnetic field, a wire carrying an electric current experiences a mechanical force. The magnetic field may be generated by a permanent magnet or, more commonly, by a second coil also carrying an electric current. Magnetic forces provide the fundamental motive power in electromagnetic machinery; powerful forces can be generated by comparatively small machines and be conveniently controlled by adjustment of the size of the currents.

3. When a coil of wire is situated in a magnetic field that is increasing or decreasing, an electrical voltage proportional to the rate of change of the field is created in the coil. This is the phenomenon of electromagnetic induction that forms the basis of the dynamo. A coil rotated in a magnetic field generates an alternating voltage, and an alternating current (ac) flows if the coil is connected to a continuous electrical circuit. By a special arrangement of connections to the rotating coil, it is possible to draw direct current (dc) instead of alternating current from the coil.

Electro-magnetic induction (margin note)

These three principles constitute the scientific basis of

the electrical power industry. Electrical power is generated by the dynamo, itself driven by a source of mechanical energy dependent on coal, oil, waterpower, or nuclear energy. The magnitude of alternating voltages and currents can be changed by a transformer, consisting of primary (input) and secondary (output) coils, the voltage being increased and the current diminished by the same factor in the secondary coil in proportion to the ratio of the number of turns on the secondary coil to the number on the primary. Such transformers operate with efficiencies of over 99 percent. Electric power is used in industry and in the home for heating and lighting and to drive electromagnetic machines of all sizes. It is used for heavy-duty traction on electrified railways and for light-duty traction in small, mobile delivery vans.

An electric current consists of moving electrical charges (usually electrons, the most elementary form of charge), and in a magnetic field the force on a conductor carrying an electric current arises from the forces exerted on the moving charges by the magnetic field. Such forces have many technical applications, such as the rapidly changing deflection of an electron beam in a television display tube, moving back and forth and up and down across the screen to form a picture. Specially designed configurations of magnetic fields are used to focus the electron beam in a cathode ray tube and in electron microscopes and to control the motion of charged particles in accelerators and other instruments used in atomic and nuclear physics.

This article is divided into the following sections:

I. General aspects

MAGNETISM: NATURAL AND APPLIED

Magnetism in nature. Magnetism plays an important role in various ways in the investigation of atomic and nuclear structures. The motion of an electron in an orbit around the nucleus of an atom is equivalent to a minute loop of electric current (Amperian current loop), which behaves as an atomic magnet, called a magnetic dipole moment. Each electron also possesses a rotation about its own axis, known as electron spin; this is again equivalent to a circulating electric current with its own magnetic dipole moment. For an atom with many electrons, the dipole moment resulting from the various orbital and spin dipole moments depends on the arrangement of the electrons within the atom, and measurement of this magnetic dipole moment gives an important clue to atomic structure. Similar but smaller dipole moments occur in nuclei and in subnuclear particles called mesons. These moments are usually measured by means of the Zeeman effect. In the Zeeman effect, an atom or nucleus subjected to a magnetic field has an additional potential (stored) energy associated with the orientation of its magnetic dipole moment in the field, and this changes the size of any quantum of energy which may be emitted as electromagnetic radiation. The frequency of the radiation is correspondingly affected, as well as its state of polarization—that is, the plane of vibration in which it occurs.

Electron spin

A body moving in a straight line has a momentum equal to the product of its velocity and mass; moving in a curved path, the angular momentum is the product of its angular velocity and moment of inertia. According to a simplified quantum theory of the atom, an electron in orbit can have an angular momentum equal only to whole multiples of the unit Planck's constant divided by two times pi ($h/2\pi$). Also, according to quantum theory, only certain orientations of the dipole are possible, the number of them being dependent on the angular momentum of the atom or nucleus. In the Zeeman effect, a line in the optical spectrum of an atom is split into a number of components. The atomic angular momentum can be deduced from the number of components, and the size of the magnetic dipole moment from the separations between the components in a known magnetic field. In terms of frequency such separations lie in the range 10^6 to 10^{11} hertz (one hertz is one cycle per second) and are most accurately measured by spectroscopic methods. Such methods are also of especial value in investigating the motion of conduction electrons (electrons free to move through a solid and thus become moving charges forming an electric current) in metals and semiconductors and the interactions of atomic magnetic moments with their surroundings in solids. A process that has become a major tool in the investigation of chemical structure and in chemical analysis, particularly in liquids in which exceptionally high accuracy and sensitivity can be attained, is called nuclear magnetic resonance; it is a technique whereby the small local change in an external magnetic field caused by the motion of the adjacent atomic electrons is detected when a nuclear dipole moment is introduced.

When atoms are chemically combined in molecules or are assembled in regular structures such as solids, they normally become ions (charged atoms or molecules) that have no resultant electronic magnetic dipole moment. Certain so-called transition groups of the periodic table, including the iron group and the rare-earth group, are major exceptions to this rule. Elements and compounds containing ions of these groups are of great technical and scientific importance, particularly because of ferromagnetism, a phenomenon that occurs when the ionic dipole moments are subject to mutual interactions that cause them to be oriented parallel to each other. This spontaneous magnetization is of macroscopic size and enormously greater than can be obtained by the orientation of atomic dipoles by an external magnetic field at ordinary temperatures. Ferromagnetism is used in making permanent magnets, in electromagnetic machinery and the electric power industry, and (to a lesser extent) in the electronics industry.

The Earth possesses a magnetic moment, ascribed to the existence of electric currents set up in its core by the revolution of the planet about its own axis. The magnetic field of the Earth affects the motions of electrons in the electrified region of the atmosphere known as the ionosphere and of charged particles approaching from outside. Magnetic rocks and particular rock formations cause local disturbances of the Earth's field, an effect exploited in geophysical exploration. The residual magnetization acquired by rocks on cooling in the Earth's magnetic field provides a record of this field in past geological time, which indicates that it has reversed its direction several times in the last few million years. On a smaller scale the clay walls of brick and pottery kilns similarly record the Earth's field at the time of the last firing, providing a method of magnetic dating based on known changes in the Earth's field in recent millennia. Around such sites, now buried, local variations in the Earth's magnetic field can be detected and form the basis of an important method of archaeological prospecting.

Earth's magnetic field

Many stars possess magnetic fields that affect the frequency and polarization of the light and radio waves emitted by them. In the case of the Sun such effects are used to map local changes in the region of sunspots and other disturbances.

Magnetism in technology. In technology, magnetism is employed on a wide-ranging scale, from enormous electromagnets used to lift massive loads to small electromagnets used for the recording of sound and television pictures on magnetic tape. The use of applied magnetic fields for the rapid reversal of the direction of magnetization of magnetic oxides or thin metallic films of iron alloys is being exploited in computer memories. The use of high magnetic fields with specially shaped configurations has been explored as a method of containing the plasma of charged ions at the temperatures of about 100,000,000° C required to produce nuclear power from controlled fusion reactions. For many such applications superconducting magnets may be used. In recent years new materials have provided superconducting compounds able to withstand high current densities without losing their superconducting property. Once established, a current continues to flow through them indefinitely without loss of energy, and a coil carrying such a current acts like a permanent magnet. The cost of refrigerating the material to a temperature well below its superconducting transition temperature (about 15° K or −258° C) is less than that of the power dissipated in the finite resistance of the electrical circuit of a conventional electromagnet. The distribution of electrical power over long distances without loss, using underground superconducting cables continuously refrigerated, has been proposed, but there are serious technical problems in avoiding temporary interruptions of the supply through breakdown in the refrigeration and other associated equipment.

Superconducting magnets (margin note)

HISTORY

First observations and uses. The mineral magnetite, a magnetic oxide of iron, appears in Greek writings from as early as 800 BC. The mineral, which even in the natural state has a strong attraction for iron, was mined in the Greek province of Magnesia, in Thessaly. According to Lucretius, the Roman author of the long philosophical poem *De rerum natura* in the first century AD, the name magnet derives from the province and its inhabitants. Pliny the Elder, however, ascribes the name to its discoverer, the shepherd Magnes, "the nails of whose shoes and the tip of whose staff stuck fast in a magnetick field while he pastured his flocks."

The name lodestone, by which the mineral was generally known in English, signifies leading stone and refers to the first application of magnetism, the compass. Some writers believe that the compass was in use in China as early as the 26th century BC; others, that it was introduced to China only in the 13th century AD, its invention being of Italian or Arab origin. The earliest extant European reference is by the Englishman Alexander Neckam (died 1217).

The first magnetic compass (margin note)

The first known experimental investigation of the lodestone is described in a Latin treatise, dated 1269, by Petrus Peregrinus de Maricourt. By mapping the direction assumed by a small rectangular piece of iron on the surface of a spherical lodestone, he obtained lines that circled the lodestone and intersected at two points in the same way as lines of longitude on the Earth intersect at the poles. By analogy, he called these two points the poles of the magnet.

In England William Gilbert repeated and extended such experiments, assembling all the available knowledge of magnetism in a treatise, *De Magnete*, published in 1600. From its similarity in magnetic behaviour to the spherical lodestone, he recognized that the Earth itself is a magnet. He also discovered that when heated to a bright red heat, lodestone loses its magnetic properties but then regains them on cooling.

Studies based on classical physics. In 1785 the French physicist Charles Coulomb, using a torsion balance, established the inverse square law of force (Coulomb's law) between both electric charges and magnetic poles. In each case, like poles repel one another, whereas unlike poles attract one another. From these results, the theory of magnetostatics, the study of steady-state magnetic fields, was developed, using the concept of a magnetic potential analogous to the electric potential. (Magnetic poles were postulated with properties analogous to electric charges.)

The origin of magnetic properties remained a mystery,

but a major step forward occurred in 1820, when a Danish physicist, Hans Christian Ørsted, observed that an electric current flowing in a wire affected a nearby magnet. (The same discovery had been made and reported by Gian Dominico Romagnosi, an Italian jurist, in *Gazetta di Trentino*, August 3, 1802, but was ignored.) Ørsted's discovery started work in many countries. In France, a physicist, François Arago, showed that a current acts like an ordinary magnet, in its ability both to attract iron filings and to induce permanent magnetism in iron needles. André-Marie Ampère, a French physicist, experimentally established quantitative laws of magnetic force between electric currents. He suggested that internal electric currents are responsible for ferromagnetism, and, with Arago, he demonstrated that steel needles become more strongly magnetic inside a coil carrying an electric current. Ampère's suggestion that there are internal circulating currents of molecular size in a metal was developed by Wilhelm Eduard Weber, a German physicist, to explain how a substance may be unmagnetized when the molecular magnets point in random directions. Under the action of an external force they turn to point in the direction of the force; when all point in this direction, the maximum possible degree of magnetization is reached, a phenomenon known as magnetic saturation.

In England, Faraday discovered that under the action of an external magnetic force all substances become magnetic to a greater or smaller degree. He named this force the magnetic field in 1845. He also found that the plane of vibration of polarized light is rotated when the light passes through a medium in a direction parallel to a magnetic field (the Faraday effect). His most celebrated discovery (made in 1831) was electromagnetic induction, in which an electrical voltage is induced in a circuit subjected to a changing magnetic field. Electromagnetic induction was also discovered independently in the United States by Joseph Henry, but it was the publication of the treatise *Experimental Researches in Electricity* by Faraday in 1839–55 that led to his ideas being cast into a mathematical form by the British scientist James Clerk Maxwell (*Treatise on Electricity and Magnetism*, 1873). This great unification of the theory of the two subjects culminated in Maxwell's discovery that his equations predicted electromagnetic phenomena with a wavelike nature; these electromagnetic waves were calculated to travel with a velocity close to (indeed, identical with) that of light. In Germany the experiments of physicist Heinrich Hertz in 1886 verified the existence of electromagnetic waves; the waves that Hertz discovered are now known as radio waves.

The work of Michael Faraday (margin note)

Maxwell's theory is the pinnacle of achievement in treating electric and magnetic fields on the macroscopic scale. At the microscopic or molecular level, progress in theory followed the discovery of the electron and the development of the electron theory of matter by a Dutch physicist, Hendrick Antoon Lorentz. A further landmark was the discovery (1896) by his pupil Pieter Zeeman of the splitting of the spectroscopic lines emitted by an atom in an intense magnetic field. Lorentz showed how such a splitting could be attributed to the change in motion of atomic electrons under the action of the magnetic field.

In the same era, the detailed and accurate researches of Pierre Curie showed how induced magnetism in paramagnetic substances (*i.e.*, with dipoles aligned in the direction of a magnetic field) varies with temperature, and that a ferromagnetic substance behaves like a paramagnetic substance above a certain characteristic temperature now known as the Curie temperature. In 1905 the temperature variation of the paramagnetism was explained by French physicist Paul Langevin on the basis of statistical theory, each molecule being assumed to possess a permanent magnetic dipole moment. Two years later another French physicist, Pierre-Ernst Weiss, extended the theory by postulating the existence in ferromagnetics of an internal field due to mutual interactions between the atomic magnets; this causes the magnets spontaneously to assume parallel orientations, giving a macroscopic magnetic moment even in the absence of an external field.

Studies based on quantum physics.   Classical physics offered no explanation of the origin or size of this internal field, enormously greater than could arise from purely magnetic forces. Even more fundamental, it offered no explanation of the existence of permanent atomic magnetic moments, a problem the solution of which depended on the discovery of a satisfactory model for the structure of the atom. The major advance came with the introduction in 1913 by Niels Bohr, the Danish physicist, of quantization (a restriction to unit quantities) of the angular momentum of electrons moving round the nucleus in the nuclear atom proposed by the physicist Ernest Rutherford in England. This orbital motion of an electron is essentially an Amperian current loop, and quantization of the angular momentum results in quantization of the magnetic moment. In 1921 Wolfgang Pauli of Austria suggested the name Bohr magneton for the fundamental unit of atomic moment, and in 1922 two physicists, Otto Stern and Walther Gerlach, in Germany, demonstrated experimentally the existence of such atomic moments and their spatial quantization, by the deflection of a beam of atoms moving through an inhomogeneous (of nonuniform intensity) magnetic field. A further advance was the suggestion (1921) of United States physicist Arthur Compton that the electron also possesses a spin about its own axis, with a corresponding magnetic moment.

The remaining discrepancies between theory and experiment disappeared in the mid-1920s after the development of wave mechanics and the new quantum mechanics. The relativistically correct quantum theory of an English physicist, Paul A.M. Dirac (1928), gave a satisfactory explanation of the intrinsic spin and magnetic moment of the electron. He and Werner Heisenberg, a German physicist, showed the existence of the previously unknown exchange forces, electrostatic in origin, that play an important role in determining the structure of atoms with more than one electron and also account for the nature and size of the internal field postulated by Weiss to explain ferromagnetism. The theory of complex atoms and of magnetic effects in solids was rapidly developed thereafter. In 1936 Louis Néel, in France, put forward the idea of antiferromagnetism, and in 1948 the idea of ferrimagnetism, in which neighbouring atomic magnets are aligned in antiparallel directions, the opposing moments being equal in the former case and unequal in the latter. Since 1945 major advances have followed from the experimental study of magnetic solids by means of magnetic resonance and neutron diffraction (rays of neutrons, the fundamental uncharged particles of atomic nuclei, may be diverted from their paths according to the magnetic properties of crystals with which they interact), with corresponding improvements in the detailed theoretical understanding of the properties of such assemblies of atomic magnets.

GENERAL PHENOMENA OF SIMPLE MAGNETIC SYSTEMS

Lodestone was the only naturally occurring magnetic material known to the ancients, but a bar of iron could be magnetized by stroking it a number of times in the same direction with a permanent magnet or even by gentle tapping with the bar oriented in a north–south direction. Such magnetization is easily diminished by rough mechanical usage; it can be reduced to zero, or even reversed, in the presence of a stronger magnet. For this reason iron is called a soft magnetic material. Iron alloys such as steel are more difficult to magnetize, but, once produced, the magnetization is also more difficult to remove and will withstand rougher handling. Such materials are known as hard magnetic materials.

With progress in chemical technology it was found that the elements cobalt and nickel and many alloys and compounds are magnetic. Lodestone, the mineral magnetite (formula [Fe_3O_4]), is one of a number of magnetic oxides. There are many elements and compounds that become strongly magnetic only at low temperatures, but for most technological applications the need is for room-temperature materials. Present-day permanent magnets are made from special alloys or oxides, and the best results are obtained through complex metallurgical and

thermal processes that increase their magnetic hardness. There are also in use a number of specially treated alloys that are magnetically much softer than iron.

Magnetic attraction and repulsion.   Some important properties of a permanent magnet can readily be demonstrated. If such a magnet is suspended or pivoted so that it can rotate about a vertical axis, it is found that one end invariably seeks the magnetic north (the direction of which, except in high latitudes, is near the geographical north) and the other the magnetic south. This well-known property of the magnetic compass is the basis of its use as an aid in navigation.

If iron filings are sprinkled over a magnet, they cling to it in a definite pattern. Each filing becomes a tiny magnet under the influence of the permanent magnet, and the attractive forces involved are those between two magnets. The filings cling most densely near the ends of the magnet, where the magnetic poles are located. Poles always occur in pairs of opposite kind, north and south, and it is not possible to have one without the other. If a magnet is broken, new poles appear near the break in such a way that each piece has two opposite poles.

If two bar magnets are placed close together, they are found either to attract one another or to repel one another. The force of attraction or repulsion is small when the magnets are far apart, and it increases rapidly as the magnets approach one another. Attractive forces appear when poles of opposite sign are close together; repulsive forces are found when poles of the same sign are close together. Briefly, like poles repel and opposite poles attract.

This result gives rise to some semantic confusion in the nomenclature for magnetic poles. The north pole of a compass needle is the pole that points toward (that is, is attracted by) the north magnetic pole of the Earth. It is more accurately known as a north-seeking pole. By analogy with electrical charges, the terms positive and negative magnetic poles may be used rather than north and south poles. These may sometimes be designated by the symbols $+q_m$ and $-q_m$, respectively, in which the subscript m denotes magnetic. Thus, poles of the same sign repel one another, and poles of the opposite sign attract one another.

The fact that forces act between magnets not in contact poses a philosophical difficulty, that of action at a distance. This difficulty is overcome by the postulates that every magnet is surrounded by a magnetic field and that a magnet placed in a magnetic field is subject to a magnetic force produced by that field. The concept of such a field of force is lent the appearance of reality by scattering iron filings over a smooth surface lying on top of a magnet. Each filing behaves as a minute compass needle, indicating the direction of the field at the point where it lies. The filings are also attracted into positions where the field is strongest, so that regions in which the density of filings is greatest are those of largest field strength—e.g., close to the poles of the magnet.

If a tiny compass needle is suspended near a magnet, the direction it assumes can be marked on a piece of paper. If the needle is moved a little in the direction in which it points, it takes up a slightly different orientation. If this process is repeated continuously, the lines that are traced out begin at one pole of the magnet and terminate at the other pole. Such lines are known as lines of magnetic force and indicate the orientation of the magnetic field in the vicinity of the magnet (Figure 1A). These lines are identical with those indicated by the use of iron filings but may be mapped more precisely with a compass. The magnetic force is greatest where the lines of force crowd most closely together.

The effects of magnetic attraction and repulsion may be ascribed to the properties of the lines of force. A tension is assumed to act along the lines of force (Figure 1B), so as to produce a pull on the poles where the lines of force terminate and a mutual repulsion between adjacent lines where they run parallel to one another, as shown in Figure 1C.

Magnetic moment.   Bar magnets may be circular, square, or rectangular in cross section without materially altering their properties. If a bar magnet is cut crosswise

Bohr
magneton

Perma-
nent
magnets
today

Concept
of the
magnetic
field

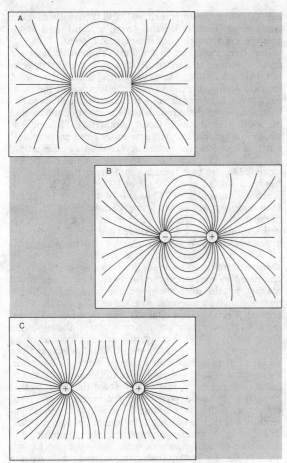

Figure 1: *Magnetic lines of force.*
(A) Lines of force of a bar magnet. (B) The attraction between two unlike magnetic charges can be attributed to tension along the lines of force. (C) The repulsion between like charges is attributed to repulsion between adjacent lines of force.

into two parts, the magnetic force exerted at large distances is proportional to the length of each portion; and if the magnet is divided longitudinally, the force exerted by each portion is proportional to the cross section of each portion. This suggests that the material possesses a fundamental property per unit volume, known as the intensity of magnetization or, more briefly, as the magnetization, denoted by the symbol M, a vector. (Vectors symbolically represent the direction and size of quantities and are often represented in drawings by arrows. Vector quantities are printed in boldface in this article.) The whole magnet has a magnetic moment m equal to the intensity of magnetization times the volume of the magnet ($M \times V$). The pole strength (the size of the magnetic charge, q_m) is equal to the magnetic moment (m) divided by the length (l), and the intensity of magnetization (M) is equal to the pole strength divided by the area (A) of the cross section. These relations are expressed in the equation

$$m = M \times (l \times A) = M \times V = q_m \times l.$$

On the right-hand side of the equation, the length is represented as a vector l to show that the magnetic moment acts along that direction; the pole strength q_m is not a directed quantity.

The inverse-square law. *Force between two magnetic poles.* The force acting between two magnetic poles separated from each other is proportional to the magnitude of each of the two poles, divided by the square of the distance between them. The force is directed along the line joining the poles; it is a force of repulsion if the poles are of the same sign (*i.e.*, both north-seeking poles or both south-seeking) and a force of attraction if they are of opposite sign (one north-seeking, the other south-seeking). In SI (International System of Units, see below) units, the force (F) is measured in newtons (a force of one newton accelerates a mass of one kilogram one metre per second per second), the distance of separation (r) in metres, and each magnetic pole (q_m and q'_m) in ampere-metres. Expressed as an equation, the law of force becomes

$$F = \frac{\mu_0}{4\pi} \frac{q_m q'_m}{r^2},$$

in which $\mu_0/4\pi$ is a constant with the magnitude 10^{-7} newton—(ampere)$^{-2}$.

Because the force on a pole q'_m is proportional to its magnitude q'_m, it is convenient to define a magnetic quantity B by the relation

$$F = q'_m B.$$

Here B is the force on unit magnetic pole; it is a vector the direction of which is that of the force F and its properties are like those of any mechanical force vector.

From the equation for the law of force (above) between two poles, it follows that at a distance r from a magnetic pole q_m the magnitude (B) of the magnetic quantity B is equal to the constant of proportionality mentioned above times the magnetic charge (q_m) divided by the distance squared, or

$$B = \frac{\mu_0}{4\pi} \frac{q_m}{r^2}.$$

Gauss's theorem. The magnetic quantity B is a vector that points away from the pole if pole q_m is positive and toward it if it is negative. The lines of force, or lines of the magnetic quantity B, from a single pole q_m spread out radially. If a sphere of radius r is drawn with its centre at the pole, the number of lines of force crossing the sphere is independent of its radius. This number is known as the magnetic flux and is denoted by the symbol N, which is simply proportional to the size of the pole q_m—*i.e.*, $N = \mu_0 q_m$. The lines of force terminate only on a magnetic pole, and the inverse-square law of force is represented geometrically by the fact that the number of lines crossing unit area of the sphere diminishes with the square of its radius. The unit of magnetic flux is known as the weber, and the value of the magnetic quantity B is given by the flux per unit area or the flux density. Its unit is the weber per square metre, or tesla.

More precisely, B, the force on unit magnetic pole, is defined as the flux per unit area normal (perpendicular) to the direction of B. Any small area dS making an angle θ with the direction of B, by the laws of trigonometry, will have an area normal to B when multiplied by the cosine of θ—*i.e.*, $dS \cos \theta$. An infinitesimal amount of flux, designated as dN, through the area will therefore be the product of B and the elemental normal area, or $dN = (B \cos \theta) \, dS$. With this definition of dN, the total flux (N) through any closed surface is defined by integrating dN, *i.e.*, $N = \int dN$; that is to say, $N = \int (B \cos \theta) \, dS$, and the relation stated above, $N = \mu_0 q_m$, holds for any closed surface surrounding the pole q_m. If more than one pole is enclosed, $N = \mu_0 \Sigma q_m$, in which Σq_m symbolizes the net total pole strength enclosed, allowing for the signs of the various poles. This relation is due to a theorem of the 18th-century German mathematician Carl Friedrich Gauss: for a magnet with poles $+q_m$ and $-q_m$, the total flux through a surface enclosing the magnet is zero. This does not imply that the value of B is everywhere zero; it implies only that in some places it acts outward through the surface and in others inward, in such a way that the total flux through the surface is zero.

Magnetic potential. In mechanics it is often more convenient to work in terms of energy (a scalar quantity having magnitude but no direction, like magnetic charge) than in terms of force (a vector quantity); and the same is true in magnetism. When a magnetic pole is moved, work must be done against any force acting on it if it is moved in the direction opposite to the force, and, conversely, work will be done (or can be extracted) by the magnetic pole when it moves in the force direction.

Thus, no work is done in moving a magnetic pole around a closed path in a magnetic field. It follows that

(Side margin notes:)
Intensity of magnetization

Magnetic flux

the work done in moving a pole q'_m from a point A to a point B is independent of the route followed. Otherwise q'_m could be returned to A by another route on which more work is extracted than was expended in the initial movement to A. The net effect would be that work could be extracted by movement around the complete path without any other change in the system, giving the possibility of a perpetual motion machine that is contrary to the laws of mechanics.

This result makes it possible to define a useful quantity, the magnetic potential. If unit pole is brought from an infinite distance to a distance r from a pole q_m, the work done is equal to a constant times the pole strength divided by the distance, or $(\mu_0/4\pi)$ (q_m/r), and is independent of the route taken. The magnetic potential (ϕ) is defined as the quotient, pole strength divided by distance, $\phi = q_m/r$; and the product of a constant times the magnetic potential, $(\mu_0/4\pi)\phi$, is the quantity of work that could be extracted by letting unit pole move from the point at r to infinity.

Magnets and magnetic forces. If a magnet consisting of two separated magnetic poles, $+q_m$ and $-q_m$, is placed in a uniform flux density B, equal and opposite forces $+q_mB$ and $-q_mB$ act on the two poles, parallel and antiparallel to B. No net translation force is exerted on the magnet as a whole, but there is a torque or couple tending to turn the magnet about its centre point. The equilibrium position of the magnet is parallel to the flux density B, and the mechanical couple is maximum when it is at right angles to the flux density.

If the magnet is pivoted and free to turn about its centre, like a compass needle, it will oscillate about the direction of B. Measurement of the period for a complete oscillation of a small magnet is used to compare the magnitudes of different flux densities B. The device is known as an oscillation magnetometer.

If the magnet is in a nonuniform flux density, the forces acting on the two poles are not equal and opposite, and there will be a net translational force on the magnet. The attraction of a permanent magnet for iron filings arises from this translational force. Each filing acquires an induced magnetic moment parallel to B and is therefore attracted toward the regions where B is largest, nearest the poles of the magnet. The magnitude of B, due to the magnet, may be calculated in a number of ways; e.g., by making use of the potential ϕ at an arbitrary point. It may conveniently be divided into two components at right angles to each other, called the angular component (B_θ) and the radial component (B_r).

The magnetic field of the Earth. As was first explicitly realized in the year 1600 by William Gilbert, the magnetic flux density at the surface of the Earth (and also outside the Earth) is very nearly that which would be created by a large magnet at the centre of the Earth, directed along a diameter joining the north and south magnetic poles. The magnetic equator is a great circle round the Earth equidistant from the two magnetic poles, and the magnetic latitude (λ) is measured from the magnetic equator in the same way as the geographical latitude is measured from the geographical equator.

The direction of the component of the magnet flux density B_θ is along the great circle from the south to the north magnetic pole passing through the point in question, so that a small magnet pivoted so as to turn in a horizontal plane will point toward magnetic north. This is the principle of the magnetic compass, the most important technological application of magnetism over many centuries.

The vertical component B_r of the Earth's field is zero at the magnetic equator ($\lambda = 0°$) and a maximum at the magnetic poles ($\lambda = 90°$). If a small magnet is pivoted about a horizontal axis so that it is free to rotate in a vertical plane containing the magnetic poles (i.e., parallel to a line of magnetic longitude), it will set at an angle to the horizontal known as the angle of dip or the magnetic inclination. This direction is that of the resultant magnetic field of the Earth at the point on its surface. The value of B is just twice as great at the poles as at the equator. At the equator the angle of dip is zero, and B is entirely horizontal, whereas at the poles the field is entirely verti-

cal. The angle of dip is then 90°, and the needle of a dip circle points directly up and down, a result used to locate the exact positions of the magnetic poles.

Short-term variations in the Earth's magnetic field are mostly ascribed to electrical currents in the ionosphere, but there are also long-term variations, in both the size of the field and its direction and in the location of the magnetic poles. In recent decades the north magnetic pole has been located in the Arctic islands north of Canada, and the south pole in Adélie Coast, Antarctica. The angle at which a magnetic compass sets away from geographical north is known as the magnetic variation or declination; the declination is small near the equator but can be extremely large in high latitudes. In Europe the declination has been west of north for about 300 years; in London it reached a maximum of 24° west in about 1800, but in the 16th century it was east of north. Because of the variation in the declination over the surface of the Earth, the magnetic compass is being superseded for navigation by the gyroscopic compass, which indicates the true geographical north (see EARTH, MAGNETIC FIELD OF).

Magnetic units. The strength of two magnets may be compared by measuring the forces they exert on a third magnet, but this does not give a unit in terms of which a quantity such as magnetic pole strength (q_m) can be expressed. Years ago this difficulty was circumvented by using the inverse-square law of force, stated above, setting the quantity ($\mu_0/4\pi$) at unity, and defining the unit of q_m as that magnetic pole which, placed at unit distance from an identical pole, repels it with unit force. In the centimetre-gram-second (or cgs) system, the unit of distance is the centimetre and that of unit force the dyne, so that two unit magnetic poles one centimetre apart repel each other with a force of one dyne. A system of magnetic units was then constructed for quantities such as flux, flux density, magnetic moment, etc., by combining the definition of unit magnetic pole with the mechanical units of the cgs system, using the relations between the various quantities as expressed in the laws of magnetism. This system is known as the centimetre-gram-second electromagnetic system of units.

A parallel system of electrical units, also using cgs units, grew up from the inverse-square law for electrical charges, defining unit electrical charge as that charge which repels an identical charge at a distance of one centimetre with a force of one dyne. The system, known as the cgs electrostatic system of units, is not independent of the cgs system of magnetic units since it may be related to the electromagnetic system through the relations (see below) that determine the magnetic forces generated by electric currents. In the electrostatic system, unit electric current arises from a flow of one unit of electric charge per second. The magnetic effect of this current can be related to the force it exerts on unit magnetic pole, and, by this means, an electromagnetic unit of electric current can be defined. Following the work of Maxwell, which showed that light waves are a form of electromagnetic radiation, it became clear that the ratios of any unit expressed in the two systems is equal to a constant c, or to c^2, in which the constant c, equal to 2.998×10^{10} centimetres, is the velocity of electromagnetic waves in vacuum. For example, the electromagnetic unit of current is greater than the electrostatic unit by a factor c. Since this factor c has the dimensions of velocity (all physical quantities can be expressed in various combinations of length, mass, and time, called dimensions), electric and magnetic units in the two systems do not have the same dimensions except for purely mechanical quantities, such as length, time, force, energy, etc.

In 1960 it was agreed internationally that a single system of units, the International System of Units (SI), should be adopted. The basic mechanical units are the metre for length, the second for time, and the kilogram for mass, all usually referred to as mks units. Other mechanical units are built up by the standard relations. For example, one unit of force (the newton $= 10^5$ dynes) will accelerate a mass of one kilogram at the rate of one metre per second per second. The unit of energy (the joule $= 10^7$ ergs) is the work done in moving a distance of one metre against a force of one newton; the unit of power (one joule per second) is the same as the watt, the practical unit of electrical power. By the addition of one electrical unit, chosen to be the unit of electric current (the ampere), a complete single set of electric and magnetic units based on the mks units has been developed: the metre-kilogram-second-ampere system (mksa).

Measurement in mksa units

The relations between electric current and magnetic force (see below) give the ampere-metre as the unit of magnetic pole strength (q_m). Because the unit of force is the newton, it follows from the inverse-square law that the quantity ($\mu_0/4\pi$) cited above is fixed and is a dimensional quantity, equal to 10^{-7} newton—(ampere)$^{-2}$. Unit magnetic flux density B exerts a force of one newton on a magnetic pole of one ampere-metre. This gives a unit for the flux density of one newton—(ampere-metre)$^{-1}$; but an equivalent unit generally employed is related to the unit (the weber, after Wilhelm Eduard Weber, a German physicist) of magnetic flux N. This unit for the magnetic flux density B is equal to a flux of one weber per square metre and is called the tesla (named in honour of the United States inventor, Nikola Tesla). A set of mksa units for magnetic quantities is given in Table 1. Two

Table 1: Some Electric and Magnetic Quantities

quantity	symbol	dimensions	mksa unit
Electric current	I	current	ampere
Electric charge	Q	current × time	coulomb
Electric voltage	V	power ÷ current	volt
Electric resistance	R	voltage ÷ current	ohm
Magnetic pole strength	qm	current × length	ampere–metre
Magnetic moment	m	current × (length)^2	ampere–(metre)^2
Magnetization	M	magnetic moment ÷ (length)^3	ampere–(metre)$^{-1}$
Magnetic flux	N	voltage × time	weber
Magnetic flux density	B	flux ÷ (length)^2	tesla
Magnetic field	H	current ÷ length	ampere–(metre)$^{-1}$
Magnetic scalar potential (magnetomotive force)	ϕ	current	ampere
Magnetic vector potential	A	flux ÷ length	weber–(metre)$^{-1}$
Self inductance	L	volt × time ÷ current	henry
Mutual inductance	M		henry

useful relations between the metre-kilogram-second-ampere and centimetre-gram-second electromagnetic systems are that the ampere is exactly one-tenth of the cgs electromagnetic unit of current, and for magnetic flux density the tesla is exactly 10^4 gauss, in which the gauss is the cgs electromagnetic unit.

II. Magnetic effects of steady electrical currents

Following the discovery in 1820 by Ørsted of the effect of an electric current on a nearby compass needle, the experiments of Ampère and others elucidated the nature of the forces between circuits carrying electric currents. They found that two long parallel wires carrying currents in the same direction attract one another, but if one current is reversed in direction the wires repel one another. Experiments on small coils showed that at large distances, not only were the forces between two such coils similar to those between two small bar magnets but also one coil could be replaced by a bar magnet of suitable size without changing the forces. The magnetic moment of this equivalent magnet was determined by the dimensions of the coil, its number of turns, and the current flowing round it.

The law governing the forces between such circuits is more complicated in its mathematical formulation than the inverse-square law between two point magnetic charges. It is simpler and more useful to approach the subject in two steps, giving, first, the formula for the magnetic flux density associated with an element of a circuit carrying a current and, second, the force exerted on such an element by a magnetic flux density due to another source.

MAGNETIC FIELDS

Magnetic flux density. The magnetic flux density at a point a distance r from an element of wire carrying a

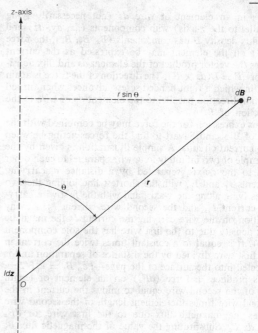

Figure 2: The law of Biot and Savart. Flux density dB is directed into page (see text).

current I is given by the law of Biot and Savart (after two French physicists, Jean-Baptiste Biot and Félix Savart). Figure 2 shows an element of wire dz, parallel to the z-axis, situated at the point O. At the point P, the element of flux density (designated as dB) is perpendicular to both the element dz and the vector r (called radius vector) joining O to P; it is directed (Figure 2) downward into the plane of the page. In magnitude dB is proportional to the current I and to the length dz, and it varies as the sine of the angle (θ) between the element of wire dz and radius vector r; it is inversely proportional to the square of the distance r. Mathematically this is expressed:

Law of Biot and Savart

$$dB = \frac{\mu_0}{4\pi} \frac{I \sin \theta}{r^2} dz.$$

For the more general case of an element of wire not necessarily parallel to the z-axis, but represented by the vector ds at the origin O with components (dx, dy, dz), the flux density at a point P can be expressed in the vector product form of the Biot and Savart law as proportional to the current divided by the distance cubed, times the vector product of the element ds and the radius vector.

$$d\boldsymbol{B} = \frac{\mu_0}{4\pi} \frac{I}{r^3} \left[d\boldsymbol{s} \times \boldsymbol{r} \right].$$

The vector product of two vectors is a vector mutually perpendicular to each; in this example, if ds is along the z-axis, and r is along the z-axis, then dH will be along the y-axis. In practice a current I cannot flow in an isolated element of wire, but the formula of Biot and Savart can be integrated along the wire to find the flux density of a complete circuit. For an infinitely long straight wire parallel to the z-axis, the integrated flux density is proportional to the current I and inversely proportional to the distance a from the wire—i.e., $B = \mu_0 I/2\pi a$. At any point P it is perpendicular both to the wire and to the line joining P to the nearest point on the wire; that is, the lines of constant flux density B are closed circles centred on the wire.

Magnetic force on a current. In the presence of a flux density B_y directed along the y-axis, a current I flowing in an element of wire dx parallel to the x-axis experiences a force dF_z parallel to the z-axis given by the product of the current, the element length dx, and the y component of the flux density, or $dF_z = IdxB_y$. The direction of the force is given by the so-called right-hand rule: if a right-handed screw is turned from the x-axis (the direction of the current element) toward the y-axis (the direction of B_y), the force is in the direction in which the screw advances (the z-axis). More generally, if the current I

flows in an element of wire ds (not necessarily lying parallel to the z-axis) with components (dx, dy, dz) and the flux density B has components (B_x, B_y, B_z), the force (dF) on the element may be expressed as the current times the vector product of the element ds and flux density, or $dF = I (ds \times B)$. The direction of the force is again that in which a right-handed screw advances when turned from a direction parallel to the element ds of wire to the direction of B.

This expression for the force may be combined with the law of Biot and Savart to find the forces acting between two current circuits. A simple illustration is given by the example of two infinitely long wires parallel to each other and to the z-axis, separated by a distance a, carrying currents I_1 and I_2, with the shortest line joining the two wires lying along the x-axis, and with the first wire carrying current I_1, and the second wire current I_2. At any position on the wire carrying the current I_2 the magnetic flux density due to the first wire has the sole component (B_y). It is equal to a constant times twice the current in the first wire divided by the distance of separation and is directed into the surface of the page—i.e., $B_y = \mu_0 I / 2\pi a$. This produces a force (dF_x) on an element of length dz_2 of the second wire equal to minus the current in the second wire times the element length of the second wire times the magnetic flux due to the first wire, or $dF_x = -I_2 dz_2 B_y$. Substituting the value of the magnetic flux B_y from above, the force on the element dz_2 is equal to minus a constant times twice the product of the two currents divided by the separation times the element length; i.e., $dF_x = -(\mu_0/4\pi)(2I_1I_2/a)dz_2$. This equation shows that there is a force per unit length on the right-hand wire equal to minus $(\mu_0/4\pi)(2I_1I_2/a)$, the negative sign meaning that the force acts towards the first wire provided that the two currents I_1 and I_2 have the same sign; that is, that they flow in the same direction along the two wires. A similar calculation shows that the first wire I_1 experiences an identical force per unit length, attracting it towards the second wire. If the two currents flow in opposite directions, the forces on the wires are forces of repulsion. Thus the forces between parallel currents differ from those between magnetic poles: like currents attract one another, but like poles repel one another.

The force between two such currents provides a method of defining the unit of current by reference to the mechanical unit of force. In SI units (mksa) the constant $(\mu_0/4\pi)$ is equal to 10^{-7} henry per metre, and two parallel wires each carrying one ampere of current at a distance one metre apart attract one another with a force of 2×10^{-7} newton per metre length of wire. The constant $(\mu_0/4\pi)$ is in fact chosen to make the unit of current identical with the absolute ampere, once defined as precisely one-tenth of the cgs electromagnetic unit of current.

Effect of a magnetic medium. The results given above apply when the current-carrying wires are in vacuum, and a modification is needed when a magnetizable medium is present. The force on a current element Ids in a field B is still given by the equation $dF = I [ds \times B]$, but the flux density produced by a current is changed by the presence of a magnetic medium. There are now two contributions: (1) a direct contribution from the current, as given above by the law of Biot and Savart; (2) a contribution from the magnetization of the medium that equals the product of a constant (μ_0) and the density of magnetization (M) or magnetic moment per unit volume of the medium; i.e., $\mu_0 M$.

The total flux density B is the sum of these two contributions. It follows that from the current alone the contribution is $B - \mu_0 M$, a quantity denoted by the new symbol $\mu_0 H$, in which the vector H is known as the magnetic field; that is, $\mu_0 H = B - \mu_0 M$. On this basis the law of Biot and Savart is rewritten as $dH = (I/4\pi r^3) [ds \times r]$, in which, as before, r is the radius vector drawn from the current element Ids to the point at which magnetic field infinitesimal dH is measured. This equation is correct in the presence of a magnetizable medium; the previous one is correct only in the absence of such a medium.

In many magnetic media the magnetization M is parallel to and proportional to the product of the field H and a quantity, χ, that is known as the magnetic susceptibility: $M = \chi H$. This equation may now be substituted into the one for the total flux density cited above; i.e.,

$$B = \mu_0(H + M) = \mu_0(H + \chi H) = \mu_0 H(1 + \chi).$$

Thus, calling the terms $(1 + \chi)$ by the symbol μ, known as the magnetic permeability, the total flux density is equal to the product of the two constants and the magnetic field; i.e., $B = \mu\mu_0 H$. In the absence of magnetic media, the magnetic susceptibility is zero and the magnetic permeability is one, and hence the total flux density can be simply written as $B = \mu_0 H$; the quantity μ_0 is sometimes called the permeability of free space, and μ is then known as the relative permeability. The quantities χ and μ are both pure numbers, but μ_0 is a dimensional quantity, as discussed previously.

In the presence of a magnetic medium, the value of dB corresponding to the law of Biot and Savart is greater by a factor μ than it would be in vacuum, and the flux density B of any circuit is increased by the same factor. Because the force on a second circuit carrying a current is determined by B, it follows that the forces between two such circuits are increased by a factor μ through the presence of the magnetizable medium. For air, μ differs from unity by about one part in 1,000,000; so that a correction is needed only for the most accurate experiments. On the other hand, in materials such as soft iron, μ can be large (as much as 10,000): this is extremely important in the phenomenon of electromagnetic induction (see below), in which the magnetic flux through a circuit is involved.

Magnetomotive force. The modified law of Biot and Savart given above may be used to calculate the magnetic field H around an infinite straight wire carrying a current I, in the same way as above. At a distance a from the wire, the magnitude of the field H is $(I/2\pi a)$ and, again, the lines of constant field are circles around the wire as centre (more accurately stated, the surfaces of constant H are circular cylinders having a common axis, the wire). The integral of H around such a circle has the value $(2\pi a)H = I$, a result that is independent of the radius of the circle. More generally, this result can be expressed as: the integral of the scalar product of magnetic field and element of path ds is equal to the current enclosed by the path; i.e., $\oint H \cdot ds = I$, whatever closed path of integration is taken, a result known as Ampère's law.

The integral $\oint H \cdot ds$ around a closed path is known as the magnetomotive force. It differs from the magnetic potential ϕ (see above) in that it is not a single-valued function of position, but increases by an amount I each time a complete path is made around the wire carrying the current I. If the path does not link (enclose) the current, then the integral $\oint H \cdot ds$ equals zero.

In general, this result can be written as: the integral, taken over a closed path, of the scalar product of magnetic field and path element is equal to the sum of all currents threading (enclosed by) the path round which the integral is taken, currents flowing in the reverse sense being counted as negative. In equation form $\oint H \cdot ds = \Sigma_n I_n$. The importance of this result is that it is independent of the presence of a magnetizable medium.

MAGNETIC MOMENT OF A CURRENT LOOP

Equivalent magnet. The size and direction of the magnetic field H set up by a system of wires or of coils carrying electric currents may be calculated from the law of Biot and Savart.

It may be shown as a general rule that a small plane coil of n turns and of area A, carrying a current I, produces the same magnetic field at distances large compared with the dimensions of the coil as a magnet of moment (nIA). The equivalent magnet is directed normal to the plane of the coil, its positive pole being on that side of the coil to which a right-handed screw would advance if rotated in the same sense as that of the current flow.

The equivalence may be completed by considering the forces on a loop or flat coil of wire carrying a current I in the presence of a magnetic flux density B. It is found that the forces acting on the coil are equal and opposite and there is no net translational force on the coil, but they do form a couple or torque, and this torque is such that the plane of the coil tends to assume a position at right angles to the direction of magnetic flux. The torque is identical to that on a magnet directed perpendicular to the plane of the coil, of moment IA (or nIA for a coil of n turns), A being the area of the coil.

Although the similarity between the inverse-square law of force for magnetic poles and the corresponding law for electrical charges might seem to suggest that there are two kinds of magnetic poles, there is a fundamental difference. Electrical charges, plus and minus, can be separated from one another, and exist independently. On the other hand a magnet broken in two will become two magnets (called magnetic dipoles), each with its own positive and negative poles, and the two magnetic poles are equal and inseparable. This result, together with the fact that a current loop behaves as a magnet, leads to the conclusion that there are no real magnetic poles, and no such pole has ever been isolated. Instead, only magnetic dipoles exist, and magnets consist of assemblies of such dipoles. Such dipoles are of atomic size, and arise from loops of current set up by the circulation of electronic charges within the atom. Thus the source of all magnetism lies in electric currents, macroscopic or microscopic.

Electric current as the source of all magnetism

An immediate consequence of this conclusion is that the lines of magnetic flux density B are everywhere continuous, since they terminate only on nonexistent true magnetic poles. From Gauss's theorem (see above) it follows also that the net flux of B through any closed surface is zero. In a vacuum, in which the magnetic field $H = B/\mu_0$, the same is true of the lines of H (provided no electric currents flow), but their behaviour is different at the surface of a magnetic medium. Here the lines of B are continuous, but the lines of H terminate on the apparent magnetic charges at the surface. At such a surface the components of B normal to the surface are the same inside and outside the medium, but the normal components of H are (B/μ_0) just outside and $(B/\mu_0) - M$ just inside. The change in the normal component of H is just equal to the apparent pole strength per unit area of the surface, which is equal to M, the density of magnetization of the magnetic medium. The components of H tangential to the surface are the same inside and outside.

Magnetic vector potential. The concept of magnetic vector potential is frequently used in mathematical derivations of magnetic fields caused by steady and time-varying electric currents. The mathematical form of the vector potential is more simple than the flux density B expressed in the Biot–Savart law. Although the vector potential will not be discussed further, it should be stated here that the magnetic vector potential and the magnetic flux density are related, but not in a simple way.

THE SOLENOID AND ITS FIELD

Although permanent magnets are convenient for many applications, they suffer from two serious disadvantages; the flux density B cannot easily be adjusted in size (or switched off), and its maximum value is limited to that of the material of the magnet. In contrast, the flux density produced by an electric current is readily adjusted by controlling the current, and much larger values can be attained if sufficient electrical power is available (see also MAGNETS and ELECTROMAGNETS).

A fairly uniform flux density of moderate size is readily produced by a solenoid, a coil of wire uniformly wound round a circular cylinder. For a solenoid of infinite length, the magnetic field is uniform inside the solenoid and is directed along the axis, being equal to the total number of turns (n) and the current (I) per unit length of the cylinder. For a solenoid of finite length, the magnetic field is not quite uniform, but the uniformity near the centre can be improved by adding extra turns at each end. In modern designs, specially shaped conductors are used instead of wires; at high current densities, flux density values over ten tesla (100,000 gauss) can be obtained,

Flux densities of modern magnets

but the power consumption exceeds one megawatt (10^6 watts) if high homogeneity, or uniformity, over a large volume such as 500 cubic centimetres is required. The

development of special alloys that retain their superconducting property even in high fields has greatly reduced the operating costs of such solenoids, a factor which generally outweighs the disadvantage of continuous refrigeration to liquid helium temperatures.

III. The motion of charged particles in magnetic and electric fields

The motion of electrical charges under the action of electric and magnetic forces is a subject of wide-ranging importance. It forms the basis of many devices developed to measure the charge, mass, and velocity of atomic particles, or to accelerate them to high energies for use as atomic projectiles. Details of atomic and nuclear structure and the magnetic fields of stars are revealed by study of their spectroscopic lines in emission or absorption. Charged particles from the Sun or from space are deflected as they enter the magnetic field of the Earth. The motion of electrons in the ionosphere (region of the upper atmosphere) profoundly influences the transmission of radio waves. Electronic devices depend on control of the movements of electrons in a vacuum tube or in a semiconducting solid.

The primary atomic particles are the electron, with a negative electric charge of -1.602×10^{-19} coulomb, and a mass (at rest) of 9.109×10^{-31} kilogram; the proton, with a positive electric charge numerically equal to that of the electron, but a mass 1,836 times greater; and the neutron, with no electric charge and a mass almost equal to that of the proton. The nucleus of an atom of atomic number Z contains Z protons and $(A - Z)$ neutrons, its mass (A) being close to A times that of the proton. The proton and neutron (and also the electron) have radii of about 10^{-15} metre, and the size of the nucleus is only a few times larger. A neutral atom contains Z electrons, at varying distances from the nucleus up to about 10^{-10} metre, which is the typical size of an atom. Ions are negatively or positively charged particles formed by the addition or removal of some of these electrons, and their charge is equal to, or is a simple multiple of, that of the electron. Electrons and nuclei may be considered as point electric charges in their interaction with external fields; for many purposes this is true also of atomic ions. The electron, proton, and neutron each possess a magnetic dipole moment; so also do many nuclei, atoms, and ions.

THE FORCE ON A MOVING CHARGE

A flow of electric current arises from the movement of electrical charge. The current I is measured by the amount of charge passing any given point in unit time; if an element of charge (dq) passes in a time dt, the instantaneous value of the current is a differential expression: $I = dq/dt$. If the charge dq has velocity v, it moves a distance ds in time dt, that is, $v = ds/dt$. Multiplying both sides of the former equation by ds, the current may thus be written in the form $I\,ds = v\,dq$, in which ds and v are vectors. This relation makes it possible to translate equations applicable to current elements into corresponding equation for moving charges. The force dF on a current element $I\,ds$ in a flux density B was given in the section above on the magnetic force on a current as the vector product $dF = I\,[ds \times B]$, and hence substituting for $I\,ds$ its equivalent, the force on the charge dq is $dF = dq\,[v \times B]$. For a charge q having dimensions so small that B is uniform over the volume occupied by the charge, this equation becomes: force equals charge times vector product of velocity and flux density; i.e., $F = q\,[v \times B]$.

The law of Biot and Savart for the magnetic field, namely, $dH = (I/4\pi r^3)\,[ds \times r]$ due to a current element $I\,ds$, may be similarly transformed to find the field of a moving charge, giving the equation that the magnetic field is equal to an elemental charge times the vector product of velocity and radius vector divided by the distance cubed; i.e., $dH = (dq/4\pi r^3)\,[v \times r]$. For an elemental charge dq moving in the plane of the page (Figure 3), the field dH at any point in the page is normal to the vector representing the velocity and to the radius vector drawn from the charge to the point. In Figure 3, the field dH is normal both to v and to r, and is directed downwards into the

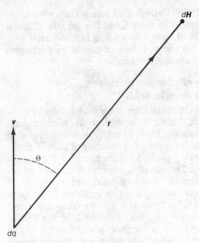

Figure 3: Magnetic field associated with a moving charge. Charge *dq* is moving with velocity **v** in the plane of the page, and the magnetic field *dH* at any arbitrary distance *r* is directed into the page.

page; its size is directly proportional to the charge, the velocity, and the sine of the angle (θ) between the two vectors, and inversely proportional to the square of the distance between the point and the charge; i.e., $dH = dq \, v \sin \theta / (4\pi r^2)$.

Two electric charges moving parallel to one another experience a magnetic force of attraction, like two parallel currents, but the magnetic force is usually small compared with the electrostatic force of repulsion between them. For two separated electric charges moving with velocity v, the ratio of the magnetic to the electric force is equal to the ratio of the square of the charge velocity to the square of the velocity of light, or v^2/c^2. Thus the magnetic forces are relatively unimportant until the velocities approach that of light. For currents flowing in wires the situation is quite different because the currents may be large (one ampere is equivalent to 6×10^{18} electrons passing per second), whereas the electrostatic forces are absent since there is no net electric charge on the wire. Thus in electric machinery large forces are generated by the use of the magnetic forces between currents, not by electrostatic forces between charges.

MOTION OF CHARGES IN A UNIFORM FLUX DENSITY

Dynamics. As stated earlier, the force (F) acting on a moving electric charge by a magnetic field is equal to the charge (q) times the vector product of velocity (v) and flux density (B)—i.e., $F = q \, [v \times B]$—and its direction is normal to both the velocity and flux vectors. Under the action of such a force the particle moves in a circle of radius r. The force necessary to hold the particle in its orbit (centripetal force) is equal to the mass (M) of the particle times its velocity squared, divided by the radius, or $M(v^2/r)$. The centripetal and magnetic forces are necessarily equal, and thus equating the two equations yields another equation of motion—i.e., mass times the quotient of velocity and radius is equal to charge times flux density, or $M(v/r) = qB$—and because the quantity (v/r) is just the angular velocity (ω_c), then angular velocity is equal to the factor, charge over mass, times the flux density, or $\omega_c = (q/M)B$. The angular velocity thus depends only on the ratio (q/M) which is a characteristic of the particle, and the flux density B. The time (τ) taken to complete a circle is the angle 2π divided by the angular velocity, which becomes $\tau = 2\pi M/qB$. The importance of this result is that the angular velocity and period are independent of the velocity of the particle. The circle in which it moves is in the plane normal to B, and its radius, from the equation of motion, is proportional to the linear momentum Mv of the particle, and inversely proportional to its charge q and the value of B, or $r = Mv/qB$. These two results form the basis of a number of methods of determining experimentally the ratio (q/M) from the angular velocity (or from the period) in a given

flux density, and also the velocity v of the particle if the ratio (q/M) is known.

In a flux density of one tesla, an electron completes one circle in a time of 3.57×10^{-11} second, corresponding to some 28,000,000,000 revolutions per second. If it has previously been accelerated through a potential drop of five kilovolts, its speed is 4.2×10^7 metres per second, and the radius of the circle is 2.4×10^{-4} metre, or about one quarter of a millimetre. Under the same conditions a proton, having the same (positive) charge as an electron, and a mass 1,836 times greater) completes a circle in 6.6×10^{-8} second (some 15,000,000 revolutions per second); its velocity is 10^6 metres per second, and the radius of the circle is about 0.01 metre (a centimetre).

At velocities approaching that of light, account must be taken of the relativistic effect which causes an increase of mass measured by an observer relative to whom the particle is moving. Already at an energy corresponding to a potential difference of 18 kilovolts, an electron reaches a velocity one quarter that of light, and the relativistic correction reduces its velocity by about 3 percent. For protons a correction of this size is reached only when the accelerating potential is greater by the ratio of the masses, a factor of 1,836.

Such corrections have important consequences in the design of accelerators and other devices for particles moving with velocities approaching that of light. The angular frequency does not remain independent of the energy of the particle, though the radius of the circle in which it travels is proportional to the linear momentum Mv, in which M is the actual mass as increased by the relativistic effect.

Applications. The circular motion of a charge in the plane normal to the flux density can be used to produce magnetic focussing, a concept that may be explained by the example of a source of charged particles, such as the electron gun of a cathode ray tube, that produces electrons moving almost parallel to the flux density vector B. A particle emerging at a small angle from this direction has a velocity component parallel to B and a transverse component perpendicular to B. This transverse component causes the particle to move in a helix, its path as viewed looking along B being a circle in the plane normal to B. After a time specified by the equation for time to complete a circle, given above—i.e., $\tau = 2\pi M/qB$—it will have completed one circle, and to the observer appears to have returned to its original point. This is true for all particles with the same value of the ratio (q/M), such as electrons, whatever the direction and magnitude of the initial transverse component. If the forward velocity is the same for all particles, in time τ they move forward a distance equal to this time times the forward velocity component, and all come together to a point at this distance from the source. In effect, they have been focussed to form an image of the original point; if they come from a number of sources, the image will be a reproduction of the object formed by the sources.

The motion of an electron in a tight helix round a high flux density can be used to keep electrons in a vacuum tube moving in a narrow beam over long distances. Even if the electrons initially travel in parallel directions, the forces caused by their mutual electrostatic repulsion tend to spread them out as the beam moves on. The magnetic force can be utilized to counteract the electrostatic forces and focus the beam at the desired position.

The deflection of a beam of charged particles through some desired angle may also be achieved by magnetic forces. When particles of mass M and charge q, travelling with velocity v, enter a region with a flux density B, normal to its path, the particles will continue in the same plane and move in an arc of a circle of radius $r = Mv/qB$. On emerging into another field-free region, the beam will continue in a straight line, thus having been deflected from its original direction. For an electron accelerated through a potential drop of five kilovolts to a velocity of 4.2×10^7 metres per second, the value of the flux density needed to produce a deflection through 45 degrees in a path length of five centimetres is about 5×10^{-3} tesla (50 gauss). In a television display tube, for which these are typical figures, the flux density is produced by two pairs of coils on either side of the neck of the tube, one pair controlling the horizontal deflection and the other the vertical deflection. The regular cycle of changes in the currents through the two pairs of coils, triggered by the incoming signal from the aerial, generates the scanning of the electron beam across the fluorescent screen at the front of the display tube.

Similar methods are used to deflect beams of protons and other charged ions in devices used in nuclear physics. If the ions are heavy the flux density must be correspondingly larger and is usually provided by the narrow gap of an iron-cored magnet with pole faces shaped to the path of the beam. The dimensions of the gap are determined by the size of the beam and of the vacuum envelope in which it moves.

MOTION OF CHARGES IN COMBINED ELECTRIC AND MAGNETIC FIELDS

Dynamics. A particle with electric charge q in an electric field E experiences a force $F = qE$, which is in the same direction as the electric field if th echarge is positive and in the reverse direction if the charge is negative. A uniform electric field is conveniently produced by a pair of plane parallel metal plates between which a voltage V is maintained. If the separation between the plates is d, the field is equal to the voltage divided by the distance, or $E = V/d$, normal to the plates; it is measured in volts per metre, unit field being produced by one volt across two plates one metre apart. In such a field the force on a charge of one coulomb is one newton.

If a magnetic flux density B is also present, the total force is given by the vector equation $F = qE + q[v \times B]$. A significant difference between the electric and magnetic forces is that the latter depend on the velocity of the particle, whereas the former do not.

Applications. This difference in forces is utilized in many devices, a simple example being a velocity filter, which selects particles of a given velocity. An electric field is produced between a pair of parallel plates, with a

Velocity filter for particles

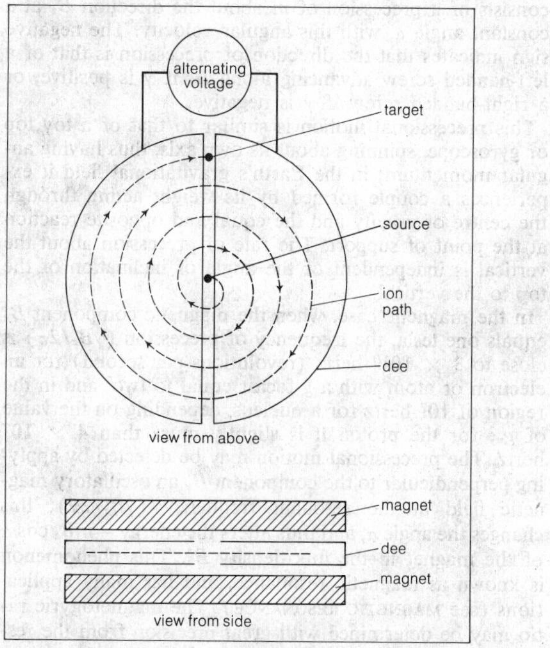

Figure 4: Acceleration of ions in cyclotron.

flux density B parallel to the plates. Particles of charge q enter in a beam parallel to the plates, but perpendicular to B. Only particles having velocities close to the ratio of magnitude of the electric field to the magnetic flux density (E/B) emerge from the plates, the range of these selected velocities being smaller the longer the plates and the narrower the gap between them.

The cyclotron, proposed in 1930 to accelerate charged particles (usually protons), also relies on the constant

time taken by an ion to complete a circle in a uniform flux density so long as the relativistic increase in mass is unimportant. Between the poles of a massive electromagnet weighing many tons, an evacuated space contains two pairs of flat semicircular plates, known from their shape as dees (Figure 4). Within either pair of plates there is no electric field, and charged particles from a source near the centre move in a semicircle because of the force exerted by the magnetic flux density, the time taken to complete a semicircle being proportional to the particle mass and inversely proportional to the charge on each particle and the flux density (but independent of the orbit radius). If a voltage V exists between the two dees, ions (charged particles) crossing from one dee to the other gain an amount qV in energy if the voltage is in the direction required to accelerate them. Because of their increase in energy and momentum, the ions move in a larger semicircle inside the other dee, but still take the same time round. Provided the voltage is reversed by the time they cross back to the first dee, they are again accelerated and gain another increment of energy qV. This behaviour of charged particles to keep step with the oscillating voltage is called cyclotron resonance. The particles complete many revolutions, until the radius of the semicircle has increased to a point at which the ions strike a target at the outside edge of the dee. Energies corresponding to falling through a potential of many million volts can be attained, though the voltage across the dees is only 50,000 to 100,000 volts. A sinusoidal oscillating voltage is maintained between the dees by power from an electronic oscillator, the frequency of which must equal (or be a multiple of) the cyclotron frequency. If the oscillator frequency is not quite equal to the cyclotron frequency, the ions may be initially accelerated but the voltage across the dees gradually changes phase relative to the time of arrival of the ions; they cease to be accelerated and are retarded at each transit when the phase error approaches 180°.

Electromagnets in cyclotrons

Such an effect occurs through the progressive change in the cyclotron frequency of an ion because of the relativistic increase in mass as its kinetic energy approaches the rest energy M_0c^2. For electrons the rest energy is equivalent to a potential drop of about 500,000 volts, or 0.5 MeV (million electron volts), but for protons it is about 1,000 MeV and they can be accelerated to some hundreds of million electron volts. The radius of the semicircle traversed by an ion is proportional to its linear momentum (Mv), and the size of a cyclotron must increase correspondingly; for high energies the magnet cost is large because of the great area over which a uniformly high value of flux density (one to two tesla) is required.

In modern high energy machines such as the synchrotron the diameter of the orbit is several hundred metres and is kept constant so that a high flux is required only at a given radius (r). When the particle velocity v is close to the velocity of light c, it remains substantially constant, and the alternating frequency (ν_0) of the accelerator voltage must satisfy the relation that the velocity of light divided by the frequency is equal to 2π times this given radius; i.e., $2\pi r = c/\nu_0$. Electrons can be injected at velocities approaching that of light when the flux density B is small, and B is then increased in time in such a way as to keep the angular velocity, which is equal to $\omega_c = qB/M$, equal to $2\pi\nu_0$ as the mass M increases. Heavy particles such as protons can be injected only with velocities considerably less than the velocity of light, and both ν_0 and B must be varied with time in a way to keep the radius of the orbit constant. Particle energies of 30,000 MeV have been achieved in proton synchrotrons; machines for energies 10 times greater are being built.

At low energies, where relativistic effects are negligible, cyclotron resonance has been used to determine the charge to mass ratio ($q/M = \omega_c/B$) of the electron and proton and as a mass spectrometer for heavy ions.

MAGNETIC DIPOLE MOMENTS

Atomic moments. A current I moving in a circular wire of radius r has an equivalent magnetic moment equal to the product of the current and enclosed area; that is, $m = I(\pi r^2)$. The current, however, arises from the motion of electric charges, and a charge moving in such a circle with velocity v also has an equivalent magnetic moment. If the charge is q, the current I is equal to the charge passing any point on the circle per unit time, $qv/2\pi r$, since the quantity $2\pi r/v$ is the time required by the charge to make one revolution. Thus the equivalent moment is the product of current and area (πr^2), or $m = qvr/2$. This expression can be related to the mechanical angular momentum, equal to the product of mass, velocity, and radius, or $G = Mvr$, in which M is the mass of the particles; thus $m = (q/2M)G$, in which both vectors m and G are normal to the plane of the coil. This relation also holds for a charge q of mass M moving in an orbit under a central force directed towards a fixed point.

In an atom, an electron of charge e and mass M_e moves in an orbit around the heavy nucleus with constant angular momentum G, but on quantum theory G is restrained to be an integral multiple of $(h/2\pi)$, h being Planck's constant. This gives a natural unit of magnetic moment for an atomic system, equal to $(e/2M_e)(h/2\pi)$ or $(eh/4\pi M_e)$, also equal to $(e\hbar/2M_e)$ if the symbol $\hbar$ is used for $(h/2\pi)$. This unit is known as the Bohr magneton, and its value is 9.273×10^{-24} ampere-(metre)^2. Because of the negative charge of the electron, its magnetic moment m is a vector parallel to but in the opposite direction to the mechanical angular momentum G, both vectors being perpendicular to the plane of the orbit.

Each electron possesses also a spin about an internal axis. The spin angular momentum for each electron is given by the equation $\frac{1}{2}(h/2\pi) = \hbar/2$, but the spin magnetic moment is given by the equation $m_s = -g_s(e/2M_e)(\hbar/2)$, in which the constant g_s is 2.0023, so that the spin moment is close to one Bohr magneton in spite of the half integral value for the angular momentum.

For an atom as a whole the resultant angular momentum ($J\hbar$) is also quantized in integral or half integral multiples of $\hbar$, but the relation between its magnetic moment and the angular momentum ($J\hbar$) is complicated by the presence of contributions from both spin and orbit of each electron. Nevertheless, the atomic magnetic moment can be written as equal to $-g(e/2M_e)$ times the atomic angular momentum ($J\hbar$), in which g is a pure number that can be calculated if details of the atomic structure are known. The term $g(e/2M_e)$ is called the magnetogyric ratio and is symbolized by the Greek letter gamma (γ).

Nuclear moments. This intimate connection between angular momentum and magnetic moment also applies to nuclei, many of which have a net angular momentum ($I\hbar$) equal to an integral or half integral multiple of $\hbar$. The nuclear magnetic moment may be written as $m_I = g_n(e/2M_p)$ times the nuclear angular momentum ($I\hbar$), in which e is now the charge on the proton and M_p its mass. The latter is 1,836 times that of the electron, and nuclear magnetic moments are smaller than those of atoms by a factor of this order. The quantity ($e\hbar/2M_p$) equals 5.051×10^{-27} ampere-(metre)^2 is used as the unit of nuclear magnetic moment, or nuclear magneton. As the nucleus is positively charged, most (but not all) nuclear moments are positive in sign; that is, the moment vector points in the same direction as the angular momentum vector. The value of the factor g_n varies widely, depending on the structure of the nucleus. Even for the elementary nuclear particles it has no simple value, being $+5.58$ for the proton and -3.83 for the neutron. These both have angular momentum $\hbar/2$, but the values of the factor g_n and the fact that the neutron has a magnetic moment but no electrical charge, indicate that they are fundamentally different from the electron.

These results illustrate the fact that, for both an atom and a nucleus, the magnetic moment m is parallel and proportional to the net angular momentum G. This is expressed in the equation $m = \gamma G$, in which the magnetogyric ratio has the dimensions of charge divided by mass. This ratio is of order $-(e/2M_e) = 8.8 \times 10^{10}$ coulombs per kilogram for an atom, and of order $(e/2M_p) = 4.8 \times 10^7$ coulombs per kilogram for a nucleus. Similar results hold for short-lived subnuclear particles, such as mesons, if the appropriate value of the mass of the particle is used in the value of the magnetogyric ratio.

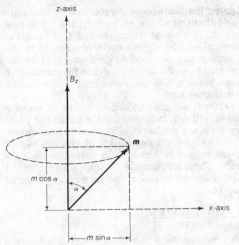

Figure 5: Precession of magnetic dipole moment m about B_z (see text).

Magnetic resonance. When a particle with a magnetic moment m is placed in a magnetic flux density B it experiences a couple (equal and opposite forces on a body form a couple) [$m \times B$], and its angular momentum changes at the rate $dG/dt = [m \times B]$. From the relation above $m = \gamma G$, and thus $dm/dt = \gamma[m \times B]$, a vector equation that can be solved using Cartesian coordinates (x, y, and z coordinates, mutually perpendicular). If the flux density has the single component B_z along the z-axis (Figure 5), the time rate of change of the magnetic moment's x-component (m_x) is equal to the magnetogyric ratio times the y-component of the magnetic moment times the flux density—i.e., $dm_x/dt = \gamma m_y B_z$; likewise, $dm_y/dt = -\gamma m_x B_z$; $dm_z/dt = 0$. The last equation shows that the component m_z is constant; if m is at an angle α to B, $m_z = m \cos \alpha$. The other two equations have solutions corresponding to a circular motion of the component $m \sin \alpha$ about the direction B_z, with angular velocity $-\gamma B_z$. The whole motion consists of a precession of m about the direction B_z at a constant angle α, with this angular velocity. The negative sign indicates that the direction of precession is that of a left-handed screw advancing along B_z if γ is positive, or a right-handed screw if γ is negative.

This precessional motion is similar to that of a toy top or gyroscope, spinning about its own axis, thus having angular momentum; in the Earth's gravitational field it experiences a couple formed by its weight acting through the centre of gravity and the equal and opposite reaction at the point of support. The rate of precession about the vertical is independent of the angle of inclination of the top to the vertical.

In the magnetic case, when the magnetic component B_z equals one tesla, the frequency of precession ($\gamma B_z/2\pi$) is close to 3×10^{10} hertz (revolutions per second) for an electron or atom with a g factor equal to two, and in the region of 10^7 hertz for a nucleus, depending on the value of g_n; for the proton it is slightly more than 4×10^7 hertz. The precessional motion may be detected by applying perpendicular to the component B_z an oscillatory magnetic field at the resonant frequency ($\gamma B_z/2\pi$); this changes the angle α, and thus alters the energy $-mB_z \cos \alpha$ of the magnet in the flux density B_z. This phenomenon is known as magnetic resonance, and has many applications (see MAGNETIC RESONANCE). The magnetogyric ratio may be determined with great precision from the resonance frequency in a known flux density; then, conversely, an unknown flux density B_z can be measured accurately. The most important technical application is in analytical chemistry, in which nuclear magnetic resonance can detect the minute variations in flux density due to local movements of the electrons characteristic of each molecule.

IV. Magnetic effects of varying currents

The discovery that an electric current is surrounded by a magnetic field, as shown by the deflection of a compass

---

The natural unit of magnetic moment in an atomic system

Precessional motion

needle, immediately raised the question of whether or not an electric current can be produced in a circuit in the neighbourhood of a magnet. A French physicist, Augustin-Jean Fresnel, argued that since a steel bar can be magnetized by passing a current through a metallic helix surrounding it, it was natural to try to see if the bar magnet would not in turn create an electric current in an enveloping helix. In the following decade many ingenious experiments were devised, but the expectation that a steady current would be induced in a coil near to a magnet had the result that any transient effect of bringing up the magnet was either accidentally missed, or its importance was not appreciated if observed.

The crucial experiment was carried out by Faraday in August 1831: two coils of wire were wound on a ring of soft iron (Figure 6). The second circuit was connected to

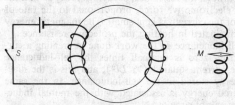

Figure 6: Faraday's magnetic induction experiment. When the switch S is closed in the primary circuit, a momentary current flows in the secondary circuit, giving a transient deflection of the compass needle M.

a copper wire extended over a compass needle so far away that it could not be affected directly by a current in the first circuit. When the first circuit was connected to a battery, Faraday observed a momentary deflection of the compass needle, followed by a damped oscillation and return to its original position. A similar deflection, but in the opposite direction, occurred when the primary current was switched off. Joseph Henry, a physicist working in Albany, New York, also recognized the momentary nature of the induced current, but his quite independent experiment was not published until after he had received the news of Faraday's work. In his paper (July 1832) Henry also reported and correctly interpreted an effect of "self-induction"—the production of sparks when a long helical conductor is disconnected from a battery.

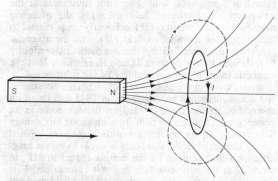

Figure 7: *Principle of Lenz's law.*
When the magnet moves towards the coil, an induced current *I* flows in such a direction that its own magnetic flux (broken lines) opposes the increase of flux through the coil from the magnet.

THE LAWS OF ELECTROMAGNETIC INDUCTION

In the following years further experiments by Faraday resulted in his enunciation of the two laws of electromagnetic induction: (1) when the flux of magnetic induction through a circuit is changing, an electromotive force (emf) is induced in the circuit; (2) the magnitude of the emf is proportional to the rate of change of the flux.

Lenz's law The sign of the emf is determined according to Lenz's law (after Friedrich Lenz, a German physicist), which states that it is such that any current flow is in the direction which would oppose the change of flux causing the emf. For example, in Figure 7, if the magnet is moved towards a closed loop of wire so that the magnetic flux

through the loop increases, the induced current flows in such a direction that its own flux circling the wire opposes the increased flux of the magnet through the loop.

These laws are expressed in an equation stating that the electromotive force (V) around the circuit is equal to minus the rate of change with time of the instantaneous value of the magnetic flux (N) through the circuit. It is expressed as $V = -(dN/dt)$. The electromotive force is the line integral of the electric field round the circuit—i.e., $V = \oint E \cdot ds$—and the flux N is equal to the integral of the normal component of B taken over a surface bounded by the circuit.

The equation of electromagnetic induction contains no arbitrary constant: an electromotive force of one volt is generated in a circuit in which the magnetic flux is changing at the rate of one weber per second.

The discovery of electromagnetic induction laid the foundation for the electric power industry. If a coil of wire is rotated with angular velocity ω in such a way that the magnetic flux (N) at any time t through the coil varies as the cosine of an angle ωt so that $N = N_0 \cos \omega t$, in which N_0 is N at its maximum, an alternating voltage $V = -dN/dt = N_0 \omega \sin \omega t$ is induced in the coil. The arrangement is an elementary form of dynamo; when current is drawn from it through an external circuit, electric power is produced, and mechanical power is consumed in driving the rotating coil.

INDUCTANCE AND MAGNETIC ENERGY

Self-inductance and mutual inductance. When a current I flows in a circuit, it sets up a magnetic field and there is a flux N of magnetic induction through the circuit arising from its own magnetic field. At every point the latter is proportional to the current I, and the flux N is therefore also proportional to I. This may be written $N = LI$, in which L is a constant that depends on the geometry of the circuit and the permeability of the medium in which it is immersed. The quantity L is called the self-inductance of the circuit and is equal to the total flux through the circuit when unit current (one ampere) is flowing. The self-inductance has unit value (one henry) if the flux is one weber when the current is one ampere.

Self-inductance of a circuit

If there is a second coil nearby, there will be a flux N_2 through the second circuit when a current I_1 flows in the first circuit. Again N_2 is proportional to I_1, and, therefore, $N_2 = M_{21}I_1$, in which M_{21} is known as the mutual inductance between the two circuits, its unit being also the henry. Conversely, a current I_2 in the second circuit creates a flux N_1 in the first circuit, given by $N_1 = M_{12}I_2$. The potential energy of the system, from the formula $U_p = -NI$, may be written either as $U_p = -N_2I_2 = -M_{21}I_1I_2$, or as $-N_1I_1 = -M_{12}I_2I_1$, showing that the mutual inductances M_{12} and M_{21} are equal to each other.

As the force between the circuits can be found from the rate of change of potential energy U_p with the distance between them, an absolute measure of current is obtained from a calculation of the mutual inductance and the measurement of the force in an instrument known as an electrodynamometer. In one design capable of a precision of one part in 50,000, two coils are attached to the beams of a balance, and these suspended coils are free to move inside two fixed coaxial coils. The same current flows through all four coils in series in such a way that the force on one coil is downward and that on the other is upward. The torque due to the current is balanced by a weight. Because the torque is proportional to the current squared, the direction of the current is unimportant, and any such electrodynamometer can also be used to measure alternating current.

For circuits of simple geometry the inductance can be found from first principles by computing the field and hence the flux due to the current flow. For an infinitely long solenoid, wound with m turns per unit length and carrying a current I, the magnetic field inside is uniform and equal to $H = mI$. If the core of the solenoid has permeability μ, the flux (N') through each turn is $N' = \mu\mu_0 AmI$, in which A is the cross-sectional area of the solenoid. The self-inductance per unit length, containing m turns, is therefore

$$L' = mN'/I = \mu\mu_0\, m^2\, A.$$

For a solenoid of length d, large compared with its diameter, this formula is still nearly correct, and the total self-inductance is

$$L = L'd = \mu\mu_0\, m^2\, Ad.$$

If a short coil of n turns, insulated from the first coil, is wound closely round the solenoid, the mutual inductance is

$$M = nN'/I = \mu\mu_0\, mnA.$$

If two coils are closely wound together, so that all the flux generated by one coil passes through the other, and vice versa, the ratio of the fluxes N_1 and N_2 through the two coils will just be equal to the ratio of the number of turns n_1 and n_2 on the two coils. For a current I_1 in the first coil $N_1/N_2 = (L_1I_1)/(MI_1) = L_1/M = n_1/n_2$; whereas for a current I_2 in the second coil, $N_2/N_1 = (L_2I_2)/(MI_2) = L_2/M = n_2/n_1$. Hence $L_1/M = M/L_2 = n_1/n_2$, and therefore the mutual inductance squared is equal to the product of the self inductances; i.e., $M^2 = L_1L_2$.

Transformer and induction coils. If the flux through the two coils is changing, the voltages induced in the two coils will be in the ratio of the two voltages (V_1 and V_2); that is, $V_1/V_2 = (dN_1/dt)/(dN_2/dt) = n_1/n_2$. Such a device is used as a transformer; if a changing voltage V_1 is applied to the primary coil, a changing voltage V_2 of a different magnitude is induced in the second coil. The voltage transformation ratio is $n_2/n_1 = V_2/V_1$, and the transformer may be used to "step up" or "step down" the voltage according to whether or not the number of turns n_2 is greater than n_1 or the reverse.

Historically, the first important application of electromagnetic induction was in the production of high voltages by the induction coil. Insulated coils of a few turns of heavy wire to carry the primary current, and many turns of fine wire for the secondary, were wound round a bundle of iron wires. A high voltage was produced in the secondary on interruption of the primary current, provided by a small battery. Early circuit breakers were cranked by hand, but an automatic circuit breaker was used in 1838. Notable improvements in construction were made so that by 1877 a spark in air 42 inches long could be produced. The induction coil was the standard method of producing high voltages in a number of fundamental experiments, including the discovery of the electron by a British physicist, J.J. Thomson (1897), and of X-rays by Wilhelm Röntgen (1895), a German physicist; the production of radio waves by Hertz (1886); and the wireless transmission of telegraphic signals by Marconi of Italy (1896). Millions of small coils have been used in automobiles to fire spark plugs, but for other purposes high voltages are now produced by electronic devices.

Betatron. The acceleration of charged particles is another application of electric field induction. In the phenomenon of electromagnetic induction a magnetic flux density that changes with time is surrounded by lines of electric field. Charged particles that move along such lines can be accelerated, and the magnetic flux density can simultaneously be used to hold them in an orbit of fixed radius. This is the principle of the betatron, first successfully used to accelerate electrons by a United States physicist, Donald William Kerst, in 1940.

For a typical betatron, in each revolution the electrons gain only about 100 electron volts in energy, and special care is needed in the design to focus them into a stable orbit in which they may travel for 10^5 to 10^6 revolutions, attaining a final energy in the range of ten to 100 million electron volts. The magnetic flux is varied sinusoidally at a low frequency of 100 to 200 hertz, acceleration taking place only during that quarter of the cycle in which the magnetic flux is increasing and in the right direction. At the end of the accelerating period extra coils are momentarily energized to expand the orbit so that the electrons strike a target, giving a copious supply of high energy X-rays.

Magnetic energy and mechanical forces. When a battery is connected to an inductive circuit, work is done by the battery in creating a flow of current against the reverse, or back, electromotive force generated by the rising current in the inductance. If there is no resistance or other source of loss in the circuit, the energy from the battery is not dissipated but is stored as magnetic energy in the inductance; this energy resembles the kinetic energy of a moving mass, which is the stored energy corresponding to the work done by a force in accelerating the mass from rest to its final velocity. When the battery is disconnected from the circuit, an induced electromotive force appears in the direction tending to maintain the current flow, and severe sparking at the switch may occur. The stored energy for a large electromagnet can be extremely high, and to avoid damage to the magnet and its associated circuits, precautions such as the provision of an electrical resistance in parallel with the switch are needed. Then, when the switch is opened, current flows instead through the resistance, decaying slowly so that the induced electromotive force, proportional to the rate of change of the current, is kept small. The magnetic energy is then dissipated in heating the protective resistance. *(margin: Energy stored as inductance)*

In a self-inductance L, the work done in creating a current I from zero is one-half times the self-inductance times the current squared ($\tfrac{1}{2}\, LI^2$), and this is the magnetic energy stored in the self-inductance. In the same way, stored energy is associated with the mutual inductance of a pair of circuits.

The energy stored in an inductive circuit carrying a current is often regarded as associated with the magnetic field round such a circuit. For a length l of an infinite solenoid, the stored energy (U) is $U = \tfrac{1}{2}\, IN = \tfrac{1}{2}\, I \times (B \times ml \times$ area of cross-section $A)$, in which m is the number of turns per unit length. The magnetic field H in such a solenoid is equal to mI. Hence, $U = \tfrac{1}{2}\, BH \times$ (area $\times$ length) $= \tfrac{1}{2}\, BH \times$ volume. This is an example of the finding that the stored energy per unit volume is $\tfrac{1}{2}\, BH$, or one-half the scalar product of the flux density (B) and magnetic field (H); i.e., $\tfrac{1}{2}\, (B \cdot H)$, if the vectors B and H are not parallel to one another.

V. General properties of magnetic materials

THE CLASSIFICATION OF MAGNETIC SUBSTANCES

All substances are magnetic to some extent; either they possess a magnetic moment in the absence of an external magnetic field, as in the case of so-called permanent magnets, or they acquire a magnetic moment when placed in a magnetic field. For most substances of the latter type, at moderate field strengths, the magnetic moment per unit volume (M) is linearly proportional to the strength of the applied field (H), and the magnetic properties are specified by the magnetic susceptibility (χ), defined by the relation $M = \chi H$, in which M is the magnetic moment per unit volume of the substance.

Faraday's original classification of magnetic substances into diamagnetic and paramagnetic in 1845 was based on observation of the force exerted on the substance in an inhomogeneous magnetic field. In a magnetic flux density B increasing in the x-direction with a gradient (spatial rate of change) dB/dx, this force is equal to m, the magnetic moment acquired by the sample (equal to MV, in which M is the magnetization per unit volume and V is the actual volume of the sample) times the field gradient dB/dx; i.e., $F = m(dB/dx) = (MV)(dB/dx)$. But $M = \chi H$ and $B = \mu_0 H$, and therefore the force from the equations above is: *(margin: Faraday's classification of magnetic substances)*

$$F = V(\chi H)\,(dB/dx) = V(\chi\mu_0)H(dH/dx).$$

This equation shows that if the magnetic susceptibility χ is positive, the force is in the direction of increasing field strength, whereas if χ is negative, it is toward the direction of a smaller field strength. Measurement of the force F in a known field H and a known gradient (dH/dx) is the basis of a number of accurate methods of determining the susceptibility.

Substances for which the magnetic susceptibility is negative are classified as diamagnetic. The susceptibility is small, of the order of -10^{-5} per unit volume (one cubic metre) of solids and liquids, and -10^{-8} for gases. A characteristic feature of diamagnetism is that the magnetic moment of unit mass in a given field is virtually constant for a given substance over a very wide range of temperature. It changes little between solid, liquid, and gas; the variation in the susceptibility (the magnetic moment per unit volume) between solid or liquid and the gas is almost entirely due to the change in the number of molecules per unit volume. This indicates that the magnetic moment induced in each molecule by a given field is primarily a property characteristic of the molecule.

Substances for which the magnetic susceptibility is positive are classed as paramagnetic. In a few cases (including most metals) the susceptibility is independent of temperature, but in most compounds it is strongly temperature dependent, increasing as the temperature is lowered. Measurements by Pierre Curie in 1895 showed that for many substances the susceptibility is inversely proportional to the absolute temperature T; that is, it is equal to a constant divided by the absolute temperature, $\chi = C/T$. This result is known as Curie's law and the constant C as the Curie constant. The laws of thermodynamics are such that Curie's law cannot be valid down to absolute zero temperature, and even at room temperature a more accurate equation in many cases is obtained by modifying the above equation using a fixed temperature (θ): $\chi = C/(T - \theta)$, known as the Curie–Weiss law. From the form of this last equation it is clear that at the temperature θ the value of the susceptibility should become infinite. This is interpreted as follows: because the susceptibility is the ratio of the magnetic moment to the applied field, $\chi = M/H$, an infinite value of the susceptibility means that a finite value of the magnetic moment per unit volume exists even when no external field is present ($H = 0$); the material has a spontaneous magnetization, and at temperatures smaller than θ it is a ferromagnet. Its magnetic properties are then very different from those in the paramagnetic or high temperature phase. In particular, although its magnetic moment can be changed by the application of a magnetic field, the value of the moment attained in a given field is not always the same and depends on the previous magnetic, thermal, and mechanical treatment of the sample.

The Curie–Weiss law

INDUCED AND PERMANENT ATOMIC MAGNETIC DIPOLES

From the atomic viewpoint, the basic distinction is between (1) substances the constituent atoms or ions of which have no permanent magnetic dipole moments, and (2) substances in which some or all of the constituent atoms do possess such permanent moments. In the first class, application of a magnetic field produces a small change in the motion of the atomic electrons, which results in the appearance of a small induced magnetic moment in each atom, proportional in size to the magnitude of the applied field. The bulk magnetic moment of a sample, representing the sum of the individual atomic moments, is thus also proportional to the applied field, giving a susceptibility equal to the magnetic moment divided by the applied field, which is independent of the field strength H and is also substantially independent of temperature. In a diamagnetic substance the induced moment in each atom is in the direction opposite to that of the applied field, giving a negative susceptibility. In fact this effect is present in all substances, but in substances of the second class it is almost always outweighed by much larger paramagnetic effects, giving an overall positive susceptibility.

In substances of the second class, when no field is present, the permanent atomic dipole moments point at random, giving no resultant magnetization of the sample. When a field is applied, the dipoles are no longer completely randomly oriented, there being an excess in the number pointing with the field over the number pointing against the field. Thus a net bulk magnetic moment in the direction of the field corresponds to a positive susceptibility.

The forces opposing alignment of the dipoles with the field are thermal in origin, and weaker at low temperatures. The excess number of dipoles pointing with the field is determined by the product of the dipole moment of the atom or ion (m) and the flux density (B), divided by the product of Boltzmann's constant ($k = 1.380 \times 10^{-23}$ joule per degree) and absolute temperature (T); that is, (mB/kT). For small values, the number is linearly pro-

portional to this quantity, giving a magnetization proportional to the flux density and inversely proportional to the absolute temperature, corresponding to Curie's law. At values of this quantity (mB/kT) sufficient to align nearly all the dipoles with the field, the magnetization approaches a saturation value corresponding to the limit where all dipoles are completely aligned.

Conduction electrons in metals form an important exception to this rule. The effect of quantum statistics is to give a constant excess number aligned with the field (except at temperatures approaching $10^4°$ K). This results in a positive susceptibility independent of temperature, small in size, and comparable with the diamagnetic contribution, so that the overall susceptibility of a metal may be positive or negative (Figure 8).

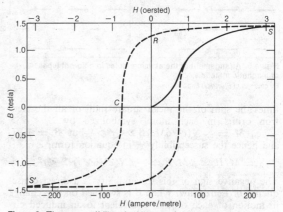

Figure 8: The susceptibility of a kilogram mole of the atomic elements. Broken lines connect the alkali metals (paramagnetic) and the rare gases of the atmosphere (diamagnetic).

In addition to the forces exerted on atomic magnets by an external magnetic field, there exist mutual forces between the atomic dipoles themselves. Such forces vary widely between different substances, but below a certain transition temperature (characteristic of each substance and primarily determined by the size of the mutual interactions) they produce an ordered arrangement of the orientations of the atomic dipoles even in the absence of an external field. The mutual forces tend to align neighbouring dipoles either parallel to one another, or antiparallel. In the former case, the spread of parallel alignment of the atomic dipoles throughout large volumes of the substance results in ferromagnetism, with a permanent magnetic moment on a macroscopic scale. On the other hand, if equal numbers of atomic dipoles are aligned in opposite directions, and the dipoles are of the same size, no macroscopic permanent moment is set up. This is known as anti-ferromagnetism. If the atomic dipoles are not of the same magnitude, and those pointing, say, to the right are all different in size from those pointing to the left, there will be a resultant permanent magnetic moment on a macroscopic scale, an effect known as ferrimagnetism. A simple schematic representation of these different possibilities is shown in Figure 9. In all cases, above the characteristic transition temperature, the material behaves as a paramagnet; it acquires a macroscopic magnetic moment only when an external field is applied, though the size of the moment is affected by the presence of the mutual forces between the dipoles.

Inter-dipole forces

MAGNETISM OF MATTER

Diamagnetism. When an electron moving in an atomic orbit experiences a magnetic flux density B, the force exerted on the moving electronic charge e produces a small change in the orbital motion, consisting of a precession of the orbit about the direction of B with an angular velocity. As a result, each electron acquires an additional angular momentum G, which, when summed over all electrons, gives a total magnetic moment (M) equal to minus the number (N) of atoms in the sample, times electronic charge (e) squared divided by six times the mass (M_e) of a single electron, times the flux density,

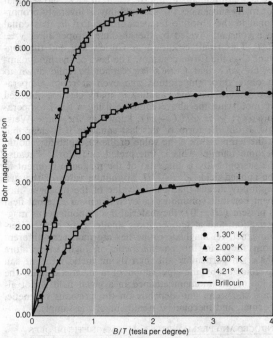

Figure 9: Arrangement of the atomic dipoles in different types of magnetic materials.
By courtesy of *Electrical Engineering*

times the sum of the mean square radii of all the electron orbits in each atom, symbolized by $\Sigma <r^2>$ —*i.e.*, $M = -N(e^2/6M_e)B\ \Sigma <r^2>$—but $B = \mu_0 H$, and hence the susceptibility χ, in equation form, is

$$\chi = M/H = \mu_0 M/B = -\mu_0 N(e^2/6M_e)\ \Sigma <r^2>.$$

The negative sign of this susceptibility is a direct consequence of Lenz's law. When B is switched on, the change in motion of each orbit is equivalent to an induced circulating electric current in such a direction that its own magnetic flux opposes the change in magnetic flux through the orbit; that is, the induced magnetic moment is directed oppositely to B.

Since the magnetic moment M is proportional to the number N of atoms (or ions), it is sometimes preferable to quote the ratio M/H for a sample not necessarily of unit volume. For unit mass, the mass susceptibility $\chi_{mass} = \chi/\rho$, in which ρ is the density (a unit mass of one kilogram occupies a volume of $1/\rho$ cubic metres). For a kilogram mole (the molecular weight in kilograms), having a mass of X kilograms, in which X is the molecular weight containing 6.023×10^{26} molecules, the numerical value of the molar susceptibility (that is, the susceptibility per unit mole) is

Molar susceptibility

$$\chi_{mole} = -3.55 \times 10^{12}\ \Sigma <r^2>.$$

For an atom the mean value of $<r^2>$ is about 10^{-21} (metre)^2, and χ_{mole} has values in the region of $-(10^{-8}$ to $10^{-9})Z$; the atomic number Z equals the number of electrons in each atom. The quantity $\Sigma <r^2>$ for each atom is almost completely independent of temperature, and so is the diamagnetic susceptibility. It is also nearly independent of the surroundings of the atom, and most substances obey a simple additive rule known as Wiedemann's rule, which states that when a mass m_1 of a salt of mass susceptibility χ_1 is dissolved in a mass m_2 of solvent of mass susceptibility χ_2, the mass susceptibility of the solution is given by $(m_1\chi_1 + m_2\chi_2) = (m_1 + m_2)$ χ, or $\chi = (m_1\chi_1 + m_2\chi_2)/(m_1 + m_2)$. This rule assumes that the susceptibilities of the isolated components are unaltered in solution, so that they can simply be added. Similar results hold approximately for ions in chemical compounds.

Paramagnetism. Paramagnetism occurs primarily in substances in which some or all of the individual atoms, ions, or molecules possess a permanent magnetic dipole moment. For a free ion this has the magnitude $m = -gJ(h/2\pi)(e/2M_e) = -gJ(eh/4\pi M_e) = -gJ\beta$, in which the quantity $J(h/2\pi)$ is the resultant angular momentum of the ion, and $(eh/4\pi M_e) = \beta = 9.273 \times 10^{-24}$ ampere-(metre)^2 is the Bohr magneton. By quantum theory, $(2J + 1)$ values (*e.g.*, 2, 3, 4, . . .), of the orientations of the dipole are allowed, and in a magnetic flux density B each has a different potential energy equal to minus the scalar product of the magnetic dipole moment

and the flux density, or $-m \cdot B = +(g\beta B)m_J$, in which m_J has the values $J, J-1, J-2, \ldots\ldots -(J-1), -J$. The fraction of dipoles with a given value of m_J (the component of J in the direction of B) is proportional to the exponential $(-g\beta Bm_J/kT)$, and the net magnetization (M) may be written in terms of the saturation value (M_s) for the magnetization as $M/M_s = f(g\beta B/kT)$. The function f is known as the Brillouin function. For values of magnetic flux equal to approximately one tesla and temperature to $1°$ K the function f approaches one; all dipoles are aligned parallel to B and the magnetization has the saturation value $M_s = Ng\beta J$ (Figure 10). At lower

Figure 10: The approach to saturation in the magnetization of a paramagnetic substance following a Brillouin curve. The curves I, II, and III refer to ions for which $g=2$ and $J=3/2$, 5/2, and 7/2, respectively, the substances being chromium potassium alum, iron ammonium alum, and gadolinium sulfate octahydrate.

values of the ratio B/T the function depends slightly on the value of J; when J equals $\frac{1}{2}$, it has the form

$$M/M_s = \frac{e^x - e^{-x}}{e^x + e^{-x}} = tanh\ x,$$

in which x has the value $\frac{1}{2}g\beta B/kT$.

When $(g\beta B/kT)$ is very much less than the value one, the function is proportional to the ratio B/T, giving $\chi = M/H = \mu_0 M/B = \mu_0 Ng^2\beta^2 J\ (J + 1)/3kT$. A plot of $1/\chi$ against temperature gives a straight line through the origin, corresponding to Curie's law; for atomic paramagnets χ is of order $10^{-2}/T$ per kilogram mole, which is much larger than the diamagnetic susceptibility at ordinary temperatures.

In substances containing nuclear magnetic dipoles there is a further contribution to the susceptibility. The size of the nuclear dipole is only about one thousandth of that of an atom, and the nuclear susceptibility χ_n can be written $\chi_n = \mu_0 Ng_n^2\beta_n^2 I(I + 1)/3kT$, in which $g_n\beta_n l$ is the nuclear magnetic moment. Per kilogram mole, χ_n is of order $10^{-8}/T$, and in solid hydrogen this just exceeds the electronic diamagnetism at $1°$ K.

Nuclear susceptibility

From its derivation, Curie's law should hold when $mB << kT$ (*i.e.*, the first term is small compared to the second) provided that no other forces act on the atomic dipoles. In many solids the presence of internal forces causes the susceptibility to vary in a complicated way with temperature. In a few compounds in which there are no permanent atomic dipoles, the application of a magnetic field may induce dipoles the sizes of which are proportional to the field, as in diamagnetism; however, such induced dipoles point with the field, giving a small positive susceptibility, constant over a wide range of temperature. The conduction electrons in metals have such a susceptibility, but for a different reason. Each carries a permanent dipole moment due to the electron spin, but the random thermal energy resisting alignment in an external field is the kinetic energy associated with the motion of the electrons within the conductor. The fractional excess of dipoles pointing with the field is a function of (mB/W), in which W is the maximum kinetic energy of the conduction electrons. At ordinary temperatures W, and hence also the susceptibility, is independent of temperature.

Ferromagnetism.   *Molecular fields.* A ferromagnetic substance contains permanent atomic magnetic dipoles, the difference from a paramagnetic substance being that the dipoles are spontaneously oriented parallel to one another even in the absence of an external field. This is due to mutual interactions between the dipoles, which, with very rare exceptions, arise from exchange forces. A simple empirical representation of the effect of such forces invokes the idea of an effective internal or molecular field H_{int}, which is proportional in size to the magnetization M; that is, $H_{int} = \lambda M$, in which λ is an empirical parameter. If this internal field is included with an external field H in the theory of paramagnetism, a magnetization M results, given by $M = \chi_p (H + \lambda M)$, in which χ_p is the susceptibility that the substance would have in the absence of the internal field λM. Assuming that the susceptibility is equal to the ratio of the Curie constant to the absolute temperature ($\chi_p = C/T$), corresponding to Curie's law, the equation $M = C(H + \lambda M)/T$ has the solution

$$\chi = M/H = C/(T - C\lambda) = C/(T - T_c).$$

This result, the Curie–Weiss law, is valid at temperatures (T) greater than the Curie temperature (T_c). At such temperatures the substance is still paramagnetic, magnetization being zero when the field is zero, but the effect of the internal field is to make the susceptibility larger than that given by Curie's law A plot of $1/\chi$ against T still gives

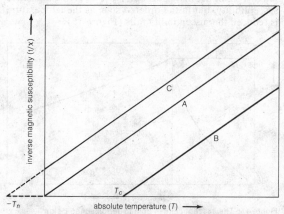

Figure 11: Plot of $1/\chi$ (the reciprocal of the susceptibility) against T (the absolute temperature). (A) Curie's law, (B) Curie–Weiss law for a ferromagnet with Curie temperature T_c, (C) Curie–Weiss law for an antiferromagnetic substance.

Curie temperature

a straight line (Figure 11), but $1/\chi$ becomes zero when the temperature reaches the Curie temperature. Inasmuch as $1/\chi = H/M$, at this temperature M must be finite even when the magnetic field is zero. Thus, below the Curie temperature, the substance has a spontaneous magnetization M in the absence of an external field—the essential property of a ferromagnet. Table 2 gives Curie temperature values for some ferromagnetic substances.

In the ferromagnetic phase below the Curie temperature, the spontaneous alignment is still ressited by the random thermal energy, and the spontaneous magnetization M is a function of temperature. The magnitude of M can be found from the paramagnetic equation for the reduced magnetization (M/M_s); i.e., $M/M_s = f(mB/kT)$ by replacing B by $\mu(H + H_{int}) = \mu(H + \lambda M)$, giving an equation that can be solved numerically if the function f is known. When H equals zero it can be written:

Table 2: Curie Temperatures for Some Ferromagnetic Substances	
	Curie temperature $^\circ$K
Iron	1,043
Cobalt	1,394
Nickel	631
Gadolinium	317
MnBi	630
MnAs	318
Fe_2O_3	893

$$\frac{M}{M_s} = f\left\{\frac{(M/M_s)}{(T/T_c)}\right\},$$

showing that the curve of (M/M_s) should be a unique function of the ratio (T/T_c) for all substances that have the same function f. Such a curve is shown in Figure 12,

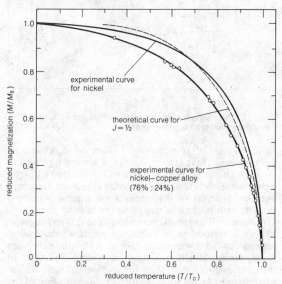

Figure 12: The reduced magnetization M/M_s as a function of reduced temperature T/T_c for a ferromagnet.

together with experimental results for nickel and a nickel–copper alloy.

The molecular field theory explains the existence of a ferromagnetic phase and the presence of spontaneous magnetization below the Curie temperature. The molecular field needed is, however, of enormous size, corresponding to a flux density of about 1,000 tesla in iron. This is far larger than can be produced by purely magnetic forces, and its origin remained a mystery until the quantum mechanical exchange forces were discovered by the physicists P.A.M. Dirac in England and W. Heisenberg in Germany. Its size also leads to the expectation that the magnetization should be little influenced by application of a comparatively small external field, but experimentally the situation is just the opposite. For iron the magnetization curve is shown in Figure 13 (solid curve) as a plot of flux density B against external field H. The variation is nonlinear, and B reaches its saturation value S in quite small fields. The relative permeability $\mu = B/(\mu_0 H)$ attains values of 10^3 to 10^4, in contrast to an ordinary paramagnet, for which $\mu = 1 + \chi$ is about 1.001 at room temperatures.

On reducing the external field H, the flux density B does not return along the magnetization curve, and even at $H = 0$ its value is not much below the saturation value (Figure 13, broken line). Its value at this point R is known as the residual flux density, and the retention of magnetization in zero field is called remanence. When the external field is reversed, the value of B falls and passes through zero (point C) at a field strength known as the coercive force. Further increase in the reverse field H sets up a reverse flux density B that again quickly reaches a saturation value S'. Finally, as the reverse field is removed and a positive field applied, the flux density traces out the lower broken line back to a positive saturation value.

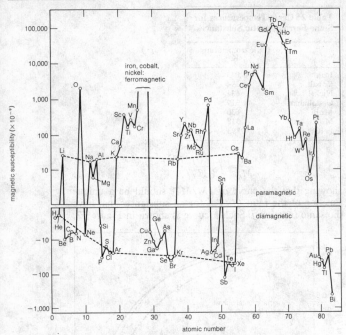

Figure 13: The magnetization curve (solid curve) and hysteresis loop (broken curve) for a ferromagnet.

Further cycles of H repeat the broken curve, known as the hysteresis curve, the change in B always lagging behind the change in H. The hysteresis curve is not unique unless saturation is attained in each direction; interruption and reversal of the cycle at an intermediate field strength results in a hysteresis curve of smaller size.

Domains. To explain these phenomena, Weiss suggested that a ferromagnetic substance contains many small regions (called domains) in each of which the substance is magnetized locally to saturation in some direction. In the unmagnetized state these directions are distributed at random or in such a way that the net magnetization of the whole sample is zero. Application of an external field produces changes in the direction of magnetization of part or all of the domains, setting up a net magnetization parallel to the field. In contrast with the microscopic scale of orientation of the atomic dipoles in a paramagnetic substance, the magnetization of a ferromagnetic substance involves re-orientation of the direction of magnetization of the domains on a macroscopic scale, giving large changes in the net magnetization when quite small fields are applied. Such macroscopic changes are not immediately reversed on reducing the size or changing the direction of the applied field, thus accounting for the presence of hysteresis and the possibility of a finite remanent magnetization even in the absence of an external magnetic field.

The technological applications of ferromagnetic substances are widespread, and the size and shape of the hysteresis curve are of overwhelming importance. A good permanent magnet must have a large spontaneous magnetization in zero field (*i.e.*, a high retentivity) and a high coercive force to prevent its being easily demagnetized by an external field. Both of these imply a "fat" hysteresis loop, typical of a hard magnetic material. On the other hand, ferromagnetic substances subjected to alternating fields, as in a transformer, must have a "thin" hysteresis loop, because of an energy loss per cycle that is determined by the area enclosed by the hysteresis loop. Such substances are easily magnetized and demagnetized and are known as soft magnetic materials.

Anti-ferromagnetism. In another class of substances, known as anti-ferromagnetics, the mutual forces between pairs of adjacent atomic dipoles are again due to exchange interactions but are of signs opposite to those in ferromagnets. As a result, adjacent dipoles tend to line up antiparallel to each other instead of parallel. At high temperatures the material is paramagnetic, but below a certain characteristic temperature there exists an ordered anti-

Marginal note: Importance of hysteresis

parallel alignment of the dipoles. The transition temperature T_n is known as the Néel temperature, after the French physicist Louis-Eugène-Félix Néel, who proposed this explanation of the magnetic behaviour of such materials in 1936.

The ordered anti-ferromagnetic state is naturally more complicated than the ordered ferromagnetic state, since there must be at least two sets of dipoles pointing in opposite directions (Figure 14). With equal numbers of

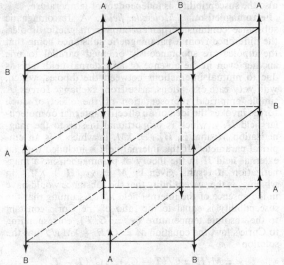

Figure 14: The antiparallel arrangement of neighbouring dipoles in an anti-ferromagnetic substance with two sublattices.

dipoles of the same size on each set, there is no net spontaneous magnetization on the macroscopic scale, and for this reason anti-ferromagnetic substances have few commercial applications. When an external field is applied, a small net magnetization is set up giving a positive susceptibility, but in the ordered state as the temperature is reduced the susceptibility falls (Figure 15).

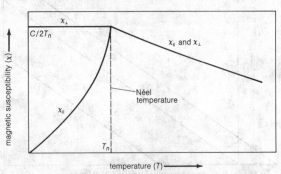

Figure 15: The susceptibility of an anti-ferromagnet. Below the Néel temperature (T_n) the susceptibility, χ_{11}, measured when an external field is parallel to the spontaneous magnetization (fixed in the crystal), falls with decreasing temperature, and perpendicular to this direction χ_1 remains constant (see text).

For the purpose of analysis such an anti-ferromagnetic arrangement is regarded as consisting of two interlocking sublattices A and B, on one of which all the dipoles point, say, upward, and on the other all point in the reverse direction. Within each sublattice there thus exists a ferromagnetic alignment that may be ascribed to the action of a molecular field. The latter is due mainly to antiparallel interaction with dipoles on the other sublattice, though there may be some interaction with other dipoles on the same lattice. If the latter is neglected, the effective field H_A acting on a dipole of sublattice A is $H - \lambda M_B$, in which H is the external field and $-\lambda M_B$ the molecular field, assumed proportional to the magnetization M_B of the other sublattice. Similarly for sublattice B the effective field H_B is $H - \lambda M_A$. In each case the negative sign is needed to represent the forces responsible for antiparallel alignment.

Above the transition temperature the magnetization of

Marginal note: Action of the molecular field in an anti-ferromagnetic arrangement each sublattice is given by the equation $M_A = \frac{1}{2}(C/T)H_A$, $M_B = \frac{1}{2}(C/T)H_B$, in which C is the Curie constant and the factor $\frac{1}{2}$ appears because each sublattice contains only half of the dipoles. The total magnetization M is $M = M_A + M_B = (C/T)(H - \frac{1}{2}\lambda M)$. Hence the susceptibility becomes $\chi = M/H = C/(T + \frac{1}{2}\lambda C) = C/(T + T_n)$, a result similar to the Curie–Weiss law for ferromagnetism except for the positive sign in the denominator. A plot of $1/\chi$ against temperature gives a straight line (Figure 11) but the intercept on the T axis is at $-T_n$.

Unlike the case of ferromagnetism, the ratio H/M does not become zero at any positive temperature, as the equation $M = M_A + M_B = 0$ always holds if $H = 0$. The criterion for the appearance of spontaneous magnetization on the two sublattices is that $M_A - M_B$ should be different from zero. From the equations above,

$$M_A - M_B = (C/2T)(H_A - H_B) =$$
$$(C\lambda/2T)(M_A - M_B),$$

or

$$(M_A - M_B)(1 - C\lambda/2T) = 0.$$

This equation is satisfied either if $M_A - M_B = 0$, which holds in the paramagnetic region, or if $(1 - C\lambda/2T) = 0$, when $M_A - M_B$ can be finite. This gives a transition temperature $T = T_n = C\lambda/2$, below which an ordered anti-ferromagnetic state exists because of the molecular fields (at $H = 0$):

$$H_A = -\lambda M_B = -\lambda(-M_0) = +\lambda M_0;$$
$$H_B = -\lambda M_A = -\lambda(+M_0) = -\lambda M_0.$$

These fields maintain a positive magnetization $+M_0$ on sublattice A and a negative magnetization $-M_0$ on sublattice B.

The exchange forces between the magnetic ions are anti-ferromagnetic in nature in the majority of insulating chemical compounds. Values of the Néel temperature for a number of typical anti-ferromagnetic substances are given in Table 3.

Table 3: Néel Temperatures for Some Anti-ferromagnetic Substances

	Néel temperature °K
Cr	311
MnF_2	67
NiF_2	73
MnO	116
FeO	198
$CuCl_2 \cdot 2H_2O$	4.3
$NiCl_2 \cdot 6H_2O$	5.3

Ferrimagnetism. Lodestone, or magnetite, has the chemical formula Fe_3O_4, and belongs to a class of substances known as ferrites. Ferrites, and some other classes of magnetic substances discovered more recently, possess many of the properties of ferromagnetic materials, including spontaneous magnetization and remanence. Unlike the ferromagnetic metals, they have a low electrical conductivity. In alternating magnetic fields this greatly reduces the energy loss due to eddy currents (see ELECTRICITY), and since these losses rise with the frequency of the alternating field, such substances have become of great technical importance in the electronics and radio industries.

A notable property of these materials is that the bulk spontaneous magnetization, even at complete magnetic saturation, does not correspond to the value expected if all the atomic dipoles are aligned parallel to each other. The explanation was put forward in 1948 by Néel, who suggested that the exchange forces responsible for the spontaneous magnetization were basically anti-ferromagnetic in nature, and that in the ordered state they contained two (or more) sublattices spontaneously magnetized in opposite directions. In contrast to the simple anti-ferromagnetic substances just considered, however, the sizes of the magnetization on the two sublattices are unequal, giving a resultant net magnetization parallel to that of the sublattice with the larger moment. For this phe-

nomenon Néel coined the name ferrimagnetism, and such substances are known as ferrimagnetic materials.

Inequality of the magnetization of the two sublattices can arise in a number of ways. A simple arrangement, in which all the atomic dipoles on one sublattice are different in magnitude from those on the other sublattice (Figure 9), seldom occurs in practice. The arrangement shown in Figure 16A, with two equal and opposite dipole

Inequality of magnetization in sublattices

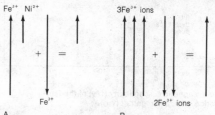

Figure 16: Division of the atomic dipoles between the two sublattices in the ordered state of (A) a ferrite such as $NiFe_2O_4$, and (B) yttrium iron garnet, $Y_3Fe_5O_{12}$. In A the net moment is that of the Ni^{2+} ion; in B it equals that of one Fe^{3+} ion.

moments but with an additional third moment on one sublattice, is typical of some ferrites, such as $NiFe_2O_4$. Here the equal and opposite moments are located on the Fe^{3+} ions, the third moment being on the Ni^{2+} ion. The net moment per formula unit $NiFe_2O_4$ is then just equal to that of the Ni^{2+} ion alone. Similarly, the formula Fe_3O_4 for magnetite should be written $Fe^{2+}(Fe^{3+})_2O_4$, the net magnetic dipole moment for this unit being just that of the Fe^{2+} ion. The values of the Néel temperature for such ferrites are well above room temperature, as shown by the examples in Table 4.

Table 4: Néel Temperatures of a Number of Ferrites of the Type MFe_2O_4

	Néel temperature (°C)
Manganese, Mn^{2+}	573
Ferrous, Fe^{2+}	858
Cobalt, Co^{2+}	793
Nickel, Ni^{2+}	858
Copper, Cu^{2+}	728

In another typical ferrimagnetic arrangement, all the atomic dipoles are equal in size, but there are more dipoles on one sublattice than on the other, as illustrated in Figure 16B. The best known example of this type is yttrium iron garnet, chemical formula $Y_3Fe_5O_{12}$. Here both the yttrium and oxygen ions carry no atomic moment, all such moments being located on the five Fe^{3+} (ferric) ions. These are divided between the two sublattices in the ratio three to two, so that the net moment per formula unit is just equal to that of a single ferric ion. The Néel temperature is 545° K, or 272° C.

Above the Néel point the susceptibility of a ferrimagnetic substance varies with temperature in a complicated manner. A simple theory due to Néel gives the relation

$$\frac{1}{\chi} = \frac{T}{C} + \frac{1}{\chi_0} - \frac{\sigma}{(T - \theta)},$$

in which C, χ_0, σ, and θ are constants. With suitable values for these constants, a reasonably good fit can be obtained to the variation of $1/\chi$ with temperature for yttrium iron garnet (Figure 17).

ATOMIC STRUCTURE AND MAGNETISM

The intimate connection between magnetic moment and angular momentum means that permanent dipole moments, of the order of the Bohr magneton in size, exist only in atoms or molecules that possess a net electronic angular momentum. Within an atom, each electron has (1) its own orbital magnetic moment associated with its orbital motion round the nucleus, and (2) its own spin magnetic moment associated with its spin about its internal axis. Each magnetic moment and each angular mo-

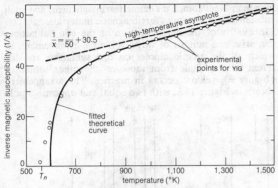

Figure 17: Inverse magnetic susceptibility ($1/\chi$) of the ferri-magnetic substance yttrium iron garnet (YIG).

mentum can be represented by a vector, and for the atom as a whole the net magnetic moment is related to the net angular momentum (orbit and spin) of all the electrons, which is a vector sum of the angular momenta of the individual electrons. This vector sum is formed in a way that depends on the forces within the atom that determine its electronic structure. Within an atom there are shells of electrons, such that each electron state within a shell has the same individual orbital and spin magnetic moment, the only difference being that the vectors representing these magnetic moments are differently oriented in space. When every such state within a shell is occupied by an electron, the net angular momentum of the filled shell is zero, and so is the net magnetic moment. This result greatly simplifies the position, making the net angular momentum and magnetic moment of the whole atom just equal to the vector sums of these quantities for the remaining electrons in the partly filled shells.

An atom or ion in which all the electron shells of lowest energy are filled with electrons and there are no electrons in partly filled shells is an especially stable structure. When atoms enter into chemical combination, they normally exchange or share electrons in such a way that all the electrons are accommodated in filled shells, giving no permanent atomic magnetic moment, but there are a number of exceptions to this rule. A molecule with an odd number of electrons, such as nitric oxide (NO) or nitrogen peroxide (NO_2), must have a permanent magnetic moment; this occurs also in a few molecules with an even number of electrons, a well-known example being oxygen (O_2). These three substances form the chief paramagnetic gases.

In the solid or liquid state, permanent atomic moments occur in ions belonging to the transition groups of the periodic table. The best known are the iron group, containing the elements titanium (atomic number or $Z = 22$) to copper ($Z = 29$), and the rare-earth group, cerium ($Z = 58$) to ytterbium ($Z = 70$); others are the palladium group, molybdenum ($Z = 42$) to palladium ($Z = 46$), the platinum group, rhenium ($Z = 75$) to platinum ($Z = 78$), and the actinide group starting with protoactinium ($Z = 91$) and continuing through uranium ($Z = 92$) to the heavier man-made transuranic elements. More precisely, the magnetic ions can be defined by the number of electrons in the partly filled shell. The iron group, with 18 electrons in closed shells, has between one and nine electrons in the $3d$ shell; the rare-earth group, with 54 electrons in closed shells, has between one and 13 electrons in the $4f$ shell. These figures refer to the ground state (the state of lowest energy) of the ion, which is the stable state at ordinary temperatures. Electrons can be excited into higher states, with a characteristic magnetic moment, but this is a transient phenomenon. Further, defects may exist in a crystal lattice or be induced by irradiation, with an abnormal electronic state carrying a magnetic moment. Such excited states or defects involve only a minute fraction of the ions in the crystal.

The paramagnetic susceptibility for a known number of ions can be found from measurements on solutions or on solid compounds (such as those in Figure 10) in which the magnetic ions are so far apart that the effect of any

mutual interactions between them is negligible. Corrections must be made for the diamagnetic susceptibility of all the ions present. For the rare-earth group, experimental values of the effective magnetic moment per ion are close to those calculated from the structure of the ions, both the orbital and the spin magnetic moments contributing in full. In the iron group the situation is more complicated, and the ionic moment is closer to that expected from the electron spin alone. The reason for this is that in a compound the magnetic electrons are subjected to electrical interactions with the neighbouring electrically charged ions. In the iron group these change the orbital motion of the magnetic electrons so drastically that their magnetic moments are practically eliminated, leaving only the spin magnetic moment. In the rare earths such effects are much smaller, though they can be seen in the behaviour of the susceptibility at low temperatures. Magnetic resonance has played a leading role in unravelling the details of these effects.

Such electrical interactions also play an important role in the ordered state of ferromagnetic, anti-ferromagnetic, and ferrimagnetic compounds. Exchange interaction between the ions determines the orientation of their dipoles relative to one another but not how they are oriented within a crystal lattice relative to the crystal axes. The latter is sometimes determined by magnetic interactions between the ions, but in many cases the electric interactions play a dominant role since their symmetry reflects the ordered array of electrically charged ions of which the crystal lattice is composed. Particularly in the rare-earth metals they give rise to a complicated three-dimensional arrangement of the atomic magnetic moments in the ordered state. Such arrangements have been determined experimentally from the scattering of beams of neutrons in these substances (neutron diffraction). The experiments are similar to the use of X-rays to reveal the detailed arrangement of ions in a crystal lattice, which acts like a three-dimensional diffraction grating. Because they possess an intrinsic spin and magnetic moment, neutrons (unlike X-rays) are sensitive to the direction of the ionic magnetic moment and are scattered in directions that are determined by the periodic nature in the ordered state of the three-dimensional array of magnetic moments.

BIBLIOGRAPHY. General college-level textbooks are: J.C. ANDERSON, *Magnetism and Magnetic Materials* (1968); F. BRAILSFORD, *Physical Principles of Magnetism* (1966); and B.I. and B. BLEANEY, *Electricity and Magnetism*, 2nd ed. (1965), which also includes the relevant electrical theory. At a more advanced level, requiring a good understanding of quantum theory, the basic text is J.H. VAN VLECK, *The Theory of Electric and Magnetic Susceptibilities* (1932); a number of later developments may be found in G.T. RADO and H. SUHL (eds.), *Magnetism*, 3 vol. (1963–65). S. CHAPMAN and JULIUS BARTELS, *Geomagnetism*, 2 vol. (1940), is a comprehensive treatment of the Earth's field; some important later developments are reviewed in TSUNEJI RIKITAKE, "Geomagnetism," in G.K.T. CONN and G.N. FOWLER (eds.), *Essays in Physics*, vol. 3 (1971). Summaries of the history of magnetism are given by Chapman and Bartels in the last chapter of vol. 2 of *Geomagnetism*; and by DANIEL C. MATTIS in the first chapter of *The Theory of Magnetism* (1965). Superconductivity and a number of other magnetic properties are discussed in C. KITTEL, *Introduction to Solid State Physics*, 4th ed. (1971); and in H.M. ROSENBERG, *Low Temperature Solid State Physics* (1963). In magnetic resonance the standard texts are A. ABRAGAM, *The Principles of Nuclear Magnetism* (1961); and A. ABRAGAM and B. BLEANEY *Electron Paramagnetic Resonance of Transition Ions* (1970). Important review articles on recent developments involving magnetic effects in the annual *Reports on Progress in Physics* are: H. ELLIOT, "The Van Allen Particles" (1963); D.B. BEARD, "The Solar Wind" (1967); and J.M. AITKEN, "Physics Applied to Archaeology, part I—Dating" (1970). Some relevant articles in the *Scientific American* are GEORGE SHIERS, "The Induction Coil," 224:80–88 (1971); ROBERT S. DIETZ and JOHN C. HOLDEN, "The Breakup of Pangaea," 223:30–41 (1970); and JOSEPH J. BECKER, "Permanent Magnets," 223:92–101 (1970). MALCOLM MCCAIG in *Attraction and Repulsion* (1967), gives an easy, readable account of the mechanical applications of permanent magnets.

(B.Ble.)

Electron shells

Neutron diffraction studies

Magnetohydrodynamic Devices

Magnetohydrodynamics is the study of the behaviour of electrically conducting fluids (either liquids or gases) in the presence of electric and magnetic fields. Magnetohydrodynamics today is primarily concerned with gases. At ordinary temperatures and pressures, gases are composed of electrically neutral atoms or molecules, and do not conduct electricity. At temperatures of several thousand degrees centigrade or above, however, the motions of the gas particles are violent enough to dislodge some of the outer electrons from the atoms. The electrons thus freed and the resulting positive ions are easily made to move by an electric field; such ionized gases (plasmas) are usually good conductors of electricity. Magnetohydrodynamic (MHD) devices generate electric current by the interaction of an electrically conducting fluid, such as a plasma, and a magnetic field. Closely related are electrogasdynamic (EGD) devices, which generate electric current by the interaction of an electrically insulating, or nonconducting, fluid carrying charged particles or ions, and an electric field.

GENERAL CONSIDERATIONS

Principles of operation. Direct energy conversion, as performed by MHD and EGD devices, involves the direct transformation of heat or radiation into electricity, rather than first to mechanical energy, and then to electricity. In a conventional power plant, the energy stored in a fossil or nuclear fuel generates heat to produce steam, which in turn drives a generator to produce electricity. By contrast, energy in MHD or EGD devices is transformed to electricity directly from the thermal and kinetic energy of the fluid. Only the fluid inside the MHD or EGD device is in motion; the device itself has no moving parts. Because of this, the device can operate at extremely high temperatures, which would destroy the metals and lubricants in a conventional steam turbine.

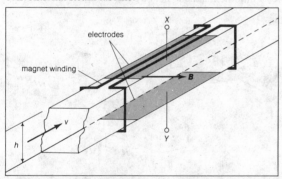

Figure 1: Operating principles of a magnetohydrodynamic electrical generator (see text).

MHD generator operation. Figure 1 illustrates the basic principles of a magnetohydrodynamic (MHD) electrical generator. The conducting fluid passes through a duct that has two opposite conducting walls (electrodes) and two opposite insulating walls. A strong magnetic field (B) is established at right angles to the duct. As the conducting fluid flows through the duct and the magnetic field with a velocity v, it generates an electrical voltage across the electrodes xy. The actual voltage generated depends on the velocity of flow, the strength of the magnetic field, and the height h (or diameter) of the duct. This voltage could measure velocity of flow, and the device would become a flowmeter.

If an electrical load of some kind, such as a light bulb, is connected across the electrodes, current will flow through the load. Inside the duct, a direct current flows between the two electrodes. This current exerts a retarding force on the fluid, and work must be done by the fluid to overcome this force. The work thus extracted from the fluid is converted to electricity. The retarding force is called electromagnetic braking.

The reverse effect can also be made to take place. If an electric current is driven through the fluid by an external battery or generator, a force is exerted on the fluid and the device becomes a pump. This technique may be applied effectively to pump liquid metals such as mercury and molten sodium.

EGD generator operation. An electrogasdynamic (EGD) device also extracts power directly from fluid flow, but the principles of operation are different (Figure 2).

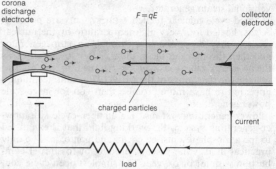

Figure 2: Operating principles of an electrogasdynamic converter (see text).

Basically, the fluid flow is used to force an electrical charge, in the form of ions or charged particles, from a region of low voltage to a region of high voltage, against an electric field E. If the ions are collected at the far end of the generator, a current, I, can flow through a load. The electrostatic retarding force, F, on the fluid is qE per unit volume, in which q is the charge density and E the collector electrode voltage divided by the distance between electrodes, and the flow does work against this force. If, instead, the electric field is reversed, the ions are forced ahead more rapidly and the device becomes a pump. The charged particles are formed by passing the fluid through an electrical discharge in which the voltage is high enough to produce ionization.

Historical background and applications. The basic principles of magnetohydrodynamics and electrogasdynamics have been known for over a century. The essential features of the interaction between an electrically conducting fluid and a magnetic field, and of electrostatics, were described by Michael Faraday in the 1830s. Practical MHD and EGD devices have had a much shorter history, however. The first large experimental MHD generator was constructed in the U.S. in 1938 by B. Karlovitz and D. Halász. These experiments were unsuccessful, however, because neither the properties of ionized gases nor the need for very high gas temperatures were sufficiently understood. By 1959, technology had progressed sufficiently so that 10 kilowatts of electric power were generated with an MHD device. Extensive research and development continues in France, Germany, Great Britain, Japan, Poland, the Soviet Union, and the U.S.

Early attempts to construct a practical high-voltage EGD generator were reported in the U.S. in 1932, and in France in 1935. Large scale work on EGD generation of electricity from fossil fuel dates from the late 1960s, with development work begun in the United States.

The magnetohydrodynamic interaction finds practical application today in flowmeters, accelerators, pumps, and generators. Electromagnetic flowmeters, in use for several decades, do not interfere with fluid flow and have no moving parts. They are used to measure liquid metal flow, flow of arterial blood, and ocean currents.

Electromagnetic or MHD pumps, easy to make corrosion-resistant, and with no moving parts, are often used in handling liquid metal. When used with gaseous working fluids, these devices are called MHD accelerators; space-flight propulsion systems based on the MHD interaction have been proposed.

MAGNETOHYDRODYNAMIC POWER GENERATION

The most important application for magnetohydrodynamics is power generation. In large public-utility plants that burn fossil fuel, significantly more efficient conversion of fuel to electricity and consequent savings in fuel and reduction of waste heat can be achieved with an open-cycle MHD generator topping (described later) a conventional steam power plant.

In open-cycle operations, the working fluid (gas) is eventually exhausted to the atmosphere; in closed-cycle systems, the fluid is reused. Topping means that the gases generated by burning the fuel (coal, oil, gas) are first passed through an MHD generator and then on to a conventional steam generator.

Closed-cycle systems

Closed-cycle nuclear-fuelled MHD systems are possible. A gas, heated to a very high temperature by the nuclear reactor, may be passed first through an MHD generator and then through the steam plant. After losing all of its (heat) energy, the gas may be returned to the nuclear reactor for reheating. In the early 1970s, MHD techniques appeared to have more promise than EGD for large-scale power generation.

Power-generating systems. In an open-cycle MHD power-er-generating system, the working fluid that is exhausted to the atmosphere must be cheap and nontoxic. The only practical fluid is the gaseous product of fossil-fuel combustion with air or oxygen. The simplest open cycle consists of a combustion chamber or furnace in which fuel burns with an oxidizer at high pressure to produce a high-temperature working fluid, a nozzle through which the combustion gases are accelerated to a high velocity of around 1,000 metres or 3,300 feet per second, and an MHD duct in which electrical power is extracted from the flow. A diffuser is used to retard the gases before they enter the atmosphere, and to raise the pressure to atmospheric.

The quantity of power that can be generated by a given amount of fluid depends in part upon its electrical conductivity. At the highest temperatures attainable with fossil fuels (about 3,000° C, 5,430° F), electrical conductivity of the combustion gases is too low to obtain adequate power yield. Consequently, the fluid is seeded with a material such as potassium, which ionizes easily and raises power yields to acceptable levels.

Seeding fluid with potassium

As the gas expands in the MHD duct and power is extracted, the gas cools and its electrical conductivity falls rapidly. At about 2,000° C (3,630° F), the MHD power-generation process ceases to be economically attractive, and the simple open-cycle system thus has a low efficiency. Since the exhausted gas is still hot in comparison with normal power-plant working fluids, the efficiency of the simple open-cycle system can be substantially increased by recovering the energy remaining in the gas stream with conventional methods.

Open cycle with heat recovery. Heat energy recovered from the MHD duct exhaust gas is used in two ways. First, it heats the high-pressure air fed to the combustion chamber. Second, the remaining heat is used to produce steam in a conventional boiler and power is generated in the conventional way.

The heat-recovery unit also recovers the seed; when the MHD exhaust gas cools, the seed material condenses on the boiler and heat-exchanger walls and is collected. Once heat recovery is complete, an electrostatic precipitator removes any remaining seed or other particulate matter and the gases are discharged through a smokestack. About 40 percent of the net thermal energy entering the heat-recovery unit can be converted into electrical power. The overall efficiency of a combined MHD-steam plant (45 to 55 percent) is thus substantially greater than that of the simple open-cycle MHD system (10 to 20 percent).

Closed-cycle systems. An alternative is the closed-cycle gas MHD system in which the working fluid, at high pressure, is heated in a nuclear reactor before it enters the MHD generator. Because the working fluid is recycled, its cost is no longer of primary concern, and the gas can be chosen for its heat-transfer and electrical properties. Helium is the most attractive gas, and cesium though expensive is the most easily ionized seed material. This system may be practical for bulk power generation because it offers a potential means of obtaining greater efficiencies from advanced-fission reactors. The top gas temperatures required are lower than peak open-cycle temperatures because certain processes can be used to increase electrical

conductivity. A heat-recovery plant is still employed, however, because the conductivity of the fluid is too low for the process to be attractive at temperatures that are high by conventional steam-plant standards.

Closed-cycle, liquid-metal systems are also being developed. These are a compromise between the higher thermal efficiency of gas-cycle MHD systems and the advantage of higher conductivity obtained by using liquid metal as the working fluid. Liquid metals have much higher electrical conductivity than seeded gases at all temperatures; power yields per given quantity of fluid can be about ten times higher than in MHD devices using ionized gases (plasma).

Many liquid-metal cycles have been proposed both for space power and central power-station applications. In these, the liquid metal is heated in a nuclear reactor; part of the flow is vapourized, and the vapour is accelerated to a high velocity in a nozzle; the vapour mixes with and accelerates the liquid flow; when the vapour and liquid are separated, the liquid enters the MHD generator where part of its kinetic energy is converted to electricity. Liquid-metal systems are less efficient than gas systems.

MHD generator geometries. For liquid-metal MHD systems, the linear duct with a single electrode on each side as shown in Figure 1 is adequate. In gaseous systems designed for bulk power generation, however, a more complicated electrode geometry is required because of the Hall effect (named after its discoverer, U.S. physicist E.H. Hall), in which the motion of the electrons that carry the current, transverse to the magnetic field, produces an additional electric field along the duct axis. This additional electric field, called a Hall field, causes axial currents that seriously decrease electrical efficiency of the generator. To prevent this, each electrode is divided into segments, each of which is connected to separate loads (Figure 3A). The result is a Faraday generator. (In Figures 3A through 3E, the load current is represented by *I* and the magnetic field by *B*.)

The Hall effect

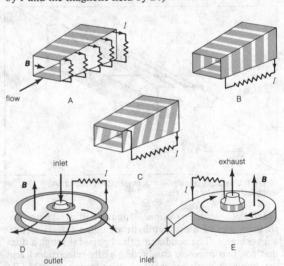

Figure 3: *Magnetohydrodynamic generator geometries.*
(A) Faraday, (B) Hall, (C) diagonal, (D) disk, and (E) vortex. The shaded areas are electrodes; the load current is represented by *I* and the magnetic field by *B* (see text).

When the Hall effect is very pronounced, the transverse currents may be short circuited in the linear duct and the axial current used to generate power with a single load (Figure 3B); this is called a Hall generator. The advantage of the Hall generator with its single load, and the higher efficiency of the Faraday generator can be combined by diagonally cross-connecting electrodes (Figure 3C).

Other duct designs or geometries have been proposed to counteract the Hall effect. One is the disk generator (Figure 3D), in which the gas flows radially outward between two disks. The short-circuited transverse currents of the linear Hall generator now flow in closed circles around the centre of the disks, and no intermediate electrodes are required. Power is generated with the radial current and radial electric field.

A vortex geometry (Figure 3E) has been proposed to reduce the wall area of the generator when the Hall effect is small. Reducing wall area of the generator makes it more efficient, lowering costs. In this vortex generator the flow spirals inwards, the magnetic field is perpendicular to the walls, and the inner and outer cylinders are the electrodes.

Performance and efficiency. The processes occurring within the MHD generator that determine its performance are power extraction and electromagnetic braking throughout the duct volume, and heat transfer and friction at the duct walls. Power extraction and heat transfer decrease the thermal energy of the fluid; electromagnetic braking force and wall friction decrease its pressure and momentum.

Heat transfer to the duct walls and friction losses must be kept small. Heat transfer lowers the fluid temperature, which, in a gas cycle, reduces the electrical conductivity and therefore increases losses due to the increased electrical resistance of the fluid. Wall friction increases the pressure required at the duct inlet for a given power output. Because the electrical conductivity decreases as pressure increases, additional resistive losses result. Since both these processes are wall effects, whereas the desired interaction, power extraction, takes place throughout the duct volume, the larger the generator the more efficient its performance will be. For this reason only large MHD generators are practicable. Even for a 2,000 MW (megawatt) unit, heat losses to the generator walls are 10 to 20 percent of the MHD power output. The heat lost is recovered in the steam plant, but at a much lower efficiency.

Only part of the work done by the flow against the electromagnetic braking force is extracted as electrical energy. The remaining part is dissipated within the generator as a result of the electrical resistance of the fluid.
Excessive dissipation is undesirable because it reduces generator efficiency. To prevent this, the external load is matched to the internal resistance of the generator, thus limiting dissipation to about one-quarter of the power generated.

Electrical losses also occur at duct inlet and exit and near the duct walls. At the entrance and exit to the magnetic-field region, closed current loops within the fluid cause additional dissipation. Since the electrode walls of the duct are cooler than the main flow, gas resistance and resulting electrical dissipation increase near the walls as well. In addition, each electrode segment short circuits the axial electric Hall field near the wall. As a result, currents flow axially in the gas and return along the electrode, again increasing resistive losses. Though each of these effects taken separately is small, together they can significantly degrade performance in a large MHD generator.

The overall cycle efficiency of a combined MHD-steam plant is equal to the net electrical power output divided by the thermal input. The net power output is the sum of the electrical output from the MHD generator and the electrical output from the steam plant, less the power required for the air compressor, the steam-plant auxiliaries, the MHD-plant auxiliaries, and the losses incurred in converting the MHD power from direct current to alternating current. For the open cycle, the thermal input is the rate at which fuel flows into the combustor multiplied by its heating value. For the closed cycle, the thermal input is the rate of heat transfer to the working fluid in the reactor.

For a large central-power generating station with a fossil-fuel thermal input of 2,000 megawatts, plant-performance design studies predict power outputs from the MHD duct varying from 600 to 800 megawatts depending on the assumptions made. With a steam-cycle efficiency of 42 percent, the efficiencies of the combined MHD-steam plant predicted for these designs lie between 45 and 55 percent.

Practical design considerations. *Production of the hot working fluid.* In gas MHD systems, an easily ionized seed material such as cesium or potassium is added to the gas stream in amounts up to 1 percent of the total gas flow. Though only about 1/1000 of the seed atoms have to be ionized to produce the required electrical conductivity within the MHD duct, gas temperatures above 2,700° C

must be attained in the open-cycle combustor. With fossil fuels such temperatures require combustion with either oxygen, air preheated to 1,200° to 1,600° C, or oxygen-enriched air at intermediate temperatures.

For central, station power generation, only preheated air is economical; a high-temperature air heater is essential. The demanding requirements of large air flow and high air-outlet temperature of at least 1,200° C, coupled with the corrosive nature of the seeded hot gas and the pressure difference between air and MHD exhaust gas, place this plant item at the limits of current technology.

In closed-cycle gas systems, acceptable electrical conductivities can be achieved at lower temperatures, but a number of significant problems are encountered in maintaining their conductivity, and extracting the MHD power. Various instabilities that occur dissipate a substantial part of the energy. Solutions to all of these problems were not yet in sight in the early 1970s.

The MHD duct. The MHD duct must operate for extended periods under extremely arduous conditions. For the linear duct one pair of walls must be electrical insulators, and the other, segmented electrode structures. All walls must be water cooled to withstand the high gas temperature, though the heat flux should be held to a minimum. In the open cycle the seed and slag-laden combustion gas is corrosive; special materials are required to withstand chemical and electrochemical erosion. The duct structure must also withstand the high electromagnetic forces on current-carrying elements.

Insulator wall designs consisting of a matrix of separately cooled metal pegs set in an insulating background have been found satisfactory. The electrodes present a more difficult materials problem. To provide efficient electron emission into the gas, the electrode surfaces must be hot, but the hotter the surface, the greater the damage from fluxing and erosion. High-temperature ceramic oxides, such as stabilized zirconia, which are conductors and electron emitters when hot, are the favoured materials. Water-cooled metal supports provide structural integrity and electrical contact to the ceramic blocks. The individual electrode segments are then separated by corrosion-resistant insulator strips and built up into a segmented electrode wall. Erosion and destruction of the ceramic are still a major problem. The only electrode structure that has operated successfully in a power-producing channel for hundreds of hours, required a replenishment system, in which zirconia added to the gas stream deposited on the electrode surface at a rate equal to the erosion.

The magnet. A magnetic field of 5 to 6 tesla (webers per square metre) is required for the MHD generator. (The weber unit of magnetic flux, in linking a circuit of one turn produces an electromotive force of one volt in it as it is reduced to zero at a uniform rate in one second.) Though higher fields would increase power density, the electric fields in the duct, the forces in the magnet windings, and the magnet costs become impractically high at fields above this value. For the linear duct, the magnet geometry is unusual; a double-saddle geometry as shown in Figure 1 is preferred since it provides an almost uniform field across the duct and allows the channel to pass straight through the magnet.

The conductor choice lies between copper at room temperature, cryogenically cooled aluminum and sodium, and superconductors such as niobium-titanium. For central-station generation, the higher initial cost of the superconducting (zero electrical resistance) winding is more than offset by the power consumption of resistive windings. Because the energy stored in the magnet is enormous, the magnet must be protected from damage during rapid shutdown. For peaking or emergency power the magnet requirements are different. Since a superconducting magnet requires continuous refrigeration, an iron-core copper magnet, self-excited by part of the generator output (and not requiring such refrigeration), may be preferred.

Steam plant and seed recovery. The heat-recovery unit contributes one-third to one-half of the combined plant output so that its capital cost and efficiency are important factors. In many respects, the steam plant topped by an

[margin note: Reducing dissipation]

[margin note: Superconducting magnets]

MHD generator is similar to a conventional plant. The major differences are: radiant heat transfer in the boiler is reduced as the MHD exhaust contains no soot; the seed-laden gas is more corrosive; seed deposits on the boiler tubes reduce heat-transfer rates; the air heater must be incorporated into the heat-recovery unit; and most of the conventional regenerative-boiler-feed water heaters are eliminated because the feed water now cools the MHD duct and combustion chamber, reducing the steam-cycle efficiency.

The heat-recovery unit also recovers the seed. Since the cost of the injected potassium seed is several times the cost of the fuel, 99 percent seed recovery is required for an economic system. The cost of cesium seed would require 99.9 percent recovery, which is probably impractical. About 80 percent of the seed is deposited in the air heater and steam plant, the remaining 20 percent is removed in an electrostatic precipitator. The seed is then processed and recycled.

Environmental factors. One benefit of increased overall efficiency is reduced heat loss to the environment. The thermal pollution of lakes and rivers caused by the discharge of condenser-cooling water from conventional fossil-fuelled and nuclear plants is a significant and increasing problem.

Conventional fossil-fuelled plants are a major source of sulfur oxides, nitrogen oxides, and particulates. The higher combustion temperatures in the MHD system substantially increase the nitrogen oxides, though the sulfur oxides remain unchanged. The need to recover the seed requires a cleaning system that removes a high percentage of all particulates, though additional gas cleaning equipment is also required.

ELECTROGASDYNAMIC DEVICES

Electrogasdynamic-generator performance. The EGD device illustrated in Figure 2 has several attractive features. Like MHD devices, it has no moving parts and high gas temperatures can be used. Since the gas must be an electrical insulator instead of a conductor, an EGD device can operate over the whole available gas temperature range. (Conductance of a gas changes with temperature.) Thus EGD is not restricted to "topping" applications, as is MHD. The electrical output is direct current, very high voltage, and is therefore suitable for long distance transmission without any need for dc/ac converters and transformers.

For a number of complex reasons, however, EGD generator performance is rather limited. For example, the electrical output of a single EGD channel (or generator) does not exceed about 50 watts. The size is limited by the electrical breakdown strength of the gas and the maximum useful voltage between electrodes. Considerable unavoidable energy loss is part of the EGD process. Thus, with today's technology, EGD generator performance still has serious drawbacks. In comparison with MHD devices, the large difference in size of the two devices is one drawback. The MHD generator size is not limited in any fundamental way; the EGD converter is limited by the very high electric fields required for high power densities.

Electrogasdynamic power generation. When an EGD device is incorporated into a power-generating cycle, high-pressure, high-temperature gas expands through the EGD generator, and power is extracted from the flow. Because the power extracted in each single EGD converter is small, however, the pressure drop across each unit is small, and many units must be connected in series and in parallel to obtain acceptable cycle efficiency and power output for bulk power generation.

Fossil-fuel-fired open-cycle systems have been proposed. In these, air would be compressed and burned with fossil fuel at high pressure in a combustor; the hot gases carrying small particles (usually fly ash) would enter the EGD generator, where the particles would be charged at the entrance to each channel. At each channel exit, the current would be collected; at the next channel entrance the ash particles would be recharged. All of the corona and collector electrodes would be connected in parallel since the voltage across each stage is high (1,000,000 volts)

(margin note: Fossil-fuel-fired open-cycle systems)

and any other connection would give a still higher voltage. Depending on the assumptions made, the efficiencies predicted for such cycles can be comparable with conventional power-generating systems, and it is expected that the capital cost of the EGD device could be much lower. The assumptions on which the design and performance calculations would have to be based had not yet been proven experimentally by the mid-1970s. A closed-cycle system with helium heated as it passes through a nuclear reactor before it enters the EGD generator has also been suggested.

PRESENT STATUS AND FUTURE PROSPECTS

Aside from MHD flowmeters and pumps for special applications, the greatest promise for MHD devices is in central-station power generation. The open-cycle system, with an MHD generator topping a conventional steam unit, has the potential for using our large fossil-fuel reserves more effectively through higher cycle efficiencies.

A number of technical problem areas remain, however, particularly in regard to the high-temperature air heater and long-life requirements for the MHD duct. It is not possible, therefore, to estimate precisely the capital costs of a central-station MHD-steam system, nor to be sure what increase in efficiency over a conventional fossil-fired plant can be attained. MHD systems must also compete with developments in the nuclear-power industry. In Great Britain and France, the economic advantages of MHD were not thought sufficient to make the substantial development costs worthwhile; their extensive MHD research programs had been discontinued by 1970. In the Soviet Union, however, which has the largest MHD effort in the world, work on a substantial scale continues with the construction of an MHD-steam pilot plant of 75-megawatt output in Moscow. In the U.S. it is expected that development of individual plant items will continue, but that construction of a complete pilot plant will await better solutions to the remaining technical problems. There are no prospects at present for developing closed-cycle MHD systems on a comparable scale. The prospects of EGD for bulk power generation are not promising. The large number of parallel and series units required for a generator of useful size makes the concept of marginal feasibility. The EGD converter may find use, however, as a small, high-voltage power supply.

BIBLIOGRAPHY. R.J. ROSA, *Magnetohydrodynamic Energy Conversion* (1968), an introductory text covering all aspects of MHD power generation; D.T. SWIFT-HOOK, "Magnetohydrodynamic Power Generation," *Direct Generation of Electricity*, ed. by K.H. SPRING, ch. 3 (1966), a review of the principles of MHD power generation; J.B. HEYWOOD and G.J. WOMACK (eds.), *Open Cycle MHD Power Generation* (1969), a comprehensive text treating all aspects of the open-cycle MHD system; PANEL ON MHD, *MHD for Central Station Power Generation: A Plan for Action*, prepared for the Executive Office of the President, Office of Science and Technology (1969), a review of the prospects for MHD central-station power generation in the U.S.; G.W. SUTTON and A. SHERMAN, *Engineering Magnetohydrodynamics* (1965), a general text on MHD, basic principles and applications; M.A. KETTARI, "Electrohydrodynamic Power Generation," *Direct Energy Conversion*, ch. 9 (1970), a concise account of principles of EGD and its applications.

(J.B.H.)

Magnets and Electromagnets

The use of the magnet and its electrical counterpart, the electromagnet, is the foundation of much of modern technology. The development of theories of magnetism was an important part of the work of the great 19th-century physicists, but a full understanding of the phenomenon had to await the development of the 20th-century ideas of quantum mechanics. Present understanding has led to the development of modern, powerful, permanent-magnet materials on the one hand and to the versatile ferrites —direct descendants of the lodestone—on the other.

This article describes electromagnets and permanent magnets and their applications in many devices, from motors and generators to computers. A more detailed description of the phenomenon of magnetism and its historical development appears in the article MAGNETISM.

MAGNETIC PROPERTIES

By the end of the 19th century all the known elements and many compounds had been tested for magnetism, and all were found to have some magnetic property. The most common was the property of diamagnetism, the name given to materials exhibiting a weak repulsion by both poles of a magnet. Some materials, for example, chromium, showed paramagnetism, being capable of weak induced magnetization when brought near to a magnet. This magnetization disappears when the magnet is removed. Only three elements, iron, nickel, and cobalt, showed the property of ferromagnetism; that is, the capability of remaining permanently magnetized. Among the known compounds of these elements, only one of iron, in particular the iron oxide Fe_3O_4, showed ferromagnetic properties; this is, of course, the lodestone.

Alongside the considerable scientific work aimed at the understanding of magnetism, there was a steady technical development producing better permanent magnets. The discovery of electromagnetism provided the means of making stronger magnets. The bar of material, usually iron, was placed in a long coil through which a heavy current was passed. It was soon discovered that among magnets produced in this way some retained their magnetism indefinitely while others lost it over a relatively short period of time. It was also found that a ferromagnetic material would exhibit saturation; i.e., there was a maximum strength attainable by the magnet that could not be exceeded, no matter how large a current was passed through the magnetizing coil.

Magnetization process. The quantities now used in characterizing magnetization were defined and named by William Thomson (Lord Kelvin) in 1850. The symbol B denotes the magnitude of magnetic flux density inside a magnetized body, and the symbol H denotes the magnitude of magnetizing force, or magnetic field, producing it. The two are represented by the equation $B = \mu H$, in which the Greek letter mu, μ, symbolizes the permeability of the material and is a measure of the intensity of magnetization that can be produced in it by a given magnetic field. The modern units of the International Standard (SI) system for B are teslas (T) or webers per square metre (Wb/m^2) and of H as amperes per metre (A/m). The units were formerly called, respectively, gauss and oersted. The units of μ are henrys per metre. (All of these terms reflect the important work on magnetism and electricity of the 19th-century German physicist Wilhelm E. Weber, the French physicist André-Marie Ampère, the 18th- and 19th-century German mathematician Wilhelm Karl Friedrich Gauss, the 18th- and 19th-century Danish physicist Hans Christian Ørsted, and the 19th-century U.S. physicist Joseph Henry.)

Hysteresis

All ferromagnetic materials exhibit the phenomenon of hysteresis, a lag in response to changing forces based on energy losses resulting from internal friction. If B is measured for various values of H and the results are plotted in graphical form, the result is a loop of the type shown in Figure 1, called a hysteresis loop. The name describes the situation in which the path followed by the values of B while H is increasing differs from that followed as H is decreasing. With the aid of this diagram, the characteristics needed to describe the performance of a material to be used as a magnet can be defined. B_s is the saturation flux density and is a measure of how strongly the material can be magnetized. B_r is the remanent flux density and is the residual, permanent magnetization left after the magnetizing field is removed; this latter is obviously a measure of quality for a permanent magnet. It is usually measured in webers per square metre. In order to demagnetize the specimen from its remanent state, it is necessary to apply a reversed magnetizing field, opposing the magnetization in the specimen. The magnitude of field necessary to reduce the magnetization to zero is H_c, the coercive force, measured in amperes per metre. For a permanent magnet to retain its magnetization without loss over a long period of time, H_c should be as large as possible. The combination of large B_r and large H_c will generally be found in a material with a large saturation flux density that requires a large field to magnetize it. Thus, permanent-magnet materials are often characterized by quoting the maximum value of the product of B and H, $(BH)_{max}$, which the material can achieve. This product $(BH)_{max}$ is a measure of the minimum volume of permanent-magnet material required to produce a required flux density in a given gap and is sometimes referred to as the energy product.

At the end of the 19th century it was known that high-carbon steel made the most permanent magnets (high H_c), and that the addition of a small amount of cobalt improved the value of $(BH)_{max}$. On the other hand, Swedish iron, a highly refined, well-annealed pure iron, made good electromagnets (high B_s, low H_c) that lost their magnetization almost completely on the removal of the magnetizing field. Nickel was a relatively poor magnetic material in its pure state, but the addition of iron greatly increased its permeability so that low values of field H produced relatively high magnetic flux density B. H_c, however, was generally low.

The 20th century has seen an enormous development in magnetic alloys and compounds, particularly from the 1930s onward. Since that time $(BH)_{max}$ has been increasing at an average rate of 3,500 to 4,000 joules per cubic metre (J/m^3) per year.

It was suggested in 1907 that a ferromagnetic material is composed of a large number of small volumes called domains, each of which is magnetized to saturation. In 1931 the existence of such domains was first demonstrated by direct experiment. The ferromagnetic body as a whole appears unmagnetized when the directions of the individual domain magnetizations are distributed at random. Each domain is separated from its neighbours by a domain wall. In the wall region, the direction of magnetization turns from that of one domain to that of its neighbour. The process of magnetization, starting from a perfect unmagnetized state, comprises three stages: (1) *Low magnetizing field*. Reversible movements of the domain walls occur such that domains oriented in the general direction of the magnetizing field grow at the expense of those unfavourably oriented; the walls return to their original position on removal of the magnetizing field, and there is no remanent magnetization. (2) *Medium magnetizing field*. Larger movements of domain walls occur, many of which are irreversible, and the volume of favourably oriented domains is much increased. On removal of the field, all the walls do not return to their original positions, and there is a remanent magnetization. (3) *High magnetizing field*. Large movements of domain walls occur such that many are swept out of the specimen completely. The directions of magnetization in the remaining domains gradually rotate, as the field is increased, until the magnetization is everywhere parallel to the field and the material is magnetized to saturation. On removal of the field, domain walls reappear and the domain magnetizations may rotate away from the original field direction. The remanent magnetization has its maximum value.

The values of B_r, H_c, and $(BH)_{max}$ will depend on the ease with which domain walls can move through the

Ferromagnetism

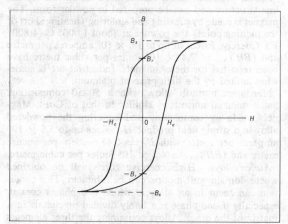

Figure 1: Typical hysteresis loop (see text).

Domain
wall
move-
ments

material and domain magnetization can rotate. Discontinuities or imperfections in the material provide obstacles to domain wall movement. Thus, once the magnetizing field has driven the wall past an obstacle, the wall will not be able to return to its original position unless a reversed field is applied to drive it back again. The effect of these obstacles is, therefore, to increase the remanence. Conversely, in a pure, homogeneous material, in which there are few imperfections, it will be easy to magnetize the material to saturation with relatively low fields, and the remanent magnetization will be small; such characteristics are required in electromagnet applications.

Demagnetization and magnetic anisotropy. So far as domain rotation is concerned, there are two important factors to be considered, demagnetization and magnetic anisotropy (exhibition of different magnetic properties when measured along axes in different directions). The first of these concerns the shape of a magnetized specimen. Any magnet generates a magnetic field in the space surrounding it. The direction of the lines of force of this field, defined by the direction of the force exerted by the field on a (hypothetical) single magnetic north pole, is opposite to the direction of field used to magnetize it originally. Thus, every magnet exists in a self-generated field that has a direction such as to tend to demagnetize the specimen. This phenomenon is described by the demagnetizing factor. If the magnetic lines of force can be confined to the magnet and not allowed to escape into the surrounding medium, the demagnetizing effect will be absent. Thus a toroidal (ring-shaped) magnet, magnetized around its perimeter so that all the lines of force are closed loops within the material, will not try to demagnetize itself. For bar magnets, demagnetization can be minimized by keeping them in pairs, laid parallel with north and south poles adjacent and with a soft-iron keeper laid across each end.

The relevance of demagnetization to domain rotation arises from the fact that the demagnetizing field may be looked upon as a store of magnetic energy. Like all natural systems, the magnet, in the absence of constraints, will try to maintain its magnetization in a direction such as to minimize stored energy; i.e., to make the demagnetizing field as small as possible. To rotate the magnetization away from this minimum-energy position requires work to be done to provide the increase in energy stored in the increased demagnetizing field. Thus, if an attempt is made to rotate the magnetization of a domain away from its natural minimum-energy position, the rotation can be said to be hindered in the sense that work must be done by an applied field to promote the rotation against the demagnetizing forces. This phenomenon is often called shape anisotropy because it arises from the domain's geometry which may, in turn, be determined by the overall shape of the specimen.

Similar minimum-energy considerations are involved in the second mechanism hindering domain rotation, namely magnetocrystalline anisotropy. It was first observed in 1847 that in crystals of magnetic material there appeared to exist preferred directions for the magnetization. This phenomenon has to do with the symmetry of the atomic arrangements in the crystal. For example, in iron, which has a cubic crystalline form, it is easier to magnetize the crystal along the directions of the edges of the cube than in any other direction. Thus the six cube-edge directions are easy directions of magnetization, and the magnetization of the crystal is termed anisotropic. In cobalt, which has a hexagonal, close-packed crystal structure, there is a single easy direction coinciding with the hexagonal axis. When the magnetization lies along an easy direction, the anisotropy energy is a minimum, and work must be done to rotate the magnetization away from this direction. This phenomenon is therefore another hindrance to domain rotation.

Magnetic anisotropy can also be induced by strain in a material. The magnetization tends to align itself in accordance with or perpendicular to the direction of the in-built strain. Some magnetic alloys also exhibit the phenomenon of induced magnetic anisotropy. If an external magnetic field is applied to the material while it is annealed at a high temperature, an easy direction for magnetization is found to be induced in a direction coinciding with that of the applied field.

The above description explains why steel makes a better permanent magnet than does soft iron. The carbon in steel causes the precipitation of tiny crystallites of iron carbide in the iron that form what is called a second phase. The phase boundaries between the precipitate particles and the host iron form obstacles to domain wall movement, and thus the coercive force and remanence are raised compared with pure iron.

The best permanent magnet, however, would be one in which the domain walls were all locked permanently in position and the magnetizations of all the domains were aligned parallel to each other. This situation can be visualized as the result of assembling the magnet from a large number of particles having a high value of saturation magnetization, each of which is a single domain, each having a uniaxial anisotropy in the desired direction, and each aligned with its magnetization parallel to all the others. It is this model that has led to the dramatic improvement in permanent magnets in modern times.

MAGNETIC MATERIALS

Powder magnets. The problem of producing magnets composed of compacted powders is essentially that of controlling particle sizes so that they are small enough to comprise a single domain and yet not so small as to lose their ferromagnetic properties altogether. Broadly, two methods have been used; these are electrodeposition and the reduction of salts or oxides of the metal. All of the early work using these methods produced spheroidal particles, and so the advantage of shape anisotropy was not obtained. Magnets were produced by compression of the powders in a protective medium such as benzene, and the final magnetic properties of the material were determined largely by the degree of compression. The most successful of the earlier materials was an iron-cobalt alloy powder magnet. The electrodeposition method was later modified to produce elongated particles, which are compressed and molded in a high magnetic field that serves to align them. The advantage of this type of magnet is that it can readily be molded and machined into desired shapes.

The disadvantage of powder magnets is that when single-domain particles are packed together they are subject to strong magnetic interactions that reduce the coercive force and, to a lesser extent, the remanent magnetization. The nature of the interaction is essentially a reduction of a given particle's demagnetizing field caused by the presence of its neighbours, and the interaction limits the maximum values of H_c and $(BH)_{max}$ that can be achieved.

More success has attended the development of magnetic alloys.

Alloys. *High anisotropy alloys.* The materials described above depend on shape for their large uniaxial anisotropy. Much work has also been done on materials having a large uniaxial magnetocrystalline anisotropy. Of these, the most successful have been cobalt–platinum (CoPt) and manganese–bismuth (MnBi) alloys.

Cobalt–platinum has a face-centred tetragonal crystalline structure and can be prepared in powder form. The magnet is made by pressing and sintering (heating short of the melting point) the powder at about 1,000° C (1,800° F). Coercive forces of up to 3.6×10^5 amperes per metre and $(BH)_{max}$ of 7.4×10^4 joules per cubic metre have been reported for these magnets. Industrial use is somewhat limited by the high price of platinum.

Manganese-bismuth alloy, with a 50–50 composition, has a uniaxial anisotropy similar to that of CoPt. Magnets made by compacting and sintering the powdered alloy in a strong field produce H_c values up to 5.6×10^5 amperes per meter with $B_r = 0.43$ webers per square metre and $(BH)_{max} = 4.2 \times 10^4$ joules per cubic metre.

Alnico alloys. High coercive force will be obtained where domain wall motion can be inhibited. This condition can occur in an alloy in which two phases coexist, especially if one phase is a finely divided precipitate in a matrix of the other. Alloys containing the three elements iron, nickel, and aluminum show just such behaviour;

Preferred
directions
of
magne-
tization

Control of
particle
size

and permanent magnet materials based on this system, with various additives, such as cobalt, copper, or titanium, are generally referred to as Alnico alloys. The addition of cobalt increases the $(BH)_{max}$ value, and one of the earlier alloys had the composition 23 percent Ni, 10 percent Al, 12 percent Co, 5 percent Cu, balance Fe. This alloy was quenched (rapidly cooled) from a temperature of 1,300° C (2,400° F), producing a single-phase form of the material, and then annealed at 650° C (1,200° F) to promote precipitation of the second phase. $(BH)_{max}$ of 1.4×10^4 joules per cubic metre was obtained.

Magnetic annealing The property of those alloys having greatest technical significance is that of magnetic annealing. If heat treatment is carried out in a magnetic field, much improved values of H_c and $(BH)_{max}$ are obtained. Heat treatment of an alloy with 14 percent Ni, 8.5 percent Al, 23 percent Co, 3 percent Cu, balance Fe, in a field of 2.4×10^7 amperes per metre produces $(BH)_{max} = 4.2 \times 10^4$ joules per cubic metre. The precipitated particles have cubic symmetry with the easy direction of magnetization along the cube edges. If the particles can be aligned with their edges parallel, an increased coercive force can be obtained. This property is achieved by a casting process in which the crystallites of the original single-phase material grow in aligned columnar form. The precipitate particles, produced by subsequent heat treatment, adopt the alignment of the matrix. One such alloy, marketed under the name Columax, has $H_c = 6.7 \times 10^4$ amperes per cubic metre and $(BH)_{max} = 6.6 \times 10^4$ joules per cubic metre.

Similar alloys with up to 4 percent titanium as an additional component are marketed under the name Ticonal, the crystal-oriented version of which is Ticonal XX. This material has $(BH)_{max} = 9 \times 10^4$ joules per cubic metre, $H_c = 10^5$ amperes per metre with $B_r = 1.18$ webers per square metre.

None of these alloys is readily machinable and generally must be cast in their final shape.

Rare-earth–cobalt alloys. Isolated atoms of many elements have finite magnetic moments; that is, the atoms are themselves tiny magnets. When the atoms are brought together in the solid form of the element, however, most of them interact in such a way that their magnetism cancels out and the solid is not ferromagnetic. Only in iron, nickel, and cobalt, of the common elements, does the cancelling-out process leave an effective net magnetic moment per atom in the vicinity of room temperature and above. The unit in which this magnetic moment is measured is the Bohr magneton, symbolized by the Greek letter beta, β, which has the value 1.165×10^{-29} weber-metres (Wb-m). The atomic magnetic moments of iron, nickel, and cobalt are respectively 2.22β, 0.606β, and 1.716β. The only other ferromagnetic solid element that shows ferromagnetic behaviour at practical temperatures is the rare-earth element gadolinium. It has the large value of 7.10β for the atomic magnetic moment, but unfortunately it loses its ferromagnetism at temperatures above 16° C (60° F) so that it is not of practical importance. Several of the rare-earth elements show ferromagnetic behaviour at extremely low temperatures, and many of them have large atomic moments. They are not, however, of great practical value at present.

Rare-earth-cobalt alloys form ferromagnetic materials, but most of them have practical disadvantages of one kind or another. Success was achieved in 1971 with the rare-earth metal samarium (Sm) alloyed with cobalt to form $SmCo_5$. This alloy has an exceptionally high magnetocrystalline anisotropy, which gives $H_c = 6.4 \times 10^5$ amperes per metre and $BH_{max} = 14.4 \times 10^4$ joules per metre with $B_r = 0.87$ webers per square metre and is a very promising permanent-magnet material.

Barium ferrites. Barium ferrite, basically $BaO:6Fe_2O_3$, is a variation of the basic magnetic iron-oxide magnetite but has a hexagonal crystalline form. This configuration gives it a very high uniaxial magnetic anisotropy capable **Tailoring magnetic properties by sintering** of producing high values of H_c. The powdered material can be magnetically aligned and then compacted and sintered. The temperature and duration of the sintering process determines the size of the crystallites and provides a means of tailoring the properties of the magnet.

For very small crystallites the coercive force is high and the remanence is in the region of half the saturation flux density. Larger crystallites give higher B_r but lower H_c. This material has been widely used in the television industry for focussing magnets for television tubes. The coercive force can be varied over the range 3.1×10^4 to 4×10^5 amperes per metre and values of $(BH)_{max} = 2.8 \times 10^4$ joules per cubic metre are claimed for commercial materials.

A further development of commercial importance is to bond the powdered ferrite by a synthetic resin or rubber to give either individual moldings or extruded strips, or sheets, that are semiflexible and can be cut with knives. This material has been used as a combination gasket (to make airtight) and magnetic closure for refrigerator doors.

The characteristics and some trade names of materials in wide use in the early 1970s is given in Table 1.

Table 1: Characteristics and Some Trade Names of Widely Used Materials

group	trade names	range of properties		
		B_r Wb/m²	$(BH)max$ J/m³ × 10⁴	H_c A/m × 10⁴
Alnico alloys, isotropic	Alnico 3 Alnico NiAl	0.5–0.66	0.96–1.12	5.4–3.8
Alnico alloys, isotropic	Alnico 2 Alnico Reco	0.65–0.8	1.36	5.4–4.0
Alnico alloys, isotropic, high H_c	Alnico 220	0.6–0.7	1.4–2.0	7.2–9.6
Alnico alloys, field treated, random grain	Alnico 5, 6 Alcomax II, III, IV Ticonal G, E Alnico 500 Ugimax	0.8–1.3	3.2–4.5	6.0–4.6
Alnico alloys, field treated, random grain, high H_c	Alnico 8 Hycomax III, IV Ticonal X	0.7–0.9	4.0–4.8	16–12
Alnico alloys, field treated, columnar grain	Alnico 5 DG Columax Ticonal GX Super Ugimax	1.3–1.4	5.2–6.8	6.7–4.8
Alnico alloys, field treated, columnar grain, high H_c	Alnico 9 Columnar Hycomax	0.95–1.05	5.6–8	16–11.6
Ba–Sr ferrite, fired, isotropic	Arnox 1 Indox 1 Ferrimag 1 Feroba I Magnadur I Caslox VI Koerox 100 Ox 100 Spinal	0.2–0.22	0.72–0.88	14.4–12.8
Ba–Sr ferrite, fired, anisotropic, high B_r	Arnox 5 Indox 5 Ferrimag 5 Feroba II Magnadur II Caslox X Westro Alpha Genox R5 Koerox 300R Spinalor B	0.36–0.4	2.6–2.9	20–12.8
Ba–Sr ferrite, fired, anisotropic, high H_c	Arnox 9 Indox 6, 7 Ferrimag 7 Feroba III Magnadur III Caslox VIII Oxit 330 Spinalor HH	0.32–0.38	2.0–2.6	26.4–20
Ba–Sr ferrite, bonded, rigid, or flexible	Arnox 3 plastiform Bonded Feroba Caslox III Ferriflex Koerox G, P Oxilit Plastoferrite	0.14–0.2	0.3–0.8	12.8–5.6

Source: J.E. Gould, of the Permanent Magnet Association.

Permeable materials. A wide range of magnetic devices utilizing magnetic fields, such as motors, generators, transformers, and electromagnets, require magnetic materials with properties quite contrary to those required

Table 2: Properties of Some Permeable Alloys

material	resistivity microhm-centimetres	μ_{RM}	B_s Wb/m²	W_H J/m³-Hz
Pure iron (99.96% Fe)	9.71	2.8×10^5	2.158	$19(B_{max} = 1.4$ Wb/m⁻²)
Iron, commercial grade (99.6% Fe)	14	5×10^3	2.12	$70(B_{max} = 0.5$ Wb/m⁻²)
Silicon iron, hot-rolled (96% Fe, 4% Si)	55	9×10^3	1.95	$35(B_{max} = 0.5$ Wb/m⁻²)
Silicon iron, cold-reduced grain-oriented (96.8% Fe, 3.2% Si)	48	7×10^4	2.0	$4.3(B_{max} = 0.5$ Wb/m⁻²)
Permalloy A (78.5% Ni, 21.5% Fe)	16	9×10^4	1.08	$5(B_{max} = 0.5$ Wb/m⁻²)
Mo-Permalloy (78.5% Ni, 17.7% Fe, 3.8% Mo)	55	7.5×10^4	0.85	$4.5(B_{max} = 0.5$ Wb/m⁻²)
Mumetal (77% Ni, 14% Fe, 5% Cu, 4% Mo)	62	9×10^4	0.80	$4(B_{max} = 0.5$ Wb/m⁻²)
Supermalloy (79% Ni, 15% Fe, 5% Mo, 0.5% Mn)	65	10^6	0.79	$0.05(B_{max} = 0.5$ Wb/m⁻²)
Hipernik (50% Ni, 50% Fe)	46	7×10^4	1.60	—
Radiometal (50% Ni, 50% Fe)	45	2.5×10^4	1.60	$22(B_{max} = 0.5$ Wb/m⁻²)
Rhometal (36% Ni, 64% Fe)	85	7×10^3	0.9	45

Source: F. Brailsford, *Physical Principles of Magnetism.*

for good permanent magnets. Such materials must be capable of being magnetized to a high value of flux density in relatively small magnetic fields and then must lose this magnetization completely on removal of the field. In terms of the hysteresis loop shown in Figure 1, such a material must have a narrow hysteresis loop (low H_c) and reach high saturation values (high B_s) with as low a remanence as possible (low B_r). Further, because the area of the loop represents a loss of energy in the material as it is magnetized and demagnetized in each direction (the hysteresis loss), the smallest possible loop area is required.

In terms of the domain model, these conditions mean that there should be few or only small obstacles to domain wall movement and as little anisotropy as possible. These requirements call for homogeneous, single-phase alloys of low magnetocrystalline anisotropy. Further, to obtain high magnetization in low fields, the material must have a high relative permeability.

Iron and silicon iron. Because iron has the highest value of magnetic moment per atom of the three ferromagnetic metals, it remains the best material for applications where a high-saturation flux density is required. Extensive investigations have taken place to determine how to produce iron as free from imperfections as possible, in order to attain the easiest possible domain wall motion. The presence of such elements as carbon, sulfur, oxygen, and nitrogen, even in small amounts, is particularly harmful; and thus sheet materials used in electrical equipment have a total impurity content of less than 0.4 percent.

The guides to magnetic quality for permeable materials are the maximum relative permeability μ_{RM} and the hysteresis loss W_H for alternating flux of a given amplitude of flux density $\pm B_{max}$. Typical values for commercially pure iron are $\mu_{RM} = 5,000$, $W_H = 70$ joules per cubic metre per hertz for $B_{max} = 0.5$ webers per square metre. Laboratory production of iron with an impurity content of 0.04 percent gives $\mu_{RM} = 280,000$ with $W_H = 19$ joules per cubic metre per hertz for $B_{max} = 1.4$ webers per square metre. The saturation flux density is in the region of 2.16 webers per square metre.

The addition of cobalt (Co) to iron (Fe) increases the saturation magnetization at the expense of a decrease in permeability. Commercial CoFe has a composition Co: 34.1 percent, Ni: 0.5 percent, C: 0.07 percent, Mn: 0.05 percent, balance Fe and gives a saturation magnetization of 2.36 webers per square metre.

Important advantages are obtained by alloying iron with a small amount (about 4 percent) of silicon. The added silicon reduces the magnetocrystalline anisotropy of the iron and hence its coercive force and hysteresis

loss. Although there is a reduction in the saturation flux density, this loss is outweighed by the other advantages, which include increased electrical resistivity. The latter is important in applications where the magnetic flux alternates because this induces eddy currents in the magnetic material. The lower the resistivity and the higher the frequency of the alternations, the higher are these currents. They produce a loss of energy by causing heating of the material and will be minimized, at a given frequency, by raising the resistivity of the material. A typical, hot-rolled silicon iron gives $\mu_{RM} = 9,000$ with $W_H = 25$ joules per cubic metre at $B_{max} = 0.5$ webers per square metre.

By a suitable manufacturing process, silicon-iron sheet material can be produced with a high degree of preferred orientation of the crystallites. The material then has a preferred direction of magnetization, and in this direction high permeability and low loss are attained. Commercially produced material has about 3.2 percent silicon and is known as cold-reduced, grain-oriented silicon steel. This material gives $\mu_{RM} = 70,000$ with $W_H = 4.3$ joules per cubic metre per hertz at $B_{max} = 0.5$ webers per square metre.

Nickel–iron alloys. Alloys of nickel and iron in various proportions are given the general name Permalloy. As the proportion of nickel varies downward, the saturation magnetization increases, reaching a maximum at about 50 percent, falling to zero at 27 percent nickel, then rising again toward the value for pure iron. The magnetocrystalline anisotropy also falls from the value for pure nickel to a very low value in the region of 80 percent nickel, rising only slowly thereafter. Highest value of permeability is at 78.5 percent nickel, which is called Permalloy A. The maximum relative permeability, which can reach a value in the region of 1,000,000 in carefully prepared Permalloy A, makes the alloy useful and superior to iron and silicon iron at low flux densities; but because of its lower value of saturation magnetization, this superiority only persists up to flux densities of 0.7 webers per square metre.

A range of commercially available permeable alloys with various additives is included in Table 2.

Ferrites. In addition to barium ferrite, which has a hexagonal crystal form, most of the ferrites of the general formula $MeO \cdot Fe_2O_3$, in which Me is a metal, are useful magnetically. They have a different crystalline form called spinel after the mineral spinel ($MgAl_2O_4$), which crystallizes in the cubic system. All the spinel ferrites are soft magnetic materials; that is, they exhibit low coercive force and narrow hysteresis loops. Furthermore, they all have a high electrical resistivity and high relative

Permalloy

permeabilities, thus making them very suitable for use in high-frequency electronic equipment. Their saturation magnetization is, however, low, compared with the alloys, and this property limits their use in high-field, high-power transformers. They are hard, brittle, ceramic-like materials and are difficult to machine. Nevertheless, they are widely used, most importantly in computer memory stores (see also FERRITES).

ELECTROMAGNETS

The magnetic circuit

Where controllable magnets are required, as for applications in which the magnetic flux is to be varied, reversed, or switched on and off, an electromagnet must be used. This device is made up of a coil of wire, through which electric current is passed. The coil is wrapped round the material to be magnetized in some suitable configuration. The engineering design of electromagnets is systematized by means of the concept of the magnetic circuit. In the magnetic circuit a magnetomotive force (mmf) is defined as the ampere-turns of the coil that generates the magnetic field to produce the magnetic flux in the circuit. Thus, if a coil of n turns per metre carries a current i amperes, the field inside the coil is ni amperes per metre and the mmf it generates is nil ampere turns, where l is the length of the coil. More conveniently, the mmf is Ni, where N is the total number of turns in the coil. The magnetic flux density B is the equivalent, in the magnetic circuit, of the current density in an electric circuit. In the magnetic circuit the magnetic equivalent to current is the total flux symbolized by the Greek letter phi, ϕ, given by BA, where A is the cross-sectional area of the magnetic circuit. In an electric circuit the electromotive force (emf) is related to the current, i, in the circuit by emf $= Ri$, where R is the resistance of the circuit. In the magnetic circuit mmf $= r\phi$, where r is the reluctance of the magnetic circuit and is equivalent to resistance in the electric circuit. Reluctance is obtained by dividing the length of the magnetic path l by the permeability times the cross-sectional area A; thus $r = l/\mu A$, the Greek letter mu, μ, symbolizing the permeability of the medium forming the magnetic circuit. The units of reluctance are ampere-turns per weber. These concepts can be employed to calculate the reluctance of a magnetic circuit and thus the current required through a coil to force the desired flux through this circuit.

Several assumptions involved in this type of calculation, however, make it at best only an approximate guide to design. The effect of a permeable medium on a magnetic field can be visualized as being to crowd the magnetic lines of force into itself. Conversely, the lines of force passing from a region of high to one of low permeability tend to spread out, and this occurrence will take place at an air gap. Thus the flux density, which is proportional to the number of lines of force per unit area, will be reduced in the air gap by the lines bulging out, or fringing, at the sides of the gap. This effect will increase for longer gaps; rough corrections can be made for taking the fringing effect into account.

It has also been assumed that the magnetic field is entirely confined within the coil. In fact, there is always a certain amount of leakage flux, represented by magnetic lines of force around the outside of the coil, which does not contribute to the magnetization of the core. The leakage flux is generally small if the permeability of the magnetic core is high.

Permeability and flux density

In practice, the permeability of a magnetic material is a function of the flux density in it. Thus, the calculation can only be done for a real material if the actual magnetization curve, or, more usefully, a graph of μ against B, is available.

Finally, the design assumes that the magnetic core is not magnetized to saturation. If it were, the flux density could not be increased in the air gap in this design, no matter how much current were passed through the coil. These concepts will be expanded further in following sections on specific devices.

Solenoids. A solenoid is generally a long coil through which current is flowing, establishing a magnetic field. More narrowly, the name has come to refer to an electro-mechanical device that produces a mechanical motion on being energized with an electric current. In its simplest form it consists of an iron frame enclosing the coil and a cylindrical plunger moving inside the coil, as shown in Figure 2. For an alternating current supply, the iron losses in a solid frame restrict the efficiency and a laminated frame is used, which is made up of a pile of thin sheets of iron cut to the appropriate shape and stacked with a layer of insulating varnish between each sheet. When the coil is energized, the plunger moves into the coil by virtue of the magnetic attraction between it and the frame until it makes contact with the frame.

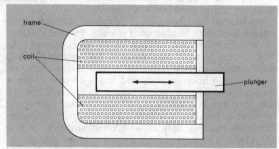

Figure 2: Elements of a solenoid.

Alternating current (ac) solenoids tend to be more powerful in the fully open position than direct current (dc) units. This result occurs because the initial current, high because of the inductance of the coil, is lowered by the air gap between the plunger and frame. As the solenoid closes, this air gap decreases, the inductance of the coil increases, and the alternating current through it falls. If an ac solenoid sticks in the open position the coil is likely to burn out.

When a solenoid is fully opened, it has a large air gap, and the high reluctance of this gap keeps the flux in the magnetic circuit low for a given mmf, and the force on the plunger is correspondingly low. As the plunger closes, the reluctance falls and the flux increases so that the force increases progressively. Manufacturers of solenoids provide force-stroke curves so that users can select the proper unit for their purpose. The curve can be modified by spring loading the plunger so that the force provided throughout the stroke may be matched to the particular mechanical load.

Relays. A relay is a device in which the solenoid principle is applied to opening and closing light-current electrical circuits. The same device applied in heavy-current circuits is called a contactor, or circuit breaker.

Because the amount of mechanical movement required is generally small, the solenoid plunger is usually stationary, and part of the frame is hinged to give the necessary movement. This arrangement is illustrated schematically in Figure 3. When the coil is energized, the hinged part of the frame is attracted to the solid iron core in the coil; this attraction pushes the contacts together. When the energizing current is removed, the hinged part is forced back to the open position by the springiness of the contact.

With the appearance of transistorized switching circuits, which use remarkably low power, a need arose for a relay that would operate reliably with a power of 100 to 300 milliwatts compared with four watts for the conven-

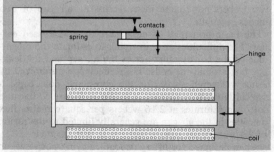

Figure 3: Elements of a relay.

tional relay. This need was met by the reed relay, or reed switch, shown in Figure 4. It consists of two flat blades of 50–50 nickel–iron alloy that overlap with a gap between them. When a magnetic field is applied along the length of the blades, opposite magnetic poles are induced in the overlapping parts, and they are attracted together, making electrical contact. On removal of the field, the springiness of the contact blade opens the contact. The overlap region is plated on each blade with gold to ensure good electrical contact, and the enclosing glass capsule is filled with dry nitrogen to prevent corrosion. The field required to operate the device is a function of the amount of overlap, and there is an optimum overlap corresponding to minimum required operating current.

Present reed switches used in telephone equipment are operated by up to 50 volts dc. Typically, the reed closes at 58 ampere-turns and releases at 15 ampere-turns, the hold current being 27 ampere-turns. The contact closes to give a stable contact resistance in two milliseconds, releases in 100 microseconds, and has a lifetime of more than 50,000,000 operations. Using a 35,000 turn coil the coil resistance is typically 18,600 ohms so that the current at 50 volts is 2.7 milliamperes. The minimum operating condition requires only about 1.7 milliamperes, so that the relay can be worked satisfactorily at lower voltage.

By the use of small, external, permanent magnets, reed switches can be made into latching relays that remain closed when the energizing field is removed. They can also be designed with three blades to give change-over contacts.

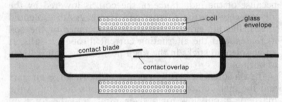

Figure 4: Elements of a reed relay.

Design of large electromagnets. Sooner or later almost every scientific research laboratory finds that it requires a facility for producing large magnetic fields. A number of advanced technologies likewise require large electromagnets; for example, a cyclotron, a device in which subatomic charged particles are accelerated by an alternating electric field in a constant magnetic field, needs a magnet to produce moderate fields but with a pole diameter that may be several metres. Some industries make use of large, high-power electromagnets for lifting purposes.

The design of large electromagnets in the past was more of an art than a science. Modern theoretical work has led to suitable approximations that allow magnet design to be carried out with the aid of some standard curves and a slide rule. For extremely high fields up to a flux density in an air gap of 25 webers per square metre, coils dissipating several megawatts of power are needed. By pulsing the current through the magnet coil with the aid of a controlled explosion, densities up to 1,400 webers per square metre have been produced experimentally. To put this high flux density in perspective, a one-ton laboratory electromagnet, with water-cooled coils passing a maximum current of about 30 amperes and with seven-inch diameter iron polefaces, could produce a density of about two webers per square metre across an air gap of two inches in length.

The basic principles of design are those discussed earlier. The difficulties arise in trying to estimate the magnitude of the fringing flux across the air gap and the leakage flux around the coils. Their effects are minimized by using a tapered shape for the cores and pole caps; a typical laboratory magnet is shown in Figure 5. Because soft iron saturates at 2.16 webers per square metre, flux densities in the air gap are generally limited to the region of 2.1 webers per square metre with iron magnets.

When designed for lifting or load-carrying purposes, an electromagnet may be required to have a single exposed

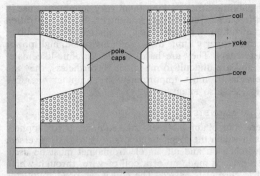

Figure 5: Elements of a typical electromagnet.

pole face to which the load to be carried will attach itself, and it will therefore have the shape of a bar magnet. The design is then dominated by the demagnetizing field. Suitably designed magnets can lift many times their own weight and are in general use in steelworks and scrapyards.

GENERAL APPLICATIONS

There are many thousands of applications of magnets and electromagnets to electromagnetic devices and it would be impossible to cite all, or even a majority, of them. A few major areas of application and the principles of operation of some of the important devices in each area are given below.

Communications. Modern and future telephone systems will undoubtedly be based on the reed relay, together with sophisticated solid circuits for complex routing of connections. The telephone receiver is basically an electromagnet with a U-shaped yoke having coils wound on each leg of the U. Passage of the electrical signal through the coils causes magnetic attraction of a soft-iron diaphragm supported a small distance from the ends of the U. The diaphragm is deflected by an amount proportional to the magnitude of the current in the coil and generates sound waves as it moves back and forth. Improvement in magnetic materials has gradually increased the sensitivity of the telephone receiver, but the basic design has remained unchanged.

In modern, high-fidelity earphones the soft-iron diaphragm is replaced by a light, nonmagnetic diaphragm that carries a coil. The magnetic field is supplied by a small permanent magnet, generally a ferrite magnet. The current through the coil causes it to experience a force caused by the magnetic field. The force deflects the diaphragm by an amount proportional to the size of the current. This design permits an extremely small physical size because of the strength of modern permanent magnets.

The loudspeaker performs the same function as the earphone but is required to displace a larger volume of air. The diaphragm comprises a flexible cone of large area carrying a coil of fine wire on a small ring located at its apex. The ring lies between the poles of a powerful cylindrically shaped permanent magnet. Audio frequency current through the coil causes deflection of the diaphragm, as in the earphone. Modern loudspeakers are much more sensitive and efficient than their predecessors because of the improvement in permanent magnet materials. The higher the flux density in the gap, the greater the sensitivity and the potential for fidelity of reproduction; modern loudspeakers use flux densities of up to one weber per square metre. Alloy magnets are usually used.

Research. Magnetic fields supply a powerful research tool without which modern physics could scarcely have grown to its present extent. A major area of application is in the interaction of magnetic fields and charged subatomic particles. A moving particle that carries a charge, such as an electron, can be regarded as an electric current and, like a current-carrying wire, experiences a force in a magnetic field. The direction of the force is perpendicular both to the direction of motion of the particle and to the magnetic field, so that the particle is deflected from its original path. This principle can be used to focus a stream of electrons into a narrow beam and to deflect the beam

Focussing a beam of electrons

by creating suitable magnetic fields, either from permanent magnets or from electromagnets. Every television receiver contains just such focussing and deflection systems to scan the face of the television tube with an electron beam.

In scientific applications the same principle is used in the electron microscope, in which the beam of electrons is passed through a series of magnetic "lenses," just as light is passed through glass lenses in a conventional microscope.

The cyclotron makes use of a magnetic field to cause charged particles to execute a circular path. On each traverse of the circle they are accelerated and finally acquire enormous kinetic energy (energy of motion). The cyclotron has been an important tool in nuclear research.

The same principle may be used to analyze materials in the mass spectrometer. The actual deflection of a moving charged particle in a magnetic field is determined by its charge, mass, and velocity. In a mass spectrometer the material under investigation is in the form of a gas of ionized particles that are accelerated by a fixed electric field. In passing through the magnetic field the particles are deflected by an amount determined by their mass, providing they all carry the same charge. By recording their arrival position at a fixed target, the mass of the particles can be deduced.

In the above description an applied voltage does work to accelerate the charged particles, and magnetic energy is expended in deflecting them. Suppose a high-velocity stream of ionized gas is produced by heating it to a high temperature (as, for example, in a jet engine) and "seeding" it with an ionizable molecule. As this ionized gas passes through a fixed magnetic field, the positive and negative ions will be deflected in opposite directions and, if they are collected on suitable electrodes, they will provide a potential difference capable of driving current around an external circuit. This is the principle of the magnetohydrodynamic (MHD) generator, which is believed to have an important future in power production (see also MAGNETOHYDRODYNAMIC DEVICES).

Electrical industry. It is no exaggeration to say that the whole of the electrical industry is founded on the generation and exploitation of magnetic fields. The electric motor is based on the force generated on a current-carrying conductor; the generator is based on the inverse effect that a conductor moving in a magnetic field has a current induced in it. In general, high-flux densities are required in the magnetic circuits of motors and generators, and this requirement has led to the use of soft iron or silicon-iron electromagnets as the source of magnetic fields in them. With the advent of modern permanent-magnet materials, however, small dc motors, in which the field is provided by permanent magnets, are finding wide applications, particularly in the toy industry.

Use of the motor principle in meters

The motor principle is also used in meters for measuring electric current. In the instrument, the design must be such that the force on the wire carrying the current to be measured is proportional to that current. In a typical design, a permanent magnet provides the field, and the pole pieces are shaped in such a way as to give a cylindrical air gap. Improved permanent magnets have led to improved instruments so that a reasonable robust meter can be made with a full-scale deflection corresponding to one microampere of current.

Magnetic recording. The principle of magnetic recording is to induce a permanent magnetization in a material by means of the signal to be recorded. The induced magnetization must be proportional to the amplitude of the signal and must remain in the material when the signal is removed. Thus, a magnetic material is required that has a high permeability, so that it will magnetize readily in a small field, a high remanent magnetization, so that the stored information can be easily "read," and not too high (but not too low) a coercive force, so that the stored information can be erased without great difficulty.

The most common type of magnetic recorder makes use of a magnetic tape. This passes at constant speed close to a recording head that may consist of a U-shaped magnet

yoke with coils wound on each limb. As the current in the coil varies in accordance with the audio-frequency signal to be recorded, a varying magnetization is induced in the tape. To play back the recorded information, the tape is passed through or near a coil so that the magnetic flux from the tape cuts the wires of the coil and induces an audio-frequency current in it. The tape may be erased by passing it through a recording head that carries a high-frequency signal, which has the effect of demagnetizing the tape.

The magnetic material used is a fine ferrite powder embedded in a plastic material comprising the tape. Manufacturers are very secretive about the precise materials and processes used in tape manufacture. A wide range of magnetic properties, however, can be obtained in the ferrites by varying the metal Me in the formula $MeO \cdot Fe_2O_3$. Further, control of coercive force is provided by the shape, size, and packing density of particles used. The ferrite is also a necessary choice because of its high resistivity. Metals and alloys would give high-eddy current losses and consequently poorer performance at the frequencies used (see also SOUND RECORDING AND REPRODUCING).

Computer information is in a particularly simple form for magnetic storage because it consists of a chain of electrical pulses of standard amplitude. Material requirements for the tape are not so stringent as for audio recording, the important feature being only that the tape should not demagnetize spontaneously; i.e., it should have an adequate value of H_c. The most modern computers have replaced tape storage by disks of magnetic alloy that rotate under the recording head. Information can be stored at a higher density (bits per unit area) than in tape, and access to the information can be made faster by traversing the "read" head in a radial direction across the disks.

Ferrite materials have found an important application in the fast memory stores of computers. A spinel ferrite is formed into a small toroidal ring with the easy direction of magnetization around its periphery. A wire passing through its centre will generate a circular magnetic field when a current is passed through it; this current magnetizes the toroidal ring. On reversal of the current the magnetization will reverse in direction, so that the information is stored as, for example, clockwise magnetization for positive current and anticlockwise for negative. The two states correspond to the binary numbers 0 or 1 used in the computer language. The basic requirement is that the material should have a rectangular hysteresis loop in which B_r will be nearly equal to B_s and that the magnetization should switch from one direction to the opposite direction when the coercive field is applied. It is often required that this switching should take place in $1/10$ to $1/100$ of a microsecond (a microsecond is $1/1,000,000$ of a second). Such a system is called a ferrite core store and the ferrite rings are often less than one millimetre in diameter. The material most frequently used is a mixed magnesium-manganese ferrite typically having a threshold field for switching of 72 amperes per metre, a remanent flux density of 0.22 webers per square metre, and a saturation flux density of 0.95 webers per square metre. The initial relative permeability is 59.

Ferrite core store

An alternative device for a fast computer store is the magnetic thin film. If a ferromagnetic alloy is prepared in the form of a film in the thickness range 100–10,000 angstroms (an angstrom is 10^{-10} metre), it can remain in a single domain state, with the magnetization everywhere in the same direction in the plane of the film. Furthermore, if the film is prepared in the presence of a magnetic field and the material used is a Permalloy, a uniaxial magnetic anisotropy is induced in it. The magnetization then has only two stable directions 180° apart, and it can be used in a way similar to the ferrite toroid in a computer store. Successful thin-film stores have employed cylindrical thin Permalloy films plated onto copper alloy wires (see also COMPUTERS).

BIBLIOGRAPHY

Historical: WILLIAM GILBERT, *De magnete* (1600; Eng. trans., *On the Magnet*, rev. ed., 1958). E.T. WHITTAKER, *A*

History of the Theories of Aether and Electricity from the Age of Descartes to the Close of the Nineteenth Century (1910), deals mainly with the discoveries leading to the understanding of electricity and devotes a whole chapter to Faraday and another to Maxwell; significant discoveries and developments in the theories of magnetism are, however, included. P.F. MOTTELAY (comp.), *Bibliographical History of Electricity and Magnetism* (1922), gives a thorough treatment of the developments in the Middle Ages and includes brief biographies of the distinguished natural philosophers of that era (up to the year 1820). H.L. HITCHINS and W.E. MAY, *From Lodestone to Gyro-Compass* (1952), is a readable account of the early history of the magnet, including its development as a mariner's compass and modern systems of navigation based on the gyro-compass.

General magnetism: J.C. ANDERSON, *Magnetism and Magnetic Materials* (1968), treats the physics of magnetism and its application to modern magnetic materials; F. BRAILSFORD, *Physical Principles of Magnetism* (1966), covers a similar field but is particularly valuable for its discursive treatment of silicon steel. J.E. GOULD, "Permanent Magnet Applications," *IEEE Trans. on Magnetics*, 5:812–821 (1969), surveys the entire field of permanent magnet applications.

General electrical engineering: R.J. SMITH, *Circuits, Devices and Systems*, 2nd ed. (1971), is a standard textbook covering the general field of electrical engineering.

Electromagnet design: D.J. KROON, *Laboratory Magnets* (1968), is a classic textbook covering the principles and calculations involved in the design of magnets, especially electromagnets, to meet specified standards. *High Magnetic Fields*, Proceedings of the International Conference on High Magnetic Fields, 1961 (1962), includes a number of articles on advanced solenoid and magnet design.

(J.C.An.)

Magnoliales

Ever since the emergence of Darwin's evolutionary theories in 1859, botanists have attempted to classify the members of the plant kingdom according to their presumed natural relationships. During the first part of the 20th century, most "natural" systems of classification of the flowering plants (angiosperms) were based primarily on similarities or differences in gross morphological (structural) features, and the emphasis was placed on the reproductive structures; *i.e.*, the flowers. More recently, however, considerable data have accumulated from investigations of wood anatomy, vegetative nodal anatomy (*i.e.*, the manner in which vascular bundles depart from stems to enter leafstalks), pollen morphology, chromosome analysis, comparative biochemistry, floral anatomy, seedling development, and embryology, which, when considered as a whole, give a much more reliable picture of the true relationships within the flowering plants. Based on the totality of these features, most students of plant evolution now regard the Magnoliales order as including the most primitive components of the angiosperms.

Magnoliales is a plant order belonging to the dicotyledonous group of flowering plants (the dicots are roughly equivalent to broad-leaved plants as opposed to the monocots that have mostly parallel-veined leaves, grasses being a familiar example) and contains 8 families, 166 genera, and about 1,800 species, all of which are woody shrubs or trees. The 8 families of the Magnoliales order include the following: (1) Magnoliaceae with 12 genera and about 210 species; (2) Degeneriaceae with 1 genus and 1 species; (3) Himantandraceae with 1 genus and 4 species; (4) Eupomatiaceae with 1 genus and 2 species; (5) Annonaceae with 122 genera and about 1,100 species; (6) Canellaceae with 5 genera and about 9 species; (7) Myristicaceae with 16 genera and about 380 species; and (8) Winteraceae with 8 genera and 88 species. These estimates indicate that approximately 80 percent of the total genera (122 of 166) in this order and 60 percent of the species (1,100 of 1,794) are included in the pantropical (*i.e.*, found throughout the tropics) family Annonaceae. The next two largest families, Myristicaceae and Magnoliaceae, include about 32 percent of the species in the Magnoliales order, with the other five families comprising the remaining 8 percent. When this many small families are found to be classified together in the same order, it is usually assumed that they represent a group of

relic families that have evolved together slowly over a long period of time—a linear evolutionary derivation of one family directly from another should not be implied.

GENERAL FEATURES

Structural diversity and distribution. All members of the order are woody; most are trees of small or intermediate size, though an exception occurs in the case of the tulip tree or tulip poplar, *Liriodendron tulipifera* (family Magnoliaceae), which reaches a height of over 150 feet (46 metres) and, in the Appalachian forests of the eastern United States, may have a base diameter of 10 feet.

Other tall trees are found in the genera *Mitrephora*, *Mezzettia*, and *Cananga* (all three of family Annonaceae) in the rain forests of Southeast Asia. The species of *Eupomatia* are shrubs, and many genera of the family Annonaceae are mostly shrubby, some being modified as climbers; *e.g.*, the genera *Ellipeia*, *Cyathostemma*, *Uvaria*, and *Phaeanthus*. Many species of Annonaceae are cauliflorous—*i.e.*, with flower buds formed from mature wood of the trunks and older branches; but the genus *Geanthemum* is unique in this order in that floral structures form on subterranean branches.

Growth forms and distributions

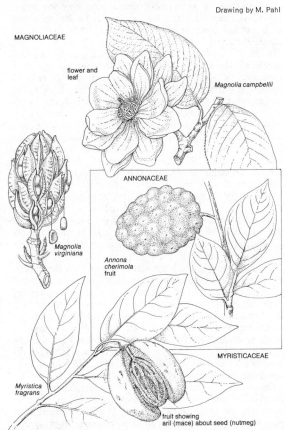

Drawing by M. Pahl

MAGNOLIACEAE

flower and leaf

Magnolia campbellii

Magnolia virginiana

ANNONACEAE

Annona cherimola fruit

MYRISTICACEAE

Myristica fragrans

fruit showing aril (mace) about seed (nutmeg)

Representative plants from three of the largest families of the magnolia order.

Most Magnoliales are tropical in distribution, with the greatest speciation occurring in Southeast Asia and Africa. *Xylopia*, which includes about 160 species in the Annonaceae family, is the only genus in the order with pantropical distribution.

Genera with some temperate species include *Magnolia* and *Liriodendron* (Magnoliaceae family), with native species growing in China, Japan, and the eastern United States. Other temperate species include the papaw tree, *Asimina*, in the Annonaceae family, which extends northward into southern Ontario, Canada; *Eupomatia* from eastern Australia; and four genera of the Winteraceae family (*Drimys*, *Tasmannia*, *Pseudowintera*, and *Bubbia*) that range from eastern Australia and New Zealand to the southern Andes in Chile.

Economic importance. The wood of the tulip tree (*Liriodendron tulipifera*) sometimes referred to as American whitewood, is one of the most valuable timber products in the United States, where more than 800,-000,000 board feet are cut each year. The wood is light yellow to tan, with a creamy white margin of sapwood. It is relatively soft, easily worked with tools, and takes paint well. Large, clear logs are well-suited to the manufacture of rotary-cut veneers, not only for furniture and cabinet-work, but also for berry and fruit boxes. Other uses are for millwork (sashes, doors, and blinds), hat blocks, and to a lesser extent, pulpwood for making paper (by the soda process).

The southern magnolia, or laurel magnolia (*Magnolia grandiflora*), has been called the most splendid ornamental tree in the American forests. The large, creamy-white flowers, together with dark green, lustrous, leathery leaves and reddish egg-shaped fruit with pendent scarlet seeds give it a striking appearance. The natural range of this stately tree (60 to 80 feet [18 to 24 metres] tall in the wild) is a strip about 100 miles (161 kilometres) wide from North Carolina, through northern Florida, along the Gulf Coast to eastern Texas. It is most abundant in Louisiana. A valuable ornamental, it is planted as far north as New Jersey on the Atlantic Coast of America and all the way to British Columbia on the Pacific Coast, where the winters are relatively mild. It also can be found in cultivation throughout most warm temperate regions of the world. Although its value as an ornamental far exceeds that as a timber producer, about 25,000,000 board feet are marketed annually in the southern United States. The majority of this wood is utilized in the manufacture of venetian blinds because of the wood's fine, uniform texture, hardness, and ability to resist warping.

The cucumber tree (*Magnolia acuminata*) reaches its greatest size (80 to 100 feet) in the narrow valleys of the Smoky Mountains of Tennessee and North Carolina. The fleshy fruit resembles a 2- to 3-inch-long cucumber, which gives the tree its popular name. The timber is not as durable as that of the related evergreen magnolia or tulip tree, but is marketed to make crates, boxes, cheap furniture, and interior flooring.

About 80 species of magnolia have been described; because of their showy flowers, which usually appear before their leaves in deciduous types, many are in cultivation in the north temperate parts of the world. Forty-six species and varieties are being grown at the Arnold Arboretum of Harvard University. The Morris Arboretum of the University of Pennsylvania has numerous American and Asiatic species, and the Royal Botanic Gardens, near London, has a magnificent living collection. Most American species have white to creamy-yellow flowers; many Asiatic species and their hybrids are characterized by pink to purplish-red flowers. A hybrid developed near Paris in 1820 is undoubtedly one of the most widely cultivated ornamentals—*M. soulangeana* is a large shrub or small tree of many varieties with large, cup-shaped, pinkish-purple flowers that appear early in the spring before the leaves. Some other well-known magnolia hybrids (indicated by the ×) in cultivation are: *Magnolia loebneri* (*kobus* × *stellata*); *M. thompsoniana* (*tripetala* × *virginiana*); *M. watsonii* (*obovata* × *sieboldii*); *M. proctoriana* (*salicifolia* × *stellata*); and *M. veitchii* (*campbellii* × *denudata*).

Another genus of the Magnoliaceae family that is widely cultivated in tropical regions is *Michelia*. Although the flowers are not as grandiose as those of the genus *Magnolia*, they more than make up this deficiency by their abundance and extreme fragrance. They also differ from the flowers of *Magnolia* in that they develop in dense clusters in the axils of leaves (the point at which the leaf stalk joins the branch), rather than singly at the ends of branches. The champac (*Michelia champaca*) is supposedly native to India, Assam, and Burma, but it has been in cultivation for so many centuries that its original natural range is difficult to determine. This tree is a handsome ornamental with evergreen leaves and profuse, highly scented yellow flowers that are the source of champak, an exotic East Indian perfume. In addition, the timber from this species has some local uses in making light furniture

Magnolia trees in cultivation

and plywood. The banana shrub (*Michelia figo*) from southern China also is cultivated to some extent as a tropical ornamental with fragrant flowers.

Because the family Annonaceae is by far the largest in the Magnoliales order, it is not surprising that this group includes the most species that yield some type of economic product. Lancewood (*Oxandra lanceolata*) from northern South America and the West Indies, is undoubtedly the most important commercial timber source in this family. The wood is yellow to olive-yellow, hard, heavy (specific gravity 0.95), of fine texture, and with an extremely straight grain. These characteristics make the wood particularly suitable for use in scientific instruments, turnery (objects shaped by lathe), tool handles, and such sporting goods as billiard cues, archery bows, and fishing rods. Solera or Colombian lancewood (*Guatteria boyacana*) has most of the same properties and uses, but is not as well known in the timber trade. Yellowwood (*Enantia chlorantha*) from Liberia, Ivory Coast, and the Cameroons of West Africa produces a sulfurous yellow dye; the wood also is used locally to make unpainted furniture and veneers. Otu (*Cleistopholis patens*) yields a soft, light (specific gravity 0.40) wood from West Africa that finds some of the same uses as balsa wood—in buoys, life rafts, floats, etc. The fibrous inner bark is of some value for cordage and coarse netting.

Polyalthia longifolia is a tall, handsome tree with pendent linear leaves, which is cultivated in most parts of Ceylon and India as an avenue tree and around temples, where it has a religious significance. Although the wood is not very durable, it is utilized to some extent in making matches, boxes, and packing crates. Other woods of the Annonaceae family in India and Burma that have some commercial value are derived from the genera *Miliusa*, *Sageraea*, *Mitrephora*, *Saccopetalum*, and *Cyathocalyx*. Because of their tough and elastic qualities, these woods are utilized in the manufacture of tool handles, wheel spokes, and sporting goods.

The wood of *Xylopia aethiopica* is quite flexible and has some local use in west central Africa for masts, boat paddles, and rudders. It has been described as termite-proof and, accordingly, is used for house posts and beams. The dried black fruits of this species are called guinea peppers and were once of commercial importance in Europe as a tangy condiment and drug. At present, the fruits are reportedly used by some African tribes as a cough medicine and purgative. The bark of several other *Xylopia* species from Brazil (*X. sericea*, *X. frutescens*, and *X. aromatica*) finds some local use in cordage and rough textiles.

The most widely known economic products of the Annonaceae family in the tropics are its edible fruits. One of the most important of these is the West Indian custard apple or bullock's heart (*Annona reticulata*). The latter common name is suggestive of the shape and general appearance of the fruits. When the fruit is ripe and the skin has begun to blacken, its white to cream-coloured flesh becomes sweet and aromatic, and resembles ice cream when chilled. It may be eaten with a spoon as a dessert. The sweetsop, or sugar apple (*Annona squamosa*), although native to northern South America, Central America and the Caribbean region, is even more widely cultivated and highly esteemed in India and Pakistan. The conical fruits break into segments when ripe and expose a cream-coloured sweet pulp in which dark brown glossy seeds are embedded. Among the natives of the tropics the sugar apple tree is of reputed medical value. Tea made from the roots is highly purgative, while that made from the leaves is mildly laxative and is also considered to have a general tonic effect on the digestive tract. Poultices of the leaves are used in dressing infected wounds.

The cherimoya is the fruit of a rather small tree, *Annona cherimola*, which is native to the cool (but frost-free) mountain valleys of Peru. Although it is grown in southern Florida, it does not produce fruit well there because of the high humidity; it is currently commercially grown on a small scale in southern California. The fruits, however, are quite perishable and ferment readily, and are thus shipped only to nearby markets. Like the

Tropical edible fruits

sugar apple, it is now well-established in the Old World tropics. Although the ripe fruit does not break into segments when ripe the way that of the sugar apple does, the flesh is of a more creamy consistency and has fewer seeds. Under ideal conditions, the fruit may attain a large size, weighing up to 16 pounds. The soursop, or guanábana (*Annona muricata*), also is native to the American tropics, but is now general throughout the Old World tropics as well. In Cuba the fruit is a favourite and the tree may be found in almost every yard planting. The fruit is large (to 10 pounds), tapering, heart-shaped, and the green skin is covered with spiny protuberances. The aromatic flesh, white and somewhat fibrous, is strained to make custards and ice cream; the acidulous juice is usually extracted to make a refreshing drink, which has been described as a combination of the flavours of strawberries, pineapples, and cinnamon. The hybrid atemoya (*Annona squamosa* × *A. cherimola*) has been established in the Caribbean region; reputedly the fruit contains the best features of both parents. The alligator apple (*A. glabra*) grows plentifully in the Florida Everglades and on the Florida Keys, where its fruits have been described as "edible but not very palatable." The tree's prime use in Florida is as a rootstock in deep, sandy soils for the grafted custard apple and the sugar apple.

Other species of *Annona* that produce comparatively inferior fruit, but which are eaten locally, include: *A. montana*, the mountain soursop (West Indies and South America); *A. longiflora* (Mexico); *A. paludosa* (Brazil); *A. testudinea* (Honduras); *A. nutans* (Paraguay); *A. senegalensis* (East and West Africa); and *A. diversifolia*, the ilama, which was first cultivated long ago by the Aztecs of Mexico.

Two species of *Rollinia* (*R. mucosa* and *R. pulchrinervia*) have edible fruits that reach four inches (ten centimetres) in length and bear some resemblance to those of the soursop, except that the spines are softer and more blunt. *R. mucosa* is a large tree native to the West Indies and northern South America, whereas *R. pulchrinervia* is restricted in the wild state to the Amazon Basin. Both species are referred to by the common name biriba and both are widely cultivated, particularly throughout Brazil, for their delicious fruits.

The papaw (*Asimina triloba*) of eastern North America produces a fruit that is sometimes eaten. The fruits of this species show considerable variability in size, colour, and palatability. Two general types have been observed: (1) large, yellow-fruited, highly flavoured, and early ripening; and (2) relatively small, white-fleshed, mild flavoured, and late ripening. A number of selected clones (groups of plants of identical genetic makeup that are vegetative divisions of one plant), propagated by grafting, are in cultivation, principally in southern Pennsylvania, Ohio, Illinois, and Indiana (where the yellowish fruits are referred to as Indiana bananas). Sometimes an alcoholic beverage is made from the papaw.

Certain Asiatic species of *Polyalthia* (*P. cerasioides*, and *P. korinthii*), *Uvaria* (*U. burahol*, *U. dulcis*, and *U. heterophylla*), and *Artabotrys* produce edible fruit, as do African species of *Uvaria* (*U. chamae* and *U. globosa*).

The ylang-ylang tree (*Cananga odorata*) has its natural range from the tropical parts of eastern India through the Malaysian regions to the Philippines and northern Australia. The name means "flower of flowers" because the yellowish-green, bell-shaped flowers yield an exceedingly delicate and evanescent fragrance that is highly valued in the manufacture of perfumes. Ylang-ylang or cananga oil is derived by simple distillation from the petals of fully opened flowers. Although the tree blossoms throughout the year, the flowers picked in May or June yield the highest amounts of the cananga oil. Long known to the peoples of the Far East, this oil first reached Europe about 1864. Although the Philippines are probably the chief producers of ylang-ylang oil, some production also comes from Malaya, Java, the Mascarene Islands, and Madagascar. The related *Artabotrys odoratissimus* (climbing ylang-ylang) is cultivated in many tropical regions for the fragrance of its flowers, but the perfume has only localized uses.

Oils and perfumes

In Ghana and the Ivory Coast regions of West Africa ethereal oils distilled from leaves of *Enneastemum capeus* are reportedly utilized in making perfume.

Cymbopetalum penduliflorum (Annonaceae family), a tree of Central America and Mexico, has flowers that, when crushed, yield an oil with a spicy odour similar to nutmeg or cubeb pepper, which has been used for several centuries to flavour chocolate and in cooking. According to one authority, this plant was called xochinacatzli—sacred ear flower of the Aztecs—because the inner petals bear some resemblance to human ears.

In the upper Amazon region, Indian tribes use an extract from the tree *Unonopsis veneficiorum* to tip their poison blowgun darts and arrows; this substance is said to have the same paralyzing effect on man and animals as that caused by curare poisons obtained from the genus *Strychnos* of the Loganiaceae family (order Gentianales).

Monodora myristica (family Annonaceae) is a large (up to 60 feet [18 metres] high) West African tree with big leaves and striking flowers; these features combine to make it an attractive ornamental in many tropical regions. Because the large ruminate (*i.e.*, folded in undulate fashion) seeds of this tree bear some resemblance to those of the true nutmeg (*Myristica*, family Myristicaceae), the tree is referred to as the Jamaica nutmeg or the calabash nutmeg. The latter name refers to the orange-sized fruit that encloses the seeds, and which has a superficial similarity to a gourd when dried. In West Africa the seeds are used to flavour cooking, as aromatic necklaces, in primitive medicinals, and (when pulverized) as a pomade.

Although many trees in the family Myristicaceae (nutmeg family) reach timber size, the wood is not of much value in world trade. Nevertheless, the following species from tropical regions of South and Central America find local uses in the manufacture of furniture, millwork, veneers, flooring, and general carpentry: *Dialyanthera otoba* (otobo), *Iryanthera lancifolia* (kirikawa), *Iryanthera sagotiana* (marakaipo), and *Virola koschyni* (banak). Wood of *Pycnanthus kombo* from West Africa is greyish-brown to pink, soft, and light (specific gravity 0.40), and is made into plywood for packing cases and low-grade interior woodwork. *Staudtia gabonensis* produces an orange to reddish-brown moderately hard and heavy (specific gravity 0.90) wood for cabinetry, tool handles, carving, and turnery in several West African countries. Chuglum (*Myristica irya*), from the Andaman Islands in the Bay of Bengal, yields light red to reddish-brown wood with darker streaks and high lustre, which is used to make musical instruments and furniture.

Both nutmeg and mace are obtained from the seeds of *Myristica fragrans*, a native of the Moluccas or Spice Islands in the Indonesian Archipelago, and is now grown in the tropics of both hemispheres. Although some of these spices are still exported from Indonesia, the greatest production today is in the British West Indies, principally the island of Grenada.

The nutmeg tree is a handsome evergreen with dark leaves and reaches a height of 30 to 60 feet (9 to 18 metres). The small, yellow, fleshy flowers are unisexual; *i.e.*, the male and female flowers are produced on separate trees. The ripe fruits are golden yellow and resemble apricots or pears. As the fruits dry out, they split open, revealing the single shiny brown seed covered with a bright red fleshy structure, called an aril. Inside the seeds are the kernels, which are the nutmegs of commerce; the aril is the source of mace. The pulverized seed finds much use for seasoning spiced fruits, sausages, pastries, puddings, egg nog, etc. Mace is one of the most delicately flavoured spices and is used in making pickles, ketchups, and sauces. Two oils are obtained from the seeds of *Myristica fragrans*, a volatile oil obtained by distillation, and a fixed oil obtained by subjecting the nutmegs to heat under pressure. The volatile oil contains myristic acid and a narcotic, myristicin; it is used medicinally as a carminative and as a flavouring agent in dentifrices tobacco, and perfumes. The fixed oil is known as nutmeg butter and is used in ointments and in candles.

Products and uses of the nutmeg

The seeds of *Gymnacranthera farquhariana* have been used in India for candlemaking. Those of *Myristica malabarica* have been used for oil and for adulterating nutmegs; its aril is marketed as Bombay mace. *Myristica argentea*, the Papua or Macassar nutmeg, is also used in oils and soaps, but is useless as a spice. The seeds of *Virola surinamensis* are used to make a commercial wax.

The family Canellaceae is of relatively little economic importance. The leaves and bark of the wild cinnamon (*Canella alba*) from the West Indies still have some use as a condiment and for medicinal purposes. The small trees of this species are cultivated to a limited extent in southern Florida, as ornamentals prized for their reddish-purple flowers and blue-black berries. The scented wood of *Cinnamosma fragrans* is exported from Zanzibar to Bombay and Thailand where it is used for religious ceremonies. *Warburgia ugandensis* is a fairly important timber producer in Uganda; the bark is utilized as a purgative and the resin for cementing tool handles.

The sole economic product from the Winteraceae family is "Winter's bark" from *Drimys winteri* of South America; it still finds some use as an astringent and a stimulant.

Distinguishing features. As classified in this treatment, the eight families included in the Magnoliales order are believed to contain many more ancient and primitive structural features than can be found in any other order of flowering plants. Some of these features follow: vessel-less woods in the Winteraceae family; *i.e.*, the water-conducting elements are all composed of primitive conducting cells called tracheids, such as those occurring in many ferns and some more primitive gymnosperms; flowers with numerous, spirally arranged, usually free parts on an elongated floral axis; the male organs or stamens often relatively broad and with pollen sacs embedded in their surfaces; the female organs or carpels often relatively unmodified from a leaflike structure; pollen grains usually with a single elongate germinal furrow such as that of the ancestral gymnosperm type; abundant ethereal oil cells in both floral and vegetative organs; and seeds bearing a small embryo embedded in copious endosperm (food storage tissue).

Pollination by beetles, believed to be a primitive condition among flowering plants, is normal for the Eupomatiaceae family and has been reported to occur commonly in many members of the Magnoliaceae, Winteraceae, and Annonaceae families. Ruminate endosperm—*i.e.*, endosperm that is fluted by the inward development of numerous ridges from the inner seed coat—is a normal feature in the Annonaceae, Myristicaceae, and Eupomatiaceae families, and at least one genus (*Cinnamosma*) in the family Canellaceae.

Since it is now recognized that evolution proceeds independently and at differing rates in both floral and vegetative organs, it is not to be expected that any one family in the magnolia order can be expected to contain only primitive characters in all their organs, and thus be selected as *the* most primitive. If the evolutionary significance of certain features is emphasized over several others, however, it is possible to suggest that either the Winteraceae or Magnoliaceae family is the most primitive living family of flowering plants.

EVOLUTION

The fossil record. Fossils representing four of the eight families of the Magnoliales order have been found. These include leaves ascribed to members of the Magnoliaceae family (*Magnolia* and *Liriodendron* from the Cretaceous Period of about 100,000,000 years ago and the Tertiary Period of about 60,000,000 years ago, and *Talauma* from the Tertiary, all of North America). Seeds (*Magnoliaespermum*) are recorded from the Tertiary brown coals of Germany, and pollen belonging to the family is widespread in the Lower Cretaceous and Tertiary deposits of both hemispheres. Fossil leaves and seeds of the Annonaceae family are known from the Cretaceous and Tertiary of both hemispheres. These have been assigned to about ten different modern genera. Seeds of the modern genus *Asimina* are known from the Tertiary brown coals of Germany, and petrified

woods (*Annonoxylon*) have been found in Tertiary deposits of North America and Austria. Fossil woods (*Myristicoxylon*) of the Myristicaceae family are known from the Tertiary of North Africa. The Winteraceae family is represented by fossil leaves (*Drimys*) from the Tertiary deposits of Australia, South America, and North America. The remaining four families have no fossil record.

Unfortunately, the fossil record is of little assistance in attempts to determine which group of flowering plants appeared first on earth. Although there are numerous scattered reports of putative angiosperm (flowering plant) fossils from pre-Cretaceous rocks—*i.e.*, deposits older than about 136,000,000 years—none of these finds has ever been indisputably accepted as belonging to the angiosperms. Indeed, possibly the best evidence is that the angiosperms arose rather suddenly during the Lower Cretaceous, about 120,000,000 years ago. Because these are the epochs when undoubted angiosperm pollen grains (which, due to the chemical nature of their coats, are extremely resistant to decay) first appeared in the fossil record, the pollen evidence is believed to be more reliable than that based on compressed leaves or leaf fragments. Nevertheless, in the absence of floral structures (which are only very rarely preserved as fossils) it is difficult to assign the Cretaceous fossils to modern families, let alone genera. Although numerous "species" of *Magnolia*, *Liriodendron*, *Drimys*, etc., have been described from leaf remains dating back to the Lower Cretaceous, only in rare instances have any of these identifications been validated by concomitant cuticular studies (*i.e.*, arrangement and types of cells on the outer cell layer of leaves), descriptions of wood anatomy, pollen morphology, fruits, or seeds preserved in the same sediments. Accordingly, most of the identifications of these supposed early remains of the Magnoliales order remain suspect. Although undoubted representatives of magnolialean families were present by the beginning of the Tertiary Period (approximately 63,000,000 years ago), so were numerous representatives of structurally much more highly evolved angiosperms; *e.g.*, the families Salicaceae (willows), Juglandaceae (walnuts), Fagaceae (oaks and beeches), and Moraceae (mulberries). Thus, the known fossil record cannot establish which angiosperm family is *the* most primitive.

CLASSIFICATION

Distinguishing taxonomic features. The features of most diagnostic value and for determining family relationships within the order include the presence or absence of stipules (leaflike appendages at the base of leafstalks); presence or degree of fusion of the carpels (simple pistil or seed-bearing organs); modification of perianth parts (tepals, the leaflike, showy parts of a flower) into sepals and petals; spiral or whorled arrangement of floral organs; free or connate (joined, fused together) stamens; pollen uniaperturate (with a single aperture, or germpore) or modified; and rumination (folded, ridged pattern of growth) of endosperm.

Annotated classification.

ORDER MAGNOLIALES

Entirely woody group; flowers hypogynous; bisexual, rarely unisexual accompanied by reduction (*i.e.*, the "other" sex parts are "reduced"; they do not develop); acyclic to cyclic; perianth obvious, tepals may not be differentiated into sepals and petals; endosperm abundant; ethereal oil cells in all organs; pollen mostly uniaperturate. Leaves alternate, simple. Eight families, 166 genera, and about 1,794 species. Mainly distributed throughout wet, tropical regions of the Old and New World, but with some temperate outliers.

Family Magnoliaceae

Trees or shrubs. Flowers terminal, except in *Michelia* and *Elmerrillia*, axillary. Leaves stipulate, evergreen, or deciduous, simple. Floral axis elongated and conelike. Tepals 6 to many, often in whorls of 3. Stamens numerous, arranged spirally. Carpels numerous to 2 with occasional species having one. Seeds numerous to 2 per carpel, often becoming pendent by the funicular threads from the ripe fruit. Pollen monocolpate (*i.e.*, with a single germinal aperture). Twelve genera and about 210 species. North America, West Indies, Central America to Brazil; also eastern Himalayas, southern India to

Primitive characteristics of the order

Problems in the fossil record

southern China, Manchuria, Japan, and Malaysia to New Guinea.

Family Degeneriaceae

Trees. Flowers solitary, subaxillary. Sepals 3, much smaller than the petals. Petals 12 to 18 in 3 to 5 whorls. Stamens 20 to 30 in 3 to 4 whorls, fleshy, flattened. Staminodes 10 to 13. Carpel 1, ellipsoid, ventral margins incompletely sealed. Ovules numerous, biseriate (*i.e.*, in two rows). Fruit indehiscent (*i.e.*, does not split open along established sutures or joints). Embryo with 3 cotyledons. Pollen monocolpate. *Degeneria vitiensis*, the only species; Fiji Islands.

Family Himantandraceae

Trees with alternate leaves, margins entire. Flowers solitary or paired on short axillary branches, at first covered by 2 leathery, deciduous stipules. Petals 5 to 7, lanceolate (*i.e.*, lance-shaped), similar in size and shape to the numerous stamens. Carpels 6 to 10, free, but soon united into a globose fruit. Ovules solitary and pendulous from each carpel. Pollen monocolpate. Single genus *Himantandra* with 3 or 4 species. Malaya, Indonesia, New Guinea, and northern Australia.

Family Eupomatiaceae

Shrubs. Flowers perigynous, with undifferentiated perianth forming a deciduous calyptra on the rim of the expanded concave receptacle. Stamens numerous, reflexed, the inner ones sterile and petaloid forming a pseudoperianth that is basally connate (*i.e.*, fused together at the base). Styles absent. Ovules numerous, endosperm ruminate. Pollen biaperturate (*i.e.*, with two apertures or germination pores). Single genus (*Eupomatia*) with two species ranging from southern New Guinea to southeastern Australia.

Family Annonaceae

Trees, shrubs or lianas. Flowers usually bisexual, actinomorphic (*i.e.*, regular, radially symmetrical), hypogynous. Sepals usually 3, free or partly connate, slightly imbricate or valvate. Petals often 6 in two series. Stamens numerous, spirally arranged; anthers (*i.e.*, male sexual parts, the pollen-producing bodies) often overtopped by fleshy, truncate connective. Carpels numerous to few, free or rarely united into a 1-locular ovary. Seeds often arillate with copious ruminate endosperm. Pollen monocolpate or inaperturate. At least 122 genera and 1,100 species. Tropics of the world, except the genus *Asimina*, which ranges to southern Ontario in America.

Family Canellaceae

Trees, seldom shrubs. Flowers bisexual, actinomorphic, solitary, cymose or racemose. Perianth imbricate (*i.e.*, overlapping like shingles), often subtended by persistent bracts. Stamens up to 20, connate (fused) in a tube. Ovary superior, 1-loculate, placentation parietal. Fruit a berry with 2 or more seeds. Endosperm ruminate only in *Cinnamosma*. Pollen monocolpate. Five genera and 9 species. Southern Florida, West Indies to Brazil; Central and East Africa, the Malagasy Republic.

Family Myristicaceae

Trees, often large, evergreen. Reddish gum ("kino") and tanniniferous tubules common in inner bark and wood. Flowers small, actinomorphic, dioecious (*i.e.*, male and female flowers are produced on separate plants), borne in fascicles or capitate. Petals absent. Calyx 3- to 5-lobed, funnel-shaped to globose, lobes valvate. Male flower with 2 to 30 stamens, filaments united into a column. Female flower with single superior ovary bearing 1 ovule. Fruit fleshy, often dehiscing by 2 valves. Seed with a thin or laciniate (*i.e.*, deeply dissected, lacerated, ragged) aril, often colored. Endosperm copious, ruminate. Pollen essentially monocolpate. Sixteen genera and about 380 species. Pantropical, often at lower elevations in rain forests.

Family Winteraceae

Trees or shrubs, woods lacking vessels (tracheids only). Flowers small, mostly cymose or fasciculate; bisexual or rarely polygamous (*i.e.*, separate male and female flowers but both produced on the same plant). Sepals 2 to 6, free and valvate or united (*Drimys*). Petals in 2 or more series, imbricate. Stamens several, hypogynous. Carpels many to one, free, seldom connate; ventral suture incompletely closed (*Tasmannia*). Fruit dehiscent or a berry. Pollen monoporate (*i.e.*, with one germination pore), shed in coherent tetrads (*i.e.*, groups of four that remain attached). Eight genera and 88 species. The Philippines, Borneo, New Guinea, New Caledonia to eastern Australia and New Zealand. Also, Mexico to Colombia, Brazil, Chile, and Argentina.

Critical appraisal. The classification presented here is a recent one that is gaining acceptance. By contrast, some authorities, in the treatment of the Magnoliales order, exclude four families recognized here (Eupomatiaceae, Annonaceae, Myristicaceae, and Degeneriaceae). Furthermore, they place the monotypic genus *Degeneria* in the Winteraceae family, the Annonaceae and Eupomatiaceae together in an order Annonales, and the Myristicaceae family in the order Laurales. To the Magnoliales order of these treatments are added the families Illiciaceae, Schisandraceae, Lactoridaceae, Trochodendraceae, and Cercidiphyllaceae, which receive no treatment here. Other authorities take an even broader view of the Magnoliales order, not only including the eight families recognized here but also adding 11 other families, which, under the treatment presented here, appear in the orders Laurales and Illiciales. Although there are grounds for criticism of all of these systems, the system presented here, circumscribing a smaller group, is probably more natural, if for no other reason than the fact that fewer genera are included, thus there are fewer "odd" morphological features to confuse the picture.

BIBLIOGRAPHY. L. CONSTANCE, "The Systematics of the Angiosperms," in *A Century of Progress in the Natural Sciences, 1853–1953* (1955), an excellent review of the influence of research in various fields of botany on ideas concerning the phylogeny of the angiosperms; A. CRONQUIST, *The Evolution and Classification of Flowering Plants* (1968), a recent text outlining the salient features of a phylogenetic system based on all available information; A.J. EAMES, *Morphology of the Angiosperms* (1961), an advanced text describing the morphological and anatomical features of presumed evolutionary significance in the angiosperms—ch. 11 includes an excellent treatment of primitive families of dicotyledons and monocotyledons, as well as an extensive bibliography; J.E. HUTCHINSON, *The Families of Flowering Plants*, 2nd ed., vol. 1, *Dicotyledons* (1959), a delineation of his earlier (1926) system, based upon two parallel linear sequences of families—one basically woody (Lignosae) and the other fundamentally herbaceous (Herbaceae); A. TAKHTAJAN, *Flowering Plants: Origin and Dispersal* (1969; Eng. trans. from the 2nd Russian ed., 1961), remarkable coverage of the literature on this subject in all languages.

(J.E.Ca.)

Mahārāshtra

India's third largest state in size and population, Mahārāshtra occupies a substantial portion of the Deccan Peninsula. It is triangular in shape, with a base running north–south for nearly 450 miles along the western shores of India and jutting out in a blunted apex toward the east about 500 miles away. It has an area of 118,637 square miles (307,269 square kilometres), and, early in the 1970s, had a population of over 50,000,000, thus taking up about one-tenth of India's land area and containing one-tenth of its population. It is bounded by the states of Gujarāt, Madhya Pradesh, Andhra Pradesh, and Mysore and the union territory of Goa, Daman, and Diu.

Mahārāshtra's capital, Bombay, is an island city, connected to the mainland by roads and railways. Aptly called the gateway of India, it is one of India's biggest commercial and industrial centres and has played a significant role in the country's social and political life.

Mahārāshtra is one of the foremost states in agricultural and industrial production, in trade and transport, and also in the growth of education and culture. Its ancient culture, at one stage considerably obscured by the dominance of the British, survives largely through the medium of a strong literary heritage. A common Marathi literature (Marathi is the predominant language) has in fact played an important role in nurturing a sense of nationality and unity among the Maharashtrians.

History. The name Mahārāshtra first appeared in a 7th-century inscription and in the account of a contemporary Chinese traveller, Hsüan-tsang. It then denoted the western upland, which has since been continuously known as Mahārāshtra. The origin of the name is still controversial. One view, however, is that it is derived from the word *rathī* (chariot driver), which refers to the skillful builders and drivers of chariots who formed a fighting force (*mahārāthis*) and migrated southward, settling in the area occupied by the modern state. Their language, intermingled with the speech of the earlier Nāga settlers, became Mahārāṣṭrī, and this by the 8th century developed into Marathi. There was also a continuous influx of people from remote Greece and Central Asia.

Emergence of Marāthā culture

The people of this early period were separated among several Hindu kingdoms: Sātavāhana, Vākāṭaka, Kalacuri, Rāṣṭrakūṭa, Cālukya, and Yādavas. After 1307 there was a succession of Muslim dynasties. Persian, the court language of the Muslims, had a far-reaching effect on Marathi. By the mid-16th century Mahārāshtra was again fragmented among several independent rulers, who waged endless wars among themselves. It was in the midst of this chaos that a great leader, Chhatrapati Śivajī, was born. Śivajī (Shivaji) showed astonishing prowess by founding a large empire that shook Mughal rule to its foundations.

During the 18th century almost all western and central India, as well as large segments of the north and east, were brought under Marāthā suzerainty. It was this empire that succumbed to the British from the early 19th century on. When India became independent in 1947, the province, long known as Bombay Presidency, became Bombay state. The following year a number of former princely states (notably Baroda) were merged into the new state, and, on November 1, 1956, a major reorganization of the states of peninsular India resulted in the addition of large parts of the former Hyderābād and Madhya Pradesh. In the north, it now comprised most of the Gujarati-speaking peoples and, in the south, most of the Marathi-speaking. As a result of the demands of the two language groups, the state was split in two on May 1, 1960, with Gujarāt, in the north, and Mahārāshtra, in the south.

The landscape. *Relief and drainage.* Mahārāshtra presents an interesting range of physical diversity.

To the west is the narrow Konkan coastal lowland. This is widest near Bombay. Numerous minor hills dominate the relief. There are numerous small, swift, west-flowing streams, most of them less than 50 miles long. The biggest, Ulhās, rising in the Bhor Ghāt, joins the sea after an 80 mile course.

The
Western
Ghāts

The Western Ghāts (which are mountains at the western edge of the Deccan Plateau; *ghāt* means "step" in Hindi) run almost continuously 398 miles north–south, the foothills reaching to within three–four miles of the Arabian Sea. Elevations increase northward to peaks of some 4,430 feet. There are a few gaps through which roads and railroads link the coast with the interior. The eastern slopes of the Ghāts descend gently to the Deccan Plateau and are sculptured by the wide, mature valleys of the Krishna, Bhīma, and Godāvari rivers.

Between Narmada Valley in the north, Krishna Basin in the south, and from the western coast as far east as Nāgpur, the Ghāts and the triangular plateau inland are covered with extensive lava outpourings called "traps." These reach a maximum thickness of 10,000 feet near Bombay. The differential erosion of lava has resulted in characteristic steplike slopes, uniform crest lines, and a table-top appearance of many hills.

East of Nāgpur, the Deccan Trap gives way to undulating uplands (890–1,080 feet high) underlain by ancient crystalline rocks. The Wardha-Wainganga Valley, part of the larger Godāvari Basin, trends southward and abounds in lakes.

The lava rock breaks down into a heavy, black, fertile soil. Very old crystalline rocks in the Wardha-Wainganga Valley have been eroded into light-coloured, sandy soils. Saline soils in the river valleys are a result of heavy evaporation.

Climate. The climate is characteristically monsoonal, with local variations. India's southwest monsoon rains break on the Bombay coast usually on June 1st and last till September, during which period they account for 80 percent of the annual rainfall. Four seasons are normal: March–May (hot and dry) June–September (hot and wet); October–November (warm and moist); and December–February (cool and dry).

The Western Ghāts and the ranges on the northern borders greatly influence the climate and separate the wet Konkan Coast from the dry interior upland, called the Desh. Rainfall is very heavy in Konkan, averaging 100 inches, with some of the wettest spots recording 250 inches rapidly diminishing to one-tenth of this east of the

Ghāts. Rainfall increases again eastward, reaching 40–80 inches in the extreme east.

The coastal districts enjoy equable temperatures, monthly averages ranging, as at Bombay, only a few degrees above or below 80° F (27° C). A range of more than 13° F (7° C) between day and night temperatures is unusual. Towns such as Pune (Poona), high up on the plateau, benefit from cooler temperatures throughout the year but remain equable.

Vegetation and animal life. Forests cover less than one-fifth of Mahārāshtra and are confined to the Sahyādri Range, its transverse ranges, the Sātpura Range in the north, and the Chandrapur region in the east. On the coast and adjoining slopes, plant forms are rich with lofty trees, variegated shrubs, and mango and coconut trees. The forests yield teak, bamboo, myrabolan (for dyeing), and other woods.

Thorny, savanna-like vegetation occurs in areas of less than 30-inch rainfall, in upland Mahārāshtra.

Subtropical vegetation is found on higher plateaus having heavy rain and milder temperatures. Bamboo, chestnut, and magnolia are common. In the semiarid tracts, wild dates are found. Mangrove vegetation occurs in marshes and estuaries along the coast.

Wild animals include tigers, leopards, and even bison. There are several species of antelope. Striped hyena, wild hog, and sloth bear occur frequently. Monkeys and snakes are of many types. Game birds, the peacock, and ducks are numerous.

Population. *Ethnic patterns.* Mahārāshtra contains a mixture of races. Ethnically, it is a conglomeration of people—indigenous and immigrant. On the Sahyādri and Sātpura perches live some 2,400,000 Australoid aboriginals—Bhīls, Warlis, Gonds, Korkus, and Gowaris. They are dark, short statured, and have long heads and flat noses. Almost ubiquitous are Kunbī Marāthās—brown, medium-statured, and supposedly descendants of waves of settlers who came from the north around the beginning of the Christian Era. Through an agelong mixture of aboriginals and immigrants, many castes have developed, most of them in the east. The tall and fair Parsis form another group, having fled from Iran, in the 11th century, to safeguard their religion.

Languages. Marathi, the state language, is spoken by over 90 percent of the people. Other important languages are Gujarati, Hindi, Telugu, Kannada, Sindhi, Urdu, and English. Sindhi has spread in urban centres as a result of an influx of refugees after the 1947 partition. English is still used in universities, in administration, and in metropolitan cities. Urdu is spoken by Muslims everywhere. There are also many dialects, such as Konkani on the west coast and Gondi and Mundari in the eastern and northern forests.

Marathi is one of India's more developed languages. Despite various regional spoken forms, its written style is uniform.

Religion. A variety of faiths is found within Mahārāshtra. Hindus predominate (over 80 percent), followed by Muslims (8 percent) and Buddhists (7 percent). There are many Christians in the metropolitan cities. Parsis (a religious minority adhering to Zoroastrianism) are mainly confined to Bombay and its environs, though some are to be found in other cities. Other religious minorities include Jains and Sikhs, who are found in small numbers everywhere.

Patterns of settlement. In 1971, Mahārāshtra's 50,-335,000 people lived in numerous villages, 289 towns (17 called cities and having over 100,000 people), and in the Bombay conurbation. Urban population was 31 percent compared to the average for India of 20 percent.

Major
urban
centres

Greater Bombay's population of 5,969,000 reflects its industrial growth and commercial success. Textiles dominate, but engineering and chemical and pharmaceutical industries are catching up. Bombay is India's best equipped port and handles an enormous foreign trade. It is a centre of business, finance, and administration.

Nāgpur (city proper over 866,000), Pune (city proper over 853,000), and Sholāpur (city proper over 398,000)

are other major cities. Its historical and cultural importance apart, Pune has developed many industries because of its proximity to Bombay. Nāgpur was once the capital of the Bhonsle kingdom and then, until 1956, of the erstwhile Madhya Pradesh. The city still enjoys status as Mahārāshtra's second capital. Nāgpur and Sholāpur have textile and other agriculturally based, market-oriented industries. Pune and Nāgpur are additionally important as educational centres. Of particular historical interest is the Mughal city of Aurangābād, which contains several forts and other historic buildings and which is in close proximity to the famous caves of Ajanta and Ellora.

Administration and social conditions. Mahārāshtra has had always three principal components: western Mahārāshtra, Vidarbha, and Marāthwādā. It is divided administratively into four divisions and 26 districts.

In common with other states, Mahārāshtra is administered by a governor and a council of ministers elected from members of the legislature and headed by the leader of the majority party.

Executive authority in the state is exercised by the cabinet in the name of the governor. The collector—responsible for collection of land revenue, special taxes, and for coordinating the work of other departments, is the key figure within the local administrative areas.

The judiciary is headed by the chief justice and a panel of judges and is based in Bombay, although there is also a bench at Nāgpur.

The legislature has two houses: Vidhan Parishad (legislative council) and Vidhan Sabha (legislative assembly). Both meet in Bombay and once annually in Nāgpur. Mahārāshtra is represented in the Lok Sabha and the Rajya Sabha (which are, respectively, the Lower and Upper Houses of the Indian parliament).

There is a Public Service Commission that selects candidates for appointment to all state services, largely by means of competitive examinations.

Health services. Health conditions improved greatly between 1947 and 1964. The death rate was reduced from 25 to 15 per 1000 and infant mortality from 162 to 91 per 1000. Life expectancy is approximately 50 years. While urban areas have one doctor for every 1,433 people, rural areas have only one for 19,393.

Medical colleges number 13, of which five are in Bombay and two in Pune. There are dental colleges in Bombay and Nāgpur. Indigenous medicine is taught at Ayurvedic colleges in Bombay and Nāgpur.

There are about 50,000 beds in 1,850 hospitals and dispensaries. Most district hospitals maintain nursing schools, and the state nursing service has over 2,500 members. Regional blood banks exist in Bombay, Pune, Aurangābād, and Nāgpur, and resuscitation centres are found in all districts. The state has three times received a national award for the best family-planning work. In Bombay the Haffkine Institute and the Indian Cancer Research Centre (located in the Tata Memorial Hospital) are well-known research centres.

Welfare services. Welfare activities are directed toward children, women, workers, and delinquent citizens but not as yet to the unemployed. A Children's Act takes care of youthful offenders, and remand homes do correctional work. About 20 state homes shelter women in distress. The aged have rest homes, and numerous hostels accommodate working women. Training facilities exist for the physically handicapped, and juvenile guidance centres function in slum areas.

Education. The average literacy percentage for Mahārāshtra is 39, as against the average for India of 30. Free compulsory education is provided for children between the ages of six and 14. During the decade 1955 to 1965 primary school enrollment increased by 80 percent and secondary school enrollment by 200 percent. Vocational and multipurpose high schools have also grown in importance.

There are six universities: two at Bombay, others at Nāgpur, Pune, Aurangābād, and Kolhāpur. Two others are projected—one in Vidarbha, the other in Khāndesh. There are also two agricultural universities and eight engineering colleges. Various other colleges impart university level education.

Economy. Mahārāshtra's per capita income is 20 percent above the Indian average. Thirty-six percent of the state's income comes from primary-agricultural activities, 35 percent from commercial and administrative services, and 29 percent from mining and manufacturing.

Agriculture. Agriculture is the bulwark of Mahārāshtra economy, and the peasantry forms 64 percent of the population.

Recent progressive measures to combat food deficits include electrifying irrigation, the use of hybrid seeds, ultra-intensive cultivation, and offering incentives to the farmer. A major continuing problem, however, is water scarcity. Millet and pulses (edible seeds) dominate the cropped area. Rice grows where rainfall exceeds 100 centimetres, and wheat is a winter crop in fields that retain moisture. Rice and wheat together occupy 12 percent of the cropped area. Cotton and groundnuts are major crops in areas having 24–39 inches of rainfall. Irrigation dams in rain-shadow areas have resulted in a rich sugarcane crop. Mangoes, cashew nuts, bananas, and oranges are popular crops. Many problems relating to soil erosion, storage, transport, and marketing have yet to be overcome.

Major crops

Forestry, fisheries, and mineral reserves. Forest products include timber, bamboo, sandalwood, and tendu leaves (for cheap cigarettes). Some 43,000 persons were thus employed early in the 1970s. The annual catch of fish is 171,000 tons, engaging 70,000 people.

Meagre mineral resources are found mostly in the eastern and, occasionally, in the western districts. Manganese, coal, iron ore, limestone, copper, bauxite, and common salt are extracted, providing employment for some 55,000 people.

Eastern Vidarbha districts are rich with reserves of coal, estimated at 5,000,000,000 tons. Mostly bituminous, it is used by railways and power stations.

Mahārāshtra produces both hydro-electricity and thermal electricity, the former in western areas, the latter in the east. There is also an atomic power station at Tārāpur, 70 miles north of Bombay.

Manufacturing. Fourteen percent of India's industrial units and 20 percent of its industrial workers are in Mahārāshtra, accounting for 24 percent of India's industrial output. The Bombay–Pune complex is the major industrial area; Nāgpur and Kolhāpur are also important.

The oldest and largest industry is the manufacture of cotton textiles. There are about 100 cotton mills and 240,000 textile workers in the state. Bombay, Nāgpur, and Sholāpur are the principal textile manufacturing centres.

Oil refining and petro-chemicals (Bombay) and the manufacture of such items as agricultural implements, electric and oil pumps, lathes, compressors, sugar-mill machinery, typewriters, refrigerators, and radio sets are assuming increasing importance. There is also an incipient automobile industry in Bombay.

Transport and communications. *Railways.* The foremost means of travel is a rail network focussing on Bombay. There is a total of 5,193 kilometres of track, both broad- and narrow-gauge. The nation's east–west and north–south trunk routes intersect between Nāgpur and Wardha.

Passenger amenities are increasing, with third class sleepers, diesel-electric engines, and air-conditioned coaches.

Roads. A 20-year plan inaugurated after independence provided for a major road within five miles of every village. Missing links on the 86 state highways were thus completed, and district roads developed in inaccessible areas. Five national highways (2,400 kilometres) connect the state with Delhi, Calcutta, Allāhābād, Hyderābād, and Bangalore.

The state transport corporation owns some 5,000 buses and carries 1,400,000 passengers daily over 5,000 routes. Recent innovations include luxury buses—including sleepers on interstate services—and a 50 percent discount for students. Special buses serve tourist, pilgrimage, and health resorts. Private motor vehicles number about 260,000.

Water transport plays a limited role in Mahārāshtra, although minor ports on the west coast handle some 1,500,000 passengers annually.

Airways. Daily air services connect Bombay with Pune, Nāgpur, Aurangābād, and Nāsik. Bombay is located on international air routes, and Nāgpur is the centre of India's airmail scheme.

Communications. More than 9,000 post and telegraph offices, 120,000 telephones, and five broadcasting stations make up the communications network. An international satellite communication centre has been commissioned at Arvi, near Pune.

Cultural life. Mahārāshtra is a distinct cultural region. Its long artistic tradition is manifested in the ancient cave paintings of Ajantā and Ellora, in medieval architectural masterpieces, in its classical and devotional music, and in its theatre. Pune, where numerous organizations sustain these great traditions, is the undisputed cultural capital. The Marathi stage is very active, plays being performed even in small communities.

Mahārāshtra's foremost diversion is *tamāshā*, combining music, drama, and dance. About seven artists form a *tamāshā* troupe. A female dancer is the central figure, a clown providing the humour.

Mahārāshtra has many festivals throughout the year: Holī is the spring festival and Ranga Panchami, which follows, is a riot of colours. The Dassera festival has a special significance, being the day on which Marāthā warriors started on their campaigns. Dīwālī, coming next, is a festival of lights and fireworks. Pola is a festival in which bullocks are given a holiday and decorated for a race. The Ganesh festival is by far the most popular in Mahārāshtra. Its public celebration was first sponsored by a nationalist political leader, B.G. Tilak. Muharram commemorates the great martyrs of Islām, although even Hindus participate. Unique to Mahārāshtra is the Hurda party, in which the farmer invites village folk to partake of fresh ears of jowar (Indian millet). Folk songs and traditional dances accompany all these celebrations.

BIBLIOGRAPHY. The GOVERNMENT PUBLICITY DIRECTOR-ATE, *Maharashtra* (1969), *Maharashtra at a Glance* (1969); and the BUREAU OF ECONOMICS AND STATISTICS publication *Statistical Abstract of Maharashtra* (annual), furnish reliable, up-to-date figures on the state. Much historical material may be found in G. YAZDANI (ed.), *The Early History of the Deccan*, 2 vol. (1960); and a brilliant socio-anthropological analysis of the population is I. KARVE, *Maharashtra Land and Its People* (1968). Resource potentials are discussed in the *Techno-Economic Survey of Maharashtra*, ed. by P.S. LOKANA-THAN (1963). A good geographical account is C.B. JOSHI and B. ARUNACHALAM, *Maharashtra: A Regional Study* (1962).

(S.Mo.)

Mahāvīra

Vardhamāna, known as Mahāvīra, Great Hero, was the last patriarch of a line of 24 Tīrthaṅkaras (prophets, or, literally, Ford-Makers), most of them legendary, who founded Jainism, a religion concentrated mainly in western India and claiming approximately 2,600,000 followers in the 1971 census. Basing his doctrines on the teachings of the 23rd Tīrthaṅkara, Pārśvanātha, a 9th-century-BC teacher from Banaras (Vārānasi, Uttar Pradesh), Vardhamāna systematized earlier Jaina doctrines —along with metaphysical, mythological, and cosmological beliefs—and also established the rules and guidelines for the monks, nuns, laymen, and laywomen of the Jaina *saṅgha,* or religious order.

Social and religious influences on Mahāvīra

Born about 599 BC into a Kṣatriya (warrior caste) family, Vardhamāna grew up in Kṣatriyakuṇḍagrāma, a suburb of Vaiśālī (modern Basarh) in Magadha (Bihār state), the area of origin of both Jainism and Buddhism. His father was Siddhārtha, a ruler of the Nāta, or Jñātṛ, clan. According to one Jaina tradition his mother was named Devanandā and was a member of the Brahmin (priestly) caste; other traditions name her Triśalā, Videhadinnā, or Priyakāriṇī, and place her in the Kṣatriya caste.

The 6th century BC was a period of great intellectual,

Mahāvīra enthroned, miniature from the *Kalpa-sūtra*, 15th-century western Indian school. In the Freer Gallery of Art, Washington, D.C.
By courtesy of the Smithsonian Institution, Freer Gallery of Art, Washington, D.C.

philosophical, religious, and social ferment in India, a period in which certain members of the Kṣatriya caste led a revolt against the Brahmins who used their positions as members of the highest caste to make demands upon the lower castes. In particular, the Brahmins demanded an increasingly large number of cattle as fees for the Vedic (ancient Aryan religious) *yajña,* or fire sacrifice. Because the strain of such demands on agriculture was intolerable to the food-producing and trading castes, attacks against animal sacrifice increased. The leaders of the anti-Brahmin sects came to be regarded as heretical. Mahāvīra and his younger contemporary Siddhārtha Gautama, the Buddha, were two of the greatest leaders in this revolt.

Though the traditions about the life of Mahāvīra vary according to the two Jaina sects (the Śvetāmbaras, or White-Clad, and the Digambaras, or Sky-Clad), he apparently was reared in luxury, though as a younger son he could not inherit the leadership of the clan. At the age of 30 (569 BC), after he had married a lady of the Kṣatriya caste and had a daughter, he renounced the world and became a monk. According to legend, his parents had died by practicing the rite of *sallekhana—i.e.,* voluntary self-starvation. Thus, when Mahāvīra joined the ascetic order of Pārśvanātha, to which his parents had belonged, self-denial was not foreign to him.

Mahāvīra's renunciation of the world

Perhaps beginning as a member of the order of Pārśvanātha, Mahāvīra used one garment for over a year, but later he went about naked and kept no possessions—not even a bowl for obtaining alms or drinking water. He allowed insects to crawl on his body and even bite him, bearing the pain with patience. People often shouted at him and hit him because of his uncouth and unsightly body. He meditated day and night and lived in various places—workshops, cremation and burial grounds, and at the foot of trees. Trying to avoid all sinful activity, he especially avoided injuring any kind of life, thus developing the doctrine of *ahiṃsā,* or nonviolence. He kept many fast periods and never ate anything that was expressly prepared for him. Though he wandered about continuously during most of the year, Mahāvīra spent the four months of the rainy season in villages and towns.

During his many wanderings he endured abusive language and physical injuries, always with patience and equanimity.

After 12 years of practicing such austerities, Mahāvīra attained, in 557 BC, *kevala-jñāna,* the highest knowledge. The school of Pārśvanātha apparently had been waning in appeal; Mahāvīra revived and reorganized Jaina doctrine and the *saṅgha,* thus being credited as the founder of Jainism. Though what he added to the teachings of Pārśvanātha is uncertain, his organization of the order and his rules for religious behaviour and practice became a landmark in Jaina history. Included in his teachings was a great interest in mathematics and the movements of celestial bodies. He taught that all that exists on earth and in other worlds is classified according to numerical categories, that objects are related to each other in a variety of ways, and that infinity and the indefiniteness of numbers are concepts significant to cosmology. In his concepts on geometry, Mahāvīra taught that lines are differentiated according to their straightness, curvature, and jaggedness and that figures are distinguished according to their angularity and curvature. Though his teachings contained philosophical complexities, he illustrated them by means of comparisons drawn from everyday life.

Religious teachings

Mahāvīra also taught that a man can save his soul from the contamination of matter by practicing extreme asceticism and that he can maintain an austere life by practicing nonviolence toward all living creatures. This encouraged his followers to become strong advocates of vegetarianism, which in the course of time helped to bring about a virtual end to sacrificial killing in Indian rituals. His followers were aided in their quest for salvation by accepting the "five great vows" that have been attributed to Mahāvīra: renunciation of killing, speaking untruths, greed, sexual pleasure, and all attachments to living beings and non-living things. Mahāvīra's predecessor Pārśva preached only "four great vows."

Mahāvīra, also called Jina, or Conqueror (*i.e.*, conqueror of enemies such as attachment and greed) among other titles, died in 527 BC at Pāvā in northern Bihār state, leaving a group of followers who influenced Indian culture by their practice of nonviolence, which, in turn, has influenced reformers down to the 20th century.

BIBLIOGRAPHY. WALTER SCHUBRING, *Der Jinismus* in *Der Religionen der Menschheit*, vol. 13, pp. 217–242 (1964; Eng. trans., *The Religion of the Jainas*, 1966), describes some important aspects of Mahāvīra's personality. MUNI NAGARAJA; *Contemporaneity and Chronology of Mahāvīra and Buddha* (1970), is a recent attempt, more convincing than earlier ones, at solving the problem of the chronology and contemporaneity of Buddha and Mahāvīra. HERMANN JACOBI's English translation of Jaina Canonical texts *Ācārāṅga*, *Uttarādhyayana*, and the *Kalpa* Sūtras, entitled *Jaina Sūtras*, 2 vol. (1884–95, reprinted 1968), supplies the earliest Jaina accounts of Mahāvīra. B.C. LAW, *Mahavira, His Life and Teachings* (1937), is an authentic account appealing to both scholars and general readers.

(U.P.S.)

Mahdī, al-

Known as al-Mahdī, or "The Divinely Guided One," Muḥammad Aḥmad ibn 'Abd Allāh created an Islāmic state extending from the Red Sea to Central Africa and founded a movement still influential in The Sudan.

Muḥammad Aḥmad was born on August 12, 1844, the son of a shipbuilder from the Dongola District of Nubia. Shortly after Muḥammad's birth, the family moved south to Karari, a river village near Khartoum. As a boy, Muḥammad developed a love of religious study. Instead of seeking an orthodox education, such as that offered at al-Azhar University in Cairo, and passing into the official hierarchy as a salaried judge or interpreter of Islāmic law, he remained in the Sudan. Increasingly, he tended to a more mystic interpretation of Islām, in the Ṣūfī tradition, through study of the Qur'ān—the sacred Muslim scripture—and the practice of self-denial under the discipline of a religious brotherhood. He joined the Sammānīyah order and grew to manhood in a wholly Sudanese religious setting, purposely separating himself from the official ruling class. By now the young man had begun to attract his own disciples and, in 1870, moved with them to a hermitage on Abā Island in the White Nile, 175 miles south of Khartoum. His highly emotional and intransigent religious observance brought him into conflict with his *skaykh* (teacher), whom he reproved for worldliness. The exasperated *skaykh* expelled him from the circle of his disciples, whereupon Muḥammad Aḥ-

mad, having vainly asked his teacher's pardon, joined the brotherhood of a rival *skaykh* within the same order.

The Sudan at this time was a dependency of Egypt, which was itself a province of the Ottoman Empire, and governed by the same multiracial, Turkish-speaking ruling class that governed Egypt. In appearance, education, and way of life the rulers contrasted starkly with their Sudanese subjects; and although the more assimilated higher officials and some of the chiefs of territories along the Nile who profited from their government connections were reconciled to the regime, the less privileged Sudanese were not. The situation was politically dangerous, for the discontented came from many different walks of life: taxpayers oppressed by fiscal injustices and enraged by the frequent floggings to which they were subject when tardy in their payments; slave traders aroused by the clumsy efforts of the government, which was hectored by the European powers, particularly Britain, to abolish the trade without delay; devout worshippers scandalized by the presence of non-Muslim Europeans as provincial governors and by their addiction to alcohol; peasants living by the Nile forced to tow government ships; warlike tribesmen, weary of the long years of enforced peace, spoiling for a fight—all these were potential enemies of the established order. It was Muḥammad Aḥmad who converted this diversified discontent into a unified movement that for a time would transcend tribalism and weld the faithful into an unconquerable military machine. Gradually, during 1880 and the first weeks of 1881, he became convinced that the entire ruling class had deserted the Islāmic faith and that the khedive, the viceroy of Egypt, was a puppet in the hands of unbelievers and thus unfit to rule over Muslims.

The political background to his ascendency

In March 1881 he revealed to his closest followers what he considered his divine mission—that God had appointed him to purify Islām and to destroy all governments that defiled it. On June 29 he publicly assumed the title of the Mahdī, who, according to a tradition cherished by the oppressed throughout Islāmic history, would appear to restore Islām.

The events that followed this announcement were among the most dramatic in the history of the Nile Valley. Within less than four years the Mahdī, who set out from Abā Island with a few followers armed with sticks and spears, ended by making himself master of almost all the territory formerly occupied by the Egyptian government, capturing an enormous booty of money, bullion, jewels, and military supplies—including Krupp artillery and Remington rifles.

By the end of 1883 the Mahdī's *anṣār* ("friends," a name first given to those people in the city of Medina who helped the prophet Muḥammad) had annihilated three Egyptian armies sent against them; the last, a force of 8,000 men with a huge camel train, commanded by Gen. William Hicks, was butchered almost to a man. El Obeid, the present-day al-Ubayyiḍ, provincial capital of Kordofan, and Bara, a chief town of that province, fell after being besieged by the Mahdī. He now committed his first acts as the head of an armed theocracy on the march: taxes were collected, not as demanded by the Egyptians but as laid down by the Qur'ān. Already his fame had reached responsive ears in Arabia to the north and as far west as Bornu, now a province of northern Nigeria. A master of the art of putting his enemies always in the wrong, he supported his military operations by an intelligent and subtle propaganda. Counterpropaganda by the governor-general, 'Abd al-Qādir Pasha Ḥilmī, a man of great resource, and by the *'ulamā'*, the learned men, of Khartoum who mocked the Mahdī's divine claims, failed miserably. The Mahdī's crowning victory was the capture of Khartoum, on January 26, 1885, after a resolute defense by its commander, Maj. Gen. Charles George Gordon, who, against the Mahdī's express order, was killed in the final assault. The Mahdī made a triumphal entry into the stricken city and led the prayers in the principal mosque. Even making allowance for the military weakness of Egypt, which during the crucial years 1881 and 1882 was torn by the nationalist revolt of Aḥmad 'Urābī Pasha, it was an astonishing feat.

Capture of Khartoum

The withdrawal of the British expedition, which had failed to relieve Khartoum, left the Mahdī free to consolidate his religious empire. He abandoned Khartoum, still heavy with the stench of the dead, and set up his administrative centre at Omdurman, an expanded village of mud houses and grass-roofed huts on the left bank of the Nile, opposite Khartoum. The site of the new capital had two advantages: it was higher and better drained, hence healthier, than Khartoum, and, by governing from the exclusively Sudanese town of Omdurman, the Mahdī avoided the evil associations of the old capital. He directed every aspect of community and personal life by proclamations, sermons, warnings, and letters. In this endeavour he was helped by the capture, intact, of the government press and an abundance of stationery. But he confined himself to the enunciation of principles; most of the routine he left to his chief officers. The political institutions, as well as the nomenclature of his government, were based insofar as practicable on those of primitive Islām. In the manner of the prophet Muḥammad he appointed four caliphs, or deputies, to be the living successors of the four earliest caliphs in Islāmic history. Three of those appointed by the Mahdī were Sudanese, including the caliph 'Abd Allāh ibn Muḥammad, the Mahdī's most trusted counsellor and chief of staff; the fourth, Muḥammad al-Mahdī ibn as-Sanūsī, head of the Sanūsīyah order in the western desert, ignored the Mahdī's invitation. The Mahdī referred to himself as "the successor to the apostle of God"—that is, successor to the prophet Muḥammad but only in the sense of continuing his work.

The Mahdī's rule was brief. He was taken ill, possibly of typhus, and died in Omdurman on June 22, 1885, only 41 years old. At his wish his temporal functions were assumed by the caliph 'Abd Allāh. Over his grave the caliph built a domed tomb similar in architecture to those customarily built over the remains of the more venerated holy men. Partially destroyed by gunfire during the battle of Omdurman in 1898, it was later rebuilt by the Mahdī's son 'Abd ar-Raḥmān and the Mahdist community.

Personality and reputation

The Mahdī made a powerful impression on his Sudanese contemporaries, and the doubters were few. Recorded recollections are capricious, but most witnesses agreed on his medium-to-tall height; his austere frame which, according to some, fattened toward the end of his life; the soft voice that a sudden access of indignation could make terrible; the sympathetic, sensitive face; the large, piercing eyes. The pious were sure that in his person he conformed to all that was traditionally expected of a *mahdī*. Understandably, European captives drew a less favourable picture. There are no portraits; a photograph in a lithographed edition (Cairo, 1342 [1923–24]) of the Mahdī's *ar-rātib* (book of devotions) is unauthentic.

The Mahdī's reputation in Europe and America has changed with the times. To the British at the time of the Mahdist wars the Mahdī was the enemy whom they associated, though wrongly, with the killing of Gordon. The war correspondents generally reported him as an ogre, cruel when he was not lascivious; in their brash assurance they dubbed him the False Prophet and a dervish, a term that the Mahdī expressly repudiated. This caricature of the Mahdī was reflected in a bulky literature of unwitting misrepresentation involving authors as different as Rudyard Kipling and George Alfred Henty (Britain), Karl May (Germany), and Henryk Sienkiewicz (Poland), which distorted the Mahdī's image for an entire generation. Ironically, it was Gen. Horatio Herbert Kitchener's conquest of the Sudan in 1896–98 that first brought Mahdists and British officials together and fostered what was to become a growing interest among European and Sudanese scholars in the study of Mahdist documents in the original Arabic. Such studies have made possible a clearer view of this modern ascetic who changed the course of African history.

BIBLIOGRAPHY. F.R. WINGATE, *Mahdiism and the Egyptian Sudan* (1891, reprinted 1968); A.B. THEOBALD, *The Mahdīya* (1951); P.M. HOLT, *The Mahdist State in the Sudan*, 2nd ed. (1970); B. FARWELL, *Prisoners of the Mahdi* (1967). The Mahdī's collected works in Arabic have been reprinted in a series of volumes under the direction of Muḥammad Ibrāhīm Aḥmad Abū Salim, director of the Sudan Government Central Archives, Khartoum.

(R.L.Hi.)

Mahler, Gustav

The stature of Gustav Mahler, the last notable exponent of the Austro-German symphony, is as yet difficult to determine, because only since about 1960 has his music, widely rejected for 50 years after his death as an extravagant consummation of what was most extreme in Romanticism, found a substantial following. He is generally admitted to have been an important forerunner of 20th-century techniques of composition; but a more significant measure of his stature in his own right is the high opinion held of him by the widely differing composers who have acknowledged his influence, including Arnold Schoenberg, Dmitry Shostakovich, Benjamin Britten, Hans Werner Henze, and Luciano Berio. More significant still, perhaps, is the devotion to his art shown by several eminent conductors, such as Bruno Walter, Otto Klemperer, Rafael Kubelík, and Leonard Bernstein, coupled with the growing response of the public, which already, wherever Mahler's music is performed regularly, accords it a popularity commensurate with that of Beethoven and Tchaikovsky.

Mahler.

Childhood influences. Born on July 7, 1860, Mahler was the son of an Austrian-Jewish tavern keeper living in the Bohemian village of Kaliště (German Kalischt), in the southwestern corner of modern Czechoslovakia; a few months later the family moved to the nearby town of Jihlava (German Iglau), where Mahler spent his childhood and youth. These simple facts provide a first clue to his tormented personality: he was afflicted by racial tensions from the beginning of his life. As part of a German-speaking Austrian minority, he was an outsider among the indigenous Czech population and, as a Jew, an outsider among that Austrian minority; later, in Germany, he was an outsider as both an Austrian from Bohemia and a Jew.

Racial and religious tensions

Mahler's life was also complicated by the tension existing between his parents. His father, a self-educated man of fierce vitality, had married a delicate woman from a cultured family; and coming to resent her social superiority, he resorted to physically maltreating her. In consequence Mahler was alienated from his father and had a strong mother fixation, which even manifested itself physically: a slight limp was unconsciously copied in imitation of his mother's lameness. Furthermore, he inherited his mother's weak heart, which was to cause his death at the age of 50. Finally, there was a constant childhood background of illness and death among his 11 brothers and sisters.

This unsettling early background may explain the nervous tension, the irony and skepticism, the obsession with death, and the unremitting quest to discover some meaning in life that was to pervade Mahler's life and music. But it does not explain the prodigious energy, intellectual power, and inflexibility of purpose that carried him to the heights as both a master conductor and a composer. The positive elements in his makeup stemmed no doubt from his father's side of the family, as did his great physical vitality. Despite his inherited heart trouble, he was an extremely active man—a ruthless musical director, a tireless swimmer, and an indefatigable mountain walker.

His musical talent revealed itself early and significantly. Around the age of four, fascinated by the military music at a nearby barracks and the folk music sung by the Czech working people, he reproduced both on the accordion and the piano and began composing pieces of his own. The military and popular styles, together with the sounds of nature, became main sources of his mature inspiration. At ten he made his debut as a pianist in Jihlava and at 15 was so proficient musically that he was accepted as a pupil at the Vienna Conservatory. After winning piano and composition prizes and leaving with a diploma, he supported himself by sporadic teaching while trying to win recognition as a composer. When he failed to win the Conservatory's Beethoven Prize for composition with his first significant work, the cantata *Das klagende Lied* (*The Song of Complaint*), he turned to conducting for a more secure livelihood, reserving composition for the lengthy summer vacations.

The next 17 years saw his ascent to the very top of his chosen profession. From conducting musical farces in Austria, he rose through various provincial opera houses, including important engagements at Budapest and Hamburg, to become artistic director of the Vienna Court Opera in 1897, at the age of 37. As a conductor he had won general acclaim, but as a composer, during this first creative period, he immediately encountered the public's lack of comprehension that was to confront him for most of his career.

Artistic director of the Vienna Court Opera

Since Mahler's conducting life centred in the traditional manner on the opera house, it is at first surprising that his whole mature output was entirely symphonic (his 40 songs are not true lieder but embryonic symphonic movements, some of which, in fact, provided a partial basis for the symphonies). But Mahler's unique aim, partially influenced by the school of Richard Wagner and Franz Liszt, was essentially autobiographical—the musical expression of a personal view of the world. And for this purpose, song and symphony were more appropriate than the dramatic medium of opera: song because of its inherent personal lyricism, and symphony (from the Wagner and Liszt point of view) because of its subjective expressive power.

First period. Each of Mahler's three creative periods produced a symphonic trilogy. The three symphonies of his first period were conceived on a programmatic basis (*i.e.*, founded on a nonmusical story or idea), the actual programs (later discarded) being concerned with establishing some ultimate ground for existence in a world dominated by pain, death, doubt, and despair. To this end, he followed the example of Beethoven's *Symphony No. 6 in F Major* (*Pastoral*) and Berlioz's *Symphonie fantastique* in building symphonies with more than the then traditional four movements; that of Wagner's music-dramas in expanding the time span, enlarging the orchestral resources, and indulging in uninhibited emotional expression; that of Beethoven's *Symphony No. 9 in D Minor* (*Choral*) in introducing texts sung by soloists and chorus; and that of certain chamber works by Schubert in introducing music from his own songs (settings of poems from the German folk anthology *Des Knaben Wunderhorn* [*The Youth's Magic Horn*] or of poems by himself in a folk style).

These procedures, together with Mahler's own tense and rhetorical style, phenomenally vivid orchestration, and ironic use of popular-style music, resulted in three symphonies of unprecedentedly wide contrasts but unified by his unmistakable creative personality and his firm com-

mand of symphonic structure. The program of the purely orchestral *Symphony No. 1 in D Major* (one of the five movements of which was later discarded) is autobiographical of his youth: the joy of life becomes clouded over by an obsession with death in the macabre "Funeral March in the Manner of Callot" (basically a parody of popular music), which is eventually routed in the arduous and brilliant finale. The five-movement *Symphony No. 2* begins with the death obsession (the first movement's "funeral ceremony") and culminates in an avowal of the Christian belief in immortality (a huge finale portraying the Day of Judgment and ending with a setting of the 18th-century German writer Friedrich Klopstock's "Resurrection" ode involving soloists and chorus). The even vaster *Symphony No. 3*, also including a soloist and chorus, presents in six movements a Dionysiac vision of a great chain of being, moving from inanimate nature to human consciousness and the redeeming love of God.

The religious element in these works is highly significant. Mahler's disturbing early background, coupled with his lack of an inherited Jewish faith (his father was a freethinker), resulted in a state of metaphysical torment, which he resolved temporarily by identifying himself with Christianity. That this was a genuine impulse there can be no doubt, even if there was an element of expediency in his becoming baptized, early in 1897, because it made it easier for him to be appointed to the Vienna Opera post. The ten years there represent his more balanced middle period. His newfound faith and his new high office brought a full and confident maturity, which was further stabilized by his marriage in 1902 to Alma Maria Schindler, who bore him two daughters, in 1902 and 1904.

Middle period. As director of the Vienna Opera (and for a time of the Vienna Philharmonic Concerts), Mahler achieved an unprecedented standard of interpretation and performance, which proved an almost unapproachable model for those who followed him. A fanatical idealist, he drove himself and his artists with a ruthless energy that proved a continual inspiration and with a complete disregard for personal considerations that won him many enemies who worked for his dismissal. At this time too, he made a number of tours and became famous over much of Europe as a conductor. He continued his recently acquired habit of devoting his summer vacations, in the Austrian Alps, to composing; and since, in his case, this involved a ceaseless expenditure of spiritual and nervous energy, he thereby placed an intolerable double strain on his frail constitution.

Importance as an interpreter

Most of the works of this middle period reflect the fierce dynamism of Mahler's full maturity. An exception is *Symphony No. 4*, which is more of a pendant to the first period: conceived in six movements (two of which were eventually discarded), it has a *Wunderhorn* song finale for soprano, which was originally intended as a movement for *Symphony No. 3* and which evokes a naïve peasant conception of the Christian heaven. At the same time, in dispensing with an explicit program and a chorus and coming near to the normal orchestral symphony, it does foreshadow the middle-period trilogy, *Nos. 5, 6,* and *7.* These are all purely orchestral, with a new, hard-edged, contrapuntal clarity of instrumentation, and devoid of programs altogether, yet each clearly embodies a spiritual conflict that reaches a conclusive resolution. *No. 5* and *No. 7* (both in five movements) move from darkness to light, though the light seems not the illumination of any afterlife but the sheer exhilaration of life on Earth. Between them stands the work Mahler regarded as his *Tragic Symphony*—the four-movement *No. 6 in A Minor*, which moves out of darkness only with difficulty, and then back into total night. From these three symphonies onward, he ceased to adapt his songs as whole sections or movements, but in each he introduced subtle allusions, either to his *Wunderhorn* songs or to his settings of poems by Friedrich Rückert, including the cycle *Kindertotenlieder* (*Songs on the Deaths of Children*).

At the end of this period he composed his monumental *Symphony No. 8 in E Flat Major* for eight soloists, dou-

Composition of *Symphony of a Thousand*

ble choir, and orchestra—a work known as the *Symphony of a Thousand*, owing to the large forces it requires, though Mahler gave it no such title. This stands apart, as a later reversion to the expansive metaphysical tendencies of the first period, and represents a consummation of them: the first continuously choral and orchestral symphony ever composed. It could be called at once a massive statement of human aspirations and a cry for illumination, from both the religious and the humanistic points of view. The first of its two parts, equivalent to a symphonic first movement, is a setting of the medieval Catholic Pentecost hymn *Veni Creator Spiritus;* part two, amalgamating the three movement-types of the traditional symphony, has for its text the mystical closing scene of Goethe's *Faust* drama (the scene of Faust's redemption). The work marked the climax of Mahler's confident maturity, since what followed was disaster—of which, he believed, he had had a premonition in composing his *Tragic Symphony, No. 6.* This work had revealed for the first time a superstitious element in his personality. The finale originally contained three climactic blows with a large hammer, representing "the three blows of fate which fall on a hero, the last one felling him as a tree is felled" (he subsequently removed the final blow from the score). Afterward he identified these as presaging the three blows that fell on himself in 1907, the last of which portended his own death: his resignation was demanded at the Vienna Opera, his three-year-old daughter Maria died, and a doctor diagnosed his fatal heart disease.

Last period. Thus began Mahler's last period, in which, at the age of 47, he became a wanderer again. He was obliged to make a new reputation for himself, as a conductor in the United States, directing performances at the Metropolitan Opera and becoming conductor of the Philharmonic Society of New York; yet he went back each summer to the Austrian countryside to compose his last works. He returned finally to Vienna, to die there, on May 18, 1911.

The three works comprising his last-period trilogy, none of which he ever heard, are *Das Lied von der Erde* (*The Song of the Earth*), *Symphony No. 9,* and *Symphony No. 10 in F Sharp Major,* left unfinished in the form of a comprehensive full-length sketch (though a full-length performing version has been made posthumously). The first of the three again revealed Mahler's superstition: beginning as a song cycle (to Chinese poems in German translations), it grew into "A Symphony for Tenor, Baritone (or Contralto) and Orchestra." Yet, he would not call it "Symphony No. 9," believing, on the analogy of Beethoven and Bruckner, that a ninth symphony must be its composer's last. When he afterward began the actual No. 9, he said, half jokingly, that the danger was over, since it was "really the tenth"; but in fact, that symphony became his last, and No. 10 remained in sketch form when he died.

This last-period trilogy, Mahler's most profoundly personal achievement, marked an even more decisive break with the past than had the middle-period trilogy. It represents a threefold attempt to come to terms with modern man's fundamental problem—the reality of death, which in his case had effectively destroyed the religious faith he had opposed to death as an imagined event. *Das Lied von der Erde*—a six-movement "song-cycle symphony" as opposed to the two-part "oratorio symphony," No. 8—views the evanescence of all things human in veiled poetic terms—sardonic, wistful, and grief stricken by turns—until it finds a sad consolation in the beauty of the Earth that endures after the individual is no longer alive to see it.

Confrontation with death in the *Ninth Symphony*

In the four-movement No. 9, purely orchestral, the confrontation with death becomes an anguished personal one, evoking horror and bitterness in Mahler's most modern and prophetic movement, the "Rondo-Burleske," and culminating in a finale of heartbroken resignation. The finales of both these works end with an extraordinary, long-drawn disintegration of the musical texture, suggesting dissolution; and the more extreme case in No. 9 was for long thought to be Mahler's final comment on human

existence. Growing familiarity with the sketch of *No. 10,* however, has suggested that he broke through to a more positive attitude: its five movements deal with the same conflict as the two preceding works, but the resignation attained at the end of the finale is entirely serene and affirmative.

Assessment. Modern critical opinion recognizes Mahler's powerful influence during a period of musical transition. In his works may be found pervasive elements foreshadowing the radical methods employed in the 20th century: these elements include "progressive tonality" (ending a work in a different key from the initial one); dissolution of tonality (obscuring the perception of key through the constant use of chromaticism or harmonies not belonging to that key); a breakaway from harmony produced by the entire orchestra in favour of a contrapuntal texture (based on interwoven melodies) for groups of solo instruments within the full orchestra; the principal of continually varying themes rather than merely restating them; ironic quotation of popular styles and of sounds from everyday life (bird calls, bugle signals, etc.); and, on the other hand, a new way of formally unifying the symphony through the adoption of techniques subtly derived from Liszt's "cyclic" method (the carrying over of themes from one movement of a work to others).

In terms of the personal content of his art, it can be said of Mahler, more than of any other composer, that he lived out the spiritual torment of disinherited modern man in his art, and that the man is the music.

MAJOR WORKS

CANTATA: *Das klagende Lied* (completed 1880).
SYMPHONIES: *Symphony No. 1 in D Major* (1888; originally subtitled *Titan*); *Symphony No. 2,* with soprano, contralto, and chorus (1894; begins in C minor and ends in E flat major, popular title *Resurrection*); *Symphony No. 3 in D Major* (1896; often wrongly said to be in D minor, originally subtitled *Eine Sommermorgentraum*); *Symphony No. 4,* with soprano (1900; begins in G major and ends in E major, popularly called *Ode to Heavenly Joy*); *Symphony No. 5* (1902; begins in C sharp minor and ends in D major, popularly called *Giant*); *Symphony No. 6 in A Minor* (1904; popular title *Tragic*); *Symphony No. 7* (1905; begins in G minor and ends in C major, often wrongly said to be in E minor, popularly called *Song of the Night*); *Symphony No. 8 in E Flat Major,* for eight soloists, double chorus, and orchestra (1907; popular title *Symphony of a Thousand*); Symphony, *Das Lied von der Erde,* for tenor, baritone (or contralto), and orchestra (1908); *Symphony No. 9* (1910; begins in D major and ends in D flat major); *Symphony No. 10 in F Sharp Major* (full-length sketch only, realized in a performing version by D. Cooke).
SONGS: *Lieder und Gesänge aus der Jugendzeit,* 14 songs for voice and piano, mainly to poems from *Des Knaben Wunderhorn* (1880–88); *Lieder eines fahrenden Gesellen,* cycle of four songs for voice and orchestra to texts by the composer (1883–85); *Des Knaben Wunderhorn,* ten songs for voice and orchestra (1888–96); "Revelge" and "Der Tamboursg'sell," two songs to poems from *Des Knaben Wunderhorn* (1899–1901); *Kindertotenlieder,* cycle of five songs to poems by Rückert (1901–04); *Fünf Lieder nach Rückert,* five songs to poems by Rückert (1901–04).

BIBLIOGRAPHY. A critical collected edition of Mahler's works is in the process of being published by the International Gustav Mahler Society of Vienna; the society possesses most of the autographs and issues a yearly bulletin. An irregular periodical, *Chord and Discord,* devoted to the study of Mahler and Bruckner, is issued by the Bruckner Society of America. The chief source book on the composer's life is that by his wife, ALMA MARIA MAHLER, *Gustav Mahler: Erinnerungen und Briefe* (1940; Eng. trans. rev. and enl. by D.C. MITCHELL, *Gustav Mahler: Memories and Letters,* 1968). Two important memoirs are B. WALTER, *Gustav Mahler* (1957; Eng. trans., 1958); and N. BAUCER-LECHNER, *Erinnerungen an Gustav Mahler* (1923; the only published volume of letters is *Briefe Gustav Mahlers* (1924). A first volume of a definitive biography (coupled with critical study) is D.C. MITCHELL, *Gustav Mahler: The Early Years* (1958); this, in conjunction with H.F. REDLICH, *Bruckner and Mahler,* 2nd ed. (1963), provides a large but not comprehensive bibliography. A notable critical study is D. NEWLIN, *Bruckner, Mahler, Schoenberg* (1947); P. BEKKER, *Gustav Mahlers Sinfonien* (1921), offers an exhaustive musical analysis of the symphonies.

(D.V.Co.)

Maḥmūd of Ghazna

A 10th–11th-century ruler of the kingdom of Ghazna (modern Ghaznī), originally comprising modern Afghanistan and the northeastern part of modern Iran, Maḥmūd made his kingdom the centre of a vast empire including at its zenith Pakistan and most of Iran. Maḥmūd also established the Afghan city of Ghazna as a cultural centre that rivalled Baghdad, which was the metropolis of Islām.

Maḥmūd was born in 971, the son of Sebüktigin, a Turkish slave, who in 977 became ruler of Ghazna. When Maḥmūd ascended the throne in 998 at the age of 27, he already showed remarkable administrative ability and statesmanship.

Early years

At the time of his accession, Ghazna was a small kingdom, comprising modern Afghanistan and the northeastern portion of modern Iran. The young and ambitious Maḥmūd aspired to be a great monarch, and in more than 20 successful expeditions he amassed the wealth with which to lay the foundation of a vast empire that eventually included Kashmir, the Punjab, and a great part of Iran.

During the first two years of his reign Maḥmūd consolidated his position in Ghazna. Though an independent ruler, for political reasons he gave nominal allegiance to the ʿAbbāsid caliph in Baghdad, and the caliph, in return, recognized him as the legitimate ruler of the lands he occupied and encouraged him in his conquests.

Maḥmūd is said to have vowed to invade India once a year and, in fact, led about 17 such expeditions. The first large-scale campaign began in 1001 and the last ended in 1026. The first expeditions were aimed against the Punjab and northeastern India, while in his last campaign Maḥmūd reached Somnāth on the southern coast of Gujarāt.

Annexation of the Punjab

His chief antagonist in northern India was Jaipāl, the ruler of the Punjab. When, in 1001, Maḥmūd marched on India at the head of 15,000 horse troops, Jaipāl met him with 12,000 horse troops, 30,000 foot soldiers, and 300 elephants. In a battle near Peshāwar the Indians, though superior in numbers and equipment, fell back under the onslaught of the Muslim horse, leaving behind 15,000 dead. After falling into the hands of the victors, Jaipāl, with 15 of his relatives and officers, was finally released. But the raja could not bear his defeat, and after abdicating in favour of his son, Ānandpāl, he mounted his own funeral pyre and perished in the flames.

Ānandpāl appealed to the other Indians rajas for help. Some replied in person, others sent armies. The Indian women sold their jewels to finance a huge army. When, at last, in 1008, Maḥmūd met the formidable force thus raised, the two armies lay facing each other between Und and Peshāwar for 40 days. The Sultan finally succeeded in enticing the Indians to attack him. A force of 30,000 Khokars, a fierce, primitive tribe, charged both flanks of the Sultan's army with such ferocity that Maḥmūd was about to call a retreat. But at this critical moment Ānandpāl's elephant, panic-stricken, took flight. The Indians, believing that their leader was turning tail, fled from the battlefield strewn with their dead and dying. This momentous victory facilitated Maḥmūd's advance into the heart of India.

After annexing the Punjab, and returning with immense booty, the Sultan set about to transform Ghazna into a great centre of art and culture. He patronized scholars, established colleges, laid out gardens, and built mosques, palaces, and caravansaries. Maḥmūd's example was followed by his nobles and courtiers, and Ghazna soon transformed into the most brilliant cultural centre in Central Asia.

In 1024 the Sultan set out on his last famous expedition to the southern coast of Kāthiāwăr along the Arabian Sea, where he sacked the city of Somnāth and its renowned Hindu temple. Maḥmūd returned home in 1026. The last years of his life he spent in fighting the Seljuq and other Central Asian tribes threatening his empire. He died in Ghazna in 1030.

Maḥmūd was the first to carry the banner of Islām into the heart of India. To some Muslim writers he was a great champion of his faith, an inspired leader endowed with supernatural powers. Most Indian historians, on the other hand, emphasize his military exploits and depict him as "an insatiable invader and an intrepid marauder." Neither view is correct. In his Indian expeditions he kept his sights set mainly on the fabulous wealth of India stored in its temples. Though a zealous champion of Islām, he never treated his Indian subjects harshly nor did he ever impose the Islāmic religion on them. He maintained a large contingent of Hindu troops, commanded by their own countrymen, whom he employed with great success against his religionists in Central Asia. Conversion to Islām was never a condition of service in the Sultan's army.

Great as a warrior, the Sultan was no less eminent as a patron of art and literature. Attracted by his munificence and encouragement, many outstanding scholars settled in Ghazna, among them al-Bīrūnī, the mathematician, philosopher, astronomer, and Sanskrit scholar, and Ferdowsī, the Persian author of the great epic poem Shāh-nāmeh. Maḥmūd's conquest of northern India furthered the exchange of trade and ideas between the Indian subcontinent and the Muslim world. It helped to disseminate Indian culture in foreign lands. Similarly, Muslim culture, which by now had assimilated and developed the cultures of such ancient peoples as the Egyptians, the Greeks, the Romans, and the Syrians, found its way into India, and many Muslim scholars, writers, historians, and poets began to settle there.

BIBLIOGRAPHY. WOLSELEY HAIG in The Cambridge History of India, vol. 3 (1965), provides a reliable account of the Ghaznavid period. RAMESH MAJUMDAR et al., An Advanced History of India, 3rd ed. (1967), includes a short sketch of this period. See also the relevant chapters in A Cultural History of Afghanistan by MOHAMMED ALI (1964); and S.M. IKRAM and PERCIVAL SPEAR, The Cultural Heritage of Pakistan (1955).

(M.Al.)

Maimonides, Moses

Moses Maimonides (Greek for Hebrew ben Maimon, "son of Maimon"), the foremost intellectual figure of medieval Judaism, made lasting contributions as a jurist, philosopher, and scientist. His epoch-making influence on Judaism extended also to the larger world. His philosophic work, after it was translated into Latin, influenced the great medieval Scholastic writers, and even later thinkers, such as Spinoza and Leibniz, found in his work a source for some of their ideas. His medical writings constitute a significant chapter in the history of medical science.

Life

He was born in 1135 to a distinguished family in Córdoba (Cordova), Spain. The young Moses studied with his learned father, Maimon, and other masters and at an early age astonished his teachers by his remarkable depth and versatility. Before Moses reached his 13th birthday, his peaceful world was suddenly disturbed by the ravages of war and persecution.

As part of Islāmic Spain, Córdoba accorded its citizens full religious freedom. But now the Islāmic Mediterranean world was shaken by a revolutionary and fanatical Islāmic sect, the Almohads (al-Muwaḥḥidūn, "the Unitarians"), who captured Córdoba in 1148, leaving the Jewish community faced with the grim alternative of submitting to Islām or leaving the city. The Maimons temporized by practicing their Judaism in the privacy of their homes, while disguising their ways in public as far as possible to appear like Muslims. The Maimons remained in Córdoba for some 11 years, and Maimonides continued his education in Judaic studies as well as in the scientific disciplines in vogue at the time.

When the double life proved too irksome to maintain in Córdoba, the Maimon family finally left the city about 1159 to settle in Fez, Morocco. Although it was also under Almohad rule, Fez was presumably more promising than Córdoba, because there the Maimons would be strangers and their disguise would be more likely to go undetected. Moses continued his studies in his favourite subjects, rabbinics and Greek philosophy, and added medicine to them. Fez proved to be no more than a short respite, however. In 1165 Rabbi Judah ibn Shoshan, with whom Moses had studied, was arrested as a practicing Jew and was found guilty and then executed. This was a sign to the Maimon family to move again, this time to Palestine, which was in a depressed economic state and could not offer them the basis of a livelihood. After a few months they moved again, now to Egypt, settling in Fostat, near Cairo. There Jews were free to practice their faith openly, though any Jew who had once submitted to Islām courted death if he relapsed to Judaism. Moses himself was once accused of being a renegade Muslim, but he was able to prove that he had never really adopted the faith of Islām and so was exonerated.

Though Egypt was a haven from harassment and persecution, Moses was soon assailed by personal problems. His father died shortly after the arrival in Egypt, and when his younger brother, David, a prosperous jewelry merchant, on whom Moses leaned for support, died in a shipwreck, taking the entire family fortune with him, Moses was left as the sole support of his family. He could not turn to the rabbinate because in those days the rabbinate was conceived of as a public service that did not offer its practitioners any remuneration. Pressed by economic necessity, Moses took advantage of his medical studies and became a practicing physician. His fame as a physician spread rapidly and he soon became the court physician to the sultan Saladin, the famous Muslim military leader, and to his son al-Afḍal. He also continued a private practice and lectured before his fellow physicians at the state hospital. At the same time he became the leading member of the Jewish community, teaching in public and helping his people with various personal and communal problems.

Maimonides married late in life and was the father of a son, Abraham, who was to make his mark in his own right in the world of Jewish scholarship.

Works   The writings of Maimonides were prolific and varied. His earliest work, composed at the age of 16, was the *Millot ha-Higgayon* ("Treatise on Logical Terminology"), a study of various technical terms that were employed in logic and metaphysics. Another of his early works, like the work on logic written in Arabic, was the "Essay on the Calendar" (Hebrew title: *Ma'amar ha-'ibur*).

The first of Maimonides' major works, begun at the age of 23, was his commentary on the Mishna, *Kitāb al-Sirāj*, also written in Arabic. The Mishna is a compendium of decisions in Jewish law that date from earliest times to the 3rd century. Maimonides' commentary clarified individual words and phrases, frequently citing relevant information in archaeology, theology, or science. Possibly the work's most striking feature is a series of introductory essays dealing with general philosophic issues touched on in the Mishna. One of these essays summarizes the teachings of Judaism in a creed of Thirteen Articles of Faith.

He completed the commentary on the Mishna at the age of 33, after which he began his magnum opus, the code of Jewish law, on which he also laboured for ten years. Bearing the name of *Mishne Torah* ("The Torah Reviewed") and written in a lucid Hebrew style, the code offers a brilliant systematization of all Jewish law and doctrine. He wrote two other works in Jewish law of lesser scope: the *Sefer ha-mitzwot* ("The Book of Precepts"), a digest of law for the less sophisticated reader, written in Arabic; and the *Hilkhot ha-Yerushalmi* ("Laws of Jerusalem"), a digest of the laws in the Palestinian Talmud that was written in Hebrew.

His next major work, which he began in 1176 and on which he laboured for 15 years, was his classic in religious philosophy, the *Dalālat al-ḥā'irīn* (*The Guide of the Perplexed*), later known under its Hebrew title as the *More nevukhim*. A plea for what he called a more rational philosophy of Judaism, it constituted a major contribution to the accommodation between science, philosophy, and religion. It was written in Arabic and sent as a private communication to his favourite disciple, Joseph ibn Aknin. The work was translated into Hebrew in Maimonides' lifetime and later into Latin. It was subsequent-

ly translated into most European languages and has exerted a marked influence on the history of religious thought.

Maimonides also wrote a number of minor works, occasional essays dealing with current problems that faced the Jewish community, and he maintained an extensive correspondence with scholars, students, and community leaders. Among his minor works those considered to be most important are *Iggert Teman* (*Epistle to Yemen*), *Iggeret ha-shemad* or *Ma'amar Qiddush ha-Shem* ("Letter on Apostasy"), and *Iggeret le-qahal Marsilia* ("Letter on Astrology," or, literally, "Letter to the Community of Marseilles"). He also wrote a number of works dealing with medicine, including a popular miscellany of health rules, which he dedicated to the sultan, al-Afḍal. A mid-20th-century historian, Waldemar Schweisheimer, has said of Maimonides' medical writings: "Maimonides' medical teachings are not antiquated at all. His writings, in fact, are in some respects astonishingly modern in tone and contents."

Maimonides complained often that the pressures of his many duties robbed him of peace and undermined his health. He died in 1204 and was buried in Tiberias, in the Holy Land, where his grave continues to be a shrine drawing a constant stream of pious pilgrims.

Posthumous reputation

Maimonides' advanced views aroused opposition in his own lifetime, and this opposition continued after his death. In 1233 one zealot, Rabbi Solomon of Montpellier, in southern France, instigated the church authorities to burn *The Guide of the Perplexed* as a dangerously heretical book. But the controversy died down after some time, and Maimonides came to be recognized as a pillar of the traditional faith—his creed became part of the orthodox liturgy—as well as the greatest of the Jewish philosophers.

BIBLIOGRAPHY. MAIMONIDES' *Guide of the Perplexed*, ed. by SHLOMO PINES (1963), a new translation from the Arabic with an introduction and notes, and with an introductory essay by LEO STRAUSS, one of the leading authorities on Maimonides today; SALO BARON, "Moses Maimonides," in SIMON NOVECK (ed.), *Great Jewish Personalities in Ancient and Medieval Times* (1959), a succinct, popular essay by a noted historian, describing the essential facts in the life of Maimonides and a characterization of his major works, and (ed.), *Essays on Maimonides* (1941), a commemorative volume marking the 800th anniversary of the birthday of Maimonides, including an essay dealing with his medical writings; BEN ZION BOKSER, *Legacy of Maimonides*, rev. ed. (1962), an interpretation of the world outlook of Maimonides, with a brief biographical sketch; A. COHEN, *The Teachings of Maimonides* (1927), a brief biographical sketch, followed by selected passages from his legal and philosophic writing, arranged according to a conceptual framework; SOLOMON ZEITLIN, *Maimonides* (1935), a biography, with a detailed characterization of his major writings.

(B.Z.B.)

Maine

Maine, the largest of the six New England states, lies at the northeastern tip of the contiguous United States. Its 33,215 square miles (86,027 square kilometres), including 2,295 square miles of water area, nearly one-half the total area of New England, are bounded on the northwest and northeast by the Canadian provinces of Quebec and New Brunswick, respectively, and on the west by New Hampshire. Its famed rocky coastline angles from southwest to northeast, along the Atlantic Ocean. Maine's capital has been Augusta since its admission, in 1820, as the 23rd state of the Union.

Location and general character

With a 1970 population of just under 1,000,000 persons, Maine is the most sparsely populated state east of the Mississippi River. More than 80 percent of its area is under forest cover. It is also, by most statistical measures, an economically depressed state; but the rugged beauty and challenge of its climate and landscape and the character of its people have given Maine an importance beyond its economic and political power. Limited economic growth, in fact, has contributed to the preservation of much of its natural appearance. Maine's economy remains largely dependent upon the extractive industries and the recreational opportunities associated with its status as a major U.S. vacationland, and the state epitomizes the increasingly difficult national choices between preservation of environmental quality or potential economic expansion. Politically, Maine was long regarded as a stronghold of the Republican Party, but it has been a two-party state in recent years. (For information on related topics, see the articles UNITED STATES; UNITED STATES, HISTORY OF THE; and NORTH AMERICA.)

THE HISTORY OF MAINE

The
Indian
natives

Algonkian Indians were the earliest known settlers in Maine. Descended from Ice Age hunters, they lived along the river valleys and the coasts, hunting and fishing and planting crops. Few of them survived the arrival of the European settlers. But the earlier tribes are remembered in numerous place-names; in the sites of their camps and burial grounds; in ancient trails and water routes; in the use of the canoe, the snowshoe, and the toboggan; in corn, beans, and squash; and in the revived concern for man's relation with the natural environment.

Explorations and disputes. The first European explorations of Maine are shrouded in mystery. Evidence that the Norsemen landed on the coast is scant and disputed, and serious questions exist about some of the early British claims based on John Cabot's voyages in the late 1490s. Portuguese, Spanish, French, and English explorers did probe the islands, the bays, and the rivers of the "maine" throughout the 16th century; and by the first decade of the 17th century, summer fisheries had been established on some of the coastal islands and fur trade had begun with the Indians.

The French and English crowns claimed the same territory; and the area was an intermittent battleground between the English, the Indians, and the French from 1615 until 1675 and a constant battleground from that date until 1763, when the British conquered the French in eastern Canada.

Maine was given separate provincial status in New England under royal patents granted by Charles I. The Puritans of Massachusetts took over the territory when the proprietor, Sir Ferdinando Gorges, backed the losing side in the British Civil War. Frontier settlers in Maine chafed under Massachusetts rule; but the merchants of the coastal towns resisted the separation movement until the War of 1812, when popular resentment against the failure of the Massachusetts Commonwealth to protect the District of Maine against British raids tipped the scales in favour of separation. Maine entered the Union as a free state under the Missouri Compromise of 1820, offsetting the simultaneous admission of Missouri without restrictions on the ownership of slaves.

Statehood. Maine intrigued entrepreneurs, who hoped to make their fortune in furs, fisheries, timber, and land development. The first three proved to be lucrative for a few; but the climate, border troubles, and the knowledge of the more fertile land of the newer territories to the west curtailed settlement of the area before and after statehood. The greatest period of economic growth came between 1830 and 1860, when lumber, ice, granite, lime (extracted from limestone), and fishing and shipbuilding dominated the state's economy. Coastal communities flourished and railroads developed as Maine men and ships traded around the world.

The Civil War and the Industrial Revolution diverted men and capital from Maine in the last decades of the 19th century. Textiles and paper products became the primary sources of manufacturing employment, while fisheries and agriculture continued as important but uncertain sources of income. The details of economic activity changed during the first half of the 20th century, but the overall picture remained one of precarious prosperity and extreme susceptibility to swings in the national economy.

Political development. Maine's social and political history has been dominated by struggles against the adversity of frontier life and economic limitations, coupled with strong drives within the state for social reform, including world peace, antislavery, prohibition, and women's suffrage. Jeffersonian and Jacksonian Democrats held sway from statehood until the rise of the Whigs and the emergence of the Republican Party. The Abolitionist movement gave the Republican Party its start in Maine in 1854, and the Grand Old Party dominated the state for almost a century. Democrats scored temporary gains in the elections of 1910 and 1912 and in the Depression elections of 1932 and 1934, but it was not until 1954 that sustained competition began to develop between the major parties.

THE NATURAL AND HUMAN LANDSCAPE

The natural environment. *Surface features.* The Appalachian Mountain chain extends into Maine from New Hampshire, terminating in Mt. Katahdin, at 5,268 feet (1,606 metres) the state's tallest peak. The western and northwestern borders adjoining New Hampshire and Quebec have the most rugged terrain, with numerous glacier-scoured peaks, lakes, and narrow valleys. South and east of the mountain areas lie rolling hills and smaller mountains and the broad river valleys of the Saco, the Androscoggin, the Kennebec, and the Penobscot. From Kittery, at the southern tip of the state, to Cape Elizabeth, just southwest of Portland, the state's largest city, long sand beaches are interrupted here and there by rocky promontories. North and east of Cape Elizabeth the coastline is a series of peninsulas, narrow estuaries, bays, fjords, and coves, once mountains and valleys that glaciers of the Ice Age pushed beneath the ocean. The Camden Hills and Mount Desert Island are the largest of the coastal mountains. The tides along this famous rockbound coast are among the strongest in the world, running between 12 and 24 feet. Off the coast lie about 1,200 islands, some no more than rocky ledges, others topped with trees and sheltering the homes of fishermen, lobstermen, and summer people. All told, the Maine coast—the bays, islands, and inlets washed by the tides—totals some 3,500 miles.

Waters and soils. Most of Maine's river systems flow from north to south. The St. John River and its principal tributary, the Allagash, are the major exceptions, flowing north and then east along the northern border of Maine and turning south through New Brunswick, Canada, to the sea. The state is dotted with 2,500 lakes and ponds, the largest of which is Moosehead Lake (120 square miles). Soils in southwestern Maine were formed primarily from granite; coastal, central, and eastern soils are composed of shale, sand, and limestone; while the soils of Aroostook County, in the northeast, which are among the most productive in the state, are largely composed of caribou loam.

Climate. Maine has three relatively well-defined climatic areas: southern interior, coastal, and northern. The southern and coastal regions are influenced by air masses from the south and west. North of the land dividing the St. John and Penobscot River basins, air masses moving down the St. Lawrence River basin tend to prevail. Mean annual temperatures range from 37° to 39° F (3° to 4° C) in the north and from 43° to 45° F (6° to 7° C) in the southern interior and coastal regions. Mean temperatures are about 62° F (17° C) throughout the state during the summer and 20° F (−7° C) during the winter. About 60 percent of the days are sunny, and annual precipitation averages 40 to 46 inches. Snowfall averages more than 100 inches in the northern area and the higher elevations.

Vegetation and animal life. Flora and fauna represent a combination of subarctic and Appalachian species. Forests include heavy stands of pine, spruce, and fir among the hardwoods. Among the fauna are the deer, moose, black bear, fox, lynx, hare, raccoon, porcupine, skunk, and woodchuck. Songbirds, lake birds, seabirds, and many game species abound throughout the state. Among the many aquatic species are the seal, whale, porpoise, lobster, shrimp, clam, haddock, cod, mackerel, Atlantic and landlocked salmon, and many freshwater game fishes.

Patterns of human settlement. *Traditional regions.* Coastal Maine is best known, from anecdotes and dialect stories, as the traditional home of the "Downeast Yankee." Many communities in that region, now relatively

Parks of Maine.
(Left) Pines along the ocean near Bar Harbour, on Mount Desert Island, site of Acadia National Park. (Right) Mt. Katahdin in Baxter State Park.
(Left) A. Devaney, Inc., (Right) Russ Kinne—Photo Researchers

isolated from the principal avenues of highway traffic, were once bustling centres of ocean commerce and river trade. Population movements have blurred some of the regional differences; but within the coastal region there are three areas, each with its own sense of identity. The southwestern coast, predominantly a resort area, extends from Kittery to the Portland metropolitan region on Casco Bay. The midcoast region, marked by a combination of fishing and maritime activities and vacation and retirement homes and resort centres, runs from Bath (long a shipbuilding centre) and the mouth of the Kennebec River to Belfast, on the western shore of Penobscot Bay. The eastern coastal region begins on the eastern shore of Penobscot Bay and ends at Calais, on the St. Croix River, at the New Brunswick border.

Central and southern Maine form a contiguous region covering the southern half of the state, from the New Hampshire border to the Penobscot River. It contains the bulk of the population and of its industrial and commercial activities. The western border areas of York, Cumberland, Oxford, and Franklin counties form a subregion, but increased mobility is eroding the distinctive community and speech patterns of those sections.

Aroostook County, a region by itself, is often referred to as "the" county. Central and southern Aroostook areas were settled by English and Irish immigrants whose speech patterns continue to resemble those of their neighbours across the border in New Brunswick more than they do the broad *a*'s and dropped *r*'s of the rest of Maine speech. The St. John Valley along the northern border of Aroostook County was settled by Acadians of French descent from Nova Scotia and New Brunswick. The communities of the valley retain their French character and speech.

Rural and small-town life. Maine's rocky terrain limited the size of farms in most areas of the state. With the exception of Aroostook County and a few broad valleys in the central region, fields are small and, in many cases, marked by old stone walls or separated by wooded lots.

Character of Maine's communities

Interior rural communities vary according to the terrain and their economic history. Some consist only of a crossroads settlement with a store, gas station, post office, and three or four homes; others have a church, school, a few stores, and small establishments clustered around a millsite; still others have the traditional village green, often with the typical white frame, single-spired New England church, as well as such social centres as a grange hall. Communities that prospered during the height of the lumber trade are marked, where the terrain permits, by broad avenues and imposing wooden homes.

Coastal communities are similar, with commercial areas on the waterfront and social, cultural, and residential centres on higher ground.

Urban centres. Maine's largest urban communities are Portland, Lewiston-Auburn, Bangor, Waterville, and Augusta. Portland is the centre of a metropolitan area (population about 107,000) spreading inland and around the harbour city, which lies on Casco Bay. It is the commercial and transportation hub of the state, whose economy has a growing and diversified industrial base, including paper manufacturing, steel fabrication, light manufacturing, and assembly. Bangor (about 33,000), an old lumbering town at the head of navigation on the Penobscot River, is the commercial centre for eastern and northern Maine. Augusta (about 22,000), the state capital, lies at the head of navigation on the Kennebec River. State government is the principal source of employment for the city, but it is also the site of textile, shoe, and paper industries.

The twin cities of Lewiston and Auburn form the second largest urban centre in the state (about 65,000). Long dependent on textile and shoe manufacturing, the two communities have pursued aggressive industrial development programs and now are diversified into electronics and light manufacturing. They also serve as a commercial and trade centre for the Androscoggin Valley and eastern Oxford County. Waterville (about 18,000), north of Augusta on the Kennebec, with its neighbouring communities of Winslow and Fairfield, is a pulp-and-paper and textile centre, a commercial and trade centre for the central and northern Kennebec Valley.

THE PEOPLE OF MAINE

The mix of peoples. The original "Downeast Yankees" were English–Scotch-Irish Protestant immigrants who made the most substantial and persistent early European settlements in Maine. They set the style of dour and taciturn industry and dry wit that is characteristic of Maine legends and stories. Their descendants dominated the political and economic life of the state during most of its development and still comprise its largest population group, particularly in the smaller communities and rural areas.

Contrary to popular impressions, however, Yankees are not the sole inhabitants of Maine. Two groups of French descent make up the second largest ethnic bloc. The Acadians, originally from Brittany and Normandy, were driven out of Nova Scotia in 1763 by the British; many of them settled in the St. John Valley, which now forms the northern border of Maine, while others made the long trip to Louisiana. The later French-Canadian migration from Quebec province began with the growth of the lumber and textile industries following the Civil War. French is the primary language in much of the St. John Valley and the second language in Maine's industrial cities. Irish immigration began in the 18th century and continued into the 20th, and the Irish and the French make up the bulk of Maine's Roman Catholic population. French Huguenot and German settlements were made early near the coast. During the 1870s the state encouraged a Swedish settlement in Aroostook County as part of a program for agricultural development and population growth.

Among the relatively small population of the state, a number of ethnic groups of significant size are identifiable. Most of the remaining 2,200 members of the original American Indian population live on state reservations. The non-white population is less than one percent of the people.

Demographic trends. Maine's general population distribution still reflects the early patterns of settlement along the coast and the river valleys, with vast sections of the interior covered with forest and virtually uninhabited, except for occasional lumber encampments. Almost one-half of the population is concentrated in four southwestern counties: Androscoggin, Cumberland, Kennebec, and York. Slightly more than one-half of Maine's residents live in what are classified as urban places; but there are only three cities with 25,000 or more inhabitants (see above); about 30 percent live in communities of more than 10,000.

Between 1960 and 1970 Maine showed increasing evidence of suburban and exurban sprawl. The proportion of urban residents dropped slightly, and the central city areas of Portland, Auburn, and Bangor lost population. Lewiston's population increased by 975, but it had a net out-migration of 2,769 during the decade. Communities around those cities, and the rural areas beyond, had substantial population increases.

Two other demographic trends were noticeable between 1960 and 1970: the northern and eastern counties of Aroostook, Piscataquis, Penobscot, and Washington lost population, as did Oxford County on the western border, whereas the central, midcoast, and southern counties gained population; and the population flow from the huge metropolitan concentrations along the northeast coast spilled northward into southern Maine, where York County had the largest numerical and proportional growth in the state.

During the 1960s Maine suffered a net loss of 70,000 persons through emigration, about 7 percent of the 1960 population. The birthrate dropped from 24 per 1,000 inhabitants to 18 per 1,000, while the death rate remained constant. The drop in the birthrate was reflected in the sharp decline in the number of children under five years of age. The post-World War II baby boom can be measured in the larger number of residents between the ages of 15 and 25, and the birthrate decline that occurred during the Depression is visible in the smaller number of 30-to-40-year-old inhabitants.

The trends of the 1960s suggest that Maine's total population will continue to grow slowly. With the exception of those areas offering attractive and accessible recreational opportunities, Maine's rural areas in the central, eastern, and northern sections will continue to have problems of emigration; the midcoast, central, and southern industrial, commercial, and recreational areas, on the other hand, will feel increasing population pressures.

THE STATE'S ECONOMY

Maine's forest and waterpower resources invited exploitation through the early years of the Industrial Revolution, and skilled, low-cost manpower gave the state a longtime advantage in the textile and shoe industries. Those advantages faded as textile and shoe companies moved their operations to new factories in low-wage areas of the South and, more recently, overseas. Rich agricultural soils are scattered; and, with the exception of Aroostook County—where the potato is the main crop

Population growth and migration

—terrain and soil conditions make large-scale farming difficult. With the exception of lobster production, fishing is a marginal industry. As a result of these factors, Maine is a relatively poor state, with the lowest per capita income in New England.

Since 1955 the state government has promoted an active economic development program through the Department of Economic Development. The state-operated Maine Industrial Building Authority, the Maine Recreation Authority, and the privately sponsored Maine Development Credit Corporation have provided industrial and commercial loan guarantees. The state also has used the services and financial assistance of the federal Economic Development Administration and the Small Business Administration.

Economic resources and components. Maine's primary natural resources are timber, sand, gravel, limestone and building stone, fish, and shellfish. There are limited deposits of copper, zinc, feldspar, and semiprecious stones. Peat is mined for horticultural use. Soils and climate have contributed to the production of high-quality potatoes, apples, blueberries, and other fruits, and dairy products.

Manufactured products represent the largest component in the market value of Maine goods and services. Pulp and paper constitute the largest item in manufactured products, potatoes and poultry in farm income, and lobsters in the fishery industry. Tourists—attracted by Maine's picturesque lakes, streams, and coast and the opportunities for swimming, boating, fishing, hunting, hiking, and winter sports—account for a large portion of retail sales and service income.

Electrical power. About 60 percent of the electrical energy generated within the state of Maine is produced in steam plants, 38 percent at hydroelectric stations, and the remainder by diesel and gas-turbine units. Most of the state's potential hydroelectric sites have been developed. Notable exceptions are the sites of the proposed Dickey-Lincoln School project on the Upper St. John River and the proposed joint U.S.–Canada tidal power project on Passamaquoddy and Cobscook bays at the eastern end of the state. Both projects have been opposed by private utility companies and the St. John project by conservation groups as well. A consortium of Maine and other New England private power companies has undertaken the construction of a nuclear power plant at Wiscasset.

Labour and management. Relatively calm labour-management relations have prevailed in Maine in spite of the state's economic difficulties. Trade unions, strongest in the textile, shoe, and pulp-and-paper industries, have successfully fought off efforts to enact so-called right-to-work legislation. Chambers of commerce and trade associations are active in economic-development projects and state legislation. The principal employer organization is Associated Industries of Maine, which has concentrated most of its efforts on influencing state legislation affecting major industries.

Continuing economic problems. Maine's serious employment and income problems encourage a continued emphasis on industrial development. By the end of the 1960s there were signs of economic expansion, in part the result of population movements into the state from the south and in part the product of the state's economic development program. The latter developments, however, faced increased resistance from those who feared environmental degradation in the state. Proposed petroleum and petrochemical projects were the immediate focus of the controversy, but the conflict is certain to increase between those who want more jobs and higher income and those who want to preserve the existing attractiveness of Maine.

Transportation. Maine depends heavily on its 21,000 miles of roads for ground transportation. The 1,800 miles of railroad track carry freight but no longer carry passengers. Buses provide interstate, intrastate, and some suburban and urban passenger transportation. Portland and Searsport are the major seaports. State and private passenger and freight ferry services operate to many of the

State and private economic promotion

Hydroelectric production and potential

coastal islands; and Portland and Bar Harbor have ferry connections with Yarmouth, Nova Scotia. An airline operates from Presque Isle, Bangor, and Portland to points outside Maine; and commuter airlines provide intrastate and interstate service to other Maine communities. Some international nonscheduled air passenger and freight traffic is routed through Bangor International Airport.

ADMINISTRATION AND SOCIAL CONDITIONS

Government and politics. *The state level.* The constitution of the state, derived from that of the Commonwealth of Massachusetts, reflects the hangover of colonial suspicions toward royal governors. The governor is Maine's chief executive officer, but he is checked by a seven-member executive council elected biennially by the state legislature. Several constitutional officers, including the attorney general, the secretary of state, the auditor, and the state treasurer, are elected by the legislature, and, until 1971, state department heads, who must be confirmed by the council, were appointed for fixed terms. Repeated efforts to abolish the council have failed. But starting with the 1958 election, the governor's term was extended to four years, with a two-term limit; and in 1971 the legislature approved the consolidation of several departments and authorized the appointment of department heads whose terms coincided with that of the governor.

Executive, legis-
lature, and judiciary

The legislature, which is comprised of a 151-member house and a 32-member senate, is elected every two years. The president of the senate is the constitutional successor to the governor. Maine has a three-tiered judicial branch, including district judges, a superior court, and a supreme court. Separate probate courts serve at the county level.

Local government. Maine's 16 counties traditionally have provided an administrative framework for the superior court system, law enforcement, land records, and probate practice and for some road maintenance and construction functions. Town government, with the annual town meeting and a board of selectmen, prevails in most communities. Twenty-one communities operate under city charters. Professional managers are used in most cities and in many towns.

Finances. Local communities depend for revenues on property, automobile excise, and poll taxes (the last a requirement for hunting, driving, and other licenses, not for voting), on state aid for education, roads, and welfare, and on federal grants-in-aid. State revenues are obtained from a corporate and personal income tax, inheritance tax, sales and use taxes, motor fuel taxes, tobacco and alcoholic beverage taxes, licenses and miscellaneous taxes, and federal grants-in-aid.

Political life. With the election of 1954, traditional Republican dominance in Maine's state offices and national representation ended. From 1954 through 1970, Democrats won six of the eight elections for governor, ten of the 22 elections for the U.S. House of Representatives, and three of the six elections for the U.S. Senate. During the same period, the Republicans controlled all but one state legislature. Registered Republicans narrowly outnumbered Democrats, and most elections turned upon the large percentage of independent voters. Party officials are elected in local caucuses and state conventions. Nominations for county and state offices are obtained through primary elections, but as of 1971 Maine had no presidential-preference primary.

The social milieu. *Education.* Local governments are responsible for public elementary and secondary education, under the general supervision of the state board of education. Most rural areas are now served by multicommunity school administrative districts. The state operates technical institutes for post-secondary-school vocational training. The University of Maine, established in 1865 in Orono as a college of agriculture and mechanic arts, has been reorganized into a nine-branch system and offers a broad range of undergraduate and graduate curricula. Private liberal arts colleges include Bowdoin (Brunswick; 1794), Bates (Lewiston; 1864), and Colby (Waterville; 1813).

Welfare. Maine's chronic economic problems are reflected in the high incidence of poverty, with about one-third of the state's population living below the poverty line as of 1970 according to the State Office of Economic Opportunity (though federal-government data show less than half this percentage). The largest proportion of poverty is found in the rural counties, particularly the eastern coastal counties and Aroostook County. Public awareness of Maine's poverty problems and of the particular difficulties faced by the state's Indian and black populations has led to more vigorous efforts by community action groups, civil rights organizations, and health and housing associations to improve economic opportunity and to deal with the related problems of housing, education, and health. Local communities provide some assistance to the poor, but most poverty assistance is administered by the State Department of Health and Welfare.

CULTURAL LIFE AND INSTITUTIONS

Folk arts and artifacts. In its culture, as in its social and economic development, Maine reveals the attributes of both a struggling frontier community and an eclectic society immersed in commerce with other cultures. Folktales, songs, local humour, and the short stories and poems of native authors are direct, earthy, and filled with a sense of the awkward absurdities of man's attempt to subdue nature.

Cultural heritage

The tools of the woodsman, farmer, and fisherman are clean and simple, as are the lines of country homes, meetinghouses, and working boats. The great mansions of the old seaports, among some of the finest memorials to an earlier America, are filled with chairs, tables, chests, books, prints, hangings, screens, pottery, and bric-a-brac gathered on the many voyages of Maine's seamen to Europe and Asia, as well as with examples of the shipbuilders' and sailors' arts of wood carving and scrimshaw. Maine has, in addition, the unique contributions of such groups as the Shakers and its own local versions of the Federal, Greek Revival, Gothic, and Victorian periods of American architecture.

In recent years Maine has had a revival in crafts production, including pottery, metalworking, block and silkscreen printing, weaving, furniture making, and carving. State agencies, historical societies, museums, and local associations are engaged in preserving historic sites and in the collection, preservation, and presentation of materials on Maine's heritage.

Fine arts. Maine has been, and continues to be, the birthplace or the permanent or seasonal home of well-known figures in the American arts. They include such writers as Henry Wadsworth Longfellow, Harriet Beecher Stowe, Sarah Orne Jewett, Edward Arlington Robinson, and Edna St. Vincent Millay; the painters Winslow Homer, John Marin, Edward Hopper, and Andrew Wyeth; and composer Walter Piston. Active cultural programs are sponsored by the state's colleges and universities, museums, community symphonies, workshops and camps, and the numerous summer theatres.

Recreation. Maine's special attractions include Acadia National Park on Mount Desert Island, the first national park east of the Mississippi River; Baxter State Park, a 200,000-acre wilderness area surrounding Mt. Katahdin; the 92-mile Allagash Wilderness Waterway; and more than 40 state parks and historic sites.

The media. One of the more important aspects of Maine's heritage is its long line of newspapers, dating back to the *Falmouth Gazette*, first published in 1785. Maine now has nine daily, more than 30 local weekly, and two statewide weekly newspapers and a number of special and general-purpose periodical publications. Twenty-seven communities have radio stations, and there are seven commercial television stations in the state. A four-station public television network serves more than 90 percent of the state's populated area.

PROBLEMS AND PROSPECTS

The people of Maine have long struggled with the pain of economic adversity, but they have enjoyed a challenging and stimulating environment. What was once merely compensation for the rigours of their own lives now has become a major attraction for other Americans who are tired of the pressures and hazards of urban living. Maine's land and waters have become thereby more valuable and the prospects for higher income brighter—and the dangers to Maine's quality of life are greater. In the 1970s the citizens of the state were endeavouring to see whether they could achieve a balance between prosperity and those natural and human qualities that have made Maine unique in the nation.

BIBLIOGRAPHY. The most authoritative general history of Maine is still LOUIS C. HATCH (ed.), *Maine: A History,* 5 vol. (1919). RONALD F. BANKS (comp.), *A History of Maine: A Collection of Readings on the History of Maine, 1600–1970* (1969), provides a good sampling of contemporaneous sources. DORRIS A. ISAACSON (ed.), *Maine: A Guide Down-East,* 2nd ed. (1970), is a valuable introduction to contemporary Maine, with travel suggestions and bibliography. STANLEY B. ATTWOOD, *The Length and Breadth of Maine* (1946), is the authoritative work on Maine's geography and natural resources. The MAINE DEPARTMENT OF ECONOMIC DEVELOPMENT, *Maine Pocket Data Book: An Economic Analysis* (1970), is a useful collection of economic facts and analysis. The *Maine Register* (annual) is filled with facts and figures on elections, state government, organizations, and businesses. ISABELLE P. CONGDON, *Indian Tribes of Maine* (1961), is a good, brief account of Maine's Indians. PHILIP T. COOLIDGE, *History of the Maine Woods* (1963), a social and economic history of a dominant part of Maine life. Among the books that give a flavour of Maine's folklore and cultural heritage are: ROBERT P. TRISTRAM COFFIN, *Lost Paradise: A Boyhood on a Maine Coast Farm* (1934); E.F. WILDER and G.A. MELLON (eds.), *Maine and Its Role in American Art, 1740–1963* (1963); FANNIE HARDY ECKSTORM and M.W. SMYTH (comps.), *Minstrelsy of Maine: Folk-Songs and Ballads of the Woods and the Coast* (1927); JOHN GOULD, *Last One In: Tales of a New England Boyhood* (1966); SARAH ORNE JEWETT, *The Country of the Pointed Firs* (1896; reprinted with other stories, 1956); and W. STORRS LEE (comp.), *Maine: A Literary Chronicle* (1968).

(E.S.M.)

Maintenon, Madame de

The second wife of Louis XIV of France and untitled queen, Mme de Maintenon (*née* Françoise d'Aubigné) rose from an obscure and poor childhood to become the favourite and, later, the secret wife of the most powerful monarch of the 17th century.

Early years   She was born at Niort, in Poitou, perhaps in the same prison where her father, Constant, was then incarcerated for debt; the infant was baptized as a Catholic on November 28, 1635. Constant, the son of Agrippa d'Aubigné, a great Huguenot soldier and companion of Henry IV as well as a poet, possessed neither his father's talents nor his virtues. His child, Françoise, received a Calvinist upbringing until the age of seven at the Château de Mursay, supervised by her aunt Villette, Agrippa's favourite daughter.

Constant was finally freed in 1645, and the Aubigné family embarked on a journey to the West Indies, for Constant believed he had been made governor of the island of Marie-Galante. The post was not vacant, however, and Constant returned to France, leaving his family in Martinique, where they were to remain for close to two years before being able to return. Constant died in France in 1647. Françoise was entrusted once more to her aunt Villette's care, but another aunt, Mme de Neuillant, a Catholic whose daughter was Françoise's godmother, claimed the child. Françoise was forced to go to this unknown relative, who raised the child sternly together with one of her own daughters.

When Françoise was 16, her mother died. Anxious to rid herself of the orphan, Mme de Neuillant arranged for her charge to live with the crippled author Paul Scarron, who was 25 years older than the girl. Françoise married him in 1652 and later said of this relationship: "I preferred to marry him rather than a convent." In addition to nursing the author, she also had to preside over his salon, where an extremely varied group was received. The marriage was probably unconsummated. The author of *Le Roman comique* was a rascal and although he may have formed his young wife intellectually, he also undoubtedly tried

Mme de Maintenon, portrait by Pierre Mignard, (1612—95). In the Louvre, Paris.
Giraudon

to corrupt her. Meanwhile, the men who frequented his salon did not hesitate to try their luck with his little wife, who skillfully practiced the art of flirtation until, at last, in 1660, she found herself a widow—free but without a sou. She was then 25 years old and beautiful. She was at first tempted to embark on a courtesan's life, but instead she took a room in a convent and, in this semi-retreat, lived the cultured and well-mannered life of a *précieuse,* zealous of her reputation. As the hostess of the Scarron salon, she had made powerful friends, with whose help she had obtained from Anne of Austria, the queen mother, an allowance of 2,000 pounds. Although later she was to be credited with many lovers, the widow remained discreet and was regarded as wise, rather devout, and even somewhat prudish.

In 1668 she was given a chance to improve her fortunes. One of her friends, the Marquise de Montespan, had become the King's mistress. Having supplanted the shy Louise de La Vallière, Mme de Montespan was soon to become pregnant. As she was already married and the king did not wish a scandal, he decided that the birth was to be kept secret. For this purpose he required a trustworthy person to receive and hide the child, a delicate task requiring both ability and discretion. Mme Scarron, displaying her prescience, agreed and thus began her surprising rise to power. She was born in March 1669 and was followed by many others. After the third, the family moved to a house in Paris, where the King made occasional visits and met the widow, then 36 years old. Louis XIV was three years younger than Mme Scarron.

The King recognized his illegitimate children by Mme de Montespan in December 1673. He gathered them around him, with their governess, at his residence in Saint-Germain. Thanks to the King's generosity, Mme Scarron was able to purchase the Château de Maintenon in December 1674. At the beginning of 1675, Louis XIV bestowed the title of her lands upon her. In December 1679, the Marquise de Maintenon was made second lady-in-waiting to the wife of the Dauphin. She was thus able to put aside her responsibilities for the royal children and to become independent from Mme de Montespan, with whom, for some time, she had been having a stormy relationship. After the Queen's death on July 30, 1683, Louis XIV was to have only one woman in his life: "la Scarron," as she was always called by her enemies. He married her, according to some, in October 1683 and according to others in April or May, 1697.

Some historians maintain that Louis XIV married Mme de Maintenon to consummate the relationship, while others believe that the King was only regularizing a liaison whose beginnings went back either to 1673 or 1678, but more likely to 1680. Whatever the date may have been, if the marriage took place in 1683, Louis XIV and his

Marriage to Louis XIV

companion had a union that lasted 32 years, 16 of them before 1700, the year in which Charles II, king of Spain, died. The latter having left his kingdom to the Duke of Anjou, Louis XIV's youngest son, France then found herself engaged in a deadly war, which was to mark the beginning of the reign's decline. The precise date of the marriage is only important for the determination of Mme de Maintenon's political role, for many have blamed her for Louis XIV's errors and faults. In reality, her influence was negligible prior to 1700 and quite prudent during the last 15 years of Louis XIV's reign. Mme de Maintenon did not have the smallest part in the Revocation of the Edict of Nantes in 1685, which denied all rights to Protestants in France. Indeed, the secret wife of Louis XIV was the only one to establish and maintain a climate of decency, dignity, and piety around her husband. Her role, all things considered, can be seen as beneficial, except for the Quietism affair, when she was to join forces with Bishop Jacques-Bénigne Bossuet in persecuting François de Salignac de la Mothe-Fénelon.

At Saint-Cyr, near Paris, she founded the Maison Royale de Saint-Louis (known simply as Saint-Cyr), an institution established for the education of impoverished young women of the nobility (1686). Racine's dramatic poem *Esther* was written for performance at the school. At first Saint-Cyr was considered fashionable. There Mme de Maintenon often sought to escape the restraints of the court and to put into practice the pedagogical talents she was convinced she possessed. To this day, many recognize that she did indeed have these talents. After the death of Louis XIV in 1715, his widow took ill and eventually died in her Saint-Cyr refuge. She survived him by four years, a stranger to the new era, and died on April 15, 1719.

Hated by some, revered by others, Mme de Maintenon never ceased to kindle violent emotions. To this day she is depicted in textbooks as greedy and evil, a narrow-minded bigot. It would be true to say that she was an ambitious woman who had an exceptional destiny, and did not do too badly with it. Her letters are still read with interest, and, in his exile at Saint Helena, Napoleon I professed to prefer them to those of Marquise de Sévigné.

BIBLIOGRAPHY. The most complete and one of the most recent studies, unfortunately not translated, is JEAN CORDELIER, *Madame de Maintenon, une femme au grand siècle* (1955), a tentative psychological explanation based on the factual and historical details known today. On the early years, EMILE MAGNE, *Scarron et son milieu*, 3rd ed. (1924), furnishes interesting details. MARCEL LANGLOIS, *Madame de Maintenon* (1932), is a slightly confused, but indispensable work in spite of the contradictions that reflect the mixed feelings of the author toward his heroine. Finally, basic to all serious study are the *Lettres* of Mme de Maintenon, published in four volumes by MARCEL LANGLOIS but incomplete (1935–39). Little has been published on the subject in English; however, MME SAINT-RENE TAILLANDIER, *Madame de Maintenon* (1920; Eng. trans., 1922), is worth reading.

Malacca, Strait of

The Strait of Malacca extends from 6° N to 1° N, running between the Indonesian island of Sumatra to the west and West Malaysia and peninsular Thailand to the east. It has an area of 25,000 square miles (65,000 square kilometres). The strait, 500 miles (800 kilometres) in length, links the Indian Ocean with the South China Sea; its width varies from 155 miles (249 kilometres) in the north to 40 miles (64 kilometres) in the south. The strait derived its name from the trading port of Malacca—which was of importance in the 16th and 17th centuries—on the Malayan coast.

Exploration

Lying on the shortest sea route between India and China, the strait, sometimes incorrectly called the "straits," is one of the most used shipping channels in the world. In early times, it helped to determine the direction of major Asian migrations of peoples through the Malayan archipelago. In the 2nd century AD, the Indianized trading kingdom of Lankasuka was based on the Malayan Peninsula shore of the strait, near Patani. The strait was later controlled successively by the Arabs; the Por-

tuguese, who established a base at Malacca, the trading port from which the strait took its name; the Dutch, who seized Malacca from the Portuguese in 1641; and the British, who took possession of the island of Penang at the northern entrance to the strait, and later, in 1819, secured Singapore in the south.

In 1826 further British holdings were added to create the Straits Settlements, a territory used to protect the British opium trade in the Orient. Pirates, who for centuries had hidden in the fringing mangrove swamps, meanwhile continued to menace shipping, using small boats of up to ten tons equipped with swivel guns. After 1837, when the first European armed steamers arrived in Southeast Asia, Anglo-Dutch forces undertook to suppress the pirates; and by 1860 the pirate strongholds had been eliminated.

In the south of the strait, water depths rarely exceed 120 feet (37 metres) and are usually about 90 feet (27 metres). Toward the northwest, the bottom gradually deepens until it reaches the 650-foot (200-metre) isobath (an imaginary line connecting all points of the same depth underwater) that marks the boundary of the Andaman Basin. Numerous islets, some fringed by reefs and sand ridges, trending northwestward for up to 30 miles (48 kilometres), hinder passage at the southern entrance to the strait. The ridges are identified as accumulations of material that have been brought down by rivers from Sumatra. Between the latitudes of Melaka (formerly Malacca) and of Port Swettenham, transverse sand dunes up to 50 feet (15 metres) high have been recorded. Many of these sand waves are asymmetrical, with steeper northern slopes. Former drainage channels are represented by valley relicts lying north off the Rokan River mouth and presumably by the 160-foot- (49-metre-) deep "hole" near Port Swettenham as well.

Geologically, the strait belongs to the Sunda Shelf, which was an extensive, low-relief land surface at the beginning of Quaternary time (about 2,500,000 years ago), and appears to have remained undisturbed by crustal movements since the Late Tertiary Period. Undeformed Quaternary terraces and a 10,000-year accumulation of peat deposit on the floor of the strait present absolute proofs of crustal stability during the most recent stage of earth's history. The strait attained its present configuration after having been inundated by the postglacial rise of the sea level resulting from the melting of land ice in higher latitudes.

Coastal swamps are common on both sides of the strait, and, in addition, at several localities in Sumatra and Malaya, hills composed of Tertiary or of Mesozoic rocks are present. Near large rivers, coastal accretion ranges from about 30 feet (9 metres) on the coast of Malaya, to about 650 feet (200 metres) annually on the east coast of Sumatra.

Various types of source rock, fluctuations of river discharge during the year, and longshore currents have produced extremely complex bottom deposits. The shallow waters are supersaturated with oxygen; pyrite (an iron sulfide that indicates reducing agents in the sediment) and glauconite (a green, pellet-like mineral of potassium iron silicate) are common within cavities of small organic remains. Decay of organic matter has probably caused these micro-reducing conditions.

The climate is hot and humid and is characterized by the northeast monsoon during the northern winter and the southwest monsoon during the northern summer. Mariners, from the earliest times, used the monsoonal wind system, scheduling their voyages to take advantage of the prevailing wind direction. The average annual rainfall varies between 76.4 inches (1,940.6 millimetres) and 101.4 inches (2,575.6 millimetres). During both monsoons the wind strength averages between 5 and 11 miles (8 and 18 kilometres) an hour. Throughout the year, the current flows northwest at rates of up to 1.7 miles (2.7 kilometres) an hour. During the earlier part of the southwest monsoon, southward currents may be evident. The net northward flow is indicated by the asymmetry of the transverse sand waves already mentioned and by the northward deflection of many river mouths on the

Climate

Malayan coast. Semidiurnal tides govern the larger part of the strait; flood currents run toward the southeast, while slightly stronger ebb currents at 21–40 inches (0.5–1.0 metres) per second flow in the opposite direction. On the Sumatran side, tidal ranges vary from 98 inches (2.5 metres) in the north to over 230 inches (5.8 metres) in the narrower southern portion. On the coast of Malaya, the tidal range averages 110 inches (2.8 metres). Surface temperatures are 30.5° C to 31° C in the east and may be as much as two degrees lower in the west. The annual variations are small and do not exceed two degrees. The bottom temperature is approximately 28° C in the region south of Pulau Pinang (formerly Penang Island); toward the north it decreases gradually to 12° C at the rim of the Andaman Basin. The close proximity of land and the occurrence of large rivers result in a low salinity.

The existence of oil wells in production on Sumatra's east coast, just off the Sunda Shelf region, has led a number of companies to prospect for petroleum in the strait. Prospects for the location of commercial tin placers off the Malayan coast are excellent.

In addition to its use as a waterway by other forms of shipping, the strait affords passage to giant oil tankers voyaging between the Middle East oil fields and ports in eastern Asia. Increasing traffic in the strait has led adjacent countries, as well as Japan, to chart the waterway in more detail.

BIBLIOGRAPHY. G.H. KELLER and A.F. RICHARDS, "Sediments of the Malacca Strait, Southeast Asia," *J. Sedim. Petrol.*, 37:102–127 (1967), an interpretation of new information on the marine geology of the strait with emphasis on bottom sediments; K. WYRTKI, *Physical Oceanography of the Southeast Asian Waters* (1961), comprehensive oceanographic information on the strait and adjacent seas.

(H.D.T.)

Malawi

A landlocked southeast African country of dramatic highlands and extensive lakes, Malawi occupies a narrow, curving strip of land along the Great Rift Valley. Stretching about 520 miles (837 kilometres) from north to south, it has a width varying from 5 to 100 miles and is bordered by the United Republic of Tanzania to the north, Mozambique to the east and south, and the Republic of Zambia to the west. Its total area of 45,747 square miles (118,485 square kilometres) includes some 9,400 square miles of lake surface dominated by the 8,900 square miles of Lake Nyasa (Lake Malawi). The federal capital was to be moved from Zomba (population about 20,000) to Lilongwe (population over 19,000).

Malawi's relatively young population of more than 4,550,000 is overwhelmingly engaged in subsistence agriculture. Most of the country's exports consist of the produce of large tea and tobacco plantations. The potential exploitation of natural resources is hindered by inaccessibility and the necessity of capital investment. The country is almost totally dependent upon Mozambique for access to the sea. Malawi attained independence on July 6, 1964, under the leadership of H. Kamuzu Banda, who became the republic's first president two years later. The leader of the Malawi Congress Party, Banda became president for life in 1971. (For coverage of associated physical features, see EAST AFRICAN LAKES and EAST AFRICAN MOUNTAINS; for historical aspects, see SOUTHERN AFRICA, HISTORY OF.)

The four basic regions

The natural environment. While the landscape is highly varied, there are four basic regions—the Great Rift Valley, the central plateaus, the highlands, and the isolated mountains.

The Great Rift Valley—by far the dominant feature of the country—is a gigantic troughlike depression running throughout the country from north to south and containing Lake Nyasa and the Shire River valley. The lake's littoral, situated along the western and southern shores and ranging from 5 to 15 miles in width, covers about 8 percent of the total land area and is spotted with swamps and lagoons. The Shire Valley stretches some 250 miles from the southern end of Lake Nyasa at

Mangochi to Nsanje at the Mozambique border and contains Lake Malombe at its northern end. The Central Region plateaus rise to an altitude of between 2,500 and 4,500 feet and lie beyond the littoral to the west; they cover about three-quarters of the total land area. The highland areas are mainly isolated tracts that rise as much as 8,000 feet above sea level. They comprise the Nyika, Vipya, and Dowa highlands and Dedza-Kirk Mountain range in the north and west and the Shire Highlands in the south. The isolated massifs (mountain masses) of Mulanje (10,000 feet) and Zomba (6,500 feet) represent the fourth physical region. Surmounting the Shire Highlands, they fall away in the east, running down to the Lake Chilwa–Phalombe Plains.

Drainage and soils. The major drainage system is that of Lake Nyasa, which covers some 61,000 square miles and extends beyond the Malawi border. It is fed by the North and South Rukuru, Dwangwa, Lilongwe, and Bua rivers. The Shire River, the lake's only outlet, flows through adjacent Lake Malombe and receives a large seasonal inflow from several tributaries before joining the Zambezi River in Mozambique. A second drainage system is that of Lake Chilwa, the rivers of which flow from the Lake Chilwa–Phalombe Plains and the adjacent highlands. An enclosed lake, its waters become distinctly saline during the dry season.

Rocks and soils. The underlying rock throughout Malawi is of Precambrian age (4,600,000,000 to 570,000,000 years old) and consists of gneisses (coarse-grained, mineral-bearing rock), schists (coarse-grained, rock-bearing mica), granite, and syenite (a rock formed deep down under heat and pressure and containing alkaline minerals). Karoo formations—sedimentary rocks 345,000,000 to 190,000,000 years old, which cover much of Africa—occur less frequently in the lake basin and the Shire Valley. Later rock formations found in the Great Rift Valley contain reptile fossils and alkaline rocks.

Soils, composed primarily of red earths, with brown soils and yellow gritty clays on the plateaus, are distributed in a complex pattern. Alluvial soils occur on the lakeshores and in the Shire Valley, while other soil types include hydromorphic (excessively moist) soils, black clays, and sandy dunes on the lakeshore.

Climate. There are two main seasons—the dry season from May to October and the wet season from November to April. Altitude has an important effect upon temperature as is clearly seen in comparison of the temperature of Nsanje (Port Herald) in the Shire River plain, which has a mean July temperature of 69° F (21° C) and an October mean of 84° F (29° C), and Dedza, which lies at an altitude of over 5,000 feet in the highlands of the Central Region and which has a July mean of 57° F (14° C) and an October mean of almost 69° F (21° C). On the Nyika Plateau in the Northern Region, at altitudes of about 8,000 feet, frosts are not uncommon in July. Annual rainfall is highest over parts of the northern highlands and on the Sapitwa Peak, of Mulanje Massif, where it is about 90 inches; it is lowest in the lower Shire Valley, where it ranges from 25 to 35 inches.

Vegetation. The natural vegetation pattern reflects diversities in altitude, soils, and climate. Various vegetation zones characterized by woodland, scrub, and grass may be distinguished. Savanna (grassy parkland) occurs in the dry lowland areas. Open woodland with bark cloth trees, or *miombo* (leguminous trees unsuitable for timber), is widespread on the infertile plateaus and escarpments. Woodland, with species of acacia tree, covers isolated, fertile plateau sites and river margins; grass-covered, broad depressions, called *madambo* (singular, *dambo*), dot the plateaus; grassland and evergreen forest are found in conjunction on the highlands and on the Mulanje and Zomba massifs. Swamp vegetation of reeds and matted grasses occurs on the edges of Lake Chilwa and along the lower Shire Valley. The vegetation is, however, being greatly altered by human settlement. Much of the original woodland has been cleared, and, at the same time, forests of softwoods are being planted in the highland areas. High population density and intensive cultivation of the Shire Highlands hinder

Diversity of vegetation

MALAWI

the natural regeneration process; wells have been sunk and rivers dammed to irrigate the dry grasslands for agriculture.

Animal life. Because of population pressures, game animals abound only in the game reserves, where antelope, buffalo, elephants, leopards, lions, rhinoceroses, and zebras occur; hippopotamuses live in Lake Nyasa. The waters of the lakes and rivers contain more than 200 species and 13 families of fish. The most common and commercially significant fish include the endemic tilapia, or *makumba* (nest-building freshwater fish); catfish, or *mlamba*; and minnows, or matemba. Birds, reptiles, and insects also occur in great variety.

The landscape under human settlement. A rural village—called a *mudzi*—is generally small. Organized around the extended family, its area is limited by the amount of water and arable land available in the vicinity. On the plateaus, which support the bulk of the population, the most common village sites are at the margins of *madambo*, which are usually contiguous with streams or rivers and are characterized by woodland, grassland, and fertile alluvial soils. In highland areas, scattered villages are located near perennial mountain streams and pockets of thin but arable land. Here, however, agriculture provides scant sustenance, and men often migrate in search

of paid employment. The larger settlements of the Lake Nyasa littoral originated as collection points for slaves and later developed as lakeside ports.

Improvements in communication and the sinking of wells in arid areas have permitted the establishment of new settlements in previously uninhabited areas. Architecture is also changing; the traditional round, mud-walled, grass-roofed hut is yielding its place to rectangular brick buildings with corrugated iron roofs.

Urban development began in the colonial era, with the arrival of missionaries, traders, administrators, and was further stimulated by the construction of the railway. The only true urban centres are Blantyre-Limbe, Zomba, and Lilongwe. Although some district centres and missionary stations have an urban appearance, they are closely associated with the rural settlements surrounding them. Blantyre, Malawi's industrial and commercial centre, is situated in a depression on the Shire Highlands at an altitude of about 3,400 feet. Zomba lies at the foot of Zomba Mountain and is purely of administrative origin. Farther north is Lilongwe, Malawi's future capital, which is the only urban centre in the Central and Northern regions.

Ethnic, linguistic, and religious groups. According to the official 1966 population census of Malawi, 99.5 percent of the country's population of 4,040,000 were Africans. The remainder were of Asian, European, or other origin. From 1945 to 1966, the population increased by nearly 100 percent, and it is estimated that it will double again by 1990.

Nine main groups are historically associated with modern Malawi—the Chewa, Nyanja, Lomwe, Yao, Tumbuka, Sena, Tonga, Ngoni, and Ngonde (Nkonde). All the African languages spoken belong to the Bantu language family. Although Chichewa and English are the official languages, English is understood by less than 10 percent of the population while Chichewa is spoken by more than 50 percent and understood by about 77 percent. Other important languages are Chilomwe, spoken by about 15 percent of the people; Chiyao, spoken by nearly as many; and Chitumbuka, spoken by 10 percent of the population.

The major religious groups are traditionalist, Christian, and Muslim. Although these groups appear to be approx-

Predominant languages

imately equal in number, their exact distribution is not known. In contrast to the other two, the traditionalist religious groups, variously called animist or nativist, lack any cohesive central organization.

Demography. No comprehensive data on birth and mortality rates are available, although there is an indication of high fertility. The median age of the population was only 18 years in 1966, indicating the relative youth of Malawi's inhabitants.

In 1968 Malawi had an average density of 118 persons per square mile. In the Northern Region the density was 48 per square mile, in the centre of the country it was 108 per square mile, and in the south it rose to 169 per square mile. This pattern reflects the preponderance of high, uninhabited plateaus and relatively inaccessible areas in the north. The figures, however, conceal marked local irregularities in distribution. Only about 5 percent of the total population was urban.

Malawi, Area and Population

	area*		population	
	sq mi	sq km	1966 census	1971 estimate
Regions				
Central	13,714	35,518	1,474,952	...
Districts				
Dedza	1,396	3,616	230,715	...
Dowa	1,250	3,237	182,000	...
Kasungu	3,037	7,866	97,472	...
Lilongwe	2,373	6,146	498,524	...
Mchinji	1,293	3,349	85,324	...
Ncheu	1,319	3,416	164,685	...
Nkhotakota	1,641	4,250	62,918	...
Ntchisi	638	1,652	66,762	...
Salima	767	1,987	86,552	...
Northern	10,376	27,884	487,481	...
Districts				
Chitipa	1,653	4,281	59,521	...
Karonga	1,292	3,346	77,687	...
Mzimba	4,018	10,407	229,736	...
Nkhata Bay	1,576	4,082	83,911	...
Rumphi	1,837	4,758	46,636	...
Southern	12,234	31,686	2,067,140	...
Districts				
Blantyre†	1,612	4,175	279,270	...
Chikwawa	1,894	4,905	158,145	...
Chiradzulu	295	764	142,197	...
Kasupe	2,298	5,952	226,506	...
Mangochi	2,417	6,260	232,692	...
Mulanje	1,329	3,442	398,881	...
Nsanje	751	1,945	101,234	...
Thyolo	644	1,668	245,824	...
Zomba	994	2,574	282,391	...
Total Malawi	36,324	94,079‡	4,039,583	4,530,000

*Land areas only. The total area, including all major inland waters is 45,747 sq mi (118,484 sq km).   †Includes figures for Mwanza district, which was created in 1970.   ‡Figures do not add to total given due to rounding.
Source: Official government figures.

As the population grows, bringing greater pressures on agriculturally productive areas, Malawians increasingly turn to emigration as a means of entering the money economy. In 1966, some 266,000 persons, excluding their dependents, were living outside the country. All but 14,000 of these were in Rhodesia, South Africa, and Zambia, where Malawi labour finds employment in the mines. Of that total, 26,000 were permanently settled, 178,000 intended to return, and the status of the remainder was unknown.

The national economy. Malawi is dependent on the export of primary agricultural products. National income data are often deficient because of the difficulty of evaluating subsistence output and the output of services. Malawi's economy is characterized by a relatively low income per capita, estimated to be about $69 U.S. a year.

Low per capita income

Mineral resources. Most of Malawi's mineral deposits are neither extensive enough for commercial exploitation nor easily accessible. Only a few have potential for future development. These include high-grade apatite (a calcium phosphate mineral used for making fertilizers), which occurs in about 3,000,000 tons of apatite-rich rock located near Lake Chilwa; bauxite deposits of about 65,000,000 tons on the Mulanje Massif; and cyanite (an

aluminum silicate mineral used for lining furnaces) on the Dedza-Kirk Range.

Biological resources. More than half of Malawi's total land area is suitable for cultivation. Some 3,200,000 acres are under field crops, with a further 1,000,000 acres lying fallow. Forests and woodlands cover nearly 9,000 square miles, of which almost 4,000 square miles are state-controlled forest reserves.

The lakes and rivers of Malawi provide a rich harvest of fish. The national herd of cattle is estimated to be about 510,000 head and grows at an average rate of 3 percent a year.

Power and water. Malawi has a vast water supply potential, although some areas have an inadequate amount of water. Most of the rivers are seasonal, but a few large ones, particularly the Shire River, have a considerable irrigation and generating potential. The total hydroelectric potential of the country is about 1,200 megawatts, of which 1,000 megawatts can be generated on the Shire alone. Present power demands, which represent less than 5 percent of potential capacity, are met by the Nkula Falls hydroelectric and diesel plants. The new 16-megawatt Tedzani Falls scheme (five miles downstream from Nkula) was scheduled for completion in 1973.

Agriculture, fishing, and forestry. The most important agricultural export products are tea and tobacco. Tea is grown on plantations on the Shire Highlands, and the industry employs the largest proportion of the country's labour force. Tobacco is raised largely on the Central Region plateau. Other important crops are maize (the major staple food), cotton, peanuts (groundnuts), cassava, sugar, coffee, and rice.

During the period from 1966 to 1968 the contribution of cash crops to the gross domestic product averaged about 15 percent a year, while that of subsistence agriculture averaged about 35 percent. The principal cash crops are marketed by the Agricultural Development and Marketing Corporation; there are also more than 100 cooperative societies that purchase and also market produce.

The amount of fish landed in 1970—mainly from Lake Nyasa—totalled almost 34,000 tons; this amount is likely to increase with the recent rise in the water level of Lake Chilwa, which had previously shown signs of drying up. Sales of forestry products yielded about $500,000 U.S. in 1968; more than 60,000 acres of the Vipya Highlands are being afforested with softwood. Sawnpoles, posts, and manufactured wooden items are produced largely for the domestic market. There are small forestry exports to Denmark and Zambia, but Malawi is a net importer of wood and wood products.

Manufacturing. The rapid growth in the number of local industries has been sufficient for Malawi to satisfy

A tea estate in Malawi.

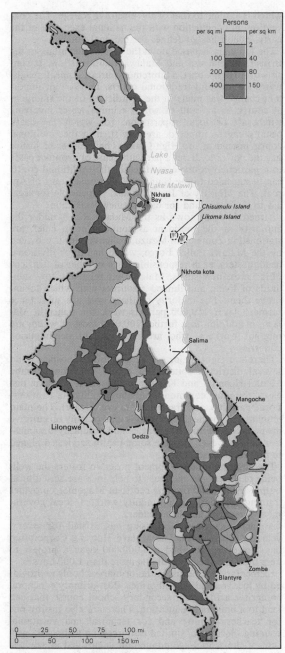

Persons

per sq mi		per sq km
5		2
100		40
200		80
400		150

Lake
Nyasa
(Lake Malawi)
Nkhata
Bay
Chisumulu Island
Likoma Island

Nkhota kota

Salima

Mangoche

Lilongwe
Dedza

Zomba
Blantyre

0   25   50   75   100 mi
0   50   100   150 km

Population density of Malawi.
Adapted from *Malawi Population Census 1966: Final Report*

Financial services. Malawi's decimal currency, introduced in February 1971, consists of the kwacha, which is divided into 100 tambala (0.84 kwacha = $1 U.S.; 2 kwachas = £1 sterling as of the beginning of April, 1971). There are two commercial banks—the National Bank of Malawi and the Commercial Bank of Malawi. The Reserve Bank of Malawi is the central bank of the country. Other financial institutions include the Post Office Savings Bank, the New Building Society, and finance houses. Among the several insurance companies, only one is locally based.

The public and private sectors. In the early 1970s the government's economic policy was anti-inflationary, arising from the need to reduce the deficit in public expenditure and to maintain the level of foreign-exchange reserves. In budgetary policies maximum restraint, consistent with development needs and planned reduction of grants-in-aid from the United Kingdom, was exercised. Estimated expenditure on the recurrent budget for 1970 to 1971 was 47,755,000 kwachas, some 12 percent higher than in 1969. Of the total, over 39,819,000 kwachas were raised from various taxes and departmental receipts; the balance is represented in grants (mainly from the United Kingdom).

The main emphasis continues to be directed toward fostering economic growth through agricultural export production and the completion of investment projects, while at the same time maintaining a satisfactory external balance. The Malawi development program is concerned with the public sector only insofar as it does not interfere with the private sector. Priority is given to transport, agriculture, education, and housing.

The development expenditure of the government and public corporations, derived mainly from external borrowing, was more than 28,500,000 kwachas in 1970. This figure represents a substantial increase over the 1969 amount of 16,000,000 kwachas.

Taxation, trade unions, and employer associations. A minimum annual tax of 3.50 kwachas is payable by all men over 18 years of age unless they are liable to other taxes. Employed men and women who earn up to 900 kwachas a year pay a graduated tax, and those with higher incomes pay an income tax. Local companies pay taxes at the rate of 40 percent of chargeable income, and companies incorporated outside of Malawi pay an additional 5 percent. Tax allowances are, however, offered as an incentive to investment.

There is no sizable industrial labour force in Malawi. Some 20 trade unions and employer associations are connected with such enterprises as the tea plantations, the building and construction industry, road transport, and railways. The Ministry of Labour plays a significant role in maintaining good relations between employers and employees.

Contemporary economic policies. The agricultural sector provides the greatest potential for increasing Malawi's national income. Consequently, the government seeks to strengthen it by encouraging integrated land use, higher crop yields, and irrigation schemes. The quality and output of subsistence agriculture is being improved by means of advisory services and educational programs. In addition, the Malawi Young Pioneers, a national youth movement, trains over 2,000 young men and women yearly in techniques of rural development.

Both higher incomes in the rural areas and continued public expenditure are likely to increase the purchasing power of the public as a whole, thus providing a stimulus for further industrial development. The government continues to promote the establishment of manufacturing industries, thus reducing reliance on expensive imported goods, and so strengthening the balance of payments situation, at the same time increasing employment opportunities.

The government, however, does not itself engage in industrial enterprise or nationalize private concerns. Through the Malawi Development Corporation, its own agency in the private sector, the government ensures local participation in agricultural, commercial, and industrial enterprises.

The growth of manufacturing industries

its domestic need for products such as cotton textiles, sugar, radios, hoes, and shoes, all of which previously had to be imported. The main demand for electric power is in the industrial areas of the Southern Region, where electricity consumption has more than trebled since 1964.

Manufacturing—together with mining and quarrying of clay, granite, limestone, and marble for building and construction—contributed about 15 percent of the gross domestic product a year in the late 1960s. Mining may expand as a result of surveys of the bauxite deposits on the Mulanje Massif and of other minerals in promising areas. In addition, it is expected that the Vipya pulpwood afforestation scheme will form the basis for a pulp and paper industry.

Foreign trade. About 95 percent of Malawi's exports are derived from agriculture. An export drive in the late 1960s, however, led to an increase in exports of manufactured products to neighbouring countries. The United Kingdom continues to provide Malawi's largest market. Zambia, Rhodesia, and the United States are also important customers. Sales to South Africa, West Germany, and the Netherlands have also increased.

Promoting higher crop yields

Any forecast of economic conditions in a country like Malawi is subject to the qualification that crop yields—hence, exports and the whole economy—are liable to be affected by weather conditions. This was demonstrated in 1968 when a poor harvest of marketable crops combined with devaluation resulted in a low growth rate. Between 1964 and 1969, however, the growth of the economy as a whole averaged about 5½ percent a year.

Transportation. The Malawi government has made substantial investments in developing its transport system. Located within the east central region of Africa, Malawi has road connections to Chipata on the Zambian border; to Salisbury, Rhodesia, via Mwanza and Tete; and to several points on the Mozambique border. In addition, there are two rail links to ports on the Mozambique coast and several air routes to east, central, and southern Africa.

Road and rail network. The backbone of the road system is represented by a road running from Blantyre in the south to Lilongwe in the west. A new lakeshore highway, roughly parallel to the inland highway from Mangochi to Karanga, was due for completion in the early 1970s. By 1970 the country had over 6,700 miles of roads, including over 460 miles of paved roads and over 520 miles of gravelled roads.

Of Malawi's two railway links to the sea, the first stretches more than 500 miles from Salima near the southwest shore of Lake Nyasa to the port of Beira on the Mozambique coast. The second railroad joins the Salima–Blantyre line at Nkaya Junction to the south of Balaka and travels due east to link with the Mozambique Railways system at Nova Freixo, from where it continues to the port of Nacala.

Lake transport. Lake Nyasa has long been used as a means of inexpensive transportation. Of the rivers, only the Shire is navigable, all other streams being broken by rapids and cataracts. A passenger and cargo service that operates on the lake is linked to Chipoka railway junction about 20 miles south of Salima. The main ports on the lake are Monkey Bay, Nkhotakota, Nkhata Bay, and Likoma Island.

Air services. Air Malawi, the national airline, operates services from the main airport at Chileka, 11 miles from Blantyre, to Lusaka, Zambia; Salisbury, Rhodesia; Beira, Mozambique; Johannesburg, South Africa; and Nairobi, Kenya.

Administration and social conditions. Under the republican constitution of Malawi promulgated in July 1966, Parliament is composed of a president, who is head of state and government and of the National Assembly. The cabinet is appointed by the president. The original number of 50 elected members of the assembly was raised to 60 in November 1969. In addition, the president can appoint no more than 15 nominated members.

The central government is composed of 14 ministries. For purposes of administration, the country is divided into 24 administrative districts. The local government system consists of district councils, the city council of Blantyre, the municipality of Lilongwe, and six town councils.

Since August 1961, when the first general elections were held, Malawi has been a de facto one-party state. This situation was formalized in the constitution of 1966 which recognizes the Malawi Congress Party—led by Pres. H. Kamuzu Banda—as the country's sole political organization.

Elections Elections for the presidency and the assembly are held every five years, the first general election since Malawi became a republic being held in 1971. For purposes of the election, the presidential candidate is nominated by an electoral college composed of party officials at the national, regional, and district levels; the League of Malawi Women; the League of Malawi Youth; members of Parliament; recognized chiefs; and all chairmen of district councils. In 1971, Banda was elected president for life. Candidates for the National Assembly may stand for election only after their nomination by the district party conferences.

There is an annual party convention, the composition of which is similar to that of the electoral college. The convention, in conjunction with the national executive of the party, establishes guidelines for national policies.

The judiciary is based upon the system prevailing in the British colonial era and Malawi traditional law. It consists of a High Court, a Supreme Court of Appeal, magistrates' courts, and traditional courts. In 1969 an important change was made in the jurisdiction of the traditional courts, as a result of which criminal cases involving witchcraft or local superstition, for which the death penalty can be imposed, are now tried in the traditional courts instead of the High Court. The minister of justice has the power to direct a particular case or group of cases to a particular court; cases tried in the traditional courts can be appealed to the National Traditional Court of Appeal. The Ministry of Justice is also responsible for legal aid to the needy and for drafting new legislation.

Armed forces, known as the Malawi Rifles, under the authority of the president as commander in chief, are stationed in Zomba and Mzuzu. Police service is provided by the Malawi Police Force, which has three divisional headquarters, each responsible for a number of districts.

Like most new states, Malawi has relatively low standards of living and limited resources with which to improve them. The majority of the people are subsistence farmers. Over 250,000 persons work for wages in Malawi, in addition to a further 200,000, most of whom are migrant workers, who are employed in neighbouring countries.

There are eight major public and private hospitals and several district hospitals and clinics, including Zomba Mental Hospital and Kochira Leprosarium. Among diseases, the most common are malaria, bilharzia (a waterborne parasite), and trachoma (an eye disease). The main emphasis of the health services is unavoidably on curative medicine. Government agencies and voluntary organizations do, however, provide some health services designed to prevent disease.

The community development program fosters the well-being of the people and seeks to help increase agricultural output. A national training centre at Magomero provides training facilities for community workers, local government personnel, and local leaders.

An acute shortage of housing has existed for several years in urban areas. The Malawi Housing Corporation has, however, launched a 3,000,000-kwacha project to help meet the need by building more than 1,000 houses.

Elementary education in the primary schools is provided by local education authorities. Post-primary education comprises a four-year secondary school course that can lead to a university education. There are also institutions for teacher training and for technical and vocational training. Because of limited resources, only about 35 percent of the school-age population is enrolled in schools. The Malawi Correspondence College caters to more than 16,000 students. In view of its central importance, agriculture is the focal point in the curricula of most primary and secondary schools and teacher-training colleges.

The University of Malawi, founded in 1965, has five constituent colleges and a total enrollment of about 900 students.

Cultural life and institutions. Though under the impact of modernization, Malawi's traditional culture is characterized by both continuity and change. The country is one of the least urbanized in Africa. Despite the geographical mobility of many Malawians, who are prepared to work for a time in the urban centres of central and southern Africa, the traditional life of the village has remained largely intact.

One of the most distinctive features of Malawi culture is the enormous variety of traditional songs and dances that use the drum as the major musical instrument. Among the most notable of these dances are *ingoma* and *gule wa mkulu* for men, and *chimtali* and *visekese* for women. There are various traditional arts and crafts, including sculpture in wood and ivory. There are two museums—The Museum of Malawi in Blantyre and a smaller one in Mangochi. While various cultural activities are organized by the Kwacha National Cultural Centre in Blantyre, radio has proved to be the most effective means of bringing traditional and modern plays to the rural population.

There are two main newspapers, both published twice a week in Blantyre-Limbe—*The Malawi News*, issued in both Chichewa and English, and *The Times*, published in English. *The African* of Lilongwe is bilingual and is issued fortnightly. There are also four monthly publications, one quarterly, and the biannual *Society of Malawi Journal*.

The Malawi Broadcasting Corporation, a statutory body, operates a radio service from Ngumbe Estate, near Blantyre. Programs are broadcast in both Chichewa and English.

Prospects for the future. Since it gained independence in 1964, Malawi has enjoyed a large measure of national unity and political stability. This circumstance has helped to create a climate conducive to economic advancement. Developments in communications and administrative services as well as improvements in agricultural productivity have contributed to an economic growth rate that has averaged more than 5 percent per year since the middle 1960s.

Malawi maintains diplomatic relations with various African countries, including the white-ruled regimes in southern Africa, with which it has close historical and economic links. Although opposed to the "apartheid" system of South Africa, its relations with that country are based on the doctrine of the sovereignty of states rather than of violent confrontation. Malawi's cooperative stance toward South Africa, while economically beneficial, may provide an alternative strategy for the solution of racial problems in southern Africa.

BIBLIOGRAPHY. The most extensive bibliography on Malawi is E.E. BROWN, C.A. FISCHER, and J.B. WEBSTER (comps.), *A Bibliography of Malawi* (1965). The following works are especially recommended: W.J. BARBER, *The Economy of British Central Africa* (1961); D.G. BETTISON, *The Demographic Structure of Seventeen Villages in the Peri-urban Area of Blantyre-Limbe, Nyasaland* (1958), rather dated; B. BINNS, *A First Checklist of the Herbaceous Flora of Malawi* (1968); E. DEAN, *The Supply Responses of African Farmers: Theory and Measurement in Malawi* (1966); F. and L.O. DOTSON, *The Indian Minority of Zambia, Rhodesia and Malawi* (1968); W.J.C. GERKE and C.J. VILJOEN, *Master Plan for Lilongwe: The Capital City of Malawi* (1968), an example of urban design, land use, and traffic planning in the context of traditional Malawi life; MALAWI GOVERNMENT, DEPARTMENT OF CENSUS AND STATISTICS, *Malawi Population Census 1966: Final Report* (1969), includes many detailed tables; J.G. PIKE, *Malawi: A Political and Economic History* (1968), covers the period up to 1965, and with G.T. RIMMINGTON, *Malawi: A Geographical Study* (1965), the most comprehensive study on the physical, historical, social, and economic geography of Malawi to date; F.E. READ, *Malawi, Land of Progress: A Comprehensive Survey*, 2 vol. (1967–69), general information on the people, economy, communications, tourism, and development projects; R.H.N. SMITHERS, *The Mammals of Rhodesia, Zambia and Malawi: A Handbook* (1966); M.M. STEWART, *Amphibians of Malawi* (1967); C.S. STRONG and D. GIBB, *A Geography of Rhodesia, Zambia and Malawi* (1966), largely an introductory text. The ECONOMIST INTELLIGENCE UNIT, *Quarterly Economic Review of Rhodesia, Zambia and Malawi*, has current data on the state of the economy, compiled from official documents and reports.

(Z.D.K.)

Malaya, History of

Malaya has been inhabited for at least 6,000 years. Archaeologists have unearthed evidence of several Stone Age cultures as well as an early Bronze Age civilization. These probably existed contemporaneously with more advanced settlements stimulated by the arrival of Indian adventurers beginning in the 2nd century BC.

Rise of Indianized states. The Malay Peninsula, and indeed most of Southeast Asia, experienced over 1,000 years of Indian or Indianized influence. Indian blood and Indian culture blended with indigenous elements to produce an amalgam, which found political expression in the creation of a number of states and several great empires. Lacking the fertile plains of Java or Cambodia, the peninsula was unable to support a great empire. Although knowledge is scanty and is based largely on Chinese written sources, it does appear that at least 30 small states, nearly all along the east coast, flourished during this millenium. These included Tun Sun, in the northeastern part of the peninsula, where in the 3rd century AD there were more than 500 Indian merchants and priests. Ch'iht'u ("Red Land," *Tanah Merah* in Malay) may have been established in the 6th century on either the Kelantan or Trengganu River. The most important of the Indianized states was Lankasuka, whose control extended at times across the whole northern part of the peninsula. The most significant complex of Indianized temple ruins in Malaya, on the slopes of Kedah Peak opposite Penang Island (now Pulaw Pinang), was at one time part of this state. Kedah, the name of a modern Malay state, was once thought to be Kalah, described by Arab sailors of the 9th through the 14th centuries. This state, it is now thought, was north of the peninsula, in present-day Thailand.

These small states, now long forgotten, have left a living legacy, traces of which are to be found even in the political structure of modern Malaysia. In religion, too, traces of Hinduism and Buddhism persist in the ritual, language, and practice of the Malay Muslims. A similar influence is seen in many of the arts and crafts still flourishing on the peninsula. *(margin: Indian influence)*

Much of the influence was imposed not directly from India but by the great Indianized empires of Southeast Asia. The small peninsula states, it would appear, were usually under the hegemony of one or the other of these empires, either in Siam (Thailand) or Cambodia to the north or Sumatra and Java to the south. On Singapore Island, for example, Tumasik, an Indianized settlement, owed allegiance in the 14th century first to Sumatra–West Malaya, under Śrivijaya; then to Majapahit, the great Javanese empire; and finally to Siam, with its capital at Ayutthaya. Paramesvara, Tumasik's Sumatran ruler near the end of the 14th century, unsuccessfully attempted to win independence for Tumasik from Ayutthaya. Tumasik was sacked, but Paramesvara found refuge at Malacca (now Melaka), at that time a small fishing village, where he established himself as ruler c. 1400.

Advent of Islām. From this precarious beginning, Malacca rose during the 15th century to become a political power of the first rank, the most important commercial mart in Southeast Asia, and the main centre for the diffusion of Islām. A fortunate set of circumstances combined to permit this. Soon after he won control of Malacca, Paramesvara secured the support of China. Chinese settlers at that time were beginning to move into the *Nanyang* ("South Seas"), or general Southeast Asian region. The Chinese admiral Cheng Ho called at Malacca in 1409 and again in 1414. In return for annual tribute, twice taken to Peking by Paramesvara himself, the Chinese emperor promised his protection to Malacca. For some decades, China's guardianship deterred other Southeast Asian states, notably Siam, from crushing Paramesvara's settlement and permitted it to develop. Its location, in addition, was attractive to traders from India, Arabia, China, and the Indonesian islands as a central, independent meeting place not for the purchase of Malaccan goods, of which there were few, but for barter and exchange. A good government and a sensible nonrestrictive policy encouraged the traders to settle and to frequent the peaceful bay in increasing numbers. The fishing village thus grew into a bustling and famous city where many of the commodities of Asia were traded. *(margin: Emergence of Malacca)*

Malacca's most important role, however, was not commercial but religious. It replaced Sumatran ports as the main centre for the transmission of Islām throughout Southeast Asia. Originally disseminated by peddlers and traders from east Bengal and other areas of the Indian subcontinent, Islām had secured a toehold in north Sumatra and east Malaya during the 14th century or earlier. With the growth of Malacca in the 15th century, however, the new faith was conveyed most effectively along Malaccan trade routes by missionaries and merchants. The ancient Hindu beliefs survived only on Bali; elsewhere the courts and the peoples accepted the new faith and helped it to spread, for the most part as a major movement for peace, to the coastal areas of West Irian and the Philippines.

On the Malay Peninsula itself, the spread of Islām was linked closely to the territorial expansion of the Malacca sultanate, which began during the reign of Muzaffar Shah (1446–59), Paramesvara's grandson. In 1456 Muzaffar Shah appointed an outstanding man, Tun Perak, as *bendahara* ("prime minister"). In that year, also, Tun Perak became the saviour of Malacca, defeating the Siamese in a fierce naval battle off South Johore. For some 40 years (1456–1498), although he never became sultan, he was the effective ruler of Malacca and promoted its expansion. The state of Perak already had become Muslim and in 1460 became a part of Malacca; Pahang, a tributary of Siam, was conquered. Islām followed and moved north to Trengganu. South Malaya also was made part of the growing sultanate. The river states in Sumatra that had been commercially linked to Malacca were acquired in 1477. In 1474 Kedah, Malaya's one granary of importance, also received a Muslim sultan.

Early European intrusions. Long before the end of the 15th century the fame of Malacca had reached Europe, attracting those interested in the spice trade. The Portuguese, who for a century had been dedicated to the national endeavour of reaching the Orient by sea, arrived at Malacca in 1509. It was the beginning, as one Asian historian has called it, of "the Vasco da Gama Era," the period of European dominance in Asia. Although the Portuguese and subsequently the Dutch did not exert the dominance exercised by the British in the 19th century, the European intrusion of the 16th century was, nevertheless, the beginning of a political movement that grew in strength for over 400 years and has only just ended.

In 1511 Malacca was captured by a Portuguese fleet led by Afonso de Albuquerque. Along with the Moluccas (Maluku) and Goa (in India), it became one of Portugal's major trading outposts in Asia. The Portuguese were, however, few in number, and although they retained defensive possession of Malacca until 1641, Malaya was more deeply influenced in the 16th century by Acheh, an aggressive state in Sumatra.

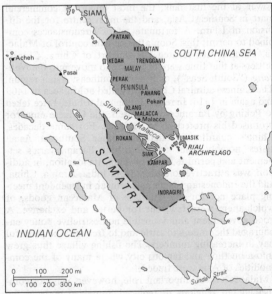

Malacca Empire in 1500.

When the Achinese first attacked Malacca in 1537, the city was saved by its new stone fort. Subsequent assaults came in 1539, 1547, 1568, 1570, and 1573. Acheh's target was not merely Malacca but all the Malay states as well. The story is complex and confused, for the allies of one decade were often the enemy in the next. The Malay states and the Portuguese sometimes fought one another, sometimes joined together. Acheh remained the aggressor until well into the 17th century. By that time the few hundred Portuguese at Malacca were a spent force. They

had to face a new opponent, the Dutch, who had secured a base in 1596 on Java. In 1607 the Dutch allied themselves with Acheh, while the Portuguese in Malacca joined with Johore. The Achinese sacked Johore, 1613–1615; Pahang in 1617; Kedah in 1619; and Perak in 1620. Acheh thus secured for 20 years an unquestioned suzerainty over the Malay states.

In Java the Dutch, in the meantime, had grown steadily in strength. They began actively meddling in the affairs of the Malay states in 1633, when they laid seige to Malacca. Year after year the few Portuguese waited in vain for relief, surrendering finally in 1641. Malacca had become a moribund town, its bustle and importance long vanished. Despite all efforts by the Dutch to revive the port and to channel the trade in tin from the west Malay states to it, Malacca never recovered its earlier glory.

The Minangkabau and the Bugis. The last 50 years of the 17th century witnessed the migration of many Minangkabau people from Sumatra. These sturdy agriculturalists settled in south Malaya, which until then had been virtually unpopulated. They brought with them an almost uniquely matrilineal outlook by which property and authority descended through the female. Their leader was freely elected (their method of election has served as the basic model for selecting the ruler of modern Malaysia), and in the late 18th century, they formed a confederation of small states, which came to be known as Negri Sembilan, or "Nine States."

During the 18th century the Dutch found that profits from dealings with Malacca could not compare with the benefits to be derived from trade with Java and the Spice Islands. Malacca was therefore neglected, a situation that permitted large-scale penetration of Malaya by the "Norseman of the East," the Bugis rovers from the Celebes (or Sulawesi). Just as the well-governed state of Normandy arose as the Norseman's contribution to Atlantic civilization, so are Selangor and Johore perhaps the best examples of Bugis occupation and organization in Southeast Asia. Hardly a member of the Johore civil service today does not have Bugis blood in his veins, and Johore's independent progress in the 19th and 20th centuries is attributable largely to the migrations of the 18th century. Although the Bugis had traded for many centuries on the Java Sea, they did not begin to settle in the relatively weak Malay Peninsula until the late 17th century. In Selangor they established their ruler as sultan as early as 1700. The Bugis leader, Raja Haji, seized Perak and sacked Alor Star, capital of Kedah, in 1770. By that time the Bugis had developed a new trading centre south of Singapore, in the Rhio (Riau) archipelago, where a policy of free trade and peaceful government attracted Asian and European merchants. Malacca was nearly captured by the Bugis in 1784.

Dutch influence in the Malay Peninsula was weakened not only by the Bugis invasions but also by the arrival of the British. Seeking a source for goods to be sold in China, the East India Company acquired Penang Island in 1786. In 1795 the British captured Malacca, and in 1819 Sir Thomas Stamford Raffles established a settlement on Singapore Island. Britain's entrenched position was clarified beyond dispute by the Anglo-Dutch treaty of 1824. Malacca, Singapore, and Penang Island, the three "Straits Settlements," came under the direct control of the British Colonial Office in 1867. Singapore, a free port, grew rapidly.

With the opening of the Suez Canal in late 1869, the full effect of European technological superiority swept over Southeast Asia. The Malay states were little prepared. With the exception of Johore, which was effectively ruled by Abubakar, the states were generally poorly administered and failed to cope with their mounting problems, chief of which was the steady immigration of Chinese in search of tin. From the mid-19th century to the present, the Chinese and the Malays have been two elements of an inadequately integrated community, prone to racial clashes and communal disorder. The clashes, which included disputes between rival Chinese groups on the newly discovered tin fields of Perak, became sufficient in 1874 to provoke British intervention.

This intervention by a European power into the internal

The Dutch

The Bugis

Chinese immigration

affairs of weak Asian states was at first crude. Malay reaction saw the murder of J.W.W. Birch, the first British resident (chief officer) in Perak (1875). Lack of understanding and incompetence also characterized the first British residents in Selangor and Sungei Ujong, one of the Negri Sembilan. They were followed, however, by more talented men. Frederick Weld (1823–91) expanded the policy of intervention to encompass all the Negri Sembilan and Pahang on the east coast. He selected competent officers to work as residents in the various states. Among these was Frank Swettenham, resident in Selangor, whose service in the Malay Peninsula culminated in his appointment as first resident general, when the four states of Perak, Selangor, Negri Sembilan, and Pahang were brought together in a federation in 1896, with Kuala Lumpur as its capital. The other sultanates in the peninsula were also induced to accept British officers as residents or "advisers" but managed to avoid joining the federation. They saw too great a loss of individuality and control despite the British policy of preserving the sultanates, the Muslim faith, and the Malay way of life. Between 1902 and 1909 Trengganu, Kelantan, and Kedah were extricated from the Siamese sphere of influence. In the south, Johore accepted a British adviser in 1914.

The genesis of the modern state of Malaya. British political control over the whole peninsula radically transformed Malaya economically and socially. As with the Romans in Britain, the British in Malaya devoted much attention to transport. Railways appeared, first from the coast to the tin fields, and then north to south down the peninsula until connections with Singapore were completed in 1924. A road network was constructed and paved to withstand the rains. Penang (Pinang), Singapore, Port Swettenham, and other ports were enlarged, improved, and given constant attention by the British.

Development of transport facilities assisted in the rapid growth of the important tin and rubber industries. During the 19th century technological developments in the U.S. and Europe created an ever increasing demand for tin. Though the Malays were indifferent to the opportunities created by this demand, thousands of Chinese migrated to Malaya during the second half of the 19th century to develop tin mining and manufacture. Vast new deposits were found, and the industry remained in Chinese hands through the 19th century. The Chinese, however, lacked capital and technological knowledge. Their open-cut, intensive labour methods of mining were replaced by the mining dredge introduced by British-financed companies in the early 20th century. Two major tin smelters were established at Penang and Singapore, and "Straits tin" became known throughout the world. The tax on the tin export became one of the two main sources of revenue for Malaya; the other was a similar levy on rubber.

The first strain of rubber, introduced from Ceylon in the 1870s, had proved unsuccessful. The planters grew coffee until the development in the 1890s of a superior strain of rubber by H.N. Ridley, the director of the Singapore Botanical Gardens. From 1896 through the early 20th century, funds from British financiers provided for the clearing of thousands of acres of virgin jungle and the establishment of new rubber plantations. Rubber production was increased also with the allotment of acreage to individual Malay and Chinese "small holders."

Whereas Chinese immigrants had been attracted in great numbers by the tin industries of Perak and Selangor in central Malaya, thousands of south Indians from 1880 through 1920 moved to the west coast of Malaya to work on the rubber estates. A plural society was thus created and was maintained largely by the educational system. One school system taught Malay to the Malays. A network of missionary schools used English to teach the Christian Chinese, Indians, and Malays. Still other schools, financed by Chinese and supported by the Chinese Communist and Kuomintang parties, instructed Chinese residents in Chinese. The status quo of the plural society, preserved by Britain, was unchallenged until 1941. The few attempts toward self-government were discouraged.

In the field of public health, the British eliminated the scourge of malaria. Beriberi and other previously incurable diseases also were eliminated.

By the close of 1941 the relations among East Asian nations had reached a critical stage. Locked in a struggle with China since 1937, and increasingly desperate for raw materials such as oil, Japan faced an embargo on raw materials from her major supplier, the U.S. To reach the oil and rubber of Java, Japan had to neutralize the great British naval base on Singapore Island. Attacks on Pearl Harbor on December 7, 1941, and on the Philippines on December 10 eliminated the U.S. presence in the Pacific, at least for several decisive months. On December 8 the Japanese had invaded Malaya and then headed south to Singapore.

The campaign was the greatest disaster the British had experienced since Cornwallis' surrender at Yorktown; the Japanese victory was complete. Singapore was captured within 70 days. Within three days Japanese aircraft had sunk the major British battleships "Prince of Wales" and "Repulse." Within a week they had swept the skies clear of the antiquated British aircraft. The troops of General Yamashita outfought and outmanoeuvred Gen. A.E. Percival and his British, Indian, Australian, and Malay troops. The Japanese scored further successes at Jitra in north Kedah, Dec. 11–12, 1942, and at Slim River in Perak on Jan. 7, 1943. Singapore fell on February 15. The Japanese lost 15,000 men. The total loss to the British Commonwealth was approximately 166,600 men.

From 1942 to 1945, when the first swift Japanese success turned to a slow, stubborn retreat, the people of Malaya received markedly different treatment from their Japanese overlords. The Malays were employed in posts of responsibility, and the Indians were assisted in forming an Indian national army to free India from British rule. The Chinese, however, were persecuted and brutally treated. Many fled into the jungle to join the Communist-organized Malayan People's Anti-Japanese Army (MPAJA).

Following the expulsion of the Japanese and the return of British rule in late 1945, an attempt by London to organize Malaya into one state deeply offended the Malays, who prized their treaty arrangements with Britain and were determined not to become a mere colony. A tremendous upsurge of Malay political feeling, led by Dato Onn Bin Jaafar, resulted in the creation in 1946 of the United Malays National Organization (UMNO). In 1948 a federation joining the Malay Peninsula and Penang was formed.

In 1948 the Malayan Communist Party (MCP), formed before the war among the Chinese community, rose in armed revolt and opposed the British from enclaves in the jungle. An Emergency was proclaimed, as Britain endeavoured to suppress the MCP and MPAJA by military means and by eliminating the political causes of their agitation. These aims finally were achieved by Gerald Templer, who arrived in 1952. Templer invigorated military measures already planned, and, as high commissioner, encouraged the attainment of *merdeka* ("independence") through political cooperation among the races. Under a new leader, Tunku Abdul Rahman, the UMNO in 1952 joined with the Malayan Chinese Association (MCA), led by Tan Cheng Lock and his son Tan Siew Sin. Both parties were anti-Communist and anticolonial. In the national election of 1955 the UMNO-MCA Alliance, led by Abdul Rahman, captured 51 of 52 seats. Britain responded by relinquishing its powers in Malaya. On Aug. 31, 1957, Malaya secured its *merdeka*, and the Emergency period ended three years later.

Independence and the federation of Malaysia. Postwar Malaya has been marked above all by the political drive of the Malays, expressed through UMNO. Only by associating with this powerful organization and its leader, Tunku Abdul Rahman, were other elements in the community able to achieve some of their goals. Malay dominance has caused bitterness, and racial antagonism found expression in the Kuala Lumpur riots of May 13, 1969. Tun Abdul Razak succeeded the Tunku in 1970.

Singapore secured full self-government in 1959. Its leader, Lee Kuan Yew, immediately pressed for "independence through merger" with Malaya. Singapore shared

Margin notes: Tin and rubber industries; Japanese invasion and occupation; Birth of Malayan nationalism; Conflict with Singapore

much with the peninsula, and Lee felt that its future could be assured only by uniting with the mainland. Tunku Abdul Rahman, who became Malaya's first chief minister in 1955, agreed to the merger in order to forestall the growth of Communist influence among Singapore's Chinese population. To offset the inclusion of the 1,000,000 Chinese of Singapore, however, Malaya suggested in 1961 that Sarawak and Sabah (North Borneo), the other British colonies in Southeast Asia, also join with Malaya and Singapore in the merger. After considerable discussion, and increasing opposition from the Philippines and Indonesia, the four states established a new, independent federation of Malaysia on Sept. 16, 1963. (August 31, the date of Malaya's founding in 1957, remains the national day.)

Within two years, however, although Malaysia was able to withstand the external pressures of Indonesian armed opposition and "confrontation," internal disagreements worsened between Kuala Lumpur and Singapore. Abdul Rahman believed that civil war was imminent, and Malay political supremacy seemed challenged. On Aug. 9, 1965, Singapore was separated from Malaysia and established as an independent republic. (For Malaysian physical features and government see the article MALAYSIA.)

BIBLIOGRAPHY. K.G. TREGONNING, *Southeast Asia: A Critical Bibliography* (1969), numerous annotated entries devoted to recent books and articles, including many bibliographical references on Malaya, *A History of Modern Malaya* (1964), a substantial survey; P. WHEATLEY, *The Golden Khersonese* (1961), a brilliant study of the historical geography of the Malay Peninsula before 1500 AD.; J.M. GULLICK, *Malaya* (1963), a comprehensive and valuable account; V. PURCELL, *The Chinese in Southeast Asia*, 2nd ed. (1965); W.R. ROFF, *The Origins of Malay Nationalism* (1967), an examination of the growth of the dominant political factor in the peninsula; LIM CHONG-YAH, *Economic Development of Modern Malaya* (1968); E. THIO, *British Policy in The Malay Peninsula, 1880–1910* (1969), a scholarly examination of the expansion of British control; C.N. PARKINSON, *British Intervention in Malaya, 1867–1877* (1960); J.B. OOI, *Land, People, and Economy in Malaya* (1963), a comprehensive geography; R. ALLEN, *Malaysia: Prospect and Retrospect* (1968), a discussion of the impact of colonial rule on Malaya.

(K.G.T.)

Malaysia

The federation of Malaysia in Southeast Asia is composed of two regions—West Malaysia, on the Malay Peninsula, and East Malaysia, consisting of the territories of Sarawak and Sabah on the island of Borneo. It has a total land area of 127,316 square miles (333,403 square kilometres) and a population of nearly 10,500,000.

West Malaysia has an area of about 51,000 square miles and occupies most of the Malay Peninsula south of latitude 6°40′ N. To the north it is bordered by Thailand, with which it shares a 300-mile land boundary. To the south, its nearest neighbour is the island republic of Singapore, with which it is connected by a causeway; to the southwest, across the Strait of Malacca, is the Indonesian island of Sumatra. East Malaysia, consisting of Sarawak and Sabah (formerly North Borneo), is separated from West Malaysia by some 400 miles of the South China Sea. Sarawak, with an area of 48,050 square miles, and Sabah, with an area of 28,460 square miles, occupy most of the northwestern coastal part of the large island of Borneo. Both these territories share common land boundaries with each other and with the Indonesian provinces of Borneo (Kalimantan). Embedded within Sarawak is the small enclave of Brunei (*q.v.*), a sultanate still under British protection, politically separate from Malaysia.

Malaysia, a member of the Commonwealth of Nations, represents the political marriage of territories formerly under British rule. When it was established on Sept. 16, 1963, Malaysia was composed of Malaya (now West Malaysia), Singapore, Sarawak, and Sabah. In August 1965 Singapore (*q.v.*) left the federation and became an independent republic. (For a detailed discussion of associated physical features, see the articles CHINA SEA; and MALACCA, STRAIT OF; for historical aspects, see the article MALAYA, HISTORY OF.)

While not large by Asian standards, Malaysia is never-theless one of the richest countries in the region. It occupies a focal position in Southeast Asia, commanding one of the major sea-lanes of the world, the Strait of Malacca. Malaysia is also unique in that it is the only country that has territory on both the mainland and insular regions of Southeast Asia. The physical separation between mainland Malaysia and insular Malaysia (Sarawak and Sabah), however, inevitably poses problems of communication. The fragmentation between West and East Malaysia is not only physical in nature. Wide disparities and differences exist as well in the degree of development and in the living standards of the population.

Malaysia inherited many long-standing problems from its colonial past. Politically the country was faced with the tasks, first of instilling a polyglot society with a sense of common identity and national purpose and, second, of resolving the tensions arising from inequalities of political and economic conditions. Economically, difficulties have included a high population growth rate (which poses the related problems of finding productive employment for an expanding labour force and of at least maintaining, if not raising, living standards); an inordinate dependence on rubber and tin production; disparities in income between rural and urban peoples and between ethnic groups; and a shortage of skilled manpower.

THE LANDSCAPE (WEST MALAYSIA)

The physical landscape.   The Malay Peninsula is a long, narrow strip of mountainous land extending southward from Burma and Thailand. West Malaysia occupies the the granite, and the remainder is covered by alluvium (de and—at its widest east–west axis—about 200 miles wide. About half of Malaya is covered by granite and other igneous rocks (*i.e.*, rocks solidified from a molten state), a third more is covered by stratified rocks older than the granite, and the remainder is covered by alluvium (deposited material). More than half of the land area is over 500 feet above sea level. Topographically, the country is dominated by its mountainous core, which consists of a number of roughly parallel mountain ranges aligned along the longitudinal grain of the peninsula. The most prominent of these is the Main Range, which has elevations of over 3,000 feet, peaks of over 7,000 feet, and is about 300 miles long. Limestone hills, with their characteristically steep, whitish-gray sides, stunted vegetation, solution caves (*i.e.*, caves eaten out by the dissolving action of water), and subterranean passages, are distinctive landmarks in central and north West Malaysia. Bordering the mountainous core are the coastal lowlands, which are 10 to 50 miles wide along the western coast of the peninsula but which are narrower and discontinuous along the eastern coast. Settlement and development have taken place primarily along the western coast. {Mountain ranges}

The peninsula is drained by an intricate network of rivers and streams. The largest river—the Sungai Pahang—is only 270 miles long. The year-round rainfall results in perennial streamflow, but the volume of water transported fluctuates considerably because of the localized and torrential nature of the rainfall. In the western part of the peninsula such heavy falls may occur at any time of year, but in the eastern part they are more likely to occur during the northeast monsoon winds that blow from November to March. Prolonged rains often cause floods, especially in areas where the natural regimes of the rivers have been disrupted by uncontrolled mining or agricultural activities in the past.

The Malay Peninsula has an equatorial climate, but its narrowness and configuration—a central mountainous core with flat flanking coastal plains—facilitate the inland penetration of maritime climatic influences. In addition, monsoonal effects further modify the climate. The country is influenced by eight or nine major airstreams, flowing from the northeast, south, and west; the advance and retreat of these are responsible for the division of the climatic year into four seasons. These are (1) the northeast monsoon (from November or December until March), (2) the first intermonsoon period (from March to April or May), (3) the southwest monsoon (from June to October), (4) the second intermonsoon period (from October

Penang, Malaysia.
T. Kautsch—Publix

to November). The onset and termination of the monsoons are not sharply defined.

The mean annual rainfall is about 100 inches. The driest location, in Kuala Kelawang (formerly Jelebu), about 30 miles east of Kuala Lumpur, receives about 65 inches of rain a year; while the wettest, Maxwell's Hill, about 25 miles northwest of Ipoh, receives 200 inches. Temperatures are uniformly high throughout the year, averaging 78° to 82° F (25° to 28° C) for most lowland areas. Relative humidities are also persistently high, averaging from 82 to 86 percent. The climate, in consequence, tends to be hot and humid.

Soils · The soils of the peninsula have been exposed for an extremely long time to intense tropical weathering, with the result that most of their plant nutrients have been leached out. The soils are typically strongly acid and coarse textured; deficient in nitrogen, phosphorus, potassium, and magnesium; and have low amounts of organic matter. Only 11 percent of the soils of West Malaysia are fertile, and of this over half are either of low or of below average fertility. Regular applications of fertilizers are therefore necessary for sustained crop yields. On slopes, such additional measures as the building of contour embankments or the planting of protective cover crops are also needed to minimize soil erosion.

The characteristic vegetation of the peninsula is the dense, evergreen rain forest—the climax vegetation of the hot, wet tropics. Rain forest still covers nearly 60 percent of the total land area; a further 9 percent is under swamp forest. The flora of the Malayan rain forest is among the richest in the world. There are about 8,000 species of flowering plants, of which at least 2,500 are trees. An acre of forest may have as many as 100 different species of trees, as well as shrubs, herbs, lianas (creepers), and epiphytes (plants that grow nonparasitically upon others, deriving nourishment from the atmosphere). The forest canopy is so dense that little sunlight can penetrate it. As a result, the undergrowth is usually poorly developed and —contrary to popular belief—is not impenetrable. Much of the original rain forest has been destroyed by wind and lightning storms, by aborigines clearing it for temporary agricultural use, or by clearances made for agricultural or commercial purposes. When such cleared land is subsequently abandoned, coarse grassland, scrub, and secondary forest develop. These types of vegetation comprise about 7 percent of the total land area.

The forests and scrubland is inhabited by a large vari-

ety of animal life. Mammals include the elephant, the tiger, the magnificent seladang (or Malayan gaur, a massive wild ox), the Sumatran rhinoceros, the tapir (a hoofed and snouted quadruped), the wild pig, and many species of deer, including the *pelandok*, or mousedeer (a small, deerlike ruminant). Crocodiles, monitor lizards, cobras, and king cobras are also indigenous to the country, while the green sea turtle and the giant leathery turtle nest regularly on the beaches of the east coast.

The landscape under human settlement. West Malaysian settlements range from the rudimentary settlements of the aborigines to modern cities. This complexity and variety reflects in part the range of economic activities, in part the cultural diversity of the inhabitants, and in part the long history of settlement in the peninsula. The first settlers were small groups of aborigines, who were later followed by peoples of Malay stock and, in recent times, by immigrants from China and India.

The Malays are predominantly a rural people. Their · Types of settlements are similar in appearance and pattern to those · rural of their rural counterparts elsewhere in Southeast Asia. · settlement The basic unit is the *kampong* (village, or community of houses), composed of dwellings on stilts, which are commonly erected beside rivers, canals, beaches, roads, and footpaths. The houses are usually built of wood and a thatched roofing called *atap*, woven from the leaves of the nipa palm (a species also used for basketry). Each house is surrounded by trees bearing coconuts, bananas, papayas, and other fruits. The four main types of Malay settlements—fishing villages, paddy (rice-field) villages, cash-crop villages, and mixed-crop villages—despite their variations, all conform to the same basic pattern.

Most other rural settlements are associated with peoples who have settled in the country within the last 150 years. The earliest of these were the mining camps, which sprang up in the tin fields on the west of the peninsula. Some of these have since grown into large towns, but others—especially in the Kinta Valley—still remain small. The British introduced the plantation system of agriculture, and the subsequent cultivation of rubber and of the oil palm has changed the face of rural West Malaysia, bringing to the landscape the plantation, or estate, settlement. This is usually a group of buildings composed of the processing factory and storehouse, the labourers' quarters, and the manager's house.

The most recent settlement type is the New Village, which originally was simply a group of buildings occupying a defensive site enclosed with barbed wire near a road. A total of about 550 New Villages were established between 1948 and 1960, during the Emergency, the formal name for the period when the administration was engaged in suppressing the Communist guerrilla uprising. They were part of a plan to resettle rural dwellers in easily defended positions, so as to prevent contact between them and the armed Communists. With the end of the Emergency in 1960, some of the New Villages were abandoned and have since disappeared. Most of them, however, took root and have now become permanent settlements. With their barbed-wire fences dismantled, they differ little from other small towns.

The cities and large towns were built up during the colonial and postcolonial periods and are distributed mainly along the tin and rubber belt on the west of the peninsula. There are at least 230 small towns with a population of 2,000 or more and over 80 with a population of 5,000 or more. The towns are associated with mining, purchasing, processing, distributing, exporting, or administrative functions, although each town usually performs not one but several of them. Some towns are located at coastal or riverine sites, emphasizing the early importance of water transport; more recently built towns are in inland areas served by road, rail, and air transport. About two-thirds of the urban population is Chinese, while Indians and Pakistanis constitute another 10 percent. Malays form only some 22 percent of the urban population, but the proportion of them is increasing.

Urban population

Except for the new satellite towns such as Petaling Jaya (outside Kuala Lumpur), the towns of West Malaysia are unplanned, having grown up around pre-urban nuclei. Urban land use is generally mixed, and buildings are put to multiple uses. Streets, built for a more leisurely era, are narrow and often congested. In the larger centres, such as Kuala Lumpur, Ipoh, and Pinang, distinct central business districts, similar to those in Western cities, have emerged. These are characterized by heavy population and traffic densities, high land values, and a concentration of shopping, banking, insurance, entertainment, and other facilities.

THE LANDSCAPE (EAST MALAYSIA)

The physical landscape. East Malaysia is an elongated strip of land approximately 670 miles long, with a maximum width of about 160 miles. The coastline of 1,400 miles is paralleled inland by a 900-mile land boundary with Kalimantan (Indonesian Borneo). For most of its length the relief is composed of three topographic features. First, there is the flat coastal plain, which in Sarawak, where the coastline is regular, averages 20 to 40 miles in width. In Sabah, where the coastline is rugged and deeply indented, it is only 10 to 20 miles in width. Inland from the coastal plain is the second topographic feature—the hill and valley region. This is generally below 1,000 feet in altitude, but isolated groups of hills reach heights of 2,500 feet or more. The terrain in this region is usually very irregular, with steep-sided hills and narrow valleys. The mountainous backbone that forms the divide between East Malaysia and Kalimantan is the third topographic feature. This backbone is both higher and nearer the coast in Sabah than it is in Sarawak. It is composed of an ill-defined complex of plateaus, ravines, gorges, and mountain ranges, all of which have been cut by erosion. The summits of the ranges are between 4,000 and 7,000 feet. Mt. Kinabalu (13,455 feet), the highest peak in the whole of the Malay Archipelago, towers above this mountain complex; no other peak in the country reaches 8,000 feet in height.

As in West Malaysia, the drainage pattern is set by the interior highlands, which also form the watershed between East Malaysia and Kalimantan. The rivers are perennial because of the year-round rainfall. They form a dense network of drainage lines covering all parts of the country. The longest river in Sarawak—the Rajang—is 350 miles long and is navigable by shallow-draft boats for about 160 miles from its mouth; its counterpart in Sabah—the Kinabatangan—is of comparable length but is only navigable to about 120 miles from its mouth.

The rivers are all of importance as they provide a means of communication between the coast and the interior. Settlement has also taken place along the rivers, as it did on the peninsula in an earlier period.

Communication by river

Both continental and insular Malaysia are in the same latitudes and are influenced by similar airstreams. They consequently experience similarly high temperatures and humidities, heavy rainfall, and a climatic year patterned around the northeast and southwest monsoons. In coastal areas in East Malaysia, minimum temperatures range from 72° to 76° F (22° to 25° C) and maximum temperatures from 88° to 92° F (31° to 33° C); temperatures are lower in the interior because of higher altitudes. As on the peninsula, rainfall variations are pronounced. Mean annual rainfall in Sabah varies from 60 inches to 120 inches, while most parts of Sarawak receive between 100 to 160 inches. The northeast monsoon brings heavy rain and rough seas to the exposed coasts of southwest Sarawak and north and northeast Sabah. The southwest monsoon, however, affects mainly the southwest coastal belt of Sabah. Floods are common, especially along the west coast of Sabah. Neither mainland nor insular Malaysia is in the typhoon belt, but their coasts

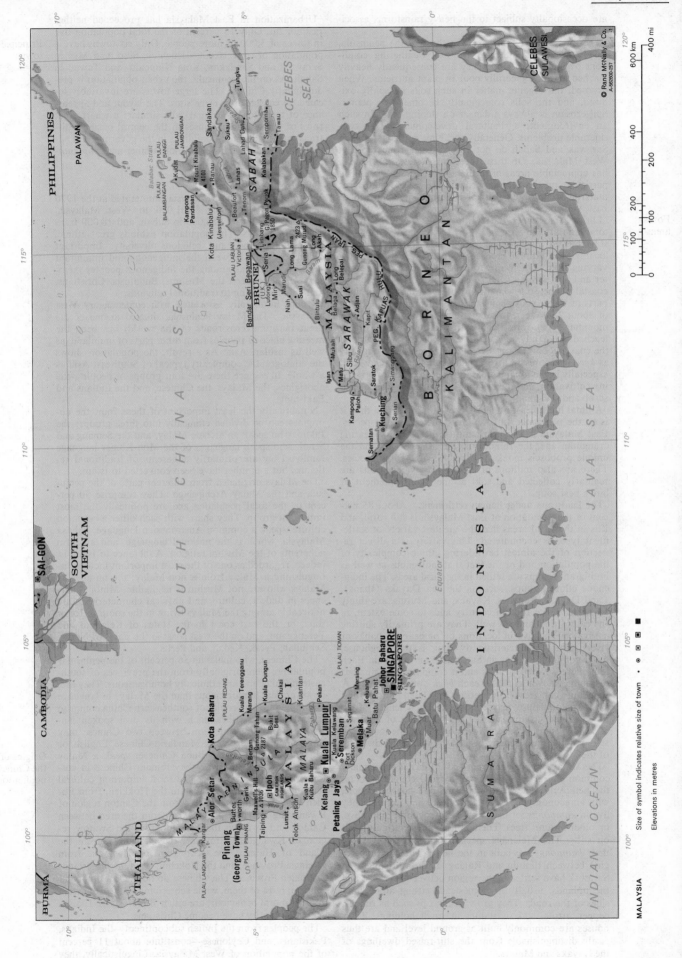

PHILIPPINES

PALAWAN

Balabac Strait

PULAU BALAMBANGAN
PULAU BANGGI

Tungku
Sandakan
Sukau
Lahad Datu
Kudat
Mount Kinabalu
4101
Ranau
SABAH
Semporna
Tawau
Kampong Pandasan
Kota Kinabalu
(Jesselton)
Beaufort
Tenom
Lanas
Kalabakan
PULAU LABUAN
Victoria
Bandar Seri Begawan
BRUNEI
(U.K.)
Seria
Labuan
Miri
Niah Marudi
Long Lama
G. Papon Pejok
1880
Gunong Mulud
PEG. IRAN
Long Akah
Long Belepai
Bintulu
Belaga
Kapit
MALAYSIA
Suai
Adjan
SARAWAK
Mukah
Igan
Matu
Sibu
Balang
PEG. KAPUAS HULU
Saratok
Simanggang
Kampong Paloh
Kuching
Serian
Sematan

BORNEO

KALIMANTAN

CELEBES
SEA

CELEBES
SULAWESI

© Rand McNally & Co.
A-56000-257

SOUTH CHINA SEA

SAI-GON
SOUTH VIETNAM
CAMBODIA

THAILAND
BURMA

PULAU LANGKAWI
Rangui
Alor Setar
Pinang
(George Town)
PULAU PINANG
Butterworth
Gerik
MALAYSIA
Maxwell's Hill
1036
Taiping
Kuala Baharu
Kota Baharu
PULAU REDANG
Kuala Terengganu
Marang
Bertam
Gunong Tahan
2187
Bukit Besi
Kuala Dungun
Chukai
MALAYA
Ipoh
CAMERON HIGHLANDS
Lumut
Telok Anson
Kuala Kubu Baharu
Kuala Kelawang
Kelang
Kuala Lumpur
Petaling Jaya
Seremban
Port Dickson
Melaka
Segamat
Muar
Batu Pahat
Kuantan
Pekan
Mersing
Keluang
PULAU TIOMAN
Johor Baharu
SINGAPORE
SINGAPORE

SUMATRA

INDONESIA

Strait of Malacca

JAVA SEA

INDIAN OCEAN

Equator

MALAYSIA

• ⊙ ◎ ■   Size of symbol indicates relative size of town

Elevations in metres

400 mi
600 km
400 200 0
200 100 0

are occasionally subject to the heavy rainstorms associated with squalls.

The soils of East Malaysia, like those of the peninsula, developed under intensive tropical weathering conditions over a long period. They are consequently heavily leached and are generally poor in plant nutrients. When exposed, the organic matter in such soils is rapidly oxidized, and the soils consequently become even poorer. Soil erosion is always a danger on sloping land. In such an environment, agricultural development poses considerable problems. Generally speaking, soil conditions in Sarawak and Sabah do not differ greatly from those in West Malaysia. Of these three territories, only Sabah has appreciable areas of fertile soils. These are found in particular on the Semporna peninsula, where the parent material from which the soil is formed is composed of basic volcanic rocks.

Forest areas

Large expanses of East Malaysia—77 percent of the total land area in Sarawak and 78 percent in Sabah—are still covered by dense, evergreen rain forest. Soil type, location, and altitude produce distinctive vegetation zones, varying from tidal swamp forest on the coast, to freshwater and peat swamp forest on the ill-drained parts of the coastal plains, to lowland rain forest on the well-drained parts of the coastal plains and foothills up to an altitude of about 2,000 feet, to submontane and montane (lower mountain-type) forest above that altitude. The highly leached and sandy soils of parts of central Sarawak and the coast support an open, heathlike forest, known locally as *kerangas* forest. Large expanses of the forested land, especially in the upland areas, have been cleared for shifting cultivation, and the original forests have given way to scrub and savanna.

Animal life in East Malaysia is even more varied than it is on the peninsula. In addition to the peninsula species, East Malaysia is also the home of the fast-disappearing orangutan ape, the rhinoceros, the honey bear, and the unique proboscis monkey—a reddish tree-living species. There are also millions of cave swifts, whose nests are regularly collected and sold as the main ingredient of bird's nest soup.

The landscape under human settlement. About 85 percent of the population of East Malaysia is still rural, and it is in the rural areas that the greatest variety of settlement types is encountered. This variety is a direct reflection of the almost bewildering ethnic complexity of the population and of the fact that indigenous as well as immigrant groups are settled in the rural areas. The indigenous ethnic groups, such as the Sea Dayaks (Ibans), Land Dayaks, Kenyahs, Kayans, and Muruts, are thinly scattered in the foothill country and, to some extent, in the coastal lowlands as well. They are primarily shifting cultivators and live in locations on or near the banks of rivers. Their characteristic dwelling is the longhouse, more commonly found in Sarawak than in Sabah. Each longhouse is raised on stilts and is composed of a number of rooms, known as *bileks;* each *bilek* houses a family. A longhouse can grow by accretions of related families, and an Iban longhouse may in time reach a length of 50 *bileks.* Some groups, such as the Melanaus of Sarawak and the Dusuns of Sabah, have abandoned the longhouse settlement form, adopting instead the individual dwelling of the Malays.

The Malays and Melanaus of East Malaysia share many common characteristics with their rural counterparts on the peninsula. They are a riverine and coastal people, with an economy based on agriculture and fishing. They live in *kampongs* set in the midst of coconut, mangrove, or other swamp trees. Their houses are invariably built on stilts. The Melanaus specialize in sago production; their *kampongs* are built in the large deltaic swamp region between Bintulu and Rajang. The rural Chinese in Sarawak have settled in the region between the coast and the uplands, usually in homesteads strung along both sides of the roads. They grow cash crops such as rubber, pepper, fruits, and vegetables in small holdings. Their houses are commonly built at ground level and are thus easily distinguishable from the stilt-raised dwellings of the Dayaks and Malays.

Urbanization in East Malaysia has proceeded neither fast nor far. Only 15 percent of the total population live in towns of 3,000 or more people. Only six towns have a population of over 10,000—Kuching, Sibu, and Miri in Sarawak, and Sandakan, Kota Kinabalu, and Tawau in Sabah. As on the peninsula, the urban population is predominantly Chinese. The large towns are invariably located on coastal or riverine sites. The layout and appearance of these towns are markedly similar: a wharf area; rows of Chinese shop-houses in the central business districts; more substantial buildings in the governmental administrative area; and one or more timber and *atap kampongs* built on the river banks.

Principal towns

PEOPLE AND POPULATION

The total population of Malaysia enumerated at the 1970 census was 10,452,000: 8,801,000 in West Malaysia, 977,000 in Sarawak, 656,000 in Sabah, and 18,000 transients and others. The population exhibits great ethnic, linguistic, cultural, and religious diversity. Important differences exist between the indigenous and immigrant peoples, as well as among the indigenous peoples themselves, and between the Muslims, Buddhists, Christians, and tribes adhering to traditional religions.

Groups historically associated with contemporary West Malaysia. The Malay Peninsula, situated at one of the great maritime crossroads of the world, has been the meeting place of peoples from other parts of mainland, as well as insular, Asia. As a result, the population shows the ethnographic complexity typical of Southeast Asia as a whole. In essence there are four groups of people—the aborigines, the Malays, the Chinese, and the Indians and Pakistanis.

Numerically the least important of these four, the aborigines can be divided ethnically into three groups: the Jakun, who speak an archaic Malay, and the Semang and Senoi, who speak languages of the Mon-Khmer language family. They are primarily adherents of traditional religions, but a number have been converted to Islām.

The Malays originated from different parts of the peninsula and the Malay Archipelago. They comprise 50 percent of the total population and are politically the most important group. They share with each other a common culture, speak a common Austronesian language, Bahasa Malaysia, which is the national language, and are firm adherents of the Muslim religion. Adherence to Islām is, indeed, regarded as one of the most important factors distinguishing a Malay from a non-Malay; the number of Malays who are not Muslim is negligible. Minor differences in dialect, culture, and physical characteristics are noticeable among the Malays living in the south in Johor state, on the east coast in the states of Kelantan and Terengganu, and on the west coast in the states of Negeri Sembilan, Perak, Kedah, and Perlis.

The Chinese, who make up 36 percent of the peninsular population, were originally from the provinces of southeastern China and are ethnically homogeneous. They are, however, less homogeneous than the Malays in language and religion. The peoples of southeastern China comprise several different tribes, each with its own spoken language. Oral communication between two Chinese may thus sometimes depend on Mandarin Chinese, English, or Malay. A minority, the Baba Chinese, speak a Malay patois, although otherwise they remain Chinese in customs, manners, and habit. The most important cultural and linguistic Chinese groups are the Hokkien, from Fukien Province; the Cantonese, from the Canton region of Kwangtung Province; the Hakka, from the area between Canton and Swatow; the Tiechiu, from the Swatow region of Kwangtung Province; the Hainanese, from the island of Hainan; the Kwongsai, or Kwangsi, from Kwangsi Province; and the Hokchiu, from the hinterlands of Fukien Province. The Chinese do not have a dominant religion; most of them, while subscribing to the Confucian code of moral behaviour, are either Buddhists or Taoists. A small minority have become Christians.

Origins of the Chinese population

The peoples from the Indian subcontinent—the Indians, Pakistanis, and Ceylonese—constitute about 11 percent of the population of West Malaysia. Linguistically, they can be subdivided into speakers of Dravidian languages (Tamil, Telugu, Malayalam *et al.*) and speakers of Indo-European languages (Punjabi, Bengali, Pashto, and Sinhalese). Numerically, the Tamil speakers are the largest group. Most of the Indians and Ceylonese are Hindus, while the Pakistanis are predominantly Muslim. Some Indians have been converted to Christianity. The Sikhs, from the Punjab, speak their own language and also adhere to their own religion, Sikhism.

The population also includes small numbers of Europeans and Americans, Eurasians, Arabs, and Thai.

West Malaysian demography. Vital statistics of West Malaysia indicate several perceptible trends in health and sanitation conditions. The average life expectancy has increased significantly in recent decades and now stands in the 60s. Crude death rates among all races dropped from about 12 per 1,000 in the late 1950s to about 7 per 1,000 in the late 1960s. Due to better health services and a more general acceptance of the methods of modern medicine, mortality rates are lower in the towns and cities. Since the Chinese are usually urban dwellers, their crude death rates have always been lower than those for the country as a whole, while the essentially rural Malays have death rates above the national average.

Crude birth rates have declined significantly only in the last decade or so. The trend toward lower birth rates is most evident among the Chinese. The rates among the Malays are higher, while those of the Indians and Pakistanis are slightly lower than those for the country as a whole. Over the years the rate of population growth has slowed down, and the average annual population increase due to the excess of births over deaths has dropped progressively from a peak of 3.5 percent in 1956 to 2.76 percent in 1968.

Restrictions on immigration

The movement of vast numbers of peoples in and out of the country, which occurred in the earlier years of West Malaysia's history, ended before World War II. A series of laws passed since 1945, and particularly after the political separation from Singapore in 1965, severely restrict the entry of immigrants from all countries. Migratory surpluses are consequently no longer significant as a cause of population growth, amounting to less than 70,000 in the decade of the 1960s.

Table 1: Malaysia, Area and Population

	area		population	
	sq mi	sq km	1957 census	1970 census
Regions				
East Malaysia	76,510	198,153	1,198,950†	1,633,000
States				
Sabah	28,460	73,709	454,421†	656,000
Sarawak	48,050	124,445	744,529†	977,000
West Malaysia	50,806	131,582	6,278,758	8,801,000
States				
Johor	7,330	18,984	926,850	1,274,000
Kedah	3,639	9,425	701,964	955,000
Kelantan	5,765	14,931	505,522	681,000
Melaka	637	1,650	291,211	404,000
Negeri Sembilan	2,565	6,642	364,524	479,000
Pahang	13,886	35,963	313,058	503,000
Pinang	399	1,033	572,100	777,000
Perak	8,110	21,004	1,221,446	1,563,000
Perlis	307	795	90,885	121,000
Selangor	3,166	8,200	1,021,929	1,629,000
Terengganu	5,002	12,955	278,269	406,000
Total Malaysia	127,316	329,736*	‡	10,452,000§

*Converted area figures do not add to total because of rounding. †Sabah and Sarawak had 1960 census. ‡No census total for Malaysia can be given because the census of Sabah, Sarawak, and West Malaysia took place at different dates. §Total is revised and includes 18,000 transients and others.
Source: Official government figures.

The pattern of population distribution consists of two areas of high population densities and one area of low density. The major area of population concentration is the tin and rubber belt, a belt 25 to 75 miles wide extending along the west of the peninsula from Perlis to Johor. Within this area, which comprises only 30 percent of the total land area, live three-quarters of the total population. Another 12 percent of the population is distributed in the Kelantan and Terengganu river deltas in the northeast of the peninsula. The remainder of the peninsula—the interior uplands and most of the east—is sparsely populated except in towns and cities and along the main rivers, roads, and railways. Approximately one-third of the population lives in towns with a population of 5,000 and over. There are over 80 such towns, and two-thirds of them are located in the tin and rubber belt.

The peninsula has a high rate of population growth, averaging about 3 percent per annum. Such a growth rate has hindered development. There are, however, indications that the rate of population growth may be slowing down. A recent survey found that within the decade 1956 to 1965 fertility among the Chinese declined by about a quarter, among the Indians by over 20 percent, and among the Malays by 13 percent.

Groups historically associated with contemporary East Malaysia. The population of East Malaysia is ethnographically even more complex. Although recent censuses have tended to oversimplify, listing 8 main ethnic groupings in Sarawak and 7 in Sabah, there are in fact 25 ethnic groups in Sarawak and 26 in Sabah, not counting minor tribal groups. In order of numerical importance, the main ethnic groups in Sarawak are the Chinese, one-third of the total population; various speakers of mutually unintelligible Austronesian languages including the Sea Dayaks or Ibans (under 30%); the Malays (under 20%); the Land Dayaks (under 10%); the Melanaus (about 5%); and other minor races (about 5%).

Ethnic diversity

The Chinese of Sarawak, drawn from the southeastern provinces of China, share common regional origins with the Chinese of West Malaysia, but the relative importance of each dialect group is different. Thus the Hakka and Foochow (Hokchiu) groups, who are less numerous than the Cantonese and Hokkien in West Malaysia, are the dominant linguistic groups and together comprise two-thirds of the Chinese population. The other important dialect groups are the Hokkien, the Cantonese, the Tiechiu, the Henghua, and the Hainanese. As in West Malaysia, the Chinese of Sarawak practice Buddhism, Taoism, and Confucianism. Only a few are Christians.

The Ibans are the largest and most important indigenous group in Sarawak. Their origins are obscure. Until fairly recently they were headhunters. They are a homogeneous people speaking a language described as a kind of pre-Islāmic Sumatran Malay. Most of them are longhouse dwellers, practicing shifting cultivation in the interior uplands. They have a distinctive culture, in which religion plays an important part; nearly every activity is influenced or governed by animist beliefs.

The Malays of Sarawak are a heterogeneous group of people, among whom only a few are of immigrant West Malaysian origin. Most are the descendants of indigenous peoples who were converted to Islām and adopted the Malay way of life some time during a period of perhaps the past 500 years. Although ethnically diverse, they are culturally homogeneous, speaking a common language and professing the Muslim faith.

The Land Dayaks live in hill country; most of them are found in the First Division. (Sarawak is divided into five divisions; these administrative units were created at different stages in the historical growth of Sarawak as a political entity.) Although all are of the same ethnic group, they speak five different but related dialects that are, nevertheless, to some extent mutually intelligible. The majority of Land Dayaks are adherents of traditional religions, but in recent years Christian missionaries have made some converts among them.

The Land Dayaks

The Melanaus differ ethnically from the Sarawak Malays, being shorter, broader shouldered, and of a lighter complexion. Their dialects, which are distinct from Malay, do not differ sufficiently to constitute a barrier to communication. Three-quarters of the Melanau population are Muslims; the rest, except for a small number of Christians, follow traditional religions. Other indigenous peoples—Kenyahs, Kayans, Kedayans, Muruts, Kelabits, Bisayas, Punans, and others—contribute much to the ethnic and cultural diversity of East Malaysia.

Sabah also has a kaleidoscopic mixture of peoples. Of

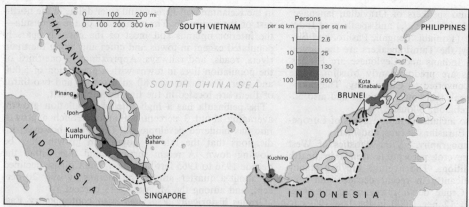

Population density of Malaysia.

the total population of 656,000, 30 percent are Dusuns (or Kadazans); 22 percent, Chinese; over 10 percent, Orang Lauts (Bajaus); almost 5 percent, Muruts; and under 20 percent is composed of such indigenous peoples as the Brunei Malays, Kedayan, Orang Sungei, Bisaya, Sulu, Tidong, and Sino-Native. Europeans, Eurasians, Malays, Indonesians, Filipinos, and Indians and Pakistanis comprise the remainder.

The Dusuns are composed of a number of tribes, each speaking a dialect that the others can understand. About a quarter of the Dusun population are Christians, about 7 percent are Muslims, and the remainder are animists. More than half of the Chinese are Hakka-speaking; the other important Chinese dialect groups are Cantonese, Hokkien, Tiechiu, and Hainanese. The Bajaus are not a cohesive community, being split into two main groups—the sedentary agriculturists, who have settled on the north coast, and those who live by the sea on the east coast. Most are Muslims, but not all of them can communicate with each other. The Muruts of Sabah are ethnically different from the Muruts of Sarawak, being descended from the same stock as the Dusuns. They are shifting cultivators. Although they are divided into subtribes, their languages are mutually intelligible. Although most follow traditional religions, approximately one-fourth are Christian.

Population growth

East Malaysian demography. The vital statistics of East Malaysia indicate that the population is increasing at an unprecedentedly rapid rate, due to increasing fertility and declining mortality. The crude birth rates of all the major ethnic groups in Sarawak and Sabah have increased steadily since 1945. The crude birth rate in both Sarawak and Sabah averages about 48 per 1,000. The crude death rates for both have fallen progressively over the last decade or so and stand at about 12 per 1,000.

Before the war there was a free flow of people to and from East Malaysia, so that the rate of population growth, although slow, was nevertheless greatly influenced by the net surplus from migration. Today neither immigration nor emigration is any longer significant as a cause of population changes. The rates of population growth in East Malaysia have nevertheless increased remarkably in recent years, averaging about 3.5 percent per annum. As in West Malaysia, this high growth rate is due almost entirely to the natural increase of population, owing little to immigration.

The population of East Malaysia is concentrated along the coasts and the rivers; the interior highlands are sparsely inhabited. Overall densities are extremely low: only 20 per square mile in Sarawak and 22 per square mile in Sabah. In Sarawak the heavy concentration of people in the southwest makes this region the most important in the country. Outside this region, every district except Miri Urban has a population density below the average. In Sabah the population is similarly clustered on the coast, but riverine settlements are less important than in Sarawak. Half of the population is distributed in the narrow west coastal zone or in Sandakan, the former capital. Large parts of the interior and of the east coast are thinly populated.

East Malaysia is still a sparsely settled land, with population densities far below the 173 persons per square mile in West Malaysia. East Malaysia can therefore afford to maintain its present high rates of population growth, as well as absorb some of West Malaysia's population in future years.

THE NATIONAL ECONOMY

Malaysia, the third richest country in Asia, is surpassed in wealth only by Japan and Singapore. The monetary unit is the Malaysian dollar. The country is the world's largest producer of two primary products: rubber and tin, and second to Nigeria in palm oil. Its economy, compared with those of most developing countries, is relatively advanced in terms of infrastructure facilities (roads, water supplies, electricity, etc.), institutional patterns, commercial and financial patterns, and management, professional, and administrative skills.

Natural resources. The mineral resources of Malaysia include tin, iron ore, bauxite (from which aluminum is made), coal, gold, china clay (kaolin), monazite (the principal ore of thorium, a malleable, radioactive metallic element), ilmenite (a common black mineral), columbite (a black crystalline mineral, the principal ore of niobium, used in making steel alloys), manganese, tantalite (a mineral used to make tantalum, a metallic element resistant to corrosion), wolframite (an important ore of tungsten, a metallic element with a high melting point), and zircon (the chief ore of zirconium, a metallic element, used in steel metallurgy) in West Malaysia; antimony (a brittle, lustrous, white metallic element, used in alloys), mercury, gold, coal, petroleum, bauxite, phosphate, and glass sand in Sarawak; and gold, coal, manganese, and copper in Sabah. Except for tin, iron ore, bauxite, petroleum, and copper, however, most of the minerals are of minor economic importance. In Sabah only copper is of importance.

Tin is by far the most important mineral in Malaysia. Found in 9 of the 11 West Malaysian states, it is distributed in two belts—western and eastern. The western tin belt runs along the flanks of the Main Range and along either side of the subsidiary granite ranges to the west of the Main Range. The less continuous, and also less rich, eastern tin belt runs from southern Terengganu to eastern Johor. Recent investigations indicate that there are 1,000,000,000 cubic yards of tin in the Malay Reservations (*i.e.*, lands set aside by law for the use of Malays and which cannot be sold to others). The search for new fields has been extended to the offshore areas of the western peninsula. Iron ore deposits along the eastern and western peninsula have been largely mined out.

Petroleum is found only in Sarawak, but offshore prospecting is being carried out in Sarawak, in Sabah, and in West Malaysia. The only oil field in Sarawak is at Miri in the Fourth Division, but in 1968 an offshore deposit was discovered in the state. Output of crude oil increased very rapidly between 1967 and 1970, reaching a total of 6,558,800 U.S. barrels in 1970.

The main biological resources of Malaysia are its forests and its fisheries. The extensive areas still under rain forest

Tin

in both West and East Malaysia are a source of various forest products used by the indigenous peoples, as well as of timber, charcoal, firewood, poles, resins, gums, and rattans, which are produced both for local consumption and for export. In recent years the exploitation of the timber resources has intensified; timber is Malaysia's third largest foreign exchange earner, after rubber and tin.

The shallow seas off the coasts of Malaysia are the principal fishing grounds. In general the nutrient level, and hence the productivity of these seas, is low, the richer portions being those fertilized by drainage waters from the land. The annual output of the fishermen who use traditional techniques and who fish in inshore waters is low. The increased use of motorized boats has extended the range of the fishermen, enabling them to tap richer offshore fishing grounds.

The power resources of Malaysia include coal, peat, wood, petroleum, and hydroelectricity. Although proved reserves of coal and peat exist, they are not economic to mine and therefore remain only of potential use. Wood and charcoal have been the traditional domestic fuels, but in the urban areas they are rapidly being displaced by bottled gas. No hydroelectric power is generated in East Malaysia, but, as on the peninsula, the abundant rainfall and steep gradients of the rivers in the interior highlands offer a good hydroelectric potential. The main hydroelectric schemes in operation in West Malaysia are at Cameron Highlands, at Batang Padang, and at Chenderoh (on the Perak River); in addition there are small plants at Ulu Langat, Sempang, and Rahman. The petroleum resources of Sarawak do not constitute a major source of fuel oil. For power generation, therefore, Malaysia continues to depend primarily on imported fuel oil.

Sources of national income. Agriculture, forestry, fishing, and mining together constitute the most important sector of the Malaysian economy, contributing more than 90 percent of the value of all exports. Slightly more than half of the work force of West Malaysia and about 80 percent of the work force in Sarawak and Sabah are engaged in these pursuits. The majority of the population continues to depend upon agriculture for a livelihood. Agriculture contributes about 30 percent of the total gross national product (GNP). About 6 percent of the land area in Sarawak, 3 percent in Sabah, and 21 percent in West Malaysia is under cultivation. The most important cash crops are rubber (the country's main foreign exchange earner), oil palm, and coconut. The main food crop is rice (called *padi* in Malay), which ranks second only to rubber in terms of the amount of land and labour devoted to its production. Cultivation systems range from the traditional shifting cultivation, still commonly practiced in East Malaysia, to the most modern forms of plantation agriculture.

Most of the land area in Malaysia, as we have seen, is still covered by forest. Forestry has assumed increased importance in recent years because of the rapid expansion of the timber industry. The sustained export demand for tropical timber has stimulated the opening up of new forest areas for timber exploitation. The output of timber has also increased as a result of the clearance of large areas of forest for land development. Timber has become Malaysia's third most important product.

Similar progress has occurred in the fishing industry. Total fish landings trebled between the late 1950s and the late '60s. The long coastlines provide Malaysian fishermen with easy access to the surrounding seas, although most of them still confine their fishing to the over-exploited shallow inshore waters. In the last decade, however, the greater use of trawlers and mechanized fishing boats has allowed the fish resources of the offshore grounds to be tapped.

The mining industry contributes about one-quarter of the total export receipts. The main minerals produced are tin, iron ore, bauxite, and petroleum. West Malaysia is the world's largest producer of tin, but intensive exploitation over the past century has led to a steady depletion of known deposits, and the tin industry is consequently searching for new deposits off the coast of the western

peninsula, as well as in Malay Reservations. The output of iron ore is also dropping due to the gradual working out of high-grade deposits. Bauxite production declined after the closure of the Sarawak mine in 1965, but an increased output from the mines in southeastern Johor had restored production to the 1,000,000-ton level by 1969. Sarawak is the only state which has petroleum resources. The first offshore well began production in Sarawak in 1968; prospecting for offshore deposits has been extended to Sabah and West Malaysia. A large deposit of copper has been discovered near Mt. Kinabalu, to be mined by a Japanese company.

Most of Malaysia's manufacturing plants are located on the peninsula. The contribution of the manufacturing sector of the economy rose from about 9 percent of the gross domestic product in 1960 to about 12 percent in 1970. Malaysia is attempting to broaden its economic base by industrialization. Efforts have been directed mainly at the production of hitherto imported consumer goods, and the range of manufacturing is also being widened to include production for export. Governmental efforts to promote industrialization include the granting of favoured treatment, including tax holidays, for selected industries; the establishment of tariff barriers for the protection of the home market; the establishment of institutions to promote industrial development; and the development of 17 industrial estates—12 in West Malaysia, 3 in Sabah, and 2 in Sarawak.

The services sector of the economy has maintained a steady growth rate over the last decade, now accounting for about half of the gross domestic product (GDP). In West Malaysia more than 30 percent of the labour force is engaged in service industries. The highest growth rates have been in electricity, water and sanitary services, banking, insurance and real estate, transport and communications, public administration and defense, and public services such as schools and hospitals.

A high percentage of Malaysia's exports is made up of raw materials. Five commodities—tin, rubber, timber, palm oil, and iron ore—account for about three-quarters of the total value of all exports. The three most important imports are food, manufactured goods and machinery, and transport equipment, which together constitute about two-thirds of the total value of all imports.

Management of the economy. The free enterprise system introduced during the British colonial era has been modified since independence. The government has embarked upon a program of planned economic development that aims at raising living standards of the population in general and of the economically weaker communities in particular. The program, however, encourages the continued participation of the private sector. Direct governmental participation is limited to the development of such infrastructural facilities as transport, public utilities, drainage and irrigation works, agricultural settlement schemes, and industrial estates, as well as of social and administrative services. The First Malaysia Development Plan, which covered the period from 1966 to 1970, was supported by both public and private investment programs.

Systems of public finance—auditing and organization of accounts, parliamentary control, and revenue collection—are based on British principles. The fiscal system—rather than being employed to manipulate the pace of economic activity, the level of employment, or price levels—is basically a mechanism for raising revenue for governmental expenditure. Heavy dependence is placed on customs and excise duties for revenue collection, while income and other direct taxes provide a comparatively small proportion of the total yield, even though in recent years higher incomes and improved methods of tax collection have increased the yield. The government is attempting, meanwhile, to distribute the tax burden equitably, by such means as sliding income tax scales, higher duties on luxury goods, and lower duties on essential commodities.

The economy of Malaysia relies heavily on a few raw materials for export. More than half the total labour force is engaged in primary production. There is a contin-

Hydro-electric potential

Mining exports

Economic development

ued dependence on imports for many manufactured goods, and the industrial sector is still insignificant. By the standards of other developing countries in Asia, Malaysia's economy is nevertheless relatively advanced, varied, and complex. The component states of Malaysia are, however, in widely different stages of economic development. West Malaysia, contributing nearly 90 per cent of the total GNP, is clearly the dominant economic partner, with Sarawak and Sabah lagging far behind.

Economically, Malaysia faces the necessity of maintaining a steady rate of economic growth despite a rapid population increase. Unemployment is growing, standing at nearly 8 percent of the total labour force of 3,200,000 in 1970. Underemployment, also, while its extent has not been accurately assessed, is widespread, especially in the agricultural sector. Most of the unemployed are in West Malaysia; Sabah, on the other hand, is short of manpower. In Sarawak, population pressure has already led to land exhaustion and to soil erosion in many areas of shifting cultivation.

In order to reduce its vulnerability to world market fluctuations, Malaysia has to diversify its economy and at the same time raise standards of living, especially in its depressed areas—in the eastern side of the peninsula and in the interior parts of Sarawak and Sabah.

TRANSPORTATION

The transport network in West Malaysia is well developed, especially in the tin and rubber belt. Both Sarawak and Sabah, however, have poor transport facilities, relying primarily on river transport for movement between the coast and the interior.

Peninsula roads
The road network in West Malaysia is considered the best in Southeast Asia. There are over 10,000 miles of road, almost all of which are hard-surfaced. The network will be further extended with the completion of the 185-mile East–West Highway, linking Kota Baharu on the east coast to Butterworth on the west via Gerik, and the 89-mile Southern Pahang road, which will open up the Pahang–Tenggara region. The road networks in Sarawak and Sabah are still skeletal in pattern, though many miles of road were added in the 1960s. There are about 1,000 miles of road in Sarawak and over 1,700 miles in Sabah. Only 200 or 300 miles in each territory are bitumen-surfaced; the rest are of poor quality.

The rail transport system is only well developed on the peninsula. Sarawak has no railway and Sabah has only a short line linking Kota Kinabalu to Beaufort, Tenom, and Melalap. Because of competition from road transport, the Malayan Railway has been operating at a loss and a reorganization has been recommended.

Traditionally, transport in both East and West Malaysia has been by water. River transport, however, is no longer important in West Malaysia except on parts of the east coast, but in East Malaysia it continues to play a major role. On the rivers of Sarawak and Sabah, which link the interior and the coast, almost all settlements are riverine and many are only accessible by water. Due to the long coastlines, the coastal and sea transport systems of Malaysia are of great importance. Over the years a number of coastal and river ports have been established at strategic locations—Pinang and Port Swettenham in West Malaysia; and Kuching, Sibu, Labuan, Kota Kinabalu, Sandakan, and Tawau in East Malaysia. Traffic at these ports has grown at a rate of between 5 and 10 percent a year.

Air transport has grown even more rapidly, with passenger traffic increasing at the rate of about 20 percent a year. The rate of increase was higher in East Malaysia, internally as well as externally, because in West Malaysia other modes of transport are available. Regular internal services fly between Kuala Lumpur, Kuching, and Kota Kinabalu and also link the component states of Malaysia. Malaysia–Singapore Airlines, the jointly owned local airline, now operates international services in the Pacific region in addition to its internal operations, using jet and propjet aircraft.

ADMINISTRATION AND SOCIAL CONDITIONS

The structure of government. Malaysia is a federal constitutional monarchy with a nonpolitical head of state (the *yang di-pertuan agong*—a title meaning literally "the supreme ruler"—who is elected from among the rulers or sultans of the nine Malay states for a five-year term of office), a legislature composed of two houses, or *dewan* (the Senate, or Dewan Negara, meaning "National Hall," and the House of Representatives, or Dewan Ra'ayat, meaning "Hall of the People"), a prime minister and cabinet, an independent judiciary, and a neutral civil service. The federal parliament is the supreme legislative body of the country. It also controls the finances of the government. A bill passed by both houses and sanctioned by the *yang di-pertuan agong* becomes a federal law.

The yang *di-pertuan* agong

The House of Representatives functions in a similar manner to the British House of Commons. It has a membership of 144, of which 104 are from West Malaysia, 24 from Sarawak, and 16 from Sabah. Members are elected to office from single-member constituencies on the basis of a simple majority. The term of office of a member is five years. The Senate has a membership of 58, of which 32 are appointed by the *yang di-pertuan agong* on the recommendation of the prime minister. The 26 elected members are made up of 2 representatives from each of the legislative assemblies of the 13 component states. Voting in either house is by a simple majority, but amendments to the constitution require a two-thirds majority.

The *yang di-pertuan agong* appoints the prime minister, who must be a citizen in law as well as a member of the House of Representatives. On the advice of the prime minister, the *yang di-pertuan agong* then appoints the other ministers who make up the cabinet. The number of ministers is not fixed, but all must be members of the federal parliament.

The powers of the federal parliament are relatively wide and include the authority to legislate in matters concerned with defense, external affairs, internal security, the administration of justice, and citizenship. The state legislatures of the 13 component states, however, retain responsibility for matters pertaining to Islāmic law and for matters pertaining to personal and family laws affecting those of the Islāmic faith, as well as for land laws. The constitution also provides that some items may be dealt with either by the federal or by the state legislature.

Each of the 13 states of Malaysia has its own written constitution and its own legislative assembly. Each state also has an executive council collectively responsible to the legislative assembly and headed by a chief minister in Pinang, Melaka, Sarawak, and Sabah and by a *mentri besar* (literally, "chief minister") in the nine other Malay states. These nine Malay states have hereditary rulers, who are entitled sultans in Johor, Kedah, Kelantan, Pahang, Perak, Selangor, and Terengganu; the raja (king) in Perlis; and the *yang di-pertuan besar* (literally, "the chief ruler") in Negeri Sembilan. The heads of the other states are appointed to office. They are known as governors in Melaka, Pinang, and Sarawak, while in Sabah the head of state is known as the *yang di-pertuan negara*. The ruler or governor of a state acts on the advice of the state government.

The constitution provides for parliamentary elections, and for elections to state legislatures, to be held at least every five years. General elections were held in May 1969, but balloting was abandoned in East Malaysia after postelection racial riots broke out in Kuala Lumpur. A halt to party politics was ordered by the emergency government (National Operations Council), which then took over the government. Elections were subsequently held in East Malaysia in July 1970. A coalition, the Alliance Government (see Table 2), was then returned to power. With the possible support of the five SUPP (Sarawak United People's Party) representatives, the Alliance Government could command a two-thirds majority in the House of Representatives, which would permit amendments to the constitution.

Elections

The constitution of the federation of Malaysia, which is the supreme law of the country, provides that the judicial power of the federation shall be vested in the High Court of West Malaysia and the High Court in East Malaysia and also in subordinate courts. Above the High

Table 2: Composition of the House of Representatives, February 1971	
party	number of seats
The Alliance	
West Malaysia (United Malays National Organization; Malaysian Chinese Association; Malaysian Indian Congress)	68
Sarawak (Parti Pesaka; Parti Bumiputra; Sarawak Chinese Association)	9
Sabah (United Sabah National Organization; Sabah Chinese Association; Sabah Indian Congress)	16
Democratic Action Party	13
Pan-Malayan Islāmic Party	12
Sarawak National Party	9
Parti Gerakan Ra'ayat (Malaysian People's Movement)	7
Sarawak United People's Party	5
People's Progressive Party	4
Total	143*

*One seat unfilled.

Courts is the Federal Court, with jurisdiction to hear and determine appeals from decisions by any High Court. The supreme head of the judiciary is the lord president of the Federal Court.

Each High Court consists of a chief justice and a number of other judges—12 in West Malaysia and 4 in East Malaysia. The High Court has unlimited criminal and civil jurisdiction and may pass any sentence allowed by law. Below the High Court are the subordinate courts, which consist of the Sessions Courts and the Magistrates' Courts. Both these lower courts have criminal and civil jurisdiction—criminal cases coming before one or the other court depending upon the seriousness of the offense and civil cases depending upon the sum involved. In addition, there are religious courts in those Malay states that are established under Islāmic law. These courts are governed by state and not federal legislation.

The armed forces and police. The Malaysian armed forces have increased in strength and capability since the formation of Malaysia in 1963. After the withdrawal of British military forces from Malaysia and Singapore at the end of 1971, a five-power defence agreement between Malaysia, Singapore, New Zealand, Australia, and Britain was concluded to ensure defence against external aggression. In the early 1970s Malaysia was engaged in internal security operations against guerrilla forces of the Malaysian Communist Party on the West Malaysia–Thai border, as well as against the clandestine Communist organization in Sarawak; the requirement that all young persons register for a national service draft to combat the guerillas was, however, ended in 1972.

The armed forces, consisting of the army, the navy, and the air force, total nearly 48,000 men (1970). The army, which is the most experienced and the largest of the three, consists of 18 infantry battalions, 2 reconnaissance regiments, 1 squadron of scout cars, 2 artillery regiments, and various supporting arms. In addition to some 38,000 men in the regular army, the ground forces also include 23,000 men in the Police Field Force and 45,000 men in the reserves. The Royal Malaysian Navy has a strength of 4,000 men and a complement of 2 frigates, 8 minesweepers, 4 fast patrol boats, and 24 other patrol boats. The emphasis is on speed and manoeuvrability for the purpose of defending the long, indented coastlines and narrow waters of Malaysia against intruders and pirates. The Royal Malaysian Air Force has 3,000 men and 30 combat aircraft (10 Sabre and 20 Tebuan jet aircraft), as well as 27 transport aircraft and a number of helicopters.

The states of Malaysia inherited from their common colonial past an internal security system based on the British model. The police force is well trained and combats not only crime but also subversive activities, including armed Communist insurrection.

Social conditions. The education system has been expanded to help to develop skills, to rectify the educational imbalance between urban and rural areas, and to foster greater national unity. Public expenditure on education increased from about 3 percent to over 6 percent of the national income in the past decade.

Education. Governmental policy is to provide nine years of education to any child who desires it. Enrollment in primary schools on the peninsula has increased by almost 40 percent in the past decade. In Sarawak in recent years, the rate of enrollment has increased even more sharply. In Sabah it more than doubled between 1960 and 1967 alone. Considerable progress has also been achieved at the secondary level, although about 90 percent of the total enrollment is in West Malaysia. Institutions of higher learning include three universities —the University of Malaya, the University of Penang, and the National University of Malaysia (Universiti Kebangsaan Malaysia)—as well as the Mari Institute of Technology, the Federal Technical College, the College of Agriculture, and a large number of teacher-training colleges and vocational training centres.

Health. The general level of health has improved in the last decade. The country is free from many of the diseases that plague tropical countries, but diseases borne by carriers, such as malaria, are still a problem in rural areas. Health conditions and health facilities vary among the component states, being better in West Malaysia than in the states of Borneo. One indicator of this difference is that the doctor-to-population ratio is one to 4,000 in West Malaysia, one to 9,000 in Sabah, and one to 14,000 in Sarawak. Within each state, health services are better in the towns and cities than in the rural areas. Segments of the rural population continue to rely on traditional rather than modern medicine for treatment. Most of the modern health services are provided by the government. Welfare services are, however, provided by both government and voluntary agencies and include relief programs for the needy, the aged, and the handicapped.

Housing. The multicultural character of the population of Malaysia is visibly reflected in the great variety of types of houses to be seen, which range from the longhouses and stilt houses of the rural peoples to examples of modern architecture in the cities. There is an abundance of forest-derived building material in the rural areas, so that no statistically measurable housing problem is evident, even though some of the dwellings in the more remote areas are often only temporary shelters. In the larger towns and cities, however, slums are common. A governmental housing authority was to be established to plan the rehousing of slum dwellers.

Wages and cost of living. As large numbers of people, especially in Sarawak and Sabah, live by hunting, gathering, fishing, and simple agriculture, wage earners form only part of the total economically active population. Because of the increasing pressure of population on the land, however, there is a growing tendency for the male labour force to seek wage employment. A major problem is, nevertheless, the shortage of skilled labour, even though high wages are offered for such labour in industrial occupations. Wages in tin mines are higher than those on the plantations. Average monthly earnings of an unskilled labourer in a tin mine may be two to three times more than the earnings of a weeder on a rubber, oil palm, coconut, or tea plantation.

The value of real wages is difficult to estimate in the absence of indexes showing the relationship between wages and cost of living. In West Malaysia, wages appeared to have risen steadily in the 1960s, especially in the tin mines and on the plantations, and to have outpaced rises in the cost of living. The cost-of-living index, for example, only rose from 100 in the base year 1963 to 110 in 1972.

CULTURAL LIFE AND INSTITUTIONS

Malaysia, with its complexity of peoples and cultures, is a melting pot of several important cultural traditions, stemming from the Malay Archipelago as well as from China, India, the Middle East, and the West. Malay culture and Bornean culture are indigenous to the area. In the first one and a half millennia AD, indigenous Malay culture in the Malay Peninsula and in other parts of Southeast Asia

Security arrangements

was strongly marked by pre-Islāmic Indian and early Islāmic influences. Indian contact with the Malay Peninsula extended over a period from about the 4th century AD to the late 14th century, exerting a profound influence upon religion (through Hinduism and Buddhism), art, and literature. Islām, introduced to Malacca (now Melaka) in the 15th century, soon became the dominant religion of the Malays. The introduction of Western cultural influences in the 19th century affected many aspects of Malay life, especially in technology, law, social organization, and economics.

Contemporary Malay culture is thus multifaceted, consisting of many strands—animistic, early Hindu, early and modern Islāmic, and, especially in the cities, Western. The collective pattern thus established is distinct from other cultures and recognizably Malay.

Unlike the early Chinese traders who settled in Malacca and Penang and were partially assimilated (at least to the extent of adopting the Malay language), the Chinese who emigrated to the Malay Peninsula in the late 19th and early 20th centuries in large numbers were usually transients who established self-contained communities. Chinese cultural influence has consequently been minimal. The Chinese immigrants themselves, moreover, did not form a homogeneous group. Their culture in Malaysia today has its roots in the culture and civilization of prerevolutionary China, with modifications brought about by local circumstances and environment.

The Indians are either immigrants or descendants of immigrants, most of whom originally came as labourers to work in the coffee and rubber plantations. Like the Chinese, they too, until World War II, were mainly transients, living in closed communities and remaining virtually unassimilated.

The communities of Malaysia have all been affected by past British colonial rule and present Western modernizing influences. Western cultural influence has been greatest in education and institutional forms. Traditions and cultural institutions have been least affected in the rural areas—in eastern West Malaysia and in the interior of East Malaysia—while the cities have been the focus of the most rapid cultural changes.

Art forms
Within Malaysian societies, external cultural influences have made the least impact in music, dancing, literature, and the decorative arts. In East Malaysia, the indigenous cultural background includes no written history or literature; architecture is little developed; and the principal art forms are dancing and handicrafts, represented notably by the textiles handwoven by the Punan tribe, cloth made by the Bajau people, patterned rattan mats and basketwork, and wood carvings. Particularly on the peninsula, the artistic manifestations of Malay culture are mainly in literature, music, dancing, and the decorative arts. Painting and sculpture are poorly developed, primarily because Islām does not encourage the representation of the human form. Distinctive and colourful examples of the Malay decorative arts include batik cloth (cloth hand dyed by using a special technique), silverware, the handmade *kris* (a short sword or heavy dagger with a wavy blade), wood carving, and basketwork. Malaysian Chinese culture is derived from Chinese civilization and is represented by literature, drama, music, painting, and architecture. In recent years some Malaysian artists, of Malay, Chinese, and Indian origin, have also begun to produce new art forms, especially in painting and architecture, that represent a new synthesis that is distinctively Malaysian in character.

Press and broadcasting. The cultural diversity of Malaysia is illustrated by the fact that newspapers, 48 (in 1969) in number, are published in 6 languages—Malay, Chinese, English, Tamil, Punjabi, and Kadazan—while Radio Malaysia broadcasts in 16 languages and dialects. The newspapers are all privately owned and vary greatly in circulation, quality of reporting, and news coverage. Among the educated groups, the press is the principal source of information. In remote rural areas, especially among illiterate groups, the radio is relied upon. Television is, however, the most popular medium among all language groups.

PROSPECTS FOR THE FUTURE

Malaysia is a federation of disparate ethnic, economic, and political components. The federation has faced difficulties and problems from the moment of its inception in 1963. The most intractable of these problems—the strained relations between West Malaysia and Singapore—was solved by a political separation. Other problems, however, no less serious, remain. Racial riots of May 1969, between the Malays and the Chinese, which led to the suspension of parliamentary rule for 21 months, were an indication of the underlying tension stemming from ethnic imbalances. Other imbalances exist—between West and East Malaysia, between urban and rural areas, and between the modern and traditional. The fact that East Malaysia takes less than 5 percent of West Malaysia's exports and supplies only 0.5 percent of its imports indicates the need for closer economic integration between the component states. Malaysia also faces the threat of armed Communism on the Thai and Sarawak borders. Within the country itself, however, the fundamental problem remains that of correcting ethnic disparities in income while fostering the growth of a Malaysian consciousness and sense of identity among the people.

BIBLIOGRAPHY. S.T. ALISJAHBANA *et al.* (eds.), *The Cultural Problems of Malaysia in the Context of Southeast Asia* (1967), articles on aspects of the culture, religion, and languages of the peoples of Malaysia; C.A. FISHER, *South-East Asia* (1964), an important work on the geography of Southeast Asia, with a substantial section on the component states of Malaysia; D.W. FRYER, *Emerging Southeast Asia* (1970), a wide-ranging analytical study of the economy of Southeast Asian countries, with a perceptive chapter on Malaysia; J.C. JACKSON, *Sarawak: A Geographical Survey of a Developing State* (1968), a comprehensive, well-documented survey; L.W. JONES, *The Population of Borneo* (1966), a demographic study of the peoples of Sarawak, Sabah, and Brunei, based on 1960 census statistics; V. KANAPATHY, *The Malaysian Economy: Problems and Prospects* (1970), a series of essays by an economist on manpower, agriculture, industrialization, financial institutions, and international trade; YONG LENG LEE, *North Borneo (Sabah): A Study in Settlement Geography* (1965), an examination of the problems and features of settlement in an equatorial environment, *Population and Settlement in Sarawak* (1970), a well-documented study of the peoples and their impact on the landscape of Sarawak; CHONG-YAH LIM, *Economic Development of Modern Malaya* (1967), a detailed study of the evolution and growth of the West Malaysian economy from 1874 to 1963; B.C. MADAY *et al.* (eds.), *Area Handbook for Malaysia and Singapore* (1965), a comprehensive compilation of basic information on the social, political, and economic background and national security of Malaysia; JIN-BEE OOI, *Land, People, and Economy in Malaya* (1963), a comprehensive study of the physical environment, resources, population, and economy of West Malaysia; N.J. RYAN, *The Cultural Background of the Peoples of Malaya* (1962), a well-written, neatly organized book on the culture of the main ethnic groups of West Malaysia; B.C. STONE (ed.), *Natural Resources in Malaysia and Singapore* (1969), proceedings of a symposium held in 1967 containing numerous articles; GUNGWU WANG (ed.), *Malaysia: A Survey* (1964), studies on the history, geography, politics, economy, and societies of Malaysia; E.L. WHEELWRIGHT, *Industrialization in Malaysia* (1965), an enquiry into the industrial structure and the industrialization policies of Malaysia (and Singapore). For current information, see the *Malaysia Official Yearbook* (annual).

(O.J.B.)

Malformation, Biological

The processes of development are regulated in such a way that few malformed organisms are found. Those that do appear may, when properly studied, shed light on normal development. The science of teratology—a branch of morphology or embryology—is concerned with the study of these structural deviations from the normal, whether in animals or plants.

In general, abnormalities can be traced to deviations from the normal course of development, often in very early embryonic stages. Such deviations may be caused by abnormal (mutant) genes, by environmental conditions, by infection, by drugs, and, perhaps most frequently, by interactions between these sets of causes. A general interpretation has been that one factor in many cases is reduction of the rate of development, the kind and degree of deformity depending upon the stage at which the retardation occurs. This interpretation is supported by the results of descriptive studies of anomalies, and especially by evidence from experimental teratology.

ANIMAL MALFORMATIONS

Among the newborn young and embryos of man and most other species of animals are found occasional individuals who are malformed in whole or in part. The most grossly abnormal of these have been referred to from ancient times as monsters, probably because the birth of one was thought to signify something monstrous or portentous; the less severely malformed are usually known as abnormalities or anomalies.

The origin of malformations

Monsters have been regarded by primitive peoples as of supernatural origin. The birth of a malformed individual was often attributed, before the rise of modern science, to intercourse between human beings and devils or animals. The mythical beings that appear in the folklore of many peoples—races of dwarfs and giants, of sirens, mermaids, and men with a single median eye (cyclops) or leg (skiapods)—were probably suggested by observations of malformed humans. Giants and dwarfs were often classed as monsters, probably because of the prominent places they occupied in mythology.

The objective study of malformations began with the English physiologist William Harvey (1651), who correctly attributed them to deviations from the normal course of embryonic development. Systematic scientific study, however, had to await the pioneer work of the French anatomists Étienne and Isidore Geoffroy Saint-Hilaire. Their *Traité de Teratologie* (1836), which laid the basis for the science of teratology, still remains a valuable source of information. Recent improvements in understanding have come from the application of experimental analytical methods and from increased knowledge of the mechanisms of inheritance—*e.g.*, from genetics.

In man certain gross defects in babies at birth have been shown to be associated with effects acting through the mother in early pregnancy: gross defects of eyes and ears caused by infection of the mother with rubella (German measles); and microcephalic idiocy with diagnostic use of X-rays on the mother. The latter observations have been confirmed by animal experimentation. It has been established that higher rates of congenital malformations occur in areas of higher natural radioactivity. The effect may be induced by fallout from atomic explosions.

The teratogenic action of many drugs has been tragically dramatized. The appearance of an alarming number of deformed, basically limbless infants, especially in Germany, in the late 1950s and early 1960s, was traced to the ingestion by pregnant women of the sedative thalidomide (known under many trade names). This drug adversely influences the developing fetus; it appears to interfere with development only in the first seven weeks of pregnancy. Hallucinogenic drugs, such as LSD, (lysergic acid diethylamide) are suspected of damaging chromosomes and their use could result in defective offspring.

According to form, two main classes of malformations may be recognized: those with defective or excessive growth in a single body, and those with partial or complete doubling of the body on one of its axes.

Repetition or deficiency of parts. *Somatic characters.* Repetition or deficiency of single parts, such as fingers or toes (polydactyly, hypodactyly, brachydactyly), is a frequent anomaly in man and other mammals. In many analyzed cases it has been shown to result from the inheritance of an abnormal gene that produces a localized disturbance of a growth process in the embryo. In the rabbit a recessive gene for brachydactyly (short digits) causes a localized breakdown of circulation in the developing limb bud of the embryo, followed by necrosis (tissue death) and healing.

Absence or abnormality of whole limbs is less common and includes, besides clubfoot, the so-called congenital amputations once thought to be caused by the strangulation of a limb by a fold of embryonic membrane (amnion). It is probable that internal abnormalities of the

bone are more frequent causes of such amputations than are strangulations. Cases are recorded of human identical twins in which both members have the same type of limb abnormality, suggesting a hereditary predisposition to this type of malformation. Besides malformed individuals with rudimentary limbs (phocomelus; having "seal-like limbs"), others have incomplete or underdeveloped extremities (hemimelus, micromelus, ectromelus).

A rare type of malformation, but one that has always attracted special interest, occurs when the lower extremities are more or less united, as in the mythical figures of sirens or mermaids. Such sirenoid individuals may have a single foot (uromelus), or limbs fused throughout their length with no separate feet (sirenomelus or symmelus).

Defects of the brain and head of man

Absence of the brain at birth (anencephaly); an abnormally small brain and head (microcephaly); and enlargement of the brain and head, sometimes to prodigious dimensions due to dilation of the ventricles by fluid (hydrocephaly), are frequent congenital defects in man. In some cases they have been traced to defective genes, although they may also arise from accidental or traumatic processes during embryonic development. Occasionally, malformed persons are found in which a part of the brain protrudes through the cranium as an encephalocoele. An extreme variant of this type is pseudencephaly, in which the whole brain is everted and rests upon the top of the cranium like a wig.

Cyclopian malformations with a single median eye occur rarely in man and other animals. More frequent anomalies are anophthalmia (absence of eyes) and microphthalmia (abnormally small eyes), both occasionally the result of abnormal heredity. Defective closure of lines of junction in the embryo produces malformations such as cleft palate, in which the ventral laminae of the palate have failed to fuse, and harelip, in which the median nasal and maxillary processes fail to unite. A frequent abnormality in human infants is spina bifida, in which the spine fails to close over and a gap is left in the vertebral column. These conditions are inherited, albeit somewhat irregularly, in man.

Sexual anomalies. In man and other vertebrates, male and female individuals usually have distinctive characters in addition to the primary one of producing either sperm or eggs. Individuals with both male and female functions are known as hermaphrodites. While this is the normal condition in some lower animals and in many flowering plants, it is so rare in mammals as to be regarded as anomalous. Individuals with mixtures of male and female characters (usually sterile) are known as intersexes. In man there occur two rare conditions that, according to recent evidence, represent partial sex reversal. Individuals with Klinefelter's syndrome are apparent males who produce no sperm. Many cases have been shown to have two X-chromosomes (the usual state determining femaleness) with an additional Y-chromosome (which carries genetic factors for maleness). Individuals with Turner's syndrome are apparent females without functional ovaries. The cases analyzed have only one X-chromosome (like the normal male with one X- and one Y-chromosome). These anomalies are clearly caused by disturbances in the mechanism for sex determination.

Complex syndromes. A remarkable feature of malformations in vertebrates including man is the association of multiple abnormalities in complex syndromes. Thus, in man harelip, spina bifida, hydrocephalus, and polydactyly may be found in the same individual; acrocephalosyndactyly (an egg- or dome-shaped skull and partial or complete fusion of digits in both hands and feet) often occurs with harelip, contractures, spina bifida, and mental abnormalities.

In man, individuals afflicted with mongolism, also known as Down's syndrome, have facial and bodily characters that permit diagnosis at or even before birth. Mongols have 47 instead of the normal 46 chromosomes. The extra chromosome is apparently responsible for the abnormal condition.

Doubling of parts. Individuals partially or wholly double, but joined together, are represented by the rare occurrence in man of Siamese twins, so-called from a famous Siamese pair exhibited for many years in the 19th century. The condition consists of identical twins joined by a bridge of tissue through which the circulatory systems communicate. Such twins probably arise by the incomplete separation of a single fertilized egg into two parts; the experimental production of such double individuals in newts has been accomplished by constricting the egg in the two-cell stage.

In man, partially double symmetrical malformations are found. They vary from those with a single head but with neck, trunk, and limbs doubled, through those with two heads and a single trunk, to others with head, shoulders, and arms doubled, but with one trunk and one pair of legs. Such double malformations probably arise following the less complete separation of the halves of the early embryo or partial separation at later stages. A rare type is one in which there is a Janus head, two faces on a single head and body. Janus malformations have been produced experimentally in amphibian embryos by a variety of treatments in early stages. A group of cases in which the hinder end of the body was doubled from the sacrum back has been found in one strain of mice and appears to be due to abnormal heredity. Doubling of whole limbs in amphibia has been produced experimentally by injuring the limb rudiment at an early, sensitive stage.   (L.C.D.)

PLANT MALFORMATIONS

Monstrosities, freaks, and other malformations have interested botanists for many years. There are numerous categories of such growth abnormalities in plants, and these are often related only loosely or not at all to one another.

Exaggerated growth. Sometimes divergence from the normal represents merely a quantitative change, which is evidenced by a harmonious but exaggerated manifestation of the normal developmental processes. This is well illustrated in the so-called *bakanae*, or foolish seedling disease, of rice. The *bakanae* disease is caused by the fungus *Gibberella fujikuroi*. Diseased plants are often conspicuous in a field because of their extreme height and pale, spindly appearance. This exaggerated growth response was found to be due to specific substances, known as gibberellins, which were produced by the fungus. Evidence is now available to indicate that gibberellins, also produced by higher plant species, participate directly as an essential growth-regulating system in all higher plant species. The gibberellins of either fungal or higher plant origin stimulate the normal development of certain genetic dwarfs of maize and peas, which cannot themselves produce the gibberellins in amounts sufficient for their normal development.

A common deformity of tobacco, called frenching, occurs in most tobacco-growing regions of the world. The advanced state of this condition is characterized by a cessation of terminal bud and stem growth. When dominance of the stem tips is lost, the buds in the axils of the leaves develop, and unusually large numbers of leaves (as many as 300) appear on a plant. The leaves are characteristically sword- or string-shaped because of the failure of the leaf blades to develop. Such plants have the appearance of a rosette. Although the cause of frenching has not yet been unequivocally established, it is thought to be due to a toxic substance produced by the nonpathogenic soil bacterium *Bacillus cereus*.

Alteration of floral parts. Under the stimulus of pathogenic organisms of the most diverse kinds, the sepals, petals, stamens, or pistils of a flower may be transformed into structures that are very different in appearance from those found normally. Certain viruses can cause enlargement of the leaflike flower parts (sepals) surrounding the base of a blossom in plants of the nightshade family. The tomato big-bud virus appears to affect the sepals of the tomato flower rather specifically. These structures enlarge greatly under the influence of the virus and fuse to form huge bladderlike structures that may be ten times or more the normal size. In the Madagascar periwinkle (*Vinca rosea*), however, viruses of this type bring about a green colouring in the petals, stamens, and styles; nor-

mally the petals are pink and the stamens and styles whitish. There is in this instance a retrograde development of floral parts into foliage leaves. (Findings such as these are of interest to the morphologist because they support the contention that the flower should be regarded as a modified leafy branch.)

Translocation of organs. Plant organs may arise in unusual places as a result of the infection by certain types of pathogenic agents. The carrot-yellows virus, for example, stimulates production of aerial tubers in the axils of the leaves of potato plants. Large numbers of adventitious roots (arising in abnormal places) appear on the stems of tomato plants infected with the bacteria *Pseudomonas solanacearum* and *Agrobacterium tumefaciens* as well as the *Fusarium* wilt fungus and the cranberry false-blossom virus.

An extreme example of adventitious shoot formation is found in *Begonia phyllomaniaca* after shock. In this instance, small plantlets develop spontaneously in incredible numbers from the superficial cell layers of the leaf blades, petioles, and stems. The adventitious shoots do not arise from preformed buds but develop from cells at the base of hairs and especially from certain glands present in great numbers in young stems and leaves of this species. Although these plantlets develop a vascular system of their own, the vast majority never succeed in connecting that system with the vascular system of the host. They must therefore be regarded not as branches but rather as independent organisms.

Witches'-brooms. Witches'-brooms, or hexenbesens, are closely grouped, many-branched structures commonly found on a number of species of trees and shrubs and caused by certain fungi. Witches'-brooms live a more or less independent existence, despite the fact that they are derived from the tissues of the host. In accordance with their independence, the witches'-brooms tend to break away from the normal correlations of the parent plant. Instead of branching out horizontally, the brooms stand as more or less erect clusters of branches. Witches'-brooms do not as a rule flower, and the vegetative buds may open several weeks earlier in the spring than do those present on healthy branches, indicating further the independence of these structures from normal controls.

Similar structures occur in certain plant species after virus infection. These appear to result from the excessive stimulation and development of secondary shoots. The witches'-broom virus in potato, for example, causes the infected plant to produce numerous buds on the above-ground stems of potato plants. Long, slender stolons resembling aerial roots that are covered with hairs develop from these adventitious buds.

Fasciation. This condition is best placed in that category of teratological abnormalities known as monstrosities. Fasciation is a term that has been used to describe a series of abnormal growth phenomena resulting from many different causes, all of which result in flattening of the main axis of the plant. Although a ribbonlike expansion of the stem is often the most striking feature of this condition, all parts of the plant may be affected. As fasciation develops, the growing point of the plant becomes broader; the unregulated tissue growth results in significant increases in the weight and volume of the plant. The apical growing point becomes linear and comblike in some instances or develops numerous growing points, producing a witches'-broom effect. In still other instances, the growing points may be coiled and resemble a ram's horn, or they may be fused and highly distorted into a grotesque tangle of coils. Fasciations found in plants such as the common cockscomb (*Celosia argentea cristata*) and in cacti are highly prized by gardeners.

There seems little doubt that nutritional changes due to disturbances in the growth-hormone relationships in a plant play an important role in fasciation. It has been suggested that maldistribution of growth hormones in the plant is also a cause of these abnormalities.   (A.C.Br.)

BIBLIOGRAPHY

Animal malformations: D. BERGSMAN (ed.), "Birth Defects Original Article Series" (1965–   ), authoritative articles on congenital malformations and abnormalities; L.C. DUNN,

"Genetic Monsters," *Scient. Am.*, 182:16–19 (1950), an illustrated account of the earliest appearance and development during embryonic life of specific abnormalities due to effects of mutated genes in vertebrates; C. STERN, *Principles of Human Genetics*, 3rd ed. (1971), illustrated descriptions of congenital abnormalities resulting from effects of mutant genes and of chromosomal aberrations; E. WOLFF, *La Science des monstres* (1948), a readable classical essay, including results of experimental teratology (in French).

Plant malformations: A.C. BRAUN, "Growth Is Affected," in J.G. HORSFALL and A.E. DIMOND (eds.), *Plant Pathology: An Advanced Treatise*, vol. 1, *The Diseased Plant*, ch. 6 (1959), a fairly comprehensive but largely descriptive account of the various types of growth abnormalities found in higher plant species; A.C. BRAUN and R.B. PRINGLE, "Pathogen Factors in the Physiology of Disease—Toxins and Other Metabolites," in C.S. HOLTON *et al.* (eds.), *Plant Pathology: Problems and Progress, 1908–1958*, ch. 9 (1959), an attempt to describe in chemical terms the specific substances involved in producing various types of abnormal growth responses in plants.

(L.C.D./A.C.Br.)

Mali

The Republic of Mali (in French, the République du Mali) is a landlocked state in central West Africa. Bounded north by Algeria, west by Mauritania and Senegal, south by Guinea and the Ivory Coast, and east by Upper Volta and Niger, it covers an area of 479,000 square miles (1,240,000 square kilometres). Mali's sparsely distributed population was about 5,000,000 in the early 1970s. Bamako is the national capital. As a part of French West Africa from 1898 to its independence in 1960, it was known as the French Sudan. Its current name, taken at the time of independence, is derived from the Mali Empire of the Upper and Middle Niger and ruled by the Mandingo (Malinke) from the 13th to the 16th century.

Mali is basically an agricultural country. Although its development has been hindered by the nature of the Sahara, which occupies about half its territory, the country nevertheless benefits from the advantages conferred by the waters of the Niger and Sénégal rivers and their tributaries: almost all of the population lives in the southern river basins, where diverse crops are cultivated. Most agricultural activity, however, is at the subsistence level, and the few cash crops grown are subject to the fluctuations of the world market. Industrial development is minimal and is largely confined to food processing. Despite its poverty, the country has long functioned as a crossroads between North and West Africa and has developed a rich cultural tradition. (For history, see WEST AFRICA, HISTORY OF. For related physical features see NIGER RIVER; SENEGAL RIVER; and SAHARA.)

THE LANDSCAPE

The natural environment. *Relief.* Mali's landscape is largely flat and monotonous. Two basic relief features can be distinguished—plateaus and plains. The highland regions are localized and discontinuous.

The plateaus of the south and southwest (extensions of the Fouta Djallon highlands of Guinea and the Guinea Highlands of Guinea and the Ivory Coast) lie between about 1,000 and 1,600 feet above sea level but attain heights approaching 2,000 feet in the Mandingue Plateau near Bamako and more than 2,100 feet at Satadougou. Composed mainly of sandstone, the plateaus are deeply incised by the Sénégal and Niger rivers and their tributaries. The plateau edges often take the form of precipitous cliffs, and their surfaces are cut by deep river valleys and waterfalls.

The plateaus of the southeast and east, also extensions of the Guinea Highlands, are a series of small, broken hills. Altitudes in the southeast range between almost 1,000 feet in the region of Sikasso and 1,739 feet (530 metres) at Mt. Mina. East of the Niger River the Dogon Plateau descends gently westward to the river valley but ends in abrupt cliffs on the southeast. These cliffs reach an altitude approaching 3,300 feet at Bandiagara.

The only marked relief feature in the north is the Adrar des Iforas. An extension of the mountainous Hoggar re-

The plateaus and the plains

gion of the Sahara, this heavily eroded sandstone plateau rises to altitudes of between 1,300 and 1,600 feet.

Northern and central Mali are composed of the plains of the Niger River basin and of the Sahara. In the north are the vast plains of the Tanezrouft and Taoudenni, which are covered with sand dunes and with areas of shifting sand known as ergs. In the central region are the alluvial plains of Meriyé and Azaouak.

Drainage. The drainage system is composed of the Sénégal and Niger rivers and their tributaries. The Sénégal River flows in a northwesterly direction across Mali for 560 miles on its course to the Atlantic Ocean. Its main headwaters—the Bafing and the Bakoye (Bakhoy) rivers—rise in the Fouta Djallon and join at Bafoulabé to form the Sénégal. The river then flows to the west across the plateau region, where it is broken by falls at Gouina and Félou. Between Kayes and the Senegalese border it receives the Kolimbiné and Karakoro rivers on the right and the Falémé—its major tributary—on the left. A tropical river, the Sénégal experiences seasonal flow. The waters are low in April and May and are high between July and October. Floods occur during the first two months of the high-water period.

For 1,010 miles, nearly one-third of its total length, the Niger River flows through Mali. Rising in the Fouta Djallon, the river is of significant size by the time it enters Mali near Banankoro. It flows to the northeast across the Mandingue Plateau, where it is broken by falls at Sotuba. Reaching Koulikoro, it spreads out in a wide valley and flows majestically to its confluence with the Banifing River at Mopti. The Niger then forms an interior delta because the land is flat and the river's descent almost nonexistent. The river breaks down into a network of branches and lakes as it continues northward. The lakes include those of Débo, Fati, Télé, and Faguibine. At Bourèm the Niger makes a great bend to the south, known as the Niger Bend, and flows past Gao and Ansongo to the Niger border at Labbezanga.

The Niger also flows intermittently. High waters occur on the Upper Niger from July to October, at the delta from September to November, and at the bend from December to January. Periodic floods and the rich alluvial soils in the central delta make the Niger Valley an important agricultural region.

Soils. The soils are generally poor. In the south, ferruginous (iron-bearing) soils are shallow and form a hard, red crust because of intense evaporation. Along the southern edge of the Sahara, the brown and reddish soils are only slightly transformed into crust because of the lack of water and chemical decomposition. The desert region is composed of sand, rock, and gravel.

Climate. Mali lies within the intertropical zone and has a hot, dry climate. The sun is at its zenith throughout most of the year. In general, there are two distinct seasons, the dry and the wet. The dry season, from November to June, is marked by low humidity and high temperatures and is influenced by the *alize* and harmattan winds. The *alize*, from the northeast from December to February, causes a relatively cold spell, with temperatures averaging 77° F (25° C). From March to June, the dry, hot harmattan blows from the east and sweeps the overheated soil into dusty whirlwinds. The wind causes temperatures between 104° and 113° F.

During the rainy season from June to October, the monsoon wind blows from the southwest. Preceded by large, black clouds, the tornado-like rainstorms are accompanied by lightning and thunder. Temperatures lessen somewhat in August, when most of the rainfall occurs.

The country can be divided into three climatic zones—the Sudanic, the Sahelian, and the desert zones. Sudanic climate occurs in almost one-third of the country, from the southern border to latitude 15° north. It is characterized by an annual rainfall of between 20 and 51 inches and average temperatures of between 75° and 86° F (24° and 30° C). The Sahel, or the area bordering on the Sahara, receives between eight and 20 inches of rain a year and has average temperatures between 73° and 97° F (23° and 36° C). In the Sahara, temperatures during the day range from 117° to 140° F (47° to 60° C), while

The Niger River

Climatic zones

at night the temperature drops to between 39° to 41° F (4° to 5° C). The scanty annual rainfall of less than seven inches is rare and irregular, and some years are rainless.

Vegetation and animal life. There are two main vegetational zones that correspond to the climatic regions of the Sudan and the Sahel. In the Sudanic zone there are localized forest corridors along the Guinean border and the river valleys. The rest of the area is covered with savanna (open grassland and scattered trees). The trees include the nere, or twoball nitta tree (*Parkia biglobosa*), the karite (*Butyrospermum parkii*), the cailcedra (Senegal khaya; *Khaya senegalensis*), and the kapioka. The incidence of trees decreases to the north as the Sudanic zone merges with the Sahel. The Sahel is characterized by steppe vegetation; drought-resistant trees such as the baobab, the doum palm, and palmyra are found. These trees also disappear to the north, however, where short, thorny plants such as the mimosa, the acacia, and cramcram (a member of the grass family) occur. All vegetation gradually disappears as one enters the Sahara region.

The animal life of the Sudan and of the Sahel is rich and varied. Large, herbivorous mammals include the gazelle, the antelope, the giraffe, and the elephant. The main carnivores are lions, panthers, and hyenas. Crocodiles and hippopotamuses inhabit the rivers, and there is a wide variety of monkeys, snakes, and birds (including the ostrich). There is a national park along the Baoulé River in the west and an animal reserve between Ansongo and Ménako in the east.

Traditional regions. Mali is traditionally divided into the nomadic region of the Sahel and the Sahara and the agricultural region of the Sudanic zone.

The landscape under human settlement. About 90 percent of the population is rural. The rural population lives in thatched dwellings grouped together in villages of between 150 and 600 inhabitants. The villages are surrounded by cultivated fields and grazing lands. The older towns, such as Djénné, Tombouctou (Timbuktu), Gao, and Ségou, are built in the characteristic Sudanese style of architecture. The newer towns, such as Bamako, Kayes, San, and Kati, consist of a central business district, around which African residential districts are grouped. The houses are built of a mixture of earth and cement.

PEOPLE AND POPULATION

Population groups. *Ethnic groups.* What is known as the "white" population includes nomadic groups of Berbers (including the important Berber subgroup of the Tuareg [Touareg]) and the Arab-Berber group known as the Moors. These groups live in the Sahelian zone and north of the Niger Bend.

The black population is composed of numerous agricultural groups, some of whom are descended from the peoples of the ancient empires of Ghana, Mali, and Songhai. The largest group are the Bambara, who number about 1,200,000 and live along the Upper Niger River. The Soninke, or Sarakole, number about 350,000; they are descended from the founders of the Ghana Empire and live in the western Sahelian zone. The 250,000 Malinke (Mandingo), bearers of the heritage of the Mali Empire, live in the southwest, while the 250,000 Songhai are settled in the Niger Valley from Djénné to Ansongo. The Dognon, who number about 180,000, live in the plateau region around Bandiagara. The Voltaic group includes the Bwa, or Bobo (70,000), the Senoufo, (about 180,000), and the Minianka (about 160,000). They occupy the east and southeast.

The Fulani, or Peul (numbering about 400,000), are nomadic pastoralists of the Sahel and Macina. Other ethnic groups of note include the Tukulors (Toucouleurs), the Kasonke (70,000), the Bozo (85,000), and the Somono.

Linguistic groups. French is the official national language. There are several indigenous languages and dialects, which roughly correspond to either ethnic groups or regions. The most important is the Mande group, which includes Bambara (spoken by 60 percent of the population), Malinke, Kasonke, and Wasulunka (Ouassoulou).

Soninke and Dogon are also related to Bambara; Dogon includes many dialects. The related but autonomous languages of the Voltaic peoples are Bwa, Senufo, and Minianka. The Fulani and Tukulor speak Fulah (Peul), and Songhaic is spoken all along the Niger Bend. The Tuareg have retained their ancient Berber language and written script, *tifinagh*, which is related to that of ancient Libya. The Moors speak Arabic.

Religious groups. There are three main religions. Islām is practiced by 65 percent of the population, animism, by about 30 percent, and Christianity, by 2 percent. Islāmization dates back to the 11th century and has eclipsed traditional animism among the Soninke, Songhai, Tukulor, Moors, Tuareg, and Fulani. Animism continues as the religion of the Voltaic peoples, the Malinke, and the Bambara.

Demography. *General distribution.* In 1969 Mali had an estimated population of 4,929,000. Because half of the country consists of uninhabited desert, the estimated average population density of ten persons per square mile is misleading. Densities ranged between 39 and 65 persons per square mile in the Niger Valley. In the less populated areas of the west and east, densities ranged from 23 persons per square mile at Nioro to ten persons at Gao and three persons at Tombouctou.

Population density

Mali, Area and Population				
	area		population	
	sq mi	sq km	1960–61 census	1969 estimate
Regions				
Bamako	34,788	90,100	...	917,000
Gao	312,306	808,870	...	606,000
Kayes	46,260	119,813	...	744,000
Mopti	34,267	88,752	...	991,000
Ségou	21,671	56,127	...	759,000
Sikasso	29,529	76,480	...	912,000
Total Mali	478,822*	1,240,142	4,100,000†	4,929,000

*Converted area figures do not add to total given because of rounding.
†Estimate based on results of a sample survey; probably including an allowance of 209,000 for nomad population and about 33,000 for persons in the zone controlled by Niger Office, not covered by survey.
Source: Official government figures; UN.

Only 10 percent of the population lived in urban areas in 1969. Bamako, with a population of 189,000, was the largest town. Other towns with populations of more than 20,000 were Mopti (34,000), Ségou (32,000), Kayes (30,000), and Sikasso (23,000).

In 1969 there were 15,000 more women than men. Almost 3,000,000 people, or 60 percent of the population, were less than 20 years of age; only about 3 percent of the Malians were over 60.

Birth rates and death rates. In 1969 the annual birth rate stood at 60 per 1,000 persons and the death rate at 30 per 1,000. These figures represented an annual growth of 30 per 1,000, a rate which would double the population in 20 years. The infant mortality rate, although reduced by improved medical and sanitary facilities, was almost 250 per 1,000.

Migration patterns. There is a constant movement of young people from the countryside to the towns, especially to Bamako. Some of the migrants return home for the planting season (May to November), but most remain in the urban areas. Employment opportunities are limited, and most of the migrants live on the income of friends and relatives.

Some Malian workers, especially members of the Soninke group, emigrate to France and other western European countries. Malian traders are found in the Ivory Coast, Liberia, and central Africa. There are also "colonies" of Malians in the Ivory Coast and Senegal whose members have adopted the nationality of their host country. The previous immigration into Mali of merchants from Libya, Syria, and Morocco has almost ceased.

THE NATIONAL ECONOMY

The extent and distribution of resources. *Mineral resources.* Iron is the most widespread mineral resource.

Found almost everywhere, its reserves are estimated at 1,000,000,000 tons. Bauxite deposits of about 800,000,000 tons are located near Kayes and on the Mandingue Plateau. There are approximately 3,500,000 tons of manganese, and the phosphate deposits in the Ansongo region are estimated at 20,000,000 tons.

There are important deposits of gold near Bambouk, on the Mandingue Plateau, and in the Adrar des Iforas. Lithium (a soft, silver-white, metallic element, the lightest of all metals) has been discovered near Kayes and Bougouni, and there are uranium deposits in the Adrar. There are also traces of tungsten, tin, lead, copper, and zinc, as well as deposits of salt, marble, kaolin (china clay), and limestone.

Biological resources. Vegetation resources are limited and are not conducive to forestry activities. The fish of the country's rivers and lakes, however, form the basis of a growing fishing and fish-processing industry. Wild animals are not economically significant.

Power resources. There are extensive possibilities for the production of hydroelectric power on the Sénégal and Niger rivers, as well as on some of their tributaries.

Sources of national income. *Agriculture and fishing.* Subsistence and commercial agriculture are the bases of the Malian economy. More than 90 percent of the working population are engaged in subsistence agriculture, and the government supports the development of commercial products. Areas of cultivation are located in the Sudanese and Sahelian zones; the most important agricultural area is the inland Niger Delta. Crops such as millet, rice, wheat, and maize, as well as potatoes, yams, and cassava, are the main subsistence crops. Cotton and peanuts (groundnuts) are the important commercial crops; sugarcane, tobacco, and tea are also grown for market. Market gardens produce a variety of vegetables and fruits, including cabbages, turnips, carrots, beans, tomatoes, bananas, mangoes, and oranges.

Agricultural products

The major areas for the raising of livestock are the Sahel and the area around Macina. There are more than 5,000,000 head of cattle and about 12,000,000 sheep and goats in the country.

Mali is the third largest producer of fish in West Africa after Morocco and Senegal, with about 29,000 fishermen producing an annual catch of about 100,000 tons. After processing (drying and smoking), about 20 percent of the annual catch is exported.

Mining and quarrying. Although mineral resources are extensive, the mining industry is minimal. The only exploited deposits are those of salt (at Taoudenni), marble and kaolin (at Bafoulabé), and limestone (at Diamou).

Manufacturing. Most industrial enterprises engage in the processing of food products. There are several rice mills, flour mills, and cotton gins. The oil and soap factory of Koulikoro satisfies domestic demands for its products. There are breweries, a tannery, and a refrigerated slaughterhouse at Bamako; fruit-preservation plants at Baguinéda; a sugar refinery at Dougabougou; and cigarette and match factories at Djoliba.

Industries and handicrafts

The Malian Company of Textiles (Comatex) produces cotton fibre and unprinted cloth, while the Textile Industry of Mali (Itema) manufactures printed cloth and blankets. A cement factory at Diamou is a basic industry. There are also shops for the construction of autocycles, the repair of machinery, and the assembly of radios.

Handicrafts are important, and the Malians are noted for their clothing, pottery, shoes, baskets, and wood carvings.

Energy. Electricity is largely produced in thermal-power stations. There are eight thermal stations, located in Bamako and other large towns. Hydroelectric power is produced at the Sotuba and Markala dams on the Niger River and at the Felou Dam on the Sénégal River. These thermal and hydroelectric stations produced about 40,000,000 kilowatt-hours of electricity in 1970. The construction of dams at Gouina on the Sénégal and at Sélingué on the Sankarani is planned. The possibility of producing solar energy is also under investigation.

Financial services. The Central Bank of Mali, managed equally by Mali and France, controls the nation's credit and the exchange rate between the Mali franc (the monetary unit of the country) and the French franc. The Development Bank of Mali finances development projects, while the Malian Bank of Credit and Deposits and the French-owned West African International Bank carry out credit and depository functions. Several French insurance companies maintain offices in Bamako.

Foreign trade. The most important export items are cotton, peanuts, live animals, and dried and smoked fish. Mali's major customers include the Ivory Coast, Senegal, and France. Imports consist largely of textiles, sugar, automobiles, iron and steel, and petroleum. The major sources of imports are France, the Soviet Union, the Ivory Coast, China, and Senegal. Foreign trade is entirely controlled by the Malian Society of Import and Export (Somiex) and operates at a deficit. Mali is a member of the Organisation pour la Mise en Valeur du Fleuve Sénégal (Organization for the Development of the Sénégal River), which also includes Senegal and Mauritania. Despite strict customs controls, smuggling—especially of cattle and fish—is considerable.

Management of the economy. *The public and private sectors.* At the time of independence in 1960, the government adopted a policy of Socialism. State companies and rural cooperative societies were organized to regulate both the production and the distribution of goods. Since the military coup d'etat in 1968, Socialist policy has been mitigated by the encouragement of private business.

Mali's form of Socialism

Taxation and foreign aid. Direct taxes include an income tax on salaries and a uniform per capita tax on those individuals who do not participate in the money economy. Most of the government's revenue is derived from indirect taxes, such as customs duties and commercial taxes.

Bilateral external aid is provided largely by China, the Soviet Union, and France. International aid is granted by such organizations as the United Nations, the FED (Fonds Européen de Développement, or European Development Fund), and the United Nations Development Programme (UNDP).

Trade unions. Trade unions were abolished by the military government in 1970.

Contemporary economic policies. Economic development is centred upon increased agricultural production and the creation of small industrial firms for the processing of agricultural products. Since 1967, when Mali rejoined the French franc zone, French businesses and advisers have become increasingly active. Private commerce is encouraged, and domestic investments in social services have been reduced.

Problems and prospects. The main economic problem is posed by a growing national debt. Imports continue to outdistance exports, while the export of agricultural products is dependent upon fluctuating world prices. There is a need to reduce reliance upon foreign aid and to make the internal civil administration more effective.

Transportation. Mali's transportation systems are concentrated in the Sudanic and Sahelian regions. Because Mali is landlocked, its major transport routes connect with those of neighbouring countries and their ports to provide it with outlets to the sea.

Roads. In 1971 there were about 7,500 miles of roads of which almost 5,000 were all-weather roads, and over 700 miles were paved. There are two main axes of paved roads radiating from Bamako. The road from Bamako to Bougouni and Sikasso connects with the Ivory Coast road running to the port of Abidjan. The second main road runs through Bamako, Ségou, San, Mopti, Gao, and Ansongo to the border with Niger.

Railways. The one railroad track runs for 400 miles from Koulikoro, a short distance northeast of Bamako, northwestward to Diboli, on the Senegal border, where it connects with the Senegalese railway to Dakar. Another railway line is planned to link Bamako with the Guinean railway, which runs to Conakry.

River transport. The Sénégal River is navigable from July to October from Kayes in the west of the country down to Saint-Louis, Senegal, at the river's mouth. The Niger River is navigable throughout its length in Mali

Inland waterways

from July to January. The Banifing River is navigable for 186 miles.

Air transport. A national airline, Air Mali, operates both domestic and international flights. The main airport is at Bamako, and another is being built at Ségou. There are domestic air routes to Ségou, Mopti, Goundam, Tombouctou, Gao, Kayes, and Nioro. Bamako is also linked by air to France, Morocco, and other West African nations.

ADMINISTRATION AND SOCIAL CONDITIONS

Structure of the government. *Constitutional framework.* Upon independence in 1960, a constitution was granted that guaranteed parliamentary democracy through universal suffrage and provided for an elected National Assembly; the provisions of the constitution were, however, not fully implemented. The military government that took power in 1968 suspended the constitution and forbade all political activity. Since then the country has been ruled by the Military Committee for National Liberation (CMLN).

Local government. The country is divided into the six regions of Kayes, Bamako, Sikasso, Ségou, Mopti, and Gao. Each of the regions is further divided into administrative units called *cercles*, which are in turn subdivided into smaller units called *arrondissements*. Each region is administered by a governor, who coordinates the activities of the *cercles* and implements economic policy. The *cercles*, directed by commanding officers, provide nuclei for the major government services; their various headquarters provide focal points for the health service, the army, the police, local courts, and other government agencies. The *arrondissement* is the basic administrative unit, and its centre usually houses a school and a dispensary. It is composed of several villages, which are headed by chiefs and elected village councils. The urban areas (or *communes*) are administered by delegates of the military committee.

The judicial system

Justice. At the head of the judicial system, the Supreme Court exercises both judicial and administrative powers; it is the court of first and last resort in matters concerning the government. The Court of Appeal, located in Bamako, tries all cases on appeal from ordinary tribunals. There are more than 50 tribunals and more than 70 magistrates. Justices of the peace have full powers to judge ordinary civil, commercial, and financial cases; they sit in the headquarters of the *cercles* and also travel to the major towns of the *arrondissements*.

Since 1960 there has been a determined attempt to mold the judicial system to the contemporary needs of the population. New law codes have liberated women from traditional restraints, defined the rights and duties of citizens, and modified the penal procedure.

The army. The army consists of 3,000 men. Its officers come from the former French colonial army or else were trained either in the Soviet Union or at Mali's École Interarme at Kati. Recruitment is by enlistment or by conscription (military service is compulsory in principle). Garrisons are located throughout the country, and the army is well equipped with Soviet arms, including jet fighter planes and tanks.

Administration. *Education.* French is the only language of instruction. In 1968 to 1969 about 22 percent of school-age children attended school. Primary and secondary education are combined in the nine-year curriculum of the *cycle fondemental* ("fundamental educational level"). The general secondary school, or *lycée*, provides the last three years of traditional secondary education. Higher education—geared directly to the needs of the government—is obtained in state colleges. These colleges include teacher-training colleges, a college of administration, an engineering institute, a polytechnic institute, and a school of medical assistants. Many of Mali's university students study abroad, especially in France, the Soviet Union, and Senegal.

Health and welfare services. In 1968 there were two national hospitals (at Bamako and Kati), six regional hospitals, more than 40 medical centres, 60 maternity centres, and 300 dispensaries. There were also infectious

disease and leprosy centres. There are not enough trained medical personnel to meet Mali's needs.

A Secretariat for Social Affairs is charged with improving the conditions of women, children, and invalids. There are more than 50 social centres, located throughout the country; they offer public-health information and provide day nurseries. There is no national social security fund. A Service for Family Allowances, however, makes loans to workers and issues pensions to retired people.

Police services. The National Gendarmerie maintains brigades in the *cercles*, and there are policemen in all the towns. The head of national security and the general staff of the gendarmerie are responsible to the Ministry of Internal Affairs, as well as to the armed forces.

Social conditions. *Wages and the cost of living.* Inflation has plagued the economy since independence and even more so since the devaluation of the Mali franc in 1967. Wages, however, have not risen as the cost of living continues to rise.

Social and economic divisions. Mali contains two distinct, stratified societies. About 90 percent of the population belong to traditional social groups, which have inherited hierarchical social structures. These groups consist of nobles, vassals, and members of various castes, all of whom acquired their status by birth.

Rural and urban society

The second Malian society is formed by the urban population. Privileged groups are the educated government officials and the traders. The middle socioeconomic group is composed of civil servants and industrial workers. The lowest group is made up of the unemployed.

CULTURAL LIFE AND INSTITUTIONS

Mali is one of the cultural crossroads of West Africa. Situated between the Arab world to the north and the black African nations to the south, it has for centuries been a cultural meeting place. The mixture of both worlds has produced an original Sudanic culture that is

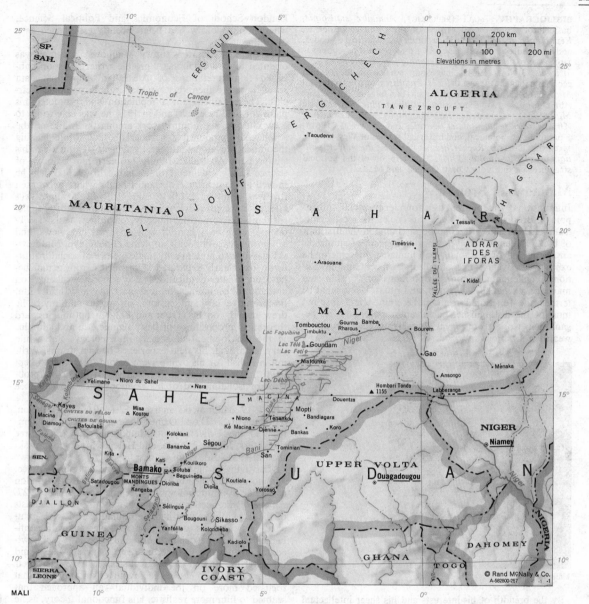

diversified according to the various ethnic groups and regions that compose it.

Cultural expression. Music and dancing are the most common cultural activities; they form an especially rich heritage among the Malinke and Songhai peoples. The Bambara and the Voltaic groups excel in the creation of wood carvings of masks, statues, stools, and objects used in animist worship. The *tiewara,* or gazelle mask, of the Bambara is remarkable for its fineness of line.

Architecture is well developed in the Niger Valley. The Sudanic style finds typical expression in the storied houses and mosques of Djénné and Tombouctou.

Localized handicrafts include jewelry making by the Mandingo people, leatherworking around the Niger Bend, the weaving of geometrical designs into cotton cloth, and the carving of statues for the tourist trade.

Cultural institutions. The Musée de l'Institut de Recherches et de Documentation at Bamako contains collections of art from most of the country's regions. The National Archives of Mali, the National Library, and the Institute of Human Sciences are also located in Bamako, as also is the Municipal Library. The Centre of Arab Documentation is located in Tombouctou, and there is a French Centre of Documentation in Bamako. The Library of the Office of Niger in Ségou contains information on agriculture, irrigation, and general science.

The government promotes the expansion of popular culture through the Committee of Youth and Sports. Youth associations organize sports, theatrical, musical, and dancing activities in every important town. Cultural competitions are presented in Bamako during the biennial Youth Week. The Malian Ballet Troupe performs throughout the world. Artists are trained at the National Institute of Arts and at the Artisan Centre of Bamako.

Press and broadcasting. The press and the broadcasting services are controlled by the government. *L'Essor* (apart from the *Journal Officiel* the country's only newspaper), is published as both a weekly and a daily. Radio Mali broadcasts from Bamako in French, English, Bambara, and several other local languages. There are no television services.

FUTURE PROSPECTS

Since 1968 the military government, which attempts to combine socialist and liberal principles, has attempted to encourage the development of Mali's economy. The main agency responsible for stimulating agricultural development is the Niger Office, although commercial crops such as cotton, sugar, and tobacco, as well as rice, are being grown by using the waters of the Sénégal River. It is anticipated that the Kayes region, which possesses important mineral reserves, including bauxite, will be the focus of future industrialization and hydroelectric development. The major economic problems confronting Mali in the early 1970s were the lack of capital investment and a well-developed transportation system.

Music, dance, and traditional crafts

BIBLIOGRAPHY. MALI (REPUBLIC), *Annuaire statistique,* basic information on all aspects of the country; *Justice en République du Mali* (1965), a study of institutions, codes, and procedures; UNION AFRICAINE ET MALGACHE DE COOPERATION ECONOMIQUE, *Étude monographique de trente et un pays africains,* 3 vol. (1964), interesting studies of the Malian economy; GERARD BRASSEUR, *Les Établissements humains au Mali* (1968), a description of the surroundings of the various ethnic groups; PAULE BRASSEUR, *Bibliographie générale du Mali* (1964), a comprehensive bibliography; J. SURET-CANALE, *Afrique noire occidentale et centrale,* 2nd ed., vol. 1 (1961), geographic, ethnological, and historical studies of West Africa; MADANI SY SEYDOU, *Recherches sur l'exercise du pouvoir politique en Afrique noire* (1965), a description of the political structures on the Ivory Coast, Guinea, and Mali.

Malinowski, Bronisław

Internationally recognized as a founder of social anthropology, Bronisław Malinowski was one of the most significant teachers and writers in the discipline in the first half of the 20th century. Developing the concept of culture as an expression of the totality of human achievement, he examined a wide range of cultural aspects and institutions, challenging existing propositions on kinship and marriage, exchange, law, myth, and ritual. Using what he termed the functional method, he trained and inspired most of the distinguished social anthropologists who began their work from Great Britain and the Commonwealth in the interwar period.

By courtesy of the Polish Library, London

Malinowski.

By the breadth of his interests and his sheer intellectual power, he also attracted the attention of prominent scientists in other disciplines, such as linguistics and psychology, and collaborated or debated with them. With a keen sense of the significance of anthropology as an analytical tool and a source of information in the study of practical problems of social relations, he participated vigorously in educational programs for administrators, missionaries, and social workers. Malinowski is thus one of the greatest historical figures in securing public recognition of the significance of anthropology in the modern world.

Bronisław Kasper Malinowski was born on April 7, 1884, in Cracow, a former capital of Poland. His father, Lucjan, a professor of Slavic philology at the Jagiellonian University in Cracow, was a linguist of some reputation who had studied Polish dialect and folklore in Silesia. His mother, Józefa, née Łącka, of a moderately wealthy landowning family, was highly cultured and a good linguist. Early afflicted by the ill health that dogged him throughout life, in his teens Malinowski travelled extensively in the Mediterranean region with his mother, who was by then widowed. Although his early education was conducted largely at home, he subsequently attended the Jagiellonian University, completing his doctorate in 1908, with highest grade honours in philosophy, with physics and mathematics as subsidiaries. Happening upon Sir James Frazer's *Golden Bough,* an encyclopaedic treatment of religious and magical practices, Malinowski was enthralled and long afterward traced his enthusiasm for anthropology to it. After contact with the newer psychologies and economics in Leipzig, he came in 1910 to the London School of Economics and Political Science, where anthropology had been recently established as a discipline.

For the next quarter-century Malinowski's career was oriented toward London. A prolific writer, he soon published reinterpretations of Australian Aboriginal data from literature then very popular in anthropological circles. These gained him a reputation and promoted his plans for field research, and in 1914 he was able to go to New Guinea. Six months' work among the Mailu on the south coast produced a monograph that, while lacking theoretical development, was sufficient—along with his study of the Australian family—to earn him a doctor of science (D.Sc.) degree from London in 1916. When he moved to the nearby Trobriand Islands, where he worked for two years in 1915–16 and 1917–18, Malinowski's talents flowered. Living in a tent among the people, speaking the vernacular fluently, recording "texts" freely on the scene of action as well as in set interviews, and observing reactions with an acute clinical eye, Malinowski was able to present a dynamic picture of social institutions that clearly separated ideal norms from actual behaviour. In later publications on ceremonial exchange, on agricultural economics, on sex, marriage, and family life, on primitive law and custom, on magic and myth, he drew heavily on his Trobriand data in putting forward theoretical propositions of basic significance and stimulus in the development of social anthropology. Yet, while very rewarding, his field experience had its strains. Writing in Polish for his own private record, Malinowski kept field diaries in which he exposed very frankly his problems of isolation and of his relations with New Guinea people.

In the Trobriand Islands

In 1919 Malinowski married Elsie Rosaline Masson, daughter of Sir David Orme Masson, professor of chemistry in the University of Melbourne; they had three daughters, Józefa, Wanda, and Helena. Mrs. Malinowski died in 1935 after a long illness.

After living in the Canary Islands and southern France, Malinowski returned in 1924 to the University of London as reader in anthropology; he became professor in 1927. As one of the intellectually most vigorous social scientists of his day, Malinowski had a stimulating and wide influence. His seminars were famous. Conversant with continental European social theory and especially acknowledging his debt to Émile Durkheim, Marcel Mauss, and others of the French sociological school, he rejected their abstract notions of society in favour of an approach that focussed more on the individual—an approach that seemed to him more realistic. His functional theory, as he himself explained,

Functionalism

insists . . . upon the principle that in every type of civilisation, every custom, material object, idea and belief fulfils some vital function, has some task to accomplish, represents an indispensable part within a working whole. ("Anthropology," in *Encyclopædia Britannica,* 13th ed., suppl., p. 133.)

Only by understanding such functions and interrelations, he held, can an anthropologist understand a culture.

Convinced of the value of functional anthropology as an aid to understanding problems of social life, he was active in sponsoring studies of social and cultural change. In the 1930s he became much interested in Africa; was closely associated with the International African Institute; visited students working among Bemba, Swazi, and other tribes in eastern and southern Africa; and wrote the introduction to Jomo Kenyatta's book *Facing Mount Kenya* (1938), prepared as a diploma thesis under his supervision. (Kenyatta became president of Kenya in 1964.)

In 1938 Malinowski went on sabbatical leave to the United States—which he had already visited in 1926 on a Laura Spelman Rockefeller Memorial Fellowship, in 1933 as a lecturer at Cornell University, and in 1936 as recipient of an honorary doctor of science degree at the Harvard University tercentenary celebrations. When World War II was declared, being by age and temperament unsuited for direct participation in the war effort, he became Bishop Museum Visiting Professor of Anthropology at Yale University, then accepted a tenured appointment there. He died unexpectedly, of a heart attack, in New Haven on May 16, 1942. His teaching career during those last years had been less remarkable than before, but he had been able to study peasant markets in Mexico in 1940 and 1941 and had plans for a study of social change in Mexican-Indian communities. A great believer in freedom, he had also been actively identified with the Polish cause in the war. In 1940 Malinowski had married again, to Anna Valetta Hayman-Joyce, an artist who paints under the name Valetta Swann and who assisted him in his Mexican studies and was primarily responsible for the publication of his *Scientific Theory of Culture* (1944) and other posthumous works.

MAJOR WORKS

The Family Among the Australian Aborigines (1913); *The Natives of Mailu* (1915); *Argonauts of the Western Pacific* (1922); *Myth in Primitive Psychology* (1926); *Crime and Custom in Savage Society* (1926); *The Father in Primitive Psychology* (1927); *Sex and Repression in Savage Society* (1927); *The Sexual Life of Savages in North-Western Melanesia* (1929); *Coral Gardens and Their Magic,* 2 vol. (1935); *The Foundations of Faith and Morals* (1935); posthumously published works include *A Scientific Theory of Culture* (1944); *Freedom and Civilization* (1944); *The Dynamics of Culture Change* (1945); *Magic, Science and Religion and Other Essays* (1948). *A Diary in the Strict Sense of the Term* (1967) is a translation of private field diaries kept in Polish during 1914–15 and 1917–18.

BIBLIOGRAPHY. ASSOCIATION OF POLISH UNIVERSITY PROFESSORS AND LECTURERS IN GREAT BRITAIN, *Professor Bronislaw Malinowski: An Account of the Memorial Meeting Held at the Royal Institution in London on July 13th 1942* (1943); RAYMOND W. FIRTH (ed.), *Man and Culture: An Evaluation of the Work of Bronislaw Malinowski* (1957), analytical studies by former students and colleagues, with bibliography; KONSTANTIN SYMMONS-SYMONOLEWICZ, "Bronislaw Malinowski: An Intellectual Profile," *Polish Review,* 3:35–67 (1958); "Bronislaw Malinowski: Formative Influences and Theoretical Evolution," *ibid.,* 4:17–45 (1959); "Bronislaw Malinowski: Individuality As a Theorist," *ibid.,* 5:53–65 (1960).

(R.W.Fi.)

Mallarmé, Stéphane

The latter part of the 19th century in France, even more than the earlier part, was a period of change and experimentation in the arts, and among the writers, painters, and musicians who extended the boundaries within which their predecessors had been confined Stéphane Mallarmé holds a high place. In terms of mere size, his achievement is relatively slight—one slim volume of poetry, a brief and obscure work enigmatically called *Un Coup de dés jamais n'abolira le hasard,* a dozen prose poems, some occasional verse, a number of short essays, and a few translations—yet the audacity of what he attempted to do, and in some measure succeeded in doing, as regards both the form and the content of poetry has ensured his reputation as one of the most remarkable figures in the history of French literature.

Mallarmé was born in Paris on March 18, 1842. He enjoyed the sheltered security of family life for only five brief years, until the early death of his mother in August 1847. This traumatic experience was echoed 10 years later by the death of his younger sister Maria, in August 1857, and by that of his father in 1863. These tragic events would seem to explain much of the longing Mallarmé expressed, from the very beginning of his poetic career, to turn away from the harsh world of reality in search of another world; and the fact that this remained the enduring theme of his poetry may be explained by the comparative harshness with which adult life continued to treat him. After spending the latter part of 1862 and the early months of 1863 in London so as to acquire a knowledge of English, he began a lifelong career as a schoolteacher, first in provincial schools (Tournon, Besançon, and Avignon) and later in Paris. He was not naturally gifted in this profession, however, and found the work decidedly uncongenial. Furthermore, his financial situation was by no means comfortable, particularly after his marriage in 1863 and after the birth of his chil-

Teaching career

dren, Geneviève (in 1864) and Anatole (in 1871). To try and improve matters he engaged in part-time activities, such as editing a magazine for a few months at the end of 1874, writing a school textbook in 1877, and translating another one in 1880. In October 1879, after a six-months illness, his son Anatole died.

Archives Photographiques

Mallarmé, 1891.

Despite these trials and tribulations, Mallarmé made steady progress with his parallel career as a poet. His early poems, which he began contributing to magazines in 1862, were influenced by Charles Baudelaire, whose recently published *Fleurs du mal* were largely concerned with the theme of escape from reality, a theme by which Mallarmé was already becoming obsessed. But Baudelaire's escapism had been of an essentially emotional and sensual kind—a vague dream of tropical islands and peaceful landscapes where all would be "*luxe, calme et volupté.*" Mallarmé was of a much more intellectual bent, and his determination to analyze the nature of the ideal world and its relationship with reality is reflected in the two dramatic poems he began to write in 1864 and 1864, *Hérodiade* and *L'Après-midi d'un faune,* the latter being the work that inspired Claude Debussy to compose his celebrated *Prélude* a quarter of a century later.

By 1868 Mallarmé had come to the conclusion that although nothing lies beyond reality, within this nothingness lie the essences of perfect forms. The poet's task is to perceive and crystallize these essences. In so doing, the poet becomes more than a mere descriptive versifier, transposing into poetic form an already existent reality; he becomes a veritable God, creating something from nothing, conjuring up for the reader, as Mallarmé himself put it, "*l'absente de tous bouquets*"—the ideal flower that is absent from all real bouquets. But to crystallize the essences of things in this way, to create the notion of floweriness, rather than to describe an actual flower, demands an extremely subtle and complex use of all the resources of language, and Mallarmé devoted himself during the rest of his life to putting his theories into practice in what he called his *Grand Oeuvre,* or *Le Livre.* He never came near to completing this work, however, and the few preparatory notes that have survived give little or no idea of what the end result might have been.

Poetics

On the other hand, Mallarmé did complete a number of poems related to his projected *Grand Oeuvre,* both in their themes and in their extremely evocative use of language. Among these are several elegies, the principal ones being to Baudelaire, Edgar Allan Poe, Richard Wagner, and the French poets Théophile Gautier and Paul Verlaine, that Mallarmé was commissioned to write at various times in his career. He no doubt agreed to do them because the traditional theme of the elegy—the man is dead but he lives on in his work—is clearly linked to the poet's own belief that, although beyond reality there is nothing, poetry has the power to transcend this annihilation. In a second group of poems, also written at various times in his career, Mallarmé wrote about poetry itself, reflecting evocatively on his aims and achievements.

Among these poems are the enigmatically entitled "Prose (pour des Esseintes)," and the sonnets "Le vierge, le vivace, et le bel aujourd'hui," "Ses purs ongles très haut dédiant leur onyx," and "À la nue accablante tu."

Sonnets to Méry Laurent

In addition to these two categories of poems related to his *Grand Oeuvre*, he also wrote some poems that run counter to his obsession with the ideal world, though they, too, display that magical use of language of which Mallarmé had made himself such a master. These are the dozen or so sonnets he addressed to his mistress, Méry Laurent, between 1884 and 1890, in which he expressed his supreme satisfaction with reality, especially in "Quelle soie aux baumes de temps," "Victorieusement fui le suicide beau," and "Le chevelure vol d'une flamme." At that time, life was becoming much happier for him, not only because of this liaison but also because his inclusion in the series of articles entitled *Les Poètes maudits* published by Verlaine in 1883 and the praise lavished upon him by J. K. Huysmans in his novel *A Rebours* led to his wide recognition as the most eminent poet of the day. A series of celebrated Tuesday evening meetings at his tiny flat in Paris were attended by well-known writers, painters, and musicians of the time, who were eager to sit at the feet of the master and listen to him expound his ideas. All this perhaps decreased his need to seek refuge in an ideal world, and in *Un coup de dés jamais n'abolira le hasard*, the work that appeared in 1897, the year before his death, he found consolation in the thoughts first that, even if he had completed his *Grand Oeuvre*, it might have been ignored by the public, and, second, that through what he considered his minor works and his discussions about his ideas, he had met with some measure of success in giving poetry a truly creative function.

Mallarmé died on September 9, 1898, at his cottage at Valvins, a village on the Seine near Fontainebleau, his main residence after retirement.

MAJOR WORKS

POETRY: A number of poems contributed to various magazines from 1862 onward and to two volumes (1866, 1869) of the anthology *Le Parnasse Contemporain; Poésies* (1887), a collection of 35 poems selected by Mallarmé; *Album de vers et de prose* (1887), a selection of nine poems from *Poésies; Vers et prose* (1893), an expansion of the above to include 21 poems; *Poésies*, 2nd enl. ed. (1899), in which Mallarmé incorporated about a dozen additional poems—published six months after the poet's death.

PROSE POEMS: Various prose poems contained in the collections *Album de vers et de prose* (1887), *Pages* (1891), and *Vers et prose* (1893); *Un Coup de dés jamais n'abolira le hasard*, published in the review *Cosmopolis* (1897).

CRITICISM: *Divagations* (1897), a collection of articles on such contemporaries as Verlaine, Villiers de l'Isle-Adam, and Wagner and a number of essays on literary matters.

OTHER WORKS: *La Dernière Mode* (1874), eight issues of a fashion magazine; *Les Mots anglais* (1877), a study of English vocabulary; *Les Dieux antiques* (1880), a study of mythology.

BIBLIOGRAPHY. STEPHANE MALLARME, *Oeuvres complètes*, ed. by HENRI MONDOR and G. JEAN-AUBRY (1945), has been reprinted many times since it was first published. *Poésies* (1970) is the latest version of the edition prepared by Mallarmé himself, to which various poems that have come to light over the intervening years have been added, along with a selection of the poet's occasional verse. *Mallarmé*, ed. with an introduction and plain prose translations by ANTHONY HARTLEY (1965), is a bilingual edition containing the *Poésies*, the occasional verse, the prose poems, some essays, and *Un Coup de dés;* Mallarmé's condensed and complex language responds badly to literal translation, and the renderings in this edition are sometimes meaningless and occasionally incorrect. The *Correspondance*, vol. 1, *1862–1871*, has been edited by HENRI MONDOR and J.P. RICHARD; vol. 2, *1871–1885*, and vol. 3, *1886–1899*, by HENRI MONDOR and L.J. AUSTIN (1959–69). HENRI MONDOR, *Vie de Mallarmé* (1941–42), is the standard biography of Mallarmé, based on the vast amount of manuscript material collected by the author. A.R. CHISHOLM, *Mallarmé's "Grand Oeuvre"* (1962), is a useful introduction (in English) to Mallarmé's work. GUY MICHAUD, *Mallarmé* (1953; Eng. trans., 1965); C. CHADWICK, *Mallarmé, sa pensée dans sa poésie* (1962); and P.O. WALZER, *Essai sur Stéphane Mallarmé* (1963), are among the best short studies.

(C.Ch.)

Malpighi, Marcello

A physician and biologist, Marcello Malpighi pioneered the use of the microscope in the study of the fine structure of plants and animals. Through his patient and systematic observations of structures never before seen, he brought about a re-examination of ancient concepts concerning the organization of living things. After Malpighi, microscopic anatomy became a prerequisite for advances in physiology, embryology, and practical medicine.

Fotofast

Malpighi, painting attributed to the School of Bologna, 17th century. In the Putti Collection, Rizzoli Institute, Bologna, Italy.

Early life

Malpighi was born on March 10, 1628, in Crevalcore, near Bologna, Italy. Little is known of his childhood and youth except that his father began his education in "grammatical studies," and that he entered the University of Bologna in 1646. Both parents died when he was 21, but he was able, nevertheless, to continue his studies. Despite opposition from the university authorities because he was non-Bolognese by birth, in 1653 he was granted doctorates in both medicine and philosophy and appointed as a teacher, whereupon he immediately dedicated himself to further study in anatomy and medicine.

In 1656, Ferdinand II of Tuscany invited him to the professorship of theoretical medicine at the University of Pisa. There Malpighi began his lifelong friendship with Giovanni Borelli, mathematician and naturalist, who was a prominent supporter of the Accademia del Cimento, one of the first scientific societies. Malpighi questioned the prevailing medical teachings at Pisa, tried experiments on colour changes in blood, and attempted to recast anatomical, physiological, and medical problems of the day. Family responsibilities and poor health prompted Malpighi's return in 1659 to Bologna, where he continued to teach and do research with his microscopes. In 1661 he identified and described the pulmonary and capillary network connecting small arteries with small veins, one of the most important discoveries in the history of science. Malpighi's views evoked increasing controversy and dissent, mainly from envy, jealousy, and lack of understanding on the part of his colleagues.

Work at Messina

Hindered by the hostile environment of Bologna, Malpighi accepted (November 1662) a professorship in medicine at the University of Messina in Sicily, on the recommendation there of Borelli, who was investigating the effects of physical forces on animal functions. Malpighi was also welcomed by Viscount Francavilla, a patron of science and a former student, whose hospitality encouraged him in furthering his career. Malpighi pursued his microscopic studies while teaching and practicing medicine. He identified the taste buds and regarded them as terminations of nerves, described the minute structure of the brain, optic nerve, and fat reservoirs, and in 1666 was the first to see the red blood cells and to attribute the colour of blood to them. Again, his research and teaching aroused envy and controversy among his colleagues.

After four years at Messina, Malpighi returned in January 1667 to Bologna, where, during his medical practice, he studied the microscopic subdivisions of specific living organs, such as the liver, brain, spleen, and kidneys, and of bone and the deeper layers of the skin that now bear his name. Impressed by the minute structures he observed under the microscope, he concluded that most living materials are glandular in organization, that even the largest organs are composed of minute glands, and that these glands exist solely for the separation or for the mixture of juices.

Malpighi's work at Messina attracted the attention of the Royal Society in London, whose secretary, Henry Oldenburg, extended him an invitation in 1668 to correspond with him. Malpighi's work was henceforth published periodically in the form of letters in the *Philosophical Transactions* of the Royal Society. In 1669 Malpighi was named an honorary member, the first such recognition given to an Italian. From then on, all his works were published in London.

Height
of his
career At the peak of his fame, Malpighi could have left his tiring medical practice and research to accept one of the many highly remunerative positions offered to him. Instead, he chose to continue his general practice and professorship. These years at Bologna marked the climax of his career, when he marked out large areas of microscopy. Malpighi conducted many studies of insect larvae—establishing, in so doing, the basis for their future study—the most important of which was his investigation in 1669 of the structure and development of the silkworm. In his historic work in 1673 on the embryology of the chick, in which he discovered the aortic arches, neural folds, and somites, he generally followed William Harvey's views on development, though Malpighi probably concluded that the embryo is preformed in the egg after fertilization. He also made extensive comparative studies in 1675–79 of the microscopic anatomy of several different plants and saw an analogy between plant and animal organization.

During the last decade of his life Malpighi was beset by personal tragedy, declining health, and the climax of opposition to him. In 1684 his villa was burned, his apparatus and microscopes shattered, and his papers, books, and manuscripts destroyed. Most probably as a compensatory move when opposition mounted against his views, and in recognition of his stature, Pope Innocent XII invited him to Rome in 1691 as papal archiater, or personal physician, such a nomination constituting a great honour. In Rome he was further honoured by being named a count, he was elected to the College of Doctors of Medicine, his name was placed in the Roman Patriciate Roll, and he was given the title of honorary valet.

Malpighi may be regarded as the first histologist. For almost 40 years he used the microscope to describe the major types of plant and animal structures, and in so doing, marked out for future generations of biologists many major areas of research in botany, embryology, human anatomy, and pathology. Just as Galileo had applied the new technical achievement of the optical lens to vistas beyond the earth, Malpighi extended its use to the intricate organization of living things, hitherto unimagined, below the level of unaided sight. Moreover, his lifework brought into question the prevailing concepts of body function. When, for example, he found that the blood passed through the capillaries, it meant that Harvey was right, that blood was not transformed into flesh in the periphery, as the ancients thought. He was vigorously denounced by his enemies, who failed to see how his many discoveries, such as the renal glomeruli, urinary tubules, dermal papillae, taste buds, and the glandular components of the liver, could possibly improve medical practice. The conflict between ancient ideas and modern discoveries continued throughout the 17th century. Although Malpighi could not say what new remedies might come from his discoveries, he was convinced that microscopic anatomy, by showing the minute construction of living things, called into question the value of old medi-cine. He provided the anatomical basis for the eventual understanding of human physiological exchanges.

Malpighi died of apoplexy in Rome on November 29, 1694. In accordance with his will, his body underwent an autopsy. He was temporarily buried in SS. Vincent and Anastasius Church, and in 1695 he was reinterred in SS. Gregorio and Siro Church, Bologna, as his will had stipulated.

BIBLIOGRAPHY. The definitive study of Malpighi is HOW-ARD ADELMANN, *Marcello Malpighi and the Evolution of Embryology*, 5 vol. (1966). It contains a complete biography of Malpighi, translations from the Latin of Malpighi's chief works with Latin on facing pages, colour reproductions of Malpighi's illustrations, and detailed essays on structure based on embryologists of the 17th, 18th, and 19th centuries with extensive translations from French, German, and Latin. ETTORE TOFFOLETTO, *Discorso sul Malpighi* (1965), provides a critical analysis (in Italian) of Malpighi both as a man and a scientist.

(E.T./Al.R.)

Malraux, André

A major novelist of the 20th century who also distinguished himself in archaeology and, notably, in political action, André Malraux can be recognized on his own admission as a man driven simultaneously by two "demons": history and art. His novels—first classed as adventure stories and for a long time regarded as disparate—reveal a unity in which the expressive forces both of an exceptional "witness of his time" and of a humanist are conjoined. Born with the 20th century in 1901, Malraux identified the stages of development not only of his own country but also of the world in his novels, breaking with those preceding generations of French writers who had confined themselves within their own frontiers.

Bruno Barbey—Magnum

Malraux, 1967.

Malraux was born in Paris on November 3, 1901 of a well-to-do family and showed an early interest in the arts and with it a longing for an exciting life.

At the age of 21 he left France accompanied by Clara Goldschmidt, whom he had married shortly before, in search of an Indochinese temple, Banteay Srei; he had read about its discovery in an archaeological bulletin. Plunging into the Cambodian forest—following an itinerary he was later to call the royal road (*la voie royale*)—he reached the temple, which was not then being considered for restoration. He had some bas-reliefs removed from it and took them back to Phnom Penh, the capital of Cambodia. He was arrested at once and sentenced to imprisonment; he appealed to Paris against the sentence and was released. But his true and historic rendezvous with the Far East was already approaching. As revolution stirred in Southeast Asia and China and the old order began to topple, Malraux organized the Young Annam League (the precursor of the Viet Minh, or Vietnam League for Independence), became a leader-writer and pamphleteer, and founded a newspaper, *L'Indochine Enchaînée* ("Indochina in Chains"). Crossing to China Malraux met—or at least has allowed it to be so be- First
revolution-
ary role lieved—Mikhail Markovich Borodin, the Soviet delegate of the Comintern, or Communist International, who sensed the revolutionary future of China and already foresaw the difference between Mao Tse-Tung's armed peasant revolution and Soviet orthodoxy.

Malraux was to return to the Far East several times. In 1929 he made important discoveries of Greco-Buddhist art in Afghanistan and Iran. In 1934 he flew over the Arabian Desert and discovered what may have been the site of the Queen of Sheba's legendary city. After his second return from Indochina in 1926 he published *La Tentation de l'Occident* (*The Temptation of the West*), in which he vainly tried to interpret to each civilization —Western and Eastern—that which the other had to offer. With his novels *Les Conquérants* (*The Conquerors*), published in 1928, *La Voie royale* (*The Royal Way*), published in 1930, and *La Condition humaine* (*Man's Fate*) in 1933, he became a literary but not a politico-philosophical success. For though he captivated Paris with his exceptional intelligence, lyrical prose, astonishing memory, and breadth of knowledge, it was not generally appreciated that his true life was elsewhere than in the salons or on the committee of the literary periodical *La Nouvelle Revue Française* (The New French Revue) or at literary congresses.

Political activities in the 1930s

History, however, beckoned Malraux again. As Fascism, in the shape of Nazism, rose in the 1930s, he recognized its threat and presided over committees pressing for the liberation of the international Communists Ernst Thälmann and Georgi Dimitrov from their imprisonment under the Nazis. He simultaneously eschewed a rigid Marxism, participated in the Ligue Nationale contre l'Antisémitisme, and in 1935—before the world in general had learned that concentration camps existed—published *Le Temps du mépris* (*Days of Contempt*)—which critics inappropriately adjudged "exotic." At the same time he began to write his *Psychologie de l'art* (*The Psychology of Art*), an activity that bore a relationship to his other interests, for, to Malraux, aesthetic ideas, like the philosophy of action expressed in his own novels, would always be part of man's eternal questioning of destiny and his response to it.

During the Spanish Civil War Malraux crossed the Pyrenees on the second day of the revolution and organized in a single week an international air squadron; he became its colonel—though he had never been a pilot. After several missions to the Madrid front, he visited the United States in order to collect money for medical assistance to Spain. (The film of his masterpeice *L'Espoir* [*Man's Hope*], which was published in 1937 and which was based on his experiences in Spain, was banned in France until after the country's liberation at the end of World War II.)

When World War II broke out and the Soviet Union's alliance with Germany shattered once and for all the old dream of a Communist International through which the whole world might be Communized, Malraux enlisted as a private soldier in a tank unit. He was captured but escaped to the free zone of France, where he joined the resistance movement under the name of "Berger"— whom he was later to make the hero of his unfinished novel *La Lutte avec l'ange* ("The Battle with the Angel"). His life in the French underground movement began in the Corrèze *département* in southwestern France. He was captured (1944) by the Germans and made to undergo a mock execution; on his liberation by the Resistance Forces Françaises de l'Intérieur, he formed the Alsace–Lorraine brigade, which he commanded during the 1st French Army's campaign against Strasbourg in Alsace. During this time of trial his ideas underwent a change, and he was able to rediscover a sense of national unity and a new promise held out by Western culture.

Participation in the French underground movement

On the Alsatian front he met Gen. Charles de Gaulle, with whom his destiny was thenceforth to be linked. He was appointed temporary minister of information (November 1945–January 1946) in de Gaulle's first government. He then followed de Gaulle into retirement, from which he emerged to deliver brilliant speeches as a national delegate to the Gaullist Rassemblement du Peuple

Français, or RPF (French Peoples' Rally). Withdrawing to his villa at Boulogne in northern France, he devoted himself to his monumental meditation on art. As a kind of preface to the historical role he would soon play as minister of cultural affairs, his *Les Voix du silence* (*The Voices of Silence*), published in 1951, sounded the notes of the first universal humanism, that of the brotherhood of works of art, through which man inherits all that is noble in the world and on whose defiance of death the foundation of his true greatness is laid.

Though he had already experienced private adventures in mass revolutions and gone through the throes of a heroic national struggle to arrive at his humanist philosophy, it was not until de Gaulle summoned him to ministerial office in 1958 that Malraux was to experience power. For ten years he was minister of cultural affairs and the intimate friend of de Gaulle. But his grand designs were limited by the means at his disposal, and, despite a promising beginning, he was less effective than might have been expected. Those works published since he quit the political scene tell much of what Malraux describes as that "historical state of grace" that he recognized at that time in France: in *Les Chênes qu'on abat* ("The Fallen Oaks"), which tells of his last conversation with de Gaulle, and likewise in *Les Oraisons funèbres* ("The Funeral Orations"), in which his principal ministerial themes are set out and his preoccupation with death is evident.

Minister of cultural affairs

André Malraux is that rare being who has lived his own legend and whose life reflects his works. His *Antimémoires* (vol. 1, 1967), the only autobiography that Malraux considers essential, has no hint of the traditions of autobiography or of confession. It records nothing of the tragic events of his own life. He makes no mention of the death of Josette Clotis, mother of his two sons, nor of their death in an automobile accident. His brother Roland's imprisonment by the Germans and death are completely ignored. The *Antimémoires* belong both to his legend and to the resurrected past in which "adventure begins by a sense of estrangement, the experience of which will eventually make of the adventurer, a madman, king, or recluse." Since the death of his companion Louise de Vilmorin, André Malraux has lived and worked in solitude at Verrières-le-Buisson, near Paris.

MAJOR WORKS

NOVELS: *Les Conquérants* (1928; *The Conquerors*, trans. by W.S. Whale, 1929); *La Voie royale* (1930; *The Royal Way*, trans. by S. Gilbert, 1935; and in *Anti-memoirs*, trans. by T. Kilmartin, 1968); *La Condition humaine* (1933; *Man's Fate*, trans. by H.M. Chevalier, 1934); *Le Temps du mépris* (1935; *Days of Contempt*, British title; *Days of Wrath*, U.S. title, trans. by H.M. Chevalier, 1936); *L'Espoir* (1937; *Days of Hope*, British title; *Man's Hope*, U.S. title, trans. by S. Gilbert and A. MacDonald, 1938); *Les Noyers de l'Altenburg*, first pub. as *La Lutte avec l'ange* (1943; *The Walnut Trees of Altenburg*, trans. by A.W. Fielding, 1952; and in *Anti-memoirs*).

WRITING ON ART: *Esquisse d'une psychologie du cinéma* (1946); *Psychologie de l'art*, 3 vol. (1947–49; *The Psychology of Art*, 1949); *Saturne, essai sur Goya* (1950; trans. by C.W. Chilton, 1957); *Les Voix du silence* (1951; *The Voices of Silence*, trans. by S. Gilbert, 1953); *Le Musée imaginaire de la sculpture mondiale*, 3 vol. (1952–54; *Museum Without Walls*, trans. by S. Gilbert and F. Price, 1967).

OTHER WORKS: *La Tentation de l'Occident* (1926; *The Temptation of the West*, first trans. in 1961, also trans. in *Anti-memoirs*); *Antimémoires* (1967; *Anti-memoirs*, 1968); *Les Chênes qu'on abat* (1971), autobiography; *Oraisons funèbres* (1971), speeches.

BIBLIOGRAPHY. Critical studies of Malraux's works (in French) include: GAETAN PICON, *Malraux par lui-même* (1953), with annotations by the subject; ANDRE and JEAN BRINCOURT, *Les Oeuvres et les lumières* (1955); PIERRE DE BOISDEFFRE, *André Malraux*, 6th ed. (1963); and ANDRE BRINCOURT, *André Malraux ou le temps du silence* (1966). English-language works particularly recommended are: R.W.B. LEWIS (ed.), *Malraux* (1964), a collection of essays representing international contemporary critical opinion; W.M. FROHOCK, *André Malraux and the Tragic Imagination* (1952), an important study of the writer by a leading American critic of modern French literature; DENIS BOAK, *André Malraux* (1968), by a more severe critic who finds much pretentiousness in the writer's work: JOSEPH FRANK, *The Widening Gyre* (1963), a lucid exposition of Malraux's artistry and personal philosophy; VICTOR H. BROMBERT, *The Intellectual Hero* (1961); and CHARLES D. BLEND, *André Malraux: Tragic Humanist* (1963), two works that concentrate on the philosophy that underlies the novels.

Literary portraits of the man include: CLAUDE MAURIAC, *Malraux; ou, le mal du héros* (1946); ROGER STEPHANE, *Portrait de l'aventurier* (1950); WALTER G. LANGLOIS, *André Malraux: The Indochina Adventure* (1966); CLARA MALRAUX, *Le Bruit de nos pas*, 3 vol. (1963–69) a candid account of Malraux by his estranged wife; VIOLET M. HORVATH, *André Malraux: The Human Adventure* (1969); and PIERRE GALANTE, *Malraux, quel roman que sa vie* (1971; Eng. trans., *Malraux*, 1971).

(An.Br.)

Malta

An independent parliamentary state, Malta consists of a small but strategically important group of islands in the central Mediterranean Sea. Throughout a long and turbulent history, the little archipelago has played a vital role in the struggles of a succession of powers for domination of the Mediterranean and in the interplay between emerging Europe and the older cultures of Africa and the Near East. As a result, Maltese society was molded by many centuries of foreign rule, with influences ranging from Arab to Norman. The withdrawal of British military and naval personnel from its famous Dockyard—associated with the achievement of independence from the U.K. in 1964—created economic and political problems. The Malta of the 1970s continues to face major problems of economic development and diversification, while its traditional social order, in which the Roman Catholic Church has played a powerful role, faces challenges from trade unionists and political movements seeking a more egalitarian society.

MALTA

There are five islands—Malta, the largest; Gozo; Comino; and uninhabited Comminotto and Filfla—lying some 58 miles south of Sicily, 220 miles north of Libya, and about 180 miles east of Tunisia, at the eastern end of that constricted portion of the Mediterranean Sea separating Italy from the African coast. The islands cover a combined land area of about 122 square miles (316 square kilometres) and supported a population of just over 322,000 in 1971. Valletta is the capital, although Sliema is the largest city. (For a related physical feature, see MEDITERRANEAN SEA; for related history, see CRUSADES; MONASTICISM.)

History. The earliest archaeological remains date from about 3800 BC. Neolithic farmers lived in caves like those at Ghar Dalam or villages, like Skorba, and produced pottery that seems to be related to that of contemporary eastern Sicily. An elaborate cult of the dead of Stone Age or Copper Age culture evolved about 2400 BC. Initially centring around rock-cut collective tombs

such as those at Ggantija and Hagar Qim, it culminated—probably through contacts with the cultures of the Cyclades and Mycenae—in the unique underground burial chamber (hypogeum) at Hal Saflieni. This culture came to a sudden end at about 2000 BC, possibly as a result of invasions. The culture which replaced it, of southern Italian flavour, is evidenced today only by fragmentary remains. Bronze Age tools and weapons have been found at Borg in-Nadur and Tarxien Cemetery, while Iron Age relics from about 1200 to 800 BC include cart ruts at Bingemma.

Authenticated News

Aerial view of Valletta with Ft. St. Elmo at the extremity of the promontory, flanked by Grand and Marsamxett harbours.

Between the 8th and 6th centuries BC contact was made with Semitic cultures. Evidence is scanty, however, and a few inscriptions found on Malta constitute the only indication of a Phoenician presence. There is more substantial proof of the Carthaginian presence in the 6th century BC; coins, inscriptions, and several Punic-type rock tombs have been found. It is certain that in 218 BC Malta came under Roman political control. Originally part of the Praetorship of Sicily, the islands were subsequently given the status of municipium and were thus allowed to coin their own money, send ambassadors to Rome, and control domestic affairs. According to tradition, St. Paul was shipwrecked in Malta in AD 60 and began to convert the inhabitants. The Maltese have been Christians uninterruptedly since that time.

Domination by Carthage and Rome

With the division of the Roman Empire, in AD 395, Malta was given to the eastern portion dominated by Constantinople. Until the 15th century, it followed the more immediate fortunes of nearby Sicily, being ruled successively by Arabs (who left a strong effect on the language), Normans (who advanced the legal and governmental structures), and a succession of feudal lords. In 1530, however, it was ceded to the Order of the Hospital of St. John of Jerusalem (the Knights Hospitallers), a religious and military order of the Roman Catholic Church. Malta became a fortress and, under the Knights' Grand Master, Jean de La Valette, successfully withstood the Ottoman siege of 1565. The new captial city of Valletta became a town of splendid palaces and unparalleled fortifications. Growing in power and wealth—due mainly to their maritime adventures against the Turks—the Knights left the island an architectural and artistic legacy. Although there was little economic and social contact between them and the Maltese, they managed to imprint their cosmopolitan character on Malta and its inhabitants.

In 1798, Napoleon Bonaparte captured the island, but the French presence was short-lived, and the Treaty of Amiens returned the island to the Knights in 1802. The Maltese protested and acknowledged Great Britain's sovereignty, subject to certain conditions incorporated in a Declara-

British rule

tion of Rights. The constitutional change was ratified by the Treaty of Paris in 1814.

Malta's political status under Britain underwent a series of vicissitudes in which successively constitutions were granted, suspended, and revoked. The economy became a function of British demands for Malta's military facilities, and the Dockyard developed into the economic mainstay.

The island flourished during the Crimean War and was favourably affected by the opening of the Suez Canal in 1869. Self-government was granted in 1921 on a dyarchical basis whereby Britain shared power and responsibility with Maltese ministers who were elected by the legislature. But the battle over the relative roles of the English, Italian, and Maltese languages took its toll and in 1936 the islands reverted to a strictly colonial regime in which full power rested in the hands of the governor. During World War II, the islands repelled the Axis powers against severe odds, having been one of the most heavily bombed targets of that conflict. As a result, it was awarded the George Cross, Britain's highest civilian decoration. Self-government was granted in 1947, revoked in 1959, and then restored in 1962. Malta finally achieved independence within the British Commonwealth on September 21, 1964.

The landscape. *Relief.* The main physical characteristic of Malta Island is a well-defined escarpment that bisects it along the Victoria Lines Fault running along the whole breadth of the island from Ra's Ir-Raheb to the coast northeast of Gharghur. The highest areas are coralline limestone uplands that comprise a triangular plateau to the west. The uplands are separated from the surrounding areas by blue clay slopes, while undercliff areas are found where the coralline plateau has fallen and forms a subordinate surface between the sea and the original shore.

Limestone and coral

Blau—Camera Press—Publix

Limestone rock and terraced plots, where shallow soil is held together by rubble walls, on the island of Malta.

To the north the escarpment is occasionally abrupt and broken by deep embayments. To the south, however, the plateaus gradually descend from a height of 600–800 feet into undulating areas of globigerina (derived from marine protozoa) limestone less than 400 feet high. On the west there are deeply incised valleys and undercliff areas, while on the east there are several valleys descending to the central plains.

The west coast of Malta presents a high, bold, and generally harbourless face. On the east, however, a tongue of high ground known as Mt. Sceberras separates the bays of Marsamxett and Grand Harbour. These deepwater harbours contribute to the strategic importance of Malta, because there are relatively few of them in the Mediterranean. The bays are associated with nine seasonal creeks that include those of Sliema, Lazaretto, Msida, and Marsa. The northern shore is again bare and craggy, charac-

terized by its coves and hills, which are separated by fertile lowlands.

In Gozo, the landscape is characterized by a broken coralline plateau to the north and by low-lying globigerina limestone plains and hills to the south.

Malta possesses favourable conditions for the percolation and underground storage of water. The impermeable blue clays provide two distinct water tables between the limestone formations. The principal source for the public supply of water has been the main sea-level water table. In the absence of permanent streams or lakes and given a considerable loss of rainfall, the water supply has often been a problem. A seawater distillation power plant, however, is now coming into operation.

Shortage of fresh water

Soils. Maltese soils are mainly young or immature and thin. By law, when soils are removed from construction sites, they must be taken to agricultural areas, and level stretches in quarries are often covered with carted soil. Organic refuse from the towns is also used. Consequently, the soils are unusual and are partly a manufactured medium.

Climate. The climate is typically Mediterranean, with hot, dry summers, warm and sporadically wet autumns, and short, cool winters with adequate rainfall. Nearly three-fourths of the precipitation falls between October and March; and June, July, and August are normally quite dry.

The temperature is very stable, the annual mean being 64° F (18° C) and the monthly averages ranging from 53° F (12° C) to 77° F (25° C). Winds are strong and frequent; the most common are the cool northwesterly (the Majjistral), the dry northeasterly (the Grigal), and the hot humid southeasterly (the Xlokk). The relative humidity is consistently high and rarely falls below 40 percent.

Vegetation and animal life. While wild vegetation is sparse, there is an abundance of cultivated potatoes, sulla (a leguminous fodder crop), onions, tomatoes, and vines. The great variety of trees includes the carob, fig, and chaste. The developed seashore vegetation includes golden and rock samphires, sea campion, spurge, saltwort, and marram grass.

Typical of the few native mammals are the hedgehog, the least weasel, the water and the white-toothed shrews, and the pipistrel and other bats. Rats, mice, and some rabbits are also found. Resident birds include the spectacled and Sardinian warblers, the Manx and Cory's shearwaters, and the blue rock thrush. Linnets, tree and Spanish sparrows, buntings, rock doves, and several kinds of owls also form breeding populations, while birds of passage include ospreys, rollers, swallows, cuckoos, bee-eaters, and vultures. Common insects are beetles, grasshoppers, flies, mosquitoes, moths, bees, wasps, cockroaches, ants, and several species of butterflies. Ladybirds migrate from Sicily.

Human settlement. Until the mid-19th century, the Maltese lived in the relative seclusion of the fields that, as they became increasingly fragmented, accentuated the individuality of the farming community. The *zuntier*, or church square, was the traditional focus of village life. With the growth of the Dockyard complex in the latter part of the 1800s, new settlements appeared around Grand Harbour, and the Sliema metropolitan region developed in the 20th century into the most fashionable part of Malta. The advent of industrial estates near major villages has somewhat stemmed the exodus from the rural areas. Higher living standards and expatriate residents are now giving rise to residential developments in several hitherto forsaken areas such as Kappara and the Gardens.

New towns

Gozo conserves its own rural character. The architecture of the new development at ta' Cenc successfully blends with the island's natural beauty and is architecturally stimulating.

Population. The islands' ethnic and linguistic composition reflects the heritage of many rulers. A European atmosphere predominates as a result of close association particularly with southern Europe. About 95 percent of the islanders are Maltese-born, about 2 percent are En-

his admission to Jesus College, Cambridge, in 1784. There he studied a wide range of subjects and took prizes in Latin and Greek, graduating in 1788. He took his master of arts degree in 1791, was elected a fellow of Jesus College in 1793, and took holy orders in 1797. He wrote a pamphlet in 1796 called "The Crisis" (not published), which, among other things, took a favourable view of newly proposed poor laws, which were to set up workhouses for the poor. This was a view that ran somewhat counter to his views on poverty and population published two years later.

The opinions and teachings that Malthus developed reflect largely a reaction, amiably conducted, to his father's views and to the doctrines of the French Revolution and its supporters. The English radical philosopher William Godwin, for example, was being widely read for such works as *Political Justice* (1793), which took for granted the perfectibility of mankind and foresaw a millennium in which rational men would live prosperously and harmoniously without laws and institutions. Unlike Godwin (or, earlier, Rousseau), who viewed human affairs from a theoretical standpoint, Malthus was essentially an empiricist, and he began from the harsh realities of his time. His reaction developed in the tradition of British economics, which would today be called sociological.

Essay on Population

In 1798 he published anonymously the first edition of *An Essay on the Principle of Population as it affects the Future Improvement of Society, with Remarks on the Speculations of Mr. Godwin, M. Condorcet, and other Writers.* The work received wide notice. Briefly, crudely, yet strikingly, Malthus argued that infinite human hopes for social happiness must be vain, for population will always tend to outrun the growth of production. The increase of population will take place, if unchecked, in a geometrical progression, while the means of subsistence will increase in only an arithmetical progression. Population will always expand to the limit of subsistence and will be held there by famine, war, and ill health. "Vice" (which included, for Malthus, contraception), "misery," and "self-restraint" alone could check this excessive growth.

Malthus was an economic pessimist, viewing poverty as man's inescapable lot. The argument in this first edition is essentially abstract and analytical. To the subsequent edition of 1803, which expanded the long pamphlet of 1798 into a longer book, part of the information for which he had gathered by reading more economic and population literature and part of which he absorbed on trips to Germany, Sweden, Norway, Finland, Russia, France, and Switzerland in the intervening years, Malthus added much factual material and illustration to his thesis. At no point, even up to the final and massive sixth edition of 1826, did he ever adequately set out his premises or examine their logical status. Nor did he handle his factual and statistical materials with much critical or statistical rigour, even though during his lifetime the sophistication of statisticians was developing remarkably in both continental Europe and Great Britain. A remark by Kingsley Davis, a United States student of population, that Malthus' theories, apparently founded on so extensive an empirical base, are yet at their weakest with respect to empiricism and at their strongest as a tight and elegant theoretical formulation, has much truth in it as both praise and blame. For better or worse, the Malthusian theory of population was, nevertheless, incorporated into current theoretical systems of economics. It acted as a brake on economic optimism, helped to justify a theory of wages that made the minimum cost of subsistence of the wage earner a standard of judgment, and discouraged traditional forms of charity.

The immediate influence of the Malthusian theory of population on social policy was very great. It had been believed that fertility itself added to national wealth; the poor laws perhaps encouraged large families by their doles. If they had "never existed," wrote Malthus, "though there might have been a few more instances of severe distress, the aggregate mass of happiness among the common people would have been much greater than it is at present." These laws limited the mobility of labour, he said, and encouraged fecundity and should be abolished. For the most unfortunate it might be licit to establish workhouses, not "comfortable asylums," but they should be places in which "fare should be hard" and "severe distress . . . find some alleviation."

Life at Haileybury and world fame. In 1804 Malthus married Harriet Eckersall and in 1805 became professor of history and political economy at the East India Company's college at Haileybury, Hertfordshire. It was the first time in Great Britain that the words political economy had been used to designate an academic office. He lived quietly at Haileybury for the remainder of his life, except for a visit to Ireland in 1817 and a trip to the Continent in 1825, for his own and his wife's health. In 1811 he met and became close friends with the economist David Ricardo.

Meanwhile, he continued publishing a variety of pamphlets and tracts on economics. In them he approached the problem of what determines price with a less rigorous analysis than Ricardo and in terms of an institutionally determined "effective demand," a phrase that he invented.

Principles of Political Economy

In 1820 in his summary *Principles of Political Economy Considered with a View to Their Practical Application*, he went so far as to propose public works and private luxury investment, as palliatives for economic distress, that would increase effective demand and prosperity. He went further and criticized thrift as a virtue knowing no limit; to the contrary, he argued, "the principles of saving, pushed to excess, would destroy the motive to production." To maximize wealth, a nation had to balance "the power to produce and the will to consume." In fact, Malthus, as an economist concerned with what he called the problem of "gluts" or, as they would be called today, the problems of slump and depression, can be said to have anticipated the economic discoveries of John Maynard Keynes in the 1930s.

In 1819 Malthus was elected a fellow of the Royal Society; in 1821 he became a member of the Political Economy Club, the number of which included Ricardo and James Mill, and in 1824 he was elected one of the ten royal associates of the Royal Society of Literature. Malthus was one of the cofounders, in 1834, of the Statistical Society of London. In 1833 he was elected to the French Académie des Sciences Morales et Politiques and to the Royal Academy of Berlin. During these later years, though he wrote various papers, he never added substantially to what he had gathered in *Essay on Population* and *Principles of Political Economy*. Malthus died on December 23, 1834, and was buried in the Abbey Church, at Bath.

BIBLIOGRAPHY. W. OTTER, "Memoir," preface to the 2nd ed. of the *Principles of Political Economy* (1836), is still a basis for any biography. J. RONAR, *Malthus and His Work* (1885, reprinted and expanded 1924), is the major work of 19th-century scholarship, illuminated by very wide learning. JOHN MAYNARD KEYNES, "Robert Malthus: The First of the Cambridge Economists," in *Essays in Biography* (1933, new ed., 1957), is charming and of great importance in the rehabilitation of Malthus as a major economic theorist. D.V. GLASS (ed.), *Introduction to Malthus* (1953), contains "A Summary View of the Principles of Population" and an important letter on the Poor Laws by Malthus, in addition to a very full bibliography on the Malthusian question in the 19th century and three useful essays discussing Malthus in historical perspective. A. FLEW, "The Structure of Malthus' Population Theory," *Australasian Journal of Philosophy*, 35:1–20 (1957), and the same author's edited version of Malthus' *An Essay on the Principle of Population* (1970), were contributed by a critic and philosopher who has brought both logical rigour and sympathy to the clarification of Malthus' analysis so that no more favourable case can be made for the Malthusian theory of population in modern terms. P.M. HAUSER and O.D. DUNCAN (eds.), *The Study of Population: An Inventory and Appraisal* (1959), though already partly out of date, is a most useful single introduction to modern population studies so far as the issues raised by Malthus are alive in the late 20th century. K. SMITH, *The Malthusian Controversy* (1951); and D.E.C. EVERSLEY, *Social Theories of Fertility and the Malthusian Debate* (1959), are two admirable and scholarly discussions of all the issues surrounding the Malthusian population theory in its long history.

(D.G.MacR.)

Malvales

Malvales, the mallow order, is a relatively small order of flowering plants (in the class Dicotyledoneae) containing nine families and about 3,000 species, most of which are woody plants, though some are herbaceous. The order is found throughout the world, except in the Arctic, in nearly all types of habitats, especially in the warm temperate and tropical regions.

A number of plants in this order are economically or aesthetically important; for example, the cotton genus (*Gossypium*), the source of chocolate (*Theobroma cacao*), and plants cultivated for their beautiful flowers (*Hibiscus, Althaea,* and others).

Fruits of a large number of species of the Sterculiaceae family are rich in caffeine and those of *Theobroma cacao* also contain the alkaloid theobromine. West African kola nuts from species of the genus *Cola* also contain the heart-stimulating glucoside kolanin. In addition, alkaloids have been detected in numerous other species, including *Waltheria indica* (family Sterculiaceae), several species of *Elaeocarpus* and *Sloanea* (Elaeocarpaceae), a number of genera of the family Malvaceae, and *Corchorus* and *Grewia* (Tiliaceae).

GENERAL FEATURES

Size range and diversity of structure. The life-forms exhibited by plants in the order Malvales are diverse, including plants with a size range from small herbs to large trees. None, however, is parasitic or normally epiphytic (not rooted in soil but living among tree branches), nor are there any particularly succulent species. In the family Bombacaceae the trees often develop swollen trunks, a feature particularly well exemplified in the baobab (*Adansonia digitata*) of tropical Africa (with related species in the Malagasy Republic and one in northwest Australia), a tree noted not for its height but for its remarkable girth, which may reach nine metres (about 30 feet) in diameter.

Importance to man. *Ochroma pyramidale* (family Bombacaceae) is the source of balsa wood, the lightest of all timbers. The trees are natives of the area from Mexico to Bolivia, in Brazil, and in the Antilles.

Source of kapok

Ceiba pentandra (Bombacaceae), the silk-cotton, or kapok, tree, is a widely buttressed tree up to 60 metres (200 feet) high, native to tropical America but now widely distributed throughout the tropics. Kapok, the resilient water-resistant hairs from the fruit capsules, is used for upholstery, lifesaving equipment, quilts, and other products. *Bombax ceiba*, the cotton tree of tropical Asia, produces an inferior kapok.

Durio zibethinus (Bombacaceae), a large buttressed tree native perhaps in Sumatra and Borneo, is now cultivated and often naturalized throughout tropical Southeast Asia for its fruit, the durian, which is famous for its delicate flavour but disagreeable odour.

The family Elaeocarpaceae contains no plants of great economic importance, although a few are sometimes grown for their horticultural merit; for example, *Muntingia calabura*, often cultivated, and naturalized in parts of Florida. Other horticultural plants include species of *Elaeocarpus* and *Crinodendron*, especially *C. hookeriana*, a native of Chile, the lantern tree. The fruits of *Aristotelia macqui*, the macqui, are eaten in Chile.

Abutilon theophrasti (Malvaceae) is cultivated in northern China for its bast fibres, Chinese jute, which are used to make ropes, twine, and other fibre products.

Althaea rosea (Malvaceae), the hollyhock, a native of the eastern Mediterranean region, is widely cultivated in temperate gardens. The well-known *Hibiscus rosa-sinensis* (Malvaceae) is grown throughout the tropics for its flamboyant flowers. *H. esculentus* (also known as *Abelmoschus esculentus*), okra, is widely cultivated in tropical regions for its edible, mucilaginous, immature fruits, much used in soups. *H. sabdariffa*, the roselle, is used for its sweet calyx or as a potherb.

Cotton is obtained from species of the genus *Gossypium* (Malvaceae) and consists of the hairs that have developed on the seeds. In addition, cottonseed oil is extracted from the seeds themselves and cottonseed-oil

cake, the residue, is used to feed cattle. There are about 20 wild species of *Gossypium*, perhaps three in Australia, seven in Africa and Southwest Asia, and eight in the Americas. All of them are lintless; that is, the individual seed hairs, even when well-developed, are without convolutions. They are perennial shrubs that occur naturally in open habitats of dry regions of the tropics and subtropics, especially on banks of creeks or stream beds that are dry during most of the year. Such habitats are preferred because the seedlings are highly susceptible to competition from other plants. The domesticated cottons, two species, bear seeds with lint that may be spun. They have double the number of chromosomes found in the wild species and arose by hybridization some time in the past between Old and New World species. At first perennial, they later developed an annual habit, as shown in the modern races.

Source of cola flavouring

The genus *Cola* (Sterculiaceae), *C. nitida* and *C. acuminata* especially, is the source of kola nuts. These two species are forest trees native to West Africa, and there they are often cultivated beyond the area of their natural distribution. Kola nuts constitute an important article of trade in West Africa and are a rich source of caffeine. They also contain the glucoside kolanin and when chewed confer considerable ability to withstand fatigue.

The species *Theobroma cacao* (Sterculiaceae), cacao, is one of about 22 species in the genus and is native from the central part of the Amazon Basin and Guyana westward and northward to southern Mexico. Its fruits are the source of cocoa, chocolate, and cocoa butter. There are two main types of cocoa trees, their distributions separated by the Isthmus of Panama. The subspecies *cacao*, from Mexico and Central America, corresponds to the "Criollo" cultivars, while the subspecies *T. cacao sphaerocarpum* of South America contains the "Forastero" varieties. The large, tough, berrylike fruits containing the seeds, or beans as they are called, are often borne directly on the tree trunks. Cocoa butter is obtained from the beans by pressing and cocoa by roasting them.

The genus *Tilia* (Tiliaceae), the lindens or limes (not to be confused with the unrelated tropical limes, *Citrus aurantiifolia* [family Rutaceae, order Rutales]), particular-

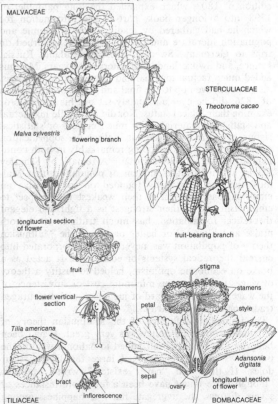

Drawing by M. Pahl based on (Tiliaceae) G.H.M. Lawrence, *Taxonomy of Flowering Plants* (1951); Macmillan & Co., and (others) H. Baillon, *The Natural History of Plants*, vol. 4 (1875); L. Reeve & Co., Ltd.

MALVACEAE

Malva sylvestris   flowering branch

longitudinal section of flower

fruit

STERCULIACEAE

Theobroma cacao

fruit-bearing branch

TILIACEAE

flower vertical section

Tilia americana

bract

inflorescence

stigma

stamens

petal   style

sepal   ovary   longitudinal section of flower

Adansonia digitata

BOMBACACEAE

Representative plants and structures from four of the largest families of the order Malvales.

ly *T. americana* and *T.* × *europaea*, are valuable as timber trees and for the fibre below the bark, the bast fibre, which is much used in country districts. The nectar secreted at the base of the sepals in the sweetly scented flowers has been much sought after by bees and produces highly prized honey.

Corchorus capsularis and *C. olitorius* (Tiliaceae) constitute the chief source of jute or gunny and—especially *C. capsularis*—are much cultivated in India and Bangladesh and, to a lesser extent, elsewhere. The plants form sparsely branched annuals up to about three metres (ten feet) high. When ready, the stems are cut, retted in water, and the fibre extracted by beating. The leaves and young shoots are also eaten as a vegetable or potherb; *C. olitorius* has been cultivated for this purpose from ancient times, especially in Egypt. The seeds, however, are poisonous and contain glycosides of the type found in the genus *Digitalis* (family Scrophulariaceae, order Scrophulariales).

NATURAL HISTORY

Pollination. Although little is known about the majority of the genera and several of the familes in this order, it appears that the flowers, with their bright colours and nectaries, are generally adapted to pollination by insects or birds. A number are pollinated by bats, especially in the family Bombacaceae. Wind pollination is rare and perhaps of only secondary importance. Flowers are commonly protandrous; that is, the male stamens develop and mature before the styles (female structures that receive the pollen) of the same flower, an adaptation that favours cross-pollination. In some weedy species in the family Malvaceae, however, the styles eventually bend over to touch the withered stamens, still bearing some pollen, and effect self-pollination, thus ensuring fertilization in case pollen from some other source has failed to reach the styles.

In the African genus *Sparmannia*, the showy flowers contain numerous fertile and sterile stamens that are sensitive to touch; they bend outward from the centre when stimulated, presumably to aid pollination.

Insect pollination

Elaborate adaptations to insect pollination are found in many members of the family Sterculiaceae. The flowers of the genus *Abroma* are a good example of "lantern-flowers," which have small "windows" in the petals that permit light to shine through, thus attracting insects. In many genera, especially *Sterculia* itself, dark-purple or chocolate-coloured flowers with a fetid odour attract flies. *Theobroma cacao*, the source of cacao and of chocolate, is pollinated by diverse types of small insects; thrips, ants, midges, and aphids have been recorded.

Pollination by hummingbirds, sunbirds, and others is widespread in many tropical species. The red flowers of *Malvaviscus*, which have a relatively narrow tube formed by the overlapping petals and have protruding stamens and styles, are an excellent example of adaptation to pollination by hummingbirds.

Hibiscadelphus, a rare native Hawaiian genus, two of four species of which are already extinct, is adapted to bird pollination. Here the natural pollinating bird may be extinct or nearing extinction too, and hand-pollination by man of the few remaining trees is necessary to ensure a good seed set.

Pollination by bats is widespread in the family Bombacaceae. In the genus *Adansonia*, for example, the drab-coloured flowers with their numerous stamens hang down below the foliage where bats can easily reach them. This association of characters is typical of flowers adapted to pollination by bats. Bat pollination has also been recorded for *Ochroma*, *Ceiba*, and *Durio* (of the family Bombacaceae).

Seed dispersal. Methods of seed dispersal are not particularly remarkable in the order Malvales. Fruits usually take the form of dry capsules or schizocarps (fruits that separate into pieces at maturity), which are sometimes hooked for dispersal by attachment to animals' coats. Drupes (stone-seeded fruits) and berries also occur; the latter are large and leathery, as in the genus *Theobroma*, or juicy, as in *Malvaviscus*.

FORM AND FUNCTION

Distinguishing characteristics. The family Bombacaceae is distinguished by a combination of characters of which the most diagnostic is perhaps the unilocular (single-chambered) anther containing smooth pollen, which distinguishes it from the very closely related family Malvaceae.

The diagnostic characters of the family Elaeocarpaceae include flowers without an epicalyx (a series of bracts close to, and resembling, the sepals), petals that are often characteristically fringed or divided at their ends, and anthers that usually open by two apical pores (small openings in the end of the pollen sac).

The family Malvaceae is identified by the characteristic combination of a united column of stamens with unilocular anthers containing spiny pollen grains, especially when combined with the possession of an epicalyx and petals convoluted in the bud.

The Huaceae is a small and little-known family in which the petals are stalked and more or less persistent. There is a single basal ovule in the genus *Hua* and six in *Afrostyrax*; the seeds in both genera smell strongly of onions.

The family Rhopalocarpaceae (Sphaerosepalaceae) has flowers with imbricate (overlapping) petals densely streaked with short resinous lines, and the numerous stamens are dotted as well.

The family Sarcolaenaceae (Chlaenaceae) has flowers with large petals, that are convolute in the bud, similar to those of many other members of the order Malvales. The stamens are usually numerous and are borne inside a disk or a cupular ring of staminodes (sterile stamens). The fruit is often surrounded by lignified (woody) bracts.

The family Tiliaceae has flowers of a somewhat generalized type for the order, with five valvate (*i.e.*, touching edge to edge in the bud; not overlapped) sepals, five convolute, imbricate, or valvate petals, usually numerous stamens that are free or united into groups, a superior ovary of united carpels, and seeds with endosperm (a starchy nutrient tissue for the developing embryo).

The family Scytopetalaceae has leaves that lack stipules (basal appendages) and that are often asymmetrical at the base. In the flower the valvate petals are either reflexed at anthesis (flower opening) or do not separate but fall as an entire cap when the flower opens. The seeds are sometimes covered with agglutinated mucilaginous hairs.

The family Sterculiaceae has leaves that are often digitately divided. The flowers are sometimes unisexual and may be without petals, the stamens are free or united into a column, and the pollen is nonspiny.

Basis of relationships between families

Anatomical characters indicate a very close affinity between the families Malvaceae, Bombacaceae, Sterculiaceae, and Tiliaceae, and, to a slightly lesser degree, the family Elaeocarpaceae. Mucilage cells are found in the tissues of all five of these families, and mucilage cavities and canals are found in the tissues of most of them. Pericyclic fibre bundles are characteristic of most families in the order. Many of these fibres are of great economic importance—*e.g.*, jute and various hemps.

The presence of stellate hairs (hairs branched in a star-like pattern) on leaves and young stems is often characteristic, especially of the families Malvaceae, Bombacaceae, Sterculiaceae, and Tiliaceae.

Pollen. Pollen grains in the order Malvales are generally three-pored (tricolpate), often with the pores sunken or sometimes with several apertures. In shape, the pollen grains are generally more or less flattened spheres. The surface is generally ridged, but in the family Malvaceae the grains are characteristically spiny. In fact, one of the factors that helps to place the genera around *Hibiscus* and *Gossypium* in the Malvaceae rather than in the Bombacaceae (in which, on fruit characters, they have been classified by some authorities) is their possession of spiny pollen.

Nonspiny pollen of a basically similar kind is common to members of the families Tiliaceae, Bombacaceae, Sterculiaceae, and Scytopetalaceae. The pollen of the Elaeocarpaceae is somewhat like that of the Tiliaceae but much smaller; however, grains that are very similar indeed are found in the family Flacourtiaceae of the order Violales, the group suggested by some as being the nearest family outside the order Malvales.

The pollen of the family Sarcolaenaceae is somewhat remarkable and has been investigated in detail. In all of the genera of that family the grains are united in firm tetrads (groups of four), sometimes with individual grains more or less degenerate and therefore smaller than the others. At first sight they appear quite dissimilar from any others in the order Malvales, yet the fine reticulations of the surface pattern show some affinity with the family Tiliaceae.

EVOLUTION

The earliest fossil remains, the petrified wood *Hibiscoxylon niloticum*, recognizable as belonging to the order Malvales date from Cretaceous deposits (about 100,000,000 years ago) in Egypt. Elsewhere, leaf impressions resembling the present-day genus *Sterculia* have been recorded from the Upper Cretaceous.

Fossil record

From the Eocene (about 50,000,000 years ago) numerous leaves and some fruits have been recognized as belonging to families in the order Malvales. A species of *Echinocarpus* (Elaeocarpaceae), for example, has been described from fruits in southern England, but other remains, not attributable to present-day genera, have been given fossil names—*e.g.*, *Sphinxia* (Sterculiaceae), and *Cantitilia* (Tiliaceae). From later Tertiary beds (about 20,000,000 years old, or less) numerous Malvalean fossils have been reported from many different parts of the world, including Europe, North and South America, Central and eastern Asia, and Australia. Leaf remains have been attributed to several modern genera—*e.g.*, *Elaeocarpus*, *Vallea*, and *Sloanea* (Elaeocarpaceae); *Bombax* and *Hampea* (Bombacaceae); *Sterculia*, *Byttneria*, *Pterospermum*, *Melochia*, and *Theobroma* (Sterculiaceae). From the Pliocene (about 5,000,000 years ago) even more numerous and recognizable leaf and fruit remains are recorded.

Fossil pollen attributed to the genus *Tilia* has been recorded from as far back as the Upper Cretaceous Period (about 65,000,000 years ago), and Bombacaceae-like pollen from Upper Cretaceous or Early Tertiary deposits in Brazil.

CLASSIFICATION

Annotated classification.

ORDER MALVALES

Trees, shrubs, or herbs, often with mucilaginous juice and fibrous stems. Leaves alternate, rarely opposite, usually with stipules. Flowers cyclical (rarely having the carpels more or less spirally arranged); hermaphroditic, sometimes unisexual. Calyx and corolla members usually 5-merous (present in groups of 5), usually distinct, rarely lacking petals, regular, rarely somewhat bilaterally symmetrical; epicalyx often present; sepals usually valvate; petals mostly convoluted in bud, sometimes imbricate or valvate. Stamens usually numerous, free, or shortly connate at the base into 5–10 bundles, or united into a staminal column surrounding the style. Carpels 2 to many, united, superior, rarely inferior, with 1 to many axile, rarely parietal (attached to ovary wall) ovules. Fruit various, seeds usually with some endosperm. Nine families, about 240 genera, and 3,000 species.

Family Bombacaceae

Trees, often large with thick trunks. Leaves simple or palmate, alternate, often containing mucilage cells. Flowers bisexual, often large, usually regular. Calyx valvate, often with an epicalyx. Petals 5, often large, sometimes absent, convoluted in the bud. Stamens 5 to numerous, free or united into a tube; anthers usually unilocular. Ovary superior, of 2–5 united carpels; style simple, capitate or lobed. Fruit a capsule, sometimes indehiscent; seeds with little or no endosperm, often surrounded by hairs from the inner wall of the capsule. About 20 genera and 180 species with worldwide distribution in the tropics, especially of the New World.

Family Elaeocarpaceae

Trees and shrubs. Leaves simple, alternate or opposite, without mucilage cells. Flowers usually bisexual and regular. Calyx valvate without an epicalyx. Petals 4 or 5, usually free, sometimes absent, often much divided at their ends, usually valvate, imbricate, never convoluted, in bud. Stamens numerous, free, arising from a disk that is sometimes developed into an an-

drophore (a structure bearing the male flower parts); anthers bilocular, usually opening by 2 apical pores. Ovary superior, with 2 to many (rarely 1) united carpels; style simple, often lobed at its apex. Fruit a capsule or drupe; seeds with abundant endosperm. About 10 genera and 350 species of wide distribution in the tropics and subtropics, centred in western Melanesia and South America but absent from continental Africa.

Family Huaceae

Trees. Leaves simple, entire, and stipulate. Flowers bisexual, regular, and small. Calyx of 3–5 valvate lobes. Petals 4–5 free, in *Hua* with a slender claw, induplicate-valvate in the bud, more or less persistent. Stamens 10, free, in one series; anthers with 4 locules, the 2 lower smaller than the upper. Ovary superior, of 5 united carpels but 1-locular; style simple; ovules 1 on a basal placenta in *Hua*, 6 basal ovules in *Afrostyrax*. Fruit relatively large, a 1-seeded capsule, dehiscent from the apex (*Hua*) or indehiscent (*Afrostyrax*); seed with copious endosperm smelling of onions in both genera. One genus, *Hua*, with 2 species or, according to some authorities, the family also contains the genus *Afrostyrax* with 5 species. Distributed in tropical Africa.

Family Malvaceae

Herbs or shrubs, rarely small trees. Leaves stipulate, alternate, simple or variously lobed, especially palmately so, mucilage cells present, also in the stem tissue. Flowers usually bisexual, regular, usually 5-merous. Calyx valvate, frequently with an epicalyx. Petals 5, free, although appearing united at the base due to junction with the filament bases, often individually asymmetrical, convoluted in bud. Stamens numerous due to branching of the inner whorl (the outer whorl usually absent), all united below to form a tube joined to the petals and surrounding the style; anthers unilocular (each consisting of half an anther by division), opening longitudinally; pollen spiny. Ovary superior with 1 to many, commonly 5, united carpels (in a few genera the several carpels are arranged in a spiral cluster); style branched above with the same number or, more rarely, twice as many branches as carpels. Fruit a dry capsule or a schizocarp (rarely in *Malvaviscus* a berry); seeds usually with a little endosperm or with none. About 75 genera and 1,000 species with wide distribution throughout the world, except in the Arctic.

Family Rhopalocarpaceae

Trees and shrubs. Leaves alternate, simple, with stipules partially encircling the stem and leaving a prominent scar on falling. Flowers bisexual, regular. Calyx of 4 (rarely 3 + 3) unequal, strongly imbricate lobes. Petals 4 (rarely 3) unequal, imbricate in the bud, densely streaked with short resinous lines. Stamens numerous, more or less connate at the base, resin dotted; anthers small, bilocular; within the stamens a large cupular disk. Ovary superior of 2 (rarely 3) united carpels; style simple, geniculate, with an entire stigma. Fruit 1- (rarely 2-) seeded, globose, densely muricate; seed large with abundant endosperm and a minute embryo. Two genera and 14 species, known only from the Malagasy Republic.

Family Sarcolaenaceae

Trees and shrubs. Leaves alternate, simple, with stipules that are often large, mucilaginous cells present. Flowers bisexual, regular. Calyx of 3–5 equal or unequal, imbricate lobes. Petals 5–6, large, convolute in bud. Stamens numerous (rarely 5 or 10) sometimes fasciculate, arising inside a disk or cupular ring of staminodes (sterile stamens); anthers bilocular, dehiscing longitudinally. Ovary superior, of 1–5 united carpels; style usually thick, more or less elongated, usually with a lobed stigma. Fruit a capsule with several-seeded locules, or 1-seeded and indehiscent; often surrounded by lignified bracts; seed with endosperm. Eight genera and about 30 species, known only from the Malagasy Republic.

Family Scytopetalaceae

Trees or shrubs. Leaves simple, alternate, often asymmetrical at their bases, without stipules. Flowers bisexual, regular. Calyx of 3–4 united persistent lobes, often petaloid or cuplike. Petals 3–16, valvate in bud, free and reflexed at anthesis or not separating and falling as an entire cap, sometimes thick in texture. Stamens numerous in 3–6 series, free or sometimes connate below; anthers bilocular, often opening by an apical pore. Ovary of 3–8 superior united carpels, the locules sometimes incomplete in the upper portion; style simple with a small stigma. Fruit usually a tardily dehiscent capsule, often woody; seeds with copious endosperm, sometimes covered with agglutinated mucilaginous hairs. Five genera and about 20 species, native to tropical Africa.

Family Sterculiaceae

Trees, shrubs, or herbs. Leaves simple or digitately divided, alternate, stipulate, often containing mucilage. Flowers unisexual or bisexual, usually regular. Calyx of 3–5 united, valvate sepals, without an epicalyx. Petals 5, in some genera often absent or small, convoluted. Stamens 5–45 in 2 whorls, the outer sometimes staminoidal or absent, the inner often branched, free or more or less united into a tube; anthers bilocular, pollen smooth. Ovary superior, usually of 5, sometimes 1–4 or 10–12 united carpels; style simple and lobed, rarely divided to the base. Fruit various, often a schizocarp; seed with or without endosperm. About 65 genera and 1,000 species, found chiefly in the tropics and subtropics.

Family Tiliaceae

Trees and shrubs, rarely herbs. Leaves simple, alternate, stipulate. Flowers usually bisexual, regular. Calyx of 5 sepals, free or united, valvate, sometimes with an epicalyx. Petals 5, rarely apetalous, convolute, imbricate or valvate in bud. Stamens usually numerous, inserted at the base of the petals or on an androphore, free or united into 5 or 10 groups; anthers bilocular, dehiscing by a longitudinal slit or an apical pore. Ovary superior with 2 to numerous united carpels; style simple with a capitate or lobed stigma. Fruit a capsule or schizocarp, rarely baccate; seed with endosperm. About 50 genera and 450 species, of which only the genera *Tilia* (50 species mainly in northern temperate areas) and *Entelea* (New Zealand, 1 species) are temperate in distribution. The remainder are tropical, especially centred in Southeast Asia and in Brazil.

Critical appraisal. All recent classifications agree on the close relationship between the families Bombacaceae, Malvaceae, Sterculiaceae, and Tiliaceae although a few authorities maintain two related orders, the Tiliales and Malvales, the latter containing only the family Malvaceae. Careful revisionary work on the order is highly desirable, and it should consider recent evidence from cytology, pollen studies, etc., and may perhaps lead to some rearrangements of a few genera among these families. The family Elaeocarpaceae, which is retained by some workers within the Tiliaceae, is separable from this close group on a number of characters and appears to be the most primitive family in the order, with a more generalized flower structure and a more primitive wood anatomy. A relationship with the family Flacourtiaceae (order Violales) is postulated by most authorities and supported by evidence from both floral and pollen-grain morphology.

Uncertain relationships of smaller families

The families included here in the order Malvales follow a recent classification system. Knowledge of the four smaller families is still inadequate. They are all confined to Africa, and two of them, the Rhopalocarpaceae and Sarcolaenaceae, are restricted to the Malagasy Republic. Some authorities classify them in an order called the Ochnales. All four are little represented in collections, and, for most of them, knowledge of their comparative anatomy, pollen morphology and comparative biochemistry is meagre or nonexistent. Clearly, they are less closely related to the larger families of the order, and even the inclusion here of the family Huaceae is somewhat speculative. Some evidence of affinity exists, but more work is required to support it or to point to true affinities.

BIBLIOGRAPHY. A. CRONQUIST, *The Evolution and Classification of Flowering Plants* (1968), a recent classification with discussion; J. HUTCHINSON, *The Genera of Flowering Plants*, vol. 2 (1967), a recent detailed and descriptive classification; G.K. BRIZICKY, "The Genera of Tiliaceae and Elaeocarpaceae in the Southeastern United States," *J. Arnold Arbor.*, 46:286–307 (1965); and "The Genera of Sterculiaceae in the Southeastern United States," *J. Arnold Arbor.*, 47:60–74 (1966), two review articles; J.B. HUTCHINSON, R.A. SILOW, and S.G. STEPHENS, *The Evolution of Gossypium and the Differentiation of the Cultivated Cottons* (1947), a classic review of the botany of cottons.

(P.S.G.)

Mamlūks

The use of Mamlūks (Mamelukes; slaves; literally, "owned men," or men of slave origin) as a major component of Muslim armies became a distinct feature of Islāmic civilization as early as the 9th century AD. The practice was begun in Baghdad by the ʿAbbāsid caliph al-Muʿtaṣim (833–842), and it soon spread throughout the Muslim world with the formation of slave armies by almost every Muslim dynasty of the Middle Ages, from the Ghaznavids of Afghanistan in the east to the Umayyads of Spain in the west. Moreover, the political result was almost invariably the same: the slaves exploited the military power vested in

Formation of slave armies

them to seize control over the legitimate political authorities, often only briefly but sometimes for astonishingly long periods of time. Thus, soon after al-Muʿtaṣim's reign the caliphate itself fell victim to the Turkish Mamlūk generals, who were able to depose or murder caliphs almost with impunity. Although the caliphate was maintained as a symbol of legitimate authority, the actual power was wielded by the Mamlūk generals; and by the 13th century, Mamlūks had succeeded in establishing dynasties of their own, both in Egypt and in India, in which the sultans were necessarily men of slave origin or the heirs of such men.

Undoubtedly the leniency recommended by Islām in the treatment of slaves helps explain the universal acceptance of a slave-based military and political institution. Both the origin and pervasiveness of such an institution, however, should be sought in the evolution of Muslim armies. Muslim rulers inevitably found the original components of their armies, whether basically tribal or regional in character, to be unreliable as loyal and effective fighting forces. Therefore, to augment or replace these components, the rulers resorted to forming corps of slaves, acquired either by purchase or capture, whose loyalty was ensured by the fact that their very existence was dependent on their owners. All too frequently, however, the loyalty of the troops was directed toward their commanders, also Mamlūks, whose power the ruler could offset only by purchasing more and more contingents of Mamlūks and thereby providing a force strong enough to usurp the power of the state.

THE MAMLUK DYNASTY (1250–1517)

History. This process of usurping power is epitomized by and culminated in the establishment of the Mamlūk dynasty, which ruled Egypt and Syria from 1250 to 1517 and whose descendants survived in Egypt as an important political force during the Ottoman occupation (1517–1798). The Kurdish general Saladin, who captured control of Egypt in 1169, followed what by then constituted a tradition in Muslim military practice by including a slave corps in his army in addition to Kurdish, Arab, Turkmen, and other free elements. This practice was also followed by his successors, the Ayyūbids, and was intensified when individual members of the royal family attempted to build up their own power in order to defend, or to capture, the throne of Egypt and Syria. Al-Malik aṣ-Ṣāliḥ Ayyūb (1240–49) is reputed to have been the largest purchaser of slaves, chiefly Turkish, as a means of protecting his sultanate both from Ayyūbid rivals and from the crusaders. Upon his death in 1249 a scramble for his throne ensued, in the course of which the Mamlūk generals murdered his heir and eventually succeeded in establishing one of their own number as sultan. Thenceforth, for more than 250 years, Egypt and Syria were ruled by Mamlūks or sons of Mamlūks.

Establishment of the Mamlūk dynasty

Historians have traditionally broken the era of Mamlūk rule into two periods—one covering 1250–1382, the other, 1382–1517. Western historians persist in calling the former the "Baḥrī" period and the latter the "Burjī," because of the political dominance of the regiments known by these names during the respective times. More meaningfully, however, the contemporary Muslim historians referred to the same divisions as the "Turkish" and "Circassian" periods in order to call attention to the change in ethnic origin of the majority of Mamlūks, which occurred and persisted after the accession of Barqūq in 1382, and to the effects that this change had on the fortunes of the state.

There is universal agreement among historians that the Mamlūk state reached its height under the Turkish sultans and then fell into a prolonged phase of decline under the Circassians. The principal achievements of the Turkish Mamlūks lay in their expulsion of the remaining crusaders from the Levant and their rout of the Mongols in Palestine and Syria; they thereby earned the thanks of all Muslims for saving Arabic-Islāmic civilization from destruction. It is doubtful, however, that such a goal figured in their plans; rather, as rulers of Egypt they were seeking to reconstitute the Egyptian Empire, which for centuries,

Mamlūk achievements

both in Islāmic and pre-Islāmic times, included the elimination of hostile forces from the eastern flank of Egypt and the maintenance of secure trade routes leading into Syria. Concomitant with their campaigns against crusaders and Mongols, and as a part of the same strategy, the Mamlūks also sought to extend their power into the Arabian Peninsula and into Anatolia and Little Armenia; to protect Egypt's rear, they strove to establish their presence in Nubia.

In order to consolidate their position in the Islāmic world and to clothe their regime in legitimacy, the Mamlūks revived the caliphate, which the Mongols had destroyed in 1258, and installed a caliph under their surveillance in Cairo. Their patronage of the rulers of the holy cities of Arabia, Mecca and Medina, served the same purpose. Spectacular success in war and diplomacy was underpinned economically by the Mamlūks' support of industries and crafts as well as by their efforts to restore Egypt's position as entrepôt in the spice trade between India and Europe. The Mamlūks' efforts were finally rewarded toward the end of the Baḥrī/Turkish period, when the inland routes of Asia were closed and Egypt once again became the principal transit route between the Orient and the Mediterranean.

The decline of the dynasty

Among the most outstanding Mamlūk sultans were Baybars I (1260–77) and al-Malik an-Nāṣir (1293–1341). The Mamlūks' failure to find an able successor after the latter's death weakened the strength and stability of their realm. But the historians of the era date the beginning of the dynasty's decline from the accession of the first Circassian sultan (Barqūq) in 1382, claiming that thereafter,

Adapted from Philip K. Hitti; *History of Syria*, Macmillan Company, New York, 1951

Mamlūk sultanate c. 1350.

advancement in the state and the army was dependent on race (*i.e.*, Circassian descent) rather than on proved skill in the art of war, which had served as the chief criterion for promotion during the Turkish period. Actually, the increased importance assigned to ethnic affiliation was but one cause of decline; equally or even more important were economic and other factors. In spite of the renewal of the flourishing spice commerce in Egypt and Syria by 1375, within the next 25 years the entire Mamlūk economy had begun to decay: agricultural revenues, tax and custom receipts, and industrial productivity had all fallen off sharply by the end of the 14th century, never to recover during the Mamlūk era. Part of the explanation undoubtedly lies in the inability of the Mamlūks, split into hostile factions, to provide necessary safeguards against the Bedouins for the peaceful conduct of trade and agri-

culture. But recent research indicates that the demographic losses caused by plagues that raged in Egypt and elsewhere in the East also contributed to economic decay. In such conditions the Mamlūks were unable to defend Syria against Timur Lenk in 1400. Under the rule of Sultan Barsbay (1422–38) internal stability was restored briefly and Mamlūk glory resuscitated by the conquest of Cyprus in 1426. Yet the increasingly higher taxes demanded to finance such ventures enlarged the Mamlūks' financial difficulties. The final economic blow fell with the Portuguese assault on trade in the Red Sea (*c.* 1500), which was accompanied by Ottoman expansion into Mamlūk territory in Syria. Having failed to adopt field artillery as a weapon in any but siege warfare, the Mamlūks were decisively defeated by the Ottomans both in Syria and in Egypt and from 1517 onward constituted only one of the several components that formed the political structure of Egypt.

Government, society, and culture. The extraordinary richness of historical sources for the Mamlūk dynasty (probably greater than that for any preceding period of Islāmic history) provides abundant details on the structure of Mamlūk government, society, and culture. Like all other Muslim governments, the Mamlūk state consisted of two classes—*ahl al-qalam* (people of the pen) and *ahl as-sayf* (people of the sword). The former consisted of scribes, judges, and legal scholars, and it staffed the vast bureaucracy that had existed in Egypt since ancient times and that was now responsible for administering the Islāmic law and the fiscal policy of the state. What distinguishes the Mamlūk from other Muslim governments is that *ahl as-sayf* consisted largely of Mamlūks who in addition to commanding and manning the army also filled the highest offices of state as a principle of policy: the sultan, the viceroy, the chief of chancery, and all the provincial governors were Mamlūks, as were numerous court officials who enjoyed considerable influence because of their intimacy with the sultan. Thus it is no exaggeration to say that Egypt and Syria were ruled for two and a half centures by an elite whose members were of slave origin or descent. The reason the Mamlūks as a class were able to maintain political control is, very obviously, the fact that they held complete and absolute control of the army.

The Mamlūk army

The Mamlūk army had three main divisions: The Royal Mamlūks were the personal property of the reigning sultan and were acquired either by purchase or inheritance; the Mamlūks of the Amirs were the property of officers (many, if not most, of whom were drawn from the Royal Mamlūks), who were ranked according to the number of Mamlūks that they owned; the *ḥalqah* was a nonslave cavalry unit that consisted of sons of Mamlūks and recruits from the free-born Muslim citizenry. These three units formed a hierarchy headed by the sultan; his ability to maintain himself on the throne depended mainly on the strength of his Royal Mamlūks who, in addition to forming the core of the army, filled all of the chief offices of state.

Military strength and the threat of force were not, of course, sufficient to give stability to the Mamlūk state. Stability was provided by a complex system of loyalties engendered by the common experience and common training required to become a Mamlūk. The aim of the system was to produce a class of skilled warriors who, being cut off from homeland, family, and religion, would be completely dependent on and loyal to the sultan or the officer who had purchased them, trained them, and then granted them freedom and enrolled them in his military service. Slave merchants, acting as agents of the Mamlūks, frequented the slave markets of western Asia and regularly delivered to Cairo consignments of adolescent boys—mainly from the Qipchak steppe and later from the Caucasus. In Egypt the boys were quartered in special barracks and enrolled in a Mamlūk school, where they were taught horsemanship and the military arts and given basic instruction in Islām. Upon graduation they were given both their freedom and their military equipment and were assigned to the ranks of their purchaser with fiefs to support them. During times of political stability and economic prosperity the system worked remarkably well in developing a strong sense of esprit de corps and loyalty toward their commanders among boys who had undergone the same experience at the same time. From the beginning, however, the system contained elements of rivalry and factionalism, which, in the absence of a strong ruler and adequate funds, could develop into anarchy.

The social hierarchy

Because the Mamlūks controlled trade, the government, and the army and owned the major part of the land, they dominated the dynamics of Egyptian and Syrian society. Besides the military elite, society was composed of two classes: civilian notables, consisting mainly of religious scholars, scribes, and merchants; and the common people, consisting of artisans, workers, and peasants. The notables served Mamlūk interests either in the governmental bureaucracy or in trade and commerce, which were directly and indirectly controlled by Mamlūk needs. The notables were assimilated into Mamlūk society; but the common people, in the absence of organized corporate life, were isolated both from the Mamlūks and from the notables and always posed the danger of violent upheaval when their needs were ignored. It is a measure of the power and skill of the Mamlūk government that violence was usually kept in check.

Culturally, the Mamlūk period is known mainly for its achievements in historical writing and in architecture and for an abortive attempt at socio-religious reform. Mamlūk historians were prolific chroniclers, biographers, and encyclopaedists; they were not strikingly original, with the exception of Ibn Khaldūn (*q.v.*), whose formative and creative years were spent outside Mamlūk territory in the Maghrib (North Africa). As builders of religious edifices—mosques, schools, monasteries and, above all, tombs—the Mamlūks endowed Cairo with some of its most impressive monuments, many of which are still standing; the Mamlūk tomb-mosques can be recognized by stone domes whose massiveness is offset by geometrical carvings. By far the most famous single religious figure of the period was Ibn Taymīyah; the stubborn attempts of this Syrian legist to rid Mamlūk Islām of superstition and foreign accretions made him a threat to public order, and the Mamlūk authorities rewarded him with imprisonment.

THE MAMLUKS UNDER THE OTTOMANS (1517–1798)

With the Ottoman victories over the Mamlūks in 1516–17, Egypt and Syria reverted to the status of provinces within an empire. Although the Mamlūk sultanate was destroyed, this did not mean the destruction of the power of the Mamlūks as a class. In fact the Ottoman sultan Selim I appointed Mamlūks as his viceroys in both Egypt and Syria. Ottoman troops were garrisoned in both provinces as a check to the viceroys' ambitions, but administrative and fiscal practice remained for a time the same as it had been under the Mamlūks, the main difference being that tax revenues were now sent to Istanbul. This arrangement lasted only until the mid-16th century; thereafter, Ottoman governors were sent from Istanbul. To assist the governors, the Ottoman government also sent military contingents and administrative personnel; from these groups an executive council (*dīwān*) was formed in Cairo, which was responsible for the formulation and implementation of state policy. Although the Mamlūks were relieved of their offices and their authority, they remained intact as a class in Egypt and continued to exercise considerable influence in the state. As had been the case during the Mamlūk dynasty, the Mamlūk elite continued to be replenished by purchases from slave markets. The slaves, after a period of apprenticeship, still formed the core of the army and were soon being appointed to offices in the Ottoman government. Thus, gradually the Mamlūks infiltrated the Ottoman ruling class and eventually were able to dominate it.

One major innovation changed the character of the Mamlūks. Earlier, during the era of the Mamlūk sultanate, the sons of Mamlūks had been excluded from serving in any but the nonslave regiments and from holding offices reserved for Mamlūks in the state. But under Ottoman rule the sons were no longer denied these privileges, so that the principles of Mamlūk loyalty and solidarity were undermined by ties of kinship. Consequently, rather than grouping themselves into military factions that lasted no longer than the lifetime of their individual members, the Ottoman Mamlūks formed "houses" that perpetuated themselves through their sons. The importance of these houses arose from the stubborn attempts of each house to dominate the others; thereby a new element of instability, perpetuated by heredity, was introduced into the Mamlūk institution. To the degree that the Ottoman governors were able to exploit Mamlūk divisiveness, they were able to retain some degree of influence in the government of Egypt. But near the end of the 17th century, when Ottoman power was in decline throughout the empire, the Mamlūks once again held virtual control over the army, the revenues, and the government. Eventually, Istanbul was reduced to recognizing the autonomy of that faction of Mamlūks that would guarantee annual payment of certain sums to the Ottomans. And thus it was that when Napoleon invaded Egypt in 1798 he was confronted by Mamlūk armies and a Mamlūk state. Their power there was finally destroyed by Egypt's new ruler, Muḥammad ʿAlī Pasha, in a massacre in 1811.

Hereditary Mamlūks

BIBLIOGRAPHY. S. LANE-POOLE, *A History of Egypt in the Middle Ages*, 4th ed. (1968), gives a reliable survey of Mamlūk history in the general context of medieval Egyptian history. I.M. LAPIDUS, *Muslim Cities in the Later Middle Ages* (1967), focusses on the structure and dynamics of political and social classes in Mamlūk Cairo, Damascus, and Aleppo. For the Mamlūks under the Ottomans, P.M. HOLT, *Egypt and the Fertile Crescent, 1516–1922: A Political History* (1966), provides a more detailed survey than that given by Lane-Poole. Three monographs by D. AYALON analyze the structure and ethos of Mamlūk institutions in meticulous detail: *L'Esclavage du mamelouk* (1951), an outline of the recruiting and training of Mamlūks; *Gunpowder and Firearms in the Mamlūk Kingdom* (1956), an examination of the result of Mamlūk reluctance to adopt new equipment and technology; and the series of articles "Studies on the Structure of the Mamlūk Army," *Bulletin of the School of Oriental and African Studies*, 15:203–228, 448–476 (1953), and 16:57–90 (1954), a description of the evolution of the Mamlūk army. R. LOPEZ, H. MISKIMIN, and A. UDOVITCH, "England to Egypt, 1350–1500," in M.A. COOK (ed.), *Studies in the Economic History of the Middle East* (1970), sets forth the economic factors that contributed to the decline of the Mamlūk state. The introductory chapter of S.J. SHAW, *The Financial and Administrative Organization and Development of Ottoman Egypt, 1517–1798* (1962), outlines the process by which the Mamlūks infiltrated the Ottoman government of Egypt.

(D.P.L.)

Mammalia

The class Mammalia is a group of back-boned animals, collectively known as mammals, in which the young are nourished with milk from special secreting glands (mammae) of the mother. Mammals are warm-blooded, four-limbed (except certain aquatic groups), and usually have hair. The word animal is often limited inappropriately to mammals (usually excluding man), but properly refers to any member of the kingdom Animalia, which includes virtually all multicellular organisms not considered plants.

GENERAL FEATURES

The evolution of the Mammalia has produced tremendous diversity in form and habits. Living kinds range in size from tiny shrews, weighing but a few grams, to the largest of all animals that has ever lived, the blue or sulphur-bottom whale, which reaches a length of more than 100 feet and a weight of 150 tons. Every major terrestrial and aquatic habitat has been invaded by mammals that swim, fly, run, burrow, glide, or climb.

There are approximately 4,000 species of living mammals, arranged in about 120 families and 20 orders. The rodents (order Rodentia) are the most numerous of existing mammals, both in number of species and number of individuals, and are one of the most diverse of living lineages. In contrast, the order Tubulidentata is represented by a single living species, the aardvark. The Proboscidea (elephants) and Perissodactyla (horses, rhinoceroses, and allies) are excellent examples of orders in which far greater diversity occurred in mid- and late-Tertiary times (from about 3,000,000 to about 30,000,000 years ago) than today.

The tropical continental areas of the world around are the places of greatest present-day diversity of mammals, although members of the order occur on (or in seas adjacent to) all major land masses and on many oceanic islands (the latter principally, but by no means exclusively, reached by bats). Major regional faunas can be identified; these resulted in large part from evolution in comparative isolation of stocks of early mammals that reached these areas. South America (Neotropics), for example, was separated from North America (Nearctic) from Paleocene through much of Pliocene times (about 2,500,000 to 65,000,000 years ago) by inundation of the Panamanian Portal and adjacent areas in Middle America. Evolution of mammalian groups that had reached South America before the break between the continents, or some that "island-hopped" in after the break, proceeded quite independently from that of relatives that remained in North America. Some of the latter became extinct as the result of competition with more advanced groups, whereas those in South America flourished, some radiating to the extent that they have successfully competed with invaders since the rejoining of the two continents. Australia provides a parallel case of early isolation and adaptive radiation of mammals (monotremes, marsupials) thus isolated, but differs in that it was not later connected to any other land mass. The more advanced mammals of the infraclass Eutheria that reached Australia (rodents, bats) did so, evidently by "island-hopping," long after the adaptive radiation of the early isolates.

In contrast, North America and Eurasia (Palearctic) are separate land masses but have closely related faunas, the result of connections several times in the Pleistocene and earlier across the Bering Strait. Their faunas frequently are thought of as representing not two distinct units, but one, related to a degree that a single name, Holarctic, is applied to it.

IMPORTANCE TO MAN

Wild and domesticated mammals are so interlocked with man's political and social history that it is impractical to attempt to assess the relationship in precise economic terms. Throughout his cultural evolution, for example, man has been dependent on other mammals for a significant portion of his food and clothing. Domestication of mammals helped to provide a source of protein for ever-increasing human populations and provided means of transportation and heavy work as well. Today, domesticated strains of the house mouse, European rabbit, guinea pig, hamster, gerbil and other species provide much-needed laboratory subjects for the study of human-related physiology, psychology, and a variety of diseases from dental caries to cancer. Recent emphasis on the study of nonhuman primates (monkeys and apes) has opened broad, new areas of research relevant to man's welfare. The care of domestic and captive mammals is, of course, the basis for the practice of veterinary medicine.

Some primitive peoples still depend on wild mammals as a major source of food, and many different kinds (from fruit bats and armadillos to whales) regularly are captured and eaten. On the other hand, the hunting, primarily for sport, of various rodents, lagomorphs, carnivores, and ungulates supports a multibillion-dollar enterprise. In the United States alone, for example, it is estimated that more than 2,000,000 deer are harvested annually by licensed hunters.

Geopolitically, the quest for marine mammals was responsible for the charting of a number of areas in both Arctic and Antarctic regions. The presence of terrestrial fur bearers, particularly beaver and several species of mustelid carnivores (*e.g.*, marten and fisher), was one of the principal motivations for the opening of the American West, Alaska, and the Siberian taiga. Sale of wild-taken furs still is an important industry in both the Old and New Worlds, but ranch-raised animals such as the mink, fox, and chinchilla now have become an important part of the fur industry, which directly and indirectly accounts for many millions of dollars in revenue each year in North America alone.

Aside from pelts and meat, special parts of some mammals regularly have been sought for their special attributes. The horns of rhinoceroses are used in concocting potions in the Orient; ivory from elephants and walruses is highly prized; and ambergris, a substance regurgitated by sperm whales, has been widely used as a base for perfumes (although now mostly replaced by synthetic substitutes).

Some mammals are directly detrimental to man and his activities. Murid rodents (house rats and mice of Old World origin) now occur in virtually all of the world's urban areas and each year cause substantial damage and economic loss. In some rural areas, herbivorous mammals eat or trample planted crops and compete with livestock for food, and native carnivores prey on domestic herds. These and other situations have led man to spend large sums annually to control populations of "undesirable" wild mammals, a practice long deplored by conservationists. Mammals are important reservoirs or agents of transmission of a variety of diseases that afflict man, such as plague, tularemia, yellow fever, rabies, leptospirosis, hemorrhagic fever, and Rocky Mountain spotted fever. The annual "economic debt" resulting from mammal-borne diseases of man and his domestic stock is incalculable.

Many large mammals that competed directly with man for food or space, or were specially sought by him for some reason, have been extirpated entirely or exist today only in parks and zoos; others are in danger of extinction, and their plight is receiving increased attention by a number of conservation agencies. Perhaps at least some can be saved. One of the most noteworthy cases of direct extirpation by man is the Steller's sea cow (*Hydrodamalis gigas*). These large (up to 12 metres, or 40 feet, long), inoffensive, marine mammals evidently lived in Recent times only along the coasts and shallow bays of the Commander Islands in the Bering Sea. Discovered in 1741, they were easily killed by Russian sealers and traders for food, their meat being highly prized, and the last known live individual was taken in 1768.

Of final note is the esthetic value of wild mammals and the relatively recent predilection of man to expend both considerable energy and resources to study and, if possible, conserve vanishing species, to set aside natural areas where native floral and faunal elements can exist in an otherwise highly agriculturalized or industrialized society, and to establish modern zoological parks and gardens. Such outdoor "laboratories" attract millions of visitors annually and will provide means by which present and future generations of humans can appreciate and study, in small measure at least, other kinds of mammals.

NATURAL HISTORY

The hallmarks of the mammalian level of organization are advanced reproduction and parental care, behavioral flexibility, and endothermy (the physiological maintenance of a relatively constant body temperature independent of that of the environment, allowing a high level of activity). Within the class, ecological diversity has resulted from adaptive specialization in food-getting, habitat preferences, and locomotion.

Throughout the past 70,000,000 years, the mammals have been the dominant animals in terrestrial ecosystems and important in nonterrestrial communities as well. The earliest mammals were small, active predacious, and terrestrial or semiarboreal. From this primitive stock the mammals have radiated into a wide spectrum of adaptive modes against the background of the diverse environment of the Cenozoic (the last 65,000,000 years). Branches of the ancestral terrestrial stock early exploited the protection and productivity of the trees, whereas other lineages added further dimensions to the mammalian spectrum by adapting to life beneath the ground, in the air, and in marine and freshwater habitats.

Radiation in South America

Influence on exploration

Extinction of Steller's sea cow

Reproduction. In reproductively mature female mammals an interaction of hormones from the pituitary gland and the ovaries produces a phenomenon known as the estrous cycle. Estrus, or "heat," typically coincides with ovulation, and during this time the female is receptive to the male. Estrus is preceded by proestrus, during which ovarian follicles mature under the influence of a follicle-stimulating hormone from the anterior pituitary. The follicular cells produce estrogen, a hormone that stimulates proliferation of the uterine lining, or endometrium. Following ovulation, in late estrus, the ruptured ovarian follicle forms a temporary endocrine gland known as the corpus luteum. Another hormone, progesterone, secreted by the corpus luteum, causes the endometrium to become quiescent and ready for implantation of the developing egg (blastocyst), should fertilization occur. In members of the infraclass Eutheria (known as placental mammals) the placenta, as well as transmitting nourishment to the embryo, has an endocrine function, producing hormones that maintain the endometrium throughout gestation.

If fertilization and implantation do not occur, a phase termed metestrus ensues, in which the reproductive tract assumes its normal condition. Metestrus may be followed by anestrus, a nonreproductive period characterized by quiescence or involution of the reproductive tract. On the other hand, anestrus may be followed by a brief quiescent period (diestrus) and another preparatory proestrus phase. Mammals that breed only once a year are termed monestrous, and exhibit a long anestrus; those that breed more than once a year are termed polyestrous. In many polyestrous species the estrous cycle ceases during gestation and lactation (milk production), but some rodents have a post-partum estrus, mating immediately after giving birth.

The menstrual cycle of higher primates is derived from the estrous cycle, but differs from it in that when progesterone secretion from the corpus luteum ceases, in the absence of fertilization, the uterine lining is sloughed. In anthropoids other than man a distinct period of "heat" occurs around the time of ovulation.

Egg-laying by monotremes

Monotremes lay shelled eggs, but the ovarian cycle is similar to that of other mammals. The eggs are predominantly yolk (telolecithal), like those of reptiles and birds. Cleavage of the egg cell in development is meroblastic (*i.e.*, the yolk does not divide) and the developing embryo lies on top of the yolk mass. The platypus lays one to three (usually two) eggs in a long nesting burrow, and the eggs are incubated for about ten days. The echidna generally produces a single egg, laid directly in a pouch developed by the female during the breeding season. It is incubated seven to ten days. Young monotremes are altricial (*i.e.*, in a relatively early stage of development and dependent upon the parent), reaching sexual maturity in about one year.

The reproduction of marsupials differs from that of placentals in that the uterine cycle of the female has no secretory phase and the uterine wall is not specialized for the implantation of the embryos. The period of intrauterine development varies from about eight days (*Dasyurus*) to 38 days (*Macropus*). After this period the young migrate from the vagina to attach to the teats for further development. Frequently the partially developed young outnumber the available teats and the excess individuals perish. In the American opossum, *Didelphis marsupialis*, litters of 25 young have been reported, but the pouch usually contains but 13 teats.

The pouch or marsupium is variously developed. Many species, such as kangaroos and opossums, have a single, well developed pouch; in some phalangerids the pouch is compartmented, with a single teat in each compartment. The South American caenolestids or rat opossums have no marsupium.

Born in an extremely altricial condition, the young of most marsupials are dependent on maternal care for considerable periods, 13 to 14 weeks in *Didelphis*. Young koalas are carried in the pouch for nearly eight months, kangaroos to ten months.

Bandicoots are unique among living marsupials in having a chorioallantoic placenta, but unlike the placentae of eutherians it does not have villi (minute projections of the wall, or chorion). Embryonic gaseous exchange in the majority of marsupials is by means of the highly vascular yolk sac.

Reproductive patterns in placentals are diverse, but in all cases a secretory phase is present in the uterine cycle and the endometrium is maintained by secretions of progesterone from the corpus luteum. The blastocyst emplants in the uterine wall. Villi are embedded in the lining of the uterus. The resulting complex of embryonic and maternal tissues is a true placenta. The uterine lining may be shed with the fetal membranes as "afterbirth" (a condition called deciduate) or may be resorbed by the female (nondeciduate). Placentae have been classified on the basis of the relationship between maternal and embryonic tissues. In the simplest nondeciduate placental arrangement the chorionic villi are in contact with uterine epithelium (the inner surface layer). In the "intimate deciduous" types, seen in primates, bats, insectivores, and rodents, the capillary endothelium (the layer containing minute blood vessels) of the uterine wall breaks down, and chorionic epithelium is in direct contact with maternal blood. In advanced stages of pregnancy in rabbits even the chorionic epithelium is eroded and the embryonic endothelium contacts the maternal blood supply. In no case, however, is there actual exchange of blood between mother and fetus; nutrients and gases must still pass through the walls of the fetal blood vessels.

The period of intrauterine development, or gestation, varies widely among eutherians, generally depending on the size of the animal, but influenced by the number of young per litter and the condition of young at birth. The gestation period of the domestic hamster (*Mesocricetus auratus*) is about two weeks, whereas that of the blue whale is 11 months and of the African elephant 21 to 22 months.

At birth the young may be well developed and able to move about at once (precocial) or they may be blind, hairless, and essentially helpless (altricial). In general, precocial young are born after a relatively long gestation period and in a small litter. Hares and many large grazing mammals bear precocial offspring. Rabbits, carnivores, and most rodents bear altricial young.

After birth young mammals are nourished by milk secreted by the mammary glands of the female. In therians (marsupials and placentals) the glands open through specialized nipples. The newborn young of marsupials are unable to suckle and milk is "pumped" to the young by the mother.

Composition of milk

Milk consists of fat, protein (especially casein), and lactose (milk sugar), as well as vitamins and salts. The actual composition of milk of whales varies widely between species. The milk of whales and seals is some 12 times as rich in fats and four times as rich in protein as that of domestic cows, but contains almost no sugar. Milk has meant an efficient energy source for the rapid growth of young mammals; the weight at birth of some marine mammals doubles in five days.

Behaviour. *Social behaviour.* The dependence of the young mammal on its mother for nourishment has made possible a period of training. Such training permits the nongenetic transfer of information between generations. The ability of young mammals to learn from the experience of their elders has allowed a behavioral plasticity unknown in any other group of organisms and has been a primary reason for the success of the mammals. The possibility of training is one of the factors that has made an increase in neural complexity selectively adaptive. Increased associational potential and memory extends the possibility of learning from experience, and the individual can make adaptive behavioral responses to environmental change. Individual response to short-term change is far more efficient than genetic response.

Some kinds of mammals are solitary, except for brief periods when the female is in estrus. In other species, however, social groups are present. Such groups may be reproductive, defensive, or may serve both functions. In those cases that have been studied in detail a more-or-less strict hierarchy of dominance prevails. Within the social group, maintenance of the hierarchy may depend on physical combat between individuals, but in many cases stereotyped patterns of behaviour evolve to displace actual combat, conserving energy, while maintaining the social structure.

Sexual dimorphism (a pronounced difference between sexes) frequently is extreme in social mammals. In large part this is because dominant males tend to be those that are largest or best armed. Dominant males also tend to have priority in mating, or may even have exclusive responsibility for mating within a "harem." Rapid evolution of secondary sexual characteristics can take place in a species with such a social structure even though the reproductive potential may be low.

A complex behaviour termed "play" frequently occurs between siblings, between members of an age class, or between parent and offspring. Play extends the period of maternal training and is especially important in social species, providing an opportunity to learn behaviour appropriate to the maintenance of dominance.

Territoriality. That area covered by an individual in his general activity is frequently termed the home range. A territory is a part of the home range defended against other members of the same species. As a generalization it may be said that territoriality is more important in the behaviour of birds than of mammals, but data for the latter are available primarily for diurnal species. The phenomenon of territoriality may be more widespread than is supposed. Frequently territories of mammals are "marked," either with urine or with secretions of specialized glands, as in lemurs, a form of territorial labelling less evident to humans than the singing or visual displays of birds. Many mammals that do not maintain territories per se nevertheless will not permit unlimited crowding and will fight to maintain individual distance. Such mechanisms result in more economical spacing of individuals over the available habitat.

Ecology.   *Response to environmental cycles.* Mammals may react to environmental extremes by acclimatization, compensatory behaviour, or physiological specialization. Physiological responses to adverse conditions include torpidity, hibernation (in winter), and estivation (in summer). Torpidity may occur in the daily cycle or during unfavourable weather; short-term torpidity generally is economical only for small mammals that can cool and warm rapidly. The body temperature of most temperate-zone bats drops near that of the ambient air whenever the animal sleeps. The winter dormancy of bears at high latitudes is an analogous phenomenon and cannot be considered true hibernation.

Hiber-
nation

True hibernation involves physiological regulation to minimize the expenditure of energy. The body temperature is lowered and breathing may be slowed to as low as 1 percent of the rate in an active individual. There is a corresponding slowing of circulation and typically a reduction in the peripheral blood supply. When the body temperature nears the freezing point, spontaneous arousal occurs, although other kinds of stimuli generally elicit only a very slow response. In mammals that exhibit winter dormancy (such as bears, skunks, and raccoons), arousal may be quite rapid. Hibernation has evidently originated independently in a number of mammalian lines and the comparative physiology of this complex phenomenon is only now beginning to be understood (see DORMANCY).

Inactivity in response to adverse summer conditions (heat, drought, lack of food) is termed estivation. Estivation in some species is simply prolonged rest, usually in a favourable microhabitat; other estivating mammals regulate the metabolism, although the effects are typically not so pronounced as in hibernation.

Behavioral response to adverse conditions may involve the selection or construction of a suitable microhabitat (such as the cool, moist burrows of desert rodents). Migration is a second kind of behavioral response. The most obvious kind of mammalian migration is latitudinal.

Migrations

Many temperate-zone bats, for example, undertake extensive migrations, although other bat species hibernate near the summer foraging grounds in caves or other equable shelters during severe weather when insects are not available. Caribou (*Rangifer tarandus*) migrate from the tundra to the forest edge in search of suitable winter range and a number of cetaceans and pinnipeds undertake long migrations from polar waters to more temperate latitudes. Gray whales (*Eschrichtius robustus*), for example, migrate southward to calving grounds along the coasts of South Korea and Baja California from summer feeding grounds in the Okhotsk, Bering, and Chukchi seas. Of comparable extent is the dispersive feeding migration of the northern fur seal (*Callorhinus ursinus*).

Migrations of lesser extent include the altitudinal movements of some ungulates, the American elk or wapiti (*Cervus canadensis*) and bighorn sheep (*Ovis canadensis*), for example, and the local migrations of certain bats from summer roosts to hibernacula. Most migratory patterns of mammals are part of a recurrent annual cycle, but the irruptive emigrations of lemmings and snowshoe hares are largely acyclic responses to population pressure on food supplies.

Populations.   A population consists of individuals of three "ecological ages"—prereproductive, reproductive, and postreproductive. The structure and dynamics of a population depend, among other things, on the relative lengths of these ages, the rate of recruitment of individuals (either by birth or by immigration), and the rate of emigration or death. The reproductive potential of some rodents (particularly muroids) is well known; some mice are reproductively mature at four weeks of age, have gestation periods of three weeks or less, and may experience post-partum estrus, with the result that pregnancy and lactation may overlap. Litter size, moreover, may average four or more, and breeding may occur throughout the year in favourable localities. The reproductive potential of a species is, of course, a theoretical maximum that is rarely met inasmuch as, among other reasons, a given female typically does not reproduce throughout the year. Growth of a population depends on the survival of individuals to reproductive age. The absolute age at sexual maturity ranges from less than four weeks in some rodents to some 15 years in the African elephant (*Loxodonta africana*).

Postreproductive individuals are rare in most mammalian populations. Survival through more than a single reproductive season is probably uncommon in many small kinds, such as mice and shrews. Larger species typically have longer life spans than smaller ones, but some bats are known, on the basis of banding records, to live nearly 20 years. Many species show greater longevity in captivity than in the wild. Captive spiny anteaters (*Tachyglossus*) are reported to have lived more than 50 years. Horses are known to live more than 60 years, and the oldest known elephant lived to be nearly 70. Man has greater potential longevity than any other known species.

Longevity

Locomotion.   Specialization in habitat preference has been accompanied by locomotor adaptations. Convergent evolution within a given adaptive mode has contributed to the ecological similarity of regional mammalian faunas. Terrestrial mammals have a number of modes of progression. The primitive mammalian stock was doubtless ambulatory and plantigrade, walking with the digits, metacarpals, and metatarsals (bones of the midfoot), and parts of the ankle and wrist in contact with the ground. The limbs of ambulatory mammals are typically mobile, capable of considerable rotation.

Mammals modified for running are termed cursorial. The stance of cursorial species may be digitigrade (the complete digits contacting the ground, as in dogs) or unguligrade (only tips of digits contacting the ground, as in horses). In advanced groups limb movement consists of a single forward and backward direction.

Saltatory (leaping) locomotion, sometimes called "ricochetal," has arisen in several unrelated groups, and typically is found in mammals of open habitats. Jumping mammals (some marsupials, lagomorphs, and several independent lineages of rodents) typically have elongate, plantigrade hind feet, reduced forelimbs, and long tails.

Mammals of several orders have attained great size and have converged on specializations for "graviportal"

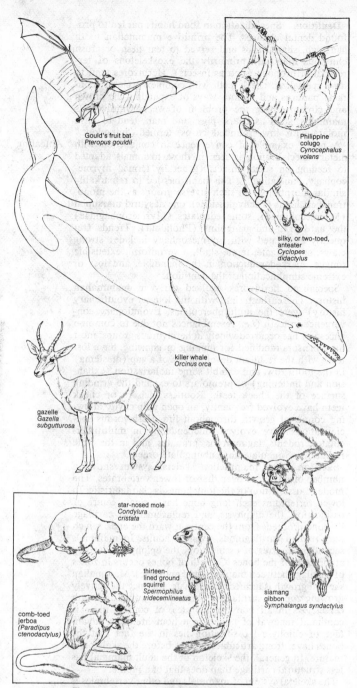

Figure 1: Range of body plans in mammals.
Drawing by R. Keane based on photographs courtesy of (Gould's fruit bat)
J. Warham, (Philippine colugo) J.N. Hamlet, (silky, or two-toed anteater)
New York Zoological Society, (comb-toed jerboa) Zeitschr. Saugetierk

Gould's fruit bat
Pteropus gouldii

Philippine colugo
Cynocephalus volans

silky, or two-toed anteater
Cyclopes didactylus

killer whale
Orcinus orca

gazelle
Gazella subgutturosa

star-nosed mole
Condylura cristata

thirteen-lined ground squirrel
Spermophilus tridecemlineatus

siamang gibbon
Symphalangus syndactylus

comb-toed jerboa
(*Paradipus ctenodactylus*)

(ponderous) locomotion. Such kinds have no digit reduction and deploy the digits in a circle around the axis of the limb for maximum support, like the pedestal of a column.

The bats are the only truly flying mammals. Only with active flight have the resources of the aerial habitat been successfully exploited. Mammals of several kinds (dermopterans, marsupials, rodents) are adapted for gliding. A gliding habit is frequently accompanied by scansorial (climbing) locomotion. Many nongliders, such as tree squirrels, are also scansorial.

Well-adapted arboreal mammals frequently are plantigrade, five-toed, and equipped with highly mobile limbs. Many New World monkeys have a prehensile tail, which is used as a "fifth hand." Gibbons have reduced the primitive, opposable anthropoid thumb as a specialization for brachiation, or "arm-walking," in which the animal hangs from branches and moves by a series of long swings. The highly arboreal tarsiers have expanded pads on the digits to improve the grasp, and many other arboreal kinds have claws (sloths) or well-developed nails.

Several groups of mammals have independently assumed aquatic habits. In some cases semi-aquatic or aquatic mammals are relatively unmodified representatives of otherwise terrestrial groups (for example, otters, muskrats, water shrews). Other kinds have undergone profound modification for natatorial locomotion and a pelagic habit. Pinniped carnivores (walruses and seals) give birth to their young on land, but cetaceans are completely helpless out of water, on which they depend for mechanical support and thermal insulation.

Food habits. The earliest mammals, like their reptilian forebears, were active predators. From such a basal stock there has been a complex radiation of trophic adaptations. Modern mammals occupy a wide spectrum of feeding niches. In most terrestrial and some aquatic communities, carnivorous mammals are at the top of the food pyramid. There are also mammalian primary consumers in most ecosystems. The voracious shrews, smallest of mammals, sometimes prey on vertebrates larger than themselves. They may eat twice their weight in food each day to maintain their active metabolism and compensate for heat loss caused by an unfavourable surface-to-volume ratio. The largest of vertebrates, the blue whale, feeds on krill, minute planktonic crustaceans.

Within a given lineage the adaptive radiation in food habits may be broad. Some of the Carnivora have become omnivorous (raccoons, bears) or largely herbivorous (giant panda). Marsupials exhibit a great variety of feeding types, and in Australia marsupials have radiated to fill ecological niches highly analogous to those of placental mammals elsewhere; there are marsupial "moles," "anteaters," "mice," "rats," "cats," and "wolves." Some bandicoots have ecological roles similar to those of rabbits, and wombats are semifossorial (*i.e.*, partially burrowing) herbivores analogous to marmots. In Australia the niche of large grazers and browsers is filled by a variety of kangaroos and wallabies.

Within the bats there has also been a remarkable adaptive radiation in food habits. Early in the history of the order there evidently was a divergence into insectivorous and frugivorous lines. The frugivorous line (Megachiroptera) has generally maintained its fruit eating habit, although some have become rather specialized nectar-feeders. The Microchiroptera have been less conservative and have undergone considerable divergence in feeding habits. A majority of living microchiropterans are insectivorous, but members of two different families have become fish eaters. Within the large neotropical family Phyllostomatidae there are groups specialized to feed on fruit, nectar, insects, and small vertebrates (including other bats). Aberrant members of the family are the vampire bats (desmodontines) with a specialized dentition to aid the blood-lapping habit.

Radiation of bats

FORM AND FUNCTION

The skin and hair. The skin of mammals is constructed of two layers, a superficial nonvascular epidermis and an inner layer, the dermis or corium. The two layers interdigitate in dermal papillae (fingerlike projections), ridges of sensitive vascular dermis projecting into the epidermis. The outermost layers of the epidermis are cornified (*i.e.*, impregnated with various tough proteins) and enucleate (lacking cell nuclei). The epidermis is composed of flattened (squamous) cells in layers and is the interface between the individual and the environment. Its primary function is defensive, and it is cornified to resist abrasion. The surface of the skin is coated with lipids and organic salts, the so-called "acid mantle," thought to have antifungal and antibacterial properties. Deep in the epidermis is an electronegative layer, a further deterrent to foreign organic or ionic agents.

The dermis lies beneath the epidermis and nourishes it. The cutaneous circulation of the dermis is variously developed in mammals but it is typically extensive, out of proportion to the nutritional needs of the tissue. The major role of the cutaneous circulations is to moderate body temperature and blood pressure by forming a peripheral shunt, an alternate route for the blood. Also in the dermis are sensory nerve endings to alert the individual to pressure (touch), heat, cold, and pain. In general, skin bearing hairs has few or no specialized sensory endings, but hairless skin, such as the lips and fingertips of man, has specialized endings. The sensation of touch on hairy skin in man depends on stimulation of the nerve fibres of the hairs.

Hair is derived from an invagination (pocketing) of the epidermis termed a follicle. Collectively, the hair is called the pelage. The individual hair is a rod of keratinized cells that may be cylindrical or more-or-less flattened. Keratin is a protein also found in claws and nails. The inner medulla of the hair is hollow and contains air; in the outer cortex layer there are frequently pigment granules. Associated with the hair follicle are nerve endings and a muscle, the arrector pili. The latter allows the erection of individual hairs to alter the insulative qualities of the pelage. The follicle also gives rise to sebaceous glands that produce sebum, a substance that lubricates the hair.

Types of hair

Most mammals have three distinct kinds of hairs. Guard hairs protect the rest of the pelage from abrasion and frequently from moisture, and usually lend a characteristic colour pattern. The thicker underfur is primarily insulative and may differ in colour from the guard hairs. The third common hair-type is the vibrissa, or whisker, a stiff, typically elongate, hair that functions in tactile sensation. Hairs may be further modified to form rigid quills. The "horn" of the rhinoceros is composed of a fibrous keratin material derived from hair. Examples of keratinized derivatives of the integument other than hair are horns, hooves, nails, claws, and baleen.

Even though the primary function of the skin is defensive, it has been modified in mammals to serve such diverse functions as thermoregulation and nourishment of young. Secretions of sweat glands promote cooling due to evaporation at the surface of the body, and mammary glands are thought to be derived from sweat glands.

In certain groups (primates in particular) the skin of the face is under intricate muscular control and movements of the skin express and communicate "emotion." In many mammals the colour and pattern of the pelage is important in communicative behaviour. Patterns may be dymantic (startling, such as the mane of the male lion or hamadryas baboon), sematic (warning, such as the bold pattern of skunks), or cryptic (concealing), perhaps the most common adaptation of pelage colour.

Hair has been secondarily lost or considerably reduced in some kinds of mammals. In adult cetaceans insulation is provided by thick subcutaneous fat deposits, or blubber, with hair limited to a few stiff vibrissae about the mouth. The naked skin of whales is one of a number of features that contribute to the remarkably advanced hydrodynamics of locomotion in the group. Some fossorial mammals also tend toward reduction of the hair. This is shown most strikingly by the sand rats (*Heterocephalus*) of northeast Africa, but considerable loss of hair has also occurred in some species of pocket gophers (Geomyidae). Hair may also be lost on restricted areas of the skin, as from the face in many monkeys, or the buttocks of mandrills, and may be sparse on elephants and such highly modified kinds as pangolins and armadillos.

Indeterminate (continuous) growth, as seen in the hair of the head in man, is rare among mammals. Hairs with determinate growth are subject to wear and must be replaced periodically—a process termed molt. The first coat of a young mammal is referred to as the juvenal pelage, which typically is of fine texture like the underfur of adults and is replaced by a postjuvenile molt. Juvenal pelage is succeeded by the subadult pelage, which in some species is not markedly distinct from that of the adult, or directly by adult pelage. Once this pelage is acquired molting continues to recur at intervals, often annually or semi-annually, sometimes more frequently. The pattern of molt typically is orderly, but varies widely between species. Some mammals apparently molt continuously, with a few hairs replaced at a time throughout the year.

Dentition. Specialization in food habits has led to profound dental changes. The primitive mammalian tooth had high, sharp cusps and served to tear flesh or crush chitinous material (primarily the exoskeletons of terrestrial arthropods, such as insects). Herbivores tend to have specialized cheek teeth with complex occlusal (contact) patterns and various ways of expanding the crown and circumventing the problem of wear. Omnivorous mammals, such as bears, pigs, and man, tend to have molars with low, rounded cusps, termed "bunodont."

Anteating

A prime example of convergence in conjunction with dietary specialization is seen in those mammals adapted to feeding on social insects (generally termed myrmecophagy, "anteating"). This habit has led to remarkably similar morphology in such diverse groups as the monotreme echidnas (Tachyglossidae), one dasyurid marsupial (Myrmecobiinae), some edentates (Myrmecophagidae) the aardvark, and pangolins (Pholidota). Trends frequently associated with myrmecophagy include: strong claws, an elongate, terete skull, a vermiform, extensible tongue, marked reduction in the mandible, and loss or extreme simplification of the dentition.

Specialized herbivores evolved early in mammalian history. The earliest (and with the longest evolutionary history) were the multituberculates. Evolutionary convergence in teeth (*i.e.*, resemblances not due to common ancestry) has occurred widely in herbivorous groups; most have incisors modified for nipping or gnawing, have lost teeth with the resultant development of a gap (diastema) in the tooth row, and exhibit some molarization (expansion and flattening) of premolars to expand the grinding surface of the cheek teeth. Rootless incisors or cheek teeth have evolved frequently, an open pulp cavity allowing continual growth throughout life. Herbivorous specializations have evolved independently in multituberculates, rodents, lagomorphs, primates, and in the wide radiation of ungulate and subungulate orders.

Skeleton. The mammalian skeletal system shows a number of advances over that of lower vertebrates. The mode of ossification of the long bones is characteristic. In lower vertebrates each long bone has a single centre of ossification, the diaphysis, and replacement of cartilage by bone proceeds from the centre toward the ends, which may remain cartilaginous, even in adults. In mammals secondary centres of ossification, the epiphyses, develop at the ends of the bones. Growth of bones occurs in zones of cartilage between diaphysis and epiphyses. Mammalian skeletal growth is termed determinate, for once the actively growing zone of cartilage is obliterated, growth in length ceases. As in all bony vertebrates, of course, there is continual renewal of bone throughout life. The advantage of epiphyseal ossification lies in the fact that the bones have strong articular surfaces before the skeleton is mature. In general, the skeleton of the adult mammal has less structural cartilage than does that of a reptile.

The skeletal system of mammals and other vertebrates is broadly divisible functionally into axial and appendicular portions. The axial skeleton consists of the braincase (cranium) and the backbone and ribs, and serves primarily to protect the central nervous system. The limbs and their girdles constitute the appendicular skeleton. In addition, there are skeletal elements derived from the gill arches of primitive vertebrates, collectively termed the visceral skeleton. Visceral elements in the mammalian skeleton include the jaws, the hyoid apparatus supporting the tongue, and the auditory ossicles of the middle ear. The postcranial axial skeleton in mammals generally has remained rather conservative during the course of evolution. The vast majority of mammals have seven cervical (neck) vertebrae; exceptions are sloths, with six or nine cervicals, and the Sirenia with six. The anterior two cervical vertebrae are differentiated as atlas and axis. Specialized articulations of these two bones allow complex movements of the head on the trunk. Thoracic vertebrae bear ribs and are variable in number. The anterior ribs converge toward the ventral midline to articulate with the sternum, or breastbone, forming a semirigid thoracic "basket" for the protection of heart and lungs. Posterior to the thoracic region are the lumbar vertebrae, ranging from two to 21 in number (most frequently four to seven). Mammals have no lumbar ribs. There are usually three to five sacral vertebrae, but some edentates have as many as 13. Sacral vertebrae fuse to form the sacrum, to which the pelvic girdle is attached. Caudal (tail) vertebrae range in number from five (fused elements of the coccyx of man) to 50.

The basic structure of the vertebral column is comparable throughout the Mammalia, although in many instances modifications have occurred in specialized locomotor modes to gain particular mechanical advantages. The vertebral column and associated muscles of many mammals is structurally analogous to a cantilever girder.

The skull The skull is composite in origin and complex in function. Functionally the bones of the head are separable into the braincase and the jaws. In general, it is the head of the animal that meets the environment. The skull protects the brain and sense capsules, houses the teeth and tongue, and the entrance to the pharynx. Thus the head functions in sensory reception, food acquisition, defense, respiration, and (in higher groups) communication. To serve these functions, bony elements have been recruited from the visceral skeleton, the endochondral skeleton, and from the dermal skeleton of lower vertebrates.

The skull of mammals differs markedly from that of reptiles because of the great expansion of the brain. The sphenoid bones that form the reptilian braincase form only the floor of the braincase in mammals. The side is formed in part by the alisphenoid bone, derived from the epipterygoid, a part of the reptilian palate. Dermal elements, the frontals and parietals, have come to lie deep to (beneath) the muscles of the jaw to form the dorsum of the braincase. Reptilian dermal roofing bones, lying superficial to the muscles of the jaw, are represented in mammals only by the jugal bone of the zygomatic arch, which lies under the eye.

In mammals, a secondary palate is formed by processes of the maxillary bones and the palatines, with the pterygoid bones reduced in importance. The secondary palate separates the nasal passages from the oral cavity and allows continuous breathing while chewing or suckling.

Other specializations of the mammalian skull include paired occipital condyles (the articulating surfaces at the neck) and an expanded nasal chamber with complexly folded turbinal bones, providing a large area for detection of odours. Eutherians have evolved bony protection for the middle ear, the auditory bulla. The development of this structure varies, although an annular (ring-shaped) tympanic bone is always present.

Bones of the ear The bones of the mammalian middle ear are a diagnostic feature of the class. The three auditory ossicles form a series of levers that serve mechanically to increase the amplitude of sound waves reaching the tympanic membrane, or eardrum, produced as disturbances of the air. The innermost bone is the stapes, or "stirrup bone." It

rests against the oval window of the inner ear. The stapes is homologous with the entire stapedial structure of reptiles, which, in turn, was derived from the hyomandibular arch of primitive vertebrates. The incus, or "anvil," articulates with the stapes. The incus was derived from the quadrate bone, which is involved in the jaw articulation in reptiles. The malleus, or "hammer," rests against the tympanic membrane and articulates with the incus. The malleus is the homologue of the reptilian articular bone. The mechanical efficiency of the middle ear has thus been increased by the incorporation of two bones of the reptilian jaw assemblage. In mammals the lower jaw is a single bone, the dentary, which articulates with the squamosal of the skull.

The limbs and girdles have been greatly modified with locomotor adaptations. The ancestral mammal had well-developed limbs and was five-toed. In each limb there were two distal (outer) elements (radius and ulna in the forelimb; tibia and fibula in the hindlimb) and a single proximal (inner or upper) element (humerus; femur). There were nine bones in the wrist, the carpals; and seven bones in the ankle, the tarsals. The phalangeal formula (the number of phalangeal bones in each digit, numbered from inside outward) is 2-3-3-3-3 in primitive mammals; in primitive reptiles it is 2-3-4-5-3. Modifications in mammalian limbs have involved reduction, loss, or fusion of bones. Loss of the clavicle from the shoulder girdle, reduction in the number of toes, and modifications of tarsal and carpal bones are typical correlates of cursorial locomotion. Scansorial and arboreal groups tend to maintain or emphasize the primitive divergence of the thumb and hallux (the inner toe on the hindfoot). Some details of limb modifications are included in the synopsis of the orders of mammals (see below *Annotated classification*).

Centres of ossification sometimes develop in nonbony connective tissue. Such bones are termed heterotopic or sesamoid elements. The kneecap (patella) is such a bone. Another important bone of this sort, found in many kinds of mammals, is the baculum or os penis, which occurs as a stiffening rod in the penis of such groups as carnivores, many bats, rodents, and some insectivores, and in many primates. The os clitoridis is a homologous structure found in females.

Muscles. The muscular system of mammals is generally comparable to that of reptiles. With changes in locomotion, the proportions and specific functions of muscular elements have been altered, but the relationships of these muscles remain essentially the same. Exceptions to this generalization are the muscles of the skin and of the jaw.

The panniculus carnosus is a sheath of dermal (skin) muscle, developed in many mammals, which allows the movement of the skin independent of the movement of deeper muscle masses. Such movement functions in such mundane activities as the twitching of the skin to foil insect pests and in some forms also is important in shivering, a characteristic heat-producing response to thermal stress. The dermal musculature of the facial region is particularly well developed in primates and carnivores, but occurs in other groups as well. Facial mobility allows expression that may be of importance in the behavioral maintenance of interspecific social structure.

Muscles of the jaw The temporalis muscle is the major adductor (closer) of the reptilian jaw. In mammals the temporalis is divided into a deep temporalis proper and a more superficial masseter muscle. The temporalis attaches to the coronoid process of the mandible (lower jaw) and the temporal bone of the skull. The masseter passes from the angular process of the mandible to the zygomatic arch. The masseter allows an anteroposterior (forward-backward) movement of the jaw and is highly developed in mammals, such as rodents, in which grinding is the important function of the dentition.

Viscera. *Digestive system.* The alimentary canal is highly specialized in many kinds of mammals. In general, specializations of the gut accompany herbivorous habits. The intestines of herbivores are typically elongate and the stomach may also be specialized. Subdivision of the gut allows areas of differing physiological environments for the activities of different sorts of enzymes and symbiotic

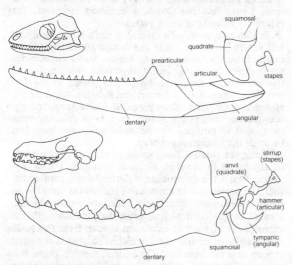

Figure 2: Comparison of lower jaw and ear region in the skull of (top) a reptile and (bottom) a mammal.

bacteria (which aid the animal by breaking down certain "indigestible" compounds). In ruminant artiodactyls the stomach has up to four chambers, each with a particular function in the processing of vegetable material. A cecum is common in many herbivores. The cecum is a blind sac at the distal end of the small intestine where complex compounds like cellulose are acted upon by symbiotic bacteria. The vermiform appendix is a diverticulum of the cecum. The appendix is rich in lymphoid tissue and in many mammals is concerned with defense against toxic bacterial products.

Hares and rabbits, the sewellel or "mountain beaver" (*Aplodontia rufa*), and some insectivores exhibit a phenomenon, known as reingestion, in which at intervals specialized fecal pellets are produced, which are taken in the mouth and passed through the alimentary canal a second time. Where known to be present, this pattern seems to be obligatory. Reingestion is poorly understood, but it is generally supposed that the process allows the animal to absorb in the upper gut vitamins produced by the microflora of the lower gut but not absorbable there.

Excretory system. The mammalian kidney is constructed of a large number of functional units called nephrons. Each nephron consists of a distal tubule, a medial section termed the loop of Henle, a proximal tubule, and a renal corpuscle. The renal corpuscle is a knot of capillaries, called a glomerulus, surrounded by a sheath, Bowman's capsule. The renal corpuscle is a pressure filter, relying on blood pressure to remove water, ions, and small organic molecules from the blood. Some of the material removed is waste, but some is of value to the organism. The filtrate is sorted by the tubules, and water and needed solutes are reabsorbed. Reabsorption is both passive (osmotic) and active (based on ion transport systems). The distal convoluted tubules drain into collecting tubules which, in turn, empty into the calyces, or branches, of the renal pelvis, the expanded end of the ureter. The pressure-pump nephron of mammals is so efficient that the renal portal system of lower vertebrates has been completely lost. Mammalian kidneys show considerable variety in structure, relative to the environmental demands on a given species. In particular, desert rodents have long loops of Henle and are able to reabsorb much water and to excrete a highly concentrated urine. Urea is the end product of protein metabolism in mammals, and excretion is therefore called ureotelic.

Reproductive system. The testes of mammals descend from the abdominal cavity to lie in a compartmented pouch termed the scrotum. In some species the testes are permanently scrotal and the scrotum is sealed off from the general abdominal cavity. In others the testes migrate to the scrotum only during the breeding season. It is thought that the temperature of the abdominal cavity is too high to allow spermatogenesis; the scrotum allows cooling of the testes.

The transport of spermatozoa is comparable to that in reptiles, relying on ducts derived from urinary ducts of earlier vertebrates. Mammalian specialities are the bulbourethral (or Cowper's) glands, the prostate gland, and the seminal vesicle or vesicular gland. Each of these glands adds secretions to the spermatozoa to form semen, which passes from the body via a canal (urethra) in the highly vascular, erectile penis. The tip of the penis, the glans, may have a complex morphology and has been used as a taxonomic character in some groups. The penis may be retracted into a sheath along the abdomen or may be pendulous, as in bats and many primates.

The structure of the female reproductive tract is variable. Four uterine types are generally recognized among placentals, based on the relationship of the uterine horns (branches). A duplex uterus characterizes rodents and rabbits; the uterine horns are completely separated and have separate cervices opening into the vagina. Carnivores have a bipartite uterus, in which the horns are largely separate but enter the vagina by a single cervix. In the bicornate uterus, typical of many ungulates, the horns are distinct for less than half their length; the lower part of the uterus is a common chamber, the body. Higher primates have a simplex uterus in which all separation

Action of the kidney (margin)

Types of uterus (margin)

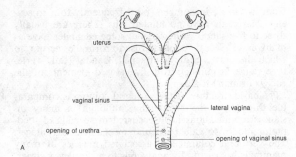

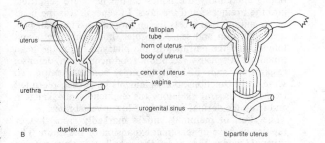

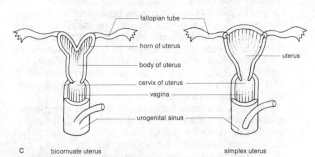

Figure 3: *Female reproductive systems.*
(A) Duplex uterus with median vaginal tube (kangaroo).
(B, C) Placental uteri.

From (A) A.S. Romer, *The Vertebrate Body*, 4th ed. (1970); W.B. Saunders Company; Philadelphia; (B, C) W.F. Walker, *Vertebrate Dissection*, 4th ed. (1970); W.B. Saunders Company, Philadelphia

between the horns is lacking, forming a single chamber.

The female reproductive tract of marsupials is termed didelphous; the vagina is paired, as are oviducts and uteri. In primitive marsupials there are paired vaginae lateral to the ureters. In more advanced groups, such as kangaroos, the lateral vaginae persist and conduct the migration of spermatozoa, but a medial "pseud-vagina" functions as the birth canal.

Monotremes have paired uteri and oviducts, which empty into a urogenital sinus (cavity) as do fluid wastes. The sinus passes into the cloaca, a common receptacle for reproductive and excretory products.

Circulatory system. In mammals as in birds, right and left ventricles of the heart are completely separated, so that pulmonary (lung) and systemic (body) circulations are completely independent. Oxygenated blood arrives in the left atrium from the lungs and passes to the left ventricle, whence it is forced through the aorta to the systemic circulation. Deoxygenated blood from the tissues returns to the right atrium via a large vein, the vena cava, and is pumped to the pulmonary capillary bed through the pulmonary artery.

Among vertebrates, contraction of the heart is myogenic; rhythm is inherent in all cardiac muscle, but in myogenic hearts the pacemaker is derived from cardiac tissue. The pacemaker in mammals (and also in birds) is an oblong mass of specialized cells called the sinoatrial node, located in the right atrium near the junction with the venae cavae. A wave of excitation spreads from this node to the atrioventricular node, which is located in the right atrium near the base of the interatrial septum. From this point excitation is conducted along the atrioventricular bundle (bundle of His) and enters the main mass of cardiac tissue along fine branches, the Purkinje fibres. Homeostatic control of the heart by neuroendocrine or other agents is mediated through the intrinsic control network of the heart.

Blood leaves the left ventricle through the aorta. The mammalian aorta is an unpaired structure derived from the left fourth aortic arch of the primitive vertebrate. Birds, on the other hand, retain the right fourth arch.

Characteristics of the blood

The circulatory system forms a complex communication and distribution network to all physiologically active tissues of the body. A constant, copious supply of oxygen is required to sustain the active, endothermous physiology of the higher vertebrates. The efficiency of the four-chambered heart is important to this function. Oxygen is transported by specialized red blood cells, or erythrocytes, as in all vertebrates. Packaging the oxygen-bearing pigment hemoglobin in erythrocytes keeps the viscosity of the blood minimal and thereby allows efficient circulation while limiting the mechanical load on the heart. The mammalian erythrocyte is a highly evolved structure; its discoid, biconcave shape allows maximal surface area per unit volume. When mature and functional, mammalian red blood cells are enucleate.

Respiratory system. Closely coupled with the circulatory system is the ventilatory (breathing) apparatus, the lungs and associated structures. Ventilation in mammals is unique. The lungs themselves are less efficient than those of birds, for air movement consists of an ebb and flow, rather than a one-way circuit, so a residuum of air remains that cannot be expired. Ventilation in mammals is by means of a negative pressure pump made possible by the development of a definitive thoracic cavity with the evolution of the diaphragm.

The diaphragm is a unique, composite structure consisting of (1) the transverse septum (a wall that primitively separates the heart from the general viscera); (2) pleuroperitoneal folds from the body wall; (3) mesenteric folds; and (4) axial muscles inserting on a central tendon, or diaphragmatic aponeurosis.

The lungs lie in separate, airtight compartments called pleural cavities, separated by the mediastinum. As the size of the pleural cavity is increased the lung is expanded and air flows in passively. Enlargement of the pleural cavity is produced by contraction of the diaphragm or by elevation of the ribs. The relaxed diaphragm domes upward, but when contracted it stretches flat. Expiration is an active movement brought about by contraction of abdominal muscles against the viscera.

Air typically enters the respiratory passages through the nostrils where it may be warmed and moistened. It passes above the bony palate and the soft palate and enters the pharynx. In the pharynx the passages for air and food cross. Air enters the trachea, which divides at the level of the lungs into primary bronchi. A characteristic feature of the trachea of many mammals is the larynx. Vocal cords stretch across the larynx and are vibrated by forced expiration to produce sound. The laryngeal apparatus may be greatly modified for the production of complex vocalizations. In some groups, for example, howler monkeys (*Alouatta*), the hyoid apparatus is incorporated into the sound-producing organ, as a resonating chamber.

Nervous and endocrine systems. The nervous system and the system of endocrine glands are closely related to one another in their function, for both serve to coordinate activity. The endocrine glands of mammals generally have more complex regulatory functions than do those of lower vertebrates. This is particularly true of the pituitary gland, which supplies hormones that regulate the reproductive cycle. Follicle stimulating hormone (FSH) initiates the maturation of the ovarian follicle. Luteinizing hormone (LH) mediates the formation of the corpus luteum from the follicle following ovulation. Prolactin, also a product of the anterior pituitary, stimulates the secretion of milk.

Control of the pituitary glands is partially by means of neurohumours from the hypothalamus, a part of the forebrain in contact with the pituitary gland by nervous and circulatory pathways. The hypothalamus is of the utmost importance in mammals, for it integrates stimuli from both internal and external environments, channelling signals to higher centres or into autonomic pathways.

The brain

The cerebellum of vertebrates is at the anterior end of the hindbrain. Its function is to coordinate motor activities and to maintain posture. In most mammals the cerebellum is highly developed and its surface may be convoluted to increase its area. The data with which the cerebellum works arrive from proprioceptors ("self-sensors") in the muscles and from the membranous labyrinth of the inner ear, the latter giving information on position and movements of the head.

In the vertebrate ancestors of the mammals the cerebral hemispheres were centres for the reception of olfactory stimuli. Vertebrate evolution has favoured an increasing importance of these lobes in the integration of stimuli. Their great development in mammals as centres of association is responsible for the "creative" behaviour of members of the class; *i.e.*, the ability to learn, to adapt as individuals to short-term environmental change through appropriate responses on the basis of previous experience. In vertebrate evolution the gray matter of the cerebrum has moved from a primitive internal position in the hemispheres to a superficial position. The superficial gray matter is termed the pallium. The paleopallium of amphibians has become the olfactory lobes of the higher vertebrates; the dorsolateral surface, or archipallium, the mammalian hippocampus. The great neural advance of the mammals lies in the elaboration of the neopallium, which makes up the bulk of the cerebrum. The neopallium is an association centre, the dominant centre of neural function, and is involved in so-called "intelligent" response. By contrast, the highest centre in the avian brain is the corpus striatum, an evolutionary product of the basal nuclei of the amphibian brain. The bulk of the complex behaviour of birds is instinctive. The surface of the neopallium tends in some mammals to be greatly expanded by convoluting, forming folds (gyri) between deep grooves (sulci).

THE EVOLUTION OF THE MAMMALIAN CONDITION

Mammals were derived in the Triassic Period from members of the reptilian order Therapsida. The therapsids, members of the subclass Synapsida (sometimes called the mammal-like reptiles), generally were unimpressive in relation to other reptiles of their time. Synapsids were present in the Carboniferous Period (about 280,000,000 to 345,000,000 years ago) and are one of the earliest known reptilian groups. They were the dominant reptiles of Permian times (about 225,000,000 to 280,000,000 years ago), and although they were primarily predacious in habit, the adaptive radiation included herbivorous species as well. In the Mesozoic (about 225,000,000 to 65,000,000 years ago), the importance of the synapsids was generally assumed by the archosaurs or "ruling reptiles," the therapsids, in general, being small, active carnivores. Therapsids tended to evolve a specialized heterodont dentition and to improve the mechanics of locomotion by bringing the plane of action of the limbs close to the trunk. A secondary palate was developed and the temporal musculature was expanded.

The several features that separate modern reptiles from modern mammals doubtless evolved at different rates.

Drawing by R. Keane based on A.S. Romer, *The Vertebrate Story*, copyright 1959; the University of Chicago Press

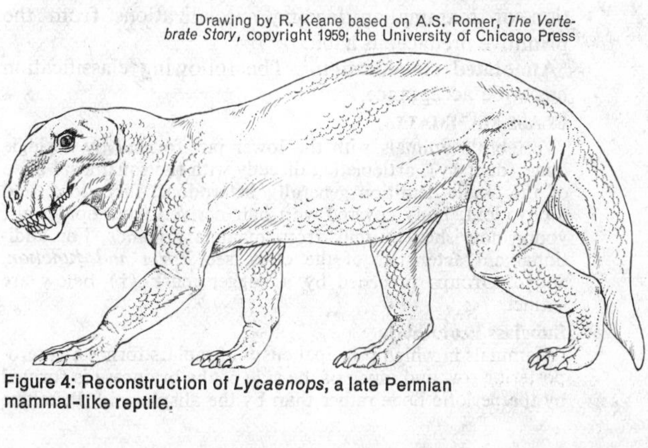

Figure 4: Reconstruction of *Lycaenops*, a late Permian mammal-like reptile.

Many attributes of mammals are correlated with their highly active habit; for example, efficient double circulation with a completely four-chambered heart, anucleate and biconcave erythrocytes, the diaphragm, and the secondary palate (which separates passages for food and air and allows breathing during mastication or suckling). Hair for insulation is a correlate of endothermy, the physiological maintenance of individual temperature independent of environmental temperature, and endothermy allows high levels of sustained activity. The unique characteristics of mammals thus would seem to have evolved as a complex interrelated system.

Because the characteristics that separate reptiles and mammals evolved at different rates and in response to a variety of interrelated conditions, at any point in the period of transition from reptiles to mammals there were forms that combined various characteristics of both groups. Such a pattern of evolution is termed "mosaic" and is a common phenomenon in those transitions marking the origin of major new adaptive types. To simplify definitions and to allow the strict delimitation of the Mammalia, some authors have suggested basing the boundary on a single character, the articulation of the jaw between the dentary and squamosal bones and the attendant movement of accessory jaw bones to the middle ear as auditory ossicles. The use of a single osteological character allows the placement in a logical classification of numerous fossil species, other mammalian characters of which, such as the degree of endothermy and nursing of young and the condition of the internal organs, probably never will be evaluated. It must be recognized, however, that were the advanced therapsids alive, taxonomists would be hard-put to decide which to place in the Reptilia and which in the Mammalia.

CLASSIFICATION

Distinguishing taxonomic features. The higher classification of the Mammalia is based on consideration of a broad array of characters. Traditionally, evidence from comparative anatomy was of predominant importance, but more recently information from such disciplines as physiology, serology, and genetics has proved useful in considering relationships. Comparative study of living organisms is supplemented by the findings of paleontology. Study of the fossil record adds a historical dimension to knowledge of mammalian relationships. In some cases, the horses for example, the fossil record has been adequate to allow lineages to be traced in great detail.

Relative to that of other major vertebrate groups, the fossil record of mammals is good. Fossilization depends upon a great many factors, most important among which are the structure of the organism, its habitat, and conditions at the time of death. The most common remains of mammals are teeth and the associated bones of the jaw and skull. Enamel covering the typical mammalian tooth is composed of prismatic rods of crystalline apatite and is the hardest tissue in the mammalian body. It is highly resistant to chemical and physical weathering. Because of the abundance of teeth in deposits of fossil mammals, dental characteristics have been stressed in the interpretation of mammalian phylogeny and relationships. Dental features are particularly well suited for this important role in classification because they reflect the broad radiation of mammalian feeding specializations from the primitive predaceous habit.

Annotated classification. The following classification has wide acceptance.

CLASS MAMMALIA

Vertebrate animals with the lower jaw formed by a single bone (dentary), articulating directly with the squamosal bone of the skull; dentition generally heterodont, thecodont, and diphyodont; body covered with hair derived from epidermis; young nourished by milk from mammary glands. For additional characteristics of the class, see *Form and function*, above. Groups preceded by a dagger mark (†) below are extinct.

Subclass Prototheria

Mammals in which principal cusps of molars form an anteroposterior row and much of the side of the braincase is formed by the periotic bone rather than by the alisphenoid. Primitive characters include uncoiled cochlea of the inner ear and absence of spine on the scapula (shoulder blade).

†Infraclass Eotheria

Fossil only; Upper Triassic to Lower Cretaceous of Eurasia and North America. Upper molars with internal and external cingula (shelves at base of crown), lower molars with internal cingulum only.

†*Order Triconodonta* (triconodonts). Fossil only; Northern Hemisphere; Upper Triassic to Lower Cretaceous. Probably carnivorous, the teeth well differentiated; molars typically with 3 prominent cusps; dentary bone lacking angular process.

†*Order Docodonta* (docodonts). Known only from fossil teeth and jaws from Upper Jurassic of Europe. Molars expanded, with transverse median furrow; angular process of mandible directed ventrally rather than posteriorly ("pseudangular").

Infraclass Ornithodelphia

Order Monotremata (monotremes). Pleistocene to Recent of Australia and New Guinea; possible record in Miocene of Australia family (Ectopodontidae). Reproduction by shelled eggs, incubated by female; no organized nipple, the milk flowing from mammary ducts onto the fur of the abdomen; cloaca present; adults toothless, rostrum covered with horny beak. Total length to 80 cm. Examples: duck-billed platypus, and echidnas or spiny anteaters (see MONOTREMATA).

†Infraclass Allotheria

†*Order Multituberculata* (multituberculates). Fossil only; Upper Jurassic to lower Eocene of North America and Eurasia. The earliest herbivorous mammals; specializations of teeth and jaws superficially rodent-like; molars elongate, with two or three longitudinal rows of cusps; lower premolars tending to become serrated shearing blades. Size larger than typical Mesozoic mammals, to about that of a woodchuck.

Subclass Theria
†Infraclass Trituberculata

†*Order Symmetrodonta* (symmetrodonts). Fossil only; Upper Jurassic to Lower Cretaceous of Eurasia and North America. Molars with 3 prominent cusps arranged in symmetrical triangles; lower molars without posterior talonid basin ("heel").

†*Order Pantotheria* (pantotheres). Fossil only; Middle Jurassic to Lower Cretaceous of North America and Europe. Molars with 3 prominent anterior cusps (trigonid), asymmetrical; posterior basin (talonid) of lower molars developed, as in higher mammals.

Infraclass Metatheria

Order Marsupialia (marsupials). Upper Cretaceous to Recent of North and South America, Europe, Australia. Placenta formed from yolk sac (simple chorio-allantoic placenta in bandicoots), the young born in a relatively undeveloped state after brief gestation, developing further attached to mammae in marsupium (pouch) or along marsupial fold; female reproductive tract bifid, uterus and vagina double, penis bifurcate, posterior to scrotum. Angular process of mandible inflected; auditory bullae (when present) formed from alisphenoid bone and thus not homologous with bullae of eutherians. Epipubis ("marsupial bone") present; length of head and body varying from about 10 cm (small opossums) to more than 160 cm (kangaroos). Examples: opossums, kangaroos, wallabies, bandicoots, wombats, phalangers, koala (see MARSUPIALIA).

Infraclass Eutheria (placental mammals)

Order Insectivora (insectivores). Upper Cretaceous to Recent, worldwide except Australia, polar regions, and many oceanic islands. A diverse group of mammals sharing certain primitive characteristics but highly specialized in several adaptive modes; dentition generally heterodont, rooted, variously modified; molars usually tuberculosectorial. Stance plantigrade to semiplantigrade; habit fossorial, terrestrial, arboreal, semiaquatic; insectivorous to omnivorous. Braincase low, rising but little above plane of rostrum; snout generally long, pointed, modified for olfaction and touch; zygomatic arch complete or incomplete. Length of head and body, 5 cm (smallest shrews) to 45 cm (largest hedgehogs). Shrews of the genera *Microsorex, Sorex,* and *Suncus* are the smallest of living mammals. Examples: shrews, moles, hedgehogs, tenrecs, solenodon (see INSECTIVORA).

Order Macroscelidea (elephant shrews). Lower Oligocene to Recent of Africa. Anteromost incisors widely spaced (incisor series forming a straight, anteroposterior row); posterior incisors caniniform; upper canine premolariform, bicuspid; posterior premolars molariform, last premolar largest tooth in dental series; molars quadrate, reduced in size or absent posteriorly; auditory bullae well developed. Stance plantigrade, hind feet elongate, modified for hopping gait; tail elongate.

Length of head and body of living species, 12 to 20 cm; tail 12 to 18 cm (see INSECTIVORA).

Order Dermoptera (colugos or "flying lemurs"). Upper Paleocene to lower Eocene of North America (Plagiomenidae), Recent of Southeast Asia (Cynocephalidae). In living species, upper incisors reduced, lower incisors procumbent, spatulate, pectinate (comb-like), molars low-crowned, used for shearing the vegetable diet. The most specialized and efficient of mammalian gliders; the patagium (gliding membrane) extends from the neck to phalanges of hand, to phalanges of foot, to tip of tail; total length of head and body, 34–45 cm.

†*Order Tillodontia* (tillodonts). Fossil only; upper Paleocene to middle Eocene of Northern Hemisphere. Omnivorous or herbivorous; incisors rootless, enlarged, molars low-crowned; perhaps superficially bearlike in appearance; total length to approximately 120 cm.

†*Order Taeniodonta* (taeniodonts). Fossil only; lower Paleocene to upper Eocene of North America, middle Eocene of Asia. Large, browsing herbivores; outer incisors rodent-like, inner incisors lost; canines well developed; cheek teeth simple, rootless pegs; length of skull to about 35 cm.

Order Chiroptera (bats). Middle Eocene to Recent in tropical and temperate regions; volant, the wings consisting of a fold of skin (patagium) supported by elongated bones of the second through fifth digits; thumb clawed in suborder Microchiroptera, thumb and index finger clawed in Megachiroptera; hind limbs variously specialized but generally weak. Incisors generally reduced, canines prominent, cheek teeth rather primitive, with prominent ectoloph. Length of head and body from about 3 to 40 cm; wing span to about 120 cm (see CHIROPTERA).

Order Primates (primates). Late Cretaceous to Recent of Eurasia, Africa, North and South America. A diverse group of generalized, generally omnivorous mammals, modified for arboreality (some secondarily terrestrial). Dentition little specialized; a pair of incisors lost above and below, canines prominent, sexually dimorphic in some species; premolars usually bicuspid, sometimes caniniform; molars typically low-crowned, tuberculosectorial to bunodont. Limbs and girdles adapted for flexibility with little loss or fusion of elements; clavicle present; digits I (hallux and pollex) divergent, tending to become opposable; stance plantigrade. Olfaction de-emphasized in favour of vision, and snout reduced; eyes rotated forward allowing trend toward stereoscopic vision; in more advanced groups cerebrum expanded to cover cerebellum, braincase expanded. Length of head and body (including extended hind limbs), 15 cm (pygmy marmosets, tarsiers) to more than 200 cm (*Homo*). Examples: lemurs, lorises, Old World and New World monkeys, marmosets, great apes, man (see PRIMATES).

Order Edentata (edentates). Lower Eocene to Recent of North and South America. Anterior teeth lost and cheek teeth reduced to simple rootless pegs without enamel, or (in anteaters) lost altogether. Secondary articulations (xenarthrous processes) present between vertebrae in addition to zygapophyses (the usual articulating surfaces); cervical vertebrae 6 to 9, in some cases fused; acromion and coracoid processes of scapula enlarged, often joining to form bony ring; claws generally stout. Several groups walk on the sides of feet and structure may be modified accordingly. Brain small, skull low, zygomatic arch usually incomplete. Total length of fossil edentates to 300 cm; living species to 185 cm (giant anteaters). Examples: sloths, armadillos, anteaters (see EDENTATA).

Order Pholidota (pangolins). Oligocene to Recent of Eurasia and Africa; possible North America representatives (Paleanodontidae) upper Paleocene to lower Oligocene. Body covered with heavy, overlapping scales with hairs only at bases of scales; tail prehensile in some species. Myrmecophagous (anteating); skull elongate, braincase low; lower jaw reduced to thin shaft of bone; feet 5-toed but only 3 toes of forefeet strongly clawed. Total length 75 to 170 cm.

Order Tubulidentata (aardvark). Miocene to Recent of Africa, Pliocene of Eurasia; possible representatives in Eocene and Oligocene of Europe. Teeth reduced to 4 or 5 simple pegs in each jaw of adults, without enamel, the dentine intersected by numerous tubules (hence the ordinal name). Four toes on forefeet, 5 behind, each bearing a strong, stout, hooflike "nail." Skull elongate and tubular; tongue vermiform; mandible not so reduced as in other "anteaters." Legs powerful, skeleton generally primitive but tibia and fibula fused. One species; total length to 200 cm.

Order Lagomorpha (lagomorphs). Upper Paleocene to Recent of Eurasia, North America, Africa, northern South America. Dentition superficially rodent-like, but with 2 pairs of upper incisors (a small pair situated behind the larger functional pair); canine and anterior premolars lost, forming prominent diastema (gap); cheek teeth high-crowned, rootless, 6 above and 5 below (more than in any rodent), and not occluding directly, so that mastication is a lateral movement; maxillary bone fenestrate (*i.e.*, with holes). Fibula articulating with calcaneum; infraorbital canal small. Scrotum anterior to penis. Total length, 15 cm (pikas) to 70 cm (hares). Examples: hares, rabbits, pikas (see LAGOMORPHA).

Order Rodentia (rodents). Lower Eocene to Recent, worldwide except Antarctica and some oceanic islands. Single pair of rootless incisors above and below; canines and anterior premolars lost forming prominent diastema; never more than 2 premolars above and 1 below; cheek teeth frequently rootless, hypsodont; cusp patterns variable, cheek teeth ranging from pegs to massive teeth with highly complex occlusal patterns. Powerful jaw musculature developed in connection with grinding dentition; angular process of mandible well developed for muscle attachment. Postorbital bar absent; infraorbital foramen variously modified, in advanced groups passing portions of masseter muscle; postcranial skeleton relatively unspecialized. Forelimbs flexible, digits clawed, little reduction in number on forefeet, some specialization of hindfeet and reduction of digits associated with saltation; stance plantigrade or semiplantigrade. Total length of living species, 10 cm (pygmy mice, some pocket mice) to 125 cm (capybara). Examples: mice and rats, squirrels, porcupines, beaver (see RODENTIA).

†*Order Creodonta* (creodonts). Fossil only; Middle Cretaceous to upper Oligocene of North America, Eurasia, Africa. Primitive carnivorous mammals; canines well developed; cheek teeth specialized for shearing, but carnassial pair farther back in tooth row than in Carnivora. Auditory bullae unossified. Distal phalanges channelled for insertion of claws; no fusion of scaphoid, lunar, and centrale bones of wrist. More than 50 genera, in about 5 families. Size to that of bear or larger.

Order Carnivora (carnivores). Middle Paleocene to Recent on all continents (probably accompanied early man to Australia). Teeth variously modified, sectorial to bunodont, but the carnassial (shearing) pair of teeth always consisting of the last upper premolar over the first lower molar; dentition simplified in advanced pinnipeds (seals), nearly homodont, with no carnassials. Auditory bullae ossified in advanced forms. Terminal phalanges not channelled for insertion of claws; scaphoid, lunar, centrale bones of wrist fused. Carnivorous, omnivorous, herbivorous. Total head and body length 15 to 370 cm. Examples: cats, dogs, bears, weasels, civets, hyenas, raccoons, seals, sea lions, walruses (see CARNIVORA).

†*Order Archaeoceti* (archaeocetes, zeuglodonts). Fossil only; lower Eocene to middle Miocene of North Africa, Europe, North America. Primitive whale-like marine mammals, dentition not highly modified; anterior teeth simple, peglike; cheek teeth sectorial as in early carnivores; teeth not exceeding basic placental number (44); nostrils placed well back on elongate snout; skull not "telescoped" as in modern whales; hindlimbs vestigial by upper Eocene; body elongate, some serpentine; total length to more than 2,000 cm (65 ft) (see WHALE).

Order Odontoceti (toothed whales). Upper Eocene to Recent in all oceans and occasionally in freshwater. Dentition generally simple, undifferentiated (homodont), exceeding the primitive placental number (to 300 teeth in some porpoises) or secondarily reduced (to a single tooth in *Monodon*, the narwhal); nostrils located on top of head, above and between eyes, forming single "blow-hole"; skull asymmetrical, markedly "telescoped," with reduction of frontals and parietals and concomitant extensive posterior expansion of maxillaries and premaxillaries. Relative to Archaeoceti, body shorter, stouter, total length 150 cm (5 ft) (small porpoises) to about 1,800 cm (about 59 ft) (male sperm whales). Examples: dolphins, porpoises, narwhal, sperm whales (see WHALE).

Order Mysticeti (baleen or "whale-bone" whales). Upper Eocene to Recent in all oceans. Teeth absent; "whale-bone" (baleen) present, consisting of ridged "curtains" of keratin extending from roof of mouth, used to strain krill (zooplankton); mouth cavernous, esophagus constricted to maximum diameter of about 20 cm; mandibular symphysis lacking; skull symmetrical, markedly "telescoped," with anterior expansion of occipitals; nostrils moved posteriorly, "blow-hole" double, anterior to orbits (eyes). Total length from 600 cm (20 ft) (pygmy right whale) to more than 3,000 cm (100 ft) (blue or sulphur-bottom whale); the blue whale, weighing to 150 tons, is the largest of all known vertebrates, living or extinct. Examples: rorquals (including blue whale), gray whales, bow-heads, right whales (see WHALE).

†*Order Condylarthra* (condylarths). Fossil only; Upper Cretaceous to lower Oligocene of Eurasia, North and South

America. Probably the basal stock from which most later ungulate groups evolved; directly descended from primitive placentals, and characteristics diverse. Tendency toward rounded molar cusps of equal height (bunodonty), formation of diastema, reduction of canine teeth, assumption of digitigrade stance and "experimentation" with hooves (ungules). About 90 genera and seven families: some species at least as large as modern bears.

†*Order Pyrotheria* (pyrotheres). Fossil only; Eocene and Oligocene of South America. Incisors enlarged, tusklike; diastema prominent; cheek teeth low-crowned and with transverse crests; nostrils on top of heavy skull, suggesting development of fleshy proboscis. About 4 genera known; as in many other ungulate groups, trend to large size (to that of elephants); length of skull to 60 cm.

†*Order Xenungulata* (xenungulates). Known only from a few fragmentary fossils from upper Paleocene of South America. Generally poorly known, but molars with tendency toward converging transverse crests as in Dinocerata of Northern Hemisphere; postcranial remains scanty but build obviously massive. Size to that of a modern rhinoceros.

†*Order Pantodonta* (pantodonts). Fossil only; Paleocene to Oligocene of North America and Asia. A varied group of herbivores, prominent in the Paleocene. Cheek teeth low-crowned, with transverse crests variously arranged, canines small or greatly developed. About a dozen genera; total length approximately 100 to 450 cm.

†*Order Dinocerata* (uintatheres). Fossil only; Paleocene and Eocene of North America and Eocene of Asia. Skull low, later representatives with bony projections on nasal, maxillary, and frontal bones. Upper incisors absent, lower incisors reduced, saber-like upper canines (evidently only in males); upper molars unique, with 2 transverse crests forming a "V." Limbs graviportal (massive); about 8 genera; size to that of large rhinoceros.

Order Proboscidea (elephants and allies). Upper Eocene to Recent in Eurasia, Africa, North and South America. Earliest known representatives characterized by low-crown molars with two transverse lophs, diastema resulting from loss of outer lower incisor, canine and first premolar, and formation of upper and lower tusks by modification of incisors. Nasal opening toward top of skull, indicating that a fleshy proboscis ("trunk") was present, but perhaps of modest size; early proboscideans relatively long-bodied and short-limbed, superficially tapir-like. Middle and later Cenozoic times saw wide radiation from basal stock; about 2 dozen fossil genera known. Two living genera (*Elephas*, the Indian elephant; *Loxodonta*, the African elephant) with high and truncate skull; massive tusks; short mandible; peculiar cheek tooth arrangement in which a single, high-crowned, lophodont tooth is exposed in each half of the jaw at any one time, and replacement occurs continually from behind; long proboscis; graviportal limbs and girdles; length of head and body to 640 cm (about 20 ft) (see PROBOSCIDEA).

Order Sirenia ("sea cows," dugongs, and manatees). Middle Eocene to Recent of Africa, Asia, North and South America. In living species: hindlimbs lacking, pelvis vestigial; front limbs modified into flippers; tail flattened, expanded; body fusiform, neck indistinct, anterior teeth reduced, replaced by horny plates used in cropping estuarine vegetation; molars of living dugongs bunodont, premolars lost; cheek teeth of manatees bilophodont, increased to 20 or more in each jaw, with 6 in each jaw at a given time and worn teeth replaced from behind as in modern proboscideans. Total length to 450 cm (15 ft) (see SIRENIA).

†*Order Desmostylia* (desmostylians). Known only as fossils from lower Miocene to lower Pliocene in shallow marine deposits of North Pacific Ocean. Skull massive, low, elongate; anterior teeth modified as tusks, 1 pair (canines) above, 2 pairs (canines and incisors) below; cheek teeth peculiar, cusps forming cylinders of enamel and replaced in a continual forward movement as in elephants and manatees; limbs and girdles massive; appearance perhaps superficially hippopotamus-like; total length to about 250 cm (about 8 ft).

†*Order Embrithopoda* (embrithopods). Known only from fossils from lower Oligocene of North Africa. Limbs 5-toed, progression graviportal; superficially rhinoceros-like, large paired horns on nasal bones and smaller horns on frontals (*i.e.*, behind the larger pair). Incisors not enlarged as in other subungulates; cheek teeth high-crowned; total length to about 330 cm (11 ft).

Order Hyracoidea (hyracoids). Lower Miocene to Recent of Africa and southwestern Asia. Most generalized of subungulates, although postorbital bar present and permanent denti-

tion reduced; last upper incisors and canine lost, forming diastema; remaining incisors rootless; molars high-crowned. Superficially rabbit- or rodent-like; herbivorous, living on rock slopes or semiarboreal. Total length of fossil species to about 200 cm (6.5 ft); living members 30 to 65 cm. Living examples: rock hyrax, tree hyrax.

†*Order Notoungulata* (notoungulates). Known only as fossils; upper Paleocene to Pleistocene of South America and Paleocene and Eocene of North America and Asia. Varied assemblage, united by dental peculiarities; accessory cusps in central valley of upper molars; lower molars with crescentric ridges, the entoconid lying within the arc of the larger posterior crescent; usually no diastema or reduction in dentition; cheek teeth tending to become rootless, high-crowned, lophodont. Tendency for reduction of toes from 5 to 3; total length approximately 30 to 300 cm (1 to 10 ft).

†*Order Astrapotheria* (astrapotheres). Known only as fossils; upper Paleocene to upper Miocene of South America. Upper incisors lost, canine enlarged, rootless; lower incisors and canine enlarged; diastema prominent; premolars reduced; molars greatly enlarged. Forelimbs stout, feet digitigrade, hind limbs relatively weakly developed, semiplantigrade. Skull truncate; position and character of nasal opening suggests presence of fleshy proboscis; absence of upper incisors suggests that heavy lower incisors may have opposed a modified upper lip to allow cropping of vegetation. Total length to about 280 cm (9 ft).

†*Order Litopterna* (litopterns). Known only as fossils; upper Paleocene to Pleistocene of South America. Hoofed herbivores with tendency toward reduced toes; from 5 to 3 or even 1. Dentition usually complete (or with some loss of incisors); no diastema; cheek teeth low-crowned, selenodont; tendency for molarization of premolars. Size to that of small horse.

Order Perissodactyla (perissodactyls). Lower Eocene to Recent; North America, Eurasia, Africa. Incisors variously modified, canines lost or specialized, diastema nearly always present, with loss of first premolars above and then below; molars primitively bunodont, becoming progressively more lophodont, hypsodont; molarization of premolars common at later stages. Hornlike projections on skull not uncommon. Trends toward lengthening of limbs, with limitation of motion to forward and backward. Feet mesaxonic (*i.e.*, with axis through toe III), reduction typically to 3 digits and later to a single digit; digits mostly hooved, but those of chalicotheres clawed. Range in body size from that of small dog (Eocene horses) to that of largest of known land mammals, *Baluchitherium*, an Oligocene rhinocerotid of Asia, nearly 600 cm (20 ft) in height at the shoulder. Examples: titanotheres, chalicotheres, tapirs, rhinoceroses, horses (see PERISSODACTYLA).

Order Artiodactyla (artiodactyls). Lower Eocene to Recent; worldwide except Australia. Dentition complete, bonodont (as in pigs) or variously reduced; incisors often reduced and upper incisors lost, vegetation cropped with lower incisors opposing gums of premaxilla; canine and first premolars frequently lost, forming prominent diastema; remaining premolars simple, not completely molariform; cheek teeth primitively low-crowned, bunodont, becoming hypsodont, selenodont (cusps expanding into crescents) in more advanced forms. Unguligrade, foot paraxonic (*i.e.*, the axis between digits III and IV); digit I lost first; digits II and V frequently rudimentary (dew claws), but more prominent in pigs and hippopotamuses; in advanced types metapodials III and IV fused to form cannon bone, adding extra functional joint to limb; astragalus distinctive, the articular surface a double pulley allowing efficient flexion and extension of hindlimb but precluding lateral movement. Parietal bones of skull reduced, frontal bones expanded, frequently bearing antlers or horns. Height at shoulder, 25 cm (10 in) in small antelope to 370 cm (about 12 ft) giraffe. Examples: pigs, cattle, sheep, goats, antelope, pronghorn, giraffe (see ARTIODACTYLA).

Critical appraisal. Three subclasses of Mammalia generally have been recognized for many years: Prototheria, the monotremes; Allotheria, the extinct multituberculates; and Theria, including marsupials and placentals as well as the extinct symmetrodonts and pantotheres. However, a number of Mesozoic groups could not be placed satisfactorily in any of these subclasses as defined. Recent evidence on the formation of the braincase in nontherian mammals has suggested that the primitive taxa may in fact constitute a more coherent group than was once supposed. All nontherian mammals are thus placed in a single subclass, Prototheria; infraordinal status is proposed for monotremes, triconodonts and symmetrodonts, and multituberculates.

Monotremes and multituberculates. Monotremes and multituberculates represent highly modified offshoots of the earliest mammalian stock. The fossil record of undoubted monotremes is limited to the Pleistocene. Surely the group is an ancient one and, although living representatives are highly specialized, represents the grade of evolution of the reptilian–mammalian transition. Their primitive organization is underscored in the relatively unspecialized brain, retention of the oviparous habit and a cloaca, incomplete homeothermy, and reptile-like frontal and pterygoid bones.

The multituberculates also were derived from the earliest mammalian stock. They were adapted early to a herbivorous diet and developed gnawing incisors and elongate, grinding cheek teeth. The fossil record of the multituberculates, from Upper Jurassic to lower Eocene, is longer than that for any other mammalian order. The extinction of multituberculates in the Early Cenozoic may have been due to competition from placental herbivores, in particular the early rodents.

Marsupials. The split between marsupials and placentals has yet to be identified with any certainty. *Pappotherium* of the Lower Cretaceous of Texas was thought for a time to represent a common ancestor of the therian infraclasses, but more recently it has been discovered that recognizable didelphoid marsupials were contemporaneous with the pappotheriids.

The earliest records of marsupials are from North America but the great adaptive radiation of this group occurred in South America and Australia. Mostly free of competition from placentals on Cenozoic island continents, marsupials converged in many cases with the specializations of placentals elsewhere. Australia has been isolated from other major land masses throughout the Cenozoic and South America was an island from Paleocene to Pliocene. Invasions by placentals in later Cenozoic times reduced the once flourishing South America marsupial fauna to the remnant extant today. The South American and Australian radiations were independent, although both assemblages had a common source in generalized didelphoid (opossum-like) groups and evolved in parallel fashion in a number of instances. In general, higher categories in the classification of marsupials are not coordinate with those of the Eutheria. Some families of marsupials, for example, encompass a range of diversity comparable to that in eutherian orders.

Drawing by R. Keane

Figure 5: Reconstruction of *Melanodon*, a shrew-sized insectivorous pantothere from the Upper Jurassic of North America.

Insectivores and colugos. Modern insectivores are divisible into several subgroups. The lipotyphlans include modern shrews, moles, and hedgehogs. The molars of hedgehogs are quadritubercular; those of shrews and moles are complicated by the development of a W-shaped external ridge or ectoloph. Lipotyphlans maintain the primitive insectivorous habits of their Mesozoic forebears. Zalambdodonts are represented by the peculiar selenodonts of the Greater Antilles, the tenrecs of Madagascar and West Africa, and the chrysochlorids—Cape golden moles—of southern Africa. The zalambdodonts may or may not represent a natural group. Their early history is obscure. All have V-shaped upper molars.

Tree shrews (tupaiids) of Southeast Asia are the sole survivors of a third insectivore group, sometimes called proteutherians, which includes a great variety of Late Cretaceous and Early Cenozoic mammals of uncertain relationships. Living tupaiids have frequently been classed as Primates, for they have remarkably advanced brains and versatile limbs. In such features as dentition, however, they remain quite primitive.

The macroscelids, or elephant shrews, are here treated as a separate order. They have frequently been grouped with tupaiids as a suborder of the Insectivora, or as a distinct Order Menotyphla. Colugos, the so-called flying lemurs, here maintained as a distinct order, Dermoptera, likewise have been considered by some authorities as insectivores.

Tillodonts and taeniodonts. The relationships of tillodonts and taeniodonts are obscure. Although apparently quite independent, both groups were evidently derived from primitive placental stocks, and both evolved rootless, rodent-like incisors. Neither group was ancestral to later, more successful mammalian types.

Bats. Bats are an ancient group; except for extensive skeletal and sensory modifications associated with flight they share many primitive characteristics with their insectivore ancestors. Bats first appear in the fossil record in the Eocene as highly adapted fliers. Were well-preserved postcranial (body and limb) remains of the earliest Cenozoic insectivores better known, some might well be found to represent intermediate stages in the evolution of flight; to date no such intermediate stages have been found. Many have thought that the Dermoptera might represent a grade through which the lineage of the bats must have passed in evolving truly volant habits; surely dermopterans and bats are not closely related, save in their retention of primitive characters of early placentals. In recent years research has brought to light important differences between the two suborders of bats, the Megachiroptera and the Microchiroptera, and some workers have suggested that the two groups be treated as separate orders, maintaining that the similarities between them are due to parallelism and convergence in adapting to the stringent demands of flight.

Primates. The Primates form a relatively coherent group, although the distinction between them and their insectivore ancestors is a difficult one and some groups, such as the tree shrews, can be placed in either order with nearly equal justification. Disagreement on classification within the order centres on the validity of the suborder Prosimii as a natural unit that includes such divergent kinds as tarsiers, lemurs, lorises, and galagos, and on the relationship between the Old World and New World monkeys. The two monkey groups may have evolved independently from prosimian ancestors; considerable convergence and parallelism no doubt are involved in the similarities between the two as both have radiated widely in response to available arboreal habitats.

Edentates and pangolins. The edentates have undergone their greatest radiation in South America. They are a highly aberrant group, of unknown ancestry, and apparently were isolated early in South America, as were the archaic South American ungulates. Edentates have commonly been subdivided into Loricata (armadillos and extinct glyptodonts), Pilosa (tree sloths and extinct ground sloths) and Vermilingua (anteaters). Each of these subgroups has had a long and independent history, but they share the unique character of xenarthrous vertebrae. The palaeanodonts of the Eocene and Oligocene of North America have been considered as nonxenarthrous edentates (a view presented in EDENTATA); they are here allocated to the order Pholidota. Little is known of the relationships of pholidotes (pangolins), once considered relatives of the Edentata; the groups are now rather generally conceded to be convergent.

Aardvarks. Aardvarks (Tubulidentata) also were thought at one time to be related to true edentates, but are now considered an independent lineage. Although they are known from Miocene deposits, no direct evidence exists of relationships with other groups. In some respects the skeleton resembles that of certain early condylarths, and it seems probable that tubulidentates descended from an early ungulate stock.

Lagomorphs. The Lagomorpha long were included (as a suborder Duplicidentata) in the Rodentia on the basis of dental similarities. Although ordinal rank for the

Lagomorpha has been firmly established, some recent classifications still include rodents and lagomorphs together in a cohort Glires, again based on dental similarities, which almost certainly represent convergence. Various other mammalian lineages of diverse affinities (multituberculates, taeniodonts, tillodonts, and certain primates, for example) have "experimented" with gnawing incisors. The earliest known fossil lagomorphs clearly represent the group and yield no clues as to origin. On the basis of serology and some dental characters, a relationship to ungulates through the condylarths has been suggested. More than likely, however, those characters held in common are primitive and lagomorphs arose directly from a primitive insectivore stock.

Rodents. In terms of numbers of individuals and numbers and diversity of species, the rodents are the most successful of living mammals and have evidently been so throughout much of the middle and later Cenozoic. The earliest known rodents (paramyids), of Paleocene age, were already highly specialized mammals. Fossil evidence indicating relationships with more primitive groups is lacking; rodents may have been derived directly from a basal eutherian stock.

The higher classification of rodents has been in a state of flux in recent years. Three suborders (Sciuromorpha, Myomorpha, and Hystricomorpha) were recognized based on the relationship of the zygomasseteric musculature to the infraorbital foramen. The sciuromorphs, or Protrogomorpha, included the earliest known rodents and also modern squirrels, beavers, and sewellels or "mountain beavers." In these taxa the masseter muscle originates from the anterior portion of the zygomatic arch or from the side of the skull in front of the orbit. The infraorbital canal is small, carrying nerves and blood vessels as in primitive mammals. In the Myomorpha, the rats and mice and their allies, the deep portion of the masseter muscle passes through the enlarged infraorbital canal. The so-called hystricomorphs, including Old World porcupines and a great variety of South American rodents, have a greatly enlarged and round infraorbital foramen, rather than a slitlike one like that of myomorphs.

Recent authors have doubted the validity of this arrangement and the utility of the infraorbital canal and zygomasseteric structure as a diagnostic feature. Many would admit the general validity of the Sciuromorpha and Myomorpha although some groups traditionally included would be reallocated. The "Hystricomorpha," on the other hand, is almost unanimously considered to be polyphyletic, and is now commonly subdivided into Caviomorpha for the complex South American "hystricomorph" radiation, and Hystricomorpha for Old World porcupines and their allies. The tendency has generally been to de-emphasize the use of subordinal classification and instead to bring together related families into a number of superfamilies. Perfection of the higher classification of rodents is difficult because fossil evidence is meager for some groups, particularly those of small or modest size, and because the successful radiation of the Rodentia has obviously led to perplexing convergence in numerous lines.

Creodonts. Creodonts were derived from the basic insectivore radiation as early carnivorous mammals, largely in response to the ecological opportunity presented by the evolution of herbivorous types.

Carnivores. True carnivores evidently are not descendants of the creodonts, but direct derivatives of Paleocene insectivores. The diversification of fissiped (terrestrial) carnivores from the basal stock (family Miacidae) occurred in the upper Eocene and lower Miocene, early dividing into arctoid or canoid (canids, ursids, procyonids, mustelids) and aeluroid or feloid (felids, hyaenids, viverrids) lines. The Pinnipedia (seals, sea lions, walruses) are here considered a suborder of the Carnivora. Appearing in the fossil record in the Miocene, the modern pinniped families already were distinct. The previous history of the group is obscure, but pinnipeds apparently were derived from arctoid fissipeds, although some have thought them to have been derived from creodonts. Some authorities have treated pinnipeds as a

distinct order, in which case they represent the most recently evolved mammalian order.

Whales. The whales and their allies have traditionally been treated as a single order, Cetacea, a reasonable arrangement on the basis of certain criteria. It is obvious, however, that cetaceans diverged early into archaeocetes, odontocetes, and mysticetes, if, indeed, the groups had a common ancestry. The earliest known fossils are perfectly good whales and clearly are assignable to one of the three groups; thus there is no concrete evidence linking the three nor is there evidence as to their ancestry. The morphological characters that whales share can be interpreted as due to parallelism resulting from stringent selection in similar habitats, or to the retention of primitive placental characteristics. Until evidence is available to establish the monophyly of cetaceans it seems preferable to treat them as representing three separate orders.

Ungulates. The term "ungulate" denotes a broad, loose association of orders including most large herbivorous mammals. The name of the group implies that its members are hoofed, but some of the ungulates (chalicotheres, for example) had clawed digits and others (such as sirenians) show considerable reduction of digits and limbs. The ungulates may be of common ancestry or may be a product of convergence from several sources among primitive placental stocks. Certain supposed early ungulates (condylarths) and early carnivorous mammals (creodonts) have many characters in common; their supposed descendants frequently have been united in a common cohort, Ferungulata.

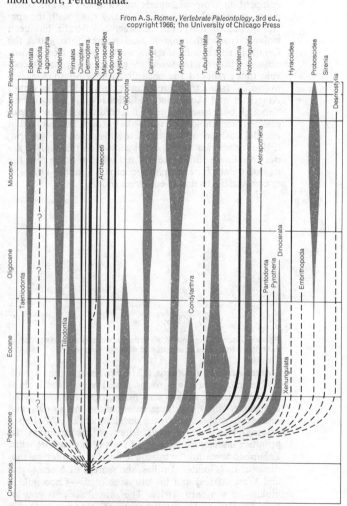

From A.S. Romer, *Vertebrate Paleontology,* 3rd ed., copyright 1966; the University of Chicago Press

Figure 6: Dendrogram of the placental mammals.

The principal characteristics shared by ungulates are those of the dentition and limbs, related to modification of the primitive placental into an efficient herbivore. There has been a tendency toward elongation of individual molar cusps to form crescentric ridges (selenodonty)

or to form ridges between adjacent cusps (lophodonty). A concomitant trend has been an increase in the height of molars from low-crowned (brachyodont) to high-crowned (hypsodont), which has allowed the efficient utilization of abrasive forage such as grass. The extent of the grinding surface has been increased by increasing the length of the molars or by "molarization" of premolars.

The radiation of large herbivores was accompanied closely by a radiation of large carnivores. The adaptive response of ungulates to predation has been varied: modified dentition (tusks), skeletal elements (horns, antlers), and behaviour have been turned to defensive purposes. Extremely large size or swift, cursorial locomotion were at a premium. Defensive gregariousness is common in extant species.

The general trend in mammalian locomotion has been plantigrade to digitigrade to unguligrade, frequently with reduction of digits. One mode of digit reduction has been mesaxonic, the axis of the foot passing through digit III (as in horses); other groups have paraxonic limbs, with the axis lying between digits III and IV. Elongation of metapodials has occurred commonly, forming a third functional segment of the limb, allowing fast cursorial gaits.

Exceptions to these trends in limb modifications occur in lineages with early trends toward extremely large size. In such groups, columnar, graviportal limbs have developed with proximal segments (femur, humerus) emphasized and metapodials de-emphasized; all digits usually are retained.

The ungulate radiation has been complex. Various subdivisions have been proposed. The condylarths may or may not be basal to the entire radiation, but they evidently gave rise to the perissodactyls.

Perissodactyls. This is a compact order, consisting of five subdivisions: horses, chalicotheres, titanotheres, rhinoceroses, and tapiroids. The history of the perissodactyls is perhaps better known than that of any other mammalian group. *Hyracotherium* ("*Eohippus*"), usually considered the base of the horse lineage, was probably near the source of the entire order.

Artiodactyls. The Artiodactyla first appear in the early Eocene. Dental characters point to an origin for the group among hypsodontid condylarths but the earliest known artiodactyls already had the unique and specialized "double-pulley" astragalus. Knowledge of transitional stages between condylarthran and artiodactyl tarsi would be of considerable interest and importance.

Archaic ungulates. A number of kinds of archaic ungulates, which generally evolved in the Western Hemisphere, have been lumped in the past in a single order, Amblypoda. Each of these groups—pantodonts, uintatheres (Dinocerata), pyrotheres, xenungulates—is here accorded ordinal rank. The relationships of these groups—if any—are obscure and their origin is unknown.

Litopterns. The Litopterna of South America were early derivatives of the condylarths, and some workers would include both in a single order. One family (Prototheriidae) closely paralleled the contemporaneous radiation of perissodactyls on the northern continents, but the macrauchenids converged toward the camels.

Notoungulates. The order Notoungulata was an early and varied assemblage, apparently restricted to South America in the Eocene, perhaps by competition with early members of more advanced ungulate groups. The greatest development of the order was in the Oligocene, after which there was a gradual decline, hastened by the entry into South America of placental carnivores and modern artiodactyls. The origin and affinities of the notoungulates are unknown, but the order may well have descended from the condylarths.

Astrapotheres. Astrapotheres were once considered to have been notoungulates. It is now generally conceded that their peculiarities recommend recognition as a separate order. This group may have had its origin among primitive notoungulates, or it may have arisen independently.

Hyracoids. The products of the early Cenozoic radiation of ungulates in Africa are commonly grouped as "subungulates." The Hyracoidea is the most generalized of these orders but the true relationships of the hyracoids to other ungulates are unknown. In common with other subungulate orders, hyracoids were more diverse in the Middle Cenozoic than they are today.

Embrithopods. The extinct Order Embrithopoda contains a single known genus, *Arsinoitherium*. Relationship with hyracoids has been suggested but concrete evidence is lacking. Aside from logical association with other subungulate groups, little can be said of the position or affinities of the Embrithopoda.

Elephants and allies. The best known of the subungulates are the Proboscidea. The later record of the order is relatively good and indicates a remarkably successful and widespread radiation in the latter part of the Cenozoic—a radiation characterized by the recurrence of several trends in separate lines. Among these trends were an emphasis on the development of the upper tusk with loss of the lower tusk in most groups, increase in the size of the skull and shortening of the neck, increase in the length of the proboscis, increase in overall size, with perfection of graviportal limbs and girdles, lengthening of the lower jaw (secondarily shortened in some groups), and reduction and specialization of cheek teeth.

Sirenians. The origin of the Sirenia is obscure. The earliest known sirenians were completely aquatic although the pelvic girdle was not so much reduced as in later forms. Dental and cranial peculiarities suggest that proboscideans and sirenians may have arisen from a common swamp-dwelling or amphibious ancestor. Concrete evidence is generally lacking regarding this and other relationships among subungulates due to a paucity of fossiliferous continental sediments of early Cenozoic age in Africa.

Desmostylians. Because of dental peculiarities and their association with shallow-water marine sediments, fossil remains of the order Desmostylia were long thought to represent aberrant sirenians; recent discoveries of massive limb bones of these mammals indicate, however, that they had quite different adaptations. The nature of the cheek teeth and their mode of replacement suggests relationships with the largely African subungulates, although desmostylians are known only from fossil deposits along the shores of the North Pacific.

BIBLIOGRAPHY. The literature on the biology of mammals is vast. The following list includes only a sample of available sources, with emphasis on those in the English language. Standard general references on the mammals are: F.E. BEDDARD, *Mammalia* (1902); W.H. FLOWER and R. LYDEKKER, *An Introduction to the Study of Mammals, Living and Extinct* (1891); and J.Z. YOUNG, *The Life of Mammals* (1957).

Less technical accounts include: F. BOURLIÈRE, *Vie et moeurs des mammifères* (1951; Eng. trans., *The Natural History of Mammals*, 1954); and L.H. MATTHEWS, *The Life of Mammals* (1970). Widely used textbooks in mammalogy are: E.L. COCKRUM, *Introduction to Mammalogy* (1962); and D.E. DAVIS and F.B. GOLLEY, *Principles in Mammalogy* (1963). The only thorough up-to-date treatment in English of the families of living mammals is S. ANDERSON and J.K. JONES, JR., (eds.), *Recent Mammals of the World: A Synopsis of Families* (1967). E.P. WALKER et al., *Mammals of the World*, 3 vol. (1964), is a semitechnical work including illustrations of representatives of most living genera; the third volume is a classified bibliography. Perhaps the most comprehensive reference on the biology of mammals is P.P. GRASSE (ed.), *Traité de zoologie*, vol. 16–17 (1967–68, 1955).

The morphology and classification of early mammals is reviewed by J.A. HOPSON and A.W. CROMPTON, "Origin of Mammals," *Evolutionary Biol.*, 3:15–72 (1969); and J.A. HOPSON, "The Classification of Nontherian Mammals," *J. Mammal.*, 51:1–9 (1970). A standard reference on the classification of mammals is G.G. SIMPSON, "The Principles of Classification and a Classification of the Mammals," *Bull. Am. Mus. Nat. Hist.*, 85:1–350 (1945); the evolution of major mammalian groups is treated by A.S. ROMER in *Vertebrate Paleontology*, 3rd ed. (1966), and *Notes and Comments on Vertebrate Paleontology* (1968).

Basic references on the status of endangered species of mammals are: F. HARPER, *Extinct and Vanishing Mammals of the Old World* (1945); and G.M. ALLEN, *Extinct and Vanishing Mammals of the Western Hemisphere with the Marine Species of All the Oceans* (1942).

Recent summaries of specialized topics in mammalogy include: H.T. ANDERSEN (ed.), *The Biology of Marine Mammals* (1969); S.A. ASDELL., *Patterns of Mammalian Reproduction,* 2nd ed. (1964); L.S. CRANDALL, *The Management of Wild Mammals in Captivity* (1964); R.F. EWER, *Ethology of Mammals* (1968); C.P. LYMAN and A.R. DAWE (eds.), *Mammalian Hibernation* (1960); W.V. MAYER and R.G. VAN GELDER (eds.), *Physiological Mammalogy,* 2 vol. (1963–64); A.G. SEARLE, *Comparative Genetics of Coat Colour in Mammals* (1968).

Some widely known journals that publish papers dealing exclusively with mammals are: *Journal of Mammalogy, Mammalia,* and *Säugetierkundliche Mitteilungen* (all issued quarterly), and *Zeitschrift für Säugetierkunde* (6/yr.). Additional technical literature is published by university and public museums and government agencies. Semitechnical and popular accounts of mammals appear in a wide variety of publications of state game departments, museums, and zoological gardens.

(J.K.J./D.M.A.)

Mammary Glands, Human

The mammary glands, a distinguishing feature of mammals, are milk-producing organs contained within the breasts. The human female breasts, important in human biology not only for their milk production, but also for their aesthetic and erotic role, are especially prone to pathological changes that are potentially lethal. In the male the mammary glands normally remain rudimentary and are less subject to pathological change.

Anatomy and physiology. *Development.* Mammary glands are derived from a modification of sweat glands. They first appear in the sixth week of fetal life as clumps of cells proliferating from a longitudinal ridge of ectoderm (the outermost of the three germ layers of the embryo) along the "milk line," from the buds, or beginnings, of the lower limbs to those of the upper limbs. The number of these clumps that ultimately become breasts, or mammae, varies with each mammalian species according to the size of its litter. In the human normally only one develops on each side of the chest. A lesser development of one or more breasts (polymastia) or nipples (polythelia) may, however, occur anywhere along the milk line. By the end of fetal life these cells are recognizable as the primitive ductal epithelium from which the future milk-bearing ducts and secretory sacs, or acini, will grow.

Anatomy of the mature breast. The mammary gland of a woman who has not borne children consists of a conical disk of glandular tissue 10–12 centimetres in diameter, 3–5 centimetres in thickness and weighing 150–200 grams. During lactation the gland weighs 400–500 grams. It is encased in variable quantities of fat that give it its characteristic shape. The glandular tissue itself is made up of 15–20 lobes composed of solid cords of ductal cells; each lobe is subdivided into many smaller lobules, separated by broad fibrous suspensory bands (Cooper's ligaments), which connect the skin with the fascia, or sheet of connective tissue, that covers the pectoral muscles which lie beneath the breast. Each lobe is drained by a separate excretory duct. These converge beneath the nipple, where they widen into milk reservoirs, before narrowing again to merge as pinpoint openings at the summit of the nipple. Circular and radiating muscles in the areola, a circular disk of roughened pigmented skin surrounding the nipple, cause the nipple to become firm and erect upon tactile stimulation; this facilitates suckling. The areola also contains sebaceous glands to provide lubrication for the nipple during nursing.

Blood is supplied to the breast through the axillary, intercostal, and internal thoracic vessels. The nerve supply is from branches of the fourth, fifth, and sixth intercostal nerves.

Hormonal relationships. Under the primary influence of estrogens from the maturing ovary at puberty, the ductal cells proliferate and form branches. After ovulation, progesterone from the corpus luteum, an organ that develops in the ovary each time an ovum has been shed and has the function of preparing the uterus for receiving the developing embryo, causes the terminal ductal cells to differentiate into the milk-producing cells, which form acini. Interspersed with these cells are smooth muscle

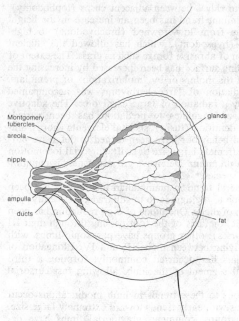

Lactating female breast.
From C. Smout, F. Jacoby, and E. Lillie, *Gynecological and Obstetrical Anatomy;* H.K. Lewis and Co., Ltd., London

cells, which can contract and assist in the ejection of milk. The acini are collapsed or filled with desquamated epithelium (epithelium that has been shed), until the stimulus of pregnancy causes proliferation of all the epithelial cells. The breast becomes enlarged, tense, and sensitive, and the areola widened and more deeply pigmented. The actual secretion of milk is induced by hormones—prolactin from the pituitary and somatomammotropin from the placenta. At the end of lactation the mammary glands and areolae return almost but not completely to their state before pregnancy (see also LACTATION, HUMAN). After the menopause the glands atrophy and are largely replaced by connective tissue and fat.

Diseases of the breast. The occurrence of supernumerary breasts and nipples has been mentioned. Absence of one or both breasts occurs, but rarely. Inequality in size is frequent, the left breast being larger more often than the right. Variations in size and shape are commonly of racial or genetic origin, but may be induced by a tight brassiere or by manipulation to cause elongation for the greater convenience of nursing an infant carried on the back.

Painful breasts may occur whenever estrogens are present in large amounts, as at puberty, during pregnancy, prior to menstruation, or after administration of the estrogens.

Fibrocystic disease, also called chronic cystic mastitis, may result in later reproductive life from the cumulative effect of the ebb and flow of endocrine stimulation with each menstrual cycle; this produces nodular fibrosis—or lumps of fibrous tissue—and cysts of various size. The condition can usually be distinguished from cancer because it is intermittently painful and tends to subside after menstrual periods. It may predispose to carcinoma, however. Early biopsy is indicated for any nodules that persist.

Precocious breast development may occur as a result of lesions in the pituitary-hypothalamic area that cause premature release of gonadotropins, or as a result of congenital anomalies of the ovaries with the autonomous production of estrogens.

Gynecomastia, or enlargement of the breast in the male, occurs whenever estrogens are present in excess. This may be physiological, during the height of male hormone production in adolescence; pathological from failure of estrogen removal by the liver, as in cirrhosis; or the result of medical treatment, as when estrogens are administered for the treatment of carcinoma of the prostate, or after the use of certain drugs such as digitalis and spironolactone. Gynecomastia occurring spontaneously in the adult male

Breast enlargement in male

suggests the existence of an estrogen-secreting tumour of the adrenal gland or testis, or of a gonadotropin-producing choriocarcinoma. Such tumours are highly malignant, and early removal is imperative. Gynecomastia may also be an indication of a sex chromatin abnormality in which an apparent male is genetically a female (Klinefelter's syndrome).

The only common infectious disease unique to the breast is acute mastitis, which occurs during lactation as the result of an invasion of pyogenic skin organisms through the nipple. The severe local inflammation, with high fever and prostration, responds promptly to antibiotics, usually without suppuration. Mastitis is ordinarily prevented by proper hygiene.

Benign
tumours;
carcinoma

Benign tumours include fibroadenoma, more common in women under 30, and intraductal papilloma, which may cause bleeding from the nipple. These tumours should be removed. Malignant tumours may arise from any of the cell types contained in the breast, but sarcomas make up only 3 percent of all breast tumours.

Carcinoma of the female breast is the commonest form of malignant tumour in the western civilized world, afflicting about 4 percent of all adult women, approximately half of whom will succumb to it. For reasons not yet clear it is less prevalent in Oriental countries. Rare under the age of 25, it increases in incidence up to the menopause, and then levels off. Hereditary factors play a role, but their exact importance has not been clearly established. The disease is more common in childless women with a late menopause, suggesting that it may be related to the total duration of ovarian activity. It is known that estrogens will stimulate the growth of mammary cancer, but there is no evidence that they will initiate it. These hormones should not be administered to women with fibrocystic disease or a family history of mammary cancer. Only 1 percent of the cases of carcinoma of the breast occur in males.

Cancer affecting the inner part of the breast is more difficult to deal with than cancer nearer the surface because of the course of the lymph channels. Lymph from the inner half of the breast drains directly through the chest wall to the internal mammary lymph nodes beneath the sternum, where metastases quickly become inaccessible. The outer half is drained by way of the pectoral, axillary, and supraclavicular nodes, where metastases can be fairly readily palpated and occasionally successfully removed.

Breast carcinoma arises more often in the ductal than the acinar cells, but may have several independent points of origin. Metastases are prone to occur early, sometimes when the original lesion is still microscopic in size, to the regional lymph nodes in the armpit or the area of the breastbone, depending upon the primary site. Further spread then occurs through the bloodstream to the skeleton, liver, lungs, brain, and generally throughout the body. Death results most commonly from destruction of the liver, less often from damage to the lungs or brain, or from hemorrhage.

An epidermoid type of carcinoma may occur in the nipple; this tumour, called Paget's disease of the nipple, may cause intermittent ulceration and bleeding.

Cancer is suspected when a painless lump in the breast is detected; the lump is firmer in consistency than the surrounding breast tissue and usually remains fixed when the overlying skin is retracted. Most lumps of this type are detected by the victims themselves as the result of self-examination, a practice that should be encouraged by gynecologists. Occasionally a bloody discharge from the nipple or retraction of the nipple will call attention to an underlying tumour.

Surgical removal of the breast before the tumour has extended beyond its primary site offers the only hope of a permanent cure. The chances of survival diminish rapidly in proportion to the distance from the origin at which lymph nodes have been invaded by tumour.

When distant metastases have become manifest, palliation may be achieved by local X-ray treatment, or by removal of the ovaries and the adrenal glands and by use of one of the chemicals that destroy cancer cells. Lesser benefit may be obtained by the administration of hormones like cortisone or testosterone, and in some elderly patients a paradoxical effect may follow large doses of estrogens.

BIBLIOGRAPHY. Additional information on this subject may be found in the following texts and journal articles: C.F.V. SMOUT, F. JACOBY, and E.W. LILLIE, *Gynaecological and Obstetrical Anatomy*, 4th ed., pp. 389–404 (1969); W.R. LYONS, C.H. LI, and R.E. JOHNSON, "Hormonal Control of Mammary Growth and Lactation," *Recent Progr. Hormone Res.*, 14:219–254 (1958); J.M.G. HARLEY, "The Endocrine Control of the Breasts," *Practitioner*, 203:153–157 (1969); H. INGLEBY and J. GERSHON-COHEN, *Comparative Anatomy: Pathology and Roentgenology of the Breast* (1960); R.L. EGAN, *Mammography* (1964); C.D. HAAGENSES, *Diseases of the Breast* (1956); K. EMERSON, JR., *Harrison's Principles of Internal Medicine*, pp. 568–573 (1970); "The First National Conference on Breast Cancer," *Cancer*, vol. 24 (1969).

(K.E.)

Ma'mūn, Al-

Al-Ma'mūn, the seventh 'Abbāsid caliph and the first to introduce elements of Greek and Hellenistic philosophy into Islām, is best remembered for his attempts to bring about a reconciliation between Shī'ites and Sunnites and to impose upon his subjects a more rationalist Muslim creed.

Early
years

The son of the celebrated caliph Hārūn ar-Rashīd and an Iranian concubine, al-Ma'mūn was born in 786, six months before his half brother al-Amīn, the son of a legitimate wife of Arab blood. When it became necessary for ar-Rashīd to choose an heir, he is said to have hesitated before deciding finally in favour of al-Amīn. In 802, on the occasion of a pilgrimage to Mecca, the Caliph formally announced the respective rights of the two brothers: al-Ma'mūn recognized al-Amīn as successor to the caliphate in Baghdad, but al-Amīn acknowledged his brother's almost absolute sovereignty over the eastern provinces of the empire, with his seat Merv in the Khorāsān.

Hārūn ar-Rashīd's death in March 809 nevertheless created discord that soon developed into armed conflict between the two brothers. Al-Ma'mūn, in effect stripped by al-Amīn of his rights to the succession, was supported by an Iranian, al-Faḍl ibn Sahl, whom he was to make his vizier, as well as by an Iranian general, Ṭāhir. Ṭāhir's victory over al-Amīn's army on the outskirts of the present Tehrān, allowed al-Ma'mūn's troops to occupy western Iran. Al-Amīn appealed in vain to new troops recruited in part from among the Arabs of Syria. He was finally besieged in Baghdad in April 812. There was desperate resistance, and the city was taken only in September 813. The Caliph, who had in the meantime been declared deposed in Iraq and Arabia, wished to surrender but was killed, contrary, it seems, to Al-Ma'mūn's orders. Thus ended one of the most merciless civil wars known to the Islāmic East. The war had originated in Hārūn ar-Rashīd's ill-advised decision, but it also revealed internal divisions in the 'Abbāsid empire. It was not merely a question of a personal rivalry between the two brothers—one of whom, al-Ma'mūn, was unquestionably of far superior intelligence—it was also a question of a clash between different politico-religious trends that had become apparent during the preceding reign, al-Amīn stressing traditionalism and Arab culture, while al-Ma'mūn, open to new movements of thought and outside influences, courted the support of Iranian figures and of the eastern provinces.

Al-Ma'mūn, having become caliph of the entire 'Abbāsid empire, decided to continue to reside at Merv, assisted by his faithful Iranian vizier al-Faḍl. It was then that al-Ma'mūn, determined to put an end to the division of the Islāmic world between Sunnites and Shī'ites—between the adherents of the 'Abbāsid caliphs, descendants of Muḥammad's uncle al-'Abbās, and the defenders of 'Alī, the prophet's cousin and son-in-law and his descendants—made a decision startling to his contemporaries and injurious to his own position. He designated as his heir not a member of his own family but 'Alī ar-Riḍā, a descendant of 'Alī. In an attempt visibly to reconcile the

Attempted
reconcilia-
tion
between
Sunnites
and
Shī'ites

two rival families, al-Ma'mūn gave 'Alī ar-Riḍā his own daughter as a wife. As a further symbol of reconciliation, he adopted the green flag in place of the traditional black flag of the 'Abbāsid family. But this spectacular measure did not achieve the anticipated result. It was not sufficient to pacify the Shī'ite extremists, while on the other hand it embittered the partisans of 'Abbāsid legitimism and of Sunnism, particularly in Iraq. In Baghdad, declaring al-Ma'mūn deposed, they proclaimed as the new caliph the 'Abbāsid prince Ibrāhīm, son of the third caliph, al-Mahdī. When news of this insurrection finally reached al-Ma'mūn, he abruptly decided to leave Merv for Baghdad. During the long journey, two dramatic events took place: the vizier al-Faḍl was assassinated in February 818; and 'Alī ar-Riḍā died in August of the same year after a brief illness that chroniclers ascribed to poisoning. Thus the man whose elevation to the position of heir presumptive had bedevilled the Caliph's rule as well as the vizier closely associated with that policy were eliminated. Notwithstanding his denials, historians have generally attributed the deaths to al-Ma'mūn.

During the following 15 years, al-Ma'mūn showed himself to be a judicious sovereign. He closely controlled his ministers and did not again appoint an all-powerful vizier. He also tried to maintain strict control over the provincial governors but was forced to allow a relative degree of autonomy to his former general, Ṭāhir, who had been named governor of Khorāsān.

Although al-Ma'mūn, on his arrival in Baghdad, abandoned his policy of reconciliation with the descendants of 'Alī, which he symbolized by reinstating the traditional black flag, he did not give up hope of attaining the same goal by a more circuitous path. He had already, at Merv, shown his sympathy for the representatives of the Mu'tazilite movement, those supporters of Islām who adopted rationalist methods and borrowed from the works of ancient Greek or Hellenistic philosophers the modes of reasoning that seemed them best suited for combatting the influence of such doctrines as Manichaeism (a dualistic religion founded in Iran). Al-Ma'mūn encouraged the translation of Greek philosophical and scientific works and founded an academy called the House of Wisdom (Bayt al-Ḥikmah) to which the translators, most often Christians, were attached. He also imported manuscripts of particularly important works that did not exist in the Islāmic countries from Byzantium. Developing an interest in the sciences as well, he established observatories at which Muslim scholars could verify the astronomic knowledge handed down from antiquity.

Not content with extending his patronage to the translators and scientific research, al-Ma'mūn imposed on all his subjects the Mu'tazilite doctrine, characterized by a purified concept of divinity, belief in free will, and full human responsibility. One of the most innovative aspects of this theodicy was the affirmation of the created and not eternal character of the Qur'ān, the word of God. Such a doctrine was likely to diminish the influence of the learned doctors, the interpreters of the sacred text, who found themselves defending 'Abbāsid legitimism; in addition, the doctrine demanded exceptional moral and religious qualities of the caliph, for it went so far as to authorize rebellion against a wicked sovereign. This tenet of the Mu'tazilite doctrine diverged from the traditional concept upon which the 'Abbāsid caliphs had based their authority, and many adherents of the doctrine manifested an avowed sympathy for Shī'ism. Al-Ma'mūn, attracted by the intellectual rigour of Mu'tazilism, also saw in it the means of encouraging public opinion to accept a new, more flexible conception of the caliphate. In fact, when he announced his adherence to the thesis of the "created Qur'ān" in 827, al-Ma'mūn also asserted the superiority of 'Alī over the other Companions of the Prophet. This position of al-Ma'mūn's manifested clear political implications.

At the beginning of 833 al-Ma'mūn decided to require adherence to Mu'tazilism from all his subjects. As the Caliph was then on an expedition against the Byzantines in the region of Tarsus, he entrusted this task to his representative in Baghdad, the prefect of police Isḥāq ibn Ibrāhīm. The latter first called together the qāḍīs (judges) to urge them to recognize the Mu'tazilite doctrine; then it was the turn of the specialists in Ḥadīth Muslim tradition; but among this group protestations were raised that the Caliph hoped to silence through the use of threats. Some resisted obstinately, refusing to pronounce the Qur'ān a "created" work. This was notably true of Aḥmad ibn Ḥanbal, the founder of the Ḥanbalite school of Islāmic law, who was to have been sent, under a heavy guard, before the Caliph, but was temporarily spared by the sudden death of al-Ma'mūn at Tarsus in August 833. This episode, called the trial (miḥnah) by the traditionalists, showed that one portion of the public opinion resisted the beliefs that al-Ma'mūn had wished to impose. The strength of this opposition serves to explain why the caliphs, a few decades later, abandoning their attempt at reorienting religious beliefs, returned to traditional dogma.

Possessed of a distinguished and sagacious mind, al-Ma'mūn set forth in the political domain very personal ideas that, in effect, ended in failure. He was never able to put an end to the divisions that were tearing the community apart; and the violence that he did not hesitate to employ at the end of his reign—to impose a doctrine he considered salutary for the Islāmic community—tarnished the image of an otherwise exceptionally openminded ruler.

BIBLIOGRAPHY. The only biography of the caliph al-Ma'mūn is found in the *Encyclopaedia of Islam*, 1st ed., vol. 3 (1936), although this article is now largely out of date. For the history of the dynasty, see the article "Abbasids," in the *Encyclopaedia of Islam*, 2nd ed., vol. 1 (1960); and also "The Abbassid Caliphate," in the *Cambridge History of Islam*, vol. 1 (1970). The problems of the relationship between al-Ma'mūn and Shī'ism are treated in F. GABRIELI, *Al-Ma'mun e gli'Alidi* (1929), which is now completed by D. SOURDEL, "La Politique religieuse du calife 'abbaside al Ma'mun" in *Revue des études islamiques*, 30:27–48 (1962).

(D.So.)

Man, Evolution of

From the point of view of the biologist, the problem of the evolutionary origin of man is only one of many problems of mammalian evolution, for, in his physical structure and physiological functions, man falls within the biologist's definition of a mammal and may be presumed to be the product of an evolutionary process similar to that which is now known from the fossil record to have occurred with other groups of mammals. At the time of the publication of Darwin's *Origin of Species* (1859), there was considerable opposition to the concept of evolution as a whole, mainly because so many people accepted the idea of the fixity and immutability of the species of animals and plants. In part, the opposition was due to the influence of the biblical story of the creation and to the fact that the hypothesis of adaptation through natural selection challenged the religious and philosophical "argument from design" for the existence of a divine intelligence. But opposition also arose because of the scientific evidence adduced by taxonomists that species are clearcut and sharply defined and usually do not interbreed with other species. In the main, the cumulative evidence advanced by Darwin and Alfred Russel Wallace, in England, and by others eventually compelled acceptance of the main hypothesis of organic evolution (see EVOLUTION). Nevertheless, general acceptance was certainly delayed by the circumstance that the hypothesis inevitably involved consideration of man's relationship to the lower animals; and the implied conclusion that if man is the product of an evolutionary process then he is not a unique and special creation dominated the minds of many anti-evolutionists for a long time to come. It is possible that some of the more bitter controversies in the early days of evolutionary discussion might have been avoided if a clear distinction had been made between what may be termed anatomical and physiological man (*i.e.*, the biological species *Homo sapiens*) and the concept of man in its wider philosophical context, for it is certain that misconceptions have arisen in the past and still arise from

Attempt to impose a rationalist form of Islām

Support of Western philosophy and science

time to time from the use and misuse of the colloquial terms man and human in the discussion of evolutionary origins.

This article is divided into the following sections:

I. Man's evolutionary relationships
    The living primates
    Fossil primates
    The Hominidae
    Homo sapiens in the fossil record
II. Evolutionary process in man
    Genetics and man
    Adaptation and genetic change
    Man's continuing evolution

I. Man's evolutionary relationships

THE LIVING PRIMATES

Taxonomic classification includes man as a member of the order Primates, which is a part of the class Mammalia. Within the Primates are included such divergent creatures as the Southeast Asian tarsiers, the Madagascan lemurs, the South American monkeys, the African monkeys, the great apes (gibbons, orangutans, chimpanzees, gorillas), and finally, man himself (see the Table). The primates that exist today comprise a remarkable gradational series that links *Homo* anatomically with small mammals of very primitive types (see PRIMATES). The most lowly representatives of the living primates are the tree shrews, small squirrel-like creatures that have a wide distribution in Southeast Asia. So primitive are the tree shrews that some authorities refuse to include them among the primates. But even these authorities would agree that tree shrews must at least be very closely related to the ancestral stock from which the primates in general have derived. In a number of their anatomical characters, the tree shrews show such a close resemblance to undoubted primates (*e.g.*, some of the lemurs) as to amount in certain details to an identity of structure. The lemurs in their more advanced anatomical structure show a mixture of characters that indicate an intermediate position between tree shrews and monkeys. The curious little tarsier (which inhabits Borneo, Sumatra, the Celebes, and the Philippines) is in some respects even more monkeylike. The various types of tailed monkeys represent a still higher grade of organization and through the gibbon, smallest of the apes, are linked with the larger tailless anthropoid apes, the chimpanzee, orangutan, and gorilla.

The manlike apes

As their name implies, the anthropoid apes are manlike in their anatomical structure. Their brains, although much smaller than a modern human brain, are relatively well developed as compared with lower primates and have the same patterns of convolutions as the human brain has (though in a simplified form); the similarities in many details of the intrinsic structure of the brain of the anthropoid ape are astonishingly precise. These anatomical resemblances in the brain have been found to be correlated with physiological similarities. Thus, the sensory and motor mechanisms fulfill functions so closely reproducing those of the human brain that for experimental studies anthropoid apes have been found to be far more reliable than any other nonhuman mammal in their application to problems of cerebral function in man. Many features of the skull and skeleton of the large apes approximate very closely to those of the Hominidae (the taxonomic family that includes living and fossil types of man), particularly if account is taken of certain extinct primitive hominids. Some of the structural similarities in the skeleton of the trunk and limbs are in part related to posture, for the chimpanzee and gorilla are capable, at times, of balancing themselves on their hindlimbs in a manner that suggests, albeit distantly, the erect posture characteristic of the Hominidae. In their dentition, particularly in the molar teeth, anthropoid apes also show a close resemblance to the Hominidae. Indeed, it is sometimes difficult to determine whether isolated fossil molar teeth belong to apes or hominids, for the distinctions that exist between the teeth of apes and those of man are in general far less obtrusive when fossil specimens are considered. Many of the muscles of the human body have the same disposition and attachments as those of the anthro-

The Classification of Man Within the Order Primates

			contained forms:
Order	Primates		prosimians, monkeys, apes, ape-men, and men
Suborder	Anthropoidea		monkeys, apes, ape-men, and men
Superfamily	Hominoidea		apes, ape-men, and men
Family	Hominidae		ape-men and men
Subfamily	Homininae		men
Genus	*Homo*		men
Species	*erectus*	*sapiens*	archaic and modern

poid apes. In the sole of the human foot, for example, are found the same muscles that are used for the mobile functions of the ape foot, even though in man the mobility is not present. The disposition of the abdominal organs in apes corresponds quite closely with that of man, and even in their microscopic details some of the organs of the body show a remarkable resemblance. These examples of anatomical and physiological similarities between the large anthropoid apes and the Hominidae could well be multiplied. Their implications for a real phylogenetic relationship are further supported by reference to similarities in serum-protein patterns, immunological responses, some of the blood groups, parasitic infestation, and susceptibility to certain diseases (see IMMUNITY; BLOOD GROUPS AND FACTORS).

Trends of primate evolutionary development. As diversified as the primates are in terms of appearance, ecological adaptations, and behaviour, through their common ancestry they share a number of distinctive characteristics. Fundamentally they have avoided extreme anatomical specializations and have, for the most part, preserved a generalized morphology, which confers on them a considerable degree of functional plasticity. The order can be defined on the basis of the prevailing trends that have dominated its evolutionary development: a generalized structure of the limbs with the replacement of sharp claws by flattened nails resulting in a grasping hand; the elaboration of the visual sense and a corresponding reduction in the sense of smell; and the progressive development of a large and complicated brain. In the Hominidae,

Primate generalized morphology

these same tendencies have manifested themselves and have progressed further than among other groups of primates. The Hominidae show also a unique specialization of the lower limb; the pelvis and leg have become adapted for support and bipedal propulsion of the body in the erect position, while the foot and toes have lost the prehensility characteristic of the primates in general.

In examining the development of the primates over a period of perhaps 70,000,000 years, the evolutionary trends that have emerged form a pattern of progressive adaptational changes largely related to arboreal life. Although a number of separate trends can be traced individually, they are largely grouped around several functional and behavioral centres. The very existence of evolutionary trends has been questioned, and some workers have suggested that they existed only in the mind of the paleontologist. But, if it is true that directed, straight-line, orthogenetic trends do not exist in nature, it is also true that within a single evolutionary lineage only certain types of variation can be accepted in a viable, reproductively successful population and that these variations, when observed in the context of geological time, will show up as evolutionary trends. While these trends in the primates are primarily related to increasing success in utilizing the arboreal environment, they have at the same time provided essential preadaptations for ground life in some primates and man.

Primate limb development

The first group of trends relates to the development of the limbs. Although some primates show a certain amount of specialization in their degree of adaptation to a specific niche, the primates have as a rule maintained a very generalized limb and hand structure. The basic pattern of pentadactylism (five digits on each hand and foot) of the early vertebrates has been retained, as have the fibula (one of two bones in the lower leg) and the radius (one of two bones in the lower arm), bones that are reduced to vestiges or are absent in some mammalian groups. The nonspecialized primate hands and feet are mobile and prehensile; the thumb and big toe remain flexible in most groups with true opposability of the thumb possible in some. Sharp claws have been replaced by flattened nails, which improve the use of the hand as a grasping instrument. The flexible, grasping hand of the primates allows use of the forelimb for nonlocomotor activities, including important primate activities such as grooming, one-handed feeding, and infant carriage. Freeing the hands from locomotion means that the body can be held upright, and this progressive development of an erect posture is another important trend in primate evolution.

A further major trend in primate evolution concerns the way in which primates perceive their environment. In most land mammals the sense of smell is the one most highly developed, as is demonstrated not only in the organization of the brain but in the more obvious development of the snout. In even the most primitive primates, however, the sense of smell has lost importance, and the visual sense has become paramount. Stereoscopic vision has been achieved by moving the eyes from the sides of the head to the front of the face, thereby allowing the visual fields to overlap and producing the ability to perceive in depth. Anatomically these changes are easy to trace in the fossil record. The importance of the eyes is demonstrated by the additional protection of a bony bar or a bony partition at the side of the head, resulting in a completely enclosed bony socket (the orbit) for the eye. This complete enclosure is absent in the closely related insectivores and in some of the most primitive living primates. The loss of importance of the olfactory sense and hence the diminution of the nose is demonstrated in the increasing orthognathism (straightness of the face) seen in the evolutionary line leading to man. The dentition has remained nonspecialized, and the occlusal (closing or biting) pattern of the molars is a simple arrangement of four or five small pointed projections (cusps). The primate dentition is composed of four distinct types of teeth: incisors (the front teeth), canines (the eyeteeth), premolars, and molars (the chewing teeth). While some groups may show specializations of

certain tooth groups (an incisor "comb" in the lemurs and enlarged canines in the baboons, for example), no group demonstrates pronounced specializations involving the entire dentition as is commonly seen in other groups of mammals.

Evolutionary trends of primate behaviour. Evolutionary trends involving behaviour are obviously difficult if not impossible to document, but observations on living primate groups suggest that certain behavioral responses are more appropriate than others to the primate way of life. From such observations workers have extrapolated that certain behavioral patterns have arisen during the course of primate evolution. Virtually all living primates demonstrate a social hierarchical structure that enables them to live together in social groups of variable composition. This social structure allows, indeed demands, prolongation of infant dependency and thereby intensifies the mother–offspring relationship. It is within the primate social structure that the roots of human behaviour are to be found.

The primate brain

Underlying and reinforcing all of these trends is the crucial development, both qualitatively and quantitatively, of the brain. The size of the brain has, during primate evolution, increased in absolute size and in size relative to body weight. That it has also increased in complexity is demonstrated by the deeper and more varied convolutions on its surface. Those areas of the brain concerned with vision, muscular coordination, memory, learning, and communication have especially shown development.

As varied as these trends may seem, none developed in isolation from the others. They form a tightly interlocking feedback system whereby advances in one area will be reinforced by and in turn necessitate changes in another area. For example, in the development of a successful adaptation to an arboreal environment, the ability to see well and to see in depth was obviously more crucial than the ability to smell acutely. The grasping hand with flat nails instead of claws is an important advantage when moving rapidly through the trees. A superior brain, stereoscopic vision, and a supremely flexible hand, along with a tendency for upright posture, were the important preadaptations (adaptations to one set of conditions that later proved to be useful or helpful under different conditions) that the ancestors of man carried with them when they left the trees for the savanna.

FOSSIL PRIMATES

Paleontology, or the study of fossils, provides the really crucial evidence concerning the evolution of the Hominidae in the past. However extensive and compelling it may be, the evidence for evolution based on the study of creatures living today can be only indirect. Further evidence of evolutionary change can be seen in the persistence of certain anatomical structures such as the vermiform appendix, which remains only as a vestige and appears to have reduced functional significance. Direct evidence of evolution must depend on actual demonstration from the fossil record of a succession of stages representing the transformation of an ancestral into a descendant type. The comparative anatomy of living forms, together with the geographical distribution of local species and varieties that exist today, suggests that evolution might have occurred. Study of the process of natural selection, experimental genetics, population statistics, and so forth establishes quite clearly how evolution could have occurred. But that evolution did occur can be scientifically established only by fossilized representative samples of those intermediate types that have been postulated on the basis of indirect evidence. The field of paleontology that is related to the study of the origin of man is called paleoanthropology. It is concerned not only with fossilized early representatives of the Hominidae and extinct primates from which this family may have been derived but also with relics of the cultural activities of ancient man and the nature of the environment in which he lived. In this article, however, attention will be confined almost entirely to the evidence of skeletal remains. Broadly speaking, the main features of the evolutionary succession of the primates are now known from the fossil rec-

Paleoanthropology

ord, and they conform in a remarkable way with inferences already reached by a consideration of living primates.

Primate development in the Early Tertiary Period. At the beginning of the geological phase now called the Tertiary Period—about 65,000,000 years ago—there were in existence the most primitive of the primates. So primitive are their anatomical characters as shown by fossils that it might be impossible to determine that they were primates but for the fact that they mark a gradation toward more highly organized creatures that definitely come within the category of primates.

The climate of the Early Tertiary Period was warm, with wide tropical and subtropical zones extending from the Equator up to the higher latitudes in both the Old and the New World. During the Paleocene Epoch, which lasted for about 11,000,000 years (c. 65,000,000–c. 54,000,000 BP [before present]), there were many primates in existence; 60 genera have been recognized and grouped into eight families. Three of these families had long chisel-shaped teeth that resembled those of the rodents with which they competed for a similar ecological niche, or habitat. It is likely that this confrontation was won by the rodents, for all of the early primate families with rodent-like teeth became extinct. It is possible that this early rodent competition was one of the factors that led the primates to occupy an arboreal habitat, but a number of groups of primates, such as the baboons, the great apes, and the hominids, later returned to the ground during the evolution of the primate order.

Early in the Tertiary Period, during the Paleocene and Eocene epochs (from about 65,000,000 to about 38,-000,000 years ago), more advanced primates appeared that belong to the same zoological groups as the modern lemurs and tarsiers. The Lemuriformes are represented in the fossil record by a widespread family, the Adapidae, divided into two subfamilies, the Adapinae and the Notharctinae. The Tarsiiformes are known from two families, the Anaptomorphidae and the Omomyidae. It would appear that the characteristic tarsioid (tarsier-like) specialization of the skull and hindlimb were already well advanced in the fossil forms that are known, but some of the European genera have some structures that indicate relationships with the early monkeys. Generally speaking, however, little is known of the Eocene ancestors of the Old World monkeys and apes; thus the Eocene Epoch terminated after about 30,000,000 years of primate evolution with lemur-like forms and tarsier-like forms but little or no evidence of anything else.

Later, in the Oligocene Epoch (38,000,000–26,000,000 BP), which followed, there came into existence primitive monkeys and exceedingly primitive anthropoid apes. Excavations into the Fayum deposits of Egypt, of Oligocene age, have disclosed a deltaic shoreline bounded by tropical bush country that supported an extensive fauna including rodents, hyraxes, pigs, small elephants, and primates. One of the earliest fossil primates from the Fayum is *Parapithecus*, known from some lower jaws; *Apidium*, which is included in the same family, the Parapithecidae, is also found there. These may be the forerunners of African monkeys, and *Apidium* in particular may be ancestral to *Oreopithecus*, a gibbon-like form from the Pliocene Epoch (c. 7,000,000–2,500,000 BP). Also derived from the Egyptian Oligocene are several fossil apes of primitive type; these include *Aeolopithecus*, which may be an ancestral gibbon, and *Aegyptopithecus*, which may be ancestral to the modern great apes. One other fossil ape from the Fayum that deserves special mention is *Propliopithecus*, formerly believed to be an ancestral gibbon. It has recently been suggested, primarily on the basis of its generalized dentition, that *Propliopithecus* is possibly ancestral to the hominids. This, however, is a speculation that requires much more evidence before it can be generally accepted.

Primate development in the Miocene Epoch. The Miocene Epoch began about 26,000,000 years ago and lasted about 19,000,000 years. It was a remarkable phase in primate evolution in which there appears to have been an increase in the numbers of larger primates that were

Early Tertiary primates

widely spread throughout the Old World, including Europe, Asia, and Africa. The large number of specimens recovered from widely separated sites over a long period of time has led to taxonomic confusion, and over 50 species have been described and classified in 20 genera. Recently this number has been considerably reduced by an overdue taxonomic revision. The first large Miocene ape found was named *Dryopithecus fontani* (the "oak ape"); it was recovered in 1856 from French middle Miocene deposits. This early ape was characterized by a special arrangement of the cusp and fissure pattern of the molar teeth, the so-called dryopithecine Y-5 arrangement. *Dryopithecus* has also given rise to the name of the subfamily that includes other Miocene specimens, the subfamily Dryopithecinae. A large group of these Miocene fossil apes is known from East Africa, where they have been found in deposits that accumulated as a result of the volcanic activity associated with the formation of the East African Rift Valley.

The primitive characters of many of the Miocene apes are particularly relevant to the problem of the origin of the Hominidae. It has been seriously argued that hominids could hardly have an anthropoid-ape (pongid) ancestry because anthropoid apes are too specialized in limb structure and limb proportions—all living anthropoid apes have quite long arms and short legs. But there is a fallacy in the assumption that extinct anthropoid apes of earlier times must have shown the same degree of structural specialization as do the living apes, which are end products of the pongid sequence of evolution, today represented by the gorilla, chimpanzee, and orangutan. The structural specialization of the pongids was certainly not always present. Indeed, on the purely morphological evidence there is no improbability in the thesis that one of the known genera of the Miocene apes may represent the common ancestral stock that gave rise, by different and contrasting kinds of adaptive modifications, to the divergent evolutionary sequences of the Pongidae (the anthropoid apes) and Hominidae. It has been proposed, and by some even taken for granted, that pongid features such as sharp, overlapping canines and certain quite minor features of the molars and premolars constitute specializations that bar these early apes from consideration as ancestors of the Hominidae. But this is to make demonstrably untrue assumptions on the irreversibility of evolution. In genetic studies it has been shown that single mutations can be reversible in direction, and in phylogenetic studies there are many examples of what may be called negative reversals (i.e., the retrocession of characters previously well developed). There are strong morphological reasons for inferring that the hominid characters of the canines and premolars have been secondarily derived from those of the pongid type.

It may be noted that paleontologists frequently need to consider whether certain extinct types had already attained such a degree of structural specialization that they should be regarded as divergent or aberrant groups with no ancestral relationship to modern types. The answer must depend on the assessment of the total morphological pattern in terms of its probable genetic constitution and the probable complexity of the selective influences that have determined its initial evolutionary development; the degree to which morphological changes have committed the group to a mode of life that has restricted the opportunities for selection in other evolutionary directions must also be gauged.

Ape–Hominidae relation-ships

THE HOMINIDAE

Ramapithecus. Exactly when the Hominidae, as a separate and independent line of evolution, became segregated from the anthropoid-ape family (Pongidae) is not certainly known; indeed, it is still the most serious gap in the fossil record of the Hominidae (q.v.). The reappraisal in 1961 of a fragment of upper jaw (*Ramapithecus*) from the Miocene–Pliocene deposits of the Siwalik Hills of India has led to the suggestion, however, that the rounded dental arcade and the short face of *Ramapithecus* could allow its inclusion in the family Hominidae, an idea originally put forward in 1934 but ignored at that time.

The earliest hominid

Later a second upper jaw and several pieces of lower jaw were referred to the same genus, *Ramapithecus*, and the genus was formally transferred to the family Hominidae. About the same time from Fort Ternan, East Africa, a portion of maxilla was reported from Pliocene deposits. The fragment was described under the name *Kenyapithecus wickerii* and later accepted as a member of the Hominidae, probably closely related to *Ramapithecus*. Subsequently the dating of this specimen was revised to the upper Miocene (perhaps 10,000,000 years ago). Despite the fragmentary nature of both the Indian and East African specimens and the complete lack of limb bones, some authorities have accepted the hominid status of these fossils and have even suggested that the two forms are specifically identical despite the temporal and geographic separation of the two sites; an assertion that is not unsupported by morphological and ecological evidence. More recently, in 1967, new material was reported again from early Miocene deposits in East Africa; material that is said to differ markedly from both the East African specimens named *Proconsul* and the dryopithecines from Europe and Asia. The new material was grouped under the name of *Kenyapithecus africanus* and was claimed as the oldest member of the family Hominidae known. This claim has, so far, not met with wide acceptance, and much more material of a better diagnostic nature will be required for its substantiation.

Although the remains of several types of apes are known from Pliocene and Miocene deposits in Europe, Africa, and Asia, they consist almost entirely of teeth and fragments of jaws. Morphologically, most of these approximate quite closely those of the modern apes, but *Ramapithecus* does show certain hominid traits, and many authorities now regard it as a very early hominid and not, properly speaking, an anthropoid ape (pongid). If this is correct, it may then be reasonably presumed that the ramapithecine phase of hominid evolution was succeeded by a phase characterized by a larger brain, in which the limb structure and dentition would show some modification in the direction of evolution that has characterized the Hominidae. The answer to the question of whether there is any fossil evidence that such a type ever existed is to be found in remarkable discoveries made in South Africa and East Africa of the remains of creatures to which (as a group) the name Australopithecinae has been given. It is difficult to give them a less pedantic name without misleading implications because of the curious mixture of anatomical features that characterize these creatures, but they are sometimes referred to as ape-men, man-apes, or near-men.

The Australopithecinae. The first fossil evidence of the existence of these creatures was obtained at Taung, in South Africa, in 1924—the skull and a natural cast of the inside of the skull of an immature individual (see AUSTRALOPITHECUS). This specimen shows a number of features (particularly in the milk teeth) in which it approximates much more closely to the Hominidae than do any of the known anthropoid apes. But, because the distinguishing characters of the skulls of adult apes and of the Hominidae are not so conspicuous in immature individuals, considerable doubt was then expressed regarding the significance of the apparently hominid features of the Taung skull.

Later, from 1937 onward, considerably more remains of the same type were discovered in the stalagmitic deposits of ancient caves and fissures formed in dolomitic limestone at sites in the Transvaal, South Africa. As the result of excavations extending over a number of years, a great quantity of important fossil material was collected, consisting of a number of skulls of immature and adult individuals, many upper and lower jaws, numerous examples of the permanent and deciduous dentition, several specimens of the limb skeleton, several parts of the bony pelvis, and the lower part of a vertebral column. The fossil material seems to fall into two categories, gracile (slender) and robust; more information is available about the anatomy of the Australopithecinae than about that of almost any other extinct group of higher primates. The outstanding characters are (1) a small cranial

The ape-man, or man-ape

capacity, equivalent to that of the modern large apes (but in some examples probably exceeding it, at any rate in relation to body size); (2) massive projecting jaws; (3) large molar and premolar (or bicuspid) teeth but remarkably small incisors and canines; and (4) pelvis and limb bones constructed on the hominid plan (but showing significant differences from those of modern *H. sapiens*). The combination of a small braincase with large jaws gives the skull a most apelike appearance; and largely for this reason some authorities at first took the view that, taxonomically, the creatures were really apes. A critical analysis of the cranial and dental characters, however, and especially the evidence of the pelvis and limb skeleton make it clear that the total morphological pattern of the remains conforms to the pattern diagnostic of hominid evolution and certainly not to the evolutionary sequence of anthropoid apes.

The australopithecine skull (Figure 1) presents a number of features that, taken in combination, are never found in apes but are characteristic of hominids. These

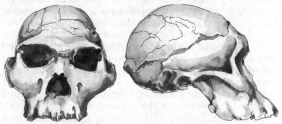

Figure 1: Skull of gracile australopithecine, "STS 5," Sterkfontein, Republic of South Africa.

include the cranial height, the low position of the occipital protuberance (the bulge at the back of the head), the detailed conformation of a number of features in the skull base, and the shape of the mandible (lower jaw). In the largest australopithecine skulls, the vertex is marked by a low median crest related to the growth of large temporal muscles that moved the massive jaws. The contour of the back of the australopithecine skull, combined with details of the cranial base, led to inferences that the Australopithecinae must have been adapted to an erect posture and gait approximating that of *Homo*. This inference received remarkable corroboration from the discovery of portions of thighbones and of the pelvic bones. The latter are of particular importance, for the total morphological pattern of the bony pelvis of the Hominidae is perhaps their most characteristic skeletal feature and, indeed, is what distinguishes them from all other primates (including the anthropoid apes). This pattern, moreover, in its major features represents an adaptation to the mechanical requirements of an upright, or erect, posture. Not one of these features is found in the ape pelvis. On the other hand, pelvic bones of the Australopithecinae all show every one of them consistently; the pelvis is constructed fundamentally on the hominid plan and was adapted for erect, bipedal posture and gait.

Until 1959 no indubitable australopithecine remains had been found outside South Africa. In that year an almost complete skull of the same group of primitive hominids was discovered in a stratum of deposits of early Pleistocene date (1,700,000 years BP) at Olduvai Gorge, Tanzania (Figure 2). It is very similar to some of the more massive skulls from the Transvaal, and the cranial vault (top of the skull) is surmounted by a sagittal crest (a bony ridge running from back to front) of the same type. This skull was at first named *Zinjanthropus*, but it does not seem to be distinct at the genus level from the South African fossils. The latter also have been multiplied by some authorities into a number of different genera (*e.g.*, *Australopithecus, Plesianthropus, Paranthropus*). But, in spite of conflicting opinion, there seems to be no compelling reason at present for recognizing more than one genus (*Australopithecus*), and the differences that *Zinjanthropus* shows are so minor that they merit a distinction equivalent to no more than a geographical variety or, at the very most, to a species distinction.

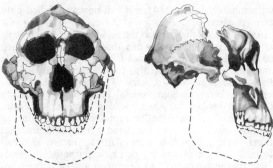

Figure 2: Skull of robust australopithecine from Bed I, Olduvai Gorge, Tanzania.

Recent discoveries from the Omo region of southern Ethiopia, from northern Kenya, and from the east of Lake Rudolf have confirmed the presence of robust australopithecines in deposits of a similar and possibly earlier date than those from Olduvai Gorge. Numerous portions of mandibles, a palate, an incomplete skull, and a complete skull are known, as well as a number of limb bones. Some of the newer fossils are remarkably robust, not to mention massive in their proportions.

At a level in the Olduvai deposits that is slightly below the remains of the robust australopithecine, a juvenile mandible was found in 1960 associated with a pair of parietal bones (from the sides of the skull), a clavicle, some hand bones, an almost complete foot, and numerous tools of the Oldowan culture. It has been claimed that the dental, cranial, and locomotor difference between these finds and the smaller or gracile australopithecines from the Transvaal were sufficient to allow them generic separation, and they were accordingly allocated to a new species of the genus *Homo, Homo habilis*. But the wisdom of this step has been seriously questioned, as has the validity of the nomenclature. Nonetheless, opinion has varied widely in designating this material as either simply a geographical variant of a gracile australopithecine or as a primitive specimen of *Homo erectus* (q.v.), the human species ancestral to *Homo sapiens*. Subsequent finds at Olduvai from Bed I and lower Bed II have proved that the smaller Olduvai form was not an isolated or aberrant individual, but so far they have done little to advance the claims of this group for membership of the genus *Homo*.

Below subfamily level the taxonomy of the Australopithecinae remains confused. According to one view, there were two species of the genus *Australopithecus, A. africanus* and *A. robustus*; the former was small, gracile, upright, and bipedal (stood on two legs) and probably omnivorous in diet, while the latter was robust, less efficiently bipedal, and more dentally specialized for a predominantly vegetarian diet. A second view maintains that there was only one species of australopithecine and that the observed differences between the known samples can be explained as being due to sexual dimorphism. A third view holds that the robust forms should be regarded as the only true members of the subfamily Australopithecinae and placed in a separate genus (*Paranthropus*) while all of the gracile material should be placed in the genus *Homo* as *Homo africanus*. Yet a fourth view would allocate all of the robust material and some of the gracile material to the genus *Australopithecus* (perhaps explaining their differences as being due to sexual dimorphism) while reallocating some of the formerly gracile material to the genus *Homo*. This view would allow representatives of the genus *Homo* to occupy the same territory as members of the genus *Australopithecus* at a relatively early date and would deny the known australopithecines any part in human ancestry. Evidence for this hypothesis is being derived from the area of Kenya to the east of Lake Rudolf, where in 1970 and 1971 mandibular and postcranial remains (body and limbs, including the jaw) were recovered from deposits alleged to be from between 1,000,000 and 2,600,000 years ago. Stone tools of the Oldowan culture have been recovered from the same area and have been attributed to the older deposits. The clear implication of the last view is that the diver-

gence between the hominids and the australopithecines must have taken place in the Pliocene, but good evidence is entirely lacking. The earliest known hominid fragments from this time range include a small piece of jaw dated at 5,500,000 years BP from Lothagam, Kenya, and a fragment of humerus dated at 4,000,000 years BP from Kanapoi, Kenya. Both have been regarded as australopithecine, but the evidence for this is slender.

The taxonomic status of a previously unknown fossil— whether it is a primitive, small-brained hominid or a member of the anthropoid-ape family—must depend on a recognition of the fundamentally different trends that have characterized the evolution of these two families and that are diagnostic of each of them as a natural taxonomic group. The indirect evidence of comparative anatomy and the direct evidence of paleontology lead to the conclusion that the anthropoid-ape family and the Hominidae represent divergent lines of evolution deriving from a common ancestry. The anthropoid-ape sequence of evolution became adapted for a quite specialized arboreal life with accompanying changes in the limbs, skull, and dentition. The hominid sequence, by contrast, became adapted for life on the ground, with profound modifications of the pelvic and limb skeleton (and also the skull) for erect bipedal posture.

The question arises whether some members of the Australopithecinae could have been the ancestors of later hominids, including *H. erectus* and *H. sapiens*. There appears to be no sound morphological argument against such an inference; indeed, the australopithecines in many ways conform very closely to theoretical postulates for the phase of hominid evolution that is presumed to have preceded the *H. erectus* phase.

Homo erectus. A variety of names have in the past been applied to members of this group (*e.g., Pithecanthropus* in Java, *Sinanthropus* in China, and *Atlanthropus* in North Africa), but the essential similarity of these middle Pleistocene (perhaps 1,000,000 to 500,000 years old) men is now widely accepted, and they are referred to as *Homo erectus*. The small differences between widely spaced members of the group are probably no more than racial variations.

Representatives of *Homo erectus* populations are now known from China, Java, Africa, and Europe. Although the known material suggests the existence of an earlier, less advanced and a later, more developed group, they all show a similar morphological pattern: mean cranial capacity of about 1,000 cubic centimetres (60 cubic inches); flat, retreating forehead; large, projecting brow ridges; flattened skull vault; low maximum skull breadth; back of the skull sharply angulate, suggesting heavy neck muscles; and no chin. The teeth and jaws show considerable variability, although they are often larger than those found in *Homo sapiens*.

The first discovery of *Homo erectus*, made at Trinil, in central Java, consisted of a skullcap found in 1891 and a femur (thighbone) found a year later. These were discovered in alluvial deposits on the bank of the Solo River at a stratigraphic level of middle Pleistocene age that probably corresponds to the time of the second (or Mindel) glaciation in other parts of the world. Although the femur and skullcap reportedly came from the same geological layer, it has been suggested that they might represent rather different levels of evolutionary development. While the skullcap is very small, its cranial capacity considerably exceeds that of any of the great apes. The femur, which shows a remarkable pathological growth, is very well preserved and shows considerable, though not total, similarity to that of modern man. Attempts to show the contemporaneity of the two specimens through chemical dating techniques have so far been inconclusive, and the question of their association remains unanswered. A considerable amount of material attributable to *Homo erectus* is now known from Java: eight fragmentary skulls (the last, VIII, demonstrates the face), numerous upper and lower jaw fragments, many teeth, and five more femurs (thighbones). The available skeletal evidence entirely supports the view that *Homo erectus* had a fully erect posture and was capable of walking bipedally.

Taxonomic classification

Java man

Homo erectus material has also been found in the beds underlying the Trinil deposits; these beds, called the Djetis, may be as much as 1,900,000 years old. Material from this level includes an infant skull found at Modjokerto; this skull is of particular interest, for, although it belonged to an individual perhaps not more than two or three years old, it shows the incipient development of some of the characteristic features of the adult *Homo erectus* skull. Also from this level is a lower jaw fragment, with three teeth, of considerable size. Although first referred to as a new genus, *Meganthropus*, there is no convincing evidence that it is other than a large *Homo erectus*. No stone tools have been found in direct association with *H. erectus* in Java.

Peking man

The Chinese representatives of *Homo erectus* are known from remains discovered at Lower Cave, Chou-k'ou-tien, near Peking. The first find, in 1927, consisted of a lower molar tooth. Two years later, a well-preserved cranium of very primitive type was found at the same site. *Homo erectus* from China is known from the very fragmentary remains of perhaps 40 individuals in all, which include portions of the facial skeleton, several mandibles, about 150 teeth, and a few limb bones. Occupation of the Lower Cave probably extended from the late second glacial period (*c.* 500,000–400,000 BP) into the second interglacial (400,000–200,000 BP); they are therefore not quite as ancient as the Javan populations and seem to represent a slight evolutionary advance. The cranial capacity has a mean value of more than 1,000 cubic centimetres, but this seems to have been remarkably variable, for in five individuals it shows a range from 915 to 1,225 cubic centimetres (55 to 75 cubic inches). The latter figure comes well within the range of variation for *Homo sapiens*. All of the skulls (see Figure 3) show a marked

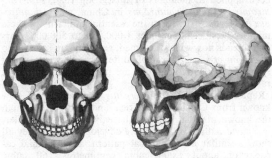

Figure 3: Skull of *Homo erectus,* Lower Cave, Chou-k'ou-tien, China.

flattening of the cranial vault (top of the skull), heavily constructed brow ridges, and thick bony walls of the braincase. The facial skeleton is strongly built, the jaws and teeth are large, and the mandible lacks a chin. The forehead region is better developed than in the Javan specimens and is probably associated with the slightly larger cranial capacity. The teeth conform in all essentials to the hominid pattern, and the canines, though in some individuals large and conical, do not project to any marked degree beyond the level of the adjacent teeth. The limb bones found at Lower Cave comprise portions of seven femora, two humeri (the bones of the upper arm), a clavicle, and one of the small bones of the wrist. Although none of the femora is complete, the preserved portions suggest a characteristic pattern: they are remarkably flattened from front to back (a condition known as platymeria), and they show relatively straight shafts and thick shaft walls with consequently narrowed marrow cavities. These features all occur in modern human groups and are certainly not inconsistent with bipedal walking; however, it is unlikely that this same pattern of features would occur in modern man. In other words, the gene frequency patterns, in this case for femoral morphology, must have been different in *H. sapiens* and *H. erectus*.

Excavations were resumed at the Lower Cave in 1958, and several more *Homo erectus* specimens have been found since that time; all of the earlier material was unfortunately lost in 1941 and can now be studied only through casts.

In the deposits that yielded the remains of *Homo erectus* at Chou-k'ou-tien, crude stone tools (cores from which flakes had been chipped) and trimmed flakes of quartz and other materials were also found, comprising a local Paleolithic stone-tool industry of an archaic but fairly uniform character. Some animal bones, which evidently had been broken for their marrow content, also were found; finally, the deposits contained the remains of hearths and quantities of charred bones, evidence that these ancient hominids were skillful hunters and had learned the use of fire for domestic purposes. It seems clear that man already had developed a very active communal life.

Possible evidence of *H. erectus* in Europe was found in a sandpit at Mauer, Germany, in 1907. It is a well-preserved, massive, chinless jaw (sometimes called the Heidelberg jaw) with teeth of a typically hominid pattern. This fossil was found in association with extinct mammals characteristic of the early part of the Pleistocene, but there were no tools. Because of the conditions of its discovery, however, its age cannot be accurately assessed; it may possibly date to the first interglacial period (approximately 700,000–500,000 BP). Three lower jaws, quite similar to the Heidelberg and Peking material, were found at Ternifine, in Algeria, in 1954, in association with stone tools of the type known as early Acheulean. A single skull bone is also known from the site; this also seems to resemble the Peking remains. A fragmentary mandible, also discovered in 1954, near Casablanca, Morocco, appears to be later than the Ternifine material, possibly third glacial (*c.* 200,000–100,000 BP), and it, too, was found with tools of Acheulean type.

The Heidelberg jaw

The important East African early-man site at Olduvai Gorge, Tanzania, has also yielded evidence of *Homo erectus*. In 1960 a skull was found in Olduvai Bed II, and, although it is somewhat larger than previously known *H. erectus* skulls, it demonstrates the large, continuous brow ridges, low maximum skull breadth, and other features characteristic of this group. It was found associated with tools of the Developed Oldowan type. A fragmentary pelvis and femur, which are known as Olduvai Hominid 28, were found in 1970 in Bed IV, also at Olduvai. Other femurs are of course known from Java and China, but the pelvis is unique in the middle Pleistocene record of fossil man. The pelvis, which is strong and robustly built, is similar to the modern human pelvis in many respects. The femur, however, is remarkably similar to the Peking femurs; it demonstrates the same front to back flattening, relatively straight shaft, and thick walls that characterize the Peking remains. The pelvis and femur are associated with numerous tools of Acheulean type and are approximately 500,000 years old.

Controversial human remains, first called *Telanthropus*, found at the South African australopithecine site at Swartkrans, have been attributed to *Homo erectus* by some workers. These remains consist of two jaws and several skull and facial pieces. It has been suggested that the large brow ridges, small jaws and teeth, and certain morphological features of the face point to a more advanced hominid, which should be included in the genus *Homo*. Others have argued that these features, because they may reflect only size differences, should not be considered as taxonomically significant; these workers would include *Telanthropus* with the australopithecines. A further possibility is that this material represents a form transitional from *Australopithecus* to *H. erectus*, but it is not possible to indicate this under present classificatory practices.

A number of crude, quartzite tools found in the Swartkrans deposits bear a close resemblance not only to tools from another South African site, at Sterkfontein, but also to those from Bed II at Olduvai. Tools of this type from Olduvai have been named Oldowan. The association at Swartkrans of the tools and the hominid remains is not clear, and none of the South African sites has yet been satisfactorily dated.

Oldowan stone-tool culture

Perhaps the most striking aspect of *Homo erectus* evolution during the middle Pleistocene is the combination of very primitive features of the skull and jaws with limb bones of nearly modern development. This phenomenon, called mosaic evolution, refers to differential rates of evolutionary progress in different parts of the body. The capability for efficient bipedal locomotion was apparently achieved at least by the earliest middle Pleistocene, yet the brain at this time was only slightly larger than that of the largest apes. Within the next few hundred thousand years, the size of the brain increased greatly. After man began to enter his own ecological niche, circumscribed only by the limits of his cultural achievements, his cranial evolution proceeded at an almost exponential rate.

The persuasive and consistent suggestion from the human fossil record is that the evolutionary pressures for a novel and almost unique method of locomotion, erect bipedalism, were at first more intense than the pressures for a large and complex brain. This is certainly not to say that these features were developing independently—quite the contrary—but the "need" for habitual bipedalism was apparently more insistent than the "need" for a larger brain in man's early evolution. Moreover, it is likely that the complete release of the forelimbs from locomotion was one of the stimuli that led to the elaboration and enlargement of human mental capacity. The freed forelimbs were then at liberty to explore and utilize the environment in unique ways.

HOMO SAPIENS IN THE FOSSIL RECORD

Geological dating methods. Before the evolutionary history of man in terms of fossil remains is traced in further detail, it is desirable to note the geological changes that marked the Pleistocene Epoch. The date of the transition from the Pliocene to the Pleistocene is an arbitrary point in time, and geologists have not found it easy to agree on its definition. Broadly speaking, it was marked by the gradual onset of a cooler climate in many parts of the world about 2,500,000 years ago and by a general lowering of temperature that finally led to the great ice ages, during which, in modern temperate zones, ice caps and glaciers originating on high levels spread out for considerable distances over lowlands. This process of glaciation was recurrent and extended throughout most of the Pleistocene Epoch; it is now generally agreed that there were four main glacial periods, of varying duration and severity, separated by interglacial periods during which the climate became warmer and in some cases (even in Europe) almost subtropical. Evidence of the successive glaciations can be detected in the characteristic geological deposits left by melting ice and also in the fossil remains of Arctic or sub-Arctic animals and plants from the glaciated regions. By the determination of the rhythmic succession of glacial and interglacial phases during the Pleistocene, geologists have provided a time scale for inferring the relative antiquity of fossil hominids and the implements they left behind.

Even in those parts of the world where there was no actual glaciation, such as the equatorial regions, there was a succession of alternating rainy and dry periods, but there is no evidence that these pluvial and interpluvial phases were closely correlated with the glacial and interglacial periods in the Northern and Southern hemispheres. The recurrent glaciations were accompanied by considerable falls in sea level, which had a profound effect on the formation of river valleys and caused the opening of land bridges that permitted migration of hominid populations and, consequently, encouraged gene flow and mixture between such populations. Similarly, the rise in sea levels during the interglacials cut these routes and produced isolation of hominid populations. With a fall in sea level, the erosive power of the rivers increased, and they cut their valleys more deeply. With the rise in sea level during the interglacial periods, the rivers flowed more sluggishly and laid down such stratified deposits as gravel and sand over their alluvial plains. As a result, series of terraces were formed along the riverbanks, and it is in these terraces that some of the oldest remains of Paleolithic (Old Stone Age) man and his stone implements have been found. The time relationship of the

The ice ages

terraces to the glaciations has been worked out in some detail by geologists, and largely on this basis the relative antiquity of the fossils can be established.

In recent years new chemical and physical methods that have been developed have assisted greatly in establishing a chronology that enables paleontologists to set their materials in a proper phylogenetic context. Relative dating, or the assessment of contemporaneity of a fossil and its layer, has been aided by the fluorine and uranium methods, while absolute dating (or age in years) has often established the sequence of fossils in the deposits. The most valuable absolute dating methods are the radioactive-carbon technique, which operates between 60,-000 years BP and the present; the potassium–argon technique, which most easily dates material older than 350,-000 years BP; and the fission-track method, which is helping to bridge the gaps between the other methods (see DATING, RELATIVE AND ABSOLUTE).

The antiquity of Homo sapiens. It is a curious fact that, although evidence for the evolution of man is extensive, direct fossil evidence of the earliest members of the species *Homo sapiens* is relatively scarce. The species *Homo sapiens* (of which the modern human races comprise a number of different geographical varieties) may be defined in terms of the anatomical characters shared by its members. The definition for prehistoric representatives of the species must be limited to skeletal characters, the only remains to be found. The definition of *H. sapiens* in terms of skeletal characteristics includes such features as a mean cranial capacity of about 1,350 cubic centimetres (82 cubic inches), an approximately vertical forehead, a rounded occipital (back) part of the skull with a relatively small area for the attachment of the neck musculature, jaws and teeth of reduced size, small canine teeth of spatulate form, the presence of a pointed or projecting chin, limb bones adapted to a fully erect posture and gait, and so forth (see HOMO SAPIENS). Any skeletal remains that conform to this pattern to an extent that precludes classification in other groups of higher primates must be assumed to belong to *H. sapiens*. In the past there was a tendency to create entirely new species of *Homo* on the basis of fragments of prehistoric human skeletons, even though the remains showed no significant differences from modern man. This tendency was prompted by the supposed antiquity of the remains or by a failure to realize how variable some features are even in modern man. One of the best examples of this kind of fallacy is the so-called Galley Hill skeleton, discovered in 1888 in the Thames Valley, in England, and supposed to be of very great antiquity. Some anatomists thought they could recognize very primitive features in this specimen, particularly in the shape of the lower jaw. An apparently exhaustive study of the femur, involving an elaborate statistical comparison of a number of measurements and indices, even led to the conclusion that it was quite distinct from modern man. But in later years it was determined, largely as a result of the analysis of its fluorine content, that the skeleton was a burial of comparatively recent date—perhaps the remains of a Neolithic man (c. 8000–2000 BC) or possibly even a later interment. The explanation of the discrepancy is an important matter, for statistical tables are apt to give an impression that conclusions based on them are final and indisputable. But it has come to be realized that the validity of statistical methods in the study of fossils depends on the actual number of measurements taken, on whether the measurements compared are really strictly equivalent in the morphological sense, on whether they are taxonomically relevant, and so forth. It also has been demonstrated that, if the individual characters of a bone or a tooth are compared independently, one by one, instead of as components of a total pattern (which can be done by a statistical method known as multivariate analysis), entirely different and sometimes very misleading conclusions may be reached. In the case of the Galley Hill femur, the statistical study was made with only a very limited sample of modern femurs, which were assumed to be representative of *H. sapiens* as a whole. Obviously the comparison must be made with adequate samples of all the main varieties

The early H. sapiens fossils

Galley Hill skeleton

of *H. sapiens* before it can be legitimately concluded that there is a distinction. The weakness of "matching typology" is particularly apparent when closely related or transitional forms are being considered, a point made by Darwin when he stated that:

In a series of forms graduating insensibly from some ape-like creature to man as he now exists, it would be impossible to fix on any point where the term "man" ought to be used.

Characters may be identified that are commonly seen in less evolved examples, yet at the same time more advanced features may be present in the same specimen, a situation that results from the mosaic evolutionary process. It is now clear that *Homo sapiens*, evolving relatively rapidly during the late middle Pleistocene, was subject to this mosaic process.

The species of the genus *Homo* that immediately preceded early *Homo sapiens* was *Homo erectus*, and it is most likely that it was from advanced members of the latter species that sapient man (*H. sapiens*) evolved. The skull of *Homo erectus* (*q.v.*) has been described as of low cranial capacity with a large face, a low maximum breadth and a sharply angulate occipital region (back of the skull). By comparison, the skulls of modern *Homo sapiens* show an expanded cranial vault, a vertical forehead, and a high maximum breadth; at the same time, the face is shortened by regression of the jaws and teeth, leaving the chin and nose as prominent features of the sapient face—a continuation of trends that are traceable well back into primate evolution. The skeleton of the trunk and lower limbs of *Homo sapiens* is characterized by its virtually complete adaptation for a fully upright posture and a striding bipedal gait. The hands of *Homo sapiens* are capable of both power and precision grips; they also possess remarkable manipulative abilities, which, with a sapient brain, can skillfully fabricate stone tools and produce art and sculpture.

Early Homo sapiens remains in Europe and Africa. Fossil remains of early *Homo sapiens* are known from sites in both Europe and Africa, and later examples have come from a wide range of sites in the Old World and later still from the New World. In 1965 some fossil human remains were found at a site named Vértesszőllős, near Budapest. The remains were derived from the third of four geological layers that showed signs of human occupation, in a quarry cut into the fourth terrace of the Danube River system. The contemporaneity of the fossil finds and the layers in which they were found was established by means of the fluorine test; radiometric dating has given a date of 350,000 years BP. The site also yielded fossil mammal bones as well as stone tools and signs of the use of fire. The find consisted of some milk teeth and an occipital bone (from the back of the skull) that is broad, thick, and well preserved. The shape of this bone is distinctive and has several features that recall the *Homo erectus* occipital; on the other hand, the estimated cranial capacity of Vértesszőllős man is 1,400 cubic centimetres (85 cubic inches), well into the normal range for *Homo sapiens*. These remains have been attributed to a *sapiens–erectus* intermediate type on the grounds that the remains show a mélange of features typical of the mosaic evolutionary process. If this assessment is correct, Vértesszőllős man must lie at the root of the *H. sapiens* evolutionary line, 100,000 years ahead of his nearest rival.

A better known early example of *Homo sapiens* comes from the Thames Middle Gravels at Swanscombe, Kent; gravels attributed to the Great Interglacial Age, about 250,000 years BP. In 1935, 1936, and 1955, three parts of a skull were unearthed that fit together to form the back of a cranial vault (braincase). The deposits at Swanscombe are well-known for their rich quantities of stone tools and fossil mammal bones; the fauna as a whole indicates warm interglacial conditions, with the river high, sluggish, and bordered by marshes and lagoons. Recent excavations have shown that animals were butchered at the water's edge with stone tools made at the site from flint transported from another location. The Swanscombe skull is generally accepted as being representative of early *Homo sapiens*, although some authorities have

Vértesszőllős man

emphasized its Neanderthal features (see NEANDERTHAL MAN).

Another skull of about the same date is from Steinheim, near Stuttgart, West Germany. It was recovered in 1933 from interglacial sands and gravels; there were no tools recovered from the site. This skull is more complete than that from Swanscombe and includes the right side of the face and some small upper teeth. Once again, the features of the skull are mixed; while the back part is reminiscent of the Swanscombe skull, the frontal region and face seem to be rather Neanderthal. Further European early sapient remains are known from Fontéchevade, Charente, France; Quinzano d'Oglio and Saccopastore, Italy; and Ehringsdorf, Germany, but none is as old as the Vértesszőllős, Swanscombe, and Steinheim finds.

The record of early *Homo sapiens* has been augmented recently by new finds in southern Ethiopia, from the banks of the Omo River, which drains southward into Lake Rudolf. Here in deposits attributed to the East African late middle Pleistocene, a skull (Omo II) and a partial skeleton (Omo I) were found. The Omo II skull is the more primitive of the two, having flattened frontal (at the front of the skull) and occipital (at the back of the skull) regions, thick walls but a rounded vault, large mastoid processes (pointed bony processes at the base of the skull behind the ears), and high cranial capacity; once again mixed features. The Omo I skull is more modern, as are its postcranial bones. The relationship of these remains to each other, assuming that their geological contemporaneity is assured, is a matter of considerable interest, as is their relationship to the other samples of the genus *Homo* from earlier deposits in East Africa. It seems likely that the Omo assemblage goes some way to bridge the gap between advanced *Homo erectus* and early *Homo sapiens* in this area.

"Neanderthaloid" remains from Asia and Africa. In passing to the upper Pleistocene for evidence of human evolution, the amount and distribution of material greatly increase. From the Far East, a group of skulls are known from the Solo area of Java. They were found in association with some stone tools and many mammalian bones. All of the skulls are thick, with divided brow ridges, sloping foreheads, and strongly marked occipital ridges, features that recall the Omo II skull or even *Homo erectus*. From southern Africa, a skull from Broken Hill, Zambia, shows similar features but has exaggerated brow ridges. Another example of this group is derived from Saldanha, near Cape Town. All of these remains have been termed Neanderthaloid because of the supposed resemblance of their principal features to those of the classic Neanderthalers of the Würm (Last) Glaciation; however, this designation is not universally accepted, for it seems to imply a close genetic association between forms that are very widely separated.

In the Near East, controversial remains are known from Mt. Carmel, Israel; two caves—Maghārat at-Tabūn and Maghārat as-Skhūl—have produced skeletal material. The Tabūn skeleton is that of a young woman with distinctly Neanderthal features, while the Skhūl material represents ten individuals of rather more modern features. This mixture of features was interpreted as being due to either a "hybridization" between a Neanderthal and a more modern sapient or to the material representing the extremes of a range of normal variation within the population at that time period. Subsequent work has shown, however, that the two sites are separated in time by as much as 10,000 years, so that the later Skhūl remains could relate to more modern forms of *Homo sapiens*, who were superseding the Neanderthals in the locality.

The taxonomic position of the whole group of early sapient remains is still somewhat problematical. For the present, therefore, it seems most appropriate to regard them all as intermediates shading off toward *Homo erectus* at the earlier end of the time range and toward Neanderthal man and modern man at the other end of the morphological spectrum.

Neanderthal man. This group consists of a widely known series of remains derived from sites arranged roughly in an arc across southern Europe and the Near

Swanscombe and Steinheim fossils

Fossils with Neanderthal-like features

East. The majority of the Neanderthal sites are from periods of glaciation and date from the Würm (Last) Glaciation. The first Neanderthaler was found in 1856 from the Neander Valley near Düsseldorf, in Germany. Subsequent finds are known from France, Italy, Belgium, Greece, Czechoslovakia, Russia, North Africa, and parts of the Middle East. They tend to show a group of quite distinctive skeletal characteristics that at one time led to their being regarded as distinct species of man. Modern taxonomists, however, tend to attribute the whole group to *Homo sapiens* and only allow subspecific differentiation (*Homo sapiens neanderthalensis*). The pattern of the Neanderthal morphology is one of a short, thickset, powerfully muscled group, well adapted to cold conditions.

The earliest assessment of their functional morphology suggested that the Neanderthalers were incompletely erect in posture and had a stooping bent-kneed gait. More recent opinion has revised this view in the light of the assessment of a wider range of Neanderthal skeletons and suggests that they were fully erect, active bipeds capable of hunting large game under almost Arctic conditions. The characteristic features of the Neanderthal morphology include large heads, large faces with receding jaws, stout and often curved long bones (arm and leg bones), and large joints (Figure 4). Neanderthalers were cave

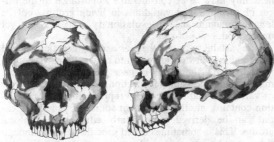

Figure 4: Male Neanderthal skull, La Ferrassie, France.

Neander-thal man and his culture

dwellers who had the use of fire and manufactured stone tools that would have permitted them to prepare skins for clothing and weapons for the hunt. The beginnings of magic or mysticism can be discerned from Neanderthal sites, for they deliberately buried their dead and on occasion provided the departed with grave goods or objects deliberately arranged around the body in the grave. The cave bear (*Ursus spelaeus*) seemed to play a part in their lives (perhaps religious), for skulls of this extinct animal are often found at Neanderthal sites.

Clearly the Neanderthalers were a successful group for many thousands of years, but their traces disappear from the fossil record, and they are superseded by other sapiens with a more advanced culture and a different morphology. In Europe these are known as the Cro-Magnon peoples (see CRO-MAGNON MAN). The reasons for the relatively sudden disappearance of the Neanderthalers are still a matter of some debate. Varying suggestions have been put forward, including catastrophic extinction due to disease, lack of adaptation to the warmer climate following the glaciation, annihilation by the more advanced sapient invaders, or genetic absorption by the new group. It is not unlikely, however, that all of these factors played a part in their demise. If absorption did take place, then it cannot be said that the Neanderthalers are an extinct side branch of the human evolutionary line, and the occurrence of Neanderthal genes in modern human populations must be allowed. This view is finding most favour at present.

Fossil examples of modern Homo sapiens. The modern distribution of *Homo sapiens* is worldwide, with indigenous populations in all the major continents except Antarctica. Within the continent of Africa, numerous discoveries of fossil sapiens have been made. These include those from Kenya (Gambles Cave, Elmenteita, Naivasha), South Africa (Homa, Boskop, Florisbad), and North Africa (Tangier, Taforalt, Mechta). Although they differ in anatomical details, the range of variability that they exhibit is in no way greater than that known for

the extant races of modern man. Similarly, in Asia the fossil record of upper Pleistocene man can be traced from Upper Cave remains described from Chou-k'ou-tien. This group was thought at first to show the racial characters of the Eskimo, the Melanesians, and the Ainu, but this seems unlikely to be the case. Other Asian fossils include Wadjak man, an upper Pleistocene or Holocene (Recent) discovery from Java; and a skull from Niah Cave in Borneo. Both of these finds have been described as having Australoid features and may represent the ancestors of the modern aboriginal Australians.

The fossil history of man in Australia has received several new finds to add to the sparse record of the past. The older specimens include the Talgai and Cohuna skulls, but more recently new acquisitions have been made from Green Gully and Lake Nitchie. The most recent dating evidence indicates a probable antiquity of man in Australia in excess of 25,000 years BP. The presence of fossil man in North America has traditionally been denied, but recent dating evidence from hearths and other archaeological sites has shown a possible antiquity of as much as 30,000 years. Skeletal evidence from both North and South America is scanty and undiagnostic, but nothing other than *Homo sapiens* remains have been identified.

Finally, in Europe the upper Pleistocene representatives of *Homo sapiens* that are most widely known are the Cro-Magnon group (see CRO-MAGNON MAN). Skeletal remains, having the same general features as those from the type site, are known from France (Abri-Pataud, Bruniquel, Chancelade, Combe-Capelle, La Madelaine), Italy (Grimaldi), Great Britain (Paviland), and many other sites. In general the skulls of these men are long with upright foreheads and jaws with well-marked chins; the postcranial skeleton indicates a tall upright people of modern skeletal form.

To attempt to identify an evolutionary centre for *Homo sapiens* would seem to be a difficult task, save for the belief that it must be within the Eurasian–African landmass. The evidence suggests that North America and Australia were peopled at about the same time (probably less than 30,000 years BP), while South America was entered later (10,000 BP?). North America was most likely colonized by groups migrating across the Bering Strait at a time of low sea level, and Australia was entered from the Southeast Asian peninsula at a similar period. Direct evidence for these migrations is lacking, but it seems the most plausible interpretation that can be advanced. The differentiation of the modern human races from an ancestral sapient stock arising within the Eurasian–African landmass is still uncertain, but several theories are available. The antiquity of human races has been the subject of considerable dispute and is a controversy that remains unabated at present.

One view is that racial differences observed in modern man originated in *Homo erectus*, remained stable through the species change, and continue today with relatively unchanged characteristics. This view sees five races arising from geographically separated groups of *H. erectus*. Support for this point of view has not been forthcoming, although some workers have commented on postulated resemblances between certain fossil specimens of *H. sapiens* and some modern racial groups (*e.g.*, between the Grimaldi fossils and the Negroids, and the Chancelade remains and an Eskimoid type). While it is possible, and even likely, that fossil populations could demonstrate some similarities to modern groups in certain adaptive features, the total gene frequency patterns would certainly differ between groups so far separated in time. Finally, although human variations must have formed in response to a variety of factors, both environmental and behavioral, these factors cannot have had the same characteristics in terms of magnitude and direction for very long periods of time; hence the racial variation of prehistoric times must have been differently distributed than at present.

An alternative view of racial origins, which incorporates those ideas, is that human races have no great antiquity and may be seen as merely transitional episodes in the history of man. This view recognizes that what appear

An evolutionary centre for *H. sapiens*

today as racial traits are adaptational features that reflect a wide range of environmental, social, and cultural pressures. These pressures must change through time not only because the environment changes but because the gene pool itself changes. Although there is no clear consensus on the number of modern races, most workers accept the existence of several major races corresponding to large geographic areas. This view recognizes the effectiveness of geographic barriers first in reducing free gene flow and second in changing the environment sufficiently to elicit different adaptive responses from the gene pool (see RACES OF MANKIND). The number of races recognized depends in part on the criteria used and in part on the reason for the classification. Six to nine major geographic races may be defined: the European Caucasoids, the African Negroids, the Asian Mongoloids, the Australoids, and the American Indians, as well as the peoples of the Pacific islands, usually divided into at least three distinct groups—the Polynesians, the Melanesians, and the Micronesians.

II. Evolutionary process in man

Evolution may be defined as change in the genetic composition of a population through time (see also GENETICS, HUMAN). It may be thought of as progressing on two levels: the production of variation and the selection of those gene combinations most "fit" in a particular environment. It would be wrong to consider that evolution is "caused" by any one factor. Indeed, the error of many earlier theories of evolution was neither intrinsic nor factual but lay in the consideration of evolutionary change solely in the light of a single process. While the modern theory of evolution relies heavily on the Darwinian concept of natural selection, many other factors unknown in Darwin's day have enlarged and enhanced man's knowledge of evolutionary process. The modern synthesis of evolutionary theory is a composite approach that views evolutionary process in the light of different scientific disciplines such as paleontology, biology, biochemistry, ecology, and many others, all of which have made significant contributions. The synthesis of fact and theory from these various fields has been the major contribution of evolutionary biology to 20th-century science.

GENETICS AND MAN

Mutation. The ultimate source of all new genetic variation is change in the genetic material itself. Genetic information is passed from parent to offspring through the complicated protein molecule known as deoxyribonucleic acid (DNA). The DNA is carried on long strands called chromosomes. Each species has a characteristic number of these strands—in man the number is 46. These 46 chromosomes comprise 23 pairs. The DNA molecules in similar positions along paired strands will code for the same feature, and, in the chemical relationships between these positions (or genes), one gene of each pair will generally be dominant, and the other will be recessive. It is usual for the activity of a gene on one strand to be masked or inhibited by its counterpart on the other strand. An important exception to this is in the determination of coloration patterns, in which the genes may appear to blend, producing colour patterns different from those of the parents.

Alteration of the genetic material is called mutation and can be of two types: point mutations, in which the molecular composition of a discrete location on the chromosome strand can be changed by a chemical process or the physical interaction of a particle (perhaps resulting from radioactivity) with the DNA molecules that make up the chromosome at that point, and mechanical mutations, in which the gross structure of the chromosome is altered, often in the process of cell reproduction. Point mutation is well documented in human populations; for example, normal hemoglobin is formed of a long chain of amino acids; if the genetic code for one of these amino acids, glutamic acid, is changed, the amino acid is replaced by another amino acid, valine, and the abnormal hemoglobin responsible for sickle-cell anemia results. This disease is of considerable importance in some human populations

and will be discussed in more detail below. Mechanical mutations do not involve chemical changes in the DNA but are physical alterations involving the body of the chromosome itself; these abnormalities usually occur during cell reproduction. One such process involves the exchange (called crossover) of material between two adjacent paired chromosomes. Other types of chromosomal mutations can be due to the inversion or translocation of chromosomal material, its loss or deletion, or the nondisjunction of chromosome pairs.

While the ultimate source of all intrinsic genetic change must occur through mutation, the vast majority of these alterations result in the death of the individual or so reduce his "fitness" that he suffers "genetic death" (*i.e.*, fails to reproduce) even though he may live to great age. The greatest source of variability is simply a change in the frequency of existing genes under various environmental and, in some cases, social stimuli. The genes themselves contain a vast reservoir of variability, only part of which can be realized in any single population. Here an important distinction must be made between the genotype—the chemical composition of the genes—and the phenotype—the external appearance—of the individual. Similar genotypes can in certain situations give quite different phenotypes, presumably because only part of the genes' activity occurs at any one time. This phenotypic flexibility may be of considerable importance in the origin of certain racial variations in living groups, but its long-term significance in evolutionary process is not yet understood.

Most variability arises, then, as existing genetic material is recombined or "reshuffled" into new patterns via sexual reproduction. Alterations in gene frequencies will occur mainly under pressure of selection. Besides the reservoir or variability that any sexually reproducing local population contains, another important source of genetic potential can be derived from interbreeding with nonlocal groups. This is sometimes called gene flow, and, although there may be a temporary disruption of the genetic equilibrium, once a balance is again obtained the hybrid population may be more "fit" than the parent generation. Heterosis, or hybrid vigour (the phenomenon whereby an organism that is the result of crossbreeding between parents of different genetic populations shows increased "fitness" and general vitality), is well documented for some human groups, most notably the people of Pitcairn Island, who are ultimately derived from crosses between Tahitian women and the British sailors from the "Bounty," groups whose ancestors were genetically separated by distance for thousands of years.

Observations on the occurrence of genetically derived traits in fossil man can be used to suggest earlier patterns of gene flow. Such observations have been made with regard to *Homo erectus*, and the suggestion has been made that genetic exchange was occurring between widely spaced members of this group during the middle Pleistocene. It has been pointed out by a number of workers that the approximately contemporaneous Ternifine mandibles (jawbones) of Algeria and the Peking mandibles of China show extreme similarities; the great similarities between the Peking femurs (thighbones) and the Olduvai Hominid 28 femur have also been noted. A reasonable explanation of this similarity is that migratory hunting patterns had brought many groups of *Homo erectus* into contact and that exogamous (marrying outside the tribal group) breeding patterns had resulted in the widespread occurrence of certain traits. These similarities are very likely too great and consistent to have resulted from separate evolution along parallel lines in isolation; and, indeed, the degree of similarity seen in the available material makes it extremely unlikely that long-term isolation was a factor in human evolution after the early middle Pleistocene.

Natural selection. Genetic variation derives from several sources and provides only the raw materials of evolution; random variation can only have a disrupting effect on genetic equilibrium unless deleterious combinations of genes are eliminated and advantageous ones are preserved. The process by which this occurs is called natural selection. Although Darwin is credited with the first full statement of the theory of evolution through natural selection, the origins of the concept are deeply rooted in European thought and may be traced to the early 17th century. Indeed, the practices of artificial selection of domesticated plants and animals, which so influenced Darwin, can be traced at least as far as the Romans and perhaps even to Neolithic times. The theory of natural selection can be stated as follows: All living things vary and reproduce themselves many times, yet the number of a given group tends to remain constant. Therefore there is a competition for survival, and only those most fitted to external conditions survive. In essence, the idea of natural selection is statistical; those members of a population who are most evolutionarily "fit" are those who will leave the greatest number of offspring. These will not be the only members of the population to leave offspring, but it is probable, in a statistical sense, that they will leave more living descendants in the long run than the less well adapted members of the population. "Fitness" therefore refers to a population's ability to cope successfully with a particular environment at a particular time; it is tied to time and place in an absolute way. The factors that help determine the course and direction of evolution are many: predation and disease; migration and conflict; behaviour and temperament; competition for breeding space and mates; competition for living space and food. Purely physical factors in the environment are no less important: stability or instability of the climate; solar radiation; natural disaster; pollution of the soil, water, and air—all will have their effect and take their toll on living groups. Evolution is not, therefore, something that has occurred and been completed. Any population is constantly evolving, assimilating changes and variations in its gene pool in response to stimuli from a large number of sources—some that are recognized and some that are not.

> Evolutionary fitness

ADAPTATION AND GENETIC CHANGE

There are a number of ways in which a population can adapt to the changing world in which it lives; under the heading of natural selection, it is possible to define several mechanisms that help maintain a viable relationship between that population and the environment of which it is a part. In a seeming paradox, natural selection can work to maintain the status quo in a changing environment while at the same time drawing on new or existing material in the gene pool to meet the demands of the environment in a new way. Natural selection is then both conservative and dynamic, with both mechanisms working to achieve the same end result, that of adaptation to the environment. Conservative, or stabilizing, natural selection basically works to eliminate detrimental genetic effects or genes harmful in a particular situation; it tends to reduce variation in the gene pool. It would appear that this aspect of natural selection has become less effective in man with the development of modern medical research and practice. Chronic and often lethal diseases caused by genetic conditions, such as diabetes mellitus, hemophilia, and phenylketonuria, are certainly more common now than several decades ago because of modern medical care, for persons with these diseases live and produce children with the disease, although they would have died or failed to reproduce under less advanced medical techniques. These individuals, however, are not less fit in a Darwinian sense than the "normal" members of the population as long as their environment includes this medical care; it is only in the absence of this care that they are less fit.

Homeostatic change. A nongenetic correlate of conservative natural selection is homeostasis. This term refers to adaptive physiological cultural flexibility that is genetically based, and it means the retention and preservation in a population of its internal equilibrium in the face of disruptive external environmental conditions. By drawing on this source of variation, a population may adapt its physiology or behaviour in response to new environmental demands without actual changes in the gene pool; because it is an immediate response, it may enhance a group's survival potential. One type of homeostatic response has been called acclimatization; the efficiency and scope of this process are genetically based, yet the full range of responses is seldom, if ever, activated. Because man occupies a wider range of habitats and is therefore exposed to more extreme conditions than any other species, the necessity for broad responsive ability to changes in environmental conditions such as climate is obvious. Homeostatic responses merge indetectably with both dynamic and conservative natural selection and cannot, indeed perhaps need not, be separated from them for most purposes. The extent of homeostatic response is unique in man, not only in the diversity of the physiological responses that deal with the extremes of the environment but also because of the added dimension of culture as an adaptive mechanism. It is this aspect, culture, that allows man not only to fully inhabit and utilize a wide range of environments but also to alter these environments to his own ends. The diversity of the ways in which man deals with environmental extremes can be seen in the various mechanisms (skeletal, physiological, and cultural) used by man in cold climates.

> Acclimatization

Blood types, abnormal hemoglobin, and disease. Diversifying, or dynamic, natural selection is one of the important and basic processes by which evolutionary changes occur. Under conditions of changing environmental pressure, advantageous genotypes will be assimilated into the gene pool, and those individuals within the population who have superior fitness will leave more numerous offspring than those without. One such adaptation is the maintenance of a potentially lethal gene for an abnormal hemoglobin in populations that are exposed to malaria. Sickle-cell anemia and several related anemias are genetically based blood disorders that can kill an individual who inherits a gene for the condition from both parents (homozygous condition); those with only a single abnormal gene (heterozygous condition) will demonstrate the disease under certain conditions but are less affected and usually do not die of it. In certain areas of tropical Africa, however, as well as around the Mediterranean and in regions of the Far East, to be without one gene for the abnormal hemoglobin can mean death or serious illness from malaria prior to breeding. The presence of the abnormal hemoglobin therefore confers protection in certain environments, while outside these areas the abnormal gene has no adaptive significance and will be selected against. The abnormal hemoglobin is virtually absent in nonmalarial areas except in the descendants of people formerly living in such areas.

> Lethal genetic disorders

Other examples of diversifying selection are to be found in the distribution patterns of the ABO blood group system (see BLOOD GROUPS AND FACTORS). Although the data is incomplete, it would appear that individuals with certain blood types are more susceptible to certain diseases and that, therefore, in areas where these diseases are common, these blood groups will be selected against. Suggestions have been made that blood group O individuals are less susceptible to syphilis, group A to plague, and group B to streptococcal infections; fieldwork seems to support statistical correlations between certain types of disorders of the gastrointestinal tract and some ABO blood groups. For example, a higher frequency of duodenal and gastric ulcers in group O and a higher incidence of cancer of the stomach of group A have been demonstrated.

Random genetic drift. Genetic drift is another mechanism by which evolutionary changes may occur. Drift can be defined as the apparently random variation of certain gene frequencies under special conditions of small population size or of isolation or both. Also called the Sewall Wright effect and non-Darwinian evolution, it has been the subject of considerable controversy in the recent literature. From these discussions it emerges that many of the features previously thought caused by drift are now known to have been the result of previously unrecognized natural selection. Central to the definition of genetic drift is the assumption that genes can be neutral and without effect in terms of evolutionary adaptation, and it is this assumption that has led to the greatest controversy. Some workers have argued that 5 to 10 percent of all mutations are selectively neutral and may be maintained in the gene pool without effect. Others have asserted that, because genetic systems have complex chemical interrelationships, with each gene contributing something to the finished product, it is unlikely that a single gene or group of genes could be totally without effect. This latter position recognizes that, while certain observable features may have little apparent effect on fitness, the genes responsible may be inextricably associated with other genetic features that do have important fitness correlations.

The near absence of blood group B in the American Indian has been attributed to genetic drift. However, B-type blood reaches its highest frequency in some Mongoloid groups thought to be ancestral to the early inhabitants of the New World. This and the probability that many incursions from Asia must have occurred in the late Pleistocene Epoch (35,000–10,000 BP) make drift a somewhat untenable explanation of the lack. A more likely explanation is that holders of B blood were faced with some as yet undefined environmental hazard in the New World that made blood type B a genetic liability and it was subsequently lost through selection.

MAN'S CONTINUING EVOLUTION

The question of man's continuing evolution may be posed on two levels, because it is possible to define two distinct yet interrelated levels of evolutionary change: the first can be called phyletic evolution; and the second, phenetic evolution.

Phyletic evolution. This term refers to cumulative and important changes in the population gene pool that lead eventually to speciation (separation into new species) and the higher levels of taxonomic differentiation. It is phyletic evolution that is usually identified in the fossil record. Phenetic evolution is more subtle, and, while it is identifiable in living populations, it is less easy to see in fossil groups. It involves changes of a lower magnitude than phyletic evolution and may be called ecotypic evolution. As with all evolutionary changes, phenetic changes occur in response to environmental stimuli, but it is the consistency of these stimuli through time that determines whether the changes will become permanently impressed on a group's phyletic record or if they will be lost within a relatively short period due to changing pressures on the gene pool. Phenetic evolution is the mechanism underlying the formation of subspecies, races, or varieties.

It is difficult to identify any unequivocal evidence of phyletic evolution in man for perhaps the last 250,000 years, and the reasons for this difficulty are not hard to find. Man's adaptations to his environment have been as broad and generalized as the ecological niche that he occupies. As a species man inhabits and uses possibly more of the Earth's surface than does any other species, and the breadth of this niche demands considerable flexibility in the human gene pool. An additional factor in man's at least temporarily arrested phyletic evolution is the intervention of culture between man and his environment. With culture, first in the form of crude tools and perhaps skin clothing and now with a variety of sophisticated technologies interposed between man and the natural environment, the environment cannot exert pressures on the human species in the same way that it has in the past. A third factor must certainly be the size of the gene pool itself and the relatively extended length of a human generation. Evolutionary changes can occur with considerable rapidity in small populations and in populations that mature and reproduce quickly; but the flow of favourable genotypes, however advantageous, must be extremely slow in man's particular circumstances. In terms of man's total morphological pattern and its component parts, then, no important changes are preserved in the fossil record since late middle Pleistocene times. The last known evidence of human phyletic evolution concerns the *H. erectus–H. sapiens* transition; this period of transition occupied a considerable period of time, and, because of the incompleteness of the fossil record, scholars can only guess at many of its details. Certainly, *H. sapiens* did not spring fully formed from his *H. erectus* ancestors but, through the process of mosaic evolution,

crossed the sapient threshold at varying times in the development of different functional complexes. The resultant combination of *H. erectus* and *H. sapiens* features is well demonstrated in a number of specimens, notably Omo II, Steinheim, and Vértesszőllős.

Phenetic evolution. The apparent arrest of man's phyletic evolution should not suggest that the environment will never affect human development again; the observed fact of his continuing phenetic evolution clearly demonstrates the possibility of further phyletic evolution. Some of the clearest evidence that man is still responding to environmental stimuli comes from studies on the distributions of ABO blood groups; this and the importance of sickle-cell anemia in this context have already been described. Further evidence for phenetic evolution is to be found in the analysis of certain general morphological patterns, such as Bergmann's rule, which states that, within a polytypic warm-blooded species, the body size of a subspecies usually increases with decreasing temperature of its habitat, and Allen's rule, which states that in warm-blooded species there tends to be an increase in the relative size of protruding organs such as the ears and tail with increasing temperature of the habitat.

Disease is an especially acute natural selective agent, and it is well recognized that many diseases recur in cyclical patterns when their virulence is increased. This may be associated with conditions in the environment favourable to the disease-producing organism (pathogen) or by changes in the organism that suffers the disease (host); plague, tuberculosis, and scarlet fever may demonstrate this sort of pattern. In addition, populations that do not have natural immunity may be decimated by a disease that is relatively mild in nonsusceptible groups. Many Polynesian peoples, for example, have been virtually annihilated by measles. It is possible, therefore, that highly lethal worldwide epidemics could act as potent selective forces; such selection could be caused by some new or previously unrecognized disease or by a new episode of high lethality in an existing one. The effects of disease are one example of how further evolution in man may occur. Although clear conclusions with regard to human populations are not yet available, experiments with laboratory animals indicate further possibilities. A number of pathologies, both social and physical, have been induced in laboratory animals under conditions of crowding: infertility, cannibalism, mental aberration, and early death have all been observed. Environmental pollution is also known to seriously damage laboratory animals, but again the application of these results to human populations is not yet defined. Clearly, in order to obtain an understanding of the course of human evolution in a modern context, it is necessary for information to be combined from a wider range of disciplines than was formerly the case. The facts of organic evolution as the overall mechanism by which man has evolved are no longer in serious dispute; undisputed too is his continuing need for reactive and progressive changes, whether evolutionary or cultural, in response to a changing world.

Marginal notes:
Levels of evolutionary change

Disease as a selection factor

BIBLIOGRAPHY. CHARLES DARWIN, *The Descent of Man and Selection in Relation to Sex*, 2nd ed. (1874), historically the foundation reference; G.G. SIMPSON, *Tempo and Mode in Evolution* (1944, reprinted 1965); THEODOSIUS DOBZHANSKY, *Mankind Evolving* (1962); and ERNST MAYR, *Animal Species and Evolution* (1963), all consider theoretical aspects of evolution as a process; while RENE DUBOS, *Man Adapting* (1965), relates man to his environment. E. GENET-VARCIN, *Les Singes actuels et fossiles* (1963); and J.R. and P.H. NAPIER, *A Handbook of Living Primates* (1967), gives good accounts of both modern and fossil primates; W.E. LE GROS CLARK, *The Antecedents of Man* (1959) and *The Fossil Evidence for Human Evolution* (1955); K.P. OAKLEY, *Frameworks for Dating Fossil Man* (1964); and M.H. DAY, *Guide to Fossil Man* (1965), provide information on the fossil history of man. JOHN BUETTNER-JANUSCH, *Origins of Man* (1966), is a modern general text; and DAVID PILBEAM, *The Evolution of Man* (1970), provides a concise account of the subject in readable form. L.S.B. LEAKEY, *Olduvai Gorge, 1951–61*, vol. 1 (1965); P.V. TOBIAS, *Olduvai Gorge*, vol. 2 (1967); and M.D. LEAKEY, *Olduvai Gorge*, vol. 3 (1971), are definitive monographs on the Olduvai Gorge site, including paleontology, anatomy of *A. boisei*, and archaeology. SHERWOOD L. WASHBURN (ed.), *Classification and Human Evolution* (1963), is an important collection of papers dealing with taxonomy. E. SIMONS and DAVID PILBEAM, "A Preliminary Revision of the Dryopithecinae," *Folia Primat*, 3:81–152 (1965); ERNST MAYR, "Taxonomic Categories in Fossil Hominids," *Cold Spring Harb. Symp. Quant. Biol.*, 15:109–118 (1950); E.L. SIMONS, "Some Fallacies in the Study of Hominid Phylogeny," *Science*, 141:879–889 (1963); G.A. BARTHOLOMEW and J.B. BIRDSELL, "Ecology and the Protohominids," *Am. Anthrop.*, 55:481–498 (1953); and F. CLARK HOWELL, "European and Northwest African Middle Pleistocene Hominids," *Curr. Anthrop.*, 1:195–232 (1960), are key papers dealing with modern views on specific areas of particular importance at the present time.

(M.H.D.)

Manchester

The Manchester of the 1970s remains one of the great regional cities of Britain, dominating much of northwest England, but it has lost that extraordinary vitality and unique influence that made it such a phenomenon of the Industrial Revolution. For Manchester was an urban prototype: in many respects it could claim to be the first of the new generation of huge industrial cities created in the Western world during the last 200 years. In 1717 it was merely a market town of 10,000 people, but by 1851 its textile (chiefly cotton) industries had so prospered that it had become a manufacturing and commercial city of over 300,000 inhabitants, already spilling out its suburbs and absorbing its industrial satellites. By the opening of the 20th century, salients of urban growth were linking Manchester to the ring of cotton manufacturing towns—Bolton, Rochdale, and Oldham, for example—that almost surround the city, and a new form of urban development, a conurbation, or metropolitan area, was evolving. By 1911 this already had a population of 2,350,000. In the following half-century, the pace of growth slowed dramatically, for by 1971 the population total was only 2,460,000. If the 19th century—when it was indisputably Britain's second city—was Manchester's golden age, the 20th century has seen it beset by increasing industrial problems associated with the decline of the textile trades (the result of foreign competition and technological obsolescence), and the city has lost much of its economic impetus.

The Manchester of the 19th century was a city of enormous vitality, not only in its economic growth but also in its political, cultural, and intellectual life. Its prosperous and influential middle class pioneered the development of the amenities and institutions of a great modern city. *The Manchester Guardian* became Britain's leading provincial newspaper, achieving an international influence, while the Hallé Orchestra was its equal in the world of music. Owens College (now known as Victoria University of Manchester) became the nucleus of the first and largest of the great English civic universities, while the academic success of the Manchester Grammar School made it something of a model in the development of selective secondary education in England. Politically, Victorian Manchester often led the nation: in the agitation for parliamentary reform and for free trade its influence was crucial. Among its intellectual achievements were John Dalton's development of the atomic theory as the foundation of modern chemistry, and the work of the "Manchester school" in the application of economic principles to the problems of commerce, industry, and government. At the end of the 19th century, Manchester made itself unique among British inland cities by becoming a port. This was accomplished by the building of the 37-mile-long (60-kilometre) ship canal leading to the Mersey estuary at Eastham and hence to the Irish Sea and the world markets beyond.

There was a price to be paid for this precocious growth; in its urban fabric, inner Manchester has remained essentially a 19th-century city, and by the second half of the 20th century it faced massive redevelopment problems. An industrial collar of obsolescent factory zones encircles the city centre, and huge areas of old slum housing survived with little renewal into the 1960s. In 1955 Manchester and its near neighbour Salford had a total of

(margin note: Nineteenth-century achievement*)*

(margin note: Twentieth-century problems*)*

80,000 houses classified as unfit. Clearance and redevelopment are nevertheless accelerating; the Hulme renewal scheme, underway in the early 1970s, is the largest project of its kind in Europe. Over 30,000 people lived in poor housing on its 350 acres, and the replacement housing will provide homes for 15,000. Manchester, then, is a city in transition: its face is being transformed by redevelopment, and its dependence on the insecure base of the textile industries is declining with the growth of a broader economic structure. The rate of population increase, on the other hand, has diminished; by the 1970s the population of the city itself was actually declining, while that of the conurbation had been virtually static in population for 50 years. This demographic trend has inevitably sapped the vitality of the city, impressive physical transformations notwithstanding.

History. Early in the Roman conquest of Britain a fort was established (AD 78–86) on a low sandstone plateau at the confluence of the Rivers Medlock and Irwell, almost a mile from the site of the medieval town. Of earth and timber, the fort was occupied intermittently, was partly rebuilt in stone by the emperor Hadrian (reigned AD 117–138), and was abandoned in the 4th century. Few traces survive: in fact, the Romans did no more than give Manchester its name, derived from Mamucium (Place of the Breastlike Hill). For the following five and a half centuries, there was no known occupation of the site, but in 919 the West Saxon king Edward the Elder sent a force to repair the ruined Roman fort and make it a defense against the Norsemen. By 1086 a manor of Manchester existed, but by then the settlement was relocated at the junction of the Rivers Irk and Irwell near the present cathedral. The Norman barony of Manchester was one of the largest landholdings in Lancashire, and its lords, the Grelley family, built a fortified hall close to the church. During the 13th century Manchester began its transition from village to town; corn and fulling mills (the latter for cloth) were established, and both a weekly market and an annual fair were held. Sometime before 1301 a charter was granted; there were then about 150 burgesses (adult male citizens) in the town. The parish served by the church was a huge one, and already the infant Manchester was acquiring a regional importance. Yet it was subordinate to its near neighbour Salford (facing Manchester across the River Irwell), which was the capital manor of the hundred (district) and had an earlier borough charter. The full development of the medieval borough followed the establishment in 1421 of a college of priests to take charge of the church. Part of the college survives as Chetham's Hospital, while a free church school set up in 1506 became the Manchester Grammar School in 1515, founded by Hugh Oldham, bishop of Exeter.

By the 16th century Manchester was a flourishing market borough already important in the wool trade, exporting cloth to Europe via London in the reign of Elizabeth I. Merchant families like the Mosleys acquired great wealth. The antiquary John Leland, who visited the town in 1538, thought it one of the "best builded" in the country. By 1620 a new industrial era had begun, with the weaving of fustians, a cloth with a linen warp (the thread extended lengthwise in the loom) but a cotton weft (the weaker cross thread). This was the origin of the cotton industry that was to transform south Lancashire after 1770. As the trade grew, the town expanded, and new "improvements" were added, including the fine square and church of St. Ann (1712).

From the 1760s onward, growth quickened with the onset of the Industrial Revolution. The first canal (the Bridgewater), bringing cheap coal from Worsley, reached the town in 1762; later extended, it linked Manchester with the Mersey and Liverpool by 1776, and so served the import–export needs of the infant cotton industry. Manchester's first cotton mill was built in the early 1780s. By 1800 Manchester was said to be "steam mill mad," and by 1830 there were 99 cotton-spinning mills. The world's first modern railway, the Liverpool and Manchester, was opened in 1830, and by the 1850s the greater part of the present railway system of the city was com-

(margin note: Early growth*)*

Manchester skyline viewed from the mathematics building of Manchester University Institute of Science and Technology.
The Guardian, Manchester and London

The
industrial
era

plete. Despite its growth to a population of over 70,000 by 1801, the town had no system of government and was still managed, like a village, by a manorial court leet (a court held semiannually by the lord of the manor or his steward to conduct local government). A police force was established in 1792, but not until 1838 did a charter of incorporation set up an elected council and a system of local government.

The economic history of Manchester during the second half of the 19th century is one both of growth and diversification. The city became less important as a cotton-manufacturing centre than as the commercial and financial nucleus of the trade; on the floor of the Royal Exchange the yarn and cloth of the entire industry was bought and sold. From an early textile-machinery industry many specialized types of engineering developed. Products included steam engines and locomotives, armaments, machine tools, and, later, those of electrical engineering. The opening of the Manchester Ship Canal (1894) gave a stimulus to this industrial diversity. By 1910 Manchester had become the fourth port of the country, and alongside the docks, at Trafford Park, the first (and still the largest) industrial estate in Britain was being developed. New industries also took sites here, with a prominent role being played by such American companies as Westinghouse and Ford, the latter moving to Essex in 1929. Ultimately, more than 50,000 workers were to be accommodated within factories of the estate.

Site and urban structure. Manchester occupies a featureless plain made up of river gravels and the glacial-transported debris known as drift. It lies at a height of 100–350 feet (30–107 metres) above sea level, enclosed by the slopes of the Pennine range on the east and the upland spur of Rossendale on the north. Much of the plain is underlain by coal measures; mining was once widespread, but only a single large newly sunk pit remains, at Agecroft. Within this physical unit, known as the Manchester embayment, the conurbation of southeast Lancashire and northeast Cheshire (often labelled by the acronym SELNEC) has evolved. Manchester, the central city, has an elongated north–south extent, the result of late 19th- and early 20th-century territorial expansion. In 1930 the city extended its boundaries far to the south beyond the Mersey, to annex nine square miles of north Cheshire, the site of what became the great Wythenshawe complex of housing estates (population more than 103,-000). Two large and independent towns adjoin Manchester on the west and southwest, the county borough of Salford (population 131,000) and the borough of Stretford (population 54,000). Together, these three administrative units form the core of the conurbation, the chief

concentration of industrial and commercial employment. From them, suburbs have spread far to the west and south, chiefly within the county of Cheshire. To the north and east of Manchester smaller industrial towns and villages, mixed with suburban development, extend as a continuous urban area to the foot of the encircling upland. Close to the upland margin lies a ring of large autonomous county boroughs, traditionally the major centres of the cotton-spinning industry—Bolton, Bury, and Rochdale on the north and Oldham, Ashton (a municipal borough), and Stockport on the east.

The urban structure of metropolitan Manchester is largely determined by its industrial zones. By far the most important of these is the one bisecting it from east to west. This contains most of the heavier industry—steel and petrochemicals on the Ship Canal near Irlam; electrical engineering in Trafford Park and Salford; and machine tools and metal fabrication in east Manchester. Industry in the south is confined to a few new, compact, largely planned factory estates, notably at Altrincham and Wythenshawe. North and east of Manchester ribbons of long-established industry follow every railway, river valley, and abandoned canal. The electrochemical industries of the Irwell valley, the dyestuffs of the Irk, and, everywhere, the old textile mills, are the dominant features.

Demography. The SELNEC (see above) conurbation is one of the world's most crowded metropolitan areas: its 2,460,000 people occupy 357 square miles at an average density of 6,891 per square mile. In the centre, densities are much higher: in Manchester they reach 15,000, and in Salford 18,400, per square mile. This overcrowding explains the chief demographic trend of the conurbation: population loss by migration. Manchester itself lost 8.3 percent of its population between 1961 and 1966 by net out-migration, and Salford 8.6 percent. These are among the highest rates of migrational loss for all British cities. Natural increase is below national average, for the migration is of young and fertile families, leaving an older population in the core cities. Thus, overall population decline is serious. Manchester has shrunk from 766,000 inhabitants in 1931 to 541,000 in 1971, a loss of almost 29 percent. This trend is also widespread in the old industrial towns of the conurbation; Bolton's population fell by 4.2 percent, and Oldham's by 8.4 percent, between 1961 and 1971.

Much of this migration is short-range, to suburban areas, and, as a result, the "dormitory" districts of the southern fringe are still growing strongly. The population trend of the metropolitan area as a whole is thus more favourable than that of its major cities. The conurbation

The
structure
of the
conurba-
tion

Migratory
loss

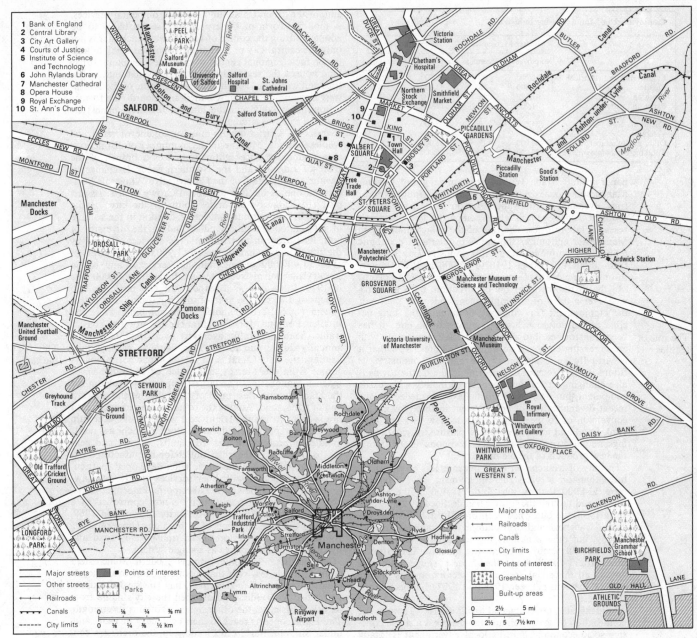

1 Bank of England
2 Central Library
3 City Art Gallery
4 Courts of Justice
5 Institute of Science and Technology
6 John Rylands Library
7 Manchester Cathedral
8 Opera House
9 Royal Exchange
10 St. Ann's Church

Major streets
Other streets
Railroads
Canals
City limits
Points of interest
Parks

Major roads
Railroads
Canals
City limits
Points of interest
Greenbelts
Built-up areas

Central Manchester and (inset) its metropolitan area.

declined by 0.9 percent during the period 1961–71; its low rate of natural increase (0.4 percent in 1970) was wholly offset by a net out-migration which reduced population by 2 percent annually during 1961–71. Increasingly, the migration from the crowded central cities is planned, as slum families are rehoused. Manchester has exported population to "overspill" estates at Middleton and Hyde, and Salford to Worsley. All of these are large schemes, involving population transfers of at least 10,000, and all lie within the conurbation. Longer range and larger scale movement to two New Town projects, at Warrington and Preston (18 miles west and 30 miles northwest, respectively, of Manchester), will commence in the 1970s. This out-migration has been partly balanced by an in-migration of migrants from Commonwealth countries, particularly those of the West Indies and the Indian subcontinent. By the early 1970s, Manchester itself had a multiracial immigrant community of at least 15,000 (probably in excess of 25,000 when children of British birth are included), chiefly concentrated in the Moss Side area. Some of the textile towns, too, have attracted Commonwealth migrants, chiefly Indian and Pakistani textile workers; Bolton has a community of at least 3,000 and Oldham 2,000. The metropolitan area as a whole has been one of the main magnets to Common-

Common-
wealth im-
migration

wealth immigrants in Britain; they total 33,000, and the non-European communities (including children born in Britain) probably have a population approaching 50,000.

Economic life. In terms of the urban economy, an initial distinction must be drawn between two areas: Greater Manchester (the city itself, together with Salford, Stretford, and the southern suburbs) and the textile towns of the north and east of the conurbation. The former area has greater economic breadth, together with most of the new growth industries; the latter has a narrow economic base, and the bulk of the declining textile sector. These contrasts are shown in the accompanying Table (1966 data).

In Greater Manchester, the engineering and electrical group is clearly the leading industry, with an output ranging from heavy generating equipment to computers and microcircuits, and from machine tools to constructional engineering. This is the only major industry still growing strongly in the area. Clothing factories (many of workshop size) are the most important employers of female labour, especially in the rainwear trade. As in the case of textiles—now a relic industry here—the clothing industry is in serious decline. The importance of paper and printing partly reflects Manchester's importance as the country's second centre of newspaper publishing, as well as its

Employment in Manufacturing Industries

	Greater Manchester		the textile towns	
	employees	percentage	employees	percentage
Engineering and electrical	118,000	33	50,000	22
Textiles	28,000	8	83,000	37
Clothing	41,000	11	10,000	4
Paper and printing	31,000	9	15,000	7
Food and drink	33,000	9	9,000	4
Chemicals	31,000	9	5,000	2
Vehicles	12,000	3	19,000	8
Other manufactures	63,000	18	35,000	15
Total factory employment	357,000		226,000	

paper products trade. Within the chemical group, Greater Manchester houses not only Imperial Chemical Industries' dyestuffs division but also (on a rural site to the south at Alderley) this giant company's fine chemicals research laboratories. The fate of the vehicle industry in Manchester epitomizes the area's problems of economic rebuilding; employment in this industry has dropped from about 130,000 in 1958 to 12,000 in 1966, largely through the closure of several railway engineering plants.

In the textile towns of the conurbation, mills still provide over a third of all employment and more than half the employment for women. Fortunately, the long decline of the cotton industry is almost at an end: it has

The role of textiles

been transformed into a general textile manufacture with an increasing emphasis on man-made fibres. Now that it is virtually an extension of the chemical industry, its future is more secure. Engineering in the textile towns is also changing. It was once concerned mainly with textile equipment, but now its products have broadened. In the recent diversification of employment in these towns, the conversion of former cotton mills to new uses has been vital. Food and tobacco products, plastics, surgical dressings, and electrical and aerospace components are among the new products of the old mills.

The city of Manchester itself depends less on manufactures than on services for employment. In 1967 there were 134,000 factory jobs, but 218,400 in the service trades; and though the former had declined by 26 percent since 1958, the latter had been broadly stable. Some services—transport and distribution, for example—are declining, but others, notably finance and the professional and scientific group, are growing quickly. The latter is now, after distribution, the largest single employer among all industrial and service sectors, and its growth rate (43 percent between 1958 and 1967) has been much the fastest.

Political and governmental institutions. Though the conurbation of metropolitan Manchester is a single cohesive socio-economic unit, its local government is totally fragmented. The dominant unit is the county borough of Manchester, which assumes the financial burden of supplying central facilities (major museums and libraries, the airport) for the area as a whole. There are six other county boroughs, each independent and able to develop its own social, educational, and planning policies. The 15 municipal boroughs have, in practice, a high degree of autonomy; but the 30 urban districts have more limited powers, and look to the county authorities for many

Political fragmentation

services. Thus three counties (Lancashire, Cheshire, and Derbyshire) share the administration of this much-divided conurbation. Division of responsibility has led to serious problems; Manchester, for example, spent 20 unsuccessful years seeking a New Town site in Cheshire (Lymm, Mobberley, and Congleton were all investigated) to absorb its surplus population. The need for a metropolitan system of government has long been recognized. In 1969 the Royal Commission on Local Government proposed a metropolitan unit of 1,043 square miles, with a population of 3,232,000, to administer the SELNEC area. Much larger than the conurbation (as a result of the enclosing of satellites and dormitories beyond the edge of continuous urbanization), this new unit was to be divided into nine metropolitan "boroughs" ranging in size from 176,000 to 979,000, each with full autonomy over community services, while the metropolitan authority would

administer general planning and environmental services. A modified form of these proposals seems likely to be adopted during the course of the 1970s. Manchester is not only the central city of a large metropolitan area but also the de facto regional capital of northwest England. It has long housed the regional offices of many national ministries and when, in 1965, it became the home of the Northwest Economic Planning Council and Board (the former a nominated body and the latter a technical panel) its regional role was strengthened.

Services. Apart from its massive volume of retail and wholesale trade, Manchester has a number of distinctions as a regional service centre. It houses a branch of the Bank of England and the Northern Stock Exchange; it has the headquarters of the Co-operative Wholesale Society and one of the few provincial Crown courts. Its airport (at Ringway, ten miles south of the city) is the leading British terminal outside of London in the volume of international traffic handled and in the diversity of both its European and transatlantic services. Owned by the city, Ringway handled nearly 1,900,000 passengers in 1970 (1,000,000 on international services) and is the country's second airfreight terminal, handling 42,000 tons in 1970. In its role as a seaport, the city possesses two groups of docks at the head of the Ship Canal. The larger system (in Salford) handles ocean shipping, while the smaller Pomona docks in Manchester are for coastal traffic. Seaborne traffic averaged over 16,000,000 tons annually during the 1960s. This figure is perhaps misleading: the Ship Canal is, in fact, a linear port along its

The role of the canal

course from the Mersey, and much of its traffic never reaches Manchester. The largest import is petroleum for the Stanlow refineries, most of it handled at the seaward end of the system. Among the other leading imports, iron ore is destined for the Irlam steel·works, and wood pulp for a paper plant at Ellesmere Port. Manchester itself handles imports of timber, foodstuffs, cotton, and general cargo, and is the chief outlet for manufactured exports. Container facilities have been developed, particularly in connection with liner services via the St. Lawrence Seaway to the Great Lakes ports. Passenger transport within the metropolitan city is now controlled by a single Passenger Transport Authority. Formed in 1969, this took over the bus fleets of 11 municipal undertakings. Its function is to develop public transport by road and by commuter rail services as a single system.

Cultural life. In some respects modern Manchester's cultural life is less rich than formerly. For example, its great newspaper, *The Guardian,* has (in the Mancunian view) fled to London and dropped the city's name from its title. Music, on the other hand, maintains its strength. The Hallé concerts reached their centenary in 1958, and, under Sir John Barbirolli's leadership, the orchestra continued its international reputation.

Of all Manchester's pioneer cultural achievements, none has prospered more than its university. After its foundation in 1851 at a site in Quay Street, the college received a charter in 1872 and began growth on its present site in 1873. By 1880 it had combined with member colleges in both Leeds and Liverpool to form a federal institution. Since becoming a separate body again in 1903, the university has grown to become one of the largest in Britain, with an enrollment of over 10,000 students. The faculty of technology has become autonomous as an Institute of Science and Technology; and with the foundation of the University of Salford in the early 1960s there are now three universities in and near the city.

A university precinct has been planned as a major feature in Manchester's redevelopment. This is to contain all the main higher educational institutions and will have a future student population of at least 25,000. The most ambitious project of its kind in Britain, it was quickly taking shape on the ground during the early 1970s. The precinct runs from the city centre southward for over a mile; at its broadest it is almost a half-mile wide. At the northern end lies the Institute of Science and Technology complex and a new Central Technical College; farther south are the sites of the Regional College of Art, the School of Music, and the Manchester Business School.

The main mass of the university occupies the southern half of the precinct, with the medical school and teaching hospitals at the southern border. Farther south still, on a 24-acre site at Fallowfield, lies the student village. The whole project reflects the growing importance of technology and research in the city's economic life.

BIBLIOGRAPHY. C.F. CARTER (ed.), *Manchester and Its Region* (1962), a collection of expert articles on the geology, history, geography, industry, and cultural life of the Manchester region; N.J. FRANGOPULO (ed.), *Rich Inheritance: A Guide to the History of Manchester* (1962), particularly strong as a survey of sources for the history of the city; T.W. FREEMAN, H.B. RODGERS, and R.H. KINVIG, *Lancashire, Cheshire and the Isle of Man* (1966), a general geography of northwest England, placing Manchester in its broader regional context; L.P. GREEN, *Provincial Metropolis* (1959), an analysis of the city and conurbation as a major urban region; S.D. SIMON, *A Century of City Government: Manchester, 1838–1938* (1938), a readable and well informed account of the development of local government in the city.

(H.B.Ro.)

Manchuria, History of

The geographical division of Manchuria into regions of forested hills and mountains, fertile plains, and semi-arid grasslands made possible the development of distinctive cultural patterns among its inhabitants. Because of its accessibility from Siberia, the Mongolian Plateau, the Korean peninsula, and China proper, many peoples have mingled and fought within its boundaries. Prior to the 17th century, the history of Manchuria was shaped by the needs and ambitions of three converging ethnic groups: the Chinese, the Tungus, and the Mongols and Proto-Mongols.

The Tungus were forest and plain dwellers. They had a mixed economy of primitive agriculture, fishing, hunting, and livestock breeding. They were known in various historical periods by such names as Su-shen, I-lou, Fu-yu, Mo-ho, Juchen, and Manchu. The Mongols and Proto-Mongols were nomadic pastoralists who occupied the grasslands of the eastern rim of the Mongolian Plateau and the eastern slope of the Great Khingan Mountains. They were known by such names as Tung-hu, Hsien-pei, Wu-huan, Shih-wei, Khitan, and Mongol. The agricultural Chinese migrated from the north of China to cultivate the soil of the rich Liao Plain in south Manchuria. The successive hegemonies and kingdoms in Manchuria resulted from violent clashes among these ethnic groups. Beginning in the late 19th century, the imperialistic expansion of Russia and Japan brought about rapid economic and political changes in the country while subjecting it to intense international rivalry.

MANCHURIA TO C. 1900

Early history. Prehistoric Manchuria was the eastern terminus of a natural highway for nomadic peoples who moved across the great Eurasian plain from the Volga to the Korean peninsula. Paleolithic and Neolithic sites in Manchuria often showed evidences of cultural diffusion from North China, the Gobi region, the Eurasian steppes, and Siberia. Of great interest is the discovery of painted ceramic wares in south Manchuria akin to the Yang-shao ware of North China and the stone-cist graves that spread from the Shantung peninsula in North China to south Manchuria and Korea.

As early as 1000 BC, certain Manchurian tribes are mentioned in Chinese sources. A pastoral tribe, the Tung-hu, made their appearance in Chinese history during the period of Warring States (481–221 BC), when they were confronted by the expanding Chinese feudal kingdom of Yen. Their defeat opened the way for the expansion of Yen territory into the Liao Plain and the settlement of Chinese colonies in south Manchuria.

Chinese immigration into south Manchuria accelerated during the period of political chaos that preceded the unification of China by the Ch'in dynasty (221–206 BC). In the succeeding Han dynasty (206 BC–AD 220), a rebel Han general, Wei Man, fled from Liao-tung into Korea, where he founded the Chosŏn kingdom with the help of Chinese colonists. After the death of Wei Man in 108 BC,

Chinese immigration (margin)

the Chosŏn kingdom and the adjacent Manchurian and Korean lands were overrun by the Han, who organized the conquered territories into military commanderies.

During the chaotic period following the collapse of the Han empire, China was able to maintain only a loose hegemony over Manchuria. Throughout the Inner Asian frontiers of China, the contest between the agricultural Chinese and the nomadic and semi-nomadic tribes of the steppes and forests often led to bloody warfare, interspersed with long periods of peaceful coexistence. The frontiers were not rigidly defined, and there was constant intermingling of populations. The Chinese learned from the nomads the art of cavalry warfare, and the nomads, in turn, learned from the Chinese the art of political organization. Both benefitted from trade.

The Tung-hu tribes that had been driven north by the Yen kingdom during the 3rd century BC regained their strength during the Han dynasty. Toward the end of that dynasty, the Tung-hu were divided into two major groups: the Wu-huan in the south and Hsien-pei in the north. The Wu-huan raided the Han frontier while China was in the throes of civil war, but they were decisively defeated in 207. Thereafter, the Hsien-pei gained ascendancy among the Tung-hu tribes. In 281 the Mu-jung branch of the Hsien-pei tribes plundered the area near modern Peking. In 285, soon after their great chief Mu-jung Hui came to power, they ravaged the Tungus Fu-yu tribes to the north, initiating a prolonged struggle between the two peoples. When China was in political disarray after 300, Mu-jung Hui moved his capital to Chi-ch'eng near the Chinese-settled Liao-tung. In 352 the Mu-jung king assumed the title of emperor and called his domain the Yen kingdom (known to historians as the Former Yen kingdom to distinguish it from other kingdoms of the same name). Further conquests enabled the Yen to control a large part of North China and to move their capital there in 359. Thereafter, the Mu-jung power began to decline, and the kingdom was overthrown in 370.

Ascendancy of the Hsien-pei (margin)

Under the Sui (581–618) and T'ang (618–907) dynasties China was able to reassert a limited control over south Manchuria. The T'ang also claimed the allegiance of many Manchurian tribes that lived beyond its frontier. As T'ang power waned, these tribes claimed independence. Ta-tso-jung, leader of the Mo-ho tribes, proclaimed the founding of the Chen kingdom in 698, which became the P'o-hai kingdom in 712. Centred in the modern province of Kirin, P'o-hai, at its height, covered nearly the whole of Manchuria and North Korea. Its population numbered over 100,000 households and included a sizeable number of Chinese and Koreans. It was through P'o-hai that Buddhism was introduced among the Tungus in Manchuria.

The P'o-hai kingdom (margin)

The Khitan and Juchen empires. With the collapse of the T'ang dynasty in 907, the Khitan, who belonged to the Yu-wen branch of the Hsien-pei tribes, gradually gained ascendancy in Manchuria. Under the leadership of their chief, A-pao-chi (872–926), the Khitan united their Hsien-pei neighbours and began expanding south against China and west against the Turkic nations. By 907 A-pao-chi was ready to have himself crowned emperor. When P'o-hai invaded a Khitan city in 924, the Khitan retaliated in 926 by overthrowing P'o-hai.

Under A-pao-chi's successor, Te-kuang, the Khitan acquired 16 strategic prefectures in northern China. In 947 Te-kuang adopted a Chinese name, Liao, for his dynasty, signifying his ambition to rule over the whole of China. Although that ambition was never realized, the Khitan did humiliate successive Chinese dynasties by requiring them to pay tribute to the Liao court. At the height of its power, the Khitan empire occupied practically the whole of Manchuria, part of North Korea, part of North China, and the greater part of the Mongolian Plateau.

The Khitan nobility preferred to reside in China, where they could enjoy a more sophisticated and luxurious life. There ensued a marked decline in administrative efficiency and military prowess toward the end of the dynasty. The non-Khitan subjects staged frequent rebellions against their overlord. Of particular importance among

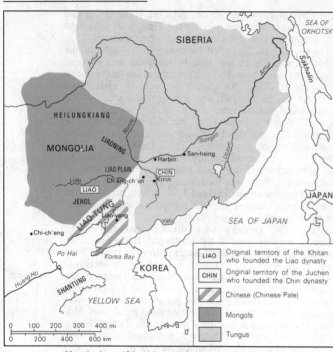

Manchuria, c. 10th–11th centuries.
Adapted from O. Lattimore, *Inner Asian Frontiers of China* (1951); American Geographical Society

The Ming Chinese, however, did not attempt to govern the tribal peoples directly. The Juchen in Manchuria, who had reverted to their ancestral way of living, were divided into three major groups: the Chien-chou, Hai-hsi, and Yeh-jen. Each group comprised a number of tribes and clans, each of which was led by a chief. The authority of the tribal chief had to be confirmed by the Ming government. The Chinese tried to keep the tribes divided into as many subdivisions as possible, in order to prevent them from uniting into a single frontier power. A similar tactic was also used in regard to the Mongol tribes near the Ming frontier. During the 15th and 16th centuries, the Mongols had regained their strength and were pressing upon the Chinese frontier. As a result, the Ming position in Manchuria gradually deteriorated, and by the 17th century the Juchen were strong enough to challenge the Ming rule.

It was the Chien-chou tribes, under the leadership of Nurhachi (1559–1626), who succeeded in forging a new and greater Juchen empire. Beginning in 1583, Nurhachi led a series of campaigns that ultimately brought all the Juchen tribes under his control. In 1616 he was proclaimed *han* (emperor) by his subjects and allies. Nurhachi named his dynasty Chin in an attempt to rekindle the desire for Imperial greatness among the Juchen people. In 1621 he captured the Ming cities of Shen-yang (Mukden) and Liao-yang in south Manchuria. After Nurhachi's death, his son and successor, Abahai, continued the task of territorial expansion. When Abahai died in 1643, Manchu arms had been carried east into Korea, north into the Amur and Ussuri valleys, west to Inner Mongolia, and south to the Great Wall. Abahai adopted the name Manchu for his people and changed the dynastic designation from Chin to Ch'ing. In 1644 the Manchus, with the help of dissident Chinese, established themselves as the new rulers of the Chinese empire.

Nurhachi *(margin)*

Sinicization of Manchuria. Although the Chinese had colonized the Liao Plain more than a thousand years before and had made it a centre of Chinese cultural influence, they had never been able to secure a foothold in central and north Manchuria, which remained predominantly a preserve of tribal groups. Paradoxically, it was during the period of Manchu ascendancy that the Chinese succeeded in penetrating the Sungari and Amur valleys.

The Manchu population had been organized by Nurhachi and Abahai into military and administrative units called banners. During and after the conquest of China, the majority of the Manchu bannermen followed the Manchu court into China. The Chinese population in Liao-tung was decimated by years of warfare, and, consequently, the whole of Manchuria was underpopulated. Until 1688 the Ch'ing government encouraged Chinese immigration to Liao-tung in order to revive its economy. After 1688 Chinese immigration was restricted. Two lines of barriers, known as the Willow Palisades, were constructed in Manchuria, separating the traditional area of Chinese settlement in Liao-tung from the tribal frontier in the west, north, and east. Chinese were prohibited from crossing the palisades without authorization.

The Willow Palisades *(margin)*

Almost from the very beginning, the Manchus had to modify their exclusion policy. The rise of Manchu power in the 17th century coincided with the eastward march of the Russian power. The might and interests of both empires clashed in the Amur Valley, and the thinly spread Manchu garrison had to be strengthened with Chinese recruits for the emergency. These recruits, chosen from the ranks of political exiles, captured rebel soldiers, and criminal convicts formed the earliest nuclei of Chinese settlements in the frontier garrison towns, such as Ninguta, Kirin, Tsitsihar, and Aigun.

Natural resources, such as ginseng (a medicinal herb), fur, gold, and fertile soil, attracted an unending stream of voluntary immigrants to Manchuria, despite the official ban. Land-hungry peasants slipped past the Willow Palisades in large numbers, and a series of great famines in the 18th century made it impossible to stem the flow of peasant refugees. The flow of immigration became a flood tide in the 19th and 20th centuries as China was torn by a series of great rebellions, and Manchuria be-

these rebels were the Juchen tribes, who lived beyond the Liao frontier but were under tributary relationship to the Liao court.

As tributary subjects, the Juchen chiefs were obliged to appear before the reigning Liao emperor, who came to fish once each year in the Sungari River. The emperor, according to custom, invited the Juchen chiefs to celebrate the occasion with a sumptuous feast and often asked them to perform their native dance for him, a gesture symbolic of the political relationships between the two peoples. In 1112 the Liao emperor, T'ien-tsu, while intoxicated, ordered A-ku-ta, the paramount chief of the Juchen, to dance before him. The proud warrior twice refused the Emperor's request. It was a dramatic signal indicating the waning of the Khitan power. In 1115 A-ku-ta proclaimed the establishment of the Chin kingdom. An alliance between the Juchen Chin kingdom and the Chinese Sung dynasty succeeded in destroying the Liao empire in 1125.

The Khitan collapse *(margin)*

After the destruction of their common enemy, the Chin turned against the Sung. In 1127 the Juchen sacked the Sung capital and the Sung court retreated to the south, where it existed as the Southern Sung dynasty. After experimenting with puppet Chinese rulers governing the occupied Sung territory, the Juchen decided to incorporate it into their own domain. In 1214 their capital was moved from Manchuria to Yen-ching (modern Peking). By then, however, the formidable Chin military machine had become moribund and was an easy prey to the Mongols, who rose to power in the Mongolian Plateau in the 12th century (see MONGOLS).

In 1210 the Mongols invaded Chin under the leadership of the great Genghis Khan, and by 1234 Chin had succumbed to the combined pressure of the Mongols and the Sung Chinese. Occupying the whole of Manchuria, the Mongols made it one province, the Liaoyang.

In 1280 the Mongols completed the conquest of China, where they established the Yüan dynasty. The Mongols, like their Juchen predecessors, located their capital in Peking, away from their steppe homeland. Although they had conquered the whole of China, the Mongols were less affected by Chinese culture than the Khitan and Juchen had been. Their harsh rule precipitated a series of rebellions among the Chinese, who overthrew the dynasty in 1368. The victorious Chinese established a native dynasty (the Ming), pursued the Mongols into the steppes, and reinstituted Chinese rule over Liao-tung.

The Ming dynasty *(margin)*

Map legend:
- LIAO — Original territory of the Khitan who founded the Liao dynasty
- CHIN — Original territory of the Juchen who founded the Chin dynasty
- Chinese (Chinese Pale)
- Mongols
- Tungus

came the target of expansionist Russia and Japan. Instead of maintaining the ineffective ban against Chinese immigration, the Ch'ing government actively sponsored planned colonization of virgin lands in Kirin and Heilung-kiang. The immigrant communities were served by merchants operating from commercial centres, such as Kirin, Mukden, Ying-kou, Tsitsihar, and San-hsing. Their economy developed from primitive self-sufficiency to an important centre of international trade.

The bandit society In this unstable frontier society Manchurian bandits preyed upon the population in the mountains and plains alike. Mounted to cover the great distances between Manchurian settlements, these outlaws moved easily from banditry to soldiering, and many military careers were built by men who rose from the outlaw ranks.

The great Manchuria frontier was thus inexorably Sinicized by Chinese colonists: the non-Manchu Tungus tribesmen of the Ussuri and Amur valleys declined in number year after year; the Manchu bannermen soon merged imperceptibly into the Chinese population; the Mongol nomads, faced with displacement from their traditional pastoral grounds, often forsook their ancestral occupation for the life of a peasant.

MANCHURIA SINCE C. 1900

Russian and Japanese aggression in Manchuria. The Russian advance into the Amur region was halted in the 17th century by Manchu arms and the 1689 Treaty of Nerchinsk, but it was resumed in the latter 19th century, when the Ch'ing empire was staggered by the great Taiping Rebellion and by humiliating defeats from the armed forces of Western nations. It meekly accepted Tsarist Russia's imposition of the Treaty of Aigun in 1858, which ceded territories to Russia on the left bank of the Amur. The Treaty of Peking in 1860 gave up the lands east of the Ussuri. Russia now looked upon Manchuria as its legitimate sphere of interest.

When China ceded the Liao-tung Peninsula to Japan at the conclusion of the Sino-Japanese War of 1894–95, Russia, supported by Germany and France, compelled Japan to return it to China for an increased indemnity. Deeply disturbed by the rising Japanese power, China concluded a secret alliance with Russia in 1896, granting the Russians the right to build the Chinese Eastern Railway across north Manchuria from Siberia to Vladivostok. Ostensibly directed against Japan, it merely opened the way for Russia to penetrate further into Manchuria.

Russian railway rights Russia's ulterior motive became apparent in 1898 when it intimidated China into granting a 25-year lease of the Liao-tung Peninsula and the right to build a connecting railway from the ports of Dairen and Port Arthur to the Chinese Eastern Railway. The Russian government thereby succeeded in establishing throughout the railway zone a system of municipal, judicial, police, and military administration that, in effect, constituted a Russian-occupied conclave within Manchuria. In 1900, under the pretext of restoring order after the Boxer Rebellion against foreigners, Russia occupied the whole of Manchuria. The withdrawal of the Russian troops, as provided by the Boxer Protocol, was deliberately delayed by the Russians in an attempt to win more political and economic privileges from the Chinese.

The clash of Russian and Japanese interests in Manchuria and Korea led to the outbreak of the Russo-Japanese War of 1904–05. After its defeat, Russia ceded to Japan all its interests in south Manchuria. Henceforth, rivalry between Russia and Japan in Manchuria was tempered by the desire of both nations to prevent Western powers, particularly the United States, from intruding into their spheres of influence. By secret agreements concluded by them in 1907, 1910, 1912, and 1916, they promised to maintain the status quo and cooperate in protecting their interests against outsiders.

The Chinese response. China responded to the new situation in Manchuria by adopting a more positive approach toward the political integration of the region with China proper. Chinese immigration was officially encouraged through the selling of public lands to individuals and to land companies at an attractive price. Mongol lands

were taken out of tribal control for sale to peasant cultivators. The hitherto predominant position of the bannermen in the political and military establishments was eroded by the introduction into Manchuria of Chinese troops and administrative personnel. The tributary relationships with the tribal peoples were dissolved in favour of direct administration of tribal areas and the eventual assimilation of tribal peoples. Toward the end of the Ch'ing dynasty, the whole of Manchuria had become a truly Chinese territory.

Further Japanese expansion. The Chinese Revolution of 1911 came to Manchuria when its armed forces were divided into two antagonistic factions: the new modernized army, whose officers were sympathetic to the republican cause, and the old provincial army, whose officers remained loyal to the old order. When confronted by a plot to detach the Manchurian provinces from Imperial control, Governor General Chao Erh-sun successfuly checkmated the revolutionaries by calling for help from Chang Tso-lin, the leader of the old provincial army. Chang Tso-lin After the dynasty was overthrown, Chang Tso-lin allied himself with the influential Chinese warlord Yüan Shih-k'ai and was able to extend his power over the whole of Manchuria.

Internal political instability in the young Chinese Republic and the outbreak of World War I in Europe provided the Japanese with a golden opportunity to advance their interest in Manchuria. Japan presented China with the notorious 21 Demands in 1915. After strenuous negotiations, the Chinese were forced to make major concessions regarding Manchuria: the extension of the Kwantung lease and the South Manchurian Railway concessions to 99 years; and the granting to Japanese subjects permission to reside, travel, engage in business, lease and own lands anywhere in Manchuria and east Inner Mongolia.

With its interests safeguarded by treaties and the might of the Kwantung Army, Japan was ready to expand its investments in Manchuria. In 1919 the Kwantung Army became a separate command. Not subject to close scrutiny by the Tokyo government, it was determined to promote the rapid development of Manchuria for the benefit of the Japanese empire, by force if necessary. The Kwantung Army The fall of the tsarist government in 1917 and agreement by the Soviet Union on joint Sino-Soviet management of the Chinese Eastern Railway and reversion of the line to China without compensation in 1936 provided future opportunity for expansion into northern Manchuria.

Rapid economic development in Manchuria encouraged Chang Tso-lin to play a decisive role in warlord politics. His ambition ran afoul not only of his fellow warlords but also of those Japanese leaders who preferred to see him as the autonomous leader in Manchuria amenable to the Japanese. When Chang Tso-lin, who had dominated the Peking government since 1926, faced defeat at the hands of the Kuomintang Army in 1928, the Japanese government advised him to withdraw his army into Manchuria to prevent hostilities from spreading north of the Great Wall. In return, Japan promised to support Chang's position in Manchuria. The radical elements in the Kwantung Army, however, wanted to disarm Chang's army and take over Manchuria. On June 4, 1928, Chang was assassinated under the direction of the senior staff officer of the Kwantung Army and with the approval of the commander in chief. The plot did not succeed in creating panic among the Chinese leaders in Manchuria nor was it approved by the Tokyo government. Consequently, the Kwantung Army had to wait for another chance to seize Manchuria.

Chang Tso-lin's son and successor, Chang Hsüeh-liang, ignoring Japanese warnings, decided to cast his lot with the Kuomintang government in Nanking. Chinese nationalism, inflamed by Japanese attempts to obstruct the unification of China, won popular support in Manchuria. Many young Japanese businessmen, fearing Japanese interests and privileges might be ousted, organized the Manchuria Youth League, which had as its objective the formation of an independent Manchuria. The Kwantung Army, on the other hand, favoured the establishment of a

Japanese puppet state and the removal of Soviet presence in north Manchuria. It also considered Manchuria as a potential base for Japanese military expansion in Asia. The stage was set for an overt clash between Chinese nationalism and Japanese imperialism.

On the morning of September 18, 1931, two explosions occurred outside Mukden. Immediately afterward, the Kwantung Army and the Japanese railway guards began attacking the Chinese barracks and the city wall. By dawn the next day, Mukden had been occupied. Honjō Shigeru, the commander in chief of the Kwantung Army, issued a proclamation saying that Chinese soldiers had dynamited the South Manchurian Railway and had attacked Japanese railway guards. The Kwantung Army, he stated, had no choice but to punish the Chinese Army by occupying the city. So began the Mukden Incident, which ultimately led to the Sino-Japanese War.

Although the invasion of Manchuria had been under discussion by the Japanese high command in Tokyo, the bombing plot was conceived and carried out by young Kwantung officers. Once firing had begun, the Kwantung Army moved forward according to predrawn plans for the occupation of Manchuria, despite restraining orders issued from Tokyo. The Nanking government directed the Manchurian leaders not to resist the Japanese. Relying upon the League of Nations to halt the Japanese aggression, it also refused to negotiate directly with Japan. This negative and passive stance enabled the Japanese to occupy all of Manchuria within five months. On March 9, 1932, the Japanese created the puppet state of Manchukuo. The last Manchu emperor, P'u-yi, was brought to Manchuria from Tientsin and made chief executive.

The League of Nations sent an International Commission of Inquiry, headed by Lord Lytton, to investigate the incident. The commission found Japan guilty of aggression and branded Manchukuo a puppet state; but it did not recommend sanction against the aggressor. The United States was unwilling to intervene, except to announce that it would not recognize the legal status of Manchukuo. The Kwantung Army then extended its conquest to Jehol. On March 27, 1933, following the issuance of the Lytton Report, Japan withdrew from the League. Realizing that there would be no foreign assistance, China agreed to sign the T'ang-ku Truce on May 31, 1933, which ended the Japanese advance toward North China and created a demilitarized zone between the Great Wall and Peking. The Japanese then enthroned P'u-yi as emperor of Manchukuo on March 1, 1934.

Manchuria under the Japanese. The creation of Manchukuo greatly enhanced the power of the Kwantung Army, whose commander in chief also served as governor of the Kwantung Leased Territory and ambassador to Manchukuo, thus concentrating all military and political powers into a single source of authority. The key official in the Manchukuo government was the director general of the General Affairs Board of the State Council, who was always a Japanese. Japanese officials were placed in key positions throughout all ministries and offices. Having succeeded in ruling Manchuria through the facade of a puppet state, the Japanese pressured the Soviet Union to sell to Manchukuo the Chinese Eastern Railway.

The Kwantung Army then proceeded to transform Manchuria into an industrial and war base for Japan's expansion in Asia. It took over direction of the South Manchurian Railway Company, which became the chief agent of Japanese economic exploitation in Manchuria. The Manchurian Heavy Industry Company, a giant holding company, was organized in 1937 to finance and direct most of the important Manchurian industries. As a result, metallurgy, mining, electric power, chemicals, transportation, and communication all made impressive gains. At the end of the war, Manchuria was the most industrialized region in China.

The agrarian policy of the Kwantung Army was also designed to implement its military objectives. First, the Kwantung Army intended to settle large numbers of Japanese and Korean farmers in Manchuria and to limit the number of Chinese immigrants. It aimed specifically at the formation of solid blocs of Japanese farmers, preferably army reservists, at strategic frontier locations as a defense measure against the Soviet Union. Second, the Kwantung Army encouraged the diversification of crops in order to achieve agricultural self-sufficiency for war purposes. Manchuria's most pressing agrarian problem, farm tenancy, remained unsolved, since the Japanese needed the cooperation of the landlord-usurer class.

Despite the Manchukuo facade, Manchuria was a land under Japanese colonial rule. The Kwantung Army was never able to completely suppress all armed resistance by the Chinese and Korean population. After the fall of Manchuria, many Manchurian soldiers, aided by armed civilians, including bandits, cooperated with the Chinese and Korean Communist underground in organizing a vast anti-Japanese guerrilla movement. In 1934 alone the Japanese reported to have suffered about 50,000 casualties in fighting the guerrillas.

The triumph of Communism.   At the Yalta Conference of February 1945, Soviet premier Joseph Stalin demanded the restoration of all former Russian rights and privileges in Manchuria as a price for Soviet entry into the Pacific war. Pres. Franklin D. Roosevelt of the United States and British prime minister Winston Churchill accepted Stalin's demand without consulting China. After Germany's surrender in May 1945, Soviet troops began to move from Europe to Asia. Thereupon, China sent T.V. Soong to the Soviet Union to negotiate an agreement before Soviet troops could enter Manchuria. Stalin offered China a 33-year treaty of friendship and alliance against future Japanese aggression. On August 9 the Soviet Union declared war on Japan and invaded Manchuria. The Sino-Soviet Treaty was signed on August 14, 1945. By August 15 the war was over. The next day, the Manchukuo emperor P'u-yi was captured by the Russians.

Having struck a good bargain for joining the war, the Soviets now plundered Manchuria as a conquered territory, systematically confiscating food, gold bullion, industrial machinery, and other stockpiles. The actual extent of Soviet looting in Manchuria is not known, but it probably ran into billions of dollars.

To the Nanking government, the political damage of the Soviet occupation was even greater than the economic ravage. Under the protection of the Soviet Army, underground Chinese Communist guerrillas united with Communist troops from North China to form the United Democratic Army. Equipped with Japanese arms turned over to them by the Russians, the Communist force blocked all land routes from China proper to Manchuria and occupied several important ports where Kuomintang troops might have landed. The Soviet Army refused to let them enter Dairen. Delayed by the Soviets and harassed by the Communists, Kuomintang progress in taking over the major Manchurian cities was exceedingly slow. It was June 1946 when the Kuomintang occupied Ch'ang-ch'un. By then the Soviets had withdrawn completely, and the countryside was in the hands of the Communists. Nearly 500,000 of the elite Kuomintang troops found themselves surrounded by Communists in Ch'ang-ch'un, Mukden, Chin-chou and Ying-kou. By the end of 1948 the Kuomintang had suffered military defeat in Manchuria.

On August 27, 1949, the Northeast People's Government was formally established. The top political figure was Kao Kang, who headed both the party and government in Manchuria. Kao led a delegation to the Soviet Union to conclude a trade agreement in August 1949. Later, in December, Mao Tse-tung visited the Soviet Union and negotiated with Stalin a 30-year treaty of friendship, alliance, and mutual assistance. In return for a Soviet pledge of military and economic assistance, China conceded the privileges granted to the Soviets in Manchuria by the Nanking government. These privileges were to be in force until a peace treaty with Japan could be concluded or, at the latest, until the end of 1952.

The Communist rehabilitation of the Manchurian economy began with the land reform in 1946, and by the end of 1949 all the lands had been redistributed among the peasants. The power of the landlords was eliminated.

Because of the existence of extensive tracts of public lands in Manchuria, a large number of state farms were set up, which were equipped with machinery and engaged in experimental farming. Otherwise, the course of agrarian reform in Manchuria, from the formation of mutual-aid teams to cooperatives and communes, did not differ from elsewhere in China proper.

Industrially, the initial task of the Communists was to reconstruct the existing industrial plants so that Manchuria could serve as a major base for the further industrialization of China. During the First Five-Year Plan of 1953–57, Manchuria received the bulk of Chinese industrial investment. Today, Manchuria is still the industrial heartland of China.

Party purges

The importance of Manchuria to the economic development of China, its proximity to the Soviet Union, its long history of political separatism, and the ambitions of Kao Kang might have been responsible for the first important purge of party leadership after the establishment of the People's Republic. Kao Kang had exercised virtually autonomous power in Manchuria and enjoyed frequent contacts with the Soviets. It was possible that he had tried to use Soviet support to gain for himself even greater power within the party and government. In 1953 Peking abolished the Northeast People's Government and replaced it with the Northeast Administrative Commission. In 1954 the commission was dissolved, and Manchuria was divided into three provinces: Liaoning, Kirin, and Heilungkiang. A Yen-pien Korean Autonomous District was created in eastern Kirin where the Korean minority congregated. The Mongol-inhabited western Manchuria became part of the Inner Mongolia Autonomous Region. Kao Kang was transferred from Manchuria to Peking, and in 1955 he was purged from the party. Since then Manchuria has been fully integrated into the political structure of China. Like the rest of China, Manchuria was buffeted by the violence and disorder of the Great Proletariat Cultural Revolution that started in 1966. By 1969 the Maoists had won, and in 1970 the reconstruction of the party structure in Liaoning was completed. It was during the turmoil of the Cultural Revolution that tensions between China and the Soviet Union, whose relations had deteriorated since 1956, reached the point of open hostility in May 1969, when a dispute over the ownership of an uninhabited island in the Ussuri led to armed clashes. The incident reminds the world that Manchuria is still the historic zone of conflict where peoples and nations have fought for its possession since the dawn of history.

BIBLIOGRAPHY. ALBERT HERMANN, *Historical and Commercial Atlas of China* (1964), dated, but still useful; WOLFRAM EBERHARD, *A History of China*, 3rd ed. rev. (1969), a general history with emphasis on Sino-barbarian relations; IMMANUEL C.Y. HSU, *The Rise of Modern China* (1970), the best recent history on modern China with good insight into Sino-Japanese relations; OWEN LATTIMORE, *Inner Asian Frontiers of China*, 2nd ed. (1951), a stimulating, theoretical discussion of China's historical relations with its nomadic and semi-nomadic neighbours; CHANG KWANG-CHIH, *The Archaeology of Ancient China* (1963); and K.H.J. GARDINER, *The Early History of Korea* (1969), some materials on prehistoric Manchuria; HSU SHU-HSI, *China and Her Political Entity* (1926), an account of the status of China's frontier territories; KARL A. WITTFOGEL and FENG CHIA-SHENG, *History of Chinese Society: Liao, 907–1125* (1949), a monumental work on the Liao society.

For Manchuria during the Ch'ing dynasty, see H.E.M. JAMES, *The Long White Mountain* (1888), an eyewitness account of Manchuria during the late 19th century; ROBERT H.G. LEE, *The Manchurian Frontier in Ch'ing History* (1970), a detailed discussion of social and political changes; GEORGE A. LENSEN, *The Russo-Chinese War* (1967), an account of the Russian occupation of Manchuria during the Boxer uprising; ANDREW MALOZEMOFF, *Russian Far Eastern Policy, 1881–1904* (1958); FRANZ H. MICHAEL, *The Origin of Manchu Rule in China* (1942, reprinted 1965), on the Sinicization of the Manchus before their conquest of China; E.G. RAVENSTEIN, *The Russians on the Amur* (1861), includes firsthand materials; BORIS A. ROMANOV, *Russia in Manchuria, 1892–1906* (1952; orig. pub. in Russian, 1928), a history of Russian imperialism in Manchuria; and KUNGTU C. SUN, *The Economic Development of Manchuria in the First Half of the Twentieth Century* (1969).

For Manchuria during the republic, see PAUL H. CLYDE, *International Rivalries in Manchuria, 1689–1922*, 2nd rev. ed. (1928); OWEN LATTIMORE, *Manchuria, Cradle of Conflict* (1932) and *Studies in Frontier History: Collected Papers, 1928–1958* (1962), sympathetic treatments of the Mongols; PETER S.H. TANG, *Russian and Soviet Policy in Manchuria and Outer Mongolia, 1911–1931* (1959); and TOA-KEIZAI CHOSAKYOKU (EAST-ASIATIC ECONOMIC INVESTIGATION BUREAU), *The Manchuria Year Book, 1931* (1931).

For the Mukden Incident, see WUNSZ KING, *China and the League of Nations: The Sino-Japanese Controversy* (1965); LIANG CHIN-TUNG, *The Sinister Face of the Mukden Incident* (1969), an abridgment of a longer Chinese work that is valuable for its discussion of the Nanking government's response to the crisis; SADAKO N. OGATA, *Defiances in Manchuria: The Making of Japanese Foreign Policy, 1931–1932* (1964), informative and perceptive; TAKEHIKO YOSHIHASHI, *Conspiracy in Mukden* (1963); and the LEAGUE OF NATIONS, APPEAL BY THE CHINESE GOVERNMENT, *Report of the Commission of Enquiry (Commonly Known As the Lytton Commission)* (1932).

For Manchuria under the Japanese, see F.C. JONES, *Manchuria Since 1931* (1949), scholarly and informative; YOSUKE MATSUOKA, *Building Up Manchuria* (1937), a justification of Japanese policy by the president of the South Manchurian Railway; and MANCHURIA, DEPARTMENT OF FOREIGN AFFAIRS, *Manchoukuo, Handbook of Information* (1933). For Manchuria under the Communists, see O. EDMUND CLUBB, *Chinese Communist Development Programs in Manchuria, with a Supplement on Inner Mongolia* (1954); and EDWIN W. PAULEY, *Report on Japanese Assets in Manchuria to the President of the United States* (1946).

(R.H.G.L.)

Manet, Édouard

In the span of French painting, rich and unbroken since the 17th century, a single artist—Édouard Manet—accomplished by himself the 19th-century transition from the Realism of Gustave Courbet to Impressionism. Lacking great imagination for the invention of themes, Manet was almost always inspired by a painting, drawing, or print either by a master or an unknown. His qualities are purely pictorial. They rise from the luminosity of his brushwork, the fine quality of his palette, and the breadth of his design. With no posterity to carry on his work, this revolutionary in spite of himself carried the light to Impressionism. His art has on its viewers the power to cleanse the dust from the eyes and wash the vision.

Giraudon

'The Studio in the Batignolles." Manet is seated at the easel in his Batignolles studio; Pierre-Auguste Renoir and Emile Zola are standing second and third from the left, respectively. Oil painting by Henri Fantin-Latour, 1870. In the Louvre, Paris. 1.74 × 2.08 m.

Early life and works. Manet was born on January 23, 1832, at 5 rue des Petits-Augustins (today rue Bonaparte) in Paris. He was the son of Auguste Manet, stern chief of personnel at the Ministry of Justice, and of Eugénie-Désirée Fournier. The child was baptized on February 2 at the church of Saint-Germain-des-Prés.

From 1839, Manet was a day pupil at Canon Poiloup's school in Vaugirard, where he began the study of French and the classics. He was later (1844–48) a boarder at the Collège Rollin, then located near the Panthéon. A poor student, he was interested only in the special drawing course offered by the school. At the Collège Rollin, he met his future biographer, A. Proust.

Although his father wanted him to enroll in law school, he could not be persuaded to do so. When his father refused to let him become a painter, he applied for the naval college but failed the entrance examination. He therefore embarked, on December 9, 1848, as an apprentice pilot on the transport vessel "Le Havre et Guadeloupe" and sailed for Rio de Janeiro, at a salary of 15 francs a month. During the crossing he wrote his parents amusing letters embellished with sketches in which his art was already apparent.

Upon his return to France in June 1849, he failed the naval examination a second time, and his parents now finally yielded to their son's stubborn determination to become a painter. In 1850 Manet entered the studio of Thomas Couture, a classical painter who had been a pupil of Antoine-Jean Gros and had painted "The Romans of the Decadence" (Louvre, Paris). Whatever may be said of him, Couture had some qualities of a great painter, and, despite faults that included both boorishness and banality, he was not a bad teacher. "I may not claim to train geniuses," he said to his pupils, "but at least I train painters to know their craft." Little as his teacher may have understood him, Manet was to owe to Couture a good grasp of drawing and pictorial technique.

The Manet family had moved to 6 rue du Mont-Thabor, where a young Dutchwoman, Suzanne Leenhoff, came to give piano lessons to Édouard. There seems to have been a love affair between the young painter and his music teacher. Indeed she later gave birth to a son whose paternity, though never acknowledged, has been attributed to Manet. The child, who was named Léon-Édouard Koëlla-Leenhoff, was represented as being Suzanne's younger brother, with Manet as the godfather.

In 1856, after six years with Couture, Manet set up a studio—which he shared with Albert de Balleroy, a painter of military subjects—in the rue Lavoisier in the Saint-Augustin quarter. There he painted "The Boy with Cherries" (c. 1858; Gulbenkian Collection, Paris), the model for which one day hanged himself from a nail in the studio. Obsessed by the child's tragic death, the artist left the rue Lavoisier and moved to 58 rue de Villiers, where he painted "The Absinthe Drinker." In 1856 he made short trips to Holland, Germany, and Italy. Meanwhile, at the Louvre he copied Titian's "Virgin with Rabbit," as well as Velázquez's "Portrait de l'Infante Marie-Marguerite," of which he left a watercolour and a recently discovered oil. At the Louvre, in 1857, Manet made the acquaintance of Henri Fantin-Latour, who was later to paint Manet's portrait.

Leaving his studio in the rue de Villiers, he moved to 58 rue de la Victoire and then to the rue de Douai, where he remained for 18 months. He met the poet Charles Baudelaire, at whose suggestion he painted "La Musique aux Tuileries" ("Concert in the Tuileries Gardens"), a picture painted outdoors, in which, it seems, the whole of Paris of the Second Empire is assembled—a smart, frivolous society composed chiefly of habitués of the Café Tortoni and of the Café Guerbois, the latter the rendezvous of the Batignolles artists. Passersby looked with curiosity at this elegantly dressed painter who set up his canvas and painted in the open air.

The following year (1861) Manet exhibited at the Salon "Spanish Singer," dubbed "Guitarero" by the French man of letters Théophile Gautier, who praised it enthusiastically in the periodical *Le Moniteur universel*. In 1862 there was "Lola de Valence" (Louvre, Paris), a dazzling portrait of a dancer who had appeared with a Spanish troupe at the Paris Hippodrome.

Mature life and works. Upon the death of his father, September 25, 1862, Manet moved to the rue Guyot. From that year until 1865 he took part in exhibitions organized by the Galerie Martinet. In 1863 the jury of the

Salon of the French Académie Royale rejected his "Déjeuner sur l'herbe" ("Luncheon on the Grass"), a work whose technique was entirely revolutionary, and Manet exhibited it at the Salon des Refusés (established to exhibit the many works rejected by the official Salon). Although inspired by works of the old masters—Giorgione's "Concert champêtre" and Raphael's "Judgment of Paris"—this large canvas, measuring 84¼ by 106¼ inches (214 by 270 centimetres), aroused loud disapproval and began for Manet that "carnival notoriety" from which he was long to suffer. His bourgeois critics were offended by the presence of a naked woman among the clothed young men.

Manet married Suzanne Leenhoff in Zalt-Bommel in The Netherlands on October 28, 1863, much to the surprise of Baudelaire and other friends, from whom he had partially concealed his intentions. In November 1864 the artist moved to a private apartment at 34 boulevard des Batignolles, where he was to remain until 1867. He began to frequent the racetrack, where he skillfully took up the theme of his friend Edgar Degas, who, in his studies of the turf, had preceded him by two years. Of the several pictures he painted on this subject, "The Races at Longchamp, Paris" is the major work.

At the Salon of 1865, "Olympia," painted two years earlier, created a scandal. This symphony in white—which the French statesman Georges Clemenceau was to install in the Louvre in 1907—was called indecent. As one 19th-century critic wrote:

Canes and umbrellas were brandished against this awakening beauty. A mob was formed which the army did nothing to disperse. The terrified administration felt obliged to have her guarded by two uniformed attendants. And that wasn't enough! Rearranging in their usual way, they hung her nudity at an enormous height where no one would see it, and from which she simultaneously defied the stares and uproar.

In his vexation, Manet left in August 1865 for Spain, but, disliking the food and frustrated by his total lack of knowledge of the language, he did not stay long. In Madrid he met Théodore Duret, who was later to be one of the first connoisseurs and champions of his work. The following year, "The Fifer," having been rejected by the Salon jury under the pretext that its modelling was flat, was displayed along with others in Manet's studio in the rue Guyot.

When a large number of his works were rejected for the Universal Exposition of 1867, Manet, in imitation of Gustave Courbet, who had had the same idea, had a stall erected at the corner of the Place de l'Alma and the Avenue Montaigne, and there in May he exhibited a group of works, including his paintings of toreadors and bullfights. "What a lot of Spaniards!" exclaimed Courbet on entering Manet's stall. And he added: "His figures are like the jack of diamonds on a playing card." When a friend reported Courbet's remark to Manet, the latter responded: "That doesn't surprise me. Courbet's ideal is a billiard ball!" In his own exhibition he showed about 50 paintings, but these were hardly received any more favourably than before. During the late 1860s his work was varied in character, but in general it seems to represent a greater concern with close relations of tone, with complexities of illumination and atmosphere, and sometimes exhibits a freedom of handling comparable with that in "La Musique aux Tuileries" (1862; National Gallery, London). "The Execution of the Emperor Maximilian of Mexico" of 1867, and "The Departure of the Folkestone Boat" (1869; Philadelphia Museum of Art) are representative of the work Manet was producing at this time.

Manet was not, however, entirely absent from the official Salon of 1867, since Fantin-Latour's portrait of him was displayed there. Wearing a top hat, his legs solidly planted, his walking stick clutched in his hands, the painter of "Olympia" is presented full face, his eyes thoughtful, his chin determined under his well-trimmed beard, and with an ambiguous smile on his lips that seems to mock the company.

Much taken by the naturalism of Manet's work, the

Entry into the studio of Thomas Couture

First Salon exhibition

Exhibition of 1867

young novelist Émile Zola undertook to defend and praise it in a long and courageous article published in the *Revue du XIXᵉ Siècle* of January 1, 1867. In the face of the hostility of the public, Zola saw Manet as representative of all artists of importance who begin by offending public opinion. "In studying in Édouard Manet the reception given to original personalities," he wrote, "I protest against this reception. I make of an individual question a question that is of interest to all true artists." "You have given me a fine New Year's present," the painter wrote in thanking the writer. Manet's gratitude was to be expressed in his portrait of Zola, shown at the Salon of 1868, where it was badly hung. "At times," Zola wrote in describing his sittings with Manet, "I looked at the artist standing before his canvas, his face tense, his eyes clear, intent on his work. He had forgotten me, he no longer knew I was there."

Along with his portrait of Zola, Manet exhibited "The Balcony," in which there appeared for the first time—in the figure of the Spanish girl seated with her elbow on the railing—a portrait of Berthe Morisot, whom he had met at the Louvre, where she was copying a work by Peter Paul Rubens. From then on, Berthe, who was to become one of the leading female French Impressionists, was a frequent visitor to Manet's studio. He painted a series of portraits of her, until her marriage to his brother Eugène Manet.

After the praise published by Zola, Duret, and the art critic Louis-Édmond Duranty (with this last the painter had fought a comic-opera duel), Manet received, at the Salon of 1870, Fantin-Latour's homage in paint—"The Studio in the Batignolles" (Louvre, Paris), a kind of manifesto on his behalf. This large canvas shows him painting, surrounded by those who were his defenders at the time: Pierre-Auguste Renoir, Zola, the painter Frédéric Bazille, Claude Monet, Zacharie Astruc. The painting was caricatured in the *Journal amusant* under the title "Jesus Painting Among His Disciples."

Involvement in the Franco-Prussian War

On July 19, 1870, the Franco-Prussian War was declared. With the advance of the Prussian troops, Manet's wife left with her mother-in-law and her son for Oloron-Sainte-Marie in the Pyrenees, where friends had offered them hospitality. Manet enlisted as a staff lieutenant in the National Guard, and his superior officer was Jean-Louis-Ernest Meissonier, the painter of musketeers. Beginning on September 26, he corresponded with his wife, the letters being carried by balloon. Provisions were short. "I wish you could see me with my artilleryman's greatcoat," he wrote to his wife on November 19. "At the same time my knapsack is equipped with everything that I need for painting." On December 1 he was present at the battle that took place between Le Bourget and Champigny: "What pandemonium!" he wrote. "Anyway I'm still alive. The shells pass over your head on all sides." But hope was sinking, and the lack of provisions became intolerable. On January 30, 1871, he wrote these despairing words to Suzanne: "It's finished. . . . We cannot hold on any longer. We are dying of hunger. . . . We are all as thin as nails."

In February 1871, Manet rejoined his family at Oloron, returning to Paris shortly before the Commune. His studio in the rue Guyot was half-destroyed, but he had taken care to store his canvases in a safe place, and these he found intact. Paul Durand-Ruel bought almost everything that Manet's studio contained, paying 50,000 francs in the currency of the time. Manet rented lodgings on the ground floor at 51 rue de Saint-Pétersbourg, the same quarter where Léon Koëlla-Leenhoff had a room, and from then on he and his friends met at the Café de la Nouvelle-Athènes, which had replaced the Guerbois. In July of the following year, the artist set up his new studio at 4 rue de Saint-Pétersbourg (today known as rue de Leningrad).

In 1872 he also visited Holland, where he became much influenced by the works of Frans Hals. As a result he painted "Le Bon Bock" (1873; Philadelphia Museum of Art), which achieved considerable success at the Salon exhibition of 1873.

Later life and works. In the Batignolles studio-salon of

Nina de Callias, a charming hostess who entertained all of the outstanding artists, writers, and personalities of the bohemian world, Manet made the acquaintance of Charles Cros, a poet and a pioneer of the phonograph and of colour photography. He illustrated Cros's *Le Fleuve* with a series of eight etchings (1874). At Nina de Callias's, he also met the poet Stéphane Mallarmé, whose work he was later to illustrate.

Friendship with Claude Monet

But the year 1874 was chiefly notable for the development of Manet's friendship (the beginning, when they had first met in 1866, had been rather cool) with the young Impressionist painter Claude Monet, with whom he painted on the banks of the Seine. Under the title "Boating," Manet painted his most luminous plein-air picture. He took as a setting Le Petit Gennevilliers, with two figures seated in the sun in a boat. It was also at Argenteuil that Manet painted "Monet Working on His Boat in Argenteuil." Monet is shown painting his wife in an old boat that he had bought secondhand (he was penniless at the time, and Manet was generous in helping him). Yet, although he was friendly with Monet and the other Impressionists, Manet would not participate in their independent exhibitions and continued to submit his paintings to the official Salon.

In 1875 Richard Lesclide published Baudelaire's translation of Edgar Allan Poe's poem "The Raven," with four illustrations by Manet—wash drawings reproduced by lithography. The following year Alphonse Derenne published Mallarmé's poem "L'Après-midi d'un faune" ("Afternoon of a Faun") with five woodcuts after drawings by Manet, who had also painted the poet's portrait. At this time Manet exhibited "The Artist" (1875) and "The Laundress," two works rejected by the Salon, along with other paintings in his studio in the rue de Saint-Pétersbourg. This exhibition at home caused such an uproar with the comings and goings of spectators that the painter's landlord refused to renew his lease. Thus, Manet took possession in April 1879 of his final studio at 77 rue d'Amsterdam.

Private collection; photograph, The Metropolitan Museum of Art, New York

"The Artist's Garden in Versailles," oil painting by Édouard Manet, 1881. In a private collection.

Earlier, in "Nana," he had given the visual version of the harlot theme touched on by Zola in his novel *L'Assommoir;* and he had painted "The Plum," one of his major works, in which a solitary woman rests her elbow on the marble top of a café table. These were followed by "La Blonde aux seins nus," in which the pearl-white flesh tones gleam with light; the "Rue Mosnier, Paris, Decorated with Flags"; and "The Conservatory," the large fresh canvas of which the 19th-century writer Théodore de Banville remarked, "One expects to see them converse, the lady in a gray dress seated on a green bench and the gentleman with the fawn-colored beard." Then came "Chez le Père Lathuille," one of Ma-

Late
pastels

net's chief works, the setting of which is a restaurant near the Café Guerbois in Clichy. It shows a coquette somewhat past her prime having lunch with her young lover.

From then on, Manet did a large number of pastels. In broad, determined strokes he captured the features of George Moore (1879; Metropolitan Museum of Art, New York), an Irish poet who was called "the Englishman of Montmartre" and who often came to join Manet and Degas at the Café de la Nouvelle-Athènes. Manet liked him, according to one critic, "for his bohemian and exotic ways, and the pallid languor of his head with its red hair."

In 1880, Manet had a one-man exhibition at the offices of *La Vie moderne,* a periodical published by Georges Charpentier, who also published Zola and other Naturalist writers. His legs already affected by the malady that was to prove fatal, he went to Bellevue for hydrotherapy. There he met the opera singer Émilie Ambre, who had had great success in the role of Carmen and who had taken with her, on her tour of the United States, Manet's "Execution of the Emperor Maximilian of Mexico," which she showed in New York and Boston.

In 1881 Manet rented a villa at Versailles, and on his return to Paris he painted "Jeanne," or "Spring" (1882; Harry Payne Bingham Collection, New York), the delightful profile posed by the actress Jeanne de Marsy. But the artist's illness was making alarming progress. The following year he went to stay in a villa at Rueil. He took part in an important exhibition of French art that was held in London at Burlington House, and at the Salon showed "A Bar at the Folies-Bergère," his last great composition. As he worked on his painting, Manet was forced to pause and sit down on a divan. "It was then that I saw," said Jeanniot, "how much his illness had affected him— he supported himself on a cane and seemed to tremble."

On April 6, 1883, after painting some roses and lilacs brought to him by his former model Méry Laurent, Manet had to take to his bed. Gangrene broke out in his left leg, which was subsequently amputated. He died on April 30 and was buried in the cemetery of Passy.

In January 1884 a posthumous exhibition was held in the Salle de Melpomène of the École des Beaux-Arts. True to his admiration for the artist, Émile Zola wrote the preface to the catalog. It was after this memorial exhibition that his paintings began to gain prominence. In the same year, the price of Manet's pictures began to rise, and his stature in the art world was assured.

MAJOR WORKS

"The Absinthe Drinker" (1859; Ny Carlsberg Glypothek, Copenhagen); "Spanish Singer" (1860; Metropolitan Museum of Art, New York); "La Musique aux Tuileries" (1862; National Gallery, London); "The Street Singer" (1862; Museum of Fine Arts, Boston); "Ballet Espagnol" (1862; Phillips Collection, Washington, D.C.); "Mademoiselle Victorine in the Costume of an Espada" (1862; Metropolitan Museum of Art, New York); "Olympia" (1863; Louvre, Paris); "Le Déjeuner sur l'herbe" (1863; Louvre); "The Races at Longchamp, Paris" (1864; Art Institute of Chicago); "Bullfight" (1866; Art Institute of Chicago); "The Fifer" (1866; Louvre); "The Execution of the Emperor Maximilian of Mexico" (1867; Städtische Kunsthalle, Mannheim); "Mme Édouard Manet au piano" (c. 1867–68; Louvre); "Portrait d'Émile Zola" (1868; Louvre); "The Luncheon" (1868; Neue Staatsgalerie, Munich); "The Balcony" (1869; Louvre); "La Brioche" (1870; David Rockefeller Collection, New York); "Gare Saint-Lazare" (1873; National Gallery of Art, Washington, D.C.); "Boating" (1874; Metropolitan Museum of Art, New York); "Monet Working on His Boat in Argenteuil" (1874; Neue Staatsgalerie, Munich); "The Laundress" (1875; Barnes Foundation, Merion, Pennsylvania); "Nana" (1877; Hamburger Kunsthalle); "The Plum" (1877; Arthur Sachs Collection, New York); "Skating" (1877; Fogg Art Museum, Cambridge, Massachusetts); "La Blonde aux seins nus" ("The Blonde with Bare Breasts"; 1878; Louvre); "Rue Mosnier, Paris, Decorated with Flags" (1878; Paul Mellon Collection, Upperville, Virginia); "The Conservatory" (1879; Nationalgalerie, Berlin); "Chez le Père Lathuille" (1879; Musée des Beaux-Arts, Tournai); "The Waitress" ("La Servante de bocks"; 1879; National Gallery, London); "The Artist's Garden in Versailles" (1881; John Barry Ryan Collection, New York); "A Bar at the Folies-Bergère" (1882; Courtauld Institute Galleries, London).

BIBLIOGRAPHY. EMILE ZOLA, "Une Nouvelle Manière de peintre, M. Édouard Manet," *Revue du XIXᵉ siècle* (January 1867, reprinted in *Mes Haines*, 1880), an important text, the first to defend and praise Manet's work; EDMOND BAZIRE, *Manet* (1884), a fine analysis (in French) of the painter's work; JACQUES DE BIEZ, *Édouard Manet* (1884), the painter as seen by an informed contemporary (in French); THEODORE DURET, *Histoire d'Édouard Manet et de son oeuvre* (1902), the first attempt to catalog Manet's work; JULIUS MEIER-GRAEFE, *Édouard Manet* (1912), an important view of Manet and his work by the great German critic; ETIENNE MOREAU-NELATON, *Manet raconté par lui-même*, 2 vol. (1926), the first concerted work on Manet, well documented and with much source material; PAUL JAMOT and GEORGES WILDEN-STEIN, *Catalogue critique de l'oeuvre de Manet*, 2 vol. (1932), —several works by Manet have been discovered since the publication of this catalog; ALAIN DE LEIRIS, *The Drawings of Édouard Manet* (1969), a scholarly compilation cataloging Manet's watercolours and drawings (good illustrations); ADOLPHE TABARANT, *Manet et ses oeuvres* (1947), the principal source for the study of Manet's life and works; PIERRE COURTHION and PIERRE CAILLER, *Manet raconté par lui-même et par ses amis*, 2 vol. (1953; Eng. trans., *Portrait of Manet by Himself and His Contemporaries*, 1960), a collection of important texts that have appeared on Manet; and PIERRE COURTHION, *Édouard Manet* (Eng. trans. 1962), a study of Manet's work, with unpublished documents on his graphic oeuvre and iconography.

(P.Co.)

Manichaeism

Manichaeism was a dualistic religious movement that arose in the 3rd century AD in Persia. Though for a long time Manichaeism was considered and treated as a Christian heresy, it was a religion in its own right. Because of the coherence of its doctrines and its rigid structure and institutions, it preserved throughout its history a unity and unique character. Moreover, in terms of its growth, but particularly in terms of its purpose and early ambition, Manichaeism should be counted among the universal religions. Indeed, it was a church, and its members referred to themselves as "the Holy Church" as well as "the Holy Religion."

HISTORY

The origin of Manichaeism. The term Manichaeism comes from the name of its founder, Mani (Manes), who was born April 14, 216, in southern Babylonia (then part of the Iranian Empire, now in Iraq). His family was perhaps related to the Arsacids, at that time the Parthian rulers of the empire. (The Arsacids were overthrown nine years after Mani's birth by Ardashīr I, and were superseded by the Sāsānids.) When Mani was four years old, his father, Pātik, who was concerned with religious ideas, sent for him to Mesene (southern Babylonia). Sometime later a mysterious voice in the temple at Ctesiphon ordred Pātik to abstain from wine, meat, and sexual intercourse, and after this experience he joined a sect called the Baptistai ("Baptists") by the Greeks, al-mughtasilah ("those who cleanse themselves") by Arabic-speaking writers, and menaqqedē ("those who are purified") and ḥallē ḥewārē ("white gowns") by Syriac writers. This sect was identical with the Elkhasaites, a Judaizing Christian sect that followed the teachings of the visionary prophet Elkhasai (Alkhasaios), who flourished about AD 100 "in the land of the Parthians." It was in a community of such Jewish-Christian influences that Mani grew, formed his doctrines, and nourished his vocation during 21 years (from AD 219/220 to 240). Apparently through this experience, Christianity—or at least a sectarian picture of Christ and the gospel teaching—had a decisive influence on him and on the elaboration of his future message. Moreover, Mani incorporated many ideas borrowed from Elkhasai.

Although for a long while he demonstrated to the members of this Judaizing-Christian sect an apparent docility and fidelity, he came to disagree with them and to criticize two of their principal practices: the use of daily and frequently repeated ablutions and the prohibition against bread, fruits, and vegetables that were grown elsewhere and were of profane origin. Relations between him and the group deteriorated. The break, according to tradition,

The life
of Mani

Fragment of wall painting depicting (left) presumably Mani, followed by members of the elect, accompanied by hearers (far right), from K'o-cha, China, 8th–9th century. In the Museum für Indische Kunst, West Berlin.
By courtesy of the Staatliche Museen zu Berlin

began to develop and then was intensified by two events. At the age of 12 (on April 7, AD 228), Mani had received an order from the angel at-Tawm ("the Twin," or "the Partner"—*i.e.*, his heavenly alter ego) to abandon the community but to delay his departure until he was older. When he was 24 years old (on April 19, AD 240), he was told to manifest himself publically from then on and to proclaim his doctrine to all. The second of these two "annunciations" marked the solemn beginning of the new religion: Mani, in whom the Holy Spirit and all knowledge were thought to have been made incarnate at that time, was confirmed in his character and vocation as the "Apostle of Light" and supreme "Illuminator" (occasionally as the "Paraclete") sent by God. His attempt to begin his work with the conversion of those nearest to him, however, was not successful. He withdrew from the religious sect, accompanied by his father and only two other believers. In his eyes, the religion of the Baptistai would henceforth be a false religion instigated by the "Spirit of Error."

Mani went first to Ctesiphon and then to the northwestern part of the Indian peninsula (present-day Baluchistan). Two years later (probably in the spring of 242), Mani returned to Persia, where an interview was arranged with the new Sāsānid king, Shāpūr I. The results of the meeting were favourable; Mani was given permission to preach his new religion freely in the empire and would have the protection of local authorities. Moreover, it seems that the King was more or less attracted to the doctrine of Mani or at least was favourably disposed toward it. During the King's reign, Mani intensified his efforts at propaganda. He preached everywhere in the empire and, at the same time, organized numerous missions to foreign lands.

After the death of Shāpūr and the short reign of his son and successor Hormizd I, the situation changed completely. Vahrām I, the younger son of Shāpūr, succeeded to the throne and yielded to the increasing influence of the representatives (the Magi) of the official orthodox Sāsānid religion—a form of Zoroastrianism—who were intolerant of heresies and foreign cults. A final journey of Mani was shortened; an unexpected obstacle—without doubt an order of the police—forced Mani to return to the city of Gondēshāpūr (Bēlapat), where he arrived on a Sunday and almost immediately appeared before Vahrām himself. Mani was condemned and thrown into prison. Beginning on a Wednesday, there were 26 days of dramatic trials making up the "Passion of the Illuminator" or—to use the term used by the Manichaeans to describe this period—Mani's "crucifixion." Cruelly chained and gradually weakening, Mani did have the strength to address a final message to his church, which he committed to several disciples who were attending to him; he then died on a Monday.

It is difficult to determine exactly the dates of these last events. There are some data available, but their interpretation is a difficult task; thus the "crucifixion" has been variously placed by scholars as between February 14 and March 2, 274; between January 19 and February 14, 276; or between January 31 and February 26, 277.

The development of Manichaeism. Mani viewed himself as the final successor of a long line of heavenly messengers or prophets sent to mankind, one after the other, and of whom, starting with Adam, the principal ones were Zoroaster, Buddha, and Jesus. The essential message of all earlier revelations—which had been restricted because they were local and which had been distorted by their disciples—was to be found in him and he could provide the key to their meaning. But beyond this, Mani felt that his message had universal meaning and value and was destined to supplant all others before the end of time. The Manichaean Church was thus dedicated from the beginning to a missionary ideal and work. Its permanent duty was to preach and convert the universe. Although it did not fulfill the grandiose plans laid out for the church, the religion of Mani did make its conquests and from the 3rd to the 15th centuries maintained or created its echoes over a large portion of the globe, from the European shores of the Atlantic to the Asian shores of the Pacific.

The beginning of this vast missionary movement goes back to the very origins of Manichaeism. From 240 on, Mani travelled extensively and established his religion at many places in the Sāsānian Empire and even converted a local ruler on his trip to India. The existence of missions organized by him during his lifetime is attested to in various reliable documents: the mission of Addā and Pāteg to Egypt, between 244 and 261, the mission of the same Addā and of 'Abzākhyā in the province of Kirkūk (northeastern Iraq), in 261/262, and, finally, the mission of Mār 'Ammo to Abharshahr and Marv in Khorāsān.

Expansion to the West. The principal effort of the young church in its endeavour to extend beyond the frontiers of the Iranian Empire seems to have been directed at first toward the West, toward the Roman Empire, where it could expect to find easier access in a Christian milieu. Manichaeism rapidly infiltrated the Roman part of Mesopotamia, then made headway in Syria, northern Arabia, and Egypt. In the middle of the 3rd century, missionaries established a centre at Hypsele (near modern Asyūt, Egypt); they made conversions all the way to Alexandria. Their success in the Nile Valley was so great that it soon provoked strong reaction from ecclesiastical authorities, from the philosophers, and even from the Roman emperor Diocletian.

From Egypt the Manichaean religion spread across North Africa where, possibly, it had already been introduced by one of Mani's disciples. The acceptance of Manichaeism by St. Augustine and his later polemic with it

The condemnation and death of Mani

Success in northern Africa

(from 373 to 382) point to the importance Manichaeism had at the end of the 4th century in this area, especially at Carthage. Even though it was to retreat just about everywhere else in the West, Manichaeism remained strong in North Africa for many centuries, perhaps in a modified and more Christianized form. The religion reached Rome during the time of Pope Miltiades (311–314), and an inscription at Salonae (near modern Split, Yugoslavia) dedicated to a "Manichaean virgin" shows that, from the beginning of the 4th century, Dalmatia had also been the object of missionary efforts. It was certainly by way of Italy that Manichaeism reached the southern part of Gaul. From there, or by way of North Africa, it passed into the Spanish peninsula.

It is rather difficult to follow the stages of the propagation of Manichaeism in the West through the vast literature of the controversialists, the multiple imperial edicts of proscription, the rare concrete details furnished by the chronicles, the biographies, and the letters of this or that bishop. Nevertheless, it is certain that the 4th century marked the apogee of Manichaeism's expansion in the Roman Empire; the fact that it was everywhere attacked and harassed indicates that it was present everywhere in a formidable manner. The decline, however, was to come quickly. Persecuted by the church and by the state, the object of repressive laws continually reinvoked and intensified, the Manichaean "heresy" seems to have disappeared almost entirely from western Europe toward the end of the 5th century and, in the course of the following century, from the eastern portion of the empire.

Development in Iran and the East. During the lifetime of Mani, the Manichaean religion had spread to the eastern provinces of the Iranian Empire. It seems, however, that prior to the fall of the Sāsānian Empire in 651, the missions had not crossed to the north of the Oxus River (Amu Darya) nor gone beyond the Pamir Mountains. Khorāsān provided a solid outpost; and it was there that, probably toward the end of the 5th century, the rigourist party of the dēnāvars was formed. Their puritanism for a long time provoked a schism with the mother church in Babylonia, but the work of converting Central Asia and China was reserved to them.

Inside Iran itself, Manichaeism managed to maintain itself, if not to develop, during the reign of the Sāsānids, despite persecutions of which it was the object. The Arab conquest in the 7th century was not a fatal blow but, in fact, stimulated a temporary renewal of Manichaeism in Babylonia and encouraged the return of several groups that had fled to Iraq and the neighbouring regions. This period saw much literary activity and even dissensions that agitated and divided the mother church. This ferment indicates that the 8th century was a flourishing period for the Manichaeans of Mesopotamia, probably the result of the generally tolerant regime of the caliphate of the Umayyads. The arrival of the 'Abbāsids in 775 brought a sudden change of attitude, and bloody persecutions were begun again. In the 10th century the Manichaeans were forced to seek refuge in Khorāsān, and the seat of the Manichaean leader was transferred from Babylon to Samarkand Province (now in Uzbek S.S.R.).

Expansion into China

In the final third of the 7th century, however, a new outlet for the expansion of the Manichaean Church had opened up in the Far East. According to a fragment of a text from Central Asia, Manichaeism made its appearance in China in 675. The conquest of eastern Turkistan by the Chinese and the re-establishment of the great caravan routes corresponded with the arrival for the first time of a Manichaean missionary in China in 694. In 731 a *fou-to-tan* (Chinese: a Manichaean "bishop"), following the orders of the Emperor, composed a catechism of the religion. It was a kind of compendium intended to inform the authorities about the doctrines, scriptures, and the discipline of the sect; it also was intended to encourage official acceptance through a skillful mixture of Taoism, Buddhism, and authentic Manichaeism. In the following year (732), an edict accorded freedom of worship to the religion, and it enjoyed extraordinary success from that point. Beginning in 745, the Uighur, a Turkic people of western China, established an immense kingdom that was

centred in northern Mongolia and extended from the Ili River in the west to the Huang Ho in the east. One of their khans, or kings, was converted in 762 and Manichaeism became the official religion of the Uighur state. According to one recent hypothesis, the religion even pushed at an undetermined date into Siberia.

But the triumph in the East was also to be rather brief. The destruction of the Uighur kingdom by the Kirghiz Turks in 840 drastically changed the situation. Weakened and dispersed, the Manichaeans survived in some of the Uighur principalities formed toward the middle of the 9th century. It is likely that Manichaeism survived in East Turkistan until the beginning of the 13th century, when the Mongol invasion led by Genghis Khan delivered the fatal blow. In China, following the downfall of Uighur power, it was forbidden in 843 and was persecuted, but some vitality remained until the 14th century, and perhaps later (especially at Fukien and Formosa).

Medieval offshoots of Manichaeism. Manichaeism survived by means of sects that developed more or less directly from the original tradition; many historians have called these sects "neo-Manichaean." Nevertheless, though the relationship of some of these sects to one another seems certain, the link of each particular sect, or its ancestor, to the authentic religion of Mani either has been or may still be cast in doubt. The fact that in their own times they were considered as "Manichaean" does not constitute a valid proof that they were, for the word was frequently applied to every movement suspected of being heterodox in both the Byzantine world and the medieval West, and even in the Islāmic world.

It is likely that three sects that appeared successively—the Paulicians, the Bogomils, and the Cathari—comprised links in the same chain. The Paulicians seem to have had their origin in Armenia in the 7th century, and they spread throughout the eastern section of the Byzantine Empire where they proved for a long time to be a formidable challenge to the religious orthodoxy in the empire and also a menace in the military and political spheres. In the eyes of Christians and contemporary witnesses, Paulicianism appeared as a resurgence of Manichaeism, but its assimilation to Manichaeism was not justified by the facts.

Paulician missionaries to Bulgaria seem to have contributed to the rise—in the first third of the 10th century—of the Bogomil movement. Bogomilism, an ascetic and revolutionary movement in revolt against the Byzantine orthodoxy, spread in the Balkan Peninsula, particularly in western Macedonia, Bosnia, and Slavonia. It reached Constantinople (modern Istanbul), was found on the coasts of Asia Minor, and then penetrated Russia, where it inspired mystical beliefs and strange rites.

Although the problem of the origin of the Cathari is far from having a definitive solution, it is no longer possible to doubt the role played by Bogomilism in the development of Catharism in the European West. According to the *Tractatus de hereticis* ("Treatise on Heretics"), written between 1260 and 1270, some French crusaders made contact in Constantinople, in 1147, with a local sect started by some of the Greek merchants of that city who had travelled to Bulgaria and had been won over to the Bogomil heresy. The French converts to the doctrine developed a separate community and, in 1149, brought the doctrine to their own land. The Cathari were commonly referred to as Albigensians after the city of Albi, one of their strongholds in Languedoc Province of southern France. A crusade undertaken against the heresy in 1209 crushed it almost definitively in 1244. Catharism lasted in Languedoc until the first half of the 14th century and continued with somewhat more vigour in Italy to the 15th century.

The Cathari

BELIEFS, PRACTICES, AND INSTITUTIONS

Doctrines and mythology. Mani intended to found a truly "ecumenical" religion, embracing all men, that could be substituted for its antecedents by integrating into it the partial truths contained in their teachings, particularly those to be found in the messages of Zoroaster, Buddha, and Jesus. This would appear to reduce the Manichaean doctrine to a simple combination of pieces joined together in a more or less coherent fashion. Although there is no doubt that in composing his writings and elaborating his doctrine he drew from a variety of sources, to make the totality of his teaching into a kind of mosaic would risk missing the originality of the system and the initial insight that gave it birth. What Mani conceived and intended to promote was, in effect, a truth that was capable of being equally translated into diverse formulas according to the different circumstances where it was to be spread. The Indian, Iranian, or Christian elements, which, with varying degrees, are revealed in Manichaean documents, appear for the most part to be less the original components of the system and more the final or outer cover that resulted from a conscious and willful effort at adaptation. In reality, Manichaeism was a particularly interesting variety of Gnosticism, a dualistic religion that postulated salvation through a special knowledge of spiritual truth.

Relationship to Gnosticism

It is not difficult to establish that Manichaeism had certain historical contacts with Gnosticism. The "Baptist" sect in which Mani lived during his formative years could not help but imbue the thought of the adolescent with Gnostic influences. It is certain that Mani was influenced by the doctrines of Marcion and Bardesanes—Christian heretics of the 2nd century who taught forms of Gnosticism. More generally, the church of Mani borrowed a good part of the apocryphal literature of Gnostic sects. When the contents of the vast number of Gnostic writings discovered about 1945 in Upper Egypt (the Naj 'Hammādī codices) are better known, the relationship between Manichaeism and Gnosticism undoubtedly will appear still stronger and clearer.

Like every form of Gnosticism, Manichaeism arose out of the anguish inherent in the human condition. The situation into which man is thrown proves to him to be alien, unbearable, and radically evil. He feels enslaved to his body, to time, and to the world; he feels entangled in evil, constantly threatened and defiled by it; and he desires to be delivered from it. But if he is capable of experiencing this need for deliverance, it is because he is essentially superior to his present condition and a foreigner to the experience of his body, of time, and of the world. His present condition seems to be some kind of fall. Moreover, as he gets to know himself as essentially a stranger in the world, he learns that God himself can also only be a stranger in it. God who is nothing other than goodness and truth can not have willed this suffering and deceit. Thus, it is necessary to attribute this responsibility to a principle that is evil and opposed to God.

As in every form of Gnosticism, this knowledge of oneself and of God also contains the certitude of salvation. To know oneself is, in effect, to know oneself again, to recover one's true self, which was previously clouded by ignorance and lack of self-consciousness because of its mingling with the body and with Matter. In Manichaeism this recognition means that one sees himself as a particle of the Light, as coming from the transcendent world, and as one who, despite his abject present condition, does not cease to remain united to that superior world by eternal and immanent bonds with it. This is an essential point. Souls share in the very nature of God; souls are nothing other than a part of God that has fallen here below. Man is thus assured that God will not lose interest in the salvation of his own members; he is assured that God will recover those members and reintegrate them into himself. Through man, God saves himself: he is both the Saviour and the one who has been saved; he is the "saved-saviour." Men, too, are "saved-saviours." The element to be saved is man's soul; the saving element is the spirit or intelligence (in Greek, the *nous*).

The interior illumination, or gnosis, that communicates to man his newly found *nous* and the manifestation that the prophets make known to him are expressed in the form of a science capable not only of explaining to man his present condition but also of linking him to an original situation prior to the fall of his soul and to a future situation that will consist in the abolition of evil and the restoration of man's primordial condition. In other words, this gnosis will make man know where he is and

what he is, where he comes from, why he has fallen, and where he is going. But inasmuch as man shares the divine nature because of his spiritual side and is one with the world because of his body, this knowledge of his nature and of his destiny implies necessarily an encyclopaedic knowledge of the nature and destinies of God and of the universe.

This gnosis is expressed in a mythical form. It is presented in the form of a complicated construction that Mani himself filled with various episodes, numerous characters, and minute details and arranged according to symmetric patterns joining all the elements in relationships that are more or less artificial. But throughout the Manichaean mythology, there is only one hero and one situation that is constantly repeated: the soul fallen into Matter and then liberated by its *nous*. The unfolding of the myth is divided into three phases: a past period or moment in which there was a separation and thus a perfect duality of the two radically separate substances—Spirit and Matter, Good and Evil, Light and Darkness; a middle moment corresponding to the present during which a mixture of the two substances begins and continues; a later moment in the future, in which the primordial division will be re-established. To accept Manichaeism is nothing more than to profess this double doctrine of "the two principles" and "the three moments."

Manichaean mythology

In the beginning, there were two antagonistic substances, the one absolutely good, the other radically evil—Light and Darkness. Both were uncreated, eternal, and equal, each one living in a separate region: the kingdom of God in the north, the east, and the west; the kingdom of Evil in the south. The kingdom of God had at its head the Father of Greatness; the kingdom of Evil, the Prince of Darkness. The former consisted of five "dwellings" or members of God (understanding, reason, thought, reflection, will) and was inhabited by innumerable "aeons." The latter consisted of five "pits," one on top of the other (the world of smoke, consuming fire, destructive wind, slime, and darkness), over which presided five chiefs, or "Archons," in monstrous demonic forms and where five different types of infernal creatures swarmed about. Here, all was disorder, stupidity, abomination, and stench, whereas the kingdom of God was characterized by peace, understanding, purity, and sweetness.

The middle moment opened with catastrophe. Darkness attempted to invade the kingdom of Light. God decided to combat the danger by means of his own soul personified in his own son whom he "evoked" from himself through the mediation of the Mother of Life; the son was the Primal Man. With his five sons (the five Light elements: air, wind, light, water, and fire) as his armour, the Primal Man went down to the infernal abyss, and his sons were devoured and swallowed up by the demons. Thus, one portion of the substance of Light was mixed with and enslaved to the substance of Matter. From that point on, God would devote himself to separating and freeing the divine substance.

It was first necessary to effect the salvation of the Primal Man himself. To accomplish this, the Father of Greatness proceeded to the second creation, which involved the successive evocations of the Friend of Lights, the Great Architect, and the Living Spirit. Accompanied by his five sons (the Ornament of Splendour, the King of Honour, Adamas of Light, the King of Glory, Atlas), the Living Spirit made his way to the frontier of the region of Darkness and made a piercing cry, which found an echo in the ardent, confident response of fallen Man. The call and the response became two divine hypostases, or persons. The Living Spirit descended again, this time to the very interior of the Darkness. He held out his right hand to the Primal Man, who grabbed it (this handclasp was to become a ritual and symbolic gesture in the Manichaean Church) and then the Living Spirit lifted the captive out of the Darkness. The Primal Man regained the paradise of Light, his heavenly country; the first to have fallen, he was thus the first to have been saved, the model of man's abasement but also of his salvation.

The salvation of the divine substance

He did, however, leave behind his soul in the Darkness, To save it, God organized the visible world. The principal worker in this enterprise was again the Living Spirit. With the assistance of his five sons, he punished the demonic Archons, making the heavens from their excoriated skin, the mountains from their bones, the earth from their flesh and their excrement, and constructed a universe made of ten firmaments and eight earths. He divided the substance of Light mixed with Matter into three portions: the part that had undergone no contact formed the sun and the moon; the part affected only slightly by the combination gave birth to the stars; the rest comprised a third mass whose liberation required more skill and time.

This was the work particularly of entities derived from a third creation, principally the Third Messenger. The Third Messenger saved the world to the extent that he was able to organize a machine to draw up, refine, and sublimate the Light buried in the Darkness. The cosmic machine consisted of the "wheels" of wind, water, fire, especially the sun and the moon. During the first 15 days of the month, the liberated substance—all those particles of Light that are souls—rose in a "Column of Glory" up to the moon, which, inflated by this force, became the full moon. During the final half of the month, the force was transferred from the moon to the sun, from which it was taken to the New Paradise. But the Third Messenger also set into motion less mechanical means of liberation. He appeared nude in the sun—in feminine form to the male Archons, in masculine form to the female demons. In this way he was able to provoke the lust of the former and make them ejaculate, and with their semen there fell to the earth the Light they had swallowed up. The seed that fell into water became a sea monster that Adamas of Light ran through with a sword; the seed that fell on land became five trees from which all vegetation sprouted. The female devils miscarried and their aborted children fell to the earth, and devoured the buds of the trees, thereby assimilating the semen and the discharged Light, and then propagated more demons. The part of the substance of Light that was not yet saved was thus gathered together on the earth but scattered and imprisoned in the plants and the bodies of demons.

To defeat the process of redemption, Matter prompted the two demons Ashaqlūn and Namraël to devour all the offspring of the abortions. Having thus increased the Light in their own bodies, the pair had intercourse and gave birth to Adam and Eve. Adam was delivered from the consciouslessness of the animal state to which he had at first been destined by a saviour, Jesus the Splendour, who awakened him to consciousness, opened his eyes, and made him aware of the divine origin of his soul. This episode, parallel to that of the salvation of the Primal Man, was conceived of as a typical example of the salvation obtained by gnosis. Unfortunately, the lineage of Adam has continued a pattern of copulation and procreation in accordance with the scheme of Matter. With the exception of those who practice an absolute continence, the shameful and painful successive imprisonment in bodily darkness that has been forced upon the luminous souls will cease only at the end of time, at the eve of the third movement of the myth. Then, after a period of apocalyptic calamities and a final judgment, the terrestrial globe will burn for 1,468 years; the last particles of Light that can still be saved will rise to the sky; the visible world will be annihilated, and Matter, with its demons, will be imprisoned in an immense pit. The absolute separation of Light and Darkness will be definitively reestablished.

The result of this cosmogony is that man shares in the divine nature in virtue of his *nous*, his living self-consciousness. Salvation consists in his regaining consciousness of himself and of his relationship with God. This is accomplished by gnosis and in a particular manner by the revelation of Mani and his church. At death, man will return to the original paradise of Light. But if he persists in keeping his soul in the impurity of the flesh and in slavery to material lusting, he will condemn himself to rebirth in a succession of bodies: thus, no fornication, no procreation, no possessions, no cultivating or harvesting, no killing, no eating of meat or drinking of wine, for

these are contaminations of self, defilements of the imprisoned Light.

The Manichaean community. Realizing that such strict prescriptions could not be observed to the same degree by all, Manichaeism insisted on their fulfillment only by the best of the faithful. The community was divided into the elect, who felt able to embrace a rigorous rule, and the hearers, who supported the elect by works and alms. The elect could expect to attain paradise at death; the hearers (with rare exceptions) could hope for salvation only after a period of reincarnation.

Although all members were thought to be an integral part of the same brotherhood, the community had a hierarchical structure. At the head of the community was its leader, Mani's successor. Under him there were five grades: 12 teachers, 72 bishops, 360 priests, the general body of the elect, and the hearers. The elect were "sealed" with the three seals of mouth and hands and breast. They were bound to chastity, poverty, and abstinence from meat and wine. All ownership, all wealth, and every occupation were condemned. They were allowed one meal of vegetables a day and one piece of new clothing a year. Because they could not harm the Light particles by plowing or reaping, kneading or baking, their meals were prepared by hearers. They had the obligation to continue living in the world but to preach the good doctrine and to carry on in strength in the battle against Evil. The chief religious duty of the hearers was to care for the elect. They were enjoined to conform to a code of ten commandments and they also took full part in the religious observances. But they lived in the world and were allowed to own, build, plant and harvest, marry or live with a mistress, have children, drink wine, and eat meat.

Critics have been inclined to accuse Manichaeans of a hostility toward the exterior forms of worship and to minimize the importance that the community attached to its ritual practices. It is true that criticisms of such forms of piety and worship can be found in Manichaean literature, but such views are rare. The Manichaean Church was essentially and organically endowed with a liturgy and must have attempted to integrate and retain members through regular communal practices. When and where the political circumstances were favourable, the Manichaeans never failed to acquire and use sanctuaries and also monasteries. Furthermore—although this statement goes contrary to the traditional opinion—the Manichaeans did not repudiate images but rather attached a sacred character to them and even had a cult of the pictures representing their Master.

Music, too, was held in high esteem and played an important role in both the liturgical services and in the religious life of the faithful; they frequently sang hymns. Music was thought to have come from the kingdom of Light and was regarded as having a purgative and liberating character by which it could cooperate in the detachment of the soul from the dimness of the body and of Matter and could contribute to its elevation.

The Manichaeans had many religious practices, but it is difficult to determine their number, their nature, and their importance. The difficulty arises because the documents are limited in number and are incomplete and unclear in their coverage. It can be said—despite the contrary opinion of some specialists—that the Manichaeans did not practice a Baptism administered with water, as in Christian practice. Their liturgy did make use of ablutions, but this use was never equated with a baptismal rite. There is greater evidence for the existence of a "baptism of oil," that is, a Baptism using oil, or chrism, in the form of an anointing. Furthermore, although the elect did celebrate a meal that involved ritual functions, strictly speaking, it was not a Eucharist in the Christian sense.

The most fundamental Manichaean rites were prayer, almsgiving, and fasting. For each of the faithful, prayer was an obligatory act that was strictly and expressly regulated. The elect were required to pray seven times daily; the hearers had four periods of prayer (at noon, in the afternoon, at sunset, and three hours after nightfall). Prayers, with prostrations, were uttered facing the sun or moon insofar as these were viewed as stages along the

The birth of Adam and Eve

The elect and the hearers

soul's journey toward God. Almsgiving involved principally the hearers, and the term was applied particularly to the gift of food that was brought to the elect and whose delivery, reception, and eating was regulated by a ritual.

Fasting and confession

Fasting was enjoined on the hearers each Sunday, on the elect each Sunday and Monday. There was a second category of fasts that lasted longer and took place only during parts of certain months—the times being calculated from solar, lunar, and zodiacal data. The first three of these fasts were each of two days' duration; the fourth fast lasted 30 days but was broken each evening at sunset. The fourth fast preceded the feast of *bēma*, the most important feast of the Manichaean year, which occurred sometime in March. The fast and feast commemorated the "Passion" of Mani and his "Ascension" to paradise. Five sets of two-day fasts called *yimki* were mentioned in fragments of Manichaean calendars written in Sogdian, an Iranian language. They seem to correspond to the four great fasts just mentioned, with the final two fasts occurring at the beginning and within the period of the 30 days in which the "Passion" was commemorated. For the hearer, the Sunday fast involved abstinence from sexual relations with one's wife, from any food comprising meat or fish, and from all material work, whether at home, in the fields, or in one's trade. For the elect, for whom strict abstinence was always the rule, the Monday fast must have meant a reinforcement of the usual observances and was an integral part of the ritual for that day.

Fasting was closely connected with another of the Manichaean rites: confession of sins. One of the purposes of the weekly fast was to prepare for the ordinary confession that hearers and elect were required to make each Monday. The hearers confessed to the elect, and the elect to one another. Likewise, once a year, the great fast of 30 days was intended to prepare members of both groups for the general communal confession that constituted one of the essential acts of the celebration of *bēma*. This confession was addressed to Mani himself. Because this event took place near the end of the year, it served to wash away the filth of the year that had passed in order that the church, purified and renewed, could begin the new year with the confidence of rediscovered innocence. The Manichaean confession poses difficult questions. There is no doubt that once they acknowledged their faults the penitents asked pardon, or absolution, for them, but it is difficult to specify in what form this pardon was granted and how the Manichaeans viewed the efficacy of the rite.

The Manichaean Church also included an elaborate initiation rite involving a group of five ritual actions—called "signs" or "mysteries"—that was used to authenticate the integration of a neophyte into the community, or the admission of a hearer into the order of the elect or any promotion to a higher grade. The imposition of hands was the most important of these actions.

The Manichaean scriptures. Mani believed that the decadence of earlier religions was caused by the fact that their founders had not written down their revelations; they had communicated these revelations only orally. Their teaching was codified only after their death; moreover, that task was undertaken by followers who had retained only a part of the revelations or who had understood it imperfectly. Thus, the scriptures that were passed on gave rise to diverse interpretations, quarrels, competition, and heresies; in brief, they caused divisions in the religion and weakened it. In an attempt to prevent such an occurrence in his church and to assure the doctrinal unity of the message it was charged to spread, Mani took it upon himself to write down his revelation with his own hand and in his own lifetime to give canonical status to the writings in which that revelation was expressed. Scribes were to copy the scriptures without alteration, and apologists were to hand them on in their literal form, for—it was thought—they contained clearly and completely the body of knowledge revealed by Mani.

Scriptures written by Mani himself

On the basis of comparative data provided particularly by Coptic documents found at al-Fayyūm in Middle Egypt and by documents found in Turfan (Chinese Turkistan)—including a version of the catechism prepared for the Chinese Emperor in 731, found in the caves of Tun-huang—it has been determined that the Manichaean canon included seven works attributed to Mani, and written originally in Syriac, one of the eastern Aramaic languages: the "Living (or Great) Gospel"; the "Treasure of Life"; the "Book of Secrets"; the "Pragmateia," or "Treatise"; the "Book of Giants"; the "Epistles"; and the "Book of Psalms and Prayers."

The Chinese catechism added a book called *Ta-men-ho-yi* (The Drawing of the Two Great Principles); possibly it corresponds to Mani's work that elsewhere was called *Ardhang* ("Image"), an album of paintings and images that was intended to illustrate the key points of the doctrine for the benefit of those who could not read. Manichaeans also included among their sacred writings the *Shābuhragān*, written by Mani in Middle Persian and dedicated to Shāpūr I. The largest of the works dug up at al-Fayyūm, the *Kephalaia* ("The Principal Points of the Teaching of the Master"), was sometimes included in canons and appeared to record meetings of Mani with his disciples. It was, however, the work of a follower and is not wholly a faithful recording of the actual teaching of Mani.

In the Middle Ages, Manichaeism became extinct and the scriptures disappeared. The 20th century led to a partial recovery of them, mainly in Chinese Turkistan and Egypt. They include some sheets from the *Shābuhragān* in the original Middle Persian in addition to a large portion of secondary religious literature. A Latin text was discovered in a cave near Tébessa, Algeria, that concerns the elect and hearers. The various finds show that the doctrinal unity of Manichaeism was preserved despite its wide areal extent.

BIBLIOGRAPHY. A bibliography, still incomplete, is in L.J.R. ORT, *Mani: A Religio-Historical Description of His Personality*, pp. 261–277 (1967). The work of P. ALFARIC, *Les Écritures manichéenes* (1918), though old, remains a most valuable bibliography, but it needs to be revised and augmented. An excellent selection of Manichaean texts or texts relating to Manichaeism is in A. ADAM (ed. and trans.), *Texte zum Manichäismus* (1954). An index of the fragments of Manichaean writings discovered in Central Asia, is in E.M. BOYCE, *A Catalogue of the Iranian Manuscripts in Manichaean Script in the German Turfan Collection* (1960). Manichaean Coptic works published or in the course of publication are: *Homilien* (1934), *Kephalaia* (since 1935), and *A Manichaean Psalm-Book*, part 2 (1939). Documentation on Manichaean iconography is collected in A. VON LE COQ, *Die manichäischen Miniaturen* (1923). General studies or comprehensive expositions of Manichaeism include: F.C. BAUR, *Das manichäische Religionssystem nach den Quellen neu untersucht und entwikelt* (1831, reprinted 1928), based above all on the testimony of St. Augustine, a classic that preserves its high value; F.C. BURKITT, *The Religion of the Manichees* (1925); H.H. SCHAEDER, *Urform und Fortbildungen des manichäischen Systems* (1927), an outstanding and epoch-making essay, with an integral and coherent interpretation of Manichaeism in all the totality and diversity of its expressions; H.J. POLOTSKY, *Abriss des manichäischen Systems* (1934), a comprehensive work; H.C. PUECH, "Der Begriff der Erlösung im Manichäismus," in *Eranos-Jahrbuch 1936*, pp. 183–286 (1937; trans. as "The Concept of Redemption in Manichaeism," in *The Mystic Vision*, "Bollingen Series," 1969); *Le Manichéisme: son fondateur, sa doctrine* (1949), copious notes and numerous references; "Le Manichéisme," in *Histoire des Religions*, vol. 2, pp. 523–645 (1972); G. WIDENGREN, *Mani und der Manichäismus* (1961; Eng. trans., *Mani and Manichaeism*, 1965); and O. KLIMA, *Manis Zeit und Leben* (1962).

(H.-C.P.)

Manila

Manila, the major city of the Republic of the Philippines, is the country's economic and cultural centre as well as its de facto national capital. Located on Luzon Island, it spreads along the eastern shore of Manila Bay at the mouth of the Pasig River and is the country's most important port. Its name is derived from the flowering *nilad* plant, a flowering shrub adapted to marshy conditions, which once grew profusely along the banks of the river. Originally called Maynilad, the name was shortened first to Maynila and then to *Manila*. The city proper covers an area of approximately 15 square miles

Downtown Manila bisected by the Pasig River. The city's post office is in the foreground.
Georg Gerster—Rapho Guillumette

(39 square kilometres) and houses a population of about 1,331,000. The greater metropolitan region—including the surrounding suburbs—has an area of 146 square miles (378 square kilometres) and a population of about 3,000,000.

Manila has been the country's principal city for four centuries and is the contemporary focus of its industrial development, as well as the international port of entry. Situated on one of the finest sheltered harbours of the Far East, it is only 600 miles east of Hong Kong. It has experienced rapid economic development since its destruction in World War II and its subsequent rebuilding; today it is plagued with such urban problems as pollution, traffic congestion, and overpopulation. Attempts are being made to ameliorate these problems, however, and Manila possesses some of the finest health facilities in the Orient.

History. In the early 16th century, Manila was a walled Muslim settlement whose ruler levied customs duties on all commerce that passed up the Pasig River. Spanish conquistadores under the leadership of Miguel López de Legaspi—first Spanish governor general of the Philippines—entered the mouth of the river in 1571. They destroyed the settlement and founded the fortress city of Intramuros ("Walled City") in its place. Outside the city walls stood some scattered villages, each of which was ruled by a local chieftain; each of these villages was centred on a marketplace. As Spanish colonial rule became established, churches were built near the marketplaces, where the concentration of population was greatest. Manila spread beyond its walls, expanding north, east, and south, linking together the market–church complexes as it did so. These early villages now form the present districts of the city.

The propagation of Catholicism began with the Augustinian friar Andrés de Urdaneta, who accompanied the expedition of 1571. He was followed by Franciscan, Dominican, Jesuit, and other Augustinian priests, who founded churches, convents, and schools. In 1574 Manila was baptized under the authorization of Spain and the Vatican as the "Distinguished and Ever Loyal City" and became the centre of Catholicism as well as the centre of the Philippines. At various periods Manila was seriously threatened, and sometimes occupied, by foreign powers. It was invaded by the Chinese in 1574, raided by the Dutch in the mid-17th century. In the 18th century the city was captured and held by the British from 1762 to 1764 during the Seven Years' War. The Treaty of Paris (1763) resulted in the restoration of the city to Spain. It was opened to foreign trade in 1832. Commerce was further stimulated by the opening of the Suez Canal of 1869.

During the Spanish-American War in 1898, the Spanish

The Spanish period

fleet was defeated at Manila Bay, after which the city surrendered to United States forces. It subsequently became the headquarters for the United States administration of the Philippines. Upon the outbreak of World War II, Manila was declared an open city and was occupied by the Japanese in January 1942. The city suffered little damage during the Japanese invasion but was levelled to the ground when it was recaptured by American forces in 1945. Rebuilt with aid from the United States, Manila was the capital of the Philippines from 1946 until 1948, when Quezon City, a suburban town northeast of Manila, was chosen as the site of the new national capital. The city remained the location of most of the government offices, however, and continues to be the Philippines' principal metropolitan area.

The contemporary city. *The physical setting.* Manila stands on the eastern shore of Manila Bay, 770 square miles (1,994 square kilometres), a large inlet with access to the sea through a channel 15 miles wide to the southwest. It occupies the low, narrow deltaic plain of the Pasig River, which flows northwestward to Manila Bay out of a large lake, Laguna de Bay, southeast of the city, which has an area of 343 square miles (888 square kilometres). Manila Bay lies to the west, the swampy delta of the southward-flowing Pampanga River to the north, the mountains of the Bataan Peninsula to the west, and Laguna de Bay to the southeast. Although the city's area is constricted, it is an excellent port site because of its sheltered harbour, its access to the inland agricultural areas by the river, and its relative proximity to the Asian mainland. The municipality itself occupies approximately 15 square miles; together with its surrounding suburbs, metropolitan Manila, as mentioned, spreads over 146 square miles.

The city site

Climate. The city is protected from extreme weather conditions by the hills of the Eastern Cordillera to the east and by the mountains of Bataan Peninsula, which lies to the west of Manila Bay. The tropical climate is characterized by a wet season that lasts from June to November and by a dry season lasting from December to May. High humidity and thunderstorms are common in July, when more rain is received than in other months. The average annual rainfall totals about 82 inches. There is little variation from the mean annual temperature of 81° F (27° C). The warmest months are from April to June, and the coolest are from November to February.

Vegetation and animal life. The city is dotted with tropical trees, including the palm, banyan, and acacia; bamboo is common in the public parks. Water buffalo, horses, dogs, pigs, and goats are common. The wealth of birdlife includes shrikes, doves, and pigeons, and Manila Bay abounds with sardines, anchovies, mackerel, tuna, snappers, and barracuda. The city's natural beauty

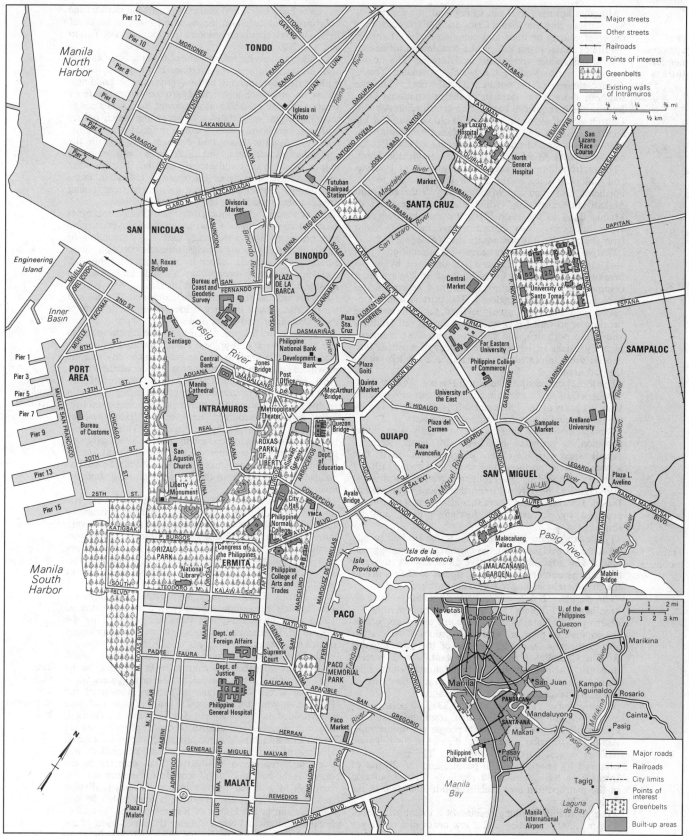

Central Manila and (inset) its metropolitan area.

is being marred, however, by air and water pollution, which is caused by the expansion of industry and the growing number of vehicles.

The city plan. The city is bisected by the Pasig River. It is divided into 14 administrative districts—seven to the north and seven to the south of the river—that have developed from the original Intramuros and the 13 vil-

lages located outside its walls. The districts of Tondo, San Nicolas, Binondo, Santa Cruz, Quiapo, San Miguel, and Sampaloc lie to the north, and Port Area, Intramuros, Ermita, Malate, Paco, Pandacan, and Santa Ana are south of the river. The two sections of the city are connected by six bridges—Jones, Quezon, Ayala, MacArthur, Roxas, and Mabini.

Although business areas are widespread, the districts of San Nicolas, Binondo, Santa Cruz, and Quiapo constitute the chief centres of trade and commerce. San Miguel is the site of Malacañang Palace, the presidential residence; several universities are located in Sampaloc. The northern shore is occupied by the heavily populated Tondo district, the site of the northern (local) port, while the southern shore is the location of the international port. Intramuros is renowned for its 16th-century San Agustin Church as well as for the ruins of its old walls and of Ft. Santiago. Ermita and Malate are choice residential districts and the sites of hotels and embassies; Paco, Pandacan, and Santa Ana are middle-income residential areas.

The metropolitan area includes the suburbs of Navotas and Caloocan City to the north, Quezon City to the northeast, San Juan and Mandaluyong to the east, and Makati and Pasay City (which stands on the shore of Manila Bay) to the south. They are mainly residential areas, but some larger industries have moved to them from the crowded city area where land values are high.

The ports. The main port area—an international port—is known as South Harbor. It is enclosed by a low breakwater and has six piers, four of which are used commercially. The Custom House and several warehouses and sheds are enclosed. The port is often congested, and ships are usually obliged to lie outside the breakwater to wait for entry. There are no rail facilities within the port area, and cargo is transported from the piers by trucks or barges. Several heavy industries that depend upon imported raw materials are located within the port area.

The local port occupies the North Harbor shore of Tondo district. Its seven piers are congested with heavy traffic from all ports in the Philippines. It is directly served by the railway and has several large warehouses.

Transportation. Within the Greater Manila area, transportation is provided principally by buses, jeepneys (small buses with the chassis of jeeps), and taxis. Bus services run to northern and southern Luzon; railroad services, operated by the Philippine National Railways, also connect the city with northern and southeastern Luzon. Interisland and international air transportation is provided by domestic and foreign airlines, and by shipping.

Traffic congestion is serious, with traffic tending to pile up at the six bridges during the morning and evening rush hours. The adjacent towns serve as dormitory suburbs, and a large number of people commute to their work in the city, thereby adding to the traffic problem.

The people. *Ethnic and religious groups.* Almost all Manilans are Filipinos. The largest foreign community is made up of Chinese, who comprise just over 6 percent of the population; there are also small groups of Americans and Europeans. About 93 percent of the population is Roman Catholic, 2 percent Protestant, and 2 percent Buddhist. The two national Christian churches—the Iglesia ni Kristo and the Aglipayan—claim the adherence of less than 3 percent of the city's inhabitants.

Demography. There are about 1,331,000 persons living within Manila's municipal area, resulting in an average population density of 89,000 people per square mile. Although Sampaloc is the largest district by area, Tondo has the largest population—434,000. The port area is occupied by fewer than 100 people, and the district of Intramuros has about 2,600 residents. The population of the metropolitan area reached about 3,000,000 in the early 1970s.

The population is young because of a high birth rate of 45 per 1,000 population and a low death rate of 11 per 1,000 population. The rate of natural increase is about three percent annually.

Housing. The city is plagued by an acute housing shortage, and tenement housing projects have been constructed by the government to help house the poor. In the early 1970s, about 40 percent of the families owned their homes, whereas the rest of the population was housed on a rental basis. There are five types of residential buildings —the single-family dwelling; the duplex for two independent households; the multistory *accessoria* whose dwell-

ing units have individual entrances from the outside; the apartment building; and the *barong-barong*, a shack of light materials that is common in the poor areas of Tondo and San Nicolas.

Architectural styles reflect American, Spanish, Chinese, and Malayan influences. Modern buildings—including multistoried commercial houses, government buildings, hotels, theatres, schools, and apartments—are made of reinforced concrete and hollow cement blocks. Houses of modern design—especially low, sprawling ranch houses with spacious lawns—are common in the districts of Ermita and Malate. Houses of Spanish design, with tile roofs, barred windows, and thick walls, were common before World War II and are still popular. The churches are American, Spanish, or European in character. Lumber, hollow cement blocks, and galvanized iron roofing are commonly used for middle-income dwellings.

The economy. *Manufacturing.* The diverse manufacturing activities include textile production, publishing and printing, food processing, and the production of paints, drugs, aluminum articles, rope and cordage, shoes, cigars and cigarettes, coconut oil, soap, and lumber. Factories generally operate on a small scale and are mostly located in the congested districts of San Nicolas (the railroad and truck terminus), Binondo, Tondo, and Santa Cruz. Heavy industry is located in the districts of Paco, Pandacan, and Santa Ana.

Commerce and finance. Manila is the centre of trade and finance in the Philippines. Trade flourishes within the Greater Manila area, as well as between the city and the provinces and with countries abroad. Most of the Philippines' imports and exports pass through the port of Manila. Banking and insurance have grown in importance in recent years. Financial institutions include such establishments as the Development Bank of the Philippines, the Philippine National Bank, the Philippine Veterans Bank, the government insurance system, the social security system, and private commercial and development banks. Private insurance companies and the Manila Stock Exchange also contribute to the mobilization of savings for investment.

Public utilities. Potable water is supplied by the National Waterworks and Sewerage Authority. Satisfactory sanitation conditions are maintained by constant surveillance of market facilities, restaurants, movie houses, recreation halls, and slaughter houses. Insecticides are sprayed regularly on open sewers, uncollected garbage, and standing water; garbage is collected by a fleet of trucks that operate night and day.

The Manila Electric Company provides electric power and lighting throughout the city and adjacent towns. Telephone and telegraph services are provided by the Bureau of Telecommunications and by several privately owned companies.

Administration and social conditions. *Government.* The city is governed by charter, with a mayor as its chief executive. He is elected by the city's voters for a four-year term. Voters must be literate citizens of the Philippines who are at least 21 years of age and who have resided in Manila for six months before the election. Legislative power and control of city appropriations are vested in a municipal board, presided over by the elected vice mayor, and composed of 20 elected councillors, five from each representative district. The secretary to the mayor is the custodian of all records and documents. For purposes of national representation, the city is divided into four districts, each of which is represented by one congressman in the House of Representatives. The city's fiscal and municipal court is under the supervision of the national Department of Justice. Although Manila is no longer the national capital, it houses such federal offices as the Malacañang Palace, the Congress of the Philippines, the Supreme Court, and various government departments, agencies, and bureaus.

Health and safety. The health facilities in Manila are among the best in the Far East. The city government maintains about 60 health centres, as well as the Lacson Memorial Hospital, at all of which patients are treated free of charge. It also subsidizes more than half a dozen government hospitals, and there are many missionary and private hospitals in the city.

Police and fire services are well organized, improved equipment and techniques are used, and personnel are comparatively well paid. With the growing population, however, additional trained men, equipment, and facilities, as well as an improved communication system, are needed. To intensify the campaign against crime, more police precincts were created in the early 1970s, and the Police Community Relation District was organized.

Education. More than 96 percent of the population is literate. More than 100 free public schools are maintained, in addition to the night vocational and secondary schools and the city-supported university. Educational opportunities are also provided for handicapped children, orphans of school age, and adults. As the education centre of the country, Greater Manila houses many of the major universities, including the University of the Philippines (with its main campus in Quezon City), the Philippine Normal College, the Philippine College of Commerce, and the Philippine College of Arts and Trades. There are several religious universities, including the University of Santo Tomas (founded in 1611), as well as nonsectarian institutions such as the University of the East and the Far Eastern University.

University education

Cultural life. The centre of the performing arts in the country is the Philippine Cultural Center, and there is an open-air theatre in Rizal Park. The many libraries and museums include the National Library and the National Museum, known for its anthropological and archaeological exhibits; the National Institute of Science and Technology, with its scientific reference library and large collections of plants and animals; the geological museum of the Bureau of Mines; the Manila Aquarium; Ft. Santiago, which houses original works by the Philippine patriot José Rizal; and the Kamaynilaan (Manila City) Library and Museum, which contains valuable carvings, paintings, and archives.

The media. There are several English-language daily newspapers, including the *Manila Daily Bulletin, The Manila Times, The Philippines Herald,* and *The Manila Chronicle. Taliba* is printed in Pilipino, the national language. Weekly magazines include the *Philippines Free Press, The Sunday Times Magazine, The Weekly Nation,* and *The Graphic.* There are many large and well-equipped publishing houses located in the metropolitan area.

In the early 1970s there were 13 radio broadcasting stations and seven television stations operating within Greater Manila. Most residents have radios, and many also have television sets.

The city's parks

Recreation. The foremost recreation area is Rizal Park. Its grounds contain a Japanese garden, a Chinese garden, an open-air theatre, a playground, a grandstand, and a long promenade adjacent to Manila Bay. Other areas include the Manila Botanical and Zoological Garden, the Mehan Garden, the Paco Memorial Park, and the Philippine-Mexican Park. Athletic facilities include the Rizal Memorial Stadium and the Pius XII Catholic Center in Manila and the Araneta Coliseum in Quezon City. Annual festivals and carnivals are held in Sunken Gardens.

Prospects for the future. Manila is destined to retain its commercial, industrial, political, and cultural importance. The city is undergoing development to improve its physical environment and standard of living. All trends point to the city's future as a modern Oriental metropolis with all the conveniences of the 20th century.

BIBLIOGRAPHY. The literature about Manila is extensive. Much valuable information may be obtained from books, magazines, newspapers, government reports, atlases, and encyclopaedias. The following references represent only some of the most recent works.

General discussions on the history, government, economy, and living conditions in Manila include: T.A. AGONCILLO and O.M. ALFONSO, *History of the Filipino People* (1967); ALFONSO J. ALUIT, *The Galleon Guide to Manila and the Philippines* (1968); ROBERT E. HUKE, *Shadows on the Land: An Economic Geography of the Philippines* (1963); RIZAL CULTURAL COMMITTEE, OFFICE OF THE PROVINCIAL GOVERNOR,

Rizal Province: A Political History (1967); D.C. SALITA, T.W. LUNA, and E.N. SALUMBIDES, *Living in Our World* (1966).

Specific treatment of population, housing, charter provisions, needs, and resources of the capital city may be found in the BUREAU OF CENSUS AND STATISTICS, *Manila 1970 Census of Population and Housing* (1971); BUREAU OF PRINTING, *Revised Charter of the City of Manila* (1950); and ANTONIO J. VILLEGAS, *Manila: Its Needs and Resources* (1962). For maps and statistical information about the city, see R.S. HENDRY, L.R. DORAN, and A. MALAY, *Atlas of the Philippines* (1959); and BUREAU OF CENSUS AND STATISTICS, *Census Atlas of the Philippines, 1939* (1941).

(D.C.S.)

Manipur

Manipur is a state of India, established in 1972 and located in the northeastern part of the country. It was previously a union territory. It is bordered by the Indian states of Nāgāland on the north and Assam to the west, by the union territory of Mizoram on the southwest, and by Burma to the south and east. It covers an area of 8,628 square miles (22,346 square kilometres) and is larger than Wales but smaller than British Honduras. Its population of almost 1,070,000 is approximately equal to that of Trinidad and Tobago. The capital, Imphāl, is the state's major trade centre.

Manipur is largely isolated from the rest of India, and the region has periodically been subject to invasions from the east. Its economy centres on agriculture and forestry, and there is lively activity in trade and cottage industries.

History. Although ancient hoes of ground stone have reportedly been found in the area, little is known of the history of the Manipur region before 1762. In that year the local prince, or raja, requested British aid to repel an invasion from Burma. Further communication was minimal until 1824, when the British were again requested to expel the Burmese. Disputed successions were a continual source of political turmoil until Chura Chand, a five-year-old member of the ruling family, was nominated raja in 1891. For the next eight years the administration was conducted under British supervision; slavery and forced labour were abolished and roads were constructed.

British intervention

In 1907 the government was assumed by the raja and the durbar, or council, whose vice president was a member of the Indian civil service. Subsequently, the administration was transferred to the raja, and the vice president of the durbar became its president. After an uprising of the Kuki hill tribes in 1917, a new system of government was adopted; the region was divided into three subdivisions, each headed by an officer from the neighbouring government of Assam.

With the accession of Manipur to India in 1947, the political agency exercised by Assam was abolished. Two years later the administration was taken over by the Indian government, and the region was ruled as a union territory by a chief commissioner and an elected territorial council. The council was abolished in 1969, and Manipur was placed under presidential rule. It became a state of India in 1972.

The landscape and environment. The state is comprised of two major physical features, the Manipur River Valley and a large surrounding tract of mountainous country. The valley extends from north to south; it covers an area of about 650 square miles and lies at an altitude of 2,600 feet above sea level. The main physical feature of the valley is the reedy Lake Loktak, which covers an area of about 25 square miles. The lake is the source of the Manipur River, which flows southward through the valley into Burma, where it joins the Myittha River, a tributary of the Irrawaddy.

The hill ranges have a general north–south trend; connecting spurs and ridges run from west to east between them. The ranges include the Nāga Hills to the north, the Manipur Hills along the eastern Burmese border, and the Lushai and Chin hills to the south. The average elevation lies between 5,000 and 6,000 feet above sea level. The hills are highest in the north, where they attain 8,427 feet (2,569 metres) in Siruhi Kashong (Siruhi Peak). In the west the mountains are broken by the valley of the Surma River. Known as the Barak River in Manipur, it rises at

Upland areas

Mount Jāpvo and flows south and west to join the Meghna River of Bangladesh.

The climate is temperate in the valley and cold in the hills. Rainfall is abundant, with about 65 inches (1,700 millimetres) of precipitation occurring annually.

The hills are densely covered with tree jungle and forests containing stands of bamboo and teak. Other trees include oak, magnolia, and chinquapin. The Luzon pine grows in the Nāga Hills. Plants include rhododendrons, primroses, and blue poppies. Animal life includes the Asiatic elephant, tiger, and leopard. The rhinoceros is hunted for its horn, which, when ground, is valued as an aphrodisiac. The brow-antlered deer is in danger of extinction; in the 1960s only 100 specimens were known to exist. Gaurs are the largest wild oxen in the world; the smaller gayals have been domesticated. There is also a fair number of wild buffalo.

The population. The population numbered about 941,000 in 1966 and 1,070,000 in 1971. In 1971 the average population density was 124 persons per square mile. About two-thirds of the people are the Meithei, who occupy the Manipur Valley and are largely Hindus. Meithei women conduct most of the trade in the valley and enjoy high social status.

The Nāga and Kuki hill tribes

The rest of the population is composed of indigenous hill tribes that are divided into numerous clans and sections. The Nāgas are found mainly in the north and the Kukis in the south. The tribesmen speak languages of the Tibeto-Burman family and practice traditional animist religions, although some of the Nāgas have been converted to Christianity. About 60 percent of the population speak Manipuri, which, together with English, is the official language of the state.

Administration and social conditions. The five states and two union territories of northeastern India—Assam, Nāgāland, Tripura, Manipur, and Meghalaya states and Arunachal Pradesh and Mizoram—share a common governor and common high court. Within Manipur the government is headed by a lieutenant governor; the state is divided into five administrative districts. In 1972 a proposal was made to create a Northeastern Council composed of representatives of each of the states and territories. The council would discuss common problems and coordinate development programs. The national Parliament has direct legislative jurisdiction over the northeast.

In 1970 educational facilities included more than 2,000 primary, 300 middle, and 120 high schools, as well as 13 colleges. There were about 230,000 enrolled students. In 1971 only one-third of the population were literate. Classes are taught in the Manipuri language, and English and Hindi are taught as well.

Major health problems include tuberculosis, leprosy, venereal disease, and filariasis. Health facilities need to be improved; in 1970 there were 12 hospitals, almost 60 dispensaries, 12 health centres, and 65 specialist clinics.

Agriculture and forestry

The economy and transport. Agriculture and forestry are the main sources of income. Rice is the major crop, and the rich soil also supports sugarcane, mustard, tobacco, fruit orchards, and pulses such as peas and beans. Terracing is common in the hills, where the tribes plow the ground with hand hoes. Among some of the hill tribes, domestic animals are kept only for meat and are not milked or used for hauling. The Nāgas are known to use intoxicants to catch fish. Teak and bamboo are major forestry products.

Manufacturing is limited to several well-established cottage industries. The designed cloth produced on handlooms is in demand throughout India. Other industries include soapmaking, carpentry, and tanning.

Manipur remains somewhat isolated from the rest of India, and communications within the state are poor. A road runs north from Imphāl to the North-Eastern Railway line at Dimāpur, and another road leads southeast from the capital to Tamu on the Burmese border. There are air links from Imphāl to Silchar, Assam, and Calcutta, West Bengal.

Cultural life. Polo and hockey are popular sports. Manipur has given birth to an indigenous form of classical dance known as Manipuri dance. It is dissimilar to other Indian dance forms; hand movements are used decoratively rather than as pantomime, bells are not accentuated, and both men and women perform communally. The dance dramas, interpreted by a narrator, are a part of religious life. Themes are generally taken from the life of Kṛṣṇa (Krishna), the pastoral god of Hinduism. Long an isolated art form, Manipuri dance was introduced to the rest of India by the poet Rabindranath Tagore in 1917.

(B.A.A.)

Manitoba

Lying midway between the Atlantic and Pacific oceans, Manitoba became the fifth province of Canada when it was admitted to the confederation in 1870. Though it is known as one of the nation's Prairie Provinces, along with Saskatchewan and Alberta, more than 50 percent of its land area is forested. Its 251,000 square miles (650,000 square kilometres) contain 39,225 square miles of water, and of its more than 38,500 lakes, Lake Winnipeg is the 13th largest in the world. The province is bounded on the north by the Keewatin District of the Northwest Territories, on the northeast by Hudson Bay, on the east by Ontario, on the south by the United States (the states of Minnesota and North Dakota), and on the west by Saskatchewan.

Overview of the province

About two-thirds of the 988,247 Manitobans counted in the 1971 census are now urban dwellers, but the province maintains the traditional conservatism of its rural days. It continues to draw the greatest proportion of its wealth from exploitation and processing of the products of its primary industries—farming, lumbering, mining, and fishing—though Winnipeg, its capital, is the focus of rapidly expanding manufacturing industries. The fourth-largest city of Canada, Winnipeg contains in its metropolitan area over one-half of the province's people and, in spite, or because of its relative isolation, is a major artistic and cultural centre. (For information on related topics, see the articles CANADA; CANADA, HISTORY OF; NORTH AMERICA; GREAT PLAINS; and HUDSON BAY.)

The history of Manitoba. *Early exploration and commerce.* When the first white man set foot in Manitoba, the province was inhabited by Cree, Assiniboin, and Ojibwa Indians and, along the shore of Hudson Bay, by Eskimos. Sir Thomas Button, an English explorer, came through the bay in 1612 and explored around the mouth of the Nelson River. In 1619 a Danish expedition wintered at the mouth of the Churchill River. The actual opening of Manitoba was the work of the Hudson's Bay Company, which was established in London in 1670. The company built northern trading posts at strategic fur-collecting points, the chief of which was York Factory at the mouth of the Nelson. From there in 1691, Henry Kelsey explored southward to the region of The Pas and to the prairies.

International and commercial conflict

As the English moved down from the north, however, the French moved in from the east, and many clashes resulted. Pierre Gaultier, sieur de La Vérendrye, arrived at the Red River in 1731 on his way to the Pacific Coast. En route he built forts from Lake Superior to the Red River valley, including Ft. Rouge on the present site of Winnipeg—at the junction of the Red and Assiniboine rivers. In 1783, with Canada under the British flag, the Montreal-based North West Company began to compete for furs with the Hudson's Bay Company, and a fur war ensued that ended only in 1821 when the two companies merged.

Settlement and provincial status. The first settlement of Manitoba came in 1812 when Thomas Douglas, 5th earl of Selkirk, received a grant of land on the Red River from the Hudson's Bay Company and brought Scots and Irishmen to farm it. Frost, flood, and grasshoppers plagued them. They also were opposed by the Métis, French-Indian half-breeds, who were in the employ of the North West Company and feared that settlement would mean the end of buffalo hunting. In the Seven Oaks massacre, near Winnipeg, the governor of the Red River colony and a score of men were killed in 1816, but the colony slowly prospered. The Dominion of Canada acquired all of the Hudson's Bay Company territory, known as Rupert's Land, in 1869. Under Louis Riel, the Métis resisted and refused to let government officials enter the territory until the government made concessions in the Manitoba Act of 1870, which made Manitoba a province.

In 1867 steamboats had linked the Red River colony with the United States. In 1878 the railway reached Winnipeg from St. Paul, Minnesota, and in 1882 from eastern Canada. With these came a flood of settlers that died down only at the outbreak of World War I. Provincial boundaries were extended westward in 1881, eastward in 1884, and northward in 1912 to give Manitoba its present dimensions. Western expansion saw the prairies broken for grain growing, while northward extension brought about exploitation of the great mineral resources; created such towns as Thompson, Flin Flon, The Pas, and Lynn Lake; and harnessed the rivers to produce cheap electrical power. The 1930s brought drought and depression, but World War II revived rural electrification and industry, beginning an expansion that has since continued.

The natural and human landscape. *Physical regions.* Extreme southern Manitoba is part of the Saskatchewan plain, a land of rich, level prairies and rolling pastures. The Manitoba Lowland to the north is the basin that once held glacial Lake Agassiz, remnants of which include Lake Winnipeg (9,230 square miles), Lake Winnipegosis (2,068), and Lake Manitoba (1,817). Upland plateaus, wooded river valleys, limestone outcrops, forests, and swamps mark the area that is drained by the Red and Assiniboine rivers into Lake Winnipeg.

To the north and east of the lowland is the geologically ancient Canadian, or Precambrian, Shield, an area of rocks, forests, and rivers. It covers three-fifths of the province and is drained by the Nelson and Churchill rivers into Hudson Bay. On the shore of the bay, the Hudson Bay Lowland extends 100 miles inland as a flat, almost treeless plain of tundra and boglike muskeg. Manitoba's highlands are on the Saskatchewan border. The Riding, Duck, and Porcupine mountains form the Manitoba Escarpment, whose high point is Baldy Mountain, at 2,727 feet (831 metres).

Climate. Manitoba has moderately dry climate with sharp seasonal temperature changes. Temperatures of −40° F (−40° C) are not uncommon in any part of the province; 100° F (38° C) is not an uncommon summer reading in the south. Average daily high temperatures at Winnipeg range from 8.8° F (−12.9° C) in January to 79.7° F (26.5° C) in July; average lows vary from −8.6° F (−22.6° C) in January to 56.8° F (13.8° C) in July. Annual precipitation varies from 13 inches to 22 inches in the southeast, (counting ten inches of snow as one inch of rain) with about 70 percent of it falling between May and October. Snow covers the ground from November to April in the south and for longer in the north.

Vegetation and animal life. Manitoba's more than 120,000 square miles of forest include open parklands of aspen, maple, elm, and oak in the south, becoming a mixed broadleaf and coniferous forest and then the true northern coniferous forest in the higher latitudes. The chief trees are spruce, aspen, jack pine, poplar, balsam, white birch, and tamarack. The southern prairies are relatively treeless except for bluffs of aspen, oak, willow, and poplar.

Caribou, moose, elk, deer, bear, beaver, fox, lynx, marten, and mink live in the northern forests; deer, coyote, rabbit, and muskrat inhabit the more southerly areas. Polar bears are found along Hudson Bay. Grouse, prairie chicken, and other game birds live in the uplands, and millions of geese and ducks breed in Manitoba's sloughs and ponds. Fish include bass, pickerel, sauger, trout, and whitefish. The Winnipeg goldeye, a whitefish that is smoked, is world-famous. Beluga whales are taken in Hudson Bay.

To conserve wildlife and waterfowl, government and private organizations cooperate in wildlife surveys and nature-management programs. Manitoba has Canada's second-largest inland fishery, but commercial fishing in some lakes was halted in 1970 because of the mercury content in fish caught. The provincial government has taken legal action against companies alleged to be responsible for water pollution.

Patterns of settlement. Manitoba's countryside has an older, more settled look than that of other Prairie Provinces, but it is marked by deserted farmhouses, dying small towns, and abandoned railway lines. Farms have become larger and more mechanized, averaging about 500 acres (200 hectares) in size, leading to a population drain to the cities and towns. Most urban dwellers are in the south, more than 80 percent of them in the six cities and six municipalities that in January 1972 were consolidated into Winnipeg. The province's other urban dwellers live in small trading centres primarily serving the farm population or in northern Manitoba at mines and transportation junctions. The main urban centres (in addition to Winnipeg) are Brandon, an industrial city serving the southwest; Thompson, a nickel-mining and -processing centre in the northern forest; Flin Flon, a northern mining centre; The Pas, a trading and communications centre on the Saskatchewan River; Portage la Prairie, the chief trading centre between Winnipeg and Brandon; Selkirk, the centre of commercial fishing and water transportation on Lake Winnipeg; and Dauphin, serving west central Manitoba.

The people of Manitoba. Scottish and Irish settlers in 1812 were the backbone of early agricultural settlement in the Red River colony, joining the Métis in the area. Between 1870 and 1900, rail and river transportation caused Manitoba's population to grow tenfold, to more than 255,000. Many of the newcomers were from Europe and from eastern Canada. After that, natural increase provided the major growth until the population drain of the depression in the 1930s and of World War II, after which the population continued its growth.

The impact of Manitoba's many ethnic groups is still evident. Store signs in Ukrainian are common in north Winnipeg. Many of the districts originally settled by specific groups remain the centres of population for those groups. Manitobans of British descent are evenly distributed. French-speaking people live mainly along the Red River, from the U.S. border to Greater Winnipeg. St. Boniface is the largest French-speaking community in Canada outside the province of Quebec. Germans settled in the south centre, Scandinavians in the original Icelandic settlements around Gimli. Some 29,000 Indians and Eskimos remain, the latter living around Churchill on Hudson Bay; the former comprise some 50 bands speaking four Indian languages. The largest religious groups are United Church of Canada, Roman Catholic, and Anglican Church of Canada, but Lutherans, Mennonites, Presbyterians, Jews, Greek Orthodox, Ukrainian Catholics, Hutterian Brethren, and other smaller groups are found across the province.

In 1971 Manitoba's preponderance of births over deaths produced a rate of natural increase of 10.5 per 1,000 inhabitants. Relatively few foreign immigrants settle in the province, which tends to lose people to Ontario, Quebec, and British Columbia when the prairie economy slows down.

The province has few racial problems. The chief one is posed by the large-scale migration of Indians from reservations into the cities, particularly Winnipeg. There they have difficulty finding jobs, are often on welfare, and are forced to live in slum squalor. Provincial, federal, and city governments are tackling the problem, but as yet they have had little real success.

The provincial economy. *Resources, products, and management.* The rich southern farmlands are a main resource of Manitoba. The Canadian Shield area accounts for more than 80 percent of mineral production. Nearly one-half of the forests are commercially productive; and the thousands of square miles of water provide sport and commercial fishing and inexpensive electrical power. Per capita income in 1969 was $2,900, compared to a national average of $2,950.

Wheat is the main crop; others include oats, barley, rye,

Marginal notes:

Topographical diversity

Wildlife and its conservation

Impact of ethnic groups

flax, rapeseed, sunflower seed, and vegetables. The major minerals are nickel, copper, gold, lead, silver, and zinc. Pulpwood for paper manufacture accounts for 60 percent of the timber cut. Main manufactures are foods and beverages, clothing, fabricated-metal goods, chemicals, space rockets, farm machinery, and cement. Among Manitoba's industrial installations are: a nuclear-research plant in Pinawa, an integrated forest-products complex in The Pas, a nickel complex in Thompson, a pulp mill in Pine Falls, and a fertilizer plant in Brandon. Large generating stations are being built on the Nelson River.

Most industry is privately owned, but the provincial government is moving into some areas. In 1971 it implemented a compulsory government-operated automobile-insurance program. Through the Manitoba Development Corporation, a government loan fund, it has acquired an interest in several businesses including the forest complex in The Pas. In 1970 about one-seventh of the labour force was covered by collective-bargaining agreements. The main labour organization is the Manitoba Federation of Labour, affiliated with the Canadian Labour Congress. Employers work through chambers of commerce and the Canadian Manufacturers' Association.

Transportation. Because of its strategic location between the east and west, Manitoba is a leading transportation centre. Main railway lines run east and west through Winnipeg, as does the Trans-Canada Highway. Changing economic conditions are lessening rail transportation's importance, and branch lines are being abandoned. Winnipeg, with nearly 50 trucking terminals, is served by 14 transcontinental carriers and is headquarters for eight of them. Four major airlines fly to all parts of Canada and to Europe and the United States. Thirty nonscheduled commercial air firms—bush fliers, freight haulers, and air taxis—are based in the province.

Churchill, on Hudson Bay, provides a short, direct sea route to Europe that is open for ten weeks in late summer. There is waterborne freight traffic on Lake Winnipeg in summer. In winter, northern mining and logging camps are supplied by sled trains hauled by tractors.

Administration and social conditions. *Structure of governments.* Manitoba derives its authority from two British statutes, the British North America Acts of 1867 and 1871, and one Canadian statute, the Manitoba Act of 1870. Power is divided between the federal government in Ottawa and the provincial government in Winnipeg. The lieutenant governor of Manitoba, appointed by the governor general in council (the federal government in Ottawa), represents the Crown; his duties are largely honorary. The functioning head of the government is the premier. The unicameral legislative assembly has 57 members and sits for five years or until dissolved by executive action. The highest court in Manitoba is the Court of Appeal, presided over by a chief justice and four associate judges. The Court of Queen's Bench hears important civil and criminal cases while lesser cases are heard in the courts of the six judicial districts.

Municipalities are creatures of the province, and local administration is under provincial control. Each of the some 200 incorporated entities is governed by a council headed by a mayor or reeve. Twenty districts are governed by provincial administrators, but there are no counties. After consolidation of Greater Winnipeg into a single administrative unit in 1972, the city was governed by a mayor and a 50-member council, all elected.

Education. Elementary, secondary, technical and vocational schools and universities are a provincial responsibility. Schools are administered by local or larger unit boards under supervision of the department of education and are financed by government grants and local taxes. The University of Winnipeg and the University of Manitoba are in Greater Winnipeg, Brandon University in Brandon. Winnipeg, Brandon, and The Pas have vocational-training schools.

Living standards and services. Manitoba is a low-wage area. Wages are well below those in eastern Canada and British Columbia, though higher than in the Atlantic provinces. Living costs are somewhat higher than the national average. The province supervises medical and

hospital insurance programs, and Manitobans participate in such federal welfare and security programs as children's allowances, old-age pensions, and the Canada Pension Plan. These are augmented by a wide provincial welfare program. Relief for indigents is administered by local councils and agencies. Most municipalities have their own police force, though provincial policing is done by the Royal Canadian Mounted Police.

Cultural life and institutions. Manitoba's mixed population gives it a rich and varied cultural life. Ethnic groups—European, Asian, Indian, and Eskimo—retain a vigorous measure of their traditional culture in customs, dance, art, music and song, language, and crafts.

Partly because of their past isolation from the rest of Canada, Manitobans have always been enthusiastic sponsors and supporters of the arts. Winnipeg is the home of the internationally famous Royal Winnipeg Ballet, the Winnipeg Symphony Orchestra, and the Manitoba Theatre Centre. One of Canada's leading theatrical companies, the Centre includes an experimental and a children's theatre and is lodged in a new downtown theatre. The Winnipeg Art Gallery, publicly supported, moved into a new building in 1971. A dozen commercial and private art galleries in Winnipeg and a large number of musical and theatrical groups operate throughout the metropolitan area. The centre of much activity is Winnipeg's downtown centennial complex, completed in 1967, which includes a concert hall, planetarium, and the Manitoba Museum of Man and Nature.

Regional activities include stampedes and roundups at Morris and Swan River, the Trappers' Festival at The Pas, the Trout Festival at Flin Flon, annual Icelandic celebrations at Gimli, and the International Music Camp at the International Peace Garden on the Manitoba–North Dakota boundary.

Manitoba has seven daily and more than 70 weekly newspapers, 17 radio stations, and nine television stations. The two largest provincial dailies, *The Winnipeg Free Press* and *The Winnipeg Tribune*, have a combined daily circulation of around 220,000. Winnipeg is also a centre of the ethnic press, with about 20 foreign-language papers published in the city.

Prospects. As befits a province lying halfway across Canada, Manitoba's population, wages, living costs, living standards, and rate of development are neither the highest nor the lowest in the country. A mixed economy balanced between primary and secondary industries but trending toward the latter, as well as the generally conservative outlook of its people, make the province sharply affected by, but less susceptible than most to, economic booms or slumps. Growth has been gradual but steady. The province's politics reflected this attitude until the election of 1969, which for the first time brought a socialist government to office. Though this may herald political changes, it is more likely that the conservative outlook of Manitobans will colour and moderate the government's policies.

BIBLIOGRAPHY. W.L. MORTON, *Manitoba: A History*, 2nd ed. (1967), is the standard and an excellent historical text on the province. His *Manitoba: The Birth of a Province* (1965), is a compendium of documents relating to the province's entry into confederation. The *Economic Atlas of Manitoba*, ed. by T.R. WEIR (1960), is a comprehensive record of economic aspects of the province; the *Atlas of Canada* (1958), includes geographical detail. A succinct but complete description of the provincial economy is *The Economy of the Province of Manitoba 1970* (1971); supplementary figures are contained in *Manitoba Facts and Figures* (1970). *The Government of Manitoba* by MURRAY S. DONNELLY (1963), is a scholarly and clear exposition of the provincial administration.

(P.McL.)

Mann, Horace

Among the educational leaders promoting the new national ideals of democracy, equality, and freedom in the years between the American Revolution and the Civil War, Horace Mann was the most influential spokesman. He is rightly called "the father of American public education," because the reforms he advocated and fought for

Provincial and local jurisdictions

Ballet, music, and theatre

constitute the basis of public schooling as it is known in that country today.

Born in Franklin, Massachusetts, on May 4, 1796, Horace Mann grew up in an environment ruled by pov-

Horace Mann.

erty, hardship, and self-denial. He was taught briefly and erratically by comparatively poor teachers, but he managed to educate himself in the Franklin town library, and, with the help of some tutoring by an itinerant schoolmaster, he gained admission at the age of 20 to the sophomore class at Brown University. He did brilliant work at Brown, manifesting great interest in problems of politics, education, and social reform; his valedictory address, on the gradual advancement of the human race in dignity and happiness, was a model of humanitarian optimism, offering a way in which education, philanthropy, and republicanism could combine to allay the wants and shortcomings that beset mankind.

Upon graduation in 1819 Mann chose law as a career. He read law briefly with a Wrentham, Massachusetts, lawyer, taught for a year at Brown, and then studied at Litchfield (Connecticut) Law School, which led to his admission to the bar in 1823. He settled in Dedham, and there his legal acumen and oratorical skill soon won him a seat in the state House of Representatives, serving from 1827 to 1833. There he led the movement that established a state hospital for the insane at Worcester, the first of its kind in the United States. In 1833 he moved to Boston, and from 1835 to 1837 he served in the Massachusetts Senate, in 1836 as president of it.

Of the many causes Mann espoused, none was dearer to him than popular education. Nineteenth-century Massachusetts could boast a public school system going back to 1647. Yet during Mann's own lifetime, the quality of education had steadily deteriorated as school control had gradually slipped into the hands of economy-minded local districts. A vigorous reform movement arose, committed to halting this decline by reasserting the state's influence over the schools. The result was the establishment in 1837 of a state board of education, charged with collecting and publicizing school information throughout the state. Much against the advice of friends, who thought he was tossing aside a promising political career, Mann accepted the first secretaryship of this board.

Endowed with little direct power, the new office demanded moral leadership of the highest order and this Mann supplied for 11 years. He started a biweekly *Common School Journal* for teachers and lectured widely to interested groups of citizens. His annual reports to the board ranged far and wide through the field of pedagogy, stating the case for the public school and discussing its problems. Essentially his message centred in six funda-

Reform program

mental propositions: (1) that a republic cannot long remain ignorant and free, hence the necessity of universal popular education; (2) that such education must be paid for, controlled, and sustained by an interested public; (3)

that such education is best provided in schools embracing children of all religious, social, and ethnic backgrounds; (4) that such education, while profoundly moral in character, must be free of sectarian religious influence; (5) that such education must be permeated throughout by the spirit, methods, and discipline of a free society, which preclude harsh pedagogy in the classroom; and (6) that such education can be provided only by well-trained, professional teachers. Mann encountered strong resistance to these ideas—from clergymen who deplored nonsectarian schools, from educators who condemned his pedagogy as subversive of classroom authority, and from politicians who opposed the board as an improper infringement of local educational authority—but his views prevailed.

Mann resigned the secretaryship in 1848 to take the seat of former Pres. John Quincy Adams in the United States Congress. There he proved himself to be a fierce enemy of slavery. In 1853, having run unsuccessfully for the Massachusetts governorship a year before, he accepted the presidency of Antioch College in Yellow Springs, Ohio, a new institution committed to coeducation, nonsectarianism, and equal opportunity for Negroes. There, amidst the usual crises attendant upon an infant college, Mann finished out his years. He died at Yellow Springs on August 2, 1859. Two months before, he had given his own valedictory to the graduating class: "I beseech you to treasure up in your hearts these my parting words: Be ashamed to die until you have won some victory for humanity."

BIBLIOGRAPHY. The most comprehensive bibliography is CLYDE S. KING, *Horace Mann, 1796–1859: A Bibliography* (1966). The definitive biography is JONATHAN MESSERLI, *Horace Mann* (1972). A recent popular biography is LOUISE HALL THARP, *Until Victory: Horace Mann and Mary Peabody* (1953). JONATHAN C. MESSERLI throws new light on Mann's early years in "Horace Mann at Brown," *Harvard Educational Review*, 33:285–311 (1963). ROBERT L. STRAKER deals authoritatively with the Antioch period in *The Unseen Harvest: Horace Mann and Antioch College* (1955). The standard work is MARY TYLER (PEABODY) MANN (ed.), *Life and Works of Horace Mann*, rev. ed., 5 vol. (1891). Excerpts from the annual reports to the Massachusetts Board of Education are in L.A. CREMIN (ed.), *Republic and the School: Horace Mann on the Education of Free Men* (1957).

(L.A.Cr.)

Mann, Thomas

The greatest German novelist of the 20th century, Thomas Mann was awarded the Nobel Prize for Literature in 1929, and by the end of his life his works had acquired the status of classics both within and without Germany. His subtly structured novels and shorter stories constitute a persistent and imaginative enquiry into the nature of Western bourgeois culture, in which a haunting awareness of its precariousness and threatened disintegration is balanced by an appreciation of and tender concern for its spiritual achievements. Round this central theme cluster a group of related problems that recur in different forms —the relation of thought to reality and of the artist to society, the complexity of reality and of time, the seductions of spirituality, eros, and death. Mann's imaginative and practical involvement in the social and political catastrophes of his time provided him with fresh insights that make his work rich and varied. His finely wrought essays, notably those on Tolstoy, Goethe, Freud, and Nietzsche, record the intellectual struggles through which he reached the ethical commitment that shapes the major imaginative works.

Early literary endeavours. Mann was born in Lübeck on June 6, 1875. His father, a prosperous grain merchant, died in 1891, and Mann moved to Munich, then a centre of art and literature, where he lived until 1933. After perfunctory work in an insurance office and on the editorial staff of *Simplicissimus*, a satirical weekly, he devoted himself to writing, as his elder brother Heinrich had already done. His early short tales, first collected as *Der kleine Herr Friedemann* (1898), reflect the aestheticism of the 1890s but are given depth by the influence of the philosophers Schopenhauer and Nietzsche and the composer Richard Wagner,

Thomas Mann.
Elliot Erwitt—Magnum

The theme of the dilemma of the creative artist

to all of whom Mann was always to acknowledge a deep, if ambiguous, debt. Most of Mann's first stories centre in the problem of the creative artist, who in his devotion to form contests the meaninglessness of existence, an antithesis that Mann enlarged into that between "spirit" (*Geist*) and "life" (*Leben*). But while he showed sympathy for the artistic misfits he described, Mann was also aware that the world of imagination is a world of make-believe, and the closeness of the artist to the charlatan was already becoming a theme. At the same time, a certain nostalgia for ordinary, unproblematical life appeared in his work.

This ambivalence found full expression in his first novel, *Buddenbrooks* (1900), which Mann had at first intended to be a novella in which the experience of the transcendental realities of Wagner's music would extinguish the will to live in the son of a bourgeois family. On this beginning, the novel builds the story of the family and its business house over three generations, showing how an artistic streak not only unfits the family's later members for the practicalities of business life but undermines their vitality as well. But, almost against his will, in *Buddenbrooks* Mann wrote a tender elegy for the old bourgeois virtues. In the partially autobiographical *Tonio Kröger* (1903), he more explicitly paid tribute to the simplicities of German bourgeois life, though as a creative artist cut off from them; and in *Tristan* (1903) the artist who repudiates the ordinary world is almost cruelly satirized as a heartless fake.

In 1905 Mann married Katja Pringsheim, daughter of a Munich professor. There were six children of the marriage, which was a remarkably happy one. It was this happiness, perhaps, that led Mann, in *Royal Highness*, to provide a fairy-tale reconciliation of "form" and "life," of degenerate feudal authority and the vigour of modern American capitalism. In 1912, however, he returned to the tragic dilemma of the artist with *Death in Venice*, a sombre masterpiece. In this story, the main character, a distinguished writer whose nervous and "decadent" sensibility is controlled by the discipline of style and composition, seeks relaxation from overstrain in Venice, where, as disease creeps over the city, he succumbs to a homosexual passion and the wish for death. Symbols of eros and death weave a subtle pattern in the sensuous opulence of this tale, which closes an epoch in Mann's work.

World War I years. The outbreak of World War I evoked Mann's ardent patriotism and awoke, too, an awareness of the artist's social commitment that was to remain central in his later work. His brother Heinrich was one of the few German writers to question German war aims, and his criticism of German authoritarianism stung Thomas to a bitter attack on cosmopolitan littérateurs. In 1918 he published a large political treatise, *Reflections of an Unpolitical Man*, in which all his ingenuity of mind was summoned to justify the authoritarian state as against democracy, creative irrationalism as against "flat" rationalism, inward culture as against moralistic civilization. This work belongs to

Mann's German patriotism

the tradition of "revolutionary conservatism" that leads from the 19th-century German nationalistic and anti-democratic thinkers Paul Anton de Lagarde and H.S. Chamberlain, the apostle of the superiority of the "Germanic" race, toward National Socialism; and Mann later was to repudiate these ideas.

With the establishment of the German (Weimar) Republic in 1919, Mann slowly revised his outlook; the essays "Goethe and Tolstoi" and "Von deutscher Republik" ("The German Republic") show his somewhat hesitant espousal of democratic principles. His new position was clarified in the long novel *The Magic Mountain*. Its theme grows out of an earlier motif: a young engineer, Hans Castorp, visiting a cousin in a sanatorium in Davos, abandons practical life to submit to the rich seductions of disease, inwardness, and death. But the sanatorium comes to be the spiritual reflection of the possibilities and dangers of the actual world. A great variety of figures, brilliantly characterized, are woven into a subtle pattern, and the issues are focussed in the long arguments between an old-fashioned democratic humanist and a totalitarian irrationalist. In the end, somewhat skeptically but humanely, Castorp decides for life and service to his people: a decision Mann calls "a leave-taking from many a perilous sympathy, enchantment, and temptation, to which the European soul had been inclined." In this great work Mann formulates with remarkable insight the fateful choices facing Europe.

Political crisis and World War II. From this time onward Mann's imaginative effort was directed primarily to the novel, scarcely interrupted by the charming personal novella *Early Sorrow*, or by *Mario and the Magician*, a novella that, in the person of a seedy illusionist, symbolizes the character of Fascism. His literary and cultural essays began to play an ever-growing part in elucidating and communicating his awareness of the fragility of humaneness, tolerance, and reason in the face of political crisis. His essays on Freud (1929) and Wagner (1933) are concerned with this, as are those on Goethe (1932), who more and more became for Mann an exemplary figure in his wisdom and balance. The various essays on Nietzsche document with particular poignancy Mann's struggle against attitudes once dear to him. In 1930 he gave a courageous address in Berlin, "Ein Appell an die Vernunft" ("An Appeal to Reason"), appealing for the formation of a common front of the cultured bourgeoisie and the Socialist working class against the inhuman fanaticism of the National Socialists. In essays and on lecture tours in Germany, to Paris, Vienna, Warsaw, Amsterdam, and elsewhere during the 1930s, Mann, while steadfastly attacking Nazi policy, often expressed sympathy with Socialist and Communist principles in the very general sense that they were the guarantee of humanism and freedom.

Attacks on Nazi policy

When Hitler became chancellor early in 1933, Mann and his wife, on holiday in Switzerland, were warned by their son and daughter in Munich not to return. For some years his home was in Switzerland, near Zürich, but he travelled widely, visiting the U.S. on lecture tours and finally, in 1938, settling there, first at Princeton, and from 1941 to 1952 in southern California. In 1936 he was deprived of his German citizenship; in the same year the University of Bonn took away the honorary doctorate it had bestowed in 1919 (it was restored in 1949). In 1944 he became a United States citizen. During World War II he broadcast many times to Germany, speaking forcefully of the crimes of Hitlerism and appealing to the "other Germany" to assert its dignity.

Mann visited both East and West Germany several times after the war and received many public honours, but he refused to return to Germany to live. In 1952 he settled again near Zürich, where he died on August 12, 1955. His last major essays—on Goethe (1949), Chekhov (1954), and Schiller (1955)—are impressive evocations of the moral and social responsibilities of writers.

Later novels. The novels on which Mann was working throughout this period reflect variously the cultural crisis of his times. In 1933 he published *The Tales of Jacob* (U.S. title, *Joseph and His Brothers*), the first part of his

The
Joseph
series

four-part novel on the biblical Joseph, continued the following year in *The Young Joseph* and two years later with *Joseph in Egypt*, and completed with *Joseph the Provider* in 1943. In the complete work, published as *Joseph and His Brothers*, Mann reinterpreted the biblical story as the emergence of mobile, responsible individuality out of the tribal collective; of history out of myth; of a human God out of the awesome unknowable. In the first volume a timeless myth seems to be re-enacted in the lives of the Hebrews. Joseph, however, though sustained by the belief that his life too is the re-enactment of a myth, is thrown out of the "timeless collective" into Egypt, the world of change and history, and there learns the management of events, ideas, and himself. Though based on wide and scholarly study of history, the work is not a historical novel, and the "history" is full of irony and humour, of conscious modernization. Mann's fundamental concern is to provide a myth for his own times, capable of sustaining and directing his generation and of restoring a belief in the power of humane reason. The novel is inexhaustibly rich in its material, in the interwoven pattern of its motifs.

Mann took time off from this work to write, in the same spirit, his *Lotte in Weimar* (U.S. title, *The Beloved Returns*). Lotte (Charlotte) Kestner, the heroine of Goethe's *The Sorrows of Young Werther*, his semi-autobiographical story of unrequited love and Romantic despair, visits Weimar in old age to see once again her old lover, now famous, and win some acknowledgment from him. But Goethe remains distant and refuses to re-enter the past; she learns from him that true reverence for man means also acceptance of and reverence for change, intelligent activity directed to the "demand of the day." In this, as in the Joseph novels, in settings so distant from his own time, Mann was seeking to define the essential principles of humane civilization; their spacious and often humorous serenity of tone implicitly challenges the inhuman irrationalism of the Nazi ideology and regime.

In *Doctor Faustus* (1947), begun in 1943 at the darkest period of the war, Mann wrote the most directly political of his novels. It is the life story of a German composer, Adrian Leverkühn, born in 1885, who dies in 1940 after ten years of mental alienation. A solitary, estranged figure, he "speaks" the experience of his times in his music, and the story of Leverkühn's compositions is that of German culture in the two decades before 1930—more specifically of the collapse of traditional humanism and the victory of the mixture of sophisticated nihilism and barbaric primitivism that undermined it. With remarkable imaginative insight Mann interpreted the new musical forms and themes of Leverkühn's compositions up to the final work, a setting of the lament of Doctor Faustus in the 16th-century version of the Faust legend, who once, in hope, had made a pact with the Devil, but in the end is reduced to anguish and hopelessness. The one gleam of hope in this sombre work, however, in which the personal tragedy of Leverkühn is subtly related to Germany's destruction in the war through the comments of the fictitious narrator, Zeitblom, lies in its very grief. No other literary work expresses the tragedy of Germany as this does. Yet it illustrates a weakness in Mann's work. For while the interpretation of intellectual and artistic trends is rich and masterly, most of the characters are oversymbolical and tend toward a certain rigidity, even to caricature. Even in Leverkühn there is a strange automatism: he lacks the warmth and fluidity of life.

The composition of the novel was fully documented by Mann in 1949 in *The Genesis of a Novel*. *Doctor Faustus* exhausted him as no other work of his had done, and *The Holy Sinner* and *The Black Swan*, published in 1951 and 1953, respectively, show a relaxation of intensity in spite of their accomplished, even virtuoso style. Mann rounded off his imaginative work in 1954 with *The Confessions of Felix Krull, Confidence Man*, the gay, often uproariously funny story of a confidence man who wins the favour and love of others by enacting the roles they desire of him.

Mann's
style

Mann's style is finely wrought and full of resources, enriched by humour, irony, and parody; his composition is subtle and many-layered, brilliantly realistic on one level and yet reaching to deeper levels of symbolism. His works lack simplicity, and his tendency to set his characters at a distance by his own ironical view of them has sometimes laid him open to the charge of lack of heart. He was, however, aware that simplicity and sentiment lend themselves to manipulation by ideological and political powers, and the sometimes elaborate sophistication of his works cannot hide from the discerning reader his underlying impassioned and tender solicitude for mankind.

MAJOR WORKS

NOVELS: *Buddenbrooks* (published 1900, dated 1901; Eng. trans. 1924); *Königliche Hoheit* (1909; *Royal Highness*, first Eng. trans. 1916); *Der Zauberberg* (1924; *The Magic Mountain*, first Eng. trans. 1927); *Die Geschichten Jaakobs* (1933; *The Tales of Jacob*, 1934; U.S. title, *Joseph and His Brothers*), first part of four-part novel entitled *Joseph und seine Brüder* (*Joseph and His Brothers*, 1 vol. 1948), and continued in *Der junge Joseph* (1934; *The Young Joseph*, 1935), *Joseph in Ägypten* (1936; *Joseph in Egypt*, 1938), and *Joseph der Ernährer* (1943; *Joseph the Provider*, 1944); *Lotte in Weimar* (1939; Eng. trans. 1940; U.S. title, *The Beloved Returns*); *Doktor Faustus* (1947; Eng. trans. 1948); *Die Bekenntnisse des Hochstaplers Felix Krull* (1954; *The Confessions of Felix Krull, Confidence Man*, 1955).

SHORT STORIES AND NOVELLAS: *Der kleine Herr Friedemann* (1898, collected early short stories; Eng. trans. in *Stories of Three Decades*, 1936; and *Stories of a Lifetime*, 1961, which contain translations of all Mann's more important short stories). NOVELLAS: *Tonio Kröger* (1903; first Eng. trans. in *Three Tales*, 1929); *Tristan* (1903; first Eng. trans. in *Three Tales*); *Der Tod in Venedig* (1912; *Death in Venice*, first Eng. trans. in *Three Tales*); *Unordnung und frühes Leid* (1926; trans. as *Early Sorrow*, 1929 and later); *Mario und der Zauberer* (1930; *Mario and the Magician*, 1930 and later); *Der Erwählte* (1951; *The Holy Sinner*, 1951); *Die Betrogene* (1953; *The Black Swan*, 1954).

PHILOSOPHICAL, POLITICAL, LITERARY PROSE WRITINGS, AND SPEECHES: *Betrachtungen eines Unpolitischen* (1918; *Reflections of an Unpolitical Man*, extracts trans. in *The Thomas Mann Reader*, 1950), political and philosophical treatise; *Goethe und Tolstoi* (1921; "Goethe and Tolstoi," first trans. in *Three Essays*, 1929), long philosophical, political, and literary essay; *Die Forderung des Tages* (1930), collected essays, mainly political; *Leiden und Grösse der Meister* (1935), collected essays, mainly philosophical and literary (including those on Freud, 1929, and Wagner, 1933), (both collections trans. in *Past Masters and Other Papers*, 1933, and *Essays of Three Decades*, 1947); *Neue Studien* (1948, collected essays; trans., with others, in *Last Essays*, 1959); *Deutsche Ansprache* (1930) and *Achtung, Europa!* (1938), collected speeches, lectures, and essays, mainly political; *Das Problem der Freiheit* (1939), long political and philosophical essay (all these, with others, trans. in *Order of the Day: Political Essays and Speeches of Two Decades*, 1942); *Deutsche Hörer* (1945), selections from broadcast talks (some trans. in *Listen, Germany! Twenty-Five Radio Messages to the German People Over BBC, 1940–42*, 1943); *Ansprache im Goethejahr* (1949), essays and lectures on Goethe (trans., with other important essays on Goethe, Chekhov, and Schiller in *Last Essays*, 1959); *Die Entstehung des Doktor Faustus* (1949; *The Genesis of a Novel*, 1961), fully documented account of the composition of *Doktor Faustus*.

BIBLIOGRAPHY

Editions and correspondence: The most complete edition is Mann's *Gesammelte Werke in zwölf Bänden*, ed. by HANS BÜRGIN (1960); vol. 1–7 contain the novels, vol. 8 the *Novellen*, vol. 9–12 the essays, addresses, and speeches. There are several other collected editions and many editions of separate works. A full bibliography is included in HANS BÜRGIN et al., *Das Werk Thomas Manns* (1959). Films have been made of *Buddenbrooks* (1959) and *Death in Venice* (1970). Recordings of Thomas Mann reading from his works have been made: from *Felix Krull* (1954) and 2 records (1959); *Das Eisenbahnunglück* and *Schwere Stunde* (1955); and the essay on Schiller (1955). There are many volumes of Mann's correspondence, the most complete being the three volumes selected and edited by his daughter ERIKA MANN, *Briefe: 1889–1936* (1961), *1937–1947* (1963), and *1948–1955* (1965). A good selection, translated, is given by RICHARD and CLARA WINSTON, *Letters of Thomas Mann, 1889–1955*, 2 vol. (1970). Other collections are *Briefe an Paul Amann, 1915–1952*, ed. by HERBERT WEGENER (1959; Eng. trans., 1960); *Thomas Mann an Ernst Bertram: Briefe aus den Jahren 1910–1955*, ed. by INGE JENS (1960); *Thomas Mann-Karl Kerényi: Gespräch in Briefen*, ed. KARL KERÉNYI

(1960); *Briefwechsel: Thomas Mann–Robert Faesi*, ed. by ROBERT FAESI (1962); *Briefwechsel: Hermann Hesse-Thomas Mann*, ed. by ANNI CARLSSON (1968); *Thomas Mann und Hans Friedrich Blunck: Briefwechsel und Aufzeichnungen*, ed. by WALTER BLUNCK (1969); *Thomas Mann-Heinrich Mann: Briefwechsel 1900–1949*, ed. by HANS WYSLING (1968).

Biography and criticism: There is no definitive biography of Thomas Mann. HANS BUERGIN and HANS-OTTO MAYER give a detailed chronicle of his life in *Thomas Mann: Eine Chronik seines Lebens* (1965; Eng. trans., *Thomas Mann: A Chronicle of His Life*, 1969). The childhood home is described by his younger brother VIKTOR MANN in *Wir waren fünf* (1949). *Thomas Mann: Autobiographisches*, ed. by ERIKA MANN (1968), contains Mann's autobiographical essays and his daughter's account (1956) of the last year of his life (trans. by RICHARD GRAVES as *The Last Year of Thomas Mann*, 1958). KLAUS W. JONAS gives a full account of critical studies on Mann in *Fifty Years of Thomas Mann Studies: A Bibliography of Criticism* (1955). HERMANN J. WEIGAND, *Thomas Mann's Novel "Der Zauberberg"* (1933), is an excellent study of a single work; while KAETE HAMBURGER skillfully uses humour as a key to the interpretation of the Joseph novels in *Der Humor bei Thomas Mann: Zum Joseph-Roman* (1965). RICHARD H. THOMAS, *Thomas Mann: The Mediation of Art* (1956), is concerned with the relation of art and reality, the artist and the moralist in Mann. ERICH HELLER, *The Ironic German* (1958), finds the clue to the many ambiguities in Mann in his irony; while KURT SONTHEIMER, *Thomas Mann und die Deutschen* (1961), is a more straightforward examination of the complex relationship of Mann to his fellow Germans. JONAS LESSER, *Thomas Mann in der Epoche seiner Vollendung* (1952), is a devoted study of the later Mann; while GEORG LUKACS' Marxist essays *Thomas Mann* (1949; rev. ed., 1957; trans. by STANLEY MITCHELL as *Essays on Thomas Mann*, 1964), are shrewdly critical as well as admiring. Various essays in CHARLES NEIDER (ed.), *The Stature of Thomas Mann* (1947); and in ERICH KAHLER, *The Orbit of Thomas Mann* (1969), may be recommended; while his position in the history of the German novel is indicated in ROY PASCAL, *The German Novel* (1956).

(Ro.Pa.)

Mansa Mūsā of Mali

Mansa Mūsā, ruler of the West African empire of Mali in the early 14th century, left a realm notable for its extent and riches, as well as its political organization. But he is best remembered for his pilgrimage to Mecca, which took place surrounded by unprecedented splendour. For almost two centuries his portrait adorned maps of Africa, and for a time he came to symbolize the continent to the European mind.

Mansa Mūsā's date of birth is not known. Either the grandson or the grandnephew of Sundiata, the founder of his dynasty, he came to the throne in 1307. In the 17th year of his reign (1324), he set out on his famous pilgrimage to Mecca. It was this pilgrimage that awakened the world to the stupendous wealth of Mali. Cairo and Mecca received this royal personage, whose glittering procession, in the superlatives employed by Arab chroniclers, almost put Africa's sun to shame. Travelling from his capital of Niani on the Upper Niger River to Walata (Oualâta, Mauritania) and on to Tuat (now in Algeria) before making his way to Cairo, Mansa Mūsā was accompanied by an impressive caravan consisting of 60,000 men including a personal retinue of 12,000 slaves, all clad in brocade and Persian silk. The Emperor himself rode on horseback and was directly preceded by 500 slaves, each carrying a gold-adorned staff weighing about six pounds. In addition, Mansa Mūsā had a baggage train of 80 camels, each carrying 300 pounds of gold.

Mansa Mūsā's prodigious generosity and piety, as well as the fine clothes and exemplary behaviour of his followers, did not fail to create a most favourable impression. The Cairo that Mansa Mūsā visited was ruled over by one of the greatest of the Mamlūk sultans, al-Malik an-Nāṣir. The black emperor's great civility not withstanding, the meeting between the two rulers might have ended in a serious diplomatic incident, for so absorbed was Mansa Mūsā in his religious observances that he was only with difficulty persuaded to pay a formal visit to the Sultan. The historian al-ʿUmarī, who visited Cairo 12 years after the Emperor's visit, found the inhabitants

Visit to Egypt

of this city, with a population estimated at 1,000,000, still singing the praises of Mansa Mūsā. So lavish was the Emperor in his spending that he flooded the Cairo market with gold, thereby causing such a decline in its value that, some 12 years later, the market had still not fully recovered.

Rulers of West African states had made pilgrimages to Mecca before Mansa Mūsā, but the effect of his flamboyant journey was to advertise both Mali and Mansa Mūsā well beyond the African continent and to stimulate a desire among the Muslim kingdoms of North Africa, and among many of European nations as well, to reach the source of this incredible wealth.

Mansa Mūsā, whose empire was one of the largest in the world at that time, is reported to have observed that it would take a year to travel from one end of his empire to the other. While this was probably an exaggeration, it is known that during his pilgrimage to Mecca, one of his generals, Sagmandia (Sagaman-dir), extended the empire by capturing the Songhai capital of Gao. The Songhai kingdom measured several hundreds of miles across, so that the conquest meant the acquisition of a vast territory. The 14th-century traveller Ibn Baṭṭuṭa noted that it took about four months to travel from the northern borders of the Mali empire to Niani in the south.

Conquest of Songhai kingdom

The Emperor was so overjoyed by the new acquisition that he decided to delay his return to Niani and to visit Gao instead, there to receive the personal submission of the Songhai king and take the King's two sons as hostages. At both Gao and Timbuktu, a Songhai city almost rivalling Gao in importance, Mansa Mūsā commissioned Abū Isḥāq as-Sāḥilī, a Granada poet and architect who had travelled with him from Mecca, to build mosques. The Gao mosque, built of burnt bricks, which had not, until then, been used as a material for building in West Africa, was still being admired as late as the 17th century.

Under Mansa Mūsā, Timbuktu grew to be a very important commercial city having caravan connections with Egypt and with all other important trade centres in North Africa. Side by side with the encouragement of trade and commerce, learning and the arts received royal patronage. Scholars who were mainly interested in history, Qurʾānic theology, and law were to make the mosque of Sankore in Timbuktu a teaching centre and to lay the foundations of the University of Sankore. Mansa Mūsā probably died in 1332.

The organization and smooth administration of a purely African empire, the founding of the University of Sankore, the expansion of trade in Timbuktu, the architectural innovations in Gao, Timbuktu, Niani, and, indeed, throughout the whole of Mali and in the subsequent Songhai Empire are all testimony to Mansa Mūsā's superior administrative gifts. In addition, the moral and religious principles he had taught his subjects endured after his death.

Assessment

BIBLIOGRAPHY. ABDERRAHMAN ES-SAʾDI, *Tarikhe es-Soudan*, trans. into French by OCTAVE HOUDAS, 2 vol. (1898–1900, reprinted 1964), written by a 17th-century Sudanese, gives a useful account of the origin of the Ghana Empire and subsequent Sudanese history based on data now lost; IBN BATTUTA, *Travels in Asia and Africa, 1325–1354,* trans. and selected by H.A.R. GIBB (1929); E.W. BOVILL, *Caravans of the Old Sahara* (1933) and *The Golden Trade of the Moors*, 2nd ed. rev. (1968), the latter contains a chapter on Mansa Mūsā; J.D. DE GRAFT-JOHNSON, *African Glory: The Story of Vanished Negro Civilizations* (1954), gives a vivid account of the great empires flourishing in the Western Sudan, including the Mali and Songhai empires; MAHMOUD KATI, *Tarikh el-Fettach*, trans. into French by OCTAVE HOUDAS and M. DELAFOSSE (1913), one of the two old histories of the Sudan published in Timbuktu; IBN KHALDOUN, *Histoire des Berbères et des dynasties musulmanes de l'Afrique septentrionale*, new ed., trans. into French by the baron DE SLANE, 4 vol. (1968–69), one of the main original sources of Sudanese history; AL-OMARI, *Masālik el-Absār* (1927), French translation of a work by a contemporary Arab scholar containing most of what is known about Mansa Mūsā's memorable pilgrimage to Mecca.

(J.C.de G.-J.)

Mansart, François

François Mansart is generally considered foremost among those who established classicism in Baroque architecture in mid-17th-century France. His works are characterized by subtlety, elegance, and harmony—the parts crisply delineated yet subordinated to the whole.

Mansart was born in Paris in January 1598, the grandson of a master mason and the son of a master carpenter. One of his uncles was a sculptor, another an architect. When his father died in 1610, Mansart's training was taken over by his brother-in-law, an architect and sculptor. Later, Mansart was apprenticed to and heavily influenced by Salomon de Brosse, a distinguished and successful architect during the reign of Henry IV and the regency of Marie de Médicis, mother of Louis XIII.

The 1600s, which saw the end of de Brosse's career and the beginning of Mansart's, could not have been more favourable for a young architect. Henry IV's entrance into Paris in 1594 as king of France signalled the beginning of a period of burgeoning political and social aspiration. Architecture reflected this aspiration, for the kings wanted their capital and their palaces to reflect the power of the crown; and the bourgeoisie commissioned châteaus (country houses) and *hôtels* (town houses) large enough for their coaches, stables of horses, and retinue of servants and splendid enough to receive the king and his entourage.

Most of Mansart's patrons were members of the middle class who had become rich in the service of the crown. They would have to have been very rich indeed to be Mansart's patrons. Not only did he draw up plans without regard to expense but refined and improved the plans—tearing down what had been built and rebuilding—as he went along. According to a contemporary, Mansart had cost one of his early patrons "more money than the Great Turk himself possesses."

Early works Mansart's career can be traced from 1623, when he designed the facade of the chapel of the Church of the Feuillants in the rue Saint-Honoré in Paris (no longer standing). Of his early works, the only one that survives is the château of Balleroy (begun *c.* 1626), near Bayeux, in the *département* of Calvados. Built for Jean de Choisy, chancellor to Gaston, duc d'Orléans, the brother of Louis XIII, the château consists of three blocks—a massive, free-standing main building to which two small pavilions are subordinated. One of the facades of the main building overlooks a court, the other a garden. The materials and treatment of the walls are characteristic of much of the work built during the reign of Henry IV. The walls are mainly of rough, brownish-yellow brick with little architectural ornament but emphasized by white stone quoins (corners) and white stone frames around the windows.

In 1635 Gaston commissioned Mansart to reconstruct his château at Blois, which had been built in the 15th and 16th centuries and used as a royal residence by three kings. Mansart proposed rebuilding it entirely, but only the north wing facing the gardens was reconstructed. The main building, flanked by pavilions, is subtly articulated by superimposed classical orders (Doric on the ground floor, Ionic on the first, and Corinthian on the second). The court entrance to the main building is approached on both sides by a curving colonnade. Mansart used the high-pitched, two-sloped roof that bears his name, mansard. (In fact, the roof had been used by earlier French architects.) The details are precise and restrained, the proportions of the masses harmonious.

In the same period, Phélypeaux de La Vrillière, an officer of the crown, commissioned Mansart to build a town house in Paris (rebuilt after Mansart's death). The building, known from engraving, was a fine example of Mansart's ability to arrive at subtle, ingenious, and dignified solutions to the problems of building on awkwardly shaped sites.

In 1642 René de Longeuil, an immensely wealthy financier and officer of the royal treasury, commissioned Mansart to build a château on his estate. The château of Maisons (now called Maisons-Laffitte, in the chief town of the *département* of Yvelines) is unique in that it is the only building by Mansart in which the interior decoration (graced particularly by a magnificent stairway) survives. The symmetrical design of the building (as well as the mansard roof) is similar to that of Mansart's earlier châteaus, but here there is a greater emphasis on relief. The central building is a free-standing

Château of Maisons

Wayne Andrews

The château Maisons-Laffitte (seen from the courtyard), *département* of Yvelines, France, designed by François Mansart, 1642.

block with a prominent rectangular frontispiece that projects from the main wall in a series of shallow steps. Two short wings, flanking the main building, standout from it in clean, unbroken rectangular sections. Extending from each of the wings is a low, one-story block. The restrained play of subtly differentiated rectangular motifs makes the building a graceful and harmonious structure.

Because it is now surrounded by roads and houses, one can only imagine how noble the château looked, in the setting of terraced gardens designed for it by Mansart, when it opened with a reception for Anne of Austria and her son, the boy king Louis XIV. At times during the construction of the château, de Longeuil must have been sorely tried by Mansart's stubborn, independent, generally difficult personality, but on this day he was surely pleased with the architect he had chosen.

Perhaps Mansart's personality was responsible for the setbacks he began to encounter, the first of which was a royal commission he received in 1645 and lost in 1646. Anne of Austria asked Mansart to draw up plans for the convent and church of the Val-de-Grâce in Paris, which the sovereign had vowed to build if she bore a son. When the costs of laying the foundation exceeded the funds provided, Mansart was replaced by Jacques Lemercier, who more or less followed the original plans.

Along with a large fortune, Mansart had accumulated many enemies who accused him of capriciousness in the building and rebuilding of his projects, of wild extravagance, and of dishonesty. In 1651 a pamphlet entitled "La Mansarade" (possibly written by political enemies of the prime minister, Cardinal Mazarin, for whom Mansart had worked) accused him of having made deals with contractors and charged him with profligacy. The attack did not prevent him from continuing to work for prominent people.

With the accession of Louis XIV to the throne in 1661, private patrons became fewer and fewer. Architects, painters, sculptors, and craftsmen were called upon to build, decorate, and furnish structures commissioned by the King. When, in 1664, Louis decided to complete the palace of the Louvre, his chief minister and *surintendant des bâtiments* (roughly, "superintendent of buildings"), Jean-Baptiste Colbert, asked Mansart to draw up plans for the east wing (the colonnaded wing). Possibly because he could not produce and keep to any final plan, Mansart lost the commission.

In 1665 Colbert again asked Mansart to produce designs—this time for a chapel for the tombs of the royal family of the Bourbons to be built at the end of the Saint-Denis basilica. Mansart planned his design (which was never executed) around a central, domed space, which later inspired his grandnephew Jules Hardouin-Mansart in his design for the dome of the church of Les Invalides.

When Mansart died in September 1666, the world was quite different from the one in which his career had begun. France had become the centre of Europe and Louis the centre of France—not only politically but also in matters of culture and taste. French architects, artists, and craftsmen were trained and employed by the crown for one end: the glorification of the state in the person of the King, who had declared himself to be the state. But the world was different, too, in that it had been enriched by the work of the independent and individualistic genius of François Mansart.

MAJOR WORKS
Château de Coulommiers (1618); Château de Berny (1623); facade of the Church of the Feuillants, Paris (1623–29); Hôtel Bouthillier, Paris (1630); Convents of the Visitation, rue Saint-Antoine, Paris (1632); Hôtel de la Vrillière, Paris (1635); Additions to château of Blois (1635); Chapel of the Dames de Sainte-Marie, Chaillot, Paris (1640); château of Maisons (Maisons-Laffitte) (1642); Val-de-Grâce, Paris (1645–46); Hôtel de Nevers, Paris (1649–50); remodelling of Hôtel Carnavalet, Paris (1655–61).

BIBLIOGRAPHY. A.F. BLUNT, *François Mansart and the Origins of French Classical Architecture* (1941), is the only monograph on Mansart published in this period (a serious work with some personal opinions). The same author's *Art and Architecture in France, 1500–1700* (1953), contains an excellent discussion of Mansart. See also the article "Mansart, François and Jules Hardouin," in the *Encyclopedia of World Art*, vol. 9, col. 478–485 (1964), a detailed biography and a bibliography of the essential works published to 1961. LOUIS HAUTECOEUR, *Histoire de l'architecture classique en France,* vol. 2 (1948; 2nd ed., vol. 1, sect. 3, 1966), is a general history that places the architect in the framework of his time.

Mansfield, William Murray, 1st Earl of

William Murray, 1st earl of Mansfield, chief justice of the king's bench from 1756 to 1788, was the first jurist to shape English law to meet the demands of the country's new industrialism, burgeoning international commerce, and colonial relations; the law offered few precedents for such "modern" problems before Mansfield's time. Only Sir Edward Coke (1552–1634) and Sir Matthew Hale (1609–76) rivalled Murray as chief justice. Parts of his work were published and became authoritative almost before he was off the bench. Mansfield's outstanding juristic ability succeeded not only in solving controversial suits but also in forming the law for future claims. His greatest contribution was in the field of commercial law.

Early life and career. William Murray was born at Scone, in Perthshire, Scotland, on March 2, 1705, the son of the 5th Viscount Stormont. Educated at Perth grammar school, Westminster School, and Christ Church, Oxford, Mansfield was called to the bar at Lincoln's Inn in 1730. In Scotland he became famous representing the city of Edinburgh when it was threatened with disfranchisement for the hanging of the English captain of the city guard by a mob. Yet his English practice remained scanty until 1737 when his eloquent speech to the House of Commons in support of a merchants' petition to stop Spanish assaults on their ships placed him in the front rank of his profession. In 1742 he was appointed solicitor general. In 1754 he became attorney general and acted as leader of the House of Commons under the Duke of Newcastle. In 1756 he was appointed chief justice of the King's Bench and was made Baron Mansfield, becoming earl of Mansfield in 1776.

Judicial decisions. As must be the case with any court in central position, politics followed Mansfield to the bench. Three cases reveal his characteristic aloofness from personal or popular prejudices in rendering decisions. After the burning of his house and library in 1780, during anti-Catholic riots, which involved mobs of 50,000 and the invasion of Parliament itself, Mansfield so fairly conducted the treason trial of the leader, Lord

Mansfield, oil painting by John Singleton Copley, 1783. In the National Portrait Gallery, London.
By courtesy of the National Portrait Gallery, London

George Gordon, that an acquittal resulted. In another case involving the prosecution of the journalist John Wilkes who had published works that were declared seditious libel by the House of Commons, he rose above both popular clamour and royal pressure by careful technical work on precedents. His investigations showed that the crown's case contained legal flaws, and he felt himself forced to discharge an agitator because due process so required. A widespread legendary view that Mansfield abolished slavery in England with one judicial decision, while it took a civil war in the United States, is unfounded. As a property-minded man of commerce, Mansfield sought, with all of his high tactical powers, to avoid any slavery issue. Even his judgment in the so-called Somersett case (1772), involving James Somersett who was bought in Virginia and attempted to run away after arriving in London, decided only that an escaping slave could not be forcibly removed from England for retributive punishment in a colony. This, as Benjamin Franklin protested, by no means implied abolition of "a detestable commerce" or of slavery in the colonies—both encouraged by the British laws until statutory changes in 1807 and 1833.

Mansfield's permanent stamp upon Anglo-American law lies in commercial law. When he mounted the bench, at the start of the Seven Years' War that was to fasten Britain's grasp upon America, India, and international trade, English law was land-centred and landbound in outlook and entrenched in professional tradition. Reform was imperative. Mansfield's vision and ambition reached beyond the continental model of a special body of rules for commerce and banking. He sought to make the international law of commerce not a separate branch but an integral part of the general law of England, both common law and equity, using the leverage thus gained to pry loose from feudalism whole blocks of other rules that had little or no direct commercial bearing. An important part of this brilliant venture succeeded.

Contribution to commercial law

In the area of bills of exchange (drafts), promissory notes, and the then still novel bank check, Mansfield, following standard international practice, shaped the law in sweeping judgments, each typically canvassing the whole relevant situation and its reasons. But Mansfield also established a new area of jurisprudence. Marine insurance, then a new industry, was centred in London and was a weapon of competition and Cold War. Mansfield did not build here on models; he created the entire discipline.

He was not always successful. In 1765, he ruled that a merchant's or banker's confirmed credit, or promise to accept drafts drawn from abroad, was enforceable "without consideration"—*i.e.*, without any bargained-for return. This decision was viewed as a flat attack on the whole legal doctrine of "consideration," and that doctrine was reaffirmed in its entirety by the House of Lords. He suffered a second defeat in his effort to make documents transferring hand interpretable by "plain intention," so that such intention could not be frustrated by technical rules giving unmeant effect to words. His decision in this area was reversed in 1772 (one of only six reversals during his 32 years of active service). But he triumphed in his expansion of the idea that a man should turn back or turn over any value received by mistake or wrongdoing or under other circumstances making it inequitable for him to retain it. The remedy he devised was a fictitious assumption of a "promise" to pay over (in modern times the fiction was discontinued and replaced by the term "restitution").

Three times during his career Mansfield held positions as a member of the cabinet, entrusting the great seal of his office to a committee, so that he could retain the chief justiceship regardless of changes in administration, but still exert political power. In 1783 he declined cabinet office, preferring to serve as speaker of the House of Lords. He resigned as chief justice in 1788 and died on March 20, 1793.

Assessment Despite his long tenure, the "father of commercial law" had almost no cases dealing with the substance of modern commercial law: mercantile contracts for the sale of wares. But he had chosen to make commercial law and general law a single whole. When commercial sales cases did arise, they came, ironically, before judges who thought in terms of haystacks and of horses, and the central area of commercial law in England was for more than a century given a flavour of land and manure rather than of commerce.

BIBLIOGRAPHY. JOHN HOLLIDAY, *The Life of William, Late Earl of Mansfield* (1797); JOHN C. CAMPBELL, *Lives of the Chief Justices . . .* , vol. 3 (1857); EDWARD FOSS, *Judges of England*, vol. 8 (1864); HORACE WALPOLE, *Letters*, ed. by P. CUNNINGHAM, 9 vol. (1857–59); EDWARD FIDDES, "Lord Mansfield and the Sommersett Case," *Law Quarterly Review*, 50:499–511 (1934); CECIL FIFOOT, *Lord Mansfield* (1936); SIR WILLIAM S. HOLDSWORTH, *A History of English Law*, 7th ed. rev. vol. 6–8 (1966).

(K.N.L.)

Mansur, al-

Abū Ja'far al-Manṣūr, the second caliph of the 'Abbāsid dynasty, which was descended from 'Abbās (an uncle of Muḥammad), is generally regarded as the real founder of the 'Abbāsid caliphate. His regnal title, al-Manṣūr, meant Made Victorious (by God).

Al-Manṣūr was born between 709 and 714 at al-Ḥumaymah, in modern Jordan, the home of the 'Abbāsid family after their emigration from the Hejaz in 687–688. His father, Muḥammad, was a great-grandson of 'Abbās; his mother was a Berber slave.

Shortly before the overthrow of the Umayyads, the first dynasty of caliphs, by an army of rebels from Khorāsān, many of whom were influenced by propaganda spread by the 'Abbāsids, the last Umayyad caliph, Marwān II, arrested the head of the 'Abbāsid family, al-Manṣūr's brother Ibrāhīm. Al-Manṣūr fled with the rest Early of the family to Kūfah in Iraq, where some of the leaders years of the Khorāsānian rebels gave their allegiance to another brother of al-Manṣūr, Abū al-'Abbās as-Saffāḥ, Ibrāhīm having died in captivity. As-Saffāḥ was the first 'Abbāsid caliph.

Because his brother died in 754, after only five years as caliph, it was upon al-Manṣūr that the main burden of establishing the 'Abbāsid caliphate fell. Al-Manṣūr had played an important part in wiping out the last remnants of Umayyad resistance. During his brother's caliphate he led an army to Mesopotamia, where he received the submission of a governor after informing him of the death of the last Umayyad caliph. In Iraq itself, the last Umayyad governor had taken refuge with his army in a garrison town. Promised a safe-conduct by al-Manṣūr

and the Caliph, the Governor surrendered the town, only to be executed with a number of his followers.

A danger to al-Manṣūr's caliphate came from a number of revolts by ambitious army commanders. The most serious of these was the revolt in 754 of al-Manṣūr's uncle, 'Abd Allāh, who thought he had better claims to the caliphate than his nephew. The danger was only averted with the help of Abū Muslim, one of the chief organizers of the revolt against the Umayyads.

Al-Manṣūr was largely responsible for cutting the 'Abbāsids free from the movement that had brought them to power. While his brother was still caliph, al-Manṣūr was involved in the murder of several leading personalities in that movement. Upon becoming caliph himself, one of his first acts was to bring about the death of the man who had helped him become caliph, Abū Muslim. These acts served both to remove potential rivals and to dissociate the 'Abbāsids from their "extremist" supporters.

Perhaps in reaction to this policy, a number of revolts broke out, in which some of the pre-Islāmic religions of Iran were involved. In 755 in Khorāsān, a certain Sunbadh, described as a magi (here probably meaning a follower of the Mazdakite heresy, not an orthodox Zoroastrian), revolted, demanding vengeance for the murdered Abū Muslim. Another group connected with the name of Abū Muslim, the Rāwandīyah, was charged with belief in the transmigration of souls and holding al-Manṣūr to be their god. Because of these excesses, al-Manṣūr had to suppress them, probably in 757–758. Finally, in 767 al-Manṣūr had to put down another revolt in Khorāsān, the leader of which was accused of claiming to be a prophet.

Probably the most frustrated of those who had worked against the Umayyads were those who had believed they were fighting for a leader from among the descendants of the Prophet Muḥammad's closest male relative, 'Alī. When it became clear that the 'Abbāsids had no intention of handing over power to an 'Alid, these groups again moved into opposition. Al-Manṣūr's consequent harsh treatment of the 'Alids led to a rebellion in 762–763, which was quickly put down.

Al-Manṣūr's achievement, however, was not based Construc-simply upon military power. His most lasting monument tion of is the great city of Baghdad, upon which work began, Baghdad at his command, in 762. The decision to build Baghdad was probably in part due to the restlessness of the chief towns in Iraq, Basra and, especially, Kūfah, but, in part, too, it was a statement by al-Manṣūr that the 'Abbāsids had come to stay. It was significant that he considered taking some material for the construction of Baghdad from the ruins of Ctesiphon, the capital of the last native Iranian dynasty.

Another reason for the construction of the new capital was the need to house the rapidly growing bureaucracy, developed by al-Manṣūr under the influence of Iranian ideas in an attempt to provide a more stable basis for 'Abbāsid rule.

By these political and military measures al-Manṣūr firmly established the 'Abbāsid caliphate. Furthermore, he arranged the succession in favour of his son, al-Mahdī, and every future 'Abbāsid caliph could trace his descent directly to al-Manṣūr.

Al-Manṣūr is described as a tall, lean man, with a brown complexion and a sparse beard. There are a number of anecdotes designed to illustrate the simplicity of his life, his tightfistedness, his love of poetry, and his objection to music. He died in October 775 on his way to Mecca to perform the pilgrimage and was buried near the holy city.

BIBLIOGRAPHY. The only study of al-Manṣūr's caliphate as a whole is in THEODOR NOLDEKE, *Sketches from Eastern History* (1892, reprinted 1963). For a general survey of the 'Abbāsid rise to power and the early years of their rule, see the article "'Abbāsids" by B. LEWIS in the *Encyclopaedia of Islam*, new ed, vol. 1, pt. 1 (1960). The *Encyclopaedia of Islam* should also be consulted for more information on specific details of al-Manṣūr's life and caliphate (see especially the articles "Baghdād" and "al-Barāmika").

(G.R.H.)

Mantegna, Andrea

Andrea Mantegna, a 15th-century painter, engraver, and possibly also a sculptor, was the first fully Renaissance artist of northern Italy. His art and his attitude toward Classical antiquity, moreover, provided a model for other artists, among them Giovanni Bellini in Venice and Albrecht Dürer in Germany. By placing the Virgin and saints of the S. Zeno altarpiece (1459) in a unified space continuous with its frame, Mantegna introduced new principles of illusionism into Sacra Conversazione paintings (i.e., paintings of the Madonna and Child with saints).

Perhaps of even greater significance were his achievements in the field of fresco painting. Mantegna's invention of total spatial illusionism by the manipulation of perspective and foreshortening began a tradition of ceiling decoration that was followed for three centuries. Mantegna's portraits of the Gonzaga family in their palace at Mantua (1474) glorified living subjects by conferring upon them the over life-size stature, sculptural volume, and studied gravity of movement and gesture normally reserved for saints and heroes of myth and history.

Anderson—Alinar

"St. James Led to Martyrdom" (destroyed during World War II), fresco by Andrea Mantegna, 1453–55. Formerly in the Eremitani Church, Padua, Italy.

Formative years in Padua. Mantegna's extraordinary native abilities were recognized early. Most likely born in 1431, the second son of a woodworker near the town of Vicenza, Mantegna was legally adopted by Francesco Squarcione by the time he was ten years old and possibly even earlier.

A teacher of painting and a collector of antiquities in Padua, Squarcione drew the cream of young local talent to his studio, which some of his protégés, such as Mantegna and the painter Marco Zoppo, later had cause to regret. In 1448, at the age of 17, Mantegna disassociated himself from Squarcione's guardianship to establish his own workshop in Padua, later claiming that Squarcione had profited considerably from his services without giving due recompense. The award to Mantegna of the important commission for an altarpiece for the church of Sta. Sofia (1448), now lost, demonstrates his

precocity, since it was unusual for so young an artist to receive such a commission. Mantegna himself proudly called attention to his youthful ability in the painting's inscription: "Andrea Mantegna from Padua, aged 17, painted this with his own hand, 1448." Altarpiece for Sta. Sofia

During the following year (1449), Mantegna worked on the fresco decoration of the Ovetari Chapel in the Eremitani Church in Padua. The figures of SS. Peter, Paul, and Christopher in the apse, his earliest frescoes in this chapel, show to what extent he had already absorbed the monumental figure style of Tuscany. In the "St. James Led to Martyrdom" in the lowest row on the left wall, painted sometime between 1453 and 1455, both Mantegna's mastery of *di sotto in su* (from below to above) perspective and his use of archaeologically correct details of Roman architecture are already apparent. The perspective scheme with a viewpoint below the lower frame of the composition exaggerates the apparent height of the scene with respect to the viewer and lends an aspect of grandiose monumentality to the triumphal arch.

In the two scenes from the life of St. Christopher united in a single perspective on the right-hand wall, Mantegna extended his experiments in illusionism to the framing element by painting a highly realistic column on the front plane. The meticulously detailed column divides the scene in two while appearing to exist in a realm totally apart from the pictorial space, a realm shared with the observer. This extension of illusionistic principles to the elements surrounding a picture anticipates Mantegna's S. Zeno altarpiece, where the carved half columns of the frame abut the painted piers (vertical members) on the front plane of the picture space, so that the frame architecture serves as the "exterior" of the temple-pavilion architecture depicted in the painting. In this way the sphere of intense ideality inhabited by the Virgin is conjoined to the beholder's own space by a brilliant combination of physical and optical devices. Unfortunately, all Mantegna's frescoes in the Ovetari Chapel except "The Assumption" and "The Martyrdom of St. Christopher" episodes were destroyed by a bomb during World War II.

The environment of the city of Padua, where Mantegna lived during the major formative years of his life (from about age 10 to about age 30), exerted a strong influence on his interests, ideas, painting style, and concept of himself. Padua was the first centre of Humanism in northern Italy, the home of a great university (founded in 1222), and renowned as a centre for the study of medicine, philosophy, and mathematics. With the influx of scholars from all over Europe and Italy, an atmosphere of internationalism prevailed. From the time of the 14th-century poet Petrarch, Padua had experienced a rapidly growing revival of interest in antiquity, and many eminent Humanists and Latin scholars had resided there. Increasing interest in and imitation of the culture of ancient Rome produced a climate in which feverish collecting of antiquities and ancient inscriptions—even if only in fragmentary form—flourished. Mantegna's friendly relations with several Humanists, antiquarians, and university professors are a matter of record, and hence he may be seen as one of the earliest Renaissance artists to fraternize from a position of intellectual equality with such men. In this way Mantegna's life-style contributed to the early 16th-century ideal of the artist as a man so intimately familiar with antique history, mythology, and literature as to be able to draw easily from these highly respected sources. Cultural influence of Padua on Mantegna

The experience of the Paduan milieu was thus decisive for the formation of Mantegna's attitude toward the classical world, which may perhaps be characterized best as double faceted. On the one hand, Mantegna's search for accurate knowledge of Roman antiquity was reflected both in his depiction of specific monuments of Roman architecture and sculpture and in his creation of a vocabulary of antique forms that became the language of antique revival for more than a generation of northern Italian painters and sculptors after the mid-1450s. On the other hand, through a process of artistic synthesis, Mantegna sensed the forces and significances below the surfaces of Roman grandeur. The architectural backgrounds Mantegna's attitude toward the classical world of pictures in the Ovetari Chapel such as the "St. James Before Herod" and the "St. James Led to Martyrdom," as well as of the two paintings of St. Sebastian in Vienna and Paris, were infused with a brooding harshness and severity against which the suffering of the Christian saints takes on the added tragic implication of an impending cultural clash that was to separate and alienate the Christian and pagan worlds. In Mantegna's century, overcoming the experience of alienation from antiquity through the study and revitalization of its architectural and sculptural vocabulary was an obsessive theme. That the Roman world still existed in Italy in ruins only served to increase the sudden sense of cultural loss that struck the 15th century. By his thoroughgoing description of antique forms coupled with an instinctive sense of the political realities that underlay their original creation, Mantegna lent great impetus to the antique revival movement at midcentury.

Mantegna's starting point had been a still earlier form of antique revival—the monumental Tuscan figure style brought to Venice by the Florentine painter Andrea del Castagno in 1442. Mantegna presumably saw Castagno's frescoes of evangelists and saints in the church of S. Zaccaria during a visit to Venice in 1447. His Venetian connections were strengthened by his marriage in 1453 to Nicolosia, daughter of Jacopo Bellini and sister of Giovanni and Gentile Bellini, who became the leading family of painters in Venice during the following decade. Jacopo Bellini's studies in perspective and drawings of fantastic architectural settings based on antique architecture would have interested his new son-in-law, who very likely had studied such drawings during his earlier visit to Venice.

Though Mantegna might have been expected to join the Bellini studio, he·preferred to pursue his independent practice in Padua, where the overwhelming artistic influence on him for the preceding few years had come from the wealth of sculpture produced by the Florentine Donatello for the high altar of S. Antonio (finished by 1450). Giovanni Bellini's response to Mantegna's style has been termed a dialogue, but Mantegna's reaction to Donatello's works might more aptly be called a struggle or even a dialectic. The frame and painted architecture of Mantegna's S. Zeno altarpiece answered the challenge posed by Donatello's Padua altar, for example. Mantegna's art always retained echoes of Donatello's sculpture in its hard, even metallic, surfaces, revealing an essentially sculptural approach that was somewhat softened only in the 1490s.

Years as court painter in Mantua. Mantegna has been characterized as strongly jealous of his independence; yet by entering the service of the marquis of Mantua, Ludovico Gonzaga, in 1459, he was forced to submit to limitations on his freedom of travel and acceptance of commissions from other patrons. Despite such limitations, Mantegna journeyed to Florence and Pisa in 1466–67, where he renewed contact with works of art by Donatello, Fra Filippo Lippi, Paolo Uccello, and Andrea del Castagno. During this decade (1460–70) Mantegna produced his finest small-scale works, such as "The Circumcision" and the Venice "St. George."

The Gonzaga patronage provided Mantegna a fixed income (which did not always materialize) and the opportunity to create what became his best known surviving work, the so-called Camera degli Sposi (Wedding Chamber), or Camera Picta (Painted Room), in the Palazzo Ducale at Mantua (1474), in which he developed a self-consistent illusion of a total environment.

Earlier practitioners of 15th-century perspective delimited a rectangular field as a transparent window onto the world and constructed an imaginary space behind its front plane. In the Camera degli Sposi, however, Mantegna constructed a system of homogeneous decoration on all four walls of the room, mainly by means of highly realistic painted architectural elements on walls and ceilings, which from ground level convincingly imitate three-dimensionally extended shapes. Though the ceiling is flat, it appears concave. Mantegna transformed the small interior room into an elegant open-air pavilion, to which the room's real and fictive occupants (actually one

and the same, since the beholders must have been members of this very court) were transported from deep within an essentially medieval urban castle.

Directly above the centre of the room is a painted oculus, or circular opening to the sky, with putti (little angels) and ladies around a balustrade in dramatically foreshortened perspective. The strong vertical axis created by the oculus locates the spectator at a single point in the centre of the room, the point from which the observer's space blends with that of the frescoed figures that are thrust out toward him by the narrow shelf of space provided for them on the fireplace wall.

The realism of the perspective handling of the oculus made it the most influential illusionistic *di sotto in su* ceiling decoration of the early Renaissance. Its implications for the future of ceiling decoration were largely unrealized, however, until the time of Correggio, a major north Italian painter of the early 16th century, who employed the same type of illusionism in a series of domes in Parma, Italy. Furthermore, the idea of total spatial illusion generated by Mantegna was not fully exploited until inventors of ingenious schemes of ceiling decoration in the Baroque era (the 17th century), such as Giovanni Lanfranco and Andrea Pozzo, utilized a basically identical concept of total illusion dependent upon the location of a hypothetical viewer standing at a single point in the room.

While at the Gonzaga court, Mantegna attained a position of great respect if not veneration. His close relations with his patron Ludovico were a unique phenomenon at such an early date. As one might expect, the signatures of Mantegna's paintings reveal intense pride in his accomplishments as a painter. Other than this there are only a few legal records of disputes with his neighbours (from which Ludovico had to rescue him) to provide tentative evidence for the painter's irascible and contentious personality during his later years. An empathetic viewer may draw many subjective conclusions as to Mantegna's thoughts and emotions by looking carefully at his paintings. But Ludovico died in 1478, followed soon after by Mantegna's son Bernardino, who had been expected to carry on his father's studio. Mantegna's financial situation was so bad that, in 1484, he was forced to ask for help from the powerful Florentine merchant Prince Lorenzo de' Medici and even contemplated moving to Florence. Ludovico's son Federico outlived his father by only a few years, and, with the accession of young Gianfrancesco II in 1484, the financial conditions of patronage improved.

Though many of Mantegna's works for the Gonzaga family were subsequently lost, the remains of nine canvases depicting a Roman triumphal procession, the "Triumph of Caesar," begun around 1486 and worked on for several years, still exist. In these paintings, reflecting the classical tastes of his new patron, Gianfrancesco, Mantegna reached the peak of his late style. Perhaps it was this new imaginative synthesis of the colour, splendour, and ritualistic power of ancient Rome that brought about Pope Innocent VIII's commission to decorate his private chapel in the Belvedere Palace, Rome (destroyed 1780), which Mantegna carried out in 1488–90.

Notwithstanding ill health and advanced age, Mantegna worked intensively during the remaining years of his life. In 1495 Gianfrancesco ordered the "Madonna della Vittoria" to commemorate his supposed victory at the Battle of Fornovo. In the last years of his life, Mantegna painted the "Parnassus" (1497), a picture celebrating the marriage of Isabella d'Este to Gianfrancesco Gonzaga in 1490, and "Wisdom Overcoming the Vices" (1502), for Isabella's *studiolo* (a small room in the Gonzaga palace at Mantua embellished with fine paintings and carvings of mythological subjects intended to display the erudition and advanced taste of its patron). A third canvas intended for this program, with the legend of the god Comus (Louvre), was unfinished when Mantegna died on September 13, 1506, and was completed by his successor at the Gonzaga court, Lorenzo Costa.

A funerary chapel in S. Andrea at Mantua was dedicated to Mantegna's memory. Decorated with frescoes, in-

Marriage to Nicolosia Bellini

The unique perspective of the Camera degli Sposi frescoes

Maturity of Mantegna's late style

cluding a dome painted (possibly by Correggio) with paradise symbols related to Mantegna's "Madonna della Vittoria," it was finished in 1516. No other 15th-century artist was dignified by having a funerary chapel dedicated to him in the major church of the city where he worked, which attests to the high stature Mantegna came to enjoy in his adopted city.

MAJOR WORKS

PAINTINGS: Ovetari Chapel frescoes (1448–55; Eremitani Church, Padua); "The Agony in the Garden" (c. 1450; National Gallery, London); "The Virgin with Sleeping Child" (c. 1450; Staatliche Museen Preussischer Kulturbesitz, Berlin); "The Man of Sorrows with the Virgin and Saints" ("The St. Luke Polyptych," 1454; Brera, Milan); "St. George" (c. 1455–60; Accademia, Venice); "Madonna Enthroned with Saints" (1456–59; S. Zeno Maggiore, Verona); "The Crucifixion" (1456–59; Louvre, Paris); "St. Sebastian" (c. 1459; Kunsthistorisches Museum, Vienna); "The Adoration of the Shepherds" (c. 1460; Metropolitan Museum of Art, New York); "Portrait of Cardinal Lodovico Mezzarota" (c. 1460; Staatliche Museen Preussischer Kulturbesitz, Berlin); "Portrait of a Man" (c. 1460; National Gallery of Art, Washington, D. C.); "Triptych with the Adoration of the Magi, the Circumcision, and the Ascension" (c. 1465; Uffizi, Florence); "The Death of the Virgin" (c. 1465; Prado, Madrid); "St. Sebastian" (c. 1465; Louvre); "The Dead Christ" (c. 1466; Jacob M. Heimann Gallery, New York); frescoes of the Camera degli Sposi (1473–74; Palazzo Ducale, Mantua); "The Mourning over the Dead Christ" (c. 1475?; Brera, Milan); "The Madonna of the Caves" (c. 1484?; Uffizi); "Triumph of Caesar" (begun c. 1486; Hampton Court Palace, England); "St. Sebastian" (c. 1490–1500; Ca d'Oro, Venice); "Madonna della Vittoria" (1495; Louvre); "Parnassus" (1497; Louvre); "Wisdom Overcoming the Vices" (1502; Louvre).

ENGRAVINGS: "Battle of the Sea Gods" (c. 1490); "Bacchanal" (c. 1490); "Madonna and Child" (c. 1490); "The Entombment" (1490s); "The Risen Christ Between St. Andrew and Longinus" (1490s). Prints of all are in the British Museum.

BIBLIOGRAPHY. PAUL KRISTELLER, *Andrea Mantegna* (1901), the first monograph on Mantegna in English, is a tremendous effort of scholarly achievement and synthesis. Many of Kristeller's conclusions remain unchallenged and all subsequent biographers have relied heavily on this book. ILSE BLUM, *Andrea Mantegna und die Antike* (1936), is a thorough analysis of the appearance of antique motifs in Mantegna's work with identification of his sources. There is some subsequent work on this aspect in English but none supplanting this. ERICA TIETZE-CONRAT, *Mantegna* (1955), is the best modern monograph in English, including a catalog of works, attributed works, drawings and engravings (fully illustrated). MILLARD MEISS, *Andrea Mantegna As Illuminator: An Episode in Renaissance Art, Humanism and Diplomacy* (1957), an essential book for evaluating Mantegna's achievement in classical revival, explores hitherto uncharted areas such as the artist's activity in the field of miniature painting and his contributions to the revival of classical epigraphy. See also the same author's "Toward a More Comprehensive Renaissance Palaeography," *Art Bulletin*, 42:97–112 (1960), a continuation of his research in this area. GIOVANNI PACCAGNINI, *Mantegna: La Camera degli Sposi* (1957), is a monograph on Mantegna's best known work by the leading Italian authority, who also wrote *Andrea Mantegna* (1961), the catalog of the Mantegna show in the Palazzo Ducale, Mantua, 1961 (with a good bibliography through 1961). See also his article in the *Encyclopedia of World Art*, vol. 9, col. 486–498 (1964), an excellent summary of the artist's life and works including accounts of disagreement among scholars and a fair reflection of the latest consensus. PHYLLIS and KARL LEHMANN, *Samothracian Reflections: Aspects of the Revival of the Antique* (1972), contains an essay on Mantegna's "Parnassus" that will most likely stand as the definitive analysis for many years to come.

(W.S.Sh.)

Manuel I of Portugal

King of Portugal from 1495 to 1521, Manuel I was called the Fortunate. His reign saw the opening of the sea route to India, the discovery of Brazil, the establishment of Portuguese power at Goa (in India), the first Portuguese contact with China, and the concentration of trade with the East at Lisbon.

Manuel was also fortunate to have reigned at all; he was the 9th child of Dom Fernando, who was the younger brother of Afonso V. Manuel was born at Alcochete on May 31, 1469; his father died a year later. King Afonso had one of Manuel's sisters married to his heir, John II, and another to the powerful Duke of Bragança. On his accession John II had Bragança executed on a charge of treason and later murdered Manuel's only surviving brother on suspicion of conspiracy. But John extended his protection to the boy Manuel, making him duke of Beja. On the death of his own son in 1491, John recognized Manuel as his heir. Although he later contemplated legitimizing his remaining son Jorge, he finally left the crown to Manuel.

As king, Manuel at once pardoned the banished Braganças and restored their confiscated estates. But the monarchy soon acquired vast new wealth as Vasco da Gama's voyage around Africa opened Portuguese trade with the East. In March 1500 Manuel sent Pedro Álvares Cabral with 13 ships to establish trade relations with the Indian princes. Cabral, sailing in the western Atlantic, sighted Brazil, sent back a ship to report the discovery, and continued around the Cape of Good Hope to India where he set up trading posts (*feitorias*) at Calicut, Cochin, and Cannanore, all on Malabar coast of southwestern India. Although half his ships were lost, the venture was profitable. In 1502 da Gama took 20 ships and brought back gold as tribute from East Africa. Manuel was already wealthy by 1503. Meanwhile, João Fernandes Lavrador reached what was probably Labrador in 1499, and Gaspar Côrte-Real discovered Newfoundland in 1500. The Brazilian coast was explored, though trade was virtually confined to the dyewood after which Brazil is named. {.marginal} Voyages to the East

Manuel's claims to these newly discovered lands were confirmed by the Papacy and recognized by the Spanish, with whom Manuel maintained close relations. His three queens were Spanish. The first was Isabella, eldest daughter of cosovereigns Ferdinand and Isabella and widow of John II's heir. As a condition of the marriage, Manuel was to expel the Jews, many thousands of whom had been admitted by John II on their expulsion from Spain in 1492. Thus in December 1496 Manuel ordered Jews and free Muslims to quit Portugal within ten months. On their assembly in Lisbon, every attempt was made to force their conversion. Some were allowed to leave, but the rest were "converted" under the promise that no inquiry should be made into their beliefs for 20 years.

Manuel and Isabella became heirs to the Spanish crowns on her brother's death. They visited Toledo and Saragossa to receive oaths of allegiance in 1498, but the possibility of the union of the crowns ended when Isabella died in the same year while giving birth to their son Miguel, who died in infancy. In October Manuel married Isabella's younger sister Maria, by whom he had nine children. {.marginal} Heir to the Spanish crown

The consolidation of Portuguese influence in the East can be dated from the foundation of the fortress at Cochin in 1503 and its successful defense by Duarte Pacheco Pereira (1504). Manuel sent Dom Francisco de Almeida as the first viceroy of Portuguese India in 1505. Albuquerque, who succeeded Almeida as governor, conquered Goa in 1510, and Malacca on the Malay Peninsula in 1511, bringing the distribution of oriental spices under Portuguese control. By 1513 the Portuguese had reached China.

The crusading aspect of the expansion reached its apogee with Albuquerque, who nourished grandiose schemes for blockading the Red Sea and capturing Mecca. Duarte Galvão's attempts to persuade other European courts to join a crusade met with little response. The arrival of an Abyssinian envoy at Manuel's court in 1514 suggested an alliance with the Christian negus (king) of that country and Manuel appointed Galvão ambassador to Abyssinia. But the mission was delayed by Galvão's death, and the crusading vision faded with the death of Albuquerque off Goa (December 1515). Manuel was no warrior. It was the Duke of Bragança who conquered Azamor in Morocco (1513).

The Indian traffic added enormously to the size and splendour of Manuel's court. John II had cowed the ambitious nobles. Manuel converted them into a palace aristocracy, paying pensions to some 5,000 persons. Despite the brilliance of his age, Manuel appears in somewhat low relief. Most of the heroes of the day had made their mark under John II. Manuel was industrious, temperate, fond of music and display, and extravagant. He resided chiefly at Lisbon where he built the waterside palace (near the present-day Terreiro do Paço) and at Sintra. The playwright-goldsmith Gil Vicente wrote for the court, which became a centre of minor poetry and painting. Manuel founded the palace-monastery of the Jerónimos and built the Tower of Belem; the architecture typical of the reign has been called "Manueline" only since the 19th century.

Under Manuel the public administration was increasingly centralized. A committee of royal officials revised town charters granted by previous rulers, standardized local privileges, and rationalized taxes. In 1515 Manuel ordered his council to revise the code of laws: his *Ordenações Manuelinas* were issued in 1512 and revised in 1521. The judiciary was enlarged and royal *corregedores* appointed to all districts. This carried forward the process of neo-Roman absolutism and assured the rise of the judicial class. Manuel also excepted the church and the military orders of knighthood from certain obligations. He severely punished those responsible for the massacre of Jews in 1506. Manuel married Eleanor of Austria, sister of the emperor Charles V, in 1518, and had one daughter by this marriage. He died at Lisbon in December 1521, and was buried in the Jerónimos.

BIBLIOGRAPHY. Chronicles of his reign were written by the humanists DAMIAO DE GOIS (1566–57), and JERONIMO DE OSSORIO (1571). There is an outline of the reign in English by ELAINE SANCEAU, *The Reign of the Fortunate King, 1495–1521* (1969).

(H.V.L.)

Mao Tse-tung

As China emerged from a half century of revolution as the world's largest nation and a compelling model of modernization for Asian and African countries, Mao Tse-tung (in Pin-yin romanization, Mao Ze-dong), its principal revolutionary thinker and, in the early 1970s, unchallenged leader, must be accorded a critical place in the story of its resurgence. To be sure, he did not play a dominant role throughout the whole struggle. In the early years of the Chinese Communist Party, he was a secondary figure, though by no means a negligible one, and even since the 1940s (except perhaps during the Cultural Revolution) the crucial decisions were not his alone. Nevertheless, looking back over the whole period since the foundation of the Chinese Communist Party in 1921, Mao Tse-tung can fairly be regarded as the principal architect of the new China.

Eastfoto

Mao Tse-tung, 1966.

Early years. Born on December 26, 1893, in the village of Shaoshan, Hunan Province, Mao was the son of a former poor peasant who had become affluent as a farmer and grain dealer. He grew up in an environment in which education was valued only as training for keeping records and accounts. From the age of eight he attended his native village's primary school, where he acquired a basic knowledge of the Confucian Classics. At 13, he was forced to leave and begin working full time on his family's farm. Rebelling against paternal authority, Mao left his family to study at a higher primary school in a neighbouring county and then at a secondary school in the provincial capital of Changsha. There he came in contact with new ideas from the West, as formulated by the political and cultural reformers such as Liang Ch'i-ch'ao, and by the Nationalist revolutionary Sun Yat-sen. Scarcely had he begun studying revolutionary ideas when a real revolution took place before his very eyes. On October 10, 1911, fighting against the Manchu dynasty broke out in Wuchang, and within 12 days the revolt had spread to Changsha.

Enlisting in a unit of the revolutionary army in Hunan, Mao spent six months as a soldier. While he probably had not yet clearly grasped the idea that, as he later put it, "political power grows out of the barrel of a gun," his first brief military experience at least confirmed his boyhood admiration of military leaders and exploits. In primary school days, his heroes had included not only the great warrior-emperors of the Chinese past but Napoleon and George Washington as well.

Enlistment in revolutionary army

The spring of 1912 saw the birth of the new Chinese Republic and the end of Mao's military service. For an entire year Mao drifted from one thing to another, trying in turn a police school, a soap-making school, a law school, a business school, studying history in a secondary school, and then spending some months reading many of the classic works of the Western liberal tradition in the provincial library. This period of groping, rather than indicating any lack of decision in Mao's character, was actually a reflection of China's situation at the time. The abolition of the official civil service examination system in 1905 and the piecemeal introduction of Western learning in so-called modern schools had left young people in a state of uncertainty as to what type of training, Chinese or Western, could best prepare them for a successful career or for service to their country.

Mao eventually graduated from the First Provincial Normal School in Changsha in 1918. While officially an institution of secondary rather than of higher education, the First Normal School offered a high standard of instruction both in Chinese history, literature, and philosophy, and in Western ideas. While at the school Mao Tse-tung also acquired his first experience in political activity by helping to establish several student organizations. The most important of these was the New People's Study Society, founded in the winter of 1917–18, some of whose members were later to join the Communist Party and to follow Mao's leadership to the final Communist victory in 1949.

From the Normal School in Changsha Mao went to Peking University, China's leading intellectual centre. The half year he spent in Peking working as a librarian's assistant was of disproportionate importance in shaping his future career, for it was then that he came under the influence of the two men who were to be the principal figures in the foundation of the Chinese Communist Party: Li Ta-chao and Ch'en Tu-hsiu. Moreover, he found himself at Peking University precisely during the months leading up to the so-called May Fourth Movement of 1919, which was to a considerable extent the fountainhead of all the changes that were to take place in China in the ensuing half century.

In a limited sense, May Fourth Movement is the name given to the massive student demonstrations which erupted in protest against the Paris Peace Conference's decision to hand over former German concessions in Shantung to Japan instead of returning them to China. But the term also evokes a period of rapid political and cultural change, beginning in 1915, that resulted in the Chinese radicals' abandonment of Western liberalism for Marxism–Leninism as the answer to China's problems and the subsequent founding of the Chinese Communist Party in

May Fourth Movement

1921. This period also saw the shift from the difficult and esoteric classical written language to a far more accessible vehicle of literary expression patterned on colloquial speech. At the same time, a new and very young generation moved to the centre of the political stage. To be sure, the demonstration on May 4th was launched by Ch'en Tu-hsiu, but the students soon realized that they themselves were the main actors. In an editorial published in July 1919, Mao wrote:

> The world is ours, the nation is ours, society is ours. If we do not speak, who will speak? If we do not act, who will act?

Since then, his generation has never ceased to regard itself as responsible for the nation's fate, and, indeed, its members are still in power today, both in Peking and in Taipei.

During the summer of 1919 Mao Tse-tung helped to establish in Changsha a variety of organizations that brought the students together with the merchants and the workers—but not yet with the peasants—in demonstrations aimed at forcing the government to oppose Japan. His writings at the time are filled with references to the "army of the red flag" throughout the world and to the victory of the Russian Revolution, but it was not until the winter of 1919–20, after fleeing from Hunan, where he had led a campaign against the military ruler there, that he became committed to Marxism. He spent that winter in Peking reading translations of Marxist writings, which, he said,

Mao's commitment to Marxism

> built up in me a faith in Marxism from which, once I had accepted it as the correct interpretation of history, I did not afterwards waver.

Mao and the Chinese Communist Party. In June 1920, after a change of governors in Changsha, Mao returned to his native province as principal of the primary school, and in September or October of that year he organized a small Communist group there. That winter he married the first of his three wives, Yang K'ai-hui, the daughter of his former ethics teacher. Although his duties at the school occupied most of his time, he managed to keep up his political activities on a part-time basis. He did attend, in the summer of 1921, a meeting of representatives from the other Communist groups in China, along with two delegates from the Moscow-based Comintern (Communist International), and helped to found the Chinese Communist Party. In 1923, when the young party entered into an alliance with Sun Yat-sen's Kuomintang (Nationalist Party) in order more effectively to fight the inefficient and oppressive regime in Peking, Mao abandoned his job as principal to become a professional revolutionary and political leader.

In 1923–24, he lived mostly with his wife and two infant sons in Shanghai, where he was a leading member of the local Kuomintang organization, as well as of the Chinese Communist Party. In the winter of 1924–25, he returned to his native village of Shaoshan for a rest. There, after witnessing demonstrations by peasants stirred into political consciousness by the shooting of several dozen Chinese by foreign police in Shanghai (May and June 1925), Mao suddenly became conscious of the revolutionary potential inherent in the peasantry. Although born in a peasant household, he had, in the course of his student years, adopted the Chinese intellectual's traditional view of the workers and peasants as ignorant and dirty. His conversion to Marxism had forced him to revise his estimate of the urban proletariat, but he continued to share Marx's own contempt for the backward and amorphous peasantry. Now, however, he turned back to the rural world of his youth as the source of China's regeneration. Following the example of other Communists working within the Kuomintang who had already begun to work with peasants, Mao began to channel the spontaneous protest movements of the Hunanese peasants into a growing network of peasant associations.

Peasants and the revolution

The Communists and the Kuomintang. Pursued by the military governor of Hunan, Mao was soon forced to flee his native province once more and returned for another year to an urban environment—this time to Canton, the main power base of the Kuomintang, then led by Chiang

Kai-shek since the death of Sun Yat-sen in March 1925. But, though he lived in Canton, Mao still focussed his attention on the countryside. Apart from editing the Kuomintang's leading organ, the *Political Weekly*, and attending the Second Kuomintang Congress in January 1926, Mao served at the Peasant Movement Training Institute, set up in Canton under the auspices of the Kuomintang, as principal of the sixth training course. Although Chiang Kai-shek still declared his allegiance to the "world revolution" and wished to avail himself of Soviet aid, he was determined to remain master in his own house. He therefore expelled most Communists from responsible posts in the Kuomintang in March 1926. Mao, however, stayed on at the institute from May to October of that year. He remained there because of the common bond of nationalism he shared with Chiang, in spite of Chiang's suspicion of the Communists. As it turned out, most of the young peasant activists Mao trained were shortly at work strengthening the position of the Communists against the Kuomintang.

In July 1926, Chiang Kai-shek set out on a Northern Expedition aimed at unifying the country under his own leadership and overthrowing the conservative government in Peking as well as other dissident warlords. At the close of the training session in October, Mao once more returned to Hunan, where, in January and February 1927, he conducted an investigation into the peasant movement, which led him to conclude that in a very short time several hundred million peasants in China would "rise like a tornado or tempest—a force so extraordinarily swift and violent that no power, however great, will be able to suppress it." Strictly speaking, this prediction proved to be false. Revolution in the shape of spontaneous action by hundreds of millions of peasants did not sweep across China "in a very short time," or indeed at all. Chiang Kai-shek, who was bent on an alliance with the propertied classes in the cities and in the countryside, turned against the worker and peasant revolution, and in April 1927 he went so far as to massacre the very Shanghai workers who had delivered the city to him. Stalin's strategy for carrying out revolution in alliance with the Kuomintang collapsed, and the Chinese Communist Party was virtually annihilated in the cities and decimated in the countryside. But in a broader and less literal sense, Mao's prophecy was justified. In August 1927 Mao led a few hundred peasants who had survived the autumn harvest uprising to a base on the Ching-kang Shan (Ching-kang Mountains) and embarked on a new type of revolutionary warfare in the countryside in which the Red Army, rather than the unarmed masses, would play the central role. But it was only because a large proportion of China's hundreds of millions of peasants sympathized with and supported this effort that Mao Tse-tung was able in the course of the civil war to encircle the cities from the countryside and thus defeat Chiang Kai-shek and gain control of the country.

Struggle with Chiang Kai-shek

The road to power. Mao's 22 years in the wilderness can be divided into four phases. The first of these is the initial three years when Mao Tse-tung and Chu Teh, the commander in chief of the army, successfully developed the tactics of guerrilla warfare from base areas in the countryside. These activities, however, were regarded even by their protagonists, and still more by the Central Committee in Shanghai (and by the Comintern in Moscow), as a holding operation until the next upsurge of revolution in the urban centres. In the summer of 1930 the Red Army was ordered by the Central Committee to occupy several major cities in south central China in the hope of sparking a revolution by the workers. When it became evident that persistence in this attempt could only lead to further costly losses, Mao disobeyed orders and abandoned the battle to return to the base in southern Kiangsi. During this year Mao's first wife was executed by the Kuomintang and he married Ho Tzu-chen, with whom he had been living since 1928 and who bore him five children.

The second phase (the Kiangsi period) centres on the founding of the Chinese Soviet Republic, November 1931, in a portion of Kiangsi Province, with Mao as

The Kiangsi period

chairman. Since there was little support for the revolution in the cities, the promise of ultimate victory now seemed to reside in the gradual strengthening and expansion of the base areas. The Soviet regime soon came to control a population of several million; the Red Army, now grown to a strength of some 200,000, easily defeated large forces of inferior troops sent against it by Chiang Kai-shek in the first four of the so-called encirclement and annihilation campaigns. But it was unable to stand up against Chiang's own elite units, and in October 1934 the major part of the Red Army, Mao, and his pregnant wife all abandoned the base in Kiangsi and set out for the northwest of China, on what is known as the Long March.

The Kiangsi period of 1931–1934 is by far the most obscure and controversial in the history of Chinese Communism and in Mao's own career. There is wide disagreement among specialists as to the extent of Mao's real power, especially in the years 1932–34, and as to which military strategies were his or other party leaders'. But the majority view appears to be that, in the last years of the Chinese Soviet Republic, Mao functioned to a considerable extent as a figurehead with little control over policy, especially in military matters, and that he achieved de facto leadership over the party (though not the formal title of Chairman of the Central Committee) only at the Tsunyi Conference of January 1935 during the Long March.

The anti-Japanese war

In any case, when a few thousand troops who had survived the perils of the Long March arrived in the northwest in the autumn of 1935, events were already moving toward the third phase in Mao's rural odyssey, which was to be characterized by a renewed united front with the Kuomintang against Japan and by the rise of Mao to unchallenged supremacy in the party. In August 1935 both the Comintern at its Seventh Congress in Moscow and the Chinese Communists from one of their halts during the Long March proclaimed the principle of an anti-Fascist united front, and in May 1936 the Chinese Communists for the first time accepted the prospect that such a united front might include Chiang Kai-shek himself, and not merely dissident elements in the Nationalist camp. The so-called Sian incident of December 1936, in which Chiang Kai-shek was kidnapped by military leaders from northeastern China who wanted to fight Japan and recover their homelands rather than participate in civil war against the Communists, accelerated the evolution toward unity. By the time the Japanese began their attempt to subjugate all of China in July 1937, the terms of a new united front between the Communists and the Kuomintang had been virtually settled, and the formal agreement was announced in September 1937.

In the course of the anti-Japanese war, the Communists broke up a substantial portion of their army into small units and sent them behind the enemy lines to serve as nuclei for guerrilla forces which effectively controlled vast areas of the countryside, stretching between the cities and communication lines occupied by the invader. As a result, they not only expanded their military forces to somewhere between 500,000 and 1,000,000 at the time of the Japanese surrender but also established effective grass-roots political control over a population which may have totalled as many as 90,000,000. It has been argued that the support of the rural population was won purely by appeals to their nationalist feeling in opposition to the Japanese. This certainly was fundamental, but Communist agrarian policies likewise played a part in securing broad support among the peasantry.

Writings, 1936–1940

During the years 1936–1940, Mao Tse-tung had, for the first time since the 1920s, the leisure to devote himself to reflection and writing. It was then that he first read in translation a certain number of Soviet writings on philosophy and produced his own account of dialectical materialism, of which the best known portions are those entitled "On Practice" and "On Contradiction." More important, Mao produced the major works which synthesized his own experience of revolutionary struggle and his vision of how the revolution should be carried forward in the context of the united front. On military matters, there was

first *Strategic Problems of China's Revolutionary War*, written in December 1936 to sum up the lessons of the Kiangsi period (and also to justify the correctness of his own military line at the time), and then *On Protracted War* and other writings of 1938 on the tactics of the anti-Japanese war. As to his overall view of the events of these years, Mao adopted an extremely conciliatory attitude toward the Kuomintang in his report entitled *On the New Stage* (October 1938), in which he attributed to it the leading role both in the war against Japan and in the phase of national reconstruction which would follow it. By the winter of 1939–40, however, the situation had changed sufficiently so that he could adopt a much firmer line, claiming leadership for the Communists. This was spelled out somewhat more openly in *The Chinese Revolution and the Chinese Communist Party*, written primarily for party members, than in *On New Democracy*, which was aimed at a wider audience, but otherwise the argument in both pieces was similar. Internationally, the Chinese revolution was a part of the world proletarian revolution directed against imperialism (whether it be British, German, or Japanese); internally, the country should be ruled by a "joint dictatorship of several parties" belonging to the anti-Japanese united front. For the time being, Mao felt, the aims of the Communist Party coincided with the aims of the Kuomintang, and therefore Communists should not try to rush ahead to socialism and thus disrupt the united front. But neither should they have any doubts about the ultimate need to take power into their own hands in order to move forward to socialism. During this period, in 1939, Mao divorced his second wife and married a well-known film actress, Lan P'ing, known today as Chiang Ch'ing.

The issues of Kuomintang–Communist rivalry for the leadership of the united front are related to the continuing struggle for supremacy within the Chinese Communist Party, for Mao's two chief rivals—Wang Ming, who had just returned from a long stay in Moscow, and Chang Kuo-t'ao, who had at first refused to accept Mao's political and military leadership—were both accused of excessive slavishness toward the Kuomintang. But perhaps even more central in Mao's ultimate emergence as the acknowledged leader of the party was the question of what he had called in October 1938 the "Sinification" of Marxism—its adaptation not only to Chinese conditions but to the mentality and cultural traditions of the Chinese people.

Mao could not claim the first-hand knowledge of how Communism worked within the Soviet Union possessed by many other leading members of the Chinese Communist Party nor the ability which some of them enjoyed to read Marx or Lenin in the original. He could and did claim, however, to know and understand China. The differences between him and the Soviet-oriented faction in the party came to a head at the time of the so-called Rectification Campaign of 1942. This program aimed at giving a basic grounding in Marxist theory and Leninist principles of party organization to the many thousands of new members who had been drawn into the party in the course of the expansion since 1937. Among the materials for study were writings by Lenin, Stalin, and Georgi Dimitrov, the Bulgarian Comintern leader. But a second and equally important aspect of the movement was the elimination of what Mao called "foreign dogmatism"—in other words, blind imitation of Soviet experience and obedience to Soviet directives.

The Rectification Campaign of 1942 has been bitterly denounced since the early 1960s by Soviet spokesmen as an attempt to purge the Chinese Communist Party of all those elements genuinely imbued with "proletarian internationalism" (*i.e.*, devotion to Moscow). It is therefore not surprising that, as Mao's campaign in the countryside moved into its fourth and last phase—that of civil war with the Kuomintang—Stalin's lack of enthusiasm for a Chinese Communist victory should have become increasingly evident. Looking back on this period in 1962, when the Sino-Soviet conflict had come to a head, Mao declared:

Fourth phase— civil war

In 1945 . . . , Stalin blocked the Chinese revolution, saying that we must not fight a civil war but must collaborate with Chiang Kai-shek. Otherwise, the Chinese nation would perish. At that time, we did not apply this, and the revolution was victorious. After the victory of the revolution, he [Stalin] again suspected that China would be like Yugoslavia, and I would turn into a Tito.

This account of Stalin's attitude is substantiated by a whole series of public gestures at the time, culminating in the fact that when the People's Liberation Army took Nanking in April 1949, the Soviet ambassador was the only foreign diplomat to accompany the retreating Nationalist government to Canton. Stalin's motives were obviously those described by Mao in the above passage; he did not believe in the capacity of the Chinese Communists to achieve a clear-cut victory, and he thought they would be a nuisance if they did.

Formation of the People's Republic of China. Nevertheless, when the Communists did take power in China, both Mao and Stalin had to make the best of the situation. In December 1949 Mao, now chairman of the Chinese People's Republic, travelled to Moscow, where, after two months of arduous negotiations, he succeeded in persuading Stalin to sign a treaty of mutual assistance accompanied by limited economic aid. Before the Chinese had time to profit from the resources made available for economic development, however, they found themselves dragged into the Korean War in support of the Moscow-oriented regime in P'yŏngyang. Only after this baptism of fire did Stalin, according to Mao, begin to have confidence in him and believe he was not first and foremost a Chinese nationalist.

Until several years after Stalin's death, the Chinese continued to go about "building socialism" in a way essentially similar to that which had been followed in the Soviet Union; i.e., based on centralized planning with an emphasis on heavy industry, especially in the form of large capital-intensive enterprises built with Soviet assistance. Mao later described this policy as unfortunate but inevitable in view of the Chinese Communists' lack of experience in economic development. In the countryside, too, the stages of land reform, followed in due course by collectivization, were similar to those in the Soviet Union, though the details were somewhat different. Throughout the first half decade of the Chinese People's Republic, Mao rarely appeared in public. Apart from speeches welcoming foreign diplomats and official decrees which he signed as Chairman of the Chinese People's Republic, very few statements were issued in his name. On July 31, 1955, however, he suddenly emerged from this ceremonial role with an important speech calling for acceleration in forming agricultural cooperatives, which differed markedly from the provisions of the five-year plan officially adopted only the day before. This marked the beginning of a four-year period during which Mao constantly and actively sought to promote his own policies in every sphere, often against the opposition of senior comrades.

Mao's re-emergence, 1955–59. In the winter of 1955–56, Mao Tse-tung edited a three-volume compilation of materials on the "Socialist High Tide" in China's countryside, designed to illustrate the advantages of rapid collectivization. In the spring of 1956, three months after Nikita Khrushchev, then first secretary of the Soviet Communist Party, made a secret speech denouncing Stalin's purges of the Party after 1934, Mao proclaimed the policy of "letting a hundred flowers bloom"—that is, the freedom to express many diverse ideas—designed to prevent the development of a similar repressive political climate in China. The uprisings of October 1956 in Poland and Hungary against Soviet domination did not induce him to retreat from this policy; instead, he pressed on even more boldly in his celebrated speech of February 27, 1957, "On the Correct Handling of Contradictions among the People." It was evident at the time that the Hundred Flowers policy was never intended as a liberalization policy in the usual sense of the term. But neither was the invitation to "bloom" merely a trap to snare those with dissident opinions. Mao's hope was that the intellectuals and specialists, whom he had hailed

in January 1956 as indispensable to the development of China's economy, would be more likely to support the regime wholeheartedly if the party demonstrated that it did not regard itself as infallible and was willing to listen to criticism. Mao soon discovered, however, that he had miscalculated. Far from contenting themselves with denouncing particular defects in the system, the critics called into question the most fundamental principle of the system itself, namely, leadership by the Communist Party.

Mao, therefore, in the autumn of 1957, turned his attention from the elite to the masses. If the specialists were not yet sufficiently "red," he would remold them by sending them to work at the grass-roots level. Meanwhile, he would rely primarily on the creativity of the rank and file as the agent of modernization. Mao was pushed in this direction by his disappointment with the intellectuals but economic necessity played an even greater role in the genesis of the new policies known as the Great Leap Forward. In the face of dwindling Soviet assistance, Mao concluded that China's economic development could best be assured by emphasizing small labour-intensive enterprises, which would require a substantial degree of local initiative, rather than capital-intensive programs. These policies were put into effect in the spring and summer of 1958 in the framework of the "people's communes," which spread rapidly throughout the Chinese countryside.

There was still an element of Leninist orthodoxy in the system that emerged at this time, namely, party leadership. The kind of leadership involved, however, went against the grain of Leninism, essentially an elitist philosophy in which the intellectuals lead the workers and the workers lead the more backward peasants. In handing over control of both political and economic affairs to party secretaries at the commune level, who were often peasants themselves, Mao made a decisive departure from Leninism. He was quite right when he said later that 1958 had marked the end of Chinese reliance on the Soviet model.

Setback and retirement. The Great Leap Forward, while its economic effects were not wholly negative, did disorganize industrial production. The disruption of the countryside caused by the overhasty introduction of the communes, combined with a series of natural disasters, also led to a severe food shortage. As a result, opposition from Mao's colleagues forced him to retreat from these bold policies and accept a more orthodox approach to economic problems, stressing centralized planning and material incentives. In the autumn of 1959 the Minister of Defense, P'eng Te-huai, was removed from his post because he had criticized Mao's economic approach too openly, but in the years 1960–1962 it was P'eng's policies rather than Mao's that were applied by the party leadership. Mao's retirement in 1959 from the post of Chairman of the Chinese People's Republic was not a consequence of these setbacks, for it had been announced within the party at the end of 1957. Nevertheless, although Mao remained Chairman of the Communist Party, he was less in the public eye until the mid-1960s. Meanwhile, Lin Piao, P'eng Te-huai's successor as Minister of Defense, was turning the People's Liberation Army into a "great school of Mao Tse-tung's thought," thereby laying the foundations for Mao's comeback.

It is from this period that one may date serious disagreement and rivalry between Mao Tse-tung and Liu Shao-ch'i, who replaced Mao as chairman of the Republic. Though, in some respects, their approach to revolution in the 1920s and 1930s was different (Liu adopting a more orthodox view stressing the role of the urban proletariat), there was clearly an effective political alliance between them from the early 1940s. In 1945, at the Seventh Congress of the Chinese Communist Party, it was Liu who made the speech hailing Mao Tse-tung's thought as the guide to all the party's work, and in 1958 he supported Mao fully on the question of rapid economic development. He did not agree, however, on the decentralized and loosely coordinated pattern of development which characterized the Great Leap Forward, and begin-

---

Margin notes:

Emphasis on centralized planning

Hundred Flowers speech

Great Leap Forward

Rivalry with Liu Shao-chi

ning in 1960 he came into conflict with Mao through his support of a more orthodox, Soviet-type model.

At the Tenth Plenary Session of the Central Committee in September 1962, Mao issued the call, "Never forget the class struggle!" In the spring of 1963 he translated this into action by launching a Socialist Education Movement, which, in his view, would prevent China from "changing colour" and becoming "revisionist" like the Soviet Union. The movement became a battlefield for the opposing concepts of revolution held by Mao, on the one hand, and the leaders of the party organization, Liu Shao-ch'i and Teng Hsiao-p'ing, on the other. In the autumn of 1963 Teng produced a new directive to guide the movement, heavily imbued with Leninist elitism as compared to Mao's original draft, and in the autumn of 1964 Liu revised the directive further in an attempt to reach a compromise between Mao's views and Teng's. In January 1965 Mao intervened once more with a new and still more radical directive, denouncing the danger of "revisionism" in the Central Committee, but he was already moving toward the idea that a completely new form of political action was required—the gigantic and unprecedented undertaking which was to be baptized Great Proletarian Cultural Revolution.

The Cultural Revolution. Mao concluded that the Socialist Education Movement had become merely another rectification movement similar to the one in 1942. There had been many such campaigns since 1949, and the party cadres were adapting themselves to them: go through the prescribed motions, produce the necessary self-criticism, then continue acting as they had before. This time the party as a whole, and not merely individual elements in it, would have to be disciplined and remolded.

It is still difficult to assess the consequences of the gigantic upheaval of the years 1966–69, although the general pattern of the movement is clear enough. First came the phase of Red Guard violence, in which the party organization was attacked and party officials beaten up by young militant zealots loyal to the Chairman, discreetly guided and supported by the army. From January 1967 to September 1968 came the "seizure of power" by revolutionary committees in the various provinces, comprising an alliance of former party cadres, young Red Guard and "revolutionary rebel" activists, and representatives of the People's Liberation Army. Then followed a period of "tidying up," symbolized by the Ninth Party Congress of April 1969, and the attempt to reanimate the party organizations at all levels by retaining most of the previous membership but altering the spirit of the party bureaucracy and its relations with the masses.

While the Cultural Revolution can hardly be seen as the logically inevitable outcome of Mao's previous ideas and career, he has so thoroughly identified himself with this attempt to transform the whole spirit and structure of Chinese society that assessment of the man and his life work today must begin here. Like many earlier episodes in Mao's life, the Cultural Revolution is full of contradictions. The most basic of these is between the extraordinary development of the Mao cult, the call to be "boundlessly loyal to Chairman Mao," on the one hand, and the effort to promote spontaneity and grass-roots initiative on the other. Mao himself would no doubt claim that, in the struggle with the entrenched party bureaucracy, he had no alternative but to throw his own personal prestige and charisma into the balance. Moreover, he would argue, if one is to extirpate the roots of bureaucracy, which lie in the attitude of arrogant superiority—which in China has always characterized those who could boast of a certain amount of book learning, from the mandarins of the past to modern Party cadres and technical experts—the only solution lies in promoting ideas simple enough to be grasped by the people, and a type of education adapted to the needs of the people.

Effects of the Cultural Revolution There is a considerable element of truth in this official Maoist view of the Cultural Revolution. But at the same time, Mao's well-intended goal of increasing the general level of education and culture has been pursued in such a way as to paralyze advanced research and humiliate those who possessed high levels of expertise, thus inhibiting the development and use of skills which Mao described as essential to China's progress. And the cult of Mao and of Mao's thought, while giving the average man the conviction that he understands the most essential philosophical truths and the confidence to speak up and participate actively in the affairs of society, also has stultifying and impoverishing effects on intellectual life as a whole. When one adds these considerations to the toll of violence of the years 1966–68, it is very hard to take a wholly positive view of the Cultural Revolution.

Assessment. In attempting to view not only Mao's recent policies but his life as a whole, his profound contribution to China's national resurgence is indubitable. Although it was not Mao's achievement alone, in view of the central role he has played since the 1940s, he must be given a large portion of the credit. To what extent the policies he has promoted during the Great Leap Forward, and subsequently during the Cultural Revolution, have contributed to China's economic development or international prestige is, of course, subject to debate. Nonetheless, there has been substantial economic progress, and the new China which he leads and symbolizes is a factor to be reckoned with in international affairs as it has not been in modern times.

More ambiguous is his message to the world at large. To Asia, Africa, and Latin America he offers China's experiences as a model of "people's war" which may be an appropriate solution in some circumstances but a source of division, dogmatic hair-splitting, and unnecessary sacrifice in others. To students and others in the advanced industrial societies of Europe and North America, he offers inspiration in the shape of a call to root out selfishness, bureaucratism, and the enslavement of man to the machine, but no infallible recipe for achieving these ends. The Chinese revolution and Mao's political theories will stand as landmarks in history but whether or not they offer to other countries an effective solution to their problems remains to be seen. Mao himself recognized this fact when he said that a thousand years hence not only he but Marx might appear somewhat out of date.

BIBLIOGRAPHY. The two best-documented biographies of Mao Tse-tung are STUART R. SCHRAM, *Mao Tse-tung*, rev. ed. (1967); and JEROME CH'EN, *Mao and the Chinese Revolution* (1965). The account of Mao's life by ROBERT PAYNE, *Portrait of a Revolutionary: Mao Tse-tung* (1961), is somewhat more impressionistic, but draws on the author's personal encounters with Mao. The most vivid account of Mao's youth is his own autobiography, as recounted to EDGAR SNOW in 1936, and published in *Red Star over China* (many editions from 1937). Other important books dealing with aspects of Mao's rise to power are BENJAMIN I. SCHWARTZ, *Chinese Communism and the Rise of Mao* (1951, reprinted in paperback 1967), dealing primarily with the late 1920s and early 1930s; and CHALMERS A. JOHNSON, *Peasant Nationalism and Communist Power: The Emergence of Revolutionary China 1937–1945* (1962). Regarding Mao Tse-tung's thought, the most complete collection of source materials available in English is to be found in the four-volume *Selected Works of Mao Tse-tung*, published by the Foreign Languages Press in Peking, supplemented by *Selected Readings from the Works of Mao Tse-tung*, published by the Foreign Languages Press in 1967, which duplicates some of the items in the *Selected Works*, but also contains several important speeches made since 1949. The official version of the *Selected Works* is incomplete, and has been extensively rewritten as compared to the original contemporary versions of many of the items included. The first attempt to compile a complete variorum edition of Mao's writings down to 1949 in Chinese was the ten-volume set of *Collected Writings of Mao Tse-tung* published in 1971–72 in Tokyo under the editorship of MINORU TAKEUCHI. Two contrasting interpretations are that of STUART R. SCHRAM (ed.), *The Political Thought of Mao Tse-tung*, rev. ed. (1969); and that of ARTHUR A. COHEN, *The Communism of Mao Tse-tung* (1964). The latter book examines Mao's ideas in the context of the Leninist and Stalinist tradition, and is primarily concerned with evaluating the extent of his original contributions to the theory and practice of revolution; the former, which also contains an anthology of extracts from Mao's writings, stresses rather the link between his thought and the Chinese tradition, as well as the circumstances of the Chinese Revolution.

(S.R.S.)

Maps and Mapping

Maps and charts are representations of features on the earth's surface drawn to scale. Globes are maps presented on the surface of a sphere. The definition can be extended to include representations of the moon, Mars, and other bodies for which increasing data are becoming available. Star charts and related celestial plats, long used for navigation and astronomical studies, might also be included.

In order to imply the elements of accurate relationships, and some formal method of projecting the spherical subject to a map plane, further qualifications might be applied to the definition. The tedious and somewhat abstract statements resulting from attempts to define maps and charts precisely are more likely to cause confusion than clarity. The terms map, chart, and plat are used somewhat interchangeably. The connotations of use, however, are distinctive: charts for navigation purposes (nautical and aeronautical), plats (in a property-boundary sense) for land-line references and ownership, and maps for general reference.

Cartography is the art and science of making maps and charts. As such, it is allied with geography in its concern with the broader aspects of the earth and its life. In early times cartographic efforts were more artistic than scientific and factual. As man explored and recorded his environment, the quality of his maps and charts improved. These lines of Jonathan Swift were inspired by early maps:

> So geographers, in Afric maps,
> With savage pictures fill their gaps,
> And o'er unhabitable downs;
> Place elephants for want of towns.

Topographic maps are graphic representations of natural and man-made features of parts of the earth's surface plotted to scale. They show the shape of land and record elevations above sea level, lakes, streams and other hydrographic features, roads and other works of man. In short, they provide a complete inventory of the terrain and important information for all activities involving the use and development of the land. They provide the bases for specialized maps, and data for compilation of generalized maps of smaller scale.

Nautical charts are maps of coastal and marine areas, providing information for navigation. They include depth curves or soundings or both; aids to navigation such as buoys, channel markers, and lights; islands, rocks, wrecks, reefs and other hazards; and significant features of the coastal areas, including promontories, church steeples, water towers, and other features helpful in determining positions from offshore.

Aeronautical charts provide essential data for the pilot and air navigator. They are, in effect, small-scale topographic maps on which current information on aids to navigation have been superimposed. To facilitate rapid recognition and orientation, principal features of the land that would be visible from an aircraft in flight are shown to the exclusion of less important details.

This article is organized into the following sections:

I. History of cartography

Centuries before the Christian era, Babylonians drew maps on clay tablets, of which the oldest specimens found so far have been dated about 2300 BC. This is the earliest positive evidence of graphic representations of parts of the earth; it may be assumed that map making goes back much further and that it began among nonliterate peoples. It is logical to assume that men very early made efforts to communicate with each other regarding their environment by scratching routes, locations, and hazards on the ground, and later on bark and skins.

Maps on clay tablets

The earliest maps must have been based on personal experience and familiarity with local features. They doubtless showed routes to neighbouring tribes; where game, water, salt and other necessities might be found; and the locations of enemies and other dangers. Nomadic life stimulated such efforts by recording ways to cross deserts and mountains; the relative locations of summer and winter pastures; and dependable springs, wells, and other vital information.

Markings on cave walls associated with paintings by primitive man have been identified by some archaeologists as attempts to show the game trails of the animals depicted, though there is no general agreement on this. Similarly, networks of lines scratched on certain bone tablets could possibly represent hunting trails, but there is definitely no conclusive evidence that the tablets are indeed maps.

There are, however, numerous examples of not yet literate peoples showing surprising aptitudes in depicting essential features of their localities and travels. During Capt. Charles Wilkes's exploration of the South Seas in the 1840s, a friendly islander drew a good sketch of the whole Tuamoto Archipelago on the deck of the captain's bridge. In North America the Pawnee Indians were reputed to have used star charts painted on elk skin to guide them on night marches across the plains. Montezuma is said to have given Cortés a map of the whole Mexican gulf area painted on cloth, while Pedro de Gamboa reported that the Incas used sketch maps and cut some in stone to show relief features. Many specimens of early Eskimo sketchmaps on skin, wood, and bone have been found.

Maps in the New World

MAPS AND GEOGRAPHY IN THE ANCIENT WORLD

The oldest maps. The earliest specimen that is indisputably a portrayal of land features thus far discovered is the Babylonian tablet previously referred to; certain land drawings found in Egypt and paintings discovered in early tombs are nearly as old. It is quite probable that these two civilizations developed their mapping skills more or less concurrently and in similar directions. Both were vitally concerned with the fertile areas of their river valleys and therefore doubtless made surveys and plats soon after settled communities were established. Later they made plats for the construction of canals, roads, and temples—the equivalent of today's engineering plans.

A tablet unearthed in Iraq some years ago shows the earth as a disk surrounded by water with Babylon as its centre. Aside from this specimen, dating from about 1000 BC, there appear to have been rather few attempts by Babylonians and Egyptians to show the form and extent of the earth as a whole. Their map making was preoccupied with more practical needs, such as the establishment of boundaries. Not until the time of the Greek philosopher-geographers did speculations and conclusions as to the nature of the earth begin to take form.

Greek maps and geography. The Greeks were outstanding among peoples of the ancient world for their pursuit and development of geographic knowledge. The shortage of arable land in their own region led to maritime exploration and the development of commerce and colonies. By 600 BC Miletus, on the Aegean, had become a centre of geographical knowledge, as well as of cosmographical speculation.

Hecataeus, a scholar of Miletus, probably produced the first book on geography about 500 BC. A generation later Herodotus, from more extensive studies and wider travels, expanded upon it. A historian with geographic leanings, Herodotus among the other things recorded an early circumnavigation of Africa by Phoenicians. He also improved on the delineation of the shape and extent of the then-known regions of the world and declared the Caspian to be an inland sea, opposing the prevailing view that it was part of the "northern oceans" (Figure 1).

Herodotus

accurate enough to show relative locations on the very small-scale, rudimentary maps that existed.

The eighth volume was a most important contribution, containing instructions for preparing maps of the world and discussions on mathematical geography and other fundamental principles of cartography. Ptolemy's map of the world as it was then known marked the culmination of Greek cartography, as well as a compendium of accumulated knowledge of the earth's features at that time (Figure 2).

The Roman period. Although Ptolemy lived and worked at the time of Rome's greatest influence, he was a Greek and essentially a product of that civilization, as was the great library at Alexandria. His works greatly influenced the development of geography, which he defined in map-making terms: "representation in picture of the whole known world, together with the phenomena contained therein." This had considerable influence in direct-

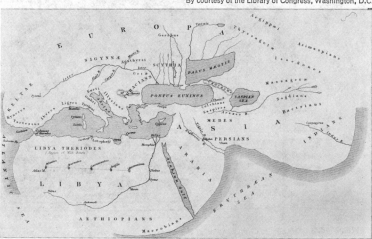

Figure 1: Herodotus' map of the world.

Although Hecataeus regarded the earth as a flat disk surrounded by ocean, Herodotus and his followers questioned the concept and proposed a number of other possible forms. Indeed, the philosophers and scholars of the time appear to have been preoccupied for a number of years with discussions on the nature and extent of the world. Some modern scholars attribute the first hypothesis of a spherical earth to Pythagoras (6th century BC) or Parmenides (5th century). The idea gradually developed into a consensus over many years. In any case by the mid-4th century the theory of a spherical earth was well accepted among Greek scholars, and about 350 BC Aristotle formulated six arguments to prove that the earth was, in truth, a sphere. From that time forward, the idea of a spherical earth was generally accepted among geographers and other men of science.

About 300 BC Dicaearchus, a disciple of Aristotle, placed an orientation line on the world map, running from west to east through Gibraltar and Rhodes. Eratosthenes, Marinus of Tyre, and Ptolemy successively developed the reference-line principle until a reasonably comprehensive system of parallels and meridians, as well as methods of projecting them, had been achieved.

The age of Ptolemy. The greatest figure of the ancient world in the advancement of geography and cartography was Claudius Ptolemaeus (Ptolemy; AD 90–168). An astronomer and mathematician, he spent many years studying at the library in Alexandria, the greatest repository of scientific knowledge at that time. His monumental work, the *Guide to Geography* (*Gēographikē hyphēgēsis*), was produced in eight volumes. The first volume discussed basic principles and dealt with map projection and globe construction. The next six volumes carried a listing of the names of some 8,000 places and their approximate latitudes and longitudes. Except for a few that were made by observations, the greater number of these locations were determined from older maps, with approximations of distances and directions taken from travellers. They were

ing scholars toward the specifics of map construction and away from the more abstract and philosophical aspects of geography.

One fundamental error that had far-reaching effects was attributed to Ptolemy—an underestimation of the size of the earth. He showed Europe and Asia as extending over half the globe, instead of the 130 degrees of their true extent. Similarly, the span of the Mediterranean ultimately was proven to be 20 degrees less than Ptolemy's estimate. So lasting was Ptolemy's influence that 17 centuries later Columbus underestimated the distances to Cathay and India partly from a recapitulation of this basic error.

Ptolemy's fundamental error

A fundamental difference between the Greek and Roman philosophies was indicated by their maps. The Romans were less interested in mathematical geography and tended toward more practical needs for military campaigns and provincial administration. They reverted to the older concepts of a disk-shaped world for maps of great areas because they met their needs and were easier to read and understand.

The Roman general Marcus Vipsanius Agrippa constructed a map of the world, prior to Ptolemy's time, based on surveys of the then-extensive system of Roman military roads. References to many other Roman maps have been found, but very few actual specimens survived the Dark Ages. It is quite probable that the Peutinger Table, a parchment scroll showing the roads of the Roman world, was originally based on Agrippa's map, as subjected to several revisions through medieval times.

The fall of Rome. The tragic turn of world events during the first few centuries of the Christian era wrought havoc to the accumulated knowledge and progress of mankind. As with other fields of science and technology, progress in geography and cartography was abruptly curtailed. After Ptolemy's day, there even appears to have been a retrogression, as exemplified by the Roman trend away from the mathematical approach to mapping.

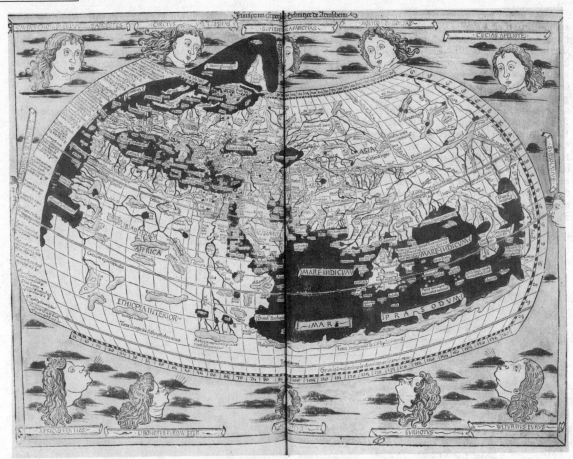

Figure 2: Ptolemy's map of the world, as printed at Ulm, 1482.
By courtesy of the Library of Congress, Washington, D.C.

Great accumulations of documents and maps were destroyed or lost, and the survival of a large part of Ptolemy's work was probably due to its great prestige and popularity. The only other major work on mapping to survive was Strabo's earlier treatise, albeit with some changes from recopying. Few of the maps and related works of the ancient world have come down to us in their original forms. The tendencies to revise and even recapitulate, when copying manuscripts, is readily understood. Doubtless, the factual content was improved more often than not, but a residual confusion remains when the specimen at hand may be either a true copy of an ancient document or a medieval scholar's version of the subject matter.

MEDIEVAL MAPS AND CHARTS

Progress in cartography during the early Middle Ages was slight. The medieval map maker seems to have been dominated by the church, reflecting in his work the ecclesiastical dogmas and interpretations of Scripture. In fact, during the 6th century Constantine of Antioch created a "Christian topography" depicting the earth as a flat disk. Thus, the Roman map of the world, along with other concepts, continued as authoritative for many centuries. A contemporary Chinese map shows that country occupying most of the world, while the Roman Empire dominates most other maps produced during early Christian times.

Later medieval map makers were clearly aware of the earth's sphericity, but for the most part, maps remained small and schematic, as exemplified by the T and O renderings, so-named from the stylized T-form of the major water bodies separating the continents and the O as the circumfluent ocean surrounding the world. The orientation with east at the top of the map was often used, as the word (orientation) suggests.

Portolan charts   Toward the end of the medieval period a significant advance in cartography was achieved in the portolan sea charts. Named for the portolano, or pilot book listing

sailing courses, ports, and anchorages, they were much in demand for the increasing trade and shipping. Genoa, Pisa, Venice, Majorca, and Barcelona, among others, cooperated in providing information garnered from their pilots and captains. From repeated revisions, and new surveys by compass, the portolan charts eventually surpassed all preceding maps in accuracy and reliability.

Many specimens of portolan charts have survived. Though primarily of areas of the Mediterranean and Black Sea, some covered the Atlantic as far as Ireland, and others the western coast of Africa. Their most striking feature is the system of compass roses (Figure 3), showing directions from various points, and lines showing shortest navigational routes.

Another phenomenon of the late Middle Ages was the great enthusiasm generated by the travels of Marco Polo in the 1270s and 1280s. New information about faraway places, and the stimulation of interest in world maps, promoted their sale and circulation. Marco Polo's experiences also kindled the desire for travel and exploration in others and were, perhaps, a harbinger of the great age of discovery and exploration.

During Europe's Dark Ages Islāmic and Chinese cartography made progress. The Arabs translated Ptolemy's treatises and carried on his tradition. Two Islāmic scholars deserve special note. Ibn Haukal wrote a *Book of Ways and Provinces* illustrated with maps, and al-Idrisi constructed a world map in AD 1154 for the Christian king Roger of Sicily, showing better information on Asian areas than had been available theretofore. In Baghdad astronomers used the compass long before Europeans, studied the obliquity of the ecliptic, and measured a part of the earth's meridian. Their sexagesimal (based on 60) system has dominated cartography since, in the concept of a 360-degree circle.

Chinese map making, like so many other aspects of art and science, developed independently. The oldest known Chinese map is dated about AD 1137. Most of the area had been mapped in crude form before the arrival of the

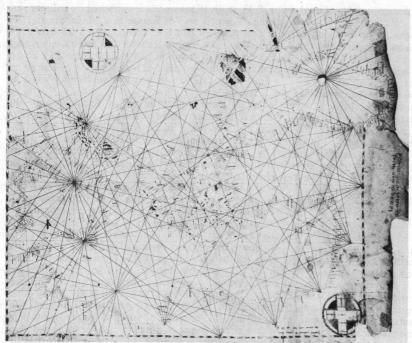

Figure 3: Portolan chart of the eastern Mediterranean area by Petrus Vesconte, 1311.
Archivio di Stato di Firenze, Carte nautiche n. 1. Autorizzazione del Ministero dell'Interno, Direzione
Generale degli Archivi di Stato (Italia), parere n. 526 del 1971

Europeans. The Jesuit missionaries of the 16th century found enough information to prepare an atlas, and Chinese maps thereafter were influenced by the West.

THE AGE OF DISCOVERY AND EXPLORATION

Revival of Ptolemy. The fall of Byzantium sent many refugees to Italy, among them scholars who had preserved some of the old Greek manuscripts, including Ptolemy's *Geography*, from destruction. The rediscovery of this great work came at a fortunate time. The recent development of a printing industry capable of handling map reproduction, made possible its circulation far beyond the few scholars who otherwise would have enjoyed access to it. This, together with a general reawakening of scholarship and interest in exploration, created a golden era of cartography.

The *Geography* was translated into Latin about 1405. Although it had not been completely lost (the Arabs had preserved portions of it) recovery of the complete work, with maps, greatly stimulated general interest in cartography. About 500 copies of Ptolemy were printed at Bologna in 1477, followed by other editions printed in Germany and Italy. The printing process, in addition to permitting the wide diffusion of geographic knowledge, retained the fidelity of the original works. By 1600, 31 Latin or Italian editions had been printed.

Maps of the discoveries. Progress in other technologies such as navigation, ship design and construction, instruments for observation and astronomy, and general use of the compass tended continuously to improve existing map information, as well as to encourage further exploration and discovery. Accordingly, geographic knowledge was profoundly increased during the 15th and 16th centuries. The great discoveries of Columbus, da Gama, Vespucci, Cabot, Magellan, and others gradually transformed the world maps of those days. "Modern" maps were added to later editions of Ptolemy. The earliest was a map of northern Europe drawn at Rome in 1427 by Claudius Claussön Swart, a Danish geographer. Cardinal Nicholas Krebs drew the first modern map of Germany, engraved in 1491. Martin Waldseemüller of St. Dié prepared an edition with more than 20 modern maps in 1513. Maps showing new discoveries and information were at last transcending the classical treatises of Ptolemy.

Characteristics of new maps. The most important aspect of postmedieval maps was their increasing accuracy, made possible by continuing exploration. Another significant characteristic was a trend toward artistic and colourful rendition, for the maps still had many open areas in which the artist could indulge his imagination. The cartouche, or title block, became more and more elaborate, amounting to a small work of art. Many of the map editions of this age have become collector's items. The first map printings were made from woodcuts. Later, they were engraved on copper, a process that made it possible to reproduce much finer lines. The finished plates were inked and wiped, leaving ink in the cut lines. Dampened paper was then pressed on the plate, and into the engraved line work, resulting in very fine impressions. The process remained the basis of fine map reproduction until the comparatively recent advent of photolithography.

The *Cosmographiae*, textbooks of geography, astronomy, history, and natural sciences, all illustrated with maps and figures, first appeared in the 16th century. One of the earliest and best known was that of Petrus Apianus in 1524, the popularity of which extended to 15 more editions. That of Sebastian Münster, published in 1544, was larger and remained authoritative and in demand until the end of the century, reflecting the general eagerness of the times for learning, especially geography.

Cartographers of the discoveries. The foremost cartographer of the age of discovery was Gerardus Mercator of Flanders. Well-educated and a student of Gemma Frisius, of Louvain, a noted cosmographer, he became a maker of globes and maps. His map of Europe, published in 1554, and his development of the projection that bears his name, made him famous. The Mercator projection (see below *Cylindrical projections*) solved an age-old problem of navigators, enabling them to plot bearings as straight lines.

Other well-known and productive cartographers of the Dutch-Flemish school are Abraham Ortelius of Antwerp, who prepared the first modern world atlas in 1570, and Jadocus Hondius. Early Dutch maps were among the best for artistic expression, composition, and rendering. Juan de la Cosa, the owner of Columbus' flagship, "Santa María," in 1500 produced a map recording Columbus' discoveries, the landfall of Cabral in Brazil, Cabot's voyage to Canada, and da Gama's route to the Indies. The first map showing North and South America clearly separated from Asia was produced in 1507 by Martin Waldseemüller. An immense map, 4½ by 8 feet, printed in 12 sheets, it is probably the first map on which the name America appeared, indicating that Waldseemüller was impressed

Printing of Ptolemy's Geography

Mercator

by the account written by the Florentine navigator Amerigo Vespucci.

In 1529, Diego Ribero, cosmographer to the king of Spain, made a new chart of the world on which the vast extent of the Pacific was first shown. Survivors of Magellan's circumnavigation of the world had arrived in Seville in 1522, giving Ribero much new information.

The first known terrestrial globe that has survived was made by Martin Behaim at Nürnberg in 1492. Many others were made throughout the 16th century. The principal centres of cartographic activity were Spain, Portugal, Italy, the Rhineland, the Netherlands, and Switzerland. England and France, with their growing maritime and colonial power, were soon to become primary map and chart centres. Capt. John Smith's maps of Virginia and New England, the first to come from the English colonies, were published in London in 1612.

18TH CENTURY TO THE PRESENT

The new cartography.   A reformation of cartography that evolved during the 18th century was characterized by scientific trends and more accurate detail. Monsters, lions, and swash lines disappeared and were replaced by more factual content. Soon, the only decorative features were in the cartouche and around the borders. The map interiors contained all the increasing information available, often with explanatory notes and attempts to show the respective reliabilities of some portions.

Appli-cation of science to map making

Where map makers formerly had sought quick, profitable output based on information obtained from other maps and reports of travellers and explorers, the new French cartographers were scientists, often men of rank and independent means. For expensive ventures, such as the triangulation of two degrees of a meridian to determine the earth's size more accurately, they were subsidized by the king or the French Academy. Similar trends were developing across Europe.

The new cartography was also based on better instruments, with the telescope playing an important part in raising the quality of astronomical observations. Surveys of much higher orders of accuracy were now feasible. The development of the chronometer (an accurate timepiece) made the computation of longitude much less laborious than before; much more information on islands and coastal features came to the map and chart makers.

The rise of national surveys.   The development in Europe of power-conscious national states, with standing armies, professional officers, and engineers, stimulated an outburst of topographic activity in the 18th century, reinforced to some extent by increasing civil needs for basic data. Many countries of Europe began to undertake the systematic topographic mapping of their territories. Such surveys required facilities and capabilities far beyond the means of private cartographers who had theretofore provided for most map needs. Originally exclusively military, national survey organizations gradually became civilian in character. The Ordnance Survey of Britain, the Institut Géographique National of France, and the Landestopographie of Switzerland are examples.

In other countries, such as the United States, where defense considerations were not paramount, civilian organizations—*e.g.*, the U.S. Geological Survey and the National Ocean Survey—were originally assigned responsibility for domestic mapping tasks. Only when World War II brought requirements for the mapping of many foreign areas did the U.S. military become involved on a large scale, with the expansion of the Oceanographic Office (navy), Aeronautical Chart Service (air force), and the U.S. Army Topographic command.

Surveys of colonies

Elaborate national surveys were undertaken only in certain countries. The rest of the world remained largely unmapped until World War II. In some instances colonial areas were mapped by military forces, but except for the British Survey of India, such efforts usually provided piecemeal coverage, or generalized and sketchy data. Some important national surveys will be outlined briefly.

France.   The work in France was organized by the French Academy, and in 1748 the *Carte Géométrique de la France*, comprising 182 sheets, was authorized. Most of the field observations were accomplished by military personnel. The new map of France as a whole, drawn after the new positions had been computed, caused Louis XV to remark that the more accurate data lost more territory than his wars of conquest had gained. Napoleon, an ardent map enthusiast, planned a great survey of Europe on a 1:100,000 scale, which was well under way when he was overthrown.

Britain.   During the 18th century Britain became the foremost maritime power of Europe, and the Admiralty sponsored many developments in charting as well as improvements in navigation facilities. Because of the Admiralty's prestige, other maritime nations accepted its proposal that Greenwich be the prime meridian for longitude reference. Other achievements in early oceanography were Edmond Halley's magnetic chart that has been continuously revised from new data. Later similar charts for currents, tides, and prevailing winds were developed.

French progress in mapping stimulated the English to start a national survey, which was completed in 1787. The Ordnance Survey was organized in 1791, and the first sheet, on the scale of one inch to the mile, was published in 1801. Over a century ago the original coverage was completed and a new series, of six inches to the mile, was begun; England was soon the best mapped country in the world. An earlier "first" was John Ogilby's *Brittania* published in 1675, an atlas of road strip maps plotted by odometer and compass, presaging the modern road map.

Other countries.   A survey of Spain was started in the 18th century. Surveys of several German principalities were combined into the Reichskarte at 1/100,000 scale after unification. A topographic survey of Switzerland was begun in 1832. An Austrian series was started in 1806, from which the Specialkarte, later considered the most detailed series of Europe, were derived. In China, under the Communist regime, survey and cartography groups have provided coverage of much of the country with a new 1:50,000-scale map series. Japan established an Imperial Land Survey in 1888. By 1925, topographical coverage of the home islands, with a scale of 1:50,000, was complete.

International Map of the World (IMW).   The International Geographical Congress in 1891 proposed that the participating countries collaborate in the production of a 1:1,000,000 scale map of the world. Specifications and format were soon established, but production was slow in the earlier years, since it was first necessary to complete basic surveys for the required data, and during and after World War II, there was little interest in pursuing the project. The intention to complete the series was recently re-established, however, and many countries have returned to the task.

World War II and after.   World War I, and to a much greater extent World War II, brought great progress in mapping, particularly of the unmapped parts of the earth; an appraisal by the U.S. Air Force indicated that less than 10 percent of the world in 1940 was mapped in sufficient detail for even the meagre requirements of pilot charts. A major program of aerial photography and reconnaissance mapping, that became known as the trimetrogen method, was developed. Vast areas of the unmapped parts of the world were covered during the war years, and the resulting World Aeronautical Charts have provided generalized information for other purposes since that time. Many countries have used the basic data to publish temporary map coverage until their more detailed surveys can be completed.

World Aeronautical Charts

International cooperation.   The Cold War atmosphere of the 1940s and 1950s promoted a continuation of militarily oriented mapping activity. Both NATO and Warsaw Pact countries continued to improve their maps; NATO developed common symbols, scales, and formats, so that maps could be readily exchangeable among the forces of member countries. Postwar economic development programs, in which maps were needed for planning road, railroad, and reservoir constructions, also stimulated much work. The United Nations provides advisory assistance in mapping to countries wishing it.

Among other collaborations, the Inter-American Geodetic Survey, in which the U.S. Army provides instruction and logistic support for mapping, was organized. Although this cooperation primarily involved Latin American countries, similar arrangements were made with individual countries in other parts of the world. Cooperation and exchange of data in hydrographic surveys, aeronautical charting, and other fields has continued.

The remaining tasks. Although some terrain data are available for practically all of the world, the data for many sectors remain sketchy. Surveys by the several countries active there are in progress in Antarctica, but the continent will not be completely mapped for some years. The goal of most countries is to achieve adequate coverage for general development needs. Much remains to be done. Even in countries like the U.S. that have not yet completed the initial coverage, many of the areas mapped in earlier years are already in need of revision. Thus, even when mapping is completed, requirements for greater detail and revision will continue to make demands upon the funds available.

Recent technology. Aerial photography, which permits accurate and detailed work within feasible cost ranges, has dominated basic mapping in recent years. During World War I aerial photography was used for reconnaissance mapping, and after the war rapid progress was made in optics, cameras, plotting devices, and related equipment. By World War II much of the highly sophisticated equipment now currently in use had been designed. Electronic distance-measuring devices have made field surveys easier and more accurate, while much improved circle graduation has made theodolites (transits) lighter as well as more precise. Computers and automation, which together have transformed the mapping procedures of yesterday, are described below in the section *Modern map-making techniques.*

II. Map making

ELEMENTS OF MAPS AND CHARTS

Design and planning. Map design is a twofold process: (1) the determination of user requirements, with attendant decisions as to map content and detail, and (2) the arrangement of content, involving publication scale, standards of treatment, symbolizations, colours, style, and other factors. To some extent, user requirements obviously affect standards of treatment, such as publication scale. Otherwise, the latter elements are largely determined on the basis of efficiency, legibility, aesthetic considerations, and traditional practices.

In earlier productions by individual cartographers or small groups, personal judgments determined the nature of the end product, usually with due respect for conventional standards. Map design for large programs such as the various national map series of today, is quite formal by comparison. In most countries, the requirements of official as well as private users are carefully studied, in conjunction with costs and related factors, when considering possible changes or additions to the current standards.

Requirements of military agencies often have a decisive influence on map design, since it is desirable to avoid the expense of maintaining both civil and military editions of maps. International organizations and committees are additional factors in determining map design. The fact that development of changes in design and content of national map series may become rather involved induces some reluctance to change, as does the fact that map stocks are usually printed in quantities intended to last for ten or more years. Also, frequent changes in treatments result in extensive overhauls at reprint time, with consequent inconsistencies among the standing editions.

Planning for the production of a national series involves both technical and program considerations. Technical planning involves the choice of a contour interval (the elevation separating adjacent contour lines, or lines of constant elevation), which in turn determines the height of aerial photography and other technical specifications for each project. The sequence of mapping steps, or operational phases, is determined by the overall technical precedures that have been established to achieve the most efficiency.

Margin note, left: Study of user requirements

The program aspects of planning involve fiscal allotments, priorities, schedules, and related matters.

Production controls also play important roles in large programs, where schedules must be balanced with capacities available in the respective phases to avoid backlogs, or dormant periods between the mapping steps. Considering that from authorization to final printing, topographic maps may require two years or more to complete, the importance of careful planning is evident. Many factors, including the weather, can converge to cause delays.

Map scales and classifications. Map scale refers to the size of the representation on the map as compared to the size of the object on the ground. The scale generally used in architectural drawings, for example, is ¼ inch to one foot, which means that one quarter of an inch on the drawing equals one foot on the building being drawn. Scale models of buildings, railroads, and other objects may be one inch to several feet. Maps cover more extensive areas and it is usually convenient to express the scale by a representative fraction or proportion, as 1/63,360, 1:63,360, or "one-inch-to-one-mile." The scale of a map is smaller than that of another map when its scale denominator is larger: thus, 1:1,000,000 is a smaller scale than 1:100,000. Most maps carry linear, or bar, scales in one or more margin or in the title blocks.

In rare instances, reference may be made to the areal scale of a map, as opposed to its more normal linear scale. In such cases, the denominator of the fractional reference would be the square of the denominator of the linear scale.

The linear scale may vary, particularly on maps of quite small scale. Variations in the scale of a map because of the spherical surface it represents may, for practical purposes, be considered as nil. On maps of very large scale, such as 1:24,000 such distortions are negligible (considerably less than variations in the paper from fluctuations of humidity). Precise measurements for engineering purposes are usually restricted to maps of that scale or larger. As maps descend in scale, and distortions inherent to their projection of the spherical surface increase, less accurate measurements of distances may be expected.

Maps may be classified according to scale, content, or derivation. The latter refers to whether a map represents an original survey or has been derived from other maps or source data. Some contain both original and derived elements, usually explained in their footnotes. Producing agencies, technical committees, and international organizations, have variously classed maps as large, medium, or small scale. In general, large scale means inch-to-mile and larger, small scale, 1:1,000,000 and smaller, leaving the intermediate field as medium scale. As with most relative terms, these can occasionally lead to confusions but are useful as one practical way to classify maps.

The nature of a map's content, as well as its purpose, provides a primary basis of classification. The terms aeronautical chart, geologic, soil, forest, road, weather, etc., map, make obvious their respective contents and purposes. Maps are therefore often classified by the primary purposes they serve. Topographic maps usually form the background for geologic, soil, and similar thematic maps and provide primary elements of the bases upon which many other kinds of maps are compiled.

Map projections. A great variety of map projections has been devised to provide for the various properties that may be desired in maps. In effect, a projection is a systematic method of drawing the earth's meridians and parallels on a flat surface. Some projections have equal-area properties, while others provide for conformal delineations, in which, for small areas, the shape is practically the same as it would be on a globe. Only on a globe can areas and shapes be represented with true fidelity. On flat maps of very large areas, distortions are inevitable. These effects may be minimized by selecting the projection best suited to the purpose of the map to be produced.

Most types of projection can be grouped according to their geometrical derivations as cylindrical, conic, or azimuthal (Figure 4). A few cannot be so related, or are combinations of these. Terms such as network, graticule, or grid might have been preferable to describe the transposition of meridians and parallels from globe to flat sur-

Margin note, right: Types of classification

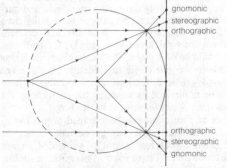

Figure 4: Derivations of basic projections.

cylindrical   conic   azimuthal

face, since few systems are actually derived by projection, and, most in fact have been formulated by analytical and mathematical processes. The term projection however, is well established and has some merit in helping the layman to understand the problems and solutions. Tables for the construction of the commonly used projections have been developed by mapping agencies.

Cylindrical projections. These projections treat the earth as a cylinder, in which parallels are horizontal lines and meridians appear as vertical lines. The familiar Mercator projection is of this class and has many advantages in spite of great distortions it causes in the higher latitudes. Compass bearings may be plotted as straight segments on these projections, which have been traditionally used for nautical charts. On cylindrical projections places of similar latitude appear at the same height. Parallels and meridians may, if desired, be omitted from the body of the map and simply indexed at the margins, while lettering can be placed horizontally rather than in a curve. Among the variations of cylindrical projections is the Transverse Mercator, in which the axis of the cylinder is parallel to the Equator, a treatment which has advantages in drawing maps that are long in the north–south direction.

Conic projections. This group is derived from a projection of the globe on a cone drawn with the point above either the North or South Pole and tangent to the earth at some standard or selected parallel. Occasionally the cone is arranged to actually intersect the earth at two closely spaced standard parallels. A polyconic projection, used in large-scale map series, treats each band of maps as part of a cone tangent to the globe at the particular latitude.

Azimuthal, or zenithal, projection. These picture a portion of the earth as a flattened disk, tangent to the earth at a specified point, as viewed from a point at the centre of the earth, on the opposite side of the earth's surface, or from a point somewhere out in space. If the perspective is from the centre of the earth the projection is called gnomonic; if from the far side of the earth's surface, it is stereographic; if from space, it is called orthographic (Figure 5).

Modified from I. Fisher and O.M. Miller, *World Maps and Globes*

gnomonic
stereographic
orthographic

orthographic
stereographic
gnomonic

Figure 5: Basis of gnomonic, stereographic, and orthographic projections.

Mercator projection (margin)

A type of projection often used to show distances and directions from a particular city is the Azimuthal Equidistant. Such measurements are accurate or true only from the selected central point to any other point of interest.

The polar projection is an azimuthal projection drawn to show Arctic and Antarctic areas. It is based on a plane perpendicular to the earth's axis, in contact with the North or South Pole. It is limited to 10 or 15 degrees from the poles. Parallels of latitude are concentric circles, while meridians are radiating straight lines.

Development of reference spheroids. Tables from which map projections of the more familiar kinds may be plotted have been available for some years and have been based on the best determinations of the size and shape of the earth available at the time of their compilation. The dimensions of Clarke's Spheroid (by the British geodesist Alexander Ross Clarke) of 1866 have been much used in polyconic and other tables. A later determination by Clarke in 1880 reflected the several geodetic surveys conducted during the interim. An International Ellipsoid of Reference was adopted by the Geodetic and Geophysical Union in 1924 for worldwide application.

Clarke's Spheroid (margin)

With the recent development of electronic distance-measuring systems, greater progress has been made in geodetic surveys. With satellite observation and international collaborations now in progress, an accurate determination of the size and shape of the earth should be made during the next few years. It will then be possible to adjust all existing primary geodetic surveys and astronomic observations to a single world datum.

Geographic and plane coordinate systems. The standard geographic coordinate system of the world involves latitudes north or south of the Equator and longitudes east or west of the Prime Reference Meridian of Greenwich. Map and control point references are stated in degrees, minutes, and seconds carried to the number of decimal points commensurate with the accuracy to which locations have been made.

Geodetic surveys, being of extensive areas, must be adjusted for the earth's curvature and reductions made to mean sea level for scale. The computations are therefore somewhat involved. As a convenience for engineers and surveyors, many countries have established official plane coordinate systems for each province, state, or sector thereof. By this means, all surveys can be "tied" to control points in the system, without transposition to geographic coordinates.

In large countries such as the United States, two basic projections are commonly selected to provide systems with minimum distortions for each state or region. For those long in N–S dimension, the Transverse Mercator is generally used, while for those long in E–W direction, the Lambert conformal (intersecting cone) projection is usually employed. In the case of large-size regions, two or more zones may be established to limit distortions. Positions of geodetic control points have been computed on the plane coordinate systems and have been made available in published lists.

Basic data for compilation. Maps may be compiled from other maps, usually of larger scale, or may be produced from original surveys and photogrammetric compilations. The former are sometimes referred to as derived maps and may include information from various sources, in addition to the maps from which they are principally drawn. Most small-scale series, such as the International Map of the World and World Aeronautical Charts, are compiled from existing information, though new data are occasionally produced to strengthen areas for which little or doubtful information, exists. Thus, compiled maps may contain fragments of original information, while those representing original surveys may include some existing data of higher order, such as details from a city plat.

Road maps, produced by the millions and familiar to everyone, are compiled from road surveys, topographic maps, and aerial photography. City maps often represent original surveys, made principally to control engineering plans and construction. Some are, however, compiled from enlargements of topographic maps of the area.

Road and city map compilations (margin)

Notations regarding the sources from which they were drawn are usually carried on compiled maps. This sometimes includes a reliability diagram showing the areas for which good information was available and those that may be less dependable. Comments regarding certain features or areas, that the editor may deem helpful to the user, may be made in the map itself.

Maps reflecting original surveys, such as a national topographic map series, carry standard marginal information. Date of aerial photography, process and instrumentation employed, notes regarding control and projection, date of field edit, and other information may be included. References to the availability of adjoining maps and those of other scales or series may also be included. Marginal ticks for intervals of plane coordinate systems, military grids, and other reference features are also shown and appropriately labelled.

Map and chart symbolization. Symbols are the graphic language of maps and charts that has evolved through generations of cartographers. The symbols doubtless had their origins as simple pictograms that gradually developed into the conventions now generally used.

Standardization. Early cartographers recognized that common usages and conventions would minimize confusion and to some extent simplify compilation and engraving. Efforts in this direction were made over the years, but cartographers, being artists of a sort, preferred to vary their styles, and effective standardization was not achieved until comparatively recent times. National agencies in most countries established conventions with due regard to practices in other countries. International Map of the World agreements, NATO conventions, the efforts of the United Nations and of international technical societies, all aid standardization.

Symbols may be broadly classed as planimetric or hypsographic, or may be grouped according to the colours in which they are conventionally printed. Black is used for names and culture, or works of man; blue for water features, or hydrography; brown for relief, or hypsography; green for vegetation classifications; and red for road classes and special information. There are variations, however, particularly in special-purpose series, such as soil and geologic maps. Symbols will also vary, perforce, due to limitations of space in the smaller scales, and the feasibility of drawing some features to actual size in maps of larger scales. Legends explain the less obvious symbols on many maps, while explanatory sheets or booklets are available for most standard series, providing general data as well as symbol information. When less familiar symbols are used on maps they are often labelled to avoid misunderstanding. The general located-object symbol, with label, is often used in preference to specific symbols for such objects as windmills and lookout towers for similar reasons.

Relief treatments. Planimetric features (those shown in "plan," such as streams, shorelines, and roads) are easier to portray than shapes of land and heights above sea level. Mountains were shown on early maps by sketchy lines simulating profile or perspective appearance as envisioned by the cartographer. Little effort was made at true depiction as this was beyond the scope of available information and existing capabilities. Form lines and hachures, among other devices, were also used in attempting to show the land's shape. Hachures are short lines laid down in a pattern to indicate direction of slope. When it became feasible to map rough terrain in more detail, Hachuring hachuring developed into an artistic speciality. Some hachured maps are remarkable for their detail and fidelity, but much of their quality depends on the skill of draftsman or engraver. They are little used now, except where relief is incidental.

Contours are by far the most common and satisfactory means of showing relief (see Figure 6). Contours are lines that connect points of equal elevation. The shorelines of lakes and of the sea are contours. Such lines were little used until the mid-19th century, mainly because surveys had not generally been made in sufficient detail for them to be employed successfully. Mean sea level is the datum to which elevations and contour intervals are generally re-

ferred. If mean sea level were to rise 20 feet the new shoreline would be where the 20-foot contour line is now shown (assuming that all maps on which it is delineated are reasonably accurate).

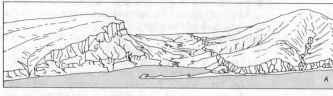

Figure 6: Landscape shown in perspective A is represented with the aid of contour lines on map B.

The quality of contour maps, until recent times, depended largely on the sketching skill of the topographer. In earlier days funds available for topographic mapping were limited, and not much time could be spent in accurate placement. Later, the accurate location of more control points became feasible. An approximate scale of reliability is therefore indicated by the date of a topographic survey, taking into account the respective situations that existed in various countries. Modern surveys, being based on aerial photos and accurate plotting instruments, are generally better in detail and accuracy than earlier surveys. The personal skill of individual topographers, long a factor in map evaluations, has therefore been substantially eliminated.

Hill shading, or shaded relief, layer or altitude tinting, and special manipulations of contouring are other methods of indicating relief. Hill shading requires considerable artistry, as well as the ability to visualize shapes and interpret contours. For a satisfactory result, background contours are a necessary guide to the artist. Hypsographic tinting is relatively easy, particularly since photomechanical etching and other steps can be used to provide negatives for the respective elevation layers. Difficulty in the reproduction process is sometimes a deterrent to the use of treatments involving the manipulation of contours.

Terrain models. In the past, three-dimensional maps were laboriously constructed for studies in military tactics and for many other purposes. They were costly to produce, as contour layers had to be cut and assembled, filled with plaster and painted, after which streams, roads, etc., had to be drawn on the surface. Lettering then was applied and models of large structures, such as buildings and bridges, were added. In view of the time and cost involved in such productions they were sparingly used until recent years when better production methods and materials became available. During and after World War I a process was developed and improved whereby an aluminum sheet was "raised" by tapping along the contours copied on its surface. When the contours selected for tapping were completed, the sheet became, in effect, a mold for shaping plastic sheets to its convolutions. The map was printed on plastic sheets prior to the thermal process of shaping them to the mold. Sets of relief maps were soon produced in this manner for use in schools, military briefings, and many other activities.

During and after World War II the production of plastic relief maps was greatly expanded, while the processes and equipment were further improved and refined. Most

Panto-
graph-
router

significant among these developments was a pantograph-router, which cuts a model from plaster or other suitable material, as the selected contours are followed by the operator on a topographic map. This eliminated the distortions inherent in shaping metal sheets by the tapping process. Selected topographic maps are now published in limited relief editions for military instruction, special displays, and general classroom instruction.

Most relief maps are exaggerated severalfold in the vertical scale. The earth is remarkably flat, when viewed in actual scale, and many significant features would hardly be distinguishable on a map without some vertical exaggeration. Mt. Everest, for example, is actually only one-seventh of 1 percent of the earth's radius in height, or only one-third of an inch at a scale of 1:1,000,000. For this reason, relief is usually shown at five, or even ten times actual scale, depending upon the nature of the area represented. This exaggerated relief scale is always explained in the map legend.

Nomenclature. All possible places and features are identified and labelled to assure maximum map usefulness. Some names must be omitted, particularly from maps of smaller scales, to avoid overcrowding and poor legibility. The editor must decide which names may be eliminated, while arranging placements so that a maximum number may be accommodated.

Geographic names are the most important, and sometimes the most troublesome, part of the map nomenclature as a whole. Research on existing maps and related documents for a given area may reveal different names for the same features, variations in spelling, or ambiguous applications of names. The field engineer often finds that local usage is confused and sometimes controversial. Various types of official organizations have been established to study the problems submitted and decide the forms and applications that are to be used in government maps and documents. This function is exercised in the U.S. by the Board on Geographic Names and in the United Kingdom by the Permanent Committee on Geographical Names.

**Topo-
nymics**

The science of place-names, or toponymics, has become a significant specialty since World War II, and efforts have been made to establish uniform usages and standards of transliteration throughout the world. Renewed interest in completing the remaining sheets of the International Map of the World, collaborations resulting from military alliances, and efforts of committees of international scientific societies and the United Nations have all contributed to these efforts.

At the local levels, however, there are different kinds of problems. The larger scales of most basic topographic map series permit the naming of quite minor hilltops, ridges, streams, and branches, for which designations can be obtained locally. In sparsely settled country, few names in actual use may be obtained for minor features, while in other areas, inquiries may reveal inconsistencies and confusions in both spelling and application of local names. In some areas, for example, local residents may tend to refer to small streams by the name of the present occupant of the headwater area. The occupants of opposite sides of a mountain sometimes refer to it by different names. In coastal areas the waterman and landsman may use different references for the same features.

A prime opportunity for resolving these problems is presented when a topographic map of an area is prepared for publication. By extensive inquiry and documentation and research of local records and deeds, the appropriate form and application of nearly all names can be determined. Publication and distribution of the map as an official document may then tend to solidify local usage and eliminate the confusions that previously existed.

Lettering

Lettering is selected by the map editor in styles and sizes appropriate to the respective features and the relative importance of each. For topographic maps and most others that follow conventional practice, four basic styles of lettering are used in the Western world. The Roman style is generally used for place-names, political divisions, titles, and related nomenclature. Italic is used for lakes, streams, and other water features. Gothic styles are usually applied to land features such as mountains, ridges, and valleys. Man-made works such as highways, railroads, and canals are usually labelled in slope Gothic capitals, but other distinctive styles are often used for these, together with descriptive notes.

The relative importance of map features is reflected in the different sizes of lettering selected to label them. The most prominent places and features are usually shown in capitals, while lesser ones are labelled with lowercase lettering. In the labelling of cities, however, uppercase lettering is often reserved for state or province capitals. County seats are also labelled in this manner on topographic maps of the U.S. For other towns, where lowercase lettering is in order, the sizes selected reflect their relative importance.

TYPES AND USES OF MAPS AND CHARTS

World status of mapping and basic data. Before World War I, only a few countries such as Britain, France, and Germany had detailed maps covering their whole national areas. Now many countries have completed coverage of their territories, while others have carried out small-scale coverage and are beginning engineering surveys in selected areas.

It has been demonstrated that the full potential of map usage in a country, state, or province is not realized until some time after complete coverage has become available. When a modern, detailed map replaces an earlier issue, annual distribution can increase dramatically.

Status of world topographic mapping. Topographic maps provide the basic data for many other kinds, as well as working bases for thematic maps showing geology, soils, and vegetation types. The progress of such mapping in the various parts of the world is therefore a primary indicator of the status of cartography in general. A United Nations survey of the status of world mapping was recently completed. Inquiries were made to the mapping organizations of all member nations regarding the extent of their respective map coverage, publication scales, and related data.

Less than 20 percent of the world's land area is now covered by maps at scales of 1:50,000 and larger. Some of such coverage is culturally obsolescent or of low structural quality. An additional 40 percent is covered by medium-scale topographic maps; *i.e.*, up to 1:250,000 (about four miles to the inch). Some of this is inferior coverage at medium scales, lacking in geodetic control and topographic detail. This is the case with much of China, but most of the mapping is quite adequate for purposes of reconnaissance and as source information for smaller scale maps.

This provides a general indication of the relative reliability of data contained in such world series maps as the 1:1,000,000 scale aeronautical charts and International Maps of the World. Areas of doubtful information are left blank or are drawn with broken lines. In spite of this dearth of reliable data, most of the IMW sheets have been compiled, and most of the aeronautical pilotage charts have been published, to provide navigation continuity across water areas as well as over unmapped parts of the world.

In some areas, however, large-scale topographic maps are not required. Australia, for example, has large-scale coverage only of its populated coastal areas, in the east; in the "outback" areas 1:250,000 scale maps are considered adequate for all foreseeable needs, and a program for their production is well under way. Likewise, large areas of tundra, as in Siberia, deserts in many parts of the world, and other sparsely populated areas may be adequately served with medium- or small-scale coverage until specific development sites require engineering maps.

Nautical charts. Nautical chart coverage of the world leaves much to be desired. Good progress has been made, however, on areas bordering the continents and islands. The Arctic, Antarctic, South Pacific, and South Atlantic oceans are the most deficient in good chart coverage. The Defense Mapping Agency, through agreement with the British Admiralty and other chart-producing countries, maintains worldwide coverage that is constantly updated.

International Hydrographic Bureau

The National Ocean Survey maintains charts of U.S. coastal waters. The International Hydrographic Bureau, based at Monaco, attempts to stimulate cooperation in improvement of hydrographic data in general. This organization's Bathymetric Chart of the Oceans shows existing knowledge and is revised from time to time, as new data are accumulated (see also HYDROGRAPHIC CHARTING).

Aeronautical charts. Coverage of reliable quality parallels the availability of topographic maps that provide the essential terrain and cultural data. For this purpose, good 1:250,000 scale maps contain sufficient information for clearance safety and position identification.

Geodetic surveys. Until recently, the progress of geodetic triangulation, the basic survey method, was more or less limited to areas either covered by good topographic maps or scheduled for mapping. Preparations for cadastral surveys, where land partition problems abound, have occasionally led to early geodetic programs. Coastal and other surveys also require good basic control to be fully effective; however, it is again the developed and heavily populated areas that are encompassed with the best geodetic surveys. Electronic distance-measuring systems have accelerated the progress of geodetic surveys during the 1960s and have extended continental schemes over many ocean areas. International cooperation on satellite triangulation is now in progress, with the prospect that existing triangulation of the continents may soon be tied together and adjusted into a single world datum. The Inter-American Geodetic Survey has made progress in the Americas.

Aerial photography. In addition to other applications, aerial photography provides a useful supplement to topographic maps. Indeed, where maps are not available, aerial photographs invariably serve as map substitutes, in spite of inherent distortions and lack of elevation data. Most of the world is covered by aerial photography.

During World War II the U.S. Air Force photographed vast areas of the world, providing reconnaissance maps that were used as bases for aeronautical charts. Much of this information now forms the basis for small-scale map coverage in still remote areas. The system of photography and mapping became known as the trimetrogon process.

Trimetrogon process

In it, three wide-angle cameras are used to photograph the terrain from horizon to horizon across the line of flight, from an elevation of 20,000 feet. Detail is usually discernible and plottable for several miles on each side of the line of flight, and occasional points, required for photo-triangulation, can be identified farther out. With higher flight capabilities, wider angle cameras, and lenses of fine resolution the progress of aerial photography has been accelerated. Films have been much improved for fineness of emulsion grain and scale stability. Satellite photography, and high-altitude flights with super-wide-angle cameras, are now under way in the remaining areas of the world. Infrared and colour film developments have greatly improved photo-interpretation capabilities, providing much better delineations for coastal charts, geologic maps, timber and soil classifications, and other thematic mapping.

Types of maps and charts available. Although the range of maps and charts now available in many countries is so wide that a complete listing is impractical, any list of principal types would have to include aeronautical (worldwide and national); congressional or political districts; population distribution; geologic (various scales); highways (national and secondary political units); historical; hydrographic (coastal areas; inland waters; foreign waters); national forests; forest types; public land survey plats; soil; topographic and related (national and foreign areas).

The National Atlas of the United States of America, published by the Geological Survey in 1970 contains contributions from all of that country's mapping agencies. Summaries are provided of all thematic and economic data of interest. The atlas also indicates where more detailed information or large-scale specialized maps may be obtained. Many countries have centres where detailed information on existing map series and related data may be obtained. In the U.S. this service is performed by the Map Information Office of the U.S. Geological Survey, which publishes and distributes indexes of each state

showing map coverage and ordering information. Summary data on geodetic control and aerial photography are also maintained.

The situation is less complex in other countries, where mapping activities are concentrated in one or two organizations; *e.g.*, Ordnance Survey in Britain and Institut Géographique National in France. The main agencies can advise where maps produced by others may be obtained. Technical societies maintain large map reference libraries and are prime sources of information, as are the map sections of national libraries and museums.

Government and other mapping agencies. The following are the primary agencies of selected countries having advanced mapping programs.

Principal Mapping Agencies of Selected Countries	
Australia	Division of National Mapping, Department of National Development
Brazil	Servico Geográfico do Exercito
Canada	Surveys and Mapping Branch, Department of Energy, Mines and Resources
Chile	Instituto Geográfico Militar
France	Institut Géographique National
Germany, West	Institut für Landeskunde Geodäsie
Iran	Army Geographic Department and National Geographic Organization
U.K.	Ordnance Survey and Directorate of Overseas Surveys
U.S.S.R.	Glavnoye Upravlenie Geodezii i Kartografii

Military agencies play large roles in the mapping activities of many countries. Frequently, a small cadre of officers administers the mapping facilities, while most of the production personnel are civilian. Many countries, such as Iran and the U.S., have both civilian and military organizations that collaborate in developing their respective programs and in performing the actual mapping.

Most countries have private and commercial organizations that produce maps. The widely distributed road maps noted earlier, are printed by a few large producers who, in cooperation with others, compile the maps. Very large-scale maps, for road construction and other engineering works, are produced under contract by a number of mapping companies. Some local highway departments have their own photogrammetric units to provide or supplement such productions. City surveys, and maps for real-estate developments, tax records, power lines, etc., are largely produced by commercial organizations.

Large societies, such as the American Geographical Society, the National Geographic Society, and the Royal Geographical Society, play important roles, in addition to being centres of reference as noted above. The National Geographic Society produces popular small-scale maps of the various regions of the world. The American Geographical Society has compiled many maps, most notably a 1:1,000,000 coverage of Hispanic America on standards similar to the International Map of the World. Technical societies, such as the American Congress on Surveying and Mapping, American Society of Photogrammetry, American Society of Civil Engineers, and others, lend their support to mapping programs and activities. They issue technical papers, and hold frequent meetings where new processes and instrumentation are discussed and displayed. *The Manual of Photogrammetry* and *Journal* produced by the American Society of Photogrammetry, *Photogrammetria*, published by the International Society of Photogrammetry, and the *Journal of Surveying and Mapping* of the American Congress on Surveying and Mapping, are prime examples of important contributions that societies make to the overall progress of mapping.

The work of geographic societies

International organizations. Many societies and other types of organizations are now engaged in activities associated with maps and mapping. In general, they encourage cooperation through meetings and articles in their journals; some are more directly concerned with the dissemination of information on the progress of particular kinds of mapping and charting. Standardizations of map treatments and conventional signs, as well as the promotion of progress in technical processes are further objectives of such groups.

The United Nations Office of Cartography. This organization plays an important role in all of the activities noted above. It maintains records of progress on the International Map of the World and performs related services formerly handled by the Central Bureau of the IMW. Technical assistance in the development of mapping facilities and programs is provided on request. Occasional regional meetings are arranged for groups of countries having similar problems while the journal *World Cartography* publishes related papers.

Inter-American Geodetic Survey. This organization is a special unit of the U.S. Corps of Engineers, organized to forward the completion of geodetic surveys and mapping in the Americas. Through technical training and assistance with programs, geodetic surveys in Central and South America have been greatly advanced in recent years. Training in photogrammetry is offered and has promoted the establishment of mapping facilities and programs in many of the collaborating countries.

Pan American Institute of Geography and History. This organization has sponsored regular meetings and consultations on cartography, much in the manner of scientific societies. The consultations are held in different countries each year.

International Hydrographic Bureau. This organization was founded in 1921 in Monaco, where it has been headquartered through the years. It serves as a clearinghouse for information related to hydrography and charting and maintains a Bathymetric Chart of the World, which is revised periodically to include data furnished by the maritime nations participating in their programs and conferences. Other organizations that promote progress in the various aspects of mapping and charting are the International Association of Geodesy, the International Cartographic Association, the International Civil Aviation Organization, the International Geographical Union, the International Federation of Land Surveyors, the International Society for Photogrammetry, and the International Union of Geodesy and Geophysics.

Bathymetric Chart of the World {.marginal}

MODERN MAP-MAKING TECHNIQUES

Compilation from existing materials. The preparation of derived maps—*i.e.*, maps that are compiled from other maps or existing data—involves the search for, and evaluation of, all extant data pertaining to the subject area. Depending on the nature of the map to be compiled, a thoroughgoing research includes boundary references, historical records, name derivations, and other materials. Selection of the most authentic items, on the frequent occasions when some ambiguities are detected, requires careful study and references to related materials. The sources finally selected may require some adjustment or compromise in order to fit properly with adjacent data. When it becomes evident that some sources are of questionable reliability, the cartographer explains this in the margin of his compilation. Sometimes this is placed in the body of the map where the doubtful features or delineations are located.

When selected materials have been assembled, they are reduced to a common scale and copied on the compilation base, often in differentiating colours for the respective features. Reductions to a common scale are usually made by photography but may be made by projection and traced directly on the drawing. Minor adjustments may have to be made, during compilation, even though the source materials are of good quality. In particular, the need to make appropriate generalizations, omitting some details in smaller scale maps, requires much study and judgment.

Except for the new methods of preparing final colour separation plates by scribing (described below), rather than by drafting or copper-plate engraving, compilation processes have changed little over the years. Automatic-focussing projectors and better illumination have made the tracing of selected data at compilation scale easier. Better and more extensive facilities for photoreduction and copying, improved light tables, and a wider choice of drafting materials and instruments have all served to facilitate compilation. The basic chores of research, selec-

tion of best data, and adjustment of these into the compilation, however, remain essentially the same.

Scale conversions. The preparation of small-scale maps from large ones is sometimes simpler than the process just described, which pertains to compilation from a miscellany of differing sources. The relatively straightforward preparation of 1:62,500 scale maps from those of the 1:24,000 scale series, for example, may require little more than photoreduction and colour-separation drafting, or scribing. Even in this case some generalizations, as well as omission of a few of the least important details, are in order. To avoid the considerable expense involved in such scale conversions, straight photoreduction of colour separation plates appears to be a promising procedure.

Straight photoreduction {.marginal}

Larger reductions from one map series to another— 1:62,500 to 1:250,000 for instance—are more of a problem, since the need for generalization is greater and the omission of many details is involved. The considerable differences in road and other symbol sizes also create displacement problems.

The component maps are reduced, and the negatives are cut and assembled into a mosaic on a clear sheet of plastic, the master negative of which provides guide copy for the several colour-separation plates required, which are then completed for reproduction as described below in *Colour-separation processes.* More often, however, it is necessary to make an intermediate compilation, rather than burden the draftsman with too many adjustments to be made while following copy on the colour-separation plates. The intermediate scale for initial reduction of the component maps provides better legibility than direct photography to reproduction scale. This negative mosaic is copied on a metal-mounted drafting board. A compiler then inks the whole map, usually in three or more contrasting colours. He also draws roads and other symbols at the intermediate size, so that they will reduce to proper dimensions at reproduction scale, and makes the necessary displacement adjustments. Minor features and terrain details to be omitted on the new map are not inked in. The drawing is now ready for photoreduction to the final colour-separation plates, providing much better copy for the draftsman or engraver than direct reduction in one step would have produced.

Most smaller scale map series are prepared from large-scale maps as described above. In earlier days, original reconnaissance surveys were made at small scales such as 1:192,000 for publication at 1:250,000. Ideally, the small-scale series of maps should be compiled progressively from those of larger scale and greater detail. Most countries, however, started their mapping programs with relatively small-scale reconnaissance surveys because of economic considerations. Later, affluence and technical competence permitted mapping at larger scales, with better accuracy.

Thematic maps. Geologic, soil, and other thematic maps usually have a topographic base from which woodland tints and road classification printings have been omitted. Such a map therefore has a topographic background printed in subdued colours, on which the geologic or soil patterns are overprinted in prominent colours. Small-scale thematic maps, showing weather patterns, vegetation types, and a large amount of economic and other information are of similar origin. Backgrounds are drawn from appropriate outline maps of provinces, countries, or regions of the world, while overlaying subject matters are compiled from specialized sources of information.

Use of topographic backgrounds {.marginal}

Generalization. The generalization of detail is a problem that frequently confronts the cartographer, both in original mapping and in reducing the scale of existing maps. There are two principal reasons for taking such liberties (or topographic license in the case of the original mapping). The primary purpose is to avoid overcrowding and the resulting poor legibility. In addition, the degree of generalization or detail should be as consistent as possible throughout the map. Generalizations in some parts, and excessive detail in others, confuse the user and make the map's reliability suspect. Effective generalization requires good judgment based on seasoned knowledge and experience.

In approaching such problems as the thousands of islets in the Stockholm archipelago, or the thousands of small lakes in the Alaskan tundra areas, when the map scale will accommodate only a small number, the cartographer may decide to draw the features in groupings that reflect the patterns shown in the large-scale source maps or aerial photos. This is difficult and at best presents the nature of the respective areas rather than a literal portrayal. There is also the possibility that the source maps may already have been generalized by some omissions to accommodate to their own scales. Another device is to note, in appropriate text or marginal references, that many minor lakes or islets are omitted because of scale. Such areas may also be symbolized and explained. The "pattern" representation noted above is actually a form of symbolization.

Intricate coastlines are also extremely difficult to generalize consistently. Here again, the purpose is to omit minor details while retaining the main features and their distinguishing characteristics. These, and many equally perplexing questions arise in preparing maps of very small scale from any source. The problems of equalization of detail are also present in such cases. The topographer of earlier days had the equalization problem between areas close at hand and those viewed distantly. In addition, the topographer had to deal with terrain on the far sides of obscuring features.

Photogrammetrists—that is, persons who compile original maps from aerial photos—have similar problems when, for example, one side of a ridge is seen in more detail than the opposite side. Indeed, in steep terrain, parts of the far sides of some mountains are not seen at all. Appropriate steps must be taken in such cases to avoid differing renditions on opposite sides of the mountain. This may be accomplished by adding in field completion of the manuscript map the segments not seen by the photogrammetrist; or additional aerial photography, patterned to cover the obscured sectors, may be requested.

Map production from original surveys. The instrumentation, procedures, and standards involved in making original surveys have all improved remarkably in recent years. Geodetic, topographic, hydrographic, and cadastral surveys have all been facilitated by the application of electronics and computer sciences. At the same time, superior optics and more refined instruments, in general, have enhanced the precision of observations and accuracies of the end products.

The improved quality of surveys has increased the reliability of maps and charts based on them. In turn, the greater output of basic data has accelerated the production of maps and charts, while parallel improvements in processing steps have increased the volume and improved the final product. In a sense, the production of maps from original surveys parallels the process steps after a compilation is made from derived sources. This phase is sometimes referred to as map finishing and involves editing, colour separation, and printing. In original surveys for topographic maps and nautical charts, however, the end products are provided for in all the process steps leading to the completed basic manuscript. The manuscript scale is, for example, selected to accommodate the plotting instruments involved, as well as the final rendering for printing. In early years, it was usual to choose a manuscript scale somewhat larger than that prescribed for publication. This was to allow for some generalization and line refinement in the final reduction. Thus, maps to be published at 1:62,500 scale were plotted in the field at 1:48,000 or thereabouts. With modern photogrammetric instruments, plotting is at reproduction scale.

Maps are not directly derived from geodetic surveys, and only land-line plats are produced from cadastral surveys. Accordingly, the primary original map and chart productions are those from topographic and hydrographic surveys. The surveys are somewhat similar, as the nautical chart is, in effect, a topographic map of the coast, with generalized topography offshore interpolated from depth soundings.

A variety of electronic devices are used to determine a survey ship's precise location while taking soundings, which are also made with electronic equipment. Both hydrographic and topographic surveys now employ aerial photography and precise plotting instruments to develop the base map. In order to simplify the description of modern map-making techniques, the process developed for topographic mapping will be described below, with comments where procedures for nautical charts differ significantly. Both processes start by expanding upon the basic control previously established from geodetic surveys.

Use of electronic devices in ship surveys

Basic control surveys, satellites. *Geodetic surveys.* These surveys involve such extensive areas that allowance must be made for the earth's curvature. Baseline measurements for classical triangulation (the basic survey method that consists of accurately measuring a base line and computing other locations by angle measurement) are therefore reduced to sea-level length to start computations, while corrections are made for spherical excess in the angular determinations. Geodetic operations are classified into four "orders," according to accuracy, the first-order surveys having the smallest permissible error. Primary triangulation is performed under rigid specifications to assure first-order accuracy.

Satellite triangulation. Efforts are now underway to extend and tie together existing continental networks by satellite triangulation so as to facilitate the adjustment of all major geodetic surveys into a single world datum and determine the size and shape of the earth spheroid with much greater accuracy than heretofore. At the same time, current national networks will be strengthened, while the remaining amount of work to be done may be somewhat reduced. Satellite triangulation became operational in the U.S. in 1963 with observations by Rebound A-13, launched that year, and some prior work using the Echo 1 and Echo 2 passive reflecting satellites. A satellite specifically designed for geodetic work, Pageos 1, was launched in 1966.

Many countries are collaborating in developing arrangements for the worldwide program underway in the early 1970s. Existing systems will be adjusted and extended to meet all needs for precise locations.

Control extension surveys. A first requirement for topographic mapping of a given area is an adequate pattern of horizontal and vertical control points, and an initial step is the assembly of all such existing information. This consists of descriptions of points for which positions of latitude and longitude and elevations above mean sea level have been determined. They are occasionally located at some distance from the immediate project, in which case it is necessary to expand from the existing work. This is usually done on second- or third-order standards, depending upon the length of circuits involved.

Between the very early maps of the U.S. and those of the early 1970s, there is a steady increase in reliability, approximately reflected by their dates of survey. The control on which mapping was based suggests a similar evolution. Some years ago, control points were much farther apart. Also on establishing the control points, and in working from them, systematic procedures .were not always followed by surveyors working under difficult conditions.

Today, extensions from existing control points are not required as frequently and can be performed much more accurately when they are required. Existing networks are being continually increased, while modern systems and instrumentation enable the photogrammetrist to bridge greater distances. Electronic distance-measuring equipment has improved the quality of second- and third-order control surveys and greatly reduced the number of traverse stations formerly required. An airborne system is one of the methods developed to facilitate the extension of existing networks of control. It involves the use of aluminum-alloy observation towers and special trucks to move them without disassembly. Helicopters are used extensively both for rapid transport and for hovering over points otherwise difficult to intersect.

Networks of control points

Similar advantages now facilitate vertical control extensions. Automatic instruments make levelling by classical methods easier and more reliable. Elevation meters extend determinations over roads at low cost, while vertical bridging enables the photogrammetrist to extend the available elevation data to the extent that further control can often be dispensed with. Refinements in altimeters, and methods of calibrating the air column with high- and low-based recording controls, permit the use of barometric means of extending vertical values.

The National Ocean Survey in recent years has hoped to increase the density of horizontal control to the extent that no location in the U.S. will be farther than 50 miles from a primary point, and advances anticipated in analytical phototriangulation suggest that the envisioned density of control may soon suffice insofar as topographic mapping is concerned. Existing densities of control in Britain and much of western Europe are already adequate for mapping and cadastral surveys.

Aerial photography. In 1851 Aimé Laussedat of France compiled some map data based upon measurements of photographs taken from a balloon, the earliest known application of photography to mapping. Little progress was made in the science, however, until World War I, by which time better lenses and cameras and better aircraft to carry them were available. By World War II most advanced countries were using photogrammetry. Since then there have been continuous advances in optics, films, and precision instruments for mapping and specialized photo-interpretations.

Precision lenses and cameras. The evolution of these important elements has increased the efficiency of plotting instruments, as well as the accuracy of the final product. For many years wide-angle lenses were not available. This focussed attention on multiple-lens arrangements, such as the trilens cameras of World War I, and three-camera devices of World War II. Other experimental arrangements included a nine-lens camera used successfully in coastal mapping. This phase of camera design tapered off with the development of lenses with a 90-degree angle of view, and particularly with the recent design and production of super-wide-angle lenses. Wide-angle lenses are important to mapping for two main reasons: first, they reduce the number of overlapping stereoscopic photographs to be oriented and plotted from, as well as the amount of control required, and second, they provide a more precise determination of vertical values and contouring because of the wider base of stereoscopic perception. At present, precision lenses are reasonably distortion free.

Photography for mapping. There is a tendency in most governments to utilize military-training efforts and expenditures to secure map photography free, or at minimum cost. This has proved to be false economy in most civilian mapping operations, because the specialized requirements of photography for mapping are better met by commercial or other civilian agencies especially equipped and experienced. Furthermore, military priorities may be such that immediate advantage cannot be taken of the few opportunities for optimum photography that are available; that is, when skies are cloudless, foliage minimum, shadows minimum, and no smog or haze is present.

Flight patterns. Stereoscopic aerial photographic coverage requires an overlap in successive exposures of about 60 percent. These overlaps form the stereoscopic models by which the terrain is mapped with any of a variety of instruments. A side overlap of 10 to 15 percent is also required along the flight lines for maximum efficiency in mapping. This assures adequate coverage and minimizes the number of supplemental control points needed, so that each one may serve in three or four models.

The flight plan is furnished to the contractor, or photographic crew, on the best existing map of the area to be covered. Later, when the actual photography is assembled, suitable controlling points in the overlap areas are selected and marked. The elevations or positions or both required for mapping are then obtained by field parties. In order to hasten the survey, a random pattern of controlling points is often obtained by the field engineers while extending the basic control. This eliminates one field operation, but the elevations of more points have to be obtained, and these are not likely to be in the best positions

for the photogrammetrist. The contour intervals designated for areas to be mapped determine the flight heights for aerial photography. The various systems have factors of capability varying from 500 to 1,200 times the contour interval. Thus, the higher order systems can draw 20-foot contours satisfactorily with aerial photographs taken at 24,000 feet above the mean ground elevation. Mapping is generally more economical at higher altitudes, since fewer models will be involved and less supplemental control required. The clarity of features diminishes with height, however, and about 25,000 feet (7,500 metres) is the current limit for cameras with six-inch focal-length lenses, used in mapping. Wider angle and shorter focal-length lenses require lower altitudes, unless their resolving powers are of higher orders.

Coastal mapping. Coastal features can be more readily identified and delineated when photography with infrared and colour films supplements the normal black and white photography. Shoals and other shallow areas are also more clearly defined and mapped. It is therefore now routine practice to obtain the additional types of photographs simultaneously.

Infra-red and colour photographs have also been found quite helpful in other activities, such as determining vegetation types and identification of areas where insects or disease may be affecting crops or woodlands. Tentative outlines of soil types and area geology can also be made through close study of aerial photographs of two or more kinds.

Photomosaics and orthophotos. Aerial photographs have always been used in field and office for a variety of purposes. Radial distortions due to relief, however, are often a great inconvenience and may render the photograph useless. Photomosaics, in which much of the distortion has been removed, are therefore assembled. This is a laborious process, involving enlargements and reductions of the photography, cutting and fitting of pieces to a controlling framework, while avoiding appreciable offsets of roads and other features.

A recently developed device known as the orthophotoscope greatly reduces distortion by producing a picture from stereoscopic models. The principle has been further developed, as part of an automatic system of mapping.

Photomaps. Aerial photos contain great amounts of detail that it is not feasible to include in a standard topographic map. Some military maps during World War II were printed with the standard topographic map on one side of the paper and the reproduction of a photomosaic of the same area on the other side. These maps were received with enthusiasm by the users. More recently, military and civilian agencies have produced some topographic maps with photo-backgrounds in colours. These have been found quite helpful to military and civilian personnel for rapid identification of position and recognition of nearby features. Thus far, civilian production has been reserved for areas difficult to portray by standard symbolization, such as swamp areas where the normal use of the swamp symbol over an extensive area would become meaningless, and some way of showing the actual variations of vegetation and swamp characteristics needs to be adopted. In view of the favourable response by both military and civilian users, it appears that this type of map will be increasingly produced, although it is more expensive than other types.

Photogrammetric mapping procedures. *Preparation of base sheets.* Manuscripts are usually prepared on coated plastic sheets which facilitate later process steps. All available controls for the area are plotted, and projection lines are drawn. Plotting is frequently done automatically by an instrument called a coordinatograph, which is directed by paper or magnetic tapes containing the coordinate values for each point and projection intersection. Edges from adjoining sheets are transferred to the base, together with pertinent notes regarding features common to both maps. If coastal areas are involved, appropriate features of the nautical chart are copied to the base so that they can be joined and duplication of work avoided. Topographic maps now carry offshore depth curves and other helpful information when it is

Wartime lens improvements

Orthophotoscope

available from charts of the area. After the quadrangle name and other identifications have been applied, the sheet is ready for stereomapping.

Preparation of diapositives. Meanwhile, the photo laboratory has prepared transparent positive prints (diapositives) of the aerial photographs on glass or film. For some instruments, the plates are made in reduction printers designed for the respective plotters. For the higher order instruments, prints are prepared by contact printing or in a one-to-one projection printer. The diapositives must be geometrically accurate and of the highest photographic quality.

Control points. Pairs of diapositives are mounted in the same relative position as that in which the pictures were taken. The overlapping projected images from the diapositives form a stereoscopic model. To compile map detail from aerial photography, each stereoscopic model must be oriented to the correct horizontal and vertical data by means of control points. Preferably, vertical control points should be available near the corners of each model, but a random pattern is usable if difficult terrain limits field operations.

Stereomapping. A variety of instruments are available for stereocompilation, from the elaborate and precise first-order instruments to those designed for reconnaissance or incidental purposes, such as, for example, the plotters using paper prints of aerial photos (see also SURVEYING).

After the relative and absolute orientations have been established for the several models in a strip of photography, the mapping proceeds, one model at a time. Planimetry (those areas having no indication of contour) is compiled first, and then the contours are plotted, so they can be fitted properly to the streams, roads, etc. Usually, the planimetry is scribed after all the models of the sheet have been plotted in pencil. The planimetry is then contact printed by the compiler onto another base on which contours are drawn. This separation simplifies later steps by providing more legible copy, in differentiating colours, for field and office operations. After all discernible roads, railroads, fences, buildings, drainage, woodland outlines (often on a separate overlay), and contours have been delineated, the bases are ready for field review. A number of spot elevation readings are also made, on mountaintops and other features, that may be shown on the final map. This is desirable for the user's convenience when rather few elevations established by control parties are available for publication. The stereoreadings are printed in brown, while those of higher order are shown in black.

Final steps in map preparation. *Field completion and editing.* After the stereo-operator has mapped all the features visible in the aerial photography, the manuscripts are contact printed on coated plastic sheets for review by the field engineer. He examines the whole map, adding such details as houses, trails, and fences that were not visible or were overlooked by the stereo-operator. Political lines such as state, county, and township limits are located, as are geographic and other names in local use. Roads are classified, and woodland outlines are checked.

Contour accuracy is tested if the operator has noted areas that may be weak. The determination of names involves extensive local inquiry, as do political lines, and both may require research of records.

In remote areas, it is more efficient to combine the above activities with supplemental control survey to avoid the extra field phase. Then, the photos must be carefully examined and annotated for the compiler, while buildings must be encircled or pricked. Roads are classified and political lines located in the usual manner and noted on the photos or overlays.

Handling corrections
Field corrections are applied to the original manuscripts. They must be scribed (engraved) on the originals so that guide copies can be prepared by contact printing for final colour-separation scribing. At this time all factual detail is carefully checked. Editing may proceed, to conserve time, while the colour-separation scribing is in progress. The editor reviews all names, boundaries, and related data, comparing them to information thereon that may be available from other sources. The editor's function is to see that the map conforms to standard conventions, is clear and legible, and free of errors.

Controversial names, or those found to be in confused or ambiguous spelling or usage, are documented and referred to an appropriate official body. The designation of type styles and sizes as well as placement of lettering is another function of the map editor.

Colour-separation processes. Because modern topographic maps are printed in several colours, separate plates must be prepared for each. Some of the earliest maps were printed from woodcuts, usually in a single colour. Various hand processes were developed through the years, culminating in the fine rendering of copperplate engraving, which dominated the map production industry for many years. The process became obsolete, however, with increased production demands and the development of efficient printing presses. After World War II engraving on glass, and later on coated plastic sheets, was developed to a point that recovered the fineness of copper engraving. These methods of engraving have become firmly established in map production throughout the world.

Scribing process
In the negative engraving or scribing process, guide copy is printed on several sheets of plastic coated with an opaque paint, usually yellow. The scriber follows copy on the respective plates, by engraving through the coating. Because arc light can pass only through the engraving scratches, the completed engravings are, in effect, negatives from which the press plates are made. The finest lines, such as intermediate contours, are engraved 0.002 inch in width, with a phonograph needle in freehand holder. Heavier lines, such as index contours, engraved at 0.007 inch may require a small tripod to assure that the scriber is perfectly vertical. Gravers for double-lined roads, others for buildings, and templates, or patterns, for a variety of symbols are used. Woodland and similar boundaries and shorelines are contact printed and etched on their respective coated sheets, and the areas of the woodland or water are then peeled off, leaving open windows for their respective features. If portions of scrub, orchard, or vineyard are contained in the "woodland" plate, negative sections for these are stripped into their respective locations. Press plates are then processed from the negatives.

A combined-colour proof is then made by successively exposing the several completed negatives to a sensitized white plastic sheet that serves for the final checking and review of all aspects of the map. After all corrections have been made the negatives are ready for the reproduction process.

Map reproduction. Nearly all map printing is now done by rotary offset presses, using flexible aluminum-alloy printing plates. The system uses surface plates (very slightly raised or recessed), as opposed to the letter-press and intaglio processes, which involve greater image heights and depths respectively. In the printing sequence inking goes from the plate to a rubber blanket to the paper. Thus, the printing plate is positive, or right reading, as is the printed map. The negatives from which the printing plates are prepared are accordingly left reading. This is the process for so-called surface plates. To retain fineness of line on very long runs (10,000 or more impressions) some map printers prefer "etched" plates, prepared from film positives. Both may be considered essentially surface plates, however, since the respective raise or recess is quite small.

Presses are of many varieties and makes. Huge multicolour types are used in large plants, printing several colours at a time. In effect, a multicolour press is several presses built into one. Each unit has three cylinders for plate, rubber blanket, and paper, as well as rollers for water and ink. Presses with automatic feed may run as many as 6,000 impressions per hour, while hand-fed types are limited to about 2,500 per hour.

Automation in mapping. During the 1960s there was much interest in the automation of mapping processes, and considerable progress was made in this area. Achievements in the fields of electronics, high-speed digital computers, and related technologies provided a favourable period for such progress. In Britain, a set of procedures utilizing automatic elements, known as the Oxford System, is in the development stage.

Automatic plotting

Some success was also achieved in the difficult area of automatic plotting. Instruments now available can automatically scan a stereo model and generate approximate profiles, from which contours may be interpolated. Some steps, however, must still be very closely monitored or else performed completely by the operator. Contouring interpolated from a profile scan is still inferior to an operator's delineation. This contouring will meet some less exacting requirements for elevation data, and there is every indication of future progress and refinement. The need for human intervention when automatic devices get "lost" is not a decisive drawback, as one operator can monitor several machines. The reduction of tedious and repetitive steps for stereo-operators offers a significant advancement.

Coordinatographs with high repeat accuracies now facilitate the automatic plotting of control points and projection intersections. Line work can also be drafted or scribed automatically by the same process, but the respective features must first be coded to provide the necessary input tapes. Automatic colour scanning and discrimination is not yet operational, so it is necessary for an operator to trace the various features on the manuscript to code them. Obviously, little is to be gained by automatic scribing until the input can be provided automatically. Coded line-work can be displayed on a cathode-ray tube and corrected with light-pen, but at present it is much simpler to check and correct the manuscript or finished drawing. Systems of automatic type placement at present offer only marginal advantages over conventional methods. In short, automation is advancing but will not be fully operational in a practical sense for some time.

An aspect of automation that is developing rapidly concerns graphic data acquisition, storage, and retrieval. Data banks are being accumulated by specialized users of topographic information, often to produce thematic maps showing soil types, vegetation classifications, and a variety of other information. Such data banks are usually organized in two parts, one for line work, such as boundaries, and the other for descriptive information, or classifications. Assuming that the necessary inputs have been made to the data bank, special plats can be generated speedily. Examples of such graphics include profiles showing elevations along a selected radio propagation path and cross sections for earthwork on roads and other construction.

Map revision and maintenance. It is well recognized by map makers and users alike that periodic revisions are necessary to maintain the usefulness of maps and charts. Aeronautical and nautical charts are revised on relatively short cycles because of changes in aids to navigation, call signals, wrecks, or channel changes. For topographic maps, however, a ten-year cycle is considered adequate, except for those areas that change rapidly.

BIBLIOGRAPHY

Techniques: Until recent years most technical dissertations on the various aspects of mapping were contained in the manuals of official producing agencies. "Topographic Instructions of the United States Geological Survey," *Bull. U.S. Geol. Surv. 788* (1928); and the *Hydrographic Manual* of the U.S. COAST AND GEODETIC SURVEY (1960), are prime examples. Bulletins of technical societies, such as *Surveying and Mapping, Photogrammetria,* and *The Military Engineer,* carry articles on all aspects of procedures and techniques. Many countries have cartographic societies whose bulletins carry current information. The following are typical of the texts available on techniques; most include comprehensive bibliographies: E.J. RAISZ, *General Cartography,* 2nd ed. (1948), *Principles of Cartography* (1962); E. IMHOF, *Gelände und Karte* (1950); T.W. BIRCH, *Maps: Topographical and Statistical,* 2nd ed. (1964); F. REIGNIER, *Les Systèmes de projection,* 2 vol. (1957); A.D. MERRIMAN, *An Introduction to Map Projections* (1947); W. CHAMBERLAIN, *The Round Earth on Flat Paper,* 2nd ed. (1947); and E. ARNBERGER, *Handbuch der thematischen Kartographie* (1966).

History: The history of cartography was somewhat neglected until the mid-19th century when the first great collec-
tions of early maps were published. Treatises on the historical aspects of cartography are enumerated in W.W. RISTOW and C.E. LEGEAR (comps.), *A Guide to Historical Cartography,* rev. ed. (1970). The essential aspects of the subject are well covered in the following; many contain references for further study: R.A. SKELTON, *Decorative Printed Maps of the 15th to 18th Centuries* (1952, reprinted 1966), and with L. BAGROW, *History of Cartography* (1964, orig. pub. in German, 1944); C. BRICKER and R.V. TOOLEY, *A History of Cartography: 2500 Years of Maps and Mapmakers* (1969); G.R. CRONE, *Maps and Their Makers,* 3rd ed. (1966); L.A. BROWN, *The Story of Maps* (1949), *Map Making* (1960); C.H. HAPGOOD, *Maps of the Ancient Sea Kings: Evidence of Advanced Civilization in the Ice Age* (1966); R. LISTER, *How to Identify Old Maps and Globes* (1965); E. LYNAM, *The Mapmaker's Art* (1953), historical essays on maps of early England through the age of discovery.

(C.F.F.)

Maranhão

Maranhão (Estado do Maranhão), one of Brazil's 22 states (*estados*), lies in the northern part of the country immediately south of the Equator and to the southeast of the Amazon Basin. It had a population of over 3,000,-000 at the 1970 census. Almost two-thirds of its 126,897 square miles (328,663 square kilometres) consists of a low, heavily wooded region, bordered by the Atlantic Ocean to the north. To the east and southeast lies Piauí state and to the west the states of Goiás and Pará (for a related physical feature see AMAZON RIVER).

Physiography. The higher plateaus in the southern section of the state are extensions of Brazil's northeastern massif (mountainous mass); the highest point, the Serra da Cinta, is 4,373 feet (1,333 metres) in altitude.

The landscape

From these highlands a number of river systems run generally northeastward into the Atlantic. Several of them form a delta region around the capital city of São Luís (population about 242,000 [1970 est.]), which stands on an island. The delta is bounded to the west by dense mangrove forests and to the east by areas of quicksand. The rivers are navigable for much of their course, cutting through arable soils that support farming and cattle raising, the economic mainstays of Maranhão. The climate is hot and moist. There is a wet and a relatively dry season but never a rainless one.

History. Tupinambá Indians inhabited the Maranhão region when Europeans first explored the coasts in 1500 and when the region was included in land grants, known as captaincies, made by the Portuguese crown in 1534. In the decades that followed, rival European powers attempted to take possession of the territory. The first settlement was established by the French in 1594; later, in 1612, they also founded a colony on São Luís Island. The French were expelled by the Portuguese in 1615, but the Dutch succeeded in holding São Luís from 1641 to 1644.

In 1621, Maranhão and adjoining regions were united as the Estado do Maranhão, which remained independent of the southern captaincies and of Portuguese colonial administration until 1774, when the territory was formally made part of the Portuguese colony of Brazil.

In 1823 Maranhão adhered to the newly independent empire of Brazil and, in 1889, to the newly proclaimed republic.

Throughout its history, Maranhão lay in the shadow of the more populous and westernized states of Brazil along the southern coast. It was settled mainly by Jesuit missionaries, who Catholicized the Tupinambás and introduced the pattern of agriculture and cattle raising that continues to characterize the domestic economy.

The contemporary state. The people of Maranhão represent a blend of Tupinambás, white Europeans (mainly Portuguese), and the descendants of African slaves. There has been considerable racial intermarriage through the centuries, though in interior regions descendants of the original Indian population, known as caboclos, remain.

Language and religion

Portuguese is the main written and spoken language, but it has been enriched by indigenous languages, just as Portuguese culture has been supplemented by local folklore. Most of the population is Catholic; São Luís is the seat of the archdiocese.

The state is administered by a governor elected for a four-year term and by a number of secretaries of state. The legislative assembly consists of 21 deputies. There is a court of justice and there are a number of lesser judges.

The economy. Maranhão is still an economically underdeveloped region, dependent largely on agriculture and cattle raising. The major industry is the extraction of oils and essences from plants. Palm oils from the babassu nut is a major export item, as is rice. A fast-growing food-processing industry employs an increasing number of persons. Deposits of the aluminum ore bauxite on Turiaçu Island are undeveloped; in 1956 oil was discovered in the interior, near the Goiás border, but has yet to be exploited. Further exploration has centred in the offshore Barreirinhas Basin east of São Luís. By 1970 this area had produced only small quantities of natural gas at Espigão.

Transportation. Itaqui Quay on São Luís Island is one of several modern shipping points on Maranhão's coasts, and the navigable river system permits extensive shipment from ports deep in the interior. A 250-mile-long railway links São Luís with Teresina, the capital of Piauí state. The road network, with a total length of about 19,000 miles, of which only about 300 are paved, is rudimentary. There are nine commercial airports, of which São Luís is by far the most important.

Health and welfare. Medical facilities and health standards are relatively good throughout the state. Occasional outbreaks of tropical disease rarely reach epidemic proportions. The state supports primary, secondary, and university education, in addition to which there are four independent colleges, a number of technical institutes, and private educational institutions at lower levels.

Culture. Cultural institutions include the Maranhão Academy of Letters and the Instituto Histórico e Geográfico do Maranhão. The most famous Maranhense writer was Antônio Gonçalves Dias (1823–64), a poet in the romantic tradition versed in Maranhense lore whose "Song of Exile" is justly renowned. The folk traditions of the state are rich and varied. The different cultural influences are typified by the blending of such elements as the native *boi-bumbá*, or "cow dance," with Catholic traditions in the festivals of the church year. (P.N.deS.)

Marat, Jean-Paul

Known during his life as a physician, surgeon, journalist, and politician, Jean-Paul Marat has been considered by later generations as a leading exponent of the most radical tendencies of the French Revolution. Marat was born at Boudry, near Neuchâtel, Switzerland, on May 24, 1743. After obscure years in France and other European countries, he became a well-known doctor in London in the 1770s, and published a number of books on scientific and philosophical subjects. His *Essay on the Human Soul* (1771) had little success, but *A Philosophical Essay on Man* (1773) was translated into French and published in Amsterdam (1775–76). His early political works included *The Chains of Slavery* (1774), an attack on despotism addressed to British voters, in which (according to some) he first expounded the notion of an "aristocratic" or "court" plot, which was to be the principal theme of so many of his great speeches and articles.

Returning to the Continent in 1777, Marat was appointed physician to the personal guards of the Comte d'Artois (later Charles X), youngest brother of Louis XVI of France. At this time he seemed mainly interested in making a reputation for himself as a successful scientist. He wrote articles and experimented with fire, electricity, and light. His paper on electricity was honoured by the Royal Academy of Rouen in 1783. At the same time, he built up a practice among upper middle class and aristocratic patients. In 1783 he resigned from his medical post, probably intending to concentrate on his scientific career. In 1780 he published his *Plan de législation criminelle* ("Plan for Criminal Legislation"). Considered subversive, it was immediately suppressed by French authorities. It may be that this episode was the origin of his bitterness against the existing system, but he had already

Early scientific work

assimilated the ideas of such critics of the *ancien régime* as Montesquieu and Jean-Jacques Rousseau and was corresponding with the American Revolutionary leader Benjamin Franklin. More serious, perhaps, was Marat's failure to be elected to the Académie des Sciences. Some historians, notably the American Louis Gottschalk, have concluded that he came to suffer from a "martyr complex," imagining himself persecuted by powerful enemies. Thinking that his work entitled him to a greater glory even than Sir Isaac Newton, he joined the opponents of the established social and scientific order. In the first weeks of 1789—the year that saw the beginning of the French Revolution—he published his pamphlet "Offrande à la Patrie" ("Offering to our country"), in which he indicated that he still believed that the monarchy was capable of solving France's problems. In a supplement published a few months later, though, he remarked that the King was chiefly concerned with his own financial problems and that he neglected the needs of the people; at the same time he attacked those who proposed the British system of government as a model for France.

Giraudon

Marat, portrait by J. Boze, 1793. In the Museum of the History of Paris.

Beginning in September 1789, as editor of the newspaper *L'Ami du Peuple* ("The Friend of the People"), Marat became an influential voice in favour of the most radical and democratic measures, particularly in October, when the royal family was forcibly brought from Versailles to Paris by a mob. He particularly advocated preventive measures against aristocrats, whom he claimed were plotting to destroy the Revolution. Early in 1790 he was forced to flee to England after publishing attacks on Jacques Necker, the King's finance minister; three months later, he was back, his fame now being sufficient to give him some protection against reprisal. He did not relent but directed his criticism against such moderate revolutionary leaders as the Marquis de Lafayette, the Comte de Mirabeau, and Jean-Sylvain Bailly, mayor of Paris (a member of the Académie des Sciences); he continued to warn against the émigrés, royalist exiles who were organizing counter-revolutionary activities and urging the other European monarchs to intervene in France and restore the full power of Louis XVI.

Attacks on the aristocracy

In July 1790 he declared to his readers:

Five or six hundred heads cut off would have assured your repose, freedom, and happiness. A false humanity has held your arms and suspended your blows; because of this millions of your brothers will lose their lives.

The National Assembly sentenced him to a month in prison, but he went into hiding and continued his campaign. When bloody riots broke out at Nancy in eastern France, he saw them as the first sign of the counter-revolution.

In 1790 and 1791, Marat gradually came to the view

that the monarchy should be abolished, but did not say so publicly before the establishment of the republic in September 1792. As a delegate to the National Convention (beginning also in September 1792), he advocated such reforms as a graduated income tax, state-sponsored vocational training for workers, and shorter terms of military service. Though he had often advocated the execution of counter-revolutionaries, Marat seems to have had no direct connection with the wholesale massacres of suspects that occurred in the same month. His articles in *L'Ami du Peuple* and his speeches before the Jacobin Revolutionary club encouraged a feeling of class consciousness among the ordinary people of Paris. He had opposed France's declaration of war against antirevolutionary Austria in April, but, once the war had begun and the country was in danger of invasion, he advocated a temporary dictatorship (probably under his fellow Parisian leader Georges Danton) to deal with the emergency.

Actively supported by the Parisian people both in the chamber and in street demonstrations, Marat quickly became one of the most influential members of the Convention. Attacks by the conservative Girondin faction early in 1793 made him a symbol of the Montagnards, or radical faction. In April the Girondins had him arraigned before a Revolutionary tribunal. His acquittal of the political charges brought against him (April 24) was the climax of his career and the beginning of the fall of the Girondins from power. On July 13, Charlotte Corday, a young Girondin supporter from Normandy, was admitted to Marat's room on the pretext that she wished to claim his protection and stabbed him to death in his bath (he took frequent medicinal baths to relieve a skin infection). Marat's dramatic murder at the very moment of the Montagnards' triumph over their opponents caused him to be considered a martyr to the people's cause. His name was given to 21 French towns and, later, as a gesture symbolizing the continuity between the French and Russian revolutions, to one of the first battleships in the Soviet Navy.

BIBLIOGRAPHY. LOUIS REICHENTHAL GOTTSCHALK, *Jean Paul Marat: A Study in Radicalism* (1927), remains the best biography. Selected articles and extracts have been recently published, with introduction and notes, by MICHEL VOVELLE, *Marat Textes choisis* (1963). Marat's scientific works are exposed in AUGUSTE CABANES, *Marat inconnu, l'homme privé, le médecin, le savant, d'après des documents nouveaux et inédits*, 3rd ed. (1920). Two other biographies of Marat (in French) provide detailed information on his political career: ALFRED BOUGEART, *Jean-Paul Marat, l'ami du peuple*, 2 vol. (1865); and JEAN MASSIN, *Marat* (1960).

(J.Vi.)

Marbles

Marbles, most simply, are rocks that are used in many classic sculptures and buildings. Though technically the term (from the Greek *marmaros*, "stone" or "boulder") is restricted to granular limestones and dolomites (*i.e.*, rocks composed of calcium–magnesium carbonate) that have been recrystallized under the influence of heat, pressure, and aqueous solutions, commercially, it includes all decorative calcium-rich rocks that can be polished, as well as certain serpentines (verd antiques).

Petrographically marbles are massive rather than thin-layered and consist of a mosaic of calcite grains that rarely show any traces of crystalline form under the microscope. They are traversed by minute cracks that accord with the rhombohedral cleavage (planes of fracture that intersect to yield rhombic forms) of calcite. In the more severely deformed rocks, the grains show stripes and may be elongated in a particular direction or even crushed.

Marbles often occur interbedded with such metamorphic rocks as mica schists, phyllites, gneisses, and granulites and are most common in the older layers of the earth's crust that have been deeply buried in regions of extreme folding and igneous intrusion (see MOUNTAIN-BUILDING PROCESSES). The change from limestones rich in fossils into true marbles in such metamorphic regions is a common phenomenon; occasionally, as at Carrara, Italy, and

at Bergen, Norway, recrystallization of the rock has not completely obliterated the organic structures.

Most of the white and gray marbles of Alabama, Georgia, and western New England, and that from Yule, Colorado, are recrystallized rocks, as are a number of Greek and Italian statuary marbles famous from antiquity, which are still quarried. These include the Parian marble, the Pentelic marble of Attica in which Phidias, Praxiteles, and other Greek sculptors executed their principal works, and the snow-white Carrara marble used by Michelangelo and Antonio Canova and favoured by modern sculptors. The exterior of the National Gallery of Art in Washington, D.C., is of Tennessee marble, and the Lincoln Memorial contains marbles from Yule, Colorado, Alabama (roof transparencies), and Georgia (Lincoln statue).

Even the purest of the metamorphic marbles, such as that from Carrara, contain some accessory minerals, which, in many cases, form a considerable proportion of the mass. The commonest are quartz in small rounded grains, scales of colourless or pale yellow mica (muscovite and phlogopite), dark shining flakes of graphite, iron oxides, and small crystals of pyrite.

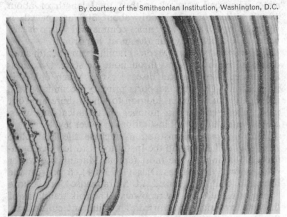

Mexican onyx marble showing concentric banding.

Many marbles contain other minerals that are usually silicates of lime or magnesia. Diopside is very frequent and may be white or pale green; white bladed tremolite and pale green actinolite also occur; the feldspar encountered may be a potassium variety but is more commonly a plagioclase (sodium–rich to calcium–rich) such as albite, labradorite, or anorthite. Scapolite, various kinds of garnet, vesuvianite, spinel, forsterite, periclase, brucite, talc, zoisite, wollastonite, chlorite, tourmaline, epidote, chondrodite, biotite, sphene, and apatite are all possible accessory minerals. Pyrrhotite, sphalerite, and chalcopyrite also may be present in small amounts.

These minerals represent impurities in the original limestone, which reacted during metamorphism to form new compounds. The alumina represents an admixture of clay; the silicates derive their silica from quartz and from clay; the iron came from limonite, hematite, or pyrite in the original sedimentary rock. In some cases the original bedding of the calcareous sediments can be detected by mineral banding in the marble. The silicate minerals (*q.v.*), if present in any considerable amount, may colour the marble; *e.g.*, green in the case of green pyroxenes and amphiboles; brown in that of garnet and vesuvianite and yellow in that of epidote, chondrodite, and sphene. Black and gray colours result from the presence of fine scales of graphite.

Bands of calc-silicate rock may alternate with bands of marble or form nodules and patches, sometimes producing interesting decorative effects, but these rocks are particularly difficult to finish because of the great difference in hardness between the silicates and carbonate minerals (*q.v.*).

Later physical deformation and chemical decomposition of the metamorphic marbles often produces attractive coloured and variegated varieties. Decomposition yields hematite, brown limonite, pale green talc, and, in particular, the green or yellow serpentine derived from forsterite and diopside, which is characteristic of the ophicalcites or verd antiques. Earth movements may shatter the rocks, producing fissures that are afterward filled with veins of calcite; in this way the beautiful brecciated, or veined, marbles are produced. Sometimes the broken fragments are rolled and rounded by the flow of marble under pressure.

Onyx marble and alabaster

The so-called onyx marbles consist of concentric zones of calcite or aragonite deposited from cold-water solutions in caves and crevices and around the exits of springs (see CAVES AND CAVE SYSTEMS; SPRINGS AND WELLS). They are, in the strict sense, neither marble nor onyx, for true onyx is a banded chalcedony composed largely of silicon dioxide. Onyx marble was the "alabaster" of the ancients, but alabaster is now defined as gypsum, a calcium sulfate rock. These marbles are usually brown or yellow because of the presence of iron oxide.

Well-known examples include the *giallo antico* ("antique yellow marble") of the Italian antiquaries, the reddish-mottled Siena marble from Tuscany, the large Mexican deposits at Tecali near Mexico City and at El Marmol, California, and the Algerian onyx marble used in the buildings of Carthage and Rome and rediscovered near Oued-Abdallah in 1849.

By courtesy of the Smithsonian Institution, Washington, D.C.

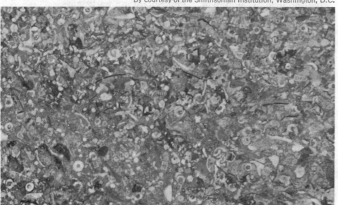

Fossiliferous marble containing fossils of crinoidal debris, bryozoans, and shell fragments.

Unmetamorphosed limestones showing interesting colour contrasts or fossil remains are used extensively for architectural purposes. The Paleozoic rocks (from 225,-000,000 to 570,000,000 years in age) of Great Britain, for example, include "madrepore marbles" rich in fossil corals and "encrinital marble" containing crinoid stem and arm plates with characteristic circular cross sections. The shelly limestones of the Purbeck Formation, England, and the Sussex marble, both of Mesozoic age (from 225,000,000 to 65,000,000 years ago), consist of masses of shells of freshwater snails embedded in blue, gray, or greenish limestone. They were a favourite material of medieval architects and may be seen in Westminster Abbey and a number of English cathedrals. Black limestones containing bituminous matter, which commonly emit a fetid odour when struck, are widely used; the well-known *petit granit* of Belgium is a black marble containing crinoid stem plates, derived from fossil echinoderms (invertebrate marine animals).

Uses of marbles

Marbles are used principally for buildings and monuments, interior decoration, statuary, table tops, and novelties. Colour and appearance are their most important qualities. Resistance to abrasion, which is a function of cohesion between grains as well as the hardness of the component minerals, is important for floor and stair treads. The ability to transmit light is important for statuary marble, which achieves its lustre from light penetrating from 0.5 to 1.5 inches from where it is reflected at the surfaces of deeper lying crystals. Brecciated, coloured marbles, onyx marble, and verd antique are used principally for interior decoration and for novelties. Statuary marble, the most valuable variety, must be pure white and of uniform grain size. For endurance in exterior use, marble should be uniform and nonporous to prevent the entrance of water that might discolour the stone or cause disintegration by freezing. It also should be free from impurities such as pyrite that might lead to staining or weathering. Calcite marbles that are exposed to atmospheric moisture made acid by its contained carbon dioxide, sulfur dioxide, and other gases maintain a relatively smooth surface during weathering; but dolomite limestone may weather with an irregular, sandy surface from which the dolomite crystals stand out.

The principal mineral in marbles is calcite, and the fact that this mineral varies in hardness, light transmission, and other properties in various directions has a number of practical consequences in the preparation of some marbles. Calcite crystals are doubly refractive—they transmit light in two directions and more light in one direction; slabs prepared for uses in which translucency is significant are therefore cut parallel to that direction. The bending of marble slabs has been attributed to the directional thermal expansion of calcite crystals on heating. Some faces of calcite crystals are less rapidly soluble than others and a number of marble tombstones from the 1800s, cut so as to expose the less soluble faces, have withstood weathering (*q.v.*) better than those not so prepared.

Quarrying

The use of explosives in the quarrying of marble is limited because of the danger of shattering the rock. Instead, channelling machines that utilize chisel-edged steel bars make cuts about two inches wide and several feet deep. Wherever possible, advantage is taken of natural joints already present in the rock, and cuts are made in the direction of easiest splitting, which is a consequence of the parallel elongation of platy or fibrous minerals. The marble blocks outlined by joints and cuts are separated by driving wedges into drill holes. Mill sawing into slabs is done with sets of parallel iron blades that move back and forth and are fed by sand and water. The marble may be machined with lathes and carborundum wheels and is then polished with increasingly finer grades of abrasive (see also MINING AND QUARRYING).

Even with the most careful quarrying and manufacturing methods, at least half of the total output of marble is waste. Some of this material is made into chips for terrazzo flooring and stucco wall finish. In various localities it is put to most of the major uses for which high-calcium limestone is suitable.

BIBLIOGRAPHY. The several uses of marble and its extraction from the earth are discussed in OLIVER BOWLES, *The Stone Industries*, 2nd ed. (1939); "Marble," *Inf. Circ. U.S. Bur. Mines 7829* (1958); and T.N. DALE, "The Commercial Marbles of Western Vermont," *Bull. U.S. Geol. Surv. 521* (1912). In a more specialized vein, the properties of carbonate minerals and the deformation that produces marbles are treated in H.W. FAIRBAIRN with supplementary chapters by FELIX CHAYES, *Structural Petrology of Deformed Rocks*, 2nd ed. (1949); and D.L. GRAF and J.E. LAMAR, "Properties of Calcium and Magnesium Carbonates and Their Bearing on Some Uses of Carbonate Rocks," *Economic Geology and the Society of Economic Geologists: Fiftieth Anniversary Volume*, pp. 639–713 (1955).

Marcel, Gabriel

A French philosopher, dramatist, and critic of literature, drama, and music, Gabriel Marcel achieved fame as a thinker by his sensitive exploration of personal experience and relations, his evocative description of the human condition, and his affirmation of communion between man and transcendent reality.

Early life and influences. Marcel was born in Paris on December 7, 1889. His father, Henry Marcel—a government official, diplomat, and distinguished curator—was a man of wide cultural interests and contacts. Gabriel's mother died suddenly when he was four, leaving him with a sense of deep personal loss and yet of a continuing mysterious presence; the event made death and the irrevocable an early urgent concern for him. He was brought up by his maternal grandmother and his aunt—a devoted woman of stern upright character, who became his father's second wife, and who had a major influence on his early development. An only child, he was, much to his distress, the centre of constant familial attention and care; and despite his brilliant scholastic achievements, his family's incessant demands for ever better academic performance, together with the rigid, mechanical quality of his schooling, filled him with a lifelong aversion toward depersonalized, forced-fed modes of education. He found some consolation in travelling to foreign places on his vacations, and when his father became French minister to Sweden he accompanied him. These vacations were the beginning of his lifelong passion for travel and of the fulfillment of a deep inner urge to make himself at home in the new and to explore the unfamiliar. In later life he became versed in several foreign languages and literatures and played a significant role in making contemporary foreign writers known in France.

H. Roger-Viollet

Gabriel Marcel, 1951.

Religion played no role in Marcel's upbringing. His father was a lapsed Catholic and cultured agnostic, who never bothered to have him baptized, and his aunt-stepmother, of nonreligious Jewish background, was converted to a liberal, humanist type of Protestantism. Reason, science, and the moral conscience were held to be sufficient guides, superseding traditional religion. Despite abundant parental love and solicitude, Marcel, in later life, looked back to this period as one of spiritual "servitude" and "captivity" that impelled him (without his knowing it) into a personal religious quest and to a philosophical inquiry into the conditions of religious faith.

Areas of his work. His search took three paths: music, drama, and philosophy. Hearing, playing, and composing music assumed an important role in the shaping of Marcel's mind from an early age, and composers such as J.S. Bach and Mozart played a more decisive role in his spiritual development than did great religious writers such as Augustine and Blaise Pascal. As a composer, his favourite mode was improvisation on the piano, for him a communion with a transcendent reality and not the mere expression of his private feelings and impressions. Only a small number of Marcel's improvisations have been transcribed or recorded; in 1945, however, he became a composer in the ordinary sense, devoting himself to the scored musical interpretation of poetry, ranging from that of Charles Baudelaire to that of Rainer Maria Rilke.

Early dramas

Playwriting provided another early and significant mode of expression. Gabriel wrote his first play at the age of eight. His father's accomplished reading-aloud of plays at home, Gabriel's own invented dialogues with imaginary brothers and sisters, or some peculiar innate cast of mind may have stimulated him to this precocious pursuit. His own family situation had provided the living matrix for his later dramatic presentations of intertwined and irreconcilable aspirations, frustrations, and conflicts of definitely individual characters. The dramatic delineation of the chaotic and unpleasant aspects of human life complemented the expression of a transcendent harmony in his music; and both touched on key experiences and themes which were to be explored later in his philosophical meditations. They were unconsciously concrete illustrations of his philosophy before the fact, not deliberately contrived examples after the fact; they dealt with what were to be Marcel's main philosophical concerns as they emerged in the dramatic spiritual crises and relations of his full-dimensioned real-life characters, not with a disingenuous manipulation of animated concepts as in the conventional "play of ideas."

Marcel dealt with themes of spiritual authenticity and inauthenticity, fidelity and infidelity, and the consummation or frustration of personal relationships in his early plays, such as *La Grâce*, *Le Palais de sable*, *Le Coeur des autres*, and *L'Iconoclaste*. In *Le Quatuor en fa dièse* his musical, philosophical, and dramatic dispositions merge to render vividly the sense of the interpenetration of persons whose lives are bound up with one another. He appended one of his most significant philosophical essays ("On the Ontological Mystery") to the play *Le Monde cassé*, in which "the broken world" of the title is displayed in the empty life and relations of the charming, despairing, and yet still hoping woman who is its protagonist.

Philosophical development. Philosophy, an early passion with Marcel, was the only subject that aroused his whole-hearted participation during his preparatory education. At 18, he was at work on his thesis for a diploma in higher studies, "The Metaphysical Ideas of Coleridge in Their Relations with the Philosophy of Schelling," and he studied philosophy at the Sorbonne. Although he passed examinations to become a teacher of philosophy in secondary schools (1910), he never completed his doctoral dissertation—on the necessary conditions for the intelligibility of religious thought. He taught philosophy only intermittently, usually earning his living as a publisher's reader, editor, writer, and critic.

At first, philosophy for Marcel meant a highly abstract type of thought that sought to transcend the everyday empirical world. Gradually, over a long period of probing and searching, he came to shape a concrete philosophy that sought to deepen and restore the intimate human experience left behind by abstract thought. This philosophical "conversion" occurred when he was working for the French Red Cross, during World War I, trying to trace soldiers listed as missing. In place of the information on file cards he came to see real, though invisible, persons—presences—and to share in the agony of their grieving relatives. What Marcel called his "metapsychical" experiments—investigations of possible communications by means of telepathy, clairvoyance, prophecy, and spiritualism—also played a role in his philosophical conversion. For him these experiences convincingly challenged the conventional naturalistic and materialistic bent of contemporary philosophy, indicating a realm beyond that of ordinary sense-experience, and promising freedom from conformist biases and prohibitions in his philosophical quest.

Originally Marcel intended to express his philosophical reflections in the conventional treatise form, but as he came to see his philosophical vocation as essentially exploratory and the philosopher's situation to be always in search and en route (*homo viator*), he abandoned this format as too didactic. Instead he published his philosophical workbooks, his day-to-day journals of philosophical investigations (such as *Metaphysical Journal*), and the later shorter philosophical diaries in *Being and Having* and *Présence et Immortalité*. He also wrote essays on particular themes and occasions (as in *Homo Viator*); these were usually a more rounded development of themes explored initially in various journal entries, such as exile, captivity, separation, fidelity, and hope, which were also a response to the particular situation of the French people during the German occupation of 1940 to 1944.

The decisive event in Marcel's spiritual life was his conversion to Roman Catholicism on March 23, 1929. The culmination of years of philosophical inquiry into the

Conversion
to
Catholicism

meanings and conditions of personal existence and faith, the action represented his realization that he had to choose a particular form of faith, that there is no faith in general. Despite his apparent affinity with Protestantism, which seemed more in keeping with his essentially nonconformist character and his need for intellectual freedom, he chose Catholicism, which he came to understand as a universal faith, not a special ecclesiastical institution or a partisan, exclusivist stance. After that decisive occasion he continued as an independent philosopher with a specific spiritual disposition, never as a theological apologist or spokesman for an official Catholic philosophy. And he continued in his plays, as well as in his philosophy, to explore and illuminate the dark and negative aspects of human existence.

Basic themes and method. Marcel's contribution to modern thought consisted of the exploration and illumination of whole ranges of human experience—trust, fidelity, promise, witness, hope, and despair—which have been dismissed by predominant schools of modern philosophy as not amenable to philosophical consideration. These explorations were buttressed by a remarkable reflective power and intellectual rigour, a metaphysical capacity *par excellence*.

His early central concept of "participation," the direct communion with reality, was gradually elaborated to elucidate everything from the elemental awareness of one's own body and sense-perception to the relation between human beings with ultimate being. The full, open relation between beings, thus conceived, is essentially "dialogical," the relation between an *I* and a *thou*, between the whole of a person and the fullness of what he confronts—another being, a "presence," and a "mystery," rather than an "object" of detached perception, thought, and expression. Such a relation requires an opening up to what is other than oneself, *disponibilité* (approximately "availability," "readiness," "permeability") and also an entering into, involvement, or *engagement*—dispositions demonstrable in everyday existence. The opposite is also ubiquitous—the refusal to open up and engage oneself, to give credit, to trust or hope, the disposition toward negation, despair, or even suicide. This possibility, for Marcel, is an essential characteristic of the human condition: man may deny as well as affirm his existence and either fulfill or frustrate his need to participate in being.

Marcel's method of thought and expression in dealing with these matters is an open, intuitive one. He probes the meaning of such terms as hope, fidelity, or witness and sketches the reality that they indicate through a sensitive description of the mind, action, and attitude of the hoper, faithful one, or witness. He makes use of concrete metaphors, and real-life instances to evoke and embody the difficult-to-express experiences and realities he is exploring.

Contributions to Phenomenology

In his own unique way, Marcel was an outstanding example of one of the central emphases of mid-20th century philosophy—Phenomenology (see PHENOMENOLOGY). Marcel's use of this intuitive method was original and was developed independently of the work of the great German Phenomenologist Edmund Husserl and his followers, just as his notion of the *I-thou* relation was developed independently of Martin Buber and other dialogical thinkers, and just as his exploration of Existential themes occurred long before his reading of Kierkegaard and the bursting forth of Existential philosophy on the mid-20th-century European scene. Marcel may justly be called the first French Phenomenologist and the first French Existential philosopher (though he deprecated the term Existentialism).

Marcel was married in 1919 to Jacqueline Boegner (died 1947), whom he called "the absolute companion of my life." Their only child was an adopted son, Jean-Marie, the relation to whom may have inspired Marcel's later reflections on "creative paternity" and the spirit of adoption.

Marcel was the recipient of many honours and awards, among them the Grand Prix de Littérature of the Académie Française (1948), membership in the Académie des Sciences Morales et Politiques (1952), and the Goethe Prize (1956). He was an officer and commander of the Légion d'Honneur. He was Gifford Lecturer at Aberdeen (1949–50), and William James Lecturer at Harvard (1961). He died October 8, 1973, in Paris.

MAJOR WORKS

PLAYS: *La Grâce* and *Le Palais de sable*, published together under the title *Le Seuil invisible* (1914); *Le Quatuor en fa dièse* (1920); *Le Coeur des autres* (1921); *L'Iconoclaste* (1923); *Un homme de Dieu* (1925, new ed. 1950; *A Man of God*, 1952); *La Chapelle ardente* (1925, new ed. 1950; *The Funeral Pyre*, 1952); *Le Regard neuf* (1931); *Le Mort de demain* (1931); *Le Monde cassé* (1933); *Le Chemin de crête* (1936; *Ariadne*, 1952); *Le Dard* (1936); *Le Fanal* (1936); *Les Points sur les i* (1938); *La Soif* (1938; retitled *Les Coeurs avides*, 1952); *L'Horizon* (1945); *Colombyre, La Double Expertise*, and *Le Divertissement posthume*, all three published, with a reprint of *Les Points sur les i*, in *Théâtre comique* (1947); *L'Emissaire* and *Le Signe de la croix*, published together in *Vers un autre royaume* (1949); *Rome n'est plus dans Rome* (1951); *A Man of God* (1952; U.S. edition, *Three Plays*, 1958) includes *A Man of God, Ariadne*, and *The Funeral Pyre*, and preface of "The Drama of the Soul in Exile"; *Mon temps n'est pas le vôtre* (1955); *Croissez et multipliez* (1955); *La Dimension Florestan* (1958); *Le Secret est dans les îles*, includes *Le Dard, L'Emissaire*, and *La Fin des temps* (1967).

WRITINGS ON THE THEATRE: *L'Heure théâtrale: de Giraudoux à Jean-Paul Sartre* (1959); *Théâtre et religion* (1959); *Regards sur le théâtre de Claudel* (1964).

PHILOSOPHICAL WRITINGS: *Journal métaphysique* (1927; *Metaphysical Journal*, 1952); "Position et approches concrètes du mystère ontologique," first published as an appendix to *Le Monde cassé* (1933, separate editions 1949 and 1967; "On the Ontological Mystery," in *The Philosophy of Existence*, 1948); *Etre et avoir* (1935; *Being and Having*, 1949), new ed. in 2 vol., *Journal métaphysique 1928–1933* and *Réflexions sur l'irréligion et la foi* (1968); *Du refus à l'invocation* (1940; *Creative Fidelity*, 1964), new ed. entitled *Essai de philosophie concrète* (1967); *Homo Viator: prolégomènes à une métaphysique de l'espérance* (1945, enlarged ed. 1963; *Homo Viator: Introduction to a Metaphysic of Hope*, 1951); *La Métaphysique de Royce* (1945; *Royce's Metaphysics*, 1945); *Le Mystère de l'être*, lectures of 1949–50 printed in 2 vol., *Réflexion et mystère* and *Foi et réalité* (1951; *The Mystery of Being*, 2 vol., 1950–51); *Les Hommes contre l'humain* (1951; *Men Against Humanity* or *Man Against Mass Society*, 1952); *Le Déclin de la sagesse* (1954; *The Decline of Wisdom*, 1954); *L'Homme problématique* (1955; *Problematic Man*, 1962); *Présence et immortalité* (1959; *Presence and Immortality*, 1967); *Fragments philosophiques 1909–1914* (1962; *Philosophical Fragments, 1901–1914*, 1965); *La Dignité humaine et ses assises existentielles* (1964; lectures pub. orig. in English, *The Existential Background of Human Dignity*, 1963); *Paix sur la terre: deux discours, une tragédie* (1965); *Pour une sagesse tragique et son au-delà* (1968).

BIBLIOGRAPHY

Biography: MARIE-MADELEINE DAVY, *Un Philosophe itinerant, Gabriel Marcel* (1959); GABRIEL MARCEL, "An Essay in Autobiography," in *The Philosophy of Existence* (1948).

Drama: JOSEPH CHENU, *Le Théâtre de Gabriel Marcel et sa signification métaphysique* (1948); EDGARD SOTTIAUX, *Gabriel Marcel, philosophe et dramaturge* (1956).

Philosophy (in English): SEYMOUR CAIN, *Gabriel Marcel* (1963); KENNETH T. GALLAGHER, *The Philosophy of Gabriel Marcel* (1962); SAM KEEN, *Gabriel Marcel* (1966); VINCENT P. MICELI, *Ascent to Being: Gabriel Marcel's Philosophy of Communion* (1965); JOHN B. O'MALLEY, *The Fellowship of Being: An Essay on the Concept of Person in the Philosophy of Gabriel Marcel* (1966). *(in French)*: MICHEL BERNARD, *La Philosophie Religieuse de Gabriel Marcel* (1952); JEAN-PIERRE BAGOT, *Connaissance et amour* (1958); ETIENNE GILSON et al., *Existentialisme chrétien: Gabriel Marcel* (1947); PIETRO PRINI, *Gabriel Marcel et la méthodologie de l'invérifiable* (1953); PAUL RICOEUR, *Gabriel Marcel et Karl Jaspers: Philosophie du mystère et philosophie du paradoxe* (1947); ROGER TROISFONTAINES, *De l'Existence à l'Être*, 2 vol. (1953).

Bibliography: Troisfontaines' work (vol. 2, pp. 381–425), contains a complete list of Marcel's writings, published and unpublished, from 1897 to January 1, 1953.

(S.C.)

Marconi, Guglielmo

Guglielmo Marconi, a distinguished Italian physicist, was the inventor of a successful system of radio telegraphy. Applying the principles of electromagnetism, as elucidated by others, to the problem of transmitting messages through space, Marconi exploited the commercial possibilities of electrical communication without wires to an unlimited number of receivers at the same time.

Marconi, c. 1908.

Marconi was born in Bologna on April 25, 1874. His father was Italian, his mother Irish. Educated first in Bologna and later in Florence, Marconi then went to the technical school in Leghorn, where, in studying physics, he had every opportunity for investigating electromagnetic wave technique, following the earlier mathematical work of James Clerk Maxwell and the electrical experiments of Heinrich Hertz, who first produced and transmitted radio waves, and Sir Oliver Lodge, who conducted experiments on lightning and electricity.

Early experiments

In 1894 Marconi began experimenting at his father's estate near Bologna, using comparatively crude apparatus: an induction coil for increasing voltages, with a spark discharger controlled by a Morse key at the sending end and a simple coherer (a device designed to detect radio waves) at the receiver. After preliminary experiments over a short distance, he first improved the coherer; then, by systematic tests, he showed that the range of signalling was increased by using a vertical aerial with a metal plate or cylinder at the top of a pole connected to a similar plate on the ground. The range of signalling was thus increased to about 1½ miles, enough to convince Marconi of the potentialities of this new system of communication. During this period, he also conducted simple experiments with reflectors around the aerial to concentrate the radiated electrical energy into a beam instead of spreading it in all directions.

Receiving little encouragement to continue his experiments in Italy, he went, in 1896, to London, where he was soon assisted by Sir William Preece, the chief engineer of the post office. Marconi filed his first patent in England in June 1896 and, during that and the following year, gave a series of successful demonstrations, in some of which he used balloons and kites to obtain greater height for his aerials. He was able to send signals over distances of up to four miles on the Salisbury Plain and to nearly nine miles across the Bristol Channel. These tests, together with Preece's lectures on them, attracted considerable publicity both in England and abroad; and in June 1897 Marconi went to La Spezia, where a land station was erected and communication was established with Italian warships at distances of up to 12 miles.

There remained, however, much skepticism about the useful application of this means of communication and a lack of interest in its exploitation. But Marconi's cousin Jameson Davis, a practicing engineer, financed his patent and helped in the formation of the Wireless Telegraph and Signal Company, Ltd. (changed in 1900 to Marconi's Wireless Telegraph Company, Ltd.). During the first years, the company's efforts were devoted chiefly to showing the full possibilities of radiotelegraph. A further step was taken in 1899 when a wireless station was established at South Foreland, England, for communicating with Wimereux in France, a distance of 31 miles; in the same year British battleships exchanged messages at 75 miles.

In September 1899, Marconi equipped two U.S. ships to report to newspapers in New York City the progress of the yacht race for the America's Cup. The success of this demonstration aroused worldwide excitement and led to the formation of the American Marconi Company. The following year the Marconi International Marine Communication Company, Ltd., was established for the purpose of installing and operating services between ships and land stations. In 1900 also, Marconi filed his now famous patent No. 7777 for Improvements in Apparatus for Wireless Telegraphy. The patent, based on earlier work in wireless telegraphy by Sir Oliver Lodge, enabled several stations to operate on different wavelengths without interference.

Founding of the American Marconi Company

Marconi's great triumph was, however, yet to come. In spite of the opinion expressed by some distinguished mathematicians that the curvature of the earth would limit practical communication by means of electric waves to a distance of 100–200 miles, Marconi succeeded in December 1901 in receiving at St. John's, Newfoundland, signals transmitted across the Atlantic Ocean from Poldhu in Cornwall, England. This achievement created an immense sensation in every part of the civilized world; and, though much remained to be learned about the laws of propagation of radio waves around the earth and through the atmosphere, it was the starting point of the vast development of radio communications, broadcasting, and navigation services that took place in the next 50 years, in much of which Marconi himself continued to play an important part.

During a voyage on the U.S. liner "Philadelphia" in 1902, Marconi received messages from distances of 700 miles by day and 2,000 miles by night. He thus was the first to discover the fact that, because some radio waves travel by reflection from the upper regions of the atmosphere, transmission conditions are sometimes more favourable at night than during the day. This is due to the fact that the upward travel of the waves is limited in the daytime by absorption in the lower atmosphere, which becomes ionized—and so electrically conducting—under the influence of sunlight. In 1902 also, Marconi patented the magnetic detector in which the magnetisation in a moving band of iron wires is changed by the arrival of a signal causing a click in the telephone receiver connected to it. During the ensuing three years, he also developed and patented the horizontal directional aerial. Both of these devices improved the efficiency of the communication system. In 1910 he received messages at Buenos Aires from Clifden in Ireland over a distance of about 6,000 miles, using a wavelength of about 8,000 metres (26,000 feet). Two years later, Marconi introduced further innovations which so improved transmission and reception that important long-distance stations could be established. This increased efficiency made it possible for Marconi to send the first radio message from England to Australia in September 1918.

In spite of the rapid and widespread developments then taking place in radio and its applications to maritime use, Marconi's intuition and urge to experiment were by no means exhausted. In 1916, during World War I, he saw the possible advantages of shorter wavelengths that would permit the use of reflectors around the aerial, thus minimizing the interception of transmitted signals by the enemy and also effecting an increase in signal strength. After tests in Italy (20 years after his original experiments with reflectors), Marconi continued the work in Great Britain and, on a wavelength of 15 metres, received signals over a range of 20–100 miles. In 1923 the experiments were continued on board his steam yacht "Elettra," which had been specially equipped. From a transmitter of one kilowatt at Poldhu, Cornwall, signals were received at a distance of 1,400 miles, much louder than those from

Investigations of short waves

Caernarvon in Wales on a wavelength several hundred times as great and with 100 times the power at the transmitter. Thus began the development of shortwave wireless communication that, with the use of the beam aerial system for concentrating the energy in the desired direction, constitutes the basis of nearly all modern long-distance radio communication. In 1924 the Marconi company obtained a contract from the post office to establish shortwave communication between England and the countries of the British Commonwealth.

A few years later Marconi returned to the study of still shorter waves of about a half metre. At these very short wavelengths a parabolic reflector of moderate size gives a considerable increase in power in the desired direction. Experiments conducted off the coast of Italy on the yacht "Elettra" soon showed that useful ranges of communication could be achieved with low-powered transmitters. In 1932, using very short wavelengths, Marconi installed a radiotelephone system between the Vatican City and the pope's palace at Castel Gandolfo. In later work Marconi once more demonstrated that even radio waves as short as 55 centimetres (22 inches) are not limited in range to the horizon or to optical distance between transmitter and receiver.

Marconi received many honours and several honorary degrees: awarded the Nobel Prize for Physics (1909) for the development of wireless telegraphy; sent as plenipotentiary delegate to the peace conference in Paris (1919), in which capacity he signed the peace treaties with Austria and with Bulgaria; created marchese and nominated to the Italian senate (1929); and chosen president of the Royal Italian Academy (1930).

Marconi died in Rome on July 20, 1937, and was accorded a state funeral by the Italian government. At his own wish he was buried in his native town of Bologna.

BIBLIOGRAPHY. W.J. BAKER, *A History of the Marconi Company* (1970), a history of the development of radio communications from early experiments over a few miles to the transmission of colour-television programs using artificial Earth satellites—includes a brief review of scientific discoveries prior to 1896 and a photograph of Marconi's first transmitter used in his earliest experiments in Italy in 1895; GEORGE G. BLAKE, *History of Radio Telegraphy and Telephony* (1926), a well-illustrated historical account of various schemes that were advanced to exploit radio communication since the earliest observations of electrical phenomena; JOHN A. FLEMING, *The Principles of Electric Wave Telegraphy and Telephony*, 4th ed. (1919), a comprehensive technical treatise describing the development of radio communications from laboratory experiments on electrical oscillations to early radio telegraphy and telephony; and "The Coming of Age of Long-Distance Radiotelegraphy and Some of Its Scientific Problems," *Jl. R. Soc. Arts*, 70:66–78, 82–96 (1921), a discussion by an associate of Marconi of early transmission experiments and of the first transatlantic signal in 1902; WILLIAM T. O'DEA, *Radio Communication*, pt. 1, *History and Development* (1934), a brief, illustrated account from experiments with spark discharges in 1780 to the development of thermionic valves and their application to sound broadcasting and television; RADIO ENGINEERING LABORATORIES, INC. (ed.), *Telecommunication Pioneers* (1963), a biographical account, with photographs, of 27 pioneers of development of radio communications.

(R.L.S.-R.)

Marcus Aurelius

Marcus Aurelius Antoninus, Roman emperor from AD 161 to 180, has symbolized, for many generations in the West the Golden Age of the Roman Empire, that period in which a thoroughly organized world state was headed by a conscientious and self-sacrificing monarch who carried out in daily practice the precepts of Stoicism, a philosophy that alone among pagan creeds provided a moral justification for a life spent in public service. His claim to the attention of subsequent ages has been the greater because, with the exception of Cicero, he is the only figure of classical antiquity whose individual personality can still be apprehended through his writings: the *Meditations,* or "soliloquies," and some of his private correspondence. Although the rosy picture of Rome's Golden Age has come under challenge in every particular and a more critical eye has been

Marcus Aurelius, bas-relief depicting his triumphal entry into Rome in a *quadriga.* In the Palazzo dei Conservatori, Rome.
Alinari

turned upon the Emperor who symbolized it, his personality and achievement, even after 18 centuries, are still worth discussing.

Period of youth and apprenticeship. His name at his birth on April 26, 121, was Marcus Annius Verus. His paternal grandfather was already consul for the second time and prefect of the city, which was the crown of prestige in a senatorial career; his father's sister was married to the man who was destined to become the next emperor and whom he himself would in due time succeed; and his maternal grandmother was heiress to one of the most massive of Roman fortunes. Marcus thus was related to several of the most prominent families of the new Roman establishment, which had consolidated its social and political power under the Flavian emperors (69–96); and, indeed, the ethos of that establishment is relevant to his own actions and attitudes. The governing class of the first age of the Roman Empire, the Julio-Claudian, had been little different from that of the late Republic—it was urban Roman (despising outsiders), extravagant, cynical, and amoral; the new establishment, however, was largely of municipal and provincial origin —as were the emperors around whom it revolved— cultivating sobriety and good works and turning more and more to piety and religiosity.

The child Marcus was, thus, clearly destined for social distinction. How he came to the throne, however, remains a mystery. In 136 the emperor Hadrian inexplicably announced as his eventual successor a certain Lucius Ceionius Commodus (henceforth L. Aelius Caesar), and in that same year young Marcus was engaged to Ceionia Fabia, the daughter of Commodus. Early in 138, however, Commodus died and later, after the death of Hadrian, the engagement was annulled. Hadrian then adopted Titus Aurelius Antoninus (the husband of Marcus' aunt) to succeed him as the emperor Antoninus Pius, arranging that Antoninus should adopt as his sons two young men, one the son of Commodus and the other Marcus, whose name was then changed to Marcus Aelius Aurelius Verus. Marcus thus was marked out as a future joint emperor at the age of just under 17, though as it turned out he was not to succeed till his 40th year. It is sometimes assumed that in Hadrian's mind both Commodus and Antoninus Pius were merely to be "place warmers" for one or both of these youths.

The long years of Marcus' apprenticeship under Antoninus are illuminated by the correspondence between him and his teacher Fronto. Though the main society literary figure of the age, Fronto was a dreary pedant whose blood ran rhetoric; but he must have been less lifeless than he now appears, for there is genuine feeling

Family

Apprenticeship under Antoninus

and real communication in the letters between him and both of the young men. It was to the credit of Marcus, who was intelligent as well as hardworking and serious-minded, that he grew impatient with the unending regime of advanced exercises in Greek and Latin declamation and eagerly embraced the *Diatribai* ("Discourses") of a religious former slave, Epictetus, an important moral philosopher of the Stoic school. Henceforth, it was in philosophy that Marcus was to find his chief intellectual interest as well as his spiritual nourishment.

Meanwhile, there was work enough to do at the side of the untiring Antoninus, with learning the business of government and assuming public roles. Marcus was consul in 140, 145, and 161. In 145 he married his cousin, the Emperor's daughter Annia Galeria Faustina, and in 147 the *imperium* and *tribunicia potestas*, the main formal powers of emperorship, were conferred upon him; henceforth he was a kind of junior co-emperor, sharing the intimate counsels and crucial decisions of Antoninus. (His adoptive brother, nearly 10 years his junior, was brought into official prominence in due time.) On March 7, 161, at a time when the brothers were jointly consuls (for the third and the second time, respectively), their father died.

Period as full Roman emperor. The transition was smooth as far as Marcus was concerned; already possessing the essential constitutional powers, he stepped automatically into the role of full emperor (and his name henceforth was Imperator Caesar Marcus Aurelius Antoninus Augustus). At his own insistence, however, his adoptive brother was made co-emperor with him (and bore henceforth the name Imperator Caesar Lucius Aurelius Verus Augustus). There is no evidence that Lucius Verus had much of a following, so that a ruthless rival could have easily disposed of him, though to leave him in being as anything less than emperor might have created a focus for disaffection. It is most probable, however, that Marcus' conscience impelled him to carry out loyally what he believed to have been the plan by which alone he himself had eventually reached the purple. For the first time in history the Roman Empire had two joint emperors of formally equal constitutional status and powers; but, although the achievement of Lucius Verus has suffered by comparison with the paragon Marcus, it seems probable that the serious work of government was done throughout by Marcus and was the more arduous in that it was done during most of his reign in the midst of fighting frontier wars and combatting the effects of plague and demoralization.

His statesmanship. For constructive statesmanship or the initiation of original trends in civil policy, Marcus had little time or energy to spare. The field most congenial to him seems to have been the law. Numerous measures were promulgated and judicial decisions made, clearing away harshnesses and anomalies in the civil law, improving in detail the lot of the less-favoured—slaves, widows, minors—and giving recognition to claims of blood relationship in the field of succession. Marcus' personal contribution, however, must not be overstated. The pattern of ameliorating legislation was inherited rather than novel, and the measures were refinements rather than radical changes in the structure of law or society; Marcus was not a great legislator, but he was a devoted practitioner of the role of "ombudsman." Moreover, there was nothing specifically Stoic about this legal activity; and in one respect the age of Antoninus Pius and Marcus signalizes a retrogression in the relationship of law to society, for under them there either began, or was made more explicit, a distinction of classes in the criminal law—*honestiores* and *humiliores*, with two separate scales of punishments for crime, harsher and more degrading for the *humiliores* at every point.

Marcus' claim to statesmanship has come under critical attack in numerous other ways; for example, in the matter of Christian persecution. Though Marcus disliked the Christians, there was no systematic persecution of them during his reign. Their legal status remained as it had been under Trajan and Hadrian: Christians were *ipso*

facto punishable but not to be sought out. This incongruous position did little harm in times of general security and prosperity, but when either of these were threatened, the local population might denounce Christians, a governor might be forced to act, and the law, as the central authority saw it, must then run its course. The martyrdoms at Lyons in 177 were of this nature, and, though it appears that Christian blood flowed more profusely in the reign of Marcus the philosopher than it had before, he was not an initiator of persecution.

His military campaigns. In 161 Syria was invaded by the Parthians, a major power to the East. The war that followed (162–166) was nominally under the command of Verus, though its successful conclusion, with the overrunning of Armenia and Mesopotamia, was the work of subordinate generals, notably Gaius Avidius Cassius. The returning armies brought back with them a plague, which raged throughout the empire for many years and —together with the German invasion—fostered a weakening of morale in minds accustomed to the stability and apparent immutability of Rome and its empire.

In 167 or 168 Marcus and Verus together set out on a punitive expedition across the Danube, and behind their backs a horde of German tribes invaded Italy in massive strength and besieged Aquileia, on the crossroads at the head of the Adriatic. The military precariousness of the empire and the inflexibility of its financial structure in the face of emergencies now stood revealed; desperate measures were adopted to fill the depleted legions, and imperial property was auctioned to provide funds. Marcus and Verus fought the Germans off with success; but in 169 Verus died suddenly, and doubtless naturally, of a stroke. Three years of fighting were still needed, with Marcus in the thick of it, to restore the Danubian frontier; and three more years of campaigning in Bohemia were enough to bring the tribes beyond the Danube to peace, at least for a time.

A more intimate contact with the thoughts pursued by Marcus during the troubling involvements of his reign, though not what would have been historically most valuable, his day-to-day political thoughts, can be acquired by reading the *Meditations*. To what extent he intended them for eyes other than his own is uncertain; they are fragmentary notes, discursive and epigrammatic by turn, of his reflections in the midst of campaigning and administration. In a way, it seems, he wrote them to nerve himself for his daunting responsibilities. Strikingly, though they comprise the innermost thoughts of a Roman, the *Meditations* were written in Greek—to such an extent had the union of cultures become a reality. In many ages these thoughts have been admired; the modern age, however, is more likely to be struck by the pathology of them, their mixture of priggishness and hysteria. Marcus was forever proposing to himself unattainable goals of conduct, forever contemplating the triviality, brutishness, and transience of the physical world and of man in general and himself in particular; otherworldly, yet believing in no other world, he was therefore tied to duty and service with no hope, even of everlasting fame, to sustain him. Sickly all through his life and probably plagued with a chronic ulcer, he took daily doses of a drug; the suggestion has been made that the apocalyptic imagery of passages in the *Meditations* betrays the addict. More certain and more important is the point that Marcus' anxieties reflect, in an exaggerated manner, the ethos of his age.

The *Meditations*, the thoughts of a philosopher-king, have been considered by many generations one of the great books of all times. Though they were Marcus' own thoughts, they were not original. They are basically the moral tenets of Stoicism, learned from Epictetus: the cosmos is a unity governed by an intelligence, and the human soul is a part of that divine intelligence and can therefore stand, if naked and alone, at least pure and undefiled, amidst chaos and futility. One or two of Marcus' ideas, perhaps more through lack of rigorous understanding than anything else, diverged from Stoic philosophy and approached that Platonism that was itself then turning into the Neoplatonism into which all pagan philosophies,

Appointment of his brother as co-emperor

Treatment of Christians during his reign

The *Meditations*

His Stoic philosophy

except Epicureanism, were destined to merge. But he did not deviate so far as to accept the comfort of any kind of survival after death.

At the same time that Marcus was securing his trans-Danubian frontiers, Egypt, Spain, and Britain were troubled by rebellions or invasions. By 175, the general Avidius Cassius, who earlier had served under Verus, had virtually become a prefect of all of the eastern provinces, including control of the important province of Egypt. In that year, Avidius Cassius took the occasion of a rumour of Marcus' death to proclaim himself emperor. Marcus made peace in the north with those tribes not already subjugated and prepared to march against Avidius; but the rebel general was assassinated by his own soldiers. Marcus used the opportunity to make a tour of pacification and inspection in the East, visiting Antioch, Alexandria, and Athens—where, like Hadrian, he was initiated into the Mysteries of Eleusis (though that esoteric religious cult does not seem to have impinged at all upon his philosophical views). During the journey the empress Faustina, who had been with her husband in the Danubian wars as well, died. Great public honours were bestowed upon her in life and in death, and in his *Meditations* Marcus spoke of her with love and admiration. The ancient sources accuse her of infidelity and disloyalty (complicity, in fact, with Avidius Cassius), but the charges are implausible.

In 177 Marcus proclaimed his 16-year-old son, Commodus, joint emperor. Together they resumed the Danubian wars. Marcus was determined to pass from defense to offense and to an expansionist redrawing of Rome's northern boundaries. His determination seemed to be winning success when, on March 17, 180, he died at his military headquarters, having just had time to commend Commodus to the chief advisers of the regime.

Criticism and evaluation. Marcus' choice of his only surviving son as his successor has always been viewed as a tragic paradox. Commodus turned out badly, though two things must be borne in mind: emperors are good and bad in the ancient sources according as they did or did not satisfy the senatorial governing class, and Commodus' rapid calling off of the northern campaigns may well have been wiser than his father's obsessive and costly expansionism. But those who criticize Marcus for ensuring the accession of Commodus are usually under the misapprehension that Marcus was reverting to crude dynasticism after a long and successful period of "philosophic" succession by the best available man. This is historically untenable. Marcus had no choice in the matter: if he had not made Commodus his successor, he would have had to order him to be put to death.

Marcus was a statesman, perhaps, but one of no great calibre; nor was he really a sage. In general, he is a historically overrated figure, presiding in a bewildered way over an empire beneath the gilt of which there already lay many a decaying patch. But his personal nobility and dedication survive the most remorseless scrutiny; he counted the cost obsessively, but he did not shrink from paying it.

Choice of Commodus as successor (margin note)

BIBLIOGRAPHY

Ancient sources: Scriptores Historiae Augustae, *Vita M. Antonini philosophi*, the standard and reasonably reliable life from the set of late Latin biographies of emperors; DIO CASSIUS, book lxxi, which survives only in Byzantine excerpts; FRONTO, *Epistulae*, which presents the correspondence (of which it is important to use the modern edition by M.P.J. VAN DEN HOUT, 1954); EUSEBIUS, *Historia ecclesiastica*, v, 1 —the account of the martyrs of Lyons; and A.S.L. FARQUHARSON (ed.), *The Meditations of the Emperor Marcus Antoninus*, 2 vol. (1944), the full annotated edition.

Modern biographies: Farquharson's edition contains a brief biography (vol. 1, pp. 256–268); the fullest treatment (in German) is by P. VON ROHDEN and H. VON ARNIM in *Pauly-Wissowa Real-Encyclopädie*, vol. 1, pp. 2279–2309 (1894), still fundamental in spite of its date. ANTHONY BIRLEY, *Marcus Aurelius* (1966), is a more recent biography in English; A.S.L. FARQUHARSON also produced a wider-ranging study: *Marcus Aurelius: His Life and His World*, ed. by D.A. REES (1951). The general history of the principate by ALBINO GARZETTI, *L'impero da Tiberio agli Antonini* (1960), places Marcus' reign in its historical setting and contains a useful bibliography. G.R. STANTON, "Marcus Aurelius, Emperor and Philosopher," *Historia*, 18:570–587 (1969), well represents a skeptical current in points of view about Marcus.

Chronological problems: For more detail on the controversial problems of the chronology of the reign, see the papers of C.H. DODD in *Numismatic Chronicle*, 11:209–350 (1911), 13:162–199, 276–321 (1913), and 14:34–91 (1914); W. ZWIKKER, *Studien zur Markussäule* (1941); and J. MORRIS, "The Dating of the Column of Marcus Aurelius," in *Journal of the Warburg and Courtauld Institutes*, 15:33–47 (1952).

(J.A.Cr.)

Margaret of Denmark, Norway, and Sweden

Margaret, queen of Denmark, Norway, and Sweden, medieval Scandinavia's most remarkable ruler, brought external and domestic peace to the three countries she united under her rule. The daughter of King Valdemar IV of Denmark, she was born in 1353 in Søborg.

By courtesy of the Nationalmuseum Arkivet, Stockholm

Margaret, detail of her tomb effigy (recumbent) in the cathedral of Roskilde, Denmark.

She was only six years old when she was betrothed to Haakon, king of Norway and son of King Magnus Eriksson of Sweden and Norway. The betrothal, intended to counter the dynastic claims to the Scandinavian thrones by the dukes of Mecklenburg and the intrigues of certain aristocratic factions within the Scandinavian countries, was imperilled by the renewal in 1360 of the old struggle between Valdemar of Denmark and Magnus of Sweden. But military reverses and the opposition of his own nobility forced Magnus to suspend hostilities in 1363. The wedding of Margaret and Haakon took place in Copenhagen in the same year.

Haakon's aspirations to become king of Sweden were thwarted when he and his father were defeated soon afterward by Albert of Mecklenburg, who bore the Swedish crown from 1364 to 1389. Haakon, however, succeeded in keeping his Norwegian kingdom, and it was there that Margaret spent her youth, under the tutelage of Märta Ulfsdotter, a daughter of the Swedish saint, Bridget. Margaret early displayed her talent as a ruler: she soon overshadowed her husband and appears to have exercised the real power. The couple's only child, Olaf, was born in 1370.

Rise to power (margin note)

After her father's death in 1375, Margaret succeeded, over the objections of the Mecklenburgian claimants, in getting Olaf elected to the Danish throne. Following her husband's death in 1380, Margaret also ruled Norway in her son's name. Thus began the Danish–Norwegian union that lasted until 1814. Margaret was successful in securing and extending her sovereignty: in 1385 she won back the economically important strongholds on the west coast of Scandia from the Hanseatic League, and for a time she was also able to safeguard Denmark's southern borders by agreement with the counts of Holstein.

Margaret and Olaf, who came of age in 1385, were on the point of making war on Albert to enforce their claims to the Swedish throne when Olaf died unexpectedly in 1387. Deploying all her diplomatic skill, Margaret consolidated her position, becoming regent of both Norway and Denmark and, in the absence of an heir, adopting her six-year-old nephew, Erik of Pomerania. She then joined forces with the Swedish nobles, who had risen against the unpopular King Albert in a dispute over the will disposing of the lands of Bo Jonsson Grip, the powerful chancellor. By the Treaty of Dalaborg of 1388, the nobles proclaimed Margaret Sweden's "sovereign lady and rightful ruler" and granted her the main portion of Bo Jonsson Grip's vast domains. Defeating Albert in 1389, Margaret took him captive and released him only after the conclusion of peace six years later. His supporters, who had allied themselves with pirate bands in the Baltic Sea, did not surrender Stockholm until 1398.

Margaret was now the undisputed ruler of the three Scandinavian states. Her heir, Erik of Pomerania, was proclaimed hereditary king of Norway in 1389 and was elected king of Denmark and Sweden (which also included Finland) in 1396. His coronation took place the following year in the southern Swedish town of Kalmar, in the presence of the leading figures of all the Scandinavian countries. At Kalmar the nobility manifested its opposition to Margaret's increasing exercise of absolute power. The two extant documents disclose traces of the struggle between two political principles: the principle of absolute hereditary monarchy, as expressed in the so-called coronation act, and the constitutional elective kingship preferred by some nobles, as expressed in the so-called union act. The Kalmar assembly was a victory for Margaret and absolutism; the union act—perhaps the medieval Scandinavian document most debated by historians—denoted a plan that failed.

Congress of Kalmar

Despite Erik's coronation, Margaret remained Scandinavia's actual ruler until her death. Her aim was to further develop a strong royal central power and to foster the growth of a united Scandinavian state with its centre of gravity located in Denmark, her old hereditary dominion. She succeeded in eliminating the opposition of the nobility, in curbing the powers of the council of state, and in consolidating the administration through a network of royal sheriffs. In order to secure her position economically, she levied heavy taxes and confiscated church estates and lands exempt from dues to the crown. That such a policy succeeded without fatal strife to the union testifies to her strong political position as well as to her diplomatic skills and her ruthlessness. By adroitly using her relations to the Holy See, she was able to strengthen her influence over the church and on the politically important episcopal elections.

Margaret's political acumen was also evident in foreign affairs. Her main goals in this area were to put an end to German expansion to the north and to extend and secure Denmark's southern borders, goals she tried to achieve through diplomatic means. An armed conflict did, however, break out with Holstein, and during the war Margaret died unexpectedly at Flensburg in 1412.

Assessment

One of Scandinavia's most eminent monarchs, she was able not only to establish peace in her realms but also to maintain her authority against the aspirations of German princes and against the superior economic power of the Hanseatic League. The united kingdom that she created and left as a legacy, whose cementing factor was a strong monarchy, remained in existence until 1523, albeit not without interruptions.

BIBLIOGRAPHY. The first study of Queen Margaret based on modern critical principles is KRISTIAN ERSLEV, *Dronning Margrethe og Kalmarunionens Grundlaeggelse* (1882), still a work of great value. The most debated event during Margaret's reign has been the foundation of the Kalmar Union in 1397. Among the contributions to this discussion the following titles are recommended: LAURITZ WEILBULL, "Unionsmötet i Kalmar 1397," *Scandia*, pp. 185–222 (1930); GOTTFRID CARLSSON, "Kalmarunionen," *Svensk Historisk Tidskrift*, pp. 405–481 (1930); and *Sveriges historia till våra dagar*, vol. 3, pt. 1 (1941); ERIK LONNROTH, *Sverige och Kalmarunionen 1397–1457* (1934); and HALVDAN KOTH *Dronning Margareta og Kalmarunionen* (1950). Margaret's financial policy is the topic of J. ROSEN, "Drottning Margaretas svenska räfst," *Scandia*, pp. 169–246 (1950). MICHAEL LINTON, *Drottning Margareta* (1971), throws new light on Margaret's methods of diplomacy.

(L.T.N.)

Maria Theresa, Empress

The archduchess of Austria, queen of Hungary, queen of Bohemia, and wife of the Holy Roman emperor Francis I, Maria Theresa was a key figure in the power politics of 18th-century Europe. To the Habsburg monarchy, a dynastic agglomeration of disparate lands, she gave a measure of unity. A princess of engaging naturalness, she was one of the most capable rulers of her house and, according to one historian, "the most human of the Habsburgs."

By courtesy of the Bild-Archiv, Osterreichische Nationalbibliothek, Vienna

Maria Theresa, oil painting by Martin van Meytens (1695–1770). In Schönbrunn Palace, near Vienna.

She was born in Vienna on May 13, 1717, the eldest daughter of the emperor Charles VI and Elizabeth of Brunswick-Wolfenbüttel. The death of an only son prompted Charles, the only living prince of his line, to promulgate the so-called Pragmatic Sanction, a royal act, eventually recognized by most powers, whereby female issue was entitled to succeed to the domains of the Habsburgs. (Since nearly every major European nation coveted some part of the Habsburg domains, their consent to the Pragmatic Sanction must be taken as nothing more than an act of convenience.) Theresa thus became a pawn on Europe's political chessboard. In 1736 she married Francis Stephen of Lorraine. Because of French objections to the union of Lorraine with the Habsburg lands, Francis Stephen had to exchange his ancestral duchy for the right of succession to the Grand Duchy of Tuscany. The marriage was a love match, and 16 children were born to the couple, of whom ten survived to adulthood.

On October 20, 1740, Charles VI died, and the war of succession he had striven so hard to forestall broke out before the end of the year. Charles left the Habsburg state at the lowest point of its prestige, its coffers empty, its capital beset by unrest. The naïve courage with which Maria Theresa assumed her heritage (and made her husband coregent) astounded Europe's chancelleries. Her

War of the Austrian Succession

refusal to negotiate with Frederick II (later the Great) of Prussia, who had invaded Silesia, her most prosperous province, appalled the senescent councillors of her late father. Her successful appearance before the refractory Hungarian Estates, ending with an appeal for a mass levy of troops, gave her a European reputation for diplomatic skill. When the elector Charles Albert of Bavaria—one of the princes who had joined Frederick in assaulting Habsburg territories—was elected emperor, Maria Theresa was mortified; that dignity, little more than titular by then, had in practice been hereditary in her family for 300 years. Upon the death of the "usurper" (1745), she secured for her husband, Francis, the imperial crown, which the law denied to women.

For some brief years she had indulged her youthful zest for horseback riding, dancing, and music making. She adored the Italian poet Metastasio and the composers who used his masques and librettos and remained partial to Italianate music throughout her life. From the mid-1740s on, however, her outlook on life became decidedly more puritanical. During the campaigns of the War of the Austrian Succession, her generals and ministers came to know both her autocratic temper and the thorough attention she gave to all matters, important or trivial. Realizing the need for a sizable standing army and in order to maintain one, she accepted the plans of Count Friedrich Wilhelm Haugwitz—the first in a succession of remarkable men of intellect she was to draw into her council. In the face of the opposition of many noblemen, she managed to reduce drastically (except in Hungary) the powers of the various dominions' estates, which had held the monarchy's purse strings since time immemorial.

Domestic reforms

In the further process of abolishing tax exemptions held by the great landowners, who dominated those assemblies, she hit on the notion of a "God-pleasing equality." Yet she did not question the justice of the manorial lord's claim on the labour of his hereditary subjects. Only many years later did peasant riots in famine-stricken Bohemia, as well as the reported cruelty of Hungarian magnates, cause her to limit the use of forced labour. "The peasantry must be able to sustain itself as well as pay taxes . . . ," she wrote. Practical, if not always fiscal, considerations, rather than doctrinaire humanitarianism, guided all of Maria Theresa's reforms. An enlarged central administration—from which the judiciary was separated in 1749—and a repeatedly reorganized treasury required knowledgeable civil servants and judges; and their training was, to her mind, the sole purpose of higher education. She approved drastic changes that her physician, the Dutchman, Gerhard van Swieten, carried through at the universities (such as the introduction of textbooks, the linking of the medical school of the University of Vienna with the embryonic public health service, and the sovereign's right to veto the election of deans by the faculties) even as he took them out of the hands of the Jesuits, to whose Society she herself was devoted. (She was the last of the Catholic monarchs to close its establishments.) Deeply pious, strictly observant, and intolerant to the point of bigotry, she was moving, nonetheless, toward subordinating the church to the authority of the state.

Neither the peace of 1745 (by which Austria ceded Silesia to Prussia) nor the peace of 1748 (which ended Maria Theresa's war with the rest of her enemies) ended her efforts to modernize the army. The dazzling ideas of her new chancellor, Wenzel Anton von Kaunitz, fired her determination to recover Silesia, indeed, to destroy Prussia. In a famous "reversal of alliances" (1756) she threw over England, the old ally and "banker" of the Habsburgs, and allied herself with France, their ancient foe. Moreover, she had entered into a treaty with Russia, a newcomer to European rivalries. She paid but scant attention to the global ramifications of the ensuing Seven Years' War. When its end sealed the loss of Silesia and left the monarchy with a mountain of debts, she became a champion of peace. As late as 1779 she single-handedly frustrated another full-scale war with Prussia, risked by her self-opinionated firstborn, Joseph II, who on his father's demise had become coregent in the Habsburg dominions (and been elected emperor).

Change of alliances

Though Francis had not been a faithful husband, Maria Theresa never wavered in her love, and his sudden death in 1765 plunged her into prolonged grief. She emerged from it, her zeal for activity nowise impaired. A new public-debt policy, the settlement of the empty spaces of Hungary, the drafting of a penal code to supplant the tangle of local systems, and a kind of poor law—these were but some of the innovations in which she herself took a hand, with her common sense doing service for the book learning she lacked. In step with the enforced retreat of the church from secular affairs, she came to feel that it was incumbent on the state to control the intellectual life of its subjects. It was she who institutionalized government censorship; on the other hand, it was she, too, who launched plans for compulsory primary education.

Although Maria Theresa pedantically supervised her children's upbringing and education, she was to experience many disappointments in connection with them. Of her sons, only Leopold of Tuscany (later Emperor Leopold II), though difficult as a child, lived up to her hopes. Her special affection belonged to Maria Christina, who was allowed to marry for love and on whom Maria Theresa showered vast gifts of money. Three of her daughters, married off to unprepossessing Bourbons—in Parma, Naples, and France—again and again irritated their mother with their strong will or their follies; to her dying day she bombarded one of these, Queen Marie-Antoinette of France, with practical advice, moral exhortations, and dire warnings of the future. But it was the running conflict with Joseph that clouded the years of her widowhood most. His flirting with the "new philosophy" of the Enlightenment frightened her, his admiration of Frederick the Great offended her, and his foreign enterprises filled her with trepidation. There were threats of abdication on both his part and hers. When Joseph, supported by Kaunitz, pressured her into agreeing to share in the (first) partition of Poland in 1772, she loudly bewailed the immorality of the action. And while she had shrugged off ridicule on such occasions as her setting up a public-morals squad (the "chastity commission" of popular parlance) or, prude though she was, her enlisting the help of Louis XV's mistress, Madame de Pompadour, in order to obtain the French alliance, the accusation of "lachrymose hypocrisy" raised in foreign courts during the Polish affair distressed her. Grown enormously stout and in poor health, she spent more and more of her time in suburban Schönbrunn, whose palace owed its reconstruction to her initiative. She was still trying to hold off the approach of the new age. Ironically, her own pragmatic reforms had smoothed the road to the enlightened despotism that was to mark the reign of her successor. She died on November 29, 1780, in the Hofburg, the vast Habsburg palace in Vienna.

BIBLIOGRAPHY. A. VON ARNETH, *Geschichte Maria Theresias*, 10 vol. (1863–79), is still the basic chronicle. Sentimental biographies abound; the most informative is EUGEN GUGLIA, *Maria Theresia: Ihr Leben und ihre Regierung*, 2 vol. (1917). J.F. BRIGHT'S primarily diplomatic study, *Maria Theresa* (1897), is useful. By far the most judicial appraisal of Maria Theresa's domestic policies is to be found on pp. 1–118 of C.A. MACARTNEY, *The Habsburg Empire 1790–1918* (1968). *Empress Maria Theresa*, by ROBERT PICK (1966), covers her life up to 1757 and contains a valuable bibliography. PRINCE J.J. KHEVENHULLER's diaries, 1748–73, published as *Aus der Zeit Maria Theresias*, 7 vol., ed. by KHEVENHULLER and SCHLITTER (1907-25), are indispensable. So are two memoirs of Maria Theresa reissued as *Maria Theresias politisches Testament* (1952). The various collections of Maria Theresa's surviving letters to her children, her friends, and some of her servants—notably *Marie Antoinette: Correspondance secrète entre Marie-Thérèse et le Cte. de Mercy-Argenteau, avec les lettres de Marie-Thérèse et de Marie-Antoinette*, ed. by ARNETH and GEOFFROY, 3 vol. (1874–75)—offer splendid views of her behaviour and her thinking.

(R.Pi.)

Marine Sediments

Marine sediments are deposits of materials that are brought to the oceans from the continents by rivers, ice, and winds. They consist of the remains of marine organisms, products of submarine vulcanism, chemical precipi-

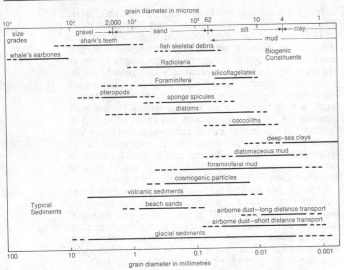

Figure 1: Grain diameters for sediment size grades and typical size ranges for biogenic constituents and typical marine sediments.

tates from sea water, sediments derived from land areas, and materials from outer space. The great bulk of marine sediments consists primarily of the residues of rock weathering and soil formation on land. Rivers contribute between 20,000,000,000 and 30,000,000,000 tons of solid sediment and 4,000,000,000 tons of dissolved material to the oceans each year. Man also contributes to the sedimentary accumulation; 10,000,000 tons of wastes are dumped annually into the Atlantic Ocean from the New York City area. This is probably the largest single source of sediment entering directly into the Atlantic from North America. Man's artifacts—in the form of beverage bottle fragments, worked wood, ships' ballast, and cinders—are found in sediment cores recovered from the ocean floor. These provide a time datum or reference surface that is used to determine sedimentation rates in areas of rapidly accumulating marine sediments.

Marine sediments presently are accumulating at various rates over two-thirds of the earth's surface. In the geologic past they occupied even more of the surface. From sedimentary rocks now exposed on land, geologists reconstruct past conditions on the earth's surface, its paleogeography. Fossils have provided most of this information, but the physical properties of the sediments themselves also provide valuable clues. The study of modern marine sediments provides information on sedimentary processes that is necessary if reasonable interpretations of ancient environments are to be made.

For further information on these ancient environments, see PALEOGEOGRAPHY and STRATIGRAPHIC BOUNDARIES; for additional details on marine sediments and their components, see CLAY MINERALS and SEDIMENTARY ROCKS; see also RIVER DELTAS, CONTINENTAL SHELF AND SLOPE, and OCEAN BASINS for treatment of the present depositional sites of marine sediments.

SEDIMENT TYPES

Marine sediments are aggregates of particles in which sea water occupies the interstices. They are classified by the grain size and the origin of the particles of which they are composed. Thus, on the basis of their dominant grain size, deposits can be characterized as boulders, gravels, sands, silts, and clays, or as such combinations of these forms as sandy silts or silty sands. Grain diameters of these size grades and the size ranges of some typical sediments are given in Figure 1. Sands are common on beaches, where boulders and gravels may also be found; but mixtures of silts and clays (muds) are the commonest sediment types over most of the ocean bottom.

Lithogenous constituents   When classified on the basis of their origins, the constituents of sediments are called lithogenous when they consist of silicate minerals and rock fragments derived from land areas; biogenic when they are the skeletal remains of

marine organisms; hydrogenous when they are the precipitates from sea water; and cosmogenic when they are primarily meteoritic in origin. Silicate minerals of lithogenous character dominate the general composition of marine sediments (Table 1). Most minerals in igneous and

Table 1: Common Minerals in Marine Sediments

silicates	oxides, oxy-hydroxides, and hydroxides	sulfides	carbonates	phosphates
Opal	Gibbsite	Pyrite	Calcite	Fluorapatite
Quartz	Boehmite	Marcasite	Aragonite	Chlorapatite
Orthoclase	Diaspore		Dolomite	Hydroxylapatite
Plagioclase	Hematite			
Zeolites	Goethite			
Clay minerals	Lepidocrocite			
Illite	Manganite			
Glauconite	Pyrolusite			
Kaolinite				
Montmorillonite				
Chlorite				
Muscovite				

metamorphic rocks form at high temperatures and pressures and are not stable when exposed to surface conditions, especially in the presence of oxygen and liquid water. Many rocks break down by means of an array of physical and chemical processes known as weathering, partially dissolve, and finally reform as more stable minerals that are transported to the ocean.

The mineral quartz is abundant in most igneous and metamorphic rocks, and because it is relatively stable it is a common constituent of sediments. Other common minerals in sediments include feldspars and micas, neither of which is as stable as quartz, and clay minerals, which are produced and altered during one or more steps of the weathering process. Table 2 lists the amounts of various

Table 2: Sources of Sediments

source of particulate matter	production	
	(grams/yr)	(000,000,000 metric tons*/yr)
Lithogenous		
River transported	2×10^{16}	20,000,000,000
Biogenic sediments		
Calcareous†	1.2×10^{14}	120,000
Siliceous†	0.4×10^{14}	40,000
Cosmogenic		
Meteorites (primarily chondrite)	7×10^{8}	700
Cosmic dust	2.5×10^{12}	2,500,000

*Metric ton = 2,204.6 pounds. †Assuming that all the silicon and calcium brought to the ocean each year are removed by organisms.

sediment types contributed annually to the sea. Most lithogenous particles are carried to the ocean by rivers; the smaller particles are transported in suspension and the coarser materials (about 10 percent of the total) are transported along the river bottom as part of the bed load. It is assumed that the annual additions of dissolved calcium carbonate and silica are removed from the ocean by organisms through shell formation.

An unknown amount of lithogenous material is carried to the ocean by winds that blow across mountains and deserts, pick up dust, and blow it out to sea. The occurrence of buff-coloured grains coated with iron oxide, in sediments downwind from deserts, attests to the local importance of wind transport. The phenomenon appears to be especially important in mid-latitudes of the Northern Hemisphere. In the Southern Hemisphere, where there is less land area and much less desert area, windblown dust is far less important as a constituent of marine sediments. High mountains without plant cover are sources of windblown dust that may contain bits of grasses or shells of one-celled plants called diatoms that grow in lakes.

Asia contributes by far the largest amount of lithogenous sediment to the ocean. This is because of its mountainous

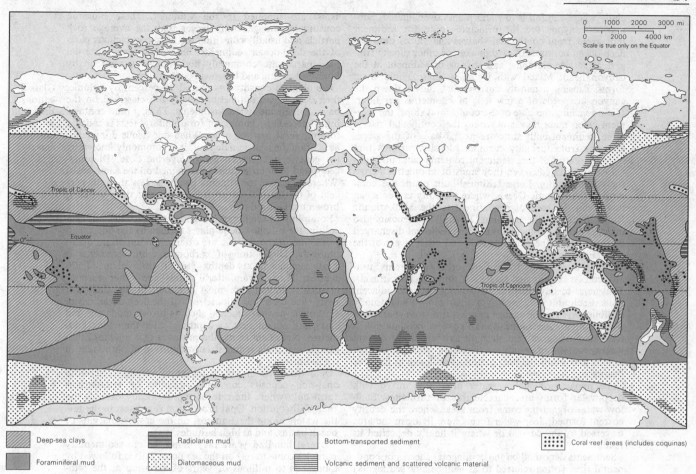

Figure 2: World distribution of marine sediments.

Legend:
- Deep-sea clays
- Foraminiferal mud
- Radiolarian mud
- Diatomaceous mud
- Bottom-transported sediment
- Volcanic sediment and scattered volcanic material
- Coral-reef areas (includes coquinas)

Scale: 0 1000 2000 3000 mi / 0 2000 4000 km. Scale is true only on the Equator

Tropic of Cancer, Equator, Tropic of Capricorn

Other constituents

terrain, relatively low rainfall, and limited plant cover. In addition, the long history of agriculture increases soil erosion, especially in semi-arid regions.

Marine organisms build their shells from dissolved silica and carbonate that originally were derived from rock weathering. These biogenic constituents are the most conspicuous components of 62 percent of the deep-ocean sediment. Wherever biogenic constituents exceed 30 percent of the total, deep ocean sediments are said to be oozes. The most abundant of the biogenic constituents are the carbonate minerals calcite and aragonite, which are precipitated by many organisms to form their shells. Calcareous or foraminiferal muds cover about 48 percent of the deep-ocean bottom (Figure 2).

Another important biogenic constituent is opal, a glass-like silicate formed by diatoms (algae) and radiolarians (protozoans). Where diatom growth is luxuriant, the sediments consist largely of their remains and are termed diatomaceous muds. Radiolarians are especially abundant in the equatorial waters of the eastern Pacific Ocean, where they form radiolarian muds (or oozes). Siliceous muds cover 14 percent of the deep-ocean floor.

Only the hard skeletal remains of marine organisms are easily recognizable in sediments. The soft flesh normally is eaten by other organisms or decomposed by bacteria. Bones and fish scales usually are broken down and only the extremely resistant sharks' teeth or rare bones, like the fist-sized earbones of whales, are recognizable.

Organic matter from these soft parts usually makes up about one percent, or less, of deep-ocean sediments and about 2 to 3 percent of nearshore sediments. Organic matter may comprise 10 percent or more of the sediment in fjords or isolated bays where sediment deposition is rapid, or where the lack of dissolved oxygen in the water keeps animals away.

Hydrogenous constituents form directly by precipitation from sea water. In areas where other types of sediment accumulate slowly, hydrogenous constituents, usually

iron-manganese nodules, form a conspicuous part of the sediment. Such nodules form extremely slowly (10^{-5} to 10^{-6} centimetres per year by some determinations), and if other materials are deposited rapidly around them, the nodules are buried before they can develop to an appreciable size.

Cosmogenic materials are recognized only in deep-ocean deposits where the supply of other constituents is extremely small. These rare particles are small spheres, usually about 30 to 60 micrometres in diameter, and have an inner nucleus of iron and an oxidized magnetic crust.

Shallow-water sediments. Most sediments are deposited initially near their sources. Most river-borne sediment, for example, is deposited near the river mouth. On open coasts, waves and tidal currents are often strong enough to hold these deposits in suspension and move them along the continental shelf. They are finally deposited in areas where currents or wave action along the bottom are too weak to keep them in suspension. If the rate of supply exceeds the capacity of coastal ocean processes to move the sediment, large deposits form river deltas. Marine sediments deposited near continents cover about 25 percent of the ocean floor, but they probably account for 90 percent (by volume) of all sediment deposits.

Modern rates of sediment transport to the ocean may be somewhat different than rates of the geological past. Lakes gouged by continental glaciers act to trap sediment and to prevent its movement to the sea. In addition, changes in sea level following the retreat of the continental ice sheets have flooded the mouths of many rivers during the past 5,000 years, forming large estuaries. Until these lakes and estuaries are filled with sediment deposits virtually no detritus can escape to the ocean.

Areas like the Atlantic coast of the United States consequently contribute little sediment. On the other hand, many land areas now stand much higher above sea level than they did during most of the earth's history; and these contribute large amounts of sediment to the ocean, espe-

Effects of density currents

cially where rainfall is low and plant cover limited. Submarine canyons are the principal route for sediment movement from continental shelves and slopes onto the deep-ocean bottom. An earthquake (or other shock) triggers a massive slumping and stirring of sediment at the canyon head. Mixed with water, a dense liquid mass forms, causing a density current that moves down the canyon at speeds of a few tens of kilometres per hour. Upon reaching the base of the continental slope, the sediment-laden mass moves out onto the continental rise, a large, sediment-built structure at the base of the slope. Deposits from turbidity currents (density currents that arise by reason of their sediment content) can build outward for hundreds, even thousands of kilometres across the ocean bottom. Large sediment-built plains are common in the Atlantic Ocean, where turbidity currents can flow from the base of a continent to the Mid-Atlantic Ridge. In the northern Indian Ocean, large deposits also occur. These deposits are built from sediment discharged by the Ganges, the Brahmaputra, and other rivers of the area (Figure 2).

Turbidites, deposits formed by turbidity currents, usually consist of silts and sands but sometimes of gravels. They tend to have distinct boundaries between adjacent units. Each unit is formed by a separate flow and usually exhibits a systematic change in grain size from coarsest at the bottom to finest at the top. This graded bedding results from decreasing current strength as the density current wanes; coarsest materials are deposited when the current is at its maximum and finer materials settle out as its force decreases.

The remains of shallow-water organisms mixed with deep-water forms are characteristic of turbidites. Shallow-water organisms come from areas where the density current formed; deep-water forms were living in the area traversed by the current or where it finally deposited its load.

Sediments deposited on the continental shelves or continental rises (often referred to as hemipelagic sediments) normally accumulate too rapidly to react chemically with sea water. Individual grains often retain characteristics imparted to them in the area in which they formed. Near a coast where soils are yellow, for example, it is common to find yellowish marine sediments.

Glaciers flowing from continents into the ocean form glacial-marine deposits. At present, this occurs off Antarctica, to a lesser extent near Greenland, and off the coasts of Alaska and South America (near Tierra del Fuego). Such sediments contain a wide range of particle sizes, ranging from silt to large boulders. In general, minerals or rock fragments in glacial deposits are little altered. Despite the richness of marine life in Antarctic waters overlying present sites of deposition, the remains of marine organisms are not conspicuous in the sediments because the accumulation of lithogenous material is rapid.

Sediments deposited near coral reefs in shallow tropical waters contain abundant carbonate material. For example, calcareous, reef-derived muds occur around atolls at the northwestern end of the Hawaiian chain, as well as in the Indonesian area.

Near volcanoes, sediments contain ash (silicate glass and fine volcanic rock fragments). In areas of island arcs (q.v.), such as Indonesia, fragments from known volcanic eruptions can be recognized in sediments. In certain places these pyroclastic materials are still being deposited or are being moved upward to the surface by organisms more than 100 years after the eruption.

Deep-ocean sediments. About 75 percent of the ocean bottom is covered by slowly accumulating deposits called pelagic sediments. Because of the great distance between the continents and the barriers that exist in the oceans' bottom topography, these areas do not receive turbidity currents and their associated coarse-grained sediment.

Because deep-ocean sediments receive relatively little lithogenous material from the continents, they commonly contain large amounts of biogenic constituents. In areas where surface waters are fertile, opal (from diatoms and radiolarians) and calcium carbonate (from foraminiferans, coccolithophorids, pteropods, and other organisms) are supplied to the sediment. These biogenic constituents are generally larger than the average rock particle and usually constitute the most conspicuous parts of the deep-ocean sediments. Shells and tests (external hard parts) are commonly dissolved or broken up by bottom-dwelling and burrowing organisms.

If biological constituents exceed 30 percent by volume, then deep ocean sediments usually are classified on the basis of their biologic constituents. Thus, a mud containing 30 percent by volume of foraminiferal tests is called a foraminiferal mud or ooze. When one genus dominates, as is often the case in a deposit, it is commonly known by the generic name, such as *Globigerina* ooze. Diatomaceous and radiolarian muds are named on the same basis. Where biogenic constituents comprise less than 30 percent of the total, the deposit is known as a deep-sea clay, brown mud, or red clay.

Foraminifera are larger and more conspicuous, but coccoliths, the minute calcite plates formed by the one-celled plant *Coccolithophorida*, are often more important quantitatively. Dissolution of carbonate from sediments is most significant at depths greater than about 4,500 metres. Thus, foraminiferal muds and other carbonate-rich sediments are most common in the shallower parts (less than four kilometres) of the deep-ocean basin. Carbonate-poor sediments, such as brown muds and red clays, are commonest at depths greater than four kilometres. Near continents, the presence of abundant lithogenous materials reduces the proportion of carbonate in the sediments.

Opal dissolves in sea water at all depths. Therefore opal-rich deposits containing diatoms or radiolarians form only where the rate of supply locally exceeds the rate of dissolution. Opal production is greatest in the fertile waters along the Equator, on the eastern margins of ocean basins, and at high latitudes.

Several hundred years may elapse before sedimentary particles come to rest on the sea floor. This is followed by thousands to millions of years of exposure at the sediment-water interface before burial. Ample time is therefore available for chemical reactions between particles and ocean waters. These waters contain abundant dissolved oxygen so that the sediments are often rust coloured and usually contain little organic matter.

The fine-grained component of deep-sea sediment consists primarily of clay minerals (q.v.), whose study requires special techniques such as X-ray diffraction. Clays come from the continents, blown by winds or carried by ocean currents. The importance of tropical areas as sediment sources is shown by the abundant kaolinite in the Atlantic Ocean and gibbsite in equatorial deep-ocean sediments. Both minerals are common in tropical soils where chemical alteration of rocks is rapid and intense. The abundance of chlorite in high latitude sediments provides a useful tracer for sediments moving from high latitude areas. Chlorite is a common constituent in high latitude soils where chemical alteration is less rapid and intense.

Clay mineral abundance in deep-ocean sediments suggests that near-bottom currents can move fine-grained sediments. After sediment has sunk through a few hundred metres of the ocean surface layers, it cannot be moved by surface currents. Subsurface currents can transport material as it sinks, and strong currents on the bottom can resuspend and transport sediment previously deposited. There is often a layer of muddy water a few hundred metres thick near the ocean floor that contains these resuspended particles. Near-bottom ocean currents (q.v.) trend north-south in all oceans, with the strongest currents paralleling continental slopes on the western side of the ocean basins. There also may be strong near-bottom currents along oceanic ridges (q.v.).

AGE DETERMINATIONS IN SEDIMENT

The ages of sedimentary deposits are determined in several ways (see DATING, RELATIVE AND ABSOLUTE). Easiest to visualize is the case in which annual layers, called varves, form as the sediment accumulates. Varved deposits (q.v.) form in basins where a low supply of dissolved oxygen prevents organisms from living in the sediments. In the

Marginal notes:

Classifications based on biological constituents

Clay minerals in deep-sea sediments

open ocean, layering of sediments due to seasonal changes in particle composition would be disrupted by the burrowing of the abundant worms and other bottom-dwelling (benthic) organisms.

It is often possible to determine when sediments form by their fossil content; the presence or absence of diagnostic species, or subspecies, whose range in time is known will indicate this. For short time intervals, it is sometimes possible to use changes in shell characteristics of a particular species to establish time markers that correlate widely separated sediment deposits. Temperature related changes in the coiling direction of certain foraminiferans are examples of such characteristics. The coiling directions have been related to glacial-interglacial fluctuations by some workers. Although the causes for such test changes are not always well understood, they can be extremely useful for studies of comparatively recent deep-ocean deposits. Radiolarians have been used to correlate sediments near the Antarctic and in the Pacific; and discoasters, remains of extinct one-celled plants similar to Coccolithophoridaceae, are useful for establishing ages of Tertiary sediments (2,500,000 to 65,000,000 years ago). Despite the utility of paleontological age determinations, these provide only relative ages or useful markers for identifying equivalent time horizons in deposits from different areas.

Radiometric dating techniques

Radiometric dating techniques utilize the decay of a radionuclide to indicate absolute age of sediments. Radionuclides decay at a fixed rate, so it is possible to determine the time elapsed since a sediment was deposited by comparing radionuclide abundance at a given depth in the sediment with the amount originally present.

Carbon-14 is often used for radiometric dating of recently deposited sediment. Formed continually in the upper atmosphere, carbon-14 occurs in a fixed amount per gram of ordinary carbon in all living things. Carbon-14 that is lost by radioactive decay while an organism is alive is made up by exchange with the atmosphere or ocean. When the organism dies, it no longer obtains carbon-14, which therefore begins to decrease at a fixed rate. After 5,600 years (the approximate half-life of carbon-14) one-half the original amount of carbon-14 remains. If analysis indicates that only one-fourth the original amount of carbon-14 remains in the sediment, the age of this carbon, and presumably the age of the sediment as well, is put at 11,200 years, or approximately two carbon-14 half-lives.

Another radiometric dating technique involves determination of the elemental abundance produced by decay of a parent radionuclide. Potassium-40, which decays to form argon-40 and calcium-40, is one example. Many minerals include potassium, of which 1.2 percent is potassium-40, a radionuclide with a half-life of 1.3×10^9 years. Eleven percent of potassium-40 decays to form argon-40, which is not incorporated in silicate minerals; thus, a comparison of the amount of argon-40 with that of potassium-40 indicates the time elapsed since the mineral formed or was last altered. To use a radiometric technique to date sediment deposition, it is essential to analyze the minerals or other material that formed at the time the sediment was lain down. Otherwise, one obtains an average age of the mineral grains rather than the age of the sediment deposit.

Two approaches have been used to date sediment deposition. One involves glauconite, a mica-like mineral that forms in sediments; the other uses volcanic material, such as ash falls that occurred while the sediment was accumulating. Because of the long half-life of potassium-40, the technique can be applied only to older sediments; under favorable circumstances, sediments as young as 100,000 years can be dated.

Most minerals and sediments also contain uranium and thorium, which are radionuclides with long half-lives. These radionuclides and their various daughter products become separated during sediment transport and deposition, so that the equilibrium relationships are disturbed. Certain of these relationships are slowly reestablished after deposition, providing a measure of the time elapsed since the sediments were deposited. This technique has been used extensively to date sediments in the age range

between the limits of carbon-14 dating (about 30,000 years) and the limits of potassium-40–argon-40 dating (greater than 100,000 years).

MARINE SEDIMENTARY ROCKS

Sediments are lithified or transformed into sedimentary rocks by several processes. These include compaction—the expulsion of water and reduction of pore space, which is especially important in muds and other fine-grained sediments; cementation—the precipitation of minerals in pores or at points of grain contact, which is important in many sediments and is quite conspicuous in sands; and diagenesis—the reactions that take place within the sediment between the contained minerals and the interstitial fluids. Solutions may bring in new materials from outside the sediment, thus precipitating new minerals and changing the chemical composition of the sediment as it lithifies.

Studies of these processes in deep-ocean sediments have been handicapped by difficulties and the expense of obtaining samples of ancient sediments far below the deep-ocean bottom. Deep-ocean drilling has provided limestones and siliceous rocks in various cores. Recovery of rocks containing unusual minerals, including zeolites, clays, and carbonate minerals, show that diagenetic alteration of sediments occurs in the deep ocean. Igneous activity at or below the ocean bottom produces fluids that react with sediments to cause diagenesis. The nature of sediment diagenesis involves the consideration of geochemical equilibria at low temperatures and pressures.

Most sedimentary rocks now exposed on the continents were originally deposited in shallow water when the ocean covered continental areas. Sedimentary rocks formed from deep-ocean sediment are rare, but some do occur in regions of crustal instability where mountain building has been active. Uplifted deep-ocean sediments are found on the islands of Timor in the Indonesian region, Barbados in the West Indies, and in the Alps.

Thickness of sediments

The thickness of sediment deposits in the ocean can be determined directly by drilling from specially constructed and equipped vessels, or indirectly by geophysical techniques. The latter, which have been used most extensively include seismic reflection and refraction techniques. Reflection techniques utilize an explosion to generate a sound signal that bounces off successive sediment layers. Precise determinations of the time elapsed between sending the signal and receiving the echo permit calculations of the layer thickness.

Seismic refraction techniques also utilize an explosion to generate a signal but employ a second station at some distance to receive the signal transmitted through the ocean bottom. Sound travels at different velocities in the various layers. Precise timing of the signal arrival from the various layers provides information about layer thickness and sound velocities in each layer. Sound velocity in turn provides information about physical properties of layers that cannot be obtained from reflected signals.

Using these techniques, geophysicists have shown that marine sediments are several kilometres thick near continents; more than three kilometres thick, for instance, in the Argentine basin off South America. Away from continents, sediments are 200 to 300 metres thick in the Pacific and about a kilometre thick in the Atlantic. Deep-ocean deposits average about 450 metres thick, lying on about 1.8 kilometres of consolidated sediments or volcanic rocks (called Layer 2, or basement) and under that, about five kilometres of basalt, in part altered (called Layer 3, or the oceanic layer). Layer 3 makes up the lowest part of the oceanic crust, which lies above the earth's mantle region.

Sea-floor spreading effects

The deep-ocean bottom seems to have been constantly renewed through a process known as sea-floor spreading. Oceanic crust apparently forms at mid-oceanic ridges by volcanic and intrusive igneous activity and moves away to be destroyed eventually at oceanic trenches. In this process, overlying sediments are carried along passively, changing both depth and position relative to the ridge crest. This affects both the type of sediment deposited and the rate at which it accumulates. Volcanic or igneous activity near ridge crests produces lithogenous material and causes a locally increased rate of sediment accumulation. Rough topography on the ridges also forms small protected areas in which these sediments collect; sediment can neither enter these small depressions at a later time nor readily escape from them. Furthermore, the shallowness of the ocean bottom near the ridges favours development of carbonate-rich sediments. Foraminiferal muds are common on the Mid-Atlantic Ridge; it is also one of the few areas where pteropods, delicate shells of planktonic gastropods, accumulate.

As the crust moves away from ridges through time, the sediment deposits are moved to greater depths where carbonate solution is most intensive, so that the most recently deposited sediment is less carbonate-rich than the older underlying sediment. The ridge topography is gradually covered by sediment accumulations. As the ocean bottom becomes deeper, turbidity currents may eventually reach the area, further changing the type of sediment deposited. Where the ocean bottom approaches a continent, the sediment deposits become thicker. Island arcs or ridges along the continental margins, as in the western Pacific Ocean, may trap sediment locally and cause an immense thickness of sediment to accumulate, up to 15 kilometres in some of the Asiatic basins. In such cases, virtually no sediment escapes to be deposited in the trench or on the deep-ocean floor seaward of the island arc (see also SEA-FLOOR SPREADING; OCEANIC RIDGES).

BIBLIOGRAPHY. M.G. GROSS, *Oceanography*, 2nd ed. (1970), an elementary text dealing with sediments and sedimentary processes in the oceans, bibliography; J. MURRAY and A.F. RENARD, *Deep-Sea Deposits* (1891), classical report on deep-ocean sediments based on the specimens collected during the voyage of H.M.S. Challenger, beautifully illustrated in colour; P.D. TRASK (ed.), *Recent Marine Sediments: A Symposium* (1939, reprinted 1968), classical picture of regional sediment distribution in the ocean, including discussion of techniques used to study unconsolidated sediments; K.K. TUREKIAN, *Oceans* (1968), chemically oriented view of marine sedimentary processes, with a bibliog. of modern studies of marine sediments; H.W. MENARD, *Marine Geology of the Pacific* (1964), sedimentary environments of the Pacific; M.N. HILL (ed.), *The Seas*, vol. 3, *The Earth Beneath the Sea* (1963), detailed descriptions of all sedimentary environments; M.N. BRAMLETTE, "Pelagic Sediments," in M. SEARS (ed.), *Oceanography* (1961), illustrates important biologic contributors to the deep-sea sediments; G. ARRHENIUS, *Sediment Cores from the East Pacific* (1952), detailed sedimentology and geochemistry of Pacific deep-sea deposits; D.B. ERICSON and G. WOLLIN, *The Deep and the Past* (1964), a popular account of the authors' study of marine sediments of the Atlantic.

(M.G.G.)

Maritime Law

Maritime law is the term commonly employed to denote the branch of jurisprudence that governs ships and shipping. In English-speaking countries, "admiralty" is sometimes used synonymously, although in a stricter sense that term relates to the jurisdiction and procedural law of courts whose origins may be traced to the office of Admiral. Although etymologically maritime law and "law of the sea" are identical, the former term is generally applied to private shipping law, whereas the latter, usually prefixed by "international," has come to signify the maritime segment of public international law.

HISTORICAL BACKGROUND

Origins of maritime law

Ancient and medieval developments. From the fact that the ancient Egyptians engaged in shipping on a wide scale, it can be inferred that they had at least rudimentary laws regulating that activity, although no trace of any has been found thus far. Nor is there anything known of any maritime laws of the Phoenicians, who succeeded the Egyptians as commercial leaders in the Mediterranean. That Rhodes was a major source of maritime law, however, is clearly indicated in two passages from the *Digest* (AD 533) of the Roman emperor Justinian. The first quotes the Emperor Antoninus (reigned AD 138–161) in a case of plunder following a shipwreck: "I am indeed lord of the world, but the Law is the lord of the sea. This matter must be decided by the maritime law of the Rhodians, provided that no law of ours is opposed

to it." The second is a statement of the basic law of "general average," which the *Digest* attributes to the Rhodians. "Average" here means any loss sustained by a vessel or its cargo. When one segment of a maritime venture is sacrificed to save the others, the average is described as general, and the owners of the property saved must help make good the loss. Thus, if cargo is jettisoned in a successful effort to refloat a grounded vessel, the owners of the vessel and of the cargo saved are obliged to bear proportionate shares of the loss sustained by the owner of the cargo singled out for sacrifice.

Rome did not become a maritime power until the Punic wars of the third century BC. From the fact that the Romans were allies of the Rhodians and from the references in the *Digest*, it is logical to assume that Roman maritime law borrowed heavily from that of Rhodes. Acknowledging Rhodes as the birthplace of maritime jurisprudence, the maritime code of the later Eastern Empire, dating from the 7th or 8th century AD, was called the "Rhodian Sea Law."

The medieval maritime codes

Because the Mediterranean, under Roman control, was not only the centre of the Western world but also its principal commercial highway, European maritime law evolved as a uniform, supranational, comprehensive body of law—a characteristic which, though sometimes threatened by the spread of nationalism, has never been lost completely. The barbarian invaders who moved south were not seafarers, and the principal Mediterranean seaports were thus able to maintain their independence. Moreover, the conquered peoples were permitted to keep the Roman law to which they had become accustomed, and in the field of maritime jurisprudence the transition into the Middle Ages was therefore gradual. As certain Italian cities began to outstrip the Eastern Byzantine Empire commercially, they formulated their own maritime laws, some dating as early as 1063. Trani, Amalfi, Venice, and other Italian port cities all offered their own collections of laws. Nevertheless, the next widely accepted body of sea laws was the *Consolat de Mar*, or "Consulate of the Sea," originally compiled at Barcelona in the 13th century. More elaborate than the earlier codes, the *Consolat* was followed in Spain, Provence, and the Italian cities and had a significant effect on the development of modern maritime law.

The earliest code to emerge beyond the Mediterranean was the "Rolls of Oléron," named for an island in the Bay of Biscay and apparently dating from the 12th century. Whether the Rolls were of French or of Anglo-Norman origin, they became the nucleus of the maritime law not only of England and France but also of Scotland, Flanders, Prussia, and Castile; and they are still occasionally cited as authority, even by U.S. courts. The Rolls were closely followed in the Laws of Wisby, headquarters of the Hanseatic League until 1361.

The effect of nationalism

Modern national developments. In Continental Europe, loss of uniformity in the maritime law began with the late Renaissance and accelerated with the rise of nationalism in the 17th century, which witnessed adoption of the Maritime Code of Christian XI of Sweden (1667), the Marine Ordinances of Louis XIV of France (1681), and the Code of Christian V of Denmark (1683). Of these, the most significant were the Ordinances, prepared under Louis XIV's finance minister, Jean-Baptiste Colbert, as part of his comprehensive though unfulfilled plan for the codification of all French law. Established customs of the sea, revised to suit the times, were made part of the national law, enforceable in the French Admiralty Court, which was granted maritime jurisdiction to the exclusion of the old consular courts, whose judges had been elected by the mariners themselves.

The individuality of the maritime law—its "separation" from other types of law—was accentuated by the Ordinances, which gathered together in one code all of the criminal, private, procedural, and public laws relating to the sea. Although the French Admiralty Court failed to survive the Revolution that began in 1789, the substantive law embodied in the Ordinances was very closely followed in the *Code de Commerce*, whose adoption in 1807 meant that the maritime law was thereafter considered simply as a branch of commercial law, with consequent diminution of the weight previously given to custom and usage. Furthermore, abolition of the Admiralty Court resulted in the trial of maritime cases by the commercial courts, on which, in the smaller ports, maritime interests might not be represented. In countries with codes based directly or indirectly on the French commercial code, civil maritime cases, as well as nonmaritime commercial disputes, are heard and decided by commercial courts.

Although the *Code de Commerce* was widely adopted in the first half of the 19th century, in some cases by choice and in others by conquest, the German Commercial Code of 1861, revised in 1897, marked a departure from French law, and revisions of the Spanish and Italian codes showed the influence of the new German law. These, in turn, had their effect in countries under Italian and Spanish influence.

Although the "Pied Poudre" courts, held primarily for the settlement of disputes at English fairs and markets, also had special jurisdiction of seamen's cases, it is probable that the first English tribunals to apply maritime law, with the Rolls of Oléron as a basis, were the courts of the Cinque Ports. The High Court of Admiralty, which sat at London, and the Vice Admiralty Courts set up in the other ports, were a later development. They were named after the admiral, an officer whose duties were at first solely administrative and military but were broadened early in the 14th century to include disciplinary proceedings in such matters as piracy. The Admiralty Court is considered as dating from 1360, when for the first time the admiral was expressly granted jurisdiction in civil maritime cases. By the end of the 16th century the admiralty courts had come to exercise an extremely wide jurisdiction, reaching far beyond saltwater transportation into many areas of commercial law. But during the first half of the 17th century, the judges of the common-law courts succeeded in divesting their competitors in the Admiralty of their commercial jurisdiction and in restricting them to the adjudication of "things done upon the sea."

The Admiralty was a royal court with valuable emoluments. It functioned without the aid of juries, following procedures borrowed from the Continent that were somewhat less dilatory and cumbersome than those of the common-law courts, and applied the laws and customs of the sea to the maritime controversies that came before it. For these reasons it was preferred by the merchants and favoured by the Crown, which depended to a considerable extent on taxation of the merchants for its revenues. Its jurisdiction therefore waxed and waned with the strength or weakness of the reigning sovereign. Thus, it enjoyed wide jurisdiction under the Tudors, but its powers were severely curtailed under succeeding monarchs and governments, and were never fully restored until the passage of the first of the Admiralty Court Acts in the 19th century.

Although the powers of the English Admiralty are today quite broad, in practice it is rare for cases other than those involving marine collisions and salvage to be brought before it. Controversies respecting charter parties, ocean bills of lading, and marine insurance, for example, are more generally brought before the Commercial Court.

In the United States, the federal district courts are by statute granted original jurisdiction, "exclusive of the courts of the States," of "Any civil case of admiralty or maritime jurisdiction, saving to suitors in all cases all other remedies to which they are otherwise entitled." This means, essentially, that if a maritime claimant wishes to have his claim litigated in accordance with admiralty procedure he must invoke the admiralty jurisdiction of the district courts. However, he is free to sue in a state court, unless the defendant is a citizen of another state, in which case the suit may be tried as an ordinary civil action in the district court.

DISTINGUISHING FEATURES OF MARITIME LAW

Maritime liens. Although admiralty actions are frequently brought *in personam*, against individual or corporate defendants only, the most distinctive feature of admiralty practice is the proceeding *in rem*, against maritime property, that is, a vessel, a cargo, or "freight," which in shipping means the compensation to which a carrier is entitled for the carriage of cargo.

Under American maritime law, the ship is personified to the extent that it may sometimes be held responsible under circumstances in which the shipowner himself is under no liability. The classic example of personification is the "compulsory pilotage" case. Some state statutes impose a penalty on a shipowner whose vessel fails to take a pilot when entering or leaving the waters of the state. Since the pilotage is thus compulsory, the pilot's negligence is not imputed to the shipowner. Nevertheless, the vessel itself is charged with the pilot's fault and is immediately impressed with an inchoate maritime lien that is enforcible in court.

Maritime liens can arise not only when the personified ship is charged with a maritime tort, such as a negligent collision or personal injury, but also for salvage services, for general average contributions, and for breach of certain maritime contracts.

In a proceeding *in rem*, the vessel, cargo, or freight can be arrested and kept in the custody of the court unless the owner obtains its release by posting a bond or such other security as may be required under the applicable law or as may be acceptable to the plaintiff. More frequently, however, the owner will post security to avoid a threatened arrest, and the property never has to be taken into custody. When the judgment is for the plaintiff in a proceeding *in rem*, there will be a recovery on the bond or other security if the owner of the property does not pay; or, if security has not been posted, the court will order the property sold, or the freight released, in order to satisfy the judgment. The sale of a ship by an admiralty court following a judgment *in rem* divests the ship of all pre-existing liens—and not merely those liens sought to be enforced in the proceeding *in rem*. By way of contrast, the holder of an *in personam* judgment against a shipowner can, like any judgment creditor, have the ship sold in execution of the judgment; but such a sale, unlike the sale under an admiralty judgment *in rem*, does not divest existing liens; the purchaser at the execution sale takes the ship subject to all such liens. Thus, an *in rem* proceeding has decided advantages over a proceeding *in personam* in a case in which the shipowner is insolvent.

Efforts have been made from time to time to increase the security value of ship mortgages, in order to encourage lending institutions to finance vessel construction, but these efforts have not been very successful, largely because of differences in national laws respecting the relative priorities of mortgages and maritime liens. (Under general maritime law there is a complex hierarchy of maritime liens; that is to say, in a proceeding that involves distribution of an inadequate fund to a number of lien claimants, liens of a higher rank will be paid in full in priority over liens of a lower rank; and in most countries a ship mortgage ranks lower than a number of maritime liens.) Attempts were made to harmonize some of these conflicts by international conventions signed in 1926 and 1968, but the first failed to win widespread support and as of the end of 1971, the second had not been ratified by any of the signatories.

Contracts for the carriage of goods. The function of ships, other than warships, pleasure craft, and service vessels of various types is of course transportation of cargoes and passengers. In the "jet age" the passenger-carrying segment of the shipping industry has lost much of its former importance, but the quantity of goods transported by water continues to grow as the world economy expands.

The great majority of the contracts governing the carriage of goods by water are evidenced either by charter parties or by bills of lading. The term charter party (a corruption of the Latin *carta partita*, or "divided charter") is employed to describe three widely differing types of contracts relating to the use of vessels owned or controlled by others. Under a "demise" or "bareboat" charter, the shipowner delivers possession of the vessel

Margin notes:

Early English maritime courts

Proceedings *in rem* and *in personam*

Ship mortgages

Charter parties and ocean bills of lading

to the charterer, who engages the master and crew, arranges for repairs and supplies, and, in general, functions in much the same way as an owner during the term of the charter. A much more common arrangement is the "time" charter, whereunder the shipowner employs the master and crew and the charterer simply acquires the right, within specified limits, to direct the movements of the vessel and determine what cargoes are to be carried during the charter period. Under both demise and time charters, the charterer pays charter hire for the use of the vessel at a specified daily or monthly rate.

The third type is the "voyage" charter, which is essentially a contract of affreightment, or carriage. Most voyage charters provide for the carriage of full cargoes on one voyage or a series of voyages, but occasionally a charterer contracts for the use of only a portion of the carrying capacity of the vessel, in which case the governing contract is described as a "space" charter. Under a voyage charter, it is customary for the master or his agent to issue a bill of lading to the shipper, who is usually the charterer, although as between shipowner and charterer the voyage charter remains the governing contract of carriage; the bill of lading serves only as a receipt and as a document of title to the goods. Ocean bills of lading are usually in order form; that is, they call for delivery to the order of the shipper or of some other designated party. Such a bill of lading may be negotiated in much the same way as a check, draft, or other negotiable instrument, which means that a bona fide purchaser of the bill of lading takes it free and clear of any defects not appearing on its face. Thus, if cargo is externally damaged on shipment but the damage is not noted on the bill of lading, the carrier will be barred from establishing that the cargo was in fact damaged before it came into the carrier's custody. Once a bill of lading issued under a voyage charter is negotiated to a bona fide purchaser, it becomes the governing contract between the carrier and the holder of the bill.

When a ship strands or collides with another vessel, substantial cargo loss or damage may result. If the casualty is found to have been caused by a sea peril or an error in navigation, there will be no liability if the goods are being carried under a statutory or contractual provision based upon the Brussels bills of lading convention of 1922, which incorporated the so-called "Hague Rules." If, however, the casualty was the result of the carrier's failure to exercise due diligence to make the ship seaworthy and to see that it was properly manned, equipped, and supplied, the carrier will be held responsible.

Limitation of liability. A distinctive feature of maritime law is the privilege accorded to a shipowner and certain other persons (such as charterers in some instances) to limit the amount of their liability, under certain circumstances, in respect of tort and some contract claims. In some countries, including the United States, the limit, except as to claims for personal injury and wrongful death, is the value of the ship and the earnings of the voyage on which it was engaged at the time of the casualty. On the other hand, in the United Kingdom and the other countries that have ratified the Brussels limitation of liability convention of 1957 or enacted domestic legislation embracing its terms, the limit is £28, or its equivalent, multiplied by the adjusted net tonnage of the vessel, regardless of its actual value. The basic condition of the privilege is that the party asserting it must be free from "privity or knowledge," in the words of the United States statute, or "actual fault or privity," in the words of the convention. This formula means, generally speaking, that the shipowner is entitled to limit his liability for the negligence of the master or crew, but not for his own personal negligence or that of his managerial personnel. In a sense the limited liability of shipowners may be compared to the limited liability that any investor may now achieve by incorporating his enterprise. The limited-liability idea in maritime law, however, long antedates the emergence or invention of the modern corporation or limited company; its early appearance in maritime law may be taken as a recognition of the extraordinary hazards of seaborne commerce and the need to

Nature of limitation of liability

protect the adventurous shipowner from the crushing burden of liability—that is, in the days before even the most primitive forms of insurance had become available. Some modern commentators have suggested that the peculiar features of maritime limitation of liability have outlived their usefulness, and that the development of insurance and of the modern limited-liability company has radically altered the conditions out of which the shipowners' privilege originally grew. Although no maritime country has yet gone to the length of abolishing limitation of liability, shipowning interests appear to have become concerned about the possibility of such a development.

In most maritime countries the principle of limitation of liability was considered to be a part of the general maritime law. As it developed in continental Europe, the idea, generally stated, was that a shipowner entitled to limitation could satisfy his liability by abandoning the ship (and its pending freight) to claimants. Since the privilege of limitation was, and is, typically invoked following a large-scale maritime disaster, the abandonment theory meant that claimants got the value of the ship as it was following the disaster. If the ship had sunk or was a total loss with no freight pending, the claimants got nothing. This theory was carried over into the law of many South American countries.

Great Britain and the United States were once the only maritime countries that refused to admit the principle of limitation as part of the general maritime law. In both countries, however, the competitive needs of the shipping industry compelled its introduction by statute.

In general, the limitation law of any country will be applied by its own courts in favour of foreign shipowners as well as of citizens. From the point of view of shipowning interests, however, a major weakness of limitation law has been the fact that limitation proceedings were not given international recognition. That has meant that a shipowner whose ships moved in international trade could find himself sued in several countries as a result of one disaster and forced to set up limitation funds in each country. The Brussels convention of 1957 makes limitation decrees delivered by admiralty courts in ratifying countries internationally effective; that is, a shipowner is required to set up only one limitation fund, out of which all claims are paid, no matter in how many countries proceedings might be instituted against him. Thus, the convention, which increases the liability of shipowners in most countries, does offer in return this considerable advantage to shipowners.

Foreign claims

Collision liability. Under maritime law responsibility for collision damage is based upon the fault principle: a colliding vessel will not be held responsible for damage to another ship or to a fixed object such as a bridge, wharf, or jetty unless the collision is caused by a deficiency in the colliding vessel or by negligence or a willful act on the part of its navigators. It is not always necessary, however, to establish fault by positive evidence; there is a presumption of fault when a moving vessel collides with a fixed object or with another vessel that is properly moored or anchored, and the burden of proving freedom from fault will lie with the moving vessel.

In countries that have adopted the International Convention for the Unification of Certain Rules Relating to Collisions between Vessels, signed at Brussels in 1910, the rule of "comparative negligence" governs: if each of two colliding vessels is to blame, the total damages will be divided between their owners or operators in proportion to the respective degrees of fault. In certain countries that have not ratified the Convention, such as the United States, the law is such that, if both vessels are to blame, the total damages are equally divided, regardless of the respective degrees of fault. In certain other countries that have not ratified the Convention, including most of the Latin American states, the principle of "contributory fault" governs: if both vessels are to blame, each owner or operator bears his own damages.

Salvage and general average. Salvage and general average are doctrines peculiar to maritime law. Under the law of salvage, strangers to the maritime venture who succeed in saving maritime property from loss or damage from perils of the sea or other waters are entitled to an award for their efforts and have a maritime lien on the salvaged property therefor. Several elements will be taken into account in fixing the amount of the award, including the extent of the efforts required; the skill and energy displayed by the salvors, the amounts involved, including both the value of the vessel or other property employed by the salvors in rendering the service and the value of the vessel, cargo, or other property salvaged; the risks incurred by the salvors; and the degree of danger from which the property was rescued. General average (defined at the beginning of this article) is a principle still universally accepted, although there is some agitation for its abolition, principally because the accounting and other expenses incurred in administering a general average are often quite out of proportion to the amounts involved and because the same underwriters sometimes insure both hull and cargo.

Marine insurance. An appreciation of the part played by marine insurance is essential to an understanding of the shipping industry and the special law that governs it. Most shipowners carry hull insurance on their ships and protect themselves against claims by third parties by means of "protection and indemnity" insurance. Waterborne cargo is almost universally insured against the perils of the seas. It is impossible in a brief outline such as this to go into any of the special intricacies, which are many, of marine insurance law. Most cases of damage to a ship or its cargo resolve themselves into settlements between insurance carriers. Proposals for changes in the maritime law must always be evaluated against this background of insurance coverage, as the imposition of liabilities that cannot be insured against can discourage all but the wealthiest ocean carriers from engaging in the affected trades.

Insured perils

Marine insurance is the oldest known form of insurance. Indeed, the institution of general average, under which the participants in a maritime venture contribute to losses incurred by some for the benefit of all, may itself be looked on as a primitive form of mutual insurance. Hull and cargo insurance today, in fact, is usually written on forms whose wording has changed little since the 18th century. The so-called "perils" clause, enumerating the risks insured against, customarily includes not only the natural hazards to which a vessel is exposed but manmade perils such as capture or destruction by enemy forces as well. In 1898, however, Lloyd's of London underwriters inaugurated the practice of adding "Free of Capture and Seizure" (F.C.&S.) clauses to the basic policy forms, the effect of which was to remove war and similar risks from coverage. The practice has since become universal, with the result that the owner of a ship or cargo must either purchase separate war-risk insurance or else pay his marine underwriters an additional premium in return for deletion of the F.C.&S. clause.

An early type of marine liability insurance was against liability for damage that the insured vessel caused to other vessels. Such insurance was effected by the addition of a "running down" or "collision" clause to the basic hull policy insuring the owner or operator of a vessel against its loss or damage. On the theory that, if given full protection, owners and operators would not be encouraged to exercise proper care in the maintenance of their vessels and the selection of their masters and crews, hull underwriters at first refused to insure against more than 75 percent of the collision liability.

Protection and indemnity associations

With the advent of steam-driven vessels of iron and steel in the 19th century, the potential liabilities of shipowners increased substantially. To protect themselves, British owners banded together in "protection and indemnity" associations, commonly known as "P. and I. Clubs," whereby they insured each other against the liabilities to which they were all exposed in the operation of their vessels. These included liability for cargo damage, personal injury, and damage to piers, bridges, and other fixed objects, and also 25 percent of the liability for damage to other vessels against which the hull underwriters refused to insure. Foreign owners soon found the P. and

I. Clubs attractive, and as of 1971 the operators of some 75 percent of the world's ocean tonnage were insured with the British clubs and their Scandinavian and Japanese affiliates.

INTERNATIONALISM OF MARITIME LAW

Maritime law is often thought of as being a species of international law rather than a branch of domestic or municipal law. It should not be denied that the international aspect of maritime law gives it a distinctive flavour; in doubtful cases courts of one country will often look to the precedents or statutes of another country for inspiration or guidance. Except to the extent that it may have bound itself by international conventions, however, each country has the right to adopt such maritime laws as it sees fit. Although many such laws are common to most maritime countries, others are not, though there is a growing tendency to restore the international uniformity in the maritime law achieved during the Middle Ages. In many areas, the lead has been taken by the International Maritime Committee, more commonly known by its French name, Comité Maritime International (CMI), which is composed of the maritime law associations of 31 nations. The work of the Comité consists principally of drafting international conventions relating to subjects of maritime law. When such a draft is prepared, it is submitted to the Belgian government, which then convenes a diplomatic conference at which the CMI draft is discussed and amended as the official delegates may decide. If the revised draft wins approval at the conference, it is then submitted to the national governments for possible ratification. Although many of these conventions have failed to be widely ratified, others have been highly successful.

International conventions

The international regulations for the prevention of collisions at sea, first adopted at an international conference held in Washington in 1889 and revised at maritime safety conferences held in London in 1914, 1929, 1948, and 1960, are recognized by all of the maritime countries. The regulations are, in effect, an international code of navigation. In other fields much has been accomplished to ensure international uniformity through private agreements voluntarily adhered to by affected interests; the York-Antwerp Rules of General Average, first promulgated in 1890 and most recently amended in 1950, are the best known example of such agreements; although they do not technically have the force of law, nevertheless, by incorporation in charter parties and bills of lading, they determine the rights and obligations of the parties as effectively as any statute.

BIBLIOGRAPHY. E. BENEDICT, *The Law of American Admiralty*, vol. 1–4, 6th ed. by A.W. KNAUTH (1940–41) and vol. 5–6B, 7th ed. by A.W. and C.R. KNAUTH (1968–69), is the standard American text on admiralty practice. Included in *British Shipping Laws* are K. MCGUFFIE, P.A. FUGEMAN, and P.V. GRAY, *Admiralty Practice* (1964); N. SINGH, *International Conventions of Merchant Shipping* (1963); and the following standard British texts: SIR JOSEPH ARNOULD, *The Law of Marine Insurance and Average*, 15th ed. by LORD CHORLEY and C.T. BAILHACHE, 2 vol. (1961); T. CARVER, *Carriage by Sea*, 11th ed. by R.P. COLINVAUX, 2 vol. (1964); R. LOWNDES and G.R. RUDOLPH, *The Law of General Average*, 9th ed. by J.F. DONALDSON, C.T. ELLIS, and C.S. STAUGHTON (1964); and R.G. MARSDEN, *The Law of Collisions at Sea*, 11th ed. by K. MCGUFFIE (1961). G. RIPERT, *Droit Maritime*, 4th ed., 3 vol. (1950–53), is the most respected modern French text on maritime law. G. GILMORE and C.L. BLACK, JR., *The Law of Admiralty* (1957), is the leading modern, single-volume text on American maritime law. SIR WILLIAM R. KENNEDY, *Civil Salvage*, 4th ed. by K. MCGUFFIE (1958), is the leading text on salvage law. J.W. GRIFFIN, *The American Law of Collision* (1949), is the standard American text on the law of marine collision. SIR THOMAS E. SCRUTTON, *Scrutton on Charter Parties and Bills of Lading*, 17th ed. by SIR WILLIAM L. MCNAIR, SIR ALAN A. MOCATTA, and M.J. MUSTILL (1964), is the best known work on the subject. M.J. NORRIS, *The Law of Seamen*, 3rd ed. (1970), is a widely used American text. F.R. SANBORN, *Origins of the Early English Maritime and Commercial Law* (1930), is an excellent inquiry into the sources of English maritime law. J.H. WIGMORE, *A Panorama of the World's Legal Systems* (1936), contains a fascinating account of the origins and early development of maritime law.

T.L. MEARS, "The History of the Admiralty Jurisdiction," in *Select Essays in Anglo-American Legal History*, vol. 2 (1907), offers a fair survey.

(N.J.H.)

Marius, Gaius

Gaius Marius, with a middle class (equestrian) background, was the first man in the late Roman Republic (Cicero, from the same town, Arpinum, was the second) to achieve striking success as what the Romans called a new man by breaking into the conservative governing class of the exclusive Roman aristocracy. The main facts of Marius' public career are certain, but the explanation is often baffling because no good history of his period survives from antiquity. What does survive is biassed, sometimes for him, more often against him.

Early career.   Born *c.* 157 BC near Arpinum, in southern Latium, he was a strong and brave soldier and a skillful general, popular with his troops; but he showed little flair for politics and was not a good public speaker. As an equestrian, he lacked the education in Greek normal to the upper classes. He was superstitious and overwhelmingly ambitious; and because he failed, despite his great military success, to force the aristocracy to accept him, he suffered from an inferiority complex that may *Rise to* help explain his jealousy and vindictive cruelty. As a *power* young officer-cadet, along with Jugurtha (later king of Numidia), on Scipio Aemilianus' staff in the Numantine War in Spain (134 BC), he, like Jugurtha, made an excellent impression on his commanding officer. Marius' family enjoyed the patronage of more than one noble family, in particular the distinguished and inordinately conceited Caecilii Metelli, then at the height of their political power; they backed his candidacy for tribune (defender) of the plebs (common people) in 119. As tribune, Marius proposed a bill affecting procedure in elections and legislative assemblies by narrowing the bridges—the gangway across which each voter passed to fill in and deposit his ballot tablet—as a result of which there was no longer room on the gangway for observers, normally aristocrats, who abused their position to influence an individual's vote. When the two consuls tried to persuade the Senate to block the bill, Marius threatened them with imprisonment, and the bill was carried.

Marius showed himself no unprincipled candidate for popular favour, for he vetoed a popular corn bill; and the following years offered him little promise of a conspicuous career. He failed to secure the aedileship (control of markets and police) and was only just elected praetor (judicial magistrate) for the year 115 after bribing heavily, for which he was lucky to escape condemnation in court. The next year he governed Further Spain, campaigned successfully against bandits, and laid a foundation for great personal wealth through mining investments. After that, he made a good marriage into a patrician family that, after long obscurity, was on the point of strong political revival. His wife was Julia, sister of Julius Caesar, father of the later dictator.

When the command in the war against Jugurtha (who was now Numidian king) was given to Quintus Metellus, brother of Metellus Delmaticus, who had opposed his election reform law, as consul in 109, Marius was invited to join Metellus' staff; his quarrel with the Metelli had evidently been patched up. After defeating Jugurtha in pitched battle, Metellus was less successful in later guerrilla warfare, and this failure was exaggerated by Marius in his public statements when at the end of 108 he returned to Rome to seek the consulship (chief magistracy) after a quarrel with Metellus that may have been exaggerated in the pro-Marian tradition. Marius was elected on *Election* the equestrian and popular vote and, to Metellus' bitter *to the* chagrin, appointed by a popular bill to succeed Metellus *consulship* at once in the African command.

In recruiting fresh troops, Marius broke with custom, because of a manpower shortage, by enrolling volunteers from outside the propertied classes, which alone had previously been liable for service. In Africa he kept Jugurtha on the run, and in 105 Jugurtha was captured, betrayed by his ally, King Bocchus of Mauretania—not to Marius

himself but to Sulla, considered a rather seedy young aristocrat, who had joined Marius' staff as quaestor in 107. Sulla had the incident engraved on his seal, provoking Marius' jealousy.

The victory, however, was Marius', and he was elected consul again for 104—at the start of which year he celebrated a triumph and Jugurtha was executed—in order to take command against an alarming invasion of the Cimbri and Teutones, who had defeated a succession of Roman armies in the north, the last in disgraceful circumstances in 105. For this war, Marius used fresh troops raised by Rutilius Rufus, consul in 105, and excellently trained in commando tactics by gladiatorial instructors. With them, Marius defeated the Teutones at Aquae Sextiae (modern Aix-en-Provence, France) in 102 and in 101 came to the support of the consul of 102, Quintus Lutatius Catulus, who had suffered a serious setback; together they defeated the Cimbri at the Vercellae, near modern Rovigo in the Po Valley, and the danger was over. This was the apex of Marius' success. He had been consul every year since 104, and he was elected again for 100. With Catulus he celebrated a joint triumph, but already there was bad feeling between them. Marius claimed the whole credit for the victory; Catulus and Sulla gave very different accounts in their memoirs.

Marius had always had equestrian support, not only because his origins lay in that class but also because wars are bad for trade, and Marius had brought serious wars to an end. The Roman populace liked him for not being an aristocrat. He had the further support of his veterans, for it was in their interest to stick closely to their general. Marius perhaps did not realize the potency of their force, one that Sulla, Caesar, and Octavian employed with overpowering effect later.

Fall from power.   The year 100 saw Marius fail disastrously as a politician. Saturninus was tribune for the *Failure* second time, and Glaucia was praetor; given the poverty *as a* of surviving sources, it is extremely difficult to under- *politician* stand either their political aims or Marius' relationship to them. The three shared a common hatred of Metellus, who, as censor in 102, had tried to remove Saturninus and Glaucia from the Senate; and in 103 Saturninus had carried a bill, evidently in Marius' interest, for the settlement of veterans in Africa. Now, with the inevitability of civil disorder—for the Roman populace opposed his measures —Saturninus introduced bills for land distribution of Cimbric territory in the north to Romans living in the country, and probably to Italians, and for the settlement of veterans, evidently including allied troops, in colonies overseas. This bill may have included a powerful command for Marius to supervise the resettlement of the veterans—empowering him to give Roman citizenship to a certain number of the new settlers in each colony.

Marius had already violated the law by granting citizenship on the battlefield to two cohorts of Italians (Camertes) who fought under him against the Cimbri in 101, and conceivably Saturninus and Marius were agreeable to a program of extensive enfranchisement of Italians by means of the new colonial settlements. A breach between them occurred, possibly because Marius, in his jealous way, thought that Saturninus was stealing some of his own thunder or possibly because Saturninus' lawlessness had reached a pitch that no self-respecting consul could tolerate.

First the land and colonial bill was passed, but with blatant illegality; it required senators to take an oath within five days to observe it. After misleading statements about his own intention, Marius took the oath. Metellus refused, however, presumably because of the way in which the bill had been carried, and, forestalling condemnation in the treason court, he retired to Greece; later he was officially exiled. At the tribunician elections for 99, Saturninus was re-elected together with a pretender who, already heavily discredited, claimed to be the son of Tiberius Gracchus. At the consular elections, with Glaucia as a candidate, Marcus Antonius, the orator, was elected, and Gaius Memmius, a man with an excellent popular record, was murdered. In the ensuing pandemonium the Senate passed the "last decree," calling on the consuls to save the state. Through Marius' action Saturninus and Glaucia were captured on the Capitol and imprisoned in the Senate house; then a mob stripped off the roof and stoned them to death. Although this was no responsibility of Marius, he was smeared as a man who betrayed not only his enemies but also his friends.

Reputation as a betrayer

Later years. Rather than attend the inevitable recall of Metellus from exile, Marius went to the east in 99 and there met Mithradates VI of Pontus. He was elected to a priesthood (the augurship) but wisely withdrew his candidature for the censorship of 97. A background figure in the not fully unravelled politics of the 90s, successfully opposing an attempt in 95 to disenfranchise men to whom he had given citizenship under the terms of Saturninus' colonial bill, though the law itself had been shelved, in 92 he supported the equites in a scandalous prosecution and condemnation of his old associate Rutilius Rufus (in fact a model administrator) for alleged misgovernment of Asia.

Marius was now beginning to show his age. In an Italian rebellion (the Social War) of 90, he campaigned under the consul Rutilius Lupus, a soldier far his inferior. In 88, when the tribune Sulpicius Rufus proposed the transfer of the Asian command from the consul Sulla to Marius, presumably on the ground that Marius alone was sufficiently experienced to conduct such a critical war, there was violent public opposition to Sulla in Rome. Sulla went to his army in Campania and marched with it on Rome. Sulpicius' measures were rescinded, and Marius was exiled.

After a series of near catastrophes, all much embroidered in the telling, Marius escaped safely to Africa. In 87, when Sulla was fighting in Greece, disorder in Rome led to the consul Cinna being dismissed. Marius landed in Etruria, raised an army, sacked Ostia, and, joining forces with Cinna, captured Rome; both were elected consuls for 86, Marius for the seventh time. Hideous massacre followed as Marius ordered the deaths of Marcus Antonius, Lutatius Catulus, Publicus Licinius Crassus, and other distinguished men whom he considered to have behaved with treacherous ingratitude toward him. By this time he was hardly sane, and his death, on January 13, 86 BC, was a godsend for both enemies and friends alike. If the outcome of his proscriptions was considered to be less disastrous than that of the later proscriptions of Sulla, it was only because they lasted for a shorter time.

Marius' only son died as consul fighting against Sulla in 82. His widow survived until 69 and received the unusual honour, for a woman, of a public funeral oration by her nephew Julius Caesar, who later won great popularity by restoring to the Capitol Marius' trophies, which Sulla had removed.

Marius was commemorated by the name Mariana given to Uchi Majus and Thibaris (two African settlements) and to a colony in Corsica, and by the Fossa Mariana, a canal dug by his soldiers at the mouth of the Rhône River.

BIBLIOGRAPHY. E. BADIAN, *Foreign Clientelae* (1958), for a general account of the period; H.M. LAST, "The Wars of the Age of Marius," in *The Cambridge Ancient History*, vol. 9, ch. 3 (1932); T.F. CARNEY, *A Biography of C. Marius* (1961), strongly biassed in Marius's favour; RONALD SYME, *Sallust* (1964), for Sallust's account of the war against Jugurtha; F.W. ROBINSON, *Marius, Saturninus und Glaucia* (1912), good on the politics; R. WEYNAND, "C. Marius," in *Pauly-Wissowa Real-encyclopädie*, suppl. 6 (1935), the most detailed biography that exists (in German); ALFREDO PASSERINI, *Caio Mario* (1941), short and readable account (in Italian).

(J.P.V.D.B.)

Marketing and Merchandising

Marketing in its most general definition is the directing of the flow of goods and services from producers to consumers or users. It is not confined to any particular type of economy, since goods must be marketed in all economies and societies except perhaps the most primitive. Nor is marketing a function only of profit-oriented business; even such service institutions as hospitals, schools, and museums, engage in some forms of marketing.

THE FUNCTIONS OF MARKETING

In Western business organizations the marketing function was once seen as encompassing only sales and advertising and perhaps, also, marketing research. The purpose of the staff engaged in marketing was primarily to maximize sales volume. More recently the marketing manager's responsibilities have broadened to include all activities relating to the firm's customers, including product development, customer communications, and customer services; in some firms, the principal marketing executives have even been given authority over credit, physical distribution, public relations, and research and development. In a few firms, the integrated marketing concept has been pushed to the point where the head of marketing becomes the chief executive officer. The emphasis on marketing has been most conspicuous in industries serving the general consumer, such as retail store chains and manufacturers of foods, toiletries, and household appliances. Service industries, such as hotels, banks, and insurance companies, have been slower in taking it up. Airline transportation companies have been notably more customer oriented than the railroads. These tendencies have been visible in most of the leading industrial countries, although they have been pushed farthest in the U.S.

The increasing scope of marketing

The activities involved in marketing account for a large proportion of consumer expenditures. Studies made in the U.S. estimate the proportion at between 40 and 60 percent of total final sales value of all tangible goods. This includes the buying and selling expenses of producers; of wholesalers' and retailers' margins; and of all other promotional, storage, and transportation expenses. The proportion has increased through the years: in 1870 in the U.S., 88 persons were employed in distribution for every 1,000 employed in production; in 1950, 407 persons were employed in distribution for every 1,000 in production. But if marketing increases in significance with the growth of an industrial economy, it also plays a large part in those less-developed economies where distribution is in the hands of myriads of small tradesmen.

Types of goods and channels of distribution. It is common to distinguish between consumer goods, which are sold directly to consumers, and industrial goods, which are used by their purchasers to produce other goods and services. Consumer goods are sometimes classified according to the way in which they are purchased. "Convenience goods" are purchased with a minimum of searching; the consumer is familiar with the assortments offered, the goods are readily accessible on shelves or in display racks, and there is little to be gained from more extended shopping. "Shopping goods" are those for which the customer searches; he compares the prices, qualities, and styles available in a number of stores, perhaps not even knowing specifically what he wants to buy. "Specialty goods" have particular characteristics that encourage customers to make special efforts to find them, and price may be a minor consideration. Some students of marketing distinguish a fourth classification of unsought goods—those customers do not want, or do not know are available, or are not looking for.

Convenience goods and shopping goods

Staple groceries, such as white bread and pancake syrup, are convenience goods in most U.S. supermarkets but might be considered specialty goods in France or Italy. Long, crusted "French" bread, or the various pastas (from *agnellotti* to *tortellini*), may be shopping goods in Nashville, Tennessee, or Fort Worth, Texas, but they are convenience goods in Rome. A common electric rice cooker is a convenience good in Tokyo but not in New York City. Major items of household furniture and appliances tend, however, to be shopping goods wherever the assortments offered are wide enough to permit a meaningful choice for the customer.

Goods move to the final consumer through various channels of distribution. Raw materials pass from the extractive industries (forestry, fishing, mining, and agriculture) to manufacturing establishments. Finished products may be sent directly to the retailer or, less often, to the consumer, but as a rule they flow from the manufacturer to one or more wholesalers before they reach the retailer and, finally, the consumer. Although legal possession of goods generally accompanies their physical transfer from one party to another, this is not always the case; in consignment selling the seller retains ownership while the goods are in the hands of the wholesaler or retailer; that is, until the merchandise is sold to the final user or consumer.

Distribution in Africa and Japan

In less developed countries, channels of distribution tend to be simpler than in the more highly industrialized nations. There are notable exceptions, however. Cacao beans in Nigeria and several other West African nations are collected by a Cocoa Marketing Board that licenses trading firms to process the commodity. Because of the large numbers of small producers, these agents work through middlemen who, in turn, employ sub-buyers who may have "runners" to bring in the produce from remote areas. Japan's marketing organization was until recently characterized by lengthy channels of distribution and a multiplicity of wholesalers. It was not unusual for a product to pass through at least five separate wholesalers before it reached a retailer: a general wholesaler, a basic product specialty wholesaler, a special wholesaler, a regional wholesaler, and a local wholesaler. A move toward efficiency and direct selling by manufacturers is compressing the length of these channels in Japan, as it is in Switzerland, Great Britain, West Germany, and most other highly industrialized nations.

Marketing as a business function. Businessmen whose primary concern is the marketing of goods usually distinguish four basic functions in their work: (1) pricing, (2) product determination, (3) distribution, and (4) promotion. More recently a fifth function has been added, marketing research. Product determination consists of establishing the assortments of goods to be produced, as well as their qualities and physical characteristics. Such determinations are usually made in concert with the company's manufacturing, engineering, and finance departments. Promotion includes both personal selling and advertising, and is intimately related to the culture in which it is found. The provision of information is an important element in promotion, but the type and degree of selling pressure varies considerably from one country to another. Marketing research is concerned with the gathering, processing, and analyzing of market information. It is an aid in the evaluation of actions already taken, as well as a guide to future planning and budgeting.

In developing its marketing strategy a firm must determine what its best potential markets are and then select the means by which it will try to sell to them. The means are various, and the individual firm will concentrate on the specific combination (or "marketing mix") that seems to yield the most successful results.

RETAILING

From peddlers to chain stores

For thousands of years most goods were sold in marketplaces or by peddlers. In tropical Africa, hawkers still walk the streets of cities and towns crying out their wares, or cycle from village to village. Marketplaces are still the chief form of retail selling in the villages of many countries. During the Renaissance, market stalls in certain localities became fixed and eventually grew into stores. Many artisans' workshops expanded their retail facilities.

Chains of retail stores are known to have operated in China several centuries before Christ. In 1643 a chain of pharmacies was founded in Japan. Mercantile operations of a chain-store character were carried on by the Fugger family of Germany in the 15th century, and a chain of outposts was developed in Canada by the Hudson's Bay Company following its charter in 1670. The chain store as it is known in much of the world today, however, is generally believed to stem from the founding of the Great Atlantic & Pacific Tea Company (A & P) in New York City in 1859.

The prototypes of present-day department stores existed in Japan as early as the 17th century, but not until horse-drawn buses encouraged the growth of central business districts did the department store take hold in the Western world. Au Bon Marché in Paris developed from a large specialty store to a department store about 1860. Retailers in the U.S. soon followed. By World War I department stores modelled after the French example existed in large cities throughout the world, including cities in Argentina, Mexico, and Egypt.

Small independent merchants, however, still form the majority of retailers in most countries of the non-Communist world. (Most retail outlets in the Communist countries are nationalized.) According to the U.S. Census of Business, 97 percent of the 1,577,302 retail firms existing in the U.S. in 1967 were single-establishment companies. They accounted for 60 percent of total sales.

Chain stores and supermarkets. Centrally managed chains of stores have many advantages over independently managed retail enterprises: they can buy at more favourable terms; employ specialized buying personnel who have a wide knowledge of the supply markets; cut operating costs by integrating wholesaling and retailing functions; maintain lower inventories relative to sales; feature special price reductions on selected items; consolidate their advertising for stores in a single area; and try out new merchandising methods in one store at a time. There are also disadvantages in the chain structure. Personal interest, drive, creativity, and the will to serve the customer are often much weaker in chain operations than among independent retailers. Public sentiment has often been hostile to chains: at one time chain-store tax laws were in effect in 29 states of the U.S.; a Danish law prohibited retailers from owning more than a single store per municipality; the Poujadist movement in France in the late 1950s and early 1960s brought political pressure to bear in favour of small business and against the retail chain.

The advantages of chain stores

The importance of retail chains varies from country to country. In western Europe in 1960, the estimated share of total retail sales made by chains (excluding consumer cooperatives and department stores) ranged from 0.7 percent in Austria to 25.6 percent in Great Britain. In Portugal, Spain, and parts of Italy, low purchasing power and the undeveloped structure of commerce and industry inhibited the growth of retail chains. In other countries, including Austria and Denmark, they were impeded by the antichain legislation of the 1930s. The strong position of consumer cooperatives in the Scandinavian countries made the spread of retail chains difficult.

Retailing in Communist countries is almost entirely in the hands of chains. The retail stores are often tied to wholesale establishments covering a municipality, a region, or even an entire country; in some cases, the integration extends back to producers. The degree of autonomy granted managers of individual stores also varies. Store managers in Hungary in the 1970s had a larger degree of operational autonomy than did their counterparts in China, where the tendency was to centralize managerial decisions.

Supermarkets do not always belong to chains, but in the U.S., Great Britain, France, Italy, West Germany, and other highly industrialized countries the chains include about 90 percent of them. Supermarkets are large stores dealing in groceries, meats, produce, dairy products, baked goods, and household sundries; they are organized departmentally and operate primarily on a self-service basis. Supermarkets in the U.S. commonly handle a broad assortment of toilet goods; those in France and Italy stock wines and other alcoholic beverages; and many Swiss supermarkets sell clothing and quantities of cut flowers.

Supermarkets

The pattern of supermarket development was set in the U.S. in 1930 when Michael Cullin opened the first unit of what was to become the King Kullen chain of supermarkets. Other independent food stores followed Cullin's lead. The major food chains gradually began to convert their service stores—most of which handled only dry groceries—into supermarkets in the mid-1930s. During the two decades following World War II, when the rate of growth of supermarket chains in the U.S. was at its peak, tens of thousands of small independent food retailers were driven out. Similar developments occurred at a later date in other countries. In France, for instance, the number of supermarkets increased from approximately 50 in 1960 to 1,500 by 1970; in the latter year, 13,000 small specialty shops were forced to close.

Many operators of individual supermarkets, superettes (small stores), and chains with only a few retail outlets have successfully fought the expansion of large chains by banding together into retail cooperatives. The cooperatives service their members by joint buying, warehousing, store delivery, and common advertising and other promotional aids. Retail cooperatives have been strong among foodstores in the Pacific coast states of the U.S., and in western Europe in nonfoods, particularly textiles.

Voluntary chains of retailers sponsored by wholesalers are common in many countries. In western Europe in the 1960s, there were at least four huge wholesaler-sponsored chains of retailers, each including 15,000 stores or more. The 30,000 "Spar" retailers were located in 10 countries, each store using the same name and, as a rule, offering the same brands of products. Wholesaler-sponsored chains offer the same types of services for their retailer clients as do the financially integrated retail chains.

Department stores and discount houses. Department stores are large retail stores that carry a wide variety of merchandise, particularly apparel and accessories, and some home furnishings. In western Europe and Japan, department stores also sell food on a large scale. They are organized in departments, each with its own merchandising, control, promotion, and service. Some departments —such as beauty parlors, restaurants, pet shops, and shoes—that have special merchandising or operational problems may be leased to outside firms.

How depart- ment stores vary

Although department stores seldom account for more than five to eight percent of total retail sales, they draw large numbers of customers in urban areas. The most influential department stores offer fashion leadership; one example is the promotion of contemporary-style furniture by the Nordiska Kompaniet (NK) department-store group of Sweden. Recreation and entertainment are often used to attract customers, as in the Japanese department stores that offer exhibitions, sideshows, and other diversions, generally without charge.

Giant department stores have also spawned chain organizations, sometimes through mergers with other department stores within the same country or by opening branch units within a region but also by expanding to other countries—for example, Sears, Roebuck and Company's operations throughout Latin America, Canada (in partnership with Simpson of that country), and Spain. Major department stores in several western European nations have branched into variety-store chains, supermarkets, specialty shops, and wholesale establishments. The laRinascente group of Italy, which began with a single department store in Milan, later developed the UPIM chain of variety stores, the SMA supermarket chain, and a buying service for other store groups, including foreign ones.

Moscow's leading department store, GUM, has a staff of well over 4,000; another Moscow department store, Childrens' World (*Detskii Mir*), selling a wide variety of children's items, employs more than 3,000 people. Other large department stores are located in some of Moscow's residential neighbourhoods.

The practice of "discounting," or selling merchandise below the manufacturer's list price, has existed among some segments of retailing for decades. In the years following World War II, large numbers of retail stores in the U.S. adopted this policy, made possible by reducing services and often locating in low-rent shopping districts. The initial growth was in "hard goods" or consumer durables, particularly electrical household appliances. Other goods were added later, until the discount houses (as these establishments came to be known) became essentially department stores featuring reduced prices and minimal services. Specialty discount operations have also grown significantly in foods, pharmaceutical items, forms of hardware, and other lines, usually through a chain-store organization. Some "closed-door"

discount houses restrict sales to a special membership, often based upon a group affiliation.

Discount houses appeared also in Canada, France, Mexico, Sweden, Great Britain, West Germany, and elsewhere. They have been most successful in countries that are well supplied with consumer goods and in which retailing is highly competitive. In some countries their growth has been inhibited by pressures from suppliers, governmental agencies, other retail organizations, and labour unions.

Consumer cooperatives. Consumer cooperatives are retail stores owned and operated by consumers for their mutual benefit. Most espouse the principles of the first cooperative store established in Rochdale, England in 1844. These include open membership, one vote per member, limited customer services, and a sharing of the profits among members in the form of rebates, generally related to the amounts of their purchases.

Consumer cooperatives have flourished in western and northern Europe, particularly in Denmark, Finland, Iceland, Norway, Sweden, and Great Britain. The Communist countries have their own forms of consumer cooperative, usually integrated into the national distributive systems. In the Soviet Union, for example, consumer cooperatives have a near monopoly of retail sales in the villages. A number of the newer countries have tried to encourage the growth of consumer cooperatives as a means of lowering prices and of counteracting foreign-business influence.

Nonstore retailing. Some retailers have no stores. The three principal types of nonstore retailers are catalog houses, itinerant retailers, and vending-machine operators.

The largest catalog houses in the world—Sears, Roebuck and Company and Montgomery Ward & Company Inc.—were founded in the U.S. during the latter part of the 19th century. They began by selling exclusively by mail order through catalogs, although today both firms do more than half their business in their retail stores. They also sell through catalog order stations in their retail stores, catalog stations located at other points, and by telephone. Other department stores and larger specialty stores frequently supplement their store operations with mail and telephone orders, often in response to advertising.

Mail- order selling

Following World War II, mail-order specialists grew rapidly in West Germany, Great Britain, and a few other highly industrialized countries. The firms of Quelle and Neckermann in West Germany also do a considerable part of their business in retail stores, in catalog service outlets, and by telephone. Development of a mail-order operation requires an efficient transportation network and a secure means of transmitting payments; in many countries these are lacking.

Itinerant retailers contact their customers in homes, at places of work, or in streets and other public places. Some sell by soliciting customers on a door-to-door basis; others work through merchandise "clubs" or personal introductions. In less-developed countries they hawk their wares in the streets. In the 1960s about 19 percent of retail businesses in Italy were itinerant in nature.

Vending-machine operations are usually carried on in sites owned by other businesses (including retail stores), by institutions, and by transportation agencies. In the U.S., vending machines deal mainly in food for immediate consumption. In other countries—Sweden, for example —vending machines have developed as a supplementary channel to retail stores where hours of business are restricted by law. High costs of manufacturing, installation, and operation have limited the expansion of vending-machine retailing.

WHOLESALING

Wholesaling consists of selling to other business firms, either for resale or for business use, usually in bulk and at less than retail prices. A wholesaler is an independent merchant operating one or more wholesale establishments. Manufacturers may engage in wholesaling through their sales branches, and retailers may also do so internally through chain-store warehouses, although they are not classed as wholesalers.

Wholesalers are of two kinds: full-service and limited-service. Full-service wholesalers are generally the more important in terms of sales volume; they perform a variety of services for their customers: stocking inventories, operating warehouses, supplying credit, employing salesmen to aid customers, and making deliveries. Full-service wholesalers who carry broad assortments of merchandise such as groceries are called general-line wholesalers; those who sell only narrow lines of goods, such as coffee and tea, or cigarettes, are called specialty wholesalers.

Limited-service wholesaling has emerged in West Germany, the U.S., and other industrialized countries as a way of reducing the costs of service. Examples of limited-service wholesalers are "cash-and-carry" outlets, usually handling only fast-moving merchandise; "drop shippers," who ship goods directly from the manufacturer to the retailer; "truck jobbers," who sell and deliver directly from their vehicles, often for cash; and the "rack jobber," who handles the requirements of supermarkets in certain nonfood lines, such as housewares or toiletries.

In less-developed countries, wholesalers often dominate trade; they are the main elements in the distribution systems of many countries in Latin America, the Far East, and tropical Africa. In those countries the business activities of wholesalers may extend to manufacturing or retailing or branch out into nondistributive ventures, such as real estate, moneylending, or transportation. Until the latter half of the 1950s Japan was a country of wholesaling where even fairly large manufacturers and retailers relied principally on wholesalers as their intermediaries, but in more recent years, as in the U.S. almost a century earlier, Japanese wholesalers have decreased in importance. Even in the most highly industrialized nations, however, wholesalers remain essential to the operations of large numbers of small retailers.

In Communist countries, wholesaling performs basically the same functions as in other economies. Some capital goods pass directly from the producer to the user; in other cases, goods may move through one or more layers of wholesalers. The latter are usually supervised by trade ministries at the national or regional level.

Manufacturers may use agents in marketing their products. Agent middlemen, unlike merchant wholesalers, do not take title to the goods they sell; nor, as a rule, do they take physical possession of them. The three principal types of agent middlemen are brokers, manufacturers' agents, and sales agents.

Brokers, most commonly found in the food industries, may represent either a buyer or a seller, but most frequently the latter. Relationships are usually temporary, and brokers often represent a number of manufacturers of noncompeting products on a commission basis.

Manufacturers' agents, on the other hand, represent their principals on a continuous basis. As a rule, they sell only part of a manufacturer's output, sometimes in areas where the manufacturer cannot support full-time salesmen. Compensation is usually by commission.

Sales agents sell all of a manufacturer's output, and generally have considerable freedom in setting prices. Sometimes they function in effect as a manufacturer's marketing department, even though they work on a straight commission basis. Sales agents often feed back market and product information to their principals and play an active role in product development.

MARKETING GOODS TO INDUSTRY

Many goods are sold for use in producing other goods and services. These include buildings, land, machinery, component parts, semifinished goods (such as textiles, steel sheets, and other products that will undergo further processing), raw materials, and such supplies as coal, oil, or janitorial services.

The marketing of goods and services to manufacturers differs markedly from marketing to final consumers. Industrial purchasers often employ professional purchasing agents backed up by engineers, testing laboratories, and production specialists. Such purchasers are generally familiar with competitive products, and are prepared to negotiate. They are also more concentrated geographically: the purchasing decisions of automobile manufacturers are made in centres such as Detroit, Paris, and Turin, Italy; data-processing equipment for large-scale financial operations is sold mainly in such cities as Tokyo, London, New York, and Geneva and Zürich, Switzerland.

The demand for industrial goods is further distinguished by its dependence upon the demand for consumer goods that are the final products. Thus, the prosperity of the steel industry depends upon conditions in the automobile industry. Similarly, the industrial demand for screws, nuts, bolts, drafting supplies, and circuits is largely derived from the purchases of the general public.

A prevalent practice in industrial marketing is reciprocity—that is, a two-way buying agreement, often inferred rather than overtly stated. It is difficult for a seller not to buy from his own customers, if they produce items he needs. Three-way reciprocal combinations also exist, generally where there are circular relations among buyers; for example, A buys from B, and B buys from C, so A places pressure on B to persuade C to buy from A. Reciprocal buying arrangements may become even more complex.

Customers for industrial goods may be classified into three groups: users, original-equipment manufacturers, and middlemen. Users make use of the goods in their businesses—for example, the manufacturer who purchases a metal-stamping press to produce parts for his finished goods. Original-equipment manufacturers incorporate the purchased goods into their final products—for example, the television manufacturer who buys his tubes and transistors. Industrial middlemen are essentially wholesalers who distribute industrial goods from the manufacturers to users, to original equipment manufacturers, and to other middlemen. Industrial goods wholesalers include mill-supply houses, steel warehouses, machine-tool dealers, paper jobbers, and chemical distributors; different industries often have different names for middlemen who perform similar functions.

MARKETING FARM PRODUCTS

Channels of distribution for agricultural products follow the same general scheme as those for other goods. Individual farmers, however, often produce in relatively small quantities for the market—e.g., cocoa beans in Ghana, or milk in Wisconsin—and therefore the production of separate farmers often has to be assembled as the first stage in marketing it. This is done by three principal types of middlemen: wholesale merchants, who buy and resell to processors or other merchants; merchandise agents and brokers, who do not take title to the goods and usually do not have possession of them; and such special types as commission buyers, auctioneers, and livestock concentration yards.

The auction is one of the more colourful features of agricultural marketing. Major auctions, as a rule, are devoted to a particular product indigenous to a region, such as cut flowers in San Remo, Italy, cheese in Alkmaar, The Netherlands, and tobacco in Winston-Salem, North Carolina. Although sellers at the auctions are usually the producers, they may be assemblers reselling to a higher echelon of assemblers or to industrial users, retailers, or even consumers.

Farmers' cooperative associations are found throughout the world. Governments have encouraged them in order to stabilize the supply of agricultural products and raise farm productivity and incomes. In addition to marketing the farms' output, these cooperatives often purchase supplies, obtain loans, encourage research, and offer a host of services ranging from irrigation to insurance. Many cooperatives pool their members' products and market them as a single batch. Swedish cooperatives handle almost all milk production, most of the output of livestock and eggs, and a large percentage of the timber. In the U.S. in the 1960s, cooperatives marketed over 20 percent of farm production and handled about 20 percent of the farm supply business.

In recent decades the less-developed countries have given particular encouragement to the development of agricultural cooperatives. Most sugarcane in India is sold to sugar factories through cooperative societies sponsored and administered by the state governments. The Commodity Marketing Boards of West African countries are government-supervised organizations regulating the buying and selling of peanuts, palm kernels and oil, cocoa, cottonseed and lint, and other exported commodities. The boards attempt to secure the most favourable terms for the purchase, grading, export, and sales of the commodities. Cooperatives are also frequently used in Communist countries to market the farms' products and to handle many of the functions of supply in rural districts.

MARKETING RESEARCH

The analysis of marketing problems

Marketing research has been defined as the application of the scientific method to the solution of marketing problems. It studies people as buyers, sellers, and consumers, examining their attitudes, preferences, habits, and purchasing power. Marketing research is also concerned with the channels of distribution, with promotion and pricing, and with the design of the products and services to be marketed. Although there is hardly a form of commercial activity that does not use marketing research with some frequency, it finds its widest application in manufacturing —probably because manufacturing is further removed from the ultimate consumer than are most service industries, public utilities, and wholesale and retail enterprises.

Kinds of marketing research. Advertising research attempts to evaluate the effectiveness of advertising expenditures and to guide future advertising efforts. Market analysis and forecasting try to identify and measure the markets for specific products and to estimate sales possibilities. Performance analysis helps a company evaluate how well it is meeting its objectives in such areas as sales, its share of the market, sales-force performance, costs, and profits. Research in physical distribution aims to increase a manufacturer's efficiency in moving products along the channels of distribution. Product research runs a gamut from identifying the needs and characteristics of product users to testing package designs.

Although the basic practices of marketing research originated in the U.S., the methods have been adopted in most parts of the world in varying degree. Western European and Japanese marketing research expanded during the 1950s and 1960s. The Soviet Union and other eastern European countries have established agencies to furnish marketing research to their nationalized industries.

Marketing research is not an exact science; it has not eliminated important areas of uncertainty in managerial decision-making and probably never will. It indicates only the conditions that exist, not what to do about them. It may also be expensive, and its value must be measured against its cost. Finally, the information provided soon becomes out of date.

Basic procedures. There are certain general procedures in marketing research, although they are not applicable to all cases. A six-step scheme for conducting research on a marketing problem is: (1) preliminary analysis, in which potentially influential factors and variables are examined, often based upon an extensive search for relevant data; (2) definition of the problem; (3) planning of the research study, which consists essentially of determining how the data will be obtained and how they will be organized in order to permit sound conclusions and recommendations; (4) collection and tabulation of data, which may be primary data gathered by observation, experimentation, or survey, or secondary data obtained from governmental or private sources; (5) interpretation of the results; and (6) presentation of the results to management, including assistance to management in following up the study's conclusions and recommendations.

Each of the six steps listed above involves serious problems of methodology and technique for the marketing researcher. In step four, for example, if the researcher wishes to gather his data by survey he must usually decide among mail, telephone, and personal interviews. He is also faced with the questions of the survey's validity (whether it measures what it is intended to measure) and of its reliability as a sample of the entire market. The researcher must further decide how much stress to put on quantitative "facts" in his survey as against the qualitative issues of motivation—that is, why respondents answer in various ways.

MERCHANDISING AND PRODUCT DEVELOPMENT

Adapting products to markets

In traditional economies, the goods produced and consumed often remain the same from generation to generation—including food, clothing, and housing. As economies develop, the range of products available tends to expand, and changes occur in the products themselves. In contemporary industrialized societies, products, like people, go through life cycles: birth, growth, maturity, and decline. This constant replacement of existing products with new or altered products is of great concern to professional marketers. The development of new products involves all the departments of a business—production, finance, research and development, even personnel administration and public relations.

Product design. When a customer purchases a product he receives not only the item itself but, along with it, labelling, branding, packaging, sometimes a warranty, and perhaps the assurance of the availability of such services as repairs. In designing the product, these other things must be considered with it. Participants in the designing of a product may include consumers, middlemen, and industrial buyers, as well as the manufacturer. In a buyer's market—that is, one in which sellers must compete actively for the consumer's patronage—the greatest influence on product design is likely to be the consumer's reaction, actual or anticipated. Because of the closeness of middlemen (particularly retailers) to the consumer, they are often in an excellent position to anticipate consumer reaction to a planned product. Some giant retailers (*e.g.*, Marks and Spencer, Ltd. in Great Britain, or Sears, Roebuck and Company in the U.S.) play major roles in designing the products they sell. Industrial users may also take an active hand in designing the items they buy because the items often fit into an existing or planned production system. The degree of patent protection offered by the government is another factor affecting product design. Manufacturers of pharmaceuticals in Italy, for instance, lacking adequate patent protection, engage in very little original product research; they tend to copy innovations in other countries. France, on the other hand, grants an unusual degree of protection to designers of fashion products, such as women's clothing, despite the fact that manufacturers in most other countries are more or less free to copy those designs.

Three main types of product design

Product design takes basically three forms: innovation, alteration of an existing product, and the development of new applications for a product that remains the same. Examples of innovation include many antibiotic drugs, a wide variety of plastics, and innumerable electrical appliances, ranging from television to electric toothbrushes. Most invention today is done by the product research and development departments of manufacturing firms, rather than by independent inventors. Examples of alteration of an existing product range from the change made in an automobile motor to reduce air pollution to such minor changes as the addition of a butter drawer to a refrigerator. Other changes merely vary the style of a product —an office typewriter, a woman's coat—to make it more attractive to the consumer. An example of a new application for an existing product may be seen in the electric blender, which was originally used to reduce soft fruits and vegetables into pulp or juices; eventually its kitchen uses were expanded so that today it is promoted as a device for chopping and mixing a wide variety of foods.

Product line and product mix. A product (or service) may be thought of merely as giving the owner basic utilitarian satisfactions, as an automobile, for example, provides transportation. On the other hand, many goods go beyond merely practical requirements: the automobile may offer aesthetic satisfaction because of its design, or enhance its owners' status, or appeal to unconscious desires for virility, power, youthfulness, or dignity. The way a product is defined may also depend on the orientation of the manufacturer. Thus, a maker of electrical refrigerators may limit his market interests to the selling of his product as narrowly defined or, on the other hand, may think of his business more broadly as the arresting of food deterioration. In defining his product, however, the manufacturer must consider the marketing, technological, financial, and even legal problems that may arise when he tries to enlarge his scope.

Marketers are continually altering their "product lines" by adding new products, changing existing ones, and dropping others. A product line is an assortment of items that have some affinity to one another, whether from the way in which the customer makes use of them or the way in which he mentally relates the products to each other. Within each product there are additional classifications by style, colour, size, or other characteristics.

In setting up a product line, the marketer must consider the whole process of selling and distribution, including the prices at which the goods are to be sold, the approach to middlemen within the channels of distribution, the personal selling efforts required, and so forth. These elements must, in turn, be integrated with production, finance, research and development, and other nonmarketing functions within the firm.

Packaging and branding. Customers in France still carry their long loaves of bread unwrapped; small produce dealers in Italy wrap their vegetables in newspapers or place them in customers' string bags; and industrial wholesalers in many countries still sell nuts, bolts, nails, and other materials in bulk. But in most industrial countries the packaging of merchandise has become a part of the selling effort; marketers now specify exactly the types of packaging that will be most appealing to prospective customers. The importance of packaging in distributing the product has increased with the spread of self-service —in wholesaling as well as in retailing. Packaging is sometimes designed to facilitate the use of the product, as with aerosol containers for room deodorants; in Europe, such condiments as mustard, mayonnaise, and catsup are often packaged in tubes. Some packages are reusable, making them attractive to customers in some of the poorer countries where metal containers, for instance, are often highly prized.

Branding is used to identify the product of a specific seller. Like packaging, a brand may become part of the product in the mind of the customer. Manufacturers' brands are found in most parts of the world, including the Soviet Union. Wholesalers' or retailers' brands (also called dealers' brands, private brands, or private labels) are employed by large department stores, large wholesale establishments, chain stores, and retail cooperatives.

Part of the marketer's product policy is his product guarantee or warranty, in which the manufacturer or middleman promises the purchaser certain services and performance standards. By explicitly stating his guarantees, the manufacturer may limit his liability, while also acquiring an additional promotion message. In most countries, large manufacturers and retailers are more likely to have specific policies on guarantees than are their smaller competitors, probably because they have more to gain or lose by the way in which their guarantees are interpreted.

Advertising. As it is handled in large organizations, advertising is one of four components of marketing promotion, the other three being personal selling, sales promotion, and public relations. If marketing is integrated into a single organizational unit, advertising usually comes under the purview of the marketing chief, along with personal selling and sales promotion. Public relations in the larger firms is usually separated from marketing in the organizational structure.

Advertising may be defined as any paid form of marketing promotion directed toward masses of potential customers (for a fuller discussion, see ADVERTISING). Manufacturers usually favour national or regional media in the effort to gain acceptance for their products and brands. Retailers, on the other hand, attempt to stimulate a more local buying response. Much advertising is not intended for the general public but for industrial buyers, and it appears in various trade publications.

Advertising is most pervasive in highly industrialized countries, where it is used to move products along the distributive channels. The Soviet Union and other east European countries have in recent years adapted advertising techniques to their socialized economies. The methods and media used in different countries vary considerably. In the U.S., for example, radio and television draw most of their revenue from advertising. France, on the other hand, does not permit advertising on its nationally operated television systems. In Japan, with its unusually high literacy rate, advertisers have access to a variety of newspapers, magazines, and other printed media; in Spain, where illiteracy is high among older women, advertisers emphasize the radio and the cinema.

WORLDWIDE TRENDS

As marketing has become more influential and pervasive in industrialized countries, its development has taken two different routes. On the one hand, channels of distribution have been compressed—that is, the number of intermediaries between the original producer and the final consumer has decreased. This has come about through a process of vertical integration up and down the marketing structure: mergers, expansion, cooperation, voluntary ties, and long-term contractual relationships among distributors have all worked to this effect. On the other hand, new marketing institutions and new ways of operating have developed. Industrialization has encouraged diversity in marketing. Developments in mass communications, for example, have increased the number of ways in which advertising and promotion may be carried on. While in some respects products have become more uniform, producers make greater efforts to cater to the individualized tastes of consumers and to tailor their products for specific segments of a market.

Marketing has not been without its critics. In the more industrialized countries, objections have been raised to the practice of inducing "forced obsolescence" of products through changes in their design; to the economic waste involved in heavy expenditures on marketing and advertising; and to the use of hard-sell techniques to make consumers buy. Along with this has gone a more general type of criticism directed at the ends of economic activity, questioning the social desirability of promoting the use of tobacco, conventional automobiles, supersonic aircraft, and even industrial growth in general.

Important changes have taken place in the marketing methods used in the Soviet Union and other Communist countries. Institutions corresponding to advertising and marketing research agencies have come into being in those countries. Branding of products is used to an increasing extent. Consumer credit is increasingly available for the purchase of major appliances. Packaging has become more attractive and more functional. Self-service techniques have been adapted to Soviet methods of retailing, although on a small scale. In the 1960s, however, Soviet citizens and knowledgeable Western visitors still complained of shoddy merchandise, the difficulty of obtaining repairs, the cumbersomeness of the three-stage cashier system used in many retail stores, and the nonprofessionalism of retail personnel.

BIBLIOGRAPHY. Among the most widely used textbooks are: THEODORE N. BECKMAN and WILLIAM R. DAVIDSON, *Marketing*, 8th ed. (1967); EDWARD W. CUNDIFF and RICHARD R. STILL, *Basic Marketing: Concepts, Decisions, and Strategies*, 2nd ed. (1971); E. JEROME MCCARTHY, *Basic Marketing: A Managerial Approach*, 4th ed. (1971); CHARLES F. PHILLIPS and DELBERT J. DUNCAN, *Marketing: Principles and Methods*, 6th ed. (1968); FREDERICK D. STURDIVANT et al., *Managerial Analysis in Marketng* (1970); and MARTIN ZOBER, *Principles of Marketing* (1971).

Several works of a more conceptual and theoretical nature are: WROE ALDERSON, *Dynamic Marketing Behavior: A Functionalist Theory of Marketing* (1965); HELMY H. BALIGH and LEON E. RICHARTZ, *Vertical Market Structures* (1967); REAVIS COX et al. (eds.), *Theory in Marketing: Second Series* (1964); JOHN A. HOWARD, *Marketing: Executive and Buyer Behavior* (1963); and DAVID B. MONTGOMERY and GLEN L. URBAN, *Management Science in Marketing* (1969).

The importance of externals

The promotion effort

Developments in the industrial countries

Books on international and comparative marketing include: DAVID CARSON, *International Marketing: A Comparative Systems Approach* (1967); JOHN FAYERWEATHER, *International Marketing*, 2nd ed. (1970); GORDON E. MIRACLE and GERALD S. ALBAUM, *International Marketing Management* (1970); and FRANKLIN R. ROOT, R.L. KRAMER, and M.Y. D'ARLIN, *International Trade and Finance*, 2nd ed. (1966).

(D.Ca.)

Markets

What economists mean by the term market

Markets in the most literal and immediate sense are places in which things are bought and sold. In the modern industrial system, however, the market is not a place; it has expanded to include the whole geographical area in which sellers compete with each other for customers. Alfred Marshall, whose *Principles of Economics* (first published in 1890) was for long an authority for English-speaking economists, based his definition of the market on that of the French economist A. Cournot:

> Economists understand by the term Market, not only particular market place in which things are bought and sold, but the whole of any region in which buyers and sellers are in such free intercourse with one another that the prices of the same goods tend to equality easily and quickly.

To this Marshall added:

> The more nearly perfect a market is, the stronger is the tendency for the same price to be paid for the same thing at the same time in all parts of the market.

The concept of the market as defined above has to do primarily with more or less standardized commodities such as wool or wheat or shoes or automobiles. The word is also used to deal with, for example, the market for real estate or for old masters; and there is the "labour market," although a contract to work for a certain wage is not quite the same thing as the sale of a packet of goods. There is a connecting idea in all of these various usages—namely, the interplay of supply and demand.

TYPES OF MARKETS

Most markets consist of groups of intermediaries between the first seller of a commodity and the final buyer. There are all kinds of intermediaries, from the brokers in the great produce exchanges down to the village grocer. They may be mere dealers with no equipment but a telephone, or they may provide storage and perform important services of grading, packaging, and so on. In general, the function of a market is to collect products from scattered sources and channel them to scattered outlets. From the point of view of the seller, dealers channel the demand for his product; from the point of view of the buyer, they bring supplies within his reach.

There are two main types of markets, in which the forces of supply and demand operate quite differently, with some overlapping and borderline cases. In the first, the producer offers his goods and takes whatever price they will command; in the second, the producer sets his price and sells as much as the market will take.

The behaviour of primary commodity markets

Markets for primary products. The first type is common among primary products—that is, those that depend upon animal, vegetable, and mineral resources. The general run of agricultural commodities is produced under competitive conditions by relatively small scale cultivators scattered over a large area. The final purchasers are also scattered, and centres of consumption are distant from regions of production. The dealer, therefore, since he is indispensable, is in a stronger economic position than the seller. This situation is markedly true when the producer is a peasant who lacks both commercial knowledge and finance so that he is obliged to sell as soon as his harvest comes in; it is true also, though to a lesser extent, of the capitalist plantation for which the only source of earnings is a particular specialized product. In this kind of business, both demand and supply are said to be inelastic in the short run—that is, a fall in price does not have much effect in increasing purchases and a rise in price cannot quickly increase supplies. Supplies are subject to natural variations, weather conditions, pests, and so forth; and demand varies with the level of activity in the centres of industry and with changes in tastes and techni-

cal requirements. Under a regime of unregulated competition such markets are, therefore, tormented with continual fluctuations in prices and volume of business. Though dealers may mitigate this to some extent by building up stocks when prices are low and releasing them when demand is high, such buying and selling often turns into speculation, which tends to exacerbate the fluctuations.

The behaviour of primary commodity markets is a serious matter when whole communities depend upon a single commodity for income or for employment and wages. The agricultural communities that form part of an industrial economy are therefore generally sheltered from the operation of supply and demand by government regulations of various types, price supports, or tariff protection. Though some attempts have been made to control world commodity markets, these are generally more talk than performance. Some nations, Australia for example, have been able to make enough profit from primary commodity exports to attract capital into the development of industry; but most of the so-called developing countries find their export earnings insecure and insufficient. Their spokesmen complain that the world market system operates in favour of the industrialized nations.

The behaviour of markets for manufactured goods

Markets for manufactures. The other type of market prevails in the sphere of manufactured goods. The market for manufactures is what economists call "imperfect," because each company has its own style, its own reputation, and its own locations; and all of the arts of advertisement and salesmanship are devoted to making it even more imperfect by attracting buyers to particular brand names. Even small businesses that depend upon outside channels of retail distribution may have the final say in what prices they will charge, and great corporations can differentiate their goods in order to create demand for them.

In this type of market, supply normally is very elastic—that is, responsive to demand—in the short run. Stocks or inventories are held at some point in the chain of distribution; while stocks are running down or building up, there is time to change the level of production, and once a price has been set, it is rarely altered in response to moderate changes in demand. Even in a deep slump, defensive rings may often be formed to prevent price cutting.

In the long run, as well as in the short, supply is responsive to demand in the market for manufactures. It is easier to change the composition of a firm's output than it is to change the production of a mine or a plantation. And when changes in demand are not too rapid, gross profits from one plant can be siphoned off and invested in something quite different. When business is good, moreover, there is continual new investment so that productive capacity is adapted to meeting changing requirements. Workers themselves may not even be aware of changes in the final commodities to which their work contributes, and the level of wages for any grade of factory labour is very little affected by the fortunes of a particular market.

Markets in Communist-governed countries

Markets under Socialism. Markets are essential to the free enterprise system; they grew and spread along with it. The propensity "to truck, barter, and exchange one thing for another" (in Adam Smith's words) was exalted into a principle of civilization by the doctrine of laissez-faire, which taught that the pursuit of his self-interests by the individual would be to the benefit of society as a whole. In the Soviet Union and other Socialist countries, a different kind of economy exists and a different ideology is dominant. There are two interlocking systems in the economy of the Soviet Union: one for industry and one for agriculture; and the same pattern is followed, with variations, in the other Socialist countries. Industrially, all equipment and materials are owned by the state, and production is directed according to a central plan. In theory, payments to workers are thought of as their share of the total production of the economy; in practice, however, the system of wages is very much like that in capitalist industry except that rates as a rule are set by decree and the managers of enterprises have little scope for bargaining. Workers may move around looking for jobs, but there is no "labour market" in the capitalist sense. Materials and equipment are distributed among enterprises by the state planning offices. (Faulty planning has given rise to intermediaries who operate between enterprises, but this is not at all the same thing as the highly developed markets in materials, components, and equipment that exist under capitalism.)

Consumption goods, on the other hand, are distributed to Soviet households through a retail market. Though some Socialist idealists, regarding buying and selling as the essence of capitalism, have advocated that money should be abolished altogether, in a large community it has proved to be most convenient to provide incomes in the form of generalized purchasing power and to allow each to choose what he pleases from whatever goods are available. Classical economists usually assert that the advantage of the retail market system is that it runs itself without excessive regulation; the housewife who goes shopping is in charge of her own money and need account to no one for what she does with it. Retail markets in Soviet-type economies are said to differ from those in capitalist economies in that while in both systems the buyer is in this sense a principal, the seller in the Soviet system is an agent. Retailers and manufacturers all serve as agents of the same authority—the central plan. Rather than making it their business to woo and cajole the customer, sellers throw supplies into the shops in a somewhat arbitrary way and the customer searches for what he wants.

Soviet agriculture is organized on principles quite different from those operative for manufacturing. Collective farms, though managed in an authoritarian way, are like cooperatives in which members share in the income of their farm in respect to the "work points" each can earn. The value of a work point is affected by the prices set for the products of the farm, and these are politically, rather than only economically, determined. In the Western industrial economies, there is also a political element involved in the setting of agricultural prices; generally the problem here is to prevent excess production from driving prices too low. For the Soviets, the problem was the opposite. There, agricultural output failed to expand rapidly enough to keep pace with the requirements of the growing industrial labour force, and prices were therefore kept down so that they would not be unfavourable to the industrial sector. At the same time, individual members of the collective farms were permitted to sell the produce of their household plots on a free market. In this specific market, the peasant was as much a principal as the buyer.

In China, cooperative farms established after 1949 were much more genuinely cooperatives than were those in the Soviet Union, and trade with the cities in China is organized through a kind of Socialist wholesaling. City authorities place contracts with neighbouring farms, specifying prices, varieties, quantities, and delivery dates, and then direct the supplies to retail outlets, which are part of the Socialist economy. A similar system controls trade in manufactured consumer goods. Through the retail shops, the authorities keep a finger on the pulse of demand and guide supply as far as possible to meet it by the contracts that they place with the Socialist manufacturers. By adapting to its own requirements a particular element in the market system—wholesale trade—the Chinese economy seems to have avoided some of the difficulties that the Soviets have encountered.

An example of socialism without a formal market was seen in the early days of the cooperative settlements known as kibbutzim in Israel, where cultivators shared the proceeds of their work without any distinction of individual incomes. (Because a kibbutz could trade with the surrounding market economy, its members were not confined to consuming only the produce of their own soil.) At the outset some of the kibbutzim carried the objection to private property so far that a man who gave a shirt to the laundry received back just some other shirt. But to dispense altogether with market relationships is apparently possible only in a small community in which all share a common ideal, and the austere standards of the original kibbutzim have softened somewhat with growing prosperity; but they still maintain a small-scale example of economic efficiency without commercial incentives.

The kibbutzim in Israel

THE MARKET IN ECONOMIC DOCTRINE

The abstract nature of traditional market theory. The key to the modern concept of the market may be found in the famous observation of the 18th-century British economist Adam Smith that "The division of labour depends upon the extent of the market." He foresaw that modern industry depended for its development upon an extensive market for its products. The factory system developed out of trade in cotton textiles, when merchants, discovering an apparently insatiable worldwide market, became interested in increasing production in order to have more to sell. The factory system led to the use of power to supplement human muscle, followed in turn by the application of science to technology, which in an ever-accelerating spiral has produced the scope and complexity of modern industry.

The economic theory of the late 19th century, which is still influential in academic teaching, was, however, concerned with the allocation of existing resources between different uses rather than with technical progress. This theory was highly abstract. The concept of the market was most systematically worked out in a general equilibrium system developed by the French economist Léon Walras, who was strongly influenced by the theoretical physics of his time. His system of mathematical equations was ingenious, but there are two serious limitations to the mechanical analogy upon which they were based: it omitted the factor of time—the effect upon peoples' present behaviour of their expectations about the future; and it ignored the consequences for the human beings concerned of the distribution of purchasing power among them. Though economists have always admitted the abstract nature of the theory, they generally have accepted the doctrine that the free play of market forces tended to bring about full employment and an optimum allocation of resources. On this view, unemployment could only be caused by wages being too high. This doctrine was still influential in the Great Depression of the 1930s.

19th-century views

Modifications of the theory. The change in view that was to become known as the Keynesian Revolution was largely an escape to common sense, as opposed to abstract theory. In a private-enterprise economy, investment in industrial installations and housing construction is aimed at profitability in the future. Because investment therefore depends upon expectations, unfavourable expectations tend to fulfill themselves—when investment outlay falls off, workers become unemployed; incomes fall, purchases fall, unemployment spreads to the consumer goods industries, and receipts are reduced all the more. The operation of the market thus generates instability. The market may also generate instability in an upward direction. A high level of effective demand leads to a scarcity of labour; rising wages raise both costs of production and incomes so that there is a general tendency to inflation.

The turn toward realism

While the English economist John Maynard Keynes was attacking the concept of equilibrium in the market as a whole, the notion of equilibrium in the market for particular commodities was also being undermined. Traditional theory had conceived of a group of producers as operating in a perfect market for a single commodity; each produced only a small part of the whole supply; for each, the price was determined by the market; and each maximized its profits by selling only as much as would make marginal cost equal to price—that is to say, only so much that to produce a little more would add more to costs than it would to proceeds. Each firm worked its plant up to capacity; *i.e.*, to the point where profitability was limited by rising costs. This state of affairs, known as "perfect competition," is quite contrary to the general run of business experience, particularly in bad times when under-capacity working is prevalent. A theory of imperfect competition was invented to reconcile the traditional theory with under-capacity working. This in its turn was attacked as unrealistic. The upshot was a general recognition that strict profit maximizing is impossible in conditions of uncertainty; that prices of manufactures are generally formed by adding a margin to direct costs, large enough to yield a profit at less than capacity sales; and that an increase in capacity generally has to be accompanied by some kind of selling campaign to ensure that it will be used at a remunerative level.

Once it is recognized that competition is never perfect in reality, it becomes obvious that there is great scope for individual variations in the price policy of firms. No precise generalization is possible. The field is open for study of what actually happens, and exploration is going on. Meanwhile, however, textbook teaching often continues to seek refuge in the illusory simplicity of the traditional theory of market behaviour.

THE HISTORICAL DEVELOPMENT OF MARKETS

Economies without markets

History and anthropology provide many examples of economies based neither on markets nor on commerce. An exchange of gifts between communities with different resources, for example, may resemble trade, particularly in diversifying consumption and encouraging specialization in production, but subjectively it has a different meaning. Honour lies in giving; receiving imposes a burden. There is competition to see who can show the most generosity, not who can make the biggest gain.

Another kind of noncommercial exchange was the payment of tribute, or dues, to a political authority, which then distributed what it had collected. On this basis, great, complex, and wealthy civilizations have arisen in which commerce was almost entirely unknown: the whole network of supply and distribution was operated through the administrative system. Herodotus remarked that the Persians had no marketplaces.

The distinguishing characteristic of commerce is that goods are offered not as a duty or for prestige or out of neighbourly kindness but in order to acquire purchasing power. It is clearly a convenience to all parties to use a single generally established currency-commodity. Once a commodity is acceptable as money, its use to store purchasing power overshadows its use for its original purpose; it ceases to be a commodity like any other and becomes the very embodiment of value.

The origin of markets. Markets as centres of commerce seem to have had three separate points of origin. The first was in rural fairs. A typical cultivator fed his family and paid the landlord and the moneylender from his chief crop. He had sidelines that provided salable products, and he had needs that he could not satisfy at home. It was then convenient for him to go to a market where many could meet to sell and buy.

The second point was in service to the landlords. Rent, essentially, was paid in grain; even when it was translated into money, sales of grain were necessary to supply the cultivator with funds to meet his dues. Payment of rent was a one-way transaction, imposed by the landlord. In turn, the landlord used the rents to maintain his warriors, clients, and artisans, and this led to the growth of towns as centres of trade and production. An urban class developed with a standard of life enabling its members to cater to each other as well as to the landlords and officials.

International markets

The third, and most influential, origin of markets was in international trade. From early times merchant adventurers (the Phoenicians, the Arabs) risked their lives and their capital in carrying the products of one region to another. The importance of international trade for the development of the market system was precisely that it was carried on by third parties. Within a settled country, commercial dealings were restrained by considerations of rights, obligations, and proper behaviour. In medieval Europe, for example, dealings were regulated in the main by the concept of the "just price," that is, a system of valuations that assured the producers and merchants an income sufficient to maintain life at a level suited to their respective positions in society. But in trade in which the dealer is not subject to any obligation at either end, no holds are barred; purely commercial principles have free play. It was in trade (for instance, the export of English wool to the weavers of Italy) that the commercial principle undermined feudal conceptions of rights and duties. As Adam Smith observed, a great leap occurred when trade released the forces of industrial production.

Throughout history the relations between the trader and the producer have changed with the development of technique and with changes in the economic power of the parties. The 19th century was the heyday of the import–export merchant. Traders from a metropolitan country could establish themselves in a foreign centre, become experts on its needs and possibilities, and deal with a great variety of producers and customers, on a relatively small scale with each. With the growth of giant corporations, the scope of the merchant narrowed; his functions were largely taken over by the sales departments of the industrial concerns. Nowadays it is common to hold international fairs at which industrial products are displayed for inspection by customers, a grand and glorified version of the village market; the business, however, consists in placing orders rather than buying on the spot and carrying merchandise home. The function of the independent wholesaler, like that of the merchant, has declined as great retail businesses have grown to a scale whereby they can deal directly with manufacturers; but specialized exchanges for primary commodities are still important.

Financial markets. Along with a growth of trade in goods, there has been a proliferation of financial markets. A stock exchange is an organized market for dealing in the securities of businesses and governments. Currently, dealings in securities that came into being in the past predominate over dealings in new issues, and the greater part of industrial investment is financed by retention of profits. Instead of serving mainly as a channel for lending to industry, the chief functions of a stock exchange are to provide a convenient way for owners of property, inherited or newly saved, to place their wealth in income-yielding form, and to provide liquidity and security for them by making a market in which financial assets can readily be realized or redeployed. Dealings in a commodity market, as noted earlier, necessarily contain a speculative element; but in the market for securities, speculation overshadows all else. The art of speculation, as Keynes said, is "to anticipate what average opinion expects average opinion to be." The notorious instability of stock exchanges, with their disturbing effects upon the availability of finance for business and upon the nominal wealth of shareholders, may have repercussions in the market for real goods and services.

Stock markets and money markets

Another kind of financial market is the so-called money market. The money market is not an organized exchange; nor is it confined to money in the ordinary sense. The phrase refers to what might be called wholesale transactions in money and short-term credit carried on mainly by large commercial banks. Through the banking system, government authorities (say, the Bank of England or the United States Federal Reserve Board) have some power to control the market for money. But the more the authorities attempt to exercise their powers, the faster the money market develops new organs for bringing lenders and borrowers together and new types of transferrable obligations that are "almost money," in order to escape from control. (An example of this is the huge Eurocurrency and Eurobond markets in which money and financial instruments are bought and sold independently of national monetary authorities.)

THE MARKETS AND SOCIAL WELFARE

The branch of academic teaching called the "economics of welfare" is nowadays generally expounded by starting with a presumption in favour of laissez-faire and free competition and then following it by a list of reservations and exceptions that destroy its validity. One is first asked to imagine a particular group of individuals, each with his tastes for a predetermined list of specific commodities, with a predetermined endowment of labour power, with specified equipment and stocks, and with a given body of technical knowledge. These individuals can produce various alternative combinations of commodities. If resources were fully utilized, it would be impossible to produce more of any one commodity without producing less of others. One could then speak of an "opportunity cost" of each commodity—that is, the cost of producing a little more of it in terms of the amounts of other commodities that would have to be sacrificed.

Conflicts of interest

On the other side of the market, the same individuals appear as consumers. If their tastes are all alike, it can be argued that there is one set of outputs and prices at which the relative subjective valuations are proportional to relative opportunity costs. This situation is the optimum in the sense that any move away from it would reduce the total satisfaction. The argument is not so simple when different consumers have different tastes. At any one pattern of prices established in the market (with full utilization of resources), each consumer can adjust his purchases so as to maximize his satisfaction at those prices. Then, starting from that set of prices, it can be shown that no one consumer could be made better off, by changing the composition of output, without making some other worse off. This is a powerful argument for the status quo, wherever it may happen to be. At every other point, there would be a different status quo, with a pattern of prices suiting some consumers better and some worse than the one that was chosen at the beginning of the argument.

The first general objection that is now admitted to this scheme (over and above some technical points within its own terms) is that it is purely static. Actual life is lived in the stream of time. In any economy, tastes, commodities, resources, and technology are continuously changing and modifying each other.

Second, there is a deep-seated inconsistency in the assumptions: when every individual pursues his own advantage, atomistic competition cannot persist, for any group of sellers or of buyers can gain by acting together and sharing the benefits among individual members of the group. Perfect competition, like free trade among nations, can persist only when there is some rule of behaviour that overrides pure self-interest.

Third, it is necessary to consider the distribution of consumption between individuals who make up the market. The purchasing power of each is limited by the receipts that he draws from his sales. His receipts depend on the amount of his original endowment and the price of the product he offers to sell. It is obvious that the distribution of the benefits of the market between individuals is quite arbitrary, and the market optimum is therefore not the same as their welfare optimum. When this objection to the laissez-faire principle is admitted, it is often suggested that inequalities might be corrected by a system of bounties and taxes; but this has never been taken seriously as a practical scheme.

A fourth set of objections comes under the heading of differences between private and social costs. The classic example is the smoke nuisance, which imposes costs upon the public that the factory concerned cannot be charged for. Examples of this phenomenon on a devastating scale are now daily coming to notice. At the same time there are many socially beneficial activities for which it is impossible to collect adequate payment from individuals in a society of unequal wealth and income—not only performances of grand opera but the whole of education and the health service.

Thus the doctrine that the free play of individual interests in a competitive market maximizes welfare for society as a whole has been demolished by its own exponents. Yet these notions still have an important influence on the formation of ideology. The rationalization grew out of the 19th-century utilitarian philosophers' hedonistic calculus, which regarded all human life as governed by the pursuit of pleasure and avoidance of pain. This train of thought identifies pleasure with consumption, leaving out of account the whole sphere of conditions in which work is carried on, and finally it sees consumption in terms of spending money. The whole economic basis of life is thus reduced to terms of commercial transactions. As the American critic Thorstein Veblen pointed out,

so great and pervading a force has this habit of pecuniary accountancy become that it extends, often as a matter of course, to many facts which properly have no pecuniary bearing and no pecuniary magnitude, as, for example, works of art, science, scholarship, and religion.

The politics of the market. The doctrines of laissez-faire are attractive in many ways. If the economy is a self-regulating mechanism and if economics is a system of scientific laws, then moral and political problems are excluded. Questions of social justice do not arise. The function of government is to be strictly neutral between interested parties. But when people come to recognize that the market, by its very nature, is necessarily a scene of conflicting interests, every element in it becomes a moral and political problem. This is distressing because one can no longer rely upon "principles of economics" to provide safe and simple rules for finding the correct solutions.

Laissez-faire as an ideal

The intrusion of politics into economic affairs increased dramatically in all the Western industrial nations after 1945. Capitalism took on a new shape, with certain characteristics that distinguish it from all former systems. The reasons for this mutation in the free market economy are numerous. Perhaps the most important was the experience of the great slump of the 1930s. After the war, public opinion, business interests, politicians, and administrators were united in resolving that massive unemployment must not be allowed to recur. Indeed, those who earlier had been the strongest adherents of laissez-faire became the strongest supporters of policies to maintain full employment, arguing that this is the best way to preserve the free enterprise system. Some observers of modern capitalism have maintained that the real purpose of the full-employment policy is to maintain profitability for the great corporations, but it cannot be denied that the results are important for all classes.

The traditional doctrines of the economists are still influential. Even John Maynard Keynes, whose critique of the traditional economics had so much to do with creating the new, gave his blessing to the old conception of the free market. He argued that if our central controls succeed in establishing full employment, there is no objection to be raised against the orthodox theory of the manner in which private self-interest will determine what in particular is produced, or how the value of the final product will be distributed.

Evidently this view owes more to sentiment than to logic. It is impossible to have a policy designed to maintain effective demand in the abstract. Every policy must have some concrete content. The instruments in the hands of government—monetary policy, the exchange rate, taxation, government expenditure—impinge in specific ways upon specific interests. Taxation may be designed to foster either investment or consumption; if the latter, it may be done either by adhering to the principle of "to him that hath shall be given" (that is, by a proportional reduction in direct tax rates) or by favouring lower income groups. Government investment cannot be neutral either; there is no criterion for allocating funds in a neutral manner between, say, armaments and hospitals.

While economic affairs grow ever more overtly political, at the same time commercial influences spread into new spheres. Old notions of loyalty, service, and proper behaviour are undermined by commercial principles. Continuous inflation and rapid technical change make it necessary for every group to defend itself against the erosion of its relative income and status. It would appear that the new capitalism, for all its benefits, may have been developing internal contradictions of its own that threaten its future stability.

Market Socialism. The approach to the market has changed in the Soviet sphere also. The Soviet style of administration and ideology was formed in the struggle for rapid and massive industrialization under Stalin's five-year plans. By the 1960s the Soviet economy had become too large and complex to be administered in the highly centralized fashion of earlier years. Some economists in Russia and eastern Europe, seeing that capitalism was providing its working class with a rising level of real earnings and an enticing variety of goods and services, came to the conclusion that the secret of its success lay in the price mechanism and the interplay of supply and demand. The notion of "market Socialism" thus came into vogue. The rigid, overcentralized administration of industry by a system of directives had, admittedly, led to considerable waste and inefficiency, and there was great scope for improvement in management. But the notion

Communist economic reforms

that a general solution could be found by introducing the criterion of profitability into Soviet enterprises turned out to be illusory. The secret of private enterprise (both for good and for ill) is that it is private; the manager of a capitalist concern acts as a principal and is able to use initiative and judgment. A Socialist manager that is told to make profits is still an agent acting under instructions, necessarily anxious to appear correct and to avoid responsibility. The profit goal may be somewhat less confusing and contradictory than the old multitude of targets handed down from above, but it is still arbitrary because it depends upon a system of prices fixed by decree. When the enterprise is granted the freedom to set its own prices (as in Yugoslavia), it is back to the anomalies of imperfect competition and of instability of markets. There is a school of thought that holds that the way ahead for the Soviet type of economy lies not in less planning but in more—in improving efficiency by intelligent application of devices such as linear programming with the assistance of modern computers. But mathematical methods can apply only in the strictly limited sphere of using pre-existing resources for predetermined ends. It is obvious that the mathematicians cannot instruct the planners on what new products to produce. There remains the problem of finding some means of bringing the needs and tastes of would-be consumers to bear upon both the design and the composition of the flow of production intended for their benefit.

Meanwhile, many of the new and developing nations find that the opening up of their resources and their markets turns out to be more advantageous for established businesses based on successful capitalist industry than for struggling newcomers in their own countries. The economic performance of the so-called developing countries does not give much support to the doctrine that the free play of market forces can be relied upon to maximize human welfare.

BIBLIOGRAPHY. ADAM SMITH'S famous discussion of the division of labour is found in the first chapter of *An Inquiry into the Causes of the Wealth of Nations* (1776). For ALFRED MARSHALL'S approach to the market, see his *Principles of Economics,* 9th ed., 2 vol. (1961). The instability of markets for primary commodities is the theme of the Argentinian economist RAUL PREBISCH, *Towards a New Trade Policy for Development* (1964). The development of the general equilibrium approach to markets by LEON WALRAS *et al.* is well recounted by JOSEPH SCHUMPETER in *A History of Economic Analysis* (1954). A critical account of the theory of imperfect competition is presented in JOAN ROBINSON, *Economics of Imperfect Competition,* preface to the 2nd ed. (1969). A slightly different approach is that of EDWARD H. CHAMBERLIN, *Theory of Monopolistic Competition,* 7th ed. (1956). Economies without markets are described in KARL POLANYI, *Primitive, Archaic, and Modern Economies* (1968), a collection of essays of great interest and originality. The classic appraisal of the market from the standpoint of social welfare is ARTHUR CECIL PIGOU, *The Economics of Welfare,* 4th ed. (1962). Recent appraisals of welfare economics include: I.M.D. LITTLE, *A Critique of Welfare Economics,* 2nd ed. (1957); J. de V. GRAAFF, *Theoretical Welfare Economics* (1957); and MAURICE DOBB, *On Economic Theory and Socialism: Collected Papers* (1955). THORSTEIN VEBLEN'S critique of the market ideology is most directly expressed in *The Place of Science in Modern Civilization, and Other Essays* (1919, reprinted 1966). The best short introduction to the Keynesian Revolution is by MICHAL KALECKI, *Studies in the Theory of Business Cycles, 1933–1939* (1966). These essays, published unnoticed in Polish, preceded the great work of JOHN MAYNARD KEYNES, *The General Theory of Employment, Income and Money* (1936). ANDREW SHONFIELD, *Modern Capitalism* (1966), is a study of the ways in which various countries have adapted their economic administration to modern requirements. A more critical view of modern capitalism is that of JOHN KENNETH GALBRAITH, *The New Industrial State* (1967). A Marxist view is set forth by PAUL BARAN and PAUL SWEEZY in *Monopoly Capital* (1968). There is no satisfactory single source on the attempts at economic reform in the Soviet Union and other countries with socialist economies. A recent summary is MICHAEL ELLMAN, *Economic Reform in the Soviet Union* (1969). The economic problems of the poor countries are examined by GUNNAR MYRDAL in *The Challenge of World Poverty* (1969), a summary of his monumental work *Asian Drama* (1968).

(J. Ro)

Marlborough, Duke of

One of England's greatest generals, John Churchill, 1st duke of Marlborough, commanded British and allied armies against the hitherto seemingly invincible forces of Louis XIV of France and secured four great victories at the battles of Blenheim (1704), Ramillies (1706), Oudenaarde (1708), and Malplaquet (1709).

By courtesy of the National Portrait Gallery, London

Marlborough, painting attributed to J. Closterman (1656–1713). In the National Portrait Gallery, London.

John Churchill was born on May 26, 1650, at Ashe, Devonshire. His father, Sir Winston Churchill, MP, possessed only a moderate property but was sufficiently influential at the court of Charles II to be able to provide for his sons there and in the armed forces. John, the eldest, advanced rapidly both at court and in the army but, marrying for love (as well as for beauty), remained throughout his life dependent upon his career in the public service for financial support. In the 17th century it was normal and honourable for a successful general to exploit his position in the manner of a modern property speculator, and war, which involved the feeding and equipping of tens of thousands of men and horses, offered an opportunity to make large profits. England, however, had withdrawn from involvement in the early wars of those European powers that feared the aggrandizement of Louis XIV, so that Churchill, although made a lieutenant general and effective commander in chief, as well as a peer of the realm, under James II, was in no sense as yet a rich man. He demonstrated his political acumen by surviving the expulsion of the Roman Catholic James II in 1688, transferring his allegiance to the Dutch prince of Orange, who was to become William III, three weeks after his landing in England, having already given William assurances that he would in all circumstances stand by the Protestant religion. He was rewarded by William with the earldom of Marlborough, membership of the Privy Council, confirmation of his military rank, and a succession of commands in Flanders and in Ireland between 1689 and 1691, in which he was uniformly successful.

Marlborough, in the prime of life by contemporary standards, appeared to be on the threshold of great achievements when, suddenly, at the end of 1691, he was removed from all his appointments. In the following May he was imprisoned in the Tower of London on suspicion of being implicated in the intrigues aiming at the restoration of James II, with the support of a French invasion to be launched from Cherbourg in the summer of that year. Released soon afterward, he yet remained wholly out of favour at court for three years and out of employment for the remainder of the war. Responsible contemporaries, however, never suspected him of treason. Although Marlborough certainly acted like all leading politicians of his age by making comforting assurances to the contender for the throne, as an insurance lest the regime be overthrown once more, as it had been twice already in

Military career

Marlborough's own lifetime, his quarrel with William did not originate in any suspicion of treason. He was dismissed, rather, because he put himself at the head of a substantial English faction opposed to the favours William bestowed on his Dutch associates.

In 1701 Louis XIV made it clear that he was again intent on advancing, through war, his claims upon the now vacant throne of Spain and the Spanish Empire. William III, now a sick man and in what turned out to be the last year of his life, appointed Marlborough to be, in effect, his successor in the struggle against the ambitions of Louis XIV, to which, in England as in Holland, William had devoted his life. On her accession, Queen Anne confirmed the appointment, and Marlborough crossed to the Continent to undertake the first of ten successive campaigns in command of the English and Dutch forces and their auxiliaries. In this first campaign he displayed all the military skill that was to bring him a reputation unrivalled until Napoleon, and a grateful sovereign made him a duke at the end of it. He was equally successful as a diplomat in first creating and then maintaining the Grand Alliance of great and small powers that combined to oppose the ambitions of Louis XIV, the ruler of the most powerful country in Europe.

Political rise and fall

At home Marlborough was an important political figure whose support was indispensable to any ministry. The key to this influence lay with his wife, the beautiful Sarah Jennings, who had been Anne's firm companion and guide through all the political upheavals of the past two decades. Anne, though a woman with decided views and prejudices of her own, was, for the time being, content to leave her affairs in the hands of Sarah's husband and his friend and political ally Sidney, earl of Godolphin, whom Anne made lord treasurer and, in effect, prime minister.

Both Marlborough and Godolphin were Tories of a traditional kind and so were staunch supporters of the crown and the court as well as of the church. They allied themselves at first with Robert Harley, later the 1st earl of Oxford, leader of a new breed of Tory hostile to the financial interests nurtured by the war. This alliance provided backing for the war against Louis XIV that produced the great victories of Blenheim (1704) and Ramillies (1706), but increasingly, as the old Tories left the government one by one, Marlborough and Godolphin could find effective and consistent support for the war only from the Whigs. Sarah strongly advocated a Whig alliance, with the result that her influence over Anne, among whose prejudices was a strong dislike of the Whig leaders, rapidly declined. A political crisis in January 1708 resulted in Harley's dismissal, and Marlborough and Godolphin were now entirely dependent upon the Whigs. Although Marlborough continued to win his battles, the Whigs proved unable to secure peace, and, by now weary of war, the people endorsed Anne's dismissal of Godolphin and his Whig colleagues in the general election of 1710. Marlborough, who had already found himself increasingly isolated and without influence during the Whig predominance, was left in command of the army for another year, but when he endeavoured to take a political stand over the terms of peace being negotiated by the new government, he was dismissed in December 1711 from all his appointments after charges of misuse of public money had been made in the House of Commons. He took no further part in public life under Anne, retiring abroad when condemned by the Commons for misappropriation of public money. Although restored to favour under George I, Marlborough was already a sick man and lived in retirement up to his death on June 16, 1722, at Windsor, near London.

Assessment

Marlborough's career therefore ended in disappointment, but that does not suffice to explain the reluctance of subsequent writers to accord due recognition of his greatness. Jonathan Swift, Alexander Pope, William Thackery, and Thomas Macaulay are among the distinguished writers who have subjected him to savage criticism. Support for such a view seems to come from the checkered nature of Marlborough's career: he deserted one monarch, James II, and was dismissed in disgrace by two others, William III and Anne. Moreover, in the public's

eye, he was suspected of treason under William and accused by Parliament of embezzlement under Anne. Many historians have made much of these episodes and of the fact that Marlborough's sister was James II's mistress and therefore perhaps the person really responsible for his rapid advance at court; and until the appearance of Sir Winston Churchill's biography of his famous ancestor in 1933, Marlborough's personal and political reputation remained largely as Macaulay had left it. Churchill, however, easily exposed Marlborough's detractors by pointing out the contrast between their assertions of treachery and dishonesty and the long-lasting friendships and political connections that Marlborough had enjoyed with the men of his day.

Most of Marlborough's contemporaries offer little assistance toward a reliable assessment of his character. For them, the magnitude of his military achievement or the fierceness of the political controversies in which he became enmeshed after 1708 overshadow everything else about him. Moreover, Sarah's quarrels, at first with Anne and subsequently with almost every one of her contemporaries, reflected adversely upon her husband's reputation. Only Marlborough's contemporary, Bishop Gilbert Burnet (1643–1715), in his *History of His Own Time*, seems to provide a convincing, if colourless, character of the duke. He points to his attractive appearance and, despite a lack of formal education, to his qualities of mind, his memory and his quick understanding of a matter. He had, therefore, all the attributes of a successful courtier, and he used them, in default of any fortune of his own, to advance his career by every means open to him. Unfortunately for Marlborough's reputation, he never discarded these policies even when he had acquired an established position in public life. "But," concludes Burnet "when allowances are made for that, it must be acknowledged that he is one of the greatest men the age has produced." That verdict would appear to remain essentially just.

BIBLIOGRAPHY. The principal biography remains that of SIR WINSTON CHURCHILL, *Marlborough: His Life and Times*, 6 vol. (1933–38), but the earlier work of WILLIAM COXE, *Memoirs of John, Duke of Marlborough*, 3 vol. (1818–19), remains valuable; and Churchill should be supplemented by the later works of IVOR F. BURTON, *The Captain-General: The Career of John Churchill, Duke of Marlborough from 1702–1711* (1968); A.L. ROWSE, *The Early Churchills, an English Family* (1956); and MICHAEL FOOT, *The Pen and the Sword* (1957).

(I.F.B.)

Marlowe, Christopher

A major poet and dramatist in his own right, Christopher Marlowe is historically important for his achievement in stimulating the astonishingly rapid growth of drama in Elizabethan England. Before him, dramatic blank verse had been wooden: he made it triumphantly flexible. His *Tamburlaine* and his *Doctor Faustus* were the first truly tragic plays in English. *Edward II* established the dramatic psychological probing that was to become a major concern of Shakespeare and the Jacobean playwrights. *The Jew of Malta* blended the violent and the grimly comic, anticipating the dramatic satires of Ben Jonson and the tragedies of Cyril Tourneur and John Webster.

The second child and eldest son of John Marlowe, a Canterbury shoemaker, Christopher was baptized on February 26, 1564. Nothing is known of his first schooling, but on January 14, 1579, he entered the King's School, Canterbury, as a scholar. A year later he went to Corpus Christi College, Cambridge. Obtaining his bachelor of arts degree in 1584, he continued in residence at Cambridge—which may imply that he was intending to take Anglican orders. In 1587, however, the university hesitated about granting him the master's degree; their doubts (arising from his frequent absences from the university) were apparently set at rest when the Privy Council sent a letter declaring that he had been employed "on matters touching the benefit of his country"—apparently in Elizabeth I's secret service—and denying that he was intending to enter the English college at Reims, in France, which was preparing Roman Catholic missionary priests to be sent to England.

Marlowe, alleged portrait by an unknown artist, 1585. In the collection of Corpus Christi College, Cambridge.
By courtesy of The Master, Fellow and Scholars of Corpus Christi College, Cambridge; photograph, Edward Leigh

Literary career. In a playwriting career that spanned little more than six years, Marlowe's achievements were diverse and splendid. Perhaps before leaving Cambridge he had already written *Tamburlaine the Great* (in two parts, both acted by the end of 1587). Almost certainly during his later Cambridge years, he had translated Ovid's *Elegies* and the first book of Lucan's *Pharsalia* from the Latin. About this time he also wrote the play *Dido, Queen of Carthage* (published in 1594 as the joint work of Marlowe and Thomas Nashe), in which he turned a humorous eye on the *Aeneid*. But it was *Tamburlaine* that made him famous, and playwriting was his major concern in the few years that lay ahead. Both parts of *Tamburlaine* were published anonymously in 1590, and the publisher omitted certain passages that he found incongruous with the play's serious concern with history: even so, the extant *Tamburlaine* text can be regarded as substantially Marlowe's. No other of his plays or poems or translations was published during his life. His unfinished but splendid poem *Hero and Leander*—almost certainly the finest nondramatic Elizabethan poem apart from Edmund Spenser's—appeared first in 1598; later in the same year it was published along with a continuation by George Chapman, different in tone but also splendid.

There is argument among scholars concerning the order in which the plays subsequent to *Tamburlaine* were written. It is not uncommonly held that *Faustus* quickly followed *Tamburlaine* and that then Marlowe turned to a more neutral, more "social" kind of writing in *Edward II* and *The Massacre at Paris*. His last play may have been *The Jew of Malta*, in which he signally broke new ground. (It is very likely that the poem *Hero and Leander* was written when the theatres had to be closed because of plague in 1592.) It is known that *Tamburlaine*, *Faustus*, and *The Jew of Malta* were acted by the Lord Admiral's Men, a company whose outstanding actor was Edward Alleyn, who certainly played Tamburlaine, Faustus, and Barabas, the Jew.

Marlowe was astonishingly learned for a man who died at the age of 29, and this learning, together with a dazzling range of imagination, is manifest in his work. In *Tamburlaine* he went outside Europe, narrated the fortunes of a Scythian shepherd who won the Persian crown, defeated the great Turk Bajazeth, conquered Damascus, defeated the Soldan of Egypt (and made the Soldan's daughter love him), sent his generals into Africa, and conquered Babylon. The scope of this play is the more astonishing as Islām was strange territory for most Elizabethans; yet he could understand that a Muslim could honour Christ, as he has one do in the second part of *Tamburlaine*. In *Faustus* he presented a man who took

the whole universe into his compass, and if he was ultimately damned still went out with more than a whimper. His understanding of theology in this play is masterly. In *Edward II* and *The Massacre at Paris* he dramatized events from English and French history. In *The Jew of Malta* he looked to a melting pot in which Christians and Turks and Jews came together and resisted union. His comic commentary in *Dido, Queen of Carthage* and in *Hero and Leander* makes the first an elegant squib and the second a masterpiece of narrative poetry.

Yet ultimately Marlowe never commits himself in his work. He was once regarded as an essentially subjective dramatist who projected himself and his dreams through his great characters Tamburlaine and Faustus so that their triumphs were his dreams for himself and their overthrow had to be by nonhuman powers, the only defeat he could recognize for himself as valid. More recently there has been an attempt to see him as an orthodox Elizabethan Christian, presenting pictures of sinners as object lessons on what should be avoided. Both views do the poet an injustice. At the end of the prologue to Part I of *Tamburlaine*, the audience is urged to

View but his picture in this tragic glass,
And then applaud his fortunes as you please.

So, too, the prologue speaker to *Faustus* declares:

Only this, gentles—we must now perform
The form of Faustus' fortunes, good or bad:
And now to patient judgements we appeal. . . .

In this second instance there is merely a hint of neutrality, for the matter was dangerous; but the emphasis on the need for "patience" suggests a repudiation of the easy response an audience of the time might be likely to make. He makes the prologue speaker to *The Jew of Malta* Machiavelli himself, who comes, he says, to "frolic with my friends" in England and who urges that the Jew should not be thought less of "Because he favours me." The line must have brought a laugh but also a shock in the theatre of Marlowe's time. *Edward II* has no prologue or epilogue, no long self-revealing speech from a major character, but of all the plays it most obviously takes its stand on "neutrality." The beholder is made to feel the shortcomings of every character, the corruption that power brings, and the strange distinction that extreme suffering can confer on even the weakest of men. This play includes a death scene that surpasses in cruelty anything else that the Elizabethans and Jacobeans can offer. The biographical documents make it plain that Marlowe was himself a violent man: he was also a man who could imagine what violence was like for its victim.

Moving to London from Cambridge in approximately 1587 and wanting to make his mark in the theatre with a serious play, he could be imagined doing as his friend Thomas Kyd did in *The Spanish Tragedie* (c. 1590) —adapting the Senecan mode of dramatic writing (the rhetorical display of intense emotion) to the English stage. But *Tamburlaine* is Senecan only in its frequent use of the long speech: in all other respects it is superficially closer to popular native plays in its concentration on a tyrant's career, its ending in that tyrant's death through natural causes (or possibly through the operation of divine anger). *Doctor Faustus* goes to the native tradition of the "morality play" (including the good and bad angels, the seven deadly sins, and the various devils that Marlowe's countrymen were used to seeing on the stage), telling a story of temptation, fall, and damnation, driving home—though with a deep and characteristically Marlovian irony—the moral lesson. In *Edward II* and *The Massacre at Paris* Marlowe's pattern was again native, influenced by Shakespeare's *Henry VI* plays. *The Jew of Malta* also drew upon the "moralities" to some extent, for Barabas is something of a "Vice"—that figure, exulting in mischief for its own sake, so commonly found in earlier 16th-century drama. But he is also a caricature of Machiavelli, as the Elizabethans saw him, as well as a caricature of the Tamburlaine or Faustus figure who dreamed of power and found absurdity.

Marlowe quickly had both imitators and detractors. Robert Greene, in 1588, in a prefatory epistle to his own

Early
works

Themes
of the
plays

Marlowe's
imitators
and
detractors

Perimedes the Black-Smith referred to the stage as "daring God out of heaven with that Atheist *Tamburlan*" and to "such mad and scoffing poets, that have propheticall spirits, as bred of *Merlins* race" ("Merlin" is a variant of "Marlowe"). In 1592 in his death-bed tract, *Greenes, groats-worth of witte, bought with a million of Repentance,* he included a warning to three dramatists against the way the theatre would treat them. One of these (there can be no doubt that it was meant to be Marlowe) he reproved for saying "There is no God" and urged him to repent. These were dangerous words to bring forward against one in 1592. Sometime after the tract was published the publisher apologized for the attack that Greene had made on Shakespeare but made it clear that he was indifferent to any resentment felt by Marlowe.

Final years. Even so, Marlowe had friends; and he was possibly still involved in "matters touching the benefit of his country" right up to his death. He may have been the "Marlin" (like "Merlin," a variant of his name) who is on record as carrying letters from France to Sir Robert Cecil (principal secretary to the Queen) in 1592. In that year, too, he was involved in a street affray in Canterbury (a similar affair in 1589 had resulted in a man's being killed, though not by Marlowe). From 1591 he was sharing a room with his friend Thomas Kyd, who was arrested on May 12, 1593, and then tortured, on suspicion of treasonable activity. His room being searched, papers were found "denying the deity of Jesus Christ." Six days later a warrant from the Privy Council was issued for Marlowe's arrest. He was found at Sir Thomas Walsingham's house at Chislehurst, Kent, but was only required to give daily attendance on their lordships "until he shall be licensed to the contrary." This was indeed an apparently lenient course to take, especially in view of what Kyd was later to declare against him—and probably had already declared under torture.

On May 30, 1593, during a long day spent in a tavern at Deptford, a suburb to the southeast of London, with Ingram Frizer, Nicholas Skeres, and Robert Poley, Marlowe was killed. He had been in dubious company indeed: Poley was a double spy; Skeres had probably been concerned with Poley in the so-called Babington Plot (against the Queen's life) in 1586; both Poley and Frizer, like Marlowe, had relations with Sir Thomas Walsingham, who was occupied with detecting and frustrating plots against the Queen's life and who had implicated Mary Stuart in the Babington Plot. The story told at the inquest on Marlowe's death was that Marlowe and Frizer quarrelled about the tavern bill, that Marlowe drew his dagger, that Frizer seized the dagger and killed Marlowe in self-defense. Marlowe was buried on June 1; Frizer was pardoned on June 28.

Kyd, as has been seen, was arrested and tortured earlier in May. Probably after Marlowe's death, Kyd wrote two letters to Sir John Puckering, the lord keeper, declaring that the blasphemous and treasonable papers found in his room were Marlowe's property. He accused Marlowe of blasphemy and violence. Soon afterward, Richard Baines, an informer, gave further evidence against the now dead poet: he was blasphemous, seditious, treasonable, a defender of homosexuality and tobacco, a man who had read an "atheist lecture." Who was really responsible for Marlowe's killing can only be wondered at: their lordships of the Privy Council may have known that Marlowe knew too much about them; his friends may have feared what he might be able to say of them under torture. The official story about a quarrel over the reckoning could, of course, be true, but the company was more than dubious and the strange leniency of the Privy Council in not keeping Marlowe as a prisoner suggests something not quite in order.

His death was seen by some people as evidence of God's vengeance on atheists—by Gabriel Harvey (who believed Marlowe died of the plague), by Thomas Beard in *The Theatre of Gods Judgments* (1597), by William Vaughan in *The Golden Grove* (1600). In Francis Meres's *Palladis Tamia* (1598) there was added the fictitious detail that Marlowe was stabbed "by a bawdy serving-man, a rival of his in his lewde love."

Marlowe's
murder

Yet there were posthumous tributes, too—from the dramatists George Peele, Michael Drayton, John Marston, and others. Most notable of all was Shakespeare's remembrance of him in *As You Like It,* in which the circumstances of his death are recalled ("a small reckoning in a little room"), and where he is quoted (a line from *Hero and Leander*) and addressed as "Dead shepherd." Shakespeare also had him in mind in the Pyrrhus speech of *Hamlet,* in an echo of "the face that launched a thousand ships" in *Troilus and Cressida,* and perhaps in the references to "Widow Dido" in *The Tempest.* Shakespeare may have had one of Marlowe's Ovid translations in his memory when he wrote "The Phoenix and Turtle."

In his own time Marlowe dominated the stage and maintained his primacy until Shakespeare came to full growth. The Victorians thought of him as a lyrical and rhetorical poet not properly at home in the theatre. But the 19th-century view of the theatre's range was less than that in the 20th century when an increasing awareness of Marlowe as a dramatist developed.

MAJOR WORKS

PLAYS (in probable order of composition, with dates of publication): *Tamburlaine the Great* (1590); *The Tragicall History of D. Faustus* (1604); *The Troublesome Raigne and Lamentable Death of Edward the Second, King of England* (1594); *The Famous Tragedy of the Rich Jew of Malta* (1633).

POEMS AND TRANSLATIONS: *Hero and Leander* (1598), long narrative poem, only the first third by Marlowe, who died before it was finished; "The Passionate Shepherd to His Love" ("Come Live with Me, and Be My Love"), Marlowe's only surviving lyrical poem, first published in the miscellany *Englands Helicon* (1600).

BIBLIOGRAPHY. S.A. TANNENBAUM, *Christopher Marlowe: A Concise Bibliography* (1937, suppl. 1947), is useful in listing early editions, biographies, and critical studies.

Editions: The standard edition is still that published in 6 volumes under the general editorship of R.H. CASE (1930–33): this includes a biography by C.F. TUCKER BROOKE (1930), along with an edition of *Dido* in the same volume, and editions of *Tamburlaine* (ed. by U.M. ELLIS-FERMOR, 1930; rev. ed., 1951), *The Jew of Malta* and *The Massacre at Paris* (ed. by H.S. BENNETT, 1931), *Poems* (ed. by L.C. MARTIN, 1931), *Doctor Faustus* (ed. by F.S. BOAS, 1932; rev. ed., 1949), and *Edward II* (ed. by H.B. CHARLTON and R.D. WALLER, 1933; rev. ed. by F.N. LEES, 1955). C.F. TUCKER BROOKE's edition of the *Works* (1910) is the standard one-volume text. SIR WALTER GREG's companion volumes, *Doctor Faustus 1604–1616: Parallel Texts* and *The Tragical History of the Life and Death of Doctor Faustus: A Conjectural Reconstruction* (both 1950), are of the first importance for the textual history of the play, although Greg's views on the dating of *Faustus* and on the question of collaboration have been challenged. The Case edition is being replaced by the Revels edition of the *Works of Christopher Marlowe,* in which *Doctor Faustus,* ed. by J.D. JUMP (1962), *Dido, Queen of Carthage* and *The Massacre at Paris,* ed. by H.J. OLIVER (1968), and *The Poems,* ed. by M. MacLURE (1968), have appeared. A complete *Marlowe* edition by FREDSON BOWERS is forthcoming.

Biography and criticism: The best biography is F.S. BOAS, *Christopher Marlowe: A Biographical and Critical Study* (1940). Valuable contributions have been made by J.L. HOTSON, *The Death of Christopher Marlowe* (1925); and P.H. KOCHER, *Christopher Marlowe: A Study of His Thought, Learning, and Character* (1946). Two outstanding works of criticism are HARRY LEVIN, *The Overreacher: A Study of Christopher Marlowe* (1954); and J.B. STEANE, *Marlowe: A Critical Study* (1964). Levin is at his best in considering the complexities of Marlowe's mind, Steane in his sensitive response to the poetic quality. The earlier view of Marlowe's outlook and of the character of his plays is well represented in U.M. ELLIS-FERMOR, *Christopher Marlowe* (1927). F.P. WILSON, *Marlowe and the Early Shakespeare* (1953), illuminatingly brings together the two major English dramatists of the 1590s. Three recent anthologies of critical essays are: *Marlowe: A Collection of Critical Essays,* ed. by C. LEECH (1964); *Critics on Marlowe,* ed. by JUDITH O'NEILL (1969); and *Twentieth Century Interpretations of Doctor Faustus,* ed. by W. FARNHAM (1969).

(Cl.L.)

Mars

Mars, the red planet, is named for the Roman god of war. The first known association of the planet with destruction was made in Babylonia about 3,000 years ago, where astronomers named the planet Nergal after their god of death and pestilence. The early Greeks named the planet Ares, for their god of battle. Mars is accompanied in its journey around the Sun by two satellites, Phobos (fear) and Deimos (terror), named after the mythical chariot horses of Mars. The astronomical symbol for Mars (♂) represents a shield with a spear.

Of the nine known planets, Mars is fourth in order of distance from the Sun and seventh in order of diminishing size and mass. It completes its orbit about the Sun once in 687 days and spins on its axis with a period only slightly longer (37 minutes) than a terrestrial day. Orbital data for Mars are listed in Table 1; physical parameters in Table 2.

Table 1: Orbital Elements of Mars*	
Mean distance from Sun (semimajor orbital axis)	227,800,000 km
Eccentricity	0.093374
Inclination	1.84989°
Mean longitude of node	49.29686°
Mean longitude of perihelion	335.43689°
Sidereal period	686.9804 mean solar days
Mean synodic period	779.94 mean solar days
Mean orbital velocity	24.1 km/sec

*For March 16, 1966; 0 hr Ephemeris Time.
Source: Mars Scientific Model, JPL Document No. 606-1, (July 15, 1968).

The telescopic view of Mars reveals dark markings on a bright red-ochre surface. Occasionally, there is clear visual evidence of a tenuous atmosphere. Meteorological phenomena in the form of local clouds and, sometimes, planet-wide obscurations of the dark surface markings are seen. The planet has white caps at both poles. These features are observed to undergo seasonal and occasionally unexpected changes.

Mars was an enigma to ancient astronomers, who were bewildered by its apparently capricious motion, sometimes direct, sometimes retrograde, across the sky. Johannes Kepler solved this problem in 1609. Using Tycho Brahe's superior observations of the planet, he was able to deduce empirically its laws of motion and so pave the way for the modern gravitational theory of the solar system. Kepler found that the orbit of Mars was an ellipse along which the planet moved with non-uniform but predictable motion. He was able to demonstrate why the planet's motion had confounded earlier astronomers who had based their theories on the older Ptolemaic idea of hierarchies of circular orbits. In the words of Kepler: ". . . Mars alone enables us to penetrate the secrets of astronomy which otherwise would remain hidden from us."

The planet has played a major role in the development of planetary astronomy. It is at the centre of considerable debate concerning the existence of extraterrestrial life and is presently one of the primary targets of the United States' planetary exploration program. High-resolution pictures and other measurements of the Martian surface and atmosphere obtained by the Mariner 4, 6, and 7 spacecraft in 1965 and 1969 have provided us with the most detailed information that exists on conditions on another planet.

Hyron Spinrad, a well-known U.S. planetary spectroscopist, has called 1963 the "year one" for modern investigations of the planet. Since then a greater effort may have been made to understand Mars than was made in all previous years, and, in any case, our knowledge of the planet, and especially of its atmosphere, has changed radically. The main stimulus has been the Mariner Planetary Fly-by Program and, in the following sections, we shall often refer to the remarkable photographs of Mars returned by Mariner 6 and 7.

MARTIAN PHENOMENA

Observing conditions: basic data. Mars moves around the Sun at a mean distance approximately 1.52 times that of the Earth from the Sun, but the large eccentricity (0.093) of its orbital ellipse brings Mars at its closest

Table 2: Physical Parameters for Mars	
Equatorial radius	3,393 ± 4 km
Polar radius (from equatorial radius and optical flattening)	3,352 km
Optical flattening	0.012
Dynamical flattening	0.00525
Area	1.43×10^8 km^2
Volume	1.62×10^{11} km^3
Mass	6.423×10^{26} gm
Density	3.96 gm per cm^{-3}
Surface gravity	371 cm per sec^{-2}
Velocity of escape	5.024 km per sec^{-1}
Martian (sidereal) day	24 hr 39 min 22.6689 sec
Mean Martian solar day	24 hr 39 min 36 sec
Direction of North Pole (1970)	
Right ascension	21 hr 08 min
Declination	+53° 05'
Pole star	BD 52° 2880
Inclination of Equator to orbit	24.936°
Visual albedo	0.159
Visual magnitude at mean opposition	−2.01
Magnetic moment	$<2.4 \times 10^{22}$ gauss cm^3

Source: From Mars Scientific Model, JPL Document No. 606-1 (July 15, 1968).

approach to 206.5 million kilometres from the Sun and at its furthest to 249.1 million kilometres. Mars completes an orbit in roughly the time Earth completes two, and, therefore, Mars spends most of its year far from the Earth in directions that are near the Sun. At closest approach, Mars is less than 56 million kilometres from the Earth but recedes to almost 400 million kilometres; thus, it is not generally available for detailed observation.

Astronomical observations of Mars are best made when the planet is at opposition—that is, when the planet is in the opposite direction in the sky to the Sun. At this time the planet culminates near local midnight and is close to the Earth. Successive oppositions occur at intervals of approximately two years and seven weeks; because this interval, called the synodic period, is not commensurate with the orbital period of Mars, an opposition may occur at any point in the orbit. Oppositions near perihelion are called favourable, or perihelic, because then the planet is closest to both the Earth and the Sun and is, therefore, brighter and appears larger than usual. The largest angular size that the planet can attain is 25 seconds of arc. Oppositions that occur near aphelion are the least favourable, for then the planet is farther from the Earth (101,000,000 kilometres) and at its greatest distance from the Sun. Such oppositions are called aphelic, the planet being less bright and smaller than at the average opposition, and it may attain an angular diameter of only 14 seconds of arc.

One further factor that critically influences the observability of Mars at opposition is that the orbital plane of Mars is inclined at an angle of 1.85° to the Earth's orbital plane. At Martian perihelion, Mars is well south of the Earth's orbital plane. Consequently, at favourable oppositions Mars is badly placed in the sky for observations in the Northern Hemisphere and is best observed from sites south of the Equator. The situation is reversed for aphelic oppositions.

The north pole of rotation of the planet is pointed in the direction of the sixth magnitude star best known by its *Bonner Durchmusterung* catalog number, BD 52°2880, which is located near the bright star Deneb in the constellation of Cygnus. BD 52°2880 is therefore the Martian "pole star" about which the apparent daily motion of the heavens takes place. As is the case with the Earth, the direction of the pole in the sky changes slowly, owing to gravitational torques exerted by the Sun on the planet's equatorial bulge. This precession causes the Martian pole to move along a small circle in the sky with a period of 97,000 Martian years.

The axis of rotation is not perpendicular to the orbital plane of the planet but is inclined at an angle of 24.936°, and, as for the Earth, the tilt gives rise to the phenomenon of seasons on Mars. The Martian year consists of 668.6 Martian (solar) days. For 371 Martian days, or a little over one-half of the Martian year, the Sun appears overhead at some northern latitude and it is spring and sum-

[margin note] Conditions at Martian opposition

[margin note] Martian "pole star"

mer in the Northern Hemisphere. The orientation and eccentricity of the orbit, however, leads to an important characteristic of the seasons on Mars: they are quite uneven in length. The summer solstice, which separates spring from summer, occurs considerably later than the midtime between the times of passage through the spring and fall equinoxes. The southern summer is short and hot while the northern summer is long and cool (see Table 3). These are important factors in understanding the seasonal behaviour of the polar caps (described below).

Table 3: Length of Seasons on Mars		
Northern Hemisphere	Southern Hemisphere	mean Martian days
Spring	Fall	194.2
Summer	Winter	176.8
Fall	Spring	141.8
Winter	Summer	155.8

Source: Mars Scientific Model, JPL Document 606-1 (July 15, 1968).

Mars is a small planet. Its equatorial radius is about half that of the Earth, and its mass only one-tenth the terrestrial value. It follows that Mars possesses four times less surface area than the Earth and its gravity is reduced by a factor of nearly 3. To escape the gravitational pull of Mars, a velocity of only 5.024 kilometres per second is required. Thus, a rocket need only supply to an object one-fifth of the energy that would be needed on Earth to free it from the gravitational attraction of the planet.

Mars is observed to be spheroidal in shape. Optical observations indicate that the polar radius of the planet is about 40 kilometres less than its equatorial radius. This surprisingly large figure exceeds, by a factor of 2, the maximum value predicted from theory. A rotating planet the surface of which is free of stress should take on the shape of an oblate spheroid. The degree of flattening should lie between two limits: an upper limit, corresponding to a homogeneous planet, and a lower limit, corresponding to a planet with the mass heavily concentrated at the centre. The upper limit for Mars, which can be computed from its known mass, radius and rotation rate is 0.00571. The observed optical value is 0.012. It would therefore appear that the surface of Mars may be under considerable stress.

Data from visual observations. The earliest telescopic observations of Mars in which the disk of the planet was seen were those of Galileo Galilei, who, in 1610, noted that the planet did not appear to be perfectly round. In 1636 the Italian astronomer Francesco Fontana produced the earliest drawings that show markings on the disk of the planet. Some of these drawings show Mars in the gibbous phase, that is, with more than half the visible disk illuminated. Unfortunately, the markings drawn by Fontana bear no resemblance to the planetary details now known, and the Dutch scientist Christiaan Huygens is credited with the first accurate drawings of surface markings. In 1659 Huygens made a drawing of the planet that shows a major dark marking on the planet now known as Syrtis Major. Polar caps on the planet were first noted by Giovanni Domenico Cassini around 1666.

The accomplishments of visual observers are many. Mars' tenuous atmosphere was first noted by the German-born British astronomer William Herschel, who also measured the tilt to the rotation axis and first discussed the seasons of Mars. The rotation of the planet was discovered by Huygens (1659) and measured by Cassini in 1666. He found the rotation period to be 24 hours and 40 minutes, which is in error by a mere three minutes, a remarkable accomplishment for that time. The moons of Mars, so important in determining the mass of Mars, were also discovered visually, by the 19th-century U.S. astronomer Asaph Hall.

Visual observations have accumulated a rich compendium of meteorological and seasonal phenomena that occur on the planet, such as numerous cloud phenomena (there are yellow, blue, white, and gray clouds), the waxing and waning of the polar caps, seasonal changes in the colour and extent of the dark areas, a "wave of darkening" in the markings that sweeps across the planet in phase with the melting of the polar caps, a green haze and bright transient spots.

Martian maps. The first map of Mars was produced in 1830 by the German astronomers Wilhelm Beer and Johann H. von Mädler. The earliest system of longitude and latitude, not too different from that in use today, was defined by these pioneers. Better maps with the first systematic attempts to name the markings were subsequently produced by three astronomers—Richard A. Proctor (1867) and Nathaniel E. Green (1877) of England and Camille Flammarion (1877) of France. The nomenclature for the markings was based on the names of prominent scientists and observers of the planet such as William Herschel, William R. Dawes, Pierre-Simon Laplace, Wilhelm Beer, Dominique Arago, and Johann Schröter.

The Italian astronomer Giovanni Schiaparelli produced the first modern map of Mars (1877), and it contained the basis of the system of nomenclature in use today. The names are in Latin and are formulated predominantly in terms of the ancient geography of the Mediterranean area in mythical and biblical times. This map also showed, for the first time, indications of a system of canals, or channels, on the bright areas, and Schiaparelli is usually credited with their first description. According to the U.S. astronomer Samuel Glasstone, however, the idea of canals originated ten years earlier in the work of the Italian astronomer Angelo Secchi.

Since Schiaparelli's time, the map of Mars has been constantly improved, and hundreds of new details have been added to it. Moreover, photography has played an increasingly important role in this process. In 1958 the International Astronomical Union adopted a formal list of place-names on Mars related to a map of Mars drawn by G. de Mottoni and based on a large number of photographs of the planet taken by the French astronomer Henri Camichel at the Pic du Midi Observatory (see Figure 1). The remarkable quality of this map is borne out by comparison with the far-encounter picture of Mars returned to Earth in 1969 from the Mariner 6 and 7 spacecraft. In a review of his own researches, the U.S. astronomer Clyde W. Tombaugh gives some interesting background information on observing Mars and the detail that appears on visual maps of Mars (he is referring in particular to one of his own):

> Unless an observer has good eyes and is willing to spend hundreds of hours looking with effective telescopes, he has little chance of seeing such detail to this extent. It is never all visible simultaneously. Not only must the terrestrial atmosphere be very steady but also colors and many details are visible only at certain Martian seasons. While a number of canals, oases, and small white spots are frequently visible, others are so rarely seen that their visibility may depend on secular causes, such as volcanic degassing in some local area, perhaps. Several details on this map have been visible to the writer for less than a total of five minutes over a span of forty years!

The above remarks are particularly cogent in relation to the long controversy over the existence of the canals, which continued from the early years of this century until finally settled by the Mariner photographs.

One of the most assiduous observers and students of Mars was the U.S. astronomer Percival Lowell, who founded the Lowell Observatory in Flagstaff, Arizona. He believed that he had identified some 500 canals and insisted that they were the work of intelligent beings on the planet rather than natural features. Lowell recorded the canals as remarkably straight, or very regularly curved, narrow filaments (sometimes double), stretching across vast areas of desert and intersecting in a seemingly organized manner at small dark spots. These spots, called oases, were discovered and named by his contemporary, the U.S. astronomer William H. Pickering of the Harvard Observatory.

The vast wealth of detail included in Lowell's maps was disputed by many of his colleagues, who were unable to locate the features or saw them with quite different characteristics. A few extremely competent observers were

marginal notes:

IAU list of Martian features

History of the canals and oases

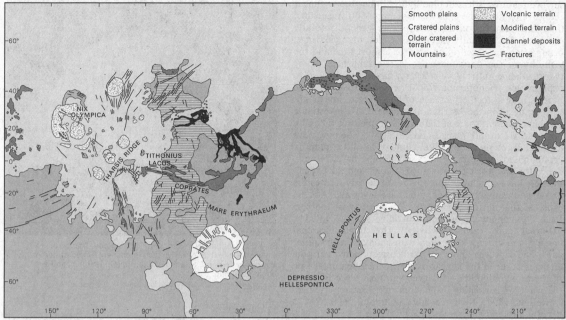

NAMES OF MARTIAN FEATURES: IAU names and traditional names (italics) are listed with their approximate 1971 coordinates.

Achillis Fons, 53°; +28° (Craneum)
Achillis Pons, 30°; +37°
Acidalium, Mare, 28°; +48°
Aeolis, 212°; −10°
Aeria, 310°; +15°
Aetheria, 240°; +40°
Aethiopis, 235°; +10°
Agathodaemon, 65°; −14° (Coprates)
Albor, 208°; +18°
Alcyonius, 260°; +50°
Alcyonius Nodus, 268°; +35°
    (Aquae Calidae, Nuba L.)
Alpheus, 280°; −40°
Amazonis, 160°; +20°
Ambrosia, 88°; −35°
Amenthes, 251°; +03°
Amphitrites, Mare, 322°; −58°
Antigones Fons, 295°; +20° (Astaborae F.)
Aonius Sinus, 105°; −47°
Arabia, 320°; +28°
Aram Regio, 12°; −05° (Thymiamata)
Araxes, 117°; −24°
Arcadia, 115°; +42°
Argenteus Mons, 40°; −70°
Argus, 10°; 00° (Brangaena)
Argyre I, 35°; −48°
Argyre II, 70°; −66°
Ascraeus Lacus, 103°; +20°
Astaboras, 305°; +26°
Astusapes, 298°; +30°
Atlantis, 173°; −30°
Aurorae Sinus, 50°; −13°
Ausonia Australis, 250°; −40°
Ausonia Borealis, 275°; −23° (Trinacria)
Australe, Mare, 90°; −65°
Azania, 185°; +30°
Bathys, 95°; −34°
Biblis Fons, 132°; +14°
Bosporus, 63°; −43° (Bosporos, Phrixi Regio)
Callirrhoes Sinus, 03°; +50° (Novem Viae.)
Candor, 75°; +05°
Capri Cornu, 45°; −15° (Protei Regio)
Casius, 275°; +43° (Wedge-of-Casius)
Cebrenia, 215°; +48°
Ceraunius, 96°; +42°
Cerberus, 212°; +09°
Chalce, 25°; −45° (Argyroporos)

Chaos, 215°; +35°
Chersonesus, 250°; −58°
Chronium, Mare, 215°; −60°
Chryse, 32°; +08°
Chrysokeras, 100°; −52°
Cimmerium, Mare, 210°; −25°
Claritas, 102°; −29°
Coloe Pons, 298°; +40°
Crocea, 293°; 00°
Cyclopia, 218°; 00°
Cydonia, 345°; +50°
Daedalia, 120°; −28°
Deltoton Sinus, 304°; −05°
Deucalionis Regio, 345°; −18°
Deuteronilus, 358°; +35°
Dia, 88°; −60°
Diacria, 170°; +47°
Dioscuria, 315°; +54°
Eden, 350°; +30°
Edom, 345°; −04°
Electris, 190°; −52°
Elysium, 215°; +25°
Eos, 37°; −15°
Erebus, 182°; +20°
Eridania, 218°; −40°
Erythraeum, Mare, 30°; −30°
Eunostos, 225°; +15°
Euripus I, 270°; −62°
Euxinus Lacus, 155°; +43°
Fastigium Aryn, 358°; 00°
Ganges, 60°; +05°
Gehon, 358°; +15°
Geryon, 78°; −15°
Gomer Sinus, 230°; −02°
Hades, 192°; +33°
Hadriacum, Mare, 265°; −40°
Hammonis Cornu, 316°; −13°
Hellas, 292°; −50°
Hellespontica Depressio, 358°; −58°
Hellespontis, 330°; −47°
Hesperia, 240°; −20°
Hiddekel, 347°; +18°
Hyblaeus, 228°; +30°
Hydrae Pons, 48°; −03°
Hyllus, 355°; −48°
Iani Fretum, 10°; −10° (Socratis Pr.)
Iapygia, Mare, 295°; −15°

Icaria, 124°; −45° (Hyscus)
Idaeus Fons, 53°; +35°
Isidis Regio, 275°; +20°
Ismenius Lacus, 335°; +42°
Jamuna, 44°; +10° (Iamuna)
Juventae Fons, 62°; −04°
Labotas, 345°; +02° (Daradux)
Laocoontis Nodus, 246°; +15° (Lacoontis)
Libya, 275°; 00°
Lunae Palus, 68°; +18° (Lunae Lacus)
Maiea Pr., 290°; −65°
Mareotis Lacus, 96°; +32°
Margaritifer Sinus, 20°; −10°
Memnonia, 142°; −20°
Meridiani Sinus, 00°; −05° (Dawes Bay)
Meroe Insulae, 290°; +30°
Mesogaea, 168°; −02°
Moab, 338°; +10°
Moeris Lacus, 278°; +08°
Nectar, 62°; −23°
Neith Regio, 275°; +30°
Nepenthes, 268°; +08° (Thoth-Nepenthes)
Nereidum Fr., 50°; −42°
Neudrus, 04°; −15°
Niliacus Lacus, 32°; +27°
Nilokeras, 55°; +28°
Nilosyrtis, 280°; +30°
Nilus, 82°; +25°
Nix Cydonia, 03°; +40°
Nix Lux, 110°; −07°
Nix Olympica, 135°; +20°
Nix Tanaica, 55°; +52°
Noachis, 355°; −40°
Novissima Thyle, 325°; −70°
Nubis Lacus, 264°; +24° (Nuba, Lethes L.)
Nymphaeum, 300°; +10°
Oceanidum, Mare, 35°; −60°
Ogygis Regio, 60°; −53°
Ophir, 65°; −10°
Oxia, 20°; +20°
Oxia Palus, 17°; +08°
Oxus, 12°; +20°
Pandorae Fretum, 345°; −25°
Peneus, 300°; −40°
Phaethontis, 140°; −50°
Phison, 308°; +35° (Phison-Vexillum)
Phlegethon, 125°; +35°

Phlegra, 190°; +45°
Phoenicis Lacus, 110°; −15°
Pontica Depressio, 85°; −47°
Promethei Sinus, 260°; −65°
Propontis I, 180°; +40°
Protonilus, 320°; +42°
Pyriphlegethon, 140°; +20°
Pyrrhae Regio, 30°; −22°
Sabaeus Sinus, 335°; −12°
Scamander, 200°; 44°
Serpentis, Mare, 320°; −28°
Sigeus Portus, 335°; −08°
Simois, 162°; −48°
Sinai, 65°; −18°
Sirenum. Mare, 140°; −40°
Sitacus, 338°; +17°
Solis Lacus, 85°; −26° (Eye-of-Mars)
Styx, 200°; +25°
Syria, 90°; −20°
Syrtis Major, 290°; +10°
Syrtis Minor, 260°; −08°
Tempe, 75°; +40°
Tempes, 63°; +47° (new—1963)
Tharsis, 103°; +08° (Tractus Albus Aust.)
Thaumasia, 75°; −35° (Martian Eye)
Thoana Palus, 256°; +35°
Thoth, 263°; +15° (Thoth-Nepenthes)
Thyle I, 160°; −65°
Thyle II, 220°; −65°
Thyles Collis, 230°; −70°
Thyles Mons, 155°; −70°
Thymiamata, 06°; +10° (Aram)
Tithonius Lacus, 80°; −05°
    (Coprates Triangle)
Tritonis Sinus, 240°; −10°
Trivium Charontis, 198°; +14°
Typhon, 322°; −04°
Tyrrhenum, Mare, 270°; −13°
Ulyxis Fr., 190°; −63°
Umbra, 290°; +49° (Nilosyrtis)
Utopia, 265°; +56°
Vulcani Pelagus, 25°; −40°
Xanthe, 50°; +15°
Xanthus, 228°; −43°
Yaonis Regio, 318°; −43°
Zea L., 288°; −46°
Zephyria, 190°; 00°

Figure 1: Mars chart based on photographs taken in 1969, North up, East to the right. The chart is a Mercator projection and extends from latitude 70° N to 70° S. It is centred on longitude 0°.
By courtesy of the U.S. Geological Survey

never able to see the canals at all: among them the U.S. astronomers Milton L. Humason and Walter Baade, who used the Mt. Wilson 100-inch reflector under almost perfect conditions. Others found that under good conditions the canals were not continuous features but broke up into a discontinuous series of lines and dots. The controversy may be considered closed, however, for the pictures of the planet returned by Mariner 6 and 7 show no obvious signs of features that could correspond to the canals seen by Lowell. It would appear that the canals are, at best, chance alignments of large craters that become visible in moments of exceptional atmospheric clarity.

Data from photographic observations. Visual observation of planets has suffered a decline in modern times following the introduction of new techniques. Photographic monitoring of Mars has largely surplanted visual observation. Surprisingly, this is not because ground-based photography can produce high-quality images but rather because the technique is far less subjective. Many Martian phenomena are in fact too delicate and subtle to

be registered on the photographic plate and are only available to the eye of the visual observer.

The chief photographic problems are blurring and rapid tremor of the image due to the time-dependent inhomogeneities in the atmospheric path through which the light must travel. The state of the atmosphere produces the phenomenon referred to as seeing. Unless exposures are short enough and made to coincide with moments of good seeing, the resulting picture will be blurred. Nevertheless, remarkable photographs of Mars, some in colour, have been made that illustrate most of the phenomena reported by visual observers. The reader is particularly referred to the monograph "A Photographic History of Mars" by the U.S. astronomer Earl C. Slipher of the Lowell Observatory, who devoted a lifetime's work to a photographic study of the planet.

A controversial phenomenon reported by many Martian observers from photographs has been called the blue haze, or violet layer. A comparison of photographs taken through blue and red filters shows that the contrast of

The blue haze and blue clearings

surface features is less in blue light. Slipher found that if the wavelength of the light was less than 4600 angstroms, then dark features on the surface were generally totally obscured. Occasionally exceptions, called blue clearings, occur when the obscuration lifts for a short time and the visibility of the dark markings is re-established. Many theories, none entirely satisfactory, have been devised to explain this phenomenon. Most presume that the blue haze is related to the presence of some scattering or absorbing agent in the Martian atmosphere. To investigate this phenomenon some of the television pictures taken by the Mariner 6 and 7 spacecraft, described below, were exposed through a blue filter similar to those used in groundbased telescopic studies of the blue haze. No evidence for any loss of contrast was found, and the experimenters have concluded that this result clearly refutes the existence of an atmospheric, blue haze layer and that the cause of the phenomenon must be a property of the surface. This conclusion has not been universally accepted.

Diurnal and seasonal activity. The major seasonal changes are closely associated with changes in the polar caps. The caps wax and wane, and corresponding periodic changes occur in the appearance of surface features. One of the more enigmatic sequences that take place is called the wave of darkening, a phenomenon first reported by Lowell in 1894. Near the edge of either polar cap, a general darkening of the surface markings appears in early spring as the cap begins to recede; then the darkening moves away from the receding polar cap, sweeps toward, and finally crosses the Equator in an indistinct band of heightened contrast to dissipate in the opposite hemisphere. The waves, one in each hemisphere, travel at an apparent speed of about 35 kilometres per day. Studies of the phenomenon were carried out by the French–U.S. astronomer Gérard de Vaucouleurs in 1939 and by the U.S. astronomer John H. Focas in 1962, using photometric techniques rather than subjective visual reports. The waves are well documented quantitatively, but no satisfactory explanation has yet been devised.

The markings are observed to undergo changes in colour and sometimes in extent. Charles F. Capen of the Jet Propulsion Laboratory, California Institute of Technology, an expert visual observer, reports the following behaviour in the Trivium Charontis region: in the spring the area is medium-dark gray with brown tints, olive drab with darkening wave, and taking on intense black later. In summer the area stays black. In fall the colour is dark gray and brown, turning to medium-dark gray and brown tints in the winter.

The reported colours of the dark features have been subject to considerable discussion, particularly because colour recognition is largely subjective. It has been questioned if the colours reported are accurate or are merely a reflection of physiological processes in the eye and mind of the observer. A straightforward answer is not entirely possible, but photoelectric spectrophotometry (a purely objective technique) of the dark areas has shown that they are actually red, although less so than the bright areas on the planet.

Diurnal changes are observed on the planet. The most striking examples are in the far-encounter pictures returned from the Mariner 6 and 7 spacecraft. These show mottled areas on the afternoon side with relatively bright, often diffuse patches, which change on a day-to-day basis. Some of the patches are striking in their geometric regularity and are presumably associated with surface features. The best example is a bright ring, 500 kilometres in diameter, associated with the region called Nix Olympica (see Figure 2). None of these patches appear to be clouds, for they show no apparent motion with respect to the surface nor any of the characteristics of clouds on the Earth (waves, cloud streets, etc.). They seem to be intimately connected with the ground, and it has been suggested that they may be fogs or ground frosts. Unfortunately, neither of these possibilities makes sense when examined carefully. Frosts of carbon dioxide are ruled out because the surface is too warm, and water-ice frosts are unlikely because of the extremely low partial pressure of water in the atmosphere.

The wave of darkening

Nix Olympica region

Figure 2: Mariner 7 far-encounter photograph, frame 76, showing the feature Nix Olympica (prominent ringed crater above centre right), a series of linear bright features, and a bright polar cap.
By courtesy of National Aeronautics and Space Administration

THE SURFACE

Appearance from the ground. To the ground-based telescopic observer, the Martian surface is characterized by red-ochre-coloured bright areas with superimposed, dark markings. It has been usual to refer to the bright areas as deserts and the majority of large dark areas as *maria* (sing. *mare*); *i.e.*, oceans or seas. It is now absolutely certain that these dark areas are not, and in all probability never were, covered by expanses of water. Nor do they appear to be closely similar to the well-known dark *maria* on the Moon. It therefore seems more reasonable to refer below simply to the dark and bright areas on the planet than to use the older terms.

The most prominent dark areas occupy a band around the planet between 10° and 40° S. Their distribution is irregular, and the Northern Hemisphere has only a single major feature, Mare Acidalium.

Dark markings cover about one-third of the total area of the planet's surface, and the best ground-based maps, such as those by G. de Mottoni and by J.H. Focas, show them to be made up of a myriad of well-developed structures, patches, and groups of spots. High resolution photographs have confirmed this description: dark regions such as Meridianii Sinus are made up of such patches pockmarked with craters. The Mariner pictures also show that the transition from dark areas to bright areas is often quite abrupt and irregular, taking place in distances of less than 10 kilometres.

The most remarkable fact about the dark areas is their ability to change. They are observed to undergo both seasonal and long-term variations in both size and colour. In the words of E.C. Slipher: "The markings are in a state of perpetual and bewildering fluctuation, the slower and more gradual ones partly through change in the illumination of the Martian air and partly through inherent change in the markings themselves." Bright areas, which represent about 70 percent of the planet's surface, are also well endowed with subtle shadings and intricate features —the so-called canals and oases.

The character of the surface. The character of the surface on linear scales below 100 kilometres was a matter of conjecture until the pictures of Mariners 4, 6, and 7 (Figures 3–6) were returned to Earth in 1965 and 1969. On scales smaller than one kilometre, speculation is still a factor, but some statements can be made. Finally, on the microscale of the individual particles that make up the surface, little can be said with certainty, but a broad picture, based on the interpretation of spectrophotometric, polarimetric, and thermal-infrared temperature measurements, can be drawn.

Mariner pictures show the surface to be composed of at least three distinct types: chaotic, cratered, and featureless terrain. The high-resolution pictures cover only a fraction

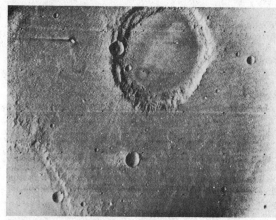

Figure 3: *Martian surface showing features similar to the Moon.*
The large flat-bottomed crater is believed to be a typical older
crater; smaller cup-shaped craters are younger. Mariner 6
photograph, frame 18.
By courtesy of National Aeronautics and Space Administration

of the surface of the planet, and the possibility remains
that types of terrain with still other characteristics may
be present on the planet.

Cratered terrain   The cratered terrain appears to be extremely old. The
number of very large craters found on the Mariner photo-
graphs implies an age of at least several billion years;
these regions of the surface could even be primordial, in
spite of the probability that the meteoric-bombardment
flux on Mars could be 25 times greater than that on the
Moon because of the greater proximity of Mars to the
asteroid belt (see Figure 5).

The craters are of two types: large and flat bottomed,
small and bowl shaped. The latter are similar to impact
craters on the Moon. A particularly striking difference
between the cratered terrain on Mars and the Moon is the
absence on Mars of the swarms of secondary craters and
ray structures often associated with large lunar craters.
This is consistent with the greater role of erosion processes on Mars as compared with that on the Moon. Ernst J.
Öpik, for example, has estimated that erosion processes
on Mars, even though only 0.03 percent as effective as
those on Earth, would cause substantial obliteration of
craters with sizes of up to 10–20 kilometres.

Chaotic terrain   Chaotic terrain appears to be much more recent in formation, and the Mariner experimenters suggest that it is
probably the result of ongoing modification processes.
This type of region is characterized by irregular areas of
chaotically jumbled short ridges and depressions (see
Figure 4). The scale of the features is typically one to
three kilometres across by two to ten kilometres long.
These regions seem to be relatively young because they
are practically uncratered. Only three possible craters
have been recognized in the million-square-kilometre
region that has been examined.

By courtesy of National Aeronautics and Space Administration

Figure 4: Chaotic terrain full of jumbled ridges unlike anything
found on the Moon or on the Earth. Detail from Mariner 6
photograph, frame 14.

A big surprise in the Mariner pictures was the discovery
of featureless terrain in the bright region called Hellas
(see Figure 5). The surface appears structureless down to
the limit of resolution and is devoid of craters. Hellas is a
large, bright, roughly circular region, some 1,900 kilometres in diameter, due south of the prominent dark area
Syrtis Major. The resolution limit of the high-resolution
cameras was 300 metres, and no craters, ridges, etc., are
seen on the floor of the region. An explanation of this
phenomenon has not yet been forthcoming.   **Feature-less terrain**

A further important observation provided by the Mariner pictures is the absence of any indications of tectonic
activity. There is no evidence for mountain ranges, folding, or volcanic activity at all in the pictures. This would
seem to imply that the interior of Mars is considerably
less active than that of the Earth.

The relationship between the classical canals and oases
and features observed in the pictures is rather sketchy,
but some oases, such as Juventae Fons and Oxia Palus,
have been identified with single, large, dark-floored
craters. Two canals, Gehon and Cantabras, appear to
coincide with "quasi-linear" alignments of several dark-
floored craters. Nix Olympica, discovered by Schiaparelli
in 1879 and observed from the Earth to be associated with
a brightening, suggestive of isolated peaks on which frost
might condense or clouds might form, has been found to
be a very large crater with a bright rim, or skirt.

By courtesy of National Aeronautics and Space Administration

Figure 5: *Featureless terrain in the region of Hellas.*
The absence of details even at the highest resolution remains
unexplained; lack of any disturbance of the region over millions
of years is highly improbable. Mariner 7 photograph, frame 28.

The composition of the surface.   The German-born
U.S. astronomer Rupert Wildt seems to have been the
first to have suggested the now popular idea that the
surface of Mars might be made up largely of iron oxides. It is argued that the surface should be rich in iron,
partly because the body of the planet is probably inactive
and therefore undifferentiated, and partly because of the
possibility of large meteoric influxes of iron-bearing material from the asteroid belt. A possible source of oxygen
could be the photodissociation of water by ultraviolet
light in the atmosphere (see below). Mars is therefore
often visualized as a "rusty planet." This hypothesis has
been tested by comparing the polarization properties of
various iron oxides—limonite, goethite, hematite—with
the observed dependence of polarization on the phase of
the planet. The French astronomer Audouin Dollfus
found that the observed dependence of the polarization
of reflected light from the planet with phase is in good
agreement with laboratory observations of pulverized
limonite. Unfortunately, such comparisons are not
unique, and it is difficult to draw specific conclusions.
The variation of the reflectivity of the surface with colour
contains information on the chemical nature and the
microscopic state of the soil. The U.S. astronomers
Thomas McCord and John B. Adams find from observational data that the mean reflective properties of the
Martian surface are duplicated by pulverized, oxidized
basalts. Probably the best that can be said is that the

photometric and polarimetric observations are not in conflict with the hypothesis of a surface consisting of an oxidized form of common terrestrial igneous rocks.

The mechanical state of the surface is similarly difficult to assess. It seems clear from polarization data and information on the rate of change of the temperature of the surface with time that the surface is covered, both dark and bright areas, with a layer of fine dust. In this respect the surface of Mars is probably much like that of the Moon. A number of features of the environment on Mars may imply significant differences in the micro-state of the surface from that of the Moon. The presence of an atmosphere should lead to effective aeolian erosion, that is, scouring by wind-borne particles; the rapid rotation of the planet compared to the Moon will make the process of thermal creep more effective on Mars than on the Moon; and finally, the presence of even minute amounts of water vapour in the atmosphere gives rise to the possibility that extensive regions of permafrost may exist on the planet. F.A. Wade and Jane de Wys have noted that in the presence of permafrost, freeze-thaw processes in the top layer may significantly modify the structure of the ground. The modification processes on Mars would presumably be similar to those that take place in cold regions on the Earth.

Possibility of permafrost

The presence of available water supplies on Mars is a matter of prime interest, and the suggestion that the Martian surface could support large areas of permafrost has been the subject of several investigations. The U.S. astronomers Robert B. Leighton and Bruce C. Murray, in a study of the thermal properties of the Martian surface, have included a discussion of the depth below the surface at which permafrost would be stable. They could not deduce the thickness of the frozen layer because factors such as the heat flow from the interior and the temperature gradient that supports it, the permeability of the surface soil, and, finally, the supply of water are unknown. Nevertheless, as water vapour is observed in the atmosphere, there must be a considerable supply. Leighton and Murray's numerical experiment showed that permafrost is likely to be present 40 centimetres below the surface above latitude 60° in the Southern Hemisphere and 20 centimetres below the surface at latitude 60° N. The ground near the North Pole would be entirely and permanently frozen.

It has been shown that liquid water is not necessary for the formation of permafrost. In a laboratory experiment simulating the Martian environment, the U.S. astronomer Richard S. Young and his collaborators have demonstrated the formation of permafrost in porous soil overlain with an atmosphere containing small amounts of water vapour. If the Martian soil is sufficiently porous, water vapour carried poleward by the atmosphere will tend to be trapped in the soil.

Thermal creep operates on slopes and is the motion of surface material that may be induced by alternate expansion and contraction caused by rise and fall of the temperature. This process may be expected to erode crater rims and other sharp surface features. It has been estimated that the rate of movement of granular surface material down a 17° slope on Mars could be as high as 1.5 centimetres per year.

Surface relief: topographic features. Early visual observers of the planet concluded that high mountain ranges of the terrestrial variety were not present on Mars. In 1906 Percival Lowell calculated that mountains with heights greater than 0.8 kilometres would have been detected as irregularities at the terminator, a probable overstatement; C.W. Tombaugh has revised the value to 8.4 kilometres. The evidence against mountain building from the Mariner pictures also seems clear, even though the coverage of the planet is far from complete. There are no signs of orogenic activity in the pictures.

There is, however, plenty of evidence for topographic relief on the surface of the planet on the continental scale. Elevation differences of as much as 10 kilometres are now known to exist over scales of thousands of kilometres. Thus, the differences in elevation, while large, only imply gentle slopes on the surface.

The history of the search for large-scale topographic relief is fascinating and has an ironic twist. In a sense, the search for large elevation differences grew out of the controversy over the nature of the dark areas. The proponents of the "vegetation" theory of the dark areas considered them to be low lying and hence warmer, moist, and therefore more conducive to life. The temperatures of dark areas are indeed a few degrees warmer than surrounding bright areas. The opponents of the above hypothesis preferred to attribute the temperature of dark areas and their curious ability to change their appearance on a seasonal basis to inorganic causes. The fact that they are warmer is simply a result of their being darker, which is just another way of saying that they absorb more energy from the Sun. Their apparent ability to change their appearance is presumed to be the result of the transport and deposition of small dust particles by the prevailing winds. The opponents of the vegetation hypothesis supposed the dark areas to be elevated with respect to the bright areas.

Radar reflections

In 1965 the U.S. astronomer Ronald A. Wells noticed that white clouds that tended to form and remain stationary over certain bright areas were aligned with the boundaries of adjacent dark areas. Wells thought of these clouds as lee clouds formed in the prevailing wind as it crossed the dark areas. He concluded that the latter must therefore be high ridges. Further circumstantial evidence was provided by the U.S. astronomers Carl Sagan, James B. Pollack, and Richard M. Goldstein in 1966. They found that surface regions with high radar reflectivity were correlated with dark areas. The regions of high reflectivity were not actually coincident with the dark areas but were always somewhat displaced in longitude. The conclusion that the above authors reached was that the dark areas were elevated regions with very low slopes. The slopes had to extend over extremely large distances, which implied that elevation differences of about 10 kilometres existed.

The 1967 and 1969 oppositions provide the final surprising chapter to this story. In 1967 precise radar-ranging methods were used by Gordon H. Pettengill and his collaborators to scan a narrow swath of the planet along latitude 22° N. The timing of the radar echoes led to the first direct and conclusive evidence that large elevation differences in fact did exist on the surface, but, ironically, there was little correlation between the dark areas and elevation. In 1969 the radar was extended to more southerly latitudes, and good data from this source is now available between the Equator and 22° N. Another investigation using an entirely different technique has confirmed and extended these measurements. The U.S. astronomers Michael J.S. Belton and Donald M. Hunten have made extensive measurements of the amount of carbon dioxide gas in the atmosphere at hundreds of points on the disk from latitudes 25° S to 40° N. If small meteorological effects are neglected, the amount of carbon dioxide is closely related to the relative elevation of the surface. These observations have therefore also provided a map of surface topography.

Elevation correlated with amount of carbon dioxide above surface

The major topographic features that have been found on the planet are as follows. The dark area Syrtis Major is part of a high ridge rising 10 kilometres above the surrounding areas and stretches for at least 4,000 kilometres north–south across the Equator. The Arabian Desert is an extensive basin running parallel to the Equator and encompassing 90° in longitude. The highest area of the planet is the bright desert Tharsis, which appears to be a vast dome 4,000 kilometres in diameter. Mare Acidalium, the only major dark area in the Northern Hemisphere, coincides with a shallow depression leading southward.

Temperatures. The temperature environment on Mars is considerably more rigorous than on the Earth for two reasons: first, the greater distance of Mars from the Sun means that less heat is received from it; and, second, the extreme thinness and composition of the atmosphere are important factors in allowing much greater diurnal fluctuations in temperature. On Earth, the atmosphere has sufficient opacity in the thermal infrared to block and slow down the rate of energy loss from the surface at night, limiting the lower extreme in temperature. On Mars, the tenuous carbon dioxide atmosphere is unimportant in this respect, and greater differences between night and day temperatures occur at the surface.

The mean temperature, averaged over the entire planet, can be estimated from the solar input and well-known radiation laws. It is found to be about 210° K, and this value has been confirmed by measurements of microwave radiation. The microwave measurement gives an average temperature that is not the instantaneous temperature of the surface but applies to some level a short distance below the surface where the diurnal variations of temperature have been damped out. The measurement is important as it indicates that there are no large sources of heat inside the planet.

Temperature changes

The actual temperature of the surface on the daylight side and just across the terminator have been measured most recently in 1954 using the 200-inch Palomar telescope and in 1969 using an infrared radiometer aboard the Mariner 6 and 7 spacecraft. In the equatorial regions the diurnal variation of temperature is found to be about 100° K. Rising rapidly at first during the early morning to a maximum of roughly 290° K at about 1300 hours and then dropping off rapidly again in the afternoon, the temperature is above freezing (273° K) for about three to four hours during the day. Temperatures fall off at higher latitudes, dropping suddenly on the polar caps to about 150° K. The dark areas are about 10° K warmer than the brighter areas. No observational data is available about nighttime temperatures, but theoretical thermal models that correctly predict the postnoon, daytime maximum indicate that the equatorial nighttime temperature will have fallen to about 175° K by dawn. The above equatorial temperatures refer to the conditions at the 1954 opposition, and because of the ellipticity of the Martian orbit the maximum daytime temperature can be expected to vary by about 30° K from perihelic conditions to those at aphelion. The 1954 opposition was approximately midway between perihelion and aphelion.

THE POLAR CAPS

The general seasonal behaviour of the polar caps is one of the more elaborately documented phenomena on Mars. Consider first the southern polar cap. In early spring the cap has its greatest dimensions and stretches from the pole to a latitude of about 50° S. As spring proceeds, the cap sublimates and begins to recede at a rate of about 1° of latitude every five days. During this time the edge of the cap takes on a ragged appearance. Eventually, gaps appear that break the cap into well-defined fragments. This process is repeated each year, and the location of the fragments is always the same. As the polar snow recedes, a dark-blue band, first noted by Wilhelm Beer and Johann von Mädler in 1830, is seen at the edge of the cap. This dark collar follows the recession of the cap. One-third of the Martian year later the cap has disappeared. A brief interlude of atmospheric clarity then follows, which terminates in early fall with the rapid formation of the polar hood. This is an atmospheric phenomenon and consists of haze and clouds that vary from day to day. Occasionally, the hood is sufficiently transparent in the red region of the spectrum to allow photographs of the new polar cap forming beneath it to be taken. The hood is far more extensive than the cap itself and has been reported to extend to within 35° of the Equator.

The polar hood

The behaviour of the northern polar cap is similar, although not exactly the same in detail. The differences are mainly due to a combination of the effects of the lengths of the seasons and the variation in distance from the Sun. Although the northern summer is longer than the southern, the northern cap never entirely disappears because the planet is at a greater distance from the Sun during the northern summer, and, correspondingly, less heat is received from the Sun. Further minor differences between the phenomena in the Northern and Southern Hemispheres, such as in the characteristics of the dark collar and the behaviour of the polar hood, have been described by Clyde W. Tombaugh.

The nature of the polar caps is a controversial subject that may soon be reconciled. An early hypothesis was that they were simply water ice. This view can be traced back to William Herschel, who imagined the polar caps of Mars to be just like those on Earth. In 1898 the Irish scientist George Johnstone Stoney pointed out that this was not necessarily so and suggested that the caps might consist of frozen carbon dioxide, though this idea remained speculation until 1947, when the U.S. astronomer Gerard P. Kuiper discovered CO_2 in the planet's atmosphere. The idea was particularly attractive because no water vapour had then been detected in the atmosphere. Nevertheless, Kuiper in 1948 was persuaded that the caps had reflection spectra that were characteristic of water ice rather than CO_2. Similar spectra, published by the Soviet astronomer V.I. Moroz in 1966, indicated the same result, and the idea that the polar caps were predominantly water ice became widely accepted. But in 1966 R.B. Leighton and B.C. Murray published an important numerical study of the thermal environment on Mars, which throws considerable doubt on the water ice hypothesis. The calculations, although based on gross simplification of the actual conditions on Mars, indicated that carbon dioxide gas would freeze out of the atmosphere. Moreover, the computations showed that polar caps so formed would behave in a way similar to that which was observed.

Composition of polar caps

Data from the Mariner 6 and 7 spacecraft now appear to have resolved the problem (see Figure 6). On board the spacecraft were an infrared radiometer that could measure the temperature of the surface and an infrared spectrometer that could look with high spatial resolution for characteristic features in the spectrum of the reflected light from the polar cap without the interference of absorption in the Earth's atmosphere. The radiometer experimenters reported that, as the field of view of their instrument swept over the polar cap, the temperature dropped to within 2° K of the predicted temperature for frozen carbon dioxide. The discrepancy may be easily accounted for, thereby demonstrating that a polar cap composed of CO_2 would be stable at the time it was observed. If the measured temperature had been, say, 10° higher, the CO_2-ice hypothesis would have been untenable. The infrared spectrometer provided conclusive evidence that frozen CO_2 does exist on the surface. The spectrum contained features at 3.0 and 3.3 microns, which are characteristic absorptions of solid CO_2.

The above evidence, plus the calculations of R.B. Leighton and B.C. Murray, has led astronomers to conclude with considerable confidence that the polar caps are predominantly solidly frozen CO_2. The presence of frozen water is not entirely excluded, for small amounts of water vapour have been observed in the atmosphere, and the polar regions will progressively collect such water. It is most likely, therefore, that the polar caps also contain some water ice. An additional possibility is that the northern polar cap, which never completely disappears, may have a solid core of water ice. Samuel Glasstone has made an estimate of the depth of the snowfall at the South Pole on Mars based on R.B. Leighton and B.C. Murray's calculations and finds that the average depth might be some three to five feet.

It has been observed and mentioned above that the caps fragment as they recede so that certain regions in which the covering remains are left isolated. Presumably, these regions are colder than the average, and the Martian snow is able to endure on them. The Mountains of Mitchel, named after their discoverer, Ormsby MacKnight Mitchel, form one such fragment in the Southern Hemisphere. The naming of this and other such features as mountains is based on a direct analogy with the Earth, where the tops of high mountains are cold regions and can support snow throughout the year. In 1967 it was pointed out that this reasoning may be quite fallacious in the case of Mars and that the area known as the Mountains of Mitchel may actually be a low-lying depression. The argument that leads to this peculiar state of affairs centres on the extreme thinness of the Martian atmosphere. It has, unlike the terrestrial atmosphere, so

Nature of the Mountains of Mitchel

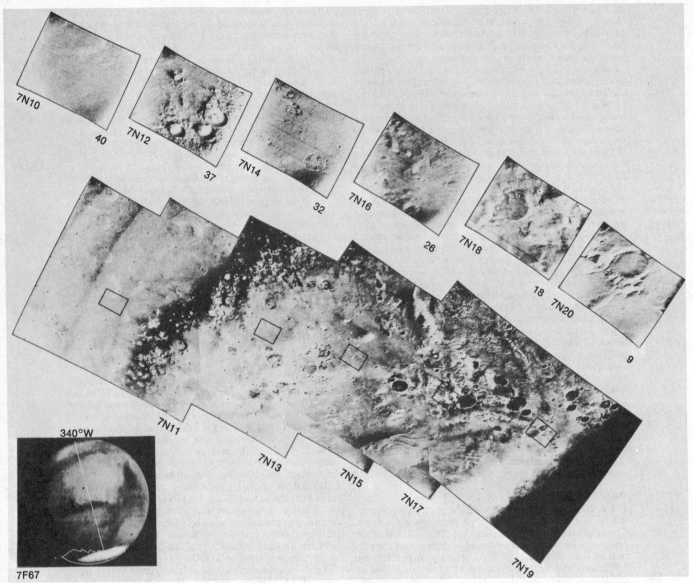

Figure 6: *Mars.*
(Centre) Mosaic from Mariner 7 frames of a region close to the edge of the south polar cap showing "snow," probably frozen carbon dioxide, lying in shadowed areas and on high ground. Outlined areas are enlarged above, and coverage relative to the planet and the central meridian (white line) are indicated bottom left.
By courtesy of National Aeronautics and Space Administration

little heat capacity and ability to block outgoing thermal radiation that temperature probably plays little role in the determining of the equilibrium of carbon dioxide snow; the equilibrium will be determined by the overlying pressure of carbon dioxide in the atmosphere. Therefore, regions on which snow lingers will be those of high atmospheric pressure—*i.e.*, low-lying areas and valleys. At present there is little observational evidence for or against this idea, but the theoretical argument seems quite sound.

THE ATMOSPHERE

Basic atmospheric data. The lower atmosphere is thought to consist mainly of carbon dioxide gas that has been released slowly from the crust and interior over times comparable with the lifetime of the planet. Water vapour and carbon monoxide have been positively identified by spectroscopic means, but only in very minute quantities. Small admixtures of spectroscopically inert gases, such as argon, also may be present in the atmosphere.

The characteristic temperature of the atmosphere, averaged over the illuminated (daytime) side, is roughly 200° K. This is colder than the mean temperature of the underlying surface, about 250° K. The difference is due to the presence of temperature gradients in the lower atmosphere that have an average value of about 4° per vertical kilometre.

The atmosphere is very thin by terrestrial standards, the surface pressure being less than one-hundredth that on the Earth. In spite of its thinness, the Martian atmosphere is observed to support clouds. One variety, the so-called yellow clouds, are most reasonably explained in terms of small dust particles. These clouds can be widespread and have been observed to move at high speeds (up to 100 kilometres per hour), indicating that the atmosphere is capable of violent large-scale motions. The study of the dynamics of planetary atmospheres is relatively new, but some highly sophisticated numerical simulations of the Martian atmosphere have been performed and are briefly reviewed below.

The atmospheric data returned by the successful Mariner 4 flyby of Mars in 1965 led to radical changes in the understanding of the Martian atmosphere. More insight is to be expected from the successful Mariner 6 and 7 experiments when the final data is released. Mariner 4 also returned the first sounding of a planetary ionosphere (other than that of the Earth) and thereby launched the special subject of Martian aeronomy, the study of the Martian upper atmosphere.

Composition and surface pressure. Before 1947 there had been no chemical identification of any of the gases in the Martian atmosphere. Its composition was postulated by a variety of arguments, including analogies with the Earth, spectroscopic upper limits on various gases, and the kinetic theory applied to escape of gases from a planetary atmosphere. The atmosphere was presumed to be composed largely of nitrogen. Between 1925 and 1963 the surface pressure was estimated by photometric measurements and arguments based on the scattering power of the atmosphere and the amount of polarization that it could induce in the reflected solar light. In 1954 Gérard de Vaucouleurs discussed all of the available data and concluded that the surface pressure was 85 ± 4 millibars, about one-tenth of the atmospheric pressure on Earth. The quoted error illustrates the confidence that was generally attributed to this determination. It is now known that the result was incorrect, being too high by a factor of about 10. The above methods led to an incorrect result for reasons that are now fairly well understood, and it was simply a misfortune that apparent agreement between results from several independent methods produced overconfidence in the value quoted above.

First detection of CO_2

The first gas to be identified, carbon dioxide (CO_2), was detected in 1947, as noted above, by Gerard P. Kuiper, who used a lead sulphide detector, developed during World War II, and what were then new techniques in infrared, astronomical spectroscopy. It was generally believed at this time that the surface pressure was about 100 millibars, and Kuiper's spectra appeared to imply that carbon dioxide was only a minor constituent. Estimates put the CO_2 content at no more than 1 or 2 percent of the total atmosphere. It was subsequently pointed out that Kuiper's spectra were consistent with an essentially pure CO_2 atmosphere with a surface pressure of 13 millibars.

The 1963 opposition brought new understanding of the Martian atmosphere. A group of three extremely faint lines near 0.87 micron was discovered in the Martian spectrum. They were immediately identified as being due to carbon dioxide, a gas already known to exist in the atmosphere. What was surprising about the three features was that, according to what was then believed to be the atmospheric composition, they should not have been visible at all. Their discovery showed that something was wrong about the established ideas.

The main result of this investigation was to reduce the estimate of the atmospheric surface pressure by a factor of nearly 4, to 25 millibars, and to show that CO_2 could be a major constituent of the atmosphere. The study also had the effect of exposing the uncertainties in the photometric and polarimetric methods that had been used previously. Considerable uncertainties, however, still remain in this work, and the succeeding oppositions in 1965, 1967, and 1969 found many groups of observers supplying new techniques to the problem of obtaining spectra of Mars. These efforts were supplemented in 1965 and again in 1969 with flyby data from Mariner 6 and 7, which proved the Martian atmosphere with radio waves. Additional unique data was obtained from the infrared and ultraviolet spectrometers on board the spacecraft.

Mean pressure of atmosphere

The net result of ground-based spectroscopic investigations into the amount of CO_2 in the planet's atmosphere is that the mean surface partial pressure of the gas is now, in the early 1970s, set at 5.5 ± 0.6 millibars. This figure is based on many diverse experiments on three separate bands of CO_2. A considerable part of the estimated uncertainty is due to the imprecision of laboratory data on the CO_2 bands, a condition that can in due course be corrected. Such diverse techniques as photographic spectroscopy, photoelectric spectrophotometry, Michelson interferometry and Fabry–Perot interferometry have been used in CO_2 studies and produce comparable results.

The amount of CO_2 is comparatively large: it is nine times the amount currently present in the Earth's atmosphere, but considering the tremendous amount of CO_2 that has been cycled through the Earth's atmosphere and is now chemically locked in terrestrial, sedimentary rocks, the Martian CO_2 content represents slightly less than 1/1000 of that on the Earth. These figures represent a rather ill-defined mean of the surface partial pressure. The amount of CO_2 above any specific point on the surface may differ considerably from it because of the large variations in altitude in the surface topography. Michael J.S. Belton and Donald M. Hunten, for example, found that they were unable to detect any CO_2 at all over the midpart of Syrtis Major, while the adjacent bright area Libya showed more than the average amount. Further, the amount of CO_2 in the atmosphere may vary considerably over the Martian year because of the alternate deposition and release of CO_2 from the polar caps. The numerical study conducted by Robert B. Leighton and Bruce C. Murray predicts that the total amplitude of the variation should be about 38 percent of the mean pressure, a very large change. Attempts have been made to detect this observationally, but the available data are too crude to make any meaningful deductions.

Spectroscopy has not been able to provide a measure of the total atmospheric pressure with any great accuracy because of technical difficulties in dealing with a spectrum integrated across the entire illuminated disk of Mars. The radio occultation experiments performed on the Mariner spacecraft are much more reliable for this purpose. Data from six occultations are now available, two from each Mariner flyby mission. As the spacecraft disappears behind the limb of the planet as seen from the Earth, the radio link between the spacecraft and the Earth cuts through the atmosphere. Corresponding changes in intensity and phase occur in the radio signal, which can be interpreted in terms of atmospheric and ionospheric properties.

A reversed but otherwise similar situation occurs when the spacecraft reappears from behind the planet at the end of the occultation. The interpretation is somewhat dependent on the assumed composition of the atmosphere, but it appears that the mean atmospheric pressure is five to seven millibars. A full analysis of all the available data pertaining to the mean atmospheric pressure on Mars is not yet available, but a value of six millibars is not likely to be changed much.

In summary, it is clear that carbon dioxide is a major constituent of the Martian atmosphere (see Table 4). At

Table 4: The Composition of the Martian Atmosphere (fraction by volume)	
Carbon dioxide	80–100%
Inert gases (argon, neon, etc.)	0–20%
Nitrogen	<1%
Oxygen	≤0.3%
Carbon monoxide	0.08%
Water vapour*	0.04%

*Variable and unevenly distributed in the atmosphere.

one extreme the atmosphere may be essentially pure CO_2, while at the other the fraction of CO_2 by weight could be no less than about 80 percent. In the latter case the balance of the atmosphere could be argon or perhaps neon. Nitrogen is also a possibility, but the ultraviolet-spectrometer experiment of Charles A. Barth and his associates on Mariner 6 and 7 showed no indications of any of the characteristic emissions of the nitrogen molecule. Barth has indicated that the amount of this gas in the atmosphere must be very small, less than 1 percent of the total atmosphere. Two other constituents that have been detected in the lower atmosphere are water and carbon monoxide. Only trace amounts are present, and the water content is highly variable. The U.S. astronomer Lewis D. Kaplan finds that the amount of carbon monoxide is about 0.08 percent of the atmosphere. The CO molecule was discovered in the infrared spectrum of Mars generated by the Michelson interferometer of Pierre and Janine Connes. The detection of oxygen has been the subject of many spectroscopic studies, but oxygen has not been positively identified. In 1968 Michael T.J.S. Belton and Donald M. Hunten reported the tentative identification of oxygen at the 0.3 percent level, but this observation has not yet been confirmed or denied.

The "water problem" is intimately connected with the possibility of life on the planet. Water in the Martian atmosphere was first identified in 1963 by Lewis D. Kaplan, Guido Münch, and Hyron Spinrad from the same photographic plate that yielded their important discoveries about CO_2. The investigation of water content is made exceedingly difficult because of the masking of weak planetary lines by strong absorptions due to water vapour in the Earth's atmosphere. The researches since 1963 by Ronald Schorn and others indicate that the atmospheric water content on Mars is always small. It is also variable and may show a seasonal dependence, though this latter behaviour has not been firmly established. The distribution of water vapour with respect to the Equator, however, has definitely been shown to be asymmetric, more water vapour being present in the summer hemisphere. Water vapour characteristically appears in amounts corresponding to about 20 or 30 microns of precipitable water. These unfortunately chosen units (which are traditional) correspond to a mean atmospheric-fractional content of about 0.04 percent. At the mean temperature of the Martian atmosphere, this corresponds to a relative humidity of about 50 percent, which is not particularly dry. Because the near surface air temperatures are considerably higher than the mean, the daytime humidity near the surface will be far lower and the lower air extremely dry.

Atmospheric water vapour molecules can be destroyed quite rapidly on Mars through the action of ultraviolet light as a result of inefficient shielding by CO_2 and the lack of ozone in the atmosphere. The light hydrogen atoms formed in the process then diffuse up through the atmosphere and ultimately escape to space. This produces a net gain of molecular oxygen in the atmosphere. Donald M. Hunten and Michael B. McElroy from the United States find that this process may explain the observed hydrogen emission in the upper Martian atmosphere, measured by Charles A. Barth with the Mariner 6 and 7 ultraviolet spectrometer. Other conclusions in Hunten and McElroy's analysis are that dissociation and the accompanying reactions could remove the entire observed amount of water vapour in the atmosphere in the relatively short time of 100,000 years, implying a continuous source of replacement water. The destruction of water will leave behind a considerable amount of oxygen which presumably oxidizes the surface material. This latter process would be facilitated by the action of ultraviolet light producing ozone and atomic oxygen near the surface.

Temperature. The vertical structure of the Martian atmosphere—that is, the relation of temperature to altitude—is determined by a complicated balance of radiative, convective, and advective energy transport. In the upper atmosphere thermal conduction also is important. A considerable amount of effort has been invested in predicting the typical structure that would occur on Mars and its dependence on the time of day.

A primary factor is the composition of the atmosphere, which is almost pure CO_2. This can quickly radiate away its heat so that the atmosphere can respond rapidly to changes of insolation and changes in ground temperature, unlike the Earth's atmosphere, in which 70 percent of the gas is radiatively inert and does not respond rapidly to thermal imbalances. Thus, on Mars, large diurnal fluctuations are predicted for the lower atmosphere. At nighttime the lower atmosphere cools off quickly, producing strong inversions in the temperature profile and strong diurnal components to the local winds. On Earth this type of inversion is limited to the first tens of metres near the ground and drives only minor local winds, such as seashore and land breezes.

In 1968 the U.S. astronomers Richard Goody and Peter Gierasch described the probable conditions in the equatorial lower atmosphere as follows: near the ground, in the first few metres, there is a turbulent boundary layer marked by very large temperature gradients. Temperature drops of as much as 70° K can take place in this layer. The noontime air temperature a few metres from the ground is always much lower than the ground temperature. (This phenomenon also occurs on the Earth.) Above the boundary layer, up to an altitude of about five kilometres, the atmospheric temperature undergoes large diurnal variations in an attempt to follow the diurnal changes in the ground temperature. At night the air is stable, but in daytime the region is characterized by strong turbulence. Above five kilometres the temperature varies much less and up to a height of about 15 kilometres falls off only at about 5° per kilometre. This region is turbulent in the daytime and stable at night. The maximum height reached by the daytime turbulence is about 15 kilometres, and this height is identified as the Martian tropopause. Michael B. McElroy has shown that from 15 to about 90 kilometres the atmosphere is nearly isothermal at a temperature of about 160° K. Above 90 kilometres, the mesopause, the temperature begins to rise again at a rate of about 4° per kilometre owing to the deposition of solar energy in the tenuous higher atmosphere.

The mean temperature of the daytime atmosphere has been measured at 200° K from the distribution of the absorption in the rotational structure of CO_2 bands. The same bands also show an indication of the temperature gradient in the lower atmosphere.

More complete data on the vertical structure at six locations on Mars are available in preliminary form from the radio occultation experiments on the Mariner spacecraft. These data appear to be in reasonable agreement with the theoretical description given above.

Atmospheric dynamics. Forecasting the weather by means of numerical models of the atmosphere is one of the largest branches of meteorology. In recent years, some of the techniques for predicting and following the dynamical state of the Earth's atmosphere have been applied to Mars. As the terrestrial techniques are generally quite reliable and bring out quite accurately the overall dynamical properties of the Earth's atmosphere, reasonable results can be expected when the same techniques are applied to the Martian atmosphere. Atmospheric motions on Mars seem to be far more violent than on the Earth for reasons connected with the thinness of the atmosphere, its ability to adjust rapidly by radiative exchange of energy to local conditions of insolation, the lack of oceans with their large storage capacity for heat, and the fact that a large fraction of the atmosphere is deposited and released from the polar caps in spring and fall.

In the winter hemisphere the zonal wind speeds in the free atmosphere reach 250 kilometres (about 160 miles) per hour in a westerly direction. The winds in the summer hemisphere are in direct contrast, being in the opposite direction with a speed of, at most, 100 kilometres (about 63 miles) per hour in equatorial and low latitudes, falling off to light speeds of perhaps 18 kilometres (about 11 miles) per hour at midlatitudes and higher. Because of the deposition of CO_2 on the winter polar cap, there is a net transport of material across the Equator, and meridional wind speeds may reach 33 kilometres (about 22 miles) per hour across the Equator. At the time of the equinoxes the wind pattern begins to resemble that seen in the Earth's atmosphere. The zonal winds in midlatitudes are westerlies in both hemispheres, with average speeds of 70 to 110 kilometres (about 45 to 70 miles) per hour. The equatorial region is marked by gentle easterly winds. The meridional wind component is very small.

This picture of motions in the Martian atmosphere is tentative; it outlines the overall characteristics in a very rough way. In particular, the calculation omits any consideration of the large-scale topography of the surface that has recently been mapped by radar and spectroscopic techniques.

THE INTERIOR OF MARS

Little is known about the interior of Mars. Models of the interior of Mars have been constructed, as they have for the other terrestrial planets, on the basis of the mass and dimensions of the planet (or, alternatively, its mean density), and the dynamical ellipticity of the planet. This latter quantity is a measure of the difference in the moments of inertia of the planet along and perpendicular to its axis of rotation. It is therefore a measure of the internal density distribution in the planet. The dynamical ellipticity generally differs from the optical ellipticity, which can be measured directly (although with great difficulty) from the image of the planet. The latter is of little use in discussion of the internal structure because its value may be strongly influenced by unrelieved strains and distortions in the upper crust of the planet. Physical data on the equation of state of materials (*i.e.*, their response to changes of pressure and temperature) are also required. In the discussion of the terrestrial planets these kinds of data are based on what is known of the behaviour of terrestrial material.

Simple models of the Martian interior There are two types of simple models. In one, the internal composition can be different from that of the Earth: the planet is visualized as being made up of certain proportions of silicate and metallic (iron) phases, and the proportions are presumed to vary from one planet to the next. The second type of model constrains the composition to be the same in all cases. The observed differences in the mean density and dynamical ellipticity are then presumed to be governed by strong phase changes in the material at certain pressures and temperatures in that material. The general conclusion from the many studies that have been carried out is that Mars possesses at most a very small core and is far more homogeneous than the Earth. The work of the U.S. astronomers Robert L. Kovach and Don L. Anderson would indicate that the Martian interior could also be similar to an undifferentiated Earth—*i.e.*, a planet with the same mean density as Earth but with no core—and satisfy the observational constraints.

It is effectively impossible to make estimates of the temperatures in the interior of the planet or of its thermal history because of the absence of factual information. Nevertheless, the consensus appears to be that the planet does not have a liquid, metallic core. This is borne out by the observed absence of a magnetic field. Mariner 4 carried a magnetometer, which implied that the dipole magnetic field on Mars was less than that of the Earth by a factor of 0.0003.

The interior of Mars appears, therefore, to be dormant. This is supported by circumstantial evidence from the Mariner pictures on which no obvious signs of tectonic activity on the planet have been found.

THE SATELLITES

The two satellites of Mars were discovered during the 1877 opposition by Asaph Hall of the U.S. Naval Observatory. Phobos, the inner and larger of the two, was discovered six days after the discovery of the fainter outer moon, Deimos. The orbit of Phobos is unique in that it is extremely close to the planet. At a mean distance of 2.8 planetary radii from the centre it approaches the so-called Roche limit of 2.4 planetary radii. This limiting distance corresponds to the range at which gravitationally bound bodies of the same mean density as the planet could be broken apart by the gravitational force of the planet. The orbital period of Phobos about Mars is 7 hours and 39 minutes. This short period means that the moon travels around Mars twice in a Martian day. Thus, an observer at a suitable point on the planet would see Phobos rise and set twice in a day.

Not all observers on the surface of Mars could see the moons, however, because of their proximity to the planet and their near Equatorial orbits. At latitudes greater than approximately 70° north or south, for example, Phobos would never be seen.

The dimensions of the satellites are difficult to judge from Earth-based telescopes because they are too small for their disks to be discerned. The area of the object is commonly estimated from the amount of light that it reflects. This procedure is uncertain to the extent that it requires an assumption about the moon's albedo; *i.e.*, its ability to reflect light. Nevertheless, the rough diameters of Phobos and Deimos have been estimated in this way at

16 and 10 kilometres, respectively. The size and shape of Phobos can now be put on a more satisfactory basis because the satellite was photographed passing between Mars and the Mariner 7 spacecraft. The shape of the satellite was resolved and found to be noticeably elongated in the plane of its orbit. The ratio of maximum to minimum diameter is at least 1.3, the apparent dimension being about 18×22 kilometres. The albedo of the satellite, 0.065, is therefore lower than was expected and turns out to be the lowest known in the solar system. To an observer close up, the surface of the satellite would appear to be black.

The discovery of the satellites was of considerable importance because the period of their motion about the planet provides basic information on the mass of the parent planet. The most accurate estimates of the mass are now derived from the orbit of the Mariner flybys. Additional information on the distribution of mass in the interior of Mars can be obtained from the rate of recession of the nodes of the satellite's orbit. This information leads to the specification of the dynamical ellipticity discussed in the previous section.

THE QUESTION OF LIFE ON MARS

Is life present on Mars? This question can be answered only in the most speculative terms in the light of present knowledge of the planet. Nevertheless, the possibility of life establishing itself on Mars and propagating can be discussed in a qualitative way. The arguments can be conveniently arranged as answers to the following series of simple questions: (1) Is there any evidence for life in the available observations of Mars? (2) Could terrestrial life forms propagate under present conditions on Mars or under probable conditions in the past? (3) Are there any simple physical modifications of terrestrial life processes that would allow terrestrial life forms to function on Mars? Positive responses to all these questions, even excluding any direct evidence for specific life forms, would amount to high probability for life being present on the planet but would not certify its presence. A direct demonstration that life exists on Mars will probably not be possible without a landing on the planet and direct sampling of any existing life forms.

Life has been defined in a general, concise way by the U.S. biologist Norman H. Horowitz: ". . . living organisms are systems that reproduce, mutate, and then reproduce their mutations." The latter property, a necessary condition for the evolution of organic life forms, does not concern us here, but a search for evidence of reproduction and the ability to grow among the observations of Mars can be made. The pertinent factors are: Martian phenomena pertinent to the determination of possible life (1) the wave of darkening, (2) the ability of dark areas to recover after apparent obliteration by Martian dust storms, (3) seasonal changes in colour of certain regions, (4) long-term changes in the markings, (5) a very weak spectral feature at 3.45 microns recorded as having been observed in the spectra of dark areas, and (6) the amount of water present on Mars. The question whether or not oceans were ever present on the planet is also important. The famous but now discredited Martian canal system historically played a central role in the concept of the possibility of intelligent life on Mars. The wave of darkening and colour changes that propagate in the dark areas across the planet as the southern polar cap disappears might be caused by the growth of Martian flora stimulated by the northern transport of water vapour released from the southern polar cap, but many of the phenomena can also be explained in terms of purely mechanical and meteorological processes.

The reported observations by the U.S. astronomer William M. Sinton of the spectral feature at 3.45 microns, which appears to be present only in the spectrum of dark areas and is listed above, is sometimes quoted as evidence for life on Mars. Absorption near this wavelength is a characteristic of all organic molecules and is connected with the fundamental vibrations of the carbon-hydrogen bond in such molecules. No alternative identification for this absorption has been offered, but a review of Sinton's evidence gives little comfort to those who would accept this observation as a demonstration that organic material is abundant in the dark areas. Absorption features actually appear on Sinton's spectra at 3.69, 3.58, and 3.45 microns. The two strongest of these (which also occurred only in the spectrum of a dark marking) have since been identified as absorption by HDO (deuterated water) in the terrestrial atmosphere. The remaining "feature" at 3.45 microns has not been similarly explained, but, as the weakest of the three, it is unlikely that it would ever have been recognized as an independent feature in the spectrum on its own.

The identification of water on Mars and the possibility that oceans might once have existed on the planet is linked to the question of whether terrestrial life forms could propagate on Mars under present conditions or under probable conditions in the past. Liquid water is generally considered to have been essential in the development of life on Earth and is the primary solvent in the metabolism of terrestrial organisms.

Water has been observed on Mars, but only in the vapour form and then only sporadically and in extremely small quantities. It was pointed out above that the atmosphere near the surface should be extremely dry in the daytime. Liquid water is not likely to exist on the planet except under special conditions. Such conditions may exist below the surface. It has been conjectured that vast amounts of water may exist beneath the surface of the planet at high latitudes in the form of a layer of permafrost, and liquid water may have a transitory existence at the surface of this layer. Other regions may be moist if heat is supplied by near surface volcanic sources. Water vapour was discovered with the help of large telescopes and spectrographs with great difficulty. No other definitive evidence for water exists, although some observers of the planet have interpreted the observations of the dark-blue collar around the polar caps as they dissipate and the occasional dark spot left on the surface after the passage of a white cloud as evidence for the transitory presence of liquid water. This interpretation is not necessarily unique, however.

The photographs of the surface of Mars returned by the Mariner spacecraft have led to rather definite limitations on the amount of water that could ever have existed on the Martian surface. The prevalence of many large craters indicates that the surface is extremely old, perhaps primordial. There are indications of many products of powerful erosion processes that would be expected if large areas of the planet had been covered with water at any time, but in all probability no oceans have existed on the planet for the last 4,000,000,000 years. It is not possible to exclude the former presence of large quantities of water entirely. Conditions at the time of the formation of the planet are unknown (see below).

A further consideration in assessing the possibility of the establishment of organisms on Mars is the radiation environment at the surface. On the Earth we are protected from harmful radiation primarily by the presence of traces of ozone gas in the stratosphere. Ozone blocks out strong ultraviolet radiation that is capable of breaking up large organic molecules, the basis of living organisms. The Martian atmosphere does not contain detectable amounts of ozone gas, and the surface of Mars, therefore, is exposed to ultraviolet radiation. Some researchers discount this as an argument against the propagation of life, pointing out that pigmentation and the availability of subsurface habitats could provide adequate protection.

Marginal conditions for life

The weight of the evidence appears to be against the development of terrestrial types of life on Mars. Nevertheless, life is extremely widespread on the Earth and can thrive under the most unlikely conditions. Plants (lichens) can live under conditions in which they are alternately frozen and thawed out. Other organisms thrive in hot springs, in strong acid solutions, and in powerful organic solvents. When such conditions are considered the Martian environment seems far less rigorous, and the evidence against the propagation of at least a sturdy and perhaps primitive form of life much less conclusive.

The possibility of the presence of intelligent life on the planet has been debated for a century, but an unequivocal answer is not possible. It was pointed out that the remote detection of life on the Earth by photographic or visual means is extremely difficult. Pictures of populated regions of the Earth taken by satellite from distances as close as 300 miles show few obvious signs of life. On the other hand, it is now at last possible to dismiss the arguments that the canals are evidence of great intelligence on the part of the Martians.

Views regarding Mars have been considerably changed as a result of an almost continuous stream of scientific data from November 1971 through late 1972. Developments include the discovery of massive tectonic activity in the Tharsis-Phoenicis Lacus area. At least four large volcanos have been found, each of which has very large caldera-like complexes at the summit. The feature on Nix Olympica is, for example, about 150 kilometres wide, much larger than any similar feature on Earth. Other major discoveries are an extremely long (greater than 2,000 kilometres), wide (200 kilometres), and deep (24 kilometres) rift valley, possibly indicating that internal convection is taking place within Mars. Also seen were many long, sinuous features which appear to be old river systems. Both polar caps have been found to have permanent cores that are likely to be frozen water. On arrival of the spacecraft Mariner 9, a major, planet-wide, dust storm was observed that obliterated the surface from view for about six weeks. The dust extended to altitudes of at least ten kilometres. Atmospheric dust has also been found to be responsible for the apparently "featureless" terrain in Hellas. Mariner 9 pictures have recorded craters in that region.

BIBLIOGRAPHY. H. STRUGHOLD, "Synopsis of Martian Life Theories," *Advances in Space Science and Technology,* 9:105–122 (1967); and F.B. SALISBURY, "Martian Biology," *Science,* 136:17–26 (1962), are two semi-technical discussions of the possibility that life forms can exist and propagate on Mars. SAMUEL GLASSTONE, *The Book of Mars,* NASA SP-179 (1969), provides a comprehensive semi-technical account of Mars data up to the flights of Mariners 6 and 7 in 1969; also has several enlightening chapters on possibilities for extraterrestrial life. N.W. CUNNINGHAM and H.M. SCHURMEIER, *Mariner-Mars 1969: Preliminary Report,* NASA SP-225 (1969); and R.B. LEIGHTON, "The Surface of Mars," *Scient. Am.,* 222:10, 26–41 (1970), describe the remarkable technical and scientific accomplishments of Mariners 6 and 7. G. DE VAUCOULEURS, *Physics of the Planet Mars* (1954), is a technical exposé of ground-based investigations of Mars up to about 1953, now very much out-of-date. Many of the conclusions have subsequently been shown to be fallacious; nevertheless, the book is valuable from a historical point of view. R.B. LEIGHTON and B.C. MURRAY, "Behavior of Carbon Dioxide and Other Volatiles on Mars," *Science,* 153:136–144 (1966), is a remarkable contribution to the understanding of the seasonal behaviour of the Martian atmosphere and its interaction with surface. E.C. SLIPHER, *The Photographic Story of Mars* (1962), is a complete photographic Earth-based study of Martian phenomena. ARTHUR KOESTLER, *The Sleepwalkers: A History of Man's Changing Vision of the Universe* (1959), gives a magnificent account of the role of Mars in the work of Brahe and Kepler.

(M.J.S.B.)

Marseille

Founded more than 2,500 years ago, the port city of Marseille can look back over a history of vigorous independence asserted against central authority in a variety of forms: Julius Caesar, Louis XIV, the Revolutionary Convention, Napoleon Bonaparte, and Napoleon III. Frenchmen elsewhere, convinced that the Mediterranean climes of Provence could never be fully integrated into either the French realm or the Gallic spirit, long looked upon Marseille as a sort of folkloric institution: a place of comic anecdote and dialect, with a seasoning of picturesque criminality; a place where the citizens played a peculiar form of outdoor bowling known as *pétanque* and concocted the glorious garlic- and saffron-flavoured fish stew known as bouillabaise.

However much the proportions of fact and myth are blended in this image, the Marseille of the early 1970s is a major element in the economic and social structure of France. It is the second largest city and the largest commercial seaport of the republic, as well as the capital of

General character of the city

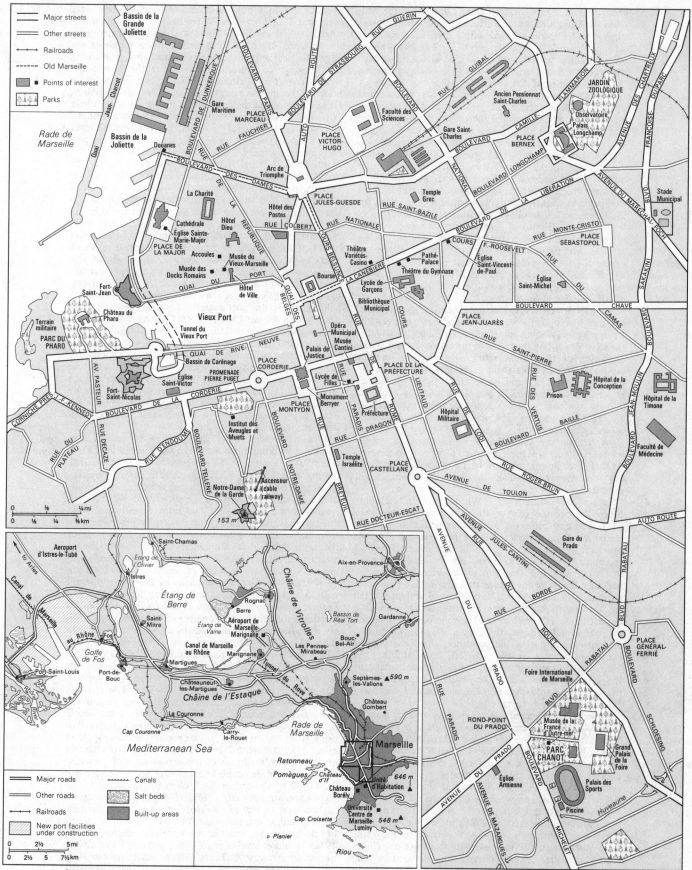

Central Marseille and (inset) its metropolitan area.

the *département* of Bouches-du-Rhône and of the Provence–Côte d'Azur region. Situated on the Mediterranean's Gulf of Lion within a semicircle of limestone hills, it lies 534 miles (859 kilometres) south-southeast of Paris by rail and 219 miles southeast of Lyon. In the

late 1960s, the city and its metropolitan area had respective populations of 889,000 and 964,000.

The history of Marseille. The oldest of the large French cities, Marseille was founded as Massalia (Massilia) by Greek mariners from Phocaea in Asia Minor about 600 BC. Archaeological finds exhibited in the Museum of Antiquities in the 18th-century Château Borély suggest that Phoenicians had settled there even earlier.

Antiquity and the Middle Ages. The Massalians spread trading posts inland as well as along the coasts, westward to Spain, and eastward to Monaco, founding the present cities of Arles, Nice, Antibes, Agde, and La Ciotat. Their coins have been found across France and through the Alps as far as the Tirol. In the 4th century BC a Massalian, Pytheas, visited the coasts of Gaul, Britain, and Germany, and a Euthymenes is said to have navigated the west coast of Africa as far south as Senegal.

When their great trade rivals, the Carthaginians, fought the Romans in the Punic Wars, Marseille (Marseilles historically) supported the Romans and received help in subduing the native tribes of Liguria. When war brought Pompey and Caesar into opposition, Marseille opted for the loser and fell to Caesar's lieutenant Trebonius in 49 BC. Although stripped of dependencies, it was permitted to retain its status as a free city in recognition of past services. For some time the university remained the last centre of Greek learning in the West, but, eventually, the city declined almost to extinction. After centuries of invasion and epidemic, it became little more than a huddle of nearly abandoned ruins.

In the 10th century, under protection of its viscounts, the area was repopulated, and it found new prosperity as a shipping and staging point for the Crusades. Gradually, the town bought up the rights of the viscounts, and, at the beginning of the 13th century, it formed a republic around the Vieux Port ("old harbour"), though the upper part of the city and its southern suburb remained under ecclesiastical jurisdiction. The counts of Provence allowed the city great independence, and only in 1245 and 1256 did Charles of Anjou force acknowledgement of his sovereignty. After Marseille was sacked by Alfonso V of Aragon in 1423, King René of Provence, whose winter residence was there, restored prosperity to the city. At this time the manufacture began of the famous laundry soap known as *savon de Marseille,* which is still produced.

Uneasy union with France. When Provence, including Marseille, became part of the Kingdom of France in 1481, the city preserved a separate administration directed by royal officials. During the wars of religion, Marseille was fanatically Catholic and long refused to recognize Henry IV as king because, until his conversion to Catholicism and accession to the French throne, he had been leader of the Protestants. During the Fronde, a movement in 1648–53 that opposed royal absolutism, the city sought to conserve its ancient liberties and rose against Louis XIV, who in 1660 came in person, breached the walls, and subdued the revolt. To discourage further manifestations of independence, the King planted Fort-Saint-Nicolas at the southern extremity of the Vieux Port. In the same year, the city pushed inland to the west beyond its walls. A few buildings constructed in this expansion still survive in the area around the Cours Belsunce and the Préfecture.

Marseille joined enthusiastically in the French Revolution. Some 500 volunteers marching to Paris in 1792 sang "The War Song of the Rhine Army," recently composed in Strasbourg. The song, which thrilled the crowds along the route of march, was renamed "La Marseillaise" and became the national anthem of France. As the early federalist concepts were washed out in the blood of the Reign of Terror, however, the city revolted against the ruling Convention. Quickly mastered by force of arms, it was officially designated as "the city without a name." When its commerce was almost destroyed by the maritime blockade of the Continent directed against Napoleon, Marseille became bitterly anti-Bonapartist and hailed the Bourbon restoration. Under Napoleon III, it remained stubbornly republican.

Building and razing. The second half of the 19th century saw the expansion of Marseille as the "port of empire," after the elimination of the Barbary pirates in 1815–35, through the conquest of Algeria in 1830, and the inauguration of the Suez Canal in 1869. The great

avenues and many of the monuments of the city were constructed in this period. A serious water problem was solved by a project (1837–48) that brought water from the Durance River. The distribution reservoir above the city was disguised as the Palais Longchamp, containing the Museum of Natural History and the Musée des Beaux-Arts. The Château du Pharo, one of the city's principal landmarks, was built as a villa for Napoleon III and Eugenie at the edge of the bay beyond the Vieux Port, but it was never occupied by the imperial couple. The Bourse (Exchange), completed in 1860 on the main street, now serves as a naval museum, overseas museum, and cultural centre.

Until 1846, the small, picturesque Vieux Port, site of the original Greek installations, was the city's only harbour. Construction of the basin of La Joliette to the north doubled the port surface, and further expansion northward along the coast continued as the need for shipping space grew. The German Army occupied the city from November 1942, but Marseille continued to be an active centre of the French Resistance movement. The Vieux Port quarter, a hillside honeycomb of ancient slums, was ideally suited to clandestine activity, which the Germans tried to arrest by dynamiting the whole district in November 1943, after ordering the evacuation of its 40,000 inhabitants. All the port installations and shipping were destroyed in August 1944 by 2,500 German mines.

Postwar expansion. After World War II, the port areas were rebuilt and extended farther north and west to the Étang de Berre, a large lagoon 17½ miles (28 kilometres) from the city. Marignane Airport, on the south bank, was extended into the lagoon in 1970 to accommodate the largest aircraft. The lagoon is connected to Marseille by canal, while another canal on the opposite shore links the Étang to Arles on the Rhône River, which has been rendered navigable in recent years.

Midway between the two cities, one of the world's most ambitious building plans has been undertaken at the village of Fos, located at the entrance to the Roman canal, the Fossae Marianae, that connects with Arles. The deepwater port of Fos, which will equal the capacity of Marseille, 35 miles away, is being developed by the Port Authority of Marseille. The Sud-Européen oil pipeline to Switzerland and Germany originates at Fos. The surrounding swampland has been filled in to receive one of the largest industrial implantations on the Continent and the greatest industrial centre on the Mediterranean. A giant steelworks, to reach a 7,500,000-ton (6,800,000,000-kilogram) capacity by 1980, is being built with Soviet participation and partial funding by the French government; a British chemical giant has built a plastics plant, and French companies are installing a variety of industries. Industrial zones are to be developed in Arles, Aix, and 11 other communities in the region.

This vast investment and alteration of the Provençal landscape has altered Marseille's conception of itself; the city now aims to be the centre of a large geographic–economic region, the Rhône–Alps–Côte d'Azur. City planning is conducted on a regional rather than a municipal scale, and economic planning embraces the whole region, with substantial financial and technical contributions from the national government. The metropolitan area, officially created in 1966, 1,100 square miles in extent, covers two-thirds of the *département* of Bouches-du-Rhône, and its population was expected to reach some 3,200,000 by the end of the 20th century.

The contemporary city. Marseille is becoming increasingly a modern city of elevated highways, vehicular tunnels (including one under the Vieux Port), and tall housing developments, but the most striking change in the 1970s is more psychological than physical: the city is becoming increasingly French. Until the enormous state investments of expertise and money in the region—as exemplified by improvements in flood control, navigation, irrigation, electricity, roads, schools, and hospitals and by promotion of and participation in industrial development—Marseille had felt as neglected by the central authorities as it was laughingly patronized by Frenchmen in other regions.

Marginal notes:

Decline and resuscitation

Marseille and the Revolution

Regional economic planning and industrial growth

The Vieux Port and the sanctuary of Notre-Dame de la Garde (centre), Marseille.
By courtesy of the French Government Tourist Office

The mythical Marseille did indeed have some small basis in fact: it was a sunny, noisy, gay place with a voluble population. Although the general standard of living ranged from modest to poor, the cynicism and tension of Paris was unknown. The port attracted a cosmopolitan population largely concentrated in the seething waterfront district noted for its gangsters and prostitutes. Until the intensified police action of 1971–72, it was a world centre for the illegal manufacture and shipping of drugs, especially heroin. The residential districts beyond the business centre consisted of spacious villas spread along broad avenues shaded by dusty plane trees. The countryside, flecked with tawny villages, began just outside the city.

The changing face of the city. The reconstruction of war-damaged neighbourhoods gave an impetus to the building trades, which continued to expand both in the private and public sectors. Le Corbusier's Unité d'Habitation, an apartment house that expressed the celebrated architect's ideal of urban family lodging, stood alone amid fields and family houses when it was built at the southern end of town in 1952. It is now surrounded by luxury apartment buildings that extend their masses through the whole district.

From 1955 the city increased the number of primary school classes from 2,500 to 6,500 and constructed 20 new secondary schools. At the southeastern extremity of the city, on the edge of the wild *calanque* ("fjord") region, stands the University Centre of Marseille–Luminy, with residences for 1,500 students. Adjoining are the National School of Architecture, the Regional School of Fine Arts, and the Marseille School of Commerce and Business Administration. The municipality's own computer is housed at this site, as is the computer centre that links the region's hospitals. The Municipal Sports Centre, with a 50,000-seat stadium and an outdoor theatre under construction in 1974, is located there as well; the Regional Institute of Physical Education is to be installed in new buildings nearby. Other university groups in Marseille are the new Saint-Joseph campus in the northeast and the older Saint-Charles in the city centre. Both are concentrated in the sciences, with numbers of specialized laboratories and study institutes. The medical and phar-

maceutical schools are served by two teaching hospital complexes, the Hôpital Nord and the Hôpital de la Timone. At the conclusion of modernization and construction programs (planned for 1980), Marseille's 12 hospitals will have about 9,000 beds.

For the 100 years preceding 1953, no important thoroughfare had been constructed in Marseille, where the average width of the streets was 19½ feet. To cope with the engulfing tide of automobiles, the city government inaugurated a program of street widening and freeway and tunnel construction that, together with the building program, has altered (and, some feel, banalized) the appearance of Marseille. In spite of such innovations designed to keep vehicular traffic flowing, municipal authorities decided in 1968 that the only solution to the problem was to go ahead with the new mass-transit Métro system, for which plans already had been drawn. Two lines, traced to make a loop around the city centre and to serve suburban areas in the north and south as well, would have 28 stations along the underground railway, a project that would take five years to complete. Work on the system had not begun in 1972 because of disagreements between local and national governments on construction costs.

The historic centre: Vieux Port and environs. Although some of the old street markets have disappeared, along the edge of the Vieux Port, fishermen and their wives still cry the virtues of their catch, which includes such local delicacies as squid and eel. From this spot, one of the most famous streets in the maritime world, La Canebière, climbs eastward up the hill. The name is a corruption of *chènevière*, a place where hemp (*chanvre*) was spun into rope during the Middle Ages. The street, which is thronged by people from around the world and unusually gay for a main business boulevard, is crowded with hotels, cinemas, shops, offices, and many broadterraced cafes. The upper half is still lined with trees. Behind the Bourse, building operations in 1967 uncovered a section of the Hellenistic ramparts of Massalia. Excavated by archaeologists, the site, dating from the 3rd and 2nd centuries BC, was found to consist of walls and towers and three sections of Roman road. The ancient port was also excavated. Nearby, close to City Hall

Innovations in transportation facilities

Ruins and
reconstructions

on the edge of the port, is the Museum of Roman Ware-houses (Musée des Docks Romains), which contains storage jars and other remains of commerce under Roman domination.

The port entrance is guarded by the Fort-Saint-Jean, a 13th-century command post of the Knights Hospitalers of St. John of Jerusalem; some ruins remain, along with a tower built in the mid-15th century by King René. The extant fortress, dating from the 17th century, was part of a nationwide system of defenses. Restored since the 1944 explosions, the fort now houses the National Centre for Underwater Archaeological Research. The other side of the harbour entrance is occupied by the Fort-Saint-Nicolas. In the harbour itself lie the Frioul Islands, on which the city has developed a large centre for water sports. Between these islands and the mainland is the Château d'If, where Alexandre Dumas's fictional count of Monte Cristo and great numbers of all-too-real state prisoners were incarcerated.

Other historic buildings are dotted around the Vieux Port. In the Place de la Major, the church of Sainte-Marie-Major, built on the ruins of a temple of Diana, dates mainly from the 12th century; it was partially dismantled to make way for the structure that in 1852 replaced it as the city's cathedral. The dome and supporting arches of the old cathedral are sterling examples of Provençal Romanesque stonemasonry.

Nearby, restored in 1971, is the Hospice de la Vieille Charité ("the old charity hostel"), built between 1660 and 1750. The interior courtyard, a series of three superimposed arcades, surrounds a chapel by Pierre Puget, regarded as the most powerful of French Baroque sculptors. Close by is the Hôtel Dieu, the oldest hospital in the city, created at the end of the 16th century. The principal building, by Jacques Hardouin-Mansart, was erected 200 years later and still serves its original function. Almost next door, the belltower of the vanished church of Accoules, a 14th-century spire mounted on a 12th-century tower, marks the centre of Old Marseille.

On the opposite side of the port stands the crenellated, square-towered church of Saint-Victor, built in the 13th century and once attached to an abbey founded about 413. The church rests on crypts dating mainly from the 11th century but also embodying architecture of the Carolingian period (c. 9th century) and of earlier centuries of the Christian Era. When Saint-Victor was built, the abbey was a temporal power of considerable extent, ruling properties in Spain, Sardinia, and the hinterlands of France.

High on the hill over the south side of the Vieux Port stands the celebrated Notre-Dame de la Garde, a sanctuary honoured from the 8th century. Its present structure was built in 1853; its steeple, crowned by a 30-foot gilded statue of the Virgin, rises 150 feet over the hillside. As la Bonne Mère ("the good mother"), the church and the illuminated figure are dear to the citizens, who, by the thousands, make the arduous climb bearing candles to implore celestial intervention on behalf of their city—as when Marseille is to play an international soccer match.

The people of Marseille. There are fewer and fewer "typical" Marseillais, as there are fewer and fewer "typical" Cockneys or Brooklynites. These are Mediterraneans of richly mixed antique strains, provincials whose province includes the sea. Of celebrated craftiness but small worldly ambition, they have meticulous interest in local food and drink and flavour their sonorous conversation with pungently phrased folk philosophy. As Marseille-the-big-village is supplanted by Marseille-the-big-city, as educational norms rise, as new industry demands new skill, as the standard of living and the level of ambition fatten, the "typical" type disappears and even the accent becomes diluted. The economically small, independent fisherman, boatman, and craftsman have become picturesque.

Prominent among recent additions to the population are young technicians drawn from other parts of France to run new industries and staff the expanding technical centres. Former colonials, spearheaded by Frenchmen pushed out of Algeria, have had a strong impact on the

community and the economy, notably because of their impatience with traditional mother-country ways of organizing and operating enterprises.

Marseille has always attracted Corsicans—including the Bonaparte family during the Revolution. It is a widespread stereotype that they gravitate to the civil service or to crime. Marseille, as all large ports, is a crime centre: smuggling, pilferage, commercial vice, and assorted illegal means of separating seamen from their money are old practices. There has always been a floating international population of men who follow the sea and women who follow sailors. Import–export trade has always provided the basis for a stable foreign colony, now growing as a consequence of increased foreign investment in the area. Manual labour is increasingly performed by North Africans and Africans who arrive from former colonies of France, mostly under group work contracts.

The city government—the usual popularly elected municipal council—keeps very much alive the historical tradition of local independence in spite of the intimate involvement of many national ministries in financing and planning of projects throughout the area.

Cultural life. Marseilles has a total of 11 museums, including a very active Children's Museum. The Museum of Old Marseille was installed in 1960 next to the City Hall in La Maison Diamantée (Diamond House), so called because of its 16th-century facade of projecting diamond-shaped stone lozenges. The Museum of Provençal Art is located at the northeastern limits of the city, in the village of Château Gombert.

Arts and recreation

The municipality contributes to the Marseille Opera, which maintains a resident company of singers and ballet dancers. The interior of its 18th-century theatre was rebuilt after a fire in 1919. The Théâtre du Gymnase was taken over in 1969 by a group known as Cultural Action of the Southwest; it presents a full season of modern theatre, dance, and music.

As building has increased within Marseille, increased attention has been paid to the conservation and development of the municipality's parks and playgrounds. There are more than 50 sports fields in Marseille, two city swimming pools, and a number of public beaches. The parks of the Château du Pharo, Château Borléy, and Palais Longchamp are extensive.

BIBLIOGRAPHY

General works: ARCHIBALD LYALL, *The Companion Guide to Southern France* (1963), includes a discussion of the typography, principal monuments, and cultural institutions of Marseille; DOUGLAS GOLDRING, *The South of France: The Lower Rhone Valley and the Mediterranean Seaboard from Martiques to Menton* (1952), contains a description of Marseille and environs; ALFRED FIRTH, *French Life and Landscape*, vol. 2, *Southern France* (1953), with a brief discussion of the city and its inhabitants; PAUL CARRERE and RAYMOND DUGRAND, *La Région Méditerranéenne* (1960), on the city's industrial region.

History: Raoul Busquet, *Histoire de Marseille*, 6th ed. (1945); RAOUL BUSQUET and REGINE PERNOUD, *Histoire du commerce de Marseille*, vol. 1 (1949).

Art: GERMAINE KRULL and ANDRE SUARES, *Marseille* (1935).

(B.E.)

Marshall, George C.

Called by Winston Churchill "the organizer of victory," General of the Army George Catlett Marshall, as chief of staff of the U.S. Army (which also included the army air forces) during World War II, raised and equipped the largest ground and air force in the history of the United States.

After his retirement, he was recalled three times by Pres. Harry S. Truman to posts normally held by civilians: head of the mission to China, secretary of state, and secretary of defense. Although a soldier in the best tradition, he successfully maintained the principle of civilian control in military matters, carefully following the political lead of presidents Franklin D. Roosevelt and Truman. So completely did he embody the ideal of the citizen soldier that he was the first professional soldier to receive the Nobel Prize for Peace.

George C. Marshall.
EB Inc.

Early years Descended on both sides of his family from settlers who had been in Virginia since the 17th century, George C. Marshall, Jr., was born in Uniontown, Pennsylvania, December 31, 1880. His father, a prosperous coke and coal merchant during his younger son's boyhood, was in financial difficulties when George entered the Virginia Military Institute, Lexington, Virginia, in 1897.

After a poor beginning at the institute, Marshall's record steadily improved, and he soon showed proficiency in military subjects. Once he had decided on a military career, he concentrated on leadership, ending his last year at the institute as first captain of the corps of cadets.

Marshall finished college in 1901. Immediately after receiving his commission as second lieutenant of infantry in February 1902, he married Elizabeth Carter Coles of Lexington and embarked for 18 months' service in the Philippines. Marshall early developed the rigid self-discipline, the habits of study, and the attributes of command that eventually brought him to the top of his profession. Men who served under him spoke of his quiet self-confidence, his lack of flamboyance, his talent for presenting his case to both soldiers and civilians, and his ability to make his subordinates want to do their best.

Somewhat aloof in manner, he seemed to some acquaintances icy cold by nature, but he had a blazing temper held under careful control and a great affection and warmth for those close to him. Happily married for 25 years to his first wife until her death in 1927, he remarried three years later, taking as his second wife a widow, Katherine Tupper Brown, whose three children gave him the family he had hitherto lacked.

After his first service in the Philippines (1902–03), he advanced steadily through the ranks, ultimately becoming general of the army in December 1944. In World War I he served as chief of operations of the 1st Division, first to go to France in 1917, and then as the chief of operations of the 1st Army during the Meuse–Argonne offensive in 1918. After the war he served for five years as aide to Gen. John J. Pershing (1919–24) and for five years as assistant commandant in charge of instruction at the infantry school, Ft. Benning, Georgia (1927–33), where he strongly influenced army doctrine as well as many officers who were to become outstanding commanders in World War II.

He was sworn in as chief of staff of the army on September 1, 1939, the day World War II began with Germany's invasion of Poland. When he entered office, the United States forces consisted of fewer than 200,000 officers and men. Under his direction it expanded in less than four years to a well-trained and well-equipped force of 8,300,000. As the chief representative of the U.S. chiefs of staff at the international conferences at Casablanca, Washington, Quebec, Cairo, and Teheran, he led the fight for an Allied drive on German forces across the English Channel, in opposition to the so-called Mediterranean strategy of the British.

A few days after Marshall resigned as chief of staff on November 21, 1945, President Harry Truman persuaded him to attempt, as his special representative, to mediate the Chinese Civil War. Though his efforts were unsuccessful, in January 1947 he was appointed secretary of state. In June of that year he proposed a European Recovery Program, which, known as the Marshall Plan, played a decisive role in the reconstruction of war-torn Europe. Also significant during his secretaryship were the provision of aid to Greece and Turkey, the recognition of Israel, and the initial discussions that led to the establishment of the North Atlantic Treaty Organization (NATO). Marshall left his position because of ill health two years later. Then, in 1950, when he was nearly 70, President Truman called him to the post of secretary of defense, in which he helped prepare the armed forces for the Korean conflict by increasing troop strength and matériel production and by raising morale. For all his services he had received unstinted praise, but, a few months before he left office, he was bitterly assailed by Sen. Joseph McCarthy and his associates, who charged him with conspiracy with President Roosevelt to keep the commanders at Pearl Harbor ignorant of Japanese plans to attack that base in December 1941; with consistently following a pro-Soviet line in strategy; and with the betrayal of Chiang Kai-shek, the leader of Nationalist China. Although the charges were disavowed by many and were refuted or softened by later careful studies, they still darkened the General's last years.

Cabinet officer

After 1951, General Marshall remained on the active-duty list as the highest ranking general of the army, available for consultation by the government. In 1953 he was awarded the Nobel Prize for Peace in recognition of his contributions to the economic rehabilitation of Europe after World War II and his efforts to promote world peace and understanding. He died at Walter Reed General Hospital, Washington, D.C., on October 16, 1959.

BIBLIOGRAPHY. The authorized biography of General Marshall is a projected four or five volume work by FORREST C. POGUE of which three volumes, *Education of a General, 1880–1939* (1963), *Ordeal and Hope, 1939–42* (1966), and *Organizer of Victory, 1943–45* (1973), have appeared. ROBERT H. FERRELL, *George C. Marshall* (1966), a volume in the "American Secretaries of State Series," written without access to unpublished State Department files, is a valuable summary of the period. JOHN ROBINSON BEAL, *Marshall in China* (1970) contains excerpts of the diary of an American news adviser to Chiang Kai-shek during the Marshall mission. H.L. STIMSON and MCGEORGE BUNDY, *On Active Service in Peace and War* (1947), draws heavily on Stimson's manuscript diary for the period 1941–45 in relation to Marshall. His papers are held in the George C. Marshall Library, Lexington, Virginia.

(F.C.P.)

Marshall, John

As fourth chief justice of the United States from 1801 to 1835, John Marshall was the principal founder of the American system of constitutional law, including the doctrine of judicial review. During his tenure Marshall participated in more than 1,000 decisions, writing 519 of them himself.

Youth. Marshall was born on September 24, 1755, near a settlement then called Germantown (now Midland), Virginia, the eldest of 15 children of Thomas Marshall and Mary Keith Marshall. His childhood and youth were spent in the near-frontier region that in 1759 became Fauquier County, later on in the more extensive properties his father acquired in the Blue Ridge mountain area. His education appears to have been largely the product of his parents' efforts, supplemented only by the instruction afforded by a visiting clergyman who lived with the family for about a year, and by a few months of slightly more formal training at an academy in Westmoreland County. His parents, however, had more learning and wider experience to transmit to their children than was common among the farmers and hunters of the backcountry of northern Virginia. Mary Keith Marshall was the daughter of a college-trained Scottish clergyman. Thomas Marshall had been an assistant surveyor to

John Marshall, crayon portrait by Févret de Saint-Mémin (1770–1852). In the Duke University Law School, Durham, North Carolina.
By courtesy of Duke University, Durham, North Carolina

George Washington, a representative in Virginia's House of Burgesses, and had held a number of other offices. This was the period when the differences between the upland counties and the tidewater aristocracy grew sharp and were paralleled by an increasing sentiment for colonial autonomy and finally for independence among the backcountry residents, whom Thomas Marshall represented.

Early career. When political debate with England was followed by armed clashes in 1775, John Marshall, as lieutenant, joined his father in a Virginia regiment of minutemen and participated in the first fighting in that colony. Joining the Continental Army in 1776, he served under Washington for three years in New Jersey, New York, and Pennsylvania, including in this service the harsh winter of 1777–78 at Valley Forge. When the term of service of his Virginia troops expired in 1779, Marshall retuned to Virginia and thereafter saw little active service prior to his discharge in 1781.

Marshall's career in law dates from 1780. His only formal training was a brief course of lectures given by George Wythe that he attended at William and Mary College early in that year. Licensed to practice in August 1780, he returned to Fauquier County and was elected to the Virginia House of Delegates in 1782 and 1784. Attending the sessions of the legislature in the capitol at Richmond, he established there both a law practice and a home, after marriage to Mary Ambler in January 1783.

For the next 15 years Marshall's career was marked by increasing stature at the brilliant bar of Virginia. He had not, in 1787, achieved a public position that would have sent him as a delegate to the Constitutional Convention in Philadelphia, but he was an active, if junior, proponent of the Constitution in the closely contested fight for ratification. Virginia was then the largest and most populous of the states. Its ratification was not only essential to the success of the proposed Constitution but was also among the most doubtful. Marshall was elected to the legislature that took the first step toward ratification by issuing a call for a convention to consider ratifying; he was also elected a delegate to the convention. On the floor of that convention the contest on behalf of the Constitution was led by men senior to Marshall—James Madison, Edmund Randolph, Edmund Pendleton, and Wilson Cary Nicholas; Patrick Henry and George Mason led the opposition. Marshall made one address in reply to a general attack by Henry. His principal effort on the floor was, perhaps prophetically, a defense of the judiciary article. It can only be assumed that his acknowledged popularity was employed with at least equal effectiveness off the floor to gain or hold the narrow margin by which Virginia's ratification was won.

With the new government under the Constitution installed, Pres. George Washington offered Marshall ap-

pointment as United States attorney for Virginia. Marshall declined. In 1789, however, he sought and obtained a further term in Virginia's House of Delegates as a supporter of the national government. As party lines emerged and became defined in the 1790s, Marshall became recognized as one of the leaders of the Federalist Party in Virginia. In 1795 Washington tendered him an appointment as attorney general. This, too, was declined, but Marshall returned to the state legislature as a Federalist leader. His first federal service came when Pres. John Adams appointed him member of a commission, with Elbridge Gerry and Charles C. Pinckney, to seek improved relations with the government of the French Republic. The mission was unsuccessful. But reports then were published disclosing that certain intermediaries, some shadowy figures known as X, Y and Z, had approached the commissioners and informed them that they would not be received by the French government unless they first paid large bribes; the reports further revealed that these advances had been rebuffed in a memorial prepared by Marshall. Marshall thereupon became a popular figure, and the conduct of his mission was applauded by one of the earliest American patriotic slogans, "Millions for defense, but not one cent for tribute."

Returned from France, Marshall declined appointment to the Supreme Court to succeed Justice James Wilson but was persuaded by Washington to run for Congress. He was elected in 1799 as a Federalist from the Richmond district, though his service in the House of Representatives was brief. His chief accomplishment there appears to have been the effective defense of the President against a Republican attack for having honoured a British request under the extradition treaty for the surrender of a seaman charged with murder on a British warship on the high seas. In May 1800 President Adams requested the resignation of his secretary of war and offered the post to Marshall. Marshall declined. The President next dismissed his secretary of state and tendered the vacant place in his Cabinet to Marshall. In an administration harassed by dissension and with uncertain prospects in the forthcoming election, the appeal of the invitation must have been addressed principally to Marshall's loyalty. After some hesitation he accepted and almost immediately became the effective head of government when the President retired to his home in Massachusetts for a stay of a few months. In the autumn of 1800, Chief Justice Oliver Ellsworth resigned because of ill health. Adams, defeated in the election of November, tendered reappointment to John Jay, the first chief justice. Jay declined. The President then turned to his secretary of state, and in January 1801 sent to the Senate the nomination of John Marshall to be chief justice. The last Federalist Senate confirmed the nomination on January 27, 1801. On February 4, Marshall accepted the appointment but, at the President's request, continued to act as secretary of state for the last month of the Adams administration.

Chief justice of the United States. It fell to Marshall, and to the Supreme Court under and beginning with Marshall, to set forth the main structural lines of the government. Whether the Constitution had created a federation or a nation was not a matter on which agreement could have been won at the beginning of the 19th century. Though judicial decisions could not alone dispel differences of opinion, they could create a body of coherent, authoritative, and disinterested doctrine around which opinion could mass and become effective. To the task of creating such a core of agreement Marshall brought qualities that were admirably adapted for its accomplishment. His own mind had apparently a clear and well-organized concept of the effective government that he believed was needed and was provided by the Constitution. He wrote with a lucidity, a persuasiveness, and a vigour that gave to his judicial opinions a quality of reasoned inevitability that more than offset an occasional lack in precision of analysis. The 35 years of his magistracy gave opportunity for the development of a unified body of constitutional doctrine. It was the first aspect of Marshall's accomplishment that he and the court he headed did not permit this opportunity to pass unrecognized.

Beginnings of his law career

The XYZ Affair

Appointment to the Supreme Court

Prior to Marshall's appointment, it had been the custom of the Supreme Court, as it was in England, for each justice to deliver an opinion in each significant case. This method may be effective where a court is dealing with an organized and existing body of law, but with a new court and a largely unexplored body of law, it created an impression of tentativeness, if not of contradiction, which lent authority neither to the court nor to the law it expounded. With Marshall's appointment, and presumably at Marshall's instance, this practice changed. Thereafter, for some years, it became the general rule that there was only a single opinion from the Supreme Court. This change of practice alone would have contributed to making the court a more effective institution. And when the opinions were cast in the mold of Marshall's clear and compelling statement, the growth of the court's authority was assured.

Marbury v. Madison

Marbury v. *Madison* (1803) was the first of Marshall's great cases and the case that established for the court its power to state and expound constitutional law in disregard of federal statutes that it found in conflict with the Constitution. President Adams had appointed a number of justices of the peace for the District of Columbia shortly before his term expired. Their commissions had been signed and the seal of the United States affixed in the office of the secretary of state, but some of them, including that of William Marbury, remained undelivered. Pres. Thomas Jefferson is believed to have ordered that some of them not be delivered. After unsuccessful application at the Department of State, Marbury instituted suit in the Supreme Court against James Madison, the new secretary. Though the matter was not beyond question, the Court found that Congress had by statute authorized that such suits be started in the Supreme Court rather than in a lower court. But the Supreme Court, speaking through Marshall, held that Article III of the Constitution did not permit this and that the court could not follow a statute that was in conflict with the Constitution. It thereby confirmed for itself its most controversial power, the function of judicial review, of finding and expounding the law of the Constitution.

Once the power of judicial review had been established, Marshall and the court followed with decisions that assured that it would be exercised, and the whole body of federal law determined, in a unified judicial system with the Supreme Court at its head. *Martin* v. *Hunter's Lessee* (1816) and *Cohens* v. *Virginia* (1821) affirmed the Supreme Court's right to review and overrule a state court on a federal question. *McCulloch* v. *Maryland* (1819) asserted the doctrine of "implied powers" granted Congress by the Constitution (in this instance, that Congress could create a bank of the United States, even though such a power was not expressly given by the Constitution). *McCulloch* v. *Maryland* well illustrated that judicial review could have an affirmative aspect as well as a negative; it may accord an authoritative legitimacy to contested government action no less significant than its restraint of prohibited or unauthorized action. *Fletcher* v. *Peck* (1810) and *Dartmouth College* v. *Woodward* (1819) established the inviolability of a state's contracts. *Gibbons* v. *Ogden* (1824) established the federal government's right to regulate interstate commerce and to override state law in doing so. It must be clearly noted, however, that many of Marshall's decisions dealing with specific restraints upon government have turned out to be his less enduring ones, particularly in later eras of increasing governmental activity and control. It is in this area, indeed, that judicial review has evoked its most vigorous critics.

Work on the circuit court and his private life

There was only one term of the Supreme Court each year, generally lasting about seven or eight weeks (a little longer after 1827). Each justice, however, also conducted a circuit court—Marshall in Richmond, Virginia, and Raleigh, North Carolina. It was in Richmond in 1807 that he presided at the treason trial of former Vice Pres. Aaron Burr, during which he successfully frustrated President Jefferson's efforts toward a runaway conviction; Burr was freed. With hardly more than three months annually engaged in judicial duties, Marshall had

much time to devote to private life. He early completed a five-volume *Life of George Washington* (1804–07). He cared for an invalid wife, who bore him ten children, four of whom died in early life. He enjoyed companionship, drinking, and debating with fellow lights in Richmond. In general, for the first 30 years of his service as chief justice, his life was largely one of contentment.

In the autumn of 1831, at the age of 76, he underwent the rigours of surgery for the removal of kidney stones and appeared to make a rapid and complete recovery. But the death of his wife on Christmas of that year was a blow from which his spirits did not so readily recover. In 1835 his health declined rapidly, and on July 6 of that year he died in Philadelphia. He was buried in Richmond.

BIBLIOGRAPHY. ALBERT J. BEVERIDGE, *The Life of John Marshall*, 4 vol. (1916–19), is the standard biography of Marshall and the most detailed and comprehensive account of his life and career; it is, however, pervasively laudatory and almost completely uncritical. JAMES BRADLEY THAYER, *John Marshall* (1901, reprinted 1967), is a biographical essay, keenly perceptive in its appraisal of Marshall's career and work as chief justice. CHARLES WARREN, *The Supreme Court in United States History*, rev. ed., 2 vol. (1937), which is a study of the Supreme Court as an institution of government, appropriately gives great emphasis to the court and the chief justiceship of John Marshall.

Marsupialia

The Marsupialia is a superorder (or order, depending on the authority) of mammals characterized by premature birth and continued development of the newborn while attached to the nipples on the lower belly of the mother. The pouch, or marsupium, from which the group takes its name, is a flap of skin covering the nipples. Although prominent in many species, it is not a universal feature among marsupials; in some species, for example, the nipples are in a well-defined area but are fully exposed or are bounded by mere remnants of a pouch. The young remain firmly attached to the milk-giving teats for a period corresponding roughly to the latter part of development of the fetus in the womb of a eutherian, or placental, mammal.

The largest and most varied assortment of marsupials—more than 100 species—is found in Australia alone: kangaroos, wallabies, wombats, the koala, and a bewildering assemblage of smaller rodent-like forms. About 70 more species are distributed more widely, in Australia (including Tasmania), New Guinea, and a cluster of nearby islands. The wide array of Australian marsupials is reflected in the extensive popular vocabulary of names, many of which are derived from descriptive Aboriginal words. Only two families of marsupials—totalling more than 70 species—are found in the Americas, vestiges of a larger group that originated there as long ago as the Cretaceous Period (from 136,000,000 to 65,000,000 years ago). The family Didelphidae comprises about 65 species of South and Central American opossums, one of which ranges as far north as southern Canada. The family Caenolestidae consists of seven species of ratlike marsupials confined to South America.

GENERAL FEATURES

Scientific and economic importance. Marsupials are of interest to zoologists for several reasons: their current geographical distribution, their remarkable evolutionary expansion in Australasia, their similarity in many respects to placental mammals, and, most obviously, their reproductive adaptations and often bizarre structure.

The question of origin and spread

Fossil evidence indicates clearly that the marsupials originated in the New World, and although the oldest fossils referable to marsupials are found in North America, it is believed that South America is equally likely as the origin of these animals. The current concentration of diverse types of marsupials in Australia and its nearby islands is thought to have occurred as a result of passage over presumed land connections with South America during a mild early geological period before the rise of the placental mammals. Later, toward the beginning of the

Tertiary Period (starting 65,000,000 years ago), Australia was isolated from all other continental masses, and the marsupials were free to evolve unrestricted by competition from other groups of mammals. Elsewhere, however, the marsupials did badly; they faced strong competition from and were supplanted by the more advanced placental mammals.

Australian marsupials provided products—meat and hides particularly—for the Aboriginal people, whose primitive hunting methods posed no threat to the continued success of the animals as a group. With the appearance of modern methods of hunting and trapping, however, several species of the kangaroo family (Macropodidae) were soon rendered extinct, and many others were brought close to that fate. For a time during the first half of the 20th century, many of the larger marsupials were slaughtered in great numbers for their pelts, which were an item of export in the fur trade; for their hides, which were made into shoes; and for their flesh, which was processed into dog and cat food. The gray kangaroo (*Macropus giganteus*), for example, is a casualty of such wholesale killing. Fortunately, in Australia most marsupials have since that time been accorded protection under law, and efforts are proceeding to conserve many species that were brought to the brink of extermination. The Tasmanian wolf, tiger, or thylacine (*Thylacinus cynocephalus*), thought to have become extinct in the 1930s, may still survive. In 1961 an expedition claimed to have found thylacine tracks in a rain forest on the west coast of Tasmania. The Tasmanian devil (*Sarcophilus harrisii*), once dangerously close to extinction, is now thriving in Tasmania. In the Americas marsupials are also hunted locally for food and other products, but, since numerous and equally desirable placental mammals abound, hunting pressure and the resulting threat of species death are not so strongly felt.

Not only man but also his introduced animals have played a part in the extinction of certain marsupials. Foxes, dogs, and cats continue to prey upon many species of marsupials, as also do the dingoes, canines introduced by the Aboriginals long ago and since gone wild. Brush and forest fires as well as climatic change and the encroachment of civilization are also factors tending to reduce the numbers of marsupial species.

Size range and diversity.   No extant marsupial even approaches the tremendous size of certain extinct forms, which apparently rivalled the mastodons in bulk. Among the largest living marsupial is *Macropus giganteus*, some individuals of which reach about two metres (six feet) in height, three metres (nine feet) from muzzle to tail tip, and weigh up to 90 kilograms (about 200 pounds); red kangaroos (*Megaleia rufa*) grow to about the same size. The smallest is the planigale (*Planigale ingrami*), a species of marsupial mice that is barely 12 centimetres (4¾ inches) in total length. The vast majority of marsupials lie in the range from the size of a squirrel to that of a medium-sized dog (Figures 1–3).

Parallels
with
placental
mammals

Structural and behavioral parallels with placental mammals are in some cases quite striking. Such resemblances are examples of convergent evolution, a tendency for organisms to adapt in similar ways to similar habitats. Thus, there are marsupials that look remarkably like moles, shrews, squirrels, and mice. Others, less in structure than in habits, are the ecological counterparts of cats, small bears, and rabbits. Even the larger grazing marsupials, which resemble no placental mammal at all, can be thought of as filling the same ecological role as deer and antelope found elsewhere.

Distribution and abundance.   There are about 175 species of marsupials native to the Australasian area, primarily in Australia (including Tasmania), New Guinea, Timor, and Celebes. Through man's agency, however, marsupials have been introduced to nearby islands of Australia and especially to New Zealand. The more than 70 native American species occur in South and Central America, with the range extended into North America by the common, or Virginian, opossum (*Didelphis marsupialis*). A number of other species extend into the southern portion of North America.

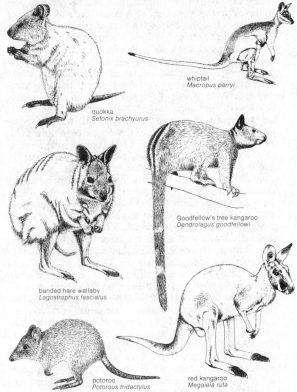

Figure 1: Representative species of the family Macropodidae.
Drawing by A.G. Lyne

whiptail
Macropus parryi

quokka
Setonix brachyurus

Goodfellow's tree kangaroo
Dendrolagus goodfellowi

banded hare wallaby
Lagostrophus fasciatus

potoroo
Potorous tridactylus

red kangaroo
Megaleia rufa

In terms of numbers of species the didelphids, or New World opossums, rank highest with 65. In sheer abundance, there are more vegetarian than carnivorous marsupials and perhaps more pouched mice than any other kind of marsupial.

The brush-tailed possums (*Trichosurus vulpecula*) exemplify marsupials that have readily adapted to changing conditions brought about by man. As recently as 1932, more than 1,000,000 pelts were sold under such names as Adelaide chinchilla. Protected for part of the year, the brush tails have now become plentiful over the vast interior of Australia and even pestiferous in urban centres. Their adaptability to different locales is attributed to their tolerance for a variety of food, including household refuse.

Koalas (*Phascolarctos cinereus*), reduced to a few thousand in the 1930s as a result of disease and logging and trapping for fur, have recovered their numbers sufficiently to be reintroduced into forested regions.

Although the red kangaroos (*Megaleia rufa*) are being killed in large numbers for commercial products and by farmers and ranchers whose grazing lands they sometimes visit during periods of drought, they are numerous in many parts of inland Australia. The total range of this species is about 2,000,000 square miles. Changes in vegetation resulting from domestic stock have improved the habitat for it in many parts of its range, and the species has increased in abundance.

NATURAL HISTORY

Life cycle.   The life cycle of marsupials exhibits the peculiarities of a mammalian group advanced over the egg-laying monotremes but primitive to the placental mammals. The gestation period of the marsupial ranges from about eight days in the native cat *Dasyurus viverrinus* to 40 days in the red-necked wallaby (*Wallabia rufogrisea*). The young, born in a vulnerable embryonic condition, make their own way to the shelter, warmth, and nourishment of the pouch; in pouchless marsupials the young simply cling to the teats. Those fortunate enough to survive this arduous journey may succeed in attaching themselves to the mother's nipples, which then swell and become firmly fastened—almost physically

Figure 2: Representative species of the families Phalangeridae, Petauridae, Peramelidae, Phascolarctidae, and Tarsipedidae.
Drawing by A.G. Lyne

strong ones reach the pouch in less than a minute, an extraordinary feat for so small and incomplete a creature. Only about 60 percent of the newborn reach the pouch; these attach themselves immediately to the teats, at which they remain for four or five weeks (Figure 4). They then begin to leave the pouch for short intervals, scampering back to it whenever danger threatens. The young stay with the mother for 90 to 100 days—toward the last not in the pouch but clinging to her fur. Shortly afterward they are weaned and begin their independent lives.

Behaviour. The marsupials are notably less intelligent than placental mammals, a fact that is attributable in part to a simpler brain (see below *Form and function*). It is not surprising, therefore, to find a repertory of behaviour that differs somewhat from that of the more advanced placentals. One peculiarity that may stem from this underdevelopment is restricted vocal ability. Although marsupials are not entirely silent, few of them emit loud sounds of excitement or distress; apparently, none utter grunts of contentment or even cries of hunger when young. What vocalizing they do is more limited and less variable than that of placentals.

There seems to be little detectable social organization among marsupials beyond the short-lived pair bonds during mating. The reproductive cycle in many marsupials is seasonally controlled, and estrus occurs in a predictable rhythm. In the quokka (*Setonix brachyurus*) and many other kangaroos and wallabies, however, the females may bear young at any time of the year. Only one young, called a joey, can be carried by the mother at a time. After suckling for about six months in the pouch, the joey begins to venture out but remains very close to the mother, plunging headfirst into the pouch when alarmed.

Drawing by A.G. Lyne

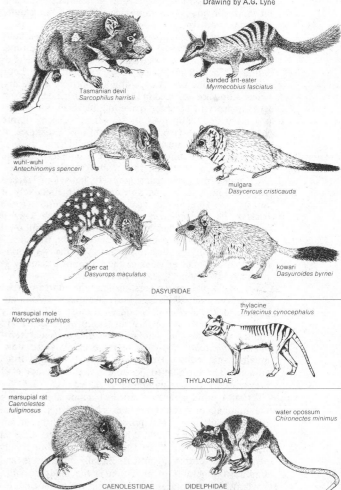

Figure 3: Representative species of the families Dasyuridae, Notoryctidae, Thylacinidae, Caenolestidae, and Didelphidae.

fused—to the mouth tissues of the young. In this condition the young continue their development for weeks or months, after which they are weaned and begin to look after themselves.

Didelphis marsupialis exemplifies one of the more primitive cycles and serves to illustrate the sequence of events in greater detail. It may have two litters yearly throughout most of its range (possibly only one in the northern reaches). The female experiences estrus (heat) and becomes receptive to the male about every 28 days during the breeding season. Heat lasts one or two days, during which an average of 22 ova are shed. Usually only ten young are born in a litter, but as many as 25 young have been reported.

During the first five or six days the embryos form very slowly, but thereafter the rate of development speeds up. The gestation period is short—about 13 days. Just before birth, the mother thoroughly cleans the pouch and her belly fur, licking a smooth path from the birth canal to the pouch. When expelled from the birth canal, the newborn are no larger than honeybees. Blind and grublike, except for their well-developed, clawed forelimbs, they emerge and immediately begin grasping and swimming-like movements along the mother's dampened fur. The

The primitive reproductive cycle of *Didelphis marsupialis*

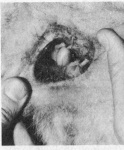
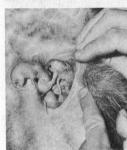

Figure 4: Development of the common opossum. (Top left) In the pouch at three weeks; (bottom left) at seven weeks; (right) mother carrying 10-week-old young.
Charles Philip Fox

The males have no interest in the young and will protect neither them nor the females against danger.

Many of the grazing marsupials, such as the kangaroos and wallabies, move in feeding groups called mobs, but these associations do not merit distinction as true herds since the individual members appear to move at liberty, without attention to any leaders or elders. One member can send the mob into a wild rout—individuals bounding off in all directions—by thumping its tail on the ground in a signal of alarm.

The larger marsupials, especially, embody nervous alertness and dull-witted consternation at the same time. A typical response of a red kangaroo when startled is to bound off in full flight—up to 65 kilometres per hour (about 30 miles per hour)—for a relatively short distance, stop short to reconnoitre the disturbance, and, in what appears to be sheer panic, double back toward its adversary and jump over it, sometimes clearing more than three metres (ten feet) in height and a distance of more than eight metres (25 feet) in a single leap.

Defensive behaviour of kanga-roos Although well equipped for escape, a boomer, or large male kangaroo, can stand fast against many of its foes. With agile arms it can spar vigorously, behaviour learned in playful bouts as a joey. But, much more effectively, it can use the forepaws to grip its enemy, while it rocks back on its tail and then swiftly drops its huge clawed hindfeet, an action that has been known to disembowel dogs and men. Despite such fearsome ability, the kangaroos are usually gentle, as are most of the vegetarian marsupials. Whatever violence they commit is usually in response to a distinct threat to themselves.

Such marsupials as the possums (families Burramyidae, Petauridae, and Phalangeridae), wombats (Vombatidae), and koala (Phascolarctidae) usually sleep by day and move about toward dusk in search of food. Except for the agile possums—notably the gliders (e.g., Acrobates, Schoinobates)—most of these animals are slow-moving and, consequently, easy prey for carnivorous animals. The bush-tailed possum, however, is not easy prey for carnivorous animals.

The most mild-mannered pouched mammal is perhaps the numbat, or banded anteater (Myrmecobius fasciatus), a small, slow forest prowler who searches out termites, its favourite food. When disturbed, the numbat hisses; if caught it neither struggles nor bites but simply vents a few grunts in protest. Equally inoffensive and similarly vulnerable to predation is the teddy-bear-like koala, which rummages about at night among eucalyptus branches munching endlessly on the only food it eats—eucalyptus leaves. Its name, an Aboriginal dialect word

meaning "no drink," refers to the koala's curious and apparently lifelong abstinence from water. Koalas provide a eucalyptus "soup" for their young at the time of weaning; it is lapped up directly from the parent's anus. The densely furred cuscuses (Phalanger) move among the trees with the same deliberation of the koalas, eating leaves as they go.

Bandicoots—whose apt name means "pig rat"—are especially fond of earthworms and insects and are only occasionally herbivorous. Although generally shy and retiring, bandicoots can at times display a surprising belligerence: with their sharp-clawed feet they can literally scratch their victims to death. Certain marsupial mice (e.g., Sminthopsis species) are so hyperactive—like shrews—that to supply their high energy needs they must devour their own weight in food, chiefly insects, each day.

A curious and effective defensive behaviour has been developed to a high degree in Didelphis marsupialis of North America: when harassed it hisses and departs, but when attacked and not able to flee, it feigns death (plays possum) so well that the aggressor may lose interest and leave.

The carnivorous marsupials are equipped with other behavioral traits. They are the fierce hunters of flesh. Although as a rule not as fast as comparable placental carnivores, they are persistent in the hunt and swift to kill. The Tasmanian devil is a stout fighter, likened in its bloodlust to the American wolverine. Yellow-footed marsupial mice (Antechinus flavipes) cling so tenaciously to their prey that they can be caught like fish on bait. The thylacine, which has been known to rise up on its hindlegs kangaroo fashion when pressed, makes up in perseverance what it lacks in speed and cunning. In sharp, foxlike snaps, thylacines have been known to dispatch an antagonist as formidable as a hunting dog.

Ecology. The niches, or ecological roles, that marsupials fill are closely associated with structure. The burrowing species, such as the marsupial mole and the wombats, have powerful foreclaws with which they can tunnel into the ground for food and for shelter. Terrestrial forms, such as the kangaroos and wallabies, possess well-developed hindlimbs that serve both as formidable weapons and catapults by which they can bound over the plains. The greater glider (Shoinobates volans) and other Australian "flying" possums have a membrane along either flank, attached to the forelegs and hindlegs, that enables these arboreal animals to glide down from a high perch. A few marsupials spend most of their lives in trees; koalas, for example, are so thoroughly arboreal that they

Life-styles

seem comfortable only when they are among the branches of trees. One marsupial is semi-aquatic, the water opossum—yapok or yapó (*Chironectes minimus*)—of Central and South America. Its thick, oily fur, partially webbed feet, and constrictable pouch opening suit it admirably for swimming and diving in search of food.

The diet of marsupials is as varied as the niches. Many live chiefly on insects and other small animals. Such are the marsupial mice and many of the smaller native cats (family Dasyuridae). The tiger cat and the Tasmanian devil feed largely on birds and small mammals. The numbat uses its remarkable wormlike tongue to lap up termites and ants. Many Australian possums, bandicoots, and American opossums have a mixed diet of plant matter and insects. Certain other marsupials are strictly vegetarian. The wombats feed on grasses, roots, and fungi, which they dig up with their clawed forepaws. The small honey possum (*Tarsipes spenserae*) is specialized to feed on the nectar of flowers.

The entire family of macropodids—the "big-footed" ones—are primarily grass eaters. They include the kangaroos and walleroo, the wallabies and pademelons, and the rat kangaroos and musk kangaroo. The walleroo, or euro (*Macropus robustus*), in particular, has a diet almost as restrictive as that of the koala: it can subsist in large part on spiky spinifex grass. Macropodids digest their vegetable food in the same manner as do sheep, cattle, and other ruminants, by relying on intestinal bacteria and protozoans to break down plant matter.

In their turn, marsupials are food for other animals. Foremost among the predators of didelphids and small dasyurids are owls and other birds of prey, snakes, and many carnivorous mammals, including dogs and cats. Some of the larger species of American opossums are eaten locally by man. The enemies of the larger marsupials, the macropodids, include the dingo, fox, eagle, pythons, goannas, and especially man.

FORM AND FUNCTION

Marsupials share with other mammals the presence of hair and the suckling of young by mammary glands. With minor differences the various systems of the body, such as the muscular and skeletal systems, are those of the placentals generally. The skull and the brain, however, differ considerably from those of placentals. Differences also exist in the dentition and in the arrangement of digits of the feet.

Bodily adaptations. In gross structure, many marsupials have hindlimbs that are larger and more powerful than the forelimbs; such an arrangement is most obvious in the large terrestrial grazing marsupials but is of wide occurrence in some degree throughout the Marsupialia. Arboreal and burrowing marsupials have forelimbs almost as well developed as the hindlimbs, understandable adaptations to their modes of living. Claws, often of considerable size, are invariably present in all marsupials and assist in climbing or digging. The tail, of tremendous size in kangaroos and wallabies, serves as an organ of stability and balance; in smaller and arboreal species it may also be prehensile (adapted for grasping), allowing the animal to hang by it.

Brain peculiarities

Compared with placentals, marsupials differ markedly in both the structure and bulk of the brain. Most notably they lack a corpus callosum, that part of the placental brain that connects the two cerebral halves. In addition, the marsupial brain is smaller relative to skull size: a marsupial cat has about half as much brain tissue as a placental cat of similar skull size. Such insufficiency may account in part for the relative backwardness of marsupials when contrasted with placental mammals.

A feature peculiar to marsupials is the presence of a pair of bones associated with the pelvic girdle. Called the epipubic, or marsupial, bones, they were earlier thought to be a supportive element for the pouch.

The teeth in marsupials are numerous—usually 40 to 50, but as few as 22 in the honey possum and as many as 52 in the numbat. The relationship of milk teeth to adult teeth is not clear; some authorities claim that a single set of teeth lasts throughout life. Typically, there are seven cheek teeth on each side of the jaw, top and bottom, which are divided into three premolars and four molars; this contrasts with the typical placental condition in which there are four premolars and three molars. Also unlike the placental condition, the number of front, or incisor, teeth differs in upper and lower jaws.

In earlier studies of marsupials much was made of the number and type of incisors (Figure 5). Marsupials with more than three incisors in the upper jaw were said to be

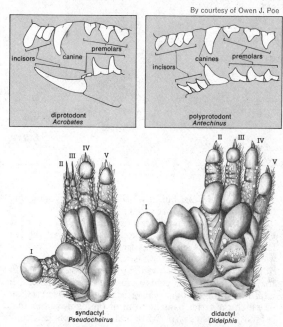

By courtesy of Owen J. Poe

Figure 5: Dentition and fusion of the digits of the hindfoot of marsupials. (Top left) Diprotodont in the pygmy gliders and (top right) polyprotodont in the broad-footed pouched mice. (Bottom left) Digits II and III syndactyl, digit I opposable, in the ring-tailed opossums and (bottom right) digits II and III didactyl, digit I opposable, in the common opossum.

polyprotodont and of a presumed more primitive type since the teeth were more or less unspecialized. Marsupials with three or fewer upper incisors and a corresponding set of modifications of the primitive condition were said to be diprotodont. Subsequent investigations disclosed a gamut of intermediate dentitions, thereby discrediting the distinction.

Another equally unsatisfactory distinction was based on the curious but minor condition in which the second and third toes of the hindfeet are covered in a common sheath of skin. Species showing that condition were syndactylous, and the remainder were didactylous. Classifications were founded on such matters, and the groups were named appropriately Polyprotodontia and Diprotodontia in one scheme, and Syndactyla and Didactyla in another (see below *Classification*).

Reproductive adaptations. The most extraordinary anatomical features of the marsupials are the specializations associated with the reproductive system. The most striking of these is the protective pouch around the nipples of the female in many species. The pouch is well developed in kangaroos, wallabies, and wombats; in the tuan (*Phascogale tapoatafa*) and some dasyurids it is poorly developed, represented by lateral abdominal folds. In several South American didelphids, in the rat opossums (family Caenolestidae), and in the numbat, the pouch is lacking entirely. Even among species that have pouches, the degree of development depends upon the breeding condition of the animal, being most obvious when the female is lactating. The pouch in most forms opens forward, especially in upright and arboreal species; in the water opossum and many quadrupedal species the pouch is directed backward. There may be as few as two nipples (as in the koala and wombats) or as many as 27 (as in *Monodelphis*, the short-tailed opossum). The number of teats does not indicate the number of young that are nursed, however; in some cases more young are born than can be

Differences in pouches

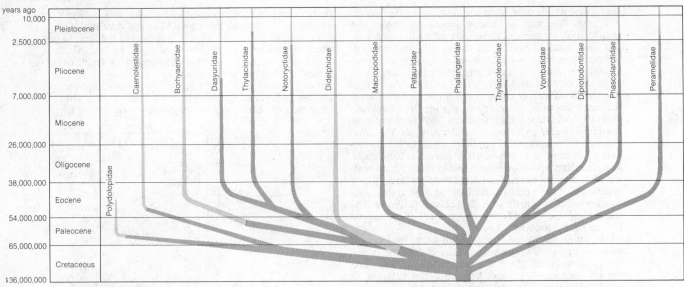

Figure 6: Dendrogram of the marsupials.

suckled at one time, but in most cases fewer young than the number of nipples are brought to full term.

The female reproductive tract is double for most of its length, becoming joined at the posterior ends of the two lateral vaginae. A birth canal, or median vagina, forms at the time of birth; copulation is accomplished by the insertion of the male's penis into the urogenital sinus of the female. The end of the penis is forked in some species. In addition to the peculiar penis, the male also has a scrotum in which the testes hang in front of the penis rather than behind; the testes are abdominal in the pouched male (*Notoryctes*). Most marsupials specialize in brief gestation, as indicated earlier. The developing embryo obtains its food chiefly from its own yolk sac, an embryonic organ provided by the mother. Typically, there is no intimate mother–fetus connection by means of a true (chorioallantoic) placenta, as in placental mammals. The bandicoots develop a rudimentary placenta, but it lacks the extensive ramifying projections (villi) that provide the close connection of mother and fetus tissue in the placentals.

EVOLUTION AND PALEONTOLOGY

Geologically, no marsupials have been discovered in Asia, and they are definitely not known from Africa. On the whole they are considered as primitive mammals, but for some 100,000,000 years they have shown a remarkable parallel and convergent evolution with placental mammals in habits, physiological processes, and structures.

Among the oldest marsupials are those represented by undisputed fossils from the Late Cretaceous strata of North America. These specimens are represented mostly by tiny isolated teeth, but parts of jaws have also been found. Until recently, all of the fragments were classified in the American opossum family, Didelphidae, but it has been observed that these early marsupials were already specialized in different directions. *Alphadon*, a genus of primarily tiny animals, is most likely a didelphid. On the other hand the group of small to medium-sized creatures, represented by the genus *Pediomys*, seem rather clearly not didelphids and are now placed in their own family, the Pediomyidae. The widely known genus *Eodelphis* is almost certainly not didelphid. Among its more conspicuous differences from the Didelphidae are the single- (not double-) rooted, much reduced first lower premolar and the presence of three, not four, lower incisors, of which the middle incisor is greatly enlarged. It is likely that this marsupial is not ancestral to any of the known later genera. Another specimen, known as *Thlaeodon*, is the largest known Cretaceous mammal. Its bulbous premolars and large canines are indicative of an adaptation to a mixed (omnivorous) diet. It appar-

ently is referable to another family. *Alphadon*, earlier thought to be nearer than any of the other Cretaceous genera to an ideal ancestral position for the marsupials as a whole, has been superseded by later finds. Fossil fragments of even earlier date (the Middle Cretaceous of Texas, about 100,000,000 years ago) have been tentatively referred to as *Holoclemensia*, a new genus in the family Didelphidae.

Evidence suggests that marsupials became widespread in the Tertiary Period, beginning 65,000,000 years ago, but they never succeeded as well on other continents as they did in South America and Australasia.

American marsupials. *Didelphoids.* Primitive marsupial characteristics in the superfamily Didelphoidea have long been recognized by mammalogists. Some of the features in the dentition, skull, and body skeleton may be reasonably expected to be remarkably like those in the Mesozoic ancestors of all later marsupials. Characters in the molars indicate that didelphoids and the South American borhyaenoids of the Paleocene Epoch (beginning 65,000,000 years ago) and Eocene Epoch (beginning 54,000,000 years ago) are closely related, but the lack of enough fossils makes it impossible to trace the lineage of all marsupial superfamilies back to the known North American Cretaceous fossils (possibly the more direct ancestors of some of the other superfamilies existed at that time). Better knowledge of the skeletons and dentitions of fossil marsupials from the Cretaceous Period and even the Early Cenozoic Era (beginning 65,000,000 years ago) may eventually alter considerably the present interpretation of their superfamily relationships.

Borhyaenoids. The oldest known South American marsupials are of the later Paleocene Epoch (about 55,000,000 years old). At that time three superfamilies, Didelphoidea, Borhyaenoidea, and Caenolestoidea, were already in existence. Patterns of the known cheek teeth of the Paleocene and early Eocene borhyaenoids and didelphoids indicate that these marsupials may have descended from a common ancestor no earlier than the Late Cretaceous.

The fossil record of the family Borhyaenidae starts in the late Paleocene and continues into the Pliocene (ending 2,500,000 years ago). No genera are known to have occurred outside South America. Borhyaenids were the flesh-eating mammals of the southern continent during nearly all the Tertiary Period. (True carnivores presumably did not reach that region until late in the Pliocene and Pleistocene.) The family name is derived from the genus *Borhyaena*, hyena-like specimens found in the early Miocene strata (about 26,000,000 years ago) of Argentina. These carnivorous marsupials had massive skulls with thick crushing teeth. Some genera—*e.g.*, *Proborhyaena* —were shorter faced and more robust.

Primitive marsupial characteristics

All borhyaenids were not hyenoid, however. There were the wolflike *Prothalycinus* and *Lycopsis* and the fox- to marten-sized *Cladosictis* and *Amphiproviverra*. One of the most specialized of all was the Pliocene sabre-toothed borhyaenid *Thylacosmilus;* it was about the size of a puma and even more specialized as a stabbing mammal than most sabre-toothed cats. In all, more than 20 borhyaenid genera have been described, revealing a long evolutionary history in South America from a Cretaceous didelphid-like mammal.

Necrolestoids. One fossil with a molelike adaptation, called *Necrolestes*, is known from the Miocene of Patagonia. It is the only known genus referable to the family Necrolestidae (superfamily Necrolestoidea), probably basically related to the Borhyaenoidea or Didelphoidea.

The early rat opossums

Caenolestoids. The South American rat opossums (superfamily Caenolestoidea) are also undoubtedly descendants of a Cretaceous group, but the oldest known caenolestoids are already too specialized to reveal affinities with any of the known Mesozoic fossils. Any resemblances they have to Australian groups apparently result from convergent evolutionary trends in certain structures.

The family Caenolestidae has been recorded from early Eocene deposits, but the genera were more numerous later in the Oligocene and Miocene periods. These little marsupials were long known from fragmentary fossils, but in 1895 this supposedly extinct family was discovered as represented in the living Andean mammalian fauna of Ecuador and Bolivia by an animal resembling a small rat in size and appearance and named *Caenolestes*. The diprotodont incisor teeth are suggestive of those in some of the Australian phalangeroids, but the hindfeet show no trace of the phalangeroid syndactylism of the second and third toes. Other genera with living species are *Orolestes* in Peru and *Rhyncholestes* in Chile.

The Polydolopidae is an Early Cenozoic family of small specialized marsupials related to the Caenolestidae. Their fossil remains are abundant in the South American strata of that time. They had transversely compressed and laterally ridged premolars, with serrated crests, and rodentlike incisors. The polydolopids, probably in a large measure, occupied the ecological niches that were later occupied by rodents.

Australasian marsupials. Although pre-Pleistocene fossils of Australian marsupials are relatively rare, representatives of the families Dasyuridae, Peramelidae, Phalangeridae, Thylacoleonidae, Macropodidae, and Diprotodontidae appear as fossils in strata as early as the late Oligocene Epoch (26,000,000 years ago). During the Miocene and Pliocene epochs that followed, fossils of the family Vombatidae were laid down. These findings suggest that the Australian families of marsupials originated in the Early Cenozic.

Dasyuroids. The oldest dasyuroid lived during the Middle Tertiary of South Australia; about the size of the present-day *Dasyurus quoll*, it was probably near the stem from which the thylacine evolved. *Glaucodon ballaratensis*, one of the most important fossil dasyurids, is possibly of Pliocene age; it bore a resemblance to both *Dasyurus* and a Pleistocene member of *Sarcophilus*. The thylacine (*Thylacinus cynocephalus*), which constitutes the family Thylacinidae, is the largest and most widely known of the dasyuroid marsupials. Although its distribution is usually recorded as being restricted to Tasmania, it was represented on the mainland of Australia less than 10,000 years ago and also lived on New Guinea.

The doubtfully extinct thylacine

The last certainly known thylacine was captured in Tasmania in 1930; however, sightings have been recorded of thylacines and their tracks as late as 1961 along a wild stretch of the west coast of Tasmania.

The family relationships of the thylacine are still not fully understood. (Its classification with the extinct Borhyaenidae of South America has almost conclusively been disproved.) Its characters, however, display a remarkable convergent evolution with the American borhyaenids. It seems reasonable to assume that the thylacine and the dasyures arose from a common ancestry. Many authorities place *Thylacinus* in the family Dasyuridae, but until its ancestry is adequately known it seems best to treat it as forming a separate family.

Without a fossil record it is not possible to conclude how closely *Notoryctes*, constituting the family Notoryctidae, is related to the basal stocks of the dasyuroids and to that of the bandicoots, but the absence of syndactyly in the hindfeet suggests they are closer to the dasyuroids. *Myrmecobius*, also lacking a fossil record, is grouped with the family Dasyuridae because of similarities.

Perameloids. Members of the superfamily Peramaloidea display one of the most primitive characters seen in any Australian marsupials: the retention of an incisor formula of $\frac{5}{3}$ (polyprotodont) in most of the genera. They have syndactylism in the hindfoot: the proximal and median phalanges (bones) of the second and third digits are enclosed in the same sheath of skin.

Among the perameloids, both *Macrotis* and *Perameles* are represented in the late Pleistocene faunas of Australia. An extinct genus, *Ischnodon*, has been found in the Pliocene strata of South Australia. The most peculiar of all peramelids is the probably extinct (it has not been seen since about 1926) pig-footed bandicoot (*Chaeropus ecaudatus*). The common name is derived from the construction of the front foot, in which the second and third digits are of equal length and closely united. The nails, of equal size and length, give the appearance of cloven hooves.

Phalangeroids. Only a very hypothetical phylogeny, indicating possible ancestral relationships of the superfamily Phalangeroidea to the other superfamilies, can be outlined until an adequate fossil record from the Late Mesozoic and Early Cenozoic has been compiled. The Phalangeroidea were probably derived from an ancestral stock that also gave rise to the Perameloidea. Evidently, in this early stock (in contrast to the Dasyuroidea) natural selection was toward syndactylism. Subsequently, one syndactyl stock led to the ancestors of the rat kangaroos, kangaroos, diprotodontids, wombats, koalas, marsupial lions, and phalangers; the other stock gave rise to the bandicoots.

Of the phalangers, *Eudromicia* is the most primitive of all the living genera. It comprises in part the dormouse possums. The retention of the fourth molars and the double-rooted first and second upper premolars distinguish *Eudromicia* from the other dormouse possums, *Cercartetus*, which they notably resemble.

The remains of a tiny marsupial called *Burramys* has been found in New South Wales, Australia. The shape of the skull and the pattern of the molars resemble those in *Cercartetus* (including *Eudromicia*), but the premolars are high and serrated. This genus is the basis for the family Burramyidae. Once thought to be extinct, several specimens of *Burramys* have been found since 1966 in northeastern Victoria.

One of the oldest fossil marsupials of Australasia is part of the skeleton of a brushtail-like possum, *Wynyardia bassiana*, found in late Eocene or Oligocene deposits near Wynyard, Tasmania. It constitutes the family Wynyardiidae. Fossils more closely related to later species occur in the Pleistocene of Australia; others much older occur in the Middle Tertiary of South Australia.

The oldest Australasian fossil

Among the most bizarre of all marsupials are the wooly possums, or cuscuses (*Phalanger*), from which the family and superfamily names are derived. *Wyulda*, the scaly-tailed possum, which is terrestrial and lives among rocks in northwestern Australia, is somewhat intermediate between the brush-tailed possums and the cuscuses. There has been much discussion about the relationships of the so-called marsupial lion (*Thylacoleo*). Most authorities agree that it belongs in a separate family, the Thylacoleonidae. Specimens of the cranium and lower jaws are well-known, and parts of the limb bones and body skeleton have been found. *Thylacoleo* was about the size of an African lion. Its teeth were even more specialized for meat shearing than those in the true cats; for example, the large posterior premolars were as long as 5.7 centimetres (2¼ inches). All the remaining teeth were greatly reduced, except the upper and lower median incisors, which apparently were utilized in capturing other animals. These great carnivorous marsupials became extinct in Australia less than 26,000 years ago.

Although the genera referred to as the rat kangaroo family (Potoroidae) are closely related to the kangaroo family (Macropodidae) and are classified by some as a subfamily of that group, they apparently have represented a distinct lineage since Eocene time. They may be distinguished from kangaroos by, among other features, several peculiarities of dentition and skull features. The female urogenital system is more specialized in the Macropodidae. A Pleistocene genus, *Propleopus*, is known, and a species of *Bettongia* and an undescribed genus occur in the Middle Tertiary of South Australia.

The most widely known marsupials are the kangaroos and their relatives (family Macropodidae). The gigantic forms during the Pleistocene were *Procoptodon*, *Sthenurus*, *Protemnodon*, and two species of *Macropus*. *Prionotemnus* is from the Pliocene, but the oldest kangaroos come from rocks probably as old as Miocene.

The macropodids are adapted for jumping. The principal digit in the hindfoot is the fourth, the fifth being somewhat reduced; the syndactyl second and third are reduced to splinters but still bear tiny claws. *Procoptodon* and *Sthenurus* differ from the other kangaroos in having lost all but the fourth digit.

Vombatoids. The superfamily Vombatoidea includes the diprotodonts, the koala, and the wombats.

The extinct family Diprotodontidae included the largest of all marsupials, *Diprotodon optatum*. It was built something like a huge ground sloth and attained the size of a large rhinoceros. Special dentition included the large, chisel-shaped median incisors and molar teeth, somewhat like those in certain kangaroos or tapirs, composed of two cross crests. *Diprotodon* was probably abundant in Australia in the late Pleistocene and subrecent time. Its remains have been found in levels contemporaneous with man. At least two other genera, *Nototherium* and *Euowenia*, representing much smaller diprotodontids, also occur in Australian Pleistocene faunas. *Palorchestes*, also of the Pleistocene, previously considered as the largest of all kangaroos, is now known to be a diprotodontid.

This family, like the Macropodidae, had a long Cenozoic history in Australia. *Meniscolophus* is known from the Pliocene, and remains of a rather primitive undescribed genus and species are thought to be as old as the Oligocene Epoch. It appears that all known diprotodontids were herbivorous. The family may have been an early offshoot of the phalangeroid stock and perhaps was distantly related to kangaroos and wombats.

One of the most famous of all Australian marsupials is the koala, family Phascolarctidae. Only one species is known, although a rather distantly related genus, *Perikoala*, from the Tertiary of South Australia, has been described. The koala, with its short tail and rather stocky body, so resembles the wombat that the two are considered by some authorities to have arisen from a common ancestor, perhaps not very far back in Cenozoic time. Others believe, however, that the koala is much closer to the ringtails and greater gliders. The wombats (family Vombatidae), which resemble koalas in having no tails, are represented by two Pleistocene fossil genera: the giant wombat, *Phascolonus*, which was as large as a black bear, and *Ramsayia*.   (Ed.)

The massive diprotodonts *(marginal note)*

CLASSIFICATION

Distinguishing taxonomic features.   Two earlier classifications of marsupials were based on the number and arrangement of the front teeth and on the appression or separateness of certain toes. Marsupials having at least four upper incisors were named Polyprotodontia; those having three or (usually) fewer upper incisors and no lower canines, Diprotodontia. Marsupials having entirely separate toes on the hindfeet were called Didactyla; those having the second and third toes of the hindfeet enclosed in a common envelopment of skin, Syndactyla. These terms no longer have taxonomic validity, but their adjectival forms are still used to describe the dentition and the character of the hindfeet.

Additional aspects, such as the pattern of hair tracts, blood chemistry, details of reproductive anatomy and physiology, chromosomal morphology, sperm morphology, and behaviour, are currently being employed to structure a new taxonomic system representing more natural units that reflect what are presumed to be fundamental phylogenetic relationships.

Annotated classification.   The time-honoured position of the Marsupialia as an order of mammals, generally unacceptable for a variety of reasons (see below *Critical appraisal*), is gradually giving way to a system first presented in 1964. As further modified, that arrangement raised the Marsupialia to the rank of a superorder and encompassed four orders, ten superfamilies, and 23 families, as given below. Wholly extinct groups are preceded by a dagger (†).

SUPERORDER MARSUPIALIA
(Metatherian, or pouched mammals)

Origin during the Cretaceous, expansion at beginning of the Tertiary, and decline with the rise of placentals thereafter. Currently established in Australia and nearby islands (introduced on New Zealand) and in the Americas. Young born after brief gestation in an embryonic condition; development completed while young are attached to teats, usually in a pouch, or marsupium. Skull elements differ from placentals; braincase small; brain relatively small and simple compared with placentals. Epipubic bones associated with the pelvic girdle. Fewer incisor teeth in lower than in upper jaws. Female reproductive tract doubled in large part (paired vaginae and uteri); testes usually in a scrotal sac and anterior to the forked penis (abdominal testes in *Notoryctes*). Comprises about 80 genera and about 240 species in 4 orders.

Order Marsupicarnivora

Comprises 3 extinct superfamilies and 2 extant superfamilies of primarily carnivorous marsupials.

†*Superfamily Argyrolagoidea*

Comprises a single family, Argyrolagidae, represented by *Argyrolagus* from the upper Pliocene to the lower Pleistocene in South America.

†*Superfamily Borhyaenoidea*

Comprises a single extinct family, Borhyaenidae, flesh-eating marsupials of South America during the late Paleocene and into the Pliocene Epoch (about 5,000,000 years ago). Many species had massive skulls and heavy crushing teeth. Named after hyaena-like specimens from Argentinian fossils. Examples: *Prothylacinus*, *Borhyaena*, *Lycopsis*, and the sabretoothed marsupial *Thylacosmilus*.

Superfamily Dasyuroidea

Primarily terrestrial carnivores that resemble the didelphids in certain anatomical features. Incisors small and unspecialized (polyprotodont). Digits in hindfeet never joined (didactylous). Marsupium not present in all species; when present it is poorly developed and opens backward. Three families ranging from Australia to nearby islands.

Family Dasyuridae.   A group widespread over Australasia and represented by marsupial mice and rats (*e.g.*, *Sminthopsis*, *Antechinus*, *Antechinomys*, *Planigale*, *Murexia*, and *Phascogale*), native cats (*Dasyurus*, *Dasyurops*), Tasmanian devil (*Sarcophilus*), numbat (*Myrmecobius*). Includes the smallest known extant marsupial, *Planigale ingrami* (about 12 centimetres in total length). About 18 genera and 48 species.

Family Notoryctidae (marsupial moles).   Mole-sized marsupials, of the deserts of central and western Australia, remarkably convergent with placental moles of other continents. Pouch opens backward, and there are epipubic bones. One genus, *Notoryctes*, and 2 species.

Family Thylacinidae (thylacines).   German-shepherd-sized wolflike marsupials. Represented on the mainland of Australia less than 10,000 years ago and in New Guinea, the thylacine was last captured in Tasmania in 1930. A single species, *Thylacinus cynocephalus*, constitutes the family.

Superfamily Didelphoidea

Primarily terrestrial American marsupials. Earliest fossils from Cretaceous strata. One extant family, Didelphidae, and 2 fossil families.

Family Didelphidae (American opossums).   Central and South America boasts many species of unusual adaptations, notably *Chironectes* (water opossum), *Philander* (4-eyed opossums), *Metachirus*, and *Lutreolina*. *Didelphis* ranges as far north as southern Canada. Includes 12 genera and about 65 species.

†*Family Pediomyidae.* One genus, *Pediomys*, from the Upper Cretaceous in North America.

†*Family Stagodontidae.*

†*Superfamily Necrolestoidea*

Comprises 1 family, Necrolestidae. Based upon molelike fossils from the Miocene (starting 26,000,000 years ago) of Patagonia. One genus, *Necrolestes*.

Order Paucituberculata
Comprises a single superfamily of marsupials.

Superfamily Caenolestoidea

South American terrestrial marsupials. Earliest fossils from the early Eocene Epoch (about 50,000,000 years ago). One extant family, Caenolestidae, and 2 extinct families.

Family Caenolestidae. Ratlike in size and appearance. Diprotodont incisors suggest relationships to Australian phalangeroids, but other evidence disputes such affinities. Includes *Caenolestes* (Ecuador and Bolivia), *Orolestes* (Peru) and *Rhyncholestes* (Chile). Comprises 3 genera and 7 species.

†*Family Groeberiidae.* One genus, *Groeberia*, from the late Oligocene.

†*Family Polydolopidae.* Known from several genera including *Polydolops* and *Amphidolops* from upper Paleocene to late Eocene in South America.

Order Peramelina
Comprises 1 extant superfamily with 1 family of primarily carnivorous marsupials. Specimens of modern species are common in Pleistocene cave deposits in various parts of Australia.

Superfamily Perameloidea (bandicoots)

Comprises 1 family, Peramelidea. Terrestrial Australian marsupials that resemble rodents, rat-sized to hare-sized. Most genera have primitive polyprotodont dentition: 5 incisors above and 3 below. Syndactylism in hindfeet. Pouch is directed backward. Eight genera and 22 species, including: *Peroryctes*, *Microperoryctes*, and *Rhynchomeles*, primitive genera restricted to New Guinea and adjacent islands; *Perameles* and *Isoödon*, of wide distribution; *Macrotis* (bilbies) and *Chaeropus* (pig-footed bandicoot), restricted to Australia. Largest of the family (weight to 7 kg, or 15 lb.) is *Peroryctes broadbenti*.

Order Diprotodonta
Comprises 3 extant superfamilies of primarily herbivorous marsupials.

Superfamily Phalangeroidea

Australasian marsupials ranging from squirrel-sized arboreal species to large terrestrial bounders. Syndactylism of the second and third digits in the hindfeet. Four extant families; 2 extinct families.

Family Burramyidae. Primarily arboreal mouse- to squirrel-sized marsupials. Includes *Acrobates* (feathertail gliders), *Burramys*, and *Cercartetus* (pigmy possums). Comprises 3 genera and 6 species.

Family Macropodidae. Primarily terrestrial medium- to large-sized Australian marsupials. Adapted for jumping, with long hindlegs and long tail for balance. Forelimbs have sharp claws, and thumbs are not opposable. Main digit in hindfoot is the fourth. Extinct giant forms occurred during the Pleistocene, but oldest forms can be traced to the Miocene. Extant macropodids include *Macropus* (gray kangaroos and wallaroos), *Megaleia* (red kangaroos), *Wallabia* (wallabies), *Thylogale* (pademelons), *Dendrolagus* (tree kangaroos), and *Setonix* (quokkas). There are about 19 genera and 47 species.

Family Petauridae. Terrestrial and arboreal marsupials. First and second digits of the forelimbs are opposable to the other digits. Molars are adapted for chewing leaves. Includes *Pseudocheirus* (ring-tailed possums), *Petaurus* (sugar gliders), *Schoinobates* (greater gliders), *Gymnobelideus* (Leadbeater's possum), and *Dactylopsila* (striped possums). About 5 genera and 25 species.

Family Phalangeridae. Squirrel-sized to cat-sized arboreal species. Includes *Trichosurus* (brush-tailed possum), *Phalanger* (cuscuses), and *Wyulda* (scaly-tailed possum). About 6 genera and 15 species.

†*Family Thylacoleonidae.* So-called Australian marsupial lions, which became extinct less than 26,000 years ago. Teeth remarkably specialized for meat shearing. One genus, *Thylacoleo.*

†*Family Wynyardiidae.* Brushtail-like possums, the oldest fossil marsupials of Australasia, from presumed late Eocene rocks of Tasmania. One species, *Wynyardia bassiana.*

Superfamily Tarsipedoidea (honey possums)

Comprises a single family, Tarsipedidae. Adapted for feeding on nectar of flowers. One species, *Tarsipes spenserae*, of southwestern Western Australia.

Superfamily Vombatoidea

Terrestrial and aboreal Australian marsupials, syndactylism of the second and third digits of the hindfeet. Two extant families; 1 extinct family.

†*Family Diprotodontidae.* Large herbivorous marsupial represented in the Australian fossil record as far back as the Miocene.

Family Phascolarctidae (koalas). Small bearlike Australian marsupials. Adapted to arboreal living and restricted to a diet of the leaves of a few species of eucalyptus. First and second digits of the forelimbs are opposable to the other digits. There is no tail. Pouch opens backward. One species along the eastern Australian coast: *Phascolarctos cinereus.*

Family Vombatidae (wombats). Woodchuck-like marsupials distinct from all others in having a single pair of ever-growing upper and lower incisors and in having rootless, high-crowned cheek teeth. The tail is very short. Includes *Phascolonus*, the giant wombat of the Pleistocene; *Vombatus* (common, or naked-nosed, wombat); *Lasiorhinus* (hairy-nosed wombat). Comprises 2 genera and 4 species.

Critical appraisal. An earlier classification, which is still encountered (see MAMMALIA), attributes ordinal rank to the marsupials. Under that system are listed 6 superfamilies and from 13 to 18 families, according to the authority followed. Various attempts to subdivide the order into suborders to accommodate necessary changes required by accumulated taxonomic findings have not been widely accepted. Along with a resurgence of interest in marsupial relationships has developed a growing body of opinion that the order rests too heavily on the presence of a pouch or its vestige. Such a foundation is as unwarranted as the reduction of all recognized orders of placental mammals into a single order because they all possess a placenta. In fact, as many variations and as great a degree of variations are found within the marsupials as are found in the placental mammals. Current opinion, therefore, favours the recognition of the Marsupialia as a superorder comprising four orders as given above.

(H.M.V.D.)

BIBLIOGRAPHY. Among general works are the following: CHARLES L. BARRETT, *Wild Life of Australia and New Guinea* (1954); CHARLES W. BRAZENOR, *The Mammals of Victoria and the Dental Characteristics of Monotremes and Australian Marsupials* (1950); ALBERT S. LE SOUEF and HARRY BURRELL, *The Wild Animals of Australasia, Embracing the Mammals of New Guinea and the Nearer Pacific Islands* (1926); BASIL J. MARLOW, *Marsupials of Australia* (1962); ELLIS TROUGHTON, *Furred Animals of Australia*, 8th ed. rev. (1966); ERNEST P. WALKER et al., *Mammals of the World*, 3 vol. (1964; 2nd ed., vol. 1, 1968); F. WOOD JONES, *The Mammals of South Australia*, 3 vol. (1923–25).
Journal and magazine articles include: J. PEARSON, "Some Problems of Marsupial Phylogeny," *Rep. Meet. Aust. N.Z. Ass. Advmt. Sci.*, 25:71–102 (1947); H.C. REYNOLDS, "Studies on Reproduction in the Opossum (*Didelphus virginiana virginiana*)," *Univ. Calif. Publs. Zool.*, 52:223–284 (1952); G.G. SIMPSON, "The Affinities of the Borhyaenidae," *Am. Mus. Novit.*, no. 1118 (1941); and "The Beginning of the Age of Mammals in South America," *Bull. Am. Mus. Nat. Hist.*, vol. 91, art. 1 (1948); G.H.H. TATE, "On the Anatomy and Classification of the Dasyuridae (Marsupialia)," *Bull. Am. Mus. Nat. Hist.*, vol. 88, art. 3 (1947); "Studies on the Anatomy and Phylogeny of the Macropodidae (Marsupialia)," vol. 91, art. 2 (1948); and "Studies in the Peramelidae (Marsupialia)," vol. 92, art. 6 (1948); D. FLEAY, "Strange Animals of Australia," *Natn. Geogr. Mag.*, 124:388–411 (1963); J.H. CALABY, "Australia's Threatened Mammals," *Wildlife*, 1:15–18 (1963); H.H. FINLAYSON, "Mitchell's Wombat in South Australia," *Trans. R. Soc. S. Aust.*, 85:207–215 (1961); A.G. LYNE, "Australian Mammals," *Aust. Mus. Mag.*, 12:121–125 (1956); J. MCNALLY, "Koala Management in Victoria," *Wildl. Circ. Vict.*, no. 4 (1957); W.E. POOLE and P.E. PILTON, "Reproduction in the Grey Kangaroo, *Macropus canguru*, in Captivity," *C.S.I.R.O. Wildl. Res.* 9:218–234 (1964); G.B. SHARMAN, "Studies on Marsupial Reproduction. III. Normal and Delayed Pregnancy in *Setonix brachyurus*," *Aust. J. Zool.*, 3:56–70 (1955); G.B. SHARMAN and J.H. CALABY, "Reproductive Behaviour in the Red Kangaroo,

Megaleia rufa, in captivity," *C.S.I.R.O. Wildl. Res.*, 9:58–85 (1964); E.M.O. LAURIE and J.E. HILL, "List of Land Mammals of New Guinea, Celebes and Adjacent Islands, 1758–1952," *Br. Mus. Nat. Hist.* (1954).

Martial

It is to Marcus Valerius Martialis, known in the English-speaking world as Martial, that most of the current knowledge of Roman society in the second half of the 1st century AD can be attributed. His poetic epigrams, numbering over 1,500, review the whole spectrum of his society. In addition, Martial recorded invaluable information on everyday life.

Early years. Martial was born on March 1 in one of the years AD 38 to 41 at Bilbilis, a Roman colony in Spain perched on a rock above the Salo River, the waters of which were used in the hardening of steel. The wild scenery of his birthplace probably affected him deeply and fostered in him that capacity for descriptive writing, which is not the least of his many talents. Proudly claiming descent from Celts and Iberians, he was, nevertheless, a freeborn Roman citizen, the son of parents who, though not wealthy, possessed sufficient means to ensure that he received the traditional literary education from a grammarian and rhetorician. In his late 50s he wrote, "My parents were stupid enough to have me taught literature, a paltry subject; but what good were teachers of grammar and rhetoric to me?" Yet this complaint should be taken with reservation, as it occurs in one of those epigrams that stress the inverse ratio of educational intensity to size of subsequent earnings.

In his early 20s, possibly not before AD 64, since he makes no reference to the burning of Rome that occurred in that year, he made his way to the capital of the empire and attached himself as client (a traditional relationship between powerful patron and humbler man with his way to make) to the powerful and talented family of the Senecas, who were Spaniards like himself. To their circle belonged Lucan, the epic poet, and Calpurnius Piso, chief conspirator in the unsuccessful plot against the emperor Nero in AD 65. After the latter incident and its consequences, Martial had to look around for other patrons. Presumably the Senecas had introduced him to other influential families, whose patronage would enable him to make a living as a poet. Yet precisely how Martial lived between AD 65 and 80, the year in which he published a small volume of poems to celebrate the consecration of the Flavian Amphitheatre, or Colosseum, is not known. It is possible that he turned his hand to law, although it is unlikely that he practiced in the courts either successfully or for long.

Recognition. By a law passed in AD 9, certain privileges were granted to fathers of three children in Rome, four children in Italy, and five children in the provinces. These privileges included exemption from various charges, such as that of guardianship, and a prior claim to magistracies. They were therefore financially profitable and accelerated a political career. As a mark of special imperial favour, they were occasionally conferred on men such as Martial and the younger Pliny who did not qualify by fatherhood. Martial was almost certainly unmarried, yet he received, probably from the emperors Titus and Domitian, this marital distinction. Moreover, as an additional mark of imperial favour, he was awarded a military tribuneship, which he was permitted to resign after six months service but which entitled him to the privileges of an *eques* (knight) throughout his life. Though he lacked the required property qualification of an *eques*, he could proudly boast that he sat in the first 14 rows of the theatre, behind the orchestra, which were reserved for the senators. As early as AD 84 the poet also owned a small country estate near Nomentum (about 12 miles [19 kilometres] northeast of Rome), which may have been given to him by Polla, the widow of Lucan. This undoubtedly was a welcome change from the city garret, three floors up, on the Quirinal Hill (one of the seven hills on which Rome stands), which he occupied until he acquired a small house of his own, also situated on the Quirinal.

Distinction and imperial favour

From each of the patrons whom Martial, as client, attended at the morning levee (a reception held when arising from bed), he would regularly receive the "dole" of "100 wretched farthings." Wealthy Romans, who either hoped to gain favourable mention or feared to receive unfavourable, albeit oblique, mention in his epigrams, would supplement the minimum dole by dinner invitations or by gifts. The poverty so often pleaded by the poet is undoubtedly exaggerated; apparently his genius for spending kept pace with his capacity for earning.

Martial's first book, *On the Spectacles* (AD 80), contained more than 30 undistinguished poems, scarcely improved by gross adulation of the emperor Titus. In the year 84 or 85 appeared two undistinguished books (confusingly numbered XIII and XIV in the collection) with Greek titles *Xenia* and *Apophoreta;* these consist almost entirely of couplets describing presents given to guests at the December festival of the Saturnalia. In the next 15 or 16 years, however, appeared the 12 books of epigrams on which his renown deservedly rests. After 34 years in Rome he returned to Spain, where his last book (numbered XII) was published, probably in AD 102. He died not much more than a year later in his early 60s.

The chief friends Martial made in Rome—Seneca, Piso, and Lucan—have already been mentioned. As his fame grew, he became acquainted with the literary circles of his day, meeting great men whose works are still studied today: Quintilian, the learned and humane professor of rhetoric and educational theorist; Pliny the Younger, a brilliant writer of letters; the incomparable satirist Juvenal; and Silius Italicus, who spread the history of the Second Punic War over 17 books of epic verse, closely modelled on Virgil. Whether he knew the historian Tacitus and the poet Valerius Flaccus is not certain. That Martial never mentions Statius, a popular author of epics on the "Seven against Thebes" (mythological warriors who led an army against Thebes, a town of central Greece), and Achilles, a hero of the Trojan War, as well as talented composer of "occasional verse," is indeed surprising, though the omission may be accounted for by Martial's expressed detestation of turgid and involved poetry dealing with the backwaters of mythology.

Assessment. Martial has been charged with two gross faults: adulation and obscenity. He certainly indulged in much nauseating flattery of the emperor Domitian, involving, besides farfetched conceits dragging his epigrams well below their usual level, use of the official title "my Lord and my God." Furthermore, he cringed before men of wealth and influence, unashamedly whining for gifts and favours. Yet, however much one despises servility, it is hard to see how a man of letters could have survived long in Rome without considerable compromise. As for the latter charge, Martial introduced few themes not touched on by Catullus and Horace (two poets of the last century BC) before him. His references to homosexuality, "oral stimulation," and masturbation are couched, at least, in a rich setting of wit, charm, linguistic subtlety, superb literary craftsmanship, evocative description, and deep human sympathy. Martial is virtually the creator of the modern epigram, and his myriad admirers throughout the centuries, including many of the world's great poets, have paid him the homage of quotation, translation, and imitation.

Creator of the epigram

Born into an age when greatness was reserved almost exclusively for the epic poet, the Spaniard from Bilbilis had the sense and the self-awareness to shun laurels manifestly beyond his grasp. He was still a true Roman poet, honouring the past and keeping to the mainstream of Greek and Roman tradition. He was, for instance, thoroughly acquainted with the great poets of Rome's Golden Age; Catullus, Tibullus, Sextus Propertius, Lucretius, Virgil, and Ovid. But in Martial's stress on the simple joys of life—eating, drinking, and conversing with friends—and in his famous recipes for contentment and the happy life, one is reminded continually of the dominant themes of Horace's *Satires, Epistles,* and *Second Epode.*

MAJOR WORKS

On the Spectacles (*Liber spectaculorum*) (AD 80), recording the opening by Titus of the Flavian Amphitheatre (Colosseum); *Xenia*, numbered as Book XIII (AD 84–85), mottoes as presents for guests; *Apophoreta*, numbered as Book XIV, mottoes as gifts to take away; Books, I, II, III, IV, V, VI, VII, VIII, IX, X, XI, XII.

The most convenient complete translation with the Latin on the facing page is in the "Loeb Classical Library," *Martial*, by W.C.A. Ker, 2 vol. (1919–20). A good selection may be found in *Martial's Epigrams: Translations and Imitations*, by A.L. Francis and H.F. Tatum (1924); and *Epigrams, with an English Translation*, by W.C.A. Ker, 2 vol. (1961).

BIBLIOGRAPHY. The basic work for an understanding and interpretation of Martial's epigrams is the volume entitled *M. Valerii Martialis Epigrammaton Libri mit erklären-den Anmerkungen*, by LUDWIG FRIEDLAENDER (1886, reprinted 1967). Most other serious work is scattered in numerous classical periodicals and rare dissertations; of this only a very small portion is in English. For the general reader the following books are recommended: the English annotated selections from the poet's work by EDWIN POST (1908, reprinted 1967), H.M. STEPHENSON (1887), and R.T. BRIDGE and E.D.C. LAKE (1906–08, reprinted 1924); A.G. CARRINGTON, *Aspects of Martial's Epigrams* (1960), a useful general study; PAUL NIXON, *Martial and the Modern Epigram* (1927), which discusses Martial's literary influence; and J. WIGHT DUFF, "Martial and Minor Flavian Poetry," in *A Literary History of Rome in the Silver Age from Tiberius to Hadrian*, pp. 498–529 (1927). See also Duff's essays "Varied Strains in Martial," in *Classical and Mediaeval Studies in Honor of Edward Kennard Rand*, pp. 87–99 (1938); and "Martial—the Epigram As Satire," in *Roman Satire*, pp. 126–146 (1936).

(H.H.Hu.)

Martinique

The island of Martinique is an overseas *département*, or administrative district, of France situated in the eastern Caribbean, about 4,400 miles (7,000 kilometres) from France and about 270 miles north of the coast of Venezuela. It forms part of the Windward Islands and is included in the Lesser Antilles island chain. Its nearest island neighbours are the British dependencies of Dominica 22 miles to the northwest and St. Lucia 16 miles to the south. The main islands of Guadeloupe, the other French overseas *département* in the Windward Islands, lie about 74 miles to the north.

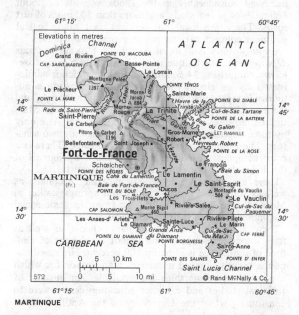

MARTINIQUE

Martinique has an area of 431 square miles (1,116 square kilometres) and, in the early 1970s, a population of about 340,000 inhabitants. The island measures about 50 miles in length and about 22 miles at its widest extent. The smallest of all the French overseas *départements*, its population density of more than 300 inhabitants per square kilometre is one of the highest in the Antilles. The administrative capital and chief town is Fort-de-France (population about 100,000).

The name Martinique is probably a corruption of the Indian name Madiana (Island of Flowers) or Madinina (fertile island with luxuriant vegetation), as reputedly told to Christopher Columbus by the Caribs in 1502. Empress Joséphine, consort of Napoleon I, was born on the island in 1763; she was the daughter of a Martinique planter named Joseph Tascher de La Pagerie (see also GUADELOUPE; for an associated physical feature, see CARIBBEAN SEA).

The landscape. *Relief and drainage.* The mountainous relief of Martinique represents the outermost edge of what remained of the original geological formation after the subsidence of the trench that became the Caribbean Sea. The relief of the island takes the form of three principal massifs (mountainous masses). These are Montagne Pelée (4,583 feet, or 1,397 metres) to the north; the Pitons (peaks) du Carbet (of which Lacroix Peak reaches 3,923 feet, or 1,196 metres) in the centre; and Montagne du Vauclin (1,654 feet, or 504 metres high) in the south. *(margin: The three principal massifs)*

The tortuous relief of the island has led to a complex drainage pattern, characterized by short watercourses. In the south, the Rivière Salée and the Rivière Pilote flow down from the scarps of Montagne du Vauclin. In the centre, the rivers flow outward from the Pitons du Carbet in a starlike pattern; they include the Lorrain, Galion, Capot, and Lézarde rivers. In the north, the Grande Rivière, the Céron, the Rivière Roxelane, the Rivière des Pères, and the Rivière Sèche are little more than irregular torrents.

The northern coastline of Martinique is characterized by steep cliffs; farther south, however, the cliffs become lower with two large bays—Fort-de-France and Le Marin—being located on the western coast. Coral reefs, headlands, and coves occur on the east coast.

Climate. The climate is remarkably constant, with the average temperature amounting to 79° F (26° C), with average minimums of about 68° to 72° F (20° to 22° C), average maximums of about 86° to 90° F (30° to 32° C), and temperature extremes of 59° F (15° C) and 93° F (34° C).

The northeast trade winds, which blow almost 300 days a year, temper the heat, but winds from the south are hot and humid and sometimes bring hurricanes.

Rainfall is abundant, especially in July and September, but is very irregularly distributed; it varies from 39 inches to more than 157 inches a year, depending upon the orientation of the relief.

The year consists of two distinct seasons—the relatively dry Lent season, which lasts from December to June, and the rainy winter season from July to December.

Vegetation and animal life. The climate, together with the volcanic soil, produces a luxuriant vegetation, which is divided, according to altitude, into four zones: the maritime zone, the lowlands, the former forest zone, and the upper mountain slopes. The maritime zone includes 7,400 acres of mangrove swamp, half of which is located in the bay of Fort-de-France. The beaches are invaded by morning glory, tropical twining herb, and sea grape. The lowland vegetation zone extends from the coast to a height of about 1,500 feet and corresponds to the chalky lands of the Sainte-Anne and Caravelle districts. Here are found ferns and orchids, as well as various trees, including mahogany, white gum, and other species. Above 1,500 feet is the former virgin forest zone, where large trees and bracken are still to be found. As the altitude increases the trees grow smaller. A transitional zone is characterized by peat moss. Above 3,000 feet the upper slopes are almost bare, except for some stunted forest. *(margin: The four vegetation zones)*

There are relatively few kinds of animals on the island. The mongoose was introduced in the 19th century in the hope of eliminating the deadly, rat-tailed viper, but without doing so. Also found are the manicon (a kind of opossum), wild rabbit, wild pigeon, turtle dove, and ortolan (a small bird about six inches long, often netted and fattened as a table delicacy).

History. Although Christopher Columbus sighted the island in 1493, it was not until 1502, on his fourth voyage, that he visited it, leaving there some pigs and goats. Neglected by the Spaniards, who sought more material rewards than those the island offered, Martinique was occupied in 1635 by a Frenchman, Pierre Belain d'Esnambuc, who established 80 settlers at Fort Saint-Pierre at the mouth of the Rivière Roxelane. A year later d'Esnambuc, who had fallen sick, entrusted Martinique to his nephew, Jacques-Dyel du Parquet, who bought the island from the Compagnie des Isles d'Amérique and developed it into a remarkably prosperous colony.

In 1654 a group of 250 Dutch Jews, chased from Brazil by the Portuguese, introduced sugarcane. In 1660 cacao trees were planted in place of cotton. After the death of du Parquet, his widow governed the island in the name of her children, but disagreed with the settlers; and in 1658 the French king, Louis XIV, resumed sovereignty over the island, paying an indemnity to du Parquet's children. In 1664 the island was placed under the authority of the Compagnie des Indes Occidentales; in 1674 it was made part of the French crown domain, being administered, according to the Pacte Colonial, a body of principles summarized in the statement: "The mother country founds and maintains the colonies; the colonies enrich the mother country." Supplies and slaves were brought out to the French Antilles by the Compagnie du Sénégal, founded in 1664; the slave ships called at Martinique before proceeding to Guadeloupe, permitting the colony first choice of the slaves. In 1723 Arabian coffee was introduced, thus further contributing to the island's prosperity. In 1787 Louis XVI granted Martinique the right to establish a Colonial Assembly.

Attacks by Dutch and British

At various times Martinique was subjected to attack by various foreign fleets. An attack by the Dutch was repulsed in 1674; further attacks by the English were repelled in 1693 and in 1759. In 1762, however, the English captured the island, only to return it to France under the terms of the Treaty of Paris in 1763. The English recaptured it in 1794, and occupied it until 1802; captured once more by the English in 1809, it was definitively restored to France in 1814. Slave uprisings occurred in 1789, 1815, and 1822. The abolition of slavery in 1848 created a labour problem, as a result of which labourers from India and China were introduced. In 1848 universal suffrage was proclaimed, but was abolished once more under Napoleon III; after 1870 the French Third Republic restored representation for the island in the French Parliament.

In 1902 the volcanic eruption of Mont Pelée destroyed the town of Saint-Pierre, killing about 30,000 people. During World War II Martinique adhered to the Vichy government for three years before rallying to the Free French cause in 1943. In 1946, Martinique was granted the status of a French *département*.

The population.   In 1658 French settlers on the island numbered about 5,000. The Carib element gradually disappeared, partly as a result of conflicts and partly as a result of assimilation. The importation of black slaves from Africa added a further ethnic component. Today the racial composition of the island is extremely mixed, although the black element is the largest. The white Creole (locally born) element, however, controls an important part of the island's economy.

Martinique, Area and Population				
	area		population	
	sq mi	sq km	1967 census	1971 estimate
Arrondissements				
Fort-de-France	302	782	243,000	...
Trinité	129	334	76,000	...
Total Martinique	431	1,116	320,000	340,000
Source: Official government figures.				

Martinique's population is rapidly increasing, at a rate of 2 percent a year. The population is youthful, with more than 50 percent less than 20 years old. A Creole dialect, similar to that spoken in Haiti, is spoken, but French, which is taught in schools, is the official language.

With the exception of a few groups within the juris-

diction of the Methodist Missionary Society, and several Adventist communities, the population is in general Roman Catholic.

The contemporary state.   *The economy.* The economy   **Agriculture and industry** of the island is primarily agricultural; sugar, bananas, and rum are the principal exports. Although about 28 percent of the population is engaged in agriculture, this activity contributes only about 20 percent to the value of the gross domestic product. The annual agricultural output includes about 30,000 tons of sugar, 10,000 tons of pure alcohol for rum making, and more than 200,000 tons of bananas. Fresh and canned pineapples are produced. Subsistence crops include yams and cassava.

Economic planning has laid emphasis on land reform, the diversification of agricultural crops, and industrialization. Local industrial plants include a plant for crushing clinkers, an oil refinery at Fort-de-France with a capacity of 600,000 tons a year, and a fertilizer plant with an output capacity of 100,000 tons a year. High hopes are placed on the development of tourism. An association has been formed that groups together ten *communes* (small administrative units) in the administrative district (*arrondissement*) of the island that is the most favourable to tourism.

Martinique receives a considerable amount of aid from FIDOM (Investment Fund for the Economic and Social Development of the Overseas Departments) as well as from European funds.

Martinique's predicament stems in part from the fact that the service sector of the economy accounts for only about one quarter of the domestic national product but employs nearly one third of the economically active population, which numbers about 90,000. Economic imbalance results in a significant deficit in the balance of trade. Overseas trade is essentially with France and the franc zone. An experiment in an adaptation of military service, consisting of road-building and repairing hurricane damage, has been undertaken.

Transportation.   Martinique maintains regular air and sea links with France and North America. Sea traffic at the port of Fort-de-France amounts to about 1,500 boats a year. There is an international airport at Lamentin, to the east of Fort-de-France. The road network, which increased considerably in the 1960s, consists of about 600 miles of paved roads, and more than 500 miles of dirt roads. There are local bus services, and small coastal steamers connect various points around the island.

Administration and social conditions.   As an overseas *département*, Martinique is divided into two *arrondissements*, comprising 34 *communes*, each of which is administered by an elected municipal council. Executive authority is represented by a prefect and other officials, and there is a legislative council of 36 elected members. Martinique is represented in the French National Assembly by three deputies and in the French Senate by two senators. The French system of justice is in force. There is a court of appeal, a judicial tribunal, and five tribunals of the first instance (the equivalent of county courts).

There are several general and maternity hospitals, as well as some dispensaries, and a hot springs station at Morne-Rouge. Martinique benefits from the same social legislation as that of metropolitan France.

There are more than 250 primary schools, as well as   **Schools** four secondary schools. The school enrollment of children of school age is virtually 100 percent. Higher education is usually pursued in metropolitan France, for which a number of scholarships are available. An institute of juridical studies and a higher education centre were to constitute part of the University of the Antilles, which was being formed.

Cultural life.   The local press consists of about a dozen daily or weekly newspapers. The ORTF (Office de Radiodiffusion Télévision Française) broadcasts radio and television programs. The Fort-de-France carnival, featuring a parade with masks, is an annual event. Voodoo ceremonies are far less important on the island than they are in Haiti. Cockfighting is a popular sport.

Prospects for the future.   The major problem faced by Martinique is demographic; it is difficult to find sufficient food and employment for a growing population. Emigration to France has been a palliative, but not a solution. Hopes for an amelioration of economic conditions depend on the development of the tourist industry.

BIBLIOGRAPHY. EUGENE REVERT, *La Martinique: étude géographique et humaine* (1949), is the best geographical work. See also the same author's *La Magie antillaise* (1951); *Les Antilles* (1954); and *Entre les deux Amériques: le monde Caraïbe* (1958); and AUGUSTE JOYAU, *La Martinique: carrefour du monde caraïbe* (1967), a good synthesis.

(R.Co.)

Marx, Karl

Karl Marx, revolutionist, sociologist, and economist, was the author (with Friedrich Engels) of *Manifest der Kommunistischen Partei* (1848), commonly known as *The Communist Manifesto*, the most celebrated pamphlet in the history of the Socialist movement, as well as of its most important book, *Das Kapital*. The body of thought and belief known as Marxism is based upon the writings of Marx and Engels.

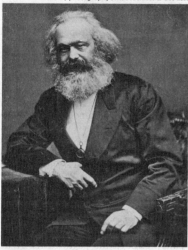

Marx.

Early years. Karl Heinrich Marx was born on May 5, 1818, in the city of Trier (formerly Trèves) in the Rhine province of Prussia, now in West Germany, one of seven children of Jewish parents. His father Heinrich, a lawyer, was a man of the Enlightenment, devoted to Kant and Voltaire, who took part in agitations for a constitution in Prussia. His mother, born Henrietta Pressburg, was from Holland and never learned to speak German properly. A year or so before Karl was born, his father —probably because his professional career required it— was baptized in the Evangelical Established Church, and Karl was baptized when he was six years old.

Marx was educated from 1830 to 1835 at the high school in Trier. Suspected of harbouring liberal teachers and pupils, the school was under police surveillance. Marx's adolescent writings exhibited a spirit of Christian devotion and a longing for self-sacrifice on behalf of humanity. In October 1835, he matriculated at the University of Bonn. The courses he attended were exclusively in the humanities, in such subjects as Greek and Roman mythology and the history of art. He participated in customary student activities, fought a duel, and spent a day in jail for being drunk and disorderly—the only imprisonment he suffered in his life. He presided at the Tavern Club and joined a poets' club that included some political activists. A politically rebellious student culture was, indeed, part of life at Bonn. Many students had been arrested; some were still being expelled in Marx's time, particularly as the outcome of an effort by students to disrupt the session of the Federal Diet at Frankfurt. The tavern clubs at Bonn were also at odds with the more aristocratic student associations. Marx, however, left Bonn after a year and in October 1836 enrolled at the University of Berlin to study law and philosophy.

Marx's crucial experience at Berlin was his introduction to Hegel's philosophy, regnant there, and his adherence to the Young Hegelians. At first he felt a repugnance toward Hegel's doctrines; when he fell sick it was partially, as he wrote his father, "from intense vexation at having to make an idol of a view I detested." But the Hegelian circumpressure in the revolutionary student culture was powerful. Marx joined a society called the Doctor Club, whose members were intensely involved in the new literary and philosophical movement. Their chief figure was Bruno Bauer, a young lecturer in theology, who was developing the idea that the Christian Gospels were a record not of history but of human fantasies arising from men's emotional needs and that Jesus had not been a historical person. Marx enrolled in a course of lectures given by Bauer on the prophet Isaiah. Bauer taught that a new social catastrophe "more tremendous" than that of the advent of Christianity was in the making. The Young Hegelians began moving rapidly toward atheism and also talked vaguely of political action.

The Prussian government, fearful of the subversion latent in the Young Hegelians, soon undertook to drive them from the universities. Bauer was dismissed from his post in 1839. Marx's "most intimate friend" of this period, Adolph Rutenberg, an older journalist who had served a prison sentence for his political radicalism, pressed for a deeper social involvement. By 1841 the Young Hegelians had become left republicans. Marx's studies, meanwhile, were lagging. Urged by his friends, he submitted a doctoral dissertation to the university at Jena, which was known to be lax in its academic requirements, and received his degree in April 1841. His thesis analyzed in a Hegelian fashion the difference between the natural philosophies of Democritus and Epicurus. More distinctively, it sounded a note of Promethean defiance:

> Philosophy makes no secret of it. Prometheus' admission: 'In sooth all gods I hate,' is its own admission, its own motto against all gods, . . . Prometheus is the noblest saint and martyr in the calendar of philosophy.

In 1841 Marx, together with other Young Hegelians, was much influenced by the publication of *Das Wesen des Christentum* (1841; *The Essence of Christianity*, 1854) by Ludwig Feuerbach. Its author, to Marx's mind, successfully criticized Hegel from the materialist standpoint, showing how the "Absolute Spirit" was a projection of "the real man standing on the foundation of nature." Henceforth Marx's philosophical efforts toward a combination of Hegel's dialectic with Feuerbach's materialism. In January 1842, Marx began contributing to a newspaper newly founded in Cologne, the *Rheinische Zeitung*. It was the liberal democratic organ of a group of young merchants, bankers, and industrialists; Cologne was the centre of the most industrially advanced section of Prussia. To this stage of Marx's life belongs an essay on the freedom of the press. Since he then took for granted the existence of absolute moral standards and universal principles of ethics, he condemned censorship as a moral evil that could have only evil consequences; it also entailed spying into men's minds and hearts and assigned to weak and malevolent mortals powers that presupposed an omniscient mind.

On October 15, 1842, Marx became editor of the *Rheinische Zeitung*. As such, he was obliged to write editorials on a variety of social and economic issues, ranging from the housing of the Berlin poor and the theft by peasants of wood from the forests to the new phenomenon of Communism. He found his Hegelian idealism of little use in these matters. At the same time he was becoming estranged from his Hegelian friends for whom shocking the bourgeois was a sufficient mode of social activity. Marx, friendly at this time to the "liberal-minded practical men" who were "struggling step-by-step for freedom within constitutional limits," succeeded in trebling his newspaper's circulation and making it a leading journal in Prussia. Nevertheless, Prussian authorities suspended it, giving in to pressures from the government of Russia. Marx went to Paris to study French Communism.

Marx, after an engagement of seven years, had been married in June 1843 to Jenny von Westphalen. Jenny

The Young Hegelians

Newspaper work

was an attractive, intelligent, and much-admired girl, four years older than Karl; she came of a family of military and administrative distinction, descended on her mother's side from the rebellious Scottish earls of Argyll. Her half-brother later became a highly reactionary Prussian minister of the interior. Her father, a follower of the French Socialist Saint-Simon, was fond of Karl, though others in her family opposed the marriage. Marx's father also feared that Jenny was destined to become a sacrifice to the demon that possessed his son.

In Paris, Marx began associating with Communistic societies of French and German workingmen. Their ideas were, in his view, "utterly crude and unintelligent," but their character moved him: "the brotherhood of man is no mere phrase with them, but a fact of life, and the nobility of man shines upon us from their work-hardened bodies," he wrote in his so-called "Ökonomisch-philosophische Manuskripte aus dem Jahre 1844" (1844; *Economic and Philosophic Manuscripts of 1844* [1959]). A venture with the liberal Hegelian Arnold Ruge in the publications of "German-French Yearbooks" proved short-lived. Marx's article "Toward the Critique of the Hegelian Philosophy of Right" appeared in their pages in 1844 with its oft-quoted assertion that religion is the "opium of the people," and it was here that he first raised the call for an "uprising of the proletariat" to realize the conceptions of philosophy. Once more the Prussian government intervened against Marx; after being expelled from France by the government of Guizot, Marx left for Brussels on February 5, 1845. That year in Belgium he renounced his Prussian nationality.

Revolutionary writings

Brussels period. The next two years in Brussels saw the deepening of Marx's lifelong collaboration with Friedrich Engels. Engels had seen at firsthand in Manchester (where a branch factory of his father's textile firm was located) all the depressing aspects of the Industrial Revolution. He had also been a Young Hegelian and had been converted to Communism by Moses Hess, who was called the "Communist rabbi." In England he associated with the followers of Robert Owen. Now he and Marx, finding that they shared the same views, combined their intellectual resources and published *Die heilige Familie* (1845; *The Holy Family*, 1956), a prolix criticism of the Hegelian idealism of the theologian Bruno Bauer. Their next work, *Die deutsche Ideologie* (written 1845–46, published 1932; *The German Ideology*, 1938), contained the first full exposition of their materialistic conception of history, but it found no publisher and remained unknown during its authors' lifetimes.

During his Brussels years, Marx developed his views and, through confrontations with the chief leaders of the working-class movement, established his intellectual standing. In 1846 he publicly excoriated the German leader Wilhelm Weitling for his moralistic appeals. Marx insisted that the stage of bourgeois society could not be skipped over; the proletariat could not just leap into Communism; the workers' movement required a scientific basis, not moralistic phrases. He also polemicized against the French Socialist thinker Pierre-Joseph Proudhon in *Misère de la philosophie* (1847; *The Poverty of Philosophy*, 1900), a mordant attack on Proudhon's book subtitled *Philosophie de la misère* (1846; *The Philosophy of Poverty*, 1888). Proudhon wanted to unite the best features of such contraries as competition and monopoly; he hoped to save the good features in economic institutions while eliminating the bad. Marx, however, declared that no equilibrium was possible between the antagonisms in any given economic system. Social structures were transient historic forms determined by the productive forces: "The handmill gives you society with the feudal lord; the steammill, society with the industrial capitalist." Proudhon's mode of reasoning, Marx wrote, was typical of the petty bourgeois, who failed to see the underlying laws of history.

An unusual sequence of events led Marx and Engels to write their pamphlet, *The Communist Manifesto.* In June 1847 a secret society, the League of the Just, composed mainly of emigrant German handicraftsmen, met in London and decided to formulate a political program. They sent a representative to Marx to ask him to join the League; Marx overcame his doubts, and, with Engels, joined the organization, which thereupon changed its name to the Communist League and enacted a democratic constitution. Entrusted with the task of composing their program, Marx and Engels worked from the middle of December 1847 to the end of January 1848. The London Communists were already impatiently threatening Marx with disciplinary action when he sent them the manuscript; they promptly adopted it as their manifesto. It enunciated the proposition that all history had hitherto been a history of class struggles, combining this with the assertion that the victory of the proletariat would be the final struggle, putting an end to class society forever. It mercilessly criticized all forms of Socialism founded on philosophical "cobwebs" such as "alienation." It rejected the avenue of "social Utopias," small experiments in community, as deadening the class struggle and therefore as being "reactionary sects." It set forth ten immediate measures as first steps toward Communism, ranging from a progressive income tax and the abolition of inheritances to free education for all children. It closed with the words, "The proletarians have nothing to lose but their chains. They have a world to win. Workingmen of all countries, unite!"

Revolution suddenly erupted in Europe in the first months of 1848, in France, Italy, and Austria. Marx had been invited to Paris by a member of the provisional government just in time to avoid expulsion by the Belgian government. In Paris he opposed an ill-fated project of Georg Herwegh, a poet, for organizing a German legion to invade and liberate the fatherland. Marx's opposition to his venture made him unpopular among most of the German exiles. As the revolution gained in Austria and Germany, Marx returned to the Rhineland. In Cologne he advocated a policy of coalition between the working class and the democratic bourgeoisie, opposing for this reason the nomination of independent workers' candidates for the Frankfurt Assembly and arguing strenuously against the program for proletarian revolution advocated by the leaders of the Workers' Union. He concurred in Engels' judgment that *The Communist Manifesto* should be shelved and the Communist League disbanded. Marx pressed his policy through the pages of the *Neue Rheinische Zeitung,* newly founded in June 1849, urging a constitutional democracy and war with Russia. When the more revolutionary leader of the Workers' Union, Andreas Gottschalk, was arrested, Marx supplanted him and organized the first Rhineland Democratic Congress in August 1848. When the King of Prussia dissolved the Prussian Assembly in Berlin, Marx called for arms and men to help the resistance. Bourgeois liberals withdrew their support from Marx's newspaper, and he himself was indicted on several charges including advocacy of the nonpayment of taxes. On this occasion Marx gave the only speech he ever made on the Cologne streets to a crowd of workers. In his trial he defended himself with the argument that the crown was engaged in making an unlawful counter-revolution. The jury acquitted him unanimously and with thanks. As the last hopeless fighting flared in Dresden and Baden, Marx was ordered banished as an alien on May 16, 1849. The final issue of his newspaper, printed in red, caused a great sensation.

Participation in the events of 1848

Early years in London. Expelled once more from Paris, Marx went to London in August 1849. Chagrined by the failure of his own tactics of collaboration with the liberal bourgeoisie, he rejoined the Communist League in London and for about a year advocated a bolder revolutionary policy. An "Address of the Central Committee to the Communist League," written with Engels in March 1850, urged that in future revolutionary situations they struggle to make the revolution "permanent" by avoiding subservience to the bourgeois party and by setting up "their own revolutionary workers' governments" alongside any new bourgeois one. Marx hoped that the economic crisis would shortly lead to a revival of the revolutionary movement; when this hope faded, he came into conflict once more with those whom he called "the alchemists of the revolution," such as August von Willich, a

Communist who proposed to hasten the advent of revolution by undertaking direct revolutionary ventures. Such persons, Marx wrote in September 1850, substitute "idealism for materialism," and regard

> pure will as the motive power of revolution instead of actual conditions. While we say to the workers: "You have got to go through fifteen, twenty, fifty years of civil wars and national wars not merely in order to change your conditions but in order to change yourselves and become qualified for political power," you on the contrary tell them, "We must achieve power immediately. . . ."

The militant faction in turn ridiculed Marx for being a revolutionary who limited his activity to lectures on political economy to the Communist Workers' Educational Union. The upshot was that Marx gradually stopped attending meetings of the London Communists. In 1852 he devoted himself intensely to working for the defense of 11 Communists arrested and tried in Cologne on charges of revolutionary conspiracy and wrote a pamphlet on their behalf. The same year he also published, in a German-American periodical, his essay "Der Achtzehnte Brumaire des Louis Bonaparte" (*The Eighteenth Brumaire of Louis Bonaparte*, 1926), with its acute analysis of the formation of a bureaucratic absolutist state with the support of the peasant class. In other respects the next 12 years were, in Marx's words, years of "isolation" both for him and for Engels in his Manchester factory.

Poverty in London
From 1850 to 1864, Marx lived in material misery and spiritual pain. His funds were gone, and except on one occasion he could not bring himself to seek paid employment. In March 1850 he and his wife and four small children were evicted and their belongings seized. Several of his children died—including a son Guido, "a sacrifice to bourgeois misery," and a daughter Franziska, for whom his wife rushed about frantically trying to borrow money for a coffin. For six years the family lived in two small rooms in Soho, often subsisting on bread and potatoes. The children learned to lie to the creditors: "Mr. Marx ain't upstairs." Once he had to escape them by fleeing to Manchester. His wife suffered breakdowns.

During all these years Friedrich Engels loyally contributed to Marx's financial support. The sums were not large at first, for Engels was only a clerk in the firm of Ermen and Engels at Manchester. Later, however, in 1864, when he became a partner, his subventions were generous. Marx was proud of Engels' friendship and would tolerate no criticism of him. Bequests from the relatives of Marx's wife and from Marx's friend Wilhelm Wolff helped to alleviate their economic distress.

Marx had one relatively steady source of earned income in the United States. On the invitation of Charles A. Dana, managing editor of *The New York Tribune*, he became, in 1851, its European correspondent. The newspaper, edited by Horace Greeley, had sympathies for Fourierist Communism. From 1851 to 1862 Marx contributed close to 500 articles and editorials (Engels providing about a fourth of them). He ranged over the whole political universe, analyzing social movements and agitations from India and China to Britain and Spain. Dana's friendship proved helpful to Marx in another personal crisis. A liberal Swiss professor, Karl Vogt, charged in 1859 that Marx was the chief of a circle of blackmailers. Marx's reply in a seldom-read book, *Herr Vogt* (1860), included a testimonial to his character by Dana.

In 1859 Marx published his first book on economic theory, *Zur Kritik der politischen Ökonomie* (*A Contribution to the Critique of Political Economy*, 1904). In its preface he described how he had arrived at the materialistic conception of history.

> The mode of production in material life determines the general character of the social, political, and spiritual processes of life. It is not the consciousness of men that determines their existence, but, on the contrary, their social existence that determines their consciousness.

Marx regarded his studies at the British Museum in economic and social history as his main task, and when the German revolutionist Ferdinand Lassalle proposed in 1862 that he join with him in organizing a new workers' movement in Germany he refused. Lassalle shortly undertook the project alone.

Role in the First International. Marx's political isolation ended in 1864 with the founding of the International Working Men's Association. Although he was neither its founder nor its head, he soon became its leading spirit. Its first public meeting, called by English trade union leaders and French workers' representatives, took place at St. Martin's Hall in London on September 28, 1864. Marx, who had been invited through a French intermediary to attend as a representative of the German workers, sat silently on the platform. A committee was set up to produce a program and a constitution for the new organization. After various drafts had been submitted that were felt to be unsatisfactory, Marx, serving on a subcommittee, drew upon his immense journalistic experience. His "Address and the Provisional Rules of the International Working Men's Association," unlike his other writings, stressed the positive achievements of the cooperative movement and of parliamentary legislation; the gradual conquest of political power would enable the British proletariat to extend these achievements on a national scale.

As a member of the organization's General Council, and corresponding secretary for Germany, Marx was henceforth assiduous in attendance at its meetings, which were sometimes held several times a week. For several years he showed a rare diplomatic tact in composing differences among various parties, factions, and tendencies. The International grew in prestige and membership, its numbers reaching perhaps 800,000 in 1869. It was successful in several interventions on behalf of European trade unions engaged in struggles with employers.

The Paris Commune
In 1870, however, Marx was still unknown as a European political personality; it was the Paris Commune that made him into an international figure, "the best calumniated and most menaced man of London," as he wrote. When the Franco-Prussian War broke out in 1870, Marx and Engels disagreed with followers in Germany who refused to vote in the Reichstag in favour of the war. The General Council declared that "on the German side the war was a war of defence." After the defeat of the French armies, however, they felt that the German terms amounted to aggrandizement at the expense of the French people. When an insurrection broke out in Paris and the Paris Commune was proclaimed, Marx gave it his unswerving support. On May 30, 1871, after the Commune had been crushed, he hailed it in a famous address:

> History has no comparable example of such greatness. . . . Its martyrs are enshrined forever in the great heart of the working class.

In Engels' judgment, the Paris Commune was history's first example of the "dictatorship of the proletariat." Marx's name, as the leader of The First International, became synonymous throughout Europe with the revolutionary spirit symbolized by the Paris Commune.

The advent of the Commune, however, exacerbated the antagonisms within the International Working Men's Association and brought about its downfall. English trade unionists such as George Odger, former president of the General Council, opposed Marx's support of the Paris Commune. The Reform Bill of 1867, which had enfranchised the British working class, had opened vast opportunities for political action by the trade unions. English labour leaders found they could make many practical advances by cooperating with the Liberal Party and, regarding Marx's rhetoric as an encumbrance, resented his charge that they had "sold themselves" to the Liberals.

The struggle with Bakunin
A left opposition also developed under the leadership of the famed Russian revolutionist, Mikhail Alexandrovich Bakunin. A veteran of tsarist prisons and Siberian exile, Bakunin could move men by his oratory, which one listener compared to "a raging storm with lightning, flashes and thunderclaps, and a roaring as of lions." Bakunin admired Marx's intellect but could hardly forget that Marx had published a report in 1848 charging him with being a Russian agent. Marx, who had various ethnic aversions, said: "I do not trust any Russian." Bakunin felt that Marx was a German authoritarian and an arrogant Jew who wanted to transform the General Council into a personal dictatorship over the workers. To Bakunin, the mission of the revolutionist was destruction; he looked to

the Russian peasantry, with its propensities for violence and its uncurbed revolutionary instincts, rather than to the effete, civilized workers of the industrial countries. The students, he hoped, would be the officers of the revolution. He acquired followers, mostly young men, in Italy, Switzerland, and France, and organized a secret society, the International Alliance of Social Democracy, which in 1869 challenged the hegemony of the General Council at the congress in Basel. Marx, however, had already succeeded in preventing its admission as an organized body into the International.

To the Bakuninists, the Paris Commune was a model of revolutionary direct action and a refutation of what they considered to be Marx's "authoritarian communism." Bakunin began organizing sections of the International for an attack on the alleged dictatorship of Marx and the General Council. Marx in reply publicized Bakunin's embroilment with an unscrupulous Russian student leader, Nechayev, who had practiced blackmail and murder.

Without a supporting right wing and with the anarchist left against him, Marx feared losing control of the International to Bakunin. He also wanted to return to his studies and to finish *Das Kapital*. At the congress of the International at the Hague in 1872, the only one he ever attended, Marx managed to defeat the Bakuninists. Then, to the consternation of the delegates, Engels moved that the seat of the General Council be transferred from London to New York. The Bakuninists were expelled, but the International languished and died in New York.

Last
years During the next and last decade of his life, Marx's creative energies declined. He was beset by what he called "chronic mental depression," and his life turned inward toward his family. He was unable to complete any substantial work, though he still read widely and undertook to learn Russian. He became crotchety in his political opinions. Increasingly, he looked to a European war for the overthrow of Russian tsarism, the mainstay of reaction, hoping that this would revive the political energies of the working classes. He was moved by what he considered to be the selfless courage of the Russian terrorists who assassinated the tsar, Alexander II, in 1881; he felt this to be "a historically inevitable means of action." When the Lassalleans and his own followers coalesced in 1875 to found the German Social Democratic Party, Marx wrote a caustic but petty criticism of their program (the so-called Gotha Program); he even objected to such proposals as that for the abolition of child labour. The German leaders put his objections aside and tried to mollify him personally. He still retained what Engels called his "peculiar influence" on the leaders of working-class and Socialist movements. In 1879, when the French Socialist Workers' Federation was founded, its leader Jules Guesde went to London to consult with Marx, who dictated the preamble of its program and shaped much of its content. In 1881, Henry Mayers Hyndman in his *England for All* drew heavily on his conversations with Marx but angered him by being afraid to acknowledge him by name. During his last years Marx spent much time at health resorts and even travelled to Algiers. He was broken by the death of his wife on December 2, 1881, and of his eldest daughter, Jenny Longuet, on January 11, 1883. He died in London, evidently of a lung abscess, on March 14, 1883.

Character and significance.   At his funeral in Highgate Cemetery, Engels declared that Marx had made two great discoveries, the law of development of human history and the law of motion of bourgeois society. But "Marx was before all else a revolutionist." He was "the best-hated and most-calumniated man of his time," yet he also died "beloved, revered and mourned by millions of revolutionary fellow-workers."

Das
Kapital Marx's masterpiece, *Das Kapital*, the "Bible of the working class," as it was officially described in a resolution of the International Working Men's Association, was published in 1867 in Berlin and received a second edition in 1873. Only the first volume was completed and published in Marx's lifetime. The second and third volumes, edited by Engels, were published in 1885 and 1894. The economic categories he employed were those of the clas-

sical British economics of David Ricardo; but Marx used them in accordance with his dialectic method to argue that bourgeois society, like every social organism, must follow its inevitable path of development. Through the working of such immanent tendencies as the declining rate of profit, capitalism would die and be replaced by another, higher, society. The most memorable pages in *Das Kapital* are the descriptive passages, culled from Parliamentary Blue Books, on the misery of the English working class. Marx believed that this misery would increase, while at the same time the monopoly of capital would become a fetter upon production until finally "the knell of capitalist private property sounds. The expropriators are expropriated."

Marx never claimed to have discovered the existence of classes and class struggles in modern society. "Bourgeois" historians, he acknowledged, had dealt with them long before he had. He did claim, however, to have proved that each phase in the development of production was associated with a corresponding class structure and that the struggle of classes led necessarily to the dictatorship of the proletariat, ushering in the advent of a classless society. It is difficult to see how he could have regarded the few paragraphs he had written on these themes as constituting proof by any scientific standard.

In his character, Marx was a combination of the Promethean rebel and the helpless intellectual. He gave most persons an impression of intellectual arrogance. A Russian writer, Pavel Annenkov, who observed Marx in debate in 1846 recalled that "he spoke only in the imperative, brooking no contradiction," and seemed to be "the personification of a democratic dictator such as might appear before one in moments of fantasy." But Marx obviously felt uneasy before mass audiences and avoided the atmosphere of factional controversies at congresses. He went to no demonstrations, his wife remarked, and rarely spoke at public meetings. He kept away from the congresses of the International where the rival Socialist groups debated important resolutions. He was a "small groups" man, most at home in the atmosphere of the General Council or on the staff of a newspaper, where his character could impress itself forcefully on a small body of coworkers. At the same time he avoided meeting distinguished scholars with whom he might have discussed questions of economics and sociology on a footing of intellectual equality. Despite his broad intellectual sweep, he was prey to obsessive ideas such as that the British foreign minister, Lord Palmerston, was an agent of the Russian government. He was determined not to let bourgeois society make "a money-making machine" out of him, yet submitted to living on the largess of Engels and the bequests of relatives. He was an affectionate father, saying that he admired Jesus for his love of children, but sacrificed the lives and health of his own. He regarded "struggle" as the law of life and existence. It pervaded his vocabulary so that he thought of learning another language as acquiring another weapon in the struggle of life. Yet he remained the eternal student in his personal habits and way of life, even to the point of joining two friends in a students' prank during which they systematically broke four or five streetlamps in a London street and then fled from the police. He was a great reader of novels, especially those of Sir Walter Scott and Balzac; and the family made a cult of Shakespeare. Of his seven children, three daughters grew to maturity. His favourite daughter, Eleanor, worried him with her nervous, brooding, emotional character and her desire to be an actress. Another shadow was cast on Marx's domestic life by the birth to their loyal servant, Helene Demuth, of an illegitimate son, Frederick; Engels as he was dying disclosed to Eleanor that Marx had been the father.

Marx's most important contribution to sociological theory was his general mode of analysis, the "dialectical" model, which regards every social system as having within it immanent forces that give rise to "contradictions" (disequilibria) that can only be resolved by a new social system. Neo-Marxists, who no longer accept the economic reasoning in *Das Kapital*, are still guided by this model in their approach to capitalist society. In this sense, The
"dialec-
tical"
model

Marx's mode of analysis, like those of Thomas Malthus, Herbert Spencer, or Vilfredo Pareto, has become one of the theoretical structures that are the heritage of the social scientist. His mode of thought has, however, been opposed by such empirically minded philosophers as Bertrand Russell, John Dewey, and Karl Popper.

MAJOR WORKS

Misère de la philosophie (1847; *The Poverty of Philosophy*, 1900); *Manifest der Kommunistischen Partei* (1848; *The Communist Manifesto*, trans. by E. and C. Paul, 1930; *Manifesto of the Communist Party*, trans. by S. Moore, new ed., 1952); *Die Klassenkämpfe in Frankreich 1848 bis 1850* (1850; *The Class Struggles in France, 1848 to 1850*, 1924); *Der Achtzehnte Brumaire des Louis Bonaparte* (1852; *The 18th Brumaire of Louis Napoleon*, trans. by E. and C. Paul, 1926); *Zur Kritik der politischen Ökonomie* (1859; *A Contribution to the Critique of Political Economy*, trans. by N.I. Stone, 1904); *Das Kapital* (vol. 1, 1867; vol. 2–3 published by Engels in 1885 and 1894; Eng. trans., *Capital: A Critique of Political Economy*, vol. 1 by S. Moore and E. Aveling, 1886; vol. 2–3 by E. Untermann, 1907 and 1909; rev. trans., 1952).

BIBLIOGRAPHY. The authoritative biography of Marx is FRANZ MEHRING, *Karl Marx: Geschichte seines Lebens* (1918; Eng. trans., *Karl Marx: The Story of His Life*, 1935; paperback edition, 1962). Mehring was an intense adherent to the left wing of German Social Democracy and his partisanship influenced his interpretation of such episodes as Marx's relations to Lassalle. BORIS NICHOLAEVSKY and OTTO MAENCHEN-HELFEN, *Karl Marx: Man and Fighter* (1936), reconstructs effectively the opposition of Marx to revolutionary adventures. OTTO RUHLE, *Karl Marx: Leben und Werk* (1928; Eng. trans., *Karl Marx: His Life and Work*, 1929), is a good general biography, especially interesting for its account of Marx's psychological sense of inferiority. Of all the literature of personal recollections, the most informative is WILHELM LIEBKNECHT, *Karl Marx, zum Gedächtniss: Ein Lebensabriss und Erinnerungen* (1896; Eng. trans., *Karl Marx: Biographical Memoirs*, 1901); DAVID RYAZANOFF (ed.), *Karl Marx: Man, Thinker and Revolutionist* (1927; orig. pub. in Russian, 1919), is a well-edited collection. The documentary evidence concerning Marx's natural son was first published in WERNER BLUMENBERG, *Karl Marx in Selbstzeugnissen und Bilddokumenten* (1962); this material and other phases of Marx's personal life are also discussed in CHUSHICHI TSUZUKI, *The Life of Eleanor Marx, 1855–1898: A Socialist Tragedy* (1967); and ROBERT PAYNE, *Marx* (1968). Marx's relations to the Young Hegelians are most fully discussed in SIDNEY HOOK, *From Hegel to Marx* (1936). H.P. ADAMS, *Karl Marx in His Earlier Writings* (1940), is a useful summary. DAVID RYAZANOFF, the most scholarly of the early Soviet students of Marx, wrote a painstaking study, *The Communist Manifesto of Karl Marx and Friedrich Engels* (1930; orig. pub. in Russian, 1922). BERTRAM D. WOLFE, *Marxism: One Hundred Years in the Life of a Doctrine* (1965), has an informative account of Marx's relations to the Paris Commune. The most thorough study of Marx's attitude to the Jews is EDMUND SILBERNER, "Was Marx an Anti-Semite?" *Historia Judaica*, 11:3–52 (1949). Marx's national and racial feelings are set forth in SOLOMON F. BLOOM, *The World of Nations: A Study of the National Implications in the Work of Karl Marx* (1941). His utopian phase and his relations to Americans are dealt with in LEWIS S. FEUER, *Marx and the Intellectuals* (1969). The best short accounts of Marx's life and work are KARL KORSCH, *Karl Marx* (1938); and ISAIAH BERLIN, *Karl Marx: His Life and Environment*, 3rd ed. (1963).

Marx's writings: The most complete bibliography of Marx's writings is MAXIMILIEN RUBEL, *Bibliographie des oeuvres de Karl Marx* (1956), and its *Supplément* (1960). A German edition of the collected works of Marx and Engels, *Werke* (1961–68), has been published in 39 volumes and two supplementary ones. A comparative index of their writings is provided by the volume *Marx Engels Verzeichnis, Werke Schriften Artikel* (1966). The volumes of D. RJAZANOV and V. ADORATSKY (eds.), *Marx-Engels, Historisch-Kritische Gesamtausgabe* (1927–35), still remain useful. The basic works of Marx have been published in English translation; the second volume of DONALD DREW EGBERT, STOW PERSONS, and T.D. SEYMOUR BASSETT, *Socialism and American Life* (1952), provides a guide to them. Many collections of Marx's pamphlets, articles, and correspondence have been edited with reference to particular historical themes: *The American Journalism of Marx and Engels: A Selection from the New York Tribune* (1966); *The Civil War in the United States* (1937); *Revolution in Spain* (1939); *On Britain* (n.d.); *Karl Marx on Colonialism and Modernization* (1968); *On Religion* (1964); *On Colonialism* (1960); *Marx on China, 1853–1860* (1951); *The Russian Menace to Europe* (1953); and *Marx and Engels on Malthus* (1953). KARL MARX and FRIEDRICH ENGELS, *Correspondence 1846–1895* (Eng. trans. 1934), is a useful collection, as are similar volumes of selected correspondence published in Moscow in 1955 and 1965, the last being the most inclusive.

(L.S.F.)

Marxism

The term Marxism is used in a number of different ways. In its most essential meaning it refers to the thought of Karl Marx, sometimes extended to include that of his friend and collaborator Friedrich Engels. There is also Marxism as it has been understood and practiced by the various Socialist movements, particularly before 1914. Then there is Soviet Marxism as worked out by Lenin and modified by Stalin, which under the name of Marxism-Leninism became the doctrine of the Communist parties set up after the Russian Revolution. An offshoot of this is Marxism as interpreted by the anti-Stalinist Leon Trotsky and his followers. There is Mao Tse-tung's Chinese variant of Marxism-Leninism. There are the post-World War II nondogmatic Marxisms that have modified Marx's thought with borrowings from modern philosophies, principally from those of Edmund Husserl and Martin Heidegger, but also from Sigmund Freud and others.

THE THOUGHT OF KARL MARX

Karl Marx was both a man of action and a thinker. Of Jewish extraction and born into a well-to-do family in Trier in the Rhine province of Prussia on May 5, 1818, he died in exile in London on March 14, 1883. His father, a distinguished lawyer converted to Protestantism, had him baptized in 1824. The conversion of his father was to have the effect on Marx of making him independent of all religions. His adolescence was spent in the enlightened liberal Rhenish environment of that period. Later, he attached himself to a group who called themselves the Berlin Young Hegelians, who acquainted him with the historical critique of established religion and the works of Ludwig Feuerbach, a young philosopher in reaction against Hegel's thought. He turned to journalism and became editor of the *Rheinische Zeitung* in October 1842.

After his marriage in the summer of 1843, he went to live in Paris. In collaboration with Friedrich Engels, whom he came to know in 1844, he undertook a critique of the Hegelianism of the Young Hegelians, which he titled sarcastically *Die hielige Familie* (1845; *The Holy Family*, 1956). He contributed to a radical weekly, *Vorwärts*, until he was expelled from France. He then took up residence in Brussels, where he wrote *Misère de la philosophie* (1847; *The Poverty of Philosophy*, 1900), an attack on Pierre-Joseph Proudhon's book subtitled *Philosophie de la Misère* (1846; *The Philosophy of Poverty*, 1888). Together with Engels he acquired a local weekly, the *Deutsche Brüsseler Zeitung*. They established close ties with the Socialist labour movement and became members of the "League of the Just," a German secret society that had branches in London, Brussels, Paris, and Switzerland. It was for this association that they wrote the famous *Manifest der Kommunistischen Partei*, commonly known as *The Communist Manifesto*, which appeared at the beginning of 1848, the year of revolutions.

Several important studies date from this period (approximately 1843–46): "Zur Judenfrage" ("On the Jewish Question"); "Zur Kritik der Hegelschen Rechtsphilosophie" ("Toward a Critique of Hegel's Philosophy of Right"); and others which did not appear during Marx's lifetime.

From 1848 onward, the life of Marx cannot be separated from his written work and his political activity. He was expelled from Prussia in May 1849 and after a brief stay in Paris took refuge in London. In 1859, at the request of Engels, he published two chapters of *Zur Kritik der politischen Ökonomie* (*A Contribution to the Critique of Political Economy*, 1904); and in 1867 he published the first volume of *Das Kapital* (*Capital*, 1886). In 1864 he took part in the founding of the International Working Men's Association, of which he be-

Marx's writings and political activity

came the leader; it broke up in 1876. He proceeded with the preparation of the other volumes of *Das Kapital* without being able to finish them before his death.

The written work of Marx cannot be reduced to a philosophy, much less to a philosophical system. The whole of his work is a radical critique of philosophy, especially of Hegel's system and of the philosophies of the left and right post-Hegelians. It is not, however, a mere denial of those philosophies. Whereas, with Hegel, reality was made philosophy, Marx declared that philosophy must become reality. One could no longer be content with interpreting the world; one must be concerned with transforming it, which meant transforming both the world itself and men's consciousness of it. This, in turn, required a critique of experience together with a critique of ideas. For Marx, all knowledge involved a critique of ideas. He was not an empiricist. His work teems with concepts (appropriation, alienation, praxis, creative labour, value, etc.) inherited from earlier philosophers and economists, including Hegel, Johann Fichte, Kant, Adam Smith, David Ricardo, and J.S. Mill. What uniquely characterizes the thought of Marx is that, instead of making abstract affirmations about a whole group of problems such as man, knowledge, matter, nature, etc., he examines each in its dynamic relation to the others and, above all, tries to relate them to historical, social, political, and economic realities.

The human agenda. To go directly to the heart of the work of Marx, one must focus on his concrete program for man. This is just as important for an understanding of Marx as are *The Communist Manifesto* and *Das Kapital*. Marx's interpretation of man begins with human need. "Man," he writes in the so-called "Ökonomisch-philosophische Manuskripte aus dem Jahre 1844" (*Economic and Philosophic Manuscripts of 1844*, 1959),

is first of all a *natural being*. As a natural being and a living natural being, he is endowed on the one hand with *natural powers, vital powers* . . .; these powers exist in him as aptitudes, instincts. On the other hand, as an objective, natural, physical, sensitive being, he is a *suffering*, dependent and limited being . . ., that is, the *objects* of his instincts exist outside him, independent of him, but are the objects of his *need*, indispensable and essential for the realization and confirmation of his substantial powers.

The point of departure of human history is therefore living man, who seeks to satisfy certain primary needs. "The first historical fact is the production of the means to satisfy these needs." This satisfaction opens the way for new needs. Human activity is essentially a struggle with nature that must furnish man the means of satisfying his needs: drink, food, clothing, the development of his powers and then of his intellectual and artistic abilities. In this undertaking, man discovers himself as a productive being who humanizes himself by his labour. Furthermore, man humanizes nature while he naturalizes himself. By his creative activity, by his labour, he realizes his identity with the nature that he masters, while at the same time he achieves free consciousness. Born of nature man becomes fully human by opposing it. Becoming aware in his struggle against nature of what separates him from it, man finds the conditions of his fulfillment, of the realization of his true stature. The dawning of consciousness is inseparable from struggle. By appropriating all the creative energies, he discovers that "all that is called history is nothing else than the process of creating man through human labour, the becoming of nature for man. Man has thus evident and irrefutable proof of his own creation by himself." Understood in its universal dimension, human activity reveals that "for man, man is the supreme being." It is thus vain to speak of God, creation, and metaphysical problems. Fully naturalized, man is sufficient unto himself: he has recaptured the fullness of man in his full liberty.

Man as an alienated being

Living in a capitalist society, however, man is not truly free. He is an alienated being; he is not at home in his world. The idea of alienation, which Marx takes from Hegel and Feuerbach, plays a fundamental role in the whole of his written work, starting with the writings of his youth and continuing through *Das Kapital*. The causes of alienation come to have an increasingly economic and social content. In the *Economic and Philosophic Manuscripts*, the alienation of labour is seen to spring from the fact that the more the worker produces the less he has to consume, and the more values he creates the more he devalues himself, because his product and his labour are estranged from him. The life of the worker depends on capital; that is, on things that he has created but that are not his, so that instead of finding his rightful existence through his labour he loses it in this world of things that are external to him: no work, no pay. Under these conditions, labour denies the fullness of concrete man. "The generic being (*Gattungwesen*) of man, nature as well as his intellectual faculties, is transformed into a being which is alien to him, into a *means of his individual existence*." Nature, his body, his spiritual essence become alien to him. "Man is made alien to man." When carried to its highest stage of development, private property becomes "the product of alienated labour . . . the *means* by which labour alienates itself (and) the realization of this alienation." It is also at the same time "the tangible material expression of *alienated human* life." Though there is no evidence that Marx ever disclaimed this anthropological analysis of alienated labour, starting with *Die deutsche Ideologie* (1932; *The German Ideology*, 1938), the historical, social, and economic causes of the alienation of labour are given increasing emphasis, especially in *Das Kapital*. Alienated labour is seen as the consequence of market product, the division of labour, and the division of society into antagonistic classes.

Alienation under capitalism. As producers in society, men create goods only by their labour. These goods are exchangeable. Their value is the average amount of social labour spent to produce them. The alienation of the worker takes on its full dimension in that system of market production in which part of the value of the goods produced by the worker is taken away from him and transformed into surplus value, which the capitalist privately appropriates. Market production also intensifies the alienation of labour by encouraging specialization, piecework, and the setting up of large enterprises. Thus the labour power of the worker is used along with that of others in a combination whose significance he is ignorant of, both individually and socially. In thus losing their quality as human products, the products of labour become fetishes, that is, alien and oppressive realities to which both the man who possesses them privately and the man who is deprived of them submit themselves. In the market economy, this submission to things is obscured by the fact that the exchange of goods is expressed in money.

Existence and consciousness

This fundamental economic alienation is accompanied by secondary political and ideological alienations, which offer a distorted representation of and an illusory justification of a world in which the relations of men with one another are also distorted. The ideas that men form are closely bound up with their material activity and their material relations: "The act of making representations, of thinking, the spiritual intercourse of men, seem to be the direct emanation of their material relations." This is true of all human activity: political, intellectual, or spiritual. "Men produce their representations and their ideas, but it is as living men, men acting as they are determined by a definite development of their powers of production." Law, morality, metaphysics, and religion do not have a history of their own. "Men developing their material production modify together with their real existence their ways of thinking and the products of their ways of thinking." In other words, "it is not consciousness which determines existence, it is existence which determines consciousness."

In bourgeois, capitalist society man is divided into citizen and economic man. This duality represents man's political alienation, which is further intensified by the functioning of the bourgeois state. From this study of society at the beginning of the 19th century, Marx came to see the state as the instrument through which the propertied class dominated other classes. "The social structure and the state issue continually from the life processes of definite individuals . . . as they are *in reality*, that is, acting and materially producing."

Ideological alienation, for Marx, takes different forms, appearing in economic, philosophical, and legal theories. Marx undertook a lengthy critique of the first in *Das Kapital* and of the second in *The German Ideology*. But ideological alienation expresses itself supremely in religion. Taking up the ideas about religion that were current in left post-Hegelian circles, together with the thought of Feuerbach, Marx considered religion to be a product of man's consciousness. It is a reflection of the situation of a man who "either has not conquered himself or has already lost himself again" (man in the world of private property). It is "an opium for the people." Unlike Feuerbach, Marx believed that religion would disappear only with changes in society.

Historical materialism. In 1859, in the preface to his *Contribution to the Critique of Political Economy*, Marx wrote that the hypothesis that had served him as the basis for his analysis of society could be briefly formulated as follows:

> in the social production that men carry on, they enter into definite relations that are indispensable and independent of their will, relations of production which correspond to a definite stage of development of their material forces of production. The sum total of these relations of production constitutes the economic structure of society, the real foundation, on which rises a legal and political superstructure, and to which correspond definite forms of social consciousness. The mode of production in material life determines the general character of the social, political, and intellectual processes of life. It is not the consciousness of men which determines their existence; it is on the contrary their social existence which determines their consciousness.

Raised to the level of historical law, this hypothesis was subsequently called historical materialism. Marx applied it to capitalist society, both in *The Communist Manifesto* and *Das Kapital* and in other writings—for example, the articles written in the *Neue Rheinische Zeitung* and collected under the title *Die Klassenkämpfe in Frankreich 1848 bis 1850* (1895; *The Class Struggles in France, 1848–50*, 1924) or the pamphlet, written in 1852, *Der Achtzehnte Brumaire des Louis Bonaparte* (1914; *The Eighteenth Brumaire of Louis Bonaparte*, 1926). But the latter two are less systematic than *The Communist Manifesto*. Although Marx reflected upon his working hypothesis for many years, he did not formulate it in a very exact manner: different expressions served him for identical realities. If one takes the text literally, social reality is structured in the following way:

1. Underlying everything as the real basis of society is the economic structure (what in late 20th-century language is sometimes called the infrastructure) that includes (a) the "material forces of production" and (b) the overall "relations of production." Though there is a correspondence between the "material forces" of production and indispensable "relations" of production, Marx never made himself clear on the nature of the correspondence, a fact that was to be the source of differing interpretations among his later followers. Moreover, he never elucidated the difference between forces of production and relations of production.

2. Above the economic structure rises the superstructure consisting of legal and political "forms of social consciousness" that correspond to the economic structure. Marx says nothing about the nature of this correspondence between ideological forms and economic structure, except that through the ideological forms men become conscious of the conflict within the economic structure between the material forces of production and the existing relations of production expressed in the legal property relations. In other words, "the sum total of the forces of production accessible to men determines the condition of society" and is at the base of society. "The social structure and the state issue continually from the life processes of definite individuals . . . as they are *in reality*, that is acting and materially producing." The political relations that men establish among themselves are dependent on material production, as are the legal relations. This reduction of the social to the economic is not an incidental point: it colours Marx's whole analysis. It is

found in *Das Kapital* as well as in *The German Ideology* and the *Economic and Philosophic Manuscripts of 1844*.

Marx puts these methods and concepts to use in *Das Kapital*, in which he analyzes the market economy system. In this work he borrows most of the categories of the classical English economists Smith and Ricardo but adapts them and introduces new concepts such as that of surplus value.

Das Kapital

Analysis of the economy. One of the distinguishing marks of *Das Kapital* is that in it Marx studies the economy as a whole and not in one or another of its aspects. His analysis is based on the idea that man is a productive being and that all economic value comes from human labour. The system he analyzes is principally that of mid-19th-century England. It is a system of private enterprise and competition that arose in the 16th century from the development of sea routes, international trade, and colonialism. Its rise had been facilitated by changes in the forces of production (the division of labour and the concentration of workshops), the adoption of mechanization, and technical progress. The wealth of the societies that brought this economy into play had been acquired through an "enormous accumulation of commodities." Marx therefore begins with the study of this accumulation. He analyzes the unequal exchanges that take place in the market. If the capitalist advances funds to buy cotton yarn with which to produce fabrics and sells the product for a larger sum than he paid, he is able to invest the difference in additional production. "Not only is the value advance kept in circulation, but it changes in its magnitude, adds a plus to itself, makes itself worth more, and it is this movement that transforms it into capital." The transformation, to Marx, is possible only because the capitalist has appropriated the means of production, including the labour power of the worker. Now labour power produces more than it is worth. The value of labour power is determined by the amount of labour necessary for its reproduction or, in other words, by the amount needed for the worker to subsist and beget children. But in the hands of the capitalist the labour power employed in the course of a day produces more than the value of the sustenance required by the worker and his family. The difference between the two values is appropriated by the capitalist, and it corresponds exactly to the surplus value realized by capitalists in the market. Marx is not concerned with whether in capitalist society there are sources of surplus value other than the exploitation of human labour—a fact pointed out by Joseph Schumpeter (*Capitalism, Socialism, and Democracy*). He remains content with emphasizing this primary source:

> Surplus value is produced by the employment of labour power. Capital buys the labour power and pays the wages for it. By means of his work the labourer creates new value which does not belongs to him, but to the capitalist. He must work a certain time merely in order to reproduce the equivalent value of his wages. But when this equivalent value has been returned, he does not cease work, but continues to do so for some further hours. The new value which he produces during this extra time, and which exceeds in consequence the amount of his wage, constitutes surplus value.

The introduction of machinery is profitable to the individual capitalist because it enables him to produce more goods at a lower cost, but new techniques are soon taken up by his competitors. The outlay for machinery grows faster than the outlay for wages. Since only labour can produce the surplus value from which profit is derived, this means that the capitalist's rate of profit on his total outlay tends to decline. Along with the declining rate of profit goes an increase in unemployment. Throughout his analysis, Marx argues that the development of capitalism is accompanied by increasing contradictions. The equilibrium of the system is precarious, subject as it is to the internal pressures resulting from its own development. Crises shake it at regular intervals, preludes to the general crisis that will sweep it away. This instability is increased by the formation of a reserve army of workers, both factory workers and peasants, whose pauperization keeps increasing. "Capitalist production develops the technique

The crises of capitalism

and the combination of the process of social production only by exhausting at the same time the two sources from which all wealth springs: the earth and the worker."

Class struggle.   Two basic classes, around which other less important classes are grouped, oppose each other in the capitalist system: the owners of the means of production, or bourgeoisie, and the workers, or proletariat. With the development of capitalism, the class struggle takes an acute form. "The bourgeoisie produces its own grave-diggers. The fall of the bourgeoisie and the victory of the proletariat are equally inevitable" (*The Communist Manifesto*). For

the bourgeois relations of production are the last contradictory form of the process of social production, contradictory not in the sense of an individual contradiction, but of a contradiction that is born of the conditions of social existence of individuals; however, the forces of production which develop in the midst of bourgeois society create at the same time the material conditions for resolving this contradiction. With this social development the prehistory of human society ends.

When man has become aware of his loss, of his alienation, as a universal nonhuman situation, it will be possible for him to proceed to a radical transformation of his situation by a revolution. This revolution will be the prelude to the establishment of Communism and the reign of liberty reconquered. "In the place of the old bourgeois society with its classes and its class antagonisms, there will be an association in which the free development of each is the condition for the free development of all."

Marx inherited the ideas of class and class struggle from Utopian Socialism and the theories of Saint-Simon. These had been given substance by the writings of French historians such as Adolphe Thiers and François Guizot on the French Revolution of 1789. But unlike the French historians, Marx made class struggle the central fact of social evolution. "The history of all hitherto existing human society is the history of class struggles."

But for Marx there are two views of revolution. One is that of a final conflagration, "a *violent* suppression of the old conditions of production," which occurs when the opposition between bourgeoisie and proletariat has been carried to its extreme point. This conception is set forth in a manner inspired by the Hegelian dialectic of the master and the slave, in *The Holy Family*. The other conception is that of a permanent revolution involving a provisional coalition between the proletariat and the petty bourgeoisie rebelling against a capitalism that is only superficially united. Once a majority has been won to the coalition, an unofficial proletarian authority constitutes itself alongside the revolutionary bourgeois authority. Its mission is the political and revolutionary education of the proletariat, gradually assuring the transfer of legal power from the revolutionary bourgeoisie to the revolutionary proletariat.

If one reads *The Communist Manifesto* carefully one discovers inconsistencies that indicate that Marx had not reconciled the concepts of catastrophic and of permanent revolution. Moreover, Marx never analyzed classes as specific groups of men opposing other groups of men. Depending on the writings and the periods, the number of classes varies; and unfortunately the pen fell from Marx's hand at the moment when, in *Das Kapital* (volume 3), he was about to take up the question. Reading *Das Kapital*, one is furthermore left with an ambiguous impression with regard to the destruction of capitalism: will it be the result of the "general crisis" that Marx expects, or of the action of the conscious proletariat, or of both at once?

The contributions of Engels.   Friedrich Engels (1820–95), the son of a manufacturer, was Marx's closest associate and most intimate friend from 1844 to 1883. He became a Communist in 1842 and discovered the proletariat of England when he took over the management of a Manchester factory belonging to his father's cotton firm. In 1844 in Paris he became a friend of Marx. Engels was finishing his "Umrisse zu einer Kritik der Nationalökonomie" ("Outline of a Critique of Political Economy") —a critique of Smith, Ricardo, Mill, and J.B. Say. This remarkable study contained in seminal form the critique

that Marx was to make of bourgeois political economy in *Das Kapital*. During the first years of his stay in Manchester, Engels observed carefully the life of the workers of that great industrial centre and described it in *Die Lage der arbeitenden Klassen in England*, published in 1845 in Leipzig (*The Condition of the Working Class in England*, 1887). This work was an analysis of the evolution of industrial capitalism and its social consequences. He collaborated with Marx in the writing of *The Holy Family*, *The German Ideology*, and *The Communist Manifesto*. The correspondence between them is of fundamental importance for the student of *Das Kapital*, for it shows how Engels contributed by furnishing Marx with a great amount of technical and economic data and by criticizing the successive drafts. This collaboration lasted until Marx's death and was carried on posthumously with the publication of the manuscripts left by Marx, which Engels edited, forming volumes 2 and 3 of *Das Kapital*. He also wrote various articles on Marx's work.

In response to criticism of Marx's ideas by a socialist named Eugen Dühring, Engels published several articles that were collected under the title *Herr Eugen Dührings Umwälzung der Wissenschaft*, which appeared in 1878 (*Herr Eugen Dühring's Revolution in Science* [Anti-Dühring], 1934) and an unfinished work, *Dialektik und Natur* (1927; *Dialectics of Nature*, 1940), which he had begun around 1875–76. The importance of these writings to the subsequent development of Marxism can be seen from Lenin's observation that he "developed, in a clear and often polemical style, the most general scientific questions and the different phenomena of the past and present according to the materialist understanding of history and the economic theory of Karl Marx." But Engels was driven to simplify problems with a view to being pedagogical; he tended to schematize and systematize things as if the fundamental questions were settled. The connections that he thus established between some of Marx's governing ideas and some of the scientific ideas of his age gave rise to the notion that there is a complete Marxist philosophy. The idea was to play a significant role in the transition of Marxism from a "critique of daily life" to an integrated doctrine in which philosophy, history, and the sciences are fused.

Anti-Dühring is of fundamental importance for it constitutes the link between Marx and certain forms of modern Marxism. It contains three parts: Philosophy, Political Economy, and Socialism. In the first, Engels attempts to establish that the natural sciences and even mathematics are dialectical, in the sense that observable reality is dialectical: the dialectical method of analysis and thought is imposed on men by the material forces with which they deal. It is thus rightly applied to the study of history and human society. "Motion, in effect, is the mode of existence of matter," Engels writes. In using materialistic dialectic to make a critique of Dühring's thesis, according to which political forces prevail over all the rest in the molding of history, Engels provides a good illustration of the "materialistic idea of history," which puts the stress on the prime role of economic factors as driving forces in history. The other chapters of the section on Political Economy form a very readable introduction to the principal economic ideas of Marx: value (simple and complex), labour, capital, surplus value, and ground rent. The section on Socialism starts by formulating anew the critique of the capitalist system as it was made in *Das Kapital*. At the end of the chapters devoted to production, distribution, the state, the family, and education, Engels outlines what the Socialist society will be like, a society in which the notion of value has no longer anything to do with the distribution of the goods produced because all labour "becomes at once and directly social labour," and the amount of social labour that every product contains no longer needs to be ascertained by "a detour." A production plan will coordinate the economy. The division of labour and the separation of town and country will disappear with the "suppression of the capitalist character of modern industry." Thanks to the plan, industry will be located throughout the country in the collective interest, and thus the opposition between town and country will disappear—to the profit of both industry

Two views of revolution

Engels' critique of Dühring

and agriculture. Finally, after the liberation of man from the condition of servitude in which the capitalist mode of production holds him, the state will also be abolished and religion will disappear by "natural death."

One of the most remarkable features of *Anti-Dühring* is the insistence with which Engels refuses to base Socialism on absolute values. He admits only relative values, linked to historical, economic, and social conditions. Socialism cannot possibly be based on ethical principles: each epoch can only successfully carry out that of which it is capable. Marx had written this in his preface of 1859.

GERMAN MARXISM AFTER ENGELS

The work of Kautsky and Bernstein. The theoretical leadership after Engels was taken by Karl Kautsky (1854–1938), editor of the official organ of the German Social Democratic Party, *Die Neue Zeit*. He wrote *Karl Marx' ökonomische Lehren* (1887; *The Economic Doctrines of Karl Marx*, 1925), in which the work of Marx is presented as essentially an *economic* theory. Kautsky reduced the ideas of Marx and Marxist historical dialectic to a kind of evolutionism. He laid stress on the increasing pauperization of the working class and on the increasing degree of capitalist concentration. While opposing all compromise with the bourgeois state, he accepted the contention that the Socialist movement should support laws benefitting the workers provided that they did not reinforce the power of the state. Rejecting the idea of an alliance between the working class and the peasantry, he believed that the overthrow of the capitalist state and the acquisition of political power by the working class could be realized in a peaceful way, without upsetting the existing structures. As an internationalist he supported peace, rejecting war and violence. For him, war was a product of capitalism. Such were the main features of "orthodox" German Marxism at the time when the "revisionist" theories of Eduard Bernstein appeared.

Doctrinal disputes

Bernstein (1850–1932) created a great controversy with articles that he wrote in 1896 for *Die Neue Zeit*, arguing that Marxism needed to be revised. His divergence widened with the publication in 1899 of *Die Voraussetzungen des Sozialismus und die Ausgaben der Sozialdemokratie* (Eng. trans., *Evolutionary Socialism*, 1909), to which rejoinders were made by Kautsky in *Bernstein und das Sozialdemokratische Programm: Eine Antikritik* (1899; "Bernstein and the Social Democratic Program") and the Polish-born Marxist Rosa Luxemburg in *Sozialreform oder Revolution* (Engl. trans. 1951, *Reform or Revolution*), both in 1899. The critique of Bernstein focussed first of all upon the labour theory of value. Along with the economists of his time he considered it outdated, both in the form expounded by British classical economists and as set forth in *Das Kapital*. He argued, moreover, that class struggle was becoming less rather than more intense, for concentration was not accelerating in industry as Marx had forecast, and in agriculture it was not increasing at all. Bernstein demonstrated this on the basis of German, Dutch, and English statistical data. He also argued that cartels and business syndicates were smoothing the evolution of capitalism, a fact that cast doubt on the validity of Marx's theory of capitalistic crises. Arguing that quite a few of Marx's theories were not scientifically based, Bernstein blamed the Hegelian and Ricardian structure of Marx's work for his failure to take sufficient account of observable reality. Finally, he appealed to the dialectic of Hegel and the philosophy of Kant.

To this, Kautsky replied that, with the development of capitalism, agriculture was becoming a sector more and more dependent on industry, and that in addition an industrialization of agriculture was taking place. Rosa Luxemburg took the position that the contradictions of capitalism did not cease to grow with the progress of finance capitalism and the exploitation of the colonies, and that these contradictions were leading to a war that would give the proletariat its opportunity to assume power by revolutionary means.

The radicals. One of the most divisive questions was that of war and peace. This was brought to the fore at the outbreak of World War I, when Social Democratic deputies in the German Reichstag voted for the financing of the war. Among German Marxists who opposed the war were Karl Liebknecht and Rosa Luxemburg. Liebknecht (1871–1919) was imprisoned in 1916 for agitating against the war. On his release in 1918 he took the leadership of the Spartacist movement, which was later to become the Communist Party of Germany. Rosa Luxemburg (1871–1919) had also been arrested for her antimilitary activities. In addition to her articles, signed Junius, in which she debated with Lenin on the subject of the First World War and the attitude of the Marxists toward it (published in 1916 as *Die Krise der Sozialdemokratie* [*The Crisis in the German Social-Democracy*, 1919]), she is known for her book *Die Akkumulation des Kapitals* (1913; *The Accumulation of Capital*, 1951). In this work she returns to Marx's economic analysis of capitalism, in particular the accumulation of capital as expounded in volume 2 of *Das Kapital*. There she finds a contradiction that had until then been unnoticed: Marx's scheme seems to imply that the development of capitalism can be indefinite, though elsewhere he sees the contradictions of the system as bringing about increasingly violent economic crisis that will inevitably sweep capitalism away. Luxemburg concludes that Marx's scheme is oversimplified and assumes a universe made up entirely of capitalists and workers. If increases in productivity are taken into account, she asserts, balance between the two sectors becomes impossible; in order to keep expanding capitalists must find new markets in noncapitalist spheres, either among peasants and artisans or in colonies and underdeveloped countries. Capitalism will collapse only when exploitation of the world outside it (the peasantry, colonies, etc.) has reached a limit. This conclusion has been the subject of passionate controversies.

Karl Liebknecht and Rosa Luxemburg

The Austrians. The Austrian school came into being when Austrian Socialists started publishing their works independently of the Germans; it can be dated from either 1904 (beginning of the *Marx-Studien* collection) or 1907 (publication of the magazine *Der Kampf*). The most important members of the school were Max Adler, Karl Renner, Rudolf Hilferding, Gustav Eckstein, Friedrich Adler, and Otto Bauer. The most eminent was Bauer (1881–1938), a brilliant theoretician whose *Die Nationalitätenfrage und die Sozialdemokratie* (1906; "The Nationalities Question and the Social Democracy") was critically reviewed by Lenin. In this work he dealt with the problem of nationalities in the light of the experience of the Austro-Hungarian Empire. He favoured the self-determination of peoples and emphasized the cultural elements in the concept of nationhood. Rudolf Hilferding (1877–1941) was finance minister of the German Republic after World War I in the Cabinets of Gustav Stresemann (1923) and Mueller (1928). He is known especially for his work *Das Finanzkapital* (1910), in which he maintained that capitalism had come under the control of banks and industrial monopolies. The growth of national competition and tariff barriers, he believed, had led to economic warfare abroad. Hilferding's ideas strongly influenced Lenin, who analyzed them in *Imperialism, the Highest Stage of Capitalism* (1916).

RUSSIAN AND SOVIET MARXISM

Das Kapital was translated into Russian in 1872. Marx kept up more or less steady relations with the Russian Socialists and took an interest in the economic and social conditions of the tsarist empire. The man who actually introduced Marxism into Russia was Georgi Plekhanov (1856–1918). But the man who adapted Marxism to Russian conditions was Lenin.

Lenin's adaptation of Marxism

Lenin. Vladimir Ilich Ulyanov, or Lenin, was born in 1870 at Simbirsk (Ulyanovsk today). He entered the University of Kazan to study law but was expelled the same year for participating in student agitation. In 1893 he settled in St. Petersburg and became actively involved with the revolutionary workers. With his pamphlet *What Is To Be Done?* (1902), he specified the theoretical principles and organization of a Marxist party as he thought it should be constituted. He took part in the second Congress of the Russian Social-Democratic Workers' Party, which was held in Brussels and London (1903), and induced the majority of the Congress members to adopt his views. Two factions formed at the Congress: the *Bolshevik* (larger) with Lenin as their leader and the *Menshevik* (smaller) with Julius Martov at their head. The former wanted a restricted party of militants and advocated the dictatorship of the proletariat. The latter wanted a wide-open proletarian party, collaboration with the liberals, and a democratic constitution for Russia. In his pamphlet *One Step Forward, Two Steps Back* (1904), Lenin opposed the organizational principles of the Bolsheviks to those of the Mensheviks. After the failure of the 1905 Russian revolution, he drew positive lessons for the future in *Two Tactics of Social Democracy in the Democratic Revolution*. He fiercely attacked the influence of Kantian philosophy on German and Russian Marxism in *Materialism and Empirio-criticism* (1908). In 1912 at the Prague Conference the Bolsheviks constituted themselves as an independent party. During the first World War Lenin resided in Switzerland, where he studied Hegel's *Science of Logic* and the development of capitalism, and carried on debate with Marxists like Rosa Luxemburg on the meaning of the war and the right of nations to self-determination. In 1915 at Zimmerwald, and in 1916 at Kiental, he organized two international Socialist conferences to fight against the war. Immediately after the February 1917 revolution he returned to Russia, and in October the Bolshevik coup brought him to power.

The situation of Russia and the Russian revolutionary movement at the end of the 19th century and the beginning of the 20th led Lenin to diverge, in the course of his development and his analyses, from the positions both of "orthodox Marxism," and of "revisionism." He rediscovered the original thought of Marx by a careful study of his works, in particular *Das Kapital* and *The Holy Family*. He saw Marxism as a practical affair and tried to go beyond the accepted formulas to plan political action that would come to grips with the surrounding world.

A plan of political action

As early as 1894, in his populist study *The Friends of the People*, Lenin took up Marx's distinction between the "material social relations" of men and their "ideological social relations." In Lenin's eyes the importance of *Das Kapital* was that "while *explaining* the structure and the development of the social formation seen *exclusively* in terms of its relations of production, (Marx) has nevertheless everywhere and always analyzed the superstructure which corresponds to these relations of production." In *The Development of Russian Capitalism* (1897–99), Lenin sought to apply Marx's analysis by showing the growing role of capital, in particular commercial capital —the exploitation of the workers in the factories, and the large-scale expropriation of the peasants. It was thus possible to apply to Russia the models developed by Marx for western Europe. At the same time Lenin did not lose sight of the importance of the peasant in Russian society. Though a disciple of Marx, he did not believe that he had only to repeat Marx's conclusions. He wrote:

> We do not consider the theory of Marx to be a complete, immutable whole. We think on the contrary that this theory has only laid the cornerstone of the science, a science which socialists must further develop in all directions if they do not want to let themselves be overtaken by life. We think that, for the Russian socialists, an independent elaboration of the theory is particularly necessary.

Lenin laid great stress upon the dialectical method. In his early writings he defined the dialectic as "nothing more nor less than the method of sociology, which sees society as a living organism, in perpetual development (and not as something mechanically assembled and thus allowing all sorts of arbitrary combinations of the various social elements) . . ." (*The Friends of the People*, 1894). After having studied Hegel toward the end of 1914, he took a more activist view. Dialectic is not only evolution; it is *praxis*, leading from activity to reflection and from reflection to action.

The dictatorship of the proletariat. Lenin also put much emphasis on the leading role of the party. On the eve of the revolution of October 1917, in *State and Revolution* he set forth the conditions for the dictatorship of the proletariat and the suppression of the capitalist state. But as early as 1902 he was concerned with the need for a cohesive party with a correct doctrine, adapted to the exigencies of the period, which would be a motive force among the masses helping to bring them to an awareness of their real situation. In *What Is To Be Done?* he called for a party of professional revolutionaries, disciplined and directed, capable of defeating the police; its aims should be to establish the dictatorship of the proletariat. In order to do this, he wrote in 1905 in *Two Tactics of Social-Democracy in the Democratic Revolution*, it was necessary "to subject the insurrection of the proletarian and *non-proletarian* masses to our influence, to our direction, to use it in our best interests." But this was not possible without a doctrine: "Without revolutionary theory, no revolutionary movement."

Lenin assigned major importance to the peasantry in formulating his program. It would be a serious error, he held, for the Russian revolutionary workers' movement to neglect the peasants, even though, of course the industrial proletariat constituted the vanguard of the Revolution. But the discontent of the peasantry could be oriented in a direction favourable to the Revolution by placing among the goals of the party the seizure of privately owned land. As early as 1903 at the third Congress of the party, he secured a resolution to this effect. Thereafter, the dictatorship of the proletariat became the dictatorship of the proletariat and the peasantry. In 1917, he encouraged the peasants to seize land long before the approval of agrarian reform by the Constituent Assembly.

Among Lenin's legacies to Soviet Marxism was one that proved to be injurious to the party. This was the decision taken at his behest by the 10th Congress of the party in the spring of 1921, while the sailors were rebelling at Kronstadt and the peasants were growing restless in the countryside, to forbid all factions, all factional activity, and all opposition political platforms within the party. This decision had grave consequences in later years when Stalin used it against his opponents.

Stalin's ideas. It is to Joseph Stalin that we owe the body of ideas that, under the name of Marxism-Leninism, constitute the doctrine of the European Communist parties. Stalin was a man of action, in a slightly different sense than was Lenin. Gradually taking over power after Lenin's death in 1924, he pursued the development of the Soviet Union with great vigour. It was by practicing Marxism that he assimilated it; but at the same time he simplified it. Stalin's Marxism-Leninism rests on the dialectic of Hegel, as set forth in *A Short History of the Communist Party of the Soviet Union* (1938) and on a materialism that can be considered roughly identical to that of Feuerbach. His work *Problems of Leninism*, which appeared in eleven editions during his lifetime, sets forth an ideology of power and activism.

Soviet dialectical materialism can be reduced to four laws: (1) History is a dialectical development. It proceeds by successive phases which supersede one another. These phases are not separate, any more than birth, growth, and death are separate. Though it is true that phase B necessarily negates phase A, it remains that phase B was already contained in phase A and was initiated by it. The dialectic does not regard nature as an accidental accumulation of objects, of isolated and independent phenomena, but as a unified, coherent whole. Furthermore, nature is perpetually in movement, in a state of unceasing renewal and development, in which there is always something being born and developing and something disintegrating and disappearing. (2) Evolution takes place in leaps, not gradually. (3) Contradictions must be made manifest. All phenomena contain in themselves contradictory elements. "Dialectic starts from the point of view that objects and natural phenomena imply internal contradictions, because they all have a positive and a negative side." These contradictory elements are in perpetual struggle: it is this struggle that is the "internal

Stalin and dialectical materialism

content of the process of development," according to Stalin. (4) The law of this development is economic. All other contradictions are rooted in the basic economic relationship. A given epoch is entirely determined by the relations of production existing among men. They are *social* relations; relations of collaboration or mutual aid; relations of domination or submission; and finally, transitory relations that characterize a period of passage from one system to another. "The history of the development of society is, above all, the history of the development of production, the history of the modes of production which succeed one another through the centuries."

From these principles may be drawn the following inferences, essential for penetrating the workings of Marxist-Leninist thought and its application: no natural phenomenon, no historical or social situation, no political fact, can be considered independently of the other facts or phenomena which surround it. It is set within a whole. Since movement is the essential fact, one must distinguish between what is beginning to decay and what is being born and developing. Since the process of development takes place by leaps, one passes suddenly from a succession of slow quantitative changes to a radical qualitative change. In the social or political realm, these sudden qualitative changes are revolutions, carried out by the oppressed classes. One must follow a frankly proletarian-class policy that exposes the contradictions of the capitalist system. A reformist policy makes no sense. Consequently (1) nothing can be judged from the point of view of "eternal justice" or any other preconceived notion and (2) no social system is immutable. To be effective, one must not base one's action on social strata that are no longer developing, even if they represent for the moment the dominant force, but on those that are developing.

Stalin's materialist and historical dialectic differs sharply from the perspective of Karl Marx. In *The Communist Manifesto* Marx applied the materialist dialectic to the social and political life of his time. In the chapter entitled "Bourgeois and Proletarians," he studied the process of the growth of the revolutionary bourgeoisie within feudal society, then the genesis and the growth of the proletariat within capitalism, placing the emphasis on the struggle between antagonistic classes. To be sure, he connected social evolution with the development of the forces of production. But what counted for him was not only the struggle but also the birth of consciousness among the proletariat. "As to the final victory of the propositions put forth in the *Manifesto*, Marx expected it to come primarily from the intellectual development of the working class, necessarily the result of common action and discussion" (F. Engels, preface to the republication of *The Communist Manifesto*, May 1, 1890).

For Stalin, on the contrary, what counted was the immediate goal, the practical result. The move was from a dialectic that emphasized both the objective and the subjective to one purely objective, or more exactly, objectivist. Human actions are to be judged not by taking account of the intentions of the actor and their place in a given historical web but only in terms of what they signify objectively at the end of the period considered.

Trotskyism. Alongside Marxism-Leninism as expounded in the Soviet Union there arose another point of view expressed by Stalin's opponent Leon Trotsky and his followers. Trotsky (1879–1940) played a leading role in both the Russian revolution of 1905 and that of 1917. After Lenin's death he fell out with Stalin. Their conflict turned largely upon questions of policy, both domestic and foreign. In the realm of ideas, Trotsky held that a revolution in a backward, rural country could only be carried out by the proletariat. Once in power the proletariat must carry out agrarian reform and undertake the accelerated development of the economy. The revolution must be a Socialist one, involving the abolition of the private ownership of the means of production, or else it will fail. But the revolution cannot be carried out in isolation, as Stalin maintained it could. The capitalist countries will try to destroy it; moreover, to succeed the revolution must be able to draw upon the industrial techniques of the developed countries. For these reasons the revolution must be worldwide and permanent, directed against the liberal and nationalist bourgeoisie of all countries and using local victories to advance the international struggle.

Tactically, Trotsky emphasized the necessity of finding or creating a revolutionary situation; of educating the working class in order to revolutionize it; of seeing that the party remained open to the various revolutionary tendencies and avoided becoming bureaucratized; and finally, when the time for insurrection comes, of organizing it according to a detailed plan.

Trotsky's tactical theories

VARIANTS OF SOVIET MARXISM

Maoism. When the Chinese Communists took power in 1948, they brought with them a new kind of Marxism that came to be called Maoism after their leader Mao Tse-tung. The thought of Mao must always be seen against the changing revolutionary reality of China, from 1930 onward. His thought is complex, a Marxist type of analysis combined with the permanent fundamentals of Chinese thought and culture.

One of its central elements has to do with the nature and role of contradictions in Socialist society. For Mao, every society, including Socialist (Communist) society, contains "two different types of contradictions": (1) antagonistic contradictions; *e.g.*, contradictions between us (the people) and our enemies (the Chinese bourgeoisie faithful), between the imperialist camp and the Socialist camp, etc. These contradictions are resolved by revolution; (2) nonantagonistic contradictions; *e.g.*, between the government and the people under a Socialist regime, between two groups within the Communist party, between one section of the people and another under a Communist regime, etc. These contradictions are resolved by vigorous fraternal criticism and self-criticism.

The notion of contradiction is specific to Mao's thought in that it differs from the conceptions of Marx or Lenin. For Mao, in effect, contradictions are at the same time universal and particular. In their universality, one must seek and discover what constitutes their particularity: every contradiction displays a particular character, depending on the nature of things and phenomena. Contradictions have alternating aspects—sometimes strongly marked, sometimes blurred. Some of these aspects are primary, others secondary. It is important to define them well for if one fails to do so, the analysis of the social reality and the actions that follow from it will be mistaken. This is quite far from Stalinism and dogmatic Marxism-Leninism.

Another essential element of Mao's thought, which must be seen in the context of revolutionary China, is the notion of permanent revolution. It is an old idea advocated in different contexts by Marx, Lenin, and Trotsky. For Mao it follows from his ideas about the struggle of man against nature (held since 1938, at least); the campaigns for the rectification of thought (1942, 1951, 1952); and the necessity of struggling against bureaucracy, wastage, and corruption in a country of 600,000,000 to 700,000,000 inhabitants, where very old civilizations and cultures still permeate both the bourgeois classes and the peasantry, where bureaucracy is thoroughly entrenched, and where the previous society was extremely corrupt. It arises from Mao's conviction that the rhythm of the revolution must be accelerated. This conviction appeared in 1957 in his speeches and became manifest in 1958 in the "Great Leap Forward," followed in 1966 by the Cultural Revolution.

The Chinese element in Maoism

Mao's concept of permanent revolution rests upon the existence of nonantagonistic contradictions in the China of today and of tomorrow. Men must be mobilized into a permanent movement in order to carry forward the revolution and to prevent the ruling group from turning bourgeois (as he asserts it has in the Soviet Union). It is necessary to shape among the masses a new vision of the world by tearing them from their passivity and their century-old habits. This is the background of the Cultural Revolution that began in 1966, following upon previous campaigns but differing from them in its magnitude and, it would seem, in the mobilization of youth against the cadres of the party. In these campaigns Mao drew upon his past as a revolutionary Marxist peasant leader, from his life in the red military and peasant bases and among the Red Guards of Yenan, seeking in his past experience ways to mobilize the whole Chinese population against the dangers—internal and external—that confronted it in the present.

The distinguishing characteristic of Maoism is that it represents a peasant type of Marxism, with a principally rural and military outlook. While basing himself on Marxism-Leninism, adapted to Chinese requirements, Mao is rooted in the peasant life from which he himself came, in the revolts against the warlords and the bureaucrats that have filled the history of China. By integrating this experience into a universal vision of history, Mao gives it a significance that overflows the provincial limits of China.

In his effort to remain close to the Chinese peasant masses, Mao draws upon an idea of nature and a symbolism found in popular Chinese Taoism, though transformed by his Marxism. It can be seen in his many poems, which are written in the classical Chinese style. This idea of nature is accompanied in his written political works by the other, Promethean idea of man struggling in a war against nature, a conception in his thought that goes back at least to 1938 and became more important after 1955 as the rhythm of the revolution accelerated.

Marxism in Yugoslavia and Cuba. The Titoist variant of Marxism-Leninism developed after the Yugoslav Communists, led by Josip Broz Tito, fell out with the Soviet Union in June 1948. It is a form of Marxist Socialism that in some respects is opposed to Stalinist Marxism-Leninism. Thus it emphasizes the struggle against bureaucracy and national chauvinism, along with the need for workers' control of the factories. In other respects it remains faithful to Stalinism in the unity of its leadership and in the monolithic nature of the League of Yugoslav Communists.

The Yugoslav Party claims that it has started on the road to the withering away of the state. It does not operationally direct economic and social life, as do other Communist parties that hold power. In foreign policy, Titoism refuses allegiance to either of the great power blocs; it favours self-determination and independence for the ex-colonial countries of the Third World.

The Marxism of Fidel Castro expresses itself as a rejection of injustice in any form—political, economic, or social. In this sense it is related to the liberal democracy and Pan-Americanism of Simón Bolívar in Latin America during the 19th century. In its liberalism, Castro's early socialism resembled the various French Socialisms of the first half of the 19th century. Only gradually did Castroism come to identify itself with Marxism-Leninism, although from the very beginning of the Cuban revolution Castro revealed his attachment to certain of Marx's ideas. But Castro's Marxism rejects some of the tenets and practices of official Marxism-Leninism: it is outspoken against dogmatism, bureaucracy, and sectarianism. In one sense, Castroism is a Marxist-Leninist "heresy." At the same time it aims to apply a purer Marxism to the conditions of Cuba: alleged American imperialism, a single-crop economy, a low initial level of political and economic development. One may call it an attempt to realize a synthesis of Marxist ideas and the ideas of Bolívar.

In the ideological and political conflicts that divide the Communist world, Castroism takes a more or less unengaged position. Castro is above all a nationalist and only after that a Marxist, much as is Tito in Yugoslavia.

The fragmentation of Marxism. By the latter part of the 20th century the ideas associated with Marx's name had been adapted to so many political and cultural conditions that it was no longer possible to define a single body of thought as Marxist. In western Europe the social democratic parties had abandoned their traditional programs and doctrines. In the Soviet Union the Leninist-Stalinist adaptation of Marxism had become the formal doctrine of a ruling party. In China, the Soviet brand of Marxism had been further modified to fit the needs of a peasant-based movement. Among certain Western intel-

lectuals Marxism enjoyed a new birth as a form of existential protest against a technological society. Some writers mixed Marxist ideas with those of other thinkers, including Nietzsche, Kierkegaard, and Freud. But the term "Marxism" in the West had come to mean certain attitudes rather than a consistent body of thought.

BIBLIOGRAPHY. General analyses of Marxism are contained in EMILE BURNS, *An Introduction to Marxism*, rev. ed. (1966); G.D.H. COLE, *The Meaning of Marxism*, 2nd ed. rev. (1948, reprinted 1964); and M.M. BOBER, *Karl Marx's Interpretation of History* (1948). R.N.C. HUNT, *Marxism Past and Present* (1954), is a valuable introductory work on Marx's social rather than economic doctrines. Studies of Marxism as a sociological doctrine may be found in KARL KORSCH, *Karl Marx* (1963); HENRI LEFEBVRE, *The Sociology of Marx* (Eng. trans. 1968); and in two works by SIDNEY HOOK, *Towards the Understanding of Karl Marx* (1933), and *From Hegel to Marx: Studies in the Intellectual Development of Karl Marx* (1936, reprinted 1950). GEORGE LICHTHEIM, in both *The Origins of Socialism* (1969), and *Marxism: An Historical and Critical Study* (1961), examines Marx's social and historical doctrines.

A.J. GREGOR, *A Survey of Marxism: Problems in Philosophy and the Theory of History* (1965), emphasizes philosophical problems in lieu of political or economic ones. The outstanding work on Marxist ethics is EUGENE KAMENKA, *The Ethical Foundations of Marxism* (1962).

Marx and Modern Economics (1968), ed. by DAVID HOROWITZ, is an excellent collection of essays by leading economic theorists. Other economic treatments of Marxism worth consulting are P.M. SWEEZY, *The Theory of Capitalist Development: Principles of Marxian Political Economy* (1942); and JOHN STRACHEY, *The Nature of Capitalist Crisis* (1935).

An account of the historical development of Marxism is HENRI CHAMBRE, *From Karl Marx to Mao-Tse-Tung: A Systematic Survey of Marxism-Leninism* (Eng. trans. 1963). G.D.H. COLE, *A History of Socialist Thought*, 6 vol. (1953–58), is a detailed study of the Marxist movement rather than the ideas; see esp. vol. 2, *Marxism and Anarchism, 1850–1890* (1954). B.D. WOLFE, *Marxism: 100 Years in the Life of a Doctrine* (1965), emphasizes the early years of the Soviet revolution; as does HERBERT MARCUSE, *Soviet Marxism: A Critical Analysis* (1958).

Of special interest is an annotated bibliography on Marxism prepared by JOHN LACHS, *Marxist Philosophy: A Bibliographic Guide* (1967).

(H.C.)

Mary

Mary, the mother of Jesus, has been an object of veneration in the Christian Church since the apostolic age and has been a favourite subject in art, music, and literature. Her humility and obedience to the message of God have made her an exemplar for all ages of Christians. Out of the sparse details supplied in the New Testament by the Gospels about the maid of Galilee, Christian piety and theology have constructed a well-developed picture of Mary that fulfills the prediction ascribed to her in the Magnificat (Luke 1:48): "Henceforth all generations will call me blessed."

Biblical references. It is impossible to assemble the biblical references to Mary into a coherent biography, even though the span of time covered by these references is, in fact, longer than the life of Jesus. The first mention of her is the story of the Annunciation, which reports that she was living in Nazareth and was betrothed to Joseph (Luke 1:26 ff.); the last mention of her (Acts 1:14) includes her in the company of those who devoted themselves to prayer after the ascension of Jesus into heaven. She appears in the following incidents in the Gospels: the Annunciation; the visit with Elizabeth, her kinswoman and the mother of John the Baptist, the precursor of Jesus, (Luke 1:39 ff.); the birth of Jesus and the presentation of him in the Temple (Luke 2:1 ff.); the coming of the Magi and the flight to Egypt (Matt. 2:1 ff.); the Passover visit to Jerusalem when Jesus was 12 years old (Luke 2:41 ff.); the marriage at Cana in Galilee, although her name is not used (John 2:1 ff.); the attempt to see Jesus while he was teaching (Mark 3:31 ff.); the station at the cross, where, apparently widowed, she was entrusted to the disciple John (John 19:26 ff.). Even if one takes these scenes as literal historical accounts, they do not add up to an integrated portrait of Mary. Only in the narratives of the Nativity and the Passion of Christ is her place a significant one: her acceptance of the privilege conferred on her in the Annunciation is the solemn prologue to the Christmas story; not only does she stand at the foot of the Cross, but in the Easter story "the other Mary" who came to the tomb of Jesus (Matt. 28:1) is not she—according to traditional interpretations, because, having kept in her heart what he was to be, she knew that the body of Jesus would not be there. On the other hand, the three incidents that belong to the life of Jesus between infancy and death all contain elements of a pronouncedly human character, perhaps even the suggestion that she did not fully understand Jesus' true mission.

Since the early days of Christianity, however, the themes that these scenes symbolize have been the basis for thought and contemplation about Mary, developing and expanding through the centuries. Christian communions and theologians differ from one another in their interpretations of Mary principally on the basis of where they set the terminal point for such development and expansion—that is, where they maintain that the legitimate development of doctrine may be said to have ended. To a considerable degree, therefore, a historical survey of that development is also an introduction to the state of contemporary Christian thought about Mary.

It should be noted that there have been various attempts to connect Christian devotion to Mary with the cult of female deities (e.g., the Great Mother of the Gods) in the Greco-Roman world. The obvious resemblances are sufficient to suggest that this was the soil in which Christian practice and thought grew, but more profound and more important than the parallels are the fundamental differences, which came from the Christian preoccupation with the historical and unrepeatable incarnation of the Son of God, as contrasted with the mythological ideas of Hellenistic religions about mother goddesses in the context of nature rather than of history.

Dogmatic titles. *Guarantee of the Incarnation.* Probably the earliest allusion to Mary in Christian literature is the phrase "born of woman" in the Letter of Paul to the Galatians (4:4), which was written before any of the Gospels. As parallels such as the Old Testament Book of Job (14:1) and the Gospel account of Matthew (11:11) suggest, the phrase is a Hebraic way of speaking about the essential humanity of a person. When applied to Jesus, therefore, "born of woman" was intended to assert that he was a real man, in opposition to the attempt —later seen in various systems of Gnosticism, a 2nd-century dualistic religion—to deny that he had had a completely human life; he was said by some Gnostics to have passed through the body of Mary as light passes through a window. It seems unwarranted to read anything further into the phrase, as though "born of woman" necessarily implied "but not of a man and a woman." Thus, the phrase made Mary the sign or the guarantee that the Son of God had truly been born as a man. For the ancient world, one human parent was necessary to assure that a person was genuinely human, and from the beginning the human mother of Jesus Christ, the Son of God, has been the one to provide this assurance. Some scholars have even maintained that the primary connotation of the phrase "born of the Virgin Mary" in the Apostles' Creed was this same insistence by the church upon the authentic manhood of Jesus. That insistence has been the irreducible minimum in all the theories about Mary that have appeared in Christian history. Her role as mother takes precedence over any of the other roles assigned to her in devotion and in dogma. Those who deny the virgin birth usually claim to do so in the interest of true humanity, seeing a contradiction between the idea of Jesus as the human son of a human mother and the idea that he did not have a human father. Those who defend the virgin birth usually maintain that the true humanity was made possible when the Virgin accepted her commission as the guarantee of the Incarnation (Luke 1:38): "Let it be to me according to your word." This is the original source of the title Coredemptrix—indicating some participa-

tion with Christ in the redemption of mankind—assigned to Mary in Roman Catholic theology, though the term has come to connote a more active role by her; the precise nature of this participation is still a matter of controversy among Catholic theologians.

Virgin mother. By far the most voluminous narratives about Mary in the New Testament are the infancy stories in the Gospels of Matthew and Luke. In their present form, both accounts make a point of asserting that Jesus was conceived in the womb of Mary without any human agency (Matt. 1:18 ff.; Luke 1:34 ff.); yet the many textual variants in Matt. 1:16, some of them with the words "Joseph begat Jesus," have caused some scholars to question whether such an assertion was part of Matthew's original account. The passages in Matthew and in Luke seem to be the only references to the matter in the New Testament. The Apostle Paul nowhere mentions it; the Gospel According to Mark begins with Jesus as an adult; and the Gospel According to John, which begins with his prehistorical existence, does not allude to the virgin birth, unless a variant of John 1:13, which reads ". . . who was born" rather than ". . . who were born," is followed. Matthew does not attach any theological significance to the miracle, but it is possible that the words of the angel in Luke 1:35 are intended to connect the holiness of the child with the virginity of the mother. In postbiblical Christian literature the most voluminous discussions of Mary have been those dealing with her virginity. On the basis of the New Testament, it was the unanimous teaching of all the orthodox Fathers of the Church that Mary conceived Jesus with her virginity unimpaired, a teaching enshrined in the early Christian Creeds and concurred in by the 16th-century Reformers as well as by most Protestant churches and believers since the Reformation. Only with the rise of rationalism in the 18th century and then of Protestant Liberalism in the 19th century did the teaching begin to lose the universal support it had enjoyed. One of the major points in the antiliberal reaction of Fundamentalism in the early 20th century was its insistence upon the literal accuracy of all the miracle stories in the Bible, including and especially those dealing with the miraculous conception and with the Resurrection of Jesus, without which his status as Son of God and Saviour was thought to be in jeopardy.

Second Eve. One of the interpretations of the person and work of Jesus Christ in the New Testament is the formulation of parallels between him and Adam: "As in Adam all die, so also in Christ shall all be made alive" (I Cor. 15:22). Decisive in the parallel is the contrast between the disobedience of Adam, by which sin came into the world, and the obedience of Christ, by which salvation from sin was accomplished (Rom. 5:12–19). Whether or not the story of the Annunciation in the first chapter of the Gospel According to Luke is intended to suggest a similar parallel between Eve and Mary, this did soon become a theme of Christian reflection. Writing at about the end of the 2nd century, the Church Father Irenaeus of Lugdunum (modern Lyon, France) elaborated the parallel between Eve, who, as a virgin, had disobeyed the word of God, and Mary, who, also as a virgin, had obeyed it;

for Adam had necessarily to be restored in Christ, that mortality be absorbed in immortality, and Eve in Mary, that a virgin, become the advocate of a virgin, should undo and destroy virginal disobedience by virginal obedience.

Irenaeus did not argue the point; he seems rather to have taken the parallel for granted, and this may indicate that it was not his own invention but belonged to tradition, for which he had a high respect. In any case, the parallel did ascribe to Mary and to her obedience an active share in the redemption of the human race: all men had died in Adam, but Eve had participated in the sin that brought this on; all men were saved in Christ, but Mary had participated in the life that made this possible.

Mother of God. The first widespread theological controversy over Mary had to do with the propriety of applying to her the title of Theotokos, "God-bearer" or "mother of God." The title seems to have arisen in devotional usage, probably in Alexandria, Egypt, sometime in

"Born of woman"

Virginity of Mary

First theological controversy over Mary

the 3rd or 4th century; it was a logical deduction from the doctrine of the full deity of Christ, which was established as a dogma during the 4th century, and those who defended that dogma were also the ones who drew the inference. Perhaps, as the 19th-century English theologian Cardinal John Henry Newman supposed, the determination of the Council of Nicaea in 325 that Christ was not merely the highest of creatures but belonged on the divine side of the line between Creator and creature was even responsible for the rapid growth of devotion and speculation attached to Mary as the highest of creatures. By the end of the 4th century, the Theotokos had successfully established itself in various sections of the church. Because it seemed to him that the supporters of the title were blurring the distinction between the divine and the human in Christ, Nestorius, the patriarch of Constantinople, objected to its use, preferring the less explicit title Christotokos, "Christ-bearer" or "mother of Christ." Along with other aspects of his teaching, Nestorius' objections were condemned at the Council of Ephesus in 431, and Theotokos was unconditionally approved.

In the devotion of Eastern Christendom, the Theotokos (Russian *Bogoroditsa*) has been very prominent; it was a favourite subject for icon painters and became one of the principal targets of the polemics levelled by the Iconoclasts—*i.e.*, opponents of the religious use of images—of the 8th and 9th centuries against the "idolatry" of the orthodox. Through its incorporation in the prayer Ave Maria ("Hail, Mary"), the title mother of God has been circulated throughout Western Catholicism as well. By the approval it received in both Lutheran and Reformed confessions during the period of the Reformation, the title assured itself a place in the official theology, though not in the popular piety, of orthodox Protestantism. It is as mother of God that Mary is also termed Mediatrix by Roman Catholics. The official teaching of the Catholic Church has sought to make clear that this latter term is intended not to detract from the glory of Christ as sole mediator but to signify that Mary mediates between Christ and mankind as she did at the marriage feast at Cana (John 2:3).

Ever virgin. Various corollaries could be deduced from the New Testament's assertion of Mary's virginity in the conception of Jesus, including the doctrine that she had remained a virgin in the course of his birth (the *virginitas in partu*) and the doctrine that she had remained a virgin after his birth and until the end of her life (the *virginitas post partum*). The Apostles' Creed appears to teach at least the *virginitas in partu* when it says "born of the Virgin Mary." Although this teaching about how Mary gave birth to Jesus occurs for the first time in the 2nd-century apocryphal, or noncanonical, *Protevangelium of James,* its origins and evolution are not easy to trace, and Roman Catholic and Protestant historians have come to contradictory conclusions. The growth of the ascetic ideal in the church helped to give support to this view of Mary as the model of the lifelong virgin. The doctrine is neither asserted nor denied but is simply ignored in the New Testament, and Old Testament passages adduced in support of it by Church Fathers (such as Ezek. 44:2 and S. of Sol. 4:12) were probably convincing only to those who already accepted the doctrine.

The doctrine also posed two problems of biblical interpretation, both of which were discussed in detail by defenders of the doctrine from St. Jerome to Luther. To the argument from words such as "until" (Matt. 1:25), "before" (Matt. 1:18), and "first-born" (Luke 2:7) that Mary must have borne further children, the defenders of the perpetual virginity have replied that none of these words speaks at all about what followed: an only child is a firstborn child, and although Pharaoh and his army, in the account of the Exodus, did not repent "before" the Red Sea had closed in on them, this did not mean that they suddenly became believers then. The other biblical problem was that of the "brothers" of Jesus referred to in I Cor. 9:5; Gal. 1:19; and several times in the Gospels and in the Acts of the Apostles. If they really were his brothers, it was obvious that Mary had given birth to other children after the birth of Jesus; this would seem to

be the natural interpretation. These, however, have been explained either as kinsmen (on the grounds that this is what "brothers" sometimes meant in Jewish society) or as children of Joseph by a previous marriage (his early death being an indication that he was considerably older than Mary) or as children of another Mary and of Clopas. Partly because of these biblical problems, the doctrine of the perpetual virginity of Mary has not been supported as unanimously as has the doctrine of the virginal conception or the title mother of God. It achieved dogmatic status, however, at the Council of Chalcedon in 451 and is therefore binding upon Eastern Orthodox and Roman Catholic believers; in addition, it is maintained by many Anglican, some Lutheran, and a few other Protestant theologians.

Immaculate. As the doctrine of the perpetual virginity of Mary implied an integral purity of body and soul, so, in the opinion of many theologians, she was also free of other sins. Attempting to prove the universality of sin against Pelagius (whose teaching was condemned as heretical by the Christian Church but who did maintain the sinlessness of Mary), Augustine, the great theologian and bishop from northern Africa, spoke for the Western Church when he wrote:

> We must except the holy Virgin Mary. Out of respect for the Lord, I do not intend to raise a single question on the subject of sin. After all, how do we know what abundance of grace was granted to her who had the merit to conceive and bring forth him who was unquestionably without sin?

It was, however, the distinction between original sin (*i.e.*, the sin that all men are born with) and actual sin (*i.e.*, the sins that men commit during their life), firmly established in Western theology by the same Augustine, that eventually compelled a further clarification of what the sinlessness of Mary meant. Certain Eastern theologians in the 4th and 5th centuries were willing to attribute actual sins to her, but most theologians in both East and West came to accept the view that she never did anything sinful, a view that found expression even among the 16th-century Reformers. But was she free from original sin as well? And if so, how? Thomas Aquinas, the most important medieval theologian in the West, took a representative position when he taught that her conception was tarnished, as was that of all men, but that God suppressed and ultimately extinguished original sin in her, apparently before she was born. This position, however, was opposed by the doctrine of the Immaculate Conception, systematized by Duns Scotus, a 13th-century British Scholastic theologian, and finally defined as Roman Catholic dogma by Pope Pius IX in 1854. According to this dogma, Mary was not only pure in her life and in her birth, but

> at the first instant of her conception was preserved immaculate from all stain of original sin, by the singular grace and privilege granted her by Almighty God, through the merits of Christ Jesus, Saviour of mankind.

Assumed into heaven. When the Immaculate Conception was promulgated, petitions began coming to the Vatican for a definition regarding the Assumption of the Virgin into heaven, as this was believed by Roman Catholics and celebrated in the Feast of the Assumption. During the century that followed, more than 8,000,000 persons signed such petitions; yet Rome hesitated, because the doctrine was difficult to define on the basis of Scripture and early witnesses to the Christian tradition. No account of the place and circumstances of Mary's death was universally accepted in the church (although paintings depicting her "dormition," or "falling asleep," in the ancient Ionian city of Ephesus were quite common); no burial place was acknowledged (although there was a grave in Jerusalem that was said to be hers); and no miracles were credited to relics of her body (although the physical remains of far lesser saints had performed many). Such arguments from silence, however, did not suffice to establish a dogma, and on the positive side even the earliest doctrinal and liturgical testimony in support of the idea has appeared relatively late in history. Finally, in 1950 Pope Pius XII made the dogma official, declaring that "the Immaculate Mother of God, the ever Virgin

Marginal notes:

Biblical problems

Recent dogmatic definitions

Mary, when the course of her earthly life was run, was assumed in body and soul to heavenly glory." As it was formulated, the doctrine left open to speculation the question whether, as most theologians have held, Mary had in fact died or whether she had been taken up into heaven, as had the patriarch Enoch (Gen. 5:24) and the prophet Elijah (II Kings 2:11), without first passing through physical death.

Cultural importance. In addition to these official prerogatives and titles given to her by Catholic Christianity, the Virgin Mary has achieved great cultural importance. Popular devotion to Mary—in such forms as feasts, devotional services, and the rosary—has played a tremendously important role in the lives of Roman Catholics and the Orthodox; at times, this devotion has pushed other doctrines into the background. Modern Roman Catholicism has emphasized that the doctrine of Mary is not an isolated belief but must be seen in the context of two other Christian doctrines: the doctrine of Christ and the doctrine of the church. What is said of Mary is derived from what is said of Jesus: this was the basic meaning of Theotokos. She has also been the type of the church, as "the first believer" and as the one in whom the humanity of the church was representatively embodied. By these emphases Roman Catholic thought has sought to reduce the extravagances of Marian cult and Mariological thought that have sometimes tended to go beyond the limits both of biblical foundation and of ecclesiastical regulations.

Mary's cultural importance, however, far transcends any dogmatic or institutional boundaries. Even the Qur'ān pays tribute to her, although it appears to have confounded her with Miriam, the sister of Moses. Both in folk piety and in the speculations of philosophers and mystics, she has served to symbolize the redemption of the entire cosmos and to provide a bridge between Christianity and those religions of nature that have spoken of such a redemption. Carl Jung, founder of analytic psychology, found in the dogma of the Assumption an *Answer to Job,* in which the exaggerated and severely masculine ideas of divine transcendence proclaimed by the Hebrew prophets had themselves been transcended. Countless paintings of the Madonna and child or of the coronation of the Virgin, as well as settings of the Annunciation, the visit with Elizabeth, and the station at the Cross of Jesus have made Mary a universal theme in the history of the arts. In the secular life and literature of the West since the Middle Ages, Mary has symbolized the nobility of woman. Although the contempt for women was often depicted by the use of the story of Eve, who had been created second but had sinned first, to prove the natural inferiority of the female, the devotion to Mary could serve at least partly as a counterbalance, proving that a woman had been the first to affirm and to help make possible the redemption of the human race. Many Protestant churches that have most vigorously criticized the "Mariolatry" they claimed to find in Roman Catholicism, especially in the dogmas of the Immaculate Conception and the Assumption, have nevertheless included in their hymnals such songs as "Ye Watchers and Ye Holy Ones," written by Athelstan Riley in 1906, in which Mary is praised as "higher than the cherubim, more glorious than the seraphim"—a praise that they would hesitate to express in the prose of their sermons or dogmatic treatises. Thus, in ways that she could never have anticipated, all generations have indeed called her blessed.

BIBLIOGRAPHY. HILDA GRAEF, *Mary: A History of Doctrine and Devotion,* 2 vol. (1963–65), is especially instructive about the early development of the doctrine. JUNIPER CAROL (ed.), *Mariology,* 3 vol. (1955–61), deals successively with the sources of Marian doctrine, theology, and devotions. LEON J. SUENENS, *Quelle est celle-ci? essai de synthèse mariale* (1957; Eng. trans., *Mary the Mother of God,* 1959), is a brief but helpful summary. Recent theological treatments by Roman Catholics include RENE LAURENTIN, *La question mariale* (1963; Eng. trans., *The Question of Mary,* 1965); and E. SCHILLEBEECKX, *Maria, moeder van de verlossing,* 3rd rev. ed. (1957; Eng. trans., *Mary Mother of the Redemption,* 1964). The Eastern Orthodox view is presented, though from a Roman Catholic standpoint, by MAURICIO GORDILLO, *Mariologia Orientalis* (1954). Critical, but sympathetic treatments by Protestants are GIOVANNI MIEGGE, *La Vergine Maria* (1950; Eng. trans., *The Virgin Mary,* 1955); and MAX THURIAN, *Marie, Mère du Seigneur, figure de l'Eglise* (1962; Eng. trans., *Mary, Mother of All Christians,* 1964). Technical problems are presented in the annual *Marian Studies* and in the proceedings of national and international Mariological congresses.

(J.J.Pe.)

Mary I of England

Queen of England from 1553 to 1558, Mary I was the first woman to rule England in her own right, but she is chiefly remembered as Bloody Mary, the instigator of a ruthless persecution of Protestants in a vain attempt to preserve Roman Catholicism in England.

Born at Greenwich Palace on February 18, 1516, daughter of King Henry VIII and the Spanish princess Catherine of Aragon, Mary as a child was a pawn in England's bitter rivalry with more powerful nations, being fruitlessly proposed in marriage to this or that potentate desired as an ally. A studious and bright girl, she was educated by her mother and a governess of ducal rank.

By courtesy of the Museo del Prado, Madrid

Mary I, painting on wood by Sir Anthony More, 1553. In the Prado, Madrid.

Betrothed at last to the Holy Roman Emperor, her cousin Charles V (Charles I of Spain), she was commanded by him to come to Spain with a huge cash dowry. This demand ignored, he presently jilted her and concluded a more advantageous match. Made princess of Wales in 1525, she held court at Ludlow Castle while new betrothal plans were made. Mary's life was radically disrupted, however, by her father's new marriage to Anne Boleyn.

As early as the 1520s Henry had planned to divorce Catherine in order to marry Anne Boleyn, claiming that, since Catherine had been his deceased brother's wife, her union with Henry was incestuous. The Pope, however, refused to recognize Henry's right to divorce Catherine, even after the divorce was legalized in England. In 1534, Henry broke with Rome and established the Church of England. The allegation of incest, in effect, made Mary a bastard. Anne Boleyn, the new queen, bore the King a daughter, Elizabeth (the future queen), forbade Mary access to her parents, stripped her of her title of princess, and forced her to act as lady-in-waiting to the infant Elizabeth. Mary never saw her mother again, though, despite great danger, they corresponded secretly.

Anne's hatred pursued Mary so relentlessly that she feared execution, but, having her mother's courage and all her father's stubbornness, she would not admit to the illegitimacy of her birth. Nor would she enter a convent when ordered to do so.

After Anne fell under Henry's displeasure, he offered to

Mary in the arts

Consequences of Henry VIII's divorce

pardon Mary if she would acknowledge him as head of the Church of England and admit the "incestuous illegality" of his marriage to her mother. She refused to do so until her cousin, the emperor Charles, persuaded her to give in, an action she was to regret deeply.

Henry was now reconciled to her and gave her a household befitting her position and again made plans for her betrothal. She became godmother to Prince Edward, his son by Jane Seymour, the third queen.

She was now the most important European princess. Although plain, she was a popular figure, with a fine contralto singing voice and great linguistic ability. She was, however, not able to free herself of the epithet of bastard, and her movements were severely restricted. Husband after husband proposed for her failed to reach the altar. When Henry married Catherine Howard, however, Mary was granted permission to return to court, and in 1544, although still considered illegitimate, she was granted succession to the throne after Edward and any other legitimate children who might be born to Henry.

Edward VI succeeded his father in 1547 and, swayed by religious fervour and overzealous advisers, made English rather than Latin compulsory for church services. Mary, however, continued to celebrate mass in the old form in her private chapel and was once again in danger of losing her head.

Upon the death of Edward in 1553, she fled to Norfolk, as Lady Jane Grey had seized the throne and was recognized as queen for a few days. The country, however, considered Mary the rightful ruler, and within some days she made a triumphal entry into London. A woman of 37 now, she was forceful, sincere, bluff, and hearty like her father but, in contrast to him, disliked cruel punishments and the signing of death warrants.

Insensible to the need of caution for a newly crowned queen, unable to adapt herself to novel circumstances, and lacking self-interest, she longed to bring her people back to the church of Rome. To achieve this end, she was determined to marry Philip II of Spain, the son of the emperor Charles V and 11 years her junior, though most of her advisers advocated her cousin Courtenay, earl of Devon, a man of royal blood.

Those English noblemen who had acquired wealth and lands when Henry VIII confiscated the Catholic monasteries had a vested interest in retaining them, and Mary's desire to restore Roman Catholicism as the state religion made them her enemies. Parliament, also at odds with her, was offended by her discourtesy to their delegates pleading against the Spanish marriage: "My marriage is my own affair," she retorted.

When in 1554 it became clear that she would marry Philip, a Protestant insurrection broke out under the leadership of Sir Thomas Wyat. Alarmed by Wyat's rapid advance toward London, Mary made a magnificent speech rousing citizens by the thousands to fight for her. Wyat was defeated and executed, and Mary married Philip, restored the Catholic creed, and revived the laws against heresy. For three years rebel bodies dangled from gibbets, and heretics were relentlessly executed, some 300 being burned at the stake. Thenceforward the Queen, now known as Bloody Mary, was hated, her Spanish husband distrusted and slandered, and she herself blamed for the vicious slaughter. An unpopular, unsuccessful war with France, in which Spain was England's ally, lost Calais, England's last toehold in Europe. Still childless, sick, and grief stricken, she was further depressed by a series of false pregnancies. She died on November 17, 1558, in London, and with her died all that she did.

BIBLIOGRAPHY. H.F.M. PRESCOTT, *Mary Tudor*, 2nd ed. rev. (1953), the best biography despite its date; FREDERIC MADDEN (ed.), *Privy Purse Expenses of the Princess Mary* (1831); JOHN E. PAUL, *Catherine of Aragon and Her Friends* (1966); ERIC N. SIMONS, *The Queen and the Rebel* (1964), a detailed account of the Wyat rebellion; J.M. STONE, *The History of Mary I, Queen of England* (1901), good, but dated; GODFREY TURTON, *The Dragon's Breed: The Story of the Tudors* (1970), contains a short account of Mary I; R.B. WERNHAM, *Before the Armada*; (1966); B.M.I. WHITE, *Mary Tudor* (1935), considered the next best life to Prescott's.
(E.N.S.)

Mary as queen

Mary, Queen of Scots

A romantic and tragic figure to her supporters, a scheming adulteress if not murderess to her political enemies, Mary, Queen of Scots, aroused furious controversy in her own lifetime, during which her cousin Queen Elizabeth I of England aptly termed her "the daughter of debate." Her dramatic story has continued to provoke argument among historians ever since, while the public interest in this 16th-century femme fatale remains unabated.

Giraudon

Mary Stuart, drawing by François Clouet, 1559. In the Bibliothèque Nationale, Paris.

Mary Stuart was born at Linlithgow on December 8, 1542, the only child of King James V of Scotland and his French wife, Mary of Guise. The death of her father six days later left Mary as queen of Scotland in her own right. Although Mary's great-uncle King Henry VIII of England made an unsuccessful effort to secure control of her (Mary inherited Tudor blood through her grandmother, a sister of Henry VIII of England), the regency of the kingdom was settled in favour of her mother.

Her mother saw to it that Mary was sent to France at the age of five. There she was brought up at the court of King Henry II and his queen Catherine de Médicis with their own large family, assisted by relations on her mother's side, the powerful Guises. Despite a charmed childhood of much luxury, including frequent hunting and dancing (at both of which she excelled) Mary's education was not neglected and she was taught Latin, Italian, Spanish, and some Greek. French now became her first language, and indeed in every other way Mary grew into a Frenchwoman rather than a Scot.

By her remarkable beauty, with her tall, slender figure (she was about 5 feet 11 inches), her red-gold hair and amber-coloured eyes, and her taste for music and poetry, Mary summed up the contemporary ideal of the Renaissance princess at the time of her marriage to Francis, eldest son of Henry and Catherine, in April 1558. Although it was a political match aimed at the union of France and Scotland, Mary was sincerely fond of her boy husband, though the marriage was probably never consummated.

The accession of Elizabeth Tudor to the throne of England in November 1558 meant that Mary was, by virtue of her Tudor blood, next in line to the English throne. Those Catholics who considered Elizabeth illegitimate because they regarded Henry VIII's divorce from Catherine of Aragon and his marriage to Anne Boleyn invalid even looked upon Mary as the lawful queen. Mary's father-in-law, Henry II of France, thus claimed the English throne on her behalf. The death of Henry in 1559 brought Francis to the French throne and made Mary a glittering queen consort of France, until Francis' premature death in December 1560 made her a widow at the age of 18.

Life in France

Returning to Scotland in August 1561, Mary discovered that her sheltered French upbringing had made her ill-equipped to cope with the series of problems now facing

Return to Scotland

her. Mary's former pretensions to the English throne had incurred Elizabeth's hostility. She refused to acknowledge Mary as her heiress, however much Mary, nothing if not royal by temperament, prized her English rights. While Mary herself was a Roman Catholic, the official religion of Scotland had been reformed to Protestantism in her absence, and she thus represented to many, including the leading Calvinist preacher John Knox, a foreign queen of an alien religion. Most difficult of all were the Scottish nobles; factious and turbulent after a series of royal minorities, they cared more for private feuds and self-aggrandisement then support of the crown. Nevertheless, for the first years of her rule, Mary managed well, with the aid of her bastard half-brother James, earl of Moray, and helped in particular by her policy of religious tolerance. Nor were all the Scots averse to the spectacle of a pretty young queen creating a graceful court life and enjoying her progresses round the country.

It was Mary's second marriage in July 1565 to her cousin Henry Stewart (Stuart), earl of Darnley, son of Matthew Stewart, 4th earl of Lennox, that started the fatal train of events culminating in her destruction. Mary married the handsome Darnley recklessly for love. It was a disastrous choice because by her marriage she antagonized all the elements interested in the power structure of Scotland, including Elizabeth, who disapproved of Mary marrying another Tudor descendant, and her half-brother James, who, jealous of the Lennox family's rise to power, promptly rebelled. Nor did Darnley's character measure up to the promise of his appearance—he was weak, vicious, and yet ambitious. The callous butchery of her secretary and confidant, David Riccio (Rizzio), in front of her own eyes when six months pregnant, in March 1566, by Darnley and a group of nobles, convinced Mary that her husband had aimed at her own life. The birth of their son James in June did nothing to reconcile the couple, and Mary, armed now with the heir she had craved, looked for some means to relieve an intolerable situation.

The next eight months constitute the most tangled and controversial period of Mary's career. According to Mary's detractors, it was during this period that she developed an adulterous liaison with James Hepburn, 4th earl of Bothwell, and planned with him the death of Darnley and their own following marriage. There is, however, no contemporary evidence of this love affair, before Darnley's death, except the highly dubious so-called Casket Letters, poems and letters supposedly written by Mary to Bothwell but now generally considered to be inadmissible evidence by historians. But Mary did undoubtedly consider the question of a divorce from Darnley, after a serious illness in October 1566, which

Darnley's murder

left her health wrecked and her spirits low. On the night of February 9, 1567, the house at Kirk o' Field on the outskirts of Edinburgh where Darnley lay recovering from illness was blown up, and Darnley himself strangled while trying to escape. Many theories have been put forward to explain conflicting accounts of the crime, including the possibility that Darnley, plotting to blow up Mary, was caught in his own trap. Nevertheless, the most obvious explanation—that those responsible were the nobles who hated Darnley—is the most likely one.

Whatever Mary's foreknowledge of the crime, her conduct thereafter was fatally unwise and showed how much she lacked wise counsellors in Scotland. After three months, she allowed herself to be married off to Bothwell, the chief suspect, after he abducted and ravished her. If passion is rejected as the motive, Mary's behaviour can be ascribed to her increasing despair, exacerbated by ill-health, at her inability to manage the affairs of tempestuous Scotland without a strong arm to support her. But in fact Bothwell as a consort proved no more acceptable to the jealous Scottish nobility than Darnley had been. Mary and Bothwell were parted forever at Carberry Hill on June 15, 1567, Bothwell to exile and imprisonment where he died in 1578, and Mary to incarceration on the

tiny island of Loch Leven, where she was formally deposed in favour of her one-year-old son James. After a brief fling of liberty the following year, defeat of her supporters at a battle at Langside put her once more to flight. Impulsively, Mary sought refuge in England with her cousin Elizabeth. But Elizabeth, with all the political cunning Mary lacked, employed a series of excuses connected with the murder of Darnley to hold Mary in English captivity in a series of prisons for the next 18 years of her life. In the meantime, Mary's brother Moray flourished as regent of Scotland.

Captivity in England

Mary's captivity was long and wearisome, only partly allayed by the consolations of religion and, on a more mundane level, her skill at embroidery and her love of such little pets as lap dogs and singing birds. Her health suffered from the lack of physical exercise, her figure thickened, and her beauty diminished as can be seen in the best known pictures of her in black velvet and white veil, dating from 1578. Naturally, she concentrated her energies on procuring release from an imprisonment she considered unjustified, at first by pleas, and later by conspiracy. Unfortunately for her survival, Mary as a Catholic was the natural focus for the hopes of those English Catholics who wished to replace the Protestant Queen Elizabeth on the throne. It was the discovery in 1586 of a plot to assassinate Elizabeth and bring about a Roman Catholic uprising that convinced Queen Elizabeth that while she lived, Mary would always constitute too dangerous a threat to her own position.

Despite the fact that she was the sovereign queen of another country, Mary was tried by an English court and condemned; her son, James, who had not seen his mother since infancy and now had his sights fixed on succeeding to the English throne, raised no objections. Mary was executed on February 8, 1587, in the great hall at Fotheringhay Castle, near Peterborough; she was 44 years old. It was a chilling scene, redeemed by the great personal dignity with which Mary met her fate. Her body ultimately came to rest in Westminster Abbey in a magnificent monument James I raised to his mother, after he finally ascended the throne of England.

BIBLIOGRAPHY. ANTONIA FRASER, *Mary Queen of Scots* (1969), the most recent comprehensive biography taking into account modern research and replacing T.F. HENDERSON, *Mary Queen of Scots*, 2 vol. (1905); PRINCE LABANOFF (ed.), *Lettres et mémoires de Marie, Reine d'Ecosse*, 7 vol. (1844), collected edition of the letters, also a useful reference book; P. STEWART MACKENZIE, *Queen Mary's Book* (1905), text and translation of all Mary's writings; CLAUDE NAU, *Memorials of Mary Stewart*, ed. by J. STEVENSON (1883), Mary's own story dictated to her secretary while in captivity; D. HAY FLEMING, *Mary Queen of Scots from Her Birth Till Her Flight into England* (1898), a well-documented account, extremely hostile; s. and M. TANNENBAUM, *Marie Stuart: Bibliography*, 3 vol. (1944), in which references to more specialized studies may be found.

(A.Fr.)

Maryland

One of the original 13 states of the United States, Maryland lies at the centre of the Eastern seaboard, astride the great industrial–population complex that stretches from Maine to Virginia. Its small size—10,577 square miles (27,394 square kilometres), about 6 percent of which is water excluding Chesapeake Bay—belies the great diversity of its landscapes and of the ways of life that they foster: from the low-lying and water-oriented Eastern Shore and Chesapeake Bay area, through the metropolitan hurly-burly of Baltimore, its largest city, to the forested Appalachian foothills and mountains of its western reaches.

General character of the state

Maryland was named in honour of the wife of King Charles I by a grateful Cecil Calvert, Lord Baltimore, who in 1632 was granted charter for the land as a haven in which his fellow Roman Catholics might escape the restrictions placed on them in England. A deep sense of history still clings to many parts of the state, most notably in the quiet charm of Annapolis, its capital since 1694, and in the white-domed, pillared statehouse, built in 1772 and today the nation's oldest statehouse in continuous use. There, a 40-block area forms the city's Colonial

Historic District, the largest in the U.S. The narrow, crooked streets, the houses abutting directly on the brickwork sidewalks, the graceful tree-covered green about the statehouse, and the myriad masts of boats at dock or anchor speak more of an earlier America than of a state with a modern industrial economy and a densely clustered population of nearly 4,000,000.

Geography, too, has provided Maryland a role in American history, as a pivot between North and South. Its northern border with Pennsylvania is the famous Mason and Dixon Line, drawn in the 1760s to settle disputes between the Penn and Calvert families and traditionally regarded as the boundary between North and South. To the south, much of the boundary with Virginia is formed by the Potomac River, a symbolic barrier during the Civil War, a contest in which the sentiments and the soil of Maryland were torn asunder. On the north bank of the Potomac lies the District of Columbia, coterminous with the city of Washington, a small enclave ceded by Maryland in 1791 for the site of the national capital. East of the Chesapeake, the Eastern Shore shares the Delmarva Peninsula with Delaware on the north and Virginia on the south. In the mountainous west, Maryland's panhandle, joined to the rest of the state by a one-and-one-half-mile-wide wasp waist, forms an interlocking handclasp with the eastern panhandle of West Virginia. (For information on related topics, see the articles UNITED STATES; UNITED STATES, HISTORY OF THE; CIVIL WAR, U.S.; NORTH AMERICA; and APPALACHIAN MOUNTAINS. For details on the parts of Maryland in the Washington metropolitan area, see WASHINGTON, D.C.)

THE HISTORY OF MARYLAND

The area's earliest human occupation is accepted as having been by roving hunters, *c.* 8000 BC, as the ice sheet made its final retreat. The records of this pre-Archaic, fluted-blade culture which left only the points of its weapons, remains imprecise. Later, the numerous Eastern Archaic and then Woodlands Indian populations practiced agriculture and left waterside middens as evidence of the shellfish that they consumed. During the early European settlement the tribes were Algonkian in language and politics, but were under heavy pressure from the Iroquois to the north. The English promise of support in these wars greatly smoothed relations in the early colonial years.

The colony. Leonard Calvert, younger brother of Lord Baltimore, landed the founding expedition on St. Clement's (now Blakistone) Island in the lower Potomac in March 1634. The first settlement and capital was St. Mary's City. Aware of the mistakes made by Virginia's first colonists, Maryland's settlers, rather than hunt for gold, made peace with the local Indians and established farms and trading posts, at first on the shores and islands of the lower Chesapeake. The field hands included indentured labourers working off the terms of their passage and, after about 1639, African slaves. The most important crop was tobacco. Roads and towns were few, and intercourse with the English-model manor houses was largely waterborne.

Religious toleration in the colony

The religious latitude stipulated by the Calvert family was formalized by the General Assembly in 1649 in an Act Concerning Religion, later famous as the Act of Religious Toleration. It granted freedom of worship, though only within the bounds of trinitarian Christianity. Commercial disputes with Anglican Virginia and boundary quarrels with Quaker Pennsylvania and Delaware did not affect this tolerance. Puritan ascendancy in England (1648–60) caused only brief turmoil, and during an interval of crown rule (1692—1715) in Maryland the Church of England was established formally. Maryland, nonetheless, remained a haven for dissidents from sectarian rigidity in other colonies.

As the population centre shifted to the north and west, the capital was moved to Annapolis, and in 1729, Baltimore was founded. Alone among royal grants, that to the Calverts was still in force at the outbreak of the Revolution, having spanned seven generations. Maryland's dominant "country party" early resisted British efforts to make the colonies bear more of the costs of government.

Repudiation of the Stamp Act occurred in Frederick County in 1765; and in 1774, the year after the Boston Tea Party, a ship loaded with tea was burned at an Annapolis dock.

Marylanders took an active part in the war, from the siege of Boston to the surrender at Yorktown. The Continental Congress, often on the move to avoid British troops, spent a winter in Baltimore. At the close of the war it convened in Annapolis, where it accepted Washington's resignation from the army and ratified the Treaty of Paris (1783) acknowledging the independence of the colonies.

The state. When harassment on the high seas and other factors brought on the War of 1812, Baltimore clippers, sailing as privateers, dealt more than equal punishment to British skippers. In 1814 the British troops who had burned the principal government buildings in Washington, D.C., were repulsed in their attempts to inflict similar punishment on Baltimore. Francis Scott Key, a Georgetown lawyer and an eyewitness of the futile bombardment of Ft. McHenry in Baltimore harbour, wrote the four eight-line stanzas that, set to music, became the national anthem, the *Star-Spangled Banner.*

With peace, Maryland and the nation became occupied with "internal improvements" in transport and communication: the National Pike, first road to cross the Appalachians; the first U.S. passenger railroad, the Baltimore & Ohio; two important canals, the Chesapeake and Ohio from Washington to Cumberland and, across the top of the Delmarva Peninsula, the Chesapeake and Delaware; and the first intercity telegraph line, from Washington, D.C., to Baltimore. In 1845, the U.S. Naval Academy was founded on the Severn River in Annapolis.

Impact of the Civil War

The Civil War, however, arrested Maryland's progress. Landed gentry and men of the Eastern Shore supported the secessionists, while workingmen and western Marylanders stood for the Union; a third faction favoured neutrality. Federal troops occupied Baltimore and Annapolis, and martial law was imposed in this border state. The new constitution of 1864 abolished slavery and removed power from the rural aristocracy. Meanwhile, three major invasions by Confederate armies in successive summers resulted in qualified defeat at Antietam, full defeat at Gettysburg, in Pennsylvania, and dissipation of a threat to Washington, D.C., in 1864. The more cautious constitution of 1867 remains in force today, though it has been amended almost beyond recognition.

Since 1865. After the Civil War, Maryland prospered: first as an entrepôt for raw materials from and consumer goods to the South and Middle West and then as a growing centre of industry that rarely was controlled from within the state. Excesses that had won Baltimore the epithet "mob town" gradually were quieted; and Marylanders settled in to vote, until recent decades, for candidates of the Democratic Party. Increasingly, however, Maryland felt the impact of its proximity to the seat of national government. It became a major centre for federal installations, both military and civilian, during both world wars and after. But most significant was the radically different face of the Maryland suburbs of Washington, D.C., which reflected change not only in the greater numbers of people but also in their unusually high educational and economic status.

THE NATURAL AND HUMAN LANDSCAPE

The natural environment. *Surface features.* The Atlantic Coastal Plain covers about one-half of Maryland's land area, yielding to the Piedmont plateau at a fall line running from the tip of the District of Columbia through Baltimore and to near the northeastern corner of the state. The Catoctin ridgeline in the west forms the gateway to the Appalachians.

To the south, the Coastal Plain is sandy; to the north, it is loamy and fertile. Its water edges, called salt marshes or wetlands, exasperate mapmakers as erosion here fills in a swamp, there deletes an entire island: Blakistone, for example, is now about one-tenth its 1634 size. The Chesapeake's 23 drowned arms, or estuarial tributaries, give the state some 3,200 miles of shoreline—subject to frequent change. The most significant of nature-made revisions was an irruption of the ocean, during a storm in 1933, through Fenwick Island into Sinepuxent Bay, just below Ocean City. The lower portion of this barrier sand reef is now a national seashore and state park known as Assateague Island, and the inlet has become a boon to Ocean City's resort fishing fleet.

The Piedmont plateau has good farming soil save for belts of clay that are mined for brick kilns: from the beginning, the exteriors of Maryland buildings have glowed with salmon-coloured brick. To the west, paralleling the fall line, the low Parr's Ridge forms a barrier between the Potomac and Chesapeake Bay.

Maryland's share of Appalachia comprises a series of forested barriers, with many of the intervening valleys still uncleared. Backbone Mountain, hugging the West Virginia line, is the highest point in Maryland, at 3,360 feet (1,024 metres).

Climate. Maryland has two climates. It is continental in the west, with temperature records from $-40°$ F $(-40°$ C) to more than $100°$ F $(38°$ C). In the east, a humid subtropical climate is dependent on the Azores High, a pressure area that moderates the weather but does not prevent ice formation almost every winter on Chesapeake Bay's northern tributaries, summer calms as high as $107°$ F $(42°$ C) and nearly 100 percent humidity. Ordinarily, rains are enough to make reservoirs spill over and to enable Baltimore and Washington, D.C., to draw all the needed soft water for drinking. Storms sweep in from the west and south, except in late summer, when the fringes of passing hurricanes often drench Maryland from the east.

Human imprints. The most salient feature of Maryland's topography is Chesapeake Bay, which makes Baltimore a world port, divides the Eastern Shore from what was once called Maryland Main, adds picturesqueness to the Maine-to-Florida Inland Waterway, and on a summer weekend may count as many as 100,000 pleasure craft, sail or power. But it has a few drawbacks: swimmers shun its brackish, murky water after the late-summer onset of billions of small, stinging jellyfish; while the cross-bay bridge, completed in 1952, is only two lanes wide, without expansion capability; and so great is the crush of summer weekenders to and from the ocean beaches that, less than 20 years later, work was begun on a parallel bridge.

Dredging is necessary to maintain the 42-foot ship channel to Baltimore and to the Chesapeake and Delaware Canal. Finally, the bay must be defended against pollution by the cities and industries in its drainage area. Once the bay was lined with oysters; today, silt and pollutants have pushed the diminished survivors into various tributary rivers. Nonetheless, the bay, called by the Baltimore sage H.L. Mencken a "great big outdoor protein factory," still affords a living to hundreds of watermen.

Sectionalism within Maryland is dictated by terrain. The Eastern Shore farmer, in modern times, concentrates on chickens, corn, and soybeans. A mercantile appendage of Wilmington and Philadelphia until the bay was bridged, the nine-county Shore is increasingly a vacation and retirement spot for the well-to-do, who appreciate the privacy of its flat, wooded, little-posted estate areas, serpentined with creeks, guts, necks, and inlets.

Southern Maryland's five counties have built a way of life around state government, tobacco-growing, and military installations. Prince Georges County in suburban Washington has become Maryland's most populous. A nuclear-power project at Calvert Cliffs attracted attention to the marine fossils of the Miocene Epoch, where the bay has exposed dense layers of shark teeth, whale vertebrae, mollusk shells, and other ocean-floor debris from possibly 15,000,000 years ago. These fossils are deemed the world's finest accessible deposit from that period.

Central Maryland's city, Baltimore, and five counties are united only by not fitting into any of the adjoining entities. Four of the counties contain most of Baltimore's suburbs; the fifth is Montgomery, on Washington, D.C.'s northwestern edge. By 1970, only 15.7 percent of Marylanders lived outside the Census Bureau's standard metro-

politan statistical areas—and central Maryland was one long, contiguous metropolitan area.

The four counties of western Maryland owe much to road, railroad, and canal builders. The barging of coal and grain ceased in 1924, but creation of the Chesapeake and Ohio Canal National Historical Park in 1971 assured a stream of excursionists. Interstate and national roads carried city dwellers to Garrett County, where mountainside ski runs complemented water sports on Deep Creek Lake, the largest man-made body of water in the state.

THE PEOPLE OF MARYLAND

Composition of the population. The white population, at first all from the British Isles, began to vary when German-speaking farmers and artisans spread down from Pennsylvania into western Maryland in the 1700s. The process accelerated from 1848 on as Germans and German Jews fled military conscription, and then Russian Jews, Poles, Czechs, Italians, Greeks, and others arrived at Baltimore, a major 19th-century immigration centre, and fanned out into the countryside. This ethnic diversity was one of the first characteristics setting Maryland apart from the regions below the Potomac River. In the years immediately following the Civil War, it was to some extent countered by an influx of Southerners who despaired of life in a defeated and devastated homeland.

Maryland's Indian population had been killed off or pushed westward by about 1700. All that remained from their centuries of occupancy were the campsite artifacts, still being unearthed by professional and amateur archaeologists, and place names, mangled by uncomprehending whites, that come out as Chesapeake, Patapsco, Potomac, Wicomico, Patuxent, Piscataway, Susquehanna, and many others.

The racial picture. African slaves were at work in Maryland under the first Calverts. The consciences of many Marylanders, particularly members of the Society of Friends (Quakers), were uneasy; and from 1783 the importation of kidnapped Africans was under prohibitive state tax. While Maryland did not formally outlaw slavery until 1864, it protected the liberty of more free blacks than any other state as slavery neared its end. After the Civil War, blacks found Maryland somewhat more congenial than the states of the Confederacy, in which, by 1900, systematic lifetime disfranchisement of blacks was under way. A corresponding effort in Maryland, led by the Democratic Party and coming to a head in 1910, was beaten in referendum by Republicans, with the aid of James Cardinal Gibbons and other leading citizens. Yet it took a U.S. Supreme Court decision in 1934 to force the University of Maryland to admit a black into its School of Law, and it was 1970 before Marylanders first sent a black to represent them in Congress—the latter in part a reflection of the fact that the population of Baltimore had become virtually half black.

Contemporary demography. Maryland's 1970 population was more than 80 percent white, however. The birthrate was 15.5 per 1,000 persons, down from 24.9 in 1960, but still far above the 1970 death rate, 8.2. Rates for nonwhites in both categories were higher than for whites.

Present and foreseeable clustering is thickest in the outskirts of Washington, D.C., and Baltimore. In the Census Bureau's 1970 list of Standard Metropolitan Statistical Areas, the two ranked seventh and 11th, respectively, up from tenth and 12th in 1960. The rural stretch between the two cities, which are only 40 miles apart, diminished, particularly as the planned, unincorporated new city of Columbia progressed toward its goal of 100,000 residents in the 1980s. Because growth outward from the cities was uneven, however, fusion into a common, uninterrupted cityscape remained an indefinite prospect. To the north and east of Baltimore, the transition from farm to suburb in Baltimore and Harford counties promised ultimate juncture with the Philadelphia–Wilmington sprawl; but Cecil County, at the head of Chesapeake Bay, remained steadfastly rural.

Baltimore, with just over 900,000 inhabitants, continues to lose people to the suburbs. Calculations for runner-up city were impeded by the 20th-century tendency of the

Chesapeake Bay

The ethnic mix

The Baltimore-Washington, D.C., corridor

state's municipalities not to incorporate, making boundaries arbitrary lines drawn by census takers.

THE STATE'S ECONOMY

The labour force and sources of income

Components. Except for high unemployment in the early 1970s, Maryland enjoyed good economic health, with personal income at an all-time high. Federal, state, and local government employed more than 300,000 members of the civilian labour force, followed closely by manufacturing. The major industries, in order of employment, were primary metal, food and kindred products, fabricated metal, transportation equipment, apparel and related products, and electrical machinery. Most of the establishments were branches of out-of-state corporations; but wages for production workers were slightly above the national average. Coal mining, however, was at its lowest ebb in a century.

Service industries bulked large in the economy, but agriculture probably directly supported fewer than 100,000 persons, including all family members. Although the number of farms had fallen from 48,000 in 1920 to 18,000 in 1970, farm income, the largest proportion from livestock, was up. Fisheries present to Maryland its one category of customary nationwide pre-eminence: oysters. The state's oyster haul rather consistently has led all others. Other saltwater staples include other shellfish, as well as perch, flounder, and other finfish.

The state has taken an increasing interest in the well being of the private sector, particularly through its Department of Economic and Community Development, which encourages outside firms to locate in Maryland, promotes tourism, and keeps close watch on the economy.

Transportation. Entering the 1970s, Maryland offered the traveller from the north three trunk highways into Baltimore and four highways south to Washington. It was possible to swing around Baltimore and Washington on beltways or to avoid them altogether by Eastern Shore routes. The state's main need was an alternate tunnel or bridge across Baltimore Harbor, where the existing tunnel often was unable to handle the flow of traffic. The chief remaining passenger rail service was the Penn Central service to Baltimore and the Capital Beltway. Baltimore's Friendship International Airport was augmented by 44 smaller airports about the state. For freight shipments, the Port of Baltimore had the skills and facilities to go with its standing as fifth in the nation in volume of foreign traffic handled. The port, supervised by a state agency, was especially adapted to bulk commodities, container shipments, and foreign-made automobiles.

ADMINISTRATION AND SOCIAL CONDITIONS

Structure of government. *The state level.* In spite of a provision for statewide voting every 20 years on whether to summon a constitutional convention, repeated attempts to scrap the 1867 document, with its unnecessary detail, obsolete concerns, and silence on points of current interest, have been failures. The existing document has been amended more than 100 times.

The form of state government is like that of most other U.S. states. The governor, who serves for four years, may be re-elected to an immediately succeeding term only once. A 1970–71 reorganization brought together in 11 new departments some 200 divisions, agencies, and facilities previously lacking in coherent direction.

Executive, legislature, and judiciary

Members of the General Assembly serve four years and may be re-elected indefinitely. Reorganization in the 1960s to assure equal voter representation in both houses brought the Senate to a membership of 43, the House of Delegates to 142. Rural domination of the legislature was effectively ended, power passing to the counties adjoining Baltimore and Washington, D.C.

Below the seven-member Court of Appeals, the highest judicial body, is an intermediate Court of Special Appeals and a series of circuit courts—known in Baltimore as the Supreme Bench. Judges are appointed by the governor and must run against their record and anyone filing in opposition—for a 15-year term—in the election following appointment.

The headquarters of the Maryland National Guard is near the Baltimore office centre, in which the offices of some 30 percent of the state's employees are located. The guard was called out in recent years for riot duty in Cambridge, to halt civil-rights disturbances; in Baltimore, where inner-city property destruction in April 1968 (following the assassination of Dr. Martin Luther King, Jr.) was so extensive that army troops quickly replaced guardsmen; and in College Park, where in 1970 and later University of Maryland students protested U.S. military and foreign policies.

Local government. To avoid the greater costs that would be entailed by incorporation as governmental bodies, many of Maryland's most populous areas remain unofficial entities, their services more efficiently and economically provided on a countywide basis. As a result, the basic agency for local administration—aside from the city of Baltimore, a separate entity—is a board of county commissioners, who are elected to four-year terms. The county commissioners' power is largely executive, and most local legislation requires an act of the state legislature. A constitutional amendment allows home rule for counties, under special charter; in 1948 Montgomery County, adjoining the District of Columbia, adopted home rule, and four other counties have since followed suit. A charter county is governed by a county executive and county council, elected to four-year terms; the council is empowered to enact all local laws.

Political life. In the 20th century, though free of the intimidation, poll tax, and other evils practiced in some places in the South, many Maryland elections have been machine dominated. The larger group of voters consistently has registered as Democrats, and their party usually, but not always, wins. Exceptions have occurred when the Democrats split internally, when a nominee's platform was outrageous, or when a Republican presidential candidate carrried the local candidates along. A Republican can usually rely on the western counties, one or two southern enclaves, and, latterly, the Eastern Shore and some affluent parts of suburbia. Baltimore, with its party-boss tradition, is a Democratic stronghold, and college-educated and consciously ethnic voters are dependably Democratic. The black vote, long staunchly Republican, switched parties during the New Deal of the 1930s.

In the early 1970s, both U.S. senators from Maryland were Republican, whereas the General Assembly remained heavily Democratic, as it had for decades. Thus, Democratic primary elections were often more important than the general election. When the nation's axis of balance was North–South, numerous presidential nominating conventions assembled in Baltimore, but none has been held there since 1912. In 1970, Marylanders chose their first Jewish governor and black congressman, but still had never elected a woman governor or member of Congress.

The social milieu. Through its revenues, largely from income and sales taxes, the state has assumed functions and responsibilities no longer within local capacity. It pays all full-time judges; the governor appoints the police commissioner of Baltimore; the construction of all new school buildings is a state matter; and Baltimore's airport is jointly operated by city and state. The state presents annual subsidies to Baltimore's leading orchestra, art museum, and resident theatre; and in 1971 the governor urged an annual subsidy to all nonpublic primary and secondary schools. In many instances, as population and industry moved outward, as old structures were demolished and property-tax assessments and yield dipped, municipalities took the initiative in this transfer of support and direction to the state. Maryland set no speed records, however, in the nationwide movement since 1954 toward racial nondiscrimination in schools, job opportunities, housing, and the like.

State assumption of local financing

Education. Control of public education is vested in the state board of education and county school boards. All positions are appointive, except in Montgomery County, which elects its board. State supervision and support of county public school systems began in 1870; yet not until 1951 were 12 years of schooling uniformly required in all counties. The state in the 1970s aided local systems particularly as regards library services, vocational and rehabilitational instruction, and utilization of federal aid; and the instructional television network opened in 1969.

In the 1960s the five state teachers' colleges were expanded into liberal arts colleges, and Morgan State College in Baltimore added a graduate school. Two-year community colleges were founded in Baltimore and in nearly one-half of the 23 counties. Crowning the state system was the University of Maryland, with its main campus in College Park and branches in Baltimore, Catonsville, and Princess Anne. Its origins date from the College of Medicine of Maryland (opened in 1807) and Maryland Agricultural College (opened in 1856). The several graduate and undergraduate schools were consolidated in 1920; and its 1970–71 enrollment made it one of the nation's ten largest universities.

Of Maryland's 22 privately operated degree-granting institutions of higher learning, the most prominent are Johns Hopkins (founded 1876), with several campuses and a world famous medical school; St. John's College (1784) in Annapolis, with its emphasis on the Great Books of the Western World; and Goucher College (1885) for women, in Towson.

Health and welfare. The Department of Health and Mental Hygiene, besides supervising county services, operates two tuberculosis hospitals, three chronic-disease rehabilitation hospitals, and seven hospitals for the mentally retarded or deranged. The department is also the focus for state efforts to prevent or remove pollution. Its environmental-health section monitors water supply and sewage, air quality, and solid-waste disposal. It also has assumed new responsibilities in the area of drug abuse.

The Department of Social Services is in charge of state welfare activities. Direct aid to families with dependent children comprises its largest outlay, followed by boarding care for children and aid to the elderly, the permanently and totally disabled, and the needy blind.

CULTURAL LIFE AND INSTITUTIONS

The cultural milieu. In the last third of the 20th century, Maryland had its full share of such nationwide phenomena as institutional uniformity, ebbing respect for local and regional distinctiveness, and transitoriness of residence. In addition, the setting contained sizable quantities of seediness, particularly in the close-packed monotony of many a residential neighbourhood, the garish commercialization of streets and highways, the urban waste spaces where torn-down buildings have not been replaced, and always the degradation of the slums—some of them rural.

At the same time, however, the high proportion of Marylanders who were long-time residents (some representing many generations) retained an unusual number of distinctive interests and activities. Echoes of landed gentry of England and of early Maryland were stirred by riding to hounds in pursuit of the fox and taking part in the Grand National Steeplechase and Maryland Hunt Cup races, by breeding Chesapeake Bay retrievers, by jousting on horseback with a spear at rings dangling from a crossbar, and even by appraising the girls making their debuts at cotillions. The out-of-doors looms large in the life of Marylanders: sailing and crabbing on the bay, and trolling for ocean marlin, shooting wild geese in the marshes of the Shore, playing the game of lacrosse (derived from an Indian sport), or hiking the 38-mile stretch of the Appalachian Trail across Maryland in a single day.

Sailboat and sports-car racing provide for both active and passive participation, while the annual Preakness Stakes, the horserace at Pimlico, and Baltimore's baseball Orioles, football Colts, and basketball Bullets have followings far beyond Maryland. The peculiar gastronomy of Maryland, similar to, but different from, that of the Atlantic Coast from Maine to Louisiana, focusses upon terrapin soup, steamed crabs, padded oysters, backfin lump crabcakes, and beaten biscuits, often washed down with Maryland rye and beer at parties ashore or afloat. In almost a different world are the communities of watermen on various islands of the bay, in which isolation has worked to preserve attitudes, ways of life, and accents directly out of the past.

Distinctive cultural remnants

The arts and letters. Among Marylanders who have made major contributions to American artistic and intellectual traditions are the critic H. L. Mencken, the Negro abolitionist-statesman Frederick Douglass, the poet and shortstory writer Edgar Allan Poe, the naturalist Rachel Carson, and the antislavery activist Harriet Tubman.

Today, Baltimore is the focus of much of the state's activity in the arts. The Baltimore Symphony Orchestra is paralleled in professional theatre by the Center Stage Theatre and numerous suburban dinner theatres. The Museum of Art and Walters Art Gallery are supplemented by similar galleries elsewhere, holding in their collections both the arts and the artifacts of the past, as well as by annual art fairs and festivals in several locations.

Historic memorabilia. Virtually all towns, cities, and rural areas in Maryland are marked by relics of the past. The state and the many county and local historical societies and museums offer only parts of the picture. Walking tours are needed to visit the innumerable private homes from the 17th and 18th centuries; the many old canal locks; the National Road in Garrett County that carried many of the early trans-Appalachian homesteaders westward; and the stone markers of the Mason and Dixon Line set at five-mile intervals. Historic festivals and tours are as numerous as those devoted to the products of the bay or to sporting or artistic events.

Pervasiveness of history

The media. Marylanders have only five morning newspapers, led by *The Sun* of Baltimore and *The Washington Post* from the neighbouring national capital, and only nine evening dailies. Several dozen radio stations and about 20 television stations can be picked up in Maryland, many of them from surrounding states.

PROBLEMS AND PROSPECTS

Entering the final decades of the 20th century, Maryland faced many of the difficulties familiar across the nation: maintaining its pleasantness as a place to live while coping with vast population growth; alleviating the deprivations of life on lower socio-economic levels; moving people swiftly between cities and between homes and jobs without paving over the entire landscape; making two-party government a working reality; reducing violent and nonviolent crime; and balancing budgets amid rising costs. The traditional evenness of Maryland ways was jeopardized still further by a clash of interests between the city, specifically Baltimore, and the bursting suburbs adjoining both Baltimore and Washington. Though steadily growing in wealth and power, the suburbs expressed unwillingness to rescue the city as its revenue sources shrank and its social-service needs expanded. Yet there was hope for a resolution of this last impasse in the visibly growing role of the state government. Assuming the role of the disinterested overseer, who requires conflicting jurisdictions to get along and promotes an all-Maryland point of view, it appeared to be leading the way toward better years to come.

BIBLIOGRAPHY. Books on all aspects of Maryland are legion. Fairly recent histories include M.L. RADOFF (ed.), *The Old Line State*, 3 vol. (1957); M.L. CALLCOTT, *The Negro in Maryland Politics, 1870–1912* (1969); C.B. CLARK, *The Eastern Shore of Maryland and Virginia*, 3 vol. (1950); and M. MITCHELL, *Annapolis Visit* (1969). Older works include M.P. ANDREWS, *History of Maryland* (1929, reprinted 1965); W.T. RUSSELL, *Maryland, the Land of Sanctuary: A History of Religious Toleration, 1634–1776* (1908); RAPHAEL SEMMES, *Captains and Mariners of Early Maryland* (1937); and J.M. WRIGHT, *The Free Negro in Maryland, 1634–1860* (1921). JOHN BARTH's novel, *The Sot-Weed Factor* (1960), is an uproarious but atmospheric tale of the 17th-century colony. Maryland's landscape comes alive in such works as the FEDERAL WRITERS' PROJECT, *Maryland* (1940); H. FOOTNER, *Rivers of the Eastern Shore: Seventeen Maryland Rivers* (1944); M.V. BREWINGTON, *Chesapeake Bay: A Pictorial Maritime History*, 2nd ed. (1956), *Chesapeake Bay Log Canoes and Bugeyes* (1963); and A.A. BODINE, *Chesapeake Bay and Tidewater*, 3rd rev. and enl. ed. (1968) and *The Face of Maryland*, 3rd ed. (1970).
The Marylanders and their institutions are covered in G. BYRON, *The Lord's Oysters* (1957); G. WOLFE, *I Drove Mules on the C and O Canal* (1969); K. SCARBOROUGH, *The Homes of the Cavaliers* (1930); H.C. FORMAN, *Maryland Architec-*

ture: *A Short History from 1634 Through the Civil War* (1968); and G.G. CAREY, *Maryland Folklore and Folklife* (1970) and *Faraway Time and Place* (1971).

(Ja.H.B.)

Masaccio

Though he was born poor and lived only 27 years, Masaccio, at the beginning of the 15th century, brought about the most important revolution the art of painting had known up to his time. Like his two great Florentine contemporaries, the architect Brunelleschi and the sculptor Donatello, Masaccio introduced Humanism into his art, putting man and the world at the centre of his works, rather than at the periphery, as in the theocentric universe of medieval art. Implicit in his work is confidence in human reason and knowledge; his subjects appear to have been drawn from the life he saw around him, rather than from the traditional models he inherited.

Anderson—Alinari

"The Trinity," fresco by Masaccio, c. 1427. In the church of Sta. Maria Novella, Florence.

In addition, fundamental technical advances, such as the first use of a central light source in painting and innovations in the use of perspective, are credited to him. The splendour of Italian Renaissance painting begins with Masaccio: all of its original currents derive from him and return to him.

Masaccio was born Tommaso di Giovanni di Simone Guidi on December 21, 1401, the son of Ser Giovanni di Mone Cassai and Monna Jacopa di Martinozzo, in Castel San Giovanni di Altura (now San Giovanni Valdarno, in the Tuscan province of Arezzo). His father was a notary and his mother the daughter of an innkeeper of Barberino di Mugello, a town a few miles south of Florence. His childhood must have been reasonably comfortable in the first years following his father's death in 1406, at the age of 26. Masaccio was then only five years old, and his brother Giovanni, who, under the nickname lo Scheggia, was also to become a painter, was born that year. The mother was remarried to an elderly apothecary who died in August 1417, when Masaccio was 16. That same year the boy moved to Florence.

Early training and influences

It is not known where Masaccio received his training in art. Sources from the 16th century indicate that he served an apprenticeship with Masolino da Panicale, his frequent collaborator, but modern criticism has, on the

whole, repudiated this claim. Masolino was from the same locality as Masaccio, and this may be why they are associated in the early texts, but their association was probably a working partnership in Florence. Close ties with the late Gothic art of Gentile da Fabriano and Arcangelo di Cola da Camerino, as well as the initial influence of such Valdarno painters as Mariotto di Cristofano, also have been surmised. On the other hand, some scholars now believe it unlikely that, given the nature of his genius, Masaccio was able to make use of any influence from the past or present; others, taking into account the chronology of his works, maintain that Masaccio's idiom derived from what had been already achieved by Brunelleschi and Donatello.

On January 7, 1422, Masaccio is known to have been enrolled in Florence in the Arte dei Medici e Speziali; this has been learned from a document in which he is specified, for the first time, as a painter in his own right. That same year, in the church of S. Giovenale in Cascia at Reggello, near Florence, he painted a now only recently discovered triptych with the Madonna enthroned, two adoring angels, and saints. This work, probably wholly executed by Masaccio, falls within the general framework of a normal Florentine tradition, though it may not completely clarify his training as an artist. There is no trace of Masolino, a sign that the meeting with his countryman had not yet occurred, but there is, instead, much of the customary Florentine tradition. There also appear new influences from Giotto and Donatello, and Brunelleschi's revolutionary new treatment of perspective—the technique of rendering objects realistically in space—is also evident.

Masaccio's second known work, the "Madonna and Child with St. Anne," in the Uffizi, was a work begun by Masolino for the church of S. Ambrogio.

Although the contributions of the two artists have been disputed, it is probable that Masaccio painted the Madonna and child and the angel in the upper right and that Masolino painted the rest. Masaccio may be considered the independent collaborator of Masolino, who had perhaps been commissioned to execute the panel. The execution of the painting can be fixed at 1424. The Renaissance biographer Giorgio Vasari seems to assert that in the interval between the "S. Giovenale Triptych" and this painting, the artist made a trip to Rome, in 1423. Such a trip might explain certain influences that are now recognized in this work from ancient Greek and Roman art, which he might have seen there. Presumably, there must have been some trace of such influence in the lost "Sagra," a fresco celebrating the consecration ceremony of the church of Sta. Maria del Carmine in Florence, on April 19, 1422, destroyed as a result of architectural alterations to the church cloister at the end of the 16th century; some indications of it survive in drawings, including a famous one by Michelangelo.

The new Madonna is defined in a more imposing sculptural way than the one of S. Giovenale, and the child, which is taken from ancient models, blesses with a broad gesture of solemnity that is almost that of a Roman consul. Most significantly, the light, for the first time in the history of painting, comes from a single source, building every aspect of form naturalistically and truthfully and immersing it in a spatial reality in which the painter's first exercises in perspective, as developed by Brunelleschi, can perhaps be seen.

Masaccio's association with Masolino grew closer. Since Masolino was planning to visit Hungary, it is possible that he needed a collaborator for both the S. Ambrogio painting and the work he had been commissioned to do in the chapel of the Carmine, so that he could deliver them in time, collect the money required for his journey, and avoid incurring penalties for default. Masaccio might well have accepted such an arrangement, because—despite their essential differences—Masolino was the Florentine painter closest to himself. Like Masaccio, he had an objective, plastic style, though softer and smoother, and both favoured naturalism, even if for Masaccio naturalism meant a compelling obligation to construct and synthesize, while for Masolino it meant sweetness and

Association with Masolino

vagueness, a feeling of springtime or the early morning to be rendered rather naïvely and with no necessary contact with the environment.

On February 19, 1426, Masaccio was commissioned, for the sum of 80 florins, to paint a large altarpiece for a chapel in the church of Sta. Maria del Carmine in Pisa. The execution of the work—as shown by the dates of various payments on account and the final settlement—took until December 26 of that year. The work was dismantled and dispersed in the 18th century, and so far 11 sections have been rediscovered and identified in museums and private collections. Essential for the partial reconstruction of the work was the discovery of the Madonna, now in the National Gallery in London, and of the Crucifixion, now in the Museo e Gallerie Nazionali di Capodimonte in Naples.

Another important presence in Pisa in the year 1426 was that of Donatello, who was working on a monument for Cardinal Rinaldo Brancacci to be sent to Naples. Various connections may be seen between Masaccio's art and the sculpture of Donatello, on which Masaccio's first experiments in plasticity and perspective were based, before he was exposed to Brunelleschi's more scientific approach to perspective. Donatello's influence may be seen especially in the central portion of Masaccio's Pisa polyptych and the Crucifixion above; in particular, certain contrasts in the modelling, by means of light, sharpen the edges in a manner characteristic of Donatello. Indeed, it appears that at Donatello's initial prompting the broad path of the Renaissance opened out before Masaccio.

On December 26, 1426, the final payment of the 80 florins agreed upon for the Pisa polyptych was made. Sometime between the end of 1424 and 1427–28, when he left Florence for Rome, Masaccio painted the most celebrated work of his brief life, the frescoes of the Brancacci Chapel in the church of Sta. Maria del Carmine in Florence, one of the supreme masterpieces of painting of all time. Masaccio and Masolino divided the work, and parts begun by Masaccio were finished by Filippino Lippi. The question of attribution of the various portions of these frescoes has been one of the most discussed artistic problems of the 19th and 20th centuries. The chronology, which remains controversial, appears to have been as follows: from the first months of 1425 and until August of that year, Masaccio executed successively the "Baptism of the Neophytes," "The Expulsion," and "The Tribute Money," while Masolino worked, respectively, on "The Sermon of St. Peter," "The Original Sin," and, aided in part by Masaccio, the "Healing of the Cripple" and the "Resurrection of Tabitha." At the end of 1425 and the beginning of 1426, Masaccio executed "St. Peter Healing the Sick with His Shadow" and "St. Peter Distributing Alms," while Masolino was in Hungary, where he remained until August 1427. Masaccio was soon taken up with work on the Pisa altarpiece, for which he might easily have obtained a release from his commitment to the Brancacci Chapel, because the work was for the same sponsors. In 1427 Masaccio began the "Resurrection of the Son of Theophilus," but work on it was interrupted.

Problems arising from the authorship of these paintings were complicated by the effects of a fire in 1771 that devastated the whole church; the frescoes were saved, except for the fall of two pieces of plaster from the left side (areas of "The Tribute Money" and "Resurrection of the Son of Theophilus"), but they were blackened by smoke. The extent of the darkening was shown only recently by the removal of two small marble projections on the sides of the altar that had covered two areas of original painting in the scenes of Masaccio's "Baptism of the Neophytes" and Masolino's "Sermon of St. Peter."

Masaccio's development can be traced in his treatment of perspective in the various paintings. In the first frescoes of the Brancacci Chapel, from the "Baptism of the Neophytes" to "The Tribute Money," it is rather similar to the intuitive perspective of Donatello, as it appears in his St. George bas-relief (c. 1415); in the final phase of the work ("Resurrection of the Son of Theophilus"), however, the feeling is more in keeping with that of Brunelleschi. This new grasp of perspective is fully realized

in "The Trinity," with the Virgin, St. John the Evangelist, and two donors, in the church of Sta. Maria Novella; the spatial scheme, showing a barrel-vaulted hall, is the first use of linear perspective in the art of fresco painting.

As has been mentioned, Masaccio seems to have returned from Pisa in 1427 to work again in the Carmine. Having begun the "Resurrection of the Son of Theophilus," he interrupted his work when he was called to Rome by Masolino, who had presumably been there since the autumn of 1427.

Attempts by critics to detect Masaccio's hand in Masolino's frescoes of S. Clemente in Rome have been unsuccessful. Nevertheless, he may have made at least a contribution to what was Masolino's polyptych of the altar in Sta. Maria Maggiore in the panel with SS. Jerome and John the Baptist, now in the National Gallery in London.

Masaccio died in Rome in the autumn of 1428. An old and unconfirmed report speaks of death by poisoning. All of his known works derive from a period of eight years.

Masaccio's significance for modern painting has never been doubted through the ages. In his own century, such eminent men of the arts as Leon Battista Alberti and Leonardo da Vinci paid homage to him, and all painters native to or working in Florence studied his Carmine frescoes in order "to learn the precepts and rules for painting well," in the words of Vasari, who specifically enumerated Fra Angelico, Filippo Lippi, Michelangelo, Raphael, and many others. Similarly, artists and writers of later periods have continued to study and to be influenced by him down to the present. Although consistently praised for the profoundly human nature of his art, he has also been variously credited with qualities that reflect the predisposition of each period or the personal biases of the critics. Thus, his work has been called pure, unadorned, and classic, on the one hand, and expressive, plastic, and highly chromatic, on the other; it has been praised by some for being rationalistic and ideologically proletarian or anti-bourgeois, while others have found it anti-intellectual and intuitive. This power to compel careful scrutiny in each succeeding age, while evading any definitive explanation, is the hallmark of only the greatest works of art.

MAJOR WORKS

"Giovenale Triptych" (dated 1422; Uffizi, Florence); "Madonna and Child with St. Anne" (c. 1424; Uffizi); Frescoes in the Brancacci Chapel, Sta. Maria del Carmine, Florence (c. 1424–28): "The Expulsion," "Baptism of the Neophytes," architecture (in the "Resurrection of Tabitha"), "The Tribute Money," "St. Peter Distributing Alms and the Death of Ananias," "St. Peter Healing the Sick with His Shadow," "Resurrection of the Son of Theophilus and St. Peter Enthroned"; "SS. John the Baptist and Jerome" (c. 1426; National Gallery, London); sections of the Pisa polyptych (1426): "St. Paul" (Museo Nazionale di San Matteo, Pisa), "Crucifixion" (Museo e Gallerie Nazionali di Capodimonte, Naples), "St. Andrew" (Lanckoronski Collection, Vienna), "St. Augustine" (Staatliche Museen Preussischer Kulturbesitz, Berlin), "St. Jerome" (Staatliche Museen Preussischer Kulturbesitz, Berlin), "The Virgin and Child" (National Gallery, London), "The Martyrdom of SS. Peter and John the Baptist" (Staatliche Museen Preussischer Kulturbesitz, Berlin), "The Adoration of the Magi" (Staatliche Museen Preussischer Kulturbesitz, Berlin); "St. Julian Murdering His Parents and the Miracle of St. Nicholas" (Staatliche Museen Preussischer Kulturbesitz, Berlin); "Prayer in the Garden and the Communion of St. Jerome" (c. 1426–27; Staatliches Lindenau-Museum, Altenburg); "The Trinity" (c. 1427; Sta. Maria Novella, Florence); "St. Julian's Story" (1427; Museo Horne, Florence).

BIBLIOGRAPHY. The extensive literature on Masaccio was gathered by O.H. GIGLIOLI in his exhaustive annotated bibliography in *Bollettino del Reale Instituto di Archeologia e Storia dell'Arte* (1929); it has been updated to 1963–64 by LUCIANO BERTI, *Masaccio* (1964). Certain contributions after 1945 are noted in ALESSANDRO PARRONCHI's small monograph, *Masaccio* (1966), in Italian. Other basic texts are MARIO SALMI, *Masaccio* (1934, 1947); UGO PROCACCI, *Tutta la pittura di Masaccio* (1951; Eng. trans., *All the Paintings of Masaccio*, 1962); UMBERTO BALDINI in the *Encyclopedia of World Art*, vol. 9, col. 509–520 (1964); and LUCIANO BERTI, *Masaccio* (1967).

(U.Ba.)

Masaccio's most celebrated work

Masaccio's continuing significance

Masaryk, Tomáš

Tomáš Garrigue Masaryk, philosopher, chief founder, and first president of Czechoslovakia, first won international fame for Czech and Slovak independence during World War I. As a philosopher Masaryk was an unrelenting critic of the Czech bourgeoisie; having rebelled against the Roman Catholic Church in his youth, he fought from the 1880s onward for the revival of the puritan ethic of the Bohemian religious reformer Jan Hus.

From the collections of the National Gallery in Prague

Tomáš Garrigue Masaryk, painting by Vojtěch Hynais, 1919. In the Národní Galerie, Prague.

The son of a Slovak coachman, Masaryk was born on March 7, 1850, on an Austrian imperial estate on the Hungarian–Moravian border near Göding (now Hodonín, Czechoslovakia). His mother, a maid, came from a Germanized Moravian family. Though he was trained to be a teacher, he briefly became a locksmith's apprentice but then entered the German high school in Brno in 1865. Continuing his studies at the University of Vienna, he obtained his doctorate in 1876. He studied for a year in Leipzig, where he met an American student of music, Charlotte Garrigue, whom he married in 1876.

He was appointed lecturer in philosophy in Vienna in 1879. Masaryk was a Neo-Kantian, but he was also strongly influenced by the English puritan ethics and the austere teaching of the Hussites. At the same time, he showed a critical interest in the self-contradictions of capitalism—e.g., in his first major work, a study of suicide as a mass phenomenon of modern civilization. In 1882 Masaryk was appointed professor of philosophy in the Czech university of Prague.

His early works on the Czech Reformation and the Czech revival of the early 19th century were intended to remind the Czechs of the "religious meaning" of their heritage. His treatise on the work of the Czech historian František Palacký, who favoured equal rights for Slavs within the Austrian state, was a profound analysis of Austrian–Czech tensions. Masaryk founded two periodicals, in one of which he proved after a bitter debate that two ostensibly early medieval Czech poems, regarded as Slavic counterparts of the German Nibelungenlied, were in fact patriotic forgeries by an early-19th-century Czech poet.

In 1889 Masaryk entered upon his political career after transforming a journal into a political review. In the early 1890s he began to turn his attention to the Slovaks in northern Hungary. By criticizing both the feudal nature of Hungarian sovereignty and the antiquated Pan-Slav tendencies of the Slovak politicians, he became the idol of the young Slovak progressives who played a decisive role in the Czech–Slovak union in 1918–19. After unmasking the forged medieval Czech poems, he demonstrated his willingness to risk unpopularity in pursuit of moral righteousness once again when he succeeded in

1899 in proving the innocence of Jews accused in a ritual-murder case. Although deeply involved in political controversies, Masaryk published two monumental works before 1914. In his work on Marxism (1898) he discussed the immanent contradictions of both capitalism and Socialism. In *Russia and Europe* (1913) he provided a critical survey of the Russian religious, intellectual, and social crises—the contradictions and confusions of the "Byzantine retardation of Russian society by the Orthodox Church and reactionary ideas.

As a politician he was at first an adherent of the federative Austro-Slavism in 1848. But as a democrat he gradually became estranged from the loyal, conservative, and Catholic concept of the Old Czech Party and accepted the invitation of the liberal, bourgeois Young Czech Party. In 1891 he was elected to the Austrian Reichsrat, but, after disagreeing with the Young Czechs' emotional nationalism, he resigned his seat in 1893. In March 1900 he founded his own Realist Party, and, after his re-election in a more democratic Reichsrat, he became an outstanding figure of the left Slav opposition there. In both the Reichsrat and the standing committee of the Austrian and Hungarian parliaments he attacked Austria–Hungary's alliance with Germany and its imperialistic politics in the Balkans. He defended the rights of the Serbs and Croats —especially at the time of the annexation of Bosnia-Hercegovina by Austria.

In early 1915, after the outbreak of World War I, Masaryk made his way to western Europe, where he was recognized as the representative of the underground Czech liberation movement and conducted a vigorous campaign against Austria–Hungary and Germany. His British and French friends helped him to establish contact with the Allied leaders, to whom he delineated the Czech aims: restitution of Bohemia's independence on a democratic basis; the establishment of Czech–Slovak unity; dismemberment of Austria–Hungary according to ethnic principles, and establishment of new states between Germany and Russia as a cordon sanitaire against German imperialism. After the overthrow of the autocratic tsarist regime in 1917, he transferred his activities to Russia in order to organize the Czechoslovak Legion, formed by Czechoslovak war prisoners, and to develop contacts with the new government. After the Bolshevik Revolution he set out for the United States, where he was welcomed by Czech and Slovak groups and negotiated the terms of Czechoslovak independence with Pres. Woodrow Wilson and Secretary of State Robert Lansing. The Lansing Declaration of May 1918 expressed the sympathy of the United States government with the Czechoslovak freedom movement, and Czechoslovakia's liberation became one of Wilson's Fourteen Points for the post-World War I peace settlement. Masaryk also concluded the so-called Pittsburgh Convention with the Slovak associations in the United States, which promised the Slovaks a large measure of home rule; the interpretation of this declaration led to controversies between the Slovak opposition and the Czechoslovak government during the life of the first Czech republic.

On June 3, 1918, Czechoslovakia was recognized as an Allied power, and its frontiers were demarcated according to Masaryk's outline. As Masaryk had promised, the new multinational state respected the minority rights of its large German and Hungarian ethnic groups. On November 14, 1918, he was elected president of Czechoslovakia and re-elected in 1920, 1927, and 1934. As a true "liberator" and "father of his country," he was constantly occupied in settling the crises resulting from the conflicts between the Czech and the Slovak parties, as well as from Slovakia's minority status. A philosopher and democrat, Masaryk was among the first to voice his anxiety over central Europe's fate after the Nazis came to power in Germany in 1933. He resigned his post in December 1935 and died in Castle Lány on September 14, 1937.

BIBLIOGRAPHY. For an anthology of Masaryk's political essays and speeches, see *Cesta demokracie*, 2 vol. (1933–34). Studies of Masaryk's life and politics include: KAREL CAPEK, *Hovory s T.G. Masarykem*, 3 vol. (1926–28; 1 vol., 1936; Eng. trans., *President Masaryk Tells His Story*, 1934, reprinted

1971; and *Masaryk on Thought and Life: Conversations with Karel Capek*, 1938, reprinted 1971); EMIL LUDWIG, *Gespräche mit Masaryk: Denker und Staatsmann* (1935; Eng. trans., *Defender of Democracy: Masaryk of Czechoslovakia*, 1936, reprinted 1971); ZDENEK NEJEDLY, *T.G. Masaryk*, 2nd ed., 2 vol. (1949–50); R.W. SETON-WATSON, *Masaryk in England* (1943); ROBERT BIRLEY, *Thomas Masaryk* (1951); and LUDWIG VON GOGOLAK, "T.G. Masaryks slowakische und ungarländische Politik: Ein Beitrag zur Vorgeschichte des Zerfalls Ungarns im Jahre 1918," in *Bohemia, Jahrbuch des Collegium Carolinum*, vol. 4, pp. 174–227 (1963). The best summation of Masaryk's views and philosophy may be found in the *Festschrift Th. G. Masaryk zum 80. Geburtstage*, ed. by B.V. YAKOVENKO, 2 vol. (1930), a collection of essays honouring him on his 80th birthday; see especially EMANUEL RADL's study.

(L.v.G.)

Mashriq, Cultures of the

The Mashriq may be defined as the region extending from the western border of Egypt through to the western border of Iran. Countries included in the area are thus Egypt, the Sudan, Saudi Arabia, Yemen (Ṣanʿāʾ), Yemen (Aden), and Oman; Kuwait and the small Persian Gulf states; and Israel, Jordan, Lebanon, Syria, and Iraq. The total land area is approximately 2,700,000 square miles (7,000,000 square kilometres) and the total population some 80,000,000. The area has, in the 20th century, been given other appellations, including Levant, Near East, and Middle East.

From the perspective of its cultural geography, the Mashriq may be divided into two types of region: the arid, infertile desert areas that are the home of the nomadic Bedouin and the fertile, cultivated river valleys of the settled agriculturalists.

The great plateau of the Arabian Peninsula comprises most of the desert area. Barren, except for occasional oases and the Najd, a pastoral tableland in the north, the peninsula is fronted to the west by mountains rising in the Hejaz, the holy land of Islām, to some 9,000 feet (3,000 metres) and further south, in the Yemen, to some 14,000 feet. The south central portion of the peninsula, an area of some 40,000 square miles (100,000 square kilometres), is known locally as ar-Rubʿ al-Khali (the Empty Quarter). Here, average summer temperatures are in excess of 120° F.

The outstanding geographical feature of the remainder of the Mashriq is the Fertile Crescent, an arc of territory stretching from the Nile Valley of Egypt through present-day Israel, Lebanon, Jordan, and Syria, into Iraq. At each horn of the Fertile Crescent there is a river valley—to the east that of the Tigris and Euphrates rivers, in Iraq, and to the west that of the Nile, in Egypt. These valleys are composed of rich and fertile masses of alluvium deposited year after year on a substratum of sand and rock. In Egypt this deposit is almost 40 feet deep. As they are annually replenished, these valleys are continually refertilized. They also provide irrigation and drinking water.

PEOPLES AND LANGUAGES

The Mashriq has the longest cultural history of any region in the world and was in fact the birthplace of human civilization. Three monotheistic religions—Judaism, Christianity, and Islām—originated there. As a land bridge connecting Asia, Africa, and Europe, it has been traversed by numerous peoples, many of whom left small groups in the region. Its cultural evolution has been such that, until recently, minority groups were permitted to retain separate and distinct entities, so that the most conspicuous fact about the Mashriq has been its demographic heterogeneity; its population is a mosaic of peoples.

Among the earliest inhabitants of the region were the Sumerians, believed to have been of an Armenoid physical type—roundheaded, of moderate height, and of heavy build. They spoke a language with certain agglutinative features suggestive of the Mongoloid family of languages. The ancient Egyptians were of the Mediterranean physical type—longheaded, dark-haired, relatively slender, and of moderate stature, speaking a separate language classified as Hamitic.

Additional early peoples in the area were the Akkadian, Babylonian, and Assyrian invaders and conquerors of Mesopotamia, the Amorites of northern Syria, the Aramaeans of inner Syria, the Canaanites of the Levant coast, and the Hebrews of the hill country. All of these peoples are generally classified as Semites—not because they possessed any unique physiological feature but because they all spoke languages assigned to the North Semitic family and because they are generally believed to have originated somewhere in the central Arabian Peninsula. Arabic, the primary contemporary South Semitic language, was apparently originally spoken by a small group of traders, townsfolk, and desert nomads in the district of Mecca and Medina. Arabic was the language of Muḥammad and his early followers, and, with the rise and expansion of Islām in the 7th century, it quickly replaced most other languages of the Mashriq. Within the region, Egyptian, Palestinian, Syrian, Iraqi, and Yemeni dialects of Arabic are spoken today. Some of these differ only in pronunciation, while in other instances the colloquial forms may be quite wide apart. Other languages spoken in the region are Hebrew, which is one of the official languages of Israel (the other is Arabic); Aramaic, which is reputed to be still spoken in a few villages of Syria; and Kurdish, an Indo-European language spoken by the approximately 1,000,000 Kurds resident in Iraq and Syria.

The Kurds, a semi-nomadic pastoral group, practice transhumance (movement between summer pastures on the mountain slopes and winter quarters in the valleys and lowlands). Kurdistan, their homeland, is a rugged mountainous region lying in Syria, Iraq, Iran, and Turkey. The Kurds have lived in the region since they invaded it, perhaps in the 2nd millennium BC, and to this day the Kurds have maintained their distinct tribal independence. Invaders of the Kurds' region—from Alexander the Great to the present-day Iraqi militia—have attested to the Kurdish reputation of being a "fierce and predatory people."

TRADITIONAL CULTURE PATTERNS

Settlement patterns and economic organization. *The fellahin ("villagers").* Agriculture has long been and still continues to be the predominant way of life of the majority of the peoples of the Mashriq. Spread along the Fertile Crescent and in the isolated oases of the deserts, the overwhelming majority of the people were—and still are—peasants. Despite widespread urbanization, more than two-thirds of the people may still be classified as fellahin.

Family solidarity and the need for security have always precluded a pattern of isolated farmsteads. Instead, the peasants gather together in villages, ranging from modern and well-off communities in Lebanon (particularly among the Christians) to the miserable mud and kerosine-can huts of semi-nomadic tribesmen. Despite such disparities, however, a broad cultural pattern can be discerned, especially in the Arabic-speaking regions.

Landownership in the Mashriq is complicated by the fact that landed property, or the right to work other people's landed property, is divided among the children, with boys sharing equally but with a girl's share equalling only half that of a boy. Complex fragmentation of agricultural land results, with the dispersed small plots, sometimes termed "dwarf holdings," rarely economically feasible. High-interest loans are often not met, and as a result the accumulation of large tracts of land in the hands of a few wealthy landowners is quite common; many debt-ridden peasants are consequently forced into sharecropping. In virtually all of the newly independent nations of the Mashriq, land reform is one of the basic tenets of revolutionary programs. Much, however, still remains to be accomplished.

Throughout the region village layout is strikingly similar. At the centre is the mosque, or church, bordered by a few small shops of the grocer, blacksmith, and cobbler. Some five to ten twisted alleys, just wide enough for a donkey with its side baskets, wind between the walls of low, flat-roofed houses and then narrow into even smaller

Linguistic basis of the Semitic ethnic classification

The traditional village

lanes that generally end where the fields begin. The village square functions as a marketplace for itinerant peddlers and is the scene of village ceremonial events.

The homes, whether of stone blocks or sunbaked bricks, consist of a few rooms and a courtyard. When a son marries, a new room is added along the side of the house, on the roof, or in the courtyard. Stables are uncommon, and the fellahin share with their animals the same dirt- and dung-littered courtyard and, in winter, the same room for sleeping.

Furniture among the peasants is limited and strictly utilitarian. Since squatting on the floor is the normal position, whether doing the housework or eating with the fingers or with a piece of bread dipped into a common bowl, there is no need for tables and chairs or forks, knives, and spoons.

A chest, a pile of bedding stored away during the day in a recess in the wall, a cradle, a few straw mats, a kerosine lamp, and perhaps one or two cheap carpets constitute the essential furniture. Kitchen needs are met by a few clay jars for keeping the drinking water, a large grain bin coated with clay and sealed at the top but open at the bottom for access to the daily need, a copper kettle, a few handwoven baskets, some locally made earthen jars, and a variety of imported bowls and basins. A few coffee cups on a tray for occasional visitors, a few photographs of the sons (daughters are rarely photographed, and their pictures are certainly not on view), some religious prints or calligraphed verses of the Qur'ān, and a newspaper photograph of the local national leader complete the inventory of the typical village home.

Water is generally a scarce commodity. If the peasants are fortunate, they may have a well in the courtyard. Generally, however, water is obtained from common village wells, springs, or ponds. When these dry up during the long arid summer months, animals and humans share the same distant, often polluted, ponds or streams. Piped water to the courtyards or to the village centre is not uncommon among wealthy villagers or in areas in which the government has embarked on special rural development programs. In some regions of Iraq and Egypt and along the rivers of the Levant, although water may be readily available, it often is a source of malaria and other diseases. Flush toilets are very rare, as are outhouses. Urine is generally disposed of in the courtyards, along the paths, or in the fields. Fecal matter is spread in the fields.

Animal dung, in treeless regions, is the prime source of fuel. Women and children carefully gather the dung, shape it, dry it in the sun, and store it on the roof or in the courtyard. The family oven, in which bread is baked, is generally in the courtyard and is a dome-shaped mud affair with a low opening.

The diet is simple and generally monotonous. Its mainstays consist of unleavened bread, accompanied by rice and a few vegetables, usually onions and garlic, and, depending on the region, olives or dates. In season, small amounts of fresh fruit and green vegetables may be added. Tea and coffee are luxury items paid for out of a limited budget. Meat and fat are eaten, by most, only at special ceremonies such as a wedding, birth of a son, or great holidays or in honour of a distinguished visitor.

Health and education among the fellahin Standards of health and education well demonstrate the poverty of the peasants. Malnutrition is chronic, and infectious diseases are endemic. It is estimated that perhaps nine-tenths of the fellahin suffer from a variety of dysfunctional or debilitating diseases such as trachoma, typhoid, dysentery, intestinal worms, and tuberculosis. Western-type medical aid is still not widely available among peasants, and their main recourse continues to be the traditional village practitioners. Schooling, despite the fact that most countries of the Mashriq have enacted compulsory-education laws, is uneven and sporadic. Illiteracy among rural adults, particularly women, is still the rule.

The way of life for the early Zionist farmers working the marginal lands of Palestine often was as difficult as that of their fellow Arabs. It was the attempt to break out of that pattern that led to the development among the Jews of collective forms of agriculture—variants of the kibbutz and the moshav—designed to maximize their financial and labour input, to raise their agricultural returns, and to improve their collective standard of living.

The Bedouin. The Bedouin, as one observer has put it, are more glamorous than numerous. They have rarely constituted more than 15 percent of the total population of the Mashriq, and in the 1970s their numbers were rapidly decreasing, even in the Arabian Peninsula, as they voluntarily migrated to the towns to work for the oil industry or to settle on government-sponsored tracts of land.

The homeland of the classical, traditional Bedouin is an area of the northern Arabian Desert, stretching into Iraq, Syria, and Jordan. The Bedouin are nomads in varying degrees, but the true Bedouin are those who possess only camels and who spend their summer months camped around wells or streams and the rest of the year ranging the desert. In kinship they trace their origin back either to Qaḥṭān, an ancient patriarch who lived before Abraham, or to Ishmael, son of Abraham and Hagar. Collectively they constitute the *aṣīlīn*, a closed circle of about 18 tribes or tribal confederations.

The material culture of the Bedouin is limited. The chief possession is the home—a long, low, black tent of woven goat hair. Men and women have separate divisions within the tent. The male side, away from the wind, is left open; it has a carpet, spread before a portable stove, or coffee hearth, with a mortar for grinding the coffee, a coffeepot, and cups. This is the social centre of the household, the meeting place for guests, and the site for the transaction of all tribal affairs.

Clothing is simple: a long robe of thick material, a large headcloth wound around the head and held in place by a black goat-hair cord and rawhide, and heelless sandals.

Water is generally too scarce to be used for washing, and sand or animal urine is substituted for use in daily ablutions. The diet is limited, consisting of a variety of milk products such as curds, buttermilk, and cheese, dried fruit, particularly dates, and, when obtainable from the fellahin, grains such as wheat, barley, or rice. Meat, as among the peasants, is a luxury eaten only when an animal has died a natural death or for a special ceremony. The meals are served first to the older men of the tent, then to the younger men and boys, and finally to the women and the girls. The sexes do not intermingle during mealtime. The inadequate diet and low standard of nutrition result in a people who are small, even stunted, and slightly built. By the age of 40, particularly among the women, old age has begun.

Raiding was the traditional means of supplementing the deficiencies of life in the arid zone. The Bedouin took by force from the peasants what they lacked in foodstuffs, material goods, and even women and children. Successful leadership in raids could be a most effective means of developing reputation and power, a practice that to this day has not been completely curtailed. **Bedouin raiding**

Social organization. In certain respects the fellahin and the Bedouin share a similar social structure, and thus the pattern traditionally common to both can be broadly sketched. The model described is that of the classical, idealized, Arab way of life.

The family. The family is the most fundamental and important feature of Arab social structure. The family is extended—that is, it is headed by an elderly man and consists of his wife, or wives, his married sons and their wives and children, his unmarried sons, and his unmarried daughters. Daughters, when they marry, leave their own extended families and become incorporated into the extended families of their husbands, even though their moral conduct continues to be the responsibility of the original family.

The extended family may total a dozen or more persons, all of whom live in one house or in a number of adjoining houses or, as among the Bedouin, in a number of tents pitched next to each other. The extended family functions as one entity in economic, political, and military ventures.

The family is patrilineal—*i.e.*, an individual belongs only to the family of his father—and patrilocal (young couples when they marry take up residence in or near the house of the bridegroom's father). It is also patriarchal: the father is the head of his family, and the elderly male who is head of the entire extended family is the absolute ruler over the entire group, traditionally. Even to this day, in certain respects, he has jurisdiction over life and death.

Pride in descent forms one of the most significant traits in the ethos of the peoples of the Mashriq. Emphasis on noble ancestry and lineage is a matter of great importance among the Bedouin and to a lesser extent among the fellahin. Tribal and village genealogists trace an individual back from his individual extended family to his sub-*ḥamūlah* (a cluster of extended families) to his *ḥamūlah* (a large group of families tied together by an actual or assumed genetic relationship) and to his subtribe (*'ashīrah*) and tribe (*qabīlah*). Beyond his tribal affiliation, a man's lineage will be traced to his supposed progenitor dating back to early biblical sources. This tribal pedigree, even among the villagers, can play a fundamental role in determining and justifying positions of traditional authority and political power.

Marriage and divorce. There is a strong tradition of endogamous marriage (that is, of marriage within a very small social circle), ideally with the father's brother's daughter or, failing that, within the same village or tribe or having the same social status. A man may be married to more than one wife simultaneously (polygyny).

Prevalence of polygyny

The prevalence of polygyny among the Arabs has been greatly exaggerated by Western commentators, and the practice has always been the exception rather than the rule, especially in modern times. The simple biological problem of acquiring a surplus of young females plus the economic cost of paying their bride-prices and then adequately supporting them and their offspring all have prevented any more than 4 to 5 percent of the married men from having more than one spouse.

Traditionally marriages are arranged and consummated when the women are still in their teens. This is considered highly proper and beneficial. An old Arab saying holds that there are only three things in life a man must do quickly: bury the dead, serve a guest, and marry off a marriageable daughter.

Great prestige is attached to the male's procreative ability and to the regular delivery of live, preferably male, children. Status is achieved through the production of large families; a childless couple is regarded with contempt. Only the extended family with many children, preferably boys, can be a strong family, providing economic and political security. The injunction to "be fruitful and multiply" thus provides a constant goal.

Term, or temporary, marriage, usually referred to as *mut'ah*, dates back to pre-Islāmic days and still survives in certain parts of the Mashriq. Term marriages were contracts made with women by soldiers, traders, and travellers under which the couple were legally married for the day, the length of the caravan journey, or for another defined time period. At the stated end of the period the contract was no longer binding. Children born of *mut'ah* marriages held all the rights of the offspring of ordinary marriages, but the term wife could not inherit from her husband nor he from her.

The announcement of the birth of a child to the father is based upon long-standing Mashriq traditions. If the infant is a boy, the father will be told *bishārah*, meaning "good tidings" or "reward." The father will ordinarily give a modest gift to the individual who first brings him this news. Among those who can afford it, a sacrifice of a sheep or a feast is also common. If the infant is a girl, no reward will be given for the announcement, neither will there be a celebration.

Traditional divorce in Arab Muslim society is extremely simple. The male is the sole initiator of such an action. The wife can neither oppose a divorce nor initiate one on her own behalf. The husband pronounces the traditional formula, "I divorce thee," in the presence of two witnesses, and the divorce is effected. The wife must return to her father's (or brother's) family and can claim only that portion of the bride-price that was stipulated in the original marriage contract to be paid in the event of such an occurrence. If a wife should leave her husband and he later agrees to a divorce, she forfeits any part of the bride-price. After the divorce a man may marry immediately, but the woman must wait three months to make sure that she is not pregnant. If she is pregnant, she cannot remarry until she has given birth to the child and reared it, during which time the father (her former husband) must support her. All children belong to the father and, in the event of a divorce, must be delivered up to him.

Among the Arab Muslims no stigma is attached to divorce, and divorced women as a rule remarry as soon as they are permitted to do so.

Socialization. Shortly after birth, the infant will be rubbed with salt and oil, not only to cleanse him but also to enable him to grow up to be modest and courteous. The infant will then be wrapped in swaddling clothes for a time period ranging from 40 days to six months.

Nursing may last for 18 months to three years. A mother is traditionally prohibited from weaning her child before two years. The extended nursing period postpones another pregnancy (suckling periods are generally connected with an abstinence from intercourse), and it is believed to make the child strong.

To mothers it is said: "pampering a girl disgraces thee; pampering a boy makes thee rich." The boy will therefore be nursed longer than the girl. As soon as the child shows the slightest signs of restlessness, he will be breast fed. As a consequence, the female is seen as sympathetic and the woman's breast as a symbol of compassion.

If for some reason, such as illness, a child is nursed by a woman other than its mother, certain protocol must be observed. A woman may not give her milk to another child or have another woman give her child milk without her husband's permission; for the child belongs to the husband's patrilineage, and that important decision rests with him. Furthermore, a boy and a girl nursed by the same woman are considered to be brother and sister and can never marry. Nursing relationships can also be a method of adoption (especially of an orphan): if a woman wishes to adopt a strange child or even an adult, she does so by offering her breast.

The religious rite of circumcision

One of the most important events in a Muslim and Jewish boy's life, not only for himself but also for his parents, is circumcision. The rite of circumcision is a religious duty, and no male can enter heaven uncircumcised. The age at which circumcision is carried out varies: it may be done shortly after birth or in childhood, but it must be done before marriage. Fathers will ordinarily have their sons circumcised soon after birth, not only because it is less painful then but also because of fear that the boy might die before the father has fulfilled the commandment of circumcising his son.

Among Muslims, the rite of circumcision proceeds in a program similar to that of a wedding. It is preceded by an evening of joy in village festivities, henna (a dye) is put on by the woman, and a new outfit is provided for the child. Festival garments decorated with flowers and leaves are worn, and, in similar fashion to a bride, the boy is led in procession around the village in his new outfit. After the ceremony there is a feast at which presents are given. Several boys may be circumcised at once, or the circumcision may be combined with a wedding to save expenses. There is a further connection between circumcision and marriage, for, as it is the duty of the father to marry his children before his death, he attempts to find a suitable mate for them as soon as possible. A boy thus often acquires his bride at his circumcision ceremony, although he will not marry her until sometime after puberty.

The early socialization of a boy and a girl into the traditional family of the Mashriq differs profoundly. The growing boy is trained to become an obedient member of his family, able to subordinate his wishes to those of his father and elder brothers. The fact is impressed upon him that the interests of his family always come first and that he must govern his actions to enhance the collective strength of his family. The girl, on the contrary, is not only weaned earlier than the boy but, by the age of five or six, is already being consciously prepared for moving out of the home of her parents and into the home of her mother-in-law. There, she will fill a subordinate and even a servant role—a role that will be improved only as she bears sons.

Religion and health. A discussion of the predominant religion of the area, Islām, can be found in such articles as ISLAM; ISLAMIC MYSTICISM; and ISLAMIC THEOLOGY AND PHILOSOPHY. But some understanding of the function of religion in the traditional Mashriq can be grasped from an analysis of its role in the peoples' approach to health, disease, and death.

Philosophy of illness. The essential philosophy underlying the traditional system of medicine in the Mashriq is that illnesses and injuries are subjective affairs arising from one's own acts or omissions or caused by someone or something possessed with power. Illnesses or injuries do not just occur—they befall a certain victim, at a given time and in a definite manner, because of specific causal actions.

Two essential elements of this philosophy are belief in animism and animatism, or, more specifically, the belief in the existence of evil spirits (animism) and of the "evil eye" (animatism), or the power of certain persons or objects to affect and influence the human body—and nature as well, in certain circumstances.

Evil spirits abound in the environment, ready to pounce on the unsuspecting victim. Strong, healthy, mature individuals are the least susceptible to such attacks; the most susceptible are infants and children, the weak, the ill, the aged, and normally healthy individuals in certain circumstances (women during menstruation, pregnancy, or while giving birth, for example).

The presence of strong, healthy, mature individuals near the susceptible person is a strong deterrent to evil spirits. As one cannot rely on such persons to be constantly on duty, however, various inanimate objects with strong power to repel the evil spirits are called into play. Common objects of this nature are the Hand of Fāṭimah (beloved daughter of Muḥammad), which may have inscribed on it holy words in Arabic or Hebrew and which is generally worn around the neck (Cochin Jews may put it around the abdomen); the shield of David (a six-pointed star); and blue beads, pieces of jewelry, or bits of cloth that are worn around the neck or attached to the clothing (blue is particularly repugnant to the evil spirits and the evil eye). Sometimes a concoction of evil-smelling herbs will be placed in a bag and worn close to the body, or various religious phrases will be written on paper and sewed into the clothing or put into a bag and worn on the body.

The Bible also possesses the power to repel evil spirits, and thus some Jewish mothers place a copy of it beneath the pillow. Another practice, but less common, is to preserve the foreskin cut off during the *ber-it mila* (the ceremony of circumcision conducted on every Jewish male child when he is eight days old), by drying the piece of skin and powdering it. It is then sewn into a piece of cloth and kept under the pillow or among the blankets of the child's bed.

Evil spirits fear the name of Allāh, which strikes terror into their hearts and weakens them and forces them to withdraw or repels them completely. Consequently, his name is uttered frequently while a person is engaged in the everyday routine of life. Otherwise healthy individuals must, in certain circumstances, be particularly careful to invoke Allāh's name. When, for example, a Muslim couple is about to engage in sexual intercourse, the male must first say a prayer: "I seek refuge in Allāh, from the accursed Satan, in the name of Allāh, the Beneficent, the Merciful." If this is not said, the evil spirit will enter the woman, and her child will be evil, bad, or a devil, or the woman herself might fall ill. A prayer to Allāh also ensures conception—the mere physical act of intercourse is no guarantee.

Vulnerability of women. From the moment of conception until the last birth pang, the pregnant woman is especially sensitive to evil spirits. Each of her actions is carefully watched by them, and, should she commit a transgression or not constantly invoke the power of Allāh, retribution will be certain to follow. The afterbirth provides powerful protection for the newborn child and must be saved. It may be left attached to the child for some hours or overnight, and it then must be preserved in or near the house.

Women during menstruation are very dangerous. They are not only considered impure and unclean but also, if not actually possessed by a spirit, likely to be transmitters of the actions of evil spirits. They must therefore be separated from others, particularly from the ill and women in labour. Women during menstruation sometimes must leave the home and live in a menstruation hut or tent for the entire period, returning to their homes only after they have been purified. When a woman is permitted to remain in the home, she is subject to numerous restrictions: She must sleep on the floor or on a low bed, must have no sexual relations with her husband, must not even touch him or his bed, and should not prepare any meals or enter a home in which there is an ill person or a woman in labour. Such restrictions are only practicable within the extended family, and disintegration of the extended family leads to forced abandonment of many such practices. The beliefs themselves, however, may persist, as may anxieties when the taboos are broken.

Safeguards against the evil eye. The prevention of illness to the inner body by the evil eye—as distinct from the prevention of illnesses caused by evil spirits—is based on the principle of misleading, deceiving, and deluding the evil eye. The evil eye is particularly feared, and more than half of all deaths are attributed to it. It is attracted to the healthy, the beautiful, the happy, and to children.

In the Mashriq, possessors of the evil eye are often women. Psychologists have argued that the evil eye is in reality an envious eye, and the entire corpus of preventive measures seems to be based upon the principle of not attracting its attention (or envy). The youngest are a particular attraction to the evil eye. Thus children, esteemed the greatest blessings, are kept dirty, ragged, and unkempt, particularly when out in public. The child may be called "Oh, dirty one" or "Oh, evil one" and similar names, in order to disguise the true feelings of the parent. The child may be given a false name, and its true name kept a secret, in order that the real name may not be overheard and utilized for negative purposes. The child will never be praised in public or boasted about; on the contrary, it will constantly be decried and complained about. A male child may be dressed as a girl and referred to in the feminine, since females have less prestige. Such practices against the evil eye are especially likely to be followed if there have been previous infant deaths in the family or if there is only one child.

To arouse disgust in the eye of the beholder is far healthier than to arouse admiration; and praise when given must be denied or deprecated. Inquiries about personal or family health, business, or status should be responded to with shaking heads and gloomy predictions. Boasting is considered the fool's way of courting disaster, as is the disclosure of one's future plans. It is possible, however, to accept praise or note good looks, good health, or good fortune if one is careful to constantly invoke the name of Allāh and to deny the force of the evil eye.

Particularly valuable as a defense against the evil eye are amulets. Blue beads are the most common type, and they may be worn on the person or placed in the house or on a dog, horse, cart, or automobile.

If, despite such precautions, evil spirits do gain access to the body and illness sets in, medicine is brought into play. Curative practices are clearly recognized, however, as being less successful ultimately than preventive measures, and their purpose is partly to provoke emotional comfort and security to the patient and his family.

The local practitioner gives the family his undivided attention, identifies and names the disease, makes a positive prognosis, and initiates certain measures to evict the evil spirits or draw away the evil eye. These include smoking, drinking, chanting, praying, burning, bloodletting, emetics, purgatives, and massages. A burning blue

(margin notes:)

Evil spirits and the evil eye

Restrictions on menstruating women

Curative practices

rag may be snuffed and the smoke inhaled to weaken or frighten out the evil spirits, especially during childbirth. Charms and holy phrases written on paper may be soaked in a liquid and then drunk in order to internalize the holy power. The spittle of a holy man may be applied to the disturbed organ of the body. The patient's name may be changed so that the evil spirit may somehow be misled and lose the patient or never find him.

Drastic, painful measures may be taken to force out the spirit. A red-hot nail may be pressed against the abdomen of an infant a number of times to force out the evil causing dysentery; it may be pressed against other parts of the skin to evict the evil spirit causing smallpox or rheumatism, or it may be pressed against a "boil" under the tongue to enable the baby to take the breast. The entire family may be required to chant special prayers, songs, or phrases or to fast or suffer other discomforts. Parents may have to abstain from sexual relations, and members of the family may have to travel on a pilgrimage. There may be bargaining on the part of the family, and precious animate or inanimate objects may be sacrificed to appease the evil spirit. The patient, recipient of this rich fund of strength, is emotionally able to endure the physical discomfort during the prescribed course of curative treatment and is mentally prepared for possible death should the treatment not succeed.

If the patient should die it is because he or his family, consciously or unconsciously, committed offenses and attracted the evil eye or permitted evil spirits to enter the body to the extent that no power was able to avert the evil and save the patient.

It is clear that both patient and practitioner operate within a cultural framework of knowledge, beliefs, and values that explain their respective actions. The patient and his family search their thoughts and actions to ascertain how the misfortune could have occurred or by whom it could have been inflicted. The practitioner, on his part, listens to the family's statements and the patient's complaint and then formulates his diagnosis and treatment. The success in such treatment in a certain number of cases inspires further faith in the system. There are few cynics among the patients and few charlatans among the practitioners.

Types of medical practitioner

Within this medical system may be distinguished three or four types of local practitioners specializing in particular areas and methods of treatment. Their sex, role, or status may vary, or they may specialize in cures for external complaints such as sores and wounds; or they may practice preventive and curative medicine for the internal body. The latter is generally a male of senior years and of religious–medical standing. To fulfill his role he must be well versed in the concepts of animism and animatism. Such knowledge alone, however, is not sufficient; he must also have a personality that will inspire confidence and elicit information from the patient and his family. In addition, he must be aware of the significance of symptoms and complaints, certain of which may or may not be expressed. He must possess to a high degree the quality of sensitivity and intuitiveness, for many of his diagnoses will be based upon implicit understanding and tacit agreement. He must have the ability to quickly analyze and evaluate the relations between the patient, his family, and his community.

MODERNIZATION OF THE CULTURES

A process of Westernization, modernization, and development has come to dominate the Mashriq. The evolution of the traditional folk culture of the fellahin and the Bedouin is being radically altered, and even rural peasants want to live the supposed good life made possible by Western technology. The town in the Mashriq is the focal centre of this Westernization process, and from there it is dispersed throughout the countryside and into the desert. It is useful, therefore, to examine the traditional town and the ways in which it is changing.

Classical urban pattern. Urban life began in this area of the world, and it is not uncommon to still find towns that have been occupied continuously or intermittently over the past 4,000 years. While the Bedouin and the

fellahin have long remained rather constant in their culture, the towns have constantly reflected the effects of political changes, military invasions, and population movements. Thus, whereas the nomads and villagers were comparatively homogeneous in both population and occupational structure, the towns contained separate quarters (*harat*) for various ethnic and religious populations and also a range of occupations and social classes.

The typical Arab town of the Middle Ages consisted of a mosque, a palace, a bathhouse, a school, a *khān* (hostelry for foreign merchants), a hospital, and a *maydān* (an open field for the horse and cattle market). Two main thoroughfares ran through the town at right angles to each other, leading from the four gates of the thick and heavily fortified walls. From the centre a network of narrow streets and alleys radiated into the residential quarters. Each of these quarters was also walled, frequently with its own bathhouse and school, as well as a mosque, church, or synagogue. The cemeteries and the *maydān* were outside the town walls.

The traditional Arab town

Such was the typical town of the Mashriq during the classical Arab period. With the conquests of the Ottoman Turks in the 16th century came urban poverty, exodus, and decay. Only within the 20th century has there been a redevelopment of the urban centres.

20th-century urbanization. Rapid, unplanned, and uncontrolled urbanization is a marked feature of the contemporary Mashriq. The 3 percent annual rate of population growth (the population of the region is apparently growing faster than any other major region of the world, except for Latin America) is causing great pressure on available agricultural land and is pushing the excess population into the urban centres. The growing difficulty in finding additional land for cultivation and the chronic weaknesses in the implementation of agricultural reforms are aggravating the already serious situation of large numbers of a redundant, underemployed rural labour force.

Other factors are also at work in accelerating the urbanization process: improved roads and transportation have made the towns increasingly accessible; increased communications, particularly by radio and television, have spread the attraction of the cities as centres of education, health, employment, recreation, and a totally different way of life; and the discovery and exploitation of oil have brought thousands of workers into the cities in search of employment. The flow of capital from oil revenues has revolutionized the cultures of some of the countries of the Mashriq, particularly Saudi Arabia and Kuwait, and has had a direct impact on the economy of cities in nearby countries—in particular, Beirut, Lebanon, which, as an oil-pipeline terminus, has benefitted greatly from Kuwait's annual oil income of over $150,000,000.

Israel holds third place in the world in proportion of urban dwellers to total population (some 76 percent). In Kuwait, some half of the total population lives in localities of 100,000 and more inhabitants, and, in Lebanon and Syria, the proportion is one-third. This large-scale urbanization has been primarily a 20th-century movement, particularly since World War II.

Growth and crowding. Urbanization has resulted in a series of physical changes and problems. The uncontrolled growth of what were for the most part medieval towns has led to their mushrooming over surrounding areas at a rapacious rate. Most cities have doubled in size within the past few decades, and some—Beirut, for example—have incorporated surrounding towns. Greater Baghdad and Kuwait have spilled over their city walls. In Israel, almost the entire coastal plains from Haifa in the north to below Tel Aviv in the south is gradually evolving into one continuous metropolitan area. The megalopolis, as well as the metropolis, is becoming a significant term in the Mashriq.

As in many other regions of the world, acute urban problems have accompanied this movement. Traffic in urban land, with building for quick, speculative profit, has become a major economic activity and has often had the result of greatly modifying traditional values and behaviour. Slums and shantytowns, a hallmark of metro-

Problems accompanying urbanization

politan growth in underdeveloped countries, are extensive. In the Mashriq, rural migrants build simple one-room shacks. Lacking sanitary amenities, these are crowded next to each other and quickly deteriorate into unhealthy and unsightly slums. Sections of greater Baghdad, for example, are ringed by slum dwellings mainly of the ṣarīfah type—a one-room house constructed mainly of reed matting. It is estimated that there are more than 44,000 ṣarīfahs in greater Baghdad—nearly 45 percent of the total number of houses. Their inhabitants are estimated at 250,000, more than a quarter of the total population of the city.

The emergence of a large and rapidly growing unskilled (and therefore underemployed or unemployed), illiterate, and unhealthy peasant population in the towns may create a new version of the lumpenproletariat. With little to lose and much to gain, these people may profoundly and radically alter traditional religious and familial values and behaviour. Juvenile delinquency, petty thievery, prostitution, and mob violence frequently accompany such changes. Violence, of course, may be aggravated by political figures. Acute xenophobia, directed particularly at traditional "imperialist" powers, and the brutal elimination of incumbent leaders are two of the more obvious by-products. During the July 1958 revolution in Iraq, for example, street mobs ran amok in Baghdad, pillaging and burning at will. Scores were slaughtered, including King Fayṣal II and Prime Minister Nuri as-Said.

In certain respects the general life of the majority of the people has been materially improved. The traditional scourges of the Mashriq—disease, poverty, and ignorance—are slowly weakening their grip. Clothing, housing, household effects, kitchen utensils, communication equipment such as radio and television, and transportation facilities are becoming increasingly available from the cities of the coast to the towns and villages of the interior and even to the peoples of the desert.

Changes in class structure. New social classes have developed, and the traditional cleavage of a small wealthy class supported by a mass of poverty-stricken peasants and nomads has been somewhat modified. The upper classes are frequently educated in the West, and their financial resources, their educational interests, and their way of life all orient them away from their own country's traditions. The wealthy of Cairo and Beirut, for example, are as much at home in Switzerland and France as in Egypt or Lebanon.

The new middle class

A new and increasingly numerous middle class has developed. The traditional class of craftsmen, merchants, artisans, and professionals has been augmented by a rapidly growing white-collar population of educated persons who go into law, politics, journalism, clerical and higher administration, and religious and teaching positions. This class frequently manifests an aversion to rural life and any type of labour associated with earning a living by one's hands.

As a result, the emerging middle class of the Mashriq, it has been argued, is lopsided when judged by Western standards. It has a profusion of white-collar workers and "intellectuals," many of whom are chronically unemployed or underemployed and underpaid. Conversely, this class lacks a sufficient number of doctors, engineers, architects, chemists, and technicians.

Disenchantment with many of their own cultural values and with many aspects of their way of life and disillusionment with much of what the West has to offer have resulted in pronounced dissatisfactions and frustrations. To the extent that such general discontent prevails, one might predict a continuation of the social and political instability characteristic of much of the area for the greater part of the 20th century.

BIBLIOGRAPHY. CARLETON S. COON, *Caravan: The Story of the Middle East,* rev. ed. (1958); MOSHE ZELTZER, *Aspects of Near East Society* (1962); GABRIEL BAER, *Population and Society in the Arab East* (1964; orig. pub. in Hebrew, 1960); and RAPHAEL PATAI, *Golden River to Golden Road: Society, Culture and Change in the Middle East,* 3rd ed. (1969), are four basic sources on the cultures of the Mashriq. Important textbooks include AILON SHILOH (ed.), *Peoples and Cultures of the Middle East* (1969); LOUISE E. SWEET (ed.), *Peoples and Cultures of the Middle East: An Anthropological Reader,* 2 vol. (1970), and *The Central Middle East: A Handbook of Anthropology and Published Research on the Nile Valley, the Arab Levant, Southern Mesopotamia, the Arabian Peninsula and Israel,* 2 vol. (1968); and ABDULLA M. LUTFIYYA and CHARLES W. CHURCHILL (eds.), *Readings in Arab Middle Eastern Societies and Cultures* (1970). STEPHAN and NANDY RONART, *The Concise Encyclopaedia of Arabic Civilization: The Arab East* (1960), is an extremely broad and useful reference text.

Specific national studies, particularly on the village ethnographic level, include HAMED AMMAR, *Growing Up in an Egyptian Village: Silwa, Province of Aswan* (1954); HENRY H. AYROUT, *Moeurs et coutumes des fellahs* (1938; rev. Eng. trans., *The Fellaheen,* 1945; as *The Egyptian Peasant,* 1963); ABDULLA M. LUTFIYYA, *Baytīn, a Jordanian Village: A Study of Social Institutions and Social Change in a Folk Community* (1966); LOUISE E. SWEET, *Tell Toqaan, a Syrian Village* (1960); JOHN GULICK, *Social Structure and Cultural Change in a Lebanese Village* (1955); ANNE H. FULLER, *Buariji: Portrait of a Lebanese Muslim Village* (1961); S.M. SALIM, *Marsh Dwellers of the Euphrates Delta* (1962); and the collected works of HILMA GRANDQUIST: *Marriage Conditions in a Palestinian Village,* 2 pt. (1931–35); *Birth and Childhood Among the Arabs: Studies in a Muhammadan Village in Palestine* (1947); *Child Problems Among the Arabs: Studies in a Muhammadan Village in Palestine* (1950); and *Muslim Death and Burial* (1965). While urbanization is considered in many of the above-cited general studies, it is important to note at least the following three works: MORROE BERGER (ed.), *The New Metropolis in the Arab World* (1963); JANE HACKER, *Modern Amman: A Social Study* (1960); and JOHN GULICK, *Tripoli: A Modern Arab City* (1967). Modernization is also considered in many of the above-cited general studies, but again, it is important to note more detailed studies, which include DANIEL LERNER, *The Passing of Traditional Society: Modernizing the Middle East* (1958); JOHN GULICK (ed.), "Dimensions of Cultural Change in the Middle East," *Human Organization,* 24:1–104 (1965); and BENJAMIN RIVLIN and JOSEPH S. SZYLIOWICZ (eds.), *The Contemporary Middle East: Tradition and Innovation* (1965). Cultural studies on selected populations of contemporary Israel include ABNER COHEN, *Arab Border-Villages in Israel: A Study of Continuity and Change in Social Organization* (1965); ALEX WEINGROD, *Reluctant Pioneers: Village Development in Israel* (1966); and EMANUEL MARX, *Bedouin of the Negev* (1967). Volumes that are regularly brought up to date and that contain a wealth of information on the general features of the contemporary Middle East include the latest editions of publications of the Royal Institute of International Affairs on this subject; *The Middle East and North Africa,* published by Europa Publications, Ltd. (annual); and W.B. FISHER, *The Middle East: A Physical, Social and Regional Geography,* 6th ed. (1971).

(An.S)

Mask

Simply defined, a mask is a form of disguise. It is an object that is frequently worn over or in front of the face to hide the identity of a person and by its own features to establish another being. This essential characteristic of hiding and revealing personalities or moods is common to all masks. As cultural objects they have been used throughout the world in all periods since the Stone Age and have been as varied in appearance as in their use and symbolism.

GENERAL CHARACTERISTICS

Masks have been designed in innumerable varieties, from the simplest of crude "false faces" held by a handle to complete head coverings with ingenious movable parts and hidden faces. Mask makers have shown great resourcefulness in selecting and combining available materials. Among the substances utilized are woods, metals, shells, fibres, ivory, clay, horn, stone, feathers, leather, furs, paper, cloth, and cornhusks. Surface treatments have ranged from rugged simplicity to intricate carving and from polished woods and mosaics to gaudy adornments.

Masks generally are worn with a costume, often so complete that it entirely covers the body of the wearer. Fundamentally the costume completes the new identity represented by the mask, and usually tradition prescribes its appearance and construction to the same extent as the mask itself. Costumes, like the masks, are made of a great

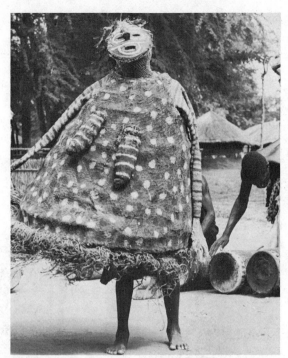

Mask worn with costume: *makishi* dancer, a masked ancestral spirit who assists at initiation rites of the tribes of the northwest region of Rhodesia.
Carl Frank

cultures it is believed that because of the close association between the mask maker and the spirit of the mask, the artist absorbs some of its magic power. A few West African tribal groups in Mali believe, in fact, that the creators of masks are even potentially capable of using the object's supernatural powers to cause harm to others.

Aesthetically, the mask maker has usually been restricted in the forms he can use since masks generally have a traditional imagery with formal conventions. If they are not followed, the artist can bring upon himself the severe censure of his social group and the displeasure or even wrath of the spirit power inherent in the mask. This requirement for accuracy, however, does not restrict artistic expressiveness. The mask maker can and does give his own creative interpretation to the traditionally prescribed general forms, attributes, and devices. The artist, in fact, is usually sought out as a maker of masks because of his known ability to give a vitally expressive or an aesthetically pleasing presentation of the required image.

The wearing of masks. The wearer is also considered to be in direct association with the spirit force of the mask and is consequently exposed to like personal danger of being affected by it. For his protection, the wearer, like the mask maker, is required to follow certain sanctioned procedures in his use of the mask. In some respects he plays the role of an actor in cooperation or collaboration with the mask. Without his performing dance and posturing routines, which are often accompanied with certain sounds of music, the mask would remain a representation without a full life-force. The real drama and power of its form is the important contribution of the wearer. When he is attired in the mask, there is a loss of his previous identity and the assuming of a new one. Upon donning the mask, the wearer sometimes undergoes a psychic change and as in a trance assumes the spirit character depicted by the mask. Usually, however, the wearer skillfully becomes a "partner" of the character he is impersonating, giving to the mask not only an important spark of vitality by the light flashing from his own eyes but also bringing it alive by his movements and poses. But it would seem that the wearer often becomes psychologically completely attached to the character he is helping to create. He loses his own identity and becomes like an automaton, without his own will, which has become subservient to that of the personage of the mask. It appears, however, that at all times there remains some important, even if *sub rosa*, association between the mask and its wearer.

The role of the spectator. It is as consecrated objects imbued with supernatural power that masks are viewed by the spectators or participants at ceremonials where their presence is required. Whatever their specific identity may be, the masks usually refer back to early times, when their initial appearance occurred. This basic aspect of the mask is understood at least in essence by everyone. A paramount role of the mask is to give a sense of continuity between the present and the beginnings of time, a sense that is of vital importance for the integration of a culture with no written history. Psychologically the spectators become associated with the past through the spirit power of the mask, and this often leads the participants to a state of complete absorption or near-frenzy. This is not, however, a consistent reaction to masked ceremonials. That depends on the character whose presence the mask represents. In some cases, the spirit or supernatural being depicted is viewed with rejoicing and almost a familiarity, which leads to gaiety that has a cathartic aspect. Even so, the mask has a spirit content that is respected and revered, even if it is not showing a being with malignant potential. All of these forms have spirit and magical qualities and are thus esteemed as agents for the accomplishing of suprahuman acts.

Some masks, however, do represent malignant, evil, or potentially harmful spirits. These are often used to keep a required balance of power or a traditional social and political relationship of inherited positions within a culture. The characters depicted are also prescribed by tradition and enact roles to achieve the desired ends. The drama involving these masks is often associated with

The mask wearer

variety of materials, all of which have a symbolic connection with the mask's total imagery. Ideally the costume should be seen with the mask while the wearer is in action.

The morphological elements of the mask are with few exceptions derived from natural forms. Masks with human features are classified as anthropomorphic and those with animal characteristics as theriomorphic. In some instances, the mask form is a replication of natural features or closely follows the lineaments of reality, and in other instances it is an abstraction. Masks usually represent supernatural beings, ancestors, and fanciful or imagined figures and can also be portraits. The localization of a particular spirit in a specific mask must be considered a highly significant reason for its existence. The change in identity of the wearer for that of the mask is vital, for if the spirit represented does not reside in the image of the mask, the ritual petitions, supplications, and offerings made to it would be ineffectual and meaningless. The mask, therefore, most often functions as a means of contact with various spirit powers, thereby protecting against the unknown forces of the universe by prevailing upon their potential beneficence in all matters relative to life.

The making of masks. With few exceptions, masks have been made by professionals who were either expert in this particular craft or were noted sculptors or artisans. In societies in which masks of supernatural beings have played a significant ceremonial role, it is presumed that the spirit power of the created image usually is strongly felt by the artist. A primary belief involved in both the conception and the rendering of these objects was that spirit power dwelled in all organic and inorganic matter, and therefore the mask will contain the spirit power of whatever material was used to make it. This power is considered a volatile, active force that is surrounded by various taboos and restrictions for the protection of those handling it. Certain prescribed rituals frequently have to be followed in the process of the mask's creation. A spirit power is also often believed to inhabit the artist's tools so that even these have to be handled in a prescribed manner. As the form of the mask develops it is usually believed to acquire power increasingly in its own right, and again various procedures are prescribed to protect the craftsman and to ensure the potency of the object. If all the conventions have been adhered to, the completed mask, when worn or displayed, is regarded as an object suffused with great supernatural or spirit power. In some

Anthropomorphic and theriomorphic masks

The mask maker

secret societies, especially in Africa, where the greatest range of mask forms and functions can be observed. These forms are often used in very restricted performances, where only select persons can view them. This is also true in other areas where masks are used, such as in Oceania, the Americas, and even in some of the folk-mask rites still performed in Europe.

Meaning and aesthetic response. On the basis of present knowledge, it would appear that there is not or has not been any set response or reaction by any one of the three groups involved with the mask: the artist, the wearer, the spectator. There is, however, a reaction of a very particular kind common to every culture, a response such as awe, delight and pleasure, fear and even terror: these are as traditionally determined as the forms and costumes of the masks themselves. This is a learned and inherent pattern of conduct for each culture. Masks, therefore, that have a closely comparable appearance in several unrelated groups in quite different parts of the world often have totally dissimilar meanings and functions. It is thus practically impossible to determine either the meaning or use of a mask by its appearance alone. For example, some masks in Africa, as well as in Oceania and East Asia, have such a grotesque or frightening appearance as to lead one to suspect that they represent evil spirits with an intent to terrorize the spectators; actually they may have the opposite character and function. The significance of masks can be determined only by reference to accounts or personal observations of the masks in the setting of their own culture.

The aesthetic effects of masks, on the other hand, since they derive from the forms and their disposition within the design, can readily be evaluated as art objects. But this evaluation is based on elements very different from those appraised within the mask's own culture. This is partly because the total artistic qualities of a mask derive both from its exterior forms and from its meaning and function within its cultural context. There exist, however, in all cultures criteria for determining the quality of objects as art. These criteria differ from one culture to another, and they may be known only from investigations carried out within the varying cultures.

Preservation and collecting. The preservation or disposal of masks is often decreed by tradition. Many masks and often their form and function are passed down through clans, families, special societies, or from individual to individual. They are usually spiritually reactivated or aesthetically restored by repainting and redecorating, without destroying the basic form and symbolism. In many instances, however, the mask is used only for one ceremony or occasion and then is discarded or destroyed, sometimes by burning.

The collecting of masks has largely been of recent origin. Not until the late 19th and early 20th century were they seriously appreciated as art objects or studied as cultural artifacts. Most masks have been obtained through archaeological excavations or in field expeditions, that is, in their place of origin.

THE FUNCTIONS AND FORMS OF MASKS

Masks are as extraordinarily varied in appearance as they are in function or fundamental meaning. Many masks are primarily associated with ceremonies that have religious and social significance or are concerned with funerary customs, fertility rites, or curing sickness. Other masks are used on festive occasions or to portray characters in a dramatic performance and in re-enactments of mythological events. Masks are also used for warfare and as protective devices in certain sports, as well as frequently being employed as architectural ornament.

Social and religious uses. Masks representing potentially harmful spirits were often used to keep a required balance of power or a traditional relationship of inherited positions within a culture. The forms of these masks invariably were prescribed by tradition, as were their uses. This type of mask was often associated with secret societies, especially in Africa, where the greatest range of types and functions can be found. They were also widely used among Oceanic peoples of the South Pacific and the

American Indians and are even used in some of the folk rites still performed in Europe.

Masks have served an important role as a means of discipline and have been used to admonish women, children, and criminals. Common in China, Africa, Oceania, and North America, admonitory masks usually completely cover the features of the wearer. It is believed among some of the African Negro tribes that the first mask was an admonitory one. A child, repeatedly told not to, persisted in following its mother to fetch water. To frighten and discipline the child, the mother painted a hideous face on the bottom of her water gourd. Others say the mask was invented by a secret African society to escape recognition while punishing marauders. In New Britain, members of a secret terroristic society called the Dukduk appear in monstrous five-foot masks to police, to judge, and to execute offenders. Aggressive supernatural spirits

Admonitory and ancestor masks.
(Left) Female *tumbuan* mask of the Dukduk secret society, New Britain. The head is of sacking with tuft of feathers and skirt of leaves. Height 1.5 m. (Right) Ancestor mask from the middle Sepik River area of New Guinea, used in clan initiation rites. Upper portion is basketwork with faces modelled of red earth mixed with coconut oil, trimmed with shells, feathers, and a skirt of bark fibres. Height 1.79 m.

of an almost demonic nature are represented by these masks, which are constructed from a variety of materials, usually including tapa, or bark cloth, and the pith of certain reeds. These materials are painted in brilliant colours, with brick red and acid green predominating.

In many cultures throughout the world, a judge wears a mask to protect him from future recriminations. In this instance, the mask represents a traditionally sanctioned spirit from the past who assumes responsibility for the decision levied on the culprit.

Rituals, often nocturnal, by members of secret societies wearing ancestor masks are reminders of the ancient sanction of their conduct. In many cultures, these masked ceremonials are intended to prevent miscreant acts and to maintain the circumscribed activities of the tribe. Along the Guinea coast of West Africa, for instance, many highly realistic masks represent ancestors who enjoyed specific cultural roles; the masks symbolize sanction and control when donned by the wearer. Among some of the Dan and Ngere tribes of Liberia and Ivory Coast, ancestor masks with generic features act as intermediaries for the transmission of petitions or offerings of respect to the gods. These traditional ancestral emissaries exert by their spirit power a social control for the community.

Particularly among Oceanic peoples, American Indians, and Negro tribes of Africa, certain times of the year are

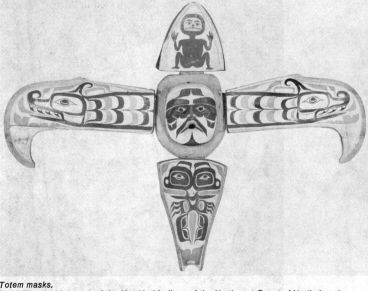

Totem masks.
(Left) Thunderbird mask of the Kwakiutl Indians of the Northwest Coast of North America.
The bird's beak and wings open to reveal a human face (mask shown open). Painted wood.
Width (open) 1.82 m. (Right) Fish mask from the Orokolo Bay area of New Guinea. Painted
bark cloth over rattan frame with fringe of dried grass. Height 1.63 m.
By courtesy of (left) the Brooklyn Museum, New York, (right) the Pitt Rivers Museum, Oxford, Eng.

set aside to honour spirits or ancestors. Among nonliterate peoples who cannot record their own histories, masked rituals act as an important link between past and present, giving a sense of historic continuity that strengthens their social bond. On these occasions, masks usually recognizable as dead chieftains, relatives, friends, or even foes are worn or exhibited. Gifts are made to the spirits incarnated in the masks, while in other instances dancers wearing stylized mourning masks perform the prescribed ceremony.

In western Melanesia, the ancestral ceremonial mask occurs in a great variety of forms and materials. The Sepik River area in north central New Guinea is the source of an extremely rich array of these mask forms mostly carved in wood, ranging from small faces to large fantastic forms with a variety of appendages affixed to the wood, including shell, fibre, animal skins, seeds, flowers, and feathers. These masks are highly polychromed with earth colours of red and yellow, lime white, and charcoal black. They often represent supernatural spirits as well as ancestors and therefore have both a religious and a social significance.

Initiation masks

Members of secret societies usually conduct the rituals of initiation, when a young man is instructed in his future role as an adult and is acquainted with the rules controlling the social stability of the tribe. Totem and spiritualistic masks are donned by the elders at these ceremonies. Sometimes the masks used are reserved only for initiations. Among the most impressive of the initiation masks are the exquisitely carved human faces of west coast African Negro tribes. In western and central Zaire, in Africa, large, colourful helmetlike masks are used as a masquerading device when the youth emerges from the initiation area and is introduced to the villagers as an adult of the tribe. After a lengthy ordeal of teaching and initiation rites, for instance, a youth of the Pende tribe appears in a distinctive colorful mask indicative of his new role as an adult. The mask is later cast aside and replaced by a small ivory duplicate, worn as a charm against misfortune and as a symbol of his manhood.

Totem masks

Believing everything in nature to possess a spirit, man found authority for himself and his family by identifying with a specific nonhuman spirit. He adopted an object of nature; then he mythologically traced his ancestry back to the chosen object; he pre-empted the animal as the emblem of himself and his clan. This is the practice of totem, which consolidates family pride and distinguishes social lines. Masks are made to house the totem spirit. The totem ancestor is believed actually to materialize in its mask; thus masks are of the utmost importance in securing protection and bringing comfort to the totem clan.

The Papuans of New Guinea build mammoth masks called *hevehe*, attaining 20 feet in height. They are constructed of a palmwood armature covered in bark cloth; geometric designs are stitched on with painted cane strips. These fantastic man-animal masks are given a frightening aspect. When they emerge from the men's secret clubhouse, they serve to protect the members of the clan. The so-called "totem" pole of the Alaskan and British Columbian Indian fulfills the same function. The African totem mask is often carved from ebony or other hard woods, designed with graceful lines and showing a highly polished surface. Animal masks, their features elongated and beautifully formalized, are common in western Africa. Dried grass, woven palm fibres, coconuts, and shells, as well as wood are employed in the masks of New Guinea, New Ireland, and New Caledonia. Represented are fanciful birds, fishes, and animals with distorted or exaggerated features.

The high priest and medicine man, or the shaman, frequently had his own very powerful totem, in whose mask he could exorcise evil spirits, punish enemies, locate game or fish, predict the weather, and, most importantly, cure disease.

The Northwest Coast Indians of North America in particular devised mechanical masks with movable parts to reveal a second face—generally a human image. Believing that the human spirit could take animal form and vice versa, the makers of these masks fused man and bird or man and animal into one mask. Some of these articulating masks acted out entire legends as their parts moved.

Funerary and commemorative uses. In cultures in which burial customs are important, anthropomorphic masks have often been used in ceremonies associated with the dead and departing spirits. Funerary masks were frequently used to cover the face of the deceased. Generally their purpose was to represent the features of the deceased, both to honour them and to establish a relationship through the mask with the spirit world. Sometimes they were used to force the spirit of the newly dead to depart for the spirit world. Masks were also made to protect the deceased by frightening away malevolent spirits.

Burial masks

From the Middle Kingdom (*c.* 2040–1786 BC) to the 1st century AD, the ancient Egyptians placed stylized masks with generalized features on the faces of their dead. The funerary mask served to guide the spirit of the deceased back to its final resting place in the body. They were commonly made of cloth covered with stucco or plaster,

Funerary masks.
(Top left) Egyptian burial mask of the Ptolemaic period. Painted stucco over cloth. (Top right)
Gold funeral mask placed over the face of an unknown Mycenaean ruler. Greece, 13th
century BC. (Bottom left) Aztec skull mask from Mexico inlaid with turquoise and lignite with
pyrite in the eye sockets. (Bottom right) Effigy mask of Edmund Sheffield, duke of Buckingham,
1735. Painted death mask with human hair, dressed in his peer's robes.
By courtesy of (top left) Museo Egizio, Turin, Italy, (top right) the National Archaeological Museum of Athens,
TAP Service (bottom left) the trustees of the British Museum; photographs, (top left) Foto Rosso, (bottom right)
Nicholas Servian/Woodmansterne Publishers

which was then painted. For more important personages,
silver and gold were used. Among the most splendid examples of the burial portrait mask is the one created *c.*
1350 BC for the pharaoh Tutankhamen. In Mycenaean
tombs of *c.* 1400 BC, beaten gold portrait masks were
found. Gold masks also were placed on the faces of the
dead kings of Cambodia and Siam. The mummies of Inca
royalty wore golden masks. The mummies of lesser
personages often had masks made of wood or clay. Some
of these ancient Andean masks had movable parts, such
as the metallic death mask with movable ears found in the
Moon Pyramid at Moche, Peru. The ancient Mexicans
made burial masks that seem to be generic representations
rather than portraits of individuals.

In ancient Roman burials, a mask resembling the deceased was often placed over his face or was worn by an
actor hired to accompany the funerary cortege to the
burial site. In patrician families these masks or *imagines*
were sometimes preserved as ancestor portraits and were
displayed on ceremonial occasions. Such masks were usually modelled over the features of the dead and cast in

wax. This technique was revived in the making of effigy
masks for the royalty and nobility of Europe from the late
Middle Ages through the 18th century. Painted and with
human hair, these masks were attached to a dummy
dressed in state regalia and were used for display, processionals, or commemorative ceremonials. From the 17th
century to the 20th, death masks of famous persons became widespread among European peoples. With wax or
liquid plaster of paris a negative cast of the human face
could be produced that in turn acted as a mold for the
positive image, frequently cast in bronze. In the 19th
century, life masks made in the same manner became
popular. Another type of life mask had been produced in
the Fayyum region of Egypt during the 1st and 2nd
centuries AD. These were realistic portraits painted in
encaustic on wood during a person's lifetime; at death,
they were attached directly to the facial area on the
mummy shroud.

The skull mask is another form usually associated with
funerary rites. The skull masks of the Aztecs, like their
wooden masks, were inlaid with mosaics of turquoise and

Death
and life
masks

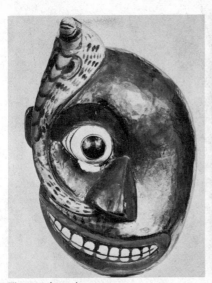 

Therapeutic masks.
(Left) Disease devil mask *(rakasa)* from Sri Lanka (Ceylon), worn to cure patients of deafness.
(Right) False Face Society mask of the Iroquois Indians of North America.

lignite, and the eye sockets were filled with pyrites. Holes were customarily drilled in the back so the mask might be hung or possibly worn. In Melanesia, the skull of the deceased is often modelled over with clay, or resin and wax, and then elaborately painted with designs that had been used ceremonially by the deceased during his own lifetime.

Therapeutic uses. Masks have played an important part in magico-religious rites to prevent and to cure disease. In some cultures, the masked members of secret societies could drive disease demons from entire villages and tribes. Among the best known of these groups was the False Face Society of the North American Iro-

quois Indians. These professional healers performed violent pantomines to exorcise the dreaded *Gahadogoka gogosa* (demons who plagued the Iroquois). They wore grimacing, twisted masks, often with long wigs of horse-hair. Metallic inserts often were used around the eyes to catch the light of the campfire and the moon, emphasizing the grotesqueness of the mask.

Masks for protection from disease include the measle masks worn by Chinese children and the cholera masks worn during epidemics by the Chinese and Burmese. The disease mask is most developed among the Sinhalese in Sri Lanka (Ceylon), where 19 distinct *rākasa*, or disease devil masks, have been devised. These masks are of fero-

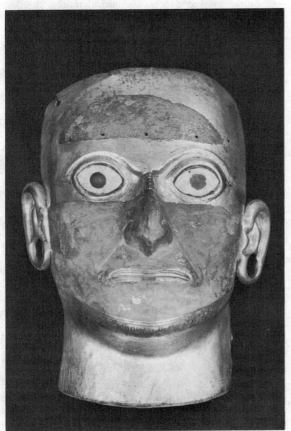 

(Left) Metallic death mask with movable ears from the Moon Pyramid in the Moche Valley, Peru, 3rd–8th century AD. (Right) Ancient Mexican mask made of porphyry found north of Texcoco, Mexico, Teotihuacán civilization, 3rd–4th century AD.

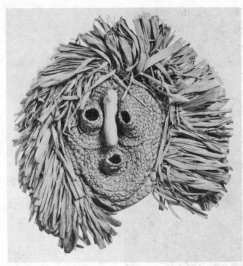

Agriculture fertility masks.
(Left) Cornhusk mask of the Seneca Indians of the Iroquois nation of New York. Height 43 cm.
(Right) Sekya, a *kachina* mask of the Zuni Indians of New Mexico. Painted leather, trimmed with feathers and hair. Height 43 cm.
By courtesy of the Museum of the American Indian, New York

cious aspect, fanged, and with startling eyes. Gaudily coloured and sometimes having articulating jaws, they present a dragon-like appearance.

SCALA, New York

Detail from "The Ridotto" by Pietro Longhi (1702–85), showing the masks popularly worn at fashionable Venetian functions of the 18th century. In the Galleria dell'Accademia Carrara, Bergamo, Italy.

Uses in warfare and sport

Masks have long been used in military connections. A war mask will have a malevolent expression or hideously fantastic features to instill fear in the enemy. The ancient Greeks and Romans used battle shields with grotesque masks or attached terrifying masks to their armour, as did the Chinese warrior. Grimacing *menpo*, or mask helmets, were used by Japanese samurai.

Many sports require the use of masks. Some of these are merely functional, protective devices such as the masks worn by fencers, baseball catchers, or even skiers. To protect their faces in sports events and tournaments of arms, horsemen of the Roman army attached highly decorative and symbolic masks to their helmets.

Perhaps the earliest use of masks was in connection with hunting. Disguise masks were seemingly used in the early Stone Age in stalking prey and later to house the slain animal's spirit in the hope of placating it. The traditional animal masks worn by the Altaic and Tungusic shamans in Siberia are strictly close to such prehistoric examples as the image of the so-called sorcerer in the Cave of Les Trois Frères in Ariège, France.

Since agricultural societies first appeared in prehistory, the mask has been widely used for fertility rituals. The Iroquois, for instance, used corn husk masks at harvest rituals to give thanks for and to achieve future abundance of crops. Perhaps the most renowned of the masked fertility rites held by American Indians are those still performed by the Hopi and Zuni Indians of the Southwest U.S. Together with masked dancers representing clouds, rain spirits, stars, Earth Mother, sky god, and others, the shaman takes part in elaborate ceremonies designed to assure crop fertility. Spirits called *kachinas*, who first brought rain to the Pueblo tribes, are said to have left their masks behind when sent to dwell in the bottom of a desert lake. Their return to help bring the rain is incarnated by the masked dancer. Cylindrical masks, covering the entire head and resting on the shoulders, are of a primal type. They are made of leather and humanized by the addition of hair and a variety of adjuncts. Eyes are represented by incisions or by buckskin balls filled with deer hair and affixed to the mask. The nose is often of rolled buckskin or corncob. Frequently the mask has a projecting wooden cylinder for a bill or a gourd stem cut with teeth for a snout. Horns are attached to some masks. Many colours are used in their painting; plumes and beads are attached, and the sex of the mask is distin-

Uses in fertility ceremonies

Alinari

Masked Roman actors in a comedy scene, 1st century relief from Pompeii.

Mask by Amleto Sartori for the character of Vanna
Scoma in Pirandello's *La favola del figlio cambiato*,
1957. Painted leather.
Antonello Perissinotto

guished by its shape: round head for male and square for
female. In the western Sudan area of Africa many tribes
have masked fertility ceremonials. The *segoni-kun* masks
of the Bambara tribes in Mali are aesthetically among
the most interesting. Antelopes, characterized by their
elegant simplicity, are carved in wood and affixed to wov-
en fibre caps that are hung with raffia and cover the wearer. The antelope is believed to have introduced agriculture, and so when crops are sown, members of Tji-wara
society cavort in the fields in pairs to symbolize fertility
and abundance.

Festive uses. Masks for festive occasions are still commonly used in the 20th century. Ludicrous, grotesque, or
superficially horrible, festival masks are usually conducive to good-natured licence, release from inhibitions, and
ribaldry. These include the Halloween, Mardi Gras, or
"masked ball" variety. The disguise is assumed to create a
momentary, amusing character, often resulting in humorous confusions, or to achieve anonymity for the prankster
or ribald reveller.

Throughout contemporary Europe and Latin America,
masks are associated with folk festivals, especially those
generated by seasonal changes or marking the beginning
and end of the year. Among the most famous of the folk
masks are the masks worn to symbolize the driving
away of winter in parts of Austria and Switzerland. In
Mexico and Guatemala, annual folk festivals employ
masks for storytelling and caricature, such as for the
Dance of the Old Men and the Dance of the Moors and
the Christians. The Eskimo make masks with comic or
satiric features that are worn at festivals of merrymaking,
as do the Ibos of Nigeria.

Theatrical uses. Masks have been used almost universally to represent characters in theatrical performances.
Theatrical performances are a visual literature of a transient, momentary kind. It is most impressive because it
can be seen as a reality; it expends itself by its very
revelation. The mask participates as a more enduring element, since its form is physical.

Ancient
Greek
and
Roman

The mask as a device for theatre first emerged in Western civilization from the religious practices of ancient
Greece. In the worship of Dionysus, god of fecundity and
the harvest, the communicants' attempt to impersonate
the deity by donning goat skins and by imbibing wine
eventually developed into the sophistication of masking.
When a literature of worship appeared, a disguise, which
consisted of a white linen mask hung over the face (a
device supposedly initiated by Thespis, a 6th-century-BC
poet who is credited with originating tragedy), enabled the
leaders of the ceremony to make the god manifest. Thus
symbolically identified, the communicant was inspired to
speak in the first person, thereby giving birth to the art of

drama. In Greece the progress from ritual to ritual-drama
was continued in highly formalized theatrical representations. Masks used in these productions became elaborate
headpieces made of leather or painted canvas and depicted an extensive variety of personalities, ages, ranks, and
occupations. Heavily coiffured and of a size to enlarge
the actor's presence, the Greek mask seems to have been
designed to throw the voice by means of a built-in mega-
phone device and, by exaggeration of the features, to
make clear at a distance the precise nature of the character. Moreover, their use made it possible for the Greek
actors—limited by convention to three speakers for each
tragedy—to impersonate a number of different characters during the play simply by changing masks and costumes. Details from frescoes, mosaics, vase paintings, and
fragments of stone sculpture provide most of what is
known of the appearance of these ancient theatrical
masks. The tendency of the early Greek and Roman artists to idealize their subjects throws doubt, however, upon
the accuracy of these reproductions. Some authorities
maintain that the masks of the ancient theatre were crude
affairs with little aesthetic appeal.

In the Middle Ages, masks were used in the mystery
plays of the 12th to the 16th century. In plays dramatiz-
ing portions of the Old and New Testaments, grotesques of
all sorts, such as devils, demons, dragons, and personi-
fications of the seven deadly sins, were brought to stage
life by the use of masks. Constructed of papier-mâché, the
masks of the mystery plays were evidently marvels of
ingenuity and craftsmanship, being made to articulate and
to belch fire and smoke from hidden contrivances. But
again, no reliable pictorial record has survived. Masks
used in connection with present-day carnivals and Mardi
Gras and those of folk demons and characters still used
by central European peasants, such as the *Perchten* masks
of Alpine Austria, are most likely the inheritors of the
tradition of medieval masks.

Medieval
and
Renais-
sance

The 15th-century Renaissance in Italy witnessed the rise
of a theatrical phenomenon that spread rapidly to France,
to Germany, and to England, where it maintained its
popularity into the 18th century. Comedies improvised
from scenarios based upon the domestic dramas of the

By courtesy of the Tropenmuseum, Amsterdam

Javanese *tupeng* mask representing the witch Rangda.
Lacquered wood, cloth, metal, and horsehair.

ancient Roman comic playwrights Plautus (254?–184 BC) and Terence (186/185–159 BC and upon situations drawn from anonymous ancient Roman mimes flourished under the title of commedia dell'arte (q.v.). Adopting the Roman stock figures and situations to their own usages, the players of the commedia were usually masked. Sometimes the masking was grotesque and fanciful, but generally a heavy leather mask, full or half face, disguised the commedia player. Excellent pictorial records of both commedia costumes and masks exist; some sketches show the characters of Arlecchino and Colombina wearing black masks covering merely the eyes, from which the later masquerade mask is certainly a development.

Modern Except for vestiges of the commedia in the form of puppet and marionette shows, the drama of masks all but disappeared in Western theatre during the 18th, 19th, and first half of the 20th centuries. In modern revivals of ancient Greek plays, masks have occasionally been employed, and such highly symbolic plays as *Die versunkene Glocke* (*The Sunken Bell*; 1897) by the German Gerhart Hauptmann (1862–1946) and dramatizations of *Alice in Wonderland* have required masks for the performers of grotesque or animal figures. The Irish poet-playwright W.B. Yeats (1865–1939) revived the convention in his *Dreaming of the Bones* and in other plays patterned upon the Japanese Nō drama. In 1926 theatregoers in the United States witnessed a memorable use of masks in *The Great God Brown* by the American dramatist Eugene O'Neill (1888–1953), wherein actors wore masks of their own faces to indicate changes in the internal and external lives of their characters. Oskar Schlemmer (1888–1943), a German artist associated with the Bauhaus, became interested in the late 1920s and '30s in semantic phenomenology as applied to the design of masks for theatrical productions. Modern art movements are often reflected in the design of contemporary theatrical masks. The stylistic concepts of Cubism and Surrealism, for example, are apparent in the masks executed for a 1957 production of *La favola del figlio cambiato* (*The Fable of the Transformed Son*) by the Italian dramatist Luigi Pirandello (1867–1936). A well-known mid-century play using masks was *Les Nègres* (1958; *The Blacks*, 1960) by the French writer Jean Genet (1910–   ). The mask, however, has unquestionably lost its importance as a theatrical convention in the 20th century, and its appearance is exceptional rather than general.

East Asian In many ways akin to Greek drama in origin and theme, the Nō drama of Japan has remained a significant part of national life since its beginnings in the 14th century. Nō masks, of which there are about 125 named varieties, are rigidly traditional and are classified into five general types: old persons (male and female), gods, goddesses, devils, and goblins. The material of the Nō mask is wood with a coating of plaster and lacquered and gilded. Colours are traditional. White is used to characterize a corrupt ruler; red signifies a righteous man; a black mask is worn by the villain who epitomizes violence and brutality. Nō masks are highly stylized and generally characterized. They are exquisitely carved by highly respected artists known as *tenka-ichi*, "the first under heaven." Shades of feeling are portrayed with beautifully sublimated realism. When the masks are subtly moved by the player's hand or body motion, their expression appears to change.

In Tibet, sacred dramas are performed by masked lay actors. A play for exorcising demons called the "Dance of the Red Tiger Devil" is performed at fixed seasons of the year exclusively by the priests or lamas wearing awe-inspiring masks of deities and demons. Masks employed in this mystery play are made of papier-mâché, cloth, and occasionally gilt copper. In Sikkim and Bhutan, where wood is abundant and the damp climate is destructive to paper, they are carved of durable wood. All masks of the Himalayan peoples are fantastically painted and are usually provided with wigs of yak tail in various colours. Formally they often emphasize the hideous.

Masks, usually made of papier-mâché, are employed in the religious or admonitory drama of China; but for the greater part the actors in popular or secular drama make up their faces with cosmetics and paint to resemble masks,

as do the Kabuki actors in Japan. The makeup mask both identifies the particular character and conveys his personality. The highly didactic sacred drama of China is performed with the actors wearing fanciful and grotesque masks. Akin to this "morality" drama are the congratulatory playlets, pageants, processions, and dances of China. Masks employed in these ceremonies are highly ornamented, with jewelled and elaborately filigreed headgears. In the lion and dragon dances of both China and Japan, a stylized mask of the beast is carried on a pole by itinerant players, whose bodies are concealed by a dependent cloth. The mask and cloth are manipulated violently, as if the animal were in pursuit, to the taps of a small drum. The mask's lower jaw is movable and made to emit a loud continuous clacking by means of a string.

Indonesian In Java and Bali, wooden masks, *tupeng*, are used in certain theatrical performances, called *wayang wong*. These dance dramas developed from the shadow puppet plays of the 18th century and are performed not only as amusement but as a safeguard against calamities. The stories are in part derived from ancient Sanskrit literature, especially the Hindu epics, although the Javanese later became Muslims. The brightly painted masks are made of wood and leather and are often fitted with horsehair and metallic or gilded paper accoutrements. They are ordinarily held in the teeth by means of a strap of leather or rattan fastened across the inside. Occasionally an actor interrupts the unseen narrator, the Dalang, who is speaking the play. The mask is then held in front of the face while the player says his line. The use of masks in Java is exceptional; for masks, being forbidden under the prohibition of images, are practically unknown in the Islāmic world.

In the 20th century, with the breaking down of primitive and folk cultures, the mask has increasingly become a decorative object, although it has long been used in art as an ornamental device. In India, Indonesia, Japan, Kenya, and Mexico, masks are largely produced for tourists. The collecting of old masks has been a part of the current interest in so-called primitive and folk arts. Masks also have exerted a decided influence on modern art movements, especially in the first decades of the 20th century, when painters in France and Germany found a source of inspiration in the tribal masks of Africa and western Oceania.

BIBLIOGRAPHY. "Masks" in the *Encyclopedia of World Art*, vol. 9, col. 520–570 (1964), a good historical survey; WILLIAM N. FENTON, "Masked Medicine Societies of the Iroquois," *Smithsonian Institution, Annual Report for 1940*, pp. 397–429 (1941), a very good general discussion of Iroquois masks, with illustrations; MARCEL GRIAULE, *Masques Dogons* (1938), a profusely illustrated classic study of the masks of the Dogon, a people of Mali, within their cultural setting; GEORGE W. HARLEY, *Masks as Agents of Social Control in Northeast Liberia*, Peabody Museum Papers 32, no. 2 (1950), a useful, illustrated article; E.A. KENNARD, *Hopi Kachinas* (1938), an important study of the masks of the Hopi, the westernmost Pueblo Indians; *Le Masque*, an exhibition catalogue, December 1959–May 1960, Musée Guimet, Paris (1959), an excellent text with superb plates; DOROTHY J. RAY, *Eskimo Masks: Art and Ceremony* (1967), one of the best studies of masks with many fine plates and bibliography; HANS HIMMELHEBER, *Afrikanische Masken, ein Brevier* (1960), a brief but good résumé, with excellent plates; F.E. WILLIAMS, *Drama of Orokolo* (1940), a classic study of masks of the Gulf of Papua, New Guinea, with fine illustrations and bibliography; LEON UNDERWOOD, *Masks of West Africa* (1948), a small book but important for the subject, with good plates.

(P.S.W.)

Masonry Construction

Masonry construction includes building and fabricating in stone, clay, brick, and concrete. Masonry materials have long been favoured by architects for their colour, scale, texture, pattern, and look of permanence. Engineers have valued them for their durability and compressive (weight-bearing) strength. Because of their own considerable deadweight and their lack of tensile strength (ability to resist pulling force), however, masonry materials now have been largely, though not entirely, replaced in structural functions by steel, reinforced concrete, wood, and plastics. Today masonry is employed chiefly as an external wall material in applications in which aesthetics and weatherability are deciding factors.

HISTORY

The art of masonry originated when early man sought to supplement his valuable but rare natural caves with artificial caves made from piles of stone. Circular stone huts, partially dug into the ground, dating from prehistoric times have been found in the Aran Islands, Ireland. By the 4th millennium BC, Egypt had developed an elaborate stonemasonry technique, culminating in the most extravagant of all ancient structures, the Pyramids.

Geological influences. The choice of masonry materials has always been influenced by the prevailing geological formations and conditions. When monumental aesthetics and durability were sought for religious and governmental buildings, natural stone was preferred. Egyptian temples were constructed of limestone, sandstone, alabaster, granite, basalt, and porphyry quarried from the hills along the Nile. The Greeks lacked Egypt's variety of natural stones, but they possessed rich quarries of unrivalled marble and coated their coarse-grained limestone with a layer of marble-stucco. The Romans, though they imported stones from both Egypt and Greece, depended heavily on their own limestone deposits, both travertine (a hard variety) and tufa (a porous variety), of which the hills of Rome are mainly composed. They also used peperino and lava stones, both of volcanic origin.

Another ancient centre of civilization, the area of western Asia between the Tigris and Euphrates, lacked stone outcroppings but was rich in clay deposits. As a result, the masonry structures of the Assyrian and Persian empires were constructed of sun-dried bricks faced with kiln-burned, sometimes glazed, units. In this area pitch or bitumen, as well as plastic, calcareous earth, was used for mortar. Both the Assyrians and Persians constructed buildings with massive brick walls, adorning the openings with alabaster or limestone masonry.

Stone and clay continued to be the primary masonry materials through the Middle Ages and later. Brick was widely employed in the lowlands of northwest Europe and in the regions of southern Europe under the influence of Byzantine architectural ideas originating in Constantinople. Special forms of clay (terra-cotta and mosaic) ornamented Byzantine and Roman buildings. Terra-cotta pieces made of a fired clay that was frequently glazed were used to create decorative cornices, gutters, or base course moldings. Mosaics, either coloured stone or glazed glassware, decorated flat surfaces.

Roman concrete and arches. A significant development in masonry construction in ancient times was the invention of concrete by the Romans. Although well-cut blocks of stone masonry could be erected without benefit of mortar, the Romans recognized the value of cement, which they made from pozzolanic tuff, a volcanic ash. Mixed with water, lime, and stone fragments, the cement was expanded into concrete. Walls of this concrete, faced with various stone or fired clay materials (see Figure 1), were more economical and faster to erect. Opus incertum required irregularly shaped stones. Opus reticulatum was arranged in diagonal lines, using tuff (limestone) studding to resemble meshes of net. Opus testaceum was faced with bricks triangular in plan. Unfaced concrete could be effectively utilized for foundation work.

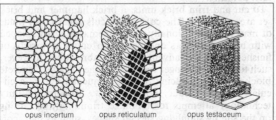

From B. Fletcher, *A History of Architecture on the Comparative Method*, 17th ed. rev., R.A. Cordingley (1961); Athlone Press of the University of London

opus incertum   opus reticulatum   opus testaceum

Figure 1: Roman methods of wall construction.

Because it provided more freedom in shaping structures, concrete helped the Romans develop the arch, long-known but little-used, into one of the great basic construction forms. Prior to the arch, all builders in stone had been handicapped by the material's fundamental lack of tensile strength—that is, its tendency to break under its own weight when supported on widely separated piers or walls. The Egyptians had roofed temples with stone slabs but had been forced to place the supporting columns close together. The Greeks had used wooden roof beams covered with thin stone; such beams were subject to weather and fire. The Roman arch avoided tension entirely, keeping all the masonry in compression, from the keystone to the piers. Stone in compression has great strength, and the Romans built huge bridges and aqueducts in large numbers. Extending their arch into a tunnel, they invented the barrel vault, with which they successfully roofed such buildings as the Temple of Venus in Rome. Several arches intersecting at a common keystone could be used to form a dome, such as that of the Pantheon in Rome. Two intersecting barrel vaults gave rise to the groin vault, which was used in some of the great public baths.

Roman arches and vaults were invariably semicircular in shape, making them massive and rigid. The shape and mass of Roman construction generally avoided problems of horizontal thrust, the horizontal pressure resulting from the arch type of construction. The Pantheon had a diameter of 142 feet, a span not equalled in magnitude until the introduction of modern steel and reinforced-concrete construction.

Gothic masonry. The Roman arch underwent a significant modification in the Middle Ages in the evolution of the pointed arch, which provided a strong skeleton resting on well-spaced piers. The massive, rigid construction of the Romans gave way to soaring vaults supported by external flying buttresses (external bracing). The use of smaller-sized stones and thick mortar joints created an elastic slender structure that stressed the masonry to its fullest. The bearing of unit upon unit required the use of mortar to distribute the contact stresses. In the Beauvais Cathedral the builders exceeded the stress limit, and the choir vault, more than 157 feet high, fell. Rebuilt after AD 1337, it remains today the loftiest structure of its kind in Europe.

With the advent of Gothic forms, masonry construction in a historic sense had solved the problem of spanning space entirely by material in compression, the only design formula suitable to stone. With the advent of the truss in the 16th century, the rise of scientific structural analysis in the 17th century, and the development of high-tensile resistant materials (steel and reinforced concrete) in the 19th century, the importance of masonry as a practical material for spanning space declined. It owes its revival largely to the invention of portland cement, the principal ingredient of concrete, which in the 20th century returned masonry to its essentially pre-Roman role of forming vertical wall enclosures, partitions, and facings.

MINING AND MANUFACTURING

Masonry construction begins with extractive materials, such as clay, sand, gravel, and stone, usually mined from surface pits or quarries. Geologically, all masonry materials come from a common source, rock, the solidified state of the molten material called magma, which still exists within the earth's interior.

Igneous rocks are created directly from the molten interior, frequently without seams, layers, or grain in massive formations that are difficult to quarry. In time, igneous rock is weathered by temperature, wind, and water, and once decomposed, it is called mantle. Particles of this rock range from fine-sized clays to large-sized gravel and stones. When deposited in compressed layers, mantle hardens into a sedimentary rock that is relatively easy to quarry because it is layered and has grain. When igneous and sedimentary rocks have been subjected to tremendous heat and pressure with the contraction and thrust of the earth's crust, they have changed into a material called metamorphic rock.

The pointed arch

Stone sources. The most widely used igneous rock is granite, a massive rock less difficult to quarry because it has grain and rift (natural seams). Typically, igneous rock is strong, hard, and durable. Composed primarily of quartz (silicon dioxide) and feldspar (aluminosilicate), it has a characteristic peppery, coarse-grained appearance predominantly gray in hue. Other igneous rocks, such as syenite (feldspar with hornblende) and diorite (feldspar with pyroxene), are excellent fine-grain rocks. Because of their massive formation (no rift and grain) and brittle behaviour, however, they cannot be commercially quarried. The porphyry rock used by the ancients is actually a form of igneous rock characterized by a dense, compact groundmass in which are embedded large, perfectly formed crystals of quartz or feldspar. Gneiss granite, a metamorphic granite form stratified during its formation, has not been commercially exploited even though its layered deposits permit easier quarrying.

Limestone and sandstone

Limestone and sandstone are the two most widely used sedimentary rocks. Limestone is primarily calcium carbonate, called calcite; most deposits are of marine origin, chiefly in the form of shells, as, for example, in a coral reef. The double carbonate of calcium and magnesium is called dolomite limestone. It is easier to quarry than the granites because it is softer, occurs in sedimentary layers, and has well-defined rift and grain. The most common colour is gray, with gradations of buff or brown. Limestone formed at the surface by precipitation from hot spring waters is called travertine. Sandstone consists of sand-sized particles of weathered rock cemented together by sedimentary action. Though the composition is frequently quartz, weathered particles of granite or feldspar have produced valuable sandstones. Hues range from white to gray, coloured with pink, red, yellow, buff, brown, or green, depending on the cementing material. Like limestone, sandstone is easy to quarry.

The major metamorphic rock of commercial value is marble, primarily a recrystallized limestone that has been subject to heat and pressure during formation. Marbles containing iron oxides display pink, red, or yellow colours; those containing carbonaceous matter (organic remains) display blue-gray, gray, or black shades. Vermont marbles, containing talc, are green.

Manufacturing. The cement used in concrete blocks is created by heating a blend of limestone and clay in rotary kilns. Clays are chemically composed of about 60 percent quartz and 20 percent aluminum oxide, with varying amounts of metallic oxides, chiefly iron, calcium, magnesium, sodium, and potassium. The aggregates in concrete blocks may be either dense, using sand and gravel, or crushed rock, or lightweight, using sand and expanded shale, pumice, cinders, or blast-furnace slag (see also CEMENT; CONCRETE).

Concrete blocks are shaped by vibrating a very dry plastic concrete mix in an automated mold. When the blocks have been hardened sufficiently to hold their shape on release from the mold, they are transferred to a curing process to minimize shrinkage. Curing may be simply slow drying over a period of two to four weeks in open sheds, with precautions against freezing. The most effective method is steam curing under high pressure. A typical concrete mix for blocks is one part cement to six parts aggregate by volume. When water is added, a chemical reaction called hydration takes place, producing a hardened mass.

Bricks and other clay construction units are essentially plastic clay fired in a fused ceramic. Screened and ground clays are blended into a mill with water to create a plastic mass called stiff-mud, which is then forced through a die. The clay column, generally cored to produce the desired geometric voids, is cut by taut, rotating wires to the desired lengths (see also BRICK AND TILE PRODUCTION). Clays that are either too wet or too harsh (nonplastic) to be formed by the stiff-mud process are subjected to a process called soft-mud, which molds wet clays. High-pressure steel molds are used on such harsh clays.

After the units are formed, they are dried in ovens and heated to moderate temperatures for one to two days. Excess water is removed, and air shrinkage of the clay mass (2 to 8 percent) takes place. The dried units are then burned in kilns. Clay properties, the type of unit, and the required specifications of the final product determine the kiln burning time and temperature, which range from two to five days and from 1,600° to 2,400° F (about 870° to 1,315° C). During firing, further shrinkage occurs, increasing the total shrinkage from 4 to 16 percent. Differential shrinkage, a major cause of rejects in older kilns, has been reduced by improved firing control in modern long-tunnel kilns that provide uniform heating.

The dimension stone industry has also adopted machine operations, but the rock mass must first be broken into pieces that can be handled by power equipment. Traditionally, rocks have been broken into sections that can be cleaved along natural seams and cracks. Today, however, wedges are inserted in pneumatic-drilled holes to cleave hard, igneous rocks. For limestone and marble, a channelling machine makes parallel cuts in the quarry face, and the channelled block is split from its bed by wedges placed in horizontal holes in the block. In another method, a wire saw (a steel cable stretched over pulleys like a band saw) cuts downward like the channelling machine. Long blocks split off from the quarry face are broken into shorter blocks by drilling and wedging. When taken to the fabricating mills, quarry blocks are generally cut into thin slabs by gang saws. To profile the stones and give them surface treatment, lathing, planing, grinding, and polishing machines are employed just as in metalworking. Hand methods employing hammers and chisels are now largely obsolete, except for special custom work.

Rock cleaving

MODERN CONSTRUCTION PRACTICE

Work methods. *Masonry tools.* The installation of masonry units is primarily a skilled hand operation. The tools needed are used for three major activities: (1) laying out the work; (2) placing the mortar; and (3) shaping the units.

The major tools are the rule, level, and line. A mason's rule, which resembles a carpenter's folding rule, has vertical coursing scales to measure the thickness of the mortar joint. The corners of a wall are constructed first, and a plumb level is used to align the work. A mason's line (a special heavy twine) is then stretched between the corners. During construction the level is continuously used to plumb the corners of window and door openings and to check the level of horizontal joints (called bed joints). Pins on a corner block hold the line in place. A support called a tingle plate is used to keep the line from sagging over a long length of wall.

Mortar is handled with a brick trowel, a tool measuring nine to 11 inches in length. To finish the joints after the units have been placed and the mortar has stiffened, the jointing tool is slid along the face of the joint. The pointing trowel fills joints to a depth of about one-half inch. On new work, this procedure makes it possible to use coloured or dense mortars. On old work, the pointing trowel is used to replace weathered mortar, to ensure greater life, and to waterproof the construction—a process called tuck-pointing.

To cut and trim brick units, a brick hammer and brick set are employed. The cold chisel cuts holes in all kinds of masonry. Traditionally, the stonemason was equipped with many hammers and chisels to create a variety of finishes. With the advent of mill fabrication, however, such tools are no longer required on the job site. Concrete block and glazed facing tile are frequently cut by a circular, diamond-blade, portable saw. Modern masonry technology attempts to minimize trimming and cutting on the site by supplying special shapes, such as half, corner, jamb, or lintel units.

Brick hammer and brick set

Mortar mixing. Mortars are generally mixed by volume, using one part cement paste and three parts sand aggregate. Sufficient water is added to provide workable consistency. The paste may vary from all cement to all lime. Cement-rich mortars are strong but difficult to work, whereas lime-rich mortars are weak but plastic to work. Masonry cements containing ground limestone blended with cement can produce a workable mortar. For an all-purpose mortar, a 1:1:6 (cement: lime: and sand aggregate) mix has proved to be both workable and relatively strong. High-bond mortars include plastic organic additives and fine aggregates (aggregate that has been pulverized), such as marble dust, to maintain workability. To reduce water permeability through the joint, stearates (fatty acids) are added for water repellency. Mortars can be safely coloured with the earthy hues of iron oxides or the black of carbon. White can be achieved with white sand and cement. Highly absorptive masonry units, such as common brick, may remove sufficient water from the mortar to reduce strength and bond measurably. Such units must be wetted prior to laying.

Bonding patterns. The common bonding patterns of brick are shown in Figure 2. The different patterns (run-

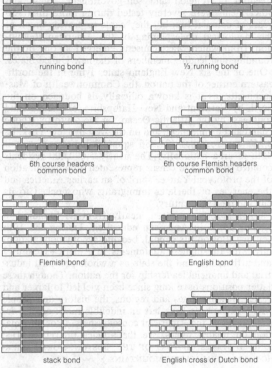

Figure 2: Common brick-bonding patterns.

ning bond, common bond, etc.) result from different arrangements of stretchers (brick with the long dimension parallel to the wall) and headers (brick with the long dimension toward the face of the wall). Where two or more vertical courses (layers) are constructed across the wall thickness, they must be tied by header units or light-gauge metal ties to provide structural stability. Mortar joints are made as narrow as the dimensional accuracy of the units will permit. Generally, this ranges from ¼ inch to ½ inch.

Physical properties of materials. Although masonry is among the oldest of building materials, only recently has it been subjected to rational engineering analysis. With the advent of modern steel and concrete, masonry has ceased to be the prime structural support and instead serves as a weather enclosure for the building system; and even this use has been challenged by modern composite material systems, such as glass walls, metal sheets, reinforced plastics, and cast architectural concrete. Since 1950 masonry industries have engaged in materials and structural testing in a search for designs based in rational engineering analysis, permitting a return to the structural use of masonry materials.

The primary physical properties of engineering interest are structural resistance; durability; volume changes; and fire, acoustical, and thermal resistance.

Structural resistance. The basic structural compressive strength of masonry materials (in pounds per square inch) ranges as follows: concrete block 1,000–5,000; clay

products 3,000–15,000; dimension stone 5,000–25,000. The tensile strength is about one-tenth the compressive value. The composite strength when used with mortar is below that of the parent masonry material, the value depending on the geometry of the unit, joint thickness, mortar strength and stiffness, and the bonding used in construction.

The deadweight of masonry varies from 90 pounds per cubic foot for lightweight concrete block, to 120 for brick masonry, to 150 for dense concrete block or natural stone. Some dense marbles and granites reach 175 pounds per cubic foot.

Durability. Traditionally, masonry materials have been valued for their permanence. The agents that cause deterioration are freezing–thawing of absorbed water, chemical action of atmospheric water containing dissolved industrial pollutants, and abrasive wear. For external use in the ground, materials of very low absorption and high strength are used, such as dense concrete block, highly fired bricks, or dense igneous rocks. The softer limestones and marbles need protection against corrosive atmospheres; they wear easily under foot and vehicular traffic.

Volume changes. Expansion and contraction due to temperature changes and to moisture changes are important concerns to the designer. Compared with most building materials, masonry materials as a class have relatively low thermal expansion. Fired clay products and igneous rocks have the least. Concrete products and sedimentary rocks approach that of mass concrete.

As a class, clay products and igneous rocks have negligible dimensional movement with moisture changes. Concrete products have substantial shrinkage upon loss of water, necessitating their careful curing, as noted earlier. Such shrinkage can be ten times greater than thermal changes. Autoclaved concrete block may reduce this movement to one-third or less. Natural stone contains "quarry sap," or absorbed water, which, when dried out, increases the strength measurably, and the stone becomes stabilized against future shrinkage. Generally, materials that shrink upon loss of absorbed water will swell and lose strength upon reabsorption.

Fire, acoustical, and thermal resistance. Fire resistance of masonry materials is generally superior to that of other building materials, even concrete. Certain igneous rocks (*e.g.*, granite) crack or spall under high temperature but do not completely disintegrate, thus providing substantial protection against collapse. Fires may reach temperatures above the softening point of steel (1,200° F). Thus, masonry is able to provide superior fire protection. Highly vitrified clay products containing fireclays can withstand temperatures in excess of 2,000° F.

The mass of masonry enhances its resistance to the transmission of airborne sound. When employed as a separating wall between noisy and quiet activities, it provides superior sound insulation. As an enclosing wall to reduce street noises, it is also effective. High-density masonry walls provide excellent protection against the noise of jets at airports.

Except for lightweight concrete blocks, most masonry materials and units are relatively poor insulators against the steady transfer of heat, as compared with rock wool, glass fibre, or Styrofoam. When the heat source is periodic, however, as during the daily summer heat-gain cycle, the high density and low specific heat of masonry acts as a heat sink of high capacity. The heat of the exterior building surface never reaches the interior before nocturnal cooling can take place. Such heat capacity (time-lag effect) explains the cool interiors of heavy fortresses or churches located in desert or tropic climates.

Modern applications. *Brick-veneer walls.* In housing, masonry is often used as a veneer over wood-stud construction. Most of the brick used in housing is applied in this manner.

Cavity walls. The most water-resistant wall construction is a masonry cavity, using an exterior course, an air space, and an interior course. Wire ties increase lateral stability. Weep holes (drainage holes) formed at the bottom of the wall allow the cavity to drain to the exterior

Dead-weight of masonry

when moisture penetrates the outside course. To reinforce the superior thermal resistance of this construction, the cavity may be filled with glass fibre or other insulation to create a degree of resistance to heat flow equal to the best of wood construction.

Concrete block foundations. House foundations are frequently built with dense concrete block as the basement wall material.

Exterior curtain walls. Brick and stone are valued aesthetically when used as weather enclosures for fenestration (window construction), particularly in high-rise commercial buildings. Such walls are usually backed up by concrete block for wind, weather, and fire resistance. They are built solid, with the exterior finish masonry bonded to the backup, using header construction, metal wire ties, or metal ladder reinforcing.

Fire walls. Most building codes require fire walls capable of resisting fire for a specified length of time, to prevent the spread of fire. The walls may be located between adjacent town houses, the major divisions of floor areas in factories, and at certain intervals in apartment construction. These walls are thick, of solid construction, and usually without openings.

Glazed-tile walls. Where low maintenance, high sanitation, and aesthetics are desired, structural glazed facing tile, a fireclay product produced in a wide colour range, is often used, typically in surgical rooms, commercial kitchens, radiation laboratories, and rest rooms. Glazed tile is not usually satisfactory for exterior use because of surface crazing (cracking) during freeze-thaw cycles.

Interior-partition walls. Lightweight concrete-block units, sometimes glazed with plastic colours, are widely used in school, commercial, and industrial walls. Economical, they provide the fire and sound resistance generally needed in such applications.

Load-bearing walls. The most significant new application is actually an old one: load-bearing use of masonry. Using modern data on material strength and modern principles of structural engineering, all interior and exterior vertical, opaque walls can be made to support floors against gravity forces. While skeleton framing of steel and reinforced concrete has dominated construction since the beginning of the 20th century, such construction has frequently employed opaque masonry materials under beams and between columns. The modern application of structural masonry can eliminate the structural frame. Eight inches of masonry can safely hold a height of ten stories. In Europe and the United States, load-bearing buildings with walls not more than 12 inches thick have been carried to about 20 stories. To withstand the horizontal forces of wind or earthquakes, load-bearing construction is braced by building high shear walls, vertical cross walls that buttress the building.

Shear walls

Reinforced walls. The resistance of unreinforced masonry walls is dependent on the tensile bond of the mortar. A low-tensile bond value is adequate for ordinary wind loads on walls one story high, but for high walls, steel reinforcing is required. In brick construction, a cavity wall is constructed and the air space is filled with grout (thin mortar) containing embedded steel bars. In concrete wall construction, bars inserted into vertical cells are grouted in position. This form of construction is common where earthquake or severe-wind resistance is needed.

Screen walls. Clay and concrete units, available in a wide variety of open-through-the-wall designs, create attractive screening walls. They are used as outside fences, inside divider walls, or above fenestration as shading against sunlight.

BIBLIOGRAPHY. J. RALPH DALZELL and GILBERT TOWNSEND, *Masonry Simplified*, vol. 1 (1948), a simplified treatment of modern workmanship practices; WHITNEY CLARK HUNTINGTON, *Building Construction: Materials and Types of Construction*, 3rd ed. (1963), an excellent treatment of masonry nomenclature, especially ch. 4; L.W. SEAKINS and S. SMITH, *Practical Brickwork* (1963), a primer text on the art of being a "do-it-yourself" mason; HARRY C. PLUMMER, *Brick and Tile Engineering*, 2nd ed. (1962), an authoritative handbook on clay masonry construction in the United States; BANISTER FLETCHER, *A History of Architecture on the Comparative Method*, 17th ed. (1963), a comprehensive architectural history text on classical masonry buildings of the past, including Oriental buildings; TALBOT HAMLIN, *Architecture Through the Ages*, rev. ed. (1953), a source that especially emphasizes primitive structures and pre-Columbian buildings; GEORGE P. MERRILL, *Stones for Building and Decoration*, 3rd rev. ed. (1903), though dated, a comprehensive statement of the geology of dimension stone in the United States; JAMES G. CROSS and HARRY C. PLUMMER, *Principles of Clay Masonry Construction* (1970), a resource text for teaching masonry to architectural and civil engineering students.

(C.B.Mo.)

Massachusetts

Like others of the 13 British colonies along America's Atlantic Seaboard in the 17th and 18th centuries, Massachusetts was founded by men seeking in a wilderness for a new way of life involving such then untried notions as freedom of religion and self-government. These and other ideals were severely tested during more than 150 years of colonial life, but they came to provide much of the ideological underpinning of the American Revolution, from which Massachusetts emerged as one of the founding and leading members of the new United States.

One of the six New England states lying in the northeastern corner of the nation, the Commonwealth of Massachusetts, as it is known officially, is bounded on the north by Vermont and New Hampshire, on the east and southeast by the Atlantic Ocean, on the south by Rhode Island and Connecticut, and on the west by New York. Its 8,257 square miles (21,386 square kilometres) rank it 45th in area nationally. The nearly 5,690,000 residents counted in the 1970 census represented an amalgamation of the prototypal Yankee spirit of an earlier America and the energies of the later immigrants who flocked to its cities in the 19th century.

Character and location of the commonwealth

Massachusetts has been, nearly from its founding, a leading force in American education. During the 19th century, Boston, its capital, became synonymous nationally with the highest attainments in America's cultural and artistic life, and the state as a whole provided industrial and financial leadership for the nation. Though these latter positions have long since been yielded to larger and faster growing states and regions, the history and people of Massachusetts have left an indelible mark on the development of the American consciousness. (For information on related topics, see the articles UNITED STATES; UNITED STATES, HISTORY OF THE; BOSTON; NORTH AMERICA; and APPALACHIAN MOUNTAINS.)

THE HISTORY OF MASSACHUSETTS

History is woven into the very fabric of life in Massachusetts and has become the state's most valuable resource. The Pilgrims' landing and the American Revolution were the most heralded events, but the elements of struggle and survival were the main lessons for posterity from those two eras.

Cornerstones of the colony. The arrival of the Pilgrims on December 21, 1620, was significant, yet the Indians had found this corner of the country some 3,500 years earlier, and Leif Eriksson and his Norsemen probably landed somewhere in the Cape Cod region in 1003. European seafarers tapped the fertile fishing areas throughout the 1500s, the French explorer Samuel de Champlain mapped the area in 1605, and in 1614 Capt. John Smith of Virginia drafted a detailed map of the New England coast from Penobscot Bay in Maine to Cape Cod. He even fought the Indians at Plymouth, stealing their canoes and trading them back in exchange for beaver skins.

At the time of the landing at Plymouth, most of the Pilgrims were at Provincetown, where they had arrived several days earlier and where the "Mayflower" was still anchored. An expedition of a dozen Pilgrims and six crewmen was sent to scout for a suitable settling place, which they found at Plymouth. The "Mayflower" did not arrive until the day after Christmas.

The Mayflower Compact, signed five weeks earlier by 41 men while still at sea, was hardly democratic. Basically, it called for rule by the elite, but it established an elective system and a basis for limited consent of the governed as the source of authority. The Compact for "the general good of ye Colonie" agreed that the "civill body politick" would abide by "just and equall lawes." Nearly 170 years later, the framers of the United States Constitution adopted that theme.

Early struggle for survival

During that first winter the Pilgrims lived aboard ship and suffered the loss of 47 colonists. Probably they were victims of the same epidemic that was believed to have killed 95,000 Indians from 1615 to 1617, leaving only about 5,000 along the coast. The "Mayflower" returned to England in the spring, leaving a hardy band atop Cole's Hill, where they buried their dead and then planted seed to conceal their tragedy.

In March a tall, nearly naked Indian named Samoset confronted the haggard settlers with the peace cry in English, "Much welcome, Englishmen! Much welcome, Englishmen!" Both races had been weakened by the plague and needed one another. Their common efforts at survival gave rise after the autumn harvests to the feast of Thanksgiving, the first and since 1621 the most characteristic celebration of the peoples of the United States. Samoset, a Pemaquid from Maine, introduced his friend Massasoit, chief of the Wampanoags, and 20 braves. Among them was Squanto, once sold into slavery in Spain and later a resident at the home of an English gentleman, where he learned English. By a quirk of history, he became the interpreter, guide, and teacher of the first white settlers.

Settlers had feared Massachusetts for its hostile Indians, but, until 1675, relative peace prevailed because of a pact with Massasoit. This accord was ended by King Philip (Metacom), Massasoit's son. His open warfare (King Philip's War [1675–76]) ended in his own death, but only after 300 settlers had been killed, 600 dwellings levelled, and 50 towns raided in southeastern and central Massachusetts.

Revolutionary period. A new struggle against new obstacles was touched off 100 years later by "the shot heard 'round the world." The colonists' fight was not so much against the British Redcoats as it was for an ideal, and the struggle actually had begun several years earlier, when a new spirit grew out of years of physical sacrifice and radical ideas involving such concepts as equality, freedom, and unity.

Leadership in fomenting the Revolution

From a tragic moment of that period—the Boston Massacre of 1770, in which British soldiers killed five civilians after a snowball-throwing incident that got out of hand—came one of the finest moments in the annals of the American judicial system. John Adams, later to be president, and Josiah Quincy successfully defended the soldiers against the outcries of an enraged citizenry bent on retribution. Three years later, another (but unrelated) Adams, Samuel, led the raid known as the Boston Tea Party, dumping chests of taxable tea into the harbour, forcing the British to close the port of Boston, and striking a kindred nerve of resistance in other colonies. Events occurred in rapid-fire sequence after that—the battles of Lexington and Concord and Bunker Hill and the evacuation of Boston, inspiring song and verse that came to typify the spirit and events of the Revolutionary era.

The state. The state's contributions to the nation were many as it was being born, and they continued as it matured. It has contributed four presidents—John Adams, John Quincy Adams, Calvin Coolidge, and John F. Kennedy—as well as many cabinet officers, career officers, diplomats, and congressional leaders. It has supported most of America's wars but opposed others, such as the War of 1812, the Mexican War (1846–48), and the Vietnamese war.

The middle and late 19th century saw pronounced changes in the state, spurred by the factories spawned by the Industrial Revolution, a golden age of literature, and immigration, particularly by the Irish. The older, established classes remained dominant during this period, taking advantage of this new, cheap work force. A large segment of the rural population migrated westward, however, where the opportunities were greater and the discrimination less.

Grass roots agitation prompted legislation in 1820 that removed property requirements for voters, and in 1833 the church was separated from the state. This set the stage for the Jacksonian Democrats, who advocated giving more power to the people. The large immigrant voting bloc soon achieved this, mainly through the Democratic Party.

New England lost its textile leadership to the South and much of its shoe business to the Middle West in the first half of the 20th century, but it continued its financial, educational, and cultural prominence while branching into the fields of electronics and communications.

THE NATURAL AND HUMAN LANDSCAPE

The natural environment. A walk along the Massachusetts coast would register about 1,500 miles, yet the cross-country distances are only 190 miles from east to west and 110 miles north to south. The jagged coast winds from Rhode Island around Cape Cod, in and out of scenic harbours along the shore south of Boston, through Boston Harbor and up the North Shore, finally swinging around the painters' paradise of Cape Ann before reaching New Hampshire.

Surface features. The indented coasts of Massachusetts were formed by the great glaciers that in places covered the land with several thousand feet of ice. Ocean tides licked away the last ice some 11,000 years ago, revealing massive chunks of rocks along the shore. Hard, flat land stretches out beyond, becoming stony upland pastures near the central part of the state and bulging into a gently hilly country in the west. Except toward the west, the land is rocky, often sandy, and not fertile.

Cape Cod and the offshore islands

In the southeast, Cape Cod juts out into the ocean. This 65-mile-long appendage is rectangular in shape except at its easternmost point, where it hooks northward. Its offshore waters are among the most treacherous in the country. Henry David Thoreau wrote that, to the people of Provincetown, at the tip of the cape, the sea is their garden, and the dog that growls at their door is the Atlantic Ocean. Tufts of grass spring up along the sand dunes, and gnarled jack pines and scrub oaks, some only head high, grow in bunches. Off the southeastern coast lie the islands of Nantucket and Martha's Vineyard, lashed by the gray Atlantic in winter but in summer alive with thousands of tourists and longtime seasonal residents.

Central Massachusetts comprises rolling plains fed by innumerable streams. Beyond lies the broad and fertile Connecticut Valley and then the Berkshire Hills. The now-paved Mohawk Trail crosses the Berkshires, the Taconic Range on the west and the Hoosac Range on the east. The state's highest point, 3,491 feet (1,064 metres), is Mt. Greylock on the Taconic side near Adams. In North Adams a natural bridge of white marble has been formed by the wind and water, and at nearby Sutton is a half-mile-long gorge that knifes through the rock, exposing 600,000,000 years of geological history.

Rivers and lakes

The land is veined with rivers—19 main systems, the best known of which are the Connecticut, Charles, and Merrimack. More than 1,200 ponds or lakes lie among the hollows of the hills, one in almost every one of the 365 communities. Many bear long Indian names, most notably Lake Chargoggagoggmauchuaggagoggchaubunagungamaugg (which, translated, means "You fish on your side; I fish on my side; nobody fish in the middle"). The best known small body of water, however, is Walden Pond, immortalized by Thoreau.

Nearly all the rivers and many lakes are now too polluted for swimming. This has long been true of the meandering Charles, which separates Boston and Cambridge and which now is favoured by college rowing crews, canoeists, and sailboat enthusiasts.

Vegetation and animal life. Despite its industrialization, Massachusetts has managed to preserve many of its forests, and it has 108 state forests and reservations.

Not far from downtown Boston is the Arnold Arboretum, which has the largest collection of trees and shrubs in the United States. Along the shores the sandpiper, blue heron, American egret, sanderling, and turnstone are seen. Water birds include the gull, scoter, cormorant, and loon, while those most often seen on land are the kingfisher, warbler, bobwhite, brown thrasher, sparrow hawk, yellow-shafted flicker, and whippoorwill. Game birds include ruffed grouse, wild turkey, and pheasant.

Public hunting grounds amount to about 23,000 acres. Three national wildlife refuges and Cape Cod National Seashore allow further contact with nature, but few animals remain. Of the larger animals, deer, snowshoe hare, red fox, woodchuck, muskrat, otter, and chipmunk still may be seen.

Climate. Statewide, a temperate climate prevails. The climate is colder but drier in western Massachusetts, although its winter snowfalls may be more severe than those nearer the coast. July and August are the hottest months, averaging about 70° F (21° C), in contrast to the 30° F (−1° C) average of winter.

Patterns of settlement. In the early days the most populated seacoast towns lay at the mouth of rivers. The settlers fanned inland along these streams, drawing on them at first for farming and later for the power to run the mills.

Today, the lure of the sea results in nearly equal popularity for all the towns along the coast, where sunbathing, swimming, yachting, and fishing are a way of life. Among these are Plymouth, with its long harbour; Duxbury, Marshfield, Scituate, and Cohasset, where the first suburbs sprang up in colonial days; the boating bays from Hingham to Boston; the beaches at Revere and Lynn; the famous fishing off Gloucester and Cape Ann; and Marblehead, the yachting capital of the world.

Boston is surrounded by communities many of whose residents work in the city by day, sleep in the suburbs by night, and clog the highways commuting back and forth. Other urban cores include Springfield, Worcester, Fall River–New Bedford, and Lowell–Lawrence. These cities, which grew large during the Industrial Revolution, continue to act as magnets to large numbers of people.

THE PEOPLE OF MASSACHUSETTS

Ethnic composition. Boston and San Francisco often are referred to as sister cities because of such similarities as busy oceanside ports, good restaurants, emphasis on culture, prominence of religion in civic and social life, fine architecture in public and private buildings, and echoes of a colourful history. Their ethnic mix is comparable as well. The blend of peoples in Boston has spread across the state. Although Boston is heavily Irish, so too are the urban areas in western Massachusetts, and the native brogue of Ireland is more likely to be heard around Springfield, Westfield, and Holyoke than in Boston. In the first half of the 20th century large numbers of Italians followed the Irish immigrations of the 1800s, while in the late 1960s and early 1970s the newcomers have been mostly Spanish speaking, from Cuba and Puerto Rico.

The English stock that still forms the backbone of the population is intermingled with Slovaks, Poles, Canadians, Russian Jews, Greek, Scandinavians, Syrians, Germans, French, and Chinese. Fall River and New Bedford are the homes of many Portuguese and Cape Verde Islanders. Descendants of the Indians are few, though the state was named by Capt. John Smith for the Massachuset tribe, whose name meant "near the great hill," believed to refer to the Blue Hill Range that rises south of Boston in an otherwise flat area. Blacks are concentrated mainly in the old and deteriorating Roxbury and Dorchester sections of Boston and in New Bedford and Springfield.

Demographic trends. Although the state's population increased by about 10.5 percent from 1960 to 1970, Boston's dipped by nearly 10 percent. Six cities had populations of 100,000 or more, while Suffolk and Middlesex counties, in and around Boston, held more than one-third of the population.

Better roads and environmental problems contributed to a growing tide of migrants away from the urban core after the early 1950s. The building of a wheellike pattern of highways with Boston at the centre started the first exodus. The second began in 1970 with the completion of a new outer rim several miles from the first one. The accessibility of both highways drew many electronics and engineering firms to these areas, providing a new nucleus for suburban and exurban employment and living.

Religious development. Massachusetts is largely Roman Catholic, with over 2,700,000 adherents, though its religious foundation was solidly Protestant. The Mayflower colonists were Separatists who fled to Amsterdam from England to practice their religion without official interference. Hardship and a desire to establish an identity free of Dutch influence prompted them to seek out America in 1620. The Puritans, who came to Massachusetts in 1630, believed in reform but only within the church structure. (They were not believers in religious freedom, a fact that other Protestant groups, such as the Anabaptists and Quakers, soon discovered, to their discomfort.)

Religious separatists and other dissenters

From this socioreligious framework evolved a theocracy in which government officials attempted to act as clergy, interpreting the will of God for the people. The arrangement fell short of its purpose. When in 1634 Gov. John Winthrop refused to call a meeting of the legislature, or General Court, the freemen demanded to see the charter. He acceded, divulging his infringement on the rights of the legislature, and a bill was quickly passed vesting governmental power in the people. The establishment religion was whittled at constantly by scores of radicals. Many of them were banished—including Roger Williams from Salem and Anne Hutchinson from Boston —for their independent views.

During its subsequent development, Massachusetts remained very religious. Following colonial patterns, churches often are found in the most prominent places of the towns and villages, symbolizing their traditional role in social life.

Social hierarchies. All the people of Massachusetts may be created equal, but some gained an edge earlier than others. The variety of peoples in the state, exceeded only by that of New York, fails to alter the fact that the major concentration of wealth and power continues to be controlled by the 800 or so families who trace their pedigrees to the "Mayflower" and the handful who in the following centuries so successfully trod the winding avenues of commerce, finance, and culture that they came to be considered among the ranks of that still relevant cadre, the Proper Bostonians. Many descendants of later immigrants also have found their way to the top of the financial—and often political—ladder. The proud tradition of family participation in the building of the state extends also to those of less exalted position: a large proportion of the residents of small-town Massachusetts, especially in the west, can claim many generations of Yankee background.

The old families and the new

THE STATE'S ECONOMY

Manufacturing. Massachusetts has been a maunfacturing state since the early 1640s, when John Winthrop, Jr. (son of Governor Winthrop), opened a saltworks in Beverly and ironworks in Saugus and Quincy. Francis Cabot Lowell was largely responsible, however, for raising the state to its manufacturing eminence, which now accounts for one-half of New England's manufacturing income. Lowell went to England to study methods of textile operations and built a power loom in Waltham in 1814. He died in 1817, but his associates developed the brick city of Lowell, with its mills driven by the Merrimack River.

Yankee ingenuity fostered much early handicraft-based industry, though the influx of unskilled, low-paid labourers from Europe during the 19th century was the necessary ingredient for the mass production that developed in the state's shoe and textile factories. One of the first and largest shoe plants in America was the United Shoe Machinery Corporation in Beverly, while the building of the Springfield armory in 1777 boosted industry in western Massachusetts at the same time that it aided the Revolutionary cause. Other well-known goods from Massachusetts factories include watches from Waltham, Salem, and Boston; rockers from Gardner; cutlery and hand tools from Greenfield; guns and motorcycles from Springfield; leather goods from Peabody; shovels (used by the '49ers in the California Gold Rush) from North Eaton; envelopes from Worcester; paper from Holyoke; silverware from Newburyport; and razor blades from Boston.

Today, the electronics and communications industries draw heavily upon the many educational institutions in and around Boston. The western suburbs of Boston have become world famous for their research-and-development facilities, which contributed significantly to space technology in the 1960s.

The sea and the soil. Foreign trade, fishing, and agriculture long buoyed the economy. Salem sailors brought exotic goods from China, the West Indies, and other faraway lands. Fishing was lucrative, adventuresome, and dangerous—more than 10,000 Gloucester fishermen have lost their lives over the centuries. Fishing and shipbuilding went hand in hand. Between 1789 and 1810 the Massachusetts fleet grew tenfold, some of it to aid in defense against British and French aggressions on the high seas. Yankee sailors also found much "black gold" in the slave trade between West Africa and Southern ports.

At the height of the whaling boom in the 19th century, 329 whaling vessels sailed from New Bedford, in addition to others from Nantucket and other ports, bringing in $10,000,000 worth of cargo each year in their holds. This great industry was not to last, however, and, by the turn of the century, its contribution to the state's economy had dwindled to only a fraction of its former importance. Fishing later suffered substantial reverses, as well. A $42,000,000 annual business in the early 1960s, fishing began to wane, late in the decade, because of foreign competition in the traditional Atlantic fishing grounds and the depletion of such species as haddock and lobster from overfishing.

The generally rocky soils support only truck gardening, although the purple sandy bogs of southeastern Massachusetts and Cape Cod produce about 60 percent of the world—and 70 percent of the U.S.—cranberry supply. Poultry accounts for about one-third of the agricultural income.

Finance. Since colonial days, Boston has been a financial centre. Its investments contributed heavily to developing the American West, while the shipping industry made it the first insurance capital of the nation.

Tourism. Tourists know Massachusetts for the haddock, cod, and shellfish of its restaurants, as well as for its rich heritage of American history. The state has some 8,500,000 visitors annually, who pump well over $1,000,000,000 into its economy.

Transportation. "Never, in these United States, has the brain of man conceived, or the hand of man fashioned, so perfect a thing as the clipper ship," wrote historian Samuel Eliot Morison in *Maritime History of Massachusetts.* All clipper ships were built between 1850 and 1855, and from then on a kind of World Series of ship racing began. The champion was Donald McKay's "Flying Cloud," which sailed to San Francisco in 89 days, went 374 miles in one day, and averaged 13.5 knots (nautical miles per hour) an hour over four days. Records were not the only motivating factor: the clippers carried 1,700 tons of cargo. Long before this, however, in 1716, Boston Light had been built off the busy port, the first lighthouse in the United States.

Water formed the Bay State's highway system for 200 years. Rivers such as the Connecticut and Merrimack and man-made canals such as the Middlesex served early needs well. The Boston Post Road and Mohawk Trail were the most heavily travelled early roadways. Opened to Boston–New York mail in 1673, the Post Road consisted of three routes. The Mohawk, an Indian footpath converted to an ox road by the settlers, became the first interstate toll-free road, called Shunpike, in 1786.

In 1826, the nation's first railroad brought granite from the quarries of Quincy and Charlestown for the building of the Bunker Hill Monument in Charlestown. The cars were horse drawn. A steam railroad connected Springfield and Worcester in 1839, and 15 systems were shut-

tling freight among western Massachusetts cities by 1855. Among the most impressive feats of early railroad building was the 4½-mile Hoosac Tunnel, drilled under the Hoosac Range between 1851 and 1875. The first electric street railway began in Brockton, and Boston had America's first passenger subway, as well as an elevated system.

Boston's Logan International Airport, stretching parallel to the harbour, is one of the few large air terminals in close proximity to a major city. It also is the nation's only airport owned and operated by the state. In spite of the general modernity of the state's transportation system, however, the sleek high-speed trains and the supersonic jets have yet to match the aesthetic perfection of the Yankee clipper.

ADMINISTRATION AND SOCIAL CONDITIONS

Government. *Traditions of self-government.* From the Mayflower Compact, drawn up by the Pilgrims in 1620 when the concept of "the divine right of kings" dominated Europe and the idea of self-government was little more than an exotic notion, a form of government evolved of which the people could feel themselves a part. In 1630, when the Puritans of the Massachusetts Bay Company settled Boston and other surrounding towns, John Winthrop and 18 assistants formed the governing body known as the Great and General Court. In a dispute over a stray pig, the Court became bicameral in 1644, the assistants forming the Senate and two deputies elected from each town making up the House.

After independence was declared, the General Court drew up a state constitution. The people rejected it, however, wanting a share in the drafting, and they elected a constitutional convention. Meeting in Cambridge in 1779, it gave the writing task to John Adams, and the people ratified his work in 1780. One of its extraordinary provisions permits the governor and his council or the legislature to seek advisory opinions on questions pertaining to the scope of gubernatorial or legislative power from justices of the Supreme Judicial Court. Today, Massachusetts is the only one of the 13 original states still governed under its first constitution, though the document has been updated many times by amendment.

The first meeting of the General Court as the legislative body of the new state took place in October 1780, exactly 150 years after the first meeting of the Puritans' Great and General Court. At present it comprises 40 senators and 240 representatives, but in the 1960s political battles began over whether the House was too unwieldy in size for efficient action. The state's judiciary mainly divides into the district courts for handling minor matters, superior courts for trial by jury, and the Supreme Judicial Court.

Local government. Another phenomenon that grew up shortly after the settlers arrived was the town meeting, which started as a forum for settling local quarrels and grew to what is in many smaller towns the community event of the year. (As the poet James Russell Lowell observed, "Puritanism, believing itself quick with the seed of religious liberty, laid without knowing it, the egg of democracy.") The first recorded meeting was in Dorchester in 1633, when citizens were summoned by the roll of a drum. A year later Charlestown organized the first Board of Selectmen, the emergence of such local government balancing the power of the colony's executive. A county system also was developed patterned after the English model, in which the greater powers reside in townships and cities rather than in the counties, which serve chiefly for judicial purposes. A major need of Massachusetts in the 1970s was in the redefinition of the roles of municipal, county, and state governments.

Political life. The legislature tends to be dominated by Democrats, but it is not surprising for Republicans to win the governorship or seats in the U.S. Congress. The Boston Irish politician has become legendary, mostly because of Mayor James Michael Curley, a skillful orator from a lowly background who was jailed twice, once while in office. During the late 19th and early 20th centuries, politics became a means to a better life—to a place alongside the "Boston Brahmins" of Mayflower heritage—for the

Margin notes: The golden age of Yankee seafarers · Waterways and highways in the past · The state constitution

Irish, who were discriminated against in employment advertisements that carried the letters "N.I.N.A."—No Irish Need Apply.

The social milieu. Discrimination was practiced from time to time in Massachusetts against such groups as the Indians, religious sects, and women, but the state also provided leaders in major fights to improve social conditions: Roger Williams and Anne Hutchinson for religious freedom; William Lloyd Garrison and Horace Greeley for the abolition of slavery; Horace Mann for public secondary education; Mary Lyon for women's education; and Francis Cabot Lowell, whose brick housing near his factories, though grim by today's standards, was better than the workers' ghettos he had seen in England.

Leaders of social consciousness

Women and children were exploited at the start of the Industrial Revolution, but Massachusetts was a pioneer in devising laws to protect them. State boards, under the supervision of the governor, later grew out of the need to improve conditions in health, education, welfare, labour, banking, insurance, prisons, and the like.

Health and welfare. Massachusetts is one of the chief medical centres of the world, particularly in the area of specialists and specialty hospitals. It also has been a leader in research, notably at Boston's Children's Cancer Research Foundation. An urgent contemporary challenge is the delivery of medical services to the poor, who have been victimized by urbanization and the gradual disappearance of the family physician. Care for the mentally ill, the alcoholic, the addict, and the juvenile delinquent remain problems, even though the state recognized its responsibility as early as 1818, when it opened an asylum for the insane.

Welfare was the province of the cities and towns until taken over by the state in 1970. Although the new program was fraught with difficulty, it was an improvement over the system that existed in the mid-19th century, when 3,000 citizens were imprisoned annually for indebtedness.

Social tensions. Except among the intellectual elite, little concern was shown for the Negroes before 1850 for fear of alienating Southern cotton producers. Boston had a separate school for blacks, but otherwise they were denied schooling. The Know-Nothing Party emerged in 1845 primarily to combat growing Irish immigration but also to fight slavery, which the party considered an outgrowth of indifference by the rich toward human rights.

In the 1960s the urban areas experienced racial unrest similar to that throughout the country. Little had been resolved by the early 1970s, but the blacks were making some advances through political and economic means. Bussing of school children was more of a dilemma in Massachusetts cities than in the South during the 1960s and 1970s. The blacks had little encouragement, however, to "pull themselves up by their bootstraps"—as they were constantly reminded that the Irish and Italians did.

The Yankees, meanwhile, continue to run most of the banks, most of the law firms, and many of the businesses. They still represent the rock-ribbed solidarity in the state, built up through generations and epitomized by their contributions to the entire nation.

Education. Close to the heart of Massachusetts' social and cultural life lies education. Harvard College (now Harvard University), founded in 1636 in New Towne (now Cambridge), was long the major factor, although it was designed originally to provide the wilderness colony with a continuing supply of trained clergy rather than an educated lay population. Its graduates became community leaders, and schooling soon was provided colony-wide. In 1647, towns with 50 householders were required to support an elementary school; those with 100, a secondary school.

Educational pioneering

Massachusetts became the pioneer as well in kindergarten and secondary education and developed a uniform state public-school system in 1840. The state has numerous private preparatory schools of national ranking. Roxbury Latin School, founded in 1645, is among the nation's oldest, while others are located in Andover, Groton, Milton, Mount Hermon and Northfield, and Deerfield.

Many of America's oldest and most prestigious institutions of higher learning, in addition to Harvard, are in Massachusetts. Some 300,000 students were in its public and private institutions in 1971, about 160,000 in Boston alone, where Boston University (1839) and Northeastern University (1898) were the largest. Nearby were the Massachusetts Institute of Technology (Cambridge; 1861) and Tufts (Medford; 1852) and Brandeis (Waltham; 1948) universities. Amherst (Amherst; 1821) and Williams (Williamstown; 1791) colleges perpetuated traditions of academic excellence at small schools, while Mount Holyoke (South Hadley; 1837), Wellesley (Wellesley; 1870), Smith (Northampton; 1871), and Radcliffe (Cambridge; 1879) colleges were pioneers in women's education. Boston College (Chestnut Hill; 1863) and Holy Cross (Worcester; 1843) are major Roman Catholic institutions. The University of Massachusetts (Amherst and Boston; 1863) has raised its academic standing significantly in recent decades.

CULTURAL LIFE AND INSTITUTIONS

The blending of an Old World heritage and a New World spirit produced a bountiful cultural environment in Massachusetts.

The arts. Literature was virtually lost in the leaden language of the early writings and sermons, though poets such as Anne Bradstreet and Edward Taylor rose well above the level of dogmatizing, and Jonathan Edwards combined taut language and a brilliant theological mind with an unemotional pulpit delivery. During what has been called the American renaissance, however, beginning around the time of the Revolution and lasting through much of the 19th century, the state nourished many writers who might be said to have founded the bases of American literature—and who brought it recognition outside the new nation.

Place in American arts and letters

The group of writers who brought fame to Concord are an indication of the inspiration of this period. A deep sense of both community responsibility and individualism may be traced through the writings of Ralph Waldo Emerson, Henry David Thoreau, Nathaniel Hawthorne, and Louisa May Alcott, all of whom were neighbours. The eloquence of Emerson, preacher, philosopher, and poet, carried his concepts of individual spiritual freedom to faraway lands while Hawthorne found tranquillity in the small town after growing up in the shadows of Salem witches near the House of Seven Gables.

The mountains of Pittsfield also provided a congenial working environment for Hawthorne as well as for Herman Melville, Oliver Wendell Holmes, and Henry Wadsworth Longfellow (the latter two combining, respectively, medicine and scholarship with their writings). Among other famous writers of the era were John Greenleaf Whittier and James Russell Lowell, as well as Emily Dickinson, today generally acclaimed as the finest American poet of the 19th century.

The universities have become central to many of the performing arts (theatre, dance, and music) in Massachusetts, although the Boston Symphony Orchestra generally is regarded as among the finest musical ensembles in the world. Its Tanglewood concerts under the stars at Lenox in the Berkshires (begun in 1937) are, with the Jacob's Pillow Dance Festival at nearby Lee, among the major attractions of the New England summer. The museums, libraries, and historical societies of Boston are among the most distinguished in the nation. These and other cultural aspects of that city are covered in greater detail in the article BOSTON.

Monuments to history. Historical sites in Boston draw the most tourists. A Freedom Trail provides a whirl through yesteryear that includes Boston Common, the old and new (1795) state houses, Park Street Church, the Old Granary Burying Ground, Old Corner Bookstore, Faneuil Hall, Paul Revere House, the Old North Church, and the USS "Constitution," better known as "Old Ironsides."

Outside the capital, the past seems still alive in three villages: Plimoth Plantation, Old Sturbridge Village, and Shaker Village in Hancock, where the sect established its

Mass Production

communal-church concept in the 1780s. Harvard Square in Cambridge is a favourite tourist stop for its potpourri of people, its proximity to Harvard and Massachusetts Institute of Technology, and the history imbedded in the cobblestone atmosphere along its narrow side streets: the Harvard Yard, Christ Church, the Fogg Art Museum, Longfellow House (one of seven making up Tory Row), and innumerable other attractions of the city.

Salem prefers to forget its witch-hunting period of the late 17th century, but visitors to the House of Seven Gables and other "haunted houses" keep the memories alive. In the elm-shrouded Chestnut Street area are Federal-style homes that reflect the days of prosperity for merchants, shipowners, diplomats, congressmen, and writers.

Along the South Shore are Quincy, where the humble homes of the eminent Adams family are next door to one another, and Hingham, where the Old Ship Church is the oldest surviving church in the 13 colonies. The Whaling Museum in New Bedford includes a half-size reproduction of a whaling vessel and some 600 log books, and the Seamen's Bethel (chapel) there was immortalized by Melville in *Moby Dick*.

Westward of Boston lies Concord and its Old Manse, home of the Emersons' grandfather and for four years, of the Hawthornes.

Historic western Massachusetts

Past the Old Mill and Longfellow's Wayside Inn in Sudbury are Worcester and then Springfield, where the armoury and arsenal are reminders of the city's famous rifle. In nearby Pelham, the Town Hall complex has the oldest continuously used meeting house in the country and a monument to Capt. Daniel Shays, who led a rebellion of poor farmers in 1786. Chesterwood in Stockbridge was the site of the studio of Daniel Chester French, sculptor of the great seated Lincoln statue in Washington's Lincoln Memorial. Some of the doors of houses in Old Deerfield bear the marks of Indian tomahawks wielded during the raids of the early 18th century.

Recreation. Private clubs, both social and athletic, long have been Massachusetts institutions, especially for golf, tennis, and yachting. Among the most exclusive were the Brookline Country Club and the Longwood Cricket Club in Brookline, the Myopia Hunt Club in Hamilton, and various yacht clubs along the North Shore above Boston, particularly in Marblehead.

Athletics have come in recent decades to form a subculture among all social classes. The professional teams—Boston's Red Sox in baseball, Bruins in hockey, and Celtics in basketball and the Foxboro-based New England Patriots in football—attract the most atttention, but the state gives considerable emphasis to high school and college activity as well.

The communications media. Boston's Freedom Trail passes the now-defunct Newspaper Row, where before World War II seven newspapers competed daily. The survivors in the early 1970s were the *Boston Globe* and *Boston Herald Traveler* and *Record American*. The *Springfield Republican* under Samuel Bowles was one of America's prominent papers during the 19th century, along with the *Worcester Telegram-Gazette,* a pioneer in modern printing technology. Both are still in operation. Among the broadcast media that blanket the state, educational television station WGBH in Boston achieved a wide reputation for its innovative programming.

PROBLEMS AND PROSPECTS

To many persons Massachusetts faces the future with a need for regeneration in many areas of its public life. Its forefathers set a straight course that resulted in prosperity and freedom, while Yankee ingenuity helped hurdle the rough places in the road. Now their ideals of freedom and equality are in practice, and the challenge that faces the beneficiaries of this groundwork is whether they can cope with the luxury bequeathed them. The physical revitalization of Boston continues, but cutbacks in federal programs hurt the defense-oriented electronics and research industries. Governmental leaders must continue to reform the political mechanisms while continuing to conform with the inspired direction of John Adams' Constitution.

BIBLIOGRAPHY. The history of Massachusetts runs back into the history of England, and the early literature is massive. Both WILLIAM BRADFORD and JOHN WINTHROP, early colonial governors, wrote journals. The early divines were prolific. The Adams family has been called "the writingest family" in American history, and their papers make up over 80 volumes without touching the 20th century. For a study of the Puritan mind, the works of PERRY MILLER are most authoritative. The intellectual history from the Puritan fathers through the Transcendentalists is thoroughly documented. Modern political history is less well covered, but it has become increasingly subject to scholarly scrutiny. A history of Harvard University is central to an understanding of the commonwealth. The following merely touches the surface of a vast literature.

General reading: FEDERAL WRITERS' PROJECT, *Massachusetts: A Guide to Its Places and People*, new ed. (1971); VAN WYCK BROOKS, *The Flowering of New England, 1815–1865* (1936) and *New England: Indian Summer, 1865–1915* (1940); CLEVELAND AMORY, *The Proper Bostonians* (1947).

History: A.B. HART (ed.), *Commonwealth History of Massachusetts: Colony, Province and State*, 5 vol. (1927–30); CHARLES M. ANDREWS, *The Fathers of New England: A Chronicle of the Puritan Commonwealths* (1920) and *The Colonial Period of American History*, 4 vol. (1934–38); SAMUEL ELIOT MORISON and HENRY STEELE COMMAGER, *The Growth of the American Republic*, 4th ed. rev. (1950); SAMUEL ELIOT MORISON, *The Maritime History of Massachusetts, 1783–1860* (1921) and *Builders of the Bay Colony* (1930); OSCAR HANDLIN, *Boston's Immigrants, 1790–1880*, rev. ed. (1959). Periodicals include *Proceedings and Collections* of the Massachusetts Historical Society, Boston; the *Proceedings* of the American Antiquarian Society, Worcester; publications of the Essex Institute, Salem; publications of the Colonial Society of Massachusetts; and the *New England Quarterly*.

Physical description: B.K. EMERSON, *Geology of Massachusetts and Rhode Island* (1917); HENRY F. HOWE, *Salt Rivers of the Massachusetts Shore* (1951); WALTER MUIR WHITEHILL, *Boston: A Topographical History* (1959); ARTHUR B. TOURTELLOT, *The Charles* (1941); WALTER R. HARD, *The Connecticut* (1947).

Government and politics: OSCAR and MARY F. HANDLIN, *Commonwealth: A Study of the Role of Government in the American Economy: Massachusetts, 1774–1861* (1947); L.A. FROTHINGHAM, *A Brief History of the Constitution and Government of Massachusetts* (1925).

(J.S.D.)

Mass Production

The term mass production refers to methods of organizing manufacturing processes so as to attain high rates of output at decreasing unit cost. Mass-production methods are based on two general principles: (1) division and specialization of human labour, and (2) the use of tools and machines in the production of standard, interchangeable parts. The term automation defines a mass production technique in which certain operations are carried on automatically under the direction of programmed controls. The following article treats mass production from the technological point of view; for a treatment in terms of economic theory, see PRODUCTION, THEORY OF.

Historical survey. The principle of the division of labour and the specialization of skills that results from its application can be found in many human activities, and there are records of its application to manufacturing in ancient Greece. The first unmistakable examples of manufacturing operations carefully designed to reduce production costs by specialized labour and the use of machines appeared in the 18th century. The French Academy of Sciences' classic work entitled "The Description of Arts and Crafts" described the manufacture of pins in 1762 and clearly illustrated the careful division of labour and the use of specialized tools to reduce production costs. In *The Wealth of Nations* (1776), Adam Smith also used pin manufacture to exemplify improvements in human productivity by the application of mass-production techniques. In 1832 Charles Babbage published "On the Economy of Machinery and Manufactures" emphasizing the economy and excellence that can be obtained by the proper planning and division of labour in producing goods.

Another major advance was made in 1798 when Eli Whitney, inventor of the cotton gin, proposed the manufacture of flintlocks with completely interchangeable parts in contrast to the older method under which each gun was the individual product of a highly skilled gunsmith, and each part was hand-fitted. Whitney obtained a contract to produce 10,000 guns; in what was perhaps one of the first examples of planned tooling for manufacture, he used standard patterns for parts, specially designed guides for tools, and jigs for holding materials during fabrication. The resulting production equipment could be run by relatively unskilled boys instead of the highly skilled gunsmiths normally required.

During the same period similar ideas were being tried out in Europe. In England, Marc Brunel, French-born inventor and engineer, established a production line to manufacture pulley blocks for sailing ships, using the principles of division of labour and standardized parts. Brunel's machine tools were designed and built by Henry Maudsley, who has been called the father of the machine-tool industry. Maudsley recognized the importance of precision tools that could produce identical parts; he and his student, Joseph Whitworth, also manufactured interchangeable, standardized metal bolts and nuts.

By the middle of the 19th century the general concepts of division of labour, machine-assisted manufacture, and assembly of standardized parts were well established. In 1881 at the Midvale Steel Company in the United States, Frederick W. Taylor began studies of the organization of manufacturing operations that subsequently were to form the foundation of modern production planning. By making detailed stop-watch measurements of the time required to perform each step of manufacture, Taylor brought a quantitative approach to the organization of production and created the "scientific management" of production functions.

At the same time, Frank B. Gilbreth and his wife, Lillian M. Gilbreth, U.S. industrial engineers, began their pioneering studies of the movements by which people carry out tasks. Using the new technology of motion pictures, the Gilbreths analyzed the design of motion patterns and work areas with a view to achieving maximum economy of effort. The "time and motion" studies of Taylor and the Gilbreths provided important tools for design of modern mass-production lines.

Much of the credit for bringing these early concepts together in a coherent form, and creating the modern, integrated mass-production operation, belongs to the U.S. industrialist Henry Ford and his colleagues at the Ford Motor Company, where in 1913 a moving-belt conveyor was used in the assembly of flywheel magnetos. With it assembly time was cut from 18 minutes per magneto to five minutes. The aproach was then applied to automobile body and motor assembly. The design of these production lines was highly analytical and sought the optimum division of tasks among work stations, optimum line speed, work height, and careful synchronization of simultaneous operations.

The success of Ford's operation led to the adoption of mass production principles by industry in the U.S. and Europe. The methods made major contributions to the large growth in manufacturing productivity that has characterized the 20th century, and produced phenomenal increases in material wealth and improvements in living standards in the industrialized countries.

GENERAL PRINCIPLES

Basic considerations. The efficiencies of mass production result from the following basic considerations:

1. The careful division of the total production operation into specialized tasks comprised of relatively simple, highly repetitive motion patterns and a minimum handling or positioning of the work piece. This permits the development of human motion patterns that are easily learned and rapidly performed with a minimum of unnecessary motion or mental readjustment.

2. The simplification and standardization of component parts to permit large production runs of parts which are readily fitted to other parts without adjustment. The imposition of other standards (*e.g.*, screw dimensions and locations, material types, stock thickness, etc.) on all

parts further increases the economies that can be achieved.

3. The development and use of specialized machines, materials, and processes. The selection of materials and development of tools and machines for each operation minimizes the amount of human effort required, maximizes the output per unit of capital investment, and reduces raw material costs.

4. The systematic engineering and planning of the total production process permit the best balance between human effort and machinery, the most effective division of labour and specialization of skills, and the total integration of the production system to optimize productivity and minimize costs.

Careful skilled production engineering is required to achieve the maximum benefits that application of these principles can provide. Planning begins with the original design of the product; component parts must be adaptable to production and assembly by mass techniques. The entire production process is planned in detail, including the flow of material and subassemblies through the line. Production volume must be carefully estimated because the selection of techniques will depend upon the volume to be produced and anticipated short-term changes in demand. Volume must be large enough first, to permit the task to be divided into its subelements and assigned to different individuals; second, to justify the substantial capital investment often required for specialized machines and processes; and third, to permit large production runs so that human effort and capital will be efficiently employed.

The need for detailed advance planning extends beyond the production line itself. The large, continuous flow of product from the factory requires equally well-planned distribution and marketing operations to bring the product to the final consumer. Advertising, market research, transportation problems, licensing, and tariffs must all be considered in establishing a mass-production operation. Thus, mass-production planning implies a complete system plan from raw material to consumer.

Continuous and batch production. There are two basic types of mass-production facilities, continuous and batch. On a continuous production line, components and subassemblies pass by steps through a series of operations and emerge at the end of the line as a completed product. The automobile final assembly line is an example.

In a batch process a given quantity is moved as a batch through one or more process steps and the total volume emerges simultaneously at the end of the production cycle. Batch processing is widely used in the chemical industry.

Many mass-production operations combine continuous and batch processes. In semiconductor integrated-circuit production, for example, many thousands of circuits are batch processed together on several slices of silicon single crystal through more than a hundred different process steps. The circuits, each a fraction of an inch (a few mm) on a side, are then separated and individually assembled with other circuit elements on a continuous line to produce a final product.

Other considerations. In addition to lowering cost, the application of the principles of mass production has led to major improvements in uniformity and quality. The large volume, standardized design, and standardized materials and processes, facilitate statistical control and inspection techniques to monitor production and control quality. This leads to a reliable assurance that quality levels are achieved without incurring the large costs that would be necessary if detailed inspection of all products was required.

Mass-production techniques are not very flexible, however. Since maximum efficiency is desired, tools, machines, and work positions are often quite precisely adapted to details of the parts produced. Changes in product design may thus render expensive tooling and machinery obsolete. One answer has been to design machinery with flexibility built in; for relatively little extra cost, tooling can be changed to adapt the machine to accommodate design changes.

Similarly, a production line is usually designed to operate most efficiently at a specified rate (Figure 1). If the required production levels fall below that rate, operators and machines are being inefficiently used; and if the rate

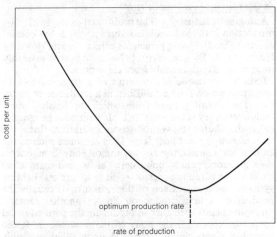

Figure 1: Curve showing relationship of unit cost to production rate.

goes too high operators must work overtime, machine maintenance cannot keep up, breakdowns occur, and the costs of production rise. Thus, it is extremely important to anticipate production demands accurately. Planning can alleviate the problems of increased demand by incorporating some excess capacity in the facilities that would require the longest time to procure and install. Then, if production loads increase, it will be easier to bring the entire line up to the new level. Similarly, if large fluctuations in demand cannot be avoided, flexibility to accommodate these changes economically must be planned into the system.

The functional relationship pictured in Figure 1 applies broadly to the economies of scale associated with mass production as a whole. At any given stage of technological development, the economies obtained by increasing production volume are largest in the initial stages of growth and level off as volumes are further increased. Indeed, if volumes grow too large, unavoidable breakdowns of facilities, failures of coordination, or other strategic factors may cause costs to rise. Advances in technology or changes in other factors can shift the optimum point to higher volume levels. For these reasons planners limit the maximum size of a single production facility and construct an independent facility if greater production is necessary.

PLANNING FOR MASS PRODUCTION

Design. Planning begins with the concept of the product and the assessment of its market. Market estimates establish the volume levels that must be initially produced, the anticipated growth of the market, and periodic changes in expected demand. Design must reflect a proper balance between the product's functional and production aspects. In the marketplace the customer is principally interested in function and appearance. Changes in detailed design may greatly simplify manufacture without affecting function or appearance. Internal parts may be shaped for easier handling during assembly. The kinds of materials readily available at low cost, and the processes available by which these can appropriately be fabricated, must also be considered during the product-design phase. The closest interaction between the product designer and manufacturing engineer from the earliest stages of design are critical in achieving a marketable product at lowest cost.

Manufacturing sequence. As the details of product design become firm, a manufacturing sequence is established. Materials are selected. Fabrication processes are chosen. Planners determine which production steps will be manual and which will be mechanized or automated (see AUTOMATION). A general layout for the production line is established on the factory floor. The manner in which material will flow through the production line is of particular importance; decisions are made between the manual transport of materials and assemblies between some production points and the mechanized or conveyorized handling of materials and parts in other areas (see MATERIALS HANDLING). Planners decide at which points in the production process control by measurement and inspection are to be required.

A critical aspect of planning is the design of information flows that insure coordination of various elements of the line, and assure that necessary materials and facilities will be available when needed. Increasingly, the information flows are provided by production control systems using electronic computers to keep track of materials and parts and plan future operations. **Information flows**

As the manufacturing sequence begins to take final form, detailed studies are made of each manual and machine operation. Manual operations are studied in minute detail in order to determine the most efficient operator position, the best design of tools and jigs, and the most effective motion patterns with which to perform the operation. The number of operators and their skill levels are defined, and the means by which parts and subassemblies are brought to, and carried from, each operator are determined.

For the mechanized operations, a detailed study is made of each machine and machine motion. This includes machines used in fabrication, in testing, and in material-transport systems. Frequently, prototypes of new machines are built and tested under simulated production conditions. The results of this testing are used to perfect the final production machinery. Machinery maintenance requirements and schedules are also determined.

The detailed integration of the various production-line components proceeds simultaneously with the specialized studies of the various operations. The rate of output of each manual and mechanized position is carefully measured; the number of positions for each operation is determined in order that the total line will be well balanced. Without this detailed line balancing, partially assembled products might accumulate at bottleneck positions so that the faster portions of the line will have to reduce speed or shut down until the slower portions are able to catch up.

Training personnel. In parallel with this planning, anticipated human-resource requirements are translated into recruiting and training programs so that a nucleus of appropriately skilled operators will be available as the machinery is installed. Specialized groups are established with responsibility for support activities such as equipment maintenance, plant services, production scheduling, and control operations, etc. Proper personnel planning is critical in assuring that expensive capital equipment will not stand idle and that early operations will not be wasteful of effort, time, and materials.

If the production line is especially complex or the production processes are new and untried, it is probable that a "pilot line" will be established to determine whether the procedures will function satisfactorily and as planned. The pilot line may be a scaled-down version of the total production process or of those portions of the process about which the greatest uncertainty may exist. Experience gained from pilot-line operation can be invaluable in assuring success of the full scale operation. Often, further changes in product design are made during this period to improve ease of manufacture. In addition, the pilot-line operations provide an opportunity to train a nucleus of operators and managers for the full-scale production line.

When planning and facilities are complete, and trained operators are ready, production may begin. Normally, the line starts up slowly with all operations working well below their planned capacities. Engineering designers constantly observe how their plans are functioning and make changes as required. As experience is gained, processes are speeded up until planned output levels have been achieved. Even a manufacturing line that has operated successfully for a considerable period requires continuing engineering attention to improve processes, layouts, and material flow and to search for cost-reduction and quality-improvement opportunities. When operators on the line find ways to improve their efficiency, these are incorporated in normal operating procedures. All of the learning processes that take place continuously on both the engineering and operating levels are major components of the continual improvements in productivity typical of well-run mass-production operations.

Manufacturing progress function

Manufacturing progress function. Because of the enormous complexity of a typical mass-production line and the almost infinite number of changes that can be made and alternatives that can be pursued, a body of quantitative theory of mass-production manufacturing systems has not yet been developed. The volume of available observational data is, however, growing, and qualitative facts are emerging that may eventually serve as a basis for quantitative theory. An example is the "manufacturing progress function." This was first recognized in the airframe industry. Early manufacturers of aircraft observed that as they produced increasing numbers of a given model of airplane, their manufacturing costs decreased in a predictable fashion. As shown in Figure 2, if the logarithm of the cost per unit is plotted as a function of the logarithm of the total number of units produced, the resulting data points almost form a straight line. Over the years similar relationships have been found for many products manufactured by mass-production techniques. The slope of the straight line varies from product to product. For a given class of products and a given type of production technology, however, the slope appears remarkably constant.

Manufacturing progress functions can be of great value to the manufacturer. It is a consequence of the mathematical relationship portrayed in Figure 2 that the cost of a unit decreases by a constant percentage every time the cumulative volume of production is doubled. The actual percentage depends on the slope of the line. (Figure 2 is a

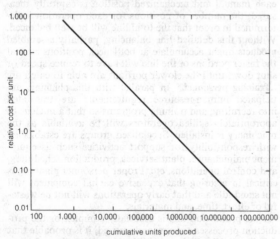

Figure 2: Manufacturing progress function relating cost per unit produced to number of units.

25 percent progress function; *i.e.*, the cost per unit decreases by 25 percent when the cumulative volume of production has doubled.) Thus the progress function can serve as a useful tool in estimating future costs. Furthermore, the failure of costs to follow a well-established progress function may be a sign that more attention should be given to the operation in order to bring its cost performance in line with expectation.

Though manufacturing progress functions are sometimes called "learning curves," they reflect much more than the improved training of the manufacturing operators. Indeed, although improved operator skill is important in the early start up of production, the major portion of the long-term cost improvement is contributed by improvements in product design, in machinery, and in the overall engineering planning of the production sequence.

In the early 1970s the manufacturing progress function was still an empirical tool. It is dangerous to place too much reliance on such a tool until there is a better basis for understanding the complex processes that give rise to this simple relationship. There exists, however, a substan-

tial incentive to develop a quantitative body of manufacturing theory that would permit more certain optimization of manufacturing systems.

EXAMPLES OF MASS PRODUCTION

Automobile industry. The traditional example of mass production is the automobile industry, which has continued to refine the basic principles originally laid down by Henry Ford. By the early 1970s automotive assembly lines differed considerably from early ones.

Today's automobile is the result of a large number of mass-production lines established in a multitude of factories. The assembly plant from which the finished automobile emerges is only the final element of a geographically distributed mass-production operation. Into the final assembly plant flow large subassemblies such as the automobile chassis, the engine, major body components such as doors, panels, upholstered seats, and many electrical and hydraulic accessories such as brakes, lighting systems, radios, etc. Each of these, in turn, is usually the product of a mass-production line in another factory. Stamping plants specialize in producing the formed metal parts that constitute the body of the automobile. Radio assembly plants, in turn, depend upon other assembly plants for components such as transistors. There are glass plants for windows, transmission plants, tire plants, and many others, each specializing in the mass production of their own product, which will, in turn, feed the final assembly plant. The control of the flow of material into and out of final assembly plants, including the scheduling of production from feeder plants and the timing of rail and truck shipments, are among the major engineering tasks that make the total mass-production system for automobiles work.

In the final assembly line one can see clearly how human effort in assembly is divided among many specialized skills. The special tooling and machinery developed to handle assembly parts and to aid operators in their tasks can also be observed. At a given point on the line an operator may specialize in mounting seats. At another position the motor is mounted on the chassis. In other places body panels and doors are assembled to the chassis, dashboard instruments and wiring are added. Each operator learns his task in detail and uses tools specialized for that task. The total operation is paced by the speed of movement of the conveyor that carries the partially assembled automobiles. The number of operators, machine stations, and the flow of materials to the conveyor have all been planned so that the conveyor can maintain an essentially constant speed with each operator and machine functioning near optimum effectiveness.

In Ford's early lines, parts and product were precisely standardized. Only one car model was manufactured, and each unit was identical to every other unit in all aspects, including colour—black. Today's automotive manufacturing engineers have learned to mass produce a highly customized product. The same assembly line may turn out a variety of models with all kinds of colours and options. This is achieved by continued insistence on standardization of critical elements such as the methods by which parts are held together internally. Thus, the operator who specializes in assembling doors can handle a variety of models and colours equally well. In addition, the flow of materials to the various line positions is carefully scheduled and controlled so that the specific part required for a given model, colour, or option list arrives at the line at the moment that the partially assembled unit requiring the part has arrived along the conveyor. The exquisitely designed production-control systems operating in the automotive and other industries make it possible for the consumer to obtain a greatly enhanced variety of product without sacrificing the cost advantages of mass-production techniques.

Product variety on single line

Telephone industry. Similar benefits have been realized in producing smaller and less expensive items. The telephone set is an example of a relatively inexpensive product that is available in a wide variety of models and colours and whose production has been carefully engineered to achieve the optimum of mass-production economies. One telephone-set manufacturing plant employs approximately 8,000 people and each year produces 6,000,000 telephone sets in more than 1,000 different varieties and colour combinations. This factory, in turn, receives materials and components from over 3,000 suppliers. The manufacturing operation consists of a varied but precisely designed mixture of manual assembly effort and mechanized production processes with major operations of both continuous and batch types. In many cases, the partially assembled product moves between operations on conveyors. In other cases, materials are moved in batches by small motorized trucks that operate along factory aisles. Again, an intricate production-control system is employed to schedule the ordering and arrival of parts and the work load of the various production sections.

Other applications. The mass-production principles of the division and specialization of labour and the use of standardized parts and processes have been applied to a wide area of productive activity. In agriculture the development of specialized machines for plowing, seeding, cultivating, and harvesting followed by factories for preparing, preserving, and packaging food products has drawn heavily on mass-production principles. There are specialized manual tasks supplementing the specialized machines both in the fields and in the processing plants.

In the service industries, such as transportation, the division and specialization of skills can be observed among ticket agents, pilots, navigators, baggage handlers, stewardesses, maintenance crews, and traffic controllers. All major engineering projects in both design and manufacture generally require a complement of engineering specialties including chemical, mechanical, and electrical engineers and further subdivisions of these professions such as semiconductor engineers, circuit designers, etc.

Thus, as industry becomes more complex at each level, the division of labour and specialization become necessary. At the same time, the need for coordination and communication between specialized members of the team becomes greater.

MASS PRODUCTION AND SOCIETY

The employee. Both the quantity and the variety of material goods in industrialized countries have resulted directly from the application of mass-production principles. At the same time the environment and circumstances of those employed by, and associated with, the production of material goods have changed. The benefits that have arisen from the greatly improved productivity made possible by mass-production techniques have been shared by employees, investors, and customers. The working environment has greatly changed, however. Similarly, the complexities of management have increased substantially and the investment requirements and risks faced by owners and investors have become much greater.

Before the introduction of mass-production techniques, goods were produced by highly skilled craftsmen who often prepared their basic raw materials, carried the product through each of the stages of manufacture, and ended with the finished product. Typically, the craftsman spent several years at apprenticeship learning each aspect of his trade; often he designed and made his own tools. He was identified with his product and his craft, enjoyed a close association with his customers, and had a clear understanding of his contribution and his position in society.

In contrast, the division of labour, the specialization of narrow skills, the detailed engineering specification of how each task is to be carried out, and the assemblage of large numbers of employees in great manufacturing plants has greatly diluted the identification of the employee with his productive function and has obscured his view of his role and position in society. In addition, the division and specialization of labour may lead to such narrowly defined skills and highly repetitive operations, paced by the steady progression of a machine or conveyor line, that tedium and fatigue may arise to reduce the sense of satisfaction inherent in productive work.

These physical and psychological factors have been the subject of numerous studies by industrial psychologists and others. Special attention has been paid to work factors that affect the psychological motivation that is a prime determinant of employee productivity. The psychological effects of the repetitive aspects of some mass-production tasks have been examined in great detail. Tasks that are precisely paced by the rhythm of machine operation or conveyor-line movement appear to be particularly fatiguing. For this reason, efforts are made to structure each job so that the operator can vary his pace by working ahead of the line for a period and then slowing down, and by interspersing work breaks with productive periods. Some individuals prefer tasks that are sufficiently repetitive and narrowly skilled that they do not require any substantial amount of mental concentration once the function is mastered. Most fatiguing are those tasks whose pace is out of the operator's control, are repetitive, but also require moderate mental concentration.

With this understanding in mind, work tasks can be structured to produce a minimum of mental and physical fatigue, an important part of the overall planning required for a successful production operation.

The highly repetitive, tightly paced production operations are usually the most easily automated. Thus, as technology advances, that part of the production operation that is most fatiguing, least satisfying, and that takes minimum advantage of the mental and physical flexibility of human effort is replaced by automatic machinery. Not only is productivity improved, but the remaining functions that require human effort can provide a more satisfying experience.

There is also increasing study of the interaction of workers with the tools and machines that assist their efforts. Working together, engineers and physicians are making quantitative biomechanical studies of how the human body functions in performing physical tasks. This has led to the improved design of tools and work positions, and is a part of the broader field of human-factors engineering, which considers the abilities and limitations of people in productive functions, and seeks out ways in which machines can be designed to provide the best allocation of function between human effort and machine assistance. These studies are especially important as automated manufacture becomes more common.

The problem of the loss of employee identification with his job has been of special concern. Progressive industrial organizations work to strengthen this identification in many ways, such as by using job rotation and educational programs to diversify the employee's experience and to acquaint him with various aspects of the manufacturing process. This can give each employee a concept of the total manufacturing task and the importance of his specific function within that task. Employee suggestion systems provide further opportunity for the individual to have a direct effect on the productive process; the employee is given other opportunities to help structure the manner in which the job is performed. Thoughtful programs of this type can substantially ameliorate the feeling of anonymity that may otherwise result. Clearly employers must be willing to compromise on the division and specialization of work tasks that technical considerations alone might suggest as desirable. Job content and employee participation must be expanded so that the employee feels significant and retains his motivation and identification.

In addition to this increased attention to the structure of the job itself, increases in productivity and resulting increases in wages have reduced working hours and provided employees with opportunities and resources to develop interests outside the work place. Forward-looking employers, aware of these needs, frequently support these activities through employees' clubs and other means.

Economic effects. Mass production, with its heavy dependence upon mechanized facilities and high levels of production volume, presents great challenges for industrial leadership. The importance of advanced planning and the coordinated control of the large human and capital resources associated with mass production have been described. The day-to-day problems of monitoring the status of a major manufacturing complex are also immense. Up-to-the-minute knowledge of status is essential

Employee fatigue factor

to effective response when difficulties such as the breakdown of a machine, the shortage of required materials or components, or the absence of important employees occurs. Many aids to management have been devised for collecting data, analyzing it, and presenting alternatives for management decision. The electronic computer, with its great capability for collecting, analyzing and comparing data, is becoming especially important as a management aid, both in the initial planning and simulation of production facilities and in computer-based production and resource-control systems. In this way, the management of mass-production operations is rapidly becoming a quantitative technology in its own right.

The need for substantial investment is another result of the application of mass-production principles. Much of the increase in productivity that has been achieved by mass production is a direct result of the development and use of automatic machinery and processes to supplement human effort. This, in turn, requires the support of a sizable technical staff in advance of production and later substantial capital investment for production facilities. Increased levels of capital, which must often be committed years before production begins, and before the true market for the product has been established, greatly increase the risks that investors must assume and have markedly affected the investment climate in manufacturing industries.

Change in
nature of
ownership
and
investment

As capital needs have grown, the nature of ownership and investment in industry has changed dramatically. Economies of scale favour large, high-volume operations that require capital investment levels often well beyond the means of an individual owner. This has been the prime stimulant for corporate ownership of major manufacturing firms. Furthermore, the direct managers of the manufacturing enterprise seldom possess ownership control of the enterprise. This has created a new spectrum of relationships between the owners, the managers, and the employees of large manufacturing firms. Frequently the owners are principally concerned with the profits on their investments and leave the planning and managerial operations to professional managers.

At the same time the large capital needs of growing industries place special emphasis on the ability to acquire the necessary capital resources. Thus, the financial markets become extremely important in determining the general directions in which manufacturing industry will grow. This emphasizes the importance of profit incentives to encourage private investment, which is vital to achieve the productivity advances possible in mass-production operations.

Similarly, industrial nations are strongly encouraged to retain and reinvest a significant fraction of their gross national product if national industries are to grow and to compete successfully in international markets. These problems of capital formation have been especially troublesome in introducing mass production in the developing nations.

Other consequences of a mass-production economy have recently become apparent. The increased consumption associated with low-cost production has created problems of conservation of natural resources and the disposal or reconversion of the wastes of production and of goods whose utility is ended. There are technological solutions for the resulting problems of solid wastes and air and water pollution, but the political and economic problems of how the costs will be distributed must be solved.

BIBLIOGRAPHY. Early studies of the organization of human effort for production are treated in classics of the 18th and 19th centuries, including *Descriptions des arts et métiers, faites ou approuvées par messieurs de l'Académie royale des sciences,* 45 vol. (1761–89); ADAM SMITH, *An Inquiry into the Nature and Causes of the Wealth of Nations* (1776); and CHARLES BABBAGE, *On the Economy of Machinery and Manufacture* (1832).

More recent historical views of developments leading to modern mass-production methods are J.K. FINCH, *Engineering and Western Civilization* (1951), *Story of Engineering* (1960); and F. KLEMM, *Technik: eine Geschichte ihrer probleme* (1954; Eng. trans., *A History of Western Technology* 1964). Technical descriptions of mass-production techniques are given by E.P. DE GARMO, *Materials and Processes in Manufacturing* (1969). The classical technical works on time and motion studies in manufacturing are F.W. TAYLOR, *The Principles of Scientific Management* (1911); and F.B. GILBRETH, *Motion Study: A Method for Increasing the Efficiency of the Workman* (1911). R.M. BARNES, *Motion and Time Study* (1968), describes modern industrial engineering methods; E.J. MCCORMICK, *Human Factors Engineering* (1964), provides a broad study of the physiological aspects of engineering design.

Books written about human and societal problems and adjustments to the industrial milieu include: R. BURLINGAME, *Backgrounds of Power* (1949), a popular history and commentary; and W.A. FAUNCE, *Problems of an Industrial Society* (1968), on the sociological effects. Others have focussed on the problems of individuals and how they may be approached. Among these are: W.J. DICKSON and F.J. ROETHLISBERGER, *Counseling in an Organization* (1966); R.N. FORD, *Motivation Through the Work Itself* (1969); F. HERZBERG, *Work and the Nature of Man* (1966); and C.R. WALKER and R.H. GUEST, *Man on the Assembly Line* (1952).

(M.T.)

Mass Society

Mass society is a term intended by its proponents to connote the main features that distinguish modern industrial societies from feudal, peasant, or tribal societies. A mass society, they argue, is one in which the most important institutions are large, centralized, bureaucratic, and impersonal; in which most human relationships are shallow, partial, and transitory; and in which individuals tend to be lonely, anxious, rootless, and in search of a sense of community.

EVOLUTION OF IDEAS CONCERNING MASS SOCIETY

Widespread use of the idea of "the mass" or "masses" originated in the ideological struggles of political and economic groups in Europe prior to the French Revolution. With the victory of the bourgeoisie, what had previously been part of the antibourgeois rhetoric of the aristocrats became transformed and redirected at the lower orders. At first, there was a happy confidence in the masses, as expressed in the essays of such radical and Utilitarian writers as Condorcet and Jeremy Bentham. But then, in the course of the 19th century, the term masses came to be used pejoratively to refer to urban industrial workers and discontented lower classes. Gradually, the demands of these "masses" for social, cultural, and political equality became identified as a threat to a stable bourgeois social order. The fear of the majority expressed in the writings of Alexis de Tocqueville and John Stuart Mill represented a retreat from the confidence of Condorcet and Bentham. Nineteenth-century liberalism became a philosophy of retrenchment and nostalgia, with concomitant fear of and disillusion with the masses. Karl Marx, too, emphasized this social division by applying the idea of the masses to that stratum of society engaged in industrial production but excluded from the ownership or control of the instruments of production—that is, the proletariat.

Liberalism
and
Romanticism
in the
idea of the
masses

In addition to its links with 19th-century liberalism, the theory of mass society also has significant roots in Romanticism. Broadly speaking, Romanticism led in two principal directions: a celebration of the free individual on the one hand and a celebration of the national, local, or folk community on the other. Sociological Romanticism combined these strands of 19th-century thought in idealizing the *Gemeinschaft,* or traditional community, and in emphasizing the unhappiness of the individual liberated from traditional society only to be thrust into the impersonal and abstract world of "the city." This theme was elaborated in the late 19th and early 20th centuries by such social scientists as Ferdinand Tönnies, Sir Henry Maine, Georg Simmel, Émile Durkheim, and Max Weber in their attempts to account for the transition from traditional to modern industrial societies. These thinkers shared a focus on "social disorganization," the breakdown of the primary, or intimate, group; the erosion of traditional social bonds of family, local community, and religion; the emergence of large-scale industrialized society, and the increasing concentration of population in urban centres. They also postulated a necessary historical development, an evolution from the simple to the complex, the homogeneous to the heterogeneous. Out of this concern for the disappearance of older forms of community, the theory of mass society emerged as

. . . a presumed scientific statement concerning the disorganization of society created by industrialization and by the demand of the masses for equality. . . . Behind the theory of social disorganization lies a romantic notion of the past that sees society as having once been made up of small "organic" close-knit communities that were shattered by industrialism and modern life, and replaced by a large impersonal "atomistic" society which is unable to provide the basic gratifications and call forth the loyalties that the older communities knew. . . . The revolutions in transport and communications have brought men into closer contact with each other and bound them in new ways; the division of labor has made them more interdependent; tremors in one part of the society affect all others. Despite this greater interdependence, however, individuals have grown more estranged from one another. The old primary-group ties of family and local community have been shattered; ancient parochial faiths are questioned; few unifying values have taken their place. Most important, the critical standards of an educated elite no longer shape opinion or taste. As a result, mores and morals are in constant flux, relations between individuals are tangential or compartmentalized rather than organic. At the same time greater mobility, spatial and social, intensifies concern over status. Instead of a fixed or known status symbolized by dress or title, each person assumes a multiplicity of roles and constantly has to prove himself in a succession of new situations. Because of all this, the individual loses a coherent sense of self. His anxieties increase. There ensues a search for new faiths. The stage is thus set for the charismatic leader, the secular messiah, who, by bestowing upon each person the semblance of necessary grace, and of fulness of personality, supplies a substitute for the older unifying belief that the mass society has destroyed. (Daniel Bell, "The Theory of Mass Society"; reprinted from *Commentary*, by permission; copyright © 1956 by the American Jewish Committee.)

The theory of mass society was prompted not only by philosophers and social scientists, however, but also by such poets as W.H. Auden, who called the modern era "the age of anxiety," and by novelists as diverse as Ernest Hemingway and Ford Madox Ford. T.S. Eliot's poems *The Waste Land* and "The Love Song of J. Alfred Prufrock" stand out as attempts to give expression to the idea of modern society as a desert and the individual within it as lost, disconnected, and insubstantial.

The presumed threats of liberty and equality

Democracy, political ideology, and culture. It was equality and the prospect of democratization that provided the opening theme for the concept of the mass and of mass society. Contemporary observers in the decades following the French Revolution and the revolutionary industrialization that began in England came to find in democracy and in the human products of industrialization a serious threat to social order. The prospect of democracy—a word that had only come into the general political vocabulary at the end of the 18th century—was not appealing. "Democracy" conjured up the picture of violent mobs. Even the authors of the United States Constitution in 1787 were uneasy about involving the people at large in the political process. One of them, Elbridge Gerry, called democracy "the worst of all political evils." Almost half a century later, when Alexis de Tocqueville, a French aristocrat and civil servant, made his celebrated observations on democracy in the United States, these sentiments were just as current. Tocqueville, like others of his time and station, saw the first two goals of the French Revolution—equality and liberty—as incompatible. He took the passion for equality to be the outstanding characteristic of democratic nations, the young American nation in particular, and, correspondingly, the preservation of liberty to be such a nation's most difficult task. He believed that people in an egalitarian society lost faith in one another and lost respect for the superior person or superior class. Instead, they placed faith only in the public as a whole and in the nation-state as its embodiment. In language that Tocqueville did not use but that he might well have used, classes became masses and the individual became all too willing to subordinate his own opinion to that of the majority. This emphasis foreshadowed contemporary thought about mass society in its concern not only for political and social life but for culture. When the individual is the object of attention in contemporary theories of mass society, there is a fear that a society of atomized individuals will lead to majority tyranny or submission to totalitarian government. When the precarious status of social and cultural elites in mass society is considered, the debasement of culture is seen as the threat. Writers such as Karl Mannheim and T.S. Eliot held that the preservation of a strong cultural tradition lay in the maintenance of a small and relatively exclusive class of persons who produce it. These fears of cultural democratization were not new. Tocqueville commented on the effect of democracy on the arts, holding that in democratic nations "the productions of artists are more numerous, but the merit of each production is diminished" (*Democracy in America*).

Whereas Tocqueville argued his fear of the majority in terms of the logical consequences of equality, others argued from their notion of the debased character and criminality of the European "masses." Recent scholarship suggests that those who participated in mobs and riots and thus elicited the fear and hostility of the powerful were actually not the criminal, the vagrant, the poorest of the city's poor but rather the sober artisans, servants, labourers, and others from stable districts and with steady jobs. But 19th-century liberals nonetheless often believed the worker and the criminal to be one and the same. They supported political and economic reforms to the extent that such reforms favoured elements of the middle class rather than the growing and presumably irresponsible urban masses. The English Reform Act of 1832 enlarged the electorate only from 4.4 to 7.1 percent of the adult population and retained property holding as a qualification for the franchise. Liberal middle class reformers in the various German states, as in England, feared the "dangerous" lower classes and, until the revolutions of 1848, looked upon the idea of manhood suffrage with horror. Socialist thinkers, of course, called these "dangerous" classes "the industrial classes" and thus portrayed in a positive light the same people whom the bourgeoisie considered so frightful.

Concept of the "dangerous" masses

It should be remembered that, in the early 19th century, ideological conflict was more significant than actual changes in social structure. Germany, France, and the United States, after all, experienced the same fears of the mob that England did and at roughly the same time, even though they lagged well behind England in the degree of industrialization. It was equality and the prospect of democratization, then, that provided an important initial element in the ideas of the mass and of mass society.

Formation of mass society and the Industrial Revolution. The rapidity of social change after the early 19th century created a world in which the major institutions affecting individual lives were quite novel. In primarily agrarian societies, work had centred on the family as the economic and social unit. When commerce and manufacturing supplanted agriculture as the focus of the economy, this changed. Although the cottage industry of the early industrial era had permitted work to be performed in the home, the development of the factory brought masses of individuals together in a single work place outside their homes. In the 19th and 20th centuries, massive shifts in population from farm to city took place in all the industrialized countries as a result of the enormous increases in agricultural productivity and the concomitant expansion of the manufacturing and services sectors of the economy.

There were more people in the world by 1900: the population of Europe had doubled in the preceding century and a half, and the population of the United States had risen from 4,000,000 in 1790 to 75,000,000. Not only did people move to the cities and work for others rather than for themselves, but the organizations they worked for grew in size, each of them employing more and more workers. Small proprietors and partnerships similarly gave way to corporations, corporations in turn grouping into cartels and monopolies. Bureaucratization every-

Urbanization and modernization

where tended to shift the emphasis in human relations from family and communal groups to impersonal, contractual groups.

Not only were there more people but they were more easily linked to one another through technological advances such as the railroad and, later, the telephone and the automobile. The invention of the printing press in the 15th century had been the beginning of a movement that spread with the growth of literacy and technological innovations in printing and marketing. The circulation of books and pamphlets spread, and literacy levels in Europe advanced markedly, both a cause and a result of the increased use of print. In England in 1841, 33 percent of bridegrooms could not sign their names to their marriage certificates; almost all could do so by 1900. In France the percentage who could not sign their names dropped from 32 percent in 1855 to 5 percent in 1900. Between 1840 and 1882 the monthly issue of newspapers in Paris jumped from 3,000,000 to 44,000,000 copies.

Sociologists, as well as poets and novelists, tried to come to grips with the contradictions of urban life as expressed in the contrast between the old German proverb that "city air makes one free" and the perception of the powerlessness of the individual in the face of urban sprawl, poverty, and corruption. Although the German sociologist Georg Simmel did argue that the city offered the individual "a kind and an amount of personal freedom which has no analogy whatsoever under other conditions," he also held that it enforced a fearful impersonality in social relations, a calculating frame of mind, a blasé attitude, an incapacity to react to new sensations, and a perception of the world as flat and grey, all of which he explained as "the faithful subjective reflection of the completely internalized money economy."

Whereas Simmel saw the city man becoming calculating and blasé, his most influential American student, Robert Park, viewed the outlook of the urban dweller as rational and practical, modelled on the machine and the application of science to life. But if this was true of the individual in the city, it was not true of the crowd. Park's pioneering textbook, *Introduction to the Science of Sociology* (1921), written in collaboration with Ernest W. Burgess, reported on the work of European psychologists who stressed the irrational aspect of the modern world and who saw modern man attaching himself to crowds that were brutal, highly emotional, and suggestible. Modern economic conditions had broken down family and local ties, freeing the individual, but "the effect," Park wrote, "has been to loosen all the social bonds and reduce society to its individual atoms. The energies thus freed have produced a world-wide ferment. Individuals released from old associations enter all the more readily into new ones. Out of this confusion new and strange political and religious movements arise, which represent the groping of men for a new social order."

Questions of rational behaviour of the masses

It would be difficult to judge whether or not, as some writers assumed, mass political action had increased and intensified. What is more certain is that the nature of collective action had changed. People were grouped into large homogeneous blocs in factories and in working class neighborhoods; special interest groups such as the labour union and the political party, capable of mobilizing people quickly, had developed; and people were concentrated in the urban seats of power, thus encouraging authorities to react more quickly to dissidence. It would also be difficult to know whether to emphasize the increased rationality of individuals in the machine age or to emphasize their increased susceptibility to collective irrationalities. It may be wiser simply to note that the context for the expression of reason and enthusiasm had changed. The great expansion of public education was instructing ever greater numbers of people in rational processes, and the great extension of the franchise was providing them the opportunity to exercise these rational processes. On the other hand, the possibility of order and rationality was being questioned. A new mood of scientific thought was denying not only the old truths of religion but the possibility of objective science as well. This was evident in the works of Kierkegaard and Nietzsche. Marx and Freud, while they remained in a scientific tradition, contributed to the skepticism of science by unearthing the social and psychological sources of human beliefs and behaviour, revealing the subjective roots even of science itself.

The mass and totalitarianism. The concept of mass society included the ideas of democratization and the splintering of community, but these in turn were deemed by some writers as prime causes of 20th-century totalitarianism, especially in Nazi Germany. The concept was fundamental in the works of such émigré German intellectuals as Hannah Arendt, Erich Fromm, and Karl Mannheim. Although critics of mass society continued to appear among aristocratic liberals and conservatives in the mid-20th century, notably José Ortega y Gasset and T.S. Eliot, the more sustained analysis appeared on the left. Indeed, it was primarily the contribution from the left that established "mass society" in the language of social science.

Presumed preconditions of totalitarianism

In trying to comprehend Nazism in Germany, the theorists of mass society emphasized the social and psychological preconditions of totalitarianism. Arendt stressed that totalitarianism built on masses, not classes—on people who "either because of sheer numbers, or indifference, or a combination of both, cannot be integrated into any organization based on common interest, into political parties or municipal governments or professional organizations or trade unions." She distinguished the 19th-century mob, which had class origins, from the 20th-century mass, which was shaped "by all-pervasive influences and convictions which were tacitly and inarticulately shared by all classes of society alike" (*The Origins of Totalitarianism*). Thus Arendt stressed not the decline of family and community so much as the isolation of huge numbers of people from participation in major social and political processes. Not all theorists would agree. Another émigré, Franz L. Neumann, did not make Arendt's sharp distinction between classes and masses but saw instead the mass as the extreme consequence of the processes of modern industrial capitalism and mass democracy. What characterized mass society in pre-Nazi Germany was not so much the psychological unwillingness of large numbers to participate in social life but the inappropriateness of the increasingly bureaucratic organs of society for satisfying human relations. To Neumann, the bureaucratic trade unions, political parties, athletic organizations, radio networks, birth-control associations, consumers' cooperatives, and food chain stores of the Weimar Republic all represented depersonalized control over the life of the individual. Such organs failed to provide proper leadership; and it was this, not the psychological susceptibility of mass man to extremism, that contributed to the rise of Hitler.

Psychological view of mass society

The theory of mass society, nevertheless, has been more closely associated with a more psychological view, emphasizing that a certain kind of social character is prominent in modern society and is unusually susceptible to the appeals of demagogues. The psychological condition of the individual in mass society has been described in terms of isolation, loneliness, yearnings for a personal or collective identity, impersonal human relations, the privatization of personal emotion. It has been suggested that whereas a communal society is regulated by shame and honour, and a liberal democratic society such as that of 19th-century England is governed by self-reliance and guilt, mass society is dominated by suggestibility and anxiety. This point of view—which was developed by such writers as Erich Fromm in a number of important works before, during, and just after World War II—had a profound influence on social science. Although these studies were primarily a response to the rise of Nazism and an attempt to explain the phenomenon, they also represented a more general approach to the psychological dimension of life in industrial society. Much influenced by Fromm was American sociologist David Riesman's evocative description of the change in the social character of the American middle class individual from "inner-directed" to "other-directed." The "inner-directed" person, broadly speaking, was the rational, individualistic person of the 19th century, driven by an internal sense of direction and destiny. The "other-directed" character, a product generally of capitalism, industrialization, and urbanization, finds his sense of direction—if he finds one at all —in cues from other people. He is not concerned with mastery of the environment; that has been taken care of. For him, *other people* are the problem" (*The Lonely Crowd*). Finally, a considerable literature on "alienation" grew out of the concern among various writers for the quality of social life under industrialism (see ALIENATION).

From another point of view, it may be that mass society is characterized more by powerful new organs of mobilization rather than by an unusual psychological readiness to be mobilized. Indeed, the enlargement of the franchise in Germany and in England at the end of the 19th century brought with it vigorous efforts to organize the new voters of the working class into political parties. Not only did parties and unions grow more important but the state itself grew more centralized and more powerful, especially through involvement in war. War, as Tocqueville observed, increases the centralization of the state, or, as a contemporary sociologist has written, "if there is any single origin of the institutional State, it is in the circumstances and relationships of war" (Robert Nisbet, *The Quest for Community*).

Here, as before, the question concerns the relationship between totalitarianism and mass society. It seems true that modern societies today are dominated by the influence of the centralized state. The expenditures of the government of the United States, for example, rose from $9,000,000,000 in 1940 to $69,000,000,000 in 1957; by 1970 the defense budget alone was $80,000,000,000. The influence of war and the military is visible not only in public expenditures but in the nature of modern institutions. The organizational techniques used in World War I provided the models for dealing with the Great Depression of the 1930s in both Europe and America. Intelligence testing, developed for classifying huge numbers of soldiers, was adopted by school systems to deal with the burgeoning school populations. Even charities were consciously organized in a military style based on war experience. Both world wars advanced the use of the mass media as systems of control—the propaganda of World War I being described as "the first modern effort at systematic, nationwide manipulation of collective passions." (Jack Roth, in *World War I: A Turning Point in Modern History* [1967]).

EVALUATIONS OF MASS SOCIETY

Criticism of the idea of mass society. The idea of mass society is open to criticism on at least two levels. First, one might ask, is modern industrial society accurately described as a mass society? In other words, are societies with large numbers of people, large cities, industrialized economies, bureaucratic organization of institutions, and widespread use of mass media of communications—are these societies characterized by the weakness of human social relations, loneliness, and the debasement of culture? Second, is the "mass-ness" of a society closely linked to tendencies to totalitarianism? In other words, are highly urbanized, industrialized, and bureaucratized societies inhabited by lonely, highly suggestible individuals who are especially prone to accept totalitarianism?

The extent to which atomism, loneliness, and anxiety characterize individuals in modern society can be questioned. Despite rapid urbanization, industrialization, and bureaucratization, close personal relationships are still basic to the individual's style of life and provide a human link between the individual and mass communications and large organizations. The now-famous Hawthorne project, spanning the late 1920s and early 1930s, offered early evidence of the possibility of creating personal ties in an industrial setting. Researcher Elton Mayo and his colleagues, studying the productivity of workers at a Western Electric Company plant outside Chicago, found that no matter what variations they made in lighting, temperature, rest periods, or working hours, the output of the workers kept rising. Only later did they realize what

Influence of war

Significance of "human relations" in modern society

had happened: the special attention that had been given to the workers in the course of the experiment had contaminated the experiment, the result being a "Hawthorne effect." The experiment had created a group among the individuals working in the test room, resulting in a new esprit de corps and mutual identification that was crucially related to the increase in output. The factory organization of work was not, as some had thought, a simple transaction between the requirements of the employer and the needs of the individual worker; rather, it operated through the work group, which established its own "informal" rules and expectations concerning behaviour, including productivity. Similarly, studies of American soldiers in World War II indicated, to the surprise of researchers accustomed to thinking of modern society as a mass society, that small-scale interpersonal relations are strong and significant even in such large-scale organizations as the military. Attachment to an informal group of "buddies" was more important as a factor in a soldier's willingness to enter combat than either ideological goals or, for that matter, the system of discipline and formal orders.

The individual in the city, too, is not as deprived of substantial personal attachments to family and small groups as the idea of mass society would suggest. Urban dwellers spend a significant share of their lives with family, friends, and relatives; many live in neighbourhoods that retain a sense of community based on ethnic, racial, or class lines. Studies in the United States, England, and elsewhere indicate that even in highly urbanized, industrialized, and bureaucratized societies there is reason to doubt that atomization and the absence of normal social relations characterize social experience.

Is the mass society totalitarianism-prone? This, too, may be questioned. Surely it would be difficult to conceive of totalitarian rule or, for that matter, of the welfare states of western Europe without cities, industry, bureaucracy, and mass communications. But to explain totalitarianism by the appeal of demagoguery to atomized masses is another matter. First, the idea of mass society, since it is designed to apply to modern industrial societies generally, is much too broad to explain why only some of these societies develop powerful extremist social movements, why such movements arise at some times and not at other times, and why only some of them succeed in gaining power. It does not explain why some societies that seem to fit the picture of mass society best —such as England or the United States—have not developed lasting extremist social movements, or why one major instance of totalitarianism, the Soviet Union, began to resemble a mass society only *after* establishing totalitarian rule.

The past and future of mass society. In his classic essay on "Urbanism as a Way of Life" (*American Journal of Sociology*, July 1938) the American sociologist Louis Wirth summarized the then prevailing view concerning the nature of urban life in a way that reflects the preoccupations of the theorists of mass society:

The distinctive features of the urban mode of life have often been described sociologically as consisting of the substitution of secondary for primary contacts, the weakening of bonds of kinship, and the declining social significance of the family, the disappearance of the neighborhood, and the undermining of the traditional basis of social solidarity.

As noted earlier, this conception has been subjected to criticism. With respect to the importance of family and kinship, for example, recent research tends to indicate that the extent and intensity of kin relationships and the frequency of interaction among kin remains quite persistent. Patterns of neighbourhood and kinship ties appear to be stronger than Wirth had supposed. On the other hand, there is perhaps at least one area to which Wirth's conceptions seem applicable, and that is to the area—sometimes referred to as the "inner city"—in which are concentrated a number of disadvantaged groups whose range of choice in housing and life-styles is restricted by income, age, ethnicity, or race and whose lives are especially subject to stress and disruption. Indeed, Wirth's formulation still seems applicable not only

Inadequacy of early views of urbanism and mass society

to residents of the American inner city, for example, but also to the citizens of some newly developing countries undergoing the strains of rapid modernization. Detribalized and declassed populations on the fringes of great urban centres in Asia, Latin America, and Africa, concentrated in shantytowns, clustered on the hillsides of Rio de Janeiro or Lima or Calcutta, may exhibit some of the same characteristics reflected in the Wirth formulation and in the classical idea of "mass society." One must therefore confront the paradox that the idea of mass society may have greatest relevance for the newly developing countries in the throes of industrialism, where the problems of 19th-century Europe are being re-created at an intensified pace over a period of time far shorter than that within which Europe and North America absorbed the strains of economic development. This also suggests that an ideology such as that represented by the idea of mass society may become most relevant to the peoples of the "Third World" precisely at the time when its relevance for the peoples of the United States, western Europe, and the other highly industrialized nations is being challenged. Both the unemployed peasant in the Brazilian shantytown, or *favela*, and the rural farm worker in Kenya who can multiply his salary six times by going to Nairobi and getting a job may ultimately find themselves enmeshed in a complex of problems envisioned by the theorist of mass society.

On the other hand, some social scientists have argued that even in newly developing countries the strains of migration to the urban centres have been exaggerated. Moreover, even though tribalism and traditionalism in Africa, Asia, and Latin America are giving way under the pressure of commercial and industrial development and the social changes associated with them, it is also true that many of these changes are giving rise to an expansion of the available alternatives that many people perceive as liberating. In reflecting on these alternatives, the British anthropologist Lucy Mair has written:

the changes that non-Western societies are going through, though they were imposed on them at the outset, are now essential for the realization of aims that they have made their own. In terms of individual actions the process can be seen as one of response to new opportunities, which include freedom to choose one's way of life and dispose of one's own earnings. Women, as well as men, seek this freedom, in the non-Western as well as in the Western world. (From *New Nations*, University of Chicago Press, 1963.)

Perpetual
elusiveness
of the
idea
of mass
society

Ultimately, the ideology of mass society emphasizes the negative effects of the rise of industrial society; and, since only a part of the answers to the questions raised by the theory of mass society can be answered by empirical research, part of the issue will always remain in the form of stubborn ideological differences concerning the good, the true, and the beautiful, and the most desirable way of life. What one thinker will deplore as the decline of the folk community might be conceptualized by another as the creation of new communities based on a new conception of the good life, new roles, and new life-styles.

In one respect, the perspective of theorists of mass society has received support from those who have pointed to a number of undesirable features of modern industrial society. Apart from the threat of nuclear, chemical, and biological warfare, there is widespread concern for the unchecked growth of population in relation to resources, giving rise to a neo-Malthusian and sometimes apocalyptic vision of the future. And considerable attention also has been given to the unanticipated consequences of technological development in the form of the pollution of the air, the earth, and the waters on a global scale. These ecological factors may be cited in the context of a discussion of mass society since they will inevitably exert a profound influence.

Finally, it should be said that precisely because of its ideological elements, the idea of mass society will continue to have appeal for social scientists interested in specific problems associated with modernization, urbanization, and industrialism. The best one may hope for is a productive tension between these ideological elements on the one hand and an empirical concern for what is really happen-

ing, what is actually the case, on the other—in the best tradition of modern social science. Freedom of inquiry concerning the nature of modern societies may be one of the important safeguards against the pessimistic view of modern life suggested by the theory of mass society.

BIBLIOGRAPHY. For an early analysis of mass society, see ALEXIS DE TOCQUEVILLE, *De la démocratie en Amérique*, 2 vol. (1835; Eng. trans., *Democracy in America*, 2 vol., 1945, reprinted 1961). For the idea of mass society at the turn of the century, see GUSTAVE LE BON, *The Crowd* (Eng. trans. 1903); GEORG SIMMEL, "The Metropolis and the Mental Life," in *The Sociology of Georg Simmel* (1950); and ROBERT E. PARK, *Human Communities* (1952). For more recent theory, see especially KARL MANNHEIM, *Man and Society in an Age of Reconstruction* (1940); HANNAH ARENDT, *The Origins of Totalitarianism* (1951); ERICH FROMM, *Escape from Freedom* (British title, *The Fear of Freedom*: 1942); and JOSE ORTEGA Y GASSET, *La Rebellión de las masas* (1929; Eng. trans., *The Revolt of the Masses*, 1932). See also RAYMOND WILLIAMS, *Culture and Society: 1780–1950* (1958), for a survey of English intellectual criticism of modern society; and RICHARD HOGGART, *The Uses of Literacy* (1957). Political aspects of mass society are the focus of WILLIAM KORNHAUSER, *The Politics of Mass Society* (1959); and ROBERT NISBET, *The Quest for Community* (1953), emphasizes the role of the state. Critical reviews of the idea of mass society may be found in DANIEL BELL, *The End of Ideology* (1960); and LEON BRAMSON, *The Political Context of Sociology* (1961). The debate concerning mass culture may be reviewed in BERNARD ROSENBERG and DAVID MANNING WHITE (eds.), *Mass Culture* (1957); DAVID RIESMAN, *The Lonely Crowd* (1950); and EDWARD SHILS, "Daydreams and Nightmares: Reflections on the Criticisms of Mass Culture," *Sewanee Review*, 65:587–608 (1957). T.S. ELIOT's essay *Notes Toward A Definition of Culture* (1948) also remains relevant. Recent works focussing on American society are PHILLIP OLSON (ed.), *America As a Mass Society* (1963); WILLIAM H. WHYTE, *The Organization Man* (1956); C. WRIGHT MILLS, *White Collar* (1951) and *The Power Elite* (1956); KENNETH KENISTON, *The Uncommitted: Alienated Youth in American Society* (1965); and ARTHUR VIDICH and JOSEPH BENSMAN, *Small Town in Mass Society*, rev. ed. (1968), and *The New American Society* (1971). The historical sociology of the masses is discussed in GEORGE RUDE, *The Crowd in History: A Study of Popular Disturbances in France and England, 1730–1848* (1964); and CHARLES TILLEY, "Collective Violence in European Perspective," in H. GRAHAM and T. GURR (eds.), *The History of Violence in America* (1969).

(L.Br./Mi.S.)

Mass Spectrometry

Mass spectrometry, or mass spectroscopy, denotes that field of physics in which the motion of ions (charged atoms, molecules or fragments of molecules) in electric and magnetic fields is used to sort ions according to their mass-to-charge ratios. The instruments used in these studies are called mass spectrometers and mass spectrographs, and they operate on the principle that moving ions may be deflected by electric and magnetic fields. The two instruments differ only in the way in which the sorted charged particles are detected. In the mass spectrometer they are detected electrically; in the mass spectrograph by photographic or other nonelectrical means, and the term mass spectroscope is used to include both kinds of devices; a person who specializes in their use is called either a mass spectrometrist or a mass spectroscopist.

Mass spectroscopes consist of five basic parts: high vacuum system; a sample handling system, through which the sample to be investigated can be introduced; an ionization chamber (ion source), in which a beam of charged particles characteristic of the sample can be produced; an analyzer, in which the beam can be separated according to its mass components; and a detector or receiver by means of which the separated ion beams can be observed or collected.

Many investigations have been conducted with the help of mass spectroscopy. These include the identification of the isotopes of the chemical elements and determination of their precise masses and relative abundances, the dating of geological samples, the analysis of inorganic and organic chemicals especially for small amounts of impurities, structural formula determination of complex organic

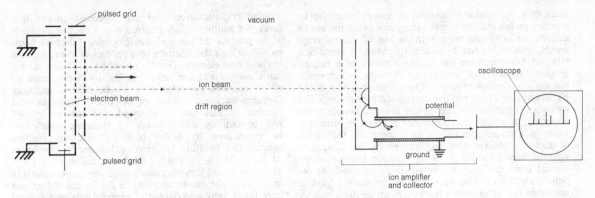

Figure 1: *Linear time-of-flight mass spectrometer.*
A pulse of electrons ionizes the sample and a pulsed grid draws ions out of ionizing region and accelerates them along a drift region. Since all ions acquire the same energy of acceleration, the lighter ions arrive at the collector first. The separated ion beams can be displayed on an oscilloscope.

substances, the strengths of chemical bonds and energies necessary to produce particular ions, the identification of products of ion decomposition, and the analysis of unknown materials, such as moon samples, for their chemical and isotopic constituents. Mass spectroscopes are employed also to separate isotopes and to measure the abundance of concentrated isotopes when used as tracers in chemistry, biology, and medicine.

HISTORY OF MASS SPECTROSCOPY

The foundation of mass spectroscopy was laid in 1898, when Wilhelm Wien, a German Nobel Prize winner, discovered that beams of charged particles could be deflected by a magnetic field. In more refined experiments carried out between 1907 and 1913 by J.J. Thomson, the great English physicist who discovered the electron, a beam of positively charged ions was passed through a combined electrostatic and magnetic field. Charged particles such as ions deflect as they pass through electrostatic and magnetic fields; the two fields in Thomson's tube were situated so that the ions were deflected through small angles in two perpendicular directions. The net result was that the ions produced a series of parabolic curves on a photographic plate placed in their paths. Each parabola corresponded to ions of a particular mass-to-charge ratio and the lengths of the parabolic curves provided a measure of the range of ion energies contained in the beam. Later, in an attempt to estimate the relative abundances of the various ion species present, Thomson replaced the photographic plate by a metal sheet in which was cut a parabolic slit. By varying the magnetic field, he was able to scan through a mass spectrum and measure a current corresponding to each separated ion species. Thus he may be credited with the construction of the first mass spectrograph and the first mass spectrometer.

The most noteworthy observation made with the parabola spectrograph was the spectrum of rare gases present in the atmosphere. In addition to lines due to helium (mass 4), neon (mass 20), and argon (mass 40), there was a line corresponding to an ion of mass 22 that could not be attributed to any known gas. The existence of different mass forms of the same element had been suspected since it had been found that many pairs of radioactive materials could not be separated by chemical means. The name isotopes was suggested by Frederick Soddy in 1913 for these different radioactive forms of the same chemical species since they could be classified in the same place in the periodic table of the elements. The ion of mass 22 was, in fact, a stable heavy isotope of neon.

Focussing spectroscopes. The spectroscopes discussed so far are analogous to the pinhole camera in optics because no focussing of the ion beams is involved. The introduction of focussing types of mass spectroscopes came in the years 1918–19 and was due to F.W. Aston and to A.J. Dempster.

In Aston's version, successive electric and magnetic fields were arranged in such a way that all perfectly collimated ions of one mass were brought to a focus independent of their velocity, thus giving rise to what is known as velocity focussing. Aston's design was the basis of his later instruments with which he systematically investigated the accurate masses of the isotopes of many of the elements. He chose ^{16}O (the isotope of oxygen of mass 16) as his standard of mass.

Dempster's spectrometer utilized only a magnetic field, which deflected the ion beam through an arc of 180°. In Dempster's machine, an ion beam homogeneous in mass and energy, but diverging from a slit, could be brought to a direction focus. This spectrometer was employed by Dempster to make accurate abundance determinations of the isotopes of magnesium, lithium, potassium, calcium, and zinc, laying the foundation for similar measurements of the isotopes of all the elements.

The resolving power of a mass spectroscope is a measure of its ability to separate adjacent masses that are displayed as peaks on the detector. If two peaks due to mass m and $(m + \Delta m)$ can just be separated, the resolving power is $m/\Delta m$. The early machines had resolving powers of only a few hundred. In 1935 and 1936, Dempster, K.T. Bainbridge, and Josef Mattauch working independently, developed instruments with electric and magnetic fields arranged in tandem in such a way that ion beams that emerged from the source slits in divergent directions and with different velocities were refocussed. Such focussing is termed double focussing. It was thus possible to achieve a resolving power of about 60,000.

Resolving power

Alternating field spectrometers. The spectrometers described so far employ steady electric and magnetic fields. In 1932 the use of alternating electric fields to separate ions of different mass was introduced by Henry D. Smyth. Instruments employing this technique are known as radio-frequency mass spectrometers, and by 1950, developments had improved them so that a resolving power of 100,000 was possible. Nonfocussed spectrometers were introduced that did not require deflecting fields but operated on the principle of the pulsed beam. Typical of these is the "time-of-flight" spectrometer, shown in Figure 1, which depends upon the fact that an accelerated bunch of ions will separate during its flight through the drift tube and arrive at the collector as a series of ion pulses, the lighter ions arriving first.

In 1953, Wolfgang Pauli and Helmut Steinwedel described the development of a quadrupole mass spectrometer. The application of superimposed radio-frequency and constant potentials between four parallel rods can be shown to act as a mass separator in which only ions within a particular mass range will perform oscillations of constant amplitude and be collected at the far end of the analyzer. This device, like the others, has the advantage of high transmission.

ION PRODUCTION AND DETECTION

Ion sources. The electron bombardment ion source was first used by Dempster. Its operation depends on the fact that an electron, when colliding with a molecule, may transfer a sufficient amount of its energy to eject one of the electrons in the molecule, thus forming a positively charged ion. A bombarding electron can transfer much more than the minimum amount of energy necessary to produce an ion and the excess energy can cause the ion to decompose in various ways with the loss of neutral fragments, thus giving rise to a mass spectrum. A simplified electron bombardment ion source consists of a heated filament, generally of tungsten or rhenium, which emits electrons in copious numbers. The electrons are attracted by slits having a high positive charge and pass through the ionization chamber containing the gaseous sample to be analyzed; here they are constrained to move in a narrow beam by a magnetic field in a direction along their lines of motion. Positive ions are formed in the ionization chamber along the length of the electron beam and are ejected from the chamber by positively charged, or repeller, electrodes. The ions leaving the source have a spread in energy of only a fraction of an electron volt. A sample is required in gaseous form at extremely low pressure, and a sample consumption of less than a thousandth of a microgram each second is typical. The source is frequently used for examination of organic compounds, which can be vaporized without decomposition, as well as for gas analysis.

Use of photons Instead of electrons, photons in the far ultraviolet region may be used, as they have sufficient energy to produce positive ions in a sample gas or vapour to be analyzed. A discharge in a capillary tube through which is passed a suitable gas, such as helium, is a good source for such radiation. Photo-ionization sources usually produce fewer ions than electron bombardment sources but have advantages when the ionization chamber must be held at low temperature.

In the vacuum spark source a pulsed, high-frequency potential of about 50 kilovolts is built up between two electrodes until electrical breakdown occurs. Hot spots appear on the electrodes, and electrode material is evaporated and sputtered, some of which is ionized by bombardment from electrons present between the electrodes. The principal merit of the vacuum spark source is its ability to produce copious quantities of ions of all elements present in the electrodes.

To obtain large ion currents a low voltage arc source can be used. The sample vapour, contained in a capillary, starts a low-current discharge in the filament chamber, the walls of which act as the anode. Electrons from this discharge ionize the vapour within the capillary and strike an arc to the anode, the ion density within the capillary being particularly high. When a magnetic field is used parallel to the direction of the primary electrons, the discharge is constrained without the use of a capillary. A weak electrostatic accelerating field extracts ions from the arc plasma and these can be collimated and focussed. Ion beams of one milliampere (a million times greater than those from the sources described above) can be obtained and collected to give usable amounts of separated isotopes. The surface ionization source depends upon the fact that when an atom of low ionization potential is heated on a surface of high work function, it is likely to evaporate as a positive ion. Neutral atoms striking the hot filament may also be re-emitted as ions. The ionization efficiency is so high in favourable cases that samples less than a millionth of a microgram (i.e., 2×10^{-13} g) may be analyzed with a precision of a few percent. This type of source has been widely used in the age determination of rocks. Substances that are adsorbed on a surface can be desorbed as positive ions under the action of a sufficiently strong electric field. Intense fields of the order of 10^8 volt per centimetre can be generated in the neighbourhood of sharp points and edges and these have been used as field emission sources. This source is becoming popular in the study of organic compounds, which can be introduced as vapours and ionized in the intense fields. The ions are formed with very little excitation energy so that there is little fragmentation of the molecular ions, making molecular formulas easier to determine.

Types of ions. When mass spectra are produced using any of the ion sources described, the various ion species can be classified into the following categories: Parent ions or molecular ions are ions that have been formed from complete molecules by removal of one or more electrons

without fragmentation. One can represent, in equation form, the addition of an electron e to a neutral molecule M to produce an ion and two electrons (electron bombardment), or the addition of a photon $h\nu$ to produce an ion and one electron (photo-ionization). Almost all organic compounds are held together by bonds, each of which contains two electrons; so the neutral molecule contains an even number of electrons. When an odd number of electrons is removed, the ion so formed will contain an odd number of electrons which can be symbolized by a dot placed beside the positive charge. The equation for electron bombardment is thus $M + e = M^{+\cdot} + 2e$, and for photo-ionization, $M + h\nu \rightarrow M^{+\cdot} + e$. These ions may contain an energy considerably in excess of the minimum required for fragmentation and may break into a variety of fragment ions and neutral species. Thus the molecular ions are the "parent" ions of the mass spectrum. Molecular ions may carry one or more charges because transfer of a large amount of energy by a bombarding electron (or photon) may expel two or more electrons from the molecule; thus, for example, processes such as are represented by the equation $M + e \rightarrow M^{2+} + 3e$, or $M + e \rightarrow M^{3+\cdot} + 4e$ can occur. These are examples of the formation of multiply charged ions.

Fragmentation of ions

Most of the research carried out in mass spectroscopy is concerned with positive ions; that is to say, ions formed by removing an electron from a neutral molecule. Electrons having a low kinetic energy can attach to molecules, forming *negative ions* and these can also be studied by mass spectroscopy.

The fragmentation of a molecular ion $ABCD^{+\cdot}$ can occur in several ways. For example, the expressions $ABCD^{+\cdot} \rightarrow AB^+ + C\cdot D\cdot$ represents simple cleavage, and $ABCD^{+\cdot} \rightarrow AC^+ + B\cdot D\cdot$ a rearrangement reaction, when the ion AC^+ is called a rearrangement ion. The fraction or moiety B has transferred during fragmentation to combine with moiety D. Such rearrangements are commonly found in the mass spectra of organic compounds and involve transfer of hydrogen atoms, or occasionally, small groups of atoms.

Ions that make up a mass spectrum also can be classified according to their stability. Ions that undergo fragmentation within the ionization chamber are classified as unstable, ions (both molecular and fragment ions) that leave the ionization chamber and reach the detector without fragmentation are classified as stable ions, and ions that undergo fragmentation between the ionization chamber and the detector are said to be metastable. Metastable ions that decompose in field-free regions of the flight tube can give rise to diffuse peaks in the mass spectrum. The positions and shapes of these "metastable peaks" can be used to give information about the individual steps in the fragmentation processes.

The detection and identification of ions. The two most widely used detection systems for energetic ions are the photographic plate and the secondary electron multiplier.

Special high-sensitivity photographic plates are employed to take account of the low penetrating power of the ions. It has proved possible with these to detect an element over a sensitivity range of 1 part in 1,000,000,000. In addition to the sensitivity, a major advantage of the photographic plate arises when it is used in a double-focussing mass spectroscope in which the whole, or a major part, of the mass spectrum is focussed in a plane (see the design of Mattauch and Richard Herzog shown in Figure 4 and described below). In this case, one can make use of the integrating action of the plate and compare the densities of lines due to different elements.

The basic electrical detector is the so-called Faraday cage. The current due to ions striking the cage is usually measured with an electrometer amplifier. The stability of electrometer amplifiers is such that the ion current issuing from the ionization chamber, minute as it is, permits intensity measurements of ten parts per million. An ion-collector system can be built with two or more slits and a corresponding number of Faraday cages that allows the simultaneous collection of two or more ion beams. Such a system allows the ratio of two ion beams to be measured continuously; it is particularly valuable in measuring the abundance ratios of the isotopes of an element and in detecting small changes in these ratios.

Secondary electron multipliers of the conventional kind are used to detect the smallest currents and to reduce the time constant, thus increasing the plotting rate of spectra. They can give a measurable current for the arrival of a single ion and be used for single ion counting. A scanning time of one second for several hundred mass peaks can be achieved if one sacrifices the accuracy of measurement of relative peak heights for the smallest peaks.

Single ion counting

Another method of detecting the positive ions in a beam is to allow them to strike a phosphor, thus producing scintillations that can be detected by a photomultiplier. A more sensitive method is to allow the ion beam to impinge upon a secondary emitting electrode, maintained at a high negative potential. The secondary electrons produced are accelerated to a phosphor that is optically coupled to a photomultiplier. In this way, high sensitivity is attained and the photomultiplier is never exposed to the atmosphere yet is conveniently located outside the vacuum system.

THE ANALYSIS OF IONS

Magnetic field analysis. Ions of mass m and charge e moving *in vacuo* with a velocity v in a direction perpendicular to a magnetic field H will follow a radius R given by

$$R = mv/He.$$

Therefore, all ions with the same charge and momentum entering the magnetic field from a common point will move in the same radius R and will come to a first order focus after 180° as shown in Figure 2, no matter what their masses. Hence, the mass spectrometer used by Dempster can be referred to as a "momentum spectrometer." If all ions of charge e enter the magnetic field with an identical kinetic energy eV, due to their acceleration through a voltage drop V, a definite velocity v will be associated with each mass and the radius will depend upon the mass. Since $eV = \frac{1}{2}mv^2$, substitution in the previous equation will give $m/e = H^2R^2/2V$. This formula shows that the radius of curvature R for ions in this spectrometer depends only on the ratio of the ions' mass to charge, as long as their kinetic energy is the same. Thus, a magnetic field can be used to separate a monoenergetic ion beam into its various mass components. A magnetic field will also exert a focussing action on a monoenergetic beam of ions of mass m as shown in Figure 2. In this figure an ion beam emerges from a point

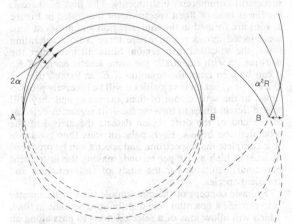

Figure 2: Paths of monoenergetic ions moving in a plane perpendicular to a magnetic field, passing through focal point B after originating at point A (see text).

A with a spread in direction 2α that then comes to an approximate focus at B after traversing 180°. When a molecular ion of mass m_1, carries a single positive charge, it may decompose in front of the magnetic sector to form a fragment ion of mass m_2 and a neutral fragment. If there is no kinetic energy of separation of the fragments, the ion m_2, and also the neutral fragment, will con-

tinue along the direction of motion of m_1 with unchanged velocity. The equation of motion for the ion m_2 entering the magnetic sector can now be written from a previous relationship, $R = m_2v/He$. In this equation v is the initial velocity appropriate to m_1 and given by $\sqrt{2eV/m_1}$. Multiplying both sides of the equation $v = \sqrt{2eV/m_1}$ by m_2, one obtains $m_2v = \sqrt{2eV}\,(m_2^2/m_1)$. Since the general momentum equation for any mass m can be written $mv = \sqrt{2eVm}$, it is apparent from the former equation that the momentum m_2v is appropriate to an ion of mass m_2^2/m_1. Thus, the decomposition of the metastable ion will give rise to a peak at an apparent mass $m^* = m_2^2/m_1$, not necessarily an integral number. This peak is known as a metastable peak. Generally, metastable peaks occur at non-integral mass numbers, and because there usually is a kinetic energy of separation during fragmentation of the polyatomic ion, they tend to be more diffuse than the normal mass peaks and thus are recognized easily. For any value of m^* a pair of integers m_1 and m_2 can be found such that $m^* = m_2^2/m_1$. Thus, the action of the magnetic field on the charged metastable-ion decomposition product can be used to give information on the individual fragmentation processes taking place in a mass spectrometer.

Metastable peaks

Electrostatic field analysis. An electrostatic field that attracts ions toward a common centre—that is, a radial field—will also exert a focussing action on a divergent beam of ions as shown in Figure 3. The radial force on

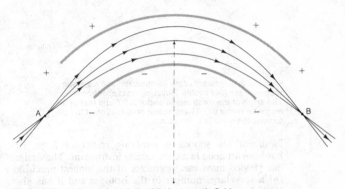

Figure 3: Focussing action of a radial electrostatic field produced by two semicylindrical charged electrodes on a monoenergetic beam of ions. The ions diverging from point A are brought to a focus at point B.

the ions due to the electrostatic field will be Ee, the product of the field E and the ionic charge e, and is equal to the centripetal force mv^2/R, of mass m moving with velocity v about a radius R. Thus, one may write the equation

$$Ee = mv^2/R \text{ or } R = \frac{1}{2}mv^2/\frac{1}{2}Ee.$$

The radius traversed by the ions will be proportional to their kinetic energy and an electric sector will thus produce an energy spectrum of the ions passing through it. Alternatively, if narrow collimating slits are placed at either end of the sector a monoenergetic beam of ions can be selected.

The possibility of using an electric wedge or sector to obtain a monoenergetic beam of ions, which is then separated for mass analysis by a magnetic sector is an obvious possibility. General equations for combined electric and magnetic sectors have been developed which show that a suitable combination of fields will give direction focussing for an ion beam of given mass-to-charge ratio, even though the beam may be heterogeneous in energy. The term double focussing is used for those combinations in which the angular and velocity aberrations effectively cancel.

Double focussing

Two of the best examples of double-focussing mass spectroscopes, both of which have been used in a variety of commercial instruments, were built by Mattauch and Herzog and by Alfred O. Nier and his collaborators. The Mattauch-Herzog geometry is shown in Figure 4 and has the remarkable property of being double focussing for all masses. Ions of all masses focus along a line that coincides with the second magnetic field boundary. Many ver-

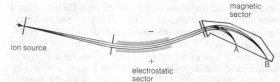

Figure 4: *Arrangement of the electrostatic and magnetic sectors in the Mattauch-Herzog double-focussing mass spectrometer.*
The ions are deflected in opposite directions in the electrostatic and magnetic fields. The divergent monoenergetic beam contains two ion species of different mass to charge ratio. All ions are brought to a focus along the plane AB.

sions of this design have been used when high resolution (up to 10^5) is desired for accurate mass and abundance measurements and general analytical work. It can give good spectra, even for a spread of 5 percent in energy of the ion beam, and can be used with virtually any ion source. The resolved ion beams can be recorded electrically or with a photographic plate.

The design due to Nier is illustrated in Figure 5. In a second instrument, Nier was able to achieve high sensitivity as well as high resolution. Using an electron-bom-

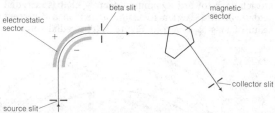

Figure 5: *Arrangement of the electrostatic and magnetic sectors in the Nier double-focussing mass spectrometer.*
The angle of the electrostatic sector is 90° and that of the magnetic sector 60°. The direction of deflection of the ion beam is the same in both sectors.

bardment ion source, a resolving power of 2×10^5 has been attained in a commercial instrument. The design has yielded mass measurements of the highest precision for a very large number of the isotopes and it has also been the most popular design for high resolution work in organic chemistry.

A few methods of attaining perfect double focussing are known. The simplest is to allow ions to move in a plane perpendicular to a homogeneous magnetic field. If the ions originate at a point, each ion will travel in a circular path appropriate to its momentum and will pass exactly through its point of origin after each revolution. In any practical system it is necessary to modify the arrangement so as to produce mass dispersion. This was first done by injecting a beam of positive ions into crossed homogeneous magnetic and electric fields. An ion moving in the plane of the electric field E and normal to the magnetic field H will describe a trochoid (the locus of a point on a wheel moving in a straight line) as shown in Figure 6, and all ions originating at the source or point A will be brought to a focus at the collector slits at point B. The

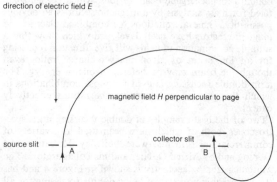

Figure 6: Ion path in the cycloidal mass spectrometer. The magnetic field H is in a direction perpendicular to the plane of the diagram.

separation distance AB of the source and collector can be written $AB = (2\pi E/H^2)\,(m/e)$. Neither the initial velocity nor direction of motion of the ions appears in this expression; so these factors do not affect the focus. In a commercial design, a resolving power of about 30,000 has been achieved.

All the designs described so far use electric and magnetic fields that are invariant with time. Several other designs, however, have been constructed in which alternating or pulsed fields are used. A method of obtaining mass separation by the use of crossed magnetic and radio-frequency fields makes use of the principle of cyclotron resonance. The "omegatron" spectrometer is illustrated in Figure 7.

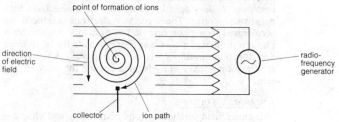

Figure 7: Path of the ions in the omegatron radio-frequency mass spectrometer. A magnetic field is in a direction perpendicular to the plane of the diagram.

Positive ions are produced by a stream of electrons moving along the direction of the magnetic field. If the time of revolution of an ion is equal to the period of the radio-frequency field (in phase), the ion can gain energy from the field and, as its energy increases, it will travel outward in an Archimedean spiral towards a collector. An ion of slightly different mass will be out of phase with the radio-frequency field and pass successively through maximum and minimum radii as it attains its maximum and minimum velocities. Ions of mass m, which are in phase, will be collected, and those ions of mass $(m + \Delta m)$ will be prevented from reaching the collector. The resolving power $m/\Delta m$ can be shown to be $\pi n/2$, in which n is the number of revolutions made by the ion before arriving at the collector. The resolving power attainable in practice is limited by ion scattering over the very long path length, which dictates a small instrument. The absence of limiting slits makes the instrument very sensitive and therefore useful in such studies as residual gas analysis.

Two other types of mass spectrometer, neither of which makes use of a magnetic field, have been developed into successful commercial instruments. The first of these is the linear time-of-flight spectrometer illustrated in Figure 1. Ions are formed in the source region and pulses of ions are injected into a region where there is no accelerating force, the so-called drift region. Since all ions enter the drift region with essentially the same kinetic energy $K.E.$, it can be seen from the equation $K.E. = \frac{1}{2}mv^2$, or $v = \sqrt{2K.E./m}$, that their velocities v will be inversely proportional to the square root of their masses m and they will take different times to traverse the drift region. A detector at the end of the drift region detects the arrival of the separated ion beams. Each pulse of ions thus gives rise to a complete mass spectrum, and spectra can be produced at rates as high as 10^5 per second, making the instrument particularly suitable for the study of fast reactions and transient species.

The basic concept of the quadrupole mass spectrometer is to provide a potential field distribution, periodic in time, which will allow ions of a selected mass to pass along an axis. The field is produced, ideally, between four hyperbolic electrodes, a cross section of the ideal arrangement being shown in Figure 8, In practice, four cylindrical electrodes are used, and combinations of dc and radio-frequency potentials are fed to opposite pairs of electrodes. Modern versions of the quadrupole mass spectrometer are compact and versatile instruments, offering a resolving power of the order of 500, plus a high ion transmission and sensitivity. It has been used to detect microscopic traces of gases and complete spectra can be obtained about once every second. The ion mass transmitted by a

Cyclotron resonance

Quadrupole field

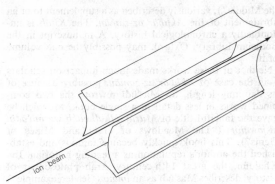

Figure 8: Quadrupole mass spectrometer, showing the four hyperbolic electrodes. Radio-frequency and direct-current potentials are applied to opposite electrodes.

quadrupole mass spectrometer can be selected with high precision merely by adjusting the radio frequency, thus making the instrument suitable for computer control and automatic data presentation.

PRINCIPAL APPLICATIONS

Studies with stable isotopes. The mass spectrometer is widely used to measure the masses of isotopes and to record the relative abundances with which they occur in nature or in artificially enriched samples. Mass spectrometers giving separated ion currents of several milliamperes are known as calutrons and these have been employed to produce relatively large and pure samples of particular isotopes. Separated isotopes are useful as targets in accelerators and reactors, and as labels in tracer studies.

A variety of compounds is commercially available in which the molecules are chemically labelled with a specific isotope. Labelling with the heavy isotopes ^2H, ^{13}C, ^{15}N, ^{17}O, and ^{18}O is of particular importance in organic chemistry and in biology and medicine. The stable isotopes of nitrogen and oxygen are used for labelling, as no suitable radioactive isotopes of these elements exist. In the so-called isotopic dilution method a known amount of a labelled compound is added to a complex mixture containing some of the same (but unlabelled) compound (see also RADIOISOTOPES, APPLICATIONS OF). Measurement with a mass spectrometer of the percentage labelling in a small sample of the compound extracted from the mixture establishes the original amount of the compound present. Important advances have been made in such fields as metabolism studies, plant respiration, photosynthesis, the direct utilization of oxygen in biological oxidations, enzymic hydrolyses, phosphate transfer reactions. Stable isotopes of elements beyond oxygen are also commonly employed. For example, ^{59}Fe has been used to follow hemoglobin cycles in the body.

Exact measurement of atomic masses. Over two-thirds of all exact atomic masses are now based on mass spectroscopic determinations. Large double-focussing mass spectroscopes are employed for the highest accuracy. The standard used is the mass of the ^{12}C isotope taken as 12 units exactly, and relative to the standard, many isotopic masses have been measured to better than 1 part in 10^7. It is possible to deduce the composition of a polyatomic ion solely on the basis of an accurate measurement of its mass. This information is of particular importance in organic chemistry and is discussed below.

Organic chemists nowadays use mass spectrometers routinely to determine the structural formulas of organic compounds. Any compound that can be heated to give a vapour pressure without decomposing can be examined by this technique. Both high-resolution (20,000 to 100,000) and low-resolution (500 to 5,000) mass spectrometers are used. With a high-resolution mass spectrometer it is possible to carry out mass measurements on the molecular ion (or any other ion in the spectrum) to an accuracy of 1 part in 1,000,000, or so. This mass provides the best index for determining ionic formulas. The accurate masses of the ions $C_6H_{12}^{+\cdot}$ and $C_4H_4O_2^{+\cdot}$ are, for example, 84.0939 and 84.0211, respectively, and these ions can easily be distinguished solely on the basis of their

masses. Once the molecular formula is known it is possible to deduce the total of rings and double bonds making up the molecular structure and to begin to speculate on possible structural formulas. In order to deduce structural formulas from molecular formulas it is essential to study the fragment ions in the mass spectrum. It is still not possible to predict fragmentation patterns for organic molecules, but many semi-empirical rules of fragmentation are known and it is usually possible to pick out peaks in the spectrum that are characteristic of particular chemical groups. The technique is valuable in that it is generally not necessary to know any details of the composition of the unknown compound in order to deduce a complete or partial structure. Only a small quantity of compound, a hundred micrograms or less, is necessary for an analysis.

Using a computer coupled to a high-resolution mass spectrometer, about 1,000 mass peaks per minute can be plotted at a resolving power of up to 20,000, accurate measurements can be made on each peak, and peak heights and ion compositions printed out in the form of an "element map" to aid in the interpretation of the spectrum. It is also possible for the computer to carry out many of the logical steps in reducing the data that lead to structural elucidation.

Continuous sampling of the materials contained in a reaction vessel, followed by analysis with a mass spectrometer, has been used to identify and measure the quantity of intermediate species formed during a reaction as a function of time. This kind of analysis is important, both in suggesting the mechanism by which the overall reaction takes place, and enabling the detailed kinetics of reactions to be resolved.

Isotopic labelling is widely used in such studies. It can indicate which particular atoms are involved in the reaction; in rearrangement reactions it can show whether an intramolecular or intermolecular process is involved; in exchange reactions it can show that particular atoms of, say, hydrogen, are exchanging between the reacting species. Labelling is also widely used in mass-spectrometric research to give information about the fragmentation reactions occurring in the mass spectrometer.

There are appreciable "isotope effects" by which isotopes may be distinguished apart from their difference in mass. It has been found, for example, that differences can be measured in the oxygen-18 content of the shells of marine animals that depend upon the temperature of the water in which the shells were formed. Such differences are preserved for millions of years and they have been used to obtain information concerning oceanic temperatures in paleolithic times.

Analysis of other chemical substances. Using the high-frequency spark source already described, many less volatile substances can be examined by mass spectrometry. The usual method of sample preparation is to construct the electrodes for the high-frequency spark source out of the pure substance to be examined, or if the sample is a powder, to mix it with, say, pure nickel powder and to compress the mixture into the form of the electrodes. The combination of high temperature and high electric field within the spark produces ions characteristic of the sample. The method has found particular application in the analysis of inorganic substances, alloys, minerals, and the highly purified materials used in atomic-energy research, and semiconductor technology. It is possible to detect impurities of the order of one part in 100,000,000, or lower by this technique.

If a monoenergetic beam of electrons or photons is used as the ionizing radiation and if the energy in the beam is slowly increased from a low value, the bombarding energy at which ions begin to appear gives the ionization potential. As the energy is increased further, fragmentation of molecular ions will occur. The energy at which a particular ion appears gives the appearance potential for that ion. Appearance potentials of fragment ions can be used in conjunction with ionization potentials and calorimetric data to estimate various thermodynamic quantities such as latent heats and bond strengths.

The absolute time scale of geologic history can be con-

Structural formulas

Isotopic labelling

Paleolithic temperatures

Appearance potentials

structed by the use of various isotopic clocks based on the radioactive decay of relatively long-lived isotopes (see DATING, RELATIVE AND ABSOLUTE). For example, uranium occasionally is found in fairly high local concentrations in radioactive rocks, along with the stable isotopes of lead-206 and lead-207, which are decay products of uranium-238 and uranium-235. Hence, knowing the decay rates of uranium-238 and uranium-235, the relative abundances of the uranium and radiogenic lead isotopes can be measured to give an estimate of age. Other natural radioactive processes that have been used in age determinations include the decay of potassium-40 to argon-40 and the decay of rubidium-87 to strontium-87.

Vacuum techniques. A type of small spectrometer adjusted for helium detection is commonly associated with vacuum systems in laboratories and industry. Connected to an evacuated system, it is an efficient and reliable aid for locating air leaks. In searching for a leak, a small jet of helium is played over the exterior of the system at the suspected joint or leakage area. When the exact point is reached, helium is sucked in along with the air, and the spectrometer sounds an alarm. The sensitivity of the technique is so great that an air leak can be detected, even if hundreds of thousands of other leaks of the same magnitude are present.

BIBLIOGRAPHY. F.W. ASTON, *Mass Spectra and Isotopes* (1933), a comprehensive account of the early work that laid the foundations of accurate mass and isotopic abundance measurements; M.G. INGHRAM and R.J. HAYDEN, *A Handbook on Mass Spectroscopy* (1954), a survey of instrument types including detailed descriptions of the physics of ion sources and detectors together with the theory of ion focussing and mass analysis; F.H. FIELD and J.L. FRANKLIN, *Electron Impact Phenomena and the Properties of Gaseous Ions* (1957), a study of the properties of gaseous ions with particular emphasis on the chemical physics of the systems; H.E. DUCKWORTH, *Mass Spectroscopy* (1958), a monograph giving good general coverage, including applications in physics, geophysics, and related sciences; J.H. BEYNON, *Mass Spectrometry and its Use in Organic Chemistry* (1960), practical information and many references to all aspects of mass spectrometry; H. BUDZIKIEWICZ, C. DJERASSI, and D.H. WILLIAMS, *Mass Spectrometry of Organic Compounds* (1967), a comprehensive account of the methods used to determine structural formulas of organic compounds.

(J.H.Be.)

Mas'ūdī, al-

Al-Mas'ūdī (full name: Abū al-Ḥasan 'Alī al-Mas'ūdī), the Arab historian and traveller known as the Herodotus of the Arabs, was the first Arabic writer to combine history and scientific geography in a single large-scale work. He thus pioneered a way of writing history that provided an alternative to the year-by-year chronology exemplified in the *Tarīkh* ("History") of aṭ-Ṭabarī (*c.* 839–923).

Born in Baghdad toward the end of the 9th century, he soon showed an extraordinary love of learning, an excellent memory, a capacity to write quickly, and a boundless curiosity that led him to study a wide variety of subjects, ranging from history and geography—his main interests—to comparative religion and science. Mas'ūdī was not content to learn merely from books and teachers but travelled widely to gain firsthand knowledge of the countries about which he wrote. His travels extended to Syria, Iran, Armenia, the shores of the Caspian Sea, the Indus Valley, Ceylon, Oman in Arabia, and the east coast of Africa as far south as Zanzibar, at least, and, possibly, Madagascar.

Extensive travels

The titles of more than 20 books attributed to him are known, including several about Islāmic beliefs and sects and even one about poisons, but most of his writings have been lost. His major work was *Akhbār az-zamān* ("The History of Time") in 30 volumes. This seems to have been an encyclopaedic world history, taking in not only political history but also many facets of human knowledge and activity. A manuscript of one volume of this work is said to be preserved in Vienna, but its projected publication has not, in the early 1970s, materialized. If this manuscript is genuine, it is all that has remained of the work. Mas'ūdī followed it with *Kitāb al-awsaṭ* ("Book of the Middle"), variously described as a supplement to or an abridgment of the *Akhbār az-zamān*. The *Kitāb* is undoubtedly a chronological history. A manuscript in the Bodleian Library, Oxford, may possibly be one volume of it.

Neither of these works made much impact on scholars —in the case of *Akhbār az-zamān*, possibly because of its daunting length. So Mas'ūdī rewrote the two combined works in less detail in a single book, to which he gave the fanciful title of *Murūj adh-dhahab wa ma'ādin al-jawāhir* ("The Meadows of Gold and Mines of Gems"). This book quickly became famous and established the author's reputation as a leading historian. Ibn Khaldūn, the great 14th-century Arab philosopher of history, describes Mas'ūdī as an *imam* ("leader, example") for historians. Though an abridgment, *Murūj adh-dhahab* is still a substantial work. In his introduction, Mas'ūdī lists more than 80 historical works known to him: but he also stresses the importance of his travels to "learn the peculiarities of various nations and parts of the world." He claims that, in the book, he has dealt with every subject that may be useful or interesting.

The Murūj adh-dhahab

The work is in 132 chapters. The second half is a straightforward history of Islām, beginning with the Prophet Muḥammad, then dealing with the caliphs down to Mas'ūdī's own time, one by one. While it often makes interesting reading because of its vivid description and entertaining anecdotes, this part of the book is superficial. It is seldom read now, as much better accounts can be found elsewhere, particularly in Ṭabarī. The first half, in contrast, is of great value, though somewhat sprawling and confused in its design. It starts with the creation of the world and Jewish history. Then it intersperses chapters describing the history, geography, social life, and religious customs of non-Islāmic lands, such as India, Greece, and Rome, with accounts of the oceans, the calendars of various nations, climate, the solar system, and great temples. Among particularly interesting sections are those on pearl diving in the Persian Gulf, amber found in East Africa, Hindu burial customs, the land route to China, and navigation, with its various hazards, such as storms and waterspouts. The relative positions and characteristics of the seas are explained.

Mas'ūdī's approach to his task was original—even eccentric. He made no attempt to write a methodical history and gave as much weight to social, economic, religious, and cultural matters as to politics. Moreover, he utilized information obtained from sources not previously regarded as reliable. He retailed what he learned from merchants, local writers, including non-Muslims, and others he met on his travels. He displayed interest in all religions, including Hinduism and Zoroastrianism, as well as Judaism and Christianity. But he tended to reproduce uncritically what he heard: thus, his explanations of natural phenomena are often incorrect. Yet he was no worse, in this respect, than medieval European travellers such as Marco Polo and Sir John Mandeville.

Historical method

Mas'ūdī had no settled abode for most of his adult life. In 945 he settled in Damascus. Two years later, he left there for al-Fusṭāṭ (old Cairo), where he remained until his death in 957.

It was there, in the last year of his life, that he wrote his "swan song," *Kitāb at-tanbīh wa al-ishrāf* ("The Book of Notification and Verification"), in which he summarized, corrected, and brought up-to-date the contents of his former writings, especially the three historical works.

BIBLIOGRAPHY. For an appreciation of Mas'ūdī as a historian within the wider context of Arabic historical writing as a whole, see FRANZ ROSENTHAL, *A History of Muslim Historiography* (1952), especially pp. 95–97 and 117–118. Little is known of Mas'ūdī's life except the little he tells us himself. About one quarter of the *Murūj adh-dhahab* can be read in English translation, with a useful preface, by ALOYS SPRENGER: *El-Mas'udi's Historical Encyclopaedia Entitled "Meadows of Gold and Mines of Gems,"* vol. 1 (1841). See also R.A. NICHOLSON, *A Literary History of the Arabs,* 2nd ed., pp. 352–354 (1930); and C. FIELD, *Tales of the Caliphs* (1909), based on Mas'ūdī.

(J.A.H.)

Materialism

Especially since the 18th century, the word Materialism has been used to refer to a family of metaphysical theories (*i.e.*, theories on the nature of reality) that can best be defined by saying that a theory tends to be called Materialism if it is felt sufficiently to resemble a paradigmatic theory that will here be called mechanical Materialism.

TYPES OF MATERIALIST THEORY

Mechanical Materialism is the theory that the world consists entirely of hard, massy material objects, which, though perhaps imperceptibly small, are otherwise like such things as stones. (A slight modification is to allow the void—or empty space—to exist also in its own right.) These objects interact in the sort of way that stones do: by impact and possibly also by gravitational attraction. The theory denies that immaterial or apparently immaterial things (such as minds) exist or else explains them away as being material things or motions of material things.

Types distinguished by departures from the paradigm. In modern physics (if interpreted realistically), however, matter is conceived as made up of such things as electrons, protons, and mesons, which are very unlike the hard, massy, stonelike particles of mechanical Materialism. In it the distinction between matter and energy has also broken down. It is therefore natural to extend the word Materialist beyond the above paradigm case (of mechanical Materialism) to cover anyone who bases his theory on whatever it is that physics asserts ultimately to exist. This sort may be called physicalistic Materialism. Such a Materialist allows the concept of material thing to be extended so as to include all of the elementary particles and other things that are postulated in fundamental physical theory—perhaps even continuous fields and points of space-time. Inasmuch as some cosmologists even try to define the elementary particles themselves in terms of the curvature of space-time, there is no reason why a philosophy based on such a geometricized cosmology should not be counted as Materialist, provided that it does not give an independent existence to nonphysical things such as minds.

Another sort of departure from the paradigm leads in the direction of what might be called a deistic Materialism. In this view it would be allowed that, although there is a spiritual Creator of the universe, he does not interfere with the created universe, which is itself describable in terms of mechanical or physicalist Materialism.

Still another departure from the paradigm is the theory that holds that everything is composed of material particles (or physical entities generally) but also holds that there are special laws applying to complexes of physical entities, such as living cells or brains, that are not reducible to the laws that apply to the fundamental physical entities. (To avoid inconsistency, such a theory may have to allow that the ordinary laws of physics do not wholly apply within such complex entities.) Such a theory, which could be called "emergent Materialism," can shade off, however, into theories that one would not wish to call Materialist, such as hylozoism, which ascribes vital characteristics to all matter, and panpsychism, which attributes a mindlike character to all constituents of material things.

Another common relaxation of the paradigm is that which allows as compatible with Materialism such a theory as epiphenomenalism, according to which sensations and thoughts do exist in addition to material processes but are nonetheless wholly dependent on material processes and without causal efficacy of their own. They are related to material things somewhat in the way that a man's shadow is related to the man. A similar departure from the paradigm is a form of what might be called "double-aspect Materialism," according to which in inner experience men are acquainted with nonphysical *properties* of material processes, though these properties are not causally effective. A form of double-aspect theory in which these properties were allowed to be causally effective would be a species of emergent Materialism.

Of course, more than one of these qualifications might be made at the same time: thus a person might wish to speak of "physicalist deistic epiphenomenalist Materialism." If no other qualifications are intended, it is convenient to use the word extreme and to speak, for example, of "extreme physicalist Materialism"—which is probably the type most discussed among professional philosophers in English-speaking countries.

Type distinguished by its view of history. In the wider world, however, the word Materialism most commonly brings to mind dialectical Materialism, which is the orthodox philosophy of Communist countries. This is most importantly a theory of how changes arise in human history, though a general metaphysical theory lies in the background. Dialectical Materialists contrast their view with what they call "vulgar" Materialism; and it does, indeed, appear that their theory is not an extreme Materialism, whether mechanical or physicalist. They seem to hold merely that mental processes are dependent on or have evolved from material ones. Though they might be akin to emergent Materialists, it is hard to be sure; their assertion that something new emerges at higher levels of organization might refer only to such things as that a wireless receiver is different from a mere heap of the same components. And if so, even an extreme physicalistic Materialist could acquiesce in this view. The distinctive features of dialectical Materialism would, thus, seem to lie as much in its being dialectical as in its being Materialist. Its dialectical side may be epitomized in three laws: (1) that of the transformation of quality into quantity, (2) that of the interpenetration of opposites, and (3) that of the negation of the negation. Nondialectical philosophers find it hard, however, to interpret these laws in a way that does not make them into either platitudes or falsehoods (see MARXISM; see also RELATED ENTRIES under MATERIALISM in the *Ready Reference and Index*).

Perhaps because of the historical determinism implicit in dialectical Materialism, and perhaps because of memories of the mechanical Materialist theories of the 18th and 19th centuries, when physics was deterministic, it is popularly supposed that Materialism and determinism must go together. This is not so. As indicated below, even some ancient Materialists were indeterminists, and a modern physicalist Materialism must be indeterministic because of the indeterminism that is built into modern physics. Modern physics does imply, however, that macroscopic bodies behave in a way that is effectively deterministic, and, because even a single neuron (nerve fibre) is a macroscopic object by quantum mechanical standards, a physicalistic Materialist may still regard the human brain as coming near to being a mechanism that behaves in a deterministic way.

Types distinguished by their account of mind. A rather different way of classifying Materialist theories, which to some extent cuts across the classifications already made, emerges when the theories are divided according to the way in which a Materialist accounts for minds. A central-state Materialist identifies mental processes with processes in the brain. An analytical behaviourist, on the other hand, argues that, in talking about the mind, one is not talking about an actual entity, whether the brain or an immaterial soul, but, rather, one is somehow talking about the way in which people would behave in various circumstances. According to the analytical behaviourist, there is no more of a problem for the Materialist in having to identify mind with something material than there is in identifying such an abstraction as the average plumber with some concrete entity. Analytical behaviourism differs from psychological behaviourism, which is merely a methodological program to base theories on behavioral evidence and to eschew introspective reports. The analytical behaviourist usually has a not too plausible theory of introspective reports according to which they are what are sometimes called "avowals": roughly, he contends that to say "I have a pain" is to engage in a verbal surrogate for a wince. Epistemic Materialism is a theory that can be developed either in the direction of central-state Materialism or in that of analytical behaviourism and that rests on the contention that the only

[margin:] Physicalistic, deistic, emergent, and epiphenomenal types

[margin:] Dialectical Materialism

[margin:] Central-state Materialism and analytical behaviourism

statements that are intersubjectively testable are either observation reports about macroscopic physical objects or statements that imply such observation reports (or are otherwise logically related to them).

Before leaving this survey of the family of Materialistic theories, a quite different sense of the word Materialism should be noted in which it denotes not a metaphysical theory but an ethical attitude. A person is a Materialist in this sense if he is interested mainly in sensuous pleasures and bodily comforts and hence in the material possessions that bring these about. A man might be a Materialist in this ethical and pejorative sense without being a metaphysical Materialist, and conversely. An extreme physicalistic Materialist, for example, might prefer a Beethoven record to a comfortable mattress for his bed; and a person who believes in immaterial spirits might opt for the mattress.

HISTORY OF MATERIALISM

Greek and Roman Materialism. Though Thales of Miletus (c. 580 BC) and some of the other Pre-Socratic philosophers have some claims to being regarded as Materialists, the Materialist tradition in Western philosophy really begins with Leucippus and Democritus, Greek philosophers who were born in the 5th century BC. Leucippus is known only through his influence on Democritus. According to Democritus, the world consists of nothing but atoms (indivisible chunks of matter) in empty space (which he seems to have thought of as an entity in its own right). These atoms can be imperceptibly small, and they interact either by impact or by hooking together, depending on their shapes. The great beauty of atomism was its ability to explain the changes in things as due to changes in the configurations of unchanging atoms. The view may be contrasted with that of the earlier philosopher Anaxagoras (c. 480 BC), who thought that when, for example, the bread that a person eats is transformed into human flesh, this must occur because bread itself already contains hidden within itself the characteristics of flesh. Democritus thought that the soul consists of smooth, round atoms and that perceptions consist of motions caused in the soul atoms by the atoms in the perceived thing (see ATOMISM).

Because Epicurus' philosophy was expounded in a lengthy poem by Lucretius, a Roman philosopher of the 1st century BC, Epicurus (died 270 BC) was easily the most influential Greek Materialist. He differed from Democritus in that he postulated an absolute up–down direction in space, so that all atoms fall in roughly parallel paths. To explain their impacts with one another, he then held that the atoms are subject to chance swerves—a doctrine that was also used to explain free will. Epicurus' Materialism therefore differed from that of Democritus in being an indeterministic one. Epicurus' philosophy contained an important ethical part, which was a sort of enlightened egoistic hedonism (see EPICUREANISM). His ethics, however, was not Materialistic in the pejorative sense of the word.

Modern Materialism. Materialism languished throughout the medieval period, but the Epicurean tradition was revived in the first half of the 17th century in the atomistic Materialism of the French Catholic priest Pierre Gassendi. In putting forward his system as a hypothesis to explain the facts of experience, Gassendi showed that he understood the method characteristic of modern science, and he may well have helped to pave the way for corpuscular hypotheses in physics. Gassendi was not thoroughgoing in his Materialism inasmuch as he accepted on faith the Christian doctrine that men have immortal souls. His contemporary, the English philosopher Thomas Hobbes, also propounded an atomistic Materialism and was a pioneer in trying to work out a mechanistic and physiological psychology. Holding that sensations are corporeal motions in the brain, Hobbes skirted, rather than solved, the philosophical problems about consciousness that had been raised by another contemporary, the great French philosopher René Descartes. Descartes's philosophy was dualistic, making a complete split between mind and matter. In his theory of the physical world,

however, and especially in his doctrine that animals are automata, Descartes's own system had a mechanistic side to it that was taken up by 18th-century Materialists, such as Julien de La Mettrie, the French physician whose appropriately titled *L'Homme machine* (1747; Eng. trans., *Man a Machine*, 1750) applied Descartes's view about animals to man himself. Denis Diderot, an 18th-century French Encyclopaedist, supported a broadly Materialist outlook by considerations drawn from physiology, embryology, and the study of heredity; and his friend Paul, baron d'Holbach, published his *Système de la nature* (1770), which expounded a deterministic type of Materialism in the light of evidence from contemporary science, reducing everything to matter and to the energy inherent in matter. He also propounded a hedonistic ethics as well as an uncompromising atheism, which provoked a reply even from the Deist Voltaire.

The 18th-century French Materialists had been reacting against orthodox Christianity. In the early part of the 19th century, however, certain writers in Germany—usually with a biological or medical background—reacted against a different orthodoxy, the Hegelian and Neo-Hegelian tradition in philosophy, which had become entrenched in German universities. Among these were Ludwig Büchner and Karl Vogt. The latter is notorious for his assertion that the brain secretes thought just as the liver secretes bile. This metaphor of secretion, previously used by P.-J.-G. Cabanis, a late-18th-century French Materialist, is seldom taken seriously, because to most philosophers it does not make sense to think of thought as a *stuff*. The Hobbesian view, also espoused by Büchner, that thought is a *motion* in the brain is usually viewed as a more promising one.

The synthesis of urea (the chief nitrogenous end product of protein metabolism), discovered in 1828, broke down the discontinuity between the organic and the inorganic in chemistry, which had been a mainstay of nonmaterialistic biology. Materialist ways of thinking were later strengthened enormously by the Darwinian theory of evolution, which not only showed the continuity between man and other living things right back to the simplest organisms but also showed how the apparent evidences of design in natural history could be explained on a purely causal basis. There still seemed to be a gap, however, between the living and the nonliving, though E.H. Haeckel, a 19th-century German zoologist, thought that certain simple organisms could have been generated from inorganic matter and, indeed, that a certain simple sea creature may well be in process of generation in this way even now. Though Haeckel was wrong, 20th-century biologists have proposed much more sophisticated and more plausible theories of the evolution of life from inorganic matter. Haeckel and his contemporary, the British zoologist T.H. Huxley, did much to popularize philosophical accounts of the world that were consonant with the scientific thought of their time, but neither could be regarded as an extreme Materialist.

Contemporary Materialism. Perhaps because recent developments in biochemistry and in physiological psychology have greatly increased the plausibility of Materialism, there has lately been a resurgence of interest in the philosophical defense of central-state Materialism. Central-state Materialists have proposed their theories partly because of dissatisfaction with the analytical behaviourism of the Oxford philosopher Gilbert Ryle. Ryle himself is reluctant to call himself a Materialist, partly because of a dislike of all "isms" and partly because he thinks that the notion of matter has meaning only by contrast with that of mind, which he thinks to be an illegitimate sort of contrast. Nevertheless, it would seem that analytical behaviourism could be used to support a physicalist Materialism that would go on to explain human behaviour by means of neural mechanisms. (Ryle himself is suspicious of mechanistic accounts of biology and psychology.) Analytical behaviourism has been felt to be unsatisfactory, however, chiefly because of its account of introspective reports as avowals (see above), which most philosophers have found to be unconvincing.

Philosophers have distinguished two forms of central-

Democ-ritus and Epicurus

Gassendi through Büchner and Vogt

Darwin, Haeckel, and Huxley

state Materialism, namely, the translation form and the disappearance form. The translation form is the view that mentalistic discourse can be translated into discourse that is neutral between physicalism and dualism, so that the truth of a man's introspective reports is compatible with the objects of these reports being physical processes. The disappearance form is the view that such a translation cannot be done and that this fact, however, does not refute physicalism but shows only that man's ordinary introspective reports are contaminated by false theories.

Feigl,
Place,
Smart,
Armstrong

Translation central-state theories. Among the philosophers who have advocated the translation form is the U.S. philosopher Herbert Feigl, earlier a member of the Vienna Circle, who, in an influential monograph (see *Bibliography*), did the most to get contemporary philosophers to treat central-state Materialism as a serious philosophical theory. Against the objection that, for example, "visual sensation" does not *mean* "process in the visual cortex," advocates of the translation form point out that "the morning star" does not mean the same as "the evening star," and yet the morning star as a matter of fact *is* the evening star. The objection confuses meaning and reference. Against the objection that a purely physical process (a dance of electrons, protons, and so on) cannot have the sensory quality of greenness that is observed in a visual experience of seeing grass, say, they reply that to talk of the sensory experience of something looking green (or having a green mental image) is not to talk of anything that is literally green, but is simply to report that some internal process is of the sort that normally goes with seeing something, such as a lawn, which really is green. Though an immaterialist might say that the sort of process in question is a spiritual process, the Materialist can equally claim that it is a material process in the brain. The analysis of the introspective report is neutral between these two contentions; the Materialist, however, opts for his contention on various grounds. The British Materialist U.T. Place does so on the ground of normal scientific methodology; and the Australian Materialist J.J.C. Smart does so with a metaphysical application of the principle (called "Ockham's razor") that entities should not be multiplied beyond necessity. A physicalistic Materialist has, of course, an obligation to go on to give a suitable account of such apparently nonphysicalist qualities as the greenness of grass. At one time Smart analyzed colours in terms of the discriminatory behaviour of human beings. Another Australian Materialist, D.M. Armstrong, holds, on the other hand, that colours are as a matter of fact properties of objects, such properties being of the sort describable in the theoretical terms of physics. Feigl, in turn, is to some extent (and rather reluctantly) a double-aspect theorist. He qualifies the position taken by the other translation theorists, conceding that the translations do leave something out, viz., the immediately introspectable properties of "raw feels," such as that of hearing the tone of middle C. He holds, however, that such properties are irrelevant to causal explanations of phenomena. The translation form of central-state Materialism thus has some affinities with the earlier epistemic Materialism of the Positivist philosophers Rudolf Carnap and Hans Reichenbach, Germans who settled in the United States. Thus Carnap has suggested that mental predicates be treated as applying to material entities: for example, "Carnap sees green" could be taken as meaning "the body Carnap is in the state of green-seeing," the state of green-seeing being a purely physical state that explains the behavioral facts that led one to ascribe the predicate "sees green" to Carnap in the first place.

Disappearance central-state theories. David K. Lewis, a United States philosopher of science and language, has developed a translation form of central-state Materialism on the basis of a theory regarding the definition of theoretical terms in science. According to this theory, entities such as electrons, protons, and neutrons are defined in terms of the causal roles that they play in relation to observational phenomena—*e.g.*, phenomena in cloud chambers—but the method of definition is able to do justice to the causal and other interrelations between the theoretical entities themselves. Lewis applies this account to com-

monsense psychology. Since mental entities, such as pains, are defined in commonsense psychology in terms of their causal roles (in relation to observable behaviour) and since there is empirical reason to ascribe the same causal roles to brain processes, Lewis identifies mental events, processes, and states with brain events, processes, and states. The disappearance form of central-state Materialism is the sort of theory held by P.K. Feyerabend, a U.S. philosopher, who denies that the Materialist can give a neutral analysis of introspective reports. In Feyerabend's view, commonsense introspective reports are irreducibly immaterialist in content. He argues, however, that this admission does not show the untenability of Materialism. Ordinary mentalistic discourse, he holds, is comparable to the medieval discourse about epileptics as being "possessed by the devil." If one now "identified" demon possession with a certain medical condition of the brain, this would really be an assertion that there is no such thing as a demon-possessed state: the medieval way of looking at the matter is thus rejected. It is in this sort of way that Feyerabend wants to "identify" the mind with the brain: he simply rejects the ordinary mentalistic conceptual scheme and so feels no obligation to show its compatibility with Materialism.

Feyerabend,
Quine,
Sellars,
Wittgenstein

The influential American philosophers W.V. Quine and Wilfrid Sellars also hold theories that could be regarded as disappearance forms of physicalistic Materialism, though there is a Kantian twist to Sellars' philosophy that makes it hard to classify. Sellars holds that mentalistic concepts cannot be eliminated from man's commonsense picture of the world, which he calls "the manifest image." In a way reminiscent of Kant he holds that, although the manifest image is inescapable, it does not give metaphysical truth about the world as it really is in itself. This truth is given, instead, by "the scientific image"—*i.e.*, by theoretical science, which is physicalist. In the case of Quine, there is a certain Platonism in that he believes in the objective reality of nonspatiotemporal entities, viz., those that are the subject matter of pure mathematics. Because he holds that the reason for believing mathematics is that it is needed as part of physical theory, his reasons for believing in numbers and the like are not in principle different from those for believing in electrons; thus Quine's Platonism does not really compromise his physicalism.

The Austrian philosopher Ludwig Wittgenstein, who lived to the mid-20th century and was professor of philosophy at Cambridge University, has sometimes been interpreted as a behaviourist, though his insistence that an inner process stands in need of outward criteria could possibly be interpreted as a sort of epistemic and central-state Materialism. Nevertheless, to count Wittgenstein as a Materialist would be to take considerable liberties with him; for, while displaying at times a certain mystical attitude, he also held very strongly that the business of a philosopher is not to put forward any metaphysical theory but to clear up conceptual confusions—to show the fly the way out of the fly bottle.

Eastern Materialism. This historical survey has been concerned with Materialism in Western philosophy. On the whole, Materialism is contrary to the spirit of both Indian and traditional Chinese philosophy, though the Cārvāka school of Materialists flourished from the 6th century BC until medieval times in India. Mention should also be made of the strong naturalistic tendency in Theravāda Buddhism, as also in certain schools of Chinese philosophy that exalt *ch'i* ("ether" or "material force") above principle and mind.

SUBSTANTIVE ISSUES IN MATERIALISM

Reductionism, consciousness, and brain. The main attraction of Materialism today is the way in which it fits in with a unified picture of science—a picture that has become very plausible. Thus, chemistry is reducible to physics inasmuch as there is a quantum-mechanical theory of the chemical bond. Biology is mainly an application of physics and chemistry to the structures described in natural history (including the natural history that one can explore through powerful microscopes). Increasingly, biological explanations resemble explanations in engineer-

Unified
science
and
physical-
mental
laws

ing, in which material structures are described and then the laws of physics and chemistry are used to explain the behaviour of these structures. (In the biological case, of course, these structures are often dynamic in the sense that their molecules are continually being replaced.) Through the influence of neurophysiology and also cybernetics (the science of information and control, which can be applied also to artificial automata), scientific psychology is also fitting well into the same mechanistic scheme. The recalcitrant residue appears in the phenomena of consciousness. Here mental events seem, indeed, to be correlated with physical events; but, if the mental events are not the very same as the physical events, one is left with apparently ultimate (or irreducible) physical–mental laws that do not fit happily into unified science, and one is thus faced with a situation unlike that of the rest of science. Looking at science generally, one expects *ultimate* laws to relate simple entities, such as fundamental particles. A physical–mental law, however, would have to refer to something very complex—a brain process involving perhaps millions of neurons, with each neuron being itself an almost fantastically complex entity. There would be a multitude of physical-mental laws, which would look like excrescences on the face of science. Because they would not fit into the network of scientific laws, Herbert Feigl has called them "nomological danglers." To get rid of these danglers is one of the chief attractions of Materialism. Of course, an immaterialist might assert that mental entities exist and also that there are no physical-mental laws. But it might be hard for him to reconcile this position with the empirical evidence; and in any case he would be faced with the problem of how to distinguish the free exercise of such anomalous physical-mental interaction from mere chance behaviour.

The development of computers and other devices to take over much of the more routine sort of human behaviour has led to attempts on the part of scientists and technologists, such as the American M.L. Minsky, to develop real artificial intelligence. So far, the success that these scientists hoped for has not been achieved. An American linguistic theorist, Noam Chomsky, has argued on the basis of his theories of generative grammar that the brain is quite unlike any already-understood type of mechanism. Indeed, any physicalistic Materialist must certainly concede that there are very deep problems about the brain, which apparently can no longer be thought of as a bundle of conditioned reflex mechanisms or the like, as it often has seemed to be to many psychologists. The physicalist can stress, however, that the investigator's ignorance need not lead him to assume that he will never be able to find an explanation of intelligence and of linguistic abilities in terms consonant with his present notion of a physical mechanism. (There is also the possibility that physical laws not yet discovered might be needed to explain the workings of the brain. So long as these turned out to be basic laws of physics, such discoveries would not imply a shift to emergentist Materialism.)

Logic, intentionality, and psychical research. Some philosophers, such as the Oxford philosopher J.R. Lucas, have tried to produce positive arguments against a mechanistic theory of mind by employing certain discoveries in mathematical logic, especially Gödel's theorem, which implies that no axiomatic theory could possibly capture all arithmetical truths. In general, philosophers have not found such attempts to extract an antimaterialist philosophy from mathematical logic to be convincing. Nevertheless, the problems of mechanizing intelligence, including the mathematical abilities of human beings, do pose unsolved problems that the Materialist is obliged to take seriously.

Perhaps the most common challenge to Materialism comes from philosophers who hold that it cannot do justice to the concept of intentionality, which Franz Brentano, a pre-World War I German philosopher, made the distinguishing mark between the mental and the nonmental (see MIND, PHILOSOPHY OF: *The search for a criterion of the mental: Intentionality*; PHENOMENOLOGY: *Origin and Development of Husserl's phenomenology:*

Basic concepts). (A related objection is that Materialism cannot do justice to the distinction between behaviour and mere bodily movements.) Brentano held that mental events and states somehow point toward objects beyond themselves (or have a "content"). Many contemporary philosophers agree with Brentano that purely physical entities cannot have this property. If it is said, for example, that punched holes on the tape of a computer can refer beyond themselves in the way that thoughts do, then it is commonly replied that, in themselves, the holes on the tape have no reference or content —for this belongs only to the thoughts in the mind of a person who reads the tape. The Materialist reply may be to argue, however, that there is a fundamental unclarity in the very notion of intentionality (this is roughly Quine's position) or else to argue that purely physical systems can, after all, possess intentionality.

The alleged spiritualistic and other phenomena reported in psychical research are sometimes adduced against Materialism. The Materialist, however, can well afford to postpone discussion of these phenomena until such time as they are accepted by the general scientific community, which on the whole still remains skeptical of them.

At present, there are reputable philosophers who accept Materialism, and there are also reputable philosophers who either reject it as false or hold that it is not the business of a philosopher to propound any sort of metaphysical system. Perhaps Materialists are still in a minority; but at any rate there is much less tendency than there was a generation ago for this type of theory to be thought philosophically naïve.

BIBLIOGRAPHY. For the period up to about 100 years ago, see F.A. LANGE, *Geschichte des Materialismus und Kritik seiner Bedeutung in der Gegenwart*, 2 vol. (1902; Eng. trans., *History of Materialism and Criticism of Its Present Importance*, 3rd ed., 3 vol. (1925). For more recent times, see JOHN PASSMORE, *A Hundred Years of Philosophy*, 2nd ed. (1966). There are excellent articles by KEITH CAMPBELL and H.B. ACTON on "Materialism" and "Dialectical Materialism" in the *Encyclopedia of Philosophy*, vol. 5, pp. 179–188 and vol. 2, pp. 389–397 (1967), which also contains excellent articles on nearly all of the noncontemporary philosophers here mentioned. Examples of work by most of the contemporary writers are given in JOHN O'CONNOR (ed.), *Modern Materialism: Readings on Mind-Body Identity* (1969); and C.V. BORST (ed.), *The Mind-Brain Identity Theory* (1970). See also HERBERT FEIGL, *The "Mental" and the "Physical": The Essay and a Postscript* (1967); J.J.C. SMART, *Philosophy and Scientific Realism* (1963); D.M. ARMSTRONG, *A Materialist Theory of the Mind* (1968); and WILFRID SELLARS, *Science, Perception and Reality* (1963), especially ch. 1. A rather difficult book defending Materialism from the difficulties about intentionality is D.C. DENNETT, *Content and Consciousness* (1969). For two very different styles of antimaterialist argument, see J.R. LUCAS, *The Freedom of the Will* (1970); and NORMAN MALCOLM, *Problems of Mind* (1971). Another interesting critique of Materialism is in JOHN BELOFF, *The Existence of Mind* (1962). A mainly mechanistic philosophy of biology is presented by the German biologist B. RENSCH in *Biophilosophie auf erkenntnistheoretischer Grundlage (Panpsychistischer Identismus)* (1968; Eng. trans., *Biophilosophy*, 1971), though Rensch's philosophy is also panpsychist.

Some classic Materialist works are: LUCRETIUS, *On the Nature of the Universe*, trans. by R.E. LATHAM (1951); THOMAS HOBBES, *Body, Mind and Citizen: Selections*, ed. by R.S. PETERS (1962); RENE DESCARTES, *Philosophical Writings*, trans. and ed. by ELIZABETH ANSCOMBE and P.T. GEACH (1954); and A. VARTANIAN, *La Mettrie's "L'Homme Machine": A Study in the Origins of an Idea* (1960), which is a critical edition with introductory monograph and notes.

For epistemic Materialism, see RUDOLF CARNAP, "Psychology in Physical Language," in A.J. AYER (ed.), *Logical Positivism* (1959); Carnap's replies to Herbert Feigl and A.J. Ayer in P.A. SCHILPP (ed.), *The Philosophy of Rudolf Carnap* (1964); and H. REICHENBACH, *Experience and Prediction* (1938).

The most relevant and important works by Ryle and Wittgenstein are: GILBERT RYLE, *The Concept of Mind* (1949); and LUDWIG WITTGENSTEIN, *Philosophical Investigations* (1953). For a Materialist critique of Ryle, see BRIAN MEDLIN, "Ryle and the Mechanical Hypothesis," in C.F. PRESLEY (ed.), *The Identity Theory of Mind*, 2nd ed. (1971).

(J.J.C.S.)

Artificial intelligence and generative grammar

Materials Handling

Materials handling is the process of applying human, animal, or other energy to the movement of raw materials from their native site to a point of use; the manipulation of materials in the production process as an aid to manufacture; and the transfer of finished goods to the final user. The major emphasis of materials handling falls at the points of contact among these three types of basic economic activities. A secondary aspect of materials handling is the transportation and storage function of industry.

In the world today, various stages of materials-handling development can be seen, often in proximity. In such countries as Turkey, ancient systems involving human and animal power interconnect with modern systems involving rail and truck facilities.

Modern trends. Modern materials handling considers the entire movement of goods from their beginnings as raw materials to processing points and to customers, in contrast to the former approach that considered each part of the system separately. In early systems, for example, vegetables might be picked one at a time, stored temporarily, placed in a package or loose in a cart, moved to an assembly point, handled again individually, put into a bag, box, or basket, placed in a larger vehicle in packaged units, moved to a wholesaler in bags, broken down into individual portions for delivery to the retailer, and, finally, sold to the consumer.

This situation still exists to a large extent in many areas, not only of the underdeveloped world but in developed countries. The only difference in the handling of many products is the level of technology applied. Australian wool is handled between 50 and 60 times before it reaches the consumer as a garment. The typical agricultural product may be handled 20 times before it reaches the store shelf.

Examples of modern techniques. The first applications of the flow concepts of materials handling occurred in large bulk industries such as those processing iron ore, coal, and petroleum. Iron ore, for example, has been moved in bulk on the Great Lakes of the United States since the beginning of the 20th century. Large earthmoving equipment removes the ore from open pits in northern Minnesota, transfers it to special trains that haul it to port, where large cranes or automatic dumping mechanisms place it in huge holding bulkheads that, in turn, transfer it by means of gravity or by cranes to the ship. The ship then steams to a lake port near a steel mill, where the process is reversed. The entire system is geared to anticipate mill needs with a continuous flow of the ore from mine to mill.

Modern materials-handling systems are also employed in assembly-line production, such as automobile manufacturing. When operating at full capacity, a large-scale auto assembly plant can produce one car every 40 seconds; a full 24-hour production schedule results in a maximum daily production of 2,160 cars. This level of production can be maintained for long periods despite differentiation in colour, style, accessories and trim that make it possible to produce a year's output of cars with no two identical. Materials handling in such productive industries must be highly organized. Arrival of raw materials at the plant site is carefully coordinated with scheduled production needs, thus reducing storage to a minimum. Finished cars cannot be economically stored at the plant and are therefore moved to distribution points as quickly as possible. Raw materials are scheduled to arrive within 96 or even 48 hours of use, and finished cars are moved away within a few hours.

The key to scheduling materials supply and handling in the assembly line for each automobile manufactured is the customer order, or purchase specification, which is converted to punch-card form and placed in the production schedule. Materials and parts necessary to complete the car in precisely the way the purchaser has specified are placed in subassembly lines; when the chassis arrives at a station, the correct part is available for assembly. Plants that employ this type of operation are not really manufacturing plants but materials-handling plants.

Handling iron ore

Practically all manufacturing of parts and components is done away from the assembly line, often at a distant point.

Another example of modern materials-handling techniques is the processing of wheat into consumer products. Harvested by large combines, the grain is moved in bulk via truck to an elevator, in which it is placed by conveyor or by an air-pressure system; from the elevator it is gravity fed to a railroad car, shipped to a flour mill, and stored again in silos. From the silos it moves to the mill via a quantity-feed conveyor or an air slide. The finished flour coming from the end of the line is either packaged for the consumer market or shipped in bulk by rail and truck to bakeries or other large industrial users. At the bakery the flour is again placed in a silo or hopper, conveyed to a mixing unit for dough preparation, baked into bread or another product, sent to an automatic wrapping machine, and wheeled to trucks for delivery. In many cases the first time the product is handled as a single unit is when the consumer takes it from the shelf. Such an integrated distribution system is made possible by meticulous attention to required materials-handling systems within each process and to the transfers of material between processes.

Automatized bread baking

TYPES OF MATERIALS-HANDLING SYSTEMS BY PROCESS

In bulk movements of any type, emphasis is on an integrated flow from source of raw materials to final user. Three principles underlie operations: (1) the best handling system involves no actual handling at all, or minimal handling; (2) the larger the volume handled the lower the unit cost; and (3) movement of materials as a unit should be maintained as far toward the ultimate point of use as possible.

Raw-materials and parts supply. Raw-materials and parts supply both have various economic and physical characteristics that affect materials handling. There are three main classes: large-volume, low-value, flowable products, such as petroleum; large-volume bulk products that do not flow, such as iron ore; and high-volume manufactured parts and components.

Flowable bulk commodities. Sources of supply for raw materials of this kind usually are located at a distance from the market. Petroleum fields in the southwest United States, in the Persian Gulf region, and in North Africa supply oil and gas to the northeast United States, Europe, and Japan—thousands of miles away. Handling of petroleum products begins with collection of crude oil in the field. Though much crude oil in the past moved by rail tank car to refineries and by tank car or truck to market, today pipelines dominate petroleum handling. Pipe of relatively small dimension is attached to each producing well. A network of these pipes serving a specified geographic area connects to bulk collecting stations, which, in turn, serve large terminal areas with storage tanks capable of holding hundreds of thousands of gallons. From these large bulk terminals, the crude petroleum is placed in a pipeline the diameter of which may reach 36 inches (91 centimetres). Since crude oil comes in various grades, minimum quantities of about 50,000 barrels (one barrel equals 55 gallons or about 220 litres) at one time are put into the pipeline system.

After refining, the finished product is either stored in bulk terminals for later pipeline delivery to smaller markets in the area or is carried by tank truck for local delivery to gasoline stations. Fuel oil moves directly to large users or distributors by pipeline.

Oil tankers typically carry petroleum and its products across large bodies of water. In the past few decades, supertankers with dead weight up to 300,000 tons have taken over most international oil movements. While increasing the risk of spills of very large magnitude, these tankers have substantially reduced the cost of handling and moving oil, acting, in effect, as extensions of the pipeline system.

Like oil, natural gas flows, and pipelines are typically employed for its transmission. Since natural gas can be compressed, it is frequently stored near markets under pressure in large circular tanks or underground. Above-ground tanks have movable upper halves that rise and fall as stored content varies. This feature of natural-gas handling allows close to 100 percent utilization of the pipeline in spite of large seasonal changes in demand. Another important feature of natural gas is its ability, when subjected to extremely low temperatures, to shrink substantially in volume. Thus, natural gas at low temperatures may be shipped in containers over long distances by rail, motor truck, or ship and may at the receiving point be permitted to expand to normal operating temperature and volume.

Moving slurries

A slurry consists of finely ground solid material suspended in a liquid carrier, usually water. Coal, pulverized and mixed with water, can be moved by pipeline. Major users of coal slurries are electric utilities. Slurries have also been moved via pipeline for short distances and can then be partially dried at terminal points before pumping onto a ship. Water is again added after the material leaves the ship so that it can be sent by pipeline to the final user. The advantage of this system is that it minimizes handling costs between pipeline and ship.

In the case of coal, gasification is sometimes employed as a basic materials-handling technique. In this process, the coal is burned in the ground and the products of combustion collected, or the coal is heated to form gas. These gases may then be burned to produce electrical energy that is transmitted over power lines. Alternatively, the gas is injected into a pipeline.

Nonflowable bulk commodities. Items in this category include iron ore, coal, limestone, cement, phosphate, potash, and sulfur. While some of the above can be made to flow, discussion here is limited to their nonflowable forms.

Most production in this category involves materials-handling systems tied to water movements by ship or barge or to rail and motor-truck movements. Because of the large volumes moving at any one time, large-scale materials-handling equipment is typical at terminal points.

Coal is handled in much the same way as iron ore. The advantage of large-scale handling systems of the type used to transport coal and iron ore is their greater efficiency. While an ordinary freight train carrying carloads of several different types of merchandise typically averages about 3 to 6 miles (5 to 10 kilometres) per hour, a train transporting coal only may average 30 to 50 miles (50 to 80 kilometres) per hour because it moves directly from the source to point of use with no intermediate stops. Thus, the use of open-pit mining methods, combined with modern materials handling, can bring a fivefold increase in the productivity of the train. Because of the higher capital cost of materials-handling equipment, however, the total system saving is considerably less, but still substantial.

Another example of this type of materials-handling system is the synthetic fertilizer industry. The principal ingredients of fertilizer—phosphate, potash, and nitrogen, plus an inert carrier—are brought together at a single processing plant and mixed to specifications. While nitrogen is extracted from the atmosphere at numerous locations, phosphate and potash are taken from mines. Furthermore, fertilizer demand is subject to wide seasonal variations. After its extraction from the earth, phosphate is moved by truck or conveyor to a rail siding for shipment to a mixing plant. The typical large fertilizer company has a network of mixing plants centred in large agricultural areas. The product is mixed close to market because rail bulk shipment of its ingredients is the cheapest part of the entire handling and distribution process. After mixing, the finished product is placed in hoppers for loading into covered railcars or trucks equipped with self-unloading equipment. Some large farms have their own fertilizer hoppers and dump the product directly into a mechanical applicator.

High-volume manufactured-parts supply. The materials-handling system for this category of goods, which typically includes automobile parts and other durable consumer goods, revolves around four basic needs: ar-

rival of the product at the processing point as close to scheduled need as possible; designing the materials-handling system, including packaging, to fit production processes as closely as possible; compatibility with transport types employed; and finished product availability at minimum cost. Great attention to the details of materials-handling equipment design is focussed in these areas, with unitization the basic principle employed. Unitization involves the handling of large volumes as a unit; thus, several thousand automobile parts may be packaged together on one warehouse pallet and not be unpacked again until they are put into the assembly line. The optimum size of package and pallet or container is crucial to handling efficiency and to the use of space in storage and transportation.

Values of unitization

Continuous-processing systems. In continuous processing, work progresses through the production system at a fixed rate. The flour and baking industries employ continuous-processing techniques, as do certain chemical producers and makers of textiles and agricultural products. The process need not depend upon the flowable characteristics of the product. The auto assembly plant is a case in point, as are steel mills. In these kinds of continuous processing, the materials-handling function is highly automated, with relatively high capital investment in automatic systems. In the most sophisticated continuous-process systems, the work function consists largely of electronically or mechanically controlling automated product flow over continuously operating equipment. Sometimes the system includes computerized control that requires simple monitoring only.

In the work-station processing system, materials move from one work station to the next in sequence, stopping at each. The role of materials handling in this type of operation involves assuring maximum productivity at each work station (see AUTOMATION; MASS PRODUCTION) and smoothing the flow of semifinished goods from one work station to the next.

MATERIALS-HANDLING EQUIPMENT

Materials-handling equipment may be classified in terms of the type of product handled, thus including machinery for bulk products in large continuous volumes; continuous processing based on industrial-parts movement; discontinuous processing of a wide variety of goods; and order filling of large varieties of goods.

A second classification relates to the mobility characteristics of the materials-handling equipment and includes both stationary and movable facilities.

A third classification, which identifies the type of equipment itself, includes wheeled carts, power and lift trucks, trailer trains, racks and pallets, bins and boxes, monorails and conveyors, containers, unit loads, and cranes and hoists.

Wheeled carts. Though they are among the more primitive materials-handling-equipment types, carts with two or four wheels are still quite widely used. A cart merely permits a man to move a larger volume of goods at one time and is generally used where distances are short and labour costs low. Shifting of a product from a storage area adjacent to the production line is a case in point. Laundries, bakeries, wholesalers, and other industries of this type characteristically use carts.

Power trucks. This equipment improves the productivity of labour by increasing both the speed and the size of load. Forklifts are among the most common power trucks now used. Trucks for general packaged merchandise usually are designed to convey from 2,000 to 4,000 pounds (900 to 1,800 kilograms). Power trucks of larger capacity are designed for special product handling. Lumber yards, for example, have large-capacity trucks usually of a straddle type that can lift 10,000 to 20,000 pounds (4,500 to 9,000 kilograms) of lumber.

Straddle trucks

Trailer trains. As their name implies, trailer trains consist of a single powered tractor with one or more four-wheeled carts attached. These usually follow a specific route covering a number of loading and unloading stations and are particularly useful where the flows of packaged materials are large and continuous.

Racks and pallets. Racks consist of stationary wood or steel frames designed to store a product. In effect, a three-tier-rack system provides three separate storage areas at one location. Material stored in racks may or may not be palletized—*i.e.*, stored on platforms for ready handling. Rack and pallet systems usually require the use of a forklift truck or a pallet jack to lift the pallet off the floor by hydraulic or electric power. Palletless systems usually are employed where products are very light and bulky, occupying a disproportionate amount of space for the weight stored. In this case, a special cleanup truck is employed; it is designed to grasp the equivalent of a pallet load of material, but without the need for the pallet itself. Products are stored one on top of the other in the storage area. Soaps and cereals typically employ this system (see STORAGE AND WAREHOUSING).

Bins and boxes. Bins and boxes find widest application in the storage of numerous small parts in one container. Nuts, bolts, and fittings are stored in bins and boxes until required. Typically, the entire bin or box is moved to the production line at a specific work station. In some industries, bins and boxes store commodities at the point of sale. Auto dealers, parts suppliers, and hardware merchants use bins and boxes for numerous small parts.

Monorails and conveyors. Animal carcasses or parts requiring painting, spraying, or dipping are typically hung on hooks or other devices and moved along on an overhead rail. Conveyors may be powered or gravity run or manually fed on belts, rollers, wheels, or hoppers; they may be fixed or portable and open to the air or closed; and they may carry loose, bulk, or packaged materials.

Conveyors typically find use in production or handling processes requiring more or less continuous operations. Post offices often use conveyors to speed mail sorting. Similarly, manufacturers and distributors find conveyors useful in sorting large numbers of parts destined for customers in different locations. In production facilities, conveyors provide a capability of scheduling work flows across work stations at optimum rates. In this case, the product is moved across a number of different work stations providing maximum employment of effort at production instead of materials handling.

For bulk products, such as sand, gravel, and ores, large-capacity conveyors frequently provide connecting links between processes. Thus, a railcar may intermittently unload coal in large quantities outdoors while a conveyor feeds the coal continuously to a furnace.

Portable conveyors find application where volumes are not large and work stations may move from one point to another. Bagged or bulk merchandise in fairly heavy weights delivered to a number of different stations in a warehouse may require portable conveyors as a loading and unloading aid.

Containers. Containers are intended to limit the number of times a product is handled. Constructed of wood, metal, or heavy corrugated paperboard, containers may consist of relatively small boxes or cages to full trailer dimensions. When a trailer is used as a container, it is typically designed for heavy stresses so that it may be lifted with its entire load and placed aboard a flatbed truck trailer, railcar, ship, or airplane. The most recent application of containers of very large size is called LASH, for Lighter Aboard Ship. In this operation, entire barges are lashed to an especially designed oceangoing ship for transfer to distant destinations. Container ships of the traditional type may carry containers that look like ordinary truck trailers. Advantages of containers include substantial increases in production (as much as 40,000 pounds [18,000 kilograms] may be handled in 30 seconds); minimized handling of individual products or packages throughout the system; and less risk of pilferage at transfer points.

Unit loads. These are similar to containers. A unit load consists of a homogeneous grouping of the same or similar commodities, moved as a unit, while freight in containers may be mixed and heterogeneous. A unit load need not be in a container; flat sheets of plywood, bound together with metal strapping and sheathed in paper, are a case in point.

Cranes and hoists. Generally employed for very heavy lifting and moving of machinery and materials, cranes and hoists may be fixed or movable.

Jib cranes, which consist of single arms attached to walls or other structures, have the capability of swinging through an angle of 180° to 360° and therefore are useful for positioning material. Jib cranes are frequently observed in high-rise building construction, where they are set on the topmost floor to move construction materials vertically to the floor that is being worked and horizontally to the place where needed.

Bridge cranes consist of heavy metal beams holding a hoist. The beams, with wheeled ends, traverse a set of guides set at an elevation. The hoist moves vertically in lifting material and horizontally across the bridge in moving it. The entire bridge may move along the girders. Thus, three-dimensional movements over large square or rectangular areas are possible. This type of crane is used in handling large electrical generators and other heavy equipment from one work station to another or in moving heavy parts to a fixed station.

Stacker cranes are used to stack and retrieve materials, usually in close quarters. Typically, they ride along an aisle and lift materials vertically on a platform or other end device up to 30-foot (nine-metre) heights. Stacker cranes have also been employed in automated storage and retrieval systems. Each stack location is given a code number that is placed on a punched card or other control device. When a shipment or order is received, the punched card is inserted to activate the system, and the stacker crane automatically finds the right location.

Gantry cranes have a movable structure similar to bridge cranes. The major difference is that the gantry legs of the crane are wheeled and set in a rail in the ground. The horizontal bar, or bridge, may extend beyond the moving legs of the crane so that clockwise unloading of ores and other materials may be accomplished by the overreach of the crane. Gantries also are used in moving industrial goods from rail cars to plant site and in lifting fully loaded containers or trailers onto a flatbed railcar.

Mobile cranes are wheeled devices with their own motive power, which enables them to move over wide areas. They are generally of the jib type with a single boom attached to the mobile body.

The endpiece of handling equipment on a crane depends upon the product moved and may be tongs, grabs, slings, hooks, magnets, or buckets.

TRANSPORTATION

Evaluating transportation alternatives. Transportation techniques can be evaluated in terms of time, space, cube, weight carried, and cost.

Time refers to the total number of hours necessary to complete a transfer of goods. An airplane, for example, which provides great transit speeds, may connect with a truck at both pickup and delivery points. Thus, although flight time may be typically 5 hours, the total time needed to complete a delivery may be as much as 24 hours.

Space refers to the coverage of pickup and delivery points that a particular form of transport offers. Most flexible in this respect is the truck, as it can reach any point where a road exists and some locations where one does not. Pipelines are least flexible.

Cube describes the efficiency with which the transport unit is utilized. Optimum utilization of cube results in maximum efficiency of movement, since waste space is held to a minimum. Cube limitations are particularly relevant in transport forms such as truck trailers and airplanes. Railroads do not suffer cube limits in the same way, as freight cars can easily be added to a train.

Weight is particularly important, as the cost of transportation is generally quoted in terms of cost per unit of weight. Weight and cube are interrelated since very light, bulky items will not result in heavy loadings and thus will show a high cost per unit of weight shipped. For this reason many items, such as bicycles, are shipped in partially disassembled form.

(margin notes:)
LASH containers

Cube as a limiting factor

Cost of transport is influenced by the four factors mentioned. Generally, the heavier the loading and the higher the density (cube), the lower the cost. Costs increase with speed, however, and with the number of deliveries (space).

The interrelationships of the four factors affecting cost and capacity of various transport types are not always readily apparent. Modern cargo jet airplanes, for example, can carry as much as 125 tons of product. An oceangoing general cargo vessel may carry 10,000 tons in one shipment. The airplane can make one trip a day between Europe and the United States, whereas the cargo vessel can at best make one round trip a week. Thus, over a two-week period, a fully loaded cargo vessel carries 20,000 tons, whereas the airplane carries 3,500 tons in the same period. From this perspective, the cargo capacity of an airplane is about 15 percent as much as a cargo vessel.

Modes of transport. The major modes of transportation are highway, rail, pipeline, ocean, inland waterway, and air.

Highway motor truck. Trucks and trailers may be of generalized or specialized design. The typical over-the-road trailer is a generalized type of vehicle capable of handling wide ranges of bulk and packaged goods. Specialized trailers, such as refrigerated, liquid-tank, dry-flowable, heavy-duty, and household-goods vans carry limited ranges of commodities.

The main point of contact between trucking and other modes of transportation is in loading and unloading. Ideally, loading and unloading facilities are arranged to keep delays to a minimum. Thus, packaged goods of general merchandise, such as groceries, are expensive to load manually and placing them upon pallets is preferred whenever possible. A higher level of development (with lower cost) is the platform-loaded unitized load, in which a movable floor on wheels is built into the truck. A winch device is used to move the whole floor in and out of the truck. The advantage of this system is that the platform can be preloaded before truck arrival, and unloaded at leisure after truck delivery.

Unitized load

In single-package unloading, the limit of movement is as much as a man can carry. In pallet movement, the limit is set by the forklift truck—usually 2,000 to 4,000 pounds —whereas in unit-platform loading, 20,000 pounds or more can be unloaded in one move.

Rail. Through restricted to a single, set rail path, the railroad is the most efficient overland method of transportation for large volumes of bulk materials over relatively long distances.

In the past, railroad freight consisted of coal, petroleum, grain, lumber, automobiles, and similar large volume products. To handle them, the railcar fleet included boxcars, flatcars, hoppers, and other basic types. Competition from larger and more efficient trucks and trailers, inland barges, ships, and pipelines and changes in the outlooks of transport users—who began to choose among alternatives in terms both of service and price—forced the rails to innovate and to design special equipment and cars for specific commodity groups. The boxcar, for example, proved a costly alternative to truck trailers. As the rails lost business, they responded by introducing the trilevel car, capable of carrying a dozen automobiles in place of the boxcar's capacity of four. Loading and unloading operations were also greatly facilitated.

Lumber and a number of other commodities are now handled in similar ways. The all-door boxcar permits side loading of long dimension products such as lumber with modern forklift trucks in bundles at a much faster rate and at lower cost than the conventional boxcar. Flatcars are also employed for unitized materials that do not need enclosed protection in shipping.

Unit trains

Another recent development in materials handling by rail is the unit train, designed to carry a single commodity from point of origin to destination. Coal, grain, and other bulk materials frequently move in unit trainloads of thousands of tons at substantially reduced rates.

Typically, the unit train requires especially designed cars as well as rather sophisticated materials-handling systems for loading and unloading. Hoppers or large cranes may be employed at the loading point. If a hopper is employed, the railcar moves under the hopper, and gravity feed is employed to load each car in turn. By this method, a single carload of coal may be loaded in less than a minute. Cranes achieve much the same result.

At the receiving end rapid unloading is achieved by gravity, dropping the product onto a storage pile. There is no need to stop the car for unloading of this type, as a simple trip device can be used to open the hopper-car chute and permit the product to fall into the storage area. Cranes and other unloading devices are also used.

Piggyback operations consist of two basic types. One provides a flatcar about 80 feet (24 metres) long that permits loading two over-the-road truck trailers with undercarriage attached. The second type consists of two containers of truck-trailer configuration without undercarriage attached, loaded on flatcars.

The economic advantage of both types lies in the substitution of lower costs of moving railcars, as opposed to trailers, over the road. Rather sophisticated loading and unloading terminal facilities are required at origin and destination. For trailer-on-flatcar operations, an asphalt apron adjacent to the tracks is required. The wheeled trailers are hauled onto the flatcar with an ordinary trailer truck.

In container trains without undercarriage attached overhead gantry cranes, capable of lifting fully loaded trailers off their undercarriage, are required. The truck trailer, in this case, consists of a flatbed truck similar to a rail flatcar.

Ocean transportation. Ocean transportation consists of two major types: self-contained vessels of bulk or general-cargo type, and general or special-purpose barges and containers of 3,000 to 5,000 tons capacity moving in especially designed oceangoing vessels.

General-cargo vessels carry a wide range of commodities, typically of the packaged or nonbulk types, and concentrate their activity on major routes where large volumes of potential freight traffic exist. These larger vessels are complemented by smaller itinerant (tramp) steamers or even sailing vessels that chiefly serve the smaller ports. Interisland steamers in the Caribbean and the Pacific and smaller sailing vessels in the Mediterranean fill local needs.

The most important oceangoing general-cargo vessels are conference carriers, which belong to a worldwide association of shipping interests that attempts to control the pricing of oceangoing general freight. Control is accomplished by requiring shippers to agree to ship on conference-member ships or pay a penalty. In return, the shipper generally receives the benefit of higher quality service in the ocean trades, including materials handling of a generally superior type, often with self-unloading devices, access to stevedoring services, customs assistance, agency assistance in ancillary services, and others.

In the bulk trades, the outstanding recent development is the construction of so-called supertankers. These very large tankers, dwarfing all other ships afloat, move large quantities of product, chiefly petroleum, over very long distances at very low unit costs. Despite these advantages, the supertankers have stirred controversy because of their potential for huge oil spills. Other bulk carriers specialize in hauling grain, fluid materials other than oil, and ores.

Combination types of vessels have recently entered the ocean trades. The three major combination types are railcars on ferry ships; container ships, carrying truck-trailer type containers below deck and above; and LASH, for transporting barges aboard a ship. Combination types permit materials handling in containers of relatively large size, which results in greater cargo security and, perhaps more important, increases the speed of port handling and thus reduces the round trip time of the vessel. On the North Atlantic trade, container ships maintain a five-day sailing schedule and a two-week round-trip transit time. A typical general-cargo ship, especially if it is making more than one port of call, takes 30 days or more.

Inland waterways. On inland waterways, barges of the pushing or pulling type predominate. The push barges common on the inland waterways of the United States employ a power push boat (tug) behind a line of barges. Pull types, common in Europe, attach a tow line to the barge. A single tow may power 10 to 20 barges.

Air transport. Though air transport is the fastest method of moving freight over long distances, trucks must be used for local delivery. Because of its high cost, air transport is generally restricted to high-value products.

Air freight moves either in converted passenger aircraft or in freighters. Carrying capacity for the smaller jets and older propeller planes is very restricted, but the larger jets can carry up to 70,000 pounds in all-freight configurations and the "jumbo jets" as much as 250,000 pounds.

Because of the high capital cost of airplanes, it is necessary to limit loading time on the ground. Large freight terminals serving jet aircraft usually use conveyor systems of various types to handle a large assortment of different types of packages. These assortments are typically placed in containers designed to fit smoothly inside the airplane so that cube may be utilized to the maximum. Containers and pallets may be loaded by forklift trucks if the airplane is side loaded, or by winches or forklifts, if tail loaded. Some of the large airplanes now flying can carry upward of 100 automobiles at one time. For specialized products such as cars, special handling systems have been developed.

BIBLIOGRAPHY. EUGENE R. SIMS, *Planning and Managing Material Flow* (1968), a comprehensive industrial engineering treatment including equipment classification and system designs; *Materials Handling Handbook* (1958, periodically updated), a comprehensive resource for techniques and equipment; *Materials Handling Manual*, 4 vol. (1955, periodically updated), detailed information on principles, cost, equipment, and applications; D.J. BOWERSOX, E.W. SMYKAY, and B.J. La LONDE, *Physical Distribution Management* (1968), a description of materials handling in the context of the total marketing, production, and distribution system of the firm; CREED H. JENKINS, *Modern Warehouse Management* (1968), on materials handling in warehouse operations; CHARLES L. HANCHETT, *Integrated Packaging and Material Handling* (1958), emphasis on the relationship of packaging to materials handling; DEAN S. AMMER, *Materials Management* (1962), written from a purchasing perspective; CHARLES A. TAFF, *Management of Traffic and Physical Distribution*, 3rd ed. (1964), a transportation-oriented text that includes materials handling considerations; WILLIAM T. MORRIS, *Analysis for Materials Handling Management* (1962), a mathematical approach to systems design; AMERICAN MANAGEMENT ASSOCIATION, *Physical Distribution Management: The Total Systems Route to New Profits* (1967), a programmed instruction approach to aid learning of handling and storage principles; NATIONAL COUNCIL OF PHYSICAL DISTRIBUTION MANAGEMENT, *Bibliography on Physical Distribution Management*, (updated annually), extensive listings of literature in the field; HARRY BRUCE, *Distribution and Transportation Handbook* (1970), references to materials handling within the distribution context of the firm.

(E.W.S.)

Materials Processing

Materials processing is the name generally used to cover those operations that are used to transform industrial materials from a raw-material state into finished parts or products. Industrial materials are defined as those used in the manufacture of "hard" goods, such as more or less durable machines and equipment produced for industry and consumers, as contrasted to disposable "soft" goods such as chemicals, foodstuffs, pharmaceuticals, and apparel.

Detailed treatment of many of these processes will be found in such other articles as METALLURGY; PLASTICS AND RESINS; and STEEL PRODUCTION. The present article provides a summary description of the wide variety of materials-processing techniques in use in modern industry.

Materials processing by hand is as old as civilization; mechanization began with the Industrial Revolution of the 18th century, and in the early 19th century the basic machines for forming, shaping, and cutting were developed, principally in England. Since then, materials-processing methods, techniques, and machinery have grown in great variety and number.

The cycle of manufacturing processes that converts materials into parts and products starts immediately after the raw materials are either extracted from minerals or produced from basic chemicals or natural substances. Metallic raw materials are usually produced in two steps: First the crude ore is processed to increase the concentration of the desired metal; this is called beneficiation. Typical beneficiation processes include crushing, roasting, magnetic separation, flotation, and leaching. Second, additional processes such as smelting and alloying are used to produce the metal that is to be fabricated into parts for assembly in the ultimate product.

In the case of ceramic materials, natural clay is mixed and blended with various silicates to produce the raw material. Plastic resins are produced by chemical methods in powder, pellet, putty, or liquid form. Synthetic rubber is also made by chemical techniques, being produced, as is natural rubber, in such forms as slabs, sheeting, crepe, and foam for fabricating into finished parts.

The processes used to convert raw materials into finished products perform one or both of two major functions: first, they form the material into the desired shape; second, they alter or improve the properties of the material.

Functions of processing

FORMING

Forming and shaping processes can be conveniently classified into two broad types—those performed on the material in a liquid state and those performed on the material in a solid or plastic condition.

Liquid-state metal processing. The processing of materials in liquid form is commonly known as casting when it involves metals, glass, and ceramics; it is molding when applied to plastics and some other nonmetallic materials.

Most casting and molding processes involve four major steps: (1) making an accurate pattern of the part; (2) making a mold from the pattern; (3) introducing the liquid into the mold; and (4) removing the hardened part from the mold. A finishing operation is sometimes needed.

Sand-casting. This technique employs molds made of sand to which varying amounts of resinous binders have been added. The process is most widely used for iron and steel castings and is applicable for parts ranging from a few pounds to several tons in weight. Sand castings of great complexity are readily produced.

Permanent-mold casting. This process makes repeated use of the same molds made in two or more parts hinged and clamped for easy removal of the finished castings. The materials that can be so cast are generally limited to aluminum and magnesium, although some kinds of iron, zinc, and lead are sometimes cast by this process. The average size of permanent-mold castings varies from about half a pound to about 12 pounds (0.2 to five kilograms).

Plaster-mold casting. This method of casting utilizes molds made from a slurry (water mixture) of gypsum. The castings have fine finishes, and surface detail is faithfully reproduced. Plaster-mold castings are usually small, up to 20 pounds (nine kilograms). The process is particularly suitable for thin wall parts—down to about $\frac{1}{16}$ inch (1.5 millimetres) thick. Though most plaster-mold castings are of copper alloys, aluminum and magnesium may also be used.

Investment casting. Frequently referred to as the lost-wax (cire perdue) process, investment casting was first used centuries ago in China. Later, such artists as Cellini employed it in the 16th century. A pattern, called an investment, is made of wax, frozen mercury, or plastic in and around a master die. The investment is then covered inside and out with a slurry of ceramic material. After the ceramic mold hardens, the investment is melted out, leaving the cavity into which the molten metal is poured. Investment casting is relatively expensive, but it is suitable for almost any fine configuration and for wall thicknesses as thin as $\frac{1}{64}$ inch (0.4 millimetre). Castings weighing up to 25 pounds (11 kilograms) and over can be produced in most castable metals.

Die-casting. This process, best suited of all the metal-casting processes for high production rates, involves forcing molten metal under pressure into closed metallic dies. Because the dies are solid, the complexity of shapes which may be handled is more restricted than with sandcasting. Most die castings are made of zinc or aluminum but other metals, including copper alloys, lead, and tin can be die-cast. Aluminum parts approaching 100 pounds (45 kilograms) and zinc parts as heavy as 200 pounds (90 kilograms) can be die-cast.

Electroforming. This is essentially a plating process. A mandrel or core pattern of the part is placed in a plating bath and metal is deposited to the desired thickness on the surface. Then the part is removed from the bath, and the core separated from the deposited metal. The finished part is a self-supporting structure with inside dimensions matching those of the mandrel, or core.

Nonmetallics casting and molding. Molding and casting of plastics is performed with the plastic material either in a hot molten state or as a liquid at or near room temperature.

Liquid casting. Liquid or sirupy plastic resins or elastomers (rubbers) to be cast are poured into molds and cured either by heating or chemical reaction. Sheets, rods, and special shapes are produced by casting.

Low-pressure molding. Reinforced plastic moldings can be made by mixing liquid resins with mats or fibres of such materials as glass or asbestos and molding at a low pressure.

Slush and rotational molding. Combinations of resins, elastomers, plasticizers, and other ingredients in liquid or paste form, called plastisols, and in the form of gels, called plastigels, are used in so-called slush and rotational molding in which the material is placed in a mold and allowed to form a layer on the mold surface. The remaining unsolidified material is then removed.

Slip casting. This technique, similar to slush molding, is widely used for making ceramic parts. A stable suspension of a mixture of clay in water is first poured or rotated in a porous mold. The porous mold sucks up the liquid, leaving a solid layer of the material. Ceramics and glass are also cast in the molten state as in metal casting.

Injection molding. In injection molding, the plastic resin is melted in a heating chamber and forced under pressure into a closed cold-metal mold, which is then opened and the finished part removed. Injection molding is primarily for thermoplastics, although it is used for molding some thermoset plastics; that is, plastics that cannot be resoftened by heat after setting. Like its diecasting counterpart for metals, this is a relatively fast, high production process and is suitable for parts weighing from around 2 to 300 ounces.

Compression molding. In this technique, commonly used for forming thermosetting plastics, resin powders or granules, after being placed in an open mold, are converted into a liquid under heat and pressure when the mold closes. The solid, finished form is produced on cooling in the mold.

Transfer molding. A modification of compression molding, this process involves heating the resin in a separate chamber and forcing it into a heated closed-mold cavity.

Processing solid materials. Materials in their solid state are formed into desired shapes by the application of a force or pressure. The material to be processed can be in a relatively hard and stable condition and in such forms as bar, sheet, pellet, or powder or it can be in a soft, plastic, or putty-like form. Solid materials can be shaped either hot or cold.

Processing of metals in the solid state can be divided into two major stages: first, the raw material in the form of large ingots or billets is hot-worked, usually by rolling, forging, or extrusion, into smaller shapes and sizes; second, these shapes are processed into final parts and products by one or more smaller scale hot or cold forming processes.

Rolling. This is the most common primary metalforming process. Hot metal ingots or billets are passed through a series of rolls that work the metal in successive stages into the desired cross-sectional shape and size. Plate, sheet, strip, bar, and rod shapes are rolled, as well as such special shapes as I-beams, channels, and angles.

Extrusion. In this process, used for producing long lengths of rod, tubing, and other cross-sectional shapes, hot or cold metal is forced through a die of the desired cross section. The process is widely used to produce intricate shapes, chiefly in copper alloys, aluminum, and magnesium.

Forging. One of the most widely used metal-forming processes, forging involves the working of either hot or cold metal into the desired shape by impact or pressing. Most metals can be forged. Forging processes are generally more expensive than casting, but they produce parts with greater strength and toughness.

The simplest and oldest method is open-die forging in which the hot metal piece is constantly turned as it is being shaped by a mechanical hammer. The method is limited to such large, heavy shapes as shafts and die and gear blanks. *Open-die forging*

Drop-forging is a refinement of the open-die process. Hot billets are forged into an open die by the repeated impact of a mechanical hammer. Often, a series of progressive dies are needed to attain the final shape. Drop forgings vary in weight from about one ounce (28 grams) to several tons.

Upset forging is used to make relatively small to medium-size parts from rod stock; that is, a long piece of raw material in the form of a rod. The end of a heated rod stock, while gripped between portions of a die, is struck by another die. The upsetting action reduces the length and increases the diameter of the rod to produce the desired shape.

In cold-heading, similar in principle to upset forging, cold wire stock is fed automatically to the dies and shaped by upsetting. Extremely high production rates are reached in the manufacture of a wide variety of such small parts as nails. Swaging, the opposite of cold-heading, is a cold-working process in which a rotary hammering action reduces the diameter and increases the length of a piece of rod or tubing.

Press-forging employs pressure rather than impact to squeeze hot metal, placed between dies, into the desired shape. As in drop-forging, progressive dies frequently are used. This process is most commonly used for forgings weighing 25 to 30 pounds (11 to 14 kilograms).

Impact extrusion can be considered either as a cold forging or as an extrusion process. A slug of metal placed in a die is subjected to the pressure of a punch, causing the metal to flow into the space between the punch and the die. The process is widely used for making collapsible tubes of soft metals.

Stamping and pressing. These two processes make up another large family of metal-forming techniques, all of which are used to cut or form metal plate, sheet, and strip. Almost all metals can be blanked and formed. The steps common to all these operations are the preparation of a flat blank and the shearing or stretching of the metal into a die to attain the desired shape. The forming process is either drawing or stamping. In drawing, the flat stock is either formed in a single operation or progressive drawing steps may be needed to reach the final form. Stamping involves placing the flat stock in a die and striking it with a movable die or punch. Besides shaping the part, the dies can perform perforating, bending, and shearing operations. In general, stampings are limited to metal thicknesses of ⅜ inch (10 millimetres) or less. Pressing and drawing operations can be performed on cold metals up to ¾ inch (19 millimetres) thick and on hot metals up to about 3½ inches (89 millimetres).

In the 1960s many new press forming and drawing techniques were developed, a number of them making use of rubber pads, bags, and diaphragms as part of the die or forming elements. Some involve stretch forming over dies; others combine forming and heat-treating operations. Still other methods, known as high energy rate forming, employ explosives, electrical energy, or magnetic energy to produce shock waves that form the material into the desired shape. *New press techniques*

Powder metallurgy processing. This involves the production of parts from metals in powder form by compacting the powder in a die to the desired form and heating (sintering) to fuse the powders together. A secondary press operation, known as coining, is sometimes performed on the sintered part. Most metals and many combinations of materials can be formed in this way. Parts ranging in size from less than an inch to around six inches in diameter (20 to 150 millimetres), and up to five or six inches long, can be produced.

Metal strip can also be produced from metal powders. The metal powder, chiefly copper or nickel, is cold-rolled into a continuous strip that passes through a sintering furnace and then through a hot-rolling mill to produce the final thickness and density.

Nonmetallic forming. Plastics, ceramics, rubber, and other nonmetallics are formed in the solid or plastic state by processes similar to many of those used for metals. In the sheet forming of thermoplastic materials, the sheet is heated above its softening point, then shaped over a mold by the application of pressure much as in metal-pressing operations. The molding pressure is applied by mechanical or hydraulic force, by preheated compressed air, or by vacuum techniques.

Calendering, widely used for producing plastic-, rubber-, and paper-sheeted products, consists of forming a continuous sheet by squeezing the softened material between two or more rolls.

In extrusion processes, the softened material is forced through a die approximating the desired cross-sectional shape. Most thermoplastics and some thermoset plastics can be extruded as well as rubber, glass, and ceramics.

Powder molding of plastics Powder molding of plastics involves the sintering or fusing of plastic powder to conform to the surface of a mold. Glass and ceramics in powder form are pressed and fused into complex shapes by much the same general techniques used in powder metallurgy. The pressing operation can be done either wet or dry. With certain refractory (high-melting, heat-resistant) ceramic powders, the pressing operation is performed at high temperatures, thus eliminating the sintering step.

Blow molding is a common method for producing hollow plastic objects. Essentially, the process involves using air pressure to force the plastic material to take the shape of the mold. Glassblowing is a somewhat analogous process for forming glass.

MATERIAL REMOVAL

In materials processing, a removal process is one that eliminates portions of a piece or body of material to achieve a desired shape. Although removal processes can be and are applied to most types of materials, they are most widely used on metallic materials. Material can be removed from a workpiece by either mechanical or nonmechanical means.

Mechanical machining (cutting). There are a number of metal-cutting processes. In almost all of them, machining involves the forcing of a cutting tool against the material to be shaped. The tool, which is harder than the material to be cut, removes the unwanted material in the form of chips. Thus, the elements of machining are a cutting device, a means for holding and positioning the workpiece, and usually a lubricant (or cutting oil). Cutting-tool materials must have a combination of strength, toughness, hardness, and wear resistance at the relatively high temperatures generated by the cutting action.

Turning The oldest and most common machining process is turning, in which the workpiece is simply rotated while a cutting tool moves parallel to its axis, cutting the material away to reduce its diameter.

Shaping and planing are used to cut material from plane surfaces. The cutting tool takes successive cuts straight across the surface of the workpiece in a predetermined pattern to achieve the desired shape. The milling process, in which the cutting is done by rotating multiple-tool cutters, is also used for facing plane surfaces and for cutting grooves and slots. Holes are cut, enlarged, and shaped by drilling, boring, and tapping operations.

Grinding, honing, and lapping remove material with abrasives, which may be bonded in belts or rotating wheels (grinding), or in a fine abrasive stone (honing), or in a soft material with abrasive particles embedded in it (lapping). In another method, ultrasonic machining, abrasive particles remove material by high-velocity bombardment of the workpiece. A mixture of air or inert gas under pressure can also be used to direct a high-velocity stream of fine abrasive particles against the workpiece.

Nonmechanical machining (chipless). There are four basic chipless removal processes: (1) in chemical milling the metal is removed by the etching reaction of chemical solutions on the metal; although usually applied to metals, it can also be used on plastics and glass; (2) electrochemical machining uses the principle of metal plating in reverse, the workpiece, instead of being built up by the plating process, is eaten away in a controlled manner by the action of the electrical current (see also ELECTROPLATING); (3) electrodischarge machining and grinding erodes or cuts the metal by high-energy sparks or electrical discharges; (4) the laser beam has limited application as a chipless cutting tool.

JOINING

Joining is the process of permanently, sometimes only temporarily, bonding or attaching materials to each other. The term as used here includes welding, brazing, soldering, and adhesive and chemical bonding.

Types of energy used in bonding In most joining processes, a bond between two pieces of material is produced by application of one or a combination of three kinds of energy: thermal, chemical, or mechanical. A bonding or filler material, the same as or different from the materials being joined, may or may not be used.

Thermal joining. Three broad groups of processes use heat (thermal energy) to bond materials together: pressure welding, fusion welding, and brazing and soldering (see also WELDING, BRAZING, and SOLDERING).

Pressure welding. Sometimes called forge welding, this oldest known welding process involves the heating of the areas to be joined to a plastic condition. The heated surfaces are placed in contact with each other and bonded together by hammering or pressing. In oxyacetylene pressure welding, a gas flame heats the abutting ends of the pieces to be joined. In resistance welding, the joint surfaces are heated by a heavy, localized electric current before mechanical pressure is applied to produce the finished bond.

Fusion welding. In fusion welding, the edges of the materials to be joined are heated to the melting point and flow together to achieve localized coalescence. On cooling, a permanent bond is produced. A filler material, the same as or different from the materials being joined, may be melted in the joint area as part of the bonding process.

The heat energy used to bring the metals to the fusion point is provided by any one of a number of sources—electric arc or current, induction heating, atomic hydrogen stream, burning fuels or gases, electron beam, exothermic chemical reaction, and laser beams.

Heat sealing Most metals can be joined by one or more fusion methods. Some thermoplastic-type plastics can also be fusion welded by a gas flame, heated tool, and friction techniques. Heat-sealing, a widely used method for joining plastic films and sheets, involves heating the adjacent surfaces and then fusing them together under pressure.

Brazing and soldering. Although this technique is used primarily to join metals, such nonmetallics as ceramics, glass, and graphite are also brazable. Soldering and brazing differ from fusion welding in that the edges or surfaces of the materials being joined are kept below their melting temperature during the bonding process. Only the filler metal, which is always used and which is different from the base metals, is in a molten condition. The part or the joint area of the metals is heated to above the melting temperature of the filler metal, which flows into the joint and coalesces with the base metals to produce the bond. Brazing, by definition, involves the use of filler metals that melt at 800° F (430° C) or higher, and soldering employs filler metals that melt below 800° F. A third method known as braze welding is the same as brazing except that it does not utilize capillary attraction to distribute the filler metal.

Many nonferrous metals, especially copper, nickel, and

the precious metals, are easily brazed or soldered. Aluminum brazing is common and some steels can be brazed. Brazing filler materials most commonly used include alloys of silver, copper, and gold. The commonly used solders include tin alloyed with antimony or silver or lead, leadsilver, cadmium alloyed with silver or zinc, and bismuth alloys. A number of heating methods can be used for brazing and soldering, including torch or flame, furnace or oven, electrical induction, molten metal or salt bath, electrical resistance, hot block or iron, and radiant lamp.

Adhesive bonding. Adhesive bonding processes make use of substances capable of holding materials together by surface attachment. Adhesives, which include cement, glue, and paste, are available or can be specially formulated to join almost any two of the same or dissimilar materials (see also ADHESIVES). In adhesive bonding the joint between materials is produced by either of two mechanisms: (1) chemical forces at the interface between an adhesive and the materials being joined, or (2) mechanical adhesion that involves an interlocking action at the molecular level of the adhesive and materials being joined.

The principal steps in adhesive bonding are: (1) preparation of the surface by chemical, mechanical, or electrical treatment; (2) application of the adhesive by spray, roller, extrusion, trowel, knife, brush coating, or film; (3) joining of the materials by application of pressure, sometimes accompanied by heat. Adhesives can be applied in a liquid, paste, powder, film, and tape form.

Solvent bonding, limited to thermoplastic plastics, uses a solvent to soften the bond areas, after which bonding is accomplished by the application of pressure.

Types of adhesives used

The major chemical classes of adhesives are natural, that is, vegetable- and animal-base adhesives and natural gums; thermoplastic, based on thermoplastic resins dissolved in solvent or emulsified in water; thermosetting, based on thermosetting resins; elastomeric, based on natural and synthetic rubbers; and alloys, adhesives compounded of resins from two or more of the other chemical classes. In addition to the above classes, a few inorganic adhesives are available for special applications.

Structural adhesives are those used in load-carrying applications as contrasted to general-purpose adhesives that are used in nonload applications, such as sealing and insulating. Elastomeric and thermoplastic adhesives are most commonly employed for general purpose or nonload-bearing uses. Most structural adhesives are thermosetting.

Adhesives classified by the curing characteristic or method include the following types: solvent release, emulsion, cold setting, hot setting, vulcanization, heat, and pressure.

PROPERTY MODIFICATION

The properties of materials can be altered by hot or cold treatments, by mechanical operations, and by exposure to some forms of radiation. The property modification is usually brought about by a change in the microscopic structure of the material.

Both heat-treating, involving temperatures above room temperature, and cold-treating, involving temperatures below room temperature, are included in this category. Thermal treatment is a process in which the temperature of the material is raised or lowered to alter the properties of the original material. Most thermal-treating processes are based on time–temperature cycles that include three steps: heating, holding at temperature, and cooling. Although some thermal treatments are applicable to most families of materials, they are most widely used on metals.

There are three major groups of heat-treating processes: annealing, stress relieving, and hardening.

1. In annealing and normalizing treatments, used to soften materials or improve ductility, the material is heated to the temperature at which the desired microstructural changes take place and then is slowly cooled; *e.g.*, for carbon steels annealing temperatures range from about 1,350° to 1,650° F (730° to 900° C).

2. Stress relieving, used to reduce or eliminate internal stresses in materials, as applied to metals, is similar to annealing except that lower temperatures are involved; for glass the term annealing is applied to the process of relieving the internal stresses that are built up during the forming and shaping of glass articles.

3. Hardening uses a wide variety of treatments to strengthen materials; the oldest and most widely used processes essentially involving the heating of material to a high temperature and suddenly quenching it with oil, water, or air, after which in some cases, a stress-relieving step follows, referred to as tempering (for glass) or drawing.

Hardening processes

A second group of hardening processes, known as precipitation, or age hardening, differ from the first group principally in that sudden changes in temperature are not usually involved and the internal hardening mechanism extends over a period of time.

A number of heat-treating processes may be used only for altering the surface of metals. In induction hardening, currents induced by radio-frequency energy generate heat in the surface of the metal. In flame hardening, the surface is heated by a flame. In both cases the part is subsequently quenched to produce a hardened surface.

Another technique involves heating the material in the presence of a substance that reacts with or diffuses into the surface and alters the surface properties, such as carburizing, in which a carbonaceous material supplies carbon to the metal surface and quenching produces a hardened surface layer. In cyaniding (carbonitriding) the metal is heated in an atmosphere containing carbon and nitrogen and then slowly cooled. A number of other such surface thermal treatments, often referred to as diffusion coating or cementation coating, each using a different diffusion substance, include aluminum (calorizing), chromium (chromizing), gaseous ammonia (nitriding), zinc (sherardizing), silicon (siliconizing), and nickel-phosphorus.

FINISHING PROCESS

Finishing processes are employed to modify the surfaces of materials in order to protect the material against deterioration by corrosion, oxidation, mechanical wear, or deformation; or to provide special surface characteristics such as reflectivity, electrical conductivity or insulation, or bearing properties; or to give the material special decorative effects.

There are two broad groups of finishing processes, those in which a coating, usually of a different material, is applied to the surface and those in which the surface of the material is changed by chemical action, heat, or mechanical force. The first group includes metallic coating, such as electroplating (*q.v.*); organic finishing, such as painting; porcelain enamelling; and others (see PAINTS, VARNISHES, AND ALLIED PRODUCTS). This article is limited to the second broad group in which the original surface of the material is altered in one way or another without the addition of a second material.

Metallic coatings

Surface modification by mechanical means. Under this heading fall such processes as cleaning and mechanical finishing.

Cleaning. Cleaning operations are usually an integral part of finishing and are used to remove dirt, grease, chemicals, scale, burrs, and other contaminants. In chemical cleaning the foreign matter is removed by the action of a chemical, which may be an acid, an alkali, an emulsifier, or a solvent. Long-established mechanical cleaning methods involve the blasting of the surface with metal shot or grit or tumbling the objects to be cleaned in barrels containing such materials as sawdust, corncobs, or glass marbles. Other cleaning methods make use of flame, ultrasonic, and electrical techniques.

Mechanical finishing. There are two broad groups of mechanical finishing processes. The first includes polishing, buffing, brushing, and barrel finishing, all of which essentially involve wearing down the ridges on the material surface or producing a pattern of fine surface scratches.

Polishing, oldest of the techniques, involves the use of wheels or belts containing such fine abrasives as pumice, rouge aluminum oxide, or emery. Buffing, which almost always follows another finishing process when a

Polishing

high lustre is desired, essentially involves finer abrasives and more flexible wheels than are used in polishing. Brushing, using either wire or nonmetallic brushes, produces decorative surfaces somewhat duller than those obtained by polishing and buffing.

In barrel finishing, parts are tumbled in a rotating drum in contact with the finishing media. There are two general tumbling methods—abrasive tumbling, and lustring or burnishing, both of which can be performed by either dry or wet techniques.

The second broad group of mechanical finishing processes are blasting, hammering, and embossing, used to produce textured finishes on metals. In blasting, metal shot or grit, sand, or other hard abrasives are directed against the metal surface at high velocity to create a pattern of small indentations. Hammering, done by hand or mechanically, produces surfaces with larger indentations. In embossing, metal sheet is passed between rolls to produce patterned decorative effects.

Chemical finishing. Sometimes called conversion coating, chemical finishing processes change the surface layer of the material by a chemical or electrochemical action. Processes involving chemical reactions without the use of an electric current include phosphate, chromate, and oxide coating, the last being applied chiefly to steels and copper and copper alloys. Chromate conversion coatings are widely used on zinc, aluminum, and magnesium. Phosphate coatings are applied to iron, steel, and zinc and to a lesser extent on aluminum and tin. Another group of chemical conversion processes, known as anodizing, produce coatings on aluminum and magnesium by electrolytic processes in which the base metal is made the anode in an electrolyte, such as sulfuric or phosphoric acid.

Other finishing processes. Many materials, especially metals, undergo property changes during certain processing operations, particularly the solid-state forming processes. A few mechanical processes are specifically designed to alter material properties; these principally involve the application of impact energy or rolling pressure to plastically deform the metal. This cold-working, as it is called, increases strength and hardness but usually reduces ductility.

Several processes have been developed that involve a combination of mechanical working and thermal, including low-temperature, treatment.

Radiation processing. Radiation in the form of light and infrared or radiant heating have long been used for certain processing techniques, but only since the 1960s has radiation been used to alter material properties. Certain plastics, specifically polyethylene, can be irradiated to raise the melting and softening points. Processes have been developed to cure coatings on automobiles by beams of electrons. Although metals can also be hardened and strengthened by radiation, so far the process does not appear to hold much promise in this application.

BIBLIOGRAPHY. H.R. CLAUSER (ed.), *The Encyclopedia of Engineering Materials and Processes* (1963), a comprehensive summary coverage of all processing methods, properties, and applications of materials; A.C. ANSLEY, *Manufacturing Methods and Processes*, rev. ed. (1968), a good treatment of modern methods of processing industrial materials; J.M. ALEXANDER and R.C. BREWER, *Manufacturing Properties of Materials* (1963), a basic review of processes with emphasis on fabricating properties of materials; D.F. EARY and G.E. JOHNSON, *Process Engineering for Manufacturing* (1962), an exposition of manufacturing engineering discipline and industrial processes; R.A. LINDBERG, *Processes and Materials of Manufacture* (1964), a basic text on materials-processing methods; AMERICAN SOCIETY FOR METALS, *Metals Handbook*, 8th ed., 3 vol. (1961–67), an extensive reference work on metalworking processes.

(H.R.C.)

Materials Salvage

The word salvage, though its roots are in the Latin *salvare* ("to save"), has in recent years taken on a much broader meaning than merely saving. Its modern usage includes the recovery and re-use, often called "recycling," of almost any material of value. The depletion of the world's natural resources such as oil, gas, coal, mineral ores, and trees had highlighted the need for new or alternative sources of such materials, to find substitutes for them, or to recycle the spent products. Recognition of the need for recycling is naturally greater in areas of the world in which raw materials are scarce.

Historically, the earliest salvage was probably military in nature. After the battle, the victors claimed the weapons of the vanquished. Almost equally ancient is salvage as the recovery of ships and their cargoes. Ships sunk in shallow harbours or broken up on the rocks of a coast often contained easily salvageable cargoes. Later, the development of the diving bell, diving suits, oxygen tanks, and modern life-support equipment all made deep marine-cargo salvage possible. Lifting equipment and other technology by the 19th century made it possible to raise the hulks themselves from shallow depths, and 20th-century developments have enabled successful operations to be carried out at depths of several hundred feet. At the same time, salvage of raw materials from the waste products of nearly every industry has become commonplace.

Ship recovery

TYPES OF SALVAGE OPERATIONS

There are, then, basically two types of material-salvage operations, one of which may be called internal, the other external. Internal salvage or recycling is the re-use in a manufacturing process of materials that are a waste product of that process. Internal recycle is common, for example, in the metals industry. The manufacture of copper tubing results in a certain amount of waste in the form of tube ends and trimmings; this material is remelted and recast. Another form of internal salvage is seen in the distilling industry, in which, after the distillation, spent grain mash is dried and processed into an edible foodstuff for cattle. External salvage or recycling is the reclaiming of materials from a product that through use has been worn out or rendered obsolete. An example of external recycle is the collection of old newspapers and magazines for the manufacture of newsprint or other paper products.

Whether the recycle or salvage operation is internal or external is of little technological significance but of considerable economic importance. The cost of reprocessing waste or recycled material must be less than the cost of new raw material. In situations of affluence and cheap natural resources there is a tendency to discard used materials. As an economic situation tightens salvage becomes attractive.

Economics of salvage

Coal has at one time or another been burned as domestic fuel in most of the world. Relatively inefficient domestic coal furnaces never burned all of the coal fed into them; when the ashes were removed, some grains of coal were lost. In times of depression, consumers often picked through the ashes to recover such coal.

More recently, new reasons for material salvage have appeared. First, there has been a widespread realization that the world's resources are not inexhaustible. Second and even more compelling was the discovery that waste materials were beginning to pollute the air, water, and land to a significant extent. Even though the salvage of materials as a pollution-abatement measure cannot always be economically justified, salvage or recycle operations have grown year by year throughout the world.

TECHNIQUES OF SALVAGING MATERIALS

It would be impossible to consider every recycle or salvage operation currently employed or considered in industry today. A number of representative examples can be cited to acquaint the reader with the general scope of present and future applications.

Ferrous metals. Ferrous products can be salvaged by both internal and external methods. Some internal-salvage operations are obvious. Metal cuttings or imperfect products are recycled by remelting, recasting, and redrawing entirely within the steel mill. The process is much cheaper than producing new metal from the basic ore.

In steelmaking, pig iron is first produced by heating the ore with coke and limestone in a vertical, cylindrical furnace (called a cupola) with tapping spouts at the bottom. Most iron and steel manufacturers produce their own coke in a device known as a coke oven, which burns bituminous coal with too little air to provide complete combustion. By-products from the coke oven include a number of organic compounds, hydrogen sulfide gas, and ammonia. The organic compounds are condensed, distilled, separated, and sold. The ammonia is concentrated and sold in aqueous form or brought into contact with a sulfuric acid solution that reacts with it to form ammonium sulfate, which is subsequently dried and sold as fertilizer. Ammonia that before development of this process was not used is now salvageable and salable.

During its manufacture, steel is pickled (treated with sulfuric or hydrochloric acid) to remove scale formed in the high-temperature drawing and rolling operations. Pickling gives the steel a smooth surface for ease in manufacture of various products. Sulfuric acid pickling solution slowly attacks the scale and removes it, forming iron sulfate in solution. Since the iron sulfate contains a large amount of usable iron, it can be transformed into iron oxide and reprocessed to make more steel. Hydrochloric acid pickling results in the formation of iron chloride, which also can be processed to reclaim iron. Either acid can also be reclaimed for future pickling operations. Blast furnace slag and, to some extent, steel slag are used by the construction industry as all-purpose aggregates for road building and in various types of concrete products. Refuse material from ore preparation from taconite mines has been converted on a research basis into a foamed building material of controlled density; similar potential exists for refuse from copper, lead, and zinc mining.

In the ferrous-metals industry there are also many applications of external salvage or recycle. A significant percentage of the feed to the open-hearth furnace, the Bessemer converter, or the basic oxygen furnace can be in the form of steel scrap, usually in bales supplied by reprocessing companies. The scrap comes from a variety of manufacturing operations that use steel as a basic material. Scrap materials are usually those either too small or of a shape that cannot be re-used in the manufacturing operation.

The second largest salvage operation in the ferrous-metal industries is the reprocessing of old automobile bodies. The average junked automobile contains about 62 percent iron and steel, 28 percent nonferrous metals, and some 10 percent rubber, plastics, and textiles. Salvage operations on automobiles actually begin before they reach the reprocessor. Parts such as carburetors and electrical components can be removed, rebuilt, and resold.

In a process developed in Belgium, liquid nitrogen (at a temperature of $-320°$ F [$-196°$ C]) is sprayed on the auto body before shredding. When steel is subjected to such temperatures, it becomes brittle; nonferrous metals, such as copper and aluminum, do not. Superchilling the auto body before shredding causes the steel to break in the shredder much as a glass bottle breaks if thrown on a concrete floor. The nonferrous metals tend to agglomerate and are therefore much more easily removed from the ferrous metals after shredding. The same basic procedures apply to washing machines, refrigerators, or other large, bulky steel or iron items.

The engine blocks of most automobiles are either cast iron or aluminum. Since cast iron is usually found in larger pieces and is, therefore, more difficult to compress and shred, it is generally remelted from its original form and recast into pigs (crude castings). Thousands of railroad freight cars are retired from service every year and dismantled for scrap and salvage. About half of these are boxcars and refrigerator cars with sides largely or wholly of wood. Generally, wooden parts are burned away, steel sections are dismantled and sold as scrap, while trucks and wheels are rebuilt.

Nonferrous metals. Nonferrous-metals salvage involves many materials, the most important of which are aluminum, copper, lead, and silver. At present, manual sorting seems to be the only practical method of separating pieces of nonferrous scrap from each other. External recycle procedures usually involve such manual sorting

with the return of the basic metal to a reprocessor who melts it down, removes impurities, and recasts it into ingots.

Secondary aluminum reprocessing is a large industry, involving salvage of machine turnings covered with oil and grease, rejected aluminum castings, aluminum siding, and even aluminum covered with decorative plastic. In these mills aluminum in all forms is thrown into a reverberatory furnace (in which heat is radiated from the roof into the material treated) and melted while the impurities are burned off. The resulting material is cast into ingots and resold for drawing or forming operations.

An internal-salvage procedure, used in aluminum mills and in secondary aluminum-recovery operations, removes aluminum from the dross or slag created in a melting process. The slag that forms on the surface of the molten metal is mixed with small amounts of aluminum. By processing this material through a hammer mill (pulverizer), the aluminum, which is malleable, can be separated from the brittle slag. Dross treated in this manner generally contains 20 to 30 percent metallic aluminum.

A salvage operation recently proposed in the copper industry involves reprocessing of the waste from copper mining and smelting operations. This waste, which consists of minute amounts of copper mixed with sand, mica, limestone, and some other minerals, is usually piled in great heaps near the mine. Since copper ore generally exists in the form of copper sulfide, it has been suggested that certain bacteria introduced to the piles of waste will cause oxidation to occur, converting the sulfide to copper sulfate. Copper sulfate is soluble in hot water; by spraying the tailings, the copper sulfate can be dissolved and recovered for processing into metal. Though the proposed method is not yet economic, rising copper prices may someday make it so. Lead recovery is also a secondary smelting operation; the primary source of used lead is discarded electric storage batteries. Lead battery plates may be smelted to produce antimonial lead (a lead–antimony alloy) for manufacture of new batteries, or pure lead and antimony as separate products.

Since photographic paper and X-ray film contain small but valuable quantities of silver, recycle methods utilizing incineration have been developed. Most of the silver salts used in photographic papers are sufficiently volatile that the vent gas from their incineration can be cooled by water sprays and then passed into an electrostatic precipitator where the silver salts are removed at efficiencies up to 99 percent. The silver may then be recycled and used for coating more photographic paper.

Ores of many nonferrous metals, such as copper, zinc, and lead, are found in the form of a sulfide. An atmospheric pollutant, sulfur dioxide, is created when the ore is roasted. The sulfur dioxide can be recovered and sold as a gas, or it can be further oxidized to sulfur trioxide, treated to make sulfuric acid, or reduced to elemental sulfur. Though smelter-gas recovery is still somewhat questionable from an economic standpoint, antipollution legislation will undoubtedly require its adoption.

Radioactive wastes. In nuclear power reactors, unwanted fission by-products are formed by the neutron bombardment of the fuel (usually uranium) and other materials within the reactor. When a reactor core (composed substantially of uranium) has reached the end of its useful life, only a small amount of the uranium has been consumed. Even so, the uranium fuel elements must be removed from the reactor and sent for reprocessing. In standard reprocessing techniques, the fuel elements are dissolved in acid and uranium is extracted from the mixture in one of several ways. The resulting acid, however, contains enormous amounts of radioactivity in the form of isotopes that are fission products of the uranium. Though production of radioactive materials in a nuclear reactor is very great, only a small portion can be salvaged and used as radioactive isotopes. The rest is usually stored deep underground.

Rubber. Though much used rubber was formerly burned, in most countries this has been greatly curtailed to avoid air pollution. Internal recycle is common in most rubber plants; the reprocessed product can be used wherever premium-grade rubber is not needed. External salvage has proved a problem over the years; the ultimate value of old or worn-out tires has been negligible. Recent experimental work, however, has indicated that destructive distillation is a viable means of disposing of scrap rubber products for reclamation of valuable chemicals, including a liquid oil that can be used in manufacturing other chemicals, a combustible gas valuable as a fuel, and a carbonaceous residue useful as a filter char or binder in concrete or asphalt roadways.

Chemicals and plastics. The chemical industry produces hundreds of waste products, many of which cannot be recovered economically at present. Because of increasing public concern with air and water pollution, however, recovery has become attractive.

Solvent recovery

Many plastics-manufacturing processes include a curing or drying operation that converts solvents into a vapour that must be vented. Vinyls, for example, used in chair coverings, automobile seats, and luggage, are usually applied to a natural or synthetic fabric in a coating operation. To cure this vinyl covering, the coated material is passed through a drying oven in which some of the solvents present in the original mixture vaporize or evaporate. Vapour from these ovens may contain valuable solvents such as methyl ethyl ketone and toluene or plasticizers such as dioctyl phthalate. Though some processors burn these noxious gases, others salvage them by passing the air-solvent mixture through a granular bed of activated carbon or charcoal. The bed recovers between 95 and 99 percent of the solvent from the airstream. Once saturated, the bed is ready for desorption or solvent removal, accomplished by flooding it with steam of a temperature higher than the vaporization temperature of the solvent. The steam flushes out almost all the solvent from the activated carbon and is then condensed, forming a mixture of solvent and water. If the solvent is miscible with the water (*i.e.*, mixes with it), then distillation follows. In many cases, however, the solvent is immiscible, separates into a layer, and can be poured off (decanted). This system accomplishes two things: it recycles a valuable solvent, and it prevents air pollution.

Residues containing chlorine

Manufacture of many insecticides and herbicides as well as polyvinyl chloride plastics results in residues ranging from water-like materials to very thick tars and sludges, all of which contain the element chlorine. Placed in natural water bodies, these by-products have caused large fish kills. Though sometimes they have been dumped far at sea, where their effect is considered to be negligible, such disposal over long periods may eventually damage the marine environment. Since most of these wastes are combustible, they are often burned; hydrogen chloride can be formed in the incinerator as one of the products of combustion. Hydrogen chloride is extremely toxic, cannot be released to the atmosphere, and must be removed from the products of combustion. Since this poisonous substance is soluble in water, it can be separated out by water scrubbing, a process that then presents the manufacturer with the problem of disposing of dilute hydrochloric acid. While the acid may be neutralized with some basic material such as lime, this does not entirely solve the pollution problem because the calcium chloride that results from the reaction of lime and hydrochloric acid is also a water contaminant. Recently, several processes have been developed that involve reclamation of the hydrochloric acid from the incinerator process either as commercial-grade muriatic acid or as anhydrous hydrogen chloride gas. Both of these products can profitably be recycled. At present, only a very large reclamation project involving many tons of residue can be economically justified for hydrogen chloride salvage, but, in the future, the value of such salvage operations may well depend on the reduction of pollution.

Sulfur, another valuable chemical, can cause serious pollution problems when in the form of hydrogen sulfide, sulfur dioxide, or sulfur trioxide. Hydrogen sulfide with its rotten-egg smell is generated in the manufacture of aviation gasoline. Though burning may destroy hydrogen sulfide, the combustion process produces sulfur dioxide, another serious pollutant. If the hydrogen sulfide is burned in insufficient air, however, a sulfur vapour is created that can be condensed into liquid sulfur, crystallized, and used by the chemical industry.

Domestic refuse. One of the biggest and most complex areas of salvage operation is the field of municipal garbage and refuse. Once ferrous and nonferrous metals have been removed from domestic refuse, along with glass and glass products if practical, what remains is essentially organic waste that lends itself to one of several salvage operations. Incineration produces potentially valuable heat energy, along with carbon dioxide and nitrogen, with some residual ash. Composting consists of biological degradation into a pathogenically pure (*i.e.*, no harmful bacteria) disposable waste. Pyrolysis (incineration with a deficiency of air) permits recovery of certain fuel gases and chemicals. Landfill allows the biological action of the earth eventually to rot away the residue and return it to the soil. Incineration appears especially promising in the light of two environmental dilemmas: a worldwide demand for more electric power and the growing mountains of organic wastes and garbage. It is now possible to burn garbage, using the heat produced to create electric power.

Burning garbage to produce electricity

The first significant work in this field was done by a Swiss company that developed an incinerator–boiler combination capable of taking 300 tons (270,000 kilograms) of municipal refuse per day, burning it at 99.5 percent combustion efficiency and generating 25,000 pounds (11,000 kilograms) of steam per hour. Another system developed in Germany achieves similar results with slightly different components.

Heat energy can be recovered from a wide variety of industrial wastes. Where it is necessary, for example, to incinerate gas or vapour emanating from an industrial process, it is often quite practical to utilize the heat from the incineration to preheat the fume before incineration. A solvent–air mixture that must be heated to 1,500° F (about 800° C) in the presence of air before it can be incinerated can use some of the heat generated in the incineration process to preheat the solvent–air mixture, thereby cutting fuel costs from 50 to 70 percent.

Power industry wastes. The power industry produces a salvageable by-product known as fly ash, which is normally created when a fossil fuel such as bituminous coal is burned. Fly ash, a finely divided powdery material composed of spheres of amorphous silica and alumina, is recovered from flue gases by electrostatic precipitators. It has been utilized in portland cement manufacture, in casting masonry cinder and concrete building blocks, in lightweight aggregate, as a base for highway material, as a filler for bituminous mix, as a filler in material for roofing and putty, as a soil conditioner, as a soil stabilizer, in oil-well grouting, and as a sand substitute in sandblasting or abrasive applications. It has also been used as a filtering medium. Sulfur dioxide is also produced by burning fossil fuels; its salvage has been described above.

Paper and other cellulose products. One of the most readily available organic materials for salvage or recycle is cellulose. Trees, vines, grasses, and straws are about one-third cellulose by weight; thus vast quantities accumulate as waste products from food processing, lumbering, papermaking, and grain harvesting. Municipal and industrial wastepaper, rags, boxes, wood, grass, and leaves also contribute to the enormous volume of cellulose waste products. Many of these wastes are currently being recovered; others are under consideration for salvage on an experimental basis. Wallboard, door cores, and mulch have been made from cereal grain straws and bagasse (a waste product of sugarcane). Chemical-grade cellulose has been made from cotton linters, wood, and similar fibres. Animal feed has been made from pea vines and other fibrous vegetable materials. Animal bedding has been made from oat, rice, and wheat straw. Furfuryl alcohol, a component of certain types of plastics, has also been made from bagasse. Chemicals have been produced from corncobs. The cellulose found in urban or municipal wastes differs from its agricultural counterpart in that it has usually been subjected to some type of processing.

In an experimental program, a food protein was developed by fermenting insoluble cellulose with bacteria. Experimental work on sugarcane bagasse has resulted in a light-brown to yellow powder with a crude protein content from 50 to 60 percent. Such research is particularly significant to the developing countries where food shortages are often severe and where protein is missing from many diets.

In the citrus industry it is possible to salvage almost all parts of the fruit not used as food. Oranges grown mainly for juice have other valuable products to offer. The peels are pressed, leached, drained, and dried as animal food. The material that has been pressed and leached out of the peels is concentrated into a heavy, nutritious molasses.

Bark, wood chips, and lignin (the basic chemical component of wood waste), from sawmills, pulp, and paper mills, constitute one of the largest classes of industrial waste. These wood wastes, a significant source of organic matter, are returned to the soil as fertilizers and soil conditioners.

In papermaking, the process known as kraft pulping produces a variety of undesirable liquid wastes. Several companies have installed devices for the purification of these wastes and recovery of such valuable chemicals as turpentine, methyl alcohol, dimethyl sulfide, ethyl alcohol, and acetone. The first commercial purification unit, developed in Sweden, commenced operation in 1963. Sludges from pulp and paper manufacture and phosphate slime from fertilizer manufacturing can be made into gypsum wallboard that utilizes the calcium sulfate content of the waste.

Glass. An easily salvageable material, but one that is difficult to recover economically, is glass. Though enormous numbers of glass containers are used throughout the world, most are not recycled. Even those that are returned by consumers in their original form sooner or later become damaged or broken, causing a disposal problem. The chief problem in recycling glass is separating it from other refuse. Direct re-use of waste glass in the glass-container industry is difficult because separation by colour is necessary before it can be recycled. If colour separation can be accomplished, fairly high percentages of recycled glass can be used in new glass production.

The glass industry now uses about 15 percent cullet (broken or refuse glass) in new glass production, but because the raw materials are so inexpensive no real attempt has been made until recently to see how much recycled glass could be used.

Waste glass has other possibilities also. By melting it and running it into cold water while molten, frit, or finely divided, glass can be formed. Frit is used as landfill, as a soil conditioner, or as a material to be mixed with asphalt for the surfacing of roads. Since glass is essentially silica or sand it may be substituted in a number of building materials that use sand as a basic substance.

Fish and animal wastes. Waste from commercial fisheries and processing plants, including parts of fish and shellfish, contains valuable oils and large amounts of protein. Methods have been developed for converting this protein into animal food, and the Food and Agriculture Organization of the United Nations is currently experimenting with the extraction of fish protein from waste materials in the hope that it can be used as a direct food supplement in underdeveloped nations. Work in Chile has indicated that fish stickwater (the water used in large fish-meal processing plants) can be reclaimed through evaporation, producing a high protein concentrate. In the early 1970s the United States Bureau of Mines announced a process for the production of a paraffinic fuel oil from animal wastes. The oil manufactured by this process is reported to have a heating value equal to about 75 percent that of domestic fuel oil and to be low in sulfur.

The large increase in livestock and poultry production in the world has created a problem in several countries of disposing of animal wastes. Processing for use as a component of animal feeds has been under intensive study, along with research on use of the wastes for large-scale composting and on possible dehydration of wastes for use as garden fertilizer.

Water. The largest domestic use for water is for human consumption and sanitation. Waste water goes to a sewage treatment plant, where it is purified and recycled to the household. In a good sewage-treatment operation, the only loss of water is evaporation. If the industrial user does not have complete water-treatment facilities, however, the water, along with associated impurities, is funnelled into a river, stream, or ocean for subsequent recycle by nature. Though nature can handle small quantities of certain wastes, temporary or permanent damage has resulted from widespread disposal of this type. In some cases, legislation has prohibited the disposal of harmful wastes, while in others, pretreatment has been required.

A waste-water recycling technique called the Living Filter was developed on an experimental basis in the early 1970s. The experiment was designed to determine if impurities in waste water could be completely filtered out by the soil while simultaneously providing nourishment to crops and developing green cover on barren land. An overwhelming success, the Living Filter has rejuvenated barren and nutrient-scarce soils while purifying waste water. Waste waters from the food and paper industries have been distributed over farm and forest acreage by spray irrigation with beneficial results to the crop and ultimate purification of the water. Experimental studies have also been made in utilization of waste sludge from sewage-treatment plants as a soil conditioner.

BIBLIOGRAPHY. R.D. ROSS (ed.), *Industrial Waste Disposal* (1968), a broadly based study of the problems of pollution and industrial salvage techniques covering both air and water pollution practices; *Kirk-Othmer Encyclopedia of Chemical Technology*, 2nd ed., vol. 21 (1970), a typical encyclopaedia coverage of pollution abatement practices in the chemical industry under the heading "Wastes, Industrial"; COCA-COLA COMPANY FEEDS DIVISION, ENVIRONMENTAL PROTECTION AGENCY, Water Quality Office Program 12060, *Treatment of Citrus Processing Wastes* (1970), examination of the value of certain wastes in the citrus-processing industry; OREGON STATE UNIVERSITY, DEPARTMENT OF FOOD, SCIENCE AND TECHNOLOGY, *Current Practice in Seafoods Processing Waste Treatment*, Report 1260ECF (1970), on the values of certain wastes in the seafood industry; GULF SOUTH RESEARCH INSTITUTE, *Polymeric Materials for Treatment and Recovery of Petrochemical Wastes* (1971), a discussion of some of the problems of pollution abatement and recycle indigenous to the petroleum industry and its products; F.J. CSERVENYAK and C.B. KENAHAN, *Bureau of Mines, Research and Accomplishments in Utilization of Solid Wastes* (1970), a review of the work of the United States Bureau of Mines relative to recycle possibilities for many waste products; UNITED STATES DEPARTMENT OF HEALTH, EDUCATION, AND WELFARE, PUBLIC HEALTH SERVICE, *An Industrial Waste Guide to the Synthetic Textile Industry* (1965), on the possibility of recovering food value from wastes in the textile industry; *Dismantling Railroad Freight Cars* (1969), on railroad car salvage; R.B. ENGDAHL and BATTELLE MEMORIAL INSTITUTE STAFF, *Solid Waste Processing* (1969), an excellent review of how solid wastes are now handled in the United States; HERBERT F. LUND (ed.), *Industrial Pollution Control Handbook* (1971), a broadly based study on the problems of pollution and industrial salvage techniques covering both air and water pollution practices; UNITED STATES DEPARTMENT OF HEALTH, EDUCATION, AND WELFARE, *Air Pollution Engineering Manual* (1969), presents engineering considerations and data unavailable in any other single text; R.L. and G.L. CULP, *Advanced Wastewater Treatment* (1971), a discussion of advanced water treatment processes in use throughout the world today; W.K. MANN and H.B. SHORTLY, *Industrial Oily Waste Control* (1970), covers some of the problems of pollution abatement and recycle indigenous to the petroleum industry and its products.

(R.D.R.)

Materials Testing

Materials testing involves measuring the characteristics and behaviour of such substances as steel or wood under various conditions. The data thus obtained can be used in specifying materials and their properties for various applications. A full- or small-scale model of a proposed machine or structure may be tested. Alternatively, investigators may construct mathematical models that utilize known material characteristics and behaviour to predict capabilities of the structure.

Materials testing breaks down into five major categories: mechanical testing; testing for thermal properties; testing for electrical properties; testing for resistance to corrosion, radiation, and biological deterioration; and nondestructive testing. Standard test methods have been established by such national and international bodies as the International Organization for Standardization (ISO), with headquarters in Geneva, and the American Society for Testing and Materials (ASTM), Philadelphia.

MECHANICAL TESTING

Structures and machines, or their components, fail because of fracture or excessive deformation. In attempting to prevent such failure, the designer estimates how much stress (load per unit area) can be anticipated, and specifies materials that can withstand expected stresses. A stress analysis, accomplished either experimentally or by means of a mathematical model, indicates expected areas of high stress in a machine or structure. Mechanical property tests, carried out experimentally, indicate which materials may safely be employed.

Static tension and compression tests. When subjected to tension (pulling apart), a material elongates and eventually breaks. A simple static tension test determines the breaking point of the material and its elongation, designated as strain (change in length per unit length). If a 100-millimetre steel bar elongates 1 millimetre under a given load, for example, strain is $(101-100)/100 = 1/100 = 1$ percent.

Elements of a static tension test

A static tension test requires (1) a test piece, usually cylindrical, or with a middle section of smaller diameter than the ends; (2) a test machine that applies, measures, and records various loads; and (3) an appropriate set of grips to grasp the test piece. In the static tension test, the test machine uniformly stretches a small part (the test section) of the test piece. The length of the test section (called the gauge length) is measured at different loads with a device called an extensometer; these measurements are used to compute strain.

Conventional testing machines are of the constant load, constant load-rate, and constant displacement-rate types (see Figure 1). Constant load types employ weights directly both to apply load and to measure it. Constant load-rate test machines employ separate load and measurement units; loads are generally applied by means of

a hydraulic ram into which oil is pumped at a constant rate. Constant displacement-rate testing machines are generally driven by gear-screws.

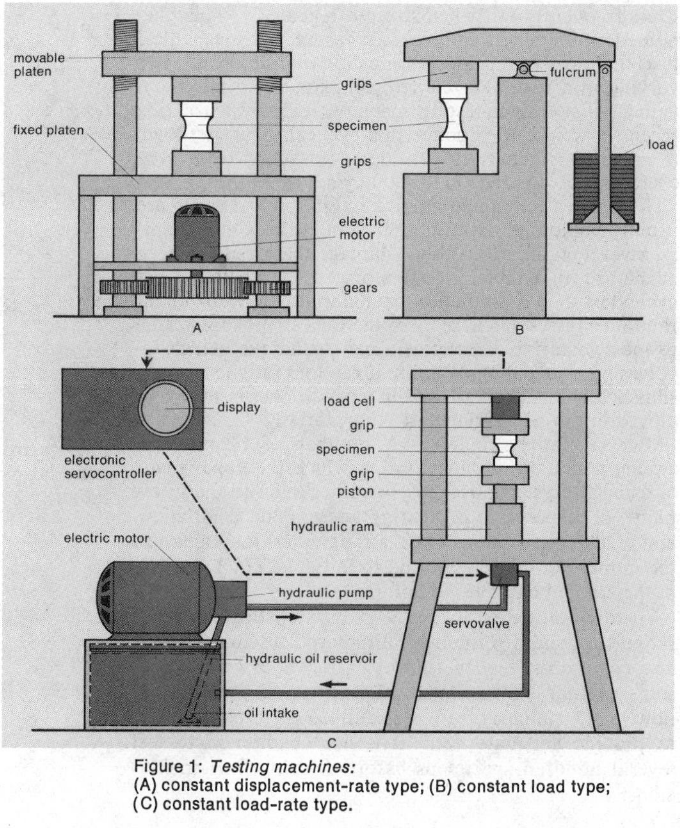

Test machine grips are designed to transfer load smoothly into the test piece without producing local stress concentrations. The ends of the test piece are often slightly enlarged so that if slight concentrations of stress are present these will be directed to the gauge section, and failures will occur only where measurements are being taken. Clamps, pins, threading, or bonding are employed to hold the test piece. Eccentric (nonuniform) loading causes bending of the sample (in addition to tension, which means that stress in the sample will not be uniform. To avoid this, most gripping devices incorporate one or two swivel joints in the linkage that carries the load to the test piece. Air bearings help to correct horizontal misalignment, which can be troublesome with such brittle materials as ceramics.

Static compression tests determine a material's response to crushing, or support-type loading (such as in the beams of a house). Testing machines and extensometers for compression tests resemble those used for tension tests. Specimens are generally simpler, however, because gripping is not usually a problem. Furthermore, specimens may have a constant cross-sectional area throughout their full length. The gauge length of a sample in a compression test is its full length. A serious problem in compression testing is the possibility that the sample or load chain may buckle prior to material failure. To prevent this, specimens are kept short and stubby.

Static shear and bending tests. Inplane shear tests indicate the deformation response of a material to forces applied tangentially. These tests are applied primarily to thin sheet materials, either metals or composites, such as fibre glass reinforced plastic.

A homogeneous material such as untreated steel casting reacts in a different way under stress than does a grained material such as wood or an adhesively bonded joint. These anisotropic materials are said to have preferential planes of weakness; they resist stress better in some planes than in others, and consequently must undergo a different type of shear test.

Shear strength of rivets and other fasteners also can be measured. Though the state of stress of such items is generally quite complicated, a simple shear test, providing only limited information, is adequate for most purposes.

Tensile testing of brittle materials

Tensile testing is difficult to perform directly upon certain brittle materials such as glass and ceramics. In such cases, a measure of the tensile strength of the material may be obtained by performing a bend test, in which tensile (stretching) stresses develop on one side of the bent member and corresponding compressive stresses develop on the opposite side. If the material is substantially stronger in compression than tension, failure initiates on the tensile side of the member and, hence, provides the required information on the material tensile strength. Because it is necessary to know the exact magnitude of the tensile stress at failure to establish the strength of the material, however, the bending test method is applicable only to a very restricted class of materials and conditions.

Measures of ductility. Ductility is the capacity of a material to deform permanently in response to stress. Most common steels, for example, are quite ductile and hence can accommodate local stress concentrations. Brittle materials, such as glass, cannot accommodate concentrations of stress because they lack ductility; they, therefore, fracture rather easily.

When a material specimen is stressed, it deforms elastically (*i.e.*, recoverably) at first; thereafter, deformation becomes permanent. A cylinder of steel, for example, may "neck" (assume an hourglass shape) in response to stress. If the material is ductile, this local deformation is permanent, and the test piece does not assume its former shape if the stress is removed. Finally, fracture occurs.

Ductility can be expressed as strain, reduction in area, or toughness. Strain, or change in length per unit length, was explained earlier. Reduction in area (change in area

Figure 1: *Testing machines:*
(A) constant displacement-rate type; (B) constant load type;
(C) constant load-rate type.

per unit area) may be measured, for example, in the test section of a steel bar that necks when stressed. Toughness measures the amount of energy required to deform a piece of material permanently. Toughness is a desirable material property in that it permits a component to deform plastically, rather than crack, and perhaps fracture.

Hardness testing. Based on the idea that a material's response to a load placed at one small point is related to its ability to deform permanently (yield), the hardness test is performed by pressing a hardened steel ball (Brinell test) or a steel or diamond cone (Rockwell test) into the surface of the test piece. Most hardness tests are performed on commercial machines that register arbitrary values in inverse relation to the depth of penetration of the ball or cone. Similar indentation tests are performed on wood. Hardness tests of materials such as rubber or plastic do not have the same connotation as those performed on metals. Penetration is measured, of course, but deformation caused by testing such materials may be entirely temporary.

Some hardness tests, particularly those designed to provide a measure of wear or abrasion, are performed dynamically with a weight of given magnitude that falls from a prescribed height. Sometimes a hammer is used, falling vertically on the test piece or in a pendulum motion.

Impact test. Many materials, sensitive to the presence of flaws, cracks, and notches, fail suddenly under impact. The The most common impact tests (Charpy and Izod) employ a swinging pendulum to strike a notched bar; heights before and after impact are used to compute the energy required to fracture the bar, and, consequently, the bar's impact strength. In the Charpy test, the test piece is held horizontally between two vertical bars, much like the lintel over a door. In the Izod test, the specimen stands erect, like a fence post. Shape and size of the specimen, mode of support, notch shape and geometry, and velocities at impact are all varied to produce specific test conditions. Nonmetals such as wood may be tested as supported beams, similar to the Charpy test. In nonmetal tests, however, the striking hammer falls vertically in a guide column, and the test is repeated from increasing heights until failure occurs.

The Charpy and Izod tests

Some materials vary in impact strength at different temperatures, becoming very brittle when cold. Tests have shown that the decrease in material strength and elasticity is often quite abrupt at a certain temperature, which is called the transition temperature for that material. Designers always specify a material that possesses a transition temperature well below the range of heat and cold to which the structure or machine is exposed. Thus, even a building in the tropics, which will doubtless never be exposed to freezing weather, employs materials with transition temperatures slightly below freezing.

Fracture toughness tests. The stringent materials-reliability requirements of the space programs of the 1960s brought about substantial changes in design philosophy. Designers asked materials engineers to devise quantitative tests capable of measuring the propensity of a material to propagate a crack. Conventional methods of stress analysis and materials-property tests were retained, but interpretation of results changed. The criterion for failure became sudden propagation of a crack rather than fracture (see Figure 2). Tests have shown that cracks occur by opening, when two pieces of material part in vertical plane, one piece going up, the other down; by edge sliding, where the material splits in horizontal plane, one piece moving left, the other right; and by tearing, where the material splits with one piece moving diagonally upward to the left, the other moving diagonally downward to the right.

Creep test. Creep is the slow change in the dimensions of a material due to prolonged stress; most common metals exhibit creep behaviour. In the creep test, loads below those necessary to cause instantaneous fracture are applied to the material, and the deformation over a period of time (creep strain) under constant load is measured, usually with an extensometer or strain gauge. In the same

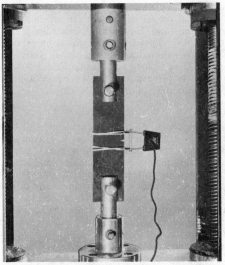

Figure 2: Typical fracture toughness test. The clip-on extensometer output signal is monitored to recognize the stress level at which the crack suddenly propagates because the extensometer will sense a sudden increase in strain without a corresponding increase in load.
By courtesy of K.E. Hofer, IIT Research Institute

test, time to failure is also measured against level of stress; the resulting curve is called stress rupture or creep rupture. Once creep strain versus time is plotted, a variety of mathematical techniques is available for extrapolating creep behaviour of materials beyond the test times so that designers can utilize thousand-hour test data, for example, to predict ten-thousand-hour behaviour.

A material that yields continually under stress and then returns to its original shape when the stress is released is said to be viscoelastic; this type of response is measured by the stress-relaxation test. A prescribed displacement or strain is induced in the specimen and the load drop-off as a function of time is measured. Various viscoelastic theories are available that permit the translation of stress-relaxation test data into predictions about the creep behaviour of the material.

Fatigue. Materials that survive a single application of stress frequently fail when stressed repeatedly. This phenomenon, known as fatigue, is measured by mechanical tests that involve repeated application of different stresses varying in a regular cycle from maximum to minimum value. Most fatigue-testing machines employ a rotating eccentric weight to produce this cyclically varying load. A material is generally considered to suffer from low-cycle fatigue if it fails in 10,000 cycles or less.

The stresses acting upon a material in the real world are usually random in nature rather than cyclic. Consequently, several cumulative fatigue-damage theories have been developed to enable investigators to extrapolate from cyclic test data a prediction of material behaviour under random stresses. Because these theories are not applicable to most materials, a relatively new technique, which involves mechanical application of random fatigue stresses, statistically matched to real-life conditions, is now employed in most materials test laboratories.

Material fatigue involves a number of phenomena, among which are atomic slip (in which the upper plane of a metal crystal moves or slips in relation to the lower plane, in response to a shearing stress), crack initiation, and crack propagation. Thus, a fatigue test may measure the number of cycles required to initiate a crack, as well as the number of cycles to failure.

Factors in material fatigue

A cautious designer always bears the statistical nature of fatigue in mind, for the lives of material specimens tested at a common stress level always range above and below some average value. Statistical theory tells the designer how many samples of a material must be tested in order to provide adequate data; it is not uncommon to test several hundred specimens before drawing firm conclusions.

MEASUREMENT OF THERMAL PROPERTIES

Thermal conductivity. Heat, which passes through a solid body by physical transfer of free electrons and by vibration of atoms and molecules, stops flowing when the temperature is equal at all points in the solid body and equals the temperature in the surrounding environment. In the process of attaining equilibrium, there is a gross heat flow through the body, which depends upon the temperature difference between different points in the body and upon the magnitudes of the temperatures involved. Thermal conductivity is experimentally measured by determining temperatures as a function of time along the length of a bar or across the surface of flat plates while simultaneously controlling the external input and output of heat from the surfaces of the bar or the edges of the plate.

Specific heat. Specific heat of solid materials (defined as heat absorbed per unit mass per degree change in temperature) is generally measured by the drop method, which involves adding a known mass of the material at a known elevated temperature to a known mass of water at a known low temperature and determining the equilibrium temperature of the mixture that results. Specific heat is then computed by measuring the heat absorbed by the water and container, which is equivalent to the heat given up by the hot material.

Thermal expansion. Expansion due to heat is usually measured in linear fashion as the change in a unit length of a material caused by a one-degree change in temperature. Because many materials expand only a few millionths of an inch with a one-degree increase in temperature, measurements are made by means of microscopes.

MEASUREMENT OF ELECTRICAL PROPERTIES

Understanding of electrical properties and testing methods requires a brief explanation of the free electron gas theory of electrical conduction. This simple theory is convenient for purposes of exposition, even though solid-state physics has advanced beyond it.

Electrical conductivity involves a flow or current of free electrons through a solid body. Some materials, such as metals, are good conductors of electricity; these possess free or valence electrons that do not remain permanently associated with the atoms of a solid but instead form an electron "cloud" or gas around the peripheries of the atoms and are free to move through the solid at a rapid rate. In other materials, such as plastics, the valence electrons are far more restricted in their movements and do not form a free electron gas. Such materials act as insulators against the flow of electricity.

The effect of heat upon the electrical conductivity of a material varies for good and poor conductors. In good conductors, thermal agitation interferes with the flow of electrons, decreasing conductivity, while as insulators increase in temperature, the number of free electrons grows, and conductivity increases. Normally, good and poor conductors are enormously far apart in basic conductivity, and relatively small changes in temperature do not change these properties significantly.

In certain materials, however, such as silicon, germanium, and carbon, heat produces a large increase in the number of free electrons; such materials are called semiconductors. Acting as insulators at absolute zero, semiconductors possess significant conductivity at room and elevated temperatures. Impurities also can change the conductivity of a semiconductor dramatically by providing more free electrons. Heat-caused conductivity is called intrinsic, while that attributable to extra electrons from impurity atoms is called extrinsic.

Conductivity of a material is generally measured by passing a known current at constant voltage through a known volume of the material and determining resistance in ohms. Total conductivity is simply the reciprocal of total resistivity.

TESTING FOR CORROSION, RADIATION, AND BIOLOGICAL DETERIORATION

Testing for breakdown or deterioration of materials under exposure to a particular type of environment has greatly increased in recent years. Mechanical, thermal, or electrical property tests often are performed on a material before, during, and after its exposure to some controlled environment. Property changes are then recorded as a function of exposure time. Environments may include heat, moisture, chemicals, radiation, electricity, biological substances, or some combination thereof. Thus, the tensile strength of a material may fall after exposure to heat, moisture, or salt spray, or may be increased by radiation or electrical current. Strength of organic materials may be lessened by certain classes of fungus and mold.

Corrosion. Corrosion testing is generally performed to evaluate materials for a specific environment or to evaluate means for protecting a material from environmental attack. A chemical reaction, corrosion involves removal of metallic electrons from metals and formation of more stable compounds such as iron oxide (rust) in which the free electrons are usually less numerous. In nature, only rather chemically inactive metals such as gold and platinum are found in pure form; most others are mined as ores that must be refined to metal. Corrosion simply reverses the refining process, returning the metal to its natural state. Corrosion compounds form on the surface of a solid material. If the compounds are hard and impenetrable, and if they adhere well to the parent material, the progress of corrosion is arrested. If the compound is loose and porous, however, corrosion may proceed swiftly and continuously.

If two different metals are placed together in a solution (electrolyte), one metal will give up ions (electrically charged particles) to the solution more readily than the other; this difference in behaviour will bring about a difference in electrical voltage between the two metals. If the metals are in electrical contact with each other, electricity will flow between them and they will corrode; this is the principle of the galvanic cell or battery. Though useful in a battery, this reaction causes problems in a structure; for example, steel bolts in an aluminum framework may, in the presence of rain or fog, form multiple galvanic cells at the point of contact between the two metals, corroding the aluminum.

Corrosion testing is performed to ascertain the performance of metals and other materials in the presence of various electrolytes. Testing may involve total immersion, as would be encountered in seawater; or salt fog, as is encountered in chemical-industry processing operations or near the oceans where seawater may occur in fogs. Materials are generally immersed in a 5 percent or 20 percent solution of sodium chloride or calcium chloride in water, or the solution may be sprayed into a chamber where the specimens are freely suspended. In suspension testing, care is taken to prevent condensate from dripping from one specimen onto another. The specimens are exposed to the hostile environment for some time, then removed and examined for visible evidences of corrosion. In many cases, mechanical tests after corrosion exposure are performed quantitatively to ascertain mechanical degradation of the material. In other tests, materials are stressed while in the corrosive environment. Still other test procedures have been developed to measure corrosion of metals by flue or stack gases.

Radiation. Materials may be tested for their reactions to such electromagnetic radiation as X-rays, gamma rays, and radio-frequency waves, or atomic radiation, which might include the neutrons given off by uranium or some other radioactive substance. Most affected by these forms of radiation are polymers, such organic compounds as plastic or synthetic rubber, with long, repeated chains of similar chemical units.

Radiation tests are performed by exposing the materials to a known source of radiation for a specific period of time. Test materials may be exposed by robot control to nuclear fuels in a remote chamber, then tested by conventional methods to ascertain changes in their properties as a function of exposure time. In the field, paint samples may be exposed to electromagnetic radiation (such as sunlight) for prolonged periods, then checked for fading or cracking.

Variation among conductors

Analogy of the galvanic cell battery

Exposure to radiation is usually, but not always, detrimental to strength; for example, exposure of polyethylene plastic for short periods of time increases its tensile strength. Longer exposures, however, decrease tensile strength. Tensile and yield strength of a type of carbon-silicon steel increase with exposure to neutron radiation, although elongation, reduction in area, and probably fracture toughness apparently decrease with exposure. Certain new wood/polymeric composite materials are even prepared by a process that employs radiation. The wood is first impregnated with liquid organic resin by high pressure. Next, the wood and resin combination is exposed to radiation, causing a chemical change in the form of the resin, producing a strengthened material.

Biological deterioration. In recent years there has been considerable activity in the new field of formulating tests to ascertain the resistance of organic materials to fungi, bacteria, and algae. Paints, wrappers, and coatings of buried pipelines, structures, and storage tanks are typical materials exposed to biological deterioration.

When biological composition of the soil in a given area is unknown, colonies or cultures of its various fungi, bacteria, or algae are isolated and incubated by standard laboratory techniques. These are then used to test materials for biological degradation, or to test the effectiveness of a fungicide or bactericide. In testing for algae resistance, for example, treated and untreated strips of vinyl film, such as might be used to line a swimming pool, are immersed in growing tanks along with seed cultures of algae plants. Within three days, luxuriant algae growths appear on untreated samples.

NONDESTRUCTIVE TESTING

The tensile-strength test is inherently destructive; in the process of gathering data, the sample is destroyed. Though this is acceptable when a plentiful supply of the material exists, nondestructive tests are desirable for materials that are costly or difficult to fabricate, or that have been formed into finished or semifinished products.

Liquids. One common nondestructive technique, used to locate surface cracks and flaws in metals, employs a penetrating liquid, either brightly dyed or fluorescent. After being smeared on the surface of the material and allowed to soak into any tiny cracks, the liquid is wiped off, leaving readily visible cracks and flaws. An analogous technique, applicable to nonmetals, employs an electrically charged liquid smeared on the material surface. After excess liquid is removed, a dry powder of opposite charge is sprayed on the material and attracted to the cracks. Neither of these methods, however, can detect internal flaws.

Radiation. Internal as well as external flaws can be detected by X-ray or gamma-ray techniques in which the radiation passes through the material and impinges on a suitable photographic film. Under some circumstances, it is possible to focus the X-rays to a particular plane within the material, permitting a three-dimensional description of the flaw geometry as well as its location.

Sound. Ultrasonic inspection of parts involves transmission of sound waves above human hearing range through the material. In the reflection technique, a sound wave is transmitted from one side of the sample, reflected off the far side, and returned to a receiver located at the starting point. Upon impinging on a flaw or crack in the material, the signal is reflected and its travelling time altered. The actual delay becomes a measure of the flaw's location; a map of the material can be generated to illustrate the location and geometry of the flaws. In the through-transmission method, the transmitter and receiver are located on opposite sides of the material; interruptions in the passage of sound waves are used to locate and measure flaws. Usually a water medium is employed in which transmitter, sample, and receiver are immersed.

Magnetism. As the magnetic characteristics of a material are strongly influenced by its overall structure, magnetic techniques can be used to characterize the location and relative size of voids and cracks. For magnetic testing, an apparatus is used that contains a large coil of wire through which flows a steady alternating current (prima-

ry coil). Nested inside this primary coil is a shorter coil (the secondary coil) to which is attached an electrical measuring device. The steady current in the primary coil causes current to flow in the secondary coil through the process of induction. If an iron bar is inserted into the secondary coil, sharp changes in the secondary current can indicate defects in the bar. This method only detects differences between zones along the length of a bar and cannot detect long or continuous defects very readily. An analogous technique, employing eddy currents induced by a primary coil, also can be used to detect flaws and cracks. A steady current is induced in the test material. Flaws that lie across the path of the current alter resistance of the test material; this change may be measured by suitable equipment.

Infrared. Infrared techniques also have been employed to detect material continuity in complex structural situations. In testing the quality of adhesive bonds between the sandwich core and facing sheets in a typical sandwich construction material such as plywood, for example, heat is applied to the surface of the sandwich skin material. Where bond lines are continuous, the core materials provide a heat sink for the surface material, and the local temperatures of the skin will fall evenly along these bond lines. Where the bond line is inadequate, missing, or faulty, however, temperature will not fall. Infrared photography of the surface will then indicate the location and shape of the defective adhesive. A variation of this method employs thermal coatings that change colour upon reaching a specific temperature.

Finally, nondestructive test methods also are being sought to permit a total determination of the mechanical properties of a test material. Ultrasonics and thermal methods appear most promising in this regard.

BIBLIOGRAPHY. J. MARIN, *Engineering Materials: Their Mechanical Properties and Applications* (1952), a classic work describing the qualitative mechanical behaviour of materials, and *Mechanical Behaviour of Engineering Materials* (1962), a comprehensive treatment of the determination and utilization of mechanical properties of materials in design; Z.D. JASTRZEBSKI, *Nature and Properties of Engineering Materials* (1959), similar to Marin's earlier work, but updated to the end of the decade; H.R. CLAUSEN et al. (eds.), *Encyclopedia of Engineering Materials and Processes* (1963); and J.M. ALEXANDER and R.C. BREWER, *Manufacturing Properties of Materials* (1963); two comprehensive and easily read texts on material properties.

Other general works include: C.W. RICHARDS, *Engineering Materials Science* (1961), a highly readable and up-to-date book; F.A. MCCLINTOCK and A.S. ARGON (eds.), *Mechanical Behavior of Materials* (1966), an excellent description of both sophisticated and conventional techniques for acquiring and utilizing modern material property data; and O.J. HORGEV (ed.), *ASME Handbook*, vol. 1, *Metal Engineering: Design*, 2nd ed. (1965), the official Mechanical Engineering Society position on the utilization of advanced material properties in design; I.E. CAMPBELL, *High-Temperature Technology* (1956); and W.D. KINGERY, *Introduction to Ceramics* (1960); books illustrating the utilization of ceramic materials and emphasizing high temperature applications; J.E. DORN (ed.), *Mechanical Behavior of Materials at Elevated Temperatures* (1961), a thorough treatment of advanced material properties, particularly of metals, as influenced by high temperature; and H.E. DAVIS, G.E. TROXELL, and C.T. WISKOCIL, *The Testing and Inspection of Engineering Materials*, 3rd ed. (1964), a highly comprehensive and easily understood work offering sufficiently detailed information on the various testing methods for use in the training of materials testing personnel.

(K.E.H.)

Mathematics, Foundations of

The study of the foundations of mathematics has dealt with the concepts and the assumptions about those concepts with which mathematics starts. Especially since 1900, foundational investigations have come to include also an inquiry into the nature of mathematical theories and the scope of mathematical methods.

THE AXIOMATIC METHOD

Geometry according to Euclid. Euclid's *Elements*, a treatise written about 330 BC on the foundations of mathematics as well as on geometry, is said to have had a greater circulation than any book in history except the Bible. Euclid employs the deductive method, which had come down from Pythagoras two centuries earlier and which is outlined in the following three stages.

Euclid's use of the deductive method

First, Euclid introduces fundamental concepts such as point, line, plane, and angle. He relates these to physical space by such definitions as "A line is length without breadth"; but, since their definitions play no further role in his system, they constitute primitive or undefined terms.

Second, Euclid asserts certain primitive propositions or postulates about these primitive terms. These are propositions that the reader is asked to accept as true immediately on the basis of the definitions of the primitive terms relative to the physical world.

Third, Euclid deduces from the postulates further propositions, called theorems, such as the theorem of Pythagoras, "The sum of the squares constructed on the arms of a right triangle is equal to the square constructed on the hypotenuse." That is, he shows that their truth follows logically from the truth of the primitive propositions. While doing so, he also introduces defined terms, such as triangle, right triangle, and hypotenuse, which are single words that can take the place of phrases using besides ordinary language only the undefined terms.

The net result is that the reader, starting with postulates of which he is supposed to be immediately convinced, is led, by a long series of simple steps each intended to be convincing, to accept the truth of other propositions, of which he would be far from convinced had they been asserted at the outset.

Non-Euclidean geometry. Euclid's parallel postulate, on which depends the theorem "Through a point P not on a line L there can be drawn exactly one line parallel to L," had long seemed less evident than his other postulates. Attempts to prove it as a theorem from the other postulates culminated in the 19th century in the independent discoveries by the Russian and Hungarian mathematicians Nikolay Ivanovich Lobachevsky and János Bolyai that a different parallel postulate can be substituted to give a non-Euclidean geometry in which instead: "For some plane, some line L in the plane, and some point P in the plane and not on L, there exist at least two distinct lines in the plane passing through point P and not intersecting line L." Bolyai was aware of the noncontradictory character of the new geometry in 1825 and Lobachevsky possibly in 1826, though the publications of both men were delayed.

Insofar as Euclidean geometry fits physical space, it is impossible to say that the geometry of Lobachevsky and Bolyai does not also fit. It is only necessary that the discrepancies between the two be too small to show up in any measurements that can be made. So, while Euclid thought of his geometry as a true description of physical space, it is necessary to regard it as one of a number of different possible mathematical models of that space.

That a theorem of Euclidean geometry be exactly true can only be a property of the geometry as a logical structure. A person who accepts Euclidean geometry as a valid logical structure is equally obliged to accept the geometry of Lobachevsky and Bolyai. For example, as the leader in German mathematics Felix Klein observed in 1871 (and an Italian, Eugenio Beltrami, in somewhat different terms in 1868), the postulates of Lobachevsky and Bolyai's plane geometry are true in Euclidean plane geometry when in those postulates the plane is interpreted to be the interior of a circle, the lines to be the chords of that circle, and congruence, distance, and angle are defined by a method given in England by Arthur Cayley in 1859.

Formal axiomatic method. Here the meaning of the undefined terms of a postulational theory has been varied while holding the deductive structure fixed, a procedure that is characteristically modern. One can deduce a theory from its postulates without saying at all what the undefined terms are to mean. The theory applies to any system of objects that when taken as supplying the meanings of the undefined terms make the postulates true.

Manipulation of undefined terms

Indeed, in a postulational theory, one should be able to perform the deductions treating the undefined terms as meaningless. For, if their meanings had to be used, whatever had to be taken from their meanings should instead be provided by additional postulates. In Euclid's *Elements* some properties of the undefined terms did in fact enter from their meanings via the figures. These hidden assumptions were brought to light and stated as postulates by the German mathematicians Moritz Pasch in 1882 and David Hilbert, the latter in his *Grundlagen der Geometrie* (1899; *The Foundations of Geometry*, 1902). Thus, Hilbert states as a postulate, "If a line L cuts the side AB of a triangle ABC and does not pass through A, B or C, then it must also cut AC or BC."

The postulational method when the undefined terms are treated as meaningless is called the formal postulational method, or formal axiomatic method. In this connection, "axiom" and "postulate" are often used synonymously, in contrast with the material axiomatic method of Euclid.

It might be thought that meaninglessness of the undefined terms would rob a theory of its interest, but the opposite can be the case. Thus, for some theories many different interpretations of their undefined terms each make the postulates true (*e.g.*, Euclidean geometry without the parallel postulate or in algebra abstract groups). The deduction of such a theory independently of any interpretation makes it a mathematical tool prepared in advance for diverse applications. If in essential respects only one such interpretation exists, the postulates are categorical; that is, admitting of no further qualifications. If there is no such interpretation, the theory is without value, and one of the problems for foundations is to exclude such theories.

THE GENETIC METHOD

Arithmetic, analysis. Systems of numbers are more often introduced by the genetic method, so called by Hilbert. In this the objects are generated or constructed in a certain orderly manner, and the theorems express properties of the system of the objects assured by this mode of generation, the term genetic being taken from biology. Of course, deductive reasoning is used, just as in the axiomatic method, to obtain unobvious properties from obvious or immediate ones, and the immediate properties can be listed as postulates. Thus, the natural numbers 0, 1, 2, $\cdots$, used in counting discrete objects, are describable genetically as the objects that are generated by starting with a first object, 0, and by proceeding from any object, n, already generated to the next object, $n + 1$, objects differently generated being distinct. A suitable selection of immediate properties constitutes the five postulates of Giuseppe Peano, an Italian mathematician and logician, expressed in 1889, which are categorical for the arithmetic of the natural numbers. By starting from these postulates, rather than from the generation, that arithmetic can then be considered as a formal axiomatic theory. But the genetic method will be used here in describing some other mathematical systems of objects.

Arithmetic has several senses; but one of them is the theory of the natural numbers and of similar systems of numbers, such as the integers (an extension of the natural numbers, by way of including negatives of natural numbers) $\cdots$, -2, -1, 0, 1, 2, $\cdots$, or the rational numbers such as $\frac{1}{2}$, $\frac{2}{3}$, $\frac{4}{5}$, which are the numbers expressible as fractions p/q in which p and q are integers with q not 0.

Analysis deals with such systems of objects as the real numbers, used in the measurement of continuously variable magnitudes. A theory of real numbers not resting on vague geometrical imagery was only achieved in the latter part of the 19th century, in Germany and France, by Karl Weierstrass, Richard Dedekind, Charles Méray, and Georg Cantor. A version using infinite decimals will suffice here. For example, $\frac{9}{4} = 2.25 = 2.24999 \cdots$, $-\frac{9}{4} = -2.25 = -3 + 0.75 = -3 + 0.74999 \cdots$, $1 = 0.99999 \cdots$, $\sqrt{2} = 1.41421 \cdots$, $\pi = 3.14159$ $\cdots$. In each example, a real number x is expressed as a sum $X + 0.x_0x_1x_2x_3x_4 \cdots$ of an integer X and a nonterminating decimal fraction $0.x_0x_1x_2x_3x_4 \cdots$ (*i.e.*, one without all digits 0 after some place). The real numbers are given genetically, each number uniquely, as all possible such sums.

Cardinal number, the theory of sets. If, in a tribe of aborigines unable to count above 20, whose chief is by custom the member with the most numerous herd, there were two contenders for the chieftaincy, the tribe could decide the winner (or that the two contenders are tied) by passing their herds, no matter how large, through a gate, a pair of animals, one from each herd, at a time.

Cantor's contribution

Cantor was the first who applied this idea systematically to the comparison of infinite collections. A one-to-one correspondence between two collections, or sets, of objects S and T is a collection of ordered pairs in which the first member of each pair belongs to S, the second member to T, and each member of S occurs as first member, each member of T as second member, of just one pair. Two sets have the same cardinal number if there is a one-to-one correspondence between them.

The natural numbers 0, 1, 2, $\cdots$, the positive integers 1, 2, 3, $\cdots$, the squares of the positive integers 1, 4, 9, $\cdots$ (an example used by Galileo in 1638), and the integers 0, 1, -1, 2, -2, $\cdots$ have the same cardinal number. Infinite sets with this cardinal are countable (or countably infinite, to distinguish them from finite sets, which are also countable), because they can be counted off or listed by using the natural numbers. A fifth example of a countably infinite set is the rational numbers; for each rational can be written as a positive or negative ratio of integers, $(-1)^n p/q$, with the least possible natural numbers n, p, q, and then the rationals can be enumerated by various techniques in order to make it explicit that they are countable. One such technique is to enumerate $(-1)^n p/q$ in the order of magnitude of the positive integers $2^n 3^p 5^q$.

A part, or subset, of a set S is a set each member of which is a member of S. As Galileo had noted, a part not the whole of an infinite set can be in one-to-one correspondence with the whole. (Dedekind in 1888 used this property to distinguish infinite sets from finite sets.) A set T is of greater cardinal number than another set S if there is a one-to-one correspondence between S and a subset of T but not vice versa.

Cantor showed in 1874 by a method now called the diagonal method that there are sets of greater cardinal number than the natural numbers (see Box, 1–4).

Thus, infinity is not simple, but indeed there are a whole host of infinite or transfinite cardinal numbers. This result is only one of many in Cantor's theory of sets, which greatly extended the mathematical horizon, besides seeming to provide the ideas for a general foundation of mathematics.

THE CRISIS IN FOUNDATIONS FOLLOWING 1900

The paradoxes. In the last decade of his scientific life Cantor became aware that his theory of sets pushed too far leads to contradictions; two may be described.

If S be the set of all sets and T the set of the subsets of S, then, since T corresponds one-to-one to itself as a subset of S, it cannot have a greater cardinal than S. Yet by Cantor's theorem it must; this is Cantor's paradox, stated in 1899.

The phrases in the English language are countable. After listing all the phrases, strike out those that do not define number-theoretic functions. Application of Cantor's diagonal method to the list remaining enables one to define in the English language a function that differs from every function definable in the English language. This paradox was found by J.A. Richard in 1905.

These modern paradoxes have a counterpart in the ancient paradox of the liar, which in one form appears in a paradoxical statement attributed to Epimenides (6th century BC) and in another is attributed to Eubulides (4th century BC), who has a person say, "What I am now saying is a lie." The quoted sentence if true must by what it says be false, and if false be true.

No one has succeeded in disposing of the paradoxes by simply pointing out a fallacy upon which all can agree.

Cantor's paradox is evidently connected with the use of too-large sets. It is difficult, however, to determine which

---

(1) A (single-valued) number-theoretic function f of one variable x is a correspondence by which, to each natural number x, there corresponds a unique natural number $f(x)$, called the value of f for x as argument. The set of these functions is uncountable, as can be shown by the following reasoning. For any infinite list $f_0, f_1, f_2, \cdots$ of such functions, the function f defined by $f(x) = f_x(x) + 1$ (so the values of f come by altering every value in the diagonal, if the values of $f_0, f_1, f_2, \cdots$ have been written in successive rows) is not in the list; for if f were f_q, the contradictory equation $f_q(q) = f_q(q) + 1$ would be obtained upon taking the value for q as argument. The set of these functions is of greater cardinal number than the natural numbers; for on the other hand, the natural numbers n are in one-to-one correspondence with the constant functions $f(x) = n$.

(2) In the generation of the real numbers using infinite decimals, the nonterminating decimals can be construed as number-theoretic functions taking values $\leqslant 9$; so the reals are uncountable, by reasoning the same as above except taking $f(x) = 8$ when $f_x(x) = 9$.

(3) A given set of natural numbers is represented by a function which takes 0 or 1 as value according as the argument is in the set or not; so the sets of natural numbers are uncountable, by reasoning the same as above except taking $f(x) = 0$ when $f_x(x) = 1$.

(4) It is not hard to show that these three uncountable sets have the same cardinal. The third illustrates Cantor's theorem, "The cardinal number of the set of the subsets of a set S is greater than the cardinal number of S."

---

sets are too large and to replace Cantor's definition "any collection of definite well-distinguished objects of our perception or our thought into a whole."

In fact, it is possible to reformulate set theory to exclude too-large sets. In doing so, axioms are listed to govern just what sets shall be allowed; and set theory becomes a formal axiomatic theory instead of a genetic one. The first system of axiomatic set theory was given in Italy by Ernst Zermelo in 1908 and improved in Germany and Scandinavia by Abraham Adolf Fraenkel and Thoralf Skolem in 1922–23. Axiomatic set theory provides probably the simplest system in which most existing mathematics, but not the paradoxes as far as is known, can be deduced. The Austrian logician Kurt Gödel in 1938 showed that Cantor's continuum hypothesis, "The cardinal number of the real numbers is the least cardinal number greater than that of the natural numbers," can be added as a new axiom to set theory without introducing contradiction, and Paul J. Cohen of the United States in 1963 showed the like for its negation (see SET THEORY).

That the paradoxes arose shows there is some defect in the methods, which hitherto had been trusted, of constructing and reasoning about mathematical objects. Transforming the theory of sets from a genetic into a formal axiomatic theory leaves over the problem of whether there is an interpretation of the undefined terms that makes the axioms in some sense true. To ignore these issues is to adopt a mathematical nihilism. Formally axiomatized mathematics cannot be all of mathematics. To draw upon another formal axiomatic theory for such an interpretation is a regress. At some level there must be a meaningful mathematics. At the very least it must be believed that the theorems of a formal axiomatic theory really do follow from the axioms. As a further example, when mathematicians say that by a certain method it can be determined in a finite number of steps whether an equation $ax + by + c = 0$ with given integral coefficients, a, b, c has a solution for x, y in integers, they certainly do not mean merely that this proposition can be deduced from certain axioms.

The great French mathematician and philosopher of

science Henri Poincaré and the outstanding English mathematician and philosopher Bertrand Russell about 1905 concluded that the explanation of the paradoxes lies in a certain circularity of definition. When a set M and an object m are so defined that m is a member of M but is defined only by reference to M, the definition of M or of m is called impredicative. An impredicative definition can be found in each of the paradoxes. Thus, the sickness of mathematics could be cured by banning impredicative definitions, if it did not inconveniently turn out that the cure would kill the patient; for, as was especially emphasized in the German-born U.S. mathematician and physicist Hermann Weyl's *Das Kontinuum* (1918; "The Continuum"), there are impredicative definitions also in analysis.   (S.C.K.)

Intuitionism. In the first quarter of the 20th century three main schools of thought, called Logicism, Formalism, and Intuitionism, arose to account for and resolve the crisis in the foundations of mathematics. Each of these is a version of a more or less traditional view of the nature of mathematics. The first is a form of Platonic Realism, according to which mathematics investigates a realm of abstract objects (such as points, numbers, sets, and the like) that "exist" external to and independent of the investigator. In Logicism it was argued that all mathematical notions are reducible to the idea of abstract property and that mathematics is derived from basic logical principles concerning properties; this is discussed in more detail below. The attempted reduction in Logicism to evident principles was not completely successful, but the work on this led to an axiomatization of Cantor's notion of set (or class) as a basis for current mathematics (see SET THEORY). Formalism holds that mathematics consists simply of the manipulation of finite configurations of symbols according to prescribed rules. Some of these configurations may have concrete meaning; others are considered as meaningless. In the Formalist view, the choice of rules is dictated by pragmatic considerations or, even better, by theoretical justification of their use in deriving concretely meaningful statements; this is also discussed below. Finally, Intuitionism is a version of the conception of mathematics as a self-sustained intellectual activity that deals with mental constructions governed by self-evident laws. These three schools of thought were principally led, respectively, by Russell, Hilbert, and the Dutch mathematician and philosopher L.E.J. Brouwer.

Mathematical logic was considerably developed in order to make these positions precise and study them more deeply. Set theory was allied with the increasingly general and nonconstructive tendency in mathematics. On the other hand, Intuitionism led to a considerable redevelopment of portions of mathematics in constructive terms, to eliminate what were regarded as philosophically untenable features. It and Formalism together bordered on the development of the important notion of mechanically computable function.

Historical background of Intuitionism. Immanuel Kant, an 18th-century philosopher who was the founder of critical philosophy, is often cited as a progenitor of Intuitionism in mathematics, inasmuch as he viewed space and time as forms that the mind imposes upon human sensibility or perception and, thus, as a priori and Idealistic. Leopold Kronecker, a 19th-century mathematician specializing in number theory and algebra, is also viewed as a progenitor because of his attitude to existence proofs. These typically give information about possible solutions to an equation or condition, such as the existence of at least one function that solves a differential equation or the existence of some point at which a continuous function achieves its maximum value in an interval. Kronecker doubted the significance of proofs, of a sort increasingly used in mathematics, that established the existence of such solutions by indirect arguments without necessarily being able to construct any one of them explicitly or even provide a finite procedure for finding one. In the beginning of the 20th century there was a French semi-Intuitionistic school of mathematics led by Émile Borel, which concentrated on explicit construc-

tions in mathematical analysis. During the same period, Poincaré was very influential through his informal writings, where he stressed the basic intuition of the sequence of integers and questioned the use of certain definitions selecting members from assumed completed infinite totalities (the so-called impredicative definitions mentioned above).

Basic features of Intuitionism. The basic concepts and results of Intuitionism in its full modern development were laid out, however, by Brouwer, who is, therefore, now considered to be the founder of the school. He regarded the starting point for mathematics to be the intuitive understanding of the generation of the sequence of (positive) integers, that is, of the repeated duplication, $|, ||, |||, \cdot \cdot \cdot$ of a single entity considered abstractly.

Brouwer believed that this was derived from a more basic inner awareness of time, whose unity is separated into a "two-ity" by the present moment; this is related to Kant's views as to the a priori status of time. Brouwer also took this idea of repeated division to be the intuitive source of the generation of sequences of rationals which make up the real number system. Thus, in contrast to the Platonic Realist position, the infinite collections considered were conceived of as potential rather than completed infinite totalities. On the Platonist view it is true to say, *e.g.*, that either the sequence 0123456789 occurs at some position in the decimal expansion $3.14159 \cdot \cdot \cdot$ of π or there exists no such position; one can further proceed to define a number n as the least position where the first case holds, if indeed it holds, and as 0 otherwise. In opposition to the Platonist conception, Brouwer restricted mathematical knowledge to that which can be known about mental constructions and proofs. For him, to know a proposition P one must have a proof of it; to know its negation not-P one must have a disproof of it; that is, a proof that P leads to a contradiction. For the proposition P that expresses that 0123456789 occurs at some position in the decimal expansion of π, there is at present neither a proof of P nor a disproof of P; for this reason there is not an explicit construction of the number n above.

More generally, on the Platonist position, one accepts for any proposition P (even ones which refer to infinite totalities) the law of the excluded middle, P or not-P; in other words, that P is true or P is false. This cannot be accepted in general by the Intuitionist in his interpretation since he cannot be sure that for every P one shall be able to find either a proof of it or a disproof of it. From this point of view, some of the most fundamental arguments and definitions in mathematical analysis and other branches of mathematics become unsupported, and these subjects require a complete re-examination.

Brouwer's work on Intuitionism falls into several distinct periods: the first, beginning with his thesis in 1907, was primarily negative, with vigorous criticisms of the Realist (Cantorian and Logicist) as well as Formalist viewpoints; and the second, in the 1920s, was positive, being occupied with the reconstruction of mathematics according to the Intuitionistic tenets. After a long period of silence, Brouwer returned to the scene in the late 1940s with his "theory of the creative subject," which was even more radically subjectivist than his previous ideas.

The criticisms of Realism and Formalism. Brouwer's criticism of the Realist position concentrated on the application therein of the so-called classical logic of propositions and predicates referring to infinite totalities. In particular, by the law of the excluded middle in classical logic, if n is used to symbolize any member of the infinite set of integers 1, 2, 3, $\cdot \cdot \cdot$ and $P(n)$ denotes a property or predicate P of n, one must admit:

(A) "Either there exists an n such that $P(n)$ holds, or, for all n, $P(n)$ fails."

One example of this has already been considered in the preceding section.

For another example, each real number that is between 0 and 1 (possibly equalling 0 or 1) has some representation $r = 0.a_1a_2a_3 \cdot \cdot \cdot$ where each $a_n = 0, 1, \cdot \cdot \cdot, 9$. If $P(n)$ is the property "a_n is less than 9," then because

$r = 1$ just in case each a_n is equal to 9 ($1 = 0.999 \cdots$), the general logical law (A) reduces to the statement in this case that $r \neq 1$ or $r = 1$. Similarly, one may use (A) to justify "r is less than s or r is greater than or equal to s" for any real numbers r and s, which is basic to the classical treatment of mathematical analysis. One may then go on to define discontinuous functions f of real numbers r, such as the so-called step function f that has the value 0 if r is less than 1 and 1 if r is greater than or equal to 1.

Of course the law (A) can be checked directly when n ranges over a given finite set of integers and $P(n)$ is a decidable property; *i.e.*, there is available a method that will tell for each n whether or not $P(n)$ holds. Brouwer argued that the assumption of (A) is based on an unjustified extrapolation of the experience with finite sets to the infinite.

Brouwer's criticism of Formalism was principally directed at Hilbert's formulation of that position, described in more detail below. Briefly, Hilbert's idea was to justify all of mathematics on the basis of the most elementary and concrete methods of finite combinatorial reasoning. The vehicle for this was to be the representation of mathematical statements as strings of symbols in formal logical systems.

The justification was to consist in giving Finitist proofs of consistency of such formal systems and, thence, of their correctness for deriving finitistically meaningful statements. Brouwer did not object to the use of Finitist reasoning, because this is just a part of what is Intuitionistically acceptable. The difference is that Finitism uses constructions only on concretely conceived objects such as the integers, whereas Intuitionism uses them also on abstractly conceived objects, such as proofs and constructions. Brouwer saw no special reason for the proposed restriction to Finitist methods. But his main objection to Hilbert's program was that in his view mere consistency of formal systems of mathematics could not justify them; only a prior understanding of the symbols of these systems and direct intuitive verification of the axioms and rules could do that. Moreover, one could not expect to pin down, once and for all, in any formal system the nature of the ongoing creative process of concept formation and discovery in mathematics. Brouwer's criticisms of Hilbert's program were in a way subsequently borne out by the famous work of Kurt Gödel in 1931, showing the inherent limitations of that program (see below *Logicism, Formalism, and the metamathematical method*).

Redevelopment of mathematics. The system of real numbers forms the basis of the calculus and more generally of mathematical analysis; this, in turn, is essential for the solution of the equations employed in scientific applications such as the differential equations of mathematical physics. It seemed to many that the Intuitionistic abandonment of classical logic would undermine a vast body of knowledge. Nevertheless, Brouwer set out to re-create mathematics in accordance with his tenets. His positive contributions to this reconstruction included a new theory of real numbers and of real functions (real-valued operations on real numbers), a theory of sets (called species), and a theory of ordinals (finite and transfinite construction stages). The groundwork was thus laid for a redevelopment of substantial portions of classical algebra, analysis, geometry, and topology. Even so, Brouwer attracted few converts to the Intuitionistic position thereby. Some of the reasons for this lie in the character of his expositions, which in the first period were polemical and in the second (technical) period were rather frequently obscure, involving unfamiliar or even "suspect" notions and familiar terminology with new meanings. This may be illustrated with Brouwer's assertion:

(B) Every real function is continuous.

This assertion is patently contradictory with the classical interpretation since, for example, the step function described above is not continuous. To understand the Intuitionistic interpretation of (B), one must first explain how real numbers are to be considered. In the classical interpretation, every real number r is the limit of a convergent sequence s of rational numbers $s_1, s_2, s_3, \cdots$; this is indicated by the symbolism $s = \{s_n\}$. There are many possible such s for each real r; one, for example, is given by the sequence $s_n = a_0 + a_1/10^1 + \cdots + a_n/10^n$ when $r = a_0.a_1a_2a_3 \cdots$ is written in decimal form. Intuitionistically, one can operate directly only with the sequences $s = \{s_n\}$, which are called real-number generators. Two such sequences $s = \{s_n\}$ and $s' = \{s'_n\}$ are said to be equivalent, and one writes $s = s'$ if the difference $s_n - s'_n$ approaches 0 as n increases without bound. (This relation is to be distinguished from that of strict identity, where, for each n, $s_n = s'_n$.) A real function f can only be given by a construction F that associates with each generator s another generator $t = F(s)$ such that if $s = s'$ (in the sense just explained) then $F(s) = F(s')$.

Now each specific real-number generator $s = \{s_n\}$ must also be given by a construction that determines s_n, given n. In practice, however, one does not make use of a rule for s when determining the terms of the generator $F(s)$, rather only the successive values $s_1, s_2, s_3, \cdots$, so to speak, as they appear. Brouwer introduced the new concept of infinitely proceeding sequence (ips); roughly speaking, this is any sequence of which one can determine as many values as desired, although at any stage not more than an initial segment need be known. Every constructively defined s is an ips, but one may also think of s that are generated by some random processes or free acts of choice. Any construction that assigns to each ips s a rational number can only make use of some finite amount of information $s_1, s_2, \cdots, s_n$ about s. Brouwer's assertion (B) easily follows from this general continuity principle. Of course there is no constructive F that determines a step function f; for otherwise it would follow that one could determine for any ips s whether or not s is less than 1 simply on the basis of some finite initial segment of s. This, of course, is absurd, because the remaining terms $s_{n+1}, s_{n+2}, \cdots$ could radically alter the situation.

With the new meanings given to the basic notions of analysis in this way, each classical theorem must be reexamined to see whether it has a correct Intuitionistic version. For example, a classical result often used is that if f is a continuous real function defined on a closed interval, then $f(r_0)$ has a maximum possible value for some r_0 in that interval (and similarly for a minimum). This is not Intuitionistically demonstrable, because one can constructively define a function f such that there is no constructive way to determine an r_0 at which f attains its maximum value. If f satisfies stronger conditions (such as differentiability) that are frequently met in applications, however, it is possible to obtain the existence of such r_0 constructively as well. When a classical result has a correct Intuitionistic version it usually requires a sharpening of the hypotheses, but for existential results one then also gets a sharpening of the conclusion.

Intuitionistic logic. The assertions that are made in Intuitionistic mathematics are supposed to be reports of completed proofs that have been carried out by a series of steps that are evident for the objects conceived when combined by suitable (mental) constructions. It is of interest to compare in general terms the type of reasoning that is admitted under this conception with that which makes use of classical logic. For this one needs an explanation of the conditions under which one has a constructive proof (or grounds) for a compound assertion; the following is based on the explanation provided by Heyting. Here P, Q denote any propositions, S is any given set, the variable x ranges over the objects of S, and $P(x)$ is a predicate of x.

Conditions for Compound Assertions

FORM OF ASSERTION	GROUNDS FOR THE ASSERTION
(a) P or Q	(a) At least one of P, Q has already been proved.
(b) P and Q	(b) Both P and Q have been proved.
(c) P implies Q	(c) One has a construction C of which it has been proved that whenever C is applied to any possible proof of P then the result is a proof of Q.

Brouwer's objection to Hilbert's program

Continuity of a real function

(d) *not P*

(d) The same as for "*P* implies $1 \neq 1$"; that is, every possible proof of *P* is shown to be transformed into a contradiction.

(e) *there exists an x such that P(x)*

(e) One has constructed an *s* in *S* and proved *P(s)*.

(f) *for all x, P(x)*

(f) One has a proof which is shown to specialize to a proof of *P(s)* for each *s* in *S*.

It should be understood that these do not constitute an explanation of the logical connectives in terms of prior, logic-free notions. They do show, however, the circumstances under which the connectives are used in practice, and they indicate the form of such an explanation in the strict sense of the word.

The conditions given do not justify the law of excluded middle *P* or not-*P*, because, as already discussed, there is no reason to expect that for any proposition *P* it is possible either to find a proof of it or to show how to derive a contradiction from it. If one accepts Brouwer's notion of ips, however, and the general continuity principle for these, one can actually disprove this classical law. This is true because, as has been pointed out, this implies the general law (A) above, of which the following is then a special case:

(C) For every ips $s = \{s_n\}$, either there exists an *m* such that $s_m = 0$ or for all *m*, $s_m \neq 0$.

A consequence is the following:

(D) For every ips $s = \{s_n\}$, there exists an *m* such that either $s_m = 0$ or for all *p*, $s_p \neq 0$.

By the general continuity principle, one should be able to associate with any *s*, two numbers *n* and *m* such that for any *s'* with $s'_1 = s_1, \cdots, s'_n = s_n$, either $s'_m = 0$ or for all *p*, $s'_p \neq 0$; one can also assume that *m* is less than or equal to *n*. If one starts with a sequence *s* of nonzero terms, however, one can always define *s'*, which agrees with *s* on the initial segment $1, \cdots, n$ but is such that $s'_{n+1} = 0$. Thus (D), and hence also the law of excluded middle, leads to a contradiction. In other words, the following has been shown:

(E) It is not the case that (C) holds.

By a similar argument the following can be shown:

(F) Not for all ips *s* and *t*, either *s* is less than *t* or *t* is less than or equal to *s*. (S.Fe.)

Logicism, Formalism, and the metamathematical method. While the philosophical debate at the foundations of mathematics was identified for many years with the debate among the three schools of thought, Logicism, Formalism, and the Intuitionism considered above, a broadened basis for reasoning followed from the work of Gödel, Church, and Turing in the 1930s. Thus, a contemporary presentation of the problems at the foundations of mathematics is coloured by the automata-based reasoning that is identified with Turing's name. Whereas Intuitionism yielded somewhat to Formalism at the hands of Heyting, the techniques made available to Logicism and Formalism were enormously broadened with the introduction of Turing's machine (see below *Turing's computing machine and formal systems*). While the lines separating the traditional three schools of thought have become less distinct since mid-20th century, it now seems natural to present the points of view with Intuitionism on the one hand and Logicism and Formalism, as transformed by the metamathematical method (in which the object of a mathematical study is a mathematical system), on the other. Such a division should not be interpreted to mean that metamathematical methods have not been fruitfully applied in studies of systematizations arising from the Intuitionistic schools.

Logicism. The Logicistic thesis is that mathematics is a branch of logic. A German logician and mathematician, Gottfried Wilhelm Leibniz, in 1666 had conceived of logic as a universal science embracing the principles underlying all others. Richard Dedekind in 1888 and, especially, Gottlob Frege in 1884 and 1893, both of Germany, derived arithmetic from logic. The thesis that all of mathematics is reducible to logic alone is due to Russell.

Russell, after rediscovering results of Frege, had to make provision against the paradoxes. This provision took the form of a ramified theory of types. Roughly described, the primary objects not being subjected to logical analysis he took to be of one type—say, type 0—properties of objects of type 0 to be of type 1, properties of properties of type 1 to be of type 2, etc.; and he excluded from use any properties not belonging to one of these types. Then, to exclude impredicative definitions within a type, he separated the types above type 0 into orders, the properties defined using the totality of properties of a given order being placed in the next higher order. Finally, to overcome the obstacle that exclusion of impredicative definitions opposes to analysis, he postulated his axiom of reducibility, which asserts that to any property belonging to an order above the lowest there is a property of order 0 possessed by exactly the same objects.

The theory of types

On this basis, mathematics was deduced from logic, in a symbolic language, in the monumental *Principia Mathematica*, by the English mathematician Alfred North Whitehead and Bertrand Russell, in 1910–13.

The use of the axiom of reducibility weakens the case for the Logicistic thesis. For, if the axiom be true, should not the reductions to order 0 be constructed instead of being merely postulated as existing? Weyl hence remarked in 1946 that in *Principia Mathematica* "mathematics is no longer founded on logic, but on a sort of logician's paradise."

Leon Chwistek in 1921 and F.P. Ramsey in 1926 introduced a simple theory of types in which the separation into orders is suppressed. This theory still allows the deduction of mathematics from logic, with the paradoxes apparently excluded, but it does not improve the philosophical position.

A fundamental objection to the Logicistic thesis is posed by the Intuitionists, who find an essential mathematical kernel in the idea of iteration, which already has to be used in establishing the hierarchy of types and even in listing the propositions in a proof.

The logician Willard Van Orman Quine of the United States in 1937 weakened the type restriction to one of stratification. The resulting system is a form of axiomatic set theory rather than of type theory. Indeed, though the Logicistic thesis did not so develop historically, it could be based as well on a set theory as on a type theory.

Formalism. Hilbert accepted that the parts of classical mathematics employing the completed infinite go beyond intuitive evidence. But, instead of rejecting those parts, he proposed in 1905 and, more specifically, after 1918 roughly to formulate classical mathematics up to a suitable point as a formal axiomatic theory and to prove this theory consistent—*i.e.*, free from contradiction.

Previous to this proposal of Hilbert, proofs of consistency had been given for axiomatic theories by interpreting their undefined terms in another theory so that the axioms become true or briefly by giving a model. Thus, the plane Lobachevskyan geometry was interpreted in Euclidean geometry by Beltrami. The consistency of geometries generally is reduced to that of analysis by René Descartes's analytic geometry of 1637, which employs real numbers as coordinates of points, so that geometrical propositions become propositions in the algebra of real numbers. For proving the consistency of analysis itself, the method of models offers no hope, because no theory is available in which analysis could be interpreted that appears safer than analysis.

Hilbert's proposal called for proving consistency by a new method, based directly on the meaning of consistency as freedom from contradiction. Not only should all the mathematical assumptions of a theory be listed but also all of the principles of logic, both the primitive propositions and the rules for drawing inferences, to be used in deducing theorems from the mathematical postulates. This listing done, it is possible to undertake to show that no two proofs in the theory terminate in theorems one of which is the negation of the other. Hilbert would thus make the proofs of the formal theory the object of an intuitive theory, called proof theory, or metamathematics. The latter should use only intuitively convincing methods, called by him finitary methods. These methods in practice are Intuitionistic methods on the level of number theory. The formal theory provides a sort of stereotyped model of the previously existing informal theory, which is called the interpretation of the formal theory. This interpretation should play no role in the metamathematics, though it motivates the choice of the particular formal theory that is the object of the metamathematics.

To guarantee that all the principles of logic used in deducing theorems have been listed as axioms and rules of inference, the meanings of all the words should be left out of account in deducing theorems, just as in a formal axiomatic theory it should be possible to leave out of account the meanings of the undefined mathematical terms. Because of the irregularities and ambiguities of the existing word languages, it is feasible to do this only by reconstructing the informal theory as a symbolic language, which can be done by combining symbolic logic with the symbolization common in modern mathematics. The resulting formal theory is called a formal system, or logistic system, a statement in it a formula (or by some writers a well-formed formula, to emphasize that it must be formed from the symbols by listed formation rules) and the method the logistic method. The description of a formal system must be given from outside in an informal theory. The method was already available, but Hilbert added the proposal to make the formal system the object of mathematical investigations in this informal theory or metamathematics.

Brouwer–
Hilbert
contro-
versy
There ensued a controversy in which Brouwer questioned how a metamathematical proof of consistency of classical mathematics would meet the objection that the propositions of classical mathematics beyond a certain elementary level lack a clear intuitive meaning. The upshot was that the Intuitionists would accept Hilbert's program as unobjectionable if the Formalists refrained from construing a consistency proof as in some manner vindicating classical mathematics intuitively. Hilbert drew an analogy with the stratagem in mathematics of adjoining ideal elements to a previously constituted system to achieve some theoretical end (*e.g.*, the irrational numbers were added to the rationals so that all convergent sequences should have limits, the imaginary numbers to the reals so that all algebraic equations should have solutions; see ANALYSIS, REAL). He called the statements of classical mathematics with an intuitive meaning real, the others ideal. The statements involving the completed infinite are ideal. So, he said, in classical mathematics the ideal statements are adjoined to the real to give the theory as a whole a simpler logical structure, and it is no more reasonable to require that each separate statement should be interpretable taken by itself than that in theoretical physics each separate statement should be verifiable by experiment. The possibility appeared that classical mathematics reinforced by a proof of consistency might even serve as a tool for the Intuitionistic proof of real statements via shortcuts through the ideal statements.

Hilbert's program was undertaken after 1920 by him and his collaborators, the German Wilhelm Ackermann and the Frenchman Paul Bernays, and by others, including the Hungarian-born U.S. mathematician John von Neumann and the Frenchman Jacques Herbrand. The start was made by investigating a formal system of classical arithmetic (with several variants), obtained by adding Peano's postulates and definitions of sum and product to the first-order functional calculus as developed by Peano and as described in Hilbert and Bernays' *Grundlagen der Mathematik* ("The Foundation of Mathematics") in 1934 and 1939. A proof by Ackermann in 1924–25 of consistency of a subsystem did not lead at once to a proof of consistency of the whole system. Then in 1931 results of Gödel appeared that clarified the situation. These results are presented below from a standpoint that was reached after 1935.

The metamathematical method proved valuable for a variety of purposes in studying formal systems generally, as well as the ones Hilbert considered. Thus, a formal system of intuitionistic logic and mathematics was described by Heyting in 1930.

Turing's computing machine and formal systems. For certain classes of questions in mathematics, a method is known that can be applied to answer by "yes" or "no" any given question of the class. For example, for any positive integers a and b, the question "Is a a multiple of b?" can be answered by dividing a by b and seeing whether the remainder is 0 or not. As a less obvious example, there is a method for deciding, for any given integers a, b, c, whether $ax + by + c = 0$ has solutions for x, y in integers. Such a method is called an algorithm, or decision procedure; and the problem of finding such a method for a class of questions is called the decision problem for that class. Similarly, for a class of questions that require for their answers not "yes" or "no" but the exhibiting of some object, one speaks of an algorithm, or computation procedure, and a computation problem.

In the logistic method, the description of a formal system must enable one to decide whether any given formula is an axiom and whether any given formula comes by a permitted inference from one or two others; so there is a decision procedure for whether a given finite list of formulas is a proof in the system. But a decision procedure is not thereby provided for whether a given formula is provable; *i.e.*, for whether there is a proof of it. The problem of finding a decision procedure for the latter is often called the decision problem for the formal system The
decision
problem and was recognized in Germany as a problem of logic by Ernst Schröder in 1895, Leopold Löwenheim in 1915 and Hilbert in 1918. In the United States Emil L. Post gave in 1921 a decision procedure for the classical propositional calculus.

A decision procedure for a formal system embracing a given portion of mathematics would make automatic the solution of any problem in that portion statable as a "yes" or "no" question. It is therefore implausible that there should be a decision procedure for a formal system embracing the usual arithmetic, in view of the experience of mathematicians in trying to solve the one particular problem whether Fermat's last theorem is true; and many other similarly refractory problems are known. (The French mathematician Pierre Fermat around 1637 claimed to have proved that the equation $x^n + y^n = z^n$ has no solution in positive integers x, y, z for any positive integer $n > 2$; but no one since then has been able to confirm or disprove this so-called "last theorem" of his.) For there to be a decision procedure would mean, so to speak, that the infinitely many arithmetical problems involve only a finite number of difficulties such that once those are overcome no further ingenuity will be required. But it might have seemed equally farfetched in 1918 to hope that mathematics could get a hold on the problem of finding a decision procedure for arithmetic, which would enable this problem to be solved by showing that there cannot be one. Exactly this latter was done in 1936 by Alonzo Church.

The consideration of the computation problems for number–theoretic functions can lead to the question of what functions can be computed or effectively calculated, in the sense that, for a given argument, the value can be found by use only of preassigned rules, applicable without ingenuity on the part of the computer. Instead of a human, it can be proposed to have a machine to do the computation, according to rules built into its structure.

As this description is somewhat vague, what is needed is an exact mathematical formulation that comes to the same end. Such a formulation was given briefly by Post in 1936 and independently in detail by Turing in 1936–37. What Turing did was to describe a kind of theoretical computing machine, not limited in use by a fixed maximum amount of storage of information nor liable to malfunctioning, as are actual computing machines. A Turing machine operates in the following manner. At discrete moments the machine assumes one of a finite list of states (fixed for a given machine), the first of which is called the passive state, the other active, of which there are k in number, in which k is 1 or a greater integer. A linear tape, potentially infinite to the right, is ruled in squares, each of which is either blank or has printed upon it one of a finite number j (one or more) of symbols

Computation of number-theoretic functions

(fixed for a given machine), including, say, the tally |; but only a finite number of squares are printed. The tape passes through the machine so that one of its squares is scanned. If at the given moment the machine is in an active state, then it can alter the condition of the scanned square (by erasing, printing, or both), and/or move the tape so that the scanned square becomes the one next right or left, and/or change to another state between the given moment and the next or any combination of the preceding; this act is determined (for a given Turing machine) by the state of the machine and the condition of the scanned square at the given moment.

Turing used his machines primarily to compute in succession the digits of decimal expansions of real numbers, but they can be adapted to compute number-theoretic functions. Let an argument x be supplied to the machine by placing a blank followed by $x + 1$ tallies on successive squares of the tape starting with the leftmost square, leaving the tape otherwise blank, and placing the tape in the machine with the rightmost tally scanned and the machine in its first active state. The machine is said to compute a value y for x as argument, if then it eventually reaches the passive state with the $x + 1$ tallies followed immediately to the right by a blank and $y + 1$ tallies, the rightmost being scanned, and the tape being otherwise blank. If, for each natural number x, the machine computes the correct value $y = f(x)$ of a function f, when supplied the argument x, it computes the function f, which is then said to be Turing-computable.

Turing advocated the thesis that any function that can be effectively calculated is Turing-computable. His arguments include showing that various operations that a human computer can perform can be analyzed into successions of the simple operations his machines perform. Church had already in 1936 proposed the thesis that every effectively calculable function is λ-definable in a sense due to himself and S.C. Kleene of the United States or, equivalently, general recursive in a sense due to Gödel, who built on a suggestion of Jacques Herbrand of France; and this thesis was subsequently proved equivalent to Turing's, so the λ-definable functions, the general recursive functions, and the Turing-computable functions are the same.

Church's theorem, logical systems without decision procedures. The pattern of behaviour of a Turing machine is completely described by a $k \times (j + 1)$ table showing the act to be performed for each of the k active states with each of the $j + 1$ conditions of the scanned square. A system for encoding such tables can be established that, to each table, gives a natural number t as code number so that a person who knows the system can from t find the table and thence the behaviour of a machine M_t with this table. If t is the code number of a machine, M_t, that computes a value for x as argument, let $f_t(x)$ be this value; and let $f_t(x)$ be undefined otherwise.

The function f may be defined by letting $f(x) = f_x(x) + 1$ if $f_x(x)$ is defined, and $f(x) = 0$ otherwise. This function f is not computable. For, if machine M_q with code number q computes a value for q as argument, that value is $f_q(q)$, not $f_q(q) + 1$, as it would have to be if M_q computes f. It follows that the property "$f_x(x)$ is defined" is undecidable. For otherwise $f(x)$ could be computed, given x, thus: first decide whether $f_x(x)$ is defined; then, if it is, imitate the behaviour of M_x to compute it and add 1; if it is not, write 0.

Thus, from Turing's thesis one has proved that there is a class of quite elementary arithmetical questions for which there is no decision procedure. This essentially is Church's theorem (1936), which he proved from his thesis using a corresponding class of questions in terms of λ-definability. For each x, the proposition "$f_x(x)$ is defined" is expressible in any formal system S that includes the usual vocabulary of arithmetic, by a formula A_x effectively determinable given x. If the quoted proposition is true, it is demonstrable intuitively by exhibiting the sequence of the acts of machine M_x in computing $f_x(x)$. If S includes ordinary arithmetical reasoning, then that demonstration can be translated into a proof in S of A_x; i.e., A_x is provable in S whenever (the proposition expressed by it is) true. Finally, if it be supposed about S that A_x is provable in S only when true, then there can be no decision procedure for provability in S; for, if there were, by answering whether A_x is provable in S, one would have a decision procedure for "$f_x(x)$ is defined."

Moreover, there is no decision procedure for the important logical system F of first-order functional (or predicate) calculus, as Church in 1936 and Turing in 1936–37 showed. For a proof of A_x in S can be arranged as a deduction by F of A_x from a suitable finite set of arithmetical axioms independent of x, the conjunction of which can be written as one formula C. If the symbolism has been suitably chosen, then A_x is provable in S, if and only if the implication C $\supset$ A_x is provable in F (the symbols C $\supset$ A_x are read "if C, then A_x"). From these beginnings, a considerable theory has grown about "unsolvable decision problems," with further contributions in the United States, Russia, England, and Poland by Post, A.A. Markov (the younger), Turing, Alfred Tarski, Andrzej Mostowski, P.S. Novikov, and others.

The effect of Gödel's theorems on Formalism. A formal system such as S is consistent if for no formula B are both B and its negation $\sim$B provable in S; complete if for each formula B without free variables (otherwise $\sim$B may not express the opposite of B) either B or $\sim$B is provable in S.

It may be further supposed that $\sim A_x$ is provable in S only when true. It is absurd that S be complete (and that $\sim A_x$ be provable in S whenever true). For, A_x is provable in S (when and) only when true. So if, for each x, either A_x or $\sim A_x$ were provable, it could be decided whether $f_x(x)$ is defined or not, by searching through all the proofs in S until one is found of A_x or of $\sim A_x$. This is Gödel's theorem of 1931 in a negative form.

Gödel's theorem

To obtain the positive form, the process can be considered, for a given x, of searching through all the proofs in S for one of $\sim A_x$ and writing 0 if one is found. A Turing machine, say machine M_q with code number q, carries out this process, when supplied with x. Now by the choice of the formulas A_x, $\sim A_q$ is true if and only if $f_q(q)$ is undefined, which by the choice of M_q is the case if and only if $\sim A_q$ is unprovable in S. In brief, $\sim A_q$ expresses its own unprovability (compare the paradox of the liar). So, were $\sim A_q$ provable, it would be false, contradicting the supposition that $\sim A_x$ is provable only when true. So $\sim A_q$ is unprovable but true, and A_q is also unprovable (since false).

Hilbert's program called for embodying classical mathematics, including arithmetic, analysis, and set theory short of the paradoxes, in a formal system and proving that system consistent by finitary methods. The part of Gödel's theorem that $\sim A_q$ is unprovable but true shows that not even the first step can be carried out fully. Despite the great value of the logistic method as a way of defining exactly the presuppositions of a given portion of mathematics, this very process of definition restricts that portion to include less of arithmetic than free use of intuitive reasoning would give, at least if what is already incorporated in the formal system is intuitively correct.

The part of the theorem that neither $\sim A_q$ nor A_q is provable in S shows the inadequacy of S to decide by proof or disproof, irrespective of the interpretation, all the statements expressible in it. Thus, A_q is said to be formally undecidable in S.

In showing $\sim A_q$ unprovable (and true), the assumption was used (for $x = q$) that $\sim A_x$ is provable in S only when true. This can be replaced by the metamathematical assumption (not ostensibly using the interpretation) that S is consistent. For, if $\sim A_q$ were provable, $f_q(q)$ would be defined, and hence, as noted above, A_q would be provable, which would contradict the consistency.

The assumption that A_x is provable only when true, used in showing A_q unprovable, can be replaced by the assumption that S is ω-consistent, in the sense that for no formula B(x) are B(0), B(1), B(2), ... and $\sim(x)$ B(x) all provable in S, when "(x)" expresses "for all x." In verifying this, B(x) will express "at the xth moment M_q has not yet computed $f_q(q)$." Adjoining A_q to S as a new axiom produces a formal system that is consistent but not ω-consistent, if S is consistent. J. Barkley Rosser of the United States in 1936 modified Gödel's formally undecidable formula so that consistency sufficed; in fact, letting M_r carry out the process of searching through all the proofs in S for one of $\sim A_x$ and writing 0 if one is found before one of A_x is found, $\sim A_r$ is unprovable but true, and A_r is unprovable, if S is consistent.

As Gödel observed in proving his theorem, the objects employed in a formal system, say S, are countable; and after correlating natural numbers (called now Gödel numbers) effectively to them, by talking about those numbers instead of the formal objects, the metamathematics of S becomes a part of arithmetic and so expressible in S. Now the implication "If S is consistent, then $\sim A_q$ is true," was obtained above as part of Gödel's theorem. If Consis be the formula of S that expresses "S is consistent" in S via the Gödel numbering, then the quoted implication translated into S becomes Consis ⊃ $\sim A_q$. Gödel claimed that, by imitating formally in S the intuitive proof of his theorem, it should be possible to prove this formula in S. (This was done in detail by Hilbert and Bernays in 1939 in their formal system of arithmetic.) But then, if Consis were also provable, $\sim A_q$ would be, which is contrary to Gödel's (first) theorem if S is consistent. Thus Gödel obtained his second theorem:

Gödel's
second
theorem if S is consistent, then the formula Consis, which says in S via the Gödel numbering that S is consistent, is unprovable in S.

Gödel's second theorem raises an obstacle to the second part of Hilbert's program. One might have supposed that the finitary methods to be used in proving consistency would be part of the methods formalized in the system, which amounts to saying that a finitary proof of consistency of S should be formalizable as a proof in S of Consis. Only such methods appear to have been used in attempts before 1931. Gödel's second theorem shows that not even all the methods incorporated in S, including the nonfinitary ones, would suffice.

Some mathematicians felt that this ended once and for all Hilbert's plan to make classical mathematics more secure by a consistency proof. Others thought it possible that methods might be found for proving consistency that, though not formalizable within S, could be construed as finitary and thus as safer than some of the methods incorporated in S. Thus, Gerhard Gentzen in 1936 gave a proof of the consistency of a system S of classical arithmetic, in which the nonelementary method (not formalizable in S) is an extension of mathematical induction from the natural number sequence to a certain segment of the transfinite ordinal numbers that Cantor had introduced for extending the counting process beyond that provided by the natural numbers.

Gödel's (first) theorem provided confirmation for the view advanced earlier by the Intuitionists on philosophical grounds that the possibilities for intuitive mathematical thinking cannot be circumscribed in advance. Taking Brouwer's interpretation of a statement "a y exists such that $P(y)$" as meaning such a y can be found and applying Church's thesis to the case the y depends on x, Kleene in 1943 proposed the further thesis that a statement "for each x, a y exists such that $P(x, y)$" is provable Intuitionistically only if such a y can be given as a computable function of x. Using this thesis, there are theorems of classical arithmetic, by Kleene in 1943, and of classical analysis, by Ernst Specker in 1949, that are unprovable Intuitionistically (not merely in some formal system but absolutely); so classical mathematics reinforced by a consistency proof cannot serve as a tool of Intuitionistic proof, except of a very restricted class of statements. Kleene in 1945 and David Nelson in 1946 together showed that the Intuitionistic formal arithmetic based on Heyting's Intuitionistic formal logic does conform to the thesis. Gödel in 1932–33 (partially anticipated by A.N. Kolmogorov in 1924–25) correlated to each arithmetical formula B a classically equivalent formula B′ that is provable in the Intuitionistic formal arithmetic if (and of course only if) B is provable in the classical formal arithmetic. In particular, the correlation proves very simply that the classical formal arithmetic is consistent if the

(5) Church's theorem exhibits an undecidable property of a very simple form. In this treatment the undecidable property is "$f_x(x)$ is defined." If "$T(t, x, y)$" abbreviates "t is the code number of a Turing machine M_t that, when supplied with x as argument, completes the computation of a value at moment y (but not earlier)," and if "(Ey)" abbreviates "there exists a y such that" or briefly "exists y" or "for some y," then $[f_x(x)$ is defined$] \equiv (Ey)T(x, x, y)$ (for all x), the symbol $\equiv$ representing "is identical to." But $T(t, x, y)$ and hence $T(x, x, y)$ is a decidable relation. So the undecidable property is of the form $(Ey)R(x, y)$ where $R(x, y)$ is a decidable relation. Using $\sim(Ey)T(x, x, y) \equiv (y)\sim T(x, x, y)$, there is also an undecidable property of the form $(y)R(x, y)$ with $R(x, y)$ decidable [where "(y)" means "for all y"]. Any decidable property $R(x)$ is expressible in both the forms $(Ey)R(x, y)$ and $(y)R(x, y)$, by taking $R(x, y) \equiv R(x)$ & $y = y$, but neither $(Ey)T(x, x, y)$ nor $(y)\sim T(x, x, y)$ is expressible in the form the other has. For, given any decidable relation $R(x, y)$, $(Ey)R(x, y) \equiv (Ey)T(p, x, y)$ where p is the code number of a Turing machine M_p that, when supplied with x as argument, searches for the least y such that $R(x, y)$. So, if $(y)\sim T(x, x, y)$ held for some decidable R, we would have $(y)\sim T(p, p, y) \equiv (Ey)R(p, y) \equiv (Ey)T(p, p, y) \equiv \sim(y)\sim T(p, p, y)$, which is absurd. By similar reasoning, to each of the two forms $(y)(Ez)R(x, y, z)$ and $(Ey)(z)R(x, y, z)$ with decidable R, there is a property, $(y)(Ez)T(x, x, y, z)$ or $(Ey)(z)\sim T(x, x, y, z)$, respectively, of that form that is not expressible in the other form and hence not in any of the simpler forms $R(x)$, $(Ey)R(x, y)$, or $(y)R(x, y)$; and likewise with three, four, $\cdots$ alternating exist-operations and all-operations. This is the (arithmetical) hierarchy theorem of Kleene.

Intuitionistic is. However, the Intuitionistic arithmetic distinguishes differing degrees of indirectness among statements classically equivalent.

Using the classical law of excluded middle, Gödel in 1930 proved a completeness theorem for the first-order functional calculus F. In one form, this says that, if a formal system obtained by adjoining mathematical axioms to F is consistent, it has a model; i.e., there is an interpretation that makes the axioms true. Indeed, the model can be constructed using the natural numbers as the objects. In another form, the theorem says that in such a system every formula is provable that is true under all the interpretations of the undefined terms that make the axioms true. In view of this, when S is based on first-order functional calculus, the unprovability in S of $\sim A_q$ implies that, while $\sim A_q$ is true under the intended interpretation of the undefined terms, there is some other interpretation that makes the axioms true (a nonstandard model) under which $\sim A_q$ is false. This illustrates the theorem of Skolem in 1933 that no list of axioms in the symbolism of the first-order functional calculus can characterize the natural numbers categorically. If higher functional calculus is used, the deductive apparatus will be incomplete. It thus appears that the logistic method is inadequate to characterize the natural numbers categorically. Peano's axioms characterize them categorically but only through an interpretation that cannot be rendered fully through the deductive possibilities. Also one sees the Gödel formal undecidability of A_q as similar to the undecidability of Euclid's parallel postulate from the other postulates of Euclidean geometry. Skolem's
theorem

Degrees of decidability in arithmetic according to Kleene and Mostowski. By Church's thesis, the decidable properties of a natural number are countable; for each decidable property P is decided by a Turing machine that computes 0 or 1 for x as argument according as x has the property P or not, and each Turing machine's behaviour is described by a code number. Thence the existence of undecidable properties follows simply by Cantor's theorem, by which the sets of natural numbers are uncountable; for each property P corresponds to the set S of the natural numbers that have the property.

Church's theorem, however, goes beyond this: it exhibits an undecidable property of a very simple form (see 5). It can also be found that the properties in arithmetic are arranged in a hierarchy, with decidable properties at the bottom and above each level another level containing new properties defined by more uses of "exist" or "all" (see 5). This is a consequence of the (arithmetical) hierarchy theorem of Kleene in 1943, abstracted in 1940, found independently in another version by Andrzej Mostowski in 1947.

Further content is lent to this theory by the notion due to Turing in 1939 of a machine that is like a computing machine except that it has access to an "oracle"; *e.g.*, such a machine may be designed to answer questions whether numbers have property P with the help of an oracle that answers questions whether numbers have property Q. This means that, in the process of answering a given question "Does x have property P?" the machine (besides performing mechanical operations) may ask and receive from the oracle answers to questions "Does y have property Q?" If such a machine exists, then it may be said that P is decidable from Q. In fact, $(Ey)T(x, x, y)$, though undecidable absolutely, is decidable from $(y)(Ez)T(x, x, y, z)$, but not vice versa; so it may be said that $(y)(Ez)T(x, x, y, z)$ is "more undecidable" than $(Ey)T(x, x, y)$.

The hierarchy has been extended upward and also applied to properties of sets. (S.C.K.)

CURRENT DIRECTIONS

Intuitionistic foundations of mathematics. Brouwer's program for the constructive redevelopment of mathematics was continued by Heyting and others. In the 1960s, the U.S. mathematician Errett Bishop carried out a substantial extension of this program. At the same time his treatment differed from Brouwer's in that he avoided the use of notions, such as ips, that classical mathematicians had viewed with suspicion. This and other work showed that Intuitionism can provide a coherent and viable alternative to the other positions for the foundations of mathematics insofar as they apply to practice.

The logical study of formal systems has also revealed the potentialities of Intuitionistic reasoning. First, proceeding from the conditions for asserting compound statements described above, Heyting set up an Intuitionistically justified formal system of logic. This was formulated in such a way that the system of classical logic can be obtained simply by adjoining the laws of excluded middle. The same was done for a system of elementary number theory. In 1932, Gödel found a translation of the systems based on classical logic into the corresponding Intuitionistic ones. This was the first step in providing a theoretical explanation for the possibility of an Intuitionistic account of significant portions of mathematics.

Much work has been done since the midcentury in setting up formal systems for Intuitionistic theories of functions, ips, species, etc., and studying their relations with classical systems. This has also served to clarify the more distinctive Intuitionistic notions and principles, especially that of ips and the associated continuity principles. The theory of Turing computable functions has also turned out to be an important tool in the study of these systems. To the classical mathematician they provide a precise substitute for the informal idea of constructive function. To the Intuitionist, however, there is no reason to believe that the mechanically computable functions exhaust the conceivable (potential) totality of constructive functions. (S.Fe.)

Recursion, proof, model, and set theory

Non-Intuitionistic studies on the foundations of mathematics. From around 1960, work on the foundations of mathematics outside the Intuitionistic school has been described as falling mainly into four areas: recursion theory, proof theory, model theory, and set theory.

Recursion theory is another name for the theory of computability and decidability. This name came into use from treatments based on the general recursive functions.

Proof theory is another name for metamathematics. One of the newer developments in proof theory is the singling out of portions of analysis formalized so as to

use only properties of sets up to a given level in the recursion-theoretic hierarchy.

Model theory deals with the interpretations, or models, that satisfy the axioms of a given formal system. For example, by Gödel's completeness theorem of 1930, if a formal system based on the first-order functional calculus F is consistent, there is a model in which the objects are the natural numbers. But the axioms might be those of an axiomatic set theory, which purport to describe an uncountably infinite totality! The model is then a "nonstandard model" of set theory (first observed to exist by Skolem in 1922–23). The opposition of Gödel's completeness and incompleteness theorems reveals that there is a nonstandard model of arithmetic.

Set theory, as a branch of foundational investigations, received great impetus from the construction in 1963 by Cohen of models that falsify the continuum hypothesis of Cantor. Cohen's and related methods are being used to show that various conjectures in set theory, analysis, and topology cannot be settled on the basis of the usual axioms of Zermelo and Fraenkel, sometimes augmented by new axioms. (S.C.K.)

BIBLIOGRAPHY. Some general references on the foundations of mathematics are HERMANN WEYL, *Philosophy of Mathematics and Natural Science* (1949 and 1963); PAUL BENACERRAF and HILARY PUTNAM (eds.), *Philosophy of Mathematics: Selected Readings* (1964); and RAYMOND L. WILDER, *Introduction to the Foundations of Mathematics*, 2nd ed. (1965). Advanced books, generally without emphasis on Intuitionism, include S.C. KLEENE, *Introduction to Metamathematics* (1952, reprinted 1971) and *Mathematical Logic* (1967); EVERT W. BETH, *The Foundations of Mathematics*, 2nd ed. rev. (1965); ALFRED TARSKI, ANDRZEJ MOSTOWSKI, and RAPHAEL M. ROBINSON, *Undecidable Theories* (1953, reprinted 1969); JOHN B. ROSSER, *Simplified Independence Proofs* (1969); and ANDRZEJ MOSTOWSKI, *Constructible Sets with Applications* (1969). An excellent source book for all the schools of thought and developments in the foundations of mathematics in the period 1879–1931 is JEAN VAN HEIJENOORT (ed.), *From Frege to Gödel: A Source Book in Mathematical Logic, 1879–1931* (1967). For the area of Intuitionism, see AREND HEYTING, *Intuitionism: An Introduction* (1956); and A.S. TROELSTRA, *Principles of Intuitionism* (1969), two general expositions.

(S.C.K./S.Fe.)

Mathematics, History of

Studies of the languages of primitive peoples and related investigations of extinct languages indicate that a process apparently as simple as counting passed through many stages before it reached a level that permitted the systematization that is essential for any mathematical procedure. Similar observations have been made in the study of early writing. Only tortuous processes led from symbols for sets of concrete objects to a general notation that can be justly called a system of numerals. Mathematics originated only in a very few areas within the framework of highly developed urban civilizations and well-organized economic conditions.

This article is divided into the following sections:

The development of mathematics
  Ancient and medieval
  Modern period
Historical development of representatve non-probabilistic areas of mathematics
  Numerals and numeral systems
  Mathematical symbols
  Calculatory science
  Geometry
  Algebra
Historical development of probabilistic areas of mathematics
  Various mathematically based probabilities
  Development of mathematical statistics

The development of mathematics

Of the great civilizations of antiquity—Babylon, Egypt, Greece, and Rome—two contributed little to the development of mathematics: neither Egypt nor Rome advanced beyond the level of elementary practical arithmetic and mensuration. Priority in the development of mathematics belongs to Babylonia, where ancient land numerical, algebraic, and geometrical methods existed at least from the Hammurabi dynasty, around 1700 BC. Little is known of the earlier or later period, until Persian times, the 6th century BC. Nevertheless, that the tradition had been kept alive is established by texts of the last three centuries BC, when Babylonia had come under Greek and then Parthian domination. By that time Babylonian astronomy, which was to become the main carrier of Babylonian arithmetical methods, but already begun developing rapidly. How widespread these arithmetical methods were is evidenced in the persistence of the division of hours and degrees using 60 as the base number.

Simple categories are no longer applicable to the modern development of mathematics, though the earliest phase followed closely the examples of antiquity. The development of analysis in the 17th century by the mathematicians Pierre de Fermat, René Descartes (both French), and Isaac Newton (English) soon left behind classical methods and problems, and an enormous wealth of new discoveries revealed an interaction between theoretical mathematics and all branches of physics and astronomy. This period of brilliant and somewhat haphazard discovery culminated in the work of the Swiss mathematician Leonhard Euler in the middle of the 18th century. Soon afterward the need for increasing rigour and abstraction became the dominant motif, and these qualities have remained characteristic for mathematics. This tendency not only profoundly influenced each of the traditional branches of mathematics; it all but obliterated the boundaries between individual fields by revealing their common logical and operational background. By the second half of the 20th century the enormous importance of mathematical physics, accompanied by the development of computing machines, furnished a new incentive to mathematical research similar to the situation at the threshold of the 19th century.

ANCIENT AND MEDIEVAL

Mesopotamia. The superiority of Babylonian mathematics is based on the place-value notation (see below) of its number system, which was equally well adapted to the expression of numbers, however large, and of fractions. The system was not an intentional invention but emerged slowly during the 3rd millennium BC. In the highly developed economic life of the period a notation evolved for recording monetary transactions in which larger and smaller units of weights of silver were expressed by simple juxtaposition of numbers, denoting units of different values, similar to the notation $5.20 as distinguished because of order of digits from $20.5. Thus the arrangement of the numbers determined their relative value. In the United States, the ratio of dollars to cents is 1 to 100; in the Babylonian monetary system it was 1 to 60. This notation was then extended to numbers in general, creating what is called a sexagesimal place-value system. In the United States, then, 5.20 means $5 + \frac{20}{100} = 5 + \frac{1}{5}$ (dollars) or $500 + 20 = 520$ (cents). Similarly 2.30 in the sexagesimal system means $2 + \frac{30}{60} = 2 + \frac{1}{2}$ or $2 \times 60 + 30 = 150$. All other arithmetical rules familiar from the decimal system have their exact counterpart in the sexagesimal place-value system. Tutoring in the decimal system produced knowledge of all products of integers up to 10 times 10; the Babylonians (and later the Greek and Islāmic astronomers) tabulated corresponding products up to 60 times 60. In this fashion all arithmetical operations—addition, subtraction, multiplication, division, squaring, cubing, and extracting roots—were carried out in Babylonian mathematics from the 2nd millennium BC on and then—beginning around the 5th century BC—by the astronomers of Mesopotamia, of Greece and Alexandria, of India, of the Islāmic world and the Byzantine world and their Western pupils to the 15th century and later.

A number system based on a place-value notation encounters the problem of the occurrence of empty places; in the sexagesimal system, the problem arises when in addition some digits total exactly 60 and are carried as 1 to the next higher place. In the earlier period of Babylonian mathematics no special symbol existed for such cases; only the relative order of the digits, which was easy to

(margin note, left column) The sexagesimal place-value system

mistake, indicated it. In the late period, however, a special sign was written for every empty place. This zero symbol was in common use in all astronomical computations and reached Hellenistic mathematicians, along with the sexagesimal place-value notation. Thus in all Greek trigonometric tables (for instance, in Ptolemy's *Almagest* of about 140 AD) a zero sign is used exactly as it is today. This condition holds for Islāmic and Byzantine tables as well; in late Greek manuscripts the form ō for zero is the most common one. When Hindu astronomy was developed under Western influence, beginning about the 5th century, the zero symbol was transferred to a decimal place-value notation. The decimal system was well-known to Islāmic scholars, although astronomical practice remained sexagesimal in most cases. In western Europe, the decimal notation gained ground very slowly, and not until the 17th century was a consistent place-value notation developed by François Viète in France and by Simon Stevin in Holland.

The facility of numerical computations, as a result of the place-value notation, is everywhere visible in Babylonian mathematics. An old Babylonian text (*c.* 1700 BC) investigates triples of Pythagorean numbers; that is, numbers satisfying the relationship $a^2 + b^2 = c^2$ (an example is 3, 4, and 5).

Many problems were of the type that requires determination of two numbers with a given sum when their difference is known. For example, if $(a + b) = 5$ and $(a - b) = 1$, then a is 3 and b is 2. This type of problem involves linear equations, in which the unknowns are not raised to higher powers than 1. Quadratic equations involve squares of unknown quantities and were involved in the problem of determining two numbers of known sum and product. For instance, if $(a + b) = 6$ and $ab = 8$, the determination of a and b requires a solution of the equation $a + 8/a = 6$. This is the quadratic equation $a^2 - 6a + 8 = 0$. Equations of fourth order (involving a^4) were obtained by squaring equations of the second order (involving a^2). A numerical algebra was developed from this insight. Similar problems in geometric formulation were handled involving concepts of similarity, the basic area relations, and volumes. The Pythagorean theorem for right triangles, the fact that a triangle inscribed in a semicircle contains a right angle, and relations in regular polygons were all known, leading to good approximations for the square roots of 2, 3, and other integers. The crude value of 3 was often used for pi, π, the ratio of the circumference of a circle to its diameter, but $3\frac{1}{8}$ was also known.

Egypt. The main source of present knowledge of Egyptian mathematics is two papryi, the so-called Rhind (or Ahmes, after the scribe who prepared it) papyrus of the British Museum, written sometime before 1700 BC, and the Golenishev papyrus in Moscow, dating from about 1900 BC. Several smaller fragments confirm impressions gathered from the two larger texts. Arithmetical operations were developed additively, repeated duplication for multiplication, with corresponding rules for division and fractions, derived from successive halvings. These often long-winded procedures were used to solve very elementary practical problems; *e.g.*, distributing bread and beer in given quotas. Also determined in the same fashion were areas of triangular or polygonal fields and volumes of solids, in particular of a truncated pyramid (probably in the special shape of a corner block of two sloping walls). The area of a circle was found by squaring $1 - \frac{1}{9}$, or $\frac{8}{9}$, of the diameter (corresponding to a value of about 3.16 for π).

Greek and Hellenistic mathematics. Late antiquity attempted to supplement the dim records of the past by associating the origin of mathematical knowledge with the early philosophical school of the 7th and 6th centuries BC in Ionia, identified with Pythagoras. These claims are not confirmed by modern research. The basic facts of elementary geometry and arithmetic had been known in Mesopotamia for many centuries. On the other hand, Greek astronomical and cosmogonic concepts in the 5th century BC were still so primitive that only a very narrow margin is left for earlier discoveries. Indeed, it seems

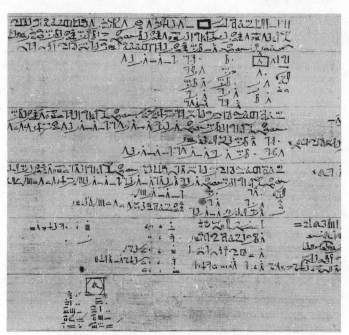

Section of the Rhind mathematical papyrus copied by the
scribe Ahmes, c. 1650 BC. In the British Museum.

more plausible to assume that the independent development of Greek mathematics began in the second half of the 5th century and the first half of the 4th century as evidenced in the earliest reliable records, namely, the determination of certain areas bounded by circular arcs by Hippocrates of Chios and the investigation of curves in space in connection with the problem of the duplication of the volume of a cube by Archytas of Tarentum. Whether this rapid development of scientific mathematical theory had anything to do with increasing contact with the Near East is unknown; it seems unlikely. Clear influence of the Oriental tradition appears much later, in the 1st- and 3rd-century-AD writings of Heron of Alexandria and Diophantus of Alexandria, although the numerical methods used in astronomy reveal Babylonian influence at least from about 150 BC and the work of Hipparchus.

Although Plato lived during the most important formative period of Greek mathematics, it seems unlikely that he played any active role in its development. Nevertheless, philosophy was of great importance for the origin of scientific mathematics, if only for the necessity of removing mathematical argumentation from the unsafe ground of philosophical discussion. The paradoxes about the infinite divisibility of space and time attributed to Zeno of Elea, 5th century BC, and the related attempts of avoiding them through the assumption of atomistic structures attributed to Democritus, c. 400 BC, led to the necessity of defining exactly the postulates to be made for the objects of mathematical discussion. These investigations soon resulted in the discovery that the rational numbers do not suffice for the measurement of geometrical quantities; thus, an independent foundation of geometry was required. As a result the mathematicians of the early 4th century BC, foremost among whom were Theaetetus and Eudoxus of Cnidus, developed a geometric theory of what are now called irrational numbers. (Rational numbers are numbers that can be expressed as quotients of integers such as 6, ⅙, ¾, etc.) The concept of area gave rise to a near rigorous theory of integration even in ancient times.

The strictly geometric formulation of these problems directed Greek mathematics away from algebraic procedures although a purely algebraic notation had been used by Aristotle in his investigation of formal logic in spite of the continuation of the Oriental tradition within elementary mathematics.

Theoretical mathematics perhaps received its original impetus from such philosophical problems as the mean-

Development of postulates

ing of infinite divisibility of lines, the meaning of area and volume, or the mutual relationship between geometrical and arithmetical ratios connected with the theory of harmonics. Two other relatively early lines of interest, however, are also discernible: namely, curves traceable by mechanical means, and conic sections (curves that are produced by taking a section of a cone). In the first group are the problems of spherical geometry as suggested by the apparent motion of the celestial bodies. The second group probably also has an astronomical origin in the theory of sundials. By the end of the 4th century BC all these areas of investigation had reached a level at which a certain codification became possible, even necessary. Eudemus of Rhodes, a pupil of Aristotle, wrote a history of mathematics, unfortunately known only in some short excerpts. Somewhat later appeared Euclid's *Elements*, concerning the most refined part of theoretical mathematics, culminating in Book X, the classification of irrationals. A work on conic sections by Euclid is lost, but some smaller writings have survived, notably a spherical astronomy that shows how far in the future a spherical geometry lay.

The theory of conic sections, however, had reached a high degree of perfection, and its significance for the solution of algebraic problems had been understood. This relation was amply attested by the use of conic sections made by Archimedes and, above all, by Apollonius of Perga, whose great work includes a systematic discussion of elementary properties of conic sections. Many theorems are also proved, but the significance of this operation was recognized only with the 19th-century development of the subject known as projective geometry. In these early sources there are theorems of duality, transformation of coordinates, a discussion of evolutes, and theorems that are related to the projective generation of conic sections from pencils of lines.

The work of Archimedes and Apollonius

With Archimedes and Apollonius, theoretical mathematics had reached its climax in antiquity. From then on, astronomical problems determined the direction of further progress. Apollonius showed that the anomalies in the motion of the Sun, Moon, and planets can be explained. It is easy to see that the apparent position of a body moving on an eccentric circle can be predicted by trigonometric relations, which in turn are always reducible to the solution of right angles. The new element brought to the problem by its astronomical application consists in the need for repetitiveness in order to describe the motion of a body by its consecutive positions. This need leads to the construction of numerical tables or to graphical or mechanical devices. In the 3rd century BC, Babylonian mathematical astronomy had reached full maturity. With Hypsicles of Alexandria and Hipparchus the Babylonian, numerical methods, with difference sequences as the main tool, appeared in Greek astronomy. Hipparchus is credited with the computation of a table of chords of circles. In the same period must belong the invention of stereographic projection, which transfers problems of spherical geometry to plane geometry under preservation of circles. Similarly, methods of descriptive geometry were invented, the so-called analemma, again with the purpose of treating spherical problems in the plane. This phase of the development was completed by the middle of the 1st or the end of the 2nd century BC.

The progress of spherical trigonometry as a method was much slower, for obvious reasons. Plane trigonometry involves no new principle beyond the Pythagorean theorem and the fact that two chords over a diameter form a right angle, both known since Old Babylonian times. Spherical trigonometry required new insight, in particular the restriction to great circle arcs (such as meridians on the surface of the Earth). The discovery of the latter fact seemed to be due to Menelaus (c. AD 100). The contrast between the work of Menelaus and the earlier *Sphaerica* of Theodosius of Bithynia in the 1st century BC shows clearly the progress made. Inequalities and qualitative considerations were replaced by accurate solutions of spherical triangles, based on the Menelaus theorem. With Ptolemy in the 2nd century AD this method became the standard procedure for spherical astronomy.

In the 4th century AD, the sciences became an object of teaching and commentaries. Pappus of Alexandria, Theon of Alexandria, and Hypatia paraphrased, commented on, and edited the great classics. Much is owed to their industry, and a work such as the *Mathematical Collection* of Pappus had great influence on the revival of mathematics in the 17th century, particularly on Descartes. The 5th-century philosopher Proclus wrote an introduction to the *Almagest* and commented on Book I of Euclid's *Elements*. Eutocius of Ascalon in the 6th century competently discussed Archimedean treatises. Unfortunately, what was left of Greek mathematical literature in Byzantium had sunk to the level of elementary summaries.

The Middle Ages. Very few details are known about the survival of ancient science during the period from the final victory of Christianity to the beginning of Islāmic science in the 9th century. Persia undoubtedly played a role in this process, not only as a refuge for exiles—non-Christian as well as Christian—from orthodox persecution, but also as an intermediary with India. In the 6th century, under Sāsānian rule, Gondēshāpūr in southwestern Iran, Khūzestān province, was a centre of learning, particularly in medicine. Under the influence of the 'Abbasid caliph al-Manṣūr a project of systematic translating was begun, centred at the House of Wisdom in Baghdad and based on a widespread search for Greek scientific literature. In the same period, Indian astronomy had reached Baghdad, thus creating the first school of Islāmic astronomy, the best known representative of which is al-Khwārizmī, who died about 850. His name still lives in the term algorithm (to designate a rule of procedure) as well as in the term algebra, which was derived from the title of one of his works, *Kitāb al-jabr wa al-maqābalah*, famous although of little originality because it closely follows the tradition of elementary mathematics traceable from Mesopotamia through the works of Heron of Alexandria and others. Yet for the revival of mathematics and astronomy, al-Khwārizmī's work was of great importance.

Indian work in trigonometry

The most significant contribution of India to medieval mathematics was in trigonometry. For a circle of unit radius the length of an arc is a measure of the angle it subtends at the centre of the circle. The Greeks, to facilitate calculations in geometry, tabulated values of the chord of arcs. This method was replaced by Hindu mathematicians with the half chord of an arc, known as the sine of the angle. The use of the decimal system, however, remained of much lesser importance, though it occurred occasionally in Islāmic, and then also in Byzantine, works. No influence on the West was exerted by the development in India in the 6th century of a theory of Diophantine equations; *i.e.*, equations with two or more variables for which the solutions are required to be integers. The origin for these investigations in all probability lay in questions related to the periodicity of planetary phenomena. Thus methods had been known in India that were not rediscovered until 1624 by the French mathematician Claude-Gaspar Bachet, sieur de Méziriac. The Hellenistic theory of numbers culminated in, among other things, the proof of the existence of an infinity of prime numbers by Euclid. What remained of Greek theory of numbers—for example, in Iamblichus or Diophantus—did not form a connected theory and had little influence during the Middle Ages.

Islāmic mathematics

The progress due to Islāmic mathematicians and astronomers probably lay mostly in the perfection of computational devices. Accurate tables for the sine and tangent function were computed, and methods were devised to modify the sine function in order to tabulate the equation of centre for planetary orbits. Spherical trigonometry was developed far beyond the level reached in antiquity. The use of the Menelaus theorem was replaced by more elegant methods; for example, the sine theorem, known since about AD 1000 and attributed to the Muslim mathematician Abū al-Wafā. At the same time the ancient tradition of descriptive geometry and graphical procedures was developed in the theory of sundials.

Abū al-Wafā and his contemporary Kūshyār ibn Labbān wrote treatises on sexagesimal computation. From them proceeds a continuous tradition to al-Kāshī, the first director of Ulūgh Beg's observatory in Samarkand in about 1400. Among these scholars, a method was developed for the determination of the nth root by means of an iteration process, one in which some standard simple procedure is repeated several times to achieve the result, such as in long division. Al-Kāshī wrote a treatise on the computation of π in which he gives approximations both in sexagesimal and decimal fractions to 9 and 16 places, respectively, based on the comparison of an inscribed and a circumscribed regular polygon of more than 8,000,-000,000 sides.

Al-Bīrūnī's 11th-century work on India or Ibn Khaldūn's 14th-century sociological studies, both masterpieces of scientific analysis, exemplify the depth of Islāmic culture that Westerners rightly regarded with the greatest of admiration. Measuring Islāmic science by its new discoveries and independent achievements, however, it is clear that the five centuries from AD 900 to 1400 cannot compete with the most creative period of Hellenistic science from 300 BC to AD 200.

The process of transmission of Islāmic science to Europe began in the 11th century with such men as the English philosopher Adelard of Bath, who visited Syria, and in the 12th century with the Italian mathematician Leonardo Pisano in north Africa and Italy at the time of Frederick II, whose court in Palermo became a centre of learning. Gerard of Cremona, working in Toledo in the 12th century, was perhaps the most prolific translator of Arabic versions of such Greek works as those of Euclid, Archimedes, and Theodosius of Bithynia. Many European scholars worked in Spain during the 12th and 13th centuries, often helped by Jewish scholars, committing to Latin an Arabic text. Their works formed the foundation on which the science of the Renaissance was built.

MODERN PERIOD

In 1545, only two years after the Polish astronomer Nicolaus Copernicus had published his *De revolutionibus orbium coelestium* ("Concerning the Revolutions of Heavenly Bodies"), which upset the Ptolemaic conception of the universe, and after the anatomist Andreas Vesalius had corrected the physiology of the 2nd-century-AD physician Galen, the Italian mathematician Gerolamo Cardano published the *Artis magnae sive de regulis algebraicis* ("The Great Art, or the Rules of Algebra"), a book that opened a new era in mathematics. Linear and quadratic equations had been solved for thousands of years, but the cubic—involving the cube of a variable—had resisted all efforts, until suddenly several Italian algebraists discovered a solution. First to succeed seems to have been Scipione del Ferro about 1510; but the formula often is named after Niccolò Tartaglia, a rediscoverer, or after Cardano, who first published it in the *Artis magnae*, together with Lodovico Ferrari's solution of the quartic. This unexpected success gave a fillip to the theory of equations, and enthusiasm for algebra, "the great art," spread to other lands. Simon Stevin of Bruges gave rules for locating roots of equations and established the systematic use of decimal fractions in 1585. In France, at the court of Henry IV, François Viète gave algebra a new name, the "analytic art," and a more general form. His use of vowels for unknown quantities and consonants for known paved the way later for the important concepts of variable (an entity standing for many possible constant values) and parameter (a variable that holds a fixed value within a given context), as well as for the rapid rise of a truly symbolic algebra. He is remembered also for his part, in 1579, in continuing the efforts of Johann Müller, whose work was published to establish trigonometry as more than a stepchild of astronomy.

Cardano's "Rules of Algebra"

17th century. Viète died in 1603, just over the threshold of the "century of genius." Brilliant discoveries were about to crowd close upon one another. In 1614 John Napier of Scotland published his discovery of logarithms (see MATHEMATICS AS A CALCULATORY SCIENCE and below *Calculatory science*). In the following year Johannes

Kepler devised infinitesimal methods, which Bonaventura Cavalieri in 1635 fashioned into a geometry of indivisibles. An example of his method is the determination of the area of an ellipse (see GEOMETRY, ANALYTIC AND TRIGONOMETRIC). It is supposed that the ellipse has a major axis of length $2a$ and a minor axis of length $2b$. A circle is drawn around the ellipse with a radius a and the same centre. Now it is supposed that a system of parallel lines is taken parallel to the minor axis. These parallel lines are intercepted to form chords of the ellipse and of the circle, and it is a property of the configuration that the ratio of the length of a circle chord to the length of an ellipse chord is a/b. Cavalieri conceived that the whole plane was divided into parallels. Each chord can then be thought of as a small rectangle of infinitesimal thickness, called an indivisible element by Cavalieri. The area of a given figure is the sum of these elements, and it follows that the ratio of the area of a circle to that of an ellipse is a/b. Hence an ellipse has an area of πab. This is the basic principle used in integration, the idea of the addition of an infinite number of infinitesimal parts.

Descartes's discovery of analytic geometry

In 1637 the French philosopher-mathematician René Descartes published, along with his *Discours de la méthode*, his greatest discovery, analytic geometry, in which a point can be represented by a pair of numbers giving its distances from two lines called axes. The numbers are known as the coordinates of the point. A function of a variable x is a mathematical expression involving x, such as x^2. Neither coordinates nor the graphical representation of functions was new at the time of Descartes, but he, with his contemporary and fellow countryman Pierre de Fermat, correlated these in the basic principle that an equation in two unknown quantities represents a curve and vice versa. For example, a general point has coordinates (x, y). The equation $y = x$ describes all points whose x coordinate equals their y coordinate. These lie on a straight line bisecting the angle between the axes.

Except for a few isolated cases (such as projective geometry), "Cartesian geometry" overshadowed "pure geometry" for almost two centuries. One of the immediate results of the new geometry was a tremendous increase in the variety of curves that came to be studied. So few curves had previously been known that no need had been felt for a general definition of tangent line; a tangent had been, with certain obvious exceptions, a line that touches the curve at one and only one point. It was Fermat, primarily, who introduced the modern idea of the tangent to a curve at any given point P. In essence, he took a second point Q on the curve, found the slope of the secant line PQ, and from this, by permitting Q to tend toward coincidence with P, he calculated the slope of the tangent. This method rightly earned for him the title of inventor of the differential calculus, in which the rate of change of a function is found. When one notes also his share, in 1654, together with the French scientist Blaise Pascal, in the founding of the theory of probability, his work on the quadrature of curves, his use of mathematical induction, and his achievements in the theory of numbers, one appreciates why Fermat, for whom mathematics was but an avocation, has been hailed as the greatest of amateurs. Fermat found the length of the semicubical parabola in 1658, the year in which the Dutch mathematician and astronomer Christiaan Huygens determined the length of the cycloid, although rectifications had been anticipated by Evangelista Torricelli, a student of Galileo, who had found the length of the logarithmic spiral in about 1640.

The work of Pierre de Fermat

Pascal and the English mathematician John Wallis also studied the cycloid, the curve traced out by a fixed point on a circle as the circle rolls along a line. Its beautiful properties led to many disputes over priority and it has been called the "Helen of Geometry." Huygens showed that the evolute (see GEOMETRY, ANALYTIC AND TRIGONOMETRIC) of a cycloid is an equal cycloid, a property that led to the concept of curvature and that was applied to the making of pendulum clocks.

Development of the calculus—Newton and Leibniz. Of all the 17-century mathematicians, none compared in power and original contributions with Sir Isaac Newton. One of his earliest discoveries was that of the binomial theorem for rational fractional exponents. The binomial theorem is the expansion of the expression $(x + y)^n$, in which n is an integer. When n is not a whole number the expression expands into an infinite number of terms. This discovery introduced Newton to the study of infinite series, which are sums of an infinite number of terms of some sequence. An example is $1 + \frac{1}{2} + \frac{1}{2}^2 + \frac{1}{2}^3 + \cdots$, with an infinite number of terms. The value of a series is obtained by the limit of partial sums. The first term here has a value of 1; the sum of the first two terms is $1\frac{1}{2}$; the sum of the first three is $1\frac{3}{4}$. As the number of terms increases, the partial sum approaches a limit of 2, this being the value of the series. Such a series is said to be convergent, as opposed to a divergent series, which does not have a limit. The ideas involved in infinite series loomed large in Newton's work on the calculus at about the same time. Areas had been found by summations by earlier mathematicians from Archimedes to Wallis; differentiations had been carried out by Fermat. Newton and the German mathematician and philosopher Gottfried Wilhelm Leibniz discovered the fundamental principle of the calculus that integrations can be performed far more easily by inverting the process of differentiation. This discovery was made possible, in the case of Newton, by his study of the methods of his teacher, Isaac Barrow, as well as by works of Fermat and Wallis; Leibniz seems to have been led to the calculus independently during the period between 1673 and 1676 by reading the works of Barrow and Pascal. Neither inventor was able to establish the calculus on a sound logical basis. Newton at first adopted a crude explanation in terms of infinitely small "moments."

The binomial theorem

Later Newton based his theory on rates of change. Briefly he used two concepts: fluents, which were changing quantities, and fluxions, which were rates of change of magnitudes. A quantity x may be considered to change uniformly with time and the rate of change of x^2, say, can be found. If x changes to $(x + h)$, x^2 changes to $(x + h)^2$ in the same time; that is, it changes to $x^2 + 2hx + h^2$, x increasing by h and x^2 increasing by $2hx + h^2$. Newton used the idea of prime and ultimate ratios. The ratio of the increments is $h : 2hx + h^2$, or $1 : 2x + h$. If h is disappearingly small, the ultimate ratio is $1 : 2x$, $2x$ being the fluxion of x^2 giving the rate at which x^2 changes when x changes. The general case of finding the fluxion of x^n involved the use of the binomial theorem for $(x + h)^n$. Newton's notation $\dot{x}$ for the fluxion of x is still used.

Leibniz used the idea of infinitesimally small differentials, denoted by dx and dy, and tried (unsuccessfully) to explain his method in terms of sums and quotients of these. The notation has been used ever since.

Newton's first publication of the calculus was in 1687 in a short offhand explanation in the *Philosophiae Naturalis Principia Mathematica* (*The Mathematical Principles of Natural Philosophy*, 1729), conceded to be the greatest of all scientific treatises. The *Principia* is written in Latin, the synthetic language of the ancients, even though the discoveries in the book were made through the new analytic devices that the author helped to develop. Newton is best known for his demonstration, in the *Principia*, of one of the greatest of scientific generalizations, the law of gravitation. Newton's discovery of the composite nature of white light was published in the *Opticks* of 1704, a treatise containing also Newton's *Quadrature of Curves* and his *Enumeration of Cubic Curves*. Whereas Newton's aim was to understand nature, the motive of Leibniz was to find a general pathway to knowledge. The Leibnizian search for a universal characteristic, which resulted in the first steps toward a symbolic logic, failed to attract a following until the publication of the English mathematician George Boole's *Investigation into the Laws of Thought* in 1854; but the method of differentials, the formal algorithmic nature of which was in accord with the aims of its inventor, became the mainspring of mathematical development during the course of the 18th and 19th centuries.

18th century. The mathematical contributions of the versatile Leibniz were more modest than those of Newton, but Leibniz' influence on the continent was far greater. The Bernoulli family in particular, great admirers of Leibniz, were fired with enthusiasm for the differential calculus; and the greatest and most influential pupil of Johann Bernoulli was Leonhard Euler, the most prolific mathematical author of all time. The 18th century saw few spectacular discoveries; yet this prosy age generated more new mathematics than had any earlier period, and most of this centred on the work of Euler. One of his treatises, the *Introductio in analysin infinitorum* ("Introduction to Infinitesimal Analysis") of 1748, may be called the foremost mathematical textbook of modern times, for it was this work that fashioned the function concept and infinite processes into the third member of the mathematical triumvirate comprising geometry, algebra, and analysis.

Euler contributed to all analytic aspects of mathematics. His treatises on the differential and integral calculus are the source from which modern authors have drawn material. He was one of the founders of two branches of mathematics: the calculus of variations and differential geometry. The former is an extension of calculus applied to cases in which a function depends on another function or a curve. Differential geometry is the application of differential calculus to studies of the general properties of curves and surfaces. Euler was also the greatest figure in the theory of numbers since Fermat; and he contributed much to mathematical physics. The vast scope of his interests accounted perhaps for a lack of soundness in his logical foundations. He based the calculus on quotients of "qualitative zeros," and he had no qualms about operating with the "sums" of series that did not converge and thus could not be used to represent numbers.

Mathematicians of the 18th century generally were connected with a university or a royal court, and Euler, no exception, found patrons at Berlin and St. Petersburg. When in 1766 Euler resigned from the Prussian academy to return to Russia, Frederick II the Great chose as his successor Joseph-Louis Lagrange of France, reputed the greatest mathematician of the century. The interests of Lagrange (algebra, analysis, the theory of numbers, and mechanics) were much like those of Euler, but his disposition was different. Lagrange published far less, but his contributions were beautifully finished products with a sound foundation. His *Théorie des fonctions analytiques* ("Theory of Analytic Functions") of 1797 made mathematicians more keenly aware of the need for rigour; but

the book that earned him greatest fame was the *Mécanique analytique* (1788), which established mechanics as a branch of mathematical analysis. Beginning with a small number of postulates, the author built up the principles of the subject without recourse to anything beyond deductive logic. The Age of Reason, typified by the French mathematician and encyclopaedist Jean Le Rond d'Alembert, may be thought of as culminating in the *Mécanique analytique*. The greatest legacy left to mathematics by the French Revolutionary period was the establishment in 1794 of the École Polytechnique, a school that boasted among its teachers the greatest mathematicians of France, including Lagrange, Pierre-Simon Laplace, and Gaspard Monge. Laplace established celestial mechanics as a branch of analysis, and it was through his work that such tools as potential theory (see ANALYSIS, COMPLEX), the Laplace transform (see ANALYSIS, FOURIER), the Laplace equation (see DIFFERENTIAL EQUATIONS), and orthogonal functions (see ANALYSIS, FUNCTIONAL) became the stock-in-trade of the analyst. His masterpiece, the *Mécanique Céleste* ("Celestial Mechanics") published in five volumes between 1799 and 1825, purported to prove the stability of the solar system, for the origin of which the author proposed a nebular hypothesis. The students of the École Polytechnique esteemed as their greatest teacher Gaspard Monge, who began an era in mathematics characterized by a resurgence of geometry. His *Géométrie descriptive* published in 1799, originally devised for military purposes, was the first significant contribution to synthetic geometry after 1639; but the author was not a single-minded synthesist, and the emphasis at the École Polytechnique upon analytic and differential geometry was in large measure the result of the successful textbook of Monge published in 1795. The key idea in his work was that each step in an analytic calculation corresponds to some geometrical construction. Lazare Carnot, the "organizer of victory" for the French Revolutionary armies, likewise made valuable contributions both to analytic and synthetic geometry, his greatest treatise being the *Géométrie de position* of 1803.

19th and 20th centuries. Carnot had sought to avert the despotism of Napoleon, but Monge and Jean-Baptiste-Joseph Fourier were friends and ardent admirers of the Emperor. Fourier's chief contribution to mathematics is typical of the originality (but not the rigour) of the new century. His classic *Théorie analytique de la chaleur* (*The Analytical Theory of Heat*) of 1822 showed that an arbitrary function can be expanded in a Fourier series of sines and cosines. In the very same year, Fourier's boldness in analysis was paralleled in projective geometry by the *Traité des propriétés projectives des figures* ("Treatise on the Projective Properties of Figures") of Jean-Victor Poncelet, a student of Monge. Poncelet became a centre of controversy over the principle of continuity and other concepts. His reckless charges of plagiarism antagonized a young German geometer, Julius Plücker, who became the greatest of analytic geometers.

In his many treatises, Plücker developed basic ideas. In Germany his work was not well received, for Jakob Steiner by 1832 had built up a strong following in synthetic geometry. Steiner hated analysis as thoroughly as Lagrange disliked geometry, arguing that calculation replaces thinking, whereas pure geometry stimulates it. His ideas were carried on by Karl G.C. von Staudt, also of Germany, who, with still sharper logic, examined the structure of pure geometry.

Non-Euclidean geometry. Probably no earlier period in the history of mathematics rivalled the 19th century either in critical spirit or originality of development, both of which are seen in the rise of non-Euclidean geometry. The parallel postulate of Euclid is that, if a point lies outside a line, then only one line can be drawn through the point parallel to the first line. This postulate seemed less fundamental than the others, but numerous attempts were made to prove it.

Between 1826 and 1832 the Russian mathematician Nikolay Ivanovich Lobachevsky and János Bolyai of Hungary showed that self-consistent geometries can be built without this principle. In 1854 Bernhard Riemann of Germany proposed the characterization of a new geometry by the quadratic differential form for arc length (see PHYSICAL THEORIES, MATHEMATICAL ASPECTS OF), involving an idea essential later in general relativity. Carl Friedrich Gauss of Germany, still another independent discoverer of non-Euclidean geometry, failed to publish his thoughts on the subject. The informed consensus is that Archimedes, Newton, and Gauss were the greatest mathematicians of all time. When he was not yet 19, Gauss discovered in 1796 that a regular polygon of 17 sides can be constructed in the Euclidean sense. Other results were entered in his diary and went unpublished until rediscovered by others. His *Disquisitiones Arithmeticae* ("Inquiries into Arithmetic") of 1801, containing the law of quadratic reciprocity and the theory of congruences (see NUMBER THEORY), is a classic in the theory of numbers; and the *Disquisitiones Generales Circa Superficies Curvas* ("General Inquiries Concerning Curved Surfaces"), of 1828, marked a new epoch in differential geometry through the exploitation of the parametric representation of surfaces and their Gaussian curvature (see GEOMETRY, DIFFERENTIAL). These books show a modern tinge in a meticulous attention to proofs. Gauss was also a prolific contributor to statistics and to applied mathematics, especially in the fields of astronomy, geodesy, and magnetism.

Theories of groups, functions, and complex variables. That the square of a positive or a negative number is a positive number and that the square root of a negative number cannot be a real number (see ANALYSIS, REAL) and is said to be imaginary were recognized by Cardano, who said that the square root of -9 is not $+3$ or -3 but is of hidden nature. The usual notation is to write, say, $\sqrt{-9}$ as $3i$, in which i is $\sqrt{-1}$. A complex number is a combination of a real number and an imaginary one $(a + ib)$.

Gauss proved in 1799 that every equation of the form $a_0x^n + a_1x^{n-1} + \cdots + a_n = 0$ has at least one root. Two contemporaries, the Norwegian mathematician Niels Henrik Abel and the French mathematician Évariste Galois, demonstrated independently that in most cases the root cannot be expressed as radicals. Abel proved in 1824 that the quintic equation cannot be solved by an explicit algebraic formula. Galois observed that every algebraic equation is associated with a certain group of substitutions and that solvability is determined by the properties of this group, thus establishing Galois theory, part of the theory of groups. Many of his findings were written down on the night before he died, in a duel in 1832 at the age of 20.

In 1872 the German mathematician Felix Klein, in his famous *Erlangen Programm*, pointed out the unifying role of the group concept (see ALGEBRAIC STRUCTURES) in geometry; and Sophus Lie of Norway, through the theory of continuous groups (see TOPOLOGICAL GROUPS AND DIFFERENTIAL TOPOLOGY) in about 1873, made it a part of analysis.

Both Gauss and his French contemporary Augustin-Louis Cauchy, the foremost mathematicians of their day, are typical exponents of 19th-century mathematics in their rigour and inventiveness. The prolific Cauchy was the successor of Lagrange in the theory of functions, to which subject he added the theory of a complex variable (see ANALYSIS, COMPLEX). The graphical representation of complex numbers by the Swiss-born mathematician Jean-Robert Argand published in 1813–14 and the discovery by Abel in 1824 of the imaginary period of elliptic functions had led up to this; but the complex variable really came into its own in 1825 with the Cauchy integral theorem. This work later was continued in two directions: Karl Weierstrass of Germany emphasized the pure analytic aspect through the analytic continuation of functions defined by power series; Riemann made greater use of geometric intuition through a study of conformal representation and Riemann surfaces (see ANALYSIS, COMPLEX).

Algebraic geometry. British mathematics had been handicapped throughout the 18th century by excessive deference to synthetic methods and the notations of Newton. In 1816, however, the Cambridge Analytical Society was formed to promote the Leibnizian methods of the calculus. Moreover, the first half of the 19th century was characterized by the rise of mathematical journals (mathematical societies being chiefly a product of the latter half of the same century), and these facilitated publication and dissemination of knowledge. Hence it was not long before England, through the voluminous work of Arthur Cayley, became the stronghold of algebraic geometry. The geometry of n dimensions (dimension higher than three) had been hinted at by the Irish mathematician and physicist William Rowan Hamilton in 1843 and by the German mathematician Hermann Günther Grassmann in 1844, but Cayley is regarded as the true founder of this branch of geometry with his publication of 1869, as well as of the theory of matrices and algebraic invariants (see ALGEBRA, LINEAR AND MULTILINEAR). Algebra, overshadowed by analysis for two centuries, again was assuming a decisive role, with the application of determinants in algebra and analysis becoming one of the most fruitful lines of development. The critical spirit of the 19th century found clearest expression in the ever-greater arithmetization of mathematics. In Italy Bernard Bolzano already had taken a step in this direction in 1817; but development of the foundations of arithmetic dates especially from 1872 when definitions of irrational number were given in Germany by Weierstrass, Richard Dedekind, and Georg Cantor. These definitions, based on the notion of infinite classes (see SET THEORY), led Cantor in his *Beiträge zur Begründung der transfiniten Megenlehre* (1895–97; *Contributions to the Founding of the Theory of Transfinite Numbers*, 1915) to one of the most strikingly original contributions of all time—the theory of transfinite numbers (see CANTOR, GEORG). After showing that the class of algebraic numbers is denumerable, Cantor was led to the startling conclusion that the number of points in space of n dimensions is not greater than that in a single dimension, a paradox confirmed by the space-filling curve of the Italian mathematician Giuseppe Peano.

Influence of science on analysis. Perhaps the most powerful impetus on the development of analysis came from mathematical physics and astronomy. The common role of extremal principles for the laws of optics as well as dynamics became clear through the work of Hamilton and his German contemporary Karl Gustav Jacobi. The geometric interpretation of the $2n$ canonic variables of the differential equations of dynamics led Sophus Lie in about 1873 to the concept of contact transformations and continuous groups that, in its abstract form, gained an important place in modern topology (see TOPOLOGICAL GROUPS AND DIFFERENTIAL TOPOLOGY). The deep interaction between analysis and mathematical physics is also visible in the work of the virtually self-taught Scottish genius James Clerk Maxwell, which ranged from the investigation of the stability of Saturn's rings to thermodynamics and his celebrated field theory of electrodynamics of 1873. The theory of statistical mechanics as developed by Maxwell, Ludwig Boltzmann of Germany, and J. Willard Gibbs of the United States opened the road to the investigation of the so-called ergodic theorems (see ANALYSIS, FUNCTIONAL), a general version of which was given in 1932 in the United States by George David Birkhoff. Through the theory of probability of Norbert Wiener of the United States, first published as a study of Brownian motion (see PROBABILITY, THEORY OF) in 1923, and the axiomatic approach to probability of A.N. Kolmogorov of the U.S.S.R. (published 1932), it had become clear that problems of statistical mechanics are essentially problems of the theory of measure, and in this form the ergodic theory has again developed into a branch of abstract mathematics. A similar development can be observed in the theory of integral equations that slowly emerged during the second half of the 19th century from problems of electrostatics and the theory of potentials (see ANALYSIS, COMPLEX: *Potential theory*). The essential turn toward a solution originated from the investigation of determinants of infinitely many rows and columns, begun by George William Hill in 1877 in connection with the perturbation theory of the lunar motion. This new type of approach led the Swedish mathematician Ivar Fredholm in 1900 to the discovery of the algebraic analogue of the theory of integral equations (equations in which a function to be determined appears as the integrand of some integral), which was crowned by the theory of eigenvalues of David Hilbert of Germany in 1906 and the related theory of spaces of infinitely many dimensions (Hilbert space and its modern generalizations; see ANALYSIS, FUNCTIONAL).

Fundamental questions. Hilbert in 1900 prophetically proposed to the second International Congress of Mathematics at Paris a series of fundamental problems that should challenge the efforts of the new century. The first problems concerned the continuum: the question of whether or not there is a transfinite number between that of a denumerable set and that of the continuum remained unanswered. Questions inquiring about the transcendence of certain numbers were partially solved in Germany by Carl Ludwig Siegel about 1930 and by Aleksandr Osipovich Gelfond of the U.S.S.R., and completed by Gelfond and Schneider (Germany) in 1934.

The problems that stimulated the most spectacular development were those in the relatively novel field of analysis situs, or topology. Certain puzzle problems of Euler were suggestive of topology, and Gauss prophesied the rise of the new subject; but the origins are more clearly apparent in the results at the beginning of the 20th

The geometry of n dimensions *(marginal note)*

Hilbert's problems of 1900 *(marginal note)*

century of Henri Poincaré of France. By the middle of the 20th century the infant prodigy had burgeoned into a major branch of mathematics. Originally an offshoot of geometry, topology became closely related also to algebra and analysis.

One of Hilbert's favourite questions concerned the compatibility of the axioms of arithmetic. The German logician and mathematician Gottlob Frege in 1879 had given a critical definition of the word "number," and just a decade later the Peano postulates for arithmetic were proposed; but by far the most ambitious effort to establish the foundations of mathematics appeared in the *Principia Mathematica*, published in three volumes between 1910 and 1913, of Bertrand Russell and Alfred North Whitehead. This *Principia*, like that of Newton, set the fashion for decades to come, so that research in symbolic logic at mid-20th century constituted a major branch of mathematics. In fact, the greatly expanded role of the axiomatic approach became possibly the most conspicuous aspect of 20th-century mathematics. Such studies in the foundations of mathematics engendered lively controversy in which varying orthodoxies are distinguishable—from the Formalists, who assert, as did Hilbert, that mathematics is a meaningless game played with meaningless symbols, to the Intuitionists, who, with the Dutch mathematician L.E.J. Brouwer, hold to a more Kantian view of the subject's "inner meaning." One factor contributing to the dilemma was the persistence of deep-rooted paradoxes. By rejecting the use of impredicative definition, Poincaré, Hermann Weyl (German-born U.S. mathematician and physicist), and Brouwer eliminated the antinomies; but this drastic solution, to which Brouwer (and later Weyl) added also the rejection of the law of the excluded middle, cut the ground out from under much of classical mathematics. Hilbert sought to save the mathematical fortunes by rejecting the idea of mathematics as necessarily true, clinging only to the criterion of self-consistency; but such efforts were dealt a shattering blow by the 1931 theorem of the Czech-born mathematician Kurt Gödel, which showed that if mathematics actually is consistent, the fact of this consistency cannot be proved within the rules of mathematics itself (see MATHEMATICS, FOUNDATIONS OF). The conclusion necessarily following from such a devastating discovery is that the ultimate foundations of mathematics must remain a mystery—at least to mathematicians. One should expect the result of this to be a deep pessimism. On the contrary, everywhere in the modern period the faith that mathematics was entering a golden age surpassing even the brightest periods of the past could be found. Theories of integration, revolutionized by the French mathematician Henri-Léon Lebesgue through his concept of measure appearing in 1902, had carried the subject far beyond Archimedes, Cauchy, and Riemann into the realm of abstract spaces; and the unification of analytic methods had led to the general analyses of E.H. Moore in 1906 and Maurice-René Fréchet of France in 1928.

Twentieth-century algebra, with its concern for such abstract axiomatic concepts as field, ring, and ideal, is far more general than in any previous age. Geometry—now encompassing spaces of infinitely many dimensions—undertakes a critical examination of its postulational basis.   (Ed.)

Historical development of representative non-probabilistic areas of mathematics

Just as the first attempts at writing came long after the development of speech, so the first efforts at the graphical representation of numbers came long after people had learned to count. Probably the earliest way of keeping record of a count was by some tally system involving physical objects such as pebbles or sticks. Judging by the habits of primitive tribes of the present as well as by the oldest trace remaining of written or sculptured records, the earliest numerals were simple notches in a stick, scratches on a stone, marks on a piece of pottery, or the like. Having no fixed units of measure, no coins, no commerce beyond the rudest barter, no system of taxation and no needs beyond those to sustain life, people had no necessity for written numerals until about the beginning of what are called historical times. Vocal sounds were probably used to designate the number of objects in a small group long before there were separate symbols for the small numbers, and it seems likely that the sounds differed according to the kind of object being counted. The abstract notion of two, signified orally by a sound independent of any particular object, probably appeared very late.

It appears that the primitive numerals were |, ||, |||, and so on, as found in Egypt and the Grecian lands, or —, =, ≡, and so on, as found in early records in the Far East, each going as far as the simple needs of the people required. As life became more complicated, the need for group numbers became apparent, and it was only a small step from the simple system with names only for one and ten to the further naming of other special numbers. Sometimes this happened in a very unsystematic fashion. In the 20th century, for example, the Yukaghirs of Siberia counted, "one, two, three, three and one, five, two threes, two threes and one, two fours, ten with one missing, ten." Usually, however, a more regular system resulted, and most of these more regular systems can be classified, at least roughly, according to the logical principles underlying them.

Table 1: Comparison of Selected Systems of Numerals

	1	2	3	4	5	6	7	8	9	0
European	1	2	3	4	5	6	7	8	9	0
Arabic	١	٢	٣	٤	٥	٦	٧	٨	٩	٠
Devanagari	୧	୨	୩	୪	୫	୬	୭	୮	୯	୦
Tibetan	༡	༢	༣	༤	༥	༦	༧	༨	༩	༠
Kashmir	३	३	३	ᒥ	५	३	∫	⅂	Ⴆ	·
Bengalese	⅃	૮	৩	8	৫	৬	৭	৮	৯	০
Siamese	๑	๒	๓	๔	๕	๖	๗	๘	๙	๐

NUMERALS AND NUMERAL SYSTEMS

Simple grouping systems.   The earliest example of a simple grouping system is that encountered in hieroglyphs that the Egyptians used for writing on stone. (Two later Egyptian systems, the hieratic and the demotic, which were used for writing on papyrus, are considered later; they are not simple grouping systems.) The hieroglyphic symbol for one was **|** and more than one was represented by aggregates of these; thus four was **||||**. An aggregate of 10 was then represented by a new symbol, **∩** , and aggregates of these were written in a similar way. Ten of these—*i.e.*, a total of 10 × 10, or 10², units—were written **℮** , and so on. Here 10 is the base of the system. The hieroglyphic symbols were

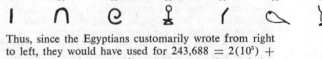

| 1 | 10 | 10² | 10³ | 10⁴ | 10⁵ | 10⁶ |

Thus, since the Egyptians customarily wrote from right to left, they would have used for 243,688 = 2(10⁵) + 4(10⁴) + 3(10³) + 6(10²) + 8(10) + 8 the symbol

Numbers of this size occur in records concerning royal estates and must have been commonplace in the logistics and engineering of the great pyramids.

In general, a simple grouping system is an assignment of special names to the small numbers, the base *b*, and powers of the base b^2, b^3, etc. Intermediate numbers are then formed by addition, each symbol being repeated the required number of times. An example of this method of formation is the Roman numeral for 23, which is written XXIII.

Cuneiform numerals.   Around Babylon, clay was abundant, and the people impressed their symbols in the damp clay tablets and then baked the tablets in the sun or in a kiln, thus forming documents practically as perma-

Diverse views concerning the nature of mathematics

Primitive representations of numbers

The Egyptian system

nent as stone. Since the pressure of the stylus gave a wedge-shaped symbol, the writings are known as cuneiform (Latin *cuneus*, "a wedge," and *forma*, "a shape") inscriptions. The symbols could be made either with the pointed or the circular end of the stylus as follows:

For numbers up to 60 these symbols were used in the same way as the hieroglyphs, except that a subtractive symbol was also used:

The cuneiform and the curvilinear numerals occur together in some documents from about 3000 BC. There seem to have been some conventions regarding their use; the cuneiform type was always used for the number of the year or the age of an animal, while wages already paid were written in curvilinear and wages due in cuneiform. For numbers larger than 60 the Babylonians used a mixed system, described in ARITHMETIC.

Greek numerals. The Greeks had two important systems of numerals besides the primitive plan of repeating single strokes, as in ||| ||| for six, one of which was again a simple grouping system. Their predecessors in culture—the Babylonians, Egyptians, and Phoenicians—had generally repeated the units up to nine, with a special symbol for 10, and so on. The early Greeks also repeated the units to nine and probably had various symbols for 10. In Crete, where the early civilization was so much influenced by Phoenicia and Egypt, the symbol for 10 was —, a circle was used for 100, and a rhombus for 1,000. But the precise forms are of less importance than the fact that grouping by 10s, with special symbols for certain powers of 10, was characteristic of the early systems of the Near East.

Greek notation

The Greeks, entering the field much later, and influenced in their alphabet by the Phoenicians, based their first elaborate system chiefly on the initial letters of the numeral names. This was a natural thing for all early civilizations, because the custom of writing out the names for large numbers was at first quite general, and the use of an initial by way of abbreviation of a word is universal. These initial numerals, in modern characters, were

Π or Γ, pi, for ΠΕΝΤΕ (pente), 5;
Δ, delta, for ΔΕΚΑ (deka), 10;
H, an old Attic breathing, like the letter h, later represented by a special symbol like ʿ, for ΗΕΚΑΤΟΝ (hekaton), 100;
X, chi, for ΧΙΛΙΟΙ (chilioi), 1,000;
M, mu, for ΜΥΡΙΟΙ (myrioi, murioi), 10,000.

These numerals were frequently combined with the symbol for 5; thus

Γ᷑ or Γ᷊, PENTE-DEKA, FOR 5 x 10, OR 50;
Γ᷉, PENTE-HEKATON, FOR 5 x 100, OR 500;
Γ᷎, PENTE-MURIOI, FOR 5 x 10,000 OR 50,000

Therefore, in this notation

36,756 = M M M Γ᷑X Γ᷉HH Γ᷑II

This system appears in records of the 3rd century BC but was probably used much earlier. Because in the 2nd century AD it was described by the grammarian Herodianus, these characters are often spoken of as Herodianic numerals, more properly called Attic numerals, being the ones always found in the Attic inscriptions.

Roman numerals. The direct influence of Rome for such a long period, the superiority of its numeral system

over any other simple one that had been known in Europe before about the 10th century, and the compelling force of tradition explain the strong position that the system maintained for nearly 2,000 years in commerce, in scientific and theological literature, and in belles-lettres. It had the great advantage that the mass of users needed to memorize the values of only five letters—I, V, X, L, and C. Moreover, it was easier to see three in III than in 3, and to see nine in VIIII than in 9, and correspondingly easier to add numbers—the simplest of all the operations.

As in all such matters, the origin of these numerals is obscure, although the changes in their forms since the 3rd century BC are well-known. Of the various theories, that of Theodor Mommsen, advanced in 1850, has had the widest acceptance. This was that the use of V for 5 is due to the fact that it is a kind of hieroglyph representing the open hand with its five fingers. Two of these gave the X for 10. Three of the other symbols, he asserted, were modifications of Greek letters not needed in the Etruscan and early Latin alphabet. These were *chi*, which appears in inscriptions not only as X but also in such forms as ⊥, ↓, and which later became the L that was arbitrarily chosen for 50; *theta* Θ, which was selected for 100, being finally changed to C under the influence of the word *centum* (hundred); and *phi* Φ, to which was assigned the value 1,000, and which finally took the forms I and M, the last being chosen because of the word *mille* (thousand).

Mommsen's theory of Roman notation

The earliest noteworthy inscription containing numerals representing very large numbers is on the Columna Rostrata, a monument erected in the Roman Forum to commemorate the victory of 260 BC over the Carthaginians. In this a symbol for 100,000, which was an early form of (((I))), was repeated 23 times, making 2,300,000. This illustrates not only the early Roman use of repeated symbols but also a custom which extended to modern times —that of using (I) for 1,000, ((I)) for 10,000, (((I))) for 100,000, and ((((I)))) for 1,000,000. The symbol (I) for 1,000 frequently appears in various other forms, including the cursive ∞. All these symbols persisted until long after printing became common. In the Middle Ages a bar (*vinculum*, *titulus*) was placed over a number to multiply it by 1,000, but this use is not found in the Roman inscriptions. When the bar appears in early manuscripts it was merely for the purpose of distinguishing numerals from nouns, as in the case ĪĪVIR for *duumviri*. In the Middle Ages such forms as |X̄| or |X| for 1,000,000 and |M̄| for one thousand hundred thousand were also used.

Of the later use of the numerals, a few of the special types are as follows:

1. c̄ · l̄xiiij · ccc · l · i, for 164,351, Adelard of Bath (*c.* 1120)
2. II. DCCC.XIIII, for 2,814, Jordanus Nemorarius (*c.* 1125)
3. MↃCLVI, for 1,656, in San Marco, Venice
4. cIↃ . IↃ . Ic, for 1,599, Leiden ed. of Capella, 1599
5. IIIIxxet huit, for 88, a Paris treaty of 1388
6. four Cli.M, for 451,000, Baker's arithmetic (1568)
7. vj.C for 600 and CCC.M for 300,000, Recorde (*c.* 1542)

The first represents the use of the bar; (2) represents the place value as it occasionally appears in Roman numerals; (3) illustrates the not infrequent use of Ↄ [like D, originally half of (I), the symbol for 1,000]; (4) illustrates the persistence of the old Roman form for 1,000 and 500, and the subtractive principle so rarely used by the Romans for a number like 99; (5) shows the use of *quatre-vingts* ("four twenties") for 80, commonly found in French manuscripts until the 17th century, and occasionally later, the numbers often being written like iiij᷎ˣˣ, vij᷎ˣˣ, and so on; (6) represents the coefficient method, "four C" meaning 400, a method often leading to forms like ijM or IIM for 2,000, as shown in (7).

The subtractive principle is seen in Hebrew number names, and in the occasional use of IV for 4 and IX for 9 by the Romans. They also used *unus de viginti* ("one from twenty") for 19 and *duo de viginti* ("two from twenty") for 18, occasionally writing these numbers as XIX (or IXX) and IIXX, respectively. The subtractive principle, however, was little used in the classical period.

Multiplicative grouping systems.   In multiplicative systems special names are given not only to 1, b, b^2, but also to the numbers 2, 3, $\cdots$, $b - 1$; the symbols of this second set are then used in place of repetitions of the first set. Thus if 1, 2, 3, $\cdots$, 9 are designated in the usual way, but 10, 100, and 1,000 are replaced by X, C, and M, respectively, then in a multiplicative grouping system 7,392 is written as 7M3C9X2. The principal example of this kind of notation is the Chinese numerical system, three variants of which are shown in Table 2. In the traditional notation, 2,605 would appear as 二千六百五 (here written from left to right rather than vertically downward, as is customary). The modern national and the mercantile systems are positional systems and use the circle ○ for zero.

Table 2: Chinese Numeral Systems

Traditional national system

Modern national system

Mercantile system

Ciphered numeral systems.   In the ciphered systems, names are given not only to 1 and the powers of the base b but also to the multiples of these powers. Thus, starting from the artificial example given above for a multiplicative grouping system, a ciphered system is obtained if unrelated names are given to the numbers 1, 2, $\cdots$, 9; X, 2X, $\cdots$, 9X; C, 2C, $\cdots$, 9C; M, 2M, $\cdots$, 9M. This requires the memorization of many different symbols, but it results in a very compact notation.

Egyptian hieratic numerals

The first ciphered system seems to have been the Egyptian hieratic (literally, priestly) numerals, so called because the priests were presumably the ones who had the time and learning required to develop this shorthand outgrowth of the earlier hieroglyphic numerals. An Egyptian arithmetical work on papyrus, employing hieratic numerals, was found in Egypt about 1855; known after the name of its finder as the Rhind papyrus, it provides the chief source of information about this numeral system. With the symbols as indicated in Table 3, which is exemplary of the kind of information to be found in the Rhind papyrus, the number 3,052 would be written (from left to right) as (the customary way of writing was from top to bottom). There was a still later Egyptian system, the demotic, which was also a ciphered system.

Table 3: Egyptian Hieratic Numerals
(mathematical papyrus, about 1600 BC)

	1	2	3	4	5	6	7	8	9
Units									
Tens									
Hundreds									
Thousands									
Tens of thousands									
Hundreds of thousands									

As early as the 3rd century BC a second system came into use in Greece, paralleling the initial-letter system but better adapted to the theory of numbers and more difficult of comprehension by the trading classes. These Ionic, or alphabetical, numerals were simply a ciphered system in which nine Greek letters were assigned to the numbers of units 1–9, nine more to the numbers of tens 10, $\cdots$, 90, and nine more to the numbers of hundreds 100, $\cdots$, 900. Since, however, there were only 24 letters in the Greek alphabet, three were added: the Phoenician *vau* (shaped like the letter F); *koph*, *qoph*, or *koppa* (shaped somewhat like Q, and indeed derived from the same source); and a character known in modern times as *sampi* (then shaped somewhat like the Greek π, but tipped about 45° to the right, and represented here by S). Only capital letters were used; lower-case letters are a relatively modern invention. The numerical values of the

Table 4: Ionic Greek Ciphered Numeral System

	1	2	3	4	5	6	7	8	9
Units	A	B	Γ	Δ	E	[F]	Z	H	Θ
Tens	I	K	Λ	M	N	Ξ	O	Π	[Q]
Hundreds	P	Σ	T	Y	Φ	X	Ψ	Ω	[S]

letters are shown in Table 4. The thousands were often indicated by placing a bar at the left of the numeral, thus:

/A = 1,000; /B = 2,000; /I = 10,000; /T = 300,000.

Such numeral forms were not particularly difficult for computing purposes once the operator was able automatically to recall the meaning of each. To be able to express 10,407 by /ITZ would have seemed to a Greek considerably simpler than the system now in use.

Other ciphered numeral systems include Coptic, Hindu, Brāhmī, Hebrew, Syrian, and early Arabic. The last three systems, like the Ionic, above, are alphabetic ciphered numeral systems. The Hebrew system is shown in Table 5.

Table 5: Hebrew Ciphered Numeral System

Units									
	א	ב	ג	ד	ה	ו	ז	ח	ט
	1	2	3	4	5	6	7	8	9
Tens									
	י	כ	ל	מ	נ	ס	ע	פ	צ
	10	20	30	40	50	60	70	80	90
Hundreds									
	ק	ר	ש	ת	ך	ם	ן	ף	ץ
	100	200	300	400	500	600	700	800	900

Positional number systems.   The modern number system is an example of a positional system in which a certain number of digits are given special names and groupings of these are represented by the position of a digit in a sequence. Thus, in the system using a base of 10, digits 1, 2, 3, 4, 5, 6, 7, 8, and 9 are used and ten is represented by 10, in which the digit 1 is displaced to the left and the symbol 0 is used for zero. In positional notation, with a base b, special symbols are not used for powers of the base b^2, b^3, etc. Instead, the information is supplied by the position of a digit, so that the example 7M3C9X2 given above (see *Multiplicative grouping systems*) is written more simply as 7,392. (Characteristics of modern numeral systems are discussed under ARITHMETIC.)   (W.J.LeV./D.E.S.)

MATHEMATICAL SYMBOLS

Mathematical symbols constitute a language in which quantities, operations with them, and their relations to each other are represented in abstract terms, clearly and concisely. As records, symbols eliminate much needless remembering, and the statements themselves frequently suggest the various procedures to be followed in mathematical thinking.

The symbols used in the earliest printed works in arithmetic and algebra were abbreviations and initial letters such as the hand copyists of earlier days had used. These shortcuts were later supplemented by signs devised for specific purposes. This was the case in the first known use of the equality sign ($=$) which the English mathematician Robert Recorde introduced in his algebra (1557) with the explanation: ". . . to auoide the tediouse repetition of these woordes: is equalle to: I will sette as I doe often in woorke vse, a paire of parallels, or Gemowe [*i.e.*, twin] lines of one lengthe, thus: $=$, bicause noe .2. thynges, can be moare equalle."

From the 15th to the 17th century there was great activity in representing unknown quantities and their powers and in indicating operations with numbers. For relationships among numbers, the symbols $<$, $=$, and $>$ (meaning less than, equal to, and greater than) sufficed. Various symbols were proposed for the same idea; in the hands of several authors, a single symbol might have as many different meanings. Some symbols seem to have survived because of the importance of the people who introduced them; others apparently persisted because they were adapted to new developments in subject matter. The result is that the symbols of elementary mathematics have been aptly described by the Italian-U.S. mathematician Florian Cajori as "a mosaic of individual signs of rejected systems."

Among 16th–17th-century mathematicians who gave serious study to the subject of mathematical symbols were François Viète, William Oughtred (English), René Descartes, and Gottfried Wilhelm Leibniz. Viète used vowels for unknown quantities and consonants for known quantities. This made possible the representation of an equation in general terms. Descartes followed this pattern but used the letters from the beginning of the alphabet as known quantities and those from the end of the alphabet as unknown quantities. Oughtred experimented with more than 150 symbols, of which only a few survive. Toward the close of the 17th century, Leibniz made a careful study of the symbols that were in use at that time, paying particular attention to their clarity and to the ease with which they could be printed. It was in the course of this work that Recorde's equality sign came to be preferred to its competitors.

The use of symbols had its detractors in this period; according to the 17th-century English philosopher Thomas Hobbes, "Symbols are poor unhandsome though necessary scaffolds of demonstration." In reference to Wallis' work, Hobbes wrote, "And for . . . your Conic Sections, it is so covered over with the scab of symbols, that I had not the patience to examine whether it be well or ill demonstrated."

The differing approaches to calculus held by Newton and Leibniz produced different notations. For more than a century, British mathematicians clung to Newton's symbols, mathematicians on the continent to those of Leibniz.

In the 18th century, Euler contributed an unusual number of symbols that lasted in mathematics; few men have been responsible for more than one. Among Euler's symbols are $f(x)$, meaning a function of x; e, the base of the natural logarithms; Σ, indicating summation; and i, standing for $\sqrt{-1}$.

As a young man Leibniz had a dream of devising a method of representing ideas in a symbolic language. He failed to implement this and the project lay dormant until the 19th century. Then, following the publication of the English mathematician George Boole's *Analysis of Logic* in 1847, the attention of mathematicians began to be directed toward the matter of symbolic logic. And in the first half of the 20th century, the study of the structure of mathematics became of prime importance. Each of these activities was accompanied by specific symbolism. Thus the modern symbolism used in the newer algebra and the symbols for symbolic logic exhibit a variety similar to that which accompanied the development of algebra and of calculus. (V.S.)

CALCULATORY SCIENCE

The history of tables. Mathematical tables appear in the earliest records of history. Thus, certain elementary numerical values connected with the combination of fractions are found in the Egyptian Rhind mathematical papyrus, the copy of a scribe named Ahmes, written some time before 1700 BC. More extensive than these are the records of the Babylonians, dated perhaps as early as 2000 BC, which contain multiplication tables and tables of reciprocal values; *i.e.*, values of $1/n$ for certain values of n.

Renewed interest in the mystery of the computation of Ahmes' table was stimulated by references to it in *Historical Topics* (edited by A.E. Hallerberg) issued in the United States in 1969 by the National Council of Teachers of Mathematics. Among both the Egyptians and the Greeks it was the custom to use fractions with unit numerators. Thus Heron of Alexandria expanded the fraction $^{31}\!/_{51}$ as the sum of the unit fractions $\frac{1}{2}$, $^1\!/_{17}$, $^1\!/_{34}$, and $^1\!/_{51}$. To aid in such representations Ahmes provided a table of fractions of the form $2/(2n + 1)$, in which n designates successively all the numbers up to and including 49, expressed as the sum of two, three, or four fractions with unit numerators, such as, for example, $^2\!/_9 = \frac{1}{8} + ^1\!/_{18}$, $^2\!/_{13} = \frac{1}{8} + ^1\!/_{52} + ^1\!/_{104}$. Florian Cajori in his *History of Mathematics* observed that if $2/x = 1/a + 1/b$, and if x is expressed as the product of p and q, that is, $x = pq$, then $a = \frac{1}{2}p(p + q)$ and $b = \frac{1}{2}q(p + q)$ will furnish a solution. Unfortunately these formulas will produce only the values in Ahmes' table when x is a prime, not, for example, the expansion of $^2\!/_9$ as given above. If $x^2 = PQ$, instead of $x = pq$, then $a = \frac{1}{2}(P + x)$ and $b = \frac{1}{2}(Q + x)$ will give all the values in Ahmes' table for sums of two fractions. This solution also provides a clue to the Ahmes mystery. The Egyptians were fully aware of the use of Pythagorean triplets such as 3, 4, 5 in the sum $3^2 + 4^2 = 5^2$, which their so-called rope-stretchers employed in orienting their temples. It is thus significant to note that the sum $2/x = 1/a + 1/b$ can be written in the form of such a triplet sum, namely, $x^2 + (a - b)^2 = (a + b - x)^2$. The solution to the Ahmes mystery follows as an immediate consequence of this formulation.

Early use of fractions

The first mathematical table in the modern sense of the word is the table of chords found in the *Syntaxis Mathematica*, or, as it is more commonly called, the *Almagest*, of Ptolemy. This remarkable table, dating from the middle of the 2nd century AD, gives the values of the chords of a circle at intervals of one-half degree to six-place approximation. In the computation of this table, Greek mathematical ingenuity reaches one of its highest points. It is probable that the table is derived from an earlier work by Hipparchus, which is mentioned by Theon of Alexandria. Three lines of this table as it appears in a Greek edition of the *Almagest* published in Basel in 1538 are given in Table 6.

Table 6: Ptolemy's Table of Chords

kanonion						translation of the canon						
κγ	κγ	νε	κζ	ο	α	α λγ	23	23	55	27	0 1 1	33
κγς″	κδ	κς	ιγ	ο	α	α λ	23½	24	26	13	0 1 1	30
κδ	κδ	νς	νη	ο	α	α κς	24	24	56	58	0 1 1	26

For the translation into Hindu-Arabic numerals the following table of equivalent symbols is necessary:

α	β	γ	δ	ε	ς	ζ	η	θ	ι
1	2	3	4	5	6	7	8	9	10

κ	λ	μ	ν	ξ	ο	π	ϙ	ρ
20	30	40	50	60	70	80	90	100

Fractions were customarily written with one accent on the numerator and two on the denominator, which was written twice. Thus $\iota\gamma' \; \kappa\theta'' \; \kappa\theta'' = ^{13}\!/_{29}$. For fractions of unit numerator the denominator only was written. Thus it is possible to interpret that $\mu\delta'' = ^1\!/_{44}$, $\gamma'' = \frac{1}{3}$, and so on. Although the usual way of writing $\frac{1}{2}$ was β'', the symbol s'' was also in common use for $\frac{1}{2}$, as in the table of Ptolemy.

The modern character of this table is seen from the fact that it contains first the values of the argument, then the tabular entries, and finally a table of differences. To interpret the table it is necessary to know only that Ptolemy used the sexagesimal system of numbers. He divided the radius into 60 parts, each of these units into 60 parts, and so on. Hence, in terms of the radius, the following is obtained:

$$\text{chord } 24° = {^{24}\!/_{60}} + {^{5}\!/_{60}}^{2} + {^{5}\!/_{60}}^{3} = 0.415824.$$

This value is equivalent to sin $12° = \frac{1}{2}$ chord $24°$ $= 0.207912$, which is correct to the last place.

Development of mathematical tables   Although mathematical tables were prepared and used both by Hindu and Arab mathematicians, it was not until the 15th century that modern development of this art began. Great tables of the natural trigonometric functions were started in the middle of the 15th century under the direction of Georg von Peurbach, who divided the radius into 600,000 parts; and his pupil Johann Müller, more generally called Regiomontanus, who computed a table of sines to every minute of arc with a radius of 1,000,000 and a table of tangents. In the first book of his *De revolutionibus orbium coelestium* ("Concerning the Revolutions of Heavenly Bodies") published in 1534, Nicolaus Copernicus gave a five-place table of sines. An improved table of tangents appeared in the *Canon foecundus* of Erasmus Reinhold in 1553 and the first table of secants in the contemporary *Tabula benefica* of Franciscus Maurolycus.

Among the greatest labours ever undertaken in table-making were those of Rhäticus, Otho, and Pitiscus. Georg Joachim von Lauchen, generally known as Rhäticus, a student of Copernicus, began the task of computing a table of the trigonometric functions to 15 decimal places for every 10 seconds of arc and for every second in the first and last degrees of the quadrant. He completed the tables of sines and began the construction of tables of tangents and secants, but died before he was able to complete them. It is said that Rhäticus kept several men in his employ as calculators for 12 years.

The great task was finished by his pupil Valentin Otho, who produced the celebrated ten-place canon *Opus Palatinum de triangulis* ("The Palatine Work on Triangles") in 1596. The 15-place table of sines was published in 1613 under the title *Thesaurus Mathematicus* by Bartholomäus Pitiscus. These works formed the basis of modern tables.

The introduction of logarithms. A logarithm is a number y appearing in the equation $x = b^y$. Here y is said to be the logarithm of x to the base b and x is the antilogarithm of y. For example, since $100 = 10^2$, 2 is the logarithm of 100 to the base 10. Similarly, since $81 = 3^4$, 4 is the logarithm of 81 to the base 3. Logarithms are useful aids to computation because two numbers can be multiplied by adding their logarithms. For example, 81 is 3^4 and 27 is 3^3. Then 81×27 is $3^4 \times 3^3$, which is $3 \times 3 \times 3 \times 3 \times 3 \times 3 \times 3$—or 3^7. Thus the logarithm of 81×27 is 7, a value obtained by addition of the logarithms of 81 and 27. In this way multiplication can be facilitated by use of a table giving the logarithms of numbers. In order to multiply numbers together their logarithms are obtained from the table and added to give the logarithm of the product. The answer is also obtained from the table by looking up the number that corresponds to this logarithm; *i.e.*, by finding its antilogarithm. This property is a consequence of the relationship $b^y \times b^z = n^{(y + z)}$.

Division and the extraction of square roots can be performed by procedures based on $b^y \div b^z = b^{(y - z)}$ and $(b^y)^z = b^{yz}$. Here y and z are powers of b and are called exponents.

The germ of the idea of logarithms goes back at least as far as a work of the German mathematician Michael Stifel that was published in 1544. Stifel, as well as Simon Stevin of the Netherlands, denoted powers (that is, repeated products) by indices, but their notation was probably not known to the originators of tables of logarithms.

With the independent publication of a table of logarithms by John Napier in Edinburgh in 1614 and a brief table of antilogarithms by the Swiss mathematician Joost Bürgi in Prague in 1620, numerical computation took a

fresh start. These men were motivated by the hope of simplifying such computations as those required in astronomy, and their invention arose from comparing arithmetic and geometric progressions. An arithmetic progression is one in which each term is derived from the preceding one by addition of a constant factor. A simple example is the progression: 0, 1, 2, 3, 4, 5, · · ·. A geometric series is one in which each term is derived by multiplying the preceding one by a constant factor; for example, 1, 2, 4, 8, 16, 32. The terms in the arithmetic series are logarithms of corresponding terms in the geometric series. Since the theory of exponents had not been worked out, the simpler modern approach was not available to them; this makes their discovery all the more remarkable.

Napier's table of logarithms extended to eight places, but his base was essentially $1/e$, $e = 2.7183 \cdot \cdot \cdot$. Although it is common to refer to tables of logarithms to the base e, namely of $\log_e x$, as tables of Naperian logarithms, they are more correctly called natural or hyperbolic logarithms. Napier's logarithms (Nap. log), given by Nap. log $y = 10^7 (\ln 10^7 - \ln y)$, were awkward for computations. For one thing, the logarithm decreased as the number increased.

Base 10 logarithms   The first table of logarithms to the base 10 was computed by the English mathematician Henry Briggs and published under the title *Arithmetica Logarithmica* in 1624. The computations were made to 14 decimal places, but included only the logarithms of numbers from 1 to 20,000 and 90,000 to 101,000.

Although Briggs had intended to complete his monumental computations, he was anticipated in this by the Dutch mathematician E. de Decker in his *Tweede Deel der Nieuwe Telkonst* of 1627 and the Dutch bookdealer, publisher, and mathematician Adriaan Vlacq in his so-called *Editio Secunda* of Briggs's *Arithmetica* in 1628. These men, who were essentially partners in the undertaking, gave ten-place logarithms together with differences over the integers 1 to 100,000.

Extensive tables of common logarithms were thus generally available before 1630. They were calculated by tedious repeated multiplications and the extraction of square roots. A clear construction of the theory came more slowly. As calculus developed, the logarithmic function appeared inevitably as the function that has a derivative of $1/x$. In 1668 the German-born astronomer Nicolaus Mercator stated a special case of the series for $\ln (1 + x)$, which could have saved much of the work of preparing tables. Wallis followed with the first general expression for the Mercator logarithmic series. The logarithmic function attracted attention, quite apart from the use of logarithms in calculation, because it is inevitably involved in applied mathematics. The differential equation $dy = ydx$, with a solution that is the exponential function (the inverse of the logarithmic function), states that the rate of change of y is proportional to y itself. Because this law of change is common to the growth of biological populations, the decay of radioactive substances, and the accumulation of money at continuous compound interest, as well as to many other phenomena, the logarithmic function has numerous applications. Moreover, the exponential function is essential in the solution of various differential equations, including all linear equations with constant coefficients.

Attempts to extend logarithms to negative numbers in the early 18th century led to considerable controversy among Leibniz, Johann Bernoulli I, and Euler. In 1742 the English mathematician William Jones gave the first systematic treatment of logarithms as exponents, and about 1747 Euler extended the theory to negative and complex numbers.

The work of de Decker and Vlacq was reprinted by George von Vega in 1794 under the title *Thesaurus Logarithmorum Completus*. Vega also included Vlacq's table of log sines and log tangents, described below, and a table of natural logarithms to 48 places computed by J. Wolfram, a lieutenant of artillery in the Netherlands. Wolfram's tables, which extended over all the numbers up to 2,200 and all the primes, together with a few numbers the least factor of which is a large prime, to 10,000, was printed for the first time in the *Sammlung* by J.C. Schulze in 1778.

Tables of the logarithmic trigonometric functions followed shortly the publication of the logarithmic tables of integers. The fundamental contributions were made by Vlacq in his *Trigonometria Artificialis* of 1633, which gave ten-place values of log sines and log tangents to every 10 seconds of the quadrant with differences, and by Briggs in his *Trigonometria Britannica* of 1633, which gave the natural sines to 15 places, tangents and secants to 10 places, log sines to 14 places, and log tangents to 10 places at intervals of 0.01° from 0° to 45°. It is interesting to observe that mathematicians have followed Vlacq's division of the degree rather than Briggs's. A new turn to this question was given at the time of the French Revolution, when weights and measures were being reduced to the metric system.

Gaspard Riche, baron de Prony, was placed in charge of a project to produce the values of trigonometric functions in centesimal units, namely divisions of the quadrant into 100 parts called grades, each grade divided into 100 minutes and each minute into 100 seconds. This vast undertaking, called the *Tables du Cadastre* from the fact that Prony was the director of the Bureau du Cadastre, was carried out on a scale that involved the calculation of the natural sine to 22 decimal places and log sine and log tangent to 14 decimal places. Although the original work was never published, tables based upon it have appeared.

With the now rapidly growing demands of science on the one hand and commerce (as shown by extensive manuals of navigation) on the other, the number of tables increased rapidly. The 18th century produced more tables than the 17th; and the 19th, by greatly expanding the number of functions tabulated, increased both the volume of tables and their variety. The first half of the 19th century, for example, originated tables of elliptic integrals, elliptic functions, hyperbolic functions, gamma functions, probability functions, Bessel functions, and many others (see ANALYSIS, COMPLEX: *Elliptic functions;* DIFFERENTIAL EQUATIONS: *Special Functions;* and PROBABILITY, THEORY OF).

With the widespread use of calculating devices, the 20th century had by 1970 increased by manyfold the total number of tables produced in all the preceding centuries. Hence the history of tables is becoming rather a history of the tables of special functions.

The bibliography of tables. In the early 19th century some systematic account of the origin, size, and accuracy of tables became necessary, and a number of excellent historical and bibliographical surveys were produced. By 1943 the need for current information became so great that the National Research Council of the United States established a special quarterly journal to review recent tables, record manuscript tables, list errata in standard tables, publish bibliographies of tables in special fields of research and of particular functions, and describe calculating machines.

With the rapid proliferation of tables it became evident that a more comprehensive and general bibliography was urgently needed. Such a work appeared in 1946: *An Index of Mathematical Tables,* by Alan Fletcher, J.C.P. Miller, and L. Rosenhead, recording the origin, range, and extent of something in excess of 2,000 tables, a monumental undertaking.

Three years later *A Bibliography and Index of Mathematical Tables,* by Harold Thayer Davis and Vera Fisher, recorded not only the titles and categories of 3,410 tables but also the production of mathematical tables by centuries from 1500—one index of the growth of scientific productivity. Thus the 16th century produced 9 tables; the 17th, 70; the 18th, 84; the 19th, 986, the 20th to 1947, 2,262, which at its mid-point had increased to something in excess of 2,800. Other bibliographies appeared in Germany and the U.S.S.R.

Since the production of mathematical tables continued to increase at a rate in excess of 100 tables per year, these bibliographies and indexes were soon found to be inadequate; Fletcher, Miller, and Rosenhead, with the assistance of L.J. Comrie, produced a second edition of their *Index* in 1962 in two volumes, more than double the original edition.

With the great increase in tables a new dimension was added to the problem, that of producing a general work that would provide, somewhat like a dictionary, a comprehensive compilation of the available values of the tabulated functions and a description of their properties. The first work of this kind had been prepared by Eugen Jahnke and F. Emde in 1909, *Funktionentafeln mit Formeln und Kurven,* which proved so useful that it reached a fifth edition in 1952. A more comprehensive work was published by the National Bureau of Standards in 1964, *Handbook of Mathematical Functions with Formulas, Graphs, and Mathematical Tables,* under the editorship of Milton Abramowitz and Irene A. Stegun. This massive work provides tables covering 29 classes of functions. The difficulty of this task is readily seen from the fact that the work is essentially an abridgment of numerous other works, some multivolumed and many devoted to the tables and properties of single functions.

A word should be said about table-makers themselves. Peter Barlow, in the preface to his classical *Tables* (1814), somewhat disparages the art of the mathematician as a computer with these words:

> Little is to be expected of mathematical reputation; nothing more being requisite for the execution of such an undertaking than a moderate skill in computation and a persevering industry and attention; which is not precisely the qualifications a mathematician is most anxious to be thought to possess.

But Barlow is wrong, because often the problems involved in computation are among the deepest and most intricate found in analysis, as is shown by the roster of table-makers including many of the greatest mathematicians: Kepler, Legendre, Euler, Gauss, Laplace, Cayley, Lord Kelvin, Lord Rayleigh, and many distinguished mathematicians of the 19th and 20th centuries.

The evolution of analogue devices. In the extraordinary expansion of the physical sciences and technology beginning in the 18th century, mathematical formulations were essential. Questions in understanding and on the design and operation of devices could be expressed in terms of analytic concepts.

Any mathematical problem may require a lengthy computation, or it may be impractical or impossible to solve directly as a mathematical problem. The scientific analysis that produced the mathematical problem, however, may also indicate methods of handling it. One method is to obtain analogous physical systems, the behaviour of which can be quantitatively observed. Examples of this are models of ships, waterways, and wind tunnel experiments on aircraft wings or fuselage shapes. To make the numerical measurements applicable, one needs dimensional theory (see PHYSICAL THEORIES, MATHEMATICAL ASPECTS OF) to indicate the significant relations.

An analogue computing device is a physical apparatus that depends on interrelated measurable quantities to deduce numbers that can serve as solutions to mathematical problems. The science of constructing analogue computers is as old as Western science itself, dating to the machines of Heron of Alexandria and of Archimedes (*q.v.*). Certain specialized analogue devices that have become important in modern times are mentioned in some detail here; most analogue devices, however, are of historical interest only since their work has been taken over by digital computers.

Harmonic analyzer. Simple harmonic motion is the motion of a body with an acceleration that is directed toward a fixed point and is proportional to its displacement from the point. An example is the swinging of a pendulum. Such motion is periodic; that is, it goes through a number of identical cycles and can be represented by an equation of the form $y = A \sin Bt$, in which y is the displacement of the body at time t and A and B are constants. The motion of bodies emitting musical sounds is the combination of many simple periodic motions of this form, hence the name harmonic motion. More complicated periodic motions, represented by some

The
role of
mysticism
in
harmonic
analysis

function $f(x)$, can be shown to be formed from a number of simple harmonic motions and $f(x)$ can be analyzed into a sum of simple harmonic functions. This is harmonic analysis, and a device for performing it is a harmonic analyzer.

Much of the history of harmonic analysis is the story of the strange marriage of mysticism and mathematics. In the 6th century BC, Pythagoras taught that the essence of harmony was inherent in the miraculous power of numbers; but his mysticism was allied with keen observation and deduction. For example, he knew that the musical note produced by a string of fixed tension was converted into its octave (vibrated at higher frequency) when the length was reduced one-half, and its fifth when reduced two-thirds. The great astronomer Johannes Kepler in the 16th and 17th centuries was imbued with the mysticism of Pythagoras, which was enjoying a revival in centres of learning, particularly in Italian universities. Kepler, while not accepting in a physical sense the "music of the spheres" of Pythagoras, believed it was possible to represent the motion of every planet in terms of musical notation. Stimulated by the quest for a basic harmony in arithmetic, geometry, and music, Kepler opened a new era of mathematics with his discovery of the laws of planetary motion. Even in his lyrical moods, Kepler maintained the mathematician's quest for precision. For example, his staff notation of the tune appropriate to Mercury indicated, in strongly accented arpeggios, that its orbit is more elliptical than that of the other planets.

Another scientist who drew his inspiration from mysticism and his technique from mathematics was Isaac Newton. Newton, who was a disciple of the mystic Jakob Böhme, wrote in the *Principia*, 1687: "Nature is pleased with simplicity, and affects not the pomp of superfluous causes."

But it was Newton, the hardheaded mathematician who said in a letter that "the best and safest method of philosophizing seems to be, first diligently to investigate the properties of things, and establish them by experiment, and then to seek hypotheses to explain them," who gave the first mathematical treatment of wave motion in the *Principia*. His calculations gave the ellipticity of the earth as 1/230; the figure accepted today is 1/297.

In connection with the study of the vibration of musical strings the Swiss Daniel Bernoulli and Leonhard Euler laid the groundwork for Fourier's elaborate mathematical structure. The equations known as the Fourier series were first published by Bernoulli in 1728.

In keeping with the ancient traditions of harmonic analysis, James Clerk Maxwell in the 19th century pronounced Fourier's *Analytical Theory of Heat* "a great mathematical poem."

In *Science and the Modern World* (1925), Alfred North Whitehead notes that

> we have in the end come back to a version of the doctrine of old Pythagoras, from whom mathematics, and mathematical physics, took their rise. He . . . directed attention to numbers as characterizing the periodicity of notes of music . . . . And now in the 20th century we find physicists largely engaged in analyzing the periodicities of atoms.

Fourier, in his study of the transmission and diffusion of heat, first made use of the simplification that often occurs when a complicated function or curve is represented as the sum of a number of simple harmonic or sinusoidal components. The importance of such a representation has increased with the years, and the measurement of the harmonic components in empirically given data is of importance to the study of communication lines, of electrical power machinery, and in the theory of prediction of statistical data.

While much of the analysis in these fields is carried out by numerical processes, some is done by harmonic analyzers. Under suitable restrictions on the function analyzed, a periodic regularly recurring function $f(x)$ can be represented by $f(x) = \Sigma (A_n \sin nx + B_n \cos nx)$, in which the amplitudes A_n, B_n are determined by integral expressions (see ANALYSIS, FOURIER).   (Ed.)

A harmonic analyzer is a device for determining the coefficients A_n and B_n. The English physicist Lord Kel-

vin in 1876 was the first to invent such an instrument by an adaptation of a device invented by his brother, James Thomson, in the same year. The first completed instrument designed by Kelvin and used for the harmonic analysis of tidal observations embodies 11 sets of a disk-sphere-cylinder mechanism, one for each harmonic to be measured. The curve to be analyzed is wound on a central cylinder, and the simple harmonic motions of the proper periods are communicated to the disks by suitable gearing. The bar to which the tracer is attached has a series of forks that embrace the spheres. In actual use, the tracer is made to follow the curve, and the readings on the different integrating cylinders give the required coefficients. The English scientists Olaus Henrici and Abraham Sharp invented an improved form of the analyzer in 1894.

A different type of harmonic analyzer, based on the English mathematician William Kingdom Clifford's graphic method, was invented by O. Mader in 1909. Essentially Mader's instrument consists of a gear and linkage that, as a pointer traces a given curve, cause a point on the gear to describe a transformed curve; the area enclosed by the transformed curve is measured by an ordinary polar planimeter (a mechanical device that integrates), and is proportional to the required harmonic coefficient. In using the Mader instrument, a guide ruler that forms part of the machine is placed parallel to the base line of the curve to be analyzed, and the tracer of the planimeter is placed in one of two holes in the gear. For each harmonic to be found there is an appropriate gear with two indentations in its face. To find the sine coefficient, the tracer of the planimeter is placed in one of the indentations while the analyzer traces the given curve, and to find the cosine coefficient, the tracer of the planimeter is placed in the other. The Mader instrument measures only one harmonic at a time, as contrasted with the Henrici analyzer, which measures several simultaneously.

Mader's
harmonic
analyzer

Several analyzers have been devised to use optical and photoelectric means. One such device was designed by H. C. Montgomery in 1939. To use Montgomery's analyzer, the curve to be analyzed is drawn or photographed on a transparent film, and the area of the film on one side of the curve is blacked out to make it opaque. A set of standard films is available in which the density varies along the length of the film. Thus when light falls on any part of the film, the fraction of the light transmitted is proportional to the function $C + D \sin nx$; C and D are constants and x is the distance from a reference mark to that part of the film where the light falls. If the film carrying the curve to be analyzed is superposed on the standard film, then the quantity of light transmitted through any transverse strip of the two superposed films is proportional to the width of the clear part of the one film multiplied by the transmission ratio of that strip of the standard film. Except for the appearance of the additive constants in the factors, this product is the integrand in the definition of the required harmonic coefficient, and the total light transmitted by the entire length of the films is the integral of the product. The total light is measured by photocells, and from this quantity the harmonic component can be deduced. The operation of the instrument is largely automatic, and 30 harmonics can be measured in about a minute and a half.

Differential analyzer. The most frequently encountered mathematical problems of engineering and physics are expressed in terms of differential equations, either ordinary or partial. The methods and theory of the solution of ordinary differential equations have received treatment at the hands of many of the masters of mathematics, but comparatively few differential equations arising in practice have solutions expressible in terms of a finite number of the elementary functions: sines, cosines, Bessel functions. In the applications of differential equations to physical systems, formal solutions may not be necessary or desirable if a numerical or graphic solution is obtainable. To calculate a graphic solution a number of differential analyzers have been constructed in the United States, Great Britain, and other countries. These have been used to solve numerous problems in design of electrical machinery, study of the scattering of electrons by

Applica-
tions
of the
differential
analyzer

atoms and determination of the paths of electrons in the field of magnetic dipoles, performance of automatic industrial control systems and of transients in electric lines, determination of the energy exchanges between gases and solids, and study of the boundary layer motion of viscous fluids; the analyzers also found extensive use in World War II in the computation of thousands of ballistic trajectories.

The development of the differential analyzer is largely due to the U.S. electrical engineer Vannevar Bush and his associates at the Massachusetts Institute of Technology in Cambridge. In 1927 Bush and others completed and described a product integraph or continuous integraph that was a forerunner to the analyzer. This device solved differential equations of the form $d^2y/dx^2 = f_a(f_1 + f_2)$ in which the f's are functions of x ordinarily given in the form of graphs.

In 1928 Bush published a description of the first differential analyzer capable of solving a broad class of differential equations. Many minor modifications have been made in the detailed mechanisms of this machine, and more or less exact copies have been produced for use at educational institutions and industrial laboratories throughout the United States, Great Britain, and Europe. The Rockefeller differential analyzer, dedicated in 1945, represented a considerable advance over the original model partly in refinement of elements but principally in the speed and convenience of means for setting up and controlling the operation of the analyzer.

The basic elementary device in the differential analyzer is the disk and wheel integrator, which appeared first in the early planimeters. Its function is to perform the integration $z = \int y \, dx$ in which, in the integrator, x is the angular displacement of the disk, y is the distance of the integrating wheel from the centre of the disk, and z is the resulting angular displacement of the integrating wheel. The addition of two quantities, x and y, each represented by the angular displacement of a shaft, is performed by a mechanical differential or adder, so arranged that a third shaft is rotated through an angle equal to the sum, z, of the first-mentioned displacements: $z = x + y$. Multiplication by a constant is accomplished in the analyzer by appropriate gearing; thus, if k is the gear-ratio between a shaft representing a variable x and another shaft representing a variable y, then $y = kx$. Arbitrary or empirical functions are introduced by means of input tables, on which are plotted the necessary functions in graphic form.

The solutions resulting from the operation of the differential analyzer appear in graphs drawn by the analyzer on output tables, or in numerical values printed by the machine at predetermined intervals.

The original differential analyzer was entirely mechanical in construction, all connections between the computing elements being made by means of shafts and gears that are mounted on a bedplate approximately 4 ft wide by 18 ft long. In using the differential analyzer, the equations to be solved are first written as a set of equations, each of which may contain an integration, an addition, a multiplication by a constant, or a functional relation like $y = f(x)$. From the equations, a working diagram is made in which symbolic representations of shafts, integrators, adders, and gears appear. The variables of the equations are equated to the rotations of corresponding shafts with suitable proportionality factors, and the performance of each mathematical operation in the equations is assigned to a particular one of the elementary mechanisms. The shafts, gears, integrators, and other elements of the analyzer are set up in accordance with their symbolic representation on the working diagram.

In the Rockefeller analyzer, shaft rotations are converted by means of rotating electrical condensers into electrical signals which control motors in such a way that the shafts driven by the motors follow very closely the positions of the controlling shafts. Electrically operated switches steer the control signals as required from place to place, thus dispensing with the necessity of connecting shafts by mechanical means. All the information needed to set up the analyzer for a given problem is coded and punched in paper tapes which automatically arrange the electrically operated switches as required, in a few minutes. (G.R.St.)

Slide rule. One of the most successful of the analogue devices, one of old origin, is the slide rule, a rule consisting of graduated scales, each movable, and by means of which simple calculations may be carried out mechanically. In ordinary slide rules these operations include multiplication, division, and extraction of square roots, as well as, in some cases, calculation of trigonometrical functions and logarithms. The slide rule has become an essential tool in the mathematics of science and engineering and is widely used in business and industry as well.

The logarithmic slide rule is a compact device for rapidly performing calculations with limited accuracy (see above *The introduction of logarithms*). Napier's early conception of the importance of simplifying mathematical calculations resulted in his invention of logarithms, and this invention made possible the modern slide rule. In 1620 an English mathematician, Edmund Gunter, plotted logarithms on a two-foot straight line. With such scales, multiplication and division were performed by addition and subtraction of lengths by a pair of dividers.

Another English mathematician, William Oughtred, according to his own statement of 1633, constructed and used as early as 1621 two of these Gunter's lines together, so as to do away with the need for dividers. The lines were used in both the straight and circular forms. In the former the scales were held against one another by the hands; in the latter, dividers were replaced by an opening index—really a pair of dividers fixed centrally on the circular scale. Oughtred's two scales were the forerunners of the C and D scales, the basic scales on nearly all slide rules from then on.

The first known slide rule in which the slide worked between parts of a fixed stock was made by Robert Bissaker of Great Britain in 1654. Others were due to the enterprise of the English surveyor and mathematical writer Seth Partridge in 1657, the English mathematician Henry Coggeshall in 1677—a slide in a two-foot folding rule adapted to timber measure—and Thomas Everard in 1683, whose rule was adapted for gauging. The usefulness of the slide rule for rapid calculation became increasingly recognized, especially in England, during the 18th century, and the instrument was made in considerable numbers, with slight modifications.

Improvements in the direction of increased accuracy in graduation were initiated by the English engineers Matthew Boulton and James Watt from about 1779 in connection with calculations in the design of steam engines.

In 1815 the English physician Peter Mark Roget invented his "log-log" slide rule for performing the involution and evolution of numbers. The fixed scale, instead of being divided logarithmically, is divided into lengths that are proportional to the logarithm of the logarithm of the numbers indicated on the scale; the sliding scale is divided logarithmically.

Amédée Mannheim, an officer of the French artillery, invented in 1859 what may be considered the first of the modern slide rules, having scales on one face only, and although quite simple is basically a type still made and designated by his name. The disposition of the scales in the Mannheim rule is the arrangement still adopted in the great majority of rules made in the 20th century. This rule, which also brought into general use a cursor, or indicator, was much used in France, and after about 1880 was imported in large numbers into other countries.

A great improvement was introduced in 1886 by Dennert & Pape in Germany by dividing the scales on white Celluloid, instead of on wood, brass, or ivory as before, which, giving a much greater distinctness in reading, was later almost universally adopted.

Before 1890 slide rules were made only in England, France, and Germany, but at that time an invention by William Cox led to the manufacture of rules in the United States. This invention introduced a revolutionary construction providing for scales on both front and back of the slide rule. An indicator with glass on both sides made

The disk and wheel integrator

The first modern slide rule

it possible to refer to all the scales on both sides of the rule simultaneously.

Many refinements in both scale arrangements and mechanical constructions have been made since that time. The decade from 1940 to 1950 saw further developments of slide rules with scales on both faces. Most important of these improvements was the arrangement of the scales, trigonometric and log-log, so that they operate together and at the same time maintain consistent relationship to the basic C and D scales. This arrangement gave added speed and flexibility to the solving of many problems, simple and complex alike, since it produced solutions by continuous operations, without the need of intermediate readings. Electronic calculators became widely available in the 1960s and 1970s; these fulfill many of the functions of the slide rule (see further MATHEMATICS AS A CALCULATORY SCIENCE).   (A.W.Ke.)

GEOMETRY

Egyptian, Babylonian, and Greek geometry. Geometry is encountered in the first written records of mankind. Fundamental formulas for measurement were known in ancient Egypt and Babylonia, and knowledge of the so-called Pythagorean theorem, which identifies the square of the hypotenuse of a right triangle with the sum of the squares of the two sides, is shown in clay tablets dating from the end of the 3rd millennium BC.

In Babylonia, geometry provided much of the language of algebra. Ancient Babylonians would state an algebraic problem like this: "Length, width. I have multiplied length and width to get the surface. I have added the excess of the length over the width to the surface: 183. I have added the length and the width: 27. Asked length, width, surface."

Today the symbols x and y are used in place of the words length and width, and the problem reads as follows: $xy + x - y = 183$, and $x + y = 27$.

Problems of truly geometrical character can also be found in cuneiform literature, and were stated in this way: "A beam, long 30, leans against a wall. The top has been lowered by 6. How far has the bottom gone away?"

More abstractly, this problem asks for the third side of a plane right triangle, given the hypotenuse (30) and another side $(30 - 6 = 24)$. From the Pythagorean theorem the third side equals $\sqrt{30^2 - 24^2}$.

The right triangle with sides ratio 3:4:5 occurs most frequently in Babylonian mathematics, which also provides an extensive table of other Pythagorean triangles. Good approximations of the ratio of diagonal and side of the square $(\sqrt{2})$ are also found in Babylonian texts. Though theoretical texts on geometry from this period have not been unearthed, some theory probably existed. Empirical methods alone do not lead to ideas like the Pythagorean theorem; some kind of genuine geometrical reasoning is needed.

According to the pre-300-BC Greek philosopher Eudemos of Rhodes the first geometrician was Thales, who is said to have predicted the solar eclipse of 585 BC, and to have proved a number of geometrical theorems. Eudemos' report has often been questioned because it seems improbable that the first geometrician could have proved theorems that presuppose deep insight, and that are not even mentioned by Euclid (flourished 300 BC). It is clear from Babylonian excavations that Thales of Miletus was not the first geometrician. Strong Babylonian influences have been shown in Greek algebra and astronomy, and doubtless reached Thales himself.

Pythagoras, who died about 490 BC, was known to his contemporaries and even later to Aristotle as the founder of a religious brotherhood in southern Italy, where the Pythagoreans played a political role in the 5th century BC (see PYTHAGOREANISM). The linking of his name to the Pythagorean theorem is rather recent and spurious. Pythagorean mathematicians developed number theory, music theory, and number mystics, and Euclid's arithmetical books (vii and viii) presumably come from a Pythagorean source. An important discovery ascribed to Pythagoras, and in any case due to his school, is that of the incommensurability of side and diagonal of the square;

The Pythagorean theorem

that is, the ratio of diagonal and side of the square is not equal to the ratio of two integers.

The proof (in Euclid's tenth book) runs as follows in modern notation: If a be the side and d the diagonal of the square, then, according to the Pythagorean theorem, $d^2 = a^2 + a^2 = 2a^2$. Given integers m and n such that $d:a = m:n$, then, $d^2:a^2 = m^2:n^2$, and hence $m^2 = 2n^2$. The integers m and n may be supposed without common divisor. From $m^2 = 2n^2$ it follows that m^2 is even. This is only possible if m itself is even. If l be half of m, then $4l^2 = m^2 = 2n^2$, hence $n^2 = 2l^2$. Thus, n^2 is even and n is even; however, then m and n would have a common divisor. Thus, there are no integers m and n such that $d:a = m:n$. This discovery of irrationality fundamentally influenced the development of Greek geometry.

In Pythagorean mathematics quadratic equations were formulated and solved by a geometrical procedure, the application of areas with excess (hyperbole) or with defect, or falling short (ellipsis). The quadratic equation $(a + x)x = P$ was interpreted as a problem of finding a rectangle of area P and with sides of length x and $(a + x)$, that is, a rectangle whose area is the sum of ax and the excess x^2. The equation $(a - x)x = P$ was interpreted in a similar way.

The Pythagorean discovery of incommensurability remodelled Greek geometry in the following way.

To prove for rectangles with the same altitude the proportionality of areas and bases, or to prove that proportional segments are cut off by parallel lines upon two fixed lines, a simple procedure may be applied as long as it is believed that two line segments always possess a common measure of which they are integral multiples. By suitable subdivisions similitude is reduced to congruency. Through the discovery of incommensurable pairs of line segments, Greek geometricians were faced with the problem of developing a satisfactory theory of proportionality. In their efforts to fill this gap, they realized that, in addition to proving theorems, inventing definitions might be a mathematical problem, especially when some field of empirical experience is to be organized mathematically. It was obvious how to define ratio and proportionality as long as the magnitudes under consideration were commensurable. It was recognized that a suitable definition of ratio and proportionality in the general case would be the clue to proving theorems.

The ultimate procedure for handling ratio, proportionality, and incommensurability in Greek mathematics is explained in Euclid's fifth and sixth books. Probably it is attributable to Eudoxus of Cnidus, a 4th-century-BC mathematician. Earlier, Aristotle had mentioned *antanairesis* or *antaphairesis* ("taking away from each other"), a procedure similar to continued fractions: If a_0 and a_1 are two magnitudes to be compared, subtract the second from the first as many times as possible, say m_1 times: if this procedure does not exhaust a_0, a remainder a_2 will be left. Continue by subtracting a_2 from a_1, m_2 times, with a remainder a_3. Generally, $a_i = m_{i+1}a_{i+1} + a_{i+2} \cdots$, $i = 0, 1, \cdots$, with positive integers m_i and $0 \leq a_{i+2} < a_{i+1}$. If this procedure stops with some $a_{p+1} = 0$, then a_p is a common measure, the largest common measure of a_0 and a_1. In this case the procedure is known as the Euclidean algorithm (first expressed in Euclid's *Elements* VII, 2 and X, 2–3). In the general case it generates an infinite number of integers m_i that in modern notations are the denominators of the expansion of $a_0:a_1$ into a continued fraction. If this development is broken off by neglecting the pth remainder, it yields an approximation of the given ratio by a ratio of integers. For instance, if a_0 is the diagonal and a_1 the side of a square, then $m_0 = 1$, and $m_1 = m_2 = \cdots = 2$, which leads to approximations for the ratio of diagonal and side $(\sqrt{2})$ by fractions $\frac{1}{1}$, $\frac{3}{2}$, $\frac{7}{5}$, $\frac{17}{12}$, $\frac{41}{29}$, $\cdots$, when any fraction s_i/t_i is computed from the preceding one by the rule $s_{i+1} = s_i + 2t_i$, and $t_{i+1} = s_i + t_i$. In his *Republic* Plato alludes to these "side-and-diagonal-numbers." By Euclid's codification, however, this Pythagorean discovery was eliminated from official mathematics.

The last pre-Eudoxian theory of proportionality must have consisted in defining two ratios to be equal if they

Discovery of incommensurability

have the same *antanairesis;* that is, if the numbers m_i appearing in the above procedure are correspondingly equal. From this definition theorems can be derived.

Eudoxus' solution (shown in Euclid's books V and VI) was more elegant. Eudoxus did not define ratio. He only said that it is a relation with respect to magnitude. Then he continued: Magnitudes are said to have a ratio if, when multiplied (by integers), they can surpass each other. This means, if a and b are magnitudes, Eudoxus' definition urged the existence of integers m and n such that $ma > b$, and $nb > a$. This property if postulated for a system of magnitudes is usually called the Archimedean axiom, though Eudoxian would be more apt. By this definition a line segment and an area have no ratio. Eudoxus' definition of equality of ratio reads in modern terminology as $a:b = a':b'$ if and only if for any pair of positive integers m and n, $ma > nb$ and $ma' > nb'$ go together as well as $ma = nb$ and $ma' = nb'$ and as well as do $ma < nb$ and $ma' < nb'$. Ratios are compared with each other by the definition: $a:b > a':b'$ if and only if there is a pair of positive integers m and n such that $ma > nb$, but $ma' < nb'$. After these three definitions the question arises whether $a < b$ implies that $a:a > a:b$. This means that positive integers m and n must be sought such that $ma > na$, but $ma < nb$. If $m = n + 1$ is tried, then $(n + 1)a < nb$. In other words, $a < n(b - a)$, which can be fulfilled if a and $b - a$ both have a ratio in the sense of Eudoxus' definition.

This axiom is the foundation of Eudoxus' theory of ratio, proportionality, and similitude. His method of combining all essential tools into a few definitions foreshadowed the most modern mathematical procedures. His approach was more elegant than that of *antanairesis*, in which an incommensurable ratio is located by comparing it with a special sequence of approximating commensurable ratios. In Eudoxus' approach it is compared with all commensurable ratios. In a certain sense *antanairesis* corresponds to defining real numbers by decimal fractions; Eudoxus' method foreshadowed modern theories in which a real number is determined by its order relation to any rational number, not only to finite decimal fractions.

Through the problem of incommensurability the Greek mathematicians learned logical analysis and mathematical rigour. These virtues, when exaggerated, finally hampered the progress of Greek mathematics. The view that the existence of incommensurable ratios cannot be granted algebraically, but only by geometry, led them to disregard algebra as developed by the Babylonians. By translating algebraic relations into geometry they created geometric algebra, a tool that could be handled by geniuses only. Genuine algebra had to be rediscovered when modern mathematics started.

Another theory that must have been highly problematic before Euclid is that of parallel lines. The uniqueness of the line through a given point and parallel to a given line is required as a postulate in Euclid's first book (whereas the existence of the parallel line is proved). Though enunciated in advance, the application of this postulate is postponed in Euclid's first book as long as possible. This delay indicates that rather than being spontaneous, the adoption of this postulate as such by Greek mathematics was probably preceded by a thorough exploration of the possibilities. It is probable that at some time before Euclid the need of adopting this postulate was under discussion and, in a comment of Aristotle's, evidence can be found for a competing theory of parallels, using points at infinity.

Euclid's activity was mainly that of a compiler. There were pre-Euclidean *Elements*, which, aside from a few fragments or vague indications, are lost. Euclid compiled pieces of different characters and qualities, and did not succeed in avoiding inconsistencies in terminology and structure. Thanks to these defects the single pieces can be isolated.

Euclid's *Elements* start with definitions, postulates, and axioms. The definitions are a strange collection of explanatory statements, loosely connected with the bulk of the work. The famous postulate of parallels is an example of his postulates; the axioms are of the type: "The whole is

greater than the part." The *Elements* have become famous as the outstanding example of a deductive theory. The claim, however, that all theorems are derived logically from the definitions, postulates, and axioms is unfounded. Modern criticism has shown essential gaps. Order notions, such as the division of the plane by its straight lines, are never mentioned, though they are implicitly used when proving the existence of parallel lines (eventually the proposition 16 stating that in a triangle an exterior angle is greater than any opposite interior angle). Even the proof of his first theorem concerning the construction of equilateral triangles is invalid, because the circles used are tacitly assumed to intersect. Postulates of congruency are lacking. The proof of the fundamental congruency theorem actually relies heavily on intuition.

It is not justifiable, however, to apply modern standards and notions of rigorous deductivity to Euclid's work. The Greek philosophy of mathematics has little in common with the modern ideal of deriving all conclusions from a few fundamental propositions (postulates or axioms). According to Plato and Aristotle, geometrical subjects are real and knowable; their properties are settled anyhow, whether they are explicitly stated or not; fundamental facts need not be announced explicitly unless they are controversial.

Nevertheless, as a deductive systematization of a field of knowledge, Greek geometry is much superior to Babylonian and Egyptian geometry. During more than 2,000 years Euclid's *Elements* were a model of deductive approach, often imitated, but never surpassed.

It should be added that after the climax of Greek mathematics the *Elements* were not adequately appreciated. The *Elements* teach geometry with a definitive approach, ignoring prior and alternative approaches, and without motivating highly sophisticated turns. Older works, which could have filled this gap, were completely lost through Euclid's authority. Thus, the problem Eudoxus solved in the theory of proportionality was not understood until Dedekind in 1871 solved the same problems independently of Eudoxus, but by the same idea. Euclid's sophisticated theory of parallels was not understood until after the invention of non-Euclidean geometry. Algebra suffered under geometrical influence, because the theoretical background of the geometrization and the subject matter could be uncovered only by modern historical research.

Euclid's unnatural and artificial methods have been taken over by many textbook writers. Geometrical transformations are changes in figures according to certain rules. A simple example is a rotation or translation of the figure in space. Other transformations involve expansion or diminution of the size of a figure or projection of it from one plane to another. Transformations do not occur in Euclid's work although they were known and used by his predecessors, especially symmetry, which played an important part in Thales' geometry (6th century BC). Possibly geometrical transformations were eliminated by Euclid because they seemed to belong to mechanics. Instead, Euclid used artificial auxiliary lines and subdivisions into congruent triangles. In elementary-school geometry his unfortunate method prevailed as late as the mid-20th century.

From Archimedes' *The Method* (a palimpsest discovered in 1906), it is known that Archimedes in the 3rd century BC did not repudiate infinitesimal and mechanical methods. Probably his finest discoveries were made in this way, but in the final editing the improved tools were eliminated in order to meet the requirements of Euclidean rigour. There are different levels of mathematical rigour that have their own functions in teaching, learning, and exploring. As long as there were written records or oral traditions of unofficial mathematics, Greek geometry could progress. After a sudden break, as by political events, the tradition could not be resumed. The level of sophistication in the surviving literature was too high for it to be used in self-instruction.

Geometric algebra was just sufficient to solve second-degree problems, corresponding geometrically to constructions with ruler and compass. When studying famous higher-degree problems, such as the duplication of the cube and the trisection of the angle, Greek geometricians had to solve the application problems of proportionality with a variable $P = y^2$ (in which y was again subjected to a quadratic relation, in order to raise the degree of the whole system). The application problem then runs $(a + x)x = y^2$, or $x^2 - y^2 + ax = 0$, which in modern terms describes an orthogonal hyperbola. After a slight generalization of the application problem, general hyperbolas appear. Other cases of the application problem provide ellipses and parabolas. (The names of these curves are simply those of the different cases of the application problem.) Greek passion for geometrization led Menaechmus, a student of Eudoxus, to the discovery that these curves are plane intersections of a cone. Menaechmus' work was continued by Archimedes and finished by Apollonius of Perga at the end of the 3rd century BC. In his formidable work he studied conics extensively, using different kinds of coordinates, though always in the clumsy language of geometric algebra.

The algebraic approach. In the period coming after the break of the tradition, genuine algebra was resumed and redeveloped by people who were unaware of Greek scruples. Following the Arabian and "rule of cross" period in the late Middle Ages, it got its final shape in the 16th and 17th centuries by the French mathematicians François Viète's and René Descartes's work. Descartes's *Geometrie* (1637) is the converse of Euclid's, the algebraization of geometry. Descartes progressed from the point where Apollonius had failed. He did not attach a coordinate system to a conic but to the plane, and he studied different figures in their mutual relations. By his method the points in the plane can be described by pairs of numbers (called coordinates) that are the distances of the point from two intersecting axes. The figures in the plane are represented by equations between these coordinates. Straight lines are represented by linear equations, $ax + by + c = 0$, and the conics by quadratic equations, $ax^2 + 2bxy + cy^2 + dx + ey + f = 0$. Problems of higher degree, and even nonalgebraic problems, can be studied with the same ease. With three coordinates the same can be done in space.

Descartes's discovery seemed to eliminate geometry theoretically. Practically, it was eliminated by the growing importance of calculus. In the 19th century, when geometry revived, a step taken that had been due during Descartes's lifetime was the invention of higher-dimensional space; it found its codification in the German mathematician Hermann Günther Grassmann's works of 1844 and 1861, in which a system of n numbers is considered as a point of n-space; the n numbers are its coordinates. Linear subspaces (corresponding to the straight lines and planes of 3-space) are defined by systems of linear equations between coordinates. Just as the distance between two points in a plane is given by Pythagoras' theorem, distance in n-dimensional space is defined by a higher-dimensional use of the theorem.

At the same time, by a slight though fundamental shift of stress, vector algebra changed the intuitive background of geometry in the work of the Italian mathematician Giusto Bellavitis and the Irish mathematician Sir William Rowan Hamilton. In mechanics many physical quantities are only completely specified by both their magnitude and their direction. The resultant of two forces, for example, depends not only on their size but on the directions in which they act. Such quantities are called vector quantities; they can be represented by arrows. Under the general name of vector, arrows (used before in mechanics to represent forces, velocities, and accelerations) were introduced in geometry. Formally, addition of points in n-space may be defined by $(\xi_1, \cdots, \xi_n) + (\eta_1, \cdots, \eta_n) = (\xi_1 + \eta_1, \cdots, \xi_n + \eta_n)$. Only if the point x is intuitively replaced by the arrow pointing from the origin to the point x does this vector addition get the intuitively significant meaning of the addition of forces, velocities, and accelerations in mechanics. The notion of inner product of two vectors, $(x, y) = \xi_1\eta_1 + \cdots + \xi_n\eta_n$ if $x = (\xi_1, \cdots, \xi_n)$ and $y = (\eta_1, \cdots, \eta_n)$, was also bor-

rowed from mechanics. The inner product (x, y) of the force vector x and the path vector y just equals the work done by x through y. Vector inspiration vivified such bloodless algebraic notions as the determinants, a formal tool for solving linear equations. For example, the volume of the parallelepiped spanned by n vectors was found to be equal to the determinant carrying the given vectors as rows or columns.

In the early 20th century the geometrical spirit of vector algebra was still enforced under the impact of the abstract algebraical school represented by the German mathematicians Ernst Steinitz and Emmy Noether and the Hungarian mathematician Frigyes Riesz. Vectors are not to be introduced by their coordinates (which have no direct geometrical meaning) but axiomatically by their intrinsic properties. This procedure leads to the definition: The set R is called an abstract vector space over the field F of numbers (scalars) and its elements are called vectors, if two operations are defined in R: adding elements $x, y, z, \cdots$ to each other, and multiplying elements $x, y, z, \cdots$ with scalars $\alpha, \beta, \gamma, \cdots$ such that certain laws are fulfilled (see ALGEBERA, LINEAR AND MULTILINEAR). The underlying field F may be that of the real numbers or complex numbers, or any other algebraic system, which are endowed with an addition and a multiplication with the usual properties.

In the (intuitive) plane two vectors e_1, e_2 can be found from which all vectors x may be combined in the form $x = \xi_1 e_1 + \xi_2 e_2$; the numbers ξ_1 and ξ_2 are called the coordinates of x with respect to this special basis e_1, e_2. In the case of ordinary space a basis of three vectors is required. R is called n-dimensional if a basis of R consists of n elements, and infinite-dimensional if no such basis is available. Infinite-dimensional spaces are important in modern analysis, which has fundamentally been influenced by this geometric terminology.

The notion of vector space is refined by requiring the existence of an inner product of vectors. When F is the field of real numbers, the laws of inner product can be quite succinctly expressed (see ALGEBRA, LINEAR AND MULTILINEAR). By one of the laws a vector length $|x| = \sqrt{(x,x)}$ can be defined with the (provable) properties $|ax| = |a| \cdot |x|$ and $|x + y| \leq |x| + |y|$.

Projective geometry. From the Greek period to the end of the 18th century two momentous geometric discoveries were made, by Desargues in 1639 and Pascal in 1640.

Briefly Desargues' theorem is concerned with perspective triangles, that is, two triangles placed so that three lines joining their corresponding vertices all intersect at a point. The theorem states that the points of intersection of pairs of corresponding sides of such triangles are collinear. Pascal's theorem is that if a hexagon is inscribed in a conic, the three pairs of opposite sides intersect in collinear points. It is sometimes named after the 3rd-century-AD Greek geometer Pappus of Alexandria who formulated a special case of the theorem, namely the case when the conic is a pair of intersecting straight lines. (A pair of lines can be regarded as a special case of a hyperbola in which the section of the cone is taken through the vertex. It is called a degenerate conic.)

Desargues' and Pascal's theorems were like erratic blocks in Euclidean geometry. The only relation that matters in their statements is that of incidence of points and straight lines. No part is played by distance, angle, congruency, or similitude (except for the definition of conic). On the other hand, in spite of the simplicity, an unusual amount of care is required in their proof—and even in their formulation—as soon as due regard is paid to the case when two or more lines are parallel. For example, if two corresponding sides are parallel Desargues' theorem states that the intersections of the other two pairs of corresponding sides both lie on a line parallel to the first sides; or that each side of one triangle is parallel to its corresponding side.

These problems were overcome by postulating points at infinity, such that every straight line is enriched with a point at infinity, and every plane with a line at infinity, this new point (line) being the same for all parallel lines

Descartes's contribution

Effect of vector algebra on geometry

Desargues' and Pascal's theorems

(planes). All infinite elements of space were supposed to lie on the infinite plane of space.

This postulate defined projective plane and "projective space" genetically. Parallelism disappeared as a relation: the only one still left from the variety of Euclid's is that of incidence (lying on). It is puzzling why this step, due to Jean-Victor Poncelet, a mathematician and general in Napoleon's army, which indicated a 19th-century revival of geometry, was not made earlier. If simplicity signifies truth, then the new geometry was much more true than Euclid's. A host of new notions and new truth, never dreamed of before, were discovered.

If a plane is considered and a point taken outside this plane, then any figure on the plane has a central projection on another plane (the plane of projection). Lines from the point (the centre of projection) through points on the figure make intersections with the projection. A conic has a central projection that is another conic, but some properties are not preserved under projection. Projective geometry can be defined as the study of those properties that are invariant under projection.

In ordinary space an intuitively important tool like central projection of one line (plane) upon another was of little use, because of the fact that at a certain point (line) the image vanished into infinity. In projective geometry, however, the central projection could be considered as a mapping of full lines (planes). The mappings resulting from repeated central projections became important under the name of projectivities. They are dealt with in the following theorems:

Fundamental Theorem of projective geometry: A projectivity of a straight line leaving three points invariant leaves invariant every point of that line. New light spread over large parts of traditional geometry thanks to the notion of harmonicity; quadruples of points on a line constructed in a certain way are called harmonic.

Theorem of Harmonicity: Three points of a harmonic quadruple determine the fourth uniquely, that is, independently of the choice of the auxiliary points of the construction.

Steiner's Theorem: The two pencils by which a conic is projected from two of its points are projectively related in the earlier defined sense of projectivity. By a converse of this theorem a purely projective definition of conics could be given, independent of their generation as plane sections of a cone. The relation of orthogonality in a pencil appeared to be a special kind of projectivity. Inverting this phenomenon, Euclidean geometry was successfully incorporated into projective geometry; assigning one line of the projective plane (to be called the line "at" infinity), and a certain projective relation in the pencil (to be called orthogonality), could produce Euclidean out of projective geometry.

A major problem was to free projective geometry from its Euclidean substrate and to found it independently. This problem seemed to be solved when the German mathematician Karl Georg Christian von Staudt in 1847 started with such incidence axioms as: two points determine one straight line; three points, not on a straight line, determine a plane; two planes intersect in a straight line, and so on. He then defined projectivity as a mapping preserving harmonicity. Taking three points on a line and constructing successively fourth harmonics, the line can be covered by a net that intuitively penetrates into any interval of the line. A projectivity leaving the given triple invariant leaves invariant every point of the net, hence, according to von Staudt, any point of the line. This condition, von Staudt said, proves the fundamental theorem of projective geometry, especially the theory of conics. Finally, von Staudt showed how to algebraize this projective geometry by geometric means.

Though von Staudt's performance was admirable, he still took the intuitive order relations in line and plane for granted without feeling the need for explicit formulations. Even worse, his process of fourth harmonics in succession was essentially the same as that of building up commensurable ratios. His transition from the net to the whole line essentially meant that things proved for commensurable ratios were believed to be valid for all

Margin note: Von Staudt's axioms

ratios. In 1847 von Staudt had not yet confronted the problems with which Greek geometry had wrestled before Euclid. In 1873 another German mathematician, Felix Klein, discovered the gap in von Staudt's reasoning. Though convinced of the possibility of founding projective geometry independently, he did not succeed in filling the gap.

A final solution for founding projective geometry independently postulates: (1) the incidence axioms; (2) cyclical order on the projective line and its preservation under projective mappings; and (3) some kind of Archimedean axiom, which permits the conclusion that a harmonic net penetrates every interval on the line (as the classical Archimedean axiom grants the possibility of fencing in incommensurable ratios by commensurable ratios).

This solution was possible under the German mathematicians Georg Cantor's and Richard Dedekind's re-examination in 1871 and 1872 of the ancient problematic. About 1880 two other German mathematicians, Moritz Pasch and Otto Stolz, a pupil of Weierstrass, recognized the import of the Archimedean axiom. In 1882 Pasch published the first rigorously deductive system of geometry in history. Through the Italian school of geometry, the formulation of the Archimedean axiom (still too Euclidean in Pasch's system) was better adapted to projective geometry.

A model of the projective plane in ordinary space is obtained by accepting a point O outside the plane and converting a point P of the plane into the line OP and a line l of the plane into the plane through O and l. The system of lines and planes through O, with its relations of incidence, then represents the system of points and lines of the projective plane. Analogously, projective n-space may be defined as the system of vector subspaces of an $(n + 1)$-dimensional vector space, every $(k + 1)$-dimensional vector subspace corresponding to a k-dimensional projective subspace. By this particular artifice the algebraization of Euclidean geometry immediately applies to projective geometry. The points of projective n-space can be described by the $n + 1$ coordinates $\xi_0, \xi_1, \cdots, \xi_n$, when two $(n + 1)$-tuples represent the same point if they are proportional.

Non-Euclidean geometry. Projective geometry toward the end of the 19th century had turned to fundamental research. Yet interest in the foundations of geometry had had an earlier modern awakening. It then centred on the celebrated parallel postulate of Euclid: that only one line can be drawn through a given point parallel to a given line. After a great many attempts to prove this postulate Gerolamo Sacheri, a Jesuit father of Milan, shifted the standpoint in 1733 by deliberately weighing alternative hypotheses and their consequences. Apparently, he was the first to do so, though possibly important work on parallel lines before Euclid may have been lost. Yet he was still strongly biassed in favour of the Euclidean postulate. The title of his major work was *Euclides ab omni naevo vindicatus* ("Euclid Vindicated from Every Flaw"). Gauss, who had very early seized upon the idea of non-Euclidean geometry (perhaps before the end of the 18th century), never published his discovery (fearing, he said in personal letters, the clamour it would arouse). His fear was unfounded. When, in the early 1830s, the Russian mathematician Nikolay Ivanovich Lobachevsky and the Hungarian mathematician János Bolyai independently made and published the same discovery, nobody was disturbed. After Gauss's death it was said that he had pursued non-Euclidean geometry. But even Gauss's name was not a strong enough incentive to invite interest in non-Euclidean geometry.

If a line l is given and a point P is outside l, then in plane Euclidean geometry a line m through P turning around fails to meet l just once. In non-Euclidean geometry as presented by Gauss, Lobachevsky, and Bolyai, it is assumed that there is an infinity of nonintersecting lines, and among them a first one and a last one. Pursuing the consequences of this assumption, they found no trouble in developing a geometry, and they did not hit upon contradictions. Gauss even considered testing the non-Euclidean hypothesis experimentally by surveying large triangles. In non-Euclidean space the sum of the angles of a triangle is not necessarily equal to 180°.

Non-Euclidean geometry was reapproached about 1868 by the mathematicians Bernhard Riemann, Hermann Ludwig von Helmholtz (both German), and Eugenio Beltrami (Italian) in another context. In 1870 Klein discovered a model of non-Euclidean geometry in Arthur Cayley's work. By this model the abstractness of non-Euclidean geometry was mitigated, and non-Euclidean geometry became familiar to mathematicians. However, the discipline was likely to be considered as a strange aberration, often confused with four-dimensional space and projective geometry.

The Cayley-Klein model

The Cayley-Klein model of non-Euclidean geometry stems from the fact that projective geometry embraces both non-Euclidean and Euclidean geometry. Instead of postulating a line at infinity, a conic K is assigned in the projective plane. Inside K the projectivities of the plane look like the rigid motions in the Euclidean plane. They preserve straightness, and if some point inside K is fixed, they carry the other points around on circlelike curves. They allow a transfer of line segments and angles that obeys the classical Euclidean congruency theorems. By the restriction to the interior of K, however, there is an infinity of lines through P that do not intersect the given line l. (Distance and angle measure have to be redefined in this geometry; the line l has an infinite length, though in the model its Euclidean length is finite.)

Into the same frame Klein fitted another non-Euclidean plane geometry, overlooked by Gauss, Lobachevsky, and Bolyai, but discovered by Riemann in 1854, published 1867. It arises if the real conic is replaced by an imaginary one. Another model of this geometry is still easier: The model of the projective plane mentioned above is taken in ordinary space as having lines through a point O considered as points and planes through O as lines of a projective plane. Intersect this model with a spherical surface S (O being its centre). It follows that to projective points correspond pairs of antipodal points of S, to projective lines correspond great circles of S. In order to avoid ambiguities, antipodal points are to be considered as one single point. Consequently, on S through two different points there is one straight line (great circle), and two straight lines (great circles) always intersect in one point. Again the rigid motions in S preserve straightness (as conceived on S) and allow the transfer of line segments (great circle arcs) and of angles under the same congruency laws as in the Euclidean plane. Now the straight lines are closed and finite.

Apart from the identification of antipodes, this system is just spherical geometry as pursued on the terrestrial or celestial sphere. The analogous model of the first non-Euclidean geometry would use a sphere with imaginary radius.

The two non-Euclidean geometries are distinguished as hyperbolic (the first) and elliptic (the second). In hyperbolic geometry the sum of the angles of a triangle falls short of 180°; in elliptic geometry it exceeds 180°, the excess or defect appearing to be proportional to the area of the triangle.

In this exposition non-Euclidean geometry has been restricted to two dimensions. Spatial elliptic geometry requires a 3-dimensional sphere in 4-dimensional Euclidean space as a model. This requirement has been and still is a difficulty if the intuitive function of a model is not really understood. A model and the thing it represents need not be alike in all aspects. The model of non-Euclidean 3-dimensional space in 4-dimensional space does not imply that a non-Euclidean universe actually needs a fourth dimension to be realized. It may be embedded in a higher-dimensional space, but its shape does not depend on that embedding.

Mathematicians themselves felt uneasy because they did not fully grasp the logical status of a model. Klein's model of non-Euclidean geometry, they said, proved nothing. It was constructed in the frame of projective geometry, which in turn depended on Euclidean geometry, the mother of all geometries. Klein replied that he had founded projective geometry independently of Eu-

clidean geometry, though his claim was not much better established than von Staudt's had been. People believed that the gap could be filled only in Euclidean geometry; though even in Euclidean geometry it remained unfilled as long as Eudoxus' solution was ignored. But the arguments in this discussion were not to the point. It does not matter whether projective geometry depends on Euclidean geometry (though in itself this is an important question). By constructing a model of non-Euclidean geometry in projective geometry (and hence by means of Euclidean geometry) it had been proved that non-Euclidean geometry was as consistent as the Euclidean version. Non-Euclidean geometry had been shown to be noncontradictory unless there were a contradiction in Euclidean geometry. This fact had been exactly proved, and no more could be done by mathematics. But this was a secret to be unveiled later when the logical status of geometry became clear.

Philosophical aspects. The philosophical view on geometry had not essentially changed since antiquity. In the realm of knowledge geometry was a peculiar problem. It was reasoned that all knowledge of the physical universe is mere opinion; it enters through the senses, which are liable to error and are to be watched by reason. Geometry was held the only exception. Geometrical truth, though dealing with the concrete world and not mere abstractions, can be proved mathematically, and was seen as beyond any doubt. Euclid's long-lasting influence is witnessed by a host of philosophers, theologians, historians, lawyers, and physicians who, imitating Euclid's method, attempted to prove their theories *more geometrico* ("in geometric fashion"). Kant, wondering how it is possible to construct *more geometrico*, with closed eyes as it were, things that prove true with one look into real space, asked the question: How are synthetic judgments a priori possible? He did not doubt that there were synthetic judgments a priori. Geometric judgments *are* synthetic according to Kant; they bring together notions that do not depend on each other by mere analysis. And, he said, they are a priori (prior to sensual experience) because otherwise they would not be sure.

It does not matter here how Kant answered his question. Philosophical discussions on space and geometry in the 19th century were heavily influenced by Kant's problem and solution. His starting point was never seriously questioned.

Pasch's first rigorous deductive system of (projective) geometry undertook to avoid any surreptitious use of intuition and he scrupulously fulfilled his program:

> Whenever geometry has to be really deductive, the process of inferring must be independent of the *meaning* of the geometrical notions as well as of the figures. The only things that matter are the *relations* between the geometrical notions, such as (have been) established in the used theorems and definitions.

Since antiquity an axiom had been considered an evident truth that neither could nor should be proved. Mostly this meant even that axioms need not be formulated. Most people spoke of axioms and never mentioned any one explicitly. If someone pointed out a gap in a geometrical proof, he was likely to be told that this was just an axiom. This was one of the usual contexts of the word "axiom." From Pasch mathematicians learned how to formulate postulates or axioms. They also learned that a complete axiomatic system of geometry must be much more involved than Euclid's, and that there were more axioms than the postulate of parallel lines worthy of special attention. In the Italian school projective planes were discovered in which the axioms of order and the Archimedean axiom cannot be satisfied.

Hilbert's resolution

The final solution of the philosophical dilemma on geometry was given by the German mathematician David Hilbert in his *Grundlagen der Geometrie* (1899; *The Foundations of Geometry*, 1902). He starts this work, after a short introduction, with the words: "Wir denken uns . . ."—"we imagine three kinds of things . . . called points . . . called lines . . . called planes . . . we imagine points, lines, and planes in some relations . . . called lying on, between, parallel, congruent . . . ," and then he enumerates the "axioms" to be fulfilled by things and relations imagined.

With "Wir denken uns" the bond with reality is cut. Geometry has become pure mathematics. The question of whether and how to apply it to reality is the same in geometry as it is in other branches of mathematics. Axioms are not evident truth. They are no truth at all in the usual sense.

Hilbert does not define what points, lines, planes are, or what "lying on," "between," "parallel," and "congruent" mean. These undefined notions are presented implicitly through the set of axioms in which they occur, as it were by rules that tell how to play the game with the things and the relations. In introducing the axioms of order Hilbert says, "The following axioms define the notion of order." When stating the axioms of congruency he states, "The following axioms define the notion of congruency or motion."

The idea that fundamental notions are defined implicitly by the axioms was the background of Pasch's work, too, though he did not say so. Whereas Pasch still believed that geometry deals with real space and anxiously stuck to what analysis may derive from sense data, in Hilbert's approach geometry was removed from sensory space. This modern idea on the logical status of geometry occurred a few years earlier to the Italian mathematician Gino Fano, and it was pronounced with even more emphasis by two of his countrymen, Mario Pieri and Alessandro Padoa, one year after Hilbert.

The clean cut between mathematics and phenomenalistic sciences became the paradigm of a new methodology. Through Albert Einstein's booklet of 1916, *Über die spezielle und die allgemeine Relativitätstheorie* ("Concerning Special and General Relativity Theory"), this doctrine made its way in the lobbies of science and philosophy. A few sentences written by Einstein in his 1921 lecture "Geometrie und Erfahrung" have grown classical:

> As far as the mathematical theorems refer to reality, they are not sure, and as far as they are sure, they do not refer to reality. . . . The progress entailed by axiomatics consists in the clean-cut separation of the logical form and the realistic and intuitive contents. . . . The axioms are voluntary creations of human mind. . . . To this interpretation of geometry I attach great importance for should I not have been acquainted with it, I would never have been able to develop the theory of relativity.

The axiomatic method. The idea on the logical status of geometry is not the only result of Hilbert's *Grundlagen*, and it is not its most important one. For the axiomatic method, which has pervaded mathematics in the 20th century, Hilbert's work was the first specimen, and a manual, in which the method is not explained in so many words but is shown instead by splendid examples.

Whoever proposes an axiomatic system has to show that it is consistent, that is, does not involve contradictions. In most cases consistency cannot be proved directly. It is done by exhibiting a so-called model that fulfills the axioms. A model of the axiomatic system of points, lines, circles and so on cannot be sought in physical nature or a pre-existent realm of Platonic ideas, which are no longer acceptable. Hilbert found his models of geometry in algebra, using Descartes's procedure. Since antiquity the relation between geometry and algebra had been inverted. Greek mathematicians were endeavouring to justify algebra by geometrization; in modern mathematics geometry is justified by algebraization.

Another concern in axiomatics is to know whether the different axioms are logically independent of each other, and what is the exact scope of any one of them. Hilbert showed how to drop axioms or to replace them by alternatives, and how to look for the consequences these changes might cause in suitable models.

In this course of thought he resumed the ancient problem of the theory of ratio and proportionality. He succeeded in getting rid of such notions and assumptions of topological character (to use modern terminology) as order and Archimedean axiom. He simply defined proportionality by means of the fundamental theorem, which was Eudoxus' first goal.

Instead of the Archimedean axiom, Desargues' and Pappus' theorems can be used as foundations of the theory of ratio and proportionality. (Actually Desargues' can still be derived from Pappus'.) This idea has surprising simplicity, and it may have occurred to Greek mathematicians. In fact, that it never arose in Greek thinking cannot be asserted. But, if it arose, it was apparently rejected, and a remark of Aristotle's reveals why.

Greek geometricians probably would not have been satisfied with this theory of ratio and proportionality that applies only to line elements instead of to all kinds of magnitudes. Hilbert, on the other hand, was allowed to stop at line elements, for meanwhile the rest of the problem had been solved by Descartes. Indeed, if some line segment OE is assigned as a unit, the product OC of two line segments OA and OB can be defined by means of the proportion OC:OA = OB:OE and by this geometry can be algebraized (the sum of line segments being unproblematic). But in algebraization all other geometrical magnitudes, such as areas and volumes, are comprehended, and no new theory of ratio is required to deal with them.

Looking to the proportion that defines the product, it can be found that Pappus' theorem actually enforces the commutativity of multiplication, that is, the law $ab = ba$. Dropping Pappus' theorem as an axiom, geometry can still be algebraized, though over a noncommutative field. Non-Pappian geometries with their algebraic matches, the noncommutative fields, have been extensively studied in modern geometry and algebra.

The algebraic equivalent of Desargues' theorem is the associativity of multiplication, the law $(ab)c = a(bc)$. The existence of non-Desarguean geometries has been shown by an example of Hilbert's. But there is a still weaker geometrical theorem than Desargues', the theorem of harmonicity. In 1933 Ruth Moufang discovered that its algebraic equivalent is a kind of weak associativity, called alternativity, $a(ab) = (aa)b$, $(ab)a = a(ba)$, $a(bb) = (ab)b$. By this discovery geometry gave algebra a new notion of major importance.

The fundamental geometric properties (harmonic, Desarguean, and Pappian) are matched by the fundamental algebraic properties of multiplication (alternative, associative, and commutative). It is remarkable that these properties are realized by the most important algebraical systems, the Hurwitz algebras, which generalize complex numbers, yet preserving the law $|ab| = |a| \cdot |b|$, in which

$$|a| = \sqrt{a_1^2 + a_2^2}$$

is the norm of the complex number $a = a_1 + ia_2$. It appears that the only Hurwitz algebras are those of the real numbers, the complex numbers, the quaternions (discovered by Hamilton in 1845), and the octaves (discovered by the English mathematician and jurist John Thomas Graves in 1829 and somewhat later by Arthur Cayley) with 1, 2, 4, and 8 basis units respectively. Real and complex numbers are commutative; quaternions are associative; octaves are alternative. The outstanding examples of Pappian, Desarguean and harmonic geometries are constructed over these algebras.

Geometrical transformations. Geometrical transformations, though a quite natural tool, were rejected by official Greek mathematics, perhaps because they were reckoned to belong to mechanics. Though this argument was refuted long ago, it is still used to oppose teaching geometrical transformations at the secondary level. Geometrical transformations belong to mechanics as little as functions do. Of course functions are used in mechanics and can be interpreted in a mechanical sense, and so can transformations.

The most perspicuous geometrical transformation (or mapping) is symmetry. Stone Age decorations witness that it was known to early mankind. Symmetry with respect to a plane maps any point of space upon its mirror image. Symmetry with respect to a straight line turns it around this line as an axis over an angle of 180°. Symmetry with respect to a point A maps every point X into the point X′ with the property that A is the midpoint of XX′.

In the plane, if first the symmetry with respect to l and then that with respect to $m(\|l)$ is applied, any point X

Symmetry

is first mapped upon its mirror image X′ with respect to *l*, and then X′ upon its mirror image X″ with respect to *m*. All the line segments XX″ are equal and parallel. The resulting mapping is a translation. If, however, *l* and *m* intersect in O, then the resulting mapping is a rotation around O. Another translation or rotation is obtained if the two symmetries are interchanged.

If two translations are applied successively, the result is a translation. Two rotations generally produce a rotation unless the rotation angles are opposite; then a translation results. Symmetries, translations, and rotations all are mappings of the plane that preserve distance, hence the rigid structure of the plane.

There are mappings of the plane that multiply all distances by the same factor; for example, the similitude mapping X upon X′ such that all lines XX′ go through a fixed point O and X divides OX′ in a fixed ratio. These mappings still preserve angles. Parallel projections of one plane upon another preserve parallelism, but generally change angles. Projectivities of projective planes preserve linearity, but not parallelism.

When two mappings are performed, first *f* and then *g*, the resulting mapping is indicated by *gf*. To any mapping *f* of the examples given, the inverse mapping (called f^{-1}) can be constructed with the property that (for every *X*, *Y*) if *f* maps *X* upon *Y*, then f^{-1} exactly maps *Y* upon *X*. A trivial case is the identity mapping *i* that carries every point into itself. Both ff^{-1} and $f^{-1}f$ are identity mappings, but generally *fg* and *gf* differ from each other.

Groups of mappings

Examples like these lead to the notion of group (of mappings). A set *G* is said to form a group if a product *fg* is specified for any couple of elements of *G* such that: for any *f*, *g*, *h* of *G*, *fg* belongs to *G* and $(fg)h = f(gh)$; there is an (identity) *i* in *G* such that for any *f* in *G*, $fi = if = f$, and for any *f* in *G* there is one f^{-1} in *G* such that $ff^{-1} = f^{-1}f = i$.

The mappings of the plane preserving distance form such a group, as do the mappings preserving the ratios of distances, the mappings preserving parallelism, the mappings of the projective plane preserving linearity (the projectivities), and the projectivities leaving invariant the non-Euclidean distance.

Lie and Klein were the first to stress the import of the notion of group in geometry. A geometry is a relational system (for example, a system of points and lines with the relation of incidence). The mappings of the system that preserve these relations form a group, the group of this geometry. In order to know whether some relation depends on some other, it is useful to determine if the mappings preserving the first one also preserve the other one. Thus, through group theory it can be decided to which kinds of geometry some notion belongs, and how different geometries are related to each other. The relationship between the non-Euclidean geometries and projective geometry was settled in this way, and a good many other geometries, discovered in the 19th century, were better understood when they were fitted into projective geometry by group-theory methods. This is, in a few words, the purport of Klein's *Erlangen Programm*, so called for the university at which he taught.

In the 20th century the French mathematician Élie-Joseph Cartan stressed the group-theory aspect even more. If *G* is the group of some classical geometry and *H* the subgroup leaving invariant a point X_0, then any point *X* can be characterized by the mappings of *G* carrying X_0 into *X*. They form what is called in group theory a coset of *H* in *G*, and *G* is the union of all these cosets. By this device the study of this given geometry reduces to a study of the set of cosets of *H* in *G*, which can be performed by group-theory methods alone. A significant part of geometrical research has since been devoted to such homogeneous spaces; that is, spaces having an associated group such that any point is carried into any other point by a suitable mapping belonging to that group.

The German mathematician Friedrich Bachmann expressed in 1959 a group-theory approach to foundations of geometry that can be sketched by the example of plane geometry: If *P* and *l* mean not only a point and a line, but also the symmetries with respect to them, then,

in the sense of group theory, $PP = i$ and $ll = i$. Then clearly $Pl = lP$ means the belonging of *P* to *l*, and $l_1l_2 = l_2l_1$ means the orthogonality of the lines l_1 and l_2, and so forth. In this language of group theory, it is possible to formulate involved relations and, especially, fundamental axioms.

The concept of space. Throughout the 19th century, the foundations of geometry were identified with the German philosopher Helmholtz' approach of 1868 (finally overshadowed by Hilbert's). Helmholtz renounced the conventional attitude toward geometry. Rather than being a logical analysis of some existing geometry, his philosophically minded attempt aims at a quest into the nature of space. To a certain degree Helmholtz was Kantian, but the a priori in space he would grant was no more than a vague topological substratum that is organized a posteriori by the knowledge of some experimental fact. This fact, he pointed out, was the existence of freely movable rigid bodies. Helmholtz' view of space

Indeed, all traditional approaches to space up to that time bore this feature, though Helmholtz was the first to recognize and analyze it mathematically. His analysis is not free from tacit assumptions and arbitrary statements. It is as rigorous as it could have been at that time, though his style, compared with today's, is vague and often admits of alternative interpretations.

Actually, to Helmholtz the whole of space was a rigid body. In modern terminology this means that it is a metric space, a space in which distance is numerically defined for pairs of points, and that the distance-preserving mappings of space on itself are considered as what should be called motions. These motions form a group. Though Helmholtz did not mention (presumably did not know) the notion of group, he extensively used group-theory notions and methods, anticipating Klein and Lie.

The free mobility of rigid bodies, or rather of space itself, according to Helmholtz, means: Any point is carried into any other by some motion. If, however, one point P_0 is fixed, then two points at the same distance from P_0 can still be carried into each other by some motion. If two points P_0 and P_1 are fixed, then the same is true of any pair of points at the same distance from both P_0 and P_1. Finally, if three points in a general situation are fixed, no continuous motion is possible. (The last assumption, which means confined rather than free mobility, probably aimed at a restriction of the dimension of space; it is redundant, because this restriction was urged before by topology.)

For *n*-dimensional space, free mobility, according to Helmholtz, goes as far as fixing $n - 1$ points, whereas immobility is reached after an *n*th point has been fixed. Helmholtz claimed that the only spaces with this property are essentially the classical Euclidean and non-Euclidean spaces, but in 1890 Lie showed that Helmholtz' methods were mathematically unsatisfactory. He improved Helmholtz' proofs, but did not remove differentiability assumptions, which are unnatural to modern taste, and represent a major obstacle. The final formulation and solution of Helmholtz' problem was not found until 1953. It is the solution of the German mathematician Jacques Tits, which after a few topological assumptions only asserts: If some triple of points can by motion be carried into any other triple with the same distances from each other, then space is Euclidean or non-Euclidean or spherical *n*-space.

Differential geometry. The classical concept of space interpreted as if it were a freely movable rigid body had been renounced by Riemann in 1854 (published in 1867) even before it was disclosed by Helmholtz. Riemann, espousing the philosophy of the German Johann Friedrich Herbart rather than Kant, did not accept a general fact such as that of rigid bodies to organize the topological substratum into space. Instead he displayed a hypothesis, the metric structure of space, not subjected to Helmholtz' restrictions, but as general as could be imagined in that time. The metric was supposed to be Euclidean up to the first approximation, with higher-order deviations from Euclidicity, which might vary from point to point. Riemann's view of space

This idea had been Gauss's earlier when he studied the differential geometry of curved surfaces. Riemann ventured to extend it to space. In order to make things clear, here it will be provisionally restricted to the two-dimensional case. Any curved surface is flat in first approximation, that is, if replaced by its tangent plane in the neighbourhood of any one of its points. In the next approximation it shows deviations from flatness, slight deviations if curvature is small and more significant deviations if curvature is stronger. To discover curvature, however, the outside view is not compulsory. A two-dimensional being (a hypothetical thinking being confined to two dimensions) confined to the surface can discover its curvature and determine it numerically while performing measurements upon the surface. Interpreting the shortest curves between any pair of points as straight, and surveying triangles, a two-dimensional being will state deviations from the Euclidean structure, such as excessive or defective totals of angles, and defective or excessive hypotenuses (as compared with those calculated according to the Pythagorean theorem). He will explain these deviations, which might vary from point to point, as caused by a positive or negative curvature of the surface he is on, and he will be able to calculate the curvature numerically.

The same train of thought applies in three dimensions. As three-dimensional beings inhabiting a three-dimensional universe, men can get information on its curvature by surveying their neighbourhood in the universe, as has been done by 20th-century astronomers. With regard to the terrestrial surface men are happier than two-dimensional beings living on it. They can learn about its curvature also from outside; they can see ships vanish behind the horizon's edge. But they cannot put their heads out of the universe to see its curvature. Men are committed to measurements within the universe. This inside view of space, though the quintessence of Riemann's theory, was barely considered in the confused discussions of the 19th century, but in the theory of relativity it has been justified in the most splendid way. The disregard paid to Riemann's theory in the 19th century resulted partly from Helmholtz' erroneous criticism. Helmholtz argued that surveying a Riemannian space requires freely movable rigid bodies as measuring tools. If this were true, Riemann would have derived no more than Helmholtz' theory yields in a more satisfactory way. Riemann's procedure, however, requires freely movable rigid rods only; as it were, one-dimensional rigid bodies. Unless two-dimensional disks are admitted as tools, Riemann's spaces are much more general than Helmholtz'.

In the 20th century Riemann's theory was supplemented by the notion of parallel transport of vectors in a curved space. The notion of parallel transport was developed by the Italian mathematician Tullio Levi-Civita in 1917 and Jan G. Schouten in 1918. What this means will again be explained here on a surface, particularly on the terrestrial surface.

Foucault's pendulum experiment A freely suspended pendulum changes its oscillation plane after a while. This is the famous experiment of the French physicist Jean-Bernard-Léon Foucault performed in 1851 that verifies the rotation of the earth. Actually the pendulum tends to preserve its oscillation plane in space. Thus, if the earth did not turn, no such change would occur. To explain this phenomenon, replace the Foucault pendulum by a point oscillating in a tangential plane of the earth. As long as this plane rests, the velocity vector of the oscillation does not change. As soon as the plane is turned around, this vector is forced to change. What happens is that it loses its component orthogonal on the plane. In the same way a being living on a curved surface is transporting his vectors over the surface by having them lose their components orthogonally on the surface. This vector transport is an inner feature of the surface, independent of its embedding, and so it can be defined in curved space too.

In the Foucault case, if a vector is moved around with the moving sphere along a parallel circle of the underlying fixed sphere, what happens can be shown quantitatively by constructing the tangential cone of the sphere along the parallel circle and spreading it upon a plane (along the two straight lines the cone was cut up; in space they are to be identified). Parallel transport along the parallel circle brings the vector back to the beginning point, but then it has undergone a turn equal to the angle of the spread cone.

This is a general feature of parallel vector transport in curved spaces. A vector moved along a closed path may appear to have changed, and the numerical value of this change depends on the value of curvature of the space.

Topology. Topology is the youngest branch of geometry but, nevertheless, its most sophisticated. In spite of important but isolated earlier results, its continuous development did not start until about 1911, when the Dutch mathematician L.E.J. Brouwer contributed general methods to topology. Since then it has developed vigorously, closely connected to modern algebra. A few very elementary examples can be used to show what topology means.

Rigidity is the main characteristic of the shapes of elementary geometry. All that Euclid could tell about straight lines, circles, spheres, cones, conics, and so on is lost under the slightest deformation of such figures. More arbitrary curves and surfaces are studied in differential geometry. If a curve is smooth enough, its curvature at any point is an important notion to differential geometry. The completely arbitrary curve, however, is an object of topology and is studied with respect to its most basic intuitive properties. In topology the circumference of a circle is not distinguished from that of an ellipse, of a square, or of the leaf of a plant. All of them, however, are topologically different from the curve suggested by the symbol 8. The capital letters D and O are topologically equivalent (closed simple curves); $C, I, J, L, M, N, S, U, V, W$, and Z are topologically in the same class (simple arcs); E, F, and T do not differ essentially from each other, and among the remaining capital letters there are a few other types.

The simple arc does not cut the plane. A simple closed curve cuts the plane into exactly two parts. These theorems, though intuitively evident, require sophisticated methods for their proof, first achieved by the French mathematician Camille Jordan in 1887.

Spheres and potatoes are topologically equivalent. But they are different from a tire, or ring, called a torus in topology. Indeed, a spherelike surface is cut into two pieces by any simple closed curve on it. On a ringlike surface, however, simple closed curves that do not cut the surface can be drawn easily. The surface of a ladder is still more involved, becoming more involved with each additional rung. This kind of surface also cuts space, as was first proved by Brouwer in 1912.

A key theorem of Brouwer's runs in intuitive terms as follows: If a wooden sphere is clothed in thin rubber, then it is impossible to uncover any point of the wooden sphere by deforming the rubber sphere, even if folding is allowed. (Tearing the rubber is forbidden; deformations should preserve the connection of the parts.)

Two closed curves in space can be located free from each other, or they can be interlaced as the links of a chain. These are topological differences. A simple closed curve can be knotted or not. It is difficult to prove that the clover knot is topologically different from its mirror image. There are infinitely many topologically different knots, but to know whether two of them are equivalent or not is difficult.

The classifying tool of topology is so-called topological mapping, which, by definition, is univalent and continuous in both directions. Topology studies those properties that are preserved under these mappings.   (Ed.)

ALGEBRA

Algebra is the expression of relationships between numbers by use of general symbols. For instance, the fact that $4 \times (2 + 1) = 8 + 4$ is an example of a general law that any numbers, denoted by x, y, and z, are related by $x \times (y + z) = x \times y + x \times z$. [This is usually written $x(y + z) = xy + xz$.] Here are x, y, and z are called variables; they are used to represent any three numbers.

In arithmetic the law could not be stated; its consequence could be demonstrated by a number of specific examples like that above. The law can also be stated in words: the product of a number and the sum of two other numbers is the sum of the products of the number with each of the other two numbers. The algebraic formulation is clearly more compact and allows the easy manipulation of such equations to give other relationships. Algebra can be defined as a generalization of arithmetic.

Babylonian, Egyptian, and Greek contributions. Algebra separated from arithmetic early in the development of mathematics, probably in Babylonia when equations and methods for reducing them were introduced. A considerable number of cuneiform mathematical tables from the period of the Hammurabi dynasty (1800–1600 BC) deal with problems now classified as algebra. The calculations of the examples from this period are presented in a way that makes clear that the general methods, and not the numerical results, are the main goal. A mastery of quadratic equations is evident; often they were presented in the standard form $x + x^{-1} = a$, which could be solved by means of tables or by reduction to a square root extraction as at present. Another normal form for quadratic problems in two unknowns was $x \pm y = a, x \cdot y = b$. More complicated problems were reduced to these. Closely related to these questions are studies of the integral solutions of Pythagorean triangles, that is, determination of integers satisfying $x^2 + y^2 = z^2$. There occur instances of fourth-degree equations (involving a variable raised to the fourth power) reducible to quadratic equations and also special cases of cubic equations, presumably solved by tables. Summation of arithmetical progressions and of the sums of squares of integers also was known.

Early use of quadratic equations

The Egyptian knowledge of algebra seems to have been much more limited than that of Babylonia and may have developed under Babylonian influence. The problems as are known from the Rhind mathematical papyrus are in the main limited to linear equations. A first approach to formal algebra is the use of a standard symbol h (aha, hau), meaning quantity, to denote the unknown to be determined.

The cultures of Asia Minor and Babylonia influenced Greece strongly, and the Greeks undoubtedly received much of their basic knowledge of algebra from these sources. Within Greek mathematics, however, algebra took on a geometric aspect, primarily, it is believed, because of the logical difficulties created by irrational numbers. In the geometric language, for instance, of Euclid's *Elements* (c. 300 BC) the quantities were represented by lengths of lines, products of two quantities by the area of rectangles, and products of three factors by volumes of rectangular solids. In this manner all problems appear in the form of homogeneous relations between quantities of the same dimension. Thus the quadratic equation can be written $b^2 = x(x \pm a)$, and the solution consists in finding a rectangle with sides x and $x \pm a$ the area of which is equal to that of a given square b^2. The actual construction can be made by right triangles or mean proportionals. In line with this geometric view of algebra is the development of the theory of conic sections, which reached its zenith in the *Conica* by Apollonius of Perga in 220 BC. The solution of such problems as the duplication of the cube and the trisection of the angle also were given in terms of the intersection of special curves.

The later Alexandrian period of Greek mathematics seems to have been closer to Babylonian sources. From the point of view of algebra the most noteworthy work is the *Arithmetica* of Diophantus of about AD 200. His problems are mostly of the so-called Diophantine type, the solutions of which are positive fractions or integers; usually the equations are linear or quadratic in several unknowns, but these are systematically reduced to a single unknown. Remarkable are the beginnings of algebraic notation or shorthand. The unknown is denoted by s (perhaps from the final letter in the Greek *arithmos*, "number") with special terms for the first powers. Terms to be added are simply written together; a special sign is used for minus.

Contributions from the Orient, India, and the Islāmic world. Concerning the development of algebra in the Orient: in India, China, and Japan there is still a good deal of dispute, some of it having a nationalistic flavour. The beginnings of algebra in these countries seem to have been influenced by the Babylonian and Greek schools. Among Hindu algebraists, Brahmagupta, whose work on indeterminate equations in about 630 in many ways goes beyond Diophantus, deserves special notice. Somewhat later, about AD 1150, are the outstanding works of Bhāskara, the *Līlāvatī* ("Arithmetic") and the *Vīja-gānita* ("Algebra"). These works give rules for dealing with negative qualities: a dot over a number was used to indicate minus. It was realized that positive numbers have two square roots, and Bhāskara also mentions that there are no roots of negative numbers. Unknowns were denoted by the names of various colours. Powers and roots were indicated by the initial letters or first syllables in the corresponding words, giving a close approach to algebraic symbolism.

The notion of negative numbers in India

With the ascendancy of Mohammedanism the Islāmic world became the centre for mathematical studies. A number of Islāmic mathematicians wrote commentaries upon Greek works in the geometric tradition, but there also were notable original algebraic contributions. The cubic equation was a favourite topic for such writers as al-Mahani and Tabit ibn Korra in the middle of the 9th century, Alhazen a hundred and fifty years later, and particularly the poet and mathematician 'Omar Khayyam in the beginning of the 12th century, who dealt with it extensively in his algebra; the solutions were obtained by intersections of conics.

The most influential algebraic work from this period was the *Kitāb al-jabr wa al-muqābalah* ("The Science of Restoration and Reduction") of al-Khwārizmī composed in Baghdad about 825. The influence of the book on Europe was so great that its name became synonymous with equation theory. The unknown was called *shai*, "the thing"; otherwise al-Khwārizmī shows little tendency to algebraic symbolism.

Islāmic algebra was introduced to Europe, especially to Italy, in the 13th and 14th centuries. Most important in this process was Leonardo of Pisa's *Liber abaci* ("Book of the Abacus") of 1202 from which later Italian algebra books borrowed freely. Under the influence of Islāmic usage the unknown was called *res* in Latin, *cosa* ("the thing") in Italian, while algebra itself became known as *l'arte della cosa*, cossic art or the rule of coss. Occasionally algebra was termed the *ars magna*, "the great art" in contradistinction to the lesser art of arithmetic.

Medieval and modern European developments. Italian algebraists, for instance Lucas Pacioli in 1494, had expressed the belief that the general cubic equation could not be solved algebraically by means of radical expressions. Thus it was a remarkable achievement when around 1515 Scipione del Ferro, professor at the University of Bologna, succeeded in solving the cubic equation in the special form $x^3 + ax = b$. Del Ferro did not reveal his formula, but after his death it passed to his pupils. In a mathematical tournament with one of them, Niccolò Tartaglia from Brescia rediscovered the method and confided it to Gerolamo Cardano, a physician in Milan, under promise of secrecy. In 1545 Cardano published his *Artis magnae* ("The Great Art"), the most important algebraic work of the Renaissance. It contained the solution of the cubic equation, still erroneously called Cardano's formula, and also the method for solving fourth-degree equations discovered by Cardano's former servant and protégé, Lodovico Ferrari. The *Artis magnae* contained novel ideas concerning the relations between roots and the coefficients of equations; Cardano even calculated formally with imaginary numbers. Publication of this work had a considerable influence on the rapid growth of algebra in Europe.

The work of Gerolamo Cardano

The presentation in the *Artis magnae* is partly geometric in the Greek tradition and partly verbal, with scant use of symbols. For problems as complicated as these, such a form became very cumbersome, and evidently a stage had been reached at which effective simplification was required. Some standard notations had already become common in arithmetic; for instance, p̄ and m̄ were used for plus and minus. The latter symbol was reduced to the bar to denote minus; the plus sign $+$ is a condensed form for the Latin *et* ("and"). The $\times$ sign for multiplication appeared in England around 1600; the radical sign $\sqrt{\ }$ may originally have been the letter *r* as an abbreviation for radix.

Cardano's compatriot Raphael Bombelli about 1560 had made some attempts at simplified writing of algebraic formulas, but the credit for a first systematic effort to introduce an algebraic sign language must go to François Viète. In his *Isagoge in artem analyticam* ("Introduction to the Analytical Art") of 1591 the quantities are denoted by letters, often vowels for the unknowns and consonants for given numbers. The powers of a number *A* were written *Aq* (*quadraticus*), *Ac* (*cubus*), *Aqq* (*biquadraticus*), and so on. The present usage of denoting unknowns by the last letters (*x, y, z*) of the alphabet and known quantities by the first letters (*a, b, c*) is attributed to Descartes; he was the first to write powers with exponents in the modern form, although this notation had been used sporadically by earlier writers. John Wallis and Isaac Newton introduced fractional exponents for roots in the second half of the 17th century. The equality sign is attributed to Robert Recorde in 1557. From the middle of the 17th century the algebraic notations were close to the modern ones. Once initiated, the advantage of symbolic writing was obvious, and the development of an effective and logical mathematical sign language has since been a continuous process.

The rapid use of algebraic technique in the 16th and 17th centuries rendered obsolete some of the medieval algebraic methods, particularly the popular rule of false position inherited from Islām. This rule was used to solve linear problems by trying out one or two particular values and adjusting them to satisfy the given conditions. As Recorde states in his *Ground of Artes* of 1542:

> Suche falsehode is so good a grounde
> that truth by it will soone be founde.

Use of determinants

The idea of solving systems of linear equations by determinants seems to have been originated by Leibniz, although Chinese and Japanese sources contain some indications of similar methods. The first systematic treatments of determinant theory were given by the French mathematicians Alexandre-Théophile Vandermonde in 1771 and Pierre-Simon Laplace in 1772, but they were not commonly used until further phases of the theory had been developed in 1812 by the French mathematician Augustin-Louis Cauchy and Karl Jacobi of Germany. A standard tool of algebra, the binomial theorem, is ancient and was quite well known by the middle of the 16th century. The more general multinomial theorem is usually ascribed to Leibniz. Interest in equation theory stimulated study of symmetric functions of roots. Fundamental facts about them were developed particularly by Newton, Wallis, Edward Waring, and other members of the English school of mathematicians studying combinatorial analysis.

The introduction of such new fields of mathematics as analytic geometry by Descartes and the calculus by Newton and Leibniz also contributed greatly to the development of algebra. The Greek idea of a geometric algebra was now reversed into an algebraic geometry. The study of algebraic curves advanced the field of algebra itself by introducing methods of reduction and elimination for general algebraic equations in several unknowns, together with various concomitant concepts such as resultants and discriminants as developed in 1764 by Étienne Bézout, a French textbook writer and mathematician.

The properties of algebraic equations indicated the desirability of recognizing complex numbers as roots on a par with real roots. Only then would the fundamental theorem of algebra be valid. The theorem states that an equation of *n*th degree always has *n* roots. This was realized as early as Cardano for third- and fourth-degree equations. It was expressed by the French mathematician

Albert Girard in 1629 and by Descartes. A fully rigorous proof was given first by Gauss in 1799 in his doctoral thesis. The representation of complex numbers graphically by coordinates in the plane is also sometimes ascribed to him, but the credit for this idea first expressed in 1795 must be awarded to the Norwegian-born Danish surveyor and mathematician Caspar Wessel.

Methods for numerical resolution of equations, in particular for extracting square and higher roots, were devised by all the ancient schools of mathematics. Leonardo of Pisa gives a numerical solution of a cubic equation with the root accurate to more than six sexagesimal places. The calculus facilitated the development of a large number of such methods; among them are those proposed by Viète in 1600, Newton, and William George Horner, an English mathematician whose method published in 1819 is still in use (see below *Computation of roots*). Various criteria were devised to determine the general locations of the roots, for instance, the number of positive roots or roots in an interval. Theorems of this kind were proved by Newton, Fourier, Jacobi, and others; most complete is a criterion by the French mathematician Charles-François Sturm that was published in 1835.

The Renaissance discovery of methods for the solution of equations of third and fourth degree left open the puzzling question of whether similar radical expressions could be found for roots of fifth- and higher-degree equations. This was a central problem in algebra in the 17th and 18th centuries, and many excellent mathematicians, notably Joseph-Louis Lagrange, expended much effort on it. A feeling that the problem was insoluble became widespread. A first proof was published by Paolo Ruffini in 1803 and 1805, but the proof by Niels Henrik Abel in 1824, 1826, is generally regarded as the first rigorous one for what has come to be known as the Abel-Ruffini theorem (see below *Evolution of the theory of algebraic equations of one variable*), which states: the general algebraic equation of degree higher than four cannot be solved by radical expressions. Abel attacked the general problem when an algebraic equation of higher degree can be solved by radicals.

Évariste Galois in 1831, independently of Abel, based his remarkable theory of equations upon the new and fundamental concept of group theory (see below *The Galois theory*). Although the importance of Galois's work was not realized until long after his death, group theory now permeates all fields of mathematics and has become one of the most important branches of algebra.

The 19th century saw a great surge in algebraic research and the creation of several new branches of algebra. Introduced were such topics as invariant theory, originally inspired by the desire to determine those algebraic quantities of a curve that are independent of the choice of the coordinate systems; the theory of algebraic functions; the theory of algebraic numbers created by the German mathematicians Ernst Kummer and Richard Dedekind, including the theory of ideals, one of the most fertile concepts of modern algebra; further extensions of the number concepts, first through the quaternions of William Hamilton and later through general hypercomplex numbers, which in turn are closely related to the theory of matrices, which is an all-pervading part of recent mathematics.

The algebraists of the 20th century have continued the work in these and many other domains. With increased knowledge in so many branches of algebra has come the realization that the various theories are related through certain general principles underlying them all, which has led to the development of a so-called abstract algebra with two chief aims: (1) A deduction problem consisting of the derivation of the properties of a system with given axioms. These axioms are of algebraic nature, and the operations on the elements correspond in some way to addition, subtraction, multiplication, and division. (2) A completeness problem consisting of the construction and classification of all systems that can exist for a given family of axioms. A typical example of an analysis of the latter kind is a work by Ernst Steinitz published in 1910 deriving all types of fields; that is, an algebraic system in

Abstract algebra

which all the ordinary axioms for the four basic operations are satisfied. The theory of rings has become equally fundamental, uniting the principles of many domains of algebra; this theory deals mainly with operations corresponding to the first three fundamental ones. Finally, intense efforts have been made in the study of groups and grouplike systems with only one operation, sometimes called an addition but more often a multiplication.

(O.Or.)

Evolution of the theory of algebraic equations of one variable. The theory of equations is concerned with determining the solvability of algebraic equations and with the development of techniques for the solution of equations that are theoretically solvable.

An equality that holds for all values of the unknowns is an identity. Thus $3x + 2 = 5$, true only for $x = 1$, is an equation; $x^2 - y^2 = (x + y)(x - y)$, holding for all values of x and y, is an identity. To distinguish identities from equations the symbol $\equiv$ is sometimes used, as in $x^2 - y^2 \equiv (x + y)(x - y)$.

The theory of equations is concerned chiefly with the properties of a single algebraic equation of the type (see Box, equation 1) in which c_0 does not have the value zero, n is a positive whole number called the degree of the equation, and the $c_0, c_1, \cdots, c_n$'s are either given numbers or numbers that are not specified but are assumed known, called the coefficients of the equation. Roughly speaking, the theory of equations discusses this

$$(1) \qquad c_0 x^n + c_1 x^{n-1} + \cdots + c_n = 0, \qquad (c_0 \neq 0)$$

problem: the coefficients being specified, find all values of x that make the equation true. Such values are called roots of the equation, and finding them is called solving the equation. More generally, there are often sets of simultaneous equations in several variables $x, y, z, \cdots$ to be solved, but the solution of these may be reduced (by eliminating variables) to solving a number of equations of the above type.

The earliest known equivalents of algebraic equations occur in the Rhind papyrus, evidently compiled from earlier works by the Egyptian Ahmes sometime before 1700 BC. For example, he proposes this problem: "A quantity and its seventh added together become 19. What is the quantity?" The problem, therefore, is to solve the equation $x + x/7 = 19$, as mathematicians would now express it. Lacking a convenient algebraic notation, he proceeded by a cumbersome method later known as that of false position.

Although the Greeks are sometimes credited with solving equations of the second degree, in general neither the Egyptians nor the Greeks made any progress that is significant from a modern point of view, and neither people rose to the abstract conception of a theory of equations as a fruitful field of mathematical science. Indian and Islāmic mathematicians achieved more, but it was not until the Renaissance, when the Italian mathematicians of the 15th and 16th centuries succeeded in solving by radicals general equations of the third and fourth degree, that any work of lasting interest was done. Similar attempts to solve equations of higher degree led nowhere, however; deeper insight into the nature of the roots of an algebraic equation was required, and this did not come until the work of Lagrange in 1770–71 and, more decisively, that of two young mathematicians half a century later, Abel and Galois.

Niels Henrik Abel at the age of 22 almost proved that equations of degree greater than 4 could not be solved by radicals. His attempt contained two oversights, however, and the definitive proof of this important fact must be credited to Évariste Galois. Killed in a duel at the age of 20, Galois spent the night before his death outlining a comprehensive theory of the roots of equations in a hastily scrawled letter to a friend. This theory, which now goes by the name of Galois theory, is a prime source of information about algebraic equations and has served as

an inspiration to much modern work in algebra and number theory.

In general, the theory of equations dates from the early part of the 19th century. The approximate solution methods developed then have remained largely unchanged, and although modern algebra has enormously simplified the theory of Galois, the basic ideas are the same.

Statement of the problem. The theory of algebraic equations discusses what is essentially a two-fold problem. In addition to ordinary real numbers, there are also complex numbers, those of the form $a + bi$, in which a and b are real and $i = \sqrt{-1}$; the real numbers are, then, those complex numbers for which $b = 0$. The algebraic equation given above can be written as $f(x) = 0$, and its coefficients can be taken to be either real or complex numbers; if all the coefficients are real, the equation is called real. This is the important case, since otherwise, multiplying $f(x)$ by $\bar{f}(x)$, in which the coefficients have been changed into their complex conjugates $(a - bi)$, gives a new equation $F(x) = 0$, which is real, of twice the degree and such that all the roots of the original equation are also roots of this new equation. The term root in this case means a complex number α such that $f(\alpha) = 0$. Even if the equation is real, it may well have complex roots.

The central problems of the theory are these:

A. The coefficients being given as definite numbers, find the roots of the equation—exactly, if possible; if not, determine how to calculate them to as many decimal places as desired.

B. Find general formulas that express the roots in terms of the coefficients. If possible the formulas should require only the operations of addition, multiplication, subtraction, division, and extractions of roots, this being called a solution by radicals. If such formulas are not possible, find the simplest functions of the coefficients that do satisfy the equation.

After the above-mentioned work of Abel and Galois, the French mathematician Charles Hermite in 1858 succeeded in solving the general equation of degree 5 by means of elliptic functions (see ANALYSIS, COMPLEX). Modern work in this direction, originating with Henri Poincaré about 1880, solves the general equation of degree n in terms of what are called Fuchsian functions. For a time, problem (A) was considered exhausted, but new methods have been developed that are especially suited to computers. Problem (B) now involves group theory and algebraic number theory, as well as special functions of a complex variable.

The fundamental theorem of algebra. A basic result applicable to both of the central problems of the theory of equations is the so-called fundamental theorem of algebra, which states that every algebraic equation has a root. It is proved either from this, or from an application of a formula of Augustin-Louis Cauchy, that an equation of degree n has precisely n roots. The remarkable feature of this theorem is that it always allows any algebraic equation to be solved without going beyond the domain of complex numbers. Although the theorem is thus so useful that the seasoned mathematician sees in it a species of fortunate miracle, the sophisticated critic views it with suspicion. The first allegedly satisfactory proof was given in 1799 by Gauss, who subsequently added three more proofs.

The first useful consequence of the theorem is the following. If $x_1, x_2, \cdots, x_n$ are the n roots of $f(x) = 0$, then f can be factored into a product of n terms, each involving a distinct root (see 2, 3). Conversely, if $f(k) = 0$, then $x - k$ is a factor of $f(x)$. More generally, if t is any complex number, $f(t)$ is equal to the remainder obtained on dividing $f(x)$ by $x - t$, and hence $f(t)$ can be calculated by division, a result of importance in the numerical solution of equations. This is called the remainder theorem.

Since $c_0, c_1, \cdots, c_n$ are any complex numbers independent of x, and $c_0 \neq 0$, the equation $f(x) = 0$ may be divided throughout by c_0. It then becomes $x^n + a_1 x^{n-1} + \cdots + a_n = 0$, in which $a_1, \cdots, a_n$ are complex numbers. This form is precisely as general as the original and

$$(2) \qquad f(x) \equiv c_0 x^n + c_1 x^{n-1} + \cdots + c_n$$

$$(3) \qquad f(x) = c_0(x - x_1)(x - x_2) \cdots (x - x_n)$$

$$(4) \qquad x^n + a_1 x^{n-1} + \cdots + a_n$$

$$(5) \qquad (x - \alpha_1)(x - \alpha_2) \cdots (x - \alpha_n)$$

is convenient to use. If the roots are $\alpha_1, \alpha_2, \cdots, \alpha_n$, the linear (first degree in x) factors of the polynomial (see 4) involve a distinct root α_k (where k is some number 1 and n) in each factor (see 5). Hence, on comparing coefficients of like powers of x, it is seen that $a_1 = (-1)$ times the sum of the roots and $\alpha_n = (-1)^n$ times the product of all the roots. This result frequently is useful in testing for rational roots an equation whose coefficients are rational numbers; by this means all the rational roots may be found.

Approximate location of roots. The problem of finding the roots of an equation, in particular calculation of the roots by an approximative method, can be confined to a discussion of the real roots of real equations; this is the significant case, because the determination of the complex roots may be reduced to locating the real roots of an auxiliary real equation. In fact, attention may even be confined to locating just the positive real roots, because the negative real roots of $f(x) = 0$ are the positive roots of $f(-x) = 0$, which is obtained from $f(x) = 0$ by changing the signs of all the terms of odd degree.

The problem divides naturally into two steps. First comes the approximate location of the real roots, which includes both determining their total number and isolating them. (A real root is said to be isolated if two real numbers α and β are known such that the equation has exactly one real root between α and β.) Once the root is known approximately, a method of calculating it to any desired degree of accuracy must be determined.

If it is assumed that $f(x)$ is real, then the most straightforward way to locate the roots approximately is to graph the equation $y = f(x)$ and to locate the points α_i where the graph crosses the x-axis. At these points $f(\alpha_i) = 0$. The problem is that because only part of the graph can be drawn, one has to decide in advance in what interval of the axis the roots will appear, and this may not be easy. Once a root is located approximately, by enlarging the scale and redrawing the graph, it can be located with any desired degree of accuracy.

A fundamental principle used in isolating the roots is this: if $f(a)$ and $f(b)$ have opposite signs, then $f(x)$ will have a root between a and b; that is, on the interval $[a, b]$ of the axis. Geometrically, if the graph of $f(x)$ is below the axis at $x = a$ and above it at $x = b$, then the graph must cross the axis somewhere in between. Mathematically, this is a consequence of the fact that the polynomial $f(x)$ is a continuous function and therefore has a graph that is unbroken.

A difficulty is that $f(x)$ may have not just one root on $[a, b]$ but three, five, or some other odd number. (A repeated root is to be counted with its multiplicity, as explained earlier.) To be sure there is only one root, it is useful to determine that the first derivative $f'(x)$ does not change sign on $[a, b]$. Geometrically, this guarantees that the graph will always be rising or falling on the interval, so that it can cross the x-axis only once within the interval.

Sturm functions More powerful tools, however, must usually be applied. Conclusive isolation of the roots is given by a method discovered in 1829 by the French mathematician Charles-François Sturm. For an equation of degree n, n auxiliary polynomials called the Sturm functions must be computed (a rather laborious task); the number of real roots (counted with multiplicities) of $f(x) = 0$ between α and β is then ascertained by inspection from the signs of the Sturm functions evaluated at α and β. Budan's theorem, named after the French physician Ferdinand-François-Désiré Budan de Boislaurent, who published it

in 1807, derives a different set of auxiliary polynomials, which are used in the same way; although they are easier to compute, they give less precise information.

Computation of roots. When a real root of a real equation $f(x) = 0$ has been isolated by any of the methods suggested, it may be calculated, digit by digit, by any one of several arithmetical processes, the most common of which are those named after William George Horner (1819), although they were known to the Chinese mathematicians of the 13th century, and Newton's method of about 1675.

Newton's method has the great advantage of being applicable to equations other than algebraic. It can be explained by using his own example, $x^3 - 2x - 5 = 0$, which has only one root between 2 and 3. To find this root, replace x by $2 + h$, in which h is necessarily between 0 and 1. The terms in h^2 and h^3 being negligible in comparison with h, in the new equation (see 6) $h = 0.1$ is clearly a first approximation to h, and hence the root is roughly 2.1. Replace h by $0.1 + k$ in the h-equation, and obtain the next approximation (see 7). Omit the k^3 and k^2 terms, which are small in comparison with k; then k is approximately -0.0054. From $h = 0.1 + k$ the result $h = 0.0946$ is obtained, giving 2.0946 as an approximate value of the required root. By repeating this process a sufficient number of times, any desired degree of accuracy is attainable.

Horner's method In Horner's method a set of equations, one for each digit of the required root, is obtained successively from the given equation. The process is a refinement of the crude graphical method, and amounts to successive shifts of the origin and magnifications of the scale. The method for positive real roots involves the successive diminution of the roots of the given equation by the smaller member in successive pairs of positive approximations; that is, a gradual approach to the root from behind. For example: a real root of $f(x) = 0$ has been isolated between 200 and 300. If an equation $f_1(x) = 0$ whose roots are those of $f(x) = 0$ each diminished by 200 is constructed, then $f_1(x) = 0$ will have one and only one root between 0 and 100. By one of the proposed methods this root is located between 60 and 70. Then $f(x) = 0$ has a root between 260 and 270. Construct an equation $f_2(x) = 0$, whose roots are those of $f_1(x) = 0$ diminished by 60, and repeat the argument. It follows that $f_2(x) = 0$ has a root between 0 and 10, which may be located as before; say it is between 5 and 6. Thus 5 is the third digit of the required root of $f(x) = 0$. Next, construct $f_3(x) = 0$, whose roots are those of $f_2(x) = 0$ diminished by 5; $f_3(x) = 0$ then has a root between 0 and 1, say 0.2. The required root so far is 265.2, and the process can be continued to any prescribed number of digits. (E.T.B./A.P.Ma.)

Formulas for solving equations of low degree. On the problem of the solution of equations by means of exact formulas for the roots in terms of the coefficients: The three equations of low degree for which such formulas exist are the quadratic (of degree 2), cubic (degree 3), and biquadratic (degree 4). Thus, the quadratic equation (see 8) has paired solutions (see 9), and so a single square-root extraction is needed to solve it. In a sense this formula, the famous quadratic formula, is only an approximate solution, since the square root can be only approximately calculated; the significant thing, however, is that the formula is universal: one formula takes care of all possible choices for the coefficients.

$$(6) \qquad h^3 + 6h^2 + 10h - 1 = 0$$

$$(7) \qquad k^3 + 6.3k^2 + 11.23k + 0.061 = 0$$

$$(8) \qquad ax^2 + bx + c = 0$$

$$(9) \qquad x = \frac{-b \pm \sqrt{b^2 - 4ac}}{2a}$$

Similar formulas for the roots of the cubic equation were first published in the *Artis magnae* in 1545 by Cardano, who obtained them from Tartaglia by questionable means; they are rather complicated, and Horner's method is in general preferable. In particular, if all three roots are real, the formulas give them in terms of complex numbers, a fact which makes the formulas quite impracticable; alternative formulas give the roots as trigonometric functions of the coefficients. Even more impracticable is the general solution to the quartic equation, found by Lodovici Ferrari at about the same time.

The Galois theory. The general theory of the roots of equations can now be discussed. The Galois theory proves the impossibility of such general formulas as the above whenever the equation is of degree greater than four.

A rational number (or common fraction) is a real number which is the quotient of two integers, so that, in particular, the sum, product, difference, and quotient of rational numbers are also rational numbers. If it be assumed that the equation $f(x) = 0$ has rational numbers for coefficients, that $f(x)$ cannot be factored as a product of polynomials of lower degree with rational coefficients, and further that $x_1, x_2, \cdots, x_n$ are the roots of this equation, then these roots are complex (or perhaps real) numbers, and all different, since $f(x)$ cannot be factored. The crucial notion is that of an admissible permutation (or substitution) of these roots. A permutation $(x_1, \cdots, x_n) \rightarrow (x_{i_1}, \cdots, x_{i_n})$ of the roots—*i.e.*, a scrambling of them—is said to be admissible if every algebraic relation holding among the roots continues to be valid after the permutation is made. Only those relations expressible in terms of sums of products of the roots, with rational numbers as coefficients, are considered here; for example, in the equation $x^4 - 2 = 0$. If x_1 is the real positive fourth root of 2, the other roots are $x_2 = ix_1$, $x_3 = -x_1$ and $x_4 = -ix_1$. The permutation $(x_1, x_2, x_3, x_4) \rightarrow (x_2, x_1, x_3, x_4)$ is not admissible, because the valid algebraic relation $x_1x_3 + x_2x_4 = 0$ goes by the permutation into $x_2x_3 + x_1x_4 = 0$, which is false. But the permutation $(x_1, x_2, x_3, x_4) \rightarrow (x_2, x_1, x_4, x_3)$ is admissible. That it does preserve the validity of the given relation is easily checked, though this check in itself would not be sufficient to prove the permutation admissible. In this case, of the 24 possible permutations, exactly 8 are admissible. If permutations are multiplied in the usual way by performing one after the other, the admissible permutations form a group.

The Galois group The set of admissible permutations is called the Galois group of the equation. Since there are n roots, the total number of all permutations is $n!$; thus the Galois group can be no larger than $n!$ and it may in fact be much smaller. Here $n!$ denotes the product $n(n-1)(n-2) \cdots 2 \cdot 1$. If it is of this maximal size, however (*i.e.*, if every permutation is admissible), then the equation is said to have the symmetric group. Loosely speaking, if an equation is written down at random, the chances are that it will have the symmetric group; the ones with smaller Galois groups are rare.

This group measures what might be called the algebraic symmetries that the roots possess, much as the group of the six possible rigid motions carrying an equilateral triangle onto itself (three rotations and three reflections) measures its sixfold geometric symmetries.

In general a finite group G is called solvable if it has subgroups $G = G_1, G_2, \cdots, G_r = \{1\}$ such that each G_{i+1} is a normal subgroup of G_i and such that G_i has p_i times as many elements as G_{i+1}, when p_i is a prime number. Such groups are very special kinds of groups. The heart of Galois's theory is the theorem that an algebraic equation is solvable by radicals if and only if its Galois group is a solvable group.

Roughly speaking, the p_i entering above into the structure of G corresponds to the solution of the equation by extraction of p_1th, p_2th, $\cdots$, p_rth roots; the possibility of solving the equation by simple root extractions is the reflection of the possibility of elucidating the structure of its Galois group by finding a sequence of subgroups of the sort indicated. Now, since it can be shown that the group of all permutations on n symbols (there are $n!$ of them)

is not solvable when $n \geq 5$, and since there are equations with rational coefficients which have these groups as Galois groups, it follows that these equations cannot be solved by radicals. Thus there cannot be any general formula for the roots in terms of the coefficients when $n \geq 5$, because such a formula would have to work regardless of what the coefficients were, and in particular would have to work for the special unsolvable equations as well.

(A.P.Ma.)

Historical development of probabilistic areas of mathematics

Of the precise meaning of probability there are conflicting views among experts (philosophers, mathematicians, statisticians). The reasons for this may be partly grasped from a survey of the various channels through which a scientific concept of probability has emerged.

Commercial insurance against risks was developed in the Italian cities of the early Renaissance. The theoretical foundations of life insurance were laid in the 17th century. The English statistician John Graunt in 1662 drew attention to the stability of statistical series obtained from registers of deaths. Soon after, the English astronomer Edmund Halley showed how to calculate annuities from mortality tables.

Another early reason for interest in probability was in connection with the weight of evidence in legal procedure. The theory of judicial evidence occupies a prominent place in probability mathematics up to the mid-19th century.

VARIOUS MATHEMATICALLY BASED PROBABILITIES

Mathematical problems relating to games of chance had been considered, though with minor success, by Luca di Paciuolo, Gerolamo Cardano, Niccolò Tartaglia, and other mathematicians of the Renaissance. The subject was developed into a "geometry of the die" (*aleae geometria*) by Blaise Pascal, Pierre de Fermat, and Christiaan Huygens in the 17th century. Fermat treated the problems within a general theory of combinations, which was further developed by the Swiss mathematician Jakob Bernoulli. The latter can be regarded as the founder of probability theory as a branch of mathematics: his posthumously published *Ars Conjectandi* of 1713 can be said to aim at a fusion of the a priori methods of combinatory probability and the a posteriori methods of early statistical theory. The research in probability done by 18th-century mathematicians culminated in the immense work of Pierre-Simon Laplace, the founder of a tradition that dominated the subject throughout the 19th century.

Laplace advocated a strictly deterministic view of the universe: an omniscient intelligence ("Laplace's demon") would be able to predict the course of nature in minutest detail with infallible accuracy. On this view, probability enters into a science of nature only as a theory of errors; that is, as a systematic study of the deviations from a mean that appear in repeated measurements of a quantity. This study was developed by Laplace, by Legendre, and by Gauss. The mathematical calculus of probability soon provided tools for handling statistical material in connection with public finance, health administration, the conduct of elections, and other social matters besides insurance. The Marquis de Condorcet and later the astronomer Adolphe Quetelet were champions of a social science based on probabilistic statistics.

From the middle of the 19th century, probability gradually gained ground as a part of physical theory. It first appeared in the theory of heat. James Clerk Maxwell in 1860 deduced gas laws from underlying probabilities for the distribution of positions and velocities of the molecules. The German physicist Ludwig Boltzmann in 1877 interpreted the irreversibility of thermal processes as a tendency toward a most probable distribution of the energies of the molecules. The rise of quantum mechanics saw the theory of radiation put on a probability basis by another German physicist, Max Planck, in the first year of the 20th century. With the further development of quantum physics, probability invaded atomic theory. By the middle of the 20th century the deterministic view of nature was thought in some quarters to be in process of being replaced by a probabilistic view. The concept of probability had become one of the fundamental notions of a modern science and philosophy of nature. This gave a new urgency to the need for clarifying the structure and meaning of the idea.

The abstract calculus of probability. In the course of the development already outlined, several definitions of probability were suggested. Accordingly, alternative methods were devised for basing the edifice of probability mathematics on those definitions. These alternative calculi take different views of the meaning of their fundamental notion, but they agree, by and large, in having a common logical structure.

These observations offer a starting point for attempts to create an abstract calculus of probability. It abstracts from various interpreted calculi their common structure, the formal properties of which it studies independently of any definition of probability.

In the abstract calculus developed by the Soviet mathematician A.N. Kolmogorov in 1933, probability figures as a function of sets. This theory, which has found much favour among mathematicians, incorporates probability mathematics within the general theory of measurable sets of points.

Abstract calculi of a type that might be called logistic were constructed by the English economist J.M. Keynes in 1921, Harold Jeffreys in 1939, the German-American philosopher Hans Reichenbach and other authors. In these systems probability figures as an undefined logical relation between propositions or attributes.

The symbol a/h can be read as "the probability of a given h." It is often convenient to speak of a as an "event" and of h as some "conditions" or "data" or "evidence." It is not necessary to assume that any pair of propositions (or attributes) determines a numerical value of the functor. If there is a numerical probability, it should, for noncontradictory data, satisfy the following four postulates: (1) $a/h \geq 0$; (2) $h/h = 1$; (3) $a/h +$ (not-a)$/h = 1$, the principle of complementarity; and (4) (a and b)$/h = a/h \times b/(h$ and a), the general multiplication principle. These four postulates suffice, with the aid of a few principles of a subordinate character, for the erection of the whole fabric of probability mathematics.

From the first, second, and third postulates it follows that all probability values are in the interval from 0 to 1 inclusive.

From the third with the aid of the fourth can be proved the general addition principle: (a or b)$/h = a/h + b/h -$ (a and b)$/h$.

If a and b are mutually exclusive alternatives, the probability of their joint occurrence is 0. Thus the equality for exclusive a and b holds: (a or b)$/h = a/h + b/h$. This is called the special addition principle.

If $a/h = a/(h$ and b), then it is said that a is independent (for probability) of b (in h). The notion of independence is of great importance to the further development of the calculus. It follows from the fourth postulate and the definition of independence that for independent a and b there is the equality (a and b)$/h = a/h \times b/h$. This is called the special multiplication principle.

The frequency theory of probability. This is the view that, popularly speaking, the probability of a given h means the relative frequency with which the event a takes place when the conditions h are fulfilled. The probability of a given h, in other words, is the proportion of h situations that lead to a events.

The frequency view of probability has a long history. Aristotle defines "a probability" as being "what men know to happen or not to happen, to be or not to be, for the most part thus and thus." A similar opinion was entertained by writers of the 17th and 18th centuries, who were interested in statistics or in a "theory of evidence."

The history of probability mathematics from Jakob Bernoulli to Laplace and his followers is allied to a different view of the meaning of probability, the range theory, discussed below. The rebirth of the frequency theory followed a criticism of the foundations of the Laplacean calculus, particularly of the use of the principle of indifference for the determination of probability values (see below *The principle of indifference*). The attack was launched by the British philosophers and economists R. Leslie Ellis, John Stuart Mill, and French economist and mathematician Antoine-Augustin Cournot in 1843. The frequency conception of probability was first worked out in a mathematical theory by John Venn in 1866.

Early proponents of the frequency theory spoke of probability as a relative frequency "in the long run." This loose way of speaking is not very satisfactory. Venn was the first to define an event's probability as the limiting value which its relative frequency approaches as the number of occasions is indefinitely increased. An improved version of this frequency-limit theory was presented by the German-American physicist and mathematician Richard von Mises in 1919; another later well-known adherent of the theory is Reichenbach.

Von Mises also thought that a probability cannot be simply the limiting value of a relative frequency, and he added the qualification that the event ought to be irregularly or randomly distributed in the series of occasions in which its probability is measured. This demand of randomness he called the principle of excluded gambling systems.

It is a great merit of von Mises to have stressed the importance of the idea of random distribution to a frequency theory of probability. With this idea, however, he introduced a considerable difficulty into the theory, the problem of defining random distribution. The definition proposed by von Mises has been challenged as inconsistent, but it is doubtful whether any of the proposed alternative definitions can be regarded as satisfactory.

The demand of randomness is relevant to the question of the adequacy of the frequency view as a proposed analysis of the meaning of probability. But randomness is not relevant to the question of the mathematical correctness of interpreting abstract probability in terms of frequencies. A frequency definition does satisfy the four postulates of the abstract calculus.

Many other objections can be raised against the frequency view. Nevertheless, some form of frequency theory is thought by many writers to offer the best account, for a large category of cases, of the relation between abstract probability and empirical reality.

The range theory of probability. Another definition of probability is given in terms of range. In its simplest form, this theory runs as follows: Analyze h into a number n of alternative conditions. That h is fulfilled means that either h_1 or $\cdots$ or h_n is fulfilled. Some of these alternatives, say m, entail the occurrence of a; the remaining ones entail the occurrence of not-a. Using a traditional terminology, the first group of alternatives is known as favourable to a and the second unfavourable to a. The probability of a given h is the ratio $m:n$ of the number of favourable alternatives and the number of all alternatives.

Omitting an important qualification discussed below, this is substantially the definition of probability that emerged from the mathematical treatment of games of chance and was canonized in the theory of Laplace; it is the classical form of the range definition.

The mutually exclusive alternatives covered by a proposition or an attribute are what is called its range. The classical definition can be generalized as follows: The probability of a given h is the ratio of the measure of the range of h-and-a and the measure of the range of h alone.

The notion of range (in German, *Spielraum*) was introduced into probability theory by Johannes von Kries in 1886. It was used to define probability as a logical relation between propositions by Ludwig Wittgenstein (1922). Substantially the same definition had been given by the Czech mathematician Bernard Bolzano as early as 1837. A generalized form of the Bolzano-Wittgenstein definition was suggested by Friedrich Waismann in 1929 and was further developed and extensively studied by Rudolf Carnap in 1950. The Waismann-Carnap definition is independent of any specific way of measuring ranges.

Early
work
on range

The range definition, both in its classical and in its generalized form, satisfies the postulates of abstract probability. The definition, no doubt, is mathematically correct. Whether it gives an adequate account of the meaning of probability is another matter.

The principle of indifference. The main difficulty confronting a range theory of probability concerns measurement of the ranges. This difficulty is allied to the question of how to analyze propositions or attributes into alternatives. Usually there are several possibilities for the choice of a measure and the analysis of the data into alternatives.

The classic workers in probability theory were aware of these difficulties; the first to discuss the matter fully was Jakob Bernoulli. He stressed that the alternatives into which *h* is analyzed ought to be equally possible; *i.e.*, "each case ought to have the same facility as any other case of coming about." This condition of equipossibility in the cases was usually added to the classical range definition of probability. The condition, it will be noted, is tantamount to a principle of measuring ranges. Jakob Bernoulli laid down a rule for the conditions in which cases can rightly be pronounced equally possible; the rule is known as the principle of insufficient reason, the principle of equal distribution of ignorance, or in Keynes's phrase the principle of indifference. In its classical version this principle states that two cases are equally possible if no reason is known why the one case rather than the other should come about.

Reliance on a principle of indifference for measuring ranges (probabilities) has a certain prima facie plausibility in games of chance, where there usually is complete agreement among experts as regards the right analysis of the situation into alternatives of equal possibility. In cases which present no obvious analogy to games of chance, reliance on the principle becomes dubious. It was the use of it made by Laplace and his followers, particularly for the notorious doctrine of inverse probability, that, in the middle of the 19th century, provoked criticism of the foundations of the entire classical fabric of probability theory. Among the notable earlier critics of the principle of indifference were R. Leslie Ellis, George Boole, Charles Sanders Peirce, and Johannes von Kries.

J.M. Keynes further discussed the principle acutely and in detail. Severely criticizing its unguarded uses, he also attempted to refashion it and to make clear its relevance to any philosophy of probability. Warranted use of the principle is tied to the question of symmetry in the unit alternatives under consideration; and the problem of symmetry in its turn is tied to the problem of an ultimate analysis of propositions or attributes into alternatives. Any judgment of symmetry or ultimacy, as it presupposes that all relevant information about the cases has been taken into account, is, negatively, a judgment of irrelevance or independence for probability among propositions or attributes. Any pronouncement on irrelevance involves, so Keynes thought, an "element of direct judgment or intuition."

The principle of indifference has usually been discussed in connection with the classical range definition, to which it was traditionally regarded as a necessary supplementation. However, the problems connected with this principle recur within any theory which defines probability in terms of the relative magnitudes of ranges.

The belief theory of probability. Many philosophers and mathematicians have spoken of probability as a degree of belief or of certainty. Frank Plumpton Ramsey in 1926 and, somewhat later, B. de Finetti in 1937 made a systematic attempt to base the mathematical theory of probability on the notion of partial belief. Both take as their point of departure an old idea, measuring a person's belief by proposing a bet and observing the lowest odds that he will accept. A person who distributes his partial beliefs (his subjective assignments of probabilities) contrary to the laws of calculus could have a so-called Dutch book made against him and would then stand to lose in any event. Because of this, the laws of probability may be called rules for consistent (coherent) sets of degrees of belief.

Ramsey, moreover, made an ingenious effort to generalize the procedure of measuring beliefs. A bet can be regarded as an option between goods, and accepting lowest odds as a reflection of an attitude of indifference in any option. A distribution of partial beliefs contrary to the laws of probability, Ramsey says, "would be inconsistent in the sense that it violated the laws of preference between options, such as that preferability is a transitive asymmetrical relation."

The ideas of Ramsey and de Finetti were later taken up by Leonard J. Savage in 1954, who became the founder of a subjectivist or personalist school in probability and statistics. The combination of probabilistic ideas with the value-theory notions of preference and utility has had fruitful applications to the mathematical study of economic and related forms of human behaviour. Acknowledgment of this fact does not exclude taking a somewhat critical view of the epistemological and logical basis of the belief theory of probability.

Probability: subjective or objective. The subjectivist conception of probability as a degree of belief is often contrasted with the objectivist conception of the notion as either a relative frequency or a ratio of measures of ranges. It is questionable, however, whether a sharp contrast can be maintained between objectivism and subjectivism in the philosophy, particularly the epistemology, of probability.

Supporters of the frequency view have found that an adequate analysis of probability requires them to combine their definition of the concept with the idea of a random distribution of events on a series of occasions. Supporters of a range theory have had recourse to some form of a principle of indifference for the determination of equipossibility in certain unit alternatives. The question may be raised whether randomness and equipossibility can be satisfactorily accounted for without reference to states of knowledge or ignorance. If the answer is negative, it shall have to be admitted that an adequate account of the meaning of probability cannot be given in purely objectivist terms.

On the other hand, the belief theory does not necessarily entail an identification of probability with belief as a psychological phenomenon. The attitudes in options between goods may be said to reveal subjective estimations of probability. But the derivation of the laws of probability within the belief theory does not confer on them the status of psychological laws of believing. It rather makes them standards of rationality (consistency) in the distribution of beliefs or in preferences. It would therefore be an oversimplification to regard the belief theory as an account of probability in purely subjectivist (that is, psychological) terms.

Bernoulli's theorem. If it is assumed that the probability for the occurrence of an event *a* on a certain occasion of *h* is not affected by its occurrence or nonoccurrence on previous occasions of *h* (that the occurrences of *a*, in other words, are independent for probability of one another), and if this probability is *p*, then the special multiplication and addition principles can be used to calculate the probability that the event *a* will, on *n* occasions of *h*, be realized with a relative frequency in the interval $p \pm \varepsilon$. From considerations about this second-order probability it can be proved that:

1. The most probable value of the event's relative frequency on *n* occasions is that value which comes nearest to its probability *p*.

2. In the long run the event will almost certainly be realized with a relative frequency corresponding to its probability; that is, the probability that the event's relative frequency on *n* occasions will deviate from its probability *p* by less than a given amount ε, however small, approaches 1 as a limit when *n* is indefinitely increased.

For example: The probability of head and tail in tossing with a normal coin is ½. The results are independent for probability: no combination of head and tail in previous tosses will influence the probability of getting head or of getting tail in the next toss. A simple calculation shows that the probability of getting 49, 50, or 51 heads in 100 tosses is approximately 0.16; the probability of getting between 490 and 510 heads in 1,000 tosses is 0.47; and the probability of getting between 4,900 and 5,100 heads in 10,000 tosses is 0.95. In other words: in 10,000 tosses it is almost certain that the proportion of heads will deviate by less than 0.01 from its probability ½.

This remarkable theorem is known as Bernoulli's theorem. It is chronologically the first of a class of propositions called the laws of large numbers, a name introduced by Siméon-Denis Poisson in 1837.

Inverse probability. In 1763 Thomas Bayes proved that, if $m:n$ is the relative frequency of an event on n independent occasions, then $m:n$ is also the most probable value of the event's probability, provided that any value of this probability is initially (a priori) as probable as any other value. The same theorem was proved independently by Laplace in 1774. Laplace also proved that, on the assumptions mentioned, it will in the long run become almost certain that the probability of the event coincides with its relative frequency.

The Bayes-Laplace theorem is the inversion of Bernoulli's theorem and the cornerstone of the classical doctrine of inverse probability for the estimation of probabilities on the basis of frequencies. The doctrine was developed and put to extensive use by Laplace and his followers. It was thought to be of great relevance to the problem of induction.

The Achilles' heel of inverse probability is its dependence on initial or a priori probabilities. These were in the classical doctrine often established by deplorably uncritical use of the principle of indifference. The doctrine was challenged in the 19th century, particularly by early proponents of the frequency view. The use of inverse probability is still a matter of debate. Some researchers, among them the British statistician Sir Ronald Fisher, have altogether rejected it.

Asymptotic probabilities and the principle of moral certitude. It was often thought in the past that, by virtue of Bernoulli's theorem, "events will, in the long run, happen in numbers proportional to probabilities" as expressed by Augustus De Morgan in 1838. But this is a serious mistake. The theorem only says that it becomes increasingly probable that the frequency coincides with the probability. And this, by itself, does not warrant any conclusion about actual frequencies, not even in the long run. The error latent in the idea that Bernoulli's theorem provides a bridge from a subjectivist conception of probability as a degree of certainty to an objectivist conception in terms of frequencies was first clearly seen and conclusively criticized by R. Leslie Ellis in 1843. There were many lapses into the error afterward, but today the correctness of the criticism is universally admitted.

There is, however, another way of using Bernoulli's theorem and other asymptotic principles of probability (laws of large numbers) as a bridge from (uninterpreted) probabilities to statistical frequencies without committing a logical error. It may be briefly indicated as follows:

Either from observations about frequencies or from considerations about ranges or from some other source, a hypothesis is framed about the probability of a given h. From this hypothesis it is calculated as "almost" or, in Bernoulli's term, "morally" certain (say probable to degree 0.95) that in a series of n trials the relative frequency of the event will deviate from its probability by less than a small fraction (say 0.01). In other words, it is "most unlikely" ("morally impossible") that the frequency will fall short of the hypothetical probability by more than this fraction. Adopting the maxim that very improbable events are "practically excluded" and that "moral certainty" should be treated as equal to full certainty, then, if the event's frequency nevertheless deviates from the hypothetical value by more than the fraction in question, it ought to be said, not that something very improbable has happened, but that the probability hypothesis has to be rejected.

The proposed maxim was in fact suggested by Bernoulli. It might be called Bernoulli's principle of moral certitude. Its adoption seems to accord with the actual use of probability calculations for scientific and other purposes.

It partially explains why, without detriment to the applications of probability, judgment can be suspended on the meaning of this controversial notion. The calculus permits transition from hypothetical probabilities to predicted frequencies. If the observed frequencies conflict with the principle of moral certitude, the hypotheses are modified or rejected. The boundaries of moral certitude are, of course, elastic; and whether they are provisionally fixed at one value rather than at another will depend upon a multitude of circumstances peculiar to each case: the amount of statistical evidence at hand, the possibilities of repeated trials, the facility with which dependencies between occurrences can be controlled, and ethical considerations relating to gains and losses from choosing one probability hypothesis over another as a basis of action.

"Probability": one or many meanings. The word "probability" can be put to many uses, as in these statements: (1) "the probability of a normal six-sided die turning up 'six' is ⅙"; (2) "the probability that Shakespeare wrote the plays commonly attributed to him is overwhelming"; (3) "Fresnel's experiment increased the probability of the undulatory theory of light."

According to Hans Reichenbach, one of the chief proponents of the frequency theory in modern times, there is only one scientific meaning of probability. A statement of the second type, which concerns the probability of an individual event, is literally meaningless, but may be reinterpreted as a statement about that which usually is the case under similar circumstances. Statements of the third type, which attribute probability to general propositions (laws of nature, theories, hypotheses) may, according to Reichenbach, be given a frequency interpretation as referring either to a proportion of successful predictions, or to a proportion of true theories within a class.

A unitary view of probability was also taken by J.M. Keynes, though on quite different grounds. According to Keynes, the difficulties presented by cases such as the second and third types exemplified above would indicate that probability is a wider notion than the concept that figures in a frequency theory or even in any theory that requires probability to be a measurable quantity. In its wide sense, probability is a degree of rational belief, not necessarily measurable. J.M. Keynes's view

Those who have advocated a dualistic view of probability have usually wished to contrast cases of the third type, or the probability of laws of nature, with other types of probability. Jakob Friedrich Fries called the probability of laws "philosophical probability" and contrasted it with "mathematical probability." This distinction was adopted by many logicians and philosophers of the 19th century such as Ernest Friedrich Apelt, Antoine-Augustine Cournot, and M.W. Drobisch. Philosophical probability was thought to be nonnumerical in principle. A similar position has found favour with many 20th-century authors: Bertrand Russell in 1948 contrasted "credibility" and "mathematical probability"; William Calvert Kneale in 1949, "acceptability" and "chance"; R.B. Braithwaite in 1953, "reasonableness" and "probability."

A dualistic view of a somewhat different nature was developed by Rudolf Carnap in his *Logical Foundations of Probability*. Of the two concepts of probability that he distinguishes, the first (which he also calls "degree of confirmation") is probability in the sense of a range theory; the second is probability in the sense of a frequency theory. Carnap tries to reconcile the rival claims of the two theories by assigning to each concept of probability its proper field of application. In view of the difficulties, however, which both theories encounter as proposed analyses of probability, it cannot be taken for granted that this reconciliation is altogether satisfactory.   (G.H.von W.)

DEVELOPMENT OF MATHEMATICAL STATISTICS

Development of the conceptual content of mathematical statistics was gradual, extending over a century and a half. As noted earlier the behaviouristic approach to problems of estimation is found in the work of Laplace and Gauss. Laplace seems one of the first to test statistical hypotheses; but at that time there was no question of mathematical statistics as an independent discipline. Laplace's criteria for testing statistical hypotheses were intuitive rather than mathematical and in no way similar to his approach to the problem of point estimators. The behavioristic approach to estimation was soon forgotten.

Mathematical statistics as an independent discipline seems to have appeared in the latter part of the 19th century in the work of the English, French, and German mathematicians Adolphe Quetelet, Gustav Theodor Fechner, Karl Pearson, George Udny Yule, and the Czech mathematician Emanuel Czuber. The then existing branches of applied mathematics (*e.g.*, analytical mechanics) were, so to speak, individualistic. Many scientific problems required a new mathematical discipline concerned with aggregates of objects, all of which satisfy a specific definition but differ in individual characteristics. Such an aggregate (population) might be all men of military age in a country; these men differ in height. Another population would be the set of gas molecules in a container; each molecule has a unique velocity as its individual characteristic.

Any population, however, has its own characteristics, conditioned by those of the individual members, but essentially different. Gas pressure is a characteristic of the population of molecules conditioned by their velocities; temperature is another such characteristic. These are examples of what Fechner called *Kollektivmass*. The average height of recruits is also a *Kollektivmass*, as is the frequency with which they are found with height between 5 ft 10 in. and 5 ft 11 in. The set of such frequencies (the frequency distribution) is also a *Kollektivmass*.

The notion of Kollektivmass

In the late 19th and early 20th centuries mathematical statistics emphasized the *Kollektivmasslehre*, a mathematical discipline concerned with collective characteristics of populations. The term descriptive statistics was introduced to mean the use of a variety of methods (including graphical and tabular methods) for describing such characteristics of populations. An important method of descriptive statistics is to consider a family of flexible curves or surfaces (depending on a moderate number of parameters) that can be used to approximate the empirical frequency distribution. A number of such families were developed, all representing interpolation formulas. The most successful system seems to be that due to Karl Pearson.

A conceptual problem studied by the German mathematician Wilhelm Lexis developed to deprive *Kollektivmasslehre* of its independent status. Lexis was concerned with the year-to-year fluctuation of sex ratio among children born in a city, and similar ratios arising in the study of vital statistics. The question was whether an empirical index of dispersion is consistent with the assumption that determination of sex is governed by a simple chance mechanism such as a toss of a coin. This renewed a continuing effort concerned with chance mechanisms acting on individuals to produce the observed collective characteristics.

Interest in flexible formulas specifically developed to fit empirical distributions gradually decreased, except for those that could be deduced from clearly defined chance mechanisms. In the 1920s the Hungarian-U.S. mathematician George Polyá constructed a system of chance mechanisms that can generate almost all the distributions of Karl Pearson's system. Thus mathematical statistics shifted from *Kollektivmasslehre* to the construction of chance mechanisms or (as they are called) stochastic models of phenomena. This idea was explicitly stated by Émile Borel of France:

The basic problem of mathematical statistics is to invent a system of simple chance mechanisms, such as throws of a coin, so that the probabilities determined by this system agree with the observed relative frequencies of the various details of the phenomena studied.

Although Borel's definition was appealing, developments following its formulation indicated that it leaves mathematical statistics without a field of its own. Depending on the attitudes of given research workers, stochastic models belong to the relevant substantive fields or to the theory of probability. Thus stochastic models of

hereditary phenomena are an integral part of genetics; stochastic models of epidemics are an integral part of epidemiology; and so on. However, considerable literature on stochastic processes developing in time (*e.g.*, birth and death stochastic process constructed to represent the growth of biological populations) is one of the most active sections of the theory of probability. Each problem of the theory of stochastic processes is reducible to that of determining probabilities (*e.g.*, that a biological population will eventually die out). While the field indicated in Borel's definition continued to grow in importance, it was claimed by other disciplines, leaving nothing to mathematical statistics.

While these ideas were in the process of dissolution, increasing effort was given to problems of estimation and of testing hypotheses. In connection with his system of curves, Karl Pearson developed a method of point estimation known as the method of moments; in 1900 he published his famous χ^2 (chi-square) test for goodness of fit. In 1908 F.Y. Edgeworth of England found that consistent use of the method of moments must yield an excessive frequency of large errors of estimation (a distinctly behavioristic approach) and proposed a new method of estimation, conjectured to be much better. Fourteen years later, Sir Ronald Fisher discussed the same ground more rigorously and intensively. He introduced the term method of maximum likelihood. The English mathematician Student (pseudonym of William Scaly Gosset) and Fisher developed a number of tests of particular hypotheses. However, studies of this kind were not yet connected by any unifying idea and were limited to particular decision functions. Problems of testing hypotheses and of estimation remained unrecognized as an independent field for systematic study.

The method of moments

Such recognition came when Fisher in 1922 gave a new definition of statistics. Stating that the object of statistical methods is the reduction of bulky data, Fisher distinguished three basic problems: those of specification of the kind of population from which the data come (*i.e.*, of the *Kollektivmass*), of estimation, and of distribution (probabilistic problems connected with point estimation). This was followed by a paper concerned specifically with the theory of estimation; the underlying ideas are distinct precursors of the behavioristic approach to mathematical statistics described earlier.   (Ed.)

BIBLIOGRAPHY

The ancient Western world: T. ERIC PEET, *The Rhind Mathematical Papyrus* (1923); OTTO NEUGEBAUER and ABRAHAM J. SACHS, *Mathematical Cuneiform Texts* (1945); OTTO NEUGEBAUER, *The Exact Sciences in Antiquity*, 2nd ed. (1957), with emphasis on Babylonian, Egyptian, and Hellenistic mathematics and astronomy; B.L. VAN DER WAERDEN, *Ontwakende Wetenschap* (1950; Eng. trans., *Science Awakening*, 1954); ARNOLD B. CHACE et al. (eds.), *The Rhind Mathematical Papyrus*, 2 vol. (1927–29) FRANCOIS THUREAU-DANGIN, *Textes mathématiques babyloniens* (1938); GEORGE SARTON, *Introduction to the History of Science*, 3 vol. (1927–48), vol. 1 up to 1400.

The medieval Western world: GEORGE SARTON (*op. cit.*), vol. 2–3; FLORENCE A. YELDHAM, *The Story of Reckoning in the Middle Ages* (1926); JOSEPH and FRANCES GIES, *Leonard of Pisa and the New Mathematics of the Middle Ages* (1969).

The modern Western world (after 1400): ISAAC TODHUNTER, *A History of the Progress of the Calculus of Variations During the Nineteenth Century* (1861; reprinted as *A History of the Calculus of Variations . . .*, 1962); OTTO TOEPLITZ, *Die Entwicklung der Infinitesimalrechnung* (1949; Eng. trans., *The Calculus: A Genetic Approach*, 1963); FLORIAN CAJORI, *A History of the Conception of Limits and Fluxions in Great Britain, from Newton to Woodhouse* (1919); DIRK J. STRUIK, "Outline of a History of Differential Geometry," *Isis*, 19:92–120, 20:161–191 (1933).

The Eastern world: G.R. KAYE, "Indian Mathematics," *Isis*, 2:326–356 (1919); YOSHIO MIKAMI, *The Development of Mathematics in China and Japan* (1913, reprinted 1961); DAVID E. SMITH and YOSHIO MIKAMI, *A History of Japanese Mathematics* (1914); *The I-Ching; or, Book of Changes*, trans. by RICHARD WILHELM, 2 vol. (1950).

The development of numerals, numeral systems, arithmetic, and number theory: DAVID E. SMITH, *History of Mathematics*, 2 vol. (1923–25), numerous facsimiles of different systems and extensive bibliography; DAVID E. SMITH and JEKUTHIEL GINSBURG, *Numbers and Numerals* (1937); OYSTEIN ORE, *Number Theory and Its History* (1948); LEONARD E. DICKSON, *History of the Theory of Numbers*, 3 vol. (1919–23, reprinted 1952); FLORIAN CAJORI, *A History of Mathematical Notations*, 2 vol. (1928–29); LOUIS C. KARPINSKI, *The History of Arithmetic* (1925, reprinted 1965); DAVID E. SMITH and LOUIS C. KARPINSKI, *The Hindu-Arabic Numerals* (1911); TOBIAS DANTZIG, *Number: The Language of Science*, 4th ed. rev. (1954).

The development of geometry and trigonometry: THOMAS L. HEATH, *A History of Greek Mathematics*, 2 vol. (1921); ANTON VON BRAUNMUEHL, *Vorlesungen über Geschichte der Trigonometrie*, 2 vol. (1900–03); JULIAN L. COOLIDGE, *A History of Geometrical Methods* (1940).

The development of algebra: DAVID E. SMITH, "Algebra of Four Thousand Years Ago," *Scr. math.*, 4:111–125 (1936); LOUIS C. KARPINSKI, *Robert of Chester's Latin Translation of the Algebra of Al-Khwarizmi* (1915); THOMAS MUIR, *The Theory of Determinants in the Historical Order of Development*, 4 vol. (1906–23; reprinted in 2 vol., 1960), with supplement, *Contributions to the History of Determinants 1900–1920* (1930).

The development of probabilistic areas of mathematics: M.G. KENDALL, "Studies in the History of Probability and Statistics: II," *Biometrika*, 43:1–14 (1956); HELEN M. WALKER, *Studies in the History of Statistical Method* (1929); ISAAC TODHUNTER, *A History of the Mathematical Theory of Probability from the Time of Pascal to That of Laplace* (1865, reprinted 1965); BAYARD RANKIN, "The History of Probability and the Changing Concept of the Individual," *J. Hist. Ideas*, 27:483–504 (1966).

Mathematics as a calculatory science: KARL PEARSON, *On the Construction of Tables and on Interpolation*, 2 vol. (1920); RAYMOND C. ARCHIBALD, *Mathematical Table Makers* (1948); FRANCIS J. MURRAY, *Mathematical Machines*, 2 vol. (1961); H.S. CARSLAW, "The Discovery of Logarithms by Napier," *Mathl. Gaz.*, 8:76–84, 115–119 (1915–16).

Miscellaneous: PAUL TANNERY, *Mémoires scientifiques*, 17 vol. (1912–50); MORITZ CANTOR, *Vorlesungen über Geschichte der Mathematik*, 2nd ed., 4 vol. (1894–1908, reprinted 1965); ERIC T. BELL, *The Development of Mathematics*, 2nd ed. (1945); FLORIAN CAJORI, *A History of Mathematics*, 2nd ed. (1919); DIRK J. STRUIK, *A Concise History of Mathematics*, 3rd rev. ed., 2 vol. (1967); GEORGE SARTON, *The Study of the History of Mathematics* (1936), an interesting introductory account, with extensive bibliographical references; RAYMOND C. ARCHIBALD, *Outline of the History of Mathematics*, 6th ed. (1949), a succinct summary, with bibliography; GANESH PRASAD, *Some Great Mathematicians of the Nineteenth Century: Their Lives and Their Works*, 2 vol. (1933–34).

(W.J.LeV./D.E.S./V.S./G.R.St./A.W.Ke./
O.Or./E.T.B./A.P.Ma./G.H.von W./Ed.)

Mathematics as a Calculatory Science

Mathematics as a logical body of knowledge can be used as a guide for arriving at precise results. If the precise results are expressible in terms of numbers or are arrived at with the use of numbers, the calculatory nature of mathematics becomes evident. Mathematics as a calculatory science includes the use of computers, as is obvious, but it includes many other things as well. In fact, a historical view of the entire mathematical literature reveals that the inclination of mathematical thought to build upon repetitious steps that submit to automation, or its inclination to reduce abstract reasoning to physical models, is not unrelated to mathematics as an abstract discipline in which it is possible to begin with unproved statements called axioms and deduce consequences. Significantly, one of the evident turning points that has affected the foundational thinking of mathematics occurred when the English mathematician Alan Turing characterized in succinct language in the 1930s precisely what is meant by an algorithm, with the use of which mathematical proofs can be constructed. Turing's work led to the modern concept of the computer, itself, and not inconsistently to a fuller understanding of mathematics as a whole (see AUTOMATA THEORY; MATHEMATICS, FOUNDATIONS OF).

Mathematics as a calculational science is then concerned with the ingredients of mathematics that characterize the automated form of the reasoning process and the methods of thought that rely upon such things as

physical models and number storage and manipulation. The end results of a mathematical calculation may be a statement, a decision, a number, a geometrical drawing, a plan, or other recorded conclusion. The calculational ingredients of mathematics are thus varied. The outline, as given below, is a guide to what is meant by the subject.

Numerical notations
  Aggregations
  Multiplication and division by doubling; Egyptian notations
  Other ancient notations
  Decimal notation
  Modern notational developments
Geometrical aids
  Applications of geometry
  Instruments for observation and navigation
  Mapping
  Spherical trigonometry
  Stereographic projections and the astrolabe
  Optical instruments
  Drawing instruments
Mathematical models
  Construction of models
  Simple polyhedra and the sphere
  Descriptive geometry
  Models that illustrate identities
  Topological models
  Surface models
  Kinematic models
Algebra and logarithms
  Algebraic notation
  Logarithms
  Slide rules
Tables
  Integral tables
  The Monte Carlo method
  Fourier series and transforms
  Function tables
  Mathematical tables
Graphs and graphical procedures
  Graphs
  Scales
  Alignment charts
  Planimeters
  Graphics
Analogue computation
  Mathematical analogues
  Analogue computers
  Resolvers
  Multipliers
  Harmonic analyzers
  Differential analyzers
  Automatic controls
  Electromechanical analogue computers
  Direct current analogue computers
  Hybrid concepts
Digital calculators
  Abacus
  Registers and adders
  Rotary calculators
Punched cards
  Cards
  Punched card machines
Programmed machines (digital computers)
  Development
  Instruction and programs
  Storage facilities
  Programming
  Circuitry
  Error detection
  Input and output
  Data processing systems
  Applications

NUMERICAL NOTATIONS

Aggregations. A numerical notation is usually directly associated with counting. The usefulness of the notation is dependent on the ease and effectiveness with which such other operations as addition, subtraction, multiplication, and division can be accomplished.

In its most elementary form, counting is based on a memorized sequence of the names of numbers. An obvious analogy is with counting by the fingers, and the advantage of aggregating the given units into larger units is clear. The Romans, for instance, grouped objects into fives, and the Roman numeral V for five is supposed to represent the hand. Aggregation by tens is the most com-

$$(1) \begin{cases} \rightarrow 1 \times 132 = 132 \\ 2 \times 132 = 264 \\ \rightarrow 4 \times 132 = 528 \end{cases}$$

mon form, but this may also appear in the so-called biquinary form in which there is an alternate aggregation by fives and by twos. Both primitive societies and advanced electronic computers aggregate by twos and threes.

Practical situations suggest a further development of aggregation. For example, retail sales in the case of certain items may be by units or dozens, but wholesale dealings may be in grosses—*i.e.*, dozens of dozens—or great grosses. Aggregation by twenties was once popular as evidenced by the term score. The Mayan culture of Central America used a system of aggregation that was basically in twenties. Aggregation by sixties apparently arose from a certain method of dividing the arc of a circle.

The aggregations that arose in the British marketplace, however, tended to be extremely *ad hoc;* for example, 16 drams equal one ounce, 16 ounces equal one pound, 14 pounds equal one stone; 12 pence equal one shilling, 20 shillings equal one pound. For such a system, only addition and multiplication by small natural numbers is at all practical. From the operational point of view, uniform aggregation by a constant factor, which may explain the British change to a decimal coinage and the metric system, both base 10, in the 1970s, is much more desirable.

Multiplication and division by doubling: Egyptian notations. An example of aggregation by a constant factor is given by the Egyptian system described in the Rhind papyrus, written by a priest, Ahmes, sometime before 1700 BC and based on sources that are believed to be much older. It is a collection of tables and problems that were used for instruction. The Ahmes notation for a number is based on assigning a symbol for each unit aggregate. These were a vertical bar, |, for one, an arch, ∩, for ten, and a C for one hundred. Symbols were assigned to these unit aggregates up to 10,000,000. A number was represented by writing down a symbol for each aggregate involved; for example, 231 was written CC∩∩∩|. This type of notation is reasonably convenient for counting, addition, and subtraction. Multiplication and division were based on doubling and tables for doubling were provided. The procedure can be illustrated by multiplying 132 by 5, for example (see Box, equations 1), in which multiplication of 132 by integers less than 5 (some distinguished with an arrow) are written on the left of the equations. The quantity 5 is expressed as $4 + 1$ (this is the significance of the arrows), and then the items on the right side are added; *i.e.*, $5 \times 132 = (528 + 132) = 660$.

The process of expressing a number (for example, 5 above) as a sum of powers of two (numbers of the form 2^n, in which n is an integer) is readily accomplished from a listing of the powers of two with values less than the given number.

Division is accomplished by repeatedly doubling the divisor. This procedure may be illustrated by dividing 2028 by 39. Again, the calculation is expressed with equations (see 2), on the left of which are products of powers of 2 times 39. In this example, 39 is the divisor and doubling has been continued up to the point at which the next result would be greater than the dividend, which is 2028. It is now possible to express 2028 as the sum of the dashed terms on the right-hand side. Thus (see 3) the dashed (or especially marked) terms involve 32, 16, and 4 as multiples of 39. The answer is 52. If the divisor were not exact, there would be an additional fraction.

The use of two as the base of the powers in this procedure is quite efficient, and, if some other quantity were used, multiples would be required that were not simply powers of the quantity. For example, if three were used instead of two, more than powers of three would be needed (see 4).

This procedure for multiplication and division persisted

a long time and became obsolete only when most people received childhood training in forming multiples of a given number by the digits one to nine. If p is such a digit, shifting the decimal point will yield $p\ 10^r \times N$ from the multiple of N by p. The modern division process chooses such an expression involving the divisor N and subtracts it from the dividend, without writing out or even obtaining multiples of N, which would not be used. In the example (2), 1×39, 2×39, and 8×39 are used only in the formation process.

On the other hand, the procedure using the powers of two can be effectively aided by a table of doubles. Thus the only other capabilities required are those of adding (or subtracting) and comparison, and the notation described can handle these latter operations.

Fractions, as often required by the Egyptian method of division, were dealt with as follows. Fractions with a numerator greater than one could only be expressed in terms of those with numerator equal to one (see 5). The sum of two fractions in this form, however, can be obtained by using a table that expresses a fraction with numerator two as a sum of fractions with numerator one. This is also true of the product of two fractions in the given form, and any numerator can be expressed as a sum of powers of two. One such table, which appeared in a manuscript written before AD 800 (the Akhmin papyrus), used a formula for $2/pq$ (see 6), in which p and q are odd. There is also a relation for $2/(2p + 1)$ (see 7), in which p may be either odd or even.

$$(2) \begin{cases} 1 \times 39 = 39 \\ 2 \times 39 = 78 \\ 4 \times 39 = 156 - \\ 8 \times 39 = 312 \\ 16 \times 39 = 624 - \\ 32 \times 39 = 1248 - \end{cases}$$

$$(3) \quad 2028 = 1248 + 624 + 156 = (32 + 16 + 4) \times 39$$
$$= 52 \times 39$$

$$(4) \quad 2 \times 3^r \times N, \quad 3^r \times N$$

$$(5) \quad \tfrac{5}{9} = \tfrac{1}{3} + \tfrac{1}{5} + \tfrac{1}{45}$$

$$(6) \quad \frac{2}{pq} = \frac{1}{q\left(\dfrac{p+q}{2}\right)} + \frac{1}{p\left(\dfrac{p+q}{2}\right)}$$

$$(7) \quad \frac{2}{2p+1} = \frac{1}{p+1} + \frac{1}{(p+1)(2p+1)}$$

Other ancient notations. Originally the Roman numeral system seems to be similar to that of the Egyptians except that it had a biquinary character. Thus, while the Egyptian notation had symbols for the powers of 10, the Romans had symbols I, V, X, L, C, D, M for 1, 5, 10, 50, 100, 500, 1,000. The indicated aggregations therefore are first by fives, then two fives to make ten, then five tens to make fifty, then two fifties to make a hundred, and so on. Some compactness was achieved by using a subtractive notation; *e.g.*, IX for nine instead of VIIII.

The Babylonians used at least two systems for expressing numbers. One of these was decimal, the other sexagesimal, with base 60. There were symbols for the digits, ten, and one hundred, but the quantities that appeared in a single decimal place were expressed by multiplication; for example, 40,000 would be expressed by a sequence of symbols for 4, 10, 10, 100, which was interpreted $4 \times 10 \times 10 \times 100$. The sexagesimal system apparently was written as a simple place system, the place on the extreme right being for units and the next for

The Babylonian system

multiples of sixties. Both of these systems were handicapped by the lack of a zero symbol.

The Babylonians (about two millennia BC) divided the circle into 360 degrees, the degree into 60 minutes, and the minute into 60 seconds. Similarly, the day was divided into 24 hours and the hour into minutes and seconds. Associated with this was a tendency to use fractions with a fixed power of sixty as a denominator. The largest such denominator appears to be 60^4, a number that was considered to have mystical significance. Division tables were constructed for those divisors that could be precisely expressed in the notation.

Greek and
Chinese
notation Greek astronomers in the 2nd century AD started to use sexagesimal fractions both to record observations and to construct trigonometrical tables, a practice that was continued until the 16th century. The Greeks also used a decimal system that was based on using the alphabet to denote the digits (see 8), the integral multiples of ten (see 9), of 100 (see 10), of 1,000 (see 11), and of 10,000 (see 12). This number system persisted in the place entries in the sexagesimal tables used in Ptolemaic astronomy. The Hebrews also used a system analogous to this.

The Chinese had a place system in which the symbols for successive places were obtained by a rotation of the symbols for the digits. Thus if |, ||, ||| stood for 1, 2, 3 in the units place, $-$, $=$, $\equiv$ would stand for 10, 20, 30 in the tens place, whereas |, ||, ||| would stand for 100, 200, and 300 in the hundreds place.

Decimal notation. The major difficulty with all these notations is their lack of compactness. The present decimal system with its place value requiring the use of zero was adapted by the Arabs from Hindu (Indian) sources in the 9th or 10th century. Hindu mathematics appears to have arisen from Babylonian and Hellenistic sources and to have been subject to Chinese influence. Indian interest in astronomy and computation, however, resulted in the development of the convenient place system with zero from an earlier native system using nine symbols and names for the powers of ten.

During the 10th century, Roman numerical procedures were reintroduced in western Europe. This was a development due to a churchman, Gerbert, who discovered a copy of the geometry of the 6th-century Roman philosopher and statesman Boethius. He also described the use of the Roman abacus, a calculating device using movable counters. About a hundred years later, a tremendous interest arose in those treasures of Hellenic classical knowledge, which were known to the Arabs and which were made available by translation from Arabic. As part of this process, Leonardo of Pisa (*q.v.*; Fibonacci) published in 1202 an account of Arabian mathematics and advocated the Arabic notation, involving place calculation with the zero. Italian merchants quickly adopted this system, which seems to have become reasonably widespread in Europe by 1300 but not particularly well accepted in learned circles. The formal procedures of commercial arithmetic, such as simple and compound interest and discount, were developed in this period by the Florentine merchants.

Decimal fractions appeared at first in a somewhat specialized form. It took a considerable time to develop a full appreciation of the fact that the decimal notation permitted both the integral and fractional part of a number to be handled in the same way arithmetically. Decimal fractions were described by Simon Stevin of Bruges in Belgium in 1585 and were used by a number of others. The notation used was relatively clumsy in most instances, and universal European use of the decimal point occurred only in the first quarter of the 18th century. With this came the standardization of today's arithmetical procedures for long division and for extracting the square root (see ARITHMETIC).

For integers, the decimal system is such that each place is treated in a similar way in addition, subtraction, multiplication, and division in which the quotient is integral. For division, in general, it is necessary to use decimal fractions, and by allowing recurring decimals it is possible to obtain a complete description of rational numbers (numbers that can be expressed as integers or as the quotient of integers) and the operations on them.

(13)	$1010, 1110, 1001$
(14)	$(2^{11} + 2^9 + 2^7 + 2^6 + 2^5 + 2^3 + 1)$
(15)	$(5 \times 8^3) + (3 \times 8^2) + (5 \times 8) + (1)$
(16)	$5.13 \times 10^{10}, -2.76 \times 10^{-8}$

Modern notational developments. The uniformity of the decimal place system permitted the development of mechanical calculators. Electronic devices, however, are most conveniently constructed to use the base two rather than ten. A number expressed in base two, however, is difficult to interpret and it is necessary either to translate into the decimal system or to use an octal (base eight) or hexadecimal (base 16) system. For example (see 13), the binary expression for the number 2793 is actually a shorthand for the coefficients multiplying the appropriate powers of 2 (see 14), but one may express it octally by grouping this expression into threes—101, 011, 101, 001—and interpreting each group as an octal digit. Octally the number is 5351, as can be found by multiplying the digits in this expression by powers of 8 and adding (see 15).

When exceedingly large or small quantities occur, it is convenient to introduce the floating point notation. A positive quantity can be expressed as a number between one and 10 multiplied by a power of 10. Examples are easily constructed (see 16).

An alternate to the floating point notation has been developed in the form of prefixes. One of these prefixes, when applied to a unit, will describe a new unit with a value that is a power of 10 times that of the original unit. For example, kilo is the prefix associated with 10^3 so that a kilometre (km) is a unit of a thousand metres. The internationally adopted set of metric prefixes are those shown below:

tera (T),	10^{12}	centi (c),	10^{-2}
giga (G),	10^9	milli (m),	10^{-3}
mega (M),	10^6	micro (μ),	10^{-6}
kilo (k),	10^3	nano (n),	10^{-9}
hecto (h),	10^2	pico (p),	10^{-12}
deca (da),	10	femto (f),	10^{-15}
deci (d),	10^{-1}	atto (a),	10^{-18}

GEOMETRICAL AIDS

Applications of geometry. Egyptian geometry was primarily constructive. It enabled straight lines to be laid out and measured and allowed for the construction of perpendiculars. The sides of the Great Pyramid, built about 2700–2300 BC, agree in length to within 0.01 per-

(8)	$\begin{cases} \alpha & \beta & \gamma & \delta & \epsilon & \varsigma & \eta & \theta \\ 1 & 2 & 3 & 4 & 5 & 6 & 7 & 8 & 9 \end{cases}$
(9)	$\begin{cases} \iota & \kappa & \lambda & \mu & \nu & \xi & o & \pi & \varphi \\ 10 & 20 & 30 & 40 & 50 & 60 & 70 & 80 & 90 \end{cases}$
(10)	$\begin{cases} \rho & \sigma & \tau & \upsilon & \phi & \chi & \psi & \omega & \lambdabar \\ 100 & 200 & 300 & 400 & 500 & 600 & 700 & 800 & 900 \end{cases}$
(11)	$\begin{cases} \alpha & \beta \\ 1{,}000 & 2{,}000 \end{cases}$
(12)	$\begin{cases} & \beta \\ M & M \\ 10{,}000 & 20{,}000 \end{cases}$

cent, and the angular errors of the corners do not exceed 12 seconds of arc.

The development of mathematics as a logically structured science occurred in the century or two before Euclid, between 500 and 300 BC. This mathematics permitted a better formulation of geographical and astronomical information as is evidenced by a considerable increase in understanding of these subjects. Aristotle (350 BC), for instance, described the Earth as spherical, and it was customary to assume that the fixed stars were on a larger sphere that rotated once a day, around an axis approximately through the North Star. The seven heavenly bodies, the Moon, Venus, Mercury, Sun, Mars, Jupiter, and Saturn, were described as moving between these. These motions were described mathematically. In the system of the 4th-century-BC Greek astronomer and mathematician Eudoxus of Cnidus (*q.v.*) a body was carried on the equator of a rotating sphere with a system of other rotating spheres, all of which were concentric with the Earth. In the system of the Greek astronomer Ptolemy (about AD 150), a body was believed to move in a circle the centre of which moved on a geometric circle. There were variations of these ideas that were regarded as empirical approximations.

These ideas, however, generated a considerable interest in trigonometry (see GEOMETRY, ANALYTIC AND TRIGONOMETRIC) and in particular in spherical trigonometry. Hipparchus (born 180 BC) worked out a table of chords as functions of angles and dealt with the theory of the projection of a sphere onto various planes, as, for example, the stereographic and gnomonic projections.

A number of estimates of the radius of the Earth were made in ancient times, the most famous of them being that of the Greek scientist Eratosthenes (flourished 3rd century BC). At the summer solstice, the Sun was directly overhead at Syene, a city in the south of Egypt, and had a meridian angular distance from zenith, at Alexandria, as determined experimentally by Eratosthenes, of 0.02 of a full circle. He assumed that these points were on the same meridian and thus the latitude difference was $7°12'$. The distance between the points was measured by professional pacers, and Eratosthenes concluded that the diameter was about 7,850 miles—about 76 miles less than the equatorial diameter as measured by modern methods.

Greek mathematics was limited in a number of ways and there were problems that they could not solve within their original frame of reference. They did, however, invent procedures that foreshadowed later mathematical developments, in particular, the infinitesimal calculus. Thus the problem of duplicating the cube was solved mechanically by Archytas (428–347 BC) and the curve of Hippias, which required a continuous mechanical construction, was used to trisect angles and "for squaring the circle." Archimedes used his knowledge of the mechanical principle of the lever to obtain heuristic evaluations of areas such as that bounded by an arc of a parabola and the corresponding chord. These evaluations were then justified by the method of exhaustion. Archimedes' mental model of the cylinder in relation to the sphere and the cone (Figure 1) is an early example of the value of the model in abstract thinking.

Instruments for observation and navigation. The value given by Ptolemy for the distance to the Moon was correct to about 3 percent, but the crude procedures for measuring angles used by the ancients yielded solar system distances that were far too small. The meridian line at an observatory could be obtained by a plumbline (the line determined by a string supporting a weight) and line of sight of the North Star. This method could also be used for surveying land. The azimuth (angular position on the horizon) of a body as it rose or set could be obtained by line-of-sight angle measurements relative to a horizontal circle. Zenith angular distances were obtained by a device called a quadrant, a representation of a quarter circle with a movable arm pivoted at the centre along which the observer could sight. In use, the quadrant was suspended in a vertical plane, and the object, the zenith angular distance of which was to be observed, was sighted along the movable arm. The quadrant then indicated the

Limitations of Greek mathematics

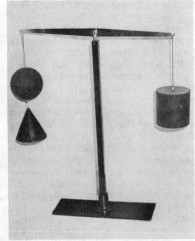

Figure 1: Model of Archimedes' theorem, showing how a balance of physical masses is used to motivate the formulation of or verify the truth of a famous mathematical relationship between the volumes of a sphere, a cone, and a cylinder.
By courtesy of the Museum of Science and Industry, Chicago

angular difference between this arm and a plumbline direction. Another ancient instrument was the planisphere, a disk with a scale of angle measure marked on its rim and having a sighting arm pivoted at its centre.

Optical instruments based on the telescope, however, were needed to obtain angular measurements precise enough to yield correct ideas concerning the size of the solar system. These devices were introduced in the early part of the 17th century and were associated with the acceptance of the concept of the solar system in which the Earth and other planets move around the Sun. This was first suggested by the Polish astronomer Nicolaus Copernicus in 1543. For navigation purposes, the horizon is a more convenient reference than a plumbline, and the sextant was invented by Thomas Godfrey of Philadelphia in 1730 to measure angular height above the horizon, which is complementary to the zenith angular distance of an object.

Invention of the sextant

The sextant determines the angle of elevation of an object. Figure 2 indicates a cross section of the instrument when held vertically. A sighting telescope T is aimed at the half-silvered piece of glass, H, which permits one to view the horizon through it and establish the instrument in a vertical plane. The component H is mounted at an angle to the line HT so that the point I is reflected in the mirrored half of H into the telescope. An upper mirror is mounted on an axis, through I, perpendicular to the plane of the diagram and has a pointer to indicate a reading on the scale OG. When the plane of the upper mirror is parallel to that of H, a point on the horizon, A, will be reflected at I to H and then to T, and the pointer indicates 0 on the scale OG. If the upper mirror is rotated through an angle x, the normal (perpendicular) n to the upper mirror makes an angle $\phi + x$ with IH and thus the point S will be reflected at I to H if SI also makes the angle $\phi + x$ with n. Thus the angle SIH has the value $2\phi + 2x$, and because AIH has the value 2ϕ, then SIA has the value $2x$. SIA, however, is the angle of elevation of S; hence its value can be read on the scale OG, which is calibrated to show $2x$. The maximum range of the scale OG corresponds to $x = 60°$ of arc—i.e., a sixth of the circle—hence the name sextant.

Astronomical assistance to navigation is based on the use of ephemeris information. For a given celestial object, say, a star, the ephemeris is the location, as a function of time in latitude and longitude, of the point on the Earth's surface for which the object is at zenith. The navigator uses the sextant to determine the angle of this object with the zenith. This determination yields the location of his vessel on a small circle of the Earth the centre of which is the ephemeris point and the angular radius of

Use of the ephemeris tables

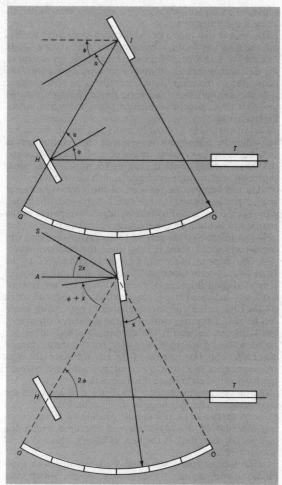

Figure 2: *Design of sextant.*
(Top) Plane of mirror *I* parallel to that of half-silvered glass *H*.
(Bottom) Plane of *I* rotated through an angle *x* (see text).

mapped onto concentric circles; these two families will yield a coordinate network for the plane. The value of the gnomonic map lies in the fact that the arcs of great circles on the Northern Hemisphere are mapped onto straight lines in the plane. This correspondence can be seen by intersecting planes through the centre of the sphere with the hemisphere and with the tangent plane. Thus the great circle course between two points on the hemisphere can be plotted by taking the two image points on the plane and drawing the straight line through these points. This permits the latitude and longitude of the division points on the course to be obtained. Similarly, a rhumb line course can be obtained from a Mercator map. This map, named after Gerardus Mercator, a Belgian mathematician and geographer, who first published the map in 1568, represents longitude as the abscissa (horizontal axis); the ordinate (vertical axis), however, is a function of latitude chosen so that straight lines correspond to rhumb line courses on the sphere. It is possible to obtain distances along a rhumb line course by a relatively simple approximate procedure.

Other projection maps can be used to solve triangles in spherical trigonometry. There are maps that yield good approximations for distances that are relatively small and good angular information for polygons of small diameter. Two such types are the Lambert conical projection and the polyconic maps of the United States Coast and Geodetic Survey.

Modern procedures for topographical mapping are based on aerial photography and the determination with great accuracy of specified reference points. The aerial photographs overlap and a stereo-optical system, a technique of photogrammetry, can position these so that one has a model of the topography and the overflight on the scale of the photographs. Measurements on the photographs and trigonometry can be used to determine heights. This system, involving the stereo-optical positioning of the photographs and measurements, was replaced in the 1960s by the digital analysis of photographs using electronic photodetectors and a computer.

Spherical trigonometry.   Modern spherical trigonometry is based on a set of formulas analogous to the formulas of plane trigonometry. Plane trigonometry is based on certain geometrical relations for solving the triangle with sides *a, b, c* and opposite angles *A, B, C*. These relations are the law of sines (see 17) and three relations in the form of generalized Pythagorean theorems (see 18) applying to non-right triangles. In a spherical triangle, the sides *a, b,* and *c* are arcs of great circles and can be measured by the angles subtended at the centre. The radian measure of these angles would correspond to the length of the arc, if the radius had unit length. There are corresponding relations in the spherical case (see 19).

In both the planar and spherical case, the basic trigonometric identities are used to transform these formulas into forms suitable for the use of logarithms (see ARITHMETIC). Because tables of high accuracy are available, they permit astronomical problems to be accurately solved. The development of this form of trigonometry occurred in the 17th and 18th centuries.

Some of the possible geometrical approaches to spherical trigonometry were given by Ptolemy. One procedure was to perform a rotation so that a desired angle could be constructed in a specified plane and thus be obtained by plane geometry. Another method was to map the sphere onto a plane by a projection that takes circles into circles or into curves that can be plotted effectively. An impor-

which is the observed zenith angle. The procedure is to obtain two such position circles and the appropriate intersection by graphical means on a chart. The ambiguity is resolved by using dead reckoning (estimation), and further geometrical adjustments may be necessary if the observations are not simultaneous. This procedure illustrates the importance of ephemeris tables and a precise determination of time. These tables required a tremendous amount of calculation and to a degree are responsible for the association of astronomy with calculation.

Mapping.   There are two aspects of the problem of mapping. One of these is to indicate the longitude (the angular distance between the points of the equator intersected by the meridians through Greenwich and the point in question) and latitude (the deviation of the visible celestial pole) of points of interest. The second problem is to establish the topography; *i.e.,* the height above sea level. The first problem is that of mapping an ideal sphere onto a plane surface. There can be no such map that preserves all distances, but there are maps that permit geometrical constructions of use in the trigonometry of the basic sphere. A specific application, however, may require more than one map.

For example, to plot a ship's course or an airplane's course between two points on the Earth, the arc of the great circle joining the two points is found and divided into smaller segments, each of which can be efficiently approximated by a course in which a constant angle or bearing is maintained with the northern direction. This is known as a rhumb line course.

Gnomonic maps   To obtain great circle courses, a gnomonic map may be used. This map is a projection of the sphere from its centre onto a tangent plane. If the point of tangency is the north pole, then the meridians are mapped onto lines radiating from the pole, and the circles of latitude are

$$(17) \qquad \frac{a}{\sin A} = \frac{b}{\sin B} = \frac{c}{\sin C}$$

$$(18) \qquad c^2 = a^2 + b^2 - 2ab \cos C$$

$$(19) \qquad \frac{\sin a}{\sin A} = \frac{\sin b}{\sin B} = \frac{\sin c}{\sin C}$$

Nomographic projection

The astrolabe

The vernier

tant example of this is the stereographic projection in which the sphere is projected from its south pole onto the equatorial plane.

The gnomonic projection of the sphere and the stereographic projection have been mentioned. A third type, the nomographic projection, is given by projecting a hemisphere on its basic plane by lines perpendicular to the base. The radius of the hemisphere is taken to be one. Given a point P on the base circle of the hemisphere, certain great circles of the hemisphere will pass through P. If the plane of such a circle makes an angle α with the base plane, the circle is projected on an ellipse with major axis vertex at P and minor axis $\cos \alpha$. The small spherical circle with centre P and radius β is projected on a straight line perpendicular to the radius for P and at a distance $(1 - \cos \beta)$ from P. Given P_0, a representation of the basic circular disk can be obtained in which these two sets of projected curves are used as coordinate lines. It is convenient to mark the angle β along the circumference of the disk. A transparent overlay for the disk may also be prepared with a representation of a similar coordinate system with origin designated Q.

This combination of disk and overlay with their coordinate systems permits the solution of spherical triangles graphically. For example, the side a and the angles β and γ are given. The overlay is placed relative to the disk so that the arc QP_0 has the value a. QP_0 is taken to correspond to the side BC of the triangle. For the overlay, at $Q = B$, the elliptic arc is chosen corresponding to β and at $P_0 = C$, the elliptic arc is chosen corresponding to $180° - \gamma$. The arc QP_0 and portions of these two arcs correspond to the projection of a spherical triangle with side a and angles β and γ. The intersection of the two elliptical arcs is the projection of the remaining vertex of the desired triangle, and the other coordinates will yield the lengths of the sides c and b. A similar construction will yield, given three sides, two angles of a spherical triangle.

Stereographic projections and the astrolabe.   The stereographic projection can be applied to the celestial sphere of the fixed stars, which appears to revolve around the North Star once a day. A stereographic mapping is taken of this celestial globe on its equatorial plane. During 24 hours, each star traces a circle on this map, and if the position is marked for each hour, a 24-hour clock is produced. Different stars will have different longitudes at the same time so that the markings will have different orientations. Furthermore, because the Sun advances on the celestial sphere one revolution per year, the set of markings for each star must uniformly rotate so as to make one complete revolution a year. For one night, however, the markings can be considered as fixed.

To read this clock, an instrument like a quadrant is used and the zenith angle of the star is determined. The zenith angle determines a spherical circle around the zenith. This circle is projected onto an ellipse in the equatorial plane by the stereographic projection. The star is then on the intersection of the ellipse and the polar circle, which is the projected path of the star. Such intersections are usually found by having one set of curves on a chart and the other set on a transparent overlay.

The stereographic projection is also the basis of the astrolabe. In its simplest form, this instrument can be regarded as consisting of two disks. The basic disk, called the mother, has a representation of the stereographic projection of geometric aspects of the sphere of the observer such as

1. The direction lines: north, east, south, and west.
2. Various circles of latitude, particularly the celestial equivalent of the Tropics of Cancer and Capricorn and the Equator.
3. The projections of the zenith circles, corresponding to number of degrees. These projections are called Almicanteras and are dependent on the latitude of the place at which the astrolabe is used. The largest of these corresponds to 90°; *i.e.*, the horizon.
4. The projections of 24 equally spaced great circles through the zenith, the azimuths.

Other geometric curves are also on the mother, but these are typical. The reverse side of the mother was usually arranged as a planisphere with a sighting arm to permit angular measurements.

The second disk, the rete, also called the spider web, is attached to the mother by a pin so that it can rotate around the north pole. It is a stereographic projection of the celestial sphere at an instant of time. It contains the projection of the ecliptic circle and the zone of the zodiac with the constellations and their limits. The rete offered an irresistible space on which to engrave fanciful astrological figures.

The astrolabe can be used in many fascinating ways, but basically the instrument represented the relationship in time between the celestial sphere of the Sun and stars and the Earth's fixed local directions of north, east, west, south, up, and down. For example, if the date and the time of day are known, the position of the various heavenly bodies can be found. On the rete is a pointer, the label, which can be adjusted so that its edge corresponds to the position of the Sun on the ecliptic circle. The label is then held fast relative to the rete and the edge of the label will correspond to 12 noon if it is along the northern direction. The edge of the label can then be considered as the hand of a 24-hour clock and the combined rete and label is rotated until the edge of the label indicates the time of day. Any indicated star is the position of a fiducial mark on the rete, and its position in azimuth and zenith angle can be read from its position on the mother. Conversely, the label can be set for the current date and either the zenith angle or azimuth of a star (or the Sun) can be observed. The rete can then be rotated until the star representation is in the observed position; the edge of the label will then indicate the time of day.

The procedure of obtaining the location of a star on the stereographic map has another application inasmuch as a position on the star circle can be considered as determining the sum of the longitude and the time within the sidereal, or star, day. If the time is known, this will yield the longitude.

Other antique instruments that are associated with Ptolemaic astronomy are the armillary sphere, which contains a simplified model of the Ptolemaic solar system, and the torquetum, which contains a sighting arm mounted on the equivalent of the equatorial mounting, permitting measurements of latitudes and longitudes on the celestial sphere.

Optical instruments.   Geometry was used initially for terrestrial measurements, such as the height of towers and the distance of ships off shore, either by the trigonometric tables or by similar triangles. The astrolabe had a U-shaped rule to permit the use of similar triangles to determine heights. The use of the telescope to establish accurately a line of sight permitted the development of instruments to measure angles more precisely. Another advance was the use of the vernier, invented in 1631 by a French mathematician, Pierre Vernier, which permits an accurate interpolation between the marks on a graduated scale. The standard surveying instrument is the theodolite (transit), which consists of a telescope mounted so that angles of azimuth and elevation can be obtained. A modern development is the use of a telescopic camera to permit fast observation and improved accuracy.

For small angles, which are of considerable interest in astronomy, a number of hairline optical instruments were developed, which were supplemented later by photographic procedures. To assist navigation, observatories correlate the celestial longitude with time. The transit telescope, a telescope mounted so that it can rotate only in the meridian plane, is used to determine the instant at which a given star passes the meridian. To correlate with modern timekeepers, other photodetectors can be used to note the instant the star is dimmed by the hairline. In another system, interpolation is used in a series of photographs.

The equatorial mounting for a telescope has a basic axis parallel to the axis of the Earth and a rotating axis perpendicular to this basic axis. This mounting permits measurement of celestial longitude and polar distance or their use to position the telescope. The vertical circle, the modern descendant of the astrolabe, will yield zenith angular distances and is equivalent to mounting a transit telescope on a vertical axis. There is an analogous type of device for measuring azimuths.

Drawing instruments. Drawings and diagrams are plane geometric figures that are used for a variety of purposes. Correspondingly, the family of drawing instruments has been developed: pens, straight edge, graduated rule, a variety of compasses for different size circles, T-squares and triangles to draw lines at given angles to one another, dividers to transfer lengths, and French curves to draw curves in a smooth fashion. In addition, the hinged quadrilateral for drawing parallel lines, the pantograph to reproduce figures on a different scale, the ellipsograph to draw ellipses based on the sum-of-distances property, and protractors all facilitate drawing. A number of these instruments are also combined into multiple function drafting machines.

So-called mechanical-drawing engineering (see DRAFTING) uses cross sections, drawings or diagrams showing materials by a code of cross hatching and cross section shapes. Such drawings show the appearance of the objects as seen from a single viewpoint. Geometrically, a drawing is a projection of the object from the point of view onto a plane not containing a line of sight. The theory of such drawings is developed in the discipline entitled descriptive geometry, which is significant not only for engineering and architecture but also for the arts of painting and sculpture. The use of perspective, a valuable technique for painting from the Renaissance on, was based on geometric principles formulated in the early 15th century by Brunelleschi, a Florentine architect.

(F.J.M.)

MATHEMATICAL MODELS

In general, the purpose of a mathematical model is to aid or simplify the description of mathematical ideas. Many mathematical models are three-dimensional equivalents of mathematical relationships that cannot easily be understood or conveniently expressed in symbolic form. Models are seldom used in mathematics to prove hypotheses, although they may serve to open up new channels of thought by clarifying difficult concepts.

Construction of models. The methods of construction of mathematical models depend very much upon the purpose for which they are required. Models in which only the external structure is to be examined can be made from opaque materials such as cardboard, wood, plaster, etc. If, however, internal structure is to be investigated without dismantling the model, the external surfaces will necessarily be made of transparent materials such as glass or clear plastic. Alternatively, they can be represented by wire, or, as in the case of ruled surfaces (formed by the motion of a straight line), by a network of stretched threads. This latter method of construction can be used, for example, to illustrate the different sections of a cone. The curved surface of the cone can either be made of a transparent material or, more simply, by a series of threads from apex to base depicting generators in the curved surface.

Solid wooden models can be constructed so that they dismantle along certain sections chosen for study (Figure 3). Sectional properties, other than general shape, include such things as area, degree of symmetry, similarity with other sections, curvature, etc. This method of construction can also be used to show how a particular solid shape may be formed from a number of smaller units. Shapes that are symmetrical about any axis can, in general, be formed by turning a block on a lathe, the surface profile being checked at intervals with a template until the final shape is produced. These can then be used as templates for molding plaster or metal replicas if required. Non-symmetrical shapes are more conveniently formed using wire skeletons or by slotting together a cross-grid of cardboard templates, the profiles of which represent the corresponding sections of the solid shape. The more closely spaced these templates are with respect to the size of the solid, then the greater is the definition of the external surface. Surfaces represented by an orthogonal grid (grid composed of curves that intersect only at right angles) of this

Figure 3: Conic sections shown in an expanded wooden model of a cone that is cut along four planes. The intersections of the planes with the surface of the cone define, from top to bottom, cases of the circle, the ellipse, the parabola, and the hyperbola.
By courtesy of Bayard Rankin

type are particularly useful for modelling quantities that are always mutually perpendicular, such as equipotentials and flow lines, which are to be found in many branches of physics.

Models may be constructed also by the use of computer graphics (see below), in which surfaces are composed of lines or dots and viewed stereoscopically to give the illusion of three dimensions. The technique is particularly useful when a mathematical configuration is animated (*e.g.*, the representation on three dimensions of a rotating, four-dimensional figure).

Simple polyhedra and the sphere. A polyhedron is a solid shape the surfaces of which consist of polygonal faces; *i.e.*, planes with three or more edges. By a simple polyhedron is meant a polyhedron with no holes in it. Such a surface could be transformed continuously into the surface of a sphere. The 18th-century Swiss mathematician Leonhard Euler was the first to discover that for a simple polyhedron, if the number of faces be designated

Computer models

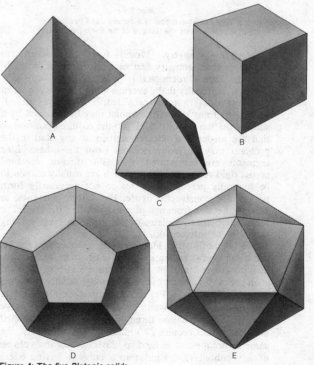

Figure 4: *The five Platonic solids.*
(A) Tetrahedron; (B) cube (hexahedron); (C) octahedron;
(D) dodecahedron; (E) icosahedron.

The five
Platonic
solids

by F, edges by E, and vertices by V, then the following relationship always holds: $V - E + F = 2$. For large polyhedra of this type, it is difficult to verify this property by counting F, E, and V from an isometric drawing (*i.e.*, a nonperspective projection), whereas the task is made much easier by using a model. By experimenting with such models, it can also be shown, as was known to the abstract thinkers of Plato's time, that there are only five regular polyhedra (the faces of which are all congruent and the angles at the vertices are all equal), namely, the cube, tetrahedron, octahedron, icosahedron, and dodecahedron (see Figure 4). These polyhedra are called the five Platonic solids.

Solid models of the sphere can be used to clarify such concepts as spherical triangles and geodesic lines (shortest arc between any two points on the surface), while wire skeleton models of a sphere may be used to study navigation problems on the surface of the Earth, angles of latitude and longitude being measured between elastic threads appropriately positioned on the model (see Figure 5).

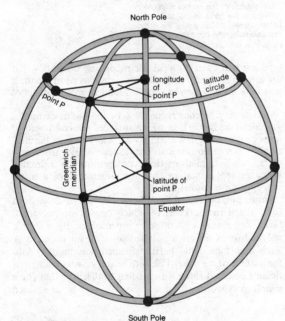

North Pole

longitude of point P

latitude circle

point P

Greenwich meridian

latitude of point P

Equator

South Pole

Figure 5: Wire skeleton model of a sphere used to study navigation problems on the surface of the Earth (see text).

Descriptive geometry. Models for use in descriptive and projective geometry find much application as teaching aids. Three-dimensional trigonometric problems present much difficulty to the average school pupil even when well-drawn diagrams are provided. A model has the advantage that any desired viewpoint may be obtained by a simple rotation of the model into the required position so that the angles and lines concerned at any step in the problem may be easily isolated from the others. Line segments are represented by elastic threads stretched across rigid reference planes, which are usually chosen to be mutually perpendicular but do not necessarily form part of the constructed figure. For certain purposes, as when projecting from one plane to another, it is useful to represent planes by plates of clear plastic hinged along their line of intersection.

Models that illustrate identities. Wooden cubes (blocks) are often useful to represent units of quantity, particularly to young children. Apart from the idea of number, such cubes can also be used to demonstrate such concepts as area and volume. For instance, if it were desired to demonstrate geometrically that $3^3 = 27$, then a large cube of edge-dimension three units would be constructed and this would require 27 unit cubes. Alternatively, the same technique can be used to illustrate how the volume of any cuboid (*i.e.*, similar to a cube in having edges mutually at right angles, but not all of the same length) is calculated from its edge dimensions. Blocks can also be

used to verify more involved identities such as the cubic identity for real values of two numbers a and b (see 20). This may be verified for positive values of a and b by arranging together a set of wooden cuboids the volumes of which are described on the right-hand side of this identity in such a way as to construct a large cube of edge dimension $(a + b)$ units. This model is better known as the binomial cube. When it is required to compare or verify the volumes of certain geometrical figures, it is also possible to use hollow shapes with an open face so that water may be decanted from one shape to another so as to provide a measure of volume. This method may be used, for example, to show that the volume of any pyramid is equal to one-third that of a prism with the same base area and vertical height.

$$(20) \qquad (a+b)^3 = a^3 + 3a^2b + 3ab^2 + b^3$$

$$(21) \qquad z^2 = 1 - x^2 - y^2$$

Topological models. Topology is a branch of geometry concerned with general transformations of shapes in which a certain correspondence between points is preserved. A general form of topological transformation is a deformation. Deformations can be shown conveniently using models of pliable materials such as clay or malleable plastic in which a basic shape may easily be molded into other shapes that are topologically equivalent; *i.e.*, having the same number of holes in the solid or the same degree of interlocking as the original.

Another field of topology that can be investigated using models concerns itself with one-sided surfaces. The simplest of such surfaces, named after its discoverer, the 19th-century German August Ferdinand Möbius, is known as a Möbius strip (Figure 6). It can be formed by pasting together the ends of a rectangular strip of paper after giving one end half a twist. By cutting such a strip along its centre line, it is found that a single strip is formed with a two-sided surface.

The
Möbius
strip

Another rather interesting one-sided surface, on which it is possible to move from the inside to the outside without crossing a boundary, is known as the Klein bottle, which is named after the 19th–20th-century German mathematician Felix Klein.

By courtesy of the Museum of Science and Industry, Chicago

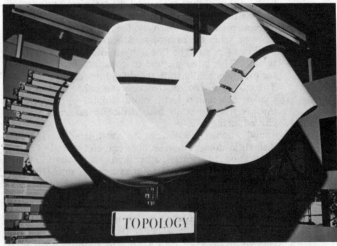

TOPOLOGY

Figure 6: Möbius strip model on which is an electrically controlled car. The motion of the car traces a closed path over the entire surface, without crossing a boundary, illustrating a basic topological property.

Surface models. Mention has already been made of the various ways in which surfaces may be represented. Elastic threads can be usefully employed for representing ruled surfaces, as for example, hyperboloids of revolution. If the boundary discs of such a model are constructed so as to rotate relative to one another, then a dynamic surface can be obtained, which passes from the curved surface of a circular cylinder to the limiting position of a double cone, intermediate positions giving various hyperboloids of revolution. Vertical threads stretched across horizontal bars that rotate relative to one another along a central vertical axis generate hyperbolic paraboloids. Thread models can be used for the most varied and beautiful surfaces (Figure 7).

Figure 7: *Thread model of a surface.*
The surface is generated by stretching threads tightly from segment to segment of a wire frame that is held in the form of a helix by a plastic cylinder.

Wooden models may be more generally used to illustrate the shapes of solids formed by the revolution of simple curves (those that do not intersect themselves) about any chosen axis. In addition to these solids of revolution, this form of model can also be used to construct three-dimensional graphs of functions defined by two independent variables. The surfaces of such graphs

Figure 8: *Stationary points on a model of the intersection of a cylinder with a hyperboloid.*
From the model it can be deduced that there are exactly four points (two not visible) on the intersection of the two surfaces that are nearest the centre of symmetry, and four points that are farthest.

are known as quadric surfaces, as, for example, the surface of a unit sphere, which may be defined with reference to the three orthogonal axes x, y, and z (see 21). Points common to two or more quadric surfaces can be deduced from models (Figure 8). Examples of less symmetrical quadric surfaces include topographical maps and three-dimensional graphs of certain physical functions such as the relationship between volume, temperature, and pressure for a fixed mass of gas.

Many minimal surface problems may be demonstrated using wire models and soap films. One classic example of this is concerned with the solution of a problem posed by the Belgian mathematician Joseph Antoine Ferdinand Plateau (c. 1830), namely, to find the surface of least area bounded by a given closed contour in space. By considerations of the condition giving minimum surface energy, it can be found that soap films naturally tend to form connecting surfaces of least area between the edges of a wire frame dipped in a soap solution (Figure 9). This fact enables Plateau's problem to be solved for general contours because a wire frame may easily be bent into the desired shape.

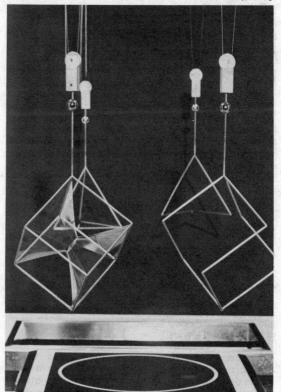

Figure 9: *Soap film model with wire boundary controlled to dip automatically into a vat of soap.*
The different boundary structures and surface tension of the soap film combine to yield minimal surfaces, the precise mathematical description of which is accomplished with the calculus of variations.

Kinematic models. There are a certain number of models that illustrate mathematical concepts in both pure and applied mathematics and that rely on the motion of one or more parts of the model during the demonstration (other than the thread models used for illustrating dynamic surfaces). Applied mathematics lends itself well to models of this kind because a large proportion of the subject concerns itself with the motion of bodies through space. The law of conservation of momentum, for example, is demonstrated effectively by a model known as Newton's cradle. This consists of a number of suspended steel balls of equal mass that are constrained to swing in their plane of contact and may be caused to collide with one another in a number of different ways. One such model is composed of five suspended balls, labelled one to five from left to right. If ball number one is swung out and released, for instance, it causes ball number five to swing outward without affecting the intermediate balls, and the motion would be exchanged between these two until the energy of the system is dissipated.

If physical phenomena are governed by mathematical laws that are not overcomplex, it is possible to construct kinematic models that illustrate with much clarity the underlying mathematical ideas. A kinematic model of the laws of celestial mechanics that govern the motion of planets in the solar system can be constructed (Figure 10).

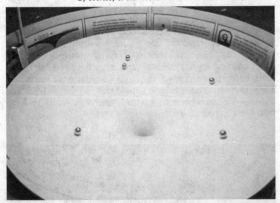

Figure 10: Celestial mechanics illustrated with a dynamic model in which the force (gravity of the Earth acting upon steel balls) and the rolling surface combine to cause an orbital motion that is similar to the motion of the planets about the Sun. When the balls are further from the centre (top), the motion is slow, as with Pluto and Neptune; when they are in an orbit of smaller diameter (bottom), the motion is more rapid, as with Venus and Mercury.

The concept of a convergent geometric series may be demonstrated to a good degree of approximation by means of a rubber ball constrained to bounce vertically within a loose fitting glass cylinder. A geometric series is a progression of numbers in which each term is obtained from the preceding one by multiplying by a constant quantity known as the common ratio; *e.g.*, 1, 2, 4, 6, 8 · · · , etc. If the numerical value of the common ratio is less than unity then the series is said to be convergent; *i.e.*, the sum of a very large number of terms approaches a finite limit. In the case of a ball bouncing vertically, the heights that the ball attains on successive bounces approximates well to the terms of a convergent geometric series and the limit of its sum will be half of the total distance that the ball travels before coming to rest.

The motion of particles in a more random fashion than the latter may be employed in models that visibly represent statistical distributions. Figure 11, for instance, shows a model that may be used to generate a curve in the form of a binomial distribution. Marbles are allowed to drop down a vertical board into which pegs have been inserted to form a grid in the shape of a rectangle. The design of the grid is such as to guide the marbles according to a statistical law, which is binomial, and is illustrated graphically by the way in which, after a large number of trials, the marbles fill the slots provided at the base of

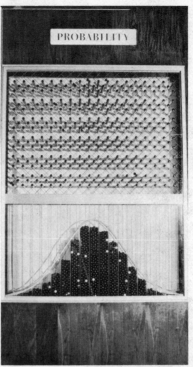

Figure 11: Probability distribution model, a prototype of the basic dispersion of random components of position that results in the binomial distribution. In this model, balls drop one after the other from the top and migrate at random through a maze of pegs to one of the lower channels. In the limit of many trials, the density of probability is described by the continuous curve known as the density function of the normal distribution.

the grid. In the limit of many trials the binomial distribution of probability can be seen to be approximated by the normal density function (see PROBABILITY, THEORY OF). (Ed.)

ALGEBRA AND LOGARITHMS

Algebraic notation. Modern elementary algebra is concerned with solving problems about numbers by reasoning and using a convenient notation that has been developed over many centuries. The numbers and operations on them are represented by letters and symbols ($+$, $-$, $\times$, $\div$) and statements about them are expressed in equation form. An unknown quantity can then be represented by a letter (traditionally x) and logical reasoning can be applied (to the statements in the form of equations) by manipulating the equations according to rules until equations are obtained which yield the values of the quantities desired.

A considerable amount of ancient non-geometrical mathematics deals with problems to which this process is immediately applicable. The Ahmes manuscript is an example, but there are many others, Egyptian, Mesopotamian, Roman, Arabic, Hindu, and Chinese. The problem is generally stated in a form in which an unknown quantity is stated as the number of a certain kind of thing (for example, loaves of bread, soldiers, bricks), and the desired property is expressed in terms of this particular situation.

It is clear also that the problem giver wishes to imply a greater generality by analogy. In general, the answer is then given by a description of the process by which it is computed. Compared to the modern process, this is equivalent to giving the first equation and then the last and omitting the intermediate reasoning steps.

It is conceivable that the intermediate process as used in antiquity was supplied by some imaginary experience with the specific situation described or it may have been obtained by trial and error or a combination of these. It was, unquestionably, not done by a sequential deductive argument.

In the case of false position, an intermediate step was supplied. When the initial information was given in a homogeneous form, a nominal value was assigned to the unknown initially and then was corrected after this value had been substituted in the equivalent of the initial equation.

In the geometry of Euclid, many constructions are equivalent to algebraic processes and include methods equivalent to solving the various cases of quadratic equations. The logic is that an analogy is established between the unknown quantity and a line segment or other geometrical quantity, and then a reasonably complete deductive discussion is possible. This analogy permits such concepts as square roots to be expressed.

Hindu mathematics emphasized computations, and systematic procedures for passing to the value of an unknown quantity were given in the work of Āryabhaṭa I (born AD 476). Brahmagupta (born AD 598) had systematic abbreviations for the arithmetical operations, including the square root, and for unknown quantities. Hindu computational procedures were adopted by the Arabs, and they were aware of many algebraic aspects of the Indian work; but they also tended to favour Greek geometric procedures for algebra. In the 16th century, Italian mathematicians solved the cubic and biquadratic equations by essentially algebraic methods; but modern notation is a later development.

Development of modern notation

The French mathematician François Viète, in the latter half of the 16th century, used letters of the alphabet to denote quantities and the plus $(+)$ and minus $(-)$ signs. The sign for equality and for the square root were also in use at this time. The multiplication signs, $\times$ and $\cdot$, and parentheses appeared in the period 1600 to 1630, and the division sign, $\div$, about 1660. The use of exponents for positive powers is due to Descartes in 1637, but the more general case of negative and fractional powers is due to the English mathematician John Wallis in 1655 and Newton in 1676. It must be admitted, however, that when these notations were introduced they were, in most cases, in competition with other notations and the standardization was really a process of the 18th century.   (F.J.M.)

Logarithms. *Basic principles.* Logarithms were invented in the early 17th century to speed up calculations, and they were basic in numerical work for more than 300 years. The perfection of the desk calculating machine in the late 19th century and the electronic computer in the 20th has made them obsolete for large-scale computation.

The operation and nature of logarithms can be seen from a table characteristic of logarithms (see 22) that identifies with the number ½ the logarithm -1, with the number 1 the logarithm 0, with the number 2 the logarithm 1, with the number 4 the logarithm 2, and so forth. Here, the constant 2 raised to any logarithmic power gives the corresponding number. A table of this type can be used for multiplication (and division)—the logarithms of the numbers to be multiplied are taken and added and the number corresponding to the answer is the result of the multiplication. For example, two numbers are taken from the first row and multiplied together; say, $2 \times 8 = 16$. The corresponding values in the second row are 1, 3, and 4; hence, when 2 is taken to the 4th power, 16 is yielded.

The reason for this is that numbers in the first row are the number 2 to the power of the corresponding number in the second. Thus $⅛ = 2^{-3}$, $1 = 2^0$, $8 = 2^3$. In the identity $32 = 2^5$ the number 2 is called the base. The exponent 5 is the logarithm of 32 to the base 2 and is written $5 = \log_2 32$. More generally, the two equations have the same meaning; the first serves to define the second. By this definition y is the logarithm of x to the

$$(22) \quad \begin{cases} \tfrac{1}{8} & \tfrac{1}{4} & \tfrac{1}{2} & 1 & 2 & 4 & 8 & 16 & 32 & 64 \\ -3 & -2 & -1 & 0 & 1 & 2 & 3 & 4 & 5 & 6 \end{cases}$$

$$(23) \quad \log_b mn = \log_b m + \log_b n$$

$$(24) \quad \log_b (m/n) = \log_b m - \log_b n$$

$$(25) \quad \log_b(n^p) = p \log_b n$$

$$(26) \quad \log_b \sqrt[q]{n} = \frac{1}{q} \log_b n$$

$$(27) \quad \log_b \sqrt{n} = \tfrac{1}{2} \log_b n$$

$$(28) \quad \begin{cases} b^x \cdot b^y = b^{x+y} \\ b^x/b^y = b^{x-y} \\ (b^x)^p = b^{px} \end{cases}$$

$$(29) \quad \begin{cases} m = b^x, & \log_b m = x \\ n = b^y, & \log_b n = y \end{cases}$$

$$(30) \quad mn = b^x b^y = b^{x+y}$$

$$(31) \quad \sqrt[q]{b^x} = b^{x/q}$$

base b if and only if $x = b^y$. The number x is also called the antilogarithm of y to the base b.

It is evidently easy to find logarithms of numbers that are simple powers of the base, and there are quite efficient methods for calculating logarithms of all numbers to as many decimal places as desired.

Use of logarithms for multiplication

Multiplication of any numbers m and n can be accomplished by adding their logarithms; *i.e.*, the logarithm of the product is the sum of the logarithms (see 23). Division of numbers can also be accomplished by subtracting the logarithms: the logarithm of the quotient is the difference of the logarithms (see 24). This is not all; powers and roots can also be found with logarithms. For example, the cube of 4 is 64 (*i.e.*, $4^3 = 64$), and from the table the logarithms of 4 and 64 are 2 and 6. Because $6 = 3 \cdot 2$, the logarithm of 4^3 can be found by multiplying the logarithm of 4 by 3. Study of the table will verify that the logarithm of a power can be found by multiplying the logarithm of the number by the index p of the power (see 25). Because logarithms transform multiplication into addition, division into subtraction, and the taking of powers into multiplication, it might be guessed that they would transform the taking of square roots into division. This is the case, for example, in computing the square root of 16, its logarithm (which is 4) is divided by 2. The result is 2, which is the logarithm of 4 as expected. In general, the logarithm of a root is the logarithm of the number divided by the index q of the root (see 26). Because $n^{1/2} = \sqrt[2]{n}$, square roots are given in the logarithmic form as ½ the logarithm of the number for which the square root is being taken (see 27). Logarithms work this way because they are exponents; and exponents are added for multiplying, subtracted for dividing, multiplied to take a power, and divided to take a root. These ideas may be expressed as laws of exponents (see 28).

The exponents in these equations can be thought of as logarithms. For example, a variable may be expressed as a power of a base (see 29), and another variable may be expressed as a power of the same base. Their product (see 30) is similarly expressible in terms of a sum. Therefore, $\log_b mn = \log_b m + \log_b n$, the relationship for the addition of logarithms (see 31).

Common logarithms. The most convenient tables for numerical calculations are those in which the logarithms are to the base 10. These are called common logarithms. They have the advantage that a table of logarithms of numbers between one and 10 can be used to find the logarithms of all other numbers. For example, from tables, $\log_{10} 2.41$ is 0.38202 (this means that $10^{0.38202}$ is 2.41; fractional powers of 10 can be found and tabulated;

$$(32) \quad \begin{cases} 2 \cdot 41 \times 10 \\ \log_{10} 24 \cdot 1 = \log_{10}(2 \cdot 41 \times 10) \\ \qquad\qquad = \log_{10} 2 \cdot 41 + \log_{10} 10 \end{cases}$$

$$(33) \quad y = \log_b x$$

$$(34) \quad e = 1 + \frac{1}{1!} + \frac{1}{2!} + \frac{1}{3!} + \cdots + \frac{1}{n!} + \cdots$$

$$(35) \quad \frac{d}{dx}\log_b x = \frac{1}{x}\log_b e$$

$$(36) \quad \frac{d}{dx}\log_e x = \frac{1}{x}$$

$$(37) \quad \log_e(1 + x) = x - \frac{x^2}{2} + \frac{x^3}{3} + \cdots$$

$$(38) \quad \log_b x = \log_a x \log_b a$$

$$(39) \quad \log_{10} x = \log_e x \log_{10} e$$

see below). The logarithm of 24.1 can then be found because 24.1 is expressible as a number between two and three times 10 (see 32). Because $\log_{10} 10 = 1$, the logarithm of 24.1 is 1.38202. Thus each common logarithm has two parts, an integer and a decimal less than one. The integral part is called the characteristic and is determined by the position of the decimal point in the number. Thus the log of 241.0 is 2.38202 and its characteristic is 2; for 2.41 the characteristic is 0, for 0.241 it is −1, and for 0.00241 it is −3. The decimal part of a common logarithm is called the mantissa and is found from a table of logarithms by disregarding the position of the decimal point in the number.

When the characteristic is negative it cannot be written with the minus sign in front of the mantissa without causing confusion. For example, the log of 0.00241 has a mantissa of 0.38202 and characteristic of −3. It cannot be written −3.38202 because it is, in fact, −3 + 0.38202 (not −[3 + 0.38202]). It is customary to write it in the form $\bar{3}.38202$.

Natural logarithms. The logarithmic function, in algebra, is defined by the relationship that identifies y with the logarithm of x (see 33). The problem of finding its derivative involves the problem of finding the limit of an expression of the form $(1 + t)^{1/t}$, as t approaches infinity. This limit is an irrational number e given by the infinite series that sums the reciprocals of factorials (see 34), in which a factorial is a product of consecutive integers beginning with 1 and ending with the integer whose factorial is being taken. The number e has a value approximated by 2.71828, given here to five decimal places. This result leads to the equation that expresses the derivative of the logarithm to an arbitrary base (see 35). If logarithms to the base e are used, the equation simplifies to the form basic to calculus, expressing the derivative of the logarithm of x as the reciprocal of x (see 36).

Logarithms to the base e are sometimes called natural logarithms. They are less useful for computation than common logarithms but are used in calculation frequently in terms of the series for the logarithm of $1 + x$ (see 37). In this way natural logarithms can be computed to any required degree of accuracy. Common logarithms can then be obtained by a change of base using the formula that converts from one logarithmic base to another through the operation of multiplication of logarithms (see 38); this follows from the law of exponents. Thus a common logarithm of x is found by the equation that identifies it with the natural logarithm times a constant (see 39). (Ed.)

History of logarithms. The invention of logarithms was foreshadowed by the comparison of arithmetic and geometric series. In the simple table used above, the top line is a geometric series and the bottom line is an arithmetic series. The first table based on this concept was published in 1620 in Prague by Joost Bürgi. The comparison between the two series was not based on any explicit use of the exponential notation; this was a later development.

John Napier, the Scottish mathematician, published his discovery of logarithms in 1614. His purpose was to assist in the multiplication of quantities that were then called sines. The whole sine was the value of the side of a right angled triangle with a large hypotenuse, say 10^7 units long. His definition was given in terms of relative rates.

The logarithme, therefore, of any sine is a number very neerely expressing the line which increased equally in the meene time whiles the line of the whole sine decreased proportionally into that sine, both motions being equal timed and the beginning equally shift.

In modern terminology, L is the logarithm and X the sine. (In modern notation X would be $r \sin \phi$.) Thus, with modern techniques derivatives can be used (see 40). At $t = 0$, $X = r$ ($\phi = 90°$), and, since the motion is "equally swift" at the beginning, $a = br$. Furthermore, the function L is known to have certain values at specific points (see 41). Thus in terms of present logarithms to the base e the function L can be expressed in terms of natural logarithms (see 42). Napier's value of r was 10^7. This expression does not have the expected property for $L(XY)$, but the relationship involving products and division (see 43) does apply.

In cooperation with the English mathematician Henry Briggs, Napier did adjust his logarithms into the form in which it is usually found. For the modern Naperian logarithm (*i.e.*, the logarithm to the base e) the comparison would be between points moving on two straight lines, marked in units of length, the L point moving uniformly from minus infinity to plus infinity, the X point moving on a half line from zero to infinity at a speed proportional to the distance from zero. Furthermore, L is zero when X is one and their speed is equal at this point. The essence of Napier's discovery is that this constitutes a generalization of the relation between the arithmetic and geometric series; *i.e.*, multiplication and raising to a power of the values of the X point correspond to addition and multiplication of the values of the L point. In modern terminology, $\frac{dL}{dt} = k_0$, $\frac{dX}{dt} = k_0 X$ correspond to $\frac{dX}{dL} = X$, $X = e^L$, $L = \log_e(X)$.

From the point of view of the user it is better to limit the L and X motion by the requirement that $L = 1$ at $X = 10$ in addition to the condition that $X = 1$ at $L = 0$. This produces the common logarithms to the base 10. These

The modern Naperian logarithm

$$(40) \quad \frac{dh}{dt} = a, \qquad \frac{dX}{dt} = -bX$$

$$(41) \quad \begin{cases} L = 0 \quad t = 0 \\ i.e., L(r) = 0 \quad \frac{dX}{dt} = \frac{-aX}{r} \end{cases}$$

$$(42) \quad \begin{cases} L(x) = r(\log_e r - \log_e x) \\ L(x) = r \log_e \frac{r}{x} \end{cases}$$

$$(43) \quad L\left[\frac{XY}{Z}\right] = L(X) + L(Y) - L(Z)$$

$$(44) \quad \begin{cases} \log\left[\frac{\sin x}{x}\right] \\ \log\left[\frac{\tan x}{x}\right] = \log\left[\frac{\sin x}{x}\right] - \log \cos x \end{cases}$$

are sometimes known as Briggsian logarithms: the natural logarithms are known as Naperian logarithms.

The calculation of logarithms. The treatment above differs from that of Napier in that the word "exactly" is applicable rather than "very neerely." This obscures the ingenious procedure used for calculating the early logarithms, in which powers of numbers such as 1.00001 were used so that multiplication was minimized and replaced by addition. Thus, $X = (1.00001)^n$, $L = n/10^5$ corresponds approximately to $L = \log_e X$, or the natural logarithm. To obtain the Briggs or base 10 table, the calculation would be continued until X exceeded 10 and then the L scale adjusted so that at $X = 10$, $L = 1$.

In addition to the discrete series procedure, Napier and Briggs suggested the calculation of logarithms by extracting roots of 10; *i.e.*, $\log \sqrt{10} = 0.5$, $\log 10^{1/4} = 0.25$. This permits the n computation of the previous paragraph to be shortened, for the Briggs logarithm can be adjusted for by taking $L = 0.25$ for $X = 10^{1/4}$. Power series were not used in the initial construction of the tables. The power series for $\log(1 + x)$ and e^x were only available in the 18th century and rigorously established in the early 19th century.

Logarithm tables. Napier died in 1617. Briggs published a table of logarithms to 14 places of numbers from 1 to 20,000 and from 90,000 to 100,000 in 1624. Adriaan Vlacq published a 10-place table for values from 1 to 100,000 in 1628, adding the 70,000 values. Both Briggs and Vlacq engaged in setting up log trigonometric tables. Such early tables were either to $\frac{1}{100}$ of a degree or to a minute of arc. In the 18th century tables were published for 10-second intervals, which were convenient for seven-place tables. In general, finer intervals are required for logarithmic functions in which the logarithm is taken of smaller numbers; for example, in the calculation of the functions log sin x and log tan x. The related functions modified by division by x in the argument of the logarithm (see 44) are easily calculated by series for small values of x.

The availability of logarithms greatly influenced the form of plane and spherical trigonometry. Convenient formulas are ones in which the operations that depend on logarithms are done all at once. The recourse to the tables then consists of only two steps. One is obtaining logarithms, the other obtaining antilogs. The procedures of trigonometry were recast to produce such formulas.

Slide rules. If a scale of numbers is taken and the values of their logarithms marked on a parallel scale, then a logarithmic scale is produced. In 1620 Edmund Gunter plotted logarithms on a two-foot straight line. With such scales multiplication and division were performed by addition and subtraction of lengths by a pair of dividers. William Oughtred, between 1620 and 1630, used two such scales sliding by each other to obviate the use of dividers. These were the forerunners of the C and D scales found on the modern slide rule. They can also be used in circular and cylindrical form. The linear slide rule may have to be reset to stay on scale, but this does not occur with the circular slide rule. Circular slide rules, however, are more difficult to make. The first known slide rule in which the slide worked between a fixed stock was made by Robert Bissaker in 1654.

Basic slide rule scales — The fundamental scales for a slide rule are the C and D scales in which 1 to 10 correspond to the full available interval in the linear slide rule or a circumference in the circular case. The scales A and B for squares are obtained by having the L length corresponding to x so that the full interval corresponds to 1 to 100. Thus, x on the D scale will be associated to $y = x^2$ on the A scale. Similarly, there is a K scale for cubes. In the centre of Figure 12 is a mid-20th-century example of a two-faced slide rule on which the K, A, and D scales are visible, as well as the S and L scales discussed below.

There may also be a facility for obtaining sines. A number of schemes are possible. There may be a single S scale on which angles are given from 34' to 90° and the sine of this angle is read on the A scale, with the maximum value of the latter corresponding to one. A variation of this is to use two S scales for the angles. One S scale lists angles

from 34' to 5°45', with the corresponding sine given on the D scale corresponding to the x interval 0.01 to 0.1. A second S scale lists angles from 5°45' to 90° with the sine on the D scale for 0.1 to 1. The tangent can also be given by two scales. For angles between 34' and 5°45', the S scale can also be used to yield tangents, with a maximum error of about one part in 200 at the very end of the scale. The second tangent scale would have angles from 5°43' to 45° and be read on the D scale for 0.1 to 1.

A log scale L may be explicitly given and a log log scale for computation with powers. A log log scale is divided into lengths that are proportional to the logarithms of the logarithms of numbers. The sliding scale has a logarithmic scale. This innovation was made by Peter Roget in 1815. Another possibility is for D and A scales replaced by log π. These yield the circumference or area of a circle from its diameter or radius in a single setting. For trigonometric purposes, a P scale is sometimes included, the value y corresponding to x on the D scale by the relation $y = \sqrt{1 - x^2}$.

Another possible shape for the slide rule is obtained by permitting the edge on which the body and slide meet to be wrapped around a cylinder so that this edge has the shape of a helix. This permits an expanded interval length and greater accuracy. The usual cylindrical slide rule is based on a folded scale principle and uses two coaxial cylinders (say D and C cylinders). The D scale is divided into a number, k, of parts of equal length and each part is laid on an element of the D cylinder; *i.e.*, on a surface line parallel to an axis. These k elements are equally spaced around the D cylinder. The C scale is set up similarly on the C cylinder. The C cylinder can be displaced along the axis of the D cylinder or rotated relative to the D cylinder around the axis by multiples of 360° k. The effect of this arrangement can be similar to that of a circular slide rule of circumference equal to k times the element length. A cylindrical slide rule designed in the 19th century and called a Thacher Calculating Instrument is shown at the top of Figure 12.

Slide rules can serve many purposes beside logarithmic calculation and can consequently assume many forms. A design of the 1970s is composed of two relatively slidable members held together by a third member that acts as a cursor (Figure 12, bottom). Contemporary uses for slide rules besides the familiar arithmetic operations in-

By courtesy of Bayard Rankin

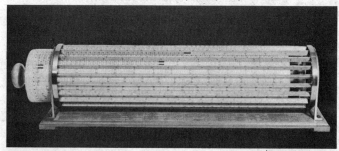

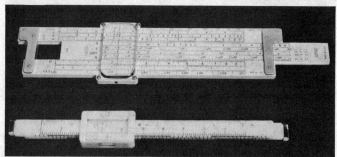

Figure 12: *Slide rules.*
A 19th-century cylindrical design (top), called a Thacher Calculating Instrument, was basically for multiplying and dividing; a mid-20th-century design (middle) is inscribed with logarithmic and trigonometric scales on both sides of a tongue and groove system; a 1970 design (bottom), composed of two relatively slidable members held together by a cursor, is inscribed with scales for generating random numbers.

clude the generation of random numbers as is the case with the last illustrated slide rule.

TABLES

Integral tables. If $y = f(x)$ is a given function, defined and positive for $a \leq x \leq b$, the definite integral of the function f from a to b (see 45) is defined by a numerical procedure as a limit of a sum in the integral calculus. The numerical value coincides with the area under the curve, $y = f(x)$, between $x = a$ and $x = b$. Many problems, such as finding the volume or surface of a solid of revolution or finding the length of an arc of a curve, can be reduced to evaluating a definite integral.

Archimedes developed procedures for evaluating areas equivalent to definite integrals and the Italian mathematician Bonaventura Cavalieri (1635) generalized the method of Archimedes. Although it did not possess an adequate logical basis, this method yielded correct results in a number of cases including the functions $y = x^n$. The calculus of Newton, however, yielded a much more general way of evaluating definite integrals, the method of indefinite integrals. A function $F(x)$ the derivative dF/dx of which equals $f(x)$ is called the indefinite integral or anti-derivative of $f(x)$. For such an anti-derivative, the so-called quadrature formula identifies the difference of F evaluated at two distinct points with the definite integral of f integrated between the same points (see 46).

$$(45) \quad \int_a^b f(x)\, dx$$

$$(46) \quad F(b) - F(a) = \int_a^b f(x)\, dx$$

In elementary calculus, methods are given for differentiating functions, including the so-called elementary functions, which include the algebraic, trigonometric, and exponential functions and functions composed of these. The derivative of an elementary function is also elementary; Joseph Liouville, however, showed that not all elementary functions are themselves derivatives of elementary functions. For example, $y = \exp(x^2)$ and, in general, square roots of cubics and biquadratics that can not be simplified are not derivative of elementary functions. In view of the quadrature formula, it became desirable to present tables of functions and their anti-derivatives. Examples of such tables are those of Peirce and of Dwight.

In general, when a function $f(x)$ has an anti-derivative, the methods of the integral calculus will yield the anti-derivative, and these tables present the result. When the anti-derivative is not an elementary function, however, it may still be possible to find the definite integral for certain values of a and b. Usually this requires advanced methods of analysis. A compilation of such results was made by D. Bierens de Hahn and published in 1858 and 1864.

The Monte Carlo method. In addition to definite integrals relative to one variable, there are definite integrals of two or more variables that are limits of weighted sums taken over areas or regions in the space of the variables. These definite integrals are, theoretically, reducible to the equivalent of integrating the process of taking integrals of one variable; and when the one variable process of integrating by finding anti-derivatives can be carried out, the problem is solved. There are many important cases in statistics, quantum mechanics, and in technology, however, in which this process is not applicable. According to the original definition of these multi-dimensional integrals, the computation required in many cases is excessive even when large-scale digital computers are available. The procedure adopted to handle this problem is to use a statistical interpretation of these integrals as the mean value of a chance variable and perform the computational analogue of an experiment in probability. This Monte

Carlo method was introduced after World War II and can be performed on a slide rule (if speed is not required) or on large-scale digital computers.

The basis of a probability experiment in a digital computer is the choice of a random number. A random number is a sample value in a sequence of statistically independent random variables. It is erroneous to believe that the intermediate digits in a long calculation are distributed randomly; for example, if a number is raised to a high power, using a floating point notation (*i.e.*, no decimal point), the sixth digit of the power may be considered to be random. But this is true only in a qualitative way. The term pseudo random numbers has been ascribed to these numbers because they do not represent the true random numbers of probability theory. Tables of true random numbers have been obtained experimentally and are available for Monte Carlo experiments. Specially designed analogue computers and slide rules have also been designed to yield random numbers (see above *Slide rules*).

Fourier series and transforms. In 1807, in his treatise on heat, Fourier proposed that an arbitrary function $f(x)$ of one variable can be expressed as a series composed of a constant and a linear expression for a trigonometric function (see 47), in which the coefficients are the definite integrals expressed in terms of the given function multiplied by trigonometric functions (see 48). The function $f(x)$ is either considered to be periodic or defined only for $-\pi \leq x \leq \pi$. This raised many questions, especially in connection with the earlier efforts of d'Alembert to analyze the vibrations of a stretched string, and is responsible for the development of much of what is termed modern analysis. Because the coefficients are given by definite integrals, the previously described tables may apply.

Thus a function $f(x)$, considered on the interval $-\pi \leq x \leq \pi$, is equivalent to two sequences of numbers: a_1, a_2, $\cdots$, b_0, b_1, $\cdots$ in the sense that $f(x)$ yields the numbers by means of the formulas using the definite integrals and the numbers yield $f(x)$ by the series expression. The equivalent of this can be obtained on any interval of finite length by a change of variable.

If, however, $f(x)$ is considered on the infinite interval $-\infty < x < \infty$, it is associated with another function $g(x)$ rather than with two sequences of numbers. The function $g(x)$ is called the Fourier transform of $f(x)$, and the relations between $f(x)$ and $g(x)$ are usually expressed by complex exponentials rather than by trigonometric functions (see 49). This concept of the Fourier transform is highly significant in many diverse fields, including mathematicial analysis, electrical circuit theory, statistics, and mathematical physics.

Because of the needs of mathematical physics, especially in quantum mechanics, the notion of the Fourier transform has been generalized to apply to a wider class of objects than functions. These objects are called distributions, and tables of distributions and their Fourier transforms appear in works on distribution theory, quantum mechanics, partial differential equations, and abstract linear spaces. For electrical circuits, an analogous transform, that of Laplace, has proved most useful and tables of these transforms appear in works on this topic.

$$(47) \quad f(x) = \tfrac{1}{2} b_0 + \sum_{n=1}^{\infty} (a_n \sin nx + b_n \cos nx)$$

$$(48) \quad a_n = \frac{1}{\pi} \int_{-\pi}^{\pi} f(x) \sin nx\, dx, \quad b_n = \frac{1}{\pi} \int_{-\pi}^{\pi} f(x) \cos nx\, dx$$

$$(49) \quad \begin{cases} g(x) = \dfrac{1}{\sqrt{\pi}} \displaystyle\int_{-\infty}^{\infty} f(y) \exp(ixy)\, dy \\[2ex] f(x) = \dfrac{1}{\sqrt{\pi}} \displaystyle\int_{-\infty}^{\infty} f(y) \exp(-ixy)\, dy \end{cases}$$

$$(50) \quad y'' + \omega^2 y = 0$$

The great practical importance of the Fourier coefficients and the Fourier transform has led to the invention of many specialized devices to perform the computations needed for their use, including the evaluation of convolution integrals.

Function tables. The mathematical procedures for handling the theories of gravity, heat, elasticity, fluid flow, electromagnetism, and quantum mechanics are based on solving or manipulating partial differential equations. The problems that are mathematically solvable are limited but of great importance. Certain techniques are based on Fourier transforms, but there is another process that reduces the problem to one involving ordinary differential equations by a method called separation of variables. The ordinary differential equations that appear in this process have as solutions functions of one variable, which have been studied intensely. Usually a parameter, a variable that distinguishes special cases, is involved in the equation; for example, ω in the second-order differential equation that describes basic vibrational problems (see 50).

These functions are analytic in general except for certain characteristic singularities. Numerical integration procedures for the differential equations have been developed and the results tabulated. Tables of these functions have been produced by the British Association for the Advancement of Science and by the Works Progress Administration in the United States.

At present, emphasis is on procedures for generating the functions in large-scale digital computers. In certain cases the procedures are used during a calculation. For example, it is more efficient to generate the values of the trigonometric functions in the computer when required than to retain stored values. Electronic computers may also function on the basis of a logarithmic routine for multiplication. Special techniques for approximating functions over fixed intervals by polynomials have been developed using values of the functions. Computers have also been used to produce tables in printed form, the typescript being set automatically by the computer, or by an intermediate punched card stage.

Mathematical tables. Printed mathematical tables are widely used in statistics, science, technology, business, numerical analysis, and investigations into number theory. Many types are available. An example of comprehensive tabular publication is the work that was published in 1964 by the National Bureau of Standards, of the United States, which was a result of a conference on mathematical tables considered in the light of electronic computers, held at the Massachusetts Institute of Technology, Cambridge, in 1952.

Tables used in statistics contain probability distributions, such as the normal, binomial, Raleigh, Student t (named after an anonymous journal contributor), and χ^2 distributions. In science and technology tables of functions are used, in particular the trigonometric, exponential, elliptic, Bessel, and Mathieu functions. There are also listings of the coefficients of polynomials, such as the Chebychev, Legendre, and Laplace polynomials, and the coefficients of series expansions.

Several types of tables are available for financial purposes. For example, tables can be obtained giving principal amounts earning compound interest, or uniform mortgage payments for specified interest rate and repayment period.

Another type of numerical table is used in number theory; for example, a table of all primes (numbers factorable only by itself and one) less than 11,000,000. There are also tables for computation purposes, such as tables of binomial coefficients, or tables of powers of two for use with binary computers. Numerical procedures such as interpolation and the step by step integration of differential equations are assisted by tables of coefficients.

GRAPHS AND GRAPHICAL PROCEDURES

Graphs. A common method of expressing a relation between two variable quantities is by a Cartesian graph (named after René Descartes). A Cartesian axis system consists of two mutually perpendicular lines usually called, respectively, the x and y axes. The coordinates of a point are obtained by projecting perpendicularly on these axes and assigning values by means of a scale on the axes. If $f(x)$ is a function of x, then for a value of x there will be a y value, $y = f(x)$, and the function $f(x)$ is graphed by marking the points with these coordinates, x, y. Such a graph permits the ready appreciation of certain characteristics of the function. Also a number of different functions can be readily compared by their graphs.

Another graphing method is represented by using polar coordinates. A point O is chosen as origin and a ray OA is also chosen. If P is a point in the plane, it has two polar coordinates, ρ, θ, in which ρ is the distance PO and θ is the angle POA. Polar graphs can be effectively used to represent functions of the time, which appears as the angle variable, whereas the radial distance, ρ, corresponds to the other variable, say, temperature. Such functions can be recorded as a polar graph by having the graph itself rotated around its origin by clockwork or by a synchronous electric motor to give an angular displacement with time, and by having the quantity to be recorded produce a linear, radial displacement of a recording pen. Cartesian graphs can be obtained by displacing a diagram in the x direction and displacing the pen in the y direction. There are commercial output devices for digital computers, in which numerical information from the computer determines both the x and y displacement of a recording pen or a beam in a cathode-ray tube.

Frequently the information recorded is of the type in which a y value is assigned to an x value only for discrete values of x. If the number of x values is relatively small, it is customary to use bar graphs, in which the quantity is represented by a rectangle of fixed base and variable height, and variables can be compared by placing the bar graphs side by side. This method is often used for quantities available on an annual basis; for example, amounts of imports, amounts of a specific crop, populations, etc. If a given quantity is made up of a sum of other quantities, these others can be indicated by shading rectangles in the graph. The last effect is also obtained by a disk graph, in which the subquantities are indicated by wedges.

Scales. It is clear that nothing is essentially changed if the values that are marked on the axes are not proportional to the distances from the origin but more or less arbitrary scales are used. Points, the coordinates of which satisfy a given equation, can be plotted as before and a curve can be drawn from which corresponding values can be read. The form of the curve can be altered and in some cases simplified. These notions were developed by Léon Lalanne in his *Anamorphose logarithmique* (1842) and further advances were made by J. Massau and Charles Lallemand in the 1880s. A basic idea is to use such scales that the graphs of the equations under consideration become straight lines, which are easy to draw. The equation that restricts a linear relationship in a function of x and a function of y (see 51) in which a, b, c are constants, becomes a straight line in an X, Y plane (see 52) if the distances X and Y along the axes to the marks x and y are determined by functions (see 53).

(51)	$af(x) + bg(y) + c = 0$
(52)	$aX + bY + c = 0$
(53)	$X = f(x), \qquad Y = g(y)$
(54)	$mY = nX + \log a$

Well-known examples based on this principle are the commercial logarithmic and semilogarithmic papers. The former papers use the scales $X = \log x$, $Y = \log y$ and are convenient for plotting the graphs of relations of the form $y^m = ax^n$. Because this may be written $m \log y = n \log x + \log a$, the graph on this paper is a straight line (see 54). The semilogarithmic papers have the scales of

(55) $\quad X = x, \qquad Y = \log y$

(56) $\quad x^2 + y^2 = z^2$

(57) $\quad X_3 = \tfrac{1}{2}(X_1 + X_2)$

(58) $\quad h(z) = f(x) + g(y)$

(59) $\quad X_1 = f(x), \qquad X_2 = g(y)$

(60) $\quad \log z = \log x + \log y$

which one is linear and the other is logarithmic (see 55). They are useful in plotting the results of experiments in which one quantity is an exponential function of the other.

A logarithmic scale can also be used to compare quantities of greatly varying size. An example of this is the line scale for the frequency of electromagnetic waves, in which the frequency of interest ranges from less than 1 hertz to 10^{19} hertz.

Another example of the use of line scales is that of graphic tables, in particular for logarithms. These serve the same purpose as the usual logarithm tables and are published in book form. In the main part of the text, a long line is depicted, broken up into segments with each segment extending the width of the text on the page. There are about 25 segments to a page. On this long line there are two scales. The upper scale gives a number N from 1 to 10, the lower scale gives the corresponding logarithm L from 0 to 1. For five-figure accuracy, a line of approximately 106 metres in total length is used. This indicates a resolution of the order of one millimetre.

(F.J.M.)

Alignment charts. The word nomogram is sometimes restricted to a special type of chart that is used by bringing the points of three scales into alignment. There is an alignment chart for the solution of a quadratic equation in three variables (see 56). On the upper and lower horizontal lines are laid off from a vertical axis the scales $X_1 = x^2$, $X_2 = y^2$ identical with those on the axes. Midway between is a line with a scale half as large, $X_3 = z^2/2$. Now let a straight line be drawn across the figure cutting the scales at points marked x, y, and z. It is seen from elementary geometry that the third coordinate is the arithmetic average of the first two (see 57), whence the equation $x^2 + y^2 = z^2$ is satisfied. The equation is solved for one of the variables by joining given values of the other two variables on the scales by a straight line and reading the solution where this line cuts the third scale.

Charts for solving equations with three variables

A chart for solving any equation containing three variables can be made in a similar manner provided the variables can be segregated into three separate terms so that a function of one variable is equal to the sum of two functions each of single variables (see 58). It is necessary merely to plot the scales that are identified with the two summed functions (see 59) on the outside lines and one-half the sum of the two functions on the middle line. Thus, a scale for multiplication, $z = xy$, could be made after first writing the equation in the form of a linear relationship between logarithms (see 60), the three plotted scales then being logarithmic.

This type of chart has certain obvious advantages. Only three scales need be drawn, and they are more easily used than a complicated diagram. Interpolation can be accurately done since the line cuts cleanly across the scale. As a practical matter the line across the chart should not be actually drawn because a few lines in pencil would mar the chart. A fine thread may be stretched across the chart. An excellent line may be stretched on a transparent ruler with the point of a knife, a little graphite being worked in to give it visibility, and this can be laid across the chart.

The principle of the alignment chart was first described in 1884 by Maurice d'Ocagne of the École Polytechnique in Paris. He developed the subject in many papers and books and particularly in his treatise of 1899, *Traité de nomographie*, in which were brought together both the general theories and a multitude of practical applications. D'Ocagne may properly be called the creator of nomography.

In its more general forms the alignment chart for the solution of an equation in three variables may employ straight scales arranged in various ways, or one or more of the scales may be curved. A curved scale may be constructed from parametric equations $X = f(t)$, $Y = g(t)$. A value of t gives a point (X, Y) on the curve. Points for suitably spaced values of t are marked and the value of t is attached. Thus, $X = \cos t$, $Y = \sin t$ gives a circular scale, since $X^2 + Y^2 = 1$. Whether the resulting scale is curved or straight depends upon the parametric equations.

Two functions of a variable x, two functions of y and two functions of z can form three scales: an x scale $X_1 = F(x)$, $Y_1 = f(x)$; a y scale $X_2 = G(y)$, $Y_2 = g(y)$; and a z scale $X_3 = H(z)$, $Y_3 = h(z)$. Three points (X_1, Y_1), (X_2, Y_2), and (X_3, Y_3), corresponding to readings x, y, and z, respectively, on the three scales lie on a line if the slope of the line joining the first two points is equal to the slope of the line joining the last two points (see 61). This condition may be put in a form involving the functions of the problem (see 62) or as a determinant (see 63). The chart will solve this equation for one of the variables when the other two are known. Conversely, an alignment chart can be made for any equation that can be written in this form.

If an equation can be solved by an alignment chart, it can be solved by an infinitude of alignment charts and by applying projective transformations (see 64).

(L.R.F.)

Planimeters. The design of a planimeter involves the production of a set of diagrams or drawings. A ship may be described by two sequences of vertical and one sequence of horizontal cross sections. A metal part for a machine may be given by longitudinal or cross sectional diagrams. Design or performance objectives such as the displacement of the vessel or the kinetic energy of a flywheel require the evaluation of certain physical characteristics of the device. Normally, these physical characteristics include volumes, areas, centres of gravity, moments, and moments of inertia. The theory and approximations of the integral calculus will yield these quantities, provided certain definite integrals associated with the diagrams can be evaluated. The quantities of interest may be defined as definite integrals of two or more dimensions, but by using Green's theorem and similar results, the evaluation can be reduced to the evaluation of one-dimensional line integrals in many important cases.

The advantage of the use of line integrals is that the quantities y and x on which the integral depends can be entered into a calculating device by tracing the curve. During the 19th century, a number of types of devices were developed for evaluating line integrals by tracing curves on a drawing board.

(61) $\quad \dfrac{Y_2 - Y_1}{X_2 - X_1} \dfrac{Y_3 - Y_2}{X_3 - X_2}$

(62) $\quad F(x)[g(y) - h(z)] + G(y)[h(z) - f(x)] + \\ \qquad + H(z)[f(x) - g(y)] = 0$

(63) $\quad \begin{cases} \begin{vmatrix} F(x) & f(x) & 1 \\ H(z) & h(z) & 1 \\ G(y) & g(y) & 1 \end{vmatrix} = 0 \end{cases}$

(64) $\quad X' = \dfrac{a_1 X + b_1 Y + c_1}{a_3 X + b_3 Y + c_3}, \qquad Y' = \dfrac{a_2 X + b_2 Y + c_2}{a_3 X + b_3 Y + c_3}$

(65) $\quad z = \int f(x)\, dx$

The ro-
tational
planimeter

One type, the rotational planimeter, was based on the disk integrator, a device in which a flat disk turns by an amount x, and a wheel driven by the disk is mounted on an axis parallel to the plane. This wheel is keyed to the axis so that its rotation is transferred to the axis, but it can be displaced an amount y along this axis. In the integrating devices, the flat disk is rotated an amount x, while the wheel is displaced an amount y, that is the function of x; i.e., $y = f(x)$. The rotating disk drives the wheel so that the rotation of the keyed shaft gives an integral z of $f(x)$ (see 65). This type of device appeared early in the 19th century and was used initially for graphical integration but later on was incorporated into other computing devices such as the mechanical differential analyzer (see below *Multipliers*).

Another type of graphical integrator was a tricycle device that could move on two balls and a steering wheel. If this device is subject to a force that is not large enough to make the wheel skid and that is applied so that the wheel will not pivot about its point of contact, the device will move instantaneously in the direction of the plane of the steering wheel. If this direction is controlled so that the slope of the curve described is the y coordinate of a given curve, the curve will also correspond to an indefinite integral. This is the principle used in the integraph of Bruno Abdank Abakanowicz and described by him in 1889.

The three-wheel design has been used in more elaborate devices to solve differential equations such as those governing the motion of a charged particle moving through a two-dimensional magnetic field (Figure 13). In a design of this type, the equations to be solved can be shown to be equivalent to $H\rho = k$, in which H is the local magnetic field, k is a constant, and ρ is the local radius of curvature. For the analogue device to operate, it is required only that the angle of the steering wheel, as the device moves over the graphical representation of the field H, be restricted to equal ρ in the above equation.

By courtesy of Bayard Rankin

Figure 13: Mechanical particle, so called because it is a particle trajectory plotter that is used to compute, by analogue methods, the orbits of charged particles in a two-dimensional magnetic field. The angle of the front wheel, if controlled according to a mathematical formula that relates to the magnetic field lines (visible), determines that the pen (between the rear wheels) draws the solution to the equations of motion.

The flat disk of the disk integrator can be replaced by any surface of revolution, provided the rotational wheel is maintained in contact with the surface. For example, a sphere can be rotated about a pole and a wheel so mounted that its displacement corresponds to colatitude. If the sphere is considered as rotating around its north pole, the take-off wheel can be mounted on a piece that has essentially the shape of a great circle and that rotates around an axis through the equator. Computation is made in the following way. The wheel axis is mounted on a pivot so that the motion of the point of contact is along a circle of latitude. If the wheel displacement is u and the sphere rotates an amount, v, the rotational output is proportional to the integral of $\sin u$ with respect to v.

Using these mechanical principles, drawing board devices have been set up to evaluate Fourier coefficients. Harmonic analyzers, based on tracing drawing board graphs, are commercially available.

The third type of planimeter is the polar planimeter invented by Jakob Amsler in 1858. The device is remarkably simple from the mechanical and operational point of view. It consists, usually, of two hinged pieces associated with an anchor piece and a scribe to follow a closed curve. On one of the hinged pieces is an integrating wheel. When a wheel is moved along a curve in a plane so that the normal to the path makes an angle α with the plane of the wheel, then the total rotation of the wheel is proportional to the integral of the $\sin \alpha$ with respect to s. It is also true that if a line segment is moved in the plane so as to return to its original position with total rotation zero, then the areas enclosed by the motion of the end points can be related to this integral. The anchoring arrangement usually ensures that the area enclosed by one end either is zero or has a fixed value.

The polar
planimeter

$$(66) \qquad dA = \ell \sin\alpha\, ds + \tfrac{1}{2}\ell^2\, d\varphi$$

The motion of a line segment PQ of length l is considered. The point P moves along a curve with differential of arc ds. The symbol α denotes the angle between PQ and the tangent to the curve, and the total rotation of PQ from a fixed position is ϕ. The change of area for an infinitesimal motion is given by a differential that can be analyzed into two component differentials, one for arc length and one for total rotation (see 66). It follows that if a motion is such that the original position is returned to $\phi = 0$, then the algebraic area covered is l times the integral with respect to s of $\sin \alpha$.

Graphics. A number of relatively simple devices establish the direction of a curve at a point or, what is equivalent, the direction of the normal. For example, if a mirror has an edge on the drawing board that crosses the curve at the point, the curve will appear to have a corner unless the mirror edge is along the normal to the curve. A triangular prism can also be used in a similar fashion, with one face on the drawing board.

One current development in the use of automatic data processing is termed computer graphics. This is a procedure by which a computer does the equivalent of drawing diagrams, producing the drawing on a cathode-ray tube. An operator controls the production of the drawing by a combination of button pushing and use of a light pen (a device that may be used to alter the display on a cathode-ray tube; see COMPUTERS). For example, the operator is able to cause a line segment to appear in the drawing by pressing a specific button and then activating the light pen at two points on the face of the cathode-ray tube corresponding to the desired end points. The completed drawing can be produced either on a plotting device or photographically.

Computer
graphics

Computer graphics permits the development of engineering drawings by the original designer without the intervention of other people, and the consequent manpower and time saving is economically significant. Another advantage is that the diagram is mathematically described in the computer, and procedures of numerical analysis can be directly applied to yield the various integrals discussed above.

ANALOGUE COMPUTATION

Mathematical analogues. The extraordinary expansion of the physical sciences and technology that began in the 18th century involved mathematical formulations in an essential manner. Questions in understanding and on the design and operation of devices could be expressed mathematically in terms of analytic concepts such as ordinary or partial differential equations, Fourier series or transforms, systems of linear algebraic equations, or definite integrals.

The mathematical problem that appears in a physical study may require a lengthy computation. Alternatively it may be impractical or impossible to solve it directly as a mathematical problem. The scientific analysis that produced the mathematical problem, however, may also indicate methods of handling it. One method is to obtain analogous physical systems, the behaviour of which can be quantitatively observed; for example, a wind tunnel experiment on an aircraft wing or fuselage shape. In this way it is possible to investigate the behaviour of an aircraft in flight.

More generally, other systems can be sought satisfying the same mathematical relations as the given system of interest. For example, the flow of heat is analogous to the flow of electricity with temperature corresponding to electric potential. Thus, the heat flow in a structure can be analyzed by means of layers of electrically conducting materials arranged to simulate the characteristics of the structure.

Engineering is frequently concerned with complex elastic structures, and methods have been developed for setting up analogies between these structures and electrical networks, with nodes arranged in two- or three-dimensional lattice patterns. The stresses, strains, displacements, and dampening effects of the original structure all have measurable electrical analogues.

Network analyzers

A more direct analogue is represented by network analyzers. These are electrical networks intended to simulate power generating and transmission line networks in order to predict possible inadequacies of a present system or to design additions. The simulation concept here is quite direct and of great practical importance.

Analogue computers. An analogue computer is a device in which numbers are represented by measured quantities and in which equations or mathematical relations are represented by distinct components corresponding to the individual mathematical operations, such as integration, addition, or multiplication.

It is customary to divide analogue computers into two classes depending on whether numbers are represented by mechanical quantities, such as linear displacements or angular rotation, or by electrical quantities, such as voltages, currents, conductances, and impedances.

If linear displacements are used to represent numbers, there are simple ways in which geometrical relations can appear in mechanical form. A line segment can correspond to a physical bar, the common end point of two line segments can correspond to a common pivot for the bars, and two intersecting lines can be represented by an arrangement of two bars, one of which has a lengthwise slot in which a pivot fixed on the other bar is constrained to move. Circular motion of a point is obtained by fixing a pivot for a bar. Linear displacement is obtained by motion in a groove, but it is frequently more practical to use the fact that a linear displacement is approximated by a circular motion of large radius.

The mathematical operations can then be realized by using a corresponding geometrical relation. For example, three linear bars are constrained to move in three parallel equally spaced grooves. The centre bar has a crosspiece attached to it by a pivot, and the crosspiece has longitudinal slots for pivots attached to the outer bars. The linear displacements x and y of the outer bars are then related to the displacement z of the central bar by the equation $2z = x + y$ (Figure 14).

The use of this sort of device is, however, limited by mechanical problems associated with the resolution of forces along certain directions and leverage effects. On the other hand, their simplicity and ease of construction makes them suitable for control devices, in which the variables involved usually have a restricted range. They have also been used in conjunction with the representation of quantities by angular rotation for certain mathematical purposes.

One advantage of the representation of quantities by angles of rotation is that total revolutions can be counted and the equivalent of a very large scale obtained. The

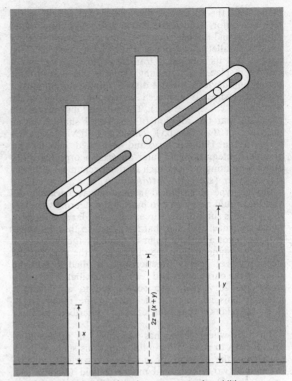

Figure 14: A simple form of analogue computer for addition. The linear displacements x and y of the outer bars are related to the displacement z of the central bar by the equation $2z = (x + y)$.

planetary gear differential permits the average of two rotations to be obtained without limit on the size of the rotations. The theory of the shape of gear teeth shows that two shafts can be connected by gears so that the rate of rotation of the driven shaft is a fixed multiple of that of the driving shaft, if the direction is not changed.

The principle of the differential can be easily understood if it is considered to be derived from the previous device in two steps. In step one, the crossbar is replaced by a wheel with an axle mounted on the centre bar. If the wheel is in non-slipping contact with the other two bars, the axle of this wheel on the centre bar will still be displaced by an amount corresponding to the average of the displacements of the two side bars. Now, if the two side bars are replaced by the perimeter of wheels on independent but coaxial axles and the axle of the centre wheel is also mounted on a rotating axle, then the centre of the wheel will rotate by an amount that is the average of the rotation of the side wheels, which in practice are the pitch circles of bevel gears.

Resolvers. A number of devices used in rotational mechanical devices depend on translating from a rotational to a linear displacement. A rack and pinion wheel combination will yield this change either way. For limited motion, a double eccentric arrangement is useful. This consists of two bars with a common pivot connection. One bar rotates around a fixed pivot and the other has an end that is constrained to move linearly. In a computer that basically represents quantities by angles of rotation, multipliers are used that involve conversion to linear displacements and the use of similar triangles for the multiplication principle. A linear harmonic displacement—*i.e.*, a linear displacement proportional to $\cos \omega t$—is obtained from a uniformly rotating shaft and a projecting bar with a pivot moving in a slot on a sliding piece that can move only in a direction perpendicular to the slot. This type of mechanism, called a Scotch yoke, is used in resolvers, devices that give the sine or cosine of their angular input as an output.

The Scotch yoke

An arrangement of gear wheels also yields a linear displacement. This corresponds to a special case of the hypocycloid, in which a circle of radius a rolls on the inner side of the fixed circle of radius $2a$. Two gear wheels can be obtained with pitch circles related in this fashion, by mounting the smaller gear on an arm that rotates around the centre of the larger circle. Then a fixed point on the smaller pitch circle moves on a straight line through the centre of the larger circle; and if α is the rotation of the arm on which the smaller wheel is mounted, the displacement from the centre is $2a \cos (\alpha + \gamma)$, in which γ is a constant. The two resolver principles described have an angular input and linear displacement output that can be converted to a rotation if required. For functions other than sines and cosines, cams can be used to produce a linear displacement that is a function of the angle of rotation of the cam.

Multipliers. A device called the pin cam produces a rotational output that is a specified function of the input. It can be considered to be derived from the disk and wheel integrator, the output of which is an integral, $z = \int y\,dx$, in which x is the rotation of the disk, y is the linear displacement of the wheel, and z is the rotation of the output shaft (Figure 15). If the displacement y of the wheel is obtained, not from an arbitrary input, but from a groove cut in the disk so that y is a specified function of x, this device will be a function generator for the function z that is an integral of the function y. If $y = 2x$, this produces essentially $z = x^2$; and if $y = 1/x$, it produces $\log x$. The first case has been used as a basis for a quarter-square multiplier with differentials being used for the additions and subtractions [*i.e.*, $xy = (\frac{1}{4})(x + y)^2 - (\frac{1}{4})(x - y)^2$].

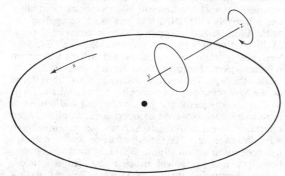

Figure 15: *Disk and wheel integrator.*
If the rotation of the disk is x and the linear displacement of the wheel is y, then the rotation z of the output shaft is the integral of y integrated with respect to x (see text).

The disk and wheel integrator normally permits two independent variable inputs x and y and yields an integral. With proper adjustments of the constants of integration, the relationship that expresses the product of two variables in terms of the sum of two integrals (see 67) is obtained. Thus two integrators with two independent variable inputs will yield a multiplier.

Harmonic analyzers. Notions and procedures relative to integrators and resolvers were introduced in the first instance for harmonic analyzers. These obtained successively the various Fourier coefficients of a curve by tracing the curve $y = f(x)$ on a drawing for each coefficient. From this it was natural to set up a more elaborate apparatus that would obtain a number of Fourier coefficients at once from a single tracing. Two such devices are those of Mader-Ott and Henrici-Conradi (Figure 16). The first name is that of the inventor, the second that of the manufacturer.

There were, however, also a relatively large number of devices that approximated the coefficients by a finite sum containing the values of $f(x)$ at equidistant points in the interval. Each of these values is multiplied by an appropriate cosine value and summed. Any consistent combination of devices can be used for the individual opera-

$$(67) \qquad xy = \int x\,dy + \int y\,dx$$

Figure 16: Harmonic analyzer, a highly refined form of a mechanical analogue computing device, with the function of extracting on read-out dials (which bear against the five crystal spheres) the first five coefficients needed, if a linear combination of trigonometric functions is to reconstitute the empirically given curve that is visible. The pointer is held to the empirical curve as the device rolls over the table and relevant motion is transferred to the spheres through wires (not shown).
By courtesy of Bayard Rankin

tions. An early example was constructed by Sir William Thomson (later Lord Kelvin) in 1878.

For a harmonic analyzer, the combined procedure must be relatively simple; a popular method for providing the sum of the quantities is the addition of torques. In an example produced by Walz, the individual term was represented by a torque obtained as follows. A balanced arm is mounted on an axis and on this arm a unit weight is placed at a distance f_r from the balance point. Now if the torque around the axis of this setup is measured at a position at which the arm makes an angle α with the horizontal, the torque is $f_r \times \cos \alpha$. The procedure for setting up the device permits appropriate α_r's to be chosen for each coefficient.

The addition of torques has also been used in devices for solving linear equations. A torque axis is used for each equation and the value of the unknowns x_i is represented by hydraulic forces that permit equalization between different torque axes.

Differential analyzers. Analogue devices for the solution of systems of ordinary differential equations are referred to as differential analyzers. The concept of this type of device was first described by Thomson in 1876, who pointed out that the output of integrators could be used as inputs for computing devices that yield the appropriate inputs for the integrators. Representation of quantities was by angular rotation, and the components included the disk and wheel integrators, gear sets for multiplying by a constant, and differentials for addition. Because the integrators have two independent inputs, it is possible to obtain an integral that is equivalent to the product of two variables. It followed that an extremely general set of systems of equations can be realized by these components.

A set up of this type, however, requires that the output of the integrators drive various other devices, and this load on the integrators introduced varying slippages resulting in errors. The general concept lay dormant until the development of torque amplifiers permitted the load on the integrators to be decreased, and the development of servo devices (see CONTROL SYSTEMS) permitted operation with negligible loads. Mechanical differential analyzers were revived around 1930, the most famous of these was that constructed at the Massachusetts Institute of Technology in the U.S. by Vannevar Bush. It had a uniform arrangement of components and shafts. Provision was made for introducing arbitrary functions by manual followers. After World War II, mechanical differential analyzers, using servo-followers to eliminate load on the integrators, were constructed, but these became obsolete with the development of electronic differential analyzers and electronic digital computation.

Automatic controls. In many circumstances automatic controls are superior to manual controls. Certain chemical manufacturing procedures of a continuous nature require input to be continuously varied. Other examples are oil refining and navigation. The gyro compass gives an electrical signal proportional to the rate of deviation of direction and thus can be used as a basis for automatic navigation for ships and aircraft and for stabilizing rockets.

A control system usually has control inputs that are adjustable to correspond to the desired output. The control inputs must be connected so as to influence the process inputs. When a straightforward functional relation is desired with variables of limited range, linkages are often used, especially because considerable force can be transmitted through such a device. When more complex control relations must be realized, however, a computer is used, supplemented by power amplification using the servo principle.

In the servo principle the purpose is to produce a power driven output with a desired value. The difference between the desired value and the power driven output is measured, and this difference is amplified and used to control the power driven output. This process is known as feedback. For example, the desired output may be given by a shaft rotation. The difference between this shaft position and a powered shaft position can be obtained by a differential, yielding a rotational value.

If rotational agreement is required, this shaft difference can be measured by using a potentiometer to produce a proportional voltage. Such a voltage can be electrically amplified to drive the powered output. If, however, the matching of rates is all that is required, the rate of this difference can be measured by a tachometer, which will also produce a directed voltage. In order to control the rate of a powered shaft the ball cage variable speed drive was used. This device is similar to the disk and wheel integrator, except that the wheel is replaced by a cage containing two spheres that transmit motion from the disk to an output cylinder. The cage can be positioned so that the output is $\int y\, dx$, but the major objective is the increase in the amount of power transmitted.

Thus, the use of servo-controlled outputs meant that an analogue computer need only indicate the desired output. This requirement was also true of subcomputations in the computer, because these could also be power amplified. An associated development was the use of voltages for computation. A potentiometer can be used to transform a shaft position to a voltage, and rotation rate can also be measured by a tachometer yielding a voltage. The difference between this voltage and a desired value of the voltage can be amplified to power the shaft position, or control its rate of rotation, by positioning the cage in a ball cage drive. Thus, a shaft position can be transformed to a voltage, and conversely either the shaft position or its rate of rotation can be made to correspond to a voltage. Thus, quantities can be represented by either shaft rotations or voltages. Nonlinear potentiometers can also be used to produce voltage-valued functions of the shaft rotations, in particular for sines and cosines.

Military applications

When artillery is to be directed at moving targets such as airplanes or ships, it is essential to predict the motion of the target. Such prediction devices were developed during World War II, using rotational analogue equipment working with voltages and servo-power amplification. The input was obtained by observing the target, relative to range, azimuth, and elevation and their rates of change. A change from polar to Cartesian coordinates was made so that uniform motion would yield constant rates for the coordinates of the target. These constant rates permit a prediction of target position and determination of time of flight for the shell by special two-dimensional cams. The angles of aim are also determined.

Electromechanical analogue computers. Bomb sights and computing devices for guns on airplanes were developed on an analogue basis. The mechanical connection of shafts and the arrangement of purely mechanical computing equipment represents a complex problem. The use of voltages greatly simplified the construction of analogue computers, and it was natural to expand this concept into what is referred to as electromechanical ana-

logue computing. Basic quantities are represented by the rotation of shafts. Potentiometers on these shafts can yield voltages corresponding to sums, products, and functions of one variable. Integration in this type of device is represented as follows. The integrand is represented by a voltage and the integral or output by a driven shaft on which is mounted a tachometer the output of which is a voltage corresponding to the rate of rotation. This voltage is compared with the input voltage and the difference used to provide a signal controlling the drive of the output shaft. There are certain advantages in the use of alternating current; for example, transformers can be used to facilitate addition.

Electromechanical analogue equipment of this type was introduced during World War II in trainers for airplane pilots. The devices contain a mathematical simulation of the motion of the aircraft in response to the control of the trainee. The output of the simulation appears on the instruments available to the trainee, and some aspects of the motion of the aircraft may also be simulated. The mathematical simulation of the motion involves computing the aerodynamical forces and solving the system of differential equations corresponding to Newtonian dynamics. Analogue activation of flight trainers was replaced by digital activation during the early 1960s.

Direct current analogue computers. During World War II, the laboratories of Bell Telephone Company in the United States introduced a computer to control anti-aircraft guns, the M-9, in which computation was accomplished by means of direct currents. This device was made practical by the development of operational amplifiers that effectively eliminated load effects on computing circuits. Addition and integration were in terms of current. Multiplication by a constant was obtained by potentiometers. Multiplication of variables and arbitrary function representations, however, were electromechanical.

The M-9 computer

After the war, commercial equipment was introduced on the M-9 principles for electronic differential analyzers. Standard components for integration and addition were introduced, each based on an operational amplifier. Multiplication was electromechanical in the potentiometer, servo-follower sense. A variety of devices were used for the generation of functions, including nonlinear potentiometers and graphical tracing by photoelectronic means. Similarly, many ways were devised to replace mechanical multiplication by various electronic methods. A certain standardization was obtained by means of the diode function generator, which represented a function by segments of linear relationships. Correspondingly, multiplication was based on the quarter-square principle, using two square function generators.

This type of device was widely used by engineering designers. A procedure was developed for basing the design of aircraft on the use of wind tunnel data for aerodynamic forces and Newtonian dynamics. There was a similar development for rockets. Basically, this type of equipment permitted simulations in which formal mathematical procedures were absent and permitted the application of scientific understanding to a wide variety of technical situations. For example, noise analysis, the design of engines, machinery, and even physical experiments were studied by this means. It was possible to use this type of equipment for harmonic analysis and also for Fourier transforms.

Systems of linear equations arise in manufacturing and economic control procedures and in obtaining the least square fit of parameters to data. A linear equation can be realized by a potentiometer or resistance network in which the unknown quantities x_i are inputs in the form of shaft rotations. A theory of appropriate feedback to position the unknowns is available and such devices have been constructed and used in manufacturing control.

Hybrid concepts. The limited precision of analogue equipment and the difficulties associated with multiplication and generation of functions suggested the possibility of using digital circuitry and procedures. Digital devices involve the use of numbers composed of discrete digits, rather than the use of quantities that can vary continuously in magnitude. One major difference between analogue and digital equipment is that the former is parallel, in the sense that for each operation in the mathematical problem, there is a component. In digital equipment, the same components are used repeatedly for the various operations.

Although some efforts have been made to introduce digital equipment in parallel fashion, in general, economic considerations make it desirable to use digital circuitry in the usual manner. Thus, normally, the analogue and digital equipment are separate and the transfer of numerical information from one group to the other is achieved by a conversion of the information from an analogue form to a digital form, or vice versa.

One possibility is the development of specialized digital equipment to perform accurate computations such as forming cosines and multiplication on a serial basis and interacting with the analogue equipment on a multiplex basis; *i.e.*, the results of the digital computation appear serially in different parts of the analogue device in a sequence fast enough to be equivalent to analogue components. The digital equipment is specialized in order to obtain maximum speed and computing capability. In the above possibility, the analogue equipment, in principle, is dominant. Another hybrid concept is to supplement a digital computation by a subsidiary analogue computation. For example, a system of differential equations may be solved by a combination of algebraic and functional computations and integrations. With suitable conversions, the computations are digital and the integrations are done by the analogue equipment. This general procedure has not been successful.

In training and control devices, both the input and output information appear in analogue form, and multiplex conversion is required as, for example, in a flight trainer activated by a digital computer. There are practical computational advantages in performing certain analogue computations on the inputs before analogue to digital conversion and on the outputs after conversion. Another type of situation in which hybrid concepts have proved successful is typified by an experiment in which large amounts of data are obtained initially in analogue form, and it is possible to process this data by analogue means so that the resulting information is more compact. Thus, the conversion to digital form and the digital processing are minimized.

DIGITAL CALCULATORS

Abacus. Probably the simplest instrument still in use to assist computation is the abacus. Decimal numbers are represented by the position of beads on wires in a frame. For each decimal place, the digits are represented in a biquinary fashion with one or two beads having the value five, and four or five beads having the value one. The framework is divided lengthwise by a partition with the beads having a value of five on one side and the beads with unit value on the other. Zero is represented by all beads pushed away from the central partition and a digit is represented by placing the appropriate value in beads against the partition. The Chinese *suan-pan* is a (2,5) abacus; *i.e.*, there are two five-value beads and five unit-value beads for each decimal place. While the Japanese *soroban* is now a (1,4) device, previously the *soroban* was a (1,5) device.

In ancient times, the Romans used a ten-bead abacus for each position with additional rows for twelfths and twenty-fourths. There was also a type of sand reckoner in which digits were represented by little cones with the digits on their base. The timing of this latter device has been the subject of considerable controversy.

In general, before paper was available, numbers had to be represented in some reusable form, for example, counters of different values, configurations of rods, marks in dust or on a waxed tablet. A more permanent record would be given by notches on a stick; *i.e.*, the tally, or knots on a cord. The early forms of the abacus consisted of a table with ruled lines on which $\times$ marks or markers were placed in a manner analogous to the beads on the abacus wires. The ruled lines could also have fractional significance.

Registers and adders. The abacus can be considered as a simple case of a register; that is, a device in which numbers are represented decimally and provision is made for indicating a digit in each place. People skilled in the use of the abacus can calculate with it at a rate comparable with a modern rotary calculator. Probably the most common type of register is one in which a cylinder corresponds to each place with ten possible positions.

A register can become a counter by providing a carry from one decimal place to another. To make a counter into an adder, it is necessary to provide some form of feed mechanism so that digits can be added into each place. Simple adding machines permit an addend to be entered, place by place, by a simple feed mechanism that may produce a carry into the next highest place but must not affect lower places. Essentially this concept is due to the 17th-century French mathematician Blaise Pascal.

In the simplest case, the feed returns to zero during the addition process and, if repeated addition is required, as in multiplication, then the addend must be entered each time. On the other hand, an effective calculator must retain the addend for repeated use as in multiplication. In addition, in order to introduce the addend simultaneously in all digits, some provision must be made to retain the carry. This might otherwise be lost because of the feed of the digit itself.

Thus, in the full adder invented by the 17th- and 18th-century German Gottfried Wilhelm von Leibniz, the carry is saved in the form of the position of a lever. After the digit feed has occurred, the carries are entered, place by place, in what is called a carry wave. Apparently the Leibniz type device was rediscovered by Charles X. Thomas de Colmar who began the commercial manufacture of this type of device in 1820 in Paris; these devices were produced for 58 years.

The Leibniz feed was based on a cylinder with teeth running lengthwise. The teeth, however, were of successively longer lengths to permit different amounts of feed, and the value of the addend digit was specified by the position of a take off wheel that determined how many teeth on this cylinder were engaged during a revolution. Many other types of feed have been introduced, for example, levers that return to their initial position by an amount of movement corresponding to a pressed key. A rather important type of feed is one in which the pressed key stops a motion at the correct amount rather than causes a motion of a certain amount.

Rotary calculators. A critical variation in these devices in which addition is accomplished in a single cycle is in the carry. In addition to the carry wave, a planetary gear carry may also be used. This makes it possible to add two motions into a given place simultaneously. In certain types of devices, it is practical to introduce a standing-on-nines carry. In this procedure, when a carry occurs into a sequence of nines, the carry bypasses the sequence into the next highest place and the nines are all advanced to zero. The principle of the standing-on-nines carry, which is due to Charles Babbage, is based on the fact that a place that stands on nines after the digit feed cannot have produced a carry. This permits all the carries to be performed simultaneously.

The major reason for retaining the addend in a cycle is to permit multiplication by repeated addition and the shifting of places. If appropriate provision is also made for negative down carries, then divisions can be performed by repeated subtractions. Initially both the repeated additions and the shifting of multiplication were done manually, and a similar procedure was used for division. It is possible, however, to incorporate electric motors into these devices so that the sequential procedure is automatic.

Variations on this have been tried at different times. One procedure was the use of the split multiplication table by Léon Bollée. In this device, the product of a digit of the multiplier by the multiplicand was added in the form of two addends. For this multiplier digit and for each digit of the multiplicand, the multiplication table yields two digits, one in the unit place and one in the tens place. One addend is constructed from the unit place digits; the other

The
Leibniz
feed

from the tens place digits with a one place shift. Another idea was to calculate the product of the multiplicand and a multiplier digit as a sum of quantities obtained by repeated doubling of the multiplicand, an idea which certainly goes back as far as Ahmes.

Immediately after World War II, rotary desk calculators were developed into devices that would automatically perform addition, subtraction, multiplication, and division and, in some cases, even extract square roots. It was also possible to enter one or more multiplier factors that could be retained during successive operations. These devices were widely used for business, technical, and scientific purposes, and special forms with printed outputs were developed for accounting. By the 1970s, however, a number of factors had tended to make them obsolete, one being the increasingly widespread use of large-scale electronic data processors for the same purposes. In addition, with the development of integrated circuitry, it has been possible to produce electronic calculators with cathode-ray tube output displays and electronic computing circuitry at a competitive price. The electronic calculators can store 16 to 48 numerical quantities and can be programmed either by card sequences or by stored programs up to 256 steps. The programming is done by going through the operations of the programmed sequence once with the calculator in what is called the learning mode.

Development of rotary desk calculator

PUNCHED CARDS

Cards. In the early forms of the desk calculator, each time a number was used it was transcribed manually into the keyboard, and for each use, therefore, there was a possibility of error. To counteract this, Herman Hollerith introduced the representation of data by holes on cards, first used in analyzing the data of the U.S. census of 1890. The cards were read by making electrical contacts through the holes. These procedures were developed by the Tabulating Machine Company, which in 1924 became the International Business Machines Corporation (IBM).

The IBM card

For the census of 1910, James Powers developed a card system in which holes in a card are sensed by plungers, which, when they penetrate a hole, act like the depressed key in a calculator relative to the mechanism below the card. This type of equipment eventually was produced by Remington Rand in the United States, Samas-Power in England, and Samas in France. It is also possible to read cards by photosensitive methods.

The standard IBM card is rectangular and measures 7⅜ by 3¼ inches (187 by 83 millimetres). The length of the card is divided into 80 columns, each of which extends the width of the card. In each column there are 12 positions for holes. These positions are named X, Y, 0, 1, · · ·, 9 beginning with the top position or that nearest the leading edge in a reading procedure (see 68). Digits are represented by a single punch in the appropriate digit position. Letters are represented by two punches. The information on such a card is represented by sets of adjacent columns called fields. These fields can contain either numerical or alphabetical information.

	A	$(X,1)$	J	$(Y,1)$		
	B	$(X,2)$	K	$(Y,2)$	S	$(0,2)$
	C	$(X,3)$	L	$(Y,3)$	T	$(0,3)$
	D	$(X,4)$	M	$(Y,4)$	U	$(0,4)$
(68)	E	$(X,5)$	N	$(Y,5)$	V	$(0,5)$
	F	$(X,6)$	O	$(Y,6)$	W	$(0,6)$
	G	$(X,7)$	P	$(Y,7)$	X	$(0,7)$
	H	$(X,8)$	Q	$(Y,8)$	Y	$(0,8)$
	I	$(X,9)$	R	$(Y,9)$	Z	$(0,9)$

The IBM card is read by electrical contacts. The movement of the card through the reading device is coordinated with the fundamental machine cycle so that the information appears in the form of time coded pulses.

Punched card machines. The original procedures in which punched cards were used involved the sorting and counting of cards. Both the Hollerith and the Powers systems were also developed for accounting purposes, which required the capability of adding the values in fixed fields into totals and subtotals. Printed outputs and machines called tabulators were developed for this purpose. As the possibility for using punched card systems for more general bookkeeping was recognized in the 1930s, machines with various other properties were introduced. The IBM equipment was electromechanical; the Samas-Powers equipment was mechanical. In addition to sorters, collators that could merge decks of cards in an order determined by specified fields were produced, as well as a multiplying punch, which could multiply the numerical values of two fields on a card and enter it in a third. In this way payrolls, insurance premiums, discounts, etc., could be calculated.

The electromechanical tabulators, collators, multiplying punches, and other devices had one advantage in that the choice of fields and operations were controlled by plug boards, with which the operator could route the electric pulses by connections with electric cables and plugs. After World War II, the electromechanical operations were replaced by electronic devices, and the use of plug boards was augmented by the ability of the device to execute a program (a logical sequence of instructions) of operations.

This programming capability was developed much further. A combination of three machines, called the card program calculator (CPC), was introduced that permitted programming by cards. The earliest really widespread electronic program data processing machine was the IBM 650, which had an internal stored program but was, in many business applications, an extremely flexible punched card processor. Even for the later and far more sophisticated large-scale data processors, cards are a desirable input and output, both for data and programs. Programs are generally devised so that new cards for additions or corrections can be added to the deck.

The card program calculator

PROGRAMMED MACHINES (DIGITAL COMPUTERS)

Development. To produce function tables or perform astronomical calculations requires a more complex mathematical capability than that of the simple arithmetical machines. The concept of devices for such purposes apparently goes back to Johann Helfrich von Müller (1786), and during the 19th century, mechanical machines were constructed with varying degrees of success. They used analytic procedures based on functional differences. The most famous effort along these lines was that of Babbage, who introduced many machine computing concepts including that of the stored program.

The technology available to Babbage was not adequate for the concepts he envisioned, but even later when mechanical procedures were sufficient, their complexity, cost, and slowness continued to limit their practicality. Another alternative for complex computing involved relays, especially those developed for telephone exchange switching. Relay machines were constructed by Bell Laboratories, by H. Aiken at Harvard University, by IBM, and in England, Germany, The Netherlands, and Sweden in the 1940s.

There had also been, however, a tremendous development of vacuum tube technology, including that of radar type circuitry in World War II, and by 1945, the Moore School of Electrical Engineering built the all electronic ENIAC for Aberdeen Proving Grounds, Maryland, for exterior ballistic calculations. This proved to be far too slavish an image of mechanical decimal computation, and succeeding machines, such as the Institute for Advanced Study computer (IAS), constructed under the supervision of John von Neumann, used the binary representation of numbers and binary arithmetic to decrease the amount of electronics and increase the speed. In binary notation a number can be represented by two symbols, 0 and 1. These can be indicated by the presence or absence of a pulse in an electric circuit or by two states of a component. A critical advance in the adaption of electronics to computation was the formulation of computer circuitry in terms of Boolean algebra by the National Bureau of Standards (1950).

In a binary system, there is also a choice between parallel arithmetic procedures in which operations in different binary positions are done simultaneously or serial procedures in which the places are treated successively. Electronically, parallel arithmetic is usually associated with flip flop circuitry in which bits are represented by the state of the circuitry, while the serial arithmetic is associated with the representation of bits by electrical pulses.

Instruction and programs. The major elements of an electronic data processing system are the central processing unit, the storage for data and instructions, and the input-output. The central processor is equivalent to a very fast desk calculator controlled by the set of instructions. The instructions are stored in sequence, and usually the next instruction executed is the next in sequence. There are, however, decision instructions in which the content of a register determines whether the next instruction is to be executed or a jump is to be made to another place for the next instruction. Loops of instructions can be executed by switching back to a previous instruction until a certain criterion is satisfied.

Various formats are used for the instructions. The instructions are stored in the form of a fixed number of binary bits; *i.e.*, zeros or ones. One subset of bits, the instruction code, determines the operation to be performed—addition or multiplication or decision. Other sets determine the address of data or instructions; that is, their location in the memory. Computers have been classified according to the number of addresses in the instructions. For example, a four-address computer is one in which there are two addresses for the operands of the operation, an address to store the result, and the address of the next instruction. A common format is the one-address instruction. These instructions operate relative to certain registers in the central processing unit (CPU). For example, in addition or multiplication one operand is already in the central register, the address of the other operand is in the instruction, and after the calculation, the result is in the register. Clearly, there is a need for load instructions to transfer the data in the address to the register and store instructions with the reverse effect.

In the computer, both data and instructions are transferred to the CPU but, in usual procedures, the paths are quite distinct. The data is associated with the numerical operational registers, the instructions with the instruction register, and the only arithmetic operations applied to the instructions refer to the addresses. This last possibility, however, may be avoided by the use of index registers, which automatically add a base number to an address in the instruction or by indirect addressing, which permits the use of addresses stored in other places.

Thus, it is reasonable to use distinct storage units for instruction and data storage and initially different media were used. The instructions in many relay machines were on a specialized type of broad paper tape that permitted one instruction to be represented on a line in a binary fashion while the numerical data was stored on relays. For special purpose machines, there are certain advantages of speed and reliability in "read only" storage for instructions, but the lack of flexibility may be a serious disability.

Storage facilities. The development of computers to the mid-1950s mainly involved a search for fast and reliable memories. Relay registers were slow and unreliable. Electronic registers, using vacuum tubes, were expensive and were limited by the tube's life. Devices, similar to cathode-ray tubes, with special electronic elements, gave memory effects by means of the electrostatic phenomena resulting from the impact of a directed stream of electrons. These proved somewhat difficult to construct, and the information had to be renewed every 50 milseconds. Another type of device was the mercury acoustic delay line storage unit in which bits were stored in the form of acoustic impulses travelling from an initial to an end

position. This was a serial device in the sense that specific information was available only periodically with intervals of nonavailability while the pulse travelled in the storage line. The temperature of this device had to be carefully controlled for proper operation. A more successful device was the magnetic drum on which pulses were stored as small magnetized areas on a rotating drum. This was also a serial device because there would usually be only one reading or writing head on a channel around the drum.

In 1953 magnetic core storage was introduced. Each bit was represented by the magnetization of a small ring of ferrite material called a core. The cores were strung on criss-crossing wires so that an electric pulse on one set of wires would cause magnetic reversals in cores corresponding to bits with value one, and these reversals would electronically pulse certain output wires. This type of storage was generally adopted as fast storage. In the 1970s, certain types of integrated circuitry were also considered for fast storage.

Magnetic drums have an access time of the order of about 17 milseconds but usually are of somewhat limited capacity. Disk devices have access times of the order of 75 milseconds but have a larger capacity. Access on magnetic tape is a matter of position, but tapes have storage advantages. For both disks and tapes, information is preferably stored in long records because, after a record has been located, it can be read very quickly.

Programming. When the fastest available storage was of a serial nature, the instruction format usually provided the address of the next instruction. This permitted optimal programming, in which the next instruction or the next operand is placed so as to be available in the serial storage at the appropriate time. To construct an optimal program manually was an onerous job, and special machine programs were devised to lay out the storage assignment for optimal timing. Instruction codes were also represented in alphanumeric mnemonic manner instead of in octal or hexadecimal form.

A program then could be written in assembler language as a sequence of instructions with mnemonic operational codes and with the operands denoted by alphanumeric names. A special program, called an assembler, would then determine the storage layout and assign to each given instruction in assembly language, an instruction in machine language. More complex computer programs were also developed, such as Algol and Fortran, which would take expressions modelled on algebraic formulas and translate these into sequences of machine instructions as well as perform the assembler function.

The programming associated with a computer system is referred to as the software as opposed to the equipment itself—the hardware. Numerous developments have made the production of software an increasingly important and financially significant aspect of data processing. A complex installation requires specialized programming for display processing, checking, and input-output control. The usual operating procedures include various language translators and monitors, which can service an arbitrary sequence of programs. Time sharing on computers by several users involves quite complex software. When a computer system is dedicated to a specific purpose, programs are usually optimized in the assembler or even in machine language form.

Circuitry. Vacuum tube electronics in computers was plagued by limited tube life, the heat generated by the filaments, and the complexity of the interconnections. In 1948 the transistor was introduced, a device that provided signal amplification by electrical field effects in certain semiconducting materials such as germanium or silicon. Because no incandescent filaments were involved, computers using transistors required far less expensive cooling systems. A reliability improvement of at least a factor of 10 also was obtained.

Plug-in units were used in the first computers for maintenance reasons. The plug-in units were electronic circuits having a considerable number of components and representing certain logical functions. Only a small number of different logical functions are represented in these units

Use of binary bits

Magnetic core storage

Computer languages

so that only a small number of different types are required. The complete logical structure of the computer is represented by using the logical functions of these units. If any component on a unit fails, there is a procedure to locate the unit; a special program is run on the machine and the logical consequence of the failure indicates the unit to be replaced. The receptacles for the plug-in units are mounted on racks. The wiring of the receptacles on the rack then corresponds to the logic of the major components. This rack wiring is designed by a computer program, and the actual wiring is done automatically by machines.

As the components developed for use in computers became faster, the size of the circuits became the limiting factor in computing speed. A consequent further development was that of large-scale integrated circuitry in which complete circuits were formed on chips of silicon by the same techniques as those used in making transistors. These techniques produced, in addition to transistors and diodes, resistors and capacitors. By the use of photographically controlled etching techniques, a remarkable reduction in size is possible so that a density of 10^5 components per square inch is possible. New storage elements, faster than those based on magnetic cores, have been developed. The indications are that integrated circuitry will permit the production of computers of extremely high speed, reliability, and perhaps lower cost.

Error detection. Digital computation must be error free. Errors can be caused by system misdesign, programming mistakes, or faulty components. The initial search for system errors and faulty components in a computer is referred to as debugging. This term is also applied to the testing of programs. When a faulty component continuously produces an incorrect output, maintenance programs based on logical analysis readily locate the plug-in unit containing the component. Intermittent faults or design mistakes that are apparent only under improbable combinations of conditions require specialized techniques such as testing with low or high voltages to maximize the possibility of errors. Even if there is no system or component fault, however, errors can occur because of thermal noise or external causes. If such an error is detected and the operation involved is repeated, it is highly probable that a second attempt will be successful.

Thus the detection of transient errors of low probability is critical. In order to detect errors that occur when data is stored or transmitted, a parity bit is used. The data is represented in the form of a word consisting of a fixed number of bits plus the parity bit, and the value of the parity bit is chosen so that the total number of bits with value one is odd. Thus, if only one bit in the word is in error, an error condition will be detected by an appropriate counter. The word length for parity checking need not be the same as that for the other computations and there has been a standardization on the eight bit plus parity unit. This is called a byte. In the correction of errors additional information must be available to locate the erroneous bit. A system has been developed such that if in a word of 2^n bits, n bits are used as parity bits, then a single erroneous bit can be detected and located.

Modulo computations

Arithmetic operations can be checked by independent modulo computations. To operate in a manner called modulo p is to ignore multiples of p so that quantities are considered equal if they differ by a multiple of p. To use modulo p relations effectively, it must be possible to reduce numbers by discarding multiples of p. For integers expressed in decimal form, this can be done for modulo 9, by replacing the integer by the sum of the digits. Thus, 4,735 can be replaced by 19, and this in turn by 1. The checking of decimal arithmetic by modulo 9 is called casting out nines. For modulo 11, the sign of the digits in the sum is alternated, with the digit in the unit place taken positive (see 69).

In a binary machine, in which an integer would be

represented with a radix (base) of two rather than ten, the concept of modulo 1 is useless for checking. Modulo 3, however, in which the bits are added with alternate signs can be used. This form of modulo 3 is readily obtained by circuitry based on Boolean algebra, in either the case of operations performed in parallel for the various binary places or serially. By grouping bits, binary expressions can also be considered as based on radix 4, 8, 16, etc. The equivalent of casting out nines for modulo 3, 7, 15, etc., is possible.

Another approach to eliminating errors is the use of duplicating circuitry. Thus, if a computation has been done by three circuits in duplicate and two answers agree, this result could be accepted if the circuits are fairly reliable. Objections have been raised to this philosophy of reliability by redundant equipment, however, because the extra equipment adds to the unreliability. Some error detection must also be available for improvement of the equipment. In practice improvements in reliability have been most effectively obtained by improving the reliability of individual components rather than by redundancy.

Input and output. The initial media for input and output were cards and paper tape. Card readers and card punches were readily adapted to input and output. Another device adapted for input or output was the tape operated typewriter in which each character corresponded to a combination of holes across the width of the paper tape, and such a combination could readily be entered as bit values into the computer or interpreted as output. Output printers were also developed.

Initially, computers were equipped with consoles in which information could be entered into the machine by switch positions and read out by lights. A later development was direct typewriter communication to the computer. There were, of course, applications requiring graphical output, and devices were developed to produce plots and diagrams by moving pens controlled by the computer.

Another graphical output was based on a cathode-ray tube (CRT). The cathode-ray tube output was also developed for military purposes, originally as part of air defense systems in which defensive aircraft are directed against attacking bombers. The CRT displays consisted of background maps with symbolic indications of the position of the various aircraft and their past and projected paths. Because much of the information and activation program of these displays does not change during the exercise, there is frequently associated with each individual CRT display, a local computer that activates the display using local program and local data storage and also information transmitted from the central computer.

CRT output

The various applications of CRT displays, including computer graphics, require the capability of manually indicating points on the display. This is done by the light pen, a photosensitive device. The display on the CRT is generated in a timing pattern in which different parts of the image are produced at different points in time during a cycle. Thus if the light pen is held against a particular point on the face of the tube, it will be pulsed only at a certain instant in the timing pattern and in this way the position can be entered into the computer. The pen is active only when a button on it is pressed so that it can be moved freely and activated only when desired.

In computer graphics, a drawing or diagram can be constructed on the face of the tube by means of the light pen and a console, consisting of buttons each of which activates a specific program. For example, a particular button will cause a straight line segment to be drawn between two points, and another button will draw a circle with an indicated centre and indicated point on it. Portions of a diagram can be constructed in different planes, and the cathode-ray tube can be used to show a rotated or rotating image of a three-dimensional diagram.

Not all cathode-ray tube displays are complex. A relatively simple display showing lines of alphanumeric characters can be used for many purposes including output without paper. Such a display can also show forms in which the alphanumeric information can be entered from a console typewriter, and these forms can be pro-

$$(69) \qquad 4735 \equiv 5 - 3 + 7 - 4 \bmod 11$$

cessed completely automatically for various business purposes.

OCR input

A number of desirable forms for input and output have been intensively studied for development, but they were in a tentative state in the 1970s. One highly desirable input procedure is to have the computer read, by a photoelectric method, a printed or written document; this is known as optical character recognition (OCR). It would permit the processing of masses of data already in existence and would be very valuable for the machine translation of natural languages. Documents that are printed with certain specific type fonts can be handled by the present state of the art. The more general problem of pattern recognition, however, appeared in the 1970s to have no economically feasible and generally acceptable solution.

By using audio-magnetic tapes, it is possible to produce a spoken output from the computer of limited vocabulary, and one can simulate the "talking down" procedure used by air controllers for instrument landings in airplane pilot trainers. On the other hand, spoken input to computers, like video input, discussed above, has an intensive development aim of getting an effective input from a specific voice.

Data processing systems. There are many applications in which information is processed in the central processor unit at rates of about a thousand times faster than it can input or output. Addition times of less than two microseconds and multiplication times of about four microseconds are now customary for larger computers, while rates of output printers based on conventional procedures are of the order of 35 milseconds per line. In addition to the difference in speed, it has proved possible to design and expand the central processor so that the registers can be used for a high fraction of the time. Thus, when relatively long arithmetic operations such as multiplication or division are being performed, other registers not involved may be used for transfers. Efforts to use thermal contact and photosensitive printing procedures to produce faster output of data have been made. To use the speed of the central processing unit for assistance in programming, procedures for eliminating routine chores have been developed. These procedures were incorporated into programming languages allowing programs to be expressed in a compact and readily understood form, which was later translated by the computer into machine language.

The CPU speed also permits time sharing, in which a larger number of remote consoles can be connected to the same central processor and communicate with it in the form of input instructions and typed output. The exchange of data with these remote terminals can be interspersed so that there is little interference between different users.

These are relatively inefficient uses of the CPU capabilities. Large amounts of data can be stored and re-entered from mass magnetic storage media such as tapes and disks at relatively fast rates, between 60,000 and 130,000 bytes per second. To the extent that data can be handled without external communication, this provides a reasonable match between computation and storage.

Elements of a modern data processing system

Thus, a modern data processing system will consist of a central processor, a hierarchy of storage facilities including magnetic cores, disks, drums, and tapes, and a complex of input-output devices under certain control units. These control units are essentially processors that execute input-output instructions. For a time, it was customary to use other computers to act as intermediaries between magnetic tape storage and devices such as printers, card readers, and punches. This allowed the central computer to deal only with magnetic tapes. This satellite-computer concept, however, has been replaced by improvements in the design of the central processor and input-output control. The objective is to permit transfers under the input-output control to occur while the longer arithmetical operations are being executed. The fast core storage is organized into subsections, each with an independent access register so that transfers can be made in and out of some sections while other sections are involved in arith-metical operations or in various operations relative to instructions.

Applications. Electronic computation has had extremely important technological, scientific, and economic consequences. The electronic developments required for computers were the main technological advances in the decades following World War II. Many complex systems were developed using the logical possibilities of digital electronic circuitry. In general, those control applications that previously had been developed with analogue computation were expanded and made more reliable by the new circuitry. In the case of airplane computers used for navigation by automatic pilots and military purposes, a considerable saving of weight was obtained. Airplane pilot trainers and similar devices were operated by digital computers rather than analogues.

In World War II, radar beams were directed by turning large dishes, but after the war, electronically directed radars were invented. Their sensitivity depended upon digital circuitry that performed statistical analyses of the radar signals. New and complex defense warning systems based on large digital computers could detect and distinguish between artificial satellites and hostile missiles and, in addition, predict their paths.

In addition to their role in activating complex systems, computers are used for modelling and simulations in designing aircraft, nuclear reactors, and other devices. Specific programs in general purpose computers permit the evaluation of Fourier coefficients and transforms and the solution of systems of algebraic or differential equations.

Modern physics often requires considerable use of computers, especially in the design and construction of devices such as the synchrotron (a device for accelerating subatomic particles; see ACCELERATORS, PARTICLE). Experiments in nuclear physics often result in large numbers of photographic plates showing the reactions of elementary particles. These can be analyzed by computer.

The ability of computers to hold and handle large amounts of information has been the basis of efforts to translate languages and considerable success has been reported. The capabilities of computers in the routine examination of alternatives has been used in programs for automatic chess playing and for dealing with formal logic, algebraic and geometrical proofs, and certain linguistic theories.

Information retrieval systems have also been introduced. Large-scale indexing of medical, scientific, and technical collections is based on the use of key words in the titles of works. Molecular structure listings have been used for patent purposes and medical research.

The application of electronic computing to business has resulted in a tremendous centralization of bookkeeping. Management control is assisted by the central processing of data about sales, stockkeeping, invoicing, shipping, billing, sales analysis, production control, inventory, and receiving. In each of these areas, up-to-date information is of considerable value. For example, maintaining inventories at the correct level avoids the objectionable extremes of overinvestment in supplies or production delays because of inadequate supplies.

Mass production bookkeeping is characteristic of public utilities and insurance companies and there has been a considerable development of business output devices suitable for billing, invoicing, and checkwriting. Airplane reservation systems use a variation of the time sharing concept with remote controls that can query airplane bookings and make reservations.

The automatic processing of accounts in large volumes has resulted in a highly significant cost reduction, even over the previously used punched card procedures. One consequence has been the widespread elimination of customer credit accounts in retail stores by means of credit cards. Charges, as represented by charge slips, are referred to customers' accounts in banks or banking subsidiaries, and handled on a mass basis by electronic equipment. This results in a considerable centralization of accounting. These systems were not free from technical difficulties initially and there has been considerable criticism directed at the mechanization and centralization.

There has also been criticism of the accumulation of information about individuals by the government in computer form. If this information were inert, in written form, rather than in computer form, it would not lend itself to possible manipulation. Part of the reaction, here and in other cases, has been a focussing on computers and data processing of a general emotional reaction against the technological explosion itself.   (F.J.M.)

BIBLIOGRAPHY. ALLEN V. ASTIN, "Standards of Measurements," *Scient. Am.*, 218:50–62 (1968), a relatively non-technical article on the nature and use of standards of length, mass, time, and temperature; PERCY W. BRIDGMAN, *Dimensional Analysis* (1922, reprinted 1963), a series of lectures giving the basic elements of the theory and a critical analysis of various application procedures; FLORIAN CAJORI, *A History of Mathematics*, 2nd rev. ed. (1938), a standard history of mathematics with emphasis on the interaction of mathematics from different geographical areas; J.L.E. DREYER, *A History of Astronomy from Thales to Kepler*, 2nd ed. (1953), describes the growth of understanding relative to the shape and motion of the earth and the structure of the solar system; GRANINO A. and THERESA M. KORN, *Electronic Analog and Hybrid Computers* (1964), standard engineering textbook on analog computation; FRANCIS J. MURRAY, *Mathematical Machines*, vol. 1, *Digital Computers*, and vol. 2, *Analog Devices* (1961), describes the principles and logic structure of analog and digital computing devices; OTTO NEUGEBAUER, *The Exact Sciences in Antiquity*, 2nd ed. (1957), a series of lectures giving a very interesting history of the understanding of ancient science, containing critical historical analyses and descriptions of many ancient procedures; WILLIAM M. SMART, *Textbook on Spherical Astronomy*, 5th ed. (1962), contains the basic mathematics associated with astronomical observation and considerable information on current practices in navigation and astronomy; DAVID E. SMITH, *History of Mathematics*, 2 vol. (1923–25, reprinted 1958), vol. 1 describes the development of mathematics in terms of people and geographical area while vol. 2 considers mathematical topics; ANTONIN SVOBODA, *Computing Mechanisms and Linkages* (1948), a precise technical and comprehensive development of the principles used in mechanical computing devices.

Two references on mathematical instruments are SEYMOUR GINSBURG, *An Introduction to Mathematical Machine Theory* (1962), and DOUGLAS R. HARTREE, *Calculating Instruments and Machines* (1949). For harmonic analyzers, see G.C. DANIELSON and C. LANCZOS, "Some Improvements in Practical Fourier Analysis and Their Applications to X-Ray Scattering from Liquids," *J. Franklin Inst.*, 233:365–380, 435–452 (1942); DAYTON C. MILLER, *Sound Waves: Their Shape and Speed; A Description of the Phonodeik and Its Applications and a Report on a Series of Investigations Made at Sandy Hook Proving Ground* (1937); "A 32–Element Harmonic Synthesizer," and "The Henrici Harmonic Analyzer and Devices for Extending and Facilitating Its Use," *J. Franklin Inst.*, 181:51–81, 182:285–322 (1916). For the theory and operation of the slide rule, see JOSEPH N. ARNOLD, *The Complete Slide Rule Handbook: Principles and Applications* (1956); JOHN P. ELLIS, *The Theory and Operation of the Slide Rule* (1961); STEFAN RUDOLF, *The Modern Slide Rule* (1959); and ALFRED L. SLATER, *The Slide Rule: A Complete Manual* (1967).

The following are references on nomography: LESTER R. FORD, *Alignment Charts* (1944); DALE S. DAVIS, *Nomography and Empirical Equations*, 2nd ed. (1962); RAYMOND D. DOUGLASS and DOUGLAS P. ADAMS, *Elements of Nomography* (1947); ALEXANDER S. LEVENS, *Nomography*, 2nd ed. (1959); DOUGLAS P. ADAMS (ed.), *An Index of Nomograms* (1950); J. REGINALD JONES and HAROLD J. ALLCOCK, *The Nomogram*, 5th ed. (1963).

ALAN FLETCHER et al., *An Index of Mathematical Tables*, 2nd ed., 2 vol. (1962), is a comprehensive and general bibliography of mathematical tables. Mathematical functions are tabulated and descriptions of their properties are given in German and English in EUGEN JAHNKE and FRITZ EMDE, *Tables of Higher Functions*, 6th ed. rev. by FRIEDRICH LOESCH (1960). A more recent work of a comprehensive nature is MILTON ABRAMOWITZ and IRENE A. STEGUN (eds.), *Handbook of Mathematical Functions with Formulas, Graphs, and Mathematical Tables* (1964), a massive work covering 29 classes of functions. Other references are HAROLD T. DAVIS et al. (comps.), *Tables of the Mathematical Functions*, rev. ed., 3 vol. (1962–63); MIECZYSLAW WARMUS, *Tables of Elementary Functions* (1960); and the CHEMICAL RUBBER COMPANY, *Handbook of Tables for Mathematics* (1962–). For statistical tables, see RONALD A. FISHER and FRANK YATES, *Statistical Tables for Biological, Agricultural and Medical Research*, 6th ed. (1963). The theory and use of logarithms in calculation is covered in the instructions accompanying many of the tables referred to above and in such elementary textbooks as ABRAHAM P. HILLMAN and GERALD L. ALEXANDERSON, *Algebra and Trigonometry* (1963). The reader interested in mathematical models may wish to consult some of the following works: H.S.M. COXETER et al., *The Fifty-nine Icosahedra* (1938); HUGO STEINHAUS, *Mathematical Snapshots*, 3rd ed. rev. (Eng. trans. 1969); MILES C. HARTLEY, *Patterns of Polyhedrons*, rev. ed. (1959); HENRY M. CUNDY and A.P. ROLLETT, *Mathematical Models*, 2nd ed. (1961); DAVID HILBERT and STEPHEN COHN-VOSSEN, *Anschauliche Geometrie* (1944; Eng. trans., *Geometry and the Imagination*, 1952).

(F.J.M./L.R.F./Ed.)

Mather Family

The prominence of the Mather family in England and the dominance of Richard, Increase, and Cotton in New England, in the 17th century, can hardly be overestimated. Though for 200 years after their time popular history labelled them witch-hunters and bigots, the fact is that they were neither. Being Puritans, with an uncompromising belief in Calvin's doctrine of the elect, who were predestined to be saved, they were men of their times; if they believed in witches, so did their contemporaries at home and abroad. Beyond this frame of reference, they were ahead of their times in many respects. They were, indeed, rebels against the prevailing establishment. Their lives spanned the reigns of many monarchs, who opposed and sometimes even persecuted advocates of Puritanism who, like the Mathers, stood courageously for their principles.

Richard Mather.   Richard Mather was born in the village of Lowton in Lancaster, England, in 1596. He was of a "credible and ancient family" of an intellectual calibre that was to be perpetuated in his descendants. He attended Winwick school under a severe taskmaster who, however, recommended him, at age 15, to be teacher at a new school at Toxteth Park. There he decided to enter the ministry, gave up his position, and entered Brasenose College, Oxford, where he greatly enjoyed the pursuit of learning. In 1618, at the request of the people of Toxteth, he left the university to become their minister and, bowing to their wishes, was ordained by the Bishop of Chester.

As a thorough Puritan, Richard Mather had rejected all pomp and ceremony retained by the Church of England from its Catholic origins, and he preached at Toxteth without a surplice for 15 years before authorities discovered it. Suspended, and then reinstated, he returned to his dissenting practices and was tried before a court, before which he admitted without apology the matter of the surplice.

Permanently "silenced from Publick Preaching the Word," he retired to private life and resolved to leave for America, where he would be free to preach and do good according to his own convictions. He and his wife (Katherine Holt, whom he had married in 1624) and their four sons sailed for America in June 1635 and arrived at Boston in August. His journal of the voyage is one of his best written works. His reputation had preceded him to New England, where several towns asked for his services. He chose Dorchester, Massachusetts, a post he held until his death. Two more sons, Eleazar and Increase, were born there.

Of Richard Mather's six sons, four became ministers. Samuel and Nathaniel, after being educated at Harvard College, returned to the British Isles in 1650, where Samuel received a degree, became a fellow at Trinity College, Dublin, and later became minister in Dublin, a post he held until his death. Nathaniel preached at Barnstaple and later succeeded Samuel in Dublin. Eleazar became minister of Northampton. Richard's first wife, Katherine, died in 1655; a year later he married Sarah Cotton, the widow of John Cotton, an eminent Puritan minister.

Richard's most respected work is his summation of principles as adopted at the Cambridge Synod of 1648 and considered to be the clearest statement of Puritan Congregationalism.

He is remembered for his part, with other ministers, in the literal translation of the Psalms for the *Bay Psalm*

Richard's refusal to wear a surplice

(Left) Richard Mather, oil painting by an unknown artist, 1853, after a contemporary portrait, c. 1660–69. In the collection of the American Antiquarian Society, Worcester, Massachusetts. (Centre) Increase Mather, portrait by Jan van der Spriet, 1688. In the collection of the Massachusetts Historical Society. (Right) Cotton Mather, portrait by Peter Pelham (1684–1751). In the collection of the American Antiquarian Society, Worcester, Massachusetts.
By courtesy of (left, right) the American Antiquarian Society, Worcester, Massachusetts, (centre) and the Massachusetts Historical Society

Book (1640), which were set to already accepted tunes; in his preface to that work, Richard excused the terrible results by explaining that the editors would not take "poeticall licence to depart from the true and proper sence of David's words."

On his deathbed, Richard Mather was troubled about two things: he was not back in his study, and he had not convinced his son Increase of the rightness of the so-called Half-Way Covenant, a plan that provided modified church membership for those who were unable to meet the rigorous tests for full membership. He died April 22, 1669.

Increase Mather. Increase Mather, the youngest and most distinguished of Richard's sons, was active at home and abroad as minister, diplomat, and president of Harvard. Born in Dorchester, June 21, 1639, he entered Harvard at the age of 12 and received his bachelor's degree at 17. At graduation, his attack on Aristotelian logic, basic to the Harvard curriculum, shocked the faculty and nearly resulted in his dismissal. On his 18th birthday he preached his first sermon in a village near his home and his second in his father's church in Dorchester. Soon he left for Dublin, where he entered Trinity College and received a master's degree the following June. At his commencement, he refused to wear a cap and gown, but the assembled scholars were so impressed with him that they hummed their approval of him. Chosen a fellow at Trinity, he refused the post. He preached at various posts in England and was at Guernsey when the Puritan Commonwealth ended and Charles II was proclaimed king (May 8, 1660). He refused to drink the King's health or sign papers expressing rejoicing. On the appointment of a new governor for Guernsey, unsympathetic to Nonconformists, Increase left a comfortable living and in a few months sailed for New England, where he became minister of North Church, Boston, in 1661, and married his stepsister, Maria Cotton, in 1662.

In 1683 Charles delivered an ultimatum to the Massachusetts colonists: to retain their charter with absolute obedience to the King or to have it revoked. Before an assembly of freemen, Mather proclaimed that an affirmative vote would be a sin against God, for only to Him should one give absolute obedience. The colonists refused submission, and the charter was subsequently revoked in 1686.

After James II became king, in 1688, Increase was sent as the representative of the colonists to thank him for his declaration of liberty to all faiths. He remained in England for several years, and on the accession of William and Mary in 1689, he obtained from them the removal of the hated governor of Massachusetts, Sir Edmund Andros, and his replacement by Sir William Phipps. Increase's petition for the restoration of the old charter

Increase's opposition to Charles II

proved unsuccessful, but he was able to get a new charter in 1691. Both the new governor and the new charter, however, turned out to be unpopular. In 1685 Increase had been made president of Harvard but resigned in 1701, in part because of opposition to the new colonial charter. He received the honorary degree of doctor of divinity in the same year.

Among his books is *An Essay for the Recording of Illustrious Providences,* 1684, a compilation of stories showing the hand of divine providence in rescuing people from natural and supernatural disasters. Some historians suggest that this book conditioned the minds of the populace for the witchcraft hysteria of Salem in 1692. Despite the fact that Increase and Cotton Mather believed in witches—as did most of the world at the time—and that the guilty should be punished, they suspected that evidence could be faulty and justice might miscarry. Witches, like other criminals, were tried and sentenced to jail or the gallows by civil magistrates. The case against a suspect rested on "spectre evidence" (testimony of a victim of witchcraft that he had been attacked by a spectre bearing the appearance of someone he knew), which the Mathers distrusted because a witch could assume the form of an innocent person. When this type of evidence was finally thrown out of court at the insistence of the Mathers and other ministers, the whole affair came to an end.

Increase's *Case of Conscience Concerning Evil Spirits Personating Men* (1693) is a clear vindication of the Mathers' part in the witchcraft trials. Yet their enemies, such as William Douglass and Robert Calef, spread denigrating rumors about them. This enmity, together with the Mathers' part in a campaign for inoculation against smallpox and the failure of their protégé Phipps to measure up to expectations, contributed to the decline of the Mathers' influence in the last decade of the century. Changing times, more than anything else, had their impact; for people like the Mathers were losing touch with the younger generation. Increase died on August 23, 1723.

Cotton Mather. Cotton Mather's heritage from his two grandfathers, Richard Mather and John Cotton, was both fortunate and unfortunate. Like them, he had an active mind and the will to use it. He lived in the shadow of their greatness and expected to carry on the tradition and to assume their role in the Puritan community. Unfortunately, he could not see that the old order was passing. As colonial communities became more secure from earlier hardships of settlements, they also became more complacent and less in need of a confining spiritual leadership. Cotton fought for the continuance of old order of the ruling clergy, sometimes with frustration, sometimes in anger.

The Mathers and the Salem witch trials

Cotton was born in Boston, February 12, 1663. He entered Harvard at 12, easily passing entrance requirements to read and write Latin and to "decline the Greek nouns and verbs." He devoted himself unremittingly to study and prayer. At 18 he received his M.A. degree from the hands of his father, who was president of the college. Unlike his father, he never went abroad but spent all his life in Boston.

He once noted that his life was "a continual conversation with heaven," but he spent agonizing hours convinced that he was damned and equal time in ecstasies that he was not. For a while, he feared he could not enter the ministry because of a speech impediment, and he considered becoming a physician; the subject of medicine was of lifelong interest to him. After a friend persuaded him "to oblige himself to a dilated Deliberation in speaking," he conquered his weakness and returned to religious studies. He preached his first sermon in his father's church in August 1680 and in October another from his grandfather John Cotton's pulpit. He was formally ordained in 1685 and became his father's colleague.

He devoted his life to praying, preaching, writing, publishing and still followed his main purpose in life of doing good. His book, *Bonifacius,* or *Essays to Do Good* (1710), instructs others in humanitarian acts, some ideas being far ahead of his time: the schoolmaster to reward instead of punish his students, the physician to study the state of mind of his patient as a probable cause of illness. He established societies for community projects.

He joined his father in cautioning judges against the use of "spectre evidence" in the witchcraft trials and in working for the ouster of Sir Edmund Andros. He was also a leader in the fight for inoculation against smallpox, incurring popular disapproval. When Cotton inoculated his own son, who almost died from it, the whole community was wrathful, and a bomb was thrown through his chamber window. Satan seemed on the side of his enemies; various members of his family became ill, and some died. Worst of all, his son Increase was arrested for rioting.

Cotton's interest in science

His interest in science and particularly in various American phenomena—published in his *Curiosa Americana,* (1712–1724)—won him membership in the Royal Society of London. His account of the inoculation episode was published in the society's transactions. He corresponded extensively with notable scientists, such as Robert Boyle. His *Christian Philosopher* (1721) recognizes God in the wonders of the earth and the universe beyond; it is both philosophical and scientific and, ironically, anticipates 18th-century Deism, despite his clinging to the old order.

Cotton Mather wrote and published over 400 works. His magnum opus was *Magnalia Christi Americana* (1702), an ecclesiastical history of America from the founding of New England to his own time. His *Manuductio ad Ministerium* (1726) was a handbook of advice for young graduates to the ministry: on doing good, on college love affairs, on poetry and music, and on style. His own style ranged from the over elaborate to the directly simple, as in his biography of Gov. William Bradford. For the most part, his prose was laden with Latinisms and quotations from ancient authorities. In one instance, the posthumously published *Political Fables,* he showed the gift of satire. His ambitious 20-year work on biblical learning was interrupted by his death.

He died on February 13, 1728, only five years after his father, whose colleague he had been for 40 years. Of 15 children by his three wives—Abigail Phillips, Elizabeth (née Clark) Hubbard, and Lydia (née Lee) George— only two survived him.

BIBLIOGRAPHY. Contemporary biographies by members of the Mather family revealing the subjects and their times, and incidentally the loyalties of one Puritan family, are COTTON MATHER, *Parentator* (1724), on Increase; INCREASE MATHER, *The Life and Death of That Reverend Man of God, Mr. Richard Mather* (1670); and SAMUEL MATHER, *The Life of the Very Reverend and Learned Cotton Mather* (1728). KENNETH B. MURDOCK, *Increase Mather: The Foremost American Puritan* (1925, reprinted 1966); and BARRETT WENDELL, *Cotton Mather: The Puritan Priest* (1891 and 1926, reprinted 1963), are definitive biographies by distinguished 20th-century writers.

(J.K.P.)

Matisse, Henri

In the general upheaval that marked the history of Western painting at the close of the 19th century and the opening of the 20th, the first element to undergo drastic change was colour, and one of the principal innovators in colour was the French painter, sculptor, and graphic artist Henri Matisse. In 1905 in Paris he helped to launch the movement known as Fauvism, which rejected chromatic naturalism and favored the use of violent hues calculated to stir the emotions of viewers. But Matisse was more than just a rebel against traditional art. He went on to become the creator of masterpieces that continue, in a modern idiom, an ancient French preference for paintings that are at once sensual and rational. He has often been bracketed with Pablo Picasso as one of the two most important artists of the 20th-century school of Paris.

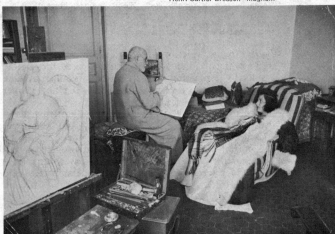

Henri Cartier-Bresson—Magnum

Matisse sketching a model, photograph by Henri Cartier-Bresson.

Henri-Émile-Benoît Matisse was born on December 31, 1869, at Le Cateau (formerly Cateau-Cambrésis), a small town in Picardy, and raised at nearby Bohain, where his parents had a grain business. He displayed little interest in art until he was 20 years old. From 1882 to 1887 he attended the secondary school in Saint-Quentin; after a year of legal studies in Paris, he returned to Saint-Quentin and became a clerk in a law office. He began to sit in on an early-morning drawing class at the local École Quentin-Latour, and, in 1890, while recovering from a severe attack of appendicitis, he began to paint, at first copying the coloured reproductions in a box of oils his mother had given him. Soon he was decorating the home of his grandparents at Le Cateau. In 1891 he abandoned the law and returned to Paris with the intention of becoming a professional artist.

Although at this period he had, in his own words, "hair like Absalom's," he was far from being a typical Left Bank bohemian art student. "I plunged head down into work," he said later, "on the principle I had heard, all my young life, expressed by the words 'Hurry up!' Like my parents, I hurried up in my work, pushed by I don't know what, by a force which today I perceive as being foreign to my life as a normal man." This 19th-century gospel of work, derived from a middle class, northern French upbringing, was to mark his entire career, and soon it was accompanied by a thoroughly bourgeois appearance— gold-rimmed spectacles; short, carefully trimmed beard; plump, feline body; conservative clothes—which was odd for a leading member of the Parisian avant-garde.

Formative years. He did not, however, become a member of the avant-garde right away. In 1891, in order to prepare himself for the entrance examination at the official École des Beaux-Arts, he enrolled in the privately run Académie Julian, where the master was the strictly, even slickly, academic Adolphe-William Bougwereau, then at the peak of a since-departed fame as a painter of bevies of naked, mildly provocative nymphs. That Matisse should have begun his studies in such a school may seem surprising, and he once explained the fact by saying that he was acting on the recommendation of a Saint-Quentin painter of hens and poultry yards. But it must be remembered that he himself was for the moment a provincial with tastes that were old-fashioned in a Paris already familiar with the Postimpressionism of Paul Cézanne, Paul Gauguin, and Vincent van Gogh. His earliest canvases are in the 17th-century Dutch manner favoured by the French Realists of the 1850s.

Training with Gustave Moreau

In 1892 he left the Académie Julian for evening classes at the École des Arts Décoratifs and for the atelier of the Symbolist painter Gustave Moreau at the École des Beaux-Arts, without being required to take the entrance examination. Moreau, a tolerant teacher, did not try to impose his own ornate, somberly fantastic style on his pupils but encouraged them rather to develop their personalities and to learn from the treasures in the Louvre. Matisse responded by turning out copies of works by, among others, Raphael, Poussin, Chardin, Fragonard, Ribera, and a Dutch still-life specialist, David de Heem. He continued, with some long interruptions, to study in the atelier until 1899, when Fernand Cormon, an intolerant painter who had become the professor after Moreau's death the previous year, insisted that he leave the École des Beaux-Arts. After that, although he was nearing 30, he frequented for a time a private academy where intermittent instruction was given by the portraitist Eugène Carrière. And as late as 1900 he was not above going to the Louvre to copy Chardin's still life "La Raie."

Few 20th-century modernists, therefore, have had as many years of solidly traditional training as Matisse had; conceivably, he could have gone on to become a favourite of the French art establishment or at least a successful muralist for town halls. But during these years he was learning some untraditional things by arguing with and working alongside sympathetic young companions. In Moreau's atelier he met Georges Rouault, Raoul Dufy, Henri Manguin, and Charles Camoin; at the École des Arts Décoratifs, Albert Marquet; in Carrière's academy, André Derain. During the summer of 1895 he went to Brittany with a Parisian friend named Émile Wéry. "At that time," he remembered, "I had nothing but yellowish browns and earth colours on my palette, while Wéry had an Impressionist palette. Like him, I undertook to work from nature. And soon I was seduced by the brilliance of pure colour. I came back from my trip with a passion for the hues of the rainbow, whereas Wéry returned to Paris in love with bitumen." Although the passion produced inconsistent results for a while, it eventually proved irresistible.

First success

In 1896 Matisse exhibited four paintings at the backward-looking Salon de la Société Nationale des Beaux-Arts and scored a triumph; he was elected an associate member of the Salon society, and his "Woman Reading" (1894), painted in relatively dark tones, was purchased by the government as decoration for the château de Rambouillet. From this point onward he became increasingly confident and venturesome, both as an artist and as a man. During the next two years he undertook two more expeditions to Brittany, met the veteran Impressionist Camille Pissarro, and discovered the series of Impressionist masterpieces in the Gustave Caillebotte Collection, which had just been donated—amid protests from conservatives —to the French nation. His colours became, for a while, lighter in hue and at the same time more intense. In 1897 he took his first major step toward stylistic liberation and created a minor scandal at the Salon with "The Dinner Table" ("La Desserte"), in which he combined a Renoir kind of luminosity with a firmly classical composition in deep red and green.

In 1898 he married a young woman from Toulouse, Amélie Parayre, and left Paris for a year, visiting London, where he studied the paintings of Turner, and working for a while in Corsica, where he received a lasting impression of Mediterranean sunlight and colour. Although he continued to revert to grays and browns, apparently out of a fear of losing control of his forms and tone values, he was no longer the provincial artist who had hoped for a conventional career via the École des Beaux-Arts and the big offical shows.

Revolutionary years. During 1898, Paul Signac, the theoretician and actively proselyting leader (after the death of Georges Seurat) of the Neo-Impressionists, or Pointillists, published in the literary review *La Revue Blanche* his principal manifesto, "D'Eugène Delacroix au Néo-Impressionnisme." Matisse, back in Paris in 1899, read the articles and, without turning into an immediate convert, became interested in the Pointillist idea of obtaining additive mixtures of colour on the retina by means of juxtaposed dots (*points* in French) on the canvas. He furthered his research into new techniques by buying, from the well-known modernist dealer Ambroise Vollard, a painting by Cézanne, "The Three Bathers"; one by Gauguin, "Boy's Head"; and a drawing by van Gogh. Often accompanied by his close friend Marquet, who was also interested in the problem of pure colour, he began to paint outdoor scenes in the Luxembourg Gardens in Paris, in suburban Arcueil, and from the open window of his apartment overlooking the Seine River near Notre-Dame Cathedral.

He also purchased from Vollard the plaster model of the bust of Henri Rochefort by Rodin, and during 1899 he began to attend an evening class in sculpture. His early work in three dimensions, the first of some 60 pieces he executed during his lifetime, reveals the influence not only of Rodin but also of Antoine-Louis Barye, generally considered the greatest of the many 19th-century French sculptors of animals. In fact, for the "Jaguar Devouring a Hare," begun in 1899, Matisse relied on copying a Barye work, with some help from a study of the anatomy of a dead cat. Later on he sometimes used modelling as a way of experimenting with motifs in his painting, and eventually he came to regard the volumes and mass of sculpture as compensating, in the interest of a full creative development, for the flatness of his pictures.

Early sculpture

After 1899 he ceased to exhibit at the Salon and gradually became a familiar figure in the Parisian circles where modern art was being produced and ardently discussed. In 1901 he showed for the first time in the juryless, eclectic Salon des Indépendants, which had been founded in 1884, by Signac among others, as a refuge for painters unacceptable to the official exhibition juries. In 1902 he was in a group show at the small gallery of Berthe Weill, and the next year he and a number of his old classmates from Moreau's atelier and the Académie Carrière were the progressive contingent in the liberal, newly created Salon d'Automne. But in spite of such recognition, he was often on the brink of financial disaster. In 1900 he was obliged to accept work on the decoration of the Grand Palais, which was being erected to house part of the new Exposition Universelle in the Champs-Élysées quarter. His wife opened a dress shop in the hope of helping to make ends meet. In 1901 an attack of bronchitis forced him to take a long rest. During part of 1902 he had to return to Bohain with his three children—Marguerite, Jean, and Pierre—and Mme Matisse. He was past 34 when, in June 1904, at Vollard's gallery, he had his first one-man show; it was a success neither with journalists nor with collectors.

Meanwhile, he was trying, partly in a series of still lifes and of views from his apartment, to advance out of the relatively dark realistic style to which he was still partly committed or at least into which he still backslid. Pushing him forward were such comparatively reckless younger contemporaries as Derain and Derain's iconoclastic friend, the painter Maurice de Vlaminck, who boasted of never having seen the inside of the Louvre. Among the older influences pushing in the same general direction were Cézanne, Gauguin, van Gogh, the Impressionists, and possibly some of the 18th-century French masters. But what appears to have been the decisive push was provided by the hues of the Mediterranean coast and by the impact of Signac, which was considerably brighter than that of the cautious, "scientific" Seurat. Matisse spent the summer of 1904 on the French Riviera at Saint-Tropez, working with Signac and producing, among other things, "Luxe, calme, et volupté"; he got the title from Baudelaire's poem "L'invitation au voyage" and the technique, rather approximately, from the Pointillists. He sent the picture to the Salon des Indépendants in the spring of 1905 and thus became, for a season, something of an official Neo-Impressionist. He was not, however, greatly pleased; he felt, he explained later, that the dabs of contrasting pigment favoured by the Seurat–Signac theory weakened dominant colours and that what was needed was a way "to exalt all colours together, sacrificing none of them." This reasoning pointed toward painting with strong, unrealistic, flat tones—toward a style that in colour, although not necessarily in drawing, was practically abstract.

Develop-
ment of the
Fauve style

He spent the summer of 1905 with Derain at Collioure, a small French fishing port on the Mediterranean, near the Spanish border. In the dazzling sunshine he rapidly freed himself from what he called "the tyranny" of Pointillism. The carefully placed little dabs required by the additive-mixture approach turned into swirls of spontaneous brushwork, and the theoretically realistic colours exploded into an emotional display of complementaries: red against green, orange against blue, and yellow against violet. Representative of this new freedom were "Open Window," which was finished at Collioure, and "Woman with the Hat," a portrait of Mme Matisse painted back in Paris in September. That fall, the two pictures were exhibited at the Salon d'Automne alongside works by a number of artists—among them Marquet, Derain, Valminck, Rouault, Manguin, and Camoin—who also had been experimenting with violent colour. The Paris critic Louis Vauxcelles called the group *les fauves* ("the wild beasts"), and thus Fauvism, the first of the important "isms" in 20th-century painting, was born. The movement was not very coherent, and Matisse was not its sole initiator and animator. But almost immediately he became its widely acknowledged leader.

Almost immediately, too, his financial situation altered for the better. The Stein family in Paris—Gertrude, her brothers Leo and Michael, and the latter's wife Sarah—became Matisse collectors, beginning with the purchase of "Woman with the Hat" at the 1905 Salon d'Automne. In 1906 the artist had a show at the Galerie Druet in Paris in addition to exhibiting again at the Salons des Indépendants and d'Automne. In 1907 a group of admirers, who included Sarah Stein and the German painter Hans Purrmann, organized for him a Left Bank art school, in which he taught off and on until 1911. In 1908 he exhibited in New York, Moscow, and Berlin; the next year he received commissions from Russia and signed a contract with the Galerie Bernheim-Jeune in Paris. From this point, his international reputation was assured, and he was on his way to becoming one of the wealthiest of 20th-century painters. But it must be remembered that in 1909 he was already 40 years old.

He invested a good deal of his new income in travel. In 1906 he visited Algeria, where he was impressed by the textiles and ceramics of the native craftsmen. The next year he went to Padova (Padua), Florence, Arezzo, and Siena in Italy. In 1908 he travelled to Germany, in 1910 to Spain, and in 1911 to Moscow and Tangier. He became an art collector himself, an intellectual capable of tossing off a quotation from Nietzsche, a lucid commentator on his own work, and a shrewd man of affairs. In 1909 the French poet and critic Guillaume Apollinaire wrote: "Bearded, sheltering behind gold glasses a look full of slyness, Monsieur Henri Matisse lives now at Paris, now at Collioure. This *fauve* is a man of refinement. He likes to surround himself with works of ancient and modern art, with precious textiles, and with those pieces of sculpture in which the Negroes of Guinea, Senegal, and Gabon have represented with a rare purity their most Pan-like passions."

Fauvism was too undisciplined to last very long, and soon its adherents were moving, according to their temperaments, toward Expressionism, Cubism, or some kind of neo-traditionalism. Matisse had no liking for these directions, and if "Fauve" is taken to mean simply a painter with a passion for pure colour, he can be said to have remained one all his life. He had, however, too much rationalism in his outlook not to wish for some order in a stylistic situation that threatened to become chaotic. In "Notes d'un peintre," an article he published in *La Grande Revue* in 1908, he explained his intentions with examples: "I have an interior scene to paint; I have before me a wardrobe that gives me a lively sensation of red, and I lay down a red that satisfies me. A relationship is set up between this red and the whiteness of the canvas. If I add a green, if I represent the floor with a yellow, there will be a still satisfactory relationship between the green or the yellow and the whiteness of the canvas. But these different colours weaken each other. The various signs I use must be balanced so as not to destroy each other. I have to put some order in my ideas . . ." The danger of becoming cold and meaningless in the course of establishing an aesthetic order was countered in a statement about painting a female nude: ". . . at first I give it grace and charm, and the problem is to give it something more. I'll condense the meaning of this body by finding its essential lines. At a first look the charm will be less apparent, but it will emerge in the long run from the new image, which will also have a larger, more fully human meaning."

His search for chromatic equilibrium and linear economy can be followed in a series of major works produced between the revelation of Fauvism in 1905 and the end of World War I. In 1906 he painted "Joy of Life"; in 1908, "The Dessert, a Harmony in Red," for the famous Russian collector of Matisses, Sergey Shchukin; in 1911, "The Red Studio"; in 1915, "Goldfish"; in 1916, "Piano Lesson"; and in 1918, "Montalban, Large Landscape."

Character-
istics of
mature
style

In such works, the list of which should be much longer, the main characteristics of Matisse's mature style recur constantly. The forms tend to be outlined in flowing, heavy contours and to have few interior details; the colour is laid on in large, thin, luminous, carefully calculated patches; shadows are practically eliminated; and the depicted space is either extremely shallow or warped into a flatness that parallels the plane of the canvas and defies academic rules for perspective and foreshortening. The total effect, although too intense and freehand to be merely decorative, may recall the patterns of the rugs, textiles, and ceramics of the Islāmic world. The choice and treatment of subject matter imply optimism, hedonism, intelligence, a fastidious sensuality, and, in spite of the many studies of pretty women, scarcely a trace of conventional sentiment. "I don't create a woman," the artist once remarked, "I make a picture."

Riviera years. He continued, although his innovations were less influential than those of the Cubists, to be regarded as a member of the band of Parisian cultural revolutionaries. In 1912 his sculpture was on view in New York and his painting in both Cologne and London. In 1913 he was represented by 13 pictures in the much discussed, much lambasted New York Armory Show, and when the exhibition arrived in Chicago he was given some useful publicity by the burning, happily merely in effigy, of his "Blue Nude." He continued to work frequently with such old companions as Marquet and Camoin; he was on friendly terms with Pablo Picasso, whom he had met through Gertrude Stein; and in 1914, at Collioure, he came to know Picasso's gifted young Cubist disciple, Juan Gris. But middle age, growing affluence, an established international reputation, the disruptions of World War I, and a distaste for public commotion gradually combined to isolate him from the centres of avant-gardism in Paris. Although he kept, after a period of absence, his Paris apartment and maintained a studio in suburban Issy-les-Moulineaux, he began to winter on the French Riviera, and by the early 1920s he was mostly a resident of Nice or its environs.

In the opinion of many art historians, his painting declined in quality during at least the first part of his so-called Nice period. Certainly his pictures became less daring in conception and less economical in means. Like many painters and composers during these years (notably Picasso and Igor Stravinsky), he relaxed into a modernized sort of classicism and into a rather evident attempt to please an art public that was a bit tired of attempts to shock it. His colours became softer, his naturalistic details more numerous, his spatial organization more conventional, and his subject matter—in particular his still lifes with flowers and his exotic nudes with densely patterned Islāmic-style backgrounds—more obviously seductive. He aimed perhaps too directly at what he once referred to as a kind of art that was "like a mental soother, something like a good armchair." But to say this is to judge by the standards of modern problem-solving art that he himself helped to erect. Judged according to less sophisticated standards, such typically Nice-period works as the "Odalisque with Magnolias" and "Decorative Figure on an Ornamental Background" are masterpieces that deserve their popularity.

Prosperity did not make him less industrious. In 1920 he did the sets and costumes for Sergey Diaghilev's Ballet Russe production of *Le Chant du Rossignol*, with music by Stravinsky and choreography by Léonide Massine. He returned to sculpture, which he had neglected for several years, and by 1930 he had completed his fourth and most nearly abstract version of "The Back" (bronzes of all four versions are in the Museum of Modern Art, New York, and the Tate Gallery, London), a monumental female nude in relief, on which he had been working at intervals since 1909. He relaxed, as he had always done, by travelling: to Étretat, on the coast of Normandy, in 1921; to Italy in 1925, and to Tahiti, by way of New York City and San Francisco, in 1930. He found time to serve on the jury of the Carnegie International Exhibition in Pittsburgh, Pennsylvania, where he had been awarded a first prize in 1927. During 1933 he visited Venice and Padova, and in Merion, Pennsylvania, completed and installed the final version of his large mural, "The Dance II" (Barnes Foundation). The first version of the mural (now in the Musée d'Art Moderne de la Ville de Paris) had turned out to be unusable because of an error in measurements, and rather than resort to patching he had done the whole work over again.

Stylistically speaking, although not in terms of actual residence somewhere else, the Nice period in easel pictures can be said to have ended definitely in 1935 with the painting of "The Pink Nude." At about this time, in a conversation with a Paris critic, Matisse made one of the most direct of his many declarations of principle, and in the course of it he implied dissatisfaction with some of his recent work. "Pictures," he said, "that are refinements, subtle shadings, delicacies without energy, need some handsome blues, some handsome reds, some handsome yellows, some substances that stir the sensual depths in men. That was the point of departure for Fauvism: the nerve to rediscover purity of means." Acting on this premise with a capacity for renewal unusual in an artist approaching 70, he turned toward simple contrasts of fresh colour enclosed in flat motifs that sometimes suggested poster patterns. Examples of this neo-Fauvist deployment of "purity of means" are "Lady in Blue," "Dancer and Armchair, Black Background," and "Large Interior in Red."

Graphic art

Matisse had been interested in etching, drypoint, lithography, and allied printmaking techniques since his first years in Paris and had produced a number of occasional prints. In 1932 he had published, as illustrations for an edition of Stéphane Mallarmé's *Poésies*, 29 etchings, in which his talent for supple contours and linear economy was subtly attuned to the "purity of means" evident in the poems. After the outbreak of World War II, he became increasingly active as a graphic artist, notably with his illustrations for Henry de Montherlant's *Pasiphaé* (published in 1944), Pierre Reverdy's *Visages* (1946), the *Lettres portugaises* (1946), Charles Baudelaire's *Fleurs du mal* (1947), Pierre de Ronsard's *Florilège des Amours* (1948), and Charles d'Orléans' *Poèmes* (1950). Along with these books in mostly black and white techniques, he published *Jazz* (1947), a book consisting of his own reflections on art and life, with brilliantly coloured

illustrations made by a technique he called "drawing with scissors": the motifs were pasted together after being cut out of sheets of coloured paper (hand-painted with gouache in order to get the desired tint). The idea, a development of the Cubist device of pasting paper into oil paintings, had been in his mind since at least 1931, when he had used cutout forms to experiment with his first designs for the Barnes Foundation murals.

During the last years of his life, he was a rather solitary man who was separated from his wife and whose grown-up children were scattered in Europe and the United States. After 1941, when he underwent an operation for an intestinal disorder, he was bedridden much of the time; after 1950 he suffered from asthma and heart trouble. Cared for by a faithful Russian woman who had been one of his models in the early 1930s, he lived in a large, sunbathed apartment and studio in the Old Hôtel Regina at Cimiez, overlooking Nice. Often he was obliged to work on his mural-sized projects from a studio bed or a wheelchair with the aid of a crayon attached to a long bamboo pole. But there are no signs of flagging creative energy or of sadness in his final achievements; on the contrary, these works are among the most daring, most accomplished, and most serenely optimistic of his entire career. At Vence, a Riviera hill town where he had a villa from 1943 to 1948, he completed in 1951, after three years of planning and execution, his Chapelle du Rosaire for the local Dominican nuns, one of whom had nursed him during his nearly fatal illness in 1941. He had begun by agreeing to design some stained-glass windows, had gone on to do murals, and had wound up by designing nearly everything inside and outside, including vestments and liturgical objects. Before the chapel was finished, he was at work on the huge coloured-paper cutouts—amplifications of what he had done in the illustrations for *Jazz* —that made him in many respects the "youngest" and most revolutionary artist of the early 1950s. Striking examples of this ultimate explosion of Fauvism are "Sorrows of the King" and "Souvenir of Oceania."

Matisse died on November 3, 1954, at Nice, within two months of his 85th birthday. He is buried in the cemetery of Cimiez.

MAJOR WORKS

PAINTINGS: "The Dinner Table" ("La Desserte"; 1897; Stavros S. Niarchos Collection, London); "Compote and Glass Pitcher" (1899; Baltimore Museum of Art, Baltimore, Maryland); "La Coiffure" (1901; Philadelphia Museum of Art, Philadelphia); "Carmelina" (1903; Museum of Fine Arts, Boston); "Luxe, calme, et volupté" (1904–05; private collection, Paris); "Joy of Life" (1905–06; Barnes Foundation, Merion, Pennsylvania); "Open Window" (1905; John Hay Whitney Collection, New York); "Woman with the Hat" (1905; Walter A. Haas Collection, San Francisco); "The Blue Nude" (1907; Baltimore Museum of Art); "Le Luxe" (1907; Musée National d'Art Moderne, Paris); "The Dessert, a Harmony in Red" (1908; Hermitage, Leningrad); "Red Madras Headdress" (1908, Barnes Foundation, Merion, Pennsylvania); "Dance" (1909; Museum of Modern Art, New York); "The Red Studio" (1911; Museum of Modern Art, New York); "Goldfish and Sculpture" (1911; Museum of Modern Art, New York); "The Blue Window" (1911; Museum of Modern Art, New York); "Goldfish" (1912; Barnes Foundation, Merion, Pennsylvania); "Goldfish" (1915; Samuel A. Marx Collection, Chicago); "Piano Lesson" (1916; Museum of Modern Art, New York); "Interior with a Violin Case" (1917–18; Museum of Modern Art, New York); "Montalban, Large Landscape" (1918; private collection); "Odalisque with Magnolias" (1924; private collection); "Decorative Figure on an Ornamental Background" (1927; Musée National d'Art Moderne, Paris); "The Dance I" (1931–32; Musée d'Art Moderne de la Ville de Paris, Paris); "The Dance II" (1932–33; Barnes Foundation, Merion, Pennsylvania); "The Pink Nude" (1935; Baltimore Museum of Art); "Lady in Blue" (1937; Mrs. John Winterstein Collection, Philadelphia); La Musique" (1939; Albright–Knox Art Gallery, Buffalo); "Dancer and Armchair, Black Background" (1942; private collection); "Large Interior in Red" (1948; Musée National d'Art Moderne, Paris); Chapelle du Rosaire (1951; Vence, France; entire decoration designed by Matisse); "Sorrows of the King" (1952; Musée National d'Art Moderne, Paris); "Souvenir of Oceania" (1953; Museum of Modern Art, New York).

SCULPTURE: (all bronze, several examples of each)—"Jaguar Devouring a Hare" (1899; private collection); "The Slave" (1900–03; Baltimore Museum of Art, and elsewhere); "Madeleine I" (1901; Baltimore Museum of Art and elsewhere); "Small Head" (1906–07); "Two Negresses" (1908); "The Back I–IV" (1909–30); "Jeanette I–V" (1910); "Seated Nude" (1925).

BIBLIOGRAPHY. ALFRED H. BARR, JR., *Matisse: His Art and His Public* (1951, reprinted 1966), is still, in spite of its date, one of the best critical analyses. A more recent general work, aimed at a wider public, is JOHN RUSSELL et al., *The World of Matisse, 1869–1954* (1969). ALBERT ELSEN, "The Sculpture of Matisse," *Artforum* (September through December, 1968), reassesses a somewhat neglected aspect of the artist's achievement. PIERRE SCHNEIDER (ed.), *Exposition Henri Matisse* (1970), is the fact-crammed catalog of the Paris retrospective show of 1970. LOUIS ARAGON, *Henri Matisse, roman*, 2 vol. (1971), is not really, as the title implies, a novel, but rather a poetic evocation by a perceptive French contemporary of the painter. Useful bibliographies are in Barr (*op. cit.*), for the period before 1951; and in JEAN LEYMARIE et al., *Henri Matisse* (1966), the catalog of the UCLA Henri Matisse retrospective, for the period 1951–66.

(R.McMu.)

Mato Grosso

Mato Grosso is an inland state (*estado*) of Brazil in the Grande Região Centro-Oeste (Grand Central-West Region). It is bounded on the northwest by the states of Rondônia and Amazonas, on the northeast by Pará, on the east by Goiás and Minas Gerais, on the southeast by São Paulo and Paraná, and on the southwest and west by the countries of Paraguay and Bolivia. One of the remaining great frontier regions of the world, its name means "great woods." The third-largest state of Brazil, after Amazonas and Pará, it has an area of 475,504 square miles (1,231,549 square kilometres). Its population has been growing rapidly since about 1950 and in 1970 was 1,600,000; nevertheless, large areas remain unsettled. The state capital is Cuiabá.

History. Mato Grosso was settled first by pioneering gold seekers from São Paulo after they had been forced to retreat by the *emboabas* (Portuguese colonists) of Minas Gerais in the so-called war of the *emboabas* in 1708, over mining rights in gold fields. With the founding of Cuiabá, where rich placer mines had been found, in 1719, Mato Grosso became a district of the captaincy of São Paulo, and in 1748 it became an independent captaincy. In 1761 the capital was transferred to Vila Bela, on the Rio Guaporé, but in 1820 it was returned to Cuiabá. During the colonial period and until deposits were largely exhausted, its placer mines supplied substantial quantities of gold and some diamonds. After the decline of mining, cattle ranching emerged as the principal activity. Mato Grosso became a province of the empire in 1822 and a state of the federal union in 1889.

The entire area's overall growth and development was long retarded by its lack of access to the sea. Until the railroad was built across southern Mato Grosso in 1914, the only means of communication except by overland trails was by way of the Paraguay and Paraná rivers, 2,000 miles (3,000 kilometres) to the Atlantic. Only in the second half of the 20th century have highways begun to offer more widespread communications. The expedition of Brazilian explorer Marshal Cândido Mariano da Silva Rondon in the early part of the 20th century furnished the first complete, accurate data about Mato Grosso; some sections of the state, however, remained virtually uninvestigated in the 1970s.

The natural environment. Most of Mato Grosso lies on the western extension of the Brazilian Plateau, across which runs the watershed that separates the Amazon Basin from the basin of the Río de la Plata system. The elevated region is known as the Planalto do Mato Grosso, or Mato Grosso Plateau, and its elevation is about 3,000 feet. Its northern slope, drained by the Rio Xingu, Rio Tapajós, and Rio Madeira, descends to the valley of the Amazon. The valley of the Rio Araguaia, an affluent of the Rio Tocantins, marks the eastern border of the state. The southern slope drains southward through a multitude of streams flowing into the Paraná in the southeast and its

Highlands, river valleys, and plains

chief tributary the Paraguay on the southwest. The general elevation in the south is much lower than in the north, ranging from 300 to 400 feet (90 to 120 metres) and large areas bordering the Paraguay are swampy. The basins of the Paraná and Paraguay are separated by low ranges extending north from Paraguay. The western part of the state, chiefly a floodplain (*pantanal*), is among Brazil's best grazing lands, and ranks as one of the great tropical grazing lands of the world.

The lowlands are hot and humid, the highlands hot and dry. The average temperature is 79° F (26° C). Average annual rainfall is 50 to 60 inches (1,300 to 1,500 millimetres). There is a distinct dry season from May to September.

Natural vegetation includes expanses of grassland, densely wooded areas, and, in the highlands, extensive plains, or *campos*, with scrub growth and light forest.

Population. The Grande Região Centro-Oeste, composed of Mato Grosso, Goiás, and the Distrito Federal, since 1950 has had the highest rate of population growth in Brazil. The population of Mato Grosso in 1950 was 522,044; in 1960 it was 910,262; and by 1970 it was 1,600,000. Historically, the state's population has been concentrated in the southeast, and the greatest growth has been in that area. The state as a whole still has a population density of less than two persons per square mile (less than 0.8 persons per square kilometre), the lowest of any Brazilian state outside Amazonas and the federal territories in the north.

Ethnically, the state includes a relatively high proportion of mestizos (persons of mixed European and Indian ancestry), as do other areas of the interior. Although many of the new immigrants also are mestizos, large numbers have come from various parts of Brazil and represent differing degrees of European, Indian, and Negro extraction, and immigrants of Japanese ancestry have settled along the railroad in the south.

The population is chiefly rural, and there are few cities, the principal ones being Corumbá, Campo Grande, and the state capital, Cuiabá. The influx of new settlers has been distributed about equally between rural and urban areas, expanding both segments of the population.

Administration and social conditions. Like the other Brazilian states, Mato Grosso has its own constitution and laws, conforming with the national constitution. The governor and the members of the legislature are elected.

Social conditions are those of an expanding frontier. Public health and welfare services are limited in the growing cities and developing rural areas of the southeast and even more limited in the sparsely settled expanses outside that region. Elementary education is free and compulsory, by law, but there are insufficient numbers of schools and teachers to supply it. Higher education is not available in the state.

Economy. Livestock raising and agriculture represent the principal economic activities of Mato Grosso. The state supports over 10,000,000 head of cattle, the principal market being São Paulo. Mato Grosso has important deposits of gold, industrial diamonds, iron, manganese, nickel, and platinum. Manganese deposits south of Corumbá have been mined since the 1940s and some iron ore and nickel are produced, but the inadequacy of transportation facilities has been a major barrier to further development.

Mineral resources

Campo Grande is the main agricultural centre in southern Mato Grosso, a position enhanced by the railroad communication with São Paulo, the movement of the coffee frontier toward the west and northwest of São Paulo state, and the concomitant shift of population. The existence of dark, purple-coloured soil, *terra rosa*, and other fertile soils in the area of Campo Grande and south into Dourados, near the southern tip of Mato Grosso, allows a wide diversity of crops to be grown. Coffee, rice, cotton, sugarcane, and corn (maize), the main commercial crops, are produced in that order. Colonization projects instituted by the federal and state governments in the vicinity of Dourados, with emphasis upon coffee cultivation, resulted in that area becoming one of the fastest growing in Brazil.

Transportation. Mato Grosso has shared with the rest of the Grande Região Centro-Oeste the isolation imposed by distance and the existence of numerous north–south ridges of watersheds that have served as barriers to transport and communications from east to west since colonial times. The only natural communications routes were along the rivers, north to the Amazon Basin, or south to the Paraná–Plata system. Overland travel was by horse or mule. The extension of the railroad across southern Mato Grosso in 1914 made Campo Grande the economic and transport centre of the region and provided the first effective overland link between the state and the national capital at Rio de Janeiro. Both Campo Grande and Corumbá are served by the railroad, and Corumbá also has rail connections with Santa Cruz, Bolivia. Cuiabá has no rail connections but is served by river boats from Corumbá and by road from Campo Grande.

Mato Grosso's 3,850 miles (6,200 kilometres) of federal roads are largely trails, many of which are impassable during the rainy season. Although paved roads are rare outside the principal cities, road transport has become increasingly important in the second half of the 20th century. While the Transamazônica road, under construction since 1970, which is to cross South America from coast to coast, passes to the north of the state, the transportation network which will be linked to it will be of particular significance for the economic development of Mato Grosso. All three principal cities are served by airports, and even remote areas have become accessible by air.

Cultural life. The state's cultural life, like many of its other characteristics, is that of an expanding frontier. Except for an academy of letters at Cuiabá, an association for cultural exchange at Guiratinga, and an ethnographic museum at Campo Grande, major cultural institutions—such as state theatres, libraries, and universities—have not yet emerged. Its traditions have been those of the cattle ranch and the farm, being transformed in the second half of the 20th century by the infusion of immigrants, many from similar parts of Brazil.

BIBLIOGRAPHY. W.L. SCHURZ, "Conditions Affecting Settlement on the Matto Grosso Highland and in the Gran Chaco," in W.L.G. JOERG (ed.), *Pioneer Settlement: Coöperative Studies by Twenty-Six Authors* (1937), is a scientific study analyzing prospects for immigration, resettlement, and colonization. VESPASIANO BARBOSA MARTINS, *Saudacão a Campo Grande* (1943), provides a brief account of the historical development of Campo Grande; see also the IBGE, CONSELHO NACIONAL DE ESTATISTICA, *Campo Grande* (1956), a statistical survey.

(J.L.Ti.)

Matter and Antimatter

The substance of every physical object in the known part of the universe is called matter. The ultimate constituents of matter are three elementary particles: the electron (e^-), the proton (p), and the neutron (n). Various combinations of neutrons and protons make up the few hundred different atomic nuclei known today. Each proton has a positive electric charge of 1.6×10^{-19} coulomb, where a coulomb is the practical (mks) unit of electric charge and a mass of approximately 10^{-24} gram. Neutrons have no electric charge; the neutron mass is almost identical to that of the proton. An electron has a negative charge equal in magnitude to that of the proton and a mass approximately $\frac{1}{2,000}$ that of a proton. The most important subatomic particles and related topics mentioned below are described in more detail in the article PARTICLES, SUBATOMIC.

Concepts and general properties. Antimatter is made up of elementary particles that have the mass and charge of electrons, protons, or neutrons, their counterparts in ordinary matter, but for which the charge is opposite in sign. Such particles are called positrons (e^+), antiprotons ($\bar{p}$), and antineutrons ($\bar{n}$), or, collectively, antiparticles. First predicted by theory, all antiparticles have been produced in the laboratory. Matter and antimatter cannot coexist at close range for more than a small fraction of a second because they annihilate each other with re-

lease of large quantities of energy. It has been suggested that some distant galaxies may be composed entirely of antimatter, but as the only known process for creating antimatter is the process called pair production, which produces equal masses of matter and antimatter from the same point at the same time, the so far insuperable difficulty of accounting for the wide separation of large quantities of matter and antimatter after production and without annihilation arises.

The concept of antimatter first arose in close connection with the duality between positive and negative charge. The work of P.A.M. Dirac on the negative energy states of the electron led to the prediction and, finally, to laboratory production of a particle identical in every respect but one to the electron, that is, with positive instead of negative charge. Such a particle, called the positron (e^+), is not found in ordinary matter. The life expectancy or duration of the positron in ordinary matter is very short. Unless the positron is moving extremely fast, it will be drawn close to a nearby electron by the Coulomb attraction, that is, the attraction between opposite charges. A collision between the positron and electron results in their simultaneous disappearance, their masses being converted into energy in accordance with the Einstein relation $E = mc^2$, where c is the velocity of light. This process is called annihilation, and the resultant energy is emitted in the form of high-energy quanta of electromagnetic radiation or gamma rays. In symbols this process is written as $e^+ + e^- \rightarrow \gamma$ rays. The inverse reaction $\gamma \rightarrow e^+ + e^-$ can also proceed under appropriate conditions, and the process is called electron-positron creation. This last process is the one commonly used to produce positrons in the laboratory.

The electron mass is so small that the discovery of the positron did not immediately suggest the existence of antimatter. The antimatter counterparts of the proton and neutron, the antiproton ($\bar{p}$) and the antineutron ($\bar{n}$), were discovered in the mid-1950s after many years of speculation on the possibility of their existence. In principle, all of the building blocks for the construction of higher antiatoms and antimatter are available. Antideuterons, the antiparticles corresponding to the nucleus of deuterium, have been produced in very high energy collisions, at the 30 GeV (gigaelectron volt) synchrotron of the Brookhaven (N.Y.) National Laboratory.

The electrical properties of antimatter are opposite to those of ordinary matter; thus, for example, the $\bar{p}$ has a negative charge, and the $\bar{n}$, although electrically neutral, has a magnetic moment opposite in sign to that of the neutron. Properties other than electrical also are reversed from matter to antimatter (see below), and, therefore, the behaviour of antimatter in contact with matter is not purely electromagnetic (with the consequent symmetry between positive and negative charge).

Antimatter, when not in contact with matter, is as stable as ordinary matter, and the existence of an anti-universe consisting of antigalaxies, antistars, and antiplanets is possible. If an antiproton, however, came within 10^{-13} centimetre of a proton for even 10^{-23} second, the proton-antiproton pair would be annihilated and their masses would be transformed into energy. One gram of antimatter on Earth would annihilate one gram of matter, releasing an energy of 5×10^7 kilowatt-hours. The energy released in this annihilation process is not emitted in the form of electromagnetic quanta but as pions (π^+, π^-, π^0), also called pi-mesons. Pions are interpreted, following the suggestion made by H. Yukawa in 1935, as the quanta of the nuclear field, by analogy with photons as the quanta of the electromagnetic field.

Historical survey. In early studies of electrical phenomena, the asymmetry between positive and negative charge was considered to be fundamental. For example, glass rubbed on silk could acquire a positive charge, hard rubber on cat's fur a negative charge. When a formal theory of electromagnetism was finally developed by the work of C.A. Coulomb, M. Faraday and A.M. Ampère, and J.C. Maxwell, its laws were symmetrical with respect to positive and negative charges. One can easily verify that Maxwell's equations are not changed in form if the sign of all charges is changed, of course simultaneously changing the

Prediction of the positron

The process of annihilation

sign of all currents and electric and magnetic fields. The deeper meaning of this symmetry was not grasped until the advent of quantum mechanics.

Advent of quantum mechanics

Dirac's contributions. In 1928 Dirac discovered the relativistic equation that now bears his name while developing his contribution to relativistic quantum mechanics. The Dirac equation correctly described the so-called spin ½ particles (which have a quantum number ½ associated with and determined by their axial spin) such as electrons and protons. The new equation led to a much better understanding of the properties of the electron, but it admitted solutions corresponding to states with negative energy. Dirac's second great contribution was to show how this apparently incorrect result could be reinterpreted to expand the scope of quantum mechanics.

The following year (1929) he proposed the hole theory, in which he assumed that almost all the negative energy states are already occupied. The few remaining empty negative energy states are called "holes." These holes were shown by Dirac to behave like electrons with positive charge. He thus predicted the existence of a new particle, identical to the electron in all properties except the charge. This particle, today called the positron, was observed for the first time by Carl David Anderson in a Wilson cloud chamber in 1932 when he found the track of a positive electron resulting from the interaction of cosmic rays with matter.

Negative energy

The entire problem of negative energy solution and of negative probability density was further clarified in 1934, when Wolfgang Pauli and Victor Weisskopf reinterpreted the Klein-Gordon equation for scalar particles as a field theory. They showed that one can associate both positive- and negative-energy particles with the same field. In other words, for scalar particles as well as for spin ½ particles, an antiparticle may be expected for each observed particle.

Positronium. The Dirac theory of electrons and positrons predicts that an e^+ and an e^-, because of Coulomb attraction, will bind together into an atom just as an e^- and a p (proton) form a hydrogen atom. The e^+e^- bound system is called positronium; its annihilation into gamma rays has been observed. The tendency of e^+ and e^- to annihilate each other when close together makes positronium extremely unstable. Its lifetime is of the order of 10^{-7} second when the total spin of the positronium is 1, and of the order of 10^{-10} second when its spin is 0. These lifetimes, computed from Dirac theory, agree well with experimental values and thus lend additional confirmation to the theory, as well as to the concept of symmetry between particles and antiparticles.

Antiproton and antineutron. Both protons and neutrons are particles of spin ½ and thus are expected to be described by the Dirac equation. If this is the case, the existence of the antiproton ($\bar{p}$) and the antineutron ($\bar{n}$) is predicted. Antiprotons can be produced according to the reaction $p + p \rightarrow p + p + p + \bar{p}$, that is, by bombarding protons with protons. In this equation two extra particles of proton mass appear as the end product of the transformation of energy into mass according to the formula $E = mc^2$ (see above). Such masses can be produced only if enough energy is available, that is, if the incident proton has a kinetic energy of at least 5.6 GeV (5.6×10^9 electron volts). Such energies became available in the 1950s at the Berkeley (Calif.) Bevatron. In 1955 a team of physicists led by Owen Chamberlain and Emilio Segré observed that antiprotons are produced by high-energy collisions. The experiment consisted mainly of a system of detectors and analyzers capable of accepting negatively charged particles whose masses were approximately equal to that of the proton. The particles originated from a target bombarded with approximately 10^{10} protons per second, the bombarding protons having been accelerated to an energy of 6.2 GeV. When the new negatively charged particles came to rest inside a detector, a tremendous release of energy was observed, giving one of the most conclusive proofs that antiprotons had indeed been discovered. Antineutrons also were discovered at the Berkeley Bevatron by observing their annihilation in matter with a consequent release of high energies.

High-energy role of the Bevatron

By the time the antiproton was discovered, a host of new subatomic particles had also been discovered; all of these particles are now known to have a corresponding antiparticle. Thus, there are positive and negative muons, positive and negative pions, the K-meson and the anti-K-meson, plus a long list of baryons and antibaryons (see PARTICLES, SUBATOMIC). As mentioned above, antideuterons have also been observed. Most of these newly discovered particles have too short a lifetime for them to be able to combine with electrons. The exception is the positive muon that together with an electron has been observed to form a muonium atom.

Production of antimatter. *Production in accelerators.* All antiparticles, except positrons, are produced only in high-energy collisions. The positrons, because of their extremely small mass, can be emitted in the disintegration of artificially produced radioisotopes. Beams of antiprotons are now available for experiments at a few accelerators. At the Brookhaven National Laboratory and CERN (Switz.) twin accelerators, some 10^9 antiprotons are produced per second. High-resolution beams giving usable intensity of 10^5 antiprotons per second have been built. A positron beam of much higher intensity can be produced by a high-energy electron accelerator. Positrons are obtained in this way by first letting the electron beam strike a target; it then produces gamma rays by *Bremsstrahlung*, that is, by emission from decelerated electrons. The gamma rays strike a secondary target producing electron-positron pairs. The positrons are then separated from the electrons by conventional magnetic methods.

Production by cosmic ray interactions. No significant flux of antiprotons due to interaction of primary cosmic rays with the upper layers of the atmosphere could reach the Earth's surfaces because of absorption in the atmosphere. The primary cosmic radiation itself is known to be free of antimatter to better than one part in 10^6.

Invariance principles. One of the most important consequences of relativistic quantum mechanics was the idea of invariance principles. One such principle of great relevance in the present context is that of invariance of the laws of physics under charge conjugation.

Operation of charge conjugation. Charge conjugation in relativistic quantum mechanics is a formal operation whose physical meaning is that of transforming every particle into its antiparticle. A reversal of the electrical properties of all known particles is associated with the particle-antiparticle conjugation, though there have been speculations that this might not always be the case. Other quantum numbers similar in their behaviour to charge (Q) are used in particle physics to describe a particle completely. Thus there is the baryon number B, which has the value of $+1$ for all baryons (particles with masses greater than or equal to that of the proton) and -1 for all antibaryons, isotopic spin T and its third component T_3, and hypercharge Y. Both Q and B for a system are absolutely conserved quantities. Y and T_3 conservation is not satisfied in weak interactions. Like Q, the quantum numbers B, Y, and T_3 change sign under charge conjugation. The absolute conservation of Q and B implies an absolute differentiation between p and $\bar{p}$, as well as n and $\bar{n}$. This is not the case for other particles. The neutral pion (π^0) is identical to its antiparticle since it carries no quantum number to distinguish it. Even more interesting is the case of the K^0 meson, which has $Y = +1$. Its antiparticle, $\bar{K}^0$, has $Y = -1$; thus it is distinct from the K^0. This distinction is very sharp for a very short time (of the order of 10^{-10} second) after the creation of either a K^0 or $\bar{K}^0$. After this period the weak interaction begins to make itself felt by inducing transitions between K^0 and $\bar{K}^0$. As a result, the states which are physically observable are neither the K^0 nor the $\bar{K}^0$ but are two states which are formed by linear superposition of K^0 and $\bar{K}^0$ and are called K^0_1, K^0_2. Because of the presence of the weak interactions, the mass degeneracy is removed and the mass of the K^0_1 and the K^0_2 now differ by one part in 10^{14}. Following an original suggestion of Abraham Pais and Oreste Piccioni, this unique situation has led to a series of unique interference and regeneration experiments, as well as to the possibility of testing the equality of the gravitational attraction of particles and antiparticles.

The definition of particles

Theory of invariance. The meaning of the invariance of the laws of physics under charge conjugation can be explained in the following way: consider a system of physical objects S and build a charge conjugate system $\bar{S}$. Let the systems S and $\bar{S}$ evolve in time, for a time interval T. Call the evolved systems $S(T)$ and $\bar{S}(T)$. If the charge conjugate of $\bar{S}(T)$ is identical with $S(T)$, then the laws of physics that govern the time evolution of the two systems are said to be invariant under charge conjugation. It is known experimentally that the most important forces governing all phenomena in the universe as it is known to man obey laws that are invariant under charge conjugation. Explicitly, these are the nuclear forces and the electromagnetic forces. It is also known experimentally that the weak interaction is not invariant under charge conjugation. This fact is extremely important because it shows that an invariance principle applicable to a certain rather wide class of phenomena does not have an absolute validity.

Absolute definition of matter

Whether or not the laws of physics are invariant under charge conjugation is relevant to the following somewhat philosophical question: can one give an absolute definition of matter and antimatter or only define one with respect to the other? The answer is, naturally, one can only define the difference between matter and antimatter if all laws of physics are invariant under charge conjugation. Since, however, the weak interaction is not invariant under charge conjugation, some delicate procedure can be prescribed to test whether some isolated system is matter or antimatter. Oddly enough, it turns out that in order to perform the test it is necessary to give an absolute definition of right-handedness. Thus, say, by mere radio communication with an intelligent being in a far galaxy, one could not reach a conclusion with regard to whether their matter would annihilate in contact with ours. This curious fact is the consequence of a more general invariance principle that is valid for nuclear, electromagnetic, and weak interactions. The physical laws governing the above interactions are invariant under the combined operations of charge conjugation and of parity transformation (*CP* transformation). An even weaker process has been observed in the decay of K^0-mesons, which is not invariant under *CP*. In principle, this gives a method for determining whether or not the visitor from outer space could be dangerous to Earth.

Cosmology and antimatter. Many attempts have been made to investigate the importance of antimatter in cosmological problems. The two main starting points are: (a) there is symmetry between matter and antimatter, (b) in all known processes there is an absolute conservation of baryon number.

Theory and experiment. Thus, it seems that theoretical and experimental knowledge of matter and antimatter is relevant to the understanding of the creation and constitution of the universe. The question of the creation of the universe really transcends cosmology, which concerns itself only with the evolution of the universe. Yet it is just the present understanding of the evolution process that makes the hypothesis of the existence of any significant amount of antimatter in the universe unlikely. Obviously no star can contain a close mixture of matter and antimatter; otherwise it would instantaneously explode with more violence than a supernova. Interstellar gas, and even intergalactic gas, cannot be a mixture, either. This is because among the annihilation products of proton plus antiproton into pions there is a certain amount of π^0 mesons, which in turn decay into two energetic gamma rays. Satellite experiments have not detected enough of such gamma rays to suggest a significant amount of antimatter annihilation. One could resort to the hypothesis that matter and antimatter are separated on the scale of clusters of galaxies. The creation of baryon-antibaryon pairs, however, is very localized, the particle and antiparticle being created at distances of approximately 10^{-13} centimetre. No present understanding of the evolution of the universe can explain the unmixing of matter and antimatter if they had been originally created together. Thus, as Hannes Alfvén has pointed out, any statement about the existence of equal amounts of matter and antimatter in the universe has to be founded on an artificial assumption that is not subject to observational tests.

Quasar hypothesis. It has been repeatedly proposed that the existence of antimatter might offer a natural explanation of the quasar phenomenon. Quasars, or quasistellar objects, if at distances comparable to those of the external galaxies as one hypothesis suggests, are pouring out energy at an enormous rate from a small volume of space; the rate is so high that ordinary processes of physics do not suffice to explain it. Annihilation of matter and antimatter is the most efficient energy-producing process and would easily provide the tremendous energy output observed for these objects. Some scientists, for example Philip Morrison, now feel that a more conventional explanation of such objects is possible without the assumption of matter-antimatter annihilation. No such assumptions are needed to explain cosmic rays and astronomical sources of X-rays. The recent discovery of pulsars (pulsating radio-astronomical sources), their probable association with neutron stars, and the subsequent study of these objects have led to a rather self-consistent picture including good agreement with X-ray and cosmic ray observations.

Amount of antimatter in universe

Nevertheless, the presence of large amounts of antimatter in the universe cannot at present be ruled out completely, nor can the possibility that some cosmic sources of intense radiation might be due to the interpenetration of matter and antimatter. But it can be shown that the total relative amount of antimatter in the Galaxy must be less than one part in 10^7.

Soon after the discovery of the antiproton the question was raised as to whether antimatter would be subject to gravitational attraction or repulsion from ordinary matter. This question is of extreme importance because gravitational repulsion between matter and antimatter is inconsistent with the theory of general relativity. The answers to such questions can be obtained experimentally because of the properties of K^0 and $\bar{K}^0$ mesons. Observation of the interference phenomena between K^0_1, and $\bar{K}^0_2$ led to the conclusion, by M.L. Good, that the gravitational interaction between matter and antimatter is identical to that between matter and matter.

BIBLIOGRAPHY. C.N. YANG, *Elementary Particles: A Short History of Some Discoveries in Atomic Physics* (1962), an excellent book for the educated layman; R.K. ADAIR and E.C. FOWLER, *Strange Particles* (1963), good descriptions of strange particles, such as the K^0 mesons, for those who know some physics; H. ALFVEN, *Worlds-Antiworlds* (1966), an interesting discourse on the unlikely supposition that matter and antimatter can be polarized.

The following articles in *Scientific American* are good expositions: E. SEGRE and C.E. WIEGAND, "The Antiproton," 194:37–41 (June 1956); P. MORRISON, "The Overthrow of Parity," 196:45–53 (April 1957); M. GELL-MANN and E.P. ROSENBAUM, "Elementary Particles," 197:72–86 (July 1957); G. BURBIDGE and F. HOYLE, "Anti-Matter," 198:34–39 (April 1958); S.B. TREIMAN, "The Weak Interactions," 200:72–78 (March 1959); and H. ALFVEN, "Antimatter and Cosmology," 216:106–112 (April 1967).

(J.L.-F.)

Matthias I Corvinus

Matthias I Corvinus, king of Hungary (1458–90), was one of the most impressive figures of his time in central and eastern Europe. An expert in diplomacy and the military art, he was also one of the first adepts of Renaissance culture among the princes north of the Alps. His reign was a period of great efforts to reconstruct the Hungarian state after decades of feudal anarchy, chiefly by means of financial, military, judiciary, and administrative reforms.

Matthias (Mátyás Hunyadi) was born in Kolozsvár (now Cluj, Romania), on February 24, 1443, the second son of a military leader, János Hunyadi. After the death of his father and elder brother, Matthias became heir to a vast landed propriety and to a great name glorified by the chroniclers of the war against Turkish conquerors. After the death of King Ladislas Posthumus of Austria (Habsburg), and despite dynastic claims of his

Matthias I Corvinus, detail from the gate tower
of Ortenburg Castle, Bautzen, now in East
Germany, 1486.
By courtesy of the Magyar Nemzeti Muzeum, Budapest

Election
as king

uncle, the Holy Roman emperor Frederick III, and other
pretenders to the throne, a general Diet held in Buda and
Pest in January 1458 elected Matthias king. This was the
first time in the medieval Hungarian kingdom that a
member of the nobility, without dynastic ancestry and
relationship, mounted the royal throne, although it happened contemporaneously in the neighbouring Bohemian
kingdom. Such elections upset the usual course of dynastic
succession. Crossing the plans of the Habsburg dynasty
(and partly those of the Jagiełłos of Poland), they caused
a long series of controversies in that part of Europe. In
the Czech and Hungarian states they heralded a new era,
characterized by the supremacy of the "estates and orders," a dietal system, and a tendency to centralization.

After struggles to stabilize his reign against repeated
attacks, mostly from baronial opposition and the foreign
dynastic pretenders, Matthias held back Turkish invad-
èrs, who had annexed the Serbian and Bosnian territories
on his southern frontiers. He reorganized a defensive
system against the Turks, taking his lack of forces into
consideration.

He did everything he could to increase state incomes
and to improve the modern elements of his army and his
warfare. One of his first steps was a reform of finances
and taxes (1467), ending special exemptions to large
proprietors. A few years later the treasury was developed
into a well-organized office, collecting regularly the "extraordinary" taxes (originally intended in case of urgent
necessity, mostly under the pressure of the Turkish peril). As a result the state income reached a considerable
sum. The high taxation burdened mostly the peasants.

The financial reforms were not easily accepted. Revolts
endangered the government, occasionally even the reign
of Matthias. The opposition, stimulated by foreign
forces, won over some old counsellors of the King. But
Matthias always succeeded, by force and diplomacy, in
calming the opposition and in re-establishing, even reinforcing, the political and social conditions of his sovereignty. Some historians have characterized him as an
early representative of modern absolutism; but this was
far beyond his possibilities. He increased the influence of
the lower nobility against the barons; he tried to oppress
or at least to moderate feudal anarchy; he protected merchants and small proprietors and even peasants, not
against their own lords but against other troubles; and he
tried to improve the system of central government (without disturbing local autonomies), mainly by increasing
the governmental role of the chancellors, the royal secretaries, and other offices. His jurists began a great work of
codification; a royal decree of 1486 was intended to summarize the main principles of law "for all times." This
meant, together with the further development of the

standing army, a certain degree of centralization, within
the limits of an essentially feudal state.

Successes in foreign politics, diplomacy, and warfare
contributed to the stabilization of his own authority and
his country's position. His diplomacy grew more active
during the second and third decades of his reign. He
maintained constant diplomatic relations with the papacy, with Venice, Naples, and other Italian states and repeatedly exchanged ambassadors with France, Burgundy,
Switzerland, and many German territories; later he tried
to establish regular contacts with Russia and, occasionally, with Persia and Egypt. His main purpose may have
been the creation of a system of alliances against actual
or possible rivals and enemies. His diplomatic activity
varied with the varying aims of his foreign policy. After
gaining suzerainty over Bosnia (1463), Matthias tried to
occupy the Bohemian kingdom. This was a grave error;
the Jagełło dynasty intervened, and a 10-year struggle
was followed by a peace that left the Bohemian crown to
Vladislav II, while Matthias retained the Moravian and
Silesian territories with the royal title.

An almost continuous rivalry with the emperor Frederick III ran through Matthias' reign. He tried repeatedly,
but without success, to induce (or coerce) the Emperor
to renounce his claims to the Hungarian throne. Following the Polish–Bohemian war, Matthias tried to annihilate
the main base of Frederick's dynastic power. After a long
series of military successes, aided by the Emperor's German and Austrian adversaries, he occupied Vienna and a
considerable part of the Habsburg family possessions.
But he could not diminish the Habsburg influence in the
German Empire or in central and western Europe. Indeed, Habsburg power began to increase as a result of
events in Burgundy. Until his death (April 6, 1490) Matthias remained in possession of his conquests; thereafter,
all of them were lost.

Hungary's political relations with the papacy and the
Italian states were connected with the interests in Turkish
wars. But they were connected also with the special rights
of Hungarian kings concerning the distribution of ecclesiastical dignities in their country. This complicated the
relations between church and kingdom. After the second
marriage of Matthias (1476), to Beatrice of Aragon,
princess of Naples, the King's diplomacy became a factor
in Italian state affairs. His connections with Florence,
Milan, and other Italian states and cultural centres reflected his interest in Italian art and humanistic culture.

Matthias deserved his reputation, mentioned by contemporaries, for being "a friend of the Muses." The knowledge of many languages, classic latinity, modern humanistic ideas, and ancient books and the support of new art
and science were all familiar to him since childhood. His
education took place partly on battlefields, partly under
the control of prominent humanists. He never ceased to
read and to learn. Supporting all kinds of art, he founded
a considerable library—the famous Corvina. He trusted,
like the majority of his contemporaries, in astrology and
other semi-scientific beliefs of his age; but he supported
many real scientists and participated eagerly in the discussions of philosophers invited to his court.

Matthias possessed high personal qualities, as reported
by friends and enemies alike. He tried to strengthen his
state, not without success. His name became later—during centuries of Turkish occupation and Habsburg oppression—a symbol of strength and independence. His
memory was glorified by statesmen and military leaders
as well as by students of cultural progress. And, despite
the heavy taxes, it was also glorified by the people, who
were reported, a few years after the King's death, as being
willing to pay still more, "if only he could rise again."
This could be explained by the general decline of the
country after Matthias' death but also by a popular saying: "Matthias is dead—justice is lost."

Foreign
successes

Intellectual
interests

BIBLIOGRAPHY. There is no modern English-language biography of Matthias I Corvinus. IMRE LUKINICH (ed.), *Mátyás
Király Emlékkönyv*, 2 vol. (1940), contains articles analyzing
the family relations, personality, political, military, and cultural activities of the king. VILMOS FRAKNOI, *Hunyadi Mátyás
király, 1440–1490* (1890); and ELEMER MALYUSZ, "Matthias

Corvinus," in *Menschen die Geschichte machten*, vol. 2, pp. 187–191 (1931), are two classic biographies; LAJOS ELEKES, *Mátyás és kora* (1956), is an essay on the social and political background of the king's activities.

(L.El.)

Maupassant, Guy de

Maupassant is "an almost irreproachable writer in a genre that is not," said the 19th-century French critic Jules Lemaître. Maupassant wrote novels, poems, plays, and travel books, but his fame rests primarily on his short stories. Their masterly style earned them the admiration of expert writers in the genre, from Henry James to W. Somerset Maugham. They owe their worldwide popularity among less sophisticated readers to a combination of brevity, slickness, and a pervasive sexuality that prompted James to say that Maupassant's work was "little else but a report of its innumerable manifestations."

Archives Photographiques

Maupassant, photograph by Nadar (Gaspard-Félix Tournachon), c. 1885.

Early life. Henry-René-Albert-Guy de Maupassant was born on August 5, 1850, the elder of the two children of Gustave and Laure de Maupassant. His mother's claim that he was born at the Château de Miromesnil near Dieppe has been disputed. (It seems probable that for snobbish reasons the parents rented the château, but it cannot be proved that Maupassant was actually born there.) The second son, Hervé, was born in 1856 at the Château Blanc at Grainville-Ymauville near Étretat.

Family difficulties

Both parents came of Norman families, the father's of the minor aristocracy; the particle "de" had been dropped during the French Revolution, but it was restored under pressure from the bride shortly before the wedding. The marriage was a failure. There was no provision for divorce in France at that time, but the couple separated for good when Guy was 11 years old, after 15 years of married life. Guy sided strongly with his mother, was a devoted son all his life and, in spite of the help that he received from him, was markedly hostile to his father. The failure of the marriage left its mark on the man and the writer. It explains Maupassant's fears of marriage and the frequent appearances in his stories of the ridiculous persecuted husband and the lonely fatherless child.

Although the Maupassants were a free-thinking family, Guy received his first education from the church. When he was 13 and had learned all he could from the parish priest, he was sent to a small seminary at Yvetot that took both lay and clerical pupils. From the start, he felt a decided antipathy for this form of life and deliberately engineered his own expulsion for some trivial offense in 1868. He moved to the lycée at Le Havre and passed his baccalaureate the following year.

In the autumn of 1869 he began law studies in Paris, which were interrupted by the outbreak of the Franco-Prussian War. Maupassant volunteered, served first as a private in the field, and was later transferred through his father's intervention to the quartermaster corps. His first-hand experience of war was to provide him with the material for some of his finest stories.

He was demobilized in July 1871 and resumed his law studies in Paris. His father came to his assistance again and obtained a post for him in the Ministry of Marine, which was intended to keep him until he qualified as a lawyer. He did not care for the bureaucracy, but was not unsuccessful and was several times promoted. His father managed to have him transferred, at his own wish, to the Ministry of Public Instruction in 1879.

Apprenticeship with Flaubert. Maupassant's mother, Laure, was the sister of Alfred Le Poittevin, who had been the most cherished friend of Gustave Flaubert's youth and who had died in 1848 at the age of 32. She remained on affectionate terms with the novelist for the rest of his life. (The suggestion has been made by more than one of Maupassant's biographers that he was the illegitimate son of Laure and Flaubert, but they have not produced any convincing evidence in support of their view.) Laure de Maupassant had sent her son to make Flaubert's acquaintance at Croisset in 1867. When he returned to Paris after the war, she asked Flaubert to keep an eye on him. This was the beginning of the apprenticeship that was the making of Maupassant the writer. Whenever Flaubert was staying in Paris, he used to invite Maupassant to lunch on Sundays, lecture him on style, and correct his youthful exercises. He also introduced him to some of the leading writers of the time, such as Émile Zola, Ivan Turgenev, Édmond de Goncourt, and Henry James, who visited Flaubert in his Paris flat on Sunday afternoons.

Influence of Flaubert on Maupassant

"He's my disciple and I love him like a son," Flaubert said of Maupassant. It was a concise description of a twofold relationship: if Flaubert was the inspiration for Maupassant the writer, he also provided the child of the broken marriage with a foster father. Flaubert's sudden and unexpected death in 1880 was a grievous blow to Maupassant, both as "disciple" and as "son."

Zola described the young Maupassant as a "terrific oarsman able to row fifty miles on the Seine in a single day for pleasure." Maupassant was a passionate lover of the sea and of rivers, which accounts for the setting of much of his fiction and the prevalence in it of nautical imagery. In spite of his lack of enthusiasm for the bureaucracy, his years as a civil servant were the happiest of his life. He devoted much of his spare time to swimming and to boating expeditions on the Seine. One can see from a story like "Mouche" (1890; "Fly") that the latter were more than merely boating expeditions and that the girls who accompanied Maupassant and his friends were usually prostitutes or prospective prostitutes. Maupassant's mother used to boast that his childhood "was absolutely chaste" and that "it was not until he was sixteen that he had his first liaison." Whether she was right or not, there can be little doubt that the early years in Paris were the start of his phenomenal promiscuity.

When Maupassant was in his early 20s, he discovered that he was suffering from syphilis, one of the most frightening and widespread maladies of the age. It is not known whether it was hereditary or caused by his promiscuity, but the fact that his brother died at an early age of the same disease suggests that it might have been hereditary. Maupassant was adamant in refusing to undergo treatment, with the result that the disease was to cast a deepening shadow over his mature years and was accentuated by neurasthenia, which had also afflicted his brother.

During his apprenticeship with Flaubert, Maupassant published one or two stories under a pseudonym in obscure provincial magazines. The turning point came in April 1880, the month before Flaubert's death. Maupassant was one of six writers, led by Zola, who each contributed a war story to a volume called *Les Soirées de Médan*. "Boule de suif" ("Ball of Fat") was not only far the best of the six; it is probably the finest story Maupassant ever wrote. Although the story is Flaubertian in conception, structure, and style, the "disciple" was a follower, not an imitator. He learned from the novelist

Flaubert but adapted what he learned to the short story, the best of which, like "Boule de suif," are characterized by economy and balance.

Mature life and works. As soon as "Boule de suif" was published, Maupassant found himself in demand by newspapers. He left the ministry and spent the next two years writing articles for *Le Gaulois* and the *Gil Blas*. Although the *Gil Blas* was ostensibly a newspaper, it found little space for news. Its primary aim was to entertain its readers with spicy stories; its sideline was the grooming of youthful courtesans, amusingly known as *horizontales*. It was not inappropriate that many of Maupassant's stories should have made their first appearance there.

Productivity of the 1880s and 1890s

The ten years from 1880 to 1890 were remarkable for their productivity. They saw the publication of some 300 short stories, six novels, three travel books, Maupassant's only volume of verse, and a fair sprinkling of miscellaneous works.

The stories can be divided into groups: those dealing with the Franco-Prussian War, the Norman peasantry, the bureaucracy, life on the banks of the Seine, the emotional problems of the different classes, and—somewhat ominously in a late story like "Le Horla" (1887)—with hallucination. Together, the stories present a comprehensive picture of French life from 1870 to 1890.

There is a strong personal element in Maupassant's work that has invited biographers to treat passages from his fiction as though they were extracts from an autobiography or diary. It is most marked in *Bel-Ami* (1885). It seems at first as though the gap between the novelist and his rascally protagonist is a wide one, that all they have in common is their womanizing. One comes to realize, however, that, in spite of a certain amount of camouflage, Maupassant does identify himself with Bel-Ami and that he would have given much to have enjoyed the same sort of outrageous triumphs as well as the same excellent health as his creation. If, in the novel itself, he camouflaged the connection, elsewhere he went out of his way to underline it. A copy of the original edition, discovered in 1932, contains a dedication to a woman friend, which reads: "To Madame B. Homage from Bel-Ami himself." And when, as a result of his prosperity, he exchanged the skiffs, which had been the delight of his youth, for yachts, he christened two of them "Bel-Ami."

The prosperity was real; he was a best-seller in several countries. He was also a tough Norman businessman. It is estimated that his earnings were the modern equivalent of something over $70,000 a year at a time when there was still no income tax. He made the most of it. He had a flat in Paris with an annex for clandestine meetings with women, a house at Étretat where he did a good deal of entertaining, and a couple of residences on the Riviera. He began to travel in 1881, visiting French Africa and Italy, and became a yacht owner two years later. In 1889 he made two balloon ascents. The same year he paid his only visit to England. While lunching in a restaurant there as Henry James's guest, he shocked him profoundly by pointing to a woman at a neighbouring table and asking James to "get" her for him.

Fascination with brothels and prostitution

The French critic Paul Léautaud called him a "complete erotomaniac." His extraordinary fascination with brothels and prostitution is reflected in stories such as "La Maison Tellier" (1881; "The Tellier House") and "L'Ami patience" (1863; "A Way to Wealth"). It is significant, however, that as the successful writer became more closely associated with women of the class of Hermine Lecomte du Nouy, marchesa d'Alligri, and the Countess Potocka, there was a change of angle in his fiction: a move from the peasantry to the upper classes, from the brothel to the boudoir. Although Maupassant appeared outwardly a sturdy, healthy, athletic man, his letters are full of lamentations about his health, particularly eye trouble and migraine headaches. With the passing of the years he had become more and more sombre. He had begun to travel for pleasure, but what had once been carefree and enjoyable holidays gradually changed, as a result of his mental state, into compulsive, symptomatic wanderings until he felt a constant need to be on the move, to rush to one of his dwellings in another part of France or to set out on a cruise in one of his yachts.

A major family crisis occurred in 1888. Maupassant's brother was a man of minimal intelligence—today one would call it arrested development—and could work at nothing more demanding than nursery gardening, undertaken in the south of France and financed by Guy. In 1888 he suddenly became violently psychotic (the family pretended that it was "sunstroke"). Guy escorted him to Paris on the pretext that he was going to a clinic to convalesce. When he discovered the true situation Hervé used words that were to prove prophetic: "But it's you who are mad, do you hear? You're the crazy one of the family." He died in an asylum on November 13, 1889.

Maupassant was reduced to despair by his brother's death; but though his grief was genuine, it cannot have been unconnected with his own condition. On January 2, 1892, when he was staying near his mother, who for her health lived on the Riviera, he tried to commit suicide by cutting his throat. Doctors were summoned, and his mother agreed reluctantly to his commitment. Two days later he was removed, according to some accounts in a straitjacket, to Dr. Blanche's establishment in Paris, where he died on July 6, 1893, one month before his 43rd birthday.

Decline of Maupassant's popularity

In the early 1970s, it was generally recognized that Maupassant's popularity as a short-story writer had declined and that he was more widely read in Anglo-Saxon countries and in the Soviet Union than in France. This does not detract from his genuine achievement: the invention of a new, high-quality, commercial short story, which has something to offer to all classes of readers.

MAJOR WORKS

STORIES: "Boule de suif," first published in *Les Soirées de Médan* (1880), also in *Boule de Suif, and Other Stories*, trans. by A.R. MacAndrew (1964); *La Maison Tellier* (1881; *The Tellier House*, trans. by D. Flower, 1964), book of short stories; *Mademoiselle Fifi* (1882, enlarged 1883), book of short stories (included in *88 More Stories*, trans. by E. Boyd and S. Jameson, 4 vol., 1932); *Contes de la bécasse* (1883), book of stories (see *The Works*, trans. by M. Laurie, 1923–29); *Clair de lune, Les Soeurs Rondoli* (see *88 Short Stories*, trans. by E. Boyd and S. Jameson, 1930), and *Miss Harriet* (all 1884; see the *Works*); *Yvette* (1885; see *88 Short Stories*); *Toine* (1885), book of stories (see the *Works*); *Le Horla* (1887; see *88 More Stories*); *Le Rosier de Madame Husson* (1888; see the *Works*); *L'Inutile Beauté* (1890; see *88 Short Stories*).

NOVELS: *Une Vie* (1883; *A Woman's Life*, trans. by H.N.P. Sloman, 1965); *Bel-Ami* (1885; trans. by H.N.P. Sloman, 1961); *Mont-Oriol* (1887; see the *Works*); *Pierre et Jean* (1888; trans. by M. Turnell, 1962); *Fort comme la mort* (1889; *The Master Passion*, trans. by M. Laurie, 1958); *Notre Coeur* (1890; see the *Works*).

OTHER WORKS: "Au bord de l'eau," first published in a periodical (1876), verse.

BIBLIOGRAPHY. Collections of Maupassant's work include the Ollendorf edition, illustrated, 29 vol. (1900–04); the Conard edition, with preface by POL NEVEUX, 29 vol. (1908–10); and the edition by RENE DUMESNIL, 15 vol., including his letters and previously unpublished writings (1934–38). In English, *The Works of Guy de Maupassant*, trans. by M. LAURIE, 10 vol., was published in 1923–29. Available correspondence and bibliography may be found in vol. 15 of the *Correspondance inédite de Guy de Maupassant*, ed. by ARTINE ARTINIAN and EDOUARD MAYNIAL (1951).

Biography: See ARMAND LANOUX, *Maupassant le "Bel-Ami"* (1967), the fullest and most-up-to-date biography; FRANCIS STEEGMULLER, *Maupassant* (1950), the only satisfactory biography in English; FRANCOIS TASSART, *Souvenirs sur Guy de Maupassant*, 3rd ed. (1911; Eng. trans., *Recollections of Guy de Maupassant by His Valet François*, 1912); and *Nouveaux souvenirs intimes sur Guy de Maupassant* (1962), two useful source books for biographers.

Criticism: See HENRY JAMES, *Partial Portraits* (1888) and also in *The Art of Fiction* (1948) and *The House of Fiction* (1957), still one of the finest essays on Maupassant; ARTINE ARTINIAN, *Maupassant Criticism in France, 1880–1940* (1941), a survey of personal judgments, French and other; E.D. SULLIVAN, *Maupassant the Novelist* (1954) and *Maupassant: The Short Stories* (1962), useful studies; and MARTIN TURNELL, *The Art of French Fiction* (1959, reprinted 1970).

(M.Tu.)

Maurice of Nassau, Prince of Orange

Soldier and statesman, Maurice of Nassau was the military architect of the emergent Dutch Republic during the years between the death of his father, William the Silent, in 1584 and the signing of the Twelve Years Truce (1609), which temporarily halted the Dutch war of independence against Spain.

Maurice of Nassau, painting by Michiel Janszoon van Mierrelt (1567–1641). In the Rijksmuseum, Amsterdam.

He was born at Dillenburg on November 13, 1567, the second son of William the Silent. Although known as the Prince of Orange, he did not actually inherit that principality until 1618, on the death of his elder half brother. A child of William's disastrous marriage to the schizophrenic Anna of Saxony and delicate as a youth, Maurice was shuffled from place to place during the most critical years of his father's struggle against Spanish tyranny. His boyhood was further overshadowed by the desertion and betrayal of his father by former allies and finally by William's assassination in 1584. It was hardly surprising that these experiences deepened his natural reserve, leaving him suspicious of friends as well as of enemies.

Stadholder of the Unified Provinces At the time of his father's death, Maurice was still a student at the newly founded University of Leiden, but the States of Holland swiftly invested him as stadholder (chief executive). He later also became stadholder of Zeeland, Utrecht, Overyssel, and Gelderland. The years 1584–86 were critical. English help for the Netherlands revolt had finally materialized in the person of the Earl of Leicester, who headed an English expeditionary force, temporarily strengthening the provinces' defenses but imperilling the cause of the rebels by political blunders. Fortunately for Maurice, he had the assistance of the master politician Johan van Oldenbarnevelt, advocate of Holland. With Maurice's cousin and loyal supporter, William Louis, stadholder of Friesland, the Advocate, and Maurice formed a powerful triumvirate. Under the three, the northern provinces steadily consolidated their position against Spain, grew progressively richer by trade and shipping, and prepared themselves for independence.

Oldenbarnevelt took charge of domestic and foreign affairs; Maurice, as federal commander in chief, attended to military matters with the aid of William Louis. Mathematics, ballistics, and military engineering had fascinated Maurice since childhood; now he was in a position to put his theories to the test. His first task was to **Military reforms** reduce the army's size and improve its organization. He did his best to remove the perpetual curse of all contem-

porary armies—mutiny—by ensuring that his soldiers were properly and promptly paid, equipped with better arms, given improved and more regular training, and instructed in the science of fortification and siege warfare. The secret of Maurice's military planning was to bring to the art of siege warfare—the dominant type of warfare of his century—those habits of steady, close observation and attention to detail so characteristic of the Dutch in all the arts and sciences of the time. He was also greatly helped by the advice of Simon Stevin—the great mathematician and philosopher of Bruges, then living in Holland—whose lectures attracted his attention.

The fruits of his efforts were harvested in the 1590s. Beginning with Breda (the Nassau family seat), Maurice captured one enemy stronghold after another. In a series of actions, remarkable less for their audacity than for cool and systematic planning, the Spanish front lines were pushed back to the north, east, and south until the republic's territory began to assume something very much like its modern shape. Joyfully the Holland towns paid homage to their saviour; Maurice was hailed (literally) as the engineer of victory.

Defeat in Flanders He had less success in the south. With great reluctance, Maurice was persuaded by the impatient Oldenbarnevelt to try to reunite the northern and southern Netherlands, divided by Spanish conquests. His attempt to invade Flanders and rouse it to repel its Spanish conquerors failed completely. After an initial victory at Nieuwpoort in 1601, Maurice was compelled to withdraw. Later, Oostende had to be surrendered. Oldenbarnevelt's optimism had proved totally misplaced. The southerners were apathetic, even hostile, to the appeals of the Hollanders. Even Maurice, with his doubts about the wisdom of undertaking such a campaign, was taken by surprise by its outcome. The defeat revealed that there was one department of military reform he had overlooked—intelligence. Unwillingly, and with bitterness, Maurice had to bow to facts. He agreed first to an armistice (1607) and then a 12-year truce with Spain (1609). The division of the Netherlands was to continue.

The problems of war had brought out the strength of Maurice's character. An English visitor noted that he was "of great forwardness, good presence and courage, flaxen haired, endued with a singular wit." With growing confidence, he stood up for his own interests as well as those of his people against the English queen, Elizabeth I, and her emissaries as well as those of France. As Maurice's stature grew to match his responsibilities, he increasingly resented the continual interference by Oldenbarnevelt in military matters. The unsuccessful foray into Flanders was a special cause of friction, and the long siege of Oostende put a heavy strain on their relations. Estrangement was made worse by the negotiations for the truce; Maurice suspected Oldenbarnevelt of sacrificing Dutch independence in his anxiety for a peace with Spain, and the Advocate suspected Maurice of attempting to acquire sovereign power.

Defeat of Oldenbarnevelt During the decade after the truce, the partnership turned into a war, as yet private and undeclared, for supremacy. Maurice's mastery of strategy again stood him in good stead. While Oldenbarnevelt was more deeply drawn into the bitter theological politics of the times, Maurice patiently waited for his moment, quietly consolidating his support in Zeeland and Amsterdam. Oldenbarnevelt, confident of his power in the Holland states, emerged as the champion of Erastianism (which advocated dominance of the state over the church) and of those moderate Protestants who wanted religious toleration, in opposition to the intolerance of the orthodox Dutch Calvinists.

It was 1617 before Maurice came out publicly as protector of the Calvinists (the so-called Counter-Remonstrants). When Oldenbarnevelt obtained authority for his supporters in the towns to raise levies of professional soldiers (*waardgelders*), Maurice acted swiftly. Marching to the Brill (in South Holland) on September 28–29, he disbanded the levies. Next, he took advantage of his legal right to approve appointments in the local governments in order to purge each *vroedschap* (council) of his opponents. By the summer of 1618 he had forcibly dismissed all the *waardgelders.* It then only remained to remove Oldenbarnevelt. On August 29, 1618, the old statesman was arrested, and on May 13, 1619, he was executed. The long political trial was marked by persistent bias, petty spite, and inexcusable cruelty and injustice. Maurice did not himself dictate the sentence, but he ostentatiously refrained from exercising his prerogative of pardon, and he personally endorsed the demand for the probably illegal forfeiture of Oldenbarnevelt's property. The trial and execution of his old ally remain a blot upon his character and career.

After this victory, Maurice wielded unprecedented power. In all but name the Stadholder was king. Yet, having forged his alliance with orthodox Calvinism, created an Orangist Party, and packed local, provincial, and federal offices with his supporters, Maurice pressed his "revolution" no further. In 1621 he ended with a flourish the truce with the Spanish that he had detested for 12 long years. Ironically, the Calvinist hero was quickly faced by a Habsburg threat so dangerous that he was compelled to conclude an alliance with Roman Catholic France. Just before he died (of a liver complaint) in 1625, Breda, the scene of his first spectacular victory against the Spanish, was again lost to the enemy.

Assessment of Maurice's life

The last ten years of his life added nothing to Maurice's reputation. He was a great soldier but not a great statesman. In peace he had little or none of those sympathetic qualities that had drawn men to his father to settle issues by advice and discussion. His greatest claim to fame was his repulsion of the Spanish from 1590 to 1609 and the extension and securing of the frontiers of the Dutch Republic. Yet his achievement fell short of reunifying the whole of the Netherlands, and his vindictive pursuit of Oldenbarnevelt helped to divide the republic permanently into Orangists and anti-Orangists. For the latter, Oldenbarnevelt's martyrdom provided a political focus and a rallying cry down to the French Revolution.

Maurice's was an involuted and contradictory character. The circumstances of his childhood left him vulnerable to fears, suspicions, and resentments; yet he was also a man of great courage, capable of magnanimity on the battlefield. His natural caution did not inhibit his capacity for swift and decisive action. Coldly logical, he enjoyed a joke, albeit a sarcastic one. His lack of passion may have prevented him from marrying but did not prevent him from fathering a brood of illegitimate children.

BIBLIOGRAPHY. G. GROEN VAN PRINSTERER, *Maurice et Barnevelt* (1875), remains the classic Dutch biography. The outstanding recent work that assesses Maurice's contribution to history is JAN DEN TEX, *Oldenbarnevelt*, 3 vol. (1960; Eng. trans., 2 vol., 1972). A shrewd appreciation of Maurice appears in *The Dutch Nation* by G.J. RENIER (1944). J.L. MOTLEY, *The Life and Death of John of Barneveld*, 2 vol. (1874), and his *History of the United Netherlands*, 4 vol. (1861–68), contain much valuable information.

(C.H.Wi.)

Mauritania

The Islāmic Republic of Mauritania (République Islamique de Mauritanie), a state in northwest Africa, forms a geographic link between the North African Maghrib (a region that includes Morocco, Algeria, and Tunisia) and the Senegal region of West Africa. Culturally, it forms a transitional zone between the Arab-Berber region of North Africa and the region to the south of the Tropic of Cancer known as the Sudan (a name derived from the Arabic and meaning "land of the blacks"). With an area of 398,000 square miles (1,030,700 square kilometres) and a population of about 1,100,000, Mauritania takes the form of an indented rectangle measuring about 930 miles from north to south and about 680 miles from east to west. It is bordered to the northwest by the Spanish Sahara, to the north by Algeria, to the east and southeast by Mali, and to the southwest by Senegal. Its Atlantic Ocean coastline, to the west, extends for 435 miles from the delta of the Sénégal River northward to the Cap Blanc Peninsula. The capital is Nouakchott (population about 35,000).

Much of Mauritania's territory forms part of the western Sahara, and a large proportion of the population is nomadic. The country's mineral wealth includes large reserves of iron ore and of copper, which are now being exploited. Mauritania, formerly French administered, became independent on November 28, 1960. By the terms of the constitution proclaimed in 1961, Islām is the religion of the Mauritanian people, and the republic guarantees freedom of conscience and religious liberty to all; Arabic is the national language, and the official languages are Arabic and French. (For associated physical features, see SENEGAL RIVER; SAHARA; for historical aspects, see NORTH AFRICA, HISTORY OF; WEST AFRICA, HISTORY OF.)

The physical and natural landscape. *Relief and drainage.* Both land relief and drainage are influenced by the aridity that characterizes the greater part of the country. The impression of immensity given by the landscape is reinforced by its flatness; the coastal plains are lower than 150 feet, while the higher plains of the interior vary between 600 and 750 feet. The interior plains form a plateau of which the culminating heights, occurring at different levels, form many tablelands joined to one another by very long, gentle slopes of about two degrees. The monotony is broken either by vestiges of cliffs (generally cuestas); or by sloping plains that terminate at one end of the slope with a steep cliff or faulted scarp, which may reach heights of 900 feet; or by inselbergs (steep-sided residual hills) of which the highest is Kediet Ijill (3,002 feet high), an enormous block of hematite.

Plains and plateaus

Structurally, Mauritania may be divided into three principal zones. The first of these, located in the north and northwest, consists of the underlying Precambrian rock (570,000,000 to 4,600,000,000 years old), which emerges to form not only the backbone of northern Mauritania's Rigaibāt ridge region but also the Akjoujt rock series which forms a vast peneplain (a land surface worn down by erosion to a nearly flat plain) studded with inselbergs. The second zone, located partly in the extreme north but mostly in the centre and east, consists of primary sandstone, which covers the Tindouf Syncline (a fold in the rocks in which the strata dip inward from both sides toward the axis), in the north, and the vast synclinal basin of Taoudeni in the centre (bounded by the Adrar, Tagant, and 'Assâba plateaus), scarcely indented to the south by the Hodh Depression, with the Affollé Anticline (a fold in which the rock strata incline downward on both sides from a central axis) lying in its centre. The third zone is formed by the Senegalese-Mauritanian sedimentary basin, which includes coastal Mauritania and the lower Sénégal River Valley of the southwest.

The Mauritanian landscape, in general, as a result of the arid phases it underwent during the Quaternary Period (*i.e.,* within the last 7,000,000 years), presents three different aspects; these are represented by skeletal soils, regs (desert surfaces consisting of small, rounded, tightly packed pebbles), and dunes.

Skeletal soils are formed where outcrops of the underlying rock have been slightly weathered, or where they have been covered with a patina or chalky crust. To these may be added the salty soils of the sebkhas (saline plains), formed from the caking of gypsum or of salt derived from the evaporation of former lakes.

The regs form plains often of great extent, carpeted with pebbles and boulders.

The dunes cover about 50 percent of the total area of the country. They are stretched out, often for several dozen miles, in long ridges known as *alâb*, which are sometimes 300 feet high; they frequently overlap with one another, forming a network of domes and basins.

It is only to the south of the ten-inch isohyet (an imaginary line connecting points with equal rainfall) that the sands bear a brown type of soil. This soil is characteristic of the steppe (treeless plains) and contains 2 percent of humus; it is also only in the extreme south of the country that the iron-bearing tropical soils of the Sudanic zone begin; in the lowest places, patches of hydromorphic soils (*i.e.,* soils that have been altered by waterborne materials) occur.

The drainage system is characterized by a lack of pattern. Normal drainage is limited to inland southwestern Mauritania where tributaries of the Sénégal River, which forms the frontier between Mauritania and Senegal, flow southward and are subject to ephemeral flooding in summer. In the greater part of the country, however, the plateaus are cut into by wadis (dry riverbeds) where the rare floods that occur dissipate their waters into a few permanent drainage basins called *gueltas*. In the wastes of the north and the east rainfall is so rare and slight that there is practically no runoff.

Climate. The climate owes its aridity to the northeast trade winds, which blow constantly north of the Tropic of Cancer, and throughout most of the year to the south of it; the drying effect produced by these winds is increased by the harmattan, or east wind. With the exception of the few winter rains that occur as a result of climatic disturbances in the polar regions, precipitation essentially results from the rain-bearing southwesterly winds, which progressively extend throughout the southern half of the country at the height of the summer. The

The arid climate

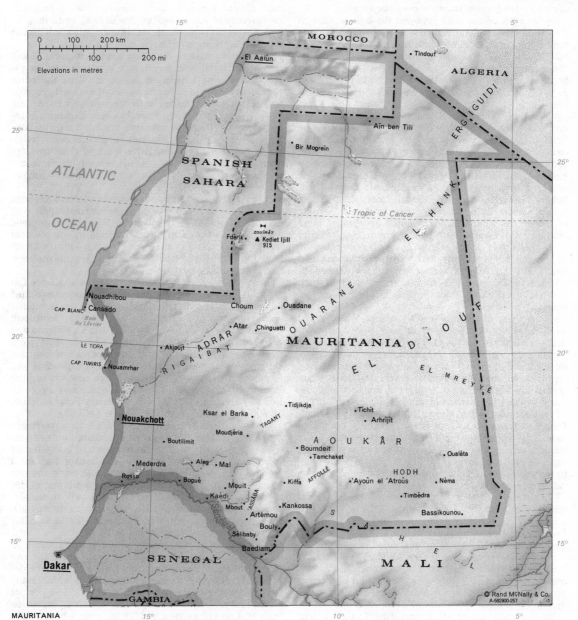

duration of the rainy season, as well as the total annual amount of rainfall, diminishes progressively from south to north. Thus, Sélibaby in the extreme south receives about 25 inches between June and October; Kiffa, further north, receives 14 inches between mid-June and mid-October; Tidjikdja receives 7 inches between July and September; Atar receives 7 inches between mid-July and September; and Nouadhibou (formerly Port-Étienne) receives between one and two inches, usually between September and November. Because of the opposition between the wet southwesterlies and the harmattan, rains often take the form of stormy showers or squalls.

The strength of the sun's rays and the lack of haze in these latitudes result in high temperatures. The average temperature in the coldest month is in the region of 68° F (20° C), while the average temperature during the hottest month rises to about 75° F (24° C) at Nouakchott in September, to about 79° F (26° C) at Kiffa in May and 81° F (27° C) at Atar in July, and to 84° F (29° C) at Néma in May.

Vegetation. Vegetational zones depend upon the degree of aridity, which increases from south to north. The Sudanic savanna (grassy parkland), studded with baobab trees and palmyra (rônier) palm trees, slowly gives way, toward 16° N, to a discontinuous belt of vegetation known as the Sahel (an Arabic word meaning riverbank or shore, which is also used to designate the southern Sahara borderlands). In the Sahel, trees are rare and consist principally of acacias, euphorbia bushes (plants of the spurge family, having a milky juice and flowers with no petals or sepals), big tufts of morkba (*Panicum turgidum*, a type of millet), or fields of cram-cram, or Indian sandbur (a bristly herb). Between the six-inch and four-inch isohyets the steppe rapidly disappears, giving way to desert. Vegetation is restricted to such places as the dry beds of wadis, beneath which water still flows, or to oases.

Animal life. In the savanna, big antelopes are hunted by lion, in the Afollé region of southern Mauritania, herds of elephants are found. The steppe is frequented by gazelles, ostriches, warthogs, panthers, and lynx; crocodiles are found in the *gueltas*. Only the addax antelope ventures out into the waterless desert. In recent years animal life has been much reduced by hunting, obliging the authorities to introduce measures for conservation.

The landscape under human settlement. The Sahara region to the north, where life is generally limited to oases, stands in contrast to the Sahelian steppelands to the south, where regular rainfall permits extensive stock raising and some agriculture. While transition occurs between one zone and another, a convenient line of demarcation is represented by the four-inch isohyet.

The heartland of Mauritania consists of the vast Adrar and Tagant plateaus, known as the Trab el-Hajra, or country of stone. Here, at the foot of cliffs, are to be found several oases among which some—such as Chinguetti, Ouadane, Tîchît, Tidjikdja, and Atar—were the sites of well-known cities in the Middle Ages. To the north and the west extend the vast desert peneplains. The exploitation of the Zouîrât mines and the development of Nouadhibou have transformed this once-abandoned region into the focus of Mauritania's economic life.

Coastal southwestern Mauritania (the former Trarza *cercle*) is covered with regularly aligned dunes and is important for stock raising; Arab-Berber culture is represented by important marabout (priestly) families.

Inland southwestern Mauritania (the former *cercles* of Brakna, Gorgol, and 'Assâba) is inhabited both by Moors and Fulani (Peuls), who engage both in stock raising and agriculture. In the extreme south (the former Guidimaka *cercle*), large villages are surrounded by fields of millet constituting the first sign of the Sudan landscape, which comes into view further south.

In the southeast, the vast Hodh Basin, with its dunes, sandstone plateaus, and immense regs, is a major stock-raising region the economy of which has many links with neighbouring Mali.

Mauritania is a country suited for nomadic life; nomads represent 78 percent of the total population. Livestock supplies the nomads with milk and meat, while transport is provided by riding camels and pack camels, and, in the south, by pack oxen and donkeys as well. The women dye sheep's wool with which they then braid long brown bands that are sewn together to make tents; they also tan goats' skins to make *guerbas* (waterskins). Movement is governed by the search for water and pasturage. In the Sahara, nomadic movements are irregular because of the extreme variability of rains; in the Sahel, however, seasonal movement occurs—to the south in the dry season, and to the north in the wet season. The size of nomadic encampments also varies from south to north. In the coastal southwest, groups of 300 tents may be found, whereas in northern Mauritania, only small groups of a few tents are to be seen.

For various reasons—including changes in political and commercial relations; a series of dry years, which resulted in a slow population movement from the north to the south; and a decrease in the camel population which has coincided with the coming of the milk cow—the nomadic way of life has been declining in recent decades. Dams to conserve floodwaters have been built in the wadis, and palm-tree culture has been considerably extended. The cumulative result of these developments has been that the nomads remain longer in the south near their millet fields and palm groves—becoming, in sum, seminomads.

Since the 1960s, a movement toward settlement has been evident, largely because of growing dissatisfaction with the harsh conditions of nomadic life; this embryonic movement has, however, been restricted by the constant lack of water. Only in the extreme south—on the banks of the Sénégal River (the Chemama)—is a normal, settled agricultural life possible.

The exploitation of the iron-ore reserves of Kediet Ijill as well as the coming of independence have transformed the urban geography of Mauritania. The ancient cities that lived by caravan traffic—*e.g.*, Tîchît, Chinguetti, Ouadane, and Oualata—and traded with Casablanca and above all with Dakar grow idler beneath their palm trees. Only Tidjikdja and Atar have maintained a certain activity. Kaédi, on the Sénégal River, is expanding and is expected to grow still larger. Three new towns have been built: Nouakchott, the capital, which had a population of 35,000 in 1971; F'Dérik (formerly Fort-Gouraud; 16,000 population); and Nouadhibou (11,000).

Nouakchott was founded in 1958 after the government decided to replace the former capital, Saint-Louis in Senegal, with an authentically Mauritanian city. Located near the sea, and providing access to the Sahara and Sahel regions alike, Nouakchott—in addition to being the seat of government and administration—has a printing works, a hospital, and numerous schools. Although it remains essentially a town for officials, its commerce is growing. Its water supply is provided by a plant that desalinizes seawater.

F'Dérik is an administrative centre situated about 15 miles from the mining town of Zouîrât, where the employees of the Miferma company (Société Anonyme des Mines de Fer de Mauritanie) live and to which many traders and unemployed have been drawn. The port of Nouadhibou, long stagnant, owes its recent expansion both to iron-ore exports and to the establishment of a fishing complex there. A few miles to the south lies a residential city, Cansado, built by Miferma.

People and population. *Ethnic and linguistic groups.* The Moors constitute 80 percent of the population; about half of them are white, or *bīdān*, Moors, and about half are black, of Sudanic origin. Moorish society is traditionally divided into a hierarchy of castes. At the head of it are the noble castes, composed of warriors and of marabouts, or people of the Book (the Qur'ān). The warriors are usually Arab, and the marabouts are usually Berber. The mass of the *bīdān* population are vassals who receive protection from the warriors or marabouts in return for tribute. There are two artisan classes—the blacksmiths and the griots (who are at once musicians and genealogists). The servant classes are formed of black Moors and are subdivided into "servants" and

The Sahara and Sahel regions

The decline of nomadism

The Moors

freedmen. Since the beginning of the century, social divisions have been modified by the disappearance of traditional insecurity and by the suppression of slavery. Members of the "servant" caste, above all, have become aware of their rights as citizens. Only by stages, however, do concepts of modern law penetrate traditional society.

The Moors speak Ḥassānīyah, a dialect that draws most of its grammar from Arabic and uses a vocabulary of both Arab and Berber words. Most of the white Moors also know literary Arabic.

The remaining 20 percent of the population consists of Tukulors (Toucouleurs), who inhabit the Sénégal River Valley; Fulani, who are dispersed throughout the south; Soninke (Sarakole), who inhabit the extreme south; and Wolof, who are found in the vicinity of Rosso in coastal southwestern Mauritania. The Tukulors and the Fulani speak Fulfulde (Poular), and the other groups their respective tribal languages. The non-Africans in Mauritania are mostly French; no more than a few thousand, they are engaged in technical assistance and in mining.

Religious groups. All Mauritanians are Muslim. Most Moors belong to the Brotherhood of the Qādirīyah, which practices the Mālikite rite. Some of the Tagant tribes, and the Tukulors, follow the Tijānīyah rite.

Demography. Precise demographic statistics cannot be compiled, because of the nomadic mode of life of much of the population. Until recently, the only statistical sources were administrative censuses held for purposes of taxation; because of nomadic mobility, however, as well as failures to report all the women, slaves, and children to the census takers, the final statistics were unreliable. A census based on sampling resulted in the 1965 population being estimated at 1,071,000, of which 802,-000 were nomadic, 158,000 were sedentary farmers, and 82,000 were urban dwellers. The birth rate was estimated at 45 per thousand, and the death rate at 29, resulting in a rate of increase of 16 per thousand. (The rate of increase among nomads was estimated at 15 and among sedentary farmers at 18 per thousand.) Between 1965 and 1970 the population movement to the towns increased. About 90 percent of the population lives south of the four-inch isohyet.

Mauritania, Area and Population

District	area sq mi	area sq km	population 1964–65 census	population 1970 estimate
Nouakchott	400	1,000	12,000	30,000
Regions				
I	64,100	166,000	183,000	192,000
II	22,000	57,000	99,000	104,000
III	18,100	46,800	176,000	184,000
IV	5,400	14,100	88,000	95,000
V	50,700	131,200	198,000	206,000
VI	43,400	112,400	209,000	218,000
VII	193,900	502,200	106,000	111,000
Total Mauritania	398,000	1,030,700	1,071,000	1,140,000

Source: Official government figures.

The national economy. In the Sahel region, a traditional subsistence economy is maintained, composed of stock raising, agriculture, crafts, and petty trading. In the Sahara region, however, a modern economy is developing, based on iron-ore and copper resources and on the fish resources of the continental shelf; the modern economy receives capital investment and technical assistance from abroad. More than 85 percent of the Mauritanian population still live by traditional activities, among which stock raising is the most significant. In 1970 the livestock consisted of about 2,600,000 cattle, more than 5,200,000 sheep and goats, more than 500,000 camels, about 225,-000 donkeys, and about 23,000 horses. The cattle are located primarily in the southern region, whereas the sheep and goats are dispersed as far north as the limits of the Sahara. The camels are found mostly in the north and the centre, especially in the Adrar region.

Stock raising

Agriculture. Agriculture is necessarily dependent upon rainfall. Where the rainfall exceeds 17 inches a year,

millet is the principal crop, supplemented by beans, yams, maize, and cotton. Seasonal agriculture is practiced on the easily flooded riverbanks, and in the wadis of the Sahelian zone, upstream from the dams. Here, too, millet, sorghum, beans, and watermelons are grown. Irrigated agriculture is practiced at oases where well water is available; corn, barley, a little millet, and some vegetables are grown. In the country as a whole, two agricultural crops predominate—millet and dates. The output of gum arabic is declining; annual production varies between 3,000 and 5,000 tons.

Mining. The iron-ore deposits of Kediet Ijill amount to 200,000,000 tons of hematite, obtainable from surface workings. A rail link 419 miles long connects the mining town of Zouîrât with the port of Nouadhibou, the only deepwater roadstead on the Saharan coastline, accommodating ships of up to 150,000 tons. Exploitation is conducted by Miferma, of which 56 percent of the financing is by French groups, the remainder by English, German, and Italian groups and the Mauritanian government. Exports increased from 1,300,000 tons in 1963 to about 9,000,000 tons in 1970.

Iron ore and copper

The copper deposits of Akjoujt amount to 500,000 tons of pure metal. Exploitation was begun in 1969 by Somima (Société Minière de Mauritanie), of which 54 percent of the shares are held by Anglo-American interests, 25 percent by the Mauritanian government, and the remainder by French interests. Processed copper is to be exported along a 173-mile highway to the wharf at Nouakchott; it was estimated that 34,000 tons were exported in 1971. Other mineral resources are minor. Salt output is declining. There are some gypsum deposits near Nouakchott. Reserves of ilmenite (the principal ore of titanium) have been located, and indications of copper have been found in the extreme south. Oil prospecting has so far yielded no results.

Fishing. Rich fishing grounds lie off Mauritania's Lévrier Bay. It is estimated that about 300,000 tons of fish are caught there each year by fishing boats of all nationalities; about 30,000 tons are landed at Nouadhibou, of which the greater part are dried. About 8,000 tons of fish are exported to other African countries each year.

Sources of national income. The gross domestic product in 1966 amounted to 41,200,000,000 CFA francs (CFA Fr.277.71=$1 U.S.; CFA Fr.666.50=£1 sterling on December 1, 1970). Of this, agriculture represented 27 percent (compared to 84 percent in 1959), and mining 38 percent (compared to 4 percent in 1959). There is no doubt that the percentage represented by mining will grow still further in future. While the proportion contributed by agriculture has declined (chiefly because of adherence to rudimentary techniques), the mining and industrial sector has greatly increased in productivity. Since 1965 income from Miferma alone has represented about 47 percent of the total budgetary receipts.

Foreign trade. Foreign trade is difficult to estimate since, while imports and exports of the modern sector are well-known, there are no statistics for the traditional sector. Mauritania is nevertheless known to import from or via Senegal quantities of millet, tea, rice, sugar, cotton goods, and hardware, while it exports to Mali and to Senegal about 100,000 cattle and 900,000 sheep and goats each year. Livestock is second in value only to iron ore as an export.

Management of the economy. The four-year plan from 1963 to 1966, which covered all aspects of social and economic development, encountered serious difficulties; it was to be followed by a second plan covering the period 1970 to 1974. In agriculture the aim is to increase the amount of irrigated land in the Sénégal River Valley and, above all, to increase production of rice, of which Mauritania is still obliged to import 20,000 tons a year; to plant fresh palm trees to replace those destroyed by the cochineal insect; to drill fresh wells; to improve the quality of dates; and to encourage the cultivation of vegetables. To promote the export of meat, two slaughterhouses are to be constructed, one at Kaédi, and one at Nouakchott. Investment in fisheries is to be concentrated on Nouadhibou, where plans include the formation of a

Mauritanian fishing fleet, establishment of a training centre for professional personnel, construction of a fishing port, and establishment of three fish-freezing depots, as well as a plant for manufacturing fish flour and fish oil, and a fish-drying factory.

Taxation. The state imposes direct taxes on the number of cattle owned and also levies an income tax. Investment by private enterprise in developmental projects is encouraged; taxes affecting concerns such as Miferma and Somima are on a long-term basis.

Transportation. Transport by pack animals—camels in the north, oxen and donkeys in the south—has retained considerable importance in a society in which a subsistence and barter economy prevails, although transport between cities and regions is increasingly by truck. Considerable hazards, however, confront road builders; among these are moving sand dunes, flash floods in the south, and steep cliffs. Only the main road running from Rosso via Nouakchott, Akjoujt, Atar, F'Dérik, and Bir Mogreïn to Tindouf, Algeria, is passable thoughout the year. The road between Rosso and Nouakchott is surfaced, as is the section between Nouakchott and Akjoujt. A road between Nouakchott, Kaédi, Kiffa, 'Ayoûn el 'Atroûs, and Néma is under construction; it will link the eastern region to the capital. A railroad from Zouîrât to Nouadhibou is used only for transporting iron ore. Cities are linked by regular air services.

The irregularity of the flow of the Sénégal River limits its use as a waterway; Kaédi can only be reached by ships drawing seven feet at the high-water season, which is from August to October. The port facilities at Nouakchott, which could accommodate 50,000 tons of shipping in 1970, were to be expanded in the early 1970s. Nouadhibou, in addition to being an iron-ore and fishing port, is also a commercial port.

Administration. The Mauritanian state has a presidential regime. The president of the republic is the head of government and the secretary general of the Parti du Peuple Mauritanien (PPM). Legislative power belongs to a national assembly of 40 elected members. The primary task of the government has been to transform a community of diverse tribes, which are hierarchical in structure and strongly differentiated, into a nation. The results have been encouraging; many local barriers to cooperation have been overcome. Traditional regional boundaries have been redrawn; seven regions and one capital district now exist, each directed by a governor, with the capital forming a separate district. One remaining difficulty consists of the latent opposition that exists between Moors and Negroes; this difference, which is cultural rather than racial, is due to the fact that the Negroes have become more educated than the Moors, who have been traditionally suspicious of nonreligious education. Consequently, the Negroes hold a large proportion of governmental positions. A campaign to Arabize the public service is now in progress.

The judicial authority is independent of both the executive and legislative branches. The legal code is inspired by the universal principles of Islām.

The army has a strength of 1,800 men, including infantry, cavalry, and parachutists.

Cultural life. Moorish society is justly proud of its Arab and Muslim heritage. Theology, poetry, and music have flourished throughout recent centuries. Architecture is inspired by that of the Maghrib, and goldsmithing is a fine art. Traditional culture, represented by the great marabout families, such as the Ahel Shaykh Sīdiyā family, is nevertheless declining. The elite are increasingly conscious that modern education taught in an international language—French—is an indispensable prerequisite of development. Primary education is making inroads, despite the enormous difficulties posed by the dispersion and mobility of the people. Instruction is given in Arabic and French alike. The government is seeking principally to promote secondary and technical education. A number of students are pursuing higher studies abroad, either at the University of Dakar in Senegal, in European (above all, French) universities, or at the University of al-Azhar in Cairo. Mauritanian society as a whole is linked

Education

by radio, which reaches the remotest encampments. There is a broadcasting station at Nouakchott.

Prospects for the future. Mauritania is pursuing the double aim of achieving internal development and of affirming its political personality. Economic growth is favoured by the existence of considerable mineral resources. Annual per capita income has risen from U.S. $65 in 1959 to U.S. $165 in 1969. But development will not realize its full potential unless professional and general education is made available, and unless the resources drawn from the Sahara permit the transformation and modernization of the traditional Sahel economy.

The Mauritanian nation is overcoming ethnic contradictions in order to become a link between Arab Africa and black Africa; it adheres to the principles of Arab policy while at the same time cooperating with other African states through the Organization of African Unity (OAU).

Since Morocco renounced its territorial claims to Saharan Mauritania in 1969, Mauritania has followed with vigilance the evolution of a neighbouring territory—the Spanish Sahara—in which it has been decided, at least in principle, that a referendum be held under United Nations' auspices. Finally, Mauritania, together with Mali, Guinea, and Senegal, is a member of the Organisation des États Riverains du Sénégal—the Organization of Senegal Riparian States—of which the purpose is the joint development of the resources of the Sénégal River Valley.

BIBLIOGRAPHY. GENEVIEVE M. DESIRE-VUILLEMIN, *Contribution à l'histoire de la Mauritanie de 1900 à 1934* (1962), text on the colonial period; CHARLES DIEGO, *Sahara* (1935), beautiful book on the life and mentality of the great wandering tribes, written by an ex-officer of the desert-raiding camel corps (or *méhariste*); PAUL DUBIE, "La Vie matérielle des Maures," *Mélanges Ethnologiques*, pp. 111–252 (1953), very useful description of different kinds of living; ALFRED G. GERTEINY, *Mauritania* (1967), the best overall survey; MOKHTAR OULD HAMIDOUN, *Précis sur la Mauritanie* (1952), description of Mauritania; JACQUES MEUNIE, *Cités anciennes de Mauritanie* (1961), interesting remarks on the architecture with beautiful illustrations; PAUL MARTY, *Étude sur l'Islam maure (Cheikh Sidia et sa voie, les Fadélia, les Ida ou Ali)* (1916), fundamental book; THEODORE MONOD, *Méharées: Explorations au "vrai" Sahara* (1937), essential book covering many aspects; JEROME PUJOS, *Croissance économique et impulsion extérieure: Étude sur l'économie mauritanienne* (1964), detailed study of the consequences of Miferma on the economy of Mauritania; R.M. WESTEBBE, *Mauritanie: esquisse d'un programme de développement quadriennal* (1968), very precise notations on the development of Mauritania.

(C.H.T.)

Mauritius

Mauritius is the central island of the Mascarene group. It is situated in the Indian Ocean about 500 miles (800 kilometres) east of Madagascar. It is 38 miles (61 kilometres) long by 29 miles (47 kilometres) wide and has an area of 720 square miles (1,865 square kilometres). The island's population is more than 800,000. The capital is Port Louis, on the northwest coast. Mauritius, an independent state, is a member of the Commonwealth of Nations. Its economy is primarily agricultural, but it is also an important link for sea and air transport in the Indian Ocean region. Its outlying territories comprise (1) the island of Rodrigues, which lies 344 miles (550 kilometres) eastward and which has an area of over 42 square miles (110 square kilometres) and a population of over 23,000; (2) the Cargados Carajos Shoals or the St. Brandon Rocks, 250 miles (400 kilometres) northeastward and consisting of a cluster of 22 islets, with a fishing station established on the largest; (3) the Agalega Islands, 580 miles (930 kilometres) northward, which are also small. They are leased to a coconut oil company. (For a detailed discussion of the physical setting, see INDIAN OCEAN.)

The natural and human setting. *Relief features, drainage, and soils.* Mauritius is volcanic, is shaped like an oyster, and is fringed by coral reefs. The northern part is a plain; the centre is a plateau rising to a height of about 2,200 feet (670 metres) and bordered by diminutive mountains, which are remnants of a huge volcano;

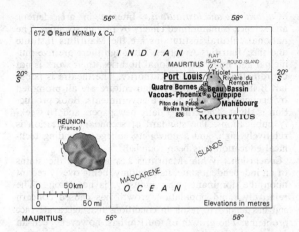

MAURITIUS

the south is largely mountainous. The highest peak on the island is the Piton de la Petite Rivière-Noire (Little Black River Peak) in the southwest, which is 2,711 feet (826 metres) high. There are many streams, generally flowing through deep ravines. During heavy rains these streams become torrents. On the plateau are two lakes, Grand Bassin and Mare aux Vacoas; the latter is the chief source of water supply. Four other large reservoirs are used for irrigation. Six major soil types are recognized. Of basaltic origin, formed from a fine-grained, dark-coloured igneous rock, they are fairly fertile but are extremely rocky.

Climate, vegetation, and fauna. The climate is maritime subtropical, with only two seasons—hot from November to April and cool from May to October. The southeast trade winds blow most of the year, and the climate is generally humid. The average temperature at Port Louis, on the coast, during the hot summer months is about 84° F (31° C), and in the cooler winter months it is about 77° F (25° C); at Curepipe, on the inland plateau, the temperature averages about 75° F (24° C) in summer and about 68° F (20° C) in winter. Heavy rains and cyclones occur during the hot season. Annual coastal rainfall varies between 35 inches (900 millimetres) on the west coast to 60 inches (1,500 millimetres) on the southeast coast. The central plateau receives about 200 inches of rain. The vegetation includes some 600 indigenous species, even though little original forest is now left. Many plants have been introduced since the 18th century, and in 1770 a botanical garden, which still exists, was formed at Pamplemousses to nurse them. The original fauna comprised insects, birds, reptiles (including chelonians, which are related to tortoises or turtles), and one mammal, the fruit-eating bat. Of particular interest were a number of wingless birds, such as the dodo and the *Aphanapteryx* (a large long-billed rail, a species of wading bird related to the crane), all now extinct. Among imported mammals are the sambar (long-tailed dark brown deer), tenrec (spiny insectivore), and mongoose. There are no venomous animals, but since 1865 the *Anopheles* mosquito, which carries malaria, was introduced and spread the disease, which remained endemic for nearly a century.

The landscape under human settlement. The island is divided into seven coastal and two inland districts. Most of the rural population still lives in the coastal districts, chiefly in the north and east, which were settled first. The original slave population lived on plantations. After emancipation in 1835 the freed slaves left to settle in coastal fishing villages. The Indian labourers who replaced them lived in estate camps until, in the 1860s, they spread out over the island, forming straggling villages. The first towns were Port Louis, on the leeward (westward) side of the island, then Mahébourg, on the windward (eastward) side. After a malaria epidemic that lasted from 1866 to 1868, the wealthier inhabitants of the towns migrated inland. Port Louis, nevertheless, remained the capital, as well as the business and administrative centre, as it is today. It is laid out on the French gridiron pattern and has a population of 139,000. It achieved city status in 1966. Some inland towns grew up

Margin note: Extinct species

in the 1870s on the Plaines Wilhems. These are Beau Bassin-Rose Hill (population 70,700), Quatre Bornes (population 45,000), Vacoas-Phoenix (population 48,-480), and Curepipe (population 51,460). All are residential and have few commercial activities. Mahébourg is now little more than a village.

People and population. The first settlers imported slaves from Madagascar and East Africa. The languages then spoken were French and Creole, a French patois. French remains the predominant European language, and Creole has become the lingua franca of the island. English, the official language, was introduced after 1810, as also were some Asian languages. The chief Indian dialect is Bhojpuri, which is associated with the Bihār region of India. Many Chinese speak Cantonese.

The largest ethnic group is Indian, comprising both Hindus and Muslims, followed by a general group composed of those who are either European, African, or Malagasy, or who are of mixed parentage. All are Christians, principally Roman Catholic. The Chinese, who are also largely Christian, form the smallest group. Despite cultural and community differences, the population tends to divide into two broad groups—one European-oriented and the other Asian-oriented. In January 1970 the population was estimated at slightly more than 800,000—an average of over 1,000 persons per square mile (380 persons per square kilometre). The crude birth rate in 1970 was over 27 per 1,000, and the crude death rate was 8. The rate of natural increase thus was over 19 per 1,000.

Margin note: Languages

Mauritius, Area and Population				
	area		population	
	sq mi	sq km	1962 census	1970 estimate
Districts				
Black River	100	259	19,000	22,000
Flacq	115	298	73,000	90,000
Grand Port	100	259	69,000	83,000
Moka	89	231	37,000	45,000
Pamplemousses	69	179	56,000	66,000
Plaines Wilhems	79	205	208,000	243,000
Port Louis	17	44	120,000	140,000
Rivière du Rempart	57	148	53,000	66,000
Savanne	94	243	46,000	56,000
Total Mauritius	720	1,865*	682,000*	811,000

*Figures do not add to total given because of rounding.
Source: Official government figures.

History. Known to Arab or Swahili seamen since the 10th century, or earlier, Mauritius and Réunion were visited by the Portuguese about 1510. Rodrigues was not visited until later. The name of Mascarenhas, first applied to Réunion, was subsequently extended to the whole group of islands. Finding Mauritius still uninhabited in 1598, the Dutch named it after their *stadhouder* (head of state) Maurice (Maurits) of Nassau. After two attempts to settle the island, made in 1638–58 and again in 1664–1710, the Dutch abandoned it, and it was then haunted by pirates. In 1721 the French East Indian Company, after annexing Réunion, sent a party to occupy Mauritius, which they renamed Ile de France. Under the rule of the company, which lasted from 1721 to 1767, the progress of settlement was slow. Port Louis was founded and was used as a base for attacking the British in India. During the Seven Years' War, from 1756 to 1763, a further attempt to use it as a base against the British again failed. In 1767 the French Ministry of Marine took over administration and a new era began. During the American Revolution, French naval units and privateers, based at Port Louis, gained many successes. Port Louis then became a vital way station, being visited by many French, Danish, and American ships. When, after the French Revolution, the government in Paris tried to abolish slavery in 1796, the island's settlers broke away from France. Even without French governmental support, however, the settlers, by conducting successful privateering expeditions and engaging in foreign trade, managed to maintain themselves. In 1810 the British captured Mauritius, restored its Dutch

Margin note: First settlement of the island

name, and occupied it with its dependencies as a crown colony. From a commercial and military outpost it was then transformed into a plantation colony, with sugar as its sole product. In language, laws, and customs, however, it remained largely French. In 1835 slavery was abolished, the slaves being replaced by Indian labourers. From 1850 to 1860, Mauritius prospered, until competition from beet sugar caused a decline. The malaria epidemic of 1866–68 caused much misery and for a time drove shipping away from Port Louis. Shipping also visited the island less frequently after the change from sail to steam and after the opening of the Suez Canal in 1869. The last years of the 19th century were difficult. World War I caused further distress, but after the war, sugar prices rose and a brief revival ensued. The economic depression of the 1930s, however, culminated in labour unrest in 1937. The situation did not improve during the uncertain years of World War II. After 1945 economic reforms were introduced. Important administrative and political reforms also were initiated; these led to self-government and independence, which was attained in 1968.

The nation. *Economy.* The economy is dominated by sugar, which accounts for about 90 percent of the export trade. A yearly average of 650,000 metric tons is processed by 23 factories. The secondary crop is tea, with eight factories producing over 3,000 tons annually. Some food crops, and tobacco, are grown, and there is a minor meat and dairy industry. Fish are caught in the lagoons, and two local companies in the Cargados area, as well as Japanese fleets with a wider range, engage in open-sea fishing. Tourism is becoming increasingly important. Mauritius is a member of the sterling area, and its currency is the rupee, which is divided into 100 cents and is worth 18 cents U.S., or 7½ new pence (sterling). The private sector of the economy is the most active, with the sugar companies, which are largely familial, overshadowing other types of enterprise. Taxation is not onerous. Efforts are being made to develop duty-free zones, as well as to provide hotel accommodation, in order to encourage foreign investment and tourism.

Transport and communications. Mauritius has 1,100 miles (1,770 kilometres) of roads, of which about 990 miles (1,590 kilometres) are tarred. Railways have been discarded, but there is an extensive bus transport system. Port Louis harbour has deepwater quays and dry-dock facilities and usually handles over a million tons of shipping a year. A government project for a second harbour at Mahébourg is under consideration. Regular cargo and passenger services to and from Europe are provided by British, French, and Scandinavian companies. A Dutch line operates a passenger and cargo service to Asian, South African, and South American ports; there are cargo services to India and South Africa. A local company links Mauritius to Rodrigues and runs ships to Madagascar, Africa, and Australia. The airport at Plaisance receives about 30,000 passengers a year. Air services are operated by eight companies. Another airport is planned in the north. The Mauritius Broadcasting Corporation runs television and radio programs.

Administration and social conditions. Queen Elizabeth II, as head of the Commonwealth of Nations, is represented by a governor general. The Legislative Assembly consists of (1) the speaker, (2) 62 elected members, (3) 8 additional members, and (4) the attorney general. The Cabinet consists of the prime minister and 20 other ministers. For electoral purposes, Mauritius is divided into three-member constituencies, of which there are 20. Rodrigues returns two members. The official language of the Assembly is English, but French may also be used. Local government is exercised at the village level by 98 village councils whose activities are coordinated by 3 district councils. In the urban areas, administration is vested in municipalities, with 24 elected members each. Port Louis has a fully elective 30-member council. There are 34 social welfare centres, mainly in the rural areas. Old age pensions, family allowances, and outdoor relief are also provided. Unemployment, however, is often high, with between 30,000 and 40,000 persons out of work.

Cultural life and institutions. Interest in arts, letters, and science is maintained chiefly by private societies. The national cultural institutions are the Mauritius Institute and the Mauritius Archives. Although there are five municipal and many institutional libraries, their work is not coordinated by a central authority. The theatre is popular. British, French, and Indian culture are all promoted by agencies of the respective governments. Book production is slight. There are 9 daily newspapers and 10 weekly publications. The standard of secondary education is relatively high, and a university college, providing technical education, has been founded.

Conclusion. While Mauritius has achieved the status of an independent state, its economy, being overly reliant upon the dominant sugar industry, is not strong. The relatively rapid population growth has caused concern and has tended to result in conditions that aggravate race problems. The growth of tourism has, however, been an encouraging development.

BIBLIOGRAPHY. PATRICK BARNWELL and AUGUSTE TOUSSAINT, *A Short History of Mauritius* (1949); BURTON BENEDICT, *Mauritius: Problems of a Plural Society* (1965); ALLISTER MACMILLAN, *Mauritius Illustrated* (1914), an extensive pre-World War I survey; JAMES E. MEADE, *The Economic and Social Structure of Mauritius*, 2nd ed. (1968); RICHARD TITMUSS, *Social Policies and Population Growth in Mauritius*, 2nd ed. (1968); AUGUSTE TOUSSAINT, *Harvest of the Sea: The Mauritius Sea Story in Outline* (1966); *Une cité tropicale: Port-Louis de l'île Maurice* (1966), the only history of Port Louis, the capital of Mauritius; and *Histoire de l'île Maurice* (1971).

(Au.T.)

Maximilian I, Emperor

One of the foremost princes of his age, the German king and Holy Roman emperor Maximilian I forged an elaborate dynastic structure that made his family, the Habsburgs, the dominant power in 16th-century Europe.

He was born at Wiener Neustadt, Austria, on March 22, 1459, the eldest son of the emperor Frederick III and Eleanor of Portugal.

By his marriage in 1477 to Mary, daughter of Charles the Bold, duke of Burgundy, Maximilian acquired the vast Burgundian possessions in the Netherlands and along the eastern frontier of France. He successfully defended his new domains against the attacks of Louis XI of France, defeating the French at the Battle of Guinegate in 1479. After Mary's death (1482) Maximilian was forced to allow the States General (representative assembly) of the Netherlands to act as regent for his infant son Philip (later Philip I the Handsome, of Castile); but having defeated the States in war, he reacquired control of the regency in 1485. Meanwhile, by the Treaty of Arras (1482), Maximilian was also forced to consent to the betrothal of his daughter Margaret of Austria to Charles VIII of France.

In 1486 he was elected king of the Romans (heir to his father, the emperor) and crowned at Aachen on April 9.

By courtesy of the Albertina, Vienna

Maximilian I, charcoal drawing by Albrecht Dürer, 1518. In the Albertina, Vienna.

With the military help of Spain, England, and Brittany, he continued his war against France and the rebellious Netherlands. In order to surround France, Maximilian in 1490 married Duchess Anne of Brittany by proxy but could not forestall an invasion of Brittany by the French. A dramatic setback occurred when Charles VIII sent his fiancée Margaret back to her father and required Anne to sever her marriage with Maximilian and to become the queen of France.

Through the archduke Sigismund, his cousin, Maximilian obtained the Tirol. Because of its favourable situation politically as well as its silver mines, its chief city, Innsbruck, became his favorite centre of operations.

By 1490 he regained control of most of his family's traditional territories in Austria, which had been seized by Hungary. He then became a candidate for the vacant Hungarian throne. When Vladislav (Ulászló) II of Bohemia was elected instead, he waged a successful campaign against Vladislav. By the Treaty of Pressburg in 1491 he arranged that the succession to Bohemia and Hungary would pass to the Habsburgs if Vladislav left no male heir.

The Treaty of Senlis (1493) ended the conflict against the Netherlands and France and left the duchy of Burgundy and the Low Countries secure in the possession of the house of Habsburg.

On the death of Frederick III in 1493, Maximilian had become sole ruler over the German kingdom and head of the house of Habsburg; he then drove the Turks from his southeast borders, married Bianca Maria Sforza of Milan (1494), and handed over the Low Countries to his son Philip (1494), reserving, however, the right of joint rule. The flourishing culture of the Low Countries influenced literature, art, government, politics, and military methods in all the other Habsburg possessions.

Charles VIII's invasion of Italy (1494) upset the European balance of power. Maximilian allied himself with the pope, Spain, Venice, and Milan in the so-called Holy League (1495) to drive out the French, who were conquering Naples. He campaigned in Italy in 1496, but although the French were expelled, he achieved little benefit from it. More important were the marriages of his son Philip to the Spanish infanta Joan (the Mad), in the same year, and of his daughter Margaret to the Spanish Crown Prince, in 1497. These marriages assured him of the succession in Spain and the control of the Spanish colonies.

At a meeting of the Reichstag (Imperial Diet) at Worms in 1495 Maximilian sought to strengthen the empire. Laws were projected to reform the Reichskammergericht (Imperial Chamber), taxation, and to give permanency to the public peace; however, no solution was forthcoming for many military and administrative problems. The princes would permit no strengthening of the central authority, and this limitation of power neutralized imperial policies. To thwart the opposition, which was led primarily by the lord chancellor Berthold, archbishop of Mainz, Maximilian set up his own extra-constitutional judicial and financial commissions.

In 1499 Maximilian fought an unsuccessful war against the Swiss Confederation and was forced to recognize its virtual independence by the Peace of Basel (September 22). At the same time, the French moved back into Italy, in cooperation with Spain, and occupied the imperial fief of Milan.

In 1500 the imperial princes at the Reichstag in Augsburg withdrew considerable power from Maximilian and invested it in the Reichsregiment, a supreme council of 21 electors, princes, and others. They even considered deposing him, but the plan miscarried because of their own apathy and Maximilian's effective countermeasures. He strengthened his European position by an agreement with France, and he regained prestige within the empire by victories in a dynastic war between Bavaria and the Rhenish Palatinate (1504). At the same time, the death of Berthold of Mainz rid him of one of his main opponents. Credit arrangements with south German business firms, such as the Fuggers, assured Maximilian of funds for foreign and domestic needs; and a campaign against

Hungary in 1506 strengthened the Habsburg claim to the Hungarian throne. Though he was German king, he had not been crowned as emperor by the pope, as was customary. Excluded from Italy by the hostile Venetians, he was unable to go to Rome for his coronation and had to content himself with the title of Roman emperor elect that was bestowed on him with the consent of Pope Julius II on February 4, 1508.

To oppose Venice, Maximilian entered into the League of Cambrai with France, Spain, and the pope in 1508. Their aim was to partition the Republic of Venice. In the war that followed, Maximilian was labelled an unreliable partner because of his lack of funds and troops. Pope Julius's severe illness prompted Maximilian to consider accepting the office of pope, which the schismatic Council of Pisa offered him. At times pious, at other times antipapal, he thought he might win financial help from the German Church if he were a rival pope; but in the end he let himself be dissuaded from this by Ferdinand II the Catholic, of Aragon. Turning away from his French alliance, he entered into a new Holy League (1511) with the pope, Spain, England, and their allies; with the help of England he scored a victory against the French in the Battle of the Spurs (1513), while his allies concentrated on regaining Milan and Lombardy. The French were victorious in Italy at the Battle of Marignano in 1515, and Maximilian's efforts to re-win Milan failed miserably. The Treaty of Brussels granted Milan to the French and Verona to the Venetians, leaving Maximilian with only the territorial boundaries of Tirol.

In the east, by making overtures to Russia, he was able to put pressure on Poland, Bohemia, and Hungary to acquiesce in his expansionist plans. In 1515, advantageous marriages were arranged between members of the Habsburg family and the Hungarian royal house, thus strengthening the Habsburg position in Hungary and also in Bohemia, which was under Hungarian influence. His intricate system of alliances, embracing both central Europe and the Iberian Peninsula, made Maximilian a potent force in European affairs.

On January 12, 1519, having spent the previous year trying to have his grandson Charles elected emperor and to raise a European coalition against the Turks, he died at Wels in Upper Austria. He was buried in Georgskirche at Wiener Neustadt. (His magnificent tomb at the Hofkirche in Innsbruck was erected later.) His plans did come to fruition when his grandson, already king of Spain, became emperor as Charles V later the same year.

Great as Maximilian's achievements were, they did not match his ambitions; for he had hoped to unite all of western Europe by reviving the empire of Charlemagne. Adhering more often to medieval patterns of thought, he was nevertheless open to new ideas, enthusiastic about promoting science as well as the arts. He not only planned a Latin autobiography but wrote two poetical allegories, *Weisskunig* ("White King") and *Teuerdank* (both largely autobiographical), and the *Geheimes Jagdbuch*, a treatise on hunting, and kept a bevy of poets and artists busy with projects that glorified his reign. His military talents were considerable and led him to use war to attain his ends. He carried out meaningful military and administrative reforms, but he was ignorant of economics and was financially unreliable.

BIBLIOGRAPHY. HEINRICH ULMANN, *Kaiser Maximilian I*, 2 vol. (1884–91, reprinted 1967), was the basic biography of Maximilian but now is completely out of date not only with respect to its sources and literature but also because of its emphatic Kleindeutsch (favouring the confederation of German states excluding Austria)–Prussian viewpoint. ROBERT W. SETON-WATSON, *Maximilian I, Holy Roman Emperor* (1902); and CHRISTOPHER HARE, *Maximilian the Dreamer, Holy Roman Emperor, 1459–1519* (1913), are the most important of the older presentations in English. GLENN E. WAAS, *The Legendary Character of Kaiser Maximilian* (1941), is primarily concerned with his character and personality; this very valuable work offers an imposing bibliography of the sources and literature as well as full scholarly apparatus. The catalogs of the *Ausstellungen Maximilian I.* (1959 and 1969), contain important contributions, especially concerning special problems of cultural history, and copious illustrations. HERMANN WIESFLECKER, *Maximilian I., Österreich, das Reich und Europa an der Wende zur Neuzeit*, vol. 1 (1971), is the first part of a projected four-volume biography of Maximilian that was prepared according to modern principles of historical research and that also contains a nearly complete bibliography of the sources and literature.

(H.Wi.)

Maxwell, James Clerk

Though familiar to every physicist, the majority of whom would rank him next to Sir Isaac Newton for the fundamental nature of his contributions to the subject, the name of James Clerk Maxwell is less well-known to the general public. To the physicist, the name Maxwell means Maxwell's equations, the basis of the field theory of electricity and magnetism. Maxwell saw the space surrounding charged bodies as the seat of an electric field, and from this view, field theories have since become of widespread importance. Though the English physicist Michael Faraday, not Maxwell, must be given the credit for the origin of the field theory, he was no mathematician, and the idea could not have developed in his hands. Had it not been for Maxwell, it would have remained imprecise and of little use. After it had left the hand of Maxwell, it had been given a precision that made it the model for all field theories to follow.

Like Newton before him, Maxwell made contributions of fundamental importance to many branches of physics. He developed a quantitative theory of colour vision—even producing one of the first, if not the first, colour photographs. His contribution to the kinetic theory of gases has been of the greatest importance. He worked out the distribution of velocities among the molecules of a gas, their mean free path between collisions with each other, and tested his conclusions by experiments on the viscosity of gases. His interest in velocity distributions may well have arisen from his early work on the rings of Saturn, which earned him the important Adams Prize at Cambridge.

Early life and education

Though born in Edinburgh, on November 13, 1831, Maxwell was brought up in the country and not as a townsman. His father inherited an estate, Glenlair, in Kirkcudbrightshire and built a substantial house there. James's mother died when he was eight years old, and he continued to live in the house with his father, to whom he became deeply attached. He thus spent his childhood surrounded by the colour of the lakes and hills of Galloway, playing in the stream that ran by his house, and even in later life always managed to spend much of his time there. He went to school at Edinburgh Academy. Joining a class of sophisticated town boys already in their second year, he became something of a misfit. His country clothes and manners quickly earned him the nickname "Dafty." Anything less appropriate can hardly be imagined, but the episode may have had much to do with his shy, introspective character. Maxwell's father mixed with the distinguished scientific circle of Edinburgh of the time, and even before he left that city at the age of 19, James had had two papers published by its Royal Society.

On leaving Edinburgh, where he had spent three years at the university, Maxwell went up to Peterhouse, Cambridge, in the autumn of 1850. A number of very able mathematicians had been attracted to this college, including P.G. Tait, a schoolfellow of Maxwell and a year his junior. Maxwell soon afterward migrated to Trinity College, where the chances of obtaining a mathematical fellowship (which he later achieved) were thought to be better. He graduated in mathematics in 1854 with high honours.

Conservative by nature and conformist in religion, Maxwell generally sided with the clerics in the arguments over evolution, which were at their height in his time. He was athletic—walking, swimming, gymnastics, rowing, and riding provided him with exercise; he was also an expert horseman. One of his simple hobbies was the "diabolo," or "devil on two sticks" as he called it; its mastery called for a measure of scientific judgment.

Maxwell was appointed to the professorship of natural philosophy at Marischal College, Aberdeen, in 1856. He

Maxwell, oil on china by an unknown artist, after a photograph. In the collection of the National Portrait Gallery, London.
By courtesy of the National Portrait Gallery London

had hoped from there to be able to spend much time with his father at Glenlair, but his father died before he took up his duties. He married Katherine Mary Dewar, the daughter of the principal of the college. After four years, Marischal College was combined with King's College to form Aberdeen University; and Maxwell, the junior partner in his department, had to seek another post. He tried unsuccessfully for a professorship that became vacant at Edinburgh, but in the summer of 1860, he was appointed to King's College, London.

He held this post for five years, during which he was at the height of his powers. He had just completed a very important paper on the kinetic theory of gases, which was published in 1860. This was later followed by other papers on the same subject, which must have remained constantly in his mind since he published his *Theory of Heat* in 1877. His electrical studies had started in Cambridge with a paper, "On Faraday's Lines of Force," read to the Cambridge Philosophical Society in two parts in 1855 and 1856. A second paper "On Physical Lines of Force," was contributed to the *Philosophical Magazine* in 1861. His electromagnetic theory was first fully set out in a paper to the Royal Society in 1864 entitled "A Dynamical Theory of the Electromagnetic Field." The best exposition of his theory, however, is to be found in the *Treatise on Electricity and Magnetism*.

Significance of work on electrical-field theory

Maxwell's work on electricity constituted his supreme achievement. It involved the extension of Faraday's ideas and their interpretation in terms of a mathematical notation. Like Faraday he looked upon the role of conductors in electricity as a minor one, since they served only as terminations of the lines of force of the surrounding electric field. He viewed all space as occupied by an ether that is capable of being electrically polarized. From this conception he postulated that a changing electric field should lead to what he called a displacement current in the ether, behaving in all respects like any other current of electricity. This concept made possible his electromagnetic theory.

The results of William Thomson (later Lord Kelvin), who calculated the velocity of a signal along an electric cable, were supported in 1857 when the German physicist Gustav Kirchhoff calculated the velocity of a signal along an isolated wire of circular cross-section. Kirchhoff found that the velocity should equal the ratio of the electromagnetic to the electrostatic unit of charge. This ratio had also been measured in 1856 by the German physicists Friedrich Kohlrausch and Wilhelm Weber and, although not of high accuracy, was very close to the measured value of the velocity of light. Kirchhoff, however, because of his view that electric current consists of positive and negative electricities, missed its significance. To Maxwell, who thought that electrical phenomena took place in the field surrounding the conductors (which merely guided the lines of force), the result was highly significant. He commented upon it in a letter to Faraday in 1861 and added that he had worked out his formula before seeing the results of Kohlrausch and Weber. Maxwell's first attempt at an electromagnetic theory of light, published in 1862, established the velocity of propagation of a signal along a wire as the ratio measured by Kohlrausch and Weber. "We can scarcely avoid the conclusion," said Maxwell, "that light consists in the transverse undulations of the same medium which is the cause of electric and magnetic phenomena." In 1868 Maxwell himself measured the ratio of the two units of charge by a better method. His theory was strikingly confirmed by the experiments of Heinrich Hertz some years later, when he demonstrated the production of electromagnetic waves. Maxwell's theory led to advances in science and technology that have transformed the modern world.

Maxwell left King's College, London, in the spring of 1865 and retired to his estate at Glenlair. His time was mainly spent in quiet country life and in perfecting his electrical theory for the writing of the treatise. He paid periodic visits to Cambridge, where he acted as moderator or examiner for the Mathematical Tripos. In 1871 he accepted, somewhat reluctantly, an invitation to become the first Cavendish Professor of Physics. It fell to him to design the Cavendish Laboratory and recruit the initial staff; and it is to Maxwell's genius that the eminence that that institution achieved by the turn of the century is due. Maxwell died after a short illness on November 5, 1879.

BIBLIOGRAPHY. LEWIS CAMPBELL and WILLIAM GARNETT, *The Life of James Clerk Maxwell* (1882, reprinted 1969), the standard biography; R.A.R. TRICKER, *The Contributions of Faraday and Maxwell to Electrical Science* (1966), on the life and electrical studies of Maxwell, including reproductions from some of his most important papers and descriptions of the development of the electromagnetic theory of radiation; C. DOMB (ed.), *Clerk Maxwell and Modern Science* (1963), a collection of essays of varying relevance to the work and life of Maxwell; SIR EDMUND T. WHITTAKER, *History of the Theories of Aether and Electricity*, 2 vol. (1960), a well-known standard work giving a full account of Maxwell's contributions and their relation to the work of his contemporaries and predecessors. Maxwell's philosophical attitude to physics as well as accounts of some of his contributions to the subject may be found in the books by Maxwell himself: *Theory of Heat*, 3rd ed. (1872), and his *Treatise on Electricity and Magnetism*, 2 vol. (1873, reprinted 1953). The latter contains the best exposition of his electromagnetic theory of radiation. For his original papers, see *The Scientific Papers of James Clerk Maxwell*, 2 vol. (1890; reprinted in 1 vol., 1965).

(R.A.R.T.)

Mayan Religion

The religion of the Maya of southern Mexico and Central America influenced the development of some of the most impressive architectural, calendrical, and mathematical accomplishments of mankind.

The Maya civilization, the most brilliant pre-Columbian civilization known to modern man, flourished from the 3rd to the 16th centuries in an approximately 125,000-square-mile (325,000-square-kilometre) area that included the peninsula of Yucatán and the eastern part of Chiapas in Mexico, most of Guatemala, the western region of the Republic of Honduras, and the territory of British Honduras. The peoples who brought this civilization to a very high level of artistic and intellectual achievement spoke dialects belonging to a common stock: the Maya language. The present-day Maya Indians speak about 20 different idioms, the most important being the Yucatec or Maya proper, the Quiché of Guatemala, the Tzeltal, Tzotzil, and Chol of Chiapas. There is no means at present, however, to determine which language or languages were in use during the Classic period (3rd–9th century). Knowledge of such Maya terms as the names of deities or of the day-signs is based on post-Columbian documents with reference mainly to Yucatec Maya or sometimes to Quiché.

Religion dominated every aspect of Maya civilization. Although external influences brought about deep changes during the post-Classic era (see below), the role of religion in the Maya cultural complex remained paramount until its collapse under the onslaught of Spanish invasion in the 16th century.

Sources. The four main categories of documents that provide knowledge of the Maya civilization and its religion are: archaeological remains; native books in hieroglyphic writing; books in native languages written in Latin script by learned Indians; and early accounts written in Spanish by conquerors or priests.

Archaeological remains. From surviving temples, tombs, sculpture, wall paintings, pottery, and carved jades, shells, and bone, a significant amount of valuable information can be gained; *e.g.*, representations of godheads and ritual scenes. The interpretation of such remains, however, is delicate, especially in regard to the Classic period, because there is no proof that more recent concepts may validly apply to it. The hieroglyphic inscriptions should supply a wealth of information, but modern scholars still cannot decipher most of them.

Native books in hieroglyphic writing. Only three of the books written in hieroglyphics have survived: the Dresden Codex (Codex Dresdensis), discovered in Vienna in 1739, then kept at the former Royal Library of Saxony (Sächsische Landesbibliothek) in Dresden; the Madrid Codex (Codex Tro-Cortesianus) of the Museo de América, in Madrid; and the Paris Codex (Codex Peresianus) of the Bibliothèque Nationale. These three remaining books deal with astronomical calculations, divination, and ritual. They appear to be relatively recent copies of early originals. Their hieroglyphic writing is a simplified form of the glyphs carved on Classic stelae (inscribed stone pillars) but similar to those that were painted on the walls of a 5th-century tomb at Tikal.

Books in native languages written in Latin script by learned Indians. After the Spanish conquest, books were written by learned Indians who transcribed or summarized hieroglyphic records. Such is the case of the *Books of Chilam Balam*, in Yucatec Maya, and of the *Popol Vuh*, in Quiché, a highland Maya language. The former consist of historical chronicles mixed with myth, divination, and prophecy, and the latter (which shows definite central Mexican influences) embodies the mythology and cosmology of the post-Classic Guatemalan Maya. The *Ritual of the Bacabs* deals with religious symbolism, medical incantations, and similar matters.

Early accounts written in Spanish by conquerors or priests. The most important of these sources is Diego de Landa's *Relación de las cosas de Yucatán* ("On the Things of Yucatán"), written about 1566. It is the best description of post-Classic religion in Yucatán and other details of late Maya history and life.

Other sources. To these sources may be added the observations recorded by modern anthropologists and ethnologists about present-day Maya, such as the Lacandones. In the Guatemalan highlands, ceremonies connected to the 260-day sacred calendar of the Maya survive, as do ancient prayers and information about Maya gods and goddesses in Yucatán and other areas.

History. *Early history.* The oldest Maya dates recorded on monuments are found at Tikal (from AD 292) and at Uaxactún (328) in the Petén rain-forest lowlands of Guatemala. Little is known of the Formative period, which must have lasted several centuries before those dates. Obvious similarities connect Maya architectural features (pyramids, sculptured altars, stelae) and chronological hieroglyphs with the Olmec civilization of the Gulf Coast (see AZTEC RELIGION), but the characteristic jaguar-baby image of the Olmecs is nowhere represented in Maya art. Early Maya religion probably revolved around rain and vegetation gods, much like that of Teotihuacán in the Mexican highlands. Apparently, an aristocracy with theocratic tendencies developed over the peasants, who retained their agricultural deities.

The Classic period. The Classic period (*c.* AD 300–900) can be accurately dated because of the most original feature of Maya religion: the stela cult; *i.e.*, the cus-

The stela cult

tom of erecting carved stelae at the end of each *katun* (a 20-year period, with each *tun*, or year, lasting 360 days). From Tikal and Uaxactún in the Petén area, the custom spread to ceremonial centres in northwestern Yucatán, Chiapas, and the Usumacinta Valley (Palenque, Yaxchilán, Piedras Negras) and to Copán between 435 and 534, then to new cities in Yucatán (Tulum, Cobá, Edzná, Jaina), to Quiriguá in the Motagua Valley, and to Tzendales, Lacanhá, and Tilá in Chiapas.

The 7th and 8th centuries can be considered the Maya Golden Age. Majestic monuments of the Copán Acropolis, exquisite sculptures and stuccos of Piedras Negras and Palenque, carved lintels of Yaxchilán, huge hieroglyphic stelae of Quiriguá, and delightful statuettes from Jaina all bear witness to the extraordinary dynamism of Maya civilization. In the year AD 790 (end of the 18th *katun* of the 9th *baktun*, 20 *katun*s each, in the Maya count), dated stelae were erected in 19 cities from Yucatán to Copán. From then on, archaeological remains show a marked decline in building and artistic activities. The last recorded dates are found in the Petén area (889 at Uaxactún). An engraved jade from Tzibanché, Quintana Roo, bears the date 909. Most of the classic centres had been abandoned by the end of the 9th century.

The post-Classic period. In the general collapse of the Classic civilization—which very well may have been caused by social and religious peasant revolts leading to the overthrow of the theocracy—the Yucatán sites such as Uxmal and Chichén-Itzá also were abandoned. In that area, however, the invasion of a foreign tribe, the Itzá, introduced (*c.* AD 1000) a completely new set of ideas and behaviours. Under the leadership of Kukulcán (Maya equivalent of the Mexican Quetzalcóatl, or Feathered Serpent god), the foreigners imposed upon the Yucatec Maya the central Mexican Toltec customs of human sacrifice and militarism and built grandiose Toltec-style monuments, such as the Temple of the Warriors at Chichén-Itzá. Other gods such as Tlalchitonatiuh, the rising sun and patron of the warrior orders of the Jaguars and Eagles, and phallic worship and other erotic practices were also introduced, all of which was not well accepted by the conquered Yucatec Maya. The alien deities little affected the peasant class. That renaissance lasted for two centuries; then the oppressive hegemony of the Mexican Maya city of Mayapán (*c.* 1200–*c.* 1450) followed by constant warfare between petty states, accelerated a cultural decline that ended only in the Spanish conquest in 1541.

The post-Spanish conquest period. Only a few Maya Indians (*e.g.*, the Lacandones) have resisted conversion to Christianity. Present-day religion of the Maya peasant, however, often combines Roman Catholic rites and beliefs with ancient cults, such as that of the Chac rain gods in Yucatán or the Year-Bearers' cult in the Guatemalan Highlands. In effect, the Maya absorbed Christianity, equating their pagan gods with Roman Catholic saints. Their moon-goddess came to be identified with the Virgin Mary, their Chacs with SS. Michael and James (depicted on horses), and the sun with Joseph or, sometimes, with Jesus. Even the cross is accorded a divine status, as both rain god and oracle.

Myths. The nature worship of the pre-Classic Maya probably began to undergo deep modifications as early as the 4th century BC with the introduction of astronomy, chronology, and hieroglyphic writing. An elaborate world view was evolved. Divinized heavenly bodies and time periods were added to the rain and maize gods.

Most deities were thought of as being simultaneously one and four, in connection with the four world directions, and as being both benevolent and malevolent. Concepts derived from priestly speculation were imposed upon the earlier pantheon, and religion became more and more esoteric, with a complex mythology interpreted by a closely organized priesthood.

Creation. The Maya, like other Middle American Indians (see AZTEC RELIGION), believed that several worlds had been successively created and destroyed before the present universe had come into being. The Dresden Codex holds that the end of a world will come about by deluge: although the evidence derived from Landa's *Relación* and from the Quiché *Popol Vuh* is not clear, it is likely that four worlds preceded the present one. Men were made successively of earth (who, being mindless, were destroyed), then of wood (who, lacking souls and intelligence and being ungrateful to the gods, were punished by being drowned in a flood or devoured by demons), finally of a maize gruel (the ancestors of the Maya). The Yucatec Maya worshipped a creator deity called Hunab Ku, One-God. Itzamná (Iguana House), head of the Maya pantheon of the ruling class, was his son, whose wife was Ix Chebel Yax, patroness of weaving.

Myths about the creation of man

Four Itzamnas, one assigned to each direction of the universe, were represented by celestial monsters or two-headed, dragon-like iguanas. Four gods, the Bacabs, sustained the sky. Each world direction was associated with a Bacab, a sacred ceiba tree, or wild cotton tree (*yaxché*), a bird, and a colour according to the following scheme: east–red, north–white, west–black, and south–yellow. Green was the colour of the centre. In one myth, the thunder god released white maize from a mountain for the benefit of man. During a blast from the thunderbolt, parts of the maize were untouched, lightly scorched, burned, or charred, hence white, yellow, red, and black ears, corresponding with the colours of the four directions.

The main act of creation, as stated in the *Popol Vuh*, was the dawn: the world and mankind were in darkness, but the gods created the sun and the moon. According to other traditions, the sun (male) was the patron of hunting and music, and the moon (female) was the goddess of weaving and childbirth. Both the sun and the moon inhabited the earth originally, but they were translated to the heaven as a result of the moon's sexual license. Lunar light is less bright than that of the sun because, it was said, one of her eyes was pulled out by the sun in punishment of her infidelity.

Because the Maya priests had reached advanced knowledge of astronomical phenomena and a sophisticated concept of time, it appears that their esoteric doctrines widely differed from the popular myths.

Cosmology. The Maya believed that 13 heavens were arranged in layers above the earth, which itself rested on the back of a huge crocodile or reptilian monster floating on the ocean. Under the earth were nine underworlds, also arranged in layers. Thirteen gods, the Oxlahuntiku (from *oxlahun*, 13), presided over the heavens; nine gods, the Bolontiku (from *bolon*, nine), ruled the subterranean worlds. These concepts are closely akin to those of the post-Classic Aztecs, but archaeological evidence, such as the nine deities sculptured on the walls of a 7th-century crypt at Palenque, shows that they were part of the Classic Maya cosmology.

According to the present-day Lacandones, the sun spends the night in the underworld, where he gets rest and food with his brother Usukunkyum, who protects him from the hostile earthquake god Kisin (Cizin). This myth reflects the strong dualistic tendency of Maya thought, which conceived the life of the universe as a struggle between benevolent and malevolent forces.

Time was an all-important element of Maya cosmology. The priest-astronomers viewed time as a majestic succession of cycles without beginning or end. All the time periods were considered as gods; time itself was believed to be divine.

The gods. Among the several deities represented by statues and sculptured panels of the Classic period are such gods as the young maize god, whose gracious statue is to be seen at Copán, the sun-god shown at Palenque under the form of the solar disk engraved with anthropomorphic features, the nine gods of darkness (also at Palenque), and a snake-god especially prominent at Yaxchilán. Another symbol of the maize god is a foliated cross or life tree represented in two Palenque sanctuaries. The rain god (Chac) appears to have been much more important in Yucatán, an utterly dry country, than in the southern rain-forest area. His mask with characteristic protruding fangs, large, round eyes, and proboscis-like nose ornates the facades of most Yucatec monuments.

Agricultural and astral deities

The three hieroglyphic manuscripts, especially the Dresden Codex, depict a number of deities whose names are known only through post-Classic documents. Itzamná, Lord of the Heavens, who ruled over the pantheon, was closely associated with Kinich Ahau, the sun, and with the moon-goddess Ixchel. Though Itzamná was considered an entirely benevolent god, Ixchel, often depicted as an evil old woman, had definitely unfavourable aspects.

The Chacs, the rain gods of the peasants, were believed to pour rain by emptying their gourds and to hurl stone axes upon the earth (the lightning). Their companions were frogs (uo), whose croakings announced the rains. Earth gods were worshipped in the highlands, and wind gods were of minor importance in Maya territory.

The maize god (left) and the rain god, Chac. Drawing from the Madrid Codex (Codex Tro-Cortesianus), one of the Mayan sacred books. In the Museo de América, Madrid.

The maize god, a youthful deity with an ear of corn in his headdress, also ruled over vegetation in general. His name, Yum Kaax, means Lord of the Forests. He is sometimes shown in combat with the death god, Ah Puch, a skeleton-like being, patron of the sixth day-sign Cimi (Death) and lord of the ninth hell. Several other deities were associated with death; e.g., Ek Chuah, a war god and god of merchants and cacao growers, and Ixtab, patron goddess of the suicides.

To these deities must be added divinized stars or planets, such as the North Star and Venus, the Oxlahuntiku and the Bolontiku (see above), and the gods of the katuns, of the months, the days, and the numerals.

In post-Classic times, central Mexican influences were introduced; e.g., the Toltec Feathered Serpent (Nahuatl: Quetzalcóatl), called Kukulcán in Yucatán and Gucumatz in the Guatemalan highlands. The Popol Vuh also mentions an important lightning god, Hurakan (One-Leg), similar to the one-legged Tezcatlipoca of central Mexico, and a deity named Ah Toltecat, the Toltec Lord. The Bacabs are represented in Toltec-Maya sculptures at Chichén-Itzá together with the Feathered Serpent.

Modern Lacandones worship Itzananohk'u (the Great God Itzana), K'in (Sun), and Kanank'ash (Protector of the Forests), which appear as recent forms of Itzamná, Kinich Ahau, and Yum Kaax. They also revere Metsabok, a cloud and rain god.

The ancient Maya's attitude toward the gods was one of humble supplication, since the gods could bestow health, good crops, and plentiful game or send illness and hunger. Prayers and offerings of food, drink, and incense (pom) were used to placate the gods. A strong sense of sin and a belief in predestination pervaded the Maya consciousness. Man had to submit to the forces of the universe. The priests, because of their astronomical and divinatory knowledge, determined favourable days for such undertakings as building houses and hunting.

Death. The Classic Maya buried the dead under the floors of their houses. High priests or powerful lords were laid to rest in elaborate underground vaults. The most striking example of the latter kind of burial is the Temple of Inscriptions crypt at Palenque, where a priest or ruler was buried in AD 633 in a wonderfully sculptured sarcophagus. The practice of cremation was introduced in post-Classic times, doubtless from central Mexico. The ashes were kept in urns or hollow statues.

Present-day Maya Indians bury their dead with mixed Catholic and native rites. Among the latter is the *bool keban*, in which the body is washed with *atole*, a maize (corn) gruel, which the family then drinks to assume the deceased's sins.

The dead were believed to descend to the nine underworlds, called Mitnal in Yucatán and Xibalba by the Quiché. There is no evidence of a belief among the Maya in a heavenly paradise, such as that which prevailed in central Mexico. The Lacandones, however, believe that the dead live forever without work or worry in a land of plenty located somewhere above the earth.

Eschatology. The present world, the Maya believed, is doomed to end in cataclysms as the other worlds have done previously. According to the priestly concept of time, cycles repeated themselves. Therefore, prediction was made possible by probing first into the past and then into the future: hence the calculations, bearing on many millennia, carved on temples and stelae. Evil influences were held to mark most of the *katun* endings. The *Chilam Balam* books are full of predictions of a markedly direful character. The priests probably believed that the present world would come to a sudden end, but that a new world would be created so that the eternal succession of cycles should remain unbroken.

The end of the world

Practices and institutions. *The calendar.* Maya mathematics included two outstanding discoveries: positional numeration and the zero. It may rightly be deemed one of the most brilliant achievements of the human mind. The same may also be said of ancient Maya astronomy. The duration of the solar year had been calculated with amazing accuracy, as well as the synodical revolution of Venus. The Dresden Codex contains very precise Venusian and lunar tables and a method of predicting solar eclipses.

Maya chronology consisted of three main elements: a 260-day sacred year (*tzolkin*) formed by the combination of 13 numbers (1 to 13) and 20 day names; a solar year (*haab*), divided into 18 months of 20 days numbered from 0 to 19, followed by a five-day unlucky period (Uayeb); and a series of cycles—*uinal* (20 *kins*, or days), *tun* (360 days), *katun* (7,200 days), *baktun* (144,000 days), with the highest cycle being the *alautun* of 23,040,000,000 days. All Middle American civilizations used the two first counts (see AZTEC RELIGION; CALENDAR), which permitted officials accurately to determine a date within a period defined as the least common multiple of 260 and 365: 18,980 days, or 52 years.

The Classic Maya Long Count inscriptions enumerate the cycles that have elapsed since a zero date in 3113 BC. Thus, "9.6.0.0.0," a *katun*-ending date, means that nine *baktuns* and six *katuns* have elapsed from the zero date to the day 2 Ahau 13 Zec (May 9, AD 751). To those Initial Series were added the Supplementary Series (information about the lunar month) and the Secondary Series, a calendar-correction formula that brought the conventional date in harmony with the true position of the day in the solar year.

Both Classic and recent Maya held the *tzolkin* as the most sacred means of divination, enabling the priests to detect the favourable or evil influences attached to every day according to the esoteric significance of the numbers and the day-signs.

Temples and ceremonial centres. Maya cities were primarily ceremonial, government, and market centres, with the temples and palaces built on pyramids or terraces. Dwellings in which people lived were thatched wooden houses or huts. The ruling class and the craftsmen probably lived close to the monuments, though this is not certain, and the peasants' settlements were scattered in clearings over the countryside. The priests lived in the ceremonial centres, usually for long periods of the isolation prior to important ceremonies. The ceremonial centre and the adjoining territory formed an independent city-state. Labour for constructing the numerous structures was supplied by the peasants, who also supported the quality of living of the ruling class.

Religion permeated the whole fabric of the social and political order. In Classic cities, governmental power seems to have belonged to the priesthood. Lay war chiefs, however, are represented on Piedras Negras stelae and Bonampak murals, but, because wars were infrequent, their power was probably limited. In post-Classic Yucatán, militaristic states were governed by rulers called "true men" (halach uinic).

Forms of sacrifice

Sacrifice. Sacrifices in return for divine favour were numerous: animals, birds, insects, fish, agricultural products, flowers, rubber, jade, and blood drawn from tongue, ears, arms, legs, and genitals. Evidence of human sacrifice in Classic times is scanty: two Piedras Negra's stelae, an incised drawing at Tikal, and some scenes in native manuscripts. Only in the post-Classic era did this practice become as frequent as in central Mexico. Toltec-Maya art shows many instances of human sacrifice: removal of the heart, arrow shooting, or beheading. At Chichén-Itzá, in order to obtain rain, victims were hurled into a deep natural well (cenote) together with copper, gold, and jade offerings. Prayers for material benefits (usually recited in a squatting or standing position), fasting and continence (often for 260 days), and drawing blood from one's body often preceded important ceremonies and sacrifices.

These practices had become so deeply rooted that, even after the Spanish conquest, Christian–pagan ceremonies occasionally took place in which men were sacrificed by heart removal or crucifixion. The last recorded case occurred in 1868 among the Chamula of Chiapas.

The priesthood. Bejewelled, feather-adorned priests are often represented in Classic sculpture. State administrators as well as scholars, astronomers, and architects, priests dominated the entire life of ancient cities. The high priests of each province taught in priestly schools such subjects as history, divination, and glyph writing. The priesthood, as described by Landa, was hereditary. *Ahkin,* "he of the sun," was the priests' general title. Specialized functions were performed by the *nacoms,* who split open the victims' breasts, the *chacs* who held their arms and legs, the *chilans* who interpreted the sacred books and predicted the future. Some priests used hallucinatory drugs in their roles as prophets and diviners.

Though the military nobility had acquired increased power in post-Classic Yucatán, the priesthood remained the most influential single group in Maya society until the Spanish conquest.

Rites. Ritual activities, held on selected favourable days, were complex and intense. Performers submitted to preliminary fasting and sexual abstinence. Features common to most rites were: offerings of incense (pom), of *balche* (an intoxicating drink brewed from honey and a tree bark), bloodletting from ears and tongues, sacrifices of animals (human sacrifices in later times), and dances. Special ceremonies took place on New Year's Day, 0 Pop, in honour of the "Year-Bearer"; i.e., the tzolkin sign of that day. Pottery, clothes, and other belongings were renewed. The second month, Uo, was devoted to Itzamná, Zec (fifth month) to the Bacabs, Xul (sixth) to Kukulcán, Yax (tenth) to Venus, Mac (13th) to the rain gods, Muan (15th) to the cocoa-tree god. New idols were made during the eighth and ninth months, Mol and Ch'en, respectively.

Every social group (priests, sorcerers, warriors, hunters, fishermen, beekeepers, and others) celebrated its own religious feast. Most ceremonies ended in feasting and heavy balche drinking.

The ritual ball game

Both the Classic and post-Classic Maya practiced a typically Middle American ritual ball game, as evidenced by numerous grandiose ball courts at Tikal, Copán, and Chichén-Itzá. No court, however, has been found at Ma-

yapán, and Landa does not mention that game. It appears, therefore, that the Yucatecs had ceased to play it, while it remained of the utmost importance in central Mexico.

Archaeological remains at Uxmal and Chichén-Itzá point to phallic rites, doubtless imported into Yucatán from the Gulf Coast. The *Chilam Balam* books strongly condemn the Mexican immigrants' sexual practices, which were quite alien to Maya tradition.

Sorcery. *Ahmen,* "he who knows," was the name given to sorcerers and medicine men, who were both prophets and inflicters or healers of disease. They made use of a mixture of magic formulas, chants, and prayers and of traditional healing methods, such as administering medicinal herbs or bleeding. Belief in witchcraft is widespread among present-day Maya Indians, as it most probably was in pre-Columbian times.

Conclusions. The evolution of Maya religion parallels that of Mexican religions from the Classic to the post-Classic era, with the sun worship and human sacrifice complex gaining importance as it did in Mexico proper.

The profoundly original feature of Maya religious thought, in comparison with that of other pre-Columbian civilizations, is the extraordinary refinement of mathematical and astronomical knowledge, inextricably mixed with mythological concepts. Even the most learned Aztec priests never reached the intellectual level of their Maya counterparts of the 1st millennium, nor did they conceive of the eternity of time and of its "bearers," the divinized time periods. The ancient Maya may be said to have been among the very few people in history (along with the Zurvanites of Iran) who worshipped time.

The simple, naturalistic religion of the maize-growing peasants, however, subsisted apart from the priesthood's abstract speculations and has partly survived to this day among the Christianized Maya Indians or the unevangelized Lacandones.

BIBLIOGRAPHY. DANIEL G. BRINTON (ed. and trans.), *The Maya Chronicles* (1882) and *The Annals of the Cakchiquels* (1885), the first attempts at a scientific interpretation of ancient Maya records; *El libro de los Libros de Chilam Balam,* ed. by A. BARRERA VASQUEZ (1948), a useful Spanish translation of important excerpts from the Chilam Balam books; WALTER KRICKEBERG, *Altmexikanische Kulturen* (1956), a highly erudite work that allows the reader to correlate Maya civilization and the other Mexican cultures; DIEGO DE LANDA, *Relación de las cosas de Yucatán,* ed. by ALFRED M. TOZZER (1941), the basic source of knowledge on recent Yucatec Maya religion; SYLVANUS G. MORLEY, *An Introduction to the Study of the Maya Hieroglyphs* (1915), one of the first and most effective attempts at deciphering Maya writing; *The Ancient Maya,* 3rd ed. rev. by G.W. BRAINERD (1956), a fundamental work by one of the foremost specialists of Maya civilization; *Popol Vuh, le livre sacré et les mythes de l'antiquité américaine,* ed. by BRASSEUR DE BOURBOURG (1861), first publication of the Quiché "Bible" with a French translation; *Les Dieux, les héros et les hommes de l'ancien Guatémala d'après le Livre du Conseil* (1925), an analysis of the Quiché sacred book; RALPH L. ROYS, *The Book of Chilam Balam of Chumayel* (1933), dealing with traditional religious and historical lore of the Maya; JACQUES SOUSTELLE, *The Ancient Civilizations of Mexico* (1969), on the relationship between the Maya and other Mexican civilizations; *Les Quatre Soleils* (1967; Eng. trans., *The Four Suns,* 1971), considerations of Mexican ethnology with reference to the ancient and present-day Maya; MORRIS STEGGERDA, *Maya Indians of Yucatan* (1941), an important study of the customs of the Yucatec Maya; J.E. TEEPLE, *Maya Astronomy* (1931), the basic work on the astronomical knowledge of Classic Maya; J. ERIC THOMPSON, *Ethnology of the Mayas of Southern and Central British Honduras* (1930), very useful comparative material in connection with other Maya areas; *Maya Hieroglyphic Writing: Introduction* (1950), an accurate study of Maya writing; *The Rise and Fall of Maya Civilization* (1954), a comprehensive record of Classic and post-Classic Maya cultures; *Maya History and Religion* (1970), a series of important studies on Maya religion, with special emphasis on the relations between the lowland and highland areas, the Mexican influences, and comparisons between myths from different Maya-speaking areas; ALFRED M. TOZZER, *A Comparative Study of the Mayas and the Lacandones* (1907), systematic comparisons between the Maya proper and the forest-dwelling Lacandones.

(Ja.S.)

Mayo Family

Probably the most famous group of physicians in the United States, three generations of the Mayo family, pioneers in the practice of group medicine, established the world-renowned Mayo Clinic and the Mayo Foundation for Medical Education and Research at Rochester, Minnesota.

By courtesy of the Mayo Clinic, Rochester, Minnesota

(From left) Charles Horace Mayo, William Worrall Mayo, and William James Mayo; photograph c. 1890.

William Worrall Mayo, father of the doctors Mayo who developed a large-scale, world-renowned practice of medicine, was born May 31, 1819, near Manchester, Lancashire. He attended Owens College in Manchester, majoring in chemistry, and, after immigrating to the United States in 1845, studied medicine with a private physician in Lafayette, Indiana, subsequently receiving degrees from Indiana Medical College, La Porte, and the University of Missouri, Columbia. In 1863 he moved to Rochester, where he soon had an extensive surgical practice. After taking care of the casualties of a disastrous tornado in Rochester, with the assistance of the Sisters of St. Francis, Mayo, his two sons, and the sisters planned to erect a new hospital. St. Mary's Hospital was opened on October 1, 1889, and Mayo and his two sons became responsible for care of the patients. After the father retired, the work was continued by his sons. William W. Mayo died in Rochester on March 6, 1911.

William James Mayo, eldest son of William Worrall Mayo, was born June 29, 1861, at Le Sueur, Minnesota. He received his M.D. degree in 1883 from the University of Michigan, Ann Arbor, and then engaged at Rochester in the private practice of medicine and surgery with his father and later with his younger brother Charles Horace Mayo. Though William J. Mayo became the administrator in the practice, no important decisions were made without the full agreement of both brothers. He and his brother performed all the surgery at St. Mary's Hospital until about 1905. From this surgical partnership of the two brothers evolved the cooperative group clinic, later known as the Mayo Clinic. William James Mayo, who became a specialist in surgery of the abdomen, pelvis, and kidney, remained active in surgery at the clinic until 1928 and in administration until 1933. From 1907 until his death, he served on the board of regents of the University of Minnesota. He died in Rochester on July 28, 1939.

The cooperative group clinic

Charles Horace Mayo, younger son of William Worrall Mayo, characterized as a "surgical wonder," was born in Rochester on July 19, 1865. He received an M.D. degree from the Chicago Medical College (later part of Northwestern University Medical School) in 1888 and in the same year began private practice of surgery with his father and brother.

Charles Mayo had the ability to work in all surgical fields; he originated modern procedures in goitre surgery and in neurosurgery; he performed highly successful operations for cataract of the eye and originated procedures for several orthopedic operations. In 1930 he retired from surgery at the clinic and three years later from administration. He was professor of surgery at the University of Minnesota Medical School from 1919 to 1936 and at the University of Minnesota Graduate School from 1915 to 1936. W.J. Mayo said about his brother, "Charlie has . . . an intuitive mind, from his knowledge of physiology and anatomy and his understanding of the personality of the patient." At one time he was a member of the advisory board of *Encyclopædia Britannica*. With his brother, he alternated as chief consultant for all surgical services in the U.S. Army during World War I, serving with the rank of colonel. After the war, each brother was commissioned a brigadier general in the medical-corps reserve. Charles Horace Mayo died in Chicago on May 26, 1939.

Charles Horace's son, Charles William, was born on July 28, 1898, at Rochester, Minnesota. He was a skilled surgeon and member of the board of governors of the Mayo Clinic, chairman of the Mayo Association, and a member (chairman 1961–67) of the board of regents of the University of Minnesota. He is still remembered for his speech given in the fall of 1953 as a member of the United States delegation at the eighth plenary session of the United Nations. He died at Rochester, Minnesota, on July 28, 1968.

The group began to grow in size in the early 1900s, when many young physicians began to apply for positions as interns and assistants. At the same time, outstanding scientists in basic medical subjects were added to the clinic's training and research programs. In 1919 the Mayo brothers transferred property and capital to the Mayo Properties Association, later called the Mayo Association, a charitable and educational corporation having a perpetual charter. About 1900 the Mayo Clinic was changed from a partnership to a voluntary association of physicians and specialists in allied fields. In the early 1970s, the clinic staff included about 500 physicians. Over 200,000 patients were seen annually, and the practice is increasing.

Expansion of Mayo Clinic

In 1915 the Mayo brothers gave $1,500,000 to the University of Minnesota to establish the Mayo Foundation for Medical Education and Research at Rochester in connection with the clinic. The foundation, which is part of the University of Minnesota Graduate School, offers graduate training in medicine and related subjects. In 1934 the endowment was increased by $500,000; by the early 1970s it amounted to more than $5,250,000. At that time, about 700 graduate physicians were attending as resident students. About 7,000 physicians have received some or all of their residency training at the Mayo Clinic and Mayo Foundation. The Mayo Graduate School of Medicine also has started an intern program, and an undergraduate medical school is in the formative stages.

BIBLIOGRAPHY. HELEN B. CLAPESATTLE, *The Doctors Mayo*, 2nd ed. (1954), an authoritative work based on printed sources and interviews; WILLIAM F. BRAASCH, *Early Days in the Mayo Clinic* (1969), written by the pioneer urologist of the Mayo Clinic; CHARLES W. MAYO, *Mayo: The Story of My Family and My Career* (1968); GUNTHER W. NAGEL, *The Mayo Legacy* (1966), written by a doctor trained in surgery at the Mayo Clinic; LUCY WILDER, *The Mayo Clinic*, 2nd ed. (1955), written by the wife of a prominent Mayo physician, Dr. Russell M. Wilder.

(T.E.K.)

Ma Yüan

Recognized as one of the most influential Chinese landscape painters, Ma Yüan (Pin-yin romanization Ma Yuan) was among the most gifted artists associated with the late-12th-century court of the Sung dynasty at Hangchow. His works and those of his contemporary, Hsia Kuei, formed the basis of a style of landscape painting called the Ma-Hsia school, which was widely imitated in eastern Asia.

Ma Yüan was born c. 1160–65 into a family of court painters: his great grandfather, Ma Fen, had been *tai-*

chao (*i.e.*, painter in attendance) at the Northern Sung Court, *c.* 1119–25; both his grandfather, Ma Hsing-tzu, and his father, Ma Shih-jung, held the same rank at the Southern Sung Court in the middle decades of the 12th century. Ma Yüan began his career under the emperor Hsiao Tsung, became *tai-chao* under Emperor Kuang Tsung, and received the highest Chinese honour, the Golden Belt, under Emperor Ning Tsung. He died in about 1225. His son, Ma Lin, the last of the Ma artistic dynasty, rose to be painter-in-waiting, *chih-hou*. Apart from these bare facts, practically nothing is known about Ma Yüan's life. Being neither a scholar nor an official, he neither left a body of his own writings nor earned a biography in the dynastic history. He seems, however, to have been in high favour at court, particularly under Ning Tsung, who, with his empress, Yang Mei-tzu, wrote poems or short inscriptions on a number of his paintings.

Ma Yüan occasionally painted flowers and figure subjects. A group of small, delicate flower paintings in the National Palace Museum, Taipei, Taiwan, are attributed to him. Typically, a single spray of blossoms lies poised in empty space across the square album leaf. One is signed, and two bear couplets written by Yang Mei-tzu. There are also three paintings of Zen masters in simple landscape settings, two of them in Tenryū-ji, Kyōto, the third in the Tokyo National Museum, which, though not signed, bear inscriptions considered to be in the handwriting of Yang Mei-tzu. They all have certain similar features of technique that have led some Japanese authorities to attribute them to Ma Yüan.

It was in landscape painting that Ma Yüan's genius lay. He executed a number of large landscape screens, all of which are now lost. He also painted tall, hanging scrolls in which, according to an early Chinese writer, "there are steep mountains rising imposingly, with streams winding around them and waterfalls partly hidden among the trees." He also wrote that Ma Yüan made his pine trees "very tall and strong as if they were made of iron wire; sometimes he painted them with a stump brush; the effect is vigorous, beautiful and elegant." Typical of this kind of picture is a tall, unsigned "Rain over Trees on a Rocky Shore" in the Seikadō Foundation, Tokyo. The monumental composition, the expressive use of monochrome ink, the powerful angularity of the brushwork, in which the artist hacks out the facets of his rocks by means of a slanting "axe-cut" stroke, are features that first had been developed by Li T'ang, the senior landscapist in the Imperial Academy in the last years of the Northern Sung dynasty. Although Li T'ang may not have lived long enough to see the Sung court re-established at Hangchow in 1136, his influence there was profound, and his style of landscape painting became the orthodox manner for Southern Academy painters, being transmitted down to Ma Yüan through a follower, Hsiao Chao, and through Ma Yüan's own forebears.

By the late 12th century, however, this style was changing, and the new elements that were appearing reflected the nostalgic and somewhat precious atmosphere of the exiled court at Hangchow. In some hanging scrolls attributed to Ma Yüan, and in many of the exquisite small album and fan paintings, the mountains are pushed to one side, creating a "one corner" composition; between the distant mountains and the strongly accented foreground rocks, where a scholar may be sitting enjoying the view, lies a vast expanse of empty space with but a suggestion of mist or water. Many of Ma Yüan's pictures are romantic night scenes. A particularly moving hanging scroll of this kind, attributed to him and bearing a long poem composed by the Emperor and written by Yang Mei-tzu, is the unsigned version of the "Banquet by Lantern Light" in the National Palace Museum, Taipei, Taiwan.

Such paintings are redolent of a poetic melancholy that hints at the decay of Sung culture, and the pictorial expression of this feeling is often rather conventional. The one-sided composition, the jutting pine tree silhouetted against empty space, the meditating scholar, the brilliant brush technique of Ma Yüan himself, all lent themselves easily to imitation. His style was very popular with late Sung painters, men and women, professionals and amateurs, and it is difficult to separate the genuine fans and album leaves from those of his followers. Among the best of them are "Early Spring" and "Two Sages and an Attendant Beneath a Plum Tree," both in the Museum of Fine Arts, Boston; "Watching the Deer by a Pine-shaded Stream," in the Mr. and Mrs. Dean Perry Collection, Cleveland; and "On a Mountain Path in Spring," a signed album leaf bearing a couplet written by the emperor Ning Tsung, in the National Palace Museum in Taiwan.

Finally, a small group of hand scrolls show another facet of Ma Yüan's genius. Most striking, and most likely to be from his hand, is the picture "The Four Sages of Shang-shan" (recluses who lived at the beginning of the Han dynasty), in the Cincinnati Art Museum. Although damaged and poorly restored, the picture presents a dramatic contrast between the vital handling of the landscape and raging torrent and the extreme delicacy and precision of the figures of the scholars and their attendants, which suggests the hand of a great master. The scroll is signed and bears 40 colophons or seals of the various owners, including one by the noted Yüan dynasty scholar-painter Ni Tsan (1301–74). A signed long scroll of mountains and pine trees in deep winter snow in the Imperial Museum in Peking, though roughly painted, is an extremely impressive work that may be a product of Ma Yüan's old age.

The romantic landscape style of the Southern Sung academicians such as Ma Yüan, his son Ma Lin, and Hsia Kuei went out of fashion after the fall of the dynasty in 1279. It was revived in the Ming dynasty (1368–1644) as a form of decorative academicism by professional painters of the so-called Che school. The style was not greatly admired by gentlemen and connoisseurs, who considered it too brilliantly professional for their taste. As a result, few high-quality paintings of the Ma-Hsia school survived in China outside the Imperial collection. Their work, however, found favour in Japan, where it was a powerful influence in forming the style of the great ink painters Shūbun (early 15th century) and Sesshū, and of the early masters of the Kanō school during the Muromachi period (1338–1573).

MAJOR WORKS

Active *c.* 1190–1225. The following are some examples of his work: "Mountains in Snow," attributed (Shanghai Museum); "A Scholar Beneath a Pine Tree" (National Palace Museum, Taipei, Taiwan) and "Through Snowy Mountains at Dawn" (National Palace Museum, Taipei, Taiwan), album leaves from the *Ming-hua chi-chen;* "Rain over Trees on a Rocky Shore" (Seikadō Foundation, Tokyo); "Scholar Contemplating the Moon" (Hakone Museum, Kanagawa, Japan); "Solitary Angler on Wintry Lake" (National Museum, Tokyo); "The Four Sages of Shang-shan" (Cincinnati Art Museum, Ohio); "Playing the Lute by Moonlight" (National Palace Museum, Taipei, Taiwan); "Early Spring: Bare Willows and Distant Mountains" (Museum of Fine Arts, Boston); "Mountains and Tall Pine Trees by a Cottage in the Snow" (National Palace Museum, Taipei, Taiwan); "An Immortal on a Dragon in Clouds and Mist" (National Palace Museum, Taipei, Taiwan); "Banquet by Lantern Light" (National Palace Museum, Taipei, Taiwan); "Ducks in the Water Beneath an Overhanging Plum Tree" (Hui-hua-kuan, Peking); "The Ch'an Monk Tung-shan Wading a Stream" (National Museum, Tokyo); "Hsiao Ssu-hua Seated Beneath a Tree Playing the Ch'in" (Museum of Fine Arts, Boston); "Two Sages and an Attendant Beneath a Plum Tree" (Museum of Fine Arts, Boston).

BIBLIOGRAPHY. OSVALD SIREN, *Chinese Painting: Leading Masters and Principles*, 7 vol. (1956–58), is the standard history of Chinese painting. There is no book in any Western language devoted to Ma Yüan, but there are sections on his work in SHUJIRO SHIMADA and YOSHIHO YONEZAWA, *Painting of Sung and Yüan Dynasties* (1952); KOJIRO TOMITA, *Portfolio of Chinese Paintings in the Boston Museum of Fine Arts*, 2nd rev. ed. (1938); SHERMAN E. LEE, *Chinese Landscape Painting*, 2nd ed. (1962); LAURENCE SICKMAN (ed.), *Chinese Calligraphy and Painting in the Collection of John M. Crawford, Jr.* (1962); JAMES CAHILL, *Chinese Painting, XI–XIV Centuries* (1960); and MICHAEL SULLIVAN, *A Short History of Chinese Art*, rev. ed. (1970). The little available evidence on his position at the Southern Sung court is discussed in CHIANG CHAO-SHEN, "The Identity of Yang Mei-

Flower and figure subjects

Hand scrolls

tzu and the Paintings of Ma Yüan," *National Palace Museum Bulletin*, vol. 2, no. 2, pp. 1–15 and no. 3, pp. 8–14 (1967).

(M.Su.)

Mazarin, Jules, Cardinal

Mazarin, successor to the great French minister the cardinal de Richelieu, completed Richelieu's work of establishing France's supremacy among the European powers and crippling opposition to the power of the monarchy at home.

By courtesy of the Musee Conde, Chantilly, France; photograph, Giraudon

Mazarin, portrait by Philippe de Champaigne (1602–74). In the Musée Condé, Chantilly, France.

Service as papal diplomat. Born a papal subject on July 14, 1602, at Pescina, in the Abruzzi, near Rome, Giulio Mazarini spent his childhood in a region whose temperament, ways of thought, and Roman Catholic outlook were to permeate his whole existence. His father, Pietro, was a romanized Sicilian in the household of the constable Filippo I Colonna; his mother, Ortensia Bufalini, of a noble Tuscan family, was related to the Colonna house by marriage. From the beginning Mazarini recognized the benefits of having powerful patrons and learned to exploit them to his advantage. Thus, in spite of financial difficulties and the expenses of a large family (another son, who became a monk, and four daughters), the Mazarini were able to send Giulio to the Jesuit school in Rome, where he was an excellent student. Accompanying a young member of the Colonna family to Spain, he completed his education at the university at Alcalá de Henares (now the University of Madrid) where he studied law and then returned to Rome eager to learn more about aristocratic ways of life and secular affairs. From the Colonna he obtained a captaincy in the papal army in 1624, and, while serving in Loreto, on Christmas night 1625 he underwent an unusual mystical religious experience, or "tranquility of soul," which was to exert a certain influence on his life. He entered the diplomatic service of the Holy See and in 1628 was appointed secretary to the papal legate of Milan, G.F. Sacchetti; in this post he had his first opportunity to play an active political role. In January 1630, during the war between Spain and France over the succession to the crown of Mantua, Sacchetti's successor, Antonio Cardinal Barberini, sent Mazarin to France to negotiate with the great Cardinal de Richelieu. The young man was fascinated by the powerful minister: "I resolved," he wrote, "to devote myself to him entirely." Soon afterward the young secretary acquired an international reputation when he dramatically galloped between the two opposing armies about to do battle at Casale in Monferrato on October 26, 1630, shouting "Peace, peace!" as if peace had been conclud-

Role in the War of the Mantuan Succession

ed. For the rest of his life he would be remembered as the intrepid knight who risked his life between two armies in order to stop the fighting. Though the Spaniards raised their siege at Casale, much remained to be done in order to bring about a general settlement. By the Treaty of Cherasco (June 19, 1631), negotiated by Mazarin, the French candidate was installed in Mantua, but the agreement settled only the differences between France and Savoy.

Mazarin's resolution to devote himself to Richelieu did not prevent him from also obtaining the patronage of Cardinal Barberini, the youngest nephew of Pope Urban VIII. After Mazarin's return to Rome in 1632, Barberini included him in a circle of artists, painters, and musicians, before obtaining for him a mission as extraordinary nuncio (ambassador) to the French court in 1634. There, at Richelieu's side, Mazarin acquired the favour of those in power and became devoted to the French nation, whose "openness of heart and of mind" impressed him. He did not forget his mission, however, which was to negotiate the peace between Spain and France sought by Urban VIII; hence it was with despair that he watched Richelieu bring France openly into the Thirty Years' War in May 1635.

Recalled to Avignon in his capacity as legate, then to Rome (December 1636), he continued to exert an influence on French politics through his correspondence with Richelieu and his adviser, Father Joseph. With his friends Cardinals Barberini, Nicholas Bagni, and Alessandro Bichi, Mazarin directed the French faction within the papal court. Louis XIII of France rewarded his efforts by recommending him as the royal candidate for a cardinalate in 1638, gave him ecclesiastical pensions and benefices (in order to be eligible for them Mazarin was granted French naturalization papers in 1639), and finally invited him to return to Paris, where he arrived on January 5, 1640. Disappointed because his ambitions in Rome had been frustrated by the Spanish faction, Mazarin left the papal service to enter the service of France. It was to France and, in particular, to Richelieu that he owed the cardinal's hat bestowed upon him by the Pope on December 16, 1641, though Urban VIII had himself been favourably impressed by the efforts his former subject was making in favour of the general peace.

Cardinalate

Career as first minister of France. Mazarin's ambition was to put an end to the rivalry between the Catholic powers of Europe. On Richelieu's death, however (December 4, 1642), and especially after that of Louis XIII (May 14, 1643), he became first minister of France, an office that the regent, Anne of Austria, entrusted to his experience and his ability in the name of the child Louis XIV. Mazarin used this new power to promote the peace negotiations that opened at Münster, in Westphalia, on April 10, 1644, although he now had to subordinate his ideal of peace to French foreign policies and ambitions. He was aided by a good diplomatic team, over which he exercised firm control, and by extremely competent generals, Louis II de Bourbon, prince de Condé, and Henri de Turenne. Their brilliant victories over the Spanish and imperial troops helped bring about the Peace of Westphalia (October 1648), a general European settlement that established peace in Germany. As the war between France and Spain still continued and as grave issues were developing in the north and east, Germany could easily have been involved again in a general war. No one believed in the power of the Emperor to safeguard the empire from this danger. Mazarin took advantage of the weakened imperial power of the Habsburgs to organize a defensive alliance between France and the German states closest to the French frontier (the League of the Rhine, August 1658). Spain, however, encouraged by the defection of the United Provinces of the Netherlands, who had signed a separate peace in January 1648, refused to agree to the peace. In order to force Spain to make a settlement, Mazarin continued the war and formed an alliance with England (March 23, 1657), surrendering to the English the fort of Dunkirk, which had been captured from the Spaniards after the Battle of the Dunes (June 14, 1658). Peace with Spain was finally negotiated in a general

treaty signed on November 7, 1659, at the Pyrenees frontier. Mazarin completed this settlement by arbitrating the
"northern peace" (the treaties of Oliva and of Copenhagen on May 3 and June 6, 1660) and by returning Lorraine to its duke (Treaty of Paris, February 28, 1661).
Thus, at his death, the former diplomat of the Holy See
could rejoice at having "returned peace to Christendom."
He would have liked to have seen Europe take advantage
of this peace by uniting in a crusade against the Turks
and, above all, to have "let these peoples enjoy the fruits
of the tranquility" they had regained now that fighting
had ended in their home territory.

France, indeed, needed a rest. Mazarin therefore had to
limit his activities within the realm to thwarting intrigues
at court and multiplying financial expedients to meet
war expenditures. The new taxes imposed upon leading
Parisians contributed to the discontent that precipitated
the revolts known as the Fronde. These rebellions, which
lasted more than five years, originated in the judicial
oligarchy of the Parlement of Paris; they spread to the
upper nobility, and soon found popular support even in
the provinces largely because of "Mazarinades," inflammatory pamphlets written against the Cardinal. Mazarin was obliged to leave the court twice and was only
able to maintain his post because he was in favour with
Anne of Austria and the boy king Louis XIV, whose education he had carefully directed. The Fronde was finally
suppressed in 1653, and Louis XIV was crowned the
following year. Mazarin increasingly involved the young
sovereign in affairs of government, encouraging him to
stand firm against the Parlement and helping him train a
staff of great administrators for his reign: Jean-Baptiste
Colbert, Nicholas Fouquet, Hughes de Lionne, and Michel Le Tellier. He re-established the role of the intendants
or commissaries of the king, who administered the provinces; they gradually assumed the power of the provincial governors who had shown themselves to be unreliable during the rebellions. He thus succeeded in sustaining
order through a policy of moderation, which he applied
even to popular revolts such as the peasant uprising of
Sologne in 1658.

Mazarin's enemies reproached him for his greed. He
had accumulated offices and benefices and had sometimes
confused royal income with his own. Yet, on several
occasions, when the state faced desperate financial situations, he put his own fortune at its disposal. A lover of the
arts, he acquired fine collections, decorated his Parisian
mansion (today the home of the Bibliothèque Nationale)
with works by Italian artists, and brought the Roman
opera into favour in France. His library remains in the
palace (now called the Institut de France) that he ordered built to house the College of the Four Nations,
intended for the education of young men from the four
provinces that had been acquired by France during his
ministry: Alsace, Roussillon, Flanders-Artois, and the
region of Pinerolo. He founded the Royal Academy of
Painting and Sculpture (1648) and gave pensions to several men of letters.

According to the Roman tradition of nepotism, Mazarin
offered rich dowries and arranged noble marriages for his
nephews and especially for his Mancini and Martinozzi
nieces. Yet he did not allow his affection as an uncle to
win out over political considerations; thus, he thwarted
the desire of Louis XIV, who by treaty was bound to
marry the Spanish infanta, to marry Marie Mancini.
Anne of Austria felt a strong attraction for him: he was a
handsome man, eloquent and charming; devoid of political experience herself, she accepted his advice unques-
tioningly. The "Mazarinades" accused them of having an
illicit relationship, but the evidence is conflicting. The
hypothesis of a secret marriage between the Regent and
her minister is also unlikely, for the cardinalate, even that
of a layman, implied the obligation of celibacy. Mazarin
was not an ordained priest (in 1632 he had received only
minor orders), though he thought of entering the priesthood on several occasions, especially in 1651 and even in
1660 shortly before his death. Faithful to the Catholicism
as he had practiced it in his youth, he had defended
Roman orthodoxy against the heterodox Jansenist move-

ment, yet without advocating persecution of the Jansen-
ists. After a painful illness, he died at the château of Vincennes on March 9, 1661.

BIBLIOGRAPHY. Mazarin's correspondence while minister
was published by ADOLPHE CHERUEL, *Lettres du Cardinal
Mazarin pendant son ministère*, 9 vol. (1872–1906); this
monumental edition is supplemented by fragmentary publications, the most important of which are those of M. RAVENEL,
Lettres du Cardinal Mazarin à la Reine . . . en 1651 et 1652
(1836), and the letters of the young Mazarin, translated
from the Italian, as an appendix to GEORGES DETHAN, *Mazarin
et ses amis* (1968; Eng. trans. in prep.). The *Carnets*, or
notebooks, in which the Minister wrote brief reflections and
guides for his conduct at court and his relations with the
Queen, have only been published in incomplete form by
VICTOR COUSIN in *Journal des Savants* (1854–56).

Standard works on Mazarin include: VICTOR COUSIN, *La
Jeunesse de Mazarin* (1865); and especially ADOLPHE CHE-
RUEL, *Histoire de France pendant la minorité de Louis XIV*,
4 vol. (1879–80), a monumental work; *Histoire de France
sous le ministère de Mazarin (1651–1661)*, 3 vol. (1882). Recent works of synthesis include: *Mazarin* (1959), a collective work with articles by Georges Mongrédien, Pierre du
Colombier, Maurice Schumann, and Georges Dethan; *Mazarin* (1961), the catalog of the *Exposition Mazarin* of the
Bibliothèque Nationale; and GEORGES DETHAN (*op. cit.*). The
chief works in English are ARTHUR HASSALL, *Mazarin* (1903);
and JAMES B. PERKINS, *France Under Mazarin*, 2 vol. (1886).

(G.Det.)

Mazzini, Giuseppe

A political thinker, writer, propagandist, and revolutionary, Giuseppe Mazzini was a champion of Italian unity
and independence, even though he lived most of his life in
exile. He gave 19th-century Italy the impetus and inspiration that were essential factors of the national movement
of liberation and unification known as the Risorgimento.

Born in Genoa, on June 22, 1805, Giuseppe Mazzini
was a doctor's son; his birthplace, formerly a republic,
was annexed to the kingdom of Piedmont in 1814. As a
child, he gave promise of high intellectual ability, fully
confirmed when he entered Genoa University at 14. Two
years later, strongly influenced by seeing a patriot fleeing
from Italy after an unsuccessful insurrection, he began to
think "that we Italians *could* and therefore *ought* to
struggle for the liberty of our country."

Mazzini, oil painting by Luigi Zuccoli, 1865. In the Museo del
Risorgimento, Milan.
By courtesy of the Museo del Risorgimento, Milan

On graduating in law in 1827, he practiced as a "poor
man's lawyer," wrote articles for progressive reviews, and
hoped to become a dramatist or historical novelist. But
his life was already shaping itself differently. His love of
freedom led him to join the Carbonari, a secret society
pledged to overthrow absolute rule in Italy; in 1830 he
was betrayed to the police, arrested, and interned at Savona, where for three months he reviewed his political
beliefs and conceived the outlines of a new patriotic
movement to replace the decaying Carbonari.

Exile in
Marseilles

When released early in 1831, he was ordered either to leave Piedmont or to live in some small town; he chose exile and went to Marseilles, where his slight figure, handsome olive features, black hair and beard, and black velvet suit were soon familiar to the other Italian exiles, who accepted him as their leader. His first public gesture was an "open letter" to Charles Albert, the king of Piedmont, urging him to give Piedmont constitutional government, to lead a national movement, and to expel the Austrians from Lombardy-Venetia and their other Italian strongholds. The letter was circulated in Italy, but Charles Albert's only reaction was to threaten Mazzini with arrest if he returned to Piedmont. As a lifelong republican, Mazzini was afterward censured for this friendly approach to an autocratic sovereign; he explained that he had meant to expose Charles Albert as one who would never fight for Italian freedom.

Foundation
of Young
Italy

At Marseilles, Mazzini spent two of his most rewarding years. He founded his patriotic movement for young men and called it Giovine Italia (Young Italy). It was designed as a national association for liberating the separate Italian states from foreign rule and fusing them into a free and independent unitary republic. Its methods were education and insurrection, and it had a moral basis derived from Mazzini's own belief in God (though he was not a Christian) and in permanent laws of progress, duty, and sacrifice. It was the first Italian democratic movement embracing all classes, for Mazzini believed that only a popular initiative could free Italy. "Neither pope nor king," he declared. "Only God and the people will open the way of the future to us."

The new movement captured the imagination of Italian youth. Branches were secretly formed in Genoa and other cities; by 1833 there were 60,000 members. Mazzini edited the propagandist journal *Giovine Italia*, which was smuggled into Italy with other revolutionary pamphlets. He also became the lover of a fellow exile, the beautiful Modenese widow Giuditta Sidoli.

Young Italy's attempted insurrections were failures. A projected rising in Piedmont in 1833 was discovered before it had begun; 12 conspirators were executed, one committed suicide, and Mazzini was tried in absence and condemned to death. He said prophetically, "Ideas ripen quickly when nourished by the blood of martyrs." A few months later, when he had moved to Switzerland to escape from the French police, he tried to rally 1,000 volunteers to invade Savoy (then part of the kingdom of Piedmont). Only 200 could be mustered, and the force was disbanded.

These failures destroyed Young Italy as an organization, though its spirit lived on. Mazzini turned to wider revolutionary plans, based on his faith in the brotherhood of man and his hopes for a world republican federation. He founded Young Europe and helped to establish Young Germany, Young Switzerland, and Young Poland, but his three years in Switzerland were unhappy and frustrated. Giuditta Sidoli had gone back to Italy to rejoin her children; he suffered an emotional crisis through doubts and disillusionment. In 1837 he went with a few Italian friends to live in London.

Stay in
England

England was now his real home. He lived in modest London lodgings, surrounded by books, papers, and the tame birds, in which he delighted; he studied at the British Museum and wrote for English periodicals. Though he had little money, he started a school for Italian boys in London and a newspaper, *Apostolato popolare* ("Apostleship of the People"), in which he published part of his essay "On the Duties of Man." In 1840, with the help of Giuseppe Lamberti in Paris, he revived Young Italy, primarily as a means of building up a national consciousness among Italians everywhere. He wrote innumerable letters to his new agents in Europe and North and South America; he also became acquainted with Thomas and Jane Welsh Carlyle and began to make many other literary and political friends.

In 1844 he was in touch with the Bandiera brothers, who made an ill-fated attempt to start a revolt in Calabria. After their execution, he told two friends, who were members of Parliament, of his fears that the British government was opening his letters and had passed on information about the Bandieras' plans to the Neapolitan authorities. The matter was raised in Parliament, and the government was compelled to admit that it opened private letters. There was much public indignation and widespread sympathy with Mazzini. The affair made him better known in England and brought him into contact with a notable liberal family, the Ashursts. Many English liberals supported him when he founded the People's International League in 1847.

In that year he wrote an "open letter" to the new pope, Pius IX, who had introduced liberal reforms in the Papal States. He urged the Pope to unify Italy, but Pius made no comment. Mazzini returned to Italy for the first time in the revolutionary year of 1848, when the Milanese drove out their Austrian masters and Piedmont began a war to expel the Austrians from Italy. Milan welcomed him, but he was soon unpopular because he wanted Lombardy to become a republic and he thought that union with the kingdom of Piedmont, as proposed by the Milanese provisional governments, was the wrong kind of pattern for the future Italy. When the Piedmontese armies withdrew and the Austrians re-entered Milan, he served briefly with an irregular force under Giuseppe Garibaldi before returning to England.

Triumvir
of
republican
Rome

Mazzini was again in Italy in 1849, first in Tuscany and then in Rome, where a revolution had driven out the Pope, and a republic had been proclaimed. He had long believed that the imperial and papal Romes would be followed by a third Rome—a Rome of the people; now his dream had come true. He was acclaimed as a great patriot, was elected a triumvir of the republic, and became the effective head of the government, showing great administrative talent in ecclesiastical and social reforms. His rule was short-lived. The Pope appealed to Catholic countries for help, and a French army landed in Italy; after heroic resistance, the republic was crushed, and Mazzini left Rome.

Back in London, he founded another society—the Friends of Italy—in 1851 and was soon involved in new revolutionary activities. In 1853 he backed the Milanese workers in their unsuccessful rising against the Austrians. In 1853–54 he sent Felice Orsini on two unproductive missions to raise revolt in Carrara. In 1856 he went secretly to Genoa to plan a number of simultaneous insurrections. The only one that was seriously attempted was Carlo Pisacane's disastrous landing in Calabria in 1857. Even the apparently futile conspiracies of this period had the useful effect, however, of keeping Italian problems before the governments of Europe. For these plots Mazzini was reviled in Piedmont, where the new moderate party was working for orderly progress without revolution. Cavour, the prime minister, called him "chief of the assassins," but this charge was unfair; Mazzini's plots were for insurrection, not assassination, and he expressly disclaimed the "theory of the dagger."

In 1858 Mazzini founded another journal in London: this was *Pensiero ed azione* ("Thought and Action"), a title reflecting his view that thought is only of value when it results in action. He had no part in the Franco-Piedmontese war against Austria in 1859, by which Cavour with the help of Napoleon III vainly sought to free Italy from the Alps to the Adriatic; nor did he belong to the "party of action," which sponsored Garibaldi's expedition to Sicily in 1860. Yet this expedition has been called "Mazzini's gift to the 'party of action,'" for it followed plans devised by himself in earlier years. He went to Naples during Garibaldi's brief dictatorship of southern Italy but was back in London when the new united Kingdom of Italy (excluding Venice and Rome) was proclaimed in 1861.

Impractical schemes for seizing Venice and Rome occupied Mazzini's mind in the 1860s. This was the decade of the Socialist First International; he had early contact with its members but soon withdrew, since the moral and religious basis of his own political thought prevented him from accepting either Marx's Communism or Bakunin's anarchism. Messina repeatedly elected him as its parliamentary deputy, but the elections were quashed by the

Accomplishments and reputation

Italian government. In 1870 he misguidedly agreed to lead a republican rising in Sicily; however, he was arrested on his way there and interned at Gaeta but was released and pardoned after the occupation of Rome by Italian troops.

Mazzini's life was ending in disappointment, even though both Venice (acquired in 1866) and Rome were now part of the new kingdom. Italy had been united by fusion, as he had always advocated against strong opposition, rather than by federation, but it was a monarchy and not the republic he had wanted. "I thought I was awakening the soul of Italy, and I see only the corpse before me," he said.

In his last years he founded another paper, *Roma del popolo* ("Rome of the People"), which he edited from Lugano, and made plans for an Italian workingmen's congress. He died from pleurisy at Pisa on March 10, 1872. He had never married.

Mazzini's reputation has fluctuated greatly. In his earlier years, he was an almost legendary hero in his own country, but he was later denounced by many of his compatriots as an enemy of the state. For two generations after his death, most historians considered that his useful work ended in 1849 and that he should then have withdrawn from conspiracy.

A different view, though, is now widely accepted. Many believe that all his plots were valuable, since they held out a permanent threat of violent revolution if Italy were not freed and united. By spurring on the Piedmontese government, and later the Italian government, to work for the national cause, he is now considered to have played an indispensable part in the making of modern Italy.

BIBLIOGRAPHY. The standard collection of Mazzini's works and letters is the comprehensive *Scritti editi ed inediti* (Edizione nazionale), 100 vol. (1906–43), but the older *Life and Writings of Joseph Mazzini*, 6 vol. (1864–70), which is partly autobiographical, is still valuable. BOLTON KING, *Mazzini* (1902); and GWILYM O. GRIFFITH, *Mazzini: Prophet of Modern Europe* (1932), are the best general biographies; his life story is told by old friends in EMILIE VENTURI, *Joseph Mazzini* (1875), which also contains the essays "Thoughts upon Democracy in Europe" and "On the Duties of Man"; and in JESSIE WHITE MARIO, *The Birth of Modern Italy* (1890). Excellent detailed studies in E.E.Y. HALES, *Mazzini and the Secret Societies* (1956), for the earlier years; SALVO MASTELLONE, *Mazzini e la "Giovine Italia," 1831–1834*, 2 vol. (1960), for Young Italy; and EMILIA MORELLI, *Mazzini in Inghilterra* (1938), for his English experiences. Mazzini's charm and humanity are delightfully revealed in the Ashurst correspondence: *Mazzini's Letters to an English Family*, 3 vol. (1920–22).

(E.C.H.)

Measurement, Principles and Instruments of

Measurement is the process used to answer the questions: how many? and how much? Measurements, broadly defined, can be made by the unaided human senses and brain —for example, in estimating distances, dimensions, temperatures, and weights; identifying and matching colours; estimating chemical composition by smell and taste; and evaluating roughness by touch. In general, however, man's capabilities need to be both extended and refined by instruments.

Some instruments, such as magnetometers and Geiger counters, measure physical quantities such as magnetism and nuclear radiation to which human senses do not respond. Some provide access to places that human senses cannot reach, for example, the space probes. Nearly all refine human capabilities by providing greater sensitivity, range, accuracy, precision, and speed. Measuring instruments are also often employed to replace human observers as a matter of convenience, as in monitoring industrial processes.

Instruments range from simple tools to large and complex systems, from the metre or yardstick to the instrument systems used in the launch and control of a space vehicle. To treat so vast a topic in detail is impossible in a brief space; the following article is intended to identify the elements and explain the principles and processes by which measuring instruments work.

A history of the development of measuring instruments and instrumentation can be found in the article INSTRUMENTATION. A list of articles containing details on specific types of measuring instruments appears at the end of this article. In what follows, the quantity being measured will be referred to as the measurand to distinguish it from other quantities and variables included in the context.

THE MEASUREMENT PROCESS

Measurement begins with a definition of a quantity, condition, property, or other characteristic that is to be determined. These definitions of measurables may be conceptual or operational. If conceptual, they must be converted to operational definitions in preparation for measurement. That is, they must be defined in terms of a sequence of steps or operations that describe a procedure for accomplishing the measurement. The measuring instrument is an embodiment of these operational steps. If the measurand is not fully defined, the measurement process becomes, itself, an essential part of the definition. An example is the measurement of hardness. Several kinds of hardness scales—*e.g.*, Brinell hardness, Knoop hardness, Rockwell hardness—are each defined by the particular method or device used to measure them. Another example is octane number of gasoline, which is determined by evaluating the fuel when used to operate an internal-combustion engine of specified design under defined conditions. In general, the translation of a conceptual definition into an operational definition is not perfect, and the measurand defined by the measurement process consequently differs in varying degree from the intended or ideal.

The information sought by the measurement process is always a comparison of the measurand with a reference quantity *of the same kind*. If a scaled series of reference quantities of all possible sizes is available, the comparison of measurand to the reference reduces to a demonstration that the measurand is equal in magnitude to a particular member of the set of reference values. Alternatively, the measurand may itself be subdivided into equal parts of uniform size shown to be equal to a unit reference magnitude, and the number of such parts is counted. Examples of scaled reference quantities are the subdivision of the metre or yard into centimetres or inches and its multiplication to kilometres or miles.

Frequently the measurand is not accessible or not suitable for direct comparison with a reference, as, for example, the radiation intensity inside a nuclear reactor. The measurand may then be transduced (converted) into an analogous measurement signal, a physical quantity of a more suitable kind that is related to the measurand in such a way that a given value of the signal represents a definite measurand magnitude. The reference quantity must then be similarly transduced to provide a reference signal of the same kind so that the measurand signal and the reference signal may be compared, after suitable multiplication or subdivision. Equality is established by opposing the measurand and reference, or the analogue signals that represent them, so that a transfer of energy occurs in one direction or the other depending on the relative magnitudes of the two. The approach to equality is then evidenced by reduction of the energy transfer to a minimum.

Because energy is required by the comparison process, there is always interaction between the observed measurand and the observing instrument. The value of the measurand observed is, therefore, not the same as that of the undisturbed measurand. If the disturbance is large enough to be significant, the exact value of the measurand must be inferred from knowledge of the disturbing process. The time required for accumulation and transfer of energy limits the capability to measure rapidly changing or dynamic phenomena.

Most measuring instruments are more or less complex systems in which a number of functional elements are joined to accomplish the desired measurement and to

Comparison with reference quantity

Instruments as systems of joining of functional elements

express the results in desired form. In some cases the functional elements are discrete units interconnected by the user to form the complete measuring instrument. In other cases the elements are so integrated that the individual functions are not readily discernible. Thus, light may be measured by connecting together a phototube, a power supply, an amplifier, and a voltmeter, or all of these may be integrated into a single instrument which is called a photometer.

Some of the measurement functions performed by the functional elements are basic to the measurement process. Thus, in any measuring instrument an element must be present that discriminates the measurand from all other conditions and senses its magnitude. In any measurement system this magnitude must be compared with the reference magnitude and the results of that comparison must be communicated to an observer or to a device that performs a control function. Other measurement functions enable the results to be presented in the desired form at a desired time and place. Examples of the latter are signal generation, excitation, modulation, demodulation, magnification, attenuation, amplification, quantizing, counting, coding, digitizing, timing, transmission, telemetering, computation, display, and recording.

Although a specific sequence of functions exists in a given system, there is no standard order in which the functions are performed. Some may even be performed more than once. Many of the functional elements are themselves measuring instruments because they accept a signal as input and produce an output signal related quantitatively to the magnitude of the input.

FUNCTIONAL ELEMENTS

Functional elements may be treated from the point of view of an ideally complete instrument system in which all measurement functions are performed without human intervention except for noting the final results. In practice, measurement systems are often only partly instrumented, some of the measurement functions being performed by operators or observers who are, therefore, participants in the measurement system. Thus, a spectrometer for measurement of chemical composition may produce a record of an infrared spectrum that must be interpreted by the observer to produce the desired composition information.

Measurands are often not measured directly but are instead inferred by combining the results of a number of separate measurements. Analogues of most instrument functions can be found in biological systems; *e.g.*, the temperature sensors of most living organisms. Conversely, most measurement functions that are performed by humans can also be accomplished by devices, although the performance of living systems has in some instances, such as in the sense of smell, not yet been equalled in nonliving systems.

Active and passive measurands

Basic functions. Measurement information is transferred throughout the instrument system by physical signals. If the measurand is itself energetic or active—for example, motion, temperature, pressure, or flow—it may provide the power required for the measurement signal. Passive measurands, such as location of an object in space, electrical resistance, and properties of materials, are not sources of signal power. To measure such phenomena, a measurement signal must be excited by causing the measurand to interact with an energetic probe or with a carrier signal.

Probes or sources of excitation signals take a variety of forms. Examples are light sources of various kinds, X-ray tubes, cathode-ray guns, particle accelerators, nuclear reactors, radioactive materials, sources of voltage and current, waveform generators, magnets, mechanical-force generators, vibration exciters, acoustic generators, and heaters.

Interaction of the carrier or probe with the measurand generates a measurement signal that carries information about the magnitude of the measurand. This information may be carried in the form of modulation of the exciting signal or carrier, a modification of a quantitative property of the carrier. If the carrier is an alternating voltage or

current, as is quite frequently the case, then amplitude, frequency, and phase-angle modulation are commonly used.

If pulsed electrical signals are used as the carrier, pulse height, pulse frequency, pulse position, pulse duration, pulse interval, or pulse time may be used to carry measurement information. The properties of the carrier or probe that affect the recovery (demodulation) of the information it carries must be accurately controlled at the source (see also RADIO; TELEPHONE AND TELECOMMUNICATIONS SYSTEMS).

A reference signal corresponding to the measurand and with which the measurand is to be compared is derived, ultimately, by a process of calibration accomplished basically by applying the instrument to measurands of known magnitude. The reference signal is often derived indirectly through a sequence of intermediate reference quantities.

Calibration may be effected automatically, but more often an operator is involved in the process. Examples of highly stable intermediate references are the cadmium standard cell and the Zener diode for voltage reference, the quartz-crystal controlled oscillator for frequency and time reference, and spectrum-line radiation emitted by elements such as sodium, cadmium, mercury, and krypton for length reference.

To effect comparison of measurand and reference, these, or the analogue signals that represent them, must be brought to equality, accomplished, for example, by subdividing or multiplying the reference to provide a series of references of suitable resolution over the ranges of interest. Detection of equality, which closes the basic measurement process, is frequently performed by the observer—*e.g.*, by noting the coincidence of a pointer and a scale graduation. It can also be performed by an instrument element.

An alternative comparison technique is quantization followed by counting. A signal is quantized by breaking it into parts, or quanta, of equal and known size. Counting the quanta then completes the measurement. Many measurands of interest occur in nature in quantized form, notably chemical species such as atoms and molecules, so that measurement of these can sometimes be accomplished by counting alone.

Amplification. The energy impressed upon or withdrawn from the measurand and from the reference quantity to provide power for the measurement signals must be kept small enough to avoid changing their magnitudes significantly. The permissible power level is frequently too small to permit performance of desired measurement functions, especially when the requirement for high accuracy is coupled with the need for high sensitivity and high speed. Amplification is the instrument function by which a signal carrying measurement information is increased in power without degrading its information content.

Use of pneumatic amplification

Electrical amplification is widely used in instrument systems. Pneumatic amplification, in which the measurement information is represented by pressure or flow of a gas, and hydraulic amplification, in which liquid pressure or flow is the information carrier, are also frequently used. Pneumatic amplification is employed in the technology of fluidics (*q.v.*), whereby pneumatic signals are manipulated rapidly and transmitted at speed of sound by means of devices of small dimensions that involve no moving parts other than the gaseous fluid itself. Hydraulic amplification finds application especially in cases in which large amounts of power are to be transmitted in a relatively small space, as for controlling the aerodynamic surfaces of aircraft, for controlling the motion of heavy machine elements, and for manipulating fluids (as in process control). Hydraulic and pneumatic amplification are also used to avoid certain hazards, such as those of electrical currents in explosive atmospheres, and, in nuclear radiation environments, to avoid the effects of radiation damage to which electronic components are sometimes susceptible.

Electrical amplification is important for measurement applications because of the extremely rapid response that can be achieved; the speed with which electrical signals can be transmitted; the relative simplicity of the physical laws involved; the relative freedom of electrical parameters, such as resistance and capacitance, from environmental influences; the availability of electrical conductors that can transmit large amounts of power with little loss within the confines of small dimensions; the ease with which electrical signals can be confined by insulators and by shielding; and the enormous versatility of the devices available for manipulation of electrical signals. Microcircuitry and integrated circuits based on semiconductor electronics have added to the already great versatility of electrical amplification.

Amplifiers function by using the low-power measurement signal to control power drawn from a relatively unlimited source other than the measurand. Electrical devices used for amplification include the vacuum electron tube, the transistor and related semiconductor devices, and the saturable core reactor, a type of transformer in which a small current in one winding controls a large amount of power in another winding. Electromechanical amplifiers include such devices as relays and magnetic clutches.

The relationship between input and output signals governed by amplifier principles and devices is, in general, only approximately correct and is subject to many environmental influences and to changes that occur in characteristics of components. If greater accuracy is required than can be achieved by isolation and correction or compensation, the principle of negative feedback, or closed-loop operation, is employed.

Negative feedback. The feedback principle is of general utility to avoid distortion of measurement signals throughout the instrument system. Its operation may be understood by noting that it involves two signal channels —an information channel and a power channel. The information channel operates at the lowest possible power level and employs signal manipulation and transmission principles and devices selected for their freedom from error and instabilities.

The output signal of the power channel, including distortions introduced by processes taking place in the channel (such as amplification, transmission, etc.) is compared with the signal from the information channel, which is assumed to be correct, and the difference between the two, the error signal, is returned to a control element in the power channel in such a way that a positive error (power channel signal greater than the information channel signal) causes a reduction in the gain, or amplification factor, of the power channel and a negative error produces the opposite effect. The result is a reduction in the error signal until the difference between the two channels becomes negligible.

Clearly, the automatic adjustment of gain of the power channel to correct the power channel signal must be effected before a significant change in magnitude of the measurand has time to occur. Lags in signal transmission in the two channels will result in incorrect adjustment of gain and unstable operation unless they are small relative to the rate at which the measurand changes (see also CONTROL SYSTEMS).

Digitalization. Another powerful tool for avoiding degradation of measurement information is conversion of the signal to coded or digital form. The analogue signals are subject to instability and to noise interference. As long as the signal remains an analogue, each operation is in essence a new measurement subject to error, so that the measurement information becomes progressively degraded at each step. Once the measurement information is represented by a number, however, such degradation is enormously reduced. Thus, if it is desired to evaluate a measurand with an error as small as one part in 1,000,000, each manipulation of an analogue signal must be performed with an accuracy of at least one part in 1,000,000. If, however, the magnitude of the measurand is represented by a decimal number, the signal simply transmits each individual digit. An accuracy of only one part in 10 permits each digit to be unambiguously identified, which is all that is required.

Furthermore, if binary-number representation is used, an accuracy of only one in two suffices. Digital signals in measurement systems are generally manipulated in binary form, by presence or absence of signal or by positive or negative direction of signal, decimal digits being represented by binary codes. The possibility of error in transmission or manipulation can be further reduced by introducing redundancy—that is, repetition of each signal as a double check.

In the manipulation of analogue signals, small errors are more probable than large, resulting in a normal (Gaussian) distribution of error. In digital signals the various digits represent different orders of magnitude, but the probability of an error in a given digit is independent of the magnitude it represents. Thus, in digital communication of measurement information, large and small errors are equally likely, but their probability of occurrence can be made as small as desired.

Techniques for high-speed manipulation of digital information in electrical form are highly developed so that digital transmission is competitive with analogue transmission even where speed or high-frequency response is important. Digital instruments are rapid enough in their response to permit their use for measurement and control of aircraft operating at supersonic speeds, of space vehicles millions of miles removed from their control centers, and of many manufacturing processes. Advantages of digital form

Many techniques are available for accomplishing conversion from analogue to digital form with high accuracy. For measurement information carried by an electrical voltage signal, a digital voltmeter may be used for the conversion. When the measurement information is a periodic signal whose frequency is the analogue of the measurand magnitude, an electronic counter that presents in digital code the number of cycles occurring during a fixed counting period provides the measurement information in digital form. When linear or angular displacement is the analogue signal to be converted (for example, the motion of a pointer), digitally coded scales are commonly used. Because of the desirability of early conversion to digital form, much attention has been given to development of so-called digital transducers, in which digitalization is immediately associated in a single device with the first conversion of the measurand magnitude into a measurement signal.

Magnification. Enlarging a measurement signal without increasing its power is called magnification. Mechanical, optical, and electrical techniques are all employed. Examples of mechanical magnifiers are the lever, the screw, pulley and gear systems, and hydraulic- and pneumatic-force multipliers. Optical magnifiers include the lenses and mirrors used to produce or modify images in microscopes, telescopes, and cameras and the optical lever used for instrument indication. Electrical magnification is provided by transformers.

The purpose of magnification is primarily to perform an interfacing function: to match the output of one element of the measurement system to the input requirements of the next. An early application (and still a major one) is to condition the measurement signal for presentation to the human senses at the interface, or point of contact, between the instrument and the observer. Its frequent function there is to match the magnitude of the readout indication to the resolution capability of the eye. It serves analogously at the interface between instrument elements, as in impedance matching between stages of an electrical measuring circuit.

Analysis. One of the most widespread characteristics of physical systems is resonance, or characteristic periodic variation. For this reason an important measurement is the determination of the resonance frequencies associated with a system. To determine these resonances, the output of the system may be subjected to harmonic analysis. This may be done by mathematical computation, or the signal may be analyzed by using resonant detection devices. Analysis of resonance frequencies

The most commonly encountered example of harmonic analysis is that of a radio receiver, in which a complex electromagnetic-field signal that is picked up by an antenna is sorted into a number of separate signals characterized by the resonant frequency of the transmitter from which the signal was broadcast. By scanning across the receiver dial and noting the points at which signals are received, a spectrum analysis of the incoming signal is performed.

Computation. General-purpose computing operations for mathematical manipulation of measurement signals include analogue computation, in which the magnitude of the signal (usually in the form of an electrical voltage) is operated upon, and digital computation, in which the magnitudes of signals are first converted to digital form and then operated upon as numbers. Both of these methods are of growing importance as components of measuring instruments.

The basic element of analogue-computing devices is the operational amplifier (opamp), a high-gain, direct-coupled, wideband amplifier available in compact modular form. Operational amplifiers are combined in various ways with other electrical-circuit elements, such as resistors, capacitors, and inductors, to perform mathematical addition, subtraction, multiplication, division, integration, and differentiation.

Digital computers combine large internal memories for storing numerical information, or any information convertible to numerical form, with arithmetic-manipulation capability. The essential characteristics of modern digital computers are very high speed operation and capability for storing and operating from a program of instructions for performing complex computation. This high-speed-computation capability, when incorporated into an instrument, permits direct automatic performance of complex measurements that would otherwise require combination by an observer of a number of separate measurement results.

The computer also identifies and monitors signals, normalizes data, linearizes or otherwise transforms instrument response, and corrects measurement data for various influences that can be measured if knowledge of their effects is programmed into the computer; in addition, it performs several different kinds of analysis, summarizes measurement data, and generates reports (see also COMPUTER).

The ability of the computer to store and manipulate instructions as well as measurement data is also used to automate the operation of instruments performing large numbers of complex measurements. Both speed and accuracy of measurement can be improved in this way. Computer generation of complex displays for presentation of interpreted data enlarges the scope of instrument communication with the observer, and it permits the observer to interact with the instrument system, as described further in the discussion of display techniques below.

Telemetry. It is often necessary for results of measurement to be presented, essentially instantaneously, at a location remote from the point of measurement. Space exploration, biomedical research, oceanography, and meteorology are fields in which such requirements are common. Telemetry (*q.v.*), or telemetering, the art of remote measurement, makes use of communication channels, especially wireless transmission, to transmit measurement data. In modern telemetry, data are frequently transmitted in digital form.

Communicating information to the observer

Display. Communication of measurement information to the observer is a function of all instruments except those that are used for automatic-control-system actuation. Even in automatic control, the results of measurement are usually displayed so that the performance of the system may be monitored. Display serves not only to present results of measurement but also to communicate with the observer when he participates in the measurement process. Display is usually visual, but presentation to the other senses is also common. Auditory display is used for alarms that indicate that some limiting value of measurand has been exceeded; *e.g.*, a fire alarm activated by a thermostat. The auditory sense is also enlisted negatively for detecting the absence of sound when a measurand signal and a reference signal are to be compared or when a feedback error signal is to be brought to zero.

The commonest visual display is the pointer moving relative to a graduated-length scale; the graduations of the scale are usually marked to read directly in measurand units. The relationship between measurand and pointer movement may be expressed as either a linear (that is, direct one-on-one relationship) or as a nonlinear relationship, such as logarithmic, in which the relationship between the measurand and the pointer deflection is exponential.

Linear relationship between measurand and pointer movement and uniform spacing of graduations facilitate interpolation between graduations. A logarithmic relationship between measurand and pointer deflection has the characteristic that the percent error of reading is uniform over the scale. Logarithmic scales permit larger ranges of measurand magnitude to be covered usefully by a given length of scale.

An important contributor to pointer-reading error is the parallax, or apparent difference in position, when the pointer and the scale are not in the same plane. Parallax is reduced by providing a mirror sector in the plane of the scale or by using a pointer configured as a thin vane rather than a needle. With the former, the eye of the observer, the pointer, and the mirror image of the pointer are aligned for reading; in using the vane, the eye is positioned for minimum pointer profile to improve consistency of reading.

Use of a beam of electrons as a pointer

A special kind of pointer, a cathode ray (beam of electrons) impinging on a phosphor screen, is used in oscilloscope and television-raster types of display. Deflection of the cathode ray is controlled by electric or magnetic fields, and its intensity may also be modulated to provide simultaneous display of the relationship among three variables. Addition of colour permits limited display of a fourth variable.

The high-speed writing capability of the cathode ray has made the oscilloscope one of the most important components of instrument systems and has contributed significantly to the desirability of using electrical signals to transmit measurement information. The oscilloscope has been developed to a very high level of sophistication for measurement of electrical variables and, hence, for any measurand that can be converted into an electrical signal. In special types of equipment, the observer can interact with the measurement system through the cathode-ray tube by use of a hand-held probe that is applied to the screen at the light spot and thereby assumes control of the cathode ray and operates upon the information being displayed.

To improve the precision obtainable by analogue display, scale expansion and zero suppression are used, the total measurement range being covered by more than one span of the scale. Unlimited precision of indication can be obtained with a digital display that relieves the observer of the measurement function involved in reading a scale.

Digital display may take the form of a set of digits arrayed in the usual way, with the significance of each digit being indicated by its position relative to a decimal point. By using a floating or movable decimal point, a wider range of values can be covered by a given number of digits.

Digital display is accomplished by mechanical, electrical, and electro-optical means. Mechanical devices may use rotatable disks or cylinders the peripheries of which carry the numerals. The automobile odometer is an example.

Another mechanical type of digital display uses a series of pointers, one for each digit, that point to numerals in a circular array, as in the common gas meter, water meter, and watt-hour meter. Analogue and digital display are frequently combined in mechanical displays, the former being used for the less significant digits. One form of this uses an analogue pointer that reads on a scale covering a full circle and one or more auxiliary pointers the indications of which count the number of full rotations performed by the analogue pointer.

Electronic and electro-optical devices for digital display frequently use illuminated numerals. Preformed numerals may be selected and illuminated electrically, numerals may be formed by selection and illumination of dots in a matrix, or numbers may actually be written, as required, by cathode-ray beams. Cathode-ray tubes and television-scan displays permit the presentation of complex information in combined analogue and digital form. Graphs, tabulations, and a great variety of symbolic information may be communicated in this way.

When large quantities of measurement information must be communicated to the human observer at high speed and with high accuracy and reliability, the display art becomes especially critical. Such situations arise, for example, in air-traffic control when the observer must assimilate large amounts of measurement information and make rapid decisions based upon it.

Recording. The recording function in instrument systems serves two distinct purposes: first, it provides a record of measurement results for future use by the observer, and, second, it stores intermediate measurement information for later automatic use by the instrument system. While the requirements of the second purpose are somewhat more restrictive than the first, records in machine-readable form can serve both purposes. It is also common to combine in a single device the functions of recording and display.

Recording techniques have a number of variable characteristics. Among these are the visibility of the record (for simultaneous display), machine readability, immediate availability of the record, permanence, erasability, susceptibility to accidental erasure, operating-power requirement, standby-power requirement, writing and reading speed, time required for access to a specific item in the record, form of the data (analogue or digital), precision of recording, number of variables accommodated, and, finally, the techniques used to achieve the characteristics desired.

The combination of recording and display is frequently accomplished by devices that produce visible markings on a surface. One very general way to do this is to substitute for the usual indicating pointer a writing stylus that produces a mark on a moving chart. The writing stylus may be an inked pen, a sharply pointed stylus used on a waxed surface, a heated stylus on a heat-sensitive surface, or electric current carried by the pointer on an electrosensitive surface.

By using a light beam as an indicating pointer, or the spot of light produced by a cathode ray, a photographic surface may be used to record the measurement information, leading to higher recording speeds. A stream of electrically charged ink particles directed to the proper point on the recording surface by an electrostatic field under control of the measurand has been used similarly to avoid recording friction.

The recording surface may be a circular disk, frequently of paper, a flat sheet, a drum, or a continuous strip. To record the measurand value as a function of time, the recording surface or chart is moved by a clock motor at adjustable or selectable speeds. To record the measurand as a function of a variable other than time, the chart may be moved under control of the independent variable, or the marking pointer may be moved in two mutually perpendicular directions: one, usually called the Y direction, being used for the measurand and the other, the X direction, indicating the independent variable.

While any readout principle that uses mechanical motion for indication may be adapted to recording if sufficient power is available, general purpose recorders are usually designed for electrical input. Some recorders operate with negative feedback, that is, a portion of the output is fed back to the input out of phase with the incoming signal; this operation serves to decrease distortion and increase stability. Though it slows the operation somewhat, it permits precision on the order of a few parts in a thousand.

The non-feedback (open-loop) type is characterized by somewhat lower precision, errors on the order of a few percent, but faster operation, with frequency response on the order of 100 hertz (0.01 second for full-scale traverse) for mechanical pointer types and several thousand

Electrical input (margin)

hertz for the photographically recording types called oscillographs.

When the measurand is the position or motion of an object that can be illuminated or is self-luminous, photographic recording is often used directly. This may be done by recording the streak produced as the object's image on the photosensitive surface moves. Alternatively, extremely short pulses of light may be used to produce separate images at the pulse-repetition rate of the light source. Electric sparks or flash-tube discharges are used as sources of light for this type of recording.

Visible recording is also accomplished in digital form by devices such as printers and teletypewriters. Very high speed printers have been developed for this purpose. When the rate at which measurement information is produced by the instrument system is beyond the capabilities of available recording means, buffers may be used to store the information temporarily.

Although techniques and devices are available to enable visible records to be read automatically into instrument systems, such records are not generally best suited for machine reading. Recording means have, therefore, been developed that have characteristics dictated primarily by the requirements of internal use in the instrument system. Such recording means are frequently called memory systems or devices. Apart from reliability, the most important of these requirements are high-speed writing capability and high-speed access to the recorded data.

Serial-recording techniques in instrument systems frequently involve magnetic recording on wires, tapes, drums, and disks. By use of multiple channels, limited partial random access is achieved with these recording media.

Serial-recording techniques (margin)

Access to the record is relatively slow not only because of serial access but also because mechanical motion is involved in the reading process. Magnetic recording with high-speed random access is provided by magnetic-core memory systems and related magnetic memories that involve no moving parts. It has been estimated that up to 90 percent of random-access memory in instrument systems is provided by magnetic cores; however, a variety of other techniques are used, and many new principles are being actively pursued in efforts to develop large-scale memories with desirable characteristics. Further information on memory systems is included in the article COMPUTER.

PERFORMANCE CHARACTERISTICS

Errors in measurement may result from imperfect definition of the measurand, from imperfect understanding of the physical laws applied to converting the measurand into a measurement signal, from failure to establish completely the conditions prescribed for performing the measurement, and from imperfect operator performance. Errors also result from deficiencies inherent in the instrument. Some of the characteristics that describe the accuracy performance of instruments on a general level that is independent of the nature of the measurand or of the specific operating principles used in the instrument are described below.

Interaction of instrument and measurand. As already mentioned, all instruments either withdraw energy from the measurand or transfer energy to the measurand. In some cases the power derived from or transmitted to the measurand is negligibly small. In other cases it contributes significantly to measurement error. The measurement-signal power reacts upon the measurand so that the magnitude of the latter differs from that of the undisturbed measurand. It is the modified value that is "seen" by the measuring instrument.

Noise. The elements of which the instrument is comprised generate internal disturbances that are indistinguishable from the signals that represent the magnitudes of measurand and reference. These disturbances are called noise by analogy with unwanted sounds. By extension the term is also applied to any unwanted signal, regardless of source. Noise interferes with the ability to evaluate the measurand. The ratio of the desired signal magnitude to the unwanted noise magnitude often sets an

Signal-to-noise ratio

upper limit on the accuracy of measurement. The signal-to-noise ratio is characteristic of a particular instrument system for noise originating within the instrument. A given level of noise is most damaging when the level of the signal is low, as in the early stages before amplification.

The first stage of amplification is therefore critical for establishing a good signal-to-noise ratio. Amplification of the measurement signal as early as possible in the sequence of functions is beneficial. Thermal agitation is an important source of noise, so that operation of the first functional elements at low temperature is often used to achieve low-noise operation.

Interference. The environment in which the instrument operates contributes influences that interfere with the measurement. Once these interfering influences enter the instrument system, they become, like any other noise, indistinguishable from the measurement signal. Unlike noise, however, they differ from the measurand before they enter the system and, hence, can be dealt with by isolating the instrument from them or by providing compensation against them. Neither the isolation nor the compensation is, in general, perfect.

Dynamic response. The physical system of the measuring instrument does not respond instantaneously to the value of the measurand. In mechanical systems inertia, elasticity or imperfect rigidity, and friction or dissipation of energy all introduce lags in response. In electrical systems analogous effects are produced by inductance, capacitance, and resistance. And in thermal systems lags are introduced by thermal capacity and by thermal resistance.

The result of these lags is that the output of the instrument is not a true representation of the instantaneous value of the measurand if the latter is changing. Instead, the indicated value may be an average that is characteristic of the instrument system. This characteristic is related to the natural frequency of the system (the frequency at which the output of the instrument would oscillate if left free after a momentary input disturbance) and to its degree of damping or internal dissipation of energy.

Drift. Unless the measuring elements in the instrument are completely stable, which is never entirely the case, the indication of the instrument will drift from the correct value in the interval between calibrations. A major cause of short-term drift is self-heating, causing changes in temperature of various parts of the instrument. It is common practice to allow a minimum warm-up time before making measurements, and instruments are often maintained in continuous operation to minimize drift for important measurements.

Changes caused by drift

Instrument drift may cause two changes: (1) change of zero indication and (2) change of sensitivity, the ratio of output to input. For accurate measurement, frequency of calibration must be appropriate to the drift characteristics of the instrument. Continuous calibration based on local reference standards that are built into the instrument system may be used in critical measurement situations.

Hysteresis. Measuring instruments may not respond equally to a measurand value that is approached from a lower value and to the same value approached from a higher value. Lagging of response behind input is called hysteresis by analogy with the similar phenomenon in magnetization of materials. More complex dependence of measurement results upon the past history of the measuring instrument may also be present. To reduce such effects, the measurement may be made in both ascending and descending directions, or the instrument may be cycled through a range of values preparatory to making the final measurement.

The dead band

A special case of hysteresis is the dead band. The output of an instrument may not respond to a change of magnitude of the measurand until that change has reached some finite magnitude characteristic of the instrument. Thus, a dead band exists that sets a lower limit to the magnitude of change that can be detected. A cause of dead band in mechanical instruments is backlash or lost motion in gear systems and other linkages.

Linearity. It is desirable that the relationship of the output to the input signal can be described by a simple mathematical statement. The actual characteristic of an instrument always departs more or less from the ideal, and the precise relationship, ascertained by the process of calibration, must usually be expressed either by a tabulation of outputs and corresponding inputs or, graphically, by a curve relating the two. A linear relationship is frequently desired because this greatly simplifies the calibration process.

Resolution. The closeness to each other with which two values of measurand may approach and still be distinguished by the measuring instrument is described as the resolution capability of the instrument.

Precision. The ability of an instrument to determine with a high degree of discrimination the relationship between two values of measurand that fall within its nominal measurement range, independently of a reference standard external to the instrument system itself, is its precision. To be capable of high precision, an instrument must be capable of a high degree of resolution, but the converse does not follow. A partial measure of precision is the dispersion or scatter of measurement results obtained when the same measurand is repeatedly measured with all conditions of measurement maintained within the range specified for proper operation of the instrument.

Precision of a measurement can be improved by averaging a number of separate readings. Precision usually increases as the square root of the number of repetitions. Similar improvement is obtained by allowing the instrument to average its measurement over a period of time during which the measurand remains constant.

Accuracy. The capability of an instrument to yield the correct (or true) value of the measurand is its accuracy. Of special importance is the accuracy with which the indications of an instrument system agree with the true value defined by international agreement. This kind of accuracy provides the most broadly significant measurement data in the sense that the widest possible range is provided for communication about the data resulting from the measurement process. The International System of Units, abbreviated SI, is a modernized version of the metric system established to provide a logical and interconnected framework for all measurement (see WEIGHTS AND MEASURES). Traceability of measurements to SI is provided by a hierarchy of intercomparisons of standards performed through the agency of the International Bureau of Weights and Measures, located at Sèvres, near Paris. National laboratories of various countries provide access to the International Bureau for the purpose of achieving international compatibility of measurements.

Dissemination of the internationally defined true values, the SI units, is accomplished in a variety of ways starting with the establishment of national standards that are the physical embodiments of the units of measurements. Methods of dissemination include calibration services, development and distribution of standard reference materials that embody measurands of known value, determination and publication of standard reference data, or best values, relating to materials and phenomena that are widely accessible for measurement, round-robin tests in which standards laboratories cooperate to compare results of measurements performed on identical measurands, and broadcast of time and frequency signals.

Basic SI units

The basic units of SI are the metre, the unit of length; the kilogram, the unit of mass; the second, unit of time; the kelvin, unit of temperature; the ampere, unit of electric current; the candela, unit of luminous intensity; and the mole, unit of quantity of matter. To these are added the radian and steradian, the units of plane angle and solid angle, respectively. From these units all other units of physical measurement are conceptually derived. Except in the case of the unit of mass, the base units are defined so that they can be realized independently of the calibration hierarchy described above. High accuracy, however, is in most circumstances more readily achieved through the hierarchy.

Safeguards against failure. A measuring instrument may fail completely, ceasing to operate, or its performance may gradually deteriorate until its accuracy degrades below the level of acceptability, without giving any indication of failure. A common safeguard in measuring instruments is visibility, as in the liquid-in-glass thermometer, in which the condition of the instrument is easily ascertained by inspection. Instrument systems in which reliable operation is critically important may have built-in self-diagnosis capabilities.

DEVELOPMENT OF MEASURING INSTRUMENTS

Five phases can be distinguished in the evolution of instrument systems: a definition phase, a research and development phase, a production design phase, a production phase, and an application phase. These phases are not clearly separable; even in the last phase, it is frequently desirable to return to earlier phases to improve operation of the instrument.

The first phase includes a definition of the measurand and a set of requirements that define performance desired and conditions of operation under which this performance is to be attained. Unless the measurand is directly observable and accessible to the human senses, it must be defined in terms of other measurables. The conversion of the measurand is called transduction, and the devices that effect the conversions are transducers. The first conversion is unique in that the measurand and the circumstances in which it occurs are not subject to choice by the instrument engineer but must be accepted as presented. The first, or primary, transducer must discriminate the measurand from among all accompanying conditions and convert it into a signal accurately related to the measurand and of such a form that it can be, in turn, measured without degradation of accuracy.

Conversion of the measurand

Next is formulation of a schematic functional design, a sequence of transductions that will provide the measurement information in the time, place, and format desired under the prescribed conditions of operation. After this, each of the functional elements is designed or selected to have the desired characteristics and to connect (or interface) appropriately with other contiguous elements and with the human observer or operator wherever he participates in the measurement process.

Detailed design is then effected and implemented by constructing a prototype. When the desired performance has been successfully demonstrated, the instrument enters the production-development stage, including design for production, selection or development of fabrication techniques, and design of the system of tests and inspections to be used for quality control. Production of the instrument is followed by application, including installation, operation, maintenance and repair, and assurance of accuracy of measurement results by standardization and calibration.

Specific measuring instruments and their applications are described in the following articles: COMPASS; HAND TOOLS (rulers and calipers); HYDROGRAPHIC CHARTING; MATERIALS TESTING (instruments for measuring such physical properties of materials as hardness, ductility, thermal conductivity, etc.); METEOROLOGICAL MEASUREMENTS (a range of instruments used in atmospheric measurement); MICROSCOPE; NAVIGATION; PHOTOGRAPHY, TECHNOLOGY OF (light meters, range finders, etc.); SEISMOGRAPH; SURVEYING (transits, theodolites); TELESCOPE; THERMOMETRY; UNDERSEA EXPLORATION (instruments for measuring salinity, temperature, wave motions, water depth); and VACUUM TECHNOLOGY (instruments for measuring low pressures).

BIBLIOGRAPHY. The very extensive literature on measuring instruments is scattered throughout science and technology—in the sciences that are the sources of instrument principles, in the technologies that provide its techniques, and in association with the fields of application of measurements. A key to these sources of information is provided by JULIAN F. SMITH and WILLIAM G. BROMBACHER, *Guide to Instrumentation Literature* (1965). BRIAN ELLIS, *Basic Concepts of Measurement* (1966), is an analytical treatment of the philosophy and logic of measurement. CHESTER H. PAGE and PAUL VIGOUREUX (eds.), *The International System of Units (SI)* (1972), describes the system of units and standards that are the internationally accepted basis for communication of the results of measurement. DOUGLAS M. CONSIDINE (ed.), *Encyclopedia of Instrumentation and Control* (1971), treats comprehensively the broad field of the applications of measuring instruments in research, development, manufacturing, medicine, etc. (emphasis is on guidance for the instrument user). CHARLES S. DRAPER, WALTER MCKAY, and SIDNEY LEES, *Instrument Engineering*, 3 vol. (1952–55), is a detailed and sophisticated treatment of principles and methods for solution of problems in measurement and control, with emphasis on the needs of the developer and designer of instrument systems. See also LESLIE W. LEE, *Elementary Principles of Laboratory Instruments*, 2nd ed. (1970). BERNARD M. OLIVER and JOHN M. CAGE (eds.), *Electronic Measurements and Instrumentation* (1971), covers many of the instrument system functions that follow conversion of a measurand to an electrical signal. THOMAS N. WHITEHEAD, *The Design and Use of Instruments and Accurate Mechanism* (1934, reprinted 1954), develops fundamental principles for achieving accuracy in the operation of measuring instruments. The NATIONAL BUREAU OF STANDARDS, *Precision Measurement and Calibration*: vol. 1, *Statistical Concepts and Procedures;* vol. 2, *Temperature;* vol. 3, *Electricity: Low Frequency;* vol. 4, *Electricity: Radio Frequency;* vol. 5, *Frequency and Time;* vol. 6, *Heat;* vol. 7, *Radiometry and Photometry;* vol. 8, *Mechanics;* vol. 9, *Colorimetry;* vol. 10, *Ionizing Radiation;* vol. 11, *Image Optics* (1968–), accumulate important papers that deal with precise, fundamental measurements. C.F. HIX and R.P. ALLEY, *Physical Laws and Effects* (1958), includes a compilation and description of the phenomena that provide the basis for conversion of measurands into instrument signals.

The following treat of the devices that perform the function of converting the measurand to instrument signals: KURT S. LION, *Instrumentation in Scientific Research: Electrical Input Transducers* (1959); HARRY N. NORTON, *Handbook of Transducers for Electronic Measuring Systems* (1969); KENNETH ARTHUR, *Transducer Measurements* (1971); GLENN F. HARVEY (ed.), *ISA Transducer Compendium*, 2nd ed., 3 vol. (1969–72).

The following treat in detail specific instrument functional elements: RICHARD F. SHEA (ed.), *Amplifier Handbook* (1966); HERMANN SCHMID, *Electronic Analog/Digital Conversions* (1970); MYRON H. NICHOLS and LAWRENCE L. RAUCH, *Radio Telemetry*, 2nd ed. (1956); CESAR A. CACERES (ed.), *Biomedical Telemetry* (1965); MISCHA SCHWARTZ, *Information Transmission, Modulation, and Noise* (1959); CLAUDE E. SHANNON and WARREN WEAVER, *The Mathematical Theory of Communication* (1949); WILLIAM R. BENNETT and JAMES R. DAVEY, *Data Transmission* (1965); C.B. PEAR, JR. (ed.), *Magnetic Recording in Science and Industry* (1967); HAROLD R. LUXENBERG and RUDOLPH L. KUEHN (eds.), *Display Systems Engineering* (1968); JOSEF CZECH, *Oszillografen-Messtechnik* (1959; rev. Eng. trans., *Oscilloscope Measuring Technique: Principles and Applications of Modern Cathode Ray Oscilloscopes*, 1965); JULIUS S. BENDAT and ALLAN G. PIERSOL, *Measurement and Analysis of Random Data* (1966).

(J.Sn.)

Measurement, Psychological

The Bible records that Gideon was instructed to reduce the number of men who were to accompany him into battle by proclaiming, "Whoever is fearful and trembling, let him return home." This constituted a test, and 22,000 left; but the 10,000 remaining still were too numerous. A further test was ordered: only those who lapped water with their tongues, as dogs do, in contrast to those who knelt to drink, were to be retained. They had passed a second test, or hurdle, thus providing an early example of what is known today as the successive-hurdles method of personnel selection.

Again, when Gileadites captured the fords of the Jordan River against the Ephraimites, a simple test was used to detect those who were attempting to masquerade as Gileadites. They were required to say "shibboleth," which Ephraimites could pronounce only as "sibboleth." It is recorded that 42,000 Ephraimites failed this simple, one-item test and were put to death.

The Greek Olympic games were of the nature of tests. And the idea of behavioral tests to reveal latent abilities is found in Plato's *Republic*:

No two persons are born exactly alike, but each differs from each in natural endowments, one being suited for one occupation and another for another . . . . It will belong to us to choose out, if we can, that special order of natural endowments which qualifies its possessors for the guardianship of the state.

Plato envisaged tests of military aptitude not unlike those used today.

Not until the end of the 19th century, however, did influences from German experimental psychology, British statistical methods for describing individual differences, and French concern for deviant individuals merge to provide a springboard for modern psychological-measurement technique and theory.

Tests: ability, aptitude, achievement, personality

The word test refers to any means (often formally contrived) used to elicit responses to which behaviour in other contexts can be related. When intended to predict relatively distant future behaviour (*e.g.*, success in school), such a device is called an aptitude test. When used to evaluate the individual's present academic or vocational skill, it may be called an achievement test. In such settings as guidance offices, mental-health clinics, and psychiatric hospitals, tests of ability and personality may be helpful in the diagnosis and detection of troublesome behaviour. Industry and government alike have been prodigious users of tests for selecting workers. Research workers often rely on tests to translate theoretical concepts (*e.g.*, intelligence) into experimentally useful measures.

GENERAL PROBLEMS OF MEASUREMENT IN PSYCHOLOGY

Physical things are perceived through their properties or attributes. A mother may directly sense the property called temperature by feeling her infant's forehead. Yet she cannot directly observe his colicky feelings nor share his personal experience of hunger. She must infer such unobservable private activities from hearing her baby cry or gurgle; from seeing him flail his arms, or frown, or smile. In the same way, much of what is called measurement must be made by inference. Thus, a mother suspecting her child is feverish may use a thermometer, in which case she infers his temperature by looking at the thermometer, rather than by directly touching his head.

Indeed, measurement by inference is particularly characteristic of psychology. Such abstract properties or attributes as intelligence or introversion never are directly measured but must be inferred from observable behaviour.

Nominal, ordinal, interval, and ratio scales

Types of measurement scales. To measure any property or activity is to assign it a unique position along some kind of numerical scale. When numbers are used merely to identify individuals or classes (as on the backs of athletes on a football team), they constitute a nominal scale. When a set of numbers reflects only the relative order of things (*e.g.*, pleasantness–unpleasantness of odours), they constitute an ordinal scale. An interval scale has equal units and an arbitrarily assigned zero point; for example, one such scale is for Fahrenheit temperature, extending well below zero. Ratio scales not only provide equal units; they also have absolute zero points; examples include measures of weight, density, and distance.

Although there have been ingenious attempts to establish psychological scales with absolute zero points, psychologists usually are content with approximations to interval scales; ordinal scales often are used as well.

Primary characteristics of methods or instruments. The primary requirement of a test is validity—traditionally defined as the degree to which a test actually measures whatever it purports to measure. A test is reliable to the extent that it measures consistently, but reliability is of no consequence if a test lacks validity. Since the person who will draw inferences from a test must determine how well it serves his purposes, the estimation of validity inescapably requires judgment. Depending on the criteria of judgment employed, tests exhibit a number of different kinds of validity, as follows:

Empirical validity (also called statistical or predictive validity) describes how closely scores on a test correspond (correlate) with behaviour as measured in other contexts. Students' scores on a test of academic aptitude, for example, may be compared with their school grades

(a commonly used criterion). To the degree that the two measures statistically correspond, the test empirically predicts the criterion of performance in school. Predictive validity has its most important application in aptitude testing (*e.g.*, in screening applicants for work, in academic placement, in assigning military personnel to different duties).

Alternatively, a test may simply be inspected to see if its content seems appropriate to its intended purpose. Such content validation is widely employed in measuring academic achievement but with increasing recognition of the inevitable role of judgment. Thus, a geometry test exhibits content (or curricular) validity when experts (*e.g.*, teachers) believe that it adequately samples the school curriculum for that topic. Interpreted broadly, content covers desired skills (such as computational ability) as well as points of information in the case of achievement tests. Face validity (a crude kind of content validity) reflects the acceptability of a test to such people as students, parents, employers, and government officials. A test that looks valid is desirable, but face validity without some more basic validity is nothing more than window dressing.

In personality testing, judgments of test content tend to be especially untrustworthy, and dependable external criteria are rare. One may, for example, assume that a man who perspires excessively feels anxious. Yet, his feelings of anxiety, if any, are not directly observable. Any assumed trait (anxiety, for example) that is held to underlie observable behaviour is called a construct. Since the construct itself is not directly measurable, the adequacy of any test as a measure of anxiety can be gauged only indirectly; *e.g.*, through evidence for its construct validity.

A test exhibits construct validity when low scorers and high scorers are found to respond differently to everyday experiences or to experimental procedures. A test presumed to measure anxiety, for example, would give evidence of construct validity if those with high scores ("high anxiety") can be shown to learn less efficiently than do those with somewhat lower scores.

Reliability

Test reliability is affected by scoring accuracy, adequacy of content sampling, and the stability of the trait being measured. Scorer reliability refers to the consistency with which different people who score the same test agree. For a test with a definite answer key, scorer reliability is of negligible concern. When the subject responds with his own words, handwriting, and organization of subject matter, however, the preconceptions of different raters produce different scores from one rater to another; *i.e.*, the test shows scorer (or rater) unreliability. In the absence of an objective scoring key, a scorer's evaluation may differ from one time to another and from those of equally respected evaluators. Other things being equal, tests that permit objective scoring are preferred.

Reliability also depends on the representativeness with which tests sample the content to be tested. If subjects' scores on some items of a test that sample a particular universe of content designed to be reasonably homogeneous (*e.g.*, vocabulary) correlate highly with those on another set of items selected from the same universe of content, the test has high content reliability. But if the universe of content is highly diverse in that it samples different factors (say, verbal reasoning and facility with numbers), the test may have high content reliability but low internal consistency.

For most purposes, the performance of a subject on the same test from day to day should be consistent. When such scores do tend to remain stable over time, the test exhibits temporal reliability. Fluctuations of scores may arise from instability of a trait; for example, one may be happier one day than the next. Or temporal unreliability may reflect injudicious test construction (*e.g.*, poor selection of items).

Reliability estimates

Included among the major methods through which test reliability estimates are made is the comparable-forms technique, in which the scores of a group of people on one form of a test are compared with the scores they earn on another form. Theoretically, the comparable-forms approach may reflect scorer, content, and temporal reliability. This ideally demands that each form of the test be constructed by different but equally competent persons, the forms being given at different times and evaluated by a second rater (unless an objective key is fixed).

In the test–retest method, scores of the same group of people from two administrations of the same test are correlated. If the time interval between administrations is too short, memory may unduly enhance the correlation. Too long an interval can result in different effects for each person of forgetting, practice, or learning. Except for very easy speed tests (*e.g.*, in which one's score depends on how quickly he is able to do simple addition), this method may give misleading estimates of reliability. Some people, for example, may look up words they missed on the first administration of a vocabulary test and thus be able to raise their scores the second time around.

Internal-consistency methods of estimating reliability require only one administration of a single form of a test. One method entails obtaining scores on separate halves of the test, usually the odd-numbered and the even-numbered items. The degree of relationship (which is expressed numerically as a correlation coefficient) between scores on these half-tests permits estimation of the reliability of the test (at full length) by means of a statistical correction.

This is computed by the use of the Spearman–Brown prophecy formula (for estimating the increased reliability expected to result from increase in test length). More commonly used is a generalization of this stepped-up, split-half reliability estimate, one of the Kuder–Richardson formulas. This formula provides an average of estimates that would result from all possible ways of separating a test into halves.

Other desirable characteristics of tests. A test that takes too long to administer will be useless for most routine applications. What constitutes a reasonable period of testing time, however, will depend in part on the decisions to be made from the test. Each test should be accompanied by a practicable and economically feasible scoring scheme, one scorable by machine or by quickly trained personnel being preferred.

A large, controversial literature has developed around response sets; *i.e.*, tendencies of subjects to respond systematically to items regardless of content. Thus, a given test taker may tend to answer questions on a personality test only in socially desirable ways or to select the first alternative of each set of multiple-choice answers or to malinger (*i.e.*, to purposely give wrong answers). Ways to correct for undesired response sets are becoming increasingly available.

TYPES OF INSTRUMENTS AND METHODS

Psychophysical scales and psychometric or psychological scales. The concept of an absolute threshold (the lowest intensity at which a sensory stimulus, such as sound waves, will be perceived) is traceable to a German philosopher, Johann Friedrich Herbart. A German physiologist, Ernst Heinrich Weber, later observed that the smallest discernible difference of intensity is proportional to the initial stimulus intensity. Weber found, for example, that, while people could just notice the difference after a slight change in the weight of a ten-gram object, they needed a larger change before they could just detect a difference from a 100-gram weight. This finding is expressed more technically in the statement that the perceived (subjective) intensity will vary mathematically as the logarithm of the physical (objective) intensity of the stimulus.

In traditional psychophysical scaling methods, a set of standard stimuli (such as weights) that can be ordered according to some physical property is related to sensory judgments made by experimental subjects. By the method of average error, for example, subjects are given a standard stimulus and then made to adjust a variable stimulus until they believe it is equal to the standard. The mean (average) of a number of judgments is obtained. This method and many variations have been used to study such experiences as visual illusions, tactual intensities, and auditory pitch.

Psychological (psychometric) scaling methods are an outgrowth of the psychophysical tradition just described. Although their purpose is to locate stimuli on a linear (straight-line) scale, no quantitative physical values (*e.g.*, loudness or weight) for stimuli are involved. The linear scale may represent one's attitude toward a social institution, his judgment of the quality of an artistic product, the degree to which he exhibits a personality characteristic, or his preference for different foods. Psychological scales thus are used for reporting one's own characteristics, as well as for rating other individuals in terms of such attributes, for example, as leadership potential or initiative.

An American psychologist, Louis L. Thurstone, offered a number of theoretical–statistical contributions that are widely used as rationales for constructing psychometric scales. One scaling technique (comparative judgment) is based empirically on choices made by people between members of any series of paired stimuli. Statistical treatment to provide numerical estimates of the subjective (perceived) distances between members of every pair of stimuli yields a psychometric scale. Whether or not these computed scale values are consistent with the observed comparative judgments is a problem that can be tested empirically.

Another of Thurstone's psychometric scaling techniques (equal-appearing intervals) has been widely used in attitude measurement. In this method, judges sort statements reflecting such things as varying degrees of emotional intensity, for example, into what they perceive to be equally spaced categories; the average (median) category assignments are used to define scale values numerically. Subsequent users of such a scale are scored according to the average scale values of the statements to which they subscribe. Another method, developed by another American psychologist, requires no prior group of judges, depends on intensive analysis of scale items, and yields comparable results. A more general technique (successive intervals) does not depend on the assumption that judges perceive interval size accurately. The widely used graphic rating scale presents an arbitrary continuum with preassigned guides for the rater (*e.g.*, adjectives such as superior, average, and inferior); for examples, see PERSONALITY, MEASUREMENT OF: *Methods of assessment: Rating scales.*

Tests versus inventories. The term test most frequently refers to devices for measuring abilities or qualities for which there are authoritative right and wrong answers. Such a test may be contrasted with a personality inventory, for which it is often claimed that there are no right or wrong answers. At any rate, in taking what often is called a test, the subject is instructed to do his best; in completing an inventory, he is instructed to represent his typical reactions. A distinction also has been made that in responding to an inventory the subject controls the appraisal, whereas in a test he does not. If a test is more broadly regarded as a set of stimulus situations that elicit responses from which inferences can be drawn, however, then an inventory is, according to this definition, a variety of test.

Free-response versus limited-response tests. Free-response tests entail few restraints on the form or content of one's response, whereas limited-response tests restrict his responses to one of a smaller number presented (*e.g.*, true-false). An essay test tends toward one extreme (free response), while a so-called fully objective test is at the other extreme (limited response).

Response to an essay question is not completely unlimited, however, since the answer should bear on the question. The free-response test does give practice in writing, and, when an evaluator is proficient in judging written expression, his comments on the test may aid the individual to improve his writing style. All too often, however, writing ability unfortunately affects judgments of how well the test taker understands content, tending to reduce test reliability. Another source of unreliability for essay

Essay and objective tests

tests is found in their limited sampling of content, as contrasted with the broader coverage that is possible with objective tests. Often both the scorer and the content reliability of essay tests can be increased, but such attempts are costly.

The objective test, which minimizes scorer unreliability, is best typified by the multiple-choice form, in which the subject is required to select one from two or (preferably) more responses to a test item. Matching items that have a common set of alternatives for matching are of this form. The true–false test question is a special multiple-choice form that may tend to arouse antagonism because of variable standards of truth or falsity.

The more general multiple-choice item is more acceptable when it is specified only that the best answer be selected; it is flexible, has high scorer reliability, and is not limited to simple factual knowledge. The ingenious test constructor can use multiple-choice items to test such functions as generalization, application of principles, and the ability to educe unfamiliar relationships.

Some personality tests are presented in a forced-choice format. They may, for example, force the person to choose one of two favourable words or phrases (*e.g.*, intelligent–handsome) as more descriptive of himself or one of two unfavourable terms as less descriptive (*e.g.*, stupid–ugly). Marking one choice yields a gain in score on some trait but may also preclude credit on another trait.

The forced-choice technique for self-appraisals is exemplified in a widely used interest inventory. Forced-choice ratings were introduced for evaluation of one military officer by another during World War II. They were an effort to avoid the preponderance of high ratings typically obtained with ordinary rating scales.

Falling between free- and limited-response tests is a type that requires a short answer, perhaps a single word or a number, for each item. When the required response is to fit into a blank in a sentence, the test is called a completion test. This type of test is susceptible to scorer unreliability.

A personality test to which a subject responds by interpreting a picture or by telling a story it suggests resembles an essay test except that responses ordinarily are oral. A personality inventory that requires the subject to indicate whether or not a descriptive phrase applies to him is of the limited-response type. A sentence-completion personality test that asks the subject to complete statements such as "I worry because . . ." is akin to the short-answer and completion types.

Verbal versus performance tests. A verbal (or symbol) test poses questions to which the subject supplies symbolic answers (in words or in other symbols, such as numbers). In performance tests, the subject actually executes some motor activity; *e.g.*, he assembles mechanical objects. Either the quality of performance as it takes place or its results may be rated.

The verbal test, requiring no special equipment and often being scorable by relatively unskilled evaluators, tends to be more practical than the performance test. Both types of devices also have counterparts in personality measurement, in which verbal tests as well as behaviour ratings are used.

Written (group) versus oral (individual) tests. In the 19th century, academic-achievement tests were usually given orally. The oral test is administered to one person at a time; written tests can be given simultaneously to a number of subjects. Oral tests of achievement, being uneconomical and prone to content and scorer unreliability, have been supplanted by written tests; notable exceptions include the testing of illiterates and the anachronistic oral examinations to which candidates for graduate degrees are liable.

Proponents of individually administered intelligence tests (*e.g.*, the Stanford–Binet) state that such face-to-face testing optimizes rapport and motivation, even among literate adult subjects. Oral tests of general aptitude remain popular, though numerous written group tests have been designed for the same purpose.

The interview may provide a personality measurement and, especially when it is standardized as to wording and order of questions and with a key for coding answers, may amount to an individual oral test. Group-administered personality inventories can be regarded as written group tests.

Appraisal by others versus self-appraisal. In responding to personality inventories and rating scales, a person presumably reveals what he thinks he is like; *i.e.*, he appraises himself. Other instruments may reflect what one person thinks of another. Because self-appraisal often lacks objectivity, appraisal by another individual is common in such things as ratings for promotions. Ordinary tests of ability clearly involve evaluation of one person by another, although the subject's self-evaluation may intrude; *e.g.*, he may lack confidence to the point where he does not try to do his best.

Projective tests. The stimuli (*e.g.*, inkblots) in a projective test are intentionally made ambiguous and open to different interpretations in the expectation that each subject will project his own unique (idiosyncratic) reactions in his answers. Techniques for evaluating such responses range from the intuitive impressions of the rater to complex, coded schemes for scoring and interpretation that require extensive manuals; some projective tests are objectively scorable.

Speed tests versus power tests. A pure speed test is homogeneous in content (*e.g.*, a simple clerical checking test), the tasks being so easy that with unlimited time all but the most incompetent of subjects could deal with them successfully. The time allowed for testing is so short, however, that even the ablest subject is not expected to finish. A useful score is the number of correct answers made in a fixed time.

In contrast, a power test (*e.g.*, a general vocabulary test) contains items that vary in difficulty to the point that no subject is expected to get all items right even with unlimited time. In practice, a definite but ample time is set for power tests.

Speed tests are suitable for testing visual perception, numerical facility, and other abilities related to vocational success. Tests of psychomotor abilities (*e.g.*, eye–hand coordination) often involve speed. Power tests tend to be more relevant to such purposes as the evaluation of academic achievement, for which the highest level of difficulty at which a person can succeed is of greater interest than his speed on easy tasks.

In general, tests reflect unknown combinations of the effects of speed and power; many consist of items that vary considerably in difficulty, the time allowed being too limited to allow a large proportion of subjects to attempt all items.

Speed tests also are used in evaluating aspects of personality. The time for responses to key words in word-association tests (which call for one to respond to a word with the first word he thinks of) may be used to infer such personality disturbances as feelings of guilt. Speed of response may suggest temperamental characteristics, particularly at the extremes, excessively slow responses typifying depressed people and extremely rapid reactions being observed among elated, manic subjects.

Teacher-made versus standardized tests. A distinction between teacher-made and standardized tests is often made in relation to tests used to assess academic achievement. Ordinarily, teachers do not attempt to construct tests of general or special aptitude or of personality traits. Teacher-made tests tend instead to be geared to narrow segments of curricular content (*e.g.*, a sixth-grade geography test). Standardized tests with carefully defined procedures for administration and scoring to insure uniformity can achieve broader goals. General principles of test construction and such considerations as reliability and validity apply to both types of test.

Special measurement techniques. Sociodrama and psychodrama were originally developed as psychotherapeutic techniques. In sociodrama, group members participate in unrehearsed drama to illuminate a general problem. Psychodrama centres on one individual in the group whose unique personal problem provides the theme. Re-

---

(margin notes)

Forced-choice items

Interviews viewed as tests

Temperament

lated research techniques (*e.g.*, the sociometric test) can offer insight into interpersonal relationships. Individuals may be asked to specify members of a group whom they prefer as leader, playmate, or coworker. The choices made can then be charted in a sociogram, from which cliques or socially isolated individuals may be identified at a glance.

Research psychologists have grasped the sociometric approach as a means of measuring group cohesiveness and studying individual reactions to groups. The degree to which any group member chooses or is chosen beyond chance expectation may be calculated, and mathematical techniques may be used to determine the complex links among group members. Sociogram-choice scores have been useful in predicting such criteria as individual productivity in factory work, combat effectiveness, and social leadership.

DEVELOPMENT OF STANDARDIZED TESTS

Item development. Once the need for a test has been established, a plan to depict the content to be covered in it may be prepared. For achievement tests, the test plan may also indicate thinking skills to be evaluated. Detailed content headings can be immediately suggestive of test items. It is helpful if the plan specifies weights to be allotted to different topics, as well as the desired average score and the spread of item difficulties. Whether or not such an outline is made, the test constructor clearly must understand the purpose of the test, the universe of content to be sampled, and the forms of the items to be used.

Planning the test

Tryouts and item analysis. A set of test questions is first administered to a small group of people deemed to be representative of the population for which the final test is intended. The trial run is planned to provide a check on instructions for administering and taking the test and intended time allowances, and it can reveal ambiguities in the test content. After adjustments, surviving items are administered to a larger, ostensibly representative group. The resulting data permit computation of a difficulty index for each item (often taken as the percentage of the subjects who respond correctly) and of an item–test or item–subtest discrimination index (*e.g.*, a coefficient of correlation specifying the relationship of each item with total test score or subtest score).

If it is feasible to do so, measures of the relation of each item to independent criteria (*e.g.*, grades earned in school) are obtained to provide item validation. Items that are too easy or too difficult are discarded; those within a desired range of difficulty are identified. If internal consistency is sought, items that are found to be unrelated to either a total score or an appropriate subtest score are ruled out, and items that are related to available external criterion measures are identified. Those items that show the most efficiency in predicting an external criterion (highest validity) usually are preferred over those that contribute only to internal consistency (reliability).

Estimates of reliability for the entire set of items, as well as for those to be retained, commonly are calculated. If the reliability estimate is deemed to be too low, items may be added. Each alternative in multiple-choice items also may be examined statistically. Weak incorrect alternatives can be replaced, and those that are unduly attractive to higher scoring subjects may be modified.

Cross validation. Item-selection procedures are subject to chance errors in sampling test subjects, and statistical values obtained in pretesting are usually checked (cross validated) with one or more additional samples of subjects. Typically, it is found that cross-validation values tend to shrink for many of the items that emerged as best in the original data, and further items may be found to warrant discard. Measures of correlation between total test score and scores from other, better known tests are often sought by test users.

Differential weighting. Some test items may appear to deserve extra, positive weight; some answers in multiple-choice items, though keyed as wrong, seem better than others in that they attract people who score high general-

ly. The bulk of theoretical logic and empirical evidence, nonetheless, is that unit weights for selected items and zero weights for discarded items and dichotomous (right versus wrong) scoring for multiple-choice items serve almost as effectively as more complicated scoring. Painstaking efforts to weight items generally are not worth the trouble.

Negative weight for wrong answers is usually avoided as presenting undue complication. In multiple-choice items, the number of answers a subject knows, in contrast to the number he gets right (which will include some lucky guesses), can be estimated by formula. But such an average correction will overpenalize the unlucky and underpenalize the lucky. If the instruction is not to guess, it is variously interpreted by persons of different temperament; those who decide to guess despite the ban are often helped by partial knowledge and tend to do better.

A responsible tactic is to try to reduce these differences by directing subjects to respond to every question, even if they must guess. Such instructions are inappropriate for some competitive speed tests, since candidates who mark items very rapidly and with no attention to accuracy will seem to excel if speed is the only basis for scoring; that is, unless wrong answers are penalized.

Norms for standardized tests. Test norms consist of data that indicate the relative standing of individuals who have taken a test. Usually, a subject's raw score (*e.g.*, the number of his answers that agree with the scoring key) is compared with the raw scores of other subjects through some system of norms. In the absence of such a comparison the raw score has little meaning.

Numerical values called centiles (or percentiles) serve as the basis for one widely applicable system of norms. From a distribution of a group's raw scores, the percentage of subjects falling below each raw score can be found. Thus, any raw score can be interpreted relative to the performance of the reference (or normative) group—eighth graders, five-year-olds, institutional inmates, job applicants. The centile rank corresponding to each raw score, therefore, will show the percentage of subjects who scored below that point. Thus, 25 percent of the normative group earn scores lower than the 25th centile; and an average called the median corresponds to the 50th centile.

Centiles; standard scores; mental age and IQ norms

Another class of norm system (standard scores) is based on how far each raw score falls above or below an average score, the arithmetic mean. One resulting type of standard score, symbolized as z, is positive (*e.g.*, $+ 1.69$ or $+ 2.43$) for a raw score above the mean and negative for a raw score below the mean; its further interpretation requires some statistical understanding, and it usually shows fractional (or equivalent decimal) values. Negative and fractional values can, however, be avoided in practice by using other types of standard scores obtained by multiplying z scores by an arbitrarily selected constant (say, 10) and by adding another constant (say, 50, which changes the z score mean of zero to a new mean of 50). Such changes of constants do not alter the essential characteristics of the underlying set of z scores.

The French psychologist Alfred Binet, in pioneering the development of tests of intelligence, listed test items along a normative scale on the basis of the chronological age (actual age in years and months) of groups of children that passed them. A mental-age score (*e.g.*, seven) was assigned to each subject, indicating the chronological age (*e.g.*, seven years old) in the reference sample for which his raw score was the mean. But mental age is not a direct index of brightness; a mental age of seven in a ten-year-old is different from the same mental age in a four-year-old.

To correct for this, a later development was a form of IQ (intelligence quotient), computed as the ratio of the subject's mental age to his chronological age, multiplied by 100. (Thus, the IQ made it easy to tell if a child was bright or dull for his age.)

Ratio IQs for younger age groups exhibit means close to 100 and spreads of roughly 45 points above and below 100. The classical ratio IQ has been largely supplanted by the deviation IQ, mainly because the spread around the average has not been uniform due to different ranges of item difficulty at different age levels. The deviation IQ, a type of standard score, has a mean of 100 and a standard deviation of 16 for each age level. Current practice with the Stanford-Binet test reflects the finding that average performance on the test does not increase beyond age 18. Therefore, the chronological age of any individual older than 18 is taken as 18 for the purpose of determining his IQ.

ASSESSING TEST STRUCTURE

Factor analysis. Test items that measure the same characteristic tend to be positively correlated with one another. A British psychologist, Charles Edward Spearman, systematically explored such intercorrelations to provide evidence that much of the variability in scores that children earn on tests of intelligence depends on a general underlying factor that he called *g*. In the United States, Thurstone developed a statistical technique called multiple-factor analysis, with which he was able to demonstrate additional (special rather than general) factors that tend to crystallize as people grow older. He provided evidence that, among adults, one specific talent (such as verbal comprehension) is distinguishable from another (*e.g.*, numerical ability).

Early computational methods in factor analysis have been supplanted by mathematically more elegant, computer-generated solutions; and the general technique is widely applicable beyond the field of psychological measurement.

Rooted in extensive applications of factor analysis, a structure-of-intellect model developed by an American psychologist, J.P. Guilford, posited a very large number of factors of intelligence. Guilford envisaged three intersecting dimensions corresponding to four kinds of test content, five kinds of intellectual operation, and six kinds of product. Each of the 120 cells in the cube thus generated was hypothesized to represent a separate ability, each as a distinct factor of intellect. Educational and vocational counselors usually prefer a substantially smaller number of scores than the 120 that are implied by this model.

Alternatives to factor analysis. Especially with respect to personality measures, simple techniques called cluster analysis have been proposed as alternatives to the statistical complications of factor analysis. In one form of cluster analysis, tables of correlation coefficients are simply inspected in an effort to find sets (clusters) of items or test scores that show high relationships among themselves.

Early forms of cluster analysis introduced in the 1930s required laborious visual inspection and time-consuming computations. With the advent of high-speed computers, new methods proliferated rapidly. Although it has been argued that clusters bear a closer relation to reality than do statistically defined factors, the correspondence appears to be at a descriptive rather than at an interpretive level. Taken separately or together, various types of cluster analysis fail to yield equivalent results; a number of authorities thus regard them as adjuncts to, rather than substitutes for, factor analysis.

Q-sort; inverse factor analysis

Techniques that are quite similar to the usual factor-analytic approach but provide different insights are those related to inverse factor analysis (based on intercorrelations among persons instead of among tests). One such method begins with what is called a *Q*-sort, in which a subject sorts words or other stimuli into categories on the basis of his preference so that they form a bell-shaped (normal) distribution.

This method is widely applicable to items from personality tests; first, correlations of data obtained from two persons' *Q*-sorts of the same items are computed. The inverse factor analysis of a matrix of such intercorrelations yields factors indicative of common ways people have of reacting to stimuli.

Another popular technique (the semantic differential) for detecting underlying variables was offered by Charles E. Osgood, an American psychologist. In this method,

the name of any object or concept (*e.g.*, religion or piety) is presented to an individual, who rates it on a series of seven-point scales defined semantically by pairs of adjectives (such as "good" versus "bad" or "valuable" versus "worthless"). When different concepts receive similar ratings on the semantic scales, they show evidence of representing the same underlying factor. The method has been applied mainly to psychological problems involving attitudes.

Profile analysis. With the fractionation of tests (*e.g.*, to yield scores on separate factors or clusters), new concern has arisen for interpreting differences among scores on the underlying variables, however conceived. Scores of an individual on several such measures can be plotted graphically as a profile; for direct comparability, all raw scores may be expressed in terms of standard scores that have equal means and variabilities. The difference between any pair of scores that have less than perfect reliability tends to be less reliable than either, and fluctuations in the graph should be interpreted cautiously. Nevertheless, various features of an individual's profile may be examined: scatter (fluctuation from one measure to another) and relative level of performance on different measures. (The particular shape of the graph, it should be noted, partly depends upon the arbitrary order in which measures are listed.) One may also statistically express the degree of similarity between any two profiles. Such statistical measures of pattern similarity permit quantitative comparison of profiles for different persons, of profiles of the same individual's performance at different times, of individual with group profiles, or of one group profile with another. Comparison of an individual's profile with similar graphs representing the means for varied occupational groups, for example, is useful for vocational guidance or personnel selection.

Prospects. Despite progress over the last century, psychological measurement warrants improvement. Brief appraisals of individual potentiality—whether in educational, vocational, or personal adjustment settings—are recognizably far from perfect. The complexities of human behaviour attributable to the myriad effects of unanticipated combinations of genes, prenatal influences, and vagaries of environmental effects make it surprising that a relatively brief test or even a full day of testing can predict future behaviour to any extent at all beyond a chance level.

Predictions are successful beyond chance expectations, however. And clearly the forecasts of psychometricians and other specialists in educational and psychological measurement have much to commend them in contrast with subjective appraisals of sooth-sayers, phrenologists, astrologers, or untrained personnel interviewers who happen to like people.

BIBLIOGRAPHY. DOROTHY ADKINS WOOD, *Test Construction* (1961), a simplified treatment of measurement principles, rules for test construction, and statistical techniques; ANNE ANASTASI, *Psychological Testing*, 3rd ed. (1968), an authoritative text and reference book with emphasis on current psychological tests; L.J. CRONBACH, *Essentials of Psychological Testing*, 3rd ed. (1970), another modern and insightful text and general reference; J.P. GUILFORD, *Psychometric Methods*, 2nd ed. (1954), a widely used book that attempts to integrate psychophysical scaling and psychological measurement methods; HAROLD GULLIKSEN, *Theory of Mental Tests* (1950), a basic theoretical reference; H.H. HARMAN, *Modern Factor Analysis*, 2nd ed. rev. (1967), an eclectic treatment of factor-analytic theory and methods; PAUL HORST, *Psychological Measurement and Prediction* (1966), a discussion of practical requirements of psychological measurement as well as of technical problems in prediction; F.M. LORD and M.R. NOVICK, *Statistical Theories of Mental Test Scores* (1968), a highly technical presentation; R.L. THORNDIKE (ed.), *Educational Measurement*, 2nd ed. (1970), contains specially prepared chapters by authorities in particular fields of measurement.

(D.C.A.)

Measurement, Theory of

Measurement theory studies the practice of associating numbers with objects and empirical phenomena. It attempts to understand which qualitative relationships lead to numerical assignments that reflect the structure of these relationships, to account for the ways in which different measures relate to one another, and to study the problems of error in the measurement process.

HISTORY AND NATURE OF MEASUREMENT THEORY

History
of
magni-
tudes
theory

An early and relatively abstract theory of magnitudes was developed in the 4th century BC by two mathematicians, Eudoxus of Cnidus, probably a member of Plato's Academy, and Theaetetus, author of the book on the regular solids and one of those on irrational numbers in Euclid's *Elements*, in which their theory of magnitudes was given its fully developed presentation. Theirs was a highly sophisticated theory of measurement. Historical evidence suggests that it was developed for purely theoretical purposes, to account for incommensurable magnitudes—pairs of numbers, such as 1 and the square root of 2, for which no third number exists of which both are even (or integral) multiples—rather than to solve any practical problems, such as those of surveying. Problems of measurement, of both a theoretical and a practical sort, continued to be discussed throughout ancient times and during the Middle Ages.

In modern times, Euclid's view of the theory of magnitudes was still relevant as late as the 18th century; it appeared, for example, in Isaac Newton's *Arithmetica Universalis* (2nd ed., 1728). The modern, axiomatic treatment of the theory—*i.e.*, its logical development from fundamental concepts and axioms—can be dated from a famous paper by Herman Ludwig Ferdinand von Helmholtz, a German philosopher and wide-ranging scientist, entitled "Zählen und Messen erkenntnistheoretisch betrachtet" (1887; Eng. trans., "Counting and Measuring," 1930). Considerable impetus was given by a classical work of Ludwig Otto Hölder, a German mathematician, entitled "Die Axiome der Quantität und die Lehre vom Mass" (1901; "The Axioms of Quantity and the Theory of Measure"), in which he provided two sets of axioms, one for the measurement (or, as he said, "the quantity") of additive attributes, such as mass, which can be built up by addition of parts to form a total bulk, and another set for nonadditive attributes involving the measurement of intervals, as in temperature or longitude. The tradition of Helmholtz and Hölder has been of importance primarily in the physical sciences.

The consideration of measurement in the social sciences, especially in economics, also has had a long history. As early as the 18th century, Jeremy Bentham, a British Utilitarian moralist, in a treatise, *The Principles of Morals and Legislation* (1789), attempted to provide a theory for the measurement of utility, or value. In the 19th century there was an effort to establish that much of economic theory could be developed solely on the basis of ordinal preferences among the economic goods being studied, without any more demanding kind of numerical measurement. The work of Vilfredo Pareto, an Italian economist and sociologist, entitled *Manuale di economia politica* (1906; "Handbook of Political Economics"), was especially important in this connection. In the mid-20th century the study of measurement in economics and in psychology was stimulated by the theory of utility set forth in *Theory of Games and Economic Behavior* (1944) by the mathematician John von Neumann, a scientist of unusual breadth, and the economist, Oskar Morgenstern. It makes use of the formation of so-called risky alternatives (see below *Economics and psychology*).

The three
basic
problems
of
measure-
ment
theory

An examination of specific examples of axiomatic measurement can lead to a general view of measurement theory. The first problem for any such theory is to justify the assignment of numbers to objects or phenomena—to pass from empirical procedures and operations to a numerical representation of these procedures. From an axiomatic standpoint, the problem—known as the representation problem—is first to characterize the formal or abstract properties of these procedures and observations and then to show mathematically that these axioms permit the construction of a numerical assignment in which familiar abstract relations and operations, such as "is greater than or equal to" (symbolized $\geq$) and "plus"

($+$), correspond structurally to the empirical (or concrete) relations and operations.

The second fundamental problem is that of the uniqueness of the representation—*i.e.*, how close it is to being the only possible representation of its type. The representation of mass, for example, is unique in every respect except the choice of unit; *e.g.*, the representation is different for pounds than for grams or grains. Ordinary measurements of temperature, however, are unique in everything except the choice of both unit and origin—the Celsius and Fahrenheit scales differ not only in the size of unit but also in the zero point. A U.S. psychophysicist, S. Smith Stevens, was among the first to place great emphasis on the uniqueness of measurement in relation to the problem of units and the consequences that this uniqueness has for data handling.

A subject closely related to the uniqueness of physical measurement is dimensional analysis, which, in a broad sense, attempts to explain why the various physical measures exhibit simple relations in the fundamental equations of classical physics. If length, time, and mass are taken to be the fundamental dimensions of mechanics, for example, then all other quantities, such as force or momentum, can be represented simply as products of powers of these dimensions—a fact that has strong implications for the forms of physical laws (see below *Universal, system, and material constants*).

A third central problem for the theory of measurement is error. In spite of the early development of precise astronomical measurement, no systematic theory of observational error appears to have been developed until the 18th century, first in an article by Thomas Simpson, an English mathematician, in 1757, and then in the fundamental work of two French mathematicians, Joseph-Louis, comte de Lagrange, who worked on the theory of numbers and celestial mechanics, and Pierre-Simon, marquis de Laplace, also an astronomer, famous for his fundamental work, *Traité de méchanique céleste* (1798–1827; *Celestial Mechanics*, 1966). Today, any really significant physical measurement is routinely reported together with some indication of the probable error, and theories are tested by confirming them within the errors of measurement. In the classical tests of Albert Einstein's general theory of relativity, for example, the discrepancies between predictions and observations fell mainly within the estimated errors of measurement (for further discussion of errors of measurement, see below *The problem of error*).

AXIOMATIC BASIS OF MEASUREMENT

Axiom systems for measurement differ in the amount and type of structure involved. All include an ordering relation, but that alone is not enough to formulate many scientific laws because its numerical representation is not closely prescribed. Additional structure and an increased uniqueness of the representation arise either by having an empirical operation of addition (extensive measurement), or by having entities that have several independent components (difference and conjoint measurement), or by other primitives that lead to a geometric representation.

Axioms of order. Whenever a measurement is made, it is done in such a way that the order induced on the objects by the assigned measure is the same as that obtained by the basic empirical operation in question. Such measures are said to be order preserving. Of course, every numerical inequality involved in measurement is transitive (*i.e.*, such that $x \geq y$ and $y \geq z$ implies that $x \geq z$) and connected (*i.e.*, either $x \geq y$ or $y \geq x$). It is therefore necessary that the empirical ordering—symbolized $\geq$ (with $\sim$ instead of $-$ to suggest real entities)—be transitive and connected in order for a representation of it to be possible by means of $\geq$. Relations exhibiting these two properties are called weak orders, in which "weak" simply means that indifference (symbolized $\sim$)—in which $x \sim y \equiv x \geq y$ and $y \geq x$—is not necessarily equality (using $\equiv$ to mean "if and only if"). Not every weak order, however, has an order-preserving numerical representation; the lexicographic

Axioms
for
binary
relations

order in the plane $(x,y) \geq (x',y') \equiv x > x'$ or $x = x'$ and $y > y'$, is a counterexample. A second, independent property of numbers, which must in turn be reflected in the empirical ordering, is that rational numbers—*i.e.*, numbers expressible as the quotient of two integers—are order-dense (*i.e.*, they are such that between any two distinct real numbers lies a rational number) and countable (*i.e.*, they can be placed in one-to-one correspondence with the integers).

In 1895 it was shown by Georg Cantor, a German mathematician, that, for any empirical ordering, the existence of a numerical representation that preserves its order is equivalent to the ordering's being a weak one that includes in its domain a countable, order-dense subset. Any two such representations are so related that one can be mapped upon the other in a strictly increasing fashion.

Though various ordinal categorizations are widely used (*e.g.*, brightness of stars, magnitude of earthquakes, hardness of minerals), the fact that equivalent ordinal representations are seldom in simple proportion to one another makes them unsatisfactory in the statement of many scientific laws. To increase the uniqueness of the representation, some structure in addition to order must be preserved by the representation.

Axioms of extension. For many physical attributes—including mass, length, time duration, and probability—the objects or events exhibiting the attribute may be combined, or concatenated, to form new objects or events that also exhibit the attribute. Both alone and combined, for example, objects have mass. Denoting the concatenation of a and b by $a \circ b$, the assignment (designated ϕ) of a given set of numbers to the objects is called an extensive representation of the empirical ordering $\geq$ and the concatenation o, provided that it is not only order preserving but also additive in the sense that $\phi(a \circ b) = \phi(a) + \phi(b)$.

Theories that are intended to account for the existence of such numerical representations must state empirical laws about ordering and concatenation separately, as well as how they interrelate. The key property of an empirical ordering is that it is a weak order, and that of a concatenation is that it is insensitive to the order of combination—concatenation is weakly commutative (*i.e.*, its order can be reversed), $a \circ b \sim b \circ a$, and weakly associative (*i.e.*, its terms can be regrouped), $(a \circ b) \circ c \sim a \circ (b \circ c)$—in which $\sim$ indicates an equivalent formulation. The key property relating them, weak monotonicity, is that the empirical ordering $a \geq b$ holds if and only if the ordering of its concatenation with any object c, $a \circ c \geq b \circ c$, also holds. As in ordinal measurement, a further and more subtle property, called Archimedean, is needed; this asserts that the elements within the structure are commensurable with one another. This property is formally analogous to the numerical Archimedean property that if $x > y > 0$, then for some integer n, $ny \geq x$ (meaning y is not "infinitesimally" small relative to x). With these stipulations, the numerical representation can be constructed.

The basic idea of the construction is simple and, in somewhat modified form, is widely used to carry out fundamental measurement. The measurer first chooses some object u, such as a foot rule, to be the unit of measurement. For any object a (say a house stud), he then finds other objects (studs) that are equivalent to a in the attribute in question (length). He concatenates these by laying them end-to-end in a straight line. Denoting by na the concatenation of any n of them, he now finds how many copies of u, say $m(n)$, are needed to approximate na; *i.e.*, $[m(n) + 1] u \geq na \geq m(n)a$. The limit toward which $m(n)/n$ tends as n approaches infinity exists and is defined to be $\phi(a)$, which is the measurement sought; it can be shown to be order preserving and additive. In contrast to ordinal measurement, such an extensive representation is almost unique: it is determined except for a positive multiplicative constant or coefficient setting the scale; or, what is the same thing, only the choice of the unit is arbitrary. As a result, such a representation is called a ratio scale.

Sequences such as na, $n = 1,2, \ldots$, being ubiquitous in measurement practice, are called standard sequences. Practical examples are standard sets of weights in multiples of a gram and the metre rule, subdivided into millimetres.

For some purposes, including the development of other kinds of measurement—*e.g.*, difference and probability measurement—it is necessary to generalize the theory to cover concatenation operations (o) that are defined only for some pairs of objects and not for others. Probability, for example, is not additive over all pairs of events, but only over those that are disjoint. Such theories, developed during the 1950s and 1960s, all assume that certain empirical inequalities have solutions. One form of such solvability is: if $a > b$, then there exists a c such that c and b can be concatenated and $a \geq c \circ b$.

Axioms of difference. Length, but not mass, may be treated also in terms of intervals (a, b) on a line. Here the empirical ordering $\geq$ is a quaternary rather than a binary relation, since it involves the comparison of two pairs, and so four points, such as the end points of two intervals; and concatenation is defined only for adjacent intervals; *i.e.*,

$$(a,b) \circ (b,c) = (a,c).$$

In addition to weak ordering, solvability, and Archimedean properties, various other axioms, depending on the exact representation to be constructed, must be satisfied. Two important representations are the algebraic difference one, in which an empirical ordering holds if and only if the differences of its elements form an ordered representation; *i.e.*,

$$(a,b) \geq (c,d) \equiv \phi(a) - \phi(b) \geq \phi(c) - \phi(d),$$

for which a key axiom is that the ordering is preserved through an interchange of arguments; *i.e.*,

$$(a,b) \geq (c,d) \equiv (a,c) \geq (b,d),$$

and the absolute difference representation, in which an empirical ordering holds if and only if the absolute values (symbolized $| \ldots |$) of such differences are ordered; *i.e.*,

$$(a,b) \geq (c,d) \equiv |\phi(a) - \phi(b)| \geq |\phi(c) - \phi(d)|,$$

for which key axioms are that any interval is at least as large as the null interval; *i.e.*, $(a,b) \geq (a,a)$ and that an interval is unordered, or the same when measured "backwards"; *i.e.*, $(a,b) \sim (b,a)$.

Such representations are called interval scales, because they are unique in every respect except for the possibilities of multiplication by a positive constant and addition of a constant; *i.e.*, both the unit and zero of the measure are arbitrary, and the equality of intervals is preserved through all transformations generated by altering these two scale factors.

Axioms of conjointness. A major hindrance to the development of fundamental measurement, other than probability, outside physics has been the failure to uncover suitable empirical concatenation operations for attributes such as utility, loudness, intelligence, or hunger. An alternative approach, implicit in much derived measurement in classical physics, has recently been made completely explicit in the behavioral sciences. It rests on the fact that many—indeed, most—attributes are defined for entities having at least two independent components, each of which affect the attribute: kinetic energy and momentum, for example, are both affected by mass and velocity; mass is varied by both changing density and volume; preference among gambles is manipulated both by outcomes and by the probabilities of their occurring; and loudness of tones depends on frequency as well as intensity. In conjoint-measurement theories, the way in which each component affects the attribute in question is studied by discovering which changes must be made in one component to compensate for changes in the other. When measures for the components already exist, the exchange relationship between the two components is often presented graphically in the form of so-called equal-attribute (or indifference) curves.

The simplest representation is additive—or, by making

Order and concatenation (left margin)

Axioms for quaternary relations (right margin)

Additive
and
poly-
nomial
represen-
tations

an exponential transformation, multiplicative (which is the way it is usually represented in physics)—in the sense that numerical functions ϕ_1 and ϕ_2 of the two components exist such that an empirical inequality holds if and only if the sums of these functions of its elements exhibit a numerical inequality in the same direction; *i.e.*,

$$(a_1,a_2) \geq (b_1,b_2) \equiv \phi_1(a_1) + \phi_2(a_2) \geq \phi_1(b_1) + \phi_2(b_2).$$

Axioms sufficient for such a numerical representation consist of weak ordering, a form of solvability, an Archimedean property, and what amount to analogues of weak monotonicity. The simplest of these, independence, states that an inequality of one component with a common value—*e.g.*, $(a_1,x) \geq (b_1,x)$—is not altered by substituting any other common value y for x. When this property is appropriately generalized to three or more components, no more stipulations are needed; for only two components, however, it must be supplemented by another property, called the Thomsen condition. In the special case when the components each have only a finite number of elements, a theoretical schema of necessary and sufficient conditions is known. Such additive measures are interval scales; but the multiplicative constant or scale factor is the same for all ϕ_i.

Other ordered representations also have been studied. Especially well understood are certain simple polynomials on several components. For three components there are four such simple polynomials: additive ($\phi_1 + \phi_2 + \phi_3$), multiplicative ($\phi_1\phi_2\phi_3$), or a combination of both, either ($\phi_1\phi_2 + \phi_3$) or $\phi_1(\phi_2 + \phi_3)$. (In these expressions the subscripted indices 1, 2, 3 can, of course, appear in any of their permutations.)

Axioms of geometry. Historically, numerical-representation and uniqueness theorems for geometry have been at least as important as those for extensive measurement and more important than the other kinds of measurement considered above. Since the discovery of analytic geometry in the 17th century, by René Descartes, the earliest important modern philosopher, the representation of geometric points by a pair of numbers (the coordinates), in the case of a plane, or a triple of numbers, in the case of space, has been of fundamental importance not only in geometry but also in much of the physical sciences.

The view that the formal adequacy of axioms for geometry is established by proving a representation theorem became explicit in the latter part of the 19th century. The most important single work may have been the classic *Grundlagen der Geometrie* (1899; *The Foundations of Geometry*, 1902), by David Hilbert. Today the distinctive feature of geometric measurement is that the representation is made in terms of pairs or triples or, in some applications in the social sciences, n-tuples of numbers, rather than in terms of simple numbers, as in extensive, difference, or conjoint measurement.

Much of the literature on the foundations of geometry has been devoted to showing the different sorts of qualitative concepts that can be taken as basic or primitive in stating the axioms of geometry. One of the simplest sets of axioms, given by Alfred Tarski, a Polish-U.S. mathematician and logician, employs the concept of equidistance and that of betweenness for three points that lie on a line. Many of the properties of the quaternary relation of absolute difference discussed above (see above *Axioms of difference*) are also properties of equidistance viewed as a quaternary relation among four points, viz., $(a,b) \sim (c,d)$ just when the distance between a and b is equivalent to that between c and d.

GENERAL PRINCIPLES AND PROBLEMS OF MEASUREMENT THEORY

Dimensions and units of measurement. Each measurable attribute constitutes a dimension; inasmuch as these are not all independent, some can be expressed as (power) functions of others—a fact that underlies both the method of dimensional analysis and the existence of coherent sets of units.

Dimensions and their algebra. Many attributes are extensively measurable. Some dimensions, however, such as density, are not extensive; and in such cases a law can be

stipulated that allows the derived, nonextensive measure to be expressed as a product of powers of two extensive measures. This possibility arises from two empirical facts. First, mass varies both with substance and volume, and the ordering that it induces over substance–volume pairs is such that a multiplicative conjoint representation exists. Thus, the conjoint measure of substance can be expressed as a product of its measure of mass and the reciprocal of its measure of volume. Both of these attributes, of course, have independent extensive measures. Second, a qualitative law, known as a law of similitude, relates concatenations of volume to those of mass via the conjoint ordering. From this law, it is possible to prove that the conjoint and extensive measures are power functions of each other; indeed, in this case, the conjoint measure of substance is, for an appropriate choice of exponent, simply the ratio of the extensive measure of mass to that of volume; *i.e.*, density. In cases such as the dependency of kinetic energy and momentum on mass and velocity, the conjoint components are both extensive and the law relating them via the conjoint ordering is called a law of exchange; interesting cases of such laws appear to involve quantities that enter laws of conservation, such as that of momentum and energy. In any event, all nonextensive measures of classical physics are expressible as products of powers of extensive ones. Some such model is the usual starting point of dimensional analysis.

Universal, system, and material constants. Sometimes two apparently distinct attributes are not independent but covariant. In the classic example of inertial mass and gravitational mass, the covariation is described by a constant known as the universal gravitational constant. This example should be contrasted with the covariation of two measures for specific systems. Mass and volume, for example, covary perfectly for any homogeneous substance, or length and force (within limits) for a specific spring. The constants describing such local covariation, called material or system constants (depending on the context), constitute a form of derived measurement.

Many more complex physical laws may be described as stating combinations of values—configurations—of certain dimensions that can obtain in a particular class of physical system. Such laws include not only measurable dimensions of the system but also system and material constants characteristic of the particular system in question. A curious and not fully understood fact of physical theory is a principle first explicitly enunciated in 1914 by the U.S. analyst Edgar Buckingham, the so-called π-theorem, according to which, when the dimensional measures and constants of some physical law are grouped into one or more terms in which the dimensions all cancel out, some function of these dimensionless quantities (or π-arguments) must equal zero for any realizable configuration of the system.

Dimensional analysis. In dimensional analysis, the investigator in part attempts to discover a particular physical law by assuming that it has the character of a π-theorem and that the relevant variables and constants are known. When they are known (an important proviso), a simple calculus permits him to discover all of the dimensionless terms. In many cases, this yields considerable insight into the law describing the system; sometimes empirical observations, as in a wind tunnel, are used to obtain an empirical approximation to the unknown function of the π-arguments.

Primary and derived units. One is free to choose the unit of measurement for each dimension, whereupon all other values are uniquely determined. Since some dimensions are related to others as products of powers, considerable simplicity is effected by choosing arbitrarily only the units of the dimensions in a maximum set of independent dimensions (base) and then letting the known dependencies determine all of the other units. Such a system of units is called coherent; those of the base are said to be primary, and all others are derived, or secondary. At the Tenth General Conference on Weights and Measures (1954), length, mass, time duration, temperature, and either charge or current were adopted as the base dimensions, with units: metre, kilogram, second, degree absolute (Kelvin), and the coulomb or ampere, respectively. This system is abbreviated MKSA.

For effective scientific communication, it is essential that each unit be specified and reproducible to some known degree of accuracy. The ideal definition of a unit is in terms of some highly invariant and readily reproduced or observable natural phenomenon, such as the wavelength of a highly reproducible, monochromatic light source. Less ideal, although still used, are carefully made and maintained unique objects, such as the standard metre in Paris, which have the drawback of being in danger of damage or deterioration.

Measurement via nonmeasurement theories. Few actual measurements are carried out in a fundamental manner using only ordering and concatenation information, because such procedures, when possible, are too slow and expensive, and in fact they are not always possible. It will be helpful to describe some of the alternative procedures employed in physics and psychology.

Indirect measure-ment

In physics. At least three kinds of indirect measurement occur in physics. First, permanent standard sequences are sometimes constructed—as for weight and length—and measurement then involves approximate matching against members of the sequence. Precision and standardization of conditions are important in making such measurements.

Second, when a law is found to hold between two or more variables, and system or material constants enter— such as the density and viscosity of a fluid—these constants are measured indirectly in terms of other measures by means of the law.

Third, various theories of specific physical phenomena may provide indirect means of measuring an attribute that may otherwise be difficult to measure; and such theories may, in some cases, lead to convenient measuring devices. A mechanical displacement in a piece of equipment—a spring balance, for example, or a voltmeter— may be systematically related to some other attribute (force or potential). In such measurement, considerable care must be taken to calibrate the apparatus in terms of fundamental measures of the two attributes. Another sort of example is provided by the measurement of astronomical distances in terms of the shift of the object's spectral lines toward the red, a technique that is based on a theory of the existence of a systematic relation between the velocity of recession and the distance of a galaxy, and one about the Doppler effect, which spreads out the waves from a receding light source and thus reduces their frequency.

In psychology. Since few, if any, psychological attributes are currently measured fundamentally, no approximate measurement using standard sequences is possible. Whether conjoint measurement will alter this situation is not yet clear.

Most formalized theory in psychology is stated in terms of physical characteristics of the stimuli and responses: various physical and temporal aspects of the stimuli, the physical nature and probability structure of the rewards provided for appropriate performance, and the time and nature of the response made. Frequently, some of the data are collapsed into relative frequencies, which are interpreted as estimates of conditional probabilities. Though, in principle, a theory could simply assert the dependence of response measures upon the various physical measures of the independent variables, this has not proved practicable; and in most theories some sort of internal representation of the stimuli is postulated to exist in the subject. Decision processes are assumed to operate on these representations, which decisions then lead to the response. Such models include free parameters that often have natural interpretations as psychological measures. If these can be estimated from the observable data, as is frequently possible, they constitute a type of indirect psychological measurement not unlike the second class of physical ones. In many cases, the parameters seem to play a role much like that of time constants in physical systems.

There is no satisfactory analogue to the third method enumerated above for physics, because no sufficiently elaborate and accepted psychological theories yet exist. Many so-called operational measures of psychological concepts—hours of deprivation for hunger or skin resistance for anxiety—pretend to be of this type, but they are not. The absence of questions of calibration is but one indication of the inadequacy of such measures.

The problem of error. Inasmuch as measurement, in practice, is always fraught with error, the types and basic theory of error must be examined.

Types of error. The classification of errors used in the theory of observations has been of great importance, both historically and practically, especially in astronomy. In that theory, four kinds of errors of observation are ordinarily distinguished. There are instrumental errors, such as those of the telescope in astronomy, that have as their source inaccuracies in the instruments used for observation. There are personal errors, sometimes called errors due to the personal equation, that arise from the different practices and reactions of human observers. Nevil Maskelyne, the fifth astronomer royal of Great Britain, provided a famous example of such personal differences in observation when he discharged his assistant in 1796 because he had observed the transits of stars and planets about a half a second later than Maskelyne himself. Systematic errors are a third kind of error of observation. A typical example of this kind would be the measurement of atmospheric pressures corrected to sea level in terms of a faulty value for the height of the station. Such an error would introduce a systematic discrepancy in all observations of atmospheric pressure for that station. The fourth and most important kind of error of observation is that of random error, so called because its causes are not understood. This type of error reflects the fact that, when observers make repeated measurements, some variation in the results will occur no matter how accurate the instruments may be.

In principle, all four types of error need to be taken into account in refining observations. In practice, however, the attention of theorists has been directed mainly to random errors. Since the end of the 18th century, the application of probabilistic methods through the estimation of random errors has been extensive.

Errors of observa-tion

Next to errors of observation, perhaps the most important kind of error is that due to sampling. If an investigator, for instance, wishes to know something about the television-viewing habits of the population, he ordinarily cannot plan to observe the viewing habits of each and every member of the population. He selects, instead, a sample of the population and from that sample infers the viewing habits of all. Errors of sampling, of course, are expected; but, the larger the sample, other things being equal, the smaller the sampling error will be. An elaborate statistical theory, both for constructing the kind of sample that should be drawn and for making inferences from the sample data to the characteristics of the population, is widely used (see STATISTICS).

Other kinds of error

Still another classification of errors involves the division into direct and indirect errors. If a surveyor, for example, measures the angles of a triangle, direct errors can arise from the measurement of the first two angles. These errors will induce errors of measurement indirectly into the value of the third angle, which he will compute instead of measuring directly. In advanced scientific practice, a large number of errors of measurement are indirect, because elaborate theory and a wide variety of ancillary measurements enter into the measurements of significant quantities, such as the velocity of light or the magnitude of the Earth's mass.

Still other kinds of errors are concerned with interpolation and extrapolation. In using mathematical tables, for example, one often wants to read a table to one more decimal place than those tabulated, and it is common to make a linear interpolation between two adjacent figures in order to extend the table. Since the curve reflected in the figures, however, may in fact be parabolic or exponential or the like, such an assumption of linearity may generate error. Similar problems arise in extrapolating beyond the limits of a given set of values. In both cases it is possible to compute the approximate error introduced.

Standard
error
and
variance

Theory of errors. The theory of errors has received a great deal of attention in the development of science and mathematics, especially in that of probability theory. Though, historically, the concept of standard error has been most widely used in reporting the results of measurement, in modern statistics the concept is of less importance. The computation of the standard error is based on the assumption that repeated observations of the same phenomenon—for example, the velocity of light—are to be assigned equal weight. It is useful to explore a case of n observations of a phenomenon, $x_1, \ldots, x_n$. If $\bar{x}$ is the mean of these observations—i.e., $\bar{x} = \frac{1}{n} (x_1 + x_2 + \cdots + x_n)$—and s is the sample standard deviation, defined as the square root of the mean squared deviation—i.e.,

$$s = \sqrt{\frac{1}{n}\left[(x_1 - \bar{x})^2 + \ldots + (x_n - \bar{x})^2\right]},$$

then the standard error of $\bar{x}$ is $s/\sqrt{n}$, and it is said that the "true" value of the observed variable lies in the interval between $\bar{x}$ plus $s/\sqrt{n}$ and $\bar{x}$ minus $s/\sqrt{n}$. A more detailed interpretation of the standard error and a critical scrutiny of the assumptions underlying its use are beyond the scope of this article (see STATISTICS; also see below *Bibliography*, the work by I. Todhunter). A few brief remarks will have to suffice here.

Under very general assumptions, it may be shown that the sum of independent random errors of observation has, as the number of terms becomes large, a normal (bell-shaped) distribution with mean μ and standard deviation σ, in which μ is the sum of the means of the individual sources of error and σ^2 is the sum of their individual variances (standard deviations squared); i.e., $\sigma^2 = \sigma_1^2 + \sigma_2^2 + \ldots + \sigma_q^2$, in which there are q sources of error. (For discussion of the normal distribution with population mean μ and variance σ, see STATISTICS.) This formulation, known as the central limit theorem, is one of the fundamental theorems of modern probability theory. Its importance lies in the fact that it is largely independent of the particular character or distribution of the individual errors. It was first stated by Laplace in 1812 and given its first rigorous proof in 1901 under fairly general assumptions by the Russian Aleksandr Lyapunov, known for his mathematical studies of stability and probability.

Probabilistic
models

In recent years different probabilistic models have been developed for the study of human behaviour, especially behaviour that expresses a choice or preference among several alternatives. Such models are devised to measure the strength of preference so as to predict the probability of choice—for experience in everyday life and in the laboratory has shown that men and animals will vary their choice of one alternative over another in what are externally identical conditions. One simple and useful model is this: if $v(x)$ is defined as the utility or value of x—i.e., the numerical measure of the strength of preference for x—and $p(x,y)$ as the probability of choosing x over y, then the model postulates that $p(x,y) = v(x)/[v(x) + v(y)]$. The problem for the theory of measurement is to show what properties the observed probabilities $p(x,y)$ must have in order for such a utility function v to exist. If a child, for instance, chooses chocolate ice cream (c) over licorice (l) with probability two-thirds, licorice over a banana (b) with probability two-thirds, and b over c with probability two-thirds, then no such strength of preference function v can be found for the set $\{b,c,l\}$.

MEASUREMENT IN SPECIAL DISCIPLINES

Classical
physics

Measurement in physics. The development of the central concepts of classical physics—such as the mechanical concepts of mass, force, momentum, and kinetic energy, and electromagnetical concepts such as those of current, voltage, resistance, and impedance—has been closely intertwined with the development of procedures for measuring quantitatively the properties of the phenomena associated with the concept. The theory and practice of extensive measurement, as discussed above (see above

Axiomatic basis of measurement), and the theory of dimensions and units (see above *Dimensions and units of measurement*) have been developed mainly in the context of classical physics.

One of the most important attitudes toward measurement in classical physics was the firmly rooted belief that, with sufficient effort, errors of measurement could be eliminated in principle and that there would be no limitation to the precision of measurement and, consequently, to the accuracy to which theories might be pushed in testing their validity. Although classical physics continues to be of major importance in applied science, a much more restrained attitude toward measurement now is customary. In the applications of classical electromagnetic theory, for example, it is customary to impose a lower limit defining the smallest admissible length to be considered: a typical restriction is to keep all lengths greater than one-tenth of a millimetre in order to avoid any atomic or subatomic effects that would fall properly within in quantum theory.

Modern
physics

A central concept of Einstein's theory of relativity and one that has had an enormous impact on modern physics is its revision of the classical concept of simultaneity, which restricts it to immediately adjacent events. There is no well-defined concept of two events at astronomical distances occurring simultaneously; this means that classical procedures for the measurement of simultaneity have been shown to be mistaken in their fundamental assumptions and that the concept of simultaneous distant events is as mistaken as that of absolute position in space.

At another level of analysis are the so-called Lorentz transformations of special relativity, which formulate the relations between two differently moving space–time frames. It is possible to give a self-contained and elementary derivation of these transformations (without any assumptions of continuity or linearity) from a single axiom asserting that the relativistic interval between any two space–time points connected by a possible inertial path of a particle remains the same in all inertial frames of reference. In other words, just two stipulations—that the macroscopic measurement of such relativistic distances be conducted along inertial paths (those followed naturally by unaccelerated particles) and that these measurements be invariant for any inertial frame of reference—are sufficient to establish the fundamental principle that any two inertial frames of reference are related by Lorentz transformations.

The theory of measurement has been important in quantum mechanics for two distinct but related conceptual reasons. One deals with the fundamental discovery that it is not possible to measure simultaneously with arbitrary precision the position and momentum of subatomic particles such as, for example, electrons or photons. The best known way of expressing this fact is in terms of the Heisenberg uncertainty principle, so-called after Werner Heisenberg, a German quantum physicist, which states that the product of the standard error of measurement of position and momentum must exceed a certain positive constant (for a more detailed discussion, see MECHANICS, QUANTUM).

The strangeness of this discovery, from the standpoint of classical physics, has been one of the most discussed problems of modern physics. Efforts to account for the theoretical uncertainties in measurement or the theoretical limits on the precision of measurement have been a central focus of conceptual discussions of the foundations of quantum mechanics. From the standpoint of classical statistical theory, perhaps what is most surprising about the Heisenberg uncertainty principle and related aspects of quantum mechanics is that one is not able to study the covariance of position and velocity measurements. The necessity of looking only at the marginal probability distributions of position and momentum and at the marginal distributions of other conjugate observables in quantum mechanics is the source of the sharpest break between the methodology of quantum mechanics and that of classical statistical theory as used both in classical physics and in other domains of science.

The second aspect of measurement that has been fundamental in quantum mechanics is the interaction between the measurement instrument and the measured object. In classical physics it was assumed that the interference of the measuring instrument can in principle be reduced to zero; in quantum mechanics the complicated and detailed analysis of the situation, in which the opposite is a fundamental assumption, has proved to be difficult and elusive.

Measurement in the social sciences and psychology. These fields pose special problems for measurement theory.

Economics and psychology. An important reason why economics is the most advanced of the social sciences—advanced in predictive power, social usefulness, and formal theory—is that the many important economic variables may be easily measured. Much of both economic theory and data are cast in terms of price and quantity. The problems associated with these concepts are not so much ones of measurement as they are of aggregation to provide representative measures for large economic units, such as an entire industry or a whole economy. Social indices, such as cost of living or gross national product, involve subtle questions of equivalence, statistical sampling, and the like.

In spite of their success in using the concepts of price and quantity, economists recognize that individuals often base their decisions on more subjective concepts. One approach is to suppose that such individuals have a numerical measure of utility, which they try to maximize. Early attempts to introduce utility into economics employed a representation that, in essence, assumed that the utility of a bundle of commodities is the sum of the utilities of the several commodities; but little attempt was made to axiomatize the representation, and, for various reasons, that hypothesis was discredited. In the 1940s it was suggested that utility could be measured by taking into account the risky character of decision alternatives. Taking a and b as the alternatives and P as a probability, these scholars symbolized by aPb the risky alternative in which one receives either a or b, the former with probability P and the latter with probability $1 - P$. They then axiomatized orderings over such structures to show that an order-preserving numerical assignment exists with the expected-utility property: $u(aPb) = u(a)P + u(b)(1 - P)$. Under these conditions, decision making becomes equivalent to maximizing expected utility. This idea has received considerable development since the end of World War II. Its main thrust has been the more careful formulation of what an alternative is in terms of various outcomes associated with different chance events and the generalization of the representation theorem to one in which, in addition to constructing the utility function, a (subjective) probability function over events is also constructed from the preference ordering of the alternatives in such a way that subjective expected utility is order preserving.

Although these ideas originated in economics and statistics, psychologists were quick to recognize the problem as one of individual preferences, and they have run numerous experiments to assess its descriptive adequacy. To oversimplify considerably, the major qualitative property known as the (extended) sure-thing principle is not valid. Roughly, this property asserts that if, no matter what possibility is realized, the outcomes of one gamble are at least as satisfactory as the corresponding ones of another, then the former gamble will be preferred or indifferent to the latter one—in the above notation, $aPb \geq a'P'b' \equiv (aPb)Qc \geq (a'P'b')Qc$. This principle is analogous to independence in additive conjoint measurement and to weak monotonicity in extensive measurement. As a postulate of rational behaviour, however, it has not been seriously questioned; thus, interest in the theory remains.

As was noted above (see above *In psychology*), some psychological theories include parameters that may be interpreted as measures of psychological attributes, parameters of which prototypic examples are found in the study of the detection and recognition of simple sensory signals. Perhaps the best known example is the theory of signal detectability, adapted from electrical engineering, which has two main parameters: d', which in effect de-

scribes how detectable the signal is against its background noise, and β, which describes how willing the subject is to interpret evidence as favouring the hypothesis that the signal is present. The former is affected by the signal-to-noise ratio, whereas the latter is manipulated by payoffs and the proportion of trials on which signals are presented. Given these two numbers, the theory specifies how to calculate the response probabilities for a variety of experimental designs.

Another type of psychological research attempts to treat the person as a null-measuring instrument—*i.e.*, as a sensor that records the point at which a difference becomes imperceptible—by having him establish equivalent intensity ratios in different sense modalities, such as sight and sound. These procedures of cross-modality matching yield approximate power relations among the usual physical measures of intensity. Various attempts are being made to place these results in either of two contexts: fundamental measurement theory or elaborations of existing theories of local psychophysics.

Sociology and demography. The main object of sociology as a science is the study of social groups and institutions and the causes of change within them. Many traditional theories in sociology have been of a speculative sort, not easily subjected to quantitative test. An increasing emphasis on quantitative theories and concepts, however, has inspired a greater concern with problems of measurement. The one part of sociology that from its beginning has emphasized quantitative data and analysis is demography, which is concerned with the quantitative study of human populations and the causes of changes in population. Though demographers are interested mainly in the measurement of factors of population change—including births, deaths, and migrations—they are also concerned with questions of population composition in terms of age, sex, and other characteristics. As in the case of sociology in general, there have been few fundamental problems of measurement of a direct sort in demography; the problems have been primarily of a statistical sort—to infer, for example, future birth trends from intensive field studies of selected samples of a population, although the trend is toward greater accuracy. Perhaps the most successful application of measurement in demography has been in the construction of the mortality tables used by insurance companies and government agencies.

BIBLIOGRAPHY. D.H. KRANTZ *et al.*, *Foundations of Measurement*, vol. 1 (1971), a comprehensive treatise in which the whole axiomatic view, including many examples of representation and uniqueness theorems, is developed extensively; JOHANN PFANZAGL, *Theory of Measurement* (1968), an earlier, briefer general treatise; R.D. LUCE and P. SUPPES, "Preference, Utility, and Subjective Probability," in R.D. LUCE, R.R. BUSH, and E. GALANTER (eds.), *Handbook of Mathematical Psychology*, vol. 3, pp. 249–410 (1965), an extensive review of preference models; P.C. FISHBURN, *Utility Theory for Decision Making* (1970), a concise mathematical summary of results in utility theory; BRUNO KISCH, *Scales and Weights: A Historical Outline* (1965), an excellent survey of the more practical aspects, with special emphasis on the history of the instruments used for scales and weights; DAVID HILBERT, *Die Grundlagen der Geometrie* (1899; Eng. trans., *The Foundations of Geometry*, 1902, reprinted 1950), one of the first fully satisfactory axiomatizations of geometry from a formal standpoint; JOHANN VON NEUMANN and OSKAR MORGENSTERN, *Theory of Games and Economic Behavior*, 3rd ed. (1953), the original treatise on the theory of games; S.S. STEVENS, "On the Theory of Scales of Measurement," *Science*, 103:677–680 (1946), his original classification of scales; ISAAC TODHUNTER, *A History of the Mathematical Theory of Probability from the Time of Pascal to That of Laplace* (1865, reprinted 1949), includes an excellent discussion of the early history of the concept of standard error; JOHANN VON NEUMANN, *Mathematische Grundlagen der Quantenmechanik* (1943; Eng. trans., *Mathematical Foundations of Quantum Mechanics*, 1955), a classical treatise containing what remains one of the best discussions of the effects of instrumentation on measurement.

(R.D.L./P.Su.

Meat and Meat-Packing

Meat, commonly defined as the edible portion and associated parts of mammals, is usually restricted to beef, veal,

---

Marginal notes:

Measurements of price, quantity, and utility

Sensation

Recent efforts at quantification

lamb, and pork, thus distinguishing meat from fish and fowl. Beef refers to meat from cattle; veal to that from calves; pork to that from pigs; lamb to that from young sheep; and mutton to that from sheep over one year old.

The meat industry purchases livestock, converts meat animals into food and nonfood products, and distributes and sells both the fresh and processed food products and the by-products of a nonfood nature. Meat-packing facilities vary in capacity. Plants range from those processing only a few head of livestock each year to those with a processing capacity of several million. Many plants conduct no slaughtering operations, buying meat at wholesale for further processing and sale to the retail and institutional trade. This group includes sausage manufacturers, meat canners, and other companies specializing in processed meat products.

World production and consumption. Perhaps the most striking statistic about world food production and consumption is that the United States produces and consumes 35 percent of the world's meat supply. Britain, the United States, and Germany are major importing countries; Argentina, Australia, New Zealand, and Denmark are major exporting countries. Many countries are both exporters and importers of meat products, importing one kind of meat and exporting another. The United States, for example, imports processed meat and canned hams and exports processed meat products to the Caribbean and United States territories. The world's major meat-exporting areas are South America, Oceania (Australia, New Zealand), and western Europe; North America and western Europe are major importing areas. The world's chief cattle-producing countries include India, with 176,-000,000 head; the United States, 109,000,000; Soviet Union, 97,000,000; Brazil, 90,000,000; and China, 63,-000,000. The leading sheep-producing countries are Australia, 167,000,000; New Zealand, 60,000,000; Argentina, 48,000,000; India, 42,000,000; Republic of South Africa, 38,000,000; United States, 22,000,000; and Ethiopia, 13,000,000. The major hog-producing countries are Brazil, 63,000,000; United States, 55,000,000; and West Germany, 19,000,000.

The major producers are also, generally speaking, the major consumers. The highest per capita red-meat consuming countries are New Zealand, 224 pounds (102 kilograms) per capita per year; Uruguay, 218 pounds (99 kilograms); Australia, 204 pounds (92 kilograms); Argentina, 220 pounds (100 kilograms); United States, 185 pounds (84 kilograms). But the United Kingdom, not a major producer, is a major consumer with 138 pounds (63 kilograms) per capita, while certain countries, like India, rank low in consumption, despite high production, apparently owing to religious prohibitions.

The meat of rabbit, horse, goat, and deer are regularly consumed in some countries, and various other mammalian species are eaten in small quantities in some parts of the world. Seal and polar bear are included in the Eskimo diet, while rhinoceros, hippopotamus, and elephant are occasionally consumed by the tribes of Central Africa.

Meat in the human diet. Meat is outstanding for its nutritive value. Based on the daily recommended allowances for a 22-year-old man, a 3½ ounce (99 gram) serving of cooked meat provides 45 percent of the needed protein, 9 percent of the calories, 36 percent of the iron, 31 percent of the thiamine, 15 percent of the riboflavin, and 26 percent of the niacin. Because of its appearance, aroma, and flavour, meat has almost universal appetite appeal. Such palatable food aids in digestion by stimulating the flow of the digestive juices. Meat has a high satiety value, giving a feeling of satisfaction and well-being that staves off hunger for longer periods than other foods.

Protein is essential to growth and life. Differences among proteins are reflected primarily in the amount and kind of amino acids they contain. Amino acids, consisting of carbon, hydrogen, oxygen, nitrogen, and sulfur, are the building blocks of proteins. Eight of the amino acids that humans cannot synthesize are essential for growth and maintenance of body tissues. Proteins containing all

of the essential amino acids in the proportions most useful to the body are described as having biological value. Meat proteins are among the most important of these. Extreme protein deficiency may result in poor muscle tone and posture, lowered resistance to disease, premature aging, anemia, stunted growth in children, tissue degeneration, edema, and slow recovery from illness or surgery. Severe cases of protein-deficiency disease in children, known clinically as kwashiorkor and often found in tropical countries, can be avoided by supplementing diets with high-quality protein.

Meat is an excellent source of B vitamins, including thiamine, one of the most important. Pork is the best source of thiamine, liver is next, and skeletal muscle, from any meat source, is third. Extreme thiamine shortage may result in beriberi, a deficiency disease common in the Far East. Liver is an excellent source of riboflavin, another B vitamin that combines with protein in the body to form important oxidative enzymes. All meats supply niacin, which helps to build and maintain a healthy skin, nervous system, and digestive system. Extreme niacin deficiency leads to pellagra. Meat also provides other essential B vitamins, such as pyridoxine, involved in amino acid metabolism, and vitamin B_{12}, needed for formation of red blood cells.

Meat is also a good source of the essential minerals iron, phosphorus, potassium, sodium, and magnesium.

MEAT STRUCTURE, CHEMISTRY, AND MICROBIOLOGY

Meat structure. Most edible meat portions are made up of skeletal muscle, connective tissue, fat, and bone.

Muscle. There are three types of muscle: involuntary muscle associated with the digestive system; involuntary cardiac muscle; and voluntary skeletal muscle. Muscle is composed of approximately 75 percent water and 20 percent protein, with fats, carbohydrates, and minerals composing the remaining 5 percent. Muscles are made up of fibres, or muscle cells, each covered by a thin membrane, the sarcolemma. Small groups of fibres, joined by connective tissue (endomysium) into bundles, or fasciculi, are sheathed, together with fatty deposits, by more connective tissue, the perimysium, to form an entire muscle.

Meat grain is determined by the size of the muscle bundles and the connective tissue, small bundles producing fine grain, and large bundles producing coarser grain. Fibre-bundle size varies in different muscles of the same animal and in different species. The number of fibres present at birth does not increase; increased size results from growth of existing fibres. Muscles receiving the greatest use, such as the neck, leg, and shoulder muscles, develop thickened cell walls and connective tissue, producing meat without the tenderness of less developed muscles but with stronger flavour. Juiciness in meat results from high water retention. Muscles vary in ability to hold water, an ability partly affected by the degree of alkalinity present.

Connective tissue. The amount and type of connective tissue, affecting meat tenderness, is increased by muscle use and age. This tissue, covering muscle fibres, fibre bundles, and the entire muscle, is primarily composed of the proteins collagen and elastin. Collagen, the major component of white connective tissue, softens during cooking and is eventually converted to gelatin, producing greater tenderness in the meat. For this reason, prolonged cooking methods are most suitable for the tougher meat cuts. Elastin, the chief component of yellow connective tissue, is tough and resistant to change and is not affected by the heat of cooking.

Fat. Fat, present in all meat, exists in the live animal as small oil droplets, increasing in number and size as fattening, or finishing, proceeds. As the animal fattens, the proportion of lean and bone is reduced and the proportion of fat increases. Fat deposits cover the organs, separate muscles, and are distributed as marbling within the muscles. Marbling increases flavour and contributes to meat tenderness and juiciness by exerting an internal basting effect during cooking.

Meat chemistry. Muscle is a colloidal system of approximately 72–73 percent water, 18 percent protein,

Major importers and exporters

Amino acids in proteins

Muscle composition

1–2 percent soluble nonprotein substances, variable amounts of fat (1–20 percent), and small amounts of ash (1 percent) and carbohydrate (1 percent).

Protein. Muscles contain two kinds of proteins: muscle-cell proteins and connective-tissue proteins. Protein percentage decreases as the amount of fat increases. Myosin, comprising the greatest portion of muscle-cell protein, is soluble in salt solutions and will gel when heated. Actin, another protein, is water soluble. Actomyosin, protein formed from the combination of actin and myosin, is the substance producing muscle contraction.

Colour
changes

Myoglobin, a water-soluble muscle protein, affects meat colour. Originally purplish-red, when combined with oxygen it forms bright-red oxymyoglobin, visible on the surface of fresh meat after exposure to oxygen. The application of heat changes the colour to brown.

Fat. As fatty tissue increases during growth and fattening, a higher proportion of the extra fat is deposited in the fatty tissue, and a smaller portion in the muscular tissue. Fats, insoluble in water but soluble in organic solvents, are composed primarily of tryglycerides, mixtures of glycerol and fatty acids. Animal fat provides arachidonic, an essential unsaturated fatty acid.

Carbohydrates. Glycogen, the principal carbohydrate in skeletal muscle, changes to lactic acid immediately after the animal is slaughtered.

Postmortem meat changes. Muscle, soft at the time the animal is slaughtered, hardens soon after, becoming extremely tough with reduced water-retention capacity. The meat is hung in a cooler for several days until the hardening passes, apparently by enzyme action, and the muscle softens and regains its water-holding ability.

Rigor
mortis

When circulation stops, absence of oxygen encourages the breakdown of the carbohydrate glycogen into glucose, which is in turn reduced to lactic acid. Rigor mortis occurs when the pH (range from acidity to alkalinity) is sufficiently lowered (high acidity), usually reaching its greatest degree within 24 hours, after which the muscle begins to soften. The amount of glycogen present in the muscle at slaughtering, because of the time required for its change to lactic acid, will affect the pH level. Rapid pH drop produces a condition called acid rigor, in which the muscle loses its water-holding capacity, becoming pale, soft, and "weepy." When the pH remains fairly high, alkaline rigor develops, and the muscle retains its dark colour and juices. Extreme alkaline rigor, however, will result in "dark cutting" meat—*e.g.*, meat that is darker in colour than normal.

Tissue changes and their causes. Relaxed muscle fibres are long; contracted muscle fibres are short. Some shortening occurs during rigor mortis, the extent varying with lactic acid accumulation and physical restraint on the muscle caused by vertical suspension of the carcass.

Cold-produced changes. Upon completion of slaughter, including removal of the viscera and the skin (beef), pelt (lamb), or hair (pig), carcasses are usually placed in coolers at 32° F (0° C) to remove body heat, and carcass temperature decreases from approximately 100° F (38° C) to the temperature of the holding cooler. Muscle temperature at the time of rigor mortis influences meat quality.

Muscle
shortening

Responses of surface-exposed muscles in a 32° F (0° C) environment vary according to species. In beef and lamb, exposed, unrestrained muscles undergo extreme "cold shortening," resulting in tough meat. Prevention of shortening is more important than actually stretching the muscle. Pork muscle, particularly, when held in a warm environment during rigor mortis development, experiences acceleration of glucose fermentation (glycolysis), decreasing meat quality. When beef is held at close to body temperature, the unrestrained muscles will shorten, although not as severely as at 32° F (0° C).

Muscle frozen before rigor and allowed to thaw in an unrestrained state, may shorten to 20–25 percent of original length. Because of this severe shortening, resulting in excessive juice loss and toughening, muscle is not immediately excised and frozen after slaughter. Although retention on the carcass prevents many of the deleterious effects, there is no assurance of prevention of localized shortening, a phenomenon that even precludes carcass freezing before rigor onset. The sudden release of calcium ions during thawing causes violent contracture; the same phenomena apparently occur during cold shortening.

Enzyme tenderization. The use of enzymes, such as papain or bromolein, produces significant meat tenderization. When these enzymes are injected in the animal before slaughter, the carcasses are sold as especially tenderized products. Some firms also inject enzymes postmortem; other establishments place the enzymes on the cut surface. The enzymes are presumably activated only over a narrow range of temperature during cooking, and although they would ideally act primarily on the connective tissues, some may also act on the muscle fibre proteins.

Aging. In aging, meat is held at 32° F (0° C) for approximately two to three weeks, or at higher temperatures for shorter periods, allowing natural tenderization. Surface spoilage or drying sometimes occurs during aging, necessitating excessive trimming.

Microbiology. *Spoilage.* The kinds and numbers of micro-organisms present on meat surfaces or within the meat are influenced by the pretreatment of the product, including: (1) kind and extent of contamination and previous opportunities for growth of certain kinds of organisms; and (2) physical properties of the meat, including the amount of exposed area. When meat is ground, the surface area is greatly increased, releasing moisture and distributing organisms throughout the meat, thereby encouraging microbial growth.

Chemical properties, such as moisture content, pH, and meat composition, affect the kind and number of organisms. Moisture content is one factor determining which organisms will predominate. When moisture is limited, molds will grow and become the dominant organism; yeasts require more moisture; bacteria growth requires even greater amounts of water. Therefore, relative humidity of the storage area is important. Since temperature is the most important factor influencing the kind of organism growth and type of spoilage occurring, meat should be stored at temperatures not far above freezing, allowing only low-temperature organism growth.

Meat discoloration and bacterial spoilage may be initiated during handling and packaging of meat for merchandising, when greater surface areas are exposed to possible juice loss and bacterial contamination. Increased handling and fluctuating temperature reduce keeping qualities. Harmful bacteria include *Pseudomonas, Achromobacter, Micrococcus, Streptococcus, Lactobacillus,* and *Clostridium.* Meat is an ideal culture medium because it is high in moisture, rich in nitrogenous foods, plentifully supplied with minerals and accessory growth factors, and usually has some fermentable carbohydrates and favorable pH for most micro-organisms.

Harmful
bacteria

Specific spoilage considerations. Molds, generally appearing dry and fuzzy to the human eye, are commonly white, green, or black, although numerous colours are possible. Molds give a musty flavour to the meat in the vicinity of their growth. The chief molds affecting meat are *Cladosporium, Mucor,* and *Alternaria* genera.

Slimes, not as readily recognized as molds, are slippery or greasy appearing in their early stages, and may be mistaken for a film of fat on the product. The early stage of sliming may be diagnosed by drawing a knife blade across the meat surface. If slime is present, a soft, creamy material will be gathered on the blade, consisting almost entirely of cells of micro-organisms that have grown extensively to produce spoilage.

Spoilage caused by pigmented bacteria appears as various coloured spots, usually red, yellow, and blue, on the meat surface. Greenish-blue to brownish-black spots, found on stored beef, are also caused by pigmented bacteria. Purple "stamping ink" discoloration of surface fat is caused by yellow pigmented cocci and rods; when the fat becomes rancid, the yellow colour changes to a greenish shade, later becoming purplish to blue.

Off odours and tastes in meat, resulting from growth of

bacteria on the surface, are often evident before other spoilage signs.

Souring, putrefaction, and taint are common types of spoilage under anaerobic conditions (without presence of air). Souring can result from the action of the meat's own enzymes during aging; from production of fatty acids or lactic acid by bacterial action; or from protein decomposition, sometimes called "stinking sour fermentation." Putrefaction, anaerobic decomposition of protein, produces such foul-smelling compounds as ammonia, hydrogen sulfide, and mercaptans. The terms bone taint or bone sour usually refer to putrefaction, and sometimes to souring, near the bone. This condition occurs commonly near the joints in hams.

Meat preservation.   Preservation is concerned with preventing development of undesirable micro-organisms, especially harmful bacteria causing spoilage or decomposition and decay. The economy of the meat industry is highly influenced by meat perishability. Most of the edible tissues of healthy pigs, beef, veal, and lambs are sterile, or contain very low micro-organism population levels. The slaughtering process, by severing the vascular system, introduces the first major contamination. Selection of a preservation method is influenced by the effect on quality, health hazards, marketing, and actual cost.

Refrigeration and freezing.   Refrigeration is the most widely used method of preserving fresh meat. Low temperatures retard microbial growth and inhibit enzymatic and chemical reaction. The shelf life of fresh meat at temperatures between 28° and 32° F (−2° and 0° C) is largely influenced by the amount of contamination that the meat has previously encountered.

When meat temperature is reduced below 28° F (−2° C), the meat will freeze, undergoing physical change and alteration of the chemical changes which occur. Fresh meat, properly prepared and frozen and stored below 0° F (−18° C), can be preserved for several months with little loss in original palatability. In meat frozen without proper wrapping, however, the surface will undergo "freezer burn," developing serious deterioration and becoming bleached and unattractive in appearance. The major problem in frozen meat is oxidation of the fat, causing a change in aroma after a long storage period. This problem is greatest in pork, which has a higher percentage of the more easily oxidized unsaturated fatty acids than found in beef, veal, or lamb.

For maximum eating quality, frozen meat should not be thawed and refrozen or stored frozen beyond a certain number of months. Refreezing produces crystal enlargement and a greater amount of ice formation and tissue damage, resulting in increased drip loss during subsequent thawing and greater cooking loss. When frozen meat is thawed and held in a thawed condition, rapidity of microbial growth and damage will be influenced by the amount of contamination present before freezing. The occurrence of fluctuating temperatures during frozen storage increases ice crystal size and, subsequently, the amount of drip loss upon thawing.

Curing.   Frozen storage has replaced curing as the major meat preservation method. Curing is now primarily used to provide flavour and a cured meat colour that is retained during cooking.

In the preservation of meat by curing, the addition of curing salts creates a selective bacteriological medium limiting the kinds of micro-organisms capable of the rapid growth that encourages spoilage. Although smoke and heat, both usually applied to cured products, reduce surface bacterial population, smoke does not play an important role in retarding meat-product spoilage.

Freeze-drying.   Meat freeze-dried by conventional methods remains frozen throughout the drying cycle, permitting moisture content reduction to less than 2 percent without appreciable alteration in form. Portions must be thin to be readily rehydratable, and this requirement somewhat limits the preservation technique. Another limitation is the need to hold the product in the absence of air and moisture.

Canning.   Meat is cooked thoroughly in preparation for canning, then packed in hermetically sealed cans, either as a single product, or in combination with other food products, forming luncheon meats. Acceptance of canned meats has increased, and highly trimmed quality cuts are now available in canned form.

MEAT TYPES

Meat quality refers to a combination of traits producing an edible product with minimum loss of constituents; without undesirable characteristics after processing and storage; remaining attractive in appearance; and appetizing, nutritious, and palatable after cooking. Meat quantity, referring to the amount of muscle in relation to bone and fat covering, is also a factor in judging meats.

Governments often establish meat quality standards based upon such highly variable properties as marbling and maturing and also upon such factors as colour, firmness, and texture. The Codex Alimentarius Commission, sponsored by the Food and Agriculture Organization and the World Health Organization, was established in 1961 to consider uniform international food standards. In the early 1970s the Codex Committee on Meat and Meat Products was working on a classification and grading system for carcasses and cuts of beef, lamb, mutton, pork, and veal and was also considering hygiene standards for fresh meat.

Beef and veal.   Beef animals ranging in weight from 1,000 to 1,200 pounds (450 to 545 kilograms) are usually preferred, although considerable variation exists among beef-consuming countries. The carcass weight of a beef animal ready for market will be about 55–60 percent of its live weight. Thickness of the body wall and degree of fatness influence yield, with old cows yielding only 45 percent of their live weight as carcass, and overly fat, adequately muscled animals yielding close to 70 percent of their weight. Beef carcasses and wholesale cuts have the greatest value when they meet high quality standards and have a high yield of preferred retail cuts, with minimum waste in the form of fat or bone.

Beef quality attributes include (1) maturity, (2) marbling, (3) texture of the lean, (4) lean and fat firmness, and (5) lean and fat colour.

In youthful beef carcasses, the split spinous processes of the vertebrae are soft, red, porous, and tipped with large amounts of soft, pearly white cartilage. Cartilage ossifies as the animal matures, and in very mature cows, all of the cartilage is completely ossified. Within wide limits, muscle colour changes as the animal matures. Texture of lean refers to the prominence of muscle bundles: all other factors being satisfactory, if the muscle bundles are fine, the muscle is likely to be tender. Firmness is important because it reflects to some extent the ability of muscle to hold its juices during cooking. Beef cuts showing coarse, soft muscle and excessive weepage are undesirable for retail marketing.

Moderate amounts of finely and uniformly dispersed marbling (intramuscular fat) in firm red muscle, from a relatively young animal, is considered ideal. Excessive marbling is not desirable, but extremely limited marbling makes beef less palatable than beef with adequate marbling. Beef from old animals is usually less tender than beef from young animals. The range in certain other muscle characteristics considered responsible for eating quality is also variable.

Beef colour varies from pale pink to the extremely dark colour, called "dark-cutting," and the average consumer cannot distinguish between dark cutting beef and beef from old animals or beef held under adverse conditions. Fat should be firm, free from greasy or oily appearance, and white to creamy white in colour. Yellow fat, sometimes appearing on beef and lamb carcasses and on the carcasses of certain breeds of dairy cows, results from concentration of fat-soluble carotinoid pigments.

Quality veal is dry, grayish-pink in colour, and firm in structure. The variety of methods normally utilized in cooking veal makes visible quality features less significant than in beef. Age and nutrition, however, greatly influence veal colour and firmness, and intramuscular fat is rarely visible. Consumers often avoid veal that is too red because of its resemblance to calf or beef.

Marginal notes: Meat quality · Carcass weight · Marbling · "Freezer burn"

Beef carcass standards often provide maturity groups ranging from the most youthful through the most advanced maturity grade, having hard, white china bones, with wide, flat rib bones, and musculature dark red and coarse in texture. Yield grades identify carcasses according to differences in yield of boneless, closely trimmed retail cuts from the round, loin, rib, and chuck.

Figure 1 shows the beef carcass with its wholesale cuts

By courtesy of the National Live Stock and Meat Board

Figure 1: Wholesale and retail cuts of beef (see text).

and lists the names given to the retail cuts commonly made from each of the wholesale cuts. A beef carcass is normally split into two sides, with each side shipped and cut separately.

Figure 2 shows wholesale veal cuts and lists the retail cuts commonly made from each. Cutting is normally accomplished at the retail sales location, and the carcasses are not usually split into sides prior to retail fabrication. The practice of centralized cutting at the packing plant or wholesale-dealer level is, however, becoming increasingly common.

By courtesy of the National Live Stock and Meat Board

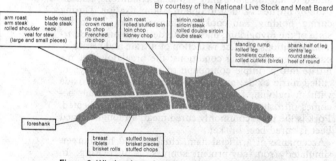

Figure 2: Wholesale and retail cuts of veal (see text).

Pork. Market pigs weigh approximately 200–300 pounds (90–135 kilograms) and yield carcasses weighing 70–74 percent of their live weight. Average back-fat thickness and area of the cross section of the longissimus muscle at the tenth rib are among the measurements used to describe quantitative carcass characteristics. These measures are intended to be estimates of the four lean cuts: ham, loin, shoulder, and butt. Yields are expressed as a percentage of the carcass weight.

Barrow (castrated male) and gilt (young female) carcasses represent the bulk of pigs slaughtered; sows (females having raised young) and boars (uncastrated males) are also marketed. The characteristic boar odour decreases desirability of boar carcasses.

The second factor in pork carcass evaluation is the quality of the lean muscle, judged by firmness of fat and lean, colour, marbling, and texture of the lean. The most desirable pork has a firm, dry surface, pinkish red in colour. The quality indicating characteristics evident on the cut surface of a major muscle, in addition to marbling, include firmness, colour, and exudation, and range in description from pale, soft, exudative (PSE) pork, to dark, firm, dry (DFD) pork.

Pork grades are primarily based on anticipated yields of the four lean cuts. Carcasses differ in lean cut yields because of differences in both degree of fatness and degree of muscling (thickness of muscling in relation to skeletal size), and these factors are considered in relation to car-

Carcass length

cass weight as the basis for assigning numbered grades. Figure 3 shows the pork carcass form with its wholesale cuts and lists the common retail cuts made from each of them.

By courtesy of the National Live Stock and Meat Board

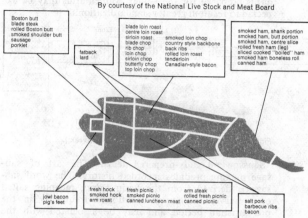

Figure 3: Wholesale and retail cuts of pork (see text).

Lamb. Lambs (wethers, castrated males; ewes, females) ready for market usually weigh between 100 and 150 pounds (45 and 65 kilograms). Regional or national preferences affect desirability. Traits associated with carcass desirability, cutability, and quality reflect the proportionate yield of preferred retail cuts and consumer acceptance, including palatability. Greater consideration is generally given to cutability, or proportion of carcass weight salable at retail level, than to quality. Desirable carcasses have a high percentage of weight in the preferred leg, loin, rack, and shoulder cuts. The internal fat of the pelvic cavity and around the kidney is extremely variable and must be estimated carefully. Ideal lamb carcass fat covering is approximately 0.1 inch (2.5 millimetres) over the centre of the rib eye.

Quality in lamb, as in other species, refers to factors influencing acceptability and palatability. Quality lamb muscle has a firm, dry surface, modest marbling, and varies in colour from light to dark pink. Dark muscle colour and yellow fat both suggest mutton-like properties and, where lamb is preferred, may be considered detrimental. Specific ages are usually defined for slaughter lambs, yearlings, and mature mutton. Estimates of maturity are based on ossification and shape of bones and colour and texture of lean. Youthful lambs have pinkish lean, and their shanks are separated at the break joints; mutton carcasses have dark-red lean and spool joints on their front shanks; yearling mutton carcasses are between these two extremes. The spool joint (round) is on the lower end of the metacarpal when the foot is removed at the ankle (next to the metacarpal bone). The break joint is located immediately above the spool joint at the zone of bone growth, the junction of the epiphysis and diaphysis. Growth in this zone stops when cartilage regeneration ceases; then the bones can no longer be separated at the break joint. Since this ossification of the break joint occurs physiologically at an age of about one year, the condition of this joint can be used to distinguish between lamb and yearling carcasses. Mutton terminology is applied to lambs two years of age or older.

Lamb carcass grades are usually based on maturity, feathering (meaning the fat streaking in muscle between the ribs), fat streaking on the inside of the flank muscles, and firmness of the fat and lean.

Yield grades for lamb and mutton carcasses are concerned with differences in cutability or expected yield of boneless, closely trimmed, major retail cuts from the leg, loin, rack, and shoulder. Yield grades are determined by considering the amount of external fat, amount of kidney and pelvic fat, and conformation grade of the legs. External fat is measured over the 12th and 13th ribs, whereas kidney and pelvic fat must be estimated. Figure 4 shows wholesale lamb cuts and the retail cuts obtained from them.

Quality factors in lamb

Although the charts shown are based on U.S. wholesale and retail cuts and exact cuts and terminology may vary among countries, methods are generally similar. Increased international trade and future acceptance of standards prepared for the Codex Alimentarius may be expected to result in greater standardization.

By courtesy of the National Live Stock and Meat Board

Figure 4: Wholesale and retail cuts of lamb (see text).

Sausage and ready-prepared meats. The art of sausage making predates recorded history. The word sausage is derived from the Latin *salsus*, meaning salted or preserved. Salami is mentioned frequently in the pre-Christian period and may be associated with the Greek city of Salamis in Cyprus. The popularity of sausage spread, and by the Middle Ages, sausage making was widely practiced commercially. Sausage makers developed individual spicing formulas, their products taking on the name of the region or city in which they originated. From Frankfurt, Germany, came the frankfurter; from Bologna, Italy, bologna; and so on. Italy's warm climate encouraged development of such dry sausage varieties as genoa; the cooler German climate led to development of such fresh and cooked sausages as bratwurst, head cheese, and blood sausage.

Many European sausage makers eventually emigrated to the United States, where over 200 different sausage varieties are produced by nearly 3,000 meat processors. The wiener and frankfurter—the hot dog—has become the most popular sausage in the United States, where some 16,000,000,000 are consumed each year—about 80 per capita.

Sausages and prepared meats are popular throughout the world, consumed not only in Europe and the U.S. but also in Africa, Asia, and Latin America.

Sausage types and standards of identity. Sausage types are classified according to processing methods. Major classifications include fresh sausage, uncooked smoked sausage, cooked smoked sausage, cooked sausage, cooked meat specialties, and dry and semidry sausage.

Fresh sausage, made from uncured pork trimmings and sometimes beef, is delicately seasoned. It is sold in links, patties, or bulk, requires refrigeration, and must be thoroughly cooked before serving. Pork sausage and bratwurst are popular varieties.

The meat materials in uncooked smoked sausage are usually cured and smoked, but not cooked. Sausages must be refrigerated and require cooking. Mettwurst and Polish sausage are examples of this classification.

Cooked smoked sausage is usually made from cured meats. These sausages are chopped, seasoned, stuffed, smoked, and then cooked. They are usually warmed before serving. Popular examples include frankfurters and bologna.

Cooked sausage, prepared from fresh, uncured meats, is cooked and ready to serve. Liver sausage, a popular variety, is a mildly seasoned mixture of livers and pork jowls.

Cooked meat specialties, cooked or baked and ready to serve, are often prepared according to the individual manufacturer's formula and may be extended with such protein materials as soy-protein concentrate. They include spiced luncheon meat, meat loaf, deviled ham, jellied corned beef, and other similar products.

The dry and semi-dry sausage group includes "summer style" products, originally made in winter for summer consumption. They are dried and then fermented with lactic acid bacteria to produce the characteristic tangy flavour. In addition to summer sausages, this group includes pepperoni, landjaeger, and mortadella.

Commercial production. Manufacturers consider consumer preference in determining the type and quality of sausage to be produced. Modern equipment provides automated mass economical production; and scientific research has led to an understanding of essential processing steps and elimination of any nonessential steps. In some wiener production, for example, computers select raw material sources daily, and these materials are fed into continuous wiener processing machines. Neither the materials nor the finished product are handled by human hands. This processing method provides for the ultimate in quality control, and a process formerly taking 9 hours is now completed in 45 minutes.

Cured and smoked meats. Curing, until the last century used for preservation, is now employed primarily for flavour and colour development. Salt-penetration rate influences the time required for curing, and the method of administration and muscle qualities will also influence the required time. Formerly, dry-salt curing mixtures were rubbed into the meat, which was then aged in curing cellars for prolonged periods. Subsequent methods have included stitch pumping, the injection of brine at different points in the muscle; artery pumping, using the arterial system to circulate the brine; and the modern injecto-cure, employing automatic, multi-needled equipment to inject the curing solution into large meat cuts.

The classic meat-curing agent is a mixture of sodium chloride, either sodium nitrite or sodium nitrate or both, and sugar. Salt inhibits microbial growth by increasing osmotic pressure and lowering water activity. The good keeping qualities of the old "country cured" hams resulted from the relatively low moisture–salt ratio. Because salts accelerate rancidity development when frozen, curing and freezing are not normally combined. Sugar is added to aid in establishing reducing conditions, and nitrate or nitrite is added to obtain colour fixation. During curing, holding, and cooking, changes occurring in the state of the myoglobin, under both desirable and undesirable conditions, include reduction of nitrate and nitrite by bacteria and reducing conditions; the breakdown of the nitrite into a simple compound of nitrogen and oxygen, called nitric oxide; and the combination of nitric oxide with myoglobin, forming nitrosomyoglobin, which becomes nitroshemochrome, pink in colour, when heated. Pork is the most commonly cured meat, although corned beef is cured beef brisket.

Acceptance of artificial ham, chicken, and hamburger, simulated from soy-protein sources, is increasing. In the U.S., "hamburger" implies ground beef with about 20 percent fat and with no pork content. The Codex Committee on Processed Meat Products has been working to establish standards for various processed meat products.

MEAT QUALITY

The ideal level of meat quality combines the capacity to retain high nutritive value in cooked form with capacity to satisfy numerous functional roles in the fabrication and processing of acceptable products.

Measurement of quality. *Colour and juiciness.* Muscle colour varies with species, beef being the darkest, lamb intermediate, and pork the lightest. Muscle colour intensity also increases with the age of the animal; differences are easily detectable between veal, market-weight beef, and old cows. This difference partially results from myoglobin concentration, generally increasing with age. Red muscles contain a majority of red (pigmented) fibres, although certain muscles have some portions which are red and other portions which are white (low in red-fibre content). The colour of fresh meat is also influenced by the state of the surface myoglobin, or the relative proportions and distributions of the three meat pigments: purple reduced myoglobin, red oxyomyoglobin, and brown metmyoglobin.

Colour is also influenced by muscle texture. Muscle having an alkaline rigor has a closed structure; the proteins are associated with large quantities of water, appearing swollen and tightly packed. This muscle scatters little

(marginal notes)
National types of sausage

Salting

Influence of muscle texture on colour

incident light and will appear dark. The other extreme is pale, soft, exudative muscle, in which the proteins are highly denatured and the structure is "open." These muscles lose large quantities of juice when cooked, and because of the association between colour and water binding, colour is indirectly related to palatability.

Tenderness. Meat tenderness is influenced by either the contractile state of the muscle (tough if the fibres have shortened) or by the amount of cross-linking in the collagen (tough if cross-linking is excessive, as in some older animals). The physiological condition of the animal influences, to some extent, the amount of postmortem shortening that will occur. The temperature at which the carcass is held is also a factor, as well as excision or cutting, which relieves physical restraint on the muscle. The chronological age and the physiological condition of the animal also influence the alterations in the connective tissue. The amount of juice retained during cooking has an indirect influence on tenderness.

Aroma and flavour. Flavours, varying with species and chronological age, are usually enhanced in older animals. The amount of time that carcasses are aged in coolers also influences flavour and aroma, and prolonged aging tends to impart an "aged flavour" to the meat.

The sex of the animal only appears to influence flavour of meat when comparing barrow and gilt (pork) meat with boar meat (uncastrated male). In some boars, the characteristic odour may be quite prominent.

Factors influencing meat quality. The quality of fresh meat is influenced by a number of factors, which include firmness, marbling, connective tissue condition, and texture.

Firmness. High quality muscle has a rigid structure. Soft muscle results from the same factors contributing to low juice retention and is therefore even more objectionable than it would be on the basis of its lack of firmness alone. For processing, fabricating, slicing, and displaying, the meat firmness is an important attribute of quality, and any tendency toward softness reduces desirability. Firmness is also influenced by the nature and firmness of the fat itself, as well as by the variation in the muscle's fat content. In pigs, soft, oily fat usually results from the diet, which tends to deposit fats as consumed. Unsaturated fats are softer at a given temperature and are more susceptible to oxidative rancidity than are saturated fats.

Intramuscular fat (marbling). Marbling is the fat present within the boundaries of a muscle and can be visibly detected as the muscle cross-sectioned surface is exposed. Fine, evenly distributed marbling apparently reduces likelihood of dissatisfaction with the cooked product. A moderate quantity of marbling appears adequate to lubricate the muscle fibres, providing a juicy and flavourful cooked product. Large, coarse strands of marbling, unevenly dispersed throughout a muscle, are unsatisfactory because they do not provide sufficient fat distribution in the entire muscle area.

Connective tissue. The proportion of connective tissue in meat varies with its anatomical origin. The distal portions of the limbs, such as the shank, illustrate the converging of several locomotion muscles, each with an increasing proportion of epimysium blending into tendons attached to the skeleton. This cut would be less tender than the posture-control muscles located in other parts of the carcass.

Texture and fibre size. The size of fibre is somewhat influenced by the contractile state and influences the size of the fibre bundle. Size of muscle bundles is positively associated with visible coarseness of a cross-sectioned area of the muscle and is related to eating quality. Increased bundle size is associated with reduced tenderness.

The qualities of the fresh meat have an influence on its response during freezing and during storage in the frozen state. Meat should be frozen as rapidly as possible and stored at a temperature well below 0° F ($-18°$ C). Freezing cannot improve quality. Low quality meat, frozen or cured under the best conditions possible, will still be low quality when consumed. High quality meat, however, can deteriorate if not frozen, stored, or cured under proper conditions.

Factors influencing grade. Carcass maturity is a significant factor influencing beef- and lamb-carcass grades. Advances in maturity are reflected by calcification of cartilagenous tips on the spinous processes and by calcification of cartilage in the sacral region. In lamb, the calcification of the break joint makes it impossible to remove the foot at this joint. A widening of the costal bones (ribs) also occurs with advancing maturity.

Coarseness and marbling distribution are major factors affecting grade. A moderate amount of fine, evenly dispersed marbling is highly desirable, and coarseness is undesirable. With advancing maturity, a higher degree of marbling is required to equal the grading of a more youthful carcass.

Dark-coloured muscle, if objectionably dark, cannot be distinguished from muscle of very old animals or from muscle which has partially spoiled and is therefore unpopular.

Yellowish, soft, oily fat is undesirable and, if present in quantity, adversely affects the grade of pork carcasses.

Muscling is a major factor affecting pork-carcass grades and is a compensating factor in establishing the final grade for beef and lamb. Excessive fat has a major influence on pork-carcass grade and on yield grade of lamb and beef.

MEAT-PACKING INDUSTRY

History. Early commercial meat-packing operations, relying on ice for refrigeration, had to restrict slaughter to winter seasons. It was not until the late 19th century that mechanical refrigeration turned the meat-processing industry into a year-round operation. About 1900, mechanized disassembly procedures and conveyor procedures were being incorporated into regular operations.

Early methods

During the 1950s, major progress was made in both plant sanitation and packaging technology, increasing shelf life significantly and contributing to the expansion of self-service retailing. During the 1960s, the meat-packing industry achieved major advances in research and development.

Slaughtering methods and equipment. *Humane slaughter.* In both the United States and Europe the desirability of stunning was recognized before the end of the 19th century, and mechanical equipment for this was developed.

As other countries have become increasingly industrialized, similar practices have been applied. Cattle may be stunned by means of a captive-bolt pistol or a pneumatic gun. Sheep and pigs may be stunned by pistol, by electric shock, or by anesthetizing in a carbon dioxide chamber. After World War II, compressed-air stunners were commonly used for cattle and gas chambers for smaller animals.

In addition to stunning devices, large modern abattoirs use a wide variety of mechanical, electrical, and pneumatic equipment for the various slaughtering and carcass dressing and processing operations. The moving chain-conveyor production-line system is widely used where the scale of operations warrants it. Special provision may be made for "ritual slaughter," or for other slaughter under the requirements of special faiths.

Hog slaughter. After stunning, pigs are bled by severing one of the large veins, the anterior vena cava, and then submerged in a scalding tank, with water temperatures between 130° and 142° F (55° and 61° C) for four to six minutes to loosen the hair. They are next subjected to a dehairer that brushes the loosened hair from the skin. The hog is then suspended vertically from a rail and shaved and singed.

The carcasses are opened by a straight cut in the centre of the belly. The viscera, including liver, heart, lungs, large and small intestines, pancreas, spleen, stomach, and bladder, are then easily removed. The intestines may be thoroughly cleaned and washed to serve as casings for specialized sausage products. The kidneys and the fat surrounding them (leaf fat) are also removed. The carcasses are then split down the centre of the backbone and, after washing, are ready to move into the cooler.

In modern slaughter plants, each pig is tattooed (producer identification) before slaughter. As the carcasses move into the cooler, a grader records the producer's identification number and the weight and grade for each, using a tape that is fed into a computer, making the information available for proper decisions.

Cattle slaughter. After stunning, the carcass is vertically suspended by one or both hindlegs, and the carotid arteries and jugular veins are severed. The carcass is then skinned with an air-operated or electrically operated skinning knife. In old or small operations this is accomplished with the aid of a "stationary bed" on which a pointed stick helps hold the carcass on its back on the floor. Large modern plants use "rail dressing," employing platforms and hide pullers.

Evisceration and splitting are similar to methods used in hog slaughter. Shrouding, performed on many beef carcasses, involves soaking a muslin cloth in warm water and stretching it tightly over the outside surface, securing it with metal pins. The carcasses are then placed in the cooler; and, after 24 hours, the shrouds are removed, and the carcass fat remains smooth and trim.

Veal slaughter. Veal slaughter is similar to beef slaughter, but the hides are frequently left on during chilling, as veal carcasses have very little fat. If the hides were removed during chilling, the carcasses would undergo excessive shrinkage.

Lamb slaughter. Lambs are slaughtered much like veal, except that the pelts (wool) are removed. The carcasses, however, are not split, but are immediately chilled in the cooler.

Processing methods and product compositions. *Wholesale cuts.* In some countries pork carcasses are cut on an assembly line. In the future much of the cutting may be performed electronically.

Beef is primarily cut on the rail, and the cuts are then resuspended. The preparation of both portion-controlled and vacuum-packed cuts at the packer level is increasing.

Product composition controls Government establishment of meat-product-composition controls is becoming increasingly important throughout the world. Many countries establish meat-product-composition controls dealing with such factors as minimum meat content and the use and acceptable quantities of such fillers as cereals, dry milk or other milk products, soybean, corn syrup, and other nonmeat ingredients. In addition to its meat content, sausage may contain other additives, which must be listed on the package. These may include salt; beet or cane sugar; maple, dextrose, or invert sugars; honey; corn-syrup solids; wood smoke; flavourings; vinegar; spices; sodium nitrite; potassium nitrite; and sodium nitrate or potassium nitrate (saltpetre). Total allowable added water is usually greater in uncooked sausage than in cooked sausage.

The allowable weight increase in hams for canning may be limited by government regulation. Such factors as the proportion of nitrite and nitrate; the ascorbic acid content of the brine; and the use of phosphates in sausage, hams, and products such as chopped ham may also be subject to government standards.

Hams may be removed, cured, boned, cooked, cooled, dipped into gelatin, inserted into casings, and sealed, or they may be pressure stuffed into casings.

A body or substance is absolutely sterile only when no vegetative micro-organisms or spores are present, either because there were none originally or because all have been killed. Since the use of sterile raw material in meat canning is not practical, the sterilization process follows as rapidly as possible the hermetic sealing of the cans.

Labelling. In various countries where modern food processing techniques are common, governments may specify the required features of a label, such as product name; ingredients, usually in decreasing order by amount; name and place of person for whom product is prepared; statement of weight; and an inspection legend. In 1970 the Codex Committee on Food Labelling submitted a general standard for labelling prepackaged foods to be considered by the member governments.

Emulsification. A meat emulsion has characteristics similar to an oil-in-water emulsion. The process is influenced by type of protein, temperature, speed of blender, and protein–water ratio. Meat from hot carcasses is usually preferred because it has not been affected by a decreasing pH (increased acidity) and is more easily increased in solubility by salt application. Mutton is restricted to 15 percent of any meat formula. If meats must be held, they are held in a frozen state. Many varieties of meats are used, including tongues, livers, hearts, kidneys, and tripe (stomach).

Manufactured casings. Cellulosic casings are manufactured from cotton. Casings made from regenerated collagen have the advantage of being consistently uniform in size and thickness.

Equipment. A meat grinder permits the worming of meat along a cylinder with sharp-edged ribs and through perforated plates, and as the meat is extruded, it is cut by revolving knives. Commercial operations employ vacuum mixers to combine the various ingredients. Cutters and emulsion mills are used as comminuters, reducing the ingredients of the mixture to minute particles, and stuffers force the mixtures into casings. Computers are major equipment in modern sausage formulation and selection of raw-materials sources.

Continuous automatic wiener process. In this process, meats are ground separately, blended with seasonings, and pumped into a final chopper. The mixture is "stuffed" under pressure, linked, and conveyed to "smoking" chambers. The wieners are then cooked, chilled, stripped of cellulose casings, and packaged. Under this process wieners are commonly produced at a rate of 36,000 per hour.

Packaging methods and equipment. Packaging is intended to protect the product and to maintain a state of freshness throughout the merchandising cycle. Factors in package-material selection include moisture and gas permeability, strength, sealability, visibility, and cost.

Cellophane, polyester, polyamide, polyolefine, and polystyrene are a few of the materials that may be used. Many packages are vacuum sealed, and most packaging processes are automated.

Packing-plant inspection. *Kosher inspection.* In kosher inspection, a member of the Jewish faith, called a "schachter," cuts the throat of the beef animal by severing the carotid arteries and jugular veins perpendicular to the axis of the neck, immediately behind the jawbone. The beef animals are not stunned before bleeding. After bleeding, the schachter examines the lungs for abnormalities. If any are present the beef is not approved and is called "trepha."

Meat inspection. Modern meat inspection is usually concerned with the state of health of the animal; the physical plant, facilities, and equipment; the use of food additives; and the use of proper labels. Inspection is frequently supervised or carried out by licensed veterinarians.

On the basis of antemortem inspection, an animal may be passed for slaughter, considered suspect, or condemned. When passed, the animal proceeds through normal processing and is subjected to routine subsequent inspection procedures. Condemnation may result when an animal plainly shows evidence of disease or a condition that obviously would result in condemnation of the carcass and its parts. If its condition is questionable, the animal may be labeled "suspect." A routine inspection of all body parts is usually conducted as the animal is slaughtered, and an inspector's mark is stamped on. In the U.S. the inspection responsibility is shared by federal and state governments.

Governments are becoming increasingly involved in meat inspection, and it may be expected that meat inspection practices throughout the world will be affected by the recommendations of the various Codex Committees concerned with establishing standards for meat and meat products, food hygiene, food labelling, and analysis and sampling.

Meat-packing industry by-products. By-products, the nonmeat materials obtained in meat processing, are used in a wide range of products.

Edible fats are used as lard or in shortenings and cooking oils; inedible fats are used in soap and candles and in various greases for industrial use. Lanolin, the fat removed from wool, is used in ointments and cosmetics. Gelatin, obtained from collagen, is used in such food products as confections and jellies and in pharmaceuticals. Sausage casings are made from intestines and from regenerated collagen, which is also being developed for use in various leather-like products. Gland extracts are used in such pharmaceuticals as insulin and cortisone.

Wool of slaughtered animals is used like any other, for yarns and textiles; hides and skins are made into leather; and hair is used in brushes, felt, and upholstery products. Bone is used principally in animal feeds and fertilizers and in glue. Blood is also used in animal feeds and fertilizers and in pharmaceuticals.

BIBLIOGRAPHY. R.A. LAWRIE, *Meat Science* (1966), a comprehensive review of basic and applied aspects of meat science, especially useful for developing a broad background in meat science; B.C. BREIDENSTEIN, *Beef Operations in the Meat Industry* (1966); D.S. MACKENZIE, *Prepared Meat Product Manufacturing*, rev. ed. (1967); and D.L. MACKINTOSH, *Pork Operations in the Meat Industry*, 7th ed. (1967), publications of the American Meat Institute on the procedures and processes involved in meat handling and manufacturing, especially pertinent for those involved in or studying meat processing; NATIONAL LIVE STOCK AND MEAT BOARD, *Lessons on Meat*, 2nd ed. (1964), a text designed to teach elementary aspects of meat and meat products; *Meat Evaluation Handbook* (1969), a text offering pictorial illustration of desirable and less desirable meat cuts and carcasses, used in teaching evaluation of meat and meat products; R.W. BRAY *et al., Techniques and Their Application to Meat Research* (1970), a detailed reference to current techniques for studying the components and structure of meat and meat products; H.A. LURIE, *Refrigeration for the Meat Processing Plant* (1966), comprehensive descriptions of the kind and magnitude of refrigeration employed in the meat processing plant; R.J. IVES, *The Livestock and Meat Economy of the United States* (1966), a survey of the economics of livestock production and processing; AMERICAN MEAT INSTITUTE FOUNDATION, *The Science of Meat and Meat Products*, 2nd ed. by J.F. PRICE and B.S. SCHWEIGERT (1971), a comprehensive text on the science of meat and meat products; E.J. BRISKEY and R.G. KAUFFMAN, "Qualitative Characteristics of Muscle as a Food," in PRICE-SCHWEIGERT (*op. cit.*), a description of quality in meat as viewed from a scientific perspective; E.J. BRISKEY, "Muscle," in S.E. HAFEZ and I.A. DYER (eds.), *Animal Growth and Nutrition* (1969), a comprehensive documented chapter on muscle, its growth, function and adaptation.

(E.J.B.)

Mecca

The holiest of Muslim cities, Mecca (in Arabic Makkah) was the birthplace of Muḥammad, the founder of Islām. Located in the Şirāt Mountains inland from the Red Sea coast of Saudi Arabia, it is a religious centre to which all Muslims attempt a pilgrimage, or *ḥajj*, during their lifetime. Mecca is also the second most populous city of Saudi Arabia, after the national capital of Riyadh. Its early 1970s population of about 300,000 occupied an area of about 10 square miles (26 square kilometres). During the month of pilgrimage, however, the city is swollen with about 1,000,000 worshippers from other parts of the country and from other Muslim nations.

An historic city closely tied to tradition, Mecca has benefitted from the Saudi Arabian oil economy of the 20th century, although income from the pilgrimage is still important. In recent decades the city has undergone vast improvements. The area around the religious shrines has been cleared, the mosque has been greatly enlarged, housing and sanitation have been improved, and transportation facilities have been greatly enhanced. As a result, Mecca can accommodate an increasing number of pilgrims, the numbers of which continually increase. (For related articles see ISLAM; ISLAM, HISTORY OF; ISLAMIC MYTH AND LEGEND; and MUHAMMAD.)

The ancient city

History. Ancient Mecca was an oasis on the old caravan trade route that linked the Mediterranean world with South Arabia, East Africa, and South Asia. Located about midway between Ma'rib in the south and Petra in the north, the town gradually developed by Roman and Byzantine times into an important trade and religious centre. It was known to Ptolemy as Macoraba.

According to Islāmic tradition, Abraham and Ishmael, his son by Hagar, built the Ka'bah as a replica of God's house in heaven. The central point of pilgrimage in Mecca before the advent of Islām in the 7th century, the cube-shaped stone building has been destroyed and rebuilt several times. During biblical times, the city was ruled by a series of Yemeni tribes. Under the Quraysh, it became a type of city-state, with strong commercial links to the rest of Arabia, Ethiopia, and Europe. Mecca became a place for trade, for pilgrimage, and for poetry festivals.

The city gained its religious importance with the birth of Muhammad about 570. Forced to flee from Mecca in 622, the prophet returned eight years later and took control of the city. He purged Mecca of idols, declared it a centre of Muslim pilgrimage, and dedicated it to Allāh. Since then, the city has remained the major religious centre of Islām. As the ancient caravan route fell into decline, Mecca lost its commercial significance and has since lived mainly on the annual pilgrimages and the gifts of Muslim rulers.

Camera Press—Pix

The central courtyard of al-Haram mosque. In the centre is the Ka'bah, the holiest shrine of Islām.

The period of foreign control

Mecca remained virtually independent, although it acknowledged the power of Damascus and later of the 'Abbāsid caliphate of Baghdad, Iraq. In 1269 it came under the control of the Egyptian Mamlūk sultans. In 1517 dominion over the holy city passed to the Ottoman Turks in Constantinople (now Istanbul). The local city rulers were chosen from the *sharīf*s, or descendants of Muḥammad, who retained a strong hold on the surrounding area. With the fall of Turkish power after World War I, control of Mecca was contested between the *sharīf*s and the Wahhābīs of central Arabia. The Wahhābī king Ibn Sa'ūd entered the city in 1925, and it became part of the Kingdom of Saudi Arabia, and the capital of Makkah *manaṭiq idārīyah* (province).

Under the Wahhābīs, a puritanical moral code and law and order were enforced, and the facilities for pilgrims were improved. With the exploitation of Saudi Arabia's oil resources since World War II, Mecca has experienced a high level of economic development.

The contemporary city. *The city site.* Mecca is situated at an elevation of 909 feet (277 metres) above sea level in the dry beds of the Wādī Ibrāhīm and several of its short tributaries. It is surrounded by the Ṣirāt Mountains the peaks of which include Jabal Ajyad, which rises to 1,332 feet (406 metres), and Jabal Abū Qubays, which attains 1,220 feet (372 metres), to the east and Jabal Qu'ayq'ān, which reaches 1,401 feet (427 metres), to the west. Jabal Hirā' rises to 2,080 feet (634 metres) on the northeast and contains a cave in which Muḥammad sought isolation and visions before he became a prophet. It was also in this cave that he received the first verse (*sūrah*) of the holy Qur'ān. South of the city, Jabal Thawr (2,490 feet [759 meters]) contains the cave in which the prophet hid from the people of Mecca before he moved to Medina.

Entrance to the city is gained through four gaps in the surrounding mountains. The passes lead from the northeast to Minā, 'Arafāt, and aṭ-Ṭā'if; from the northwest to Medina; from the west to Jidda; and from the south to Yemen (Ṣan'ā'). The gaps have also defined the direction of the contemporary expansion of the city.

Because of its relatively low-lying location, Mecca is threatened by seasonal flash floods despite the low amount of annual precipitation. There are less than five inches of rainfall during the year, mainly in the winter months. Temperatures are high throughout the year and in summer may reach 113° F (45° C). Vegetation and animal life are scarce and consist of species that can withstand the high degree of aridity and heat.

Natural vegetation is sparse, and includes tamarisks and various types of acacia. Wild animals include wild cats, wolves, hyenas, foxes, mongooses, and kangaroo rats (jerboas).

The city plan. The city centres upon the al-Ḥaram mosque and the sacred well of Zamzam, located inside the mosque. The compact built-up area around the mosque comprises the old city, which stretches to the north and southwest but is limited on the east and west by the nearby mountains. The main avenues are al-Mudda'ah and Sūq al-Layl to the north of the mosque and as-Sūq as-Saghīr to the south.

Since World War II, Mecca has expanded along the roads through the mountain gaps to the north, northwest, and west. Among the new residential areas are Al-'Azīzīyah and al-Faysalīyah along the road to Minā and aẓ-Ẓāhir, az-Zahra'ā, and Shāri' al-Manṣūr along the roads to Jidda and Medina. Expansion has been accompanied by the construction of new streets in the old city and by the transformation of Mecca into a modern city, with fountains, built since the 1950s, in its four main squares. The square mosque is magnificent in its size and architecture. Enlarged from 313,520 to 1,724,032 square feet (29,127 to 160,168 square metres), it can accommodate more than 300,000 worshippers at one time. Houses near the mosque have been razed, and it is now surrounded by open spaces and wide streets, which can be crossed through underground walkways, built to ease traffic.

Mecca's more than 35,000 houses are more compacted in the old city than in the newly developed residential areas. Traditional buildings of two or three stories are built of local rock. The villas in the new areas are constructed of concrete. Slum conditions can still be found in various parts of the city; the slum inhabitants are mainly poor pilgrims who remained in Mecca after arriving on pilgrimage in past years.

The people. The population of about 300,000 lives in an area of about 10 square miles (26 square kilometres). The average population density is about 30,000 persons per square mile (12,000 persons per square kilometre); most of the people are concentrated in the old city, while densities in the new residential areas may drop to only 7,300 per square mile (2,800 per square kilometre). There are slightly more males than females. About one-third of the population is under 10 years of age, and about two-thirds are under 30 years of age.

Residence in Mecca is permitted only to followers of Islām. It is, however, one of the most cosmopolitan cities in the world, containing people from the various Islāmic countries in Asia and Africa. People of the same national origin tend to live together in certain parts of the city. There is, however, no racial discrimination.

The economy. Arable land and water are scarce, and food must be imported. Vegetables and fruits are brought in daily from the surrounding *wadi*s, such as Wādī Fāṭimah, from the Ṭā'if area to the east-southeast, and from the southern agricultural areas, such as Bilād Ghāmid and Bilād Zahrān. Foodstuffs are imported from abroad mainly through the port of Jidda, 45 miles to the west on the Red Sea.

Industry is limited (it includes the manufacture of textiles, furniture, and utensils), and the overall urban economy is commercial. The number of commercial establishments grew from almost 2,300 in 1959 to about 7,000 in 1969. Transportation and facilities related to the pilgrimage are the main service industries.

Mecca has no airport nor water or rail services. It is well served, however, by the Jidda seaport and airport and by truck, bus, and taxi services. Asphalt roads link Mecca with the main cities of Saudi Arabia and neighbouring countries.

Because of the improvement of services, the number of foreign pilgrims increased from 61,000 in 1946 to about 480,000 in 1972. There is also a similar number of Saudi pilgrims. This annual influx brings a good income to the city, but it also results in a population of about 1,000,000, all of whom need accommodations, food, water, electricity, transportation, and medical services. In a normal month Mecca consumes about 173,000,000 gallons of water, but, in the month of Dhū al-Ḥijjah (the month of pilgrimage), the amount of water consumed rises to 552,000,000 gallons.

The main problem is transportation. In accordance with the prescribed route, all pilgrims have to be transported from Mecca to 'Arafāt, a distance of about 12 miles (19 kilometres), during the early morning of the 9th day of the month of Dhū al-Ḥijjah. During the night of the same day, they must travel to Minā, which is almost two miles from Mecca; after three days, all are returned to Mecca. This problem has been met by the construction of a good road network, an adequate supply of vehicles, and traffic control.

Administration and social conditions. The governor of the city is the amir of Makkah *manāṭiq idārīyah,* who is responsible for the maintenance of law and order in both the city and the *manāṭiq;* appointed by the king, he is immediately responsible to the Minister of the Interior. The municipal council is responsible for the functioning of the municipality; the council was formed after World War II, and has 14 members, who are locally elected and are then approved by the Minister of the Interior. Mecca is also the capital of Makkah *manāṭiq idārīyah* which includes the cities of Jidda and aṭ-Ṭā'if.

Free education is provided for both girls and boys from primary to university level. There are two university-level colleges—the Sharī'ah College of Islamic Jurisprudence, and the College of Education (a teacher training college).

Health services and medical care are free and adequate. There are more than 800 hospital beds and about 70 physicians. Police and fire service is modern and effective. A major sewer project was under construction in the early 1970s. Despite careful checking at points of entry into Saudi Arabia, pilgrims may bring various illnesses, particularly cholera, smallpox, and cerebro-spinal infections, into the city; the health services, however, have been able to keep such problems under control.

Mecca depends upon the surrounding *wadi*s for drinking water. The waters of 'Ayn Zubaydah (Zubaydah Spring), built in the 8th century, flow through tunnels from Wādī Nu'mān, about 20 miles (30 kilometres) to the southwest. 'Ayn al-'Azīzīyah sends its waters through pipelines from Wādī ash-Shāmīyah, about 60 miles (100 kilometres) to the northeast. Water and electricity have reached almost all houses. Electricity is generated at an oil-fuelled power station located on the road to Medina.

Mecca's religious shrines

The problems of the pilgrimage

Education services

Cultural life. Mecca has a number of cultural and sporting clubs and public libraries. In summer, its residents travel to the nearby resort of aṭ-Ṭa'if, 50 miles (80 kilometres) to the southeast.

Daily newspapers are available in Arabic, and there is a daily English newsletter. Radio and television programs are broadcast from Jidda.

BIBLIOGRAPHY. Literature about Mecca is available mainly in Arabic. For pre-Islāmic and early Islāmic times, see M.A.A. AL-AZRAQI, *Akhbăr Makkah,* written in the 9th century (1875, reprinted 1969); and A.I. AL-SHARIF, *Makkah wa-al- Madīnah* (1965). For the Middle Ages, see IBN JUBAYR, *Travels . . . (1183–1185 A.D.),* written in the 12th century, trans. by R.J.C. BROADHURST (1952); and IBN BATUTA, *Travels,* A.D. *1325– 1354,* written in the 14th century, trans. by H.A.R. GIBB (1958). Other English-language accounts include JOHN L. BURCK-HARDT, *Travels in Arabia* (1829); JOHN F. KEANE, *Six Months in Meccah* (1881); C. SNOUCK HURGRONJE, *Mekka,* 2 vol. (1888–89); Eng. trans. of vol. 2, *Mekka in the Latter Part of the 19th Century: Daily Life, Customs and Learning* (1931); SIR RICHARD BURTON, *Personal Narrative of a Pilgrimage to El-Medinah and Meccah,* 5th ed., 3 vol. (1906); AR-THUR WAVELL, *A Modern Pilgrim in Mecca and a Siege in Sanaa* (1912); ELDON RUTTER, *The Holy Cities of Arabia* (1928); and J.B. PHILBY, *A Pilgrim in Arabia* (1946). For statistics, see the *Statistical Yearbook* (annual), published by the Central Department of Statistics, Riyadh, Saudi Arabia.

(A.S.A.)

Mechanical Engineering

Mechanical engineering is the branch of engineering that deals with machines and the production of power. It is particularly concerned with forces and motion.

History. The invention of the steam engine in the latter part of the 18th century, providing a key source of power for the Industrial Revolution, gave an enormous impetus to the development of machinery of all types. As a result a new major classification of engineering, separate from civil engineering and dealing with tools and machines, developed, receiving formal recognition in 1847 in the founding of the Institution of Mechanical Engineers in Birmingham, England.

Mechanical engineering has evolved from the practice by the mechanic of an art based largely on trial and error to the application by the professional engineer of the scientific method in research, design, and production.

The demand for increased efficiency, in the widest sense, is continually raising the quality of work expected from a mechanical engineer and requiring of him a higher degree of education and training. Not only must machines run more economically but capital costs also must be minimized.

Fields of mechanical engineering. *Development of machines for the production of goods.* The high material standard of living in the developed countries owes much to the machinery made possible by mechanical engineering. The mechanical engineer continually invents machines to produce goods and develops machine tools of increasing accuracy and complexity to build the machines.

The principal lines of development of machinery have been an increase in the speed of operation to obtain high rates of production, improvement in accuracy to obtain quality and economy in the product, and minimization of operating costs. These three requirements have led to the evolution of complex control systems.

The most successful production machinery is that in which the mechanical design of the machine is closely integrated with the control system, whether the latter is mechanical or electrical in nature. A modern transfer (conveyor) line for the manufacture of automobile engines is a good example of the mechanization of a complex series of manufacturing processes. Developments are in hand to automate production machinery further, using computers to store and process the vast amount of data required for manufacturing a variety of components with a small number of versatile machine tools. One aim is a completely automated machine shop for batch production, operating on a three-shift basis but attended by a staff for only one shift per day.

Development of machines for the production of power. Production machinery presupposes an ample supply of power. The steam engine provided the first practical means of generating power from heat to augment the old sources of power from muscle, wind, and water. One of the first challenges to the new profession of mechanical engineering was to increase thermal efficiencies and power; this was done principally by the development of the steam turbine and associated large steam boilers. The 20th century has witnessed a continued rapid growth in the power output of turbines for driving electric generators, together with a steady increase in thermal efficiency and reduction in capital cost per kilowatt of large power stations. Finally, mechanical engineers acquired the resource of nuclear energy, whose application has demanded an exceptional standard of reliability and safety involving the solution of entirely new problems. The control systems of large power plants and complete nuclear power stations have become highly sophisticated networks of electronic, fluidic, electric, hydraulic, and mechanical components, all of these involving the province of the mechanical engineer.

Complex control systems

The mechanical engineer is also responsible for the much smaller internal combustion engines, both reciprocating (gasoline and diesel) and rotary (gas-turbine and Wankel) engines, with their widespread transport applications. In the transportation field generally, in air and space as well as on land and sea, the mechanical engineer has created the equipment and the power plant, collaborating increasingly with the electrical engineer, especially in the development of suitable control systems.

Development of military weapons. The skills applied to war by the mechanical engineer are similar to those required in civilian applications, though the purpose is to enhance destructive power rather than to raise creative efficiency. The demands of war have channelled huge resources into technical fields, however, and led to developments that have profound benefits in peace. Jet aircraft and nuclear reactors are notable examples.

Bioengineering. Bioengineering is a relatively new and distinct field of mechanical engineering that includes the provision of machines to replace or augment the functions of the human body and of equipment for use in medical treatment. Artificial limbs have been developed incorporating such lifelike functions as powered motion and touch feedback. Development is rapid in the direction of artificial spare-part surgery. Sophisticated heart–lung machines and similar equipment permit operations of increasing complexity and permit the vital functions in seriously injured or diseased patients to be maintained.

Environmental control. Some of the earliest efforts of mechanical engineers were aimed at controlling man's environment by pumping water to drain or irrigate land and by ventilating mines. The ubiquitous refrigerating and air-conditioning plants of the modern age are based on a reversed heat engine, where the supply of power "pumps" heat from the cold region to the warmer exterior.

Many of the products of mechanical engineering, together with technological developments in other fields, have side effects on the environment and give rise to noise, the pollution of water and air, and the dereliction of land and scenery. The rate of production, both of goods and power, is rising so rapidly that regeneration by natural forces can no longer keep pace. A rapidly growing field for mechanical engineers and others is environmental control, comprising the development of machines and processes that will produce fewer pollutants and of new equipment and techniques that can reduce or remove the pollution already generated.

Mechanical engineering functions. Four functions of the mechanical engineer, common to all the fields mentioned, can be cited. The first is the understanding of and dealing with the bases of mechanical science. These include dynamics, concerning the relation between forces and motion, such as in vibration; automatic control; thermodynamics, dealing with the relations among the various forms of heat, energy, and power; fluid flow; heat transfer; lubrication; and properties of materials.

Second is the sequence of research, design, and development. This function attempts to bring about the changes necessary to meet present and future needs. Such work requires not only a clear understanding of mechanical science and an ability to analyze a complex system into its basic factors, but also the originality to synthesize and invent.

Third is production of products and power, which embraces planning, operation, and maintenance. The goal is to produce the maximum value with the minimum investment and cost while maintaining or enhancing longer term viability and reputation of the enterprise or the institution.

Fourth is the coordinating function of the mechanical engineer, including management, consulting, and, in some cases, marketing.

In all of these functions there is a long continuing trend toward the use of scientific instead of traditional or intuitive methods, an aspect of the ever-growing professionalism of mechanical engineering. Operations research, value engineering, and PABLA (problem analysis by logical approach) are typical titles of such new rationalized approaches. Creativity, however, cannot be rationalized. The ability to take the important and unexpected step that opens up new solutions remains in mechanical engineering, as elsewhere, largely a personal and spontaneous characteristic.

Education and professional societies. Education in engineering has also reflected the growing professionalism of the practice. Until World War II, most universities in Europe and the U.S. had curricula involving a considerable degree of specialization into mechanical, electrical, or other engineering. With the rapid growth of these fields of technology, students were becoming more and more specialized. At the same time, the increasing complexity of technical projects required from the professional engineer not only a knowledge of his own specialty but an understanding of the other branches of engineering. Widespread revision of university curricula has more recently aimed at providing a broad, fundamental knowledge of engineering science, leaving the specialized training to industry.

Another approach, considered more practical and less intellectual, is the sandwich, or cooperative, system of education, comprising alternating periods of six months spent in industry and at college. British engineering schools have been prominent in pioneering this arrangement.

In the Soviet Union, university courses in mechanical engineering last about five and one-half years, of which the first three are applied to the fundamentals of the subject with a strong mathematical content, while the remaining period provides a wide choice of specialist training. Similarly, in most of the countries of Continental Europe and Japan, engineering courses run for five years and, while of a general nature for the first two years or so, become specialized and practical thereafter. The student is expected to obtain experience in industry during his vacation, so that, after graduation, he is able to take a professional post of responsibility without further training.

The professional societies have been the main instrument in raising the status of mechanical engineering to that of an important profession grounded in a lengthy training in mechanical science.

For the various grades of membership of the major societies it is necessary to attain specified academic qualifications, practical experience, and defined levels of responsibility. In the British Institution of Mechanical Engineers a member of either of the two most senior grades, "Fellow" and "Member," is designated "Chartered Engineer"—a title denied by law to those who have not achieved the necessary qualifications and membership.

Although in the majority of Western countries it is not necessary to attain formal registration before practicing as an engineer, the achievement of a senior grade of membership of a professional society is generally important in seeking a responsible engineering post.

The growth of membership of the Institution of Mechanical Engineers has been almost uniform over 120 years. The mean rate of increase has been 5.2 percent per year, a figure that indicates the rapid and continuing increase in the size and importance of the mechanical engineering profession. The growth rate of the American Society of Mechanical Engineers has been similar.

Societies of professional mechanical engineers have long been established in European countries; in Japan (1897), in India (1920), in China (1951), and in most other countries that have significant strength in this field. The primary function of these societies is to promote mechanical engineering by publishing technical papers and arranging conferences. Unlike the British Institution, however, they do not in general regulate, by their conditions of membership, the qualifications and status of professional engineers.

With the broadening and changing content of mechanical engineering, specialized groups have been organized within the national societies—*e.g.*, groups concerned with automatic control, combustion engines, heat transfer, and lubrication technology.

National societies are also often subdivided on a geographical basis and have links with similar societies in other countries and with their fellow societies in other fields of engineering and science.

The future of mechanical engineering. The number of mechanical engineers continues to grow as rapidly as ever, while the duration and quality of their training increases. There is a growing awareness, however, among engineers and in the community at large that the exponential increase in population and living standards is raising formidable problems in pollution of the environment and the exhaustion of natural resources; this clearly heightens the need for all of the technical professions to consider the long-term social effects of discoveries and developments. There will be an increasing demand for mechanical engineering skills to provide for man's needs while reducing to a minimum the consumption of scarce raw materials and maintaining a satisfactory environment.

BIBLIOGRAPHY. For general reading, see *Engineering Heritage: Highlights from the History of Mechanical Engineering*, 2 vol. (1963–66), issued by the INSTITUTION OF MECHANICAL ENGINEERS. The history of this society is given in R.H. PARSONS, *A History of the Institution of Mechanical Engineers, 1847–1947* (1947). For information on educational requirements, see the *Britannica Review of Developments in Engineering Education*, ed. by NEWMAN A. HALL (1970–   ); and for salaries, the ENGINEERING MANPOWER COMMISSION OF THE ENGINEERS JOINT COUNCIL (New York), *Professional Income of Engineers, 1968–1969* (1969); and the *Survey of Professional Engineers 1968* (HMSO, 1970). Machine-tool trends are discussed in W.H.P. LESLIE (ed.), *Numerical Control Users' Handbook* (1970).

(J.F.Br./P.McG.R.)

Mechanics, Celestial

Celestial mechanics is a branch of astronomy pertaining to the motion of natural and artificial bodies in space. The application of mathematics to the motion of artificial satellites, space crafts, space probes, rockets, even missiles, is often called astrodynamics, and is considered a branch of astronautics. Dynamical astronomy deals with the forces and motions of celestial bodies and includes stellar and planetary dynamics. The terminology of these scientific areas is not well defined, and there is an undesirable and restrictive traditional association of celestial mechanics with the dynamical study of the solar system. In this article, a systematic treatment of the pertinent dynamical and mathematical principles is applied to the motion of bodies in space, regardless of their origin.

The laws of dynamics are described by differential equations and an understanding of these laws is fundamental to the study of celestial mechanics. The close relation between dynamics and celestial mechanics suggests that Sir Isaac Newton may be the founder of celestial mechanics because his laws of motion, which express the principles of mechanics, are applicable to any force field. His universal law of gravitation is one example of how his formulation and application of the calculus to dynamical problems permits an orderly and scientific treatment of the behaviour of celestial bodies. In fact, this is the only known language for treating problems in celestial mechanics, and without it the computation of orbits of space vehicles would not be possible (see MECHANICS, CLASSICAL).

A century before Newton, Johannes Kepler (1571–1630) obtained his three laws of planetary motion empirically, but they may be derived from Newton's laws of motion and gravitation; the brilliant contributions to celestial mechanics of Nicolaus Copernicus (1473–1543), Tycho Brahe (1546–1601), and Galileo (1564–1642) also include special cases of Newton's results, anticipating Newton, though it was he who comprehended and formulated the abstract laws.

Operational processes of celestial mechanics The operational processes of celestial mechanics use as input either observations or, in the case of space vehicles, certain mission requirements. Next, the equations are formulated and solved. The output may be the time dependence of the position of a satellite, a set of initial conditions applicable to firing tables, the prediction of the orbit of a comet, or the location of a planet at any given time. In 3000 BC the Babylonian priest-astrologers made naked eye observations of what was then considered to be the planetary motions (the five visible planets, the Moon, and the Sun were all considered to be planets of the Earth) in order to keep nations and kings out of trouble, to regulate the calendar, and to aid travellers. Modern preparation of lunar and planetary ephemerides (listings of locations of celestial bodies for regular time intervals), of nautical almanacs, of guidance and firing tables, of refined relativity corrections is fundamentally the same kind of output that Mesopotamia requested from its high priests of celestial mechanics. The computations they performed might be considered clumsy today, but even the modern—but precomputer—use of E.W. Brown's (1866–1938) lunar theory allowed hardly enough time for prediction of the Moon's motion. Two men were fully occupied in establishing one new position of the Moon every 12 hours. The balance between observations and computations has always been precarious, and today the enormous number of radar observations and their high precision may overload the most advanced electronic computers.

Historical review. Early celestial mechanics concentrated attention on the behaviour of the major members of the solar system. Observations were relatively crude, and even completely erroneous dynamical ideas, or models devoid of dynamics, could offer fairly satisfactory predictions—at least for short times. This situation has a counterpart today: inadequate knowledge of the gravitational field of the Moon prevents long-term predictions of the orbits of lunar satellites.

The early Babylonian priest-astrologers were mainly observers. They invented the signs of the Zodiac and recognized the precession of the vernal equinox, but there seems to be no evidence that either they or the early Egyptian astronomers established a consistent theory of planetary motions. The Greek period (from about 400 BC) of celestial mechanics is of more interest to philosophers than to astronomers. Plato's problem regarding the representation of the motion of celestial bodies by combining uniform circular motions had, at that time, two philosophical solutions: one culminating in Aristotle's 55 spheres, and the other in the Ptolemaic system. Plato's problem is now seen as one of Fourier analysis, which, using trigonometric series as approximations, is today still the basic tool in treating planetary and lunar theories. The concept of the rotating celestial sphere with the Earth at its centre (even now, occasionally, a useful convention) and the concept of concentric shells used by Aristotle (384–322 BC) were attempts to represent planetary as well as stellar motion relative to the Earth. The model was intended to describe the geometry of the motion without reference to causes. Hipparchus (approximately 130 BC), inventor of spherical trigonometry, emphasized the importance of observations and made Claudius Ptolemaus' (c. AD 200) system feasible. The Ptolemaic system was still a purely kinematic approach to celestial mechanics, being devoid of dynamical concepts. The Ptolemaic

representation of the apparent planetary motions by epicycles centred at the Earth is approximate and somewhat complicated since the motions of the planets actually centre around the Sun.

Arguments favouring a heliocentric system were mentioned by some early Greek astronomers, notably Aristarchus (c. 270 BC), but the first consistent theory with the Sun placed centrally in the solar system was accomplished in the 16th century by Nicolaus Copernicus. Tycho Brahe later proposed the somewhat irrelevant view that the Sun and Moon moved on circles centered at the Earth, all other planets revolving around the Sun; nevertheless Brahe's excellent observations were fundamental to Kepler's (1571–1630) work.

Kepler's laws Kepler's contributions may be considered the last of purely kinematic significance in celestial mechanics. His laws describe the motions of the planets without reference to the governing forces. His original three laws, formulated in 1609, were the ones numbered (1) and (2) below, together with a statement according to which the planes of motion of the planets pass through the Sun. His original fourth law, proposed in 1618, is shown as (3) below. The laws are as follows: (1) the orbit of each planet is an ellipse, with the Sun at one focus of the ellipse; (2) the line joining the Sun to the planet sweeps through equal areas in equal times; (3) the squares of the periods of revolution of any two planets are in the same proportion as the cubes of their mean distances from the Sun.

The first and second laws are true only if perturbations (that is, disturbances caused by additional forces) of the two-body problems are neglected. The third law is only approximately true even when perturbations are not present since it assumes that the masses of the planets may be neglected as compared to the mass of the Sun.

The ellipse of the first law (Figure 1) is a plane curve such that for any point, G, on the ellipse, the sum GS + GS' is the same. In fact, S'G + SG = AP. The point P on the orbit closest to the Sun, S, is called the perihelion. The furthest, A, is the aphelion. The focuses are S and S'. The semimajor axis of the ellipse is half the distance between A and P; that is, AC or CP, usually denoted by a; C is the centre of the ellipse. The eccentricity of the ellipse, e, is the focal length CS divided by the semimajor axis CP. The *line of apsides* is defined by the major axis. The *mean distance* of a planet from the Sun is the length of its semimajor axis.

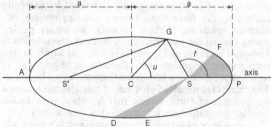

Figure 1: Orbital element in plane (see text).

The second law reveals empirically that the shaded areas on Figure 1 are equal, provided the same time has elapsed between corresponding locations of the planet. In other words, consider a planet located at perihelion P and a month later at point F. Now, if the planet is (at a later time) at point D and one month later at E, then the areas of the sectors SPF and SDE are equal. Inasmuch as points F and P are closer to S than D and E, it can be concluded that the velocity of the planet is greater at perihelion than anywhere else. (Aphelion passage is the slowest and perihelion the fastest.) The angular velocity of the planet (rate of change of its angular position) varies on its orbit; the average angular velocity is called the mean motion of the planet.

The third law relates the semimajor axes of the planets to their mean motions or periods of revolution around the Sun. Once the period of revolution of a planet is known, its mean distance from the Sun can be computed relative to another planet's mean distance. The Earth's mean distance, the astronomical unit (A.U.), is used as the scale of the solar system. Consequently, any planet's mean distance in astronomical units may be obtained by computing the ⅔ power of its period of revolution expressed in years. Thus, Jupiter's orbital period is approximately 11.86 years, the ⅔ power of which is 5.2. The mean distance of Jupiter from the Sun (its semimajor axis) is 5.2 times that of Earth.

Kepler's contemporary, Galileo (1564–1642), well-known for his observations, which included the discovery of four of Jupiter's satellites, made his major contribution by introducing concepts of modern dynamics. Newton's first two laws of motion were anticipated by Galileo, whose observations uncovered the fact that bodies maintain uniform motion (or are at rest) when no force is acting on them. To demolish the Aristotelian myth that rest was a "natural state" and motion per se required force were major steps made by Galileo before Newton's discoveries.

Newton's three laws of motion are concerned with the effect of force on motion. They are: (1) every body continues in its state of rest, or of uniform motion in a straight line, unless compelled by a force to change that state; (2) the rate of change of momentum (velocity × mass) is proportional to and along the line of the force; (3) to every action corresponds an equal and opposite reaction. The first law may be considered a corollary of the second. The force acting on a body is proportional to the rate of change of momentum; consequently, if there is no force, the body's momentum is constant.

Newton's laws

Newton's law of universal gravitation states that two bodies attract each other with a force that is along the line connecting the bodies, is proportional to the product of the masses of the bodies, and is inversely proportional to the square of the distance between the bodies. The law is universal since it is applicable to the motion of a planet around the Sun as well as to the falling of a stone (or apple). The law of gravitation speaks about two bodies, the Sun and a planet, or the Earth and the stone, but the law is valid for computing the interactions of any number of bodies. The motion of two (isolated) bodies subject to mutual gravitational forces can be computed by solving the pertinent differential equations. The solution in the planetary case is an ellipse on which the motion takes place according to Kepler's laws. But this result is no longer empirical; it does not follow from observations as in Kepler's case, but it is obtained by analytical tools using the force as input. In fact, the motion of double stars, of comets, or of satellites might be computed by carefully evaluating the forces and solving the appropriate differential equations. If there are only two bodies participating (called the problem of two bodies), the solution is known to be either an ellipse, hyperbola, or parabola, but such general statements about the solution of problems in which more than two bodies participate cannot be made. The celebrated unsolved problem of celestial mechanics is the problem of three bodies; that is, when three bodies interact gravitationally with each other (see below).

Progress in celestial mechanics after Newton's work was rapid, since the basic force law, as well as the equations to be solved, were now ready for application. Powerful analytic methods have been developed in the last two centuries.

The Newtonian approach to dynamics is to solve the equations of motion by finding *explicit expressions* of the positions of the bodies as functions of the time, but such satisfying and luxuriously elegant results can be obtained only for the simplest problems of celestial mechanics. In practice, one must resort to successive approximations and *series solutions*, since the simple closed-form solutions are not available. Often these series represent solutions valid only for a short interval of time or, in the language of mathematics, the series are either not convergent or have a small radius of convergence. The other fundamental difficulty of series solutions is that they are unable to furnish the properties of the general solution. Nevertheless, the success of classical series solutions in obtaining approximate representations of the motion is unquestionable.

The next step in the development of dynamics was the application of *qualitative methods*. The unsurpassed master of such methods was H. Poincaré (1854–1912), who revolutionized the fundamental concepts of celestial mechanics. The qualitative approach does not furnish numerical descriptions of the motion; consequently, Poincaré's contributions—and those of G.D. Birkhoff (1884–1944), A. Wintner (1903–58), and A.N. Kolmogorov (1903–)—were of more theoretical than of immediate practical or observational interest.

Qualitative methods of Poincaré

Modern method. The qualitative, quantitative, and formalistic methods of celestial mechanics have clearly defined places in the aforementioned development of dynamics. The most powerful mathematical methods belong to the modern qualitative approach, and the use of computers permits the full utilization of the quantitative and formalistic approaches. The formalistic approach is the classical series solution of problems of celestial mechanics used by the great mathematicians from L. Euler (1707–83) to D. Brouwer (1902–66). The capability of high-speed computers to perform algebraic manipulations, series expansions, multiplications of series (in addition to numerical work) makes the classical formalistic approach once again fashionable, since high order expansions may be obtained with high reliability and with great speed. The quantitative approach is popular with astronomers and space engineers because often a particular solution of a problem is sought rather than the general behaviour of the dynamical system. Examples are planetary ephemerides, representing particular solutions of the astronomers' *n*-body problems (when any number, *n*, of bodies interact) and lunar trajectories, representing particular solutions of the engineers' problem.

The recent popularity and importance of celestial mechanics are due not only to the great advances made in the development of electronic computers but also to successful launching of space probes and satellites. Computers perform computations that some years ago would have taken lifetimes of hard labour with desk calculators. The concept of experimentation in its original and numerical sense has entered celestial mechanics. Physical experimentation in classical astronomy was not possible; the universe could be observed only. But it is now possible to launch satellites on orbits designed to obtain information regarding the Earth's gravitational field, and this is an experiment in astronomy. Modern computers permit *numerical* experiments also. From the point of view of dynamics, it is essential to survey the totality of possible motions and thereby to establish information about the future behaviour of a system of interest. For instance, a stone thrown with various initial velocities will have different orbits. Once a method is established whereby the orbit can be predicted from the direction and speed with which the stone was thrown, the possible motions that result can be surveyed. In space research this concept may assume the greatest interest, as the following example demonstrates.

Space missions as experiments

The orbit of an Apollo space vehicle is designed so that the astronauts may land on the Moon and safely return. There are many possible ways to do this; in other words, there are many possible orbits satisfying the mission requirements (hitting a can with a stone and a target with a missile are similar types of "missions"). Knowing the totality of such orbits permits selection of the optimum path: the shortest flight time, minimum amount of fuel used, largest payload delivered, etc. So, from theoretical and practical viewpoints, comprehension of all possible orbits is essential. The computer furnishes just such information when analytical methods fail.

The problem of three bodies (Earth, Moon, space vehicle) is an unsolved one in celestial mechanics; that is, there are no closed-form formulas describing the orbit of the space probe, but computers offer numerical solutions and help to find the totality of orbits. The dynamical system (in the case of an Apollo flight) consists of the three bodies, the motions of two of which are known since the orbits of the Earth and of the Moon are available from precomputed ephemerides. The motion of the space vehicle may be numerically integrated (*i.e.*, the differential equations may be solved) for any specific set of initial conditions knowing the firing date, the location, and the direction and magnitude of the initial velocity. Thousands of such trajectories can be calculated in minutes on a computer, and the "best" may be chosen.

In fact, it is possible to experiment numerically to see which planetary or satellite orbits are stable, what initial conditions result in orbits that repeat themselves (periodic orbits), or under what conditions a triple-star system will break up into a binary and an escaping star. The last example refers to the case when two of three stars form a two-body system, revolving around each other, while the third star departs from this binary.

Orbits with close approaches. New developments in computational techniques are necessary to satisfy the operational requirements imposed by attempts to solve new problems. An outstanding new problem resulting from space-probe activities is related to the accurate computation of orbits with *close approaches.* Close approaches are common occurrences—in fact, often they are operational requirements—for space probes, while natural celestial bodies seldom have close approaches. The consequence is far-reaching, and it can be comprehended when the structure of the Newtonian gravitational force field is considered. The force acting between two bodies becomes large when their mutual distance decreases. The relative velocities and accelerations also become large, and computational inaccuracies might occur just at the time when increased accuracy is usually mandatory. When the space probe is in the immediate vicinity of a target planet, the accuracy of the orbit prediction must be great; while it is coasting between centres of gravitation, the preciseness of its orbit is not critical. Close approaches may occur sometimes with asteroids or with comets, and ingenious ad hoc methods have been devised for accurate orbit computations by modifying the classical methods. Hansen's (1795–1874) *method of partial anomalies*, one such technique, splits the orbit into segments, and the motion is described by different variables on each segment. Changes of relative distances between bodies in the solar system are not as great as in the case of space probes. The Newtonian force field shows a "singular" behaviour when the participating bodies are close, in that the force becomes large and the slightest computational errors are amplified. Such a singularity may be eliminated in most problems in celestial mechanics by using properly selected variables to describe the motion. This process of mathematical regularization was investigated by T. Levi-Civita (1873–1941), H. Poincaré, and K.F. Sundman (1873–1942).

These mathematical methods were not used much in classical celestial mechanics until the peculiar orbit requirements of space exploration made their applications essential. The theory of regularization, or smoothing of the singular behaviour of the force field, has now become a characteristic approach to celestial mechanics. It stabilizes computational processes, speeds up computer solutions, and simultaneously reduces computational errors. In a special form, the method was already known to Kepler, who made use of the eccentric anomaly (see the angle GCS = u in Figure 1), in addition to the true anomaly (BSP = f) and to the mean anomaly. (This latter is the angular measurement of time expressed in radians along the orbit, so that after the planet completes one orbit around the Sun, its mean anomaly increases by 2π.) Introducing the eccentric anomaly as a variable (instead of the time) to describe the motion is the basic method of regularization. Sophisticated regularization techniques may be considered generalizations of the use of the eccentric anomaly and consist of the introduction of new dependent as well as independent variables. These methods have been applied with considerable success to calculations of lunar trajectories as well as to other problems in modern space dynamics.

The problem of two bodies and perturbations. The orbits of two gravitationally attracting bodies are ellipses, hyperbolas, or parabolas, depending on the initial conditions of the motion. The orbits of natural and artificial planets and satellites would be ellipses if perturbations did not influence these orbits; any effects that result in devia-

tions from the elliptic orbits are called perturbations. The gravitational effect of Jupiter, for instance, on the motion of the Earth around the Sun is a perturbation; because if the Earth's motion were only under the Sun's influence, its orbit would be an ellipse. One of the classical triumphs of celestial mechanics was the discovery of the planet Neptune in 1846 from perturbations of Uranus (see NEPTUNE).

Deviations from elliptic orbits may be caused by effects other than that of a third body. The orbit of an Earth satellite is a perturbed ellipse because the Earth does not consist of homogeneous, concentric, spherical shells, and its mass distribution is distorted. Such *oblateness* perturbations on the elliptic orbits of natural and artificial satellites can be evaluated today without difficulty, and it is known that the orbits are not stationary ellipses. Another perturbation on the orbits of close Earth satellites is caused by the atmosphere. Atmospheric effects tend to circularize elliptic orbits and progressively reduce the satellite's altitude until it hits the surface of the Earth, or is destroyed by heat upon re-entering the lower atmosphere. Solar radiation pressure is another perturbation that may become important for large, light, balloon-type satellites. An originally circular orbit is distorted by the radiation effect into an ellipse with decreasing perigee distance until the satellite is destroyed.

In order to describe the effects of perturbations, it is necessary to introduce the conventional parameters describing a satellite orbit in space (see Figures 1 and 2). In

Calculating pertur-bations

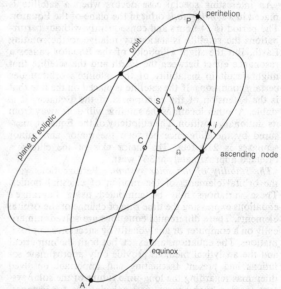

Figure 2: Orbital elements in space (see text).

addition to the previously mentioned orbital elements, the semimajor axis (a) and the eccentricity (e), which together determine the shape and size of the elliptic orbit, four more quantities (also called parameters) are needed. The inclination (i) of the orbital plane to a fixed plane such as the equatorial or the ecliptic plane (in which the Earth moves) and the location of the ascending node Ω on the ecliptic define the plane of the orbit. The fifth orbital element, ω, determines the orientation of the ellipse in its plane by the location of the pericentre, the point of the orbit closest to the centre of attraction. The last parameter specifies the location of the body on its orbit by the time, T, of its perihelion (or perigee, etc.) passage or the time when any other position along the orbit is occupied. The ascending node Ω is the point where the body in orbit passes from north to south of the ecliptic plane, and it is described by its angular position measured from a point on the ecliptic plane, such as the vernal equinox, at a given time. The six quantities a, e, i, Ω, ω, and T, or any equivalent set, define the unperturbed orbit of a planet around the Sun or of a satellite around a planet. Perturbations will result in changes in these orbital parameters. At any instant one may think of the body moving on a specially varying ellipse called the osculating ellipse that stimulates the actual momentary path quite closely. If the perturbations suddenly stopped, the body would then continue travelling on the same ellipse.

Those changes in the shape and position of the two-body orbit that progress always in the same direction with time are called *secular*, while certain others, varying in intensity and direction, are called *periodic*. Secular effects are of great importance as they accumulate with time. The term secular in astronomy refers to effects continuing through centuries and ages.

The principal effects of the oblateness of a planet on the motion of its satellites are a backward motion of the node Ω and a motion of the apsidal line ω. Hence, by carefully measuring satellite orbits, the gravitational field of planets can be determined. Especially designed satellites are observed to obtain information about the internal mass distribution of the Earth. This procedure is called satellite geodesy.

A few numerical results concerning an artificial Earth satellite may be of interest. Consider an orbit inclined at 30° to the Earth's equatorial plane, with perigee altitude of 100 miles and with apogee altitude of 520 miles. The eccentricity is 0.05 and the semimajor axis is 4,273 miles. The orbital period of this satellite is 92 minutes; therefore, it performs 15.7 revolutions per day. The angle of the ascending node changes 7° per day (*i.e.*, the nodal line regresses by 7° per day), or in 51.4 days the orbital plane precesses 360° (*i.e.*, it makes a complete revolution). The argument of the perigee changes 11° per day.

An interesting special case occurs when a satellite is placed in a *synchronous* orbit in the plane of the Equator. The period is 24 hours and consequently without perturbations the satellite is stationary relative to the rotating Earth. But the slight ellipticity of the Equator causes a resonance effect between the Earth and the satellite that might result in instability of the satellite's orbit under certain conditions. If the satellite is placed on the line that is the extension of the minor axis of the Equator, it is stable. At other locations the satellite will drift away from its stationary position. The ellipticity of the Equator measured by the difference between the major and minor semiaxes is 210 feet. The major axis of the ellipse is oriented approximately at 36° west.

The stability of the solar system. Perturbations vary the orbital elements of the motion of celestial bodies. These variations may be computed using Lagrange's equations expressing the time rate of change of the orbital elements. These differential equations are solved numerically on a computer or analytically by successive approximations. The equations are exact, but both the numerical and the analytical methods provide only approximate solutions and present fascinating and important unsolved dilemmas regarding the long-time future of the solar system. If, from such approximate calculations, for instance, the eccentricity of the Earth's orbit is shown to increase proportionally with time, the calculations will predict that the orbit eventually will change so much that the Earth may depart from the solar system or fall into the Sun. But when higher order approximations are computed, an opposite or compensating trend may be seen. It is essential to realize the limitations of the analytical methods, as well as the restricted applicability of computers when long-time effects are to be evaluated. At present, questions that are related to the long-time stability of the solar system cannot be answered either analytically or computationally.

These questions involved the fundamental unsolved problem of celestial mechanics, and also of dynamics: whether or not some characteristics of unperturbed, highly idealized elliptic orbits will survive slight perturbations that last for a long time. Recent mathematical results (1954) allow an approach, in principle, to the stability problem for long-time periods in an entirely different manner, according to which the quasi-periodic behaviour of the solar system will prevail. Very small perturbations will not disturb its stability provided that conditions excluding certain resonances in the system are satisfied. Unfortunately, the application of this principle to celestial mechanics encounters two serious difficul-

ties. First, the theory contains certain assumptions whose validity for the solar system is questionable. Second, Newtonian gravitational forces are not the only effects influencing the orbits of the members of the solar system. Atmospheric drag, radiation pressure, relativity effects, and others must be considered also. These forces are negligible at any instant, but their cumulative actions for several times 10^9 years may influence planetary motions significantly. In addition, there may be unknown effects and perturbations; these naturally cannot be expressed or represented in the equations, and it must be emphasized that such unknown factors can have only very small instantaneous effects; that is, practically speaking they cannot be detected.

The classical problem of three bodies. Because of its historical, dynamical, astronomical, and astronautical significance, the problem of three bodies, the "most celebrated of all dynamical problems" (E.T. Whittaker, 1904), is described separately. This is a strikingly simple problem to state, but its solution is still not available. Three bodies attract each other according to the Newtonian gravitational law. The bodies are thought of as point masses; that is, their gravitational fields correspond to those of the concentric homogeneous spheres mentioned previously. These bodies are free to move in space and are initially supposed to be moving in any given manner. The problem is to determine their subsequent motion. The solution cannot yet be expressed mathematically in finite terms. The number of articles and memoirs published on this problem is well over 1,000 and includes contributions of the greatest mathematicians from Newton to the present. The motion of the Moon in the field of the Sun and the Earth is a classical example. The motion of a planet around the Sun as perturbed by Jupiter, the motions of the satellites of the planets perturbed by the Sun, and, in astronautics, the orbits of space vehicles to the Moon as affected by the Moon and the Earth are others.

A version of the three-body problem of practical importance occurs when one of the three participating bodies is much less massive than the other two. The approximate ratios of the masses of the Sun, Earth, and Moon are 300,000:1:0.01. The mass ratios of the Earth, Moon, and a space vehicle are about $100:1:10^{-19}$; that is, the mass of a six-ton space vehicle is represented in this ratio by 18 zeroes and a one following a decimal point. When one of the participating bodies has such a small mass, its effect on the other two bodies may be neglected. In this way, the problem is split into a two-body problem (which is solvable) and the problem of determining the motion of the third (small) body. Once the first problem is solved, the third body is introduced into the known and moving (time dependent) gravitational fields of the two large bodies, often called primaries, and an attempt is made to determine the motion of this single small body. The motions of the primaries will not be measurably influenced by the small body; the motion of the small body is governed entirely by the primaries. This problem, originated by L. Euler in the 18th century is known as the *restricted three-body problem*, but even in this simplified form, the problem is not solved.

Unsolved problems in dynamics may have certain characteristics, which, even though the complete solutions are unknown, will promote the understanding of the behaviour of the system. Such characteristics are usually either qualitative or are given in closed form mathematical expressions, representing *some* relations between the variables involved. For instance, in the gravitational problem of any number of bodies, the total energy (the sum of the kinetic and potential energies) is constant, for there is no dissipation of energy. This is the principle of the conservation of energy, and its mathematical expression is known as the integral of energy. The kinetic energy is proportional to the masses and to the squares of the velocities of the participating bodies; the potential energy is related to the relative positions of the bodies. Therefore, the conservation of energy principle can be expressed by an equation relating the velocities to the positions of the participating bodies at any instant. While it does not represent the

Influences
on orbits

Conservation of
energy

solution of the problem, it does contribute to the understanding of the behaviour of the bodies. Using such an expression, G. Hill arrived at the conclusion that the Moon will never depart from the Earth, provided the assumptions of the restricted problem of three bodies are valid. Regions limiting possible motions of the bodies may be established in this way without solving the problem.

An interesting application of the three-body problem is Lagrange's prediction (1772) of the existence and location of the *Trojan planets*, which, 134 years later, were actually observed. These minor planets are found around the triangular (equilibrium) points of a three-body system, Jupiter and the Sun occupying the other corners of an equilateral triangle. At the points, there are no resultant forces acting on the asteroids, so they are in equilibrium.

The configuration is shown schematically in Figure 3. The line of syzygies is L_1L_3, connecting the primaries (m_1 = Sun and m_2 = Jupiter). Point C is the fixed centre of

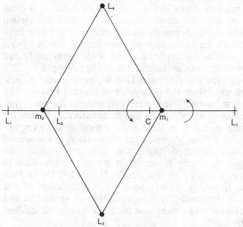

Figure 3: The Lagrangean Points L_1–L_5. $L_1L_2L_3$ is a straight line. $L_4m_1m_2$ and $L_5m_1m_2$ are equilateral triangles (see text).

mass around which the Sun and Jupiter revolve approximately in circles. As a consequence, the rigid triangles $m_1L_4m_2$ and $m_1L_5m_2$ also revolve, and L_4 and L_5 also describe circles. The minor planets "librate" (oscillate) around L_4 and L_5 in stable orbits. Lagrange also showed that if the third particle is placed at any of the three collinear points (L_1, L_2, L_3), the ever-present perturbations will eject it; in other words, these points represent unstable solutions. The stability of L_4 and L_5 when m_1 = Earth and m_2 = Moon is influenced by the Sun, among other perturbing effects. Mathematical and observational evidence for the possible existence of material particles around the Earth-Moon triangular libration points is still lacking.

Other famous special solutions of the problem of three bodies are *periodic solutions*, in which the three bodies periodically return to their original position with their original velocities and repeat their motion. Poincaré's unproved conjecture in celestial mechanics states that all solutions may be approximated by periodic solutions. This lends considerable importance to the numerical and analytical investigation of periodic orbits. The planetary, lunar, and satellite theories are all based on the idea of using trigonometric functions and periodic solutions as reference orbits, which, when improved, may represent the actual solutions.

When such periodic terms are used in the solution, they introduce small divisors resulting in large amplitude motions. This phenomenon, described by Laplace in 1780, is related to resonance, and one of the most famous examples is "the great inequality" in the motion of Jupiter and Saturn. These planets are nearly in resonance since their mean motions are approximately in the ratio of 5:2.

Another important problem of celestial mechanics is connected with the possibility of *capture*. This formidable mathematical problem may be stated in a variety of ways depending on the orientation of interest. A practical appli-

cation is the origin of the Earth-Moon system. From the point of view of celestial mechanics, it is essential to know if the Moon could have been captured by the Earth, being originally an independent planet with an orbit around the Sun close to the orbit of the Earth. If the assumptions of the restricted problem are valid, this could not have happened, but with tidal effects or dissipative mechanisms operating, the answer could be affirmative.

The systematic numerical survey of the totality of possible solutions in the restricted problem began in 1913 by E. Strömgren at the Copenhagen Observatory. The corresponding survey for the much greater variety of possible motions in the general three-body problem was made possible only by the use of high-speed electronic computers, and it is in progress at the present time.

The problem of *n* bodies. This is a generalization of the three-body problem for the case when the number of bodies (n) is larger than three. All participating bodies attract each other according to the Newtonian law of gravitation and are free to move in space. Initially all bodies have arbitrary positions and velocities. The problem is to find their subsequent motions.

Equations like the integral of energy are again available to establish certain properties of the motion. Nevertheless, the mathematical complications limit the possibility of finding explicit solutions analytically and once again numerical solutions become of considerable interest. Elaborate electronic computers have been used to attack the problem when n = 10, 25, 50 and up to several hundred. The complexity of these programs is revealed when it is realized that for 100 bodies the simultaneous solution of 600 first order differential equations is required. At every step of the computation almost 5,000 mutual distances and the corresponding inverse squares must be computed. Any time two or more of the participating bodies perform close approaches, the accuracy of the computational process is jeopardized. Such computations could not have been performed before the use of electronic computers.

Depending on the number of bodies and on the initial conditions, the *n*-body problem corresponds to various physical systems. The solar system has been modelled in this way, and planetary ephemerides have been obtained for thousands of years. If n is sufficiently large (the order of a hundred), the problem corresponds to the motion of stars in a globular cluster. Computations have shown the dynamical formation of binaries and the phenomenon of escaping stars. Trends regarding the stability of the system also are indicated. It is known that, due to close approaches, a large inherent instability is present in the calculations that makes the results of the numerical integrations questionable.

BIBLIOGRAPHY. Modern introductory treatments of celestial mechanics include: J.M.A. DANBY, *Fundamentals of Celestial Mechanics* (1962); S.W. MCCUSKEY, *Introduction to Celestial Mechanics* (1963); H. POLLARD, *Mathematical Introduction to Celestial Mechanics* (1966); and J. KOVALEVSKY, *Introduction à la mécanique céleste* (1963; Eng. trans., *Introduction to Celestial Mechanics*, 1967). Applications to space dynamics and astrodynamcis are offered by K.A. EHRICKE, *Space Flight*, vol. 1, *Environment and Celestial Mechanics* (1960); R.H. BATTIN, *Astronautical Guidance* (1964); and R.L.M. BAKER and M.W. MAKEMSON, *An Introduction to Astrodynamics*, 2nd ed. (1967).

Two volumes of collected papers written by authorities in the field are V.G. SZEBEHELY (ed.), *Celestial Mechanics and Astrodynamics* (1964); and, edited with R.L. DUNCOMBE, *Methods in Astrodynamics and Celestial Mechanics* (1966).

Advanced standard references are by P.S. LAPLACE, *Mécanique céleste*, 4 vol. (1829–39); F.F. TISSERAND, *Traité de mécanique céleste*, 4 vol. (1889–96); H. POINCARE, *Les Méthodes nouvelles de la mécanique céleste*, 3 vol. (1892–99); C.V.L. CHARLIER, *Die Mechanik des Himmels*, 2 vol. (1902–07); G.W. HILL, *Collected Mathematical Works*, 4 vol. (1905–07); H.C. PLUMMER, *An Introductory Treatise on Dynamical Astronomy* (1918); E.W. BROWN and C.A. SHOOK, *Planetary Theory* (1933); P. HERGET, *The Computation of Orbits* (1948); W.M. SMART, *Celestial Mechanics* (1953); K. STUMPFF, *Himmelsmechanik*, 2 vol. (1956–65); D. BROUWER and G.M. CLEMENCE, *Methods of Celestial Mechanics* (1961); G.A. CHEBOTAREV, *Analytical and Numerical Methods of Celestial Mechanics* (1967; orig. pub. in Russian, 1965); V.G. SZEBEHELY, *Theory of Orbits: The Restricted Problem of Three*

Bodies (1967); G.N. DUBOSHIN, Celestial Mechanics (1968); and Y. HAGIHARA, Celestial Mechanics (1971).

The mathematical and dynamical principles are treated by J.L. LAGRANGE, Mécanique analytique (1788); E.T. WHITTAKER, Analytical Dynamics (1904); A. WINTNER, The Analytical Foundations of Celestial Mechanics (1941); C.L. SIEGEL, Vorlesungen über Himmelsmechanik (1956); and L.A. PARS, A Treatise on Analytical Dynamics (1965).

(V.G.S.)

Mechanics, Classical

Classical mechanics is the physical science that deals with the motions of material bodies of ordinary size moving at speeds that are small compared with the speed of light. It differs from quantum mechanics, which describes the behaviour of atoms and subatomic particles, and from relativistic mechanics, which deals with high-speed phenomena. In the 1970s classical mechanics applies to the behaviour of supersonic jet planes and artificial satellites.

Classical mechanics, also known as Newtonian mechanics, is a basic part of physics and astronomy and the foundation of most branches of engineering; all rational procedures for the design of machines and structures are based on the laws of classical mechanics. The subject is also of interest to mathematicians because some basic mathematical procedures, such as the differential calculus, were invented for solving mechanical problems.

The bodies dealt with in classical mechanics are assumed to be so stiff that their deformations have no effect on their motions. The effects of deformations are treated in the mechanics of deformable bodies or elasticity; fluid mechanics deals with liquids and gases.

Classical mechanics is usually subdivided into statics, which deals with bodies at rest, and dynamics, which deals with bodies in motion. Dynamics is further subdivided into kinematics, which treats of motions without considering the forces involved, and kinetics, which seeks the relation between the forces and the motions.

Classical mechanics is the oldest of the physical sciences. It grew out of man's search for an explanation of natural physical phenomena and his curiosity regarding the conditions necessary for a state of rest or of motion. Another motivating factor was the urge to create more effective tools and mechanical devices.

This article is divided into the following sections:

I. The origins and foundations of mechanics

HISTORY

The foundations of statics were laid in the 3rd century BC by the Greek mathematician Archimedes, who derived formulas for the equilibrium of simple levers and centres of gravity. These derivations were restricted to parallel forces, which were only slightly more difficult to deal with than collinear forces. The treatment of nonparallel forces presented difficulties that were not overcome until force was conceived as a vector quantity, having both magnitude and direction, and describable by a directed line segment (arrow). About 2,000 years after the death of Archimedes, the Dutch mathematician and inventor Simon Stevin, who flourished in the 16th century, solved the lever problem with nonparallel forces and by observation and intuition alone demonstrated the equilibrium of bodies on a double inclined plane; he showed how to add force vectors by constructing a parallelogram using the force vectors as the sides.

Forces as vectors

In his writings, Stevin makes the statement that what a simple machine gains in force it loses in distance, a clear indication that he understood the principle of virtual work, which was formally enunciated by the Swiss John Bernoulli in the 18th century. The work of Stevin gave a new impetus to the study of statics, which previously had only the theory of the lever as a working principle.

Although the pre-Christian Greeks, particularly Aristotle, tried to explain the behaviour of moving bodies, they were unsuccessful. There were two reasons for their failures: in the first place, they had no satisfactory means for measuring distance or time and, consequently, were unable to check their formulas experimentally; in the second place, they laboured under the false assumption that force was necessary to maintain motion rather than to change its direction or magnitude. It was left for Galileo early in the 17th century to lay the foundation of the science of dynamics, by a combination of analytical and experimental procedures that is characteristic of the best scientific work.

One of Galileo's contributions deals with the motion of falling bodies; he disproved the Aristotelian theory that heavy bodies fall faster than light bodies. To verify his theory that the height fallen would be proportional to the square of the time and independent of the weight, he experimented with a smooth ball rolling down an inclined plane; he measured the time of the motion by weighing the water that flowed through a small hole at the bottom of a large tank filled with water.

Galileo developed the equation of motion of a projectile and showed that, neglecting the air resistance, the curved path was the result of two independent motions, namely, a horizontal motion at a constant speed and a vertical motion at a varying speed under the action of the force of gravity. In this case he utilized the principle of compounding motions in accordance with the parallelogram law for force vectors introduced by Stevin.

Galileo anticipated the law of inertia, formulated by the English physicist Isaac Newton at a later date, when he stated that a body in motion and free from external influences would keep on moving at a constant speed in a straight line; he was the first to recognize that it was acceleration (the rate of change of velocity) and neither velocity nor position that was determined by the external forces.

The effects of forces

Following Galileo in the 17th century, the next important contributor to the science of dynamics was the Dutch physicist Christiaan Huygens, who developed the equations of motion of the pendulum and invented the pendulum clock. He was the first to obtain the acceleration of gravity by pendulum observations and the first to encounter the term now known as the moment of inertia—that is, the measure of the inertia of a body in rotary motion.

Isaac Newton was born the year Galileo died, and, apart from his important discoveries of the law of universal gravitation, the mathematics of the calculus, and his work in optics, he introduced the concepts of force and mass and formulated the three laws of motion that summarize, clarify, and extend the principles introduced by

Galileo. The magnitude of his contributions is reflected in the fact that "Newtonian" and "classical" are synonymous terms in the field of mechanics.

Newton's second law equates the force acting on a body to the product of the mass of the body and the acceleration; because the latter is the time rate of change of the velocity, the resulting equations of motion are differential equations and require mathematical techniques for their solution. When possible, Newton used geometrical methods, believing that they would be more easily understood by readers. The Swiss mathematician Leonhard Euler in the 18th century wrote a series of textbooks on mechanics in which he used the analytical methods of the calculus to solve the differential equations of motion. Euler also showed that any motion of a rigid body can be separated into a translation followed by a rotation about a chosen point, and he extended Newton's second law, which applies to bodies with mass but negligible dimensions (particles), to rigid bodies.

The French mathematician Jean Le Rond d'Alembert was the author in the same century of a famous textbook on mechanics and the discoverer of a principle that bears his name. This was an entirely new and original method of solving problems in dynamics by applying the principles of statics. When a body is being accelerated, the forces acting on it are unbalanced, but by Newton's second law they are equal to the product of the mass and the acceleration of the body. By the simple expedient of reversing the mass-acceleration terms, the body is placed in equilibrium, and unknown forces can be determined by the equations that apply to bodies at rest.

Dynamics reduced to statics

One hundred years after the publication of Newton's laws, the French mathematician Joseph-Louis Lagrange developed a formula for deriving the equations of motion that is more universal in its application and for certain types of problems easier to use than Newton's equations. Lagrange's equation is a differential equation that deals with energy rather than force, and with velocity rather than acceleration; the resulting equations of motion are the same as those derived by Newton's second law. Equations of a similar type were developed by the Irish mathematician Sir William Rowan Hamilton in the 19th century. Both Lagrange's and Hamilton's equations have proved invaluable in the more advanced and theoretical treatments of dynamics.

THE FUNDAMENTAL CONCEPTS AND QUANTITIES OF MECHANICS

The descriptions of the states of rest or of motion of bodies that Newton's laws provide are inherently mathematical, and, consequently, the quantities appearing in the equations require explanation and in some cases precise definition.

A description of motion requires a frame of reference and means for locating bodies in the frame. The reference frames used in mechanics are known as coordinate systems, with mutually perpendicular axes (lines) emanating from a point known as the origin; for motion parallel to a fixed plane two axes are required, while for motion in space three are required. Strictly speaking, Newton's laws of motion are valid only in a coordinate system with origin at the centre of the solar system; this is known as a Newtonian, or inertial reference, frame. Although it rotates, the Earth can be considered an inertial reference frame in most cases.

The principal units of length used to describe the position of bodies are the metre in the International System (SI) and the foot in the engineering (English) system. With time measured in seconds, the derived units of velocity (directed speed) are metres per second and feet per second. Acceleration, which is the time rate of change of velocity, is expressed as metres per second per second or feet per second per second.

The concept of mass

The mass of a body is a measure of its inertia, or the resistance that it offers to having its speed changed; as an illustration of the difference between mass and weight, consider the following example. If a smooth, heavy body were resting on a flat sheet of ice, the mass of the body would influence the time taken to bring it up to a given speed by pushing it and also the time taken to stop it; the greater is the mass, the longer is the time. On the other hand, the weight of the body would influence the effort required to lift it.

Newton's second law states that the acceleration a imparted to a body by a given force is equal to the force F divided by the mass m; i.e., $a = F/m$. This means that, because acceleration has the dimensions distance per second per second, the quotient F/m must have the same dimensions; either F or m can be chosen as the fundamental unit, and the other will be the derived unit.

The SI system is known as an absolute system, and mass in kilograms is the fundamental unit; the derived unit of force is known as a newton, and from the expression for a it is the force that acting on a one-kilogram mass will produce an acceleration of one metre per second per second.

The engineering system is known as a gravitational system, and force in pounds is the fundamental unit; the derived unit of mass is known as a slug, and it is that mass that, when acted on by a one-pound force, will have an acceleration of one foot per second per second.

The relation between mass and weight can be obtained by applying Newton's equation to a falling body. The force acting on the body is W, the weight, and the average value of the acceleration of gravity g on the surface of the Earth is 9.81 metres per second per second in the SI system and 32.2 feet per second per second in the engineering system. Then, in the SI system $W/m = 9.81$, which means that a kilogram weighs 9.81 newtons; in the engineering system $W/m = 32.2$, which means that a slug weighs 32.2 pounds.

The SI and the engineering systems are related in the following way; one pound force equals 4.4 newtons, and one slug mass equals 14.59 kilograms.

The acceleration of gravity varies slightly from place to place on the surface of the Earth, and in interstellar space it may approach zero. Thus, whereas the mass of a body at the speeds considered in classical mechanics is a constant, the weight of a body will vary with its position relative to the centre of the Earth. At the same place, the masses of bodies are proportional to their weights so that weighing is a convenient means of measuring masses.

Newton's equations of motion deal with the gross motion of a body; i.e., the motion of the body as a whole. There is one point in a body the motion of which is characteristic of the gross motion; it is called the centre of mass. If the body rotates, the rotation can always be referred to the centre of mass, and additional equations must be deduced to deal with the rotation. When the gross motion of a body is more significant than its rotary motion, the body may be treated as a particle. The Earth, for example, can be treated as a particle when describing its motion around the Sun; it cannot be treated as a particle when dealing with terrestrial problems.

II. Statics

The forces in the members of a machine or structure must be known before the dimensions required to carry them can be calculated; thus, methods for determining such forces are of extreme importance to all designers of mechanical devices. Assuming that the main loads that a machine or structure is expected to carry are specified, the forces acting in the connected elements of the machine and the reactions from the supports can be determined by various analytical and graphical procedures. When a machine or structure is in a state of equilibrium (at rest), the science of statics provides the means for calculating a limited number of the unknown forces.

The science of statics assumes that the bodies with which it deals are perfectly rigid and asserts that when at rest the resultant (sum) of all the forces acting on a body must be zero and that there must be no tendency for the forces to turn the body about any axis. These conditions are independent of one another, and their expression in mathematical form constitutes the equations of equilibrium. When all the forces lie in the same plane there are only three equations so that only three unknown forces can be calculated. If there are more than three unknown forces, it signifies either that there are more restraints than are necessary to keep the body from moving or that there are more members (as in a structure) than are necessary to support the applied loads; the unnecessary restraints and members are said to be redundant. In such cases, the rigid-body assumption must be discarded, and the elastic properties of the members must be considered. Although the procedures for finding the forces in structures with redundant members are strictly static rather than dynamic in nature, it is customary to designate such structures as statically indeterminate. Unless otherwise noted, the following material deals with rigid-body statics only.

FORCE

In statics a force may be defined as any action that tends to maintain or alter the position of a body or to distort it. There are many kinds of forces, such as a push or a pull, gravity (which is manifested as weight), steam or gas pressure in an engine cylinder, atmospheric pressure, wind pressure on a building, resistance to motion in air or water, magnetic and electrostatic attraction, nuclear attraction, and pressure and friction between contacting bodies.

The effect of a force on a body is determined by its point of application, its direction, and its magnitude. Because it has direction as well as magnitude, force is a vector quantity and can be shown graphically as a directed line segment; *i.e.*, a line with a length equal to the magnitude of the force, to some scale (such as one inch equals 100 pounds), inclined at the proper angle, and with an arrowhead at one end to indicate sense (one of two opposite directions). When it is necessary to emphasize the vectorial nature of a quantity it will be indicated in boldface type.

The representation of forces by vectors implies that they are concentrated at a single point or along a single line. Physically this is impossible; even when two metallic spheres are pressed together, the contacting surfaces flatten, and the force is distributed over a small area. On a loaded member of a machine or structure, the force produces an internal force or stress that is distributed, in some manner, over the cross section of the member. The force of gravity is distributed throughout the volume of a body. Nevertheless, when the equilibrium of a body is the main consideration, it is usually valid as well as convenient to assume that the forces are concentrated at a point. In the case of the gravity force, the total weight of a body is assumed to be concentrated at its centre of gravity.

Internal forces

Basic principles. There are three main principles or axioms that facilitate the solution of problems in statics, namely, the parallelogram of forces, action and reaction, and the transmissibility of a force.

The parallelogram of forces, formulated by Stevin in 1586, states that, if two forces whose lines of action intersect are acting on a body, their action is equivalent to the action of a single force whose vector representation is the diagonal of the parallelogram of which the two original force vectors are sides.

In Figure 1A the flexible cords AB and BC are attached to a ring at point B from which the weight W is suspended by the cord BD. The forces acting on the ring are the tension in the cord BD (acting down and equal to the weight W) and the tensions T_1 and T_2 in the cords AB and BC, respectively. Because it is in equilibrium, the resultant force acting on the ring—*i.e.*, the sum of W, T_1, and T_2—must be zero. This requirement enables T_1 and T_2 to be determined as functions (*i.e.*, in terms of) of W. In Figure 1B the vector W is drawn to any convenient length to represent the tension in the cord BD; to complete the triangle of forces, T_1 and T_2 are drawn parallel to AB and BC, respectively. When vectors are added, they are placed tail to tip so that knowing the sense of W the arrowheads can be placed on T_1 and T_2 to satisfy this requirement.

In Figure 1A the vector BE, acting upward, is the diagonal of the parallelogram formed by T_1 and the parallel side GE and T_2 and the parallel side FE. Because triangle BEF is similar to the triangle in Figure 1B, the

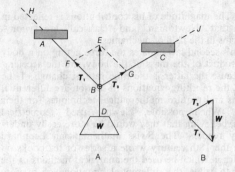

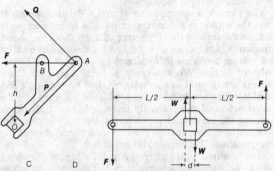

Figure 1: *Equilibrium of forces and their turning effects.*
(A) Parallelogram of forces, (B) triangle of forces, (C) moments, (D) couples (see text).

vector BE must be equal in magnitude to W. It is shown acting upward to indicate that it is the resultant of T_1 and T_2 and could serve as their replacement as far as their effects on the ring at B are concerned. The ring would then be in equilibrium under the action of two forces, namely, W acting upward and W acting down.

The principle of action and reaction, which is also known as Newton's third law of motion, states that, when one body exerts a force on another body, the second body exerts a force on the first body; the two forces are collinear (act along the same line), equal in magnitude but opposite in sense.

The weight W in Figure 1A pulls down on the ring B while the ring pulls up on the weight with an equal and opposite force. Contact forces between bodies always occur in pairs; a book resting on a table pushes down on the table with a force that is equal and opposite to the upward force of the table on the book. The principle is also true for some of the forces that act at a distance, such as gravitational attraction; a flying airplane pulls up on the Earth with a force equal and opposite to its weight.

The principle of transmissibility states that the equilibrium of a body is not altered when the point of application of a force is moved to some other point on its line of action; *i.e.*, the line along which the force acts. In Figure 1A the position of the weight W would be unaltered if the cord BD were lengthened and attached to W at its centre or if A and C were moved to points such as H and J or F and G.

The principle of transmissibility

Moment of a force and a couple. The concept of moment, or torque, as it is used in mechanics is the tendency of a force to rotate the body to which it is applied about a point or axis. Of the three forces of equal magnitude applied to the wrench in Figure 1C, the force Q, which acts at right angles to OA, is clearly the most effective in tending to turn the square bolt head to which the wrench is applied about the point O; force P is completely ineffective. The moment of a force about a point O is equal to the product of the magnitude of the force and the length of a line from O at right angles to the line of action of the force. Thus the moment of the force F in Figure 1C is equal to Fh, and from the principle of transmissibility F would have the same effect if applied at either point A or point B.

A more effective wrench than the one in Figure 1C is shown in Figure 1D. If the forces F are equal, they constitute a "couple," and the turning effect, or moment, of the couple is FL. To keep this wrench in equilibrium, another couple, Wd, the reaction from the bolt head, must be acting and must be equal to FL. On the other hand, because the torque is applied to the wrench in Figure 1C by a force, there must be a force equal and opposite to F (or Q) acting on the wrench in addition to a balancing couple.

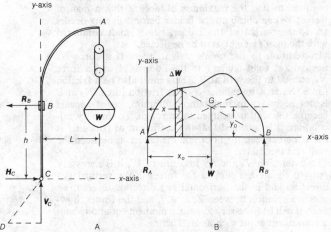

Figure 2: *Supporting reactions on stationary bodies.*
(A) Lifeboat davit, (B) flat plate (see text).

Application of equilibrium equations. Figure 2A shows one of the two davits used to suspend a lifeboat. The load applied to the davit at A by the boat is W, the reaction R_B at B is assumed to be horizontal because the support is frictionless, and the support at C is a ball-and-socket joint that can carry both horizontal and vertical reactions, such as H_C and V_C. It is required to find the reactions as functions of W, h, and L.

When applying the condition that when a body is in equilibrium the resultant force acting on the body must be zero, it is usually convenient to resolve (separate) the forces into sets of orthogonal (mutually perpendicular) components and assert that the summation of the forces in each orthogonal direction must be zero. Because the direction of a vector involves both inclination and sense, a vector or the component of a vector along or parallel to any fixed line, such as the axis of a coordinate system, has a fixed inclination and can be described by a number, either positive or negative, to indicate its magnitude and whether it points in one or the other of two opposite directions (sense). Consequently, such vectors, although they are shown as directed lines, can be considered as scalars; *i.e.*, quantities that require only a number for their specification. In the following examples, force components along chosen directions will be taken as scalars and be added, subtracted, multiplied, and divided like ordinary numbers.

For the davit, using the x and y coordinate axes as convenient directions, Σ for summation, F as a general term for forces, and F_x and F_y for the forces acting along x and y, the two force equations of equilibrium would be $\Sigma F_x = 0$ and $\Sigma F_y = 0$. An additional moment equation, expressing the requirement that the davit must not rotate about any chosen point in the plane of the forces, must be written; choosing point C and using M to designate moment, the moment equation would be $\Sigma M_C = 0$. In Figure 2A the reaction R_B and the two components of the reaction at C, namely, H_C and V_C, are shown acting in assumed directions; the correctness of these assumptions will be verified later. Because positive directions for x and y are to the right and up, respectively, R_B is negative, while H_C and V_C are positive. Clockwise moments will be considered positive.

From $\Sigma F_y = 0 = V_C - W$ it follows that $V_C = W$;

from $\Sigma M_C = 0 = WL - R_B h = 0$ it follows that $R_B = WL/h$; and from $\Sigma F_x = 0 = H_C - R_B$ it follows that $H_C = R_B = WL/h$. Because all three unknown forces came out positive, it proves that the assumed directions were correct; if H_C, for example, had been assumed in the negative x direction, it would have come out negative in $\Sigma F_x = 0$. The total force at C, which is the resultant of V_C and H_C, is a vector DC, pointing up and to the right.

Centre of gravity. Figure 2B shows a plate of weight W resting on horizontal supports at A and B. If the reactions R_A and R_B were required, the summation of vertical forces F_V would yield only $\Sigma F_V = R_A + R_B - W = 0$; to find R_A and R_B it would be necessary to write a moment equation about either A or B that would include the moment of the weight of the plate. The moment of the plate about A could be obtained by adding up the moments of a large number of small slices of the plate, symbolized by ΔW (delta W), whose moment arms x are taken at the centre lines of the slices. It would be more convenient if a point such as G, the centre of gravity, could be found at which the entire weight of the plate could be concentrated. The distance x_0 from A to the line of action of W can be found by equating the moment Wx_0 to the sum of the moments obtained by the slicing method; this gives $Wx_0 = \Sigma(\Delta W)x$, in which the summation is taken over the whole body. Solving this equation for x_0 yields $x_0 = \Sigma(\Delta W)x/W$. The vertical coordinate y_0 of G can be obtained by slicing the plate parallel to AB. The coordinate of G perpendicular to the plane of the paper would be half the thickness of the plate from either surface of the plate.

If the upper surface of the plate were a curve that could be described by a mathematical equation, the coordinates of G could be obtained by the integral calculus. The summation sign Σ becomes an integral sign $\int$, the slices become infinitesimally thin, and the calculated value of x_0 is exact. For a plate of any shape the centre of gravity can be obtained by suspension. If the plate in Figure 2B were suspended from A, the line AG would be vertical, while if suspended from B the line BG would be vertical; point G is at the intersection of these two lines.

For bodies with three planes of symmetry, such as a sphere or a circular cylinder, the centre of gravity is at the geometric centre of the body. For bodies with geometric shapes, such as cones, segments of a circle, and triangles, formulas for the centre of gravity are to be found in handbooks.

Centre of gravity by suspension

FRICTION

Friction is of considerable importance in everyday life as well as in mechanics. Without friction, walking would be impossible, no ladder would stand against a wall, an automobile could not be driven or stopped.

Between two bodies in direct contact there is always some friction, which tends to hinder, or even prevent, the sliding of one body on the other. Consider the steel block resting on the steel table in Figure 3A. The weight W, acting down, and the reaction N from the table, acting up, must be equal and opposite. If a small horizontal force P is applied to the block and the block does not move, there must be a friction force F, equal and opposite to P at the surface of contact between the block and the table. If the force P is increased, it will eventually cause the block to slide on the table.

Experiments show that when slipping impends, the value of F is always a fixed ratio of the normal force N and that this ratio depends on the materials and the roughness of the contacting surfaces. Thus, when slipping impends, $F = fN$, in which f is the coefficient of static friction. For dry steel on steel the value of f is given as 0.15 in some handbooks, but it varies greatly with surface roughness and whether or not surface films such as oxides are present.

The value of f can be determined experimentally by means of an adjustable inclined plane, as in Figure 3B. The angle θ (theta) is slowly increased until the block starts to slide down the plane. There are two forces acting on the block: the weight W and the reaction R from the plane, both of which must pass through the centre of

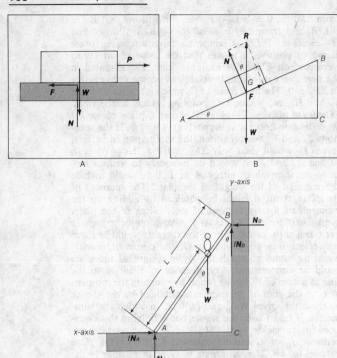

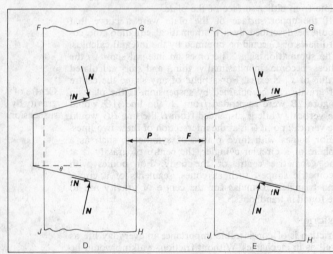

Figure 3: *Friction forces and their effects.*
(A) Sliding block, (B) the angle of repose, (C) a sliding ladder,
(D,E) a wedge (see text).

friction, to distinguish it from viscous friction, which occurs in oil films.

In the operation of machines, friction may be either a useful agent or the cause of lost power. The operation of brakes and clutches, the grip of belts on pulleys, and the tractive effort of wheels on rails are all applications in which the maximum amount of friction is desired. In bearings and sliding connectors the friction, which causes heat and loss of power, is reduced to a minimum by the addition of lubricants whose main function is to minimize metal-to-metal contact.

The ladder. A ladder AB of length L in Figure 3C rests on a horizontal floor at A and a vertical wall at B. It is required to find the maximum distance Z that a man of weight W can climb up the ladder before slipping occurs at A; the weight of the ladder, being small compared with the man's weight, is to be neglected.

In addition to the man's weight, there is a force N_A normal (at right angles) to the floor at A and a force N_B normal to the wall at B. There must also be a friction force fN_A at A to balance N_B; the friction force fN_B at B is not necessary to maintain equilibrium, but it appears because the wall is assumed to be rough. To simplify calculation, it is assumed that the coefficient of friction f is the same between the floor and the ladder as between the wall and the ladder.

To determine N_A and N_B in terms of W, it is necessary only to equate the sum of the forces in the vertical (y) direction and in the horizontal (x) direction to zero. To obtain a relation between Z, L, θ, f, and the forces, however, it will be necessary to write a moment equation about a convenient point such as A. Then:

$$\Sigma F_y = N_A + fN_B - W = 0,$$
$$\Sigma F_x = N_B - fN_A = 0.$$

The summation of moments is given by:

$$\Sigma M_A = WZ \sin\theta - N_B L \cos\theta - fN_B L \sin\theta = 0$$

(sin, cos, tan, and cot are ratios of the various sides of a right-angled triangle). Solving these equations yields the following:

$$\frac{Z}{L} = \frac{f \cot\theta + f^2}{1 + f^2}.$$

As long as $f \cot\theta$ is equal to or greater than one, Z/L will be equal to or greater than one, and the man can climb to the top of the ladder without fear of the ladder slipping. When slipping impends, $f \cot\theta = 1$ or $f = 1/\cot\theta = \tan\theta$. From Figure 3C, $\tan\theta = AC/BC$ so that as long as AC/BC is less than f the ladder will not slip. For timber on stone f is approximately 0.40, which corresponds to an angle θ of 21°48'; if θ is greater than this, the ladder will slip. On rough ground f could be 1.0, which corresponds to a safe angle θ of 45°. It is worth noting that θ is the same as the angle of repose, in Figure 3B, at which friction just holds the block from sliding down.

The wedge. In Figure 3D a tapered plug is being driven into a matching hole in the member $FGHJ$ by a force P; the progress of the plug is opposed by the two normal (at right angles) reactions N and the two friction forces fN. The summation of forces in the horizontal direction yields the equation $P - 2N \sin\theta - 2fN \cos\theta = 0$, which, solved for N/P, gives

$$\frac{N}{P} = \frac{1}{2(\sin\theta + f \cos\theta)}.$$

The ratio N/P is the mechanical advantage, a measure of the force-amplifying property of a wedge. The magnitude of the ratio increases as the denominator of the previous equation decreases. The magnitude of the denominator depends on both the angle θ and the coefficient of friction f; the smaller is the angle and the smaller is the friction coefficient, the smaller is the denominator. As θ approaches zero, $\sin\theta$ approaches zero and $\cos\theta$ approaches unity. This means that no matter how small θ becomes, the term $f \cos\theta$ can only be reduced by lowering f.

If the plug in Figure 3D is to be pulled out, the force

The angle of repose

gravity G. Resolving R into the components N and F and noting that triangle ABC and the triangle formed by R, N, and F are similar, $BC/AC = F/N = \tan\theta$, which by definition is equal to f; the angle θ is known as the angle of repose.

Between a rubber tire and a dry concrete road f could reach a value of 1.00 so that $F = N$, and in Figure 3B, BC would equal AC and θ would equal 45°. This means that an automobile with locked brakes could stand on an incline of 45°, but for greater angles it would slide downhill.

The first complete investigation of dry friction was made by the French physicist Charles-Augustin Coulomb in 1781; he discovered that the total amount of friction that can be developed between two contacting bodies is proportional to the normal pressure and independent of the area of contact. If a brick is pulled along a table, the frictional force is the same whether the brick is lying flat, on its side, or on its end. Coulomb also found that after slipping has started, the frictional force is less than the friction when slipping impends. Later experiments indicate that at extremely high pressures abrasion may alter the surface conditions and cause f to reach unpredictable values. Dry friction is usually called Coulomb

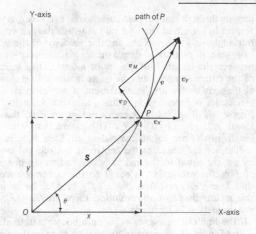

A

P (now labelled *F*) and the frictional forces will be reversed, as shown in Figure 3E. For this case it can be shown that $F = 2N(f \cos \theta - \sin \theta)$.

When $f \cos \theta = \sin \theta$, or $f = \tan \theta$, the magnitude of *F* is zero. This means that the plug will fall out of its own accord when *P* is removed. For all angles for which $\tan \theta$ is less than *f*, the taper is a "sticking" one, and *F* in the previous equation will be greater than zero. Sticking tapers are used for holding such cutting tools as drills and reamers in machine-tool spindles.

Wedges that stick

III. Dynamics

KINEMATICS

The position vector and motion. Motion is change of position, and to describe the motion of a body *A*, for example, relative to another body *B*, it is necessary to establish a reference frame on body *B* and means for describing the position of any point in body *A* in this frame. A convenient frame is a system of rectangular coordinate axes; *i.e.*, graduated lines emanating from a point called the origin and at right angles to one another. For three-dimensional (space) motion three axes are necessary, for two-dimensional (plane) motion two are required, while for one-dimensional (line) motion only one axis is necessary.

In Figure 4A the position of point *P* on its path in the *OXY* coordinate system can be described either by the coordinates *x* and *y* or the length of the vector *S* and the angle *θ*. Like all vectors, *S* has both magnitude, as given by its length, and direction, which is a combination of inclination and sense (one of two opposite directions). When a vector, such as *S*, is used to describe the position of a point, it is known as a position vector.

As the point moves on its path, the head of vector *S* will move with it, and the magnitude and direction of *S* will change. These changes are the only two that a vector can experience. The coordinates *x* and *y* will change in magnitude as the point moves and serve as orthogonal components of the vector *S*.

Velocity. The speed of the point *P* is the time rate at which the point moves along the path; the velocity of the point is a vector quantity and as such has both magnitude, which is equal to the speed, and direction, which, as shown in Figure 4A by the vector *v*, is tangent to the path and pointing in the direction in which the point is moving.

By definition, the velocity of point *P* can be expressed either as the time rate of change of the vector *S* or the vector sum of the changes in *x* and *y*. Because *S* changes in both magnitude and direction, the velocity *v* must be the vector sum of these changes. As will be shown below, changes in the magnitude of a vector are always collinear with the vector, whereas changes in direction are at right angles to the vector.

The vector v_M in Figure 4A represents the rate at which the magnitude of *S* is changing and v_D the rate at which its direction is changing. Both of these changes are functions of *S*; *i.e.*, they are expressed mathematically in terms of *S*.

The coordinates *x* and *y* are quantities that have magnitude and sense only; they are positive when they lie above and to the right of the origin *O* and negative when they lie below or to the left of *O*. Because they do not rotate and change in magnitude only, *x* and *y* can be considered as scalars or directed lines or one-dimensional position vectors. The velocities resulting from their rates of change are usually called the scalar components of *v*. Velocities obtained from scalar quantities, or the magnitude of a velocity vector, are usually indicated by *v*. Then v_x and v_y are the velocities resulting from the changes in *x* and *y* and their resultant is the vector *v*.

Acceleration. Being a vector, the velocity *v* may change in both magnitude and direction as the point moves, and the vector sum of these changes is defined as the acceleration *a* of *P*. The acceleration can also be defined in terms of the sum of the changes in v_D and v_M, or the changes in v_x and v_y. Because v_D and v_M move with *S*, they may change in both magnitude and direction, and the acceleration vector will have four components if they are used, and they will all be functions of *S*; if v_x and v_y are used,

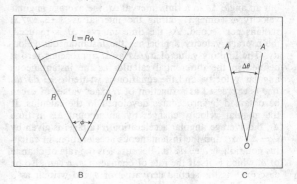

B   C

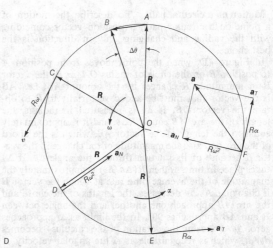

D

Figure 4: *Motion of a point on a plane (flat) curve.*
(A) Position and velocity vectors, (B) radian measure, (C) rotary motion, (D) motion on a circle.

there will be only two components, parallel to the *X* and *Y* axes, and functions of *x* and *y*. These scalar components, like the magnitude *a* of *a*, are written as a_x and a_y. If a point moves on a curved path, the direction of its velocity must change, and its acceleration can never be zero, even if the speed is constant.

Scalar components of acceleration

Because the coordinate system in Figure 4A can be located in any position relative to the path, there are an infinite number of coordinates and position vectors that can be used to describe the position of the point; the choice must be made by the analyst. For a straight path, a directed line lying in the path and changing only in magnitude is obviously the best choice. For a point moving on a circle, a position vector with its tail at the centre of the circle and changing only in direction is most suitable. The use of position vectors that change in both magnitude and direction is to be avoided, if possible.·

Rotation about a fixed axis. When a body rotates about a fixed axis, the angular position of any line on the body passing through and perpendicular to the axis changes with respect to time, and the time rate at which the line sweeps out angles is known as the angular velocity of the body.

Because it permits a simple mathematical relationship between the length L of the arc of a circle (*i.e.*, segment of the circumference) and the angle subtended (enclosed) at the axis by the arc, measurement of angles in classical mechanics is expressed in radians, as explained below. In Figure 4B if ϕ (phi) is measured in radians, the arc length L is given by $L = R\phi$. This means that, when the length of the arc equals the radius, or $L = R$, ϕ is one radian, or the angle at the centre of a circle subtended by an arc equal to the radius is one radian. In one revolution the arc length is equal to the circumference so that $L = 2\pi R$, and thus $2\pi R = R\phi$ or $\phi = 2\pi$ radians; this means that in one revolution there are 2π (*i.e.*, approximately 6.28) radians.

If the line OA in Figure 4C is on a body rotating about a fixed axis O perpendicular to the page and sweeps out an angle $\Delta\theta$ in a time interval Δt, the average angular velocity ω (omega) during the interval is $\omega = \Delta\theta/\Delta t$ radians per second. As the time interval Δt is reduced, the average velocity approaches the instantaneous velocity. The limiting value of $\Delta\theta/\Delta t$ as Δt approaches zero is defined in the differential calculus as the instantaneous angular velocity, and the equation is written $\omega = d\theta/dt$. If θ is expressed as a function of t, exact values of ω can be obtained by procedures developed in the calculus. If the angular velocity changes by an amount $\Delta\omega$ in time Δt, the average angular acceleration α (alpha) is given by $\alpha = \Delta\omega/\Delta t$, and the instantaneous acceleration, in calculus notation, is $\alpha = d\omega/dt$. Because α is the rate of change of ω, which is itself the rate of change of θ, α can also be described as the second derivative of θ and written as $\alpha = d^2\theta/dt^2$.

Motion on a circular path. To describe the motion of a point on a circular path, a position vector coinciding with the radius and changing only in direction is the best choice.

In Figure 4D, when the point moves from position A to position B on the circle of radius $OA = R$, the vector R of magnitude R changes by the amount AB; *i.e.*, AB is the vector that must be added vectorially to R to obtain the vector OB. If $\Delta\theta$ is measured in radians, the length of the arc AB equals $R\Delta\theta$, and it is approximately equal to the length of the vector AB, which is the chord of the arc, and also the magnitude of the change in the vector R because of its rotation through the angle $\Delta\theta$. If $\Delta\theta$ takes place in time Δt then $R(\Delta\theta/\Delta t)$ is approximately the magnitude of the average time rate at which the vector R is changing. As $\Delta\theta$ decreases, the lengths of the chord and the arc AB approach one another and the angle between R and AB approaches $90°$. In the limit, as Δt approaches zero, $\Delta\theta/\Delta t$ (using the notation of the calculus) becomes $d\theta/dt$, which is recognizable as ω, the angular velocity of R in radians per second. Then $R\omega$ is the magnitude of the vector that represents the instantaneous time rate of change of R; this is the magnitude of the velocity, or the speed, of the moving point and is written as $v = R\omega$. The velocity vector v is inclined at $90°$ to R, with a sense compatible with the direction of ω. At point C in Figure 4D, a position vector R rotating in a counterclockwise direction and the corresponding velocity vector v of magnitude $R\omega$, are shown in the proper relationship. As shown below, this relationship can be described in a more convenient way.

Vectors that rotate When a vector rotates, its time rate of change resulting from the rotation is a vector whose magnitude is equal to the product of the magnitude of the rotating vector and its angular velocity; the direction of the vector is found by turning the rotating vector through $90°$ in the direction of the angular velocity. This procedure applies to all rotating vectors regardless of the kinematic property that they represent. As shown below it can be used to find the acceleration resulting from the rotation of v.

The vector v in Figure 4D must always change in direction, and because it is always at right angles to R its angular velocity is ω. The vector that represents the rate at which its direction changes will have a magnitude equal

to $R\omega \times \omega$ or $R\omega^2$ and its direction will be obtained by turning v through $90°$ in the direction of ω. As shown at D in Figure 4D, this vector, labelled a_N and with magnitude $a_N = R\omega^2$, is collinear with R but with the opposite (inward) sense. If R rotated clockwise, v would point up at point C and when rotated clockwise it would point toward the centre of the circle, just like a_N at point D.

The vector a_N always points toward the centre when a point moves on a circular path. The subscript N signifies that the vector lies along the normal (at right angles) to the tangent to the path; a_N is also known as the centripetal acceleration.

The relation $v = R\omega$ when solved for ω yields $\omega = v/R$, and, if this is substituted for ω in $R\omega^2$, the magnitude of the normal acceleration can be written as v^2/R. When a point moves on a curved but noncircular path, the normal component of acceleration has a magnitude v^2/ρ, in which ρ (rho) is the radius of curvature of the path; *i.e.*, the radius of the circle that matches the curve at the point.

Any changes in the speed of the point in its orbit about O must come from changes in ω, which are measured by the angular acceleration α of R. Consequently, the magnitude of the other component of the acceleration of the point is $a_T = R\alpha$, because it represents a change in the magnitude of v, it must be collinear with v; *i.e.*, tangent to the path and with a sense compatible with the direction of α, as shown by a_T at point E in Figure 4D. The resultant (total) acceleration a of the point, as shown at F, is the vector sum of a_N and a_T.

Simple harmonic motion. The device shown in Figure 5A is a Scotch yoke; it consists of a T-shaped yoke with

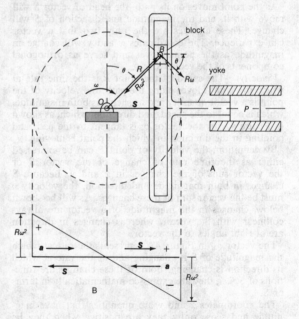

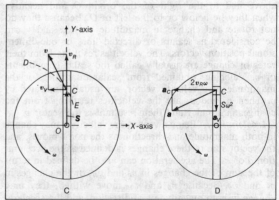

Figure 5: *Harmonic and relative motion.*
(A) Scotch yoke, (B) harmonic motion, (C) relative velocity, (D) relative acceleration.

a slot in which the block can slide and an integral piston P that slides in a cylinder in the frame, which is shown crosshatched. The crank of radius R is pivoted to the frame at O and to the block at B. Rotation of the crank about O with an angular velocity ω causes the block to slide up and down in the slot and the yoke to move back and forth (left and right in the Figure) with a translatory motion while being guided by the piston.

The directed line S, with its tail at O and head at the centre of the slot, is convenient for describing the position of the yoke on its straight path. From the Figure it is clear that the length of S measured from O depends on the length of R and the angle θ and that S will point to the left when θ exceeds $180°$; to distinguish between the directions of S it will be assumed that S is positive $(+)$ when it points to the right and negative $(-)$ when it points to the left.

From trigonometry the relation between S, R, and θ is given by $S = R \sin \theta$. When θ is zero and $180°$, $\sin \theta$ and S are zero; when $\theta = 90°$, $\sin \theta = 1$ and $S = R$; when θ is between $180°$ and $360°$, $\sin \theta$ is negative. Consequently, the magnitude and direction of S are taken care of automatically by $\sin \theta$.

Because the vector S does not rotate, its time rate of change, which is the velocity of the yoke, can be obtained from the calculus by taking the derivative of $S = R \sin \theta$ with respect to time. The velocity can also be obtained by utilizing the relationships shown in Figure 4D for a point moving on a circular path. Point B in Figure 5A moves on a circular path of radius R, and its velocity, of magnitude $R\omega$, is perpendicular to R and pointing down. The velocity of the yoke is the horizontal component of $R\omega$, namely, $v = R\omega \cos \theta$, pointing to the right in the position shown and collinear with S.

If ω is constant, the acceleration of B has a magnitude $R\omega^2$ and is collinear with R and pointing toward O. The acceleration of the yoke is the horizontal component of $R\omega^2$, namely, $a = -R\omega^2 \sin \theta$, pointing to the left in the position shown and collinear with S.

Because $S = R \sin \theta$, the horizontal component of the acceleration can be expressed in terms of S, as $a = -S\omega^2$. This important relationship is illustrated in Figure 5B. The motion of the yoke, which is known as a simple harmonic motion, can be described in words as follows: if the displacement (S) of a reciprocating point is measured from the centre of its path and the acceleration is proportional to the displacement and in the opposite sense, then the motion is called simple harmonic. In Figure 5B, when the displacement S is to the right $(+)$ the acceleration is to the left $(-)$, and when S is to the left $(-)$ the acceleration is to the right $(+)$.

Simple harmonic motion is an important form of periodic motion; it is the motion of a point on the prong of a tuning fork, the bob of a simple pendulum swinging on a small arc, and a weight hung from a spring and vibrating vertically.

Motion of a tuning fork

The period, or time required for one complete to-and-fro motion of a body executing simple harmonic motion, is equal to the time required for one revolution of the crank in Figure 5A. Because there are 2π radians in one revolution, the speed of the crank in revolutions per second is $\omega/2\pi$ and the time for one revolution $T = 2\pi/\omega$ seconds. Then, from $a = -S\omega^2$, $\omega = \sqrt{-(a/S)}$ and $T = 2\pi/\sqrt{-(a/S)}$ or $T = 2\pi\sqrt{-(S/a)}$. Because S and a are always of opposite sign, the quantity under the radical is always numerically positive.

Relative motion. Although all motion is relative, the term is usually reserved for motion on a moving path or, in other words, relative to a moving coordinate system. In Figure 5C, a large horizontal table rotating at a constant (nonvarying) speed ω about a vertical axis O carries a radial track on which a car C is moving away from the axis at a constant speed. The track is a moving path, and the OXY axes attached to the table form a moving coordinate system. Because the car is being carried around counterclockwise by the table as it moves outward along the radial track, the path that it traces in space will be a spiral curve, like ED. The motion of the car on its space path—i.e., its absolute motion—can be described as the

sum of its motion relative to the table and the motion of the table, and for this purpose the position vector S is convenient. Relative to the table, S changes only in magnitude at a time rate appropriately designated as the relative velocity v_R. Because it rotates with the table, S also changes in direction at a rate that, as shown previously, is given by a vector, of magnitude $S\omega$, perpendicular to S and pointing to the left because of the direction of ω. All points on the table have circular space paths, and their speeds are equal to the products of their distances from the centre of the table and the angular velocity ω. Consequently, $S\omega$ can be interpreted as the speed of the point on the table that coincides with C at the instant considered; the corresponding vector is called the vehicle velocity v_V, the table being the vehicle. The absolute velocity v of the car is equal to the vector sum of v_R and v_V, and, as shown in Figure 5C, it is tangent to the space path.

Because the car is moving at a constant speed there is no relative acceleration, and, consequently, v_R remains constant in magnitude; it does change in direction, however, because it rotates with the table at an angular velocity ω. The vector v_V also changes in direction, but, in addition, it changes in magnitude because S is increasing in magnitude. Thus the acceleration of the car is the sum of the three changes in the components of the velocity, namely, the changes in the direction and magnitude of v_V and the change in the direction of v_R.

The directional change in v_V is obtained by turning v_V through $90°$ in the direction of ω; because $v_V = S\omega$ its magnitude is $S\omega \times \omega = S\omega^2$ and it is collinear with S and in the opposite sense; because of its similarity to a_N in Figure 4D, it can be interpreted as the acceleration of the point in the table coinciding with C at the instant considered; this is the vehicle acceleration a_N.

Because $v_V = S\omega$ and ω is constant, the change in the magnitude of v_V is the result of the change in the magnitude of S, which has already been shown to be v_R. Consequently, the magnitude of this change in v_V is $v_R\omega$ and it is collinear with and has the same sense as v_V because S is increasing.

The directional change in v_R is obtained by turning v_R through $90°$ in the direction of ω; its magnitude is $v_R\omega$ and it will coincide with v_V in Figure 5C. It can be shown that the two vectors of magnitude $v_R\omega$, one resulting from the change in magnitude of v_V and the other from the change in direction of v_R will always coincide. The sum of these two components is the Coriolis component of acceleration a_C, and its magnitude is $2v_R\omega$. In Figure 5D the absolute acceleration of the car a is shown as the vector sum of a_V and a_C. If the car were moving at a variable speed, there would be a relative acceleration vector, collinear with S and pointing in the same direction as S if the relative velocity were increasing. If the table were being accelerated, there would be another component of vehicle acceleration, perpendicular to S and of magnitude $S\alpha$, in which α is the angular acceleration of the table.

Summarizing, the absolute velocity is always equal to the sum of the relative and vehicle velocities. The absolute acceleration is the sum of the relative and vehicle accelerations, and, if the vehicle rotates, there is an added term, the Coriolis component (discovered in 1835 by the French mathematician Gustave-Gaspard Coriolis).

Coriolis component of acceleration

In the case considered, it is clearly convenient to describe the absolute motion in terms of the relative motion and the vehicle motion. To find v and a using absolute quantities, it would have been necessary to know the precise nature of the absolute (space) path. There are many applications, particularly in the analysis of machinery, for which either absolute or relative quantities can be used. In some cases absolute quantities provide the simpler solution.

KINETICS

Newton's laws of motion. Newton's three laws are the basic postulates (self-evident truths) governing the relations between the forces acting on a body and the motion of the body. Although they were formulated for the first time in usable form by Isaac Newton, they had been discovered experimentally by Galileo about four years before Newton was born. The laws cover only the overall motion of a body—i.e., the motion of its centre of mass—and not any rigid-body motion such as a rotation. This is equivalent to assuming that the body is a particle.

The law of inertia. The first law states that, if a particle is at rest or moving at a constant speed in a straight line, it will remain at rest or keep moving at a constant speed in a straight line unless it is acted upon by a force. This postulate is known as the law of inertia, and it is basically a description of one of the properties of a force, namely, that it can change rest into motion or motion into rest or one kind of motion into another kind.

Before Galileo's time it was thought that bodies could move only as long as a force acted on them and that a body free from external influences would come to rest. Those who sought to find the forces that kept the planets moving did not realize that no force was necessary to keep them moving at a practically uniform rate in their orbits; gravitational force was necessary only to change the direction of motion.

The most common impediment to steady motion is friction. A power-driven vessel is quickly brought to rest by fluid friction when the driving engine is stopped; after being struck, a hockey puck will keep on moving for a longer time on smooth ice than on a rough road. No moving body is entirely free from the effects of friction, but it seems reasonable to assume that, if a moving body were free from all external influences, it would move at a constant speed in a straight line. When a body is at rest the forces acting on it form a balanced system; i.e., the **Bodies** net or resultant force is zero. **at rest**

The law of force. Newton's second law is a quantitative statement of the changes that a force can produce in the motion of a particle. It states that the time rate of change of the velocity—i.e., the acceleration—is directly proportional to the force and inversely proportional to the mass of the particle. The larger the force (F) is, the larger is the acceleration (a), and the larger mass (m) is, the smaller is the acceleration; thus $a = F/m$.

Both force and acceleration are vector quantities and as such have both magnitude and direction. The acceleration produced by a force is in the same direction as the force; if several forces act on a body, it is their resultant (sum), obtained by adding the vectors tail to tip, that produces the acceleration.

The mathematical expression of the second law can be established by considering the results of Galileo's experiments with falling bodies; he found that the force of gravity W, acting alone on a body, produces a constant acceleration equal to g. If a force F acts on the same body instead of W and produces an acceleration equal to a, it follows from the second law that the ratio of a to g is the same as the ratio of F to W; i.e., $a/g = F/W$, from which $a = F/(W/g)$. The quantity W/g is equal to m, the mass of the particle, and a measure of its inertia or reluctance to having its speed changed. As stated in the law, the larger the mass is, the smaller is the acceleration produced by a given force. The second law is usually expressed in the form

$$F = ma. \qquad (1)$$

If the force acting on a body is resolved into components along coordinate axes, each component force equals the mass multiplied by the corresponding component of the acceleration.

The law of action and reaction. Newton's third law, frequently referred to as the law of action and reaction, asserts that forces, being the result of interactions of two **Forces** bodies, always appear as equal and opposite pairs. For **in pairs** bodies in direct contact with one another the proposition seems obvious; it is also true for some forces that act at a distance, such as gravitational attraction. As noted previously, the property of forces expressed by the third law is particularly useful in statics.

Motion under a constant force. According to Newton's second law—namely, $F = ma$—if the force acting on a body passes through the body's centre of mass and remains constant in magnitude and direction, the body will

move in a straight line with a constant acceleration. This means that the body will acquire equal increments of velocity in equal time intervals. Figure 6A shows how the velocity of the body increases from zero at the beginning of a time interval t to v at the end of the interval.

Because the line *odf* is straight, the ratios cd/oc and ef/oe, which represent the slope of the line, are equal, and either may be used to find the acceleration, which is the rate of increase of velocity per unit of time, or v/t. Using ef/oe, $a = v/t$; solving this equation for v yields $v = at$, which states that, if the velocity is zero at the beginning—i.e., when $t = 0$—the velocity at the end of any time interval t is equal to the acceleration multiplied by the time.

The distance travelled in a given time by a body moving at a constant velocity is equal to the velocity multiplied by the time. When the speed varies, it is equal to the product of the average velocity and the time. In Figure 6A the average velocity is $v/2 = at/2$ so that the distance S travelled during the interval is the average velocity times the time: $S = at/2 \times t = \frac{1}{2}at^2$, which is half the product of the acceleration and the square of the time; it is also equal to the area of the triangle in Figure 6A.

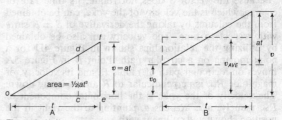

Figure 6: *Uniformly accelerated motion.*
(A) Initial velocity zero, (B) initial velocity v_0 (see text).

If the body were moving with an initial velocity v_0 before the force were applied to it, the relation between velocity and time—i.e., the velocity–time (v, t) curve— would look like Figure 6B. In this case v is equal to the initial velocity v_0 plus the added part at; i.e., $v = v_0 + at$. The distance travelled, S, is the area under the curve, which is the sum of the rectangle v_0t and the triangular piece, which is the same as the one in Figure 6A, namely, $\frac{1}{2}at^2$. The distance travelled can also be expressed as the average velocity $v_{AVE} = (v_0 + v)/2$ multiplied by t. Summarizing:

$$v = v_0 + at \qquad (2)$$
$$S = v_0t + \frac{1}{2}at^2 \qquad (3)$$
$$S = \left(\frac{v_0 + v}{2}\right)t. \qquad (4)$$

If air resistance is neglected, these equations are valid for a falling or a rising body that is sufficiently close to **Falling or** the Earth that the acceleration of gravity g may be taken **rising** as a constant. For a body falling from rest, $v_0 = 0$ and **bodies** $a = g$; for a body projected vertically upward with an initial velocity v_0,

$$v = v_0 - gt \qquad (5)$$
$$S = v_0t - \frac{1}{2}gt^2. \qquad (6)$$

At the top of the rise $v = 0$, and setting $v = 0$ in equation (5) and solving for t yields the corresponding time

$$t = \frac{v_0}{g}. \qquad (7)$$

Substituting this value of t in equation (6) gives $S = v_0^2/2g$, which is the height to which the body will rise.

Motion of a projectile. Consider a projectile of mass m fired from a gun with an initial velocity v_1 at an angle θ to the horizontal (Figure 7A). The projectile's motion may be considered as consisting of a horizontal part and a vertical part, the initial horizontal component of velocity being $v_H = v_1 \cos \theta$ and the initial vertical component $v_V = v_1 \sin \theta$. If air resistance is neglected, the only force on the projectile after firing is its weight, W, acting downward; there is no force in the horizontal direction. Consequently, the horizontal component of velocity will remain

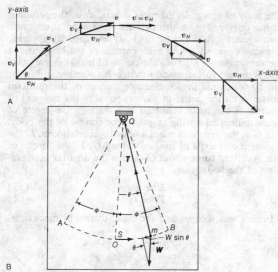

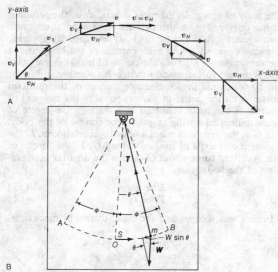

Figure 7: *Motion of a projectile and a pendulum.*
(A) Projectile, (B) simple pendulum.

unaltered throughout the motion, while the vertical component will change because of the force of gravity; *i.e.,* the weight.

It is clear that the projectile will rise and then fall back to Earth after describing a curved path. During its travel the velocity v will remain tangent to the path, while v_H will remain constant, and v_V will vary as shown in Figure 7A.

The distance covered in a given time by a body moving with a constant velocity is equal to the velocity multiplied by the elapsed time. Therefore x, the horizontal distance traversed in time t by the projectile, is given by $x = (v_1 \cos \theta)t$.

The vertical motion of the projectile is governed by the action of gravity and is entirely independent of the horizontal motion. It is an example of a body projected vertically upward with a velocity $v_1 \sin \theta$ and, consequently, equations (5) and (6) will apply. Letting $S = y$, $v = v_V$, and $v_0 = v_1 \sin \theta$

$$v_V = v_1 \sin \theta - gt \qquad (8)$$
$$y = (v_1 \sin \theta)t - \tfrac{1}{2}gt^2. \qquad (9)$$

From equation (8) it may be seen that the projectile will have reached its greatest height when $v_V = 0$ and $t = (v_1 \sin \theta)/g$ and returned to Earth when $t = (2v_1 \sin \theta)/g$. Substituting this value of t in the equation for x gives $x = (2v_1^2 \sin \theta \cos \theta)/g$, which can be written $x = v^2 \sin 2\theta/g$.

Because $\sin 2\theta$ has its maximum value of unity when $2\theta = 90°$—that is, when $\theta = 45°$—it follows that the greatest horizontal range for a given initial velocity is obtained when $\theta = 45°$.

Ballistic calculations such as the foregoing are of little practical value when the initial velocities and the ranges are large. A precise calculation of the trajectory of a *Long-range* long-range projectile or guided missile must take into ac-*projectile* count air resistance, the variation in the value of g, the *motion* rotation of the Earth, and any spin of the projectile.

Simple pendulum. A simple pendulum (Figure 7B) consists of a small, heavy body of mass m called the bob, suspended from a fixed point Q by a cord of length l and of mass so small compared with m that it can be neglected.

If the bob is raised to position A in Figure 7B and let go, it will oscillate (swing back and forth) in a vertical plane through the angle ϕ on each side of the equilibrium position OQ. The forces acting on the bob are the tension T in the cord, acting upward, and the weight of the bob W, acting down. The cord tension keeps the bob on its circular-arc path AB, and the resulting centripetal acceleration a_N, which is a consequence of the changing direction of the velocity of the bob, is directed toward Q. The tangential component of the acceleration a_T, which results from changes in the magnitude of the velocity, is

produced by the component of the weight of the bob acting tangent to the path.

In Figure 7B the bob is shown in an intermediate position defined by the angle θ in radians, measured, for convenience, from the midposition OQ; the corresponding displacement S along the arc is given by $S = l\theta$, and it is arbitrarily considered positive when pointing to the right.

From Newton's second law, the summation of forces along the cord yields $T - W \cos \theta = ma_N$; from this equation the cord tension T can be calculated, but only after a_N has been determined by other means. Along the tangent the only force acting is the component $-W \sin \theta$ of W, which is negative because it points to the left; then, from Newton's second law, $-W \sin \theta = ma_T$. Now a_T can be expressed as a function of θ, namely, the second derivative of θ with respect to time, as described above under *Rotation about a fixed axis*. If this replacement for a_T is made, the previous equation becomes a differential equation; it is difficult to solve, but, if the oscillation of the pendulum is restricted to small angles, which it usually is, a simple solution can be obtained by replacing $\sin \theta$ by the angle θ in radians. On pendulum clocks the half oscillation ϕ is usually less than $10°$, and for that angle the difference between $\sin \theta$ and θ in radians is never more than one-half of 1 percent.

Because $S = l\theta$ in Figure 7B, then $\theta = S/l$, and, if this is substituted for $\sin \theta$ in the previous equation and m is expressed as W/g, the weight W, being on both sides of the equation, will cancel out, and the equation will reduce to $-S/l = a_T/g$ or $a_T = -(g/l)S$.

The term g/l is a constant; *i.e.,* it does not vary during the motion. Thus the tangential acceleration of the bob is proportional to its displacement (S) from the midposition and in the opposite sense. By definition, this is a simple harmonic motion, and the formula for the period (time for a complete cycle of two swings) of such a motion, previously derived for a Scotch yoke, is applicable. For the Scotch yoke $T = 2\pi \sqrt{-S/a}$; for the pendulum $S/a_T = -l/g$ so that $T = 2\pi \sqrt{l/g}$.

A seconds pendulum is one that takes one second to *The* make one swing (one-half cycle); then $T = 2$ seconds *seconds* or $l = g/\pi^2$. Because g varies slightly on the surface of *pendulum* the Earth, the length of a seconds pendulum will be different at the North Pole than at the Equator. An average value for l for a seconds pendulum is slightly more than 39 inches, or about one metre. By measuring the length and period of a pendulum the value of g can be calculated; this is one of the most accurate methods of determining g at any place on the surface of the Earth.

Force required for motion on a circle. When a particle moves on a circular path with a velocity that is changing in both magnitude and direction, it is convenient to treat these effects separately when seeking the forces that are their causes.

In Figure 8A, a particle of mass m in the form of a

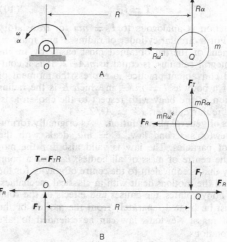

Figure 8: *Forces required for motion in a circle.*
(A) The acceleration, (B) the forces.

circular plate is attached at Q to a rigid bar of length R that rotates about a fixed axis at O with an angular velocity ω and an angular acceleration α. The mass of the bar is assumed to be so small compared with the mass of the particle that it can be neglected, while the total mass of the particle is assumed to be concentrated at Q. From Figure 4D the two components of the acceleration of the particle are $R\omega^2$, the centripetal or radial component directed inward along the bar, and $R\alpha$, the tangential component at right angles to the bar and with a sense compatible with a counterclockwise α (Figure 8A).

To determine the forces that are acting on the particle and on the bar, it will be convenient to draw free-body diagrams. A free-body diagram is a sketch showing a body isolated from all adjacent bodies and with all the forces acting on it that are significant to the problem under consideration.

From Newton's second law the components of the acceleration of the particle are caused by the forces $F_R = mR\omega^2$ and $F_T = mR\alpha$; in Figure 8B these forces are shown acting on a free-body diagram of the particle.

From Newton's third law, action and reaction are equal and opposite. The forces F_R and F_T are exerted by the bar on the particle, and, consequently, the particle must exert equal and opposite forces on the bar; they are shown at point Q on a free-body diagram of the bar in Figure 8B. Because the mass of the bar is to be neglected, there are no inertial effects, and the forces on the bar must balance. The force F_R at Q is easily balanced by an equal and opposite force at O. To balance F_T there must be an equal and opposite force at O, but, because these forces are equal, opposite, and separated by a distance R, they constitute a clockwise couple that, for balance, requires that a counterclockwise couple or torque, $T = F_TR$, be applied (by some means) to the bar at O. Because $F_T = mR\alpha$, the torque can be expressed as $T = mR^2\alpha$.

If another particle of mass m were located diametrically opposite to the first particle on a bar at the same distance R from O, the forces created at O would be equal and opposite to those shown in Figure 8B, and they would cancel each other. The torque T, however, would be twice as much, namely, $2mR^2\alpha$.

Rotational inertia   The quantity mR^2 is a measure of the rotational inertia of a particle, in the same way that m is a measure of its translatory inertia. Each particle in a rigid body has rotational inertia about any chosen axis, and the sum of all these inertias is called the moment of inertia, I, of the body.

For a rigid body $I = \Sigma mR^2$, or, using the calculus notation, $I = \int r^2 dm$, which means that every particle in the body is to be multiplied by the square of its distance from the chosen axis and the products added together. For a rigid body rotating about a fixed axis, for which its moment of inertia is I, the relation between the torque T and the resulting angular acceleration is given by

$$T = I\alpha \qquad (10)$$

This equation is analogous to $F = ma$ for translatory motion. For a circular cylinder of radius A and mass m, the moment of inertia, obtained most easily by means of the integral calculus, is equal to $mA^2/2$. It is a common and convenient practice to express the moment of inertia of a body as $I = mK^2$, in which K is the radius of gyration of the body with respect to the chosen axis; for the circular cylinder, $K^2 = A^2/2$.

Kinetics of general plane motion.   As originally formulated, Newton's second law, $F = ma$, deals with the motion of particles. The law is valid also for the motion of the centre of mass of all bodies; i.e., for a point in a body that is equivalent to the centre of gravity for the bodies and the motions dealt with in classical mechanics. When a body rotates, the causes and effects of the rotations must be treated separately from the motion of the centre of mass; Newton's law can be extended to take care of rotations.

If the resultant of all the forces acting on a body passes through the centre of mass of the body, it will not cause the body to rotate. In the most general case, the resultant force does not pass through the centre of mass, and, consequently, it will cause the body to rotate. By applying Newton's second law to each particle of the body, it can be shown that in all cases the centre of mass behaves as if the resultant force passed through it (whether it does or does not), while the moment, or torque, of the resultant force about the centre of mass is equal to the moment of inertia of the body about an axis through the centre of mass multiplied by the angular acceleration of the body. If G is the centre of mass and a_G its acceleration, I_G the moment of inertia of the body about G, T_G the torque of the resultant force about G, and α the angular acceleration of the body, then

$$F = ma_G \qquad (11)$$
$$T_G = I_G a. \qquad (12)$$

Forces and torques are the basic causes in mechanics,

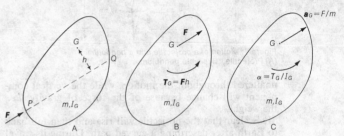

Figure 9: *Causes and effects in plane motion.*
(A) Prime cause, (B) resulting cause, (C) effects.

while accelerations are their effects. In Figure 9A, the resultant force F acting along the line PQ on the body of mass m creates a torque, $T_G = Fh$, about the centre of mass G. The equivalent force and torque system are shown in Figure 9B, whereas the effects are shown in Figure 9C. It should be noted that, while equations (11) and (12) express relationships that exist at any instant during the plane motion of a rigid body, the magnitudes and directions of a_G and α may be changing continuously on account of changes in F.

Since the position of point P relative to G in Figure 9A affects the magnitude and direction of T_G and α but not the magnitude and direction of a_G, it follows that the motion of the centre of mass of a body is entirely independent of any rotation of the body. This means that the centre of mass moves as if it were a particle with the mass of the entire body and acted upon by the resultant force. Neglecting air resistance, any rotational motion of a projectile, for example, will not affect the motion of its centre of mass. Even after the projectile explodes, the centre of mass of the fragments will continue moving on the same path the shell was travelling before the explosion.

Equations (11) and (12) were derived by specifying the instantaneous acceleration of one point in a body and the angular velocity and acceleration of the body and then determining the resultant of the force system required to produce the accelerations. A similar procedure is necessary when making a dynamic analysis of the mechanism of a machine.

Motion of centre of mass

PRINCIPLES OF MOMENTUM AND ENERGY

Newton's second law, $F = ma$, describes the relation between the acceleration of a particle and the force acting on it. This equation works both ways; i.e., if the acceleration is known, the force required to produce it can be calculated, while if the force is known, the acceleration that it produces can be calculated. The relationship defined by the equation is a causal one between the force, which is the cause, and the acceleration, which is the effect.

Although the acceleration a of a particle at any instant can be calculated directly from the formula if F and the mass of the particle are known, this instantaneous value of acceleration gives no information regarding the velocity of the particle. To obtain an adequate description of a particle's motion—i.e., its velocity and displacement (position)—the manner in which F varies must be known. In general, F may vary with the elapsed time or with the distance that it moves or with its velocity.

If F is known as a mathematical function of t, S (distance), or v, it may be possible to integrate the equation $F = ma$ (which is basically a differential equation) by the methods of the integral calculus and so obtain equations for the displacement and velocity of the particle. When the force is constant (nonvarying), the velocity and displacement can be found without using the calculus; when the force varies with time or distance, the results of the integration are embodied in two important and useful relations. One of the relations, known as the principle of impulse and momentum, describes what a force can do in a given time; the other, the principle of work and energy, describes what a force can do in a given distance. Both of these principles are extensions of Newton's second law, and they can be derived in a fairly satisfactory manner without using the calculus.

Impulse and momentum. When a constant force is applied for a time t to a particle moving with a velocity v_0, the velocity of the particle increases to some value v, as shown in Figure 6B. From this figure, if a is the acceleration of the particle, $v - v_0 = at$. From Newton's second law, $F = ma$ or $a = F/m$. Substituting F/m for a in the previous equation gives $v - v_0 = (F/m)t$, which can be written $Ft = m(v - v_0)$. The term Ft, which is the product of the force and the time during which it acts, is called the impulse of the force. The product of the mass of a particle and its velocity is known as the momentum of the particle so that $m(v - v_0)$ is the change in momentum. Hence, the impulse of a force equals the change in momentum produced by it; this is the principle of impulse and momentum, and it simplifies the solution of many problems that would be difficult to solve by $F = ma$.

The margin: **The impulse of a force**

The impulse Ft can be visualized as the area of a rectangle t units of time long and F units of force high. When the force F is not constant, the impulse is the average force during the time interval multiplied by the time interval; this average is the imaginary (constant) force whose impulse equals the impulse of the real (varying)

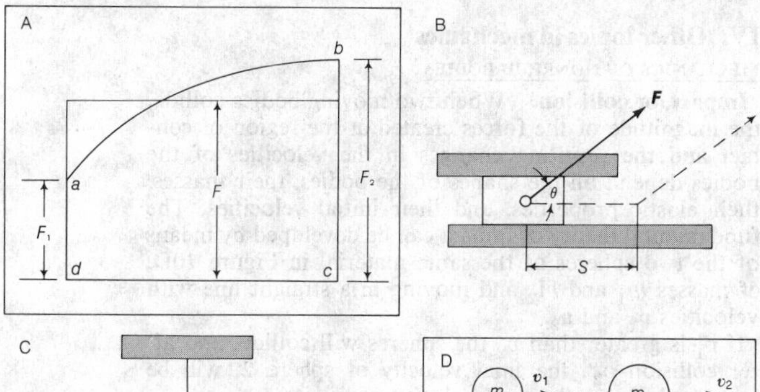

Figure 10: *Work, energy, and impact.*
(A) Average force F, (B) work done by a force, (C) potential energy, (D,E) impact, or collision.

force. In Figure 10A, the force varies from F_1 at the beginning of the time interval dc to F_2 at the end of the interval. The average force F is the force that when multiplied by dc gives the area enclosed by $abcd$. Consequently, the impulse of a force is the area under the force–time (F, t) curve.

The impulse–momentum equation is especially useful

in dealing with the interactions between pairs of particles since in such cases it may not be necessary to calculate the impulse. As an example, consider a projectile of weight W_1 and a gun of weight W_2, which is free to recoil. During the short interval of the explosion, the equal and opposite forces F acting on the gun and projectile, produced by the gas pressure, vary in an unknown manner, and it would be difficult to calculate the impulses of these forces. Because the forces and the times are equal, however, the impulses on gun and projectile must be equal and opposite. Thus, if the initial velocities are zero and the final velocities v_1 and v_2 for the projectile and gun, respectively, then $Ft = (W_1/g)v_1 = (W_2/g)v_2$, from which $v_1/v_2 = W_2/W_1$. Thus the velocities of the projectile and gun after firing are in opposite directions and inversely proportional to their weights.

The projectile and the gun can be thought of as a system of two particles on which no external force acts; the forces F are internal forces. In general, when no external force is applied to a system of particles, the momentum of the system remains unchanged. This is known as the principle of conservation of momentum; the solar system furnishes an illustration of this principle. Because the nearest stars exert no appreciable attractions, the members of the system move under the action of their mutual attractions only, and the momentum of the system does not change. Consequently, the mass centre of the system moves in a straight line with a uniform velocity, just like a particle with a mass equal to the sum of the masses of the Sun and planets.

Work and energy. When a force moves a body through a given distance in the direction in which it acts, the changes in the velocity of the body that result from this action are easily calculated if the force is constant. From equation (4), $S = \frac{1}{2}(v + v_0)t$; solving this equation for t yields $t = 2S/(v + v_0)$. If this value of t is substituted in the impulse–momentum equation, $Ft = m(v - v_0)$, the result is $FS = \frac{1}{2}m(v^2 - v_0^2)$.

The quantity FS is the work done by the force. One-half the product of the mass of a body and the square of its velocity is called the kinetic energy of the body, or K.E. $= \frac{1}{2}mv^2$. The quantity of $\frac{1}{2}m(v^2 - v_0^2)$ is, therefore, the gain in kinetic energy of the body, and, from the previous equation, the work done on a body is equal to the gain in kinetic energy; this is the principle of work and energy, and it simplifies the solution of many problems difficult to solve by $F = ma$.

The margin: **The work done by a force**

The work FS can be visualized as the area of a rectangle S units of distance long and F units of force high. If the force F varies, the work is the average force for the distance multiplied by the distance moved; this average is the imaginary (constant) force that would do the same work as the real (varying) force. In Figure 10A, the force varies from F_1 at the beginning of the displacement dc to F_2 at the end of the movement. The average force F is the force that when multiplied by dc gives the area enclosed by $abcd$. Consequently, the work done by a force is the area under the force–distance (F, S) curve.

When a force does not act in the same direction in which it moves, it is only the component of the force in the direction of the motion that performs work. In Figure 10B, work $= FS \cos \theta$. If a force moves in a direction opposite to that in which it acts, it does negative work.

In the treatment of impulse and momentum, it was shown that the momenta of a projectile and gun are equal and opposite because they are acted upon by equal and opposite forces for the same length of time. Because the mass of the gun greatly exceeds the mass of the projectile, however, the final velocity of the gun will be considerably less than that of the projectile. This means that the distance that the gun moves during recoil will be less than the distance that the projectile moves during the firing period. Consequently, the force, acting for a longer distance on the projectile than on the gun, will do more work on it, and the kinetic energy of the projectile will be greater than that of the gun.

A particle that is in such a state that it can do work is said to possess energy; this energy may be kinetic and the result of the particle's motion or it may be the result of other circumstances, such as position above the Earth's surface or elastic deformation.

Potential energy

Consider, for example, the weight of mass m and weight W suspended by a cord at a height h above the ground (Figure 10C). If the cord were cut, the weight would fall to the ground, and the gravity force would do work. Thus, by virtue of its position above the ground, the weight has the capacity for doing work. This is known as its potential energy relative to the ground.

The work done by gravity on the weight must be equal to the kinetic energy of the weight just before it strikes the ground. If, as shown in Figure 10C, the initial position of the suspended weight is designated by 1, an intermediate position by 2, and the final position by 3, then $Wh = \frac{1}{2}mv_3{}^2$.

It is worth noting that the previous equation provides the most direct method of determining the final velocity of a freely falling body in terms of the initial height. Substituting W/g for m, $Wh = \frac{1}{2}(W/g)v_3{}^2$ and solving for v_3 yields

$$v_3 = \sqrt{2gh}. \tag{13}$$

In position 2 in Figure 10C, the weight will have a potential energy of Wx relative to the ground and kinetic energy of $\frac{1}{2}mv_2{}^2$, which must be equal to the work done by gravity as the weight fell from position 1 to position 2, namely, $W(h - x)$. If E represents the total energy, P potential energy, and U kinetic energy, then at position 2,

$$E_2 = P_2 + U_2 = Wx + W(h - x) = Wh.$$

Now $E_1 = Wh$ and $E_3 = \frac{1}{2}mv_3{}^2 = Wh$, so that in all three positions of the weight its total energy is the same. In position 1 the energy is all potential, in position 2 it is partly potential and partly kinetic, while in position 3 it is all kinetic. A system of particles in which the sum of the potential and kinetic energies remains constant is said to be a conservative system and to satisfy the law of conservation of mechanical energy; the forces involved are said to be conservative forces. When the motion of a body is opposed by friction, mechanical energy is lost; because the energy is not conserved, the force of friction is said to be a nonconservative force.

The "force" of a blow

The work-energy equation can be used to approximate the force required to stop a moving particle or the "force" of a blow. If a wooden pile is being driven into the ground by successive blows of a hammer of weight W falling from a height h on the head of the pile, the "force" of the blow will depend on the nature of the ground and the amount that the pile penetrates the ground on each blow. If the penetration d is small compared with the height h and the weight of the pile is small compared with the weight of the hammer, then the average "force" of the blow, or resistance to penetration R, will be obtained by equating the kinetic energy of the hammer to the work done by the force R during the penetration. The kinetic energy of the hammer when it strikes the pile is equal to its potential energy at the height h, namely, Wh, and the work done on the pile is Rd. Then $Wh = Rd$, from which $R = Wh/d$. This result shows that for given values of W and h the force R depends on d, which depends on the nature of the ground; the harder it is to penetrate the ground, the larger the value of R. If the ground acted like a compressed coil spring, the maximum force would be doubled.

Momentum and energy in rotary motion. Because it is applicable only to the motion of particles or the centres of mass of bodies, the equation $Ft = m(v - v_0)$ is known as the linear impulse–momentum equation. In much the same way that $F = ma$ for particles was shown to become $T = I\alpha$ when applied to the rotary motion of bodies, the linear impulse-momentum equation can be adapted to rotating bodies. In order to do this in a simple way, it will be expedient to utilize the perfect analogy between the mathematical description of motion on a straight path and rotation about a fixed axis.

If the position of a particle on a straight path is described by a position vector that lies in the path, the vector will change only in magnitude as the particle moves, the first time rate of change being the velocity and the second the acceleration of the particle; all vectors will lie in the path.

The angular position, relative to a fixed radial line, of a line on a body rotating about a fixed axis can be described by a vector that lies along the axis and points in a direction that a right-hand screw would advance in a fixed nut if it were attached to and rotated with the body. As the body rotates the vector will change in length, the first rate of change being the angular velocity of the body and the second change the angular acceleration, just like the vectors for a point moving on a straight path.

As a consequence of the similarity of their vector representation, θ (in radians) in rotary motion is analogous to S in linear motion, ω is analogous to v, and α to a. The diagrams in Figure 6 can be adapted for rotation by a constant torque by changing v to ω and a to α. From equations (11) and (12), T is analogous to F and I to m.

Using these relationships, the angular impulse–momentum equation can be written as $Tt = I(\omega - \omega_0)$. If the angular impulse Tt imparted to a rotating body for an interval of time is zero, then the angular momentum of the body must remain constant during the interval. This is known as the conservation of angular momentum. A figure skater may start to revolve slowly at a speed ω_1 and a moment of inertia I_1 with arms extended. By drawing the arms in close, the moment of inertia is reduced to I_2 and the speed increased to ω_2. From the previous equation, with zero impulse $I_1\omega_1 = I_2\omega_2$ or $\omega_2 = (I_1/I_2)\,\omega_1$.

The conservation of momentum

The dimensions of linear impulse are force multiplied by time, and those of angular impulse, moment multiplied by time. Consequently, the linear momentum and the angular momentum of a body cannot be added.

The equation for work and kinetic energy of rotation can be written down at once by using the analogies; it is $T\theta = \frac{1}{2}I(\omega^2 - \omega_0{}^2)$. The work done by a torque is equal to the torque multiplied by the angle that it turns through in radians. Because θ is dimensionless, $T\theta$ has the same dimension as FS, and the kinetic energy of rotation can be added to the kinetic energy of translation.

IV. Other topics in mechanics

MECHANICS OF NONRIGID BODIES

Impact, or collision. When two moving bodies collide, the magnitude of the forces created at the region of contact and the resulting changes in the velocities of the bodies depend on the shapes of the bodies, their masses, their elastic properties, and their initial velocities. The fundamental theory of impact can be developed by means of the two spheres of the same material in Figure 10D, of masses m_1 and m_2 and moving in a straight line with velocities v_1 and v_2.

If v_1 is greater than v_2 the spheres will collide, and after collision v_2', the final velocity of sphere 2, will be greater than v_1', the final velocity of sphere 1.

During the short period of contact the forces on the spheres will be equal and opposite, and, because they act for the same length of time, their impulses will produce equal and opposite changes in the momentum of the spheres. Hence, the law of conservation of momentum applies, and the total momentum after impact equals the total momentum before impact, or

$$m_1v_1' + m_2v_2' = m_1v_1 + m_2v_2. \tag{14}$$

In order to determine the velocities after impact, the energies of the spheres must be considered. At the moment of impact the energy is all kinetic; during impact some of this energy is lost as a result of permanent deformation of the spheres and the generation of vibrations and sound waves. If there are no losses, it can be shown that the velocity difference of approach $(v_1 - v_2)$ is equal to the velocity difference of separation $(v_2' - v_1')$. By experiment, Isaac Newton discovered that $(v_2' - v_1')$ is always less than $(v_1 - v_2)$ and that the relation between these velocity differences is given by

$$v_2' - v_1' = e(v_1 - v_2), \tag{15}$$

The coefficient of restitution

in which the numerical factor e, the coefficient of restitution, has values between zero and unity that depend only on the material of the bodies and not on their masses or velocities. Knowing v_1, v_2, and e, the final velocities v_1' and v_2' can be calculated from equations (14) and (15).

If the spheres were lead, putty, or some other soft material, e would be almost zero, and from equation (15), $v_2' = v_1'$, which means that after impact the spheres would move on together with a common speed that can be calculated by equation (14). This is known as inelastic impact.

For the special case of equal masses and purely elastic impact—i.e., $e = 1$—it can be shown, by solving equations (14) and (15) simultaneously for v_1' and v_2', that $v_1' = v_2$ and $v_2' = v_1$, which means that the spheres will exchange velocities after impact. If sphere 2 is stationary when sphere 1 strikes it—i.e., if $v_2 = 0$—then $v_1' = 0$, and sphere 1 will stop dead on impact, while sphere 2 will move on with the speed of sphere 1 before impact. This effect can be demonstrated by suspending the spheres on cords, as shown in Figure 10E. If sphere 1 is moved through the angle θ and let go, it will stop dead when it collides with sphere 2, which instantaneously will acquire the velocity of sphere 1 and swing up through an angle slightly less than θ on account of energy losses. Isaac Newton is reported to have used this apparatus with cords 10 feet long to confirm his third law.

If a small ball is dropped on the horizontal surface of a large mass of the same material, the coefficient of restitution can be calculated by comparing the height h to which the ball bounces with the height H from which it is dropped. Assuming that the large mass is stationary before and after impact, then v_2 and v_2' are both zero, and from equation (15) $-v_1' = ev_1$ or $e = -v_1'/v_1$.

From equation (13) $v_1 = +\sqrt{2gH}$ in a downward (assumed positive) direction, and $v_1' = -\sqrt{2gh}$ in an upward (assumed negative) direction; then $e = \sqrt{h/H}$.

Mechanics of elastic bodies. There are several reasons, even in a treatment of classical mechanics, which deals largely with so-called rigid bodies, for considering the deformations of these bodies. It has already been pointed out that the number of unknown forces in the members of a machine or structure that can be determined by the equations of rigid-body statics is limited and that the elastic properties of the members must be taken into account if the forces in redundant members or supports are to be found.

Most structural members may be classified as either bars or beams; bars are usually subjected to longitudinal (axial) loads that tend to stretch or shorten them, while beams usually support transverse loads that bend them. In machine construction, shafts are usually bent by transverse loads and twisted by torques. The type of stress (internal force) and the deformations that these three types of forces produce form the subject matter of "strength of materials" and "theory of elasticity," but, to the extent that the nature of these stresses and deformations influences the reactions on the members, their consideration in this article is justified.

The tension in a flexible cable (rope or chain) hanging freely between two horizontal supports and the shape of the curve assumed by the cable can be found by the equations of statics, but only under the assumption that the cable cannot offer any resistance to bending.

Interchanges of energy

The mechanical oscillations of bodies and the vibration of strings and membranes are all maintained by interchanges in kinetic energy and elastic strain energy; i.e., the energy stored in an elastic body when it is deformed.

When the shape of a solid body is changed by the application of a force, the body may be elastic and assume its original shape when the force is removed or be plastic and retain much or all of its loaded shape when unloaded. Most metallic bodies are elastic if the load to which they are subjected does not exceed a limiting value.

The simplest loaded state, and the one to which all other loaded states are referred when the limiting loads in these states are being investigated, is the state of simple tension; a wire fixed at one end and supporting a weight hung on the other end is in this state.

If the load is applied to a suspended wire by attaching a container to the free end and gradually filling it with water, there will be a measurable relation between the stretch of the wire and the weight of the water in the container. In order to make the results of such measurements applicable to all wires of the same material regardless of their length and cross-sectional area, it is convenient to designate the stretch of the wire as a fraction of its original length and the load as the weight of the water divided by cross-sectional area of the wire.

If L is the original length of the wire, A its area, and L' the length under a load P, then $(L' - L)/L = \varepsilon$ is known as the unit strain corresponding to the stress $\sigma = P/A$. If the wire is made of steel, the relation between σ and ε will remain constant as long as the limiting value of σ (the elastic limit) is not exceeded. This relationship is known as Hooke's law and is given by $\sigma = E\varepsilon$, in which E is the modulus of elasticity (a measure of a material's resistance to being stretched) of steel. Materials such as steel, which obey Hooke's law up to the elastic limit, are said to be linearly elastic; i.e., if the stress is doubled, the strain is doubled. It should be noted that strain is a measurable quantity, while stress is a concept and is not directly measurable.

Hooke's law

A useful form of Hooke's law can be derived by noting that $L' - L = \Delta$ is the deflection at the loaded end of the wire, so that $\varepsilon = \Delta/L$. Substituting Δ/L for ε and P/A for σ in the equation defining Hooke's law yields $\Delta = PL/AE$.

Stiffness. In addition to being strong enough to carry the imposed loads without failure, a structure or a machine component must also satisfy certain requirements regarding deflections. In most cases a structure should be rigid, whereas a spring should be flexible. Stiffness is also important in all forms of mechanical vibration.

Within the limits of elastic behaviour the deformations of solid metallic bodies are extremely small. For unhardened steel, for example, the allowable unit tensile strain ε is about 0.001 inch per inch, or centimetre per centimetre, or metre per metre. This means that a bar one inch long could be stretched to no more than 1.001 inches, or one centimetre to 1.001 centimetres, and so on. To obtain the flexibility that is characteristic of a spring from a bar stressed in simple tension, it would be necessary to use a very long bar. By loading the bar in a different way, however, or by changing its geometry—i.e., by making its axis curved instead of straight—the flexibility of the bar can be increased and its stiffness reduced.

The deflection (Δ) of an axially loaded wire or bar has been shown to be $\Delta = PL/AE$, which, solved for P/Δ, given $P/\Delta = AE/L$. The quantity P/Δ is the ratio of the load to the corresponding deflection, while AE/L depends only on the dimensions of the bar and its material; these equivalent quantities, expressed in different ways but having the same dimension, namely, load per unit of deflection, are measures of the stiffness of an axially loaded bar. The stiffness of any elastic body or structure depends on the way in which it is loaded—i.e., on whether it is pulled, bent, or twisted—but it is always equal to the load divided by the corresponding deflection. If the structure is complex, the stiffness may have to be determined experimentally by simultaneous measurements of load and deflection. The stiffness is usually designated by K, which has the dimension pounds per inch, or newtons per metre, or any other load-detection ratio.

For simple structures or bodies loaded in a simple way, such as an axially loaded bar, the stiffness can usually be obtained analytically and expressed by a formula as a function of the dimensions of the structure and the modulus of elasticity of the material.

If a bar of length L, a circular cross section of diameter D, and an area A were fixed at one end in a horizontal position and loaded at the free end like a cantilever beam with a transverse load P, its stiffness would be $K = (AE/L) (3D^2/16L^2)$. Comparing this formula with that for an axially loaded bar, it is seen that the fraction $3D^2/16L^2$ is a measure of the reduction in stiffness obtained by using the bar as a cantilever beam; for $L = 12D$ the reduction is 1/768. Because of the way in which it is loaded, the bending stress in the cantilever bar would be almost 100 times greater than the tensile stress in the axially loaded bar for the same load P. This means that the limiting elastic load on the cantilever bar would be about one-hundredth of that for the axially loaded bar. Nevertheless, as long as the limiting load is not exceeded, the cantilever bar will satisfy Hooke's law—i.e., the deflection under the load will be proportional to the load. In some cases Hooke's law may not be valid for certain configurations of elastic components; this is usually the result of changes in the geometry of the assemblage as the load is increased.

INERTIA FORCES AND THE CORIOLIS FORCE

It was pointed out by Jean Le Rond d'Alembert that Newton's second law could be interpreted in a different way by writing it in the form $F + (-ma) = 0$ and treating the term $(-ma)$ as if it were a force. In this form $(-ma)$ is called an inertia force to distinguish it from such real forces as the force of gravity or the force exerted by one body on another by direct contact. The inertia-force concept makes it possible to reduce a problem in dynamics to a problem in statics by writing the second law in the form $\Sigma F = 0$ and including the inertia forces in the summation. The term $(-ma)$ is sometimes called a reversed effective force and also a fictitious force.

Fictitious forces

When a particle is moving on a curved path at a constant speed, the force and the centripetal acceleration are both directed toward the centre of curvature of the path. The corresponding outward inertia force, equal in magnitude to the centripetal acceleration, is called the centrifugal force. Neglecting gravity, a stone whirling in a circle in a horizontal plane at the end of a string has only one real force acting on it, namely, the tension in the string. The string tension keeps the stone on its circular path, and, because it continually alters the direction of the velocity of the stone, it creates the centripetal acceleration. Using the inertia-force viewpoint, the stone is in equilibrium—i.e., has zero acceleration—under the influence of the inward string tension and the outward centrifugal force. A real force, however, equal to the centrifugal force in both magnitude and direction, is acting on the member at the centre of the circle to which the string is attached.

When a body is at rest, the external forces (loads and reactions) acting on it are in equilibrium. If the body is assumed to be cut in a region that is stretched, bent, or twisted, the stresses acting on the cut cross section must balance the external forces on the portions of the body on either side of the cross section. When a machine or structural member is being accelerated, the external forces are not in equilibrium, and the stresses on any cross section do not balance the loads and reactions. By employing d'Alembert's principle this difficulty can be overcome, and a problem in dynamics becomes a problem in statics, for which the equations of equilibrium can be used.

D'Alembert's principle is particularly useful in deriving the equations for the stresses in bodies rotating about fixed axes. On a disk rotating at a constant speed, for example, each cubical element of the disk is assumed to be in equilibrium under the action of the stresses acting on its sides and the outwardly directed centrifugal (inertia) force. To a person standing on it, the particles of the disk do appear to be in equilibrium because they do not move relative to the disk. In the theory of elasticity (q.v.), inertia forces and gravitational forces are classified as body forces; in the rotating disk, the centrifugal forces, because they vary with the distance of the element from the axis, have the same effect on the stresses as varying gravitational forces. From a similar point of view, a centrifuge or a cream separator is a system in equilibrium to an observer rotating with it and can be more easily explained in terms of centrifugal force than in terms of centripetal force.

In the treatment of relative motion in Figure 5D, the absolute acceleration a is shown as the resultant of the Coriolis component $2v_R\omega$ and the centripetal component $a_V = S\omega^2$, in which S is the magnitude of the vector S. If m is the mass of the car, the track must be exerting a force on the car equal to $m2v_R\omega$, collinear with the acceler-

ation vector and in the same direction; this is the Coriolis force. There must also be a centripetal force ma_V, collinear with a_V and in the same direction, generated by the mechanism that drives the car on the track.

The Coriolis force is always present when a particle moves on a rotating body or when a body rotates about an axis that is fixed on another rotating body. The torque in a fluid coupling or converter is created by the Coriolis forces that result from the relative motion of the fluid; on an automobile making a turn to the right, elements in the upper half of the rotating flywheel experience a Coriolis acceleration forward and those in the lower half an acceleration backward. The Coriolis forces corresponding to these accelerations are produced in the crankshaft bearings; they are known as gyroscopic couples. The behaviour of gyroscopes can be explained in terms of Coriolis forces.

Because of its rotation about an axis joining the poles, the Earth is a rotating frame of reference, and the Coriolis and centripetal components will appear in the acceleration equations for particles moving in certain directions and in certain locations on and near the Earth's surface. Because the Earth rotates at only 0.000694 revolution per minute (0.0000729 radian per second), the forces associated with these accelerations are small and can usually be neglected; they do have some geophysical importance, however.

Like the expansion of a rotating disk caused by the centrifugal forces, the centrifugal forces on the Earth's crust are responsible for the equatorial bulge; the forces are greatest at the Equator because the centrifugal force $(-mR\omega^2)$ depends on the distance R from the polar axis.

The Earth's equatorial bulge

In Figure 5D, the real Coriolis force from the track is pushing to the left on the car; the inertia force from the car is pushing to the right against the track, and if the track were not there the car would slide to the right. This deviation is known as the Coriolis drift, and it has a marked effect on the paths of long-range projectiles and the direction of trade winds and ocean currents.

To complete the treatment of relative motion and the corresponding forces, it will be helpful to re-examine the implications and validity of Newton's second law, $F = ma$. As stated, the law applies to the absolute motions of particles—i.e., their motions in a reference frame or coordinate system attached to the fixed stars. This is called either a Newtonian frame or an inertial frame. If the motion of the particle is described in terms of a moving coordinate system—i.e., one attached to a moving vehicle—it may be necessary to modify Newton's equation.

In general, when a particle moves on a nonrotating vehicle, its absolute acceleration can be expressed as the vector sum of the absolute acceleration of the point on the vehicle coinciding with the particle at the instant considered (a_V) and the acceleration of the particle relative to the vehicle (a_R). Thus $a = a_V + a_R$, it being understood that the plus sign signifies a vector addition. Then Newton's second law takes the form $F = m(a_V + a_R)$.

If the vehicle is moving with a uniform velocity—i.e., on a straight line at a constant speed—then $a_V = 0$ and $F = ma_R$. This means that Newton's law applies without correction to, for example, motions relative to a train moving on a straight track at a constant speed.

If the vehicle is accelerating, then a_V is the same for all points in the vehicle and can be added vectorially to a_R to obtain the absolute acceleration a. Newton's equation, however, can be written as $F - ma_V = ma_R$; in this form it signifies that the law applies to accelerations relative to an accelerating nonrotating vehicle, provided an inertia force of magnitude $-ma_V$ is added to the left side of the equation.

If the vehicle rotates, the Coriolis component a_C appears, and the absolute acceleration $a = a_V + a_R + a_C$. When Newton's law is written in the form $F - ma_V - ma_C = ma_R$, it signifies that the law applies to acceleration relative to a rotating vehicle, provided the inertia forces $-ma_V$ and $-ma_C$ are added to the left side of the equation.

In Figure 5D, there is no relative acceleration a_R, and the vehicle acceleration a_V is simply the centripetal acceleration $S\omega^2$; if the vehicle were being accelerated, there would be another component $S\alpha$. Consequently, $F - ma_V - ma_C = 0$, and to an observer on the table the inertia forces $- ma_V$ and $-ma_C$ balance the two components of F, one from the bottom of the track and one from the side of the track; i.e., the car is in relative equilibrium.

On the surface of the Earth $-ma_V$, the centrifugal force, and $-ma_C$, the reversed Coriolis force, are both small and can usually be neglected. Then $F = ma_R$, and Newton's second law can be applied, without correction, to motions relative to the Earth.

MECHANICS OF COMPLEX SYSTEMS

The principle of virtual work. The solution of problems in statics by the equations of equilibrium—i.e., by force and moment summations—can become tedious for complex structures and mechanisms. To determine forces by the equilibrium method it is usually necessary to dismember the structure and treat each component separately; when the number of components is large, many equations must be solved. In addition, even if only one or two unknown forces are to be found, in moving from one component to the next, many unwanted forces may appear and require evaluation. The method of virtual work is an alternate approach to statics problems that is well suited for complex systems and for cases in which only a few unknown forces are to be found. It can also be used for the dynamic analysis of mechanisms, provided the inertia-force concept of d'Alembert is utilized to create a state of equilibrium in each component.

The principle of virtual work, formulated by Johann Bernoulli in 1717, states that, if a rigid body or a system of connected rigid bodies is in equilibrium, then the total virtual work of the external forces acting on the body or system of bodies is zero for any arbitrary virtual displacement of the body or the system consistent with the constraints.

When the force F moves a very short distance, ΔS, in the direction in which it is acting, the mechanical work done is $F\Delta S$. The displacement ΔS is "virtual" if it is not actually experienced but merely imagined in the course of an analysis; it is usually assumed to be infinitesimal in order that the geometry of the system be maintained and that F and ΔS be always in the same direction. The product of F and a virtual displacement is virtual work. The principle can be illustrated by means of the simple lever in Figure 11A.

Virtual displacements [margin note]

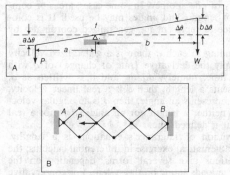

Figure 11: *Applications of virtual-work principle.*
(A) Simple lever, (B) linked structure.

For the lever, a virtual displacement consistent with the constraints is a rotation through a small angle $\Delta\theta$, in radians, about the fulcrum f. The virtual displacements of P and W are $a\Delta\theta$ and $b\Delta\theta$, respectively. Because P goes down during the displacement, its virtual work is positive; the work of W is negative because W and $b\Delta\theta$ are in opposite directions. The sum of the virtual works is thus given by $P(a\Delta\theta) - W(b\Delta\theta) = 0$, from which $P/W = b/a$. In this case, the principle of virtual work offers no real advantage; it seldom does for a single rigid body.

The device in Figure 11B consists of eight weightless pin-connected bars that are held at A and B and subjected to a load P; the reactions at A and B are required. When

point B is displaced a distance Δ to the right by a force Q, the displacement will be consistent with the restraint at A. Then, from the nature of the device, the corresponding displacement of P will be $\Delta/3$ to the right. The sum of virtual works is $Q\Delta - P\Delta/3 = 0$, from which $Q = P/3$, pointing to the right. By similar means the reaction at A can be shown to be $2P/3$, pointing to the right. This problem would be more difficult to solve by any other means.

The principle of virtual work, or, as it is sometimes called, the principle of virtual displacements, was originally known as the principle of virtual velocities. Because all of the displacements are simultaneous, their relative magnitudes are unaltered if divided by equal time intervals; the resulting quotients are average velocities that become instantaneous velocities when the time interval approaches zero. The use of instantaneous velocities instead of displacements has many advantages when the principle is applied to machine mechanisms and leads to a basic velocity–force–power relationship in machines.

If a virtual displacement ΔS takes place in a time interval Δt, then $F(\Delta S/\Delta t)$ is the average time rate at which the work is being done—or the average power—while $\Delta S/\Delta t$ is the average velocity of the force. In the limit, as Δt approaches zero, $\Delta S/\Delta t$ becomes v, the instantaneous velocity, and Fv the instantaneous power.

On such simple machines as the lever, the wheel and axle, and the screw, the ratio of the load (output force) to the effort (input force) is called the mechanical advantage (MA). The ratio of the motion of the effort to the motion of the load is known as the velocity ratio (VR). If friction is neglected, the mechanical advantage is the reciprocal of the velocity ratio. Because of friction, the mechanical advantage is always less than the velocity ratio, and the ratio MA/VR is the mechanical efficiency of the machine. The efficiency of machines that rotate continuously is most easily obtained by measuring the instantaneous output and input powers and dividing the output by the input.

Mechanical advantage [margin note]

The principle of virtual work can also be applied to rotating bodies; it is only necessary to replace the force F by the torque T and ΔS by $\Delta\theta$ (in radians). Then the virtual work is $T(\Delta\theta)$, and instantaneous power becomes $T\omega$. In the case of the lever in Figure 11A, the torques are Pa and Wb, in which a and b are the lever arms, so that $(Pa)(\Delta\theta) - (Wb)(\Delta\theta) = 0$, which leads to the same result as before.

Spinning tops and gyroscopes. In the previous sections the force systems and the motions of the particles and bodies were confined to parallel planes. There were two reasons for restricting the treatment to two dimensions; in the first place, most of the problems of interest to physicists and engineers can be solved by the equations of plane mechanics; in the second place, solutions to spatial (three-dimensional) problems in statics can be effected most easily by the formalized procedures of vector analysis, while some of the problems in spatial dynamics are so complicated that solutions have not yet been obtained.

In three-dimensional space, as in two-dimensional space, the centre of mass of a body moves as if it were a particle with the resultant of the external forces acting on it. In plane motion the sum of the torques about the centre of mass equals $I_G\alpha$, which is equivalent to assuming that the body rotates about an axis passing through the centre of mass and perpendicular to the plane of motion. In space motion there are three planes and three axes through the centre of mass about which the body may be rotating simultaneously; this is the reason for the complexity of space motion. In special cases, such as the motion of spinning tops and gyroscopes, satisfactory explanations of dynamic behaviour can be obtained by making simplifying assumptions.

It has been shown that when a body rotates about a fixed axis the torque impulse Tt is equal to the change in the angular momentum $I(\omega - \omega_0)$. Because t is the time interval during which the torque acts, it may be written as Δt, and, because $I(\omega - \omega_0) = I\omega - I\omega_0$ is the corresponding change in the angular momentum, it may be written as $\Delta(I\omega)$. Then $T(\Delta t) = \Delta(I\omega)$, from which

$T = \Delta(I\omega)/\Delta t$, or the torque is the time rate of change of the angular momentum. When a body rotates about a fixed point, a similar equation applies; in this case, T is replaced by M, the moment of the external forces about the point, and $I\omega$ is the resultant angular momentum of the body. Then, in the limit, as Δt approaches zero, $M = d(I\omega)/dt$.

In Figure 12A, a top in the form of a disk of weight W, mounted on a shaft with a pointed end, is held in a frictionless support at O in the frame. The shaft rotates at a high speed ω in a clockwise direction viewed from O. If the top were stationary, the moment of the weight W, which is $M = WC \sin \alpha$, would cause it to fall. Because the top rotates, however, the spin axis OS sweeps out the surface of a cone as the line QS (which is at right angles to OQ) rotates at an angular speed Ω in a counterclockwise direction, viewed from above, about point Q.

The right-angled triangle OQS forms a plane that sweeps out the volume of the cone at the speed Ω, which is called the angular velocity of precession of the top.

The angular momentum $I\omega$ of the top is represented by the vector OS, coinciding with the axis of the top and pointing in the direction that a right-handed screw would advance if it were attached to the rotating axis. The vector OS of magnitude $I\omega$, is changing in direction only, and, because its rate of change must equal the velocity v_S of point S on the circular path, it is also equal to the rate of change of QS, of magnitude $I\omega \sin \alpha$. Then $v_S = QS\Omega = (I\omega \sin \alpha)\Omega$ is the time rate of change of $I\omega$.

As the top rotates about its axis, the axis also rotates, and $I\omega$ is not the total angular momentum of the top; there are two other components of the momentum, and they would have to be considered for a complete description of the motion. If ω is very large compared with Ω, however, a satisfactory explanation of the motion can be obtained by assuming that $I\omega$ is the resultant momentum.

Using the right-hand screw rule, the moment M, of magnitude $WC \sin \alpha$, is a vector acting through O, at right angles to the plane OQS and, therefore, parallel to v_S. Then, equating the moment to the rate of change of momentum, $WC \sin \alpha = (I\omega \sin \alpha)\Omega$, from which $WC = I\omega\Omega$. This result shows that the velocity of precession is the same for all values of α. Because of the attraction of the Sun and the Moon on the Earth's equatorial bulge, the Earth's axis has a small velocity of precession. It requires 26,000 years for a complete revolution and was first explained by Isaac Newton.

A gyroscope is a small, accurately made flywheel that is usually supported in encircling rings known as gimbals in such a way that it can rotate freely about any axis. This is equivalent to mounting it at its centre of mass so that the distance C in Figure 12A is zero and the axis of spin remains immovable (theoretically) in space.

In Figure 12B a circular disk of moment of inertia I, rotating at a high angular velocity ω, is supported in bearings at A and B in the U-shaped frame. The frame is rotating about a vertical axis at C with a clockwise

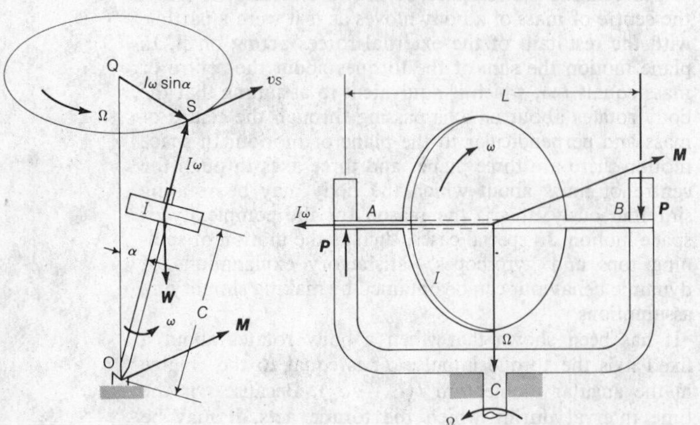

(viewed from above) angular velocity Ω, indicated, according to the right-hand rule, by a vector pointing down. This is a forced precession, and the change in the angular momentum vector $I\omega$, like the change in any vector caused by rotation, will be perpendicular to $I\omega$ and pointing into the paper for the given direction of Ω. The magnitude of the change in $I\omega$ is $I\omega\Omega$, and the moment M that produced the change must have the same magnitude and direction; it is shown by the vector M in Figure 12B. The additional loads on the bearings, the equal and opposite forces P that create the moment M, are obtained from $PL = I\omega\Omega$. Note that the spin, precession, and moment axes are mutually perpendicular and that the spin axis, when precessing, always rotates toward the moment axis.

On some ships the controlled precession of a large gyroscope is used to produce a moment to counteract the rolling of the ship at sea. There are many other applications of the gyroscope.

Lagrange's and Hamilton's equations. As the complexity of the problems in classical dynamics increases, it becomes more and more difficult either to formulate the equations of motion or to solve them. In many cases, the forces acting on the particles may be difficult to ascertain, and Newton's second law, which expresses a causal relationship between force and acceleration, may be difficult to formulate. Among the more powerful and more universal methods that have been developed for deriving the equations of motion for these more complicated situations, the equations of Lagrange and Hamilton are the most generally useful. These equations do not represent new theories, but only new ways of looking at dynamics, and the resulting equations of motion are the same as those derived by Newton's law.

Because it emphasizes the vectorial characteristic of the quantities involved, Newtonian dynamics is largely geometric; Lagrangian and Hamiltonian dynamics, on the other hand, require only analytical operations and deal with scalar (nonvectorial) quantities that require no geometric representation.

In Newtonian dynamics force and acceleration are the basic components, and in the coordinate systems only lengths and angles are used to describe the position of particles. In the Lagrange and Hamilton equations, the components are kinetic and potential energy, and the coordinates are generalized; $i.e.$, they are not restricted to lengths and angles but may be any quantities that describe the state of a mechanical system and can be varied independently of one another. In some cases, areas or combinations of lengths and angles may be used. It is common practice to represent the generalized coordinates by $q_1, q_2, q_3, \cdots q_n$.

Corresponding to each q there is a generalized velocity that is simply the derivative (rate of change) of q with respect to time, namely, dq/dt, and it is written as $\dot{q}$. If q represents a length, then $\dot{q}$ is a real linear velocity, while if q represents an angle, then $\dot{q}$ is an angular velocity. If q is neither a length nor an angle, $\dot{q}$ is not a real velocity but a defined one.

The derivation of Lagrange's equations is a lengthy, abstract mathematical exercise in differential calculus; the basic equations take several forms, depending on the nature of the loads acting on the system. For conservative systems—$i.e.$, systems for which the law of conservation of energy is valid—the following equation holds for each generalized coordinate q:

$$\frac{d}{dt}\left(\frac{\partial L}{\partial \dot{q}}\right) - \frac{\partial L}{\partial q} = 0.$$

The quantity $L = (T - V)$, in which T is the kinetic energy and V the potential energy of the system in generalized coordinates, is called the Lagrangian function. The term $\partial L/\partial \dot{q}$ is the derivative (rate of change) of L with respect to $\dot{q}$ when all other variables in the expression for L are held constant; it is called a partial derivative and written with ∂ instead of d, to distinguish it from $dq/dt = \dot{q}$, which is called an ordinary derivative.

When $\partial L/\partial \dot{q}$ has been evaluated, the first term in Lagrange's equation is obtained by taking its derivative

(A)

(B)

Figure 12: *Gyroscopic action.*
(A) Spinning top, (B) forced precession.

with respect to time. The terms $\partial/\partial q$ and d/dt can be thought of as operators that are to be applied to L and $\dfrac{\partial L}{\partial \dot{q}}$, respectively. If the position of a point moving on a straight path is described by its distance s from a fixed point on the path then ds/dt is the velocity of the point. In general, dy/dx, the derivative of y with respect to x, can be applied to any function of x such as, for example, $y = x^n$, in which n is any number such as 0.5, 1, 2, and so on, but the physical interpretation of the derivative depends on the nature of the function.

There are simple algebraic rules for taking derivatives; for the power function $y = x^n$, the derivative $dy/dx = nx^{n-1}$ so that, if $y = x^2$, then $dy/dx = 2x$. Since dy/dx is also a function of x, the derivative of dy/dx with respect to x, namely, d^2y/dx^2, is equal to 2; this is the second derivative of y with respect to x.

As an example of the application of Lagrange's equation, consider a freely falling body of weight W and mass m at a height y above the ground and assume that the differential equation of motion is required; i.e., an equation containing the second derivative of y with respect to time, namely, $\ddot{y}$.

The velocity of the body is given by $\dot{y}$ and the kinetic energy T by $\frac{1}{2}m\dot{y}^2$; the potential energy V is Wy and $L = T - V = \frac{1}{2}m\dot{y}^2 - Wy$. The obvious generalized coordinate is $q = y$, $\partial L/\partial y = -W$, $\partial L/\partial \dot{y} = m\dot{y}$, and $d(m\dot{y})/dt = m\ddot{y}$. Substituting these values in Lagrange's equation gives $m\ddot{y} + W = 0$, from which $\ddot{y} = -W/m$ and since $m = W/g$ this reduces to $\ddot{y} = -g$. This is the differential equation of motion for a falling body, which may be written as $d^2y/dt^2 = -g$ and expresses the acceleration of the body in terms the second derivative of y with respect to time. The velocity equation, $v = \dfrac{dy}{dt}$, is the function of time that when differentiated will yield the acceleration. This process is known as integration, and it is the inverse of differentiation. It is easy to see that $v = \dfrac{dy}{dt} = -gt + v_0$, in which v_0 is the velocity of the body when $t = 0$; because v_0 is a constant, its derivative is zero. Integrating the velocity equation yields $y = -\frac{1}{2}gt^2 + v_0 t + y_0$, in which y_0 is the position of the body when $t = 0$. This is the complete equation for a falling body, which was obtained previously by more elementary methods; differentiating it twice yields $d^2y/dt^2 = -g$.

When using Lagrange's equations the differential equations of motion are derived in the same way for each generalized coordinate. Because kinetic energy involves velocities only, accelerations do not have to be considered; in addition, the velocity terms are squared so that the kinetic energy is always positive, and difficulties with algebraic signs are avoided.

Degrees of freedom

Lagrange's equations are particularly useful when the number of generalized coordinates is two or more or, in other words, when the number of degrees of freedom—i.e., the ways in which the system can move—is two or more. The differential equations of motion for vibrating systems with multiple masses and springs are most easily obtained by Lagrange's equations.

The equations of Hamilton contain another generalized quantity, namely, generalized momentum p and the Hamiltonian function H. The generalized momentum p associated with the generalized coordinate q is defined as $p = \partial L/\partial \dot{q}$. If q is a length, then $p = m\dot{q}$, which has the dimensions of linear momentum, mv; if q is not a length, it does not have this dimension, and the generalized momentum is strictly a mathematical definition. The function H is defined as $H = \Sigma p\dot{q} - L$, in which $\Sigma p\dot{q}$ is the sum of the $p\dot{q}$ terms for all generalized coordinates in the system and L is the Lagrangian function. For each generalized coordinate, Hamilton's canonical equations are

$$\dot{q} = \frac{\partial H}{\partial p}, \qquad \dot{p} = -\frac{\partial H}{\partial q}.$$

Because Hamilton's equations utilize both generalized coordinates and momenta, whereas Lagrange's equations use only generalized coordinates, there is more freedom in choosing the variable when Hamilton's equations are used.

It should be noted that, although Lagrange's equations are useful for finding the differential equation of motion of a dynamic system, Newton's equations are still unrivalled when the forces acting on the system are required.

BIBLIOGRAPHY. The PHYSICAL SCIENCE STUDY COMMITTEE, *Physics* (1960); and SIDNEY ROSEN, ROBERT SIEGFRIED, and JOHN M. DENNISON, *Concepts in Physical Science* (1965), contain well-illustrated elementary treatments of the principles of mechanics suitable for a beginner; they are the only books in this list that do not utilize calculus. JAMES L. MERIAM, *Mechanics*, 2nd ed., 2 vol. (1971); and JACOB P. DEN HARTOG, *Mechanics* (1948), are both designed for undergraduate engineering students and contain a large number of worked and exercise problems dealing with machine and structural components. SIR CHARLES INGLIS, *Applied Mechanics for Engineers* (1951), is noteworthy in both style and content and is based on lectures given by the author to students working for honour degrees in engineering at the University of Cambridge, England; it assumes some knowledge of the principles of mechanics. JAMES H. JEANS, *An Elementary Treatise on Theoretical Mechanics* (1907, reprinted 1967); and WILLIAM F. OSGOOD, *Mechanics* (1937, reprinted 1965), are paperbacks that are more theoretical in their approach than the previous three books and cover more advanced topics. JOHN L. SYNGE and BYRON A. GRIFFITH, *Principles of Mechanics*, 3rd ed. (1959); HERBERT GOLDSTEIN, *Classical Mechanics* (1950); GEORGE W. HOUSNER and DONALD E. HUDSON, *Applied Mechanics*, 2nd ed., 2 vol. (1959–61); JAMES W. BROXON, *Mechanics* (1960); KEITH R. SYMON, *Mechanics*, 3rd ed. (1971); LAWRENCE E. GOODMAN and WILLIAM H. WARNER, *Dynamics* (1963); and JERRY B. MARION, *Classical Dynamics of Particles and Systems*, 2nd ed. (1970), are all of an intermediate level and, in keeping with the modern trend, utilize algebraic rather than geometric methods in the treatment of vectors. In most cases an introductory chapter on vector analysis is included. F.P. BEER and E.R. JOHNSTON, JR., *Vector Mechanics for Engineers*, 2 vol. (1970), like practically all modern texts for undergraduate engineering students, employs the full vector treatment and contains a large number of practical problems. EDMUND T. WHITTAKER, *Treatise on the Analytical Dynamics of Particles and Rigid Bodies*, 4th ed. (1959), is a well-known classic that presents an exhaustive and strictly analytical treatment of dynamics. It does not, however, use vector notation, and the scarcity of diagrams makes it difficult to follow. ROBERT B. LINDSAY and HENRY MARGENAU, *Foundations to Physics* (1936), is a work that contains a concise treatment of the foundations of classical mechanics. A.G. WEBSTER, *The Dynamics of Particles . . .* (1904), is a classic work containing an extensive treatment of the dynamics of rigid bodies.

(A.Co.)

Mechanics, Fluid

Fluid mechanics, one of the engineering sciences, is concerned with gases and liquids at rest or in motion. A fluid is any gas or liquid, and, as such, a mass the shape of which yields to pressure (a more formal definition will be given below in the section *Properties of ideal and actual fluids*). Fluid mechanics deals with the forces exerted on a fluid to hold it at rest, as well as with the interplay of forces between a fluid and boundaries that cause motion of the fluid. It uses methods of analysis that have evolved from the application of basic principles, concepts, and laws such as: Isaac Newton's law of motion and viscosity (the resistance to flow); the first and second laws of thermodynamics; the principle of conservation of mass; and equations of state relating fluid properties of pressure, temperature, and density, all of which will be elaborated on below.

The importance of fluid mechanics

Fluid mechanics is important in that it supplies the theoretical foundation for many disciplines: meteorology, the global study of the atmosphere, which takes into account the dynamics of its motion caused by heating and cooling effects and changes in the amount of water content; hydrology, which deals with the processes governing the depletion and replenishment of water resources of the land areas of the Earth and which is also concerned with rainfall, consumptive uses of water, and runoff of water in rivers and through the ground; hydraulics, the technology dealing with flow of fluids in pipes, rivers and channels, and the confinement of fluids by dams and tanks; aerodynamics, the study of the flow of gases and its application to design of objects acted upon by the force of air and wind, such as aircraft, rockets, automobiles, ships, bridges, and tall buildings; magnetohydrodynamics, the science dealing with relationships between magnetic fields and plasmas (a state of matter in which single electrons and positive particles, in about equal proportions, form a gas); and cryogenics, the physics of low temperatures, which includes the study of superfluids (*e.g.*, the flow of liquid helium at high velocity through tiny holes and capillaries impervious to the flow of ordinary liquids).

This article is divided into the following sections:

Studies before the 20th century. The control of water has been practiced by man from prehistoric times. He has constructed irrigation works including dams, canals, and other control structures and has been able to take advantage of wind and water by the use of windmills and sailing vessels.

Archimedes, who studied under the disciples of Euclid in Alexandria, Egypt, in the 3rd century BC, was the first to develop the principles of buoyancy and flotation. He derived the following three basic theorems of hydrostatics: (1) Any solid lighter than a liquid of equal volume will be immersed to such an extent that the weight of the solid is equal to the weight of displaced liquid. (2) If a solid lighter than a liquid of equal volume be immersed in it, the fluid will exert a force upward on the solid equal to the weight of displaced fluid. (3) A solid heavier than a fluid of equal volume will descend to the bottom of the fluid if immersed in it. When weighed in the fluid, it will be lighter by the weight of displaced fluid.

These findings are as relevant now as they were in the time of Archimedes, and they form the basis for flotation and stability analysis with substantially no change up to the present time. Archimedes is also credited with inventing a pump known as Archimedes' screw, which consists of a pipe wound around an inclined shaft with the lower end open and submerged in water. Rotation of the shaft causes water to be picked up and carried to the upper end of the pipe, from which it is discharged into a trough.

The Romans made use of the hydraulics of both pipes and open channels for water supply and transport of sewage, although the laws associated with the resistance of pipes and channels to the flow of liquids were completely unknown at that time.

In the 15th and 16th centuries Leonardo da Vinci of Italy was aware of the earlier accomplishments of fluid flow engineering and referred to them in his copious notes. He strongly urged that observation and experiments be performed before trying to analyze the problem and discover the basic laws. He wrote on the following subjects of fluid mechanics: water waves, eddies, floating bodies, falling water, flow in pipes, destructive force of water, efflux, and mills and hydraulic machinery. He was the first to propose the parachute, the anemometer (which measures wind speed), and the centrifugal pump. He recognized and stated the principle of continuity (discussed below) and also the principle of force involved in the hydraulic press.

Simon Stevin, a Dutch mathematician of the 16th and 17th centuries, apparently unaware of Leonardo da Vinci's work, also wrote a book on hydrostatics, in which he developed the correct analysis for forces on plane surfaces and so proved that pressure is a function of distance below the free surface of a liquid. Evangelista Torricelli, who occupied Galileo's chair of mathematics at Florence later in the 17th century, stated the hypothesis that liquid issuing from an outlet in a tank would have the same speed as if it were dropped from the free surface to the outlet; this hypothesis is now known as Torricelli's theorem. He is credited with the discovery of the barometer as well.

Blaise Pascal, 17th-century French mathematician and scientist who influenced the development of the calculus, is best known in hydraulics for the axiom that for fluids at rest, pressure is transmitted equally in all directions, now known as Pascal's law. An English contemporary, Isaac Newton, recognized the nature of resistance to fluid flow and developed his law of viscosity relating shear force or stress, viscosity, and relative motion of one layer of fluid adjacent to another layer.

Henri Pitot, who practiced civil engineering in southern France in the 18th century, building bridges and aqueducts and providing flood protection for his district, is remembered today primarily for the invention of a velocity-measuring device for fluids that is now called the Pitot tube. By determining the impact of the pressure of flowing water, as measured by the height the column would rise in a vertical tube, Pitot was able to calculate the water's velocity.

Daniel Bernoulli and Leonhard Euler, Swiss mathematicians of the 18th century, contributed greatly to the formulation of hydrodynamics. Bernoulli is best known for his development of energy principles, and Euler developed the general nonviscous equations of motion in terms of the acceleration components of a fluid particle. Euler also developed the equations for analysis of the reaction turbine. In the 18th and 19th centuries Joseph-Louis Lagrange of France contributed to hydrodynamic theory by introducing the concepts of velocity potential and stream function. In the 18th and 19th centuries Pierre-Simon Laplace of France worked with waves and tides but is best known for his mathematical operator, called the Laplacian operator, symbolized by ∇^2, a partial differential operator of calculus that expresses how a mathematical or physical variable (*e.g.*, curvature or pressure) changes with respect to spatial coordinates. It represents one of the most important relationships in theoretical fluid mechanics.

In the 18th and 19th centuries Giovanni Battista Venturi, an Italian physicist who studied the flow of fluids through conical reducing tubes and through expanding tubes, for the purpose of reducing the turbulence and losses caused by such velocity changes, devised the venturi meter, a device that allows computation of flow volume by a measurement of the pressure drop through a conical reducing section. Claude-Louis-Marie Navier, a 19th-century French engineer who was primarily a builder of bridges, made a major contribution to hydrodynamics by extending the Euler equations to include the attraction of adjacent molecules.

The French engineer Adhémar-Jean-Claude Barré de Saint-Venant in the 19th century developed the equations of motion of a fluid particle in terms of the shear and

Margin notes:

Archimedes' theorems

Pascal's law

normal (perpendicular) forces exerted on it. Sir George Gabriel Stokes, a 19th-century English physicist, made the final derivation of the equations of motion in terms of the coefficient of viscosity, now called the Navier–Stokes equations.

Developments during the 20th century. Fluid mechanics is based today on the experimental approach of hydraulics over the past 200 years plus the mathematical developments over the same period. These two approaches did not converge until the 20th century. Valuable contributions to the experimental approach to understanding were made by Jean-Louis-Marie Poiseuille, a 19th-century French physiologist interested in blood flow, who determined the equation for laminar flow (flow without turbulence) through capillary tubes. A 19th-century German engineer, Julius Weisbach, included hydraulics in a treatise on engineering mechanics; he also made contributions to the knowledge of flow over weirs (dams) and of losses caused by sudden contractions in a pipeline. Osborn Reynolds, a 19th-century British physicist, made important advances both analytically and through experimentation, notably his development of the dimensionless parameter, now called the Reynolds number, that distinguishes the type of flow, laminar or turbulent, in a closed conduit. He also expressed the Navier–Stokes equations in a form introducing the concepts of turbulent shear stress.

The Reynolds number

Important contributions to vortex (whirling) motion, free streamlines, and dynamic similarity were made by a 19th-century German physicist, Hermann von Helmholtz, and studies of vortex motion, irrotational flow, and open-channel waves were made by the 19th-century British physicist Lord Kelvin. The first correct analysis of the water-hammer effect, a pressure wave that travels the water with the speed of sound, was made by the 19th- and 20th-century Russian aerodynamicist Nikolay Yegorovich Zhukovsky, who made a thorough, large-scale experimental confirmation of the effect in 1897. The 19th- and 20th-century English mathematician and physicist Sir Horace Lamb's six editions of *Hydrodynamics* (1895–1932) made available a great amount of work on fluid motion.

Ludwig Prandtl, a German physicist, by statement of his boundary-layer hypothesis in 1904, was able to bridge the gap between empirical hydraulics and hydrodynamics. His hypothesis holds that for fluids of low viscosity, the effects of viscosity may be considered to be limited to a narrow region surrounding the boundaries of the flow. Outside this region, irrotational (nonrotatory) flow exists (practically). Through his great insight into the mechanics of fluid flow and his ability to perform pertinent simple experiments, he contributed greatly to understanding of the boundary layer, turbulent velocity distributions, and separation of flow at boundaries. Theodore von Kármán, a student of Prandtl, made important advances in the knowledge of velocity distributions, open channel flow, and aerodynamics and jet propulsion. The British meteorologist and physicist Geoffrey Ingram Taylor, through his ingenious experiments and profound insight into flow phenomena, has contributed strongly to understanding of fluid turbulence and to diffusion caused by turbulence.

During the first three quarters of the 20th century, the number of investigators in fluid mechanics multiplied and the fields of research broadened.

Properties of ideal and actual fluids

A fluid is a substance, the parts of which cannot remain at rest relative to one another when subjected to a shear force, no matter how small that force may be. A shear force is defined as a force exerted along a direction parallel to an area, and it is distinguished from a compressive force exerted at right angles to an area. Thus a shear force—or, simply, shear—can produce a sliding motion of one block on another, whereas a compressive force only squeezes them together. A plastic substance does not, however, satisfy the definition of a fluid; it needs a definite shear exerted on it to exceed what is known as its yield strength and produce the movement of one layer

Shear force

with respect to another, and hence the shear force is not infinitesimally small. Similarly, a granular material cannot fit the definition of a fluid because it requires a finite force to overcome Coulomb (dry) friction between its parts.

When a fluid is placed between two closely spaced parallel plates, with one in motion at a velocity relative to the other and at a fixed distance from it, the fluid will be subjected to shear by the plate motion. If the shear force as measured is proportional to the relative velocity of the plates, then the fluid is defined as a Newtonian fluid. All other fluids are known as non-Newtonian fluids, and their study is known as rheology. Most gases and thin liquids tend to be Newtonian fluids. If the shear force exerted on the fluid varies with the amount of prior motion of the plates (*i.e.,* prior work done on the fluid by a shear force), then the fluid is said to be thixotropic. Printer's ink and thick paints are well-known examples of thixotropic fluids.

Both gas and liquid flow study are included in fluid mechanics. Gas flow regimes (behaviours) may be classified by the ratio of average distance that gas molecules travel between collisions to a characteristic length for a confining body or conduit. For small values of the ratio, the flow regime is called gas dynamics; the next regime is called slip flow; and for large values of the ratio it is called free molecule flow. The properties of fluids are treated below in two categories, mechanical properties and thermodynamic properties.

THE MECHANICAL PROPERTIES OF FLUIDS

Fluid pressure and solubility of gases. Average pressure of a static, or resting, fluid in contact with a plane area is defined as the normal, or perpendicular, force exerted against the area divided by the area. The pressure at a point is the limit of the normal force divided by the area as the area approaches zero size at the point. The pressure is the same in all directions at a point within a static fluid at rest.

The pressure and temperature of a liquid affect its ability to hold gases in solution. The greater the external pressure on a liquid, the more gas may be held in solution; and the lower the temperature, the more gas may be held in solution. Changes in pressure and temperature of a flowing liquid may affect its compressibility and acoustic behaviour (sound-conducting property), as a result of gases coming out of solution and being carried along as fine bubbles.

Changes in acoustic behaviour

Liquids may sustain extremely high pressures without much change in volume. In general, they cannot sustain tensile forces, forces that extend them, unless they are indeed pure, for otherwise vapour bubbles will form and rupture the liquid.

Density-related terms. The density, symbolized by the Greek letter rho, ρ, of a fluid is the ratio of the mass of a portion of the fluid to the volume of that portion. Density at a point is the limit of the ratio as the mass and volume shrink to zero (mathematically) at the point. Density in SI (International System) units is expressed in kilograms per cubic metre; in the English system it is expressed either in pounds mass per cubic foot or in slugs (32.174 pounds mass) per cubic foot. The specific weight, symbolized by the Greek letter gamma, γ, of a fluid is the weight of a unit volume of the fluid. In the SI system it is newtons per cubic metre; in the English system it is pounds force per cubic foot.

The specific volume of a fluid (V_s) is the reciprocal of its mass density; *i.e.,* its volume per unit mass $V_s = 1/\rho$. The specific gravity of a substance is the ratio of its weight to the weight of an equal volume of water at standard conditions.

Compressibility and elasticity. The compressibility of a liquid is usually expressed by the value of its bulk modulus of elasticity. If a volume (V) of liquid is subjected to an additional increment of pressure (Δp; an incremental change in a variable hereafter will be represented by the delta symbols Δ and δ), its volume will be reduced by an amount $-\Delta V$. The ratio of pressure change to volume change per unit volume is the bulk modulus of elasticity K, which is equivalent in the case when the volume shrinks to zero to the density (ρ) times the rate of change of pressure with density, expressed as the differential $dp/d\rho$. Thus, as noted below, the equation can be written as:

$$K = -\frac{\Delta p}{(\Delta V/V)} = \frac{\rho dp}{d\rho}.$$

As the ratio $\Delta V/V$ is dimensionless (*i.e.*, is not expressed in terms of physical units), the bulk modulus of elasticity (K) has the units of pressure. Water has a value for the bulk modulus of about 2×10^9 newtons per square metre (300,000 pounds per square inch [psi]) for ordinary pressures and temperatures. As the pressure increases, the bulk modulus of elasticity of water increases. At about 50,000 atmospheres pressure, the value of K will be doubled. Although the compressibility of gases may be expressed by use of the bulk modulus, it is considered customary to use the perfect gas law to express the relations among temperature, pressure and specific volume, or density. The perfect gas law is examined below under the main heading of *The thermodynamic properties of fluids*.

Surface tension and capillarity. A quasi-film forms at a liquid–gas or liquid–liquid interface because of the mutual attraction of liquid molecules near that region. The formation of a film at an interface may be considered from the basis of surface energy, or the work per unit area required to bring the interior molecules to the interface (or surface in a liquid–gas system). The film has a resistance to tension (that is, to having its area increased), called the surface tension of the liquid. The surface tension of a water–air interface may be demonstrated in a simple manner by floating a steel needle on the surface of water.

The surface tension of water varies from 0.073 newton per metre (0.005 pound force per foot) at 20° C (68° F) to 0.059 newton per metre (0.004 pound force per foot) at 100° C (212° F). Surface tension is the same phenomenon that causes small liquid droplets to tend to be spherical, because a sphere has the least area per unit volume of any closed shape.

The action of surface tension of a liquid that partially fills a vertical tube is to draw the liquid up into the tube if the liquid wets the tube, and to depress the liquid surface (meniscus) if it does not wet the tube. This effect is called capillarity. The adhesion of water to glass at an air–water–glass interface is greater than the cohesion of water, and hence water is said to wet the glass. On the other hand, at an air–mercury–glass interface, the cohesion of mercury is greater than its adhesion to glass and it does not wet the glass. Hence a mercury column is seen to be depressed.

The height to which a liquid column rises in an open tube is used as a measure of pressure at the base of the tube. For small diameter tubes (less than a centimetre [0.4 inch] in diameter) the effects of capillarity should be taken into account.

THE THERMODYNAMIC PROPERTIES OF FLUIDS

Thermodynamic relations of particular value in fluid flow situations include the concepts of temperature, work, and thermal energy, as well as the first and second laws of thermodynamics.

Temperature, heat content, and work. The temperature of a substance is a measure of its molecular activity. In dealing with gases, absolute temperature scales are used, because molecular activity approaches zero as the absolute temperature approaches zero. The internal energy of a substance is the sum of its potential and kinetic energies, plus its intrinsic energy (u), which is related to its molecular spacing and forces. The relation between intrinsic energy and temperature is given by a partial derivative (denoted by the symbol ∂, which means that all variables except one are held constant) stating that the rate of change of the intrinsic energy with absolute temperature, the volume of the substance being held constant, is equal to a constant known as the specific heat at constant volume; *i.e.*, is given by $c_V = (\partial u/\partial T)_V$, in

which c_V is the specific heat at constant volume and T is the absolute temperature. In other words, if a unit mass of a pure substance held at constant volume has its temperature raised one degree by addition of thermal energy (*e.g.*, heat transfer across its boundaries), the amount of thermal energy addition is its specific heat c_V.

Another kind of specific heat is c_p, the amount of thermal energy per unit mass added to cause the temperature to rise one degree when the substance is held at constant pressure. Specific heat depends on the enthalpy per unit mass, which is a property of the substance defined as the sum of the intrinsic energy and the ratio of pressure to density; *i.e.*, $h = u + p/\rho$. In equation form, specific heat at constant pressure is equal to the partial of the enthalpy per unit mass (h) with respect to absolute temperature, the pressure remaining constant, or $c_p = (\partial h/\partial T)_p$.

Many of the common gases, such as air, oxygen, hydrogen, and water vapour, have specific heat values, c_V and c_p, that are substantially constant over a wide temperature range. They may be taken as constants in solving practical problems. The specific heat at constant pressure is always greater than the specific heat at constant volume because of the work done by the gas in expanding its boundaries at constant pressure.

The term system refers to a definite mass of material and distinguishes it from all other material, referred to as its surroundings. A system is said to do work on its surroundings when the sole effect on the surroundings is equivalent to the lifting of a weight. Work or energy is measured in joules in the SI system and in foot-pounds in the English system.

Definition of system

The first and second laws of thermodynamics. According to the first law of thermodynamics, a statement of the conservation of energy, the heat added to a system, minus the work done by the system, depends only upon the initial and final energy states of the system. The difference in the initial and final states of the system, being independent of the path (the means by which it changes) from initial to final state, must be a property of the system and is called the internal energy (E) of the system (the internal energy per unit mass is represented by a quantity e). In equation form, the heat added to a system minus the work done by a system is equal to the difference in energy between the final and initial states, or, $Q_H - W = E_f - E_i$, in which Q_H is the heat added, W is the work done by the system, and E_f and E_i are the final and initial internal energies.

The first law of thermodynamics may also be written for a control volume; *i.e.*, a fixed volume in space through which fluid may flow. The heat (δQ_H) added to the control volume (V) per unit time (δt) minus the shear work (δW_s) done by the fluid within the control volume on its surroundings per unit time must just equal the time rate of increase of internal energy per unit mass (e) in the control volume plus the work done by the boundaries and the efflux of internal energy across the boundaries. By shear work one means the export of work from the control volume, as by a rotating turbine shaft or by electric power leaving the control volume. In equation form, the first law states:

$$\frac{\delta Q_H}{\delta t} - \frac{\delta W_s}{\delta t} = \frac{dE}{dt} = \frac{\partial}{\partial t}\int \rho e dV + \int\left(\frac{p}{\rho} + e\right)\rho v \cdot dA,$$

in which dV is an element of volume within the control volume, and the density (ρ) times the scalar product of the vectors v and dA, or, $\rho v \cdot dA$, is the mass per unit time flowing with velocity v out of an element δA of the control surface comprising the boundary. The first integral is throughout the volume and the second integral is over the boundary surface.

Before developing relationships pertaining to the second law of thermodynamics, some definitions are needed. A process is known as a succession of states through which a system passes, such as changes in temperature, pressure, density, and elevation. When a process takes place in such a manner that it can be reversed (that is, return to its original state without a change in the surroundings) the process is called reversible. Any actual process is irrever-

Capillarity

sible. The difference in the amount of work a process can accomplish and the amount of reversible work is called the irreversibility of the process. This irreversibility of the process is also called the losses, the loss of ability to do work. Losses do not refer to lost energy but to a transformation of energy to a form not available to do work directly.

An important thermodynamic property is entropy, defined for a reversible process as the ratio of the heat added to a system to the absolute temperature, that is, in differential form,

$$ds = \left(\frac{dq_H}{T}\right)_{rev}, \qquad (1)$$

in which ds is the change in entropy per unit mass caused by the addition of dq_H units of heat per unit mass at absolute temperature T.

The first law of thermodynamics, in the absence of shear work, may be expressed as: heat added is equal to the sum of two terms, the first being the product of the pressure and the change in specific volume, and the second, the change in intrinsic energy:

$$dq_H = pd\left(\frac{1}{\rho}\right) + du. \qquad (2)$$

The first term on the right is work done by the fluid on its boundaries. For a reversible process, the heat term dq_H may be completely eliminated in the above equations (1) and (2), thus giving the relationship that the change in entropy per unit mass times the absolute temperature is equal to the work done by the fluid plus the change in intrinsic energy, or

$$Tds = pd\left(\frac{1}{\rho}\right) + du. \qquad (3)$$

Equation (3) is a well-known and important version of the second law of thermodynamics; although it was primarily developed for reversible processes, because every term is a property, it must also hold for real, or irreversible, processes.

The Clausius inequality The Clausius inequality (so called for the 19th-century German physicist Rudolf Clausius) states that the entropy change per unit mass is equal to or greater than the heat change divided by the absolute temperature; i.e., $ds \geq dq_H/T$, or $Tds \geq dq_H$. The equality of the two terms applies only for reversible processes. By defining losses in terms of an inequality of the two terms, that is, the losses being equal to the absolute temperature times the entropy change per unit mass, minus the amount of heat added to the system, or

$$d(\text{losses}) = Tds - dq_H, \qquad (4)$$

it is an important fact that losses are zero for the reversible case. It is also to be remembered that, in the absence of heat transfer out of a process, the entropy of a system cannot decrease, and with processes in real systems it can only increase.

Equation (3) is one form of the second law of thermodynamics. In the section on compressible fluid flow below, it will be extended to other useful forms.

The perfect gas law. Any fluid that substantially obeys the law that its pressure is proportional to its mass density and the absolute temperature, or

$$p = \rho RT, \qquad (5)$$

in which R is known as the gas constant, is called a perfect gas and the formula is the perfect gas law. Here, p is the absolute pressure; i.e., pressure measured from absolute zero, such as that of a complete vacuum. The mass density, symbolized by the Greek letter rho (ρ), may be written as the ratio of the mass of gas (m) to its volume (V)—that is, m/V—with the result that the pressure times volume of a gas is equal to its mass, times the gas constant, times the absolute temperature: $pV = mRT$. In this form the relations among pressure, volume, and temperature are exposed. The formula contains both Boyle's law and Charles's law. Boyle's law is an isothermal (constant temperature) law and states that at constant temperature the volume of a given mass of gas varies inversely as the pressure. Charles's law states that for constant pressure the volume of a given mass of gas varies directly with the absolute temperature. The gas constant (R) depends upon the molecular weight (M) of the gas and upon the units of pressure, temperature, volume, and mass used in the formula. In the International System of Units it is $R = 8.31434$ joules per degree Kelvin per mole.

Flow processes. Real flow processes are generally complicated, involving the effects of many kinds of forces caused by gravity, viscosity, surface tension, compressibility, pressure, and shear, and the effects of heat transfer and friction. To analyze and design systems, one usually tries to simplify the interaction of forces by neglecting those forces that have a minor effect upon the process. Other assumptions may be made to simplify the analysis; then practical corrections must be made to improve the accuracy of the final result. Some of the flow processes used are:

Isothermal flow. The flow is assumed to take place with no change in its temperature; this condition requires heat transfer to take place if the pressure is changing. An example of such a flow process is the transmission of natural gas through pipelines.

Adiabatic flow. In insulated pipes, for instance, or in flow systems in which heat transfer is minimized, the system may be analyzed as if no heat transfer (adiabatic condition) takes place. However, during rapid changes in properties, as through a flow nozzle, when little time is available for heat transfer, the flow is assumed to be adiabatic.

Isentropic flow. When flow of a fluid may be assumed to take place without heat transfer and by neglecting frictional effects (reversible-adiabatic), it is said to be isentropic flow. Flow through the test section of a wind tunnel (in the absence of shock waves) is an example of isentropic flow.

Polytropic flow. An actual flow process with little frictional loss that obeys the relation, pressure divided by density raised to some power n is equal to a constant ($P/\rho^n = $ constant), is called a reversible-polytropic process. The air in an air chamber on the discharge side of a reciprocating pump would approximately obey the equation for a power of $n = 1.2$. In general, heat transfer takes place during a polytropic process.

Fluid statics and equilibrium

BASIC EQUATION OF FLUID STATICS

By consideration of the fluid forces acting on a small element of fluid, as in Figure 1, with gravity acting in the vertical, or $-y$ direction, equations for rate of change of pressure in the coordinate directions are obtained. The pressure is p at the centre of the element and is assumed to vary continuously in any direction. The equation for the sum of forces acting on the element in the x-direction, $\Sigma f_x = 0$, has only the two forces, the pressure forces on the faces normal (perpendicular) to x, which must then be equal and opposite, yielding the partial derivative of pressure with respect to distance x equals zero, $\partial p/\partial x = 0$. Similarly for the z-direction, $\partial p/\partial z = 0$. For the vertical direction, however, the body force, or weight, of the element must be included, resulting in the partial derivative of pressure with respect to vertical distance (y) equals minus the specific weight, or $\partial p/\partial y = -\gamma$.

The partial derivative expressions, $\partial p/\partial x$, $\partial p/\partial z$, equal to zero, are one of several forms of Pascal's law, which state that two points at the same elevation in the same continuous mass of fluid at rest have the same identical pressure.

Inasmuch as the pressure is a function of the vertical direction only, then the partial derivative becomes a total derivative of pressure with respect to vertical distance; i.e.,

$$\frac{dp}{dy} = -\gamma, \qquad (6)$$

which is the relation for determination of pressure variation in a static fluid, liquid, or gas.

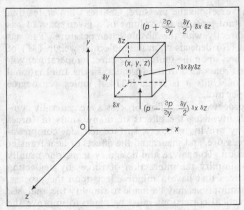

Figure 1: Fluid forces acting on a rectangular parallelepiped element of fluid at rest at point (x, y, z) (see text).

From V.L. Streeter, *Fluid Mechanics*, copyright 1971; used with permission of McGraw-Hill Book Co.

For a liquid, the specific weight may usually be considered to be constant, and so integration of equation (6) gives the relationship that pressure equals minus specific weight times vertical distance, plus a constant of integration:

$$p = -\gamma y + \text{constant.}$$

This equation states that the pressure increases linearly with depth, or $-y$. If $y = 0$ is taken at the free liquid surface at atmospheric pressure (gauge pressure zero, $p = 0$) and h is measured vertically downward from the free surface, then the pressure is equal to specific weight, symbolized by a Greek gamma, γ, times depth, or

$$p = \gamma h, \qquad (7)$$

a simple form of the fluid static law for liquids. Under ordinary conditions the specific weight for water is about 9,800 newtons per cubic metre (62.4 pounds per cubic foot). The pressure variation for perfect gases requires that the specific weight be expressed in terms of the perfect gas law, equation (5). From the relation density is equal to specific weight divided by g, the acceleration of gravity ($\rho = \gamma/g$; g is approximately 9.8 metres, or 32.2 feet, per second per second), it follows that the specific weight is equal to pressure times the acceleration of gravity, divided by the gas constant times absolute temperature, $\gamma = pg/RT$; then from equation (6), the total derivative of the pressure with respect to vertical distance is equal to minus pressure times acceleration of gravity, divided by the gas constant times absolute temperature, or

$$\frac{dp}{dy} = \frac{-pg}{RT}. \qquad (8)$$

If the gas is at constant temperature (*i.e.*, $T =$ constant), the isothermal case, the equation may be integrated as the natural logarithm (ln) of pressure equals minus a quantity, acceleration of gravity times the vertical distance (y), divided by the gas constant times absolute temperature, plus a constant of integration (C), namely,

$$\ln p = \frac{-gy}{RT} + C.$$

If the pressure is p_0 at a vertical distance $y = 0$, the equation becomes: pressure equals the pressure at zero vertical distance times the exponential constant ($e = 2.718$) raised to a negative power of acceleration of gravity times vertical distance divided by the gas constant times absolute temperature, or

$$p = p_0 e^{-gy/RT}, \qquad (9)$$

showing that the gas pressure reduces exponentially with vertical distance in the isothermal case.

The atmosphere near the Earth's surface, called the troposphere, experiences a drop in temperature with elevation, on the average, which may be expressed as minus beta, β, per unit distance ($-\beta$/metre, $-\beta$/foot). The constant β is called the temperature lapse rate. Hence,

measured from sea level, the absolute temperature (T) is equal to the absolute temperature at sea level (T_0) minus the temperature lapse rate times elevation (vertical distance); that is, $T = T_0 - \beta y$. By substituting this relation in equation (8), the total derivative of pressure with respect to elevation is equal to minus the pressure times the acceleration of gravity divided by the quantity, gas constant times the difference between the absolute temperature at sea level and the temperature lapse rate times elevation, or

$$dp/dy = -pg/R\,(T_0 - \beta y).$$

This equation may be integrated for constant β, yielding the variation of pressure with elevation for a gas with a constant temperature gradient, that is, the pressure is equal to the pressure at sea level times a quantity, one minus the temperature lapse rate times elevation divided by the absolute temperature at sea level, all raised to the power: acceleration of gravity divided by the gas constant times the temperature lapse rate, or

$$p = p_0 \left(1 - \frac{\beta y}{T}\right)^{g/R\beta}. \qquad (10)$$

Equation (10), together with the isothermal equation (9), may be used to calculate pressure and density relations in the stratosphere. For the defined standard atmosphere, $\beta = 0.0065°$ C per metre ($\beta = 0.0036°$ F per foot).

FLUID FORCES ON PLANES AND CURVED SURFACES

Pressure measurement: manometers. Local atmospheric pressure is the datum for gauge pressures. It varies from one location to another and from one time to another. The barometer measures the local atmospheric pressure in terms of its difference from absolute zero pressure, a complete vacuum. A standard atmosphere is the average sea level pressure, about 1.01×10^6 dynes per square centimetre, or 1.01×10^5 newtons per square metre (14.7 pounds force per square inch). As equivalents, it will support a column of mercury of a height of 760 millimetres (30 inches) or a column of water of a height of 10.3 metres (33.8 feet). A bourdon gauge, which measures gauge pressures, consists of a closed hollow curved member with its inside exposed to the pressure to be measured. Pressure causes the member to tend to straighten, thereby actuating a pointer that moves along a calibrated dial. The gauge is adjusted so that its reading is zero when exposed to the same pressure inside and outside the curved member. Common gauge pressure units in the metric system are the barye, one dyne per square centimetre, or 0.1 newtons per square metre; the megabarye, also called the bar, 10^6 dynes per square centimetre, or 10^5 newtons per square metre; and millimetre of mercury (in the English system, the units are pounds per square inch, inches of mercury, and feet of water). When a pressure is negative, called suction or vacuum, it is measured from the gauge pressure zero datum and is less than local atmospheric pressure. By adding the barometric pressure, in the proper units, to a gauge pressure, the absolute pressure is easily obtained. The standard atmosphere is considered to be a unit of absolute pressure only and is always measured from an absolute vacuum.

The simple manometer (Figure 2) is used to measure gauge pressures. It generally is composed of a transparent tube containing liquid, with one end connected to the pressure source and the other end, known as the meniscus, open to the local atmosphere. By use of equation (7), the hydrostatic law for liquids, the pressure change from the known zero gauge pressure to the unknown pressure is given by the product of the vertical distance (h) and the specific weight (γ). In some cases, two or more liquid columns may be used; then the algebraic sum of the pressure changes caused by the liquid columns is calculated to determine the unknown pressure.

In certain situations, as with rate measuring instruments such as a venturi meter, a difference in pressure between two points of unknown pressure is needed. Figure 3 illustrates the differential manometer used to measure pres-

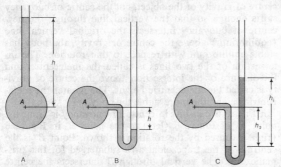

Figure 2: *Examples of simple manometers used for measuring the pressure in a liquid at point A (atmospheric pressure neglected). (A) Elementary type. (B) Type for determining small negative or positive pressures. (C) Type for determining large negative or positive pressures.*

From V.L. Streeter, *Fluid Mechanics*, copyright 1971; used with permission of McGraw-Hill Book Co.

sure differences. It also utilizes equation (7) as the measure of pressure change from one meniscus to another. For example, in Figure 3A, the difference in liquid pressures between bulbs B and A, $(p_A - p_B)$, in terms of specific weight times vertical distance, is $p_A - p_B = \gamma_1 h_1 + \gamma_2 h_2 - \gamma_3 h_3$. There are many kinds of manometers, such as inclined manometers and micromanometers, but all use the same basic concepts in determining pressure differences.

From V.L. Streeter, *Fluid Mechanics*, copyright 1971; used with permission of McGraw-Hill Book Co.

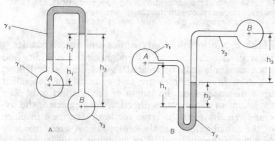

Figure 3: Differential manometers (see text).

Analysis of fluid forces. By Pascal's law, pressure (p) is constant over a horizontal area submerged in a static fluid. The force (F) on such a surface would then be equal to pressure times surface area (A) or $F = pA$. For an inclined plane area submerged in a liquid, the pressure changes linearly with elevation, and a simple expression can be obtained for magnitude of the force by summing up the product pdA over the surface by the calculus method of integration. With reference to Figure 4A using the strip element of area δA of width δy, the elemental force δF on the strip is $\gamma h \delta A$, or specific weight times depth times element of area, or $\gamma y \sin \theta \delta A$, in which $h = y \sin \theta$. The angle symbolized by the Greek letter theta, θ, that the plane B'A' makes with the horizontal, and the specific weight are constant. The force is therefore given by the specific weight times sine of the slope angle times the integral of ydA taken over the total area (A); as shown by

$$F = \gamma \sin \theta \int_A ydA = \gamma \sin \theta \, \bar{y} A = \gamma \bar{h} A = p_{cg} A, \tag{11}$$

in which $\bar{y}$ is the distance from the axis Ox to the centre of mass G (centroid) of the area and $\bar{h}$ is the vertical distance from the centroid of the area to the liquid free surface. The last form of the expression, equation (11), is particularly convenient in that p_{cg}, the pressure at the centroid (centre of mass) of the area, may be found by any available means and does not, in fact, imply a free surface.

The force F, however, does not act at the centroid if it is to be equivalent to the distributed force and replace its action. Because it must be an equivalent force, it has the same moment of force (torque) about any axis, say the

Ox axis. Then the product y_pF is equal to the integral, taken over the area A, of the elemental force dF times the distance y ($dF = \gamma \sin \theta \, ydA$), or

$$y_pF = \int_A ydF,$$

in which y_p, the distance in the y-direction from Ox to the line of action of the resultant force, is sought. Similarly, to find the location of the line of action of F in the x-direction, the moment equation about Oy is

$$x_pF = \int_A xdF.$$

These equations may be solved for the two distances x_p and y_p; then by placing the force F at this x_p, y_p location, called the pressure centre, the action of the distributed liquid force on the area has been replaced with F, its resultant force. Pressure centre

If the action of liquid pressure on a submerged curved surface is desired, it is convenient to decompose the liquid forces into horizontal and vertical components at right angles, then combine them as vectors. (Vectors are quantities that may be symbolized by arrows to show their magnitude and direction.) The horizontal component of force in the x-direction on a curved surface, Figure 4B, may be shown to be equal to the force on a projection of the curved surface onto a plane normal to x. The force on a small area element exerted by pressure p on an elemental area δA is $p\delta A$, and the x-component of this elemental force is $p\delta A \cos \theta$. The quantity $\delta A \cos \theta$, however, is the projection of the area element onto the normal plane. By summing up all such elemental forces it is noted to be equivalent to finding the force on the projected vertical plane area. The pressure centre for the projected area gives the location of line of action of this component. By taking the horizontal axis at right angles to x, the force component is found in magnitude and location in the same way. After combining these two forces as vectors the resultant horizontal component of force on the curved surface has been determined.

The vertical component of force on a curved surface is found in a rather similar manner, Figure 4C, by considering the force element $p\delta A$ and taking its vertical component $p\delta A \cos \theta$. The quantity $\delta A \cos \theta$ is the projection of the elemental area δA onto a horizontal plane and is the area of the base of the liquid prism of height h (for which $h = p/\gamma$) extending up to the free surface. By summing up all such volume elements the vertical component of force on the curved surface equals the weight of liquid vertically above the curved surface. For situations in which there is no free surface, an imaginary free surface may be constructed such that it would yield the same pressure at each point on the curved surface. It may be shown that the line of action of the resultant vertical force acts through the centroid of the liquid volume (real or imaginary) above the curved surface. By adding the vertical component force to the horizontal resultant vector, the single force replacing the distributed liquid force on the curved area is found. Determination of the vertical component of force

A body submerged or floating in a static liquid can have no horizontal component of force exerted on it due to the fact that the projection on a vertical plane is always zero.

Buoyant force. The resultant force exerted by static liquid on a body floating or submerged in it is called the buoyant force. It must be vertical (that is, acting in a direction opposite to the force of gravity), and its magnitude can be found by application of the relations for finding the vertical component of force on a curved surface, applied to its lower and upper surfaces. This operation results in the simple relationship that the buoyant force is equal to the weight of fluid displaced by the body (γV), and its line of action is through the centroid of the displaced volume. In equation form, $F_B = \gamma V$, in which F_B is the buoyant force and V the displaced volume of fluid. This equation is a statement of Archimedes' principle.

The hydrometer uses this principle in determining the specific gravity of a liquid. The less the specific weight of a liquid, the farther downward a floating object sinks before equilibrium is reached. Marks on the body may be

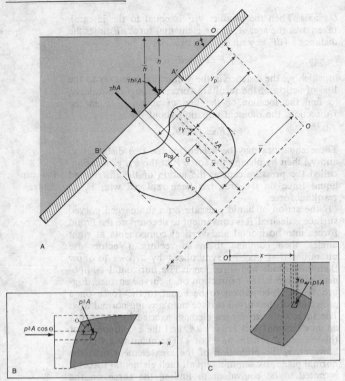

Figure 4: *Three aspects of liquid force.*
(A) On one side of a plane inclined area. (B) Horizontal component of force on a curved surface. (C) Vertical component of force on a curved surface (see text).
From V.L. Streeter, *Fluid Mechanics*, copyright 1966; used with permission of McGraw-Hill Book Co.

made at the liquid contact line designating the specific gravity of the liquid.

Stability of floating and submerged bodies. A body floating in a liquid has vertical stability. Any tendency for it to become further submerged results in a greater buoyant force that returns it to its equilibrium position, and any tendency for it to rise higher causes a reduction in the buoyant force so that the weight of the body returns it to its original position.

The centre of buoyancy is the centroid of the displaced liquid volume, and the buoyant force always acts vertically through the centre of buoyancy. The weight of a body acts vertically downward through its centre of gravity. A body has rotational stability if any rotational displacement sets up a rotational force, called a couple, tending to return the body to its original position. If a couple tends to increase the displacement, then the body is unstable, and if no couple is set up it is said to have neutral equilibrium. In Figure 5A a light piece of wood has a weight attached to one end; it is stable as shown. Figure 5B shows unstable equilibrium and Figure 5C is a case of neutral stability.

Any submerged body must have the centre of gravity vertically below the centre of buoyancy to be in stable rotational equilibrium. In the case of floating bodies, however, such is not the case. When a floating body is rotated slightly there is a shift in the centre of buoyancy toward the portion of the object moving deeper into the liquid. In effect, a wedge-shaped volume of fluid is displaced on the low side, and an equal volume wedge-shaped portion on the high side is removed from below the liquid surface. If the centre of buoyancy is below the

From V.L. Streeter, *Fluid Mechanics*, copyright 1966; used with permission of McGraw-Hill Book Co.

Figure 5: Examples of equilibria (see text).

centre of gravity of the object, but the centre of buoyancy shifts enough so that the vertical line through the new centre of buoyancy intersects the original vertical line (equilibrium) above the centre of gravity, the body has stable equilibrium with respect to that rotation. The intersection of the two lines is called the metacentre, and the distance of the intersection above the centre of gravity is called the metacentric height. The greater the metacentric height, the more stable the body.

In Figure 6 the shift in centre of buoyancy is from the point B_o of Figure 6 (left) to the point B' in Figure 6 (right), caused by the rotation θ shown. Point B' is the centroid of the trapezoidal area submerged for this prismatic case. The vertical through B' intersects the centre line PG at M, which is above the centre of gravity at G. If the metacentre is at G, neutral stability is indicated; and if the metacentre is below G, the body is unstable and will not remain in a vertical position. MG is the metacentric height.

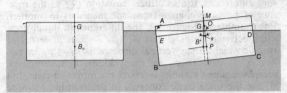

Figure 6: *Stability of prismatic body.*
(Left) A cross section of a body with all other parallel cross sections identical. (Right) When the body is tipped, the centre of buoyancy is at the centroid B' of the trapezoid ABCD. The buoyant force acts upward through B', and the weight acts downward through G, the centre of gravity of the body.

Fluids in motion: hydrodynamics and aerodynamics

Flow of liquids and gases through closed conduits and open channels may be treated as one-dimensional flow; *i.e.*, flow in which pressure and velocity are dependent upon distance along the length of the conduit only. The variations in a transverse direction are neglected, the average velocity over the cross section being used in place of the actual velocity at the centre line. A great majority of engineering applications of fluid flow to design may be carried out using the one-dimensional analysis. Compressible flow is considered in a separate section. The flow in general is assumed to be steady; *i.e.*, not to vary with time at any point.

FRICTIONLESS ONE-DIMENSIONAL FLUID FLOW

Many frictionless flow problems may be analyzed by use of three equations: the continuity equation, Euler's equation, and Bernoulli's equation. The continuity equation, one of the most fundamental equations of fluid dynamics, is derived for one-dimensional flow from the general law of conservation of mass, whereas the Euler equation and the Bernoulli equation are consequences of applying Newton's second law of motion to a fluid particle. A few definitions are needed before the following equations can be stated.

A streamline is a line drawn through a fluid in such a manner that it has the direction of the fluid velocity at every point. If the flow is steady, the streamline is fixed in space and is the path a fluid particle would follow. If all the streamlines through a small closed curve were constructed for a steady flow, these streamlines would form a stream tube, fixed in space that completely separates the flow inside the tube from the flow outside the tube. Obviously, no flow can take place through the wall of the tube.

The continuity equation. For a steady stream tube (Figure 7A), the mass flow rate through section 1 must just equal the mass flow rate through section 2. If this were not so, some fluid would be added to storage or taken out of storage between the two sections, and this change would require a change in conditions (density) with time that contradicts the assumption of steady flow. If a stream tube, Figure 7A, has end sections of elemental area δA_1 and δA_2, then the mass flow per unit time at section 1 is equal to its density (ρ) times flow velocity

Equations used in frictionless flow problems

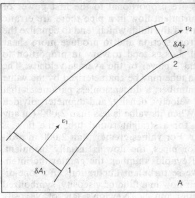

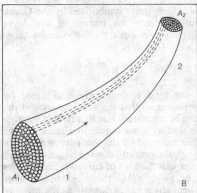

Figure 7: *Steady flow.*
(A) Through a stream tube. (B) A collection of
stream tubes between fixed boundaries (see text).

From V.L. Streeter, *Fluid Mechanics*, copyright 1966; used
with permission of McGraw-Hill Book Co.

(v_1) times sectional area (δA_1), and similarly at section 2; or in equation form, which is the continuity equation for the stream tube of elemental area, δA, $\rho_1 v_1 \delta A_1 = \rho_2 v_2 \delta A_2$. If all the stream tubes comprising a flow situation, such as those shown in Figure 7B, are summed up, the continuity equation states that the product of density, velocity, and cross-sectional area (A) is the same at ends 1 and 2, or $\rho_1 v_1 A_1 = \rho_2 v_2 A_2$, in which ρ_1 and v_1 are the average density and velocity over cross section A_1, and similarly over cross section A_2. For the incompressible flow case, with $\rho_1 = \rho_2$, the equation reduces to a simpler form such that Q, the discharge rate (volume per unit time) passing any cross section in the collection of stream tubes comprising the flow, is equal to the velocity of the fluid times the cross-sectional area, or $Q = v_1 A_1 = v_2 A_2$.

Euler's equation. By applying Newton's second law, the equation of motion, to a fluid particle in the direction along a streamline in steady, incompressible, frictionless flow, a differential equation is obtained, called Euler's equation. In Figure 8, a particle having an elemental area δA and length δs is acted on by three forces along the path indicated by s: a force acting uphill, equal to pressure times area, or $p \delta A$; a force acting downhill equal to minus the pressure, which has changed by the increment $\dfrac{\partial p}{\partial s} \, \delta s$, or $(p + \dfrac{\partial P}{\partial s} \delta s)\delta A$; and a second force acting downhill, the component of weight $\rho(\delta s \delta A)\,g$, or $-\rho g \delta A \delta s \cos \theta$. The sum of these forces, according to Newton's second law, is equal to the mass of the particle times its acceleration (a_s) along path s, giving $p\delta A - (p + \dfrac{\partial p}{\partial s} \delta s)\delta A - \rho\,g\,\delta A\,\delta s \cos \theta = \rho\,\delta A\,\delta s\,a_s$. Because $\cos \theta$ may be expressed as the ratio $\delta z/\delta s$, in which z is measured vertically upward, the equation reduces to: the change in pressure divided by the density, plus the acceleration of gravity times change along vertical direction, plus the particle acceleration times change of path length along path, equals zero, or $\dfrac{dp}{\rho} + g\,dz + a_s\,ds = 0$. The ac-

celeration component, being the change of velocity with time (dv/dt), may be written as the product of the change of velocity with distance along the path (dv/ds) and the velocity along the path ($v = ds/dt$), or $a_s = (dv/dt) \times (ds/dt) = v\,(dv/ds)$.

Substituting $v\,(dv/ds)$ for a_s in the preceding equation yields a relationship such that the sum of three terms is zero, namely, change of pressure divided by density, acceleration of gravity times change in vertical distance, and velocity times change in velocity, or $dp/\rho + g\,dz + v\,dv = 0$, which is the Euler equation.

Bernoulli's equation. Euler's equation may be integrated, for constant density, yielding the Bernoulli equation: pressure divided by density, plus acceleration of gravity times total vertical distance moved along the path, plus one-half the velocity squared, equals a constant, or

$$p/\rho + gz + v^2/2 = \text{constant}.$$

By dividing each term by the acceleration of gravity it takes the form: pressure divided by specific weight plus vertical distance, plus one-half the velocity squared divided by the acceleration of gravity, equals a constant, or

$$\frac{p}{\gamma} + z + \frac{v^2}{2g} = \text{constant}. \qquad (12)$$

The term p/γ may be interpreted as flow work, or as a portion of the potential energy term that the fluid is capable of yielding because of its sustained pressure. The term may also be called the pressure energy; z is the potential energy, and $v^2/2g$ is the kinetic energy, each term having the dimensions of a length that is interpreted as energy per unit weight. In the International System of Units each term is in metres, or in joules per newton (in English units feet, or foot-pounds per pound).

From V.L. Streeter, *Fluid Mechanics*, copyright 1971;
used with permission of McGraw-Hill Book Co.

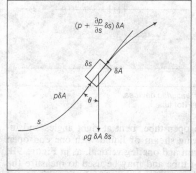

Figure 8: Force components on a fluid particle
(see text).

The Bernoulli equation aids in solving problems in which the losses may be neglected or corrected for by application of an experimentally determined coefficient. Three applications of the equation are given:

Torricelli's theorem. The Bernoulli equation states that the energy is the same at any two points along a streamline in steady, frictionless, incompressible flow. In the case of a tank of liquid having a nozzle (point 2) on the side at a distance H below the surface (point 1), one may consider that a streamline connects points 1 and 2, and applying equation (12) to each point,

$$v_1^2/2g + p_1/\gamma + z_1 = v_2^2/2g + p_2/\gamma + z_2.$$

The velocity at the surface of the reservoir is almost nil, in which case v_1 is approximately zero and the pressure is zero ($p_1 = 0$). At point 2 the pressure is substantially zero, neglecting surface tension effects, because the streamlines are parallel and surrounded by zero-pressure air.

The elevation difference is $z_1 - z_2 = H$, and therefore the square of the velocity of the liquid issuing from the spout divided by twice the acceleration of gravity is equal to the head, or distance of the liquid level above the spout: $v^2/2g = H$, or $v_2 = \sqrt{2gH}$. This speed is the same as that attained by a particle in dropping the distance H

under the acceleration of gravity. This result is known as Torricelli's theorem.

The venturi meter. The venturi meter shown in Figure 9A is used to measure the rate of flow of a fluid in a closed conduit. It consists of a converging portion from 1 to a throat section at 2, followed by a gradually diverging reach that converts most of the kinetic energy at 2 back into pressure. Pressure connections are attached at sections 1 and 2 so that the pressures may be determined. The Bernoulli equation for points 1 and 2 may be written $p_1/\gamma + v_1^2/2g = p_2/\gamma + v_2^2/2g$ after eliminating z; as $z_1 = z_2$. By use of the continuity equation $v_1 A_1 = v_2 A_2$, the equations may be solved for $v_2 A_2$, equal to the discharge rate (Q), which is equal to the product of the two areas times the square root of twice the acceleration of gravity times the difference of the two pressures divided by the specific weight times the difference of the square of the two areas, or

$$Q = v_2 A_2 = A_1 A_2 [2g(p_1 - p_2) / \gamma (A_1^2 - A_2^2)]^{1/2}.$$

This result is a little high, in general, because of the neglect of friction. An experimentally found coefficient may be applied as a multiplier to make the equation yield correct results.

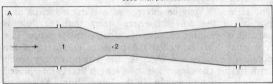

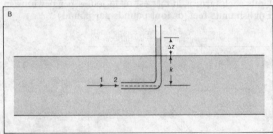

Figure 9: *Fluid flow measuring devices.*
(A) Venturi meter. (B) Pitot tube.

Pitot tube. An open tube, bent at right angles and inserted into a flowing stream of liquid with one end open and facing upstream and one leg vertical, as in Figure 9B, is a form of pitot tube and may be used to measure the velocity of a flowing stream. At point 2, the liquid is forced into the open end until the impact of the flow is just balanced by the column height ($\Delta z + k$) in the tube. Point 2 is a stagnation point, at which the velocity is zero ($v_2 = 0$). By writing Bernoulli's equation from point 1, an undisturbed point having velocity v, there results $v^2/2g + p_1/\gamma = p_2/\gamma = p_1/\gamma + \Delta z$, using manometer principles. A solution of this equation gives for the velocity, $v = \sqrt{2g\Delta z}$.

Energy equation. The energy equation for steady, incompressible, one-dimensional flow takes the form of the Bernoulli equation with a correction term for losses. If section 1 is upstream of section 2, then

$$v_1^2/2g + p_1/\gamma + z_1 = v_2^2/2g + p_2/\gamma + z_2 + losses_{1-2}.$$

In words, the energy equation, in joules per newton (or foot-pounds per pound) states that the available energy at 1 is equal to the available energy at 2, plus all the losses between the two sections. If a pump were in action between the sections, its total dynamic head would appear in the loss term as a negative quantity. Similarly a turbine would be treated as a loss.

FLOW IN PIPES AND CHANNELS

Laminar flow: the Poiseuille equation. In laminar flow, fluid particles move in laminas, or layers; *e.g.*, in a pipe, each concentric cylindrical shell of fluid moves faster than its next outer layer, with the fluid at rest at the

pipe wall. Losses are proportional to the first power of the velocity. In turbulent flow in a pipe there are erratic transverse motions of the fluid, which tend to equalize the velocity over a cross section and to produce more shear stress at the wall. Losses tend to vary in proportion to about the 1.85 and 2 power of the average velocity. The nature of flow in a tube may be characterized by the value of the Reynolds number, a dimensionless parameter that is the product of velocity, density, and diameter, divided by the viscosity. When its value is less than 2,000 (in any consistent units) for a straight round tube, the flow is generally laminar. For values greater than 2,000 in ordinary situations for pipes, the flow is usually turbulent. The greater the Reynolds number, the greater the intensity of the transverse turbulent fluctuations. For one-dimensional laminar flow in a fluid of viscosity, symbolized by the Greek letter mu, μ, Newton's law of viscosity states that the fluid shear stress symbolized by the Greek letter tau, τ, resulting from the motion of one layer adjacent to another layer, is equal to the viscosity times their relative velocity (du/dy), or

$$\tau = \mu\left(\frac{du}{dy}\right). \tag{13}$$

The viscosity of the fluid is frequently determined by setting up an experiment so that the shear stress and the relative velocity can be measured. For steady flow through a circular tube of radius a, as shown in Figure 10, the pressure drop is just balanced by the shear force on a free body of the fluid; *i.e.*, the pressure drop (a negative value) times the end area equals the area of curved cylinder times the shear stress, or $(-dp/dl)\delta l\pi r^2 = 2\pi r\delta l\tau$; or, after simplifying, the shear stress varies directly as the pressure gradient and as the radius of cylinder (r), or $\tau = -(dp/dl)r/2$, in which the shear stress is considered positive as shown. If equation (13) is written $\tau = -\mu(du/dr)$ and is substituted into the last equation, then

$$\mu\left(\frac{du}{dr}\right) = \left(\frac{dp}{dl}\right) r/2.$$

The term dp/dl is not a function of r, and hence the equation may be integrated so that $u = 1/4\mu \ (dp/dl)r^2 +$ constant. Because the velocity of a real fluid must be zero at a stationary boundary, $u = 0$ when $r = a$; the constant may thus be determined, yielding $u = -[(a^2 - r^2)/4\mu] \ (dp/dl)$. This equation shows that the velocity is a maximum at the centre line, and varies parabolically to zero at the wall. The maximum velocity is $u_{max} = -(a^2/4\mu) \ (dp/dl)$, and the average velocity is $u_{av} = -(a^2/8\mu) \ (dp/dl)$. The discharge rate Q, volume per unit time, is the product of the average velocity by the area πa^2 of the tube; that is,

$$Q = -\frac{\pi a^4}{8\mu}\frac{dp}{dl}, \tag{14}$$

Poiseuille's equation. The Poiseuille equation states that the laminar flow through a circular tube varies as the fourth power of the radius, inversely as the viscosity and directly as the pressure drop per unit length; *i.e.*, as given in equation (14). The discharge is independent of the density of the fluid and of the roughness of the tube wall.

The differential dp/dl is sometimes expressed as ($p_2 - p_1)/l$, in which p_1 and p_2 are the pressures at points 1 and 2, and l is the distance between them.

Turbulent flow. *Prandtl mixing length.* In order to obtain some measure of the turbulent fluctuations and their relation to shear stresses, Prandtl developed the concept of a mixing length l that a molar fluid particle might move transversely in a turbulent flow before it became identified with the fluid around it. The concept is analogous to the mean free path of a molecule. He obtained an expression ($y =$ distance from the boundary) that the shear stress (τ) equals the product of density (ρ), square of the mixing length, and square of the velocity gradient (du/dy), or $\tau = \rho l^2(du/dy)^2$.

By further reasoning the mixing length was taken to be proportional to the distance from a pipe wall, which leads to equations for the variation of velocity across a pipe in

Bernoulli's equation with losses

Laminar flow through a circular tube

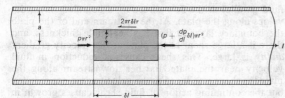

Figure 10: Free-body diagram for steady flow through a round tube.

From V.L. Streeter, *Fluid Mechanics*, copyright 1966; used with permission of McGraw-Hill Book Co.

turbulent flow, and also leads to an expression for energy loss in turbulent flow through pipes.

The Darcy–Weisbach equation. Laminar flow through pipes is calculated by the Poiseuille equation, as stated above. For turbulent flow in pipes the Darcy–Weisbach equation is frequently used, which states that the head loss (energy difference between two sections of a pipe) is proportional to the product of length of pipe and the square of the velocity divided by the diameter and by twice the acceleration of gravity, or $h_f = f\ Lv^2/2Dg$, in which h_f is the head loss (energy loss in joules per newton, or foot-pounds per pound) for the length L of pipe of inside diameter D and average velocity v. For turbulent flow the dimensionless factor f is dependent upon the pipe wall roughness and the fluid properties of density and viscosity; it also is a function of the velocity and pipe diameter, because the losses are not always proportional to the square of the velocity and inversely proportional to the diameter.

For closed conduits of other than circular cross section, an equivalent diameter D may be approximated by four times the cross-sectional area (A) divided by the wetted perimeter (P), or $D = 4\ A/P$; by wetted perimeter is meant the length of the boundary of the cross section in contact with the flowing fluid.

Complex steady flow piping systems may be analyzed by use of the Darcy–Weisbach equation, plus the continuity equation which states the flow into a junction of pipes must equal flow out of the junction. For networks of pipes an additional criterion is needed, namely, that the pressure difference around any closed loop in the network must be zero. These problems are generally too complex for a direct analytical solution and procedures are used that improve the solution with repeated trials.

Special types of flow. *Unsteady flow.* Unsteady flow in pipes is much more complicated than steady flow, because conditions may be changing with time at any point within the system. Unsteady flow problems are usually calculated by use of the digital computer. The basic partial differential equations of motion and continuity are converted into algebraic finite difference equations that are applied repeatedly to individual reaches of the conduits making up the flow system. Extremely complex problems may be solved by these methods, such as the calculation of pressures and flows through a network of pipes when power to a pumping station supplying the system is interrupted.

Flow in open channels and rivers. Uniform flow occurs when the velocity vector is everywhere the same throughout the flow at an instant. This strict definition is relaxed for real fluids so that when the average velocity at every cross section of the flow is the same at any instant the flow is called uniform. A widely used empirical equation for steady-uniform flow in open channels is the Manning formula in English units, $v = 1.49\ R^{2/3}S^{1/2}/n$, in which v is the average velocity in feet per second, S is the slope of the bottom of the channel, R is the hydraulic radius, defined as the ratio of the cross-sectional area of the flow to the wetted perimeter (liquid–solid contact line) of the cross section, and n is an absolute roughness factor. In SI units the constant 1.49 becomes 1.

Because the Manning formula is empirical it is essential that the velocity be in feet per second, the radius in feet, and the slope be dimensionless. The equation may be written in terms of the discharge, Q, by multiplying both sides by the area A: $Q = 1.49\ AR^{2/3}S^{1/2}/n$.

The value of n for water and concrete is 0.012, and for water and corrugated metal it is 0.022. These values are reasonably satisfactory for other low viscosity liquids as well.

For natural rivers the flow may be fairly steady for some periods of time, but the flow is never uniform because of the variation of cross-sectional area and the changing direction of the river bed. The flow in a river is usually determined by measuring the velocity at many positions over a cross section, then multiplying the velocity by the appropriate area for each measurement and summing up the resulting discharges for the total area. The flow may be approximated by measuring the cross-sectional area at each end of a fairly uniform reach, and by measuring the slope of water surface and estimating the channel roughness. These values are substituted into the Manning formula to calculate the discharge.

In general, for gradually varying flow in the river with time, the differential equations of continuity and momentum are written, using the Manning formula above as a basis for estimating losses (or wall shear stresses). Solutions to the equations are usually carried out with the aid of a digital computer.

GENERAL TWO- AND THREE-DIMENSIONAL FLOW

Two- and three-dimensional flow must be approached from a mathematical viewpoint, resulting in complicated equations not appropriate to this article.

Mathematical conditions. The conditions to be satisfied are:

1. Continuity principles, derived from the general law of conservation of mass, which states that the net mass inflow into any small volume must just equal the time rate of increase of mass within the volume. For incompressible fluids this condition guarantees that fluid will not pile up at a point, or that gaps will not occur in a fluid.

2. Newton's second law of motion, which states that the net force acting on any small particles of fluid (mass) will cause it to be accelerated in proportion to the force and in inverse proportion to its mass. For real (viscous) fluids, shear forces must also be taken into account.

3. Boundary conditions, which are statements that the velocity component of a fluid normal to a solid boundary must just equal the velocity of the boundary normal to itself. For real fluids the velocity of a particle of fluid in contact with a boundary has the same velocity as the boundary; *e.g.*, fluid particles in contact with a solid boundary at rest have no velocity.

4. Irrotational (nonrotatory) conditions for nonviscous fluids, which state that a portion of fluid with each particle moving or at rest without rotation cannot be set into rotation. The amount of rotation of a fluid particle about an axis through it is defined as the average of the angular velocities of two line segments mutually at right angles to the axis.

Each of these basic concepts leads to equations that must be satisfied by the flow. This field of study is referred to as hydrodynamics, which was developed primarily during the 19th century.

The irrotational flow concepts lead to the definition of a velocity potential, which is a scalar function of time and space the derivative of which with respect to any direction is the negative of the velocity component in that direction. The combination of the irrotational concept with the continuity equation in frictionless incompressible flow leads to the Laplace equation. When this equation is satisfied by any function of space and time, say a function of the rectangular coordinates x,y,z, and time t —i.e., $f(x,y,z,t)$—then this function is the velocity potential for some fluid flow case. The determination of which case this may be requires a detailed examination of the possible boundary conditions that it can satisfy.

By use of the irrotational condition plus Newton's second law of motion (through development of Euler's equations of motion), it is possible to obtain an energy equation that states that in any steady, irrotational flow of a frictionless, incompressible fluid, the energy throughout the fluid must be constant. This equation is known as the Bernoulli equation.

Vorticity. By considering that a fluid has particles that have rotation about their axes, another field of study called vortex flow has been evolved. No velocity potential exists for this flow. A single line through a fluid may be

The Manning formula

Hydrodynamics

considered to have vorticity, and this condition affects the motion of fluid around it that may be irrotational.

If a long cylindrical body is rotated in a real fluid, it tends to pull fluid particles around it, thereby setting up some rotation. If a line is drawn in the fluid that contains the cylinder within it, the sum of the products of the velocity component tangent to the line by an element of length of line is called the circulation about the cylinder. It may be shown that when fluid flows across such a cylinder having a circulation, a force at right angles to the approaching flow develops that is called the lift force. It is proportional to the circulation, the approach velocity, and the fluid density. An example of this was an experimental vessel that sailed the Atlantic Ocean, called the Flettner rotorship after its inventor, a German engineer, Anton Flettner. It had two large vertical cylinders mounted on deck that were rotated mechanically, and thus had a thrust at right angles to the wind's directions.

Viscous three-dimensional flow theory must take into account the shear stresses exerted on the fluid particles by their angular deformation. The equations of motion are called the Navier–Stokes equations, and are extremely complicated, having been solved only for cases in which great simplifications could be made.

The Navier–Stokes equations apply directly to low Reynolds number flow (laminar flow), such as creeping flow between surfaces or small clearance; e.g., flow through journal bearings (called hydrodynamic lubrication).

The equations may be applied to the steady flow case of two horizontal closely spaced plates, with separation a, the lower plate being fixed in position and the upper one being free to move parallel to the lower plate at velocity U in the x-direction. The pressure of the fluid contained between the two plates may change in the x-direction because of the conditions at the boundaries (see Figure 11). The z-axis is vertical, z being the distance above the fixed plate. For this case the velocity u for any point is a function of z only. An equation for the velocity u may be derived, yielding $u = U z/a - (dp/dx)(az - z^2)/2\mu$, in which the Greek letter mu symbolizes the viscosity.

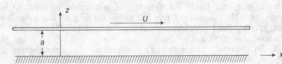

Figure 11: Flow between parallel plates with one plate in motion.

The term dp/dx is the change in pressure per unit length in the direction of flow. If this pressure gradient dp/dx is zero, the equation shows the velocity to be zero at the fixed plate, varying linearly with z to U at the moving plate. For two fixed plates ($U = 0$) the velocity distribution is parabolic; i.e., the velocity is a parabolic function of the distance z. The discharge per unit width (measured normal to the page) is given by $Q = U a/2 - a^3(dp/dx)/12\mu$. This equation is useful in determining leakage between small clearances, as in a piston pump.

To apply the Navier–Stokes equations to turbulent flow cases, they must be altered to bring in turbulent shear stresses.

Boundary layers. In 1904 Prandtl stated his boundary-layer hypothesis: For fluids having relatively small viscosity, the effect of internal friction in a fluid is appreciable only in a narrow region surrounding the fluid boundaries. This statement implies that the flow outside of the narrow region surrounding fluid boundaries may be considered as irrotational (nonrotatory) fluid flow. The boundary-layer hypothesis permitted the vast theory in potential flow to become useful in practical flow situations, joining the empirical approach of hydraulics with the mathematical theory of irrotational flow. The Navier–Stokes equations may be applied to the boundary regions, and the Euler equations to nonboundary regions of flow.

The boundary layer is defined as that portion of the flow that has had its velocity affected by fluid shear at the boundary. If a flat, smooth plate is immersed in a moving fluid parallel to the flow direction, a boundary layer develops along the plate. At the upstream end of the plate the boundary layer at first has negligible thickness, and there is a large shear at the plate as the velocity gradient du/dy is large. This shear causes a reduction in fluid velocity near the plate. Farther downstream along the plate the shear is reduced as the velocity gradient reduces, but the continuing action of fluid shear causes growth in the thickness of the fluid layer of reduced velocity in the downstream direction. Near the upstream end of the plate, the layer is called a laminar boundary layer, because the fluid particles move in smooth paths substantially parallel to the plate; as the layer becomes thicker, however, the laminar flow becomes unstable and transverse fluctuations develop within the layer changing the flow to turbulent flow. This portion of the flow is called the turbulent boundary layer. The thickness of laminar boundary layer grows as the square root of distance along the plate, whereas the shear stress varies as the inverse square root of the distance. For the turbulent boundary layer, it grows in thickness proportional to distance to the ⅘ power, and the shear stress varies inversely as distance to the ⅕ power.

For the case of a flat plate, parallel to the flow, the boundary layer continues to grow in the downstream direction indefinitely. If the flow boundaries are such that the pressure is increasing downstream, as with flow between diverging plates or in a conical diffusor, the action of the pressure is to hasten the growth of the layer and to bring the momentum of the flow in the layer to zero near the boundary. When this occurs, the boundary layer separates from the boundary and a region of backflow, called the wake, develops near the boundary. Separation of the boundary layer and the ensuing wake adds to increased losses in the flow. In flow around airfoil sections, as in airplane wings, and through the vanes of hydraulic machines such as propellers, pumps, or turbines, the separation of boundary-layer flow is the principal factor in poor performance. By altering the shape and thickness of airfoil sections or flow passages, the advent of transition to turbulent boundary layer may be delayed in such a manner as to reduce losses; or in some cases, by causing the turbulent boundary layer to develop before separation occurs, the size of the wake may be reduced and efficiency improved. In some practical cases momentum may be added to the boundary layer, as by drawing off the slow-moving fluid near the boundary, allowing high-momentum fluid from the main flow to replace it, and thus retarding separation.

Drag. An object submerged in a flowing fluid is subjected to a fluid force component on it in the direction of the approach velocity, called the drag. The drag force is caused by skin friction drag, which is caused by shear stress components in the flow direction, and by form, or profile, drag, caused by the lower pressure on the downstream side of the object. Drag, in general, must be determined experimentally, and it is convenient to use a drag coefficient C_D, which depends on the object shape and the fluid viscosity. An equation for drag therefore includes a drag coefficient and is proportional to the area (A) presented to the flow and velocity squared; i.e., drag $= C_D A \frac{\rho}{2} U^2$, in which C_D is dimensionless, A is usually the projected area of the object onto a plane normal to the flow direction, the Greek letter rho, ρ, symbolizes the mass density, and U is the velocity of the approaching fluid relative to the object. The drag coefficient for a given body is a function of Reynolds number, Ul/ν, in which l is a characteristic length of the body and the Greek letter nu, ν, symbolizes the fluid kinematic viscosity. Figure 12 is a plot of drag coefficients versus the Reynolds number R (in which $R = UD/\nu$) for spheres and circular disks on a log–log scale. The line marked Stokes is a representation of the Stokes law, drag $= 6\pi a\mu U$, for a sphere of radius a in laminar flow. The critical Reynolds number of laminar flow around a sphere is $UD/\nu = 1$, with D the diameter of sphere. The results shown in the plot were determined by experiment. The sudden drop in the drag coefficient for the sphere at $R = 250,000$ is caused by the

Lift force (margin)

Prandtl's hypothesis (margin)

Flow around airfoils (margin)

Drag coefficient (margin)

laminar boundary layer changing to a turbulent boundary layer which delays separation and causes a smaller wake. The disk, normal to the flow, has its separation at the edge of the disk, and hence does not have such a sudden reduction in the drag coefficient.

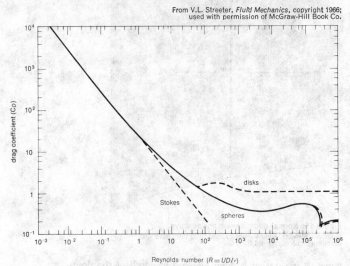

Figure 12: Drag coefficients for spheres and circular disks.

A disk that rotates while submerged in a real fluid has a drag moment, or torque, exerted on it by boundary shear forces. In hydraulic machinery this disk drag contributes to losses. A circular cylinder, rotating while submerged in a real fluid flowing around it at right angles to the cylinder axis, suffers a drag force component as well as the lift force component, known as the Magnus effect.

COMPRESSIBLE FLUID FLOW

The equations of gas dynamics. The perfect gas law, $p = \rho RT$, equation (5), has been defined, as well as the definitions of specific heats c_V and c_p. Also, enthalpy has been defined as $h = u + p/\rho$. The specific heat ratio k is given by the ratio of the two specific heats, namely, $k = c_p/c_V$. The gas constant R and k, c_p and c_V are related by the equations $c_p = kR/(k-1)$; $c_V = R/(k-1)$, in which consistent heat units or work units must be employed. Equation (3) states: $T ds = du + p d(1/\rho)$. By using $du = c_V dT$ and the perfect gas law, it becomes $ds = c_V(dT/T) + R\rho d(1/\rho)$. This equation may be integrated, yielding the difference in entropy per unit mass for the two states, 1 and 2; i.e., $s_2 - s_1 = c_V \ln[(p_2/p_1)(\rho_1/\rho_2)^k]$. These equations are forms of the second law of thermodynamics.

If a process is reversible, the entropy differential $ds = dq_H/T$; furthermore if the process is also adiabatic (no heat transfer), the heat-added differential $dq_H = 0$. Thus $ds = 0$, for an isentropic, or reversible-adiabatic, process. From the equation, for $s_2 - s_1 = 0$, the relation $p_1/\rho_1{}^k = p_2/\rho_2{}^k$ results, which describes the relationship of pressure to density for an isentropic process. The enthalpy change for an isentropic process is

$$h_2 - h_1 = c_p(T_2 - T_1) = c_p T_1 [(p_2/p_1)^{(k-1)/k} - 1].$$

Isentropic (reversible-adiabatic) flow. *Speed of a sound wave: Mach number.* The speed of a sound (acoustic) wave in a one-dimensional flow may be determined by use of the continuity and momentum (one form of Newton's second law) equations. The question of the possible conditions that would permit a consideration of small change in velocity, pressure, and density at a fixed position in a prismatic channel in steady flow leads to the following expressions for speed c of a sound wave: $c = \sqrt{dp/d\rho} = \sqrt{K/\rho} = \sqrt{kp/\rho} = \sqrt{kRT}$, in which K is the bulk modulus of elasticity, k is the specific heat ratio, and R is the gas constant. The last two expressions are for isentropic (reversible-adiabatic) conditions. A sound wave through air closely approximates isentropic flow.

The ratio of velocity at a point to the local wave speed v/c, is called the Mach number M, a dimensionless number. It is a measure of the importance of compressibility. The acoustic speed in air at sea level and at 20° C (68° F) is 0.343 kilometre (1,125 feet) per second, and the acoustic speed in water at ordinary pressure is 1.442 kilometres (4,730 feet) per second. For an incompressible fluid, the acoustic speed approaches infinity and M is equal to zero.

Flow in ducts and nozzles. Although isentropic (reversible-adiabatic) flow is unattainable with real fluids, it is approached in flow through transitions, nozzles, and venturi meters in which friction effects are small and heat transfer is minor. By use of Euler's equation and the continuity equation, an expression of interest may be derived for duct flow: $dA/dv = A(\text{M}^2 - 1)/v$, in which A is the cross-sectional flow area, v the average velocity, and M the local Mach number.

This equation is for steady, one-dimensional frictionless flow in the duct of varying cross sectional area. If the Mach number is less than unity (one), the situation for subsonic flow, dA/dv is always negative, and hence for acceleration of flow the area must reduce. The Mach number can be unity (i.e., sonic flow will prevail) only when $dA/dv = 0$ (at a throat or minimum section). For Mach numbers greater than unity (supersonic flow) dA/dv is positive; hence for acceleration of the flow the cross-sectional area must increase. In order for supersonic flow from a reservoir through a duct to occur, the flow is accelerated in the subsonic regions from zero to sonic flow through a converging duct leading to a throat, or minimum cross section. Then the duct must expand in area to accommodate supersonic flow. Whether or not supersonic flow actually occurs depends upon downstream conditions.

Isentropic flow, because it is frictionless and does not allow for heat addition or heat loss, is flow with constant energy. This kind of flow permits the energy, momentum, and continuity equations, as well as the perfect gas law and the constant entropy condition, $p\rho^{-k} = $ constant, to be applied to any problem. For flow through a duct of varying cross sections from a reservoir, simple equations may be developed for changes in pressure, density, and temperature, p, ρ, and T, from their respective values in the reservoir, p^0, ρ^0, and T^0, all in terms of the local Mach number v/c. These equations are:

$$\frac{p^0}{p} = \left(1 + \frac{k-1}{2}\text{M}^2\right)^{k/(k-1)},$$

$$\frac{\rho^0}{\rho} = \left(1 + \frac{k-1}{2}\text{M}^2\right)^{1/(k-1)},$$

$$\frac{T^0}{T} = 1 + \frac{k-1}{2}\text{M}^2.$$

For flow with sonic conditions at the throat (M = 1) in which the area is A^*, the value of Mach number at any other cross section A (for air or diatomic gases having $k = 1.4$), there results

$$\frac{A}{A^*} = \frac{1}{\text{M}}\left(\frac{5 + \text{M}^2}{6}\right)^3.$$

The area A must always be greater than the throat area A^*. The maximum flow rate $\dot{m}$, the change of mass per unit time, through a duct system (for $k = 1.4$), is given by $\dot{m} = 0.685\, A^*\, p_o/\sqrt{RT_o}$; i.e., the flow $\dot{m}$ is directly proportional to the throat area A^*, and to the reservoir pressure p_0, and inversely proportional to the square root of the temperature in the reservoir.

Figure 13 shows the relations among Mach number, pressure ratio p/p_0, and area ratio A^*/A for $k = 1.4$. At point r on the curve the fluid would be at rest with the Mach number M = 0. As the pressure is reduced, say at point t, subsonic flow occurs. At the throat, for critical (sonic) flow at point t^*, the Mach number is unity. Then for supersonic flow in the diverging portion of the tube; say at s, the area ratio is shown related to pressure ratio and Mach number.

Figure 14 illustrates the various possible flow cases for isentropic flow through a converging–diverging nozzle, including the possibility of a normal shock wave. If the

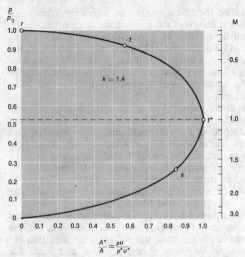

Figure 13: Isentropic relations for a converging–diverging nozzle.

From *Elements of Gas Dynamics* by H. Liepmann and A. Roshko, copyright 1957. By permission of John Wiley & Sons, Inc.

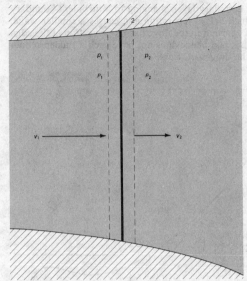

Figure 15: Normal compression shock wave.

From V.L. Streeter, *Fluid Mechanics*, copyright 1966; used with permission of McGraw-Hill Book Co.

downstream pressure is p_c or greater, isentropic subsonic flow occurs throughout the duct. If the pressure is at j on the graph, isentropic flow occurs throughout, with supersonic flow in the diverging portion. For downstream pressure between c and f, a normal shock wave occurs within the tube, causing a non-isentropic sudden jump from supersonic to subsonic conditions. For pressure p_f a normal shock wave occurs at the exit, and for pressures between p_f and p_j, oblique shock waves occur at the exit.

wave. It is a rather sudden increase in depth of the flowing stream [Figure 16].) Losses occur across a shock wave so the flow is not isentropic; *i.e.*, there is an increase in entropy from 1 to 2 in Figure 15. The velocity always changes from supersonic to subsonic.

From V.L. Streeter, *Fluid Mechanics*, copyright 1966; used with permission of McGraw-Hill Book Co.

Figure 16: Hydraulic jump in a rectangular channel. A liquid jet stream of specific weight γ that flows in an open channel with depth y_1 and velocity v_1 expands to a slower moving stream (velocity v_2) of depth y_2 and the same width, giving steady non-uniform flow.

From *Elements of Gas Dynamics* by H. Liepmann and A. Roshko, copyright 1957. By permission of John Wiley & Sons, Inc.

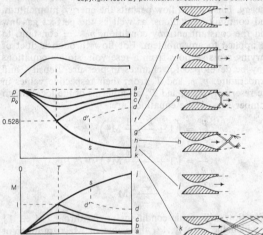

Figure 14: Various pressure and Mach number configurations for flow through a nozzle.

Fanno and Rayleigh lines. The normal shock wave has been analyzed by means of the continuity, energy, and momentum equations applied to a situation of constant area. Valuable conclusions can be obtained by use of the continuity and energy equations only, applied to a constant area situation for steady adiabatic, frictional flow. The line obtained by plotting enthalpy against entropy is called a Fanno line (Figure 17). Similarly, a plot resulting from use of the momentum and continuity equations is called a Rayleigh line. Because neither includes the complete physics of shock wave formation, it is necessary to draw conclusions from both lines.

Shock wave formation

Shock waves. The one-dimensional steady shock wave (*i.e.*, the normal shock wave) occurs under certain conditions in a converging–diverging duct. The normal shock wave consists of a sudden change in pressure, density, and velocity, always from supersonic flow to subsonic flow. The thickness of the shock wave is of the order of the molecular mean free path (average distance between collisions of molecules) of the gas, and hence the cross-sectional area on each side may be considered the same. Losses occur in flow through the shock wave. The continuity equation, the energy equation, and the momentum equation must be satisfied.

Figure 15 portrays a normal shock wave. If the conditions of the supersonic flow, ρ_1, p_1, v_1 are known, by solution of the three equations, the values of ρ_2, p_2, v_2 may be calculated for the shock wave to occur. These values are $p_2 = [1/(k + 1)] [2\rho_1 v_1^2 - (k - 1)p_1]$, $v_2 = (p_1 - p_2 + \rho_1 v_1^2)/\rho_1 v_1$, and $\rho_2 = \rho_1 v_1/v_2$.

(In open channel flow, under certain conditions, a hydraulic jump occurs that is analogous to the normal shock

From V.L. Streeter, *Fluid Mechanics*, copyright 1966; used with permission of McGraw-Hill Book Co.

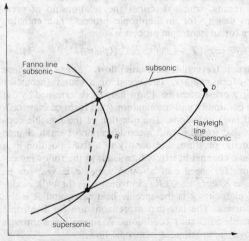

Figure 17: Fanno and Rayleigh lines.

Point *a* on the curve can be shown to be the sonic condition on the Fanno line, and point *b* the sonic condition on the Rayleigh line. The intersection of the Fanno and Rayleigh lines satisfies all three equations for the normal shock wave. Because no heat transfer has taken place, and by the second law of thermodynamics the entropy cannot decrease, the shock wave must occur from the supersonic point 1 to the subsonic point 2.

Sonic boom. When an aircraft flies at a speed faster than the speed of sound, it creates shock waves in the air around the plane. Under certain conditions these shock waves reach the ground and are heard and felt as explosions, or sonic booms. The stronger booms are caused by an airplane diving to accelerate through the sonic speed range. As the plane pulls out of its dive the shock waves continue, striking the ground, buildings, or the listener's ears, with one or two explosive booms.

BIBLIOGRAPHY. HUNTER ROUSE and SIMON INCE, *History of Hydraulics* (1957), treats the development of hydraulics and hydrodynamics from early Roman days to the middle of the 20th century. SIR HORACE LAMB, *Hydrodynamics*, 6th ed. (1932), is a widely used treatise on the theory and applications of hydrodynamics. A.H. GIBSON, *Hydraulics and Its Applications*, 4th ed. (1934), is an outstanding practical book on fluid flow; and LUDWIG PRANDTL and O.G. TIETJENS, *Hydro- und Aeromechanik nach Vorlesungen* (Eng. trans., *Fundamentals of Hydro- and Aeromechanics*, 1934), is the pioneering book on fluid mechanics. V.L. STREETER, *Fluid Dynamics* (1948), is a simple presentation of some aspects of hydrodynamics; JAMES M. ROBERTSON, *Hydrodynamics in Theory and Application* (1965), presents an intermediate level treatment; and CHIA-SHUN YIH, *Fluid Mechanics* (1969), an advanced treatment of fluid flow. V.L. STREETER, *Fluid Mechanics*, 5th ed. (1971), is a widely used elementary text.

(V.L.S.)

Mechanics, Quantum

Quantum mechanics is the branch of mathematical physics that deals with the motion of electrons, protons, neutrons, and other subatomic particles in atoms and molecules. The subject is entirely a product of researches made in the 20th century, particularly resulting from major contributions, which are treated in this article, by the physicists Werner Heisenberg, Louis de Broglie, Erwin Schrödinger, Max Born, and Paul A.M. Dirac since 1925. The ideas and methods of quantum mechanics have dominated all progress in atomic, nuclear, and molecular physics and chemistry since that year. In the first quarter of the century the principal initial discoveries were made by Max Planck, Albert Einstein, and Niels Bohr.

Before the principles of quantum mechanics were discovered, physicists had taken for granted that motions at the atomic level should be described in terms of the classical mechanics of Isaac Newton, perhaps with relatively minor modifications. This form of mechanics (see ME-CHANICS, CLASSICAL) was initially developed in connection with the study of motions of bodies, such as planets and satellites of the solar system, projectiles moving near the Earth's surface, or, in general, bodies of all kinds that are large compared with the atoms of which they are composed. Newtonian mechanics is even found to be applicable with high accuracy to the motion of subatomic particles under certain circumstances, such as the beam of electrons in a cathode-ray tube (*e.g.*, television picture tube) or the beams of protons in cyclotrons or high-energy accelerators.

The use of classical Newtonian mechanics to describe electronic motions within atoms was initiated by Bohr in 1913 and found to have considerable success, proving to be a great stimulus to further developments. But by 1925 this approach had run into difficulties; physicists realized that the principles of quantum mechanics differ drastically from those of Newtonian mechanics, even when used in the relativistic form developed by Einstein in 1905. Despite the great differences in outlook between classical and quantum mechanics, they are, of course, closely related. The relationship is much like that already known from 19th-century optics. Here much of the theory of reflection and refraction as used in optical instruments can be handled by methods of geometrical optics, which

trace rays of light through the instruments as if these are the paths of particles of light. But after the phenomena of interference and diffraction were discovered it was necessary to modify such treatments to obtain greater accuracy by describing light as a propagated wave motion that was recognized in the late 19th century as being electromagnetic in character. Quantum mechanics also recognizes that material particles in motion need a related wave motion for their description, and in consequence the subject is sometimes called wave mechanics.

There is another and deeper sense in which classical and quantum mechanics are related. Science is a human enterprise, carried out by human beings, employing sense organs, muscular structure, and a nervous system, as well as auxiliary tools of manipulation and observation, which are enormously large compared to the atoms of which they consist. When scientists seek to learn details of atomic structure by observation, they are limited to what can be learned through observations made with such large instruments. Some of the features of quantum mechanics have to be understood in terms of this limitation on human observational powers.

Need for quantum mechanics

This article is divided into the following sections:

I. Development of quantum theory

CLASSICAL MECHANICS

Because of the close relation between classical and quantum mechanics, concepts employed in the former also occur in the latter, with the same names but often with greatly altered meanings, a fact that can be confusing to the beginner. Space and time are dealt with classically in nonrelativistic forms of the theory, to which attention here is largely confined. Also, particles will be thought of as being subatomic. Space being three-dimensional, three coordinates (x,y,z) are needed to specify the location of a point at an instant of time (t). Each and every particle has an attribute called its mass (m), a measure of its inertia. The velocity and acceleration of a particle each require three components (*i.e.*, their values along the directions of the coordinates x, y, and z) for their description: (v_x,v_y,v_z) and (a_x,a_y,a_z), respectively, in which each component of velocity is the time rate of change of the associated space coordinate, and each component of acceleration is the time rate of change of the corresponding component of the velocity. The product of mass by each component of velocity gives the three components of the momentum (p) so that $p_x = mv_x$, $p_y = mv_y$, and $p_z = mv_z$.

The classical equations of Newton say that each component of the time rate of change of the momentum is equal to the corresponding component of the total force (F_x,F_y,F_z) acting on it due to the influences of neighbouring particles. Thus, to describe the motions of planets in the solar system (for which the theory was originally designed), there are three such differential equations of motion for each body, so $3N$ simultaneous differential equations for a system of N bodies. The general solution of these describes all possible forms of motion of the system represented. It involves $6N$ arbitrary constants. To complete the specification of the motion in a particular case it is necessary to determine the particular values of these $6N$ constants. Usually this is done by choosing them to represent the $3N$ position coordinates and the $3N$ velocity coordinates at some initial instant of time. With the particular solution so determined, the exact positions of the bodies at all future times can be in principle exactly calculated.

Thus classical mechanics has a fully deterministic char-

The deter-
ministic
nature of
classical
mechanics
acter: given the masses and the forces and the initial positions and velocities exactly, exact predictions of future (and past) behaviour can be found by the method outlined. In complicated cases, the finding of accurate solutions is a matter of great computational difficulty, but when carried out with sufficient care such solutions are always found in large systems to predict the motions in a way agreeing with later observations of the highest precision. Such a procedure receives one of its severest tests in predicting the orbital motions, from Earth to Moon and return, of manned spacecraft that have been made to travel to a specified place on the Moon and return to a specified place on the Earth.

This fully deterministic character has played an important role in the philosophy of determinism and free will. It was particularly stressed by a French mathematician, Pierre Simon de Laplace, in the 18th century (and for this reason is often sometimes called Laplacian determinism) in an oft-quoted passage:

> We ought then to regard the present state of the universe as the effect of its antecedent state and the cause of the state that is to follow. An intelligence knowing, at any given instant of time, all forces acting in nature, as well as the momentary positions of all things of which the universe consists, would be able to comprehend the motions of the largest bodies in the world and those of the smallest atoms in one single formula, provided it were sufficiently powerful to subject all data to analysis: to it, nothing would be uncertain, both future and past would be present before its eyes.

The point here is not so much whether or not such an intelligence exists but the supposed attribute of the universe to run on like a machine with no capacity for caprice or free choice in any of its behaviour, including that of the living beings who are also supposed to be subject to Newtonian mechanics.

HEISENBERG UNCERTAINTY PRINCIPLE

Importance
of
knowledge
of original
positions
and
velocities
An essential feature of the classical procedure just outlined is the need to know precisely initial positions and velocities of all the particles in a system in order fully to determine the applicable special solution of the equations of motion. This step requires observation of all the positions over a small time interval to get also the velocities, or momentum components. Ordinarily this could be done by illuminating them and observing them by means of the light that they scatter into the eyes or optical instruments of the observer. The validity of this procedure depends thus on the tacit assumption that the motion of the bodies being observed is not disturbed by the fact of their having scattered the light with which they are observed. The actual success of classical mechanics when applied to large objects is thus an indication of the lack of appreciable disturbances of motion by the light scattering.

The situation is otherwise when this general procedure is applied in an attempt to study motions of electrons within atoms and molecules. It is known that the light from a point source is not brought to a point focus in the image plane of a telescope or microscope. The image is always somewhat blurred by the property called diffraction, and this blurring gives rise to a corresponding uncertainty in the measurement of the direction of the light source from the instrument. Diffraction is an inherent and inescapable feature associated with the wave nature of light, over and above any blurring that may be caused by imperfections of workmanship in making the instrument.

The simplest form of wave motion is sketched in Figure 1. The amplitude Ψ (the Greek letter psi) is drawn as a function of x, a coordinate in the direction of wave propagation, as a sinusoidal curve for a particular instant of time, t. At a time t' later, the wave will have progressed to the right without change of form by a distance ct', in which c is the wave velocity. This is the speed of travel of some particular feature of the wave, such as one of the crests. The distance from crest to crest is called the wavelength, λ, and its reciprocal, $1/\lambda$, or λ^{-1}, is called the wave number, giving the number of crests found in unit length. The number of crests passing a stationary observer in unit time is called the frequency (ν) and is equal to

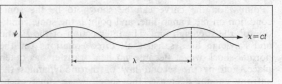

Figure 1: Sinusoidal wave motion at an instant of time t. Ψ is a measure of amplitude at any position x along the curve (see text).

the velocity of the wave (i.e., the crest) times the wave number, or $\nu = c\lambda^{-1}$. These relations apply to wave motions of all kinds. In a sound wave, Ψ is the deviation of the gas pressure from its mean value, and in radio or light waves it is the electric vector, E, that gives the measure of the electric force exerted by the wave on unit electric charge.

When light from a point source is brought to a focus with a lens of aperture A as shown in Figure 2 (A is the angle at the focus subtended by the half-diameter of the lens), the blurred diffraction image gives rise to a positional uncertainty (within the image) of what is commonly regarded as a point image by the amount $(\lambda/2\pi)/\sin A$. Thus, to reduce the uncertainty it is desirable to use the shortest wavelength possible and make the lens opening as large as possible. This is done in microscopy by using ultraviolet light instead of visible light and using an objective with a wide aperture. But there is no actual way possible to reduce to zero the blurring of an image. For visible light of the shortest wavelength the uncertainty of position location is necessarily about 6×10^{-8} metre, which is about 600 times the radius of most atoms. Hence visible light is wholly unsuitable for following the details of position changes of electrons within single atoms. Conditions
for
accuracy
of location

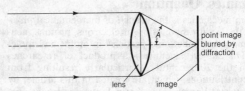

Figure 2: Diffracted image formed by lens of half-diameter A (see text).

Light has attributes other than those described by regarding it as a wave motion. In interacting with matter (emission, scattering, absorption) it also behaves in some respects like a stream of particles, called light quanta or photons. Each photon carries an amount of energy (W) equal to a constant (h) times its corresponding frequency (ν), or $W = h\nu = hc\lambda^{-1}$, and an amount of momentum (p) in the direction of propagation of the light beam, equal to this same constant (h) times the wave number, or $p = h\lambda^{-1}$. Here h is called Planck's constant, equal to 6.625×10^{-34} joule second. Planck's constant h is the fundamental parameter of quantum mechanics, occurring in every quantitative expression relating to quantum phenomena. In the example above it appears in a way that relates the dual aspects of light as a wave motion and as a stream of photons.

When an electron is exposed to a light beam (i.e., stream of photons), there is a fundamental indeterminacy about the light-scattering processes that take place. Some photons go by unaffected. Others are scattered through various angles. Change in direction of motion of a photon so scattered necessarily involves a change in its momentum (Compton effect; see following sections). Because of conservation of momentum, this necessarily involves a change in the momentum of the scattering electron. This alteration occurs in a statistically random way; thus, there is an uncertainty in the electron's momentum after scattering even if there had been none before. This uncertainty in momentum is less with photons of small wave number (long wavelength) observed over a wide range of scattering angles.

Thus, the conditions needed for accuracy in observation of the electron's momentum are in direct conflict with those needed for accuracy in observation of its position.

Detailed analysis along these lines shows that the product of the position uncertainty, Δx, and the associated momentum uncertainty, Δp_x, must always be greater than $h/4\pi$, and similarly for the other components of position and momentum.

This basic result was first recognized by Heisenberg in 1927. It is known as the Heisenberg uncertainty (or indeterminacy) principle. It provides the fundamental reason why Newtonian mechanics cannot be applied at the atomic level: it is impossible to know both position and momentum with sufficient accuracy at the same time. Thus the Newtonian laws, with their exactly deterministic solutions, must be replaced by different laws of quantum mechanics. These laws of quantum mechanics do not describe detailed orbital motions. They describe alternative possible happenings and give numerical values for the relative probabilities of occurrence of the different alternatives, in much the same way that actuarial tables give the probability of a person's death at each age, without making any assertion about the life span of a particular individual.

WAVE-PARTICLE DUALITY

The preceding section considered the dual aspects of the nature of light whereby it exhibits properties of a wave motion in some respects and of a stream of particles (photons) in others. The energy and momentum of photons increase with the frequency so that photons are extremely small for light of long wavelengths, and therefore the wave aspect is most pronounced; photons are large for X-rays and gamma rays, for which wavelength is short, and therefore with these radiations the particle aspect is the more pronounced. In reality, however, both aspects play a role at all frequencies or wavelengths.

Historically this duality was first recognized by Planck in 1900. He was studying the distribution in wavelengths of the radiation from a black body (an ideal solid postulated to absorb all the light falling on it, having zero reflectivity). In colloquial terms this is the problem of quantitatively describing how hot bodies become redder and brighter as their temperature is increased. To explain the observed distribution he had to assume that emission and absorption of radiation occurs in quanta of energy, now called photons, each quantum having an energy (W) equal to the constant h times its frequency, or $W = h\nu$. Thus was h, Planck's constant, first introduced into physics. Planck's reasoning was somewhat complicated, and the concept of quanta was not accepted by physicists at first.

In 1905 Einstein firmly established the photon concept by using it to interpret the photoelectric effect (*q.v.*), which is the ejection of electrons from a metal when illuminated particularly by ultraviolet light or X-rays. He postulated that, when light falls on a metal, the photons are absorbed by individual electrons, giving their energy to them, one by one. Thus the photon energy has to be more than enough to free an electron from the forces binding it to the metal, accounting for the observed fact that light must have more than a threshold frequency to be able to cause emission of electrons. This also accounts for the observed fact that greater intensity of light results in the emission of more electrons, but the energy of each individual electron is not increased with increasing intensity. For this work, not that on the theory of relativity, Einstein received the Nobel Prize for Physics in 1921.

The inverse of the photoelectric effect occurs when X-rays are generated in an X-ray tube. Here a beam of electrons is given energy by applying a high negative voltage (around 10,000 to 1,000,000 volts) to the cathode, a hot filament that emits electrons. These electrons are accelerated toward the anode because of its positive field; they strike and enter the anode, losing their energy in various kinds of collisions with its atoms and electrons, a small fraction of them radiating their energy as X-rays. From the photon view, the maximum energy that could be radiated by an electron would be all that it had gained in the tube. This energy in joules is the product of the voltage (V) applied to the tube and the electronic charge

Planck's constant

(e) in coulombs, Ve. Hence the shortest wavelength (λ_{min}) of the X-ray photons is given by $Ve = hc\lambda_{min}^{-1}$. X-rays of longer wavelength than λ_{min} are also emitted: these come from emission by those electrons that lose part of their energy by other processes before radiating. This short-wave limit of the X-ray spectrum is observed experimentally and accords with what is expected on assuming that X-rays consist of photons.

In 1923 Arthur Holly Compton of the United States studied the scattering of a beam of X-rays by solid matter, using mostly graphite (carbon) because the electrons are less tightly bound to atoms of carbon and other elements with low atomic number than is the case with elements that have medium or high atomic number. Using an incident monochromatic beam of wavelength λ_0, he found that the scattered radiation consists of two wavelengths: unmodified λ_0 and modified λ_1, in which λ_1 is greater than λ_0 by an amount that increases with the angle of scattering A, as indicated in Figure 3. This indi-

The work of A.H. Compton

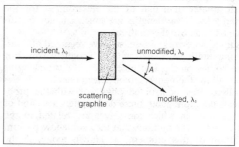

Figure 3: Compton effect in scattering of X-rays. The modified wavelength (λ_1) is greater than the unmodified (λ_0) and increases with angle of scattering (A).

cates clearly that there are two distinct processes by which X-rays are scattered. The unmodified photons are interpreted as having been scattered by those electrons that are tightly bound to atoms in the graphite. The modified photons are interpreted as arising from the loosely bound electrons, which can be regarded as moving almost freely within the graphite.

To account for the shift of wavelength to larger values and hence to photons of smaller energy, Compton assumed this to be a consequence of the photons having momentum as well as energy, of amount $p = h\lambda^{-1}$ in their direction of motion. In being scattered through angle A, the momentum is changed and some of the energy of the scattered photon is transferred to the scattering electron, which recoils because of the momentum given to it. The theory also predicts the direction and speed of the recoil electron for each angle of scattering. These recoil electrons have been studied experimentally and found to have properties expected from the theory.

The photoelectric effect and the Compton effect point to the existence of photons of energy $W = h\nu$, and of momentum $p = h\lambda^{-1}$. The connecting link between W and p, which describe the particle aspect, and ν and λ, which describe the wave aspect, is the Planck quantum constant, h.

DE BROGLIE WAVES

In 1924 a suggestion was put forward by de Broglie that the duality shown by light might extend to particles other than photons. In particular, he postulated that the behaviour of electrons is somehow governed by an accompanying wave motion (which later became known as de Broglie waves) of which the wavelength is related to the classical momentum by the same relation, $p = h\lambda^{-1}$, that applies to photons.

Because the kinetic energy of an electron accelerated by a voltage V is Ve, this postulate gives for the de Broglie wavelength of electrons accelerated through V the expression

$$\lambda = \frac{h}{\sqrt{2meV}}.$$

Substitution of known values for h, m, and e shows that an electron for which $V = 150$ volts has a de Broglie wavelength of 10^{-10} metre, which is of the order of usual X-ray wavelengths and also of the same order as the spacing between atoms in most crystals. This suggested that a beam of electrons when scattered by a crystal would be diffracted by the regularly spaced atoms in the crystal, in much the same way as a German physicist, Max von Laue, observed in 1912 in an experiment that laid the basis for the wave aspect of X-rays and that, as X-ray diffraction, provided a powerful tool for the study of crystallography (*q.v.*). In short, de Broglie's idea led to the prediction of the probable existence of the analogous electron diffraction phenomenon by Walter Elsasser, born in Germany. Experimental proof of the actual existence of electron diffraction by crystals came in 1927.

Subsequently, de Broglie's wave-particle idea was extended to other particles, such as protons, hydrogen and helium atoms, and neutrons, for which diffraction was also found experimentally. The masses of these particles are much greater than that of the electron; so for the same energy their wavelengths are much smaller in fulfilling the basic de Broglie relation, $\lambda = h/p$.

In all subsequent work, physicists have regarded all matter as being dually associated with de Broglie waves. For the large bodies of classical mechanics, the wavelengths are too small for their effects to be detectable.

These discoveries confronted physicists with the problem of learning more about these de Broglie waves and of finding the ways in which the waves are related to the particle aspect of the motions that they somehow govern. The solution of this problem, as known today, is the principal content of quantum mechanics.

Principal content of quantum mechanics

The revolutionary development of quantum mechanics (of which wave mechanics and matrix mechanics are specialized partial formulations) occurred with breathtaking rapidity in the years 1925–30. It is an essentially mathematical subject that can scarcely be described without using mathematical concepts that are usually unknown to persons whose education is limited to humanistic studies. The far-reaching importance of the results requires, nevertheless, an attempt to give such persons a glimpse of how physicists understand these questions. In doing so some compromise with accuracy must be made: the process is somewhat analogous to an attempt to convey an appreciation of classical literature while making no mention of Greek or Latin and while using only the Anglo-Saxon part of the vocabulary of the English language.

As indicated above, physicists took the radical step of giving up the strict determinism of Newtonian mechanics. Instead they postulated strict deterministic propagation only for the waves involved in the wave aspect of matter. They then introduced a looseness of connection between the waves and the motion of the associated particles, whereby the waves merely tell what may happen among a number of alternatives, together with predictions of the relative probabilities of the various alternatives actually occurring in a particular set of observations.

This loose, or partial, determinism, as contrasted with the strict determinism of classical physics, is now quite generally accepted as fundamental in theoretical physics. But a long struggle preceded this acceptance. The indeterministic probabilistic interpretation is often called the Copenhagen interpretation, because it was largely developed in the school headed by Bohr. This view was not accepted by Einstein, and it has been strongly criticized by experts on quantum theory, notably de Broglie, David Joseph Bohm, and others.

It is important to be clear on the nature of this difference of opinion. Einstein and other critics of the Copenhagen interpretation accept, of course, the positive content of the computational methods of quantum mechanics, including the indeterminisms inherent in present knowledge. Where the two schools differ is in their attitude toward the indeterministic qualities. The Copenhagen view is that these qualities are ultimate and fundamental. The anti-Copenhagen view is that they are evidences of incompleteness of present knowledge that are

likely to be eliminated at some future date by new fundamental discoveries, the nature of which cannot at present be foreseen.

In this sense the dispute is more concerned with feelings about possible future developments in quantum mechanics than with implications of present knowledge. The Copenhagen view leads to seeking detailed knowledge concerning these uncertainties wherever they manifest themselves. The anti-Copenhagen view motivates its adherents to a quest for modifications of present theory so that the elements of strict determinism will be restored.

The following quotation from a 1936 essay by Einstein serves to illustrate his attitude about expectations or preferences in this field. After briefly expounding the orthodox uncertainty principle view, he writes:

> But now I ask: Is there really any physicist who believes that we shall never get any inside view of these important alterations in the single systems, in their structure and their causal connections, and this regardless of the fact that these single happenings have been brought so close to us, thanks to the marvelous inventions of the Wilson chamber and the Geiger counter? To believe this is logically possible without contradiction; but it is so very contrary to my scientific instinct that I cannot forego the search for a more complete conception.

A possible future revolution in physics

This quest for elimination of indeterminacy has been followed diligently but fruitlessly by a minority of physicists for some four decades. Although this failure does not prove the incorrectness of the anti-Copenhagen view, it has tended to make many physicists adhere to the Copenhagen view. If, at some time in the future, discoveries are made that restore strict determinism to quantum mechanics, this will mean a new revolution in physics at least as momentous as that of 1925–30, which introduced indeterminacy into present-day physics.

BOHR'S THEORY OF ATOMIC SPECTRA

When the light emitted by a gas discharge at low pressure (such as in a neon sign) is analyzed in a spectrograph, it is found to consist of a large number of lines, the frequencies of which can be precisely measured, usually at least to an accuracy of six decimal places. These are called lines because of their appearance in the spectrograph as sharp images of the linear slit in the spectrograph. The ensemble of the lines emitted or absorbed by a particular element, in a particular stage of ionization, is called its spectrum. Thousands of such lines may be involved in the spectrum of each kind of atomic ion, although different elements give rise to spectra of widely differing degrees of complexity. The simplest spectra are those emitted by atomic hydrogen and the alkali elements: lithium, sodium, potassium, rubidium, and cesium.

Experimental study of atomic spectra was well started by 1860, and the first numerical regularities between the frequencies observed were found in the 1880s. Bohr gave the first successful interpretation of atomic spectra in 1913, and the study since of the many lines and their relative intensities has proved by far the richest source of observational material contributing to knowledge of atom structure and guiding the development of quantum mechanics.

Bohr adopted Einstein's idea that light is emitted and absorbed in photons or quanta of energy, $W = h\nu$. He also postulated that atoms are capable of existing only in discrete quantized energy levels, W_1, W_2, W_3, . . . , which are characteristic of the atomic number (Z, charge on its nucleus) and the total number (N) of electrons in the ion, in which $N = Z$ for the usually neutral atom. He then postulated that a photon of radiation is emitted when an atom makes a transition from a higher initial level, W_i, to a lower final level, W_f, the energy difference going into the energy content of the emitted photon, thus giving the relation

$$h\nu = hc\lambda^{-1} = W_i - W_f.$$

An absorption line occurs at the same frequency when an atom picks up a photon to make a transition from a lower energy level to a higher energy level. This picture of the origin of spectral lines is fundamental to all subsequent developments and applies to spectra of molecules and of nuclei, as well as to that of atoms.

Furthermore, Bohr provided a model of the hydrogen atom in which the single electron, acted on by the electrical (inverse square) attraction of the proton, would go around the proton in circular orbits (later generalized to include elliptic orbits and hyperbolic orbits). According to Newtonian mechanics, orbits of all radii and eccentricities are possible. Bohr had to add a rule of quantization, as an additional postulate, in order to pick out a discrete set of orbits from this continuum of possible orbits to get the discrete energy levels needed to describe the line spectrum of atomic hydrogen.

For the circular orbits he proposed the rule that the orbital angular momentum (L) of the electron motion is equal to a number (k) of units of $h/2\pi$, in which h is Planck's constant and the angular momentum is equal to the product of the velocity of the electron (v) in the circular orbit, its radius (r), and its mass (m); i.e.,

$$L = mvr = k(h/2\pi), \qquad k = 1, 2, 3, \ldots.$$

When elliptic orbits are considered, a slightly more complicated expression for orbital angular momentum is involved, but it is still assumed to be constant and equal to an integral multiple of $h/2\pi$. For elliptic orbits, in which the electron moves in and out radially instead of staying always at the same distance from the proton, another rule is needed, as the actual ellipticities are also restricted. This rule introduces another integer, n, called the principal quantum number, whereas k is called the azimuthal quantum number. In general, each integer (sometimes half an odd integer) that occurs in labelling a quantum level, which represents a distinctive energy state, is called a quantum number.

Spectral series The most conspicuous feature in the visible spectrum of hydrogen is the Balmer series, a series of lines that a Swiss physicist, Johann Jakob Balmer, represented by a simple empirical formula as early as 1885,

$$\lambda_n^{-1} = R\left(\frac{1}{2^2} - \frac{1}{n^2}\right), \qquad n = 3, 4, 5, \ldots,$$

in which R is called the Rydberg constant and has the observed value of 109,677 waves per centimetre. The observed wave numbers of the Balmer lines agree to high accuracy with the Balmer formula on supposing that these arise from transitions from higher states down to the final $n = 2$ state. From Bohr's theory one would expect another series of lines lying in the deep ultraviolet, which were not known at the time but were soon found by a United States physicist, Theodore Lyman, and are now known as the Lyman series. These lines correspond to transitions to the final $n = 1$ state. Similarly, other series of lines corresponding to transitions to final $n = 3$, 4, and 5 states from higher levels lie in the infrared. They too were found experimentally within a few years under the stimulus provided by Bohr's ideas. The various lines of the spectrum of the one-electron ions with Z greater than unity lie in the deep ultraviolet. These too were soon studied and found to agree with Bohr's theory.

Ordinarily in a gas at room temperature all the atoms are in their state of least energy, called the ground state, or normal state, and therefore cannot radiate, as this would require transitions to still lower levels. When a gas is excited to radiate, this is usually done by having free electrons accelerated in the gas so that they gain enough energy to put the atoms into excited states by collisional exchange of energy. Many experiments were performed to verify the quantum nature of this energy exchange of electrons with atoms in gases, largely under the leadership of the German physicists James Franck and Gustav Ludwig Hertz. This provided a valuable additional triumph for Bohr's ideas, as well as a new tool for the experimental study of atomic structure.

Immediately after the end of World War I, there followed a tumultuous period of extending Bohr's hydrogen theory to other atoms, which brought forth successes and difficulties, and was the principal activity of physicists in the early 1920s.

Bohr's rule of quantization for the circular orbits can be stated in another way in terms of de Broglie waves, as de Broglie recognized in 1924. For the kth orbit the relation $mv_k r_k = k (h/2\pi)$ can be rewritten

$$2\pi r_k = k (h/mv_k), \qquad k = 1, 2, 3, \ldots.$$

In this form it is recognized as the requirement that the circumference $(2\pi r)$ of the allowed orbit be such as to contain an integer (k) number of de Broglie wavelengths, (h/mv_k).

In this form the rule is suggestive of the kinds of relations involving integers that occur in musical instruments in which vibrations of stretched strings (violin, guitar, etc.) or vibrations of air columns in tubes (flute, clarinet, etc.) are involved. On an indefinitely long stretched string it is possible to have travelling waves of any frequency. But, when the two ends are stopped, as in a violin, the wave is reflected at each end to give a standing wave, and these two waves must be of such a frequency that the length (L) of the string between stops is exactly equal to an integer multiple of half wavelengths for the allowed frequencies. This gives the relation,

$$L = m(\lambda_m/2), \qquad m = 1, 2, 3, \ldots,$$

in which $m = 1$ is called the fundamental mode of the string, and higher values of m are called harmonics. More complicated analysis is needed to describe the modes of vibration of a vibrating drumhead, but this case also resembles the stretched string in that there is a discrete set of allowed vibrational patterns that are distinguished by integer labels like the quantum numbers of the Bohr theory.

SCHRÖDINGER'S WAVE MECHANICS

This analogy with acoustic devices led Schrödinger in 1926 to carry the de Broglie wave idea much further than de Broglie had done. Schrödinger postulated the existence of a wave amplitude, $\Psi(x,y,z,t)$, varying with position **Wave amplitude** and time for the de Broglie wave associated with a single moving particle. His next task was to postulate a suitable partial differential equation governing Ψ, reasoning by analogy with the earlier (19th-century) work on the mathematics of wave motion.

This procedure has a certain analogy with what had happened earlier in the development of optics. At first, light was supposed to travel in paths given by geometrical optics. Then wave theory was substituted to give a more accurate account of the actual distribution of light intensity as influenced by interference and diffraction. Similarly here, Schrödinger supposed that the motion as given by Newtonian equations is an approximation analogous to that of geometrical optics, to be supplanted by a wave theory of higher accuracy, for the motion of the represented particle.

Most wave theory as it had been developed up to that time was restricted to the case of homogeneous media, in which the wavelength remains the same from point to point, except for the abrupt changes that take place at the boundary between two different homogeneous materials. When a particle moves classically in a force field, its momentum is continually changing, and therefore the de Broglie wavelength changes with position; so the forms of wave propagation involved in such problems as the wave version of the hydrogen atom and others are mathematically more complicated than the cases usually treated in acoustics or wave optics.

For a single particle of mass m, moving under forces such that its potential energy is $V(x,y,z)$ at location (x,y,z), the relation from classical mechanics between the kinetic energy (equal to $p^2/2m$, in which p is momentum), the potential energy, and the total energy (W) is

$$\frac{p^2}{2m} + V(x,y,z) = W.$$

Because kinetic energy is essentially positive, this equation indicates that the particle's motion is confined within a region of space in which $V(x,y,z)$ is less than the total energy, W. Schrödinger postulated that this relation could be used to give the value of momentum p and hence of de Broglie's wavelength $\lambda = h/p$ at each point in space, and he used this expression for λ varying with position in an equation for the wave amplitude that was known from classical acoustics.

The result is called Schrödinger's equation and can be written in the following form:

$$-\frac{(h/2\pi)^2}{2m}\left(\frac{\partial^2\Psi}{\partial x^2} + \frac{\partial^2\Psi}{\partial y^2} + \frac{\partial^2\Psi}{\partial z^2}\right) + V\Psi = W\Psi.$$

Schröding-er's equation

The properties of this equation are fully discussed in books on quantum mechanics. Here it must suffice to say that in certain cases, with regard to choice of potential energy V, the equation has solutions for only certain discrete values of the total energy W. This happens whenever the region of space in which V is less than W is finite so that the waves are confined to a finite region, as they are, for example, with a violin string or a vibrating drumhead. The general character of the solution for the amplitude, or wave function, Ψ, is that it is oscillatory (but more complicated than sinusoidal) inside the region where W is greater than V but dies off rapidly (but not abruptly) at places outside this region. Schrödinger postulated that this new procedure gives the allowed energy levels and that the Ψ associated with any one of the allowed values of W provides the new wave mechanical description of the particle's orbital motion when it has that energy. This rule replaces the old Bohr rule for quantization of the classical mechanical orbits. The quantized classical orbits of Bohr now are regarded as a historical stepping-stone to the more accurate methods of wave mechanics.

In the hydrogenic atoms (a single electron outside a closed or completed electron shell), the potential energy is a function only of r, the distance of the electron from the nucleus, varying as the inverse first power because the force varies as the inverse square of the distance. The problem therefore has spherical symmetry with

$$V(r) = -Ze^2/r.$$

The solutions of the wave equation of Schrödinger correspond to the values of the total energy (W) derived by Bohr and require three quantum numbers (n, l, m) for their specification, in which n is the total quantum number introduced above. Here $l = k - 1$ of the Bohr theory and is the measure of resultant orbital angular momentum of the state in units of $h/2\pi$, whereas m in the same unit gives the z component of the angular momentum. Two angles (θ, ϕ) are used to specify the direction in space of the line from nucleus to electron. The wave function has the form of a product of a radial function $P_{nl}(r)/r$ multiplying into a set of functions $Y_{lm}(\theta, \phi)$ that specify the dependence of the wave function on direction. These angular functions are called spherical harmonics and occur in nearly all problems of classical mathematical physics that have spherical symmetry.

Schrödinger first supposed that the electron is actually spread out and distributed in space in such a way that the square of the wave function (Ψ^2) in his equation gives the fractional density of the total at the place for which it is calculated. This view soon proved untenable and was replaced by Max Born's interpretation, now generally accepted, that Ψ^2 gives the probability of finding the electron in unit volume, the electron itself remaining a tiny charge that is itself much smaller in extent than the region of space over which there is a reasonable probability of finding it. Because of this probability interpretation, the wave function, Ψ, is often called the probability amplitude. Because of the dependence of the quantity Ψ^2 on the angles θ and ϕ, the location of an electron with respect to the nucleus in a hydrogen-like atom is equally probable in any direction only when it is in the quantum state $l = 0$. If the atom changes to other values of l, the probability pattern may take the form of rings, multiple lobes, etc., and thus this atom would not have the simple appearance of a sphere.

Study of the fine structure of atomic spectral lines finally led in 1925 to the realization that an electron requires another coordinate for the description of its motion. This was called spin and can be visualized by supposing that each electron rotates on its axis with an amount

$\frac{1}{2}(h/2\pi)$ of spin angular momentum, which is capable of being oriented either parallel or antiparallel to any direction in space. This discovery was made in The Netherlands by physicists George Uhlenbeck and Samuel Abraham Goudsmit as the culmination of a long and confusing period of study of fine structure by many physicists. Introduction of the spin brings with it the need for the introduction of a fourth quantum number, m_s, which is restricted to the two values $\pm \frac{1}{2}$, so that with a given nl the number of distinct quantum states is $2(2l + 1)$.

Spin quantum number

For an atom consisting of several, say N, electrons, the wave function Ψ becomes a function of the locations and spin of each of them, hence it depends on $3N$ positional coordinates and N spin coordinates. In an analogous way, the classical potential energy (V), which appears in the Schrödinger equation to represent the electric interactions, becomes a function of all $3N$ positional coordinates. Likewise, there have to be N terms, such as the first term in the wave equation representing one particle, to represent the sum of the kinetic energies of each of the electrons.

The resulting wave equation is too complicated to be solved exactly, even for the very next case, $N = 2$, the helium-like atoms and ions. (This is also true of those equations governing the planetary orbits in celestial mechanics.) A large part of the subject is therefore concerned with finding techniques for obtaining approximate solutions of such complicated wave equations. Such methods go by the general name of perturbation theory. An attempt is first made to discover a problem that resembles but is simpler than the more complicated one and one that can be solved exactly. Using this simpler solution as a starting point, an attempt is then made to estimate quantitatively the difference between the allowed levels and wave functions of the actual problem and the simpler problem. Most of the actual results that are obtained in quantum mechanics are obtained in this manner, since the relevant problems that can be exactly solved are relatively few in number.

The theory of atomic structure is entirely based on a special case of perturbation theory known as the central field approximation. Each electron in an atom is attracted to the nucleus of charge Ze in a way described by a potential energy term $-Ze^2/r$ in which r is the distance from the electron to the nucleus. Each electron is also repelled by the other $N - 1$ electrons. These are distributed in a nearly spherically symmetric way around the nucleus. As a result, the repulsion also acts approximately as a central field. The part of the $N - 1$ electrons at greater distance than r do not give rise to a net repulsion; so the screening, or weakening, of the nuclear attraction by the presence of the part closer than r can be taken into account by supposing each electron to be acted on by a central field of the form $V(r) = -Z(r)e^2/r$, in which $Z(r) = Z$ very close to the nucleus and decreases to $Z(r) = Z - N + 1$—that is, to 1 for neutral atoms—at distances outside the radius of a sphere in which the $(N - 1)$ electrons are almost certain to be found. Figure 4 gives as an example some calculated curves of how the effective field decreases for various values of Z as the distance r increases. A log-log plot is used in which the logarithm of $Z(r)$ is the ordinate and the logarithm of (r/a) the abscissa, a being the Bohr radius as already defined. These curves were calculated for neutral atoms by what is known as the Thomas–Fermi method and illustrate how the central field $Z(r)$ decreases to its limiting value of unity in every case for $r = 3a$. For large $Z(r)$, the more tightly bound are the electrons, especially those of smaller values of the principal quantum number n. Another effect of the departure from the inverse-square law of effective central force is that now the energy depends on l as well as on n by an amount that increases as the atomic number Z increases, as shown in Figure 5.

The dependence of the effective field $Z(r)$ on r is a consequence of the radial distribution of density of the electrons, which in turn is a consequence of the way in which $Z(r)$ depends on r; thus, ways of calculation of $Z(r)$ have to be devised that are self-consistent, which

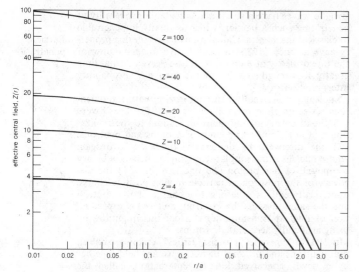

Figure 4: Log-log plot showing variation with r/a (ratio of separation to Bohr radius) of the effective central field $Z(r)$ in neutral atoms having various values of Z.

Radial wave functions

means that the $Z(r)$ leads to radial wave functions that give a density distribution that is consistent with the assumed $Z(r)$.

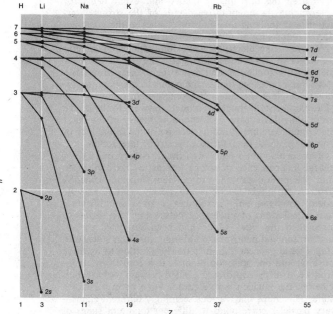

Figure 5: Some observed energy levels (indicated by circles) in hydrogen and in the alkali metals, showing the increasing dependence of W_{nl} on l as Z increases and as the effective central field departs more strongly from the Coulomb field. (The W_{1s}, not shown, is four times that of W_{2s}.) Total quantum numbers n are shown on the ordinate.

Because each electron requires four quantum numbers (n, l, m, m_s) to specify its state, an atom or ion containing N electrons requires N such sets of four quantum numbers to specify the quantized state of the N electron system. Starting with a bare nucleus, the electrons are successively captured into the lowest available energy state that determines the quantum numbers of the N electrons in the normal or ground state.

PAULI EXCLUSION PRINCIPLE

Wolfgang Pauli, an Austrian physicist, discovered in 1924 the rule that governs the states that are available to be filled in adding electrons to a nucleus. It is known as the Pauli exclusion principle. At first it was found as an empirical rule; later it was found to be a consequence of the then newly discovered principles of quantum mechanics. The Pauli principle may be stated as the rule that no

two of the N sets of four quantum numbers can be fully alike. Here the rule is discussed in relation to the isolated atoms of elements. It also plays a role of great importance in controlling the behaviour of electrons in molecules, and hence the energy of chemical bonds, as well as controlling the behaviour of electrons in solid bodies, particularly determining whether the solid in question is a metal, semiconductor, or insulator. (For details of how the exclusion principle is used to build up the periodic system of the elements, see PERIODIC LAW; ATOMIC STRUCTURE; and SPECTROSCOPY, PRINCIPLES OF.)

The basis for the Pauli principle in quantum mechanics is a property of the Schrödinger equation called equivalence degeneracy. This is a consequence of the fact that each of the N electrons in the atom is exactly alike with respect to mass, charge, and other basic attributes. Therefore, the Schrödinger equation is unaltered by permuting any two of the electrons, say the ith and the jth. Consequently, the N sets of different one-electron quantum numbers can be assigned to the N electrons in any one of $N!$ ($e.g.$, if $N = 4$, $N! = 4 \times 3 \times 2 \times 1 = 24$) permuted orders. The wave functions resulting from various linear combinations of the wave functions in different permutations are also solutions of the Schrödinger equation. Among these possibilities there is always one that is totally antisymmetric, which means that it reverses sign everywhere if any two electron indices in the equation are interchanged. Such a wave function vanishes identically when any of the two individual sets of four quantum numbers are alike, and so the empirical fact that Pauli's principle holds indicates that it is the totally antisymmetric wave function that occurs for systems of electrons.

Particles for which the wave function must be totally antisymmetric in the several coordinates are called fermions and are said to obey the Fermi–Dirac statistics (that is, the particles obey the Pauli exclusion principle, which means that no two particles may be in the same energy state). In addition to electrons, the protons and neutrons of which nuclei are composed are also known to be fermions.

II. Applications of quantum mechanics

MOLECULAR STRUCTURE

Molecules emit and absorb light by transitions between quantized energy levels to give spectra that are vastly more complicated than those of atoms. When interpreted, these complicated spectra give a great deal of quantitative information about the way in which electrons are shared between atoms to form the chemical bonds by which molecules are held together. This application of quantum mechanics has revolutionized the science of chemistry in the past half century, giving rise to a new borderline science known as chemical physics (see MOLECULAR STRUCTURE; CHEMICAL BONDING).

The richness of molecular spectra arises from the fact that, in addition to possessing quantized electronic energy levels, the molecule as a whole may have quantized amounts of rotational and vibrational motion. Changes in these can occur simultaneously with (or without) changes in the electronic state to give many hundreds of lines associated with a single electronic change. From their spacing it is possible to learn exact distances between atoms in a molecule and also the forces that develop when a chemical bond is stretched and that govern the modes of vibration (see SPECTROSCOPY, PRINCIPLES OF).

The possibility of an analysis in which rotation and vibration of the molecule as a whole are treated somewhat separately from the theory of the electronic states owes its validity to the fact that the masses of the nuclei are thousands of times greater than the mass of each electron. This permits a treatment (known as the Born–Oppenheimer approximation after Max Born and J. Robert Oppenheimer) in which it is first assumed that the nuclei do not move at all. The electronic energy levels of such a system are then found to depend on the assumed distances of separation of the nuclei. The variation with nuclear coordinates of the electronic energy (including electric repulsion of the nuclei) then can be used as the potential energy function that determines the equilibrium size and shape of the molecule, and hence its rotational energy levels, and also its modes of vibration about this equilibrium shape. The guiding idea here is that the nuclei in fact move so slowly compared to the electrons in a molecule that in the first approximation the dynamical effects of their actual motion can be neglected in analyzing the electronic states.

Thus the problem of molecular structure is effectively separated into two parts: (1) the study of electronic states for quasi-stationary nuclei and (2) the study of the slow nuclear motions that arise from the variations in the energy of the electronic states due to nuclear motions.

Orbitals

The one-electron wave functions of isolated atoms are often called atomic orbitals. As two or more atoms approach each other so closely that there is appreciable "overlap" (a condition in which orbitals of different atoms have appreciable values in a region of space close to both of them), the atomic orbitals become distorted into forms called molecular orbitals. This distortion results from the fact that under these conditions the outer electrons formerly belonging distinctly to a particular atom come under the influence of more than one nucleus and its attendant electrons, thereby affecting, through the Schrödinger equation, the distribution in space of the wave amplitude and also the associated electronic energy level.

The computations involved in using quantum mechanics for molecular structure problems are exceedingly complex. Much use is made of automatic digital computers. But even so, in many cases the results so far have been only semi-quantitative. Nevertheless, the overall result has been to give a theoretical framework for the correlation of many of the known facts of chemistry.

NUCLEAR STRUCTURE AND PARTICLE PHYSICS

Nuclear physics as a major discipline is treated more fully elsewhere (see NUCLEUS, ATOMIC); here, only the major connections with quantum mechanics are outlined. Atomic nuclei have radii about $1/10,000$ of the radii of the atomic orbitals of the electrons—that is, about 10^{-15} metre. Nuclear binding energies are of the order of 1,000,000 times greater than those of the outer atomic electrons. Accurate mass measurements show that the masses of compound nuclei are less than the sum of the masses of the nucleons of which they are composed. This result provided the first direct experimental support for Einstein's famous mass equivalence relation ($E = mc^2$).

The first major application of quantum mechanics to the nucleus was the barrier leakage interpretation of the natural radioactive decay of those elements that emit alpha particles or helium nuclei. This was done in 1928 independently by physicists George Gamow in Germany and R.W. Gurney and Edward Condon in the United States. The theory used a mathematical property of the Schrödinger equation that had been first noticed a few months earlier by Oppenheimer.

In the disintegration of uranium-238, for example, the alpha particle, a helium-4 nucleus, is emitted with a kinetic energy of 4.25 MeV (million electron volts). The instant at which a particular nucleus disintegrates is apparently a matter of pure chance, the statistical disintegration rate in this case being exceedingly slow. Of a given quantity of uranium only half of it disintegrates in 4.5 $\times 10^9$ years.

The fact that an alpha particle can remain in the uranium nucleus for 10^9 years shows that when inside it is attracted by strong forces that are effective only over a distance comparable in size to that of the nuclear radius. When the alpha particle is just outside what was the parent uranium-238 nucleus, its two positive charges are strongly repelled by the 90 positive charges in the resulting daughter nucleus, thorium-234. The emitted alpha particle gains its kinetic energy by the action of this electric repulsion. Thus the alpha particle can be inside the nucleus or outside, the two regions being separated by a potential wall. It cannot be inside, according to classical mechanics, for to be there its kinetic energy would have to be negative; in quantum mechanics, however, the de

Barrier penetration

Broglie waves have a small and calculable probability of penetrating such a barrier, which is totally impenetrable in classical mechanics. Calculations based on this property gave at once (1928) a quantitative understanding of the rate of decay of α-emitters. It also served at that time greatly to strengthen faith in the then new probability interpretation of Ψ^2.

Nuclear physics really came into being with a momentous series of discoveries all made in 1932. These were (1) the discovery of the neutron, leading to the realization that nuclei are compounds of protons and neutrons; (2) the discovery of deuterium, or heavy hydrogen, whose nucleus is the simplest compound nucleus, a binary compound of one proton and one neutron; (3) the discovery of the positron, a particle having positive charge numerically equal to the negative charge of the electron and the same mass as the electron; and (4) the production of nuclear transmutations in copious quantities by using artificially accelerated protons.

In 1935 a Japanese physicist, Hideki Yukawa, showed that neutrons and protons, or nucleons, are held together by a newly conceived kind of interaction, called the strong interaction because the force is much stronger than the electrical repulsions between protons at distances corresponding to nuclear radii. These interactions are short-range in character, the forces falling to zero rapidly when the nucleons are separated by distances greater than usual nuclear radii. Among the central problems of nuclear physics in the past three decades have been the devising of theory and experiments for determining the quantitative details of the strong interaction and applying quantum mechanics to the construction of models for all of the observed nuclei.

Nucleons, like electrons, have individual spin angular momenta of $h/4\pi$ and also require the use of antisymmetric wave functions, and hence there exists in nuclei a controlling influence that is analogous to the Pauli exclusion principle in the outer electronic structure.

Development of nuclear models proved to be much more difficult than the corresponding theory of the outer electronic structure of atoms because of the initial lack of knowledge about the nature of the strong interaction.

Of particular importance was the discovery in 1937 of charge-independence of strong interaction. According to this, the proton–proton, proton–neutron, and neutron–neutron strong interactions are nearly, if not exactly, equal. This not only introduces a great simplification into calculations of nuclear structure but also serves to strengthen the view, which had been suspected earlier, that proton and neutron are different quantum states of a single basic particle, the nucleon. In addition to its three position and one spin coordinates, it is convenient to introduce a fifth coordinate, called isospin, which tells whether the nucleon is in a proton state or in a neutron state. This view, that various seemingly different elementary particles correspond to different quantum states of some other particle, has played an increasingly important role in particle physics in the past two decades.

This view of interconvertibility of proton and neutron found its first fruitful application in the theory of beta radioactivity as developed in 1934, principally by Fermi. When a radioactive atom emits a high-energy electron or positron, the emitted particle must have been created in the emission process, because there are strong grounds for believing that there can be no electrons or positrons in nuclei. This process is analogous to the creation of the emitted photon when light is emitted in radiative transitions, there being no preformed photons in the atom waiting to be emitted. In beta decay, one electronic charge is emitted, and, as total charge is conserved, this is accompanied by the change within the nucleus of one nucleon from the neutron state to the proton state. Conversely, emission of a positron involves the change in the nucleus of one nucleon from a proton state to a neutron state. The total nucleon number A is unchanged in these processes. With electron emission atomic number Z changes to $Z + 1$, and with positron emission Z changes to $Z - 1$. Writing P and N, respectively, for a nucleon in a proton or neutron state, the changes could be written

$$N \rightarrow P + e \qquad \text{(electron emitted)}$$
$$P \rightarrow N + e^+ \qquad \text{(positron emitted)}.$$

As the changed nucleon is part of a compound nucleus, the energy change involved in these transformations is that of the entire nucleus of which the nucleon is a part.

If this were a correct formulation, then the emitted electron or positron, respectively, would come out with a definitely calculable amount of kinetic energy, the energy equivalent of the mass difference of the parent and daughter nuclei involved in the change. It had long been known, however, especially from studies on the naturally beta-active elements, that the emitted electrons are ejected with a broad continuous distribution of kinetic energies, in seeming violation of the principle of conservation of energy. This difficulty was resolved by Pauli in 1933 with the suggestion that the total available energy is divided between two emitted particles, so the preceding equations become

The neutrino hypothesis

$$N \rightarrow P + e + \nu$$
$$P \rightarrow N + e^+ + \nu',$$

in which ν and ν' symbolize the new particles that elude detection in the experiments carried out in the usual way. To account for the fact that the new particles, called neutrinos by Fermi, escape detection, they have to be without charge and without rest mass and thus able to pass through solid matter for great distances without interaction.

In 1934 Fermi took the neutrino idea and developed a quantum mechanical theory of beta decay based on it. This used some relatively new mathematical methods for treating processes of creation and destruction of new particles in quantum transitions. This led to the discovery of mathematical forms for processes, now called weak interaction, that describe the overall rate at which beta decay occurs and details concerning the way in which the total available energy is statistically distributed between the emitted particles.

All subsequent work on beta decay is based on extensions of the general pattern of Fermi's theory. The neutrino hypothesis has been experimentally confirmed in many ways, such as measurement of the recoil of the decaying nuclei, detection of the momentum carried off by the elusive neutrino, and direct detection of the neutrinos themselves.

Development of these ideas has opened up a large field of study concerned with the nature of the weak interaction. Whether or not weak interaction is fundamentally connected with the strong interaction between nucleons, in the sense that the existence of one quantity implies the existence of another, remains an open question.

OTHER APPLICATIONS

Allusion only is made here to some other topics of great importance in which quantum mechanics plays a role in modern physics but that cannot be treated because of space limitations.

Going beyond the application of quantum mechanics to molecular structure is its application to the theory of matter in the solid state. It is concerned, among other things, with the forces that determine crystal structure, the behaviour of electrons in states that permit motion over large distances in a crystal (metals and semiconductors), and the physical factors that determine magnetic properties. Also of great importance is the quantum mechanical treatment of special interactions of electrons in those metals that give rise to superconductivity.

Quantum mechanics has also been widely applied to the study of electron–atom collision processes; that is, of the details of the mechanisms by which an electron colliding with an atom can raise it to an excited quantum level or even knock free one or more of its electrons (ionization). Atom–atom and molecule–molecule collisions are treated by the quantum mechanics of collision processes to investigate ways in which atoms and molecules dissociate and re-form and the elementary processes that determine the rate at which chemical reactions occur (chemical kinetics).

Quantum mechanical collision theory also finds a wide range of important applications in the analogous treatment of nuclear reactions in which compound nuclei are transformed. Further applications occur in the description of the processes by which electron–positron pairs are created and annihilated and the many analogous processes involving the creation of mesons and strange particles that are studied in high-energy physics.

Another major development is that of quantum electrodynamics. Initially it was assumed that the electromagnetic field could be handled mainly by the classical methods of the British physicist-chemist James Clerk Maxwell. But it was soon realized (initially by Dirac in 1926) that the equations of the electromagnetic field must be reformulated to take explicit account of quantum phenomena. This has led to some important corrections to energy levels not covered by the ordinary treatment and confirmed by experimental observation (Lamb–Retherford shift; see ELECTRON).

Quantum electro-dynamics

Among the most important practical consequences of quantum electrodynamics has been the development of lasers, which permit the generation and study of beams of coherent light. In these, light beams are produced that are millions of times more intense than with any previously known light source. This is a consequence of a feature, first noted by Einstein in 1917, whereby atoms that are exposed to a coherent light beam are stimulated to emission at a greater rate than that of their spontaneous emission. Production of such intense light beams has opened up a large field of study of new optical properties of matter that are manifested when such intense beams go through it (see LASER AND MASER).

BIBLIOGRAPHY. For a general descriptive survey, VICTOR GUILLEMIN, *The Story of Quantum Mechanics* (1968), is recommended. Also relatively non-mathematical are WERNER HEISENBERG, *Die physikalischen Prinzipien der Quantentheorie* (1930; Eng. trans., *The Physical Principles of Quantum Theory*, 1930) and *Physics and Philosophy* (1958); HANS REICHENBACH, *Philosophic Foundations of Quantum Mechanics* (1944); and STEPHAN KORNER (ed.), *Observation and Interpretation: A Symposium of Philosophers and Physicists* (1957). Good elementary texts that are more mathematical than this article are V.B. ROJANSKY, *Introductory Quantum Mechanics* (1938); and DAVID BOHM, *Quantum Theory* (1951). More advanced works are P.A.M. DIRAC, *The Principles of Quantum Mechanics*, 4th ed. (1958); and L.D. LANDAU and E.M. LIFSHITZ, *Quantum Mechanics: Nonrelativistic Theory*, 2nd ed. (1965). On the historical side, MAX JAMMER, *The Conceptual Development of Quantum Mechanics* (1966); and TED BASTIN (ed.), *Quantum Theory and Beyond* (1971), are recommended. A relatively elementary introduction to the applications to atomic and molecular structure is UGO and L. FANO, *Basic Physics of Atoms and Molecules* (1959). Basic works on the more advanced phases are E.U. CONDON and G.H. SHORTLEY, *The Theory of Atomic Spectra* (1935); J.C. SLATER, *The Quantum Theory of Atomic Structure*, 2 vol. (1960); C.A. COULSON, *Valence*, 2nd ed. (1961); and LINUS PAULING, *The Nature of the Chemical Bond, and the Structure of Molecules and Crystals*, 3rd ed. (1960). A good general work on application to nuclear structure is R.D. EVANS, *The Atomic Nucleus* (1955). More specialized in this field are M.G. MAYER and J.H.D. JENSEN, *Elementary Theory of Nuclear Shell Structure* (1955); and B.L. COHEN, *Concepts of Nuclear Physics* (1971).

(E.U.C.)

Mechanoreception

Sensitivity to mechanical stimuli is a common endowment among animals. In addition to mediating the sense of touch, mechanoreception is the function of a number of specialized sense organs, some found only in particular groups of animals. Thus, some mechanoreceptors act to inform the animal of changes in bodily posture, others help detect painful stimuli, and still others serve the sense of hearing (see SOUND RECEPTION).

Slight deformation of any mechanoreceptive nerve cell ending results in electrical changes, called receptor or generator potentials, at the outer surface of the cell; this, in turn, induces the appearance of impulses ("spikes") in the associated nerve fibre. Laboratory devices such as the cathode-ray oscilloscope are used to record and to observe these electrical events in the study of mechanoreceptors. Beyond this electrophysiological approach, mechanoreceptive functions are also investigated more indirectly—*i.e.*, on the basis of behavioral responses to mechanical stimuli. These responses include bodily movements (*e.g.*, locomotion), changes in respiration or heartbeat, glandular activity, skin-colour changes, and (in the case of man) verbal reports of mechanoreceptive sensations. The behavioral method sometimes is combined with partial or total surgical elimination of the sense organs involved. Not all the electrophysiologically effective mechanical stimuli evoke a behavioral response; the central nervous system (brain and spinal cord) acts to screen or to select nerve impulses from receptor neurons.

Man experiences sharp, localized pain as a result of stimulation of "pain spots" (probably free nerve endings) in the skin, and dull pain, usually difficult to localize, associated with inner organs. The sensory structures of pain spots in the skin differ from other receptors in that they respond to a wide range of harmful (noxious or nociceptive) stimuli. Excessive stimulation of any kind (*e.g.*, mechanical, thermal, or chemical) may produce the human experience of pain. Apart from eliciting this subjective feeling of pain, stimulation of pain receptors in the human skin is objectively characterized by such signs of emotional expression as weeping and by efforts to withdraw from the stimulus. The reflex withdrawal of his hand from a burning stimulus may begin even before the person becomes conscious of the pain sensation (see PAIN, THEORIES OF).

Experience of pain in animals Judging from objective criteria, responses to painful stimuli also occur in nonhuman animals, but, of course, any subjective experience of pain sensation cannot be directly reported. Still, the question of painful experience among animals is of considerable interest because investigators (*e.g.*, medical researchers) are often obliged to subject laboratory animals to treatments that would elicit complaints of pain from a man. If a cat's tail is accidentally stepped on, the pitiful screeching and efforts to withdraw are so strikingly similar to human reactions that the observer is led to attribute the experience of pain to the animal. If one treads accidentally on an earthworm and observes the animal's apparently desperate struggles to get free, he might again be inclined to suppose that the worm feels pain. This sort of "mind reading," however, is inherently uncertain and may be grossly misleading.

The following observations illustrate some of the difficulties in making judgments of the inner experiences of creatures other than man. After the spinal cord of a fish has been cut, the front part of the animal may respond to gentle touch with lively movements, whereas the trunk, the part behind the incision, remains motionless. A light touch to the back part elicits slight movements of the body or fins behind the cut, but the head does not respond. A more intense ("painful") stimulus, however (for instance, pinching of the tail fin), makes the trunk perform "agonized" contortions, whereas the front part again remains calm. To attribute pain sensation to the "painfully" writhing (but neurally isolated) rear end of a fish would fly in the face of evidence that persons with similarly severed spinal cords report absolutely no feeling (pain, pressure, or whatever) below the point at which their cords were cut.

Aversive responses to noxious stimuli nevertheless have a major adaptive role in avoiding bodily injury. Without them, the animal may even become a predator against itself; bats and rats, for instance, chew on their own feet when their limbs are made insensitive by nerve cutting. Some insects normally show no signs of painful experience at all. A dragonfly, for example, may eat much of its own abdomen if its tail end is brought into the mouthparts. Removal of part of the abdomen of a honeybee does not stop the animal's feeding. If the head of a blow fly (*Phormia*) is cut off, it nevertheless stretches its tubular feeding organ (proboscis) and begins to suck if its chemoreceptors (labellae) are brought in touch with a sugar solution; the ingested solution simply flows out at the severed neck.

At any rate, responsiveness to mechanical deformation is a basic property of living matter; even a one-celled organism such as an amoeba shows withdrawal responses to touch. The evolutionary course of mechanoreception in the development of such complex functions as gravity detection and sound-wave reception leaves much room for speculation and scholarly disagreement.

RECEPTION OF EXTERNAL MECHANICAL STIMULI

The sense of touch. Sensitivity to direct tactual stimulation—*i.e.*, to contact with relatively solid objects (tangoreception)—is found quite generally, from one-celled organisms up to and including man. Usually the whole body surface is tangoreceptive, except for parts covered by thick, rigid shells (as in mollusks). Mechanical contact locally deforms the body surface; receptors typically are touch spots or free nerve endings within the skin, often associated with such specialized structures as tactile hairs. The skin area served by one nerve fibre (or sensory unit) is called a receptive field, although such fields overlap considerably. Particularly sensitive, exposed body parts are sometimes called organs of touch—*e.g.*, the tentacles of the octopus, the beak of the sandpiper, the snout of the pig, or the human hand.

Stimulation of the human skin with a bristle reveals that touch (pressure) sensation is evoked only from certain spots. These pressure spots, especially those on hairless parts (*e.g.*, palm of the hand, or sole of the foot), are associated with specialized microscopic structures (corpuscles) in the skin. Pressure spots are most densely concentrated on the tip of the human tongue (about 200 of them per square centimetre), roughly twice their concentration at the fingertip. A characteristic feature of many tactile sense organs is their rapid and complete adaptation (*i.e.*, temporary loss of sensitivity) when stimulated. Still, in man a distinction can be made between transient and more prolonged pressure sensations.

Relatively little research has been done with regard to the physiology of individual tangoreceptors in vertebrates. The Pacinian corpuscle of higher vertebrates, however, has been studied in isolation (see SENSORY RECEPTION, HUMAN for illustrations). These corpuscles, found under the skin, are scattered within the body, particularly around muscles and joints. Local pressure exerted at the surface or within the body causes deformation of parts of the corpuscle, a shift of chemical ions (*e.g.*, sodium, potassium), and the appearance of a receptor potential at the nerve ending. This receptor potential, on reaching sufficient (threshold) strength, acts to generate a nerve impulse within the corpuscle. Among insects, movements of tactile hairs have been shown (sometimes specifically) to affect the receptor potential and the impulse frequency in the connected nerve fibre.

Many vertebrates and invertebrates can localize with some precision points of tactual stimulation at the body surface. People typically can still distinguish two sharpened pencil points, or similar pointed stimuli, when the points are separated by as little as about one millimetre at the tip of the tongue. (When moved closer together, the two points are perceived as one.) The human two-point threshold is about two millimetres at the finger tip, reaching six or seven centimetres at the skin of the back. Such tactual ability serves blind people when they read raised type (Braille) with their fingers. Closely related functions Reading Braille include the ability to distinguish between tactile stimuli that differ qualitatively; for example, between a rough and a smooth surface. This ability is even observable in the ciliate *Stylonychia* (a one-celled relative of *Paramecium*).

Sensory contact with the ground below often informs animals about their spatial position. Nocturnal animals (for example, some eels) find shelter during the day by keeping as much of their skin as possible in contact with solid objects in the surroundings (thigmotaxis). Animals that live in running water usually maintain their position as they turn and swim head-on against the current (rheotaxis). Study of rheotaxic behaviour reveals that the sensory basis almost exclusively depends on visual or tactile stimuli (or both) arising from the animal's movements relative to the solid bottom or surroundings. The long antennae of many arthropods (*e.g.*, crayfish) and the lengthened tactile hairs (vibrissae) on the snouts of nocturnally active mammals (*e.g.*, cat, rat) serve in tactually sensing objects in the vicinity of the animal's body, extending and enriching the adaptive function of the sense of touch.

Lateral-line organs. *Mechanoreceptor function.* All of the primarily aquatic vertebrates—cyclostomes (*e.g.*, lampreys), fish, and amphibians—have in their outer skin (epidermis) special mechanoreceptors called lateral-line organs. These organs are sensitive to minute, local water displacements, particularly those produced by other animals moving in the water. In this way, approaching organisms are detected and localized nearby before actual bodily contact takes place. Thus the lateral lines are said to function as receptors for touch at a distance, serving to perceive and locate prey, approaching enemies, or members of the animal's own species (*e.g.*, in sexual-display behaviour).

Each epidermal organ, called a sense-hillock or neuromast (Figure 1C), consists of a cluster of pear-shaped sensory cells surrounded by long, slender supporting

From *Experientia* (1952)

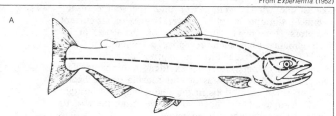

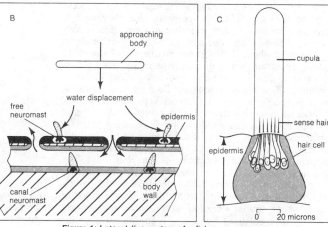

Figure 1: *Lateral-line system of a fish.*
(A) Bodily location of lateral lines; (B) longitudinal section of a canal; (C) superficial neuromast.

cells. The sense hairs on top of the sensory cells project into a jellylike substance (the cupula) that bends in response to water displacement. The cupula stands freely in the surrounding water, grows continuously (*e.g.*, as a human fingernail), and wears away at the top. Sense organs of this type are distributed along definite lateral lines on the head and body of the animals (Figure 1A), developing in the outer layer of cells (ectoderm) of the embryo from a thickening called the lateral placode. From the central part of the same placode the sensory cells of inner-ear structures (the labyrinth) arise. The common embryologic origin and structural similarities of mature neuromasts and labyrinthine cell groups have led to the designation of all of these organs as the acoustico-lateralis system. The nerves to all the sense organs of the system arise from a common neural centre (called the acoustic tubercle in the wall of the brain's medulla oblongata). Among such amphibians as frogs, lateral-line organs and their neural connections disappear during the metamorphosis of tadpoles; as adults they no longer need to feed under water. The higher land-inhabiting vertebrates—reptiles, birds, and mammals—do not possess the

lateral-line organs; only the deeply situated, labyrinthine sense organs persist.

The sensory cell of a neuromast bears one relatively long hair (kinocilium) and about 50 shorter ones (stereocilia). The kinocilium is inserted eccentrically on top of the sense cell; the stereocilia are arranged in parallel rows. In about half of the hair cells of a neuromast, the kinocilium is found on one (and the same) side of the cell; in the remaining hair cells it is found on the opposite side. In most cases these are cranial and caudal side, respectively. In the toad *Xenopus*, each group of hair cells in a neuromast connects to its own nerve fibre; hence there are two fibres per sense organ. The hair cells send a continuous series of neural impulses toward the acoustic tubercle in the absence of adequate external stimulation. A longitudinal water current along the toad's body surface, however, selectively increases or decreases the frequency of impulses from the cranial and caudal cells, depending on whether the flow is from head to tail or vice versa; current directed at right angles to such neuromasts has no effect. The impact of the moving water moves the cupula to deform the sensory hairs. Even minute cupula displacements of less than one thousandth of a millimetre are clearly effective in altering the impulses.

In *Xenopus*, as well as in other animals that have lateral-line organs, there are also some neuromasts with their hair cells asymmetrical at right angles to the head–tail axis. These add directional sensitivity so that other animals moving nearby in the water are well distinguished and localized. The postulated function of the lateral-line organs in the reception of low-frequency propagated pressure waves ("subsonic sound") has not been verified behaviorally. At very short distances, however, a vigorous low-frequency sound source stimulates the lateral-line system on the basis of acoustical near-field effects (water particle displacements), just as does any moving or approaching object.

Cyclostomes, many bony fishes, and all the aquatic amphibians studied have only superficial ("free") neuromasts of the kind described above. In the development of most fish, however, a number of structures called lateral-line canals (Figure 1B) are formed as a secondary specialization. They begin as grooves that develop in the epidermis along the main lateral lines; thus, a number of formerly free neuromasts are taken down to the bottom of each groove. The walls of the grooves then grow together above the neuromasts. Eventually the grown-together walls form canals under the epidermis, containing in their walls a series of canal neuromasts and a chain of openings to the outside (canal pores) along the lateral lines. The cupulae are changed in form, fitting the canal somewhat like swinging doors. The canal is filled with a watery fluid. Stimulation occurs essentially in the same way as with free neuromasts: local, external water displacement is transmitted via one or more canal pores to produce a local shift of the canal fluid to move cupulae. The sense cells in the canal neuromasts are polarized in the direction of the canal.

Canal specialization is particularly well developed in lively species of fish that swim more or less continuously and in bottom dwellers that live in running or tidal waters. Canalization has been interpreted as a case of adaptive evolution, serving to avoid the almost continuous, intense stimulation of free neuromasts by water flowing along the fish body during swimming or, in the case of relatively inactive bottom dwellers, by the external currents. These coarse water displacements probably mask subtly changing stimuli from detection by the lateral-line organs on the surface of the animal's body. Canal neuromasts are shielded in large degree from these masking currents.

The lateral-line organs function mainly in locating nearby moving prey, predators, and sexual partners. Usually these objects must be much closer than one length of the animal's body to be detected in this way; even intense stimuli are hardly ever detected beyond five body lengths away. Lateral-line function in rheotactic orientation against currents is restricted mainly to inhabitants of

Detection of water currents

Locating prey, predators, and sexual partners

small currents such as mountain brooks, where marked differences of water-flow velocity affecting the fish body locally are likely to occur. Compared to their use of other sensory functions (*e.g.*, vision) the animals depend little on ability to sense extremely close, resting objects (obstacles) through the lateral lines. Obstacle detection of this kind does not arise from reflection of water waves; rather, the pattern of water displacement around the moving fish abruptly undergoes deformation at the near approach of an obstacle as the result of compression; the fish encounters a sudden rise in water resistance in the immediate vicinity of the obstruction. Nor do the lateral-line organs function to regulate or coordinate the animal's movements on the basis of the water flow or pressure variations along its body produced by swimming; neither do they serve for the reception of water-transmitted propagated sound waves (hearing).

Ampullary lateral-line organs (electroreceptors). Perhaps the most interesting specialization of the lateral-line system is the formation in several groups of fish of deeply buried, single electrically sensitive organs. Such structures, for example, are found on the head of all the elasmobranchs (*e.g.*, sharks and rays), and are called ampullae of Lorenzini. Similar organs include those on the head of *Plotosus*, a marine bony fish (teleost); structures called mormyromasts in freshwater African fish (mormyrids) and in electric eels (gymnotids); what are named small pit organs of catfishes (silurids); and possible related organs in several other fish groups. These are known as ampullary lateral-line organs, and they have features in common. The sensory cells are withdrawn from the body surface, lack kinocilia, and have no mechanical contact with the surrounding water through a cupula. The latter attribute, indeed, is typical for all the acousticolateral end organs, except ampullary sense organs, in which the sense cells lie within the wall of a vesicle (or ampulla) that opens to the surface through a tubelike duct. Ampulla and duct are filled with a gelatinous substance that has excellent electrical conductivity.

Fish with ampullary sense organs are found to be remarkably sensitive to electrical stimuli—*i.e.*, minute, local potential differences in the surrounding water at their body surface. In behavioral experiments with sharks and rays, sensitivity to changes of 0.01 microvolt per centimetre (one microvolt = 1/1,000,000 of a volt) along the body surface has been found for the ampullae of Lorenzini. Similar, though somewhat higher, values have been recorded from the ampullary nerve fibres. A decrease in voltage at the opening of the ampulla causes an increase of the spontaneous nerve-impulse frequency; an increase in voltage at the opening produces the opposite response. Through their electrical sensitivity, such fish can detect and locate other organisms in darkness, in turbid water, or even when these organisms are hidden in the sand or in the mud of the bottom.

Sharks, rays, and most catfishes are able to detect electrical changes (biopotentials) emanating from other organisms. The freshwater mormyrids and eels, on the other hand, have special signal-emitting electric organs. They produce a series of weak electric shocks (up to a few volts), sometimes quite regularly and frequently; for example, about 300 shocks per second in the mormyrid fish *Gymnarchus*. In this way, a self-generated electric field is created in the immediate surroundings. Any appropriate object (for example, a prey animal with good conductivity in relation to freshwater) will cause a deformation of the electric field and can thus be detected in a radar-like manner through the sensitive ampullar electroreceptors.

Some theorists suggest that initially mechanoreceptive lateral-line organs evolved into electroreceptors. At any rate, evidence of a certain double sensitivity—to mechanical and to electrical stimuli—has been observed in electrophysiological experiments with Lorenzinian ampullae. This double sensitivity has not been found, however, in behavioral experiments; alterations in behaviour indicate that ampullary lateral-line organs merely serve the animal as electroreceptors in adapting to the environment.

Electrical "radar"

Other varieties of mechanoreception. *Surface waves.* Several species of animals living at or near the water surface use surface waves or ripples emanating from potential or struggling victims to locate their prey quickly: examples are the toad *Xenopus*, several fish species, and such insects as the back swimmer (*Notonecta*) and the water strider (*Gerris*). The whirligig beetle (*Gyrinus*) also uses surface ripples to avoid collisions with obstacles and companions. The sensory structures involved range from specialized tactile hair receptors (trichobothria) to internally located cells (proprioceptors) in movable body appendages and lateral-line organs.

Water and air currents. Special water-displacement receptors found in lobsters (*Homarus*) are most reminiscent of the lateral-line organs in vertebrates. Water-current receptors also enable several kinds of bottom-dwelling invertebrates to orient themselves (rheotaxis) in rivers and tidal currents. Many predators among these animals also respond chemically (see CHEMORECEPTION), moving against the current (positive rheotaxis) until the prey is reached. In this way, for example, certain marine snails easily find their particular prey (sea anemones). Similarly among insects, the chemical "smell" of prey or of potential sex partners elicits a tendency to move against the wind (anemotaxis) until the source of the chemical stimulus is found. Several types of air-current receptors (true mechanoreceptors) on the heads of insects enhance such chemoreceptive behaviour. In flying locusts, an air current directed appropriately toward the head elicits compensatory reflex flight movements. The receptors involved (groups of hair sensilla on the head) mediate small corrections in the maintenance of straight flight; major guidance, however, derives from the insect's visual contact with the ground below.

Vibration reception. Adaptation and recovery occur most rapidly among touch receptors, and they tend to respond well to repeated stimulation, even of relatively high frequency. Thus, a person can feel whether an object is vibrating; above a threshold frequency of about 15 cycles per second (cps), discretely perceived tactual stimuli seem to fuse into a quite new and distinct vibratory sensation. The upper frequency limit of this vibration sense is found at several thousand cps among normal individuals, with sensitivity being maximal in the range of 200 cps (above a threshold amplitude of about 100 millimicrons). Just as pitch is discriminated in hearing, differences of about 12 to 15 percent in vibration frequencies can be distinguished by most people.

Vibration sensitivity is not limited to man; fish, for instance, also may respond to low-frequency water vibrations with tactile receptors. In addition, several kinds of animals have special vibration receptors. In some insects, a group of specialized structures (chordotonal sensilla) in the upper part of each tibial segment of the leg signal vibrations from the ground below. In the cockroach, the threshold amplitude for vibrational stimuli of this kind has been found to be less than 0.1 millimicron. Birds have special receptors (corpuscles of Herbst in the tibiotarsal bone of the leg) with which they can detect slight vibrations of the twig or branch on which they sit. Perhaps birds are alerted at night in this way to approaching predators; maximal sensitivity is at about 800 cps, and the threshold amplitude is close to 20 millimicrons. Spiders also use their vibration sense to locate prey in the web.

Generalized hydrostatic pressure. Several types of aquatic animals are sensitive to small changes of hydrostatic, or water, pressure. Among fish, this applies particularly to the order Ostariophysi (Cypriniformes), which includes about 70 percent of all the freshwater species of bony fishes. The swimbladder in these animals is connected with the labyrinth (sacculus) of the inner ear through a chain of movable tiny bones, or ossicles (weberian apparatus). Alterations in hydrostatic pressure change the volume of the swimbladder and thus stimulate the sacculus. These fish can easily be trained to respond selectively to minute increases or decreases in pressure (for example, to a few millimetres of water pressure), indicating that they have a most refined sense of water depth. All of these fish are so-called physostomes, which means that

Specialized vibration receptors

they have a swimbladder duct through which rapid gas exchange with the atmosphere can occur; many live in relatively shallow water. The hydrostatic-pressure sense can function to inform the animals about their distance from the surface or about the direction and velocity of their vertical displacement. It also appears that improvement and refinement of the sense of hearing arises through the swimbladder's connections via the weberian apparatus with the labyrinth.

The sensitivity of several kinds of crustaceans to relatively small hydrostatic-pressure changes (as low as five to ten centimetres of water pressure) is most remarkable because these animals have no gas-filled cavity whatsoever. The mechanism by which the stimuli are detected remains a puzzling question, although information about changing water depth during tidal ebb and flow clearly would seem to have adaptive value.

RECEPTION OF INTERNAL MECHANICAL STIMULI

Some proprioceptors (internal receptors) for mechanical stimuli provide information about posture and movements of parts of the body relative to each other; others contribute to an undisturbed course of coordinated muscular actions (*e.g.*, in locomotion). Best known from studies of vertebrates and arthropods, some are tonic proprioceptors (serving to maintain muscle tone in posture); others are of the phasic type (serving movement); still others have a mixed phasic–tonic character. In principle, proprioceptors can be stimulated adequately by pressure or stretching during active movements of the animal (reafferent stimulation) as well as through passive external pushing and pulling (exafferent stimulation). One passive factor, particularly in land-inhabiting animals, is gravity as it acts on bodily tissues or organs. Proprioceptors thus not only serve reflex adjustments in posture and relatively automatic movements of parts of the body with respect to each other (as in driving an automobile) but they also provide gravitational information about the position of limbs or of the whole body in space. To the extent that they are gravity detectors, these sensory structures are properly called external receptors (exteroceptors instead of proprioceptors). For receptors that are diffusely located within the body, a clean distinction between proprioceptive and possible exteroceptive function (gravity reception) is experimentally practicable only under conditions of weightlessness, as in space travel.

Vertebrates. *Muscle spindles.* Well-known proprioceptors of all the four-limbed vertebrates studied are the muscle spindles occurring in the skeletal (striate) muscles; fish muscles show structurally simpler but functionally comparable receptors. Each muscle spindle in mammals consists of a few slender, specialized (intrafusal) muscle fibres that are surrounded by a sheath of connective tissue filled with lymph fluid (Figure 2). The muscle spindle itself is surrounded by and arranged parallel to the ordinary (extrafusal) muscle fibres. Each intrafusal fibre consists of contractile (motor) parts at both ends and a noncontractile sensory midsection that serves as a receptor for stretch (changes of length and tension). There is double (primary and secondary) sensory innervation in mammals, but the secondary endings are lacking in lower vertebrates. Even when the animal is at rest, both types of endings are active (under the tension of normal muscle tonus). Additional stretch (lengthening) of the intrafusal midsection increases the nerve impulse frequency, and relaxation (shortening) causes a decrease. The primary (phasic-tonic) ending responds quickly; responses of the secondary (tonic) endings are slower.

The length of the muscle spindle as a whole varies with the contraction phase and the length of the muscle to which it belongs. The length of the sensory midsection, however, may change more or less independently because its motor nerve endings function apart from the innervation of the extrafusal muscle fibres. Thus the ratio of extrafusal–intrafusal contraction determines whether or not a change of length in the midsection will occur during muscle activity. There are reasons to suppose that midsection stretch remains more or less unchanged dur-

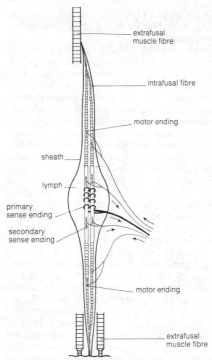

Figure 2: Mammalian muscle spindle.

ing self-initiated ("voluntary") movements; reafferent stimulation of muscle spindles would be avoided in this way. But as soon as an unexpected (exafferent) stretch of a muscle occurs—for example, when a leg pushes against an obstacle during locomotion—the midsections stretch to produce an increase of impulse frequency. This neural activity elicits a compensatory reflex contraction of the stretched muscle, as in the knee jerk during medical examinations: a blow beneath the kneecap causes stretch of a thigh muscle, stimulation of its muscle spindles, and a compensatory jerking contraction of the same muscle. Knee jerk

Tendon organs. Branched nerve endings on vertebrate tendons (not far from their point of attachment to muscle) also respond to stretch; however, they are decidedly less sensitive than are muscle spindles. These tendon organs produce no impulses under the stretch of normal, resting muscle tonus. Neither is there a mechanism preventing reafferent stimulation of tendon organs, nor does it make any difference whether the stretch is brought about by active muscle contraction or passively following external influence. In both cases tendon receptors respond according to the intensity of the stretch; their response causes relaxation of the attached muscle and may serve (among other functions) to prevent anatomical damage.

Human awareness of posture and movement of parts of the body with respect to each other (kinesthetic sensations) is attributable neither to muscle spindles nor to tendon organs. The sensations are based on stimulation of sensory nerve endings of various types at the joint capsules and of stretch receptors in the skin. There are also mechanoreceptors in the walls of some blood vessels (*e.g.*, in the aorta and the carotid sinus); these are sensitive to blood-pressure changes and play a regulatory role in the circulatory system.

Invertebrates. Among invertebrates, the arthropods exhibit the most readily distinguished proprioceptors, called muscle-receptor organs and chordotonal proprioceptors. Both types of structure occur in crustaceans as well as in insects. Adequate stimuli are variations in length and tension (stretch).

Muscle receptor organs. Although they structurally and functionally resemble the muscle spindles of vertebrates, arthropod muscle receptor organs are always situated outside of the muscles proper. Numerous branches of multipolar primary nerve cells are connected with the noncontractile midsection of specialized muscle fibres, both ends of which are contractile and have an efferent (motor) innervation. In crustaceans, the muscle receptor organ contains two elements: a slowly contracting, nonadapting tonic fibre and a quickly contracting, rapidly adapting phasic element.

Chordotonal proprioceptors. Widely distributed among arthropods, chordotonal receptor organs are thin, elastic, innervated strands of connective tissue, stretched between adjacent segments of the body or of leg joints. The sensory endings of a few bipolar primary nerve cells, each provided with a spiny sensillum (scolopidium), are attached to the strand. Chordotonal proprioceptor organs generate neural impulses that show them to contain both phasic movement receptors and tonic pressure receptors; sometimes two varieties of each. Thus there are receptors that selectively respond only during flexion, only in the flexed position, only during stretch, or only in the stretched state of the given strand. Several kinds of insects, apart from their clearly proprioceptive-chordotonal functions, have other chordotonal elements that serve as typical exteroceptors. Sense organs of this type (tympanic and subgenual organs in legs, organs of Johnston in the antennae) may function in the reception of sound waves, of vibrations in the ground, or of other external mechanical stimuli. Many insects also have a special type of chordotonal-proprioceptor structure (campaniform sensilla) not found in crustaceans. Sensory endings of primary nerve cells are connected with thin, dome-shaped (campaniform) spots on the exoskeleton. These campaniform sensilla respond to local tensions and deformations of the body surface. They function in the regulation of such movements as the beating of wings in locusts. Similarly functioning proprioceptors (lyriform organs) are also observed among spiders.

In insects, posture and movements of body parts with respect to each other can be detected through groups of external tactile hairs implanted near the joints between adjacent skeletal elements. Some function as rotation receptors or exteroceptors to detect the direction of gravity.

Among other invertebrates, the cephalopod *Octopus* clearly exhibits proprioceptive abilities, though specific receptors have not yet been identified. These animals, however, seem unable to integrate proprioceptive data in the central nervous system with other sensory information in learning. Thus an octopus readily can be taught to discriminate between two small cylindrical objects (both provided with longitudinal ribs) if the ribs on one of them are somewhat coarser than those on the other. But the animal cannot learn to distinguish between cylinders of the same size if the ribs are equally coarse and if they are longitudinal on one and transverse in the other; nor can it learn to discriminate between small objects of different form or different weight. This indicates that an octopus cannot learn any discrimination that depends on sensory information about the position of the arms and suckers making contact.

Octopus learning

EQUILIBRIUM

Active maintenance of equilibrium during bodily movement (*e.g.*, in locomotion) requires appropriate sensory functions. Although many animals usually maintain their bodies with the long axis horizontal (backside up), man being a notable exception, there are frequent departures from the usual position. A fish may dive steeply downward; a spiny lobster may crawl along a perpendicular cliff, and a man may alter his normal orientation by lying down at full length. In no case, however, need there be any loss of equilibrium. Every deviation from the actively pursued posture means an equilibrium disturbance and evokes compensatory reflex movements, not only a deviation from the usual position as in most laboratory experiments.

Maintenance of equilibrium is based upon contact of the animal with the external world; several sensory systems may play a role in this context. When an animal moves over a solid surface, tactile stimuli usually predominate as cues. It has been noted above how proprioceptors in vertebrates and arthropods can also contribute to spatial orientation; bodily tissues under gravity weigh vertically down and stimulate internal mechanoreceptors in a way that depends on, and varies with, the animal's spatial position. When they are out of contact with the ground, many animals orient themselves in space by keeping their back (dorsal) side turned up toward the light. Visual cues also can serve equilibration; for example, through compensatory body movements (optomotor reflexes) brought about by the shifts of the image of the environment over the retina of the eye. For the receptors mentioned thus far, however, equilibration is not the unique function. There are other sensory structures that are genuine organs of equilibrium in that they primarily and exclusively serve orientation of posture and movement in space.

Gravity receptors. Because of the constancy of its magnitude and direction, gravity is most suitable in providing animals with cues to their position in space. The sense organs involved (statoreceptors) usually have the structure of a statocyst, a fluid-filled vesicle containing one or more sandy or stonelike elements (statoliths). Sensory cells in the wall of the vesicle have hairs that are in contact with the statolith, which always weighs vertically down. Hence, depending on the animal's position, different sense cells will be stimulated in statocysts with loose statoliths (Figure 3A); or the same sense cells will be stimulated in different ways in statocysts with a statolith loosely fixed to the sense hairs (Figure 3B).

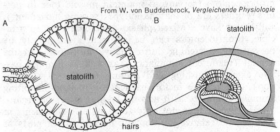

From W. von Buddenbrock, *Vergleichende Physiologie*

Figure 3: *Statocyst gravity receptors.*
(A) With a free-moving statolith, as in a mollusk (scallop), and (B) with statolith loosely fixed to hair cells, as in a crustacean (opossum shrimp).

Statocysts are found in representatives of all of the major groups of invertebrates: jellyfish, sandworms, higher crustaceans, some sea cucumbers, free-swimming tunicate larvae, and all the mollusks studied thus far. Analogous receptors that occur generally in vertebrates are the ear's utriculus and probably (to a degree) also two other otolith organs (sacculus and lagena) of the ear (labyrinth). Statocysts (including vertebrate labyrinthine statoreceptors) develop embryologically from local invaginations of the body surface. In primitive evolutionary forms, the interior of the statocyst is in open communication with the surrounding sea and thus is filled with water; statoliths usually are sand particles taken up from outside. In a few animal groups, this developmental stage is only found during the larval phase, the initial opening to the exterior being closed in the adult animal. In more advanced forms, the liquid content (statolymph) and the statoliths are produced by cells in the wall of the organ. This specialized type of closed statocyst is found in many snails, in all the cephalopods such as the squid (except *Nautilus*), and in the vast majority of vertebrates (from bony fishes up to and including mammals).

Statocyst function may be studied by observing compensatory reflexes under experimental conditions. When the position of a laboratory animal is appropriately changed, movements of such body parts as the eyes, head, and limbs can be observed. Such movements tend to counteract the imposed change and to restore or to maintain the original position. Evidence of statoreceptor function is provided if these reflexes are abolished after surgical elimination of both statocysts. Many animals exhibit locomotion that is gravitationally directed vertically down or up (positive or negative geotaxis, respectively). Geotactic behaviour may be experimentally altered by whirling the animal in a centrifuge to change the direction and to increase the intensity of the force exerted on the sensory hairs by the statoliths. Molting crustaceans shed the contents of their statocysts along with their exoskeleton.

Geotactic behaviour

If such an animal is placed in clean water containing iron filings, it takes up new iron statoliths instead of the usual sand grains. By moving a magnet to vary the direction of the force exerted by the metal statoliths, the animal can be made to adopt any resting position, even to stay upside down. Statoliths can be washed out of the open statocysts of a shrimp without damaging the sensory hairs. When the hairs are pushed in different directions with a fine water jet, the shrimp exhibits compensatory reflexes. In this way, it has been shown that each statocyst signals a change of position around the animal's long axis; the same reaction is found to occur after removal of the statocyst on one side only. Electrical impulses in the statocyst nerve can be recorded while the animal is in different spatial positions, or during experimental deflection of the sensory hairs. Such experiments reveal that both vertebrates and decapod crustaceans (*e.g.*, shrimp) exhibit spontaneous and statolith-induced neural activity in the lining (epithelium) of the gravity receptor.

Spontaneous activity. The sensory epithelium of a statocyst is spontaneously active, initiating a continuing series of impulses directed toward the central nervous system (even when the statoliths are experimentally removed from the statocyst). This resting frequency of neural activity is fairly constant and completely independent of the animal's position in space. In vertebrates and in crustaceans, spontaneous activity of the left statocyst affects the central nervous system to produce a tendency of the animal to roll to the right about its long axis; spontaneous activity of the right statocyst prompts a tendency to roll to the left. Normally, these rolling tendencies neutralize each other in the central nervous system, not becoming manifest unless the statocyst on one side of the body is functionally eliminated by complete surgical removal, by destruction of its sensory epithelium, or by cutting its nerve. This intervention permits the influence of the spontaneous activity generated in the remaining statocyst to be felt, and the animal tends to roll toward the operated side. Unilateral (one-sided) removal of the statoliths alone, however, does not produce such an effect so long as the sensory cells in the epithelium remain intact. The rolling tendency of a unilaterally operated animal usually diminishes little by little in the course of hours or days, until it finally disappears completely. If the remaining statocyst is then removed, rolling occurs again, but this time to the other (last operated) side. This tendency also diminishes and disappears with time. Apparently the unbalancing effect of the spontaneous influx from a statocyst is gradually counteracted in some unknown way by the central nervous system.

Statolith influences. Vertebrates and crustaceans have statoliths that are loosely connected to the sensory hairs by a sticky substance. With such a mechanical arrangement, the statolith stimulates the sensory cells by parallel (shearing) motion rather than by pressure or pull at right angles to the epithelium. The effects are demonstrable in experiments with fish, based on the dorsal-light orientation noted above. In a laboratory darkroom, if light shines at a fish from one side, the animal assumes an oblique position. While the fish tends to turn on its side (with its back side to the light), gravity tends to keep it vertical; the oblique position is the resultant. In a whirling centrifuge, the pressure exerted by the statoliths may be increased. When this is done, the fish rights itself almost precisely to the degree that the shearing force exerted by the statoliths is held constant.

In vertebrates, statoreception is localized in the head within the labyrinth, particularly within the utriculus, one of the three statolith (or otolith) organs (Figure 4). The statolith is surrounded by a gelatinous substance akin to the cupula of the lateral-line organs. In most higher vertebrates, the head moves rather flexibly because it is not rigidly connected to the trunk. Thus information coming from the utriculi has to be neurally integrated centrally with impulses from proprioceptors that signal the position of the head with respect to the limbs and trunk (for example, neck receptors), if the animal is to orient its head and body appropriately in space.

The roles played by the remaining otolith organs of the

Otolith organs in vertebrates (margin)

labyrinth (sacculus and lagena) in statoreception remain unclear. Their sensory epitheliums (maculae) are roughly at right angles to each other and to that of the utriculus. In view of their arrangement, it was once supposed that the three otolith organs of the labyrinth would serve to detect position in three spatial planes (indeed, the three semicircular canals do serve to detect rotation in different planes). It has been found, however, that the sacculus and the lagena (as far as it is present) can be put out of function bilaterally in representatives of all the classes of vertebrates without causing overt equilibration disturbances. On the other hand, some secondary statoreceptor function has been demonstrated for these otolith organs in all the animals from fish up to and including man.

In the special case of flatfishes (*e.g.*, halibut, sole, flounder), the normal upright position in the juvenile stage changes to one of swimming and lying on one side as an adult. The eye from that side migrates to the upper surface; but the situation of both labyrinths remains unchanged. Hence, the originally horizontal maculae of the utriculi are now oriented vertically. In these fish, the sacculi (usually the major organs of hearing in bony fishes) indeed may be shown to serve as statoreceptors. At any rate, the same otolith organ may function in one fish species as an organ of hearing and in another as a gravity receptor; clearly, both functions depend on basically identical mechanical stimulation.

As receptors belonging to the acousticolateralis system, the otolith organs of vertebrates have hair cells of the same type that is found in lateral-line neuromasts. Under the electron microscope, the sensory hair cells show a pattern of polarization (arrows in Figure 4) throughout

From Cold Spring Harbor Symposia on Quantitative Biology (1965)

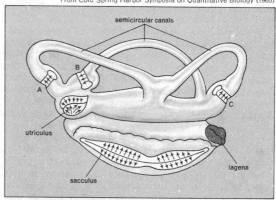

Figure 4: Right labyrinth of a codlike fish called the burbot, seen from above. Ampullae of anterior, horizontal, and posterior semicircular canals are lettered A, B, and C, respectively. Arrows show direction of hair-cell polarization.

the macula, indicating the directions in which the shearing otolith should have an activating or an inhibiting influence. Results of physiological investigations thus far performed agree well with these deductions.

Among the invertebrates, most statocyst research has been done with such decapod crustaceans as lobsters. The working mechanism of their statocysts conforms with the physiological principles of vertebrate statoreception discussed above. The results of electrophysiological investigations support the conclusions drawn from behavioral observations. In some crustacean statocysts (for example, in the lobster, *Homarus*), special statoreceptors are found that signal the same bodily position differently, depending on the direction of movement through which it was reached (hysteresis effect). The part played by the statocyst in equilibration has been investigated in several other invertebrate groups, among them jellyfish, sandworms, and such mollusks as scallops, common snails, sea hare, and octopus. Each sensory cell from the vertical macula in a statocyst of the octopus bears up to 200 kinocilia, and all the cilia of each cell are polarized in the same direction. On the macula as a whole, there is a radiating polarization pattern, the activating direction pointing everywhere from the centre to the margin. Compensatory eye reflexes resulting from tilting the animal

Statocyst research among crustaceans (margin)

head down or head up around a transverse axis reveal a hysteresis effect. After unilateral-statocyst removal, mollusks do not tend to roll toward the operated side (as do vertebrates and crustaceans) but toward the side of the remaining statocyst.

The almost complete absence of statocysts in insects is remarkable in view of evidence that many of them have a high degree of sensitivity to the direction of gravity. Receptors involved are specialized tufts of tactile hairs at the external body surface; in the honeybee, such groups of hairs are notably found between head and thorax and between thorax and abdomen. The adaptive function of these static (gravity) receptors becomes manifest in the honeybee "dance language" performed on a vertical comb in the hive. The angle between the dancing bee and the perpendicular seems to direct other bees to sources of nectar and pollen.

Rotation receptors. In addition to having tonic statoreceptors (signalling position with respect to gravity), several groups of animals have purely phasic rotation receptors that respond only to angular acceleration or deceleration, as produced on a turntable. Vertebrates, cephalopods (*e.g.*, squid), and decapod crustaceans (*e.g.*, lobsters) have special rotation receptors at the inner surface of the fluid-filled organ of equilibrium (labyrinth or statocyst). This fluid lags inertially with respect to the wall of the organ at the onset and arrest of every rotation. Among crustaceans, such as crabs or lobsters, the rotation receptors incorporate relatively long, delicate hairs that extend more or less at right angles to the wall freely into the statocyst fluid. The hairs respond quickly to fluid motion, swaying around their point of attachment and returning slowly through their elasticity to resting position. Their stimulation causes compensatory reflexes of the eyestalks or of the whole animal.

Eyestalk reflexes can be readily observed when a blinded, legless crab is rotated while flat on a turntable. These reflex movements are called nystagmus. At the onset of rotation to the right, both eyestalks move at about the rotation rate to the left by way of compensation until they reach their maximal deviation. In most cases, one or more jerky movements of the eyestalks in the opposite direction are observed per rotation during the initial period (quick, restoring nystagmus phases). In general, however, the eyestalks remain deviated opposite to the direction of rotation for several revolutions of the turntable. During prolonged constant-velocity rotation, the crab's eyestalks return to their symmetrical position; at this point, inertial lag in the statolymph is reduced to the degree that the fluid finally rotates together with the statocyst wall. Sudden arrest of the turntable under these circumstances causes afternystagmus: the eyestalks move promptly to the right (at about the same velocity as they moved to the left at the onset of rotation) until their maximal deviation toward this side is reached. After a quick jerk in the opposite direction, the eyes continue their slow movement to the right, and in this way as many as three or more afternystagmus jerks may occur with decreasing intensity. Such aftereffects may last many seconds, but finally the eyestalks return slowly to their symmetrical position. All of these nystagmic effects from such horizontal rotation are abolished in a blinded crab, however, after bilateral elimination of the long, delicate statocyst hairs by their denervation or by cauterization of the hair bases.

In vertebrates, rotation reception occurs within the labyrinth. Each labyrinth has three semicircular canals arranged in planes at right angles to each other (Figure 4); the canals communicate with the utriculus. One end of each canal is widened into an ampulla, and the sensory cells (hair cells) are arranged in a row on a ridge (crista) of the ampullar wall. The crista is oriented at right angles to the plane of the canal, and the extended hairs of its sensory cells are imbedded in a jellylike cupula that reaches to the opposite wall of the ampulla. Endolymph displacement through a canal makes the cupula move aside, as if it were a swinging door. In vertebrates, the inertial lag of the endolymph at the onset of rotation is very brief, the fluid catching up with the angular velocity

of the labyrinth within a fraction of a second. An ampulla with its crista and cupula is reminiscent of a lateral-line canal neuromast, except that all of the hair cells of a crista are polarized in the same direction. In the cristae belonging to the vertical semicircular canals the kinocilium is implanted at the side facing the canal; in the horizontal cristae all of the sensory cells are polarized toward the opposite side (facing the utriculus). This structural arrangement is in keeping with differences between the vertical and the horizontal canals observed in behavioral and electrophysiological experiments.

A turn of the animal's head around the vertical axis to the left increases the neural-impulse frequency (activation) in the left horizontal crista; a turn of the head to the right causes a frequency decrease (inhibition). Opposite effects occur at the same time in the right horizontal crista. Recordings from the different crista nerves, while the animal is being rotated successively around all three major body axes, show the horizontal crista to respond only to rotation of the animal around its vertical axis; the vertical cristae, however, respond to rotation about all three axes. Behavioral data (compensatory eye reflexes) provide similar results, except that the eyes fail to exhibit an observable response associated with the vertical semicircular canals during rotation around the vertical axis. Stimulation of the vertical cristae under these circumstances gives rise to the simultaneous contraction of antagonistic pairs of eye muscles; hence the absence of a compensatory eye rotation.

In decapod crustaceans, particularly crabs, the statocyst is anything but a simple spherical vesicle; it has a very complicated shape with several curved invaginations and projections. In a small corner in the lowest (most ventral) part of the crab statocyst, a cluster of minuscule sand particles (statoliths) is found in contact with specialized (hooked) hairs. Apart from these hook-hair gravity receptors, there is a single, slightly curved row of relatively straight "thread" hairs atop an oval invagination in the middle of the lower statocyst wall. These hairs are the rotation receptors described above in the blinded crab revolving on a turntable. Bilateral elimination of the thread hairs alters the reflexes of the eyestalks. Instead of reacting immediately, at the very onset of rotation, in the absence of thread hairs on both sides, the eyes initially maintain their symmetrical position. They start their compensatory movement only after rotation has begun or at the end of rotation after the animal has reached a new, steady position. Furthermore, the velocity of this compensatory eye movement seems to be independent of the rate of angular acceleration or deceleration. The delayed nature of the response suggests that loss of rotation sensitivity about horizontal axes results from thread-hair elimination.

That the thread hairs are indeed responsive to rotation about all three major body axes is supported by a number of observations. Bilateral elimination of the impulses from the statolith hairs (position receptors) by selective nerve cutting, for example, does not affect the animal's response to rotation around the vertical axis. Despite their loss of impulses from position receptors, crabs subjected to angular acceleration or deceleration about either horizontal axis exhibit the normal compensatory eyestalk reflexes at the very onset of rotation. When a new (inclined) position of the animal is maintained, the eyestalks again become symmetrical, although complete return to symmetry may require several minutes. On the other hand, when both thread hairs and statolith hairs are eliminated, all such rotation and position reflexes of the eyestalks and related aftereffects are abolished. After unilateral elimination of the thread hairs or removal of one entire statocyst in a blinded crab, both eyes still react to rotation around the vertical axis in both directions. When electrical recordings are made of the activity of the primary sensory neurons innervating the thread hairs, similar results are obtained, the receptors responding only to angular acceleration and deceleration. They are spontaneously active, and the neural response to rotation that is superimposed upon the spontaneous background consists of a coded sequence of impulse-frequency increases and

Rotation of a blinded crab

Eyestalk reflexes

decreases. The same reception unit responds to acceleration about all three major axes.

The statocysts of cephalopods (nautilus, squid, octopus) rival the complexity of crab statocysts. In addition to the perpendicular macula with its statolith (for gravity reception), the octopus has three cristae (containing many hair cells with two-directionally polarized kinocilia) arranged approximately at right angles to each other. Rotation (turntable) experiments and surgical removal of statocyst receptors have shown that the octopus cristae function as rotation receptors. Nystagmus and afternystagmus persist almost unchanged after unilateral statocyst removal, but they are completely abolished after the additional removal of the second statocyst in a blinded octopus. In the cuttlefish (*Sepia*), the statocyst is structurally even more complicated; besides three cristae, it has three maculae (statolith organs) also arranged in different planes.

Rotation receptors of quite a different type are found in some groups of insects. Dragonflies (for example, *Aeshna*) have external hair receptors between the head and thorax. If a gust of wind turns the animal around its long axis during flight, the relatively heavy head lags with respect to the thorax. The resulting stimulation of the hair receptors in the neck region elicits compensatory flight reflexes and restores the insect to a normal position. These receptors do not respond to static head displacements. In the Diptera (true flies), the posterior knobbed "wings" (halteres) serve as flight stabilizing rotation receptors. During flight, the halteres beat in a vertical plane, synchronously with the forewings. Rotational instability as the insect flies is gyroscopically counteracted by the beating action. Receptors are campaniform sensilla at the base of the haltere.

BIBLIOGRAPHY. J. FIELD (gen. ed.), *Handbook of Physiology*, sec. 1, *Neurophysiology*, 3 vol. (1959–60), chapters on nonphotic receptors, posture and locomotion, vestibular mechanisms, initiation of impulses at receptors, touch and kinesis, and pain; J.D. CARTHY and G.E. NEWELL (eds.), *Invertebrate Receptors* (1968), chapters on mollusk statocysts, invertebrate proprioceptors, chordotonal organs, and mechanoreceptive transduction; P.H. CAHN (ed.), *Lateral Line Detectors* (1967), contributions of 35 investigators; M.J. COHEN and S. DIJKGRAAF, "Mechanoreception," in T.H. WATERMAN (ed.), *The Physiology of Crustacea*, vol. 2 (1961); S. DIJKGRAAF, "The Functioning and Significance of the Lateral-Line Organs," *Biol. Rev.*, 38:51–105 (1963); E. VON HOLST, "Die Arbeitsweise des Statolithenapparates bei Fischen," *Z. Vergl. Physiol.*, 32:60–120 (1950), a classical study on statoreception in the labyrinth; I.P. HOWARD and W..B TEMPLETON, *Human Spatial Orientation* (1966), extensive coverage of the regulation of body posture; O. LOWENSTEIN, "Labyrinth and Equilibrium," pp. 60–82 in *Physiological Mechanisms in Animal Behaviour*, in *Symp. Soc. Exp. Biol.*, no. 4 (1950); D. MELLON, *The Physiology of Sense Organs* (1968); C.L. PROSSER and F.A. BROWN, *Comparative Animal Physiology*, 2nd ed. (1961), a textbook survey of mechanoreception and equilibrium; A.V.S. DE REUCK and J. KNIGHT (eds.), *Myotatic, Kinesthetic, and Vestibular Mechanisms* (1967), deals primarily with mammals; J SCHWARTZKOPFF, "Mechanoreception," in M. ROCKSTEIN (ed.), *The Physiology of Insecta*, vol. 1 (1964).

(S.Di.)

Medical Education

Medical education is directed toward imparting to persons seeking to become physicians the knowledge and skills used in the prevention and treatment of disease and also toward developing the methods and objectives appropriate to the study of the still unknown factors that produce disease or favour well-being. Medical education may be classified as (1) the basic training, (2) the training of specialists, and (3) the continuing education of the practicing physician. Attention in this article is focussed primarily on the basic education.

BACKGROUND

The Greeks' spirit of rational inquiry may be considered the starting point of medical education because it introduced the practice of observation and reasoning regarding disease. Rational interpretation and discussion lend themselves to teaching and thus to the formation of schools such as that at Cos, where the Greek physician Hippocrates taught in the 5th century BC. Later, the Christian religion greatly contributed to both the learning and the teaching of medicine because it favoured as acts of Christian piety not only the protection and care of the sick but the establishment of institutions where collections of sick people encouraged observation, analysis, and discussion among physicians by furnishing excellent opportunities for comparison. With the rise of the universities in Italy and later in Cracow, Prague, Paris, Oxford, and elsewhere in western Europe, the teachers of medicine were in some measure drawn away from the life of the hospitals and were offered the attractions and prestige of university professorships and lectureships. As a result, the study of medicine led more often to a familiarity with theories about disease than with actual sick persons. The establishment in 1551 of the Royal College of Physicians of London, however, largely through the energies of Thomas Linacre, who in 1518 had obtained from Henry VIII the original letters patent for a body of regular physicians, produced a system of examination of medical practitioners. The discovery of the circulation of the blood by William Harvey provided the necessary stimulus to the scientific study of the processes of the body, so that gradually the emphasis upon theory and doctrine decreased, although it lasted well into the 18th century. The Royal College of Physicians

Little by little, in the 17th and 18th centuries, the value of hospital experience and the training of the students' sight, hearing, and touch in studying disease were reasserted. In Europe, medical education began slowly to assume its modern character in the application of a gradually increasing knowledge of natural science to the actual care of patients. This return to the bedside aided the hospitals in their long evolution from dwelling places of the poor, the diseased, and the infirm, maintained by charity and staffed usually by religious orders, to the well-equipped, efficient places of today, used by every part of the community, maintained by charity or at public expense, and staffed by trained nurses, physicians, surgeons, and lay assistants.

The 19th-century discoveries of Louis Pasteur, which showed the relation of micro-organisms to certain diseases, Joseph Lister's application of Pasteur's concepts to surgery, and the studies of Rudolf Virchow and Robert Koch in cellular pathology and bacteriology brought immense stimulus to the practice of medicine and surgery. The passage of the Medical Act of 1858 has been termed the most important event in British medicine. It established the General Medical Council, which thenceforth controlled admission to the medical register and thus had great powers over medical education and examinations.

In the United States, medical education was greatly influenced by the example set in 1893 by the Johns Hopkins Medical School in Baltimore. It admitted only college graduates with a year's training in the natural sciences. Its clinical work was superior because the school was supplemented by the Johns Hopkins Hospital, created expressly for teaching and research carried on by members of the medical faculty. The number of inadequate medical schools in the United States was reduced after the Carnegie Foundation for the Advancement of Teaching published in 1910 a report by Abraham Flexner. The report attracted attention to the need of medical schools for better laboratory facilities, better access to patients in hospitals, and larger, better trained teaching staffs. Aided by the General Education Board, the Rockefeller Foundation, and a large number of private donors, U.S. and Canadian medical education was characterized by substantial improvements from 1913 to 1929 in the matters of endowments, buildings, laboratories, clinical facilities, teaching staffs, and methods of instruction. Advances at Johns Hopkins Medical School

PATTERN ESTABLISHED IN THE FIRST HALF OF THE 20TH CENTURY

General characteristics. As medical education developed after the Flexner report was published, the distinctive feature was the thoroughness with which theoretical and scientific knowledge were fused with what experience teaches in the practical responsibility of taking care of human beings. The clinical teacher has an immediate and absolute responsibility.

The premedical courses required in most countries emphasized the subjects of physics, chemistry, and biology. Graduation from a recognized secondary school was required. The courses in physics, chemistry, and biology were required in order to make it possible to present subsequently the subjects of anatomy, physiology, biochemistry, and pharmacology with precision and economy of time to minds prepared in scientific method and content. Each of the required courses included laboratory periods ranging from two hours to six hours a week for a full academic year. The extent of the student's familiarity with the use of instruments and laboratory procedures varied widely from country to country, however.

The medical schools began their work with the study of the structure of the body and its formation: anatomy, histology, and embryology. Concurrently, or soon thereafter, came the studies related to function—*i.e.*, physiology, biochemistry, pharmacology, and, in most schools, biophysics. Usually after the microscopic study of normal tissues (histology) had begun, the student was introduced to pathological anatomy, bacteriology, immunology, parasitology—in short, to the agents of disease and the changes that they cause in the structure and function of the tissues. Courses in medical psychology, biostatistics, and public health sometimes were given in the first two or two and a half years of the medical course, but this was not common before 1935. Wide differences were observed from country to country and from decade to decade in the sequence and emphasis given the courses in the above-named medical sciences and in the balance between laboratory work, lectures, and seminars.

The
clinical
years The two or more clinical years of an effective curriculum were characterized by active student participation in small group conferences and discussions, a decrease in the number of formal lectures, and an increase in the amount of contact with patients in teaching hospitals and clinics. Through work with patients, under the supervision and guidance of experienced teachers, students learned methods of obtaining comprehensive, accurate, and meaningful accounts of illness, how to conduct physical examinations, and how to develop judgment in the selection and utilization of laboratory diagnostic aids. During this period they learned to apply the knowledge gained in their pursuit of the basic medical sciences to the study of general medicine and the medical and surgical specialties.

On completion of medical school, the physician usually sought graduate training and experience in a hospital under the supervision of competent clinicians and other teachers. In Britain after 1953, a year of resident hospital work was required after qualification and before admission to the medical register. In North America, the first year of such training is known as an internship. Persons seeking further graduate education and training to qualify themselves as specialists or to fulfill requirements for a higher academic degree subsequently became hospital residents or fellows for periods of from one to four or five years.

The second type of advanced training is known as postgraduate education. It consisted of courses and training opportunities of from a few days to several months in duration, designed to enable physicians to learn of new developments within their special areas of concern. Such courses, fostering the continuing education of physicians, were offered by medical schools, hospitals, and medical societies in many parts of the world.

Pedagogical aspects. Abraham Flexner rightly insisted that medical education is a form of education and not a mysterious process of professional initiation or apprenticeship. In terms of educational methods the following points deserve mention:

In the United States, Great Britain, and the Commonwealth countries, medical schools were inclined to limit the number of students admitted so that each student might have a reasonably good opportunity. In western

Europe, South America, and most other countries, no exact limitation of numbers of students was effected, though there was a trend toward such limitation in some of the western European schools. Some medical schools in North America were able to show ratios of teaching staff to students as high as 1 to 1 or 1 to 2, in contrast with 1 teacher to 20 or even 100 students in certain European universities. Limitation
of number
of
students

As applied to clinical teachers the term full time originally implied an educational ideal: that a clinician's salary from the university should be large enough to relieve him of any reason for seeing private patients for the sake of supplementing his salary by professional fees. Full time came to be applied, however, to a variety of modifications; it could mean that a clinical professor might supplement his salary as a teacher up to a defined maximum, might see private patients only at his hospital office, or might see such patients only a certain number of hours per week. The intent of full time has always been to place the professor's capacities and strength entirely at the service of his students and the patients entrusted to his care as a teacher and investigator.

Courses in the medical sciences commonly followed the formula of three hours of lectures and six to nine hours of laboratory work per week for a three-, six-, or nine-month course. Instruction in the clinical subjects, though retaining the formal lecture, tended to diminish the time and emphasis allowed to lectures in favor of experience with and attendance on patients. Nonetheless, the level of lecturing and formal presentation in continental Europe remained high. Formality and a considerable measure of emphasis on status also characterized the relationship between professor and student in European schools.

In the United States, the fifth, or intern, year was of special importance and value, though it was not usually directly controlled by the medical school and ordinarily followed the award of the M.D. degree. The intern usually lived in an approved hospital and in any case devoted his entire time to the work of the hospital. Often the intern year led to a second year called assistant residency or residency, a continuation of this extremely valuable practical experience. In the United States, approximately three-fourths of graduate physicians entered residency training for a period of two to five years after the internship.

The clinicopathological conference is a distinctive feature of medical education in North America. As a public exercise, a clinician comments upon the record of a case of fatal illness in a patient he has not seen and discusses from this record the probable cause and nature of the illness. The pathological anatomist who examined the organs of the deceased then reports upon the actual findings. The lessons are vivid, and the effect upon the fullness and accuracy of hospital records is excellent. The
clinico-
path-
ological
conference

In Great Britain, Canada, Australia, New Zealand, South Africa, and Ireland, the academic degrees given at the end of five years of study were the M.B. and B.Ch. (bachelor of surgery). Only after considerable further study was the M.D. given, and only to a few persons; only these persons are entitled to be addressed as "doctor." It is customary in Great Britain and the British Commonwealth to address all physicians as "doctor," however, whether or not they hold the M.D. degree; but surgeons, including holders of the M.D. degree, prefer to be called "mister," although in northern England and in Scotland they are called doctor.

In some countries of western Europe, in South America, North America, China, and the Philippines, the M.D. was given at the end of four to six years of study and was not, therefore, an advanced degree.

The quality of medical education is supervised in the English-speaking countries by councils appointed by the profession as a whole—*e.g.*, the Council on Medical Education and Hospitals of the American Medical Association in the United States—or, in the case of Great Britain, by a statutory body, the General Medical Council, most of whose members are from the profession, although only a minority of the members are appointed by it. In other countries this is a function of the Ministry of Public

Instruction with, in some cases, the help of special councils to represent professional knowledge and experience.

Social factors. In the United States, licensure to practice medicine is controlled by boards of licensure in each of the states. These boards set and conduct examinations of applicants to practice within the state, and they examine the credentials of applicants who wish licences obtained in other states to be accepted in lieu of examination. In 1915 the National Board of Medical Examiners was created as a voluntary organization with two representatives each from the army, navy, and Public Health Service, three representatives from state licensure boards, and seven other physicians to hold examinations leading to a diploma that would be acceptable to all the state boards. National laws regulating professional practice cannot be enacted in the United States.

In Canada, the Medical Council of Canada conducts examinations and enrolls successful candidates on the Canadian medical register. The provincial governments accept the certificate of this registration as the main requirement for licensure. In Great Britain, the medical register is kept by the General Medical Council, which supervises the licensing bodies; unregistered practice, however, is not illegal. In most European countries graduation, on conditions set by law, from the state-controlled university or medical school in effect serves as a licence to practice; and the same is true for the Union of Soviet Socialist Republics and Japan.

After 1920 there was a steady growth and improvement of preventive medicine and public health in the United States, in terms of its importance in the medical curriculum as well as in the number and qualifications of professional personnel employed by cities, counties, states, and the U.S. Public Health Service. A similar development characterized many other countries, especially the Union of Soviet Socialist Republics.

It became apparent that it is of special advantage to a patient to obtain care in a teaching hospital because, if his case is to be used for discussion or teaching, there is every likelihood that the examination, diagnosis, and treatment will receive particular care and repeated attention; hence, a hospital's affiliation with a medical school for research and teaching purposes is highly desirable. This was realized by the U.S. Veterans Administration in 1945, when the deans' committee assured collaboration between the medical schools and the hospitals of the Veterans Administration. Collaboration between school and hospital has given rise to the so-called medical centres.

Economic aspects. The income of a medical school is derived from four principal sources: (1) tuition and fees; (2) endowment income or appropriation from the government (taxation); (3) gifts from private sources; and (4) donation of teachers' services. Tuition or student fees are large in the English-speaking countries (except in United States state universities) and small throughout the rest of the world. Only rarely does income from tuition exceed 50 percent of a school's total income. The total cost of maintaining a medical school, if prorated among the students, would give a figure from three to 50 times the tuition or other charges paid by the student.

The expenses of medical education fall into two groups: those of the instruction given in the medical sciences and those connected with hospital teaching. In the medical sciences, costs of building maintenance, laboratory equipment and supplies, research expenses, salaries of teachers, and wages of employees are heavy but comparable to those in other departments of the university. In the clinical subjects all expenses in connection with the care of patients usually are considered as hospital expenses and are not carried from the medical school budget, which is normally reserved for expenses of teaching and research. Here the heavy expenses are salaries of clinical teachers and the cost of studying cases of illness with a thoroughness appropriate to their use as teaching material.

To a considerable degree in all capitalist countries, the cost of securing an adequate medical education has tended to exclude the student whose family cannot contribute a large share of his living expenses and tuition for a period of four to ten years. This difficulty is offset in some medical schools by loan funds and scholarships, but these aids are commonly offered only in the second or subsequent years. In Britain, scholarships and maintenance grants are available, through both state and local educational authority funds, so that a clever boy or girl can have the opportunity of a medical education even though the parents may not be able to afford its cost.

Scientific aspects. Medical education has the double task of passing on to students what is known and of attacking what is still unknown. The cost of research is borne by a few; the benefits are shared by many. There are countries whose inhabitants are too poor to support physicians or use them; countries that can support a few physicians but are too poor to maintain a good medical school; countries that can maintain medical schools where what is known can be taught but no research can be carried out; and a few countries in which teaching and research in medicine can be carried on to the great advantage of the world at large.

A medical school having close geographical as well as administrative relationships with the rest of the university of which it forms a part usually profits by this intimate and easy contact. Medicine cannot wisely be separated from the biological sciences, and it continues to gain immensely from chemistry, physics, mathematics, and psychology. The social sciences have a contribution to make in helping physicians provide a better distribution of medical care. Contact with teachers and the advancing knowledge in other faculties of the university would extend and improve the chances of progress in medicine.

International aspects. With the development of the World Health Organization and the World Medical Association after World War II, there has been increasing international interest in medical education. World War II showed the advantages and economy derived from satisfactory systems of medical education. Defects and diseases were more widely and accurately detected among recruits than ever before, health and morale were effectively maintained among combatants, and disease and battle injuries were effectively treated only in the armed forces of those nations whose medical schools had been of high quality. As a result of the war, however, the medical schools of Norway, Finland, the Union of Soviet Socialist Republics, Poland, Czechoslovakia, Germany, Austria, the Balkan states, Italy, France, Belgium, The Netherlands, and Britain, as well as those of China, Japan, the Philippines, Java, and Thailand, suffered either physical destruction of laboratories, hospitals, and libraries or serious losses of teaching personnel and students. (Al.Gr./E.L.T.)

THE SITUATION SINCE 1960

The essential features of the medical education that was established in the early 20th century survived in much of the world during the 1960s and early 1970s, especially in the developed countries of the West; but need for more physicians, desire for improvement in the quality of medical care, and efforts to relate medical care more closely to the needs of the populace to be served brought some changes and many plans for change. The most dramatic changes occurred in China.

People's Republic of China. In 1966 the medical schools of the People's Republic of China were closed. The students, then accepted as graduates, and the faculty were sent out to give medical care where it was needed, particularly in the rural areas.

The medical schools remained closed until December 1970. Meanwhile, the administrative structure of the schools (like the administrative structures of other organizations) was placed under the control of revolutionary committees consisting of representatives of the People's Liberation Army, of workers or students, and of the administration or faculty. The chairman of the committee in each school was an army officer.

The curriculum was still undergoing discussion, but when the schools reopened in December 1970, the contemplated three-year program was as follows:

The first nine months are academic and include instruction in anatomy, physiology, biochemistry, Chinese traditional medicine, political education, pharmacology, and microbiology. Then, after two months devoted to military and physical training and manual labour, the student has one month of vacation before six months of training, consisting of lectures and clinical demonstrations in internal medicine, surgery, obstetrics, and gynecology. After a second sequence of two months of military and physical training and manual labour followed by a month's vacation, nine months are devoted to on-the-job training. Faculty and students form medical teams that serve the rural populace during the day. They also do manual labour. During the evenings students and faculty repair to local classrooms, where lectures are given in clinical practice and basic science. During this same period the students learn the science of acupuncture—the elaborate system of pricking precise points on the body in diagnosis and treatment of disease—and the recognition, collection, and use of herbs.

Three months of intensive training at a teaching hospital and three months of military and physical training, labour, and vacation complete the course.

Africa. In the developing countries of Africa, a number of medical schools were established after 1960, but there were still too few institutions to train an adequate number of qualified personnel. A majority of the practicing physicians in the area were still non-nationals who had received their training elsewhere.

African medical students abroad and at home

A survey of the region carried out by the World Health Organization in 1967 indicated that about 1,300 African medical students were studying abroad and that about 1,800 were attending African medical schools. The report of the survey stated that there was at that time one physician for 20,000 people in the countries surveyed, one registered nurse for 12,000 people, and one sanitary engineer for 2,000,000 people. Furthermore, 70 percent of the faculty members in the medical schools were non-nationals; this may account in part for the fact that the medical education given in Africa was deemed unsuitable for the situations in which the physicians were to practice.

India. The number of physicians graduating annually from the medical schools of India increased ninefold in the period from 1947–48 to 1968–69, but the physician–population ratio still remained far behind that of Europe and North America. The medical schools remained conservative in their methods and were criticized on the ground that their curricula were overloaded with details; that preclinical and clinical training were inadequately related; and that in the clinical course too much time was spent in lectures and too little in demonstrations. In certain institutions, however, efforts were begun to acquaint students with the problems of the rural areas, where eight-tenths of the Indian population resided.

United States. In the United States, in response to the need for more physicians, many medical schools changed their program leading to a medical degree from four years to three. Responses to a questionnaire sent in 1968 to the deans of all the medical schools in the United States indicated that 19 schools had started three-year programs or would soon do so and that 14 other institutions were studying the possibility of making this change.

Various methods were used to achieve the reduction in time spent in education. In some institutions, the fourth year, which had been devoted to elective work in research laboratories, for example, or to gaining clinical experience in a hospital, was simply dropped, and the student received his degree after completion of three years at the medical school and one year of internship. In other schools, the conventional curriculum was preserved and the four-year course was compressed into three by elimination of summer vacations. Still another program eliminated from the curriculum courses in subjects in which students had been adequately prepared before entering medical school. One program, based on careful coordination between premedical and medical training, achieved a five-year program from high school graduation to receiving an M.D. degree.

In the 1960s the first steps were taken toward computer-assisted medical education. In one such program, funds for which were supplied by the Division of Physician Manpower of the National Institutes of Health, the computer served as a "patient" and the medical student as a physician in a simulated situation. In interviewing the patient, for example, the student typed out his questions and the computer answered on a television-like screen.

The questions and answers might relate to the symptoms, to the results of laboratory tests, or to the physical examination. After making his diagnosis, the student typed out his course of treatment, and the patient recovered or died, depending upon the suitability of the treatment chosen.

In 1968 the Lister Hill Center for Biomedical Communications was established as one of the five major divisions of the National Library of Medicine. A committee of the Council of Academic Societies of the Association of Medical Colleges recommended that the Lister Hill Center

The Lister Hill Center

should have as its eventual goal the development of educational methods which will render obsolete the current systems of libraries, textbooks, medical school curricula, and total dependence on memory and pattern recognition in clinical decision-making and problem-solving. These major changes will come only with the development of new sources and new types of manpower ready to devise new approaches to the problems of medical education and the delivery of health care. Their long-term objective will not be limited to improving existing systems but will include devising newer systems using a different mix of men and machines than now familiar. This revolution will require a faculty who have mastered communications technology and who are eager to sail in yet uncharted educational waters. (From *Journal of Medical Education*, July 1971, part 2.) (T.F.R.)

BIBLIOGRAPHY. For new developments in medical education and for recent accounts of the situation prevailing in particular countries and regions, the periodicals *Journal of Medical Education*, *British Journal of Medical Education*, and *WHO Chronicle* are recommended. Also of interest are JULIUS B. RICHMOND, *Currents in American Medicine: A Developmental View of Medical Care and Education* (1969); FREMONT J. LYDEN, H. JACK GEIGER, and OSLER L. PETERSON, *The Training of Good Physicians: Critical Factors in Career Choices* (1968); and JOHN H. KNOWLES (ed.), *Views of Medical Education and Medical Care* (1968). For earlier developments the following sources are suggested: ABRAHAM FLEXNER, *Medical Education: A Comparative Study* (1925); *J.A.M.A.*, educational numbers (beginning in August 1903); *Report* of the Commission on Medical Education of the Association of American Medical Colleges (1932); *Report* of the Interdepartmental Committee on Medical Schools, Ministry of Health (1944); GENERAL MEDICAL COUNCIL, *Recommendations as to the Medical Curriculum* (1947); RAYMOND B. ALLEN, *Medical Education and the Changing Order* (1946); H.E. SIGERIST, *American Medicine* (1934); First World Conference on Medical Education, *Proceedings* (1953); and WILLIAM F. NORWOOD and GEORGE MILLER, "Medical Education and the Rise of Hospitals," *J.A.M.A.*, vol. 186, no. 10–12 (1963).

(Al.Gr./E.L.T./T.F.R.)

Medical Jurisprudence

Medical jurisprudence, or forensic medicine, is, in the strict sense, the application of the science of medicine in courts of law. In practice the subject includes many other matters that are not necessarily concerned with court proceedings. These include the medical aspects of proceedings before administrative or quasi-judicial bodies (such as pensions tribunals, industrial injuries boards, and medical appeal tribunals) and medicolegal aspects of administrative law (such as the control of dangerous drugs and poisons, the disposal of dead bodies and stillbirths, and the exercise of compulsory powers of admission to a hospital over persons of unsound mind). Legal and ethical aspects of medical practice itself are included, such as the functions of professional disciplinary bodies, medical registration and licensing of doctors, professional negligence, medical certification, and the code of medical ethics. The European practice of referring to the subject as "legal medicine" (*médecine légale* in French, *gerichtliche Medizin* in German) is, therefore, a more correct description of its scope, and the term legal medicine is increasingly used in the United States.

The broad canvas that the subject now covers is a reflection of the increasing part played by medicine in the social life of the community. Inevitably there is overlap into subjects such as public health, industrial medicine, criminology, drug dependence, and into the wider field of forensic science. In some European countries, university chairs of legal medicine are combined with criminology or with social or insurance medicine.

Growth of medical jurisprudence. Although instances of medical evidence being given in courts of law can be cited back to classical antiquity, the basis of modern medical jurisprudence cannot be traced beyond the 13th century, when the laws of the north Italian states first provided for the appointment of medical experts to advise the courts and laid down the requirements necessary to qualify as an expert medical witness. About the same time the first appointments as police surgeons were made. Postmortem examinations (autopsies) were carried out for medicolegal purposes, particularly in cases of suspected poisoning. It was this practice that revived the interest in anatomical dissection, itself to have a profound effect on the development of modern European medicine.

By the 16th century, the procedure for assembling medical evidence and presenting it in courts of law in criminal cases was well developed. It found expression in the penal codes promulgated by the bishop of Bamberg (1507), the elector of Brandenburg (1516), and Charles V of the Holy Roman Empire (1533). At the same time the procedure for investigating cases of violent or sudden deaths was also laid down. Centuries were to pass before these principles were accepted in Britain, where the development of medical jurisprudence was apparently unaffected by the important events taking place on the European continent. Until 1836 the coroner in England had no power to pay for medical evidence in inquests, and it was even doubted whether he could order a postmortem examination.

Acceptance as part of medical education. Similarly, the teaching of medical jurisprudence at British universities lagged behind the Continent. More than 150 years elapsed between the presentation of lectures on legal medicine at Leipzig (1642) and at Edinburgh University (the elder Andrew Duncan was the lecturer in 1801). Meanwhile, chairs of legal medicine, often combined with public health and hygiene, had been set up in many universities on the Continent. The first chair in the United Kingdom was established by crown commission in 1807 and was held by the younger Andrew Duncan. At about the same time, James S. Stringham delivered a course of lectures in New York at Columbia College (1804); he was appointed, in 1813, to the first chair of medical jurisprudence in the United States, instituted by the College of Physicians and Surgeons in New York city. Other courses were given by Charles Caldwell at Philadelphia Medical College in 1812–13 and by T.R. Beck at the College of Physicians and Surgeons for the Western District at Fairfield, New York. Since that period the majority of medical schools in the United States have included the subject in their courses of instruction.

Post-graduate instruction — Postgraduate instruction in legal medicine has been available on the continent of Europe for a considerable time. From the beginning of the 19th century attendance at courses at the medicolegal institute in Vienna was a condition of appointment as police surgeon in many European countries. Recognition as an expert in the subject on the Continent is dependent upon a long course of postgraduate instruction at a medicolegal institute or a university department of forensic medicine. This contrasts favourably with the position in British and American courts, where any medically qualified person may give evidence in court as an expert witness. In parts of England and of the United States, coroners' postmortem examinations may be carried out by any qualified doctor, irrespective of his experience in medicolegal work; in other parts only experienced pathologists are employed for the purpose; *e.g.*, in London, and in particular in Los Angeles, where coroners' autopsies may be carried out only by official autopsy surgeons. Concern has been expressed that there was no mention at all of legal medicine in a report of the British Royal Commission on Medical Education (1968).

Medical evidence in courts of law. Both criminal and civil courts receive medical evidence. In criminal courts such evidence is concerned chiefly with the identification and interpretation of injuries in support of charges of crimes such as murder, manslaughter, infanticide, woundings, poisonings, assaults (both sexual and nonsexual), rape, and criminal abortion. The identification of human remains, the distinction between injuries received before death and after death, the time elapsed since death, the distinction between live birth and stillbirth, the signs of drowning, traumatic asphyxia, hanging, strangulation, suffocation, throttling, electrocution, burning, and wounds received from instruments or firearms are but a few of the wide range of matters upon which medical evidence may be required in criminal courts.

The sensational nature of this kind of evidence usually overshadows the importance of medical evidence in the civil courts, where it may be needed in common-law actions based on negligence that results in personal injuries; *e.g.*, traffic accidents and nervous shock cases. In such cases medical evidence may be relevant, both as to the cause and extent of the injuries and to their possible consequences in terms of assessing damages. Medical evidence may also be needed by the courts in connection with such considerations as the mental capacity to make a will disposing of property (testamentary capacity), presumption of survivorship, inability to consummate a marriage, the state of mind of one or other spouse, duration of pregnancy, and illegitimacy. In England the president (senior judge) of the probate, divorce, and admiralty division of the high court appoints special medical inspectors to examine the parties in nullity (annulment) cases. Courts may also require medical evidence in the exercise of their jurisdiction over the property of persons of unsound mind (in England, court of protection orders). Other civil cases in which medical evidence may be required include paternity orders, maintenance orders, and noncohabitation orders, which are often dealt with by lower courts of summary jurisdiction. Jurisdiction in civil cases in the United States varies considerably from state to state.

Investigation of sudden death. Coroners have jurisdiction over violent, unnatural, or sudden deaths of unexplained cause, and it is in these cases that medical evidence is essential. In some areas coroners themselves are medically qualified, and in those parts of the United States where coroners have been replaced by medical examiners, a medical qualification is a condition of appointment. The coroners in London are qualified both in medicine and in law. The main evidence received by the coroner is the report of the autopsy carried out on the body of the deceased person, and in many areas such examinations are carried out in nearly every case. Corresponding, though less comprehensive, investigations are carried out by the procurator fiscal in Scotland. There is no corresponding procedure for investigating sudden death on the continent of Europe. Deaths attract investigation in such cases only where there is manifest suspicion of crime or wrongdoing. They are often notified to the police or local public prosecutor (*e.g.*, *procureur de la république*). Unlike the coroner, neither the police nor public prosecutors have power to order medicolegal autopsies, and the authorization of an investigating judge (*juge d'instruction*) may have to be obtained. Exceptions include Denmark, Finland, and Portugal, where the police are so authorized, and The Netherlands and the Union of Soviet Socialist Republics, where the local public prosecutor may authorize an autopsy. In some countries (*e.g.*, the Federal Republic of Germany), the judge must be present at the autopsy. Finally, the right, and in some cases duty, of the coroner to hold a public inquest, at which persons can be examined under oath and a verdict of a jury can be obtained on the cause of death, is peculiar to the Anglo-American coroner system and does not exist under the medical examiner or continental systems of medicolegal investigation. The coroner system, therefore, secures a far more comprehensive check on sudden deaths. In England investigation was undertaken in 1964 of the entire system of death certification and of coroners, under a governmental committee.

Two types of medical evidence. Two kinds of medical evidence may be given in courts of law. Evidence can be given as to facts that have come within the doctor's knowledge in the course of his practice, and in respect of which he is in the same position, in principle, as other witnesses to fact; he can also be called to give expert evidence on facts that have been presented to him for his opinion and have not come within his knowledge in the course of his practice, or on facts that he has secured from making special examinations or investigations for the specific purpose of providing the evidence.

Confidential information The question whether information obtained in a professional capacity should be disclosed without prior consent of the patient may bring the physician into conflict with the law. The international code of medical ethics that has been adopted in principle by all countries whose medical associations are affiliated to the World Medical Association embodies the Declaration of Geneva (1949), which states: "I will respect the secrets which are confided in me." In circumstances in which the court requires disclosure of information, the physician may risk imprisonment for contempt of court if he declines to give the information. This is the position in Great Britain and in about 15 states of the United States. In about 35 states, however, varying degrees of privilege, precluding disclosure of confidential information obtained in the course of treating a patient, are allowed, but the privilege can be waived in certain circumstances; *e.g.*, if the patient offers himself or his physician as a witness, although this is not the invariable rule. The tendency is to allow privilege to physicians.

As a general rule, evidence as to opinion is excluded from the courts on the grounds that it is for the court to form its own opinion on the facts that are before it, and the admission of expert evidence based on opinion would, therefore, trespass on the function of the judge and jury. In cases in which the matter before the court is complicated or technical in nature, however, it has become customary for the courts to admit evidence of expert opinion in order to assist it to reach its conclusions on the facts before it. Accordingly, specialists in various branches of medicine may be called to assist the courts. It is in the field of pathology that expert medical evidence is most frequently required. Expert psychiatric opinion is also sought increasingly in connection with the state of mind of persons who have been accused of committing criminal offenses or in other circumstances that have been mentioned above. The frequent need for courts to obtain evidence in these two fields has led to the development of specialties in forensic pathology and forensic psychiatry.

Other specialties on which the courts frequently require expert opinion include forensic odontology, which is concerned with the identification of persons or their remains through examination of their teeth; forensic immunology and serology, concerned with the identification of persons from examination of blood stains or of other secretions of the body such as spermatozoa, and with related problems such as disputed paternity; and forensic toxicology, concerned with the unlawful or accidental use of poisons or drugs and their identification by analysis of specimens. Specialists in these fields are not necessarily medically qualified. The interpretation of a bullet wound may depend on a knowledge of ballistics, for example, and the question whether a person is fit to have control of a motor vehicle may depend on the concentration of alcohol in the body tissues. Expert medical evidence in courts of law has become associated increasingly with supporting evidence of investigations carried out in the field of forensic chemistry, such as spectrophotometry, chromatography, activation analysis for minute amounts of various elements, and the identification of fibres, soils, or other substances.

The handling of expert medical evidence by continental courts (based on civil-law "inquisitorial" procedure) is very different from the procedure in English and United States courts (based on common-law "accusatorial" procedure), and the difference is most marked in criminal or quasi-criminal (delictual) cases. In England, documentary evidence is admitted only subject to strict limitations, whereas on the Continent the expert medical evidence is almost entirely documentary and is included in the dossier. Either side in an English trial may call expert medical witnesses, who may frequently disagree in their opinions, and who may be examined, cross-examined by the other side, and re-examined. Under the classical continental system, expert medical evidence is given only by the court's officially recognized expert, who will appear in person only when it is necessary to explain any doubtful points in his written evidence. Even then, he may be examined only by the presiding judge and cannot be questioned by counsel for the parties to the action. The limitation of medical evidence to experts recognized by the courts means that the spectacle of medical witnesses giving directly contrary evidence on behalf of either side—the so-called battle of the experts—is not a feature of continental courts. In most continental countries medicolegal institutes have been set up by the state to provide the courts with the best evidence; the more famous ones being in Vienna (founded 1803), Berlin, and Leipzig. In Denmark the courts are advised by the State Medico-Legal Council, which examines about 4,000 cases each year. Each case referred by the courts is examined by three members of the council. These institutes are equipped to carry out investigations covering the whole field of forensic sciences and may deal with matters such as the examination of individuals injured in industrial accidents, in addition to court work. They may also arrange for operations such as castration or sterilization of certain offenders when the laws of the country permit it. Their nearest equivalent in English-speaking countries is the forensic science laboratories that have been set up by the Home Office in England on a regional basis, but their scope is limited and restricted mainly to the field of chemical analysis.

Medical certification. A physician in any country will be asked to give certificates required by law for various purposes. Medical certification, in terms of legal duty, forms an important part of a doctor's practice, and the consequences of inaccurate certification are serious. In many cases, international forms of medical certificates have been introduced; *e.g.*, death certificates and certificates of vaccination. Stillbirth certification by doctors or midwives is obligatory in most countries, and the detention of a person of unsound mind in a hospital or under guardianship must always be supported by a medical certificate. Methods of disposal of dead bodies other than earth burial (*e.g.*, cremation), which destroy all evidence of the cause of death, must generally be authorized by special medical certificates. An increasing number of countries now require a medical examination and report on the child as well as the prospective adoptive parents before legal adoption of a child is permitted. Certain infectious diseases, depending on the country concerned, must be reported by physicians to public-health authorities. Certificates of incapacity for work on account of illness or injury are universally required from physicians, while many medical certificates are required in the insurance field in support of prospective policy holders or of claims for sickness or injury benefits.

Medical discipline and conduct. Most countries have introduced regulations to enable the public to distinguish between duly qualified physicians and unqualified practitioners, and this is achieved by licensing or registration procedure. In the United States, licensing is administered by the various states and may be either general or limited. General licenses are issued to duly qualified physicians after scrutiny of their qualifications, character, and experience. No license to practice medicine is required in Great Britain, but it is an offense for a person to pretend to the public that he is a registered medical practitioner, as by willfully and falsely using certain titles calculated to deceive (*e.g.*, in Britain, M.D.). Licenses to practice

U.S. and English practices contrasted with continental

Types of medical certificates

are required in the United States. Persons who are not licensed or registered are prohibited from various functions for which licensed or registered doctors are empowered; *e.g.*, prescribing dangerous drugs (narcotics), treating venereal disease, giving medical certificates, or attending maternity cases (except for certified midwives). Reciprocal recognition of degrees or diplomas is not extensive, but it forms an important part of the so-called Brussels Directives, which will regulate the practice of medicine in countries belonging to the European Economic Community (Common Market).

Disciplinary measures The various registration and licensing bodies have power to suspend registration or a license upon proof of professional misconduct in certain circumstances. For example, in Great Britain conviction of certain offenses or the judgment of the disciplinary committee of the General Medical Council is grounds for removal from the register. Professional misconduct can include adultery or other improper conduct with patients, procuring illegal abortions, drunkenness or drug dependence, advertising, and canvassing. The standards of professional conduct, however, vary greatly in different countries. Adultery with patients, for example, is not generally regarded as grounds for prohibiting a doctor from practicing in most European countries, with the exception of Britain. An increasing number of countries have introduced state health services, and disciplinary bodies have been set up to pronounce upon alleged breaches by doctors of their terms of service with the state health service. Finally, national medical associations may expel from membership physicians who are found guilty of infringing their association's own code of medical ethics, and many associations (*e.g.*, the British Medical Association [B.M.A.]) have set up means to deal with such cases.

Law relating to medical practice. Finally, medical jurisprudence is concerned with the relationship of medical practice itself to the laws of the country. The legality of certain practices such as termination of pregnancy, sterilization, castration, artificial insemination, transplantation, contraception, animal experiments, anatomical dissection, and euthanasia is a matter of very considerable importance to doctors, and their position in law in relation to many of these practices is often obscure; *e.g.*, it is an offense in parts of the United States to run a birth control clinic, yet the supply of contraceptives for prophylaxis against venereal disease may be allowed. Sterilization is permitted in some states and not in others. The grounds on which pregnancy can be terminated in different countries vary from absolute prohibition to almost any medical, eugenic or social consideration.

The physician is in exactly the same position as any other professional man, in that failure to exercise reasonable care may result in an action being brought against him in negligence if the patient suffers damage as a consequence. The same rules as to presumptive and contributory negligence apply. Both in England and in the United States a mistaken diagnosis or treatment is not per se actionable in negligence; it must be shown that the physician omitted or committed some procedure that a reasonable physician in his position would have done or not done; *e.g.*, failure to X-ray head injuries or omission to give antitetanic serum in the appropriate cases. Physicians will also be liable in trespass (assault) for carrying out procedures without the express or implied consent of the patient. The age at which consent can be given became a subject of much controversy with the increased demand by adolescent girls for induced abortion. Finally, patients may sue their physicians in contract for inadequate or faulty provision of services.

BIBLIOGRAPHY

General reference works: F.E. CAMPS (ed.), *Gradwohl's Legal Medicine,* 2nd ed. (1968), a comprehensive, fully illustrated text incorporating sections by British and American experts that deal specifically with the credibility of scientific evidence—differences in American and British legislation are brought out; W.J. CURRAN and E.D. SHAPIRO, *Law, Medicine, and Forensic Science,* 2nd ed. (1970), a comprehensive text containing detailed studies of some major conflicts over scientific and medical proof in American courts; R.P. BRITTAIN, *Bibliography of Medico-Legal Works in English* (1962), a complete list of medico-legal works in English.

Sudden death: J.D.J. HAVARD, *The Detection of Secret Homicide* (1960), a historical and comparative review of systems of investigation; W.B. PURCHASE and H.W. WOLLASTON, *Jervis on the Office and Duties of Coroners,* 9th ed. (1957), a comprehensive work on the law relating to coroners in England; BRITISH MEDICAL ASSOCIATION, *Medico-Legal Investigation of Deaths in the Community* (1964), a concise report of the situation in England, with recommendations for improvements.

Medical evidence in courts of law: BRITISH MEDICAL ASSOCIATION, *Medical Evidence in Courts of Law* (1965), a report by a joint committee of organizations representing the bar, solicitors, and the medical profession that reviews the arrangements for obtaining and giving medical evidence in courts of law in England and that makes recommendations for improvements; LAW REFORM COMMITTEE, *Privilege in Civil Proceedings* (HMSO 1967), report of an official committee that reviews "privilege" in English civil actions and makes recommendations for change in the law.

Abortion, sterilization, and euthanasia: G.L. WILLIAMS, *The Sanctity of Life and the Criminal Law* (1957), a critical account of the legal aspects of abortion, artificial insemination, sterilization, birth control, and euthanasia, with special reference to English and American legislation; WORLD HEALTH ORGANIZATION, *Abortion Laws* (1971), a survey of legislation on induced abortion in different countries.

Legal aspects of medical practice: GENERAL MEDICAL COUNCIL, *Professional Discipline* (1971), disciplinary rules issued by the body responsible for registering medical practitioners in the United Kingdom; MEDICAL DEFENCE UNION, *Consent to Treatment* (1971), a concise review of position at English law, with model forms for obtaining consent or providing proof of refusal to consent in various circumstances; BRITISH MEDICAL ASSOCIATION, "Memorandum of evidence to the Monopolies Commission on Restrictive Practices in the Medical Profession," *Brit. Med. J.,* suppl. (April 13, 1968), a detailed account of legal and ethical rules governing medical practice in the United Kingdom and the justification for their existence.

(J.D.J.H.)

Medici Family

Medici is the name of the Italian family that ruled Florence, and later Tuscany, for more than three centuries, from 1434 to 1737, except for two brief intervals (from 1494 to 1512 and from 1527 to 1530). Unique in the history of dynasties, their founder was not a "soldier of fortune," and consequently their entourage and their court continually showed an astonishing lack of men of the sword. The basis of their power was gold, accumulated by a long succession of shrewd merchants and bankers, Basis of the family's power whose genius consisted in taking the greatest possible advantage of the economic renaissance of Europe after the 12th century. Yet in time these financiers desired to exercise real power, instead of operating behind the scenes as did so many of their kind. Although they tried to avoid becoming involved in politics, they eventually recognized that, in a city as jealous of rank and position as was republican Florence they were at the mercy of spoliatory laws voted by the popular assemblies under pressure from either various demagogues or their competitors. The most illustrious of the Medici, Lorenzo the Magnificent, wrote in capital letters in his diary: "One cannot live in wealth in Florence without the state."

ORIGINS OF THE MEDICI

The three lines. Three lines of Medici successively approached or acquired positions of power (see the Table). In the 14th century, the attempt ended in failure. In the 15th century, the Medici set up a hereditary principate in Florence but without legal right or title, hence subject to sudden overthrow; crowns burgeoned, however, on the last branches of their genealogical tree, for two of them were dukes outside Florence, their last heir in a direct line became queen of France, and their final offspring, a bastard, was duke of Florence. In the 16th century, a third line renounced republican notions, imposed its tyranny, and its members made themselves grand dukes.

The differences between these three collateral lines are

due essentially to circumstances, for there was, in all the Medici, an extraordinary persistence of hereditary traits. In the first place, not being soldiers, they were constantly confronting their adversaries with gold-bearing mules rather than with battalions of armed men. In addition, the early Medici resolutely courted favour with the middle and poorer classes in the city, and this determination to be *popolani* ("plebeian") endured a long time after them. Finally, all were consumed by a passion for arts and letters and for building. They were more than beneficent and ostentatious patrons of the arts; they were also enlightened and were probably the most magnificent such patrons that the West has ever seen.

The line of Chiarissimo II. The Medici were originally of Tuscan peasant origin, from the village of Cafaggiolo in the Mugello, the valley of the Sieve, north of Florence. Their descendants never forgot that they were of rustic stock, and this possibly accounts for their love of gardens that may correctly be included among their hereditary characteristics. Some of these villagers, in the 12th century perhaps, became aware of the new opportunities afforded by commerce and emigrated to Florence. There they settled near the Church of San Lorenzo, at that time still outside the walls of the city. The Medici would always remain faithful to their parish and even to the name of its patron saint. They were neither doctors nor apothecaries, in spite of the false stories later circulated at the French court when Catherine de Médicis married Henry II. The balls on their coat of arms, the famous *palle*, represent not pills but a Byzantine coin—the bezant—heraldic symbol of their true trade, money changing.

In 1201 the name of a Medici was mentioned for the first time in a notarial document, that of Chiarissimo, son of a certain Giambuono. By the following century, the Medici were counted among the wealthy notables, although in the second rank after leading families of the city. After 1340, an economic depression throughout Europe forced these more powerful houses into bankruptcy. The Medici, however, were able to escape this fate and even took advantage of it to establish themselves among the city's elite. But their policy of consolidating their position by controlling the government—the work of the grandsons of Chiarissimo II (himself the grandson of the first known Medici)—resulted in 50 years of serious misfortunes for the family (1343–93). Giovanni, one of the grandsons, persuaded the Florentines to seize Lucca, but the plan failed, and he paid for the debacle with his life. His cousin Salvestro took up his policy of alliance with the *popolo minuto* ("common people") and was elected gonfalonier, head of the *signoria*, the council of government, in 1378. Salvestro more or less willingly stirred up an insurrection of the *ciompi*, the artisans of the lowest class, and, after their victory, was not above reaping substantial monetary and titular advantages. But in 1381, when the popular government fell, he had to go into exile. His memory, however, was still alive in 1393, when the *popolo magro* ("lean people") once more thought it possible to take over the *signoria*. The mob hastened to seek out his first cousin, Vieri, who was, however, able to fade away without losing face. With Vieri this branch of the Medici was to disappear definitively from history.

THE LINE OF COSIMO THE ELDER, THE PRINCIPATE

The restoration of the Medici fortune was the work of Giovanni di Bicci, who was descended from Averardo, a brother of Chiarissimo II. Giovanni's father, Averardo III, had acquired the surname Bicci. Nothing is known about the first 40 years of Giovanni's life. His name first appears in 1401 on the list of those judging the open competition for the door of the Baptistery of San Giovanni, of which he was also a donor. He must certainly have lived dangerously, for the Medici name did not ring favourably in the ears of the Albizzi-Capponi-Uzzano oligarchy that had ruled Florence since 1381; and he had done nothing to re-establish himself in their good graces, for he had remained a *popolano*. To them he was at once dangerous and elusive, for experience had taught him to act with the utmost prudence. The oligarchs thought they

Giovanni di Bicci

must overthrow him before he was elected gonfalonier in 1421, but Niccolò da Uzzano made them realize that it was already too late: his popularity and his wealth, reinforcing each other, elicited respect. His bank had realized enormous profits from its management of the Council of Constance's finances. And although so much wealth risked arousing the envy of a fiercely egalitarian proletariat, Giovanni was protected from it by his simple life-style, his inexhaustible largesse, his support of an income tax plan (the *catasto*, based on landed property), and finally, his patronage. He had recognized the genius of Filippo Brunelleschi and provided him with the means to employ it by building the Ospedale degli Innocenti and reconstructing the church of San Lorenzo. Giovanni's portrait, the first of a Medici still extant, shows a small and somewhat stoutish man whose restrained smile masks an ill-concealed anxiety. He died on February 28, 1429, warning his two sons to "take no more from the state than man and law allow, if you wish to live in safety." One of these sons, Cosimo the Elder, was destined to establish an uncrowned monarchy in Florence, while the younger son, Lorenzo, would much later become the ancestor of the grand-ducal dynasty. Thus, Giovanni must be considered the real founder of the family.

Cosimo the Elder. Cosimo, born in 1389, resembled his father very little in physical appearance. He was tall and lean, with a hooked nose and a wide mouth in an emaciated face. But here the differences between them ended. The son possessed his father's prudence, patience, and talent for sharp speculation and was to achieve even greater success than he. Cosimo had been initiated into affairs of high finance in the corridors of the Council of Constance, where he represented the Medici bank. He went on from there to manage the papacy's finances and in 1462 filled his coffers to overflowing by obtaining from Pius II the Tolfa alum mines monopoly, alum being indispensable to Florence's famed textile industry. He was certainly the wealthiest man of his time, not only in terms of bullion but also in the amount of bank and promissory notes payable to his bank in Florence and to its branches operating in all the important financial markets of Europe. Such great power alone would have been sufficient to set the oligarchy against him; his "popular" policies rendered him completely intolerable. The death of Niccolò da Uzzano in 1431 left the Albizzi, one of the other leading families, free to attempt a coup. Cosimo was vacationing in Cafaggiolo when he received a summons to reply to his indictment for the capital crime "of having sought to elevate himself higher than others." He could have taken refuge in Bologna, but instead he chose to let himself be incarcerated in a small dungeon in the Palazzo Vecchio. Although the Medici may have been somewhat lacking in valour, they often evinced a calm audacity. The Albizzi soon discovered that so wealthy a man could not be assassinated so easily. The jailer was bribed to taste Cosimo's food beforehand, and the gonfalonier, assuaged by the famous gold-bearing mules, arranged to have the usual death sentence reduced to banishment. Cosimo retired to Padua (Padova) and Venice, where he was received like a sovereign. Exactly one year later, a sudden and unexpected move by the Medici, in which they doctored elections, gave them back the *signoria*. Cosimo triumphantly re-entered the city; and his enemies went into exile, never to return. The Medici principate had begun (1434).

Cosimo traditionally has been accused of destroying Florentine liberties; but these ancient liberties, more of an illusion than a reality, had already ceased to exist in the Florence of the Albizzi. Cosimo only had to perpetuate the formula of those he was evicting, in other words, to maintain the appearance of a constitutional régime. But, in order not to be taken by surprise like the Albizzi, he perfected the system. He made no changes in the law's actual administration, but in the spirit of the law he changed everything. Previously, it was the rule to fill high official positions by drawing lots. The process was now manipulated so that only the names of men who could be depended upon were drawn. The independent mood of

Cosimo's wealth

Political manipulation

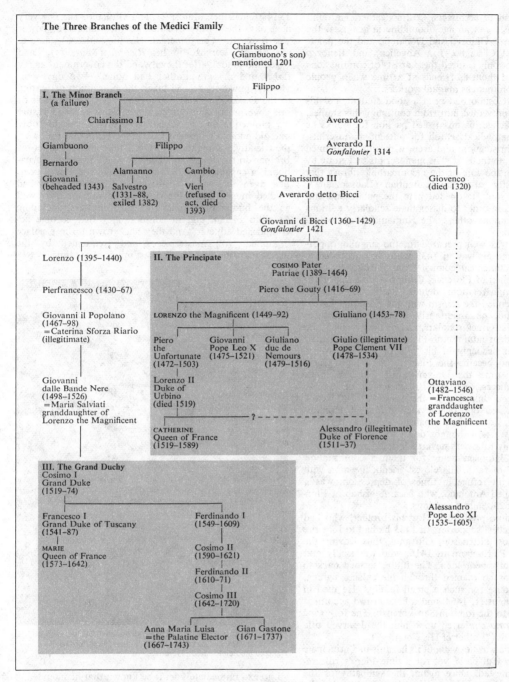

The Three Branches of the Medici Family

Chiarissimo I
(Giambuono's son)
mentioned 1201

Filippo

I. The Minor Branch
(a failure)

Chiarissimo II

Averardo

Giambuono   Filippo

Bernardo   Averardo II
                                            Gonfalonier 1314

Giovanni   Alamanno   Cambio
(beheaded 1343)   Chiarissimo III   Giovenco
                  Salvestro   Vieri   (died 1320)
                  (1331–88,   (refused to   Averardo detto Bicci
                  exiled 1382) act, died
                               1393)
                                            Giovanni di Bicci (1360–1429)
                                            Gonfalonier 1421

Lorenzo (1395–1440)   **II. The Principate**
                                            COSIMO Pater
                                            Patriae (1389–1464)

Pierfrancesco (1430–67)   Piero the Gouty (1416–69)

Giovanni il Popolano   LORENZO the Magnificent (1449–92)   Giuliano (1453–78)
(1467–98)
=Caterina Sforza Riario
(illegitimate)   Piero   Giovanni   Giuliano   Giulio (illegitimate)
                       the   Pope Leo X duc de   Pope Clement VII
                       Unfortunate (1475–1521) Nemours   (1478–1534)
                       (1472–1503)   (1479–1516)
Giovanni
dalle Bande Nere   Lorenzo II   Ottaviano
(1498–1526)   Duke of   (1482–1546)
=Maria Salviati   Urbino   =Francesca
granddaughter of   (died 1519)   ?   granddaughter
Lorenzo the Magnificent   - - - - - -   of Lorenzo
                       CATHERINE   Alessandro (illegitimate) the Magnificent
                       Queen of France   Duke of Florence
                       (1519–1589)   (1511–37)

III. The Grand Duchy
Cosimo I
Grand Duke
(1519–74)
                                                            Alessandro
                                                            Pope Leo XI
Francesco I   Ferdinando I   (1535–1605)
Grand Duke of Tuscany (1549–1609)
(1541–87)
MARIE   Cosimo II
Queen of France   (1590–1621)
(1573–1642)
                      Ferdinando II
                      (1610–71)

                      Cosimo III
                      (1642–1720)

Anna Maria Luisa   Gian Gastone
=the Palatine Elector (1671–1737)
(1667–1743)

the two municipal assemblies was neutralized by making the exceptional procedure of the Balìa—the committee of magistrates—the rule: it now granted dictatorial powers for a fixed term that was always renewed. The people, Cosimo believed, would not soon forget the flood of assistance, free distributions, and benefices dispensed by a man "who reckoned only in order to give away." Cosimo had unquestionably won the hearts of his countrymen, but he realized that his machinations were barely tolerated. He understood that a return to power of the *fuorusciti* ("exiles") continued to constitute a threat. In his own words, a state could not be kept under control with paternosters: a sword was necessary. The sword he managed to obtain was that of Francesco Sforza, duke of Milan, whom he won over in 1450 by tirelessly refurbishing the chronically depleted ducal finances. This alliance permitted him to crush the rising opposition by a coup d'état in August 1458 and to create a Senate composed of 100 loyal supporters (the Cento, or Hundred); thus he was able to live out the last six years of his life in security. "Although Cosimo is practically the lord of the city," wrote Pope Pius II, "he conducts himself so that he appears to be a private citizen, preferring actions to appear-

ances." Such was this strange principate that had no equivalent in Europe at that time and can only vaguely be compared with the "dictatorship of influence" enjoyed by Pericles.

Cosimo required undivided power in order to carry out his plans as well as to satisfy his passions, above all, his passion for building. "Fifty years will scarcely pass," he would say, "before we are chased out, but the buildings will remain." He continued to rely on Brunelleschi and discerned the genius of Michelozzo. Brunelleschi completed the "marble hat" of his famous cupola by a happy coincidence, at the time of Cosimo's return in 1434; in addition, he almost completed the work on San Lorenzo and on the Sagresta Vecchia and began work on the strange rotunda of Santa Maria degli Agnoli. He drew up plans for a princely palace for Cosimo; but the latter preferred the less lofty plans of Michelozzo, although Michelozzo's Medici Palace (the modern Palazzo Medici-Riccardi) was only slightly less grandiose and provided the first break with the family's traditional stance of humility. Under the patronage of Cosimo, Michelozzo also built the convent of San Marco, the Medici Chapel at Santa Croce, and a chapel at San Min-

Patron of the arts

iato. In addition to architects, Cosimo gathered around him all the masters of an age abounding in geniuses: the sculptors Lorenzo Ghiberti and Donatello and the painters Andrea del Castagno, Fra Angelico, and Benozzo Gozzoli. He not only assured these artists of commissions but also treated them as friends at a time when people still looked upon them as manual workers.

In his youth Cosimo had been a good student, but his active life had prevented him from continuing his studies. In order to assuage his unsatisfied passion for books he organized a methodical search for ancient manuscripts, both within Christendom and even, with Sultan Mehmed II's permission, in the East. The manuscripts picked up by his agents form the core of the incomparable library that is rather unjustly called the Laurentian (Laurenziana), after his grandson. He opened it to the public and employed copyists in order to disseminate scholarly editions compiled by, among others, the Humanists Poggio and Marsilio Ficino.

In short, he was well prepared for the singular opportunity that came his way in 1439 when he succeeded in enticing the ecumenical council from Ferrara to Florence. The Council of Florence, Cosimo's most important success in foreign relations, deluded itself into believing it had finally ended the schism with the Eastern Church. As for Cosimo, he assiduously attended the lectures delivered by the Greek scholars, and at the age of 50 he became an ardent admirer of Plato. He then re-created Plato's ancient academy in his villa of Careggi, where Marsilio Ficino became the Platonic cult's high priest. At the same time the University of Florence, with conspicuous success, resumed the teaching of Greek, which had been unknown in the West for 700 years. Thus Cosimo was one of the mainsprings of Humanism and of a form of rationalistic thinking that has distinguished Western thought down to the present age. Cosimo and his followers nevertheless did not renounce Christianity, Platonism being for them a confirmation and a renewal of faith. His closest friend, the man with whom he sought refuge in times of depression, was a Dominican called Antonino, who became bishop of Florence and, in 1523, Saint Antoninus.

Piero the Gouty　In 1440 Cosimo prematurely lost his brother, who had been his staunchest supporter. In 1463 he had to face the loss of his most gifted son, Giovanni, thus leaving the succession to Piero, born in 1416, who was sickly and almost constantly bedridden. The future seemed dark to the old man as he roamed through his palace, sighing, "Too big a house for such a small family." He died in Careggi on August 1, 1464, and a huge crowd accompanied his body to the tomb in San Lorenzo. The following year, the *signoria* conferred upon him the deserved title of Pater Patriae ("Father of His Country").

The succession was not without its hazards in a principate lacking any lawful basis, yet for a time Piero's rule remained uncontested. Once again, the sympathy of the little people for a *popolano* played its role. Most of the notables, the *ottimati*, were favourable, and the support of Milanese arms caused the malcontents to hesitate before launching a coup. Piero did not lack opponents, for, badly advised, he provoked a panic by calling in credits granted in profusion by his father, which the beneficiaries had regarded as gifts. On the other hand, his gout forced him to live the life of a recluse and gave his enemies a free hand. Luca Pitti, formerly a bulwark of the regime, organized the opposition that had been encouraged by the death of Duke Francesco Sforza of Milan in 1466. But Piero, supported by the new duke of Milan, Galeazzo Maria, took the offensive by convoking a Balia that re-established and strengthened his authority. In the five years of his rule, he mainly assured the transmission of power from one great Medici, his father, to one even greater, his son. He was not unworthy of either of them. He acted as patron of the Platonic Academy and provided work for such great artists as Donatello, Antonio and Piero Pollaiuolo, Andrea del Verrocchio, and Sandro Botticelli.

Lorenzo the Magnificent.　Piero died on December 2, 1469, leaving two young sons, Lorenzo, born on January 1, 1449, and then almost 21, and Giuliano, 16. The very next day, the thorny question of the transfer of power was resolved. "The *principati* (leading citizens) came to me," wrote Lorenzo in his *Ricordi* (Memoirs), "and urged me to look after the city and the government as my father and my grandfather had done." Two days previously, however, he had taken the precaution of writing to the Duke of Milan: "You have been the bulwark of our government and our greatness. May you now assure my protection and preservation." Lorenzo was the only one old enough to govern, but, in the years that followed, the friendly and lighthearted Giuliano continued to let his brother do the governing. Their mother, Lucrezia Tornabuoni, a capable woman with a certain talent as a poet, had given her sons a well-balanced education. They had studied music, under the organist Squarcialupi, as well as the humanities, under the best masters, including Marsilio Ficino, and in addition they had become accomplished athletes. And they had grown up in a palace crammed with masterpieces and frequented by the greatest artists as well as the best minds of the time.

Brogi—Alinari

Lorenzo the Magnificent, detail from the fresco "The Procession of the Magi" by B. Gozzoli (1420–97). In the chapel of the Palazzo Medici-Riccardi, Florence.

Lorenzo immediately let it be known that he intended to follow his father's and grandfather's example and "use constitutional methods as much as possible." In saying this, he was, however, keeping up appearances. In 1471 the popular assemblies lost their financial powers, and the Cento, which had demonstrated independence, was severely purged. The Milanese ambassador was able to reassure his master, who had taken Lorenzo's constitutional intentions literally: "Lorenzo will always have the *signoria* he wants." According to the historian Francesco Guicciardini's apt definition, Lorenzo's regime was "that of a benevolent tyrant in a constitutional republic." It was, moreover, a tyranny tempered by the festivals that Florentines always loved passionately: carnivals, balls, tournaments, weddings, and princely receptions. During these golden days in the early years of the "reign," it seemed that "youth was permanently in the prow and pleasure at the helm." The Pazzi Conspiracy in 1478 came as a rude shock to a carefree city.

The Pazzi bank, in the course of a treacherous war in which the adversaries did not scruple to use the most disgraceful methods, had taken the business affairs of the papacy away from the Medici. Sixtus IV, his nephew Riario, and Francesco Salviati, the archbishop of Pisa,

The Pazzi Conspiracy

supported the Pazzi and in the end formed one of the most lamentable conspiracies in modern history with them. They decided to assassinate Lorenzo and Giuliano in the cathedral during Easter mass on April 26, while the Archbishop was to take over the *signoria*. They were counting on Florence to rise up at the old cry of *popolo e libertà* ("people and liberty"). Giuliano was indeed killed in front of the altar, but Lorenzo succeeded in taking refuge in a sacristy. The Archbishop clumsily accosted the Medici gonfalonier, a harsh and suspicious man who immediately had him hanged from a window of the Palazzo Vecchio wearing his episcopal robes. The crowd stood by the Medici, seized the conspirators, and tore them limb from limb. Sixtus IV, forgetting the murder in the cathedral—in which two priests had taken part— refused to consider anything else than the hanging of a prelate and threatened Florence with interdiction unless it handed over Lorenzo to him. The city and its clergy rejected the proposal. The situation was all the more critical because Ferdinand I, king of Naples, was supporting the papacy. Florence's ruler could count on nothing more than very limited aid from Milan and the encouragement of the King of France. Lorenzo thereupon went, alone, to Naples. In his situation it required unusual audacity to present himself before one of the cruelest rulers of the century. But Lorenzo's boldness was crowned with success. Ferdinand, disconcerted, perhaps intimidated, yielded and concluded a peace; and Sixtus IV, now isolated, could only comply with it.

Lorenzo the Wise

Lorenzo emerged from the conflict with greatly increased prestige. From then on he was considered the Wise, "the needle on the Italian scales." He did not take advantage of his position by imitating the Sforza and making himself a duke. He contented himself with creating a Council of Seventy that he hoped would be even more manageable than the Cento. This amazed Europe, for he had all the attributes of a true sovereign. Louis XI of France called him "his noble cousin" and sought his advice, and the timorous humility of his forebears had given way to an assurance and ostentation worthy of a king. His new villa, at Poggio a Caiano, had all the majesty of a royal residence, as the emperor Charles V noted half a century later.

Thus, step by step, the Medici were approaching the status they continued to refuse. Earlier, Louis XI had authorized Piero the Gouty to unite their coats of arms by decorating one of his *palle* with three fleurs-de-lis; and Lorenzo had married an Orsini, of the high Roman nobility. His daughter Maddalena was married to a son of Pope Innocent VIII (born before his father's entry into religious orders), and his eldest son Piero married another Orsini. When his son Giovanni was 13, Lorenzo obtained a cardinal's hat for him from Innocent VIII, that, in the words of Machiavelli, "was the ladder upon which the Medici climbed to heaven." To be sure, Lorenzo remained a simple citizen, and yet he was called "the Magnificent." In Italy during this period, this was a title of commonplace obsequiousness used in addressing the great; but it was Lorenzo who raised it to its current high stature.

There was, however, one difference between Lorenzo and titled kings, who are able to live in pomp and ceremony even when their treasury is empty. Lorenzo could not do so, and the stream of florins that fed his munificence was becoming less abundant. This was partially his own fault for, with the Medici, the aptitude for business diminished as the thirst for power increased. In addition, economic conditions were deteriorating. New competitors were appearing in Europe and the branches in London, Bruges, and Lyons became insolvent. But the recurrent accusation that the Medici bank was kept solvent at the expense of the public treasury is not borne out by the facts. The movement of funds between the Medici bank and the treasury of the *signoria* was the equivalent of that occurring between private and public banks in modern states. The family's patronage of artists, architects, and writers also imposed a considerable burden upon its resources. When Lorenzo the Magnificent made an accounting of these expenses going back as far as 1434, the date of Cosimo's re-entry into the city, he found the total expenditure "unbelievable" and added,

Many deem that it would have been preferable to keep part of the funds in the treasury; I think that our patronage was the great splendor of our regime and, in my opinion, the money was well spent.

Posterity has agreed with him. He himself contributed more than anyone to the flowering of Florentine genius during the second half of the 15th century. As a Venetian writer felicitously put it, "Literature owes much to the Florentines, but among these, most of all to the Medici, and among these, most of all to Lorenzo."

He continued collecting ancient texts, and in his villas in Careggi, Fiesole, and Poggio a Caiano he assembled what is called the Platonic Academy but was more like a circle of good friends: his teacher Marsilio Ficino, the Humanist Pico della Mirandola, and the man who was always closest to his heart, Politian (Angelo Poliziano), the poet, who had saved his life on the day of the Pazzi Conspiracy. Lorenzo's reputation did not rest on lavish hospitality alone. He was also respected as a poet of great talent. His preference for the Tuscan dialect over Latin was remarkable for this time. Equally rare was his custom of treating artists with "the affectionate and warmhearted familiarity that allows a protégé to stand erect at the side of his protector, as man to man." The artists under his protection included Giuliano da Sangallo, Botticelli, Verrocchio, and Verrocchio's pupil Leonardo da Vinci. Toward the end of his life, Lorenzo opened a school of sculpture in his garden of San Marco. There a 15-year-old pupil attracted his attention and was brought up in the palace like a son of the family; it was Michelangelo.

Savonarola and Lorenzo

On the recommendation of Pico della Mirandola, Lorenzo permitted the Dominican monk Girolamo Savonarola to preach at San Marco in 1490. He mounted the pulpit on August 1 and henceforth launched an unceasing deluge of denunciations of the Medici, the papacy, and the whole of Christianity. The Florentines, who had grown weary of festivities, listened feverishly to his appeals for asceticism and to his terrifying prophecies, among which was the imminent death of the "tyrant." But it was easy for him to be thus prophetic, for Lorenzo's health had been declining for three years, and the secret had not been well kept. His condition grew rapidly worse. Suffering from "intolerable stomach pains," he awaited death at Careggi, spending his last days chatting with his friends, or reading Virgil, Homer, or Plato with them. On his deathbed, he sent for Savonarola who, according to a doubtful tradition, called upon him to "give Florence back her freedom," and in the face of the dying man's silence, refused to grant him absolution. Lorenzo's obsequies were simple, as he had requested; but the presence of the entire population of Florence, sincerely moved by his premature death (April 9, 1492)—he was 43—took on the character of a plebiscite. He was buried in San Lorenzo, where the grandiose tomb that his son Giovanni, who later became Pope Leo X, had planned was never executed. His tombstone passes almost unnoticed at the side of the monuments erected by Michelangelo to Giuliano, one of his sons, and to his grandson Lorenzo, both very insignificant persons.

Lorenzo the Magnificent died at the very moment when a new historical era was beginning. Six months later Christopher Columbus was to reach the New World. And two years later the foolish Italian expedition of the French king Charles VIII was to plunge the peninsula into a half century of suffering from which it could only have been saved, according to Machiavelli, by Lorenzo. The opinion of such an astute observer, more than a handsome eulogy, merits the historian's most serious attention.

TWO EXILES—TWO RETURNS (1494–1530)

Piero the Unfortunate. Like his father, Piero, born in February 1471, came to power too young—at the age of 21. Nevertheless, the succession took place without difficulty, and the régime appeared to have a firm foundation. The King of Naples thought that the time had come to make the offer of a baron's crown, but Piero refused it, preferring, like his forebears, no title other than that of "simple private citizen." He had been endowed with beautiful features, notoriously denied to Lorenzo the Magnificent; and he could turn a pretty verse. And when forced by circumstance, he showed himself a good soldier, a new trait in the family. But unfortunately, he was painfully lacking in political sense; and if he has gone down in history with the surname of "the Unfortunate," it is above all because of his errors of judgment. Threatened domestically by Savonarola's denunciations and by the intrigues of the younger branch of the Medici family and abroad by the imminence of a French invasion of Italy, he made the foolish and dangerous decision of abandoning the old French alliance in favour of one with Naples. Suddenly realizing the danger when the "barbarians" from beyond the Alps poured into Tuscany under Charles VIII, Piero thought he could save the day by imitating his father and hastened to meet the invader. The disastrous agreement—the only one possible under the circumstances—that he obtained from Charles aroused a wave of indignation in Florence. A revolt broke out, and Piero was forced to flee while the populace sacked the Medici Palace; only at the risk of his life did the cardinal Giovanni succeed in saving the most precious manuscripts. Piero henceforth led the restless life of a *fuoruscito*. He never again saw Florence and was drowned in the shipwreck of an armed galley in 1503.

Giovanni (Leo X) and the problem of the succession. After having plunged with splenetic joy into the mortifications of the flesh decreed by Savonarola's theocracy, mercurial Florence burned its prophet in 1498. But it did not recall the Medici. Furthermore, Donatello's "Judith and Holofernes" had been removed from the Medici Palace and placed in front of the *signoria* "as a salutary example to tyrants"; and in 1504, for the same purpose, Michelangelo's "David" was placed at its side. Yet in 1512, when the Spanish troops, allied with the papacy, entered Florence, bringing Giovanni Cardinal de' Medici with them, he was received enthusiastically. When Giovanni was elected pope—as Leo X—the following year, he had to content himself with keeping a watchful eye from Rome on his nephew Lorenzo, the son of Piero the Unfortunate, to whom he had left the government of the city (it was to him that Machiavelli dedicated *The Prince*). Faithful to the Medici tradition, Leo X did not grant Lorenzo a princely title in Florence but preferred to seize the duchy of Urbino and give it to his nephew, who, however, was unable to maintain himself there. Lorenzo climbed one more rung of the nobility ladder when, in 1518, he married Madeleine de La Tour d'Auvergne, a relative of the Bourbons. Two years earlier, at the French court, his uncle Giuliano had charmed Francis I with his elegant manners and had married the sovereign's young aunt, receiving the duchy of Nemours as a dowry.

Apogee of the Medici age These few years are often considered to be the apogee of the Medici age. The period has even been called "the century of Leo X." From 1513 to 1521, surrounded by five nephews and cousins whom he had named cardinals, Leo X reigned less over Christianity than over arts and letters in the style of his father, the Magnificent, too occupied with patronage to pay sufficient attention to an unimportant monk by the name of Martin Luther.

Just when the future of the dynasty seemed assured, death struck two irreparable blows. Giuliano, duc de Nemours, died in 1516, one year after his marriage, and Lorenzo, duke of Urbino, died a year after his marriage as well (and only a few days after the birth of his daughter Catherine), the last scion of Cosimo the Elder's line. The succession was now in question, for it seemed more than improbable that a woman would ever be admitted to the principate. But apart from Catherine, only bastards remained: Giulio, posthumous son of Giuliano, the brother of Lorenzo the Magnificent, who had been assassinated in the cathedral; Ippolito, son of the Duc de Nemours; and Alessandro, a mulatto whom the Medici tried to pass off as the son of the Duke of Urbino but who was very probably Giulio's son by a Nubian slave

girl. It is said that illegitimacy did not constitute a major obstacle at this time. In fact, the French statesman and historian Philippe de Commynes noted that "in Italy they do not make a great distinction between bastards and legitimate children." There were, however, certain reservations. First of all, the church refused ecclesiastical honours to bastards. This is why Leo X had hastened to declare his cousin Giulio born of a secret marriage before appointing him cardinal. And then, for purposes of nobiliary succession, in Italy as elsewhere, the illegitimate branch did not count. When the cardinal Giulio installed Ippolito and Alessandro in the Medici Palace, their aunt Strozzi protested loudly that the family home was not a "stable for he-mules" (bastards). Even so, the two adolescents were the nominal rulers of Florence, at first under the guardianship of the cardinal Giulio, who showed a marked preference for Alessandro, and later under that of Silvio, Cardinal Passerini, when the cardinal Giulio donned the tiara under the name of Clement VII in 1523.

Florence, usually turbulent and ungovernable, seemed to be mired in resignation when the news arrived in 1527 of Rome's sacking by imperial bands and of Clement's undignified flight. A republican uprising immediately expelled the unpopular Cardinal Passerini and his two wards. For the second time in 33 years the Medici lost control of Florence. But not for long. The emperor Charles V came to terms with Clement VII and sent an army to besiege Florence, which capitulated in August 1530. The Emperor and Clement VII then decided to destroy the Florentine hornet's nest of republican insurgents. Alessandro was given the ducal crown that his ancestors had so long refused. On May 1, 1532, the 1,572nd and last gonfalonier surrendered his powers to him.

Clement thus kept Ippolito from the succession but in compensation made the unwilling Ippolito a cardinal. He then turned his attention to the legitimate heir, Catherine. In order to balance the imperial influence, he married Catherine to the Duc d'Orléans, second son of the King of France, who in 1547 after the unexpected death of the Dauphin, became king of France as Henry II. Duke Alessandro

As for Alessandro, unlettered, perverse, and debauched, he reigned by terror over a city that resigned itself to its fate. Upon the death of Clement VII in 1534, a shade of opposition emerged around Ippolito, who died by poisoning shortly thereafter. All indications were that the new duke would perpetuate his dynasty when he married Margaret of Austria, the illegitimate daughter of Charles V. Then the younger branch of the Medici intervened.

THE GRAND DUKES

Descending from Lorenzo the Elder, the son of Giovanni di Bicci and brother of Cosimo Pater Patriae (see Table), this branch had taken an active part in Medici affairs but had played no political role. In the third generation, however, the brothers Lorenzo and Giovanni appealed for popular support, took the name of Popolano, and contributed to the downfall of Piero the Unfortunate. Their grandsons were to complete the ruin of the family's older branch. Lorenzo's grandson, a puny fellow called Lorenzino, should by all rights have received the succession when the older branch was reduced to a girl and a few bastards. But ousted by Clement VII, he kept his silence and even misled people regarding his intentions by joining Alessandro in his dissolute life. But in January 1537 he suddenly ambushed Alessandro and killed him in hand-to-hand combat. He then fled without asserting his rights. This enigmatic Medici, the author of the *Aridosio*, a play displaying much talent, was later to attract the attention of the Romantics and in fact become the model for the tragedy *Lorenzaccio* by the French poet Alfred de Musset. Cosimo, a grandson of Giovanni, then took up matters where his cousin had left them. Cosimo's father had been Giovanni dalle Bande Nere (John of the Black Bands), the single great military leader among all the Medici; and his mother was a granddaughter of Lorenzo the Magnificent. Thus the blood of the two lines was united in him. As soon as The Popolano he heard of Alessandro's assassination, he rushed off to Florence. This young man, born on June 12, 1519, was regarded as relatively inoffensive and was warmly welcomed. The notables handed the government over to him after having proclaimed the deposition of Lorenzino; and Charles V even named him duke and his son-in-law's successor. Some *fuorusciti* were dispersed or captured as soon as they set foot in Tuscany in July 1537.

Cosimo I. It did not take long to determine what sort of master Florence had acquired. Prisoners were mercilessly executed, and the opponents of the régime were secretly liquidated throughout his reign. The historian Francesco Guicciardini, who let his disillusionment show too clearly, died of poisoning, according to general opinion; and Lorenzino, pursued from Paris to Constantinople and overtaken in Venice was assassinated there in 1548. On the other hand, Cosimo created the Order of Santo Stefano for the loyal nobility and took care to assure his subjects of equitable justice. The European wars were now bypassing Tuscany, except for Siena, which had to surrender to the imperial forces in 1555 after a memorable siege. Cosimo, allied with the emperor Charles V, annexed Florence's ancient rival. He himself had not been present at the siege, for this son of a courageous captain was singularly lacking in bravery. Immediately after the surrender, however, he hastened to the city and saved the survivors from the customary atrocities.

In 1539 Cosimo had married Eleonora de Toledo, the daughter of the Spanish viceroy of Naples, by whom he had eight children. In 1562 Eleonora and two of their young sons died within a few days of each other. Subsequently, it was claimed that one of the boys had assassinated his brother, that Cosimo had killed the assassin on the spot, and that their mother had died of grief. The true cause of these deaths was malaria; and these rumours merely belong to the tradition of "Medicean tragedies" that holds that "never was there a race more iniquitous." An examination of the archives and of the tombs, in which the bodies repose in an excellent state of preservation, refutes these tales. Cosimo did not poison his daughter Maria, and it is doubtful that he had incestuous relations with another daughter, Isabella. Neither was his daughter Lucrezia poisoned by her husband, Alfonso of Ferrara.

Sovereign ruler of a unified Tuscany, Cosimo believed that he should be crowned king; but neither the emperor Charles V nor Ferdinand I after him encouraged him in these ambitions. So he turned toward the papacy. In 1559 a Medici from Milan, elected pope as Pius IV, appropriated the Medici coat of arms, even though he was not related to the family. Cosimo did not protest, and Pius IV, pleased with what he considered his adoption into the family, offered to make him a grand duke. But the offer seemed untimely and was reluctantly refused. A new occasion presented itself under Pius V. Cosimo handed over to him Pietro Carnesecchi, a suspected Lutheran who had taken refuge at his court. In return, Pius V proclaimed Cosimo "grand duke of the province of Tuscany" in August 1569 and crowned him at Saint Peter's the following February. But this constituted a usurpation of the rights of the Emperor who, followed by Spain, refused to recognize the pontifical action.

Cosimo amazed Europe by displaying the old Medici traits, particularly those of the shrewd and mercenary banker, insatiable for big profits. In his administration of Tuscany he showed that he was energetic and concerned with exactitude and economy in his accounts; and his passion for efficiency inspired him with the idea, extremely advanced for the times, of uniting all public services into a single building, the Uffizi (or offices), which was built for him according to Giorgio Vasari's grandiose yet practical design. In order to satisfy his taste or, better said, his Medici passion for buildings, he made Vasari his superintendent of buildings and had him redecorate the interior of the Palazzo Vecchio. He then adopted as his residence the Pitti Palace, which Eleonora had purchased unfinished in 1549. Here he entrusted the extensive work of enlargement to the architect and sculptor Bartolommeo Ammannati. In 1564 Cosimo and Vasari boldly

built the gallery that permits convenient passage from one palace to the other by utilizing the Ponte Vecchio. Behind the Pitti Palace, the vast expanses of the hill of Boboli enabled Cosimo to indulge still another of his hereditary passions in designing, with Tribolo's help, the plan of the famous gardens.

Yet in his patronage of the arts, Cosimo was increasingly frustrated, for the great period of the *officina*, the workshop of Florentine masterpieces, was drawing to its close. Michelangelo could no longer be induced to stay on. In 1534 he departed for Rome, leaving the Sagrestia Nuova tombs and the Laurentian Library unfinished. But Cosimo had the artist's body brought back in 1564 and buried it himself with great pomp at Santa Croce. On the other hand, he kept Jacopo Pontormo and Bronzino, the official court portraitists, and Ammannati, who was also an engineer and who had rebuilt the bridge of Santa Trinità after the disastrous flood of 1557 according to a design that must be considered a stroke of genius. Cosimo, an archaeologist by temperament, was a true forerunner in this field. He opened up excavations on Etruscan sites from which such world-renowned pieces as the "Orator" and the "Chimera" were taken. Finally, he established the Florentine Academy, which engaged in serious linguistic studies.

According to his portraits, Cosimo was of athletic build, with harsh features lit by the dark velvety eyes of the Medici. He had aged prematurely and in 1571 handed over effective power to his eldest son, Francesco, born on March 25, 1541. He retired to the villa of Castello, where his childhood had been spent and where he died on April 21, 1574. Though a ruthless despot, he must be considered one of the great Medici.

Francesco I. Francesco's regency ended with his father's death. Like Cosimo, Francesco was a crafty and brutal tyrant to those opposing him. But Tuscany was well governed; it remained out of the wars that were dividing Europe and suffered mainly from the burden of taxes. Francesco married Joanna, archduchess of Austria, sister of Emperor Maximilian II, who consented in 1576 to officially proclaim his brother-in-law grand duke, at the same time raising Tuscany to the status of a grand duchy. Francesco I's work was along the lines of Medici tradition. He had Bernardo Buontalenti build the Tribuna of the Uffizi; he assembled the first collections of the celebrated gallery; and, at his new villa of Pratolino, he freely indulged his love of artistically designed gardens. In addition, his interest in philology prompted him to found the Accademia della Crusca and to entrust it with compiling a dictionary of the Tuscan language in its purest form. But—and this was a sign of the times—his real passion was of a scientific nature. He spent the greater part of his time in his chemical laboratory, where he was the first to make a porcelain somewhat similar to the Chinese model.

In spite of all his accomplishments, Francesco largely lives on in the romantic popular memory because of his love affair with Bianca Cappello. While he was still heir presumptive, he had taken this young patrician as his mistress—after she had been abandoned by the lover with whom she had fled from Venice. Nothing could ever deflect Francesco from this passion—neither the marriage with Joanna of Austria, nor the reproaches of his family and of the Emperor, nor public censure. When Joanna died, after giving him three children, he married Bianca and had her solemnly crowned in the Palazzo Vecchio. Their end was such as famous lovers wish for; they died within a few hours of each other in 1587. Perhaps consumption, but certainly malaria, caused their deaths. Popular imagination refused to believe this. It was said that Bianca had prepared a poisoned tart intended for her brother-in-law Ferdinando, that Francesco had eaten some of it by mistake, and that Bianca in desperation then ate some of it in order not to survive her lover and husband.

Ferdinando I. Ferdinando, born on July 30, 1549, succeeded his brother. A cardinal at 14, he had been living in Rome in the midst of his collections of antiques, among which was the "Venus de' Medici." In order to succeed

Annexation of Tuscany

Cosimo's support of the arts

Francesco's affair with Bianca Cappello

his brother Francesco, who had no children by Bianca and was survived only by a daughter, Maria, the child of Joanna of Austria, Ferdinando renounced the purple and perhaps even the tiara, for he had been spoken of as eligible for the papacy. He tried to rule as a just prince and came close to his ideal, for the conspiracies of the exiled Strozzi family became more rare. Certain of his acts, however, astonished his contemporaries: he had Alfonso Piccolomini, an old-fashioned *condottiero* who was ravaging Tuscany, hanged as a criminal but had his daughter brought up in an aristocratic convent; he also promulgated a constitution that welcomed to Leghorn (Livorno), a city founded by Cosimo I, all immigrants, with no distinction as to religion. His foreign policy leaned toward France. He married Christine of Lorraine, the granddaughter of Catherine de Médicis, and loans from his bank, as well as his influence in Rome, played no small part in Henry IV's accession to the French throne. Naturally enough, he married his niece Maria to the new king and made her the second Medici to become queen of France. Five years later, in 1605, Alessandro, a great-grandson of Lorenzo the Magnificent and a grandnephew of Leo X, became the third Medici to ascend the throne of Saint Peter. He took the title of Leo XI; he died, however, 27 days after his election. The Medici dynasty was thus keeping pace with the great royal houses of Europe. To place the tombs of past and future grand dukes under one roof, Ferdinando undertook to build the Cappella dei Principi from the designs of Don Giovanni, a natural son of Cosimo I. And on Belvedere Hill near the Pitti Palace, Buontalenti, the greatest architect of the day, built a fortress that was intended as a place of refuge but was never used. But Ferdinando's great desire to be a patron of the arts was thwarted by the impoverishment of the Florentine genius, which became increasingly evident. Giambologna, who executed the equestrian statues of Cosimo I and of Ferdinando, was Flemish.

Ferdinando died on February 7, 1609, after a prosperous reign of 22 years.

Cosimo II. Cosimo II, born on May 12, 1590, was 19 years old when he succeeded his father. Less than a year later, on January 7 and 13, 1610, Galileo discovered four satellites of Jupiter that he named the Medicea Sidera. Cosimo had been Galileo's pupil at Padova and had called him to his court as "first mathematician." He had just closed the family bank, feeling that after 400 years of such business the Medici had no further need to demean themselves. Tuscany still cut a rather mediocre figure in comparison to the great western monarchies, even though Cosimo's father had married into the French court. To keep on good terms with the imperial court at Vienna, Cosimo on his part married Emperor Ferdinand II's sister Maria Magdalena. The court at the Pitti Palace continued to be a brilliant one: the favourite portrait painter was the Fleming Sustermans. Although in his youth Cosimo had shown great promise, illness prevented him from fulfilling it. He died before he was 31, on February 28, 1621.

Later Medici rulers. Many of the Medici had come to power very young, but regencies had always been avoided. This time one was inevitable, for Cosimo's son Ferdinando, born on July 14, 1610, was only 10 years old when his father died. His grandmother Christine and his mother, Maria Magdalena, together squandered the treasures so wisely amassed by Cosimo. But they inculcated in their ward such complete submission to the Holy See that he let Urban VIII take over the duchy of Urbino to the detriment of his future wife, Vittoria della Rovere; and he also showed a distressing lack of initiative in the trial by the church of his father's friend Galileo. When Ferdinando married Vittoria della Rovere she brought him as a dowry, in place of the duchy of Urbino, her rich collections of paintings. His 49-year reign (1621–70) at least saw Leopoldo, Ferdinando's brother, act like a true Medici. It was he who founded the Accademia del Cimento, one of the first European scientific academies, who collected the *autoritratti* (self-portraits) of the great painters and assembled in the Pitti Palace and in the Uffizi many of the masterpieces that had been scattered

Ferdinando II

among the various Medici residences. He died on May 24, 1670.

Cosimo, Ferdinando's eldest son, was born on August 14, 1642. He reigned for 53 years (1670–1723), longer than any other Medici. Dull-witted and solitary, he limited his patronage to musicians. During Louis XIV's wars, he maintained a benevolent neutrality toward the empire and was rewarded with the title of Royal Highness in 1695. He had appeased the Bourbons by marrying Marguerite-Louise d'Orléans, a niece of Louis XIV. Unfortunately, she had been forced into this marriage and, being a gay, cultured, and worldly woman, felt repugnance toward her husband. Although long rebuked by the court at Versailles and even temporarily confined in the villa of Poggio a Caiano, she finally returned to France. As she had given the crown two sons and a daughter, there was no reason to foresee the extinction of the dynasty: but these children were all to be without posterity.

Cosimo III

Ferdinando, the eldest, married Violante of Bavaria. Charitable and a patron of the arts (he assembled a famous collection of musical instruments), he died before his father in 1713. Gian Gastone, the youngest, lived apart from the court, occupying himself with archaeology and natural history. Cosimo forced him to marry the widow of a count palatine, Anne of Saxe-Lauenburg, an eccentric woman who refused to leave her Reichstadt castle in Bohemia. Gian Gastone, losing his patience, returned alone to Florence. Cosimo then procured a ruling from the Florentine Senate that the succession would pass to his daughter Anna Maria Luisa. But the European powers rejected this stratagem and, over Cosimo's protests, in 1718 chose Don Carlos, the son of Isabella of Parma, queen of Spain, as heir presumptive of Tuscany. Then, in 1735, the choice fell on Francis, duke of Lorraine, who was to marry Maria Theresa of Austria, who became empress in 1740.

Born in May 1671, Gian Gastone was 52 at the time of his accession in 1723. A liberal intellectual, he loosened the hold of the clergy on Tuscany, but, disheartened by the impatience of those who were waiting for him to die, he quickly slipped into debauchery. Even so, he had the energy to insist that the Medici property be exempted from the escheat of the Grand Duchy. Following his death on July 9, 1737, Francis of Lorraine was installed in the Pitti Palace. In October, Gian Gastone's sister bequeathed the enormous mass of masterpieces accumulated by the Medici to the House of Lorraine, on condition that nothing be removed from it or transported outside of Tuscany. She died on February 18, 1743, and on her tomb in the Cappella dei Principi (Chapel of the Princes) was engraved *Ultima della stirpe reale dei Medici* ("Last of the royal Medici line").

Gian Gastone

BIBLIOGRAPHY. Among many historians and memorialists contemporary with the Medici, Niccolò Machiavelli, Francesco Guicciardini, and, to a lesser degree, Scipione Ammirato cannot be dispensed with. Modern works, for a general view, include G.F. YOUNG, *The Medici*, 2 vol. (1909, reprinted 1933; Italian trans., 1935; French trans., 1969), dated but still useful; ALBERT JOURCIN, *Les Médicis* (1968; German trans., 1969); GAETANO PIERACCINI, *La stirpe de' Medici di Cafaggiolo*, 2nd ed., 3 vol. (1947), extensive researches on the hereditary features and diseases that run in the Medici family; and MARCEL BRION, *Le Siècle des Médicis* (1969; Eng. trans., *The Medici: A Great Florentine Family*, 1969). More specialized monographs are CURT S. GUTKIND, *Cosimo de' Medici, Pater Patriae, 1389–1464* (1938); ALISON M. BROWN, "The Humanist Portrait of Cosimo de' Medici. . . ," *Journal of the Warburg and Courtauld Institutes*, 24:186–221 (1961); and ANDRE ROCHON, *La Jeunesse de Laurent de Médicis* (1963). On institutions and banking, NICOLAI RUBINSTEIN, *The Government of Florence Under the Medici, 1434 to 1494* (1966), based on a masterly examination of the Florentine archives, is fundamental; while RAYMOND DE ROOVER, *The Rise and Decline of the Medici Bank, 1397–1494* (1963), excellently clears up a difficult matter. The story of the dynasty of the grand dukes has been less thoroughly investigated. Nevertheless, three good titles cannot be omitted: LUIGI CARCERERI, *Cosimo I Granduca*, 3 vol. (1926–29); HAROLD ACTON, *The Last Medici*, rev. ed. (1958); G.E. SALTINI, *Tragedie medicee domestiche, 1577–87* (1898), a cool restatement of the traditional story of Medicean crimes and turpitude.

(A.Jn.)

Medicine, History of

The history of medicine and surgery is the account of man's efforts to deal with human illness and disease, from the primitive attempts of preliterate man to the present complex array of specialties and treatments.

An article on so vast a subject can trace only an outline of the rise and development of medical thought and practice from the earliest times. No rigid classification can be applied to the history of medicine, and the story cannot be unfolded as a steadily progressive series of events. It has had many developments and setbacks and is best understood as a simple narrative, rather than as a chapter of epochs. It is often stated that medicine, like so many other arts and sciences, had its origin in ancient Greece, but that is only a partial truth. There were many great men before the ancient Greeks, and, even before the tale could be written down, the healing art was taught and practiced.

This article is divided into the following sections:

Extensive supplementary material on the history of medicine and surgery appears in other articles, including those on the major subdivisions of medicine and surgery, the major concepts of illness and treatment, the chief therapeutic agents, and most of the persons mentioned in this article.

I. Medicine and surgery before 1800

PRIMITIVE AND PREHISTORIC MEDICINE

Unwritten history is not easy to interpret, and, although much may be learned from a study of the drawings, bony remains, and surgical tools of early man, it is difficult to reconstruct his mental attitude toward the problems of disease and death. It seems probable that man, as soon as he had reached the stage of reasoning, discovered, by the process of trial and error, which plants might be used as foods, which of them were poisonous, and which of them had some medicinal value. Folk medicine or domestic medicine, consisting largely in the use of vegetable products, or herbs, originated in this fashion and still persists.

But that is not the whole story. Man did not at first regard death and disease as natural phenomena. Common maladies, such as colds or constipation, he accepted as part of existence and dealt with by means of such herbal remedies as were available. Serious and disabling diseases, however, he placed in a very different category. These were of supernatural origin, the work of a malevolent demon or of an offended god who had either projected some object—a dart, a stone, a worm—into the body of the victim or had abstracted something, usually the soul of the patient. The treatment then applied was to lure the errant soul back to its proper habitat within the body or to extract the evil intruder, be it dart or demon, by suction, incantations, or other means. One curious method of providing the disease with means of escape from the body was by making a hole in the skull of the victim —*i.e.*, the practice of trepanning, or trephining. Trepanned skulls of prehistoric date have been found in Brit-

Belief in supernatural causes of illness

ain, France, and other parts of Europe and in Peru. The practice still exists among primitive people in parts of Algeria, in Melanesia, and perhaps elsewhere, though it is fast becoming extinct.

Magic and religion played a large part in the medicine of prehistoric or primitive man. Administration of the vegetable drug or remedy by mouth was accompanied by incantations, dancing, grimaces, and all the tricks of the magician. Thus, the first doctors, or "medicine men," were witch doctors or sorcerers. The use of charms and talismans, still prevalent in modern times, is of ancient origin. Apart from the treatment of wounds and broken bones, the folklore of medicine is probably the most ancient aspect of the art of healing, for primitive physicians showed their wisdom by treating the whole man, soul as well as body.

BABYLONIAN AND EGYPTIAN MEDICINE

The establishment of the calendar and the invention of writing marked the dawn of recorded history. The clues to early knowledge are scanty, consisting of clay tablets bearing cuneiform signs and seals that were used by Babylonian physicians about 3000 BC. In the Louvre, in Paris, there is preserved a stone pillar on which is inscribed the Code of Hammurabi, an early king of Babylon. This code includes laws relating to medical practice; the penalties for defaulters were severe. For example, "If the doctor, in opening an abscess, shall kill the patient, his hands shall be cut off"; if, however, the patient was a slave, the doctor was simply obliged to supply another slave. The Greek historian Herodotus in his *History* states that every Babylonian was an amateur physician, since it was the custom to lay the sick in the street so that anyone passing by might offer advice. Divination, from the inspection of the liver of a sacrificed animal, was widely practiced and applied to foretell the course of a disease. Little else is known regarding Babylonian medicine, and the name of not a single physician has survived.

It is only with the study of the medicine of ancient Egypt that the picture becomes clearer. The first physician to emerge was Imhotep, grand vizier to King Djoser (Zoser) of Egypt (2980–2900 BC), who designed one of the earliest pyramids, the Step Pyramid at Saqqārah, and who, as the Egyptian god of medicine, rivals the Greek god Asclepius, or Aesculapius, with whom he is sometimes confused. Knowledge becomes surer with the study of Egyptian papyri, especially the so-called Ebers and Edwin Smith papyri discovered in the 19th century. The former is a list of remedies, with appropriate spells or incantations, while the latter is a surgical treatise on the treatment of wounds and other injuries. One might imagine that the widespread practice of embalming the dead body would have stimulated the study of human anatomy, but that was not so.

Medicine of ancient Egypt

The search for information regarding ancient medicine leads naturally from the papyri of Egypt to Hebrew literature. Strangely enough, the Bible contains little on the subject of the medical practices of Old Testament times. It is, however, a mine of information on social and personal hygiene. The Jews were indeed pioneers in matters of public health.   (D.J.G.)

TRADITIONAL MEDICINE AND SURGERY IN THE ORIENT

India. Indian medicine is ancient. Its earliest concepts are set out in the sacred writings called the Vedas, especially in the metrical passages of the Atharvaveda, which may possibly date as far back as the 2nd millennium BC. According to a later writer, the system of medicine called Ayurveda was received by a certain Dhanvantari from Brahma, and Dhanvantari was deified as the god of medicine. In later times his status was gradually reduced, until he was credited with having been an earthly king who died of snakebite. Legend tells of Dhanvantari's relations with snakes and illustrates the skill with which early Indian practitioners treated snakebite.

The period of Vedic medicine lasted until about 800 BC. The Vedas are rich in magical practices for the treatment of diseases and in charms for the expulsion of the demons traditionally supposed to cause diseases. The chief conditions mentioned are fever (*takman*), cough, consumption, diarrhea, dropsy, abscesses, seizures, tumours, and skin diseases (including leprosy). The herbs recommended for treatment are numerous.

The golden age of Indian medicine, from 800 BC until about AD 1000, may be termed the Brahmanistic period. It is marked especially by production of the medical treatises known respectively as the *Caraka-saṃhitā* and *Suśruta-saṃhitā*, attributed, respectively, to the physician Caraka and Suśruta, traditionally a surgeon. Both these works were formerly regarded as being of great antiquity, and hence claims arose for the priority of Indian scientific medicine over its Greek counterpart. Another school asserted that these works were written many centuries after the beginning of the Christian Era. The most recent estimates place the *Caraka-saṃhitā* in its present form as dating from the 1st century AD, and there were earlier versions. The *Suśruta-saṃhitā* probably originated in the last centuries of the pre-Christian Era and became fixed in its present form in the 7th century AD at the latest. Other medical treatises of lesser importance are those attributed to Vagbhata (*c.* 8th century). All later treatises were based on these works.

Because the Hindus were prohibited by their religion from cutting the dead body, their knowledge of anatomy was limited. The *Suśruta-saṃhitā* recommends that a body be placed in a basket and sunk in a river for seven days. On its removal the parts could be easily separated without cutting. As a result of these crude methods, the emphasis in Hindu anatomy was given to the bones, and then to the muscles, ligaments, and joints. The nerves, blood vessels, and internal organs were very imperfectly known.

The Hindus believed that the body contains three elementary substances, microcosmic representatives of the three divine universal forces, which they called spirit (air), phlegm, and bile. These were comparable with the humours of the Greeks. Health depends on the normal balance of these three elementary substances. The spirit has its seat below the navel, the phlegm above the navel, and the bile between the heart and the navel. The seven primary constituents of the body—blood, flesh, fat, bone, marrow, chyle, and semen—are produced by the action of the elementary substances. Semen was supposed to be produced from all parts of the body and not from any individual part or organ.

Both Caraka and Suśruta state the existence of a large number of diseases (Suśruta says 1,120). Rough classifications of diseases are given. In all texts "fever," of which numerous types are described, is regarded as important. Phthisis (wasting disease, especially pulmonary tuberculosis) was apparently common, and the Hindu physicians knew the symptoms of cases likely to terminate fatally. Smallpox was common, and it is probable that smallpox inoculation was practiced.

In diagnosis the Hindu physicians used all five senses. Hearing was used to distinguish the nature of the breathing, alteration in voice, and the grinding sound produced by the rubbing together of broken ends of bones. They appear to have had a good clinical sense, and their sections on prognosis contain acute references to symptoms that are of grave import. Magical beliefs still persisted, however, until late in the classical period; the prognosis could be affected by such fortuitous factors as the cleanliness of the messenger sent to fetch the physician, the nature of his conveyance, or the types of persons whom the physician met on his journey to the patient.

Indian therapeutics was largely dietetic and medicinal. Dietetic treatment was important and preceded any medicinal treatment. Fats were much used, internally and externally. The most important methods of active treatment were referred to as the "five procedures": the administration of emetics, purgatives, water enemas, oil enemas, and sneezing powders. Inhalations were frequently employed, as were leeching, cupping, and bleeding.

The Indian materia medica was extensive and consisted mainly of vegetable drugs, all of which were from indigenous plants. Caraka knew 500 medicinal plants, and Suśruta knew 760. But animal remedies (such as the milk

of various animals, bones, gallstones) and minerals (sulfur, arsenic, lead, copper sulfate, gold) were also employed. The physicians collected and prepared their own vegetable drugs. Among those that eventually appeared in Western pharmacopoeias are cardamom and cinnamon.

As a result of the strict religious beliefs of the Hindus, hygienic measures were important in treatment. Two meals a day were prescribed, with indications of the nature of the diet, the amount of water to be drunk before and after the meal, and the use of condiments. Bathing and care of the skin were carefully prescribed, as were cleansing of the teeth with twigs from named trees, anointing of the body with oil, and use of eyewashes.

In surgery, ancient Hindu medicine reached its zenith. Detailed instructions about the choice of instruments and the different operations are given in the classical texts. It has been said that the Hindus knew all ancient operations except the arrest of hemorrhage by the ligature. Their operations were grouped broadly as follows: excision of tumours; incision of abscesses; punctures of collections of fluid in the abdomen; extraction of foreign bodies; pressing out of the contents of abscesses; probing of fistulas; and stitching of wounds.

The surgical instruments used by the Hindus have received special attention in modern times. According to Suśruta the surgeon should be equipped with 20 sharp and 101 blunt instruments. The sharp instruments included knives of various patterns, scissors, trocars (instruments for piercing tissues and draining fluid from them), saws, and needles. The blunt instruments included forceps, specula (instruments for inspecting body cavities or passages), tubes, levers, hooks, and probes. The *Suśruta-saṃhitā* does not mention the catheter, but it is referred to in later writings. The instruments were largely of steel. Alcohol seems to have been used as a narcotic during operations.

In two types of operations especially, the ancient Hindus were outstanding. Stone in the bladder (vesical calculus) was common in ancient India, and the surgeons frequently carried out the operation of lateral lithotomy for removal of the stones. They also introduced plastic surgery. Amputation of the nose was one of the prescribed punishments for adultery, and repair was carried out by cutting from the patient's cheek a piece of tissue of the required size and shape and applying it to the stump of the nose. The results appear to have been tolerably satisfactory, and the modern operation is certainly derived indirectly from this ancient source. The Hindu surgeons, also performed an operation for the cure of anal fistula, and in this they were definitely in advance of the Greeks.

In the past there has been much speculation as to whether the Greeks derived any of their medical knowledge from the Hindus. Mid-20th-century opinion held that there was certainly intercommunication between Greece and India before the time of Alexander the Great.

China. The Chinese system of medicine is of great antiquity and is independent of any recorded external influences. According to legend it commenced with Fu Hsi (*c.* 2953 BC) and was continued by the emperors Shen Nung (died 2698 BC) and Huang Ti (died 2598 BC). The latter, the Yellow Emperor, was always regarded as the author of the canon of internal medicine called the *Nei Ching,* but there is some evidence that in its present form it does not date from earlier than the 3rd century BC. Most of the Chinese medical literature is founded on the *Nei Ching,* and it is still regarded as a great authority. Other famous works are the *Mo Ching* (known in the West as the "Pulse Classic"), composed *c.* AD 300; and the *Golden Mirror,* a compilation, made about AD 1700, of medical writings of the Han dynasty (202 BC–AD 221). Chinese medicine continued to make substantial progress until about AD 170, and, until about AD 960, some progress was made; then, after a static period, it degenerated because progress was considered simply as the detailed elaboration of the ancient themes. European medicine began to obtain a footing in China early in the 19th century, but the native system is still widely practiced.

Basic to traditional Chinese medicine is the dualistic cosmic theory of the Yin and the Yang. The Yang, the male

principle, is active and light and is represented by the
heavens; the Yin, the female principle, is passive and dark
and is represented by the earth. The human body, like
matter in general, is made up of five elements: wood, fire,
earth, metal, and water. With these are associated other
groups of five, such as the five planets, the five conditions
of the atmosphere, the five colours, and the five tones.
Health, character, and the success of all political and
private ventures are determined by the preponderance, at
the time, of the Yin or the Yang. In the body their
proportions can be controlled, and this is the great aim of
ancient Chinese medicine.

The teachings of the religious sects forbade the mutilation of the dead human body; hence traditional anatomy
rests on no sure scientific foundation. One of the most
important writers on anatomy, Wang Ch'ing-jen, gained
his knowledge from the inspection of dog-torn children
who had died in a plague epidemic in AD 1798. Traditional Chinese anatomy is based on the cosmic system, which
postulates the presence of such hypothetical structures as
the 12 channels. Anatomical knowledge is therefore simply a corroboration of the system; when there is a contradiction, the system is assumed to be right. The body
contains five organs (heart, lungs, liver, spleen, and kidneys), which store up but do not eliminate; and five
viscera (such as the stomach, intestines, gallbladder, and
bladder), which eliminate but do not store up. Each organ is associated with one of the planets, colours, tones,
smells, and tastes. There are 365 bones and 365 joints in
the body. There are also three so-called burning spaces,
but there is little agreement concerning the form and
position of these hypothetical structures.

According to the physiology of traditional Chinese medicine, the blood vessels are supposed to contain blood and
air, in proportions varying with those of the Yin and the
Yang. These two cosmic principles circulate in the 12
channels and control the blood vessels and hence the
pulse. The *Nei Ching* says that "the blood current flows
continuously in a circle and never stops. It may be compared to a circle without beginning or end." On this insubstantial evidence it has been claimed that the Chinese
anticipated Harvey's discovery of the circulation of the
blood. Tears are supposed to be secreted by the liver, and
there are two kinds of salivary secretion, one arising
from the heart and the other from the kidneys.

Traditional Chinese pathology is also dependent on the
theory of the Yin and the Yang; this led to an elaborate
classification of diseases in which most of the types listed
are without any scientific foundation.

In diagnosis, detailed questions are asked about the history of the illness and the patient's taste, smell, dreams,
etc. Attention is paid to the quality of the voice, and
far-reaching conclusions are drawn from it. Note is made
of the colour of the face and of the tongue. The most
important part of the investigation, however, is the examination of the pulse.

The doctrine of the pulse is ancient. Some say that it was
introduced about 255 BC; Wang Shu-ho, who wrote the
"Pulse Classic," lived about AD 280. This work (with
innumerable commentaries) asserts that health depends
on the harmonious balance of the Yin and the Yang. If
the flow of one of these principles is obstructed, disharmony and disease result. The state of the pulse indicates
the point at which obstruction in the hypothetical channels has occurred. Feeling the pulse is the most important
aspect of diagnosis. Three fingers are used to feel the
radial artery (serving the forearm, wrist, and hand); and,
as there are six pulses, each of which must be felt three
times with strong, medium, and weak pressure successively, the number of possible variations is large. Several
other qualities of the pulse at any point are also noted,
and the pulses on the two sides differ. The pulse also
varies according to the time of day and season of the
year. These comments refer only to the radial pulse at the
wrist; but there are ten other places at which the pulse can
be, and often is, felt. The minimum time necessary to feel
the pulse is ten minutes, and the operation may take three
hours. It is often the only examination made, and it is
used not only for diagnosis but also for prognosis. Some

say that from it the organs that are diseased can be ascertained and the time of death or recovery foretold.

For the Western observer, traditional Chinese medical
treatment has three points of interest: the materia medica, moxibustion, and acupuncture.

The materia medica has always been extensive and consists of vegetable, animal (including human), and mineral remedies. There were famous herbals from ancient
times; but all these, to the number of about 1,000, were
collated, correlated, corrected, and used by Li Shih-chen
in the compilation of *Pen-ts'ao kang-mu* (AD 1552–78;
"Great Pharmacopoeia"). This work, in 52 volumes, has
been frequently revised and reprinted and is still authoritative. The use of drugs is mainly to restore the harmony
of the Yin and the Yang. The drugs are also related to
such matters as the five organs, the five planets, and the
five colours. The art of prescribing is therefore complex.
Almost every conceivable natural substance has at one
time or another been used therapeutically. In addition, in
prescribing there are often the elements of sympathetic
magic, and the doctrine of signatures, long since abandoned by Western medicine. (The doctrine of signatures
held that the shapes of plants or natural marks on them
indicated their proper use by man.) Various plasters are
often applied, sometimes far from the seat of the pain.

Among the drugs taken over by Western medicine from
the Chinese are rhubarb, iron (for anemia), castor oil,
kaolin, aconite, camphor, and *Cannabis sativa* (Indian
hemp). Chaulmoogra oil was used by the Chinese for
leprosy from at least the 14th century, and about a century ago it began to be used for this purpose by Western
physicians. The herb mahuang has been used in China for
at least 4,000 years. Botanically it is *Ephedra vulgaris* (or
E. sinica), and the isolation of the alkaloid ephedrine
from it has greatly improved the Western treatment of
asthma and similar conditions. The most famous and
expensive of Chinese remedies is ginseng. Western
methods have shown that it has diuretic and other properties but is of doubtful value.

In recent years reserpine, the active principle of the
Chinese plant *Rauwolfia*, has been isolated; it is now
effectively used in the treatment of high blood pressure
and some emotional and mental conditions.

Hydrotherapy is probably of Chinese origin, since cold
baths were used for fevers as early as 180 BC. The inoculation of smallpox matter, in order to produce a mild but
immunizing attack of the disease, was practiced in China
from ancient times and came to Europe about 1720.

Moxibustion consists in making a small, moistened cone
(moxa) of powdered leaves of mugwort, or wormwood
(*Artemisia* species), applying it to the skin, igniting it,
and then crushing it into the blister so formed. Other
substances are also used for the moxa. Dozens of these
are sometimes applied at one sitting. The practice is often
associated with acupuncture.

Acupuncture consists of the insertion into the skin and
underlying tissues of a metal needle, either hot or cold.
The theory is that the needle will affect the distribution of
the Yin and the Yang in the so-called burning spaces and
in the hypothetical channels of the body. The site of the
insertion is chosen to affect a particular organ or organs.
The practice of acupuncture dates from before 2500 BC
and is peculiarly Chinese. Little of practical importance
has been added since that date, although there have been
many well-known treatises on the subject.

A bronze model, *c.* AD 860, shows the hundreds of specified points for the insertion of the needle; this was the
forerunner of the innumerable models and diagrams that
were later produced. The needles used are three to 24
centimetres (about one to nine inches) in length. They
are often inserted with considerable force and after insertion may be screwed to the left or right. One Western
observer saw unsterilized needles driven up to 15 centimetres (six inches) into solid organs such as the liver.
Acupuncture, often combined with moxibustion, is still
widely used for many diseases, including fractures.

Japan. The most interesting features of Japanese medicine are the extent to which it was derivative and the
rapidity with which, after a slow start, it became Western-

ized and scientific. In the early pre-Christian Era disease was regarded as sent by the gods or produced by the influence of evil spirits. Treatment and prevention were based largely on religious practices, such as prayers, incantations, and exorcism. At a later date drugs and bloodletting were also employed.

The first known intrusion of a foreign influence occurred in AD 458, when a Korean physician settled in Japan. His stay there did not have much influence, but, a century and a half later (AD 608), young Japanese physicians were sent for a long period of study in China, and that episode marks the real beginning of Chinese influence on Japanese medicine. In 984, Tamba Yasuyori completed the 30-volume *Ishinhō*, the oldest Japanese medical work still extant. This work discusses diseases and their treatment, classified mainly according to the affected organs or parts. It is based entirely on older Chinese medical works. During the next 600 years, the influence of China was paramount, and the Yin and the Yang played a marked role in the theory of disease causation. In 1528 the first medical book to be printed in Japan was published; it was a Chinese work.

In 1570 a 15-volume medical work was published by Menase Dōsan, who, in the next ten years, published at least five other works. In the most significant of these, the *Keiteki-shū* (a manual of the practice of medicine, 1574), diseases—or sometimes merely symptoms—are classified and described in 51 groups. For the period in which the work was written, the descriptions of symptoms, signs, and treatment are reasonably good; the work is also unusual in that it includes a section on the diseases of old age. Another distinguished physician and teacher of the period, Nagata Tokuhun, whose important books were the *I-no-ben* (1585) and the *Baika mujinzo* (1611), held that the chief aim of the medical art was to support the natural force, and consequently that it was useless to persist with stereotyped methods of treatment unless the physician had the cooperation of the patient.

During the 16th century, important cultural and social changes occurred. The Portuguese first landed briefly in Japan about 1530, and in 1549 the Jesuit missionary Francis Xavier brought Christianity to the country. In 1556 a hospital was established in Funai for the treatment of lepers and the poor; the care of the patients was entrusted to Louis Almeida, a member of the Jesuit mission, who was the first European to practice medicine in Japan. At about the same time a Japanese named Pohl, who had been taught the art of medicine by the Portuguese, began medical practice. This date marks the introduction of European medicine to Japan.

In 1568 a church, named Namban-ji (Church of the South Barbarians—*i.e.*, the Portuguese), was built in Kyōto by order of the government. Two native physicians who had learned medicine from the Portuguese were attached to the church; they treated the poor, performed operations, and founded hospitals. Then a reaction set in, and, within 20 years, the Portuguese had been exiled and Christianity had been stamped out. These events were succeeded by the foundation of several Japanese schools of medicine, all based on Chinese works.

The Dutch, who had first visited Japan in 1597, formed in 1641 a trading colony at Deshima, an island near Nagasaki. A few years later their physician, Caspar Schambergen, arrived at Nagasaki, and, during the next 50 years, other Dutch physicians resided at the Dutch embassy there and taught Japanese students. One of these students published, in 1706, an abstract in Japanese of the works of the French surgeon Ambroise Paré. Within 40 years the court librarian and the court physician were ordered by the shogun to learn Dutch.

Maeno Ryotaku was a well-known physician who knew Dutch thoroughly. In 1771 he and three colleagues dissected the body of a female subject and compared their findings with the plates in a Dutch anatomical work. They decided that the plates were correct and that the Chinese and Japanese works were wrong. In consequence they made a translation of the Dutch book, which was published in 1773. This work had great influence. It was later followed by translations of other European books

Chinese influence *(margin)*

European influences *(margin)*

on anatomy and internal medicine. It was not until 1836 that a work on physiology, written in Japanese, appeared. It was based on the German work by Blumenbach, and it opened new horizons.

In 1791 a medical academy—the Igakukan—had been founded in Edo (in 1868 renamed Tokyo). The Dutch also had a medical school, described as the European Medical School. In 1849 there came a sudden change of official policy, the study of European medicine—except surgery—was forbidden, and medical books could only be published with the permission of the Igakukan. This state of affairs was soon changed, for in 1857 a group of Japanese physicians, trained in the European School, founded a medical school in Edo. Three years later it was taken over by the government, and it is regarded as the beginning of the medical faculty of the Imperial University of Tokyo. In 1868 the European Medical School was reorganized and a large hospital was built. But in 1871 the government suddenly decided that thenceforth all medical instruction was to be after the German model, and two German military surgeons, Müller and Hoffman, arrived in Tokyo to organize the new education. As a result of the government's eagerness to westernize Japanese medicine, very great progress was made in the foundation of medical schools and the encouragement of research. The first important medical discovery by the Japanese was that of the plague bacillus, in 1894. This was followed by the discovery of a dysentery bacillus in 1897; the isolation of adrenaline in crystalline form in 1901; the first experimental production of a tar-induced cancer in 1918; and other discoveries in the field of tropical medicine.   (E.A.U.)

EARLY GREEK AND ROMAN MEDICINE

Before Hippocrates.   The transition from magic to science was a gradual process that lasted for centuries, and there is little doubt that ancient Greece inherited much from Babylonia and Egypt, and even India and China. Twentieth-century readers of the Homeric tales the *Iliad* and the *Odyssey* may well be bewildered by the narrow distinction between gods and men among the characters and between historical fact and poetic fancy in the story. Two characters, the military surgeons Podaleirius and Machaon, are said to have been sons of Asclepius. Asclepius, the god of medicine, may have originated in a human Asclepius who lived about 1200 BC and is said to have performed many miracles of healing. The divine Asclepius was worshiped in hundreds of temples throughout Greece, the remains of which may still be seen at Epidaurus, Cos, Athens, and elsewhere. To these resorts or hospitals many sick persons went for the healing ritual known as incubation, or temple sleep; they lay down to sleep in the dormitory, or *abaton*, and were visited in their dreams by Asclepius or by one of his priests, who gave advice. In the morning the patient often departed cured. There are at Epidaurus many inscriptions recording the cures, but there seem to have been no failures and no deaths. Diet, baths, and exercises played their part in the treatment, and it would appear that these temples were the prototype of modern health resorts. Each had its theatre for amusements and its stadium for athletic contests. The cult of incubation continued far into the Christian Era. In Greece some of the Aegean islands, Sardinia and Sicily, sick persons are still taken to spend a night in certain churches in the hope of a cure.

It was, however, the work of the early Greek philosophers, rather than that of the priests of Asclepius, that provided the impetus that led men to refuse to be guided solely by supernatural influence and to seek out for themselves the causes and reasons for the strange ways of nature. The 6th-century philosopher Pythagoras, whose chief discovery was the importance of numbers, also investigated the physics of sound. In the 5th century BC Empedocles set forth the view that the universe is composed of four elements—fire, air, earth, and water; this conception led to the doctrine of the four bodily humours: blood; phlegm; choler, or yellow bile; and melancholy, or black bile. The maintenance of health was held to depend upon the harmony of the four humours.

Cure by incubation *(margin)*

Hippocrates. Medical thought had reached this stage and had partially discarded the conceptions based upon magic and religion by 460 BC, the year that Hippocrates is said to have been born. Little is known of his life, and there may, in fact, have been several men of this name, or Hippocrates may have been the author of only some, or none, of the books that make up the *Hippocratic Collection*, or the *Corpus Hippocraticum*. Ancient writers held that Hippocrates taught and practiced medicine in Cos, the island of his birth, and in other parts of Greece, including Athens, and died at an advanced age.

Whether Hippocrates was one man or several seems immaterial. The works attributed to him were written by someone, and they do indicate a stage in the progress of medicine. For convenience, Hippocrates is referred to in the following material as if he were known to be one man who wrote all the works of the *Hippocratic Collection*. Some of the works, notably the *Aphorismi* (*Aphorisms*), were used as textbooks until the 19th century. Admittedly they contain much that is obsolete, but they embody a code of teaching and principles that are surprisingly modern. The first aphorism is, "Life is short, and the art long; opportunity fleeting; experiment dangerous, and judgment difficult." This is followed by a large number of brief comments on diseases and symptoms, many of which remain true. The thermometer and the stethoscope were not then known. Employing only his own powers of observation and of logical reasoning, Hippocrates had an almost uncanny ability to foretell the course of the malady, laying more stress upon the expected outcome, or diagnosis.

On the mainland, close to Cos, was a rival school of Cnidus, the members of which were apt to confuse symptoms and diagnosis; they insisted upon naming the disease and treating it and were not concerned with prognosis or with causes. Hippocrates had no patience with the idea that disease was a punishment sent by the gods. Writing of epilepsy, then called "the sacred disease," he said, "It is not any more sacred than other diseases, but has a natural cause, and its supposed divine origin is due to man's inexperience. Every disease," he continued, "has its own nature, and arises from external causes." He noted the effect of food, of occupation, and especially of climate in causing disease, and one of his most interesting books, entitled *De aëre, aquis et locis* (*Air, Waters and Places*), would today be classed as a treatise on human ecology. Pursuing this line of thought, Hippocrates stated that "Our natures are the physicians of our diseases" and that this tendency to natural cure should be fostered; he laid much stress on diet and the use of few drugs. He knew well how to describe illness clearly and concisely and recorded failures as well as successes; he viewed disease with the eye of the naturalist and studied the entire patient in his environment.

The oath of Hippocrates

Perhaps the greatest legacy of Hippocrates was the charter of medical conduct known as the oath of Hippocrates, which has been adopted as a pattern by medical men throughout the ages and is still used during the ceremony of graduation at many universities and schools of medicine:

I will look upon him who shall have taught me this Art even as one of my parents. I will share my substance with him, and I will supply his necessities, if he be in need. I will regard his offspring even as my own brethren, and I will teach them this Art, if they would learn it, without fee or covenant. I will impart this Art by precept, by lecture and by every mode of teaching, not only to my own sons but to the sons of him who has taught me, and to disciples bound by covenant and oath, according to the Law of Medicine.

The regimen I adopt shall be for the benefit of my patients according to my ability and judgment, and not for their hurt or for any wrong. I will give no deadly drug to any, though it be asked of me, nor will I counsel such, and especially I will not aid a woman to procure abortion. Whatsoever house I enter, there will I go for the benefit of the sick, refraining from all wrongdoing or corruption, and especially from any act of seduction, of male or female, of bond or free. Whatsoever things I see or hear concerning the life of men, in my attendance on the sick or even apart therefrom, which ought not to be noised abroad, I will keep silence thereon, counting such things to be as sacred secrets.

The term oath should not be interpreted too narrowly. It was, rather, an ethical code or ideal and in no sense a law. It is an appeal for correct conduct but contains no threat of punishment. In one or other of its many versions, it has guided the practice of medicine for more than 2,000 years.

Between Hippocrates and Galen. In the following century, Aristotle flourished, the first great biologist, whose work was of inestimable value to medicine. A pupil of Plato at Athens and tutor to Alexander the Great, Aristotle studied the entire world of living things, laying the foundations of comparative anatomy and of embryology.

After the time of Aristotle, Greek culture began to fade in the land of its birth. The scene shifted to Alexandria, where a famous medical school was established *c.* 300 BC. There, the two best medical teachers were Herophilus, whose treatise on anatomy may have been the first of its kind, and Erasistratus, regarded by some as the founder of physiology, who noted the difference between sensory and motor nerves but thought that the nerves are hollow tubes containing fluid and that air enters the lungs and heart and is carried through the body in the arteries. Alexandria continued as a centre of medical teaching even after the Roman Empire had attained supremacy over that of Greece, and medical knowledge remained predominantly Greek.

Herophilus and Erasistratus

Aulus Cornelius Celsus, the Roman nobleman who wrote *De medicina* about AD 30, based his knowledge on Greek medicine. His book, overlooked in his day, became well known after it was printed at Florence, in 1478. Celsus followed the teaching of Asclepiades of Bithynia (born 124 BC), who differed from Hippocrates in that he denied the healing power of nature and insisted that disease sould be treated safely, speedily, and agreeably.

An opponent of the humoral theory, Asclepiades drew upon the atomic theory of the 5th-century Greek philosopher Democritus in advocating a doctrine of *strictum et laxum*—the attribution of disease to the constricted or relaxed condition of the solid particles that he believed make up the body. To restore harmony among the particles and thus effect cures, Asclepiades used typically Greek remedies: massage, poultices, occasional tonics, fresh air, and corrective diet. He gave particular attention to mental disease, clearly distinguishing hallucinatory conditions from those marked by delusions. He released the insane from confinement in dark cellars and prescribed a regimen of occupational therapy, soothing music, soporifics (especially wine), and exercises to improve the attention and memory. Asclepiades did much to win acceptance for Greek medicine in Rome. After his death came a period of much disputation as to the nature of disease. This period was brought to a close by the career of Galen, who began practising in Rome in AD 164.

Galen. During the early centuries of the Christian Era, Greek doctors thronged to Rome. The most illustrious of them was Galen, who acknowledged his debt to Hippocrates and followed the Hippocratic method, accepting the doctrine of the humours. He laid stress on the value of anatomy, and he virtually founded experimental physiology. Galen recognized that the arteries contain blood and not merely air and showed how the heart sets the blood in motion in an ebb and flow fashion, but he had no idea that the blood circulates. Dissection of the human body was at that time illegal, so that he was forced to base his knowledge upon the examination of apes and pigs. A voluminous writer who stated his views forcibly and with confidence, he remained for centuries the undisputed authority from whom no one dared to differ.

Although the contribution of Rome to the practice of medicine was negligible compared with that of Greece, it must be admitted that in matters of public health Rome set the world a great example. The city of Rome had an unrivaled water supply. Gymnasiums and public baths were provided, and there was even domestic sanitation and adequate disposal of sewage. The Roman army had its medical officers; public physicians were appointed to attend the poor; and hospitals were built; in fact, a Roman hospital excavated near Dusseldorf, Germany, was found to be strangely modern in design.

ARABIAN TEACHING AND THE SCHOOL OF SALERNO

After the fall of Rome, learning was no longer held in high esteem, experiment was discouraged, and originality became even a dangerous asset. During the early Middle Ages medicine passed into the widely contrasting hands of the Christian Church and the Arab scholars.

The Christian reservoir of learning. It is sometimes stated that the early Christian Church had an adverse effect upon medical progress: disease was regarded as a punishment for sin, and such chastening demanded only prayer and repentance. Furthermore, the human body was held sacred and dissection was forbidden. It seems probable, however, that the infinite care and nursing bestowed upon the sick by the Christian Church far outweighs any intolerance shown toward medicine in the early days. Perhaps the greatest service rendered to medicine by the church was the preservation and transcription of the classical Greek medical manuscripts. This work was carried on in many medieval monasteries and was also pursued by the Nestorian Christians (an Eastern church not affiliated with the Patriarchy of Constantinople), who established a school of translators to render the Greek medical texts into Arabic. This famous school, and also a great hospital, were located at Jundi Shāhpūr in southwest Persia, where the chief physician was Jurjīs ibn Bukhtīshūʿ, the first of a dynasty of translators and physicians that lasted for six generations. A later translator of great renown was Ḥunayn ibn Isḥāq, or Johannitus (born AD 809), whose translations were said to be worth their weight in gold.

About this time there appeared a number of saints whose names were associated with miraculous cures. Among the earliest of these were twin brothers, Cosmas and Damian, who suffered martyrdom (c. AD 303) and who became the patron saints of medicine. The Christian Church sought to replace the signs of the zodiac, to which parts of the human body were referred, by various patron saints: St. Blaisius dominated the throat and lung; St. Apollonia, the teeth; St. Erasmus, the abdomen; SS. Lucia and Triduana, the eyes. Other saints were powerful healers of certain diseases: St. Vitus, for example, was invoked for chorea, or St. Vitus' dance, and St. Anthony for erysipelas, or St. Anthony's fire. The cult of these saints was widespread in medieval times, and a later cult, that of St. Roch for plague, was widespread in the 15th century when that disease was prevalent.

The Arabian medical reservoir. The second reservoir of medical learning during those early times was the great Muslim Empire, which extended from Persia to Spain. Although it is customary to speak of Arabian medicine in describing this period, it must be remembered that the physicians were not all Arabs or natives of Arabia. Nor, indeed, were they all Muslims: some were Jews, some Christians, and they were drawn from all parts of the great empire, extending along the entire northern coast of Africa and invading Spain. Only a few of the leading figures need be mentioned. One of the earliest was Rhazes, a Persian born in the last half of the 9th century near the modern Teheran, who wrote a voluminous treatise on medicine, *Kitāb al-hāwī* ("Comprehensive Book"), but whose most famous work, *De variolis et morbillis* (*A Treatise on the Smallpox and Measles*), deals with the distinction between these two diseases and gives a clear description of both.

Of later date was Avicenna (980–1037), who has been called the prince of physicians. Like Rhazes, Avicenna was a Persian. Born near Bukhara, he could repeat the Koran before he was ten years old and at the age of 18 became court physician. His principal medical work, *Al-Qānūn fi'l-Tibb* (*The Canon of Medicine*), became a classic and was used at many medical schools—at Montpellier, France, as late as 1650—and is still said to be used in the East. Avicenna died at Hamadan, where his tomb is a place of pilgrimage.

The greatest contribution of Arabian medicine was in chemistry and in the knowledge and preparation of medicines; many drugs now in use are of Arab origin, as also are such processes as distillation and sublimation. Often the chemistry of that time was mainly a search for the philosopher's stone, which supposedly would turn all common metals to gold. Astronomers were astrologers and chemists were alchemists. It is, therefore, surprising that, despite all this, the physicians of the Muslim empire did make a noteworthy contribution to medical progress.

At that period and, indeed, throughout most historical times, surgery was regarded as inferior to medicine. One Arab surgeon, however, Abū al-Qāsim (Albucasis) of Córdoba, wrote the first illustrated book on surgery, which was widely used. He was a careful and conservative surgeon who did much to raise the status of surgery in Córdoba, an important centre of commerce and culture with a hospital and medical school equal to those of Cairo and Baghdad.

Another great doctor of Córdoba, born in the 12th century, just as the sun of Arabian culture was setting, was a Jew, the philosopher Maimonides. Banished from the city because he would not become a Muslim, he eventually went to Cairo, where the law was more lenient and where he acquired a reputation so high that he became physician to Saladin, the Saracen leader. He was the original of El Hakim in Sir Walter Scott's *Talisman*. A few of his works, written in Arabic, were eventually translated into Latin and printed; perhaps the best known is *Yad-Hachazakah* (*The Code of Maimonides*), an ethical code still esteemed in Jewish medical circles.

Salerno. At about the same time that Arabian medicine flourished, there was established at the city of Salerno, in southern Italy, the first organized medical school in Europe. Although the school of Salerno produced no brilliant genius and no startling discovery, it was the parent of the great medieval schools soon to be founded at Montpellier and Paris, in France, and at Bologna and Padua, in Italy. The Salerno school owed much to the enlightened Holy Roman emperor Frederick II, who decreed in 1221 that no one should practise medicine until he had been publicly approved by the masters of Salerno.

Salerno drew scholars from near and far. One of the earliest was the 11th-century physician Constantine the African, who, after years of wandering in the East, sought refuge in Salerno. (He later retired to Monte Cassino, the monastery founded by St. Benedict in the 6th century, there to translate from Arabic into Latin many of the Greek classic writings.) The Salernitan school also produced a literature of its own; the best known work, of uncertain date and of composite authorship, was the *Regimen Sanitatis Salernitanum* ("Salernitan Guide to Health"). Written in verse, it has appeared in numerous editions and has been translated into many languages. The *Regimen* is said to have been written as a handbook of domestic medicine for Robert, duke of Normandy, a crusader who visited Salerno for the treatment of a wound, but the most authentic contemporary manuscript is that of Arnald of Villanova. Among its oft-quoted couplets is the following:

Use three physicians still, first Doctor Quiet,
Next Doctor Merryman, and Doctor Diet.

REFORM AND REVIVAL IN MEDICINE

The spread of new learning. Salerno yielded its place as the premier medical school of Europe to Montpellier in about 1200. John of Gaddesden, the model for the "doctour of physick" in Chaucer's *Canterbury Tales*, was one of the English students there. That he relied upon astrology and upon the doctrine of the humours is evident from Chaucer's description:

Well could he guess the ascending of the star
Wherein his patient's fortunes settled were.
He knew the course of every malady,
Were it of cold or heat or moist or dry . . . .

Among the teachers of medicine in the medieval universities there were many who clung to the past, but there were not a few who determined to explore new lines of thought. The new learning, or Renaissance, born in Italy, grew and expanded slowly. Two great 13th-century scholars who influenced medicine were Roger Bacon, an active observer and tireless experimenter, and Albertus Magnus. About this time, also, Mondino de'Luzzi taught at Bologna, Italy, performing his own dissections rather than

Preservation of Greek medical manuscripts

Abū al-Qāsim and Maimonides

The "Salernitan Guide to Health"

following the then usual procedure of entrusting the task to a menial. Although he perpetuated the errors of Galen, his anatomy, published in 1316, was the first practical manual of anatomy.

Foremost among the surgeons of the day was Guy de Chauliac, a good physician as well as a surgeon and one who based his writing on observation and experience. His *Chirurgia magna* ("Great Surgery") had a profound influence upon the progress of surgery.

The Renaissance, a movement of the 14th, 15th, and 16th centuries, was much more than merely a reviving of interest in Greek and Roman culture; it was rather a change of outlook, an eagerness for discovery, a desire to escape from the limitations of tradition and to explore new fields of thought and action. In medicine, it was perhaps natural that anatomy and physiology, the knowledge of the human body and its workings, should be the first aspects of medical learning to receive attention from those who realized the need for reform.

The work of Vesalius

It was in 1543 that Andreas Vesalius, a young professor of anatomy at the University of Padua, published *De humani corporis fabrica* ("On the Fabric of the Human Body"). The work, the fruit of his own observations, showed that Galen could no longer be regarded as the final authority from whom none dared to differ; Vesalius corrected many of Galen's errors. His good work at Padua was continued by Gabriel Fallopius and, later, by Hieronymus Fabricius ab Aquapendente, whose work on the valves in the veins, *De venarum ostiolis*, published in 1603, suggested to his pupil William Harvey the idea of the circulation of the blood.

Surgery profited from the new outlook in anatomy, and a great surgical reformer, Ambroise Paré, now appeared on the scene. Paré was surgeon to four kings of France in succession, and he well earned for himself the title of "the father of modern surgery." In his autobiography, written after he had retired from 30 years of service as an army surgeon, Paré described how he had abolished the painful cautery for gunshot wounds and used soothing dressings instead; his favourite expression, "I dressed him; God healed him," is characteristic of this humane and careful surgeon.

Medical colleges in Britain.   At about the time of these developments in Italy and France, surgery, which was ahead of medicine in the establishment of organizational controls, underwent reorganization in Britain. As early as 1505 a decree, or "seal of cause," was granted to the Incorporation of Barber-Surgeons of Edinburgh; it was confirmed by King James IV of Scotland a year later. In 1540, King Henry VIII of England granted a royal charter to Thomas Vicary, the first master of the Barber-Surgeons Company, which became the Company of Surgeons of London in 1745, the Royal College of Surgeons in 1800, and still later the Royal College of Surgeons of England. Thus were founded the bodies that became the Royal Colleges of Surgeons in Scotland and in England. At the end of the century, in 1599, Peter Lowe obtained from King James VI of Scotland a charter for the Faculty (now Royal College) of Physicians and Surgeons of Glasgow to control practice in and around the city. Lowe had the foresight to include all who practised medicine or surgery and thus sought to unite the two aspects of the healing art that had long been separated.

Another event of great importance during the 16th century was the foundation of the College of Physicians in London, which received its charter from Henry VIII in 1518. The College had the sole privilege of permitting persons to practise as physicians in London and the surrounding district. The first president was Thomas Linacre, the leading Oxford scholar of his day. He was succeeded by John Caius, honoured by inclusion of his name in that of the modern Gonville and Caius College, Cambridge, and author of an excellent account of the curious disease called sweating sickness, which ravaged the country in a series of epidemics attended by a high mortality. The Royal College of Physicians of Edinburgh was founded in 1681. Edinburgh University was the first British university to found (1726) a medical faculty and to provide a complete training in medicine.

Paracelsus.   No account of Renaissance medicine can afford to omit some mention of the strange man, the alchemist known as Paracelsus. Theophrastus Bombastus von Hohenheim, who called himself Phillipus Aureolus Paracelsus, was the son of the country doctor of Einsiedeln, near Zürich. He travelled extensively in Europe, practising and teaching as he went. Eager for reform, he allowed his intolerance to outweigh his discretion, as when he prefaced his lectures at Basel by publicly burning the works of Avicenna and Galen. The authorities were understandably annoyed. To this day, Paracelsus is highly regarded by some and as strongly decried by others. He remains an enigma. There is no doubt, however, that he simplified prescribing and introduced chemical drugs in place of vegetable remedies.

Fracastoro.   A contemporary of Paracelsus, Girolamo Fracastoro, of Verona, Italy, was a scholar of very different mold. His account of the disease syphilis, entitled *Syphilis sive morbus Gallicus* (1530; "Syphilis or the Gallic Disease"), was written in verse. Fracastoro called syphilis the French disease; others called it the Neapolitan disease, for it was said to have been brought to Naples from America by the sailors of Columbus; its origin is still questioned. Fracastoro was also interested in epidemic infection, about which his ideas were surprisingly modern. In 1546 he published his great work, *De Contagione*, in which he theorized that the seeds of certain diseases are imperceptible particles carried by air or by contact.

Fracastoro on syphilis

MEDICINE IN THE 17TH CENTURY

William Harvey and the experimental method.   The medical progress of the 17th century can now be considered, together with the leading part played by William Harvey, whose classic little book *Exercitatio anatomica de motu cordis et sanguinis in animalibus* ("An Anatomical Experiment Concerning the Movement of the Heart and Blood in Animals"), often called for short *De motu cordis*, was printed at Frankfurt am Main in 1628.

Born at Folkestone, Kent, the eldest of the seven sons of the mayor, Harvey studied at Caius College, Cambridge, and then spent several years at Padua, where he came under the influence of Fabricius. By the time that Harvey began to lecture in London, in 1616, he had already reached his conclusion regarding the circulation of the blood, although he waited for 12 years before printing his views. That the book aroused much controversy is not surprising. There were still many who adhered to the ancient teaching of Galen and affirmed that the blood follows an ebb and flow movement in the blood vessels. Harvey's work was the result of many careful experiments, but few of his critics took the trouble to repeat the experiments; instead, they simply argued in favour of the older view, in their bookish and scholastic fashion. His second great book, *Exercitationes de generatione animalium* ("Experiments Concerning Animal Generation"), published in 1651, laid the foundation of modern embryology. Harvey's discovery of the circulation of the blood was a most important landmark of medical progress; the new experimental method by which the results were secured was as noteworthy as the work itself. He drew the truth from experience and not from authority, following the method described by the philosopher Francis Bacon.

There was one gap in Harvey's argument—he was obliged to assume the existence of the capillary vessels that conveyed the blood from the arteries to the veins at the periphery. This link in the chain of evidence was supplied by Marcello Malpighi of Bologna, who was born in 1628, the year of publication of *De motu cordis*. With a primitive microscope Malpighi saw a network of tiny blood vessels in the lung of a frog. Harvey also failed to show why the blood circulated. After Robert Boyle had shown that air is essential to animal life, it was Richard Lower who traced the interaction between air and the blood. Eventually the importance of oxygen, which masqueraded for a time as phlogiston, was revealed, but it was not until 1775 that Antoine Laurent Lavoisier discovered the nature of oxygen and solved a problem that had puzzled many.

Invention and development of microscope

The invention of the compound microscope is usually attributed to a spectacle maker named Zacharias Janssen, in Holland, but its development, like that of the telescope, was the work of Galileo, who was the first to lay stress upon the value of measurement in science and in medicine, thus replacing theory and guesswork with accuracy. One of the greatest of the early microscopists was Anton van Leeuwenhoek of Delft, who devoted his long life to microscopical studies and who was probably the first to see and describe bacteria, reporting his results to the Royal Society of London. In England, Robert Hooke, who was Boyle's assistant and curator to the Royal Society, published his classic book *Micrographia* in 1665.

The futile search for an easy system. It was during the 17th century that several attempts were made to discover an easy system as a clue to the problems of medical practice. A substratum of superstition still remained at this time; *e.g.*, Richard Wiseman, surgeon to Charles II, affirmed his belief in the "royal touch" as a cure for king's evil, or scrofula, while even the learned English physician Sir Thomas Browne stated that witches really existed. There was, however, a general desire to discard the past and to adopt new ideas.

The view of the 17th-century French philosopher René Descartes that the human body is a machine had its repercussions in medical thought. One group adopting this explanation called themselves the iatrophysicists; another school, preferring to view life as a series of chemical processes, were called iatrochemists. Sanctorius, at Padua, an early exponent of the iatrophysical view, did much pioneer work in what is now called metabolism, being especially concerned with the measurement of what he called "insensible perspiration," described in his book *De statica medicina*, published in 1614. Another Italian who developed the idea still further was Giovanni Alfonso Borelli, a professor of mathematics at Pisa University, who busied himself with the mechanics and statics of the body and with the physical laws that govern its movements. The iatrochemical school was founded at Brussels by Jan Baptista van Helmont, whose writings are tinged with the mysticism of the alchemist. A more logical and intelligible view of iatrochemistry was advanced by Franciscus Sylvius, at Leiden, while in England a leading exponent of the same school was Thomas Willis, who is better known for his description of the brain in his *Cerebri anatome nervorumque descriptio et usus* ("Anatomy of the Brain and Descriptions and Functions of the Nerves"), published in 1664 and illustrated by Sir Christopher Wren.

The iatrochemical school

It soon became apparent that no easy road to medical knowledge was to be found along these channels and that the best method is the age-old system of straightforward clinical observation originally initiated by Hippocrates. The need for a return to Hippocratic views was strongly urged by Thomas Sydenham, well named "the English Hippocrates." Sydenham was not a voluminous writer and, indeed, had little patience with book learning in medicine, but nevertheless he gave excellent descriptions of the phenomena of disease. His greatest service, much needed at the time, was to divert men's minds from speculation and to lead them back to the bedside, for there only could the art of medicine be studied.

MEDICINE IN THE 18TH CENTURY

Brown and Hahnemann. Sydenham's praiseworthy appeal for a return to Hippocratic methods was not accepted by everyone. Even in the 18th century the search for a simple way of healing the sick continued. In Edinburgh a writer and lecturer named John Brown expounded, at the Royal Medical Society (of which he was president three times), his Brunonian system. In his view, there were only two diseases, sthenic (strong) and asthenic (weak) and two treatments, stimulant and sedative. Lively and heated debates took place between Brunonians and the more orthodox Cullenians (followers of William Cullen), and the disturbance spread to Europe. Meantime, the unfortunate Brown, at war with all his colleagues, became a victim of his own system and died in debt and poverty, his end hastened by his two chief reme-

The Brunonian system

dies, opium and alcohol. At the opposite end of the scale, at least in regard to dosage, was Samuel Hahnemann, of Leipzig, the originator of homeopathy, a system of treatment involving the administration of minute doses of drugs whose effects resemble the effects of the disease being treated. His ideas had a salutary effect upon medical thought at a time when prescriptions were lengthy and doses were large; his system has had many followers.

Medical teaching in Britain. Before the 18th century, there was little organized medical teaching in Britain. Those who wished to become doctors first became apprentices; they could then also attend classes in anatomy, botany, and chemistry, the tripod of learning upon which medicine was then founded. Those who could afford it studied and even graduated at one of the European universities, as William Harvey did at Padua in 1602. When the centre of medical learning shifted from Padua to Leiden, many students were attracted there from abroad. Among them was John Monro, an army surgeon, who resolved that his native city of Edinburgh should have a similar medical school. He specially educated his son Alexander with a view to having him appointed professor of anatomy, and the bold plan was successful. Alexander Monro studied at Leiden under Hermann Boerhaave, the central figure of European medicine and the greatest clinical teacher of his time, and on returning to Edinburgh was appointed professor of anatomy. Monro was followed in the chair by his son Alexander Monro II, and he, in turn, by the grandson Alexander Monro III; although in the third generation the high standard was not maintained, the three Alexander Monros taught anatomy in Edinburgh University over a continuous period of 126 years. Robert Sibbald and Archibald Pitcairne, who had helped to found the Royal College of Physicians of Edinburgh in 1681, were now gone; but medicine was brilliantly taught by Robert Whytt, then by the Gregorys, John and James, and still later by William Cullen, who in 1747 founded the faculty of medicine in Glasgow.

Surgery and obstetrics. In the early years of the 18th century the leading surgeons of London were William Cheselden and Percivall Pott, although their work tends to be overshadowed by their more famous pupil, John Hunter. John left his home in Lanarkshire in 1748 to assist his elder brother, William, who was already well established in London as an obstetrician and anatomist. Although he made no great single discovery, John, by his vast researches in comparative anatomy and physiology, raised surgery to the level of a definite branch of science and was actually the founder of surgical pathology. After his death, the museum that he had laboriously collected eventually became the property of the Royal College of Surgeons, which honours his memory with the Hunterian oration, although the museum was mostly destroyed by German air raids in World War II. Just as John Hunter raised the status and prestige of surgery, so his contemporary William Smellie performed a similar service for midwifery. Like the Hunters, Smellie was a native of Lanarkshire. After practising medicine in the town of Lanark for 16 years, he settled in London, in 1739. He soon became the leading obstetrician, or man midwife, as specialists of this kind were then called. He placed midwifery on a sound scientific footing. His well-known *Treatise on the Theory and Practice of Midwifery* was published in three volumes in 1752–64.

The work of John Hunter and William Smellie

Pathology and diagnosis. In the 18th century, too, the science of modern pathology was created. Giovanni Morgagni, of Padua, in 1761 published the great work *De sedibus et causis morborum* ("On the Sites and Causes of Diseases"), a description of the appearances found by postmortem examination of almost 700 cases, revealing many new facts.

On the basis of work begun in the 18th century, René Laënnec, a native of Quimper, Brittany, who became a physician in Paris, invented the stethoscope, or *cylindre*, as it was originally called. In 1819 he wrote a treatise, *De l'auscultation médiate* ("On Indirect Auscultation"), describing many of the curious sounds in the heart and lungs that are revealed by the stethoscope.

Meanwhile a Viennese physician, Leopold Auenbrugger, discovered another method of investigating diseases of the chest, that of percussion. The son of an innkeeper, he is said to have conceived the idea of tapping with the fingers when he recalled that he had used this method to gauge the level of the fluid contents of his father's casks.

Public health. Public health and hygiene began to attract attention in the 18th century, although a more lively awakening was later to accompany the Industrial Revolution. Toward the end of his life, early in the 18th century, Bernardino Ramazzini wrote the first work on occupational diseases, *De morbis artificum diatriba (On the Diseases of Artificers)*, a most interesting book of the period. At this time, too, Johann Peter Frank evolved his scheme of health legislation and attempted to awaken a health consciousness in the people and in their rulers. In his *System einer vollständigen medicinischen Polizey* ("System of a Complete Medical Policy"), published in 1779, he was one of the first to suggest that a government should be responsible for the health of its people.

First book on occupational diseases

Smallpox and digitalis. One important discovery of the 18th century was vaccination. Smallpox, disfiguring and often fatal, was then prevalent. Inoculation, which had been practiced in the East, was popularized in England in 1721–22 by Lady Mary Wortley Montagu, who is best known for her letters. She observed the practice in Turkey; it produced a mild form of the disease, thus securing immunity, although not without danger. The next step was taken by Edward Jenner, a country practitioner of Berkeley, Gloucestershire, who had been a pupil of John Hunter. He observed that those who became infected with cowpox (the bovine form of the disease) did not become infected with smallpox. In 1796 he performed the first vaccination on a certain James Phipps; he found, on inoculating Phipps with smallpox eight weeks later, that the disease did not appear. The advantage of the method became apparent everywhere.

William Withering's discovery of the value of foxglove, or digitalis, as a remedy for dropsy and for heart disease is another example of the good work of a general practitioner. Withering, who practised in Shropshire, noted that the country folk often used a decoction of foxglove leaves. After many experiments, he wrote his classic *An Account of the Foxglove*, in 1785.

Phrenology and mesmerism. Phrenology and mesmerism first emerged in the 18th century. Phrenology was a belief that one could judge the development of any faculty by the configuration of the skull over the point on the brain where the faculty was thought to be centred, while mesmerism, a belief in animal magnetism, probably owed any success that it had to suggestions given while the patient was under hypnosis. The first owed its birth to Franz Joseph Gall and his pupil Johann Kaspar Spurzheim. Mesmerism, another product of Vienna, was sponsored by Franz Anton Mesmer.

Scurvy and military hospitals. No account of 18th-century medicine would be complete without a reference to two important advances affecting the health of the navy and of the army. Observing the prevalence of scurvy among English sailors, James Lind, a graduate of Edinburgh who had entered the navy, recommended the use of lemon juice, which caused survy to disappear. He probably adopted the practice from the Dutch, who, in the 16th century, had discovered the value of citrus fruits in the diet of sailors. Several years passed before Lind's advice was put to use in England. Lind's account of his researches, *A Treatise on the Scurvy*, was published in 1754.

In 1752 there was published another medical classic entitled *Observations on the Diseases of the Army*. The author was Sir John Pringle, who had been professor of moral philosophy at Edinburgh before embarking upon his military career and who rendered valuable service by his recommendations for the health and comfort of the troops. During the War of the Austrian Succession, he had suggested, at the battle of Dettingen, in 1743, that military hospitals on both sides should be regarded as sanctuaries. This plan eventually led to the establishment of the Red Cross organization, although the first Geneva convention was not assembled until 1863, at the instigation of the Swiss banker Jean Henri Dunant.

II. The rise of scientific medicine in the 19th century

The portrayal of medical history becomes more difficult as modern times are approached. Discoveries multiply and the number of eminent doctors is so great that the story is apt to become a mere string of biographies. This synopsis selects some of the leading trends in medical thought in order to provide a scaffolding upon which the reader may build.

By the beginning of the 19th century, the structure of the human body was almost fully known, thanks to new methods of microscopy and of injections. Even the minute structure of the body was understood. Much more important than anatomical knowledge was the knowledge of physiological processes that was becoming rapidly elucidated, especially in Germany. There, physiology became established as a distinct science under the guidance of Johannes Müller, who was professor at Bonn and then at the University of Berlin. An energetic worker and an inspiring teacher, he described his discoveries in a famous textbook, *Handbuch der Physiologie des Menschen* ("Manual of Human Physiology"), published 1833–40. Among his pupils were Hermann von Helmholtz, who made great discoveries relating to sight and hearing and who invented the ophthalmoscope, and Rudolf Virchow, also of Berlin, whose greatest achievement was his conception of the cell as the centre of all pathological changes. Virchow's work, *Die Cellular-pathologie*, published in 1858, gave the deathblow to the outmoded "humoral" pathology.

The work of Johannes Müller and his students

In France, the leading physiologist of the time was Claude Bernard, all of whose work was the outcome of carefully planned experiments. His first researches were directed to digestion. Next, he explained the presence of the carbohydrate glycogen in the liver, while his third discovery was that of the vasomotor mechanism, the system of controls of the contraction and expansion of blood vessels. Toward the end of his life, in 1865, he expounded his methods and principles in his *Introduction à l'étude de la médecine expérimentale* ("Introduction to the Study of Experimental Medicine"), a classic still worthy of study by all who undertake research. Meantime, physiology had made progress in Britain under the leadership of Marshall Hall, whose greatest discovery was that of reflex action; William Sharpey, the first in Great Britain to devote his exclusive attention to physiology, separating it from anatomy and physics and placing it among the sciences; and Sir Charles Bell, whose researches on the nervous system yielded notable advances in that field. His *Idea of a New Anatomy of the Brain,* first expounded in 1811, has been called the Magna Carta of neurology, although it is true that François Magendie of France gave a more complete demonstration of the functions of motor and sensory nerves.

VERIFICATION OF THE GERM THEORY

Perhaps the greatest medical advance of the 19th century, certainly the most spectacular, was the conclusive demonstration that certain diseases, as well as the infection of surgical wounds, were directly caused by minute living organisms. This discovery changed the whole face of pathology and effected a complete revolution in the practice of surgery.

The idea that disease was caused by the entry into the body of tiny imperceptible particles was of ancient date. It had been expressed by the Roman encyclopedist Varro as early as 100 BC, by Fracastoro in 1546, by Athanasius Kircher and Pierre Borel about a century later, and by Francesco Redi, who in 1684 wrote his *Osservazioni intorno agli animali viventi che si trovano negli animali viventi* ("Observations on Living Animals Which Are to Be Found Within Other Living Animals"), in which he sought to disprove the idea of spontaneous generation. Everything must have a parent, he wrote; only life produces life. Another worker in this field, regarded by some as founder of the parasitic theory of infection, was Agostino Bassi, who showed that a disease of silkworms was caused by a fungus that could be destroyed by chemical agents.

Ancient parallels to the germ theory

Nevertheless, the main credit for the establishment of

the science of bacteriology must be accorded to Louis Pasteur. It was Pasteur who, by a brilliant series of experiments, proved that fermentation, or putrefaction, was not a chemical process but was caused by the living organisms known as bacteria. He solved one problem after another during his strenuous life—problems concerning the fermentation of wine, the prevention of anthrax in sheep and cattle, of chicken cholera, and, finally, of rabies in man and dogs. The later was a bold experiment that resulted in the widespread establishment of Pasteur institutes.

Lister's introduction of antiseptics

From Pasteur, Joseph Lister borrowed, with full acknowledgment, the idea that led to his introduction of the antiseptic system in surgery. Lister, who was born close to London, at Upton, Essex, made known in 1865, while professor of surgery at Glasgow University, his great discovery, the placing of an antiseptic barrier between the wound and the germ-containing atmosphere. Though Lister did not at first realize that infection not only is airborne but also can be carried by the hands, skin, or instruments, he left a noble example and a priceless heritage. Besides creating a complete revolution in the surgical outlook, he is to be remembered as one of the founders of bacteriology.

Obstetrics had already been robbed of some of its terrors by Alexander Gordon at Aberdeen, Scotland, Oliver Wendell Holmes at Boston, and Ignaz Semmelweiss (1818–65) at Vienna and Pest (Budapest), who advised disinfection of the hands and clothing of midwives and students who attended confinements.

Another pioneer of bacteriology was Robert Koch, who showed how bacteria could be cultivated and stained and how their specificity could be proved. Koch discovered the tubercle bacillus in 1882 and the vibrio of cholera in 1883. Before the turn of the century many other disease-producing organisms had been identified.

MEDICINE AND ANESTHESIA

There was a danger at this time that in the feverish search for bacteria, other causes of disease would escape detection. Physicians of slightly earlier date, who worked along other lines, deserve to be remembered. Among them were physicians attached to Guy's Hospital, London: Richard Bright, Thomas Addison, and William Gull. Bright made important advances in the knowledge of diseases of the kidneys, including so-called Bright's disease, while Addison gave his name to a disease. Gull, a great clinical teacher, left a legacy of pithy and helpful aphorisms that might well rank alongside those of Hippocrates.

In Dublin, two eminent physicians were Robert Graves and William Stokes (1804–78), while, in Paris, Pierre-Charles-Alexander Louis was attracting many students from the United States by the excellence of his teaching. By this time, the United States—having drawn from Leiden, Edinburgh, and London the learning that went to found in the 18th century the first medical schools at Philadelphia and elsewhere, under the guidance of such pioneers as John Morgan, William Shippen, and Benjamin Rush—was now ready to send back the results of its own researches. Daniel Drake founded medical schools at Cincinnati and described the diseases of the Ohio River Valley; Ephraim McDowell performed a bold ovariotomy (removal of an ovary) in a small Kentucky village in 1809; and William Beaumont, in treating a gunshot wound of the stomach, was led to make many original observations that were published in 1833 as *Experiments and Observations on the Gastric Juice and the Physiology of Digestion.*

Early developments in United States

The most famous contribution by the United States to medical progress at this period was undoubtedly the introduction of general anesthesia, a discovery that was marred by controversy. Crawford Long, Gardner Colton, Horace Wells, and Charles Jackson are all claimants for priority: some used nitrous oxide gas, and others employed ether, which was less capricious. There is little doubt, however, that it was William Thomas Morton who, on October 16, 1846, at Massachusetts General Hospital, first demonstrated before a gathering of physi-

cians the use of ether as a general anesthetic. News of the discovery soon reached Europe. In Edinburgh, the professor of midwifery, James Young Simpson, had been experimenting upon himself and his assistants, inhaling various vapours with the object of discovering a general anesthetic. In November 1847 chloroform was tried with complete success. Within a few days it was tested in an operation, and soon it was preferred to ether and became the anesthetic of choice. Although Simpson is remembered mainly as the discoverer of chloroform, he did a great deal more to enhance the reputation of Edinburgh, and was created a baronet in 1866.

ADVANCES AT THE END OF THE CENTURY

While antisepsis and anesthesia placed surgery on an entirely new footing, similarly important work was carried out in other branches of medicine. Sir Patrick Manson showed in Amoy, China, in 1877, how insects may carry disease and how the embryos of the little worm *Filaria*, which causes elephantiasis, are transmitted by the mosquito. Manson explained his views to the young doctor who became Sir Ronald Ross, then working on the problem of malaria, and Ross discovered the malarial parasite in the stomach of the *Anopheles* mosquito in 1897. Carlos Finlay in Cuba expressed the view, in 1881, that yellow fever is carried by the *Stegomyia* mosquito; following him, Walter Reed, William Gorgas, and others conquered the scourge of yellow fever and made possible the completion of the Panama Canal by reducing the death rate there from 176 per 1,000 to 6 per 1,000.

Cures for malaria, yellow fever, and typhoid

An event of equally startling significance was the control of typhoid by the method of inoculation devised by Almroth Wright. There were other victories in preventive medicine because the maintenance of health had now become as important a duty as the cure of disease; and the 20th century was to witness the evolution and progress of national health services in a number of countries. In addition, spectacular advances in diagnosis and treatment followed the discovery of X-rays by Wilhelm Conrad Röntgen, in 1895, and of radium by Pierre and Marie Curie in 1898. The new field of psychiatry was opened up by Sigmund Freud. The development of chemotherapy, immunology, endocrinology, and the science of nutrition, which were later advances, are described below.

(D.J.G.)

III. Medicine in the 20th century

The first six decades of the 20th century witnessed such a plethora of discoveries and advances that in some ways the face of medicine was changed out of all recognition. In 1901, for instance, the standardized mortality ratio (*i.e.,* the ratio of observed deaths to expected deaths for the whole population, expressed as a percentage) in England and Wales was 266; in 1962 it was 92. For tuberculosis the standardized mortality ratio in the decade 1901–10 was 649; in 1962 it was 22. Even more striking was the position with regard to diphtheria in children. In the decade 1901–10 the death rate per 1,000,000 population at ages under 15 years was 571; in 1969 it was zero. Indeed, the outlook was so altered that, with the notable exception of cancer, attention became focussed on morbidity rather than mortality, and the emphasis has changed from keeping people alive to keeping them fit.

Declining death rate

In the medical kaleidoscope of this era, four main trends may be distinguished: the first and the most important was the development of chemotherapy; the second, and closely associated, was the development of immunology; the third was progress in endocrinology; and the fourth was progress in nutrition.

CHEMOTHERAPY

Development of arsphenamine. At the turn of the century, Germany was well to the forefront in medical progress. The scientific approach to medicine had been developed there long before it spread to other countries, and postgraduates flocked to German medical schools from all over the world. The opening decade of the 20th century has been well described as the "golden age" of German medicine. Outstanding among its leaders was Paul Ehrlich. While still a student at Strasbourg, Ehrlich carried out some work on lead poisoning from which he evolved the theory that was to guide all his subsequent work—that certain tissues have a selective affinity for certain chemicals. A quarter of a century was to pass before he gained success. By his discovery of arsphenamine, once sold under the commercial names of Salvarsan and 606, he inaugurated the chemotherapeutic era, which revolutionized the treatment and control of infectious diseases. Salvarsan is a synthetic arsenical preparation that is lethal to the micro-organism responsible for syphilis. Until the introduction of penicillin, Salvarsan or one of its modifications remained the standard treatment of syphilis and went far toward bringing this social and medical scourge under control.

Sulfonamide drugs. In 1932, a quarter of a century later, the German scientist Gerhard Domagk announced that the dye Prontosil rubrum is active against streptococcal infections in mice and in man. Soon afterward French workers showed that the active antibacterial agent is sulfanilamide. In 1936, the English physician Leonard Colebrook and his colleagues provided overwhelming evidence of the efficacy of both Prontosil and sulfanilamide in streptococcal septicemia (bloodstream infection), thereby ushering in the sulfonamide era. New sulfonamides appeared with almost embarrassing rapidity—with greater potency, a wider antibacterial spectrum, or lower toxicity. Some stood the test of time; others, like the original sulfanilamide and its immediate successor, sulfapyridine, were replaced by safer and more potent successors.

Antibiotics. *Penicillin.* Finally came the era of the antibiotics—in some ways the most dramatic episode in modern medicine. It was in 1928 that Alexander Fleming noticed the inhibitory action of a stray mold on a plate culture of staphylococci in his laboratory at St. Mary's Hospital, Paddington, London. Many another bacteriologist must have made the observation, but none had realized the possible implications. The mold was a strain of *Penicillium—P. notatum*; from this name was derived the term penicillin, which became known throughout the whole world. In spite of his conviction that penicillin is a potent antibacterial agent, Fleming was unable to carry his work to fruition, mainly because biochemists at the time were unable to isolate it in sufficient quantities or in a sufficiently pure form to allow its use on patients. Ten years later Howard Florey, Ernst Chain, and their colleagues at Oxford took up the problem again and solved it. By the time that Florey and his team had isolated penicillin in a form that was relatively pure by standards then current, though hopelessly crude by modern ones, and had demonstrated its potency and relative lack of toxicity, World War II had begun. In some ways this was an advantage because, if it had not been for the top priority given to commercial production, penicillin would not have become available in adequate amounts in such an amazingly short time.

Antituberculous drugs. While penicillin is the most useful and the safest antibiotic, it suffers from certain disadvantages. The most important of these is that it is not active against *Mycobacterium tuberculosis*, the bacillus of tuberculosis. In view of the importance of tuberculosis as a public health hazard, this is a serious defect, but the position was rapidly rectified when, in 1944, Selman A. Waksman and his colleagues announced the discovery of streptomycin from cultures of a soil organism, *Streptomyces griseus*, and stated that it is active against *Mycobacterium tuberculosis*. Subsequent clinical trials amply confirmed this claim. Unfortunately, streptomycin suffers from the great disadvantage that the *Mycobacterium tuberculosis* tends to become resistant to it. Fortunately, other drugs became available that compensated for this, the two most important being para-aminosalicylic acid (or PAS, as it is usually referred to) and isoniazid. With a combination of two or more of these preparations, the outlook in tuberculosis was revolutionized. Tuberculosis was not conquered but—provided reasonable precautions were taken—it was well under control.

Apart from its inadequacy as an antituberculosis drug, the other main disadvantage of penicillin is that its antibacterial spectrum does not cover the entire field of micro-organisms pathogenic to man. The pharmaceutical companies of the world—and particularly those of the United States—devoted a large part of their energies during the 1950s to a search for antibiotics to fill this gap. The search was amazingly successful and resulted in a steady stream of antibiotics, some with a much wider antibacterial spectrum than penicillin (the so-called broad-spectrum antibiotics) and some capable of coping with those micro-organisms that are inherently resistant to penicillin or have developed resistance through exposure to penicillin.

Derivatives of penicillin. This tendency of micro-organisms to develop resistance to penicillin at one time threatened to become almost as serious a problem as the development of resistance to streptomycin by the bacillus of tuberculosis. Fortunately, early appreciation of the problem by clinicians, resulting in more discriminate use of penicillin, combined with the availability of new antibiotics for general use, brought the problem largely under control.

Further developments related to penicillin occurred. The chemical synthesis of penicillin is possible but not practical on a commercial scale. The alternative method —by fermentation—is practical but cumbersome. Hence a search was made for a more effective means not only of production but also of producing a variety of penicillins, some of which might overcome the problem of the development of resistance in micro-organisms and at the same time might also be active when given by mouth. The fact that benzylpenicillin (the major penicillin) must be given by injection is one of its minor handicaps.

In 1959, British research workers achieved a major breakthrough by the isolation of 6-aminopenicillanic acid, the penicillin "nucleus." As a result, it became possible to introduce a new series of what became known as semisynthetics, some of which are active when given by mouth, while others are active against micro-organisms resistant to benzylpenicillin. Within a decade, over 2,000 new penicillins were produced in this way, six of which proved of clinical value.

IMMUNOLOGY

Dramatic though they undoubtedly were, the advances in chemotherapy still left one point vulnerable, that of the viruses, and it was in bringing them under control that advances in immunology—*i.e.*, the study of immunity—played such a striking part. It is one of the paradoxes of medicine that the first large-scale immunization against a virus disease was instituted and established long before viruses were discovered. When Edward Jenner introduced smallpox vaccination, as it is now known, against the virus that causes smallpox, the identification of viruses was still 100 years ahead, and almost another half century had to pass before an effective method was discovered of producing antiviral vaccines that were both safe and effective. In the meantime immunization against bacterial diseases made rapid progress.

Developments through World War II. *Typhoid and paratyphoid.* In 1897 the English bacteriologist Almroth Wright introduced a vaccine prepared from killed typhoid bacilli as a preventive of typhoid. Preliminary trials in the Indian army produced excellent results, and typhoid vaccination was adopted for the use of the troops serving in the South African War. Unfortunately, the method of administration was inadequately controlled, and all the War Office would sanction was that only such men would be inoculated as "voluntarily presented themselves for this purpose prior to their embarkation for the seat of war." The result was that, according to the official records, only 14,626 men volunteered out of a total strength of 328,244 who served during the three years of war. Although later analysis showed that inoculation had had a beneficial effect, there were 57,684 cases of typhoid —approximately one in six of the British troops engaged —with 9,022 deaths. In the subsequent embittered discussions, Karl Pearson, a statistician, challenged the valid-

Tetanus
antitoxin

Immuni-
zation
against
tuber-
culosis

ity of the claims put forward by Wright. To settle the matter an anti-typhoid commission was set up. On the strength of its report, published in 1913, the British Army officially adopted immunization against typhoid, Lord Kitchener decreeing that no man would be sent abroad who had not been inoculated. The result was that almost 100 percent of the British Expeditionary Force was immunized by the end of 1915. If figures mean anything, those for the South African War and World War I provide striking confirmation of the value of anti-typhoid inoculation, even when all due allowance is made for better sanitary arrangements in World War I. In the South African War the annual incidence of enteric infections (typhoid and paratyphoid) was 105 per 1,000 strength, and the annual death rate was 14.6 per 1,000 strength. The comparable figures for World War I were 2.35 and 0.139 respectively.

It is perhaps a sign of the increasingly critical outlook that developed in medicine in the post-1945 era of therapeutic advance that in the 1970s the experts still differed on some of the aspects of typhoid immunization. There was no question as to its fundamental efficacy, but there was considerable variation of opinion as to the best vaccine to use and the most effective way of administering it. A theoretical point that also worried the purist was that in many instances it was difficult to decide to what extent the decline in typhoid is due to improved sanitary conditions and what to the greater use of the vaccine.

Tetanus. The other great hazard of war that was brought under control in World War I was tetanus. This was achieved by the prophylactic injection of tetanus antitoxin into all wounded men. The World War I use of this serum, which was originally prepared by the bacteriologists Emil von Behring and Shibasaburo Kitasato in 1890–92, was the first large-scale trial of tetanus antitoxin, and the results amply confirmed its efficacy. (Tetanus antitoxin is a sterile solution of antibody globulins—a type of blood protein—from immunized horses or cattle.) But it was not until the 1930s that an efficient vaccine, or toxoid, as it is known in the cases of tetanus and diphtheria, was produced against tetanus. (Tetanus toxoid is a preparation of the toxin—or poisons—produced by the micro-organism. Injected into humans, the toxoid stimulates the body's own defenses against the disease, thus bringing about immunization). Again, a war was to provide the opportunity for testing on a large scale, and experience with tetanus toxoid in World War II indicated that it gave a high degree of protection.

Diphtheria. The story of diphtheria is comparable to that of tetanus, though even more dramatic. First came the preparation of diphtheria antitoxin, as in the case of tetanus antitoxin, by Behring and Kitasato in 1890. As diphtheria antitoxin came into general use for the treatment of cases, the death rate began to decline. There was no significant fall in the number of cases, however, until a toxin–antitoxin mixture, introduced by Behring in 1913, was used to immunize children. A more effective toxoid was introduced by the French bacteriologist G. Ramon in 1923, and with subsequent improvements this became one of the most effective vaccines available in medicine. Where mass immunization of children with the toxoid has been practiced, as in the United States and Canada beginning in the late 1930s and in England and Wales in the early 1940s, cases of diphtheria and deaths from the disease became almost nonexistent. In England and Wales, for instance, the number of deaths fell from an annual average of 1,830 in 1940–44 to zero in 1969.

BCG vaccine. If, as is universally accepted, prevention is better than cure, immunization is the ideal way of dealing with diseases caused by micro-organisms. An effective, safe vaccine protects the individual from disease, whereas chemotherapy merely copes with the infection once the individual has been affected. In spite of its undoubted value, however, immunization was a recurring cause of controversy. Reference has already been made to the controversy surrounding the introduction of typhoid immunization; the later controversy over poliomyelitis (infantile paralysis) immunization was another

example. Yet another form of immunization, or vaccination, that evoked widespread controversy was that for tuberculosis. In 1908 Albert Calmette, a pupil of Pasteur, and Camille Guérin produced an avirulent (attenuated) strain of the bovine *Mycobacterium tuberculosis*. About 13 years later, vaccination of children against tuberculosis was introduced, with a vaccine made from this avirulent strain and known as BCG (bacillus Calmette-Guérin) vaccine. Although it was adopted in France, Scandinavia, and elsewhere, British and United States authorities frowned upon its use on the grounds that it was not safe and that the statistical evidence in its favour was not convincing. One of the stumbling blocks in the way of its widespread adoption was what came to be known as the Lübeck disaster. In the spring of 1930, 249 infants were vaccinated with BCG vaccine in Lübeck, Germany; by autumn, 73 of the 249 were dead. Criminal proceedings were instituted against those responsible for giving the vaccine; the final verdict was that contamination of the vaccine had occurred, and BCG vaccine was exonerated from any responsibility for the deaths. A bitter controversy followed, but in the end the protagonists of the vaccine won when a trial sponsored by the Medical Research Council showed that the vaccine was safe and that it protected four out of five of those vaccinated.

Recent virus advances. So far as viruses were concerned, with the exception of smallpox, it was not until well into the 20th century that efficient vaccines became available. This is scarcely surprising when it is realized that it was not until the 1930s that much began to be known about viruses. The two advances that contributed most to the rapid advance in knowledge since then were the introduction of tissue culture as a means of growing viruses in the laboratory and the development of the electron microscope. Once the virus could be cultivated with comparative ease in the laboratory, the research worker could study it with care and evolve methods for producing one of the two desiderata for a safe and effective vaccine: either a virus that was so attenuated that it could not produce the disease for which it was responsible in its normally virulent form or a dead virus that retained the faculty of inducing a protective antibody response in the vaccinated individual.

The first of the viral vaccines to result from these advances was for yellow fever, developed by the microbiologist Max Theiler in the late 1930s. About 1945, the first relatively effective vaccine was produced for influenza; in 1954, the American physician Jonas E. Salk introduced a vaccine for poliomyelitis; and in 1960, an oral poliomyelitis vaccine, developed by the virologist Albert B. Sabin, came into wide use. These vaccines went far toward bringing under control three of the major diseases of the time although, in the case of influenza, a major complication was the disturbing proclivity of the virus to change its character from one epidemic to another. Even so, sufficient progress was made to ensure that a pandemic of the order of the one that swept the world in 1918–19, killing more than 15,000,000 people, is unlikely to occur again. In guarding against such a tragic eventuality, one of the most potent safeguards was the World Influenza Centre, which was established in London by the World Health Organization. Thither information about outbreaks of influenza anywhere in the world is immediately sent, together with samples of the causative virus. This means that the identity of the virus can quickly be established and that, if necessary, steps can be taken to produce an effective vaccine. If the virus is a new one, a vaccine may not be ready for the early stages of the epidemic, should one occur, but it will be available for the later stages.

During the 1960s effective vaccines came into use for measles and rubella (German measles). Both evoked a certain amount of controversy. In the case of measles in Western civilization, it was contended that, if acquired in childhood, it is not a particularly hazardous disease, and the naturally acquired disease evokes permanent immunity in the vast majority of cases. Conversely, the vaccine induces a certain number of reactions, and the duration of the immunity it produces is problematical. In the end the official view was that universal measles vaccination is

Polio-
myelitis
vaccine

to be commended. The problem in the case of rubella vaccine was different. This is a fundamentally mild disease, and the only cause for anxiety is its proclivity to induce congenital deformities should a pregnant woman acquire the disease. Once an effective vaccine was available, the problem was the extent to which it should be used. Ultimately the commonsense compromise was achieved that all girls who had not already had the disease should be vaccinated around the age of 12 years.

The isolation of the virus of trachoma by Chinese and British workers raised hopes for the possibility of evolving a vaccine that would be effective in curbing the ravages of the greatest blinding disease in the world. In the early 1970s these hopes had not yet been realized.

Up until the turn of the century, for all practical purposes immunology was used in the narrow sense of the study of the means of resistance of an animal to invasion by a parasite or micro-organism. Around the midcentury, however, there came a growing and clearer realization of the fact that immunity, and the study thereof, cover a much wider field and are concerned with mechanisms for preserving the integrity of the individual (or animal). The introduction of organ transplantation, with its dreaded complication of organ rejection, brought this wider field of immunology to the fore. At the same time, research workers and clinicians began to appreciate the far-reaching implications in endocrinology, genetics, cell biology, tumour biology, and a range of so-called autoimmune diseases. In thus stretching out into the unknown, the searching mind in medicine began to probe mysteries of great magnitude.

ENDOCRINOLOGY

At the beginning of the 20th century, endocrinology was in its infancy. Indeed, it was not until 1905 that Ernest H. Starling, one of the many brilliant pupils of Sir Edward Sharpey-Schafer, the dean of British physiology during the early decades of the century, introduced the term hormone for the internal secretions of the endocrine glands. In 1891 the English physician George Redmayne Murray was the first to treat myxedema (the common form of hypothyroidism) successfully with an extract of the thyroid gland. Three years later, Sharpey-Schafer and George Oliver demonstrated in extracts of the adrenal (suprarenal) glands a substance that raised the blood pressure, and in 1901 Jokichi Takamine (1854–1922), a Japanese chemist working in the U.S., isolated this active principle: epinephrine (as it is known in the *United States Pharmacopeia*) or adrenaline (as it is known in the *British Pharmacopoeia*).

Isolation of epinephrine

Discovery of insulin and cortisone. During the first two decades of the century, steady progress was made in the isolation, identification, and study of the active principles of the various endocrine glands, but the outstanding event was the discovery of insulin by Sir Frederick Banting, Charles H. Best, and John James Rickard Macleod in 1921. Almost overnight the lot of the diabetic patient was changed from a sentence of almost certain death to a prospect not only of survival but of being able to lead a long and healthy life. As so often happens with the great discoveries in medicine, this one came from a most unexpected source. For more than 30 years, some of the greatest minds in physiology had been seeking the cause of diabetes mellitus. In 1889, the German physicians Joseph von Mering (1849–1908) and Oskar Minkowski (1858–1931) had shown that removal of the pancreas in dogs produced diabetes. In 1901, the American pathologist Eugene L. Opie described degenerative changes in the clumps of cells in the pancreas known as the islets of Langerhans, thus confirming the association between failure in the function of these cells and diabetes. Sharpey-Schafer concluded that the islets of Langerhans secrete a substance that controls the metabolism of carbohydrate. In 1921 Banting, then a young Canadian orthopedic surgeon interested in physiology, working with Best, a medical student, in the laboratory of Macleod at the University of Toronto, succeeded in isolating the elusive hormone and gave it the name of insulin. Insulin was available in a variety of forms, but synthesis on a commercial scale was

not achieved, and the only source of the hormone was the pancreas of animals. One of its practical disadvantages is that it has to be given by injection, and, during the subsequent years, an intense search was conducted for some alternative preparation that would be active when taken by mouth. Various preparations—oral hypoglycemic agents, as they are known—appeared that were effective to a certain extent in controlling diabetes, but all the available evidence indicated that these were only of value in relatively mild cases of diabetes. For the person with advanced diabetes, a normal healthy life remained dependent upon the continuing use of insulin injections.

Another major advance in endocrinology came with an announcement from the Mayo Clinic, in Rochester, Minnesota. In 1949 Philip S. Hench and his colleagues announced that a substance isolated from the cortex of the adrenal gland has a dramatic effect upon rheumatoid arthritis. This was compound E, or cortisone, as it came to be known, which had been isolated by Edward Calvin Kendall and his colleagues at the Mayo Clinic in 1935. The subsequent course of events showed that cortisone is not the answer to the problem of rheumatoid arthritis, but ample evidence was forthcoming to show the potent influence of cortisone and its many derivatives as anti-inflammatory agents. It is not a cure for rheumatoid arthritis, but as a temporary measure it can often control the acute exacerbation caused by the disease, just as it can aid in such other diseases as acute rheumatic fever, certain kidney diseases, certain serious diseases of the skin, and some allergic diseases, including acute exacerbations of asthma. Of even more long-term importance is the valuable role it has as a research tool.

Isolation of cortisone

Use of sex hormones. Not the least of the advances in endocrinology was the increasing knowledge and understanding of the sex hormones. This ultimately culminated in the application of this knowledge to helping solve the world population problem. After an initial stage of hesitancy, the contraceptive pill, with its basic rationale of preventing ovulation, was accepted by the vast majority of family-planning organizations and a not inconsiderable number of gynecologists as the most satisfactory method of contraception. Its risks, practical and theoretical, introduced a note of caution, but this was not sufficient to detract from the wide appeal induced by its effectiveness and ease of use.

ADVANCES IN OTHER FIELDS

Nutrition. *Discovery of vitamins.* In the field of nutrition, the outstanding advance of the 20th century was the discovery and the appreciation of the importance of the "accessory food factors," or vitamins. Although various workers had shown that animals did not thrive on a synthetic diet containing all the correct amounts of protein, fat, and carbohydrate and even suggested that there must be some then-unknown ingredients in natural food that were essential for growth and the maintenance of health, little progress was made in this field until the classical experiments of the English biologist F. Gowland Hopkins were published in 1912. So conclusive were these that there could be no doubt that what he termed "accessory substances" were essential for health and growth. The name vitamine was suggested for these substances by the biochemist Casimir Funk in the belief that they were amines, certain compounds derived from ammonia. In due course, when it was realized that they were not amines, the term was altered to vitamin.

Identification of vitamins. Once this concept of vitamins was established on a firm scientific basis it was not long before their identity began to be revealed; soon there was a long series of them, best known by the letters of the alphabet after which they were originally named when their chemical identity was still unknown. Deficiency diseases such as rickets (due to deficiency of vitamin D) and scurvy (due to lack of vitamin C, or ascorbic acid) practically disappeared from Western communities, while deficiency diseases such as beriberi (caused by lack of vitamin B_1, also called thiamine or aneurin), which were endemic in Eastern countries, either disappeared or could be remedied with the greatest of ease.

Vitamin
B₁₂ and
pernicious
anemia

The last of this group of essential factors to be isolated —vitamin B_{12}, or cyanocobalamin—was of particular interest because it rounded off—or almost rounded off—the fascinating story of how pernicious anemia was brought under control. Throughout the first two decades of the century, the diagnosis of pernicious anemia, like that of diabetes mellitus, was almost equivalent to a death sentence. Unlike the more common form of so-called secondary anemia, it did not respond to the administration of suitable iron salts, and no other form of treatment touched it; hence, the grimly appropriate title of pernicious anemia. In the early 1920s, George R. Minot, one of the many brilliant investigators whom Harvard University contributed to medical research, became interested in work being carried out by the American pathologist George H. Whipple into the beneficial effects of the administration of raw beef liver in severe experimental anemia. With a colleague at Harvard, William P. Murphy, he decided to investigate the effect of raw liver in patients with pernicious anemia, and in 1926 they were able to announce that this form of therapy was successful. The validity of their findings was amply confirmed, and all fears of pernicious anemia were ended. As so often happens in medicine, many years were to pass before the rationale of liver therapy in pernicious anemia was fully understood. In 1948, however, almost simultaneously in the United States and in Britain, the active principle was isolated from liver. It was originally known as vitamin B_{12} but came to be known as cyanocobalamin. It became the standard treatment for pernicious anemia.

Malignant disease. While progress was the hallmark of medicine after the beginning of the 20th century, there was one field in which a gloomier picture must be painted, that of malignant disease, or cancer. It was the second most common cause of death in most Western countries early in the second half of the 20th century, being exceeded only by deaths from heart disease. Some progress, however, was achieved. The cause of cancer was not known, but many more methods were available for attacking the problem; surgery remained the great therapeutic standby, but radiotherapy and chemotherapy played increasingly important parts.

Radiation
treatment
of cancer

Soon after the discovery of radium was announced, in 1898, its potentialities in treating cancer were realized; in due course it assumed an important role in therapy. Simultaneously, deep X-ray therapy was developed. Finally, with the atomic age came the use of radioactive isotopes. (A radioactive isotope is an unstable variant of a substance that has a stable form; during the process of breaking down, the unstable form emits radiation.) High-voltage X-ray therapy and radioactive isotopes largely replaced radium. Whereas irradiation had long depended upon X-rays generated at 250 kilovolts, machines that were capable of producing X-rays generated at 8,000 kilovolts and betatrons of up to 22 million electron volts (MeV) were in clinical use. In the application of radioactive isotopes to the treatment of malignant disease, the most important development was the use of radioactive cobalt. Telecobalt machines (*i.e.*, those that hold the cobalt at a distance from the body) were available containing 2,000 curies or more of the isotope, an amount equivalent to 3,000 grams (100 ounces) of radium (an unheard-of amount of radium), and sending out a beam equivalent to that from a 3,000-kilovolt X-ray machine.

Of even more significance were the developments in the chemotherapy of malignant disease. Nothing remotely resembling a chemotherapeutic cure was achieved, but in certain forms of malignant disease, such as leukemia, which cannot be treated by surgery, palliative effects were achieved that prolonged life and allowed the patient in many instances to lead a comparatively normal existence. Fundamentally, however, perhaps the most important advance of all in this field was the increasing appreciation of the importance of prevention. The discovery of the relationship between cigarette smoking and cancer of the lung was the classic example. Less publicized, but of equal import, was the continuing supervision of new techniques in industry and food manufacture to ensure that they did not involve the use of cancer-causing substances.

Tropical medicine. In the field of tropical medicine, the first six decades of the 20th century witnessed the virtual conquest of three of the major diseases of the tropics: malaria, yellow fever, and leprosy. At the turn of the century, as for the preceding two centuries, quinine was the only known drug to have any appreciable effect on malaria. With the increasing development of tropical countries and rising standards of public health, it became obvious that quinine was not completely satisfactory. Intensive research between World Wars I and II indicated that several synthetic derivatives in the acridine and quinoline groups of organic compounds, as well as other synthetic aromatic compounds, were more effective than quinine. The first of these to become available, in 1934, was quinacrine (mepacrine, Atabrine, or Atebrin), an acridine derivative. In World War II it amply fulfilled the highest expectations and helped to reduce disease among Allied troops in Africa, Southeast Asia, and the Far East. Other effective antimalarial drugs that subsequently became available included chloroquine (Aralen), a 4-aminoquinoline, 1939; chlorguanide (Paludrine or Proguanil), 1946; primaquin, an 8-aminoquinoline, 1946; amodiaquin (Camoquin), 1948; hydroxychloroquine (Plaquenil), 1950; and pyrimethamine (Daraprim), 1951.

DDT and
malaria

An even brighter prospect—the virtual eradication of malaria—was opened up by the introduction, during World War II, of the insecticide DDT (chlorophenothane in the *U. S. Pharmacopeia*, dicophane in the *British Pharmacopoeia*). It had long been realized that the only effective way of controlling malaria was to eradicate the anopheline mosquitoes, which transmit the disease. The older methods of mosquito control, however, were cumbersome and expensive. The lethal effect of DDT on the mosquito, its relative cheapness, and its ease of use on a widespread scale provided the answer. An intensive worldwide campaign, sponsored by the World Health Organization, was planned and went far toward bringing malaria under control. The major problem encountered with respect to effectiveness was that of the developing resistance of the mosquito to DDT, but the introduction of other insecticides, such as dieldrin and lindane (BHC), helped to overcome this difficulty. In recent years the use of these and other insecticides has been criticized by ecologists.

Reference has already been made to the important part that the introduction of an effective vaccine played in bringing yellow fever under control. Since this is another mosquito-transmitted disease, the prophylactic value of the introduction of modern insecticides was almost as great as in the case of malaria. The forest reservoirs of the virus present a more difficult problem than in the case of malaria, but the combined use of immunization and insecticides did much to bring this disease under control.

Until the 1940s, the only drugs available for treating leprosy were the chaulmoogra oils and their derivatives. These, though helpful, were far from satisfactory. In the 1940s the group of drugs known as the sulfones appeared; it soon became apparent that they were infinitely better than any other group of drugs in the treatment of leprosy. Several other drugs that later became available proved of promise. Although it was clear that there was as yet no known cure—in the strict sense of the term—for leprosy, the outlook so changed that there were good grounds for believing that this age-old scourge could be brought under control and the victims of the disease saved from those dread mutilations that gave leprosy such a fearsome reputation throughout the ages.   (Wm.A.R.T.)

IV. Surgery in the 20th century

THE OPENING PHASE

Three seemingly insuperable obstacles beset the surgeon in the years before the mid-19th century: pain, infection, and shock. Once these were overcome, he believed he could burst the bonds of centuries and become the master of his craft. Unfortunately life is not that simple. There is more to anesthesia than putting the patient to sleep. Infection, despite first antisepsis (destruction of microorganisms present) and later asepsis (avoidance of contamination), is still an ever-present menace; and shock continues to perplex. But, in the 20th century, surgery has progressed further, faster, and more dramatically than in all preceding ages.

The situation encountered.   The shape of surgery that entered the new century was clearly recognizable as the forerunner of today's, blurred and hazy though the outlines may now seem. The operating theatre still retained an aura of the past, when the surgeon played to his audience and the patient was little more than a stage prop. In most hospitals it was a high room lit by a skylight, with tiers of benches rising above the narrow, wooden operating table. The instruments, kept in glazed or wooden cupboards around the walls, were of forged steel, unplated, and with handles of wood or ivory.

Antisepsis and asepsis

The means to combat infection hovered between antisepsis and asepsis. Instruments and dressings were mostly sterilized by soaking in dilute carbolic acid (or other antiseptic), and the surgeon often endured a gown freshly wrung out in the same solution. Asepsis was gaining ground fast, however. It had been born in the Berlin clinic of Ernst von Bergmann where, in 1886, steam sterilization had been introduced. Gradually, this led to the complete aseptic ritual, which has as its basis the bacterial cleanliness (as opposed to social cleanliness) of everything that comes in contact with the wound. Hermann Kümmell, of Hamburg, devised the routine of "scrubbing up." William Stewart Halsted, of Johns Hopkins, in 1890 had rubber gloves specially made for operating, and, in 1896, Johannes von Mikulicz-Radecki, a Pole working at Breslau, invented the gauze mask. Many surgeons, brought up in a confused misunderstanding of the antiseptic principle—believing that carbolic would cover a multitude of sins, many of which they were ignorant of committing—failed to grasp what asepsis was all about. Thomas Annandale blew through his catheters to make sure that they were clear, and another Scottish surgeon periodically removed his pince-nez for a closer inspection of his work. Many an instrument, dropped accidentally, was simply given a quick wipe and returned to use. Tradition died hard, and asepsis had an uphill struggle before it was fully accepted—"I believe firmly that more patients have died from the use of gloves than have ever been saved from infection by their use," wrote W.P. Carr, an American, in 1911—but over the years a sound technique was evolved as the foundation for the growth of modern surgery.

Anesthesia at the turn of the century

Anesthesia, at the turn of the century, was progressing slowly. Few physicians made a career of the subject, and frequently the patient was rendered unconscious by a student, a nurse, or a porter wielding a rag and bottle. Chloroform was overwhelmingly more popular than ether, on account of its ease of administration, despite the fact that it was liable to kill by stopping the heart. Although by the end of the first decade, nitrous oxide (laughing gas) combined with ether had displaced—but by no means entirely—the use of chloroform, the surgical problems were far from ended. For years to come the abdominal surgeon besought the anesthetist to deepen the level of anesthesia and thus relax the abdominal muscles; the anesthetist responded to the best of his ability, acutely aware that the deeper he went, the closer the patient was to death. When other anesthetic agents were discovered, the anesthetist came into his own, and many advances in spheres such as brain and heart surgery would have been impossible without his skill.

The third obstacle, shock, is perhaps the most complex and the most difficult to define satisfactorily. The only major cause properly appreciated at the start of the 20th century was loss of blood, and once that had occurred nothing could, in those days, be done. And so, as the years passed, the study of shock, its causes, its effects on human physiology, and its prevention and treatment, became all important to the progress of surgery.

Thus, in the latter part of the 19th century, surgeons had been liberated from the age-old bogies of pain, pus, and hospital gangrene. Hitherto, operations had been restricted to amputations, cutting for stone in the bladder, tying off arterial aneurysms (bulging and thinning of ar-

tery walls), repairing hernias, and a variety of procedures that could be done without going too deeply beneath the skin. But the anatomical knowledge, a crude skill derived from practice on dead bodies, and, above all, the enthusiasm were there, waiting. Largely ignoring the mass of problems they uncovered, surgeons launched forth into a mighty exploration of the human body.

They acquired a reputation for showmanship; much of their surgery, though speedy and spectacular, was rough and ready. A few there were who developed a supreme skill and dexterity and could have undertaken a modern operation with but little practice—indeed, some devised the very operations still in use today. One such was Theodor Billroth, head of the surgical clinic at Vienna, who collected a formidable list of successful "first" operations. He represented the best of his generation—a surgical genius, an accomplished musician, and a kind, gentle man who brought the breath of humanity to his work. Moreover, the men he trained, including von Mikulicz, Vincenz Czerny, and Anton von Eiselsberg, consolidated the brilliant start that he had given to abdominal surgery in Europe.

Billroth's influence

Changes before World War I.   The opening decade of the 20th century was a period of transition. Flamboyant exhibitionism was falling from favour as surgeons, through experience, learned the merits of painstaking, conscientious operation—treating the tissues gently and carefully controlling every bleeding point. The individualist was not submerged, however, and for many years the development of the various branches of surgery rested on the shoulders of a few clearly identifiable men. Teamwork on the grand scale arrived only after World War II. The surgeon, at first, was undisputed master in his own wards and theatre, but as time went on and he found he could not solve his problems alone, he called for help from specialists in other fields of medicine and, even more significantly, from his colleagues in other scientific disciplines.

The increasing scope of surgery led to specialization. Admittedly, most general surgeons had a special interest, and for a long time there had been an element of specialization in such subjects as ophthalmology, orthopedics, obstetrics, and gynecology, but before long it became apparent that, to achieve progress in certain areas, surgeons had to concentrate their attention on that particular subject.

By the start of the 20th century, abdominal surgery, which provided the general surgeon with the bulk of his work, had grown beyond infancy thanks largely to Billroth. In 1881 he had performed the first successful removal of part of the stomach for cancer. His next two cases were failures, and he was stoned in the streets of Vienna; yet, he persisted and by 1891 had carried out 41 more of these operations with 16 deaths—a remarkable achievement for that era. Peptic (gastric and duodenal) ulcers appeared on the surgical scene (perhaps as a new disease, but more probably because they had not been diagnosed previously), and in 1881 Ludwig Rydygier cured a young woman of her gastric ulcer by removing it. Bypass operations—gastro-enterostomies—soon became more popular, however. Gastro-enterostomies enjoyed a considerable vogue that lasted into the 1930s, even though fresh ulcers at the site of the juncture were not uncommon. The other end of the alimentary tract was also subjected to surgical treatment; cancers were removed from the large bowel and rectum with mortality rates that gradually fell from 80 to 60 to 20 to 12 percent as the surgeons learned their lessons. In 1908 the British surgeon Ernest Miles carried out the first abdomino-perineal resection for cancer of the rectum; that is, the cancer was attacked both from the abdomen and from below through the perineum (the area at the base of the trunk between the anus and the genital organs), either by one surgeon, who really did two operations, or by two working together. This technique formed the basis for all future developments.

Abdominal surgery

Much of the new surgery in the abdomen was for cancer, but not all. Appendectomy became accepted treatment for appendicitis (in appropriate cases) in the United

States before the close of the 19th century, but in Great Britain surgeons were reluctant to remove the organ until King Edward VII's coronation (1902) was dramatically postponed on account of appendicitis. The publicity attached to his operation caused the disease and its surgical treatment to become fashionable—despite the fact that the royal appendix remained in the King's abdomen; the surgeon Frederic Treves merely drained the abscess.

Neurosurgery, probably the most demanding of all the surgical specialties, was nevertheless one of the first to emerge. The techniques and principles of general surgery were inadequate for work in such a delicate field. William Macewen, a Scottish general surgeon of outstanding versatility, and Victor Alexander Haden Horsley, the first British neurosurgeon, showed that the surgeon had much to offer in the treatment of disease of the brain and spinal cord. Macewen, in 1893, recorded 19 patients operated on for brain abscess, 18 of whom were cured; at that time most other surgeons had 100 percent mortality rates for the condition. His achievement remained unequalled until the discovery of penicillin. An American, Harvey Williams Cushing, almost by himself consolidated neurosurgery as a specialty. From 1905 on, he advanced neurosurgery and neurology every time he picked up his scalpel to operate or his pen to write. Tumours, epilepsy, trigeminal neuralgia, and pituitary disorders were among the conditions he treated. (Trigeminal neuralgia, tic douloureux, is sharp pain along branches of the trigeminal nerve, particularly those serving the jaws and the eyes.)

Impor-
tance
of the
discovery
of X-rays
In 1895 a discovery in Würzburg had far-reaching effects in medicine and surgery, opening up an entirely fresh field of diagnosis and study of disease and leading to a new form of treatment (radiation therapy). Wilhelm Conrad Röntgen, professor of physics, discovered X-rays. Within a matter of months of the discovery there was an extensive literature on the subject—Robert Jones, a British surgeon, had localized a bullet in a boy's wrist before operating; stones in the urinary bladder and gallbladder had been demonstrated; fractures had been displayed; and experiments had started on introducing radiopaque substances into the body to outline the normal and the abnormal. Walter Bradford Cannon, a Boston physiologist, used X-rays in 1898 in his studies of the alimentary tract. Friedrich Voelcker, of Heidelberg, devised retrograde pyelography (introduction of the radio-opaque medium into the kidney pelvis by way of the ureter) for the study of the urinary tract in 1905; in 1921, in Paris, Jean Athanase Sicard X-rayed the spinal canal with the help of an oily iodine substance, and the next year he did the same for the bronchial tree; and in 1924 Evarts Ambrose Graham, of St. Louis, used a radio-opaque medium in viewing the gallbladder. Air was also used to provide contrast; in 1918, at Johns Hopkins, Walter Edward Dandy injected air into the ventricles (liquid-filled cavities) of the brain. The problems of injecting contrast media into the blood vessels took longer to solve, and it was not until 1927 that António Egas Moniz, of Lisbon, succeeded in obtaining pictures of the arteries of the brain. Eleven years later, George Porter Robb and Israel Steinberg of New York overcame some of the difficulties of cardiac catheterization (introduction of a small tube into the heart by way of veins or arteries) and were able to visualize the chambers of the heart on X-ray film. After much further research, the final refinement came in 1962, when Frank Mason Sones and Earl K. Shirey of Cleveland, Ohio, showed how to introduce the contrast medium into the coronary arteries (the arteries that supply oxygen-rich blood to the heart muscle).

WORLD WAR I

The battlefields of the 20th century stimulated the progress of surgery and taught the surgeon innumerable lessons, which he subsequently applied in civilian practice. Regrettably, though, the principles of military surgery and casualty evacuation, which can all be traced back to Dominique-Jean Larrey in the Napoleonic Wars, had to be learned over and over again.

World War I broke, quite dramatically, the existing surgical hierarchy and rule of tradition. No longer had the European surgeon to waste his best years in apprenticeship before seating himself in his master's chair. Suddenly, young surgeons began conquering problems that would have daunted their elders. Furthermore, their training had been in "clean" surgery performed under aseptic conditions. Now they found themselves confronted by the need to treat large numbers of grossly contaminated wounds in improvised theatres. They rediscovered débridement (the surgical excision of all dead and dying tissue and the removal of all foreign bodies whatever their nature). The cry of the older surgeons was "back to Lister," but antiseptics, no matter how strong, were no match for putrefaction and gangrene. One method of antiseptic irrigation—devised by Alexis Carrel and Henry Drysdale Dakin and called the Carrel-Dakin treatment—was, however, beneficial, but only after the wound had been adequately débrided. The scourges of tetanus and gas gangrene were controlled to a large extent by antitoxin and antiserum injections, yet surgical treatment of the wound remained an essential requirement.

Treat-
ment of
contam-
inated
wounds

Abdominal casualties fared badly for the first year of the war, because experience in the utterly different circumstances of the Boer War had led to a belief that these men were better left alone surgically. Fortunately, the error of continuing with such a policy 15 years later was soon appreciated, and every effort was made to deliver the wounded men to a suitable surgical unit with all speed. Little progress was made with chest wounds beyond more extensive operations to drain pus from the pleural cavity (i.e., from between the membrane lining the chest and that covering the lungs).

Perhaps the most worthwhile and enduring benefit to flow from the war of 1914–18 was rehabilitation. For almost the first time, surgeons realized that their work did not end with a healed wound. In 1915 Robert Jones set up special facilities for orthopedic patients, and at about the same time Harold Delf Gillies founded British plastic surgery in a hut at Sidcup, Kent. In 1917 Gillies popularized the pedicle type of skin graft (the type of graft that consists of skin and subcutaneous tissue that is attached for nourishment as long as necessary to the site from which the graft was taken). Since then the specialty has given freely of its techniques and principles to other branches of surgery.

BETWEEN WARS

The years between the wars may conveniently be regarded as the time when surgery consolidated its position. A surprising number of surgical firsts and an amazing amount of fundamental research had been achieved even in the late 19th century, but the knowledge and experience could not be converted to practical use because the human body could not survive the onslaught. In the years between World War I and World War II, it was realized that physiology (in its widest sense, including biochemistry and fluid and electrolyte balance) was of major importance along with anatomy, pathology, and surgical technique.

The problem of shock. The first problem to be tackled was shock, which was, in brief, found to be due to a decrease in the effective volume of the circulation. To combat shock, the volume had to be restored, and the obvious substance was blood itself. In 1901 Karl Landsteiner, there in Austria, discovered the ABO blood groups, and in 1914 sodium citrate was added to freshly drawn blood to prevent clotting. Blood was occasionally transfused during World War I, but three-quarters of a pint was considered a large amount. These transfusions were given by directly linking the vein of a donor with that of the recipient. The continuous drip method, in which blood flows from a flask, was introduced by Hugh Leslie Marriott and Alan Kekwick at the Middlesex Hospital, London, in 1935.

Restora-
tion of
blood
volume
after
shock

As blood transfusions increased in frequency and volume, blood banks were required. Although it took another world war before these were organized on a large scale, the first tentative steps were taken by Sergey Sergeyevich Yudin, of Moscow, who, in 1933, used cadaver blood, and by Bernard Fantus, of Chicago, who, four years later, used living donors as his source of supply. Saline solution, plasma, artificial plasma expanders, and other solutions are now also used in the appropriate circumstances.

Sometimes after operations (especially abdominal operations) the gut becomes paralyzed. It is distended, and quantities of fluid pour into it, dehydrating the patient. In 1932 Owen Hardy Wangensteen, at the University of Minnesota, advised decompressing the bowel, and in 1934 two other Americans, Thomas Grier Miller and William Osler Abbott, of Philadelphia, invented apparatus for this purpose, a tube with an inflatable balloon on the end that could be passed into the small intestine. The fluid lost from the tissues was replaced by a continuous intravenous drip of saline solution on the principle described by Rudolph Matas, of New Orleans, in 1924. These techniques dramatically improved abdominal surgery, especially in cases of obstruction, peritonitis (inflammation of the membrane lining the abdomen and pelvis and covering the viscera) and acute emergencies generally, as they made it possible to keep the bowel empty and at rest.

Anesthesia and thoracic surgery. The strides taken in anesthesia from the 1920s onward allowed surgeons much more freedom. Rectal anesthesia had never proved satisfactory, and the first improvement on the combination of nitrous oxide, oxygen, and ether was the introduction of the general anesthetic cyclopropane by Ralph Milton Waters of Madison, Wisconsin, in 1933. Soon afterward, intravenous anesthesia was introduced; John Silas Lundy of the Mayo Clinic brought to a climax a long series of trials by many workers when he used Pentothal (thiopental sodium, a barbiturate) to put a patient peacefully to sleep. Then, in 1942, Harold Randall Griffith and G. Enid Johnson, of Montreal, produced muscular paralysis by the injection of a purified preparation of curare. This was harmless since, by then, the anesthetist was able to control the patient's respiration.

Methods for prevention of lung collapse

If there was one person who was aided more than any other by the progress in anesthesia, it was the thoracic (chest) surgeon. What had bothered him previously was the collapse of the lung, which occurred whenever the pleural cavity was opened. Since the end of the 19th century, many and ingenious methods had been devised to prevent this from happening. The best known was the negative pressure cabinet of Ernst Ferdinand Sauerbruch, then at Mikulicz' clinic at Breslau; the cabinet was first used clinically in 1904 but destined soon to become obsolete. The solution lay in inhalational anesthesia administered under pressure. Indeed, when Théodore Tuffier, in 1891, successfully removed the apex of a lung for tuberculosis, this was the technique that he used; he even added an inflatable cuff around the tube inserted in the windpipe to ensure a gas-tight fit. Tuffier was ahead of his time, however, and other surgeons and research workers went wandering into confused and complex byways before Ivan Whiteside Magill and Edgar Stanley Rowbotham, working at Gillies' plastic-surgery unit, found their way back to the simplicity of the endotracheal tube and positive pressure. In 1931 Waters showed that respiration could be controlled either by squeezing the anesthetic bag by hand or by using a small motor.

These advances allowed thoracic surgery to move into modern times. In the 1920s, operations had been performed mostly for infective conditions and as a last resort, but the operations necessarily were unambitious and confined to collapse therapy—thoracoplasty (removal of ribs), apicolysis (collapse of a lung apex and artificially filling the space), or phrenic crush (this paralyzed the diaphragm on the chosen side)—to isolation of the area of lung to be removed by first creating pleural adhesions; and to drainage. The technical problems of surgery within the chest were daunting, and despair was never far away until Harold Brunn of San Francisco reported six lobectomies (removals of lung lobes) for bronchiectasis with only one death. (In bronchiectasis one or more bronchi or bronchioles—small bronchi—are chronically dilated and inflamed, with copious discharge of mucus mixed with pus.) The secret of Brunn's success had been intermittent suction after operation to keep the cavity free of secretions until the remaining lung could expand to fill the space. In 1931 Rudolf Nissen, in Berlin, removed an entire lung from a girl with bronchiectasis. She recovered to prove that the risks were not as bad as had been feared.

Throughout the 20th century the pattern of disease has continually been changing, whether in the natural course of events or because man has disturbed the balance. Tuberculosis and bronchiectasis still exist but are nowhere near the problems that they were. In their place has come cancer of the lung—maybe a genuine increase, maybe modern techniques of diagnosis reveal it more often. As far back as 1913 a Welshman, Hugh Morriston Davies, had removed a lower lobe for cancer, but the start of the present era was Evarts Graham's removal of a whole lung for cancer, in 1933. The patient, a doctor, was still alive at the time of Graham's death in 1957.

Cancer of esophagus

The thoracic part of the esophagus, or gullet, was particularly difficult to reach, but in 1909 the British surgeon Arthur Henry Evans operated successfully for cancer. The results were generally poor until, in 1944, John Harry Garlock, of New York, showed that it is possible to excise the esophagus and to bring the stomach up through the chest and join it to the pharynx. Lengths of colon are also used as grafts to bridge the gap.

WORLD WAR II AND AFTER

Once the principles of military surgery were relearned and applied to modern warfare, instances of death, deformity, and loss of limb were reduced to levels previously unattainable. This was due largely to a thorough reorganization of the surgical services, adapting them to prevailing conditions, so that the casualty received the appropriate treatment at the earliest possible moment. Evacuation by air (first used in World War I) helped greatly in this respect. Diagnostic facilities were improved, and progress in anesthesia kept pace with the surgeon's demands. Blood was transfused in adequate—and hitherto unthinkable—quantities, and the blood transfusion service as it is known today came into being. Surgical specialization and teamwork reached new heights with the creation of units to deal with the special problems of injuries to different parts of the body. But the most revolutionary change was in the approach to wound infections brought about by the use of sulfonamides and (after 1941) of penicillin. The fact that these drugs could never replace meticulous wound surgery was, however, another lesson learned only in the bitter school of experience.

When the war ended, surgeons returned to civilian life feeling that they were at the start of a completely new, exciting era, and indeed they were, for the intense stimulation of the past few years had led to developments in many branches of science that could now be applied to surgery. Nevertheless, to keep matters in correct perspective, it must be remembered that these developments merely allowed surgeons to realize the dreams of their fathers and grandfathers; they opened up remarkably few original avenues. The two outstanding phenomena of the 1950s and 1960s—heart surgery and organ transplantation—both originated in a real and practical manner at the turn of the century.

At first, perhaps, the surgeon tried to do too much himself, but before long his failures taught him to share his problems with experts in other fields. This was especially so with respect to difficulties of biomedical engineering and the exploitation of new materials. The relative protection from infection given by antibiotics and chemotherapy allowed the surgeon to become far more adventurous than hitherto in repairing and replacing damaged or worn-out tissues with foreign materials. Much research was still needed to find the best material for a particular purpose and to make sure that it would be acceptable to the body. Plastics, in their seemingly infinite variety, were used for almost everything from suture material to heart valves; for strengthening the repair of hernias; for replacement of the head of the femur (first done by the French surgeon Jean Judet and his brother Robert Louis Judet, in 1950); for replacement of the lens of the eye after extraction of the natural lens for cataract; for

Use of plastics in surgery

valves for use in draining fluid from the brain in patients with hydrocephalus; and for many other applications. A far cry, indeed, from the unsatisfactory use of celluloid to restore bony defects of the face by the German surgeon Fritz Berndt in the 1890s. Inert metals, such as vitallium, have also found a place, largely in orthopedics for the repair of fractures and the replacement of joints.

The scope of surgery was further expanded by the introduction of the operating microscope. This brought the benefit of magnification in particular to neurosurgery and to aural (ear) surgery. In the latter it opened up a whole field of operations on the drum and within the middle ear. The principles of these operations were stated in 1951 and 1952 by two German surgeons, Fritz Zöllner and Horst Wullstein; and in 1952 Samuel Rosen of New York mobilized the footplate of the stapes to restore hearing in otosclerosis—a procedure attempted by the German Jean Kessel in 1876. (The stapes, or stirrup bone, is the innermost of the three minute bones in the middle ear which, linked together, convey sound vibrations from the eardrum membrane to the liquid in the inner ear; in otosclerosis the stapes becomes rigidly fixed to the sides of the opening into the inner ear and can no longer transmit the vibrations.)

Although surgeons aim to preserve as much as disease permits, they are sometimes forced to radical measures to save life; for instance, when cancer affects the pelvic organs. Pelvic exenteration (surgical removal of the pelvic organs and nearby structures) in two stages was devised by Allen Oldfather Whipple of New York, in 1935, and in one stage by Alexander Brunschwig, of Chicago, in 1937. Then, in 1960, Charles S. Kennedy, of Detroit, after a long discussion with Brunschwig, put into practice an operation that he had been considering for 12 years: hemicorporectomy—surgical removal of the lower part of the body. The patient died on the 11th day. The first successful hemicorporectomy (at the level between the lowest lumbar vertebra and the sacrum, the fused vertebrae that form the back portion of the bony pelvis) was performed 18 months later by J. Bradley Aust and Karel B. Absolon, of Minnesota; this operation would not have been possible without all the technical, supportive and rehabilitative resources of modern medicine.

Heart
operations
of early
20th
century

The attitude of the medical profession toward heart surgery was for long overshadowed by doubt and disbelief. Wounds of the heart could be sutured (first done successfully by Ludwig Rehn, of Frankfurt am Main, in 1896); the pericardial cavity—the cavity formed by the sac enclosing the heart—could be drained in purulent infections (as had been done by Larrey in 1824); and the pericardium could be partially excised for constrictive pericarditis when it was inflamed and constricted the movement of the heart (this operation was performed by Rehn and Sauerbruch in 1913); but little beyond these could find acceptance. Yet, in the first two decades of the 20th century, much experimental work had been carried out, notably by the French surgeons Théodore Tuffier and Alexis Carrel. Tuffier, in 1912, had operated successfully on the aortic valve. In 1923, Elliott Carr Cutler of Boston had used a tenotome, a tendon-cutting instrument, to relieve a girl's mitral stenosis (a narrowing, that is, of the mitral valve, which is between the upper and lower chambers of the left side of the heart), and in 1925, at The London Hospital Henry Sessions Souttar used a finger to dilate a mitral valve in a manner that was 25 years ahead of its time.

Despite these achievements, there was too much experimental failure, and heart disease remained a medical matter. Resistance, however, began to crumble in 1938, when Robert Edward Gross successfully tied off a persistent ductus arteriosus (a fetal blood vessel between the pulmonary artery and the aorta), and was finally swept aside by Dwight Emary Harken's wonderful record in World War II (134 missiles—13 in the heart chambers—removed from the mediastinum [the area between the two lungs] without the loss of one patient). After the war, advances came rapidly, with the initial emphasis on the correction or amelioration of congenital defects. Gordon Murray, of Toronto, made full use of his amazing technical ingenuity to devise and perform many pioneering operations. And Charles Philamore Bailey of Philadelphia, adopting a more orthodox approach, was responsible for establishing numerous basic principles in the growing specialty. Until 1953, however, the techniques all had one great disadvantage—they were done "blind." The surgeon's dream was to stop the heart so that he could see what he was doing and be allowed more time in which to do it. In 1952 his dream began to come true when Floyd John Lewis, of Minnesota, used hypothermia (artificial reduction of the temperature of the body) so as to lessen its need for oxygen while he closed a hole between the two upper chambers, the atria. The next year John Haysham Gibbon of Philadelphia brought to fulfillment the research he had begun in 1937, by using his heart–lung machine to supply oxygen while he closed an interatrial septal defect—a hole in the partition between the atria. Unfortunately, neither method alone was ideal, but intensive research and development led, in the early 1960s, to their being combined as extracorporeal cooling. That is, the blood circulated through a machine outside the body which cooled it (and, after the operation, warmed it); the cooled blood lowered the temperature of the whole body. With the heart dry and motionless, the surgeon operated on the coronary arteries, he inserted plastic patches over holes, he sometimes almost remodelled the inside of the heart, but when it came to replacing valves destroyed by disease he was, and still is, faced with a choice between human tissue and man-made valves (and even valves from animal sources).

Heart
trans-
plantation

In 1967 surgery arrived at a climax that made the whole world aware of its medicosurgical responsibilities when the South African surgeon Christiaan Neethling Barnard transplanted the human heart. Reaction, both medical and lay, contained more than an element of hysteria. Yet, in 1964, two prominent research workers, Richard Rowland Lower and Norman E. Shumway, had written: "Perhaps the cardiac surgeon should pause while society becomes accustomed to resurrection of the mythological chimera." And, again in 1964, James Daniel Hardy, of the University of Mississippi, had transplanted a chimpanzee's heart into a man. And, finally, research has been remorselessly leading up to just such an operation since Charles Claude Guthrie and Carrel, at the University of Chicago, had perfected the suturing of blood vessels in 1905 and had then carried out experiments in the transplantation of many organs, including the heart.

Other organs had already been transplanted clinically with varying degrees of failure. For instance, the lung (first by James Daniel Hardy, in 1963); liver (Thomas Earl Starzl, in 1963); the pancreas (Richard Carlton Lillehei, in 1966); and the kidney (since 1902, although the operation that advanced the procedure beyond the experimental stage was performed in Boston in 1954 between identical twins). The transplanting of a kidney has been the most successful of these, but it is exceptional in that there is an artificial kidney machine (invented by Willem Johan Kolff in wartime Holland) to prepare the patient for operation and to support him in times of crisis. Such a machine does not exist for the liver or the heart (despite research since 1960 to invent an artificial heart that will support life for a reasonable length of time). Moreover, the kidney is a paired organ. Nevertheless, the major problem of transplantation of organs between different individuals is rejection by the body of the patient of the transplanted organ. And until this highly complex problem is overcome, there is small prospect of worthwhile progress in this area.   (R.G.R.)

BIBLIOGRAPHY

Medicine and surgery to 1900: S.G.B. STUBBS and E.W. BLIGH, *Sixty Centuries of Health and Physick* (1931), a history of the concepts of medicine from primitive notions of health and disease to the beginnings of modern medicine; R.H. MAJOR, *A History of Medicine,* 2 vol. (1954), a comprehensive, well-organized study of the major contributors to the development of the science of medicine from primitive times to the mid-20th century; W.H.R. RIVERS, *Medicine, Magic, and Religion* (1924), a comprehensive treatise on primitive medicine; W.G. BLACK, *Folk-Medicine: A Chapter in the History of Culture* (1883, reprinted 1970); W.R. DAWSON, *Magician and Leech* (1929), a history of early medicine, with emphasis on ancient Egypt; T.C. ALLBUTT, *Greek Medicine in Rome* (1921); JOHN SCARBOROUGH, *Roman Medicine* (1969), a well-documented, readable study; E.G. BROWNE, *Arabian Medicine* (1921), a study of the major Islāmic, particularly Persian, contributions to the development of medicine; J.F. PAYNE, *English Medicine in Anglo-Saxon Times* (1904); J.D. COMRIE, *History of Scottish Medicine*, 2nd ed., 2 vol. (1932), a detailed study of Scottish medicine from the Stone Age to the early 20th century; G.T. BETTANY, *Eminent Doctors: Their Lives and Their Work*, 2nd ed., 2 vol. (1885); MICHAEL FOSTER, *Lectures on the History of Physiology During the Sixteenth, Seventeenth and Eighteenth Centuries* (1901); ARTHUR NEWSHOLME, *The Evolution of Preventive Medicine* (1927); E.R. LONG, *A History of Pathology*, rev. ed. (1965), a history of pathology from antiquity to the early 1960s; H.H. SCOTT, *A History of Tropical Medicine*, 2 vol. (1939). (*Oriental medicine*): K.C. WONG and WU LIEN-TCH, *History of Chinese Medicine*, 2nd ed. (1936), the most complete treatise on Chinese medicine from its beginnings; W.R. MORSE, *Chinese Medicine* (1934), a very useful small book on the subject; E.H. HUME, *The Chinese Way in Medicine* (1940), not a history, but contains interesting historical material; PIERRE HUARD and MING WONG, *La Médecine des Chinois* (1967; Eng. trans., *Chinese Medicine*, 1968); JEAN FILLIOZAT, *La Doctrine classique de la médecine indienne* (1949; Eng. trans., *The Classical Doctrine of Indian Medicine*, 1964), the most scholarly work on the subject; H.R. ZIMMER, *Hindu Medicine* (1948), a very valuable work for certain aspects; P. KUTUMBIAH, *Ancient Indian Medicine* (1962); J.Z. BOWERS, *Western Medical Pioneers in Feudal Japan* (1970), deals mainly with Dutch and German doctors working in Japan.

Medicine and surgery from 1900: LEONARD COLEBROOK, *Almroth Wright, Provocative Doctor and Thinker* (1954); RICHARD H. SHRYOCK, *The Development of Modern Medicine: An Interpretation of the Social and Scientific Factors Involved* (1947, reprinted 1969); F.H. GARRISON, *An Introduction to the History of Medicine*, 4th ed. rev. (1929, reprinted 1960), with bibliography; DOUGLAS GUTHRIE, *A History of Medicine*, rev. ed. (1958), comprehensive; CHARLES SINGER and E. ASHWORTH UNDERWOOD, *A Short History of Medicine*, 2nd ed. (1962); F.F. CARTWRIGHT, *The Development of Modern Surgery* (1967); and R.G. RICHARDSON, *Surgery: Old and New Frontiers* (1968), two adequate surveys for the general reader; R.H. MEADE, *An Introduction to the History of General Surgery* (1968), excellently documented but deals with the subject by organs; R.G. RICHARDSON, *The Scalpel and the Heart* (1970; British title, *The Surgeon's Heart: A History of Cardiac Surgery*, 1969); M.H. ARMSTRONG DAVISON, *The Evolution of Anaesthesia* (1965); T.E. KEYS, *The History of Surgical Anesthesia* (1963), with good bibliography and illustrations; JUSTINE RANDERS-PEHRSON, *The Surgeon's Glove* (1960), a short but well-documented story showing how a discovery evolved; C.C. GUTHRIE, *Blood-Vessel Surgery and Its Applications* (1912); and V.P. DEMIKHOV, *Experimental Transplantation of Vital Organs* (Eng. trans. 1962), intriguing accounts of their authors' experiments—in the United States and Russia—on organ transplantation, remarkable more for their similarities than their differences.

Medicine and Surgery, Practice of

Until the great scientific discoveries of the 19th and 20th centuries, physicians were almost helpless before nearly all maladies. Though the best they could do was to comfort the patient until nature cured him, they often gave remedies recommended by authority and dependent on false theory that worsened the chances of recovery. The most important development in the 19th century was in the field of public health; water supplies were made safe, and waterborne diseases such as cholera were largely eliminated. Surgery also made great strides in the same century with the discovery of anesthetics and measures to prevent wound infection. But, leaving aside malaria (for which quinine or its precursor cinchona bark has been a known cure for centuries), only in the last 50 years have physicians possessed effective remedies for more than a minute proportion of the ills of mankind. Even now little can be done for many important maladies, including most of the degenerative conditions related to arterial disease, many kinds of cancer, most rheumatic conditions, the virus infections, and many kinds of psychological disorders.

Until modern times medicine was little unified. In the medieval period, separate bodies of physicians, barber-surgeons, and apothecaries developed in Britain and other countries of western Europe. The physicians were educated men, mostly graduates of universities; in England, of Oxford and Cambridge. The barber-surgeons were unlettered craftsmen whose skills were often handed on from father to son. The apothecaries, who made their physics from herbs, were usually members of the Grocers' Company.

By the beginning of the 19th century, the distinction between physicians, surgeons, and apothecaries was breaking down, and most medical men were becoming general practitioners. Indeed, any physician was competent to deal with almost every medical problem, because nothing useful could be done for the vast majority of patients. Some general practitioners had partners, but most worked in isolation, though perhaps with an arrangement with a colleague. They went into practice where they believed they could make a living, either by buying a practice from a retiring physician or "putting up a plate" in an expanding area. They worked from surgeries in their own houses with a minimum of equipment and dispensed their own usually valueless physics. Their greatest contribution to the community was, no doubt, to be wise men who could give help and advice to people in distress.

From about 1920 the proportion of medical practitioners in general practice has steadily declined in all the developed countries. In the Union of Soviet Socialist Republics general practice as it is known in Britain hardly exists, and in the United States and many western European countries, a high proportion of medical practitioners to whom the public has direct access are specialists of some kind.

(In this article the terms medical practitioner and physician are used interchangeably of a person who is qualified to practice medicine, without implications as to specialization.)

This article is divided into the following sections:

I. The kinds of medical practice
    General practice and first-contact care
    Hospital and specialist practice
    Industrial medicine
    Governmental practice
    Clinical research
II. Maintenance of professional standards
    Ethical basis of medical practice
    Licensure requirements for practice
    Legal restrictions on practice
    Professional organizations
    and the maintenance of standards

I. The kinds of medical practice

GENERAL PRACTICE AND FIRST-CONTACT CARE

In countries in which the general practitioner does still exist, it is sometimes said that he is an obsolescent figure, that medicine covers an immense, rapidly changing, and complex field, and no physician can possibly master more than a small fraction of it. The very concept of the general practitioner who tries to know a little about everything, it is thus argued, may, therefore, seem absurd.

The obvious alternative to general practice is the direct access of patient to specialist. If a patient cannot see, he goes to an eye specialist, and, if he has a pain in his chest (which he fears is due to his heart), he goes to a heart specialist. One objection to this plan is that the patient often cannot know which organ is responsible for his symptoms, and the most careful physician, after doing many investigations, may remain uncertain as to the cause of the pain in the chest. And the severity of all pain is influenced by the patient's state of mind as well as by the nature of the bodily disease that is causing it. Breathlessness—a common symptom—may be due to heart disease, to lung disease, to anemia, or to emotional upset. The inability of the patient to know why he is unwell provides one overriding reason for the doctor of first contact to be a generalist.

A large proportion of maladies provide a general, not a specialist, problem. Among the commonest symptoms

The need for generalists

are a general malaise—feeling run-down or always tired; others are headache, chronic low backache, rheumatism—the meaning of which often is aches and pains in various places—and abdominal discomfort, poor appetite, constipation, and wind, or gas. Many persons are also overtly anxious or depressed. Among the most subtle medical skills is the ability to assess people with such symptoms and to distinguish between symptoms that are caused predominantly by emotional upset and those that are predominantly of bodily origin and, if there is a physical basis for the symptoms, to decide whether there is some benign process or some more serious disease that require investigation. A specialist may be capable of such a general assessment; but, if he is, he succeeds by virtue of his general qualities and not his specialized knowledge. Too often the specialist, with his inevitable emphasis on his own subject, fails at this point. The man best fitted to make this kind of assessment is the generalist.

It is usually felt that there are also great practical advantages for the patient in having "my doctor," who knows about his background, who has seen him through various illnesses, and who has often looked after his family as well. This personal physician is in the best position to decide when he himself can take full charge and when the patient should be referred to a consultant—and, if so, which consultant.

The advantages of general practice and specialization are combined when the physician of first contact is a pediatrician. Although he sees only children and so can acquire a special knowledge of childhood maladies, he remains a generalist who looks at the whole patient, and the patient (or his mother) does not have to decide which organ is responsible for the symptoms. On the other hand, this kind of specialization implies that parents and children have a different physician, a situation that many people believe has disadvantages.

Another method of attempting to combine the advantages of general practice and specialization is by what has come to be called a group practice, the members of which partially specialize. All are general practitioners, but one may be also a surgeon, a second an obstetrician, a third a pediatrician, and a fourth an internist with a particular interest in obscure medical disorders. In isolated communities group practice may be a satisfactory compromise, but in advanced countries, where nearly everyone can be sent quickly to hospital by motor vehicle or airplane, the specialist surgeon working in a fully equipped hospital is in a far better position to treat persons needing operation than is a part-time general practitioner surgeon in a small clinic hospital. Moreover, partial specialization in general practice implies that there is no individual who is, to the patient, "my doctor."

Britain. Before 1948, general practitioners in Britain settled where they could make a living. Patients fell into two main groups: weekly wage earners, who were compulsorily insured, were on a doctor's "panel" and were given free medical attention (for which the doctor was paid quarterly by the government); and the remainder, who mostly paid the doctor a fee for service at the time of the illness. In 1948 the National Health Service started. Under its provisions, everyone was entitled to free medical attention with a general practitioner with whom he registered. Though general practitioners in the National Health Service were not debarred from also having private patients, these must be people who are not registered with them under the National Health Service. Any physician was free to work as a general practitioner entirely independent of the National Health Service, though outside the West End of London there were few who did so. Ninety-seven percent of the population were registered with a National Health Service general practitioner, and the vast majority automatically saw this physician, or one of his partners, when they required medical attention. A few people, mostly rich, while registered with a National Health Service general practitioner, regularly saw another physician privately; and a very few, although they usually saw their National Health Service general practitioner, might occasionally seek a private consultation with another physician because they were dissatisfied.

National Health Service

A general practitioner under the National Health Service remained an independent contractor, paid by capitation fee; that is, according to the number of people registered with him. He might work entirely from his own house in premises modified by himself, and he provided and paid his own receptionist, secretary, and other ancillary staff. Most general practitioners had one or more partners and worked more and more in premises built for the purpose. Some of these structures were erected by the physicians themselves, but many were provided by the local authority, the physicians paying rent for using them. Health centres, in which up to 20 or more general practitioners worked, were steadily increasing in number in the 1970s.

In Britain only a small minority of general practitioners can admit patients to a hospital and look after them personally. Most of this minority are in country districts, where, before the days of the National Health Service, there were cottage hospitals run by general practitioners; many of these hospitals continued to function in a similar manner. All general practitioners use such hospital facilities as X-ray departments and laboratories, and many general practitioners work in hospitals in casualty departments or as clinical assistants to consultants.

Although general practitioners are spread more evenly over the country than formerly, when there were many in the richer areas and few in the industrial towns, physicians (or their wives) may still be unwilling to settle in the larger and less pleasant industrial towns, even though they can be assured of a larger income there than in other places. The maximum allowed list of National Health Service patients per doctor in the early 1970s was 3,500; the average was about 2,500. Patients had free choice of physician with whom they registered, with the proviso that they could not be accepted by one who already had a full list and that a physician could refuse to accept them (though such refusals were rare). In remote country places there would be only one physician within a reasonable distance.

In the past, upper class patients expected physicians to visit them when they were unwell, but recent trends have been for more work to be done in the doctor's office, usually by appointment. Many home visits were still needed to care for patients who were acutely ill, frail, or crippled and whose going to the surgery would be unpleasant or dangerous. In some large towns during evenings and weekends, it could at times be difficult to obtain a physician for a home visit. The problem was met in some places by the development of off-duty deputizing services that chiefly employed young physicians, usually for short periods between hospital appointments. By paying to this service, a general practitioner could be assured that his patients would be seen in emergency in his absence and that a report about the situation would be given to him. The system was much less satisfactory for the patient than the usual one in which partners take turns in doing evening and weekend work.

United States. Whereas in Britain the doctor of first contact is regularly a general practitioner, there is no such uniformity in the United States. In country districts far from the big cities, there are still many family general practitioners, and there have been many voices deploring the demise of this kind of physician in the cities. The American Academy of General Practice and the Section on General Practice of the American Medical Association in 1969 created the American Board of General Practice, but to date few young graduate physicians have been attracted back to this field, and the decline of general practice has not been halted, though it may have been delayed.

In the larger cities the needs of the poor for first-contact medical attention were largely met in the early 1970s by hospital emergency rooms mainly staffed by newly qualified physicians seeking experience. The care provided under such methods, although it might be the best possible in the circumstances and satisfactory for trivial injuries and brief self-limiting infections, cannot deal properly with maladies for which prolonged treatment is indicated.

Medical care of the poor

The middle and upper classes in the cities had many

varieties of primary medical care. Children were mostly taken to pediatricians. Many adults went to internists, whose field is mainly that of medical (as opposed to surgical) illnesses; many others went directly to the narrower specialists such as dermatologists, allergists, gynecologists, ophthalmologists, and abdominal surgeons. Critics believed that some inevitably went to the wrong specialist. The specialist who has seen someone through an illness may, especially if he is young, continue to give the patient care of a more general kind in the future. Indeed, whereas in the usual sense there was much less general practice in the United States than in Britain in the 1970s, in another sense there was more, for in Britain the specialist or consultant did not give primary medical care; in the United States he often did.

Most physicians in the United States giving primary medical care worked entirely independently; partnerships were uncommon. Doctors provided their own equipment, often very lavish, and paid their own ancillary staff. Some had their own X-ray equipment. In smaller cities they mostly had full hospital privileges, but in larger cities these privileges were more likely to be restricted to certain types of case and certain types of procedures, and some primary physicians had no access to hospital beds.

In the early 1970s the complaint was often heard that it was impossible to persuade some physicians in the large cities to make home visits to the sick. Reluctance to make such visits could to some extent be justified on the grounds that the physician worked more effectively in his office and that the patient too ill to come to the office was better off in hospital.

Medicare and Medicaid, government-supported programs, enabled the elderly and the poor to have medical attention that they previously lacked; in the early 1970s these services did not appear to have changed the general pattern of medical care.

Soviet Union. In the Union of Soviet Socialist Republics, there are no general practitioners covering every aspect of medicine except in the most thinly populated rural areas. Pediatricians deal with children up to the age of 15. Internists look after the medical ills of adults, and occupational physicians deal with the workers, sharing care with the internists. Patients have no free choice of physician, but, if there is friction between patient and physician, it may be possible for a change to be made at the instigation of either. Attention is free, though some drugs have to be paid for.

Soviet poly- clinics Physicians work from polyclinics, clinics at which many types of diseases are treated. In small towns there was usually one polyclinic for all purposes in the early 1970s, but in large cities there were separate polyclinics for children and adults, as well as clinics for special purposes such as women's diseases, mental illnesses, and venereal diseases. Polyclinics usually had X-ray apparatus and facilities for examination of tissue specimens, facilities associated with the departments of the district hospital.

Home visits were common, and much of the physician's time was spent in doing routine checkups for preventive purposes. This was of value because tuberculosis—a malady for which early diagnosis and immediate treatment are important—was still comparatively common in the Soviet Union.

Some patients in sparsely populated rural areas were first seen by feldshers, nurses, or midwives who worked under the supervision of a polyclinic or hospital physician. The feldsher was once a lower grade physician in the army or peasant communities, but, by the 1970s, he had become a paramedical worker acting in cooperation with a physician. There were also some feldshers in the towns.

Japan. In Japan, with less rigid legal restriction of the sale of pharmaceuticals than in the West, there was formerly a strong tradition of self-medication and self-treatment. This was modified by the institution, in 1961, of health insurance programs that covered a large proportion of the population; there was then a great increase in visits to the outpatient clinics of hospitals and to private clinics and individual physicians.

When Japan abandoned traditional Chinese medicine and adopted Western medical practices in the 1870s, Germany became the chief model. As a result of German influence and of their own traditions, Japanese physicians tended to prefer professorial status and scholarly research opportunities at the universities or positions in the national or prefectural (*i.e.*, district) hospitals to private practice. There were some pioneering physicians, however, who brought medical care to the ordinary people and who cared for seriously ill patients in their homes.

In December 1969, the number of private general clinics registered had reached 68,305. Most of these clinics had several physicians on their staffs, and 40 percent of the clinics had beds (in accordance with the Medical Service Law medical clinics are classified as hospitals if the number of beds is 20 or more).

In 1970 in Japan there were approximately 128 physicians per 100,000 people, but the physicians tended to cluster in the urban areas. The Medical Service Law of 1963 had been amended to empower the Ministry of Health and Welfare to control the planning and distribution of future public and nonprofit medical facilities, partly to redress the urban–rural imbalance. Meanwhile, mobile services were being expanded. More fundamental medical reforms were under way.

The influx of patients into hospital and private clinics after the passage of the national health insurance acts of 1961 had, as one effect, a severe reduction in the amount of time available for any one patient. Perhaps in reaction to this situation, there has been a modest resurgence in the popularity of traditional Chinese medicine, with its leisurely interview, its dependence on herbal and other "natural" medicines, and its other traditional diagnostic and therapeutic practices. One practice that has shared in this growth of popularity is acupuncture, a form of surgery consisting in the insertion of needles into one or more of 365 precise points on the trunk, the extremities, and the head. In the People's Republic of China, since 1957, acupuncture has also been employed in anesthesia.

Other developed countries. On the continent of Europe there are great differences both within single countries and between countries in the kinds of first-contact medical care. General practice, while declining in Europe as elsewhere, is still rather common even in some large cities, as well as in remote country areas, where it always tends to be the norm.

In The Netherlands, departments of general practice are run by general practitioners in all the medical schools— an exceptional state of affairs—and general practice flourishes. In the larger cities of Denmark, general practice on an individual basis is usual and popular, because the physician works only during office hours, there being a duty doctor service for nights and weekends. In the cities of Sweden, primary care is given by specialists. In the remote regions of the north of Sweden, district doctors act as general practitioners to patients spread over huge areas and delegate much of their home visiting to nurses.

In France there are still general practitioners, but their number is declining. Many medical practitioners advertise themselves directly to the public as specialists in internal medicine, ophthalmologists, gynecologists, and other kinds of specialist. As elsewhere, there is said to be tension at times between specialists and general practitioners, who feel that their status has declined. Even when patients have a general practitioner, they may still go directly to a specialist. Attempts to stem the decline in general practice are being made by the development of group practice (in place of the single-handed practice that used to be the norm in France) and of small rural hospitals equipped to deal with less serious illnesses, where general practitioners can look after their own patients.

Although Israel has a high ratio of physicians to population (about one to 450), there is a shortage of general practitioners, and only in rural areas is general practice common. In the towns many people go directly to pediatricians, gynecologists, and other specialists. In the early 1970s there was a reaction against this direct access to the specialist. Since then more general practitioners have been trained than in the recent past, and the Israel Medical Association has recommended that no patient should be referred to a specialist except by the family physician or on instructions given by the family nurse. At Tel Aviv University there is a department of family medicine. In some newly developing areas, where the doctor shortage is greatest, there are medical centres at which all patients are initially interviewed by a nurse. She herself deals with many minor ailments, thus allowing the physician to occupy his time on the more seriously ill. This system is popular with the nurses because it gives them more responsibility and is said to work well.

Nearly half the medical doctors in Australia are general practitioners—a far higher proportion than in most other advanced countries—though, as elsewhere, the proportion is declining. They tend to do far more for their patients than in Britain, many performing such operations as removal of appendix, gallbladder, or uterus, operations that elsewhere would be carried out by a specialist surgeon. Group practices with some degree of specialization are common. Most general practitioners have access to hospital beds.

The developing world. In the rich countries most people can obtain some kind of medical care; in the poor countries most cannot do so. Few developing countries spend more than one dollar per year for each inhabitant on medical care. In Northern Nigeria and Nepal, there was, according to the latest available figures, about one physician per 100,000 people, in India one per 6,000, and in Brazil one per 3,000, whereas in Britain there was one per 1,000, in the United States one per 800, and in the Soviet Union and Israel one per 450. In those developing countries in which the proportion of medical practitioners is comparatively high, nearly all are concentrated in the towns. In Kenya, for example, the overall ratio of physicians to patients was one per 10,000, but in the rural areas it was one per 50,000.

Medical needs in developing countries Along with the shortage of physicians, there is a shortage of everything else needed to provide medical care—of equipment, of drugs, of suitable buildings, and of nurses, technicians, X-ray technicians, and all other grades of staff, whose presence is taken for granted in the affluent societies. Yet medicine has far more to offer to the sick in the poor countries than in the rich countries. In the poor countries a high proportion of people are young, and all are liable to many infections, including tuberculosis, syphilis, typhoid, and cholera (which, with the possible exception of syphilis, are now rare in the rich countries), and also malaria, yaws, worm infestations, and many other conditions occurring primarily in the warmer climates. Nearly all these infections respond to the antibiotics and other drugs that have been discovered since the 1920s. There is also much malnutrition and anemia, which can be cured if money is available. Many people have goitres, cysts, cataracts, and other disorders remediable by surgery. Preventive medicine can achieve much by ensuring clean water supplies, destroying insects that carry infections, teaching hygiene, and showing how to make the best use of meagre resources.

Urban and rural differences In most poor countries there is a small number of rich people, usually living in the cities. They can afford to pay for medical care, and in a free market system the physicians go where they can make a living; this situation explains why the doctor–patient ratio is so much higher in the towns than in country districts. A physician in Bombay or in Rio de Janeiro may have equipment as lavish as that of a physician in the United States and can earn an excellent income. The poor, both in town and country, can get satisfactory medical attention only if it is paid for by the state, by some supranational body, or by a mission or other charitable organization. In practice, hospitals run by a mission may cooperate closely with state-run health centres.

The gross national product of the developing countries is only about one-twentieth that of the rich countries. In Britain, where most of the cost of medical care is provided by public funds, around 4 percent of the gross national product is spent on health. Few developing countries expend this proportion of their small gross national product on health. With such an enormous amount to be done

with so small an expenditure, the overriding consideration is to concentrate on what can be provided most cheaply.

It is now generally believed that, because physicians are scarce, their skills must be used to best advantage; that most of the work normally done by physicians in the rich countries has to be delegated to various kinds of auxiliaries or nurses, who have to diagnose the common conditions, give treatment, take blood samples, help with operations, supply simple posters containing health advice, and carry out many other tasks. In such places the doctor has time only to perform major operations and deal with the more difficult medical problems.

Because hospital care is expensive, people are treated as far as possible on an outpatient basis from health centres housed in simple buildings. Few people can travel except on foot, and, if they are more than five miles or so from a health centre, they tend not to go there. Health centres are also used as centres for propaganda to the local inhabitants, who can perhaps be persuaded to improve their hygiene—by the better disposal of excrement, by improving the water supply, and by the destruction of some insects—and can be taught to improve their dietary habits, mainly by being shown how their protein intake can be increased.

The developing countries vary widely in the medical care that they have made generally available. In some, such as Kenya, there has been extensive development of simple health centres providing medical care to most of the population; in others, vast numbers have no medical care at all. There is also a tendency to spend too much of the little money available on expensive hospitals, where elaborate investigations and complicated operations are performed.

<u>HOSPITAL AND SPECIALIST PRACTICE</u>

In the Middle Ages, hospitals were places of refuge for the aged poor, the crippled, and the destitute and were attached to monasteries. In the 18th and 19th centuries, hospitals under religious auspices persisted, but many other voluntary hospitals were founded all over the Western world as independent secular organizations financed by subscriptions and endowments. In the 19th century these voluntary hospitals increasingly restricted their clientele to the noninfectious acutely sick. The needs of the mentally and chronically sick and of the tuberculous and those with other infections were met by the erection of public hospitals financed by government or local authorities.

Whereas there are great differences between and within the Western countries in the kinds of primary medical care, there is more uniformity in hospital care. The new hospitals in the poorer countries are largely modelled on those in the West. Most patients in or attending hospital are looked after by a specialist.

Principal surgical and medical specialties The main specialties are, in surgery: general surgery; gynecology and obstetrics; orthopedic and traumatic surgery; neurosurgery; thoracic and cardiac surgery; ear, nose, and throat surgery; and ophthalmic surgery. In medicine they are: general or internal medicine; dermatology; physical medicine or rheumatology; neurology; pediatrics; geriatrics; and psychiatry. The important nonclinical specialties are anesthetics, radiology, and pathology, which is usually subdivided into morbid histology (study of diseased tissue), biochemistry, bacteriology, and hematology (which is concerned with blood disorders).

The trend is to more and more specialization, largely as a result of the vast increase in knowledge in recent years. But specialization in clinical medicine can lead to problems: patients cannot be separated into categories, each to be looked after by a particular specialist; they are sick people who should be looked at as a whole. A patient with heart disease is not necessarily given better advice by a cardiologist than by a general physician. The general physician is widely held to be an obsolescent figure who should be replaced by specialists in the various systems of the body, but there are good reasons for the existence of general physicians. A large proportion of the patients for whom the general practitioner wishes a second opinion are not clearly affected by a disease of some organ; they are obscurely unwell.

Specialization in surgery can be much better justified than can specialization in medicine, because the practice of surgery implies technical skills. Wisdom and understanding are important qualities in the cardiac surgeon, but they are not enough; he must also have a knowledge of the heart and of the craft of heart operations that only regular practice can give.

Radiation therapy, also known as radiotherapy, is unique in that it is a specialty of treatment, patients being given X-rays or radium. It can be justified because the apparatus and the methods of treatment are so complicated that only a specialist can master them.

There are few objections to increasing specialization in nonclinical spheres. The bacteriologist is likely to give a better bacteriology service than the general pathologist can, and the radiologist who has made a special study of X-ray views of the alimentary tract will probably give a better opinion of this tract than will the radiologist who covers the whole body.

Organization of the specialist's work. Clinical specialists divide their time between dealing with inpatients in a hospital or nursing home and dealing with patients who attend at the outpatient department of a hospital or in private consulting rooms. They may also visit patients in their own homes occasionally.

In remote districts and developing countries, specialists may work with little help. In the rich countries, many specialists have junior medical staff who handle much of the emergency work, carry out various procedures such as blood transfusions, help at operations, and accompany their chief on his ward rounds and carry out his instructions. This kind of work is an important part of the young doctor's education.

The work of nonclinical specialists is largely determined by their equipment. The radiologist must have his massive and expensive X-ray machines, with technicians to help him and with equipment to process his films. The anesthetist inevitably works largely in operating rooms, though he may occasionally give anesthetics to outpatients with trivial conditions. In the past his equipment was simple; now it is elaborate. The pathologist needs his laboratory, with its equipment and technical staff.

Medical schools. The most sought after posts in the hospital world are in the hospitals with medical schools. Newly qualified physicians wish to work there because doing so will aid their future careers, though the actual experience may be wider and better in a hospital without a medical school. Senior physicians hope to make their careers in hospitals with medical schools, because consultant, specialist, or professorial posts there usually carry the highest prestige of any that the medical profession can offer. When the posts are salaried, the salaries are sometimes, but not always, higher; and, when the consultant makes all or part of his living by private practice, he is likely to earn far more when on the staff of a medical school.

In many medical schools, especially on the European continent, there are clinical professors in each of the major specialties, such as surgery, internal medicine, obstetrics and gynecology, psychiatry, and often of the smaller specialties as well. There are also professors of pathology, radiology, and radiotherapy. Whether professors or not, all senior doctors in teaching hospitals have the two functions of caring for the sick and educating students. They give lectures and seminars and, when doing ward rounds, are accompanied by students with whom they discuss the patients' problems.

Britain. Before the National Health Service the most famous hospitals were the voluntary teaching hospitals. The senior medical staff gave their services free, deriving their income from seeing well-to-do patients privately. Most patients were in local-authority hospitals, many of which developed in the 19th century from workhouses controlled by boards of guardians of the poor. The local authorities also built large mental hospitals, infectious-diseases hospitals, and tuberculosis sanatoriums. In 1928 the boards of guardians were abolished, and their hospitals were taken over by the local authorities. During World War II, nearly all hospitals were incorporated in the Emergency Medical Service.

When the National Health Service began in 1948, virtually all hospitals became part of it. They are administered centrally by the Ministry (later the Department) of Health and locally by regional boards (responsible for a population of several million people) through management committees responsible for individual hospitals or groups of hospitals. The pattern of hospitals varies widely, but the plan in the early 1970s was that district hospitals of some 600 beds would in time largely replace smaller hospitals and provide the basic hospital services, including some care for the mentally sick and those with infectious diseases. In addition, some hospitals, especially the teaching hospitals, had departments for highly specialized treatment, such as cardiac surgery and radiotherapy, and there would continue to be hospitals especially for long-term mentally disturbed, mentally subnormal, and geriatric patients. Hospitals under National Health Service

As a rule, the only part of a hospital to which the public has direct access is the casualty department, which is usually staffed by doctors of intermediate status. Consultative outpatient departments are under the charge of consultants, who sometimes run them single-handedly but more often are assisted by a registrar, to whom some patients are delegated. Patients have to be referred by a general practitioner, another consultant, or a casualty officer. After examination and investigation, many are referred back to their general practitioners with a letter giving the consultant's suggestions. Other patients, especially those requiring surgery, are admitted or placed on a waiting list for admission when a bed is available. The acutely sick are admitted directly to the hospital by arrangements between the general practitioner and the admissions officer.

Although the vast majority of all the patients in hospital are treated free, in most hospitals there are a small number of private beds. Patients who occupy them make payments to the National Health Service and also pay the consultant's fee.

United States. There are federal, state, local government, church, nonprofit voluntary, and proprietary hospitals in the United States. The federal hospitals, which have 10 percent of all beds and are staffed by full-time federal employees, include military, Veterans Administration, and Public Health Service hospitals. The state hospitals, mostly of more than 1,000 beds each and containing 42 percent of all beds, care for the mentally and chronically sick and the tuberculous. Many are widely believed to be understaffed in both nurses and physicians, who are full-time state employees. Local government hospitals, with 13 percent of all beds, are run by the local municipalities and councils. They are the district general hospitals for those who cannot afford the fees of the private institutions and mostly provide care for the usual acute and chronic illnesses. Some of their staff are full-time employees, and others are part-time. The voluntary nonprofit community hospitals, which contain 19 percent of all the beds, range from the world-renowned teaching hospitals to small community hospitals with fewer than 20 beds. Most of the community hospitals have a few beds for highly specialized work and are staffed by the local physicians. Among the staff of the teaching hospitals are most of the most eminent specialists. They also have a large number of junior physicians. Proprietary hospitals, with 3 percent of all beds, are mostly small, are privately owned, and are organized to make profit for their shareholders.

Most of the voluntary nonteaching hospitals and all the proprietary hospitals offer open access to beds and other facilities for all local physicians who satisfy certain—and not always very exacting—criteria. There may thus be an extremely large medical staff, each member of which may have only one or two patients in the hospital at any time. Whereas in poor rural areas there may be a shortage of facilities, in prosperous districts there is sometimes an excess, with resultant competition for patients.

About 75 percent of the United States population contribute to insurance schemes that provide some cover for hospital costs. These schemes tend to encourage admission to hospital for brief periods while investigations, which would be feasible on an ambulatory basis, are done. In 1964, 14.8 percent of all American citizens were admitted to hospital, by comparison with 10.5 percent in Britain. Investigations that in Britain would be done in the outpatient department are in the United States more often done in the physician's office. There are outpatient facilities in some American hospitals, mainly for the indigent. The emergency rooms of larger hospitals also provide first-contact care for the U.S. poor.

Japan. In the era after World War II, the technology and language employed in the Japanese laboratories have been predominantly American, but the educational philosophy, with teaching through the lecture and with emphasis on research, still shows the influence of the German professors who helped to found the modern Japanese medical system. Efforts have begun to give greater emphasis to clinical laboratory instruction and bedside teaching.

In 1971, research institutions included 118 associated with universities, of which 57 were national, 17 prefectural or municipal, and 44 private, and 111 medical institutes not affiliated with universities; of the 111 about one-half were privately financed.

Japan is especially advanced in the study of radiation-induced cancer through the work of the Atomic Bomb Casualty Commission, organized in 1947 by the National Academy of Sciences of the United States to study the long-term effects of the atomic bombing of Hiroshima and Nagasaki. Japanese researchers also work closely with the World Health Organization committees that study prevention or treatment programs for such diseases as cancer, leprosy, and tuberculosis.

The National Cancer Centre in Tokyo (founded in 1956) includes Asia's largest cancer hospital and sophisticated research facilities. There are also nine regional cancer institutes and some 160 prefectural and municipal cancer clinics supplemented by more than 300 mobile units equipped for examinations.

A number of contagious diseases have yielded in some measure to research and prevention programs. Tuberculosis, for example, the leading cause of death in Japan in 1950, had been reduced, by 1968, to eighth place in the order of causes. Pneumonia and bronchitis, which caused 8.6 percent of deaths in 1950, caused 4.6 percent in 1968.

In 1969 there were approximately 8,000 hospitals in Japan, with somewhat more than 1,000,000 beds. The governmental hospitals (national, prefectural, and municipal) were about one-third the total number and had somewhat less than two-thirds of the beds. Of the remaining hospitals, 85, with about 43,000 beds, were associated with universities.

Other countries. Most hospitals in the Soviet Union are of standard types, ranging from small general hospitals of 15 to 100 beds—located in remote rural areas and staffed by pediatricians, internists, surgeons, and sometimes pathologists and radiologists—through district hospitals, of 250–500 beds; to regional and republic hospitals. Medical schools are associated with the last, and specialists tend to be concentrated in the regional and republic hospitals. Mental and tuberculosis hospitals are separate from the other hospitals.

INDUSTRIAL MEDICINE

The Industrial Revolution greatly changed, and as a rule worsened, the health hazards caused by industry, while the numbers at risk vastly increased. In Britain, where the Industrial Revolution began, the first small beginnings of efforts to ameliorate the lot of the workpeople in factories and mines began in 1802, with the passing of the first factory act, the Health and Morals of Apprentices Act. The second factory act, in 1819, stipulated nine years as the minimum age for employing children. The factory act of 1838 was the first really effective measure in the industrial field. It forbade night work for children and

restricted their hours to 12 per day. Children under 13 were required to attend school. A factory inspectorate was established, the inspectors being given powers of entry into factories and power of prosecution of recalcitrant owners. Thereafter, there was a succession of acts with detailed regulations about safety and health in all industries. Industrial diseases were made notifiable, and those who develop any one of the 40 prescribed industrial diseases are entitled to industrial injuries benefit.

In Britain the industrial physician is, then, bound by all sorts of legal restrictions and must report those who develop the specified industrial diseases. The situation is similar in other developed countries. The industrial physician's most important function, however, is to prevent industrial diseases. Many of the measures to this end have evolved over the years and become standard practice, but, especially in new industries working with new substances, the physician may be able to detect evidence that the workers are being damaged and suggest measures to prevent this. He will be able to advise management about industrial hygiene and the design of buildings so as to minimize health hazards. He should ensure that individual workers are aware of the risks they are running and that they have the means to minimize these risks.

In many factories there are arrangements for giving first aid in case of accidents. In practice, the facilities range from one simple first-aid box to a large suite of rooms lavishly equipped with all kinds of first-aid equipment and also X-ray and physical-therapy equipment, with a staff of qualified nurses and physiotherapists. In the larger places one or more full-time physicians may be on duty.

Periodic medical examination. Physicians in industry carry out many medical examinations, especially on recruits and on employees returning to work after sickness or injury. In addition, those liable to health hazards may be examined regularly in the hope of detecting evidence of incipient damage. In some organizations every employee may be offered a regular medical examination. When a potential employee is medically examined, the physician may advise whether he should be accepted and, if he is, the kind of work for which he is fit.

The industrial and the personal physician. There may be doubt as to which physician bears the main responsibility for someone's health, especially in such countries as Britain, where most people consult a general practitioner. In the United States the problem is less likely to arise because few have a single personal physician. In the Soviet Union the occupational physician acts to some extent also as a general practitioner.

Dealing with the health hazards of industry is clearly within the province of the industrial physician. When someone has an accident or becomes acutely ill at work, the first aid is given or directed by him. Subsequent treatment may either be given at the clinic at work or be arranged by the personal physician. Difficulties may arise when an employee returns to work after an illness. He may feel that, whereas his own personal physician is a friend, the industrial physician represents the organization and is not to be trusted.

Industrial health services. Only in the Soviet Union and other Communist countries is there a fully developed state industrial health service. At the larger industrial establishments in the Soviet Union employing 5,000 or more workers, there are polyclinics that provide both occupational and general care to the workers and their families. Each occupational physician is responsible for about 1,000 workers. His work includes the prevention of occupational diseases and injuries, health screening, immunization, and health education. He may be assisted by feldshers who have been specially trained in this work.

Industrial
health
service
in the
Soviet
Union

In the Western countries there is no fixed pattern of industrial health service. Legislation impinges upon health in various ways, including the provision of safety measures, the restriction of pollution, and the enforcement of minimum standards of lighting, ventilation, and space per person. This legislation started in Britain in 1802 and has continued in all developed countries ever since.

Even in Britain, which has the most comprehensive health service in the non-Communist world, there is no occupational health service as a general bureau of service of the government. There is, instead, an infinite variety of schemes financed and run by individual firms or, equally, by huge nationalized industries, such as the Coal Board and the Gas Council. The smaller firms usually have no scheme of any kind, some intermediate firms may employ a general practitioner for a few hours a week, and, in a few industrial estates, firms have joined forces in promoting a local industrial health service. There is a similar variety in the United States and throughout the Western world.

GOVERNMENTAL PRACTICE

Public health practice. The physician working in the field of public health is mainly concerned with the environmental causes of ill health and in their prevention. Bad drainage, polluted water and atmosphere, noise and smells, infected food, bad housing, and poverty in general are all his especial concern. Perhaps the most satisfying title he can be given is that of community physician. In Britain he has been customarily known as the medical officer of health and, in the United States, as the health officer.

Public
health
measures
of the
19th
century

The spectacular improvement in the expectation of life in the affluent countries has been due far more to public health measures than to curative medicine. These public health measures were largely put into operation in the 19th century. At the beginning of that century, drainage and water supply systems were all more or less primitive; nearly all the cities of that time had poorer water and drainage systems than Rome had possessed 1,800 years previously. The drains regularly infected the water supply, and vast outbreaks of typhoid, cholera, and other waterborne infections were common. By the end of the century, at least in the larger cities, water supplies were usually safe, and wastes were carried away in underground drains, though often to pollute the rivers lower down. Food-borne infections were also drastically reduced by the enforcement of laws concerned with the preparation, storage, and distribution of food. Insect-borne infections, such as malaria and yellow fever, which were common in the southern United States and in other hot countries, were eliminated by the destruction of the responsible insects, chiefly by getting rid of the pools where they bred. Fundamental to this improvement in health has been the diminution of poverty, for most public health measures are expensive. The peoples of the developing countries fall sick and die from infections that the affluent countries have almost abolished.

Britain. Whereas the general practitioner and hospital services are part of the National Health Service, public health services are organized locally, under the county and county-borough councils and the smaller local councils. This separation between the largely preventive local health services and the national curative health service has been widely criticized. In the near future there may be a fusion of all these services, accompanied by a widespread change in the local government areas.

Medical
officer
of
health

The medical officer of health is employed by the local council and is their expert adviser in health matters. The larger councils employ a number of medical officers with a hierarchical structure under a chief. Most are full-time employees, but, in some small rural areas, a general practitioner may be employed part-time as medical officer of health.

The medical officer of health has various statutory powers conferred by acts of Parliament, regulations and orders, such as food and drugs acts, milk and dairies regulations, and factories acts. He supervises the work of sanitary inspectors in the control of health nuisances. The compulsorily notifiable infectious diseases are reported to him, and he takes appropriate action, such as X-raying persons who have come in contact with tuberculosis and tracing the source of infection of typhoid.

The medical officer of health is involved with the work of the district nurse, who carries out nursing duties in the home, and the health visitor, who gives advice on health matters, especially to the mothers of small babies. He has other duties in connection with infant welfare clinics,

crèches, day and residential nurseries, the examination of schoolchildren, child guidance clinics, foster homes, factories, problem families, and the care of the aged and the handicapped.

United States. Federal, state, county, and city governments all have public health functions. Under the United States Department of Health, Education and Welfare is the Public Health Service, headed by the surgeon general. The commissioner of health, usually a physician, is the head of the state health department and is often in the governor's cabinet. He usually has a board of health that adopts health regulations and holds hearings on their alleged violations. A state's public health code is the foundation on which all county and city health regulations must be based. A city health department may be independent of its surrounding county health department, or there may be a combined city–county health department. The physicians of the local health departments are usually called health officers, though occasionally people with this title are not physicians. The larger departments may have a public health director, a district health director, or a regional health director.

The minimal complement of a local health department is a health officer, a public health nurse, a sanitation expert, and a clerk who is also a registrar of vital statistics. There may also be sanitation personnel, nutritionists, social workers, laboratory technicians, health educators, and others.

Japan. Japan's Ministry of Health and Welfare directs public health programs at the national level, maintaining close coordination among the fields of preventive medicine, medical care, and welfare and health insurance. The departments of health of the prefectures and of the 29 largest municipalities operate health centres that totalled 832 in 1970. The integrated community health programs of the centres encompass maternal and child health, communicable disease control, health education, family planning, health statistics, food inspection, and environmental sanitation. The national government meets one-half of the cost of a new health centre and provides for one-third of the operating expenses. Private physicians, through their local medical associations, help to formulate and execute particular public health programs needed by their localities.

About 80 relevant laws are administered through the Ministry's ten bureaus and agencies, which range from Public Health, Environmental Sanitation, and Medical Affairs to the Children and Families Bureau. The approximately 20 categories of institutions run by the Ministry, in addition to the national hospitals, include research centres for cancer and leprosy, homes for the blind, rehabilitation centres for the physically handicapped, and the port quarantine services.

Military practice. The medical services of armies, navies, and air forces are geared to war. During campaigns the first requirement is the prevention of sickness. In all wars before the 20th century, many more combatants died of disease than of wounds. And even in World War II, although few died of disease, vast numbers became casualties from disease, especially in the tropical theatres.

The main means of preventing sickness that have been highly successful in temperate theatres are: the provision of food and pure water, thus eliminating starvation, avitaminosis, and dysentery and other bowel infections, which used to be particular scourges of armies; the provision of proper clothing and other means of protection from the weather; the elimination from the service of those likely to fall sick; the vaccination of all against various infections, notably typhoid and smallpox; in malarious areas, provisions for the regular taking of suppressive drugs to prevent the symptoms of the disease; and the education of all in hygiene. In addition, the maintenance of high morale has a striking effect on the casualty rates, for, when morale is poor, men are likely to suffer psychiatric breakdowns, and malingering is more prevalent.

Most of these preventive methods are the concern of the service as a whole. The medical branch may provide advice about disease prevention through the proper preparation of food, the provision of water, the disposal of

Military
prevention
of
sickness

excrement, the elimination of insects, and the taking of suppressive drugs, but the actual execution of this advice is through the ordinary chains of command. It is the duty of the colonel, not of the medical officer, to ensure that the troops do not drink infected water and that they take tablets to suppress malaria.

When army casualties occur during war, the supreme requirement is rapid evacuation of the wounded from the front. A sick or wounded man at the front interferes with his comrades' activities. The general principle is to give first aid on the spot and then to evacuate quickly to the rear. Air transport has revolutionized the means of achieving this. The situation in air forces and navies considerably differs from that of armies. When a man is wounded in a plane, little can be done except by the self-application of dressings, but, if he gets to base alive, he can immediately go to a well-equipped hospital. In a naval action there may be massive casualties that overwhelm the available medical services, especially in isolated small ships. On the other hand, the action is usually brief, and, when it is over, casualties are evacuated to hospital ships or land-based hospitals.

Army medical organization. The medical doctor of first contact to the soldier is an officer in the medical corps, usually fairly junior. He may be designated battalion or regimental medical officer. In peace conditions, he sees the sick and has functions similar to those of the general practitioner. He prescribes drugs and dressings and may have a sick bay where lightly sick men can remain for a few days. He is usually assisted by orderlies. If a further medical opinion on a soldier is required, the patient can be referred to a specialist at a military hospital or, when occasion demands, to a civilian hospital.

Dealing with the wounded
In war conditions, the regimental medical officer has a regimental aid post where, with the help of one or more orderlies, he applies first aid to the walking wounded and to the more seriously wounded who are brought in by the stretcher-bearers. The casualties are evacuated as quickly as possible by field ambulances, of which there are usually three to each division. Each field ambulance has two companies and a headquarters. The companies have medical officers, stretcher-bearer officers (nonmedical), and men of the medical corps who man an advanced dressing station. There, further treatment may be given before evacuation to the main dressing station at the headquarters of the field ambulance, where a surgeon may perform emergency operations. Thereafter, evacuation may be to casualty clearing stations, to advanced hospitals, or to base hospitals, but no general description can be given, because circumstances vary. Air evacuation, which can immediately take men thousands of miles, is widely used.

In peace conditions most of the intermediate medical units exist only in skeleton form; the active units are at battalion and hospital level. A military hospital is much the same as a civilian hospital, with various specialists, laboratory, X-ray department, physical therapy department, and so on.

When a physician joins the medical corps, he may join with specialist qualifications, or he may obtain such qualifications while in the army, sometimes by secondment to a civilian hospital. A feature of army medicine is promotion to administrative positions. The commanding officer of a hospital and the medical officer at headquarters may have no contacts with actual patients. This practice is often held to be an unsatisfactory feature of a military doctor's life.

Although the medical officer in peacetime has some choice of the kind of work he will do, he also expects to be moved at intervals. He is in a hierarchical organization with a chain of command.

The medical officer is a soldier and under military discipline in ordinary matters, but, when dealing with patients, he is in a special position. He cannot be ordered by a superior officer to give some treatment or take other action that he believes is wrong. The medical officer also does not bear or use arms, except when patients under his care are being attacked.

Naval medicine. Naval medical services are run on similar lines to those of the army. Junior Medical officers are attached to ships or to shore stations and deal with most cases of sickness in their units. When at sea, the medical officer has an exceptional degree of responsibility in that he is working alone, unless he is on a very large ship. In peacetime, only the larger ships carry a medical officer; in wartime, destroyers and other small craft may also carry medical officers. Medical organization in the navy

In a navy there is no need, even in war, for intermediate medical units corresponding to the field ambulances and casualty clearing stations of the army. The main requirements are a doctor of first contact, who has a sick bay, and either a shore-based hospital or a hospital ship. When war comes, an increase in medical facilities, though with no great change in organization, is needed.

Air force medicine. Flying has many medical repercussions. Cold, oxygen lack, and the changing of direction at high speed all have important effects on bodily and mental functions. These problems are studied in special institutes devoted to aviation medicine.

Most armies and air forces share the same medical service; others have air force medical services entirely separate from those of their armies. The organization is similar to that of the navy, in that there is no need for intermediate medical units. Air bases have medical units where minor cases are dealt with. Major cases are sent to hospitals.

A recent development is aerospace medicine. This involves medical problems such as have never been known before, for the main reason that men in space are not under the influence of gravity, a situation that has profound physiological effects. Aerospace medicine is dealt with in a separate article.

CLINICAL RESEARCH

When any new treatment is introduced, someone must be the first on whom it is tried; this trial is an important kind of clinical research. The practical problem is to advance medicine without appreciable risk for the patients.

Although the most spectacular changes in the medical scene during the 20th century, and the most widely heralded, have been the development of potent drugs and elaborate operations, another striking change has been the abandonment of most of the remedies of the past. In the mid-19th century, persons ill with numerous maladies were starved (partially or completely), bled, purged, cupped (by applying a tight-fitting vessel filled with steam to some part and then cooling the vessel), and rested, perhaps for months or even years. Much more recently they were prescribed various restricted diets and were routinely kept in bed for weeks after abdominal operations, for many weeks or months when their hearts were thought to be affected, and for many months or years with tuberculosis. The abandonment of these measures may not be thought of as involving research, but the physician who first encouraged persons who had peptic ulcers to eat what they wanted (rather than to live on the customary mince and slops) and the physician who first got his patients out of bed a week or two after they had had minor coronary thrombosis (rather than insisting on a minimum of six weeks of strict bed rest) were as much doing research as is the physician who first tries out a new drug on a patient. This research by observing what happens when remedies are abandoned has been, indeed, of inestimable value, and the need for it has not yet gone, for practice is still to some extent shackled by the past. Abandonment of remedies of the past

Many controlled clinical trials of traditional remedies have been performed, alternate patients being given them and the others denied them, and these trials have often shown which remedies should be abandoned.

Drugs. The commonest kind of clinical research is the trial of new drugs. The usual course of events in developing a new drug is about as follows: a compound is synthesized in the laboratory or isolated from some natural source; endless laboratory observations are made, including vast numbers of animal experiments. Only a minute proportion of compounds pass these preliminary tests. The few survivors that seem likely to be superior to existing drugs must then be tried on patients.

The justification for using a new drug depends on the nature of the malady from which the patient is suffering. If he has far advanced cancer, remedies with serious side effects can properly be used. If he has a common cold, a drug likely to have any but the most trivial side effects must not be used.

When one deals with progressive or little-changing maladies, useful conclusions can be drawn from observing the effect of treatment in single cases. But, when maladies have a short and usually favourable course (as do colds, influenza, and lumbago) or a recurrent and unpredictable course (as do duodenal ulcer, multiple sclerosis, and colitis), observations on single cases, or even on large numbers when all are treated alike, are of little value. In such situations controlled series are needed, certain patients being given the drug to be tested and alternate patients being denied it. Best of all is the double blind trial in which neither patients nor observers know who is having the drug to be tested and who are having dummy tablets. The effect of suggestion, which can be important, is thus eliminated. If the patients given the drug regularly do better than those who have the dummy tablets, there is evidence of the drug's value.

In dealing with minor maladies such as colds or boils, there are few ethical problems in doing controlled trials, but, when there is a risk of death or permanent disability, it is justifiable to give dummy tablets only when evidence is lacking that any remedy will improve the outcome. Frequently, a number of drugs are all known to be effective for a certain malady, but there is doubt as to which is the best. It is then justifiable to perform a controlled trial in which certain patients are given one of the drugs and alternate patients are given another.

Before patients take part in a trial, they are told of the implications, and their permission is obtained. In practice, nearly all patients agree. Difficulties arise when patients are unconscious or mentally confused—and so cannot validly give consent—or when they are children. The legal position in most countries appears to be obscure in these situations. According to British law, parents probably cannot give consent to experimental procedures on their children that involve risk, though there seems some doubt about this.

However much care is taken in research with new drugs, disasters can occur. This is especially so when the drugs appear harmless to all experimental animals, when only very few patients are harmed, and when there is delay before the harm becomes manifest. There can indeed be extreme difficulty in deciding whether a drug has been responsible for some disorder. An example of the difficulty is provided by the thalidomide disaster. Only after a long time and after numerous deformed babies had been born all over the world did it become clear that thalidomide taken by the mother as a sedative had been responsible.

Hospital ethical committees

In hospitals in which clinical research is carried on, ethical committees often consider each research project. Then, if the committee believes that the risks are not justified, the project is rejected. Official bodies give general advice on this matter.

Surgical operations. In drug research the essential steps are taken by the chemists who synthesize or isolate new drugs in the laboratory; clinicians play only a subsidiary part. In developing new operations clinicians play a more important role, though laboratory scientists and others in the background may also contribute largely. Many new operations have been made possible by advances in anesthesia, and these in turn depend upon engineers who have devised machines and chemists who have produced new drugs. Other operations are made possible by new materials, such as the alloys and plastics that are used to make artificial hip and knee joints.

Whenever practicable, new operations are tried on animals before they are tried on patients. This practice is particularly relevant to organ transplants. Surgeons themselves—not experimental physiologists—transplanted kidneys, livers, and hearts in animals before attempting these procedures on patients. But experiments on animals are of little or no value in developing some operations. This may be because no animal suffers from a malady similar to that of the patient. An important advance after World War II was valvulotomy, dilation of the mitral valve of the heart that had become narrowed from rheumatic disease. The need for the operation had long been obvious; it had not been devised because anesthesia had not advanced enough. When machines and drugs enabled the heart to be approached without the lungs' collapsing, valvulotomy became possible. The essential research could be done only by a surgeon operating on a patient.

Observing the natural history of maladies. The one kind of clinical research that any physician can carry out single-handedly with little or no equipment and with no ethical repercussions, is the long-term observation of patients with certain maladies. This type of research is not popular. Those who conduct research mostly aim to achieve results quickly; a lapse of 20 or 30 years before a paper can be published is unattractive. Yet, this kind of research can yield valuable information. What happens to persons with many common maladies, including such relapsing conditions as peptic ulcer, colitis, and multiple sclerosis, is still not known. Any hospital physician knows of the variety of relapses that the victims of these conditions may have, but he does not know how many patients never have relapses, because they do not consult him. Little is known as to how many of those who develop these maladies in their 20s are alive and free of symptoms in their 60s. Careful observations by a number of general practitioners lasting throughout their careers and published when they retire would be most valuable.

Even longer term research of this kind can usefully be done for hereditary maladies. Few families have been properly observed for two generations, and virtually none for three, and yet only by such studies can satisfactory knowledge be obtained of an important range of human maladies, and only with such knowledge can sound genetic counselling be given to people with hereditary conditions.

II. Maintenance of professional standards

ETHICAL BASIS OF MEDICAL PRACTICE

The first great exposition of the ethical basis of medicine was the Hippocratic oath. No one knows how and when the oath was formulated. It is part of the large Hippocratic collection, of which the earliest complete manuscript is of the 9th century AD. Some of the ideas behind the oath date back long before Hippocrates (who lived in the 5th century BC). The most important part of the oath is usually rendered:

Hippocratic oath

> The regimen I adopt shall be for the benefit of my patients according to my ability and judgment, and not for their hurt or for any wrong. I will give no deadly drug to any, though it be asked of me, nor will I counsel such, and especially I will not aid a woman to procure abortion. . . . Whatsoever house I enter, there will I go for the benefit of the sick, refraining from all wrongdoing or corruption, and especially from any act of seduction, of male or female, of bond or free. Whatsoever things I see or hear concerning the life of men, in my attendance on the sick or even apart therefrom, which ought not to be noised abroad, I will keep silence thereon, counting such things to be as sacred secrets.

Many of the precepts in the oath express noble ideals, and yet such is the difficulty of laying down criteria to cover any eventuality that in practice exceptions have to be allowed. Few would insist that in no circumstances should a woman procure an abortion, and occasionally it may be justifiable to disclose a patient's secrets to others.

In the everyday practice of medicine, physicians spend little time in considering the ethical basis of their work. They simply take for granted a few moral principles—whether they believe these are derived from Hippocrates, from the natural law, from the divine law, or just from plain common sense. They do their best to benefit their patients, by curative methods, if possible, and otherwise by relieving symptoms and by kindness and reassurance; they tell the truth (except when the truth is too wounding); and they do not reveal their patients' confidences. Ethical problems are likely to arise in only a few special circumstances.

One such circumstance is when the doctor is employed by a corporation to examine potential and actual employees. He then must decide to whom his allegiance lies—whether to the corporation or to the individual. When the individual is applying for a job in which his ill health may endanger others (as in the case of an airplane pilot) and if the physician finds evidence of some disorder likely to cause sudden incapacity, he is, without doubt, morally entitled to advise the corporation not to employ the person. When the question of danger to others does not arise and the physician finds some abnormality, he will, if he abides strictly by the Hippocratic oath, advise hiring the applicant.

A widely discussed moral dilemma is presented by the patient who is artificially kept alive by a machine. The question then may be whether the machine should be switched off. The frequency of this situation has been greatly exaggerated by some popular writers. In practice, most of the persons who are so maintained are young people with severe brain injuries. When they are first admitted to hospital, the extent of brain damage may be impossible to assess. Because many profoundly unconscious people recover, the patient is rightly attached to a machine. If, as time passes, it becomes clear that his brain is damaged beyond hope of recovery, the machine may properly be switched off, though the decision to do so is repugnant to make.

The commonest ethical problems involving doctors in the Western world relate to abortion and religious scruples against it.

LICENSURE REQUIREMENTS FOR PRACTICE

There are wide variations between countries in the requirements for practice, and a license to practice in one country only occasionally implies the right to practice in another. Even within some countries that have a federal system of government, there may be no equivalence of medical qualifications. The physician who qualifies in one state of the United States or in a province of Canada is not automatically entitled to practice in another state or province.

Throughout the world the most important requirements for practice are the taking of a prescribed course of study in a medical school and the passing of examinations. Most medical schools are faculties of universities, and the qualifying examinations are usually run by the universi-

ties. After passing the final examination, the successful candidate becomes a doctor of medicine (M.D.) in most countries; he becomes a bachelor of medicine and bachelor of surgery or chirurgery (M.B., B.S., or M.B., Ch.B.) in Britain and many Commonwealth countries, where M.D. is a higher qualification. In some countries, bodies other than universities may hold qualifying examinations. In Britain many medical students take the examination of the conjoint board of the Royal Colleges of Physicians and Surgeons, becoming members of the Royal College of Surgeons and licentiates of the Royal College of Physicians (M.R.C.S., L.R.C.P.).

Britain. The General Medical Council was established by the Medical Act of 1858. The preamble to the act began: "It is expedient that persons requiring medical aid should be enabled to distinguish qualified from unqualified practitioners." The chief duties of the council are to keep a register of duly qualified doctors and to ensure that the educational standard of entry to the register is maintained. All except three of the 49 council members are physicians; eight are nominated by the crown, and the remainder either by the Royal Colleges of Physicians, of Surgeons, and of Obstetricians and Gynaecologists, in the universities, or directly by the medical profession.

The council influences medical education mainly by issuing recommendations to universities and medical schools on such matters as the range of subjects in the curriculum and the scope of the examinations. Since 1953, students who have passed their final examinations have been placed on a provisional register; only after they have spent a year as a resident house officer are they placed on the full register.

The council also places overseas graduates on the full or provisional register. By law it can do so only for graduates of countries that have reciprocal arrangements for registration with Britain. Such arrangements have been made with most Commonwealth countries and with the Republic of South Africa. Graduates from other countries may be placed on a temporary register, entitling them to work only in certain approved hospitals.

The function of the council that brings it most to public notice is in medical discipline. The council's primary duty here is to protect the public. The chief varieties of "serious professional misconduct" that may cause a physician to be summoned before the council are addiction to drugs or alcohol, the abuse of his professional position (as by having sexual relations with a patient or by revealing confidential information), advertising, and canvassing for patients. The disciplinary committee of the council derives its information from lawcourt proceedings or by direct written complaints from individuals. If the committee finds that a physician has been guilty of "serious professional misconduct," it may warn him as to his future behaviour, put him on probation, advise him to have treatment (especially for addiction), suspend him from duty immediately (this is chiefly used when a physician appears mentally deranged), or, as the supreme penalty, direct the registrar to erase his name from the register.

United States. Each state has the constitutional right to grant licenses to practice medicine within its boundaries. In consequence, the policies and legislature provisions concerning the practice of medicine vary from state to state. A citizen of the United States who has qualified in medicine in one state is not automatically entitled to practice in any other state.

In the state of Illinois, for example, the Medical Practice Act lays down that no person may receive a license to practice medicine unless he has passed an examination of the Department of Registration and Education. The candidate must be a citizen of the United States or be in process of becoming one, and he must prove that he has had the preliminary general and professional education required by the act, detailed provisions as to the medical training required being laid down.

The Illinois Department of Registration and Education may, without examination, issue a license to a person who has been licensed in another state or country, provided he is a United States citizen or in process of becoming one and is a graduate of a medical college of good standing. The state or country in which the candidate was licensed must accord the same privileges to physicians licensed in Illinois. The department may also issue a limited license entitling the holder to practice only under supervision in certain hospitals.

In addition to the examinations of the individual states, there is a National Board of Medical Examiners, which holds regular examinations. Success in these entitles a physician to practice without further examination in all except five of the states. Only graduates of approved medical schools in the United States or Canada are allowed to take the national board examinations.

The State Department has ordered that visas not be issued to foreign physicians unless they have passed the examination held by the Educational Council for Foreign Medical Graduates. This examination includes a test in English. When the foreign physician has passed this examination, he must also satisfy the authorities in the state where he wishes to practice by either passing the examination held by the state examination board or by other means (such as the method just described for Illinois).

Other countries. In France, the medical practitioner must hold the French state diploma of doctor of medicine (unless he is covered by special provisions relating to Alsace and Lorraine and the Saar) and must, in general, be a French citizen. A citizen of a state that has granted the right of French citizens to practice on its territory may be authorized to practice medicine in France provided that an agreement to this effect with the state concerned has been reached and that the standing of the diploma is recognized by the minister of national education.

In the Federal Republic of Germany (West Germany),

the medical practitioner must be a German citizen, must have passed the qualifying examination, and must have completed a two-year period of internship. In principle no foreigner may practice medicine in West Germany, though exceptionally a permit to do so may be granted to a person who has fulfilled the training requirements of the Federal Republic.

In other countries of western Europe, the situation is similar to that in France and Germany, though it is usually easier for foreign physicians to practice in the small countries than in the large ones. Italy has limited reciprocity arrangements with Germany, Portugal, and Spain, and physicians may obtain licenses to practice throughout the Scandinavian countries.

In India, a Medical Council maintains the Indian Medical Register, and any person on this register may practice anywhere in India. There are also state medical registers for the individual states, and people in these registers are also in the Indian Medical Register. Those who have obtained a degree from a university, usually M.B., B.S., or the qualification of licensed medical practitioner (L.M.P.) are entered in these registers. Qualifications from many foreign countries, including Britain, Australia, Burma, Canada, Pakistan, Ceylon, and Italy, are also recognized for entry to the registers.

LEGAL RESTRICTIONS ON PRACTICE

In most countries most physicians are only rarely conscious of legal restrictions on their activities. These restrictions are mainly concerned with procedures performed on minors and mentally disordered patients, operations for abortion and sterilization, the notification of certain maladies, death from unnatural causes, and the use of certain drugs.

Procedures are not usually done on minors without the agreement of the parents. The legal position when a parent is unavailable is, in Britain and the United States, not clear, but, if the physician does what he thinks best, there seems no risk of his being later taken to court. Legal difficulties with children largely arise when parents refuse to allow some action that the physician considers necessary.

Issuance of death certificate

When a patient dies, a death certificate must be issued by a physician who has been in attendance. If the physician suspects that death has been due to other than natural causes, he must by law report the matter to some official person. In England and most of the United States, this person is the coroner; and in Scotland, the procurator fiscal. The coroner is appointed in England, always has a legal qualification, and frequently also is a qualified physician. In most of the United States the coroner is elected, often on the party political ticket. Some states, starting with Massachusetts in 1888, have a medical examiner instead of a coroner. The coroner or medical examiner usually orders a postmortem examination. If this shows that death was due to natural causes, the coroner signs the death certificate. If death is found to be due to violence or other unnatural cause, an inquest is held, and, if appropriate, criminal proceedings follow. On the continent of Europe, no single executive officer is responsible for dealing with cases of sudden death. When there is a suspicion of crime, the death is reported to the police, who may inform the public prosecutor.

In civilized countries the only people other than criminals who can be legally incarcerated are those affected by so grave a degree of mental disorder that they are a danger to themselves or others. Physicians are concerned in this incarceration, for they have to sign appropriate certificates, though various legal officials may also be involved.

In most countries the physician has a legal obligation to report certain maladies. These requirements vary from place to place and time to time, but the main maladies involved are certain infections (which may result in epidemics) and certain industrial diseases.

There are legal restrictions on the use of certain drugs nearly everywhere. The sale of a few drugs is totally prohibited in some countries. Thus, heroin is prohibited in the United States and most other countries apart from Britain and West Germany, because addiction to it is particularly likely. The sale of other dangerous or addictive drugs may be severely restricted. In Britain there is a Dangerous Drugs Act, under which there are stringent regulations as to the prescription, storage, and issuing of morphine and other drugs of addiction. Radioactive substances are also subject to severe restrictions.

In some countries there are laws compelling citizens to accept certain measures to prevent disease. Smallpox vaccination used to be compulsory for all children in Britain, though there was a clause excepting the children of conscientious objectors to vaccination. In a law of 1966, compulsory immunization against poliomyelitis was introduced for all infants in Italy.

There are laws restricting the termination of pregnancy in all countries. In most of the Communist countries and in Japan, a woman is entitled to have an abortion early in pregnancy if she wishes it, but abortion is illegal later than about the fourth month. In all other countries, there must be some specified ground for abortion, and the wish of the patient is not of itself a ground. In most of the predominantly Roman Catholic countries, such as Ireland and Italy, abortion is illegal except when the woman has a diseased womb that needs to be removed but that incidentally contains a fetus. The penalty for breaking the law may be a long term of imprisonment. In many predominantly Protestant countries, the abortion laws have been made more liberal in the second half of the 20th century, notably in Britain by an act of 1967. In these countries the decision for or against abortion is in practice more an ethical than a legal matter. If a physician's ethical views allow him to advise abortion, the law is such that he can usually recommend it legally on the practical ground that he believes it is in the woman's best interest to have it.

Suicide used to be a crime in all countries of Christendom, but this is no longer so in many countries, including Britain and many states of the United States. The doctor who deals with patients who have taken overdoses of drugs need not, therefore, consider the legal aspects of the matter.

Suits for malpractice

Perhaps the way in which the physician is most likely to become involved with the law in most countries today is in suits for malpractice. Such actions are especially common in the United States. Those most likely to be sued are surgeons, since malpractice is much more easy to prove when a surgical operation is done. When, for example, a surgeon has left an instrument or a swab behind in the wound, he is clearly liable at law. The surgeon is also liable to be sued because a patient is dissatisfied with the result of the operation. Plastic surgeons are most of all at risk; many of their operations are done solely to improve the patient's appearance, and, if he does not like the result, he may sue. Consequently, plastic surgeons in the United States may find it prohibitively expensive, or even impossible in some states, to obtain insurance coverage against malpractice suits.

Internists and general practitioners are, by contrast, comparatively rarely sued for malpractice. They may make serious errors, especially by prescribing the wrong drug and occasionally by failing to prescribe the right drug, but such errors rarely come to light. Even if a patient or his relatives suspect that such errors have been made, it can hardly be proved in a court of law that the physician was criminally negligent. An error of judgment by a physician is not a crime.

In the United States, because of fear of suits for malpractice, many persons, both physicians and others, have been slow to go to the aid of victims of traffic accidents. In response to this problem, a number of states enacted legislation, so-called good samaritan laws, to protect physicians and others from such suits.

PROFESSIONAL ORGANIZATIONS
AND THE MAINTENANCE OF STANDARDS

From medieval times there have been professional medical organizations concerned with maintaining standards. In England the physicians established their college in 1518, and candidates for admission were required to read certain books and were set examinations. The United

Company of Barber-Surgeons was established in 1540, and apprentices had to serve for seven years as other apprentices did, attend lectures and dissections, and pass an examination before being allowed to practice on their own account.

American and British medical associations

The American and British medical associations, to which most physicians belong, publish weekly journals in which appear original articles and review articles. Both associations also publish numerous specialist journals. There are many other medical journals. The prime means by which most physicians keep up to date is by regularly reading their journals.

The medical associations hold meetings and conferences and run courses. There, papers are read, demonstrations made, and discussions held. All these practices help in the continuing education of the physician throughout his career. Participation in continuing medical education has been made a requirement for membership in some organizations.

In Britain the Royal Colleges also maintain standards by holding examinations. Medical doctors must pass the fellowship examination of the Royal College of Surgeons of England or the membership examination of the Royal College of Physicians of London (or of the sister colleges in Scotland and Ireland) before they can hope to become consultant surgeons or physicians. Gynecologists must pass the membership examination of the Royal College of Obstetricians and Gynaecologists. The British system is sometimes criticized because it involves too many examinations.

Most hospitals in the United States are assessed by the Joint Commission of Accreditation of Hospitals, set up by the American Medical Association, the American Colleges of Surgeons and Physicians, and the American Hospital Association. This assessment involves a triennial inspection of buildings, equipment, patients' records, and internal hospital organization. This accreditation process has a great effect in improving hospital standards.

Within the voluntary community hospitals, there are committees for the maintenance of standards. The credentials committee investigates the credentials of all applicants for membership of the medical staff. The tissue committee maintains an individual audit on all surgeons and investigates all cases of removal of normal tissue, discrepancies between preoperative and postoperative diagnosis, and cases of possibly unjustified surgery. General practitioners on the staffs of the hospitals are appointed to the department of medicine or surgery, depending on their experience and interest, and their staff privileges are exactly delineated. Thus, it may be specified that a doctor may perform appendectomy, but no other abdominal operation. In certain situations, such as a first cesarean section or sterilization operation, it is laid down that consultation with another doctor, preferably a specialist in the condition concerned, must be held. These detailed specifications have no counterpart in most other countries.

The situation in other developed countries is similar in other respects to that in Britain and the United States.

BIBLIOGRAPHY. JOHN FRY, *Medicine in Three Societies* (1969), compares hospital care and other medical facilities in the United States, Britain, and the Soviet Union. DONALD HUNTER, *Health in Industry* (1959), gives a succinct account, intended for the general reader, of the health problems of industry throughout the world, and includes a historical section. MAURICE H. KING (ed.), *Medical Care in Developing Countries* (1966), describes the grave health problems in the developing countries and discusses means of solving them.

(J.W.T.)

Mediterranean Folk Cultures, Western

The western Mediterranean folk cultures include the peoples of southern Portugal, southern Spain, and southern Italy—the dry zone in the south of Europe bordering on the Mediterranean. It forms in its entirety a region linking Europe with North Africa. In the past the societies on the southern shore of the Mediterranean have made incursions into the area to the north and left behind important elements of their culture. The Arabic expressions, words, and place names abounding throughout the area bear witness to more than 200 years of domination by Arabic culture. So also does the architecture, notably the Moorish palaces and forts of southern Spain and Sicily. The seclusion of women, so customary in this area, probably also derives from Arabic influence.

In other respects the area shows a remarkable unity of European culture elements deriving from the Hellenic, Roman, and Christian traditions. The Mediterranean has always provided the communication necessary for the diffusion and maintenance of distinct cultural elements, and it has acted as a barrier to easy penetration from the south.

Though the area today is economically marginal to the rest of Europe because of its impoverished agricultural system, it has not always been poor. Once it was rich in agricultural and mineral resources. The mountains and hills, today eroded, were at one time densely forested. The countryside was sunny and reasonably well watered. It provided a fertile agricultural milieu that invited incursions from the Greeks, Romans, and Arabs, all of whom sought additional resources to sustain their expanding populations. This led to large-scale exploitation of the forest for wood and to the establishment of grain and livestock farming. The transformation had important consequences for the local climate and drainage: as the vegetation disappeared, the summers became relatively drier and the winter rains washed the soil from the eroding slopes, creating unhealthy marshes along the coast. The progressive deterioration of the terrain is one of the characteristic long-term processes in the area, continuing from ancient times to the present. National governments have recently sought to restrain it, but without success. One characteristic of the area is that central government has always been weak.

CULTURAL PATTERNS

The gulf between town and country

The folk societies in the western Mediterranean all show a strong urban orientation and a pronounced polarization between landowners and peasants. The urban orientation is evident in the settlement pattern. Hill-top villages and huge farm towns predominate in much of the region, and in between them lies the empty countryside. Profit from the chief crops—cereals, wines, olive oil, and livestock products—does not flow back to the countryside in the form of investment in roads, farm buildings, irrigation, and general improvements on the land. Instead, it is spent by the absentee landlords living in towns and cities, often outside the area. This pattern of capital accumulation widens the gap between the elite and the peasantry, between town and country. There is a general disdain for manual work, and those who labour on the land are looked down upon. The countryside is regarded as devoid of civilized life. This social and geographical distance has made room for a rural middle class between the landowners and the peasants.

The gulf between city and country corresponds to the distribution of political power. Until recently there were few ties linking the various regions into a comprehensive whole. Because landowning elites held local and regional power, central government has had to find some form of accommodation with them in order to maintain peace and collect its revenues.

In the absence of effective state control, the people have been largely dependent upon themselves. They could not rely on organized corporate kinship groups, such as clans and tribes, for the dominant residential and productive unit throughout the area has been the small nuclear family. Instead, they have traditionally turned to particular kinsmen, friends, and powerful local strong men to settle conflicts and to right wrongs. This has meant a high level of open violence: banditry and feuding have been endemic, and until recently peasant rebellions were frequent. These conditions buttressed the local enclaves of power and set strong limits on the development of central control.

Mass emigration to the Americas in the period around 1900 reinforced this distribution of power, for it reduced the number of potential malcontents. In the period since

World War II, the migration of workers to industrial areas in the north has altered the balance of power at local and regional levels. Wages earned in northern industries have given the peasants alternative resources, making them less dependent upon the local power holders.

Social organization. All western Mediterranean folk societies belong to larger political units or states. In each country there is considerable cultural, economic, and political variation from region to region. Such differences are often expressed in rivalry and competition between region and state. These decentralizing forces have recently been granted formal recognition in Italy. In Spain, on the other hand, such regional autonomy has been resisted by the authoritarian regime.

Throughout the whole area, states rather than nation-states have been predominant. People see themselves as subjects of rulers rather than as citizens of a nation.

Farm towns

To protect themselves from bandits and outlaws, not to mention Arab and Turkish pirates in search of booty and slaves, the population long ago crowded together in tightly knit villages and towns for mutual protection. Feudal lords, most notably in Sicily, founded a number of such farm towns to facilitate their control over the peasants as well as to extend the area of cultivated land. Cereal production and livestock breeding did not necessitate permanent settlement on scattered farms. With the growth of population in the 19th century, increasing numbers of peasants became landless and had to live near the labour market, which was located in the town's central square. Scarcity of water, the prevalence of malaria, and the absence of usable roads also encouraged concentration in towns. The political status of these communities for a long time was feudal, and even after feudalism ended in the early 19th century they remained dependent upon groups of local landowners.

The last century has seen a movement from inland areas to the coast, where a number of new settlements have been established. Following World War II the increasingly efficient state apparatus, aided by the World Health Organization, eliminated malaria in the western Mediterranean. The states also have succeeded in eliminating banditry in a number of areas. These factors have enabled many peasants to settle on the land. Scattered farms have been increasing, except in western Sicily and inland Sardinia where banditry is still rife.

Economy. The principal crops in the western Mediterranean are the same today as they were in Roman times: wheat, wines, and olive oil produced in conjunction with extensive cattle, sheep, and goat breeding. The agricultural structure is still highly polarized: on the one hand, small family farms produce a variety of products, both for consumption and for the market, but cover little of the total area; on the other hand, large holdings (*latifundia*) produce cereals and livestock for the market. Until the 19th century the *latifundia* covered most of the arable land.

Latifundia and small holdings

The fields are rotated among wheat, pasturage, and fodder crops. On the large holdings there are various forms of sharecropping, in which both the cultivator and the owner-manager share the output. Sharecropping contracts are renewed annually. This form of tenure does not encourage capital investment by either of the parties involved. Harvest hands are recruited chiefly from the growing category of landless peasants.

The impact of recent land reforms has been slight; they have contributed more to the fragmentation of land holdings than to increased production. Cultivation methods are still traditional, despite the introduction of labour-saving machinery. The increasing scarcity of agricultural labour, which since 1955 has been migrating to north European industrial regions, and the abolition of protective tariffs had by 1970 seriously inhibited grain production. Marginal lands were increasingly being used to pasture livestock.

Under the traditional inheritance laws, property is divided equally among all heirs. With the growth of population, this has brought about a progressive division of the smaller holdings into very small plots. The heirs of small holders do not inherit economically viable units. Wealthy landowners, on the other hand, often have fewer children, and their superior education enables them to take up alternative pursuits such as the church and the professions. Many also stay unmarried to maintain the family patrimony.

Family and kinship patterns. Western Mediterranean countrymen live primarily in small nuclear families—that is, in households consisting of married couples with their unmarried children. The family is also the primary production unit. The kinship structure is bilateral, the children having equal access to both the father's and the mother's relatives. Godparenthood and friendship are important in cementing relationships outside the household, for people cannot rely upon public institutions to protect their interests.

Authority over the economic activities of the family is vested in the father, who serves as business manager of the family and represents it in the public sphere. Unmarried children work under his supervision. The dominant position of the father is reinforced by the teachings of the Roman Catholic Church. A man's social status as a person with honour is closely linked to his ability to maintain or improve the economic position of his family and to safeguard his wife and daughters. His women constitute a permanent danger to his honour, being regarded as morally weak. The preoccupation of men with honour is a strong element in the culture of the area.

Role of the father

Women, although subordinate to the men and more or less confined to the household, are by no means without influence. The woman administers the household finances. Among the western Mediterranean peasants, the relatives of the mother are visited more often and tend to play a more important role in family affairs than those of the father. In fact, a landless labourer who is not tied by property considerations to his own place of birth frequently moves upon marriage to the village of his wife so that the latter can be near her own relatives. This clustering of female relatives is consistent with a marked segregation between the sexes.

The distribution of power. Beginning in the early 19th century, a rural middle class gradually emerged from the leaseholders and supervisors of large estates and from the millers and waggoners, who formed an intermediary category between landowners and peasants. This new class derived its power from its control of the links between the main social strata, between the regions, and between town and country. Its strategic position enabled it to attract a following of peasants who depended upon the members of this middle class for access to land and for protection. Their local power basis also enabled them to perform important services for the urban elite, who needed them to run the estates and to mobilize the voters at election time. The urban elite depended upon these rural entrepreneurs not only for success in the national political arena but also for prestige and standing in the city.

The rural middle class

Where government was especially weak, respect and prestige tended to belong to individuals who were successful in the use of violence. In mountainous areas in Greece, inland Sardinia, and Sicily, this pattern of respect for violence still holds.

During the past century the power of the landowning classes has been threatened by mass parties of the left in parliamentary elections. To defend their interests, the landed elite have often entered into coalition with other conservative forces and supported right-wing dictatorships such as that of Benito Mussolini in Italy. In fact, the only conservative dictatorships in Europe in 1970 were in Portugal, Spain, and Greece. In postwar Italy, however, pressure from mass parties led to certain land-reform measures and to more favourable contracts for peasant labourers. These to some extent reduced the power of the rural elite.

Religion and art. The established religion is Roman Catholicism. Not surprisingly, the church has been closely associated with the interests of the landowners, who have supported it by their financial contributions and their participation in church-run lay associations. The peasants, on the other hand, have been generally unsympathetic to the church, when not openly hostile. This latent anti-clericalism has sometimes assumed extreme forms, as in the desecration of churches and the assassination of priests during the Spanish Civil War of the 1930s. The cult of the saints is particularly strong. There is a striking similarity between the role of saints as intermediaries between God and man and the role of the patron who intercedes with a powerful person on behalf of his client.

Belief in magic Although nominally practicing the established religion, many peasants also adhere to other beliefs and practices. Many of these involve the use of love potions and the recitation of incantations and spells to cure ills, most often administered by wise old women who function as informal priestesses. The established religion generally condemns such practices, but in most rural areas they are firmly entrenched. Everywhere one finds belief in the evil eye and in the power of envy to do evil. This is related to the peasant notion that one person's gain must necessarily be at the expense of someone else.

The music of the peasants is often extemporaneous, played on simple stringed instruments and sung as a lament or a satirical attack on a rival. Much folk music still bears traces of Arabic influence. Everywhere, however, this traditional music is rapidly being replaced by the popular music of western Europe, which penetrates via television, transistor radio, and record player to even the most remote hamlet.

LONG-TERM TENDENCIES

The general social and cultural patterns sketched above are being modified by long-term developments in the wider societies in which the peasant communities are embedded. These long-term processes include the rising level of education, the growing division of labour, increasing centralization, and the growing economic dependence of southern Europe on the north. At the same time, modernization is eroding the traditional basis of peasant society and reducing the relative importance of the resources on which the traditional elite based its power.

The increasing dependence of Mediterranean Europe on its industrialized northern neighbours does not offer a fundamental solution to the economic problems of the area. Migrating peasants have become industrial labourers abroad. The vast sums of money that they send back to their families cannot be productively invested in the transformation of the economy because that would require a coordination of groups and regions that is still far from being realized. The funds are mainly spent on consumption goods and on the purchase of fragments of land.

The odd-job man of Europe The growing integration of Europe has made the south increasingly dependent upon the north. A sharp economic recession in the north not only would affect the industries in the Mediterranean countries, forcing them to lay off local workers, but also would send hundreds of thousands of migrant labourers back to the south. Such a recession would also severely curtail the flow of northern tourists. The south European, in short, is still the odd-job man of Europe: he cleans up after the Dutchman, the German, the Swiss, and the Belgian in their home countries, performing the tasks they no longer want to do, and waits upon them when they come to the Mediterranean on holiday. He is likely to be the first to suffer in time of economic difficulty. Peasants and post-peasants in the western Mediterranean are still among the most marginal men of Europe.

BIBLIOGRAPHY. General works include: ANTON BLOK, "South Italian Agro-Towns," *Comparative Studies in Society and History*, 11:121–135 (1969); N. ELIAS, "Processes of State Formation and Nation Building," *Transactions of the 7th World Congress of Sociology* (1972); S.H. FRANKLIN, *The European Peasantry* (1969); D.S. PITKIN, "Mediterranean Europe," *Anthrop. Q.*, 36:120–129 (1963); JANE SCHNEIDER, "Of Vigilance and Virgins: Honor, Shame and Access to Resources in Mediterranean Societies," *Ethnology*, 10:1–24 (1971); and E.R. WOLF, *Peasants* (1966).

Detailed case studies include: E.C. BANFIELD, *The Moral Basis of a Backward Society* (1958), for Italy; JEREMY BOISSEVAIN, *Hal-Farrug: A Village in Malta* (1969); JOSE CUTILEIRO, *A Portuguese Rural Society* (1971); MAURICE LE LANNOU, *Pâtres et Paysans de la Sardaigne* (1971); CARMELO LISON-TOLOSANA, *Belmonte de Los Caballeros: A Sociological Study of a Spanish Town* (1966); E.E. MALEFAKIS, *Agrarian Reform and Peasant Revolution in Spain* (1970); J.A. PITT-RIVERS, *The People of the Sierra* (1971), for Spain; and RENE ROCHEFORT, *Le Travail en Sicile* (1961).

(Je.Bo./A.Bl.)

Mediterranean Sea

The Mediterranean Sea, the great expanse of waters that, stretching from the Atlantic Ocean on the west to Asia on the east, separates Europe from Africa, often has been called the incubator of Western civilization.

This ancient "sea between the lands" occupies a deep, elongated, and almost landlocked irregular depression lying between 30° and 46° N and between 5°50′ W and 36° E. Its east–west extent is approximately 2,500 miles (4,000 kilometres), while its average north–south extent is about 500 miles. The Mediterranean Sea, including the Sea of Marmara and the Black Sea, occupies an area of 1,145,000 square miles (2,966,000 square kilometres); its area excluding the Black Sea is close to 970,000 square miles.

The western extremity of the Mediterranean connects with the Atlantic Ocean by the narrow and shallow channel of the Strait of Gibraltar, which is only eight miles wide at its narrowest point and the depth of the sill, or submarine ridge separating the basins, is 1,050 feet (320 metres). To the northeast the Mediterranean Sea is connected with the Black Sea through the Dardanelles (with a sill depth of 230 feet) the Sea of Marmara, and the strait of the Bosporus. To the southeast it is connected with the Red Sea by the Suez Canal. (For further details, see EUROPE; ADRIATIC SEA; AEGEAN SEA; BLACK SEA.)

THE PHYSICAL ENVIRONMENT

Natural divisions. A submarine ridge between the island of Sicily and the African coast, with a sill depth of about 1,200 feet, divides the Mediterranean Sea into western and eastern parts. The western part, in turn, is subdivided into three principal submarine basins. The Alborán Basin is east of Gibraltar, between the coasts of Spain and Morocco. The Algerian (sometimes known as the Algero-Provençal, or Balearic, Basin, east of the Alborán Basin, is west of Sardinia and Corsica, extending from off the coast of Algeria to off the coast of France. The Tyrrhenian Basin, that part of the Mediterranean known as the Tyrrhenian Sea, lies between Italy and the islands of Sardinia and Corsica. The eastern Mediterranean is subdivided into two major basins. The Ionian Basin, in the area known as the Ionian Sea, lies to the south of Italy and Greece, where the deepest sounding in the Mediterranean, about 16,000 feet (4,900 metres), has been recorded. A submarine ridge between the western end of Crete and Barqah (Cyrenaica) separates the Ionian Basin from the Levantine Basin to the south of Asia Minor, and the island of Crete separates it from the Aegean Sea, which comprises that part of the Mediterranean Sea north of Crete and bounded on the west and north by the coast of Greece and on the east by the coast of Turkey. The Aegean Sea contains numerous islands known as the Grecian archipelago. The Adriatic Sea (*q.v.*), northwest of the main body of the Mediterranean Sea, is bounded by Italy to the west and north and by Yugoslavia and Albania to the east.

Geology and physical geography. The Mediterranean is the main existing fragment of the Tethys Sea, which formerly girdled the Eastern Hemisphere. The structure and present form of the basin and its bordering mountain system have been determined by the convergence and recession of the relatively stable continental blocks of Eurasia and Africa. The interpretation of geological data suggests that there are, at present, areas of constriction between Africa and Eurasia the amplitude of which appears to be several centimetres a year. The use of laser tellurometry has demonstrated the intermittent nature of this phenomenon.

The western Mediterranean. The Tyrrhenian Basin of the western Mediterranean has two exits into the eastern

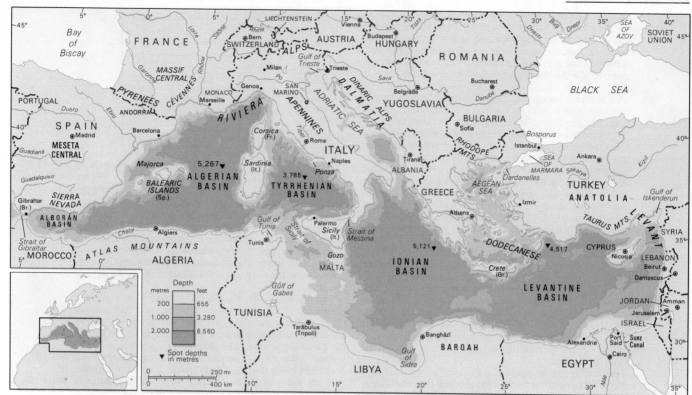

The Mediterranean Sea and its basin.

Continental shelves and coasts

Mediterranean, the Strait of Sicily and the Strait of Messina, both of which were of great strategic importance throughout Mediterranean history. The submarine relief of the Sicilian channel is rather complicated; the group of islands composed of Malta, Gozo, and Comino, all of which are of Tertiary limestone, stands on a submarine shelf that extends southward from Sicily.

The widest of the continental shelves is off Spain's Ebro Delta, where it extends to 60 miles. Similarly, west of Marseille the shelf widens off the Rhône Delta area to 40 miles. Off the Italian peninsula the shelf is narrow, and the slopes are mostly quite low. The narrow shelves continue along the French Riviera, but the slopes show a marked increase where they are cut by many canyons and troughs.

Along the Atlas Mountain coast of North Africa, a narrow shelf bordered by slopes is found from the Strait of Gibraltar to the Gulf of Tunis. The slopes are cut by many canyons or troughlike indentations.

The coasts of the western Mediterranean, just as those of the eastern basin, have been subjected in recent geological times to the uneven action of deposition and erosion. This action, together with the movements of the sea and the emergence and submergence of the land, resulted in a rich variety of types of coasts. The Italian peninsula underwent considerable uplift in post-Pliocene times (the last 2,000,000 or so years), as a result of which a strip of Late Tertiary rocks has been exposed on the Adriatic flank of the Apennines. The Italian Adriatic coast exemplifies a coast owing much to emergence. Examples of coasts the outline of which is due to submergence are the granite coast in northeast Sardinia and the Dalmatian coast where the eroded land surface has been sunk, producing elongated islands parallel to the coast. The deltas of the Rhône, Po, Ebro, and Nile rivers are good examples of coasts resulting from the deposition of silt.

The eastern Mediterranean. The Sicilian straits scarcely exceed 1,500 feet in depth, so that there is essentially a shelf from Tunisia to Sicily separating the Mediterranean into two parts. South of the straits the shelf widens to as much as 170 miles off the Gulf of Gabes on the eastern coast of Tunisia. The first mud appears on the approach to the Nile Delta, and the shelf widens again to 70 miles off Port Said at the entrance to the Suez Canal. The shelves continue to be narrow along most of

the northern shore of the Mediterranean. An exception is the broad shelf extending for 300 miles along the inner portion of the Adriatic Sea. Relatively deep water is found along much of the coast of Yugoslavia and along the Italian coast, in contrast to the gentle slopes of the Po Valley.

The northern shores of the eastern Mediterranean are very complex and, unlike the southern shores, have variable fold mountains that offered favourable sites for the development of the Mediterranean civilizations.

The north coast of Africa bordering the eastern Mediterranean is low-lying and of monotonous uniformity except for the Barqah highlands in Libya, which lie to the east of the Gulf of Sidra.

The largest islands of the eastern Mediterranean are Crete and Cyprus, both of which are mountainous.

Hydrology. The hydrological conditions in the Mediterranean are dominated by the presence of three layers of water masses: the surface layer, the intermediate layer, and the deep layer that continues down to the bottom, a separate bottom layer being absent.

The surface layer has a thickness varying between 250 and 1,000 feet. This variable thickness is determined in the western basin by the presence of a minimum temperature at its lower limit. In the eastern basin the temperature minimum is generally absent, and a layer of low temperature decrease is found instead.

The intermediate layer is accompanied by warm and saline water coming from the eastern Mediterranean and characterized by temperature and salinity maxima at 1,300 feet. This layer is situated at depths between 1,000 and 2,000 feet.

The deep layer occupies the remaining zone between the intermediate layer and the bottom. The approximate temperatures in this zone are: 55.2° F (12.9° C) at 3,000 feet and 55.6° F (13.1° C) at 8,200 feet; its salinity is 38.40 parts per thousand or slightly less. In general, the water of this layer is very homogeneous.

Currents. The Mediterranean Sea receives from the rivers that flow into it only about one-third of the amount of water that it loses by evaporation. In consequence there is a continuous inflow of surface water from the Atlantic Ocean. After passing through the Strait of Gibraltar, the main body of the incoming surface water flows eastward along the north coast of Africa. This current is the most constant component of the circulation of the Mediterranean. It is most powerful in summer, when evaporation in the Mediterranean is at a maximum. This inflow of Atlantic water loses its strength as it proceeds eastward, but it is still recognizable as a surface movement in the Sicilian channel and even off the Levant coast.

A small amount of water also enters the Mediterranean from the Black Sea as a surface current through the Bosporus, the Sea of Marmara, and the Dardanelles.

By evaporation, the Mediterranean water becomes more saline, with a corresponding increase in density. It therefore sinks, and the excess of this denser bottom water emerges into the Atlantic Ocean over the sill forming the shallow Strait of Gibraltar, as a west-going subsurface current below the inward current. The latter extends from the surface down to 230 or 260 feet. The Mediterranean has been metaphorically described as breathing, inhaling surface water from the Atlantic and exhaling deep water in a countercurrent below.

The fundamental surface circulation of the Mediterranean consists of separate counterclockwise movement of the water in each of the two basins.

Because of the complexity of the northern coastline and of the numerous islands, many small eddies and other local currents form essential parts of the general circulation. Tides, although only significant in range in the Gulf of Gabes and in the northern Adriatic, add to the complications of the currents in narrow channels such as the Strait of Messina.

Historically, large seasonal variations in the Nile discharge influenced the hydrology, productivity, and fisheries of the southeastern part of the Mediterranean. It reduced the salinity of the coastal waters and increased both the stratification and productivity of these waters. The Aswān High Dam (1970) stopped the seasonal fluctuation of the discharge of the Nile water into the Mediterranean.

The Suez Canal between the Mediterranean and Red seas passes negligible amounts of Red Sea water into the Mediterranean.

The general water budget of the Mediterranean is given in Table 1.

Table 1: Water Budget in the Mediterranean Sea

gains	cu ft/sec	cu m/sec	losses	cu ft/sec	cu m/sec
Inflow from the Atlantic	61,800,000	1,750,000	Outflow to the Atlantic	59,330,000	1,680,000
Inflow from the Black Sea	445,000	12,600	Outflow to the Black Sea	215,000	6,100
Precipitation	1,115,000	31,600	Evaporation	4,075,000	115,400
Runoff	260,000	7,300			
Total	63,620,000	1,801,500	Total	63,620,000*	1,801,500

*Totals do not correspond because of rounding.

Seawater temperature. The 40° N parallel runs through the middle of the western basin, whereas the corresponding latitude of the eastern basin is 6° farther south, a fact that explains the higher surface temperature of the latter.

The highest temperature of the Mediterranean is met within the Gulf of Sidra, off the coast of Libya, where the mean temperature in August is around 88° F (31° C). This is followed by the Gulf of Iskenderun, Turkey (mean temperature about 86° F [30° C]). The lowest sea temperatures are found in the extreme north of the Adriatic, where the mean temperature in February falls down to 41.4° F (5.2° C) in the Gulf of Trieste. In this region ice occasionally forms in the depth of winter.

Salinity. Just as in all other seas and oceans, chlorides constitute more than half of the total ions present in the Mediterranean water, and the proportions of all the principal salts in the water are constant.

Assuming that in Mediterranean waters the average salinity (weight of dissolved ions per 1,000 parts; *i.e.*, grams per kilogram) is 38, usually expressed as 38 per mille (thousand) or 38 ‰ (3.8 percent), as compared with 35 ‰ for the oceans, then the composition of the major ions in the Mediterranean would be as given in Table 2.

Table 2: Major Ions Dissolved in One Kilogram of Mediterranean Seawater

(salinity = 38 parts per thousand)

	gm/kg		gm/kg
Chlorides	20.815	Magnesium	1.402
Sulfates	2.918	Calcium	0.437
Bicarbonates	0.156	Potassium	0.418
Sodium	11.636	Others*	0.218
Total			38.000

*Present in minute quantities.

Dissolved oxygen. The distribution of oxygen is in agreement with the origin of the different water masses. The surface layer down to 700 feet shows a high oxygen content all over the Mediterranean. The intermediate layer that is formed by the sinking of the surface layer in the eastern basin has a high oxygen content where it is freshly formed in this basin; but, as it moves westward, it loses some of its oxygen content, the lowest values occurring in the Algerian Basin. The transition layer between the intermediate and the deep water is characterized by an oxygen minimum.

Plant nutrients. In the Mediterranean Sea, plant nutrients such as phosphates, nitrates, and nitrites are scarce. Just as in all other seas, these nutrients show seasonal fluctuations, generally with a rise in the spring, the blooming season. The scarcity of nutrients in Mediterranean waters is attributed to several factors, the most important being that the Mediterranean receives its main bulk of water from the surface water of the Atlantic Ocean, which is itself not rich in these nutrients.

In the western basin below 3,000 feet the contents of phosphates and nitrates are less than one-half of the amounts in the open ocean at the same depths.

The shortage of phosphates and nitrates in Mediterranean Sea water, so vital for the creation and the maintenance of the marine life cycle, results in the limited productivity of the region in terms of the life-forms it supports.

Climate. The flow of the air into the Mediterranean Sea takes place through gaps in the mountain ranges, except over the southern shores east of Tunisia. Strong winds funnelled through the gaps are the most important. The mistral, a cold, dry, northwesterly wind, passes through the Alps–Pyrenees gap, the strong northeasterly bora passes through the Trieste gap, and the cold easterly levanter and the westerly vendaval pass through the Strait of Gibraltar. The warm, dusty southeasterly that blows from Saharan Africa is known as the gibleh or khamsin. In the eastern Mediterranean the estian winds are steady, dry northwesterlies and northerlies; the sirocco, from Africa, is dry and hot.

The Mediterranean weather is characterized by windy, mild, wet winters and relatively calm, hot, dry summers. Spring, however, is a transitional season and is changeable. Autumn is relatively short.

The amount and distribution of rainfall in the Mediterranean cannot be generalized. Along the North African coast from Qābis (Gabes) in Tunisia to the Arab Republic of Egypt, more than ten inches (250 millimetres) of rainfall per year is rare, whereas, on the Dalmatian coast of Yugoslavia, there are places with 100 inches.

ANIMAL LIFE AND VEGETATION

Because the primary productivity of life-forms depends to a large extent on the concentration of the plant nutrient salts, it is, as would be expected, generally low in the Mediterranean Sea. The effective potential productivity in various regions of the Mediterranean as measured by radioactive methods using carbon-14 to determine the amount of carbon produced in milligrams of carbon per cubic metre of water (expressed as mg C/m^3) per 24 hours, varies from five to 150 mg C/m^3 per 24 hours. The lowest values are observed in the Levant, ranging from five to 30 mg C/m^3 per 24 hours, and also in the Ionian Basin, where values ranging between seven and 21 mg C/m^3 per 24 hours are observed.

The highest primary-production values in the Mediter-

Scarcity of nutrients

ranean Sea are observed in springtime (March–May) off the Egyptian coast in areas under the influence of the Nile. There primary-production values as high as 700 mg C/m³ per 24 hours are found.

Fish stocks and fisheries. The environmental conditions of the Mediterranean already described, namely, the low concentration of phosphates and nitrates so necessary for the maintenance of marine pastures, together with the poor standing crop of bottom-dwelling organisms, provide no opportunity for the evolution of a big fisheries industry.

Although the general lack of large concentrations of fish has prevented the development of large-scale operations, the high prices of fresh fish in most Mediterranean countries have favoured the development of a large number of small-scale fisheries. Though the boats used are rather small, rarely exceeding 70 feet long, their numbers are sufficient to deplete the local stocks through overfishing. The tendency to overexploitation is strengthened by the use of trawl nets with very small mesh size that retain the smallest individuals.

The fish fauna of the Mediterranean is basically related to the fauna of the subtropical Atlantic with a large variety of species. Of the demersal (bottom-living) fishes, flounders, sole, turbot, whiting, congers, croakers, red mullet, gobies, gurnards, lizard fish, redfishes, sea bass, groupers, combers, sea breams, pandora, and jacks and cartilagenous fishes such as sharks, rays, and skates are all caught by the trawlers. Among the demersal fish, hake is one of the more important in all countries bordering the Mediterranean Sea. It is caught in deeper waters.

Rocky coasts provide a valuable harvest of lobsters, crabs, shrimp, and prawns. Oysters are more common on shallower alluvial coasts. The brackish lagoons and deltas provide eels, anchovies, and gray mullets.

Pelagic species

About half of the Mediterranean and Black Sea catches are of pelagic species (those caught in the upper layers of the sea). Sardines constitute the main catch in the western and northeastern parts of the Mediterranean. Occasionally sardines also appear in relatively small quantities in the southeastern part of the Mediterranean. The total yearly catch from the Mediterranean amounts to 366,000 tons. Closely related fishes (*Sardinella aurita* and *S. maderensis*), however, occur in considerable quantities in the southern and southeastern region of the Mediterranean. The sprat is taken in some quantities in the most northern parts of the Mediterranean such as the northern Adriatic. It also occurs in commercial quantities in the Black Sea. Anchovy is important in most of the regions of the Mediterranean and the Black Sea.

Of the really large fish there is one of great commercial value, the bluefin tuna that moves into the Mediterranean from the Atlantic and disperses in several directions, toward the southern and eastern coasts of Spain, the coasts of the Balearic Islands, the northern coast of Morocco, and the coasts of Sardinia, Sicily, Algeria, Tunisia, and Libya. Related species of economic value are the bonitos and the mackerels. They are caught in various quantities in practically all the countries of the region.

Of the nonedible products of the Mediterranean, the most important are the corals of Naples and the sponges of the Dodecanese, the Gulf of Gabes, and the western coasts of Egypt.

Annual catch

According to statistics of the Food and Agricultural Organization (UN), the total annual catch for the Mediterranean and Black seas' fisheries amounted in the early 1970s to about 1,200,000 tons. In terms of tonnage the leading catches are herrings, sardines, sprat, and anchovies over 300,000 tons; redfishes, basses, and congers, 100,000 tons; shads and milkfishes, 90,000 tons; and jacks and mullets, 70,000 tons. Catches of tunas, bonitos, and skipjack, of mackerels and bluefishes, and of cods, hakes, and haddocks are in the 25,000- to 30,000-ton range. Lesser amounts of sharks and rays, flounders, halibuts, and soles, river eels, porpoises, and sturgeons and paddlefishes are caught. Unsorted, or unclassified, fish account for almost 200,000 tons. Mollusks account for over 90,000 tons, and other crustaceans account for more than 25,000 tons.

Vegetation. The natural vegetations of the lands bordering the Mediterranean can be classified into six general types, one of which is the typical Mediterranean forest. The olive tree provides a satisfactory criterion for the distribution of Mediterranean climate. The holm (or holly) oak and the cork oak provide a better criterion. They tolerate low rainfall and a few months of drought. The conifers, especially the domestic pine, the maritime pine, and the Aleppo pine, are the remnants of the typical Mediterranean forests that suffered from extensive destruction by man. A characteristic feature of the landscape is provided by the macchia (or maquis, evergreen shrubs with hard, leathery leaves), which has widely replaced the conifers. Garigue in its different forms, including sage, prostrate prickly plants, and tuberous perennials, is commonly found in Greece, Spain, and Italy, especially where the soil is limey.

Another type of natural vegetation is the mixed green and deciduous forest, which occupies large areas in Greece, Albania, the north Aegean region, Spain, Portugal, the Alps, and the Apennines. It is made up of species adapted to short periods of drought and to cool winters, hence the presence of evergreens and also the deciduous oak.

A third type is the deciduous forest found in central Italy, where chestnuts occur between 2,000 and 3,000 feet. It extends to the Alps, Cévennes, and Pyrenees. The beech follows the chestnut in altitude.

Other vegetation types are the high coniferous zone, characterized by the white fir, widespread throughout the mountains of central Europe, the high pastures, and the arid zone.

Many plants have been introduced and cultivated in the Mediterranean lands by the Arabs and Spaniards. The more successful introductions include rice, cotton, oranges, sugarcane, maize, tobacco, potatoes, and sisal.

EARLY MEDITERRANEAN CULTURES

Some of the world's earliest civilizations originated in the Mediterranean and spread throughout the greater part of the world. The first of these was the ancient Egyptian civilization in the Nile Valley. Egypt and Babylonia long before the dawn of history struggled with their irrigation problems. They grew grain on a large scale and used the rivers for navigation. In the calm waters of the Aegean Sea, the Minoans (2800–1500 BC) learned the great lessons of navigation and were able to compete with the Phoenicians on equal terms so that they were ultimately driven from the east and established themselves more firmly in the west, and Carthage grew great along the north coast of Africa.

Then the Hellenic civilization assured a wide dissemination of art, literature, and science. The Greek culture faded under the impact of imperial Rome, which grew in everwidening circles, overwhelming the Greeks and destroying Carthage and making the Mediterranean area one unit. The people of Europe reacted, however, and, under the impact of Goths and Vandals, with the Arabs advancing along the southern shores of the Mediterranean, Rome went down. From Asia Minor new armies appeared to menace the Levantine coast, and the Turks advanced both into Europe and down the coasts of Syria and Egypt.

A study of history in the lands surrounding the Mediterranean shows that a period of splendour was always followed by confusion and outburst, and then a new grouping presented itself.

HISTORY OF SCIENTIFIC STUDY

Although well known to the geographers of antiquity and the Middle Ages, the Mediterranean Sea was scarcely subjected to any thorough modern study until the Danish expedition in the "Thor" undertook such a task in 1908–10. The investigations carried out covered as much of the Mediterranean Sea as possible with regard to pelagic (open-sea) animal life and its dependence on hydrographical (flow) conditions and also studied the seasonal circulation between the western and eastern basins and between the Balearic and Tyrrhenian seas.

The expedition of the "Thor"

Not until the end of World War II were major scientific surveys resumed when, in 1948, several surveys were made in the western basin. More systematic studies were carried out there (by the French) from 1957 to 1963.

The eastern basin has received less attention. Mention should be made, however, of investigations into the sources of the formation of deep water in the eastern basin (1957), studies of the vertical circulation of the Mediterranean Sea (1960, 1961), and studies of the hydrographic conditions of the bottom water during summer, using the observations of the French vessel "Calypso" (1955–60).

Cooperative investigations in the Mediterranean were initiated in 1969 by the Intergovernmental Oceanographic Commission (IOC/UNESCO), the International Commission for the Scientific Exploration of the Mediterranean Sea (ICSEM), and the General Fisheries Council for the Mediterranean (GFCM/FAO). Twenty-four nations agreed to cooperate in implementing these programs that cover physical, chemical, geophysical, biological, and fisheries research. Operations were started in 1969 by the German research vessel "Meteor." These operations covered seismic research, continuous seismic reflection measurements, geothermal measurements, radiological and petrophysical investigations, bathymetric measurements, volcanological studies, investigations of marine geology, biological investigations, studies regarding recent ore formation, and analysis for cosmic dust. The Mediterranean Sea, in which the continental transition between Europe and Africa takes place, still poses many unsolved geological problems, and it is hoped that Mediterranean scientific institutions can take part in tackling them within the IOC framework.

International cooperation

BIBLIOGRAPHY. General works include D.S. WALKER, *The Mediterranean Lands*, 3rd ed. (1965); V.M. ALAVEDRA, *Contribution à la connaissance des régimes fluviaux Méditerranéens* (1949); and PIERRE BIROT and JEAN DRESCH, *La Méditerranée et Le Moyen-Orient*, vol. 1, *La Méditerranée Occidentale*, vol. 2, *La Méditerranée Orientale et Le Moyen-Orient* (1953–56). See also M.I. NEWBIGIN, *The Mediterranean Lands* (1924), a general treatment of countries bordering the Mediterranean, with emphasis on human geography; and *Southern Europe*, 3rd ed. rev. (1949); E.C. SEMPLE, *The Geography of the Mediterranean Region* (1932); M. SORRE and J. SION, "Méditerranée," in *Géographie universelle*, vol. 7, pt. 1 (1934); and GEORG WUST, "On the Vertical Circulation of the Mediterranean Sea," *J. Geophys. Res.*, 66:3261–3271 (1961), which deals with Mediterranean currents studied from data already published.

(S.G./M.M.Sa.)

Meghalaya

Meghalaya, literally Abode (*ālaya*) of the Clouds (*megha*), situated in the northeast corner of India, was inaugurated as a full-fledged state of the Indian Union in 1972. Occupying a mountainous plateau of great scenic beauty, it is bounded on the south and west by Bangladesh (formerly East Pakistan) and on the north and east by the Indian state of Assam.

The area of Meghalaya is 8,666 square miles (22,445 square kilometres). Its population in 1971 was about 1,000,000. Its capital is the beautiful hill town of Shillong, which is also the temporary capital of Assam, from which Meghalaya was formed. (For an associated physical feature, see BRAHMAPUTRA RIVER.)

History. Meghalaya consists of two districts, the Gāro Hills and the Khāsi and Jaintia Hills. It is inhabited mainly by tribal people, many of whom trace their origins to pre-Aryan times in India. Though the Aryan invaders drove the inhabitants from the plains to the surrounding hills, these people never really came under the rule of any alien group and largely managed to preserve their way of life in seclusion. Even the British, who established their sway over all of India, did not really conquer them and, in return for acceptance of overall British control, left the tribes alone. After Indian independence, the control and rule of the central government was slowly extended and expanded. But India's first prime minister, Jawaharlal Nehru, evolved a policy to preserve and protect the way of life of the tribal peoples. With other tribal areas, the Gāro Hills and the Khāsi and Jaintia Hills were given special protection in the Indian constitution, and, while included within the state of Assam, the two districts retained a great deal of autonomy.

Even this did not prove enough, however, and when Assam, in 1960, introduced Assamese as the state's official language, agitation for autonomy and self-rule gathered strength. After several commissions and committees had studied the question, in April 1970 the government of India created Meghalaya as an autonomous state within Assam, and in December 1971 the Indian Parliament enacted a law making the area a separate state and bringing within its ambit the town of Shillong.

Physical geography. Geologically, Meghalaya is a detached extension of the Indian plateau. From west to east, the Gāro Hills rise abruptly from the Brahmaputra Valley to about 1,000 feet and merge with the Khāsi Hills and Jaintia Hills, two adjacent highland systems that form a single massif consisting of a series of eastward-trending ridges with tablelands between. The massif rises to 4,000–6,000 feet, declining toward the east. There are steep slopes on the southern faces of the plateau and comparatively gentle slopes toward the Brahmaputra Valley in the north. The central plateau acts as a watershed for the many rivers and streams traversing the state, the most important being the Umiam-Barapani, which is the source of hydroelectric power for the whole of Assam and Meghalaya.

One of the world's wettest regions is found in the state —Cherrapunji, with an average of 500 inches (13,000 millimetres) of annual rainfall, is, however, outclassed by Mawsynram, with an average of 700 inches (18,000 millimetres) (previously there had been no observation station at Mawsynram and the amount of rainfall was thus unknown).

Rainfall

The climate is mild, with an average minimum temperature in the Gāro Hills of 39° F (4° C) and in the Khāsi and Jaintia Hills, 54° F (12° C). The average maximum temperatures are 93° F (34° C) and 74° F (23.3° C), respectively.

The state is rich in forests—pines, sals, and bamboo are plentiful. Among the other trees are oaks, birches, beeches, and magnolias. The state abounds in elephants, tigers, leopards, deer, wild pigs, wild buffalo, mithun (wild oxen), wolves, anteaters, monkeys, apes, squirrels, snakes, hares, and sambar deer. Peacocks, partridges, pigeons, hornbills, jungle fowls, mynas, parrots, and other birds are found in the forests.

Population. According to the 1971 census, the state had a population of 983,336. Most of the inhabitants of Meghalaya are Tibeto-Burman (Gāros) or Mon-Khmer (Khāsis) in origin, and their languages and dialects belong to these groups. Whether the Mon-Khmers originally belonged to this region and were subsequently driven away to Southeast Asia or migrated from there, they are the only people in India speaking languages of the Mon-Khmer group. The most commonly spoken languages and dialects are Khasi and Garo, followed by Pnar-Synteng, Nepali, Jaintia, and Haijong, in addition to the plains languages of Bengali, Assamese, and Hindi.

Christianity, Hinduism, and animistic forms of Hinduism are the major religions in the area. There are also some Muslims (about 30,000) and a few Buddhists (about 1,800).

The population is predominantly rural and the state has few industries. The important urban centres are Shillong, Jowai, Nongthymmai, and Tura.

Administration. Like other states of the Indian Union, Meghalaya has a governor, appointed by the president of India, and a council of ministers, headed by a chief minister. The ministers are collectively responsible to the legislature, which is elected on the basis of adult franchise. Meghalaya shares with Assam a common governor, high court, and other administrative organs.

Administrative associations with other Indian states

The states of Assam, Manipur, Meghalaya, Nāgāland, and Tripura, and the union territories of Arunachal Pradesh and Mizoram all belong to the Northeastern Council, which coordinates plans and schemes for economic

development of the region as a whole. In Shillong, where Assam also has its temporary capital, the government of India has temporary overall control of police and law and order, to obviate any friction between Meghalaya and Assam.

Social conditions. The state is one of the most backward and least developed areas of the country. Only about 28 percent of the people are literate. The 1947 partition of the subcontinent into India and Pakistan disrupted the tribal populations, many of whom suddenly found themselves on different sides of the international frontier between India and what was then East Pakistan. There were also tribal migrations from East Pakistan into India. In 1971, consequent on the troubles in East Pakistan and as part of the huge refugee influx into India, refugees, who outnumbered the total population of Meghalaya, took shelter in that state, completely disrupting for 11 months the political, economic, and social fabric of the state. With the creation of the new country of Bangladesh, however, the refugees returned to their homes.

Mineral resources

Economy. Meghalaya is blessed with abundant natural but untapped resources. It has rich mineral resources —coal, limestone, kaolin, feldspar, quartz, mica, gypsum, bauxite, and other minerals. The deposits of sillimanite (a source of high-grade ceramic clay) are reputedly the best in the world. Agriculture is the mainstay of the populace—71 percent of the people are cultivators. Land is owned in common, but the primitive *jhum* form of shifting cultivation (burning of trees and planting the clearings in a cyclical operation) has left the people very poor and has eroded the soil. The main products are rice, millet, maize (corn), potatoes, pepper, chilies, cotton, ginger, jute, betelnuts, oranges, mangoes, bananas, pineapples, and other vegetables.

Transport and communications. There is little communication between the two districts, and within the districts many of the valleys are isolated. The state has about 600 miles of surfaced roads, 900 miles of gravelled roads, 500 miles of earth roads, and 300 miles of bridle paths. High priority is being given by the state's development plan to the building, improvement, and surfacing of roads, bridges, and other facilities.

Cultural life. The area is rich in tribal culture and folklore. The advent of Christianity and its strict rules of Judeo-Christian ethics and morality have disrupted many of the tribal and communal institutions, however. The folk dances and music of the area are rich and colourful. Drinking and dancing to the accompaniment of music from buffalo horn *singa*s, bamboo flutes, and drums are integral parts of religious ceremonies and social functions. Marriages are exogamous. One of the most curious and extraordinary customs among the Gāros is that after marriage the son-in-law comes to live in his wife's parents' house and becomes the father-in-law's *nokrom,* or a representative of the father-in-law's clan in the mother-in-law's family. After the death of the father-in-law, the *nokrom* marries (and the marriage has to be consummated) the widowed mother-in-law, thus becoming the husband of both mother and daughter. Enlightened Gāros are now discarding this custom. The Khāsis once practiced human sacrifice, but this is no longer so.

There are no daily newspapers, though there are some weeklies. The Shillong station of All-Indian Radio serves the region.

BIBLIOGRAPHY. *The Tribes of Assam,* a National Book Trust publication (1969), gives in a very concise form detailed information about the various tribes of Assam and among them the Gāros and Khāsis. KAMALESHWAR SINHA, *Meghalaya* (1970), contains a great deal of information about history and other information on the state; the *Meghalaya Year Book* provides a variety of statistical and other information about the state.

(C. Ra.)

Mehmed II

Mehmed II (1432–81), Ottoman sultan from 1444 to 1446 and again from 1451 to 1481, styled Fatih ("the Conqueror") by the Turks, was the true founder of the

Ottoman Empire and an outstanding military leader. He captured Constantinople (Istanbul) and created his empire, in Anatolia and the Balkans, around it. The territories that he conquered and organized remained for four centuries the empire's solid heartland. The conqueror reorganized the Ottoman government and, for the first time, codified the criminal law and the laws relating to his subjects in one code, whereas the constitution was elaborated in another, the two codes forming the nucleus of all subsequent legislation. In the utterly autocratic personality of the conqueror, the classical image of an Ottoman padishah (emperor) was born. He punished with the utmost severity those who resisted his decrees and laws, and even his Ottoman contemporaries considered him excessively hard.

Mehmed II, miniature by Sinan Bey, late 15th century. In the Topkapı Sarayı Museum, Istanbul.

Nevertheless, Mehmed may be considered the most broadminded and freethinking of the Ottoman sultans. After the fall of Constantinople, he gathered Italian humanists and Greek scholars at his court; he caused the patriarch *Gennadius* to write a credo of the Christian faith and had it translated into Turkish; he collected in his palace a library of works in Greek and Latin. He called Gentile Bellini from Venice to decorate the walls of his palace with frescoes as well as to paint his portrait (now in the National Gallery, London). Around the grand mosque that he constructed, he erected eight colleges, which, for nearly a century, kept their rank as the highest teaching institutions of the Islāmic sciences in the empire. At times, he assembled the *'ulamā',* or learned Muslim teachers, and caused them to discuss theological problems in his presence. In his reign, mathematics, astronomy, and Muslim theology reached their highest level among the Ottomans. And Mehmed himself left a divan (a collection of poems in the traditional style of classical Ottoman literature).

Mehmed as patron of the arts

Early years and first reign. Mehmed was born on March 30, 1432, at Edirne (Adrianople), the fourth son of Murad II by a slave girl; at the age of 12 Mehmed was sent, as tradition required, to Manisa (Magnesia) with his two tutors. The same year, his father set him on the throne at Edirne and abdicated. During his first reign (August 1444–May 1446), Mehmed had to face grave external and internal crises. The king of Hungary, the pope, the Byzantine Empire, and Venice—all eager to take advantage of the accession of a child to the Ottoman throne—succeeded in organizing a crusade. Edirne was the scene of violent rivalry between the powerful grand vizier Çandarlı Halil, on the one hand, and the viziers Zaganos and Şihâbeddin, on the other, who claimed that they were protecting the rights of the child sultan. In September 1444 the army of the crusaders crossed the Dan-

Abdication of Murad II

ube. In Edirne this news triggered off a massacre of the Christian-influenced Hurūfī sect and conjured up an atmosphere of panic and arson. When the crusaders laid siege to Varna, the reigning sultan's father was urged to come back from retirement in Bursa and lead the army. The Ottoman victory at Varna under Murad II (November 10, 1444) put an end to the crises. Mehmed II, who had stayed in Edirne, maintained the throne, and after the battle his father retired to Manisa. Zaganos and Şihâbeddin then began to incite the child sultan to undertake the capture of Constantinople, but Çandarlı engineered a revolt of the Janissaries and called Murad II back to Edirne to resume the throne (May 1446). Mehmed was sent once more to Manisa with Zaganos and Şihâbeddin, newly appointed as his tutors. There Mehmed continued to consider himself the legal sultan.

Second accession in 1451. On his father's death, Mehmed ascended the throne for the second time in Edirne (February 18, 1451). His mind was filled with the idea of the capture of Constantinople. Europe and Byzantium, remembering his former reign, were then not concerned much about his plans. Neither was his authority firmly established within the empire. But he was not long in showing his stature by severely punishing the Janissaries who had dared to threaten him over the delay of the customary gift of accession. Yet he reinforced this military organization, which was destined to be the instrument of his future conquests. He devoted the utmost care to all the necessary diplomatic and military preparations for the capture of Constantinople. To keep Venice and Hungary neutral, he signed peace treaties favourable to them. He spent the year 1452 mainly in building the fortress of Boğazkesen (later Rumeli Hisarı) for the control of the Bosporus, in building a fleet of 31 galleys, and in casting new cannon of large calibre. He made the Hungarian master gunsmith, Urban, cast guns of a size unknown as yet even in Europe. Meanwhile, the grand vizier Çandarlı argued against the enterprise and during

Siege and fall of Constantinople

the siege of Constantinople (April 6–May 29, 1453), the opposing views were voiced in two war councils convened at critical moments. Zaganos vehemently rejected the proposal to raise the siege. He was given the task of preparing the last great assault. The commander in chief, Mehmed II himself, on the day of the attack personally directed the operations against the breach opened in the city wall by his cannon. The day after the capture of the city, Çandarlı was arrested and soon afterwards was executed in Edirne. He was replaced by Zaganos who had become Mehmed's father-in-law. Mehmed had had to consent to a three-day sack of the city, but, before the evening of the first day after its capture, he countermanded his order. Entering the city at the head of a procession, he went straight to Hagia Sophia and converted it into a mosque. Afterward he established charitable foundations and provided 14,000 gold ducats per annum for the upkeep and service of the mosque.

One of the tasks on which Mehmed II set his heart was the restoration of the city, now called Istanbul, as a worthy capital of a world-wide empire. To encourage the return of the Greeks and the Genoese of Galata (the trading quarter of the city), who had fled, he returned their houses and provided them with guarantees of safety. In order to repopulate the city, he deported Muslim and Christian groups in Anatolia and the Balkans and forced them to settle in Istanbul. He restored the Greek Orthodox Patriarchate (January 6, 1454) and established a Jewish grand rabbi and an Armenian patriarch in the city. In addition, he founded, and encouraged his viziers to found, a number of Muslim institutions and commercial installations in the main districts of Istanbul. From these nuclei, the metropolis developed rapidly. According to a survey carried out in 1478, there were then in Istanbul and neighbouring Galata 16,324 households and 3,927 shops. Fifty years later, Turkish Istanbul had become the largest city in Europe.

Mehmed's empire. The capture of Istanbul bestowed on Mehmed incomparable glory and prestige and immense authority in his own country, so that he began to look upon himself as the heir of the Roman Caesars and

the champion of Islām in holy war. It is not true that he had preconceived plans for his conquests, but it is certain that he was intent upon resurrecting the Eastern Roman Empire and upon extending it to its widest historic limits. His victory over the Turkmen leader Uzun Ḥasan at the Battle of Bashkent in Erzincan (August 11, 1473) marked in Mehmed's life a turning point as important as the capture of Istanbul, and sealed his domination over Anatolia and the Balkans.

The Battle of Bashkent

Mehmed had assumed the title of Kayser-i Rum (Roman Caesar) and, at the same time, described himself as "the lord of the two lands and the two seas" (*i.e.,* Anatolia and the Balkans, the Aegean and the Black seas), a designation that reflected his idea of the empire. During the quarter-century after the fall of Constantinople, he undertook a series of campaigns or expeditions in the Balkans, Hungary, Walachia, Moldavia, Anatolia, the island of Rhodes, and even as far as the Crimea and Otranto in southern Italy. This last enterprise (1480) indicated that he intended to invade Italy in a new attempt at founding a world empire. The following spring, having just begun a new campaign in Anatolia, he died (May 3, 1481) at Hunkârçayırı near Maltepe, 15½ miles (25 kilometres) from Istanbul. Gout, from which he had suffered for some time, in his last days had tortured him grievously, but, there are indications that he was poisoned.

During the autocrat's last years, his relations with his eldest son Bayezid became very strained, as Bayezid did not always obey his orders. Mehmed's financial measures resulted, toward the end of his reign, in widespread discontent throughout the country, especially when he distributed as military fiefs about 20,000 villages and farms that had previously belonged to pious foundations or the landed gentry. Thus, at his death, the malcontents placed Bayezid on the throne, discarding the Sultan's favourite son, Cem (Jem), and initiated a reaction against Mehmed's policies.

BIBLIOGRAPHY. FRANZ BABINGER, *Mehmed der Eroberer und seine Zeit* (1953), is the most detailed account of the subject by an authority, reviewed by HALIL INALCIK, "Mehmed the Conqueror (1432–1481) and His Time," in *Speculum,* 35:408–427 (1960). See also *Cambridge History of Islam,* pp. 295–308 (1970); and STEVEN RUNCIMAN, *The Fall of Constantinople, 1453* (1965). The main sources on the subject are given in H. INALCIK, "Mehmed II," in *Islam Ansiklopedisi,* 7:506–535 (in Turkish).

(H.I.)

Mekong River

The Mekong, 2,500 miles (4,000 kilometres) long, is the longest river in Southeast Asia and the seventh longest in all of Asia. Rising in Tsinghai Province, China, it flows through the Yunnan Province, after which it forms part of the international border between Burma and Laos, as well as between Laos and Thailand, also flowing through Laos, Cambodia, and South Vietnam before draining into the South China Sea to the south of Saigon, capital of South Vietnam. Vientiane, capital of Laos, and Phnom Penh, capital of Cambodia, both stand on its banks.

About 77 percent of the drainage area of the Mekong lies within the four countries traversed by its lower basin —Laos, Thailand, Cambodia, and South Vietnam; the lower basin is inhabited by about 30,000,000 people. The four countries are cooperating in the Mekong River Development Project, which, when completed, will provide facilities for the generation of hydroelectric power, irrigation, flood control, drainage, improvements in navigation, water management, and water supply. The project, which was initiated by the United Nations Economic Commission for Asia and the Far East (ECAFE), is being carried out by the four countries with the assistance of 21 governments and 11 United Nations agencies. (For historical aspects, see CAMBODIA, HISTORY OF; LAOS, HISTORY OF; SIAM AND THAILAND, HISTORY OF; and VIETNAM, HISTORY OF.)

The Mekong—a physical conspectus. The Mekong River drains more than 307,000 square miles (795,000 square kilometres) of land, stretching from the Tibetan Plateau to the South China Sea. Among Asian rivers, only the Yangtze, Ganges, and Irrawaddy have larger minimum flows. The Mekong River's small width in the first 1,150 miles of its course and the contrast between the physical conditions that prevail above and below the reach where it flows down off the Yunnan highlands, divide it into two major parts.

The Upper Mekong is a long, narrow valley comprising roughly 26 percent of the total area, cutting through the mountains and plateaus of the People's Republic of China. The Lower Mekong, below the point where it forms the border between Burma and Laos, is a stream 1,454 miles in length that claims the drainage from the Korat Plateau of Thailand, from most of Cambodia, and from the westward slopes of the Chaîne Annamitique (Annamite mountain chain) in Laos and North Vietnam before reaching the sea through the distributary channels of its delta.

Origin of the river

In its upper reaches the Mekong is one of the cluster of great streams rising in the plateau between the Salween and the Yangtze; the stream bed has cut deeply into the rugged landscape through which it flows. Where it flows between Burma and Laos, it drains about 8,000 square miles of Burmese territory, all of which consists of rough and relatively inaccessible terrain. In its more gentle lower stretches, where for a considerable distance it constitutes the boundary between Laos and Thailand, it forms a subject of both friction and cooperation among the four countries of Cambodia, Laos, Thailand, and the Republic of Vietnam.

Physiography. *The Upper Mekong.* The upper sources, known locally as the Pam and the Dzi Chu, rise at elevations of more than 16,000 feet in the Tibetan highlands on the southern border of Tsinghai. They flow southeasterly through the Chamdo region of Tibet. The main stream, called the Lan Ts'ang Chiang, descends in a southerly direction across the highlands of Yunnan, which are cut by erosion into hills and valleys, to a point south of Yiin-ching Hung, where it becomes the border between Burma and China. The river then moves in a southwesterly direction; over a reach of more than 125 miles it forms the Burmese–Laotian border. Although two great roads cross it—the caravan route from the southeast to Lhasa, and the K'un-ming-to-Burma road —much of the river valley in the high plateau and in the Yunnan Mountains is extremely inaccessible and sparsely populated.

The Lower Mekong Basin. Below Burma, the river basin may be divided into six major sections—the northern mountains, Korat Plateau, eastern highlands, southern lowlands, southern highlands, and delta sections. All these sections have somewhat similar landforms, vegetation, and soils. Most of the vegetation in the lower basin is of the tropical broad-leaf variety, although the occurrence of individual species varies with latitude and topography.

The northern mountains section has highly folded mountains reaching elevations of about 9,000 feet above sea level, many with slopes slanting at steep angles. As far south as the latitude of Vientiane, these dissected uplands (*i.e.,* cut by erosion into hills and valleys) are covered with dense deciduous forest that has deteriorated as a result of inroads made by shifting cultivation. To the south of the east–west course of the river above Vientiane lies the Korat Plateau, which embraces almost all of the Thai portion of the basin as well as the lower parts of the Mekong's Laotian tributaries. This is an area of flat or gently rolling plains traversed by relatively flat valley bottoms. Soils and deciduous vegetation on the uplands are thin, and much of the original forest has been replaced by grassland as a result of grazing and repeated burning.

The Korat Plateau

The eastern highlands form part of the Chaîne Annamitique of mountains, from which streams drain west into the Mekong. Throughout most of the distance between Muong Sen in North Vietnam and Krâchéh in Cambodia the watershed forms the border between Vietnam to the east and Laos and Cambodia to the west. There is greater relief in the northern than the southern parts of the watershed, but the highlands in general are characterized by rapid streams that flow through narrow valleys before entering the Korat Plateau or other lowlands. Forest degradation, that has resulted from lumbering, the temporary use of land for cultivation, and grazing, is widespread.

The southern lowlands border both sides of the Mekong below Paksé in Laos. The part of the river that flows through Cambodia has wide stretches of alluvium in its floodplain. Near Phnom Penh, the Cambodian capital, a junction occurs between the Mekong and the Tonle Sap river, which connects it to the Tonle Sap lake, sometimes called the Great Lake. The direction of flow of the Tonle Sap river varies according to the season. In midsummer, when the Mekong is in flood, waters flow down the Tonle Sap to the lake, which at this time increases its area from about 1,000 square miles to about 3,000 square miles. In midwinter when the floods subside, the Tonle Sap reverses its flow to drain southeastward into the Mekong. Tonle Sap lake is one of the most productive fishing grounds in the world, producing as much as 26 tons of fish a year per square mile.

The Great Lake of Tonle Sap

Along the southern border of the basin in Cambodia, the Éléphant and Cardamon mountains form a string of southern highlands that drain northward into the southern lowlands.

The river divides into two streams—the Mekong and the Bassac—below Phnom Penh. From this point onward the delta spreads out to the sea. The delta, which has a total area of about 25,000 square miles, has three major sections. The upper section, above Chau Phu, has strong natural levees (embankments built on either side of the river by accumulated deposits of silt) behind which are low, wide depressions. The middle section has some

The Lower Mekong River Basin.

areas that are well drained, others that are poorly drained and swampy. Along the lower section, formed by the river mouths and by the area to the southwest, sediment is in the process of being deposited, and the flooding is less extreme than in the upper sections of the delta.

Hydrology. The mean annual flow of the river at Krâchéh in Cambodia is about 500,000 cubic feet per second (cusecs), making a total annual discharge for the year of about 378,000,000 acre-feet. The recorded minimum at Krâchéh is about one-twelfth of the mean, and the annual peak flow about four times the mean. Below Krâchéh the peak flows diminish as the water spreads out into the distributary channels and backswamps. Flow comes chiefly from rainfall in the lower basin and reflects the variation in seasonal rainfall caused by the monsoon winds; this variation generally forms a regular annual pattern: in April the flow is ordinarily at its lowest; in May or June the flow begins to increase, doing so most rapidly in the eastern highlands and northern mountains; the highest water levels are reached as early as August or September in the upper reaches and as late as October in the southern reaches. The northeast monsoon wind, beginning ordinarily in November in the southern areas, brings dry weather until May.

The annual sediment load is recorded as being highest at Paksé, where it amounts to 132,000,000 tons; it is about half that amount at the Burmese border and about two-thirds at Phnom Penh. The dominant hydrologic fact affecting agriculture is the long dry period in which rice cultivation is impossible without irrigation.

The riverain populations. In 1970 the inhabitants of the lower basin amounted to half the population of the four riparian countries, a total of 30,000,000 people. About 80 percent were engaged in agriculture, and rice was the major crop. Heaviest population concentrations are in the delta and on the Korat Plateau. The small urban population has been growing rapidly, chiefly through migration to the capital cities. There is no common ethnic tie among the basin populations. Ethnic groups range from Sino-Tibetan, including Karen and Meo mountain groups, in the Upper Mekong region, to Khmer, Cham, Tai, Mon, and Vietnamese lowland groups in the Lower Mekong Basin. The Vietnamese are heavily concentrated in the delta, and the Khmer and Tai are the most widely distributed in the lower basin.

Ethnic groups

The river's resources. *Irrigation and flood control.* In the lower basin the management of water offers major opportunities to increase the economic productivity of the tributary lands. Farmers practicing shifting cultivation on the uplands and the rice growers on the rain-fed lowlands are able, under normal conditions, to grow only one crop a year, taking advantage of wet season precipitation. Half the cultivated land is dependent upon some form of inundation by flood flows. Control of water, however, makes it possible to store water during the dry season, and thus permits the harvesting of a second or third crop. If irrigation is combined with flood control, the losses and delays caused by floods pouring over the river's banks can be reduced. Where storage facilities and the degree of downward slope are favourable, hydroelectric power can be generated. If navigational conditions on the Mekong's main stream and on some of its tributaries were to be improved, transport costs for landlocked areas could be reduced.

The actual development of the river's resources has, however, been modest. By 1971 only about 3 percent of the cultivated area was being irrigated. Only three small hydroelectric plants were in operation. Flood control and drainage works have been constructed in the delta to deal with smaller inundations in limited areas.

Navigation. In the Vietnamese part of the delta there is an elaborate system of canals. Smaller seagoing vessels can sail upstream as far as Phnom Penh and vessels drawing almost 15 feet can reach Kompong Cham during high water. Continuous water transport is blocked chiefly by the barriers of the Khone Falls and other falls between Sâmbor and Paksé, and upstream uses of the river are limited to local traffic.

In 1926, Thailand and France—which then adminis-

tered Indochina (Cambodia, Laos, and Vietnam)—entered into an agreement that neither would obstruct navigation of the river. In 1949, Cambodia, France, Laos, and South Vietnam executed a Convention on Maritime and Inland Navigation on the Mekong and on water routes to Saigon. A convention to coordinate action on navigation, river construction and other projects, and fiscal regulations affecting river commerce was signed in 1954 by Cambodia, Laos, and South Vietnam.

The Mekong River Development Project. After the Bureau of Flood Control of the United Nations Economic Commission for Asia and the Far East (ECAFE) had recommended study of the Lower Mekong, surveys were carried out by ECAFE and by the U.S. Bureau of Reclamation. This led to the adoption by Cambodia, Laos, Thailand, and South Vietnam of a 1957 statute creating the Committee for Coordination of Investigations of the Lower Mekong. By 1971 the four riparian countries had sponsored a series of preinvestment investigations and had undertaken construction of multiple-purpose water projects costing $143,000,000. They had continued to cooperate despite the political stresses produced by the war in Vietnam and had enlisted the assistance of other countries. The United Nations Development Program provided assistance in the technical and administrative organization of the studies. Financial contributions toward the work had been made by 25 nations, the larger sums coming from the United States, France, Japan, and West Germany. Sixteen international specialized agencies, including the World Bank and the United Nations Food and Agriculture Organization, had also given assistance to the projects.

Investigations undertaken included basic mapping, hydrologic observations, soil surveys, fisheries studies, health studies, engineering-feasibility studies, power-market surveys, agricultural research and pilot farms, and many other inquiries. The engineering studies had provided for reconnaissance appraisal of all of the tributary basins and for more detailed examination of selected projects. Flood forecasting was begun and river navigation was improved. Mineral surveyors explored possible opportunities for bauxite and iron development.

An irrigation and hydroelectric installation was completed at Nam Pung in Thailand in 1968, and a larger irrigation and power project at Nam Phong, also in Thailand, was under construction in the early 1970s. A small power plant on the lower Done in Laos was completed in 1970. Five other water projects were under construction: on the Ngum River in Laos a power, flood-control, and irrigation scheme was under way, and Laos was negotiating with Thailand for sale of power from the 105-megawatt plant; on the Tnâot River in Cambodia, an irrigation project was being financed by the cooperation of 12 countries; a small power plant was scheduled for the Done River in Laos; and two irrigation and power projects were begun on the Dom Noi and Phrom rivers in Thailand.

Recent irrigation and power projects

Meanwhile, the focus of the Mekong Development Project as a whole was shifting to the planning of comprehensive programs for agricultural and community development in areas where water supply was available, with each country working out its individual financial arrangements with donor nations. No formal negotiations with the two upstream riparian countries, Burma and the People's Republic of China, or with adjacent countries that might be markets for power, had as yet taken place.

Prospects for the future. The provision of water control on the Mekong has entailed risks as well as benefits. If the engineering works are not accompanied by suitable measures to build canals, construct farm ditches, level fields, supply new seeds and fertilizers, improve farm-to-market roads, organize markets, and establish agricultural credit, no gain will be made in agricultural production, as was the case with several score small reservoirs constructed on the Korat Plateau during the 1950s. If resettlement from reservoir areas is slow or inadequate, as happened at Nam Pung, the social costs may be heavy. Water storage and irrigation may promote the spread of schistosomiasis (a water-borne parasitic disease) and malaria or may interfere with fisheries. The Mekong Committee has been studying these problems as well as investigating other agricultural and water-management programs.

So long as military conflict continues in the region the preparation of comprehensive plans will be curtailed. Whenever that constraint is removed the countries will be obliged to consider new arrangements with their neighbours. At that time, too, the need to coordinate Lower Mekong planning with broader national programs will become more urgent.

BIBLIOGRAPHY. UNITED NATIONS, *Selected Bibliography: Lower Mekong Basin,* 2 vol. (1969), provides the most comprehensive list of references to the literature on the lower basin. The basic maps of resources, with descriptive text, are compiled in the UNITED NATIONS, *Atlas of Physical, Economic, and Social Resources of the Lower Mekong Basin* (1968). Two general reviews of planning for the lower basin are found in C. HART SCHAAF and RUSSELL H. FIFIELD, *The Lower Mekong: Challenge to Cooperation in Southeast Asia* (1963); and W.R.D. SEWELL and GILBERT F. WHITE, *The Lower Mekong* (1966). *Principal Rivers in Communist China,* JPRS, no. 33,880, *National Technical Information Service* (1966), contains English translations of Chinese publications describing major river systems, including the Mekong.

(G.F.W.)

Melanchthon, Philipp

The first systematic theology of the Protestant Reformation, the Protestant public school system, and the basic Protestant creed all originated with Philipp Melanchthon, theologian and educator who, though he was for 28 years a co-worker of Martin Luther, is today often denigrated as a traitor, the source of an allegedly "alien," rationalistic element in Lutheranism.

By courtesy of the Staatliche
Museen Kuperstichkabinett, Berlin

Melanchthon, engraving by Albrecht Dürer, 1526.

Early influences and humanistic education

Born Feb. 16, 1497, in Bretten (Germany), Melanchthon inherited from his parents, Barbara Reuter and Georg Schwartzerd, a deep sense of piety that never left him. From his Bretten surroundings (where five citizens were burned as witches in 1504) he absorbed a sense of the occult that combined later with biblical references to stars, dreams, and devils to make him a firm believer in astrology and demonology. In 1508, within a period of 11 days, both his grandfather Reuter and his father died, his father after four years of invalidism.

Humanism predominated in Melanchthon's education, his studies having been directed by a great-uncle, Johannes Reuchlin, famed Hebraist and humanist. Philipp's first tutor instilled in him a lifelong love of Latin and classical literature, and, at the Pforzheim Latin school, he received further humanistic training and had his name changed from Schwartzerd ("black earth") to its Greek equivalent, Melanchthon. While at the universities of Heidelberg (1509–11, B.A.) and Tübingen (1512–14, M.A.), Melanchthon explored Scholastic thought in depth, steeped himself in the rhetoric of the Dutch humanist Rudolf Agricola and the Nominalism of the En-

glish philosopher William of Ockham and the ecclesiastical reformer John of Wesel, studied Scripture, and read classical works with a fellow student. On receiving the M.A. degree, he lectured, with conspicuous success, on the classics and soon had six books to his credit, including "Rudiments of the Greek Language" (1518), a grammar that was to go through many editions. He was praised by the great Dutch humanist Erasmus, and his name became known in England. In the best tradition of the time, Melanchthon was a humanist.

In 1518 Melanchthon accepted an invitation, relayed through Reuchlin, to become the University of Wittenberg's first professor of Greek. Only four days after his arrival, he addressed the university on "The Improvement of Studies," boldly setting forth a humanistic program and calling for a return to classical and Christian sources in order to regenerate theology and rejuvenate society.

Luther, the founder of the Protestant Reformation, and Melanchthon responded to each other enthusiastically; and their deep friendship developed, with Melanchthon committing himself wholeheartedly to the new evangelical cause, initiated the previous year when Luther nailed his Ninety-five Theses to the door of the castle church in Wittenberg. By the end of 1519 he had already defended scriptural authority against Luther's opponent Johann Eck, rejected (before Luther did) transubstantiation—the doctrine that the substance of the bread and wine in the Lord's Supper is changed into the body and blood of Christ—made justification by faith the keystone of his theology, and openly broke with Reuchlin. During this time he had also published seven more small books and had earned the Bachelor of Theology degree at Wittenberg. His energy was phenomenal. He began his day at 2 AM, with lectures, often to as many as 600 students, at 6. In addition, he found time to court Katherine Krapp, whom he married in 1520 and who bore him four children—Anna, Philipp, Georg, Magdalen.

At Luther's urging, Melanchthon lectured on Paul's Letter to the Romans and in 1521 published the *Loci communes,* the first systematic treatment of evangelical doctrine. Sin, law, and grace were the principal topics, with free will, vows, hope, confession, and other doctrines subsumed. Drawing on Scripture, Melanchthon argued that sin is more than an external act; it reaches beyond reason into man's will and emotions so that man cannot simply resolve to do good works and earn merit before God. Original sin is a native propensity, an inordinate self-concern tainting all man's actions. But God's grace consoles man with forgiveness, and his works, though imperfect, are a response in joy and gratitude for divine benevolence. Three editions of the *Loci* appeared before the end of the year, 18 editions by 1525, in addition to printings of a German translation. The last edition in 1558 was much enlarged and changed. Luther declared that the *Loci* deserved a place in the canon of Scriptures; the University of Cambridge in England later made it required reading, and Queen Elizabeth I (1533-1603) virtually memorized it so she could converse about theology.

Despite an imperial decree of death to those who supported Luther, in 1521 Melanchthon sharply answered the Sorbonne's condemnation of 104 statements of Luther with "Against the Furious Decree of the Parisian Theologasters." His "Passion of Christ and Antichrist," in the same year, utilized woodcuts by Lucas Cranach (1472–1553) in a scathing criticism of the pope's lifestyle as diametrically opposed to Christ's. When Melanchthon hesitated to publish his lectures on Corinthians, Luther stole a copy and published them in 1521 with a preface saying, "It is I who publish these annotations of yours, and send you to yourself." In 1523 Luther did the same with Melanchthon's notes on John.

While Luther was safely confined at the Wartburg after his confrontation with papal authorities at the Diet of Worms and his subsequent status as an outlaw, troubles erupted in Wittenberg over the issue of clerical marriage, granting the laity the right to use wine in the Lord's Supper, and abolition of the mass. A radical Reformer, Karlstadt (c. 1480–1541), wanted to abolish all educa-

Involvement in the Reformation

tion because Christ and the Apostles were not educated, and radical prophets of Zwickau said that God had told them to eliminate infant Baptism. Melanchthon was unable to control the mobs that demonstrated in the streets, intimidated priests, destroyed side altars, despoiled gravestones, and broke images. Early in March 1522, Luther returned, preached eight sermons on love, and quelled the disturbances.

Although Melanchthon did not relinquish his views on justification by faith and scriptural authority, the disruptions at Wittenberg, the caustic interchange between Luther and Erasmus on free will, and the Peasants' War in 1524–1525 caused him to put more emphasis on humanism as a moderating influence in religion. This is revealed in the revised editions of the *Loci* that made more use of reason, in his educational endeavours, and in his various commentaries. In 1528 Saxony enacted into law Melanchthon's "Visitation Articles," which were guidelines for churches and schools, and established the first public school system since that of ancient Rome. At least 56 cities asked his advice in founding schools. Through him, his textbooks, and the teachers he trained, virtually the whole educational system in Germany was reorganized. He helped found the universities of Königsberg, Jena, and Marburg and reformed those of Greifswald, Wittenberg, Cologne, Tübingen, Leipzig, Heidelberg, Rostock, and Frankfort-on-the-Oder. He believed that without education, religion would decline and mankind would be reduced to animality.

The Augsburg Confession

Melanchthon's greatest triumph was the Augsburg Confession of 1530, in which for unity's sake he sought to be as inoffensive to the Catholics as possible but forcefully stated the evangelical stance. In the ensuing negotiations over adoption of the confessional statement, he seemed to compromise, but the vigour of his Apology of the Confession of Augsburg (1531) belied any change. The Apology and Confession quickly became official Lutheran symbols (authoritative statements of faith), as did one other Melanchthon treatise, his "Appendix on the Papacy," which was an addition to the Schmalkald Articles of 1536–37, another Lutheran confessional statement. In the "Appendix," Melanchthon refuted historically and theologically any papal primacy by divine right but accepted papal jurisdiction as a human right for the sake of peace, if the Gospel were permitted.

The evangelical movement suffered setbacks in 1546 with the death of Luther and, in 1547, with the defection of Duke Maurice of Saxony to the side of the Holy Roman emperor Charles V and the military defeat of the Lutherans at Mühlberg. The University of Wittenberg was dissolved. Melanchthon and his family fled. But before the year ended, Maurice (needing the support of his Lutheran subjects) invited Melanchthon to restore the university. Recognizing that Wittenberg symbolized the evangelical cause and receiving assurances that pure doctrine would be allowed, Melanchthon returned and gathered a faculty—only to incur the hostility of theologians who regarded his actions as a betrayal. Melanchthon opposed the Augsburg Interim of 1548 (a doctrinal formula weighted toward the Catholic position, which Charles V tried to impose on Saxony to settle religious matters), but when he realized that the princes were about to adopt the nonevangelical Leipzig Interim to avoid war with Charles, he salvaged the key doctrine of justification by faith, eliminated the idea of a mass that granted merits to the worshipper, and said that the adiaphora (nonessentials, such as liturgical dress) could be accepted even though they added nothing to doctrinal integrity. His opponents protested that in time of stress nothing could be yielded and that pure forms were integral to pure biblical doctrine. Maurice, in 1552, turned against the Emperor and ended the interim with the Treaty of Passau, which was superseded in 1555, by the Peace of Augsburg with its formula of *cujus regio, ejus religio* ("whose region, his religion"), enunciating the principle that a region's religion is that of its ruler.

Melanchthon's reputation was badly tarnished, and several controversies beclouded his final years. In a controversy over the role of man as a cooperating participant with God in the matter of salvation, Melanchthon seemed to undercut the doctrine of justification by faith alone by maintaining that three concurrent causes operate in conversion—the Word (Christ), the Holy Spirit, and man's will. Melanchthon's maintaining of the third use of the law—referring to the three uses of the law, such as the Ten Commandments, to maintain civil peace and order, show man what a sinner he really is, and serve as a guide for living—as a guideline for Christians seemed to be a return to legalism. His turning toward a spiritual view (similar to the Reformed view) of the Lord's Supper, as evidenced in the *Variata* (altered) edition of the Augsburg Confession in 1540 (Article X), seemed to be crypto-Calvinistic (*i.e.*, though Lutheran in name, apparently Calvinist, or Reformed, in tendency). These controversies diminished his influence in Lutheranism. Succeeding generations have questioned Melanchthon's approval of the death penalty for the radical Reformers, the Anabaptists, and an anti-Trinitarian, Michael Servetus; his approval of war to defend the Gospel; his condoning of polygamy for the English king Henry VIII and Philip the Magnanimous, landgrave of Hesse; and his extension of reason to support revelation.

Melanchthon died April 19, 1560, and was buried in Wittenberg beside Luther.

BIBLIOGRAPHY. C.L. MANSCHRECK, *Melanchthon: The Quiet Reformer* (1958), is the fullest biography to date; see also R. STUPPERICH, *Der unbekannte Melanchthon* (1961; Eng. trans. by R.H. FISCHER, *Melanchthon*, 1965). M. ROGNESS, *Philip Melanchthon: Reformer Without Honor* (1969), contains aspects of Melanchthon's thought. His basic works and letters may be found in K.G. BRETSCHNEIDER and E. BINDSEIL (eds.), *Corpus Reformatorum*, 28 vol. (1834–60); W. PAUCK (ed.), *Melanchthon and Bucer* (1969), contains the 1521 *Loci*; and C.L. MANSCHRECK (ed.), *Melanchthon on Christian Doctrine* (1965), the 1555 *Loci*. For information on Lutheran symbols, see T.G. TAPPERT (ed.), *The Book of Concord* (1959); for educational endeavours, C. HARTFELDER, *Philipp Melanchthon als Praeceptor Germania* (1889), with bibliography. W. HAMMER, *Die Melanchthonforschung im Wandel der Jahrhunderte*, 2 vol. (1967–68), has a good bibliography to 1965; for a discussion of Melanchthon's relation to patristics, see P. FRAENKEL, *Testimonia Patrum* (1961).

(C.L.Ma.)

Melanesian Cultures

Melanesia has no firm geographical boundaries. It is generally held to include the island of New Guinea and a number of island groups to the north and east: the Bismarck Archipelago, the Solomon, New Hebrides, and Torres Straits islands, New Caledonia, Fiji, and intervening groups. All of the islands lie in the central Pacific between the Equator and the Tropic of Capricorn. (For a map of the area, see OCEANIAN PEOPLES AND CULTURES.) The term Melanesia (black islands) was introduced in 1832 by a French navigator, Dumont d'Urville, to describe those areas of the Pacific inhabited by dark-skinned peoples. There is considerable variation in skin colour, ranging from light brown in the Trobriand Islands to almost black in the northwestern Solomons.

PEOPLES AND LANGUAGES

The people of Melanesia have been classified as belonging to the Oceanic Negroid division of mankind. Three main physical types have been distinguished: Melanesians in the anthropological and linguistic sense, Papuans, and Pygmies—the latter two only on New Guinea.

The Melanesians, who inhabit the southeast peninsula of New Guinea and the other islands eastward to Fiji, tend to have broad noses and little body hair. Their head hair is generally frizzy, although it may be wavy or curly. The Papuans are mostly of medium stature, ranging from five feet seven inches (170 centimetres) for those living at the head of the Gulf of Papua to about five feet (152 centimetres) for some mountain tribes. Their facial and body hair is often abundant and woolly in texture. Their heads tend to be long in relation to breadth; their noses are sometimes hooked and prominent; they have marked brow ridges and high, receding foreheads; and their skin colour ranges from dark to very dark.

The Pygmies inhabit the central mountains of New Guinea; two groups are the Tapiro of Irian Barat (now in Indonesia, formerly called West Irian) and the Aiome of the Trust Territories. The average height of the adult male Tapiro is four feet nine inches. The Pygmies often have abundant body and facial hair, round heads, and broad noses; their skin colour varies from yellow to dark brown. The origin of the Pygmy peoples is unclear; it has been suggested that they may have been the aboriginal inhabitants of New Guinea, driven into the mountains by invading peoples, or, alternatively, that they may derive from a Papuan stock. Several of the mountain peoples have both Pygmy and Papuan characteristics.

Micro-
nesian and
Polynesian
influence

The Melanesians may also be a mixture of immigrant strains with a basically Papuan stock. Micronesian and Polynesian influence can be discerned in the culture and physical characteristics of some of them. Small islands near the Solomon and Santa Cruz groups have been colonized by Polynesians; there is a strong Polynesian influence in the Loyalty Islands and the Lau Islands of the Fiji group, and some Polynesian mixture occurs in New Caledonia and parts of the New Hebrides. Micronesian influence can be traced in certain areas of the Bismarck Archipelago.

More than 700 distinct languages are spoken in Melanesia. In the interior of the Solomons, New Britain, and New Guinea, the languages are collectively called Papuan, although their relations to one another are largely unknown. On the coasts of these islands and throughout the rest of Melanesia, the languages (usually called Melanesian) all belong to the Austronesian (Malayo-Polynesian) family, which includes the languages of Indonesia, the Philippines, aboriginal Taiwan, Malaysia, and Madagascar (see PAPUAN LANGUAGES; AUSTRONESIAN LANGUAGES). The distribution is complex, and the two major groups are often present on the same island. There is no precise correlation between language, physical type, and culture. As a rule, each language is spoken in a limited area, although some, such as Motu in Papua, are understood outside their district of origin. Pidgin English is still in use as a lingua franca.

It is not known precisely how Melanesia was first populated, although ethnologists assume that the earliest inhabitants came in successive waves from the west. No common cultural pattern is discernible today; rather, there is tremendous diversity in every aspect of social life among the peoples of Melanesia. Their societies have been described as classless, meaning that power and status are matters of individual achievement, not of inheritance or of membership in a particular group. The "big man" in Melanesian society acquires his position of leadership through his success in the acquisition of wealth and sometimes by some skill, such as oratory (as among the peoples of the Mount Hagen area in the New Guinea highlands). In this respect Melanesian society differs markedly from the Polynesian, where there is a strong emphasis on rank and chieftainship.

TRADITIONAL CULTURE PATTERNS

Economic patterns. *Settlement patterns and housing.* Village settlements are usually small, ranging between 50 and 200 inhabitants, although on river estuaries or along the seacoasts they sometimes exceed 1,000. The villages may consist of scattered hamlets, as among the Chimbu of eastern New Guinea, or they may be concentrated, as in the villages of the Orokaiva in Papua. Some villages in the Trobriand Islands are built on a circular plan, the houses facing inward to a cleared space; in the space are storehouses for yams and the chief's house. Mountain villages are often sited on easily defensible ridges; coastal villages are set back from the shore; and lowland villages are located near rivers or streams.

Houses vary in design and construction, depending on the local materials and other factors. Some have earthen floors; others are built on piles. Pile dwellings are found in various places in New Guinea and in the Bismarck Archipelago, often in locations that are subject to flooding; they are also used on dry ground, particularly where

it is uneven. The space underneath the pile house provides a useful storage area, helps to improve ventilation, and makes the house easier to defend. The height of a pile house ranges from one or two feet above the ground, as among the Mafulu of central Papua, to as much as 15 feet for men's houses—social and ceremonial centres of many villages. The ordinary village house is built for a single family; occasionally, joint or extended families occupy a single dwelling, as in the Sepik Basin and among the Kiwai of western Papua.

Some houses are circular, with a roof supported by a single central post. The more common rectangular houses have a ridgepole supported at either end and sometimes in between by central posts. Rafters stretch from the ridgepole to the top of the wall plates; the roof thatch, usually grass or palm leaves, is lashed to horizontal members running across the rafters. Kiwai communal houses have two rows of posts on each side of the centre line, supporting rafters that are joined at a ridgepole in the centre. In larger houses, tie beams are often lashed to opposite wall plates or between rafters partway up the slope of the roof to counter the outward pressure of the roof timbers.

Decoration is widely applied on men's houses, clubhouses, and chiefs' houses. In New Caledonia, chiefs' houses have carved human-shaped boards flanking the doorways. In the Trobriand Islands, the yam houses are adorned with carved and painted boards.

Most Melanesian dwellings are dark and poorly ventilated; doors are small and there are no windows. The simple furnishings include bed mats, headrests, and a few personal belongings, such as pots, baskets, tools, fishing equipment, and weapons. A fire often burns all night, the smoke escaping through the roof.

Food. For many Melanesians, gardening provides the main source of food. The so-called swidden type of agriculture is practiced, whereby the land, after it lies fallow for a number of years to restore its fertility, is cleared by burning off the vegetation. The system is believed to have originated in Southeast Asia. Agriculture has had a long history in New Guinea. Pig bones have been found in the remains of inhabited sites dated at about 3000 BC. The findings suggest that the pigs were domesticated and that crops must have been grown to feed them. Systems of water-control ditches existed in the western Wahgi Valley of eastern New Guinea as early as 350 BC, indicating that intensive agriculture had been established by then.

Gardening
and
gathering

The three most important staple crops are yams, taro, and sweet potatoes. Yams are grown in the dry regions, such as the leeward slopes of high islands covered with savanna or savanna woodland; taro grows well in areas of high rainfall; and in the highlands the sweet potato predominates. The sweet potato is of South American origin and may have reached New Guinea from the Philippines after Spanish colonization. Other crops include bananas, plantains, coconuts, manioc, maize, cassava, breadfruit, pineapple, and tomatoes.

The gathering of wild and semicultivated plants and fruits, either for medicinal purposes or as a supplement to the diet, is common. The sago palm, which grows well in the freshwater swamps of New Guinea and the Solomon Islands, is one of the most important wild food plants.

Pigs provide the main supply of animal protein. Some crops are grown specifically for them, and they also scavenge around the villages and root in the gardens. Other domesticated livestock include chickens and dogs, which are sometimes eaten and are also used for hunting. Cassowary birds are sometimes caught and reared in pens. Cattle and horses have been introduced in Fiji and New Caledonia, and goat herds have been established in some places. The hunting and trapping of wild pigs, marsupials, and birds provides a small amount of additional protein.

Coastal peoples eat a lot of fish. The reefs of eastern Papua, the Torres Straits, the northern Solomon Islands, Fiji, and the areas surrounding New Caledonia yield shellfish, crabs, octopus, sea snails, and mussels; in the lagoons, mullet, bream, grouper, small sharks, and turtles can be caught. The bonito is an important food fish on the

Dietary customs

north coast of New Guinea and around the Solomons. Fish in river pools and lagoons are sometimes drugged with a fluid from pounded plants of the genus *Derris*. Spears, harpoons, traps, nets, and hooks are also used.

The main meal of the day is usually cooked and eaten in the late afternoon. The Melanesians use an earth oven, consisting of a pit with hot stones. The stones are covered with a layer of leaves, on which the food is placed. Water is sprinkled over everything, and the pit is covered with leaves and earth to prevent the steam from escaping. The size of the pit depends on the quantity of food being prepared. In Fiji, the pit is sometimes 50 feet (15 metres) in circumference and up to eight feet deep. Food is also cooked on fires above ground or boiled in pots; in the interior of New Guinea it is cooked in sections of bamboo. Vegetables are usually scraped and then cut up with tools made from shell, coconut, or bamboo. The meat of coconuts is gouged out, and the liquid is expressed and added to vegetable dishes. Staples such as taro are mashed after cooking to make a kind of pudding.

The preservation of food is a problem in Melanesia. Taro can be left in the ground for fairly long periods. In the Trobriand Islands yams are stored in specially constructed houses. Breadfruit is preserved by drying it over a fire or by fermenting it in a pit covered with earth and leaves. Baskets of vegetable food are often hung on wooden hooks inside the huts.

Betel chewing is common. The chewer uses a mixture of the nut of the areca palm (*Areca catechu*), the fruit or leaves of the betel pepper (*Piper betle*), and lime made either by burning coral or shells or by grinding limestone. A small piece of nut is wrapped in a leaf of the betel pepper with a pellet of lime, or the lime may be mixed with the nut and pounded in a small mortar. Betel chewing has a mildly stimulating effect; it induces salivation, and its prolonged use stains the mouth red.

Tobacco is grown and smoked widely. Several kinds of pipes are used; in Irian Barat some have bowls made from nuts. One popular pipe in Irian Barat and New Guinea consists of a tube of bamboo closed at one end, near which a hole is bored. Tobacco in a piece of leaf or a wooden bowl is fitted in the hole. Cigarettes are made with banana leaves.

In eastern Melanesia, where betel is not chewed, an infusion is made from the root of the pepper plant *Piper methysticum*. It is known as kava and has a mildly stimulating effect like that of betel. The root is grated, and the pulp is placed in a bowl. Water is added, and the solution is put into a strainer of hibiscus fibre, which is wrung out like a sponge into a coconut kava cup. Drinking is usually ceremonial, every stage regulated by a precise code of behaviour.

Food taboos are numerous for nursing mothers, young children, fighting males, and others. The Tsembaga of the Bismarck Range in New Guinea eat a large quantity of heavily salted pig fat before fighting; this, together with a taboo on drinking, has the effect of shortening the fighting day because after a certain period everyone becomes unbearably thirsty.

Division of labour. Men do the heavy work of clearing, planting, and fencing. Women generally do the weeding, tending, and digging; they also collect wild food plants and shellfish and feed the pigs. Women prepare the everyday family meals, but the men dig earth ovens and often do large-scale cooking for feasts. Both sexes make their own tools and utensils, men producing axes and adzes and the women making baskets, mats, armbands, ornaments, or shell disks for currency.

Work roles of children

Children start to help their parents from a very young age. In Wogeo, boys participate in fishing expeditions from the age of about four or five. Small girls often begin by carrying vegetables home from the gardens, and by the age of 10 or so they may be entrusted with their own garden areas.

The crafts are not highly specialized. In some areas, however, certain work is undertaken by specialists. The *malanggan* carvings of New Ireland, used in mortuary rituals, are made by specialist carvers; the rights to individual designs are transferable property. The builders of large seagoing canoes in Fiji are a distinct group with their own chief. In fields such as dentistry and medicine, particular individuals tend to acquire a reputation for competence. Most specialization is on the level of the village or area. Extensive trading networks exist throughout Melanesia, and goods produced in one part are often to be found far away from their place of manufacture.

Where larger work forces are needed for specific tasks such as building houses, an individual has a special call on his kin. Most labour is provided reciprocally, with a good deal of cooperation at the village level. In a few areas, such as parts of the central highlands of New Guinea, labour is a salable commodity, and a man may hire himself out for a specific task, such as building a fence.

Tools. While a Bronze Age culture existed prehistorically in Melanesia, by the time the Europeans came the Melanesians were not using metal. Tools are made of stone and shell. The adze (in which the blade is set at right angles to the haft) and the axe are used in woodworking. Their blades are made from fine-grained tough stone, ground on sandstone. They are hafted in various ways; one typical form is the elbow haft: a handle-length piece of wood is cut from the fork of a tree and the blade lashed to the shorter, stubby end from the major limb, the longer, slimmer branch forming the handle. Axe and adze blades are also fashioned from the shell of the giant clam *Tridacna*.

Knives are made from bamboo all over Melanesia. Cutting implements are also made from stone in Irian Barat and from obsidian in the Admiralty Islands; many groups simply use sharp-edged flakes without refining them. Drills are made of stone. Other tools include stone or shell blades hafted as chisels and pigs' tusks used for burnishing wood or, when sharpened, as chisels. Engraving tools are made from the incisor teeth of rodents; the jawbones serve as handles. Rasps are made from the skin of sharks and rays, and awls and needles from the bones of birds or rodents.

Clothing and ornament. Everyday clothing is fairly simple. Men wear a strip of bark cloth, vegetable fibre, or pandanus leaf between their legs. This can be looped under a waistband and may be painted or decorated. Penis wrappers and sheaths made from bamboo or gourd are worn in the northern New Hebrides, Irian Barat, and New Caledonia. On the border of Papua and New Guinea, the common dress is a bark-cloth apron hanging down the back and a series of triangular fibre fringes in front.

Women's clothing

Women's dress is most commonly a skirt made from shredded leaf or string attached to a waist cord. The skirt may be only a few inches long as in the Loyalty Islands or ankle length as in parts of the New Hebrides, but it usually reaches to about the knees. Skirts of fine matting are worn in the New Hebrides, and in parts of inland Papua women wear a band of bark cloth or matting similar to that of men. Women often remove their skirts while working and wear only a few leaves tucked into a waist cord. For both men and women in parts of New Guinea, bark-cloth cloaks protect them from the rain and provide warmth at night. Belts made from long strips of bark are also worn.

Ornaments of some kind are worn by all Melanesians. Generally, those worn by males and females are distinct. Leg bands and armbands made of plaited vegetable fibre are widely distributed in New Guinea, the Bismarck Archipelago, and the Solomon Islands and are worn by both sexes. Head ornaments include combs, some of which are fairly elaborate, such as those of the Admiralty Islands that have handles of red-painted resin with geometric patterns. Feather headdresses are worn for ceremonial occasions in many parts of New Guinea. An ornament known as a *kap-kap*, of the Solomon Islands and the Bismarck Archipelago, consists of a piece of fretwork carving, sometimes painted, attached to a disk of white shell and worn on the forehead or breast. Ears and noses are commonly pierced to take ornaments of carved bone, shell, bamboo, wood, and vegetable fibre. Necklaces are made from shells, teeth, bone, seeds, and vegetable fibre. Shell arm rings have a wide distribution; in some areas they are narrow and are worn in sets. Wooden arm rings are made in the New Hebrides.

Some ornaments indicate status; thus, breast ornaments of shell and cachalot ivory are worn by Fijian chiefs, while other types show that a man has taken a life or accomplished a certain number of ceremonial exchanges.

Hairdress varies. It may be allowed to grow in ringlets, as in New Guinea and parts of the Solomons. It is shaved off as a sign of mourning in the Trobriand Islands. Some coastal peoples in New Guinea draw their hair through a tapering cylinder of plaited cane, decorated with shells and teeth. Hair may also be decorated with lime or flowers.

Body painting and tattooing

Elaborate body painting is undertaken for ceremonial occasions. The practice of tattooing is widespread. Cicatrization, or the production of scar tissue, is common in New Guinea and the Solomons, where cuts are emphasized by rubbing some foreign matter into the wound. The heads of children are constricted to make them longer in parts of southern New Britain and in southern Malekula.

Handicrafts. Many articles are made from string, produced by rolling vegetable fibres in the palm of the hand or on the thigh. Before the fibres are twisted they may be prepared by soaking, scraping, or chewing. For thicker string or rope, several strands are twisted or plaited together. The string is used for nets, bags, bowstrings, and for lashing adze blades. It also has many constructional purposes; *e.g.*, in house or canoe building and rigging.

Weaving is not common in Melanesia except where there is some Polynesian or Micronesian cultural influence, as in the small islands stretching from the Bismarck Archipelago to the Santa Cruz group. It is done with the single-tension loom, with no frame.

Use of bark cloth, however, is widespread. Fijian bark cloth, the finest, is made by soaking the inner bark of the paper mulberry (*Broussonetia papyrifera*) and beating it. It may be painted, rubbed with pigment, or stencilled. The bark cloth produced in the rest of Melanesia is generally coarser than that of Fiji.

Baskets are woven by practically all groups. The materials used include coconut leaves, pandanus, grass, rushes, and rattan. In the Admiralty Islands baskets are waterproofed with crushed putty nut. Mats, made from similar materials, provide bed and floor coverings, clothing, currency, canoe sails, and even house walls.

Pottery is made in all the main island groups and in most areas of New Guinea. No wheel is used. Firing is done in the open, without kilns or ovens. Pots are decorated in various ways, without glazing. Fijian pots are rubbed with resin while they are hot, giving them a shiny appearance.

Transportation. The lack of roads, vehicles, and pack animals in Melanesia means that travelling in the interior is usually done on foot. Dugout canoes made from tree trunks carry people and goods on rivers and streams.

Melanesian water craft

Oceangoing outrigger canoes ply between islands. Canoes from the Santa Cruz Islands have a balancing platform on the side opposite the outrigger. Double-outrigger craft, with a float on each side of the hull and generally held to be an Indonesian type of craft, are to be seen in western Irian Barat, in the Torres Straits islands, and in the Nissan group. Catamarans, consisting of two hulls side by side, are made in the Fiji group, New Caledonia, and on the south coast of Papua. The Fijian catamaran sometimes exceeds 100 feet in length and can carry 200 men. The *lakatoi* of the Port Moresby area of New Guinea is a large cargo-carrying craft composed of a number of dugout hulls lashed side by side, with a deck covering them.

Some boats in the Solomon Islands and in southern New Ireland are constructed of planks, which are hand hewn by splitting tree trunks and adzing the surfaces. They are lashed together, held in place by U-shaped ribs, and the seams caulked with crushed putty nut. They are often lavishly decorated; the bows and sides are covered with pearl shell inlay, and a carved figurehead of a guardian spirit is attached to the bow.

Canoes for sailing generally have one mast, although two-masted forms occur in New Guinea. Sails were formerly made of vegetable fibre or matting, now replaced in most areas by canvas. Paddles are manned both for moving and steering the canoes. Some are decoratively carved or painted.

Property and exchange. In Melanesia, property is usually vested in kinship groups rather than individuals. These groups tend to be either patrilineal (descent traced through the male line) or matrilineal (descent traced through women; for example, from a mother's brother to her son). Among the Trobriand Islanders, landholdings are vested in matrilineal subclans. The head of the subclan, who has the formal title of ownership, is the eldest male of the eldest lineage in the subclan. All members of the subclan have a share in the joint ownership and work as much of the land as they need or are able to use. They may pass on plots to their heirs but have no rights of disposal outside the subclan. Groups may also have vested rights to areas of beach for fishing or storing canoes, and rights to areas of uncultivable bush and even to particular trees. Patterns of kinship are not always rigid, and in a patrilineal society an individual may also have claims on his matrilateral kin; in certain circumstances he may exert his right to work land owned by his matrilineage.

Kinship basis of property

Some kinds of property are held individually, as personal possessions: tools, weapons, artifacts of all kinds, and garden produce. A man's wealth is usually distributed on his death. His pigs may be slaughtered for his funeral rites, leaving very little to his immediate heirs.

The exchange of goods is an important part of life in Melanesia. Great emphasis is placed upon reciprocity. Within any local group the bartering of such small objects as baskets and pots goes on continually. More formalized exchanges occur both within and between communities. Among the people of Mount Hagen in New Guinea, ceremonial exchange is one of the means by which status is achieved. The transactions take place between partners (usually of different subclans), who exchange pigs and pearl shells. It is status enhancing to give back more than one has received, so that if a man gives his partner two pearl shells and one pig (worth four pearl shells), he may expect to receive eight to 10 pearl shells in return. Wealth is thus kept in circulation.

Exchanges between relatives are common; a man is under an obligation to give a clansman an object he may need or covet, but there is an understanding that a reciprocal gift will be made at some future date. One way of celebrating a marriage is by an exchange of goods between the prospective in-laws.

At feasts and on ceremonial occasions, gifts of food and valuables are brought and then redistributed, often by a chief or big man. At these times specific obligations may be discharged. The settlement of disputes between warring groups frequently involves gift exchange, in addition to any compensation paid for death or injury.

Exchanges also take place with more distant communities. Elaborate trade networks have been established in the interior of New Guinea. The Kapauku of the central highlands form an important link in a trade route that originates at the coast and goes northward and then east into the mountains. Cowrie-shell necklaces, steel axes, and machetes move from the coast to the interior; red ochre, stone axes and knives, decorated net bags, and palm wood move in the opposite direction. Traders in each region acquire the goods, carry them a certain distance, and sell them to the next group in the chain.

Trade networks of New Guinea

The famous *kula* networks that cover a large area of the Massim district of eastern Papua handle two classes of goods. Each class always travels in the same direction around the *kula* area; thus, arm rings go counterclockwise and necklaces clockwise, so that a man receives necklaces from his partners in one direction and gives them arm rings he has received from the other direction. The valuables are highly prized, particularly old and finely made ones that have completed many circuits. A *kula* expedition requires a great deal of preparation, including magical ceremonies to ensure that all goes well. The canoes travel in fleets, carrying ordinary goods as well as valuable ones, although prestige and status come with the acquisition of *kula* objects.

Numerous objects serve as currency. To qualify for such use, an object must have a relatively stable value for all who use it, and the value of other objects must be easily calculable in terms of it. Some currency objects, such as tobacco and pigs, have an intrinsic practical use; others are employed only in transactions, and some are limited to particular kinds of transactions, such as the marriage payment. The stylized ornamental fishhooks of the Torres Straits islands fall into the last category. Shell disks, shell ornaments, pigs, pig tusks, mats, teeth, and many other objects serve as currency.

Social and political life. *Kinship.* Clan membership is determined by descent from a common ancestor. Some clans are fairly loose in organization, but most are exogamous—that is, marriage to another clan member is forbidden. Clansmen do not necessarily live in the same village; they cooperate with each other in various ways but tend to meet only on ceremonial occasions.

Some clans are totemic, believing themselves to be mystically associated with or descended from a particular animal or vegetable species; taboos may prohibit the killing or eating of one's totem. Some totemic clans believe they are able to increase or control the totem species.

Totemic clans and taboos

Certain types of marriage are often preferred. A common preference is for marriage with a cross-cousin. (Cross-cousins are the children of siblings of the opposite sex; for example, one's cross-cousins are the children of one's mother's brother or one's father's sister.) Marriage with the children of the mother's brother is generally preferred, especially if they are also the children of the father's sister—which may be the case if cross-cousin marriage has been practiced over several generations.

The customs of kinship and marriage vary greatly in Melanesia. In some societies certain relationships are characterized by avoidance, notably that between a man and his mother-in-law. The man will aim to reduce all contact with his mother-in-law as far as possible. The degree of avoidance may depend on how closely he is related to her in other ways; it becomes attenuated with genealogical distance, so that avoidance is characteristically strongest where a man's mother-in-law is also his father's sister.

Many kinship systems are of the classificatory type in which a person calls various relatives by the same name. Thus, the term father may be used in addressing all of one's father's relatives of the same generation, such as his brothers and cousins. The children of these classificatory fathers then become "brothers" and "sisters." This is presumably an expression of the social ties and obligations that exist between kin and does not imply any confusion on the part of the Melanesians.

Polygyny is widespread. Since it is the wives who tend the gardens, such marriages have economic advantages. Although a particular group may be strongly patrilineal (as the Fijians) or matrilineal (as the Trobriand Islanders), it may stress kinship ties on both sides in different contexts. A man may wish to call on supporters or helpers in a range of situations—*e.g.*, to help him pay for a wife or clear a patch of forest—and his kin are under a special obligation to him. In societies where matrilineal ties are particularly important, a man can expect to inherit from his mother's brother. Tensions may arise in such cases if the father favours his own children rather than those of his sister.

Political leadership. Hereditary chieftainship is the rule in certain areas (for example, in Fiji and the Trobriand Islands), but it is not a typical institution in Melanesia. A big man or chief acquires his position by achieving prestige in his society. This may be done in a variety of ways, not merely by the accumulation of wealth; skill in oratory may be one requirement. Theoretically, the way to leadership is open to anyone with sufficient perseverance. Informal government by old men is common in much of Melanesia, the elders deciding group policy and arbitrating in internal and external disputes. It is recognized, however, that no individual has the right to compel anyone to do anything against his will.

Fiji, where there has been Polynesian influence, has powerful chiefs, and its society can be called highly stratified. Even there, however, sanctions curb the abuse of power, and commoners may withhold their cooperation in communal enterprises.

Political units are generally small and do not always have a specific head, although the leaders of component groups may confer together. Men's organizations constitute an important social institution. The men's house, usually a large building in the village, serves as a social centre where men meet, sleep, eat, and talk; it may also have political, religious, or economic functions. Membership is often based on the clan. The senior and most influential members tend to be lineage elders who have prestige in the society as a whole. Ceremonial and sacred objects are prepared and stored in the men's house to keep them away from the gaze of women and uninitiated males. When members give feasts, they distribute food and goods to each other. Some clubs are graded, as in the northern New Hebrides: an entrance fee has to be paid, and promotion through the grades is gained by purchase and by giving feasts. Most men join the clubs. There are also various secret societies whose members wear masks and impersonate spirits. A man may belong to several of them.

Functions of the men's house

The life cycle. Ideas about conception vary in Melanesia, and it has been suggested that some peoples are ignorant of the nature of the relationship between sexual intercourse and pregnancy. In most of the societies, however, it is understood that both parents play a part in the process. On the island of Wogeo the man is likely to suffer morning sickness; he is treated as an "expectant father." Pregnant women observe various taboos such as restraining from sexual intercourse to ensure the health of the child. During birth a woman may go into seclusion, perhaps in a specially built hut. Female relatives assist with the process.

The weaning of children takes place late by Western standards, sometimes delayed until the end of the third year, although supplementary solid foods are given at an early stage. It is common for a mother to take her baby to the garden with her, carrying it in a bag on her back or suspending it from a tree in a basket while she works. Older children are left in the village with relatives and friends. Babies in Wogeo are discouraged from crawling, as the parents feel they should be old enough to look after themselves before having freedom of movement. Small children of both sexes play together but normally form separate groups at puberty or earlier. By the early teens young people tend to be preoccupied with adult concerns. The Wogeo people set aside property for a child, such as a garden plot, and both boys and girls are expected to assist their elders according to their capacity. The education of children is taken seriously. Much time and trouble are expended on imparting knowledge and teaching technical skills. Moral training is also emphasized, including learning to cooperate with others. Myths and stories are used in teaching.

Weaning and care of young children

Initiation rites are held for both boys and girls, although they are generally of greater significance for boys. The boys may spend a period in seclusion, where they learn about the male role in society or are given secret knowledge not available to women and uninitiated males. Initiation is often done in fairly large groups; it may involve circumcision or some other form of physical marking.

Ceremonies at birth, initiation into manhood, marriage, and death usually include a feast and the exchange of gifts. Sometimes ceremonies are combined, as in New Ireland, where funeral rites may include the initiation of a group of boys.

Some ceremonies take place regularly every year, notably those connected with gardening. In the Trobriand Islands the garden magician is an important figure at every stage of the horticultural cycle. At harvest time piles of yams are displayed, the storehouses are filled, and feasting and distribution of food take place.

Law and justice. In many Melanesian societies, certain offenses are thought to be punished automatically by spirits or ancestral ghosts. Other punishment takes different forms, depending on the seriousness of the offense. Failure to cooperate with one's kin and fellow villagers may lead to ostracism. For more violent offenses such as homicide, the culprit may be required to leave the community for a space of time. "Big men" sometimes act as arbitrators in disputes, using their position and influence to encourage the parties to settle their differences. Such a settlement may be marked by an exchange of goods to show that the parties have resumed relations. Members of the same lineage tend to support each other in disputes with those of other groups. In general, within political units the tendency is to settle quarrels; if skirmishes occur, nonlethal weapons are used.

Warfare between groups was formerly endemic in Melanesia and still persists in some areas. The situation among the Siane of the eastern highland of New Guinea may be taken as fairly typical. A clan normally maintains friendly relations among its members and is formal or hostile with members of other clans. But since other groups are possible sources of husbands or brides, alliances are made between clans. Disputes usually concern such matters as the seduction of a wife, theft of a pig, or perhaps a death blamed on sorcery. Resort to force may take the form of ambush and murder of a single victim from the offending clan, or it may involve a bout of ceremonial warfare. Neutral clans may be brought in to mediate in the settlement of hostilities; they estimate on which side the balance of damages lies, so that compensation can be made. A peacemaking feast usually follows the settlement.

Headhunting was formerly practiced in western Papua, in large areas of Irian Barat, in the Sepik River basin, and in the central Solomon Islands. It usually had some ritual significance. In some cases a male had to obtain a head before he could be initiated into manhood. The Kiwai of southwest Papua took heads as a sign of achievement and kept them as trophies.

Warfare on a large scale occurred only in Fiji, where mercenaries from Tonga took service with the Fijian chiefs.

Religion and art. *Beliefs.* Melanesian believe in a wide range of supernatural phenomena. These include spirit beings, non-personalized forces, and sometimes totems. It is often difficult to make a distinction between magic and religion.

Spirit beings are of various kinds. There are spirits of the dead, both remote and recent. There are spirits that have some creative or regulative function and others that have no such function, including demons or tricksters. The latter two groups are often associated with a particular place, such as a river or sea. Totems, which are species of animals or vegetables, fall into two categories: they may be believed to be ancestors of a particular descent group, or they may be regarded as symbols for such groups.

All Melanesians perform rituals to coerce or propitiate the dead. The Mae Enga of the western New Guinea highlands often dedicate the pigs they kill to potentially dangerous ancestors. If a man falls ill or is injured, a pig is killed immediately; if the patient fails to recover, divination is made by specialists to see where the ritual was at fault.

Ancestors, souls of the dead, and spirits are often thought to inhabit a world similar to that of living beings. Existing social customs are generally validated through myths about ancestors or spirit beings, including how they set the precedents for current forms of behaviour.

The concept of mana, or supernatural power, is a recurrent theme in Melanesian religion, particularly among the eastern groups. Mana can benefit a man or be dangerous to him; it may be contained in inanimate objects or be infused into them by experts. It seems to originate from spirits or ghosts of the dead.

Magical techniques are used to achieve health, wealth, good looks, or resistance to alien sorcery. Most persons possess a few charms and spells, but there are also specialists who practice the more important kinds of magic such as garden or healing magic, sometimes for a fee. Serious illness or death is often ascribed to sorcery within or outside the group, and sorcerers are greatly feared.

Art and music. The Melanesians have a rich and varied artistic life. The principal medium of the artist is wood; other materials include seashells, turtle shells, vegetable fibres, feathers, flowers, leaves, and string. In most areas a great many masks, figures, and other ceremonial objects are produced. They may be made of carved wood, bark cloth, or basketry and are painted with red, white, and black earth pigments. Houses are often decorated; in New Caledonia, chiefs' houses are carved and painted in black and red, the designs incorporating enormous human faces. A lot of decorative work is done on everyday objects such as lime boxes, spatulas, and food bowls. In the Massim district of eastern Papua, the curvilinear patterns carved in low relief on canoe prows, dance ornaments, ornamental boards for yam houses, and war clubs are derived from birds (especially the frigate bird) and other natural objects. The human figure is a dominant theme in many areas. The *malanggan* carvings of northern New Ireland, made for funeral rituals, are complex wooden figures in the shape of men, pigs, birds, snakes, and fish, painted in various colours, often with areas of openwork.

Music and dancing are practiced both ceremonially and for amusement. Learning dances is sometimes part of a young man's initiation. Men and women tend to dance separately. Dancing is accompanied by skin drums beaten by hand and wooden slit gongs played with sticks. Rhythm is also supplied by seed rattles attached to the wrists or ankles. Panpipes, mouth harps, and bamboo or reed flutes are widely used. Bull-roarers are whirled to simulate the voices of the spirits. In the New Hebrides, enormous slit gongs are played for elaborate ballet-type dances.

Singing and storytelling are important in many ceremonies. The songs are made up, often describing recent events, with the audience singing a refrain. The impersonation of spirits, mythological characters, and ancestors is widespread. The Elema of the Gulf of Papua region have a dramatic cycle taking 20 to 30 years to complete. It involves much complex ritual; central to it is the production of masks, which are ritually killed after the ceremonies are completed. A segment of dancing and drama may last a month, during which the characters and actions of a number of sea spirits are portrayed to the accompaniment of drums.

Children's games such as hide-and-seek, cat's cradle, "hunt the nut," and chasing games are played. One adult game in the New Hebrides is played by throwing reeds on the ground so that they rise in the air and fly some distance; the winner is the one whose reed goes the farthest. Contests between villages often end in blows.

MODERN MELANESIA

European settlers, chiefly missionaries at first, came to Melanesia in the 19th century. The Dutch took possession of western New Guinea in 1828; the French gained New Caledonia in 1853; Fiji was ceded to the British in 1874; the British and Germans partitioned New Guinea and the Bismarck Archipelago in 1884; a British protectorate was established over the Solomon Islands, with the exception of Buka and Bougainville, in 1893; Anglo-French competition for influence in the New Hebrides led to the establishment of a condominium there in 1906; the Australians began to administer Papua in 1909 and all of eastern New Guinea after World War I. West New Guinea (Irian Barat) became part of Indonesia in 1969.

Europeans and their civilization had a powerful impact upon the Melanesians. The Europeans introduced plantation agriculture and indentured labour, metal tools, and many new crops. They also introduced various infectious diseases, including measles, from which many people died. Another product of the European influx was the cargo cult. It was based on the idea of a coming millennium. One of the early cargo cults was the Tuka movement in Fiji, first observed in 1885. Ndugumoi, a hereditary priest, claimed to have received word that all ancestors would soon return, the whites would be driven away, and quantities of goods would be provided for everyone. He rallied many followers, but the government arrested

Spirit
beings

Music and
dancing

The
European
impact on
traditional
Melanesia

him and he died in exile. The Tuka movement lasted until after World War I.

There have been numerous other cargo cults, all arising out of the Melanesian astonishment at the vast amount of goods available to the white men, which they assume to be provided by some supernatural agency. One version of the central myth is that God (or Jesus or angels) has been sending goods to the Melanesians but that the white people have been intercepting them. In some of the cults that developed after World War II, the participants even built airstrips and warehouses to receive the cargo. In recent times the cults have acquired political overtones, and some observers have suggested that they represent emergent nationalist movements.

In the 1970s Melanesia seemed to be moving rapidly into the modern world. Fiji had become independent; the Solomon Islands had a Governing Council with a Melanesian-elected majority, and nationalist movements were becoming stronger in the territories of Papua, New Guinea, New Caledonia, and the New Hebrides. Melanesians were being increasingly employed in jobs formerly held by Europeans. Education was continually increasing; there were universities at Port Moresby (in eastern New Guinea) and on Fiji.

The culture of Melanesia as described is disappearing; only in areas without intensive contact with Europeans do the old ways continue without much change.

BIBLIOGRAPHY. Not many books deal with the Melanesian region as a whole. LEWIS L. LANGNESS and JOHN C. WESCHLER (eds.), *Melanesia: Readings on a Culture Area* (1971), includes materials dealing with a range of Melanesian societies. A comprehensive treatment of the region and its geography is H.C. BROOKFIELD with DOREEN HART, *Melanesia: A Geographical Interpretation of an Island World* (1971). The Melanesian economy is treated in JACQUES BARRAU, *Subsistence Agriculture in Melanesia* (1958), which correlates different types of subsistence economies with five ecological zones. LEOPOLD POSPISIL, *Kapauka Papuan Economy* (1963), is a description of the economy of the West New Guineans. BRONISLAW MALINOWSKI'S works on the Trobriand Islands are classics; his *Argonauts of the Western Pacific* (1922), contains a full account of the *kula* exchange of eastern Papua. B.A.L. CRANSTONE, *Melanesia: A Short Ethnography* (1961), is a clear, concise, and well-illustrated treatment of all aspects of material culture and technology. Recent economic changes are discussed in RICHARD F. SALISBURY, *From Stone to Steel: Economic Consequences of a Technological Change in New Guinea* (1962). There are numerous monographs and articles dealing with social organization in various parts of the Melanesian region. J.A. BARNES, "African Models in the New Guinea Highlands," *Man*, 62:5–9 (1962), is an important essay. M.J. MEGGITT, *The Lineage System of the Mae-Enga of New Guinea* (1965), describes a Melanesian segmentary lineage system but has led to much controversy. Another recent view of patterns of kinship is PHYLLIS M. KABERRY, "The Plasticity of New Guinea Kinship," in MAURICE FREEDMAN (ed.), *Social Organization: Essays Presented to Raymond Firth* (1967). A description of the way in which "big men" achieve their status in the Hagen area of New Guinea is ANDREW STRATHERN, "Despots and Directors in the New Guinea Highlands," *Man*, 1:356–367 (1966). H. IAN HOGBIN'S studies of socialization among the Wogeo include "A New Guinea Infancy: From Conception to Weaning in Wogeo," *Oceania*, 13:285–309 (1942–43); "A New Guinea Childhood: From Weaning till the Eighth Year in Wogeo," *ibid.*, 16:275–296 (1945–46); and "Puberty to Marriage: A Study of the Sexual Life of the Natives of Wogeo, New Guinea," *ibid.*, 16:185–209. Some general characteristics of Melanesian religions are examined in PETER LAWRENCE and M.J. MEGGITT (eds.), *Gods, Ghosts, and Men in Melanesia: Some Religions of Australian New Guinea and the New Hebrides* (1965). For a historical and analytical account of cargo cults in Melanesia, see PETER WORSLEY, *The Trumpet Shall Sound* (1957). Useful books on Melanesian art include P.H. LEWIS, *The Social Context of Art in Northern New Ireland* (1969); DOUGLAS NEWTON, *Art Styles of the Papuan Gulf* (1961); and FRANCIS E. WILLIAMS, *Drama of Orokolo: The Social and Ceremonial Life of the Elema* (1940).

(C.J.U.)

Melbourne

Although the officially defined city was the home of only some 75,000 people in the early 1970s, Melbourne is the core of an extensive metropolitan area and the world's most southerly multimillion-peopled urban area. It is situated on the southeastern coast of Australia, at the head of Port Phillip Bay and is the capital of the state of Victoria; from 1901 until 1927 it was the capital of the Commonwealth of Australia. In Australia, it is second only to Sydney in size, and there is an intense rivalry between the two cities, to whom history and geography have bequeathed quite diverse characteristics. Though Melbourne's flat site has led to the regular development of a rectangular pattern of streets, the city has many beautiful parks, and the person with an eye for architectural detail and history can find much that is varied and attractive. Melbourne also has a reputation for conservatism and financial soundness—attributes that many feel were revealed in the early 1970s by the burgeoning skyline of the central city and the rapidly expanding eastern suburbs. Related information may be found under VICTORIA; AUSTRALIA, HISTORY OF.

The city's character

History. Melbourne is distinguished from the other state capitals by the fact that it was founded unofficially, by individual enterprise. The site of Melbourne was discovered in February 1803, but settlement was delayed until 1835, when the pioneer settler and entrepreneur John Batman and his associates purchased 600,000 acres on the northern shores of Port Phillip Bay from aboriginal groups. Before returning to Tasmania, Batman left a party to protect this new interest near Geelong. A second, independent party from Tasmania, organized by another pioneer land speculator, John Fawkner, arrived two months later and established stores and houses. Though there was disagreement between the two early groups, they were both agreed that the New South Wales government should recognize the settlement. One year later, the first administrator of Port Phillip arrived, and in 1837 the new settlement between the Yarra River and the Maribyrnong River was named Melbourne, after the British Prime Minister, Lord Melbourne.

The first settlement measured one mile in length along the north bank of the river and half a mile in width; it became a town in 1842 and a city in 1847, but the first spurt in development followed the discovery (1857) of gold around Bendigo and Ballarat, less than 100 miles away. These discoveries at first depopulated the city, but immigrants from overseas soon began to arrive, and good business was done in satisfying their needs. In 1852 alone, 100,000 people arrived at the gold fields, and in three years the population of the city itself had increased fourfold to 80,000. Melbourne quickly capitalized on its central position and port facilities to capture most of the region's trade: railways were built to other important centres such as Geelong (1856); Ballarat and Bendigo (1862); Echuca (1864); and Wodonga (1873); a link with the New South Wales system at Albury was made in 1883. In recognition of the importance of the city's port facilities the Melbourne Harbour Trust was created in 1887, and the course of the lower Yarra was redirected through the Goode Canal to the south to improve navigation and reduce silting problems. During the 1870s manufacturing industries flourished under the protection of a high tariff wall, and progress in most areas continued until 1889 when financial problems and the collapse of many firms began to shake public confidence. In the decade before 1891 the population of the city increased by nearly 200,000; in the following decade only 6,000 were added.

19th-century expansion

The 20th century, however, brought new confidence with the establishment of the Commonwealth of Australia and the short-lived selection of Melbourne as the national capital. During the two World Wars, and in the period after 1945, manufacturing industry in Melbourne increased dramatically. The expansion in the latest period was accompanied by the influx of thousands of British and European immigrants.

The contemporary city. For census and planning purposes the Melbourne of the 1970s has two boundaries. The outer boundary, defining the Melbourne Statistical Division, includes all areas in close economic and social contact with the central city. It begins on the west shore

Administrative definitions

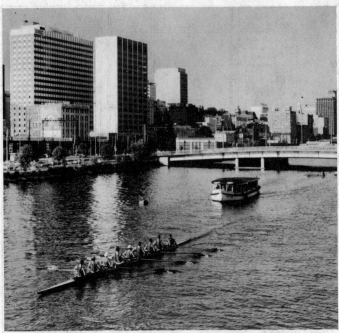

Melbourne, where Kings Bridge fronts the Customs House
(centre left), on the Yarra River.
Charles May—Black Star

of Port Phillip Bay and arches north and east of the bay to the north shore of Western Port Bay; the area enclosed is 2,368 square miles (6,133 square kilometres). The inner boundary encloses the Melbourne metropolitan area; i.e., those areas, which, at the time of a census, have a density of at least 500 persons per square mile. By 1966, this area occupied 21 percent of the statistical division.

The metropolitan area occupies a flat site at the northern end of Port Phillip Bay. Most of it is less than 400 feet high. The shape of the area displays a strong correlation with the geology and drainage of the site. The central city is built close to the Yarra River on firm foundations of ancient sandstones and mudstones. Similar rocks underlie some of the higher eastern areas that command the best views and are occupied by more expensive housing. To the north and west, a plain underlain by basalt rocks encouraged the early establishment of low-cost housing and industry but has proved less attractive in recent times. To the south, the mouth of the Yarra and Maribyrnong rivers consists of soft alluvium, which has been easily excavated to provide excellent docks and industrial sites close to the city centre. The metropolitan area is drained by the River Yarra and its main tributaries—the Maribyrnong River, and the Merri, Darebin, Diamond, and Gardiner creeks. These watercourses interrupt the urban areas, and their valleys are used mainly for drainage, sports grounds, parks, and principal railways and highways. The city has developed in an asymmetric pattern around the bay. The western shores of the bay are comparatively underdeveloped, while most of the eastern shores have been subdivided for commuters' homes in Frankston, and for holiday homes in Mornington and Flinders. Development toward building sites in the eastern hills at Eltham, Lilydale, and Sherbrooke was further distorting the shape of the city in the early 1970s.

Demographic trends. At the start of the 1970s, the population of the Melbourne Statistical Division was estimated to be over 2,380,000, or almost 70 percent of the population of the entire state of Victoria. Even as far back as 1921, Melbourne had contained more than half the state's population. Ninety-five percent of Melbourne's population lives in the metropolitan area and the city's population is growing at an annual rate of about 2 percent. This is slower than it was in the decade following the 1954 census, when immigration accounted for well over half the annual increase. Immigration and natural increase were making equal contributions to population growth in 1970. The distribution of population within the metropolitan area is slowly changing. Some rehabilitation of the poorer residential inner areas has occurred. The Housing Commission supervises the completion of about 1,500 houses and apartments each year.

Economic life. That Melbourne dominates the economic life of Victoria is not surprising in view of the fact that the city is at the centre of the communications network linking the rest of the state to Australia and the world, that it contains the bulk of the state's population, and is the seat of government and of major financial institutions.

Melbourne port occupies 10½ square miles of level, easily excavated land at the mouth of the Yarra River. Particular sections of the port specialize in different types of cargo, using the most modern loading and unloading techniques. Main imports are bulk oils, newsprint and paper, phosphatic rock, iron and steel, chemicals, timber, and coal. Main exports are wool, scrap metal, meat, fruit, flour, and dairy products. Passenger terminals handle some 100,000 travellers each year.

The Melbourne Statistical Division includes three-quarters of the state's factories, employing 83 percent of its industrial workers. Although 60 percent of the factories employ fewer than ten people, 55 percent of the work force is employed in large factories with more than 100 employees. The earliest clothing and metal factories were established in the inner suburbs of Collingwood, Richmond, Fitzroy, Brunswick, Melbourne, and Footscray. Newer and larger industries—producing motor cars, rubber goods, chemicals, and refined oils—are being established in such outer suburbs as Moorabbin, Altona, Broadmeadows, and Dandenong, areas which offer cheaper land in more extensive sites, an increasing population, and fewer traffic congestion problems. The most important Melbourne industries, in terms of numbers employed, are: metal processing; textile and clothing manufacture; food preparation; and paper making and printing. The reduced industrial importance of the inner city is paralleled by its declining share of the retail trade. New, large, regional shopping centres have been established in the rapidly growing eastern and southern suburbs.

Administration and services. The Melbourne Statistical Division consists of 41 cities and 13 shires, each with its own council. The councils have the responsibility of collecting taxes (rates) and using these and other funds to provide local services, notably the maintenance of roads and the provision of libraries. While uniform building regulations apply to the Melbourne Statistical Division, local councils may make specific bylaws dealing with such subjects as subdivisions and apartment building. There are also certain statutory authorities that control aspects of metropolitan government. The Melbourne and Metropolitan Board of Works is responsible for a master planning scheme, the construction of main roads and bridges, the provision of water, and the disposal of sewage. A Tramways Board controls tram and bus services; a Harbour Trust is responsible for the large port area; and a Housing Commission, created in 1938, coordinates slum clearance and urban renewal. *(margin: Local government)*

Melbourne is well equipped to provide the services expected of a major city. Adequate public transport is provided by electric trains, buses, and old-fashioned—but nevertheless efficient—tramcars. Increasing numbers now travel by car, however, and all three services were showing declining numbers of passengers and rising deficits at the beginning of the 1970s. The emphasis on car travel has created problems of road congestion at peak hours, and efforts were being made by the 1970s to provide a system of freeways, clear ways, and a major high-level bridge over the lower Yarra to link the eastern and western industrial areas. An international airport near suburban Tullamarine opened in 1970, and a well-equipped port serves overseas passengers. Melbourne maintains excellent telecommunication links with the world's major cities.

Cultural life. Opportunities to appreciate all forms of art and culture and to enjoy other types of recreation are plentiful in and around Melbourne. The Victorian Arts Centre, opened in 1968, houses art galleries, theatres,

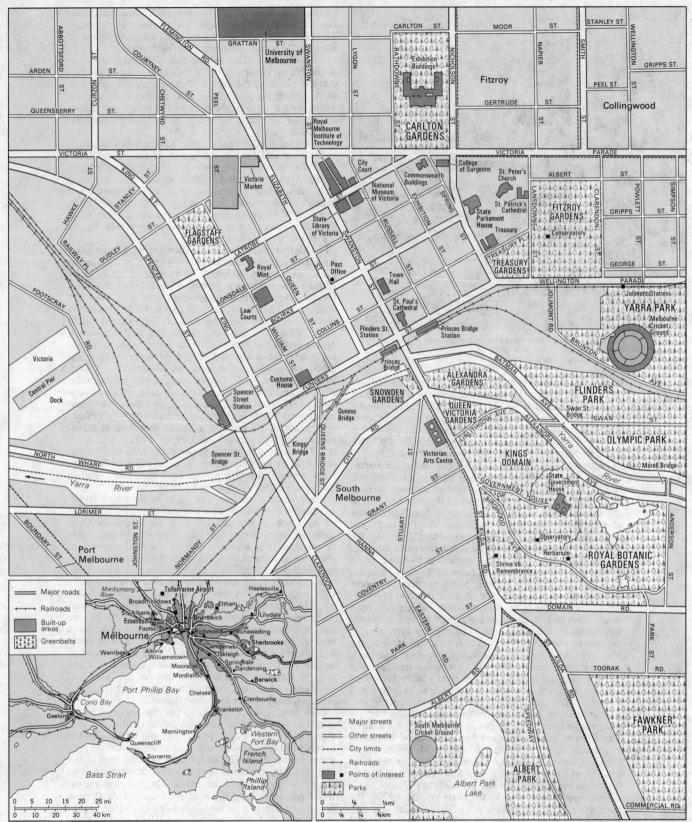

Central Melbourne and (inset) the Port Phillip Bay area.

auditoriums, studios, and study areas on a central site. Each year seasons of opera, ballet, and concerts include performances by international artists. Live theatres and cinema complexes present contemporary and popular plays and films. There are hundreds of sports grounds, tennis courts, swimming pools, and golf courses for active sportsmen, while spectators find good accommodations at the famous Melbourne Cricket Ground, which holds crowds of more than 110,000, and at the Kooyong tennis courts. Sailing and fishing on the bay and surfing on the ocean beaches are also available, and the winter ski fields around Buller are within easy reach.

BIBLIOGRAPHY. W.H. NEWNHAM, *Melbourne* (1956), a good, general, historical account; MELBOURNE, COMMONWEALTH BUREAU OF CENSUS AND STATISTICS, *Victorian Year Book* (annual), invaluable for recent statistics and developments; also contains a detailed bibliography.

(J.R.V.P.)

Melville, Herman

In his life as well as his work, Herman Melville was a symbol of the conflicts inherent in the new American nation in which he wrote. He was a man at odds with the heady idealism of his age, which saw the young nation as an image of moral regeneration, liberated from the corrupting traditions of Europe. He wanted to believe, with Ralph Waldo Emerson, in the greatness of America's and humanity's future, and, unlike his friend Nathaniel Hawthorne, he longed to cling to an idealistic vision of the human being. But he was unable to reconcile such ideals with the reality he experienced. Instead of finding in the explosive growth of the country in the 19th century a sign of regeneration, he saw the brutal acquisitiveness of its commerce, the misery of the exploited immigrants, and the contrast between human profession and human act.

Melville, oil painting by Joseph Oriel Eaton. In the Houghton Library, Harvard University.

Heritage and youth. Melville's heritage and youthful experiences were perhaps crucial in forming the conflicts underlying his artistic vision. He was born on August 1, 1819, in New York City, the third child of Allan and Maria Gansevoort Melvill, in a family that was to grow to four boys and four girls. His forebears had been among the Scottish and Dutch settlers of New York and had taken leading roles in the American Revolution and in the fiercely competitive commercial and political life of the new nation. One grandfather, Maj. Thomas Melvill, was a member of the Boston Tea Party in 1773, and subsequently a New York importer. The other, Gen. Peter Gansevoort, was a friend of James Fenimore Cooper and famous for leading the successful defense of Ft. Stanwix, in upstate New York, against the British.

In 1826 Allan Melvill wrote of his son as being "very backward in speech and somewhat slow in comprehension . . . of a docile and amiable disposition." In that same year, scarlet fever left the boy with permanently weakened eyesight, but he attended Male High School. When the family import business collapsed in 1830, the family returned to Albany, where Herman enrolled briefly in Albany Academy. Allan Melvill died in 1832, leaving his family in desperate straits. The eldest son, Gansevoort, assumed responsibility for the family and took over his father's felt and fur business. Herman joined him after two years as a bank clerk and some months working on the farm of his uncle, Thomas Melvill, in Pittsfield, Mass. About this time, Herman's branch of the family altered the spelling of its name. Though finances were precarious, Herman attended Albany Classical School in 1835 and became an active member of a local debating society. A teaching job in Pittsfield made him unhappy, however, and after three months he returned to Albany.

Wanderings and voyages. Young Melville had already begun writing, but the remainder of his youth became a quest for security. A comparable pursuit in the spiritual realm was to characterize much of his writing. The crisis that started Herman on his wanderings came in 1837, when Gansevoort went bankrupt and the family moved to nearby Lansingburgh (now Troy). In what was to be a final attempt at orthodox employment, Herman studied surveying at Lansingburgh Academy to equip himself for a post with the Erie Canal project. When the job did not materialize, Gansevoort arranged for Herman to ship out as cabin boy on the "St. Lawrence," a merchant ship sailing in June 1839 from New York for Liverpool. The summer voyage did not dedicate Melville to the sea, and on his return his family was dependent still on the charity of relatives. After a grinding search for work, he taught briefly in a school that closed without paying him. His uncle Thomas, who had left Pittsfield for Illinois, apparently had no help to offer when the young man followed him West. In January 1841 Melville sailed on the whaler "Acushnet," from New Bedford, Mass., on a voyage to the South Seas.

In June 1842 the "Acushnet" anchored in the Marquesas Islands in present-day French Polynesia. Melville's adventures here, somewhat romanticized, became the subject of his first novel, *Typee* (1846). In July Melville and a companion jumped ship and, according to *Typee*, spent about four months as guest-captives of the reputedly cannibalistic Typee people. Actually, in August he was registered in the crew of the Australian whaler "Lucy Ann." Whatever its precise correspondence with fact, however, *Typee* was faithful to the imaginative impact of the experience on Melville. Despite intimations of danger, Melville represented the exotic valley of the Typees as an idyllic sanctuary from a hustling, aggressive civilization.

Typee

Although Melville was down for a 120th share of the whaler's proceeds, the voyage had been unproductive. He joined a mutiny that landed the mutineers in a Tahitian jail, from which he escaped without difficulty. On these events and their sequel, Melville based his second book, *Omoo* (1847). Lighthearted in tone, with the mutiny shown as something of a farce, it describes Melville's travels through the islands, accompanied by Long Ghost, formerly the ship's doctor, now turned drifter. The carefree roving confirmed Melville's bitterness against colonial and, especially, missionary debasement of the native Tahitian peoples.

These travels in fact occupied less than a month. In November he signed as a harpooner on his last whaler, the "Charles & Henry" out of Nantucket, Mass. Six months later he disembarked at Lahaina, in the Hawaiian Islands. Somehow he supported himself for over three months, then in August 1843 he signed as an ordinary seaman on the frigate "United States," which in October 1844 discharged him in Boston. *White-Jacket* (1850) conveys an idea of the tensions embodied for Melville in that voyage home, among them his feeling for the democratic fraternity of the seamen, about which he had mixed feelings, and his opposition to savage shipboard discipline. (Over 160 floggings were recorded on that voyage of the "United States.") The book demonstrated comradeship undermined by alienation and a faith in human perfectibility that was unsettled by an awareness of human corruption.

The years of acclaim. Melville rejoined a family whose prospects had much improved. Gansevoort, who after James K. Polk's victory in the 1844 presidential elections had been appointed secretary to the U.S. legation in London, was gaining political renown. Encouraged by his family's enthusiastic reception of his tales of the South Seas, Melville wrote them down and attempted to publish them. Harper and Brothers, skeptical of their authenticity, rejected the manuscript. Gansevoort had more success; though also dubious, the London publisher John Murray accepted it. Wiley and Putnam agreed to an American edition. The years of acclaim were about to begin for Melville.

Typee provoked immediate enthusiasm and outrage. Was it to be believed? The companion of Melville's Polynesian idyll appeared and verified its truth, but his corroboration was poorly detailed. Doubts persisted. Missionaries protested loudly against the criticism of their

Early novels

activities, and the second edition deleted offensive passages. But for Melville it was unquestionably fame, confirmed by the identical response to *Omoo*, published by a still uneasy Murray. Gansevoort, dead of a brain disease, never saw his brother's career consolidated, but the bereavement left Melville head of the family and the more committed to writing to support it. Another responsibility came with his marriage in August 1847 to Elizabeth Shaw, daughter of the chief justice of Massachusetts. He tried unsuccessfully for a job in the U.S. Treasury Department, the first of many abortive efforts to secure a government post.

In 1847 Melville began a third book, *Mardi*, and, through Evert Duyckinck, a Wiley and Putnam editor, was introduced into the literary and artistic circles of New York City. He became a regular contributor of reviews and other pieces to a literary journal. To his new acquaintances he appeared the character of his own books—extrovert, vigorous, "with his cigar and his Spanish eyes," as one writer described him. Melville resented this somewhat patronizing stereotype, and in her reminiscences his wife recalled him in a different aspect, writing in a bitterly cold, fireless room in winter. He enjoined Murray not to call him "the author of *Typee* and *Omoo*," *Mardi* for his third book, *Mardi* (1849), was to be a different cast.

The quests begun. When *Mardi* appeared, public and critics alike found its wild, allegorical fantasy and medley of styles incomprehensible. It began as another Polynesian adventure but quickly set its hero in pursuit of the mysterious Yillah, "all beauty and innocence," a symbolic quest that ends in anguish and disaster. Concealing his disappointment at the book's reception, Melville wrote to Richard Bentley, now his English publisher, that the book, "judged only as a work meant to entertain," had been misapprehended by the critics and added, darkly, that "*Mardi*, in its larger purposes, has not been written in vain."

Financially it had been. To repair his popular reputation, Melville quickly wrote *Redburn* (1849) and *White-Jacket* (1850) in the manner expected of him. Richard Bentley in England and Harper and Brothers in New York brought out *Redburn*, which was an elaboration of Melville's 1839 voyage on the "St. Lawrence," with an invented melodramatic sequence in England. In October 1849 Melville sailed to England to resolve Bentley's doubts about *White-Jacket*. Rewarded by Bentley's acceptance of *White-Jacket*, he visited the Continent, kept a journal, and arrived back in America in February 1850. The critics acclaimed *White-Jacket*, and its powerful criticism of abuses in the U.S. Navy won it strong political support.

But both novels, however much they seemed to revive the Melville of *Typee*, had passages of profoundly questioning melancholy. It was not the same Melville who wrote them. He had been reading Shakespeare with "eyes which are as tender as young sparrows," particularly noting sombre passages in *Measure for Measure* and *King Lear*. This reading struck deeply sympathetic responses in Melville, counterbalancing the Transcendental doctrines of Emerson, whose general optimism about human goodness he had heard in lectures and some of whose attitudes pervaded *White-Jacket*. A fresh imaginative influence was supplied by Hawthorne's *Scarlet Letter*, a novel deeply exploring good and evil in the human being that Melville read in the spring of 1850. On Duyckinck's encouragement, he made Hawthorne's *Mosses from an Old Manse* the basis of a eulogistic essay that was published in Meeting a journal. That summer, Duyckinck introduced him to with Hawthorne, who was living near Pittsfield. Melville Hawthorne bought a nearby farm, which he christened "Arrowhead," and the two men became neighbours physically as well as in sympathies.

Moby Dick and Pierre. Melville had promised his publishers for the autumn of 1850 the novel first entitled *The Whale*, finally *Moby Dick*. His delay in submitting it was caused less by his early-morning chores as a farmer than by his explorations into the unsuspected vistas opened for him by Hawthorne. Their relationship reani-

mated Melville's creative energies. On his side, it was dependent, almost mystically intense—"an infinite fraternity of feeling," he called it. To the cooler, withdrawn Hawthorne, such depth of feeling so persistently and openly declared was uncongenial. The two men gradually drew apart. They met for the last time, almost as strangers, in 1856, when Melville visited Liverpool, where Hawthorne was American consul.

Moby Dick was published in London in October 1851, and a month later in America. It brought its author neither acclaim nor reward. Basically its story is simple. Captain Ahab pursues the white whale, Moby Dick, which finally kills him. At that level, it is an intense, superbly authentic narrative of whaling. In the perverted grandeur of Captain Ahab and in the beauties and terrors of the voyage of the "Pequod," however, Melville dramatized his deeper concerns: the equivocal defeats and triumphs of the human spirit and its fusion of creative and murderous urges. In his private afflictions, Melville had found universal metaphors.

Increasingly a recluse to the point that some friends feared for his sanity, Melville embarked almost at once on *Pierre*. It was an intensely personal work, revealing the sombre mythology of his private life framed in terms of a story of an artist alienated from his society. In it can be found the humiliated responses to poverty that his youth supplied him plentifully and the hypocrisy he found beneath his father's claims to purity and faithfulness. His mother he had idolized; yet he found the spirituality of her love betrayed by sexual love. The novel, a slightly veiled allegory of Melville's own dark imaginings, was rooted in these relations. When published in 1852, it was another critical and financial disaster. Only 33 years old, Melville saw his career in ruins.

The losing of faith. Near breakdown, and having to face in 1853 the disaster of a fire at Harper's that destroyed most of his books, Melville persevered with writing.

Israel Potter, plotted before his introduction to Hawthorne and his work, was published in 1855, but its modest success, clarity of style, and apparent simplicity of subject did not indicate a decision by Melville to write down to public taste. His other contributions to *Putnam's Monthly Magazine*, "Bartleby the Scrivener" (1853), "The Encantadas" (1854), and "Benito Cereno" (1855), reflected the despair and the contempt for human hypocrisy and materialism that possessed him increasingly following the failure of *Pierre*. The clerk Bartleby was typical. The germ of his experience—isolating himself from his duties, from society, in the end from life itself—was Melville's own. Bartleby was the casualty of a society indifferent to his mute, passive protest. The tormented writer knew that these stories were not the way back to his audience but a private pursuit. As he wrote to Hawthorne, "What I feel most moved to write will not pay."

In 1856 Melville set out on a tour of Europe and the Levant to renew his spirits. The most powerful passages of the journal he kept are in harmony with *The Confidence-Man* (1857), a despairing satire on an America corrupted by the shabby dreams of commerce. This was the last of his novels to be published in his lifetime. Three American lecture tours were followed by his final sea journey, in 1860, when he joined his brother Thomas, captain of the clipper "Meteor," for a voyage around Cape Horn. He abandoned the undertaking in San Francisco.

The years of withdrawal. Around these years Melville abandoned the novel for poetry, but when he came home the prospects for publication were not favourable. With two sons and daughters to support, Melville sought government patronage. A consular post he sought in 1861 went elsewhere. On the outbreak of the Civil War, he volunteered for the Navy, but was again rejected. He had apparently returned full cycle to the insecurity of his youth, but an inheritance from his father-in-law brought some relief and "Arrowhead," increasingly a burden, was sold. By the end of 1863, the family was living in New York City. The war was much on his mind and furnished the subject of his first volume of poetry, *Battle-Pieces and*

Aspects of the War (1866), published privately. Four months after it appeared, an appointment as a customs inspector on the New York docks finally brought him a secure income.

Despite poor health, Melville began a pattern of writing evenings, weekends, and on vacations. In 1867 his son Malcolm shot himself, accidentally the jury decided, though it appeared that he had quarrelled with his father the night before his death. His second son, Stanwix, who had gone to sea in 1869, died in a San Francisco hospital in 1886 after a long illness. Throughout these griefs, and for the whole of his 19 years in the customs house, Melville's creative pace was understandably slowed from the amazing fertility of the 1840s.

Final writings His second collection of verse, *John Marr, and Other Sailors; With Some Sea-Pieces*, appeared only in 1888, again privately published. By then he had been in retirement for three years, assisted by legacies from friends and relatives. His new leisure he devoted, he wrote in 1889, to "certain matters as yet incomplete." Among them was *Timoleon* (1891), a final verse collection. More significant was the return to prose that culminated in his last work, the novel *Billy Budd*, which remained unpublished until 1924. Provoked by a false charge, the sailor Billy Budd accidentally kills the satanic master-at-arms. In a time of threatened mutiny he is hanged, going willingly to his fate. Evil has not wholly triumphed, and Billy's memory lives on as an emblem of good. Here there is, if not a statement of being reconciled fully to life, at least the peace of resignation. The manuscript ends with the date April 19, 1891. On the following September 28, Melville died.

Melville's was a life neither happy nor, by material standards, successful. By the end of the 1840s he was among the most celebrated of American writers, yet his death evoked but a single obituary notice.

In the internal tensions that put him in conflict with his age lay a strangely 20th-century awareness of the deceptiveness of realities and of the instability of personal identity. Yet his writings never lost sight of reality. His symbols grew from such visible facts, made intensely present, as the dying whales, the mess of blubber, and the wood of the ship, in *Moby Dick*. For Melville, as for Shakespeare, man was ape and essence, inextricably compounded; and the world, like the "Pequod," was subject to "two antagonistic influences . . . one to mount direct to heaven, the other to drive yawingly to some horizontal goal." It was Melville's triumph that he endured, recording his vision to the end. After the years of neglect, modern criticism had secured his reputation with that of the great American writers.

MAJOR WORKS

NOVELS: *Typee: A Peep at Polynesian Life* (1846); *Omoo: A Narrative of Adventures in the South Seas* (1847); *Mardi and a Voyage Thither* (1849), a political and philosophical allegory; *Redburn, His First Voyage* (1849); *White-Jacket; or, The World in a Man-of-War* (1850); *Moby Dick; or, The Whale* (1851, as *Moby Dick; or, The White Whale* in some later-19th-century editions); *Pierre; or The Ambiguities* (1852); *Israel Potter: His Fifty Years of Exile*, (1855), a historical novel of the American Revolution; *The Confidence-Man: His Masquerade* (1857), a satirical allegory; *Billy Budd, Foretopman*, a short novel written 1888–91 and found after Melville's death; first published in *Billy Budd, and Other Prose Pieces* (1924).

SHORT STORIES, SKETCHES, AND JOURNALS: *The Piazza Tales* (1856), includes "The Piazza," "Bartleby the Scrivener," "Benito Cereno," "The Encantadas, or, Enchanted Isles," and "The Lightning-Rod Man"; *The Apple-Tree Table and Other Sketches* (1922), contains 10 sketches first published in periodicals, 1850–56; *Journal up the Straits, October 1, 1856–May 5, 1857* (1935); *Journal of Melville's Voyage in the Clipper Ship, "Meteor"* (1929).

VERSE: *Battle-Pieces and Aspects of the War* (1866); *Clarel: A Poem and Pilgrimage in the Holy Land* (1876); *John Marr, and Other Sailors; With Some Sea-Pieces* (1888); *Timoleon* (1891), a collection. Poems unpublished during Melville's lifetime are included in later collections and selections.

BIBLIOGRAPHY

Editions: The standard edition is *The Works of Herman Melville*, 16 vol. (1922–24); Hendricks House undertook a new complete edition in 1947; the Northwestern-Newberry edition, ed. by HARRISON HAYFORD, HERSHEL PARKER, and G. THOMAS TANSELLE, began in 1968; *Collected Poems of Herman Melville*, ed. by HOWARD P. VINCENT (1947); *Melville's Billy Budd*, ed. by F. BARRON FREEMAN, corrected by ELIZABETH TREEMAN (1956); *The Complete Stories of Herman Melville*, ed. by JAY LEYDA (1949); *Journal of a Visit to London and the Continent, 1849–1850*, ed. by ELEANOR MELVILLE METCALF (1949); *Journal of a Visit to Europe and the Levant, 1856–1857*, ed. by HOWARD C. HORSFORD (1955); *Letters*, ed. by MERRELL R. DAVIS and WILLIAM H. GILMAN (1960).

Biographical: RAYMOND M. WEAVER, *Herman Melville: Mariner and Mystic* (1921), interesting as the first biographical study; LEWIS MUMFORD, *Herman Melville* (1929), an early life, now a little outmoded, but still a sensitive appreciation of the man; NEWTON ARVIN, *Herman Melville* (1950), a critical biography, judiciously combining life and works; LEON HOWARD, *Herman Melville: A Biography* (1951), the most complete factual account of Melville's life, perceptively analytic; JAY LEYDA, *The Melville Log: A Documentary Life of Herman Melville* (1951), a fascinating collection of documents, photographs, and letters; WILLIAM H. GILMAN, *Melville's Early Life and Redburn* (1951), a thorough record of Melville's youth and the relationships between fact and fiction in *Redburn*.

Critical: F.O. MATTHIESSEN, *American Renaissance* (1941), a brilliant short analysis of Melville in relation to his contemporaries and his times; WILLIAM E. SEDGWICK, *Herman Melville: The Tragedy of Mind* (1944), one of the best studies of Melville's ideas as they appear in his novels; VAN WYCK BROOKS, *The Times of Melville and Whitman* (1947), useful for general historical background; RONALD MASON, *The Spirit Above the Dust* (1951), straight, interpretive criticism, illuminating on *Pierre* and *Moby Dick;* LAWRENCE THOMPSON, *Melville's Quarrel with God* (1952), an interesting case for Melville's Christian unorthodoxy; ELEANOR MELVILLE METCALF, *Herman Melville: Cycle and Epicycle* (1953), an important addition to Melville studies; RICHARD CHASE, *Herman Melville: A Collection of Critical Essays* (1962), a well-chosen selection of criticism; A.R. HUMPHREYS, *Melville* (1962), an excellent introductory study; D.E.S. MAXWELL, *Herman Melville* (1968), representative excerpts from the works, with explanatory and critical comment.

(D.E.S.M.)

Membrane, Biological

Biological membranes are the thin layers of material that form the outer limits of living cells and their various inner components. Membranes are ubiquitous structures in living matter. They differ greatly in structure and properties, however, and statements on membranes may be generalized only to a certain limited degree.

Every cell, including the most primitive micro-organism, is surrounded by a membrane called the plasma membrane. This membrane separates the cell from its environment, thereby fostering the maintenance of a constant milieu in which intracellular reactions occur. The plasma membrane, however, does not isolate the cell completely from the external world. Instead, it allows a highly controlled exchange of matter across the barrier it poses; some special compounds are able to pass through the membrane easily; others are completely blocked. This screening effect on the substances that enter and leave the cell is perhaps the most important function of the cell membrane.

External and internal membranes Within cells, many additional membranes can be distinguished. These membranes surround, or themselves comprise, the various structural units, called, as a group, organelles. Prominent among these are the nucleus, or central body of the cell, and the mitochondria, or energy-storing units. Photographs taken with an electron microscope reveal that membranes from different cell types have certain common structural features (see Figure 1). Most prominent of these is a three-layered structure, which, after staining by a chemical agent, becomes visible as two dark layers separated by an intermediate light one. This three-layered structure appears to be a fundamental feature of almost all biological membranes. Both the plasma membrane and some of the intracellular membranes are believed to be parts of a continuous membrane system that extends through much of the body of the cell.

Certain biochemical processes are known to occur in

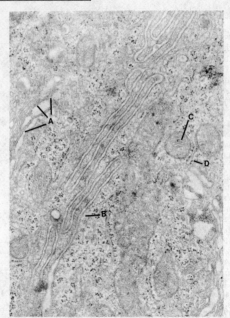

Figure 1: Electron micrograph of columnar epithelial cells of the mouse intestine showing (A) Golgi membranes, (B) plasma membrane, (C) mitochondrion, and (D) ribosomes (magnified 24,600 X).
F.S. Sjostrand

close association with membranes. This is especially true of those sequences of reactions associated with energy production in the mitochondria. In bacteria, the protein-synthesizing units (ribosomes) and the genetic material (DNA) are attached to the plasma membrane.

Comparison of the cells of a series of organisms of increasing complexity—such as bacterial, yeast, plant, and animal cells—reveals that the number of cellular structures containing membranes increases with the increasing complexity of the organism. In the cells of the bacterium *Escherichia coli,* the chromosomes are simply embedded in the cytoplasm, whereas in yeast cells they are enclosed in a nuclear membrane. Such membrane-containing organelles as mitochondria and chloroplasts, photosynthetic structures occurring in plant cells, are found only in the more highly organized cells of animals and plants.

During the lifetime of every multicellular organism, primitive cells undergo differentiation and specialization, with the result that a diverse population of highly differentiated and specialized cells is formed; associated with this process is the development of different kinds of membranes in the differentiated cells. The degree of development in embryonic liver cells of the complex membrane structure called the endoplasmic reticulum may, for instance, be correlated with the stage of growth of the cells. In some cases, highly specialized membrane structures are formed in specialized cells; examples are the brushlike membrane surface (brush border) of certain epithelial cells and the membrane structures (myelin sheaths) wound round the extensions (axons) of nerve cells.

Surrounding the membranes of bacterial and plant cells is an additional structure, the rigid cell wall, whose chemical composition is quite different from that of the proper cell (cytoplasmic) membranes. The walls of these cells appear to play chiefly a protective and structural role, leaving to the cell membrane the task of regulating the passage of materials into and out of the cell. This conclusion is supported by the finding that removal of the cell wall does not increase the permeability of the cell membrane to various materials.

The nature of membranes

BIOCHEMICAL CONSTITUENTS OF MEMBRANES

Most of current knowledge about the biochemical constituents of membranes originates in studies of red blood cells (erythrocytes) of animals. Less is known about the

molecular composition of bacterial and plant cells. The chief advantage of red blood cells for experimental purposes is that they may be obtained easily in large amounts. In addition, the red blood cells contain no typical membrane structures other than the plasma membrane, a situation that facilitates study of that structure. Generally speaking, the chief biochemical components of membranes are fats (lipids) and proteins; lesser amounts of carbohydrates and nucleic acids are found in certain membranes.

Lipids. The amount of lipid in the cell membrane varies considerably among different cell types. For example, the lipid content of the myelin sheath of the nerve cells is about 70 percent of the total membrane material; whereas that of the liver mitochondrial membrane is about 30 percent, and that of the liver endoplasmic reticulum is about 50 percent.

The composition of the lipids in the membranes of various kinds of cells also differs greatly. For example, cholesterol, a lipid material that is not a true fat, is a major component of most varieties of animal-cell membranes; whereas in several internal membranes of liver cells, it is present in only minor amounts, and it is almost entirely absent from bacterial membranes. Even the lipid composition of red-blood-cell membranes varies among different animal species. There are, however, some common features: on the average, cholesterol makes up about 27 percent of the total lipids, and the lipids bearing phosphate groups (phospholipids) account for about 60 percent. The amount of a particular phospholipid, lecithin, shows considerable variation among red-cell membranes of different species: it is hardly detectable in red-cell membranes of the sheep, whereas its content in those of the pig is about 25 percent, and in those of the rat 50 percent. Lipids containing carbohydrates (glycolipids) have not been found in intracellular membranes; they appear to occur exclusively in plasma membranes. The pattern of the fatty acids incorporated in the fats of biological membranes also varies within a wide range. More than three quarters of the total of fatty acids in human erythrocytes are made up by the following five species: palmitic acid (30 percent of the total), oleic acid (17 percent), stearic acid (16 percent), linoleic acid (10.5 percent), and arachidonic acid (10 percent).

A number of external factors have been found to affect the lipid content of membranes. In the micro-organism *Mycoplasma laidlawii,* for example, cholesterol may or may not be present depending on the composition of the growth medium. Within mammalian cells of any one type, the ratio between the amounts of the different lipid classes is relatively constant, but the pattern of fatty acids they contain may vary with such factors as diet and the external temperature.

Proteins. Evidence suggests that a protein layer covers the lipid core of the membrane on each side. Less is known about the composition of the protein than about that of the lipid fraction of the membrane. The proteins probably account for special biological functions of the membrane, such as transport of material into and out of the cell. Both the stability and the flexibility of biological membranes are maintained by special lipid–lipid and lipid–protein interactions, but little is known about the specific forces involved.

Carbohydrates. The carbohydrates found in membranes are bound chemically to the lipids (producing glycolipids) and to the proteins (giving glycoproteins). Glycoproteins appear chiefly in the outer protein layer of the membrane.

Nucleic acids. Although adsorption of foreign ribonucleic acid (RNA) to membranes during laboratory separations cannot be excluded, it appears that some RNA is a genuine component of the plasma membranes of rat liver cells. The amount present seems to be very small, of the order of five micrograms for every milligram of protein. Larger amounts of RNA have been found in bacterial membranes.

Arrangement of the biochemical constituents. Ideas concerning the molecular arrangement of the membrane components are based to a considerable extent on obser-

Variable compositions of lipid membranes

vations of the behaviour of similar molecules at the surface of a water solution exposed to air. Experiments of this kind suggest that the lipid molecules are packed together as closely as possible, like pickets in a picket fence. Since the minimum surface area occupied by all lipids extractable from erythrocytes exceeds the surface of the cells, the lipids are assumed to be present in a double layer. The concept of a double lipid layer, covered on both sides by proteins, was put forward in 1935 as the first significant model of membrane architecture, and has subsequently come to be known as the unit-membrane concept. Since membranes may be isolated without alteration of the molecular arrangement, the organization of the biological membrane appears to be more stable than that of a lipid film at a water surface.

Layered models of membranes

Studies of various membranes (such as those of the myelin sheath) by means of the electron microscope have revealed a three-layered structure, in agreement with the proposed membrane model. The thickness of plasma membranes is of the order of 70–90 angstrom units, the double-layered lipid core alone being about 50 angstroms. Later modifications of the original membrane model included the ideas that the proteins were spread out over the lipid surfaces and that those on the inside of the cell membrane differ from those on the outside (see Figure 2).

From M. Locke (ed.), *Cellular Membranes in Development*

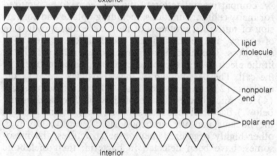

Figure 2: Unit membrane concept (see text).

Many results of recent experiments are difficult to reconcile with the concept of the unit membrane. Consequently, alternative models of membrane structure have been proposed. According to some of these, called "subunit models," the membrane may be considered as a two-dimensional aggregation of separate lipoprotein subunits, rather than discrete layers of lipid and protein. For 30 years concepts of membrane structure have been dominated by the unit-membrane model, but some of the early arguments supporting it have lost much of their force, and subunit models now are likely to receive more serious consideration.

PROPERTIES OF MEMBRANES

Properties attributable to lipid components. At the end of the 19th century it was postulated that lipids were located at the cell surface. This assumption was based on studies of the penetration into cells of compounds known to be readily dissolved in lipid materials. Extension of these studies established a close correlation between the lipid solubility of substances and their ability to penetrate the plasma membrane. On the other hand, a negative correlation could be established between the ability of substances to form hydrogen bonds (secondary associations involving hydrogen atoms) with suitable materials and their ability to penetrate the cell membrane. Lipid materials generally do not form hydrogen bonds. Thus, although lipids are no longer considered to form the surface of the cell membrane, they do nonetheless appear to be involved in the process that admits or excludes materials from the cell.

Largely because of the lipid component of the cell membrane, its electrical resistance is high. The electrical resistance may be lowered by special substances, for instance, certain antibiotics and detergents. The antibiotics are known to interact with cholesterol and possibly with other membrane components. The detergents generally appear to weaken protein–lipid interactions.

Properties attributable to protein components. Even after almost all lipids have been removed from mitochondrial membranes, the membranes do not collapse. It has been assumed, therefore, that protein bridges cross the lipid core to connect the outer and inner protein layers and maintain the membrane structure with or without the lipid materials.

The physical properties of the cell surface appear to be due largely to the effect of the membrane proteins. The surface tension of cells suspended in an aqueous medium, for example, is very low compared to the tension of a water–air or of a water–oil interface. Since the adsorption of proteins onto oil droplets considerably decreases the surface tension, it was initially concluded that a lipid layer covered by proteins would best account for the low surface tension of the cell membrane. But this conclusion does not take into consideration the fact that for a double layer of lipids only the difference between two opposing surface tensions is measured; this should be much lower than that of any single layer measured separately, and therefore the introduction of protein to explain the result may not be necessary. A bimolecular layer of pure lipid, however, cannot account for the structural elasticity of the cell surface. The presence of an elastic protein in this region is considered the likely explanation.

Surface tension and elasticity

Membranes, especially the plasma membrane, incorporate various specific proteins, such as enzymes and antibodies, that play active and specific roles in the functioning of the cell. The enzyme pattern of the cell membrane varies greatly from cell type to cell type. Proteins at the surface of cell membranes also are believed to be involved in the transport across the membrane of specific chemical substances, such as amino acids, sugars, and ions of various kinds. Partial disruption of the cell membrane leads to the separation of specific "binding" proteins that manifest the properties expected of such transport materials.

Various glycolipids and glycoproteins seem to be located at the cell surface. This is known to be true of the blood-group substances, specific materials that are responsible for the existence of the various blood types. Similar substances can be isolated from bacteria. As shown by immunological techniques, plasma membranes of rat liver cells have a structural pattern different from that of other membranes within the same cell, and also from the plasma membranes of liver cells of other animal species.

Electrical properties. Most, possibly all, membranes of living cells manifest a difference in electrical potential between the two sides of the membrane. With suitable electrodes a fairly constant electrical current can be drawn from such membranes. The electrical activity of biological membranes clearly depends upon active metabolism in the cell, because it disappears upon chemical inhibition of metabolism and after the death of the cells. Electrical activity also appears to be associated closely, either directly or indirectly, with the active transport of ions, such as sodium and potassium, across the membrane.

Potential difference across the cell membrane

There are two ways in which an electromotive force might be produced in a biological membrane: (1) by the maintenance of an unequal distribution of one or more ions on the two sides of the membrane, or (2) by the action of a so-called ion pump, which moves a single ion type directly across the membrane. Some insight into the first possibility has been obtained from observations with artificial membranes, such as collodion, or cellophane, separating two solutions of the same salt, at varying concentrations. Such studies show that a difference in electrical potential between the two sides of the membrane will appear if the concentration of the salt on both sides of the membrane is unequal and if the membrane is preferentially permeable (selectively permeable) to either positively charged ions (cations) or negatively charged ions (anions).

The electrical potentials associated with many biological

membranes can be partly accounted for by the maintenance of unequal distributions of ions and by the selectively permeable nature of the particular membrane. Since biological membranes are not "ideally" selectively permeable, this kind of potential difference is a nonequilibrium condition; *i.e.*, it will tend to cancel, unless the unequal ion distribution is maintained by the metabolic activity of the cell. Thus the electrical potential disappears upon metabolic inhibition.

Figure 3 shows the relationship between potassium ions (K^+) and sodium ions (Na^+) on either side of a semipermeable membrane, such as occurs in cells, in a resting state. It can be seen that potassium ions have a greater tendency to diffuse outward through the membrane (top channel with arrow directed to the exterior—to the left). Sodium ions, however, tend to diffuse inward through the membrane (bottom channel with arrow directed to the interior—to the right). The steepness of the sodium-ion channel, from exterior to interior, indicates the relative ease with which sodium ions would pass inward through the membrane in the absence of the Na^+-K^+ pump, whose directional nature is shown by the arrows in the circle. The mechanism of operation of the pump is indicated by the arrows in the channels directly above the pump (for potassium) and below it (for sodium). Thus, the pump, which requires metabolic energy to function, actively pumps the inward-diffusing sodium outward and, by pumping some potassium inward, helps to maintain a relatively constant interior potassium-ion concentration. This concentration is responsible for the so-called resting potential of cell membranes. (The widths of the channels indicate the relative quantities of ions passing through the membrane either by diffusion or by the operation of the pump.)

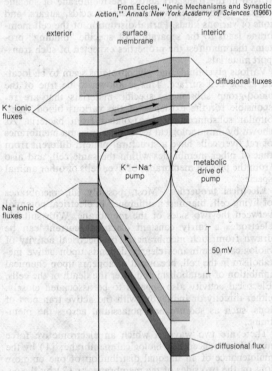

From Eccles, "Ionic Mechanisms and Synaptic Action," *Annals New York Academy of Sciences* (1966)

exterior   surface   interior
             membrane

diffusional fluxes

K^+ ionic fluxes

K^+-Na^+ pump   metabolic drive of pump

Na^+ ionic fluxes

50 mV

diffusional flux

Figure 3: Potassium (K^+) and sodium (Na^+) fluxes through the surface membrane in the resting state (see text).

In biological systems special potential differences occur because of an unequal distribution of the proteins, which as a rule are polyanions unable to penetrate the cellular membranes. These potential differences also contribute to the overall potential difference measured between the intercellular fluid and the external medium. They often persist after metabolic inhibition or death. Their contribution to the overall potential difference, however, is small compared to the previously mentioned potential differences.

In addition to the potential differences mentioned above, which primarily depend on the unequal distribution of ions, an electrical potential difference also may be directly produced by the active transport of a single ion type, even in the absence of unequal distribution of ions. Such an ion pump is unidirectional; *i.e.*, it pumps only one ion species in one direction. This is different from the exchange of ions associated with the maintenance of the unequal distribution. The potential difference produced by an ion pump in a membrane between identical electrolyte solutions depends on the power of the pump to move ions and on the general ability of the membrane to carry ions of all types.

Generally it is difficult to decide whether a potential difference observed in a biological membrane is due to the combined effect of an unequal distribution of ions and a selectively permeable membrane, or to the operation of a unidirectional ion pump.

Functions of membranes

COMPARTMENTALIZATION OF CELLS

Cells contain various internal structures, or organelles, each of which is enclosed by a membrane. Functionally, these organelles are separate metabolic compartments, specialized to carry out distinct sequences of enzyme-catalyzed reactions. They are protected from one another's enzymatic activities, and those of the ground substance of the cell, by membranes of limited permeability.

A compartmentalization of the cell seems to be required for many cellular functions, including uptake and conversion of nutrients, synthesis of new molecules, production of energy, and regulation and coordination of metabolic sequences. The subcellular particles generally are visible in the electron microscope after appropriate treatment of the cell. The best known of these particles are: (1) the nucleus, (2) the mitochondria, (3) the lysosomes, and (4) the microbodies. (Each of these is discussed briefly below.) Bacterial cells lack some of these organelles; *e.g.*, the nucleus and the mitochondria. Recently, however, other highly organized membrane structures, the mesosomes, have been detected in bacteria; their metabolic functions are not yet known.

The nucleus. Because the nucleus of the cell has the highest specific density of all subcellular particles, it can be isolated easily by differential centrifugation (a separation method based on spinning a solution in a centrifuge). The nucleus may occupy anywhere from 10 percent to nearly 100 percent of the total volume of the cell. It contains the genetic material of the cell, or DNA (deoxyribonucleic acid), as well as the associated basic proteins, glycolytic enzymes, and several varieties of cation. The nucleus is surrounded by a double membrane, the outer layer of which is connected with the membranes of the endoplasmic reticulum (the membrane material that traverses the cytoplasm of the cell). The nuclear membrane disappears during cell division. It apparently does not represent a real barrier to most of the cellular and nuclear substances; pores as large as 500 angstroms in diameter have been observed in this membrane, but the size varies with the condition of the cell. Thus, the interior of the nucleus is in complete communication with the cytoplasm during cell division (when the nuclear membrane is gone) and partially so at other times (by way of pores in the membrane).

Mitochondria. Mitochondria are constituents of most cells that undergo respiration (oxygen uptake). They are enclosed by an outer membrane; the interior contains two compartments, a granular matrix, which is surrounded by a folded membrane (the inner membrane) and an intermembrane space or outer compartment. In mitochondria, many substances are oxidized, and adenosine triphosphate (ATP), the energy-storing chemical of the cell, is produced. These biochemical functions are carried out chiefly by enzyme complexes situated in (or in close association with) the mitochondrial membranes. The outer membrane is readily permeable to substances of low molecular weight, with the result that the outer compartment is in equilibrium with the cytoplasm with respect to these substances. Evidence has been presented that distinct

Organelles

Compartmentalization

translocating systems for ions and metabolites (biochemical transformation products) are constituents of the inner membrane. The compartment enclosed by this membrane contains all the enzymes responsible for the energy-producing metabolic transformations associated with cellular oxidation processes. It is evident that the high efficiency of the energy-generating enzyme complexes is made possible by the special organization of the inner mitochondrial membrane.

Lysosomes. A distinct variety of subcellular organelles in the cells of various tissues, because it serves a degradative function, has been given the designation lysosome (Greek: *lysis*, dissolve; *sōma*, body). These particles contain enzymes that are able to degrade nearly all cellular macromolecules, such as nucleic acids, proteins, and polysaccharides. That lysosomes are not structurally uniform is indicated by the fact that they sediment at different rates in an ultracentrifuge (a device that separates materials on the basis of their weight and shape). Each lysosome is surrounded by a single membrane of low permeability, which protects the other cellular material from the degrading enzymes of the lysosomes. Lysosomes play a role in the decomposition of cell components after the death of the cell (autolysis), and they are also involved in the degradation of small particles that have been taken up by pinocytosis (see below *Pinocytosis*).

Microbodies. Another group of membranous subcellular particles has been isolated from mammalian cells and named microbodies or peroxysomes. These particles are minute spheres composed of a granular matrix enclosed by a single membrane. Peroxysomes are characterized by their content of a series of enzymes that produce hydrogen peroxide, as well as the enzyme catalase, which splits the peroxide produced by the other enzymes to give oxygen and water. The peroxysomes obtained from animal liver or kidney cells are closely related to similar particles isolated from protozoans, yeasts, and plant cells. They all have similar sedimentation constants and similar structures. They also contain, as a rule, catalase and other enzymes. In some cases, microbodies contain enzymes of the glyoxylic acid cycle, which plays an important role in cellular metabolism. Hence the name glyoxysome also has been proposed for this group of organelles.

MOVEMENT OF WATER ACROSS CELL MEMBRANES

All biological membranes appear to be permeable to water, but permeability varies widely among different membranes. The flow of water across biological membranes, as compared to the flow of dissolved materials (solutes), shows certain peculiarities that result from the continuous and semicrystalline arrangement of the water molecules. In dilute solutions, the solute particles are far enough apart not to influence each other's movements. Consequently, their behaviour follows the laws that govern the behaviour of gas molecules in free space. In contrast, the molecules of water form a continuum, each molecule remaining in immediate contact with its neighbours in a semicrystalline lattice. Though this lattice tolerates distortions and rearrangements, contact between the molecules is always maintained. At the boundary with air, vacuum, or other, immiscible liquids, single water molecules may leave the continuum to pass into the contiguous phase. Hence water may penetrate a membrane in two different ways: (1) as a continuum, by bulk flow, or (2) as a solute—that is, molecule by molecule, by diffusional flow. Diffusional flow occurs if water molecules pass across a lipid membrane or into a gaseous phase. Bulk flow, on the other hand, predominates if water moves through pores or through a membrane made of material easily penetrated by water. Diffusional flow is very slow as compared to bulk flow. Across artificial nonlipid membranes, such as collodion or cellophane membranes, water has been shown to move almost exclusively by bulk flow, no matter what drives it across the membrane. Across purely lipid membranes, which presumably lack pores, bulk flow should not occur at all. Across biological membranes, which consist of both lipid and, possibly porous, nonlipid material, both bulk and

Bulk flow and diffusional flow

diffusional flow are believed to occur in parallel. Bulk flow may be considerably influenced by interaction with solutes, owing chiefly to frictional forces between the flowing water and the solute molecules. Accordingly, water passing through narrow pores will tend to drag solute molecules along with it, and the flow of water may be slowed down if the solute particles penetrate the pores less readily because of their size or electric charge. Conversely, solutes diffusing through narrow pores will tend to carry water with them in the direction opposite to that in which it would normally move.

The flow of water across the cell membrane is determined by two factors: the osmotic pressure and the hydrostatic pressure. The former is an effect brought about by different concentrations of dissolved substances on the two sides of the membrane. In effect, this results from the replacement of water molecules by solute molecules on the side of the membrane with the more concentrated solution. The flow of water across the membrane acts to neutralize this concentration difference. The flow of water also is proportional to the difference between the hydrostatic pressure on the two membrane sides. In this respect, the behaviour of water differs from that of solutes, since the immediate influence of a hydrostatic pressure difference on the diffusion of solutes is negligible. The two driving forces, the osmotic and the hydrostatic pressure differences, are additive, so that the movement of water between two solutions of the same solute across a membrane is almost proportional to the sum of the two effects.

Osmotic and hydrostatic pressure

The modification of the water flow due to interaction with the flow of solute depends on the permeability of the membrane for the solute. This may be illustrated for some extreme cases by a simplified model, consisting of two solutions of the same solute separated by a membrane. In a highly selective, so-called semipermeable membrane, which permits the passage of water, but not that of any solute present, the flow of water, which cannot interact with any solute flow, is proportional simply to the sum of the hydrostatic and osmotic effects. A directly opposite situation would be represented by a coarse membrane, which owing to the width of its pores lets all solutes penetrate as easily as water. In this case no osmotic pressure difference would develop and any volume flow of water would have to be attributed to the hydrostatic pressure difference only. More interesting and relevant are the intermediate cases, represented by selectively permeable or "leaky" membranes. These are permeable to solutes but less so than to water; consequently, frictional forces between water and solute within the pores will greatly alter the rate of movement of both. Thus, the osmotic pressure difference, which will steadily decrease, can at no time exert its full effect in these cases. The effect of leaky membranes may be different for different solutes, because the same membrane may be more permeable to one solute than to another. The concept of selective permeability is especially important in the study of biological membranes.

MOVEMENT OF SOLUTES THROUGH MEMBRANES
IN RESPONSE TO A CONCENTRATION GRADIENT

Methods of studying permeability. The rate of uptake of solutes by a cell or a cellular tissue is usually obtained either from the rate of disappearance of the solute in the medium, or from the rate of its appearance in the cellular mass. The exit of solutes from cells is studied in an analogous way—that is, by the rate of their appearance in the medium, or the rate of their disappearance from the cell. In special cases the entry of solutes is measured indirectly by the changes in the cell volume brought about as water follows the solute by osmosis. Most of the methods do not tell reliably whether the substance has truly entered the cells or whether it is adsorbed to the cellular surface. Adsorption may be significant with very large molecules, like those of certain dyes, but not with such small molecules as inorganic ions, sugars, and amino acids (as has been shown by fluorescence and studies with radioactive isotopes). If these substances disappear from the medium or appear in the cellular mass, it usually can be taken for granted that they have entered the cell. Measuring the disappearance from the medium has the disadvantage that the medium is often of greater volume than the cellular mass, so that changes in concentration of the solute there may be small. On the other hand, the rate of appearance of a solute inside the cell may be misleading if the solute is metabolized or otherwise altered inside the cell. In special cases, however, if the reaction is rapid enough and the product can be measured easily, the alteration may be useful as an indirect determination of the rate of entry of the original material. For example, the rate of entry of sugar into muscle cells can be estimated satisfactorily by the appearance of the transformation product, lactic acid.

Theoretically, the rate of uptake should be referred to the total cellular surface area. The assessment of this surface area, however, is very difficult, especially if, for example, the cellular shape is not spherical. For this reason, the rate of penetration is usually related either to volume of water in the cells or their dry weight. Relating it to the cellular water volume may be ambiguous, because the water content of a cell can change during the penetration of the solute. If such volume changes are not taken into account, the true entry (or exit) rates may be greatly obscured. Its relation to cellular dry weight, therefore, often is more meaningful than its relation to cellular water. The dry weight presumably stays constant during the experiment and also may have a constant relation to the total cellular area or to the total number of transport sites or permeability channels in the cell membranes.

The rate at which a solute enters or leaves a cell is called a flux (influx and efflux, respectively). It is important to distinguish between net, or overall, flux and unidirectional flux, either influx or efflux. The net flux is the total observed shift of a given solute from the extracellular into the intracellular compartments, or *vice versa*. Unidirectional fluxes, of a given substance, can be measured only by the use of radioactive isotopes that behave just as the ordinary atoms of an element do, but are easily detected because of their radioactivity. The movement of molecules carrying such atoms (called labelled molecules) can be followed by means of the radioactivity. The difference between influx and efflux, as determined by labelling experiments, must be equal to the net flux as measured by chemical means. Knowledge of unidirectional fluxes may be helpful, for instance, in testing for active transport (see below). Furthermore, the unidirectional fluxes may reveal special phenomena, which may give relevant information concerning the mechanism by which transport occurs (see below *Facilitated diffusion* and *Exchange diffusion*). Unidirectional fluxes may be determined even in the absence of net transport—for example, when the rates of influx and efflux are exactly in balance.

To study the transport rates, or kinetics, of rapidly penetrating substances, the time allowed for transport to occur must be short and sharply terminated, circumstances that can be provided, for instance, by separating the cells rapidly from the extracellular medium. To carry out such separations in a short enough period compared to the incubation time is often very difficult, if not impossible. Many bacteria, because of their stiff walls, can be filtered through membrane filters and subsequently washed. In such cases separation between cells and incubation medium is complete in a few seconds. Many mammalian cells, however, cannot be filtered and, therefore, must be centrifuged, a procedure that may take a minute or more. The transport experiment usually is terminated by the sudden cooling of the incubated cells or by the addition of certain chemicals, usually mercury salts, that supposedly stop all transport. Other methods to allow a more rapid termination of the experiments and hence shorter incubation times are under development.

The problems just mentioned refer chiefly to suspensions of cells, such as red blood cells, or bacteria. Other problems arise if whole tissue or tissue fragments are studied. Such tissue always contains some extracellular space, enclosed within the tissue but actually between the cells. In order to determine the exact cellular content of the tissue, the fraction of the trapped extracellular space must be precisely determined. This can be done with the help of materials that do not penetrate the cell, such as iodinated proteins or certain higher polysaccharides (complex sugars). Determining the concentration of such substances in the tissue mass and assuming that their concentration in the trapped extracellular space equals that in the external medium makes it possible to estimate the size of the trapped extracellular space.

Factors that influence permeability. The permeability of the plasma membrane to various solutes ranges widely, from extremely high permeability to complete impermeability. It often is difficult to state a reliable correlation between the permeability and the chemical and physical properties of the solute. Usually, however, lipid-soluble substances penetrate cellular membranes easily. The rate at which these substances move through the membrane seems to be directly related to their solubility in lipids relative to that in water (partition coefficient) and to their molecular size. For many water-soluble substances the penetration seems to depend greatly on the molecular weight and, in the case of ions, on the number of electrical charges per ion. For neutral substances the ease of penetration decreases with increasing molecular size. It is assumed, therefore, that water-soluble substances (neutral and ionic) penetrate the cellular membrane through charged pores of an appropriate size. Very often there is a sharp limit of molecular size, above which solutes are quite unable to penetrate the cellular membrane. Water-soluble organic compounds containing more than three to five carbon atoms, for example, seem to be unable to penetrate the membrane of the red cell. On the basis of these results, it would seem that there are two major channels for passive penetration of cell membranes, one through the lipid part of the membrane (used by lipid-soluble substrates) and the other across preformed pores (used by water-soluble substances). There is, however, a great number of organic compounds to which the above rules do not apply; *e.g.*, many substances of physiological importance, such as sugars, amino acids, nucleotides, and other materials. These substances are not soluble in lipids, and their size exceeds by far the limit of permeability mentioned above. For these and other reasons, it is generally assumed that such compounds penetrate the plasma membrane by special transport mechanisms.

As a rule, the presence of more than one electrical charge per molecule seems to hinder penetration; hence polyvalent ions, such as calcium ions and sulfate ions, appear to penetrate cells very slowly, if at all. With monovalent ions, oppositely charged particles often behave very differently. It is well established, for instance, that the red-blood-cell membrane is selectively permeable for anions, but not cations. Small anions, such as chloride and bicarbonate, penetrate the membrane about a million times faster than cations of similar size. The ability of the membrane to discriminate between positively and negatively charged solutes is reportedly due to the presence of fixed positive charges inside the membrane, perhaps on the surfaces of water-filled pores. Such regions of high positive-charge density could act as barriers to cations but, at the same time, could favour the penetration of anions. The positive charges in membranes could result from the attachment of protons (positively charged hydrogen ions) to basic amino-acid residues in membrane proteins. As a consequence of the presence of fixed charges, equilibria will be established between the membrane proteins and the suspension fluid. Because of these equilibria, it might be expected that the passage of anions through the red-cell membrane would be highly dependent upon the acidity and the ionic strength of the suspending medium. In fact, the flux of the sulfate ion has been shown to increase as the hydrogen-ion concentration in the medium is increased, as could be expected on the basis of the expected equilibrium.

Facilitated diffusion. As has been mentioned, certain substances, including sugars and amino acids, easily penetrate the plasma membrane of many, or all, cells, although they are neither soluble in lipids nor small enough to penetrate the membrane pores. It is therefore assumed that the transport of these substances across the plasma membrane is brought about by a special mechanism. This mechanism, called facilitated diffusion, has the following characteristics not found in free diffusion:

1. It can be saturated; *i.e.*, the rate of penetration does not increase with the concentration difference but tends toward a maximum value, which cannot be exceeded by a further increase of the concentration gradients. In other words, the mechanism behaves as if the membrane had only a limited number of transport sites which, once occupied, cannot accommodate other molecules.

2. It is subject to competitive inhibition; *i.e.*, closely related molecules seem to compete with each other for the available sites, because the transport rate of any one substance is depressed in the presence of the other.

3. It shows a considerable degree of specificity; *i.e.*, a limited number of compounds are "recognized" and admitted, and others are rejected. This selection is not on the basis of gross chemical or physical properties, because molecules that greatly resemble one another may be treated quite differently. For instance, D-glucose (a common sugar) readily enters red blood and muscle cells, whereas its isomer, L-glucose, which is hardly distinguishable from it by chemical or physical means, enters these cells hardly, if at all.

4. Some systems of facilitated diffusion undergo the peculiar phenomenon of counterflow or countertransport. In this phenomenon, the movement of a certain substance across the membrane is accelerated by the presence of a closely related substance on the other side of the membrane. Such behaviour has been shown by amino acids and sugars in various cells. Often a compound that competitively inhibits the transport of another compound when it is on the same side of the membrane may enhance it when it is on the other side.

All these characteristics, or at least the first three, are very similar to those of enzymatic reactions and are best explained in terms of a carrier substance, which combines with the transported substrate on the one side of the membrane, carries it through the membrane, and delivers it on the other side. Nearly all observations that have been made are compatible with this concept. But only speculations as to the nature of such a carrier are possible. The fact that it enables a substance to penetrate a lipid membrane has led some authors to believe that any such carrier is of a lipid nature. On the other hand, the high degree of specificity toward the transportable substance can only be accounted for by a protein, because only a protein molecule could show the required specificity of shape that would permit it to function as required. Many investigations assume that such a carrier must be a lipoprotein.

Exchange diffusion. Exchange diffusion may be considered a special case of facilitated diffusion with the additional feature that the solute molecule penetrates the membrane only in exchange for another molecule, either of the same species (homoexchange) or of a different but closely related one (heteroexchange). The second molecules cross the membrane in a direction opposite to that of the first. Obviously homoexchange does not permit net transport of the solute concerned; it can be detected, therefore, only by isotopic labelling of the solute on one side of the membrane. Exchange diffusion is not to be confused with electrostatic exchange, in which one ion species cannot penetrate a membrane for electrostatic reasons, unless another charged particle of the same charge moves in the opposite direction. Electrostatic exchange is unspecific, whereas true exchange diffusion shows a high degree of specificity with respect to both exchange partners.

Pure exchange diffusion is rare. A typical example is the penetration of phosphate ions into the cells of staphylococci, a process that requires exchange by another phosphate ion or, specifically, the similar arsenate ion. More frequently, there occurs a so-called partial exchange diffusion, in which a solute can penetrate without an exchange partner but does so much more readily in the

presence of one. Such instances are found in the transport of sugars and amino acids into various cells. Partial exchange diffusion can lead to the temporary movement of one solute from a volume of low concentration into one of high concentration but such a concentration gradient of the other solute must be present, if the process is to occur at all.

Exchange diffusion is usually interpreted in terms of a carrier substance, which is mobile only when it carries a solute molecule (and, therefore, immobile in the empty form). In explanation, it can be hypothesized that the unloaded carrier is loosely bound to some membrane constituent, and is released upon the attachment of a solute molecule. In partial exchange diffusion the unloaded carrier is thought to be not entirely immobile, merely less mobile than the loaded one.

Comparison of permeability properties of different kinds of cells. The permeability properties of biological membranes vary widely among the different classes of cells and tissues, but many features seem common to the membranes of all cells. The variations may be due partly to differences between membranes with respect to their basic structure—for example, size of pores, presence or absence of fixed electrical charges, and the nature of the lipid components. Other differences may concern the presence or activity of special transport systems. As mentioned above, the red-cell membrane is almost impermeable to cations but highly permeable to anions. For certain cancer cells the opposite is true. These differences are attributed to fixed electrical charges of the membrane. Within the same organism variations among the membranes of various cells also are observed; for example, liver cells supposedly are far more permeable to almost all solutes than are other cells. The activity of the different transport systems may change during the development of a given cell. The red cell, for instance, loses some of its transport systems for amino acids during maturation. During cell division, membrane permeability also changes. In addition, it would appear that a normal cell becomes more permeable to certain amino acids, and possibly other solutes, after infection with cancer-producing virus. Many transport systems in various cells also can be controlled by hormones, metabolites, and other physiological substances, as has already been mentioned.

The permeability pattern of the membranes of subcellular organelles greatly differs from that of the plasma membrane of the same cell. For instance, the mitochondrial membrane is impermeable to chloride ions, but permeable to phosphate ions and to the coenzyme adenosine triphosphate, whereas the opposite is true for the cellular membrane. Furthermore, the mitochondria and also the sarcoplasmic reticulum of muscle cells are able to transport calcium ions (the former one in exchange for hydrogen ions), whereas the plasma membrane is practically impermeable to calcium ions.

MOVEMENT OF SOLUTES INDEPENDENT OF CONCENTRATION GRADIENTS: ACTIVE TRANSPORT

Requirements. Transport of a solute across a membrane is called active if it occurs "uphill"—that is, against a concentration gradient and if the solute is electrically charged (ionic), against an electric field. In chemical terms "uphill" means from a lower to a higher thermodynamic potential—that is, from a system of lower energy to one of higher content. The true significance of active transport, then, is that it occurs in seeming violation of simple chemical and physical laws; it is a process made possible only by the active participation of processes occurring within the cell.

The difference in the thermodynamic potential of a solute on two sides of a membrane (a comparison that makes it possible to judge whether transport processes are active or passive) is the sum of a chemical and an electrical term and, therefore, is also called the electrochemical potential difference. The chemical term contributing to the electrochemical potential difference is given by multiplying a constant factor (the gas constant) by the absolute temperature and by the natural logarithm of the ratio of the concentrations of the solute on the two sides of the

Partial exchange diffusion

"Uphill" transport

membrane. The electrical term is equal to another constant (the Faraday constant) multiplied by the electrical potential difference across the membrane. In equation form, these relationships are written as:

$$\Delta\mu = RT \ln (C_2/C_1) + FE,$$

in which $\Delta\mu$ is the electrochemical potential difference (the Greek letter delta, Δ, indicating difference, and the Greek letter mu, μ, representing potential); R is the gas constant; T, the absolute temperature; ln indicates natural logarithm; C_1 and C_2 are the concentrations of solute on the two sides of the membrane; F is the Faraday constant; and E is the electrical potential difference across the membrane.

If the electrochemical potential difference ($\Delta\mu$) is positive, the flow of the solute in the direction from side one to side two is uphill, or, by definition, active. This is so because an additional driving force not expressed in the equation, but greater than the electrochemical potential difference, must be present to enforce the uphill flow of the solute. If the electrochemical potential difference is negative, the flow of solute is "downhill" and may be passive. Active transport would, however, not be excluded, for an active force could still be present, and, according as it is directed parallel to, or against, the electrochemical potential difference, accelerate or retard the flow. One way to test for the presence of such a force would be to vary the electrochemical potential difference arbitrarily and see whether uphill transport does occur. If such variations are not feasible, the ratio of unidirectional fluxes may be determined and related to the electrochemical potential difference. To do this, however, the influx and efflux must be determined separately using different radioactive isotopes. Fortunately, in biological transport, this problem rarely arises since the question usually is whether a clear difference in concentration or in electrochemical potential of a given solute is, or is not, due to active transport.

In true active transport the necessary energy to drive the process uphill is derived directly or indirectly from a chemical reaction of cellular metabolism, most likely from the splitting of energy-rich compounds (such as ATP). Accordingly, active transport should have an additional criterion, namely the dependence of the transport rate, or of the accumulation of solute on one side of the membrane, on metabolism. This dependence usually is tested by withholding oxygen (anoxia) or cellular nutrients from the cells, or by adding metabolic inhibitors. To the extent that transport or accumulation is independent of metabolism, active transport can be excluded. Dependence on metabolism, on the other hand, suggests, but does not prove, active transport.

Dependence on metabolism

It follows from the foregoing that active transport involves an energetic coupling between the movement of the solute and a chemical reaction. In some systems this coupling between the two processes appears to be direct. In that case the active transport is said to be "primary." On the other hand, there are systems of active transport in which the coupling is indirect, the uphill transport being driven not immediately by metabolism but by the gradient of another solute. In these cases, the actively accumulated solute is, in effect, dragged along with the downhill movement of the other solute. In this case the active transport is said to be "secondary." A typical example of secondary active transport is the accumulation of amino acids and sugars in animal cells, a process that requires that the electrochemical potential difference ($\Delta\mu$) of sodium ions is higher outside the cell than inside. In order to maintain this relationship sodium ions must be actively extruded from the cells by the so-called sodium-ion pump, a metabolic process leading to transfer of sodium ions across the membrane. Hence, secondary active transport ultimately also depends on metabolism, unless the appropriate electrolyte gradient is artificially maintained.

The kinetics of active transport closely resembles that of facilitated diffusion (see above) except for the capability of uphill movement (pumping). Both systems show saturation kinetics, competitive inhibition, specificity toward the transported substrate, and, in some cases, countertransport phenomena. Each may be considered a special case of a more general process called "mediated transport."

Substances transported. Active transport of inorganic and organic solutes occurs in all living cells and tissues. It may serve several purposes, one of them being to maintain a constant composition of solutes inside the cell (homocellular transport). This may be achieved by replacing solutes lost by metabolism and leakage, or by removing solutes entering the cell in excess. A typical example is the maintenance of a high level of potassium ions and a low level of sodium ions inside the cell. Another purpose of active transport is to move large amounts of certain solutes through cellular layers, as in reabsorption and excretion (transcellular transport) by the epithelial layers of the intestine, the kidney tubules, and the various secretory glands. Both homocellular and transcellular transport are believed to operate according to the same general principles, because in either case the essential process takes place in the cellular membrane. In transcellular transport, however, unlike homocellular transport, the transporting cell membrane must be "polar"; that is, the transport capacities in one region of the membrane must be different from those in different regions of the membrane. For example, the epithelial cell of the intestine seems to reabsorb sugars or amino acid actively only at the part of the cell next to the space through which the food moves (lumen), whereas the movement of these solutes across the part of the cell membrane facing the body interior (serosa) seems to be passive, following the concentration gradient. For the active extrusion of sodium ions the opposite behaviour seems to be the case, the active pump being isolated only in the serosal border, whereas across the luminal border sodium ion enters passively. In essence, then, transcellular transport also is homocellular.

Homocellular and transcellular transport

Sodium and potassium ions.   One of the longest known and most extensively studied transport systems is the sodium-ion–potassium-ion pump, which accounts for the homocellular transport of potassium ions into, and sodium ions out of, the cell. This pump is present in all cells of animals, plants, and micro-organisms, in which it maintains the typical distribution of these ions: high cellular potassium; low cellular sodium. Even in the few apparent exceptions, such as the red blood cells of some animal species, which have a higher level of sodium ions than of potassium ions, the sodium-ion–potassium-ion pump is present, only it is much less effective than in other cells.

The uptake of potassium ions seems to be linked with the extrusion of sodium ions, but the nature of the linkage is not completely understood. Accordingly, the uptake of potassium ions is greatly enhanced by an increase in intracellular sodium ions, and the extrusion of sodium ions by an increase in extracellular potassium ions. It has been assumed that a single pump is responsible for both movements, a so-called exchange pump. To the extent that this pump exchanges one potassium ion for one sodium ion, it does not cause a net shift of electric charges. Some authors postulate two separate pumps, which are linked to each other in an unknown way. In some cells, such as those of muscle and nerve tissue, a potassium-ion pump need not be postulated, since the accumulation of potassium ions is almost entirely accounted for by the electric potential difference as measured across the cell membrane. This potential difference would then have to be attributed to a sodium-ion pump. In other words, the electrochemical potential of potassium is about equal on both sides of the membrane. This does not entirely rule out a potassium-ion pump or a sodium-ion–potassium-ion exchange pump. In this case, however, active potassium-ion transport, if it occurs, is abortive, for it does not show any effects.

Sodium-ion and potassium-ion pumps

Perhaps the passive permeability of the muscle-cell membrane to the potassium ion is so great as to prohibit any sizable electrochemical potential difference for potassium ions to be established. In other cell types, such as red cells, cancer cells, and others, the assumption of active transport of both potassium and sodium ions seems inescapable.

Transcellular transport of sodium ions occurs in the reabsorption of this ion by the intestine and by the kidney tubules. As has already been mentioned, the transcellular transport of sodium ions seems essential for the net movement of water across tissue membranes of animals. In animal cells, the same pump mechanism seems to be involved in homocellular distribution of both sodium and potassium ions as well as for the net transport of sodium ions, potassium ions, and water in the intestine and the kidneys.

As to the energy requirements of the sodium-ion–potassium-ion pump, a direct coupling with metabolism is suggested by considerable evidence. In all cellular material containing membranes with sodium-ion pumps so far investigated, an enzyme has been found that splits ATP into ADP (adenosine diphosphate) and inorganic phosphate, thus catalyzing the reaction generally assumed to supply energy for transport. The behaviour of this enzyme has many features in common with the transport of sodium and potassium ions; it is activated, for instance, by sodium and potassium ions, and it is inhibited by certain substances such as digitalis and strophanthin. It is therefore assumed that this enzyme, the so-called transport adenosine triphosphatase, is an essential component of the transport systems concerned, or of their coupling to metabolism. Although details of the molecular mechanism of the enzyme reaction have been elucidated, the nature of its connection with the transport process itself is still a matter of controversy. Some investigators believe that the enzyme itself is the carrier of sodium ions, but this opinion is not shared by all workers in the field.

Other inorganic ions. By contrast to the transport of sodium and potassium ions, that of other ions is quantitatively less conspicuous and mostly restricted to special tissues or cells. An active transport of magnesium and sulfate ions in many cells is considered likely in view of the high concentration of these ions in most cells, but this has not been proven. Nor is it known why calcium ions have a much lower concentration in most cells than in the extracellular fluid. That the ions magnesium, sulfate, and calcium, because of their double electric charge, penetrate cellular membranes less readily than do singly charged ions, such as sodium and potassium ions, may be of importance, but the calcium ion seems indisputably transported actively during its reabsorption from the intestine. This transport seems to be promoted by vitamin D, but this vitamin seems to act by an indirect and obscure mechanism. Of special physiological importance is the active transport of calcium ion in subcellular particles, such as mitochondria and the endoplasmic reticulum (see above). The latter system of fine tubular vesicles within muscle cells is able to accumulate calcium ions from the cytoplasm, thereby causing relaxation of the muscles. Conversely, during muscle contraction, calcium is released from these vesicles, and the resulting rise in cytoplasmic level of calcium seems to initiate the contraction of muscular protein. Here also a special enzyme, an adenosine triphosphatase activated by calcium ions, appears to be involved.

Active transport of hydrogen ions (protons) is involved in the formation of acidic fluids, such as gastric juice and urine. The active transport of hydrogen ions in the gastric mucosa is extremely powerful. The power of gastric acid secretion is very high, of the same order as that of the heart muscle in its most active state. The acidification of the urine is very important for the maintenance of the acid–base balance in the organism—*e.g.*, during excessive acid formation.

Transport of anions

Transport of anions (negatively charged ions) is less frequent in animal cells than is cation (positively charged ion) transfer. Chloride ion, however, is actively transported by stomach cells in connection with the formation of gastric acid. It also seems to occur in the cornea of the eye, and possibly in other tissues. Active transport of sulfate ion is found in certain bacteria, such as *Salmonella typhimurium*, in which the sulfate ion serves as a precursor for the synthesis of sulfur-containing amino

acids. Anion transport seems to have a paramount transport function in the absorption of water by plant roots. In this case, nitrate ions are thought to be the predominant ions. While nitrate ions are being absorbed by the surrounding fluid into the inner parts of the root, water also moves there, following an osmotic gradient between the root sap and the extracellular fluid. Very high hydrostatic pressures within the root can be produced in this way and may cause the flow of water from the roots to the upper parts of the plant. The transport of nitrate ions, and other anions, is closely connected with the respiration of the root (anion respiration). This is in accord with the assumption that the transport of these ions, depending on energy supply, is linked to cellular metabolism.

Organic substances. In addition to inorganic ions, various organic solutes are actively transported by many cells and tissues. Sugars, however, usually enter mammalian cells, such as muscle cells and red blood cells, merely by facilitated diffusion. Only in the intestine and in the kidney tubule does active accumulation of sugar occur, probably driven by a sodium-ion concentration gradient, as has been mentioned above. Various amino acids are accumulated by single cells, as well as by the intestinal mucosa and by the kidney tubules. The mechanism in all cases seems to be based on the same principle. Apparently there are different systems of amino-acid transport, with differing—but overlapping—specificities. This transport is also, at least in part, driven by a sodium gradient. Various other organic solutes, such as nucleotides, also seem to be accumulated by cells by the intestine, or by the kidney tubules. Knowledge of the properties of such transport processes is very scanty.

Transport of organic solutes

Mechanisms of active transport. The mechanism of active transport has not been elucidated. The most common view is that a mobile carrier is involved, just as in facilitated diffusion. In order to perform active transport, however, the carrier, after having delivered solutes to the final compartment, must undergo a change of such type that it can no longer bind the transported solute. Then, on its return trip it somehow must be reactivated, possibly with the expenditure of metabolic energy. This may be illustrated in Figure 4. In this figure, X is the carrier in

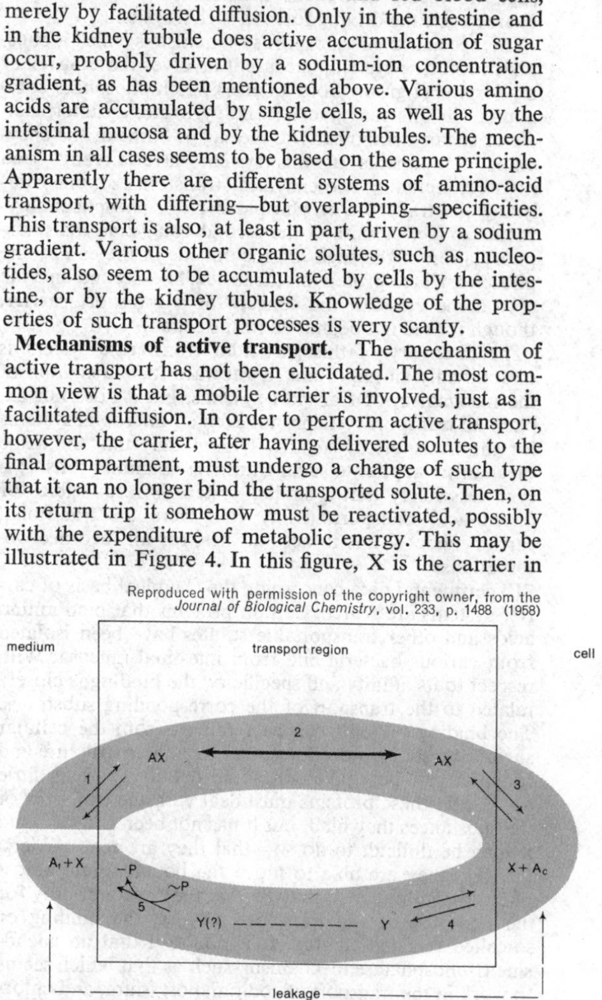

Figure 4: Schematic model of active transport, associated with exchange diffusion (see text).

the activated and Y the carrier in the inactivated form. Only X binds the substrate A; it carries A across the membrane and after delivering it at the other side, X itself is catalytically transformed into Y. Later Y must be reactivated by a reaction that presumably involves energy-rich phosphates. Even though most observations can be easily reconciled with this model, it has not yet been proven by direct experimental evidence. The model does not necessarily imply that the carrier as a whole moves freely within the transport region; it would suffice if only a binding group of the carrier molecules were shuttled back and forth across the osmotic barrier. Other models have been based on immobile systems, with the assumption of binding sites lining the transport pores. If the affinity of these binding sites is shifted, the molecule to be transported may be moved across the channel. Such a model would account for many observations in connection with active transport and facilitated diffusion. It would, however, not be easily compatible with the phenomena of countertransport and exchange diffusion. The principle of such a schematic model is also depicted in Figure 4.

Sugar transport in bacteria

A transport system of a special kind seems to be involved in the transport of sugars in certain species of bacteria. In these bacteria, the sugar is not transported as such but as a phosphate ester. The phosphorylation reaction appears to take place simultaneously with transport, for it can be shown with isotopic labelling that the sugar portion of the phosphate esters derives exclusively from the extracellular sugar, whereas the phosphate unit is entirely of intracellular origin. Presumably, an enzyme located in the membrane catalyzes the reaction between the sugar and the phosphoryl donor, thereby pulling the sugar molecule across the membrane. It is difficult to characterize the driving force in such a system.

This special sugar-transport system also is called a phosphotransferase system, because it involves the transfer of a phosphoryl group from an energy-rich phosphate compound (in this case phosphoenolpyruvate, an intermediate of sugar metabolism) to the sugar. Some of the enzymatic components of this system have already been isolated, including two enzymes (transferases), one catalyzing the transport of phosphate from phosphoenolpyruvate to a protein, and the second catalyzing the phosphorylation of the sugar on the outside of the cell by the phosphorylated protein on the inside. The second enzyme may come close to the concept of a transport carrier, though it need not be mobile for its action.

The discovery of this particular transferase system is undoubtedly an important step toward the elucidation of the mechanism of transport systems, but it does not explain all transport systems, not even all microbial systems for the transport of sugars. It is unlikely that the same mechanism applies to sugar transport in animal cells. It is even less likely that a similar system is responsible for amino-acid transport in any cell. Here the traditional carrier model seems to account best for all recorded observations.

Experimental data concerning the chemical basis of carrier systems are scarce. Certain proteins that bind amino acids and other transportable solutes have been isolated from various bacteria and from intestinal mucosa. With respect to its affinity and specificity, the binding is closely related to the transport of the corresponding substrates. The binding proteins can be removed from the cellular surface by shock procedures, and thus their structure and function can be studied in some detail. There is little doubt that these proteins must deal with the transport of the substances they bind, but it has not been shown—and it may be difficult to do so—that they are real carriers; *i.e.*, that they are able to move the bound solute across plasma membranes. It may be that they account only for the first step of the transport process, the binding or so-called recognition step. It is doubtful that an adenosine triphosphatase mechanism, such as that which seems to work in the transport of sodium, potassium, and chloride ions, is involved in amino acid and sugar transport. No such adenosine triphosphatase has been shown to be activated by amino acids, sugars, or any other of the transported organic solutes.

Oxidation–reduction models

Little is known about the underlying mechanism of electrolyte transport, as has already been mentioned, apart from the likely participation of the transport adenosine triphosphatase. An older but revived hypothesis is that of an oxidation–reduction (redox) pump. It is known that, in oxidation–reduction reactions within the respiratory chain, electrons are transferred between reacting molecules or ions. It has been surmised that this electron transfer is spatially orientated in membranes so that the resulting shift of electrical charges may entail the equivalent movement of oppositely charged ions, such as sodium and potassium ions or hydrogen ions. The direct linkage between electron transfer and active ion transport, thus postulated, is hardly compatible with the concept of an adenosine triphosphatase. For this reason the older versions of the redox models, formerly much in vogue, have been abandoned. With additional assumptions, however, the implementation of redox processes in electrolyte transport can still be defended. In this connection, however, it is not known whether the transfer of energy from a chemical reaction, such as the splitting of an energy-rich phosphate bond, to a transport process is reversible. It is possible that such a reversible transfer may be involved (according to the so-called chemi-osmotic hypothesis) in oxidative phosphorylation; *i.e.*, in the synthesis of energy-rich phosphates in connection with the oxidative degradation of metabolites in the respiratory chain.

Pinocytosis. Pinocytosis, which means "cell drinking," is often considered to be a special device for the transport of material into and across cells, which is used by the cells in addition to, or even instead of, active transport. In this process single molecules or ions alone are not transported, but rather a droplet of the medium surrounding the cell is caught and engulfed by the cellular membrane and taken as a vesicle into the cell. The appearance of little vesicles within leucocytes,· and their movements there, were observed about forty years ago. Later it was shown that the formation of these vesicles is initiated by prior binding or absorption of a solute or protein to the cellular surface, which then invaginates and forms the little vesicles. These remain, apparently floating freely in the cytoplasm. The borders of these vesicles are thought to be similar to the cellular membranes, with the result that the material trapped in them has not really mixed with the cellular contents. The further fate of these vesicles is uncertain. They may serve to carry a part of the extracellular fluid across the cell, finally being emptied on the opposite side by reverse pinocytosis. In this way extracellular fluid could be moved across a cellular layer without actually entering the cytoplasm. Such a process might be involved in the reabsorption of certain insoluble materials from the intestine or in the movement of plasma across the capillary membranes. On the other hand, all or part of the solutes present in the vesicular fluid could be transported across the vesicular membrane into the cell. This would, of course, be a real transport process, such as has been discussed above. It has been suggested that the cellular membrane, once it has been transformed into the boundaries of the pinocytosis vesicle, changes its permeability so as to become more permeable to otherwise nonpermeating solutes. A sugar molecule, for example, could be taken up by the cell in two steps, first by pinocytosis, and second by modified transport from the vesicle into the cytoplasm. It has been shown that pinocytosis is an energy-consuming process and that it is involved in the secretion of large molecules and particles, such as proteins, lipid droplets, micelles, and crystallites, from the cell. It probably is not involved in the transport and uptake of small molecules and ions, such as sugars, amino acids, and electrolytes. Thus, pinocytosis and membrane transport may exist side by side and serve different purposes.

BIBLIOGRAPHY. R.M. DOWBEN (ed.), *Biological Membranes* (1969), a series of articles discussing modern problems in membrane biology; D. CHAPMAN (ed.), *Biological Membranes: Physical Fact and Function* (1968), an outline of the composition and functions of biological membranes, including modern techniques used in investigations; J.L. KAVANAU, *Structure and Function in Biological Membranes*, 2 vol. (1965), a comprehensive textbook with an extended bibliography; H.N. CHRISTENSEN, *Biological Transport* (1962), a useful introduction to the problems of permeability of biological membranes and active transport; W.D. STEIN, *The Movement of Molecules across Cell Membranes* (1967), a modern, comprehensive textbook dealing especially with membrane permeability and solute migration; W. WILBRANDT and E. HEINZ, *Biological Transport* (1971), a brief, general introduction to the subject of biological membrane transport and permeability.

(E.H./K.R./W.Gr.)

Memling, Hans

Hans Memling (Memlinc) was one of the most prolific and accomplished masters of Flemish painting at the end

"Diptych with Madonna and Martin van Nieuwenhove"
(left wing), oil on panel by Hans Memling, 1487. In the
Memling-Museum, Brugge, Belgium. 44.1 x 33 cm.
By courtesy of the Memling-Museum, Brugge, photograph, © A.C.L., Brussels

of the 15th century. Though heavily influenced by contemporary painters, Memling's art displays better than that of any other Flemish master (except his follower Gerard David) the general tenor of that interlude in Netherlandish art known as the détente, the mellowing and relaxation of expression that followed the first generations of painters and provided a bridge to the new Italianizing styles of the 16th century in the north. Memling painted portraits and devotional pictures—well-balanced, restrained compositions, often full of charm and colourful detail. Rather than displaying drama or pathos, Memling's paintings render figures that are withdrawn into calm idealism, with faces demonstrating gentle, sweet piety.

Memling was born about 1430/35 in or near Seligenstadt in the region of the Middle Rhine. He was apparently first schooled in the art of Cologne and then travelled to the Netherlands (c. 1455–60), where he probably trained in the workshop of the painter Rogier van der Weyden. He settled in Bruges (modern Brugge) in 1465; there he established a large shop and executed numerous altarpieces and portraits. Indeed, he was very successful in Bruges: it is known that he owned a large stone house and by 1480 was listed among the wealthiest citizens on the city tax accounts. By 1484 he had enrolled at least three apprentices, and the number of his imitators and followers testifies to his widespread popularity throughout Flanders. Sometime between 1470 and 1480 Memling married Anna de Valkenaere (died 1487), who bore him three children.

Difficulties of dating Memling's works

A number of Memling's works are signed and dated, and still others allow art historians to place them easily into a chronology on the basis of the patron depicted in them. Otherwise it is very difficult to discern an early, middle, and late style for the artist. His compositions and types, once established, were repeated again and again with few indications of any formal development. His Madonnas gradually become slenderer, more ethereal and self-conscious, and a greater use of Italian motifs such as putti, garlands, and sculptural detail for the settings marks the later works. His portraits, too, appear to develop from a type with a simple neutral background to those enhanced with a loggia or window view of a landscape, but these, too, may have been less a stylistic development than an adaptation of his compositions to suit the tastes of his patrons.

A good example of the difficulties of dating encountered by scholars is the triptych of "The Virgin and Child with Saints and Donors" that Memling executed for Sir John Donne (National Gallery, London), which until recently had been dated very early—around 1468—because it was believed that the patron commissioned the work while visiting Bruges for the wedding of Charles the Bold (duke of Burgundy) to Margaret of York and that he died the following year (1469) in the Battle of Edgecote. It is now known that Sir John lived until 1503 and that it is probably his daughter Anne (born 1470 or later) who is portrayed as the young girl kneeling with her parents in the central panel, thus indicating that the painting was commissioned about 1475.

Memling's art clearly reveals the influence of contemporary Flemish painters. He borrowed, for example, from the compositions of Jan van Eyck, the famed founder of the Bruges school. The influence of Dirck Bouts and Hugo van der Goes can also be discerned in his works—for example, in a number of eye-catching details such as glistening mirrors, tile floors, canopied beds, exotic hangings, and brocaded robes. Above all, Memling's art reveals a thorough knowledge of, and dependence on, compositions and figure types created by Rogier van der Weyden, the painter with whom he had probably apprenticed. In Memling's large triptych (a painting in three panels, generally hinged together) of the "Adoration of the Magi" (Prado, Madrid), one of his earliest works, and in the altarpiece of 1479 for Jan Floreins (Memling-Museum, Brugge), the influence of Rogier's last masterpiece, the "Columba Altarpiece" (1460–64; Alte Pinakothek, Munich), is especially noticeable. Some scholars believe that Memling himself may have had a hand in the production of this late work while still in Rogier's studio. He also imitated Rogier's compositions in numerous representations of the half-length Madonna with the Child, often including a pendant with the donor's portrait (the "Madonna and Martin van Nieuwenhove"; Memling-Museum, Brugge). Many devotional diptychs (two-panel paintings) such as this were painted in 15th-century Flanders. They consist of a portrait of the "donor"—or patron—in one panel, reverently gazing at the Madonna and Child in the other. Such paintings were for the donor's personal use in his home or travels.

Most of Memling's patrons were those associated with religious houses, such as the Hospital of St. John in Bruges, and wealthy businessmen including burghers of Bruges and foreign representatives of the Florentine Medicis and the Hanseatic League (an association of German merchants dealing abroad). For Tommaso Portinari, a Medici agent, and his wife, Memling painted portraits (Metropolitan Museum of Art, New York) and an unusual altarpiece that depicts over 22 scenes from the Passion of Christ scattered in miniature in a panoramic landscape encompassing a view of Jerusalem (Galleria Sabauda, Turin). Such an altarpiece, perhaps created for new devotional practices, became very popular at the end of the 15th century. His best known work with extensive narration is the sumptuous Shrine of St. Ursula in the Hospital of St. John. It was commissioned by two nuns, Jacosa van Dudzeele and Anna van den Moortele, who are portrayed at one end of the composition kneeling before Mary. This reliquary, completed in 1489, is in the form of a diminutive chapel with six painted panels filling the areas along the sides where stained glass would ordinarily be placed. The narrative, which is the story of Ursula and her 11,000 virgins and their trip from Cologne to Rome and back, unfolds with charm and colourful detail but with little drama or emotion. Other patrons of the same hospital commissioned Memling to paint a large altarpiece of St. John with the mystical marriage of St. Catherine to Christ as the central theme (Memling-Museum, Brugge). Elaborate narratives appear behind the patron saints John the Baptist and John the Evangelist painted on the side panels, while the central piece is an impressive elaboration of the enthroned Madonna between angels and saints (including Catherine) that one

Altarpieces and portraits

finds in innumerable other devotional pieces attributed to Memling. His last great monumental commission that is recorded is the "Passion Triptych", including the Crucifixion Panel (St.-Annen-Museum, Lübeck), a work executed in 1491 for Heinrich Greverade, a merchant of Lübeck, and widely copied.

Because Memling's work was so strongly influenced by that of other painters, it often has been harshly dealt with by 20th-century critics. Yet in his own lifetime he was acclaimed. Recording his death on August 11, 1494, the notary of Bruges described him as "the most skillful painter in the whole of Christendom."

MAJOR WORKS

"The Martyrdom of St. Sebastian" (c. 1470; Musées Royaux des Beaux-Arts, Brussels); "Portinari Triptych" (c. 1470; Metropolitan Museum of Art, New York); "Portrait of Gilles Joye" (1472; Sterling and Francine Clark Art Institute, Williamstown, Massachusetts); "The Last Judgment" (c. 1473; Marienkirche, Danzig); "Triptych: The Virgin and Child with Saints and Donors" (c. 1475; National Gallery, London); "The Deposition" (c. 1475; Museo de la Capilla Real, Granada, Spain); "The Virgin and Child" (c. 1475; Museo de la Capilla Real, Granada, Spain); "The Mystic Marriage of St. Catherine of Alexandria" (c. 1475; Louvre, Paris); "Christ Surrounded by Angel Musicians" (c. 1475; Musée Royal des Beaux-Arts, Antwerp); "Mystic Marriage of St. Catherine of Alexandria" (1479; Memling-Museum, Brugge); "Adoration of the Magi" (1479; Memling-Museum, Brugge); "The Descent from the Cross" (1480; Memling-Museum, Brugge); "Scenes from the Life of Christ and the Virgin" (c. 1480; Alte Pinakothek, Munich); "Madonna and Child with Angels" (c. 1480–85; National Gallery of Art, Washington, D.C.); "Moreel Triptych" (1484; Groeninge Museum, Brugge); "Bathsheba" (c. 1485; Staatsgalerie, Stuttgart); "Diptych with Madonna and Martin van Nieuwenhove" (1487; Memling-Museum, Brugge); "St. Benedict" (1487; Uffizi, Florence); "Portrait of Benedetto Portinari" (1487; Uffizi, Florence); "The Virgin and Child" (1487; Staatsliche Museen Preussischer Kulturbesitz, Berlin); St. Ursula Shrine (1489; Memling-Museum, Brugge); "Resurrection" (c. 1490; Louvre, Paris); "Passion Triptych" (Crucifixion Panel, 1491; St.-Annen-Museum, Lübeck).

BIBLIOGRAPHY. Lengthy bibliographies on the artist appear in A. WURZBACH, *Niederländisches Künstler-Lexikon*, vol. 2 (1909); and V. DENIS, *Encyclopedia of World Art*, vol. 9, col. 729–735 (1964). Among the earlier studies of Memling, see especially J.A. CROWE and G.B. CAVALCASELLE, *The Early Flemish Painters* (1857); L.J. KRAMMERER, *Memling* (1899); F. BOCK, *Memling Studien* (1900); W.H.J. WEALE, *Hans Memling* (1901); and K. VOLL, *Memling* (1909). For the relationships with Rogier van der Weyden, see especially G. HULIN DE LOO "Hans Memling in Rogier van der Weyden's Studio," *Burlington Magazine*, 52:160–177 (1928); and M.J. FRIEDLANDER, "Noch etwas über das Verhältnis Roger van der Weydens zu Memling," *Oud-Holland*, 61:11–19 (1946). The standard references are L. VON BALDASS, *Hans Memling* (1942); and M.J. FRIEDLANDER, *Memling* (1950); and his *Die Altniederländische Malerei*, vol. 6 (1928; Eng. trans., *Early Netherlandish Painting*, vol. 6, 1971). Also very useful are the discussions of Memling's works that have appeared in the series *Les Primitifs flamands*, especially vol. 9, J. BIALOSTOCKI, *Les Musées de Pologne* (1966); and vol. 11, M. DAVIES, *The National Gallery-London-III* (1970).

(J.E.Sn.)

Memory, Abnormalities of

Disorders of memory must have been known to the ancients and are mentioned in several early medical texts; but it was not until the closing decades of the 19th century that serious attempts were made to analyze them or to seek their explanation in terms of brain disturbances. Of the early attempts, the most influential was that of a French psychologist, Théodule Armand Ribot, who, in his *Diseases of Memory* (1881, English translation 1882), endeavoured to account for memory loss as a symptom of progressive brain disease by embracing principles describing the evolution of memory function in the individual, as offered by an English neurologist, John Hughlings Jackson. Ribot wrote:

The progressive destruction of memory follows a logical order—a law. It advances progressively from the unstable to the stable. It begins with the most recent recollections, which, being lightly impressed upon the nervous elements, rarely repeated and consequently having no permanent associations, represent organization in its feeblest form. It ends with the sensorial, instinctive memory, which, having become a permanent and integral part of the organism, represents organization in its most highly developed stage.

The statement, amounting to Ribot's "law" of regression (or progressive destruction) of memory, enjoyed a considerable vogue and is not without contemporary influence. The notion has been applied with some success to phenomena as diverse as the breakdown of memory for language in a disorder called aphasia and the gradual return of memory after brain concussion. It also helped to strengthen the belief that the neural basis of memory undergoes progressive strengthening or consolidation as a function of time. Yet students of retrograde amnesia (loss of memory for relatively old events) agree that Ribot's principle admits of many exceptions. In recovery from concussion of the brain, for example, the most recent memories are not always the first to return. It has proved difficult, moreover, to disentangle the effects of passage of time from those of rehearsal or repetition on memory.

A Russian psychiatrist, Sergey Sergeyevich Korsakov, (Korsakoff), may have been the first to recognize that amnesia need not necessarily be associated with dementia (or loss of the ability to reason), as Ribot and many others had supposed. Korsakov described severe but relatively specific amnesia for recent and current events among alcoholics who showed no obvious evidence of shortcomings in intelligence and judgment. This disturbance, now called the Korsakoff syndrome, has been reported for a variety of brain disorders aside from alcoholism and appears to result from damage in a relatively localized part of the brain.

The neurological approach may be combined with evidence of psychopathology to enrich understanding of memory function. Thus, a French neurologist, Pierre Janet, described amnesia sufferers who were apparently very similar to those observed by Korsakov but who gave no evidence of underlying brain disease. Janet also studied people who had lost memory of extensive periods in the past, also without evidence of organic disorder. He was led to regard these amnesias as hysterical, explaining them in terms of dissociation: a selective loss of access to specific memory data that seem to hold some degree of emotional significance. In his experience, reconnection of dissociated memories could as a rule be brought about by suggestion while the sufferer was under hypnosis. Freud regarded hysterical amnesia as arising from a protective activity or defense mechanism against unpleasant recollections; he came to call this sort of forgetting repression, and he later invoked it to account for the typical inability of adults to recollect their earliest years (infantile amnesia). He held that all forms of psychogenic (not demonstrably organic) amnesia eventually could resolve after prolonged sessions of talking (psychotherapy) and that hypnosis was neither essential nor necessarily in the amnesiac's best interest. Nevertheless, hypnosis (sometimes induced with the aid of drugs) has been widely used in the treatment of hysterical amnesia, particularly in time of war when only limited time is available.

Ribot's "law"

Repression

ORGANIC DISORDERS OF MEMORY

Defect of memory is one of the most frequently observed symptoms of impaired brain function. It may be transitory, as after an alcoholic bout or an epileptic seizure; or it may be enduring, as after severe head injury or in association with brain disease. When there is impaired ability to store memories of new experiences (up to total loss of memory for recent events) the defect is termed anterograde amnesia. Retrograde loss may progressively abate or shrink if recovery begins, or it may gradually enlarge in scope, as in cases of progressive brain disease. Minor grades of memory defect are not uncommon aftereffects of severe head injury or infections such as encephalitis; typically they are shown in forgetfulness about recent events, in slow and insecure learning of new skills, and sometimes in a degree of persistent amnesia for events preceding the illness.

Transient global amnesia. Apparently first described in 1964, transient global amnesia consists of an abrupt loss of memory lasting from a few seconds to a few hours, without loss of consciousness or other evidence of impairment. The individual is virtually unable to store new experience, suffering permanent absence of memory for the period of the attack. There is also a retrograde loss that may initially extend up to years preceding the attack. This deficit shrinks rapidly in the course of recovery but leaves an enduring gap in memory that seldom exceeds the three-quarters of an hour before onset. Thus the person is left with a persisting memory gap only for what happened during the attack itself and in a short period immediately preceding. Such attacks may be recurrent, are thought to result from transient reduction in blood supply in specific brain regions, and sometimes presage a stroke.

Traumatic amnesia. On recovery of consciousness after trauma, a person who has been knocked out by a blow on the head at first typically is dazed, confused, and imperfectly aware of his whereabouts and circumstances. This so-called posttraumatic confusional state may last for an hour or so up to several days or even weeks. While in this condition, the individual appears unable to store new memories; on recovery he commonly reports total amnesia for the period of altered consciousness (posttraumatic amnesia). He also is apt to show retrograde amnesia that may extend over brief or quite long periods into the past, the duration seeming to depend on such factors as severity of injury and the sufferer's age. In the gradual course of recovery, memories are often reported to return in strict chronological sequence from the most remote to the most recent, as in Ribot's law. Yet this is by no means always *Hap-* the case; memories seem often to return haphazardly and *hazard* to become gradually interrelated in the appropriate time *recovery* sequence. The amnesia that remains seldom involves *of memory* more than the events that occurred shortly before the accident though in severe cases careful inquiry may reveal some residual memory defect for experiences dating from as long as a year before the trauma. It is thought by some that, after recovery, the overall period of time for which there is no recollection may indicate the degree of severity of the head injury.

Traumatic automatism. Posttraumatic amnesia sometimes is observed after mild head injury without loss of consciousness and with no apparent change in ordinary behaviour. A football player who is dazed but not knocked out by a blow on the head, for example, may continue to play and even score a goal. But he may be going through these motions automatically and may later have no memory whatever of the part of the game that followed his injury. The phenomenon is known as traumatic automatism and seems similar to, if not identical with, transient global amnesia.

Memory defect after electroconvulsive therapy. Electroconvulsive treatments have been widely used in psychiatry, particularly for depressed people. A seizure or convulsion is induced by passing current through electrodes placed on the forehead. Each treatment is followed by a period of confusion for which the person is subsequently amnesic; at this time there is also a rapidly abating amnesia of some seconds for events that immediately preceded the shock. After a number of treatments, however, some individuals complain of more persistent memory defect, shown mainly in exaggerated forgetfulness for day-to-day events. These difficulties nearly always clear up within a few weeks after treatment ends. Experimental evidence tentatively suggests that electroshock administered to only one side of the head produces therapeutic results equal to those of the standard procedure but with significantly reduced impairment of memory.

Korsakoff syndrome. First described in cases of chronic alcoholism, Korsakoff's psychosis, or syndrome, occurs in a wide variety of toxic and infectious brain illnesses, as well as in association with such nutritional disorders as deficiency of the B vitamins. The syndrome also has been observed among people with cerebral tumours, especially those involving the third ventricle (one of the fluid-filled cavities in the brain). The main psychological feature is gross defect in recent memory, sometimes so severe as to produce "moment-to-moment" consciousness; such people can store new information only for a few seconds and report no continuity between one experience and the next. They seem incapable of learning, even after many trials or repetitions. Although cases of such severity are relatively rare, the ability to store experience only briefly is quite characteristic of the Korsakoff syndrome.

In addition, sufferers almost always show evidence of retrograde amnesia that can span as little as a few weeks past to as much as 15 or 20 years before onset of the disorder. These extensive retrograde amnesias are seldom total or uniform, and "islands" of memory often can be found by persistent interrogation. The person's memory function depends heavily on circumstances; for example, a man with Korsakoff's syndrome who recognizes his *Extensive* wife instantly when she visits may in her absence vehe- *retrograde* mently deny that he is married. Commonly, there is dis- *amnesia* orientation in place and time; the individual often underestimates his own age, sometimes grossly. Some sufferers characteristically confabulate; *i.e.*, they remember experiences they never personally had or they falsely localize their memories in time. Not uncommonly, these people deny being ill or that their memory is in any way affected. Otherwise, they can exhibit good intelligence and, apart perhaps from some lack of spontaneity, may show little or no personality change.

While Korsakoff's syndrome is commonly encountered as a transitory sign of brain disorder, it can be chronic, remaining effectively unimproved over many years. Even with improvement, however, an appreciable weakness in recent memory, particularly in regard to sequence in time, is quite apparent.

Persistent defect after encephalitis. Attention repeatedly has been drawn to severe and persistent memory defect following attacks of a form of brain inflammation called acute inclusion body encephalitis. The individual's behaviour closely resembles that of Korsakoff's syndrome except that his insight into the memory disorder is usually good and confabulation is infrequent or absent. Indeed, the memory disorder is sometimes so limited and specific as to raise the possibility of a psychogenic (*i.e.*, hysterical) amnesia. In cases of this kind there may be little or no impairment of intelligence or judgment.

Defect following brain surgery. Surgical operations on the sides of the brain (the temporal lobes) to remove tissues that produce symptoms of epilepsy are routine. While good results are often achieved, a degree of memory defect ensues. Operations on the dominant (usually left) temporal lobe tend to hamper one's ability to learn verbal information by hearing or reading. Usually observable even before surgery, the defect tends to be more marked after operation and has been reported to persist for up to three years before eventual recovery. Operations on one temporal lobe when there is unsuspected damage to its fellow on the other side of the brain (or on both lobes, in surgery very rarely undertaken) produce severe and persistent general memory defect, altogether comparable to postencephalitic amnesia. There is gross defect in recent memory and in learning (except perhaps in motor learning), with retrograde amnesia that initially may involve several years of the person's past. Intelligence otherwise appears to be well preserved; the individual shows insight into his memory difficulty, and seldom, if ever, confabulates.

Diffuse brain diseases. Some memory failure is almost universal during old age, particularly in forgetfulness for names and in the reduced ability to learn. Many people of advanced age, nevertheless, show adequate memory function if they suffer no brain disease. Impairment of memory is a characteristic early sign of senility, as well as of hardening of the brain arteries (cerebral arteriosclerosis) at any age, with exaggerated forgetfulness for recent events and progressive failure in memory for experiences that preceded the disorder. As arteriosclerotic brain dis- *Senility* ease progresses, amnesia tends to extend further into the past, embracing personal experience and general or common information. When the symptoms are almost those of the Korsakoff syndrome, the disturbance is called presbyophrenia. In most cases the amnesia is complicated by failure in judgment and changes in character. It has been suggested that severe memory defect in an elderly person carries a poor prognosis, being related to such factors as a shortened survival time and an increased death rate.

A Swiss psychiatrist, Eugen Bleuler, held that amnesia results only from a diffuse disorder of the outer layers (cortex) of the brain and suggested that memory depends on the integrity of the cortex as a whole. Indeed, the removal of brain tissue from rats and monkeys in experimental studies has indicated that retention of complex habits by the animals depends on the total amount of cortex that remains. It was claimed that the degree to which memory is lost depends not on where the brain is injured but on the extent of the damage. (This is the "law" of mass action, which asserts that the brain functions in a unitary manner; *i.e.*, as a whole.) While the extent of diffuse brain damage is roughly related to the severity of memory defect, the principle of mass action is nevertheless manifestly inadequate. It would seem that, whatever its physical basis, memory depends on the integrity of relatively limited parts of the brain, rather than on that organ (or even the cortex) as a whole.

Severe and highly specific amnesic symptoms principally stem from damage to such brain structures as the mammillary bodies, circumscribed parts of the thalamus, and of the temporal lobe (*e.g.*, the hippocampus). (For illustrations and descriptions of these structures, see NERVOUS SYSTEM, HUMAN.) While the ability to store new experience (and perhaps in some degree to retrieve well-established memories) appears to depend on a distinct neural system involving the temporal cortex and limited parts of the thalamus and hypothalamus, understanding of the neuroanatomy of memory remains sketchy enough to generate major differences of opinion. French and German workers tend to stress the role of the mammillary bodies, while United States investigators are more prone to implicate the thalamus. It has been pointed out that circumscribed damage to the mammillary bodies is not invariably associated with memory defect; cases of amnesia evidently occur in which these structures are spared. Nevertheless, implication of the mammillary bodies in a large number of verified cases of Korsakoff's syndrome seems incontrovertible. Injury to other neural tissues (*e.g.*, the so-called fornix bundle deep within the brain) that anatomically might be expected to produce severe memory disorder rarely does so. While evidence for amnesia as a sign of localized brain damage is impressive, much remains to be understood about the physical system that sustains memory.

Brain structures in amnesia

PSYCHOLOGICAL STUDIES OF AMNESIA

Short-term memory. It has long been known that so-called short-term memory (see MEMORY: RETENTION AND FORGETTING) is typically intact among amnesia sufferers. Such victims usually can repeat a short phrase or a series of words or numbers from immediate memory as adequately as anyone of comparable age and intelligence. Such an amnesic person can retain the gist of a question or request long enough to respond appropriately, unless, of course, there is enough delay in performance or attention is diverted. Evidently the ability to register information is intact, if this means availability of data in short-term memory. For this reason, experimental psychologists who favour a sharp distinction between short-term and long-term storage systems contend that the primary deficit in amnesia is an inability to transfer information from short-term to long-term storage.

Associative learning. It has been argued that the basic deficit in the amnesic state is a loss of learning ability. In a series of experiments with amnesic patients, using, for the most part, verbal material, the subjects evidenced failure to link new with old associations, rapid fading of new associations, and great difficulty in reproducing whatever associations might have been formed. These findings have been amply confirmed by later work; in one view, however, the weakness resides less in the failure to establish new associations than in their rapid decay (*i.e.*,

accelerated forgetting). On the other hand, it has often been noticed that if a Korsakoff patient can once succeed in learning an item, he may be able to reproduce it correctly after an appreciable interval of time. Further experiments, using a variety of techniques for assessing learning and retention, have suggested that it is retrieval rather than learning that is at fault.

Motor skill. Attention has been drawn to the fact that the acquisition of manual skill in Korsakoff patients is less impaired than either verbal learning or the solution of puzzles or mazes. This is confirmed in the observation that a severely amnesic patient who had undergone an extensive operation on the temporal lobes could perform rotary-pursuit and tracking tasks at a level not greatly inferior to that of healthy control subjects. A second case of the same kind has recently been described, in which memory for motor tasks such as maze learning or the rendering of new compositions on the piano is said to have been completely preserved. These observations suggest that the acquisition of motor skill may remain relatively unaffected by lesions that give rise to a severe defect of general memory. What is commonly called global or generalized memory defect may, therefore, become increasingly subject to fractionation.

Generalized versus specific memory loss

Residual learning capacity. Korsakov himself pointed out that a patient who consistently denies that he has seen his doctor before does not necessarily react to him on each successive encounter as a total stranger. It would thus appear that, in spite of gross amnesia, some learning, perhaps implicit, can still take place. This view has gained considerable support from both clinical and experimental studies. About 1900 it was reported that even severely affected Korsakoff patients show appreciable savings in relearning verbal material after an interval of several hours or days, thus indicating minimal retention. Some Korsakoff patients, in spite of gross amnesia, eventually learn their way about the hospital. Again, some patients who disown any knowledge of their whereabouts may nevertheless give the correct name of the hospital, when asked to guess or to select it correctly from a list containing the names of several hospitals. Thus, while learning capacity is seldom, if ever, wholly destroyed, there is failure to integrate new knowledge within the total personality. It is apparently a lack of mental cohesion that lies at the basis of Korsakoff's psychosis.

Forgetting. While some clinicians have attributed memory defect largely, if not exclusively, to defective registration of experience (*i.e.*, failure to form memory traces), the widely accepted view is that it results primarily from a greatly increased rapidity of forgetting (*i.e.*, rapid decay of memory traces). With some exceptions, this view has also been held by the great majority of experimental psychologists who have worked with amnesic people. The consensus is that amnesia sufferers characteristically lose much of the memory they once had. This conclusion finds support in the very rapid extinction of conditioned eyeblink responses to a buzzer. It is notable that, in Korsakoff states, forgetting appears to be due to the passage of time (oblivescence) rather than to retroactive inhibition or some kindred interference effect (see LEARNING THEORIES).

Time disorders. Estimation of time is typically poor in amnesic states. The individual is prone to underestimate grossly the duration of an interview or the time in which he has been engaged on any particular activity. Conversely, he may equally grossly overestimate the time that has elapsed since a particular event (*e.g.*, the visit of a relative) of which he has preserved some recollection. Indeed, amnesic patients exhibit a remarkable want of coherence in their thought processes, suggesting that a lack of temporal synthesis underlies, and may indeed in large part explain, the defect of memory. Nevertheless, although difficulties in dating particular past events and in building a coherent time framework are quite characteristic of amnesic states and may persist after otherwise good recovery, an explanation couched wholly in terms of time disturbance is scarcely convincing.

Retrograde amnesia. Inasmuch as retrograde amnesia relates to memory for events that took place at a time when brain function was unimpaired, it clearly cannot be ascribed to failure of registration—with the exception, perhaps, of the very brief permanent amnesias following electroconvulsive shock or head injury. Retrograde amnesia otherwise would appear to be wholly due to a failure of retrieval, though this failure is evidently selective. That recent memories are generally harder to evoke than those more remote is usually explained on the basis of consolidation; *i.e.*, progressive strengthening of memory traces with the passage of time. Yet, recency is not the only factor governing the vulnerability of memory traces, and in some cases memory for a relatively recent event may still be preserved while that for one more remote is inaccessible. Much depends, too, on the method used to test retrieval; recognition, for example, may succeed when voluntary recall entirely fails. By and large, the availability of information in memory would seem to depend to a considerable extent on its relation to the person's current interests and preoccupations. When these are severely curtailed by an amnesic state, the links connecting present and past are severed, with a consequent failure of reproduction.

Consolidation of the memory trace

PSYCHOGENIC AMNESIA

It long has been known that some forms of amnesia appear to be quite different from those associated with detectable injury or disease of the brain. These comprise, first, amnesias that can be induced in apparently normal individuals by means of suggestion under hypnosis; and secondly, amnesias that arise spontaneously in reaction to acute conflict or stress, and which are commonly called hysterical. Such amnesias are effectively reversible and have been explained wholly in psychological terms. Nevertheless, organic factors are not infrequently involved to some extent, and the distinction between organic and psychogenic amnesia may well turn out to be a good deal less absolute than has been traditionally supposed.

Hypnotic amnesia. Memory of a hypnotic trance is often vague and fragmentary, as in awakening from an ordinary dream. This may be due in part to defect of registration during the period of altered consciousness. At the same time, very much more complete posthypnotic amnesia can be induced if an individual is told that, when he awakens, he will remember nothing of what went on during the period of hypnosis. This is clearly a psychogenic phenomenon; memory is fully regained if the patient is rehypnotized and an appropriate countersuggestion given. It may also be regained if the person is persistently interrogated in the waking state, again suggesting that the amnesia is apparent rather than real. This observation led Freud to seek access to ostensibly forgotten (repressed) memories in his patients without the use of hypnosis.

Hysterical amnesia. Hysterical amnesia is of two main types. One involves the failure to recall particular past events or those falling within a particular period of the patient's life. This is essentially retrograde amnesia but it does not appear to depend upon an actual brain disorder, past or present. In the second type there is failure to register—and, accordingly, later to recollect—current events in the patient's ongoing life. This is essentially anterograde amnesia and, as an ostensibly psychogenic phenomenon, would appear to be rather rare and almost always encountered in cases in which there has been a pre-existing amnesia of organic origin. Very occasionally, amnesia appears to cover the patient's entire life, extending even to his own identity and causing him to fail to recollect all particulars of his whereabouts and circumstances. Although most dramatic, such cases are extremely rare and seldom wholly convincing. They usually clear up with relative rapidity, with or without psychotherapy.

Hysterical amnesia differs from organic amnesia in a number of important respects. As a rule it is sharply bounded, relating only to particular memories, or groups of memories, often of direct or indirect emotional significance. It is also usually motivated in that it can be understood in terms of the patient's needs or conflicts; *e.g.*, the need to seek financial compensation after, say, a road accident causing a mild head injury or to escape from the memory of an exceptionally distressing or frightening event. Hysterical amnesia also may extend to cover basic school knowledge, such as spelling or arithmetic, which is never seen in organic amnesia unless there is concomitant aphasia or a very advanced state of dementia. A most distinctive feature of hysterical amnesia is that it can almost always be relieved by such procedures as hypnosis. Although the task of distinguishing organic and psychogenic amnesia is not always easy, it can usually be achieved on the basis of such criteria, especially when there is no reason to suspect actual damage to the brain.

Relief of amnesia through hypnosis

Legal implications. The differentiation of organic from functional amnesia not uncommonly assumes legal importance, as in cases in which compensation is sought for disability held to be due to industrial or road accidents causing head injuries. If there is a complaint of defective memory, it is legally important to ascertain what part of it can be ascribed to the aftereffects of the head injury and what part of it to subsequent psychogenic elaboration. Similar issues may also arise on occasion in criminal cases, as in a trial in England (1959) in which it was contended that the accused man had a total amnesia for the circumstances of his alleged offense—the murder of a police officer—and should therefore be regarded as unfit to plead. After much discussion as to whether the amnesia was organic, hysterical, or feigned, the jury found it not to be genuine and the trial proceeded to conviction.

Mixed amnesic states. Students of amnesia have been increasingly impressed by the frequency with which psychogenic factors appear to reinforce, prolong, or otherwise complicate an organic memory defect. Hysterical reactions appear to be far from uncommon in brain-damaged patients: conversely, there is little or nothing in the pathology of hysterical amnesia that has not been observed in the organic syndrome. A particularly interesting case reported in the German literature in 1930 aroused great controversy. This was the case of a young man who developed severe and persistent amnesia following accidental carbon monoxide poisoning. His consciousness was virtually restricted to a second or two and no lasting memory traces could apparently be formed. While the original defect of memory may have been largely, if not wholly, organic, it was sustained thereafter on a hysterical basis. Conversely, a case has been reported in which the diagnosis, originally hysterical amnesia, had to be altered in light of the discovery that the patient had suffered from progressive disease of the brain. In such cases, organic and psychogenic factors appear to interact to produce complex and atypical symptoms.

Fugue states. The fugue is a condition in which the individual wanders away from his home or place of work for periods of hours, days, or even weeks. One celebrated case was that of the Rev. Ansell Bourne, described most eloquently by the U.S. psychologist William James. This clergyman wandered away from home for two months and acquired a new identity. On his eventual return, he was found to have no memory of the period of absence, though it was eventually restored under hypnosis. In not all cases, however, is the basis of the fugue so manifestly psychogenic. Indeed, close observation in some instances may reveal minor alterations in consciousness and behaviour that suggest an organic basis, probably epileptic. According to one view, pathological wandering with subsequent amnesia is due to a constellation of factors, among which are a tendency toward periodic depression, history of a broken home in childhood, and predisposition to states of altered consciousness, even in the absence of organic brain lesion. Psychoanalysts, on the other hand, see in the fugue a symbolic form of escape from severe emotional conflict.

Possible basis in epilepsy

PARAMNESIA AND CONFABULATION

The term paramnesia was introduced by a German psychiatrist, Emil Kraepelin, in 1886 to denote errors and illusions of memory. He distinguished three main varieties; one he called simple memory deceptions, as when one remembers as genuine those events imagined or hallucinated in fantasy or dream. This is not uncommon among confused and amnesic people and may also occur in paranoid states. Kraepelin also wrote of associative memory deceptions, as when a person meeting someone for the first time claims to have seen him on a variety of previous occasions. This has since been renamed reduplicative paramnesia or simply reduplication. Lastly there was identifying paramnesia, in which a novel situation is experienced as duplicating an earlier situation in every detail; this is now known as déjà vu or paramnesia *tout court*. The term confabulation denotes the production of false recollections generally.

Déjà vu. The déjà vu experience has aroused considerable interest, and is occasionally felt by most people, especially in youth or when they are fatigued. It has also found its way into literature, having been well described by, among other creative writers, Shelley, Dickens, Hawthorne, Tolstoy, and Proust. The curious sense of extreme familiarity may be limited to a single sensory system, such as the sense of hearing, but as a rule it is generalized, affecting all aspects of experience including the subject's own actions. As a rule, it passes off within a few seconds or minutes, though its repercussions may persist for some time. For some epileptics, however, déjà vu may continue for hours or even days and can provide a fertile subsoil for delusional elaboration.

In view of its occurrence among organically healthy individuals, déjà vu commonly has been regarded as psychogenic and as having its origin in some partly forgotten memory, fantasy, or dream. This explanation has appealed strongly to psychoanalysts; it also gains support from the finding that an experience very similar to déjà vu can be induced in normal people by hypnosis. If a picture is presented to a hypnotized person with the instruction to forget it and then is shown with other pictures when he is awake, the subject may report an intense feeling of familiarity that he is at a loss to justify. The déjà vu phenomenon also is attributable to minor neurophysiological abnormality; it is frequent in epilepsy. Indeed, déjà vu is accepted as a definite sign of epileptic activity originating in the temporal lobe of the brain and may occur as part of the seizure activity or frequently between convulsions. It seems to be more frequent in cases in which the disorder is in the right temporal lobe and has on occasion been evoked by electrical stimulation of the exposed brain during surgery. Some have been tempted to ascribe it to a dysrhythmic electrical discharge in some region of the temporal lobe that is closely associated with memory function.

Reduplicative paramnesia. Reduplication is observed mainly among acutely confused or severely amnesic people; for example, a patient may say that he has been in one or more hospitals that are very similar to his present location and that all bear the same name. The effect also can be induced by showing the person an object such as a picture and by testing him for recognition of the same picture a few minutes later. He is apt to say that he has seen a similar picture but definitely not the one now being shown. This effect appears to depend on loss of a sense of familiarity and on failure to treat a single object seen on a number of occasions as one and the same. It has been reported that reduplication of this kind is typically associated with confabulation, speech disorder (paraphasia), disorientation, and denial of illness.

Confabulation. Spurious memories or fabrications are very common in psychiatric disorders and may take on an expansive and grandiose character. They may also embody obvious elements from fantasy and dream. At a more realistic level, the production of false memories (confabulation) is best studied among sufferers of the Korsakoff syndrome, for whom consciousness and reasoning remain clear. When asked what he did on the previous day, such a person may give a detailed account of a typical day in his life several months or years earlier. Evidently his retrograde amnesia and his disorientation in time provide fertile soil for false reminiscence. When the confabulation embodies dramatic, fanciful elements, it is the exception rather than the rule.

Confabulation once was regarded as one's reaction to the social embarrassment produced by a memory defect; *i.e.*, as an attempt to fill memory gaps plausibly. Despite this possibility, many severely amnesic patients confabulate little, if at all; and there appears to be no relation between the severity of amnesia and frequency of confabulation. In consequence, individual differences in preamnesic personality have been stressed, particularly in regard to suggestibility. While many patients who confabulate are obviously highly suggestible, precise tests of suggestibility have not been used in most clinical evaluations. It also has been claimed that the superficially sociable, but basically secretive, individual is particularly prone to confabulate. The most critical factor appears to be the sufferer's degree of insight into his disorder; it has been observed that the amnesia sufferer who most strongly denies any lapse in memory is most prone to confabulate. By contrast, it also has been claimed that in chronic Korsakoff states the individual's insight into his condition is no guarantee of freedom from confabulation.

While confabulation is pathological by definition, all people include an inventive, imaginative (and therefore spurious) element in their remembering. Indeed, it seems valid to say that all remembering depends heavily on reconstruction rather than on mere reproduction alone. Among amnesiacs, reconstruction is especially drastic, inventive, and error prone, particularly in regard to chronological sequence. The difference, therefore, between normal and grossly amnesic confabulation may well be one of degree rather than kind.

HYPERMNESIA

Enhancement of memory function (hypermnesia) under hypnosis and in some pathological states was frequently described by 19th-century medical writers; for example, cases were recorded of delirious people who would speak fluently in a language they had not had occasion to use for up to 50 or more years and apparently had forgotten. It was then categorically claimed that anyone under hypnosis would recollect events with invariably greater efficiency than in the waking state. It is true that experience inaccessible to ordinary recall sometimes can be recollected under hypnosis; some have attributed this effect to release from emotional inhibition. Nevertheless, evidence indicates that previously memorized material (*e.g.*, poetry) in many cases is reproduced no better under hypnosis than in the waking state.

Memory prodigies. Few individuals who exhibit exceptional gifts of memory have been studied extensively. The case of a Russian mnemonist (memory artist), "S," was studied over a period of 30 years, and his story has been delightfully written by a Soviet psychologist (see *Bibliography*). This man's exceptional mnemonic ability seemed largely to depend on an outstandingly vivid, detailed, and persistent visual memory, almost certainly eidetic ("photographic") in nature. "S" also reported an unusual degree of synesthesia, though whether this helped or hindered his feats of memory is not entirely clear. (A person shows signs of synesthesia when he reports that stimulation through one sense leads to experiences in another sense; for example, such a person may say that he sees vivid flashes of colour when he hears music or speech.) Although "S's" highly developed power of concrete visualization made possible feats of memory far beyond the ordinary, he exhibited genuine weakness in abstract thinking.

Exceptional memory capacity is occasionally observed among mathematicians and others with exceptional talent for lightning calculation. A mathematics professor at the University of Edinburgh, for example, was reported to be capable of remarkable feats of long-term memory for personal experiences, music, and verbal material in either English or Latin. This talented mathematician has been said to recall with complete accuracy a list of 25 unrelated words after only a brief effort to memorize, and to recite the value of pi (an endless number) to a thousand places or more. Likewise, some composers and musicians appear to possess exceptional auditory memory, though no systematic study of their attainments appears

Inventive memory

Photographic memory

to have been made. The anatomical or physiological basis of hypermnesia remains most incompletely understood.

BIBLIOGRAPHY. A.R. LURIA, *The Mind of a Mnemonist* (1968), a fascinating account of a "memory prodigy" studied over many years by an outstanding Soviet psychologist; B. MILNER (ed.), "Disorders of Memory After Brain Lesions in Man," *Neuropsychologia*, 6:175–291 (1965), a symposium on memory disorders with major emphasis on psychological aspects; T. RIBOT, *Les maladies de la mémoire* (1881; Eng. trans., *Diseases of Memory*, 3rd ed., 1885); the classical text on disorders of memory. G.A. TALLAND, *Deranged Memory: A Psychonomic Study of the Amnesic Syndrome* (1965), a thorough historical, clinical, and experimental study of memory defect associated with chronic alcoholism, *Disorders of Memory and Learning* (1968), a popular survey of memory and some of its disorders; G.A. TALLAND and N.C. WAUGH (eds.), *The Pathology of Memory* (1969), the proceedings of an international symposium on the topic; C.W.M. WHITTY and O.L. ZANGWILL (eds.), *Amnesia* (1966), a review of amnesia considered from the neurological point of view.

(O.L.Z.)

Memory: Retention and Forgetting

That experiences influence subsequent behaviour is evidence of an obvious but nevertheless remarkable activity called remembering. Learning could not occur without the function popularly named memory. Practice results in a cumulative effect on memory leading to skillful performance on the tuba, to recitation of a poem, and even to reading and understanding these words. So-called intelligent behaviour demands memory, remembering being prerequisite to reasoning. The ability to solve any problem or even to recognize that a problem exists depends on memory. Typically, the decision to cross a street is based on remembering many earlier experiences.

Practice (or review) tends to build and maintain memory for a task or for any learned material. Over a period of no practice what has been learned tends to be forgotten; and the adaptive consequences may not seem obvious. Yet, dramatic instances of sudden forgetting (as in amnesia) can be seen to be adaptive. In this sense, the ability to forget can be interpreted to have survived through a process of natural selection in animals. Indeed, when one's memory of an emotionally painful experience leads to severe anxiety, forgetting may produce relief. Nevertheless, an evolutionary interpretation might make it difficult to understand how the commonly gradual process of forgetting survived natural selection.

In speculating about the evolution of memory, it is helpful to consider what would happen if memories failed to fade. Forgetting clearly aids orientation in time; since old memories weaken and the new tend to be vivid, clues are provided for inferring duration. Without forgetting, adaptive ability would suffer; for example, learned behaviour that might have been correct a decade ago may no longer be. Cases are recorded of people who (by ordinary standards) forgot so little that their everyday activities were full of confusion. Thus, forgetting seems to serve the survival of the individual and the species.

Another line of speculation posits a memory storage system of limited capacity that provides adaptive flexibility specifically through forgetting. In this view, continual adjustments are made between learning or memory storage (input) and forgetting (output). Indeed, there is evidence that the rate at which individuals forget is directly related to how much they have learned. Such data offer gross support of contemporary models of memory that assume an input-output balance.

Whatever its origins, forgetting has attracted considerable investigative attention. Much of this research has been aimed at discovering those factors that change the rate of forgetting. Efforts are made to study how information may be stored; that is, to discover the ways in which it may be encoded. Remembered experiences may be said to consist of encoded collections of interacting information; and interaction seems to be a prime factor in forgetting.

MEASURING RETENTION

Standard sentences, prose passages, and poems have been used to control input in studies of retention; but discrete verbal units (such as words or sets of letters) are most frequently employed. The letters usually comprise lists of consonant syllables (three consonants; *e.g.*, RQK) or so-called nonsense syllables (consonant-vowel consonant; *e.g.*, ROK). The order in which verbal units are to be learned and to be recited may be left to the subject (free recall). A schoolboy who can recite the names of all African countries probably has learned such a free-recall task. Units also can be presented serially (in a constant order), the subject being asked to recite them in that order; reciting the alphabet in the usual way represents such serial learning.

Pairs of words may be offered; in such paired-associate tasks the subject eventually is asked to produce the missing member of each pair when only one word is shown. This is akin to learning English equivalents for words from another language.

For these and similar tasks investigators commonly permit subjects enough practice trials to reach some preselected criterion or level of performance. This level effectively defines an immediate retention score against which later forgetting may be measured. Subsequent tests of retention are then made to investigate the rate at which forgetting proceeds. This rate tends to vary with the methods used, basically those of recall, recognition, or relearning.

Recall. Subjects may be asked to reproduce (recall) previously learned data in any order or in the original order in which they were learned.

In a free-recall test the instructions might be: "Yesterday you learned a list of words; please write as many of those words as you possibly can as they occur to you." For the paired-associate task the subject may be told: "Yesterday you learned some pairs of words; I will show you one word from each pair and you try to give the other." He may be paced, being limited to a few seconds to produce each word; or he may be unpaced, being given no rigidly specified limits.

If retention of any kind is to be measured over different periods (*e.g.*, an hour, a day, a week) a separate group of individuals should be used for each period. The reason is that the very act of remembering constitutes practice that keeps memory lively, tending to give misleading underestimates of the rate of forgetting if the same subjects are tested over successive intervals.

Recognition. The subject's task is simpler in tests of recognition, since reproduction or retrieval (as in recall) is not required. The subject simply is asked to remember previously presented information when it is offered to him again. For example, he may be given a list of words for study; on the subsequent test of retention these are mingled with additional words, the subject being asked to identify (recognize) the original words. Apparently the recognition test stresses ability to choose between "old" (studied) data and "new" words, although this need not mean that choices are based only on temporal discrimination (awareness of time distinctions).

In an alternative variety of recognition test, each word studied might be paired with a new one, the task being to choose the old member of each pair. Or, the test words might be presented one at a time for identification as old or new. Sometimes learning and testing are combined: a very long list of words may be presented one at a time, some being repeated; the task is to recognize the repeats.

Some recognition tests stress memory of the order of presentation. The subject learns a serial list (reciting in a prescribed order); the list then is scrambled, and he is tested on his ability to rearrange it appropriately. Order may be based on how units are arranged in space (*e.g.*, printed on a page) or on their numerical position in a series or on associative information. Thus, if a paired-associate list has been learned, the test may consist of the unmatched presentation of all units with a request to pair them properly. This sort of recognition seems to emphasize associative attributes. If some elements on the test were not presented originally, the temporal attribute also may be involved.

Relearning. The number of successive trials a subject takes to reach a specified level of proficiency may be

Free recall, serial learning, paired-associate tasks

compared with the number of trials he later needs to attain the same level. This yields a measure of retention by what is called the relearning method. The fewer trials needed to reach the original level of mastery, the better the subject seems to remember. The relearning measure sometimes is expressed as a so-called savings score. If ten trials initially were required, and five relearning trials later produce the same level of proficiency, then five trials have been saved; the savings score is 50 percent (that is, 50 percent of the original ten trials). The more forgetting, the lower the savings score.

Although it may seem paradoxical, relearning methods can yield both sensitive and insensitive measures of forgetting. Tasks have been devised that produce wide differences in recall but for which no differences in relearning are observed. (Some theorists attribute this to a form of heavy interference among learned data that has only momentary influence on retention.) Six months or a year after initial learning, some tests may give zero recall scores but can show savings in relearning.

Short-term and long-term memory

When relatively long retention intervals (usually hours or days) are used, the methods are said to involve long-term memory. In a sense, methods for studying short-term memory are miniaturized versions of these. A list may be as short as one item, level of proficiency is very low, and retention intervals are in seconds (or minutes at most).

For example, the subject may be shown a single non-sense syllable for a few seconds' study. Next he is given a simple task (such as counting backward) to occupy him for a half minute so that he cannot rehearse, and then is asked to recall the syllable. Forgetting is observed to occur over such short intervals, tending to be greater when length of interval increases, as in long-term memory. The same procedure can be used with a single paired-associate item or with a short list of four or five pairs. In a short-term counterpart of serial learning, a string of about eight single-digit numbers or letters is presented very rapidly (say, two per second), and the subjects are asked to recall them in the order in which they were presented. Recognition tests also can be adapted for measuring short-term retention. When only one presentation is used for learning, however, relearning measures are obviously unfeasible.

TIME-DEPENDENT ASPECTS OF RETENTION; STORAGE AND RETRIEVAL

Some workers theorize a distinct short-term memory system of sharply limited capacity that can retain information perhaps only a few seconds and a long-term system of relatively unlimited capacity and retention.

Among typical people, short-term function seems limited to about seven separate units (e.g., seven random letters or unrelated common words). Thus, one may consult a telephone directory and forget the number before dialing is completed. Information seems to enter long-term storage by such processing as rehearsal and encoding, as if short-term retention is a way station between incoming information and more enduring memory.

Other theorists do not distinguish short- and long-term systems as inferred from observed differences in capacity and retention. Positing only one storage system, they attribute short-term phenomena to very low levels of learning. Those who postulate distinct systems point to the results of injury to a specific brain region (the hippocampus): (1) information stored prior to hippocampal damage seems to be retained; (2) sufferers seem incapable of new long-term storage; (3) the short-term functions appear to be unimpaired and subjects perform as well as ever in tests of immediate memory (e.g., for a set of random numbers). It is as if new information no longer can be transferred from some sort of short-term system to relatively enduring storage.

Other data that bear on the controversy among theorists come from studies of people without known brain injury. When one has just seen a new list of words one at a time, the initial words in the list tend to be recalled best (primacy effects), those at the end next best (recency effects), while items from the middle are least likely to be recalled.

This is quite consistently found as long as recall begins immediately following presentation of the last word. If, however, a short interval follows, during which the subject is otherwise occupied to prevent rehearsal, the recency effect may completely disappear; words at the end are no better recalled than those in the middle. Primacy effects are essentially undisturbed, while a delay as short as perhaps 15 seconds is enough to abolish the recency phenomenon. Although some suggest that recency effects depend on a separate short-term memory system and that primacy effects are mediated by a long-term system, a single memory function also may be invoked to accommodate the findings. Nevertheless, interest is growing in multisystem theories on the grounds that they enhance appreciation of the processes involved in establishing relatively enduring memory.

Investigators concerned with physiological bases for memory seek a kind of neurochemical code with enough stability physically to produce a structural change or memory trace (engram) in the nervous system; mechanisms for decoding and retrieval also are sought. Efforts at the strict behavioral level similarly are directed toward describing encoding, decoding, and retrieval mechanisms as well as the content of the stored information.

One way to characterize a memory (or memory trace) is to identify the information it encodes. A learner may encode far more information than is apparent in the task as presented. For example, if a subject is shown three words for a few seconds and (after 30 seconds of diversion from rehearsal) is asked to recall and then another triad of words is given under the same procedure, then another, and so on, then if all triads share some common element (e.g., all are animal names), poorer and poorer recall is observed on successive trials. Such findings may be explained by assuming that the learner encodes this animal category as part of his memory for each word. Initially, the common code might be expected to aid recall by sharply delimiting the word population. Successive triads, however, should tend to be encoded in increasingly similar ways, blurring their unique characteristics for the subject. An additional step provides critical supporting evidence for such an interpretation. If a final triad of vegetable names is unexpectedly presented, recall recovers dramatically. The subject tends to reproduce the vegetable names much better than he does those of the last animal triad; recall is about as efficient as it was for the first three animal names. This particular shift clearly seems to provide escape from earlier confusion or blurring, and it may be inferred that a common conceptual characteristic was encoded for each animal name.

Any characteristic or attribute of a word may be investigated in this way to infer whether it is incorporated in memory. When recall does not recover it would seem that the manipulated characteristic has little or no representation in memory. For example, grammatical class typically does not appear to be encoded; decrement in recall produced after a series of triads consisting of verbs tends to continue when a shift is made to three adjectives. Such an experiment does not indicate what common encoding characteristic might be responsible for the decrement, suggesting only that it is not grammatical class.

Encoding mechanisms

Encoding mechanisms also may be inferred from tests of recognition. For example, subjects study a long list of words, being informed of a multiple-choice memory test to follow. Each word studied is made part of a test item that includes other carefully chosen new words (distractors). Distractors are selected to represent different types of encoding the investigator suspects may have occurred in learning. If the word presented for study is chosen by the subject, little can be inferred about the nature of the encoding. Any errors, however, can be most suggestive. Thus, if the word presented for study was TABLE, the multiple-choice item might be TABLE, CHAIR, ABLE, FURNITURE, PENCIL. If CHAIR is incorrectly selected, it may be suspected that this associatively related word occurred to the subject implicitly during learning and became so well encoded that the subject later could not determine whether it or TABLE had been presented. If the wrong choice is ABLE, acoustical resemblance to

TABLE may have contributed to the confusion. If FURNITURE is erroneously chosen, perhaps conceptual category was prominent in the encoding.

Since it is not related in any obvious way to TABLE, the word PENCIL may be intended as a control, unlikely to be a part of the memory for TABLE. If this is the case, subjects should be more likely to select distractor words other than PENCIL (if indeed they have been encoded along with TABLE).

Although a subject may have encoded in ways suggested by particular distractors, he still may be able to choose the correct word. Or he may have encoded in ways not represented by the distractors.

Evidence has been accumulating to suggest that a long-term memory is a collection of information or of attributes that can serve in discriminating it from other memories and can function as retrieval cues. In addition to verbal attributes, visual images may be a part of the memory; emotional responses produced at the time the memory is established may be incorporated.

The common experience of having a name or word on the tip of the tongue seems related to specific perceptual attributes. In particular, people who report the "tip-of-the-tongue" feeling tend to identify the word's first letter and number of syllables with an accuracy that far exceeds mere guessing. There is evidence that memories may encode information about when they were established and about how often they have been experienced. Some seem to embrace spatial information; e.g., one remembers a particular news item to be on the lower right-hand side of the front page of a newspaper. Research indicates that the rate of forgetting varies for different attributes. For example, memories in which auditory attributes seem dominant tend to be more rapidly forgotten than those with minimal acoustic characteristics.

If a designated (target) memory consists of a collection of attributes, its recall or retrieval should be enhanced by any cue that indicates one of the attributes. For example, on failing to recall the term horse (included in a list he has just seen), one may be told that there was an animal name among the words. Or he may be asked if an associate term (say, barn or zebra) helps him think of a word he missed. While some additional recall has been observed with this kind of help, failures are common even with ostensibly relevant cues. Though it is possible that the cues frequently are inappropriate, nevertheless, if words were not learned (encoded or stored) with accompanying attributes, cuing of any kind should be ineffective.

THEORIES OF FORGETTING

When memory of past experience is not activated for days or months, forgetting tends to occur; and any theory of forgetting must cope with this primitive observation. Such auxiliary phenomena as differences in the rates of forgetting for different kinds of information also must be accommodated.

It has been theorized that as time passes the physiological bases of memory tend to change. With disuse, it is held that the neural engram (the memory trace in the brain) gradually decays or loses its clarity. While such a theory seems reasonable, it would, if left at this point, do little more than restate behavioural evidence of forgetting at the nervous-system level. Decay or deterioration does not seem attributable merely to the passage of time; some underlying physical process needs to be demonstrated. Until a neurochemical basis for memory can be more explicitly described, any decay theory of forgetting must await detailed development.

Interference theory; retroactive and proactive inhibition

A pre-eminent theory of forgetting at the behavioral level is anchored in the phenomena of interference; in what are called retroactive and proactive inhibition. In retroactive inhibition, new learning interferes with retention of the old; in proactive inhibition, old memories interfere with the retention of new ones. Both phenomena have great generality in studies of any kind of learning, although most research among humans has considered verbal learning.

People may, for example, learn two successive verbal lists; the next day some are asked to recall the first list and others to recall the second. Still a third (control) group learns only one list and is asked to recall it a day later. People who learn two lists almost unfailingly will recall much less than do the control group. The amount by which controls exceed those who recall the first list is a measure of retroactive inhibition; the degree to which they are better than those who recall the second list is a measure of proactive inhibition. While retroactive inhibition usually will be observed in relearning, it is unusual to detect proactive deficit under such circumstances.

Theorists attribute the loss produced by these procedures to interference between list-learning tasks. When lists are constructed to exhibit varying differences, the degree of interference seems to be related to the amount of similarity. Thus loss in recall will be reduced when two successive lists have no identical terms. Maximum loss generally will occur when there appears to be heavy (but not complete) overlap in the memory attributes for the two lists. One may recall parts of the first list in trying to remember the second and vice versa. (This breakdown in discrimination may reflect the presence of dominant attributes that are appropriate for items in both lists.) Discrimination tends to deteriorate as the number of lists increases, retroactive and proactive inhibition increasing correspondingly, suggesting interference at the time of recall.

In retroactive inhibition, however, all of the loss need not be attributed to competition at the moment of recall. Some of the first list may be lost to memory in learning the second; this is called unlearning. If one is asked to recall from both lists combined, first-list items are less likely to be remembered than if the second list had not been learned. Learning the second list seems to act backward in time (retroactively) to destroy some memory for the first. So much effort has been devoted to studying conditions that affect unlearning that it has become a major topic in interference theory.

Retroactive and proactive effects can be quite gross quantitatively. If one learns a list one day and tries to recall it the next, learns a second list and attempts recall for it the following day, learns a third and so on, recall for each successive list tends to decline. Roughly 80 percent recall may be anticipated for the first list; this declines steeply to about 20 percent for the tenth list. Learning the earlier lists seems to act forward in time (proactively) to inhibit retention of later lists. These proactive phenomena indicate that the more one learns the more rapidly one will forget. Similar effects can be demonstrated for retroactive inhibition within just one laboratory session.

Such powerful effects have led some to theorize that all forgetting is produced by interference. Any given memory is said to be subject to interference from others established earlier or subsequently. Interference, theoretically, may occur when memories conflict through any attributes. With a limited group of attributes and an enormous number of memories, it might seem that everyday attempts to recall would be chaotic. Yet even if all of the memories shared some information, other attributes not held in common could still serve to distinguish them. For example, every memory theoretically is encoded at a different time and temporal attributes might serve to discriminate otherwise conflicting memories. Indeed, when two apparently conflicting lists are learned several days apart, proactive inhibition is markedly reduced. Assuming memories to be multiple-encoded, interference theory need not predict utter confusion in remembering.

Sources of interference are most pervasive and should not be considered narrowly. For example, any memory seems to be established in specific surroundings or context, and subsequent efforts to remember tend to be less effective when the circumstances differ from the original. Alcoholics, when sober, tend to have trouble finding bottles they have hidden while intoxicated; when they drink again, the task is much easier. Some contexts also may be associated with other memories that interfere with whatever it is that one is trying to remember.

Each new memory tends to amalgamate information already in long-term storage. Encoding mechanisms invariably adapt or relate fresh data to information already present, to the point that what is coded may not be a direct representation of incoming stimuli. This is particularly apparent when input is relatively meaningless; the newly encoded memory comes to resemble those previously established (*i.e.*, it accrues meaning). For example, a nonsense word such as LAJOR might be encoded as MAJOR.

To recall any nonsense word correctly requires that an appropriate decoding rule be a part of the memory; but coding rules are subject to forgetting (interference) in the same way that any attribute is. Qualitative changes in memory may result when the information presented does not allow precise decoding; thus, when one sees a drawing of a jagged figure that resembles a star he might encode it as a star, knowing full well that it is not perfect. Subsequent decoding in recall (or recognition) thus produces only an approximation of the original jagged figure; it may well be influenced by other equally imprecise decoding rules already stored. In like fashion, somewhat incoherent sentences may become more reasonable during encoding; they tend to be reproduced in memory tests more coherently. When the learner has trouble making sense of any new stimulus (when he cannot specify encoding and decoding rules with precision) the decoded memory tends to resemble previously established memories.

Although interference has attracted wide support as an account of forgetting, it must be placed in perspective. Interpretations that emphasize distinctions between short- and long-term memory and that posit control processes for handling information are potentially more comprehensive than is interference theory. Behavioral evidence for interference eventually may be explained within such systems.

In addition, a number of deductions from interference theory have not been well supported by experiment. The focus of difficulty lies in the hypothesis that interference from established memories is a major source of proactive inhibition. The laboratory subject is asked to learn tasks with attributes that have varying degrees of conflict with memories established in daily life. Theoretically, the more conflict, the greater the proactive interference to produce forgetting. Yet a number of experiments have failed to provide much support for this prediction.

Interference theory also fails to account for some pathological forms of forgetting. Repression as observed in psychiatric practice, for example, represents almost complete, highly selective forgetting; far beyond that anticipated by interference theorists. Attempts to study repression through laboratory procedures have failed to yield systematic data that could be used to test theoretical conclusions.

CORRELATES OF RATE OF FORGETTING

Remi-
niscence

Although forgetting normally is expected to begin as soon as practice ceases, at times an exception (known as reminiscence) has been reported. In reminiscence, memory seems to improve without practice; retention is even better if tested after a rest period than if tested immediately after learning trials stop. Observed only over periods of a few minutes, this elusive phenomenon produces very small improvements, and forgetting follows. Scores of studies designed to elicit reminiscence have failed to do so, yielding only evidence of forgetting. Reasons for the conflicting findings have not been identified.

Degree of learning.   The degree of learning is found to be directly associated with the amount of practice. In a metaphoric sense, specific memory may be said to grow stronger and stronger as practice proceeds. Even after a task can be performed or recited perfectly, continued practice (sometimes called overlearning) increases the "strength" of the memory. The rate of forgetting is slower when the degree of learning is greater. If there were one universal prescription for resisting forgetting, it would be to learn to a very high level initially; results seem even better when learning trials are not bunched together. Practice trials may be given en masse in a single session or the same number of trials may be distributed in sessions held on different days. The interrupted schedule is far superior to massed practice in that the rate of forgetting that follows distributed practice is much slower. The

laboratory evidence also confirms the belief that cramming for an examination may produce acceptable performance shortly afterwards, but that such massed study results in poor long-term retention. Information learned in widely distributed practice appears less susceptible to interference; memories established under distributed schedules also are less likely to produce proactive inhibition than are those learned in massed trials.

Mnemonic systems.   The principle that new information is encoded to previously stored data has been used in an effort to aid memory function. When encoding techniques are formally applied, they are called mnemonic systems or devices. (The popular rhyme that begins "Thirty days hath September . . ." is an example.) Verbal learning can be enhanced by providing an appropriate mnemonic system (even to a bright college student who may have devised efficient systems of his own). Thus, paired associates (*e.g.*, DOG-CHAIR) will be learned more rapidly if they are included in a simple sentence (*e.g.*, The dog jumped over the chair.) Imagery that can relate different words to be learned (even in a bizarre fashion) has been found beneficial. Some investigators hold that pure rote learning (in which no use is made of established memories except to directly perceive the stimuli) is rare or nonexistent. They suggest that all learning elaborates on memories already available. This could be taken to mean that the rate of forgetting would be the same whether or not a formal mnemonic system were used in learning.

Indeed, there seem to be no experimental results in which formal mnemonic instruction has resulted in forgetting more rapidly than when such special training is not given. Yet, while there often is no difference in the rate of forgetting, a number of studies indicate slower forgetting following instruction in a mnemonic system. These discrepancies may mean that some mnemonic systems are more subject to interference than are others. Perhaps the methods used fail to adequately distinguish between learning and forgetting.

Factors that influence rate of learning should be distinguished from those that affect rate of forgetting. For example, nonsense syllables are learned more slowly than are an equal number of common words; if both are studied for the same length of time, the better learned common words will be forgotten more slowly. But this does not mean that rate of forgetting *intrinsically* differs for the two tasks. Degree of learning must be held constant before it may be judged whether there are differences in rate of forgetting. Rates of forgetting can be compared only if tasks are learned to an equivalent degree. Indeed, when degree of learning is experimentally controlled, different kinds of information are forgotten at about the same rate. Nonsense syllables are *not* forgotten more rapidly than are ordinary words. In general, factors that seem to produce wide differences in rate of learning show little (if any) effect on rate of forgetting. (Despite discrepant evidence, mnemonic systems may prove an exception.)

Individual differences.   Experimental findings seem to contradict the common intuition that people inherently differ in the rate at which they forget. This intuitive belief appears largely to derive from definite, wide individual differences in rate of learning; some people do learn faster than others. Thus, given the same number of trials or identical time in which to study, people will vary widely in the level of learning they achieve. Individual differences in forgetting then can be predicted efficiently, merely on the basis of how well each person has learned. This powerfully indicates that ordinary estimates of one's rate of forgetting are spurious, being obscured by uncontrolled differences in learning ability. One's talent for learning seems to swamp efforts to assess his inherent tendency to forget. Under less ordinary circumstances, however (*e.g.*, selective brain injury, stroke, neurotic amnesia), the degree of learning does seem to be almost completely irrelevant to the rate at which one forgets. An amnesia sufferer may forget his own name and still may be able to remember that Sofia is the capital of Bulgaria (see MEMORY, ABNORMALITIES OF).

BIBLIOGRAPHY. J.A. ADAMS, *Human Memory* (1967), provides a well-considered account of memory as viewed from laboratory findings. A somewhat more abbreviated account is J. JUNG, *Verbal Learning* (1968). Two versions of formal models of memory are given in K.W. and J.T. SPENCE (eds.), *The Psychology of Learning and Motivation*, 3 vol. (1967–69), one by G. BOWER, "A Multicomponent Theory of the Memory Trace," 1:229–325 (1967); the other by R.C. ATKINSON and R.M. SHIFFRIN, "Human Memory: A Proposed System and its Control Processes," 2:89–195 (1968). The most comprehensive account of interference in long-term memory is provided by G. KEPPEL, "Retroactive and Proactive Inhibition," in *Verbal Behavior and General Behavior Theory* ed. by T.R. DIXON and D.L. HORTON, pp. 172–183 (1968). A parallel analysis for short-term memory is given by L. POSTMAN, "Short-term Memory and Incidental Learning," in *Categories of Human Learning* ed. by A.W. MELTON, pp. 145–201 (1964). B.J. UNDERWOOD, "Attributes of Memory," *Psychol. Rev.*, 76:559–573 (1969), summarizes evidence that memory can be described as a collection of information.

(B.J.U.)

Memphis (Egypt)

Memphis, the capital of ancient Egypt during the Old Kingdom (*c.* 2686–*c.* 2160 BC), was located south of the Nile Delta, on the west bank of the river. Closely associated with the city site are the cemeteries, or necropolises of Memphis, where the famous pyramids of Egypt and the Great Sphinx are located. From north to south, the main pyramid fields are: Abū Ruwaysh, Giza, Zawayet el-Aryan, Abū Ṣīr, Ṣaqqārah, and Dahshūr.

History. *Foundation and Early Dynastic Period.* According to a commonly accepted tradition, Memphis was founded around 3100 BC by Menes, who supposedly united the two prehistoric kingdoms of Upper and Lower Egypt. The precise historical identity of this king is still in question, but there is little doubt as to his connection with Memphis or of the importance of the city from the earliest period. The site had obvious political advantages, being located at the junction of the boundaries of the two formerly separate kingdoms. The local god of Memphis was Ptah, patron of craftsmen and artisans and, in some contexts, a creator god as well. The Great Temple of Ptah was one of the city's most prominent structures. According to an Egyptian document known as the Memphite Theology, Ptah created mankind through the power of his heart and speech; the concept, having been shaped in the heart of the creator, was brought into existence through the divine utterance itself. In its freedom from the conventional physical analogies of the creative act and in its degree of abstraction, this text is virtually unique in Egypt, and it testifies to the philosophic sophistication of the priests of Memphis.

The White Wall

The original name of the city was the White Wall, and the term may have referred originally to the king's palace, whose walls would have been built of whitewashed brick. The colour also had significance politically; white was the colour of the Lower Egyptian crown.

No remains of the period of Menes have come to light in the city site itself, but the evidence of the Memphite necropolises confirms the traditional age of the city. The large, elaborately niched tombs of the 1st and 2nd dynasties (*c.* 3100–*c.* 2686 BC) found at Ṣaqqārah have been claimed as royal tombs, but some scholars doubt that Memphis was the sole, or even the primary, capital of Egypt under those dynasties. According to the 3rd-century-BC historian Manetho, the 1st and 2nd dynasties originated at Tjene, or Thinis, in Upper Egypt. Thinis is near Abydos, and excavations at Abydos uncovered rectangular cut-stone tombs (mastabas) of this period that were long believed to be the royal burials of the first dynasties. To complicate the matter still further, there are equally important tombs of the period at other sites, such as Tarkhan and Abū Ruwaysh. Scholars disagree as to which of these are actually royal tombs, which are simply memorials, and which are tombs of important courtiers.

The Old Kingdom. By the 3rd dynasty the pre-eminence of Memphis is unquestioned. Manetho calls the 3rd and 4th dynasties (*c.* 2686–2494) Memphite, and the huge royal pyramid tombs of this period, in the necropolises of Memphis, confirm this. Djoser, the second king

of the 3rd dynasty, was the builder of the Step Pyramid of Ṣaqqārah, the first large monument to be constructed entirely of stone. Imhotep, the King's architect and adviser, is credited with this architectural feat; his reputation as a wise man and physician led, in later times, to his deification and his identification with the Greek god Asclepius.

The remains of several unfinished or badly ruined pyramids near Memphis have been attributed to other 3rd-dynasty kings. The first king of the 4th dynasty, Snefru, built two pyramid tombs at Dahshūr. The three great pyramids of Giza belong to Khufu, Khafre, and Menkaure, later-4th-dynasty monarchs. The Great Sphinx at Giza dates from the time of Khafre. The last legitimate king of this dynasty, Shepseskaf, built his tomb at South Ṣaqqārah. It was not a pyramid but a distinctive oblong structure with sloping sides, now called the Maṣṭabat Firʿawn.

The Pyramids of Giza

The royal pyramids are surrounded by large cemeteries where the courtiers and officials who had served the king during his lifetime were buried. The beautiful reliefs in certain of these tombs include scenes of daily life and thus give some idea of the crafts, costumes, and occupations of the royal court of Memphis. Since little has survived of domestic architecture and household furnishings, these reliefs are a valuable source of information on such subjects. A notable exception to the general rule of loss and destruction is the hidden tomb of Queen Hetepheres, the mother of Khufu, which was discovered near the Great Pyramid of Giza. Though the Queen's body was unaccountably missing from her sarcophagus, her funerary equipment and furniture survived. The exquisite taste and craftsmanship of these objects testify, as do the splendid low reliefs of the tombs, to the high development of the arts and crafts of the period. Indeed, it is believed by some scholars that the Old Kingdom, influenced by the craftsmen of the Memphite court and the philosopher-theologians of Ptah, reached a peak of "classic" culture that was never surpassed in Egypt.

The kings of the 5th dynasty (*c.* 2494–*c.* 2345) moved south of Giza to build their funerary monuments; their pyramids, at Abū Ṣīr, are much smaller than those of the 4th dynasty, but the pyramid temples and causeways were decorated with fine reliefs. This dynasty was probably marked by a decline of Memphite influence paralleling the rise of a sun cult centred at Heliopolis. The major monuments of the period are not the pyramids but the sun temples, which were, however, also part of the so-called Memphite pyramid area, not far from Abū Ṣīr.

During the 6th dynasty (*c.* 2345–*c.* 2181), which Manetho also designates as Memphite, the funerary monuments, in the pyramid field of Ṣaqqārah, continue to decline in size and workmanship; a curious fact is that the modern name of Memphis is ultimately derived from Men-nefer, the name of the pyramid city of the 6th dynasty king Pepi I. This relatively small and obscure pyramid thus gave its name to the entire region. At this time the influence of the centralized government at Memphis began to wane, as is indicated by the increased prominence of provincial cities and the number of fine tombs located away from the Memphis area. This process of decentralization ended in the First Intermediate Period, a time of internal breakdown. Manetho's 7th and 8th dynasties are both called Memphite, but it is believed that both dynasties together comprised a very short period and that the old Memphite house lost its control over the provincial princes soon after the end of the 6th dynasty.

The last Memphite dynasties

Later history. Memphite influence continued during the Middle Kingdom, (*c.* 2040–1786) when Egypt was once more reunited, but the official residence of the 12th dynasty (1991–1786) was at Lisht, near the entrance to al-Fayyum. Several 12th-dynasty monarchs erected pyramids at Dahshūr, the southernmost of the Memphite pyramid fields, but the majority of Middle Kingdom monuments were located nearer to Lisht. Yet the predominant artistic and administrative influences during this period seem to be Memphite, and virtually every 12th-dynasty ruler added to the Great Temple of Ptah.

Another period of political and social chaos followed

Recumbent colossus of Ramses II photographed at Memphis in the early 1900s. The statue is now housed for display near the ancient site.
Foto Marburg

the 12th dynasty. This Second Intermediate Period (1786–1567) is characterized by the presence in Egypt of the Asian Hyksos peoples. According to the 1st-century-AD historian Josephus, the Hyksos king, whom he calls Salitis, made his capital at Memphis and from there ruled both Upper and Lower Egypt. Inscriptional and archaeological evidence, though scanty, tends to confirm the assumption that the invaders controlled northern Egypt, but their capital is generally supposed to have been located at Avaris, near Tanis, in the Delta. Records left by Kamose, the 17th-dynasty king who began the reconquest of Egypt from the Hyksos, describe his holdings as running from Elephantine to Hermopolis Magna but note that he "could not pass by (the invader) as far as Memphis."

With the final expulsion of the Hyksos and the restoration of a united kingdom under the 18th dynasty, based at Thebes in Upper Egypt, Memphis entered on a new period of prosperity. Some scholars claim that Memphis never lost its political pre-eminence and that during the New Kingdom, as in earlier times, the city was the actual political capital of Egypt, with Thebes merely the religious centre. Such a hypothesis is impossible to prove, and it may well be that such distinctions, with their rigidity and exclusiveness, are meaningless in terms of Egyptian culture.

The importance of Memphis was based to a considerable extent upon its venerable religious role. Certain of the coronation ceremonies were traditionally enacted in Memphis, as was the Sed festival, a re-enactment of the coronation that restored and restated the supernatural powers of the kingship.

Memphis in the New Kingdom
During the New Kingdom (1567–1085), Memphis probably functioned as the second, or northern, capital of Egypt. At one time it seems to have been the principal residence of the crown prince. Several 18th-dynasty (1567–1320) inscriptions mention royal hunting parties in the desert near the Sphinx. Amenhotep II (reigned 1450–1425) was born at Memphis and held the office of high priest there. Both he and his son, Thutmose IV (reigned 1425–1417), left inscriptions at Giza.

Despite the rise of the god Amon of Thebes, Ptah remained one of the principal gods of the pantheon. The Great Temple was added to or rebuilt by virtually every king of the 18th dynasty. Chapels were constructed by Thutmose I and Thutmose IV, and by Amenhotep III. The latter's son, Prince Thutmose, was high priest of Ptah. Amenhotep III's son, the religious reformer Akhenaton, built a temple to his god Aton in Memphis. A number of handsome private tombs dating from this period in the Memphite necropolis testify to the existence of a sizeable court.

During the New Kingdom the city shared the increasingly cosmopolitan character of the nation, as trade, foreign conquest, and travel developed. Though Memphis was not on the Nile, it was connected with it by a canal, and it was probably important as a commercial centre. Specific quarters of the city were named after the foreign colonies—slaves, prisoners of war, or merchants—who resided there. A section called the "Field of the Hittites" is known, as are, in later periods, sections inhabited by Carians and Phoenicians.

Under the 19th dynasty (1320–1200) a new royal residence was built farther north at Per-Ramessu in the Delta, but Memphis continued to be important. The Great Temple was rebuilt. The kings of that period pillaged the monuments of their predecessors for building materials, and some of the reused blocks come not only from structures in the city but also from temples and pyramid complexes in the Memphite necropolises. Ramses II (reigned 1304–1237) erected several colossi in the temple. The Sarapeum, dedicated to the cult of Apis, the bull-god, and built in the form of a labyrinth, was begun under the son of Ramses II, Khaemwese, high priest of Ptah.

By the end of the 20th dynasty the united kingdom had begun to break down once again. The official capitals were Tanis and Thebes, but the royal palace at Memphis continues to be mentioned. The growing popularity of the Apis cult led to further enlargement of the Sarapeum. In the 8th century BC, the Nubian king Piankhi conquered Egypt and restored its unity. Nubia (or Kush), to the south of Egypt, had been under Egyptian political and cultural influence for centuries. An inscription describing Piankhi's campaign has survived, and it mentions a siege of Memphis. The city had fortified walls and was surrounded by water, presumably from its encircling canals. Piankhi took the city, but it was left to his brother and successor, Shabaka, to claim the royal title. There are some indications that this king made Memphis his capital. But the Kushite dynasty was overthrown shortly thereafter, when the Assyrians invaded Egypt. Records left by the Assyrian king Esarhaddon (680–669 BC) refer to the siege and destruction of Memphis, the royal residence of one Tarku, king of Egypt, who is probably to be identified with Taharqa, who became pharaoh in 689 BC. After the death of Esarhaddon, Taharqa regained Memphis, but he was driven out of the city again by Ashurbanipal of Assyria, in 667 BC.

Kushite occupation

The collapse of Assyria (612 BC) led to brief Egyptian independence under the 26th dynasty, but it was not long before new invaders appeared. The Persian Cambyses took Memphis by siege in 525 BC. After years of Persian rule Egypt was ready to welcome Alexander the Great in 332 BC. The conqueror used Memphis as his headquarters while making plans for his new city of Alexandria. After his death at Babylon, his body was brought to Egypt and was laid to rest temporarily in Memphis before being buried at Alexandria.

Under the Hellenistic Ptolemaic dynasty (305–30 BC), Memphis retained its cosmopolitan character and had a sizable Greek population. Some of the diversified racial types to be found in the city during Greco-Roman times are depicted in a series of striking terra-cotta heads dating from this period.

At the beginning of the Roman period (1st century BC) Memphis was still considered an important provincial capital. The serious decay of the ancient city began after the rise of Christianity, when zealots of that faith defaced and destroyed the remaining pagan temples. In the 5th century AD the Christian monastery of Apa Jeremias rose among the venerable tombs of Ṣaqqārah. The capital continued to deteriorate, receiving its death blow during the Muslim conquest of Egypt in AD 640. A garrison and fort called Babylon occupied the eastern end of the bridge that crossed the Nile from Memphis, and after a long siege the fortress was taken by the Arab general 'Amr ibn al-'Aṣ. Memphis was abandoned, and later the few remaining structures were dismantled so that the stone might be reused in the neighbouring villages and in Cairo, after that city's foundation in the 10th century.

Archaeology. The ancient city of Memphis lies near the modern village of Mīt Ruhaynah. At the beginning of the 20th century some ruined walls were still to be seen, but these have now disappeared, and the only monument above ground is a colossal statue of Ramses II, which once adorned the Great Temple of Ptah. Few city sites in Egypt have been excavated, and, like so many other ancient Egyptian sites, Memphis is known primarily from the exploration of its necropolises, which tend to yield more dramatic finds than the city itself.

The site of the city

The first archaeologist to work at the city site for any prolonged period was Flinders Petrie, who excavated between 1908 and 1913, uncovering sections of the Great Temple of Ptah. These remains, left exposed, soon disappeared under the effects of weather and the depredations of the nearby villagers. In recent times expeditions have been led by Ahmad Badawi, in 1942, and by Labib Habachi, in 1950. A University of Pennsylvania expedition worked at the site in 1917, finding foundations of a palace of Merneptah (1236–1223 BC) east of the temple of that king. The University sponsored further digging in 1955 and 1956, excavating parts of the Great Temple and a small temple of Ramses II.

For the past century there has hardly been a season when archaeological activity was not proceeding at one or another of the pyramid sites. Almost all of the pyramids, and a majority of the large private tombs, were entered by treasure hunters before the beginning of scholarly excavation. One of the earliest scholars to work in the Memphite area was Auguste Mariette, who discovered the Sarapeum in 1851. Among the most important of Mariette's successors were G.A. Reisner and Hermann Junker, who excavated at Giza; Ludwig Borchardt, who excavated the sun temples and the 5th-dynasty pyramids at Abū Sīr; Ahmad Fakhry, who worked in the pyramids of Snefru at Dahshūr; and Zakaria Goneim, who discovered a previously unknown pyramid, probably of the 3rd dynasty, to the southwest of the Step Pyramid at Ṣaqqārah. Also noteworthy are the excavations of J.P. Lauer in the Step Pyramid complex. In the 1930s, W.B. Emery began the excavations that uncovered the great 1st-dynasty tombs. His work in the archaic cemetery disclosed another huge labyrinth resembling that of the Sarapeum, the precise function of which is as yet undetermined. Extensive as the work has been in these necropolises, it is certain that new discoveries are waiting to be made. Yet of all these areas it is unlikely that any deserves painstaking excavation more than does the city site of Memphis itself.

BIBLIOGRAPHY. JEAN CAPART, *Memphis: À l'ombre des pyramides* (1930), a popular tour of the necropolises; WALTER EMERY, Reports on the excavations at Ṣaqqārah in the *Journal of Egyptian Archaeology* (1965–69); HERMANN KEES, "Memphis and Heliopolis," in *Das alte Ägypten* (1955; Eng. trans., *Ancient Egypt: A Cultural Topography*, 1961), the most useful general work; W.M.F. PETRIE, *Seventy Years in Archaeology*, pp. 226–246 (1932, reprinted 1969), a general and interesting account of the author's work, *Memphis I–V* (1909–13);

I.E.S. EDWARDS, "The Early Dynastic Period in Egypt," in *Cambridge Ancient History*, rev. ed., vol. 1, ch. 11 (1964); RUDOLPH ANTHES, *Mit Rahineh 1955 and 1956* (1959, 1965), excavation report; A.H. GARDINER, *Egypt of the Pharaohs* (1961), for general historical background.

(B.G.M.)

Mencius

The Chinese philosopher and follower of Confucius, Mencius has long been considered the second Sage by the Chinese (Confucius being the first). Although his surname is Meng and his personal name K'o, the philosopher is usually referred to by his honorific title, Meng-tzu (in Pin-yin romanization Meng-zu; "Master Meng"); Mencius is its Latinized form. Among all of the philosophers and teachers of China, only Confucius and Mencius have had their names Latinized.

By courtesy of the National Palace Museum, Taipei, Taiwan, Republic of China

Mencius, ink and colour on silk by an unknown artist. In the National Palace Museum, Taipei, Taiwan.

Of noble origin, the Meng family settled in the state of Tsou, a minor state about the size of a county in the present province of Shantung. Mencius was born there about 371 BC. In several respects his life was similar to that of Confucius. Tsou and Lu (the state of Confucius' origin) were adjacent states. Like Confucius, Mencius was only three when he lost his father. Mencius' mother paid special attention to the upbringing of her young son. A traditional story tells of her moving their home several times and finally settling near a school, so that the boy should have the right kind of environmental influence, and of her cutting up the cloth on her loom in order to teach her son an unforgettable lesson about perseverance and devotion in his studies. Among the Chinese, the mother of Mencius has been for ages upheld as the model Chinese mother.

Early life

As a young scholar Mencius had for his mentor a pupil of Tzu Ssu, the grandson of Confucius. Thus, the continuity of the Confucian orthodoxy in all its purity was assured. In due time Mencius became a teacher himself and for a brief period served as an official in the state of Ch'i. He spent much time travelling, offering his advice and counsel to the various princes on government by *jen* ("human heartedness"), or humane government. The effort was foredoomed because the times were chaotic, and the contending princes were interested not in humane government but in power.

The Chou dynasty (c. 1122–221 BC) was founded on the feudalistic principle of a sociopolitical hierarchy, with clearly defined prerogatives and obligations between those of high and low status. As time went on, however, ambition and intrigue resulted in usurpations and impositions, eroding the feudalistic system at the root and bringing on a condition of political and moral disorder. This trend, which caused alarm to Confucius, continued to worsen at an accelerating rate, and the age in which Mencius lived is known as the period of Warring States in Chinese history (481–221 BC). Under such conditions, Mencius' preachments to the princes on virtuous personal conduct and humane government fell on deaf ears; yet, he continued to speak his mind, even though he knew that he was championing an unpopular cause.

Philosopher for the people

According to Mencius, the ruler was to provide for the welfare of the people in two respects: material conditions for their livelihood and moral and educational guidance for their edification. Mencius had worked out a definite program to attain economic sufficiency for the common people, and it is recorded in the book of *Mencius* three times. He also advocated light taxes, free trade, conservation of natural resources, welfare measures for the old and disadvantaged, and more nearly equal sharing of wealth. It was his fundamental belief that "only when the people had a steady livelihood would they have a steady heart."

While Mencius patiently exhorted the princes to cultivate the way of moral power and to forsake the way of force and intrigue, he also reminded them emphatically of the responsibility that came to them with the mandate of Heaven to govern for the good of the people. With unusual courage, Mencius declared: "The people are the most important element in a nation; the spirits of the land and grain come next; the sovereign counts for the least." He also quoted for all to hear from the *Shu Ching* ("Classic of History"), one of the Five Classics of Confucianism, the saying "Heaven sees as the people see; Heaven hears as the people hear." The outspoken sympathies of Mencius made him a champion of the common people and an advocate of democratic principles in government.

Mencius' sojourn covered several states, but nowhere did he find a prince willing to put his lofty principles of government into practice. His sense of disappointment grew with the years and finally brought him back to his native state of Tsou, where he devoted the remaining years of his life to the instruction of his pupils. The work *Mencius* is a collection of the records of the doings and sayings of the master by his disciples, arranged in seven books with two parts to each book.

Doctrine of human nature

The philosophic ideas of Mencius might be regarded as an amplification of the teachings of Confucius. Confucius taught the concept of *jen*, love or magnanimity, as the basic virtue of manhood. Mencius made the original goodness of human nature the keynote to his system. That the "four beginnings," or "four principles" (*ssu tuan*)—the feeling of commiseration, the feeling of shame, the feeling of courtesy, and the feeling of right and wrong—are all inborn in man was a self-evident truth to Mencius; and the "four beginnings," when properly cultivated, will develop into the four cardinal virtues of *jen*, righteousness, decorum, and wisdom. This doctrine of the goodness of human nature on the part of Mencius has become an enduring topic for debate among the Chinese thinkers throughout the ages.

Mencius went further and taught that man possessed intuitive knowledge and intuitive ability and that personal cultivation consisted in developing one's mind. Mencius said: "He who has developed his mind to the utmost, knows his nature. Knowing his nature, he knows Heaven." Hence, all men could become like the great sage-kings Yao and Shun, the legendary heroes of the archaic past, according to Mencius.

While Mencius has always been regarded as a major philosopher, special importance was attributed to him and his work by the Neo-Confucianists of the Sung dynasty (AD 960–1279). For the last 1,000 years, Mencius has been revered among the Chinese people as the cofounder of Confucianism, second only to Confucius.

Mencius died in about 289 BC.

BIBLIOGRAPHY. Among the several translations of the *Mencius* into the English language, the one by JAMES LEGGE, *The Chinese Classics*, vol. 2, *Mencius*, 2nd ed. (1893–95; 3rd ed., 1960), is the standard one. W.A.C.H. DOBSON's translation, *Mencius: A New Translation Arranged and Annotated for the General Reader* (1963), is also worth consulting. ALBERT F. VERWILGHEN, *Mencius: The Man and His Ideas* (1967), is the only general treatise on the subject in English. For the philosophy of Mencius, see FUNG YU-LAN, *A History of Chinese Philosophy*, 2nd ed., vol. 1 (Eng. trans. 1952).

(Y.P.M.)

Mendel, Gregor Johann

Gregor Johann Mendel, the Austrian monk whose discoveries of the first laws of heredity laid the foundation of the science of genetics, was born Johann Mendel, in Heinzendorf, which was then in Austrian Silesia, on July 22, 1822. His interest in natural science developed early. After two years' study at the Philosophical Institute at Olmütz (now Olomouc, Czechoslovakia), he entered the Augustinian monastery at Brünn, Moravia (later Brno, Czechoslovakia), in 1843, taking the name Gregor. He was ordained a priest in 1847. During the period of his monastic training he taught himself a certain amount of science. From 1849 he acted for a short time as a substitute teacher of Greek and mathematics in the secondary school at Znaim (Znojmo), near Brünn. In 1850 he took the examination for certification as a regular teacher but failed, his lowest marks being given, ironically, in biology and geology. He was then sent by his abbot to the University of Vienna, where he studied physics, chemistry, mathematics, zoology, and botany (1851–53). In 1854 Mendel returned to Brünn and taught natural science in the technical high school there until 1868, although he never succeeded in passing the examination for a teacher's license. In that year he was elected abbot of his monastery.

Mendel, etching by August Potuczek (1917-   ).

First experiments

The experiments that led to his discovery of the basic principle of heredity and, subsequently, to the science of genetics were begun in the small monastery garden in 1856. He worked for himself but in an atmosphere conducive to scientific interests. Among his colleagues at the high school were several men engaged in science, some of whom founded in Brünn, in 1862, the Natural Science Society, in whose meetings Mendel took an active part. The libraries of both monastery and school contained essential scientific books, especially on agriculture, horticulture, and botany, subjects in which Mendel's interest had been aroused by experience in his father's orchard and farm. That Mendel himself bought new books in these fields as they appeared is shown by his marginal notes in the works of Charles Darwin that appeared in the 1860s and 1870s. But it is also certain that he had begun his experiments before Darwin's first book was published and before the essential role assigned to heredity as the basis of evolutionary change had been widely recognized. In fact, when he reported the results of his experiments to the Brünn Society for the Study of Natural Science on February 8 and March 8, 1865, he referred to his field of interest as "plant hybridization," and after indicating his familiarity with the work of his predecessors in this field, he boldly stated that

> among all the numerous experiments made, not one has been carried out to such an extent and in such a way as to make it possible to determine the number of different forms under which the offspring of hybrids appear, or to arrange these forms with certainty according to their separate generations, or definitely to ascertain their statistical relations.

It was this formulation by Mendel of the essential requirements for the experimental study of heredity and his provision of experimental data satisfying these requirements—both original achievements—that led him to the solution of a problem that underlies not only the understanding of heredity and of evolution but of biological processes generally.

Mendel crossed varieties of the garden pea that had maintained, under his observation, constant differences in such single alternative characters as tallness and dwarfishness, presence or absence of colour in the blossoms and axils of the leaves, and similar alternative differences in seed colour, seed shape, position of the flowers on the stem, and form of the pods. He theorized that the occurrence of the visible alternative characters of the plants, in the constant varieties and in their descendants, is due to the occurrence of paired elementary units of heredity, now known as genes. (For the behaviour of these units in heredity, see HEREDITY.) The novel feature of Mendel's interpretation of his data, amply confirmed by subsequent observations on other organisms, including man, is that these units obey simple statistical laws. The principle of these laws is that in the reproductive cells of the hybrids, half transmit one parental unit and half transmit the other. This separation of alternative characters in the reproductive cells, now known as Mendel's first law, or the principle of segregation, adequately accounts for the results when single pairs of alternative characters are observed through several generations and serves reliably as a basis of prediction. Mendel showed, moreover, that when several pairs of alternative characters are observed, the several pairs of elements enter into all possible combinations in the progeny. In the pea varieties at his disposal he observed that the seven pairs of differentiating characters recombined at random, according to the law, or principle, of independent assortment, and he worked out the statistical consequences of this principle and confirmed them by experiment.

It is known now that Mendel's second principle (independent assortment) applies only to genes that are transmitted in different "linkage groups" or chromosomes in which genes are organized. Likewise the appearance (or dominance) in the hybrid of one of the alternative characters, which was true of all seven pairs observed by Mendel, proves, on wider experience, not to be true of all alternative characters. But neither of these limitations affects the fundamental truth of the system of particulate heredity by units or genes, which he was the first to prove. In the early years of the 20th century, while it was being tested and confirmed, this system was called Mendelism; it proved to be of general application and is one of the basic principles of biology.

This theory and the description of the experimental results from which it was deduced were presented in two papers that Mendel read at meetings of the Natural Science Society early in 1865 and published in detail in the transactions of the society in 1866. The article, entitled "Versuche über Pflanzenhybriden" ("Experiments with Plant Hybrids"), seemed to have had no effect whatever on the biological thinking of his time in Brünn or elsewhere, although his publication reached the major libraries in Europe and America. Perhaps typical of the reception given Mendel's monumental publication was that of the eminent botanist Karl Wilhelm von Nägeli, at the University of Munich; from his correspondence with Mendel it appears that Nägeli neither fully understood the spare, mathematical logic of Mendel's paper nor adequately appreciated the implications of the monk-scientist's revolutionary discoveries.

Nevertheless, Mendel continued his research, attempt-

ing to test his theory by experiments with other plants. He published one further paper in 1869, but the plant he chose to investigate—the hawkweed (*Hieracium*), which Nägeli encouraged Mendel to work with—was inherently unsuited to serve as test material and no corroboration of Mendel's principles was obtained because in this genus the embryo is formed from the ovum without fertilization (somatic parthenogenesis). Although Mendel's interest and work in botany, bee culture, and meteorology continued almost until his death, science ceased to occupy the central position in his life, for his election as abbot of his monastery in 1868 brought with it a host of administrative duties and a protracted struggle with the Austrian government over the taxation of the monastery.

Mendel died on January 6, 1884, respected and loved by his fellow monks and townsmen but unknown as the great biological scientist that he was.

Fame came to him only after his death. In 1900 three other European botanists, Carl Erich Correns, Erich Tschermak von Seysenegg, and Hugo de Vries, independently obtained results similar to Mendel's and in searching the literature found that both the experimental data and the general theory had been published 34 years previously. What followed is now a part of the history of genetics: confirmation and extension of his theory by biologists in many countries and its incorporation as the basis of a rapidly developing science with primary influence on the understanding of evolution, development, physiology, biochemistry, medicine, agriculture, and social science.

BIBLIOGRAPHY. H. ILTIS, *Gregor Mendel: Leben, Werk und Wirkung* (1924; Eng. trans., *Life of Mendel*, 1932), the standard biography; L.C. DUNN, "Mendel, His Work and His Place in History," *Proc. Am. Phil. Soc.*, 109:189–198 (1965), a description of Mendel's life and an evaluation of his work prepared for the commemoration of the publication of Mendel's pioneer experiments in genetics; and (ed.), *Genetics in the 20th Century* (1951), essays on the progress of genetics following the rediscovery of Mendel's work in 1900; C. STERN and E.R. SHERWOOD (eds.), *The Origin of Genetics: A Mendel Source Book* (1967), a work containing English translations of Mendel's papers of 1865 and 1869, his letters to Karl von Nägeli, 1866–73, papers reporting the rediscovery of Mendel's work in 1900, and later commentaries on his work.

(L.C.D./Ed.)

Mendeleyev, Dmitry Ivanovich

Dmitry Ivanovich Mendeleyev made a basic contribution to the study of chemistry by proving that all chemical elements are related members of a single ordered system. Mendeleyev arranged all the known elements according to their atomic weights on what he called a periodic table and by his periodic law proved that the chemical properties of the elements are periodic functions of their atomic weights. His work was the culmination of a search for a relation between the elements that had been foreshadowed in classical times, a search that had been resumed since the beginning of scientific chemistry in the early 18th century. Mendeleyev, by establishing a periodic classification of the elements, merits a place with Antoine Lavoisier, who clarified the concept of an element as the ultimate chemical species resisting further analytical breakdown, and with John Dalton, who showed how each element can be considered as constituted of identical atoms characterized by a determinable atomic weight.

Mendeleyev was born at Tobolsk, Siberia, on February 7 (January 27, old style), 1834, the 17th and last child of the director of the gymnasium there. In the same year his father became blind, and, in order to support the family, his mother leased and operated a glass factory in a town 20 miles (32 kilometres) away. At school Dmitry excelled in mathematics, physics, and geography but fared badly in the compulsory classical languages.

In 1847 his father died, and the next year fire destroyed the glass factory. Faced with these disasters, his mother made a brave decision: she turned her back on Tobolsk and, with her only two dependent children (Dmitry and his sister), set out for Moscow to place her son in the university.

Notwithstanding her good connections, she could not

Discovery
of laws
of heredity

prevail in the face of the inflexible regulations that restricted admission according to place of origin: Siberia was outside the academic pale. She pressed on to St. Petersburg, but the university there, too, was closed to her son. Dmitry was also refused admission to the medical school, but, ten weeks before her death, his mother finally secured him a place in the Pedagogic Institute.

In 1855 he qualified as a teacher, winning a gold medal for his academic achievements. On account of his health, he was posted, at his own request, to the Crimea, where he continued his chemical studies at Odessa; he returned to St. Petersburg in 1856 to obtain an advanced degree in chemistry. In 1857 he received his first university appointment.

In 1859 the government sent him for further study to the University of Heidelberg. Although Robert Bunsen, the chemist and inventor, and the physicist Gustav Kirchhoff were then the dominant figures in the natural sciences at Heidelberg, Mendeleyev preferred to work independently. His study of molecular cohesion was begun at this time, and while at Heidelberg he attended the celebrated Karlsruhe conference (September 1860) and made valuable contacts with French chemists and with the Italian chemist Stanislao Cannizzaro, whose insistence on the distinction between molecular and atomic weights influenced Mendeleyev considerably.

In 1861 Mendeleyev returned to St. Petersburg. The lack of a permanent position led him to take up editing

By courtesy of the Mendeleyev All-Union Research Institute of Metrology, Moscow

Mendeleyev.

and scientific writing. In 1864 he became professor of chemistry at the Technical Institute, and three years later he was made professor of general chemistry at the university there. Since he could not find a textbook that met his needs, he set about writing his own: the result was *The Principles of Chemistry* (1868–70), a classic textbook.

In the course of writing the book, Mendeleyev probed deeply into the relationship between the properties of elements in an attempt to devise a system of classifying them. Other scientists had also tried to construct such a system of classification. After the English chemist and physicist John Dalton had developed the idea of atomic weights, chemists sought arithmetic connections between them, partly to see whether there was any likelihood of all elements being composed of a simple, common substance and partly to see whether occasional similarities in their properties pointed to similarities in structure. Johann Döbereiner and William Odling, both of whom had also done work with atomic weights, were the most prominent among the chemists who attempted to devise a logical order for the elements. It was Mendeleyev, however, who formulated the periodic law, according to which, when all known elements are arranged in order of increasing atomic weight, the resulting table shows a periodicity of properties and allows one to observe the many types of chemical relation hitherto studied only in isolation. The new system did not win wide acceptance at first,

Formulation of the periodic law

its validity becoming apparent only with time. The table of elements had gaps, but Mendeleyev predicted that they would be filled by elements not yet discovered; three were discovered within 20 years, and they possessed the properties he had predicted. Gradually the table became the framework for a great part of chemical theory and proved to be most useful in the interpretation of the processes of the natural transformation of one element into another, called radioactive decay, more than 20 years after the table's conception.

Although Mendeleyev's textbooks ran to many editions in many languages, the periodic theory remained his chief monument. Mendeleyev's mind however, was not, limited to theory and to classroom teaching. He was also by nature a practical man, aware of the necessity to use science in solving the problems of the world. In 1865, he farmed a small estate and improved the yield and quality of crops by the application of his scientific knowledge, a measure he knew was essential to the improvement of the general agricultural condition of Russia.

In 1867 he was sent to organize the Russian pavilion at the Paris Exposition of that same year. His study of the French chemical industry during his stay helped him improve the Russian soda industry, and, later, he spent much time working on the problems of the Russian petroleum industry. During a visit to the United States in 1876, he criticized the manner in which American oil interests concentrated on mere expansion of production without giving attention to scientific improvements of either the efficiency of the industry or the quality of its products. At home he was equally critical of the way Russian oil was exploited by foreign interests, and he constantly urged that Russia develop its own oil for its own profit. His interest in aeronautics led him to make balloon ascents for scientific observation and to encourage his colleagues to pursue the possibilities of heavier-than-air flight.

Work in applied chemistry

Politically, Mendeleyev held progressive views and was much interested in social reform. The tsarist regime did not approve of his political views, and, although a man of his stature could not be suppressed, he was often snubbed —as, for example, in 1880, when he was ostentatiously refused advancement from corresponding to full membership of the Imperial Academy of Sciences. In 1890 Mendeleyev's transmittal of a request from students at the university for alleviation of unjust conditions led to an open clash between him and the government. For this allegedly improper action he was retired from the university. He held no further major academic post.

He was too useful, however, to be left idle. In 1891 he was officially employed in setting up a new system of import duties on heavy chemicals, and in 1893 he headed the Bureau of Weights and Measures, a post he filled efficiently until his death.

His last years were saddened not only by declining health but by the political events that preceded the uprising of 1905. He died on February 2 (January 20, O.S.), 1907. He had been greatly honoured by colleagues of many countries as a guest lecturer and as an honorary member of academies. He was recognized in his day as a leader of the movement to systematize and make cohesive the study of chemistry. He is recognized now as the discoverer of the interrelationship of chemical elements, which not only underlies most of chemistry but also unifies a great deal of modern physics.

Death

BIBLIOGRAPHY. The definitive biography is that of N.A. FIGUROVSKY, Дмитрий Иванович Менделеев, 1834–1907 (1961). The only substantial biography in English is D.Q. POSIN, *Mendeleyev: The Story of a Great Scientist* (1948), a fanciful and romanticized version. An excellent brief bibliography may be found in a popular but well-presented account of his life by P. KOLODKINE, *Dmitri Mendeleïev et la loi périodique* (1963). Studies of Mendeleyev's scientific work are included in J.R. PARTINGTON, *History of Chemistry*, vol. 4, ch. 21 (1964), which also gives biographical notes on and estimates of the work of his principal contemporaries, with many references. Mendeleyev's works were collected in 25 volumes (1934–52). A 3rd English language edition of *Principles of Chemistry*, 2 vol., trans. from the 7th Russian edition was published in 1905.

(F.Gre.)

Mendelssohn, Felix

The work of Felix Mendelssohn, composer, pianist, and conductor, was pivotal in the history of music by largely observing classical models and practices while initiating key aspects of Romanticism—the late 18th-century movement that exalted feelings and the imagination at the expense of rigid forms and traditions. Born at Hamburg on February 3, 1809, of Jewish parents, Jakob Ludwig Felix Mendelssohn-Bartholdy was the grandson of the philosopher Moses Mendelssohn and son of Abraham Mendelssohn. His mother was Lea Salomon, from whom he took his first piano lessons. Though the Mendelssohn family was proud of their ancestry, they considered it desirable, in accordance with 19th-century liberal ideas, to mark their emancipation from the ghetto by adopting the Christian faith. Accordingly Felix, together with his brother and two sisters, was baptized in his youth as a Lutheran Christian. The name Bartholdy, a family property on the river Spree, was held by a wealthy maternal uncle who had embraced Protestantism. When the fortune of this relative passed to the Mendelssohns his name was adopted by them.

Mendelssohn, watercolour by James Warren Childe, 1829. In a private collection.

In 1811, during the French occupation of Hamburg, the family had moved to Berlin, where Mendelssohn studied the piano with Ludwig Berger and composition with K.F. Zelter, who, as a composer and teacher, exerted an enormous influence on his development. Other teachers gave the Mendelssohn children lessons in literature and landscape painting, with the result that at an early age Mendelssohn's mind was widely cultivated. His personality was nourished by a broad knowledge of the arts and was also stimulated by learning and scholarship. He travelled with his sister to Paris where he took further piano lessons and where he appears to have become acquainted with the music of Mozart. He wrote numerous compositions during this boyhood period, among them five operas, 11 symphonies for string orchestra, concerti, sonatas, and fugues, most of which, long preserved in manuscript in the Preussische Staatsbibliothek, Berlin, are believed to have been lost in World War II. He made his first public appearance in 1818—at the age of nine—in Berlin.

In 1821 Mendelssohn was taken to Weimar to meet Goethe, for whom he played works of Bach and Mozart and to whom he dedicated his *Quartet in B Minor*. A remarkable friendship developed between the aging poet and the 12-year-old musician. In Paris in 1825 Cherubini discerned his outstanding gifts. The next year he reached his full stature as a composer with the *Overture to A Midsummer Night's Dream*. The atmospheric effects and

Boyhood works

the fresh lyrical melodies in this work revealed the mind of an original composer, while the animated orchestration looked forward to the orchestral manner of Rimsky-Korsakov. Mendelssohn also became active as a conductor. On March 11, 1829, at the Singakademie, Berlin, he conducted the first performance since Bach's death of the *St. Matthew Passion*, thus inaugurating the Bach revival of the 19th and 20th centuries. In the meantime he had visited Switzerland and had met Weber, whose opera *Der Freischütz*, given in Berlin in 1821, encouraged him to develop a national character in music. The greatest work of this period was the *Octet* (1825), displaying not only technical mastery and an almost unprecedented lightness of touch but great melodic and rhythmic originality. Mendelssohn developed in this work the genre of the swift-moving scherzo (a playful musical movement), also shown in the incidental music to *A Midsummer Night's Dream*.

In the spring of 1829 Mendelssohn made his first journey to England, conducting his *Symphony in C Minor* at the London Philharmonic Society. In the summer he went to Scotland, of which he gave many poetic accounts in his evocative letters. He went there "with a rake for folksongs, an ear for the lovely, fragrant countryside and a heart for the bare legs of the natives." At Abbotsford he met Sir Walter Scott. The literary, pictorial, and musical elements of Mendelssohn's imagination are often merged. Describing, in a letter written from the Hebrides, the manner in which the waves break on the Scottish coast, he noted down, in the form of a musical symbol, the opening bars of the *Hebrides Overture*. Between 1830 and 1832 he travelled in Germany, Austria, Italy, and Switzerland and, in 1832, returned to London, where he conducted the *Hebrides Overture* and where he published the first book of his *Lieder ohne Worte* (*Songs Without Words*), completed in Venice in 1830. Gradually Mendelssohn, whose music in its day was held to be remarkable for its charm and elegance, was becoming the most popular of 19th-century composers in England. His main reputation was made in England, which, in the course of his short life, he visited no less than ten times. At the time of these visits the character of his music was held to be predominantly Victorian, and indeed he eventually became the favourite composer of Queen Victoria herself.

Mendelssohn's subtly ironic account of his meeting with the Queen and the Prince Consort at Buckingham Palace in 1843, to both of whom he was affectionately drawn, shows him also to have been alive to both the pomp and sham of the royal establishment. His *Scottish Symphony* was dedicated to Queen Victoria. And he became endeared to the English musical public in other ways. The fashion for playing the "Wedding March" from *A Midsummer Night's Dream* at bridal processions originates from a performance of this piece at the wedding of the Princess Royal after Mendelssohn's death, in 1858. In the meantime he had given the first performances in London of Beethoven's *Emperor* and *G Major* concerti. He was among the first to play a concerto from memory in public —Mendelssohn's memory was prodigious—and he also became known for his organ works. Later the popularity of his oratorio *Elijah*, produced at Birmingham in 1846, established Mendelssohn as a composer whose influence on English music equalled that of Handel. After his death this influence was sometimes held to have had a stifling effect. Later generations of English composers, enamoured of Wagner, Debussy, or Stravinsky, revolted against the domination of Mendelssohn and condemned the sentimentality of his lesser works. But there is no doubt that he had, nevertheless, succeeded in arousing the native musical genius, at first by his performances and later in the creative sphere, from a dormant state.

Many new experiences marked the grand tour that Mendelssohn had undertaken following his first London visit. Lively details of this tour are contained in his long series of letters. On Goethe's recommendation he had read Laurence Sterne's *Sentimental Journey*, and, inspired by this work, he recorded his impressions with great verve. In Venice he was enchanted by the paintings of Titian and Giorgione. The papal singers in Rome, how-

First journey to England

Impact on English music

ever, were "almost all unmusical," and Gregorian music he found unintelligible. In Rome he describes a "haggard" colony of German artists "with terrific beards." Later at Leipzig, where Berlioz and Mendelssohn exchanged batons, Berlioz offered an enormous cudgel of lime tree covered with bark, whereas Mendelssohn playfully presented his brazen contemporary with a delicate light stick of whalebone elegantly encased in leather. The contrast between these two batons precisely reflects the violently conflicting characters of the two composers.

In 1833 he was in London again to conduct his *Italian Symphony* and in the same year became music director of Düsseldorf, where he introduced into the church services the masses of Beethoven and Cherubini and the cantatas of Bach. At Düsseldorf, too, he began his first oratorio, *St. Paul*. In 1835 he became conductor of the celebrated Gewandhaus Orchestra at Leipzig, where he not only raised the standard of orchestral playing but made Leipzig the musical capital of Germany. Chopin and Schumann were among his friends at Leipzig, where, at his first concert with the Gewandhaus Orchestra, he conducted his overture *Meeresstille und glückliche Fahrt* (*Calm Sea and Prosperous Voyage.*)

In 1835 Mendelssohn was overcome by the death of his father, Abraham, whose dearest wish had been that his son should complete *St. Paul*. He accordingly plunged into this work with renewed determination and the following year conducted it at Düsseldorf. The same year at Frankfurt he met Cécile Jeanrenaud, the daughter of a French Protestant clergyman. Though she was ten years younger than himself, that is to say, no more than 16, they

Marriage   became engaged and were married on March 28, 1837. His sister Fanny, the member of his family who remained closest to him, wrote of her sister-in-law: "She is amiable, childlike, fresh, bright and even-tempered, and I consider Felix most fortunate for, though inexpressibly fond of him, she does not spoil him, but when he is capricious, treats him with an equanimity which will in course of time most probably cure his fits of irritability altogether." This was magnanimous praise on the part of Fanny, to whom Mendelssohn was drawn by musical as well as emotional ties. Fanny was not only a composer in her own right—she had herself written some of the *Songs Without Words* attributed to her brother—but she seems to have exercised, by her sisterly companionship, a powerful influence on the development of his inner musical nature.

Works written over the following years include the *Variations sérieuses*, for piano, the *Lobgesang* (*Hymn of Praise*), *Psalm CXIV*, the *Second Piano Concerto*, and chamber works. In 1838 Mendelssohn began the *Violin Concerto*. Though he normally worked rapidly, throwing off works with the same facility as one writes a letter, this final expression of his lyrical genius compelled his arduous attention over the next six years. Later, in the 20th century, the *Violin Concerto* was still admired for its warmth of melody and for its vivacity, and it was also the work of Mendelssohn's that, for nostalgic listeners, enshrined the elegant musical language of the 19th century. Nor was its popularity diminished by the later, more turgid, and often more dramatic, violin concerti of Brahms, Bartók, and Alban Berg. It is true that many of Mendelssohn's works are cameos, delightful portraits or descriptive pieces, held to lack the characteristic Romantic depth. But occasionally, as in the *Violin Concerto* and certain of the chamber works, these predominantly lyrical qualities, so charming, naïve, and fresh, themselves end by conveying a sense of the deeper Romantic wonder. In 1843 Mendelssohn founded at Leipzig the conservatory of music where, together with Schumann, he taught composition. Visits to London and Birmingham followed, entailing an increasing number of engagements. These would hardly have affected his normal health; he had always lived on this feverish level. But at Frankfurt in May 1847 he was greatly saddened by the death of Fanny. It is at any rate likely that for a person of Mendelssohn's sensibility, living at such intensity, the death of this close relative, to whom he was so completely bound, was calculated to undermine his whole being. In fact, after the death of his sister, his energies deserted him, and, following the

rupture of a blood vessel, he died at Leipzig on November 4, 1847.

Though the music of Mendelssohn, stylish and elegant,   **Assessment** does not fill the entire musical scene, as it was inclined to do in Victorian times, it has elements that unite this versatile 19th-century composer to the principal artistic figures of his time. In the *Midsummer Night's Dream* music, with its hilarious grunting of an ass on the bassoon and the evocative effect of Oberon's horn, Mendelssohn becomes a partner in Shakespeare's fairyland kingdom. The blurred impressionist effects in *Fingal's Cave* foreshadow the later developments of the painter J.M.W. Turner. Wagner understood Mendelssohn's inventive powers as an orchestrator, as is shown in his own opera *The Flying Dutchman*, and, later, the French composers of the 20th century learned much from his grace and perfection of style.

In recent times the appeal of Mendelssohn's work has not dwindled. It is true that *Elijah* is not so frequently performed as it was and some of his fluent piano works are now overshadowed by the more enduring works of Beethoven and Schumann. But the great pictorial works of Mendelssohn, the *Scottish* and *Italian* symphonies, repeatedly yield new vistas. Mendelssohn was one of the first of the great 19th-century Nature composers, and in this sense he remains even today a figure to be rediscovered.

MAJOR WORKS
Orchestral works

SYMPHONIES: *No. 1 in C Minor*, op. 1 (1824), really *No. 13*, as twelve symphonies for strings were written earlier; *No. 2* (see ACCOMPANIED CHORAL MUSIC); *No. 3 in A Minor–Major* (*Scottish*), op. 56 (1830–42); *No. 4 in A Major–Minor* (*Italian*), op. 90 (1833); *No. 5 in D Major* (*Reformation*), op. 107 (1829–30).

OVERTURES: *A Midsummer Night's Dream*, op. 21 (1826); *The Hebrides*, also known as *Fingal's Cave*, op. 26 (1830–32); *Meeresstille und glückliche Fahrt* (*Calm Sea and Prosperous Voyage*), op. 27 (1828–32); *Die schöne Melusine* (1833), overture for opera, libretto by Grillparzer.

CONCERTI: *Piano Concerto No. 1 in G Minor*, op. 25 (1831); *Piano Concerto No. 2 in D Minor*, op. 40 (1837); *Violin Concerto in E Minor–Major*, op. 64 (1844).

INCIDENTAL MUSIC: *A Midsummer Night's Dream*, op. 61 (1842).

Chamber music

STRING QUARTETS: *E Flat Major* (1823); *No. 1 in E Flat Major*, op. 12 (1829); *No. 2 in A Major*, op. 13 (1827); *No. 3 in D Major*, op. 44, no. 1 (1838); *No. 4 in E Minor*, op. 44, no. 2 (1837); *No. 5 in E Flat Major*, op. 44, no. 3 (1838); *No. 6 in F Minor*, op. 80 (1847).

STRING QUINTETS: *No. 1 in A Major*, op. 18 (1826; second version 1832); *No. 2 in B Flat Major*, op. 87 (1845).

PIANO QUARTETS: *No. 1 in C Minor*, op. 1 (1822); *No. 2 in F Minor*, op. 2 (1823); *No. 3 in B Minor*, op. 3 (1825).

PIANO TRIOS: *No. 1 in D Minor*, op. 49 (1839); *No. 2 in C Minor*, op. 66 (1847).

OTHER CHAMBER MUSIC: *String Sextet in D Major*, op. 110 (1824); *String Octet in E Flat Major*, op. 20 (1825); *Sonata for Violin and Piano in F Minor*, op. 4 (1825); *Four Pieces for String Quartet*, op. 81 (1827–47).

Vocal music

OPERAS: *Die Hochzeit des Camacho*, op. 10 (1825); *Die Heimkehr aus der Fremde*, op. 89 (1829), operetta.

CHURCH MUSIC: *Three motets*, op. 39 (1830); eight psalms; six anthems for eight-part chorus, op. 79 (1843–46); hymn, *Hear My Prayer*, for soprano chorus and organ (1844).

ACCOMPANIED CHORAL MUSIC: (ORATORIO): *St. Paul*, op. 36 (1836); *Elijah*, op. 70 (1846). (CANTATA): *Lobgesang* (*Hymn of Praise*), op. 52 (1840; always counted as *Symphony No. 2*); *Lauda Sion*, op. 73 (1846).

Piano music

Five fantasies; eight books of *Lieder ohne Worte* (*Songs Without Words*); seven preludes and fugues; three sonatas; *Kinderstücke*, op. 72 (1842); five sets of variations including *Variations sérieuses*, op. 54 (1841).

Organ music

Three preludes and fugues, op. 37 (1833–37); six sonatas, op. 65 (1844–45).

BIBLIOGRAPHY. FELIX MENDELSSOHN-BARTHOLDY, *Briefe*, vol. 1, *Briefe an deutsche Verleger*, ed. by RUDOLF ELVERS with an introduction by HANS HERZFELD (1968), the first volume of the complete correspondence of Mendelssohn to be published in nine volumes; *Letters*, ed. by G. SELDEN-GOTH (1945); *Felix Mendelssohn im Spiegel eigener Aussagen und zeitgenössischer Dokumente*, ed. by WILLI REICH (1970), a valuable source reference.

Biography and criticism: E. WERNER, *Mendelssohn* (1963); H.E. JACOB, *Felix Mendelssohn und seine Zeit* (1959; Eng. trans., *Felix Mendelssohn and his Times*, 1963); J. HORTON, *The Chamber Music of Mendelssohn* (1946); F. HORSLEY, *Mendelssohn and His Friends in Kensington* (1934), an account of Mendelssohn's social life in London; SIR GEORGE GROVE, *Beethoven, Schubert, Mendelssohn* (1951), a valuable Victorian appraisement; MAX F. SCHNEIDER, *Reisebilder aus der Schweiz, 1842* (1954), an evaluation of Mendelssohn's work as an artist, with reproductions from his sketchbooks.

(E.L.)

Menelik II of Ethiopia

Menelik II, creator of the modern Ethiopian state, was emperor of Ethiopia in the decades preceding World War I, a period during which Ethiopia, alone of the polities of Africa, maintained its independence in the face of European colonialism.

Menelik, or Sahle Mariam as he then was, was born on August 17, 1844, at Ankober, one of the capitals of the Ethiopian kingdom of Shewa. His father was Haile Malakot, later negus (or king) of Shewa. His mother was a court servant who actually married Haile Malakot shortly after Menelik was born. Menelik II's forefathers had been rulers of Menz, the heartland of Shewa, since the 17th century, and it has been claimed that further back they were related to the so-called Solomonic line of emperors who ruled Ethiopia between 1268 and 1854 (alternate dates 1270–1855). The name Menelik was significant: Menelik I was a legendary son of Solomon and the Queen of Sheba.

By courtesy of the Senat, Paris; photograph, J.E. Bulloz

Menelik II, oil painting by Paul Buffet, 1897. In the Senate Palace, Paris.

In 1855 the vigorous emperor of Ethiopia, Tewodros II, invaded the then semi-independent kingdom of Shewa. Early in the subsequent campaigns Menelik's father died, and Menelik was captured and taken to the Emperor's mountain stronghold, the Amba Magdela. Menelik, in nearly ten years of captivity, had opportunity to observe Tewodros' dedication to the unification and modernization of the empire and also the heavy-handed and often violent methods that ultimately led to the Emperor's failure and suicide.

Menelik contrived to escape from Magdela in 1865 and returned to Shewa, which had remained in a state of sporadic unrest and revolt against Tewodros. Although only 21 years of age, Menelik was able to displace Bezebeh, a ruler appointed by the Emperor in 1859, who had subsequently declared himself negus of the province.

King of Shewa

Menelik stood six feet tall and had a very dark complexion and fine white teeth, but smallpox had left its marks on his face. He usually wore traditional dress—*a shamma*. As a diplomat he was very courteous and made a great impression on the many foreign emissaries who visited his court. With their help he steadily imported firearms, the better to equip his armies and the garrisons and settlers that he planted in their wake.

On the death of Tewodros, Menelik, as negus of Shewa, aspired to the position of emperor. But he was not the only claimant and had to submit first to Tekle Giorgis (1868–72) and then Yohannes IV (1872–89). Before Yohannes died fighting the Sudanese in 1889, he obliged Menelik to direct his ambitions mainly to the south and east. Menelik subsequently incorporated Arusi, Harer (Harar), Jimma, Kaffa, and the several kingdoms and states of southern Ethiopia within his domains. By the time of Yohannes' death, Menelik had emerged as the strongest man in Ethiopia and was able to assume the imperial crown for which he had waited so long.

A circular letter sent to the heads of state of Britain, France, Germany, Italy, and Russia in 1891 provides a good illustration of Menelik's aims and attitudes as emperor:

> . . . tracing today the actual boundaries of my Empire, I shall endeavour, if God give me life and strength, to re-establish the ancient frontiers (tributaries) of Ethiopia up to Khartoum, and as far as Lake Nyanza with all the Gallas. Ethiopia has been for fourteen centuries a Christian land in a sea of pagans. If Powers at a distance come forward to partition Africa between them, I do not intend to be an indifferent spectator. As the Almighty has protected Ethiopia up to this day, I have confidence He will continue to protect her, and increase her borders in the future. I am certain He will not suffer her to be divided among other Powers.

During the period of his rivalry with Emperor Yohannes and the latter's son, Mengesha, Menelik appeared to befriend the Italians, but a quarrel soon developed. The Italians interpreted Article XVII of the Treaty of Wachile (Uccialli), concluded in 1889 by the Italians and Menelik, as giving Italy a protectorate over Ethiopia. It is quite inconceivable that Menelik would have agreed to his historic country becoming a protectorate. When he learned of the Italian interpretation, which was gaining some acceptance in Europe, he at once denied it and, in 1893, renounced the whole treaty.

The Italians had established themselves along the Red Sea coast, and the governor of the Italian colony of Eritrea, after much intrigue and several minor military skirmishes, risked a major confrontation. His army was crushingly defeated by the Ethiopians in one of the greatest battles in the history of Africa—the Battle of Adowa, on March 1, 1896.

Defeat of Italy at Adowa

A settlement cancelled the Treaty of Uccialli and acknowledged the full sovereignty and independence of Ethiopia, but the Italians were allowed to retain Eritrea.

After Adowa, Menelik's Ethiopia was at once accepted by the European powers as a very real political force. The crushing defeat of a European army greatly enhanced Menelik's international reputation, causing a host of foreign advisers, ambassadors, emissaries, and pure adventurers to flow into the country.

Menelik's later activities as emperor included the creating of ministries, the initiating of modern education, and the constructing of telephone and telegraph systems and of a railway from Djibouti to the highlands of Shewa. But, beginning in 1906 or 1907, he suffered a series of paralytic strokes, and power passed to his wife, the empress Taitu; to Ras Tesemma, who became regent; and to Lij Iyasu, the grandson who was to succeed him. The striken emperor finally died in 1913. (The exact date is disputed, but December 12 is usually given.)

BIBLIOGRAPHY. GUEBRE SELLASSIE, *Chronique du Règne de Ménélik II*, 2 vol. (1930–32), was written by a court chronicler, traditionally uncritical of his monarch. This is thus a biased though standard work. See also KOFI DARKWAH, *Menelik of Ethiopia* (1971); and HAROLD MARCUS, *The Life and Times of Menilek II of Ethiopia, 1844–1913* (in press).

(Ri.G.)

Mennonites

The Mennonites, named after Menno Simons (1496–1561), are a Christian denomination of approximately 460,000 members located in many countries of the world, with heaviest concentrations in the United States and Canada. They are an offshoot of the 16th-century Anabaptists, a radical reform movement of Europe.

NATURE AND SIGNIFICANCE

Anabaptist and Mennonite thought has been characterized by a separation between religion and the world. Under the impact of severe persecution in the 16th century, Anabaptism was driven to a strategy of withdrawal from society in its attempt to survive, a strategy that became central in Mennonite theology. Consequently, most Mennonites have possessed a strong cultural cohesion that they maintained externally by withdrawal and internally by rigorous group discipline. This isolation encouraged the sectarian virtues of frugality, hard work, piety, and mutual helpfulness but frequently also led to schism. By the mid-20th century, however, Mennonites were deeply involved in the social, educational, and economic world around them, an involvement that led to revolutionary changes in their life and thought. It also led to a new search for identity as a distinct group in the modern world, through a study of their denominational history, sociological analysis, and theological interaction with other groups.

Mennonites are trinitarian (believing in the doctrine of the Trinity—*i.e.*, Father, Son, and Holy Spirit), affirm the Scriptures (especially the New Testament and the teachings of Jesus) as their final authority for faith and life, and appeal to the pattern of the early church as their congregational model. They stress the importance of Baptism on confession of faith and a symbolic understanding of the Lord's Supper. Some practice foot washing, a practice based on an act of Jesus with his disciples. The doctrines of nonconformity to the world, nonwearing of oaths, nonresistance in lieu of military service, and church discipline are generally affirmed but not practiced universally.

HISTORICAL DEVELOPMENT

Reformation origins. Mennonites trace their origins back to the 16th-century Anabaptists, particularly to those known as the Swiss Brethren, who formed their first congregation on January 21, 1525, in the face of imminent persecution for their nonconformity to the demands of the state church led by the Reformation theologian Huldrych Zwingli (1484–1531). Though these demands centred on infant Baptism, which Anabaptist leaders Conrad Grebel, Felix Manz, and others questioned on the basis of biblical studies, the real issue was the nature of the church. Christ, according to their view, is Lord of the church. Only those who submit to that lordship can be true members of his body. Furthermore, the body of Christ receives its guidance from Christ himself through the Scriptures and the Holy Spirit, not from or through the civil magistracy. Persecution soon scattered the Swiss Brethren across Europe; their doctrinal views found quick response among many people, and for a time the movement grew.

Menno Simons. Though Mennonites are the direct descendents of the Anabaptists of the 16th century, the two movements are not identical. Menno Simons, a Dutch priest who joined the Anabaptist movement in 1536, gathered the scattered Anabaptists of northern Europe into vital congregations that were soon called by his name. These congregations led by Menno Simons were similar to another Anabaptist-related group organized in Strassburg under Melchior Hofmann in 1530. Initially, Menno Simons was not directly influenced by the Swiss Brethren; but with the death of the first Swiss and south German Anabaptist leaders soon after the defeat of the peasant forces led by some radical revolutionary Anabaptists—such as Thomas Müntzer (*c.* 1490–1525)—in the Peasants' War (1525), Simons began to consolidate and institutionalize the work that the moderate Anabaptist

(margin) Anabaptist view of the church

leaders of Europe had begun. He represents a second generation of leaders in which the emerging tradition determined basic faith and doctrine.

Hutterites. Another Anabaptist movement flourished in central Germany under the leadership of Hans Hut (died 1527), Hans Denk (*c.* 1500–27), and especially Pilgram Marpeck (*c.* 1492–1556), a major early lay theologian. Still another movement came to be known as the Hutterian Brethren because of the coordinating leadership of Jakob Hutter (died 1536). The Hutterites were soon known for their communal living and for an intense missionary zeal that continued into the 17th century, after all other Anabaptist groups had found relative physical security by withdrawing geographically and socially from the mainstream of European life.

Developments from the 17th century to the 19th. Mennonites found political freedom first in The Netherlands, after their last martyr died there in 1574. Before that date, however, many had emigrated from there to the Vistula River area in what is now northern Poland, where their communities became large and flourishing. By 1700 there were 160,000 baptized members in the Mennonite churches of The Netherlands. Because many of the professions were legally closed to them, they turned to business and in the process became wealthy and urbanized. In matters of faith, they followed the Enlightenment, a 17th- and 18th-century intellectual movement that placed its hope for human betterment on the use of right reason. They became well known as artists, writers, and patrons of social programs; but membership declined to about 15,300 in 1837.

Persecutions that continued in Switzerland into the 18th century drove many Mennonites to south Germany, Alsace, The Netherlands, and the United States. A major schism occurred (1693–97) when the Swiss Mennonite bishop left the Mennonites to form the Amish Church in an attempt to preserve biblical discipline among the membership. From the 17th to the 20th centuries, most Mennonites in Switzerland, south Germany, and Alsace lived in semiclosed rural communities with a simple agrarian economy. Religiously, they were influenced by Pietism, a Lutheran-based movement that emphasized personal religious experience and reform.

(margin) The Amish Church

In 1788 the first of a long stream of Mennonites left the Vistula Delta of northern Poland (Prussia) to settle in the Ukraine, where they acquired land and escaped military conscription. By 1835 about 1,600 families had settled in 72 villages with landholdings amounting to about 500,000 acres. By World War I, these settlements had grown to over 120,000 members living in autonomous communities where religious, educational, social, economic, and even political affairs were under their own control. All Mennonite communities in Russia were either destroyed during World War II or dissolved by the Soviets soon after 1945. Mennonites today live scattered among the Russian population.

Beginning in 1663, Mennonites emigrated to North America to preserve the faith of their fathers, to seek economic opportunity and adventure, and especially to escape European militarism. Until the late 19th century, most Mennonites in North America lived in rural communities and engaged successfully in farming. They retained their German language, partly as a religious symbol and partly as insulation against their environment. Their main concern was to be left alone to worship God according to their conscience and tradition. In 1775 they addressed a statement to the Pennsylvania Assembly that read:

(margin) Emigration to North America

> It is our principle to feed the hungry and give the thirsty drink; we have dedicated ourselves to serve all men in everything that can be helpful to the preservation of men's lives, but we find no freedom in giving, or doing, or assisting in anything by which men's lives are destroyed or hurt.

In 1783 Mennonites in Lancaster County were accused of treason for feeding destitute British soldiers. During the U.S. Civil War, rather than fight, some hired substitutes or paid an exemption fee of $300 in the North and $500 in the South. Those who fought in the armed forces were usually excommunicated for doing so.

20th-century developments. Mennonite migrations continued during the 20th century, primarily from Russia to North and South America—to Brazil, Paraguay, Uruguay, Bolivia, Mexico, and British Honduras. By 1970 about 92 families from The Netherlands had located in Australia and New Zealand. Mennonite missionaries from North America and Europe planted still more churches in Latin America, Africa, India, and other parts of Asia. In 1970 there were approximately 60,000 members in eight nations of Africa, 70,000 in six nations of Asia, 100,000 in ten European nations, including the U.S.S.R., 200,000 in the United States and Canada, and 30,000 in 12 nations of Latin America, giving a worldwide total of 460,000 members of which nearly one-third were nonwhite. The fastest growing Mennonite Church in 1970 was in Indonesia.

In the 20th century, the Mennonites of North America gave new emphasis to higher education, especially by supporting their own colleges and seminaries, while continuing to maintain secondary and Bible schools. New interest in the faith of early Anabaptists was fostered by the scholarly work of both Mennonite and non-Mennonite historians. This activity not only offered new insights for the renewing of church life but accented the disparity between the 16th-century Anabaptist ideals and present Mennonite beliefs and practices. A rediscovery of their history also gave new meaning to urban social relationships; witness, service, discipleship, and evangelism became household words and shaped Mennonite identity. Instead of withdrawal, they found in witness and service a new way of relating to the world.

TEACHING, ORGANIZATION, AND PRACTICE

Teaching. In describing the Anabaptists, the historian Walther Köhler wrote: "The Anabaptists are the Bible Christians of Reformation history, distinguished from the Reformers through the extension of the Biblical norm beyond the purely religious into economic and social life" (*Religion in Geschichte und Gegenwart;* Tübingen, J.C.B. Mohr, 1931). This "extension" has often been described as discipleship that, together with brotherhood and love, is frequently considered to be the central theme of the movement.

The first "Brotherly Union," called the Schleitheim Confession (1527), or common confession of faith, adopted seven articles of faith. Article I taught that Baptism was only for those who asked for it and were willing to "walk in the resurrection" and participate in (not imitate) the life of Christ. Article II taught that church discipline was necessary for salvation and for being a witness of the church because members voluntarily joined the group and asked in Baptism for help and admonition. Article III taught that the Lord's Supper celebrated the unity of the church and was intended only for true believers. Article IV taught separation from unbelievers in daily life, including separation from secular, social, and governmental organizations. Article V taught the need for support of pastors and outlined their place within the congregation. Article VI taught love and the way of the cross as the believer's only legitimate response to violence and evil. Article VII taught honesty in word and deed, thereby making the swearing of oaths unnecessary and sinful.

Such early Mennonites as the Anabaptists insisted that they were not teaching new doctrines but restoring biblical church practices. Baptism of believers implied a willing witness to others that made Mennonites the only missionaries of the Reformation movement. Voluntary church membership implied discipline and mutual helpfulness to one another. The way of the cross meant nonresistance and implied suffering; it meant the renunciation of power in all relationships. Separation of church and state implied differing views of man and the world. For Mennonites, the church was gathered around the confession that "Jesus Christ is Lord," while the state proclaimed that "Caesar is Lord." The place of the state was "outside of the perfection of Christ."

The uniqueness of Anabaptism, and some Mennonitism, centres in their understanding of the Bible and of the work of Christ. Both Old and New Testaments are truly the word of God but follow a progressive order of promise and fulfillment. The New Testament, especially the words of Christ, are God's final revelation to man but can be rightly understood only when read and studied within the circle of believers under the guidance of the Holy Spirit. And Christ, it is believed, did not come simply to change man's condition in a mysterious way by dying for him but to reconcile him to God by redeeming him morally from slavery to sin. This redemption thus gives to man a new ethical possibility, thereby establishing communion again without destroying man's freedom or by making of God a pagan deity who needs a human sacrifice to be appeased.

Organization and practices. All Mennonites are congregational in polity: they call their own ministers, decide their own priorities, and even write their own statement of faith, if they so desire. These congregations are joined together into many conferences, seven of which are in North America. The Amish, Hutterian Brethren, and some conservative Mennonites do not form conferences. Since 1925 there has been a Mennonite World Conference that meets every five years for fellowship, study, and inspiration but does not make decisions binding on its member bodies.

The desire to express positively the ethic of love and nonresistance has historically given Mennonites a deep social concern. An emergency relief committee for national and international aid, founded by the Dutch Mennonites in 1725, is still active. In 1920 North America Mennonites founded the Mennonite Central Committee (MCC) for the same purpose, initially to relieve famine in Russia. By 1970 this work was carried on in 35 countries, through approximately 700 volunteer workers with an annual budget of just over $4,000,000.00.

Worship. Mennonite worship services are sermon-centred. A simple, almost austere, liturgy surrounds the Gospel proclamation. By the 1970s, however, there were many signs of experiment in worship similar to those found in other denominations. Mennonites have traditionally practiced the lay ministry, but many congregations are served by fully trained and salaried pastors. Most congregations have one or more deacons or elders, sometimes selected for life, but the contemporary pattern of committee organization is dominant. Baptism was traditionally observed once each year but is increasingly administered as candidates ask for it. The Lord's Supper is normally observed from two to four times annually. In some congregations, the love-feast pattern, involving a meal from which some bread and wine is reserved for the Lord's Supper, is observed. Foot washing is practiced by some congregations.

Social, political, and cultural attitudes. Because of their historical experience of suffering and because of a basic church–world dualism in their theology, Mennonites have, for most of their history, been content to live as "the quiet of the land." Today, this pattern has been shattered by the revival of an earlier sense of mission and by growing urbanization. Except in certain parts of North and South America, Mennonites have become an integral part of their environment on various levels of accommodation or even assimilation. Many Mennonites are entering the helping professions in society, and some have been elected to political office. Earlier political conservatism is breaking down, especially in North America, under the impact of growing concern over the great social issues of race, war, and poverty.

BIBLIOGRAPHY. *The Mennonite Encyclopedia,* 4 vol. (1955–59), is the standard reference work in English. C.J. DYCK (ed.), *An Introduction to Mennonite History* (1967), is a popularly written general history of the Anabaptist-Mennonite movement. ANNI DYCK (ed.), *Mennonites Around the World* (1967), gives a short interpretive overview. Two comprehensive treatments of wider Anabaptist relationships to other movements, together with a thorough analysis of these movements are G.H. WILLIAMS, *The Radical Reformation* (1962); and D.F. DURNBAUGH, *The Believers' Church* (1968). LEONARD VERDUIN, *The Reformers and Their Stepchildren* (1964), compares Anabaptism to other movements in the history of the church. The theological and contemporary

Biblical interpretation

Experimentation in worship

Schleitheim Confession

significance of the movement is explored in G.F. HERSHBERGER (ed.), *The Recovery of the Anabaptist Vision* (1957); and J.H. YODER, *The Christian Witness to the State* (1964). Further detailed bibliographies may be found in H.J. HILLERBRAND (ed.), *A Bibliography of Anabaptism, 1520–1630* (1962), and continued in *A Mennonite Bibliography, 1631–1961*, 2 vol. (in prep.).

(C.J.D.)

Menno Simons

Menno Simons, the 16th-century Dutch priest who became a member of the radical reform group known as the Anabaptists after some revolutionary Anabaptists had failed to establish the Kingdom of God by force at Münster in 1535, is known as the leader of those who formed the Mennonite Church. Through his writings and courageous leadership, the peaceful wing of Dutch Anabaptism became normative and grew rapidly. His influence has been significant in the life of the Mennonite Church and in the area of pacifism to the present time.

By courtesy of the Mennonite Library and Archives, North Newton, Kansas

Menno Simons, engraving by Christopher van Sichem, 1605–08.

Education and conversion

Little is known about his early life. He was born into a Dutch peasant family in Witmarsum, in the province of Friesland, in 1496. At an early age Menno was enrolled in a monastic school, possibly at the Franciscan monastery in Bolsward, to prepare for the priesthood. In March of 1524, at the age of 28, he was ordained at Utrecht and assigned to the parish at Pingjum near the place of his birth. Seven years later, in 1531, he became the village priest in his home parish at Witmarsum.

Though Menno was to become a major spokesman of ethical Christianity, his initial concern was doctrinal. During his first year as priest he began to question the real presence of Christ in the bread and wine of the Eucharist (Lord's Supper). This was probably due largely to the anti-sacramental tendencies prevalent in the Netherlands at that time, tendencies that grew in the fertile soil of Erasmian Humanism and the ethical concerns of the Brethren of the Common Life, leading ultimately to the *Epistola Christiana* of Cornelius Hoen. These doubts led Menno to read both the Bible and the writings of Martin Luther for the first time. At first he read the Bible with real fear, for he knew this step had driven Luther and the Swiss reformer Huldrych Zwingli (1484–1531) out of the Roman Church, but he soon confessed with them that biblical authority ought to be primary in the life of the believer and in the church. By 1528 he was known as an evangelical preacher, though he continued as parish priest.

From doubts about the Eucharist, Menno moved gradually to questions about infant Baptism and the meaning of church membership. His discovery of the New Testament led him to the firm conviction that the church was the body of Christ, called to holiness and purity. This meant, according to Menno's interpretation, that only persons of mature faith, who acknowledged Jesus as Lord and had counted the cost of following him, could be eligible for membership. Only such persons could be baptized as a seal (sign of guarantee) of the covenant and a witness to all the world. Little children were indeed sinners with all mankind, but, Menno claimed, the grace of Christ was sufficient for them until they reached the age of accountability and made a conscious choice either for or against him. The experience of conversion came to be central to all of Menno's life and theology.

Meanwhile, the revolutionary wing of early Dutch Anabaptism continued its agitation. On April 7, 1535, the Olde Klooster near Bolsward, which had been occupied by them as a staging area for aid to Münster, fell before the onslaught of the state militia. Among those killed were members of Menno's congregation and Peter Simons, who may have been his brother. This prompted him to preach openly against the errors of the revolutionaries. In doing so he articulated with increasing clarity what he believed to be the true nature of a believers' church: pure doctrine, scriptural use of sacraments, ethical obedience, love of neighbour, a clear and open witness to the faith, and a willingness to suffer. The fall of Münster on July 25, 1535, increased pressure within him to help those whom he considered to be misguided spirits. This bold and outspoken ministry soon jeopardized his safety, and in January 1536 he went into hiding after a spiritual struggle of 11 years.

In describing his decision he wrote,

Pondering these things my conscience tormented me so that I could no longer endure it. . . . If I through bodily fear do not lay bare the foundation of the truth, nor use all my powers to direct the wandering flock who whould gladly do their duty if they knew it, to the true pastures of Christ— oh, how shall their shed blood, shed in the midst of transgression, rise against me at the judgment of the Almighty and pronounce sentence against my poor, miserable soul!

Menno spent a quiet year in hiding, finding a sense of direction for his future work. During this time he wrote "The Spiritual Resurrection," "The New Birth," and "Meditation on the Twenty-third Psalm." Late in 1536 or early 1537, he was rebaptized, called to leadership by the peaceful Anabaptist group founded in 1534 by Obbe Philips, and ordained by Obbe. He also married Gertrude. From this time on his life was in constant danger as a heretic. In 1542 the Holy Roman emperor Charles V (1500–58) himself issued an edict against him, promising 100 guilders reward for his arrest. One of the first Anabaptist believers to be executed for sheltering Menno was Tyaard Renicx of Leeuwarden, in 1539.

From 1543 to 1544 Menno worked in East Friesland, where in January 1544 he had a major interview or debate with the Polish reformer Johannes à Lasco (1499–1560). The following two years, 1544–46, were spent in the Rhineland, after which he travelled from his new home base in Holstein, near Oldesloe, northeast of Hamburg, until his death on Jan. 31, 1561. Here he found time for extensive writing and established a printing press to circulate Anabaptist writings. His travels not only took him back to The Netherlands but also to Danzig.

Menno was not the founder of the Mennonite Church nor the most articulate spokesman of early Anabaptist theology. His greatness lay rather in the leadership he gave to northern Anabaptism during its formative first generation, a leadership maintained through his calm, biblically oriented approach and through his writings, which consolidated the insights of the movement. Though these writings often seem tedious and excessively polemical, they delineated the Anabaptist faith he defended against both Catholic and Protestant attacks on the one hand and distortions by zealots from within the movement on the other. During the last years of his life he was troubled particularly by some of his own brethren who pressed for great rigour in the application of the ban (expulsion from the church) and other measures of discipline. His more than 40 extant writings are all prefaced with I Cor. 3:11 "No other foundation can any one lay than that which is laid, which is Jesus Christ."

Menno's concept of the believers' church

BIBLIOGRAPHY. J.A. BRANDSMA, *Menno Simons Van Witmarsum* (1960), a biography containing a careful evaluation of stories and legends about Menno Simons; C.J. DYCK (ed.), *A Legacy of Faith: The Heritage of Menno Simons* (1962), a discussion of Dutch Anabaptism with three chapters devoted to Menno Simons; I.B. HORST, *A Bibliography of Menno Simons, ca. 1496–1561* (1962), the definitive bibliography of his writings; C. KRAHN, "Menno Simons," *Mennonite Encyclopedia*, vol. 3 (1957), a major interpretive article by one of the foremost scholars of Dutch Anabaptism; F.H. LITTELL, *A Tribute to Menno Simons* (1961), a discussion of the significance of the theology of Menno Simons; H.W. MEIHUIZEN, *Menno Simons* (1961), a biography giving particular attention to the place of Menno Simons in the life and culture of his time; MENNO SIMONS, *Opera Omnia Theologica* (1681; Eng. trans., *The Complete Writings of Menno Simons*, ed. by J.C. WENGER, 1956), the definitive English language edition; K. VOS, *Menno Simons, 1496–1561* (1914), the standard work (in Dutch).

(C.J.D.)

Menopause

Description and causation

"Menopause" (female climacteric) is a term that implies the final cessation of menstruation and therefore the end of a woman's reproductive life. The popular term "change of life" is neither descriptive nor accurate for it tends to indicate a physical, mental, and sexual deterioration, whereas deterioration does not occur.

In about half of all women, menopause begins between the ages of 45 and 50 years. Although the average age for onset is about 48 years, menopause may begin as early as age 40 or be delayed to the early 50s. Although the age of onset is probably determined by the hereditary background of the individual, good nutrition and health habits tend to postpone onset.

A premature menopause—*i.e.*, one that takes place spontaneously before the age of 40—occurs in about 8 percent of women. An artificial menopause may be induced by removing the ovaries by surgery or by destroying them with X-rays or radium.

The natural life of the ovaries is about 35 years. The menopause is brought on by a progressive decline in ovarian function. This decline is a normal result of aging and is accelerated as the menopause approaches. During the reproductive years follicles in the ovaries mature and release their ova periodically under hypothalamic-pituitary stimulation. In the years immediately preceding the menopause, however, first some follicles and later all follicles fail to rupture and release their ova. The failure to ovulate results in a disturbed menstrual pattern. A woman may miss a period or two and suspect pregnancy. A medical examination, however, will establish the proper diagnosis. The continued decline in ovarian activity may provoke prolonged intervals between periods or irregular bleeding episodes. The length of the periods may vary, and the flow may become either more scant or profuse. In a fortunate small minority the periods cease abruptly.

As the ovaries decline in function, they produce smaller and smaller amounts of the hormone estrogen; this decline in estrogen initiates subtle rearrangements in the hormonal activity of the glands that control the reproductive function. The decrease in output of estrogen disturbs the neurovascular mechanism of the hypothalamus and probably initiates the vasomotor changes that may provoke the characteristic "hot flashes" of the menopause. The metabolism of the pituitary gland is altered and increasing amounts of follicle stimulating hormone (FSH) appear in the blood and urine. Rearrangements in the hormonal activity of the adrenal and thyroid glands also take place, for the metabolic activities of all these glands are interrelated. These adjustments are usually made without physical or mental disturbances in most women.

Hot flashes are the only characteristic symptoms of the menopause. They often appear before its obvious onset and their duration is usually limited to two or three years. The young woman who has her ovaries removed for disease or other reasons will develop flashes within a week following the operation.

The hot flash usually begins as a sense of warmth over the upper chest. It then spreads to the neck and face and may extend over the entire body, sometimes giving rise to a prickling sensation. The woman is acutely aware of blushing, which usually is disturbing to her, particularly in company. The flashes may recur frequently during the night and may interfere with sleep. She may awaken because of a chilly sensation and may perspire freely.

A variety of other symptoms can and do occur, although many are entirely unrelated to the changes incidental to the menopause. Nervousness, headaches, and dizziness are common complaints. The fear of aging, the altered pattern of life, and changing family relationships also may precipitate many disturbing symptoms.

Many women complain of weight gain during the menopause. Occasionally this is related to decreased thyroid function. In most cases, however, it is brought about by decreased physical activity and by increased food intake as a substitute for many emotional and social satisfactions. The menopause need not be associated with any unusual changes in physical appearance and fitness.

Medical management

There are three principal aspects to the medical management of the menopause: (1) education, (2) periodic examination, and (3) the substitution of estrogenic hormone when this is desirable.

Providing information to women concerning the physiologic function of their reproductive organs will make them aware of the limited duration of their reproductive years and prepare them for the important transitional years leading into the menopause. The menopause need not be a harbinger of old age. The woman in the climacteric, because of her makeup and the vicissitudes of her environment, enters middle life with an uneasy and uncertain tread. It is a time for introspection, of inventories, of soul searching. It is a period of boredom, of phobias, and fears. An intelligent understanding of the problems she may face and the proper medical guidance, if necessary, will prevent serious sequelae.

Every woman, including those of menopause age, should have a health examination at least once a year. At this time she should be screened for cancer by having a smear taken for uterine cancer and by receiving an examination for breast cancer. She also should be instructed on the proper method for self-examination for breast cancer.

Finally, the administration of estrogenic hormones may be indicated and desirable for the prompt relief of symptoms. Estrogen should be taken only under the direction of a physician but can be taken indefinitely without harmful side effects. It will stop flashes and will retard the shrinkage of the tissues of the external genitalia, which otherwise may become irritated and infected. Studies indicate that estrogen also may slow the development of atherosclerosis and osteoporosis, bone decalcification, and may influence the aging process favourably (see also HORMONE; REPRODUCTIVE SYSTEM, HUMAN).

BIBLIOGRAPHY. Additional information on this subject may be found in the following articles: M.E. DAVIS, "Symposium on Gynecology and Obstetrics: The Therapeutic Role of the Estrogens," *Surg. Clin. N. Amer.*, 23:113–131 (1943), "Long-Term Estrogen Substitution After the Menopause," *Clin. Obstet. Gynec.*, 7:558–572 (1964), "Estrogen and the Aging Process," in J.P. GREENHILL (ed.), *Year Book of Obstetrics and Gynecology*, pp. 339–358 (1964–65), and with N.M. STRANDJORD and L.H. LANZL, "Estrogens and the Aging Process," *JAMA*, 196:219–224 (1966); S. WALLACH and P.H. HENNEMAN, "Prolonged Estrogen Therapy in Postmenopausal Women," *JAMA*, 171:1637–1642 (1959); H.E. and S. MEEMA, "Prevention of Postmenopausal Osteoporosis by Hormone Treatment of the Menopause," *Canad. Med. Ass. J.*, 99:248–251 (1968).

(M.E.D.)

Menstruation

Menstruation is the periodic discharge from the vagina of blood, secretions, and disintegrating mucous membrane that had lined the uterus.

The biological significance of the process can best be explained by reference to the reproductive function in other mammals. In a number of species of wild sheep, for example, there is only one breeding season in the year; during this season a cycle of changes takes place in the reproductive organs, characterized by ripening and release of ova from the ovaries, increased blood supply to the genital tract, growth of the uterus, and proliferation of its lining. There is a discharge of blood and mucus from the uterus and vagina, and this is the time when coition may take place. Pregnancy normally follows, but if the ewe is not served by the ram the changes retrogress until the next breeding season. This cycle of changes is termed the estrous cycle (see REPRODUCTION; REPRODUCTIVE SYSTEMS, ANIMAL).

In many domesticated sheep there is more than one estrous cycle in the breeding season. If the ewe does not become pregnant in the first cycle there is a short resting phase; then ovulation is repeated and another cycle of activity of the reproductive system takes place. After each breeding period, with its succession of estrous cycles, there is a relatively long resting phase.

In most female primates, including women, there is no resting phase; an unbroken series of estrous cycles occurs throughout the year, and pregnancy can occur in any one of them.

In some animals a variety of external stimuli act through the central nervous system on the hypothalamic region of the brain. The hypothalamus controls the release from the pituitary gland of hormones that induce ripening of ovarian follicles—ova and the cellular structures that enclose them. These pituitary hormones, called gonadotropic hormones, are carried to the ovaries by way of the bloodstream. In primates the hypothalamic mechanism normally is independent of external stimuli, and regular discharge of ova into the tubes leading to the uterus occurs even in the absence of coitus. Under the influence of the pituitary gonadotropic hormones, the ovary produces other hormones, which cause growth and increased vascularity of the uterus and vagina. These hormones are estrogens—chiefly 17 beta-estradiol—and progesterone. It is as though the ovary prepares the uterus for the reception of the ovum that is released in the particular cycle.

Menstrual cycle. The normal human menstrual cycle is 28 days, but no woman is always precisely regular, and cycles as short as 21 days or as long as 35 days are not abnormal. It is customary to call the first day of the menstrual period the first day of the cycle, although menstruation is the end rather than the beginning of a process. On this basis the cycle is described as starting with about

From *Ciba Collection of Medical Illustrations*, vol. 4, J. & A. Churchill, Ltd.

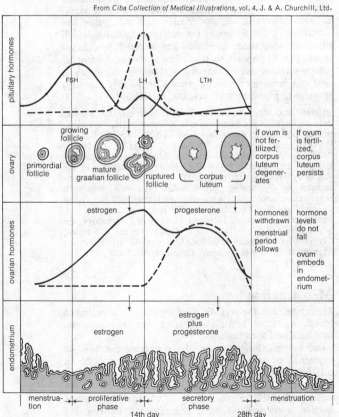

Menstrual cycle.

five days of menstruation, followed by a proliferative phase that lasts to about the 14th day, and then a secretory phase that lasts until the next menstruation. The external manifestation of menstruation depends upon cyclical change in the lining of the body of the uterus. The lining, called endometrium, consists of tubular glands that open into the uterine cavity. The glands lie in a vascular framework, or stroma, and are separated by it.

At the end of menstruation, just at the beginning of the proliferative phase, the endometrium is thin, with short, straight glands, and the ovary is quiescent. Under the influence of the gonadotropic hormones from the pituitary gland an ovarian follicle (occasionally more than one) ripens in one of the ovaries. This ovarian follicle contains the ovum, which is a cell about 0.14 millimetre in diameter, surrounded by a group of smaller cells, called granulosa cells. The granulosa cells multiply, with the ovum situated in the wall of the rounded structure that they form, and secrete an estrogenic hormone, estradiol (see HORMONE). This hormone causes proliferative changes in the endometrium, so that the glands become taller and the whole endometrium becomes thicker and more vascular. *The proliferative phase*

At about midcycle ovulation occurs: The ovum is discharged out of the follicle and from the surface of the ovary, to be received into the fallopian tube, down which it is carried to the uterus. After ovulation the granulosa cells lining the follicle from which the ovum has been extruded accumulate yellow lipid and are therefore called lutein cells, from the Latin word *luteus,* "saffron-yellow." The altered follicle is called corpus luteum. The corpus luteum continues to secrete estrogens but now also secretes progesterone; this additional hormone induces the secretory phase in the endometrium. The endometrial glands are distended with secretion and become very tortuous, while the stromal cells are swollen. The appearance of the endometrium at the end of the menstrual cycle is indistinguishable from that of early pregnancy, and this endometrial change is a preparation for the reception of the ovum. If it is fertilized, the ovum liberated at midcycle reaches the uterine cavity at a time when the endometrium is in the secretory phase, and the ovum embeds itself in the endometrium and starts its growth. If the ovum is not fertilized the endometrium breaks down and menstruation occurs. Menstruation has therefore been described as the outward evidence of the abortive close of one cycle and the hopeful commencement of the next. *The secretory phase*

When the ovum dies, the corpus luteum degenerates and ceases to produce hormones. On the withdrawal of estrogens and progesterone there is sudden spasm of the endometrial blood vessels, and all but the basal layer of the endometrium dies. The disintegrating endometrium is shed, together with some blood. The endometrium contains plasmin, an enzyme that dissolves blood clot, so that the menstrual discharge is normally fluid. The total blood loss does not ordinarily exceed 50 millilitres.

After menstruation the endometrium regenerates from the residual basal layer during the proliferative phase of the next cycle.

Hormonal control of menstrual cycle. The ovarian hormones circulate in the blood and are excreted in modified forms in the urine. Estimation of the urinary output by chemical methods gives an indication of the blood levels and of the total production of these substances. There are several natural estrogens, and numerous synthetic modifications of these and of progesterone have been devised; many are active when taken by mouth and are used for treatment of hormonal disorders and as oral contraceptives.

The cyclic events in the ovary that have already been mentioned depend on gonadotropic hormones secreted by the anterior lobe of the pituitary gland; this gland is situated in a small recess at the base of the skull. There are two, and possibly three, gonadotropic hormones: follicle-stimulating hormone (FSH), luteinizing hormone (LH), and, possibly, luteotropic hormone (LTH).

FSH is secreted in greatest amount in the first half of the menstrual cycle, and LH has its peak of secretion at midcycle. It is believed that the sequential action of FSH and

LH causes ripening of the follicle and ovulation. In some animals LTH is necessary for maintenance of the corpus luteum, but in women under treatment for infertility ovulation has been successfully induced with FSH and LH alone. Multiple births, as the result of multiple ovulation, have occurred after excessive doses of FSH have been given.

Inhibitory effect of estrogens and progesterone

The pituitary gland stimulates the ovary to produce estrogens and progesterone, but there is a "negative feedback" by which the estrogens inhibit the output of FSH from the pituitary gland (and probably stimulate the output of LH). In addition, progesterone is believed to inhibit the further output of LH. In this process, in which the pituitary first stimulates the ovary, and the ovary then inhibits the pituitary, the basic rhythm is under the control of the hypothalamus; nevertheless, ovulation can be inhibited by oral contraceptives, which contain estrogens and progestogens—modifications of progesterone.

The anterior lobe of the pituitary gland is connected by its stalk to the hypothalamic region of the brain. The anterior lobe secretes many important hormones, including those that control the activity of the adrenal and thyroid glands, the growth hormone, and the gonadotropic hormones. From the hypothalamus substances are carried in the veins in the pituitary stalk that cause release of hormones from the pituitary, including FSH and LH, but also a factor that inhibits release of LTH. The higher brain centres no doubt affect the hypothalamic function; this explains the temporary disturbances of menstruation that may follow emotional stress.

Ovulation and the fertile phase. Ovulation occurs at about the midpoint of each normal cycle, and the ovum is probably capable of fertilization for only about two days after this. In the majority of women the time of ovulation is fairly constant. In women with cycles of irregular length the date of ovulation is uncertain; in these women the long menstrual cycles are usually due to prolongation of the proliferative phase; the secretory phase tends to remain normal in length. In some animals, ovulation only follows coitus; this mechanism has been used to explain cases in which human pregnancy has apparently followed coitus early or late in the menstrual cycle, but there is no definite evidence for such a mechanism in women.

The rhythm method of contraception is based on the fact that ovulation normally occurs at midcycle, but the date of ovulation may vary unexpectedly even in women whose menstrual cycle were previously regular.

The menarche. The first menstruation, or menarche, usually occurs between 11 and 13 years of age, but in a few otherwise normal children menstruation may begin sooner or may be delayed. If the menstrual periods have not started by the age of 16 gynecological investigation is indicated. The menarche is preceded by other signs of estrogenic activity, such as enlargement of the breasts and the uterus and growth of pubic hair. The ovarian response to gonadotropic hormones may be erratic at first, so that irregular or heavy bleeding sometimes occurs, but this irregularity nearly always disappears spontaneously.

Normal menstruation. Each menstrual period lasts for about five days, but the duration and amount of the flow vary considerably even in perfect health.

Discomfort in normal menstruation

In some women there may be premonitory symptoms such as pelvic discomfort, soreness of the breasts (because of the response of these organs to estrogens), and emotional tension. Ovarian hormones cause retention of sodium and water in the tissue fluids; premenstrual tension may be partly due to this and in some cases can be relieved by diuretics, drugs that increase the production of urine. When the menstrual flow starts the uterus contracts to expel the blood and disintegrating endometrium. These contractions may be painful, especially in young women who have never been pregnant.

Menstrual discomforts such as those that have been mentioned vary greatly in degree from woman to woman and from time to time but ordinarily do not interfere with normal activities.

The menopause. Just as puberty is a gradual process, so are the changes leading to the termination of the reproductive period. Before the final cessation of the menstrual cycles—known as the menopause—there is a gradual decline in ovarian activity, and fertility declines because ovulation does not take place in every cycle. The menopause generally occurs between ages 47 and 52, but in a few otherwise normal women it may occur earlier or later. An early onset of menstruation is often followed by a late menopause, and this may be an inherited characteristic. In some women the periods cease abruptly; in others they gradually diminish or occasionally are missed. Irregular or heavy bleeding at this time is not normal and calls for investigation.

After the menopause atrophic changes occur in the breasts, uterus, vagina, and vulva, but many women continue to have normal intercourse. A common symptom at this time is flushing of the face and body with sweating, which may occur several times a day. The flushes are thought to be due to a temporary excess of pituitary gonadotropic hormone. In troublesome cases the flushes can be controlled by administration of estrogens, but the flushes usually cease spontaneously after a few months (see MENOPAUSE).

Menstrual disorders. Abnormalities of menstrual function include absence of menstruation, called amenorrhea; excessive blood loss at each period, known as menorrhagia; irregular cycles, or metrorrhagia; and painful menstruation, or dysmenorrhea. In addition, there may be premenstrual tension, and in a few women, pain at the time of ovulation. As a sexual and reproductive function, menstruation has deep emotional significance, but the popular belief that regular menstrual flow is necessary for health is unfounded. The belief arises in part from the fact that in any severe illness, and during emotional disturbances and psychiatric illness, the cycles may be disturbed. This is particularly true of diseases of the endocrine system, not only of the pituitary gland but of other glands, such as the thyroid and the adrenal, as well.

Menstrual abnormality may also be a symptom of local disease of the pelvic organs. Irregular bleeding, bleeding after intercourse, and bleeding at or after the menopause may be early signs of uterine malignant disease.

Ovulatory pain, premenstrual tension, dysmenorrhea

A few women have transient abdominal discomfort at the time of ovulation because of slight bleeding from the follicle into the peritoneal cavity. Oral administration of estrogens and progestogens will remedy the condition by suppression of ovulation, but the discomfort seldom recurs in every cycle or is severe enough to merit such treatment.

Premenstrual tension has already been mentioned. When it is due to fluid retention there is increase in weight before menstruation, and diuretics such as chlorothiazide give relief. In most instances emotional tension is the main complaint, and relief is attained by the use of mild sedatives or tranquilizers. Objective studies of women who do fine work show a reduction in accuracy and in concentration at this time, and outbursts of emotion may occur. The claim that relief is obtained by administration of progestogens is not generally accepted.

Painful menstruation in young women who have not borne children is a common complaint; the pain is sometimes so severe as to interfere with daily occupations. There is, as a rule, no endocrine or anatomical abnormality, and fertility is normal. The pain occurs during the active menstrual flow and is due to colicky contractions of the uterus. Minor degrees of pain are adequately controlled with analgesic drugs. In the past severe cases were often treated by surgical dilation of the cervix, and occasionally by severing the nerves that carry the pain impulses from the uterus, but now hormonal treatment is more usual. This type of dysmenorrhea usually does not persist after birth of a child.

Another type of dysmenorrhea results from pelvic disease such as inflammation of the tubes and ovaries, or from endometriosis. In endometriosis, deposits of endometrium, which undergo cyclic response to the ovarian hormones, are found in the ovaries and in other sites outside their normal location; these deposits form blood-filled cysts, and pain and excessive bleeding result. In painful menstruation secondary to pelvic disease there is, before menstruation, pain associated with a feeling of congestion, and the menstrual bleeding is often excessive. Surgical treatment may be required, although the symptoms of endometriosis can be suppressed by use of progestogens.

Excessive or irregular menstrual bleeding, intermenstrual bleeding

Excessive or irregular menstrual bleeding may be due to an imbalance of the pituitary and ovarian hormones, but it may also be the result of local disease of the pelvic organs. This local disease may be inflammation due to infection; it may be a benign tumour such as a fibromyoma, or fibroid; it may be a polyp, or projecting mass of endometrium; or it may be a cancer, especially after age 35. Some types of local pelvic disease may require removal of the uterus or treatment by irradiation but polyps and some fibroids can be removed without loss of the uterus.

Irregular or excessive bleeding often results from emotional disturbance; this type of abnormality tends to disappear spontaneously.

As the menopause approaches, extremely heavy bleeding may occur, causing anemia, tiredness, and ill health. Menorrhagia in this instance is due to overdevelopment of the endometrium as a result of excessive or unbalanced action of estrogens. Younger or childless women can be treated with progestogens; for others removal of the uterus may be necessary.

Bleeding between periods or after intercourse is frequently due to some abnormality of the cervix; in women who have borne children the possibility of cancer must be borne in mind. Such bleeding may also come from a simple polyp on the cervix or a cervical erosion. The latter is a rather common condition in which the glandular lining of the canal of the cervix extends out onto its surface. Treatment is often unnecessary, but erosions are easily dealt with by cauterization. Polyps require removal.

Irregular bleeding also may occur during pregnancy when there is danger of abortion; if any menstrual periods have been missed this possibility must be considered.

Amenorrhea

Amenorrhea, or absence of menstruation, is normal during pregnancy and for a variable time after delivery. If the mother is breast-feeding her baby, as much as six months may pass before return of menstruation; earlier return of menstruation is not abnormal and is to be expected if the mother is not producing milk. Pregnancy is the commonest cause of amenorrhea during the reproductive years.

The term primary amenorrhea refers to the absence of menstruation in a woman who has never previously menstruated. In rare cases, primary amenorrhea is due to gonadal dysgenesis, the failure of the ovaries to develop normally, and may be associated with chromosomal abnormalities. Instead of the normal female complement of 46 chromosomes in each cell, including two X-chromosomes, a patient may have only one X-chromosome, or even a male pattern of an X- and a Y-chromosome (see BIRTH DEFECTS AND CONGENITAL DISORDERS). In such persons the uterus and tubes often are absent, although the general physique may be female.

Even with normal ovaries, absence of the uterus occasionally occurs. A less rare abnormality is vaginal atresia, or closure, an obstruction of the vagina by a membrane just above the level of the hymen; menstruation occurs, but the discharge cannot escape and distends the vagina. This condition, called false amenorrhea or cryptomenorrhea, is easily corrected by an incision in the membrane.

Cessation of periods after menstruation has been established, but before the normal time for the menopause, is usually the result of some general illness, some emotional disturbance, or a psychiatric illness. It may also be due to disease of the endocrine system, not only of the pituitary gland but of other endocrine glands as well. Secondary amenorrhea results if the ovaries are removed or are irradiated but is unlikely to be caused by ovarian disease, as both ovaries would have to be totally destroyed to stop all function. There is a functional disorder of the ovaries, described by I.F. Stein and M.L. Leventhal, in which production of estrogens is disturbed. Symptoms of this disorder include abnormal growth of facial hair because of abnormal androgenic—that is, masculinizing—activity. An ovarian tumour, arrhenoblastoma, that secretes an-

drogenic hormone, is another extremely rare cause of amenorrhea and abnormal growth of hair.

Most cases of secondary amenorrhea are temporary, and spontaneous improvement is to be expected, especially when the cause is some general illness or emotional disturbance. Treatment of amenorrhea serves no purpose unless pregnancy is ultimately desired and is possible. The feasibility of treatment with hormones is determined by a general medical examination and a complete pelvic examination, including various hormonal assays and inspection of a specimen of endometrium.

Menstruation without discharge of an ovum

In some women who complain of infertility but apparently have normal periods, it has been found that the cycles are anovular. Estrogens are produced in each cycle in amounts sufficient to cause endometrial proliferation, but ovulation does not occur and the corpus luteum is not formed, so that there is no secretion of progesterone. The endometrium breaks down and bleeds in each cycle as the estrogens are withdrawn. Cycles of this type occur in women who are using oral contraceptives.

A simple way to determine whether ovulation is occurring is to record the woman's early morning temperature daily. In a normal cycle the temperature is about 0.5° C lower in the first than in the second half of the cycle, and the rise in temperature occurs at the time of ovulation. No rise occurs in anovular cycles. Another test is to remove and inspect a fragment of endometrium in the late part of the cycle; if microscopic examination shows that normal secretory changes are present ovulation must have taken place.

In persons with anovular cycles and in some with amenorrhea it is now possible to induce ovulation by injection of FSH or of a synthetic drug, clomiphene, followed by injection of a luteinizing hormone.

BIBLIOGRAPHY. Additional information may be found in the following textbooks: S.G. CLAYTON, D.B. FRASER, and T.L.T. LEWIS (eds.), *Gynaecology by Ten Teachers*, 12th ed. (1971); E.R. NOVAK, E.S. JONES, and H.W. JONES, *Novak's Textbook of Gynecology*, 7th ed. (1965); S.L. ISRAEL, *Menstrual Disorders and Sterility*, 5th ed. (1967); R.B. GREENBLATT (ed.), *Ovulation* (1966); W. CALDWELL, *Sex and Internal Secretions*, 2 vol., 3rd ed. (1961); and A. MCLAREN (ed.) *Advances in Reproductive Physiology* (1969).

(S.G.C.)

Mental Health and Hygiene

Since the founding of the United Nations the concept of mental health has achieved international acceptance. As defined in the 1946 constitution of the World Health Organization, "health is a state of complete physical, mental, and social well-being, and not merely the absence of disease or infirmity." The term mental health represents a variety of human aspirations: rehabilitation of the mentally disturbed, prevention of mental disorder, reduction of tension in a conflict-laden world, and attainment of a state of well-being in which the individual functions at a level consistent with his mental and physical potentials. As noted by the World Federation for Mental Health, the concept of optimum mental health refers not to an absolute or ideal state but to the best possible state insofar as circumstances are alterable. Mental health is regarded as a condition of the individual, relative to his capacities and to his social-environmental context. Mental hygiene includes all measures taken to promote and to preserve mental health. Community mental health refers to the extent to which the organization and functioning of the community determines, or is conducive to, the mental health of its members.

HISTORY OF TREATMENT

Throughout the ages the mentally disturbed have been viewed with a mixture of fear and revulsion. Their fate generally has been one of rejection, neglect, and ill treatment. Though, in medical and biblical writings there are ancient references to mental disturbance that display views very similar to modern humane attitudes; interspersed in the same literature are instances of socially sanctioned cruelty based upon the belief that mental disorders have supernatural origins such as demonic possession. Even reformers sometimes used harsh methods of treatment; for example, Benjamin Rush (see below) endorsed the practice of restraining mental sufferers with his once notorious "tranquilising chair."

Early institutions. The history of care for the mentally ill reflects man's cultural diversity. The earliest known hospitals in the Arab world were established in Baghdad (AD 918) and in Cairo with that special consideration traditionally given disturbed people, the "afflicted of Allāh." Some contemporary African tribes benignly regard hallucinations as communications from the realm of the spirits; among others, Hindu culture shows remarkable tolerance for what is considered to be bizarre behaviour in Western societies. Belief in demonic possession reached its height during a prolonged period of preoccupation with witchcraft (15th through 18th century) in Europe and in colonial North America.

So-called madhouses such as Bedlam (founded in London in 1247) and the Bicêtre (the Paris asylum for men) were typical of institutions in which sufferers were routinely shackled during the 18th century. Inmates of these places often were believed to be devoid of human feeling and their management was indifferent if not brutal; the primary consideration was to isolate the mentally disturbed from ordinary society. In British colonial America, *Inhumane* mentally deranged persons frequently were auctioned off *treatment* to be cared for (or exploited) by farmers; some were driven from towns by court order, and others were placed in almshouses. Only after more than a century of colonization was the first colonial asylum for the insane established in Williamsburg, Virginia, in 1773. In the 1790s, the French reformer Philippe Pinel scandalized his fellow physicians by "striking the chains" from 49 inmates of the Bicêtre. At about the same time, William Tuke, a Quaker tea and coffee merchant, founded the York (England) Retreat to provide humane treatment. Benjamin Rush, the physician-signer of the Declaration of Independence, also advocated protection of the rights of the insane. Despite this progress, more than half a century of independence passed in the U.S. before Dorothea Dix, a teacher from Maine, discovered that in Massachusetts the insane were being jailed along with common criminals. Her personal crusade in the 1840s led to a flurry of institutional expansion and reform in her own country, in Canada, and in Great Britain.

While these pioneering humanitarian efforts tended to improve conditions, one unplanned result was a gradual emphasis on centralized, state-supported facilities in which sufferers were sequestered, often far from family and friends. Largely kept from public scrutiny, the unfortunate inmates of what fashionably were being called mental hospitals increasingly became victims of the old forms of maltreatment and neglect.

Modern approaches. The modern mental-health movement received its first impetus from the energetic leadership of a former mental patient in Connecticut, Clifford Whittingham Beers. First published in 1908, his account of what he endured, *A Mind That Found Itself,* continues to be reprinted in many languages, inspiring successive generations of students, mental-health workers, and laymen to promote improved conditions of psychiatric care in local communities, in schools, and in hospitals. With the support of prominent persons, including distinguished professionals, Beers in 1908 organized *The* the Connecticut Society for Mental Hygiene, the first *modern* association of its kind. In its charter, members were *mental-* charged with responsibility for the same pursuits that *health* continue to concern mental-health associations to this *movement* day: improvement of standards of care for the mentally disturbed, prevention of mental disorder and retardation, the conservation of mental health, and the dissemination of sound information. In New York City less than a year later, on February 19, 1909, Beers led in forming the National Committee for Mental Hygiene, which in turn was instrumental in organizing the National Association for Mental Health in 1950.

While philosophic and scientific bases for an international mental-health movement were richly available, Beers seems to have served as a catalytic spark. Charles Darwin and his contemporaries already had shattered traditional beliefs in an immutable human species with fixed potentialities. By the time Beers began his public agitation, it was beginning to be understood that developing children need not suffer some of the crippling constraints imposed on their parents. A newly emerging scientific psychology had revealed some of the mechanisms by which the environment had its effects on individual adjustment, fostering hopes that parents and community could provide surroundings that would enhance the growth and welfare of children beyond levels once thought possible. In this spirit, the mental-health movement early inspired the establishment of child-guidance clinics and programs of education for parents and for the public in general.

Psychiatric and psychological developments during and after World War I provided fresh impetus to the movement. Over the same period, the European development of psychoanalysis, initiated by Sigmund Freud in Vienna, placed heavy emphasis on childhood experiences as major determinants of psychiatric symptoms and led worldwide to increasing public awareness of psychological and social-environmental elements as primary factors in the development of mental disorders.

International. Beers formed an International Committee for Mental Hygiene in 1919. By 1930, the time of the *Mental-* First International Congress of Mental Hygiene in Wash- *health* ington, D.C., there were mental-hygiene societies in 25 *organi-* countries. In London at the third international congress *zations* in 1948, the World Federation for Mental Health was formed. By 1970 it had more than 160 member associations in more than 50 countries. It provides consultants and shares informal reciprocal functions with several United Nations agencies, including the World Health Organization (in which a mental-health unit was established in 1949). The federation has convened international study groups and expert committees, held regional and international meetings, and developed close contacts with mental-health workers in more than 100 countries. The 20th anniversary of the federation was celebrated at the Seventh International Congress of Mental Health in London in 1968. The public throughout the world is aware of mental health as a major social issue. In almost every country there is increasing recognition of the interrelationship between mental health, population pressures, and social unrest. With growing urgency, people almost everywhere seek to promote mental health and to educate the public to pursue conditions conducive to individual growth and peaceful development.

National. For more than a century before World War II, the mental hospitals of many countries had been the responsibility of local government. Under the British National Health Service Act of 1946, however, the task of providing hospital care fell almost completely on the national government through boards of hospital administration acting as regional agencies for the Ministry of Health. In the same year, existing privately supported mental-health organizations combined to form the (U.K.) National Association for Mental Health. This voluntary national group provides resident facilities for disturbed persons, offers follow-up services, and trains mental-health personnel, in addition to carrying on educational *Mental-* programs. The Mental Health Act of 1959 nullified earli- *health laws* er British laws governing policies toward psychiatric disturbance and retardation. The act provided that a person requiring treatment for a psychological disorder could obtain it in a hospital on the same basis as any medical complaint. Community mental-health services were placed under the jurisdiction of local health authorities working in close association with hospital and outpatient centres. British research into mental-health problems is mainly under the direction of the government-financed Medical Research Council.

Provisions for treating and caring for mentally disturbed persons and for encouraging mental hygiene are generally organized in this manner over most of the continent of Europe. In such countries as the Soviet Union, the state, either through the central or regional governments, has the task of providing and maintaining facilities for disturbed or retarded persons. In other European countries, including members of the Common Market, government shares its mental-health function with religious groups or with other nongovernmental agencies. Many innovative mental-health services have been initiated in Europe, including the concept of integrated community services, the use of tranquillizing drugs, the sheltered workshop, and the employment of nonprofessional workers in positions of responsibility.

Imported European ideas combined with the traditional reliance on self-improvement and adjustment already present in Canadian and U.S. culture to give the mental-health movement in those countries additional momentum in the 1930s and early 1940s.

World War II and the postwar problems of returning veterans stimulated further public interest in mental health. The mental-health movement and the mass media discovered each other, and a flood of exposés swept Canada and the U.S., notably Albert Deutsch's *The Shame of the States* in 1948. Published in 1946, Mary Jane Ward's *The Snake Pit* became a Hollywood film success, followed by many more honestly realistic portrayals of mental problems on screen and television. A psychodynamic approach to the understanding and guidance of children infused North American popular culture. The introduction of pharmacotherapy (*e.g.*, tranquillizing and mood-elevating drugs) stimulated further progress.

In 1946 the passage of the National Mental Health Act in the U.S. made possible the creation of the National Institute of Mental Health (NIMH) in 1949 within what became the Department of Health, Education, and Welfare. State hospital systems were reorganized with increased budgets, while significant federal funds were made available for research, training, and clinical facilities. NIMH is the major funding resource in the U.S. for basic and applied research in mental health and in the behavioral sciences, for demonstration projects, and for the training of mental-health professionals. It has developed special programs in a broad range of social problem areas, from drug addiction to suicide prevention. The National Clearinghouse for Mental Health Information, operated by NIMH, is a valuable resource, as is the periodical publication *Mental Health Digest*. Additional sources of support for mental health in the U.S. include the National Institute of Child Health and Human Development, the Veterans Administration, the Office of Education, the Social and Rehabilitation Service, the National Science Foundation, and the medical sections of the Department of Defense. Charitable foundations also have provided generous support over the years. Meanwhile, the National Association for Mental Health continues to grow; by 1970 more than 800 state and local associations were affiliated with the association, bringing to more than 1,000,000 the number of volunteers in the mental-health movement in the U.S.

The situation in Australia and New Zealand is similar to that of North America and Europe. Developments in Latin America, Africa, and Asia commonly have been hampered by a shortage of trained institutional staff members and of local sources of support. In many so-called developing countries, mental health and hygiene depend heavily on missionaries, intergovernmental aid programs, and the efforts of agencies of the United Nations.

PREVALENCE AND TYPES OF MENTAL DISTURBANCE; TREATMENT

Few countries provide reliable statistics on which to base valid judgments concerning the prevalence of mental disorder or of emotional instability. As a result, there are considerable difficulties in comparing the actual incidence of psychiatric problems in different geographic areas and at various levels of society throughout the world. Reports of the World Health Organization do suggest, however, that the per capita incidence of severe or major mental disturbance (psychosis) is much the same in most countries. While some varieties of mental distress may manifest symptoms related to specific cultures (*e.g.*, Haitian voodoo bewitchment), the relative number of people likely to develop signs of schizophrenia, for example, does not seem to vary significantly from one population group to another (see PSYCHOSES).

Much has been written about an alleged increase in anxiety and in other neurotic symptoms (see PSYCHONEUROSES) both in the highly industrialized nations and in those developing lands where professional mental-health manpower is very scarce. It may be understandable that under the changing culture patterns of any country, psychotic conditions may seem to be occurring more frequently, but it has also been suggested that these are simply being recognized more often. Previously, persons suffering even major mental disturbance could remain in large family or tribal groups, thus escaping official attention.

One of the commonest factors invoked as a producer of pathological anxiety is fear of failure. Faster communication, new industries, and mechanized agriculture bring stresses with them that seem to lead to anxiety. In many regions of the world there is additional psychiatric strain as tribes or other groups shift from economies based on barter to those founded on money.

The quality of mental-health facilities is variable throughout the world. Contemporary improvements include the introduction of day hospitals, where patients still living at home can be treated during ordinary working hours in a pleasant and welcoming atmosphere; the provision of night hospitals for those working in the community; and growing experience with transient facilities such as "halfway" houses for partially treated drug addicts, as well as outpatient clinics and vocational rehabilitation. These developments have led in many countries to much greater demand for earlier treatment; typically the result has been the rapid return home of about 75 percent of people admitted to hospitals for the first time.

Children and youth. The mental-health movement long has fostered the establishment of better services for children. In the U.S., with the support of congressional funds, a Joint Commission on Mental Health of Children was organized in 1965. In its 1970 report, *Crisis in Child Mental Health: Challenge for the 1970's*, the commission noted a large number of emotionally disturbed children in the U.S. who need care. It viewed as a "national tragedy" the lack of any unified commitment to children and youth. The tendency "to rely on a proliferation of simple, one-factor, short-term and inexpensive remedies and services" was deplored. To alter this situation, the commission called for a "commitment to change" to bring about a truly "child-oriented society."

As part of its work, the commission surveyed worldwide practices in mental-health care. What emerged from the information gathered was that in most advanced countries of the world child mental-health services are an integral part of, or are closely affiliated with, formal health and welfare programs. These usually are perceived as being more of a public than a private or voluntary responsibility. The expenditure of government monies for children's services is widely accepted, generally in addition to any programs sponsored by private sick-benefit insurance funds. In the U.S. there exists a confusing array of overlapping and professionally competitive mental-health services. Most Scandinavian nations, Israel, Great Britain, The Netherlands, and the socialist countries of eastern Europe, present a different picture. Mental-health services are planned on a nationwide basis, with integration and coordination on the local level. By contrast, in the U.S. rarely is there a central organizing authority with power to coordinate the maze of local or regional programs or to cut through a complex network of eligibility requirements. County services compete with city services, and private agencies vie with state facilities; schools often are self-isolating, and county chapters of professional organizations seldom participate in planning integrated community services.

By comparison, in many other developed countries, a broader and better integrated range of services is more readily available to all socio-economic strata of the population. Greater responsibility and status are accorded to members of the child-care staff who have limited formal qualifications. There is less emphasis on formal evaluation or cost and more concern with finding practical solutions to immediate problems. Perhaps most noteworthy

Mental-health training and research (marginal note)

World-wide practices (marginal note)

is a considerable emphasis on the therapeutic meaning of work and on vocational training of adolescents. Industrial workshops are fully staffed and supervised, and institutional training and work assignments are made meaningful; there is no "make-do" work.

Responsibility for disturbed children in western and northern Europe varies by law and by custom. At one pole is Switzerland, which takes a position most similar to that of the U.S. in emphasizing individual responsibility in choosing and in paying for private services; the family is viewed as the primary social unit, and the state is relegated to a minor role in mental health and hygiene. At the opposite pole is Denmark, where the state assumes almost the complete burden of seeing to the economic and social well-being of its citizens. In Denmark the state can and does assume the functions of parents; local councils examine evidence of parental neglect and are empowered to prescribe a course of action after parents are given a hearing.

In sharp contrast with current U.S. practice are those welfare-oriented, sometimes collectivist societies that have established central planning, state-directed coordination of mental-health services, including some control over manpower training and placement, coupled with a strong tradition of comprehensive social security and sick-benefit insurance. These tendencies are increasingly displayed along a continuum that includes The Netherlands and the United Kingdom, through the Scandinavian countries and Israel, to the managed economies of the socialist countries of eastern Europe and Asia.

Mental-health practices in the Soviet Union

Particularly informative are reports prepared by the 1967 U.S. Mission on Mental Health to the Soviet Union. These describe an elaborate array of services that has been developed in the Soviet Union, including creches, nurseries, boarding schools, forest schools, sanitariums, and invalid houses. Children are accommodated days, evenings, or on a residential basis. After a mother delivers her child to the facility, the district children's "policlinic" is immediately notified by the hospital. These district policlinics are the medical hub of all services for children; there is one in each Soviet district serving approximately 15,000 children. They also provide most of the medical and mental-health services for kindergarten and school children, including physical and psychological examinations. When he grows older, the Soviet child and his record are transferred to centres for adolescents or adults, including the aged. With this procedure, continuity of service is maintained; waiting lists are rare; and there is no need to initiate new records at every health agency consulted during the individual's life.

The U.S. mission to the Soviet Union noted a continuing Soviet effort to identify gaps in services and to fill them by swelling the ranks of existing medical and supporting personnel and by increasing the number and variety of facilities. Delivery of health care was observed to be a highly organized process, functioning through a coordinated network of prevention-oriented, readily available, and geographically accessible services, free of cost to all Soviet citizens. The mission reported a strong social commitment to the needs of children in the hierarchy of Soviet values.

Juvenile delinquency. Among the most baffling social maladies of the 20th century is that of juvenile delinquency. A worldwide phenomenon, it varies in quality and frequency from country to country. Again, the U.S. seems unique, showing at least one significant difference between its juvenile statistics and those of other countries. Nearly everywhere else, a youngster is taken into court only if charged with breaking a law that also would define a crime when violated by an adult. In the U.S., legal definitions of juvenile delinquency have become so all-encompassing that children enter official statistical records for such "offenses" as truancy from school, stubbornness, leaving home, and curfew violations.

Despite extensive surveys and reports, a precise estimate of the extent to which mental-health principles actually have been applied to work with delinquent youth does not seem feasible. Efforts in this direction vary considerably among countries and among types of institutions within

any given nation, and nearly all who are concerned with problems of delinquency reflect dissatisfaction with progress made so far. Workers in countries that have relatively high ratios of staff to inmates in institutions for treating delinquents and that boast a comparatively extensive complement of mental-health specialists are no more content than are their counterparts in countries still aspiring to such levels of effort.

Well-intentioned endeavours had limited effect on a rising worldwide rate of juvenile delinquency in the 1970s. The mere construction of housing developments and playgrounds, the organization of boys' clubs, reduction in the number of working mothers, the mending of broken homes, and the widespread use of child-guidance clinics failed to show far-reaching effects. Still unsatisfactory but more encouraging experiences reported from some countries suggest that some results can be obtained by providing meaningful jobs; by lowering the age at which some children can leave academically oriented schools to enter vocational training programs; and by improving and expanding the work of police, parole, and volunteer agencies with youngsters. Regardless of local legal definitions of delinquency, there appears to be an international consensus that correctional institutions should stress rehabilitation and therapy, rather than punishment. There is, nevertheless, considerable evidence of wide divergence between institutional aspirations and actual practices in terms of requests for staff and operating personnel and in the application of new concepts of treatment.

Often enough, promising methods for rehabilitating delinquents have been developed locally by highly motivated groups of workers, but they have failed to inspire imitative programs either in their own country or abroad. Though change may be advocated by administrators of facilities for youthful offenders, those involved in daily operations tend to be more concerned with problems of inmate control and restriction. Change is feared in itself and often is misunderstood. Neither a growing variety of available services nor an increasing sophistication in pioneering programs seemed to have a marked effect on the worldwide rise in delinquency.

Group care. A major issue facing mental-health specialists and others entrusted with caring for children is the so-called deprivation syndrome, a combination of intellectual retardation, personality defect, and social maladaptation. The syndrome generally is found among children who are deprived of nutritional and other environmental elements necessary for normal growth and development, usually in association with gross social disturbance in the community.

Deprivation syndrome

Worldwide evidence reflects the predictable results of economic deprivation and maternal ill health, of poor prenatal and infant care, and of malnutrition. Numerous studies have shown personality defects and delinquent behaviour patterns to be especially common among deprived youth. Such children tend to receive little intellectual stimulation at home; often barely motivated to attend school, they commonly are crowded into inadequate classrooms. They are likely to live in enclaves of decay, neighbourhoods rich only in opportunity for trouble and characterized by values and ethical standards often in conflict with those of dominant surrounding culture.

Many of these children contribute to the statistics on delinquency and disorder; they become premature and inadequate parents themselves and impose similar lives of deprivation on a succeeding generation. To stop this pernicious cycle, increasing consideration is being given in almost all modern societies to substitutes for parental care. The Western world, strongly influenced since the turn of the century by Freudian concepts and laissez-faire philosophy, has leaned toward parental substitution in the form of individual child care in foster homes. Manpower shortages, a scarcity of housing, and considerable employment of mothers in agriculture and industry have combined with ideological considerations to favour the practice of group care in the predominantly Roman Catholic lands of Europe and Latin America, in Israeli collective settlements (kibbutzim), and in socialist societies of Asia and eastern Europe.

Infant group care

Under some group-care programs, newborn infants are placed directly in residential institutions; *e.g.*, in special facilities established for the babies of graduate students at Soviet universities. Children of working parents may spend five days a week in an institution and the weekend at home. Other youngsters go directly to the nursery from about three months of age onward and continue in day care throughout their preschool years. While the concept of infant group care remains a subject of controversy, its proponents hold that it might well open the way for breaking the vicious circle that perpetuates damage to mental health. Socio-economic and cultural deprivation are widespread even in some of the most industrially advanced countries; for example, nearly a quarter of all children in the United States are reported to suffer these conditions.

Manpower problems. A shortage of professional and nonprofessional mental-health and child-care workers is recognized almost everywhere. In some countries, it is particularly acute in residential facilities for emotionally disturbed, culturally deprived, or delinquent youngsters. The treatment model in most North American children's centres places primary emphasis on diagnosis and group and individual therapy conducted by professional workers.

Unfortunately, those professionals who have the least contact with the daily lives of children tend to accumulate the highest status and rewards and to exercise major control over therapy; those who deal most closely with the children and with their immediate behaviour frequently receive the least formal recognition for their work. While child-care workers as a group enjoy minimal prestige in the U.S., newer, more respected roles have emerged more rapidly in Europe.

Particular attention has focussed on professionals called *éducateurs* in France and on persons identified as *orthopedagogues* in The Netherlands. By 1970 the training of *éducateurs* had been well developed in France for more than two decades. The graduate *éducateur* is in considerable demand throughout Europe; he is recognized as a representative of an independent discipline that is not subordinate to medicine, psychology, social work, or education. His training does not stress diagnosis or therapy; neither is he a teacher who is expected to raise a maladjusted child to a particular academic level; nor is he a houseparent or attendant preoccupied with policing the behaviour of his wards. Rather, the *éducateur* is a highly trained professional youth worker who is assigned primary concern for the total life process of individual children with whom he works. He is expected to stimulate, during the child's leisure time, activities that will facilitate physical, moral, social, and intellectual development.

In many institutions for disturbed youngsters (in France and elsewhere on the Continent), *éducateurs* are the central adult figures in the lives of the children. Deeply involved in day-to-day re-education and resocialization, *éducateurs* work in and frequently manage institutions for such maladapted children as delinquents, the mentally retarded, the physically handicapped, the socially and emotionally disturbed, and the homeless and neglected.

They also are trained to function as street workers in slum areas. These functions are applied to integrate the traditional professional roles of psychiatrists, psychologists, social workers, and teachers who may operate within an institution under the daily management and leadership of an *éducateur-directeur* and his *éducateur* colleagues.

During the 20 years after 1950 there was more socio-economic and technological change in the Western world than there had been in the previous century and a half; and during those 150 years more change occurred than had occurred in the preceding 2,000. The rate of change seems likely to accelerate even more. In North America especially, statistics demonstrate starkly that existing systems for organizing and delivering mental-health care, typically demanding individual payment for services, are outmoded and that they fail to meet the health, education, and welfare requirements of millions of children. There are differing approaches and ideologies in diverse geo-graphic regions; however, no one country, no one profession, and no one ideology has a monopoly on innovative programs.

For additional details on the mental-health problems of the aged see also HEALTH AND SAFETY LAWS; HEALTH AND DISEASE, ECONOMICS OF; and OLD AGE, SOCIAL ASPECTS OF: *The aged individual.*

BIBLIOGRAPHY. C.W. BEERS, *A Mind That Found Itself: An Autobiography* (1908); A. DEUTSCH, *The Mentally Ill in America: A History of Their Care and Treatment from Colonial Times* (1937); and N. RIDENOUR, *Mental Health in the United States: A Fifty Year History* (1961), are good historical references. The concept of mental health is well discussed in M. JAHODA, *Current Concepts of Positive Mental Health* (1958). The wide scope of mental health is delineated in A. DEUTSCH (ed.), *The Encyclopedia of Mental Health* (1963). Of special interest are the report of the JOINT COMMISSION ON MENTAL HEALTH OF CHILDREN, *Crisis in Child Mental Health: Challenge for the 1970s* (1970); and the chapter by R.N. SANFORD on the prevention of mental illness in B.B. WOLMAN (ed.), *Handbook of Clinical Psychology* (1965). For international trends in mental health, see H.P. DAVID, *International Resources in Clinical Psychology* (1964), *International Trends in Mental Health* (1966), and *Child Mental Health in International Perspective* (1971). The U.S. DEPARTMENT OF HEALTH, EDUCATION, AND WELFARE issued a report on *The First U.S. Mission on Mental Health to the U.S.S.R.* (1969). Topical reference lists are available from the National Association for Mental Health, New York; and from the National Institute of Mental Health, Rockville, Maryland.

(H.P.D.)

Mercator, Gerardus

Gerardus Mercator, the greatest cartographer of the 16th century, produced maps and globes that exhibited the best scientific knowledge of his time, and were so well-designed that they remain a pleasure to the eye today. His achievement rested on a unique combination of qualities: a thorough knowledge of mathematics and land-surveying; competence in astronomy and instrument-making; the ability to seek out, digest, and apply reliable information; and a consummate talent for graphic design, engraving, and calligraphy. He developed the technique known today as "Mercator's projection" for drawing the map of the world, and invented the term "atlas" for a collection of maps.

Mercator, portrait attributed to H. Goltzius, 1574. In the Bibliothèque Royale Albert Ier, Brussels.

Mercator was born on March 5, 1512, at Rupelmonde in Flanders, of a German family that had recently moved from that country. The family name was probably de Cremer, but Mercator invariably used the Latinized version. His formal education began at a school of the Brothers of the Common Life at 's Hertogenbosch, where he received training in Christian doctrine, dialectics, and Latin. In 1530 he entered the University of Louvain (Belgium) to study the humanities and philosophy and graduated with a master's degree in 1532.

Religious doubts assailed him about this time, for he could not reconcile the biblical account of the origin of the universe with that of Aristotle. After two years of study which led him to Antwerp and Mechelen he emerged from his personal crisis, fortified in his faith, with less enthusiasm for philosophical speculation. Moreover, he brought back to Louvain a freshly acquired taste for geography, which may have been inspired by conversations with scholars in Mechelen, and he may have studied engraving at Antwerp, where good copper plates were manufactured.

A poor youth who had to make his way in life unaided, Mercator now immersed himself in study, often neglecting food and sleep. Under the guidance of Gemma Frisius, the leading theoretical mathematician in the Low Countries, who was also a physician and astronomer, Mercator mastered the essentials of mathematics, geography, and astronomy. Frisius and Mercator also frequented the workshop of Gaspar a Myrica, an engraver and goldsmith. The combined work of these three men soon made Louvain an important centre for the construction of globes, maps, and astronomical instruments. In 1534 Mercator married Barbara Schellekens, by whom he had six children.

By the time he was age 24, Mercator was a superb engraver, an outstanding calligrapher, and a highly skilled scientific-instrument maker. In 1535-36 he cooperated with Myrica and Frisius in constructing a terrestrial globe, and in 1537 its celestial counterpart. Here, for the first time, may be seen the free and graceful italic lettering with which Mercator was to change the face of 16th-century maps. He now began to build his reputation as the foremost geographer of the century with a series of printed cartographic works: in 1537 a map of Palestine, in 1538 a map of the world on a double heart-shaped projection, and about 1540 a map of Flanders. In 1540 he also published a concise manual on italic lettering, the *Literarum Latinarum quas Italicas cursoriasque vocant scribende ratio*, for which he engraved the wood blocks himself. He produced a terrestrial globe in 1541 and a celestial globe in 1551.

Mercator's career was interrupted suddenly in 1544 when he was arrested and imprisoned on a charge of heresy. His inclination to Protestantism, and frequent absences from Louvain to gather information for his maps, had aroused suspicions; he was one of 43 citizens trapped in this affair. But the university authorities stood behind him, and he was released after seven months. Mercator was able to resume his former way of life. He obtained a privilege to print and publish books, and was free to continue his scientific studies, such as his calculations concerning magnetic variation.

In 1552 Mercator moved permanently to Duisburg in the Duchy of Cleve (now in West Germany). One attraction was the more tolerant religious attitude in Germany. Another was a possible appointment as professor at a university Duke Wilhelm was planning. Soon he became a well-known figure, for he was frequently called upon to give professional opinions in land disputes, and he assisted the Duke in establishing a grammar school by helping to design its curriculum. After establishing a cartographic workshop and engaging his own engravers, he was able to return to his lifework.

In 1554 he published a map of Europe that he had begun at Louvain, and between 1559 and 1562 he further assisted the Duke by teaching mathematics in the grammar school. During these busy years he also undertook genealogical research for the Duke, drew up a Concordance of the Gospels, and composed a detailed commentary on the first part of the Letter of Paul to the Romans. In 1564 he completed a map of Lorraine (now lost) and another of the British Isles. Public recognition of his accomplishments came in 1564 with his appointment as court "cos-

mographer" to Duke Wilhelm of Cleve, to whom Mercator dedicated some of his works. During these years he perfected his cylindrical projection, which enabled mariners to steer a course over long distances by plotting straight lines without continual adjustment of compass readings. This technique immortalized his name in the "Mercator projection," which he used on his map of the world in 1569.

The Mercator projection

Mercator now embarked on a series of publications to realize his long-planned design of describing the creation of the world and its subsequent history. He called his new work his *Atlas* (*Atlas sive Cosmographicae meditationes de Fabrica Mundi et fabricati figura*)—the term still used today for a collection of maps—for he saw in the Greek demigod a symbol of the study of celestial and terrestrial events. He planned, however, something more ambitious than a useful collection of maps such as those published in 1570 by Abraham Ortelius, who had acted on his suggestion. But Mercator's ambitious scheme was never completed.

In 1569, as the first section, he published a chronology of the world from the Creation to 1568. He then published 27 of the maps originally prepared by the Greek geographer Ptolemy, with corrections and commentary in 1578, under the title *Tabulae Geographicae C. Ptolemei ad mentem autoris restitutae et emendatae*. The next part of the *Atlas*, consisting of a set of new maps covering France, Germany, and the Netherlands, came out in 1585, with maps of Italy, "Sclavonia" (now the Balkan countries) and Greece following in 1589. A last section, on the British Isles, was included in an edition with the previous sections, which was seen through the press after his death by his son in 1595. Another printing followed in 1602, and further maps were added in a subsequent edition of 1606, usually known as the "Mercator-Hondius Atlas."

A contemporary described Mercator as a highly respected citizen of Duisburg, a hardworking, modest, and frugal man, fond of serious conversation, yet congenial and witty when the occasion called for it and a good neighbour who always helped the poor. Mercator suffered a series of strokes beginning in 1590, which led to his death in 1594.

BIBLIOGRAPHY. GUALTERUS GHYMMIUS (WALTER GHIM), *Vita . . . Gerardi Mercatoris* (1595), the principal original source for Mercator's life; J. VAN RAEMDONCK, *Gérard Mercator, sa vie et ses oeuvres* (1869), a biography now out of date but still worth consulting; H. AVERDUNK and J. MUELLER-REINHARD, *Gerhard Mercator* (1914), the standard full-length biography (in German); *Correspondance Mercatorienne*, ed. by M. VAN DURME (1959), the only complete collection of Mercator's letters—inaccurate in some details; *Duisburger Forschungen*, vol. 6 (1962), a collection of essays to mark the 450th anniversary of Mercator's birth that is essential reading, especially de Smet's contribution on Mercator's activity at Louvain; A.S. OSLEY, *Mercator* (1969), a work dealing with Mercator as calligrapher, containing facsimile and English translation of Mercator's writing-book, English translation of Ghim's *Vita*, and a general bibliography. De Smet's article in *Catalogus van de mercatorverzameling van de Oudheidkundige Kring van het Land van Waas te Sint-Niklaas* (1971, in Flemish), is also valuable.

Mercury

Mercury, designated ☿ in astronomy, the planet closest to the Sun, revolves around it in a flood of sunlight. Its average distance from the Sun is 58,000,000 kilometres, compared with 150,000,000 kilometres for the Earth, and therefore it always appears close to the Sun. Its greatest elongation (angular distance from the Sun), 27° 45′, occurs only near aphelion (when it is furthest from the Sun). The brightness of the daytime sky prevents Mercury from being seen with the naked eye except as a morning "star," just before sunrise, or as an evening "star," just after sunset. At these times Mercury is never far from the horizon, and the long optical path through mist and haze compounds the difficulties of observation. As the orbit of Mercury is interior to the Earth's, the planet exhibits phases, as do Venus and the Moon, during its 88

Carto-graphic training

(Earth) day period of revolution about the Sun. Near inferior conjunction (when it is at its closest approach to the Earth, some 92,000,000 kilometres on the average) it may be seen through the telescope as a thin crescent, some 6″ (seconds of arc) in angular extent. At greatest elongation the apparent disk of Mercury is half-illuminated. At superior conjunction (when the planet, the Sun, and the Earth are practically in line and the fully illuminated face of Mercury is most distant) it has its smallest angular diameter, 2″ or 3″, compared to 1,800″ for the Moon. The planet is so difficult to observe as a naked-eye object that there is a story (probably apocryphal) that Nicolaus Copernicus, who devised a self-consistent heliocentric theory of planetary motions before the invention of the telescope, regretted on his deathbed only that he had never seen the planet Mercury. Probably no more than a few dozen people have ever seen the surface features of Mercury through a telescope, and photographs showing reliable surface detail on Mercury are still extremely rare.

Mercury was known as a planet in Sumerian times in the 3rd millenium BC. In classical Greece, as a morning star designated Apollo, it was distinguished from its apparition as an evening star designated Hermes, the Greek equivalent of the Roman Mercury. That these two apparitions were of the same body was known to classical astronomers; Heraclitus, a pre-Socratic Ionian philosopher, used the small angular elongations of Mercury and Venus from the Sun to argue that these two planets revolved about the Sun and not the Earth—an important forerunner of the Copernican theory.

Next to that of Pluto, Mercury's orbit among the planets departs most markedly from a circle, with an eccentricity of 0.2056. It is at 46,000,000 kilometres from the Sun at perihelion (closest approach to the Sun) and recedes to 70,000,000 kilometres from the Sun at aphelion. The average orbital speed is 48 kilometres per second, somewhat less near aphelion, somewhat more near perihelion. Mercury is named appropriately after the fleet messenger of the gods.

Mass and radius. The inclination of its orbit to the invariable plane of the solar system is 7°, the second largest for any planet, after Pluto. Mercury's diameter, measured optically, is around 4,840 kilometres, but more reliable radar measurements make it 4,868 ± 2 kilometres. Mercury is the smallest planet in the solar system, with the possible exception of Pluto. The innermost and outermost planets thus share aberrant qualities. Mercury is only a little larger than the Moon and is comparable in size to the largest moons of Jupiter, Saturn, and Neptune. A planet's mass is usually calculated from the orbits and speeds of its satellites or its perturbing effects on the orbits of other planets. Mercury has no satellite, and its small mass hardly disturbs the orbits of other planets; the best determination of its mass has been made from the perturbations it has caused in the orbit of the minor planet (asteroid) Eros, which sometimes passes relatively near Mercury. Mercury's mass is 3.2×10^{26} grams, or 0.054 times the mass of the Earth.

Loss of atmosphere

The escape velocity—the speed that any planet, molecule or space vehicle, must have to escape from a planet's gravitational field—at the surface of Mercury, calculated from the mass and radius, is 4.2 kilometres per second (compared with 11.2 kilometres per second for escape from the Earth). The low escape velocity on Mercury and the high temperature due to its proximity to the Sun imply that any atmosphere once held by Mercury has long since escaped to space. Only gases of very high molecular weight, such as carbon dioxide (one molecule of which is 44 times as heavy as a hydrogen atom) or argon (40 times as heavy) have any chance of being retained by Mercury—except for very small amounts of hydrogen retained between capture from the solar wind streaming out from the Sun past Mercury and rapid gravitational escape from Mercury into space. The results of observational searches for an atmosphere on Mercury are described below.

The mean density of Mercury, calculated from the mass and radius, is about 5.2 grams per cubic centimetre, near

that of the Earth, which is 5.5 grams per cubic centimetre. But the Earth, much more massive than Mercury, contains regions in its interior of high pressure and thus of high compression. In the smaller Mercury, the high mean density must imply a larger abundance of intrinsically high-density material—probably iron–nickel—in its interior. The high density makes understanding of the mean densities of Mercury, Venus, the Earth, the Moon, and Mars on a common basis very difficult, if identical interiors, with the differences in mean density attributed to differences in compression and to phase transitions, are assumed.

The question of separation of an iron or any other core from a silicate mantle on Mercury is also undecided. Mercury may have originally had amounts of silicate and iron–nickel quite similar to the primitive Earth, and the planet would have been more intensely bombarded by solar electromagnetic and corpuscular radiation in the earliest phases of the evolution of the Sun. This radiation may have been intense enough to vaporize and drive off much of the upper silicate mantle of Mercury. Johannes Kepler, in his *Astronomia Nova* (published in 1609), suggested that Mercury had the highest density of all the planets—although he proposed that the planet had the same density as the element Mercury, 13.6 grams per cubic centimetre, a curious conclusion of no more than alchemical significance.

Table 1 shows basic data for Mercury.

Table 1: Planetary Data for Mercury

Average distance from Sun	58,000,000 km (36,250,000 mi)
Eccentricity of orbit	0.2056
Inclination of orbit to invariable plane of solar system	7°
Sidereal period of revolution (year)	87.969 Earth days
Rotation period	59 ± 3 Earth days or 58.65 Earth days
Mean synodic period	116 Earth days
Mean orbital velocity	48 km/sec (30 mi/sec)
Inclination of equator to orbit	less than 10°
Mass (Earth = 1)	0.054
Diameter	4868 ± 2 km (about 3,050 mi)
Density (water = 1)	5.2 (5.2 gm/cm³)
Satellites	none known

Mercury and theories of gravitation. The proximity of Mercury to the Sun and the eccentricity of its orbit makes it useful for studying the Sun's gravity. The orbit of a planet is not fixed in space but responds to the net gravitational influence of bodies in its environment. Through combinations of many small effects, the long axis (the line of apsides) in Mercury's orbit is in slow movement around the Sun. The perihelion point moves eastward almost 10′ per century. Most of this procession is due to the gravitational influence of the other planets; but a residual of 35″ per century, not readily explained, was found in 1845 by Urbain-Jean-Joseph Le Verrier, the codiscoverer of Neptune. Subsequently this value was improved to about 40″ per century. Le Verrier attributed this discrepancy to the effect of hypothetical planets between Mercury and the Sun. Marginal observations in the 19th century had suggested that such a planet might exist; it was even named Vulcan. Some such objects were reportedly observed in transit across the face of the Sun, but very complete and careful observations of the Sun and its neighbourhood at times of total eclipse during the last century have not confirmed their existence. Another idea, that the residual in the perihelion advance is due to small particles responsible for the zodiacal light in the vicinity of the Sun, has also been shown to be untenable.

Advance of perihelion

In 1915 Albert Einstein showed that the general theory of relativity, a generalization of the Newtonian equations of motion, predicted a perihelion advance of Mercury of 43″ per century that the classical Newtonian theory did not. Thus the motion of Mercury's orbit has been considered as an important observational verification of the general theory of relativity. A third gravitational theory, the Brans–Dicke scalar-tensor theory, predicts yet another value of the perihelion advance. Robert Dicke of Princeton University, one of the originators of this theory, proposes that the difference in the observed perihelion motion is due to the Sun's mass distribution rather than to the correctness of Einstein's theory. The matter is not yet settled.

There is, however, a further test of the general theory of relativity for which Mercury is important. A ray of electromagnetic radiation—for example, visible light or radio waves—will travel a longer path when it passes close to a massive body, according to general relativity. A radar signal from the Earth bounced off Mercury when Mercury is at inferior conjunction or at greatest elongation does not pass close to the Sun and is not a good experimental situation for this test of the general theory of relativity. But when Mercury is near superior conjunction, a radar ray reaching it and reflected back to the Earth must pass very close to the Sun. Radar observations made at the Lincoln Laboratory of the Massachusetts Institute of Technology in 1967, when Mercury was near superior conjunction, showed a time delay in approximate accord with the predictions of the general theory of relativity.

Transits of Mercury. Roughly 15 times per century, Mercury crosses, or transits, the Sun's disk as seen from the Earth. It then appears as about the same size as a modest sunspot, but much sharper in definition. Some of the evidence against Mercury having an extensive atmosphere is obtained on such occasions. As Mercury's orbit is inclined to the ecliptic plane by 7°, at most of the inferior conjunctions the planet passes north or south of the Sun. But inferior conjunction sometimes occurs near one of the nodes of Mercury's orbit—where its orbit crosses the ecliptic plane—and on these occasions transits are observed. Table 2 lists the dates of transits of Mercury be-

Table 2: Transits of Mercury from 1677 to 2003

(Times given are Greenwich Mean Time)

year	month and day	hour	year	month and day	hour
1677	Nov. 7	0	1845	May 8	8
1690	Nov. 9	18	1848	Nov. 9	2
1697	Nov. 2	18	1861	Nov. 11	20
1707	May 5	11	1868	Nov. 4	19
1710	Nov. 6	11	1878	May 6	7
1723	Nov. 9	5	1881	Nov. 7	3
1736	Nov. 10	22	1891	May 9	14
1740	May 2	11	1894	Nov. 10	7
1743	Nov. 4	22	1907	Nov. 14	0
1753	May 5	18	1914	Nov. 7	0
1756	Nov. 6	16	1924	May 7	14
1760	Nov. 9	10	1927	Nov. 8	18
1776	Nov. 2	10	1940	Nov. 11	11
1782	Nov. 12	3	1953	Nov. 14	5
1786	May 3	18	1957	May 5	13
1789	Nov. 5	3	1960	Nov. 7	5
1799	May 7	1	1970	May 8	20
1802	Nov. 8	21	1973	Nov. 9	23
1815	Nov. 11	15	1986	Nov. 12	16
1822	Nov. 4	14	1993	Nov. 5	16
1832	May 5	0	1999*	Nov. 15	9
1835	Nov. 7	8	2003	May 6	19

*Mercury grazes the Sun's limb.

tween 1677 (the first accurately observed transit) and 2003, giving Greenwich Mean Time for the middle of the transit; the hours are reckoned from noon. All 44 of the observed transits occur in the first half of May or the first half of November. The Earth passes near the line of nodes of Mercury's orbit only near May 7 and November 9, and consequently transits can occur only near these two dates.

The rotation of Mercury. *Early studies of surface features and rotation period.* In the late 1960s dramatic new developments in the study of Mercury occurred. In order to understand these developments it is first necessary to consider the earlier theories and observations of the surface of the planet.

Composite prints have been made with several photo-

graphs of Mercury at a variety of telescopes, in New Mexico, Texas, and France, in the 1960s. They were taken under conditions of excellent atmospheric steadiness or "seeing," as is indicated by the sharp definition of the edge of the planet. Nevertheless, detail is fuzzy (though better than on the original photographic plates from which the composites were made). Much more detail can on occasion be seen by a trained human eye at the focus of the telescope, because the human eye can recall fleeting moments of clarity and good "seeing" during exceptional atmospheric steadiness that the photographic plate cannot. But this superior definition is often offset by vexing questions of human judgment; and visual observers have differed among themselves as to just what features on Mercury—an object of very small angular size seen very close to the horizon and obscured by sunlight scattered from the sky—are real. By watching true surface details move across the disk of the planet it would be possible to determine the period of rotation (that is, the length of the day) of Mercury and the tilt of the axis of rotation to the orbital plane. But, in practice, great difficulties were encountered.

At the beginning of the 19th century Johann Hieronymus Schröter, a German astronomer, published drawings of Mercurian surface features from which the celebrated German astronomer Friedrich Wilhelm Bessel derived a period of rotation of 24 hours 0 minutes and 53 seconds, with an axis of rotation lying 20° out of the orbital plane—a very large axial tilt. As the Earth and Mars have rotation periods near 24 hours, and it had been erroneously deduced that Venus had a similar rotation period, this produced an agreeable but incorrect uniformity in the length of the day for all of the inner or terrestrial planets.

Bessel's result was accepted for some 75 years, until the Italian planetary astronomer, Giovanni Schiaparelli, demonstrated conclusively from visual observations that the rotation period must be much longer than 24 hours. Schiaparelli concluded that Mercury rotated once every 87.96 terrestrial days, a period exactly equal to the length of the Mercurian year. Schiaparelli's conclusion implied that Mercury was rotating synchronously, making one rotation for each revolution (except for a relatively small effect due to libration, which is an apparent oscillation of the planet as seen from the Sun, due chiefly to the eccentricity of its orbit). This implied that one hemisphere of Mercury was forever bathed in intense sunlight, the other hemisphere being forever averted from the Sun. Mercury was thus considered to be at the same time both the hottest and the coldest place in the solar system. It is now known that it is neither of these.

A synchronously rotating Mercury fitted well with the tidal-evolution theory of planets then being developed by the British physicist Sir George Howard Darwin. The Moon raises tides not only in the Earth's oceans but also very small ones in the solid body of the Earth. Darwin showed that tidal friction in the Earth and the Moon, acting in accord with the conservation of energy and angular momentum in the two bodies, leads to slow changes in the period of rotation of the Earth, as well as in the distance, period of revolution, and period of rotation of the Moon. He showed that a stable situation arises when the Moon has a period of rotation equal to its period of revolution about the Earth. The length of the lunar day equals the length of the month: our natural satellite is in synchronous rotation. It seemed plausible that the much greater solar tides raised in the solid body of Mercury had also brought that small planet into synchronous rotation about the Sun.

After Schiaparelli, several observers made systematic visual studies of the Mercurian surface features, all concluding that the rotation period was synchronous with the period of revolution to high accuracy. The Franco-Greek astronomer E.M. Antoniadi gave names rich in Latin and Greek classical allusions to the features that he observed, many of the names having some mythological association with the god Mercury. For example, Caduceata refers to the caduceus, the double helix of snakes

Attempts to determine rotation period from surface details

that was the staff of Mercury; and the large feature Solitudo Hermae Trismegisti is the Solitude of Thrice-Great Hermes.

Difficulties with synchronous rotation. The first hint that something was amiss in the view of a synchronously rotating Mercury came in 1962, when the first successful detection of radio emission from Mercury was made at the University of Michigan. Mercury cannot be resolved by a single ground-based radio telescope because of its small angular size, and the Michigan observations made near 3 centimetre wavelength were of the radio emission from the entire disk of Mercury. At the time of the observations Mercury showed only a thin crescent; the bulk of the radio-wave emission must have been from the presumably very cold dark side. Earlier infrared measurements at Mt. Wilson Observatory had shown the illuminated hemisphere of Mercury to be at a temperature near 620° K (347° C; Celsius temperatures are 273° lower than Kelvin temperatures). With only a thin sliver of crescent visible and a dark side temperature near absolute zero, the Michigan investigators should have observed much less microwave radiation than they did. Either the bright or the dark side of Mercury had to be hotter than had been assumed up to that time. If the culprit was the bright side, the temperature had to be about 1,100° K, in disaccord with the infrared measurements—and indeed much hotter than even a perfectly absorbing solid body at Mercury's distance from the Sun should be. The alternative was that the dark-side subsurface, at least at the level from which the radiowaves were coming, was at a temperature above 300° K, much too high a temperature to be maintained by starlight and heat conducted from the interior of a synchronously rotating Mercury. It was then proposed that winds in a thin Mercurian atmosphere might carry heat from the illuminated to the unilluminated hemisphere, but because Mercury could have at most only a very thin atmosphere, the velocities required were very large indeed, almost supersonic.

But there was a difficulty even with a thin Mercurian atmosphere, although some spectroscopic and polarimetric observations of Mercury had suggested the presence of an atmosphere of carbon dioxide or argon with total pressure of one to ten millibars (1 millibar = 1/1,000 atmosphere). The surface properties of Mercury appeared to be very similar to those of the Moon; Table 3 shows

Temperatures on bright and dark sides

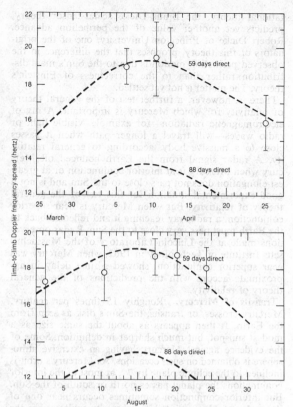

Figure 1: Radar observations (circles with vertical bars of Mercury made in 1965 at Arecibo Ionospheric Observatory, Puerto Rico. The limb-to-limb Doppler frequency spread is a function of the date. The theoretical curves (dashed lines) were computed for sidereal rotation periods of 59 and 88 days, assuming no inclination of the rotation axis.
By courtesy of Arecibo Observatory, Puerto Rico

Table 3: Comparison of Optical, Thermal, and Electrical Properties of Mercury and the Moon

property	Mercury	Moon
Blue geometric albedo, p(B)	0.076	0.088
Yellow geometric albedo, p(V)	0.100	0.115
Red geometric albedo, p(R)	0.145	0.16
Near infrared geometric albedo, p(I)	0.179	0.17
Yellow phase integral, q(V)	0.563	0.585
Yellow Russell-Bond albedo, A(V)	0.056	0.067
Radar reflectivity, 3.8 to 70 cm, R	$\simeq 0.06$	0.060 ± 0.003
Density of surface material, ρ	1.5 ± 0.4 gm cm⁻³	1.5 gm cm⁻³
Dielectric constant, ε	$\simeq 3$	$\simeq 3$
Loss tangent, tan Δ	$9(\pm 4) \times 10^{-3}$	10^{-2}
Thermal parameter, γ	$2(\pm 1) \times 10^{-3}$ cal cm⁻² sec⁻¹/²	2.5×10^{-3} cal cm⁻² sec⁻¹/²
Thermal conductivity, K	$4(\pm 2) \times 10^{2}$ erg cm⁻¹ sec⁻¹	2×10^{2} erg cm⁻¹ sec⁻¹

photometric and radar-reflecting properties of the two bodies. Similarly, the polarization phase curve of Mercury—which measures the polarization (asymmetry in the directions of lightwaves) produced in the previously unpolarized sunlight by reflection from the planetary surface, in terms of the angle between the Sun and the observer (the phase angle)—closely resembles that of the Moon. It is now known that the early polarimetric data had been erroneously interpreted in terms of a Mercurian atmosphere. (A range of recent attempts to measure the infrared spectrum of various carbon dioxide bands on Mercury has not met with success, one of the upper limits being 10^{-2} millibar of carbon dioxide set in 1970.) With no atmosphere there would be no way of heating the dark side by winds. If this argument and the Michigan observations had both been taken seriously, it might

have been possible to conclude that Mercury did not rotate synchronously. But no one was willing to take such a step at the time.

The two-thirds spin-orbit coupling with the orbital period. The decisive evidence was provided directly in 1965 when Rolf Dyce and Gordon Pettengill of Cornell University's Arecibo Observatory in Puerto Rico attempted to measure the rotation period of Mercury by radar techniques. The principle used was the Doppler effect, familiar through the change in pitch of an automobile horn moving towards or away from a listener, and in the red shift observed in the light from galaxies moving away from the Earth. The Arecibo radar telescope sent a pulse of radio waves out toward Mercury, a small portion of which was intercepted by the planetary surface and reflected back to Earth. The part of the pulse reflected from the edge of Mercury receding, because of planetary rotation, from Earth was shifted to longer wavelengths; the fraction of the pulse reflected from the approaching edge of the planet was shifted to shorter wavelengths. The Doppler spread of the returned signal is directly proportional to the speed of rotation of the planet. When many such pulse reflections were made, over a period of some months, to resolve possible ambiguities, the results shown in Figure 1 were obtained. The most recent radar data show that Mercury rotates in a direct sense (that is, in the same sense as it revolves around the Sun) with a sidereal period of 59 ± 3 days, and with an inclination of the rotation axis to a vertical through the planetary orbit of less than 10°.

How could this radar finding be reconciled with the tidal theory and with optical observations that seemed to point unambiguously to 88 days? The idea of a stable synchronous rotation was based on the assumption of a circular orbit. But Mercury has an extremely eccentric orbit; the present rotational velocity could be the result of the average torque exerted by the Sun on the tidal bulge it rises on Mercury. The eccentricity of Mercury's orbit causes this torque to vary greatly between aphelion and perihelion.

Rotation period measured by radar

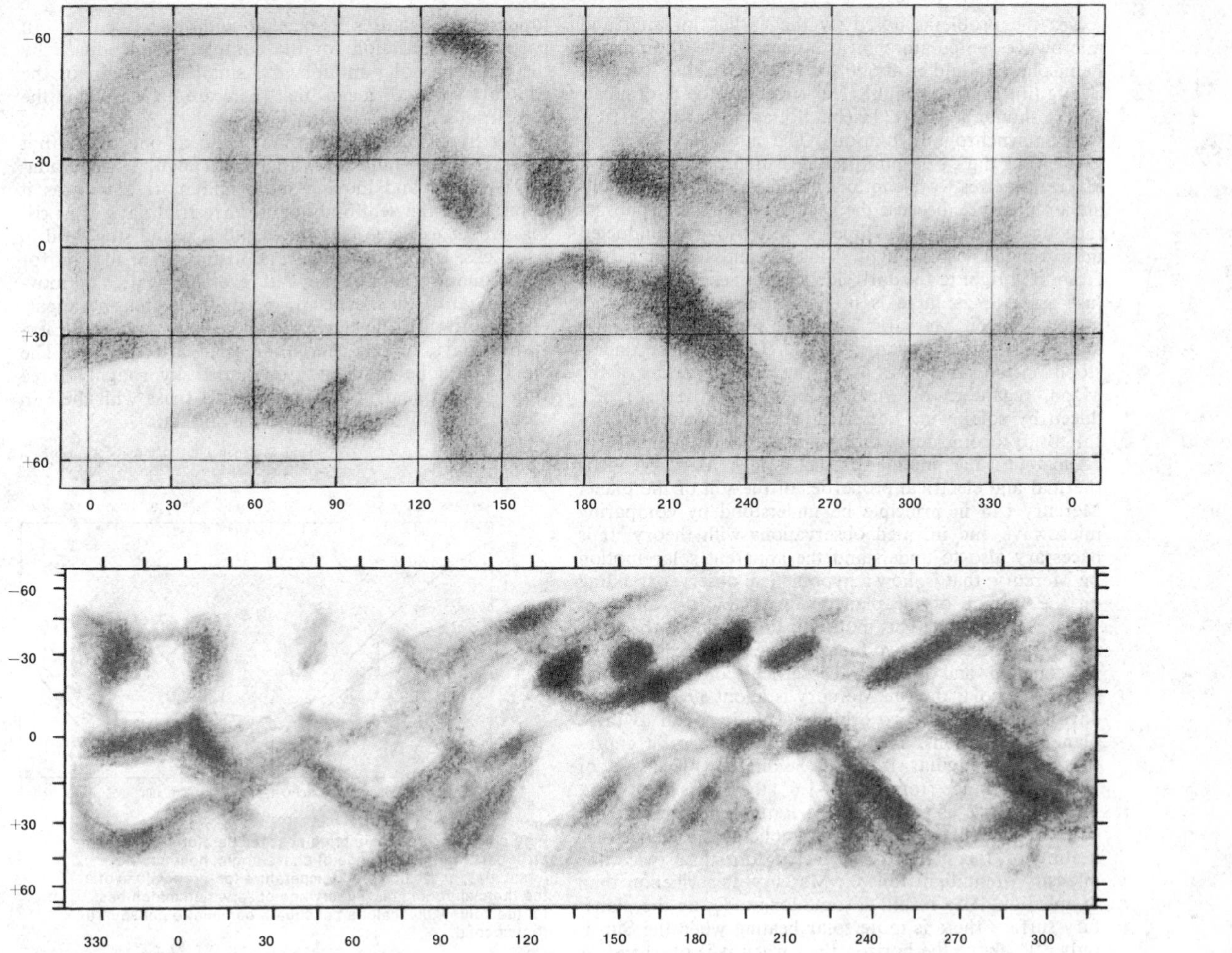

Figure 2: *Modern maps of Mercury.*
The maps are based on the assumption that the rotation period is exactly ⅔ of the orbital period and that the axis of rotation is perpendicular to the orbital plane. The coordinate scales of the maps are different. The feature resembling a script figure 5 at the extreme right of the upper map corresponds to the comparable figure at the extreme left of the lower map. (Top) Drawn by H. Camichel and A. Dollfus from photographic and visual data. (Bottom) Compiled by C. Chapman from 130 selected drawings and photographs by many observers.
By courtesy of (top) C. Chapman and (bottom) the Observatoire de Paris, Meudon

An Italian astronomer, Giuseppi Colombo, of the University of Padua and the Smithsonian Astrophysical Observatory, quickly pointed out that two-thirds of Mercury's precisely determined orbital period of 87.969 days is 58.656 days, close to the period found with radar. Colombo and Shapiro then showed that, provided Mercury had a permanent asymmetry in its mass distribution, the two-thirds resonance lock—*i.e.*, the ratio of three rotations to two revolutions maintained by the tidal effects of the Sun—would be stable. The only puzzling aspect of the tidal theory for Mercury, for a two-thirds resonance lock between rotation and revolution, is that although the condition is stable the probability of ever getting into it from some other rotation period seems to be low.

There being little difficulty with the present version of the tidal theory, how can the optical period have been so wrong? If both hemispheres of Mercury see the Sun, why are there no early maps of the "other" hemisphere? The time between successive apparitions of the same phase of Mercury—for example, full phase—is 116 Earth days and is called the synodic period. The solar day on Mercury is the time between successive sunrises at a given spot on Mercury. If the rotation period is two-thirds the period of revolution, then the solar day on Mercury is 176 terrestrial days and exactly two Mercurian years. A day two years long is quite different from terrestrial experience. Moreover, the solar day is very close to 1½ synodic periods. Thus the same side of Mercury is seen at the same phase after every three synodic periods. But since three synodic periods is close to one terrestrial year, the most favourable times for observing Mercury also recur every three synodic periods (see last section). At such times, the same surface markings are seen at the same phase, at least for a period of years. Thus every observer who draws pictures of surface markings on Mercury over a period of years will always see the same markings at the same phase and will be sorely tempted to conclude that the planet is in synchronous rotation. But astronomers observing at some different epoch should see different hemispheres of Mercury, because three synodic periods do not exactly equal one Earth year, and the stroboscopic effect gradually slips out of phase. Indeed, markings seen by the older observers appear to be not in perfect accord. The earlier observers were delinquent in not pointing out that other rotational periods besides 88 days were consistent with their observations. Indeed, the whole episode is a cautionary tale: observations that are consistent with a given hypothesis do not necessarily demonstrate its correctness.

Length of "day" and "year" on Mercury

Now that the period of rotation is established with some reliability, it is possible to combine the best earlier observations with excellent recent observations to produce Mercury cartography. Two recent attempts at such cartography are shown in Figure 2, which should be compared with the earlier drawings. Most recent visual observations give a period of 58.650 ± 0.006 days, and it has been estimated that the rotation axis is within 3° of perpendicular to the orbital plane. Thus the most recent optical work is in excellent agreement both with the radar data and with the stable two-thirds resonance lock of tidal theory.

The two-thirds spin-orbit coupling of Mercury then resolves the problems posed by the earlier infrared and microwave temperature measurements. The illuminated hemisphere should be at 600° or 700° K because it spends a long time in the sunlight. The surface of the dark hemisphere should be very cold (but not as cold as if Mercury were in synchronous rotation). The subsurface temperature on the dark side, emitting measured radiowaves of a few centimetres wavelength, should be at some intermediate temperature, because the heat delivered to the subsurface by sunlight in daytime is only slowly conducted outward and lost at night. Violent winds carrying heat from the bright to the dark side are not needed—which is just as well, as there is no evidence whatever for an atmosphere on Mercury. Thus the surface photometric and polarimetric properties of Mercury could be understood on the same basis as the surface properties of the Moon, regardless of whether these properties are produced by solar wind bombardment, micrometeoritic infall, or by a coincidence of basaltic chemistry.

Apparent solar motion in the sky of Mercury. The thermal and electrical properties of the soil of the planet Mercury can in principle be understood by comparing microwave and infrared observations with theory. It is necessary also to understand the apparent solar motion on Mercury; that is, how a hypothetical observer standing on the surface of the planet would view the apparent motion of the Sun. This motion is unique in all the solar system as a result of two factors—the two-thirds spin-orbit coupling and the high eccentricity of the Mercury orbit. The solar day on Mercury is about 176 terrestrial days long, equal to two orbital revolutions and to three planetary rotations. The eccentricity of the orbit causes the apparent angular size of the Sun in the (black) sky of Mercury to range from 1.1° to 1.6°; the Sun is about 0.5° in angular size as seen from the Earth. The combination of these two effects leads to a complicated periodic solar heating of the planetary surface. More than twice the intensity of sunlight falls on Mercury at perihelion than at aphelion. As a result, at some longitudes on the planetary surface there is more solar heating when the Sun is only 30° above the horizon than when it is overhead. A diagram of the apparent motion of the Sun in the Mer-

From *Nature* (1967)

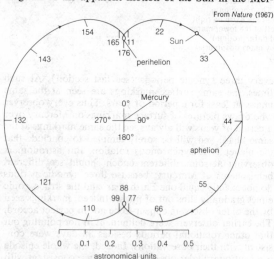

Figure 3: Apparent path of the Sun as seen from Mercury. Positions and distances are drawn to scale, with time marked in 11-day intervals. The two loops occur at perihelion, when the Sun briefly seems to move in a retrograde sense.

Strange behaviour of Sun as seen from Mercury

curian sky is shown in Figure 3. The two longitudes on the Mercurian surface marked 0° and 180° in the figure, where the Sun is overhead at perihelion, receive more than twice the energy received at the longitudes marked 90° and 270°. The intersections of these longitudes with the equator may be called the "hot poles" and the "warm poles" of Mercury, respectively. These temperature non-uniformities are permanently locked to specific locales on the surface, and it will be interesting to see, when better photographs of Mercury become available from space vehicle missions, whether there are any characteristic

topographic features associated with these "poles." In partial compensation for the complexity introduced by the apparent solar motion, the small inclination of the Mercury spin axis means that there are no seasons in the terrestrial sense on Mercury.

To a hypothetical Mercurian living at one of the hot poles, the Sun would rise with a small angular size, gradually swelling and moving more and more slowly as it approached the zenith about 44 terrestrial days after rising. About a degree past the zenith it would stop dead in its tracks. It then would reverse its apparent motion for about one degree, stopping and reversing again, and moving forward with increasing speed and decreasing apparent size toward the horizon, where it would set 88 terrestrial days, or one Mercurian year, after sunrise. The stars would be moving through the sky roughly three times as fast as the Sun, and stars that rise with the Sun would set and rise again before the Sun set.

From C. Sagan and D. Morrison, *Astrophysical Journal* (1967); University of Chicago Press

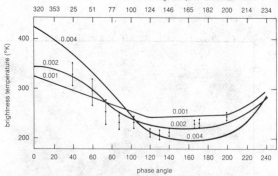

Figure 4: Measured radio brightness temperature shown with error bars for a given range of phase angle, heliocentric longitudes, and calculated temperature for three values of the thermal parameter. Theory and observation match best for the value 0.002 calorie per square centimetre per square root second.

An observer situated at one of the warm poles of Mercury would have quite a different story. He would see a large Sun rise slowly, stop at the horizon, and ponderously set again. It would then rise in earnest, shrinking in angular size and increasing in angular speed; a small Sun would speed through the zenith, swelling as it set, and very slowly sinking below the horizon. It would slowly rise again and finally set—not to rise again for an entire Mercurian year. At longitudes that are intermediate between the hot poles and the warm poles, a somewhat more complex but equally unearthly solar choreography would be observed.

Mercury's surface material. With various assumptions about the thermal and electrical properties of the Mercurian surface and subsurface material, the corresponding variations of subsurface temperature with time or phase angle (see above) can be calculated. Radio telescopes measure the temperature from the whole disk, not from a particular point, so that calculated surface temperatures must be appropriately averaged or integrated before being compared with observations. The combined effects of spin-orbit coupling and orbital eccentricity make the temperatures dependent on phase angle and also on heliocentric longitude (the actual position of Mercury in its orbit). Figure 4 shows radio temperatures for three different values of a thermal parameter. Putting this parameter equal to 0.002 calorie per square centimetre per square root second agrees best with the observations. The predicted temperature variation at the equator of Mercury at both a hot pole and a warm pole are shown in Figure 5 for two different thermal parameters, both close to the value mentioned above. The mean night equatorial surface temperature is a little more than 100° K. Infrared observations of the night side of Mercury show a disk-averaged temperature of about 110° K. This agreement in turn tends to confirm the choice of thermal parameter as well as the other assumptions in this theory.

Temperatures on the surface

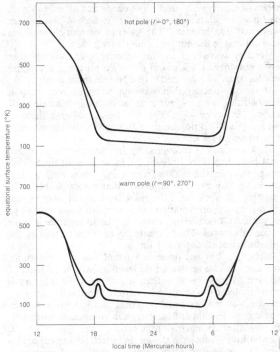

Figure 5: Computed temperature variations during a day on Mercury at a hot pole and a warm pole. One "hour" is 1/24 of Mercury's "day" and 176 times longer than on Earth. The two curves are shown for slightly different values of the thermal parameter.

From D. Morrison, *Space Science Reviews* (1970); D. Reidel Publishing Company

In theory, heat may be transferred through the surface in two ways—by contact conduction or by radiation conduction, in which adjacent particles that are not in contact in the soil of Mercury may nevertheless exchange heat by radiation. Radiation conduction is usually assumed proportional to something like the third power (the cube) of the temperature. This leads to a kind of solid-surface "greenhouse effect" analogous to the atmospheric greenhouse effect well known for planetary atmospheres. Radiation falling into a glass greenhouse, or an atmosphere, may be retained as heat if it is converted to infrared energy that cannot readily pass out again through the glass or air. In daytime on Mercury the surface and immediate subsurface temperatures are high, the radiative conductivity is high, and therefore the solar heat is rapidly transported to some depth. At night, however, the temperatures are lower, the conductivity is lower, and the heat of regions slightly below the surface does not escape to the surface so easily. As a result the temperatures of the radiation coming from longer wavelengths coming from greater depths within the surface (see next paragraph) tend to be higher; this does not hold for depths great enough to be unaffected by daytime heating. Observations seem on the whole to favour an important contribution from radiation conduction but are not yet good enough for this to be certain. All models so far have been homogeneous in depth, ignoring, for example, the possibility of looser packing of dust at the surface than at depth.

Temperatures just below the surface

Table 3 also compares lunar and Mercurian surface properties deduced from such radio information and shows that Mercury is remarkably like the Moon at all wavelengths observed. The thermal skin depth of the Mercurian surface is about 10 centimetres; that is, the diurnal temperature variation produced by the rising and setting Sun on Mercury is damped to about 37 percent of its surface amplitude at a depth of about 10 centimetres. The electrical skin depth, a measure of the depth from which radiowave radiation is observed, is approximately 10 wavelengths. So radiation at 10-centimetre wavelength is coming from approximately one metre below the Mercurian surface. From the average 10-centimetre temperatures it appears that at about a metre below the surface of Mercury the temperatures must be quite Earth-like.

But because of the absence of an atmosphere and the searing effect of the electromagnetic and charged-particle radiation from the Sun, the prospects for life on Mercury appear very bleak.

Mercury's peculiar periods. The synodic period of Mercury is the time required for swiftly moving Mercury to gain one lap on the Earth in their orbits around the Sun. If the orbital periods (in Earth days) of the two planets are designated P_M and P_E, Mercury will be seen on the average to move $1/P_M$ of a revolution per day, while the Earth moves $1/P_E$ of a revolution in pursuit. Mercury's daily gain on the Earth is $(1/P_M - 1/P_E)$ of a revolution, so that the time for Mercury to gain one complete revolution on the Earth, the synodic period S, is given by:

$$\frac{1}{S} = \frac{1}{P_M} - \frac{1}{P_E}; \text{ or } S = \frac{P_M \times P_E}{P_E - P_M}.$$

In units of terrestrial days, the synodic period is:

$$S = \frac{88 \times 365}{277} = 116 \text{ days.}$$

To find the length of the solar day on Mercury, it must be noted that the planet's rotation and revolution are both in a counterclockwise direction as viewed by a hypothetical observer from the direction of the North Star. Assuming the position of a Mercurian living in northern latitudes and facing south, one notes that the effect of Mercury's rotation, acting alone, is to cause the Sun to rise on the left and set on the right, as on Earth, while the effect of revolution acting alone is to move the Sun across the sky in the opposite direction, from right to left. In the special case of equal periods of rotation and revolution, the Sun would stand still in the sky. It is clear, then, that the apparent angular velocity of the Sun is the difference between the axial and orbital angular velocities of the planet:

$$\frac{1}{P_{sun}} = \frac{1}{P_{rot}} - \frac{1}{P_{rev}}; \text{ or } P_{sun} = \frac{P_{rot} \times P_{rev}}{P_{rev} - P_{rot}}.$$

With the radar rotational period of 59 terrestrial days, the solar day on Mercury is:

$$P_{sun} = \frac{88 \times 59}{29} = 176 \text{ days.}$$

Thus, for $P_{rot} = \frac{2}{3} P_{rev}$, $P_{sun} = 3P_{rot} = 2P_{rev}$, so that a day on Mercury is two years long. There is also the numerical coincidence that $2P_{sun}$ and $3S$ are each approximately one terrestrial year.

BIBLIOGRAPHY. V. DE CALLATAY and A. DOLLFUS, *Atlas des planètes* (1968), a popular well-illustrated book in French, with many telescopic drawings of Mercury; C. SAGAN and D. MORRISON, "The Planet Mercury," *Sci. J.*, 4:72–77 (1968), a popular survey of new data; P. GOLDREICH and S.J. PEALE, "The Dynamics of Planetary Rotations," *A. Rev. Astr. Astrophys.*, 6:287–320 (1968), a detailed technical discussion on the spin-orbit coupling of Mercury; D. MORRISON, "Thermophysics of the Planet Mercury," *Space Sci. Rev.*, 11:271–307 (1970), a review of heat transfer in the subsurface of Mercury and its connection with radio and infrared observations; D. MORRISON and C. SAGAN, "The Microwave Phase Effect of Mercury," *Astrophys. J.*, 150:1105–1110 (1967), one of the first papers to explain the microwave observations of Mercury successfully in terms of the planet's spin-orbit coupling and orbital eccentricity; G.H. PETTENGILL and R.B. DYCE, "A Radar Determination of the Rotation of the Planet Mercury," *Nature*, 206:1240 (1965), an important paper that announced the discovery that Mercury was not in synchronous rotation about the Sun; C. SAGAN, "The Photometric Properties of Mercury," *Astrophys. J.*, 144:1218–1220 (1966), an article on similar light-scattering properties of Mercury and the Moon; S.L. SOTER and J. ULRICHS, "Rotation and Heating of the Planet Mercury," *Nature*, 214:1315–1316 (1967), a paper that first showed the Soter diagram of the apparent motion of the Sun in the sky of Mercury. Only the first two references are nontechnical.

(C.Sn.)

Mercury Products and Production

Mercury, also known as quicksilver, and its principal ore mineral, cinnabar, have been known and used by man for

Cinnabar

more than 2,300 years. In early times, mercury was used in religious ceremonies, in medicinal ointments and cosmetic preparations, and in the recovery of gold and silver by the process of amalgamation. Mercury readily forms alloys (amalgams) with gold, silver, and many other metals. Since the 17th century the importance of mercury has steadily increased with advancing science and industry.

Metallic mercury, symbol Hg, is a silvery-white liquid at ordinary temperatures. Its unique combination of physical properties includes high specific gravity, high surface tension (mercury does not wet glass), low electrical resistivity, constant volume expansion over the entire temperature range of its liquid state, and the ability to amalgamate with other metals.

Of the more than 25 known minerals that contain mercury, the principal ore mineral is cinnabar—a soft red to reddish-brown mercury sulfide. Mercury is found in the elemental state in some deposits. Cinnabar has been found in all types and ages of rock, usually alone, but sometimes in association with antimony, gold, iron, and zinc.

Air samples taken in the vicinity of sulfide and precious metal ores have shown a mercury content several times greater than that found in samples taken over non-mineralized areas, and such air sampling for mercury content promises to become an important tool in exploration for mercury and associated minerals.

Mining.   Mercury deposits are small and irregular, usually veinlets but sometimes small disseminated deposits, a situation that precludes large-scale, highly mechanized mining methods.

Most of the ore comes from underground mines in which the ore is broken by conventional drilling and blasting and is removed by scrapers or is mechanically loaded into cars. Surface mining is also carried on.

Important sources.   Despite the widespread occurrence of mercury, only a few commercial-size deposits have been found. The largest of these so far known is at the Almadén Mine in Spain, which has produced more than one-third of the world's total output since production first began about 400 BC. The next largest producer is the Idria Mine in Yugoslavia, followed by the Monte Amiata district in Italy. The fourth largest producer, the Santa Barbara Mine, Huancavelica, Peru, was the world's major producer during the 17th century. The next largest producer, the New Almadén Mine in California, helped make the United States the world's largest producer for a few years following 1875, though today two-thirds of U.S. needs are supplied by imports from Canada, Spain, Italy, Mexico, Yugoslavia, and the Philippines. Mercury is also produced in China, Japan, Turkey, and the U.S.S.R.

Secondary mercury, that is, mercury that has been recovered after primary uses, is a significant source in most developed countries.

Recovery and refining.   The recovery of the metal from the ore is one of the more simple of the metallurgical extraction processes. Mercury is separated by roasting the ore as mined or as a concentrate at temperatures near or above 580° C (1,080° F), the temperature near which mercury sulfide sublimes (changes from solid to vapour directly). The mercury sulfide vapours react with oxygen in the air to form mercury and sulfur dioxide and are then passed through a dust collector and into a series of condenser pipes.

Because concentrates and some ores contain relatively large amounts of sulfur, various substances are added to assist in oxidizing the sulfur and to prevent the formation of a synthetic cinnabar or free sulfur in the condenser pipes. Brine, iron filings, and scrap iron are some of the substances used.

Cinnabar is roasted in a variety of furnaces. The most common is a retort or tube, ranging in size from 10 to 20 inches (25 to 50 centimetres) in diameter and 6 to 12 feet (1.8 to 3.6 metres) in length, supported by some type of masonry construction with a firebox below or beside the retort. A number of other types of furnaces are used to provide greater capacity and continuous operation.

The upper end of the furnace is connected to a condenser system. The typical condenser system consists of a series of vertical cast-iron pipes connected at the top with cast-iron or glass fibre return bends and at the bottom with cast-iron hoppers. The gaseous mercury condenses and collects in the hoppers under a water seal.

Mercury recovered in this manner, pure enough for most commercial uses, is of prime virgin grade averaging not less than 99.9 percent bright and clean mercury.

Mercury is packaged in cast-iron, wrought-iron, or spun steel bottles or flasks four to seven inches in diameter and about 12 inches high. The net weight of one flask of mercury is 34.5 kilograms, or 76 pounds, the commercial unit of world trade.

Most mercury is recovered by furnace treatment of ore that has come directly from the mine without processing other than crushing. Ore from some mines may be low grade or may contain impurities that create problems in roasting. In such cases the mercury content may be upgraded by the ore flotation process, which takes advantage of mercury's nonwetting characteristic to separate it from other substances. The concentrates are then treated by the roasting process described above.

Although it is not done in current mining operations, mercury can be recovered by leaching with a solution of sodium hydroxide and sodium sulfide. Metallic mercury is precipitated from solution by adding aluminum.

Generally neither flotation concentration prior to furnacing nor leaching of mercury can compete economically with direct furnacing of the ore.

Laboratory tests have shown that electrochemical oxidation in a brine slurry is a promising method of recovering mercury from low-grade ore.

The metal and its alloys and amalgams.   Perhaps the best known use for mercury is the "mercury" thermometer, which is based on mercury's property of constant volume expansion over its entire range in the liquid state. Mercury is also used in many measurement and control instruments, including barometers, manometers, flow meters, and pressure gauges. These instruments utilize mercury's high surface tension, high density, and low vapour pressure.

But by far the greatest usage of mercury is in electrical applications. The largest single application is in the production of chlorine and caustic soda by the electrolysis of brine in a mercury cell. This process makes use of mercury's electrical conductivity, as well as its ability to amalgamate with other metals. As a moving cathode, mercury amalgamates with the liberated sodium, which immediately reacts with water to form metallic mercury and sodium hydroxide. Chlorine is recovered at the anode. Investigations have shown the feasibility of using mercury cathode cells in the recovery of uranium and vanadium by electrolysis. Mercury is used in an electrolytic process to remove impurities from metals.

The next largest use is the mercury dry cell battery. These batteries operate under conditional high temperature and humidity, have long life, deliver the same ampere-hours of service at the rated current range whether operated continuously or intermittently, and have large power output per unit size. The mercury battery is used in hearing aids, guided missiles, communications equipment, and other applications in which a constant output of electric current is required.

Mercury-vapour arc lamps are compact and have high wattage and high lumens-per-watt output. They are used particularly for industrial floodlighting and street lighting. Other uses for mercury lamps are in motion-picture projection, photography, dental examination, and heat therapy. Electrical applications also include rectifier bulbs, oscillators, power-control switches, and home-type wall switches.

In precision casting, patterns have been made of frozen mercury, a technique used particularly for the casting of complex parts. A possible space-age use of mercury is as the propellant in a low-thrust ionic engine for long journeys in deep space. Another possible space application is a mercury-filled flywheel for spacecraft stabilization.

Mercury amalgamates readily with many metals. Gold and silver are recovered by amalgamation. Amalgams of sodium and potassium are used as reducing agents. A

Electrical applications

Amalgams

mercury-thallium amalgam with a melting point of $-60°$ C ($-76°$ F) is used as a low-temperature thermometer. Mercury-silver amalgams are used in dentistry for repairing cavities.

Although prime virgin grade mercury is satisfactory for most uses, it may have to be purified to meet the special requirements of dental and medical instrument and battery applications. Mercury is purified by redistilling or treatment with nitric acid.

Mercury vapour boilers have been tried for power generation but were found uneconomical.

Chemical compounds. Mercury compounds are used in the chemical industry, in pharmacology, in the paint industry, and in agriculture. Mercury sulfate is used as a catalyst in the production of glacial acetic acid, methyl styrene, and vinyl chloride. Bichloride of mercury, mercurochrome and ointments of metallic mercury, yellow mercuric oxide, and ammoniated mercuric chloride are used as skin antiseptics. Mercurous chloride (calomel) has been used as a diuretic and a cathartic.

Phenylmercury compounds, predominately the acetate, are used for treating and storing seeds, for spraying fruit trees, for weed control, and as textile preservatives. Though mercury compounds were once widely used for slime control in the production of pulp and paper, this use has declined considerably in recent years because of the potential health hazard in paper used for food products.

A growing use for mercury is in mildew-proofing paints. The use of mercury for antifouling paints—*i.e.*, paints resistant to marine growth—has declined in recent years. Mercury as a solid solution of mercury sulfide and cadmium sulfide is used in producing heat- and light-fast red pigments.

Mercury fulminate, resulting from a reaction of alcohol and mercuric nitrate, explodes on impact and is used in percussion caps as a detonator for other explosives.

Health hazards. Exposure to metallic mercury or mercury compounds, even in small amounts, over a period of time can result in mercury poisoning. Mercury can enter the body by inhalation of fumes or dust, by ingestion, or by absorption through the skin. Early symptoms of chronic mercury poisoning are weakness, fatigue, inflammation of the mouth, loosening of teeth, excessive salivation, body tremours, and emotional instability. Acute poisoning causes nausea, abdominal pain, vomiting, headaches, diarrhea, and occasionally cardiac weakness.

Industrial safety measures

Working areas in mines, furnaces, and industrial plants can be made relatively safe by taking such preventive measures as providing proper ventilation, personal hygiene, and plant cleanliness. Large exhaust fans to draw clean air over workers and the maintenance of negative pressures in furnaces or heating equipment reduce the pollution of the air by fumes and dust. Smooth, impervious plant floors and work benches slope to a point where spillage can be collected and removed. All surfaces require frequent washing, and personnel are trained to wash hands and rinse mouth before eating and to take hot showers at the end of the workday. Clothes must fit snugly at neck, wrists, and ankles, and are changed at the end of work, and washed frequently. Because leather absorbs liquids containing mercury, rubber boots, or at least rubber-soled shoes, are worn. Mercury-vapour detectors are used to indicate the level of contamination, and periodic physical and dental examinations monitor the occurrence of poisoning.

Economic importance. There are few satisfactory substitutes for the applications of mercury that depend on mercury's high specific gravity, fluidity at room temperatures, or electrical conductivity. In the pharmaceutical field, sulfa drugs, iodine, and various antiseptics and disinfectants can be substituted for mercury. Plastics, porcelain, and other metals may replace mercury-silver amalgams for some dental uses. Other types of dry-cell batteries may replace mercury batteries for other than specialized uses.

During the 1960s, mercury was in short supply in much of the world due to large increases in demand, in the U.S., Europe, the U.S.S.R., and China, and declining production in many countries. As a result, the price rose from a previously stable rate of about $190 for a 76-pound flask

to $710 per flask in 1965. Since 1967 the price has ranged from $450 to $500 per flask.

Since it is indispensable for many military and other essential uses during defense emergencies, some governments stockpile mercury.

World Production and Reserves of Mercury (flasks)		
country	production in 1969*	reserves
Canada	20,000	300,000
Italy	48,733	700,000
Mexico	22,500	125,000
Spain	64,406	1,000,000
U.S.	29,360	825,000
Other Free World	19,014	150,000
China†	20,000	900,000
U.S.S.R.†	47,000	1,000,000
Yugoslavia	14,330	400,000
World total	285,343	5,400,000

*Preliminary. †Estimate.
Source: U.S. Department of the Interior, Bureau of Mines, *Minerals Yearbook 1969*.

BIBLIOGRAPHY. R.C. WEAST (ed.), *Handbook of Chemistry and Physics*, 50th ed. (1969), a compilation of the chemical and physical properties of elements and compounds; C.J. SMITHELLS (ed.), *Metals Reference Book*, 4th ed., 3 vol. (1967), a comprehensive reference work on the properties and uses of metals and alloys; D.M. LIDDELL, *Handbook of Nonferrous Metallurgy*, vol. 2, *Recovery of the Metals*, pp. 473–515, a textbook describing the metallurgical processing of ores and concentrates to recover nonferrous metals; N.I. SAX, *Dangerous Properties of Industrial Minerals*, 3rd ed. (1968), a reference work on the hazards and toxicity of industrial materials and medical treatment following exposure; J.W. PENNINGTON, *Mercury: A Materials Survey*, Bureau of Mines Information Circular 7941 (1959), a useful summary of resources, processing, and uses of mercury; *U.S. Bureau of Mines Minerals Yearbook* (annual), a statistical series reporting production, trade, and uses of metals and minerals; S.H. WILLISTON, "Mercury in the Atmosphere," *J. Geophys. Res.*, 73:7051–7055 (1968), a discussion of a modern geophysical technique for the discovery of ore deposits.

(J.E.S.)

Meredith, George

Unlike most of his fellow novelists in the England of the last half of the 19th century, George Meredith considered himself primarily a poet and was impatient of the mechanics and skills of constructing a conventional novel; he achieved his often magnificent effects mainly by the brilliance of his dialogue and by building up grand scenes with all the wit, intellect, and poetry at his command. His novels are also distinguished by psychological studies of character and a highly subjective view of life that, far ahead of his time, regarded women as fully independent individuals, as truly the equals of men.

Origins and early years. George Meredith, the son and grandson of tailors, was born above the family tailor shop in Portsmouth, Southampton, on February 12, 1828. The name Meredith is Welsh in origin, and family tradition held that its bearers were descendants of Welsh kings and chieftains. In keeping with this tradition, the young Meredith was proud and patrician in his bearing. A small inheritance from his mother, who died when he was five, enabled him to attend a superior local seminary and thus early to assume the role of a young "gentleman." Yet the sensitive boy must gradually have become conscious of the contrast between this role and his actual social status. And the reality was to become even harsher with the bankruptcy of the tailoring shop when he was about 11 and his father's subsequent marriage to the girl who had been their housekeeper.

A second legacy, this time from an aunt in 1840, enabled him to go first to a boarding school and then, in 1842, to the Moravian School at Neuwied on the Rhine River, which was to leave its stamp upon the remainder of his life. The picturesque Rhineland, with its cliffs, its ruined castles, and its legends, stimulated the fancy of the already romantic youth. Tolerant religious in-

Meredith, oil painting by G.F. Watts, 1893. In the National Portrait Gallery, London.
By courtesy of the National Portrait Gallery, London

struction was combined with humanism: the boys were taught to think for themselves, to respect truth and scorn falsehood, to admire courage and abhor cowardice, to love nature, and to live in peace and amity with their fellows. The monotony of study was broken by daily sports, storytelling, playacting, and in vacations by week-long expeditions or boating trips down the Rhine. All of these influences except the religious remained with Meredith throughout life. After "a spasm of religion which lasted about six weeks," he later said, he never "swallowed the Christian fable" and thereafter called himself a freethinker.

Meredith's return to England in 1844, at the age of 16, ended his formal education. Like all of the other great Victorian novelists, he was to be largely self-educated. After several false starts, he was apprenticed at 18 to a London solicitor named Richard Charnock and was ostensibly launched upon a career in law. There is no evidence, however, that he ever pursued it. Probably like the writer and politician Benjamin Disraeli, the novelist William Makepeace Thackeray, and others before him, he found it intolerably dull and abandoned it at the start. But if not the law, what profession offered hope to a young man who was brilliant but untrained, ambitious but without means? If to be a poet seems an unlikely choice, it nevertheless accorded with his romantic nature and was the one he made. He was steeped in *The Arabian Nights* and German legends and literature; he had already written verse, and he soon found that Charnock's interests were more literary than legal and that he had gathered around him a coterie of young friends whose interests were also literary. Perhaps all of these were influences. At any rate, among the Charnock circle was Edward "Ned" Peacock, son of Thomas Love Peacock, the eccentric author; and through Edward he met Edward's sister, Mary Ellen Nicolls, then a widow with a small daughter. She was brilliant, witty, handsome, and about eight years older than he. Not unnaturally, in the course of editing and writing for a manuscript literary magazine conducted by the Charnock circle, he fell in love with her. Shortly after he reached his majority and came into the remainder of his little inheritance, they were married and spent their honeymoon on the Continent.

Beginnings as poet and novelist. On their return, the Merediths took lodgings at Weybridge, Surrey, near Peacock's house at Lower Halliford, Middlesex, and George busied himself writing poems and articles and making translations. Unfortunately, they brought in little money. Somehow, nevertheless, he managed to pay the publication costs of a little collection of verse, entitled *Poems*, in 1851. Though the writer and critic William Michael Rossetti praised it, Charles Kingsley, the novelist, found "very

Literary influences [margin note]

high promise" in it, and the poet Alfred Tennyson said kindly that he wished he might have written the beautiful "Love in the Valley," praise added nothing to the family coffers.

Beset by creditors, the Merediths had to take refuge in Peacock's house, where their only child, Arthur, was born in 1853. Understandably, Peacock soon preferred to rent a cottage for them across the village green from him. As poetry did not pay, Meredith now in desperation turned his hand to prose, writing a fantasy entitled *The Shaving of Shagpat: An Arabian Entertainment*, published in 1855. Original in conception but imitative of *The Arabian Nights* in manner, it baffled most readers, who did not know whether to regard it as allegory or fairy tale. But the most perceptive of the critics, the novelist George Eliot, praised it as "a work of genius, and of poetical genius."

Poverty, disappointment, and the growing antagonism between two highly strung, critical natures placed an unbearable strain upon the marriage of the Merediths. Little more is known of this period in their lives, except that Mrs. Meredith was in Wales, in the company of an artist friend of the couple, Henry Wallis, during the summer of 1857. In April 1858 she gave birth to a son, whose father was registered as "George Meredith, author," but whose paternity Meredith always denied. Subsequently, Mrs. Meredith and Wallis went off to Capri together. She died in 1861, leaving Meredith with his eight-year-old son Arthur.

Work was Meredith's only solace, and he was feverishly working upon a novel, *The Ordeal of Richard Feverel* (published in 1859), with which he hoped to win fame and fortune. It was characteristic of his best work in many respects: in form it is a romantic comedy (but with a tragic ending, as is frequent in Meredith); it deals with the relationship between a baronet and his son; the son falls in love with a lower class girl and is subjected to an ordeal—a recurring motif in Meredith—by his father; the novel is rich in allusion, image, and metaphor; the dialogue is sparkling, witty, and elliptical as in life; there are frequent intrusions by the author; three of the chapters are written in highly lyric prose; and the psychology of motive and rationalization is explored in depth. Father and son suffer from excessive pride and self-delusion (regarded by Meredith as forms of egoism), which it is the purpose of comedy, as he later said in his "Essay on Comedy," to purge and replace with sanity. Though not without faults, the novel nevertheless remains Meredith's most moving and most widely read novel. But delicate readers found it prurient and had it banned by the influential lending libraries, scattering Meredith's hopes of affluence. He was forced to accept employment as a reader of manuscripts for a publisher and as a writer of editorials and news items for a provincial newspaper. His own writing had to be done in what spare time remained.

Feverel was followed by *Evan Harrington* (1860), an amusing comedy in which Meredith used the family tailoring establishment and his own relatives for subject matter. The hero is the son of a tailor who has been brought up abroad as a "gentleman" and has fallen in love with the daughter of a baronet. His ordeal comes when he returns home to find his father dead and himself heir to the tailor shop and a considerable debt. Taking up poetry again, Meredith next published a volume of poems, *Modern Love, and Poems of the English Roadside, with Poems and Ballads*, in 1862. If *Evan Harrington* had exorcised the tailor demon that haunted him, "Modern Love" doubtless served a similar purpose for his own disastrous marriage. Semi-autobiographical, it is concerned with the tragedy of marital infidelity and its nemesis, though his own wound was now sufficiently healed for him to write compassionately. The poem deserves a place among his permanent contributions to English poetry.

After a walking tour on the Continent, he once more turned to prose. The theme of his next novel, *Emilia in England* (later renamed *Sandra Belloni*), was the contrast between a simple but passionate girl and some sentimental English social climbers—an excellent theme for

First novels [margin note]

Meredithian comedy. Its publication in 1864 was made the occasion of the first general consideration of all his works up to this point in an article in the *Westminster Review* by the Irish journalist and writer Justin M'-Carthy. A second event of importance in 1864 was his remarriage. Arthur had been placed in boarding school, and Meredith's own loneliness was intensified. Luckily, he met an attractive, well-bred young woman of Anglo-French descent, Marie Vulliamy, fell in love with her, and, after undergoing his own ordeal in persuading her father of his respectability, married her in September 1864. Thus ended a period in his life: he was no longer unknown and no longer lonely.

A son was born to the couple in 1865 and a daughter in 1871. With a family to support and popularity still elusive, Meredith had to keep hard at work for the next 15 years, with only occasional walking expeditions on the Continent. In 1866, however, he was sent out by *The Morning Post* to report the Italian campaign in the Austro-Prussian War, which lasted only seven weeks but enabled him to spend three months in his beloved Italy. After his return he was able to purchase a comfortable cottage near the bottom of Box Hill, Surrey, where he was to live quietly until his death. It stands today much as when he lived in it.

Mature works. During the next 20 years, from 1865 to 1885, Meredith continued the drudgery of reading manuscripts but substituted weekly readings to an elderly rich widow for the newspaper work. It was, however, a period marked by the birth of the children, the publication of seven novels and a volume of poems, and, in the 1880s, by growing public recognition. The next two novels, *Rhoda Fleming* (1865) and a sequel to *Emilia*, entitled *Vittoria*, added nothing to his reputation. With *The Adventures of Harry Richmond* (1871), however, Meredith returned to what was his forte—romantic comedy. Once more he wrote a close study of a father–son relationship, only this time the father is an impostor who out-Micawbers Dickens' Mr. Micawber in his belief that something will "turn up" to make his fortune. The son's ordeal is that he must perceive and reject the world of fantasy in which his father lives and achieve maturity through painful experience. After an interval of about four years came *Beauchamp's Career*. Its hero is a self-deluded idealist who is converted to radicalism and whose ordeal is both political and personal. It is one of Meredith's better novels and confirmed what was clear by now, that one of his greatest strengths was the creation of spirited, flesh and blood women who think for themselves.

The next two novels of consequence, *The Egoist* (1879) and *Diana of the Crossways* (1885), marked the beginning of Meredith's acceptance by a wider reading public and a more favourable reception by critics. Both are comedies, full of Meredithian wit and brilliant dialogue and notable for women characters who prove their right to be accepted as individuals, equal with men, rather than puppets. In *The Egoist* the enemy is egoism, and the egoist is tested by a succession of ordeals before joining the ranks of humanity. While that novel is concerned with the dangers of wrong choice before marriage, *Diana* is the first of a series of studies of mismating in marriage. Diana herself is a memorable character of spirit and brains, although Meredith is less successful in persuading readers that she could naïvely be guilty of a grave breach of confidence. In both novels, however, the men that Meredith approves of and hands the heroines over to are rather flat and uninteresting.

A new period now began in Meredith's life. Fame, if not popularity, and financial independence had come at last. Yet his enjoyment of them was to be tempered by the death of his wife in 1885 and of Arthur in 1890, by the beginning of deafness, and by the onset of ataxia that was first to limit his ability to walk and finally to render him immobile. Honours and testimonials came in plenty: an honorary LL.D. degree from the University of St. Andrews, Fife, Scotland; election to the prestigious office of President of the Society of Authors; and in 1905 the Order of Merit, strictly limited to 24 members, was conferred upon him by order of the King. Meredith had

become a public institution, his home at Box Hill almost a literary shrine.

After 1885 his work was done except for three novels and five volumes of poems that were increasingly more philosophic than poetic. *One of Our Conquerors* (1891) is probably the most difficult of his novels because of the indirect and cryptic style, metaphor, and long passages of interior monologue. *Lord Ormont and His Aminta* (1894), unlike its predecessor, was praised for the brilliancy and clarity of its style. The final novel, *The Amazing Marriage* (1895), repeats the theme of *Lord Ormont* —that a wife is free to leave a husband who does not recognize her as an equal.

In person Meredith was slightly built but athletic, remarkably handsome, and aristocratic in manner. Because of his concern with upper class life in his novels, he has sometimes been accused of being ashamed of his lowly birth and of being at heart a snob. The charge hardly bears inspection: he chose the fashionable world as a subject because it was fittest for his brand of comic treatment. His own tastes and manner of living were almost spartanly simple, his greatest pleasures being long walks and communion with nature. His friends, for the most part, were not aristocrats; they were chiefly writers and artists, along with a few professional men. It is true that in the years of his fame he was taken up by various fashionable ladies—usually young ones whom he had fascinated—and that journalists began to beat a path to his door. If he was not the oracle with all the answers, he was willing to play the role. A brilliant talker, he delighted in expressing radical and startling ideas to journalists —that the Boers should have been given their freedom; that Britain should join the United States; that marriage should be for a ten-year trial period, renewable by mutual consent; that there was no future life; and that Britain should arm itself against impending German aggression. On his 80th birthday he was presented with another testimonial, with 250 signatures of the great ones of the world, and both King Edward VII and President Theodore Roosevelt sent congratulations. After a short illness he died on May 18, 1909.

Reputation and influence. On his 80th birthday the newspapers of the world saluted Meredith as "the Dean of English Writers," the "last Great Victorian," the "Grand Old Man of Letters," and the "Sage of Box Hill." Shortly after his death, *The Times Literary Supplement* said that his mind was "so rich, so full, that one wonders where there is another mind so rich, outside Shakespeare, in English literature." As not infrequently happens, however, his great reputation went into eclipse, and other gods—Henry James, James Joyce, Joseph Conrad, and D.H. Lawrence—replaced him. Ardent Meredithians remained, but the pendulum of popular taste has not swung back. *The Ordeal of Richard Feverel* and *The Egoist* will continue to have a share in college and university curricula, *The Adventures of Harry Richmond* and *Beauchamp's Career* may have limited appeal, and for the rest, Meredith will be left to scholars and the intellectual elite.

The influence of Meredith on the novel has been indirect rather than direct. Although his highly personal style was incapable of imitation, his extensive use of interior monologue anticipated the stream-of-consciousness technique of James Joyce and others. Moreover, with George Eliot he was creating the psychological novel and thus was an important link between his 18th-century precursors and 19th- and 20th-century followers. Among later novelists influenced by him the Marxist critic Jack Lindsay cites George Robert Gissing, Thomas Hardy, Henry James, and Robert Louis Stevenson; and the writer and critic J.B. Priestley points to Virginia Woolf, D.H. Lawrence, and E.M. Forster.

MAJOR WORKS

POETRY: *Poems* (1851), including the first version of "Love in the Valley"; *Modern Love, and Poems of the English Roadside, with Poems and Ballads* (1862); *Poems and Lyrics of the Joy of Earth* (1883), including "The Woods of Westermain," "A Ballad of Past Meridian," "The Day of the Daughter of Hades," "The Lark Ascending," "Phoebus with Admetus," final version of "Love in the Valley," "Earth and Man," "Lucifer in Starlight," and "The Spirit of Shakespeare"; *Bal-*

Second marriage

Final years

lads and Poems of Tragic Life (1887), including "The Nuptials of Attila" and "Pháethón"; A Reading of Earth (1888), including "The Thrush in February," "Hymn to Colour," and "Meditation Under Stars"; Poems. The Empty Purse. With Odes to the Comic Spirit, to Youth in Memory, and Verses (1892); Odes in Contribution to the Song of French History (1898); A Reading of Life, with other Poems (1901); Last Poems (1909).

NOVELS: The Shaving of Shagpat: An Arabian Entertainment (1855, dated 1856); Farina: A Legend of Cologne (1857); The Ordeal of Richard Feverel: A History of Father and Son (1859); Evan Harrington; or, He Would Be a Gentleman (1860); Emilia in England (1864; renamed Sandra Belloni, 1889); Rhoda Fleming (1865); Vittoria (1867); The Adventures of Harry Richmond (1871); Beauchamp's Career (1875, dated 1876); The Egoist: A Comedy in Narrative (1879); The Tragic Comedians (1880); Diana of the Crossways (1885); One of Our Conquerors (1891); Lord Ormont and His Aminta (1894); The Amazing Marriage (1895); Celt and Saxon (1910; unfinished).

OTHER WORKS: The House on the Beach (1877); The Case of General Ople and Lady Camper (1890); and The Tale of Chloe (1890), three short stories; An Essay on Comedy (1897).

BIBLIOGRAPHY. M. BUXTON FORMAN, A Bibliography of the Writings in Prose and Verse of George Meredith (1922, suppl. 1924) and C.L. CLINE, "George Meredith," in LIONEL STEVENSON (ed.), Victorian Fiction: A Guide to Research (1964), provide a fairly complete listing of works by and about Meredith. The Altschul Collection at Yale University and the Morgan Library in New York hold most of his manuscripts and papers. The University of Texas at Austin holds several hundred Meredith letters. The Memorial Edition of the Works of George Meredith, 27 vol. (1909–11), is the standard edition. Vol. 2, The Ordeal of Richard Feverel, however, reprints the revised edition of 1896, to which reprints of the original edition of 1859 are preferable. Good reprints of the 1859 edition are available in the Modern Library editions (ed. by LIONEL STEVENSON) and the Houghton Mifflin Riverside editions (ed. and annot. by C.L. CLINE). The Letters of George Meredith, 2 vol., ed. by his son, W.M. MEREDITH, was published in 1912. C.L. CLINE, The Letters of George Meredith, 3 vol. (1970), is now the standard edition. LIONEL STEVENSON, The Ordeal of George Meredith (1953), is the standard biography; see also J.B. PRIESTLEY, George Meredith (1926) a biographical and critical study.

(C.L.Cl.)

Merovingian and Carolingian Age

The period of the Merovingian and Carolingian Frankish dynasties (476–887) marked the transition from antiquity to what can properly be called the Middle Ages. In the 4th and 5th centuries, Germanic peoples penetrated within the Roman Empire and brought the existence of that Mediterranean state to an end. The Franks played a key role in Gaul, reunifying it under their rule. Merovingian and, later, Carolingian monarchs created a kingdom centred in an area between the Loire and Rhine but extending beyond the Rhine into large areas of Germany.

ORIGINS

Early history of the Franks. In the second half of the 4th century the Salian Franks, who lived along the lower bank of the Rhine, occupied the Toxandria—an area west of the Meuse, along and on both sides of the modern Belgium–Netherlands border, that had formerly been Roman and had become depopulated—with the permission of the imperial authorities. Later, in the second quarter of the 5th century, all of the Franks moved southward toward the middle Rhine area (Cologne), the lower branches of the Moselle and Meuse, and the coastal region. In the latter area they took possession of Tournai and Cambrai and reached the Somme. These Franks along the coast were divided into many small kingdoms. One of the most important of the kingdoms was Tournai, the earliest known king of which was Childeric (died c. 481/482). Traditionally regarded as the son of Merovich (Merovée or Merowe), eponymous ancestor of the Merovingian dynasty, Childeric placed himself in the service of the Roman Empire. Clovis was his son.

Gaul and Germany at the end of the 5th century. Other Germans had already entered Gaul. The area south of the Loire was divided between two tribes. One, the

Ancestor of the Merovingian dynasty

Visigoths, occupied Aquitaine, Provence, and most of Spain. Their king, Euric (ruled 466–484), seems to have been the principal monarch in the West. The other tribe, the Burgundians, were masters of most of the Rhône Valley. In northern Gaul, the Alemanni occupied Alsace and moved westward into the area between the Franks and Burgundians, while the first British immigrants established themselves on the Armorican Peninsula (now Brittany). A territory that continued to call itself Roman remained within these areas of Gaul. An imperial functionary, Syagrius, was installed in Soissons and shared power with the local bishops.

In spite of the German influx, Gaul, which had been part of the Roman Empire for 500 years, remained basically romanized. While most of its administrative institutions could not withstand the crisis of the 5th century, Gaul's traditional Roman civilization survived, especially among the aristocratic classes. In addition, the Germans themselves were, to varying degrees, affected by this civilization. This influence was stronger among the Burgundians and the Visigoths, who had lived within the empire for a longer time and had intermingled with other Germanic peoples to a great extent, than it was among the Franks and Alemanni, who had only recently entered the empire. The Burgundians and Visigoths adopted a heretical form of Christianity—Arianism. The Franks and Alemanni remained pagan and preserved limited contracts with free Germany.

In effect, the Germanic peoples who penetrated into Roman Gaul were only the advance guard of the Germanic world. The northern Germans (Angles, Jutes, Saxons, Frisians) still occupied the coastal regions of the North Sea east of the Rhine; the Thuringians and Bavarians divided the territory between the Elbe and Danube; the Slavic world began on the opposite bank of the Elbe.

THE MEROVINGIANS

Clovis. Clovis (ruled 481/482–511) unified Gaul with the exception of areas in the southeast.

Frankish expansion and the unification of Gaul. During the years following his accession Clovis consolidated

From R. Grousset and E. Leonard (eds.), *Histoire Universelle*

The division of the Frankish kingdom among the sons of Clovis at his death in 511.

the position of the Franks in northern Gaul. In 486 he defeated Syagrius and occupied an area situated between the Frankish kingdom of Tournai, the Visigothic and Burgundian kingdoms, and the lands occupied by the Rhenish (Ripuarian) Franks and the Alemanni, removing it from Roman control once more. It was probably during this same period that he eliminated the other Salian kings. In a second phase, he attacked the other Germanic peoples living in Gaul, with varying degrees of success. An Alemannian westward push was blocked, probably as a result of two campaigns—one conducted by the Franks of the kingdom of Cologne in about 495–496 at the Battle of Tolbiac (Zülpich), the second by Clovis in about 506, after the annexation of Cologne. Clovis thus extended his authority over most of the territory of the Alemanni. Some of the former inhabitants sought refuge in Theodoric's Ostrogothic kingdom. Despite his marriage to a niece of Gundobad, one of the Burgundian kings, Clovis plotted (c. 500–501) with Godigisel, another Burgundian king. Gundobad, however, succeeded in foiling the plot and reuniting the kingdom. Clovis then turned against the Visigothic kingdom and, reconciled with Gundobad, defeated Alaric II at Vouillé (507). He annexed Aquitaine, between the Loire, Rhône, and Garonne, as well as Novempopulana, between the Garonne and the Pyrenees. Opposed to a Frankish hegemony in the West, Theodoric intervened on behalf of the Visigothic king and prevented Clovis from annexing Septimania, on the Mediterranean between the Rhône and the Pyrenees, which the Visigoths retained, while Theodoric occupied Provence. In the west, the eastern section of Amorica (the bishoprics of Nantes, Rennes, and Vannes) appeared to have submitted to Clovis. In addition, in the east Clovis eliminated the kingdom of Cologne and united the Frankish people under his own leadership.

Clovis established Paris as the capital of his new kingdom, and in about 507–508 he received from the Emperor an honorary consulship and the right to use the imperial insignia. These privileges gave the new king legitimacy of sorts and were useful in gaining the support of his Gallo-Roman subjects.

The conversion of Clovis. According to tradition, substantiated by Gregory of Tours, Clovis converted, under the influence of his wife Clotilda and Remigius, bishop of Reims, because of a vow taken during the campaign against the Alemanni. Avitus, bishop of Vienne, and Nicetus, bishop of Trier, also mention the conversion in their correspondence; historians disagree, however, as to the location of the Baptism (Reims or Tours) and the date (496 or 506). Because the other Germans in Gaul were Arians (anti-Trinitarian Christians), Clovis' conversion assured the Frankish king of the support of the Catholic hierarchy and, generally, of Catholic opinion. It also ensured the triumph in Gaul of Catholicism over paganism and Arianism and spared Gaul lengthy conflicts that punctuated the history of other Germanic kingdoms.

The sons of Clovis. Following the death of Clovis (511) the kingdom was divided among his four sons. This partition was not made according to ethnic, geographic, or administrative divisions. The only factor taken into account was that the portions be of equal value. Boundaries were poorly defined. The territory was divided into two general areas: one was the territory north of the Loire (that part of Gaul that was conquered earliest); the other, to the south in Aquitaine, was a region not yet assimilated. Theuderic I received lands around the Rhine, Moselle, and upper Meuse, as well as the Massif Central; Chlodomer, the Loire country on either side of the Rhine (this kingdom was the only one not composed of separated territories); Childebert I, the country of the English Channel and the lower Seine and, probably, the region of Bordeaux and Saintes; Chlotar I, the old Frankish country north of the Somme and an ill-defined area in Aquitaine. Their capitals were centred in the Paris Basin, which was divided among the four brothers; Theuderic I used Reims; Chlodomer, Orléans; Childebert I, Paris; Chlotar I, Soissons. As each brother died, the survivors

partitioned the newly available lands among themselves. This system resulted in bloody competition until 558, when Chlotar I succeeded in reuniting the kingdom under his own rule.

The conquest of Burgundy and southern Germany. In spite of these partitions, the Frankish kings continued their conquests. One of their primary concerns was to extend their dominion over the whole of Gaul. It took two campaigns to overcome the Burgundian kingdom. In 523 Chlodomer, Childebert I, and Chlotar I, as allies of Theodoric, moved into Burgundy, whose king, Sigismund, Theodoric's son-in-law, had assassinated his own son. Sigismund was captured and killed. Godomer, the new Burgundian king, defeated the Franks at Vézeronce and forced them to retreat; Chlodomer was killed in the battle. Childebert I, Chlotar I, and Theudebert, the son of Theuderic I, regained the offensive in 532–534. The Burgundian kingdom was annexed and divided between the Frankish kings. Following Theodoric's death (526), the Franks were able to gain a foothold in Provence by taking advantage of the weakened Ostrogothic kingdom. The Franks were thus masters of all southeastern Gaul and had reached the Mediterranean. But in spite of two expeditions (531 and 542: the Siege of Saragossa), they were unable to gain possession of Visigothic Septimania. Also, at least a portion of Amorica in the northwest remained outside the Frankish sphere of influence. During this period, British colonization of the western half of the Armorican Peninsula was at its height.

To the east, the Franks extended their domain in southern Germany, bringing Thuringia (in c. 531 Chlotar I carried off Radegunda, a niece of the Thuringian king), the part of Alemannia between the Neckar and the upper Danube (after 536), and Bavaria under subjection. The latter was created as a dependent duchy in about 555. The Franks were less successful in northern Germany; in 536 they imposed a tribute on the Saxons (who occupied the area between the Elbe, the North Sea, and the Ems), but the latter revolted successfully in 555.

Conquests of Thuringia and Bavaria

Theudebert and his son, Theudebald, sent expeditions into Italy during a struggle between the Ostrogoths and Byzantines (535–554), but they achieved no lasting results.

The grandsons of Clovis. The Frankish kingdom was partitioned once more in 561 and again in 567. At the death of Chlotar I (561) the Frankish kingdom, which had become the most powerful state in the west, was once again divided, this time between his four sons. The partition agreement, based on that of 511, dealt with more extensive territories. Guntram received the eastern part of the former kingdom of Orléans, enlarged by the addition of Burgundy. Charibert's share was fashioned from the old kingdom of Paris (Seine and English Channel districts), augmented in the south by the western section of the old kingdom of Orléans (lower Loire Valley) and the Aquitaine Basin. Sigebert received the kingdom of Reims, extended to include the new German conquests; a portion of the Massif Central (Auvergne) and the Provençal territory (Marseilles) were added to his share. Chilperic's portion was reduced to the kingdom of Soissons.

The death of Charibert (567) resulted in a new partition. Chilperic was the principal beneficiary; he received the lower Seine district, which gave him a large tract of the English Channel coast. The remainder, most notably the Aquitaine Basin, was divided in a complex manner; and Paris was subject to joint possession. These two partitions, which served to reaffirm the division of Gaul, were the sources of innumerable intrigues and family struggles, especially between, on the one hand, Chilperic I, his wife Fredegund, and their children, who controlled northwestern Gaul, and, on the other hand, Sigebert I, his wife Brunhilda, and their descendants, the masters of northeastern Gaul.

Intrigues and family struggles

The shrinking of the frontiers and peripheral areas. These events undermined the Frankish hegemony. In Armorica the Franks maintained control of the eastern region, but had to cope with raids by the Bretons, who had established heavily populated settlements in the western part of the peninsula. To the southwest the Gas-

Triumph of Catholicism in Gaul

cons, a highland people from the Pyrenees, had been driven northward by the Visigoths in 578 and settled in Novempopulana; in spite of several Frankish expeditions, this area was not subdued. In the south the Franks were unable to gain control of Septimania; they tried to accomplish this by means of diplomatic agreements, which were buttressed by dynastic intermarriage, and by military campaigns occasioned by religious differences (the Visigothic kings were Arians). In the southeast the Lombards, who had recently arrived in Italy, made several raids on Gaul (569, 571, 574); Frankish expeditions into Italy (584, 585, 588, 590), led by Childebert II, were without result. Meanwhile the Avars, an Asian people who settled along the Danube in the second half of the 6th century, threatened the eastern frontier; in 568 they took Sigebert prisoner, and in 596 they attacked Thuringia, forcing Brunhilda to purchase their departure.

The parcelling up of the kingdom.   Internal struggles unleashed centrifugal forces. At the time of the partitions of 561 and 567, new political geographical units began to appear within Gaul. Austrasia was created from the Rhine, Moselle, and Meuse districts, which had formerly been the kingdom of Reims; Sigebert I (died 575) transferred its capital to Metz. Neustria was born out of the partition of the kingdom of Soissons; a portion of the kingdom of Paris was added to it, thus endowing the area with a broad coastal section and making the lower Seine Valley its centre. Its first capital, Soissons, was returned to Austrasia following the death of Chilperic; its capital was later moved to Paris, which had been controlled by Chilperic. The kingdom of Orléans, less its western territory but with part of the old Burgundian lands added to it, eventually became Burgundy; Guntram fixed its capital at Chalon-sur-Saône. Aquitaine submitted to the Frankish kingdoms centred farther north in Gaul; it was the object of numerous partitions made by sovereigns who regarded it as an area for exploitation. Aquitaine did not enjoy political autonomy during this period.

The failure of reunification (613–714).   Territorial crisis was partially and provisionally averted during the first third of the 7th century.

Chlotar II and Dagobert.   Chlotar II, king of Neustria since 584, inherited Burgundy and Austrasia in 613 upon the death of Brunhilda, and thus the kingdom was reunited. He fixed his capital at Paris and, in 614, convoked a council there that, by increasing the powers of the church and the nobility, proved to be the most important meeting of the Merovingian epoch. His son Dagobert (ruled 629–639) was able to preserve this unity; and he journeyed to Burgundy, where the office of mayor of the palace was maintained, to Austrasia, and to Aquitaine, which was given the status of a duchy.

Dagobert had only limited success along the frontier. In 638 he placed the Bretons and the Gascons under nominal subjection, but ties with these peripheral regions were tenuous. He intervened in dynastic quarrels of Spain, entering the country and going as far as Saragossa before receiving tribute and quitting the country. Septimania remained Visigothic. On the eastern frontier there were incidents involving Frankish merchants and Moravian and Czech Slavs; after the failure of a campaign conducted by Dagobert, with the assistance of the Lombards and Bavarians (633), the Slavs attacked Thuringia. The King reached an agreement with the Saxons, who would protect the eastern frontier in return for remission of a tribute they had paid since 536.

The hegemony of Neustria.   The territorial struggles began anew after 639. In both Neustria and Austrasia power was in the hands of aristocratic leaders, called the mayors of the palace. Ebroin, mayor of the palace in Neustria, attempted to unify the kingdom under his leadership but met with violent opposition. Resistance in Burgundy was led by St. Leodegar, who was assassinated in either 677 or 679. In Austrasia Ebroin was opposed to the Pepinid mayors of the palace; Pepin I of Landen was succeeded by Grimoald, who tried unsuccessfully to have his son, Childebert the Adopted, crowned king, and by Pepin II of Herstal (or Heristal), whom Ebroin was briefly able to keep from power (c. 680).

Frankish hegemony was once more threatened in the peripheral areas, especially to the east where Austrasia was endangered. The Thuringians (640–641) and Alemanni regained their independence. The Frisians reached the mouth of the Schelde and controlled the towns of Utrecht and Dorestat; the attempted conversion of Frisia by Wilfrid of Northumbria had to be abandoned (*c.* 680). In southern Gaul, Duke Lupus changed the status of Aquitaine from that of a duchy to an independent principality.

Austrasian hegemony and the rise of the Pepinids.   The murder of Ebroin (681 or 683) reversed the situation in favour of Austrasia and the Pepinids. Pepin II, who defeated Neustria at Tertry (687), reunified northern Gaul under his own control. Austrasia and Neustria were reunited, theoretically under the Merovingian dynasty, but actually under Pepin II, who governed through his position as mayor of the palace. At the same time, Pepin II partially restabilized the frontiers by driving the Frisians north of the Rhine and by restoring Frankish suzerainty over the Alemanni. But control of southern Gaul continued to elude the Franks. In the early 8th century, Provence became an autonomous duchy, while power in Burgundy was divided.

From G. Fournier, *L'Occident de la fin du Ve siecle a la fin du IXe siecle*

The Frankish domains in the time of Charles Martel (boundaries approximate).

THE CAROLINGIANS

Representatives of the Merovingian dynasty continued to reign, at least in title, during most of the first half of the 8th century. They were slothful monarchs, according to a contemporary biographer of Charlemagne. In actual fact, power was in the hands of the Pepinids, who, thanks to their valuable land and loyal retainers, maintained a monopoly on the office of mayor of the palace. Because of their familial predisposition for the name Charles, and because of the significance of Charlemagne in the family's history, modern historians have called them Carolingian.

Charles Martel and Pepin III the Short.   Pepin II's death in 714 jeopardized the Austrasian hegemony. His heir was a child of six. There was a revolution in Neustria, and Eudes, duke of Aquitaine, used the occasion to increase his holdings and make an alliance with the Neustrians. The Saxons crossed the Rhine and the Arabs crossed the Pyrenees.

Charles Martel.   The situation was rectified by another of Pepin's sons, Charles Martel. Defeating the Neustrians at Amblève (716), Vinchy (717), and Soissons (719), he made himself master of northern Gaul. He then re-established Frankish authority in southern Gaul, where the local authorities could not cope with the Islāmic threat; he stopped the Muslims at Poitiers (732) and used this opportunity to subdue Aquitaine (735–736); the Muslims then turned toward Provence, and Charles Martel sent several expeditions against them. At the same time, he succeeded in re-establishing authority over the dissident provinces in the southeast (737–738). Finally, he re-established Frankish influence in Germany. In his numerous military campaigns he succeeded in driving the Saxons across the Rhine, returned the Bavarians to Frankish suzerainty, and annexed southern Frisia and Alemannia. He also encouraged missionary activity, seeing it as a means to consolidate the Frankish empire; this undertaking was supported by the papacy, which was beginning to seek support in the West. Missionaries, most of whom were Anglo-Saxon (*e.g.*, Willibrord and Winfrid, also known as Boniface), made definite progress in their task.

Charles Martel had supported a figurehead Merovingian king, Theuderic IV (ruled 721–737), but upon the latter's death he felt his own position secure enough to leave the throne vacant. His chief source of power was a strong circle of followers, who furnished the main body of his troops at a time when cavalry was becoming the most important element in the army. He attached them to himself by concessions of land, which he obtained by drawing on the considerable holdings of the church. This gave him large tracts of land at his disposal, which he granted for life (*precaria*). He was thus able to recruit a larger and more powerful circle of followers than that surrounding any of the other influential magnates.

Pepin III the Short. At the death of Charles Martel (741), as was the custom, the kingdom was divided between his two sons, Carloman and Pepin III the Short. This partition was followed by insurrections in the peripheral countries—Aquitaine, Alemannia, and Bavaria.

Carloman's abdication in 747 reunited the country. Pepin the Short was crowned king of the Franks with the complicity of the papacy, which, threatened by the Lombards and having problems with Byzantium, sought a protector in the West. The usurpation was accomplished in two stages: in 750, after obtaining the support of Pope Zacharias, Pepin deposed Childeric III; he then had himself elected king by an assembly of magnates and consecrated by a bishop, thus ending the nominal authority of the last Merovingian king, Childeric III, who had been placed on the throne in 743. The new pope, Stephen II, sought aid from Gaul; in 754 at Ponthion he gave Pepin the title patrician of the Romans, renewed the King's consecration, and consecrated Pepin's sons, thus securely establishing the line.

As king, Pepin limited himself to consolidating Frankish influence in Gaul, thus paving the way for later Carolingian expansion. Despite Pepin's efforts, the situation at the German frontier was unstable. The duchy of Bavaria, which the Franks had given to Tassilo III as a benefice, gained its independence in 763; several expeditions were unable to subdue the Saxons. On the other hand, Pepin achieved a decisive victory in southern Gaul by capturing Septimania from the Muslims (752–759). He broke down Aquitaine's resistance, and it was reincorporated into the kingdom (760–768). Pepin intervened in Italy twice (754–755; 756) on the appeal of the Pope and laid the foundations for the Papal States. He exchanged ambassadors with the great powers of the eastern Mediterranean—the Byzantine Empire and the caliphate of Baghdad.

Charlemagne. Pepin III, faithful to ancient customs, divided his kingdom between his two sons, Charles (Charlemagne) and Carloman. On Carloman's death in 771 the kingdom was reunited. Charlemagne established the base of his kingdom in northeastern Gaul (his preferred residence was Aachen [Aix-la-Chapelle]).

The conquests. He extended the territory controlled by the Franks considerably and unified a large part of the Christian West; he followed no devious policy of expansion, taking advantage, instead, of situations as they arose.

Charlemagne consolidated Frankish authority up to the geographic limits of Gaul. Though he put down a new insurrection in Aquitaine (769), he was unable to bring the Gascons and the Bretons under submission. Charlemagne pursued an active policy toward the Mediterranean countries. In Spain he attempted to take advantage of the emir of Córdoba's difficulties; he was unsuccessful in western Spain, but in the eastern area he was able to establish a march south of the Pyrenees. Pursuing Pepin's Italian policy, he intervened in Italy, for at the request of Pope Adrian I, who was threatened by the Lombards, he took possession of Pavia and had himself crowned king of the Lombards; in 774 he fulfilled Pepin's promise and created a pontifical state; the situation on the peninsula remained confused, and many expeditions were necessary (in Friuli, in Istria, against the Lombards in Spoleto and Benevento). This enlargement of his Mediterranean holdings led Charlemagne to establish a protectorate over the Balearic Islands in the western Mediterranean to hold Muslim pirates in check (798–799).

Charlemagne conquered more German territory and secured the eastern frontier. By means of military campaigns and missionary activities he brought Saxony and northern Frisia under control; the Saxons, led by Widukind, offered a protracted resistance (772–804), and Charlemagne deported part of the population. To the south, Bavaria was brought under Frankish authority and annexed. Frankish conquests in the east brought them into contact with new peoples—Charles was able to defeat the Avars in three campaigns (791, 795, 796), from which he obtained considerable booty; he was also able to establish a march on the middle Danube, and the Franks undertook the conversion and colonization of that area. Charles held fast against the Slavs along the Elbe frontier; he constructed a march at the border of Jutland, facing the Danes, who in turn constructed a great fortification, the Danewirk, across the peninsula on their own shore. He also founded Hamburg on the banks of the Elbe. These actions gave the Franks a broad face on the North Sea.

The Frankish state now appeared to be the principal power in the West. Charlemagne claimed to be defender of Roman Christianity and, acting on this title, intervened in the religious affairs of Spain. Problems arose over doctrinal matters that, along with questions concerning the Italian border and the use of the imperial title, brought him into conflict with the Byzantine Empire; a peace treaty was signed in 810–812. Charles continued his peace policy toward the Muslim East: ambassadors were exchanged with the caliph of Baghdad and Charles received a kind of eminent right in Jerusalem.

The restoration of the empire. When, by the end of the 9th century, Charles was master of a great part of the West, he re-established the empire in his own name. He was crowned emperor in Rome (Christmas Day, 800), in the presence of Pope Leo III, but under uncertain circumstances. His new title replaced the ambiguous patrician of the Romans. Charles's powers in Rome and in relation to the pontifical state, which was incorporated, with some degree of autonomy, into the Frankish empire, were clarified. Above all, his new title, which did not replace King of the Franks or King of the Lombards but took precedence over them, was well suited to Charles's preponderant position in the old Roman West. The restoration of the empire discloses a will to unify the West; nevertheless, Charlemagne had to make concessions to certain national bodies—he preserved the kingdom of Italy, giving the crown to one of his sons, Pepin, and made Aquitaine a kingdom for his other son, Louis.

Louis the Pious. Only chance ensured that the empire remained united under Louis the Pious, the last surviving son of Charlemagne (the latter had anticipated the partitioning of his empire among his three sons). The era of great conquests had ended and, on the face of it, Louis's principal preoccupation was his relations with the countries to the north. In the hope of averting the threat posed by the Normans, who had begun to raid the coasts of the

(margin left:) Pepin III's usurpation

(margin right:) Charlemagne's coronation as emperor

The Carolingian Empire and (inset) divisions after the Treaty of Verdun, 843.

Adapted from p. 104, *The Middle Ages, 395–1500*, 5th ed., J.R. Strayer and D.C. Munro, copyright © 1970;
by permission of Appleton-Century-Crofts, Educational Division, Meredith Corporation

North Sea and the Atlantic, Louis proposed to evangelize the Scandinavian world. This mission was given to St. Ansgar but was a failure.

During Louis's reign, the imperial offices were systematized. He saw the empire, above all, as a religious ideal, and in 816 the imperial coronation, originally a secular ceremony, was complemented by a religious ceremony, the anointment, at which the pope presided. At the same time, Louis the Pious took steps (*Ordinatio Imperii*, 817) to regulate the succession so as to maintain the unity of the empire. His oldest son, Lothair, was to be sole heir to the empire, but within it three small dependent kingdoms were maintained: Louis's younger sons, Pepin and Louis, received Aquitaine and Bavaria, respectively; his nephew Bernard was given Italy.

The remarriage of Louis the Pious and the birth of a fourth son, Charles the Bald, upset this project. In spite of opposition from Lothair, who had the support of a unitarian faction drawn from the ranks of the clergy, the emperor's principal concern was to create a kingdom for Charles the Bald. These divergent interests led to conflicts that weakened imperial prestige (in 833, abandoned by his followers at the Field of Lies, Louis the Pious was forced to make public penance at Saint-Médard in Soissons). The question of Aquitaine arose at the death of Pepin I, ruler there since 814; the emperor gave this subordinate kingdom to Charles, but the magnates rose up and proclaimed Pepin II, the son of the dead king.

The partitioning of the Carolingian Empire. After the death of Louis the Pious (840), his sons continued their plotting to alter the succession. Louis the German and Charles the Bald united against Lothair (Oath of Strasbourg, 842).

The Treaty of Verdun. Later the three brothers came to an agreement in the Treaty of Verdun (843). The empire was divided into three kingdoms arranged along a north–south axis: Francia Orientalis was given to Louis, Francia Media to Lothair, and Francia Occidentalis to Charles the Bald. The three kings were equal among themselves. Lothair kept the title of emperor, but this title had completely lost its universal character and had meaning only in a portion of the old empire.

The kingdoms created at Verdun. Until 861 the clerical ranks imposed a government of fraternity on the three brothers, manifested in the numerous conferences they held; but centrifugal forces destroyed it.

Francia Media proved to be the least stable of the kingdoms, and the imperial institutions bound to it suffered as a result. In 855 the death of Lothair I was followed by a partition of his kingdom among his three sons: the territory to the north and west of the Alps went to Lothair II (Lotharingia) and to Charles (kingdom of Provence); Louis II received Italy and the imperial title. At the death of Charles of Provence (863), his kingdom was divided between Lothair II (Rhône region) and Louis II (Provence). When Lothair II died in 869 Lotharingia was divided between his two uncles, Louis the German and Charles the Bald; the latter was made master of the Rhône regions of the ancient kingdom of Provence. Louis II (died 875) devoted most of his attention to fighting the Muslims who threatened the peninsula and the papal territories.

In Francia Occidentalis Charles the Bald was occupied with the struggle against the Normans, who ravaged the countryside along the Schelde, Seine, and Loire rivers. More often than not, the King was forced to pay for their departure with silver. Aquitaine remained a centre of dissension. For some time (until 864) Pepin II continued to have supporters there, and Charles the Bald attempted to pacify them by installing his sons—first Charles the Young (ruled 855–867) and then Charles the Stammerer (ruled 867–877)—on the throne of Aquitaine. The problems in Aquitaine were closely connected to general unrest among the magnates, who wished to keep the king under their own tutelage. By accumulating countships and creating dynasties, the magnates succeeded in carving out vast principalities at the still unstable borders: Robert the Strong and Hugh the Abbot in the west; Eudes, son of Robert the Strong, in this same region and in the area around Paris; Humfred, Vulgrin, Bernard Plantevelne, count of Auvergne, and Bernard of Gothia in Aquitaine and the border regions; Boso in the southeast; and Baldwin II in Flanders. Nevertheless, Charles the Bald appeared to be the most powerful sovereign in the West, and in 875 Pope John VIII bestowed upon him the imperial crown. But an expedition that he organized in Italy on the appeal of the pope failed, and the magnates of Francia Occidentalis rose up. Charles the Bald died on the return trip (877). Charles's son, Louis II, the Stammerer, reigned for only two years. At his death in 879 the kingdom was divided between his sons Louis III and Carloman. In the southeast, Boso, the count of Vienne, appropriated the royal title to the kingdom of Provence. The imperial throne remained vacant. The death of Louis III (882) permitted the reunification of Francia Occidentalis (except for the kingdom of Provence) under Carloman.

In Francia Orientalis, royal control over the aristocracy was maintained. But decentralizing forces, closely bound to the existence of strong ethnic communities, made themselves felt in the form of revolutions led by the sons of Louis the German. The latter partitioned his kingdom in 864, Bavaria going to Carloman, Saxony to Louis the Younger, Alemannia (Swabia) to Charles the Fat. Although Louis the German managed to gain a portion of Lotharingia in 870, he was unable to prevent Charles the Bald's coronation as emperor (875).

When Louis the German died in 876, the partition of his kingdom was confirmed. At the death of Charles the Bald, Louis the German's son Carloman seized Italy and intended to take the imperial title, but ill health forced him to abandon his plans. His youngest brother, Charles the Fat, benefitted from the circumstances and restored the territorial unity of the empire. The deaths of his brothers Carloman (880) and Louis the Younger (882) without heirs allowed him to acquire successively the crown of Italy (880) and the imperial title (881), and to unite Francia Orientalis (882) under his own rule. Finally, at the death of Carloman, son of Louis the Stammerer, Charles the Fat was elected king of Francia Occidentalis (885); the magnates had bypassed the last heir of Louis the Stammerer, Charles the Simple, in his favour.

Charles the Fat avoided involving himself in Italy, in spite of appeals from the pope, and concentrated his attention on coordinating resistance to the Normans, who had resumed the offensive in the valleys of the Schelde, Meuse, Rhine, and Seine. He was unsuccessful, however, and in 886 had to purchase the Normans' departure: they had besieged Paris, which was defended by Count Eudes. The magnates of Francia Orientalis rose up and deposed Charles the Fat (887).

THE FRANKISH WORLD

Society. *Germans and Gallo-Romans.* The settlement of Germanic peoples in Roman Gaul brought people from two entirely different worlds into contact. Linguistic barriers were quickly overcome, for the Germans adopted Latin. At the same time, German names were preponderant. Although there were religious difficulties in those regions settled by peoples converted to Arianism (Visigoths, Burgundians), Clovis' conversion simplified matters. In keeping with the Roman principle of hospitality, the Germans who settled in Gaul were able to preserve their own judicial institutions. The first sovereigns committed the customs of the people to writing (Code of Euric, *c.* 470–480; Salic Law of Clovis, *c.* 507–511; Law of Gundobad, *c.* 501–515) and occasionally had summaries of Roman rights drawn up for the Gallo-Roman population (Papian Code of Gundobad; Breviary of Alaric); this system of individual law, certain aspects of which survived until the 9th century, did not prevent the eventual triumph of German judicial concepts. Multiple contacts in daily life produced an original civilization composed of a variety of elements, some of which were inherited from antiquity, some brought by the Germans, and all strongly influenced by Christianity.

Social classes. The collapse of the Roman Empire and the influx of Germans did not destroy the old Roman senatorial and landed aristocracy; the 6th-century kings called on its members to serve in their administrative bodies. A sort of military aristocracy had existed among the Germans: at the time of their settlement within the empire, its members were given lands confiscated from the Gallo-Roman aristocracy or awarded the fisc (royal treasury). The two groups fused rapidly. They shared a common life, discharging public and religious duties and frequenting the court. By the beginning of the 7th century there arose an aristocracy of office, whose signs of prestige were the possession of land and service to the king and church. This aristocracy increased in importance during the conflicts between the Merovingian sovereigns. The ascendance of the Pepinids, Carolingian rule, and the power struggles in the 9th century furnished these magnates, on whom those in power were dependent, with a means of enriching themselves and augmenting their political and social influence.

Parallel to this class of lay magnates was an ecclesiastical aristocracy, which was one both of office and of land. The church found itself in possession of a vast landed fortune. At the beginning of the 7th century, at least, the church frequently benefitted from immunity, and regalian rights were conferred on abbots or bishops.

A class of small and middle-sized landholders apparently existed, about which little is known. It appears that both the power of the magnates and the practices born of the ancient patronage system had the effect of diminishing the size of this class. In fact, many free peasants appear to have been *coloni* who worked tenures.

During the Merovingian epoch, slavery, inherited from antiquity, was still a viable institution. Slaves continued to be obtained in war and through trade. But the number of slaves decreased under the influence of the church, which encouraged manumission and sought to prohibit the enslavement of Christians. Under the Carolingians, the slaves in Gaul formed only a residual class, although the slave trade was still active. Taken increasingly from the Slavic territories (the term *slavus* replaced the traditional *servus*), slaves were a commodity for trade with the Muslim lands of the Mediterranean.

The origins of feudalism. During the period of insecurity and turbulence that marked the end of the Merovingian epoch, bonds of personal dependence, which originated in earlier Roman and Germanic institutions, were formed with increasing frequency. In the 7th century this bond took one of two forms: recommendation (a free man placed himself under the protection of a more powerful lord for the duration of his life); precarious contract (a powerful lord received certain services in return for the use of his land for a limited time under advantageous conditions). In the 8th century, the Pepinids had to form a circle of followers, and cavalry began to assume a preponderant role in armies, increasing the expense of military service. This situation encouraged feudal practices, which then began to take their definitive form. Charlemagne attempted to encompass the entire population of his empire within the feudo-vassal relationship. He encouraged the development of feudal institutions and gave them administrative functions. During the 9th-century power struggles, however, these institutions were distorted. Enfeoffment became hereditary, though it was not originally meant to be so. In addition, before the end of the century a man could place himself in vassalage to several lords. Finally, the feudal bond allowed for the usurpation of regalian powers; and this led to the formation of territorial principalities, resulting in the disintegration of royal authority.

Institutions. The institutions of government underwent great changes under the Frankish monarchs.

Kingship. Kingship was the basic institution in the Merovingian kingdom. Since Clovis' reign, the power of the king had extended not only over a tribe or tribes but also over a territory inhabited by Germans of divergent backgrounds and by Gallo-Romans as well. The king exercised absolute power without legal limitations; the only possible curbs on him were civil war, assassination, and a belief in God and the saints. So constituted, royal power was dynastic and patrimonial. The Frankish kings successfully eliminated the common Germanic practice of the magnates electing the king (the Frankish king was content to present himself to the magnates who acclaimed him) and accepted the hereditary principle as a personal right. The kings had to concede, however, to the partition of the kingdom at each succession. Royal power, as was the case in all German monarchies, also had a sacred aspect; under the Merovingians the external sign of this was long hair.

Changes in the Frankish monarchy

The nature of the Frankish monarchy was profoundly changed during the Carolingian epoch. When Pepin III the Short restored the office of king in his own name, he had himself consecrated first by a bishop and then by the pope. This rite, of biblical origin, had already been adopted by the Visigoths; it gave a new foundation to royal authority because it reinforced the religious character of the monarchy and signified the king's receipt of special grace from God. The king was permitted to reign and was given stature above the common level because of this grace. Acclamation by the magnates became a pledge of obeisance to a king whom God had invested with power.

To this new royal status Charlemagne added the title of emperor, which had not been used in the West since 476. He adopted this title as a concession to the situation at the time. It was conferred in the course of a ceremony that, in spite of the presence of the pope, was of secular character. Perhaps Charlemagne felt that it was only a provisional dignity, which would not survive him. But among the clerical ranks that formed the entourage of the new emperor, the revival of the empire was regarded as a magistracy conferred by God in the interests of Western Christianity and the church; imperial authority was considered a kind of priesthood, and its bearer was obligated to lead and protect the faithful. This idea reached fruition under Louis the Pious, who introduced the ceremony of anointment as part of the investiture; this ritual furnished the pope with the means for gaining a dominant role in the designation of the emperor. His role increased because, in spite of all the efforts of the clergy to maintain the integrity of the empire, the imperial title was returned to Italy. Later Carolingian emperors were designated on the basis of the interests and actions of the papacy.

The central government. By the time of Clovis, the ancient Germanic assembly of free men no longer participated in the conduct of affairs and was consigned to a military role. Within each kingdom, the king was surrounded by a court. This court had been a Roman imperial institution, which the Frankish sovereigns had adopted, modifying it to suit their own needs. The court encompassed domestic services (treasury, provisioning, stables, clergy), a bureau of accounts, and a military guard (antrustion). It was presided over by three men—the seneschal, the count of the palace, and the mayor of the palace—who travelled with the king who, while having various privileged places of residence, did not live at a fixed capital.

Local institutions. Except in the north, which was divided into regions called *pagi*, the Merovingians continued to use the city (the Roman *civitas*) as the principal administrative division. A count was installed in each *pagus* and town and given financial, military, and judicial authority. Groups of counts were placed under the authority of a duke, whose responsibilities were primarily military.

The development of institutions in the Carolingian age. The Carolingians contented themselves with refining their administrative system in order to strengthen royal control and to solve the problems posed by a large empire. The kingdom's cohesion was augmented by an oath of fidelity, which Charlemagne exacted from every free man (789, 793, 802), and by the publication of legislation—the capitularies—which regulated the administration and exploitation of the kingdom. While he did not forgo the itinerant life, Charlemagne did wish to make Aachen, where he constructed a vast palace, the centre of his state.

At the local level, a broad government—the march—was formed in the most exposed areas. In order to counterbalance the absolute power of the counts, the episcopate was given a central role in the administration. Charlemagne extended the use of the *missi dominici*—i.e., envoys who served as liaisons between the central government and local agents, and who were responsible for keeping the latter in line. In order to strengthen his control over the population, Charlemagne attempted to develop intermediary bodies; he tried to use both vassalage and immunity as means of government—in the first instance by creating royal vassals and feudalizing public offices, in the second, controlling protected institutions (monasteries, etc.) through the person assigned to defend them (the *advocatus*).

Economic life. Agriculture was the principal economic activity, and during the entire Frankish age the great estate, inherited from antiquity, remained the predominant characteristic of rural life. These estates were the residence and principal source of income of the aristocracy. The estates appear to have long been placed under direct cultivation by servile labour, which was abundant at the time. The heavy work was done with the assistance of day labourers; a portion, however, was given to the tenants—the *coloni*—who were compelled to pay annual charges. With the decline in slavery at the end of the Merovingian era, the number of tenancies was increased and tenants were compelled to render significant amounts of forced labour to cultivate land held directly by the lord. This system was not adopted throughout the Frankish empire (it was most widespread between the Seine and the Rhine), and it soon fell into disuse.

Predominance of the estate

Trade. Most scholars formerly believed that the Germanic invasions had destroyed the ancient economy, the foundation of which was Mediterranean trade. Others, notably the great French historian Henri Pirenne, have maintained that the ancient economic system lasted until the Muslim invasions of the 7th–8th centuries. While the matter is not yet settled, the following facts are definite. Commerce did not decline abruptly—in Gaul, such goods as papyrus, oil, and spices were imported from the East, and there were numerous colonies of Syrians; currency continued to be based on the gold standard, and imperial units were still used; and all signs point to the existence of manufacturing for trade (marble from Aquitaine, Rhenish glass, ceramics).

During the Carolingian age the Mediterranean, although not completely closed (Italy was the single Western port of trade with the East), no longer occupied its long-standing place in the economy. The adoption of a new monetary system based on silver and a reduction in the number of Oriental goods and merchants are signs of the change. After the 7th century, trade among the countries bordering the English Channel and the North Sea and in the Meuse Valley increased steadily. In the north, trade continued among the Scandinavians, expanding until in the 9th century it brought them to Russia. The Vikings, with their great commercial centres at Birka in Sweden and Hedeby in Denmark, were both pirates and traders; they established new contacts between East and West.

In addition to this large-scale commerce there was agriculturally based local trade. The number of markets increased, and market towns (as opposed to the former Gallo-Roman cities, which survived mainly as fortresses and religious centres) began to appear.

Frankish fiscal law. The Frankish fiscal system reflected the evolution of the economy. Frankish kings were unable to continue the Roman system of direct taxation. Their principal sources of income were the exploitation of the domains of the fisc (royal treasury), war (booty, tribute), the exercise of power (monetary and judicial rights), and the imposition of *telonea* (taxes collected on the circulation and sale of goods), the number of which was increased by the kings.

The church. The episcopate and the diocese were practically the only institutions to survive the collapse of the Roman Empire. During the German conquest many bishops played important roles in defending the population. During the Frankish era bishops and abbots occupied a socially prominent position because of both their great prestige among the people and their landed wealth.

Institutions. The organization of the secular church took its final form under the Merovingian and Carolingian kings. The administrative bodies and hierarchy of the early Christian church were derived from institutions existing during the late Roman Empire. In principle, a bishop was responsible for the clergy and faithful in each town (*civitas*). The bishop whose seat was in the metropolitan city had pre-eminence and was archbishop over the other bishops in his district. During the Merovingian era, the episcopate became more discernibly national in character. By the 7th century, the practice of the king appointing bishops had become common. This was to have many consequences—in the first place, kings most often appointed bishops from among their followers without regard for religious qualifications; in the second, the metropolitan see was often fragmented in the course of territorial partitions and tended to lose its importance; and finally, the church in Gaul tended to withdraw more and more from papal control, despite papal attempts to re-establish ties.

The first Carolingians re-established the ecclesiastical hierarchy. They restored the authority of the archbishops and generalized the institution of cathedral chapters in order to have the clergy living around a bishop submit to a communal life. They did not renounce their right to nominate bishops, however, whom they considered more then ever to be agents of the monarchy.

During the 4th and 5th centuries, success at converting the countryside made it necessary for the bishops to divide the dioceses and create branches of the episcopal churches in the most important places. The first generation of these great parish churches was limited to between 15 and 40 per diocese. They were further divided in the Carolingian era and replaced by small parish churches better suited to the conditions of rural life.

Monasticism. Monasticism originated in the East. It was introduced in the West during the 4th century and was developed in Gaul, mainly in the west (St. Martin) and southeast (St. Honoratus and St. John Cassian). The earliest monasteries were not organized according to any definite system. In spite of efforts to impose a communal form of discipline, eremitism was the most widespread practice. Beginning in the 6th century, the number of monasteries throughout Gaul increased and efforts were made to regularize this kind of religious life. The Irish monasticism introduced by St. Columban (543–615) was very influential in the 7th century, but it was later superseded by the Benedictine rule, introduced from Italy. The monasteries suffered from the upheavals affecting the church in the 8th century. The Carolingians attempted to reform the monasteries. Louis the Pious, acting on the advice of St. Benedict of Aniane, imposed the Benedictine rule; its usage became general, and from that point on the Benedictine rule was a characteristic feature of western monasticism. On the other hand, the Carolingians continued the practice of having lay abbots.

Education. In the 6th century, especially in southern Gaul, the aristocracy and, consequently, the bishops drawn from it preserved an interest in traditional classical culture. Beginning in the 7th century, however, a new culture issued forth from the Columbanian monasteries based not on a study of the authors of antiquity but on the study of the Bible and the celebration of the liturgy. These new principles were triumphant in the Carolingian era.

Religious discipline and piety. One characteristic of the church in the 6th century was the frequent convening of councils to settle questions of doctrine and discipline. The conciliar institution declined, however, resulting in a struggle that was aggravated by intervention on the part of the secular powers, leading to liturgical anarchy and a moral and intellectual crisis among the clergy. At the same time that they were re-establishing discipline in the clergy, Charlemagne and Louis the Pious attempted to impose a uniform liturgy, inspired by the one used at Rome. They also took measures to raise the standard of education of both clerics and the faithful.

One of the most original aspects of faith during the Frankish epoch was the development of the cults of saints and relics. The desire to possess the greatest possible number of relics of distinguished saints became a permanent concern of clerics and the faithful. Beginning in the Carolingian era a veritable commerce in relics developed, with Rome as one of the key centres. The number of pilgrimages thus increased. The desire on the part of the faithful to be buried near relics upset funeral practices. Ancient cemeteries, peripherally located, were abandoned and burials in or near churches (burials *ad sanctos*) increased.

In spite of progress in conversions, the continuing influence of German paganism provoked a pagan reaction. During the 6th and 7th centuries, religious authorities were constantly denouncing pagan practices.

The influence of the church on society and legislation. The progressive Christianization of society influenced Frankish institutions significantly. The introduction of royal consecration and the creation of the empire afforded the clergy an opportunity to elaborate a new conception of power based on religious principles. The church was involved in trying to discourage slavery and in ameliorating the legal condition of those enslaved. It was during the Carolingian period that, in reaction to the polygamy practiced in German society, Christian doctrines of marriage were formulated.

Merovingian literature and arts. During the entire 6th century many writers, inspired by classical tradition, produced works patterned on antique models; such writers included Sidonius Apollinaris (died *c.* 488), Gregory of Tours (died 594), and Fortunatus (died 599). The writing of saints' lives—hagiography—became the most widespread literary genre of the period. Nevertheless, the standard of literature continued to decline, becoming more and more conventional and artificial. The use of popular Latin became common among writers.

Religious architecture remained faithful to the early Christian model (churches of basilican type, baptisteries and vaulted mausoleums with central plans). Because of the development of the cult of saints and the practice of burying *ad sanctos*, mausoleums became common in churches. As had been the case in antiquity, marble was the principal sculptural material. In the Pyrenees, sculptors produced capitals and sarcophagi in antique style, which they exported throughout Gaul; these workshops reached their zenith in the 7th century. The development of the art of metal work (fibulae, buckles) was another characteristic of the Merovingian age. As a result of Germanic influences, new techniques came to the fore (*e.g.*, *cloisonné* and damascene work). A new aesthetic standard, characterized by the play of colour and the use of stylized motifs, eventually predominated.

Carolingian literature and arts. A renaissance movement occurred during the general work of renovation undertaken by the Carolingian monarchs; they supported the movement as an aid to religious reform and as a means to enhance their own prestige. The origins of the

[left margin] Development of the secular church

[right margin] The cults of saints and relics

[right margin] The Carolingian renaissance

movement lie deep in the 7th and 8th centuries. It received great stimulus, however, when the growth of the empire brought the Franks into contact with lands where a higher cultural standard had been maintained and the antique tradition was still viable (Ireland, Italy, and Anglo-Saxon England). The Carolingian sovereigns attracted foreigners (*e.g.*, the Anglo-Saxon Alcuin, the Italian Paul the Deacon) who played a decisive role in this renewal.

After raising the standard of the clergy, Charlemagne founded a new group of scholars. Even if, contrary to legend, there was no school established in the imperial palace, there were numerous schools opened in the vicinity of churches and monasteries. An attempt was also made to reform handwriting. Research was carried on simultaneously under the auspices of several monastic centres (most notably Tours) for the purpose of standardizing writing; this effort resulted in the adoption of a regular and uniform script (Carolingian minuscule). Improved teaching and a desire to imitate classical antiquity helped to revivify the Latin used by writers and scribes.

The imperial court was a hub of intellectual life, and from it came works dedicated to the glory of the emperors. Based on the examples of ancient authors, they were a characteristic product of this literary group; important works include Einhard's *Vita Karoli imperatoris* ("Life of Charlemagne"), the Astronomer's *Vita Hludowici imperatoris* ("Life of Louis the Pious"), Nithard's *Historiarum libri IV* ("History of the Sons of Louis the Pious"), and Hincmar's *De ordine palatii*.

Beginning in the mid-9th century, however, the kingdoms formed from the partitions of the empire saw a renaissance of national cultures. The fact that the Oath of Strasbourg was drawn up in Romance and German is an early indication of this development. There is a striking contrast between the *Annales Bertiniani* ("Annals of St. Bertin"), written at the court of Charles the Bald, and the *Annales Fuldenses* ("Annals of Fulda"), written at the principal intellectual centre in Francia Orientalis. They are, respectively, the French and German narratives of the same events.

Some of the great imperial monuments erected during the Carolingian age (palace of Ingelheim, place of Aachen) reveal the permanence of ancient tradition in their regular plans and conception. The churches were the subjects of numerous architectural experiments; while some were constructed on a central plan (Germigny-des-Prés, Aachen), most remained faithful to the traditional basilican type. Liturgical considerations and the demands of the faith, however, made certain modifications necessary: crypts on the east, a westworks or second apse on the west. These church buildings afforded architects an opportunity to make definitive experiments in balancing the arches. The extension of the vaults over the entire church, and the more rational integration of the annexes and church proper, gave rise to Romanesque architecture.

The buildings of the period were richly decorated with paintings, painted stucco, and mosaics in which figural representation increasingly replaced strictly ornamental decoration. North Italian ateliers were popularizing the use of interlace in chancel decoration. Sumptuary arts became more common, especially illumination, ivory work, and metalwork for liturgical use (reliquaries).

BIBLIOGRAPHY. The works listed on the general history of the period in this bibliography are rather general in nature. More detailed studies will be found in the bibliographies of these works.

General works: A chronological framework and an introductory approach to the subject may be found in *The Cambridge Medieval History*, 2nd ed., vol. 1–2 (1966); F. LOT, C. PFISTER, and F.L. GANSHOF, *Les Destinées de l'Empire en Occident de 395 à 888*, 2nd ed. (1940–41); and MARGARET DEANESLY, *A History of Early Medieval Europe, 476 to 911* (1956).

The invasions: The two works by LUCIEN MUSSET, *Les Invasions: les vagues germaniques* and *Les Invasions: le second assaut contre l'Europe chrétienne (VIIᵉ–IXᵉ siècles)* (both 1965), constitute the best and most recent restatement of this subject.

The Merovingians: The works of EUGEN EWIG, *Die fränkischen Teilungen und Teilreiche (511–613)* (1953) and *Die fränkischen Teilreiche im 7. Jahrhundert, 613–714* (1954), have significantly revised the political history of Merovingian Gaul.

The Carolingians: LUCIEN HALPHEN, *Charlemagne et l'Empire carolingien*, new ed. (1949, reprinted 1968), remains the classic work. DONALD BULLOUGH, *The Age of Charlemagne* (1965), reflects the latest scholarship.

The civilization: CHRISTOPHER DAWSON, *The Making of Europe: An Introduction to the History of European Unity* (1932), remains a good essay on the development of medieval civilization. See also J.M. WALLACE-HADRILL, *The Barbarian West, 400–1000*, 3rd rev. ed. (1967), and *Early Germanic Kingship in England and on the Continent* (1971).

(G.Fo.)

Meso-American Civilization, History of

The term Meso-America means that part of Mexico and Central America that was civilized in pre-Spanish times. In many respects, the American Indians who inhabited Meso-America were the most advanced native peoples in the Western Hemisphere. The northern border of Meso-America runs west from a point on the Gulf Coast of Mexico just above the modern port of Tampico, then dips south to exclude much of the central desert of highland Mexico, meeting the Pacific coast opposite the tip of Lower California. On the southeast, the boundary extends from the mouth of the Motagua River on the Caribbean across to the Pacific shore just south of Costa Rica's Nicoya Peninsula. Thus, about half of Mexico; all of Guatemala, British Honduras, and El Salvador; and parts of Honduras and Costa Rica are included in Meso-America.

Geographically and culturally, Meso-America consists of two strongly contrasted regions: highland and lowland. The Mexican highlands are formed mainly by the two Sierra Madre ranges that sweep down on the east and west. Lying athwart them is a volcanic cordillera stretching from the Atlantic to the Pacific. The high valleys and landlocked basins of Mexico were important centres of pre-Spanish civilization. In the southeast part of Meso-America lie the partly volcanic Chiapas-Guatemala highlands. The lowlands are primarily coastal. Particularly important was the littoral plain extending south along the Gulf of Mexico, expanding to include the Petén-Yucatan Peninsula, homeland of the Mayan peoples. *The two major regions*

Agriculture in Meso-America was advanced and complex. A great many crops were planted, of which maize (corn), beans, and various squashes were the most important. In the highlands, hoe cultivation of more or less permanent fields was the rule, with such intensive forms of agriculture as irrigation and *chinampas* (the so-called "floating gardens" reclaimed from lakes or ponds) known in some regions. In contrast, lowland agriculture was usually of the slash-and-burn type; *e.g.*, a patch of jungle is selected, felled and burned toward the end of the dry season, and planted with a digging stick in time for the first rains. After a few years, the field is abandoned to the forest, as weed competition and declining fertility result in diminishing yields. Demographic potential was very different in the two regions, and true cities were fairly well confined to the highlands.

The extreme diversity of the Meso-American environment produced what has been called symbiosis among its subregions. Interregional exchange of agricultural, luxury, and other products led to the development of large and well-regulated markets in which chocolate beans were used for money. It may have also led to large-scale political unity and even to states and empires. High agricultural productivity resulted in a nonfarming class of artisans who were responsible for an advanced stone architecture featuring the construction of stepped pyramids, and for highly evolved styles of sculpture, pottery, and painting.

The Meso-American system of thought, recorded in folding-screen books of deerskin or bark paper, was perhaps of even greater importance in setting them off from other New World peoples. This system was ultimately

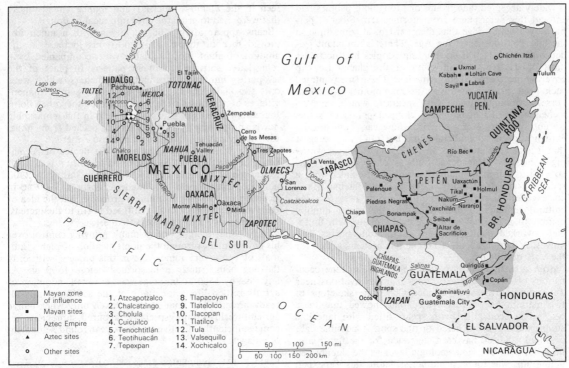

Principal sites of Meso-American civilization.
Adapted from *Grosser Historischer Weltatlas*, vol. II, *Mittelalter* (1970); Bayerischer Schulbuch-Verlag, Munich

based upon a calendar in which a cycle of 260 (13 × 20) days intermeshed with a "vague year" of 365 days (inter-calculations or leap years were not used), producing a 52-year Calendar Round (see CALENDAR). The entire religious life was geared to this cycle, which is unique to them. The Meso-American pantheon was closely associated with the calendar and featured an old, dual creator-god; a god of royal descent and warfare; a sun god and moon goddess; a rain god; a culture hero called Feathered Serpent; and many other deities. Also characteristic was the notion of a layered system of 13 heavens and 9 under-worlds, each with its presiding god. Much of the system was under the control of the priesthood that also maintained an advanced knowledge of astronomy.

Language groups

As many as 14 language families were found in Meso-America, but these can be grouped into six large "phy-la": Utoaztecan, Macromayan, Otomanguean, Taras-can, Huavean, and Xinca-Lencan. A dominant role was played by Utoaztecan, particularly by speakers of the Nahua groups of languages of which Náhuatl, official tongue of the Aztec Empire, was the most important. While Macromayan includes Zoquean and Totonacan, its largest member is Mayan, with 10 mutually unintelli-gible languages, at least some of which were spoken by the inhabitants of the great Maya ceremonial centres. The Mexican state of Oaxaca is the centre of the extremely heterogeneous Otomanguean phylum, but the only lin-guistic groups that played any great part in Meso-Ameri-can civilization were the Mixtec and Zapotec, both of which had large, powerful kingdoms at the time of the Spanish Conquest. Still a linguistic puzzle is Tarascan, mother tongue of an "empire" in western Mexico that successfully resisted Aztec encroachments; it has no sure relatives. Huavean and Xinca-Lencan are little-known language groups of southeastern Meso-America.

The story of what happened in pre-Spanish Meso-Ameri-ca is part of the larger picture of New World culture history, although the Meso-Americans reached stages of development unknown away from those areas.

This article is divided into the following sections:

Pre-Classical and Classical periods

EARLY HUNTERS (TO 6500 BC)

The time of the first peopling of Meso-America remains a puzzle, as it does for that of the New World in general. It is widely accepted that groups of Mongoloid peoples had entered this hemisphere from northeastern Siberia, perhaps by a land bridge that then existed, at some time in the late Pleistocene, or Ice Age. There is abundant evidence that, by 11,000 BC, hunting peoples had occupied most of the New World south of the glacial ice cap covering northern North America. These men hunted such large grazing mammals as mammoths, mastodon, horse, and camel, armed with spears to which were attached finely made, bifacially chipped points of stone. Recent finds in Meso-America, however, confirm the existence of a "prebifacial-point horizon" and suggest that it is of very great age. In 1967, archaeologists working at the site of Tlapacoya, southeast of Mexico City, uncovered a well-made blade of obsidian associated with a radiocarbon date of about 21,000 BC. Near Puebla, Mexico, excavations in the Valsequillo region have revealed cultural remains of human groups that were hunting mammoth and other extinct animals, along with unifacially worked points, scrapers, perforators, burins, and knives. A date of about 21,800 BC has been suggested for the Valsequillo finds.

Tepexpan finds

More substantial information on late Pleistocene occupations of Meso-America comes from excavations near Tepexpan, northeast of Mexico City. The skeletons of two mammoths were excavated that showed that these beasts had been killed with spears fitted with lancelike stone points and butchered on the spot. A possible date of about 8000 BC has been suggested for the two mammoth kills. In the same geologic layer as the slaughtered mammoths was found a human skeleton; this Tepexpan "man" has been shown to be female and rather a typical American Indian of modern form. While the association with the mammoths was first questioned, fluorine tests have proved them to be contemporary.

The environment of these earliest Meso-Americans was quite different from that of today's, for volcanoes were then extremely active, covering thousands of square miles with ashes. Temperatures were substantially lower, and local glaciers formed on the highest peaks. Conditions were ideal for the large herds of grazing mammals that roamed Meso-America, especially in the highland valleys much of which consisted of cool, wet grasslands not unlike the plains of the northern United States. All of this changed around 7000 BC, when worldwide temperatures rose and the great ice sheets of northern latitudes began their final retreat, bringing to an end the successful hunting way of life that had been followed by Meso-Americans, although man probably also played his role in bringing about the extinction of the large game animals.

INCIPIENT AGRICULTURE (6500–1500 BC)

The three major food plants

The most crucial event in the prehistory of Meso-America was man's capture of the food energy contained in plants. This process centred on three plants: maize (Indian corn), beans, and squashes. Since about 90 percent of all food calories in the diet of Meso-Americans eventually came from maize, archaeologists for a long time sought the origins of this plant, which has no wild forms existing today, in order to throw light on the agricultural basis of Meso-American civilization. This search has successfully ended in the dry Tehuacán Valley, in the state of Puebla, Mexico, where a number of caves and rock shelters on the edge of the valley produced a long sequence of occupations from the Early Hunters stage through the Conquest. Preservation of plant remains is remarkably good, and from these it is evident that shortly after 6500 BC the inhabitants of the valley were selecting and planting seeds of chili peppers, cotton, and one kind of squash.

Most importantly, between 5000 and 3500 BC they were beginning to plant mutant forms of maize that already were showing signs of the husks characteristic of domestic corn. Stands of truly wild maize, however, were also exploited. In terms of food energy available, there is little difference between the wild and early domesticated forms, but it has been estimated that there is more energy present in a single kernel of some modern races than in an ear of this ancient Tehuacán maize. Possibly some of this was popped, but a new element in food preparation is

seen in the *metates* (querns) and *manos* (handstones) that were used to grind the corn into meal or dough.

Beans appear after 3500 BC, along with a much improved race of maize. This enormous increase in the amount of plant food available was accompanied by a remarkable shift in settlement pattern. In place of the temporary hunting camps and rock shelters, which were only seasonally occupied by small bands, semipermanent villages of pit houses were constructed on the valley floor. Increasing sedentism is also to be seen in the remarkable bowls and globular jars painstakingly pecked from stone, for pottery was as yet unknown in Meso-America.

Pottery, which is a good index to the degree of permanence of a settlement (because of its fragility it is difficult to transport), was made in the Tehuacán Valley by 2300 BC. Fired clay vessels were made as early as 3000 BC in Ecuador and Colombia, and it is probable that the idea of their manufacture gradually diffused north to the increasingly sedentary peoples of Meso-America.

The picture, then, is one of man's growing control over his environment through the domestication of plants; animals played a very minor role in this process, with only the dog being surely domesticated before 1500 BC. At any rate, by 1500 BC the stage was set for the adoption of a fully settled life, with many of the sedentary arts already present. The final step was taken only when native agriculture in certain especially favoured subregions became sufficiently effective to allow year-round settlement of villages.

EARLY FORMATIVE PERIOD (1500–900 BC)

Early village life. It is fairly clear that the Mexican highlands were far too dry during the much warmer interval that prevailed from 5000 to 1500 BC for agriculture to supply more than half of a given population's energy needs. This was not the case along the alluvial lowlands of southern Meso-America, and it is no accident that the best evidence for the earliest permanent villages in Meso-America comes from the Pacific littoral of Chiapas (Mexico) and Guatemala, although comparable settlements probably existed along the Gulf Coast.

Ocós and Cuadros phases

The Ocós (c. 1500–1200 BC) and Cuadros (1100–900 BC) phases on the Pacific coast of Guatemala are good examples of these early village cultures. From the rich lagoons and estuaries in this area, the villagers obtained oysters, mussels, clams, crabs, many kinds of fish, and turtles. They were productive corn farmers as well, raising a small-eared race of maize called Nal-Tel, which their wives and daughters ground on *metates* and *manos* and cooked in globular jars. Their villages were small, with perhaps 10 to 12 thatched-roof houses arranged haphazardly.

Ocós pottery is highly developed technically and artistically. Something of the mental life of the times may be seen in the tiny, handmade clay figurines produced by the Ocós villagers. These, as in Formative cultures generally throughout Meso-America, represent nude females and may have something to do with a fertility cult. The idea of the temple-pyramid may well have taken root by this time, for one Ocós site has produced an earthen mound about 26 feet (8 metres) high that must have supported a perishable building. The implication of the site is that with increasing prosperity, some differentiation of a ruling class had taken place, for among the later Meso-Americans the ultimate function of a pyramid was as a final resting place for a great leader.

Eventually, the highlands also saw the appearance of effective village farming with nucleated settlements occupied throughout the year. But perhaps from the very beginning of Formative life there were different cultural responses directed toward both kinds of environment. In the highlands, divided into a number of mutually contrasting environments no one of which could have provided sufficient resources for the subsistence of a single settlement, villages were presumably linked to each other symbiotically. In the lowlands, particularly in the littoral, one especially favourable environment, such as the lagoon–estuary system, may have been so rich in resources that villages within it would have been entirely self-sufficient. In effect, the former would have resulted in a cultural integration based upon trade, while the latter would have been integrated, if at all, by a unity of likeness. The two kinds of civilization that eventually arose in each region, urban and non-urban, reflect the same contrast.

The rise of Olmec civilization. Until recent years, it was assumed that the Formative stage was characterized only by simple farming villages. It is now realized, however, that coexisting with these peasant-like cultures was a great civilization, the Olmec, that had arisen in the humid lowlands of southern Veracruz and Tabasco, in Mexico.

The Olmec were perhaps the greatest sculptors of ancient Meso-America. Whether carving tiny jade figures or gigantic basalt monuments, the great artistry of their work has led a number of archaeologists to doubt their considerable antiquity, although a number of radiocarbon dates from the type site of La Venta showed that Olmec civilization was indeed Formative, its beginning dating to at least 1,000 years before the advent of Maya civilization.

The San Lorenzo site

San Lorenzo is now established as the oldest known Olmec centre. In fact, excavation has shown it to have taken on the appearance of an Olmec site by 1150 BC and to have been destroyed, perhaps by invaders, around 900 BC. Thus, the Olmec here had already achieved considerable cultural heights within the Early Formative, at a time when the rest of Meso-America was at best on a Neolithic level. The reasons for its precocious rise must have had something to do with its abundant rainfall and the rich alluvial soil deposited along the broad, natural levees that flank the waterways of the southern Gulf Coast. Thus, the ecological potential for corn farmers in this counterpart of Mesopotamia's Fertile Crescent was exceptionally high. The levee lands, however, were not limitless, and increasingly dense populations must inevitably have led to competition for their control. Out of such conflicts would have crystallized a dominant landowning class, perhaps a group of well-armed lineages. It was this elite that created the Olmec civilization of San Lorenzo.

In appearance, the San Lorenzo site is a compact plateau rising about 160 feet (50 metres) above the surrounding plains. Cutting into it are deep ravines that were once thought to be natural but that are now known to be man-made, formed by the construction of long ridges that jut out from the plateau on the northwest, west, and south sides. Excavations have proved that at least the top 26 to 33 feet (8 to 10 metres) of the site was built by the labour of men. There are about 200 small mounds on the surface of the site, each of which once supported a dwelling house of pole and thatch, which indicates that it was both a ceremonial centre, with political and religious functions, and a minuscule town.

San Lorenzo is most noted for its extraordinary stone monuments. Many of these, perhaps most, were deliberately smashed or otherwise mutilated c. 900 BC and buried in long lines within the ridges and elsewhere at the site. They weighed as much as 44 tons and were carved from basalt from the Cerro Cintepec, a volcanic flow in the Tuxtla Mountains about 50 air miles to the northwest. It is believed that the stones were somehow dragged down to the nearest navigable stream and from there transported on rafts up the Coatzacoalcos River to the San Lorenzo area. The amount of labour involved must have been enormous and so would have the social controls necessary to see the job through to its completion.

The "Colossal Heads"

Most striking are the "Colossal Heads," human portraits on a stupendous scale. Seven of these are now known for San Lorenzo, the largest of which is nine feet high. The visages are flat-faced, with thickened lips and staring eyes. Each has a headgear resembling a football helmet, and it is entirely possible that these "helmets" were in fact protective coverings in a rubber-ball game that is known from Olmec figurines to have been played at San Lorenzo.

The central theme of the Olmec religion is a pantheon of deities each of which usually is a hybrid between jaguar and human infant, often crying or snarling with open mouth. This "were-jaguar" is the hallmark of Olmec art,

and it was the unity of objects in this style that first suggested to scholars that they were dealing with a new and heretofore unknown civilization. There is actually a whole spectrum of such were-jaguar forms in Olmec art, ranging from the almost purely feline to the human in which only a trace of jaguar can be seen.

These Olmec monuments were generally carved in the round with great technical prowess, even though the only methods available were pounding and pecking with stone tools. Considerable artistry can also be seen in the pottery figurines of San Lorenzo, which depict nude and sexless individuals with were-jaguar traits.

Olmec trade

Exotic raw materials brought into San Lorenzo from distant regions suggest that the early Olmec controlled a large trading network over much of Meso-America. Obsidian, used for blades, flakes, and dart points, was imported from highland Mexico and Guatemala. Most items were obviously for the luxury trade, such as iron ore for mirrors and various fine stones like serpentine employed in their lapidary industry. One material that is conspicuously absent, however, is jade, which does not appear in Olmec sites until after 900 BC and the fall of San Lorenzo.

There is growing evidence that the Olmec themselves had sent groups from their Gulf Coast "heartland" into the Meso-American highlands toward the end of the Early Formative, in all likelihood to guarantee that prestige goods needed by the elite of San Lorenzo would reach their destination. San Lorenzo-type Olmec ceramics and figurines have been found in burials at several sites in the Valley of Mexico, such as Tlapacoya, and in the state of Morelos. The Olmec involvement with the rest of Meso-America continued into the Middle Formative and probably reached its peak at that time.

San Lorenzo is not the only Olmec centre known for the Early Formative. Laguna de los Cerros, just south of the Cerro Cintepec in Veracruz, appears to have been a large Olmec site with outstanding sculptures. La Venta, just east of the Tabasco border, was another contemporary site, but it reached its height after San Lorenzo had gone into decline.

MIDDLE FORMATIVE PERIOD (900–300 BC)

Horizon markers. Once ceramics had been adopted in Meso-America, techniques of manufacture and styles of shape and decoration tended to spread rapidly and widely across many cultural frontiers. These rapid diffusions are called horizons, which enable archaeologists to link different cultures on the same time level. For the Early Formative, complex methods of rocker stamping (a mode of impressing the wet clay with the edge of a shell); the *tecomate* or globular, neckless jar; and Olmec excised pottery are good horizon markers. The beginning of the Middle Formative over much of Meso-America is marked by the diffusion of a very hard, white pottery, decorated with incised lines, and by solid pottery figurines with large, staring eyes formed by a punch. The people who replaced and probably overthrew the Olmec of San Lorenzo at about 900 BC had such pottery and figurines, the ultimate origins of which are still a puzzle.

During the Middle Formative, cultural regionalism increased, although the Olmec presence can be widely detected. The transition to fully settled life had taken place everywhere, and burgeoning populations occupied hamlets, villages, and perhaps even small towns throughout Meso-America, both highland and lowland.

Olmec civilization at La Venta. La Venta was located on an almost inaccessible island, surrounded at that time by the Tonalá River, which divides the states of Veracruz and Tabasco. As San Lorenzo's fortunes fell, La Venta's rose, and between 800 and 400 BC it was the most important site in Meso-America.

At the centre of La Venta is a 100-foot-high mound of earth and clay that may well house the tomb of a great Olmec ruler. Immediately north of the Great Mound is a narrow north–south plaza flanked by a pair of long mounds. Beyond the plaza is a ceremonial enclosure surrounded by a "fence" made entirely of upright shafts of columnar basalt.

A low, round mound on the north side of the ceremonial enclosure contained several tombs, one of which was surrounded and covered by basalt columns. In this tomb were found the bundled remains of two children, accompanied by magnificent ornaments of jade. Offerings were made not only to be placed with the dead but were also deposited as caches in the site, especially along the north–south axis of the ceremonial centre.

Among the most beautiful objects manufactured by the Olmec were the concave mirrors of iron ore, which were pierced to be worn around the neck. These can throw pictures on a flat surface and can probably start fires on hot tinder. Olmec leaders at La Venta, whether kings or priests, undoubtedly used them to impress the populace with their supernatural powers. Olmec sculptors continued to produce basalt monuments, including Colossal Heads and "altars," at La Venta. Significantly, an increasing number of monuments were carved in relief, and some of these were stelae with rather elaborate scenes obviously based upon historical or contemporary events.

Olmec colonization in the Middle Formative. In the Middle Formative there are important Olmec sites located along what seems to have been a highland route to the west to obtain the luxury items that seemed to have been so desperately needed by the Olmec elite; *e.g.*, jade, serpentine, iron ore for mirrors, cinnabar, and so forth. Olmec sites in Puebla, the Valley of Mexico, and Morelos are generally located at the ends of valleys near or on major passes; they were perhaps trading stations garrisoned by Olmec troops. The most impressive of these sites is Chalcatzingo, Morelos, a cult centre located among three denuded volcanic peaks rising from a plain. On a talus slope at the foot of the middle peak are huge boulders on which have been carved Olmec reliefs in La Venta style. The principal relief shows an Olmec woman, richly garbed, seated within the mouth of a cave; above her, cumulus clouds pour down rain.

Similar Olmec reliefs, usually narrative and often depicting warriors brandishing clubs, have been located on the Pacific plain of Chiapas (Mexico) and Guatemala. Within the last decade, spectacular Olmec cave paintings have been found in Guerrero, offering some idea of what the Olmec artists could do when they worked with a large spectrum of pigments and on flat surfaces.

There is a conspicuous absence of Olmec remains in the lowland Maya area. In fact, there is no sure evidence of any kind of human occupation there until after 800 BC, and the nonexistence of Olmec sites or carvings may simply reflect that the San Lorenzo and La Venta elite were uninterested in the region, perhaps because of even poorer agricultural potential than exists today.

It used to be thought that the Olmec worshipped only one god, a rain deity depicted as a were-jaguar, but a recent study has shown that there were at least 10 distinct gods represented in Olmec art. Surely present were several important deities of the later, established Meso-American pantheon, such as the Fire God, Rain God, Maize God, and Feathered Serpent. Other aspects of mental culture are less well-known; some Olmec jades and a monument from La Venta have noncalendrical hieroglyphs, but none of this writing can as yet be deciphered. To sum up the Olmec achievement, not only was this the first high culture in Meso-America—one that had certainly achieved political statehood—but either it or cultures influenced by it lie at the base of every other Meso-American civilization.

Early Monte Albán. Monte Albán is a prominent series of interconnected hills lying near Oaxaca, Mexico. One of these was completely levelled off in Middle Formative times to serve as the base for a site that was to become the Zapotec people's most important capital. A peculiar group of reliefs carved on sandstone slabs is believed to date from this earliest epoch, Monte Albán I. These slabs were affixed to the front of a rubble-faced platform mound and around a contiguous court.

The reliefs are usually called "Danzantes," a name derived from the notion that they represent human figures in dance postures. Actually, almost all of the "Danzante" sculptures show Olmecoid men in strange, rubbery postures as though they were swimming in honey. From their open mouths and closed eyes, it can be assumed with great certainty that they are meant to represent dead persons. On many "Danzantes" one or more unreadable hieroglyphs appear near the heads of the figures, most likely standing for the names of the sacrificed lords of groups beaten in combat by the Zapotec. Several slabs also bear calendrical notations, and it can be firmly stated that the Middle Formative elite of Monte Albán were the first in Meso-America to develop writing and the calendar (at least in written form).

Village cultures of the Middle Formative. When Europe had not yet emerged from Neolithic barbarism, the Near East had already entered Bronze Age civilization. A similar culture lag is to be found in those parts of Meso-America not strongly touched by the Olmec spark. On the western shores of the great lake filling the Valley of Mexico, for instance, remains of several simple villages have been uncovered that must have been not unlike small settlements that can be found in the Mexican hinterland today. The people who lived at El Arbolillo and Zacatenco had simply terraced off village refuse to make platforms on which their pole-and-thatch houses were built. *Metates* and *manos* are plentiful; pottery is relatively plain with the abundant hard, white-slipped ware of the Middle Formative, and amusing little female figurines are present by the thousands. Subsistence was based upon corn farming and upon hunting. In contrast to the nearby site of Tlatilco, which flourished under an Olmec-influenced elite in the Early and Middle Formative, there is virtually no evidence of ceremonial life for these two villages, which probably followed popular fertility cults.

In the Maya highlands, the key archaeological region has always been the broad, fertile Valley of Guatemala around present-day Guatemala City. The earliest substantial occupation of the valley is called Las Charcas, a Middle Formative culture known largely from the contents of bottle-shaped pits found dug into the subsoil on the western edge of the capital. In them have been excavated extremely fine ceramics, including red-on-white bowls with animal figures, effigy vessels, three-footed cups, and peculiar three-pronged incense burners. Solid female figurines are also present, but there are no detectable gods to be seen among them.

It has been mentioned that the Maya lowlands, in spite of extremely intensive archaeological survey, have no sure occupation at all before 800 BC. At about this time, the early Middle Formative culture known as Réal-Xe appears at certain sites in the western part of the Maya area, such as Seibal and Altar de Sacrificios. The problem of the origin of the Mayan-speaking people has not been solved, but one possibility is that the *ur*-Mayans were the Olmec of the Gulf Coast "heartland." With the collapse of San Lorenzo about 900 BC, some Olmec groups may have begun colonizing the empty lowlands to their east. Another group could have moved north along the Gulf Coast to become the Huaxtec, who were also Mayan speakers. Thus, Olmec and Maya would have been the same people.

The succeeding Middle Formative culture, Mamom, has been found all over the Maya lowlands, from the central Petén Peninsula to northern Yucatan. It is known only from deeply buried refuse layers underneath the plazas of Maya ceremonial centres and is not very different from Las Charcas in its main features. Pottery is almost entirely monochrome—red, orange, black, and white—and figurines are female with the usual punched and appliqué embellishments. Little or nothing is known of Mamom architecture, perhaps because whatever might have existed is covered with towering masses of Late Formative and Classic Maya temple and palace structures. But from what is known, Maya culture of the Middle Formative was on the peasant level and in the cultural shadow of the Olmec civilization to the west.

LATE FORMATIVE PERIOD (300 BC–AD 100)

Probably the most significant features of the Late Formative are (1) the transformation of Olmec civilization in southeastern Meso-America into something approaching the earliest lowland Maya civilization and (2) the abrupt appearance, toward the end of the Late Formative, of fully urban culture at Teotihuacán in the Valley of Mexico. Most of the distinctive cultures that were to become the great Classic civilizations began to take shape at this time. There was no unifying force in the Late Formative comparable to the earlier Olmec; rather, regionalism and local cultural integration were the rule. There were, however, horizon traits, particularly in pottery, that were almost universal. Ceramics became highly involved in shape, often with composite or recurved outlines, hollow, bulbous feet, and flange-like protrusions encircling the vessel. The use of slips of several different colours as pottery decoration at times approached the elaborate polychromes of Classic times.

The idea of constructing temple-pyramids was probably also a general trait. It was a Meso-American custom to bury a dead person beneath the floor of his own house, which was often then abandoned by the bereaved. As an elite class of noble lineages became distinguished from the mass of the people, the simple house platforms serving as sepulchres might have become transformed into more imposing structures, ending in the huge pyramids of the Late Formative and Classic, which surely have funerary functions. The deceased leader or the gods from which he claimed descent, or both, would then have been worshipped in a "house of god" on the temple summit. These pyramids became the focal point of Meso-American ceremonial life, as well as the centres of their settlements.

Valley of Mexico. The Cuicuilco-Ticomán culture succeeded the Middle Formative villages of the valley but retained many of their traits, such as the manufacture of solid, handmade figurines. Of considerable interest is the type site of Cuicuilco, located on the southwestern edge of the valley. Lava from a nearby volcano covers all of Cuicuilco, including the lower part of the round "pyramid" for which it is best known. Ceramic analysis and radiocarbon dating, however, have proven the flow to have occurred at about the time of Christ. Rising up in four tiers, the Cuicuilco pyramid has a clay-and-rubble core faced with broken lava blocks. The summit was reached by ramps on both sides. Circular temples were traditionally dedicated in Meso-America to Quetzalcóatl, the Feathered Serpent, and he may have been the presiding deity of Cuicuilco.

In the Valley of Teotihuacán, a kind of side pocket on the northeastern margin of the Valley of Mexico, Cuicuilco-Ticomán culture eventually took on a remarkable outline, for there is evidence that by the beginning of the Christian Era a great city had been planned. There is little doubt that by the Proto-Classic stage (AD 100–300) it had become the New World's first urban civilization (see below).

Valley of Oaxaca. Occupation of the Monte Albán site continued uninterrupted, but ceramic evidence for Monte Albán II culture indicates that cultural influences from southeastern Mexico were reaching the Zapotec people. On the southern end of the site's main plaza is a remarkable stone structure called Building J; this is shaped like an arrow pointing southwest and is honeycombed with galleries. Some believe it to have been an astronomical observatory. Incised slabs are fixed to its exterior; these include some older "Danzantes" as well as depictions of Zapotec place glyphs from which are suspended the inverted heads of dead chiefs—surely again the vanquished enemies of Monte Albán. Dates are given in the 52-year Calendar Round, with coefficients for days and months expressed by bar-and-dot numerals, a system that is first known for Monte Albán I and that became characteristic of the Classic Maya. Throughout its long Formative and Classic occupation, the dominant ware of Monte Albán is a fine gray pottery, elaborated in Monte Albán II into the usual Late Formative shapes.

Veracruz and Chiapas. La Venta suffered the fate of San Lorenzo, having been destroyed by violence around 400 BC. Olmec civilization subsequently disappeared or was transformed into one or more of the cultures of the southeastern lowlands.

One centre that retained a strong Olmec tradition, however, was Tres Zapotes, near the Tuxtla Mountains in the old Olmec "heartland." Its most famous monument, the fragmentary Stela C, is clearly epi-Olmec on the basis of a jaguar-monster mask carved in relief on its obverse. On the reverse is a column of numerals in the bar-and-dot system, which was read by its discoverer, Matthew W. Stirling, as a date in the Maya calendar corresponding to 31 BC; this is over three centuries earlier than any known dated inscription from the Maya area itself. Thus, it is highly probable that this calendrical system, formerly thought to be a Maya invention, was developed in the Late Formative by epi-Olmec peoples living outside the Maya area proper.

Izapan civilization. Izapa, type site of the Izapan civilization, is a huge temple centre near Tapachula, Chiapas, on the hot Pacific coast plain. Its approximately 80 pyramidal mounds were built from earth and clay faced with river boulders. A large number of carved stone stelae have been found at Izapa, almost all of which date to the Late Formative and Proto-Classic. Typically, in front of each stela is a round altar, often crudely shaped like a toad.

These stelae are of extraordinary interest, for they contain a wealth of information on Late Formative religious concepts prevalent on the border of the Maya area. Izapan stelae are carved in relief with narrative scenes derived from mythology and legend; among the depictions are warfare and decapitation, ceremonies connected with the sacred world tree, and meetings of what seem to be tribal elders. Many deities are shown, each of which seems derived from an Olmec prototype.

Sites with Izapan-style sculpture are distributed in a broad arc extending from Tres Zapotes in the former Olmec region, across the Isthmus of Tehuantepec into coastal Chiapas and Guatemala, and up into the Guatemalan highlands. Izapan civilization is definitely the intermediary between Olmec and Classic Maya in time and in cultural content, for the following early Maya traits are foreshadowed by it: (1) the stela–altar complex, (2) long-lipped deities, (3) hieroglyphic writing and Long Count dates on some monuments, (4) such iconographic elements as a U-shaped motif, and (5) a cluttered, baroque, and painterly relief style that emphasizes narrative.

Perhaps it was not Izapa itself but the great site of Kaminaljuyú, on the western edge of Guatemala City, that transmitted the torch of Izapan civilization to the lowland Maya. This centre once consisted of more than 200 earth and clay mounds, most of which have been destroyed in recent years. The major occupation is ascribed to the Miraflores phase, the Late Formative culture of the Valley of Guatemala. Some of these huge Miraflores mounds contained log tombs of incredible richness. In one, the deceased lord was accompanied by sacrificed followers or captives. As many as 340 objects were placed with him, including jade mosaic masks, jade ear spools and necklaces, bowls of chlorite schist, and pottery vessels of great beauty. Also present in the tombs are peculiar "mushroom stones," which may actually have been used in rites connected with hallucinogenic mushrooms.

The earliest Maya civilization. By the Late Formative, the lowland Maya had begun to shape a civilization that was to become the greatest in the New World. The Petén-Yucatan Peninsula lacks many raw materials and has a relatively low agricultural potential. But what it does have in limitless quantities is readily quarried limestone for building purposes and flint for stoneworking. Cement and plaster could easily be produced by burning limestone or shells.

The heart of the Maya civilization was always the northern Petén, in Guatemala, where the oldest dated Maya stelae are found. The Late Formative culture of the Petén is called Chicanel, evidence of which has been found at many Maya centres. Chicanel pottery includes dishes with wide-everted and grooved rims, bowls with composite silhouette, and ice-bucket-like vessels. Figurines are curiously absent.

[margin note: Horizon traits]

[margin note: Tres Zapotes]

[margin note: Kaminaljuyú]

Early
architec-
ture

Architecture was already quite advanced and had taken a form peculiar to the Maya. Temple-platforms were built by facing a cemented-rubble core with thick layers of plaster. At the site of Uaxactún, Structure E-VII-sub affords a good idea of a Chicanel temple-platform. It is a four-sided, stucco-covered, stepped pyramid with pairs of stylized godmasks flanking stairways on each side. On its summit was a thatched-roof temple. At Tikal, the giant among Maya ceremonial centres, the so-called Acropolis was begun in Chicanel times, and there was a great use of white-stuccoed platforms and stairways, with flanking polychromed masks as at Uaxactún. Most importantly, there is evidence from Tikal that the Maya architects were already building masonry superstructures with the corbel vault principle; *i.e.*, with archlike structures the sides of which extend progressively inward until they meet at the top.

Chicanel-like civilization is also known in Yucatán, where some temple-pyramids of enormous size are datable to the Late Formative. An outstanding site is the cave of Loltún in Yucatán, where a relief figure of a standing leader in pure Izapan style is accompanied by a number of unreadable hieroglyphs as well as a notation in the 260-day count. This inscription raises the question of writing and the calendar among the lowland Maya in the Late Formative. On the whole, the evidence is negative and suggests that several important intellectual innovations considered to be typically Maya were developed beyond the Maya area proper and only appeared there at the close of the Formative. Izapan civilization played the crucial role in this evolutionary process.

EARLY CLASSIC PERIOD (AD 100–600)

Definition of the Classic. In the study of the Classic stage, there has been a strong bias in favour of the Maya; this is not surprising in view of the fact that the Maya have been studied far longer than any other people in Meso-America. But the concept of a "Classic" period is a case of the Maya tail wagging the Meso-American dog, since the usual span given to that stage—AD 300–900—is the period during which the Maya were erecting dated stone monuments. This brackets the Maya apogee, but for most areas of non-Maya Meso-America only the first half of the period may be accurately called a "golden age." While the famous and yet mysterious Maya collapse took place at about AD 900, in many other regions this downfall occurred almost three centuries earlier.

From a qualitative point of view, there is little to differentiate the Classic from the Late Formative that preceded it. One can only say that various tendencies that were crystallizing in the last centuries before Christ reached fulfillment in the Classic. Two cultures stand out beyond all others. One is that of Teotihuacán, which during the Early Classic played a role in Meso-America similar to that which Olmec had performed in the Early Formative. The second is the lowland Maya civilization, which during its six centuries of almost unbroken evolution in the humid forests reached cultural heights never achieved before or since by New World natives. The curious contrast between the two—one urban and expansionist, the other non-urban and non-expansionist—exemplifies well the cultural results of the ecological possibilities offered by highland and lowland Meso-America.

Teotihuacán. Teotihuacán, which was located in the Valley of Teotihuacán, a pocket-like extension of the Valley of Mexico on its northeastern side, was probably the largest city of the New World before the arrival of the Spaniards. At its height, toward the close of the 6th century AD, it covered about eight square miles (20 square kilometres) and may have contained more than 150,000 people. The city was divided into quarters by two great avenues that crosscut each other at right angles, and the entire city was laid out on a grid plan oriented to these avenues. The Avenue of the Dead, the main north-south artery of the city, is aligned to a point 16° east of true north, which must have had astrological meaning.

Layout
of the
city

Because irrigation plays some part in the present-day agricultural economy of the Valley of Teotihuacán, it has been suggested that the Early Classic city also was based upon this subsistence system. It is almost inconceivable, however, that a city of such proportions could have relied upon the food production of its own valley or even upon the Valley of Mexico, whether irrigated or not.

Planning and construction of Teotihuacán began, according to radiocarbon dates, about the beginning of the Christian Era, in the Tzacualli phase. At this time, the major avenues were laid out and construction begun of the major ceremonial structures along the Avenue of the Dead. Figurines and potsherds extracted from fill inside the 200-foot (60-metre) high Pyramid of the Sun, the most prominent feature of Teotihuacán, prove that this was erected by the end of the Tzacualli phase. The pyramid rises in four great stages, but there is a fifth and much smaller stage between the third and fourth. An impressive stairway dramatically rises on its west side, facing the Avenue of the Dead. A recent re-examination suggests that there is a huge tomb at its base, but this has never been excavated.

On the northern end of the Avenue of the Dead is the Pyramid of the Moon, very similar to that of the Sun, but with an additional platform-temple jutting out on the south. This exhibits the *talud-tablero* architectural motif that is typical of Teotihuacán culture: on each body or tier of a stepped pyramid is a rectangular frontal panel (*tablero*) supported by a sloping batter (*talud*). The *tablero* is surrounded by a kind of projecting frame, and the recessed portion of the panel usually bears a polychrome mural applied to the stuccoed surface.

Near the exact centre of the city and just east of the Avenue of the Dead is the Ciudadela (Citadel), a kind of sunken court surrounded on all four sides by platforms supporting temples. In the middle of the sunken plaza is the so-called Temple of Quetzalcóatl, which is dated to the second phase of Teotihuacán, Miccaotli. Along the balustrades of its frontal stairway and undulating along the *talud-tablero* bodies of each stage of this stepped pyramid are sculptured representations of Quetzalcóatl, the Feathered Serpent. Alternating with the Feathered Serpents on the *tableros* are heads of another monster that can be identified with the Fire Serpent—bearer of the Sun on its diurnal journey across the sky.

The temple
of Quetzal-
cóatl

On either side of the Avenue of the Dead are residential palace compounds (probably occupied by noble families), which also conform to the Teotihuacán master plan. Each is a square, 60 metres on a side, and is surrounded by a wall. The pedestrian would have seen only the high walls facing the streets, pierced by inconspicuous doors. Within the compounds, however, luxury was the rule. Roofs were flat, constructed of large cedar beams overlaid by brush and mortar. Interior walls were plastered and magnificently painted with ritual processions of gods and various mythological narratives. Interconnected apartments were arranged around a large central court that was open to the sky.

These dwellings were the residences of Teotihuacán's elite. Toward the periphery of Teotihuacán, however, the social situation may have been quite different. One excavation on the eastern side of the city disclosed a maze-like complex of much tinier and shoddier apartments that recall the poorer sections of Near Eastern cities. It may be guessed that here lay the crowded dwellings of the artisans and other labourers who made the city what it was. There is also evidence that certain peripheral sections were reserved for foreigners.

Teotihuacán must have been the major manufacturing centre of the Early Classic, for the products of its craftsmen were spread over much of Meso-America. The pottery, particularly during the Xolalpan phase, which represents the culmination of Teotihuacán as a city and empire, is highly distinctive. The hallmark of the city is the cylindrical vessel with three slab legs and cover, often stuccoed and then painted with scenes almost identical to those on the walls of buildings. There are also vessels shaped like modern flower vases and cream pitchers. Thin Orange ware is a special ceramic type produced to Teotihuacán specifications, perhaps in southern Veracruz, and exported by its own traders. Figurines were produced by the tens of thousands in pottery molds.

Manu-
facturing
and
trade

Among its many commercial specializations, obsidian was probably pre-eminent, for the Teotihuacanos had gained control of the mines of green obsidian above the present-day city of Pachuca, in Hidalgo. They also had a local but poorer quality source. Millions of obsidian blades, as well as knives, dart points, and scrapers, were turned out by Teotihuacán workshops for export.

The name Teotihuacán meant Place of the Gods in Aztec times, and although the city had been largely deserted since its decline, the Aztec royal house made annual pilgrimages to the site. Teotihuacán culture exerted a profound influence on all contemporary and later Meso-American cultures. Many Aztec gods, such as Tlaloc, his consort Chalchiuhtlícue, and Quetzalcóatl, were worshipped by the Teotihuacanos. Like the Aztec, the Teotihuacanos generally cremated their dead. In fact, there are so many congruences between Teotihuacán practices and those of the later Toltec and Aztec that some authorities believe them to have been speakers of Nahua language and the precursors of those people. It is not known whether the people of the city were literate like the Maya.

Not only was Teotihuacán the greatest American Indian city in this hemisphere, it was probably the capital of the largest empire ever seen in Meso-America. Whatever the economic impetus that started it on the road to urbanism, the evidence both of its immense size and of its strong cultural presence in far-flung regions make it likely that Teotihuacán must have embarked upon imperial expansion after AD 400. At its absolute height it may well have controlled all of Meso-America, an achievement the Aztec never could have claimed. The Aztec never managed to subdue the Maya, or never tried. Apparently the Teotihuacanos did, and their interference in Maya affairs is a characteristic feature of Early Classic Maya culture. This universal spread of Teotihuacán traits truly constitutes an Early Classic horizon.

Cholula. The broad, fertile plains surrounding the colonial city of Puebla, to the southeast of the snowcapped volcanoes that border the Valley of Mexico, were from very ancient times an important centre of pre-Hispanic population. As the modern traveller approaches the city, he sees to its west, in the distance, what looks like a sizable hill rising from the plain. In actuality this is the pyramid of Cholula, the largest single structure in Mexico before the conquest.

Archaeological exploration of the Cholula pyramid has shown that it was built from adobe in four great construction stages. In its final form, the pyramid covers 28 acres (11 hectares) and has a height of 180 feet (55 metres). By Late Post-Classic times the pyramid had been abandoned for so long that the Spaniards who subdued (and massacred) the residents of Cholula considered it a natural prominence. All four superimposed structures within the pyramid were carried out according to strict Teotihuacán architectural ideas. The earliest structure, for instance, has the usual *talud-tablero* motif, with stylized insect-like figures painted in black, yellow, and red appearing in the *tableros*. Similar decoration, also in Teotihuacán style, is to be found in the later structures.

Great quantities of ceramics and pottery figurines have been recovered from the excavations, and these demonstrate a near archaeological identity between Early Classic Teotihuacán and Cholula. Because of the staggering size and importance of its pyramid, it has been suggested that Cholula was some kind of sister city to Teotihuacán. Cholula was surely part of the Teotihuacán culture sphere and may well have participated in the administration of its empire.

Recent excavations at the base of the pyramid have produced a previously unsuspected cultural element. Several enormous slabs were uncovered, two of which were a kind of altar, while the third was set upright as a stela. All are rectangular, but with borders carved in low relief in the complex interlace motif that is the hallmark of the Classic Central Veracruz style.

Classic Central Veracruz. The Meso-American ball game has been mentioned several times above. It was played all over the area and still survives in attenuated form in northwestern Mexico. On the eve of the conquest, games took place in a rectangular court bordered along the long sides by walls with both sloping and vertical rebound surfaces. There were two teams, each comprised of a small handful of players. The ball was of solid rubber, of substantial size, and travelled with considerable speed around the court. It could not be hit or touched with the open hands or with the feet; most times the player tried to strike it with the hip. Consequently, fairly heavy protective padding was necessary to avoid injuries, which in some cases were fatal. Leather padding was worn over the hips, and pads were placed on the elbows and knees. A heavy belt was tied around the waist built up from wood and leather, while in some parts of the Maya region and in Late Formative Oaxaca, gloves and something resembling jousting helmets were worn.

The Classic Central Veracruz style is almost purely devoted to the paraphernalia of the ball game and to the ball courts themselves. At the site of El Tajín, which persists through the end of the Late Classic, elaborate reliefs on the walls of the courts furnish details on how this equipment was used. *Yugos* (or "yokes") were the stone counterparts of the heavy protective belts. During the post-game ceremonies, which may have featured the sacrifice of the captain and other players on the losing side, these U-shaped objects were worn about the waists of the participants. On the front of the *yugo* was placed an upright stone object that may originally have functioned as a ball-court marker and that took two forms: *hachas* ("axes") or thin stone heads, and *palmas* ("palms"). All are carved in an extremely elaborate low-relief style in which life forms are enmeshed in undulating and interlaced scroll designs with raised borders. All of these items, and the style itself, may have evolved out of very late Olmec art on the Gulf Coast.

Very often the *yugos* represent the marine toad, a huge amphibian with swollen poison glands on the head; in its jaws is a human head. The earliest *hachas*, which are characteristically notched to fit on the *yugos*, are quite thick human heads and may well date to the Late Formative or Proto-Classic. In time, these become very thin and represent human heads wearing animal headgear. *Palmas* are paddle-shaped stone objects with trilobate bases and exhibit a much richer subject matter than either *hachas* or *yugos*, quite often illustrating brutal scenes of sacrifice and death, two concepts that were closely associated with the ball game on the Gulf Coast.

Despite the definite presence of the style at Teotihuacán and Cholula, Classic Central Veracruz is focussed upon north central Veracruz, where the type site of El Tajín is located, and contiguous parts of Puebla. Today, this region is dominated by speakers of Totonac, a distant relative of Mayan, and the Totonac themselves claim that they built El Tajín. Whether or not Classic Central Veracruz culture was a Totonac achievement, the style persisted through the Classic period and strongly influenced developments in distant regions.

Southern Veracruz. On the southern Gulf Coast plain, Olmec traditions seemed to have lasted into the Early Classic and merged with Teotihuacán artistic canons to produce new kinds of art. Cerro de las Mesas, lying in the plains of the Papaloápan River not far from the coast, is one of these hybrid sites. Dozens of earthen mounds are scattered over the surface in a seemingly haphazard manner, and the archaeological sequence is long and complex. The site reached its apogee in the Early Classic, when the stone monuments for which it is best known were carved. Most important are 15 stelae, some of which are carved in a low-relief style recalling Late Formative Tres Zapotes, early lowland Maya, and Cotzumalhuapa (on the Pacific Coast of Guatemala).

Cerro de las Mesas pottery, deposited in rich burial offerings of the Early Classic, is highly Teotihuacanoid, with slab-legged tripods predominating. At this and other sites in southern Veracruz, potters also fashioned large, hollow, handmade figures of the gods. An especially fine representation of the Old Fire God was found at Cerro de las Mesas. The most spectacular discovery, however, was a cache of 782 jade objects. Many of the specimens in this treasure trove are of Olmec workmanship, obviously heirlooms from the much earlier Olmec civilization, while some are clearly Early Classic Maya.

The entire coastal plain from Cerro de las Mesas north to the borders of Classic Central Veracruz culture is famed for Remojadas-style pottery figurines, which must have been turned out in incredible quantity for use as burial goods. The Remojadas tradition goes back to the Late Formative and lasts until the Early Post-Classic. Figurines are hollow and largely mold-made in the Late Classic, while they were fashioned by hand in the Early Classic. The best known Classic representations are the "smiling figures" of grinning boys and girls wearing loincloths, skirts, or nothing at all. All kinds of genre scenes are represented, including even lovers in swings, as well as more grim activities such as the heart sacrifice of victims tied down in what look like beds.

Classic Monte Albán. Monte Albán III-A and III-B mark the Classic occupation of this major site in the Valley of Oaxaca. There can be little doubt that the people of Monte Albán were Zapotec speakers, who during Classic times had unequalled opportunity to develop their civilization unaffected by the major troubles that disturbed Teotihuacán and the Maya at the close of the Early Classic. Instead of the 18 or 19 sites known for the valley during the Late Formative, there now were more than 200, a testimony to Zapotec prosperity.

There is, however, a chronological problem. Monte Albán III-A is very closely linked with Teotihuacán, which may have exercised hegemony over the Zapotec between AD 300 and 600. But there is almost no difference between the products of III-A and those of III-B, suggesting that the latter cannot be substantially later than AD 600. Furthermore, radiocarbon dates on Monte Albán IV, supposedly belonging to the Early Post-Classic, fall within the Late Classic. Thus, "Classic" Monte Albán may be purely a product of the earlier period.

The Classic site of Monte Albán is quite impressive. Stone-faced platforms are fronted by stairways with flanking balustrades and exhibit a close counterpart of the *talud-tablero* motif of Teotihuacán. The temple superstructures had colonnaded doorways and flat beam-and-mortar roofs. One of the best preserved ball courts of Meso-America can be seen at Monte Albán, with a ground plan fashioned in the form of a capital "I." Spectators watched the game from stone grandstands above the sloping playing surfaces.

Subsurface tombs were dug in many parts of the site as the last resting places of Monte Albán's elite. The finest are actually miniature replicas of the larger temples on the surface, complete with facade and miniature painted rooms. The style of the funerary wall paintings is quite close to Teotihuacán, in which areas of flat colour are contained within very finely painted lines in red or black. Teotihuacán presence can also be seen in the finer pottery of Classic Monte Albán, but the manufacture is local as can be proved from the predominance of the fine gray ware that has always typified Monte Albán.

The tradition of literacy goes back to Monte Albán I. By Classic times, inscriptions are abundant, appearing on stelae, lintels, slabs used as doors, and wall paintings. The 52-year Calendar Round was the only form of writing dates. The subject matter of these inscriptions can be related to the scenes that they accompany: quite often it is a bound captive standing on a place-glyph, presumably an enemy leader taken in war—an old Monte Albán preoccupation.

The Zapotec of Monte Albán, like the Maya, never exerted much cultural or other pressure on peoples beyond their lands. They did, however, control lands from the Tehuacán Valley in Puebla as far south as the Pacific shore of Oaxaca. Whether they themselves were also controlled by Teotihuacán cannot yet be demonstrated, but it is likely.

The Maya highlands and Pacific Coast. Little is known about the Guatemalan highlands between the demise of the Late Formative Miraflores culture and the onset of the Early Classic. But at the ancient site of Kaminaljuyú, on the western side of Guatemala City, a group of in-

vaders from Teotihuacán built a miniature replica of their capital city. This happened about AD 400, when Teotihuacán was at the height of its power.

This implanted Teotihuacán culture is called Esperanza. Mexican architects must have accompanied the elite, for Kaminaljuyú structures copy the older prototypes down to the last detail, including the support of the lower moldings around *tableros* with slate slabs. The abundant volcanic building stone, however, so freely used at Teotihuacán, was not present, so that Esperanza temple-platforms are built from clay instead.

Each temple-platform was rebuilt several times, the later structures being raised over the earlier. Within the stairways fronting each successive platform a great leader was buried. The rich burial furniture in the tombs is quite informative, for it included three classes of goods: (1) items such as Thin Orange pottery manufactured in Teotihuacán or in one of its satellite areas, (2) hybrid Teotihuacán-Maya pottery and other objects, probably made in Kaminaljuyú, and (3) pottery imported from the Petén and of Early Classic Maya manufacture. Also discovered in one tomb was a slate mirror carved in Classic Central Veracruz style. Jade objects occur in abundance in the Esperanza tombs, and in one structure an enormous boulder was recovered; it had been imported from the Maya source along the Motagua River in the southeastern lowlands. The Esperanza elite were enormously wealthy.

What were they doing in the Maya highlands in the first place? Among the Aztec of the Late Post-Classic, there was an institution called the *pochteca*, a hereditary guild of armed merchants who travelled into distant lands looking for luxury goods to bring back to the royal house. Quite often the *pochteca* would seize lands of hostile peoples through which they passed, or they would provoke an incident that led inevitably to the intervention of the regular Aztec army.

It has been suggested that the Teotihuacanos in Kaminaljuyú were also *pochteca*. They had clear access to the Petén-Yucatán Peninsula and probably exercised political control over it. Kaminaljuyú may have been one of their principal bases of operations in the inclusion of the Maya, both highland and lowland, within the Teotihuacán state.

Within a restricted zone only 75 miles (120 kilometres) long and 30 miles (50 kilometres) wide, on the Pacific coast plain of Guatemala, is a cluster of nine compactly built ceremonial centres that together form the Cotzumalhuapa civilization. It forms a real puzzle, for there are strong affiliations with most other contemporary civilizations in Meso-America. Stylistic influence from the lowland Maya, Classic Central Veracruz, and Teotihuacán can be detected among others. While Cotzumalhuapa takes form by the Early Classic, it continues into the Late Classic, but there are great problems in dating individual sculptures.

The Cotzumalhuapa problem has been linked with that of the Pipil, a shadowy people living in the same region on the eve of the conquest, who spoke Nahua rather than Maya. It is possible that these Classic sites were actually Pipil capitals, but the case cannot be proved. There is some hieroglyphic writing on Cotzumalhuapa sculptures, mainly dates within what seems to be a 52-year Calendar Round, the glyphs for days being Mexican rather than Maya. There are no real texts, then, to help with the problem.

Classic civilization in the Maya lowlands: Tzakol Phase. Archaeologists have divided the entire area occupied by speakers of Mayan languages into three subregions: (1) the Southern Subregion, essentially the highlands and Pacific Coast of Guatemala, (2) the Central Subregion, which includes the department of Petén in northern Guatemala and the immediately adjacent lowlands to the east and west, and (3) the Northern Subregion, consisting of the Yucatán Peninsula north of the Petén proper. Between AD 300 and 900 the most brilliant civilization ever seen in the New World flourished in the forested lowlands of the Central and Northern subregions.

Lowland Maya civilization falls into two chronological

Zapotec prosperity

The pochteca

phases or cultures: Tzakol culture, which is Early Classic and began shortly before AD 300, and the Late Classic Tepeu culture, which saw the full florescence of Maya achievements. Tepeu culture began about AD 600 and ended with the final downfall and abandonment of the Central Subregion about AD 900. (These dates, based on the correlation of the Long Count system of the Maya calendar with the Christian calendar, are the most generally accepted; but there is a very slight chance that a rival correlation espoused by Herbert J. Spinden, which would make these dates 260 years earlier, may be correct.)

One of the earliest objects inscribed with the fully developed Maya calendar is the Leiden Plate, a jade plaque, now housed in the Leiden Museum, depicting a richly arrayed Maya lord trampling a captive underfoot. On its reverse side is a Long Count date corresponding to AD 320. Although it was found in a very late site on the Caribbean coast, stylistic evidence suggests that the Leiden Plate was made at Tikal, in the heart of the northern Petén. More recently, the University of Pennsylvania's ambitious field program at the Tikal site has produced Stela 29, erected 28 years before, in AD 292. Both objects and, in fact, almost all early Tzakol monuments draw heavily upon a heritage from the older Izapan civilization of the Late Formative, with its highly baroque, narrative stylistic content.

Because of the Maya penchant for covering older structures with later ones, Tzakol remains in the Central Subregion have to be laboriously dug out from their towering Late Classic overburdens. Nevertheless, it is clear that at sites like Tikal, Uaxactún, and Holmul, Maya civilization had reached something close to its final form. Enormous ceremonial centres were crowded with masonry temples and "palaces" facing onto spacious plazas covered with white stucco. The use of the corbel vault for spanning rooms—a trait unique to the lowland Maya —was by this time universal. Stelae and altars (a legacy from Izapa) are carved with dates and embellished with the figures of men and perhaps gods. Polychrome pottery, the finest examples of which were sealed in the tombs of honoured personages, emphasizes stylized designs of cranes, flying parrots, gods, and men. These often occur on bowls with a kind of apron or basal flange encircling the lower vessel. Along with these purely Maya ceramics are vessels that show the imprint of distant Teotihuacán: the cylindrical vase supported by three slab legs, the "cream pitcher," and the *florero* ("flower vase").

Wall painting had already reached a high degree of perfection in the Central Subregion, as attested by an extremely fine mural at Uaxactún depicting a palace scene in which two important lords confer with each other. This mural art is quite different from that of Teotihuacán, being very naturalistic instead of formal, and including a definite interest in portraiture. Nonetheless, recent excavations in Petén sites have shown that Teotihuacán influence was quite pervasive. At Tikal, for example, a stela has been found depicting a richly garbed Maya lord, festooned with jade ornaments, standing between two warriors from Teotihuacán. These foreigners carry shields that bear the visage of the Teotihuacán rain god, Tlaloc. It is certain that there was a three-way trading relationship between Tikal, Kaminaljuyú, and Teotihuacán in Early Classic times.

Thus, the Teotihuacán involvement with Tikal and the Central Subregion may have taken, as at Kaminaljuyú, the form of *pochteca* trading colonies that more or less exerted military control over the lowland Maya. The lord on Stela 31 may have been a puppet ruler manipulated by tough merchant-warriors. It will be remembered that Teotihuacán as a city and capital of an empire began to weaken toward the close of the 6th century AD. It could therefore be expected that the disruptions that effectively ended the life of the great Mexican capital would be reflected in the Maya area. This is exactly the case. In the Guatemalan Highlands, Kaminaljuyú declined rapidly after AD 600, and the entire Southern Subregion was to play little part in Maya culture until the Late Post-Classic. The lowland Maya suffered even greater reverses; no stelae whatsoever were erected between 534 and 692 AD, and there is evidence of international mutilation of already existing monuments at that time. The great Teotihuacán crisis brought down most of the Early Classic cultures, most of which were never to recover. The Maya were the only important exception.

LATE CLASSIC NON-MAYA MESO-AMERICA (600-900)

The cultural situation in Late Classic Meso-America is the reverse of that prevailing in the Early Classic: Central Mexico now plays only a minor role, while the lowland Maya reach intellectual and artistic heights unattained by any other native peoples of the New World. In contrast to the old Teotihuacanos, however, the Maya were not expansionistic, surely a reflection of their lack of mercantile interests. It is true that Maya cultural influence can be detected along the Gulf Coast and in distant Morelos, but this surely was not the result of military takeover. The outcome of this state of affairs, with no one people powerful enough or sufficiently interested in dominating others, was a political and cultural fragmentation of Meso-America after AD 600. It was not until the great Toltec invasions of the Early Post-Classic that anything approaching an empire was to be seen again.

The decline in fortunes of the Valley of Mexico, and especially of Teotihuacán, cannot now be explained. Climatic deterioration, resulting in drier conditions and thus a diminished subsistence potential, may have been a factor.

Nevertheless, Teotihuacán was never completely abandoned, even though its great palaces had been burned to the ground and its major temples abandoned. People continued to live in some sections, but their houses were mere hovels compared to the dwellings of the Early Classic. In general, the Valley of Mexico was a cultural and political vacuum in Late Classic times.

One of the very few centres of the Late Classic in Central Mexico to amount to much was Xochicalco, Morelos. Strategically located on top of a hill that was completely reworked with artificial terraces and ramparts, Xochicalco was obviously highly defensible, an indication of the unsettled times then prevailing in Central Mexico. The site shows a bewildering variety of cultural influences, particularly Maya. The principal structure of Xochicalco is a temple substructure of masonry that has been completely carved in relief with undulating Feathered Serpents, indicating that it was dedicated to the cult of Quetzalcóatl. All indications are that Xochicalco was a cosmopolitan and very powerful centre, perhaps the most influential west of Veracruz and northwest of the Maya area. It was literate and civilized at a time when most other parts of Central Mexico were in cultural eclipse.

The nature of the Late Classic occupation of Oaxaca, especially of the Valley of Oaxaca, is still a matter of debate. Monte Albán III-B is supposed to fall within the AD 600–900 range, but radiocarbon dates on the Monte Albán IV culture, said to be Early Post-Classic, also fall within this span. Until these contradictions are resolved, little can be said about Zapotec civilization on the eve of the Mixtec invasions, which probably began in earnest around AD 900. The Mixtec occupied the hilly, northern part of Oaxaca. Their own records extend back to the 7th century AD and show them to have been organized into a series of petty states headed by aggressive, warlike kings. By the Post-Classic, they became the dominant force throughout Oaxaca and in part of Puebla.

The tendencies in Central Veracruz art and architecture that began in the Late Formative culminated in the Late Classic at the great centre of El Tajín, placed among jungle-covered hills in a region occupied by the Totonac Indians, whose capital this may well have been. Its most imposing structure is the Pyramid of the Niches, named for the approximately 365 recesses on its four sides. In this and other buildings at El Tajín, the dominant architectural motif is the step-and-fret. There are a number of other temple-pyramids at the site, as well as palace-like buildings with flat, concrete roofs, a tour de force of Meso-American engineering knowledge. El Tajín's three

Ceremonial centres

Decline of Teotihuacán

The Pyramid of the Niches

major ball courts are remarkably important for the reliefs carved on their vertical playing surfaces, for these give valuable information on the religious connotations of the sacred game. Like Xochicalco, El Tajín was in some way linked to the destiny of the lowland Maya, and the collapse of Maya civilization around AD 900 may have been reflected in the demise of the Veracruz centre.

Further down the Gulf Coast plain, the Remojadas tradition of hollow pottery figurines continued to be active in the Late Classic, with a particularly large production of the mysterious smiling figures of dancing boys and girls, which were intended as funerary offerings. But in addition, there was a great deal of pottery and figurines that were fashioned under very strong Maya influence. In fact, much of southern Veracruz at this time was a cultural extension of the lowland Maya. There is no indication, however, that these peoples had any acquaintance with Maya literacy or with Maya building techniques.

LATE CLASSIC LOWLAND MAYA (600–900)

Settlement pattern. There is still controversy over whether the Late Classic sites built by the lowland Maya were actually cities or whether they were relatively empty ceremonial centres staffed only by rulers and their entourages.

The common people built their simple pole-and-thatch dwellings on low earthen mounds to keep them dry and comfortable during the summer rains. Thus, total mapping of a particular site should always include not only masonry structures but also house mounds as well. So far, only a few Maya sites have been so mapped. The mightiest Maya centre of all, Tikal in the northern Petén, has a total of about 3,000 structures ranging from the tiny mounds up to gigantic temple-pyramids; these are contained, however, within an area of six square miles (16 square kilometres). The Tikal population has been estimated from this survey to be 10,000–11,000 persons, but perhaps as many as 50,000 souls within an even wider area could have belonged to Tikal.

This sounds very much like a city, but the evidence actually can be differently interpreted. First, at the time of the conquest the Maya generally buried their dead beneath the floors of houses, which were then abandoned. Thus, an increase in number of house mounds could just as easily indicate a declining population in which the death rate exceeded the birth rate. Second, the appearance of even such a tremendous centre as Tikal is quite different from that of such true cities as Teotihuacán. An ordinary Maya family typically occupied two or three houses arranged around a rectangular open space. These were grouped into unplanned hamlets near good water and rich, well-drained soils. A survey of the Petén has shown that for every 50 to 100 dwellings there is a minor ceremonial centre; this unit has been called a zone. Several zones formed a district for which a major centre like Tikal acted as the ceremonial and political nucleus. Neither Tikal nor any other such centre shows signs of town planning or neatly laid-out streets.

There are also ecological factors that set stringent limits upon the potential for urban life in the Maya lowlands. There is little or no possibility of intensive forms of agriculture, such as irrigation farming, or *chinampas*, in the tropical forest of the Petén-Yucatán Peninsula. While it is true that in good soils, shifting cultivation could support fairly large populations, these would have had to be relatively dispersed as weed competition and declining fertility forced farmers to seek new fields farther and farther from the settlement. In addition, the monotonous uniformity of the lowland environment made interregional exchange of subsistence products of little use; thus, there was little development of the intense trade that entered into the early rise of cities in central Mexico. The Maya cities, therefore, were actually organizational centres mainly occupied by the rulers and nobility, along with their followers, servants, and slaves. Nonetheless, these centres were the foci of a civilization that had no rivals elsewhere in the New World.

Major sites. While there are some important differences between the architecture of the Central and North-

ern subregions during the Late Classic, there are many features shared between them. A major Maya site generally includes several types of masonry buildings, usually constructed by facing a cement-and-rubble core with blocks or thin slabs of limestone. Temple-pyramids are the most impressive, rising in a series of great platforms to the temple superstructure above the forests. The rooms, coated with white stucco, are often little more than narrow slots because of the confining nature of the corbelled vaults, but this was probably intentional, to keep esoteric ceremonies from the public.

The so-called palaces of Maya sites differ only from the temple-pyramids in that they are lower and contain a great many rooms. Their purpose still eludes discovery; many scholars doubt that they really served as palaces, for the rooms are damp and uncomfortable, and there is little or no evidence of permanent occupation. The temples and palaces are generally arranged around courts, and often have inscribed stelae and altars arranged in rows before them. Leading from the central plazas are great stone causeways, the function of which was probably strictly ceremonial. Other features of lowland sites (but not universal) are sweathouses, ball courts, and possibly even marketplaces.

There are more than 50 known sites that deserve to be called major. Most are in the Central Subregion, with probably the greatest concentration in the northern Petén, where Maya civilization had its deepest roots. Tikal is the largest and best known site of the Central Subregion, and may well have been the capital for much of the Maya lowlands. It is dominated by six lofty temple-pyramids, one of which is 229 feet (70 metres) high, the tallest structure ever raised by the Meso-American Indians. Lintels of sapodilla wood still span the doorways of the temple superstructures and are carved with reliefs of Maya lords enthroned amid scenes of great splendour. Some extraordinary Late Classic tombs have been discovered at Tikal, the most important of which produced a collection of bone tubes and strips delicately incised with scenes of gods and men. Causeways connect outlying temple-pyramids with the centre of the site. Ten large reservoirs, partly or entirely artificial, supplied the scarce drinking water for the residents of Tikal.

Other important sites of the northern Petén include Uaxactún, Naranjo, Nakum, and Holmul, of which only the first has been adequately excavated. To the southeast of the Petén are two Maya centres—Copán and Quiriguá —that show interesting differences with the Petén sites. Copán is located above a tributary of the Motagua River in western Honduras in a region now rich in tobacco. Its architects and sculptors had a ready supply of a greenish volcanic tuff far superior to the Petén limestone. Thus, Copán architecture is embellished with gloriously baroque figures of gods, and its stelae and other monuments are carved with an extraordinary virtuosity. Copán also has one of the most perfectly preserved ball courts in Meso-America. Quiriguá is a much smaller site 30 miles (48 kilometres) north of Copán. While its architectural remains are on a minor scale, it is noted for its gigantic stelae and altars carved from sandstone.

The principal watercourse on the western side of the Central Subregion is the Usumacinta River, originating in the Guatemalan highlands and emptying into the Gulf of Mexico. For much of its course the Usumacinta is lined with such great Maya ceremonial centres as Piedras Negras and Yaxchilán. Even more renowned is Bonampak, a satellite of Yaxchilán located on a tributary of the Usumacinta. The discovery in 1948 of the magnificent murals embellishing the rooms of an otherwise modest structure astounded the archaeological world. From floors to vault capstones, its stuccoed walls were covered with highly realistic polychrome scenes of a jungle battle, the arraignment of prisoners, and victory ceremonies. These shed an entirely new light on the nature of Maya society, which up till then had been considered peaceful.

In the hills just above the floodplain of the Usumacinta lies Palenque, the most beautiful of Maya sites. The architects of Palenque designed graceful temple-pyramids and "palaces" with mansard-type roofs, embellished with

[margin notes]
Tikal

Ecological factors

The Bonampak murals

delicate stucco reliefs of rulers, gods, and ceremonies. The principal structure is the Palace, a veritable labyrinth of galleries and with interior courts; over it looms a four-story square tower that may have served as both lookout and observatory. A small stream flowing through the site was carried underneath the Palace by a long, corbel-vaulted tunnel. The Temples of the Cross, Foliated Cross, and Sun were all built on the same plan, the backroom of each temple having a kind of sanctuary designed like the temples of which they were a part. It can be supposed that all three temples served the same cult. The most extraordinary feature of Palenque, however, was the great funerary crypt discovered in 1952 deep within the Temple of the Inscriptions. Within a sarcophagus in the crypt were the remains of an unusually tall ruler, accompanied by the richest offering of jade ever seen in a Maya tomb. Over his face had been fitted a mask of jade mosaic, while a treasure trove of jade adorned his body.

As one moves north from the Central Subregion into the drier and flatter environment of the Yucatán Peninsula, the character of lowland Maya civilization changes. Just north of the Petén is the Río Bec zone, as yet little explored but noted for temple-pyramids and palaces with flanking false towers fronted by unclimbable "stairways" reaching dummy "rooms" with blank entrances. Río Bec structures are carved with fantastic serpents in deep relief, a feature that becomes even more pronounced in the Chenes country to the northwest, in the state of Campeche. At Chenes sites, Maya architects constructed frontal portals surrounded by the jaws of sky serpents and faced entire buildings with a riot of baroquely carved grotesques and spirals.

This elaborate ornamentation of buildings is far more restrained and orderly in the style called Puuc, so named from a string of low hills extending up from western Campeche into the state of Yucatan. The Puuc sites were for the Northern Subregion what the Petén sites were for the Central, for they are very numerous and clearly were the focal point for Maya artistic and intellectual culture. Uxmal is the most important Puuc ceremonial centre and an architectural masterpiece. It has all of the characteristics of the Puuc style: facings of thin squares of limestone veneer over a cement-and-rubble core; boot-shaped vault stones; decorated cornices around columns in doorways; engaged or half-columns repeated in long rows; and lavish use of stone mosaics in upper facades, emphasizing sky-serpent faces with long, hook-shaped noses, as well as frets and latticelike designs of crisscrossed elements.

The nearby centre of Kabah, connected to Uxmal by a ceremonial causeway, has an extraordinary palace completely faced with masks of the sky serpent. Other major Puuc sites are Sayil, with a multistoried palace, and Labná. The Puuc style reaches east across the Yucatán Peninsula, for at Chichén Itzá, a great site that was to occupy centre stage during the Toltec occupation of the Northern Subregion, there are several buildings strongly Puuc in character.

It was formerly believed that the Puuc sites represented a "New Empire" formed by survivors of the great collapse that took place in the Central Subregion at the close of the 9th century. Archaeological research, however, has shown that the ceramics associated with Puuc architecture are not only pre-Toltec but partake of many features typical of Late Classic Maya pottery elsewhere. Nevertheless, it is also clear, both on stratigraphic grounds and upon certain dates painted on Puuc capstones, that these centres were built in their present form in the final decades of the 9th century and probably were occupied until the latter half of the 10th, when the Toltec invaders ended the Late Classic in the Northern Subregion. As well as being late in the Classic sequence, the Puuc sites were under several influences from non-Maya Mexico, particularly from central Veracruz.

Maya art of the Late Classic. Maya art, at the height of its development, was fundamentally unlike any other in Meso-America, for it was highly narrative, baroque, and often extremely cluttered, unlike the more austere styles found elsewhere. It is essentially a painterly rather than sculptural tradition, and it is quite likely that even stone reliefs were first designed by painters. Much of this art has disappeared for all time because of the ravages of the wet, tropical environment on such perishable materials as wood, painted gourds, feathers, bark, and other substances. There must have been thousands of bark-paper codices, not one of which has survived from Classic times.

Following the downfall of Teotihuacán, Maya artists were free to go their own way. Magnificently carved stelae and accompanying altars are found at most major sites, the greatest achievement in this line being found at Copán, where something approaching three-dimensional carving was the rule. Palenque and Yaxchilán specialized in graceful bas-reliefs placed as tablets or lintels in temple-pyramids and palaces. In the Northern Subregion, however, the sculptor's art was definitely inferior in scope and quality and shows strong influence from alien, non-Maya cultures.

A few wooden objects have miraculously survived. Particularly noteworthy are the massive wooden lintels of Tikal, with scenes of lords and their guardian deities, accompanied by lengthy hieroglyphic texts. In ancient times, wood carvings must have been vastly more common than sculptures. The wet climate has also destroyed innumerable examples of mural art.

Maya pottery can be divided into two groups: (1) the pots and pans of everyday life, usually undecorated but sometimes with geometric designs, and (2) grave offerings. Vessels meant to accompany the honoured dead were usually painted or carved with naturalistic and often macabre scenes. To achieve polychrome effects of great brilliance, the Maya potters painted in semi-translucent slips over a light background, then fired the vessels at a very low temperature. Relief carving was carried out when the vessels were leather-hard, just before firing.

The most precious substance of all to the Maya was jade, to which their craftsmen devoted great artistry. Jade was mainly fashioned into thin plaques carved in relief, or into beads. In the absence of metal tools, jade was worked by applying abrasives and water with cane or perhaps other pieces of jade.

The Maya calendar and writing system. It is their mental life that established the cultural superiority of the Maya over all other American Indians. Much of this was based upon a calendrical system that was partly shared with other Meso-American groups but that they perfected into a tool capable of recording important historical and astronomical information. (For an extended discussion of the Mayan calendar, see CALENDAR; CHRONOLOGY.) Most Maya inscriptions that have been interpreted are calendrical inscriptions. Since the late 1950s, it has been learned that the content of Classic Maya inscriptions was far more secular than had been supposed. For many years specialists believed that the inscriptions recorded little more than the passage of time and that, in fact, the Mayans were time worshippers. Since 1958 it has been shown that certain inscriptions recorded the birth, accession, marriage, and military victories of ruling dynasties. Yet it would be misleading to contend that the hurly-burly of Maya court affairs and conquests was all that mattered, for some texts must have been sacred and god-oriented. At Palenque, in the similar Temples of the Cross, Foliated Cross, and Sun, the dates inscribed on the tablets in the sanctuaries fall into three groups. The very latest seem to refer to events in the lives of reigning monarchs. An earlier group must deal with distant but real ancestors of those kings, while the very earliest fall in the 4th millennium BC and apparently describe the birth of important gods to whom the respective temples were dedicated and who may have been regarded as the progenitors of Palenque's royal house.

The meaning of many noncalendrical signs and even of complete clauses is not known, but there is a difference between this and assigning an actual Maya word to an ancient glyph or a sentence to a glyphic clause. While it is certain that the language of the Classic inscriptions was Mayan, it is also certain that it was more archaic than any

Uxmal

Wood carvings

of the Mayan languages spoken at the time of the conquest, six centuries after the Classic downfall. The three extant Maya codices, none dating earlier than AD 1100, contain a strong phonetic component, in fact a kind of syllabary, which can be successfully read as Yucatec-Maya, but the Classic peoples of the Central Subregion more likely spoke an ancestor of the Cholan branch of Maya. Furthermore, Maya hieroglyphic writing covers the entire span from c. AD 300 to the conquest, during which time both the language or languages and the writing system itself must have undergone extensive evolution.

In writing systems in general, there is usually a development from pictographic signs, in which a picture stands for a word or concept, through logographic systems in which words are still the basic unit but phoneticism is employed to reduce ambiguities (as in Chinese), to phonetic syllabaries, and finally to alphabets. Probably most Classic Maya hieroglyphs are logograms with a mainly ideographic orientation, and it seems that there was a considerable degree of flexibility in how the words and sentences could be written. By the Post-Classic, this had been codified into a much more rigid system closely resembling that of Japanese, in which a well-defined syllabary can supplement or even replace logograms. There are approximately 300 to 500 logograms in Classic Maya (the number varies according to how one separates affixes from so-called main signs), but it will probably be several years before the majority of these are satisfactorily deciphered. One can, however, expect great progress in unravelling their meaning in specific contexts.

Classic Maya religion.   Most of what is known about ancient Maya religion is inferred from the descriptions that the Spanish friars have left of Maya life and thought on the eve of the conquest. All modern scholars have stressed the deep religious conservatism and resistance to change of the Maya, and it is highly likely that the 16th-century picture was not appreciably different from that prevailing in the Late Classic, in spite of centuries of Mexican contact.

Their view of the universe was essentially that of all Meso-Americans; there were four world directions, each associated with a colour and with a tree on the summit of which sat a particular bird. The heavens were 13-layered, and the underworld was stratified into nine layers. Classic Maya art indicates that the Earth was thought of as the back of a great saurian, floating in a pond with water lilies and fish.

The world directions were reached by four roads emanating from the "green tree of abundance," a gigantic silk-cotton tree at the Earth's centre. The counterparts of these divine roads are probably the great limestone causeways at such sites as Tikal. In the 16th century, important ceremonies were held for the impending New Year, at which time there were processions to shrines at the four entrances to a settlement. Perhaps the temple-pyramids found at the ends of causeways in Classic cities were the prototypes for such shrines.

It has been denied that there was any such thing as a pantheon of deities in Classic times, the idea being that the worship of images was introduced by the Toltec or Itzá invaders, or both, in the Post-Classic. Several gods who play significant roles in the Post-Classic codices, however, can be identified on Maya monuments. The most important of these is Itzamná, the supreme Maya deity, who functioned as the original creator-god, as well as lord of the fire and therefore of the hearth. In his serpent form, he appears on the ceremonial bar held in the arms of Maya rulers on Classic stelae. Another ophidian deity recognizable in Classic reliefs is the Feathered Serpent, known to the Maya as Kukulcán. Probably the most ubiquitous of all is the being known only as God K, a deity with a baroquely branching nose who may have functioned as a god of royal descent; he is often held as a kind of sceptre in rulers' hands.

The Classic Maya lavished great attention on their royal dead, who almost surely were thought of as descended from the gods and partaking of their divine essence. Many reliefs and all of the pictorial pottery found in tombs deal with the underworld and the dangerous voyage of the soul through that land. Classic Maya funerary ceramics show that this dark land was ruled by a number of gods, including several sinister old men often embellished with jaguar emblems, the jaguar being associated with the night and the nether regions.

Contrary to what has often been claimed, the Classic Maya practiced human sacrifice on an extensive scale. Torture followed by decapitation was probably most common, on the evidence of pictorial ceramics, but heart sacrifice has also been depicted on the monuments. The victims were probably captives, as in non-Maya Mexico. Remains found in the passage leading to the tomb of the Temple of the Inscriptions at Palenque show that this practice was sometimes carried out to ensure companions for the deceased king in the other world. Self-sacrifice or mutilation was also a common practice; blood drawn by jabbing spines through the ear or penis, or by drawing a thorn-studded cord through the tongue, was spattered on paper as an offering to the gods.

Society and political life.   There is a vast gap between the lavishly stocked tombs of the Maya elite who ran the ceremonial centres and the simple graves of the peasantry. Careful measurements of the skeletons found in tombs and graves have also demonstrated that the Maya ruling class was much taller than the tillers of the soil who provided them tribute. It is likely that this gulf was unspannable, for throughout Meso-America the rulers and nobility were believed to have been created separately from commoners.

The most astonishing testimony to this royal cult is the temple-pyramid itself, for in almost every one explored there is a great tomb hidden in its base. On death, each ruler might have been the object of ancestor worship by members of his lineage, the departed leader having become one with the god from whom he claimed descent. Ancestor worship, in fact, seems to be at the heart of ancient and modern society and religion among the Maya.

The ordinary folk may have participated in the ceremonies of even the greatest Maya centres. The modern highland Maya have a complex ceremonial life in which a man advances through a series of increasingly prestigious *cargos*, or "burdens," each one of which costs him a great deal of money and requires that he reside in the otherwise nearly empty centre for a year at a time carrying out his religious duties. The same may have prevailed in Classic times, but it should be remembered that all activities were then under the direction of a hereditary and divine elite class, long since destroyed throughout Maya land by the Spaniards.

Apparently, warfare was a continuing preoccupation of the Maya lords, but it was carried out not so much for territorial aggrandizement as to gain captives for slavery and sacrifice. It is not yet known whether any one centre dominated the others, but the inscriptions will some day throw light on Maya territorial organization during the Late Classic.

It has often been said that the Maya realm was a theocracy, with all power in the hands of the priests. That this is a misconception is apparent from the monuments themselves, which show kings, queens, heirs, and war prisoners, but no figures surely identifiable as priests. In 16th-century Yucatán, the priesthood was hereditary, and it is reported that younger sons of lords often took on that vocation. Quite probably such a class was also to be found among the Late Classic Maya, but neither for the Maya nor for any other Classic civilization of Meso-America can the term theocracy be justified.

The collapse of Classic Maya civilization.   In the last century of the Classic, Maya civilization went into a decline from which it never recovered. Beginning about AD 790 in the western edge of the Central Subregion, such ceremonial activity as the erection of stelae virtually came to a standstill. During the next 40 years this cultural paralysis spread gradually eastward, by which time the great Classic civilization of the Maya had all but atrophied. A date in the Maya calendar corresponding to AD 889 is inscribed on the last dated monuments in the Central Subregion; soon after the close of the 9th century it is clear that almost all of this region was abandoned.

For this event, which must have been one of the greatest human tragedies of all time, there are few convincing explanations. It now seems that the Classic Maya civilization in the region of its greatest development went out "not with a bang but a whimper." Massive foreign invasions can be discounted as a factor, but non-Maya elements did appear in the west at the same time as ceremonial activity terminated. These became the inheritors of whatever was left of the old civilization of the Central Subregion after AD 900, having established trading colonies and even a few minor ceremonial centres on its peripheries.

Whatever incursions did take place from the west were piecemeal and probably the result of the general decline, rather than its cause. Similarly, there is little reason to believe that there were peasant revolts on a general scale. The only real fact is that most of the inhabitants of the Central Subregion went elsewhere. Probably some were absorbed by such still flourishing ceremonial centres of the Northern Subregion as Uxmal and Kabah, while others might have migrated up into the congenial highlands of Chiapas. Although a population explosion and severe ecological abuse must have played their role in the tragedy, the full story of the decline and fall of this brilliant aboriginal civilization will only be told when the last Maya inscriptions can be read.   (M.D.C.)

Post-Classic Period (900–1519)
DEFINITION OF THE POST-CLASSIC
The final period of Meso-American history is referred to as the Post-Classic. Its beginning is usually placed at 900, and it terminates with the arrival of the Spanish conquistador Hernán Cortés in 1519 or his conquest of the Aztecs in 1521. The 900 date is based on two considerations: first, the 10th century witnessed the catastrophic collapse of the Lowland Maya civilization and the cessation of the custom of erecting monuments dated by the Long Count; second, it was also the approximate date of the founding of the city of Tula in central Mexico and the rise of a people called the Toltecs, who, according to the historical annals, built the first great empire in Meso-America. At one time it was thought that the date marked the collapse of all of the regional Classic civilizations of the area as the result of massive population dislocation. But it now appears that some Classic civilizations declined as early as 750, whereas others persisted until as late as 1200. The period is usually divided into two phases: Early Post-Classic (900–1200) and Late Post-Classic (1200–1519), the former equivalent with the period of the Toltecs, the latter with that of the Aztecs.

The Post-Classic period as a whole has also been distinguished from the Classic on the basis of assumed major changes in Meso-American political, economic, and social institutions. It has been asserted, for example, that the Classic period was one of relatively peaceful contact between polities, of the absence of large imperialistic states and empires (and of the militaristic élan and organization that accompanies such states). The Classic has been further characterized by the absence of true cities, by theocratic rather than secular government, and by an overall superiority of arts and crafts, with the exception of metallurgy, which appears for the first time in the Post-Classic period. In contrast, the Post-Classic was characterized as a period of intense warfare and highly organized military organization, of empires and cities, of secular government, and of overall artistic decline.

Recent research, however, has cast considerable doubt on these conclusions. Many of the contrasts were drawn from events in the Lowland Maya area and applied to the entire culture area; others were concluded essentially by a comparison of the Classic Maya of the lowland tropical forest of northern Guatemala and the Yucatán Peninsula with the Post-Classic Aztec living in Central Mexico in a dry mountain basin 7,000 feet above sea level. The differences, in part, are the product of separate culture evolution, conditioned by ecological factors. Cities and large states comparable to those built by the Toltecs and Aztecs were present in Early Classic times at Teotihuacán in Central Mexico and probably at Monte Albán in Oaxaca.

Militarism was at least significant enough to be a major artistic theme throughout the Classic period, even among the Lowland Maya. One could also question the criterion of artistic decline, since a number of Post-Classic crafts were highly developed, such as Aztec sculpture, Mixtec ceramics and metallurgy, and Zapotec architecture.

The separation between Post-Classic and Classic is therefore little more than a convenient way of splitting up the long chronicle of Meso-American cultural development into manageable units for discussion and analysis. It is a period also in which historical traditions combine with archaeological data, whereas the Classic essentially lacks a written history. Perhaps this is the best rationale for definition of the period.

At the time of the Spanish conquest, Meso-America was occupied by a number of peoples speaking languages as distinct from each other as English is from Chinese. On the Central Gulf Coast and adjacent escarpment were the Totonac; in Oaxaca and adjacent portions of Puebla and Guerrero, two major ethnic groups, the Mixtec and the Zapotec, shared the western and eastern portions of the area, respectively; and in Michoacán lived the Tarascans. Various peoples of the Maya linguistic family occupied most of Guatemala, the Yucatán Peninsula, eastern Tabasco, highland Chiapas; a detached group, the Huastec, occupied the North Gulf Coast. An equally widespread family, the Nahua (to which the Aztec belonged) occupied most of the Central Plateau, a huge area in the northwest frontier, portions of Guerrero, the Pacific Coast of Chiapas and Guatemala (where they were known as the Pipil), and the South Gulf Coast. Some detached groups had spread beyond the frontier of Meso-America into Nicaragua and Panama. The linguistic family to which the Nahua belong (the Uto-Aztecan) is the only Meso-American family with affinities to languages north of the Rio Grande, including those of such western United States Indians as the Hopi, Paiute, and Shoshoni. *The Nahua peoples*

One of the Nahua-speaking nations, the México or Tenochcas (or the Aztecs, as they are commonly called), were the dominant people in Meso-America in 1519, having conquered an empire estimated as covering 80,000 square miles and having a population of 5,000,000 to 6,000,000 people.

All of these diverse ethnic groups shared a common cultural tradition, but separate historical origins and environmental factors had also produced a substantial degree of regional differentiation. Most of the cultural characteristics of the area go back at least to the beginning of the Post-Classic, and many appeared in Classic times. The various regional cultures and languages have great time depths and were undoubtedly present during the Classic period. Common institutional characteristics included organization into centralized polities, including populations minimally in the tens of thousands, with a formal government, supported by a highly organized taxation system; stratification into social classes (including slave and serf classes); occupational specialization—in some areas full time with a guildlike organization; highly organized local and interregional trade involving professional merchants and regularly meeting markets; and a professional priesthood.

The technological base of this elaborate institutional structure seems weak by western European standards, since the primary technology (*i.e.*, the tools used to manufacture other technology) was based on chipped and ground stone (metal being reserved primarily for ornaments). Since draft animals were absent, all power was based on human energy. The economic base of the civilization was a highly productive agriculture, but the basic tool kit was primitive—stone axes for clearing vegetation and a number of wooden digging tools for working the soil. The crop complex was a rich one, with maize serving as the staple food and beans an important source of protein. But the list of secondary crops is impressive: chili peppers, tomatoes, squashes, sweet potatoes, manioc, cotton, tobacco, cacaos, pineapples, papayas, maguey, nopales, zapotes, peanuts, avocados, paper figs, and many others. *Post-Classic technology*

Many crops were limited to particular environmental zones, thus acting as a major stimulus to trade. In many areas, particularly the tropical lowlands, the system of farming was swidden; *i.e.*, a system in which forests are cleared, planted for up to three years, and rested for longer periods to restore fertility and eliminate the more difficult weeds. This regular rotation of fields resulted in high production per capita but had low demographic potential because in any given year most of the land lay fallow. In some lowland areas permanent grain and orchard cropping were practiced. In the drier highlands, a number of specialized techniques were used, and agriculture was more intensive. Particularly important were terracing, irrigation, and swamp reclamation. The per capita productivity of highland agriculture was probably less (because of the higher labour input), but the demographic capacity was considerably greater than in the lowlands. As a result of these highly effective approaches to farming, the population was dense when compared to western Europe in the 16th century. Population estimates for the conquest period have varied from 3,000,000 to 30,000,000; a reasonable estimate is between 12,000,000 and 15,000,000.

The diet of the average Meso-American was one of those cultural aspects that was relatively uniform throughout the area. Dried maize was boiled in lime-impregnated water to soften the hull, ground into a dough on milling stones (*manos* and *metates*), and then either made into pancakes (*tortillas*) or mixed with water and drunk as a gruel (*pozol*). The tortillas were eaten with sauces prepared from chili peppers and tomatoes, along with boiled beans. This was essentially the diet of the peasant, with the addition of pulque, the fermented sap of the maguey, at higher altitudes. To this were added the other crops in minor quantities and combinations depending on the specific local environment. Luxury foods included chocolate drinks, meats (from game or from the only two domestic animals of significance, the hairless dog and the turkey), and fish. The diet of the peasant, as is the case even today, was low in animal protein; but apparently the quantity of vegetable protein ingested made up for this deficiency.

Post-Classic arts and crafts

Major Post-Classic Meso-American crafts were cotton and maguey fibre weaving; ceramics for pottery vessels, figurines, and musical instruments; stone sculpture; featherwork used for personal and architectural ornament; lapidary work (jadeite, jade, serpentine, and turquoise); metalwork (using gold, copper, and, more rarely, silver) for ornaments and a few tools; woodworking, the products including large dugout canoes, sculpture, magnificently made drums, stools, and a great variety of household items; baskets for containers and mats; painting; and, most particularly, stone and lime concrete masonry architecture.

On the intellectual, ideological, and religious levels, although some diversity and certain elaborations occurred in some regions, there was a fundamental unity to the Meso-American area, the product of centuries of political and economic ties. The religion was pantheistic, with numerous gods specialized along the lines of human activities. There were gods for basic activities such as war, reproduction, and agriculture; cosmogenic gods who created the universe and invented man's culture; gods of craft groups, social classes, political systems and their subdivisions. Gods were all-powerful and had to be constantly propitiated with offerings and sacrifices, a concept reaching its peak in personal bloodletting and human sacrifice. Certain gods, such as the god of rain (called Tlaloc in Central Mexico), were found throughout the area. A fundamental concept was that of a quadripartite multilevel universe that, by 1519, had gone through five creations and four destructions. Meso-American religion heavily emphasized the astral bodies, particularly the Sun, the Moon, and Venus, and the observations of the movement of these bodies by the astronomer-priests were extraordinarily detailed and accurate. The major purpose of these observations was astrological, and the Meso-American priests had developed a number of time counts, or calendrical rounds, based in part on these observations. Two

basic calendars, a 260-day divinatory calendar and one based on the solar year of 365 days, were found all over the area (see CALENDAR: *Pre-Columbian*).

One of the great intellectual achievements of Meso-American civilization was writing; in Post-Classic times books were made from the inner bark of the paper-fig tree and used to record calendars, astronomical tables, dynastic history, taxes, and court records.

Religion was a pervasive force in Meso-American life, as the art demonstrates; and considerable surplus energy was devoted to it (*e.g.*, temple construction, support of a numerous professional priesthood). Many writers have stated that the major focus of Meso-American culture was in this sphere. In fact, the contrast between Post-Classic and Classic was in part based on the presumed even greater emphasis on religion in the art and architecture of the latter period.

THE HISTORICAL ANNALS

The rise of the Aztecs. A major characteristic of the Post-Classic in contrast to the Classic is the abundant historical documentation available for the former. The Aztec record is particularly rich, and much of it is undoubtedly genuine, although there is always the possibility that records were rewritten or doctored for political reasons. One of the functions of Meso-American writing was to record the succession and achievements of dynastic lines, and consequently it served as a validation of power. Virtually all of the dynasties of the local states recorded their history. A problem in the utilization of these documents, other than the low number of survivals, is the fact that many of them have strong mythological overtones. The Aztecs themselves, for example, as creators of a great empire, explained their rise in part to the fact that they were the chosen people of the sun god Huitzilopochtli, or Tonatiuh. They started their history as a poor, nomadic tribe from the north, who entered the Basin of Mexico, led by a magician priest, and ultimately settled on the lake islands because of a series of astrological predictions and signs. They lived for a while as a subject people and then embarked on their destined role as conquerors and priests of the sun god. Virtually all historic traditions of local groups begin with a migration, a period of trials, and ultimate success—and some records even claim that the people were hunters and gatherers during the early part of their history.

On the northern frontier of Meso-America, in the arid north Mexican plateau, true hunters and gatherers, referred to as the "chichimeca" by the civilized peoples, did actually reside in 1519. The name chichimeca was frequently applied to the migrant groups. It is difficult to see how hunting and gathering bands could successfully invade areas of dense civilized populations; but agricultural barbarians, during periods of dynastic weakness, undoubtedly could. In fact, the term chichimeca was also applied to agricultural but less civilized peoples (such as the Otomí in Central Mexico) and thus connoted a lack of polish or a rustic life-style. Since the northwest portion of Meso-America was occupied by such people and since they were Nahua in speech, the legends of periodic north to south migrations of invaders may have a factual basis but probably refer to movements of agricultural rather than hunting and gathering peoples.

The chichimeca peoples

The histories of these invading groups take on a more convincing historical character after the legends of migration. In the Aztec case they record the founding of Tenochtitlán in 1325. By 1376 the Aztecs had increased in numbers and prestige sufficiently to obtain a member of the ruling family of Culhuacan, a neighbouring state, to rule as their tlatoani, or king. His name was Acamapichtli. The Aztecs at this time were paying tribute to another state, Azcapotzalco, on the lake shore; and they remained under this obligation through the reigns of his two successors, Huitzilhuitl (1391–1415) and Chimalpopoca (1415–26). During the reign of Chimalpopoca, Maxtla, the ruler of Azcapotzalco, attempted to secure tighter control over subject states by replacing their tlatoanis with his own men. He succeeded in arranging the assassination of Chimalpopoca and the exile of Nezahualcóyotl, ruler of Texcoco, a state on the east shore of Lake Texcoco. In response to these acts, a coalition was formed between Nezahualcóyotl, Itzcóatl (Chimalpopoca's successor), and another small state (Tlacopan), and the power of Azcapotzalco was broken.

The triple alliance

A triple alliance was then formed between Tenochtitlán, Texcoco, and Tlacopan, which by 1519 resulted in the dominance of Aztec Tenochtitlán. Under the Aztec rulers Itzcoatl (1428–40), Montezuma I (1440–69), Axayacatl (1469–81), Tizoc (1481–86), Ahuitzotl (1486–1503), and Montezuma II (1502–20), and the two Texcocan rulers—Nezahualcóyotl (1431–72) and Nezahualpilli (1472–1516)—the triple alliance succeeded in conquering the vast domain previously described. Tlacopan seems to have been relegated to an inferior political role early in the history.

The records of the Aztecs and neighbouring states in the Basin of Mexico between 1300–1519 are relatively free from mythological tales and have sufficient cross-referencing to present a reasonably clear picture of military events, dynastic succession, institutional changes, and economic development. The period from 1200 to 1300 is essentially one of migration legends of the dynasties of the various states, the historical traditions of which are discussed below.

The question of the Toltecs. The historical traditions also state that these migrations were responsible, along with a series of natural disasters, for the collapse of a great empire ruled by a people called the Toltecs from their capital of Tollan, or Tula. Many of the conquest period dynasties, not only in Central Mexico but even as far afield as highland Guatemala and Yucatán Peninsula, claimed descent from the Toltecs, apparently as a result of their dispersion after the fall of Tula.

The traditions describe the Toltecs as the first civilizers, the first city builders, and the originators of craft skills and astrological knowledge. The major questions are: Did the Toltecs really exist as a people? Where was Tollan? Did these people actually play the extraordinary political and cultural role ascribed to them?

To begin with, the annals themselves are in fundamental disagreement with respect to dates and the lists of Toltec kings. There are at least three major chronologies of the Toltec Empire (see the chart).

Ixtlilxóchitl		Anales de Cuauhtitlan		Codex Ramirez	
Chalchiuhtlanetzin	510–562	Huetzin	869–?		
Ixtlilcuechahauac	562–614	Totepeuh	?–887	Mixcoatl	900–947
Huetzin	614–666	Ihuitimal	887–923		
Totepeuh	666–718	Topiltzin	923–947		980–999
Nacoxoc	718–770	Matlacxochitl	947–983		1000–34
Mitl-tlacomihua	770–829	Nauhyotzin	983–997		1034–49
Xihuiquenitzan	829–833	Matlaccoatzin	997–1025		1049–77
Iztaccaltzin	833–885	Tlilcoatzin	1025–46		1077–98
Topiltzin	885–959	Huemac	1047–1122		1098–1168

Ixtlilxóchitl's dates place the Toltecs well within the Classic period of Meso-American archaeology, but the others would correlate them with the early portion of the Post-Classic. Most writers favour the later dates, but this would mean that the Toltecs were not the first civilized peoples in Meso-America, or at least in Central Mexico, as they claim.

Mythic evidence

Adding further doubt to the veracity of the Toltec history is the admixture of myth and magic in the annals, not only at the beginning (which, like the histories of later dynasties, begins with a migration under a magician priest) but throughout the narrative. The ruler Topiltzin, for example, is also called Quetzalcóatl (the name of a god); another ruler, Ce Acatl, is opposed by Tezcatlipoca (also a god) and is driven out of Tula. He flees with his followers to the Gulf of Mexico and embarks on a raft of serpents. The story sounds like a duplicate of the cosmic myth or conflict between the two gods. Interestingly, the Maya in Yucatán had a tradition of a landing on the west coast made by foreigners, under a leader named Kukulcán (which in Maya means Feathered Serpent, the meaning also of the Nahua Quetzalcóatl), who founded a city at Chichén Itzá and ruled over the Maya.

In spite of all the objections, the traditions of a great empire and of the city of Tula are so persistent that they must refer to some historical event and, indeed, have some archaeological support.

ARCHAEOLOGICAL REMAINS OF POST-CLASSIC CIVILIZATION

The early Post-Classic period (900–1200) in Central Mexico is associated with three major sites, all of which probably began in Classic times: Cholula in Puebla, Xochicalco in Morelos, and Tula in Hidalgo. Cholula was a major centre as far back as Early Classic times, probably as a political dependency of Teotihuacán. It reached its maximum growth in Late Classic times, following the collapse of Teotihuacán, when the largest structure ever built by Meso-Americans was erected—a pyramid platform nearly 200 feet (60 metres) high and with a base measuring 1,000 feet (300 metres) to a side. In Post-Classic times Cholula continued as a major religious and cultural centre. Xochicalco probably was of minor significance in Early Classic times; but it went through a phase of explosive growth in the Late Classic and was probably abandoned by 1200, possibly earlier. Tula, on the other hand, a small centre in the Late Classic, went through a rapid growth during the period 900–1200 and then declined to a provincial centre in the Late Post-Classic. There is a strong suggestion that the demise of Classic Teotihuacán was in part related to the emergence of one or all of these major centres.

Tula. The location of the Toltec capital of Tollan, or Tula, is not certain. The archaeological site located on a low ridge near the contemporary town of Tula has been the persistent choice of all historians since the conquest, in part because of the coincidence of place-names. There is further support for this identification in that the annals provide a great number of place-names that have persisted since the conquest. There is also support for the identification in that the glyph Ce Acatl, the birthday and birth name of the great Toltec leader Quetzalcóatl Topiltzin has been found carved on a hill near Tula. Moreover, the sculpture from the site is heavily loaded with symbolism that relates to the Quetzalcóatl cosmology and cosmogony. It clearly was the city of the god Quetzalcóatl. The confusion between the god and the ruler can be ascribed to the fact that the name Quetzalcóatl may have served as a title of office carried by all Toltec rulers. The archaeological dates are in agreement with the *Anales de Cuauhtitlan* and the Codex Ramirez (see below *The nature of the sources*).

The question of Tula's existence

The major factors that have made some researchers reluctant to accept this identification lies in the claim that Tula was the capital of a great Pan-Meso-American empire and that the Toltecs were the first civilizers in Central Mexico. Archaeologically, it is quite clear that Tula was preceded by the great Classic centre of Teotihuacán. Tula as a site does not really approach the earlier Teotihuacán or the later Tenochtitlán in size, in the number of public buildings, or in estimated population. Furthermore, although some generic stylistic elements of the art and architecture of Tula are widespread, the style, in an integrated specific sense, is limited (with one notable exception) to a small area in Central Mexico. These facts make it difficult to accept Tula as the capital of a great empire. But archaeological evidence of even the Aztec Empire is skimpy. In both cases, this may mean that the expansion was a rapid, explosive one that failed to last long enough to register these effects. But at least in the case of Tenochtitlán it did result in the rapid growth of a truly gigantic urban centre.

Because of these objections and because Teotihuacán fits better the description of the Toltecs as the builders of the first truly civilized society in Central Mexico, that site must still be considered a possible candidate.

The art and architecture of Tula shows a striking similarity to the later art and architecture of Tenochtitlán, and the themes represented in the art indicate a close approximation in religious ideology and behaviour. The symbols of sun sacrifice and the marching predators represented in sculpture both suggest that the Aztecs' concept of themselves as the warrior priests of the sun god was directly borrowed from the people of Tula.

On the basis of the symbolism represented in the carvings at Structure B it has been concluded that it was dedicated to the god Quetzalcóatl, lending further support to the identification of the site as the Toltec capital.

Chichén Itzá. Also in support of the identification of Tula as the Toltec capital are the architectural characteristics and stylistic features of the sculpture of a large site in northern Yucatan called Chichén Itzá. The resemblance between the two sites is extraordinarily close. At Chichén are found flat beam and masonry roofs (contrasting sharply with the typical Maya corbelled vault), serpent columns, colonnaded halls attached to the bases of temples, altars with Atlantean figures, sculptured representations of skulls and crossbones, marching felines, canines and raptorial birds devouring human hearts, and depictions of warriors with typical Toltec accoutrements. Furthermore, there are even scenes showing Toltec and Maya warriors in combat. The Temple of the Warriors at Chichén Itzá looks like an attempt to duplicate a temple pyramid at Tula.

Tula and
Chichén
Itzá
compared

One of the puzzling aspects of the relationship between the two sites is that the public architecture of Chichén Itzá is actually more monumental than that at Tula, leading at least one Meso-American specialist to believe that Tula's style was derived from Chichén. Many of the stylistic features themselves, however, have prototypes in Classic Teotihuacán, whereas there is little in Classic Maya culture that could be considered as the source. What is more probable, and this agrees with the Toltec version of the relationship, is that the Toltec state in Yucatan was politically independent from Tula. The presence of rival states in central Mexico such as Xochicalco and Cholula may have kept the core of the Toltec polity relatively restricted in space. The much larger area and population controlled by the Toltec state at Chichén would explain the differences in the scale of architecture. The superior military organization and equipment of the Toltecs might explain their apparent success in Yucatán.

Archaeological unity of the Post-Classic. The Post-Classic period of Meso-American archaeology generally is a period characterized by considerable regionalism combined with a certain degree of uniformity. To a great extent, the latter was the product of the large states and extensive trade networks centred in the central plateau region. The Early Post-Classic in some areas may be described as a continuation of the Late Classic; on the Gulf Coast, for example, sites like Tajin continued to be occupied, while in the Valley of Oaxaca (although Monte Albán was abandoned) the Zapotec tradition continued with the new centre at Mitla. In other areas, new styles either begin or reach their climactic development, such as the Mixteca-Puebla style in painting, ceramics, and metallurgy, which either evolved in western Oaxaca or more probably at Cholula in Puebla. On the Guatemalan Pacific piedmont and in Tabasco, two specialized ceramic traditions (both of which begin in Late Classic times) evolved and were widely traded: (1) plumbate (so called because of its slip, which has an unusually high iron content in the natural clay that fires to a lead colour glaze); and (2) Fine Orange (so called because of its fine-grained temperless paste).

Ceramic
traditions

The unity of the Post-Classic consists primarily of the diffusion of religious ideology, particularly the sun god-warfare-sacrificial complex and of the related institutional development such as the military orders (the latter probably originated at Classic Teotihuacán). This ideology clearly originated in Central Mexico, either at Cholula or Tula or both. The specific artistic style of representation of the themes in painting and sculpture spread as well. Along with this was diffused a specific style of representation of the social calendar and writing generally and much greater emphasis on the 52-year cycle. The specific style most probably originated at Cholula.

In the highland areas of Meso-America the Late Post-Classic was a period of maximum population growth. The Early Post-Classic was, however, the period of maximum expansion of sedentary peoples on the northern frontier, probably the product of minor changes in climate as a result of increased rainfall. This frontier retracted substantially in Late Post-Classic times, possibly because the rainfall decreased. This was perhaps the major factor in the precipitation of barbarous tribes into the plateau, as the annals state.

The Post-Classic, over large areas of the lowlands, on the other hand, was strikingly different. One of the most intriguing problems of Meso-American archaeology is the peculiar sequence of events in the Lowland Maya area. At the time of European contact much of the northern portion of the Yucatán was well settled. A narrow band of densely settled country also extended along the east coast south to Belize City and along the entire length of the west coast (where it joined another area of substantial settlement in the south Gulf Coast). Most of the heart of the peninsula, the department of Petén in Guatemala, and large portions of Campeche and Quintana Roo in Mexico (the most densely settled portion of the Classic Maya territory) were virtually abandoned.

One of the major problems of Meso-American archaeology is the explanation of this massive population decline. The immediate causes are clear: it must have been the product of migrations out of the area or a set of internal factors that caused an in situ decline or both. Various hypotheses as to processes and causes have been suggested. These may be grouped in the following categories: natural disasters (earthquakes, famines, epidemics, and hurricanes have all been suggested); ecological processes (primarily the deterioration of the natural environment by overintensification of land use in response to population pressure); and sociopolitical processes (internal warfare, invasion from outside, peasant revolts, breakdown of critical trade networks). Some of these are clearly derivations from others or are not explanations but descriptions of events that were produced by other processes. It seems certain that the causes were multiple and in some way interrelated.

Reasons
for the
decline in
population

Of great interest is the fact that at least one other lowland area, the Pacific Coastal plain of Guatemala, experienced a comparable Post-Classic decline.

AZTEC CULTURE TO THE TIME OF THE SPANISH CONQUEST

The nature of the sources. At the time of the Spanish conquest the dominant people of Meso-America was the Aztec. This description is based primarily on written documents from the 16th century but also includes some archaeological data. The literature, both published and unpublished, of the 16th century is enormous and takes in all aspects of Aztec culture. Much of it covers the period within a few decades after the conquest; and it is uncertain how much change had occurred because of the introduction of Spanish culture. Some Aztec institutions, such as the military orders, were immediately abolished by the Spaniards; and the sources, therefore, give only the barest outline of their organization. The sources can be classified by content and purpose into five categories:

First, there are the eyewitness accounts of Aztec culture on the eve of the conquest. These, of course, are the most directly pertinent sources because they describe Aztec culture before it became transformed by the Spanish conquest, but they are the least detailed of the sources.

Second, there are the post-conquest histories of the Aztec written in Spanish. Within a few decades of the conquest, a series of histories had been written in the Spanish language, based in part on Aztec books and in part on upper class informants.

Third, there are post-conquest ethnographic accounts written in Spanish and Nahua. They are comparable in methodology and subject matter to the kinds of studies of native peoples conducted by present-day anthropologists. One of them, Bernardino de Sahagún's monumental *Historia general de las cosas de Nueva España*, covers virtually all aspects of Aztec culture. It is particularly detailed in religion, ethnobotany, folk medicine, and economics. As a source, it has the added value of being written in the Aztec language.

Fourth, there are the native books, or codices. Because of their religious content only a small fraction of these escaped destruction by the Spaniards. What few have survived usually come accompanied by Spanish nota-

The
codices

tions. These sources are limited in scope and subject matter but nevertheless are valuable documents, particularly with respect to history and calendrics. Among those that were prepared in Central Mexico are the Codex Chimalpopoca (also called the *Anales de Cuauhtitlan*), the Codex Ramirez (also called the *Historia de los mexicanos por sus pinturas*), both historical texts. Other native books include the Codex Borbonicus, a calendar; the Codex Badianus, a herbal with magnificent drawings of medicinal plants; the Codex Mendoza and the *Matrícula de tributos*, both tax documents of the Aztec Empire.

A fifth source is comprised of official ecclesiastic and government records. Much of this literature is unpublished. Its purpose was administrative rather than intellectual, but it has provided an extraordinarily rich source of information for all 16th-century ethnic groups. The documents vary from tax lists, censuses, and marriage and baptismal records to broad geographic–economic surveys. One of the most valuable of the last type are the *Relaciones geográficas* of 1579–80, a survey ordered by Philip II of all of his overseas possessions. A formal questionnaire was drawn up that demanded information from each town in the empire on virtually all aspects of Meso-American life: questions on the natural environment and resources, crops, population history, settlement patterns, taxes paid, markets and trade, the language, native history and customs, and progress of the missionization program.

This information, combined with archaeological data, gives a fairly detailed picture of Aztec culture at the time of the Spanish conquest.

Agriculture. The homeland of the Aztecs, from which they ruled their vast domain, was a large (about 3,000 square miles, or 8,000 square kilometres), mountain-rimmed, basin with a floor at approximately 7,000 feet (2,200 metres) above sea level. The surrounding ranges reached a maximum elevation of 18,000 feet (5,500 metres) with the volcano of Popocatépetl. The annual rainfall varied from 20 to 35 inches (500 to 900 millimetres) in the valley floor to a maximum of 50 inches (1,300 millimetres) on the southern escarpment. Approximately 80 percent of the rain fell between May 1 and October 1. Because of the high elevation, the area suffered from severe winter frosts that normally began in mid-October and lasted until the end of March. Normally, the rainfall was adequate for maize, even in the drier portions of the basin; but a major problem was the timing of the rains and the frosts. A delay of the rainfall to mid- or late June, accompanied by early autumn frosts, could produce crop disasters.

Another major problem for the pre-Hispanic cultivator was the paucity of level land. Much of the land surface is sloping, and the problem of soil erosion was acute. Furthermore, of the 1,600 square miles (4,150 square kilometres) of relatively level land, 400 square miles were occupied by a chain of lakes; and much of the immediate lakeshore plain was waterlogged.

Because of the effect of elevation on the growing season, the areas above 8,300 feet (2,800 metres) were also unsuitable for cultivation, removing an additional 400 square miles from the agricultural resource. Even within zones of cultivation, the presence of steep slopes and thin soil reduced even further the area of cultivation. It is doubtful that more than 50 percent of the basin was suitable for labour-extensive methods of cultivation. Yet in 1519 it supported a population of 1,000,000 to 1,-500,000; *i.e.*, a density of 500 people per square mile (200 per square kilometre), the densest population in Meso-American history. This was achieved by an extraordinarily intensive system of farming that involved a number of specialized techniques. Soil fertility was maintained by plant and animal fertilizers, by short-cycle fallowing, and by irrigation. In gently sloping terrain, erosion was controlled by earth and maguey terraces, in steeper areas by stone terracing. The problem of humidity was solved by canal irrigation of both the floodwater and permanent type. Much of the irrigation was done just before planting in April and May in order to give the crop a head start and hence avoid the autumn frosts. Terracing functioned

also as a method of conserving humidity. There is also evidence that dry-farming techniques were applied to store moisture in the soil. The most impressive achievement of Aztec agriculture, however, was that of swamp reclamation, even including colonization of the lakes. This system of farming, called chinampa, was first applied to Lake Chalco. The lake covered approximately 60 square miles and apparently varied in its character from swamps to ponds of fairly deep, open water. By a process varying from digging drainage ditches to artificial construction of land from lake mud and vegetation, most of the lake was converted to highly productive agricultural land. A series of masonry causeway dikes were constructed across the lake to control flooding. By a system of dikes and sluice gates the Aztecs even managed to convert a portion of saline Lake Texcoco, the largest and lowest lake in the basin to a freshwater bay for further chinampa colonization.

The total area colonized was probably in the neighbourhood of 30,000 acres (12,000 hectares); and much of the food base for Tenochtitlán, the Aztec capital, depended on these lands. By a comparable method, much of the waterlogged lakeshore plain was also converted into agricultural land. Particularly impressive is the fact that all of these techniques of food production were achieved by human power and simple hand tools.

Aside from agriculture, the basin had a number of major resources, some of which were exploited not only for local consumption but also to supply other areas of Meso-America. Obsidian, a kind of natural glass, was a superb material for a great variety of stone tools; and the northeastern ranges of the basin contained one of Meso-America's major deposits. Basalt for *manos* and *metates* (milling stones) was also abundant. Lake Texcoco was a major source of salt, and the lakes generally provided waterfowl, fish, and other aquatic foodstuffs. The great pine forests above the limits of agriculture were a major source of lumber. On the other hand, the basin, because of its high elevation, was unsuitable for a great variety of tropical products including cotton, paper, tropical roots and fruits, tobacco, copal incense, rubber, cacao, honey, precious feathers and skins, and such prized goods as metal, jade, and turquoise. The major motivation of Aztec conquest was to obtain control of these resources.

Social and political organization. Technologically, the Aztecs differed little from other Meso-American groups. One of the distinctive aspects of Aztec technology was its differentiation by status levels. The use of most of the extra-local resources noted above was limited to a small upper and middle class; and there were striking differences in dress, housing, and diet by social class. Commoners, for example, wore clothing woven from maguey fibre, while the upper classes wore cotton garments. The use of imported foods, at least on a regular basis, was limited to the upper and middle classes. Commoners lived in small adobe or stone and mud huts, the upper and middle class in large multi-roomed palatial houses of cut stone, lime plaster, and concrete.

Aztec social and political organization can be divided into a number of levels of increasing size and complexity of organization. The nuclear family—that is, a pair of cohabiting adults and their unmarried children—formed the lowest level of organization. The nuclear family functioned in procreation, education of children, and as a unit of food preparation and consumption with a well-defined division of labour between husband and wife. Among the Aztecs, however, a number of nuclear families usually resided together in a single cooperating household, or extended family. Such a family usually consisted of a man, his married sons or brothers, and their families. The average peasant household of this type was small. Up to three nuclear families occupied a small multi-room house divided into apartments for each family. The houses were usually placed within a courtyard fenced with organ cactus or adobe walls, forming a compound. The extended family household probably functioned as a unit of land use and food production. In the towns, however, some households could be considerably larger; and the household of Montezuma included several thousand people.

Factors limiting cultivation

Other resources of the basin area

The nuclear family

The calpulli.   A number of households, varying from a few score to several hundred, were organized into an internally complex corporate group referred to as a calpulli by the Aztecs and translated as a barrio ("ward") by the Spaniards. Questions about the structure and function of this level of Aztec organization have caused a great deal of debate among Meso-American specialists. It is clear, however, that it was a physical and territorial unit as well as a socially organized one. It was a unit of land tenure. Calpulli lands were owned communally but were distributed among various households. The household retained the right of usufruct, but only the calpulli as a whole could sell or rent lands. The calpulli rural communities varied considerably in physical appearance. Some were isolated, tightly nucleated physical settlements surrounded by their agricultural land, whereas in others houses were dispersed through the land holdings. In a few cases, they were physically attached as wards to one or more other calpulli. These differences correspond to ecological, economic, and political factors. Rural, dispersed settlements were found on terraced hillsides in which houses were tightly integrated with the terrace; in the chinampa area, each house was placed on its chinampa holding. On the other hand, nucleated, isolated calpulli were found in areas of level land, and the ward type was usually found in the towns and cities. In the latter case, many lost their agricultural character and became units of craft specialization.

The calpulli was a unit of political administration within the larger unit that will be referred to here as the state. It was ruled by a council of household heads presided over by a chief selected by the council from within a particular lineage. The calpulli functioned as a unit of taxation to the central government, as a unit of corvée labour, and as a military regiment.

Structure of the calpulli

The structure of the calpulli is open to question. Some sources call it a kin group, "a lineage" with a common ancestor; and as a result some anthropologists have referred to it as a clan, or sib. There is no evidence, however, of either exogamy or unilineal descent; in fact, marriage records from the post-conquest period show a strong tendency toward endogamy. There is some evidence of internal ranking and significant status differentiation, another non-clanlike feature. The sources also mention smaller territorial subdivisions, referred to as *barrios pequeños,* or "little wards." If these are descent lines, then the calpulli resembles quite closely a type of kin group called by anthropologists a ramage, or a conical clan. This is a group with a myth of common descent, divided up into ranked senior and junior lineages based on the seniority of older versus younger brother in the group genealogy. In support of this reconstruction is the statement that the calpulli god was a deified ancestor.

The calpulli also functioned as a unit of education as each possessed a school for young men—the telpochcalli —primarily for military and moral instruction.

The Aztec state.   Above the level of the calpulli was the state. With the exception of those historical periods when larger polities, such as the Aztec Empire, emerged, such states in Meso-America, including the Basin of Mexico, were small. Just prior to the Aztec expansion there were 50 or 60 such states in the basin with an average size of about 50 to 60 square miles. In 1519 these once independent domains had an average population of 25,000 to 30,000 people. In less densely settled areas, the territories were larger and populations smaller. The range of size was from a few thousand up to 100,000.

The average small state included a central town with a population of several thousand, the balance of the population consisting of the rural calpulli. The central town was divided up into wards that corresponded in size and to a certain degree in structure to the rural calpulli but were clearly different in function; they in turn were divided into *barrios pequeños.* At the head of the state was an official called the tlatoani, or tlatoque, to whom all household heads owed allegiance, respect, and tax obligations. The tlatoani's position was fixed within a particular lineage, the particular choice varying from state to state. In some areas, succession passed from

Functions of the tlatoani

father to son; in others, the succession went through a series of brothers and then passed to the eldest son of the eldest brother. In still other states, the office was elective; but the choice was limited to sons or brothers of the deceased ruler. The office was accompanied by all of the trappings and sumptuary behaviour typical of despotic states. The ruler resided in a large, multi-room masonry palace inhabited by a great number of wives, servants, and professional craftsmen. He was carried in a sedan chair in public and treated with exaggerated respect by his subordinates. The tlatoani held considerable power: he appointed all lesser bureaucrats, promoted men to higher military status, organized military campaigns, and was the distributor of booty and tribute; he collected taxes in labour, military service, and goods from his supporters; he owned private estates manned by serfs; he was the final court of appeal in judicial cases; and he was titular head of the religious cult and head of the town market.

Many of these functions were delegated to a large staff of professional administrators: priests, market supervisors, military leaders, judges, tax collectors, and accountants. The tax collectors, or calpixque, were especially important administrators because they acted as the rulers' agents in collecting goods and services from the calpulli chiefs.

Class structure.   Most of these positions were appointed and selected from two classes—the pilli and the professional warriors. Society was divided into three well-defined castes. At the top were the pilli, nobles by birth and members of the royal lineage. Below them was the macehual class, the commoners who made up the bulk of the population. At the base of the social structure were the mayeques, or serfs, attached to private or state-owned rural estates. Within these three castes, a great number of social classes could be differentiated, according to wealth, occupation, and political office. The Aztec system made a distinction between ascribed and achieved status. By a system of promotions, usually as a reward for military deeds, commoners were appointed to such political offices as calpixque and judges. Many pilli held no political office and, unless they had inherited private estates, were forced to live off the largess of the ruler. Commoners who had captured four enemy warriors in combat were promoted to the rank of tecuhtli, entered one of the military orders, were assigned a private estate with serfs for their maintenance, and acted as an elite professional army. The children of both pilli and tecuhtli could enroll in the religious college, or calmecac, where they could be trained as priests or political administrators. The calmecac apparently was also open to certain other commoners, such as wealthy and influential merchants and craftsmen.

The three social castes

Aside from the commoner-warriors, the macehual class was further differentiated into class levels. Certain occupations were accorded higher prestige than others (merchants, lapidarians, goldsmiths, and featherworkers are mentioned, and the list probably included stone sculptors); and all urban occupations were assigned higher status as compared with rural farming. Since occupations were restricted to calpulli membership and since the calpulli were kin groups, it follows that crafts tended to be hereditary. In small towns the craft specializing group would have to be the small barrios. In the cities it was definitely the larger unit, but in either case crafts would be found within hereditary corporate groups.

The system of social stratification emphasized ascribed status but also permitted considerable vertical mobility. The land-tenure system was an important aspect in maintaining both processes, as could be expected in a basically agrarian society. Although most of the land was held in common by the calpulli, private estates with serfs helped to maintain the prestige of the pilli class and similar estates assigned to political office; and the tecuhtli positions freed able commoners from the necessity of subsistence procurement.

The taxation system also helped to maintain the social system. All heads of households owed military service to the tlatoani. For the pilli and tecuhtli, this was the only tribute demanded. Urban craftsmen also paid tribute in their craft products but were exempt from corvée labour. That obligation, plus taxes in agricultural products, were the burdens of the rural peasants, and the mayeques owed their labour and agricultural produce to their overlord.

Pawns and slaves Two other elements in the Aztec social system were pawns and slaves. The former were poor men who could sell themselves or members of their household for a specified period of time. Their rights were carefully defended by Aztec law, and they were not slaves but more like indentured servants. True slaves did exist and in some parts of Meso-America were used as workers or servants. Among the Aztec, the mayeques were their counterpart. Slaves were bought in lowland markets and used primarily for human sacrifice.

The high development of craft specialization—much of it full-time—in Aztec towns has already been noted. But many rural communities also had part-time specialties, a feature due in part to the heterogeneity of the highland environment, with its highly local distribution of resources. Foreign goods were brought into the Aztec homeland by great caravans of professional merchants called pochteca, who frequently undertook journeys exceeding a year in length. As a group the merchants enjoyed very high prestige and even had their own tribunals. Various merchant wards of a great number of towns and cities in central Mexico were organized into one great trading guild that had its centre at Tenochtitlán. They also organized and administrated the town markets, another highly evolved aspect of Aztec institutions. These markets were held in great open plazas—in smaller towns every fifth day, in larger towns and cities daily, although in the latter case the market population reached a peak every fifth day.

Organization of the empire. The centres and the political organization of large states such as the Aztec Empire were fundamentally similar in character to small ones; but the vast differences in size (Tenochtitlán, the Aztec capital, may have had 140,000 to 200,000 inhabitants in 1519) demanded some changes. Generally, when one central Mexican state conquered another, the ruler of the conquering town extorted an annual tribute; but there was little attempt at political integration. In the case of the Aztecs, this policy was generally maintained, but many conquered states were replaced with Aztec governors. Furthermore, conquest was usually accompanied by an exchange of women from the two ruling lineages (conqueror and conquered), and successors to the throne of the conquered states were through these women, from the royal lineage of Tenochtitlán. As a result, the ruling class gradually tended toward a single kin group. Because of the great number of states conquered by the Aztecs (400 to 500), some form of intermediate level territorial and administrative organization became imperative. The land conquered by the Aztecs was grouped into 38 provinces. One of the towns served as capital for each prov-Organiza-
tion of the
provincesince; and an Aztec tax collector-governor was placed there to supervise the collection, storage, and disposition of the tribute. In many provinces, the Aztecs established garrisons. These consisted of warriors and their families culled from all of the towns of the Basin of Mexico, and they were assigned lands in the conquered province. Since they supported themselves, they were colonists as well as troops. The planting of colonists, combined with such factors as the merchant guild and royal family intermarriage, suggests that the Aztec elite were attempting to integrate more closely the population of the Basin of Mexico as a kind of core nationality for the empire. Other indications that the Aztecs were in the process of achieving further political integration are statements in several *relaciones* that the tax collectors served as courts of appeals in serious judicial cases and also that the Aztecs introduced the cult of their national god Huitzilopochtli to conquered provinces.

Tenochtitlán. Tenochtitlán itself was a huge metropolis covering more than five square miles (13 square kilometres). It was originally located on two small islands in Lake Texcoco; but it gradually spread into the surrounding lake by a process, first of chinampa construction, then of consolidation. It was connected to the mainland by several causeway dikes that terminated in smaller lakeside urban communities. The lake around the city was also partly covered with chinampas with numerous rural settlements. Together, the complex of settlements—the city, the chinampa villages, and the settlements along the lakeshore plain—must have appeared from the air as one gigantic settlement. The population in 1519 was in the neighbourhood of 400,000 people, the largest and densest concentration in Meso-American history.

The majority of the people in the city were non-food-producing specialists; *i.e.*, craftsmen, merchants, priests, warriors, and administrators. In Tenochtitlán, as in other larger towns, the larger calpulli formed craft guilds. Guild organization was internally complex, an economic development related to the higher level of political integration and the greatly expanded trade and tax base that accrued from it. The great market in the barrio of Tlatelolco is reported by the Spaniards as having 60,000 buyers and sellers on the main market day. The Spaniards also describe the enormous canoe traffic on the lake moving goods to the market. There is even evidence that many chinampa cultivators, in response to the expanded market, were shifting to truck gardening rather than toward the production of staple crops.

The Aztec capital was originally two separate cities, Tlatelolco and Tenochtitlán, merged into one through the conquest of Tlatelolco. The division was maintained for administrative purposes, however, and with further growth it became necessary to divide Tenochtitlán into four great wards (confusingly referred to as calpulli also). Each ward contained 12 to 15 calpulli, 50 to 60 in all. Tlatelolco must have had 10 to 20 calpulli as well, bringing the total up to perhaps 80.

With this enormously expanded tax base, the central government became internally complex. The Spaniards describe Montezuma's palace as containing 300 rooms Montezu-
ma's palace grouped around three courts. Land titles dating from after the conquest give it an area of 10 acres. Aside from the private apartments of the king, the palace included libraries, storehouses, workshops for royal craftsmen, great halls for justice and other councils, and offices for an army of accountants. The sources even describe a royal zoo and aviary and a number of country retreats. The internal organization of the taxation, military, and judicial departments must have been far more complex than in small states; but precise data is lacking.

Within the city there were literally hundreds of temples and related religious structures. There were at least two large complexes, religious centres of the dual cities of Tenochtitlán and Tlatelolco. Each of the four great wards of Tenochtitlán, as well as each calpulli, had smaller temple complexes, so that the total number must have run into the hundreds. The great temple complex of Tenochtitlán consisted of three large pyramid-temples (the principal temple platform, dedicated to Huitzilopochtli and Tlaloc, was 100 feet high and measured 300 feet on a side at its base). There were also six small pyramid-temples, three calmecac buildings (dormitories and colleges for priests), a ball court, a great wooden rack for the skulls of sacrificed victims, a sacred pool, a sacred grove, and several large open courts. All of these structures were placed within a vast walled enclosure, 400 yards on a side. The temple complex at Tlatelolco was at least half as large.

Aztec religion. Perhaps the most highly elaborated aspect of Aztec culture was the religious system. The Aztecs derived much of their religious ideology from the earlier cultures of Meso-America or from their contemporaries. This was particularly true during the final phase of their history, when their foreign contacts broadened. Indeed, much confusion about Aztec religious ideology stems, in part, from the fact that Aztec civilization was still in a process of assimilation and reorganization of these multi-stranded religious traditions. Moreover, as the empire expanded and Tenochtitlán evolved into a heterogeneous community, the religious needs correspondingly changed from those of a simple agrarian society. The ruling class, particularly, demanded a more intellectual and philosophical ideology. (For a detailed discussion of the Aztecs' religion, cosmology, and calendar see AZTEC RELIGION; CALENDAR.)

The great ceremonial rites

The Aztec approach to contact with the supernatural was through a complex calendar of great ceremonies held at the temples and performed by a professional priesthood that acted as the intermediary between the gods and man. Many of these were public in the sense that the populace played the role of spectators. Elements in all the ceremonies were very similar and included ritual ablutions to prepare the priests for the contact; offerings and sacrifices to gain the gods' favour; and theatrical dramas of myths by masked performers in the form of dances, songs, and processionals. Each god had his special ceremony that, considering the richness of the pantheon, must have filled the calendar. These ceremonies must have played a significant recreative function, as do ceremonies held in honour of patron saints in present-day Mexico.

Aztec religion heavily emphasized sacrifice and ascetic behaviour as the necessary preconditions for approaching the supernatural. Priests were celibate and were required to live a simple, spartan life. They performed constant self-sacrifice in the form of bloodletting as penitence (by passing barbed cords through the tongue and ears). This pattern of worship reached its climax in the practice of human sacrifice; it was in this aspect of Aztec culture that religion, war, and politics became closely interrelated.

The Aztecs believed that, as a people, they had a divine mission to prevent the fifth destruction of the Earth. They believed that the previous destructions were caused by the death of the Sun and that therefore the way to prevent his death was by sustaining him with human hearts and blood. Ideologically at least, Aztec warfare was waged for the purpose of obtaining sacrificial victims. The tribute lists, of course, demonstrate that there was a more mundane purpose as well; and it would be a serious mistake to think of Aztec warfare as functioning primarily in the religious sphere.

The priesthood

The cult of the gods required a large professional priesthood. Spanish documents indicate that the priesthood was one of the most elaborate of Aztec institutions. Each temple and god had its attendant priestly order. At Tenochtitlán the high priests of Tlaloc and Huitzilopochtli served as heads of the entire priestly organization. Within the orders were priests in charge of ceremonies, of the education of novices, of astrology, and of the temple lands. (These consisted of specific rural communities assigned by the state to particular temples.) Furthermore, there were several grades of priests. As noted above, the priests maintained a number of schools, or calmecacs, where sons of the nobility and certain commoners were given instruction. Most of these novices ultimately left the priesthood and occupied economic and political statuses; others remained, joined the priesthood on a permanent basis, and lived at the calmecac.

Probably much of Aztec religion was practiced at home at special household altars. Common archaeological artifacts are small baked-clay idols or figurines, representing specific gods apparently used in these household ceremonies, along with incense burners.

The Post-Classic civilizations of Meso-America came to an abrupt end with the coming of the Spanish in the early 16th century. (For the history of the Spanish Conquest, see LATIN AMERICA AND THE CARIBBEAN, COLONIAL.)

(W.T.Sa.)

BIBLIOGRAPHY

Pre-Classical and Classical periods: MIGUEL COVARRUBIAS, *Indian Art of Mexico and Central America* (1957); WILLIAM T. SANDERS and BARBARA J. PRICE, *Mesoamerica: The Evolution of a Civilization* (1968); and ERIC R. WOLF, *Sons of the Shaking Earth* (1959), are good general introductions to Meso-America and its prehistory. Two books dealing with the Olmec civilization are MICHAEL D. COE, *America's First Civilization* (1968); and IGNACIO BERNAL, *The Olmec World* (1969). JOHN PADDOCK (ed.), *Ancient Oaxaca* (1966), deals with the Monte Albán civilization, among other matters.

Two up-to-date books on the Maya are J. ERIC S. THOMPSON, *The Rise and Fall of Maya Civilization*, 2nd ed. (1966); and MICHAEL D. COE, *The Maya* (1966). J. ERIC S. THOMPSON, *Maya Hieroglyphic Writing: An Introduction*, 2nd ed. (1960), is a monumental survey of Maya calendrics and writing. For a contrasting view of the nature of Maya script, see YURI V. KNOROZOV, *Selected Chapters from the Writing of the Maya Indians* (1967; orig. pub. in Russian, 1963).

Post-Classic Period, 900–1519: MICHAEL D. COE, *Mexico* (1962) and *The Maya* (1966), are the most recent syntheses on Meso-American archaeology as a whole and provide much descriptive information with a minimum of theoretical interpretation. WILLIAM T. SANDERS and BARBARA J. PRICE (*op. cit.*), has little descriptive detail and is essentially a theoretical interpretation of Meso-American archaeology from an evolutionary and ecological point of view. BERNARDINO DE SAHAGUN, *Florentine Codex*, trans. by CHARLES E. DIBBLE and ARTHUR J.O. ANDERSON, 9 vol. (1950–63), is the first full translation of this 16th-century Spanish writer of Aztec culture and is particularly full on Aztec religion. J. ERIC S. THOMPSON, *Mexico Before Cortez* (1940), and *The Rise and Fall of Maya Civilization*, 2nd ed. (1966), remain the best detailed descriptions of Aztec culture. GEORGE C. VAILLANT, *The Aztecs of Mexico*, rev. ed. (1966), now somewhat out of date, still is the best archaeological and ethnohistoric syntheses of the culture history of the Basin of Mexico.

(M.D.C./W.T.Sa.)

Meso-American Indian Cultures

Indigenous to Mexico and Central America (roughly between latitudes 14° N and 22° N), Meso-American Indian cultures had a common origin in the pre-Hispanic civilizations of the area (see MESO-AMERICAN CIVILIZATION, HISTORY OF). Most Meso-American peoples belong to one of three linguistic groups: the Macro-Mayan, the Oto-Manguean, or the Uto-Aztecan. Macro-Mayan peoples, with the exception of a northeastern enclave, the Huastecs, live at the southeastern extremity of Meso-America. Oto-Mangueans are to be found in a wide area of Meso-America between Uto-Aztecan peoples to the north and east and Mayan and other peoples to the south. Oto-Manguean languages (now extinct) were spoken south of the Mayan area along the Pacific coasts of El Salvador, Honduras, and Nicaragua; and one Oto-Manguean language, North Pame, spoken in the central desert of highland Mexico, is outside Meso-America to the north. The main branches of the Oto-Manguean family are Oto-Pamean, Amuzgoan, Popolocan, Chinantecan, Mixtecan, Zapotecan, Manguean, and perhaps Huave and Tlapanec. The Tlapanec and Chontal languages of Oaxaca, spoken on the Pacific coast of Mexico, are held by some scholars to be related to the Hokan Coahuiltecan (sometimes termed the Hokaltecan) languages farther north. As a result of the expansion of the Aztec Empire centred in the valley of Mexico, Uto-Aztecan enclaves are found throughout the area. Tarascan, a language the filiation of which is still in doubt, is spoken in the highlands of Michoacán, Mexico.

Main linguistic groups

Settlement patterns. The territorial unit that has prime importance for most Meso-American peoples is the *municipio*, a unit roughly corresponding to a county in Great Britain or the United States. Each *municipio* has a municipal centre where most civic, religious, and marketing activities take place. In the modern pattern, this centre is the largest settlement in the area. The usual elements, which vary according to the size and importance of the community, are laid out according to the standard pattern imposed by early Spanish administrators throughout New Spain: a plaza surrounded by public edifices (church or chapel, curacy, jail, perhaps a school, and a meeting place for civil authorities). Houses nearest the plaza are those of the principal persons. Larger communities are often divided into sociopolitical enclaves called barrios.

An older pattern, still found in some areas (as among some Mayan peoples of the south and among the Huichol of the north), is for the *municipio* centre to be an empty town, occupied continuously only by civil and religious authorities and perhaps a few merchants. The bulk of the population resides in hamlets or on individual farms most of the year, moving to town residences only for

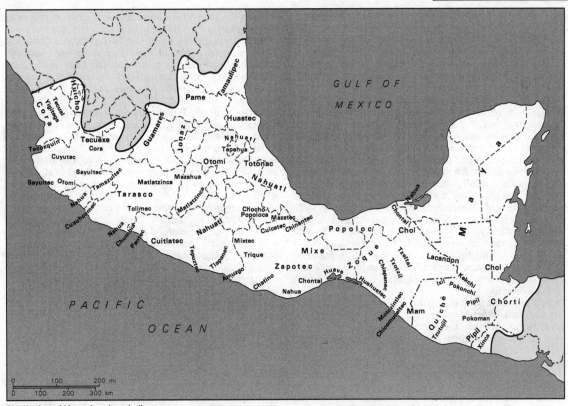

Distribution of Meso-American Indians.
From H. Driver *et al*, *Indiana University Publications in Anthropology and Linguistics* (1953)

short periods either to transact business or to participate in a religious festival.

Social, political, and religious institutions. The basic social and economic unit of Meso-America is the extended family of from two to four generations. There is a strong tendency for the extended family to fragment into individual nuclear families, each consisting of one couple and their children. Kinship is reckoned bilaterally, no distinction being made between kinsmen related through males and those related through females. Such distinctions are made in a few Mayan and Zoque communities, and they are common immediately north of Meso-America. These and other facts have led some anthropologists to suggest that small preconquest communities were patrilineal clans or lineages. Named clans and lineages have actually been reported in a few present-day Tzeltal (Mayan) communities.

Throughout Meso-America generally, newly married couples tend to locate near the groom's family in a slight majority of cases. Inheritance also generally favours the male line, including family names, which are almost invariably inherited from males. Inherited names are now most commonly of Spanish origin, but native surnames are known among some Mayan groups. In certain Mixtec (Oto-Manguean) communities, a man's first name becomes the surname of his offspring.

Marriage, traditionally an alliance between two families, is initiated by the groom's parents and arranged by them directly or through the services of a go-between. A period of bride service by the groom, often involving at least temporary residence with the bride's family, is not uncommon. Polygyny is known and socially acceptable but is not common.

Political and religious institutions are traditionally bound together into a complex of hierarchically arranged year-long offices through which adult males may attain status and power in the community. All males must serve in the lower ranked offices at one time or another, but only the most successful attain the highest positions.

Progress through the ranks typically involves an alternation between civil and religious offices. Successful passage to the highest ranks results in election to the position of elder. Elders form a more or less informal group of senior men to whom the community looks for experienced guidance in policy matters and in times of crisis.

Meso-American religion, called Christo-pagan by anthropologists, is a complex syncretism of indigenous beliefs and the Christianity of early Roman Catholic missionaries. A hierarchy of indigenous supernatural beings (some benign, others not) have been reinterpreted as Christian deities and saints. Mountain and water spirits are appeased at special altars in sacred places by gift or animal sacrifice. Individuals have companion spirits in the form of animals or natural phenomena, such as lightning or shooting stars. Disease is associated with witchcraft or failure to appease malevolent spirits.

Economic patterns. The cultivation of Indian corn, as well as of a number of secondary crops, provides basic subsistence for all Meso-America. Secondary crops include the bean, the squash or pumpkin, the chili pepper for seasoning, and tomatoes of both cooking and eating varieties. Additional foods with a limited distribution because of differing climates and terrain are the pineapple, sweet potato, manioc, chayote, vanilla, maguey, nopal, mesquite, cherimoya, papaya and avocado. Pre-Hispanic commercial plants included cotton, tobacco, henequen for its fibre, and cocoa beans, which served as a medium of exchange. Important commercial crops that have been introduced since European contact include Old World cereals (wheat, barley, oats), bananas, coffee, sugarcane, sesame, and the peanut.

Traditional slash-and-burn agriculture persists in the most isolated areas, but plow agriculture has replaced it in many places. *Chinampa* agriculture is limited to the valley of Mexico: small artificial islands are built up about one foot above the level of shallow waters of a freshwater lake, formed from the mud and vegetation of the lake floor. After settling, this serves as a rich bed for mixed-crop rotation, nurseries, and seed plots.

All Meso-American communities are tied to national and international markets, but the extent of this relationship varies considerably. The Lacandones of the Chiapas lowland jungles bordering Guatemala lie at one extreme. If the machete, axe, rifle, matches, and similar items from the outside became unavailable to the Lacandones through some catastrophe, they, of all Meso-Americans,

Agricultural methods

would have perhaps the least difficulty in adjusting to the challenge of their ecological situation. Living members of the community still retain personal knowledge of working flint and stone and of the making of fire, cloth, and pottery. The Cora and Huichol, Uto-Aztecans of northwestern Meso-America, are also reported to be only marginally dependent upon outside markets.

A larger segment of Indian populations is tied to the outside cash economy by one or more products, such as coffee, citrus, vanilla, livestock, or manufactured goods. Specialization is not the norm, but from pre-Hispanic times certain communities have developed products and skills that depend upon trade relations. An entire community may be known for its pottery, weaving, or basketry.

Markets are typically organized into a network in which each of several towns hosts the market in its central plaza, a different town each day of the week. The network may or may not include a central market that is held every day of the week. Such a market consists of a core of local merchants the ranks of which are swollen once a week by merchants from the outlying hamlets of the area. All of the merchants, whether from the central market or from outlying markets, tend to be organized in single household units.

Arts and crafts Craft specializations that figure in marketing operations are also widely practiced to meet family needs only. Before the appearance of inexpensive commercial cloth, it was the norm throughout Meso-America for every young girl to learn to weave cotton cloth and, as a married woman, to provide clothing materials for her family. This skill is declining in the face of easy access to materials of cotton, wool, silk, and synthetic materials and blends. The introduction of the treadle loom by the Spaniards brought men into the weaving industry, especially as a commercial operation.

Both men and women are hat and basket weavers. Commercial products are produced from grasses, reeds, and palms, and lowland peoples also produce baskets of vine for local use.

A variety of pottery-making techniques is known in Meso-America. Before Hispanization, female potters made most ware, forming vessels by hand modelling, by building with coils, or by using a wooden paddle or molds. The Spaniards introduced the potter's wheel. Present-day techniques are a synthesis of indigenous and Spanish methods.

A lacquering art, now an integral part of the tourist trade, was practiced at the time of the conquest. A variety of gourd vessels of many sizes and shapes are artistically painted, using local materials and techniques. The beautifully decorated vessels serve a range of purposes, from simple utilitarian items, such as dippers, to elaborate ceremonial bowls.

The life cycle. Christian baptism is the first major event in the life of an individual. Indeed, among Chinantecs, a child is not considered fully human until the rite has been performed. If an unbaptized infant dies, the body is buried immediately without the usual ritual observances—ringing of the church bells, burning of incense, and reading and singing of prayers in the home, at the church, and at the graveside.

Nursing may continue for as long as three or four years, and childhood is a period of little discipline except for the responsibility placed on older children to care for their younger siblings while the parents work. **Formal education** Formal schooling is now available in most areas for at least a few years, but monolingualism in less acculturated areas severely limits the efficacy of the training, which is almost always conducted in Spanish only. There is no puberty rite, so that the transition from infancy to adolescence is unmarked ritually.

A girl becomes an adult at marriage, but a boy becomes an adult in two ways: through marriage and through citizenship attained when he reaches the proper age, usually 14 or 15 years. At this time he must enter the labour pool of adult men who maintain community property and must contribute his share of any assessment the citizenry may impose upon itself to cover community expenses. He becomes eligible (and obligated) to serve in the lowest ranking offices of the political and religious institutions of the community.

Death is marked by ritual and burial within 24 hours of death, with repetition of the ritual at periodic intervals after death, sometimes ending on the ninth day, sometimes repeated on the anniversary. An All Saints feast of several days' duration is prepared annually in the fall of the year for all of the dead.

Modernization. Indigenous communities have in most cases made a healthy adjustment to the larger non-Indian community around them. Although this has and will continue to involve many kinds of cultural change, the indigenous communities have been able to maintain their cultural integrity with little sign of the kind of disorganization leading to cultural collapse that is often found when two cultures meet. And though the Spanish-speaking community has come to accept (even to take pride in) its Indian heritage, its direct attempts to bring the Indian way of life more in line with that of its own have met with much resistance. While it has been possible to introduce technological changes that have improved the economic position of Indian communities, attempts to change those parts of the culture that have symbolic value—political and religious ideologies that tend to preserve indigenous social systems—have met with less success.

BIBLIOGRAPHY. SOL TAX (ed.), *Heritage of Conquest: The Ethnology of Middle America* (1952, reprinted 1968), includes Paul Kirchhoff's ground-breaking article "Mesoamerica" and is the best early synthesis of ethnographic information on the area. A comprehensive statement on all aspects of the subject is found in ROBERT WAUCHOPE (ed.), *Handbook of Middle American Indians* (1964–), a projected 16-volume reference work and bibliographic sourcebook of which 9 volumes have appeared. Volumes 4 and 11 of THOMAS A. SEBEOK (ed.), *Current Trends in Linguistics* (1968 and 1972), provide the latest syntheses of linguistic relationships. Ethnographic material includes: RALPH L. BEALS, *The Ethnology of the Western Mixe* (1945); GEORGE M. FOSTER, *Empire's Children: The People of Tzintzuntzan* (1948); ROBERT REDFIELD, *A Village That Chose Progress: Chan Kom Revisited* (1950, paperback 1962); WILLIAM MADSEN, *The Virgin's Children: Life in an Aztec Village Today* (1960); OSCAR LEWIS, *Life in a Mexican Village: Tepoztlán Restudied* (1963); EVON Z. VOGT, *Zinacantan: A Maya Community in the Highlands of Chiapas* (1969); and PHILLIP BAER and WILLIAM R. MERRIFIELD, *Two Studies on the Lacandones of Mexico* (1971). Linguistic descriptions include: RICHARD S. PITTMAN, *A Grammar of Tetelcingo (Morelos) Nahuatl* (1954); VELMA B. PICKETT, *The Grammatical Hierarchy of Isthmus Zapotec* (1960); JOSEPH E. GRIMES, *Huichol Syntax* (1964); MARVIN K. MAYERS (ed.), *Languages of Guatemala* (1966); H. HARWOOD HESS, *The Syntactic Structure of Mezquital Otomi* (1968); WILLIAM R. MERRIFIELD, *Palantla Chinantec Grammar* (1968); and MARION M. COWAN, *Tzotzil Grammar* (1969).

(W.Me.)

Meso-American Indian Languages

Meso-American, or Middle American, Indian languages are spoken in Meso-America; *i.e.*, an area of the aboriginal New World that includes central and southern Mexico, Guatemala, British Honduras, El Salvador, parts of Honduras and Nicaragua, and part of northwest Mexico. Though various centres of civilization have flourished in the area, sometimes concurrently, from 1000 BC down to the time of the Spanish conquest of Mexico in 1519, Meso-America as a whole has had a more or less common cultural history for 2,500 years.

Treatments of the languages of Meso-America are customarily organized on the basis of their genetic relationships, and only secondarily on that of geographical distribution. Thus, some languages treated as Meso-American are not in fact spoken in Meso-America proper but form linguistic families with languages that are spoken there. For information about languages of northeast, north central, and northwest Mexico that are not dealt with in this article, see NORTH AMERICAN INDIAN LANGUAGES. For languages of Central America not treated here, see SOUTH AMERICAN INDIAN LANGUAGES.

Numbers of languages and speakers Some 70 Indian languages are spoken today in Meso-America by perhaps 6,000,000 people. When the Span-

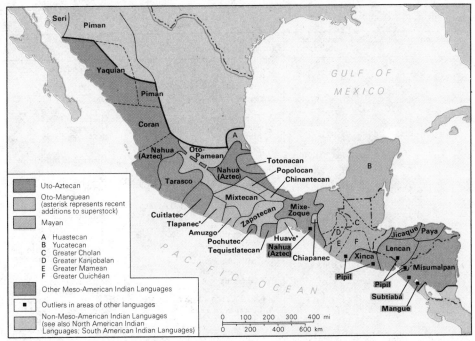

Distribution of Meso-American Indian languages c. AD 1500. Boundaries are schematic.

ish conquered Mexico in 1519, there may have been 20,000,000 people in Meso-America. Within 100 years of the conquest, the Indian population had decreased by 80 percent as a result of war, disease, forced labour, and starvation. Since then, the Indian population has gone back to a higher level, but several languages—about ten such are documented—have become extinct. Meso-American languages with the greatest number of speakers in the mid-20th century are:

language	number of speakers	family
Aztec	1,000,000	Uto-Aztecan
Yucatec	350,000	Mayan
Quiché-Tzutujil-Cakchiquel	900,000	
Mam	350,000	
Kekchí	300,000	
Mixtec	250,000	
Zapotec	300,000	Oto-Manguean
Otomí	300,000	

The study of the Meso-American languages. During the 16th and 17th centuries, some Dominican and Franciscan missionaries devoted themselves to the study of native languages so that priests could deal in religious matters with monolingual Indians. They wrote grammars following a Latin model, devised orthographies applying values used in Spanish or Latin (occasionally inventing new letters), made dictionaries (usually vocabularies or glossaries), and translated Christian texts (confessionals, sacraments, and sermons) into Indian languages. Except for one heroic figure, the Spanish missionary priest Bernardino de Sahagún, they neither collected nor fostered the collection of folklore. During this period grammars and dictionaries were written for such languages as Aztec, Zapotec, Mixtec, Tzeltal, Yucatec, Quiché-Tzutujil-Cakchiquel, Chortí, and Northeastern Otomí. These collections of data served the successors of the first missionaries. During the 18th century, the momentum of such work decreased, and, after Mexican independence in the first part of the 19th century, Spanish clerics were ousted, leaving further work on indigenous languages to travellers and gentlemen scholars—mostly people poorly qualified for such a task.

Modern linguistic techniques for the description of languages were not applied to Meso-American languages until North Americans turned their attention to the area in the 1930s (Protestant missionaries) and 1940s (secular academic linguists). Since then, much professional linguistic work has been done on these languages, especially those of Mexico. Almost every language of Meso-Ameri-

ca has been worked on by at least one linguist, but the time spent and the level of linguistic competence of the investigators have varied greatly. For most of the languages, grammatical and lexical data have been collected, much of which remains unpublished. A number of competent grammars and dictionaries have appeared; none of them, however, is exhaustive or definitive. Folktales have been collected for a smaller number of languages. Spanish-based orthographies have been devised for most of the Meso-American languages in the 20th century, but not much reading matter is available in them. In short, much work remains to be done.

CLASSIFICATION OF THE MESO-AMERICAN LANGUAGES

Modern genetic groupings. The classification of Meso-American Indian languages presented here reflects generally accepted genetic groupings (as of the early 1970s), based on similarities in vocabulary and grammar and on the establishment of regular correspondences between sounds in cognate (related) words among the several languages. The languages grouped together are presumed to have developed from a common ancestor, called a protolanguage. Not all of the languages of Meso-America have been convincingly assigned to a specific group. A few are currently thought to be unrelated to any of the established genetic groupings and are listed individually; these are called isolates.

Within a given genetic grouping, there may be several levels of relatedness. Glottochronology (or lexicostatistics), developed by two United States linguists—Morris Swadesh and Robert Lees—is a controversial and not universally accepted procedure for measuring degrees of difference between related languages in terms of years of separation. Based on the assumption that all languages change more or less to the same degree in a given period of time, the method employs a list of 100 items of "basic" or "noncultural" concepts, which are assumed to be expressible by vocabulary items in any language. Over a period of 1,000 years, different words will have been substituted to express 14 percent of the notions on the list, thus leaving fewer cognate (related) words. Since every language replaces 14 percent of the 100 concepts every 1,000 years, two languages that separated 1,000 years ago will share 74 percent cognates (86 percent of 86 is 74 percent). The following are terms and categories for degree of relatedness, correlated with glottochronological time depths, that will be used to describe the various Meso-American language groups. The figures given are minimal bounds.

Extent of the studies of Meso-American languages

Meso-American Indian Languages

family, branch (or group), language	location	number of speakers	family, branch (or group), language	location	number of speakers
1. Uto-Aztecan (Uto-Nahuan) family 48c*			**5. Jicaque isolate**	NW Honduras	?
			(several dialects or languages)		
Shoshonean (Yutan, Oregonian) division† 34c			**6. Tlapanec (Subtiaban, Tlapanecan) complex 8c**		
A. *Plateau group* 18c			A. Tlapanec (Yope)	Guerrero	24,000
1. Mono, N Paiute–Bannock (complex?)			B. Subtiaba (Nagrandan)‖	Nicaragua	extinct?
2. Shoshoni–Goshiute, Comanche (complex?)			Maribio‖	El Salvador	extinct?
3. Ute-Chemehuevi, S Paiute (complex?)			**7. Oto-Pamean stock 55c**		
B. Tubatulabal			A. Chichimec (Meco, Jonaz)	Guanajuato (Mex.)	1,000
C. *Southern California branch* 24c			B. *Pamean group* 18c		
1. Serrano			N Pame	San Luís Potosi (Mex.)	
2. Luiseño, Juaneño			S Pame	Hidalgo (Mex.)	2,000
3. *Gabrieleño complex* 10c			C. *Matlatzinca complex* 10c		
Gabrieleño			Matlatzinca (Pirinda)	State of Mexico	2,000
Fernandeño			Ocuiltec (Atzingo)	State of Mexico	a few
4. *Cahuilla complex‡*			D. *Otomian group* 16c		
Cahuilla			1. *Otomí complex* 9c		
Cupeño			NW Otomí		
D. Hopi			NE Otomí	Hidalgo, Guanajuato,	300,000
Sonoran (Mexican) division 39c			SW Otomí	State of Mexico,	
E. *Piman group*			Ixtenco Otomí	Querétaro (Mex.)	
1. *Piman complex* 8c			2. Mazahua	Michoacán and	100,000
Papago (Pima)	Arizona; Sonora (Mex.)	13,000		State of Mexico	
Lower Pima (Nevome)	Sonora	a few	**8. Popolocan (Olmecan) family 25c**		
Tepecano§	Jalisco (Mex.)	a few	A. *Chochoan group* 13c		
2. *Tepehuán complex‡*			1. Ixcatec	NW Oaxaca (Santa María Ixcatlán)	?
N Tepehuán§	Sonora	?			
S Tepehuán§	Jalisco	?	2. *Chocho complex* 8c		
F. *Yaquian (Taracahitian) branch* 23c			Popoloc	SE Puebla, NW Oaxaca	15,000
1. *Tarahumara complex* 7c					
Tarahumara (Rarámuri)	Chihuahua (Mex.)	12,000	Chocho	NW Oaxaca	1,000
Guarijío		several hundred	B. *Mazatec complex* 10c		
2. Tubar		extinct	Mazatec (1)		
3. *Cáhita complex* 15c			Mazatec (2)	SE Puebla, N Oaxaca	85,000
Eudeve (Heve)		extinct	**9. Mixtecan family 42c**		
Opata, Jova		extinct	A. Amuzgo	E Guerrero, W Oaxaca	12,000
Yaqui, Mayo (Cáhita)§	Arizona; Sonora, Sinaloa (Mex.)	13,000	B. *Greater Mixtecan branch* 25c		
G. *Coran group* 15c			1. *Mixtec group* 15c		
Cora§		?	Mixtec (1)	E Guerrero,	
Huichol§	Nayarit (Mex.)	5,000	Mixtec (2)	S Puebla,	250,000
H. *Nahuan group* 15c			Mixtec (3)	W Oaxaca	
1. *Aztec complex* 11c			2. Cuicatec	NE Oaxaca	12,000
C, N Aztec (Náhuatl)§	State of Mexico, Puebla, Hidalgo (Mex.)		C. Trique	W Oaxaca	5,000
W Aztec (Náhual)§	Michoacán (Mex.)	1,000,000	**10. Zapotecan family 24c**		
E Aztec (Náhuat)§	Veracruz (Mex.)		A. *Zapotec group* 14c		
Pipil§	C America	2,000	Juárez Zapotec	Ixtlán	
2. Pochutec§	Oaxaca Coast (Mex.)	extinct	Villalta Zapotec	Yatzachi	300,000
2. Cuitlatec (Teco) isolate	Guerrero (Mex.)	extinct	S Mountain Zapotec	Cuixtla	
3. Seri isolate	Sonora coast	a few	Valley Zapotec	Mitla, Tehuantepec	
4. Tequistlatec complex or group	SE Oaxaca		B. Papabuco	Elotepec, Oaxaca	extinct
Huamelultec	coast	5,000	C. Chatino	SW Oaxaca	18,000
Tequistlatec	mountains	5,000			

*Indicates centuries of separation.　†Not spoken in Meso-America.　‡There is some doubt whether these groups should be given the status of complexes. §Sonoran languages spoken in Meso-America.　‖Varieties of the same language spoken in different countries (and having different names).

term	centuries of separation	percentage of cognates
dialects	0–5	86–100
language complex	7–11	71–81
language group	13–17	60–68
branch (or family if there is no super-ordinate category)	19–26	46–56
language family	35–45	26–35
stock or phylum	55–65	14–19

In the Table every family (group) and isolate has a separate number from 1 to 21. Each of the 21 headings specifies the name of a grouping, with alternate names. Numbers in parentheses following language names indicate that there are several closely related languages all referred to by the same name. For each language grouping the various levels of relatedness are specified, including glottochronological figures (c = centuries), which are Swadesh's, except for Mixe-Zoque, Mayan, and Xincan, which are by the U.S. linguist Terrence Kaufman. Family and stock names are formed in the following ways: (1) A typical language, usually the most widely spoken, is suffixed with -an (e.g., Mixtecan). (2) Two typical names are chosen and compounded (e.g., Mixe-Zoque). (3) Parts of two or more language names are joined, and -an is suffixed (e.g., Oto-Manguean, Oto-Pamean, Mis-Uluan/Misumalpan). Group names end in -an if the groups are further subgrouped but do not end in -an if they are immediately divided into discrete languages.

The map gives the approximate geographical distribution of the 21 language groupings and isolates of Meso-America. None of the extinct undocumented languages is indicated. Except for some outliers, separate languages within a grouping are not localized. An outlier is a language that has been carried into a foreign cultural and linguistic context by migration; e.g., Mangue is a Chiapanec outlier in Misumalpan territory, Subtiaba is a Tlapanec outlier in Misumalpan territory, Pipil is a Nahua (Aztec) outlier in Quichéan, Xinca, Lencan, and Misumalpan territories.

In the following paragraphs the numbers in parentheses refer to groupings in the Table.

Uto-Aztecan (1). The Uto-Aztecan family consists of some 27 languages that are universally recognized to fall into eight groups or branches—the Plateau group, Tubatulabal, the Southern California branch, Hopi, the Piman group, the Yaquian branch, the Coran group, and the Nahuan group. Tubatulabal and Hopi contain just one language each. The first four groups are commonly, but not universally, recognized as forming a Shoshonean division within the family. None of the Shoshonean languages is spoken in Meso-America, and no distribution or population data is cited for them in the Table (see NORTH AMERICAN INDIAN LANGUAGES). There are two common ways of grouping the remaining languages, depending on

Meso-American Indian Languages (continued)

family, branch (or group), language	location	number of speakers	family, branch (or group), language	location	number of speakers
11. Chinantecan group 15c*			2. *Greater Kanjobalan branch 21c*		
Chinantec (1)			a. *Chujean group 16c*		
Chinantec (2)			Tojolabal (Chaneabal)	Chiapas	12,000
Chinantec (3)	N Oaxaca	25,000	Chuj	NW Guatemala	13,000
Chinantec (4)			b. *Kanjobal proper group 15c*		
12. Manguean (Chorotegan, Chiapanec-Mangue) group 13c			i. *Kanjobal complex 7c*		
A. Chiapanec	Chiapas (Mex.)	extinct	Kanjobal (Conob, Solomec)	NW Guatemala	27,000
B. Mangue (Dirian, Nagrandan)‖	Nicaragua	extinct	Acatec	NW Guatemala	13,000
Chorotega‖	Honduras	extinct	Jacaltec	NW Guatemala	12,000
Nicoya (Orotiña)‖	Costa Rica	extinct	ii. Motozintlec, Tuzantec (Cotoque)	SE Chiapas	600
13. Huave isolate	SE Oaxaca	6,000	D. *Eastern division 34c*		
14. Mixe-Zoque (Zoquian, Mixean, Zoque-Mixe) family 36c			1. *Greater Mamean branch 26c*		
A. *Zoquean group 14c*			a. *Mamean proper group 15c*		
Zoque	Tabasco, Chiapas, Oaxaca	20,000	Teco	SE Chiapas, W Guatemala	3,000
Sierra Popoluca	Veracruz	12,000	Mam		350,000
Texistepec	Veracruz	1,000	b. *Ixilan group 14c*		
B. *Mixean group 13c*			Aguacatec	NW Guatemala	10,000
1. Sayula	Veracruz	1,000	Ixil	NW Guatemala	20,000
Oluta	Veracruz	1,000	2. *Greater Quichéan branch 26c*		
E, W Mixe	E Oaxaca	48,000	a. Uspantec	NW Guatemala	2,000
2. Tapachultec	SE Chiapas coast	extinct	b. *Quiché complex 10c*		
15. Totonacan family 26c			Quiché, Achí	C Guatemala	500,000
Totonac	Veracruz, Puebla	130,000	Sacapultec	C Guatemala	3,000
Tepehua	Veracruz, Hidalgo	4,000	Sipacapa	C Guatemala	3,000
16. Mayan family 41c			Cakchiquel	C Guatemala	400,000
A. *Huastec complex 9c*			Tzutujil	C Guatemala	20,000
Huastec	San Luís Potosí, N Veracruz	60,000	c. *Pocom complex 10c*		
Chicomucelcec (Coxoh)	Chiapas	a few?	Pocomam	EC Guatemala	17,000
B. *Yucatec (Maya) complex 10c*			Pocomchí	EC Guatemala	25,000
Yucatec	Yucatán, Campeche, Quintana Roo, N Guatemala, Brit. Honduras	350,000	d. Kekchí	EC Guatemala	300,000
			17. Tarasco isolate	SW Michoacán	60,000
Lacandón	Chiapas	200?	**18. Xinca complex 10c**		
Itzá	N Guatemala	500	Xinca A	Yupiletepeque, Jutiapa	extinct?
Mopán	N Guatemala, Brit. Honduras	2,000	Xinca B	Guazacapán, Chiquimulilla, Sinacantán	200?
C. *Western division 30c*			**19. Lencan family 20c**		
1. *Greater Cholan branch 19c*			Lenca	SW Honduras	extinct?
a. *Cholan proper group 14c*			Chilanga	E El Salvador	a few
Chontal (Yocotán)	Tabasco (Mex.)	20,000	**20. Paya complex 10c**	N Honduras	?
Chol	Tabasco, Chiapas	30,000	**21. Misumalpan (Misuluan) family 43c**		
Chortí	Honduras, E Guatemala	33,000	A. *Mísquito*	Nicaragua, Honduras	?
b. *Tzotzilan group 14c*			B. *Matagalpa complex 10c*		
Tzotzil (Quelén)	Chiapas	120,000	Matagalpa	Nicaragua, Honduras	a few?
Tzeltal	Chiapas	80,000	Cacaopera	El Salvador	?
			C. *Sumo complex 11c*		
			Sumo, Úlua, Tahuajca	Nicaragua	?

*Indicates centuries of separation. †Not spoken in Meso-America. ‡There is some doubt whether these groups should be given the status of complexes. §Sonoran languages spoken in Meso-America. ‖Varieties of the same language spoken in different countries (and having different names).

the position assigned the Nahuan group. Either Nahuan is considered as separate and the rest as forming a Sonoran division, thereby producing three divisions—Shoshonean, Sonoran, and Nahuan—or else Nahuan is included within Sonoran, thereby producing a Shoshonean versus Sonoran dichotomy, which is the arrangement used in this article. Several scholars believe that the "division" concept is faulty here and that Uto-Aztecan contains eight groups and branches that are not to be further grouped in any special way.

Only some Sonoran languages are spoken in Meso-America (indicated by asterisks [*] in the Table). The extinct Tubar belongs to the Yaquian branch, but whether to the Tarahumara complex, the Cáhita complex, or neither, is not clear. The Nahuan group includes the extinct Pochutec, formerly spoken on the coast of Oaxaca, Mexico, and poorly documented; Pochutec is clearly very divergent from the rest of the group. The Aztec complex is considered by some to be a single language with several dialects. The three Aztec languages were spoken within the Aztec Empire as it was constituted in 1519. Pipil speakers, who also refer to their language as *nawat*, were not a part of the Aztec culture and probably represent a Toltec expansion from several centuries earlier.

In 1859, Johann Karl Buschmann, a German philologist, correctly identified all the then-known Uto-Aztecan languages as forming a family. In 1883 a French philologist, Hyacinthe de Charencey, divided Uto-Aztecan into Oregonian (=Shoshonean) and Mexican (=Sonoran), and, in 1891, in the United States, anthropologist Daniel Brinton recognized Shoshonean and divided the Sonoran division (of this article) into Nahuatlan (=Nahuan) and Sonoran (=the Sonoran of this article minus Nahuan). Brinton's division was followed by the United States biologist John Wesley Powell in his classification of North American languages.

Buschmann in 1859 and United States anthropological linguist Edward Sapir in 1915 contributed to the comparative study of Uto-Aztecan by assembling sizable numbers of cognate sets.

A number of now-acculturated and racially absorbed Indian ethnic groups of northern Mexico are believed by many to have spoken Uto-Aztecan languages, although only the language names are known, and not the languages themselves. These are: Suma, Jumano, Lagunero, Cazcán, Tecuexe, Guachichil, and Zacatec.

Uto-Aztecan is generally accepted by specialists as related to the Kiowa-Tanoan family of North America and with it to form the Aztec-Tanoan stock (or phylum).

Cuitlatec (2). The now extinct Cuitlatec language has not been linked convincingly with any other language or family, though the idea that it might be related to Uto-Aztecan has been entertained.

The Hokan hypothesis (3–5). In 1919 two United States anthropologists, Roland Dixon and Alfred Kroeber, tried to improve on an older North American classi-

Various scholars' work on Uto-Aztecan

fication by reducing the multiplicity of language groupings in California (about 50) to a manageable number of families and stocks. Working over a period of several years, they developed the hypothesis that most California languages belong to one of two great groupings (called phyla or superstocks), Hokan and Penutian. The formulation was accepted and extended by others. Hokan included Shasta, Achumawi, Atsugewi, Chimariko, Karok, Yanan, Pomoan, Washo, Esselen, Yuman, Salinan, and Chumashan. By 1891/92 it had been suggested that Yuman, Seri (3), and Tequistlatec (4) were related. In 1915 the matter was re-examined in the light of the Hokan hypothesis, and it was concluded that all of the languages named above are related. Since then most scholars familiar with Yuman languages have believed that Seri and Yuman are related, and many who accept the Hokan hypothesis believe that Seri and Yuman form a special group within Hokan.

Jicaque (5), which is very poorly documented, though still spoken, has plain, aspirated, and glottalized stops (different varieties of consonant sounds), as do many Hokan languages. In 1953 it was suggested that Jicaque is a Hokan language. The general acceptance of the proposition may have been uncritical, because the available data on Jicaque is hardly reliable.

Extinct languages of northeast Mexico. All but one
Documented dead languages
(Tonkawa) of the several languages once spoken in northeast Mexico and South Texas have become extinct. Documented languages of Mexico are: Coahuilteco, Comecrudo, Cotoname, Naolan, and Maratino (or Tamaulipec). Those of Texas are Karankawa (and Klamkosh), Atakapa, and Tonkawa. John Wesley Powell classified the first three as forming a Coahuiltecan family. The other Mexican languages were unknown until recently. Each of the three Texan languages was considered by Powell to be an isolate. In 1920 Coahuiltecan was redefined to include Karankawa and Tonkawa and to be coordinate with Hokan in a Hokan-Coahuiltecan (=Hokaltecan) superphylum.

Tlapanec (6). The Tlapanec complex was first correctly identified by Walter Lehmann, a German physician, in 1920. In 1925 Edward Sapir tried to establish Subtiaba as a Hokan language, proposing some Proto-Hokan reconstructions that could account for the Subtiaba forms. This classification is generally accepted. More recently, however, Calvin Rensch, a U.S. missionary linguist, tried to validate the Oto-Manguean hypothesis (see below) by means of full-scale phonological reconstruction. He believed Tlapanec to be Oto-Manguean; others considered it to be intermediate between Oto-Manguean and Hokan. It must be kept in mind that most of the specialists who have immersed themselves in the study of large numbers of American Indian languages believe that almost all of them are genetically related to one another. This relationship derives from a period, perhaps 20,000 to 30,000 years ago when some of the languages were still spoken in Asia. With such a point of view, correct grouping (or degree of relationship) is a more interesting question than genetic relatedness.

Oto-Pamean (7). The Oto-Pamean stock contains four groups and complexes, Chichimec, Pamean, Matlatzinca, and Otomían, of which only the last two are spoken within Meso-America. The exact number of languages within the Otomí complex is not yet determined, though there seem to be four. Oto-Pamean was first correctly identified in 1892.

Popolocan (8). The Popolocan family (which might more appropriately be called Mazatecan) was correctly identified in 1926. The exact number of languages within the Mazatec complex has not yet been determined, though there are at least two.

Mixtecan (9). There is some difference of opinion as to how the various languages here included within Mixtecan are to be grouped. The main problem is whether
Problem of classifying Amuzgo
Amuzgo is Mixtecan or a separate branch within Oto-Manguean. It has been included within Mixtecan in some systems and excluded from it in others. There seem to be three languages within the Mixtec group, a subdivision of Mixtecan.

Zapotecan (10). The Zapotecan family was correctly identified by William Mechling in 1912, but only Francisco Belmar, a Mexican philologist, correctly recognized that Papabuco is a separate language, neither Zapotec nor Chatino (in 1905). Belmar, however, incorrectly included Chinantec within Zapotecan. The Chatino language has several dialects. Within the Zapotec complex there are at least four languages, and perhaps more.

Chinantecan (11). The Chinantecan group contains approximately four languages, the exact number as yet undetermined. The separateness of Chinantecan within Oto-Manguean was recognized in 1912.

Manguean (12). The Manguean group was correctly identified by Belmar in 1905. Its members, formerly spoken in Chiapas (Mexico), and in Nicaragua, Honduras, and Costa Rica, are now extinct.

The Oto-Manguean hypothesis (7–12 or 6–13). Ever since 1891, it has been proposed that two or more of the above families (7–12) should be linked. Since about 1925, it has been generally accepted by specialists that the Oto-Pamean, Popolocan, Mixtecan, Zapotecan, Chinantecan, and Manguean groups form a larger genetic grouping (phylum), commonly labelled Oto-Manguean. This may be called the "classical Oto-Manguean formulation." Since 1950, work has been going on in the reconstruction of parent languages for each of the constituent families and groups. Since 1961, two revisions have been proposed in the formulation of what constitutes Oto-Manguean: the Tlapanec language complex has been recognized as included in or closely related to Oto-Manguean, and Huave has been proposed as an Oto-Manguean language. In the early 1970s, therefore, most Oto-Manguean specialists considered the grouping to consist of groups 6–13.

The comparative study of the Oto-Manguean phylum
Reconstruction of Oto-Manguean phonology
has resulted in the first case in the Western Hemisphere in which the remote common ancestor of several language families has been phonologically reconstructed. Comparative linguistics at the phylum level has been largely unsuccessful with other postulated superstocks because of the relatively small number of cognates that can be identified. Except for Manguean, all Oto-Manguean languages are spoken in central Mexico.

Huave (13). Early proposals linked Huave to Mixe-Zoque and Mayan. Although this has not been generally accepted by many specialists, it has been uncritically repeated in most compilations. Recently, Morris Swadesh presented a reasonably well documented proposal for Huave as an Oto-Manguean language.

Mixe-Zoque (14). The Mixe-Zoque family consists of eight languages, which, comparative phonology and grammar suggest, form two branches—a Zoquean group, and a Mixean group including Tapachultec. Glottochronological figures, however, suggest a three-way division, as shown in the Table. The Mixe-Zoque family was correctly identified by Hyacinthe de Charencey in 1883. The Texistepec, Sayula, and Oluta languages of this family are all locally called Popoluca.

Totonacan (15). The Totonacan family contains just two languages, of which one (Totonac) has at least three dialects. Possibly, Totonac is a complex.

Mayan (16). The Mayan family was correctly identified by a German ethnographer, Otto Stoll, in 1884. This family, with 24 languages and nearly 2,500,000 speakers, is the most diversified and populous language family of Meso-America. The Huastec language is separated by more than 1,000 miles from the nearest other Mayan language. Taken with the fact that the Huastecs did not share in the Classic Maya civilization, this requires a historical explanation involving the separation of Huastec from the rest of the family more than 2,500 years ago. Though the geographical extent of the Mayan languages is considerable, the Mayan peoples, languages, and cultures (as contrasted with those of the Aztecs), have never been particularly expansionist.

A number of attempts have been made to classify the Mayan languages, each one availing itself of more data than the last. The classification given here as of 1971 recognizes, at the lowest level, ten groupings. Specialists have disagreed on the precise positions of Tojolabal and

Chuj, Motozintlec, Aguacatec, Uspantec, and Kekchí and have held no firm opinions about the Yucatec or Huastec complexes. Not much comparative work on the Mayan family has seen print, but much data has recently been collected. The main contributors to Mayan comparative studies have been the U.S. linguists Norman McQuown (1950s and 1960s) and Terence Kaufman (1960s).

The Macro-Mayan and Macro-Penutian hypotheses. In 1931 L.S. Freeland, a U.S. anthropological linguist, tried to show that Mixe (Zoque) is related to the "Penutian" languages, a superstock that up until then had been limited to California, Oregon, Washington, and British Columbia. In 1935 it was suggested that the similarities between Uto-Aztecan, Tanoan, Kiowa, Penutian, Mixe-Zoque, and Mayan were such as to indicate the existence of a superstock, which it was proposed to call Macro-Penutian. This hypothesis had favour for a period but was never demonstrated nor taken very seriously by specialists. Since then the first three have been generally joined in Aztec-Tanoan. In 1942 it was suggested that Mixe-Zoque and Totonacan might be related genetically to each other and the two in turn might be related to Mayan, the resultant superstock to be called Macro-Mayan. Recently it has been claimed that Tarasco (17) probably belongs in Macro-Mayan as well, though the attempt to prove this has not been convincing to most Mayanists, to whom, minus Tarasco, the Macro-Mayan hypothesis seems as reasonable as the Hokan hypothesis.

Tarasco (17). Tarasco has been linked genetically by some not only to Macro-Mayan but also to both Zuni (in North America) and Quechua (in South America), but without general scholarly acceptance.

Xinca and Lencan (18–19). It has been suggested that Xinca and Lencan are related and that one or both of them is related to Mayan (16), Chibchan (in South America), or Uto-Aztecan (1). None of these hypotheses has been demonstrated as probable.

Languages outside Meso-America proper. The Paya language (20) and the Misumalpan family (21) are Central American languages spoken outside of the cultural area of Meso-America proper, though they have Meso-American outliers in their territory. Paya (20) has been linked in hypotheses to Chibchan and Cariban (both in South America), and perhaps to others, but not convincingly. The Misumalpan family (21) has been recognized since 1895. Since that date some scholars have believed that the three languages and complexes listed are coordinate, and others have believed that the first two constitute one group and the other constitutes a second group. Although the family relationship can be verified on inspection, no supporting comparative work has been published. Previous comprehensive classifications of the Meso-American Indian languages were presented by the U.S. anthropologists Cyrus Thomas and John R. Swanton in 1911 in *Indian Languages of Mexico and Central America and Their Geographical Distribution*, by Edward Sapir in the 14th edition of *Encyclopædia Britannica* (1929), and by Morris Swadesh in 1967 in *Handbook of Middle American Indians*.

Newly discovered languages and reconstructions. Although there are probably no uncharted areas in Meso-America, it is not necessarily the case that all the Indian languages of Meso-America have been correctly identified, and there are probably some multilingual Indian communities as well that are not known to be such. In 1967 Terrence Kaufman discovered a hitherto undocumented Mayan language spoken by several hundred Indians in four or five towns in southeast Chiapas and west central Guatemala. Although it appears to be closely related to Mam, Kaufman considered it a separate language and christened it Teco. Kaufman identified two more new Mayan languages in the course of a linguistic survey of Guatemala. These two new languages—Sacapultec (formerly considered Quiché) and Sipacapa (formerly assumed to be Mam)—are not documented in print and both belong to the Quiché complex.

Reconstruction of earlier forms of the Meso-American Indian languages has focussed primarily on phonology and vocabulary. Phonological and lexical comparative

studies as well as reconstruction have been done for the following groups: Uto-Aztecan; Oto-Manguean—Oto-Pamean, Popolocan, Mixtecan, Zapotecan, Chinantecan, Manguean; Mixe-Zoque; and Mayan (in part). A small amount of grammatical comparison has been done within Oto-Manguean and Mixe-Zoque. In addition, some studies have been done of reconstructed vocabulary for the purpose of hypothesizing about the culture of the speakers of the protolanguages.

RELATION OF LANGUAGES TO HISTORICAL AND CULTURAL INFLUENCES

Pre-Columbian diffusion. The following are some of the important civilizations that have flourished in Meso-America:

civilization	period	location
Olmec	1200 BC–400 BC	Gulf Coast, Mexico
Monte Albán	400 BC–AD 700	Oaxaca, Mexico
Teotihuacán	AD 100–600	Central Mexico
Classic Maya	AD 300–900	Chiapas, Mexico; Petén, Guatemala
Toltec	900–1200	Central Mexico
Aztec	1300–1500	Central Mexico

The Aztecs spoke Nahuatl, as did the Toltecs. The Classic Maya probably spoke two or three Mayan languages, and the people of Monte Albán probably spoke one or more Zapotecan languages. No one knows what either the Teotihuacán people or the Olmecs spoke, but it has been surmised that at least some Olmecs spoke Mixe-Zoque languages and that the Teotihuacán people may have spoken Otomían languages (though an Aztec tradition says Totonac).

In the pre-Columbian period, there was naturally contact among Meso-American languages and occasional borrowing of vocabulary and other linguistic features. Partly because of the unavailability of grammars and dictionaries, actual cases of such diffusion have not been much studied.

Some of the known contacts resulting in borrowing are the following: (1) Mixe-Zoque languages (Olmecs?) have given words to Mayan, Mixtecan, Zapotecan, Otomían, Aztec, Lencan, Xinca, and Jicaque; (2) Zapotecan languages (Monte Albán) have given words to Huastec and Yucatec; (3) Mayan languages (Mayas) have given words to Xinca, Lencan, and Jicaque; and (4) Nahuatl (Toltecs and Aztecs) has given words to Mayan, Lencan, other Uto-Aztecan languages, as well as to other Meso-American languages. Words diffused from these sources provide evidence that contact took place. Scholars know that contact must have taken place at particular times and places, and therefore can form hypotheses about where certain languages may have been spoken in the more remote past.

External relationships and contacts. Various scholars have suggested that some Meso-American language or family is related to a language or family (other than Uto-Aztecan) outside of Meso-America. These suggestions are mostly parts of larger attempts to synthesize the language classification of the New World, or of the whole world, and are usually based on the sometimes unexpressed view that all the languages of the Western Hemisphere or even of the whole world are ultimately genetically related. Although the assumption may be true, the proposed connections have been unconvincing to specialists in Meso-American languages. The only generally accepted larger groupings are Hokan and Penutian. Most scholars do not have the breadth of knowledge to be able to evaluate these vast proposals.

One proposal of external relationship probably has some merit. In 1961 it was suggested that Chipaya—a language spoken on the shores of Lake Titicaca in Bolivia—is genetically related to the Mayan languages. The hypothesis, proposed by Ronald Olson, a U.S. missionary linguist, was based on 120 sets of lexical comparisons between Chipaya and Proto-Mayan. The data cited are subject to more than one interpretation, because many of the comparisons involve semantic notions and word forms that are widespread in the Western Hemisphere; also, Chipaya has been so influenced grammatically

Marginal notes:
Hypotheses concerning superstocks

Known contacts between various Indian groups

by Aymara (which all Chipayas can speak) that any grammatical peculiarities it may once have shared with Mayan have disappeared. Because a core of data showing regular sound correspondences remains, it is probably necessary to assume that there is a historical connection between Chipaya and Mayan, possibly, but not demonstrably, a genetic relationship. The connection may have been direct—presumably from Meso-America to Bolivia via land—or there may be other languages in western South America that show prehistoric contacts with Mayan. The acceptance of a prehistoric linguistic connection, neither extremely remote nor extremely recent, between Meso-America and the Andes is quite provocative, inasmuch as other evidence exists for early culture contact between Meso-America and the Andes, Meso-America generally being the donor and the Andes generally being the beneficiary; *e.g.*, in the case of corn. Later diffusion from South America to Meso-America also occurred; *e.g.*, witness the transference of peanuts, metallurgy, hammocks.

Interaction between Spanish and Indian languages. In modern Meso-America, the dominant European language is Spanish. The speakers of all Meso-American Indian languages include some who are bilingual; and a few languages are spoken by almost totally bilingual populations. Most Indian languages spoken by sizable populations have at least 50 percent monolingual speakers. All Meso-American languages with a significant number of bilingual speakers have been influenced by Spanish, primarily in the areas of vocabulary, particles, and word order. Since the Spanish conquest, Meso-American languages have been borrowing words from Spanish, and, because the kind of Spanish spoken has changed somewhat over the years, both in vocabulary and pronunciation, different historical periods are usually distinguishable in lexical borrowings. For a variety of reasons, certain function words, primarily conjunctions and adverbs, are frequently borrowed from Spanish; *e.g.*, *ya* "already," *pero* "but," *hasta* "until," *y* "and," *o* "or," *ni* "not even," *hasta* "even," *si* "if," *cuando* "when," *porque* "because," *por eso* "therefore, so," *entonces* "then." Some languages have assimilated the Spanish word order of subject–verb–object.

Conversely, the Spanish of Meso-America has been the recipient of vast amounts of lexical material from local languages, primarily Nahuatl. The borrowing has provided names of plants, animals, artifacts, and social forms indigenous to Meso-America and lacking names in Spanish. Among the reasons that Nahuatl has been the primary source is that the Aztecs were the first Meso-American people conquered by the Spaniards; the Aztecs had outposts in many parts of Meso-America; the Spaniards recruited Aztecs, particularly as guides, into their military force to assist their venture of subduing the rest of Meso-America; and, for several decades, Aztec, written in Roman orthography, was used in many parts of Meso-America to keep official records, such as deeds, wills, and censuses.

Many of the words borrowed into Spanish from Aztec have since passed in turn into English; *e.g.*, chili, chile, or chilli (Spanish *chile*), avocado (Spanish *aguacate*), chicle, chocolate, peyote, coyote, tomato (Spanish *tomate*), ocelot (Spanish *ocelote*), guacamole, mescal.

In some parts of Meso-America, because of economic and social conditions, an Indian may speak one or more Indian languages besides his own. This is common in Guatemala, where some areas have been recently colonized by speakers of more than one language, or some communities have received outside settlers in the more remote past.

The names used in this article for the Meso-American Indian languages are English versions of the Spanish terms for them. Only in a few cases are these names the ones actually used by the people who speak the languages in question. First, most of the names are of Aztec origin, because at the outset the Spanish learned of local phenomena primarily via Aztec. Secondly, some languages have no special name of their own, simply being called "our language."

Pre-Columbian writing. Most of the Meso-American cultures shared a mathematical notation and calendrical system that had been developed and diffused in the distant past, probably before 500 BC. At the time of European contact the Aztecs, Zapotecs, Mixtecs, Otomís, Mayans, and perhaps some others were all producing records on stone (inscriptions) and on a type of homegrown paper (produced from the amate tree, *Ficus glabrata*), these latter being commonly called codices. Except for the Mayan system, which probably originated before AD 1, the records cannot properly be called writing, in that it was not possible to represent all of speech, but only numbers, dates, and names (pictographically). The Mayan system, besides representing all these, was also used to represent morphemes (words and word elements) and phonemes (distinctive sounds). Presumably the symbols used in this system (called glyphs) represent individual phonemes, syllables, and morphemes; and they give semantic information as well to take the ambiguity out of homophonous readings. Several scholars have devoted much time to the study of Mayan writing, but, to date, the results have not been very impressive. A few scholars outside the Meso-American field believe the Mayan writing system is purely ideographic and hence inherently undecipherable without a bilingual inscription or text in a known language. All specialists within the Mayan field hold that the Mayan is a mixed ideographic and phonological system.

What may be delaying progress in the deciphering of Mayan writing is the absence of reconstructions for intermediate groupings within the Mayan family (*e.g.*, Proto-Yucatecan, Proto-Cholan, and others) and ignorance of Mayan languages other than colonial Yucatec on the part of the investigators. Efforts are being made to correct these deficiencies, particularly by Mexican specialists. It is not known whether Mayan writing was used to write more than one language and, if so, what the languages were. If only one, it was probably either Proto-Cholan or Proto-Yucatecan. The symbols used in all the pre-Columbian notation systems are obviously pictographic in origin, as was the case in the ancient Egyptian, Sumerian, ancient Chinese, and Indus Valley writing systems.

LINGUISTIC CHARACTERISTICS
OF THE MESO-AMERICAN LANGUAGES

In general, all the languages of a particular family are typologically similar to one another both in phonology and grammar. Among the 21 language groupings in Meso-America, there are several types of sound systems and grammatical systems. Because study in this area has hardly begun, nothing very secure can be asserted here, but some general characteristics can be outlined on the basis of data for the following reasonably well-documented languages: Tequistlatec, Otomí, Mazatec, Mixtec, Zapotec, Chinantec, Aztec, Zoque, Totonac, Quiché, and Tarasco.

Phonologically, there is a wide diversity among Meso-American languages. Voiced spirants—*i.e.*, sounds like English *v*, *z*, or *th* in "then"—are missing from all Meso-American languages. Other phonological features in these languages include a voiceless lateral spirant sound, *lh* (in Tequistlatec and Totonac); a lateral affricate, *tl* (in Aztec and Totonac); a postvelar stop, *q*, in contrast with a velar stop, *k* (in Quiché and Totonac); glottalized vowels (in Zapotec, Zoque, Aztec, and Totonac); glottalized consonants (in Tequistlatec, Quiché, Otomí, and Mazatec); aspirated stops (in Tarasco, Otomí, and Mazatec); voiced stops (in Tequistlatec, Otomí, Mazatec, and Chinantec); prenasalized stops (in Otomí, Mazatec, and Mixtec); nasalized vowels (in Otomí, Mazatec, Mixtec, and Chinantec); a labiovelar stop, *kw*, sometimes contrasting with a bilabial stop, *p* (in Otomí, Mazatec, Mixtec, Aztec); tone and stress accent (tone in Otomí, Mazatec, Mixtec, Chinantec, Zapotec; stress in Tarasco and Tequistlatec); and initial and final consonant clusters (in Tequistlatec).

Grammatically, Meso-American languages are rather diverse, but, according to available data, they fall into three main types: Type A, an Oto-Manguean type, is

*Pre-
historic
linguistic
connection
between
Meso-
America
and the
Andes*

*Bilingual-
ism
among
Indians*

*Diverse
types of
sound
systems
and
grammars*

Gram-
matical
generaliza-
tions

rightward expanding (*i.e.*, modifiers follow the elements they modify) and synthetic to a low degree (*i.e.*, characterized by relatively few morphemes per word). It employs prefixes and prepositions, and it seldom uses compounding to form words. Type B, an intermediate type, is prepositional, like A, and averagely synthetic, making some use of prefixes (subjects, objects, and possessors) and much use of suffixes. It is mildly leftward expanding (*i.e.*, modifiers precede the elements they modify) and is mainly represented by Mayan and Uto-Aztecan languages but partially by Mixe-Zoque and Totonacan. Type C, a leftward expanding type, is highly synthetic with great use of suffixes and postpositions and active ablaut (an interchange among consonants and vowels for the purpose of derivation or inflection). It is represented by Tarasco and, partially, by Totonacan and Mixe-Zoque.

There are a number of grammatical generalizations that can be made about all or most Meso-American Indian languages. (1) The genitive relationship between nouns or noun phrases is (except for Tarasco) expressed by means of a possessive pronoun with the possessed noun; *e.g.*, "the dog's fleas" is expressed as "his fleas the dog." (2) Locative notions, such as "above," "below," "in," "on," "beside," are not expressed by prepositions and adverbs, as in European languages, but by means of location nouns (meaning "aboveness," "belowness," "belly," "surface," "side," and so forth), which are always combined with a possessive pronoun, the function of which is to indicate the "object" of the prepositional–adverbial notion. Most languages, however, have at least one generic relational particle that is combined in a phrase with a location noun and its object and has "generic prepositional" function; thus "on the table" is expressed "at (generic particle) its-top the table," or "in the box" is expressed "at its-inside the box." Whereas in most languages the generic relational particles are prepositions, Zoque and Tarasco have postpositions, which are in part related to location nouns.

(3) Within the verbal system, aspect (type of action—*e.g.*, ongoing, habitual, finished, potential, and so forth) is well developed, and tense (time—*e.g.*, now, in the past, in the future) is generally weakly developed. (4) The copula, or equational verb "be," is not expressed in most Meso-American languages. (5) Case suffixes are generally absent, being present in just three languages: Tarasco has a genitive case, an objective case, and various locational cases; Aztec and Zoque have only locational cases, and these are usually related to location nouns. (6) A relative clause that modifies a noun follows it in all the languages of the sample above; *e.g.*, "the man whom I saw (on the street yesterday)." (7) Some Oto-Manguean languages and some Mayan languages distinguish an inclusive pronoun "we" ("I and you") from an exclusive "we" ("I and he/they").

(8) Gender, or inflectional agreement of other word classes in the noun phrase with the noun itself, is rare in Meso-American languages and is limited to some Oto-Manguean languages. (9) Noun subclassification in the context of possession is not uncommon. In some languages, some nouns undergo form changes when possessed; these languages, therefore, have at least two classes of nouns. In other languages, the possessive pronouns differ in form according as they are associated with different classes of nouns. In languages in which the semantic motivation for such a subdivision is clear, the main kind of distinction is between intimate possession (body parts, kinship terms, articles of clothing) and casual possession (domestic animals, tools). (10) Some languages (Mayan, Mixe-Zoque) distinguish between the subject (actor) of a transitive verb and that of an intransitive verb by the form of the associated affixed pronoun. (11) Most Meso-American languages average more than one morpheme per word, and Tarasco and Totonac average more than two morphemes per word. (12) Most Meso-American languages (except Aztec) have consonantal or vocalic ablaut, or else show in their vocabulary sets of words that seem to be related through a formerly functional ablaut system.

(13) The numeral systems are vigesimal–decimal; that is, counting is from 1 to 10, then from 11 to 20, then from 21 to 40 (adding 1–20 to 20), then from 41–60 (adding 1–20 to 40), and so on, with special terms for 400 (20 × 20), 8,000 (20 × 20 × 20), 16,000 (20 × 20 × 20 × 20), and so on. In most languages (except Mayan) the numeral expressions for 6 through 9 (sometimes 5 through 9) are compounds of $5 + 1, 5 + 2, 5 + 3, 5 + 4$, or the like. (14) In all the languages referred to here, a numeral precedes the noun it quantifies.

BIBLIOGRAPHY. Few books ever appear treating the Meso-American Indian languages as a group, although many dictionaries and grammars for individual languages have been prepared. The most up-to-date overview can be gotten from three articles in the *Handbook of Middle American Indians*, vol. 5, *Linguistics* (1967): MARIA TERESA FERNANDEZ DE MIRANDA, "Inventory of Classificatory Materials," which is an annotated bibliography; MORRIS SWADESH, "Lexicostatistic Classification," in which the author applies glottochronology to the classification of all the Meso-American Indian languages; and ROBERT LONGACRE, "Systematic Comparison and Reconstruction," a review of what has been accomplished in the historical-comparative field to date. For linguistic characteristics of Meso-American languages, see TERRENCE KAUFMAN, "Areal Linguistics and Middle America," *Current Trends in Linguistics*, vol. 11 (1972). For Uto-Aztecan, see CHARLES F. and FLORENCE M. VOEGELIN and KENNETH L. HALE, *Topological and Comparative Grammar of Uto-Aztecan* (1962); and WICK R. MILLER, *Uto-Aztecan Cognate Sets* (1967). For Mayan and "new languages," see TERRENCE KAUFMAN, "Teco—A New Mayan Language," *Int. J. Am. Linguistics*, 35:154–174 (1969). For "external contacts," see RONALD D. OLSON, "Mayan Affinities with Chipaya of Bolivia," *ibid.*, 30:313–324 (1964) and 31:29–38 (1965).

(Te.K.)

Mesopotamia and Iraq, History of

Mesopotamia, most of which is contained within the present Republic of Iraq, was the home of some of the earliest, if not the earliest, civilized (urban and literate) communities in the world. This article, which covers the area's 5,000-year history, is divided into the following sections:

I. Mesopotamia until 1600 BC

THE ORIGINS OF HISTORY

The Mesopotamian background. In the narrow sense, Mesopotamia is the area between the Euphrates and Tigris rivers, north or northwest of the bottleneck at Baghdad; it is al-Jazīrah (The Island) of the Arabs. South of this lies Babylonia, named after the city of Babylon. But in the broader sense the name Mesopotamia has come to be used for the area bounded on the northeast by the Zagros Mountains and on the southwest by the edge of the Arabian Plateau and that stretches from the Persian Gulf in the southeast to the spurs of the Anti-Taurus Mountains in the northwest. Only from the latitude of Baghdad do the Euphrates and Tigris truly become twin rivers, the *rāfidān* of the Arabs, which have constantly changed their courses over the millennia. The low-lying plain of the River Kārūn in Persia has always been closely related to Mesopotamia; but it is not considered part of Mesopotamia as it forms its own river system.

Mesopotamia, south of ar-Ramādī (about 70 miles, or 110 kilometres, west of Baghdad) on the Euphrates and the bend of the Tigris below Sāmarrā' (about 70 miles north-northwest of Baghdad), is flat alluvial land. Between Baghdad and the mouth of the Shatt al-Arab (the mouth of the Tigris and Euphrates) there is a difference in height only of about 30 feet (or 10 metres). As a result of the slow flow of the water, there are heavy deposits of silt; and the river-beds are raised. Consequently, the rivers often overflow their banks (and may even change their course) when they are not protected by high dikes or—in recent times—can be regulated above Baghdad by the use of escape channels with overflow reservoirs. The extreme south is a region of extensive marshes and reed swamps, *hawrs*, which, probably since early times, have served as an area of refuge for oppressed and displaced peoples. The supply of water is not regular: as a result of the high average temperatures (at Baghdad, July–August 93° F [34° C], December–January 52° F [11°C]) and a very low annual rainfall (less than eight inches—200 millimetres—in southern Mesopotamia), the ground of the plain of latitude 35° S is hard and dry and unsuitable for plant cultivation for at least eight months in the year. Consequently, agriculture without risk of crop failure, which seems to have begun in the higher rainfall zones and in the hilly borders of Mesopotamia in the 10th millennium BC, began in Mesopotamia itself, the real heart of the civilization, only when artificial irrigation had been invented, bringing water to large stretches of territory through a widely branching network of canals. Since the ground is extremely fertile and, with irrigation and the necessary drainage, will produce in abundance, southern Mesopotamia became a land of plenty that could support a considerable population. The cultural superiority of north Mesopotamia, which may have lasted until *c.* 4000 BC, was finally overtaken by the south when men there had responded to the challenge of their situation.

The present climatic conditions are fairly certainly similar to those of 8,000 years ago. An English survey of ruined settlements in the area 30 miles—about 50 kilometres—around ancient Hatra (180 miles northwest of Baghdad) has shown that the southern limits of the zone in which agriculture is possible without artificial irrigation has remained unchanged since the first settlement of al-Jazīrah.

The availability of raw materials is a historical factor of great importance, as is the dependence on those materials that had to be imported. In Mesopotamia, agricultural products and those from stock breeding, fisheries, date-palm cultivation, and reed industries—in short, corn, vegetables, meat, leather, wool, horn, fish, dates, and reed and plant-fibre products—were available in plenty and could easily be produced in excess of home requirements to be exported. There are bitumen springs at Hīt (90 miles west of Baghdad) on the Euphrates (the Is of Herodotus). On the other hand, wood, stone, and metal were rare or even entirely absent. The date palm—virtually the national tree of Iraq—yields a wood suitable only for rough beams and not for finer work. Stone is completely lacking in southern Mesopotamia, although limestone is quarried in the desert about 35 miles to the west; and "Mosul marble" is found not far from the Tigris in its middle reaches. Metal can only be obtained in the mountains, and the same is true of precious and semiprecious stones. Consequently, southern Mesopotamia in particular was destined to be a land of trade from the start. Only rarely could "empires" extending over a wider area guarantee themselves imports by plundering or by subjecting neighbouring regions.

The raw material that epitomizes Mesopotamian civilization is clay: in the almost exclusively mud-brick architecture and in the number and variety of clay figurines and pottery artifacts, Mesopotamia bears the stamp of clay as does no other civilization; and nowhere in the world but in Mesopotamia and the regions over which its influence was diffused was clay used as the vehicle for writing. Such phrases as cuneiform civilization, cuneiform literature, and cuneiform law can apply only where men had held the idea of using soft clay not only for bricks and jars and for the jar stoppers on which a seal could be impressed as a mark of ownership but also as the vehicle for impressed signs to which established meanings were assigned—an intellectual achievement that amounted to nothing less than the invention of writing.

The character and achievements of ancient Mesopotamia. Questions as to what ancient Mesopotamian civilization did and did not accomplish, how it influenced its neighbours and successors, and what its legacy has transmitted of value are posed from the standpoint of 20th-century civilization and are in part coloured by ethical overtones, so that the answers can only be relative. Modern scholars assume the ability to assess the sum total of an "ancient Mesopotamian civilization"; but, since the publication of an article by Benno Landsberger, an Assyriologist, on "Die Eigenbegrifflichkeit der babylonischen Welt," it has become almost a commonplace to call attention to the necessity of viewing ancient Mesopotamia and its civilization as an independent entity.

Mesopotamia has many languages, many cultures, is broken up into many historical periods, has no real geographical unity, and above all no permanent capital city, so that by its very variety it stands out from other civilizations with greater uniformity, particularly that of Egypt. The script and the pantheon constitute the unifying factors, but in these also Mesopotamia shows its predilection for multiplicity and variety: written documents turned out in quantities and a pantheon consisting of more than 1,000 deities, even though many names may apply to different manifestations of a single god. Throughout 3,000 years of Mesopotamian civilization, each century gave birth to the next. Thus classical Sumerian civilization influenced that of the Akkadians; and the Ur III Empire, which itself represented a Sumero-Akkadian synthesis, exercised its influence on the first quarter of the 2nd millennium BC. With the Hittites, large areas of Anatolia were infused with the culture of Mesopotamia from 1700 BC onward. The contacts between Syrian and Palestinian scribal schools and Babylonian civilization during the Amarna period (14th century BC) must have led to the enrichment of the literature of the west Semitic lands: this, and not direct borrowing, is the explanation of the similarity of themes in cuneiform literature and the Old Testament, such as the story of the Flood or the motif of the righteous sufferer.

The world of mathematics and astronomy owes much to the Babylonians: for instance, the sexagesimal system for the calculation of time and angles, which is still practical because of the multiple divisibility of the number 60; the Greek day of 12 "double-hours"; and the zodiac and its signs. But often the origins and routes of borrowings are obscure, as in the problem of the survival of ancient Mesopotamian legal theory.

The achievement of the civilization itself may be expressed in terms of its best points—moral, aesthetic, scientific, and, not least, literary. Legal theory flourished and was sophisticated early on, being expressed in several collections of legal decisions, the so-called codes, of which the best known is the Code of Hammurabi. Throughout these codes recurs the concern of the ruler for the weak, the widow, and the orphan—even if, sometimes, the phrases were regrettably only literary clichés. The aesthetics of art are too much governed by subjective values to be assessed in absolute terms; but certain peaks stand out above the rest, notably the art of Uruk IV, the seal engraving of the Akkad period, and the relief sculpture of Ashurbanipal. Nonetheless, there is nothing in Mesopotamia to match the sophistication of Egyptian art. Science the Mesopotamians had, of a kind, though

The impetus of artificial irrigation

The importance of clay

Unique variety of the Mesopotamian civilization

Scientific
achieve-
ments

not as the word is understood of Greek science. From its beginnings in Sumer before the middle of the 3rd millennium BC, Mesopotamian science was characterized by endless, meticulous enumeration and ordering into columns and series, with the ultimate ideal of including all things in the world but without the wish or ability to synthesize and reduce the material to a system. Not a single general law has been found and only rarely the use of analogy. Nevertheless, it remains a highly commendable achievement that Pythagoras' law (that the sum of the squares on the two shorter sides of a right-angled triangle equals the square on the longest side), even though it was never formulated, was being applied as early as the 18th century BC. Technical accomplishments were perfected in the building of the ziggurats (temple towers like pyramids), with their huge bulk, and in irrigation, both in practical execution and in theoretical calculations beforehand. At the beginning of the 3rd millennium BC an artificial stone in use at Uruk (160 miles south-southeast of modern Baghdad) constitutes a forerunner of concrete, but the secret of its manufacture apparently was lost in subsequent years.

Writing pervaded all aspects of life and gave rise to a highly developed bureaucracy—one of the most tenacious legacies of the ancient East. Remarkable organizing ability was required to administer huge estates, in which, under the 3rd dynasty of Ur, for example, it was not unusual to prepare accounts for thousands of cattle or tens of thousands of bundles of reeds. Above all, the literature of Mesopotamia is one of its finest cultural achievements. Though there are many modern anthologies and chrestomathies (compilations of useful learning), with translations and paraphrases of Mesopotamian literature, as well as attempts to write its history, it cannot truly be said that "cuneiform literature" has been resurrected to the extent that it deserves. There are partly material reasons for this: many clay tablets survive only in a fragmentary condition, and duplicates that would restore the texts have not yet been discovered, so that there are still large gaps. A further reason is the inadequate knowledge of the languages: insufficient acquaintance with the vocabulary and, in Sumerian, major difficulties with the grammar. Consequently, another generation of Assyriologists will pass before the great myths, epics, lamentations, hymns, "law codes," wisdom literature, and pedagogical treatises can be presented to the reader in such a way that he can fully appreciate the high level of literary creativity of those times.

The classical and medieval views of Mesopotamia; its rediscovery in modern times. Before the first excavations in Mesopotamia, around 1840, nearly 2,000 years had passed during which knowledge of the ancient Near East was derived from three sources only: the Bible, Greek and Roman authors, and the excerpts from the writings of Berosus, a Babylonian who wrote in Greek. In 1800 very little more was known than in AD 800, although these sources had served to stir the imagination of poets and artists, down to *Sardanapalus* by the 19th-century English poet Lord Byron. Apart from the building of the Tower of Babel, the Old Testament mentions Mesopotamia only in those historical contexts in which the kings of Assyria and Babylonia affected the course of events in Israel and Judah: in particular Tiglath-pileser III, Shalmaneser V, and Sennacherib, with their policy of deportation, and the Babylonian Exile introduced by Nebuchadrezzar II. Of the Greeks, Herodotus of Halicarnassus (5th century BC, a contemporary of Xerxes I and Artaxerxes I), was the first to report on "Babylon and the rest of Assyria"; at that date the Assyrian Empire had been overthrown for more than 100 years. The Athenian Xenophon took part in an expedition, during 401–399 BC, of Greek mercenaries who crossed Asia Minor, made their way down the Euphrates as far as the vicinity of Baghdad, and returned up the Tigris after the famous Battle of Cunaxa. In his *Cyropaedia* Xenophon describes the final struggle between Cyrus II and the Neo-Babylonian Empire. Later, the Greeks adopted all kinds of fabulous tales about King Ninos, Queen Semiramis, and King Sardanapalus. These stories are described mainly in

Greek
views of
Mesopota-
mia

the historical work of Diodorus Siculus (1st century BC), who based them on the reports of a Greek physician, Ctesias (405–359 BC). Herodotus saw Babylon with his own eyes, and Xenophon gave an account of travels and battles. But all later historians wrote at second or third hand, with one exception, Berosus (born *c.* 340 BC), who emigrated at an advanced age to the Aegean island of Cos, where he is said to have composed his three books of *Babylōniaka*. Unfortunately, only extracts from them survive, prepared by one Alexander Polyhistor (1st century BC), who, in his turn, served as a source for the church father Eusebius (who died AD 342). Berosus derided the "Greek historians" who had so distorted the history of his country. He knew, for example, that it was not Semiramis who founded the city of Babylon; but he was himself the prisoner of his own environment and cannot have known more about the history of his land than was known in Babylonia itself in the 4th century BC.

Berosus' first book dealt with the beginnings of the world and with a myth of a composite being, Oannes, half fish, half man, who came ashore in Babylonia at a time when men still lived like the wild beasts. Oannes taught them the essentials of civilization: writing, the arts, law, agriculture, surveying, and architecture. The name Oannes must be derived from the cuneiform U'anna (Sumerian) or Umanna (Akkadian), a second name of the mythical figure Adapa, the bringer of civilization. The second book of Berosus contained the Babylonian king list from the beginning to King Nabonassar (Nabu-naṣir, 747–734 BC), a contemporary of Tiglath-pileser III. Berosus' tradition, beginning with a list of primeval kings before the Flood, is a reliable one; it agrees with the tradition of the Sumerian king list, and even individual names can be traced back exactly to their Sumerian originals. Even the immensely long reigns of the primeval kings, which lasted as long as "18 sars" ($= 18 \times 3,600 = 64,800$) of years, are found in Berosus. Furthermore, he was acquainted with the story of the Flood, with Cronus as its instigator and Xisuthros (or Ziusudra) as its hero, and with the building of an ark. The third book is presumed to have dealt with the history of Babylonia from Nabonassar to the time of Berosus himself.

Diodorus made the mistake of locating Nineveh on the Euphrates, and Xenophon gave an account of two cities, Larissa and Mespila, which, it is suspected, represented the ancient Kalakh (20 miles southeast of modern Mosul) and Nineveh (just north of modern Mosul), Mespila probably being nothing more than the word of the local Aramaeans for ruins: there can be no clearer instance of the rift that had opened between the ancient Near East and the classical West. In sharp contrast, the East had a tradition that the ruins opposite Mosul (in north Iraq) conceal ancient Nineveh. When a Spanish rabbi from Navarre, Benjamin of Tudela, was travelling in the Near East between 1160 and 1173, Jews and Muslims alike knew the position of the grave of the prophet Jonah. The credit for the rediscovery of the ruins of Babylon goes to an Italian, Pietro della Valle, who correctly identified the vast ruins north of modern al-Ḥillah (60 miles south of Baghdad); and he must have seen there the large rectangular tower that represented the ancient ziggurat. Previously, other travellers had sought the Tower of Babel in two other monumental ruins: Birs Nimrūd, the massive brick structure of the ziggurat of ancient Borsippa (near al-Ḥillah), vitrified by lightning, and the ziggurat of the Kassite capital, Dūr Kurigalzu, at Burj 'Aqarqūf, 22 miles west of Baghdad. Pietro della Valle also brought back to Europe the first specimens of cuneiform writing, stamped brick, of which highly impressionistic reproductions were made. Thereafter, European travellers visited Mesopotamia with increasing frequency, among them Carsten Niebuhr (an 18th-century German traveller); Claudius James Rich (a 19th-century Orientalist and traveller); and Ker Porter (a 19th-century traveller).

In modern times, a third Near Eastern ruin drew visitors from Europe—Persepolis, in the land of Persia east of Susiana near modern Shīrāz. In 1602 reports had filtered back to Europe of inscriptions that were not in Hebrew, Arabic, Aramaic, Georgian, or Greek. In 1700 an English-

The work
of Pietro
della
Valle

man, Thomas Hyde, coined the term "cuneiform" for these inscriptions, and by the middle of the 18th century it was known that the Persepolis inscriptions were related to those of Babylon. Carsten Niebuhr distinguished three separate alphabets (Babylonian, Elamite, and Old Persian cuneiform). The first promising attempt at decipherment was made by G.F. Grotefend in 1802, by use of the kings' names in the Old Persian versions of the trilingual inscriptions, although his later efforts led him up a blind alley. Thereafter, the efforts to decipher cuneiform gradually developed in the second half of the 19th century into a discipline of ancient Oriental philology, which was based on results established through the pioneering work of Emile Burnouf, Edward Hincks, Sir Henry Rawlinson, and many others.

Today this subject is still known as Assyriology, because at the end of the 19th century the great majority of cuneiform texts came from the Assyrian city of Nineveh, in particular, from the library of King Ashurbanipal in the mound of Kouyunçik at Nineveh.

Modern archaeological excavations. One hundred and thirty years separate the first excavations in Mesopotamia —adventurous expeditions involving great personal risks and far from the protection of helpful authorities—from those of the present day with their specialist staffs, modern technical equipment, and objectives wider than the mere search for valuable antiquities. The progress of five generations of excavators has led to a situation in which less is recovered more accurately; in other words, the finds are observed, measured, and photographed as precisely as possible. At first digging was unsystematic, with the consequence that although huge quantities of clay tablets and large and small antiquities were brought to light, the findspots were rarely described with any accuracy. Not until the beginning of the 20th century did excavators learn to isolate the individual bricks in the walls that had previously been erroneously thought to be nothing more than packed clay; the result was that various characteristic brick types could be distinguished, and successive architectural levels established. Increased care in excavation does, of course, carry with it the risk that the pace of discovery will slow down. Moreover, the eyes of the local inhabitants are now sharpened and their appetite for finds is whetted, so that clandestine diggers have established themselves as the unwelcome colleagues of the archaeologists.

Problems of mud-brick buildings

A result of the technique of building with mud brick (mass production of baked bricks was impossible because of the shortage of fuel) was that the buildings were highly vulnerable to the weather and needed constant renewal; layers of settlement rapidly built up, creating a *tall*, a mound of occupation debris that is the characteristic ruin form of Mesopotamia. The word itself appears among the most original vocabulary of the Semitic languages and is attested as early as the end of the 3rd millennium BC. Excavation is made more difficult by this mound formation, since both horizontal and vertical axes have to be taken into account. Moreover, the depth of each level is not necessarily constant, and foundation trenches may be dug down into earlier levels. A further problem is that finds may have been removed from their original context in antiquity. Short-lived settlements that did not develop into mounds mostly escape observation, but aerial photography can now pick out ground discolorations that betray the existence of settlements. Districts with a high water level today, such as the reed marshes (*hawr*s), or ruins that are covered by modern settlements, such as Arbīl, some 200 miles north of Baghdad, or that are surmounted by shrines and tombs of holy men are closed to archaeological research altogether.

Excavations in Mesopotamia have been almost exclusively national undertakings (France, England, the United States, Germany, Iraq, Denmark, Belgium, Italy, Japan, and the Soviet Union) and the "joint expedition" first sent to Ur (190 miles south-southeast of Baghdad) in the 1920s has remained a rare exception. The history of archaeological research in Mesopotamia falls into four categories, represented by phases of differing lengths: the first, and by far the longest, begins with the French expe-

dition to Nineveh (1842) and Khorsabad (the ancient Dur Sharrukin, 20 miles northeast of modern Mosul; 1843–55) and that of the English to Nineveh (1846–55) and Nimrūd (ancient Kalakh, biblical Calah; 1845; with interruptions until 1880). This marked the beginning of the "classic" excavations in the important ancient capitals, where spectacular finds might be anticipated. The principal gains were the Assyrian bull colossuses and wall reliefs and the library of Ashurbanipal from Nineveh, whereas the ground plans of temples and palaces were quite as valuable. While these undertakings had restored to life the remains of the Neo-Assyrian Empire from the 1st millennium BC, new French initiatives in Tello (Arabic Tall Lūḥ), 155 miles southeast of Baghdad, from 1877 onward reached almost 2,000 years further back into the past. There they rediscovered a people whose language had already been encountered in bilingual texts from Nineveh—the Sumerians. Tello (ancient Girsu) yielded not only inscribed material that, quite apart from its historical interest, was critical for the establishment of the chronology of the second half of the 3rd millennium BC but also a large number of artistic masterpieces. Thereafter, excavations in important cities spread to form a network, including Susa, 150 miles west of Isfahan in Iran (France; 1884 onward); Nippur, 90 miles southeast of Baghdad (the United States; 1889 onward); Babylon, 55 miles south of Baghdad (Germany; 1899–1917 and again from 1957 onward); Ashur, modern ash-Sharqāṭ, 55 miles south of Mosul (Germany; 1903–14); Uruk (Germany; 1912–13 and from 1928 onward); and at Ur (England and the United States; 1918–34). Mention should also be made of the German excavations at Boğazköy in central Turkey, the ancient Hattusas, capital of the Hittite Empire, which have been carried on, with interruptions, since 1906.

Investigations after 1925

The second phase began in 1925 with the commencement of U.S. excavations at Yorgan Tepe (ancient Nuzu), 140 miles north of Baghdad, a provincial centre with Old Akkadian, Old Assyrian, and Middle Assyrian/Hurrian levels. There followed, among others, French excavations at Arslan Tash (ancient Hadatu; 1928); Tall al-Aḥmar (ancient Til Barsib; 1929–31); and above all at Tall Harīrī (ancient Mari; 1933 onward); and U.S. excavations in the Diyālā region, 90 miles northeast of Baghdad: Tall al-Asmar (ancient Eshnunna), Khafājī, and other sites. Thus, excavation in Mesopotamia had moved away from the capital cities to include the "provinces." Simultaneously, it expanded beyond the limits of Mesopotamia and Susiana and revealed outliers of "cuneiform civilization" on the Syrian coast at Ras Shamra (ancient Ugarit; France, 1929 onward) and on the Orontes of northern Syria al'Aṭshānah (ancient Alalakh; England, 1937–39, 1947–49), whereas Danish excavations on the islands of Bahrain and Faylakah, off the Tigris–Euphrates Delta, since 1954 have disclosed staging posts between Mesopotamia and the Indus Valley civilization.

In its third phase, archaeological research in Mesopotamia and its neighbouring lands has probed back into prehistory and protohistory. The objective of these investigations, initiated by U.S. archaeologists, was to trace as closely as possible the successive chronological stages in the progress of man from hunter and gatherer to settled farmer and, finally, to city dweller. These excavations are strongly influenced by the methods of the prehistorian, and the principal objective is no longer the search for texts and monuments. Apart from the United States investigations, Iraq itself has taken part in this phase of the history of investigation, as has Japan since 1956.

Finally, the fourth category, which runs parallel with the first three phases, is represented by "surveys," which do not concentrate on individual sites but attempt to define the relations between single settlements, their positioning along canals or rivers, or the distribution of central settlements and their satellites. Since shortage of time, money, and an adequate task force preclude the thorough investigation of large numbers of individual sites, the method employed is that of observing and collecting finds from the surface. Of these finds, the latest in date will give a rough termination date for the duration of the settlement, but, since objects from earlier, if not the earliest, levels work their way to the surface with a predictable degree of certainty or are exposed in rain gullies, an intensive search of the surface of the mound allows conclusions as to the total period of occupation with some degree of probability. If the individual periods of settlement are marked on superimposed maps, a very clear picture is obtained of the fluctuations in settlement patterns, of the changing proportions between large and small settlements, and of the equally changeable systems of riverbeds and irrigation canals—for when points on the map lie in line, it is a legitimate assumption that they were once connected by water courses. During the four phases outlined, the objectives and methods of excavation have broadened and shifted. At first the chief aim was the recovery of valuable finds suitable for museums, but at the same time there was, from early on, considerable interest in the architecture of Mesopotamia, which won for it the place it deserves in architectural history. Alongside philology, art history also made great strides, building up a chronological framework by the combination of evidence from stratigraphical and stylistic criteria, particularly in pottery and cylinder seals. The discovery of graves and a variety of burial customs threw new light on the history of religion, stimulated by the interest of Old Testament studies. Later, an increasing interest from neighbouring disciplines emerged. While pottery had been collected previously for purely aesthetic motives or from the point of view of art history, attention came to be paid increasingly to the everyday wares, and greater insight into social and economic history was based on knowledge of the distribution and frequency of shapes and materials. Finally, the observation and investigation of animal bones and plant remains (pollen and seed analysis) supplied invaluable information on the process of domestication, the conditions of animal husbandry, and the advances in agriculture; such studies demand the cooperation of both zoologists and paleobotanists.

The emergence of Mesopotamian civilization. *The Late Neolithic period and the Chalcolithic period.* Between about 10,000 BC and the genesis of large permanent settlements, the following stages of development are distinguishable, some of which run parallel: (1) the change to sedentary life, or the transition from continual or seasonal change of abode, characteristic of hunter-gatherers and the earliest cattle breeders, to life in one place over a period of several years or even permanently; (2) the transition from experimental plant cultivation to the deliberate and calculated farming of grains and leguminous plants; (3) the erection of houses and the associated "settlement" of the gods in temples; (4) the burial of the dead in cemeteries; (5) the invention of clay vessels, made at first by hand, then turned on the wheel and fired to ever greater degrees of hardness, at the same time receiving almost invariably decoration of incised designs or painted patterns; (6) the development of specialized crafts and the distribution of labour; and (7) metal production (the first use of metal—copper—marks the transition from the Late Neolithic to the Chalcolithic period).

These stages of development can only rarely be dated on the basis of a sequence of levels at one site alone. Instead, an important role is played by the comparison of different sites, starting with the assumption that what is simpler and technically less accomplished is older. In addition to this type of dating, which can be only relative, over the last 20 years the carbon-14 method has been of great assistance. By this method the known rate of decay of the radioactive carbon isotope (carbon-14) in wood, horn, plant fibres, and bones allows the time that has elapsed since the "death" of the material under examination to be calculated. Although a plus/minus discrepancy of up to 200 years has to be allowed for, this is not such a great disadvantage in the case of material 6,000 to 10,000 years old. Even when skepticism is necessary because of the use of an inadequate sample, carbon-14 dates are still very welcome as confirmation of dates arrived at by other means.

The first agriculture, the domestication of animals, and the transition to sedentary life took place in regions in which animals that were easily domesticated, such as sheep, goats, cattle, and pigs, and the wild prototypes of grains and leguminous plants, such as wheat, barley, bitter vetch, pea, and lentil, were present. Such centres of dispersion may have been the valleys and grassy border regions of the mountains of Iran, Iraq, Anatolia, Syria, and Palestine; but they could also be, for example, the northern slopes of the Hindu Kush. As settled life, which caused a drop in infant mortality, led to the increase of the population, settlement spread out from these centres into the plains—although it must be remembered that this process, described with the phrase Neolithic revolution, in fact took thousands of years.

Representative of the first settlements on the borders of Mesopotamia are the adjacent sites of Zawi Chemi and Shanidar, which lie northwest of Rawāndūz. They date from the transition from the 10th to the 9th millennium BC and are classified as "pre-pottery." The finds included querns (primitive mills) for grinding grain (whether wild or cultivated is unknown), the remains of huts about 13 feet in diameter, and a cemetery with grave goods. The presence of copper beads is evidence of acquaintance with metal, though not necessarily with the technique of working it into tools; and the presence of obsidian (volcanic glass) is indicative of the acquisition of nonindiginous raw materials by means of trade. The bones found testify that the sheep were already domesticated at Zawi Chemi-Shanidar.

At Karīm Shahir, a site that cannot be accurately tied chronologically to Shanidar, clear proof was obtained both of the knowledge of grain cultivation, in the form of sickle blades showing sheen from use, and of the baking of clay, in the form of lightly fired clay figurines. Still in the hilly borders of Mesopotamia, a sequence of about 3,000 years can be followed at the site of Qalʿat Jarmo, east of Kirkūk, some 150 miles north of Baghdad. The beginning of this settlement can be dated to around 6750 BC; and excavations uncovered 12 archaeological levels of a regular village, consisting of about 20–25 houses built of packed clay, sometimes with stone foundations, and divided into several rooms. The finds included types of wheat (emmer and einkorn) and two-row barley, the bones of domesticated goats, sheep, and pigs, and obsidian tools, stone vessels, and, in the upper third of the levels, clay vessels with rough painted decorations, providing the first certain evidence for the manufacture of pottery. Jarmo must be roughly contemporary with the sites of Jericho (13 miles east of Jerusalem) and of Çatal-hüyük in Anatolia (central Turkey). Those sites, with their walled settlements, seem to have achieved a much higher level of civilization; but too much weight must not be placed on the comparison, as no other sites in and around Mesopotamia confirm the picture deduced from Jarmo alone.

About 1,000 years later are two villages that are the earliest so far discovered in the plain of Mesopotamia: Hassūna, near Mosul, and Tall Ṣawwān, near Sāmarrāʾ. At Hassūna the pottery is more advanced, with incised and painted designs; but the decoration is still unsophisticated. One of the buildings found may be a shrine, to judge from its unusual ground plan. Apart from emmer there occurs, as the result of mutation, six-row barley, which was later to become the chief grain crop of southern Mesopotamia. In the case of Tall Ṣawwān, it is significant that the settlement lay south of the boundary of rainfall agriculture; thus, it must have been dependent on some form of artificial irrigation, even if this was no more than the drawing of water from the Tigris. This, therefore, gives a date after which the settlement of parts of southern Mesopotamia would have been feasible.

The emergence of cultures. For the next millenium, the 5th, it is customary to speak in terms of various "cultures" or "horizons," distinguished in general by the pottery, which may be classed by its colour, shape, hardness, and, above all, its decoration. The name of each horizon is derived either from the type site or from the place where the pottery was first found: Sāmarrāʾ on the

The spread of early settlements

Pre-urban stages of development

Identification of cultural stages through pottery

Tigris, Tall Ḥalaf in the central Jazīrah, Ḥassūna Level V, al-'Ubaid near Ur, and Ḥājj Muḥammad on the Euphrates, not far from as-Samāwah (some 150 miles south-southeast of Baghdad). Along with the improvement of tools, the first evidence for water transport (a model boat from the prehistoric cemetery at Eridu, in the extreme south of Mesopotamia, c. 4000 BC), and the development of terra-cottas, the most impressive sign of progress is the constantly accelerating advance in architecture. This can best be followed in the city of Eridu, which in historical times was the centre of the cult of the Sumerian god Enki.

Originally a small, single-roomed shrine, the temple in the Ubaid period consisted of a rectangular building, measuring 80 by 40 feet (24 by 12 metres), that stood on an artificial terrace. It had an "offering-table" and an "altar" against the short walls, aisles down each side, and a facade decorated with niches. This temple, standing on a terrace probably originally designed to protect the building from flooding, is usually considered the prototype of the characteristic religious structure of later Babylonia, the ziggurat. The temple at Eridu is in the very same place as that on which the Enki-ziggurat stood in the time of the 3rd dynasty of Ur (c. 2112–c. 2004 BC), so the cult tradition must have existed on the same spot for at least 1,500–2,000 years before Ur III itself. Remarkable as this is, however, it is not justifiable to assume a continuous ethnic tradition. The flowering of architecture reached its peak with the great temples of Uruk, built around the turn of the 4th to 3rd millennium BC (Levels Uruk VI to IV).

In extracting information as to the expression of mind and spirit during the six millennia preceding the invention of writing sketched above, it is necessary to take account of four major sources: decoration on pottery, the care of the dead, sculpture, and the designs on seals. There is, of course, no justification in assuming any association with ethnic groups.

The most varied of these means of expression is undoubtedly the decoration of pottery. It is hardly coincidental that in regions in which writing had developed, high-quality painted pottery was no longer made. The motifs in decoration are either abstract and geometrical or figured, although there is also a strong tendency to geometric stylization. An important question is the extent to which the presence of symbols, such as the bucranium (a sculptured ornament representing an ox skull), can be considered as expressions of specific religious ideas, such as a bull cult, and, indeed, how much the decoration was intended to convey meaning at all.

It is not known how ancient is the custom of burying the dead in graves nor whether its intention was to maintain communication (by the cult of the dead) or to guard against the demonic power of the unburied dead left free to wander. A cemetery, or collection of burials associated with grave goods, is first attested at Zawi Chemi-Shanidar. The presence of pots in the grave indicates that the bodily needs of the dead person were provided for, and the discovery of the skeleton of a dog or, at Eridu, of a model boat in the cemetery suggests that it was believed that the activities of life could be pursued in the hereafter.

Early statuettes The earliest sculpture takes the form of very crudely worked terra-cotta representations of women; the "Ubaid horizon," however, has figurines of both women and men, with very slender bodies, protruding features, arms akimbo and the genitals accurately indicated, and also of women suckling children. It is uncertain whether it is correct to describe these statuettes as idols, whether the figures were cult objects, such as votive offerings, or whether they had a magical significance, such as fertility charms, or, indeed, what purpose they did fulfill.

Seals are first attested in the form of stamp seals at Tepe Gawra, north of Mosul. Geometrical designs are found earlier than scenes with figures, such as men, animals, conflict between animals, copulation, or dance. Here again, it is uncertain whether the scenes are intended to convey a deeper meaning. Nevertheless, unlike pottery, a seal has a direct relationship to a particular individual or group; for the seal identifies what it is used to seal (a

vessel, sack, or other container) as the property or responsibility of a specific person. To that extent, seals represent the earliest pictorial representations of persons. The area of distribution of the stamp seal was northern Mesopotamia, Asia Minor, and Iran. Southern Mesopotamia, on the other hand, was the home of the cylinder seal, which was either an independent invention or was derived from stamp seals engraved on two faces. The cylinder seal, with its greater surface area and more practical application, remained in use into the 1st millennium BC. Because of the continuous changes in the style of the seal designs, cylinder seals are among the most valuable of chronological indicators for archaeologists.

In general, the prehistory of Mesopotamia can only be described by listing and comparing human achievements, not by recounting the interaction of individuals or peoples. There is no basis for reconstructing the movements and migrations of peoples unless one is prepared to equate the spread of particular archaeological types with the extent of a particular population or the change of types with a change of population or the appearance of new types with an immigration.

The only certain evidence for the movement of men beyond their own territorial limits is provided at first by material finds that are not indigenous. The discovery of obsidian and lapis lazuli at sites in Mesopotamia or in its neighbouring lands postulates the existence of trade, whether it consisted of direct caravan trade or of a succession of intermediate stages.

Just as no ethnic identity is recognizable, so nothing is known of the social organization of prehistoric settlements. It is not possible to deduce anything of the "government" in a village nor of any supraregional connections that may have existed under the domination of one centre. Constructions that could only have been accomplished by the organization of men in large numbers are first found in Uruk Levels VI to IV: the dimensions of these buildings suggest that they were intended for gatherings of hundreds of people. As for artificial irrigation, which was indispensable for agriculture in south Mesopotamia, the earliest form was probably not the irrigation canal. It is assumed that at first floodwater was dammed up to collect in basins, near which the fields were located. Canals, which led the water farther from the river, would have become necessary when the land in the vicinity of the river could no longer supply the needs of the population.

Mesopotamian protohistory. Attempts have been made by philologists to reach conclusions as to the origin of the flowering of civilization in southern Mesopotamia by the analysis of Sumerian words. It has been thought possible to isolate an earlier, non-Sumerian substratum from the Sumerian vocabulary by assigning certain words on the basis of their endings to either a Neolithic or a Chalcolithic language stratum. These attempts are based on the phonetic character of Sumerian at the beginning of the 2nd millennium BC, which is at least 1,000 years later than the invention of writing. Quite apart, therefore, from the fact that the structure of Sumerian words themselves is far from adequately investigated, the enormous gap in time casts grave doubt on the criteria used to distinguish between Sumerian and "pre-Sumerian" vocabulary.

Analyses of Sumerian words

The earliest peoples of Mesopotamia who can be identified from inscribed monuments and written tradition—people in the sense of speakers of a common language—are, apart from the Sumerians, Semitic peoples (Akkadians or pre-Akkadians) and Subarians (the predecessors or near relatives of the Hurrians, who appear in northern Mesopotamia around the end of the 3rd millennium BC). Their presence is known, but no definite statements about their past or possible routes of immigration are possible.

At the turn of the 4th to 3rd millennium BC, the endlessly long span of prehistory is over, and the threshold of the historical era is gained, captured by the existence of writing. Names, speech, and actions are fixed in a system that is composed of signs representing complete words or syllables. The signs may consist of realistic pictures, abbreviated representations, and perhaps symbols selected at random. Since clay is not well suited to the drawing of curved lines, a tendency to use straight lines rapidly gained ground. When the writer pressed the reed in harder at the beginning of a stroke, it made a triangular "head," and thus "wedges" were impressed into the clay. It is the Sumerians who are usually given the credit for the invention of this, the first system of writing in the Near East. As far as they can be assigned to any language, the inscribed documents from before the dynasty of Akkad (c. 2334–c. 2154 BC) are almost exclusively in Sumerian. The extension, moreover, of the writing system to include the creation of syllabograms by the use of the sound of a logogram (sign representing a word), such as *gi*, "a reed stem," used to render the verb *gi*, "to return," can only be explained in terms of the Sumerian language. It is most probable, however, that Mesopotamia of the 4th millennium BC, just as in later times, was composed of many races. This makes it likely that, apart from the Sumerians, the interests and even initiatives of other language groups may have played their part in the formation of the writing system. A strong argument in favour of this is afforded by the system of numbers and measures, which, in contrast to the rudimentary methods of writing words, was very precise and complex from the beginning. In addition to the sexagesimal system indigenous to Sumerian, which has a progression of alternating tens and sixes (1, 10, 60, 600, 3,600, 36,000, and so on), there is the decimal system (1, 10, 100, and so on). Since the number 100 had no special significance for the Sumerians but was expressed in words as 60 + 40, the decimal system was probably intended to do justice to the numerals of a second, non-Sumerian language.

Sumerian is an agglutinative language: prefixes and suffixes, which express various grammatical functions and relationships, are attached to a noun or verb root in a "chain." Attempts to identify Sumerian more closely by comparative methods have as yet been unsuccessful and will very probably remain so, as languages of a comparable type are only known from AD 500 (Georgian) or AD 1000 (Basque)—that is, 3,000 years later. Over so long a time the rate of change in a language, particularly one that is not fixed in a written norm, is so great that one can no longer determine whether apparent similarity between words goes back to an original relationship or is merely fortuitous. Consequently, it is impossible to obtain any more accurate information as to the language group to which Sumerian may once have belonged.

Urban development in the 4th millennium BC

The most important development in the course of the 4th millennium BC was the birth of the city. There were precursors such as the unwalled prepottery settlement at Jericho of c. 7000 BC, but the beginning of cities with a more permanent character came only later. There is no generally accepted definition of a "city." In this context, it means a settlement that serves as a centre for smaller places, one that possesses one or more shrines of one or more major deities, has extensive granaries, and, finally, displays an advanced stage of specialization in the crafts.

The earliest cities of southern Mesopotamia, as far as their names are known, are Eridu, Uruk, Bad-tibira, Nippur, and Kish (35 miles south-southeast of Baghdad). The archaeological surveys of Robert McCormick Adams and Hans Nissen have shown how the relative size and number of the settlements gradually shifted: the number of small or very small settlements was reduced overall, whereas the number of larger places grew. The clearest sign of urbanization can be seen at Uruk, with the almost explosive increase in the size of the buildings. Uruk Levels VI to IV had rectangular buildings covering areas as large as 275 by 175 feet; they are described as temples, since the ground plans are comparable to those of later buildings whose sacred character is beyond doubt.

The major accomplishments of the period Uruk VI to IV, apart from the first inscribed tablets (Level IV B), are masterpieces of sculpture and of seal engraving and also of the form of wall decoration known as cone mosaics. Together with the everyday pottery of black or red burnished ware, there is a very coarse type known as the *Glockentopf* ("bell pot"). These are vessels of standard size whose shape served as the original for the sign *sila*, meaning "litre." It is not too rash to deduce from the mass production of such standard vessels that they served for the issue of rations. This would have been the earliest instance of a system that remained typical of the southern Mesopotamian city for centuries: the maintenance of part of the population by allocations of food from the state.

Historians usually date the beginning of history, as opposed to prehistory and protohistory, from the first appearance of usable written sources. If this is taken to be the transition from the 4th to the 3rd millennium BC, it must be remembered that this only applies to part of Mesopotamia: the South, the Diyālā region, Susiana (with a later script of its own invented locally), and the district of the Middle Euphrates. It does not apply to regions that remained without writing for a longer time, such as the Middle Tigris region (Assyria), Syria, Asia Minor, and Iran.

SUMERIAN CIVILIZATION

The Sumerians down to the end of the Early Dynastic period. Despite the Sumerians' leading role, the historical role of other races should not be underestimated. While with prehistory only approximate dates can be offered, historical periods require a firm chronological framework, which, unfortunately, is not yet established for the first half of the 3rd millennium BC. The basis for the chronology after about 1450 BC is provided by the data in the Assyrian and Babylonian king lists, which can often be checked by dated tablets and the Assyrian lists of eponyms (annual officials whose names served to identify each year). But it is still uncertain how much time separated the middle of the 15th century BC from the end of the 1st dynasty of Babylon, which is therefore variously dated to 1594 BC ("middle"), 1530 BC ("short"), or 1730 BC ("long" chronology). As a compromise, the middle chronology will be used. From 1594 BC several chronologically overlapping dynasties reach back to the beginning of the 3rd dynasty of Ur, c. 2112 BC. From this point to the beginning of the dynasty of Akkad (c. 2334 BC) the interval can only be calculated to within 20–30 years, via the ruling houses of Lagash and the rather uncertain traditions regarding the succession of Gutian viceroys. With Ur-Nanshe (c. 2520 BC), the first king of the 1st dynasty of Lagash, there is a possible variation of 50–60 years, and earlier dates are a matter of mere guesswork: they depend upon factors of only limited relevance, such as the computation of occupation or destruction levels, the degree of development in the script (paleography), the character of the sculpture, pottery, and cylinder seals, and their correlation at different sites. In short, the chronology of the first half of the 3rd millennium is largely a matter for the intuition of the individual author. Carbon-14 dates are at present too few and far between to be given undue weight. Consequently, the turn of the 4th to 3rd millennium is to be accepted, with due caution and reservations, as the date of the flourishing of the archaic civilization of Uruk and of the invention of writing.

Problems in chronological reconstruction

In Uruk and probably also in other cities of comparable size, the Sumerians led a city life that can be more or less reconstructed as follows: temples and residential districts; intensive agriculture, stock breeding, fishing, and date-palm cultivation, forming the four mainstays of the economy; highly specialized industries, carried on by sculptors, seal engravers, smiths, carpenters, shipbuilders, potters, and workers of reeds and textiles. Part of the population was supported with rations from a central point of distribution, which relieved people of the necessity of providing their basic food themselves, in return for their work all day and every day, at least for most of the year. The cities kept up active trade with foreign lands.

That organized city life existed is chiefly demonstrated by the existence of inscribed tablets. The earliest tablets contain figures with the items they enumerate and measures with the items they measure, as well as personal names and, occasionally, probably professions. This shows the purely practical origins of writing in Mesopotamia: it did not begin as a means of magic or as a way for the ruler to record his achievements, for example, but as an aid to memory for an administration that was ever expanding its area of operations. The earliest examples of writing are very difficult to penetrate because of their extremely laconic formulation presupposing a knowledge of the context and because of the still very imperfect rendering of the spoken word. Moreover, many of the archaic signs were pruned away after a short period of use and cannot be traced in the paleography of later periods, so that they cannot be identified.

One of the most important questions that has to be met when dealing with "organization" and "city life" is that of social structure and the form of government. But it can only be answered with difficulty, and the use of evidence from later periods carries with it the danger of anachronisms. The Sumerian word for ruler *par excellence* is *lugal*, which etymologically means "big man." The first occurrence comes from Kish around 2700 BC, since an earlier instance from Uruk is uncertain because it could simply be intended as a personal name: "Monsieur Legrand." In Uruk the ruler's special title was *en*. In later periods this word (etymology unknown), which is also found in divine names such as En-lil and En-ki, has a predominantly religious connotation that is translated, for want of a better designation, as "en-priest, en-priestess." *En*, as the ruler's title, is encountered in the traditional epics of the Sumerians (Gilgamesh is the "*en* of Kullab," a district of Uruk) and particularly in personal names, such as "The-*en*-has-abundance," "The-*en*-occupies-the-throne," and many others.

It has often been asked if the ruler of Uruk is to be recognized in artistic representations. A man feeding sheep with flowering branches, who is a prominent personality in seal designs, could thus represent the ruler or a priest in his capacity as administrator and protector of flocks. The same question may be posed in the case of a man depicted on a stele aiming an arrow at a lion. But these questions are purely speculative: even if the "protector of flocks" were identical with the *en*, there is no ground for seeing in the ruler a person with a predominantly religious function.

Literary and other historical sources. The picture offered by the literary tradition of Mesopotamia is clearer but not necessarily historically relevant. The Sumerian king list has long been the greatest focus of interest. This is a literary composition, dating from Old Babylonian times, that describes kingship (*nam-lugal* in Sumerian) in Mesopotamia from primeval times to the end of the 1st dynasty of Isin. According to the theory—or rather ideology—of this work, there was officially only one kingship in Mesopotamia, which was vested in one particular city at any one time; hence the change in dynasties brought with it the change of the seat of kingship:

Kish–Uruk–Ur–Awan–Kish–Hamazi–Uruk–Ur– Adab–Mari–Kish–Akshak–Kish–Uruk–Akkad– Uruk–Gutians–Uruk–Ur–Isin.

The king list gives as coming in succession several dynasties that now are known to have ruled simultaneously. It is a welcome aid to chronology and history, but, so far as the regnal years are concerned, it loses its value for the time before the dynasty of Akkad: for here the lengths of reign of single rulers are given as more than 100 and sometimes even several hundred years. One group of versions of the king list has adopted the tradition of the Sumerian flood story, according to which Kish was the first seat of kingship after the Flood, whereas five dynasties of primeval kings ruled before the Flood in Eridu, Bad-tibira, Larak, Sippar, and Shuruppak. These kings all allegedly ruled for multiples of 3,600 years (the maximum being 64,800 or, according to one variant, 72,000 years). The tradition of the Sumerian king list is still echoed in Berosus.

It is also instructive to observe what the Sumerian king list does not mention. It lacks all mention of a dynasty as important as the 1st dynasty of Lagash (from King Ur-Nanshe to Uru'inimgina, formerly known as Urukagina) and appears to retain no memory of the archaic florescence of Uruk at the beginning of the 3rd millennium BC.

Besides the peaceful pursuits reflected in art and writing, the art also provides the first information about violent contacts: cylinder seals of the Uruk IV Level depict fettered men lying or squatting on the ground, being beaten with sticks or otherwise maltreated by standing figures. They may represent prisoners of war being killed in order to dispose of them. It is unknown from where these captives came or what form "war" would have taken or how early organized battles were fought. Nevertheless, this does give the first, albeit indirect, evidence for the wars that are henceforth one of the most characteristic phenomena in the history of Mesopotamia; and it makes it all the more surprising that the Mesopotamian cities at the beginning of the 3rd millennium BC were not walled. The earliest city wall so far known, that of Uruk, dates only to 2700–2650 BC.

Just as with the rule of man over man, with the rule of higher powers over man it is difficult to make any statements about the earliest attested forms of religion or about the deities and their names without running the risk of anachronism. Excluding prehistoric figurines, which provide no evidence for determining whether men or anthropomorphic gods are represented, the earliest testimony is supplied by certain symbols that later became the cuneiform signs for gods' names: the "gatepost with streamers" for Inanna, goddess of love and war, and the "ringed post" for the moon god Nanna. A scene on a cylinder seal—a shrine with an Inanna symbol and a "man" in a boat—could be an abbreviated illustration of a procession of gods or of a cultic journey by ship. The constant association of the "gatepost with streamers" with sheep and of the "ringed post" with cattle may possibly reflect the area of responsibility of each deity. The Sumerologist Thorkild Jacobsen sees in the pantheon a reflex of the various economies and modes of life in ancient Mesopotamia: fishermen and marsh dwellers, date-palm cultivators, cowherds, shepherds, and farmers all have their special groups of gods.

Both Sumerian and non-Sumerian languages can be detected in the divine names and place-names. Since the pronunciation of the names is known only from 2000 BC or later, conclusions as to their linguistic affinity are not without problems. Several, for example, have been reinterpreted in Sumerian by popular etymology. It would be particularly important to isolate the Subarian components (related to Hurrian), whose significance was probably greater than has hitherto been assumed. For the south Mesopotamian city HA.A (the noncommittal transliteration of the signs) there is a pronunciation gloss shubari, and non-Sumerian incantations are known in the language of HA.A, which have turned out to be Subarian.

There have always been in Mesopotamia speakers of Semitic languages (which belong to the Hamito-Semitic group and also include ancient Egyptian, Berber, and various African languages). This element is easier to detect in ancient Mesopotamia, but whether people began to participate in city civilization in the 4th millennium BC or only during the 3rd is unknown. Over the last 4,000 years Semites (Amorites, Canaanites, Aramaeans, and Arabs) have been partly nomadic, ranging the Arabian fringes of the Fertile Crescent, and partly settled; and the transition to settled life can be observed in a constant, though uneven, rhythm. There are, therefore, good grounds for assuming that the Akkadians (and other pre-Akkadian Semitic tribes not known by name) also originally led a nomadic life to a greater or lesser degree. Nevertheless, they can only have been herders of domesticated sheep and goats, which require changes of pasturage according to the time of year and can never stray more than a day's march from the watering places. The traditional nomadic life of the Bedouin makes its appearance only with the domestication of the camel at the turn of the 2nd to 1st millennium BC.

The question arises as to how quickly writing spread and by whom it was adopted about 3000 BC or shortly thereafter. At Kish, in north Babylonia, almost 120 miles northwest of Uruk, clay tablets have been found with the same repertoire of archaic signs as at Uruk itself. This fact demonstrates that intellectual contacts existed between north and south Babylonia. The dispersion of writ-

Complexities in unravelling the nature of the power structure

The Sumerian king list

Early religious beliefs

The spread of writing

ing in an unaltered form presupposes the existence of schools in various cities that worked according to the same principles and adhered to one and the same canonical repertoire of signs. It would be wrong to assume that Sumerian was spoken throughout the area in which writing had been adopted: it is linguistically significant that even the earliest of the Uruk texts use a sexagesimal and a decimal system side-by-side. Moreover, the use of cuneiform for a non-Sumerian language can be demonstrated with certainty from the 27th century BC.

First historical personalities. The specifically political events in Mesopotamia after the flourishing of the archaic culture of Uruk cannot be pinpointed. Not until about 2700 BC does the first historical personality appear—historical because his name, Enmebaragesi (Me-baragesi), was preserved in later tradition. It has been assumed, although the exact circumstances cannot be reconstructed, that there was a rather abrupt end to the high culture of Uruk Level IV. The reason for the assumption is a marked break in both artistic and architectural traditions: cylinder seals were replaced by others with an entirely new style; the great temples were abandoned—flouting the rule of a continuous tradition on religious sites—and on a new site a shrine was built on a terrace, which was to constitute the lowest stage of the later Eanna ziggurat. On the other hand, since the writing system developed organically and was continually refined by innovations and progressive reforms, it would be overhasty to assume a revolutionary change in the population.

In the quarter or third of a millennium between Uruk Level IV and Enmebaragesi, southern Mesopotamia became studded with a complex pattern of cities, many of which were the centres of small independent city-states, to judge from the situation in about the middle of the millennium. In these cities, the central point was the temple, sometimes encircled by an oval boundary wall (hence the term temple oval); but nonreligious buildings, such as palaces serving as the residences of the rulers, could also function as centres.

Enmebara-
gesi

Enmebaragesi, king of Kish, is the oldest Mesopotamian ruler about whom there are authentic inscriptions. These are vase fragments, one of them found in the temple oval of Khafājī. In the Sumerian king list, Enmebaragesi is listed as the penultimate king of the 1st dynasty of Kish; a Sumerian epic, *Gilgamesh and Agga of Kish,* describes the siege of Uruk by Agga, son of Enmebaragesi. The discovery of the original inscriptions was of great significance because it enabled scholars to ask with somewhat more justification whether Gilgamesh, the heroic figure of Mesopotamia who has entered world literature, had actually been a historical personage. The indirect synchronism notwithstanding, the possibility exists that even remote antiquity knew its "Ninos" and its "Semiramis," figures onto which a rapidly fading historical memory projected all manner of deeds and adventures. Thus, though the historical tradition of the early 2nd millennium believes Gilgamesh to have been the builder of the oldest city wall of Uruk, such may not have been the case. The palace archives of Shuruppak (modern Tall Fa'rah, 125 miles southeast of Baghdad), dating presumably from shortly after 2600, contain a long list of divinities, including Gilgamesh and his father Lugalbanda. More recent tradition, on the other hand, knows Gilgamesh as judge of the nether world. However that may be, an armed conflict between two Mesopotamian cities such as Uruk and Kish would hardly have been unusual in a country whose energies were consumed, almost without interruption from 2500 to 1500, by clashes between various separatist forces. The great "empires," after all, formed the exception, not the rule.

Emergent city-states. Kish must have played a major role almost from the beginning. After 2500, southern Babylonian rulers, such as Mesannepada of Ur and Eannatum of Lagash, frequently called themselves king of Kish when laying claim to sovereignty over northern Babylonia. This is not to agree with some recent histories in which Kish is represented as an archaic "empire." It is more likely to have figured as a representative of the

north, calling forth perhaps the same geographical connotation later evoked by "the land of Akkad."

Although the corpus of inscriptions grows richer both in geographical distribution and in point of chronology in the 27th and increasingly so in the 26th century, it is still impossible to find the key to a plausible historical account. Besides, history cannot be written on the sole basis of archaeological findings. Unless clarified by written documents, these findings contain as many riddles as they seem to offer solutions. This applies even to as spectacular a discovery as that of the royal tombs of Ur with their hecatombs (large-scale sacrifices) of retainers who followed their king and queen to the grave, not to mention the elaborate funerary appointments with their inventory of tombs. It is only from *c.* 2520 to the beginnings of the dynasty of Akkad that history can be written within a framework, with the aid of reports about the city-state of Lagash and its capital of Girsu and its relations with its neighbour and rival, Umma.

Sources for this are, on the one hand, an extensive corpus of inscriptions relating to nine rulers, telling of the buildings they constructed, of their institutions and wars, and, in the case of Uru'inimgina, of their "social" measures. On the other hand, there is the archive of some 1,200 tablets—insofar as these have been published—from the temple of Baba, the city goddess of Girsu, from the period of Lugalanda and Uru'inimgina (first half of the 24th century). For generations, Lagash and Umma contested the possession and agricultural usufruct of the fertile region of Gu'edena. To begin with, some two generations before Ur-Nanshe, Mesilim (another "king of Kish") had intervened as arbiter and possibly overlord in dictating to both states the course of the boundary between them; but this was not effective for long. After a prolonged struggle Eannatum forced the ruler of Umma, by having him take an involved oath to six divinities, to desist from crossing the old border, a canal. The text that relates this event, with considerable literary elaboration, is found on the Stele of Vultures. These battles, favouring now one side, now the other, continued under Eannatum's successors, in particular Entemena, until, under Uru'inimgina, great damage was done to the land of Lagash and to its holy places. The enemy, Lugalzaggesi, was vanquished in turn by Sargon of Akkad. The rivalry between Lagash and Umma, however, must not be considered in isolation. Other cities, too, are occasionally named as enemies, and the whole situation resembles the pattern of changing coalitions and short-lived alliances between cities of more recent times. Kish, Umma, and distant Mari on the Middle Euphrates are listed together on one occasion as early as the time of Eannatum. For the most part, these battles were fought by infantry, although mention is also made of war chariots drawn by onagers (wild asses).

Intercity
rivalry
between
Lagash
and Umma

The lords of Lagash rarely fail to call themselves by the title of *ensi,* of as yet undetermined derivation; "city ruler," or "prince," would only be approximate translations. Only seldom do they call themselves *lugal,* or "king," the title given the rulers of Umma in their own inscriptions. In all likelihood, these were local titles that were eventually converted, beginning perhaps with the kings of Akkad, into a hierarchy in which the *lugal* took precedence over the *ensi.*

Territorial states. More difficult than describing its external relations is the task of shedding light on the internal structure of a state like Lagash. For the first time, a state consisting of more than a city with its surrounding territory came into being because aggressively minded rulers had managed to extend that territory until it comprised not only Girsu, the capital, and the cities of Lagash and Nina (Zurghul) but also many smaller localities and even a seaport, Guabba. But it is not clear to what extent the conquered regions were also integrated administratively. On one occasion Uru'inimgina uses the formula "from the limits of the Ningirsu [that is, the city god of Girsu] to the sea," having in mind a distance of up to 125 miles. It would be unwise to harbour any exaggerated notion of well-organized states exceeding that size.

For many years views were conditioned by the slogan of

the Sumerian temple city, used to convey the idea of an organism whose ruler, as representative of his god, theoretically owned all land, privately held agricultural land being a rare exception. The image of the temple city had its origin partly in the overinterpretation of a passage in the so-called reform texts of Uru'inimgina, which state that "on the field of the *ensi* [or else, his wife and the crown prince], the city god Ningirsu [or else, the city goddess Baba and the divine couple's son]" had been "reinstated as owners." On the other hand, the statements in the archives of the temple of Baba in Girsu, dating from Lugalanda and Uru'inimgina, were held to be altogether representative. Here is a system of administration, directed by the *ensi*'s spouse or by a *sangu* (head steward of a temple), in which every economic process, including commerce, stands in a direct relationship to the temple: agriculture, vegetable gardening, tree farming, cattle raising and the processing of animal products, fishing, and the payment in merchandise of workers and employees.

The conclusion from this analogy proved to be dangerous because the archives of the temple of Baba provide information about only a portion of the total temple administration and that portion, furthermore, is limited in time. Understandably enough, the private sector, which of course was not controlled by the temple, is scarcely mentioned at all in these archives. The existence of such a sector is nevertheless documented by bills of sale for land purchases of the pre-Sargonic period and from various localities. Written in Sumerian as well as in Akkadian language, they prove the existence of private land ownership or, in the opinion of some scholars, of lands predominantly held as undivided family property. Although a substantial part of the population was forced to work for the temple and drew its pay and board from it, it is not yet known whether it was year-round work.

It is probable, if unfortunate, that there will never exist a detailed and numerically accurate picture of the demographic structure of a Sumerian city. It is assumed that in the oldest city the government was in a position to summon sections of the populace for the performance of public works. The construction of monumental buildings or the excavation of long and deep canals could be carried out only by means of such a levy. The large-scale employment of indentured persons and of slaves are of no concern in this context. Evidence of male slavery is fairly rare before Ur III, and even in Ur III and in the Old Babylonian period slave labour was never an economically relevant factor. It was different with female slaves. According to one document, the temple of Baba employed 188 such women; the temple of the goddess Nanshe, 180, chiefly in grinding flour and in the textile industry; and this continued to be the case in later times. For accuracy's sake it should be added that the terms male slave and female slave are used here in the significance they possessed around 2000 and later, designating persons in bondage who were bought and sold and who could not acquire personal property through their labour. A distinction is made between captured slaves (prisoners of war and kidnapped persons) and others who had been sold.

In one inscription, Entemena of Lagash boasts of having "allowed the sons of Uruk, Larsa, and Bad-tibira to return to their mothers" and of having "restored them into the hands" of the respective city god or goddess. Read in the light of similar but more explicit statements of later date, this laconic formula represents the oldest known evidence of the fact that the ruler occasionally endeavoured to mitigate social injustices by means of a decree. Such decrees might refer to the suspension or complete cancellation of debts or to exemption from public works. Whereas a set of inscriptions of the last ruler from the 1st dynasty of Lagash, Uru'inimgina (possibly the correct reading in lieu of the former "Urukagina"), has long been considered a prime document of social reform in the 3rd millennium, the designation "reform texts" is only partly justified. Reading between the lines, it is possible to discern that tensions had arisen between the "palace"—the ruler's residence with its annex, administrative staff, and landed properties—and the "clergy"; that is, the

stewards and priests of the temples. In seeming defiance of his own interests, Uru'inimgina, who in contrast to practically all of his predecessors lists no genealogy and has therefore been suspected of having been a usurper, defends the clergy, whose plight he describes somewhat tearfully. If the foregoing passage about restoring the *ensi*'s fields to the divinity is interpreted carefully, it would follow that the situation of the temple was ameliorated and that palace lands were assigned to the priests. Along with these measures, which resemble the policies of a newcomer forced to lean on a specific party, are found others that do merit the designation of "measures taken toward the alleviation of social injustices"—for instance, the granting of delays in the payment of debts or their outright cancellation and the setting up of prohibitions to keep the economically or socially more powerful from forcing his inferior to sell his house, his ass's foal, and the like. Besides this, there were tariff regulations, such as newly established fees for weddings and burials, as well as the precise regulation of the food rations of garden workers, called blind men.

These conditions, described on the basis of source materials from Girsu, may well have been paralleled elsewhere; but it is equally possible that other archives, yet to be found in other cities of pre-Sargonic southern Mesopotamia, may furnish entirely new historical aspects. At any rate, it is wiser to proceed cautiously, by keeping to analysis and evaluation of the available material rather than to construct generalizations.

This, then, is the horizon of Mesopotamia shortly before the rise of the Akkadian Empire. In Mari, writing was introduced at the latest around the mid-26th century BC; and from that time this city, situated on the Middle Euphrates, forms an important centre of cuneiform civilization, especially in regard to its Semitic component. Reaching out across the Diyālā region and the Persian Gulf, Mesopotamian influences extended to Iran, where Susa is mentioned along with Elam and other, not yet localized, towns. In the west, the Amanus Mountains were known; and under Lugalzaggesi, the "upper sea" in other words, the Mediterranean, is mentioned for the first time. To the east, the inscriptions of Ur-Nanshe of Lagash already name the isle of Tilmun (modern Bahrain), which may have been even then a transshipment point for trade with the Oman coast and the Indus region, the Magan and Meluhha of more recent texts. Trade with Asia Minor and Afghanistan was nothing new to the 3rd millennium, even if these regions are not yet listed by their names. It was the task of the Akkadian dynasty to unite, within these boundaries, a territory that transcended the dimensions of a state of the type represented by Lagash.

Sumer and Akkad in 2350–2000 BC. There are several reasons for taking the year 2350 as a turning point in the history of Mesopotamia. For the first time, an empire arose on Mesopotamian soil. The driving force of that empire was the "Akkadians," so called after the city of Akkad, which Sargon chose for his capital (it has not yet been identified but was presumably located on the Euphrates between Sippar and Kish). The name Akkad becomes synonymous with a population group that stands side-by-side with the Sumerians. The "land of Sumer and Akkad" becomes a name for southern Mesopotamia; "Akkadian" becomes the name of a language; and the arts rise to new heights. But even this turning point was not the first time the Akkadians had emerged in history. Semites—whether Akkadians or a Semitic language group that had settled before them—perhaps had had a part in the urbanization that took place at the end of the 4th millennium. The earliest Akkadian names and words occur in written sources of the 27th century. The names of several Akkadian scribes are found in the archives of Tell Abu Ṣalābīkh near Sippar, synchronous with those of Shuruppak (shortly after 2600). The Sumerian king list places the 1st dynasty of Kish, together with a series of kings bearing Akkadian names, immediately after the Flood. In Mari, Akkadian script was probably used from the very beginning. Thus, the founders of the dynasty of Akkad were presumably members of a people who had been familiar for centuries with Mesopotamian culture in all its forms.

Sargon's reign. According to the Sumerian king list, the first five rulers of Akkad (Sargon, Rimush, Manishtusu, Naram-Sin, and Shar-kali-sharri) ruled for a total of 142 years; Sargon alone ruled for 56. Although these figures cannot be checked, they are probably trustworthy, because the king list for Ur III, even if 250 years later, did transmit dates that proved to be accurate.

As stated in an annotation to his name in the king list, Sargon started out as a cupbearer to King Ur-Zababa of Kish. There is also an Akkadian legend about Sargon, who is supposed to have been exposed after birth, brought up by a gardener, and beloved of the goddess Ishtar. Nevertheless, there are no historical dates about his career. Yet it is feasible to assume that in his case a high court office served as springboard for a dynasty of his own. The original inscriptions of the kings of Akkad that have come down to posterity are brief, more informative for geographical distribution than content. The main source material for Sargon's reign, with its high points and catastrophes, are copies made by Old Babylonian scribes in Nippur, from the very extensive originals that presumably had been kept there. They are in part Akkadian, in part bilingual Sumerian–Akkadian texts. According to these texts, Sargon is said to have fought against the Sumerian cities of southern Babylonia, thrown down city walls, taken prisoner 50 *ensi*s, and have "cleansed his weapons in the sea." He is also supposed to have captured Lugalzaggesi of Uruk, the former ruler of Umma, who had vigorously attacked Uru'inimgina in Lagash, forcing his neck under a yoke and leading him thus to the gate of the god Enlil at Nippur. "Citizens of Akkad" filled the offices of *ensi* from the "nether sea" (the Persian Gulf) upward, which was perhaps a device used by Sargon to further his dynastic aims. Aside from the 34 battles fought in the south, Sargon also tells of conquests in northern Mesopotamia: Mari, Tuttul on the Balīkh, where he venerated the god Dagan (Dagon), Ebla (Tall Mardīkh of Syria), the "cedar forest" (Amanus or Lebanon), and the "silver mountains"; battles in Elam and the foreshore of the Zagros are mentioned. Sargon also relates that ships from Meluhha (Indus region), Magan (possibly the coast of Oman), and Tilmun (Bahrain) made fast in the port of Akkad.

Impressive as they are at first sight by way of a terse synopsis, these reports have only a limited value because they cannot be arranged chronologically, and it is not known whether Sargon built a large empire. Akkadian tradition itself saw it in this light, however, and a learned treatise of the late 8th or the 7th century lists no fewer than 65 cities and lands belonging to that empire. But even if Magan and Kapturu (Crete) are given as the eastern and western limits of the conquered territories, it is impossible to transpose this to the 3rd millennium.

Sargon appointed one of his daughters priestess of the moon god in Ur. She took the name of Enkheduana and was succeeded in the same office by Enmenana, a daughter of Naram-Sin. Enkheduana must have been a very gifted woman; two Sumerian hymns by her have been preserved, and she is also said to have been instrumental in starting a collection of songs dedicated to the temples of Babylonia.

Sargon died in very old age. The inscriptions, likewise preserved only in copies, of his son Rimush are full of reports about battles fought in Sumer and Iran, just as if there had never been a Sargonic empire. It is not known in detail how rigorously Akkad wished to control the cities to the south and how much freedom had been left to them; but they presumably clung tenaciously to their inherited local autonomy. From a practical point of view, it was probably in any case impossible to organize an empire that would embrace all of Mesopotamia.

Since the reports (that is, copies of inscriptions, as was their later elaboration into legend) left by Manishtusu, Naram-Sin, and Shar-kali-sharri speak time and again of rebellions and victorious battles and since Rimush, Manishtusu, and Shar-kali-sharri are themselves said to have died violent deaths, the problem of what remained of

Source materials on Sargon

Sargon's daughter

Akkad's greatness obtrudes. Wars and disturbances, the victory of one and the defeat of another, and even regicide constitute only one of the aspects suggested to us by the sources. Whenever they extended beyond the immediate Babylonian neighbourhood, the military campaigns of the Akkadian kings were dictated primarily by trade interests instead of being intended to serve the conquest and safeguarding of an empire. Akkad, or more precisely, the king, needed merchandise, money, and gold in order to finance wars, buildings, and the system of administration that he had instituted.

On the other hand, the original inscriptions that have been found so far of a king like Naram-Sin are scattered over a distance of some 620 miles as the crow flies, following the Tigris downriver: Diyarbakır on the Upper Tigris, Nineveh, Tall Birāk on the upper Khābūr (which had an Akkadian fortress and garrison), Susa in Elam, as well as Marad, Puzurish-Dagan, Adab (Bismāyah), Nippur, Ur, and Girsu in Babylonia. Even if all this was not part of an empire, it surely constituted an impressive sphere of influence.

Also to be considered are other facts that weigh more heavily than high-sounding reports of victories that cannot be checked. After the first kings of the dynasty had borne the title of king of Kish, Naram-Sin had himself addressed as "king of the four quarters of the earth"; that is, of the universe. As if he were in fact divine, he also had his name written with the cuneiform sign "god," the divine determinative that was customarily used in front of the names of gods; furthermore, he assumed the title of "god of Akkad." It is legitimate to ask whether the concept of deification may be used in the sense of elevation to a rank equal to that of the gods. At the very least it must be acknowledged that in relation to his city and his subjects, the king saw himself in the role played by the local divinity as protector of the city and guarantor of its well-being. In synchronous judicial documents from Nippur, the oath is often taken "by Naram-Sin," with a formula identical with that used in swearing by a divinity. Documents from Girsu contain Akkadian date formulas of the type "in the year in which Naram-Sin laid the foundations of the Enlil temple at Nippur and of the Inanna temple at Zabalam." As evidenced by the dating procedures customary in Ur III and in the Old Babylonian period, the use of such formulas presupposes that the respective city acknowledged as its overlord the ruler whose name is invoked.

Ascendancy of Akkad. Under Akkad, the Akkadian language acquired a literary prestige that made it the equal of Sumerian; under the influence, perhaps, of an Akkadian garrison at Susa, it spread beyond the borders of Mesopotamia. After having employed for several centuries an indigenous script patterned after cuneiform writing, Elam adopted Mesopotamian script during the Akkadian period and with a few exceptions used it even when writing in Elamite rather than Sumerian or Akkadian. The so-called Old Akkadian manner of writing is extraordinarily appealing from the aesthetic point of view; as late as in the Old Babylonian era, it served as a model for monumental inscriptions. This bears out the fact that the plastic and graphic arts, especially sculpture in the round, relief work, and cylinder seals reached a high point of perfection.

Thus the reign of the five kings of Akkad may be considered one of the most productive periods of Mesopotamian history. Although separatist forces opposed all unifying tendencies, Akkad brought about a broadening of political horizons and dimensions. The period of Akkad fascinated historiographers as did few other eras; having contributed its share to the storehouse of legend, it has never disappeared from memory. With a phrase such as "There will come a king of the four quarters of the earth," liver omens (sooth-saying done by analyzing the shape of a sheep's liver) of the Old Babylonian period express the yearning for unity at a time when Babylonia had once again disintegrated into a dozen or more small states.

The end of the dynasty. Of the kings after Shar-kali-sharri (*c.* 2217–*c.* 2193), only the names and a few brief

Divine kingship

inscriptions have survived. Quarrels arose over the succession, and the dynasty went under, although modern scholars know as little about the individual stages of this decline as about the rise of Akkad. Two factors contributed to its downfall: the invasion of the nomadic Amurrus (Amorites), called Martu by the Sumerians, from the northwest, and the infiltration of the Gutians, who came, apparently, from the region between the Tigris and the Zagros Mountains eastward. This argument, however, may be a vicious circle, as these invasions were provoked and facilitated by the very weakness of Akkad. In Ur III, the Martu, in part already sedentary, form one ethnic component along with Sumerians and Akkadians. The Gutians, on the other hand, played only a temporary role, even if the memory of a Gutian dynasty persisted until the end of the 17th century BC. As a matter of fact, the wholly negative opinion that even some modern historians have of the Gutians is based solely on a few stereotyped statements by the Sumerians and Akkadians, especially on the victory inscription of Utu-khegal of Uruk (2116–10). While Old Babylonian sources give the region between the Tigris and the Zagros Mountains as the home of the Gutians, these people probably also lived on the Middle Euphrates during the 3rd millennium. According to the Sumerian king list, the Gutians held the "kingship" in southern Mesopotamia for about 100 years. It has long been recognized that there is no question of a whole century of undivided Gutian rule and that some 50 years of this rule coincided with the final half century of Akkad. From this period there has also been preserved a record of a "Gutian interpreter." As it is altogether doubtful whether the Gutians had made any city of southern Mesopotamia their "capital" instead of controlling Babylonia more or less informally from outside, scholars cautiously refer to "viceroys" of this people. The Gutians have left no material records, and the original inscriptions about them are so slight that no binding statements about them are possible.

The Gutians' influence probably did not extend beyond Umma. The neighbouring state of Lagash enjoyed a century of complete independence, between Shar-kali-sharri and Ur III, during which time it showed expansionist tendencies and had widely ranging trade connections. Of the *ensi* Gudea (*c.* 2144–*c.* 2124) there are extant writings, exclusively Sumerian in language, which are of inestimable value. He had the time, power, and means to carry out an extensive program of temple construction during his reign; and in a hymn divided into two parts and preserved in two clay cylinders 12 inches (30 centimetres) high he describes explicitly the reconstruction of Eninnu, the temple of the god Ningirsu. Comprising 1,363 lines, the text is second in length only to Eannatum's Stele of Vultures among the literary works of the Sumerians up to that time. While Gudea forges a link, in his literary style, with his country's pre-Sargonic period, his work also bears the unmistakable stamp of the period of Akkad. Thus, the regions that furnish him building materials reflect the geographical horizon of the empire of Akkad, and the *ensi*'s title "god of his city" recalls the "god of Akkad" (Naram-Sin). The building hymn contains interesting particulars about the work force deployed. "Levies" were organized in various parts of the country, and the city of Girsu itself "followed the *ensi* as though it were a single man." Unfortunately, synchronous administrative archives of sufficient length to provide less summarily compiled information about the social structure of Lagash shortly before the 3rd dynasty of Ur are lacking. After the great pre-Sargonic archives of the Baba temple at Girsu, only the various administrative archives of the king of Ur III give a closer look at the functioning of a Mesopotamian state.

The 3rd dynasty of Ur. Utu-khegal of Uruk is given credit for having overthrown Gutian rule by vanquishing their king Tiriqan along with two generals. Utu-khegal calls himself lord of the four quarters of the earth in an inscription; but this title, adopted from Akkad, is more likely to signify political aspiration than actual rule. If another inscription has been correctly restored, Utu-khegal was a brother of the Ur-Nammu who

founded the 3rd dynasty of Ur ("3rd" because it is the third time that Ur is listed in the Sumerian King List). Under Ur-Nammu and his successors Shulgi, Amar-Su'en (Amar-Sin), Shu-Sin, and Ibbi-Sin, this dynasty lasted for a century (*c.* 2112–2004). Ur-Nammu was at first "governor" of the city of Ur under Utu-khegal. How he became king is not known, but there may well be some parallels between his rise and the career of Ishbi-Erra of Isin or, indeed, that of Sargon. By eliminating the state of Lagash, Ur-Nammu caused the coveted overseas trade (Tilmun, Magan, and Meluhha) to flow through Ur. As evidenced by a new royal title that he was the first to bear—that of "king of Sumer and Akkad"—he had built up a state that comprised at least the southern part of Mesopotamia. Like all great rulers, he built much, including the very impressive ziggurats of Ur and Uruk, which acquired their final monumental dimensions in his reign.

Assyriologists have given the name of Codex of Ur-Nammu to a literary monument that is the oldest hitherto-known example of a genre extending through the Code of Lipit-Ishtar in Sumerian to the Code of Hammurabi, written in Akkadian. It is a collection of sentences or verdicts mostly following the pattern of "If A [assumption], it follows that B [legal consequence]." The collection is framed by a prologue and an epilogue. The original was most likely a stele, but all that is known of the Code of Ur-Nammu so far are Old Babylonian copies. The term code as used here is conventional terminology and should not give the impression of any kind of "codified" law; furthermore, the content of the Code of Ur-Nammu is not yet completely known. It deals, among other things, with adultery by a married woman, the defloration of someone else's female slave, divorce, false accusation, the escape of slaves, bodily injury, the granting of security, as well as with legal cases arising from agriculture and irrigation.

Before its catastrophic end, under Ibbi-Sin, the state of Ur III does not seem to have suffered setbacks and rebellions as grievous as those experienced by Akkad. There are no clear indications pointing to inner unrest, although it must be remembered that the first 20 years of Shulgi's reign are still hidden in darkness. But from that point on until the beginning of Ibbi-Sin's reign, or for a period of 50 years at least, the sources give the impression of peace enjoyed by a country that lived undisturbed by encroachments from abroad. Some expeditions were sent into foreign lands, to the region bordering on the Zagros, to what later became Assyria, and to the vicinity of Elam, in order to secure the importation of raw materials, in a fashion reminiscent of Akkad. Force seems to have been employed only as a last resort; and every attempt was made to bring about peaceful conditions on the other side of the border through the dispatch of embassies or the establishment of family bonds, for example, by marrying the king's daughters to foreigners.

Shulgi, too, called himself king of the four quarters of the earth. Although he resided in Ur, another important centre was in Nippur, whence—according to the prevailing ideology—Enlil, the chief god in the Sumerian state pantheon, had bestowed on him the royal dignity. Shulgi and his successors enjoyed divine honours, as Naram-Sin of Akkad had before them; by now, however, the process of deification had taken on clearer outlines in that sacrifices were offered and chapels built to the king and his throne, while the royal determinative turned up in personal names. Along with an Utu-khegal (The Sun God Is Exuberance) there appears a Shulgi-khegal (Shulgi Is Exuberance), and so forth.

Administration. The highest official of the state was the *sukkal-makh*, literally "supreme courier," whose position may be paraphrased with "(state) chancellor." The empire was divided into some 40 provinces ruled by as many *ensis*, who, despite their far-reaching authority (civil administration and judicial powers), were no longer autonomous, even if only indirectly, although the office was occasionally handed down from father to son. They could not enter into alliances or wage wars on their own. The *ensis* were appointed by the king and could

The Gutians' obscure role

The Codex of Ur-Nammu

probably also be transferred by him to other provinces. Each of these provinces was obliged to pay a yearly tribute, the amount of which was negotiated by emissaries. Of special significance in this was a system called *bala*, "cycle" or "rotation," in which the *ensi*s of the southern provinces took part; among other things, they had to keep the state stockyards supplied with sacrificial animals. Although the "province" often corresponded to a former city-state, many others were no doubt newly established. The so-called land-register text of Ur-Nammu describes four such provinces north of Nippur, giving the precise boundaries and ending in each case with the statement: "King Ur-Nammu has confirmed the field of the god XX for the god XX." In some cities, notably in Uruk, Mari, or Der (near Badrah, Iraq), the administration was in the hands of a *shakana*, a man whose title is rendered partly by "governor" and partly by "general."

The available histories are practically unanimous in seeing in Ur III a strongly centralized state marked by the king's position as absolute ruler. Nevertheless, some caution is indicated. For one thing, the need to deal as tactfully as possible with the *ensi*s must not be underestimated. A further question arises from the borders between and relative extent of the "public" and the "private" sector; the latter's importance may have been underrated as well. What is meant by "private" sector is a population group with land of its own and with revenues not directly granted by a temple or a "palace," such as by the king's or an *ensi*'s household. The traditional picture is derived from the sources, the state archives of Puzurish-Dagan, a gigantic "stockyard" situated outside the gates of Nippur, which supplied the city's temples with sacrificial animals but inevitably also comprised a major wool and leather industry; other such archives are those of Umma, Girsu, Nippur, and Ur. All these activities were overseen by a finely honed bureaucracy that stressed the use of official channels, efficient administration, and precise accounting. The various administrative organs communicated with one another by means of a smoothly functioning network of messengers. Although almost 23,000 documents referring to the economy of Ur III have so far been published, they are still waiting to be properly evaluated. Nor is there yet a serviceable typology for them; only when that has been drawn up will it be possible to write a book entitled "*The Economic System of Ur III*." Represented in the main by contracts (loans, leases of temple land, the purchase of slaves, and the like), the "private" sector makes up only a small part of this mass of textual material. Neither can the sites at which discoveries have been made so far be taken as representative; in northern Babylonia, for example, scarcely any contemporary written documents have yet been recovered.

Ethnic, geographic, and intellectual constituents. From the ethnic point of view, Mesopotamia was as heterogeneous at the end of the 3rd millennium as it had been earlier. The Akkadian element predominated, and the proportion of speakers of Akkadian to speakers of Sumerian continued to change in favour of the former. Some scholars consider it altogether wrong to speak of "Sumerians" and "Akkadians" at this point, since the Sumerians had been living in southern Mesopotamia for at least 1,000 years, without any contact with possibly related peoples, whereas the Semitic population regenerated itself continually from the ranks of nomads who became sedentary. The third group, first mentioned under Sharkali-sharri of Akkad, are the Amorites. In Ur III, some members of this people are already found in the higher echelons of the administration, while the bulk, organized in tribes, still led a nomadic life. Their great days came in the Old Babylonian period. While clearly differing linguistically from Akkadian, the Amorite language, which can be reconstructed to some extent from hundreds of proper names, is fairly closely related to the so-called Canaanite branch of the Semitic languages, of which it may in fact represent an older form. The fact that King Shu-Sin had a regular wall built clear across the land, the "wall that keeps out the Tidnum" (name of a tribe), shows how strong the pressure of the nomads was in the 21st century and what efforts were being made to

check their influx. The fourth major ethnic group comprised the Hurrians, who were especially important in northern Mesopotamia and in the vicinity of modern Kirkūk.

It is likely that the geographical horizon of the empire of Ur III did not materially exceed that of the empire of Akkad. No names of localities in the interior of Asia Minor have been found, but there was much coming and going of messengers between Mesopotamia and Iran, far beyond Elam. There is also one mention of Gubla (Byblos) on the Mediterranean coast. Oddly enough, there is no evidence of any relations with Egypt, either in Ur III or in the Old Babylonian period. It is odd if no contacts existed at the end of the 3rd millennium between the two great civilizations of the ancient Near East.

Intellectual life at the time of Ur III must have been very active in the cultivation and transmission of older literature, as well as in new creations. Although its importance as a spoken tongue was diminishing, Sumerian still flourished as a written language, a state of affairs that continued into the Old Babylonian period. As shown by the hymn on the deified king, new literary genres arose in Ur III. If Old Babylonian copies are any indication, the king's correspondence with leading officials was also of a high literary level.

In the long view, the 3rd dynasty of Ur did not survive in historical memory as vigorously as did Akkad. To be sure, Old Babylonian historiography speaks of Ur III as *bala-Shulgi*, the "(reigning) cycle of Shulgi"; but there is nothing that would correspond to the epic poems about Sargon and Naram-Sin. The reason is not clear, but it is conceivable that the later, purely Akkadian population felt a closer identification with Akkad than with a state that to a large extent still made use of the Sumerian language.

Ur III in decline. The decline of Ur III is an event in Mesopotamian history that can be followed in greater detail than other stages of that history. There are some clear sources, such as the royal correspondence, two elegies on the destruction of Ur and Sumer, and an archive from Isin that shows how Ishbi-Erra, as usurper and king of Isin, eliminated his former overlord in Ur. Ibbi-Sin was waging war in Elam when an ambitious rival came forward in the person of Ishbi-Erra from Mari, presumably a general or high official. By emphasizing to the utmost the danger threatening from the Amorites, Ishbi-Erra urged the King to entrust to him the protection of the neighbouring cities of Isin and Nippur. Ishbi-Erra's demand came close to extortion, and his correspondence shows how skillfully he dealt with the Amorites and with individual *ensi*s, some of whom soon went over to his side. Ishbi-Erra also took advantage of the depression that the King suffered because the god Enlil "hated him": a phrase presumably referring to bad omens resulting from the examination of sacrificed animals, on which procedure many rulers based their actions (or, as the case may be, their inaction). Ishbi-Erra fortified Isin and, in the 10th year of Ibbi-Sin's reign, began to employ his own dating formula on documents, an act tantamount to a renunciation of loyalty. Ishbi-Erra, on his part, believed himself to be the favourite of Enlil, the more so as he ruled over Nippur, where the god had his sanctuary. In the end, he claimed suzerainty over all of southern Mesopotamia, including Ur.

While Ishbi-Erra purposefully strengthened his domains, Ibbi-Sin continued for 14 more years to rule over a decreasing portion of the land. The end of Ur came about through a concatenation of misfortunes: a famine broke out; and Ur was besieged, taken, and destroyed by the invading Elamites and their allies among the Iranian tribes. Ibbi-Sin was led away captive, and no more was heard of him. The elegies record in moving fashion the unhappy end of Ur, the catastrophe that had been brought about by the wrath of Enlil.

THE OLD BABYLONIAN PERIOD

Isin and Larsa. During the collapse of Ur III, Ishbi-Erra established himself in Isin and founded a dynasty there that lasted from 2017 to 1794; his example was fol-

[margin notes]

The bureaucracy

Literature of Ur III

Ur's end

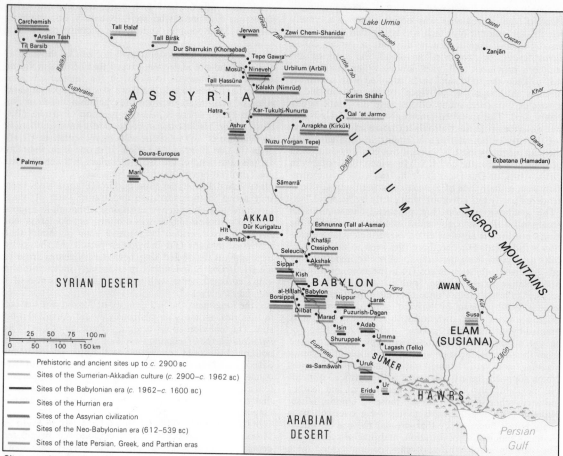

Sites associated with ancient Mesopotamian history.

Map legend:

Prehistoric and ancient sites up to *c.* 2900 BC
Sites of the Sumerian-Akkadian culture (*c.* 2900–*c.* 1962 BC)
Sites of the Babylonian era (*c.* 1962–*c.* 1600 BC)
Sites of the Hurrian era
Sites of the Assyrian civilization
Sites of the Neo-Babylonian era (612–539 BC)
Sites of the late Persian, Greek, and Parthian eras

lowed elsewhere by local rulers, as in Der, Eshnunna, Sippar, Kish, and Larsa. In many localities an urge was felt to imitate the model of Ur; Isin probably took over unchanged the administrative system of that state. Ishbi-Erra and his successors had themselves deified, as did one of the rulers of Der on the Iranian border. For almost a century Isin predominated within the mosaic of states that were slowly re-emerging. Overseas trade revived after Ishbi-Erra had driven out the Elamite garrison from Ur, and under his successor, Shu-ilishu, a statue of the moon god Nanna, the city god of Ur, was recovered from the Elamites who had carried it off. Up to the reign of Lipit-Ishtar (*c.* 1934–*c.* 1924), the rulers of Isin so resembled those of Ur, so far as the King's assessment of himself in the hymns is concerned, that it seems almost arbitrary to postulate a break between Ibbi-Sin and Ishbi-Erra. As a further example of continuity it might be added that the Code of Lipit-Ishtar stands exactly midway chronologically between the Code of Ur-Nammu and the Code of Hammurabi. Yet it is much closer to the former in language and especially in legal philosophy than to Hammurabi's compilation of judgments. For example, the Code of Lipit-Ishtar does not know the lex talionis (or "an eye for an eye and a tooth for a tooth"), the guiding principle of Hammurabi's penal law.

Political fragmentation. It is probable that the definitive separation from Ur III came about through changing components of the population, from "Sumerians and Akkadians" to "Akkadians and Amorites." An Old Babylonian liver omen states that "He of the steppes will enter, and chase out the one in the city." This is indeed an abbreviated formula for an event that took place more than once: the usurpation of the king's throne in the city by the "sheikh" of some Amorite tribe. These usurpations were regularly carried out as part of the respective tribes became settled, although this was not so in the case of Isin because the house of Ishbi-Erra came from Mari and was of Akkadian origin, to judge by the rulers' names. By the same linguistic token the dynasty of Larsa was Amor-

ite. The fifth ruler of the latter dynasty, Gungunum (ruled *c.* 1932–*c.* 1906), conquered Ur and established himself as the equal and rival of Isin; at this stage—the end of the 20th century BC—if not before, Ur had certainly outlived itself. From Gungunum until the temporary unification of Mesopotamia under Hammurabi, the political picture was determined by the disintegration of the balance of power, by incessant vacillation of alliances, by the presumption of the various rulers, by the fear of encroachments by the Amorite nomads, and by increasingly wretched social conditions. The extensive archive of correspondence from the royal palace of Mari (*c.* 1810–1750) is the best source of information about the political and diplomatic game and its rules, whether honoured or broken: treaties, the dispatch and reception of embassies, agreements about the integration of allied armies, espionage, "situation reports" from "foreign" courts. Devoid of exaggeration or stylization, these letters, dealing as they do with everyday events, are preferable to the numerous royal inscriptions on buildings even when the latter contain historical allusions.

Literary texts and increasing decentralization. Another indirect but far from negligible source for the political and socio-economic situation in the 20th–18th centuries BC is the literature of omens. These are long compendiums in which the condition of a sheep's liver or some other divinatory object (for instance, the behaviour of a drop of oil in a beaker filled with water, the appearance of a newborn baby, and the shape of rising clouds of incense) are described at length and commented on with the appropriate prediction: "The king will kill his dignitaries and distribute their houses and property among the temples"; "A powerful man will ascend the throne in a foreign city"; "The land that rose up against its 'shepherd' will continue to be ruled by that 'shepherd' "; "The king will depose his chancellor"; and "They will lock the city gate and there will be a calamity in the city."

Beginning with Gungunum of Larsa, the texts allow greater insight into the private sector than in any other

The literature of omens as a source

previous period. There is a considerable increase in the number of private contracts and private correspondences. Especially frequent among the private contracts are those concluded about loans of silver or grain (barley), illustrating the common man's plight, especially when driven to seek out a creditor, the first step on a road that in many instances led to ruin. The rate of interest, murderously high at 20 percent in the case of silver and 33 percent in that of grain, increased further if the deadline for repayment, usually at harvest time, was not kept. Insolvency resulted in imprisonment for debt, slavery by mortgage, and the sale of children and even the debtor's own person. Many private letters contain entreaties for the release of family members from imprisonment at the creditor's hands. Yet considerable forutnes were also made, in "liquid" capital as well as landed property. As these tendencies threatened to end in economic disaster, the kings prescribed as a corrective the liquidation of debts, by way of temporary alleviation at least. The exact wording is known of one such decree from the time of Ammisaduqa of Babylon.

Until the Ur III period, the only archives so far recovered dealt with temples or the palace. But belonging to the Old Babylonian period, along with documents pertaining to civil law, were an increasing number of administrative records of privately managed households, inns, and farms: settlements of accounts, receipts, and notes on various transactions. Here was clearly a regular bourgeoisie, disposing of its own land and of means independent of temple and palace. Trade, too, was now chiefly in private hands; the merchant travelled (or sent his partners) at his own risk, not on behalf of the state. Among the civil-law contracts there was a substantial increase in records of land purchases. Also significant for the economic situation in the Old Babylonian era was a process that might be summarized as "secularization of the temples," even if all the stages of this development cannot be traced. The palace had probably possessed for centuries the authority to dispose of temple property, but, whereas Uru'inimgina of Lagash had still branded the tendency as leading to abuses, the citizen's relationship to the temple now took on individual traits. Reve-

Changing relationship between religious institutions and individuals

nues from certain priestly offices—benefices, in other words—went to private individuals and were sold and inherited. The process had begun in Ur, where the king bestowed benefices, although the recipients could not own them. The archives of the "canonesses" of the sun god of Sippar furnish a particularly striking example of the fusion of religious service and private economic interest. These women, who lived in a convent called *gagûm*, came from the city's leading families and were not allowed to marry. With their property, consisting of land and silver, they engaged in a lively and remunerative business by granting loans and leasing out fields.

The tendency toward decentralization had begun in the Old Babylonian period with Isin. It concluded with the 72-year reign of the house of Kudur-Mabuk in Larsa (*c.* 1834–*c.* 1763). Kudur-mabuk, sheikh of the Amorite tribe of the Jamutbal, despite his Elamite name, helped his son Warad-Sin to secure the throne. This usurpation allowed Larsa, which had passed through a period of internal unrest, to flourish one more time. Under Warad-Sin and in the long reign of his brother Rim-Sin, large portions of southern Babylonia, including Nippur, were once again united in one state of Isin in 1794. Larsa on its part was conquered by Hammurabi in 1763.

Early history of Assyria. In contrast to southern Mesopotamia or the mid-Euphrates region (Mari), written sources in Assyria do not begin until very late, shortly before Ur III. By Assyria—a region that does not lend itself to precise geographical delineation—is understood the territory on the Tigris north of the river's passage through the mountains of the Jabal Ḥamrīn to a point north of Nineveh, as well as the area between Little and Great Zab (a tributary of the Tigris in northeast Iraq) and to the north of the latter. In the north, Assyria was later bordered by the mountain state of Urartu; to the east and southeast, its neighbour was the region around the old Nuzu (near modern Kirkūk, "Arrapachitis" [Ar-

rapkha] of the Greeks). In the early 2nd millennium the main cities of Assyria were Ashur (160 miles north-northwest of modern Baghdad), the capital (synonymous with the city god and national divinity); Nineveh, lying opposite modern Mosul; and Urbilum, the later Arbela (today Arbīl, some 200 miles north of Baghdad).

In Assyria, inscriptions were composed in Akkadian from the beginning. Under Ur III, Ashur was the provincial capital. Assyria as a whole, however, is not likely to have been a permanently secured part of the empire, since two date formulas of Shulgi and Amar-Su'ena mention the destruction of Urbilum. Ideas of the population of Assyria in the 3rd millennium are necessarily very imprecise. It is not known how long Semitic tribes had been settled there. The inhabitants of southern Mesopotamia called Assyria Shubir in Sumerian and Subartu in Akkadian; these names may point to an older Subarean population that was related to the Hurrians. Gasur, the later Nuzu, belonged to the Akkadian language region about the year 2200 but was lost to the Hurrians in the first quarter of the 2nd millennium. The Assyrian dialect Language differences of Akkadian found in the beginning of the 2nd millennium differs strongly from the dialect of Babylonia. These two versions of the Akkadian language continue into the 1st millennium.

In contrast to the kings of southern Mesopotamia, the Assyrian rulers styled themselves, not king but partly *iššiakum*, in short, the Akkadian for the Sumerian word *ensi*, partly *rubā'um*, or "great one." Unfortunately, the rulers cannot be synchronized precisely with the kings of southern Mesopotamia before the Assyrian Shamshi-Adad I (*c.* 1813–*c.* 1781 BC). For instance, it has not yet been established just when Ilushuma's excursion into Babylon, recorded in an inscription, actually took place. Ilushuma boasts of having freed of taxes the "Akkadians and their children." While he mentions the cities of Nippur and Ur, the other localities listed were situated in the region east of the Tigris. The event itself may have taken place in the reign of Ishme-Dagan of Isin (*c.* 1953–*c.* 1935 BC), although how far Ilushuma's words correspond to the truth cannot be checked; in the Babylonian texts, at any rate, no reference is made to Assyrian intervention. The whole problem of dating is aggravated by the fact that the Assyrians did not, unlike the Babylonians, use date formulas that often contain interesting historical details; instead, every year was designated by the name of a high official (eponymic dating). The conscious cultivation of an old tradition is mirrored in the fact that two rulers of 19th-century Assyria called themselves Sargon and Naram-Sin, after famous models in the Akkadian dynasty.

Aside from the generally scarce reports on projected construction, there is at present no information about the city of Ashur and its surroundings. There is, however, unexpectedly rewarding source material from the Assyrian trading colonies in Asia Minor. The texts come mainly from Kanesh (near modern Kayseri, in southeast Turkey) and from Hattusas (also southeast Turkey), the later Hittite capital. In the 19th century BC three generations of Assyrian merchants engaged in a lively commodity trade (especially in textiles and metal) between the homeland and Anatolia, also taking part profitably in internal Anatolian trade. Like their contemporaries in southern Mesopotamia, they did business privately and at their own risk, living peacefully and occasionally intermarrying with the "Anatolians." As long as they paid taxes to the local rulers, the Assyrians were given a free hand.

It is obvious that these forays by Assyrian merchants led to some transplanting of Mesopotamian culture into Asia Minor. Thus the Anatolians adopted cuneiform writing and used the Assyrian language as a means of communication. While this influence doubtless already affected the first Hittites arriving in Asia Minor, a direct line from the period of these trading colonies to the Hittite Empire cannot yet be traced.

From *c.* 1813 to *c.* 1781 Assyria was ruled by Shamshi-Adad I, a contemporary of Hammurabi and a personality in no way inferior to him. Shamshi-Adad's father—an

Amorite, to judge by the name—had ruled near Mari. The son, not being of Assyrian origin, ascended the throne of Assyria as a foreigner and on a detour, as it were, after having spent some time as an exile in Babylonia. He had his two sons rule as viceroys, in Ekallatum on the Euphrates and in Mari, respectively, until the older of the two, Ishme-Dagan, succeeded his father on the throne. Through the archive of correspondence in the palace at Mari, scholars are particularly well informed about Shamshi-Adad's reign and many aspects of his personality. Shamshi-Adad's state had a common border for some time with the Babylonia of Hammurabi; in the west, it reached to the Mediterranean. Soon after Shamshi-Adad's death, Mari broke away, regaining its independence under an Amorite dynasty that had been living there for generations; in the end, Hammurabi conquered and destroyed Mari. After Ishme-Dagan's death, Assyrian history is lost sight of for over 100 years.

The Old Babylonian Empire. *Political fortunes.* Hammurabi (*c.* 1792–50 BC) is surely the most impressive and by now the most popular figure of the ancient Near East of the first half of the 2nd millennium BC. He owes his posthumous reputation to the great stele into which the "Code of Hammurabi" has been carved and indirectly also to the fact that his dynasty has made the name of Babylon famous for all time. In much the same way in which pre-Sargonic Kish exemplified the non-Sumerian area north of Sumer and Akkad lent its name to a country and a language, Babylon became the symbol of the whole country that the Greeks called Babylonia. This term has already been used anachronistically as a geographical concept in reference to the period before Hammurabi. Originally the city's name was probably Babilla, which was reinterpreted in popular etymology as Bab-ilu (Gate of the God).

The 1st dynasty of Babylon rose from insignificant beginnings. The history of the erstwhile province of Ur is traceable from about 1894 onward, when the Amorite Samu'abum came to power there. What is known of these events fits altogether into the modest proportions of the period when Mesopotamia was a mosaic of small states. Hammurabi played skillfully on the instrument of coalitions and became more powerful than his predecessors had been. But it was only in his 30th year, after his conquest of Larsa, that he gave concrete expression to the idea of ruling all of southern Mesopotamia by "strengthening the fundament of Sumer and Akkad," in the words of that year's dating formula. In the prologue to the Code of Hammurabi the King lists the following cities as belonging to his dominions: Eridu near Ur, Ur, Lagash and Girsu, Zabalam, Larsa, Uruk, Adab, Isin, Nippur, Keshi, Dilbat, Borsippa, Babylon itself, Kish, Malgium, Mashkan-shapir, Kutha, Sippar, Eshnunna in the Diyālā region, Mari, Tuttul on the lower Balīkh (a tributary of the Euphrates), and finally Ashur and Nineveh. This was on a scale reminiscent of Akkad or Ur III. Yet Ashur and Nineveh cannot have formed part of this empire for long because at the end of Hammurabi's reign mention is made again of wars against Subartu—that is, Assyria.

Decline of Babylonia under Samsuiluna

Under Hammurabi's son Samsuiluna (*c.* 1749–*c.* 1712 BC) the Babylonian Empire greatly shrank in size. Following what had almost become a tradition, the south rose up in revolt; Larsa regained its autonomy for some time, and the walls of Ur, Uruk, and Larsa were levelled to the ground. Eshnunna, which evidently had also seceded, was vanquished in *c.* 1730. Later chronicles mention the existence of a state in the Sealand, with its own dynasty; by "sealand" is understood the marshlands of southern Babylonia. Knowledge of this new dynasty is unfortunately very vague, only one of its kings being documented in contemporary texts. In *c.* 1741 Samsuiluna mentions the Kassites for the first time; in *c.* 1726 he constructed a stronghold, "Fort Samsuiluna," as a bulwark against them on the Diyālā near its confluence with the Tigris.

Like the Gutians before them, the Kassites were at first prevented from entering Babylonia and pushed into the mid-Euphrates region; there, in the kingdom of Khana (centred on Mari and Terqa, both below the junction with the Khābur), a king appears with the Kassitic name of Kashtiliashu, who ruled toward the end of the Babylonian dynasty. From Khana the Kassites moved south in small groups, probably as harvest workers. After the Hittite invasion under Mursilis I, who is said to have dethroned Samsuditana, the last king of Babylon, in 1595, the Kassites assumed the royal power in Babylonia. So far, the contemporary sources do not mention this epoch, and the question arises as to how the Kassite rulers named in king lists mesh with the end of the 2nd millennium BC.

Babylonian law. The Code of Hammurabi is the most frequently cited cuneiform document in specialized literature. Its first scholarly examination in 1902 led to the development of a special branch of comparative jurisprudence, the study of cuneiform law. Following the division made by the first editor, Jean-Vincent Scheil, the Code of Hammurabi contains 280 judgments, or "paragraphs," on civil and criminal law, dealing in the main with cases from everyday life in such a manner that it becomes obvious that the "lawgiver" or compiler had no intention of covering all possible contingencies. In broad outline, the themes treated in the Code of Hammurabi are: libel; corrupt administration of justice; theft, receiving stolen goods, robbery, looting, and burglary; murder, manslaughter, and bodily injury; abduction; judicature of tax lessees; liability for negligent damage to fields and crop damage caused by grazing cattle; illegal felling of palm trees; legal problems of trade enterprises, in particular, the relationship between the merchant and his employee travelling overland, and embezzlement of merchandise; trust monies; the proportion of interest to loan money; the legal position of the female publican; slavery and ransom, slavery for debt, runaway slaves, the sale and vindication of slaves, and disclaimer of slave status; the rent of persons, animals, and ships and their respective tariffs, offenses of hired labourers, and the vicious bull; family law: the price of a bride, dowry, the married woman's property, wife and concubine, and the legal position of the respective issue, divorce, adoption, the wet nurse's contract, and inheritance; and the legal position of certain priestesses.

The Code of Hammurabi

A similar if much shorter compendium of judgments, probably antedating that of Hammurabi by a generation or two, has been discovered in Eshnunna.

Hammurabi, who called his own work *dīnāt mīšarim,* or "verdicts of the just order," states in the epilogue that it was intended as legal aid for persons in search of advice. It is nevertheless doubtful whether these judgments were meant to have binding force in the sense of modern statutes. The Code of Hammurabi differs in many respects from the Code of Lipit-Ishtar, which was written in Sumerian. Its most striking feature lies in the extraordinary severity of its penalties and in the principle of the lex talionis. The same attitude is reflected in various Old Babylonian treaties in which defaulters are threatened with bodily punishment. It is often said, and perhaps rightly so, that this severity, which so contrasts with Sumerian judicial tradition, can be traced back to the Amorite influence.

There is yet another way in which the Code of Hammurabi has given rise to much discussion. Many of its "paragraphs" vary according to whether the case concerns an *awīlum,* a *muškēnum,* or a *wardum.* A threefold division of the populace had been postulated on the basis of these distinctions. The *wardum* is the least problematical of them all: he is the slave—that is, a person in bondage who could be bought and sold, unless he was able to regain his freedom under certain conditions as a debtor-slave. The *muškēnum* were, under King Hammurabi at least, persons employed by the palace who could be given land in usufruct without receiving it as property. *Awīlum* were the citizens who owned land in their own right and depended neither on the palace nor the temple. As the scholar I.M. Diakonoff points out, the distinction cannot have been very sharply drawn because the classes *awīlum* and *muškēnum* are not mutually exclusive: a man in high palace office could fairly easily purchase land as private property, whereas the free citizen who got into debt as a result of a bad harvest or some other misfortune had one foot in the slave class. Still unanswered is the question as to which segment of the population could be conscripted to do public works, a term that included the levy in case of war.

Ammisaduqa (c. 1646–c. 1626 BC) comes a century and a half after Hammurabi. His edict, already referred to, lists, among others, the following social and economic factors: private debts in silver and grain, if arising out of loans, were cancelled; also cancelled were back taxes that certain officials owed the palace and that had to be collected from the people; the "female publican" had to renounce the collection of outstanding debts in beer and barley and was, in turn, excused from paying amounts of silver and barley to the king; taxes on leased property were reduced; debt slaves who had formerly been free (as against slaves made over from debtor to creditor) were ransomed; and high officials were forbidden on pain of death to press those who held property in fee into harvest work by prepayment of wages. The phrase "because the king gave the land a just order" serves as a rationale for many of these instances. In contrast to the "codes," about whose binding force there is much doubt, edicts such as those of Ammisaduqa had legal validity since there are references to the edicts of other kings in numerous legal documents of the Old Babylonian period.

Babylonian literature. The literature and the literary languages of Babylonia during the three centuries following Ur III deserve attention. When commenting on literary and historical texts such as the inscriptions of the kings of Akkad, it was pointed out that these were not originals but copies of Old Babylonian vintage. So far, such copies are the main source for Sumerian literature. But, while the Old Babylonian period created much literature itself (royal hymns of the kings of Isin, Larsa, and Babylon and elegies), it was above all a time of intensive cultivation of traditional literature. The great Sumerian poems, whose origins or first written version, respectively, can now be traced back to about 2600, were copied again and again. After 2000, when Sumerian as a spoken language rapidly receded to isolated regions and eventually disappeared altogether, texts began to be translated, line by line, into Akkadian until there came to be bilingual versions. An important part of this, especially in the instructional program in schools, were the so-called lexicographic texts. Sumerian word lists are almost as old as cuneiform writing itself because they formed the perfect material for those learning to write. In the Old Babylonian period, the individual lexical entries were translated and often annotated with phonetic signs. This led to the creation of "dictionaries," the value of which to the modern philologist cannot be exaggerated. Since Sumerian had to be taught much more than before, regular "grammatical treatises" also came into being: so far as it was possible, in view of the radically different structure of the two languages, Sumerian pronouns, verb forms, and the like were translated into Akkadian, including entire "paradigms" of individual verbs.

In belles-lettres, Sumerian still predominates, although there is no lack of Akkadian masterpieces, including the oldest Akkadian version of the *Epic of Gilgamesh.* The very high prestige still enjoyed by Sumerian should not be underestimated, and it continued to be used for inscriptions on buildings and the yearly dating formulas. Aside from being the language of practical affairs (letters and contracts), there was a high incidence of Akkadian in soothsaying and divinatory literature. To be sure, the Sumerians also practiced foretelling the future from the examination of animal entrails, but as far as is known they did not write down the results. In Akkadian, on the other hand, there are extensive and "scientifically" arranged compendiums of omens based on the liver (as well as other omens), reflecting the importance that the divination of the future had in religion, in politics, and in all aspects of daily life.

Judging by its continually more refined juridical thought, its ability to master in writing ever more complicated administrative procedures, its advanced knowledge of mathematics, and the fact that it marks the beginning of the study of astronomy, the Old Babylonian period appears to have been a time of exceedingly active intellectual endeavour—despite, if not because of, its lack of political cohesiveness.

The Hurrians. The Hurrians enter the orbit of ancient Near Eastern civilization toward the end of the 3rd millennium BC. They arrived in Mesopotamia from the north or the east, but it is not known how long they had lived in the peripheral regions. There is a brief inscription in Hurrian language from the end of the period of Akkad, while that of King Arishen (or Atalshen) of Urkish and Nawar is written in Akkadian. The language of the Hurrians must have belonged to a widespread group of ancient Near Eastern languages. The relationship between Hurrian and Subarean has already been mentioned, and the language of the Urarteans, who played an important role from the end of the 2nd millennium to the 8th century BC, is likewise closely related to Hurrian. Soviet scholars claim to be able to show that the "Veinakh" group of north-eastern Caucasian languages is an offspring of the Hurrian–Urartean group.

It is not known whether the migrations of the Hurrians ever took the form of aggressive invasion: 18th-century-BC texts from Mari speak of battles with the Hurrian tribe of Turukku south of Lake Urmia (some 150 miles from the Caspian Sea's southwest corner); but these were mountain campaigns, not the warding off of an offensive. Proper names in cuneiform texts, increasing in the period of Ur III, constitute the chief criterion for the presence of Hurrians. Nevertheless, there is no clear indication that the Hurrians had already advanced west of the Tigris at that time. An entirely different picture results from the 18th-century palace archives of Mari and from texts originating near the upper Khābūr. Northern Mesopotamia, west of the Tigris, and Syria now appear settled by a population that is mainly Amorite and Hurrian; and the latter have already reached the Mediterranean littoral, as shown by texts from Alalakh on the Orontes. In Mari, literary texts in Hurrian have also been found, indicating that Hurrian had by now become a full-fledged written language as well.

The high point of the Hurrian period was not reached until about the middle of the 2nd millennium. In the 15th century, Alalakh was heavily Hurrianized; and in the empire of Mitanni the Hurrians represented the leading and perhaps the most numerous population group.

(D.O.E.)

II. Mesopotamia from 1600 BC to AD 630

THE KASSITES, THE MITANNI, AND THE RISE OF ASSYRIA

About 150 years after the death of Hammurabi, his dynasty was destroyed by an invasion of new peoples. Because there are hardly any written records of this era, the time from about 1600 BC to about 1450 BC (in some areas until 1400 BC) is called the dark ages. The remaining Semitic states, such as the state of Ashur, became minor states within the sphere of influence of the new states of the Kassites and the Hurrians-Mitanni. But the languages of the older cultures, the Akkadian and Sumerian, continued or were soon re-established. The cuneiform script persisted as the only type of writing in the entire area. Cultural continuity was not broken off, either, particularly in Babylonia. A matter of importance was the emergence of new Semitic leading classes from the ranks of the priesthood and the scribes. These gained increasing power.

The Kassites in Babylonia. The Kassites had settled by 1800 BC in what is now western Iran in the region of Hamadan-Kermanshah. The first to feel their forward thrust was Samsuiluna, who had to repel groups of Kassite invaders. Increasing numbers of Kassites gradually reached Babylonia and southern Mesopotamia. There they founded principalities, of which little is known. No inscription or document in the Kassite language has been preserved. Some 300 Kassite words have been found in Babylonian documents. Nor is much known about the social structure of the Kassites or their culture. There seems to have been no hereditary kingdom. Their religion was polytheistic; the names of 30 gods are known.

Margin notes:

Economic legislation

The people and the language of the Kassites

The beginning of Kassite rule in Babylonia cannot be dated exactly. A king called Agum II ruled over a state that stretched from western Iran to the middle part of the Euphrates Valley; 24 years after the Hittites had carried off the statue of the Babylonian god Marduk, he regained possession of the statue, brought it back, and renewed the cult, making the god Marduk the equal of the Kassitic equivalent god, Shuqamuna. Meanwhile, native princes continued to reign in southern Babylonia. It was Ulamburiash who finally annexed this area around 1450 and began negotiations with Egypt in Syria. Karaindash built a temple with bas-relief tile ornaments in Uruk (Erech) around 1420. A new capital west of Baghdad, Dur Kurigalzu, was named after Kurigalzu I (c. 1415–c. 1390). His successors Kadashman-Enlil I (c. 1390–c. 1375) and Burnaburiash II (c. 1375–c. 1347) were in correspondence with the Egyptian rulers Amenhotep III and Akhenaton (Amenhotep IV). They were interested in trading their lapis lazuli and other items for gold as well as in planning political marriages. Kurigalzu II (c. 1345–c. 1324) fought against the Assyrians but was defeated by them. His successors sought to ally themselves with the Hittites in order to stop the expansion of the Assyrians. During the reign of Kashtiliash IV (c. 1242–c. 1235), Babylonia waged war on two fronts at the same time—against Elam and Assyria—ending in the catastrophic invasion and destruction of Babylon by Tukulti-Ninurta I. Not until the time of the kings Adad-shum-nasir (c. 1218–c. 1189) and Melishipak (c. 1188–c. 1172) was Babylon again able to experience a period of prosperity and peace. Their successors were again forced to fight, facing the conqueror, King Shutruk-Nahhunte of Elam (c. 1185–c. 1155). Cruel and fierce, the Elamites finally destroyed the dynasty of the Kassites during these wars (about 1155). Some poetical works lament this catastrophe.

Babylonia under the Kassites   Letters and documents of the time after 1380 show that many things had changed after the Kassites took power. The Kassite upper class, always a small minority, had been largely babylonized. Babylonian names were to be found even among the royalty, and they predominated among the civil servants and the officers. The new feudal character of the social structure showed the influence of the Kassites. Babylonian town life had revived on the basis of commerce and handicrafts. The Kassitic nobility, however, maintained the upper hand in the rural areas, their wealthiest representatives holding very large landed estates. Many of these holdings came from donations of the king to deserving officers and civil servants, considerable privileges being connected with such grants. From the time of Kurigalzu II these were registered on stone tablets or, more frequently, on boundary stones. After 1200 the number of these increased substantially, because the kings needed a steadily growing retinue of loyal followers. The boundary stones had pictures in bas-relief, very often a multitude of religious symbols, and frequently detailed inscriptions giving the borders of the particular estate; sometimes the deserts of the recipient were listed and his privileges recorded; finally, trespassers were threatened with the most terrifying curses. Agriculture and cattle husbandry were the main pursuits on these estates, and horses were raised for the light war chariots of the cavalry. There was an export trade in horses and vehicles, in exchange for raw material.

The decline of the Babylonian culture at the end of the Old Babylonian period continued for some time under the Kassites. Not until approximately 1420 did the Kassites develop a distinctive style in architecture and sculpture. Kurigalzu I played an important part, especially in Ur, as a patron of the building arts. Poetry and scientific literature developed only gradually after 1400. The existence of earlier work is clear from poetry, philological lists, and collections of omens and signs that were in existence by the 14th century or before and have been discovered in the Hittite capital of Hattusas, in the Syrian capital of Ugarit, and even as far away as Palestine. Somewhat later, new writings appear—medical diagnoses and recipes, more Sumero–Akkadian word lists, and collections of astrological and other omens and signs with

their respective interpretations. Most of these works are known today only from copies of more recent date. The most important of them all is the Babylonian epic of the creation of the world, *Enuma elish*. Composed by an unknown poet, in all probability in the 14th century, it tells the story of the god Marduk. He began as the god of Babylon and was elevated to be king over all other gods after having successfully accomplished the destruction of the powers of chaos. For almost 1,000 years this epic was recited during the new year's festival in the spring as part of the Marduk cult in Babylon. The literature of this time contains hardly any Kassitic words. Many scholars believe that the essential groundwork for the development of the subsequent Babylonian culture was laid during the later epoch of the Kassite era.

Kingdom of the Hurrians and the Mitanni.   The weakening of the Semitic states in Mesopotamia after 1600 enabled the Hurrians to penetrate deeper into this region, where they founded numerous small states in the eastern parts of Asia Minor, Mesopotamia, and Syria. The Hurrians came from northwestern Iran, but their early history is almost unknown. After 1500, isolated dynasties appeared with Indo-Aryan names, but the significance of this is disputed. The fact that Old Indian technical terms appear in later records about horse breeding and that the names of Indian gods are used in some compacts of state led many scholars to assume that numerous groups of Aryans, closely related to the Indians, pushed into Asia Minor from the northeast. They were also credited with the introduction of the light war chariot with spoke wheels. This conclusion, however, is by no means established fact. So far it has not been possible to appraise the quantity and the political and cultural influence of the Aryans in Asia Minor relative to that of the Hurrians.

Shortly after 1500 the kingdom of the Mitanni arose near the sources of the Khābūr River in Mesopotamia. Since no record or inscription of their kings has been unearthed, there is hardly anything known about the development and history of the Mitanni before King Tushratta. The Mitanni were known to the Egyptians under the name of Naharina, and Thutmose III fought frequently against them after 1468 BC. By 1440 the domain of the Mitanni king Saustatar (Saushatar) stretched from the Mediterranean all the way to the Zagros Mountains, in western Iran, including Alalakh, in northern Syria, as well as Nuzu and Arrapkha. The northern boundary dividing the Mitanni from the Hittites and the Hurrians was in all probability not fixed even under his successors Artatama and Shuttarna II, who married their daughters to the pharaohs Thutmose IV (1425–1417) and Amenhotep III (1417–1379). Tushratta (c. 1390–c. 1340), the son of Shuttarna, was able to maintain the kingdom he had inherited from his predecessors for many years. In his sometimes very long letters to Amenhotep III and Akhenaton he writes about commerce, his desire for gold, and marriage. Weakened by internal strife, the Mitanni kingdom eventually became a pawn between the rising kingdoms of the Hittites and the Assyrians.

The kingdom of the Mitanni was a feudal state led by a warrior nobility of Aryan or Hurrian origin. Frequently horses were bred on their large landed estates. Documents and contract agreements in Syria often mention a chariot-warrior caste that also constituted the social upper class in the cities. The aristocratic families usually received their landed property as an inalienable fief. Consequently, no documents on the selling of landed property are to be found in the great archives of Akkadian documents and letters discovered in Nuzu, near Kirkūk. The prohibition against selling landed property was often dodged, however, with a stratagem: the previous owner "adopted" a willing buyer against an appropriate sum of money. The wealthy lord Tehiptilla was "adopted" almost 200 times, acquiring tremendous holdings of landed property in this way without interference by the governmental authorities. He had gained his wealth through trade and commerce and in agriculture. For a long time, a prince was in charge of the royal governmental administration in the district capital. Society was highly struc-

Empire of the Mitanni

tured in classes, ranks, and professions. The judiciary, patterned after the Babylonian model, was well organized; the documents place heavy emphasis on correct procedure.

Temple monuments of modest dimensions have been unearthed; in all probability, specific local traditions played a deciding factor in their design. The dead were probably buried outside the settlement. There is evidence that members of the royal family were cremated. Small artifacts, particularly seals, show a peculiar continuation of Babylonian and Assyrian traditions in their preference for the naturalistic representation of figures. There were painted ceramics with finely drawn decorations (white on a dark background). The strong position of the royal house was evident in the large palaces, existing even in district capitals. The palaces were decorated with frescoes. Because only a few settlements of the Mitanni have been unearthed in Mesopotamia, knowledge of the Mitanni arts and culture is as yet insufficient.

Assyria under Mitanni rule

The rise of Assyria. Very little can be said about northern Assyria during the 2nd millennium BC. Information on the old capital, Ashur, located in the south of the country, is somewhat more plentiful. The old lists of kings suggest that the same dynasty ruled continuously over Ashur from about 1670 on. All the names of the kings are given. But little else is known about Ashur before 1420. Almost all the princes had Akkadian names, and it can be assumed that their sphere of influence was rather small. Although Assyria belonged to the kingdom of the Mitanni for a long time, it seems that Ashur retained a certain autonomy. Located close to the boundary with Babylonia, it played that empire off against the Mitanni whenever possible. Puzur-Ashur III concluded a border treaty with Babylonia in 1490 as did Ashur-bel-nisheshu in 1415. Ashur-nadin-akhe II (c. 1402–c. 1393) was even able to obtain support from Egypt, which sent him a consignment of gold.

Ashur-uballit I (c. 1365–c. 1330) was at first subject to King Tushratta of the Mitanni. After 1350, however, he attacked Tushratta, presumably together with Suppiluliumas of the Hittites. Taking away from the Mitanni parts of northeastern Mesopotamia, Ashur-uballit I now called himself "Great King" and socialized with the King of Egypt on equal terms—arousing the indignation of the King of Babylonia. Ashur-uballit was the first to name Assyria the Land of Ashur, because the old name, Subartu, was often used in a derogatory sense in Babylonia. He ordered his short inscriptions to be partly written in the Babylonian language rather than the Assyrian, since this was considered refined. Marrying his daughter to a Babylonian, he intervened there energetically when Kassite nobles murdered his grandchild. Future generations came to consider him rightfully as the real founder of the Assyrian Empire. His son Enlil-nirari (c. 1328–c. 1320) also fought against Babylonia. Arik-den-ili (c. 1319–c. 1308) turned westward where he encountered Semitic tribes of the so-called Akhlamu-group.

Still greater successes were achieved by Adad-nirari I (c. 1307–c. 1275). Defeating the Kassite king Nazimaruttash, he forced him to retreat. After that he defeated the kings of the Mitanni, at first Shattuara I, then Wasashatta. This enabled him for a time to incorporate all of Mesopotamia into his empire as a province, although in later struggles he lost large parts to the Hittites. In the east, he was satisfied with the defense of his lands against the mountain people.

Adad-nirari's inscriptions were more elaborate than those of his predecessors and were written in the Babylonian language. In them he declares that he feels called to these wars by the gods, a statement that was to be repeated by other kings after him. Assuming the old title of great king, he called himself "King of All." He enlarged the temple and the palace in Ashur and also developed the fortifications there, particularly at the banks of the Tigris River. He worked on large building projects in the provinces.

His son Shalmaneser I (c. 1274–c. 1245) attacked Uruatru (later called Urartu) in southern Armenia, which had allegedly broken away. But Shattuara II of Hanigalbat

put him into a difficult situation, cutting his forces off from their water supplies. With courage born of despair, the Assyrians fought themselves free. They then set about reducing what was left of the Mitanni kingdom into an Assyrian province. The king claimed to have blinded 14,400 enemies in one eye—psychological warfare of a similar kind was used more and more as time went by. The Hittites tried in vain to save Hanigalbat. Together with the Babylonians they fought a commercial war against Ashur for many years. Like his father, Shalmaneser was a great builder. At the juncture of the Tigris and the Great Zab rivers he founded a strategically situated second capital, Kalakh (biblical Calah; modern Nimrūd).

His son was Tukulti-ninurta (c. 1244–c. 1208), the Ninos of Greek legends. Gifted but extravagant, he made his nation a great power. He carried off thousands of Hittites from eastern Anatolia. He fought particularly hard against Babylonia, deporting Kashtiliash IV to Assyria. When the Babylonians rebelled again, he plundered the temples in Babylon, an act regarded as a sacrilege, even in Assyria. The relationship between the king and his capital deteriorated steadily. For this reason the king began to build a new city, Kar-Tukulti-Ninurta, on the other side of the Tigris River. Ultimately, even his sons rebelled against him and laid siege to him in his city; in the end he was murdered. His victorious wars against Babylonia were glorified in an epic poem, but his empire broke up soon after his death. Assyrian power declined for a time, while that of Babylonia rose.

Assyria had suffered under the oppression of both the Hurrians and the Mitannis. Its struggle for liberation and the bitter wars that followed had much to do with its development into a military power. In his capital of Ashur, the king depended on the citizen class and the priesthood, as well as on the landed nobility that furnished him with the war-chariot troops.

Organization of the Assyrian state

Documents and letters show the important role agriculture played in the development of the state. Assyria was less dependent on artificial irrigation than was Babylonia. The breeding of horses was carried on intensively; remnants of elaborate directions for their training are extant. Trade and commerce were also of notable significance: metals were imported from Asia Minor or Armenia, tin from northwestern Iran, and lumber from the west. The opening up of new trade routes was oftentimes a cause and the purpose of war.

Assyrian architecture, derived from a combination of Mitannian and Babylonian influences, developed early quite an individual style. The palaces often had colourful wall decorations. The art of seal cutting, taken largely from the Mitanni, continued creatively on its own. The schools for scribes, where all the civil servants were trained, taught both the Babylonian and the Assyrian dialects of the Akkadian tongue. Babylonian works of literature were assimilated into Assyrian, often reworked into a partially different form. The Hurrian tradition remained strong in the military and political sphere while at the same time influencing the language.

ASSYRIA AND BABYLONIA AT THE END OF THE 2ND MILLENNIUM

Babylonia under the 2nd dynasty of Isin (c. 1156–c. 1025). In a series of heavy wars about which not much is known, Marduk-kabit-akheshu (c. 1156–c. 1139) established what came to be known as the 2nd dynasty of Isin. His successors were often forced to continue the fighting. The most famous king of the dynasty was Nebuchadrezzar I (c. 1124–c. 1103). He fought mainly against Elam, which had conquered most of Babylonia. His first attack miscarried because of an epidemic among his troops, but in a later campaign he conquered Susa, the capital of Elam, and returned the previously stolen statue of the god Marduk to its proper place. Soon thereafter the king of Elam was assassinated, and his kingdom fell apart into small states. This enabled Nebuchadrezzar to turn west, using the later years of peace to complete extensive building projects. After him, his son became king, succeeded by his brother Marduk-nadin-ahhe (c. 1098–c. 1081). At first successful in his wars against

Assyria, he later experienced heavy defeat. A famine of catastrophic proportions triggered an attack from Aramaean tribes, the ultimate blow. His successors made peace with Assyria, but the country suffered more and more from repeated attacks by Aramaeans and other Semitic nomads. Even though some of the kings still had grand titles, they were unable to stem the progressive disintegration of their empire. There followed the era known as the 2nd dynasty of the Sealand (c. 1024–c. 1004), which included three usurpers. The first of these had the Kassitic name of Simbar-shikhu (c. 1024–c. 1007).

Toward the end of its reign, the dynasty of the Kassites became completely babylonized. The changeover to the dynasty of Isin, actually a succession of kings from different families, brought no essential transformation of the social structure. The feudal order remained. New landed estates came into existence in many places through grants to deserving officers; many boundary stones (*kudurru*) have been found that describe them. The cities of Babylonia retained much of their former autonomy. The border provinces, however, were administered by royally appointed governors with civil and military functions.

This was a period of creativity in the literary arts. The successes of Nebuchadrezzar I provided new material. One heroic epic, modelled upon older epics, celebrates his deeds, but unfortunately little of this is extant. Other material came from ancient myths. The best known poet is Sinleqeunnini (c. 1100–?) of Uruk (Erech), the poet of the later version of the *Epic of Gilgamesh* known as the Twelve-Tablet Poem. This version is distinguished by its greater stress on the human qualities of Gilgamesh and Enkidu, making it one of the great works of world literature. Another poet working at about the same time was the author of verses meditating on the workings of divine justice, a matter that had acquired vital importance in the contemporary religion of Babylon. This poem elaborates on the great suffering of a high official and his subsequent salvation by the god Marduk. Other religious poems have been preserved, but their time of origin is not certain. The later Babylonians with good reason regarded the time of Nebuchadrezzar I as one of the great eras of their history.

Assyria between 1200 and 1000. After a period of decline following Tukulti-Ninurta I, Assyria was consolidated and stabilized under Ashur-dan I (c. 1179–c. 1134) and Ashur-resh-ishi I (c. 1133–c. 1116). Several times forced to fight against Babylonia, the latter was even able to defend himself against an attack by Nebuchadrezzar I. According to the inscriptions, most of his building efforts were in Nineveh, rather than in the old capital of Ashur.

The reign of Tiglath-pileser I His son Tiglath-pileser I (Tukulti-apal-Esharra, c. 1115–c. 1077) raised the power of Assyria to new heights. First he turned against a large army of the Mushki that had entered into southern Armenia from Asia Minor, defeating them decisively. After this he forced the small Hurrian states of southern Armenia to pay him tribute. Trained in mountain warfare themselves and helped by capable pioneers, the Assyrians were now able to advance far into the distant valleys of the interior. Their main enemies were the Aramaeans, the Semitic camel Bedouins whose many small states often combined against the Assyrians. Tiglath-pileser I also went to Syria and even reached the Mediterranean, where he took a sea voyage. After 1100 these campaigns led to conflicts with Babylonia. Tiglath-pileser conquered northern Babylonia and plundered Babylon, without decisively defeating Marduk-nadin-ahhe. In his own country the King paid particular attention to agriculture and fruit growing, improved the administrative system, and developed more thorough methods of training scribes.

Three of his sons reigned after Tiglath-pileser, including Ashur-bel-kala (c. 1074–c. 1057). Like his father, he fought in southern Armenia and with Babylonia as his ally, against the Aramaeans. Disintegration of the empire could not be arrested, however. The grandson of Tiglath-pileser, Ashurnasirpal I (c. 1050–c. 1032), was sickly and unable to do more than defend Assyria proper against his enemies. Fragments of three of his prayers

to the goddess Ishtar are preserved; among them is a penitential prayer in which he wonders about the cause of so much adversity. Referring to his many good deeds but admitting his guilt at the same time, he asks for forgiveness and health. According to the king, part of his guilt lay in neglecting to teach his subjects the fear of god in sufficient measure. After him, little is known for 100 years.

State, law, and justice under Tiglath-pileser State and society during the time of Tiglath-pileser were not essentially different from those of the 13th century. Collections of laws, drafts, and edicts of the court exist that go back as far as the 14th century BC. Presumably, most of these remained in effect. One tablet defining the marriage laws shows that the social position of women in Assyria was lower than in Babylonia or Israel or among the Hittites. A man was allowed to send away his wife at his own pleasure with or without divorce money. In case of adultery, he was permitted to kill or maim her. Outside of her house the woman was forced to observe many restrictions, such as the wearing of a veil. It is not clear whether these regulations carried the weight of law, but they seem to have represented a reaction against practices that were more favourable to women. Two somewhat older marriage contracts, for example, grant equal rights to both partners, even in divorce. The women of the king's harem were subject to severe punishment, including beating, maiming, and death, along with those who guarded and looked after them. The penal laws of the time were generally more severe in Assyria than in other countries of the East. The death penalty was not uncommon. In less serious cases the penalty was forced labour after flogging. In certain cases there was trial by ordeal. One tablet treats the subject of landed property rights. Offenses against the established boundary lines called for extremely severe punishment. A creditor was allowed to force his debtor to work for him, but he could not sell him.

The greater part of Assyrian literature was either taken over from Babylonia or written by the Assyrians in the Babylonian dialect, who modelled their works upon Babylonian originals. The Assyrian dialect was used in legal documents, court and temple rituals, and collections of recipes—as, for example, in directions for manufacturing perfumes. A new art form was the picture tale: a continuing series of pictures carved on square steles of stone. The pictures, showing war or hunting scenes, begin at the top of the stele and run down around it, with inscriptions under the pictures explaining them. These and the finely cut seals show that the fine arts of Assyria were beginning to surpass those of Babylonia. Architecture and other forms of the monumental arts also began a further development, such as the double temple with its two towers (ziggurat). Colourful, enamelled tiles were used to decorate the façades.

ASSYRIA AND BABYLONIA C. 1000–750 BC

Assyria and Babylonia until Ashurnasirpal II. The most important factor in the history of Mesopotamia in the 10th century was the continuing threat from the Aramaean seminomads. Again and again, the kings of both Babylonia and Assyria were forced to repel their invasions. Even though the Aramaeans were not able to gain a foothold in the main cities, there are evidences of them in many rural areas. Ashur-dan II (934–912) succeeded in suppressing the Aramaeans and the mountain people, in this way stabilizing the Assyrian boundaries. He was the first to use the Assyrian dialect in his written records.

The reign of Adad-nirari II Adad-nirari II (c. 911–891) left very detailed accounts of his wars and his efforts to improve agriculture. He led six campaigns against Aramaean intruders from northern Arabia. In two campaigns against Babylonia he forced Shamash-mudammiq (about 930–904) to surrender extensive territories. Shamash-mudammiq was murdered, and a treaty with his successor, Nabu-shum-ukin (904–888) secured peace for many years. Tukulti-Ninurta II (890–884), the son of Adad-nirari II, reigned only for a short time. He preferred Nineveh to Ashur. His wars led him to southern Armenia. He was portrayed on steles in blue–yellow enamel in late Hittite style, showing him under the winged sun—a theme adopted from Egyptian art. His son Ashurnasirpal II (883–859) continued the policy of conquest and expansion. He left a very detailed account of his campaigns, which were impressive in their cruelty. Defeated enemies were impaled, flayed, or beheaded in great numbers. But mass deportations were found to serve the interests of the growing empire better than terror. Through the systematic exchange of native populations, conquered regions were denationalized. The result was a servile, submissive, mixed population in which the Aramaean element became the preponderant majority. This provided the labour force for the various public works in the metropolitan centres of the Assyrian Empire. Ashurnasirpal II rebuilt Kalakh, founded by Shalmaneser I, and made it his capital. Ashur remained the centre of the worship of the god Ashur—in whose name all the wars of conquest were fought. A third capital was Nineveh.

The reign of Ashurnasirpal II

Ashurnasirpal II was the first to use cavalry units to any large extent in addition to infantry and war-chariot troops. He was also the first to employ heavy, mobile battering rams and wall breakers in his sieges. Following after the conquering troops came officials from all branches of the civil service, because the king wanted to lose no time in incorporating the new lands into his empire. The supremacy of Assyria over its neighbouring states owed much to the proficiency of the government service under the leadership of the minister Gabbilani'-er-esh. The campaigns of Ashurnasirpal II lead him mainly to southern Armenia and Mesopotamia. After a series of heavy wars, he incorporated Mesopotamia as far as the Euphrates River. A campaign to Syria encountered little resistance. There was no great war against Babylonia. Ashurnasirpal, like other Assyrian kings, may have been moved by religion not to destroy Babylonia, which had almost the same gods as Assyria. Both empires must have profited from mutual trade and cultural exchange. The Babylonians, under the energetic Nabu-apal-iddin (c. 887–855) attacked the Aramaeans in southern Mesopotamia and occupied the valley of the Euphrates River to about the mouth of the Khābūr River.

Ashurnasirpal, so brutal in his wars, was able to inspire architects, structural engineers, and artists and sculptors to heights never before achieved. He built and enlarged temples and palaces in several cities. His most impressive monument was his own palace in Kalakh, covering a space of 25,000 square metres (269,000 square feet). Hundreds of large limestone slabs were used in murals in the state rooms and living quarters. Most of the scenes were done in relief, but painted murals have also been found. Most of them depict mythological themes and symbolic fertility rites, with the king participating. Brutal war pictures were aimed to discourage enemies. The chief god of Kalakh was Ninurta, god of war and the hunt. The tower of the temple dedicated to Ninurta served also as an astronomical observatory. Kalakh soon became the cultural centre of the empire. Ashurnasirpal claimed to have entertained 69,574 guests at the opening ceremonies of his palace.

Shalmaneser III and Shamshi-Adad V of Assyria. The son and successor of Ashurnasirpal was Shalmaneser III (858–824). His father's equal in both brutality and energy, he was less realistic in his undertakings. His inscriptions, in a peculiar blend of Assyrian and Babylonian, record his considerable achievements but are not always able to conceal his failures. His campaigns were directed mostly against Syria. While he was able to conquer northern Syria and make it a province, in the south he could only weaken the strong state of Damascus and was unable, even after several wars, to eliminate it. In 841 he laid unsuccessful siege to Damascus. Also in 841 King Jehu of Israel was forced to pay tribute. In his invasion of Cilicia, Shalmaneser had only partial success. The same was true of the kingdom of Urartu in Armenia, from which, however, the troops returned with immense quantities of lumber and building stones. The king and, in later years, the general Daian-Ashur, went several times to western Iran, where they found such states as Mannai in northwestern Iran and, further away in the

Conquest of northern Syria

southeast, the Persians. They also encountered the Medes during these wars. Horse tribute was collected.

In Babylonia, Marduk-zakir-shumi I ascended the throne around the year 855. His brother Marduk-bel-usate rebelled against him, and in 851 the king was forced to ask Shalmaneser for help. Shalmaneser was only too happy to oblige; when the usurper had been finally eliminated (850), Shalmaneser went to southern Babylonia, which at that time was almost completely dominated by Aramaeans. There he encountered, among others, the Chaldeans, mentioned for the first time in 878 BC, who were to play a leading role in the history of later times; Shalmaneser made them tributaries.

During his long reign he built temples, palaces, and fortifications in Assyria as well as in the other capitals of his provinces. His artists created many statues and steles. Among the best known is the Black Obelisk, which includes a picture of Jehu of Israel paying tribute. The bronze doors of Imgur-Enlil in Assyria portray the course of his campaigns and other undertakings in rows of pictures, often very lifelike. Hundreds of delicately carved ivories were carried away from Phoenicia, and many of the artists along with them; these later made Kalakh a centre for the art of ivory sculpture.

In the last four years of the reign of Shalmaneser, the crown prince Ashur-danin-apal led a rebellion. The old King appointed his younger son Shamshi-Adad as the new crown prince. Forced to flee to Babylonia, Shamshi-Adad V (823–811) finally managed to regain the kingship with the help of Marduk-zākir-shumi I under humiliating conditions. As king he campaigned with varying success in southern Armenia and Azerbaijan, later turning against Babylonia. He won several battles against the Babylonian kings Marduk-balassu-iqbi and Baba-aha-iddina (about 818–12) and pushed through to Chaldea. Babylonia remained independent, however.

Adad-nirari III and his successors. Shamshi-Adad V died while Adad-nirari III (810–783) was still a minor. His Babylonian mother, Sammu-ramat, took over the regency, governing with great energy until 806. The Greeks, who called her Semiramis, credited her with legendary accomplishments, but historically little is known about her. Adad-nirari later led several campaigns against the Medes and also against Syria and Palestine. In 804 he reached Gaza, but Damascus proved invincible. He also fought in Babylonia, helping to restore order in the north.

Shalmaneser IV (c. 783–773) fought against Urartu, then at the height of its power under King Argishti (about 780–755). He successfully defended eastern Mesopotamia against attacks from Armenia. On the other hand, he lost most of Syria after a campaign against Damascus in 773. The reign of Ashur-dan III (772–755) was shadowed by rebellions and by epidemics of plague. Of Ashur-hirari V (754–746) little is known.

In Assyria, the feudal structure of society remained largely unchanged. Many of the conquered lands were combined to form large provinces. The governors of these provinces sometimes acquired considerable independence, particularly under the weaker monarchs after Adad-nirari III. Some of them even composed their own inscriptions. The influx of displaced peoples into the cities of Assyria created large metropolitan centres. The spoils of war, together with an expanding trade, favoured the development of a well-to-do commercial class. The dense population of the cities gave rise to social tensions that only the strong kings were able to contain. A number of the former capitals of the conquered lands remained important as capitals of provinces. There was much new building. A standing occupational force was needed in the provinces, and these troops grew steadily in proportion to the total military forces. The civil service also expanded, the largest administrative body being the royal court, with thousands of functionaries and craftsmen in the several residential cities.

The cultural decline around the year 1000 was overcome during the reigns of Ashurnasirpal II and Shalmaneser III. The arts in particular experienced a tremendous resurgence. Literary works continued to be written in

Assyrian and were seldom of great importance. The literature that had been taken over from Babylonia was further developed with new writings, although one can rarely distinguish between works written in Assyria and works written in Babylonia. In religion, the official cults of Ashur and Ninurta continued, while the religion of the common people went its separate way.

In Babylonia, not much was left of the feudal structure; the large landed estates almost everywhere fell prey to the inroads of the Aramaeans, who were at first half nomadic. The leaders of their tribes and clans slowly replaced the former landlords. Agriculture on a large scale was no longer possible except on the outskirts of metropolitan areas. The predominance of the Babylonian schools for scribes may have prevented the emergence of an Aramaean literature. In any case, the Aramaeans seem to have been absorbed into the Babylonian culture. The religious cults in the cities remained essentially the same. The Babylonian Empire was slowly reduced to poverty, except perhaps in some of the cities. In 764, after an epidemic, the myth of pest god Erra was written by the poet Kabt-ilani-Marduk.

THE NEO-ASSYRIAN EMPIRE (746–609)

Tiglath-pileser III and Shalmaneser V. The decline of Assyrian power after 780 was notable; Syria and considerable lands in the north were lost. A military coup deposed king Ashur-nirari V and raised a general to the throne. Under the name of Tiglath-pileser III (746–727) he brought the empire to its greatest expanse. He reduced the size of the provinces in order to break the independence of the governors. He also invalidated the tax privileges of cities such as Ashur and Haran, in order to distribute the tax load more evenly over the entire realm. Military equipment was improved substantially. In 746 he went to Babylonia to aid Nabu-nasir (747–734) in his fight against Aramaean tribes. Tiglath-pileser beat the Aramaeans and then made visits to the large cities of Babylonia. Here he tried to get the support of the priesthood by patronizing their building projects. Babylonia retained its independence.

His next undertaking was to throw back Urartu. His campaigns in Azerbaijan were designed to drive a wedge between Urartu and the Medes. In 743 he went to Syria, defeating there an army of Urartu. The Syrian city of Arpad, which had formed an alliance with Urartu, did not surrender so easily. It took Tiglath-pileser three years of siege to conquer Arpad, whereupon he massacred the inhabitants and destroyed the city. In 738 a new coalition formed against Assyria under the leadership of Samal of northern Syria. It was defeated, and all the princes from Damascus to eastern Anatolia were forced to pay tribute. Another campaign in 735, this time directed against Urartu itself, was only partly successful. In 734 Tiglath-pileser invaded Palestine, going as far as the Egyptian border. Damascus and Israel tried to organize resistance against him, seeking to bring Judah into their alliance. But Ahaz of Judah asked Tiglath-pileser for help. In 733 Tiglath-pileser devastated Israel and forced it to surrender large territories. In 732 he advanced upon Damascus, first devastating the gardens outside the city and then conquering the capital and killing the king, whom he replaced with a governor. The Queen of southern Arabia, Samsia, was now obliged to pay tribute, being permitted in return to use the harbour of the city of Gaza, which was in Assyrian hands.

The death of King Nabonassar of Babylonia caused a chaotic situation to develop there, and the Aramaean Ukin-zer crowned himself king. In 731 Tiglath-pileser fought and beat him and his allies, but he did not capture Ukin-zer until 729. This time he did not appoint a new king for Babylonia but assumed the crown himself under the name Pulu (Pul in the Old Testament). In his old age he abstained from further campaigning, devoting himself to the improvement of his capital Kalakh. He rebuilt the palace of Shalmaneser III, filled it with treasures from his wars, and decorated the walls with bas-reliefs. The latter were almost all of warlike character, as if designed to intimidate the onlooker with their presentation of gruesome executions. These pictorial narratives on slabs have also been found in several provincial capitals of Assyria.

Tiglath-pileser was succeeded by his son Shalmaneser V (726–722), who continued the policy of his father. As king of Babylonia he called himself Ululai. Almost nothing is known about his enterprises, since his successor destroyed all his inscriptions. The Old Testament relates that he marched against Hoshea of Israel in 724 after Hoshea had rebelled. He was probably assassinated during a three-year siege of Samaria. His successor maintained that the god Ashur had withdrawn his support of Shalmaneser V for acts of disrespect.

Sargon II (721–705) and Marduk-apal-iddina of Babylonia. It was probably a younger brother of Shalmaneser who ascended the throne of Assyria. Assuming the old name of Sharru-kin (Sargon in the Bible), meaning Legitimate King, he assured himself of the support of the priesthood and the merchant class by restoring privileges they had lost, particularly the tax exemptions of the great temples. The change of sovereign in Assyria triggered another crisis in Babylonia. An Aramaean prince from the south, Marduk-apal-iddina II (the biblical Merodach-Baladan), seized power in Babylon in 721 and was able to retain it until 710 with the help of Humanigash I of Elam. A first attempt by Sargon to recover Babylonia miscarried when Elam defeated him in 721. During the same year the three-year siege of Samaria was brought to a close. The Samarian upper class was deported, and Israel became an Assyrian province. Samaria was repopulated with Syrians and Babylonians. Judah remained independent by paying tribute. In 720 Sargon squelched a rebellion in Syria that had been supported by Egypt. Then he defeated both Hanunu of Gaza and an Egyptian army near the Egyptian border. In 717 and 716 he campaigned in northern Syria, making the hitherto independent state of Carchemish one of his provinces. He also went to Cilicia in an effort to prevent further encroachments of the Phrygians under their king Midas.

In order to protect his ally, the state of Mannai, in Azerbaijan, Sargon embarked on a campaign in Iran in 719 and incorporated parts of Media as provinces of his empire. But in 716 another war became necessary. At the same time, he was busy preparing a major attack against Urartu. Under the leadership of the crown prince Sennacherib, armies of agents infiltrated Urartu, which was also threatened from the north by the Cimmerians. Many of their messages and reports have been preserved. The longest inscription ever composed by the Assyrians about a year's enterprise (430 very long lines) is dedicated to this Urartu campaign of 714. Phrased in the style of a first report to the god Ashur, it is interlaced with stirring descriptions of natural scenery. The strong points of Urartu must have been well fortified. Sargon tried to avoid them by going through the province of Mannai and attacking the Median principalities on the eastern side of Lake Urmia. In the meantime, hoping to surprise the Assyrian troops, Rusas of Urartu had closed the narrow pass lying between Lake Urmia and Sahand Mount. Sargon, anticipating this, led a small band of cavalry in a surprise charge that developed into a great victory for the Assyrians. Rusas fled and died. The Assyrians pushed forward, destroying all the cities, fortifications, and even irrigation works of Urartu. They did not conquer Mannai itself but took possession of the mountain city of Muṣaṣir. The spoils were immense. The following years saw only small campaigns in Media, eastern Asia Minor, and against Ashdod, in Palestine. King Midas of Phrygia and some cities on Cyprus were quite ready to pay tribute.

Sargon was now free to settle accounts with Marduk-apal-iddina of Babylonia. Abandoned by his ally Shutruk-Nahhunte II of Elam, Marduk-apal-iddina found it best to flee: first to his native land on the Persian Gulf and later to Elam. Because the Aramaean prince had made himself very unpopular with his subjects, Sargon was hailed as the liberator of Babylonia. He complied with the wishes of the priesthood while at the same time putting down the Aramaean nobility. The modest title of governor of Babylonia was enough for him.

At first Sargon resided in Kalakh, but he then decided to

Assyria at its peak

Sargon II's military campaigns

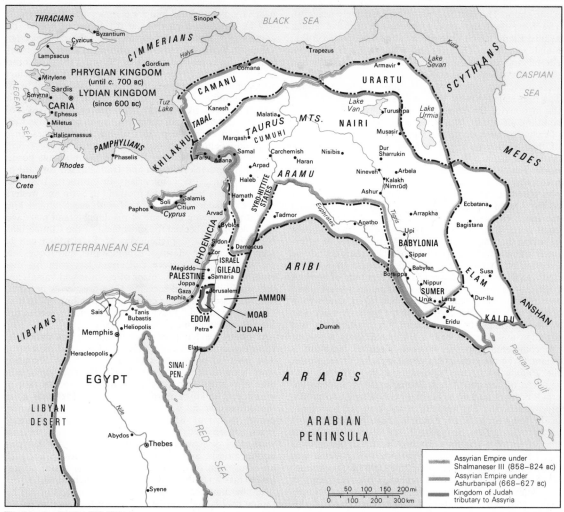

The Assyrian Empire, 858–627 BC.

From W. Shepherd, *Historical Atlas;* Harper & Row, Publishers (Barnes & Noble Books), New York; revision
copyright © 1964 by Barnes & Noble, Inc.

The
founding
of Dur
Sharrukin

found an entirely new capital north of Nineveh. He called
the city Dur Sharrukin—Sargonsburg (now Khorsabad).
He erected his palace on a high terrace in the northeastern part of the city. The temples to the main gods, smaller
in size, were built within the palatial rectangle, which was
surrounded by a special wall. This arrangement enabled
Sargon to supervise the priests better than had been possible in the old, large temple complexes. One consequence
of this design was that the figure of the king pushed the
gods somewhat into the background, thereby gaining in
importance. Wanting his palace to match the vastness of
his empire, the King planned it in monumental dimensions. Stone reliefs of two winged bulls with human heads
flanked the entrance—much larger than anything comparable built before. The walls were decorated with long
rows of bas-reliefs showing scenes of war and festive
processions. A comparison with a well-executed stele of
the Babylonian king Marduk-apal-iddina shows that the
fine arts of Assyria had far surpassed those of Babylonia.
Sargon never completed his capital, though from 713 to
705 BC tens of thousands of labourers and hundreds of
artisans worked upon the great city. Yet, with the exception of some magnificent buildings for public officials,
only a few durable edifices were completed in the residential section. In 705, in a campaign in northwestern Iran,
the King was ambushed and killed. His corpse remained
unburied, food for birds of prey. His son Sennacherib,
who had quarrelled with his father, was inclined to believe with the priests that the death of the King was a
punishment from the gods.

Sennacherib. Sennacherib (Assyrian Sin-akhkhe-eriba;
704–681) was well prepared for his position as sovereign.
With him Assyria acquired an exceptionally clever and

gifted, though often extravagant, ruler. His father, interestingly enough, is not mentioned in any of his many
inscriptions. He left the new city of Dur Sharrukin at
once and resided in Ashur for a few years, until in 701 he
made Nineveh his capital.

Sennacherib had considerable difficulty with Babylonia.
In 703 Marduk-apal-iddina again crowned himself king
with the aid of Elam, proceeding at once to ally himself
with other enemies of Assyria. After nine months he was
forced to withdraw when Sennacherib defeated a coalition army consisting of Babylonians, Aramaeans, and
Elamites. The new puppet king of Babylonia was Bel-ibni
(702–700), who had been raised in Assyria.

In 702 Sennacherib undertook a predatory raid into
western Iran, then moved against Syria and Palestine in
701 to smash a coalition of Phoenicians, Palestinians, and
Egyptians. Sidon immediately expelled its ruler, who was
hostile to Assyria. The other allies surrendered or were
beaten. One Egyptian army was defeated at Eltekeh.
Only Hezekiah of Judah did not surrender, fearing grave
judgment and retribution. Failing in their efforts to incite
the people of Jerusalem against their king, the Assyrians
laid siege to the city. The Old Testament relates these
events in great detail. The most likely reconstruction of
events is that, when an epidemic broke out among the
Assyrian troops during the siege of Jerusalem, Sennacherib found it advisable to return to Assyria. In the course
of time several generations of storytellers in Judah
swelled the number of Assyrian dead to 185,000. Hezekiah nevertheless paid tribute to Nineveh.

Bel-ibni of Babylonia seceded from the union with Assyria in 700. Sennacherib moved quickly, defeating Bel-ibni
and replacing him with Sennacherib's oldest son, Ashur-

The
siege of
Jerusalem

nadin-shum. The next few years were relatively peaceful. The King used this time to prepare a decisive attack against Elam, which time and again had supported Babylonian rebellions. The overland route to Elam had been cut off and fortified by the Elamites. Sennacherib had ships built in Syria and at Nineveh. The ships from Syria were moved on rollers from the Euphrates to the Tigris. The fleet sailed downstream and was quite successful in the lagoons of the Persian Gulf and along the southern coastline of Elam. The Elamites launched a counteroffensive by land, occupying Babylonia and putting a man of their choice on the throne. Not until 693 were the Assyrians again able to fight their way through to the north. Finally, in 689, Sennacherib had his revenge. Babylon was conquered and completely destroyed, the temples plundered and levelled with the ground. The waters of the Arakhtu Canal were diverted over the ruins, and the inner city remained almost totally uninhabited for eight years. Even many Assyrians were indignant at this, believing that the Babylonian god Marduk must be grievously offended at the destruction of his temple and the carrying off of his image. Marduk was also an Assyrian deity, to whom many Assyrians turned in time of need. A political–theological propaganda campaign was launched to explain to the people that what had taken place was in accord with the wish of most of the gods. A story was written in which Marduk, because of a transgression, was captured and brought before a tribunal. Only a part of the commentary to this botched piece of literature is extant. Even the great poem of the creation of the world, the *Enuma elish*, was altered: the god Marduk was replaced by the god Ashur. Sennacherib's boundless energies brought no gain to his empire, however, and probably weakened it. The tenacity of the king can be seen in his building projects: for example, when Nineveh needed water for irrigation, Sennacherib had his engineers divert the waters of a tributary of the Great Zab River. The canal had to cross a valley at Jerwan. An aqueduct was constructed, consisting of about 2,000,000 blocks of limestone, with five huge, pointed archways over the brook in the valley. The bed of the canal on the aqueduct was sealed with cement containing magnesium. Parts of this aqueduct are still standing today. The King wrote of these and other technological accomplishments in minute detail, with illustrations.

Sennacherib built a huge palace in Nineveh, adorned with reliefs, some of them depicting the transport of colossal bull statues by water and by land. Many of the rooms were decorated with pictorial narratives in bas-relief telling of war and of building activities. Considerable advances can be noted in artistic execution, particularly in the portrayal of landscapes and animals. Outstanding are the depictions of the battles in the lagoons, the life in the military camps, and the deportations.

In 681 BC there was a rebellion. Sennacherib was assassinated by one or two of his sons in the temple of the god Ninurta. This god, along with the god Marduk, had been badly treated by Sennacherib, and the event was widely regarded as punishment of divine origin.

Esarhaddon. Ignoring the claims of his older brothers, an imperial council appointed Esarhaddon (Ashur-akhiddina, 680–669) as the successor. The choice is all the more difficult to explain in that Esarhaddon, quite unlike his father, was friendly toward the Babylonians. It can be assumed that his energetic and designing mother, Nakija, who hailed from Syria or Judah, used all her influence in his behalf to override the national party of Assyria. He may very well have been a partner in plotting the murder of his father; at any rate, he was able to procure the loyalty of his father's army. His brothers had to flee to Urartu. In his inscriptions, Esarhaddon always mentions both his father and grandfather.

Defining the destruction of Babylon explicitly as punishment by the god Marduk, the new king soon ordered the reconstruction of the city. He referred to himself only as governor of Babylonia and by his policies obtained the support of the cities of Babylonia. At the beginning of his reign the Aramaean tribes were still allied with Elam against him, but Urtaku of Elam (675–664) signed a peace treaty and freed him for campaigning elsewhere. In 679 he stationed a garrison at the Egyptian border, because Egypt, under its Ethiopian king Taharqa, was intervening in Syria. He put down with great severity a rebellion of the combined forces of Sidon, Tyre, and other Syrian cities. The time was ripe to attack Egypt, which was suffering under the rule of the Ethiopians and by no means a united country. Esarhaddon's first attempt in 674/673 miscarried. In 671 BC, however, his forces took Memphis, the Egyptian capital. Assyrian consultants were assigned to assist the princes of the 22 provinces, their main duty being the collection of tribute.

Occasional threats came from the mountainous border regions of eastern Anatolia and Iran. Pushed forward by the Scythians, the Cimmerians in northern Iran and Transcaucasia tried to get a foothold in Syria and western Iran. Esarhaddon allied himself with the Scythian king Partatua by giving him one of his daughters in marriage. In so doing he checked the movement of the Cimmerians. Nevertheless, the apprehensions of Esarhaddon can be seen in his many offerings, supplications, and requests to the sun-god. These were concerned less with his own enterprises than with the plans of enemies and vassals and the reliability of civil servants. The priestesses of Ishtar had to reassure the King constantly by calling out to him, "Do not be afraid." Previous kings had never needed this kind of encouragement.

At home the King was faced with serious difficulties from factions in the court. His oldest son had died early. The national party suspected his second son Shamash-shum-ukin of being too friendly with the Babylonians; he may also have been considered unequal to the task of kingship. The king's third son, Ashurbanipal, was given the succession in 672, Shamash-shum-ukin remaining crown prince of Babylonia. This arrangement caused much dissension, and some farseeing civil servants warned of disastrous effects. Nevertheless, the Assyrian nobles, priests, and city leaders were sworn to just such an adjustment of the royal line; even the vassal princes had to take an oath of allegiance to Ashurbanipal.

Another matter of deep concern for Esarhaddon was his failing health. He regarded eclipses of the moon as particularly alarming omens, and in order to prevent a fatal illness from striking him at such times he had substitute kings chosen who ruled during the three such critical periods that occurred during his 12-year reign. The replacement kings died or were put to death after their brief term of office. During his off terms Esarhaddon called himself "Mister Peasant." This practice implied that the gods could not distinguish between the real king and a false one—quite contrary to the usual assumptions of the religion.

Esarhaddon enlarged and improved the temples in both Assyria and Babylonia. He also constructed a palace in Kalakh, using many of the picture slabs of Tiglath-pileser III. The works that remain are not on the level of those of either his predecessors or of Ashurbanipal. He died while on an expedition to put down a revolt in Egypt.

Ashurbanipal (668–627) and Shamash-shum-ukin (668–648). Although the death of his father occurred far from home, Ashurbanipal assumed his kingship as planned. He may have owed his fortunes to the intercession of his grandmother Nakija, who had recognized his superior capacities. He tells of his diversified education by the priests and his training in armour making as well as in other military arts. He may have been the only king in Assyria with a scholarly background. As crown prince he had also studied the administration of the vast empire. The record notes that the gods granted him a record harvest during the first year of his reign. There were also good crops in subsequent years. During these first years he was also successful in foreign policy, and his relation to his brother in Babylonia was good.

In 668 he put down a rebellion in Egypt and drove out the Ethiopian king, Taharqa. But in 664 the nephew of Taharqa, Tanutamon, gathered forces for a new rebellion. Ashurbanipal went to Egypt, pursuing the Ethiopian prince far into the south. His smashing victory moved

(margin notes)
The destruction of Babylon

Esarhaddon's policies

Ashurbanipal's education and early years

Tyre and other parts of the empire to resume regular payments of tribute. Ashurbanipal installed Psamtik as prince over the Egyptian region of Sais. In 656 Psamtik dislodged the Assyrian garrisons with the aid of Carian and Ionian mercenaries, making Egypt again independent. Ashurbanipal did not attempt to reconquer it again. A former ally of Assyria, Gyges of Lydia had now aided Psamtik in his rebellion. In return, Assyria did not help Gyges when he was attacked by the Cimmerians. Gyges lost his throne and his life. His son Ardys decided that the payment of tribute to Assyria was a lesser evil than conquest by the Cimmerians.

Graver difficulties loomed in southern Babylonia, which was attacked by Elam in 664. Another attack came in 653, whereupon Ashurbanipal sent a large army that decisively defeated the Elamites. Their king was killed, and some of the Elamite states were encouraged to secede. Elam was no longer strong enough to assume an active part on the international scene. This victory had serious consequences for Babylonia. Shamash-shum-ukin had grown weary of being patronized by his domineering brother. He formed a secret alliance in 656 with the Iranians, Elamites, Aramaeans, Arabs, and Egyptians, directed against Ashurbanipal. The withdrawal of defeated Elam from this alliance was probably the reason for a **Defeat of** premature attack by Shamash-shum-ukin at the end of **Shamash-** the year 652, without waiting for the promised assistance **shum-** from Egypt. Ashurbanipal, taken by surprise, soon pulled **ukin** his troops together. The Babylonian army was defeated and Shamash-shum-ukin was surrounded in his fortified city of Babylon. His allies were not able to stand on their own against the Assyrians. Reinforcements of Arabian camel troops were also defeated. The city of Babylon was under siege for three years. It fell in 648 amid scenes of horrible carnage, Shamash-shum-ukin dying in his burning palace.

After 648 the Assyrians made a few punitive attacks on the Arabs, breaking the forward thrust of the Arab tribes for a long time to come. The main objective of the Assyrians, however, was a final settlement of their relationship with Elam. The refusal of Elam in 647 to extradite an Aramaean prince was used as pretext for a new attack that drove deep into its territory. The assault on the solidly fortified capital of Susa followed, probably in 646. The Assyrians destroyed the city, including its temples and palaces. Vast spoils were taken. As usual, the upper classes of the land were exiled to Assyria and other parts of the empire, and Elam became an Assyrian province. Assyria had now extended its domain to southwestern Iran. Cyrus I of Persia sent tribute and hostages to Nineveh, hoping perhaps to secure protection for his borders with Media. Little is known about the last years of Ashurbanipal's reign.

Ashurbanipal left more inscriptions than any of his predecessors. His campaigns were not always recorded in chronological order but clustered in groups according to their purpose. The accounts were highly subjective. One of his more remarkable accomplishments was the founding of the great library in Nineveh, which is today one of the most important sources for the study of that era. The King himself supervised its construction. Important works were kept in more than one copy, some intended for the King's personal use. The work of arranging and cataloging drew upon the experience of centuries in the management of collections in huge temple archives such as the one in Ashur. In his inscriptions Ashurbanipal tells of becoming an enthusiastic hunter of big game, acquiring a taste for it during a fight with marauding lions. In his palace at Nineveh the long rows of hunting scenes show what a masterful artist can accomplish in bas-relief; with these reliefs Assyrian art reached its peak. In the series picturing his wars, particularly the wars fought in Elam, the scenes are overloaded with human figures. Those portraying the battles with the Arabian camel troops are magnificent in execution.

One reason for the durability of the Assyrian Empire was the practice of deporting large numbers of people from conquered areas and resettling others in their place. This kept many of the conquered nationalities from re-

gaining their power. Equally important was the installation in conquered areas of a highly developed civil service under the leadership of trained officers. The highest ranking civil servant carried the title of *tartan*, a Hurrian word. The *tartan*s also represented the king during his absence. In descending rank were the palace overseer, the main cupbearer, the palace administrator, and the governor of Assyria. The generals often held high official positions, particularly in the provinces. The civil service numbered about 100,000, many of them former inhabitants of subjugated provinces. Prisoners became slaves but were later often freed.

State and culture in the Neo-Assyrian Empire

No laws are known for the empire, although documents point to the existence of rules and standards for justice. Those who broke contracts were subject to severe penalties, even in cases of minor importance: the sacrifice of a son or the eating of a pound of wool and drinking of a great deal of water afterward, which led to a painful death. The position of women was inferior, except for the queen and some priestesses.

Good estimates of the economic situation of the period do not exist. The arts and crafts experienced a golden age in Assyria; many qualified artists and artisans went there, bringing renewed creativity and new ideas. Finds of Aramaic texts from the Assyrian era are notably few because neither papyrus nor parchment preserved well in the climate; evidence of literary efforts in other languages is lacking, except of course in the border areas of Syria–Palestine and Judah.

Babylonia lagged behind Assyria during the period. Many small wars severely hampered the development of the country, undermining agricultural production and commerce. The temples fared best because many Assyrians supported them, but they left no document—a fact that can hardly be regarded as accidental. The continuing existence of scholarly study can be inferred from extant letters and the continuation of old traditions. The pictorial arts, however, were neglected, and the Babylonian artists may have found better jobs in Assyria. This period saw the first use of ancestral names as family appelations.

The era apparently was not fruitful for literary accomplishments either in Babylonia or Assyria. The large inscriptions of the kings were the most important achievements in Assyria; there were also hymns and prayers, executed mostly in the traditional style, and unusual oracle texts in the Assyrian language. Both countries saw the beginnings of a historical literature, going far beyond the ordinary chronicals.

Decline of the Assyrian Empire. Few historical sources remain for the last 30 years of the Assyrian Empire. There are no extant inscriptions of Ashurbanipal after 640 BC, and the few surviving inscriptions of his successors contain only vague allusions to political matters. In Babylonia the silence is almost total until 625 BC, when the chronicles resume. The rapid downfall of the Assyrian Empire was formerly attributed to military defeat, although it was never clear how the Medes and the Babylonians alone could have accomplished this. More recent work has established that after 635 a civil war occurred, weakening the empire, so that it could no longer stand up against a foreign enemy. Ashurbanipal had twin sons. Ashur-etel-ilani was appointed successor to the throne, but his twin brother Sin-shar-ishkun did not recognize him. The fight between them and their supporters forced the old king to withdraw to Haran, in 632 at the latest, perhaps ruling from there over the western part of the empire until his death in 627. Ashur-etel-ilani governed in Assyria from about 633 on, but a general, Sin-shum-lisher, soon rebelled against him and proclaimed himself counterking. Some years later (629?) Sin-shar-ishkun finally succeeded in obtaining the kingship. In Babylonian documents dates can be found for all three kings. To add to the confusion, until 626 there are also dates of Ashurbanipal and a king named Kandalanu. In 626 the Chaldean Nabopolassar revolted from Uruk and occupied Babylon. There were several changes in government. King Ashur-etel-ilani was forced to withdraw to the west, where he died sometime after 625.

Internal struggles in the last years of the empire

Around the year 626 the Scythians laid waste to Syria and Palestine. In 625 the Medes became united under Cyaxares and began to conquer the Iranian provinces of Assyria. One chronicle relates of wars between Sin-shar-ishkun and Nabopolassar in Babylonia in 625–623. It was not long until the Assyrians were driven out of Babylonia. In 616 the Medes struck against Nineveh, but, according to the Greek historian Herodotus, were driven back by the Scythians. In 615, however, the Medes conquered Arrapkha (Kirkūk) and in 614 the old capital of Ashur, looting and destroying the city. Now Cyaxares and Nabopolassar made an alliance for the purpose of dividing Assyria. In 612 Kalakh and Nineveh succumbed to the superior strength of the allies. The revenge taken on the Assyrians was terrible: 200 years later Xenophon found the country still sparsely populated.

Sin-shar-ishkun, king of Assyria, found death in his burning palace. The commander of the Assyrian army in the west crowned himself king in the city of Haran, assuming the name of the founder of the empire, Ashuruballit II (611–609 BC). Ashuruballit had to face both the Babylonians and the Medes. They conquered Haran in 610, without, however, destroying the city completely. In 609 the remaining Assyrian troops had to capitulate. With this event, Assyria disappeared from history. The great empires that succeeded it learned a great deal from the hated Assyrians, both in the arts and in the organization of their states.

THE NEO-BABYLONIAN EMPIRE (626–539)

The Chaldeans, who inhabited the coastal area near the Persian Gulf, had never been entirely pacified by the Assyrians. About 630 Nabopolassar became king of the Chaldeans. In 626 he forced the Assyrians out of Uruk and crowned himself king of Babylonia. He took part in the wars aimed at the destruction of Assyria. At the same time, he began to restore the dilapidated network of canals in the cities of Babylonia, particularly those in the city of Babylon. He fought against the Assyrian Ashuruballit II and then against Egypt, his successes alternating with misfortunes. In 605 Nabopolassar died in Babylon.

Nebuchadrezzar (Nabu-kudurri-usur) II. Nabopolassar had named his oldest son after the famous king of the second dynasty of Isin, had trained him carefully for his prospective kingship, and had shared responsibility with him. When the father died in 605, Nebuchadrezzar was with his army in Syria; he had just crushed the Egyptians in a cruel, bloody war and pursued them into the south. On receiving the news of his father's death, Nebuchadrezzar returned immediately to Babylon. In his numerous inscriptions he tells but rarely of his many wars. The Babylonian chronicle is extant only for the years 605–594, and not much is known from other sources about the later years of this famous king. He went very often to Syria and Palestine—at first to drive out the Egyptians. In 604 he took the Philistine city of Ashkelon. In 601 he tried to push forward into Egypt but was forced to pull back after a very bloody, undecided battle and to regroup his army in Babylonia. After smaller incursions against the Arabs of Syria, he attacked Palestine at the end of 598. Joiakin of Judah had rebelled, counting on help from Egypt. According to the chronicle, Jerusalem was taken on March 16, 597, and King Joiakin, together with at least 3,000 Jews, were led into exile in Babylonia. They were treated well there, according to the documents. Zedekiah was appointed the new king. In 596, when danger threatened from the east, Nebuchadrezzar marched to the Tigris River and induced the enemy to withdraw. After a revolt in Babylonia had been crushed with much bloodshed, there were other campaigns in the west.

According to the Old Testament, Judah rebelled again in 589; Jerusalem was under siege. The city fell after 18 months of siege and was completely destroyed. Many thousands of Jews were forced into "Babylonian exile," and their country was reduced to a province of the Babylonian Empire. The revolt had been caused by an Egyptian invasion that pushed as far as Sidon. Nebuchadrezzar laid siege to Tyre for 13 years without taking the city,

The Chaldean kings

Campaigns in Syria and Palestine

because there was no fleet at his disposal. In 568/567 he attacked Egypt, again without much success, but from then on the Egyptians refrained from further attacks on Palestine. Nebuchadrezzar lived at peace with Media throughout his reign and acted as a mediator after the Median–Lydian war of 590–585.

The Babylonian Empire under Nebuchadrezzar extended to the Egyptian border. It had a well-functioning administrative system. Though he had to collect extremely high taxes and tributes in order to maintain his armies and carry out his building projects, Nebuchadrezzar made Babylonia one of the richest lands in western Asia —the more astonishing because it had been rather poor when it was ruled by the Assyrians. Babylon was the largest city of the "civilized world." The King maintained the existing canal systems and built many supplementary canals, making the land even more fertile. Trade and commerce flourished.

Nebuchadrezzar's building activities surpassed those of most of the Assyrian kings. He fortified the old double walls of Babylon, adding another triple wall outside the old wall. In addition, he erected another wall, the Median Wall, north of the city between the Euphrates and the Tigris rivers. According to Greek estimates, the Median Wall may have been about 30 metres (100 feet) high. He enlarged the old palace and added many wings, so that hundreds of rooms with large inner courts were now at the disposal of the central offices of the empire. Colourful glazed-tile bas-reliefs decorated the walls. Terrace gardens, called hanging gardens in later accounts, were added. Hundreds of thousands of workers must have been required for these projects. The temples were objects of special concern. He devoted himself first and foremost to the completion of the Tower of Babel. Its base measured 91 metres (about 300 feet) on each side and 91 metres in height. There were five terrace-like gradations surmounted by a temple, the whole tower being about twice the height of those of other temples. The wide street used for processions led along the eastern side by the inner city walls and crossed at the enormous Ishtar Gate with its world-renowned bas-relief tiles. The King also built many smaller temples throughout the country.

The Tower of Babel

The last kings of Babylonia. Awil-Marduk (in the Old Testament Evil-Merodach, 561–560), the son of Nebuchadrezzar, was unable to win the support of the priests of Marduk. His reign did not last long, and he was soon eliminated. His brother-in-law and successor, Nergalshar-usur (in classical sources, Neriglissar, 559–556), was a general who undertook a campaign in 557 into the "rough" Cilician land, which may have been under the control of the Medes. His land forces were assisted by a fleet. His still-minor son Labashi-Marduk was murdered not long after that, allegedly because he was not suitable for his job.

The next king was the Aramaean Nabonidus (555–539) from Haran, one of the most interesting and enigmatical figures of ancient times. His mother, Addagoppe, was a priestess of the god Sin in Haran, who came to Babylon and managed to get responsible offices for her son at court. The god of the moon rewarded her piety with a long life—she lived to be 102—and she was buried in Haran with all the honours of a queen in 547. It is not clear which powerful faction in Babylon supported the kingship of Nabonidus; it may have been one opposing the priests of Marduk, who had become extremely powerful. The King raided Cilicia in 555 and secured the surrender of Haran, which had been ruled by the Medes. He concluded a treaty of defense with Astyages of Media against the Persians, who had become a growing threat since 559 under their king Cyrus II. He also devoted himself to the renovation of many temples, taking an especially keen interest in old inscriptions. He gave preference to his god Sin and had powerful enemies in the priesthood of the Marduk temple. Modern excavators have found fragments of propaganda poems written against Nabonidus and also in support of him. Both traditions continued in Judaism.

Internal difficulties and the recognition that the narrow strip of land from the Persian Gulf to Syria could not be

Nabonidus and Belshazzar

defended against a major attack from the east induced Nabonidus to leave Babylonia around 552 and to reside in Taima in northern Arabia. There he organized an Arabian province with the assistance of Jewish mercenaries. His viceroy in Babylonia was his son Bel-shar-usur, the Belshazzar of the Book of Daniel in the Bible. Cyrus turned this to his own advantage by annexing Media in 550. Nabonidus, in turn, allied himself with Croesus of Lydia in order to fight Cyrus. But, when Cyrus attacked Lydia and annexed it in 546, Nabonidus was not able to help Croesus. Cyrus bode his time. In 542 Nabonidus returned to Babylonia, where his son had been able to maintain good order in external matters but had not overcome a growing internal opposition to his father. Consequently, Nabonidus' career after his return was of short duration, though he tried very hard to regain the support of the Babylonians. He appointed his daughter to be high priestess of the god Sin in Ur, thus returning to the Sumerian-Old Babylonian religious custom. The priests of Marduk looked to Cyrus, hoping to have better relations with him than with Nabonidus; they promised Cyrus the surrender of Babylon without a fight if he would grant them their privileges in return. In 539 Cyrus attacked northern Babylonia with a large army, defeating Nabonidus, and entered the city of Babylon without a battle. The other cities did not offer any resistance, either. Nabonidus surrendered, receiving a small territory in eastern Iran. Tradition has confused him with his great predecessor Nebuchadrezzar II. The Bible refers to him as Nebuchadrezzar in the Book of Daniel.

Babylonia's peaceful submission to Cyrus saved it from the fate of Assyria. It became a territory under the Persian crown but kept its cultural autonomy. Even the racially mixed western part of the Babylonian Empire submitted without resistance.

Culture of the Neo-Babylonian Empire

The Babylonians by 620 had grown tired of Assyrian rule. They were also weary of internal struggle. They were easily persuaded to submit to the order of the Chaldean kings. The result was a surprisingly quick social and economic consolidation, helped along by the fact that after the fall of Assyria no external enemy threatened Babylonia for over 60 years. In the cities, the temples were an important element of the economy, having vast benefices at their disposal. The business class regained its strength, not only in the trades and commerce but also in the management of agriculture in the metropolitan areas. Livestock breeding—sheep, goats, beef cattle, and also horses—flourished, as did poultry farming. The cultivation of corn, dates, and vegetables grew in importance. Much was done to improve communications, both by water and by land, with the western provinces of the empire. The collapse of the Assyrian Empire had the consequence that many trade arteries were rerouted through Babylonia instead. Another consequence was that the city of Babylon became a world centre.

The immense amount of documentary material and correspondence that have survived has not yet been fully analyzed. No new system of law or administration seems to have developed during that time. The Babylonian dialect gradually became Aramaicized, still written primarily on clay tablets that often bore added material in Aramaic lettering. Parchment and papyrus documents have not survived. There is no evidence of much artistic creativity. Aside from some of the inscriptions of the Kings, especially Nabonidus, which were not comparable from a literary standpoint with those of the Assyrians, the main efforts were devoted to the rewriting of old texts. In the fine arts, only few monuments have any suggestion of new tendencies.

MESOPOTAMIA UNDER THE PERSIANS

Cyrus as king of Babylonia

Cyrus united Babylonia with his country in a personal union, assuming the title of "King of Babylonia, King of the Lands." His son Cambyses was appointed vice king and resided in Sippar. The Persians relied on the support of the priests and the business class in the cities. In a Babylonian inscription, Cyrus relates with pride his peaceful, bloodless conquest of the city of Babylon. At the same time, he speaks of Marduk as the king of gods.

His moderation and restraint were rewarded: Babylonia became the richest province of his empire. There is no indication of any national rebellion in Babylonia under Cyrus and Cambyses (529–522). That there must have been an accumulation of discontent became clear at the ascension to the throne of Darius I (522–486), when a usurper seized the throne of Babylonia under the name of Nebuchadrezzar (III), only to lose both the throne and his life after ten weeks. Darius waived any punitary action. He had to take more drastic measures in 521, when a new Nebuchadrezzar incited another rebellion against him. This usurper's reign lasted for two months. Executions and plundering followed; Darius ordered the inner walls of Babylon to be demolished and reformed the organization of the state. But Babylon remained the capital of the new satrapy and also became the administrative headquarters for the satrapies of Assyria and Syria. One result was that the palace had to be enlarged.

Babylonia remained a wealthy and prosperous land, in contrast to Assyria, which was still a poor country. At the same time, the administration was more and more in the hands of the Persians, and the tax burdens grew heavier. This produced discontent, centring especially on the large temples in Babylon. Xerxes (486–465) had his residence in Babylon while he was crown prince and knew the country very well. When he assumed his kingship, he immediately curtailed the autonomy of the satrapies. This, in turn, gave rise to many rebellions. In Babylonia there were two short interim governments of Babylonian pretenders during 484–482. Xerxes retaliated by desecrating and partially destroying the holy places of the god Marduk and the Tower of Babel in the city of Babylon. Priests were executed, and the statue of Marduk was melted down. The members of the royal family still resided in the palaces of the city of Babylon, but Aramaic became more and more the language of the official administration. One source of information for this period are the clay-tablet archives of the commercial house of Murashu and Sons of Nippur for the years of 455–403, which tell much about the important role the Iranians played in the country. The state domains were largely in their hands. They controlled many minor feudal tenants, grouped into social classes according to ancestry and occupation. The business people were predominantly Babylonians and Aramaeans, but there were also Jews. The documents became increasingly sparse after 400. The cultural life of Babylon became concentrated in a few central cities, particularly Babylon and Uruk; Ur and Nippur were also important centres. The work of astronomers continued, as evidenced in records of observations. Nabu-rimanni, living and working around 500, and Kidinnu, 5th or 4th century BC, were also known to the Greeks; both astronomers are famous for their methods of calculating the courses of the Moon and the planets. In the field of literature, religious poetic works as well as texts of omens and Sumero–Akkadian word lists were constantly copied very often with commentaries.

(W.T.v.S.)

BABYLONIA UNDER ALEXANDER, THE SELEUCIDS, AND THE PARTHIANS

The end of Babylonian culture

Babylonia was once more to become the centre of the civilized world. Alexander the Great decided to make Babylon one of the capitals of his empire after he conquered the Persians. He began to build a large harbour. In 331 he ordered the restoration of the Marduk temples, among them also the high temple of Etemenanki; Marduk was henceforth recognized as the equal of the Greek god Zeus. After Alexander's death, Babylon lost its position of importance. In 312 Seleucus I Nicator entered Babylon. But soon he founded a new capital, Seleucia, on the Tigris River. Babylon's temples and scholarly institutions continued to receive the care and consideration of the kings of the Seleucid dynasty as well as of some of the later Parthian kings. Antiochus I Soter (281–261) even ordered a Babylonian inscription to be included in the walls of the Temple of Nabu when he undertook the rebuilding of the city of Borsippa. Babylonian business documents from the time of the Seleucids, written on clay tablets, are still extant. Greek and Aramaean documents did not survive. The city of Uruk was second in importance to Babylon as a cultural centre at this time. Uruk's god Anu—the god of the heavens—was recognized along with Marduk as the equal of the Greek Zeus. Two large temples were built for Anu and Ishtar. Written rituals indicate that the cult had remained true to the old traditions. The citizens of Uruk participated in these rituals in various functions, lucrative as well as honourable and respected. Some documents indicate that religious benefices were handled as stock and often sold in shares. Other documents deal with the selling of promises. The exact measurements and markings of the boundary lines are stated on these. While the names of the parties are mostly Babylonian, it is not unusual to find a second, Greek name added to the original Babylonian one.

The Babylonian astronomers

An important result of the mixture of Babylonian and Greek culture in Babylon and Uruk was the further development of the science of astronomy. The Babylonians contributed their methods of mathematical calculation, as well as an accumulation of observations covering several centuries. The Greeks contributed their training in logical thinking. Many documents of the Hellenistic princes who ruled in Asia Minor and along the Aegean Sea during this time show the cooperative efforts of the Greek and Babylonian astronomers. They laid the basis upon which astronomers of later times were able to build. One of them deserves particular mention: the Marduk priest Berosus, who founded a school for astrology and astronomy on the island of Kos around the year 280. He was also the author of a book about Babylonia, its history, and its religion (*Babylōniaka*). The book was written in Greek, and fragments of it still exist.

The decline of the empire of the Seleucids after 150 led to the incorporation of Babylonia into the empire of the Parthians in eastern Iran between 141 and 129. The result was by no means a great political catastrophe. Nevertheless, it hastened the decline of the late Babylonian city culture. There had been no new creative or cultural ideas for a long time, and the old schools for scribes slowly became extinct. Few literary texts and documents survive from the time between 140 BC and 80 BC. The knowledge of the cuneiform script was lost under the Greeks, who were hardly interested in foreign languages. Not until the 19th and 20th centuries did the discovery of tens of thousands of cuneiform texts lead to the decoding of this entirely forgotten writing. This permitted scholars to repossess a large part of the lost literature of Mesopotamia.

Parthian and Sāsānian periods. Mesopotamia (especially the district of Nisibis) was attached to the growing dominions of Armenia temporarily in the 1st century BC but was recovered for Parthia by Phraates III (reigned 70–58/57 BC). With the rise of Roman power in the Near East, it assumed the character of a border territory between the Roman and Parthian spheres of influence, though it usually remained under Parthian control. The Roman leader Crassus led an army into Mesopotamia in 54 BC but was defeated by the Parthians at Carrhae in 53. In AD 114–117 the emperor Trajan conquered the area and made it a Roman province, but it was abandoned once again to Parthia by Hadrian after Trajan's death. Beginning in 165, the Romans once more occupied the northwest portion of Mesopotamia.

During most of the period from the early 3rd century until the rise of Islām in the early 7th century, Mesopotamia remained a battleground between the Romans (in the 6th and 7th centuries, the Byzantines) and the Sāsānian successors of the Parthians. As during the Parthian period, Roman influence was for the most part confined to the extreme northwestern part of the country—the area around Carrhae, Edessa, and Nisibis, near the Syrian and Anatolian borders. The Sāsānian kings made their capital at Ctesiphon, near the midpoint of the Tigris, and their influence predominated in the rest of Mesopotamia. During this period, Mesopotamia became one of the chief centres of Nestorian Christianity and had a sizable Jewish community. (For the history of the Parthian and Sāsānian empires, see IRAN, HISTORY OF.)   (Ed.)

III. Iraq from the Arab conquest to 1918

From the Arab conquest in the 7th century to the second decade of the 20th century, Iraq existed not as an independent state but as a geographical expression for the flatlands between Baghdad and the Persian Gulf—an area of unavoidable passage between Central Asia and the Mediterranean. The history of Iraq in this period is dominated by the rivalry of the three strongest ethnic elements of the Muslim world: the Arabs, the Iranians, and the Turks. During this period Iraq was also a great centre of Islāmic culture as well as the place of origin of several religious sects that divided the community of Islām. The political history of the area may be summarized as follows: after being the metropolitan province of the Arabo-Islāmic Empire under the caliphs' more or less effective authority, Iraq fell successively under the control of the Būyid dynasty of Iran and the Seljuq Turks; and then, after the Mongol invasion, which hastened its decline, it became a dominion of Mongol and later Turkmen and Persian dynasties established in Iran and remained for almost four centuries under Ottoman rule, to emerge again as an independent state as a result of World War I. Further information about Iraq's history during this period is contained in the following articles: IRAN, HISTORY OF; CALIPHATE, EMPIRE OF THE; SELJUQS; MONGOLS; OTTOMAN EMPIRE AND TURKEY, HISTORY OF THE.

THE ARAB CONQUEST

From the 3rd century AD, the Lakhmids, a small dynasty of South Arabian origin, ruled al-Ḥīrah, on the Euphrates, as vassals of the Sāsānid rulers of Iran, who had entrusted them with keeping the Bedouins in check and holding the borders of Iran against the Byzantines; the Lakhmid capital was a flourishing centre of trade between Persia and Arabia as well as a focus of Arabic culture. In addition, some elements of such important Arab tribes as the Taghlib, the Bakr, and the Tamīm had taken the steppes of Lower Mesopotamia for pastureland, and, relations had been established between the Prophet and those Bedouins, perhaps with a view to subsequent operations in the area.

The rich area stretching south of al-Ḥīrah was protected by strongholds that were easily reduced on the occasion of mere reconnaissances made by Arab parties under al-Muthannā ibn Ḥārithah, a leader of the Bakr, who is said to have called in the famous general Khālid ibn al-Walīd to help him. Khālid seized Al-Ḥīrah in 633–634, but he was sent to Syria. Al-Muthannā was left in charge of the Arab forces in Lower Iraq. For three years, the progress of the conquest proceeded slowly, until 637, when Sa'd ibn Abī Waqqāṣ won a decisive victory over the Sāsānids at al-Qādisīyah, 20 miles (32 kilometres) southeast of al-Ḥīrah. The Arabs sacked Ctesiphon, the Persian capital, and seem to have been welcomed by the native population of the region. Those successes marked the beginning of the collapse of the Sāsānid Empire and made it possible for the Arabs to spread eastward. In 641 both Nineveh and Mosul fell to the Arabs. Sāsānid power was eventually destroyed in 642 at the battle of Nehāvand. This victory enabled the Arabs to control western and central Persia in addition to Mesopotamia.

Establishment of Basra and Kūfah

At that time two military camps, Basra and Kūfah, had been established, the former on the right bank of the Shatt al-Arab in 638 and the latter on the right bank of the Euphrates, near al-Ḥīrah, in 638–639. Both camps were to develop into large cities and play an outstanding part in the history of Iraq until the foundation of Baghdad in 762. Both towns received new inhabitants either from Arabia or the East as a result of conquests that brought them captives and booty as well as revenue from two Persian provinces (*māh al-Baṣrah* and *māh al-Kūfah*) within their scope. The area to the east of Basra and Kūfah was called as-Sawād (the Black Region), in reference to its fertility. The mixing of various ethnic elements promoted economical and intellectual development in the rival cities, while political events gave rise to the great politico-religious parties that were to divide Islām into discordant groups. Moreover, it was in Basra and Kūfah that all literary, philological, and historical materials that were to form the basis of Arabo-Islāmic culture were collected from Bedouins: it was there that Islāmic sciences such as grammar and lexicography came into existence. Qur'ānic exegesis and science of traditions developed, while several schools of thought, particularly Mu'tazilism (see below), took shape. It is true that Kūfah did not outlive for long the founding of Baghdad, but Basra was far enough from the capital to retain its identity. The whole history of Islām has been to some extent conditioned by events that occurred at Basra and Kūfah or were in connection with either city. 'Uthmān ibn 'Affān, the third orthodox caliph, was murdered in 656. 'Ā'ishah, a Prophet's widow, set out for Basra with her followers with the object of avenging the caliph and fighting 'Alī ibn Abī Tālib, the latter's successor. With the help of troops from Kūfah, 'Alī defeated the rebels in the so-called Battle of the Camel (for 'Ā'ishah was riding a camel) fought in Basra in December of 656. Here two parties of Muslims struggled against each other for the first time. In the following year 'Alī tried to subdue Mu'āwiyah, the powerful governor of Syria who had refused to obey an order of dismissal. Leaving Kūfah, where he had established the seat of his government, he met his rival at Ṣiffīn, on the right bank of the Euphrates. When 'Alī was about to win the day, Mū'āwiyah's troops raised leaves of the Qur'ān on their spears, meaning that they wished to leave it to God's decision. 'Alī agreed to stop fighting and both parties agreed to arbitration. On his return to Kūfah, 'Alī had to suppress a rebellion instigated by some soldiers who contested the very principle of arbitration, and he crushed these Khārijites ("Seceders") on July 17, 658, in an-Nahrawān. The survivors, however, continued the movement, scattering in various areas and recruiting new followers; thus, it was in Iraq that Khārijism, the earliest sect to rise within Islām, came into existence.

THE UMAYYADS

After being deposed in January 659 by the arbitrators met in Adhruḥ, 'Alī tried to preserve the caliphate, but he was murdered by a Khārijite on January 24, 661, and Mu'āwiyah, who had asserted his dominion over Syria and Egypt, was proclaimed in the Arabian province of Hejaz. Mu'āwiyah moved the seat of the Umayyad caliphate to Damascus in Syria. Iraq became a single province but a privileged one, as it developed into a military base for the Muslim conquest of Eastern countries. Iraq continued to play a major political role in the empire of the caliphate.

Movement of the caliphate to Damascus

In Umayyad times and afterward, the limits of Iraq were roughly marked out by a line running some distance to the west of the Shatt al-Arab and the Euphrates up to al-Anbār (sometimes up to al-Ḥadīthah), thence to Takrīt on the Tigris, then on through Ḥulwān to the Persian Gulf east of 'Abbādān (now Abadan, in Iran); al-Jazīrah and Mosul were not included in Iraqi provinces except during certain periods.

Under the Umayyads, Kūfah inclined toward 'Alī and his party; it was there that revolts raised by his descendants or their followers, the Shī'ah, broke out. Basra seemed to be in favour of a more democratic regime, but it was anxious to preserve independence and scarcely accepted governors sent from Damascus. It was at Basra that the Khārijites, the most vehement opponents to the established order, caused disturbances. After the murder of 'Alī and the failure of a plot woven simultaneously by them against Mu'āwiyah and the Governor of Egypt, they constantly threatened Iraq and especially Basra during the following decades. While Iraqi troops were launched to the conquest of Oriental areas as far away as India, Basra had to defend itself against the rebels. Mu'āwiyah publicly recognized Ziyād (an alleged illegitimate son of his father) as his brother and appointed him governor of Basra in 665 and then of Basra and Kūfah from 670 to 675. Ziyād fought both Khārijites and Shī'īs with efficiency and, by promoting important drainage projects, did much to restore the economic life of Lower Iraq. His son, 'Ubayd Allāh, continued to rule firmly in Iraq, but, when Mu'āwiyah died in 680, the succession of his son

engendered further revolts. Al-Ḥusayn, 'Alī's second son, was invited by his followers to Kūfah, where a revolt had been initiated in his support; on October 10, 680, al-Ḥusayn was intercepted at Karbalā', near Kūfah, and slaughtered, together with his small escort. This event had an enormous impact on the Muslim world: it inspired unspeakable abhorrence among the Shī'ah and other orthodox Muslims toward the Umayyads. A few years after Karbalā', in January 685, the so-called Penitents (Tawwābūn) tried, with little success, to foster disturbances in Iraq with a view to avenging the murder of al-Ḥusayn; next, a rebellion broke out under al-Mukhtār, who backed the cause of Muḥammad, another son of 'Alī. Al-Mukhtār succeeded in winning the support of some 'Alids (supporters of 'Alī) and *mawālī* (non-Arabs who had accepted Islām) and gained control over Kūfah for a few months. At that time, the anti-caliph 'Abd Allāh ibn az-Zubayr, who had revolted in Medina and established himself in Mecca, had appointed Muṣ'ab, his brother, as governor of Basra. Muṣ'ab suppressed the uprising, and al-Mukhtār was killed in 687. Four years later, the Umayyads recovered their control over Iraq.

Despite this internecine warfare, Iraq prospered. The province profited by remote conquest, carried out by its armies, and witnessed an important development. In 694, the caliph 'Abd al-Malik ibn Marwān appointed an outstanding statesman, al-Ḥajjāj, as governor of Kūfah. With the support of Syrian forces, he established respect for the caliphal authority and restored order throughout the country. Eager to achieve some sort of a balance between the two cities of Basra and Kūfah, he founded a new city, which he called Wāsiṭ (intermediary), and made it the seat of his governorship. At the same time, important public utility works were undertaken: canals were dug, swamps drained, and agriculture revitalized. Arabic replaced Persian as the official language of government administration. New coins with Arabic inscriptions were minted at Wāsiṭ to replace Sāsānid money.

The founding of Wāsiṭ

A serious problem arose concerning the tax system. According to a general rule, those lands that had been left to their non-Muslim owners were subjected to the *kharāj* (land tax), while Muslim landowners paid only the tithe; thus, a large number of peasants embraced Islām in order to escape paying the *kharāj*. But some tax collectors continued to levy the land tax; this caused a mass movement of the peasantry into the towns. Al-Ḥajjāj forcibly resettled them on the land, and their embittered discontent erupted into several revolts against the Umayyads. Under the caliph Hishām ibn 'Abd al-Malik (724–743) it was decided that land tax should be imposed independently of the religion of *kharāj* landowners.

After al-Ḥajjāj's death (714), Yazīd ibn al-Muhallab, one of his successors, who had been put in jail and escaped, fomented a rebellion that was crushed in 721; order was temporarily restored by Khālid ib 'Abd Allāh al-Qasrī, but increasing disturbances stirred up by Khārijites and 'Abbāsid followers as well brought the Umayyad rule to an end. In Khorāsān a campaign aiming at overthrowing the Umayyads in favour of the 'Abbāsids, who inclined more toward the Persian element, was successful; the example of Khorāsān was followed in other areas; Kūfah was the first town to rise, and it was in its great mosque that as-Saffāḥ, the first 'Abbāsid caliph, was proclaimed on October 30, 749. Thenceforth, the history of Iraq intermingles with the 'Abbāsids'.

THE 'ABBASIDS

The reign of Abū al-'Abbās as-Saffāḥ (749–754) was taken up with fighting the last Umayyads and asserting 'Abbāsid power. His successor, al-Manṣūr (754–775), ruthlessly harried the Shī'īs, whose revolts he suppressed in 755 and 762–763; in 755 he put to death Abū Muslim, to whom the 'Abbāsids were principally indebted for their accession to power. His fame rests on his founding of the new capital, Baghdad, completed in 766, and in laying the foundations on which his successors were to build an elaborate administration. Al-Mahdī (775–785) distinguished himself in fighting the so-called *zanādiqah* —*i.e.*, heterodox sects and individuals, especially Mani-

The founding of Baghdad

chaeans. He was succeeded by al-Hādī (785–786) and Hārūn ar-Rashīd (786–809). The latter's image has been somewhat idealized by the *Thousand and One Nights*.

The Umayyads had been an Arab dynasty; the 'Abbāsids, however, who often had Iranian blood on their mothers' side, naturally turned east and organized their administration and court on the same lines as the Sāsānids'. The first 'Abbāsid period was the golden age of Persian officials. Although deeply Arabicized, they did not fail to remember the old glory of their fatherland and to assume hostile attitudes toward the Arabs, which produced a racial movement known as Shu'ūbīyah and various conflicts between Arabs and non-Arabs. On the other hand, it is obvious that converts to Islām were not always absolutely sincere, and many of them secretly retained their own faiths. That is the reason al-Mahdī hunted out the *zanā-diqah* and put a great many of them to death. Al-Mahdī acted in self-defense; it is not preposterous to discern a feeling of the same kind in ar-Rashīd's reaction against the Barmakids.

As-Saffāḥ had taken as his chief associate Khālid ibn Barmak, a noble Persian who remained in the service of the caliphs. Yaḥyā, Khālid's son, became the vizier of ar-Rashīd, while al-Faḍl and Ja'far, Yaḥyā's sons, were entrusted with high government offices. Suddenly, ar-Rashīd decided to execute Ja'far (January 803). He imprisoned Ja'far's father and brothers and seized the property of the whole family. The reason for ar-Rashīd's actions is not quite made clear by the sources, which speak of an affair between Ja'far and 'Abbāsah, ar-Rashīd's sister; whether this was so or not, such an act of cruelty was regarded as an unbearable slur cast on Persians, at a time when the Shī'īs, after some unsuccessful attempts at seizing power, fostered deep resentment against the 'Abbāsids.

On ar-Rashīd's death, his succession gave rise to bloody conflicts between his sons al-Amīn (809–813) and al-Ma'mūn (813–833); the latter defeated his brother but was compelled to besiege Baghdad to recover the throne. Aiming at reconciling Shī'īs and Sunnīs, al-Ma'mūn contemplated the designation of 'Alī ar-Riḍā, the eighth Shī'ī *imām*, or leader of the community of Islām, as heir apparent; he was forced, however, to go back on his decision in view of the strong Sunnī opposition in Baghdad, a fact that was again jeopardizing the balance between Arabs and Persians, the latter supporting the Shī'īs; such policy was all the more a failure as Shī'īs suspected the caliph of having poisoned ar-Riḍā (died 818). In 815, Abū as-Sarāyā, allegedly backing the 'Alids Ibn Ṭabāṭabā and Muḥammad ibn Zayd, occupied Kūfah, where he minted money, seized Wāsiṭ, Basra, and other towns; and set out for Baghdad. He was eventually defeated and was beheaded on October 18, 815.

Later, however, the political power of the caliphate asserted itself. Economic prosperity grew, and the Arabo-Islāmic civilization centred in Baghdad radiated far beyond the limits of the empire. The seventh 'Abbāsid caliph, al-Ma'mūn, founded, or at least developed, in Baghdad the Bayt al-Ḥikmah (The House of Wisdom), where Greek philosophical and scientific works were translated into Arabic. A rich library was attached to the House of Wisdom, as were several astronomical observatories. A harmonious blending of cultural factors, borrowed from Greece, Persia, and India, enabled Arabo-Islāmic culture to rise to a high degree of refinement in such fields as medicine, mathematics, philosophy, theology, literature, and poetry. Iraq came to regard itself as a kind of privileged heir to all former civilizations and felt bound to accept, sort out, and develop their legacies. Aristotle was considered the master by an intellectual elite fascinated by his method of logical reasoning. The influence of Aristotle was reflected in Mu'tazilism, a school of thought that flourished in Basra before reaching its peak in Baghdad. Without breaking with orthodoxy, the Mu'tazilīs aimed at harmonizing reason and faith; therefore, they assigned free will to man and regarded the Qui'ān as created by God, unlike strict orthodox Sunnīs, who hold it uncreated, coeternal with God. Anticipating that he could rely on the support of the

The House of Wisdom

intellectual elite against his opponents, al-Ma'mūn embraced the Mu'tazilī doctrine, but he came up against difficulties when he wanted to enforce the createdness of the Qui'ān as a formal tenet. Al-Ma'mūn's religious policy alienated both the Shī'īs and the Sunnīs, and in order to maintain his precarious position he inaugurated a severe inquisition (*miḥnah*).

In ordering the *miḥnah* al-Ma'mūn had proved that the 'Abbāsid caliph could become an *imām*, a spiritual ruler, although without any right of legislation on purely religious matters such as worship and canon law; in addition, he was a monarch whose powers were fixed by the Sharī'āh, the Islāmic law. Though these powers were held in the person of the caliph, he frequently delegated them to a vizier placed at the head of the hierarchical central administration, which included the army, the chancery, the ministry of finance, the postal system, and the intelligence service. A great *qāḍī*, with his seat at Baghdad, headed the administration of justice. Provincial towns often were governed by 'Abbāsid princes, who were closely connected with the central government, the orders of which they carried out.

Powers of the caliph

From the economic point of view, the founding of Baghdad shifted international trade toward Iraq and developed Basra as an emporium and transit centre. The capital was the hub of Middle Eastern trade. From Baghdad, merchants sailed to India, Ceylon, and even China, while overland trade routes converged on Baghdad from Asia Minor, Syria, Egypt, Arabia, and Persia.

It was not long, however, before Iraq shared in the political and economic decline of the caliphate. Religious conflicts had to some extent weakened the authority of the caliph and divided the Muslim community. Yet a powerful administration for some time kept up a semblance of cohesion, in spite of centrifugal forces tending to detach several outlying provinces from Baghdad.

When al-Mu'taṣim (833–842) succeeded to power, he enrolled a number of foreign mercenaries, mainly Turkish slaves, in his bodyguard. The officers of the new Turkish guard rapidly distinguished themselves in war and rose to influential positions. Since the excesses of these troops created a dangerous state of tension in Baghdad, al-Mu'taṣim in 836 moved his residence to a new city, Sāmarrā', about 60 miles (97 kilometres) north of Baghdad. Henceforth, Turkish mercenaries dominated the empire and controlled the succession of caliphs. Under al-Wāthiq (842–847), the commander of the Turkish guard was even given the title of sultan. Al-Mutawakkil (847–861) succeeded to the throne with the help of two Turkish chiefs. In a desperate attempt to restore the caliph's authority, al-Mutawakkil endeavoured to conciliate the orthodox Muslims (Sunnīs). He persecuted not only the Mu'tazilites but also the Shī'īs and imposed severe restrictions on Jews and Christians, compelling them to wear distinctive dress.

These measures did not prevent the decline of the dynasty. Between 861 and 870 four caliphs appeared in succession; they were to suppress a revolt of the Turks leading to the siege of Baghdad in 865–866 and, more especially, a serious uprising of Negro slaves (the Zanj) settled in the swamps of Lower Mesopotamia; the operations launched against them during 15 years (869–883) wore out the resources of the government. Basra was sacked (871), Lower Iraq occupied, Wāsiṭ taken (878), and the country devastated. This social revolt threatened the caliphate, which at the same time was faced with other rebellions in Khorāsān, Egypt, Ṭabaristān, and in other areas.

About 890 Lower Iraq was again shaken by revolt, this time by Ḥamdān Qarmat, whose followers won tremendous victories and gained control over parts of Iraq, Syria, and Palestine. Al-Mu'tamid (870–892) re-established the seat of the caliphate in Baghdad (892) shortly before he died, and his successors did not return to Sāmarrā'. Al-Muktafī (902–908) stopped the Qarmaṭian movement temporarily, but the rebels resumed their activity and plundered Kūfah in 925.

In addition to such factors of internal decay, centrifugal forces compelled the 'Abbāsids to grant independence to some provinces, even on the borders of Iraq. As early as

'Abbāsid decline

890, the Ḥamdānids, who were to come into prominence in Aleppo during the 10th century, created an independent amirate in Mosul, and the Caliph himself was sometimes induced to ask their help. Less than two centuries after the beginning of 'Abbāsid rule, Iraq became practically the sole possession of the caliphate. Struggles among the Turkish commanders and between the Turks and the Daylamite and other elements of the army reduced even Baghdad and the neighbourhood to anarchy.

THE BUYIDS

In 936 the caliph ar-Rāḍī (934–940) introduced the title of amīr al-umarā', (amir of the amirs) and bestowed it on Muḥammad ibn Rā'iq, governor of Basra, retaining for himself only the religious leadership of the Muslim community. The new title brought about serious rivalries between several pretenders to it, until the Būyids, a Shī'ī family from Daylam, a mountainous region in Iran, made themselves masters of Basra, Wāsiṭ, and Baghdad, ushering in a new stage and giving the caliphate, which had retained part of its previous prestige, a still unknown character. Although it reached its lowest ebb during the period of Būyid supremacy, the caliphate was not entirely eliminated by the Būyids, who probably hoped to use such glamour as the 'Abbasids still possessed. Moreover, the survival of a sunnī caliphate left them with a free hand for their own political and religious aims. They were content with the rank of amīr al-umarā' and with honorary titles ending with ad-Dawlah ("of the dynasty," e.g., "friend of the dynasty," or "support of the dynasty"), but it is obvious that they held all powers in their hands.

The reign of the first of them, Mu'izz ad-Dawlah (945–967), was largely occupied by internal rebellions and a series of expeditions against the Ḥamdānids; confiscations of the property of officials on death or dismissal were common, and offices were put up to the highest bidder. The Amīr al-Umarā' did nothing to improve conditions and had no care for the local population; he also made grants of land to his troops, the result of which was to bring agriculture into a hopeless state of disorganization. Under his successor 'Izz ad-Dawlah (967–977), Turkish mercenaries revolted and seized power. In 977 'Aḍud ad-Dawlah became the chief of the family; he ruled first in Fars, and then in Fars and Iraq (977–983). A capable ruler, 'Aḍud ad-Dawlah kept up some prosperity, improved roads, dug canals, reorganized the postal system, stamped out brigandage, and fostered trade. After his death the Būyid dynasty rapidly declined; the western provinces of their dominions were torn by internecine strife, the administrative system collapsed, and agriculture fell into decay.

In the field of finance, reforms initiated by the Būyids were connected with the pay of troops: the caliphs had tended to grant to the military an increasing amount of lands subject to the tithe. When the treasury proved unable to cover the cost of the army, the Būyids introduced the practice of granting iqṭā's, or lands hitherto subject to land tax (kharāj). The beneficiaries of iqṭā's levied the revenue of the kharāj themselves and paid nothing to the treasury. The debilitating consequences of such a system contributed to the political disintegration of the empire.

As for religion, the Būyids did not fail to spread their Shī'ī doctrines and practices, erecting in particular mausoleums on the tombs of the imāms. In spite of their Daylamite origin, the Būyids were eager supporters of Arabic culture, although they also favoured the development of new Iranian influences. It was at that time that rhymed prose gained ground in the Chancery and literature, the maqāmah appeared, and a new style was initiated in epistolography, yet most of that activity took place beyong Iraq. Baghdad, where Arabic culture had reached its height—with prose writers such as al-Jāḥiẓ, Ibn Qutaybah, al-Mas'ūdī, and many others; historians such as al-Ya'qūbī, aṭ-Ṭabarī, or ad-Dīnawarī; poets such as Abū Nuwās, Abū Tammān, al-Buḥturī, and others; philosophers such as al-Fārābī; and scientists such as al-Khwārizmī—was not quite superseded, but it was challenged by other centres, such as Shīrāz and Isfahan, let alone Cairo, where the Faṭimids established themselves in 969, attract-

ing a large part of the flow of trade that previously had converged on Iraq.

In fact, a large district of Iraq escaped Būyid control; just as Mosul was in the hands of the 'Uqaylids, so, as early as 1012, the Mazyadids were recognized as amīrs over an area extending from Basra to Hīt; they threatened Baghdad itself, where the 'ayyārūn were terrorizing the inhabitants, being actually the masters of the capital. The activities of the 'ayyārūn lasted until 1055—when the Seljuq ruler, Toghrïl Beg, entered Baghdad—and perhaps a little longer.

THE SELJUQS

A former high official of the Būyids, al-Basāsīrī, who had risen to power in Baghdad, fled on Toghrïl's coming, but it was not long before he marched on the city, occupied it on December 27, 1058, and proclaimed the Fāṭimid al-Mustanṣir caliph; the 'Abbāsid al-Qā'im took refuge with the 'Uqaylids, and al-Basāsīrī extended his control over Basra and Wāsiṭ, with Mazyadid support. In 1059 Toghrïl reconquered Baghdad, and the caliph returned.

While the power of the Būyids had been usurped, that of the Seljuq Turks was given a legal basis. Unlike the Būyids, the Seljuqs were Sunnī, hence the caliph recognized them as sultans and delegated all his powers to them, entrusting them with eradicating Shī'īsm from Iraq and other parts of the empire. With their eagerness to restore and assert Sunnism, they must be credited with the founding of madrasahs—high colleges intended for training future officials in both religious and secular matters. The most famous among those madrasahs is the Niẓāmīyah, founded at Baghdad in 1067. Nevertheless, the Seljuqs did not take Baghdad as their capital, since they lived at Isfahan and later (from 1157 onward) at Hamadan. During the Seljuq period, the history of Iraq is that of a succession of Turkish sultans who regarded the ancient centre of the Islāmic Empire as a kind of protectorate under religious leadership of the caliph, who was not more than a local ruler, certainly less powerful, in the political and military field, than the Zangids in Mosul or the Mazyadids in Lower Iraq. The Arab dynasty of the Mazyadids came to prominence in al-Jāmi'ān (called al-Ḥillah from 1101 onward); they were Shī'ī, as were the majority of the Arab tribes in the region, and ready to support 'Alid movements against the Seljuqs or play off some of them against the others. Profiting by the struggles between Berk-yaruq and his brother Muḥammad, Ṣadaqah ibn Manṣūr extended his power over almost all Iraq by the end of the 11th century; the towns of Hīt, Wāsit, Basra, and Takrīt fell into his hands, but he was killed in a battle against the Seljuqs in 1108, and the dynasty of the Mazyadids eventually came to an end in 1163.

In 1118 there came to power a branch of Seljuqs who established an autonomous principality in Iraq that lasted until 1194. During this period the caliphs made some attempts to dispute the supremacy of the sultans and shake off their tutelage, but these actions resulted in struggles, notably in the reign of Sultan Mas'ūd (1134–52). Al-Mustarshid (1118–35) was the first caliph in Seljuq times to assemble an army and lead it in person. But al-Mustarshid was executed in 1135, as was his successor, ar-Rashīd, in 1136. Subsequently, on the death of Mas'ūd, al-Muqtafī (1136–60) established himself as the legitimate sovereign in Iraq, exercising both temporal and religious power. Later, the caliph an-Nāṣir (1180–1225) tried to restore some importance to the caliphate by conciliating Sunnīs and Shī'īs and using associations of various kinds (grouped under the general name of futūwah) as instruments of moral and social education, hoping to restore the moral and political unity of the 'Abbāsid Empire. Furthermore, about 1192, he appealed to the khwārezm-shāh Tekesh for help against Toghrïl III, the last of the Seljuq sultans of Iraq, who was defeated in 1194 and his dynasty overthrown. An-Nāṣir contended with Tekesh for Seljuqs' spoils and succeeded in taking Khuzistan and other Persian provinces. But Tekesh proved a more dangerous rival than Toghrïl; shortly

Rise of 'Aḍud ad-Dawlah *(margin)*

Daylamite culture *(margin)*

Reform organizations *(margin)*

before his death (1200), he demanded that the *khuṭbah* (the Friday sermon in the great mosques) should be read in Baghdad in the name of the Khwārezm-Shāh. An-Nāṣir refused, and in 1196 fighting took place between the Khwārezm-Shāh's army and the Caliph's, to the disadvantage of the latter. Some years later, Muḥammad ibn Tekesh reiterated his father's demand and met with an uncompromising refusal. The conflict culminated in 1216, when the Caliph had a former official of Tekesh assassinated. In the following year Muḥammad ibn Tekesh set out for Baghdad but was unable to take the city, his army being annihilated by the Kurds. An-Nāṣir played off the Mongol leader Genghis Khan against the Khwārezm-Shāh, and the latter was defeated in 1219.

THE MONGOLS

Unfortunately, an-Nāṣir's successors, aẓ-Zāhir (1225–26), al-Mustanṣir (1226–42), and al-Mustaʿṣim (1242–58), were weak and unable to carry on his policy. In the meantime, Hülegü, a descendant of Genghis Khan, who established Mongol power in Iran, invited the caliph al-Mustaʿṣim to surrender and, on his refusal, marched on Baghdad, which he took on February 10, 1258, after a siege of some seven weeks. Al-Mustaʿṣim and several members of his family were put to death; the city was sacked and its inhabitants slaughtered. Iraq, the core of the ʿAbbāsid Empire, was devastated and depopulated. It did not recover for centuries.

Until 1339 the province of Iraq remained under the domination of the Īl-Khāns, a Mongol dynasty founded in Persia by Hülegü. Under the Īl-Khāns, the western frontier of Mesopotamia was the political boundary of Persia, Baghdad being the capital of Lower Mesopotamia and Mosul the seat of another government. In 1295, Baydu, a grandson of Hülegü and governor of Iraq, seized power, but he was overthrown in the same year by Ghāzān, governor of Khorāsān. When Abū Saʿīd, the 9th Īl-Khān, died in 1335, Ḥasan Buzurg (died 1356) founded in Baghdad the dynasty of the Jalāyirids, who achieved some success, chiefly in Fars and Upper Mesopotamia, but they were compelled to suppress a succession of revolts in Baghdad. Restless Bedouin tribes in the south and Turkmens and Kurds in the north complicated the state of affairs and hastened the decline of a moribund country. This small dynasty of Mongol origin ruled from 1339 to 1410 and incorporated Mosul into its dominions in 1364. On two occasions, however, in 1393 and particularly in 1401, Timur (Tamerlane) took and sacked Baghdad, slaughtered its inhabitants, and pulled down a great part of the town. Aḥmad the Jalāyirid (died 1410), driven out by Timur, recovered Baghdad in 1394 and again in 1405 and tried to make good the damages. Until 1432, Jalāyirid rulers retained some power in Lower Mesopotamia (al-Ḥillah, Basra, Khuzistan) but were unable to preserve Baghdad, which fell (1411) into the hands of the Kara Koyūnlu (the Black Sheep), a Turkmen dynasty that ruled Asia Minor from 1375 to 1468. This period is also marked by political fragmentation and rivalries between Baghdad and Mosul. The rule of the Turkmens was challenged by the politico-religious movement of the Mushaʿshaʿ, who came into prominence in Khuzistan, attempted to extend their control over Lower Iraq, and harried the Kara Koyunlu as far as the outskirts of Baghdad, which they were not able to take. In 1468, the Ag Koyunlu (the White Sheep) took over from the Kara Koyunlu, ruling from Tabriz; in 1503, the last member of the dynasty was compelled to seek refuge at Baghdad, where he ruled till 1508, when Iraq, including Mosul, fell under the sway of the Shīʿī Ṣafavids and remained in their possession until the Ottomans conquered it. In spite of the weakness of the local government, Iraq enjoyed a fairly prosperous economy during this short period.

The Jalāyirids

THE OTTOMANS

Although Sultan Selim I (1512–20) had crushed the Ṣafavid armies at Chāldirān in 1514 and taken Tabriz, Mosul, Diyarbakır, and several Kurdish areas east of the Tigris in 1515–17, Iraq proper remained under Persian control for some time. In Baghdad, the Kurdish leader Dhū al-Faqār raised a revolt in 1527 that induced Shāh Ṭahmāsp (1524–76) to assert Persian authority over central Iraq more firmly than ever, but hostilities started again between him and Süleyman (Sulayman the Magnificent, 1520–66); the latter entered Baghdad in 1534, and Iraq remained in the possession of the Ottomans until March 1917, though not without trouble: the peace was somewhat disturbed by intermittent struggles between Turks and Iranians, resulting in the occupation of Baghdad by the Ṣafavids from 1623 to 1638; the Turkish communications were at the mercy of turbulent tribesmen; and parts of the country were semi-independent at one time or another. The long period of Ottoman rule, however, witnessed some revival of Baghdad, improvement of living conditions, and administrative reorganization on Western lines as well as the beginning of European penetration.

Süleyman the Magnificent

The Ottomans had assumed the title of caliph, and the capture of the last ʿAbbāsid puppet in Cairo (1517) had emphasized their feeling that they were the successors of the great Baghdadian dynasty; therefore, the conquest of Baghdad increased Süleyman's prestige, but it had another consequence: on the one hand, it temporarily brought to an end the rivalries between Shīʿīs and Sunnīs and materialized the triumph of Sunnism in the country where such religious conflicts were frequent; on the other hand, the conquest of Egypt had made the Ottomans the masters of the Red Sea, which retained, in spite of the discovery of the Cape route around Africa at the end of the 15th century, much of its former importance in international trade. As masters of the Persian Gulf, the Ottomans could control all the traffic in the Middle East. Last but not least, Iraqi territories were a kind of buffer against not only the rulers of Iran but also the restless tribes of Kurds and Arabs.

Basra, always eager to preserve independence, played a certain part under the Ottoman rule. At first a vassal of the Sultan, it tried to shake his suzerainty, but two expeditions sent from Baghdad in 1546 resulted in its incorporation into the Ottoman possessions in Iraq, which was divided at the time into five *eyalet*s: Baghdad, Basra, Mosul, Shahrazūr, and al-Ḥasā, on the western shore of the Persian Gulf.

For almost two centuries the Ottomans tried to exercise a sort of direct rule over Iraq. Süleyman organized local administration, made a survey of the lands, appointed governors, sent Janissaries, and displayed some building activity, mainly in Baghdad, which became a prosperous centre of trade much admired by European travellers. Early in the 17th century, however, a Janissary officer named Bakr Ṣū Bāshī revolted, held sway over Baghdad —which he terrorized—and entered upon negotiations with Shāh ʿAbbās I (1587–1629) in order to strengthen his position, but Iraq was taken by the Ṣafavids in 1623, the Ottomans being able to preserve only Mosul and Shahrazūr. The Persians destroyed many buildings, including Sunnī mosques, and several thousands of inhabitants were killed or sold as slaves.

Just as in al-Ḥasā a family of governors ruled from the late 16th century until 1663, so in Basra Afrāsiyāb an army officer of unknown origin purchased the governorship from the local pasha in 1612 and founded a small dynasty of governors who ruled the town until 1668 and favoured European penetration by opening the doors to English, Portuguese, and Dutch merchants trading in the Persian Gulf. Afrāsiyāb offered strong resistance to the Ṣafavids but did not support Baghdad against them.

Beginning of European penetration

In the meantime, Baghdad had been retaken in 1638 by Sultan Murad IV (1612–40), and a great many Shīʿīs were massacred. A treaty concluded in 1639 at Qaṣr-e Shīrīn between the Ottomans and Ṣafavids fixed the boundaries of the two states.

This Ottoman victory did not bring stability to Iraq, and the rulers had to suppress many disturbances caused by the turbulent garrison troops and unruly Arab and Kurdish tribes. In Lower Iraq, after the Afrāsiyāb dynasty was overthrown, the Arab tribes of al-Muntafiq and Ḥuwayza threatened the Ottoman supremacy, while Iranians penetrated into this region. After the Treaty of Karlowitz

(1699) with Austria, Russia, Poland, and Venice, the Ottomans were able to send some troops to Iraq and recover Basra. In spite of the 1639 settlement, Baghdad was still the stake of struggles betweeen Turks and Persians because of its being the most important city in the east of the Ottoman possessions.

From 1704 a new government system was introduced in Iraq by Hasan Paşa (governor from 1704 to 1724), his son Ahmad Paşa (1724–1747), and their successors. Themselves of Georgian origin, they relied on young Georgian slaves, trained in a special school, to become the chiefs of the main administrative services; those *mamlūk*s (slaves), known in Turkish as *kölemen*, sometimes reached governorship in Baghdad and applied personal policies; they suppressed revolts, restored order, annexed Basra, and promoted some prosperity in the country. In 1733, however, Nāder Shāh (later ruler of Iran from 1736 to 1747) besieged Baghdad but was compelled to withdraw from the capital; in 1742, he also failed to seize Mosul, governed by a native pasha, ʿAbd al-Jalīl, whose family, the Jalīlīs, ruled there from 1726 to 1834, and an agreement in 1746 confirmed the terms of the Qaṣr-e Shīrīn settlement. In 1775, Basra, where an agency of the British East India Company had been established as early as 1763, was lost for five years to Ṣādiq Khān, a brother of Karīm Khān Zand, the ruler of Persia. Süleyman Paşa (later known as Büyük the Great), governor of Basra, was transported to Shīrāz and came back on Karīm's death, took possession of Baghdad, and was given the governorship of Baghdad, Basra, and Shahrazūr by the Sultan. Under Büyük (1780–1802), the *kölemen* rule reached its zenith. He fostered agriculture and trade, built several monuments, and, in 1798, permitted a permanent British resident to be appointed in the capital. Shortly before he died, however, Iraq was attacked by the Wahhābīs of Arabia, who penetrated into al-Ḥasā and, with their iconoclastic zeal, raided and sacked in 1802 Karbalāʾ, the holy city of Shīʿīs, despite the support of the Muntafiq confederacy to Baghdad.

The *kölemen* regime lasted until 1831, when Sultan Mahmud (1730–54) turned out Dawud Paşa from Baghdad after famine and flood had devastated and depopulated the city. From 1831, the Sublime Porte had high hand over Iraq, the history of which is henceforth characterized by administrative, economic, and social reform, together with European penetration. English, French, and Italian agencies and consulates were established in Basra. A company for river traffic between Basra and Baghdad was created; a telegraphic line linked Istanbul with Baghdad; but the Ottoman authority over the tribesmen was still weak. A new stage came with the governorship of Midhat Paşa (1869–72), who enforced the Ottoman law of *vilayet*s, introduced a new administrative system, including an elected town council, created a press and the earliest Iraqi newspaper (*az-Zawrāʾ*, 1869), founded primary and secondary military schools, and inaugurated the Baghdad–Kāẓimayn tramway line. This was a meritorious attempt at modernizing the country, at least Baghdad. Progress continued until the early 20th century, when Arabic-speaking Iraqi leaders began to lose confidence in the Ottomans and to dream about independence within the framework of a Pan-Arab and anti-Ottoman movement.

On November 20, 1914, an Anglo-Indian expeditionary force occupied Basra; Gen. Charles Townshend seized Kūt al-ʿAmārah in 1915 but was compelled to surrender on April 29, 1916; finally, the British took possession of Baghdad in March 1917, Mosul remaining in the hands of the Ottomans until the armistice of Mudros (October 30, 1918).   (C.L.P.P.)

IV. Iraq since 1918

BRITISH OCCUPATION AND THE MANDATORY REGIME

The merging of the three provinces of Mosul, Baghdad, and Basra into one political entity and the creation of a nation out of the diverse religious and ethnic elements inhabiting these lands was accomplished by the events and circumstances following World War I. Action undertaken by the British military authorities during the war and the upsurge of nationalism after the war helped determine the shape of the new Iraqi state and the course of events during the postwar years, until Iraq finally emerged as an independent political entity in 1932.

British control of Iraq, however, proved to be short-lived. After the war Britain debated both its general policy in Iraq and the specific type of administration to establish. Two schools of thought influenced policy makers in London. The first, advocated by the Colonial Office, stressed a policy of direct control to protect British interests in the Persian Gulf and India. Assessing British policy from India, this school may be called the Indian school of thought. The other school, hoping to reconcile Arab nationalism, advised indirect control. In Iraq itself, British authorities were divided on the issue. Some, under the influence of Sir Arnold Wilson, the acting civil commissioner, advocated direct control; others, alarmed by growing dissatisfaction with the British administration, advised indirect control and suggested the establishment of an indigenous regime under British supervision. Britain was still undecided on which policy it should follow in 1920 when external events in other Arab countries radically changed the internal conditions of Iraq.

Early in 1920 the *amīr* Fayṣal I, son of the *sharīf* Ḥusayn, who had led the Arab Revolt in 1916, established an Arab government in Damascus and was proclaimed king of Syria. Meanwhile, a group of Iraqi nationalists met in Damascus to proclaim the *amīr* ʿAbd Allāh, older brother of Fayṣal, as king of Iraq. Under the influence of nationalist activities in Syria, nationalist agitation followed first in northern Iraq and then in the tribal areas of the Middle Euphrates. By the summer of 1920 the revolt had spread to all parts of the country except the big cities of Mosul, Baghdad, and Basra, where British forces were stationed.

Amīr ʿAbd Allāh proclaimed king

In July 1920, Fayṣal came into conflict with the French authorities over control of Syria. France had been given the mandate over Syria and Lebanon in April and was determined to obtain Fayṣal's acceptance of the mandate. Nationalists urged Fayṣal to reject the French demands, and conflict ensued between him and the French, resulting in his expulsion from Syria. Fayṣal went to London to complain about the French action.

Although the revolt in Iraq was suppressed by force, it prompted both Iraq and Great Britain to reconcile their differences. In Britain a segment of public opinion wanted to "get out of Mesopotamia" and urged relief from further commitments. In Iraq, the nationalists were demanding independence. When Fayṣal arrived in London, the question of Iraq had been the subject of discussion between the Colonial and Foreign offices. In 1921 Britain offered the Iraqi throne to Fayṣal along with the establishment of an Arab government under British mandate. Fayṣal wanted the throne if it were offered to him by the Iraqi people. He also suggested the replacement of the mandate by a treaty of alliance. These proposals were accepted by the British government, and Winston Churchill, then colonial secretary, promised to carry them out. He was advised by T.E. Lawrence, known for his sympathy for the Arabs.

In March 1921 a conference presided over by Churchill was held in Cairo to settle Middle Eastern affairs. Fayṣal was nominated to the Iraqi throne, provided that a plebiscite be held to confirm the nomination. Sir Percy Cox, recently appointed a high commissioner for Iraq, was entrusted with carrying out the plebiscite before Fayṣal's accession to the throne. A provisional government set up by Cox shortly before the Cairo Conference passed a resolution on July 11, 1921, declaring Fayṣal king of Iraq, provided that his "Government shall be constitutional, representative and democratic." The plebiscite confirmed this proclamation, and Fayṣal was formally crowned king on August 23, 1921.

The establishment of the monarchy was the first step in the establishment of a national regime. Two other steps followed immediately: the signing of a treaty of alliance with Great Britain and the drafting of a constitution. It was deemed necessary that a treaty should precede the constitution and define relations between Iraq and

Britain. The treaty was signed on October 10, 1922. Without direct reference, it reproduced most of the provisions of the mandate. Iraq undertook to respect religious freedom and missionary enterprises and the rights of foreigners, to treat all states equally, and to cooperate with the League of Nations. Britain was obligated to offer advice on foreign and domestic affairs, such as military, judicial, and financial matters (defined in separate and subsidiary agreements). Although the terms of the treaty were open to periodic revision, they were to last 20 years. In the meantime, Britain agreed to prepare Iraq for membership in the League of Nations "as soon as possible."

It soon became apparent that the substance, though not the form, of the mandate was still in existence and that complete independence had not been achieved. Strong opposition to the treaty in the press made it almost certain it would not be ratified by the Constituent Assembly. Nor was British public opinion satisfied with the commitments to Iraq. During the general elections of 1922 there was a newspaper campaign against British expenditures in Iraq. In deference to public opinion, both in Britain and Iraq, a protocol to the treaty was signed on April 30, 1923, reducing the period of the treaty from 20 to four years. Despite the shortening of British tutelage, the Constituent Assembly demanded complete independence when the treaty was put before it for approval. Ratification of the treaty was accomplished on June 11, 1924, after England's warning that nonapproval would lead to the referral of the matter to the League of Nations.

The Constituent Assembly then moved to consider a draft constitution drawn up by a constitutional committee. The committee tried to give extensive powers to the king. Discussion on the draft constitution by the Constituent Assembly lasted a month, and, after minor modifications, it was adopted in July 1924. The Organic Law, as the constitution was then called, went into effect right after it was signed by the King on March 21, 1925. It provided for a constitutional monarchy, a parliamentary government, and a bicameral legislature. The latter was composed of an elected House of Representatives and an appointed Senate. The lower house was to be elected every four years in a free manhood suffrage. The first Parliament met in 1925. Ten general elections were held before the downfall of the monarchy in 1958, and over 50 Cabinets formed during the same period reflected the instability of the system.

From the establishment of a national government, there was keen interest in organizing political parties. Three parties, organized in 1921, one by the group in power and two by opposition parties, had similar social and economic views and essentially the same political objective: termination of the mandate and the winning of independence. They differed, however, in the means of achieving the objective. After the achievement of independence in 1932, these parties dissolved, because their *raison d'être* had disappeared. It was only when social issues were discussed that new political groupings, even if not formally organized as political parties, began to emerge. The power struggle among these groups became exceedingly intense after World War II.

The Iraqi nationalists, though appreciating the free expression of opinion permitted under a parliamentary system, were far from satisfied with the mandate. They demanded independence as a matter of right, as promised in war declarations and treaties, rather than as a matter of capacity for self-government as laid down in the mandate. Various attempts were made to redefine Anglo-Iraqi relations, as embodied in the 1926 and 1927 treaties, without fundamentally altering Britain's responsibility. The British treaties were deemed by the nationalists as not only impeding the realization of Iraq's nationalist aspirations, but also inimical to the economic development of the country. The nationalists viewed the situation as a "perplexing predicament" (al-waḍ 'ash-shadh) —a term that became popular in Parliament and the press. It referred to the impossibility of government by the dual authority of the mandate. The nationalists argued that there were two governments in Iraq, one foreign and the other national, and that such a regime was

an abnormality that, though feasible in theory, was unworkable in practice.

In 1929 Britain decided to end this stalemate and reconcile its interests with Iraq's national aspirations. It notified Iraq that the mandate would be terminated in 1932 and a new treaty of independence negotiated. A new government was formed, headed by Gen. Nūrī as-Saʿīd, who helped in achieving Iraq's independence.

The new treaty was signed on June 30, 1930. It provided for the establishment of a "close alliance" between Britain and Iraq, with "full and frank consultation between them in all matters of foreign policy which may affect their common interests." Iraq would maintain internal order and defend itself against foreign aggression, supported by Britain. Any dispute between Iraq and a third state, involving the risk of war, was to be discussed with Britain in the hope of a settlement in accordance with the Covenant of the League of Nations. In the event of an imminent menace of war, the two parties would take a common defense position. Iraq recognized that the maintenance and protection of essential British communications was in the common interest of both parties. Air-base sites for maintaining British troops were therefore granted and installed near Basra and west of the Euphrates, but these forces "shall not constitute in any manner an occupation, and will in no way prejudice the sovereign rights of Iraq." This treaty, valid for 25 years, was to come into effect after Iraq had become a member of the League of Nations. On October 3, 1932, Iraq was admitted to the League of Nations as an independent state.

INDEPENDENCE, 1932–39

Since conflict among Iraq's political leaders centred essentially on how to end the mandate rather than on the right of independence, King Fayṣal sought the cooperation of opposition leaders after independence. Shortly after Iraq's admission to the League, General Nūrī, who had been prime minister since 1930, resigned. After an interim administration, King Fayṣal invited Rashīd ʿAlī al-Gaylānī, one of the opposition leaders, to form a new government. For a short while it seemed that all the country's leaders would close ranks and devote all their efforts to internal reforms.

But internal dissension soon developed. The first incident was the Assyrian uprising of 1933. The Assyrians, a small Christian community living in Mosul Province, were given assurances of security by both Britain and Iraq. When the mandate was ended, the Assyrians began to feel insecure and demanded new assurances. Matters came to a head in the summer of 1933 when King Fayṣal was in Europe. The opposition, now in power, wanted to impress the public through a high-handed policy toward a minority group. In clashes with the Iraqi troops several hundred Assyrians were brutally killed. The incident was brought to the attention of the League less than a year after Iraq had given assurances that it would protect minority rights. Had King Fayṣal been in the country, he would have counselled moderation. Upon his hasty return to Baghdad, he found deep-seated divisions and events beyond his control. Suffering from heart trouble, he returned to Switzerland, where he died in September 1933. The Assyrian incident brought about the fall of Rashīd ʿAlī and his replacement by a moderate government.

Fayṣal was succeeded by his son, King Ghāzī (1912–39), who was still young and inexperienced—a situation that gave political leaders an opportunity to compete for power. Without political parties to channel their activities through constitutional processes, politicians resorted to extraconstitutional, or violent, methods. One extraconstitutional method involved clever political manoeuvring. Opposition leaders tried to embarrass those in power by press attacks, palace intrigues, or incidents that would cause Cabinet dissension and force the prime minister to resign. The first five governmental changes after independence, from 1932 to 1934, were produced by these methods.

The second device used was the incitement of tribal

uprisings in areas where there were tribal chiefs unfriendly to the group in power. Tribes, though habitually opposed to authority, had been brought under control and remained relatively quiet after 1932. When opposition leaders began to incite them against the government in 1934, however, they rebelled and caused the fall of three governments from 1934 to 1935.

The third method was military intervention. The opposition tried to obtain the loyalty of army officers, plan a coup d'etat, and force those in power to resign. This method, often resorted to by the opposition, proved to be the most dangerous because, once the army intervened in politics, it became increasingly difficult to re-establish civilian rule. From 1936 until the army was defeated in a war with Britain, in 1941, the army dominated domestic politics. The army again intervened in 1958, and it continues to dominate the political scene.

The coup d'etat of 1936

Two different sets of opposition leaders produced the first military coup d'etat in 1936. The first group, led by Ḥikmat Sulaymān, was a faction of old politicians who sought power by violent methods. The other was the Ahalī group, composed mainly of young men who advocated Socialism and democracy and sought to carry out reform programs. It was Ḥikmat Sulaymān, however, who urged Gen. Bakr Ṣiqī, commander of an army division, to stage a surprise attack on Baghdad, in cooperation with another military commander, and forced the cabinet to resign. It seems that young King Ghāzī had also been disenchanted with the group in power and so allowed the government to resign. Ḥikmat Sulaymān became prime minister in October 1936, and Bakr Ṣidqī was appointed chief of the general staff. Neither the Ahalī group nor Ḥikmat Sulaymān could improve social conditions, however, because the army gradually dominated the political scene. Supported by opposition leaders, a dissident military faction assassinated Bakr Ṣidqī, but civilian rule was not re-established. The significance of this first military coup lies in the fact that it introduced a new factor in politics. Lack of leadership after the assassination of Bakr Ṣidqī left the army divided, while jealousy among leading army officers induced each faction to support a different set of civilian leaders. The army continued to influence political decisions behind the scenes and became virtually the deciding factor in Cabinet changes from 1936 to 1941.

Despite political instability, material progress continued under King Ghāzī's short reign: the Kūt al-'Amarah irrigation project, begun in 1934, was completed; other projects, to be financed by oil royalties, were laid down; the pipelines from the Kirkūk oil fields to the Mediterranean were opened in 1935; the railroads, still under British control, were purchased in 1935, and the Ba'ijī–Tal Kü-çük section, the only missing railway link between the Persian Gulf and Europe, was completed in 1938; and there was a noticeable increase in construction, foreign trade, and in educational facilities. Several outstanding disputes with Iraq's neighbours were settled, including the dispute with Iran over the Shatt al-Arab in 1936 and the boundary with Syria, which was settled in Iraq's favour to include within its boundary the Jabal Sinjār. A nonaggression pact, called the Sa'dābād Pact, between Turkey, Iran, Afghanistan, and Iraq was signed in 1937. Arab cooperation was stressed in a nonaggression agreement with Saudi Arabia and Yemen. In 1939, shortly before the outbreak of World War II, King Ghāzī was killed in a car accident and his son Fayṣal II ascended the throne. As Fayṣal was only four years old, Fayṣal's uncle, Amīr 'Abd al-Ilāh, was appointed regent and served in this capacity for the next 14 years.

WORLD WAR II AND BRITISH INTERVENTION, 1939–45

General Nūrī, author of the 1930 treaty, was prime minister when World War II broke out. Believing that the Anglo-Iraqi alliance was the best guarantee for Iraqi security, he wanted to declare war on Germany, but his ministers counselled caution as British victory was then in doubt. General Nūrī accordingly declared Iraq nonbelligerent and severed diplomatic relations with Germany. When Italy entered the war, however, Nūrī, then

Minister of Foreign Affairs in Rashīd 'Alī al-Gaylānī's Cabinet, was unable to persuade the Cabinet to break off diplomatic relations with Italy. Under the influence of Pan-Arab leaders, public opinion in Iraq radically changed after France's fall, becoming especially hostile to Britain because other Arab countries remained under foreign control. Pan-Arabs urged Iraqi leaders to free Syria and Palestine and achieve unity among Arab countries. Extremists advocated alliance with Germany as the country that would foster independence and unity among Arabs.

Hostility toward Britain

Rashīd 'Alī was at first unwilling to side with the extremists and gave lip service to the Anglo-Iraqi alliance. But dissension among the Iraqi leaders forced Rashīd 'Alī to side with the Pan-Arabs. Leading army officers also fell under Pan-Arab influences and encouraged Rashīd 'Alī to detach Iraq from the British alliance. During 1940 and 1941 Iraqi officers were unwilling to cooperate with Britain, and the Pan-Arab leaders began secret negotiations with the Axis Powers. Britain decided to send reinforcements to Iraq. Rashīd 'Alī, while allowing the landing of a small British force in 1940, was overthrown from power early in 1941, but he was reinstalled by the army in April and refused further British requests for reinforcements.

British contingents entered Iraq from the Persian Gulf as well as from the Ḥabbānīyah air base during April and May 1941; armed conflict with the Iraqi forces followed. The hostilities lasted only 30 days, during which period a few Iraqi leaders, including the regent and General Nūrī, fled the country. By the end of May the Iraqi Army capitulated, and Rashīd 'Alī and his Pan-Arab supporters left the country.

The return of the regent and moderate leaders through British intervention had far-reaching consequences. Britain was given what it demanded: the use of transportation and communication facilities and a declaration of war on the Axis Powers in January 1942. Rashīd 'Alī's supporters were dismissed from the service and some of them interned for the duration of the war. Four officers who were responsible for the war were hanged.

POSTWAR RECONSTRUCTION AND SOCIAL UPHEAVALS, 1945–58

During World War II, liberal and moderate Iraqi elements began to play an active political role. The entry of the United States and the Soviet Union into the war on the side of Britain and their declarations in favour of democratic freedoms greatly enhanced the position of the Iraqi democratic elements. The people endured shortages and regulations restricting personal liberty and the freedom of the press, trusting that the end of the war would bring the promised better way of life. The government, however, paid no attention to the new spirit, and the wartime regulations and restrictions continued after the war. The regent called a meeting of the country's leaders in 1945 and made a speech in which he attributed public disaffection to the absence of a truly parliamentary system. He called for the formation of political parties and promised full freedom for their activities and the launching of social and economic reforms.

The immediate reactions to the regent's speech were favourable, but, when political parties were formed in 1946 and certain regulations abolished, the older politicians and vested interests resisted, and the new government formed in January 1946 to honour the regent's promises was overthrown within a few months of its inception. General Nūrī then became prime minister and tried to enlist the cooperation of political parties, but the general elections held under his government's supervision were no different from previously controlled elections. The parties boycotted the elections. General Nūrī resigned in March 1947, and Ṣāliḥ Jabr formed a new government.

Ṣāliḥ Jabr's government

Jabr, the first Shī'ī politician to become a prime minister, included in his cabinet a number of young men, but he himself was unacceptable to some liberal and nationalist elements who had been roughly handled when he was wartime Minister of Interior. Jabr tried to help the Arabs in Palestine in order to improve his image in nationalist circles, but he mishandled opposition leaders. Most damaging was his attempt to replace the Anglo-Iraqi treaty of 1930 by another—without consultation with the country's leaders. When his attention was called to the need for consultation, he consulted only with older politicians and excluded younger leaders.

Jabr entered into negotiations with Britain with the intention of enhancing his own position. When he found that Britain wanted to retain control of its air bases in Iraq, he insisted that Britain accept the principle of Iraqi control of the bases and allow Iraq the use of the bases for defensive purposes. He threatened to resign if Britain refused his proposals. It was with this understanding that Jabr proceeded to London early in 1948 to negotiate a new treaty. Jabr and Ernest Bevin, the British foreign secretary, quickly came to an agreement and signed a new 20-year treaty at Portsmouth on January 15, 1948. It provided for a new alliance between Iraq and Britain on the basis of equality and complete independence and stated "each of the high contracting parties undertake not to adopt in foreign countries an attitude which is inconsistent with the alliance or which might create difficulties for the other party." The annex to the treaty stressed the importance of the air bases as "an essential element in the defense of Iraq," but Britain's use of the air bases in the event of war, or threat of war, would be dependent on Iraq's invitation. The treaty also provided for the establishment of "a joint defence board," equally represented by Britain and Iraq, for common defense and consultation. Both parties agreed to grant each other necessary facilities for defense purposes. An improvement of the 1930 treaty, this treaty sought an alliance on the basis of mutual interests. The two air bases, which were often the subject of criticism, were returned to Iraq. British forces were to be evacuated, and Iraq would be supplied with arms and military training.

Anti-British rioting

Despite these advances, the treaty was repudiated immediately in a popular uprising. Street demonstrations had been going on before the treaty was signed, in defense of Arab rights in Palestine, but, when the news of the signing of the new treaty was broadcast in London, rioting and demonstrations in Baghdad led to clashes between students and the police. The regent called a meeting at the royal household on January 21, which was attended by the country's leaders. After deliberations, it was decided to repudiate the treaty. Jabr returned to Baghdad to defend his position but to no avail. Rioting, demonstrations, and clashes with the police increased, and Jabr was forced to resign. Obviously the new treaty was not the root cause of the uprising. The uprising was the culmination of events in a struggle between the liberal and young leaders who wanted to participate in political activities and the older leaders who insisted on excluding the younger elements from public affairs. The conflict between the older and younger leaders continued after the treaty had been rejected. The older politicians returned to power under General Nūrī's leadership. By 1952 another popular uprising, stirred by opposition leaders and carried out by students and extremists, again manifested itself in rioting and street demonstrations. The police were unable to control the mob, and the regent called on the army to maintain public order. The chief of the general staff governed the country under martial law for more than two months. Civilian rule was restored at the beginning of 1953, but there was no sign that the country's older leaders were prepared to share authority with their opponents. Meanwhile, King Fayṣal II, who had come of age, began to exercise his formal powers, and the period of regency came to an end. It was hoped that the regent would withdraw from active politics and allow the political forces of the country to create a new order. The former regent, who became the crown prince, continued to control political events from behind the scene. The struggle for power among the leaders continued with increasing intensity until the downfall of the monarchy in 1958.

Despite political instability, Iraq achieved material progress during the 1950s, thanks to a new oil agreement that increased royalties and the establishment of the Develop-

ment Board. The oil agreement between the Iraqi government and the Iraq Petroleum Company (IPC), originally signed in 1925, had yielded relatively modest royalties, owing to certain technical limitations, such as construction of pipelines, and to war conditions. It was not until 1952 that construction of pipelines to Banias was completed. There were certain points of dispute between the government and the IPC that were not entirely resolved. The nationalization of the oil industry in Iran and the announcement of the 1950 agreement between Saudi Arabia and Aramco (Arabian American Oil Company), on a half-and-half basis of payment, induced the Iraqi government and IPC to negotiate a new agreement on the new pattern of the division of profits. Some of the opposition leaders demanded the nationalization of the oil industry, but the Iraq government and IPC, forestalling any serious move for nationalization, agreed to negotiate on the basis of the fifty-fifty formula, to the mutual advantage of Iraq and the company. The new agreement was signed in 1952, allowing Iraq to take in kind as part of its share and to receive an increasing amount of royalties specifically agreed upon between the two parties. It was then estimated that Iraq would receive no less than £30 million in 1953 and 1954 and no less than £50 million in 1955 and subsequent years.

Development of Iraq oil in the 1950s

In 1950 the government created the independent Development Board, an agency immune from political pressures and responsible directly to the prime minister. This agency provided for a body of six executive members, three of whom were to be experts in some branch of the development program. The prime minister, as chairman, and the minister of finance were ex-officio members. An amendment to the law increased membership by two and provided for a minister of development responsible directly to the head of the Cabinet. These members were appointed by the Cabinet, given equal voting rights, and might not hold any other official position. Two foreign members held positions as experts, and the Iraqi members were selected on merit and past experience. The board was composed of a council and ministry. Its staff was divided into technical sections and the ministry into a number of departments. The technical sections were for irrigation, flood control, water storage, drainage, transportation, and industrial and agricultural development. The board was financed from 70 percent of oil royalties and from loans and revenues from the board's own projects. The estimated expenditure of the first six-year program (1951–56) was £155,000,000, and in 1950 the World Bank provided a loan of $12,800,000 for the Wādī ath-Tharthār flood-control project.

Creation of the Development Board

The Tharthār project, completed in 1956, connects the River Tigris at Samarrā' (some 60 miles north of Baghdad) with the Wādī ath-Tharthār Depression. A barrage was constructed on the Euphrates at Ramādī, making it possible to divert water into Lake Ḥabbānīyah. Other flood-control plans, such as that at Bakhma (completed after the revolution of 1958), were laid down. Extensive work on bridges and public buildings, including schools, hospitals, a new Parliament building, and a royal house, was started, and it was completed after 1958. This work, especially the work on dams and irrigation projects, was a long-term investment, and many short-term projects of more direct benefit to the population were neglected. Opposition leaders attacked the Development Board for the stress on long-term projects whose beneficiary, they held, were the vested interests—landowners and tribal chiefs. Despite criticism, the board maintained an independent status rarely enjoyed by any other government department. Nevertheless, the public remained unaware of the far-reaching effects of the projects undertaken, while the opposition attacked the board for squandering funds on contracts given to wealthy landlords and influential politicians.

THE REVOLUTION OF 1958

Despite material progress, the monarchy failed to win public support and, in particular, the confidence of the younger generation. Before the revolution, Iraq lacked an enlightened leadership capable of achieving progress and inspiring public confidence. The new generation offered such leadership, but the older leaders resisted. Moreover, the older leaders embarked on an unpopular foreign policy, including an alliance with Britain and participation in a regional security plan, the Baghdad Pact. Above all, Iraq's opposition to the establishment of the United Arab Republic (U.A.R.) was viewed in Iraqi nationalist circles as opposed to Arab nationalist aspirations. These conflicts created a climate of opinion favourable to revolutionary change as the older leaders tried to suppress this opposition.

The failure of younger civilians to obtain power aroused the concern of the young officers, whose sympathies lay with their own age group. The young officers, watching the struggle among civilian leaders, began secretly to engage in underground activities to overthrow the old leaders. Required by military discipline to take no part in politics, these officers, calling themselves the Free Officers, began to organize in small groups and to lay down revolutionary plans. The number of officers who took part in clandestine activities was relatively small, but a considerably larger number of sympathizers, either directly or indirectly, supported the Free Officers movement. The officers worked in cells, and the identity of the participants was kept secret. Only the Central Organization, which supplied leadership of the movement, was known to all the Free Officers. The Central Organization was composed of 14 officers, headed by ʿAbd al-Karīm Qāsim, who held the highest military rank. The officers were secretly in touch with some of the civilian leaders, but the plot was laid down by the officers themselves. In secret meetings the Free Officers made several decisions concerning the regime to be established by the revolution, such as the abolition of the monarchy and the establishment of a republic and a new democratic and representative, rather than authoritarian, system.

Several plots were laid down to overthrow the monarchy but were called off because circumstances seemed unfavourable; the plan that was laid down by Qāsim and his close collaborator ʿAbd as-Salām ʿĀrif proved the most appropriate. The general staff issued an order to one of the brigades, in which ʿĀrif served, to proceed to Jordan on July 14, 1958, to reinforce the Jordanian forces against alleged threats by Israel. Brigadier Qāsim, in command of another brigade, was to protect the brigades going to Jordan. Qāsim and ʿĀrif agreed that as the brigade proceeding to Jordan passed through Baghdad it would capture the city.

On July 14 the Iraqi forces captured the capital by surprise and declared the downfall of the monarchy and the proclamation of a republic. A faction of the army took control of the radio-broadcasting building and other key government buildings; another surrounded the royal palace and put to death the leading members of the royal house, including the King and Crown Prince. Still another small force proceeded to surround the house of General Nūrī. Nūrī left his house from a back door and remained hiding in the city for two days; he was found and shot while he was trying to escape. Qāsim, head of the revolutionary force, proceeded to the Ministry of Defence and established headquarters. He formed a Cabinet, over which he presided, and appointed himself Commander of the National Forces. He also assumed the portfolio of defense and appointed ʿĀrif both Minister of the Interior and Deputy Commander of the National Forces. The vacancy created by the destruction of the monarchy was filled by a Council of Sovereignty, composed of three persons, to act as head of state.

The initial public reaction was favourable, and there were demonstrations in support of the revolutionary change. Qāsim responded by releasing political prisoners and allowing those in exile to return to the country. All parties and political groupings that had been banned were allowed to resume activities. A provisional constitution was promulgated until a new one could be drawn up by a national assembly. This constitution declared that Iraq formed an integral part "of the Arab nation," and "Arabs and Kurds are considered partners in this homeland." Iraq was declared a republic, Islām the religion of

the state, and all executive and legislative powers entrusted to the Sovereignty Council and the Cabinet during the transitional period. It soon became clear that power rested in Qāsim's hands, supported by the army whose immediate command was entrusted to Brigadier Ahmad Salih al-Abdi, one of Qāsim's protégés, and ultimately under Qāsim's own control. A military court, presided over by Colonel Fadil Abbas al-Mahdawi, another protégé, was designed to try political leaders of the old regime and others who conspired against the new regime.

Conflicts among the officers developed, first between Qāsim and ʿĀrif, and then between Qāsim and his supporters. ʿĀrif championed the Pan-Arab cause and advocated Iraq's union with the U.A.R. Qāsim rallied the forces against Arab unity—Kurds, Communists, and others—and stressed Iraq's own identity and internal unity. These forces supported Qāsim's drive against joining Egypt in an Arab union. ʿĀrif was dropped from power in December, but in the following year Qāsim became deeply involved in a power struggle with other factions. Qāsim's military opponents tried first to oust him through a plot in Baghdad and then by a military uprising in Mosul; both failed because Qāsim was able to manipulate forces and liquidate one opponent after another. He dealt ruthlessly with his foes and went so far as to execute some of his closest military supporters. He survived a plot to assassinate him in October 1959 by rallying Communist against nationalist factions. Qāsim might have committed himself to one ideological group and ruled the country in its name. He was, however, distrustful of both nationalists and Communists and tried to play off one against the other. In the last analysis, he had to rely on the army and tried to purge from it unreliable elements. Qāsim tried to divert public opinion from domestic conflicts to foreign affairs by putting forth Iraq's claim to Kuwait's sovereignty in June 1961. This claim brought him into conflict not only with Britain and Kuwait but also with the other Arab countries. He opened negotiations with the Iraq Petroleum Company to increase Iraq's royalties, but his extreme demands resulted in the breakdown of negotiations in 1961. A law, called Public Law 80, was enacted to prohibit the granting of concessions to any foreign company and to transfer control over all matters connected with oil to an Iraq National Oil Company (INOC).

By 1963 Qāsim had become isolated internally as well as externally. Even the Communists, who enjoyed more freedom under him than before, had certain reservations about him. He also came into conflict with most of Iraq's neighbours and with the Western powers. The only great power with which he remained on friendly terms was the Soviet Union because of financial assistance he had received. When one faction of the army, in cooperation with one nationalist group—the Baʿth—started a rebellion in February 1963, the Qāsim regime suddenly collapsed, and Qāsim was executed.

RECURRENCE OF MILITARY COUPS, 1963–68

The military faction that brought about the collapse of the Qāsim regime preferred to remain behind the scenes rather than to assume direct responsibility. The Baʿth Party, a group of young nationalists who advocated nationalism and socialism, was entrusted with power. Baʿth leaders invited ʿAbd as-Salām ʿĀrif, an officer retired by Qāsim, to assume the presidency of the republic. A National Council for Revolutionary Command (NCRC), composed of civil and military leaders, was established to assume legislative and executive powers. The premiership was entrusted to Col. Ahmad Hassan al-Bakr, a Baʿthist officer, with whom a number of civil and military leaders cooperated.

At the outset the Baʿth Party disclosed no new revolutionary principles, since its main purpose was to discredit Qāsim and to win over public opinion. The NCRC issued a set of proclamations to enforce public order, and the National Guard, a civil militia, was instructed to pursue Communists and their sympathizers who had persecuted Arab nationalists. Like the militia under Qāsim, the National Guard often committed excesses that reflected on Baʿthist leadership. The Baʿth Party tried to infuse new

Margin notes:

Rise of the Free Officers

Proclamation of a republic

Pan-Arabism versus Iraq nationalism

The Baʿth Party

blood in the administration by appointing Ba'thist members to high posts but most of the appointees were very young—some had hardly completed high school—and obviously lacked experience.

Some of the Ba'th leaders wanted to carry out Ba'th Socialist ideas; others advised more caution. A compromise was finally reached in which the party's goals—Arab unity, freedom, and Socialism—were reaffirmed in principle, but it was decided to adopt a transitional program to prepare the country for Ba'th principles. In this program, the industrialization and economic development of Iraq were stressed, and the role of the middle class recognized. These steps were regarded as necessary prerequisites to the adoption of Socialism. A number of influential Ba'th leaders, however, pressed for immediate implementation of certain measures that caused dissension among the leaders.

'Arif's alliance with the military

President 'Arif, whose powers were initially restricted by the Ba'th leaders, seized the opportunity by rallying the military to his side. On November 18, 1963, in agreement with Tahir Yahya, chief of the general staff, he placed the leaders of the Ba'th Party under arrest and took over control. 'Arif became in fact, as in name, the real ruler of the country. From November 1963 until his accidental death in April 1966, 'Arif governed the country through Cabinets that were directly responsible to him, while the army, which he was able to manipulate, was completely dominated by him. Before he was appointed president, 'Arif was known in nationalist circles as an advocate of Pan-Arabism, but after he became president he was in no great hurry to join the U.A.R. Negotiations with Egypt stressed the need for preparing Iraq step by step for unity, and it was made clear that before Iraq joined the U.A.R., it should adopt Arab Socialism. In May 1964, a new provisional constitution was promulgated in which the principles of Arab unity and Socialism were adopted, and, in July, Socialist decrees were issued in which the banks and a number of the country's industries were nationalized. These steps were followed by the establishment of a Socialist union, like Egypt's Arab Socialist Union, to prepare the country for Arab unity. Despite these measures, unity was not forthcoming.

The idea of Arab Socialism attracted only a small group in Iraq, and 'Arif began to discover its unfavourable effects on the country. 'Arif himself had never been a believer in Socialism, but he had adopted it under the influence of Egypt. The adverse impact of nationalization gave 'Arif an excuse to replace the ideological group that supported Socialism with others who would pay attention to the reality of Iraq's economic conditions. Nor had 'Arif been happy with the group of officers who had elevated him to power. 'Arif must have realized that a stable regime would have to depend on popular rather than military support, and he began to prepare the way to entrust power to civilian hands willing to be guided by him as chief executive.

Return to civilian rule

In September 1965 'Arif invited Abd ar-Rahman al-Bazzaz to form a new government. Bazzaz had distinguished himself as an able lawyer and a writer on Arab nationalism, and he had served as Iraq's ambassador to Egypt and England. Bazzaz did not feel that he should abolish Arab Socialism, but he offered to increase production and create a balance between public and private sectors. He also offered to establish a permanent regime by holding general elections and setting up a parliament.

'Arif died in a helicopter accident in April 1966, and Bazzaz, though continuing in office until August under the presidency of 'Arif's older brother, Abd ar-Rahman, was forced to resign under military pressure. Abd ar-Rahman 'Arif owed his election as president to army support, and, therefore, he had to listen to the officers' complaints when it became evident that Bazzaz was intent on keeping the army out of politics. Bazzaz was succeeded by an officer who was active in military circles, and the premiership remained in military hands until July 1968, when the Ba'th, supported by a dissident military faction, staged a coup d'etat that eliminated both 'Arif and his military supporters. Ahmad Hasan al-Bakr, a Ba'thist officer, assumed the presidency.

THE KURDISH QUESTION

The Kurds were given the opportunity to form a separate political entity under the Treaty of Sèvres (1920), before Iraq was created as a state. The Kemalist movement, however, shattered their hopes by rejecting the Treaty of Sèvres, and the Treaty of Lausanne (1923), which superseded the Sèvres arrangement, made no room for Kurdish nationhood. After the national regime was established in Iraq, the Kurds were persuaded to live under the Iraqi political system.

But neither the Arabs nor the Kurds were prepared to merge into one nationality and create a new Iraqi nation. The Arabs, divided into two unequal communities on religious grounds (Sunnīs and Shī'īs), were consciously discouraged to move too swiftly to form an Iraqi nation. The merging of the Kurds—a solidly Sunnī community—with the Sunnī Arabs was considered by the Shī'ah to weaken their position and therefore was resisted by almost half of the population of the country. Moreover, the Sunnī Arabs themselves were reluctant to merge with the Kurds by the upsurge of Arab nationalism. This move discouraged the Kurds from uniting with a people unprepared to maintain Iraq as a separate national identity distinct from Arab nationalism, and it encouraged Kurdish leaders to advocate Kurdish nationalism for survival. Thus, both Arab and Kurdish nationalism grew in strength in the last days of the monarchy.

Arab-Kurd religious differences

The Kurds welcomed the revolution of 1958 since they had suffered certain restrictions imposed on their national activities. The Free Officers sympathized with the Kurds, and Qāsim offered to cooperate with their leaders as co-partners with Arabs within the framework of Iraqi unity. The Kurds formed a Kurdish Democratic Party, advocating Kurdish nationalism and Communism. The party became active in politics and hoped that the new regime would sympathize with Kurdish national aspirations.

The Qāsim regime, however, failed to give assurances that the Kurds would be free and equal partners with the Arabs. The Kurds hoped for administrative autonomy in the Kurdish provinces, for a fair share of economic development projects and social services, and for promotion of Kurdish language and cultures. Qāsim did little or nothing to improve the social and economic conditions of the Kurds, and their leaders despaired of any improvement under the new regime.

Mulla Mustafa of Barzan, a Kurdish leader exiled under the monarchy for political activities, returned in 1958 to lead the Kurdish nationalist movement. At first he offered to cooperate with Qāsim but soon found Qāsim instigating rival leaders against him. In June 1961 matters came to a head, and a clash between a few Kurds and the Iraqi Army took place in Rānyah, a small Kurdish town. Mulla Mustafa, who was not directly involved in the Ranya incident, supported Kurdish demands and led a protracted war against Qāsim. Unable to defeat Mulla Mustafa's forces, the successor Ba'th government decided to come to terms with the Kurds, having been in touch with some of their leaders before Qāsim's fall in 1963. It was agreed that a democratic regime would be established and the Kurds would enjoy autonomy but not independence. No sooner had Qāsim been overthrown than Mulla Mustafa sent a telegram to the Ba'th government congratulating its leaders and ordering a cease-fire. Mulla Mustafa's action was premature, as negotiations led to no agreement on Kurdish autonomy, even after the Mulla's acceptance of administrative decentralization instead of autonomy. In resumed fighting, the Kurds inflicted heavy damages on the Iraqi Army. It was only when Bazzaz came to power and realized the strength of Kurdish nationalism that a settlement of the Kurdish question was possible. Negotiations were resumed, and an agreement was reached, embodied in a public declaration made by Bazzaz on June 29, 1966. The agreement, among other things, included the following points:

Outbreak of civil war in 1961

1. The Iraq government recognized Kurdish nationality and the national rights of the Kurds within one Iraqi homeland, and Arabs and Kurds were to enjoy equal rights and duties.

2. Kurdish nationality and national rights were to be

implemented in a provincial law based on the principle of decentralization. Each province was to have an elected council that would exercise wide power on education, health, and local affairs.

3. The Iraq government would recognize the Kurdish language as an official language, in addition to Arabic, in regions where the majority of the population is Kurdish.

4. The Kurds were to be represented in proportion to their numerical strength in the parliamentary system that would be established in forthcoming general elections for both national and provincial councils. The Kurds would also be adequately represented in all the departments of government.

5. The Kurdish provinces would have their share in all social and economic reconstruction to be undertaken by the government. Moreover, the government was to compensate all those who had suffered damage during the military operations.

Before Bazzaz had an opportunity to implement this agreement, his government fell, and its provisions were never fully carried out. There were complaints of violations on both sides, but in reality Mulla Mustafa remained in control of the Kurdish provinces. Attempts were made to resume negotiations to implement the agreement but to no avail. The Ba'th government announced, in March 1970, that it had reached an agreement on points of difference that would allow the Kurds to maintain their own forces and give them adequate representation in high government posts. Since Kurdish forces in the early 1970s were in de facto control of the Kurdish provinces, it was likely that Kurdish national demands would increase. Unless an assurance of Kurdish autonomous rule is given, conflict with the Iraq government is likely to continue. Continuation of the conflict might eventually push the Kurds toward independence, to the disadvantage of both Arabs and Kurds. (M.Kh.)

BIBLIOGRAPHY

Mesopotamia until 1600 BC: See the relevant chapters of *The Cambridge Ancient History,* rev. ed. (1962–68), each written by an individual author and richly documented; *Fischer Weltgeschichte, Die Altorientalischen Reiche,* 3 vol. (1965–67; Eng. trans., *The Near East: The Early Civilizations,* 1967), with contributions by JEAN BOTTÉRO (Akkad), D.O. ED-ZARD (Early history, Ur III, and Old Babylonian Period), and A. FALKENSTEIN (Prehistory and Protohistory), which gives a balanced picture of political, social, and economic history; ROBERT W. EHRICH (ed.), *Chronologies in Old World Archaeology* (1965), with contributions on Mesopotamia by R.H. DYSON, JR., E. PORADA, and P.J. WATSON; J.B. PRITCHARD (ed.), *Ancient Near Eastern Texts Relating to the Old Testament,* 3rd ed. with suppl. (1969), a collection of important literary sources in English translation with bibliography; A. FALKEN-STEIN, "La Cité-temple sumérienne," in *Cahiers d'histoire mondiale,* 1:784–814 (1954), a description and discussion of Sumerian temple economy and its political implications; I.M. DIAKONOFF (ed.), *Ancient, Mesopotamia: Socio-Economic History* (1969), English translation of representative articles by the editor and others on Mesopotamian history, with emphasis on social and economic aspects; W.W. HALLO, "Gutium-lex-icon" article (English) in *Reallexikon der Assyriologie,* vol. 3, pp. 708–720 (1957–71), the best résumé available of the state of knowledge on the Gutians; D.O. EDZARD, *Die zweite Zwischenzeit Babyloniens* (1957), detailed monograph (the title is misleading) on the history of the Old Babylonian Period from Ur III to the end of Hammurabi; PAUL GARELLI, *Les Assyriens en Cappadoce* (1963), a standard work on the Old Assyrian trade colonies in Asia Minor; I.J. GELB, *Hurrians and Subareans* (1944), still the best book on the third cultural element in ancient Mesopotamian history.

Mesopotamia from 1600 BC to AD 630: See the relevant chapters of *The Cambridge Ancient History;* H.W.F. SAGGS, *The Greatness That Was Babylon* (1962), which deals with history and civilization; *Fischer Weltgeschichte* (*op. cit.*), an up-to-date paperback account by different authors; A. LEO OPPENHEIM, *Ancient Mesopotamia: Portrait of a Dead Civilization* (1964), including some controversial views; WOLFRAM VON SODEN, *Herrscher im alten Orient,* ch. 6–14 (1954), treats the more important kings; HARTMUT SCHMÖKEL (ed.), *Kulturgeschichte des alten Orient* (1961), a good general account; and FIORELLA IMPARATI, *I Hurriti* (1964), a short synopsis in Italian. Standard works, now partly out of date, include A.T. OLMSTEAD, *History of Assyria* (1923, reprinted 1960); and BRUNO MEISSNER, *Babylonien und Assyrien,* 2 vol.

(1920–25). J.A. BRINKMAN, *A Political History of Post-Kassite Babylonia, 1158–722 B.C.* (1968), is an extensive special study, with complete documentation.

Iraq from the Arab Conquest to 1918: There is no comprehensive history of medieval Iraq in English; some periods or towns form the subject of special works: GUY LE STRANGE, *Baghdad During the Abbasid Caliphate* (1900, reprinted 1924); REUBEN LEVY, *A Baghdad Chronicle* (1929); STEPHEN H. LONGRIGG, *Four Centuries of Modern Iraq* (1925). Travellers' accounts are of some importance: J.-B. TAVERNIER, *Les Six Voyages,* 2 vol. (1675; Eng. trans., 3 vol., 1677–78); ED-WARD IVES, *Journey from Persia to England by an Unusual Route* (1773); KER PORTER, *Travels in Syria, Persia, Armenia, Ancient Babylonia,* 2 vol. (1817–20); JAMES S. BUCK-INGHAM, *Travels in Mesopotamia* (1827); J.R. WELLSTED, *Travels to the City of the Caliphs . . . ,* 2 vol. (1840); HENRY SOUTHGATE, *Narrative of a Tour Through Armenia, Kurdistan, Persia and Mesopotamia,* 2 vol. (1840). For Iraq during World War I, see the ADMIRALTY NAVAL STAFF, *A Handbook of Mesopotamia,* 4 vol. (1916–17); and also *The Encyclopaedia of Islam,* new ed. (1960–), in which articles on almost all persons, places, and dynasties mentioned in this article are to be found.

Iraq since 1918: The most comprehensive history of Iraq since World War I is STEPHEN H. LONGRIGG, *Iraq, 1900–1950* (1953). The period of the Mandate is adequately treated in PHILIP W. IRELAND, *Iraq: A Study in Political Development* (1937). A study of the political development of Iraq after independence is covered in considerable detail in MAJID KHADDURI, *Independent Iraq, 1932–1958: A Study in Iraqi Politics,* 2nd ed. (1960) and *Republican Iraq: A Study in Iraqi Politics Since the Revolution of 1958* (1969). For the economic development of Iraq, see the INTERNATIONAL BANK FOR RECONSTRUCTION AND DEVELOPMENT, *The Economic Development of Iraq* (1952); KATHLEEN M. LANGLEY, *The Industrialization of Iraq* (1961); and FAHIM QUBAIN, *The Reconstruction of Iraq, 1950–1957* (1958).

(D.O.E./W.T.v.S./C.L.P.P./M.Kh.)

Mesopotamian Religions

The term Mesopotamian religions serves generally to designate the religious beliefs and practices of the Sumerians and Akkadians, who inhabited ancient Mesopotamia (modern Iraq) in the millennia before the Christian era. These beliefs and practices form a single stream of tradition. Sumerian in origin, it was added to and subtly modified by the Akkadians (Semites immigrating into the country from the West at the end of the 4th millenium BC), whose own beliefs were in large measure assimilated to, and integrated with, those of their new environment.

NATURE AND SIGNIFICANCE

As the only available intellectual framework that could provide a comprehensive understanding of the forces governing existence and also guidance for right conduct in life, religion ineluctably conditioned all aspects of ancient Mesopotamian civilization. It yielded the forms in which that civilization's social, economic, legal, political, and military institutions were, and are, to be understood, as well as providing the significant symbols for poetry and art. In many ways it even influenced peoples and cultures outside of Mesopotamia, such as the Elamites to the east, the Hurrians and Hittites to the north, and the Aramaeans and Israelites to the west. Of lesser importance in evaluating the degree of such influence are, perhaps, the direct or indirect borrowings of individual Mesopotamian gods or myths, and the adjustments and subtle reinterpretations that the gods and myths have undergone to fit into the borrowing culture and its special system of values and meanings. Far more significant is the aspect of new religious insights and attitudes that arose in Mesopotamia and that spread from there to neighbouring cultures, modifying their religious beliefs and practices and indigenous cultures.

SOURCES

Present knowledge of ancient Mesopotamian religion rests almost exclusively on archaeological evidence recovered from the ruined city-mounds of Mesopotamia during the last century or so. Most significant is the literary evidence, texts written in cuneiform (wedge-shaped) script

Uruk Vase decorated with an offering scene to a goddess, rows of porters, and animals and plants; bas-relief, early 3rd millennium BC. In the Iraq Museum, Baghdad.
By courtesy of the Directorate General of Antiquities, Baghdad

on tablets made of clay or, for monumental purposes, on stone. Central, of course, are the specifically religious texts comprising god lists, myths, hymns, laments, prayers, rituals, omen texts, incantations, and other forms; but since religion permeated the culture, giving form and meaning to all aspects of it, any written text, any work of art, or any of its material remains, are directly or indirectly related to the religion and may further scholarly knowledge of it.

Impor- Among the archaeological finds that have particularly
tance helped to throw light on religion are the important discov-
of eries of inscribed tablets with Sumerian texts in copies of
archaeo- Old Babylonian date (c. 1800–c. 1600 BC) at Nippur and
logical Ur, the Sumerian and Akkadian texts of the 2nd and 1st
discoveries millennia from Ashur and Sultantepe, and particularly the
all-important library of the Assyrian king Ashurbanipal
(reigned 668–627 BC) from Nineveh. Of nonliterary remains, the great temples and temple towers (ziggurats) excavated at almost all major sites—e.g., Eridu, Ur, Nippur, Babylon, Ashur, Calah, Nineveh—as well as numerous works of art from various periods, are important sources of information. The Uruk Vase, with its representation of the rite of the sacred marriage, the Naram-Sin stele (inscribed commemorative pillar), the Ur-Nammu stele, and the stele with the Code of Hammurabi (Babylonian king, 18th century BC), which shows at its top the royal lawgiver before the sun god Shamash, the divine guardian of justice, are important works of art that may be singled out. Also among important sources are the representations on cylinder seals and on boundary stones (kudurrus), both of which provide rich materials for religious iconography in certain periods.

In working with, and seeking to interpret, these varied sources two particular difficulties stand out: the incompleteness of the data, and the remoteness of the ancients from modern man, not only in time but also in experience and in ways of thought. Thus, for all periods before the

3rd millennium scholars must rely on scarce, nonliterary data only, and even though writing appears shortly before that millennium, it is only in its latter half that written data become numerous enough and readily understandable enough to be of significant help. It is generally necessary, therefore, to interpret the scarce data of the older periods in the light of survivals and of what is known from later periods, an undertaking that calls for critical acumen if anachronisms are to be avoided. Also, for the later periods, the evidence flows unevenly, with perhaps the middle of the 2nd millennium the least well documented and hence least known age.

Difficulties
in
interpreta-
tion of
sources

As for the difficulties raised by differences in the ways of thinking between modern man and the ancients, they are of the kind that one always meets in trying to understand something unfamiliar and strange. A contemporary inquirer must keep his accustomed values and modes of thought in suspension and seek rather the inner coherence and structure of the data with which he deals, in order to

Detail of the stele inscribed with Hammurabi's code, showing the king before the god Shamash; bas-relief from Susa, 18th century BC. In the Louvre, Paris.
Giraudon

enter sympathetically into the world out of which they came, just as, for example, in entering the sometimes intensely private world of a poem, or, on a slightly different level, in learning the new, unexpected meanings and overtones of the words and phrases of a foreign language.

HISTORICAL DEVELOPMENT

Cultural background. Human occupation of Mesopotamia—"the land between the rivers" (i.e., the Tigris and Euphrates)—seems to reach back furthest in time in the north (Assyria) where the earliest settlers built their small villages some time around 6000 BC. The prehistoric cultural stages of Hassuna-Samarra and Halaf (named after the sites of archaeological excavations) succeeded each other here before there is evidence of settlement in the south—Sumer. There, the earliest settlements, such as Eridu, appear to have been founded around 5000 BC, in the late Halaf Period. From then on the cultures of the north and south move through a succession of major archaeological periods that in their southern forms are known as Ubaid, Warka, Protoliterate (during which writing was invented), and Early Dynastic, at the end of which —shortly after 3000 BC—recorded history begins. The historical periods of the 3rd millennium are, in order: Akkad, Gutium, 3rd dynasty of Ur; those of the 2nd millennium: Isin-Larsa, Old Babylonian, Kassite, and

Periodiza-
tion of
Mesopota-
mian
history

Middle Babylonian; and those of the 1st millennium: Assyrian, Neo-Babylonian, Achaemenian, Seleucid, and Parthian.

Politically, an early division of the country into small independent city-states, loosely organized in a league with the centre in Nippur, was followed by a unification by force under King Lugalzaggesi (*c.* 2400 BC) of Uruk, just before the Akkad Period (2371–2230 BC). The unification was maintained by his successors, the kings of Akkad, who built it into an empire, and—after a brief interruption by Gutian invaders—by Utuhegal (2120–2114) of Uruk and the rulers of the 3rd dynasty of Ur (*c.* 2112–*c.* 2004 BC). When Ur fell, around 2000 BC, the country again divided into smaller units, with the cities Isin and Larsa vying for hegemony. Eventually Babylon established a lasting national state in the south, while Ashur dominated a similar rival state, Assyria, in the north. From the middle of the 1st millennium onward, Assyria built an empire comprising, for a short time, all of the ancient Near East. This political and administrative achievement remained essentially intact under the following Neo-Babylonian and Persian kings down to Alexander's conquest (331 BC).

Stages of religious development. The religious development—as indeed that of the Mesopotamian culture generally—was not significantly influenced by the movements of the various peoples into and within the area—the Sumerians, Akkadians, Gutians, Cassites, Hurrians, and Aramaeans (or Chaldeans). Rather it forms a uniform, consistent, and coherent Mesopotamian tradition changing in response to its own internal needs of insights and expression. It is possible to discern a basic substratum involving worship of the forces in nature—often visualized in nonhuman forms—especially those that were of immediate import to basic economic pursuits. Many of these figures belong to the type of the "dying god" (a fertility deity displaying death and regeneration characteristics as in agriculture) but show variant traits according to whether they are powers of fertility worshipped by marsh men, orchard growers, herders, or farmers. This stage may be dated tentatively back to the 4th millennium BC and even earlier. A second stage, characterized by a view of the gods as human in shape and organized in a polity of a primitive democratic cast in which each deity had his or her special offices and functions, overlaid and conditioned the religious forms and characteristics of the earlier stage during the 3rd millennium BC. Lastly, a third stage, characterized by a growing emphasis on personal religion involving concepts of sin and forgiveness, and by a change of the earlier democratic divine polity into an absolute monarchical structure dominated by the god of the national state—to the point of pious abstention from all human initiative, in absolute faith and reliance on divine intervention—characterizes the 2nd and 1st millennia BC. As a result of this development, since the ancient Mesopotamians were intensely conservative in religious matters and unwilling to discard anything of a hallowed past, the religious data of any period, and particularly those of the later periods, are a condensed version of earlier millennia that must be carefully analyzed and placed in proper perspective before it can be evaluated.

Characteristics of the stages of religious development

WORLD VIEW

Myth: its role in the expression of the world view. The more completely a given culture is embraced, the more natural will its basic tenets seem to the people involved. The most fundamental of its presuppositions are not even likely to rise into awareness and be consciously held but are tacitly taken for granted. It takes a degree of cultural decline, of the loosening of the culture's grip on thought and action, before its most basic structural lines can be recognized and, if need be, challenged. Since culture, the total pattern within which man lives and acts, is thus not likely to be conceived of consciously and as a whole until it begins to lose its obvious and natural character, it is understandable that those myths of a culture that may be termed existential—in the sense that they articulate human existence as a whole in terms of the culture and show

its basic structure—are rarely encountered until comparatively late in the history of a culture. Before that occurs, it is, rather, the particular aspects and facets of existence that are apt to claim attention.

In ancient Mesopotamia the oldest known materials, the Sumerian myths, have relatively little to say about creation; scholars must, for the most part, turn to the introductions of tales and disputations to infer how things were believed to be in the beginning. Thus, a story about the hero Gilgamesh refers in its introductory lines to the times: "after heaven had been moved away from earth, after earth had been separated from heaven." The same notion that heaven and earth were once close together occurs also in a bilingual Sumero-Akkadian text from Ashur about the creation of man. The actual act of separating them is credited to the storm god Enlil of Nippur in the introduction to a third tale that deals with the creation of the first hoe. From similar passing remarks scholars have inferred that the gods, before man came into being, had to labour hard at the heavy works of irrigation agriculture and dug out the beds of the Tigris and the Euphrates.

Not creation but the ordering of the cosmos gave rise to separate myths. In one such myth, "Enki and World Order," the god Enki organized the cosmos on behalf of Enlil much as a steward would organize a large estate, ordering its various economic functions—herding, agriculture, building, and other operations—and appointing gods to oversee them. Another, but rather differently oriented myth, "Lugal-e," viewed the ordering of the world under the image of the reorganization of a conquered province by a victorious young king, Enlil's son, the god Ninurta. The "Eridu Genesis" is a myth that presumably began with an account of the creation of the world by the deities An, Enlil, Enki, and Ninhursag. As preserved, it relates stories about the creation of man and animals, the founding of the first cities, and the sending of the flood. In all of these myths, except the last, a single god is the hero, and the "horizon" of the story—*i.e.*, the kind of creative acts with which it deals—is limited by his particular character and powers.

Myths of the ordering of creation

Cosmogony and cosmology. Though the "Eridu Genesis" may have come close to treating existence as a whole, a true cosmogonic and cosmological myth that deals centrally with the origins, structuring, and functional principles of the cosmos does not actually appear until Old Babylonian times, when Mesopotamian culture was entering a millennium and a half of doubts about the moral character of world government and even of divine power itself. Yet, the statement is a positive one, almost to the point of defiance. *Enuma elish*, the Babylonian creation story, tells of a beginning when all was a watery chaos and only the sea, Tiamat, and the sweet waters under ground, Apsu, mingled their waters together and the original watery form that was personified served as Apsu's page. In their midst the gods were born. The first pair, Lahmu and Lahamu, represented the powers in silt; the next, Anshar and Kishar, those in the horizon. They engendered the god of heaven, Anu, and he in turn the god of the flowing sweet waters, Ea.

The tradition here used is known in a more complete form from an ancient list of gods known as *An: Anum*. There, after a different beginning, Lahmu and Lahamu give rise to Duri and Dari, "the time-cycle"; and these in turn give rise to the powers for a circle to be Enshar and Ninshar, "Lord and Lady Circle." Enshar and Ninshar engender the concrete circle of the horizon, Anshar and Kishar, probably conceived of as silt deposited along the edge of the universe. Next on the list is the horizon of the greater heaven and earth, and then—omitting an intrusive line—heaven and earth, probably conceived as two juxtaposed flat disks formed from silt deposited inward from the horizons. *Enuma elish* truncates these materials and violates their inner logic considerably. Though they are clearly cosmogonic and assume that the cosmic elements and the powers informing them come into being together, *Enuma elish* seeks to utilize them for a pure theogony (account of the origin of the gods). The creation of the actual cosmos is dealt with much later. Also, the intro-

Enuma elish, the Babylonian creation story

duction of Mummu, the personified "original form," which in the circumstances can only be that of water, may have led to the omission of Ki, "Earth" who—as nonwatery—did not fit in.

The gods, who in *Enuma elish* come into being within Apsu and Tiamat, are viewed as dynamic creatures, who contrast strikingly with the older generation. Apsu and Tiamat stand for inertia and rest. This contrast leads to a series of conflicts in which first Apsu is killed by Ea; then Tiamat, who was roused later to attack the gods, by Ea's son Marduk. It is Marduk, the hero of the story, who creates the extant universe out of the body of Tiamat after he kills her. Marduk cuts her, as a dried fish, in two, making one-half of her into heaven—appointing there sun, moon, and stars to execute their prescribed motions —and her other half into the earth. He pierces her eyes to let the Tigris and Euphrates flow forth, and then, heaping mountains on her body in the east, he makes the various tributaries of the Tigris flow out from her breasts. The remainder of the story deals with Marduk's organization of the cosmos, his creation of man, and his assigning to the gods their various cosmic offices and tasks. The cosmos is viewed as structured as, and functioning as, a benevolent absolute monarchy.

The gods and demons. The gods were, as mentioned previously, organized in a polity of a primitive democratic cast. They constituted, as it were, a landed nobility, each god owning and working an estate—his temple and its lands—and controlling the city in which it was located. On the national level he attended the general assembly of the gods, which was the highest authority in the cosmos, to vote on matters of national import such as, for example, election or deposing of kings. The major gods also served on the national level as officers having charge of cosmic offices. Thus, for example, Utu, the sun god, was, in addition to taking care of the sun, the judge of the gods and in charge of justice and righteousness generally.

Highest in the pantheon—and presiding in the divine assembly—ranked An (Akkadian Anu), god of Heaven and responsible for the calendar and the seasons as they were indicated by their appropriate stars. Next came Enlil of Nippur, god of winds and of agriculture, creator of the hoe. Enlil executed the verdicts of the divine assembly. Equal in rank to An and Enlil was the goddess Ninhursag (also known as Nintur and Ninmakh), goddess of stony ground: the near moutain ranges in the east and the stony desert in the west with its wildlife—wild asses, gazelles, wild goats, etc. She was also the goddess of birth. With these was joined—seemingly secondarily—the god Enki (Ea), god of the sweet waters of rivers and of the fertile male semen; he was the cleverest of the gods and a great troubleshooter often appealed to both by gods and by men. Of other gods may be mentioned Enlil's sons: the moon god Nanna or Sîn; the god of thunderstorms, floods, and the plough, Ninurta; and the underworld figures Meslamtaea, Ninazu, and Ennugi. Sîn's sons were the sun god and judge of the gods, Utu (the Akkadian Shamash), the rain god Ishkur (the Akkadian Adad), and his daughter, the goddess of war, love, and morning and evening star, Inanna (the Akkadian Ishtar). Inanna's ill-fated young husband was the herder god Dumuzi (the Akkadian Tammuz). The dread Nether World was ruled by the goddess Ereshkigal and her husband Nergal, a figure closely related to Meslamtaea and Ninurta. Earlier tradition mentions Ninazu as her husband.

Demons played little or no role in the myths or lists of the Mesopotamian pantheon. Their domain was that of incantations. Mostly, they were depicted as outlaws; the demoness Lamashtu, for instance, was hurled from Heaven by her father An because of her wickedness. The demons attacked man by causing all kinds of diseases and were, as a rule, viewed as wind and storm beings. Consonant with the classical view of the universe as a cosmic state, it was possible for a person to go to the law courts against the demons; *i.e.*, to seek recourse before Utu and obtain judgments against them. Various rituals for such procedure are known.

Man: his origin, nature, and destiny. Two different notions about man's origin seem to have been current in

Marduk as creator

Hierarchy of the gods

ancient Mesopotamian religions. Brief mentions in Sumerian texts indicate that the first men grew forth from the earth in the manner of grass and herbs. One of these texts, the "Myth of the Creation of the Hoe," adds a few details: Enlil removed heaven from earth in order to make room for seeds to come up and, after he had created the hoe, he used it to break the hard crust of earth in Uzumua ("the flesh-grower"), a place in the Temple of Inanna in Nippur. Here, out of the hole made by Enlil's hoe, man grew forth.

The other notion presented the view that man was created by Enki, or by Enki and his mother Nammu, or by Enki and the birth goddess called variously Ninhursag, Nintur, and Ninmakh. In a Sumerian myth known as "Enki and Ninmakh," Enki made man from the "engendering clay of the Apsu"—*i.e.*, of the waters underground —and was borne by Nammu. The Akkadian tradition, as represented by the "Myth of Atrakhasis," had Enki advise that a god—presumably a rebel—be killed and that the birth goddess Nintur mix his flesh and blood with clay. This was done, after which 14 womb goddesses gestated the mixture and gave birth to seven human pairs. A similar—probably derived—form of this motif is found in *Enuma elish*, in which Enki (Ea) alone fashioned man out of the blood of the slain rebel leader Kingu. The creation of man from the blood shed by two slain gods is yet another version of the motif that appears in a bilingual myth from Assur.

Man's nature, then, is part clay (earthly) and part god (divine). The divine aspect, however, is not that of a living god but rather that of a slain, powerless divinity. The Atrakhasis story relates that the *etemmu* (ghost) of the slain god was left in man's flesh and thus became part of man. It is this originally divine part of man, his *etemmu*, that was believed to survive at his death and to give him a shadowy afterlife in the Nether World. No other trace of a notion of divine essence in man is discernible; in fact, man by himself was viewed as being utterly powerless to act effectively or to succeed in anything. For anything he might wish to do or achieve, man needed the help of a personal god or goddess, some deity in the pantheon who for one reason or other had taken an interest in him and helped and protected him, for "Without his personal god a man eats not."

About man's destiny all sources agree. However man may have come into being, he was meant to toil in order to provide food, clothing, housing, and service for the gods, so that they, relieved of all manual labour, could live the life of a governing upper class, a landed nobility. In the scheme of existence man was thus never an end, always just a means.

The divine and earthly nature of man

INSTITUTIONS AND PRACTICES

City-state and national state. In early dynastic times, probably as far back as historians can trace its history, Mesopotamia was divided into small units, the so-called city-states, consisting of a major city with its surrounding lands. The ruler of the city—usually entitled *ensi*—was also in charge of the temple of the city god. The spouse of the *ensi* had charge of the temple of the city goddess, and the children of the *ensi* administered the temples of the deities who were regarded as children of the city god and the city goddesses. After the foundation of larger political units, such as leagues or empires, contributions were made to a central temple of the political unit, such as the temple of Enlil at Nippur in the Nippur league. On the other hand, however, the king or other central ruler might also contribute to the shrines of local cults. When, in the 2nd and 1st millennia, Babylonia and Assyria emerged as national states, their kings had responsibility for the national cult and each monarch supervised the administration of all temples in his domain.

Cult. In the cultic practices man fulfilled his destiny: to take care of the gods' material needs. Man therefore provided the gods with houses (the temples) that were richly supplied with lands, which man cultivated for them. In the temple the god was present in—but not bounded by—a statue made of precious wood overlaid with gold. For this statue the temple kitchen staff prepared daily meals from

The purpose of man in relation to the gods

victuals grown or raised on the temple's fields, in its orchards, in its sheepfolds, cattle pens, and game preserves, brought in by its fishermen, or delivered by farmers owing it as a temple tax. Not only was the statue fed but it was also clad in costly raiments, bathed, and escorted to bed in the bedchamber of the god, often on top of the temple tower, or ziggurat. To see to all of this the god had a corps of house servants; *i.e.*, priests trained as cooks, bakers, waiters, and bathers, or as encomiasts (singers of praise) and musicians to make the god's meals festive, or as elegists to soothe him in times of stress and grief. Diversions from the daily routine were the great monthly festivals, and also a number of special occasions. Such special occasions might be a sudden need to go through the elaborate ritual for purifying the king when he was threatened by the evils implied in an eclipse of the moon, or in extreme cases there might be a call for the ritual installation of a substitute king to take upon himself the dangers threatening, and various other nonperiodic rituals.

Partly regular, partly impromptu, were the occasions for audiences with the god in which the king or other worshippers presented their petitions and prayers accompanied by appropriate offerings. These were mostly edibles, but not infrequently the costly containers in which they were presented, stone vases, golden boat-shaped vessels, etc., testified to the ardour of the givers. Appropriate gifts other than edibles were also acceptable—among them cylinder seals for the god's use, superhuman in size, and weapons for him, such as maceheads, also outsize.

To the cult, but as private rather than as part of the temple cult, may be counted also the burial ritual, concerning which, unfortunately, there is little known. In outgoing early dynastic times in Girsu two modes of burial were current. One was ordinary burial in a cemetery; the other, laying the body "in the reeds of Enki," is not clear, perhaps it denoted the floating of the body down the river into the canebrakes. Elegists and other funerary personnel were in attendance and conducted the laments seeking to give full expression to the grief of the bereaved and propitiate the spirit of the dead. In later times burial in a family vault under the dwelling house was frequent.

Sacred times. During most of the 2nd millennium each major city had its own calendar. The months were named from local religious festivals celebrated in the month in question. Only by the 2nd millennium did the Nippur calendar attain general acceptance. The nature of the festivals in these various sacred calendars sometimes reflected the cycle of agricultural activities, such as celebrating the ritual hitching up of the plows and, later in the year, their unhitching, or rites of sowing, harvesting, and other activities. The sacred calendar of Girsu at the end of the early dynastic period is rich in its accounting of festivals. During some of these festival periods the queen travelled through her domain to present funerary offerings of barley, malt, and other agricultural products to the gods and to the spirits of deceased charismatic human administrators.

The cycles of festivals celebrating the marriage and early death of Dumuzi and similar fertility figures in spring are structured according to the backgrounds of the various communities of farmers, herders, or date growers. The sacred wedding—sometimes a fertility rite, sometimes a harvest festival with overtones of thanksgiving—was performed as a drama: the ruler and a high priestess took on the identity of the two deities and so ensured that their highly desirable union actually took place. In many communities the lament for the dead god took the form of a procession out into the desert to find the slain god in his gutted fold, a pilgrimage to the accompaniment of harps and heart-rending laments for the god.

New Year Festival

Of major importance in later times was the New Year Festival, or Akitu, celebrated in a special temple out in the fields. Originally an agricultural festival connected with sowing and harvest, it became the proper occasion for the crowning and investiture of a new king. In Babylon it came to celebrate the sun god Marduk's victory over Tiamat, the goddess of the watery deep. Besides the yearly festivals there were also monthly festivals at New Moon, the 7th, the 15th, and the 28th of the month. The last—when the moon was invisible and thought to be dead—had a distinctly funereal character.

Administration. Supreme responsibility for the correct carrying out of the cult, on which the welfare of the country depended, was entrusted to the city ruler, or, when the country was united, the king. The city ruler and the king were, however, far more than administrators; they also were charismatic figures imparting their individual magic into their rule, thus creating welfare and fertility. In certain periods the king was deified; throughout the 3rd millenium, he became, in ritual action, the god Dumuzi in the rite of the sacred marriage and thus insured fertility for his land. The rulers of the entire 3rd dynasty of Ur (*c.* 2112–*c.* 2004 BC) and most of the dynasty of Isin (*c.* 2020–*c.* 1800 BC) were treated as embodiments of the dying god Damu and invoked in the ritual laments for him. As a vessel of sacred power the king was surrounded by strict ritual to protect that power, and he had to undergo elaborate rituals of purification if the power became threatened.

The role and functions of the priesthood

The individual temples were usually administered by officials called *sanga* ("bishops"), who headed staffs of accountants, overseers of agricultural and industrial works on the temple estate, and *gudu* (priests), who looked after the god as house servants. Among the priestesses the highest ranking were termed *en* (Akkadian *entu*). They were usually princesses of royal blood and were considered the human spouses of the gods they served, participating as brides in the rites of the sacred marriage. Other ranks of priestesses are known, most of them to be considered orders of nuns. The best known are the votaries of the sun god, who lived in a cloister (*gagu*) in Sippar. Whether, besides nuns, there were also priestesses devoted to sacred prostitution is a moot question; what is clear is that prostitutes were under the special protection of the goddess Inanna (Ishtar).

Sacred places. Mesopotamian worshippers might worship in open-air sanctuaries, chapels in private houses, or small separate chapels located in the residential quarters of town; but the sacred place par excellence was the temple. Archaeology has traced the temple back to the earliest periods of settlement, and though the very early temple plans still pose many unsolved problems, it is clear that from the early dynastic period onward the temple was what the Sumerian (*e*) and Akkadian (*bitum*) terms for it indicate; *i.e.*, the temple was the god's house or dwelling. In its more elaborate form such a temple would be built on a series of irregular artificial platforms, one on top of the other; by the 3rd dynasty of Ur, near the end of the 3rd millennium, these became squared off to form a ziggurat. On the lowest of these platforms a heavy wall—first oval, later rectangular—enclosed storerooms, the temple kitchen, workshops, and other such rooms. On the highest level, approached by a stairway, were the god's living quarters centred in the cella, a rectangular room with an entrance door in the long wall near one corner. The god's place was on a podium in a niche at the short wall farthest from the entrance; benches with statues of worshippers ran along both long walls, and a hearth in the middle of the floor served for heating. Low pillars in front of the god's seat seem to have served as stoppers for a hanging that shielded him from profane eyes. Here, or in a connecting room, would be the god's table, bed, and bathtub.

The structure and function of the temple

At a later time in Babylonia the dimensions of the cella with its adjoining rooms were greatly enlarged so that it became an open court surrounded by rooms. Only the section separated by the hanging remained roofed and became a new cella, entered from the middle of its long side and with the god in his niche in the wall directly opposite. The development in Assyria took a slightly different course. Here the original door in the long side moved around the corner to the short side opposite the god, creating a rectangular cella entered from the end wall.

The function of the temple, as of all of the other sacred places in ancient Mesopotamia, was primarily to ensure the god's presence and to provide a place where he could be approached. The providing of housing, food, and service for the god achieved the first of these purposes. His presence was also assured by a suitable embodiment—the cult statue, and, for certain rites, the body of the ruler. To achieve the second purpose, greeting gifts, praise hymns as introduction to petitions, and other actions were used to induce the god to receive the petitioner and to listen to, and accept, his prayers.

In view of the magnitude of such an establishment provided for the gods and the extent of lands belonging to them and cultivated for them—partly with temple personnel, partly by members of the community holding temple land in some form of tenure or another—it was unavoidable that temples should vie in economic importance with similar large private estates or with estates belonging to the crown. This importance, one may surmise, would lie largely in the element of stability that an efficiently run major estate provided for the community. With its facilities for producing large storable surpluses that could be used to offset bad years and with its facilities—such as its weaveries—the temple estates could absorb and utilize elements of the population, such as widows, waifs, captives, and others, who otherwise would have perished or become a menace to the community in one way or other. The economic importance of the temple primarily was local. The amount of foreign trade carried on by them apparently was small. The power behind foreign trade seems rather to have been the king.

The magical arts. In the ancient Mesopotamian view, gods and humans shared one world. The gods lived among men on their great estates (the temples), ruled, upheld law and order for men, and fought their wars. In general, knowing and carrying out the will of the gods was not a matter for doubt: they wanted the practice of their cult performed faultlessly, work on their estates done willingly and well, and they disapproved, in greater or lesser degree, of breaches of the moral and legal order. On occasion, however, man might well be uncertain: did a god want his temple rebuilt or did he not? In all such cases, and others like them, the Mesopotamians sought direct answers from the gods through divination, and conversely the gods might take the initiative and convey specific wishes through dreams, signs, or portents.

Belief in divination and astrology

There were many forms of divination. Of interest to students of biblical prophecy is recent evidence that prophets and prophetesses were active at the court of Mari on the Euphrates in Old Babylonian times (*c.* 1800–*c.* 1600 BC). In Mesopotamia as a whole, however, the forms of divination most frequently used seem to have been incubation—*i.e.*, sleeping in the temple in the hope that the god would send an enlightening dream—and hepatoscopy; *i.e.*, examining the entrails, particularly the liver, of a lamb or kid sacrificed for a divinatory purpose, to read what the god had "written" there by interpreting variations in form and shape. In the 2nd and 1st millennia large and detailed handbooks in hepatoscopy were composed for consultation by the diviners. Though divination in historical times was regularly presented in terms of ascertaining the divine will, there are internal indications in the materials suggesting that it was originally less theologically elaborated. Apparently it was a mere attempt to read the future from "symptoms" in the present, much as a physician recognizes the onset of a disease. This is particularly made clear in that branch of divination that deals with unusual happenings believed to be ominous. Thus, if a desert plant sprouted in a city—indicating that desert essence was about to take over—it was considered an indication that the city would be laid waste.

Related to the observation of unusual happenings in society or nature, but far more systematized, was astrology. The movements and appearance of the sun, the moon, and the planets were believed to yield information about future events affecting the nation or, in some cases, the fate of individuals. Horoscopes, predicting the character and fate of a person on the basis of the constellation of the stars at his birth, are known to have been constructed in the late 1st millennium, but the art may conceivably be older.

Belief in witchcraft

Witchcraft was apparently at all times considered a crime punishable by death. Frequently, however, it probably was difficult to identify the witch in individual cases, or even to be sure that a given evil was the result of witchcraft rather than of other causes. In such cases the expert in white magic, the *ashipu* or *mashmashshu*, was able to help both in diagnosing the cause of the evil and in performing the appropriate rituals and incantation to fight it off. In earlier times the activities of the magicians seem generally to have been directed against the lawless demons who attacked man and caused all kinds of diseases. In the later half of the 2nd, and all through the 1st millennium, however, the fear of man-made evils grew, and witchcraft vied with the demons as the chief source of all ills.

RELIGIOUS ART AND ICONOGRAPHY

The earliest periods in Mesopotamia have yielded figurines of clay or stone, some of which may conceivably represent gods or demons; certainty of interpretation in regard to these figurines is, however, difficult to attain. With the advent of the Protoliterate period toward the end of the 4th millennium BC, the so-called cylinder seal came into use. In the designs on these seals—often, it would seem, copies from monumental wall paintings now lost—ritual scenes and divine figures, recognizable from what is known about them in historical times, make their first appearance. To this period also belongs the magnificent Uruk Vase, with its representation of the sacred marriage rite. Until the early centuries of the 2nd millennium the cylinder seal remains one of the most prolific sources of religious motifs and representations of divine figures, but larger reliefs, wall paintings, and sculpture in the round greatly add to modern historians' understanding of who and what is rendered. In the 2nd and 1st millennia, the humble categories of clay plaques and clay figurines often contained representations of deities, and the numerous sculptured boundary stones (*kudurru*s) furnish representations of symbols and emblems of gods, at times identified by labels in cuneiform. To the 1st millennium belong also the magnificent colossal statues of protective genii (spirits) in the shape of lions or human-headed bulls that guarded the entrances to Assyrian palaces, and also, on the gates of Nebuchadrezzar's (died 562 BC) Babylon, the reliefs in glazed tile of lions and dragons that served the same purpose.

CONCLUSION

A religious development covering four millennia such as one finds in ancient Mesopotamian religions is obviously of interest in and of itself. The tendencies that lead from a central concern with salvation from famine to salvation from attack, and finally to salvation from a sense of personal guilt, with the attendant deepening and enriching of the concept of the divine, invites close study. So also do the many moving and profound expressions of religious faith in the hymns, laments, and prayers of these religions. As one of the earliest religious systems in history to structure, and be itself structured by, the complexities of a high civilization, Mesopotamian religions are of significant interest to historians, historians of religion, and theologians. As a source from which religious insights, attitudes, and problems flowed into all of Western tradition, Mesopotamian religions are of lasting and great interest beyond themselves.

BIBLIOGRAPHY. E.P. DHORME, *Les Religions de Babylonie et d'Assyrie* (1945), the standard survey of data on ancient Mesopotamian religions; H. FRANKFORT, *Kingship and the Gods* (1948), on the theme of the king as intermediator between men and gods, and *et al.*, *Before Philosophy* (1951), an attempt at synthesis and religious interpretation; T. JACOBSEN, *Toward the Image of Tammuz*, ed. by W.L. MORAN (1970), a more detailed attempt at synthesizing, ordering, and interpreting data; J.B. PRITCHARD (ed.), *Ancient Near Eastern Texts Relating to the Old Testament*, 3rd ed. (1969), major sources in reliable translations; C.J. GADD, *Ideas of Divine Rule in the Ancient Near East* (1948), on the problems of divination and the communication between men and gods; S.A. PALLIS, *The Babylonian Akitu Festival* (1926), the first and only attempt to understand the meaning and function of the ritual drama; S.N. KRAMER, *The Sacred Marriage Rite: Aspects of Faith, Myth, and Ritual in Ancient Sumer* (1969), on the fertility cult.

(T.J.)

Mesopotamian Religious Literature and Mythology

The large body of written remains that has been preserved from ancient Mesopotamian civilization is here termed religious literature, because its core, the part of it that by form and expressiveness qualifies as literature in the strict sense (*belle lettres*), is predominantly religious in nature. This core comprises the genres (literary kinds or forms) of myth, epic, hymn, lamentations, penitential psalm, incantation, and wisdom literature. Outside the core literature there are several more practically oriented handbook genres. Only two of these, those dealing with rituals and omina (signs, or omens), are clearly religious; the rest, consisting of historical, juridical, economical, mathematical, astronomical, lexical, grammatical, and epistolary collections, tend toward the secular. Because religion provided the only total view of existence in ancient Mesopotamian civilization, however, religious themes, attitudes, and presuppositions turn up quite frequently in these quasi-secular writings.

NATURE AND SIGNIFICANCE

Sumerian literature. Mesopotamian literature originated with the Sumerians, whose earliest known written records are from the middle of the 4th millennium BC. It constitutes the oldest known literature in the world; moreover, inner criteria indicate that a long oral-literary tradition preceded, and probably coexisted with, the setting down of its songs and stories in writing. It may be assumed, further, that this oral literature developed the genres of the core literature. The handbook genres, however, in spite of occasional inclusions of oral formula— *e.g.*, legal or medical—may generally be assumed to have been devised after writing had been invented, as a response to the remarkable possibilities that writing offered for amassing and organizing data.

The purpose underlying the core literature and its oral prototypes would seem to have been as much magical as aesthetic, or merely entertaining in origin. In magic, words create and call into being what they state—the more vivid and expressive they are the more they are believed to be efficacious—so by its expressiveness literature forms a natural vehicle of such creativity. In ancient Mesopotamia its main purpose appears to have been the enhancement of what was seen as beneficial. With the sole exception of wisdom literature, the core genres are panegyric in nature (*i.e.*, they praise something or other), and the magical power and use of praise is to instill, call up, or activate the virtues presented in the praise.

That praise is of the essence of hymns, for instance, is shown by the fact that over and over again the encomiast, the official praiser, whose task it was to sing these hymns, closed with the standing phrase: "O [the name of a deity], thy praise is sweet." The same phrase is common also at the end of myths and epics, two further praise genres that also belonged in the repertoire of the encomiast. They praise not only in description but also in narrative, by recounting acts of valour done by the hero, thus sustaining and enhancing his power to do such deeds, according to the magical view.

In time, possibly quite early, the magical aspect of literature must have tended to fade from men's consciousness, yielding to more nearly aesthetic attitudes that viewed the praise hymns as expressions of allegiance and loyalties, and accepted the narrative genres of myth and epic for the enjoyment of the story and the values expressed, poetic and otherwise.

Hymns, myths, and epics all were believed to sustain existing powers and virtues by means of praise, but laments were understood to praise blessings and powers lost, originally seeking to hold on to and recall them magically, through the power in expression of intense longing for them and vivid representation of them. The lamentation genre was the province of a separate professional, the elegist. It contained dirges for the dying gods of the fertility cults and laments for temples and cities destroyed and desecrated. The laments for temples—which go back no earlier than to the 3rd dynasty of Ur (*c.* 2112–*c.* 2004

BC)—were used to recall the beauties of the lost temple as a kind of inducement to persuade the god and owner of the temple to restore it.

Penitential psalms lament private illnesses and misfortunes and seek to evoke the pity of the deity addressed and thus to gain divine aid. The genre apparently is late in date, most likely Old Babylonian (*c.* 19th century BC), and in it the element of magic has, to all intents and purposes, disappeared.

The core genres of Mesopotamian literature were developed by the Sumerians apparently as oral compositions. Writing, which is first attested at the middle of the 4th millennium BC, was in its origins predominantly ideographical (picture or symbol writing) and long remained a highly imperfect means of rendering the spoken word. Even as late as the beginning of the Early Dynastic III Period in south Mesopotamia at the end of that millennium, the written literary texts preserved have the character of mnemonic (memory) aids only and seem to presuppose that the reader has prior oral knowledge of the text.

As writing developed more and more precision during the 3rd millennium BC, more and more oral compositions seem to have been put into writing and with the 3rd dynasty of Ur (*c.* 2112–*c.* 2004 BC) a considerable body of literature had come into being and was being added to by a generation of highly gifted authors. Fortunately for its survival, this literature became part of the curriculum in the Sumerian scribal schools, studied and copied by student after student so that an abundance of such copies, reaching a peak in old Babylonian times, duplicated and supplemented each other as witnesses to the text of the major works. As many as 50 or more copies or fragments of copies of a single composition may support a modern edition, and many thousands more such copies probably still lie unread, buried in the earth.

Akkadian literature. The first centuries of the 2nd millennium BC witnessed the demise of Sumerian as a spoken language and its replacement by Akkadian. Because of its role as bearer of Sumerian culture, as the language of religion, literature, and many arts, however, Sumerian (much as Latin in the Middle Ages) continued to be taught and spoken in the scribal schools throughout the 2nd and 1st millennia BC. New compositions were even composed in it, grammatically more and more barbarous the greater the distance in time from when it was still alive.

Akkadian, when it supplanted Sumerian as the spoken language of Mesopotamia, was not without its own literary tradition. Writing, to judge from Akkadian orthographical peculiarities, was very early borrowed from the Sumerians. By old Babylonian times (*c.* 19th century BC), the literature in Akkadian, partly under the influence of Sumerian models and Sumerian literary themes, had developed myths and epics of its own, among them the superb Old-Babylonian Gilgamesh epic (dealing with the problem of death) as well as hymns, disputation texts (evaluations of elements of the cosmos and society), penitential psalms, and not a few independent new handbook genres—*e.g.*, omina, rituals, laws and legal phrasebooks (often translated from Sumerian), mathematical texts, and grammatical texts. A noticeable amount of translations from Sumerian is observable: incantation series like the *utukke limnuti* ("The Evil Spirits"), laments for destroyed temples, penitential psalms, and others. The prestige of Sumerian as a literary language, however, is indicated by the fact that translations were rarely, if ever, allowed to supersede the original Sumerian text. The Sumerian text was kept with an interlinear translation to form a bilingual work.

The continued study and copying of literature in the schools, both Sumerian and Akkadian, by the middle of the 2nd millennium led to a remarkable effort of standardizing, or canonizing. Texts of the same genre were collected, often under royal auspices and with royal support, and were then sifted and finally edited in series that from then on were recognized as the canonical form. Authoritative texts were established for incantations, laments, omina, medical texts, lexical texts, and others. In

---

The significance of writing

Canonization of Mesopotamian religious literature

Functions of Mesopotamian religious literature

myths and epics, such major and lengthy compositions as the Akkadian creation story *Enuma elish*, the Erra myth, Nergal and Ereshkigal, the Etana legend, the Gilgamesh epic, and the Tukulti-Ninurta epic were reworked or re-created.

Of special interest are philosophical compositions, in Akkadian called *Ludlul bel nemeqi*, "Let me praise the expert," and theodicies (justification of divine ways) that deal with the problem of the just sufferer, similar to the biblical Job. They constitute a high point in the genre of wisdom literature. From the 1st millennium BC the rise of factual historical chronicles and a spate of political and religious polemical writings reflecting the rivalry between Assyria and Babylonia deserve mention. Very late in the millennium, the first astronomical texts appeared.

The influence of Mesopotamian literature. That Mesopotamian literature influenced the later literatures that grew up in surrounding countries (*e.g.*, Syria, the land of the Hittites, Israel, Phoenicia, and Greece), is unmistakable, but little work has been done to trace its influence in detail. The Mesopotamian story of the flood told in the old Babylonian Atrahasis (hero of the flood) myth and secondarily incorporated in the Gilgamesh epic shows such close correspondence in details with the biblical account of Noah and the Flood that direct influence must be assumed, even though the setting of the story and its ultimate significance was viewed very differently by the Mesopotamian and the biblical narrators. The Babylonian account of the ruling generations of gods—the dynasty of Dunnum—is traceable to Phoenicia and from there on to Greece, in which it underlies Hesiod's Theogony (birth of the gods). A variant form found its way to the Hittites. Not only individual works and literary motifs seem to have spread but also borrowings of literary forms may be assumed in the case of the biblical book of Lamentations, which clearly stands in the tradition of the Mesopotamian genre of lamentations for temples and cities. A similar case is the genre of penitential psalm developed in Mesopotamia early in the 2nd millennium, spreading to the Hittites and to Egypt in the middle and latter half of that millennium, and then continuing in Israel as a type of psalm. More easy to trace—though the cuneiform (wedge-shaped writing) original has not yet been uncovered—is the distribution of the book about the wise Achiqar, a minister of the Assyrian king Sennacherib (died 681 BC), which was spread in its Aramaic form throughout the Near East. The spread of fables about animals and trees is traceable from Mesopotamia to Greece in the West and to India in the East.

Besides core literature, "handbook" literature also *Handbook literature* spread, but it is often difficult to distinguish whether what was borrowed was literature, or content and data only. Here must be mentioned first of all the early and broad spread of written legal and business forms, contracts, account types, legal phraseology, and other Sumerian and Akkadian forms to ancient Iran in the East, and to Syria and Asia Minor in the West. Clear links with the earlier Mesopotamian legal tradition are also evident in the laws of the Hebrews. In the 2nd and 1st millennia Babylonian mathematics and astronomy also spread. Babylonian terms, formulations, and inventions found their way to Egypt and Greece and—transmitted by the Greeks—to India. Further evidence and further study will most likely amplify and clarify much, in the matter of the diffusion of Mesopotamian cultural achievement, both literary and otherwise, to its neighbours and heirs.

THE LITERATURE AND ITS TEXTS

Present knowledge of ancient Mesopotamian literature is due almost exclusively to archaeological excavations, which began probing the ruined city-mounds of ancient Mesopotamia—present-day Iraq—around the middle of the 19th century. Thousands of ancient documents have been exhumed.

Of greatest importance was the early discovery of the Assyrian king Ashurbanipal's library in Nineveh in 1849, at a time when the decipherment of cuneiform writing was still in its infancy. This library, collected by Ashurbanipal (668–627 BC), contained speimens of al-

most all genres of Ancient Mesopotamian literature and apparently had copies—unfortunately not always completely recovered—of most of its greatest works. Of particular practical importance were the lexical texts found in it. Without them and the information about the many different possible values of each cuneiform sign that the ancient scribes had here organized, it is doubtful that cuneiform could ever have been fully deciphered. Similar though less extensive libraries of about the same period have been found in Nimrud (Assyria) and Sultan Tepe. In ancient Ashur (ash-Sharqāṭ) German excavators unearthed a number of private libraries in which literary texts were well represented.

The importance of the library at Nineveh

Whereas the Ashurbanipal library was a true library, another large find of texts, the so-called temple library at Nippur in Mesopotamia, constituted the waste from scribal schools of the Old Babylonian Period. These texts and fragments of texts were found in the foundations of private houses and apparently had been carted there from the school's waste heaps to serve simply as fill, for which they were, of course, eminently well suited. Since the first finds of literary texts in Nippur (1889–1900), similar finds in Old Babylonian private houses have been made on other sites, most extensively by the archaeologist Leonard Woolley at Ur (1930–31). The Old Babylonian literary texts from Nippur and elsewhere represent copies of Sumerian literature as it was preserved and handed on in the scribal schools of the period. A majority of its greatest works apparently date back to the time of the 3rd dynasty of Ur and the centuries immediately preceding and following it; but relatively few copies of that period have yet been found. The famous Cylinders of Gudea (rulers of Lagash *c.* 2050 BC) from Tello and an as yet unpublished group of literary texts of the Ur III Period from Nippur may be mentioned. The oldest collections of literary works so far discovered were found at Fara and at Ishan Abu Salabikh; they date to the borderline between Early Dynastic II and III (*c.* 2750–*c.* 2334 BC).

Tablet recounting the Sumerian story of the Flood, *c.* 2000–1500 BC, excavated from Nippur, Iraq. In the University Museum, University of Pennsylvania, Philadelphia.

Relatively little is known about the verse style of ancient Mesopotamian literary compositions. The Sumerians, it seems, often used syllabic verse with a constant or regularly alternating number of syllables to each line. Often the line appears to be divided by a medial caesura (poetical interruption). The lines are usually grouped into stanzas consisting of strophe (two or more lines repeated as a unit) and antistrophe (distich), or strophe and two antistrophes (tristich). Stanzas of four or six lines also occur. A much used device is the "particularizing" stanza in which a person or thing is mentioned under a general term in the strophe, to be then named or similarly particularized in the otherwise identical antistrophe. Larger sections, or

Use of verse styles

"cantos," with short responses following them are often indicated in hymns and laments by the following notations: *ki-ru-gu* ("place in which to counter") after the canto, and *gis-gi-gal-bi-im* ("is its antiphone") after the antiphon. Occasionally, very elaborate patterns were developed, such as in the myth of "Inanna and Bilulu" in which the lines are grouped in stanzas as strophe and antistrophe, or strophe and two antistrophes. These stanzas are themselves grouped into larger "megastrophes" (great strophes).

In Akkadian, the verse is accentual verse. The line is usually divided by a medial caesura into halves, each of which has two stresses. All lines end in a trochee; *i.e.*, metrical unit of one stressed and one unstressed syllable. As in Sumerian poetry, distichs and tristichs are frequent and may be enlarged to four- or six-line stanzas. The tristichs and longer stanzas seem to be characteristic of the later periods after old Babylonian times. To these later times belong also lines with more than four stresses. In the last millennium BC the highly artificial form of the acrostic came into use and enjoyed a fair measure of popularity.

REPRESENTATIVE TYPES OF LITERATURE

Myths. The genre of myths in ancient Mesopotamian literature centres on praises that recount and celebrate great deeds. The doers of the deeds (creative or otherwise decisive acts), and thus the subjects of the praises, are the gods.

Sumerian myths. In the oldest myths, the Sumerian, these acts tend to have particular rather than universal relevance, which is understandable since they deal with the power and acts of a particular god with a particular sphere of influence in the cosmos. An example of such myths is the myth of "Dumuzi's Death" that relates how Dumuzi (the Quickener of the Young), the power in the fertility of spring, dreamed of his own death at the hands of a group of deputies from the Nether World and how he tried to hide himself but was betrayed by his friend after his sister had resisted all attempts at making her reveal where he was.

A similar, very complex myth, "Inanna's Descent," relates how the goddess Inanna (Lady of the Date Clusters) set her heart on ruling the Nether World and tried to depose her older sister, the queen of the Nether World, Ereshkigal (Lady of the Greater Earth). Her attempt failed, she was killed, and changed into a piece of rotting meat in the Nether World. It took all the ingenuity of Enki (Lord of the Earth) to bring Inanna back to life, and even then she was released only on condition that she furnish a substitute to take her place. On her return, finding her young husband Dumuzi feasting instead of mourning for her, Inanna was seized with jealousy and designated him as that substitute. Dumuzi tried to flee the force of deputies who had accompanied Inanna, and with the help of the sun god Utu ("Sun"), who changed Dumuzi's shape, he managed to escape, was recaptured, escaped again, and so on, until he was finally taken to the Nether World, where the fly told his little sister Geshtinanna where he was, and she went in search of him. The myth ends with Inanna rewarding the fly and decreeing that Dumuzi and his little sister could alternate as her substitute, each of them spending half a year in the Nether World, the other half above with the living.

A third myth built over the motif of journeying to the Nether World is the myth of "The Engendering of the Moongod and his Brothers," which tells how Enlil (Lord Wind), when still a youngster, came upon young Ninlil (the Varicoloured Ear; goddess of grain) as she—disobeying her mother—was bathing in a canal. He lay with her in spite of her protests and thus engendered the moon god Suen. For this offense Enlil was banished from Nippur and took the road to the Nether World. Ninlil, carrying his child, followed him. On the way Enlil took the shape first of the Nippur gatekeeper, then of the man of the river of the Nether World, and lastly of the ferryman of the river of the Nether World. In each such disguise Enlil persuaded Ninlil to let him lie with her to engender a son who might take Suen's place in the Nether World and

leave him free for the world above. Thus three further deities, all underworld figures, were engendered: Meslamtaea (he who comes out of temple), Ninazu (Water Knower), and Ennugi (the God who returns not). The myth ends with a paean to Enlil as a source of abundance and to his divine word, which always comes true.

Most likely all of these myths have backgrounds in fertility cults and concern the disappearance of nature's fertility with the onset of the dry season or with the underground storage of food.

As Enlil is celebrated for engendering other gods that embody other powers in nature, so also was Enki in the myth of "Enki and Ninhursag," in which myth Enki lay down with Ninhursag (Lady of the Stony Ground) on the island of Dilmun (modern Bahrein), which had been allotted to them. At that time all was new and fresh, inchoate, not yet set in its present mold. There Enki provided water for the future city of Dilmun, lay with Ninhursag, and left her. She gave birth to a daughter, Ninshar (Lady Herb), on whom Enki in turn engendered the spider Uttu, goddess of spinning and weaving. Ninhursag warned Uttu, but Enki, proffering marriage gifts, persuaded her to open the door to him. After Enki had had his will of her and abandoned her, Ninhursag found her and removed Enki's semen from her body. From the semen seven plants sprouted forth. These plants Enki later saw and ate and so became pregnant from his own semen. Unable as a male to give birth, he fell fatally ill, until Ninhursag relented and—as birth goddess—placed him in her vulva and helped him to give birth to seven daughters, whom Enki then happily married off to various gods.

Not only the birth of gods but also the birth, or creation, of man is treated in the myths. The myth of "Enki and Ninmakh" relates how the gods originally had to toil for their food, dig irrigation canals, and perform other acts until, in their distress, they complained to Enki's mother Nammu, who took the complaints to Enki. Enki remembered the engendering clay of the Apsu (*i.e.*, the fresh underground waters that fathered him) and from his clay, with the help of the womb goddesses and eight midwife goddesses led by Ninmakh (another name for Ninhursag) he had his mother become pregnant with, and give birth to man so that he could relieve the gods of their toil. At the celebration of the birth, however, Enki and Ninmakh both drank too much beer and began to quarrel. Ninmakh boasted that she could impair man's shape at will and Enki countered that he could temper even the worst that she might do. So she made seven freaks, for each of which Enki found a place in society and a living. He then challenged her to alleviate the mischief he could do, but the creature he fashioned (one suffering from all the ills and debilities of extreme old age) was far beyond her powers to cope with. Thus the many imperfections in man came into being.

The ordering, rather than the creation, of the world is the subject of another myth about Enki, called "Enki and World Order." Beginning with long praises and self-praises of Enki, it tells how he blessed Nippur (Sumer), Ur, Meluhha (Ethiopia), and Dilmun (Bahrein) and gave them their characteristics, after which he turned his attention to the Euphrates and the Tigris rivers, to the marshes, the sea, and the rains, and then to instituting one facet after another of the economic life of Sumer: agriculture, housebuilding, herding, and so forth. The story ends with a complaint by Enki's granddaughter Inanna that she has not been given her due share of offices, at which he patiently pointed to various offices she had in fact been given and kindly added a few more.

Another myth about the world order but dealing with it from a very different point of view is about Enlil's son, the rain god Ninurta, called from its opening word "Lugal-e" (O King). This myth begins with a description of the young king, Ninurta, sitting at home in Nippur when, through his general, reports reach him of a new power that has arisen in the mountains to challenge him—*i.e.*, Azag, son of Anu (Sky) and Ea (Earth), chosen king by the plants and raiding the cities with his warriors, the stones. Ninurta sets out in his boat to give battle, and a fierce engagement ensues in which Azag is killed. After-

Fertility myths

The ordering of the world: cosmological myths

Shamash, the sun god, rising in the morning from the eastern mountains between (left) Ishtar (Sumerian Inanna), the goddess of the morning star, and (far left) Ninurta, the god of thunderstorms, with his bow and lion, and (right) Ea (Sumerian Enki), the god of water, with (far right) his vizier, the two-faced Usmu.

ward Ninurta reorganizes his newly won territory, builds a stone barrier, the *hursag*, the near mountain ranges, gathers the waters that used to go up into the mountains and directs them into the Tigris to flood it and provide plentiful irrigation water from Sumer. The *hursag* he presents as a gift to his mother, who had come to visit him, naming her Ninhursag, Lady of the Hursag; and lastly he sits in judgment on the stones who had formed the Azag's army. Some of them, who had shown special ill will toward him, he curses, and others he trusts and gives high office in his administration. These judgments give the stones their present characteristics so that, for example, the flint is condemned to break before the much softer horn, as it indeed does when the horn is pressed against it to flake it. Noteworthy also is the way in which order in the universe, the yearly flood and other seasonal events, is seen—consonantly with Ninurta's role as "king" and leader in war—under the pattern of a reorganization of conquered territories.

Other myths about Ninurta are "An-gim dim-ma" and a myth of his contest with Enki. The first of these tells how Ninurta, on returning from battle to Nippur, was met by Enlil's page Nusku, who ordered him to cease his boastful clamor and not scare Enlil and the other gods. After long speeches of self-praise, by Ninurta, further addresses to him calmed him and made him enter Nippur gently. The second tale relates how he conquered the Thunderbird Ansud with Enki's help but missed the powers it had stolen from him, and how, resentful at this, he plotted against Enki but was outsmarted and trapped. Another Sumerian myth, the "Eridu Genesis," tells of the creation of man and animals, of the building of the first cities, and of the flood.

Akkadian myths. The Akkadian myths are in many ways dependent on Sumerian materials, but they show an originality and a broader scope in their treatment of the earlier Sumerian concepts and forms; they address themselves more often to existence as a whole. Fairly close to Sumerian prototypes is an Akkadian version of the myth of "Inanna's Descent." An old Babylonian myth about the Thunderbird Ansud, who stole the tablets of fates, was conquered by Ninurta, and who was guided by Enki's counsel, is probably closely related to the Sumerian story of Ninurta's contest with Enki.

Also important is an old Babylonian "Myth of Atrahasis," which, in motif, shows a relationship with the account of the creation of man to relieve the gods of toil in the "Enki and Ninmakh" myth, and with a Sumerian account of the flood in the "Eridu Genesis"; but the myth treats of these themes with noticeable originality and remarkable depth. It relates, first, how the gods originally had to toil for a living, how they rebelled and went on strike, how Enki suggested that one of their number—apparently the ringleader who "had the idea," one We—be killed and mankind created from clay mixed with his flesh and blood, so that the toil of the gods could be laid on man and the gods left to go free. But after Enki and the birth goddess Nintur (another name for Ninmakh) had created man, man multiplied at such a rate that the din he made kept Enlil

sleepless. At first Enlil had Namtar, the god of death, cause a plague to diminish mankind's numbers, but the wise Atrahasis, at the advise of Enki, had man concentrate all worship and offerings on Namtar, and Namtar, embarrassed at hurting people who showed such love and affection for him, stayed his hand. Next Enlil had Adad, the god of rains, hold back the rains and thus cause a famine, but because of the same strategem, Adad was embarrassed and released the rains. After this, Enlil, next planned a famine by divine group action that would not be vulnerable as the earlier actions by individual gods had been. Anu and Adad were to guard the heavens, he himself earth, and Enki the waters underground and the sea so that no gift of nature could come through to man. The ensuing famine was terrible. By the seventh year one house consumed the other and people began eating their own children. At that point Enki—accidentally he maintained—let through a wealth of fish from the sea and so saved man. With this, however, Enlil's patience was at an end and he thought of the flood as a means to get rid of humanity once and for all. Enki, however, warned Atrahasis and had him build a boat in which he saved himself, his family, and all animals. After the flood had abated and the ship was grounded, Atrahasis sacrificed, and the hungry gods, much chastened, gathered around the offering. Only Enlil was unrelenting until Enki upbraided him for killing innocent and guilty alike and—there is a gap in the text—suggested other means to keep man's numbers down. In consultation with the birth goddess Nintur, Enki then developed a scheme of birth control by inventing the barren woman, the demon Pashittu who kills children at birth, and the various classes of priestesses to whom birth giving was taboo.

The myth uses the motif of the protest of the gods against their hard toil and the creation of man to relieve it, which was depicted earlier in the Sumerian myth of "Enki and Ninmakh," and also the motif of the flood, which occurred in the "Eridu Genesis." The import of these motifs here is, however, new: they bring out the basic precariousness of man's existence and man's usefulness to the gods will not protect him unless he takes care not to annoy them, however innocently. He must stay within bounds; there are limits set for his self-expression.

A far more trustful and committed attitude to the powers that rule existence finds expression in the seemingly slightly later Babylonian creation story, *Enuma elish*, which may be dated to the later part of the 1st dynasty of Babylon (*c.* 1894–*c.* 1595 BC). Babylon's archenemy then was the Sealand, which controlled Nippur and the country south of it—the ancestral country of Sumerian civilization. This lends political point to the battle of Marduk (thunder and rain deity), the god of Babylon, with the Sea, Tiamat; it also accounts for the odd, almost complete silence about Enlil of Nippur in the tale.

The myth tells how in the beginning there was nothing but Apsu, the sweet waters underground, and Tiamat, the sea, mingling their waters together. In these waters the first gods came into being and generation followed generation. The gods represented energy and activity, and thus differed markedly from Apsu and Tiamat, who stood for rest and inertia. True to their nature the gods gathered to dance, and in so doing, surging back and forth, they disturbed the insides of Tiamat. Finally, Apsu's patience was at an end, and he thought of doing away with the gods, but Tiamat, as a true mother, demurred at destroying her own offspring. Apsu, however, did not swerve from his decision and he was encouraged in this by his page Mummu, "the original (watery) form." When the youngest of the gods, the clever Ea (Sumerian Enki), heard about the planned attack he forestalled it by means of a powerful spell with which he poured slumber on Apsu, killed him, and built his temple over him. He seized Mummu and held him captive by a nose rope.

In the temple thus built the hero of the myth, Marduk, was born. From the first he was the darling of his grandfather, the god of heaven, Anu, who engendered the four winds for him to play with. As they blew and churned up waves, the disturbing of Tiamat—and of a faction of the gods who shared her desire for rest—became more and

The role of Atrahasis as the hero of the flood

The *Enuma elish*

more unbearable. At last these gods succeeded in rousing her to resistance and she created a mighty army with a spearhead of monsters to destroy the gods. She placed her consort Kingu ("Task[?]") at the head of it and gave him absolute powers.

When news of these developments reached the gods there was consternation. Ea was sent to make Tiamat desist, and then Anu, but to no avail. Finally Anshar, god of the horizon and king of the gods, thought of young Marduk. Marduk proved willing to fight Tiamat but demanded absolute authority. Accordingly, a messenger was sent to the oldest of the gods, Lahmu and Lahamu ("Silt[?]"), to call the gods to assembly, and in the assembly the gods conferred absolute authority on Marduk, tested it by seeing whether his word of command alone could destroy a constellation and then again make it whole, hailed him king, and set him on the road of "security and obedience," a formula of allegiance that placed his power and authority on the pressing need for protection of the moment.

In the ensuing encounter with Tiamat's forces Kingu and his army lost heart when they saw Marduk. Only Tiamat stood her ground, seeking first to throw him off his guard by flattery about his quick rise to leadership, but Marduk angrily denounced her and the older generation: "The sons (had to) withdraw (for) the fathers were acting treacherously, and (now) you, who gave birth to them, bear malice to the offspring." At this Tiamat, furious, attacked, but Marduk loosed the winds against her, pierced her heart with an arrow, and killed her. Kingu and the gods who had sided with her he took captive.

Having thus won a lasting victory for his suzerain, King Anshar, he gave thought to what he might do further. Cleaving the carcass of Tiamat, he raised half of her to form heaven, ordered the constellations, the calendar, the movements of sun and moon, and, keeping control of atmospheric phenomena for himself, made the earth out of the other half of her, arranging its mountains and rivers. Having organized the various administrative tasks, he put their supervision in Ea's hands; to Anu he gave the tablets of fate he had taken from Kingu. His prisoners he paraded in triumphal procession before his fathers, and as a monument to his victory he set up images of Tiamat's monsters at the gate of his parental home. The gods were overjoyed to see him; Anshar rushed toward him and Marduk formally announced to him the state of security he had achieved. He then bathed, dressed, and seated himself on his throne, with the spear "Security and Obedience," named from his mandate, at his side. By now, however, the situation had subtly altered. The old fear and urgent need for protection was gone, but in its stead had come a promise held out by Marduk's organizational powers; so when the gods reaffirmed their allegiance to him as king they used a new formula: "benefits and obedience." From then on Marduk would take care of their sanctuaries and they, in turn, would obey him.

The
building
of
Babylon

Marduk then announced his intention of building a city for himself, Babylon, with room for the gods when they come there for assembly; and his fathers suggested that they move there themselves to be with him and help in the administration of the world he had created. Next, he pardoned the gods who had sided with Tiamat and had been captured, charging them with the building tasks. Grateful for their lives, they prostrated themselves before him, hailed him as king, and promised to do the building.

Pleased with their willingness, Marduk magnanimously wanted to relieve them even from this chore and planned to create man to do the toil for them. At the advice of his father Ea, he then had them indict Kingu as instigator of the rebellion. Kingu was duly sentenced and executed, and from his blood Ea created man. Then Marduk divided the gods into a celestial and a terrestrial group, assigned them their tasks in the cosmos, and allotted them their stipends. Thus freed from all burdens, the gods wanted to show their gratitude to Marduk and as a token they took, of their own free will, for one last time, spade in hand to build Babylon and Marduk's temple Esagila. In the new temple the gods then assembled, distributed the celestial and terrestrial offices, the "great gods" went into

session and permanently appointed the "seven gods of destinies," or better "of the decrees," who would formulate in final form the decrees enacted by the assembly. Marduk then presented his weapons and Anu adopted the bow as his daughter and gave it a seat among the gods. Lastly, Marduk was enthroned, and after the gods had prostrated themselves before him they bound themselves by oath—touching their throats with oil and water—and formally gave him kingship, appointing him permanently lord of the gods of heaven and earth. After this they solemnly named his 50 names expressive of his power and achievements. The myth ends with a plea that it be handed on from father to son and told to future rulers, that they may heed Marduk: it is the song of Marduk who bound Tiamat and assumed the kingship.

The motifs from which this myth is built up are in large measure known from elsewhere. The initial generation of the gods is a variant form of the genealogy of Anu in the great god list *An: Anum;* the threat to annihilate the disturbances of sleep are known from the Atrahasis and the Sumerian flood traditions; the battle of Marduk with Tiamat seems to stem from western myths of a battle between the thunder god and the sea; the organization of the universe after victory recalls the organization of conquered territory in "Lugal-e"; and the killing of a rebel god to create man to take over the gods' toil is found in the Atrahasis myth and—without the rebel aspect—in a bilingual creation myth found in Assur. New and original, however, is the way in which they have all been grouped and made dependent on the figure of the young king. The political form of the monarchy is seen as embracing the universe; it was the prowess of a young king that overcame the forces of inertia; it was his organizational genius that created and organized all; and it is he that—as his counterpart on earth, the human king—grants benefits in return for obedience. The high value set on the monarchy as a guarantor of security and order in the *Enuma elish* can hardly have seemed obvious in Babylonia in the first troubled years of Assyrian rule in the second quarter of the 1st millennium BC. From this period (*c.* 700 BC) comes a myth usually called the Erra epic, which reads almost like a polemic against *Enuma elish.* It tells how the god of affray and indiscriminate slaughter, Erra, persuaded Marduk to turn over the rule of the world to him while Marduk was having his royal insignia cleaned, and how Erra, true to his nature, used his powers to institute indiscriminate rioting and slaughter. Royal power here stands no longer for security and order, but for the opposite: license to kill and destroy.

The
value
of the
monarchy

Two other Akkadian myths may be mentioned—both probably dating from the middle of the 2nd millennium —the myth of the "Dynasty of Dunnum" and the myth of "Nergal and Ereshkigal." The first of these tells of succeeding divine generations ruling in Dunnum, the son usually killing his father and marrying, sometimes his mother, sometimes his sister, until—according to a reconstruction of the broken text—more acceptable mores came into vogue with the last generation of gods, Enlil and Ninurta. This myth, as has been mentioned, underlies the Greek poet Hesiod's Theogony. The myth of Nergal and Ereshkigal relates the unorthodox way in which the god Nergal became the husband of Ereshkigal and king of the Nether World.

Epics. The genre of epics appears generally to be younger in origin than that of myths and apparently was linked—in subject matter and values—to the emergence of monarchy at the middle of the Early Dynastic Period. The works that have survived seem, however, all to be of later date. A single short epic tale, "Gilgamesh and Agga of Kish," is told in the style of primary epic. It deals with Gilgamesh's successful rebellion against his overlord and former benefactor, Agga of Kish. More in the style of romantic epic are the stories of "Enmerkar and the Lord of Aratta," "Enmerkar and Ensuhkeshdanna," and the "Lugalbanda epic," all of which have as heroes rulers of the 1st dynasty of Uruk (*c.* 3500 BC) and deal with wars between that city and the fabulous city of Aratta in the eastern highlands. Gilgamesh, also of that dynasty, figures as the hero of a variety of short tales;

some, such as "Gilgamesh and Huwawa" and "Gilgamesh and the Bull of Heaven" in romantic epic style, and others, such as "The Death of Gilgamesh" and "Gilgamesh, Enkidu and the Nether World," concern the inescapable fact of death and the character of afterlife.

A much later dynasty, which similarly inspired epic tales, was the dynasty of Akkad (c. 2334–c. 2154 BC). The quick rise of its founder Sargon from obscurity to fame and his victory over Lugalzaggesi of Uruk form the theme of several tales. The sudden eclipse of the Akkadian empire under Naramsin, attributed to that ruler's pride and the gods' retaliation, is the theme of "The Fall of Akkad." Akkadian epic tradition continues and gives focus to the Sumerian tales of Gilgamesh.

The Gilgamesh epic The Akkadian *Epic of Gilgamesh* seems to have been composed in old Babylonian times but was reworked by a certain Sin-liqi-unninni later in the 1st millennium BC. It tells how Gilgamesh, the young ruler of Uruk, drives his subjects so hard that they appeal to the gods for relief. The gods create a wild man, Enkidu, who at first lives with the animals in the desert but is lured away from them and becomes Gilgamesh's friend. Together they vanquish the terrifying Huwawa, set by Enlil to guard the cedar forest in the West, and when on their return the goddess of Uruk, Ishtar, falls in love with Gilgamesh, is jilted by him, and sends the dread "bull of heaven" to kill him, he and Enkidu manage to kill the bull. At this point, however, their fortunes change. Enlil, angered at the killing of Huwawa, causes Enkidu to fall ill and die, and Gilgamesh, inconsolable at the death of his friend and terrified at the realization that he himself must someday die sets out to find eternal life.

After many adventures he reaches an ancestor of his, Utnapishtim, to whom the gods have granted eternal life, but his case proves to be a unique one and so of no help to Gilgamesh. Utnapishtim was rewarded for having saved human and animal life at the time of the great flood. Eventually, just as Gilgamesh is ready to return home he is told about a plant that rejuvenates and makes old men children again. Gilgamesh finds it and begins his return journey. But as the day is warm, when he passes an inviting pool, he leaves his clothes and the plant on the shore and goes in for a swim. A serpent smells the plant, comes out of its hole and eats it. Thus Gilgamesh's quest comes to naught. Eternal life is beyond man's grasp. The Gilgamesh epic is perhaps the most moving work in Ancient Mesopotamian literature with its sharp contrast of values: the warrior's disdain of death and danger, which informs the early parts of the epic, and the haunting fear that drives Gilgamesh in the later parts.

Other Akkadian epics that deserve to be mentioned are the Etana epic, which tells how Etana, the first king, was carried up to heaven on the back of an eagle to obtain the plant of birth, so that his son could be born; and epic tales about Sargon of Akkad, one of which, the birth legend, tells of his abandonment in a casket on the river by his mother—much as the Hebrew Moses was abandoned —and his discovery by an orchardman, who raised him as his son. Another Sargon tale is "The King of Battle," which tells about conquests in Asia Minor to protect foreign trade. Naramsin is the central figure in another tale dealing with that king's pride and also relating the destructive invasions by barbarous foes. A late flowering of primary epic is the Assyrian Tukulti-Ninurta epic that deals with that king's wars with Babylonia. He reigned from 1245 to 1208 BC.

Other genres. In addition to the genres of myth and epic, ancient Mesopotamian literature comprises much else of note, which should be at least briefly touched upon. The genre of cult literature reaches its high point in **Cult literature** the Tammuz compositions; i.e., love songs and descriptive compositions accompanying the rite of the sacred marriage, and, often deeply moving, laments—narrative or purely lyrical—used in the yearly ritual of wailing for the dead god. Of different character, practical rather than literary, are cult texts meant as instructional guides, outlining the sequence and nature of ritual acts. The earliest known text of this type is from Sumer (c. 2000 BC), but the great majority of what is known is relatively late.

Outstanding among them is a detailed description of the great New Year festival in Babylon.

Hymns and prayers, sometimes meant for public, sometimes for private, worship may also be considered as cult texts. Among the hymns the superb poem in praise of the temple Eninnu in Girsu, known as Gudea's Cylinders A and B, must rank foremost. Among hymns to the gods, the great Sumerian hymn to Enlil stands out. Prayers, both Sumerian and Akkadian, are often remarkable in the intensity of religious feeling they convey. Another cult genre is that of lamentations for temples and cities. Here the "Lament for the Destruction of Ur" is the masterwork, unequalled for poignancy and power of expression.

It remains to mention the more secular genres of didactic and wisdom literature. Besides proverbs and fables, this genre has characteristic "disputation texts," serving as vehicles of evaluation of various elements in the cosmos or in society: summer and winter, copper and silver, shepherd and farmer, a father and his wayward son, and other opposing elements argue their respective merits. Sometimes—e.g., in disputes between schoolboys or between common scolds (those addicted to reprimand harshly) —sheer enjoyment of the slanging match seems to take over. The genre of juridical literature—i.e., extensive and varied collections of formulas for contracts, records of lawsuits, law codes, and other juridical works—is perhaps best represented by the famous Reform Texts of Urukagina (24th century BC) and the even more famous Code of Hammurabi (1792–1750 BC), both of which stand in a tradition of equity over against the common law.

Lastly, the genre of historical texts must be briefly mentioned. It may perhaps be thought of as including building and votive inscriptions, especially the Assyrian annalistic inscriptions of the 1st millennium BC, although these are commemoratively rather than historically oriented in the strict sense. Of truly historical works the earliest known example is the Sumerian king list composed around 2300 BC and chronicles that—though perhaps they are earlier in origin—appear fully developed in the 1st millennium BC. The most impressive example is the Babylonian Chronicle that presents a remarkably concise, factual, and unbiased account of contemporary events.

CONCLUSION

The wealth and the richness of ancient Mesopotamian literature makes it impossible to deal with it here in any great degree of detail. Nor can its works—even at best— be given in other than outline. It seems proper, however, that in conclusion at least one sample of its powers of expression should be quoted in translation. The lines below are from a lament for the dying god, whose mother is seeking for him in the desert as he speaks from the grave:

> I am not one who can answer my mother,
>   who cries for me in the desert,
> Who makes the cry for me echo in the desert,
> She will not be answered.
> I am not the grass, may not grow up (again) for her,
> I am not the waters, may not rise (again) for her,
> I am not the grass sprouting in the desert,
> I am not the new grass, growing up in the desert.
>   (From *Most Ancient Verse*; selected and translated by T. Jacobsen and J.A. Wilson, The University of Chicago Press, 1963, p. 29.)

BIBLIOGRAPHY. A. LEO OPPENHEIM, *Ancient Mesopotamia* (1964), provides a good general account of the cultural background. Reliable translations of most of the relevant texts may be found in J.B. PRITCHARD (ed.), *Ancient Near Eastern Texts Relating to the Old Testament*, 3rd ed. (1969). Special groups of texts, such as hymns and prayers, are covered in A. FALKENSTEIN and W. VON SODEN, *Sumerische und Akkadische Hymnen und Gebete* (1953); and in W.G. LAMBERT, *Babylonian Wisdom Literature* (1960). Both of these works have introductions dealing with the history of that particular branch of literature. T. JACOBSEN and J.A. WILSON, *Most Ancient Verse* (1963), seeks to render the poetic qualities of ancient passages. Interpretative works include: H. FRANKFORT *et al.*, *Before Philosophy* (1951); T. JACOBSEN, *Toward the Image of Tammuz*, ed. by W.L. MORAN (1970); and S.N. KRAMER, *Sumerian Mythology* (1944) and *The Sumerians* (1963).

(T.J.)

Mesozoa

In 1876 the name Mesozoa was proposed for dicyemids, a group of minute multicellular parasites that seem to represent a true "missing link" between the Protozoa and the Metazoa. There is no sign, in either the adult or embryonic stages of dicyemids, of the discrete systems (*e.g.*, muscular, reproductive, digestive) typical of metazoans. Although all dicyemid functions are carried out at the cellular level, as in protozoans, dicyemids are too complex to be colonial protozoans. The name Mesozoa and the concepts associated with it have persisted. Sometimes the term mesozoan is expanded to include another parasitic group, the orthonectids.

From *The Encyclopaedia of the Biological Sciences* by Peter Grey © 1961 by Litton Educational Publishing, Inc. Reprinted by permission of Van Nostrand Reinhold Co.

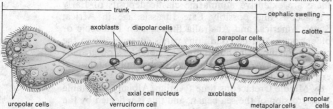

Young dicyemid.

General features. Mesozoans, minute, wormlike parasites of marine invertebrates, range from less than a millimetre to a few millimetres in length. Orthonectids, often considered mesozoans, occur as multinucleate ameboid masses (known as plasmodia) in the incubatory pouches of ophiuroids, such as brittle stars, as well as in the tissue spaces of diverse groups that include turbellarian, nemertean, and polychaete worms, and gastropod and bivalve mollusks. The plasmodia of orthonectids give rise to free-swimming sexual adults. Dicyemid mesozoans occur only in the renal chambers of cephalopods. A single, long reproductive cell, the axial cell, is surrounded by a single layer of ciliated somatic cells, those at the anterior end forming a sort of head (the calotte) by which the dicyemid clings to the renal tissue of its host.

In both the dicyemids and the orthonectids, the number and arrangement of cells is relatively constant for any given species. This definitive cell number is attained during embryonic development. Growth, therefore, consists of the enlargement and differentiation of existing cells. In both groups chromatin (the material that comprises chromosomes) elimination occurs during early cleavage divisions from the cell line that will give rise to somatic cells.

Both groups are very widely distributed wherever appropriate hosts occur in shallow bottom environments of the sea. They are not found in hosts in open sea environments, nor have they been found in hosts from tropical coral islands. In many regions dicyemids infect entire populations of bottom-dwelling cephalopods, such as squids and octopuses. On the other hand, orthonectids infect only a small percentage of their hosts in a given region. In orthonectids agametes (asexual reproductive cells), formed during the plasmodial stage, give rise to sexual adults that leave the host for a brief free-swimming period, during which the females are impregnated. The zygotes develop into ciliated larvae that infect new hosts, giving rise to new plasmodia. While in the host, the plasmodia pass through a period of asexual reproduction forming agametes before adults appear once more.

Dicyemids have a more complex life cycle, one that is not yet fully understood. Two reproductive phases occur in the cephalopod host. During a phase called the nematogen phase, agametes give rise to wormlike larvae similar to their parents. These nematogens remain in the same host, thus increasing the parasite population. In the next phase, known as the rhombogen phase, a few axoblasts give rise to minute organisms known as infusorigens; these are reduced hermaphroditic individuals that remain in the axial cell of the rhombogen and give rise to sperm and egg cells. The zygotes develop into ciliated infusoriforms, or swarm larvae, which escape from the parent rhombogen and from the cephalopod. Their fate is unknown.

Life cycle

In some species the first nematogens, infecting very young cephalopods, have three (or two) axial cells. These stem nematogens give rise to ordinary nematogens.

Phylogeny and evolution. Studies of orthonectids in 1969 revealed them to be more complex than formerly supposed. In addition to reproductive cells, they contain specialized internal contractile and supportive cells. These studies emphasized the uniqueness of orthonectids rather than any relationship with another group and led to the possible conclusion that resemblances between dicyemids and orthonectids are superficial, and that, rather than grouping them together in one phylum, the Mesozoa, they should perhaps be considered separate groups of uncertain systematic position.

The unique structure, complex life cycle, wide distribution, and host specificity of dicyemids indicate that the cephalopod-dicyemid association has been a very long one. In addition, some zoologists feel that the basic features of mesozoan morphology are primitive rather than derived. If these hypotheses are true, the Mesozoa are of great phylogenetic significance.

BIBLIOGRAPHY

General treatments of Mesozoa: L.H. HYMAN, *The Invertebrates,* vol. 1, *Protozoa Through Ctenophora* (1940); H.W. STUNKARD, "The Life-History and Systematic Relations of the Mesozoa," *Q. Rev. Biol.,* 29:230–244 (1954).

Orthonectida: C. JULIN, "Contribution à l'histoire des Mesozoaires: recherches sur l'organisation et le développement embryonnaire des Orthonectides," *Archs. Biol., Paris,* 3:1–54 (1882); E.N. KOZLOFF, *Morphology of the Orthonectid Rhopalura ophiocomae* (1969).

Dicyemida: B.H. MCCONNAUGHEY, "The Life Cycle of the Dicyemid Mesozoa," *Univ. Calif. Publs. Zool.,* 55:295–335 (1951); "Mesozoa," in *The Lower Metazoa: Comparative Biology and Phylogeny,* ed. by E.C. DOUGHERTY (1963); and with E.I. MCCONNAUGHEY, "Strange Life of the Dicyemid Mesozoans," *Sci. Mon.,* 79:277–284 (1954); H. NOUVEL, "Les Dicyémides," 2 pt., *Archs. Biol., Paris,* 58:59–220 (1947) and 59:147–223 (1948).

(B.H.McC.)

Mesozoic Era

The Mesozoic Era is the time period from about 225,-000,000 to 65,000,000 years ago, and it embraces the Triassic, Jurassic, and Cretaceous periods. The term Mesozoic was proposed in 1841 on the basis of the existing knowledge of fossils in Great Britain. The vast amount of data accumulated since that time has served to confirm the quality of this judgment, because the Mesozoic Era is characterized by many groups of organisms that are quite different from those in the Paleozoic and Cenozoic eras. It is now widely believed that continental drift (*q.v.*), the separation of the continents from a primordial landmass, was initiated during this era.

This article provides an overview of the rocks, life, and environments of Mesozoic time. For additional detail on these topics see TRIASSIC PERIOD; JURASSIC PERIOD; and CRETACEOUS PERIOD. See also EARTH, GEOLOGICAL HISTORY OF for the relation of Mesozoic events and those of other eras during earth history; and FOSSIL RECORD and STRATIGRAPHIC BOUNDARIES for relevant information on Mesozoic stratigraphy and paleontology.

MESOZOIC ROCKS

Mesozoic rocks are widespread in every continent, and marine deposits occupy progressively greater areas with each successive period. There were initially two major continental shield areas, Laurasia, including most of North America and Asia, and Gondwanaland, in the Southern Hemisphere. These were separated by the Tethys, an ocean that extended from the present central Atlantic region, through the Mediterranean and Middle East, to Indonesia and New Zealand. Marine deposits also were laid down throughout the era in a geosynclinal belt around the margins of the Pacific Ocean. Subsequently, the world paleogeography was complicated by the opening of the Atlantic and Indian oceans by sea-floor spreading (*q.v.*). The shield areas were emergent as land or were covered by continental or shallow marine sediments, and deeper water marine sediments were laid down in the

Tethys and circum-Pacific zone intermittently. In both cases, there is a widespread tendency for Mesozoic rocks to rest unconformably upon Paleozoic rocks that were deformed by the Hercynian orogeny (major episode of mountain building, which occurred during Carboniferous–Permian time).

Triassic deposits

Triassic marine deposits are substantially confined to the Tethyan and circum-Pacific zones, but they also occur in parts of the Arctic coastlands. The best known marine rocks are those around the Mediterranean, where they consist usually of thick limestones and dolomites with subordinate red beds, mainly of older Triassic age. The carbonates include massive reef limestones that contain corals and calcareous algae, and bedded limestones containing stromatolites (distinctive fossil algae deposits). The circum-Pacific marine Triassic deposits consist dominantly of clastic and volcanic sediments. Continental Triassic deposits are much more widespread and consist mainly of red shales, marls, and sandstones with subordinate conglomerates, and salt deposits (gypsum, anhydrite, and halite). Gray beds with coals also are known, as in some localities of Central Asia, the southern Appalachian Mountains, and Australia. In areas of central and southern Europe, marine limestones and dolomites are interbedded with typical red continental beds.

Jurassic deposits were laid down conformably on the Triassic almost everywhere, and they occupy approximately the same areas, but marine deposits are more widespread. Within the Tethyan zone of southern Europe, limestones and dolomites are predominant, as in the Triassic. In the early Jurassic, shallow-water reefoid and stromatolitic limestones are common; but toward the end of the period, deeper water, fine-grained, pelagic limestones composed of calcareous microplankton were laid down over wide areas. Of special interest are certain red nodular limestones, often with black iron manganese oxide incrustations, and layers of bedded chert. In northern Europe, the marine beds commence with the Rhaetic shales, sandstones, and limestones, now considered to be uppermost Triassic. They are followed by variable thicknesses of marine deposits in which terrigenous clastic sediments, namely, shales, siltstones, and sandstones, predominate. Generally, the more northerly the occurrence of the deposits, the greater is the proportion of terrigenous clastic sediments to biogenic and chemically precipitated rocks such as limestones. Of considerable economic importance and academic interest are the minette-type oolitic ironstones, which occur mainly in the Lower and Middle Jurassic. In the course of time the pattern of sedimentation changed; the area of marine deposition spread somewhat, as did the area covered by limestones; but at the close of the period, lagoonal deposits, including calcium sulphate salts, were laid down and continental sedimentation occurred over wide areas.

Sedimentation

The pattern of sedimentation in North America during the Jurassic is similar to the European. Calcareous deposits are more abundant in the south, in areas such as Mexico, the Gulf Coast, and New Mexico. Marine deposits in the western interior region of the United States are Middle Jurassic in age. Jurassic sedimentation in this region began and ended with continental clastic deposits. The Western Cordillera received thick clastic deposits, consisting primarily of volcanic material, in what was clearly an unstable geosynclinal belt. This type of sedimentation is known from Alaska to the Andes, in Japan and New Zealand, and elsewhere around the Pacific. Thick salt deposits that are presumed to be of Early or Middle Jurassic age are known from subsurface drilling in Arkansas and Louisiana.

Continental clastic deposits, including coal, are widespread throughout Asia, where marine deposits are confined mainly to the oceanic margins or the Tethyan zone, excepting northeast Siberia. Upper Jurassic marine limestones are relatively widespread, and important salt deposits of this age occur in the southern U.S.S.R. and the Middle East. Jurassic sediments of the southern continents are largely continental, but marine limestones and clastics occur on the east coast of Africa, western Madagascar, and the west coast of Australia.

In Early Cretaceous time the same broad patterns of Jurassic sedimentation persisted. Shallow-water reefoid and deeper water pelagic limestones were laid down in the Mediterranean countries and Middle East. Elsewhere in Europe, nonmarine sandstones and shales of Lower Cretaceous (Neocomian) age are widespread in northern Spain, southern England, and northern France and Germany; but marine clays are found farther north, from England to the Moscow region. In North America, marine deposits of the Early Cretaceous are confined to the Western Cordilleran region and parts of the Arctic; nonmarine deposits are known on the Atlantic seaboard, where they lie unconformably on much older rocks. The areas of nonmarine sedimentation extended considerably from Jurassic times. Besides large areas in Central Asia, there are extensive nonmarine clastic deposits of Early Cretaceous and possibly Late Jurassic age in Africa, South America, and Australia that rest on Paleozoic or older rocks. Marine conditions persisted generally in the circum-Pacific belt, but there are notable stratigraphic gaps, as in New Zealand, that signify that uplift and orogeny occurred.

Cretaceous deposits

By Middle Cretaceous time (Aptian/Albian), a notable transgression of the sea began, and this is reflected by the fact that in many parts of the world marine deposits of this age overlie continental deposits. This is the case, for example, in northern Europe, the western interior of North America, and the coastlands of West Africa, Brazil, and southern Australia. In Europe, the characteristic deposits of this age are greensands (rich in the green iron silicate mineral, glauconite), clay, and sandy rocks with a silica cement (gaize). The dominant deposits of the western Tethys region are still carbonates, and those of the circum-Pacific geosynclinal zone are clastic rocks.

Marine deposits of Late Cretaceous age cover a vastly greater area than do older Mesozoic rocks; they occur extensively, for example, over the old shield areas of northern Africa and the western interior of North America. Hardly anywhere are marine deposits of the earlier Cretaceous overlain by continental Upper Cretaceous. Chalk is an interesting variety of limestone that occurs widely in northern Europe and parts of southern and central United States. In its pure state chalk is composed largely of coccoliths, the minute calcareous plates of a group of planktonic algae, and it is uncemented and therefore soft and friable. The widespread ironstones and manganese beds of the Jurassic substantially gave way to extensive phosphorites (q.v.), deposits that are of great commercial importance in some of the Mediterranean countries. With respect to clay minerals, montmorillonite first becomes dominant in Mesozoic time, at least in the Northern Hemisphere. Within the Alpine fold belts of southern Europe, Upper Cretaceous deposits are marked by the sudden appearance of flysch sediments—alternations of sandstones and shales that are thought to signify deposition in rather deep troughs into which the sand was carried by density currents.

Toward the close of the Cretaceous, a return to continental conditions is indicated in many areas, either by a break in deposition, as in England, or by the presence of nonmarine, clastic sediments, as in the Rocky Mountain region. Continuous sequences of marine deposits from the Cretaceous to the Paleocene, the oldest unit of the Cenozoic Era, do occur in Denmark, the Pyrenees and a few other continental areas, and in many deep-sea cores.

<u>MESOZOIC LIFE</u>

The vertebrate terrestrial life of the Mesozoic Era was dominated by reptiles. Faunas changed considerably during the course of the era, however. In Triassic times, a common and widely distributed animal group was the labyrinthodonts, large clumsy amphibians with an aquatic mode of life. They suddenly became extinct at the end of the period. The more advanced toads and frogs, Order Anura, arose in Late Triassic times and continued to flourish. The oldest known salamander is Cretaceous in age.

Vertebrate groups

Amphibians had declined, as early cotylosaurs, "stem reptiles," developed during Late Carboniferous through Permian time. The cotylosaurs are considered to be the group from which major reptile lines became differentiated. In Permian time, forms leading to turtles, marine groups such as plesiosaurs and ichthyosaurs, mammal-like therapsids, and thecodonts could be defined. The thecodonts are limited to the Triassic and include small bipedal forms (*e.g.*, *Pseudosuchia*) and the crocodile-like, 20-foot-long phytosaurs. Thecodonts gave rise to such disparate groups as pterosaurs, birds, and dinosaurs. The dinosaurs first appeared in the Late Triassic, and they clearly are derived from thecodont ancestors. From small bipedal animals such as *Coelophysis* evolved the huge and spectacular creatures of the Jurassic. These include the herbivorous *Brontosaurus* and *Diplodocus* (Saurischia), and *Stegosaurus* and the carnivorous, bipedal *Allosaurus* (Saurischia). The best known carnivore of the Cretaceous was the huge saurischian *Tyrannosaurus*. Cretaceous dinosaurs were even more abundant and diversified than those of the Jurassic. They include large herbivores like *Iguanodon*, the armoured *Ankylosaurus*, and the horned *Triceratops*, together with the duckbill hadrosaurs and small, lightly built, bipedal forms as *Ornithomimus*. The sudden extinction of the flourishing Late Cretaceous dinosaur fauna is one of the major mysteries of paleontology.

The Mesozoic is also characterized by the existence of other interesting groups of reptiles that became extinct at or near the close of the era. The pterosaurs, capable of limited gliding flight, might have become extinct through competition with birds. These had evolved from reptiles by Cretaceous times as evidenced by *Archaeopteryx*, a primitive Jurassic bird with major reptilian characters. Even more characteristic of the Mesozoic are those reptiles that became well adapted to swimming in the sea, such as the nothosaurs (Triassic), placodonts (Triassic), ichthyosaurs (Triassic to Cretaceous), plesiosaurs (Jurassic to Cretaceous), and mosasaurs (Cretaceous), the last being huge marine lizards.

Therapsid reptiles are of especial interest and are best known from abundant fossil remains in the Permo/Triassic Karroo deposits of South Africa. In the Triassic they consist of diversified forms including dicynodonts, tritylodonts, and ictidosaurs. The last group shows an impressive evolutionary series culminating in animals that are virtually indistinguishable in bone structure from mammals; hence, they give a clear indication of the origin of modern mammals.

Mesozoic mammals belong to several extinct orders; all were of small size. Late Triassic groups were triconodonts (to Middle Cretaceous), docodonts (to latest Jurassic), and symmetrodonts (to Middle Cretaceous). To these were added pantotheres and multituberculates by Late Jurassic. The latter became extinct in Early Cenozoic time, but the pantotheres gave rise to marsupials, known from the Cretaceous of North America, and to small, primitive placentals that are found in the Cretaceous of North America and Mongolia.

Mesozoic marine vertebrates also include several important groups of fish. The most primitive of the bony fish, the chondrost fishes, represented today by the sturgeon, were dominant in Triassic times but declined in importance at the end of that period. They were replaced by the holost fishes, characterized by heavy rhombic scales. This group of fish ranged throughout the Mesozoic but declined in Late Cretaceous times; they are represented today by only a few species, such as the garpike of the Mississippi River. Their decline probably resulted from competition by the most advanced group, the teleost (bony) fishes, which arose from the holosteans in the Jurassic and became dominant in Late Cretaceous times. Other Mesozoic fish include crossopterygian fishes and sharks.

Inverte-
brate
groups The marine invertebrate faunas of the Mesozoic are of greater importance to stratigraphers than the vertebrate faunas. A progressive increase in diversity of invertebrates occurred throughout the era. Perhaps the best known, and certainly the most useful for stratigraphic correlation because of their rapid evolution, are the cephalopod mollusca with (usually) plane spiral, chambered shells known as ammonites. These are as characteristic of

Mesozoic faunas as the dinosaurs and, like them, the ammonites became extinct at the end of the Cretaceous. From a solitary family that survived the widespread extinction of invertebrates at the close of the Paleozoic Era, there evolved a highly diversified series of ammonites in Triassic time. The group barely survived a further period of extinction at the close of the Triassic and underwent another major phase of radiation in the Jurassic. Cretaceous ammonites include a variety of interesting forms with shells showing varying degrees of deviation from the plane spiral pattern (*e.g.*, *Scaphites*, *Baculites*, *Turrilites*). The total extinction of ammonites at the end of the Mesozoic Era is as great an enigma as the extinction of the Mesozoic reptile groups. The belemnites are another group of cephalopods that are quite characteristic of the Mesozoic; they also disappeared at the end of the Cretaceous.

Other important groups of mollusca are the bivalves (lamellibranchs) and gastropods. The bivalves became one of the dominant invertebrate groups from Triassic time onward. This is partly the result of the evolution of siphons, which allowed them to colonize a new ecological niche, namely, the muddy sediments of the sea floor. Among the numerous genera, *Gryphaea*, *Inoceramus*, *Spondylus*, *Trigonia*, *Pholadomya*, and the peculiar, coral-like rudists are especially characteristic of the era. The principal change among gastropods in the course of the Mesozoic was the rise in Late Cretaceous time of the siphonate order, Neogastropoda, many of which are carnivores.

Echinoderms are best represented by crinoids and echinoids. The former were abundant in shallow waters, and free-living, stalkless forms evolved later in the era. The early echinoids were of the more primitive, regular type; but Jurassic faunas included irregular, modern echinoids such as *Clypeus*. The heart urchins (*e.g.*, *Micraster*) are very characteristic of the Cretaceous. Brachiopods, though less dominant than in the Paleozoic, were much more abundant and varied than today; the most abundant are members of the Rhynchonellida and Terebratulida, two of the three surviving groups. Among the larger Arthropoda, abundant crustaceans left their record preserved both as exoskeletons and fossil tracks and burrows. Corals are represented by the still thriving Scleractinia, which originated in the Triassic. These reef builders occurred most abundantly in the Tethyan zone. The so-called ahermatypic forms, which can live in the deep sea, appear to have evolved by Late Jurassic time. Calcareous and siliceous sponges are also well represented in the fossil record.

The invertebrate microfaunas are represented by abundant foraminifera, radiolaria, and ostracods, all of which are of great value to oil companies in correlation studies. The nodosarid family of benthonic foraminifera was dominant throughout most of the era, together with the more complex Lituolacea in the Tethys. Appearing first in the Late Jurassic and expanding rapidly in the Cretaceous, planktonic foraminifera such as *Globigerina* are a notable component of Late Mesozoic pelagic deposits.

Although far less diverse than the marine faunas, Mesozoic invertebrates lived also in continental environments such as lakes and rivers. They include a few genera of bivalves, gastropods, and ostracods. The Triassic insect fauna seems modern in aspect because few now extinct orders survived the Permian. Grasshoppers, earwigs, flies, ants, bees, and wasps appeared before the Cretaceous. With regard to the plant kingdom, the Mesozoic may be called the age of Pteridophytes. This group comprises the ferns, the gymnosperm orders of cycads, ginkgos and conifers, and the angiosperms, which became well established by the end of the era. Cycadean plants, which were rare in Late Paleozoic and Early Triassic time, became common at the end of the Triassic, and the true Cycadales survived in reduced numbers to the present day. Conifers were widespread, and they provide most of the fossil logs that have been preserved as "petrified forests." Ginkgos, first abundant in Late Triassic, became particularly common in Arctic floras and are represented today by a solitary survivor, the maidenhair tree. A rich Paleozoic holdover Major
plant
groups flora of ferns and horsetails is also known in the Mesozoic fossil record. The most striking evolutionary event in the era was the sudden rise to dominance of the angiosperms, or flowering plants, in the Late Cretaceous. Their ancestry is obscure; the first undisputed record is in the Lower Cretaceous, but they must have evolved somewhat earlier in the era. With the rise of the angiosperms, land flora took on a modern aspect before the close of the Mesozoic.

For more primitive plants, the best record is preserved in marine deposits. The most primitive algae, the Cyanophyta, or blue greens, are represented by the wavy banding in limestones known as stromatolites. Lime-secreting red and green algae form an important component of many limestones in the Tethyan zone. Planktonic algae (diatoms and coccolithophorids) and dinoflagellates are also known. Many Late Jurassic and Cretaceous limestones are composed largely of coccoliths. Solution of siliceous diatoms, which appeared in the Jurassic, radiolarian skeletons, and the spicules of siliceous sponges, must have provided the major source for the bedded and nodular cherts that occur frequently in many younger Mesozoic rocks.

STRATIGRAPHIC CORRELATION OF MESOZOIC UNITS

The world standard for the correlation of Mesozoic strata is provided in the Table. The stages are based upon fossils found in marine deposits in classical European sections.

Stratigraphic Correlation of Mesozoic Units	
Maestrichtian	
Campanian	
Santonian	
Coniacian	
Turonian	
Cenomanian	
Albian	Cretaceous
Aptian	
Barremian	
Hauterivian	
Valanginian	
Berriasian	
Tithonian/Volgian	
Kimmeridgian	
Oxfordian	
Callovian	
Bathonian	
Bajocian	Jurassic
Aalenian	
Toarcian	
Pliensbachian	
Sinemurian	
Hettangian	
Rhaetian	
Norian	
Carnian	
Ladinian	Triassic
Anisian	
Scythian	

Though this is the generally accepted scheme, agreement on the stratigraphic boundaries (q.v.) is not universal. Some stratigraphers would include the Danian stage, here accepted as part of the Paleocene, in the Cretaceous. Precise correlation of the Tithonian and Volgian, which contain very different ammonite faunas, has not yet been achieved, and Berriasian ammonite faunas seem to show closer affinities to the Tithonian than to the Valanginian. A third topmost Jurassic stage, the Portlandian, has been widely used; but its lower boundary is somewhat higher in the ammonite sequence, and thus it affects the local definition of the Kimmeridgian. The Aalenian stage generally has not been recognized by British stratigraphers. There has been considerable difficulty in applying the scheme of stages for the Triassic in areas other than Europe.

The scheme given in the Table is based essentially on ammonite faunas, which provide by far the best means of correlation when they are available. Where ammonites are sparse or absent, recourse must be had to other groups. As far as marine deposits are concerned, Triassic pteriomorph bivalves, such as *Halobia, Daonella, Mono-*

tis, and *Rhaetavicula,* and the Jurassic and Cretaceous *Buchia* and *Inoceramus,* have proved useful. Belemnites, echinoids, and crinoids also have been used in the Cretaceous. In recent years much success has been obtained by correlating planktonic foraminifera of Cretaceous age, and oil companies in particular have used a variety of microfossils. Nonmarine deposits are much harder to correlate. A series of reptile zones has been established in the South African Karroo deposits, but vertebrates generally are much too scarce to be helpful. Pollen stratigraphy (*q.v.*) has been utilized with some success in recent years, but it does not always allow precise correlation. The same is true of attempting to correlate nonmarine bivalves.

MESOZOIC ENVIRONMENTS

At the beginning of the Mesozoic Era, the seas were at their most restricted; and more or less continuous marine transitions from the Permian were confined to very few areas, such as East Greenland, the Caucasus, the Salt Range of Pakistan, and parts of the circum-Pacific region. Subsequently, in later Triassic time, the seas spread widely over the Tethyan and circum-Pacific zones; but, except for a limited incursion of the Muschelkalk Sea in northern Europe and marginal marine incursions along the Arctic coastlands, the main continental-shield areas remained emergent. Thus, the shield areas were dry land or, perhaps, were covered by nonmarine or lagoonal sediments in some instances.

The marine transgression extended further in the Jurassic. In the early part of the period (and even in the latest Triassic) a shallow sea spread widely in northern and western Europe, and a marine gulf was established along the eastern side of Africa to Tanzania and Madagascar. There was also an extensive transgression in northeastern Siberia. In Middle Jurassic times, extensive parts of the western interior of North America were flooded, and shallow gulfs became established in western Australia. The Jurassic seas reached their maximum extent toward the close of the period; marine conditions prevailed continuously from the British Isles to European Russia and into the lands around the Gulf of Mexico. At the end of the Jurassic, however, a widespread regression set in. The sea retreated from much of northern and western Europe, from the western interior of North America, and also from most of northeastern Siberia.

The paleogeographic conditions of the Early Cretaceous resembled closely those of the latest Jurassic, but the seas began to transgress once more. By the middle of the period the seas reached for the first time coastlands of the South Atlantic, southern Australia, eastern India, and the eastern United States. In Late Cretaceous times the seas attained their maximum extent in the era, and the proportion of shield areas covered compares with that of the Early Paleozoic. The most spectacular changes took place in North America, where a wide seaway extending from the Arctic to the Gulf of Mexico split the subcontinent into two major landmasses, and in northern Africa, where the sea crossed the Sahara to establish a marine link between the Gulf of Guinea and the Mediterranean. Regression set in over large areas at the close of the period.

Although there is not an exact synchronism of major transgressions and regressions in all cases, the movements of sea level relative to the continents on a worldwide basis during the Mesozoic cannot be doubted.

If one accepts the abundant evidence favouring continental drift, then such drift must be taken into account in reconstructions of Mesozoic paleontology. Opinions differ as to when the major continental dispersal began. The evidence from the distribution of terrestrial animals, marine sediments along the margins of the southern continents, rock magnetism, and oceanography appears to favour a relatively late breakup, initiated no earlier than the Middle Jurassic. This would imply that in Early Mesozoic time the Atlantic and Indian oceans did not exist.

The evidence of orogeny and volcanism is consistent with this picture because both were more widespread and intense in the later Mesozoic. Volcanic activity was persistent throughout the era only in the circum-Pacific geosynclinal zone, where many basaltic and andesitic lavas

Continental drift

and tuffs are intercalated with clastic sediments, which themselves often have a significant volcanic component. During the Triassic, important eruptions of basalts took place in central Siberia, North Africa, and the northern Appalachians. In the Jurassic, the most important centres of volcanic activity in the shield areas were southern Africa, East Antarctica, and eastern Australia; Jurassic granites are known in West Africa, New England, and in parts of the circum-Pacific region. The vast flood basalts of southern Brazil and peninsular India are largely Cretaceous in age, as are widespread ultrabasic rocks in the western Tethys. Also belonging to the Cretaceous are the vast granite batholiths of the Andes, the western Cordillera of North America, and eastern Asia.

The Triassic and Early Jurassic generally are time periods of orogenic quiescence, but tectonic movements in geosynclinal and shield areas occurred in the Middle Jurassic. The most important orogenic phase in the Jurassic occurred at the close of the period, with events recorded in several continents. This heralded more intense disturbances, involving strong folding, thrusting, metamorphism, and intrusion in the Cretaceous Period throughout the circum-Pacific and Tethyan geosynclines.

Mesozoic climates
With respect to the evidence for climatic change, both rocks and fossils clearly indicate more equable conditions than exist today; polar ice caps were almost certainly absent. In consequence, Mesozoic floras and faunas tend to be cosmopolitan, with many of the same genera and species ranging from Greenland and Spitsbergen to Antarctica. In particular, the existence of large reptiles and reef corals in high latitudes of both hemispheres suggests relatively mild minimum temperatures. Major faunal realms existed, but it is by no means clear that they always relate to climate rather than to paleogeographic configurations and sedimentary facies. Research on oxygen isotopes in fossil shells has suggested the possibility of widespread temperature fluctuations in the Late Cretaceous, but this has yet to be confirmed by other evidence. Geochemical methods have added little to other evidence for the earlier Mesozoic.

Widespread aridity over the continents in Triassic time is suggested by extensive salt deposits and by fossil sand dunes (in South Africa). Ancient desert deposits also are known in the Jurassic of the western United States, and salt deposits in various parts of the Tethyan and adjacent regions indicate some aridity during this period. The northern continents at this time must have been more humid, as evidenced by coals and ironstones. There is no indication of extensive aridity during the Cretaceous.

BIBLIOGRAPHY. B. KUMMEL, *History of the Earth*, 2nd ed. (1970), a general, well-illustrated account of changing paleogeography and animal life on the whole globe; W.J. ARKELL, *Jurassic Geology of the World* (1956), a standard scholarly text on the Jurassic, indispensable for serious students of the subject; H. and G. TERMIER, *Atlas de paléogéographie* (1960), a series of paleographic maps for Phanerozoic time, with the Mesozoic well represented; W.B. HARLAND et al. (eds.), *The Fossil Record* (1967), essentially a piece of massive documentation by many specialists of the stratigraphical ranges of all important fossil groups; E.H. COLBERT, *Evolution of the Vertebrates*, 2nd ed. (1969), a general account of fossil vertebrates, easily assimilable by the non-specialist; BRITISH MUSEUM (NATURAL HISTORY), *British Mesozoic Fossils*, 3rd ed. (1967).

(A.H.)

Messiah and Messianic Movements

The term messianism, derived from the Hebrew word *mashiah* ("anointed") and denoting the Jewish religious concept of a person with a special mission from God, is used in a broad and at times very loose sense to refer to beliefs or theories regarding an eschatological (concerning the last times) improvement of the state of man or the world, and a final consummation of history.

NATURE AND SIGNIFICANCE

Origins. The term messiah has been applied to a variety of redeemer figures, and many movements with a markedly eschatological or utopian-revolutionary character or message have been termed messianic. Though messianic movements have occurred throughout the world, they seem to be especially characteristic of the Jewish and Christian traditions. Hence, not only the word messiah but also other terms relating to the messianic type of phenomena are derived from biblical religion and from the history of Jewish and Christian beliefs—*e.g.*, "prophetic," "millenarian," and "chiliastic" movements—the last two terms referring to a 1,000-year reign of Christ and his saints before the final end of history. Moreover, the scientific study of messianic beliefs and movements—originating, as it did, in the Western theological and academic tradition—was directed mainly to phenomena occurring either in Christian history or in cultures exposed to Western colonial, missionary, and modernizing influences. These Western origins of messianic terms and concepts give discussions of the subject an almost unavoidable Judeo-Christian slant. Hence, many present-day sociologists and anthropologists have attempted to develop a more neutral terminology—*e.g.*, nativistic movements, religious movements of liberty and salvation, renewal movements, revitalization movements, crisis cults—but many of these terms emphasize incidental and adventitious aspects of the phenomenon and miss its essential features.

Development of neutral terminology

Relationship of messianism to concepts of time. Basic to messianism is a certain relationship to the time dimension; the time process is expected to lead to a major change—or even to a final consummation—as a result of which a happier, better, or perfect state of things will take the place of the imperfect present. Intrinsic to messianism is the negative evaluation of the present. If the present is satisfactory and right, it need not be "fulfilled" and transcended, but rather perpetuated or renewed and rejuvenated in accordance with a pattern set by myth and ritual. Because, however, the present is viewed as unsatisfactory and blighted by suffering, death, sin, and other evils, it has to be changed and superseded by a new age. Such a new age may be conceived either as something utterly new or as a return to a past golden age. Messianism thus tends to develop in situations of stress, suffering, and frustration. It is also most conspicuous in cultures whose time concept permits an historic orientation; *i.e.*, instead of a constant pattern of cyclical returns, a repetition as in natural processes, there is a linear time process leading to a fulfillment and end that is possibly predestined. A certain historical dimension is thus an essential feature of the fully developed messianic complex.

Messianism as ideology and as movement. A distinction must be made between messianism as a complex of ideas, doctrines, hopes, and expectations on the one hand, and messianic movements on the other. Messianism is the potentiality of messianic movements; messianic movements are messianism in action. Even the "facts" of suffering and frustration require ideas and social symbolism before they can assume cultural shape and historical reality (*i.e.*, before they can appear, be expressed, or function as such in a particular time and culture). Conversely, beliefs and doctrines require a specific constellation of facts in order to pass from potentiality to actuality. The student of the subject is therefore faced with two distinct problems: (1) how do messianic ideas arise and how do they function in the culture and history of specific societies? and (2) what situations or events precipitate messianic movements—that is, turn a messianic ideology into an active social and historical movement? Related to these problems is the question of the relationship of the social and religious context to the role of the charismatic personality (one having spiritual power and influence) and messianic leader.

Messianic ideologies and movements are not necessarily centred on a messianic figure, though there is a tendency for such movements to personify the messianic ideal and to have a personal messiah play the central role in its realization. Very often messianic movements, envisaging a decisive improvement in the spiritual and practical affairs of man, are initiated by strong charismatic personalities. Messianic movements being, by definition, movements concerned with radical changes for the better (*e.g.*, salvation, redemption, liberation), they have played a significant role in the history of mankind. Before the modern secular age and in premodern societies (in which most cultural values have a religious sanction of one kind or another), messianism was one of the chief ideological and practical vehicles for radical cultural, social, political, or religious change.

MESSIAH AND MESSIANIC MOVEMENTS IN JUDAISM AND CHRISTIANITY

Judaism. *Biblical messianism and messianic movements.* In biblical Hebrew the adjective or noun *mashiah* is used of material objects (*e.g.*, the shield of Saul in II Sam. 1:21) as well as of consecrated persons, such as anointed priests (*e.g.*, Lev. 4:3) and kings (*e.g.*, Saul, in I Sam. 10:1; David, in I Sam. 16:13 and II Sam. 5:3; and Solomon, in I Kings 1:39). The latter are also called the Lord's anointed (*e.g.* II Sam. 1:14; Lam. 4:20), the title expressing the charismatic character and divine sanction of their office as well as the unique inviolability of their status (*e.g.*, I Sam. 26:8–11 and II Sam. 1:14). In usage during and after the Babylonian Exile (6th century BC) the term "anointed" could denote anyone with a special mission from God: prophets (*cf.* Isa. 61:1), the patriarchs (Abraham, Isaac, and Jacob), and even Gentile kings (*e.g.*, the 6th-century-BC founder of the Persian Empire, Cyrus II the Great, in Isa. 45:1). The Old Testament never speaks of an eschatological messiah—one inaugurating the last times—and even the "messianic" passages containing prophecies of a future golden age under an ideal king never use this term. Nevertheless, many modern scholars hold that Israelite messianism grew out of beliefs connected with kingship. Comparisons with the forms of divine or sacral kingship current among Near Eastern peoples (Egypt in particular) suggests that in Israel, too, kingship had a definitely sacral character. Though not in any sense divine, the anointed king of Israel would be called the "son of God," and messianic hopes and functions would be ascribed to him. Many prophecies and psalms (*e.g.*, Ps. 2) have been interpreted in this sense, and this alleged kingship ideology has been connected with the messianic doctrines of early Christianity. When the vicissitudes of actual reality and the careers of particular historic kings proved more and more disappointing, the messianic kingship ideology was projected onto the future. With the declining national fortunes of Israel, whose political kingdoms were conquered or even abolished by the great empires (Assyria, Babylonia, etc.), the notion developed of the eschatological messiah-king.

After the Babylonian Exile, and under the influence of apocalyptic literature—a type of literature that flourished from *c.* 2nd century BC–*c.* 2nd century AD and was concerned with the dramatic intervention of God into history in behalf of the elect—the prophetic vision of a future restoration and of the universal establishment of God's Kingdom became firmly associated with the ingathering of Israel under a scion of David's (king of United Israel, beginning his reign *c.* 1000 BC) house, one who would be the Lord's anointed. Hence the Hebrew word *mashiah* (*messias* in Greek, and messiah in English) came to mean the anointed one *par excellence*; *i.e.*, the ultimate redeemer and expected king of the Davidic line who would deliver Israel from foreign bondage and restore the glories of its golden age.

In Hellenistic Judaism. In the period of Seleucid (Syrian Greek dynasty ruling Palestine *c.* 200–165 BC) and later Roman and Byzantine (63 BC–AD 638) rule and oppression, the expectation of a personal messiah acquired increasing prominence and became the centre of a number of other eschatological concepts held by different groups in different combinations and with varying emphases. The Qumrān sect, a Jewish monastic group known in modern times for its preservation of the Dead Sea Scrolls, held a doctrine—found also in later Jewish sects—of a messianic pair: a priestly messiah of the House of Aaron (the brother of Moses) and a royal messiah of the House of David. This messianic detail, incidentally, shows that these "anointed ones" were not thought of as saviours—as in later Christian thought—but rather as ideal lead-

(margin note: Emergence of Davidic messianic hopes)

ers presiding over an ideal, divinely-willed, and "messianic" socioreligious order. The "son of David" messianism, with its political implications, was overshadowed by apocalyptic notions of a more mystical and mythological character. Thus it was believed that a heavenly being called the "son of man" (the term is derived from Daniel 7:13) would descend to save his people (*e.g.*, as in the apocryphal books of Enoch). The messianic ferment of the period, attested by contemporary Jewish-Hellenistic literature, is also vividly reflected in the New Testament.

The destruction of the Temple at Jerusalem by the Romans (AD 70), exile, persecution, and suffering only intensified Jewish messianism, which continued to develop theoretically in theological and semimythological speculations and to express itself practically in messianic movements. In popular apocalyptic literature another messianic figure gained some prominence: the warrior-messiah of the House of Joseph (or Ephraim) who would precede the triumphant messiah of the House of David—but would himself fall in the battle against Gog and Magog, two legendary powers under Satan and opposed to the people of God (Ezek. 38:2; Rev. 20:8). The notion seems to have developed toward the end of the 2nd century, after the failure of the last revolt against the Romans (AD 132–135), led by Bar Kokhba, who was hailed as the messiah, but it is connected with a more basic notion of apocalyptic messianism; that is, the belief that the messianic advent is preceded by suffering and catastrophe. In some versions of apocalyptic messianism, the notion of a messianic age merges with that of an end of days and last judgment: the "new heaven and new earth" are ushered in amid destruction and catastrophe.

(margin note: Apocalyptic messianism)

In medieval and modern Judaism. Messianic faith tended to develop into mass enthusiasm, frequently fed by calculations based on the Book of Daniel and other biblical passages. Almost every generation had its messianic precursors and pretenders; *e.g.*, Abū 'Īsā al-Iṣfahānī and his disciple Yudghan in 8th-century and David Alroy in 12th-century Persia; the propagandists of the messianic agitation in the Jewries of western Europe in the 11th and 12th centuries; and—perhaps the most notorious of all—the 17th-century pseudomessiah Shabbetai Tzevi (Sabbatai Zevi) of Smyrna. Belief in, and fervent expectation of, the messiah became firmly established tenets of Judaism and are included among the great Jewish medieval philosopher Maimonides' Thirteen Articles of Faith. There was much variety in the elaboration of the doctrine—from the early apocalyptic visionaries and later Kabbalistic (Jewish esoteric) mystics at one end of the scale to the rationalist theologians on the other. The latter (including Maimonides) emphasized the unmiraculous nature of the messianic age.

Modernist movements in Judaism tended to maintain the traditional faith in an ultimately redeemed world and a messianic future for mankind, without insisting on a personal messiah figure. Judaism undoubtedly owes its survival, to a considerable extent, to its steadfast faith in the messianic promise and future. Jewish messianism, in spite of its spiritual and mystical connotations, never relinquished its basically this-worldly orientation and its understanding of the messianic order in historical, social, and political terms. Hence, many writers consider the participation of Jews in so many secular reform, liberation, and revolutionary movements (both political and social) as a secularized version of traditional Jewish messianism. Similarly, the ideology of Zionism, as a movement for Jewish national emancipation and liberation, is not devoid of messianic features.

Christianity. *Messianism and messianic movements in the New Testament period.* The preaching and ministry of Jesus of Nazareth and the activities of his followers in the 1st century AD can be properly understood only in the context of contemporaneous Jewish messianic and eschatological beliefs. Though the precise nature of Jesus' beliefs about himself and about the nature of the "messianic" task that he attributed to himself are still a matter of scholarly controversy, there is little doubt that already at an early date his followers saw in him the promised "anointed one" (Greek *christos,* whence the English

Christ) of the Lord, the son of David. This view is evident in the Gospel accounts that attempt to trace the ancestry of Jesus back to David, evidently for the purpose of legitimizing his messianic status. According to Luke 2:11 his messiahship was also proclaimed by angels at his birth. Jesus himself seems to have rejected the term—possibly because of its political implications—in favour of other eschatological titles (*e.g.*, the "Son of Man"), but the early community of his followers, believing, as they did, in his Resurrection after the crucifixion, evidently held this term to be expressive more than any other of the role and function that they attributed to their master and "Lord" (Greek *kyrios*). In due course the title ("Jesus, the Christ") became synonymous with the proper name, and the word Christ was used by believers as the name of the risen Jesus (*cf.* Gal. 1:6; Heb. 9:11).

With the adoption of the Greek word "Christ" by the church of the Gentiles (non-Jewish believers), the nationalist and political implications of the term "messiah" vanished altogether in Christianity, and the "Son of David" and the "Son of Man" motifs, to which subsequently was added that of the "suffering Servant" (Isa. 52–53), could merge in a politically neutral and religiously original messianic conception. Subsequently, the doctrine of the messiahship of Jesus (*i.e.*, Christology) also had to take into account other features of evolving Christian dogma (the Messiah as the Son of God; the Trinity, of God the Father, Son, and Holy Spirit; the incarnation of the Word), and thus came to assert that Jesus as the Messiah, Saviour, and Redeemer was essentially divine. In due course the concept of salvation was radically spiritualized, and the Messiah, through his sacrificial death, was viewed as having delivered man from his bondage to sin and having restored him to communion with God. Meanwhile, Christians asserted that the present world order would provisionally continue until the Second Coming (the Parousia) of Christ in power and glory to judge the living and the dead.

The early Christians held this Second Coming to be imminent, but as time went on this particular expectation shifted to the eschatological horizon. Some early Christian circles also believed that, after his return, Christ would reign on earth for 1,000 years (*cf.* Rev. 20:1–5). This belief easily combined with that in a fifth kingdom (*cf.* Dan. 2:44)—*i.e.*, the Kingdom of Christ following the four empires (Assyrian, Persian, Greek, and Roman) of this world. (It was from this belief that the Fifth Monarchy Men, an extreme English Puritan sect of the middle of the 17th century, derived their name.) Emphasis on the expected Second Coming introduced an element of messianic unrest in addition to questioning the validity of the present order; it was soon repudiated by the church as "unspiritual," since it envisaged a messianic kingdom upon earth—rather in the manner of the Jews—instead of a heavenly kingdom.

In early Christianity. Belief in the Second Coming of Christ and the establishment of his reign upon earth continued to exist as an undercurrent known as millenarianism or chiliasm (from Latin *millenarias* and Greek *chilioi*, "a thousand"), and occasionally came to the surface in sectarian, revolutionary, or heretical movements. The heretical element, though not inherent in millenarianism as such, resided in the tendency of radical religious or social criticism to use chiliast-messianic terminology when such criticism propagated the notion that the present rulers—and even the very forms—of church and state would be superseded by a perfect order.

It is necessary, therefore, to distinguish between early Christian and later, post-4th-century, messianism. Original Christianity was a messianic movement from its very beginning, and the millenarianism of the early Christians was an extension of their belief in the imminent Parousia, or Second Coming. Later medieval chiliasm by definition implied disappointment with what was supposed to be an already redeemed world, and the eager expectation of the passing away of the present order. The difference is due to an inner, theologico-religious development on the one hand, and an outer, politico-religious event on the other. The fact that the Second Coming had not taken place

caused the gradual liquidation of imminent messianism. The emphasis was placed on the Saviour who had come and redeemed the world from sin, rather than on his final Parousia. The granting of toleration to Christianity by the Roman emperor Constantine the Great (died 337), and its becoming subsequently the religion of the Roman Empire, heralded a development in which the church became an ally of the present order rather than the harbinger of its passing away.

In medieval and modern Christianity. The speculations of the 12th-century Italian theologian Joachim of Fiore, which evisaged the imminent supersession of the present age (the second age of the world, the dispensation of the Son, which had replaced the first age, of the Father) and church by the age of the Holy Spirit and by a "spiritual church," exerted considerable influence on subsequent messianic movements. These increased in the 15th century and in the Reformation and post-Reformation periods. The extreme wing of the Bohemian Hussite movement, known as the Taborites, sought to establish the Kingdom of God by force of arms. The left-wing Protestant Anabaptists as well as the Bohemian and Moravian Brethren were millenarians. The great Peasants' War in Germany (1524–25), in which the radical reformer Thomas Müntzer and the radical Zwickau prophets took a leading part, and the Anabaptist "Kingdom of God" in the German city of Munster (1534–35)—ruled over by the fanatical John of Leiden—are examples of millenarian-apocalyptic movements or of social movements with a messianic dimension.

In England, the Independents (those who separated themselves from the Church of England) thought of ushering in the Kingdom of God, and groups such as the Fifth Monarchy Men believed that revolution was necessary to prepare the way for the reign of Christ and his saints. The revolutionary Puritan leader Oliver Cromwell's (1599–1658) sober common sense and his dissolution of the so-called Parliament of Saints prevented apocalyptic enthusiasm from dominating the Commonwealth. The millenarian element also was strong in 17th- and 18th-century German Pietism, and it played a major role in the doctrines of many sects that arose in the 19th century in the United States and Great Britain (*e.g.*, Irvingites, Mormons, Adventists, Jehovah's Witnesses, Christadelphians, and others). Many of these sects, however, are more correctly described as entertaining messianic expectations than as actual messianic movements.

Secular movements. Western civilization, even in its modern secularized forms, is heir to a long tradition of Christian patterns of thought and sensibility. Thus, it is not surprising that many movements of social reform as well as ideologies regarding an ideal future should bear traces—conscious or unconscious—of Christian influence. Both the 18th- and 19th-century Enlightenment and the Romantic versions of the idea of the progress of humanity to an ideal state of peace and harmony betray their descent from messianic-millenarian beliefs. The 18th-century German philosopher Immanuel Kant, when speaking of the ideal state of eternal peace, describes this concept as a "philosophical chiliasm." The indebtedness of presocialist, utopian thinkers—such as the French social reformer Henri de Saint-Simon, the English reformer Robert Owen, and the French reformer Charles Fourier—to Christian millenarianism was recognized by Karl Marx and Friedrich Engels, who, in their *Communist Manifesto* (1848), contemptuously referred to the utopias of these writers as "duodecimo editions of the New Jerusalem." Some early socialist movements, including Christian socialism, exhibited messianic features. Marxist Communism, in spite of its explicit atheism and dogmatic materialism, has a markedly messianic structure and message. Some of the analogies with traditional Christian eschatology have been described, in a slightly ironical vein, by the English philosopher Bertrand Russell, who contends that Marx adapted the Jewish messianic pattern of history to socialism in the same way that the philosopher-theologian St. Augustine (AD 354–430) adapted it to Christianity. According to Russell, the materialistic dialectic that governs historical development

Marginal notes (left column):

Messianic conceptions of Jesus

The Second Coming of Christ

Marginal notes (right column):

Reformation messianic movements

Analogies of Marxist Communism with Christian messianism

corresponds—in the Marxist scheme—to the biblical God, the proletariat to the elect, the Communist Party to the church, the revolution to the Second Coming, and the Communist commonwealth to the millennium.

Whether or not Socialism and Communism, as well as certain national liberation movements, are described as secularized messianism, pseudomessianism, "substitute" messianism, and the like, is partly a matter of semantics, partly an attempt to use evaluative instead of descriptive language. The differences between secular ideologies and traditional messianic expectations are obvious. The similarities are founded on actual historic contacts and derivation (as in the history of reform and revolutionary movements in the West as well as of liberation movements in countries colonized by the West), and also on the fact that they are variations of the same social dynamisms and of a basic myth, expressing in powerful imagery certain elemental human experiences and aspirations.

MESSIANIC MOVEMENTS IN OTHER RELIGIONS

Primitive religions. Messianic movements have occurred in many primitive societies all over the world. Most of the movements studied and described in scholarly literature arose in societies that had been exposed to contact with the white, or Western, man. This presence frequently had traumatizing and disintegrating effects on many levels of primitive society (economic, cultural, religious), creating new tensions, pressures, deprivations, and frustrations. The factors contributing to this situation were not only the political and economic aspects of Western colonization but also the disintegration of traditional cultural values and religious symbols by the Christian missionaries who formed, as it were, part of the colonial "establishment." Hence, many primitive messianic movements—even when antiwhite and anticolonialist—exhibit markedly Christian features both in the details of their symbolism as well as in their overall messianic ideology. Some messianic movements (e.g., that of Simon Kimbangy in the former Belgian Congo from 1921, or that of Isaiah Shembe from 1911, among the South African Bantu, as also several movements in Brazil), in fact, appeared outwardly as Christian revivalist sects with an eschatological character. The movement of Simon Kimbangy has been admitted to the World Council of Churches as a member.

Nativistic messianic movements

A variety of names has been applied to these movements that emphasize various messianic characteristics. "Nativistic" movements expect salvation from a revival of native values and customs and a rejection of everything alien; e.g., many of the North American Indian movements from the 17th century on, including the Pueblo Indian Revolt led by Popé in 1680; the anonymous Delaware prophet (1762) and Pontiac; the religious revival and politico-military revolt led by Tenskwatawa and Tecumseh in 1807; the Ghost Dance outbreaks of 1870 and subsequent years among Southwestern and Plains Indians. The many messianic movements in Melanesia focussing on the arrival—in ships or airplanes—of "cargo" (i.e., the coveted wealth and riches that symbolize power, well-being, and salvation) are generally referred to as cargo cults. Some anthropologists speak of "revitalization movements," whereas others emphasize the connection between acculturation and primitive messianic movements. Since it is not acculturation as such that produces messianism but the crises and dislocations caused by certain forms of culture contact, many scholars now prefer the more neutral and objective term "crisis cults." Since many movements are started or propagated by the activity and preaching of prophet-like leaders, they are also spoken of as "prophetic movements."

There is a tendency among modern anthropologists to consider primitive messianisms as forms of protonationalism in non-European and premodern societies. Though Christian influence and Christian symbols often play a major role in the crystallization of messianic ideologies, they are by no means their only source. The ideological starting point of a messianic movement can be supplied by native traditions and mythologies, by Christian ideas, or by motives that are born under the pressure or circum-

stance. (For a fuller discussion of these various movements, see TRIBAL RELIGIOUS MOVEMENTS, NEW.)

Islām and Zoroastrianism. Islām is not a messianic religion and has no room for a saviour-messiah. Nevertheless, there gradually developed—and probably under Christian influence—the notion of an eschatological restorer of the faith, identified as a descendant of the Prophet or as the returning 'Isā (i.e., Jesus). He is usually referred to as the mahdī; i.e., the "[divinely] guided one." In Sunnī (traditional) Islām the whole subject is one of folklore rather than of dogmatic theology, though all orthodox Muslims believe in the coming of a final restorer of the faith. In times of crisis and of political or religious ferment, mahdistic expectations have increased and have given rise to many self-styled mahdīs, the best known of all being Muḥammad Aḥmad, the Mahdī of Sudan, who raised a revolt against the Egyptian administration in 1881 and after several spectacular victories established the mahdist state that existed until defeated by the English military leader Kitchener at Omdurman (Sudan) in 1898. In the Islāmic Shī'ah sect (which holds a belief in the transference of spiritual leadership through the family of 'Ali, Muḥammad's cousin and son-in-law), the doctrine of the mahdī is an essential part of the creed. Among the Twelvers, the main Shī'ah group, the expected mahdī is believed to be the hidden 12th imām, or religious leader, who will reappear from his place of occultation. The notion of a mahdī also played a role in the foundation of new religions or Shī'ah sects—e.g., the belief of the Druzes that the Egyptian caliph of the Fāṭimid dynasty al-Ḥākim (reigned 996–1021), who is thought to be the last prophet and divine incarnation, would return at the end of days (1,000 years after his appearance at the end of the 9th century AD) to establish his rule over the world. Other Islāmic-based messianic figures include the founder of the Indian Ahmadiya sect, Mirza Ghulam Ahmad, who in the late 19th century declared himself to be the Christ and the Mahdī; and the founder of the religion that subsequently became known as Bahā'ism, the Iranian Mirzā 'Alī Moḥammad of Shīrāz, who proclaimed himself in 1844 to be the Bāb ("gate") on the 1,000th anniversary of the disappearance of the 12th imām.

The role of the mahdī

Zoroastrianism is a religion with a thoroughly eschatological orientation: for it world history is a battlefield on which the forces of light and good fight the powers of darkness and evil. Though the notion of a personal saviour figure is not essential to the Zoroastrian system, it did nevertheless arise. The Iranian prophet Zoroaster's ministry (6th century BC) is said to have opened the last of the history of the world's four periods of 3,000 years each. He is followed, at intervals of 1,000 years, by three "saviours," considered to be posthumous sons of Zoroaster. The last of these, the soshyans (or saoshyant), will appear at the end of days, and God will entrust to him the task of the final rehabilitation of the world and the resurrection of the dead.

Religions of the East. Hinduism and Buddhism, unlike Zoroastrianism, lack historical and eschatological orientation. Certain "messianic" elements, however, are recognizable. The Hindu belief in a progressive deterioration of the world cycles and in the saving manifestations of the divine at the critical moments is a case in point. Yet it would be a misrepresentation of the facts to describe the expected return of the god Viṣṇu (Vishnu) at the end of the present cycle in his tenth avatāra ("incarnation"), Kalkin, as a messianic hope. In Mahāyāna (the Greater Vehicle) Buddhism the figure of the bodhisattva (future Buddha) Maitreya has a certain messianic quality: Maitreya will ultimately descend from his present abode in one of the heavens and bring the faithful to paradise. Some scholars believe that Zoroastrian eschatology may have influenced Buddhist Maitreya beliefs. A great many insurrections and peasant revolts in China had religious-sectarian and eschatological overtones. In the best known of these politico-religious movements, the Taiping (Great Peace) Rebellion of 1851–64, which was led by Hung Hsiu-ch'üan, Christian influence and messianic elements are obvious.

TYPES AND FUNCTIONS OF MESSIANISM

The preceding survey of messianic beliefs and movements indicates that they are not amenable to hard-and-fast classifications. Nevertheless, it should be possible to point out several major features and types. There is a distinction—as noted before—between eschatological beliefs and doctrines, and messianic movements. The latter need not arise even where the former exists of old.

Restorative and future oriented. The messianic ideal, on the one hand, may be the return to an original state of bliss that has been forfeited for one reason or another and the restoration to a pristine perfection (the Paradise Lost–Paradise Regained theme). Connected with this notion is the idea of the messiah as a *returning* saviour: the Second Coming of Christ; the reappearing *imām*; the awakening and return of the sleeping monarch or hidden emperor of many legends (*e.g.,* King Arthur or Frederick Barbarossa in medieval Europe and King David in some Jewish legends); the returning culture hero or the returning ancestor spirits, as in the North American Ghost Dance movements. On the other hand, there is the idea of the messianic future as a radically new state of being, the like of which has never been before. This viewpoint is that of the utopian-revolutionary form of messianism ("a new heaven and a new earth"), and it tends to be present, at least to some extent, even in essentially restorative ideologies and movements. The expectation of a radically new state of being often expresses itself in antitraditional and antinomian (against divine or moral law) behaviour: the destruction of traditional symbols or cult objects and the transgression of traditional laws and taboos signify that the old things have passed away and that a new era of freedom has dawned. Thus, in Christianity the old (Mosaic) Law, according to St. Paul, is fulfilled in Christ; in Judaism the 17th-century messiah Shabbetai Tzevi solemnly broke the prohibitions of the Judaic law in his mystical rituals; in many Melanesian cargo cults there was destruction of cult objects; and the North American Ojibwa threw away their sacred medicine bundles on the shores of Lake Superior. Conversely, many movements are extremely conservative and hold the messianic advent to be conditional on strict traditional observance, ascetic rigour, and penitential discipline: they are hypernomian (excessively legalistic) rather than antinomian. There is, very often, a conflict between conservative and revolutionary tendencies in many messianic movements.

Eschatological and reformative. The role and function of the messianic leader depends on a variety of sociocultural and individual factors. Many messianic movements have no messiahs at all, only prophets and precursors who announce the impending salvation and give instructions how to prepare for it. These prophets may be of the eschatological type, predicting a cosmic catastrophe and subsequent mighty deeds of salvation, or they may be of the moral and reforming type, exhorting their followers to qualify for salvation by adhering to strict codes of belief and behaviour. The 16th-century radical reformers Thomas Müntzer and the Zwickau prophets considered themselves prophets and apostles only; the leader of the Münster prophets, John of Leiden, however, considered himself a messianic king; the English Quaker James Nayler entered Bristol in 1656 to the shouts of "Hosannah to the Son of David" from a crowd of enthusiastic followers. Similarly, leaders of many primitive messianic cults have claimed to be divine.

Not all millenarian sects are founded by prophetic, visionary, inspired, or illuminate enthusiasts. Some groups are extremely "rationalist" in their approach; their messianic expectations are based not on mystical experiences but on their interpretation of Holy Scripture. Many adventist and millenarian sects (*e.g.,* the Christadelphians, Jehovah's Witnesses) are of this kind. A very literalist and "rational" exegesis (interpretation) of prophecies (*e.g.,* the statements in the books of Daniel and Revelation) provides the leader of such groups and sects with the date and details of the expected messianic advent. The understanding of prophecy in the literalistic sense also implies that the course of history is strictly predetermined and that the messianic hour is fixed and can therefore be computed.

Active and passive messianisms. Closely related to the above distinction is that between active and passive messianism. Passive messianism holds the end to be preordained. The believers do not make the revolution but prepare for its advent. On the active end of the scale are the aggressive and militant movements that believe themselves called to be instrumental in ushering in the new order. In many cases the activity is not of the military-revolutionary but rather of the ritual-magical type. The believers engage in cultic or other preparatory (*e.g.,* penitential) activities in order to hasten the advent or to prove that they are worthy of it—*e.g.,* the Jewish movement that centred on Shabbetai Tzevi, the North American Ghost Dance, and the Melanesian cargo cults. Some millenarian groups are very outspoken in their rejection of the present order and refuse to cooperate with it, but they desist from active steps to establish the Kingdom, as the latter will be established by God himself in his own time.

Immediate and distant messianisms. Messianic movements imply the imminent occurrence of some decisive event. They have therefore been called short-range messianisms. Long-range messianism, on the other hand, is a matter of beliefs and doctrines rather than of ferment and agitation; the expected advent is a dim and often colourless dogma on a far-away horizon rather than the life-giving power of a dynamic movement. Short-range messianisms may turn into long-range beliefs as a result of initial failure and disappointment. When the expected event has failed to materialize at the appointed time or the messianic promises have not been fulfilled, then the messianic date may be postponed or the present time declared to be an interim period pending the final consummation.

Other messianic types. Messianisms can also be distinguished according to the contents of their expectations. Mention has already been made of the distinction between restorative and innovative messianisms, as well as of the dialectical relationship between catastrophic and messianic redemption. In Jewish eschatology, for example, the advent of the messiah is preceded by a period of terrible suffering and tribulation, the so-called "birth pangs of the messianic age"; and in Christian eschatology the final consummation of history is preceded by the rule of the Antichrist. Messianism may be particular or universal, or exhibit different combinations of these two characteristics. Most messianisms tend to be particularistic and exclusive, at least in the sense of distinguishing between the elect who accept the messianic message or who otherwise qualify, and who hence will be saved, and the others who do not, and who will be lost. The community of the saved may be identical with a particular and ascriptively defined group (people, race) or part thereof, or with an electively defined part of mankind.

Messianism also can broaden its scope beyond a particular group and even mankind so as to embrace the whole cosmos. The messianic era is then described as one of cosmic rejuvenation and perfection. Very often this element is so strong that the new reality can no longer be described in ordinary language and in categories taken from historical experience. The new reality is of a mythological and symbolic order, and its inauguration presupposes the passing away or even cataclysmic annihilation of the old order. The transition from historical to mythological symbolism can be made in many different ways, and messianic movements exhibit great variety in the forms of interrelationship between history and myth. Particular historical and geographical symbols can become "mythologized" and universalized (*e.g.,* the "New Jerusalem" or the heavenly Jerusalem in Christian symbolism) and, conversely, universal symbols—such as those exhibited in Christianity—can be reinterpreted in a particularistic fashion (*e.g.,* "Jesus" or "Christ" in some African movements and sects).

Related to, though not identical with, the myth-history differentiation (see above *Relationship of messianism to concepts of time*) is that between politico-social and spiritual messianism. Predominantly historical messianisms

(margin notes:)
The messianic ideal as restorative

Millenarian approaches

Exclusive and inclusive messianisms

tend to focus on social and political hopes; these, in their turn, may become partly or wholly spiritualized. The issue played a prominent role in medieval Christian-Jewish polemics. Christian authors accused the Jews of a gross, carnal, and materialistic understanding of the messianic prophecies. The Jews considered the accusation as a compliment, believing that whatever the spiritual, cosmic, or inner aspects of salvation, it had to be vindicated primarily on the concrete historical level of national, social, and political realities. Where spiritual deliverance becomes altogether detached from social and political utopianism, it is doubtful whether the term messianism can still be legitimately applied, as the phenomena concerned belong to a different type of doctrine of salvation.

Interpretation. Although messianic movements are, almost by definition, doomed to failure, not all of them dissolve completely. Reinterpretation or spiritualization of the original message often enables a movement to survive apparent failure. The study of messianic movements, therefore, has to pay attention not only to the causal character of their origins and the dynamics of their development and survival but also to their capacity for transformation and survival. From a sociological point of view it has been argued that messianic movements, even where they appear to have failed, have had an integrative function in situations of social stress and cultural change. Thus, many primitive messianisms have been interpreted as connecting links between prepolitical and political activity; *i.e.*, from premodern religious revolt to modern revolutionary movement. Whether messianic movements play an integrative or, to the contrary, an impairing or nonadaptive role in society depends on a variety of factors as well as on a variety of criteria of interpretation, and not necessarily on the nature of the messianic message as such. The fact that messianic doctrines and beliefs exist, that messianic movements arise, and that the messianic hope is projected on individual messiah figures, seems to testify to some basic human predispositions, among which are orientation to the time process, capacity to negate the present but not to be crushed by this negation, ability to "hope" (*i.e.*, to envisage a future that is congruous with the ideals and values that the human mind can project), and the faculty of projecting these orientations, hopes, and values in mythical symbols.

BIBLIOGRAPHY

General: W.D. WALLIS, *Messiahs: Their Role in Civilization* (1943); Y. TALMON, "Millenarian Movements," *European Journal of Sociology*, 7:159–200 (1966), an excellent critical survey of the major modern studies on messianic movements; W. LA BARRE, "Materials for a History of Studies of Crisis Cults: A Bibliographical Essay," *Current Anthropology*, 12:3–44 (1971), a recent survey, with full bibliography.

Jewish and Christian Messianism: H. GRESSMANN, *Der Messias* (1929); S.O.P. MOWINCKEL, *Han som kommer* (1951; Eng. trans., *He That Cometh*, 1956); A. BENTZEN, *Messias-Moses Redivivus-Menschensohn* (1948; Eng. trans., *King and Messiah*, 1955); R.J. ZWI WERBLOWSKY, "Messianism in Jewish History," *Journal of World History*, 11:30–45 (1968), bibliography; ALBERT SCHWEITZER, *Von Reimarus zu Wrede* (1906; Eng. trans., *The Quest of the Historical Jesus: A Critical Study of Its Progress from Reimarus to Wrede*, 1910; 3rd ed., 1954); A.E.J. RAWLINSON, *The New Testament Doctrine of the Christ* (1926); N.R.C. COHN, *The Pursuit of the Millennium*, 2nd ed. (1961; rev. paperback ed., 1970); W. NIGG, *Das ewige Reich, Geschichte einer Sehnsucht und einer Enttäuschung* (1944).

Others: E. ABEGG, *Der Messiasglaube in Indien und Iran* (1928); D.B. MACDONALD, "al-Mahdī," in the *Encyclopaedia of Islam*, vol. 3 (1936), full bibliography; V.Y. SHIH, "Some Chinese Rebel Ideologies," *T'oung Pao*, 44:150–226 (1956); J.L. TALMON, *Political Messianism* (1960).

(R.J.Z.W.)

Metabolism

Metabolism is a term that embraces all of the chemical changes that occur in the cells of living organisms, enabling them to grow, to maintain their identity, and to reproduce. Each chemical change is catalyzed by a specific protein called an enzyme. Cellular metabolism is a highly integrated, purposeful activity for which, even in a single cell, many hundreds of enzymes are needed; me-

tabolism effects the exchange of matter and energy between the cell and its environment. Metabolism is so finely controlled that there is neither extensive overutilization nor underutilization of food materials nor overproduction nor underproduction of energy derived from them. This article concentrates on the nature of the cellular processes involved in metabolism and the manner in which they are regulated.

The first section of the article, *A summary of metabolism*, presents an overview of the entire subject. Its purpose is to provide the reader with a brief discussion of the salient features of metabolism. The succeeding sections of the article deal in detail with the individual metabolic pathways, reactions, and regulatory mechanisms involved in metabolism. The physical and chemical properties of the components of living things dealt with in this article are found in various other articles: CARBOHYDRATE; LIPID; NUCLEIC ACID; VITAMIN; NUCLEOTIDES; and PROTEIN. For details of enzymatic action, see ENZYME.

This article is divided into the following major sections:

I. A summary of metabolism

All living organisms ultimately derive their energy from sunlight; however, only green plants and photosynthetic micro-organisms can directly utilize light energy to synthesize cellular components from simple sources such as carbon dioxide (CO_2), water (H_2O), and ammonia (NH_3). Most other organisms must use the products of photosynthesis as food, either directly (by consuming plant material) or indirectly (by consuming organisms that have consumed plant material). The chemical reactions undergone by the components of the food—mostly proteins, carbohydrates, and lipids (fats)—serve two main purposes: they provide, from complex starting materials, the simpler fragments from which cell constituents are synthesized; and they yield the energy needed for such chemical syntheses and for the many other energy-requiring life processes. An understanding of metabolism thus requires knowledge not only of the manner in which the fragmentation of food materials yields energy and of the manner in which that energy is conserved for the performance of useful work but also of the manner in which these events are integrated.

BIOLOGICAL ENERGY EXCHANGES

The energy changes associated with physico-chemical processes are the province of a subdiscipline of physics termed thermodynamics. The first two laws of thermodynamics state, in essence, that energy can neither be created nor destroyed and that the effect of physical and chemical changes is to increase the disorder, or randomness (*i.e.*, entropy), of the universe. Although it might be supposed that biological processes—through which organisms grow in a highly ordered and complex manner, maintain order and complexity throughout their life, and pass on the instructions for order to succeeding generations—are in contravention of these laws, this is not so. Living organisms neither consume nor create energy: they can only transform it from one form to another. From the environment they absorb energy in a form useful to them; to the environment they return an equiva-

Free energy and heat

lent amount of energy in a biologically less useful form. The useful energy, or free energy, may be defined as energy capable of doing work under isothermal conditions (conditions in which no temperature differential exists); free energy is associated with any chemical change. Energy less useful than free energy is returned to the environment, usually as heat. Heat cannot perform work in biological systems because all parts of cells have essentially the same temperature and pressure.

The carrier of chemical energy. Although energy can be made available to cells in a variety of forms, it is usable by them largely in only one form. The situation is analogous to lighting an electric lamp: the energy for illumination may be derived from the burning of coal, from the disintegration of radioactive nuclei, or from the kinetic energy of a waterfall, but the lamp cannot be lighted unless the various forms of energy—heat, nuclear, or kinetic—are transformed into an electric current, the only form of energy usable by the lamp. Similarly, although photosynthetic organisms harness the radiant energy of sunlight directly, by converting it to chemical energy in the pigment chlorophyll, and non-photosynthetic organisms tap the chemical energy stored in the food materials synthesized through photosynthesis, both types of organism use one specific chemical compound for energy exchange: adenosine triphosphate (ATP; Figure 1). Adenosine triphosphate functions as the major carrier of chemical energy in all forms of living matter. As it transfers its energy to other molecules, ATP loses its terminal phosphate group as inorganic phosphate (P_i), or two of its phosphate groups as inorganic pyrophosphate (PP_i), becoming adenosine diphosphate (ADP) or adenosine monophosphate (AMP), respectively. These

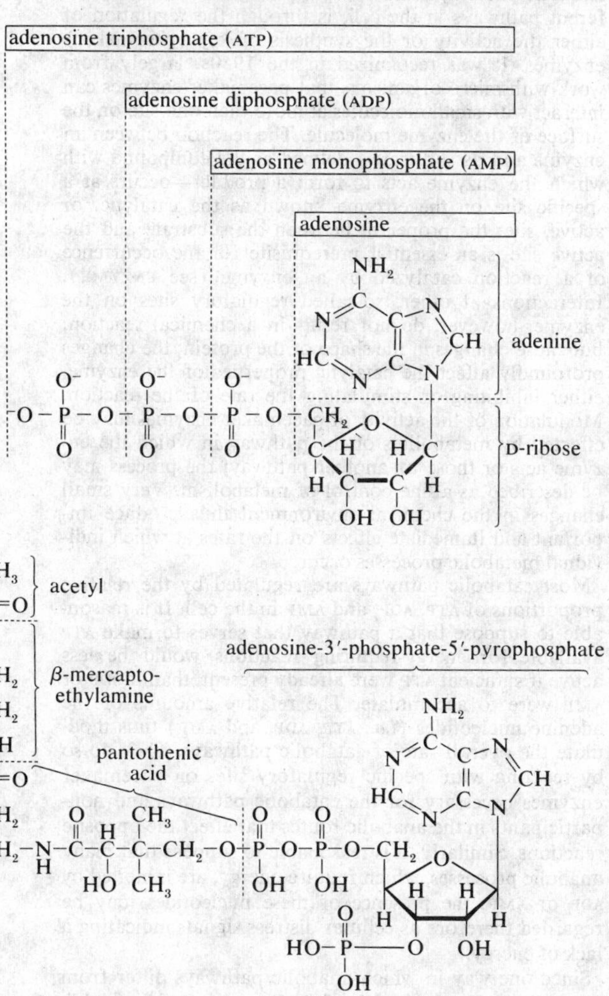

Figure 1: *Biological energy carriers.*
(Top) ATP, ADP, and AMP. (Bottom) Acetyl coenzyme A (acetyl CoA).

products can, directly or indirectly, be reconverted to ATP by regaining phosphate groups in reactions coupled to the utilization of either light energy (in photosynthetic cells) or chemical energy (in nonphotosynthetic organisms).

Metabolism may thus be viewed as a network of cellular processes in which reactions called catabolic reactions—the occurrence of which is accompanied by a decrease in free energy—are coupled to the synthesis of ATP from ADP and inorganic phosphate, whereas energy-requiring reactions, called anabolic reactions, are coupled to the energy-yielding reactions by which ATP is split to ADP and inorganic phosphate or to AMP and pyrophosphate (see below, *Biological energy transduction*, for a discussion of the mechanisms by which ATP is synthesized from ADP and inorganic phosphate).

Catabolism. *Formation of small molecules.* The release of chemical energy from food materials essentially occurs in three phases. In the first phase (phase I), the large molecules that make up the bulk of food materials are broken down into small constituent units: proteins are converted to the 20 or so different amino acids of which they are composed; carbohydrates (polysaccharides such as starch in plants and glycogen in animals) are degraded to sugars such as glucose; and fats (lipids) are broken down into fatty acids and glycerol. The amounts of energy liberated in phase I are relatively small: only about 0.6 percent of the free, or useful, energy of proteins and carbohydrates, and about 0.1 percent of that of fats, is released during this phase. Because this energy is liberated largely as heat, it cannot be utilized by the cell. The purpose of the reactions of phase I, which, in animals, occur mainly in the intestinal tract and in tissues in which reserve materials are prepared, or mobilized, for energy production, is to prepare the foodstuffs for the energy-releasing processes.

Incomplete oxidation. In the second phase of the release of energy from food (phase II), the small molecules produced in the first phase—sugars, glycerol, a number of fatty acids, and about 20 varieties of amino acids—are incompletely oxidized (in this sense, oxidation means the removal of electrons or hydrogen atoms), the end product being (apart from carbon dioxide and water) one of only three possible substances: the two-carbon compound acetate, in the form of a compound called acetyl coenzyme A (Figure 1); the four-carbon compound oxaloacetate; and the five-carbon compound α-oxoglutarate. The first, acetate in the form of acetyl coenzyme A, constitutes by far the most common product—it is the product of two-thirds of the carbon incorporated into carbohydrates and glycerol; all of the carbon in most fatty acids; and approximately half of the carbon in amino acids. The end product of several amino acids is α-oxoglutarate; that of a few others is oxaloacetate, which is formed either directly or indirectly (from fumarate). These processes, represented diagrammatically in Figure 2, show what happens in the bacterium *Escherichia coli*, but remarkably similar processes occur in animals, plants, fungi, and other organisms capable of oxidizing their food materials wholly to carbon dioxide and water.

Complete oxidation. Total oxidation of the relatively few products of phase II occurs in a cyclic sequence of chemical reactions known as the tricarboxylic acid (TCA) cycle, or the Krebs cycle, after its discoverer, Sir Hans Krebs; it represents phase III of energy release from foods. Each turn of this cycle (see below *The tricarboxylic acid [TCA] cycle*) is initiated by the formation of citrate, with six carbon atoms, from oxaloacetate (with four carbons) and acetyl coenzyme A; subsequent reactions result in the reformation of oxaloacetate and the formation of two molecules of carbon dioxide. The carbon atoms that go into the formation of carbon dioxide are no longer available to the cell. The concomitant stepwise oxidations—in which hydrogen atoms or electrons are removed from intermediate compounds formed during the cycle and, via a system of carriers, are transferred ultimately to oxygen to form water—are quantitatively the most important means of generating ATP from ADP and inorganic phosphate. These events are known as

The three possible end products of incomplete oxidation

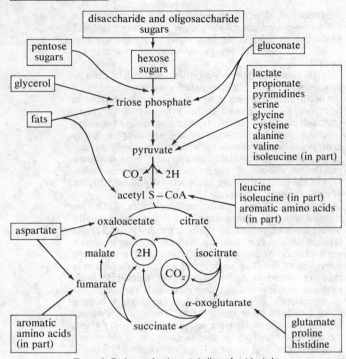

Figure 2: Pathways for the catabolism of nutrients by *Escherichia coli.*

terminal respiration and oxidative phosphorylation (for details of this process, see below *Biological energy transduction*).

Some micro-organisms, incapable of completely converting their carbon compounds to carbon dioxide, release energy by fermentation reactions, in which the intermediate compounds of catabolic routes either directly or indirectly accept or donate hydrogen atoms. Such secondary changes in intermediate compounds result in considerably less energy being made available to the cell than occurs with the pathways that are linked to oxidative phosphorylation; however, fermentation reactions yield a large variety of commercially important products. Thus, for example, if the oxidation (removal of electrons or hydrogen atoms) of some catabolic intermediate is coupled to the reduction of a substance called pyruvate or of acetaldehyde derived from pyruvate, the products formed are lactic acid and ethyl alcohol, respectively.

Anabolism.   Catabolic pathways effect the transformation of food materials into the interconvertible intermediates of the pathways shown in Figure 2. Anabolic pathways, on the other hand, are sequences of enzyme-catalyzed reactions in which the component building blocks of large molecules, or macromolecules (*e.g.*, proteins, carbohydrates, and fats), are constructed from the same intermediates. Thus, catabolic routes have clearly defined beginnings but no unambiguously identifiable end products; anabolic routes, on the other hand, lead to clearly distinguishable end products from diffuse beginnings. The two types of pathway are linked through reactions of phosphate transfer, involving ADP, AMP, and ATP as described above, and also through electron transfers, which enable reducing equivalents (*i.e.*, hydrogen atoms or electrons), which have been released during catabolic reactions, to be utilized for biosynthesis. But, although catabolic and anabolic pathways are closely linked, and although the overall effect of one type of route is obviously the opposite of the other, they have few steps in common. The anabolic pathway for the synthesis of a particular molecule generally starts from intermediate compounds quite different from those produced as a result of catabolism of that molecule; for example, micro-organisms catabolize aromatic (*i.e.*, containing a ring, or cyclic, structure) amino acids to acetyl coenzyme A and an intermediate compound of the TCA cycle. The biosynthesis of these amino acids, however, starts with a compound derived from pyruvate and an

The differences between catabolic and anabolic pathways

intermediate compound of pentose (a general name for sugars with five carbon atoms) metabolism. Similarly, histidine is synthesized from a pentose sugar but is catabolized to α-oxoglutarate.

Even in cases in which a product of catabolism is used in an anabolic pathway, differences emerge; thus, fatty acids, which are catabolized to acetyl coenzyme A, are synthesized not from acetyl coenzyme A directly but from a derivative of it, malonyl coenzyme A (see below *The biosynthesis of cell components: Lipid components*). Furthermore, even enzymes that catalyze apparently identical steps in catabolic and anabolic routes may exhibit different properties. In general, therefore, the way down (catabolism) is different from the way up (anabolism). These differences are important because they allow for the regulation of catabolic and anabolic processes in the cell.

In eucaryotic cells (*i.e.*, those with a well-defined nucleus, characteristic of organisms higher than bacteria) the enzymes of catabolic and anabolic pathways are often located in different cellular compartments. This also contributes to the manner of their cellular control; for example, the formation of acetyl coenzyme A from fatty acids, referred to above, occurs in animal cells in small sausage-shaped components, or organelles, called mitochondria, which also contain the enzymes for terminal respiration and for oxidative phosphorylation. The biosynthesis of fatty acids from acetyl coenzyme A, on the other hand, occurs in the cytoplasm.

INTEGRATION OF CATABOLISM AND ANABOLISM

Fine control.   Possibly the most important means for controlling the flux of metabolites through catabolic and anabolic pathways, and for integrating the numerous different pathways in the cell, is through the regulation of either the activity or the synthesis of key (pacemaker) enzymes. It was recognized in the 1950s, largely from work with micro-organisms, that pacemaker enzymes can interact with small molecules at more than one site on the surface of the enzyme molecule. The reaction between an enzyme and its substrate—defined as the compound with which the enzyme acts to form a product—occurs at a specific site on the enzyme known as the catalytic, or active, site; the proper fit between the substrate and the active site is an essential prerequisite for the occurrence of a reaction catalyzed by an enzyme (see ENZYME). Interactions at other, so-called regulatory sites on the enzyme, however, do not result in a chemical reaction, but cause changes in the shape of the protein; the changes profoundly affect the catalytic properties of the enzyme, either inhibiting or stimulating the rate of the reaction. Modulation of the activity of pacemaker enzymes may be effected by metabolites of the pathway in which the enzyme acts or those of another pathway; the process may be described as a fine control of metabolism. Very small changes in the chemical environment thus produce important and immediate effects on the rates at which individual metabolic processes occur.

Most catabolic pathways are regulated by the relative proportions of ATP, ADP, and AMP in the cell. It is reasonable to suppose that a pathway that serves to make ATP available for energy-requiring reactions would be less active if sufficient ATP were already present, than if ADP or AMP were to accumulate. The relative amounts of the adenine nucleotides (*i.e.*, ATP, ADP, and AMP) thus modulate the overall rate of catabolic pathways. They do so by reacting with specific regulatory sites on pacemaker enzymes necessary for the catabolic pathways and nonparticipants in the anabolic routes that effect the opposite reactions. Similarly, it is reasonable to suppose that many anabolic processes, which require energy, are inhibited by ADP or AMP; the presence of these nucleotides may be regarded therefore as cellular distress signals indicating a lack of energy.

Since one way in which anabolic pathways differ from catabolic routes is that the former result in identifiable end products, it is not unexpected that the pacemaker enzymes of many anabolic pathways—particularly those effecting the biosynthesis of amino acids and nucleotides

—are modulated by the end products of these pathways or, in cases in which branching of pathways occurs, by end products of each branch. Such pacemaker enzymes usually act at the first step unique to a particular anabolic route. If branching occurs, the first step of each branch is controlled. By this so-called negative feedback system, the cellular concentrations of products determine the rates of their formation, thus ensuring that the cell synthesizes only as much of the products as it needs.

Coarse control. A second and less immediately responsive, or "coarse," control is exerted over the synthesis of pacemaker enzymes. The rate of protein synthesis reflects the activity of appropriate genes, which contain the information that directs all cellular processes. Coarse control is therefore exerted on genetic material rather than on enzymes. Preferential synthesis of a pacemaker enzyme is particularly required to accommodate a cell to major changes in its chemical milieu. Such changes occur in multicellular organisms only to a minor extent, so that this type of control mechanism is less important in animals than in micro-organisms (see HOMEOSTASIS). In the latter, however, it may determine the ease with which a cell previously growing in one nutrient medium can grow after transfer to another. In cases in which several types of organism compete in the same medium for available carbon sources, the operation of coarse controls may well be decisive in ensuring survival.

Alterations in the differential rates of synthesis of pacemaker enzymes in micro-organisms responding to changes in the composition of their growth medium also manifest the properties of negative feedback systems. Depending on the nature of the metabolic pathway of which a pacemaker enzyme is a constituent, the manner in which the alterations are elicited may be distinguished. Thus, an increase in the rates at which enzymes of catabolic routes are synthesized results from the addition of inducers—usually compounds that exhibit some structural similarity to the substrates on which the enzymes act. A classic example of an inducible enzyme of this type is β-galactosidase. *Escherichia coli* growing in nutrient medium of a certain composition do not utilize the milk sugar, lactose (glucose-4-β-D-galactoside); however, if the bacteria are placed in a growth medium containing lactose as the sole source for carbon, they synthesize β-galactosidase in very large amounts. The reaction catalyzed by the enzyme is the hydrolysis (*i.e.*, breakdown involving water) of lactose to its two constituent sugars, glucose and galactose; the preferential synthesis of the enzyme thus allows the bacteria to utilize lactose for growth. Another characteristic of the process of enzyme induction is that it continues only as long as the inducer (in this case, lactose) is present; if cells synthesizing β-galactosidase are transferred to a medium containing no lactose, synthesis of β-galactosidase ceases, and the amount of the enzyme in the cells is diluted as they divide, until the original low level of the enzyme is re-established.

In contrast, the differential rates of synthesis of pacemaker enzymes of anabolic routes are usually not increased by the presence of inducers. Instead, the absence of small molecules, which act to repress enzyme synthesis, accelerates enzyme formation. Similar to the fine control processes described above is the regulation by coarse control of many pacemaker enzymes of amino acid biosynthesis. Like the end product inhibitors, the repressors in these cases also appear to be the amino acid end products themselves.

It is useful to regard the acceleration of the enzyme-forming machinery as the consequence, metaphorically, of either placing a foot on the accelerator or removing it from the brake. Analysis of the mechanisms by which gene activity is controlled suggest, however, that the distinction between inducible and repressible enzymes may be more apparent than real (see below *Regulation of metabolism*).

THE STUDY OF METABOLIC PATHWAYS

There are two main reasons for studying a metabolic pathway: (1) to describe, in quantitative terms, the chemical changes catalyzed by the component enzymes of the route; and (2) to describe the various biological controls that govern the rate at which the pathway functions.

Studies with whole organisms or organs can provide information that one substance is converted to another and that this process is localized in a certain tissue; for example, experiments can show that urea, the chief nitrogen-containing end product of protein metabolism in mammals, is formed exclusively in the liver. They cannot reveal, however, the details of the enzymatic steps involved. Clues to the identity of the products involved, and to the possible chemical changes effected by component enzymes, can be provided in any of four ways involving studies with either whole organisms or tissues.

First, under stress or the imbalances associated with diseases, certain metabolites (*i.e.*, products of metabolism) may accumulate to a much greater extent than normal. Thus, during the stress of violent exercise, lactic acid appears in the blood, while glycogen, the form in which carbohydrate is stored in muscle, disappears. Such observations do not, however, prove that lactic acid is a normal intermediate of glycogen catabolism; rather, they show only that compounds capable of yielding lactic acid are likely to be normal intermediates. Indeed, in the example, lactic acid is formed in response to abnormal circumstances, and is not directly formed in the pathways of carbohydrate catabolism. On the other hand, the abnormal accumulation of pyruvic acid in the blood of vitamin B_1-deficient pigeons was a valuable clue to the role of this vitamin in the oxidation of pyruvate.

Second, the administration of metabolic poisons may lead to the accumulation of specific metabolites. If fluoroacetic acid or fluorocitric acid is ingested by animals, for example, citric acid accumulates in the liver. This correctly suggests that fluorocitric acid administered as such, or formed from fluoroacetic acid via the tricarboxylic acid (TCA) cycle, inhibits an enzyme of citrate oxidation.

Third, the fate of any nutrient—indeed, often the fate of a particular chemical group or atom in a nutrient—can be followed with relative ease by administering the nutrient labelled with an isotope. Isotopes are forms of an element that are chemically indistinguishable from each other but differ in physical properties.

The use of a non-radioactive isotope of nitrogen in the 1930s first revealed the dynamic state of body constituents. It had previously been believed that the proteins of tissues are stable once formed, disappearing only with the death of the cell. By feeding amino acids labelled with isotopic nitrogen to rats, it was discovered that the isotope was incorporated into many of the amino acids found in proteins of the liver and the gut, even though the total protein content of these tissues did not change. This suggested that the proteins of these tissues exist in a dynamic steady state, in which relatively high rates of synthesis are counterbalanced by equal rates of degradation. Thus, although the average liver cell has a life-span of several months, half of its proteins are synthesized and degraded every five to six days. On the other hand, the proteins of the muscle or the brain, tissues that (unlike the gut or liver) need not adjust to changes in the chemical composition of their milieu, do not turn over as rapidly. The high rates of turnover observed in liver and gut tissues indicate that the coarse controls, exerted through the onset and cessation of synthesis of pacemaker enzymes, do occur in animal cells.

Finally, genetically altered organisms (mutants) fail to synthesize certain enzymes in an active form. Such defects, if not lethal, result in the accumulation and excretion of the substrate of the defective enzyme; in normal animals, the substrate would not accumulate, because it would be acted upon by the enzyme. The significance of this observation was first realized in the early 20th century when the phrase "inborn errors of metabolism" was used to describe hereditary conditions in which a variety of amino acids and other metabolites are excreted in the urine (see METABOLISM, DISEASES OF). In micro-organisms, in which it is relatively easy to cause genetic muta-

Inducers in microbial systems

Identification of metabolites

tions and to select specific mutants, this technique has been very useful. In addition to their utility in the unravelling of metabolic pathways, the use of mutants in the early 1940s led to the postulation of the one gene–one enzyme hypothesis by the Nobel Prize winners G.W. Beadle and E.L. Tatum; their discoveries opened the field of biochemical genetics and first revealed the nature of the fine controls of metabolism.

Because detailed information about the mechanisms of component enzymatic steps in any metabolic pathway cannot be obtained from studies with whole organisms or tissues, various techniques have been developed for studying these processes—e.g., sliced tissues, and homogenates and cell-free extracts, which are produced by physical disruption of the cells and the removal of cell walls and other debris. The sliced-tissue technique was successfully used by the Nobel Prize winner Sir Hans Krebs in his pioneer studies in the early 1930s on the mechanism of urea formation in the liver. Measurements were made of the stimulating effects of small quantities of amino acids on both the rate of oxygen uptake and the amount of oxygen taken up; the amino acids were added to liver slices bathed in a nutrient medium. Such measurements revealed the cyclic nature of the process; specific amino acids acted as catalysts, stimulating respiration to an extent greater than expected from the quantities added. This was because the added material had been re-formed in the course of the cycle (see below *The catabolism of proteins: Disposal of nitrogen*).

The use of homogenates

Homogenates of tissue are useful in studying metabolic processes because permeability barriers that may prevent ready access of external materials to cell components are destroyed. The tissue is usually minced, blended, or otherwise disrupted in a medium that is suitably buffered to maintain the normal acid–base balance of the tissue, and contains the ions required for many life processes, chiefly sodium, potassium, and magnesium. The tissue is either used directly—as was done by Krebs in elucidating, in 1937, the TCA cycle from studies of the respiration of minced pigeon breast muscle—or fractionated (*i.e.*, broken down) further. If the latter procedure is followed, homogenization is often carried out in a medium containing a high concentration of the sugar sucrose, which provides a milieu favourable for maintaining the integrity of cellular components. The components are recovered by careful spinning in a centrifuge, at a series of increasing speeds. It is thus possible to obtain fractions containing predominantly one type of organelle: nuclei (and some unbroken cells); mitochondria, lysosomes, and microbodies; microsomes (*i.e.*, ribosomes and endoplasmic reticulum fragments); and—after prolonged centrifugation at forces in excess of 100,000 times gravity—a clear liquid that represents the soluble fraction of the cytoplasm. The fractions thus obtained can be further purified and tested for their capacity to carry out a given metabolic step or steps. This procedure was used to show that isolated mitochondria catalyze the oxidation reactions of the TCA cycle and that these organelles also contain the enzymes of fatty acid oxidation. Similarly, isolated ribosomes are used to study the pathway and mechanism of protein synthesis.

The final procedure in the elucidation of a reaction in a metabolic pathway usually involves isolation of the appropriate enzyme. The reaction catalyzed by that enzyme and the factors that control the rate of catalysis are then measured.

It should be emphasized that biochemists realize that studies on isolated and highly purified systems, such as those briefly described above, can do no more than approximate biological reality. The identification of the fine and coarse controls of a metabolic pathway, and (when appropriate) other influences on that pathway, must ultimately involve the study of the pathway in the whole cell or organism. Although some techniques have proved adequate for relating findings in the test tube to the situation in living organisms, study of the more complex metabolic processes, such as those involved in differentiation and development, may require the elaboration of new experimental approaches.

II. The fragmentation of complex molecules

Food materials must undergo oxidation in order to yield biologically useful energy. Oxidation does not necessarily involve oxygen, although it must involve the transfer of electrons from a donor molecule to a suitable acceptor molecule; the donor is thus oxidized and the recipient reduced. Many micro-organisms either must live in the absence of oxygen (*i.e.*, are obligate anaerobes) or can live in its presence or its absence (*i.e.*, are facultative anaerobes).

If no oxygen is available, the catabolism of food materials is effected via fermentations, in which the final acceptor of the electrons removed from the nutrient is some organic molecule, usually generated during the fermentation process. There is no net oxidation of the food molecule in this type of catabolism; that is, the overall oxidation state of the fermentation products is the same as that of the starting material.

Organisms that can use oxygen as a final electron acceptor also use many of the steps in the fermentation pathways of food catabolism to fragment molecules; the fragments, instead of serving as electron acceptors, are fed into the TCA cycle, the pathway of terminal respiration.

In this cycle all of the hydrogen atoms (H) or electrons (e^-) are removed from the fragment and are channelled through a series of electron carriers, ultimately to react with oxygen (O; see below *Energy conservation*). All carbon atoms are eliminated as carbon dioxide (CO_2) in this process. The sequence of reactions involved in the catabolism of food materials may thus be conveniently considered in terms of an initial fragmentation (fermentation), followed by a combustion (respiration) process.

THE CATABOLISM OF GLUCOSE

Glycolysis. *The transformation of glucose.* Quantitatively, the most important source of energy for cellular processes is the six-carbon sugar, glucose ($C_6H_{12}O_6$). The structure of glucose is shown in Figure 3, in which the carbon atoms are numbered consecutively. (See CARBOHYDRATE for a discussion of the chemical nature of glucose and other carbohydrates.) Glucose is made available to animals through the hydrolysis of polysaccharides, such as glycogen and starch, the process being catalyzed by digestive enzymes. In animals, the sugar thus set free passes from the gut into the bloodstream and from there into the cells of the liver and other tissues. In micro-organisms, of course, no such specialized tissues are involved.

The fermentative phase of glucose catabolism (glycolysis) involves several enzymes; the action of each is summarized below. In living cells, many of the compounds that take part in metabolism exist as negatively charged moieties, or anions, and are named as such in most of this article; *e.g.*, pyruvate, oxaloacetate.

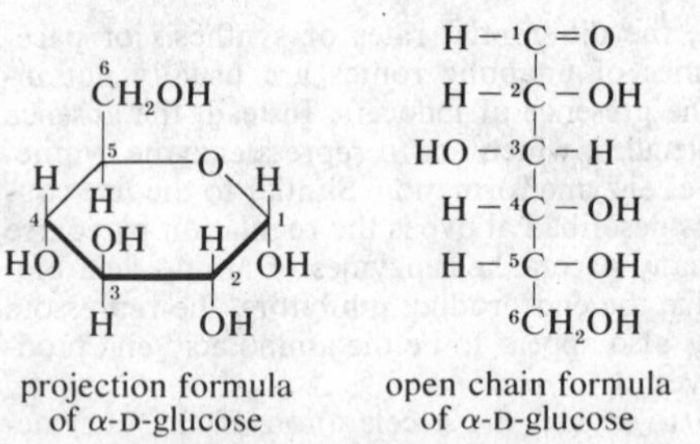

projection formula
of α-D-glucose

open chain formula
of α-D-glucose

Figure 3: The structure of α-D-glucose.

In order to obtain a net yield of ATP from the catabolism of glucose, it is first necessary to invest ATP. During step [1] the alcohol group (CH_2OH at position 6 of the glucose molecule) readily reacts with the terminal phosphate group of ATP, forming glucose-6-phosphate and ADP. For convenience, the phosphoryl group (PO_3^{2-}) is represented by (P). Because the decrease in free energy is so large during this reaction, it is virtually irreversible under physiological conditions.

The formation of glucose-6-phosphate

$$
\begin{array}{c}
\text{1} \quad HC=O \\
\text{2} \quad HCOH \\
\text{3} \quad HOCH \\
\text{4} \quad HCOH \\
\text{5} \quad HCOH \\
\text{6} \quad CH_2OH
\end{array}
\; + \; ATP \longrightarrow
\begin{array}{c}
HC=O \\
HCOH \\
HOCH \\
HCOH \\
HCOH \\
CH_2O\,\textcircled{P}
\end{array}
\; + \; ADP \qquad [1]
$$

glucose   glucose-6-phosphate

In animals, this phosphorylation of glucose, which yields glucose-6-phosphate, is catalyzed by two different enzymes. In most cells, a hexokinase with a high affinity for glucose—*i.e.*, only small amounts of glucose are necessary for enzymatic activity—effects the reaction. In addition, the liver contains a glucokinase, which requires a much greater concentration of glucose before it reacts. Glucokinase functions only in emergencies, when the concentration of glucose in the blood rises to abnormally high levels.

Certain facultative anaerobic bacteria also contain hexokinases but apparently do not use them to phosphorylate glucose. In such cells, external glucose can be utilized only if it is first phosphorylated to glucose-6-phosphate via a system linked to the cell membrane that involves a compound called phosphoenolpyruvate (formed in step [9] of glycolysis), which serves as an obligatory donor of the phosphate group; *i.e.*, ATP cannot serve as the phosphate donor in the reaction.

The reaction in which glucose-6-phosphate is changed to fructose-6-phosphate is catalyzed by phosphoglucoisomerase [2]. In the reaction, a secondary alcohol group

$$
\begin{array}{c}
HC=O \\
HCOH \\
HOCH \\
HCOH \\
HCOH \\
CH_2O\,\textcircled{P}
\end{array}
\; \rightleftharpoons \;
\begin{array}{c}
CH_2OH \\
C=O \\
HOCH \\
HCOH \\
HCOH \\
CH_2O\,\textcircled{P}
\end{array}
\qquad [2]
$$

glucose-6-phosphate   fructose-6-phosphate

($-\overset{|}{\underset{|}{C}HOH}$) at the second carbon atom is oxidized to a keto-group (*i.e.*, $-\overset{|}{C}=O$), and the aldehyde group ($-CHO$) at the first carbon atom is reduced to a primary alcohol group ($-CH_2OH$). Reaction [2] is readily reversible, as is indicated by the double arrows.

The formation of the alcohol group at the first carbon atom permits the repetition of the reaction effected in step [1]; that is, a second molecule of ATP is invested. The product is fructose-1,6-diphosphate [3]. Again, as in

$$
\begin{array}{c}
CH_2OH \\
C=O \\
HOCH \\
HCOH \\
HCOH \\
CH_2O\,\textcircled{P}
\end{array}
\; + \; ATP \longrightarrow
\begin{array}{c}
CH_2O\,\textcircled{P} \\
C=O \\
HOCH \\
HCOH \\
HCOH \\
CH_2O\,\textcircled{P}
\end{array}
\; + \; ADP \qquad [3]
$$

fructose-6-phosphate   fructose-1,6-diphosphate

the hexokinase reaction, the decrease in free energy of the reaction, which is catalyzed by phosphofructokinase, is sufficiently large to make this reaction virtually irreversible under physiological conditions; ADP is also a product.

The first three steps of glycolysis have thus transformed an asymmetrical sugar molecule, glucose, into a symmetrical form, fructose-1,6-diphosphate, containing a phosphoryl group at each end; the molecule next is split into two smaller fragments that are interconvertible. This elegant simplification is achieved via steps [4] and [5], which are described in the next section.

The aldolase reaction. In [4], the enzyme catalyzes the breaking apart of the six-carbon sugar fructose-1,6-diphosphate into two three-carbon fragments. The

$$
\begin{array}{c}
\text{1} \quad CH_2O\,\textcircled{P} \\
\text{2} \quad C=O \\
\text{3} \quad HOCH \\
\text{4} \quad HCOH \\
\text{5} \quad HCOH \\
\text{6} \quad CH_2O\,\textcircled{P}
\end{array}
\qquad [4]
$$

fructose-1,6-diphosphate

$$
\rightleftharpoons
\begin{array}{c}
CH_2O\,\textcircled{P} \\
C=O \\
CH_2OH
\end{array}
\; + \;
\begin{array}{c}
CHO \\
HCOH \\
CH_2O\,\textcircled{P}
\end{array}
$$

dihydroxyacetonephosphate   glyceraldehyde-3-phosphate

molecule is split between carbons 3 and 4. Reversal of this cleavage—*i.e.*, the formation of a six-carbon compound from two three-carbon compounds—is possible. Because the reverse reaction is an aldol condensation—*i.e.*, an aldehyde (glyceraldehyde-3-phosphate) combines with an alcohol (dihydroxyacetonephosphate)—the enzyme is commonly called aldolase. The two three-carbon fragments produced in step [4], dihydroxyacetonephosphate and glyceraldehyde-3-phosphate, are also called triose phosphates. They are readily converted to each other by a process [5] analogous to that in step [2].

$$
\begin{array}{c}
CH_2O\,\textcircled{P} \\
C=O \\
CH_2OH
\end{array}
\; \rightleftharpoons \;
\begin{array}{c}
CHO \\
HCOH \\
CH_2O\,\textcircled{P}
\end{array}
\qquad [5]
$$

dihydroxyacetonephosphate   glyceraldehyde-3-phosphate

The enzyme that catalyzes the interconversion [5] is triose phosphate isomerase, a different enzyme than that catalyzing step [2].

The formation of ATP. The second stage of glucose catabolism comprises reactions [6] through [10], in which a net gain of ATP is achieved through the oxidation of one of the triose phosphate compounds formed in step [5]. One molecule of glucose forms two molecules of the triose phosphate; both three-carbon fragments follow the same pathway, and steps [6] through [10] must occur twice to complete the glucose breakdown.

Step [6], in which glyceraldehyde-3-phosphate is oxidized, is one of the most important reactions in gly-

Conversion of energy of oxidation into ATP

$$
P_i \; + \;
\begin{array}{c}
CHO \\
HCOH \\
CH_2O\,\textcircled{P}
\end{array}
\; + \; NAD^+ \longrightarrow
\begin{array}{c}
COO\,\textcircled{P} \\
HCOH \\
CH_2O\,\textcircled{P}
\end{array}
\; + \; NADH \; + \; H^+ \qquad [6]
$$

glyceraldehyde-3-phosphate   1,3-diphosphoglycerate

colysis; it is during this step that the energy liberated during oxidation of the aldehyde group ($-CHO$) is conserved in the form of a high-energy phosphate compound; namely, as an anhydride of a carboxylic acid and phosphoric acid, 1,3-diphosphoglycerate. The hydrogen atoms or electrons removed from the aldehyde group during its oxidation are accepted by a coenzyme (so called because it functions in conjunction with an enzyme) involved in hydrogen or electron transfer; the coenzyme, nicotinamide adenine dinucleotide (NAD+), is reduced to form NADH + H+ in the process. The NAD+ thus reduced is bound to the enzyme glyceraldehyde-3-phosphate dehydrogenase, catalyzing the overall reaction, step [6].

The 1,3-diphosphoglycerate produced in step [6] reacts with ADP in a reaction catalyzed by phosphoglycerate kinase, with the result that one of the two phosphoryl groups is transferred to ADP to form ATP and 3-phosphoglycerate. This reaction [7] is highly exergonic (*i.e.*, it

$$
\begin{array}{c}
COO\,\textcircled{P} \\
HCOH \\
CH_2O\,\textcircled{P}
\end{array}
\; + \; ADP \longrightarrow
\begin{array}{c}
COOH \\
HCOH \\
CH_2O\,\textcircled{P}
\end{array}
\; + \; ATP \qquad [7]
$$

1,3-diphosphoglycerate   3-phosphoglycerate

proceeds with a loss of free energy); as a result, the oxidation of glyceraldehyde-3-phosphate, step [6], is irreversible. In summary, the energy liberated during oxidation of an aldehyde group (—CHO in glyceraldehyde-3-phosphate) to a carboxylic acid group (—COOH in 3-phosphoglycerate) is conserved as the phosphate bond energy in ATP during steps [6] and [7]. This step occurs twice for each molecule of glucose; thus the initial investment of ATP in steps [1] and [3] is recovered.

The 3-phosphoglycerate in step [7] now forms 2-phosphoglycerate, in a reaction catalyzed by phospho-

$$
\begin{array}{c}
\text{COOH} \\
| \\
\text{HCOH} \\
| \\
\text{CH}_2\text{O}\,\textcircled{P}
\end{array}
\rightleftharpoons
\begin{array}{c}
\text{COOH} \\
| \\
\text{HCO}\,\textcircled{P} \\
| \\
\text{CH}_2\text{OH}
\end{array}
\qquad [8]
$$

3-phosphoglycerate   2-phosphoglycerate

glyceromutase [8]. During step [9] the enzyme enolase reacts with 2-phosphoglycerate to form phosphoenolpyruvate (PEP), water being lost from 2-phosphoglycerate in the process. Phosphoenolpyruvate acts as the second

$$
\begin{array}{c}
\text{COOH} \\
| \\
\text{HCO}\,\textcircled{P} \\
| \\
\text{CH}_2\text{OH}
\end{array}
\underset{-\text{H}_2\text{O}}{\overset{+\text{H}_2\text{O}}{\rightleftharpoons}}
\begin{array}{c}
\text{COOH} \\
| \\
\text{CO}\,\textcircled{P} \\
|| \\
\text{CH}_2
\end{array}
\qquad [9]
$$

2-phosphoglycerate   phosphoenolpyruvate

source of ATP in glycolysis. The transfer of the phosphate group from PEP to ADP, catalyzed by pyruvate kinase [10], is also highly exergonic and is thus virtually irreversible under physiological conditions.

$$
\begin{array}{c}
\text{COOH} \\
| \\
\text{CO}\,\textcircled{P} \\
|| \\
\text{CH}_2
\end{array}
+ \text{ADP} \longrightarrow
\begin{array}{c}
\text{COOH} \\
| \\
\text{C}=\text{O} \\
| \\
\text{CH}_3
\end{array}
+ \text{ATP} \qquad [10]
$$

phosphoenolpyruvate   pyruvate

Reaction [10] occurs twice for each molecule of glucose entering the glycolytic sequence; thus the net yield is two molecules of ATP for each six-carbon sugar. No further molecules of glucose can enter the glycolytic pathway, however, until the NADH + H+ produced in step [6] is reoxidized to NAD+. In anaerobic systems, this means that electrons must be transferred from (NADH + H+) to some organic acceptor molecule, which thus is reduced in the process. Such an acceptor molecule could be the pyruvate formed in reaction [10]. In certain bacteria (e.g., so-called lactic acid bacteria) or in muscle cells functioning vigorously in the absence of adequate supplies of oxygen, pyruvate is reduced to lactate via a reaction catalyzed by lactate dehydrogenase (reaction [11a]); i.e., reduced NAD+ gives up its hydrogen

$$
\begin{array}{c}
\text{CH}_3 \\
| \\
\text{C}=\text{O} \\
| \\
\text{COOH}
\end{array}
+ \text{NADH} + \text{H}^+ \longrightarrow
\begin{array}{c}
\text{CH}_3 \\
| \\
\text{CHOH} \\
| \\
\text{COOH}
\end{array}
+ \text{NAD}^+ \qquad [11a]
$$

pyruvate   lactate

atoms or electrons to pyruvate, and lactate and NAD+ are formed. Alternatively, in organisms such as brewers' yeast, pyruvate is first decarboxylated to form acetaldehyde and carbon dioxide in a reaction catalyzed by pyruvate decarboxylase [11b]; acetaldehyde then is reduced

$$
\begin{array}{c}
\text{CH}_3 \\
| \\
\text{C}=\text{O} \\
| \\
\text{COOH}
\end{array}
\longrightarrow
\begin{array}{c}
\text{CH}_3 \\
| \\
\text{CHO}
\end{array}
+ \text{CO}_2 \qquad [11b]
$$

pyruvate   acetaldehyde

by (NADH + H+) in a reaction catalyzed by alcohol dehydrogenase [11c], yielding ethanol and oxidized coenzyme (NAD+).

$$
\begin{array}{c}
\text{CH}_3 \\
| \\
\text{CHO}
\end{array}
+ \text{NADH} + \text{H}^+ \longrightarrow \text{CH}_3\text{CH}_2\text{OH} + \text{NAD}^+ \qquad [11c]
$$

acetaldehyde   ethanol

Many variations of reaction [11] occur in nature. In the heterolactic (mixed lactic acid) fermentations carried out by some micro-organisms, a mixture of reactions [11 a, b, and c] regenerates NAD+ and results in the production, for each molecule of glucose fermented, of a molecule each of lactate, ethanol, and carbon dioxide. In other types of fermentation, the end products may be derivatives of acids such as propionic, butyric, acetic, and succinic; decarboxylated materials derived from them (e.g., acetone); or compounds such as glycerol.

The phosphogluconate pathway. Many cells possess, in addition to all or part of the glycolytic pathway that comprises reactions [1] through [11], other pathways of glucose catabolism that involve, as the first unique step, the oxidation of glucose-6-phosphate [12] instead of the formation of fructose-6-phosphate [2]. This is the phosphogluconate pathway, or pentose-phosphate cycle. During reaction [12], hydrogen atoms or electrons are re-

The oxidation of glucose-6-phosphate

$$
\begin{array}{c}
\text{CHO} \\
| \\
\text{HCOH} \\
| \\
\text{HOCH} \\
| \\
\text{HCOH} \\
| \\
\text{HCOH} \\
| \\
\text{CH}_2\text{O}\,\textcircled{P}
\end{array}
+ \text{NADP}^+ + \text{H}_2\text{O} \longrightarrow
\begin{array}{c}
\text{COOH} \\
| \\
\text{HCOH} \\
| \\
\text{HOCH} \\
| \\
\text{HCOH} \\
| \\
\text{HCOH} \\
| \\
\text{CH}_2\text{O}\,\textcircled{P}
\end{array}
+ \text{NADPH} + \text{H}^+ \qquad [12]
$$

glucose-6-phosphate   6-phosphogluconate

moved from the carbon atom at position 1 of glucose-6-phosphate in a reaction catalyzed by glucose-6-phosphate dehydrogenase. The product of the reaction is 6-phosphogluconate. The reducing equivalents (hydrogen atoms or electrons) are accepted by nicotine adenine dinucleotide phosphate (NADP+), a coenzyme similar to but not identical with NAD+. A second molecule of NADP+ is reduced as 6-phosphogluconate is further oxidized; the reaction is catalyzed by 6-phosphogluconate dehydrogenase [13]. The products of the reaction also include ribu-

$$
\begin{array}{ll}
1 & \text{COOH} \\
2 & \text{HCOH} \\
3 & \text{HOCH} \\
4 & \text{HCOH} \\
5 & \text{HCOH} \\
6 & \text{CH}_2\text{O}\,\textcircled{P}
\end{array}
+ \text{NADP}^+ \longrightarrow
\begin{array}{ll}
2 & \text{CH}_2\text{OH} \\
3 & \text{C}=\text{O} \\
4 & \text{HCOH} \\
5 & \text{HCOH} \\
6 & \text{CH}_2\text{O}\,\textcircled{P}
\end{array}
+ \text{CO}_2 + \text{NADPH} + \text{H}^+ \qquad [13]
$$

6-phosphogluconate   ribulose-5-phosphate

lose-5-phosphate and carbon dioxide. (The numbers at the carbon atoms in step [13] indicate that carbon 1 of 6-phosphogluconate forms carbon dioxide.)

Ribulose-5-phosphate can undergo a series of reactions in which two-carbon and three-carbon fragments are interchanged between a number of sugar phosphates; this sequence of events can lead to the formation of two molecules of fructose-6-phosphate and one of glyceraldehyde-3-phosphate from three molecules of ribulose-5-phosphate (i.e., the conversion of three molecules with five carbons to two with six and one with three). Although the cycle, which is outlined in Figure 4, is the main pathway in micro-organisms for fragmentation of pentose sugars, it is not of major importance as a route for the oxidation of glucose. Its primary purpose in most cells is to generate reducing power in the cytoplasm, in the form of reduced NADP+. This function is especially prominent in tissues—such as the liver, mammary gland, fat tissue, and the cortex (outer region) of the adrenal gland—that actively carry out the biosynthesis of fatty acids and other fatty substances (e.g., steroids). A second function of reactions [12] and [13] is to generate from glucose-6-phosphate the pentoses that are used in the synthesis of nucleic acids (see below The biosynthesis of cell components).

In photosynthetic organisms, some of the reactions of the phosphogluconate pathway are part of the major route for the formation of sugars from carbon dioxide; in this case, the reactions occur in a direction opposite

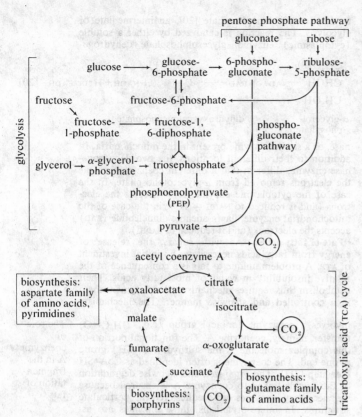

Figure 4: Pathways for the utilization of carbohydrates.

to that in which they occur in non-photosynthetic tissues (see PHOTOSYNTHESIS).

A different route for the catabolism of glucose also involves 6-phosphogluconate; it is of considerable importance in micro-organisms lacking some of the enzymes necessary for glycolysis. In this route, 6-phosphogluconate (derived from glucose via steps [1] and [12]) is not oxidized to ribulose-5-phosphate via reaction [13] but, in an enzyme-catalyzed reaction [14], loses water, forming the compound 2-keto-3-deoxy-6-phosphogluconate (KDPG).

$$
\begin{array}{ccc}
\text{COOH} & & \text{COOH} \\
\text{HCOH} & & \text{C=O} \\
\text{HOCH} & & \text{CH}_2 \\
\text{HCOH} & \longrightarrow & \text{HCOH} \quad + \ \text{H}_2\text{O} \quad [14] \\
\text{HCOH} & & \text{HCOH} \\
\text{CH}_2\text{O}\ⓅP & & \text{CH}_2\text{O}\ⓅP \\
\text{6-phosphogluconate} & & \text{KDPG}
\end{array}
$$

This is then split into pyruvate and glyceraldehyde-3-phosphate [15] both of which are intermediates of the glycolytic pathway.

$$
\begin{array}{cccc}
\text{COOH} & & & \\
\text{C=O} & & \text{COOH} & \text{CHO} \\
\text{CH}_2 & \longrightarrow & \text{C=O} \ + \ & \text{HCOH} \\
\text{HCOH} & & \text{CH}_3 & \text{CH}_2\text{O}\ⓅP \quad [15] \\
\text{HCOH} & & & \\
\text{CH}_2\text{O}\ⓅP & & & \\
\text{KDPG} & \text{pyruvate} & \text{glyceraldehyde-} \\
& & \text{3-phosphate}
\end{array}
$$

THE CATABOLISM OF SUGARS OTHER THAN GLUCOSE

The main storage carbohydrate of animal cells is glycogen, in which chains of glucose molecules—linked end to end, the C1 position of one glucose being linked to the C4 position of the adjacent one—are joined to each other by occasional linkages between a carbon at posi-

tion 1 on one glucose and a carbon at position 6 on another. Two enzymes cooperate in releasing glucose molecules from glycogen. Glycogen phosphorylase catalyzes the splitting of the 1,4-bonds by adding the elements of phosphoric acid at the point shown by the broken arrow in [16], rather than water, as in the digestive hydrolysis of polysaccharides such as glycogen and starch. The products of [16] are glucose-1-phosphate and chains of sugar molecules shortened by one unit; the chains are degraded further by repetition of step [16]. When a bridge linking two chains, at C1 and C6 carbon atoms of adjacent glucose units, is reached, it is hydro-

[16]

lyzed in a reaction involving the enzyme $\alpha (1 \rightarrow 6)$ glucosidase. After the two chains are separated, reaction [16] can occur again. The glucose-1-phosphate thus formed from glycogen or, in plants, from starch, is converted to glucose-6-phosphate by phosphoglucomutase [78], which catalyzes a reaction very similar to that effected in step [8] of glycolysis; glucose-6-phosphate can then undergo further catabolism via glycolysis [2–10] or via either of the routes involving formation of 6-phosphogluconate [12].

Other sugars encountered in the diet are likewise transformed to products that are intermediates of central metabolic pathways. Lactose, or milk sugar, is composed of one molecule of galactose linked to one molecule of glucose. Sucrose, the common sugar of cane or beet, is made up of glucose linked to fructose. Both sucrose and lactose are hydrolyzed to glucose and fructose or galactose, respectively. Glucose is utilized as already described, but special reactions must occur before the other sugars can enter the catabolic routes. Galactose, for example, is phosphorylated in a manner analogous to step [1] of glycolysis. The reaction, catalyzed by a galactokinase, results in the formation of galactose-1-phosphate; this product is transformed to glucose-1-phosphate by a sequence of reactions requiring as a coenzyme uridine-triphosphate (UTP). Fructose may also be phosphorylated in animal cells either via hexokinase [1], in which case fructose-6-phosphate is the product, or in liver tissue via a fructokinase that gives rise to fructose-1-phosphate [17]. Adenosine triphosphate supplies the phosphate group for the phosphorylation of fructose in both cases.

Fructose-1-phosphate is also formed when facultative anaerobic micro-organisms use fructose as a carbon source for growth; in this case, however, the source of the phosphate is phosphoenolpyruvate rather than ATP. Fruc-

Fragmentation of lactose and sucrose

$$\begin{array}{c}
\text{CH}_2\text{OH} \\
\text{C}=\text{O} \\
\text{HOCH} \\
\text{HCOH} \\
\text{HCOH} \\
\text{CH}_2\text{OH}
\end{array} + \text{ATP} \longrightarrow \begin{array}{c}
\text{CH}_2\text{O}\,\text{P} \\
\text{C}=\text{O} \\
\text{HOCH} \\
\text{HCOH} \\
\text{HCOH} \\
\text{CH}_2\text{OH}
\end{array} + \text{ADP} \quad [17]$$

fructose　　　　　　　　fructose-1-phosphate

tose-1-phosphate can be catabolized by one of two routes. In the liver, it is split by an aldolase enzyme [18] abun-

$$\begin{array}{c}
\text{CH}_2\text{O}\,\text{P} \\
\text{C}=\text{O} \\
\text{HOCH} \\
\text{HCOH} \\
\text{HCOH} \\
\text{CH}_2\text{OH}
\end{array} \rightleftharpoons \begin{array}{c}
\text{CH}_2\text{O}\,\text{P} \\
\text{C}=\text{O} \\
\text{CH}_2\text{OH}
\end{array} + \begin{array}{c}
\text{CHO} \\
\text{HCOH} \\
\text{CH}_2\text{OH}
\end{array} \quad [18]$$

fructose-1-phosphate   dihydroxyacetone-   glyceraldehyde
phosphate

dant in that tissue (but lacking in muscle); the products are dihydroxyacetonephosphate and glyceraldehyde. It will be recalled that dihydroxyacetonephosphate is an intermediate compound of glycolysis. Although glyceraldehyde is not an intermediate of glycolysis, it can be converted to one in a reaction involving the conversion of ATP to ADP; the product, glyceraldehyde-3-phosphate, is an intermediate of glycolysis.

In many organisms other than mammals, fructose-1-phosphate does not have to undergo reaction [18] in order to enter central metabolic routes. Instead, a fructose-1-phosphate kinase, distinct from the phosphofructokinase that catalyzes step [3] of glycolysis, effects the direct conversion of fructose-1-phosphate and ATP to fructose-1,6-diphosphate and ADP.

THE CATABOLISM OF LIPIDS (FATS)

Although carbohydrates are the major fuel for most organisms, fatty acids are also a very important energy source. In vertebrates, at least half of the oxidative energy used by the liver, kidneys, heart muscle, and resting skeletal muscle is derived from the oxidation of fatty acids; in fasting or hibernating animals or in migrating birds, fat is virtually the sole source of energy.

Neutral fats or triglycerides, the major components of storage fats in plant and animal cells, consist of the alcohol glycerol linked to three molecules of fatty acids (see LIPID). Before a molecule of neutral fat can be metabolized, it must be hydrolyzed to its component parts. Hydrolysis [19] is effected by intracellular enzymes

$$\begin{array}{c}
\text{O} \\
\| \\
\text{CH}_2\text{OC(CH}_2)_x\text{CH}_3 \\
\text{O} \\
\| \\
\text{CHOC(CH}_2)_y\text{CH}_3 \\
\text{O} \\
\| \\
\text{CH}_2\text{OC(CH}_2)_z\text{CH}_3
\end{array} + 3\text{H}_2\text{O} \longrightarrow \begin{array}{c}
\text{CH}_2\text{OH} \\
\text{CHOH} \\
\text{CH}_2\text{OH}
\end{array} + \begin{array}{c}
\text{CH}_3(\text{CH}_2)_x\text{COOH} \\
\text{CH}_3(\text{CH}_2)_y\text{COOH} \\
\text{CH}_3(\text{CH}_2)_z\text{COOH}
\end{array} \quad [19]$$

triglyceride　　　　　　　　glycerol　　fatty acids

or gut enzymes, and forms phase I of fat catabolism. Letters x, y, and z represent the number of —CH₂— groups in the fatty acid molecules.

As is apparent from [19], the three molecules of fatty acid released from the triglyceride need not be identical; a fatty acid usually contains 16 or 18 carbon atoms but may also be unsaturated; that is, containing one or more double bonds (—CH=CH—). Only the fate of saturated fatty acids, of the type $CH_3(CH_2)_nCOOH$ (n can be an even or an odd number), is dealt with here.

Fate of glycerol. It requires but two reactions to channel glycerol into a catabolic pathway (see Figure 2). In a reaction catalyzed by glycerolkinase, ATP is utilized to phosphorylate glycerol; the products are α-glycerolphosphate and ADP. Alpha-glycerolphosphate then is oxidized

to dihydroxyacetonephosphate [20], an intermediate of glycolysis. The reaction is catalyzed by either a soluble (cytoplasmic) enzyme, glycerolphosphate dehydroge-

$$\begin{array}{c}
\text{CH}_2\text{O}\,\text{P} \\
\text{CHOH} \\
\text{CH}_2\text{OH}
\end{array} + \text{NAD}^+ \text{ or FAD} \longrightarrow \begin{array}{c}
\text{CH}_2\text{O}\,\text{P} \\
\text{C}=\text{O} \\
\text{CH}_2\text{OH}
\end{array} + \text{NADH} + \text{H}^+ \text{or FADH}_2 \quad [20]$$

α-glycerol-　　　　　　dihydroxyacetonephosphate
phosphate

nase, or a similar enzyme present in the mitochondria. In addition to their different locations, the two dehydrogenase enzymes differ in that a different coenzyme accepts the electrons removed from α-glycerolphosphate. In the case of the cytoplasmic enzyme, NAD⁺ accepts the electrons (and is reduced to NADH + H⁺); in the case of the mitochondrial enzyme, flavin adenine dinucleotide (FAD) accepts the electrons (and is reduced to FADH₂).

Fate of fatty acids. As with sugars, the release of energy from fatty acids necessitates an initial investment of ATP. A problem unique to fats is a consequence of the relative insolubility in water of most fatty acids. Their catabolism thus requires mechanisms that fragment them in a controlled and stepwise manner. The mechanism involves a coenzyme for acyl group (e.g., $CH_3\overset{|}{C}=O$) transfer, namely, coenzyme A. The functional portion of this complex molecule is the sulfhydryl (—SH) group at one end. The coenzyme is often identified as CoA–SH (see step [21]). The organized and stepwise degradation of fatty acids linked to coenzyme A is ensured because the necessary enzymes are sequestered in particulate structures. In micro-organisms, these enzymes are associated with cell membranes, and in higher organisms with mitochondria.

Fatty acids are linked to coenzyme A (CoA–SH) in one of two main ways. In higher organisms, enzymes in the cytoplasm called thiokinases catalyze the linkage of fatty acids with CoA–SH to form a compound that can be called a fatty acyl coenzyme A [21]. This step requires

The role of coenzyme A in the fragmentation of fats

$$\begin{array}{l}
\text{CH}_3(\text{CH}_2)_n\text{COOH} + \text{ATP} + \text{CoA}-\text{SH} \\
\quad \text{fatty acid}
\end{array} \qquad [21]$$

$$\longrightarrow \underset{\substack{\text{fatty acyl} \\ \text{coenzyme A}}}{\text{CH}_3(\text{CH}_2)_n\overset{\overset{\text{O}}{\|}}{\text{C}}\text{S}-\text{CoA}} + \text{AMP} + \text{PP}_i$$

ATP, which is split to AMP and inorganic pyrophosphate (PP$_i$) in the process. In this series of reactions, n indicates the number of hydrocarbon units (—CH₂—) in the molecule. Because most tissues contain highly active pyrophosphatase enzymes [21a], which catalyze the vir-

$$\begin{array}{c}
\text{O} \quad\quad \text{O} \\
\uparrow \quad\quad \uparrow \\
\text{O}^- - \text{P} - \text{O} - \text{P} - \text{O}^- + \text{H}_2\text{O} \longrightarrow 2\left[\begin{array}{c} \text{O} \\ \uparrow \\ \text{O}^- - \text{P} - \text{OH} \\ | \\ \text{OH} \end{array}\right] \\
\text{OH} \quad\quad \text{OH}
\end{array} \quad [21a]$$

tually irreversible hydrolysis of inorganic pyrophosphate (PP$_i$) to two molecules of inorganic phosphate (P$_i$), reaction [21] proceeds overwhelmingly to completion; i.e., from left to right. In obligate anaerobic bacteria, the linkage of fatty acids to coenzyme A may require the formation of a fatty acyl phosphate; i.e., the phosphorylation of the fatty acid using ATP. ADP is also a product [21b]. The fatty acyl moiety [CH₃(CH₂)ₙCOO] is then

$$\underset{\text{fatty acid}}{\text{CH}_3(\text{CH}_2)_n\text{COOH}} + \text{ATP} \longrightarrow \underset{\substack{\text{fatty acyl} \\ \text{phosphate}}}{\text{CH}_3(\text{CH}_2)_n\text{COO}\,\text{P}} + \text{ADP} \quad [21b]$$

transferred to coenzyme A [21c], forming a fatty acyl coenzyme A compound and P$_i$.

$$\text{CH}_3(\text{CH}_2)_n\text{COO}\,\text{P} + \text{CoA}-\text{SH}$$

$$\longrightarrow \underset{\substack{\text{fatty acyl} \\ \text{coenzyme A}}}{\text{CH}_3(\text{CH}_2)_n\overset{\overset{\text{O}}{\|}}{\text{C}}\text{S}-\text{CoA}} + \text{P}-\text{OH} \quad [21c]$$

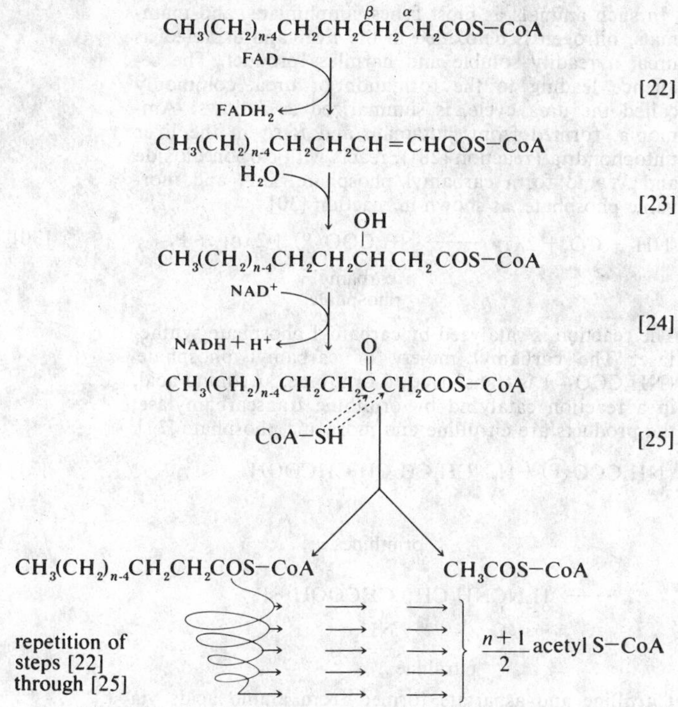

$$CH_3(CH_2)_{n-4}CH_2CH_2\overset{\beta}{C}H_2\overset{\alpha}{C}H_2COS-CoA$$

$$FAD \searrow$$
$$FADH_2 \nearrow \qquad [22]$$

$$CH_3(CH_2)_{n-4}CH_2CH_2CH=CHCOS-CoA$$

$$H_2O \searrow$$
$$\qquad [23]$$
$$\overset{OH}{|}$$

$$CH_3(CH_2)_{n-4}CH_2CH_2CH\,CH_2COS-CoA$$

$$NAD^+ \searrow$$
$$NADH+H^+ \nearrow \qquad [24]$$
$$\overset{O}{\underset{\|}{}}$$

$$CH_3(CH_2)_{n-4}CH_2CH_2C\,CH_2COS-CoA$$

$$CoA-SH \qquad [25]$$

$$CH_3(CH_2)_{n-4}CH_2CH_2COS-CoA \qquad CH_3COS-CoA$$

repetition of
steps [22]
through [25]
$$\left.\begin{array}{c}\end{array}\right\} \dfrac{n+1}{2} \text{ acetyl } S-CoA$$

Figure 5: Fragmentation of acyl coenzyme A with an even number of carbon atoms (see text).

In either case, it is the fatty acyl coenzyme A molecules that are fragmented in the sequence of events summarized in Figure 5.

Initially (step [22], Figure 5) two hydrogen atoms are lost from the fatty acyl coenzyme A, resulting in the formation of an unsaturated fatty acyl coenzyme A (i.e., with a double bond, $-CH=CH-$) between the α- and β-carbons of the acyl moiety—the α-carbon is the one closest to the carboxyl ($-COOH$) group of a fatty acid; the next closest is the β-, and so on to the end of the hydrocarbon chain). The hydrogen atoms are accepted by the coenzyme FAD (flavin adenine dinucleotide), which is reduced to $FADH_2$. The product of step [22], α,β-unsaturated fatty acyl coenzyme A, is enzymatically hydrated [23]; i.e., water is added across the double bond. The product, called a β-hydroxyacyl coenzyme A, can again be oxidized in an enzyme-catalyzed reaction [24]; the electrons removed are accepted by NAD^+. The product is called a β-ketoacyl coenzyme A.

The next enzymatic step [25] enables the energy invested in step [21] to be conserved. The β-ketoacyl coenzyme A that is the product of reaction [24] is split, not by water, but by coenzyme A. The process, called thiolysis (as distinct from hydrolysis), yields the two-carbon fragment acetyl coenzyme A and a fatty acyl coenzyme A having two fewer carbon atoms than the molecule that underwent reaction [22]; otherwise the two are similar.

The shortened fatty acyl coenzyme A molecule now undergoes the sequence of reactions again, beginning with the dehydrogenation step [22], and another two-carbon fragment is removed as acetyl coenzyme A. With each passage through the process of fatty acid oxidation, the fatty acid loses a two-carbon fragment as acetyl coenzyme A and two pairs of hydrogen atoms to specific acceptors. The 16-carbon fatty acid, palmitic acid, for example, undergoes a total of seven such cycles, yielding eight molecules of acetyl coenzyme A and 14 pairs of hydrogen atoms, seven of which appear in the form of $FADH_2$ and seven in the form of $NADH+H^+$. The reduced coenzymes, $FADH_2$ and reduced NAD^+, are reoxidized when the electrons pass through the electron transport chain, with concomitant formation of ATP (see below *Biological energy transduction*). In anaerobes, organic molecules other than FAD and NAD^+ are electron acceptors; thus the yield of ATP is reduced. In all organisms, however, the acetyl coenzyme A formed from the breakdown of fatty acids joins that arising from the catabolism

The products of fatty acid oxidation

of carbohydrates (see below *The oxidation of pyruvate*) and many amino acids (see below *The catabolism of proteins*); Figure 2 shows the interrelationships.

Fatty acids with an odd number of carbon atoms are relatively rare in nature but may arise during microbial fermentations or through the oxidation of amino acids such as valine and isoleucine. They may be fragmented through repeated cycles of steps [22] to [25] until the final five-carbon acyl coenzyme A is split into acetyl coenzyme A and propionyl coenzyme A, which has three carbon atoms. In many bacteria, this propionyl coenzyme A can be transformed either to acetyl coenzyme A and carbon dioxide or to pyruvate. In other micro-organisms and in animals, propionyl coenzyme A has a different fate: carbon dioxide is added to propionyl coenzyme A in a reaction requiring ATP. The product, methyl malonyl coenzyme A, has four carbon atoms; the molecule undergoes a rearrangement, forming succinyl coenzyme A, which is an intermediate of the TCA cycle.

THE CATABOLISM OF PROTEINS

The amino acids derived from proteins function primarily as the precursors, or building blocks, for the cell's own proteins and (unlike lipids and carbohydrates) are not primarily a source of energy (see PROTEIN for a discussion of amino acids and classes of proteins). Many micro-organisms, however, can grow on amino acids as the sole carbon and nitrogen source; under these conditions, they derive from them all of their energy and all of the precursors of the macromolecules that comprise cell components. Moreover, it has been calculated that a man of average weight (70 kilograms, or 150 pounds) turns over about 0.4 kilogram of protein per day. About 0.1 kilogram is degraded and replaced by dietary amino acids; the remainder is recycled as part of the dynamic state of cell constituents. Plants contain and metabolize many amino acids in addition to the 20 or so normally found in proteins; discussion of these special pathways is outside the scope of this article, however.

Before proteins can enter cells, the bonds linking adjacent amino acids (peptide bonds) must be hydrolyzed; this process releases the amino acids constituting the protein. The utilization of dietary proteins thus requires the operation of extracellular digestive enzymes; i.e., enzymes outside the cell. Many micro-organisms secrete such enzymes into the nutrient mediums in which they are growing; animals secrete them into the gut. The turnover of proteins within cells, on the other hand, requires the functioning of intracellular enzymes that catalyze the splitting of the peptide bonds linking adjacent amino acids; little is known about the mechanism involved.

Amino acids may be described by the general formula $RCH(NH_2)COOH$, in which R represents a specific chemical moiety. The catabolic fate of amino acids involves (1) removal of nitrogen, (2) disposal of nitrogen, and (3) oxidation of the remaining carbon skeleton.

Removal of nitrogen. The removal of the amino group ($-NH_2$) generally constitutes the first stage in amino acid catabolism. The amino group usually is initially transferred to one of three different α-keto compounds (i.e., of the general structure $RCOCOOH$): pyruvate, which is an intermediate of carbohydrate fragmentation; or oxaloacetate or α-oxoglutarate, both intermediates of the TCA cycle. The products are alanine, aspartate, and glutamate (reactions [26a, b, and c]).

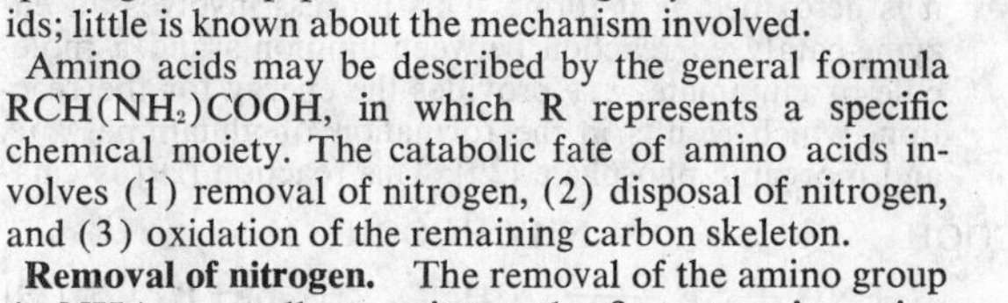

$$\underset{\text{an amino acid}}{\overset{COOH}{\underset{R}{\overset{|}{H_2NCH}}}} + \underset{\text{pyruvate}}{\overset{CH_3}{\underset{COOH}{\overset{|}{C=O}}}} \rightleftharpoons \underset{\alpha\text{-keto acid}}{\overset{COOH}{\underset{R}{\overset{|}{C=O}}}} + \underset{\text{alanine}}{\overset{|}{\underset{CH_3}{\overset{|}{H_2NCHCOOH}}}} \qquad [26a]$$

$$\underset{\text{an amino acid}}{\overset{COOH}{\underset{R}{\overset{|}{H_2NCH}}}} + \underset{\text{oxaloacetate}}{\overset{COOH}{\underset{COO^-}{\underset{CH_2}{\overset{|}{C=O}}}}} \rightleftharpoons \underset{\alpha\text{-keto acid}}{\overset{COOH}{\underset{R}{\overset{|}{C=O}}}} + \underset{\text{aspartate}}{\overset{H_2NCHCOOH}{\underset{COO^-}{\overset{|}{CH_2}}}} \qquad [26b]$$

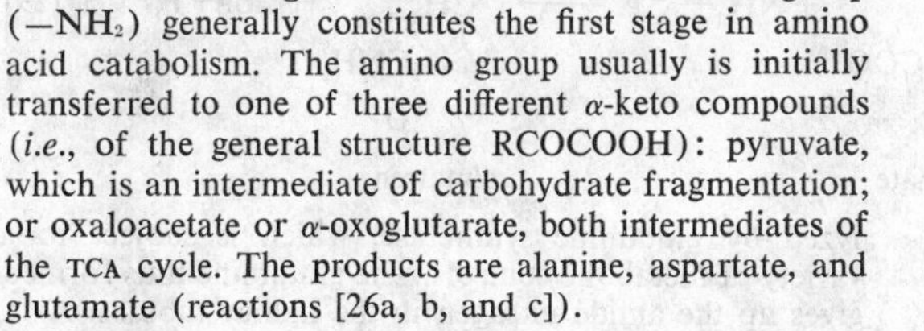

$$
\underset{\text{an amino acid}}{\overset{\text{COOH}}{\underset{\text{R}}{\overset{|}{\underset{|}{\text{H}_2\text{NCH}}}}}} + \underset{\alpha\text{-oxoglutarate}}{\overset{\text{COOH}}{\underset{\text{COO}^-}{\overset{|}{\underset{|}{\overset{\text{C=O}}{\underset{\text{CH}_2}{\overset{|}{\text{CH}_2}}}}}}}} \rightleftharpoons \underset{\alpha\text{-keto acid}}{\overset{\text{COOH}}{\underset{\text{R}}{\overset{|}{\text{C=O}}}}} + \underset{\text{glutamate}}{\overset{\text{H}_2\text{NCHCOOH}}{\underset{\text{COO}^-}{\overset{|}{\underset{|}{\overset{\text{CH}_2}{\text{CH}_2}}}}}} \qquad [26c]
$$

Since the effect of these reactions is to produce n amino acids and n keto acids from n different amino acids and n different keto acids, no net reduction in the nitrogen content of the system has yet been achieved. The elimination of nitrogen occurs in a variety of ways.

In many micro-organisms, ammonia (NH₃) can be removed from aspartate via a reaction catalyzed by aspartase [27]; the other product, fumarate, is an intermediate of the TCA cycle.

$$
\underset{\text{aspartate}}{\overset{\text{NH}_2\text{CHCOOH}}{\underset{\text{CH}_2\text{COO}^-}{\overset{|}{|}}}} \rightleftharpoons \text{NH}_3 + \underset{\text{fumarate}}{\overset{\text{HOOCCH}}{\underset{\text{CHCOO}^-}{\overset{\|}{}}}} \qquad [27]
$$

A quantitatively more important route is that catalyzed by glutamate dehydrogenase, in which the glutamate formed in [26c] is oxidized to α-oxoglutarate, another TCA cycle intermediate [28]. Either NADP⁺ or both NADP⁺ and NAD⁺ may serve as the hydrogen or electron acceptor, depending on the organism; and some organisms synthesize two enzymes, one of which prefers NADP⁺ and the other NAD⁺. In reaction [28], NAD(P)⁺ is used to indicate

$$
\underset{\text{glutamate}}{\overset{\text{NH}_2\text{CHCOOH}}{\underset{\text{CH}_2\text{COO}^-}{\overset{|}{\underset{|}{\text{CH}_2}}}}} + \text{NAD(P)}^+ \rightleftharpoons \underset{\alpha\text{-oxoglutarate}}{\overset{\text{O=CCOOH}}{\underset{\text{CH}_2\text{COO}^-}{\overset{|}{\underset{|}{\text{CH}_2}}}}} + \text{NAD(P)H} + \text{H}^+ + \text{NH}_3 \quad [28]
$$

that either NAD⁺, NADP⁺, or both may serve as the electron acceptor.

The occurrence of the transfer reactions [26] and either step [27] or, more importantly, step [28] allows the channelling of many amino acids into a common pathway by which nitrogen can be eliminated as ammonia.

Disposal of nitrogen. In animals that excrete ammonia as the main nitrogenous waste product (*e.g.*, some marine invertebrates, crustaceans), it is derived from nitrogen transfer reactions [26] and oxidation via glutamate dehydrogenase [28] as described above for micro-organisms. Because ammonia is toxic to cells, however, it is detoxified as it forms. This process involves an enzyme-catalyzed reaction between ammonia and a molecule of glutamate; ATP provides the energy for the reaction, which results in the formation of glutamine, ADP, and inorganic phosphate [29]. This reaction [29] is cata-

$$
\underset{\text{glutamate}}{\overset{\text{NH}_2\text{CHCOOH}}{\underset{\text{CH}_2\text{COO}^-}{\overset{|}{\underset{|}{\text{CH}_2}}}}} + \text{NH}_3 + \text{ATP} \longrightarrow \underset{\text{glutamine}}{\overset{\text{NH}_2\text{CHCOOH}}{\underset{\text{O}}{\overset{|}{\underset{\|}{\underset{\text{CH}_2\text{CNH}_2}{\overset{|}{\text{CH}_2}}}}}}} + \text{ADP} + \text{P}_i \quad [29]
$$

lyzed by glutamine synthetase, which is subject to a variety of metabolic controls. The glutamine thus formed gives up the amide nitrogen in the kidney tubules. As a result glutamate is formed once again, and ammonia is released into the urine.

In terrestrial reptiles and birds, uric acid rather than glutamate is the compound with which nitrogen combines to form a nontoxic substance for transfer to the kidney tubules. Uric acid is formed by a complex pathway that begins with ribose-5-phosphate and during which a so-called purine skeleton (see Figure 11) is formed; in the course of this process, nitrogen atoms from glutamine and the amino acids aspartic acid and glycine are incorporated into the skeleton. These nitrogen donors are derived from other amino acids via amino group transfer [26] and the reaction catalyzed by glutamine synthetase [29].

In such animals as most fishes, amphibians, and mammals, nitrogen is detoxified in the liver and excreted as urea, a readily soluble and harmless product. The sequence leading to the formation of urea, commonly called the urea cycle, is summarized as follows: Ammonia, formed from glutamate and NAD⁺ in the liver mitochondria (reaction [28]), reacts with carbon dioxide and ATP to form carbamyl phosphate, ADP, and inorganic phosphate, as shown in reaction [30].

$$
\text{NH}_3 + \text{CO}_2 + 2\text{ATP} \longrightarrow \underset{\substack{\text{carbamyl}\\\text{phosphate}}}{\text{NH}_2\text{COO}\,\textcircled{P}} + 2\text{ADP} + \text{P}_i \qquad [30]
$$

The reaction is catalyzed by carbamyl phosphate synthetase. The carbamyl moiety of carbamyl phosphate (NH₂COO—) is transferred to ornithine, an amino acid, in a reaction catalyzed by ornithine transcarbamylase; the products are citrulline and inorganic phosphate [31].

$$
\text{NH}_2\text{COO}\,\textcircled{P} + \underset{\text{ornithine}}{\overset{\text{H}_2\text{NCH}_2\text{CH}_2\text{CH}_2\text{CHCOOH}}{\underset{\text{NH}_2}{\overset{|}{}}}} \qquad [31]
$$

$$
\longrightarrow \underset{\text{citrulline}}{\overset{\text{H}_2\text{NCNH(CH}_2)_3\text{CHCOOH}}{\underset{\text{O}\quad\quad\quad\text{NH}_2}{\overset{\|}{}}}} + \text{P}_i
$$

Citrulline and aspartate formed from amino acids via step [26b] react to form argininosuccinate [32]; arginino-

$$
\underset{\text{citrulline}}{\overset{\text{H}_2\text{NCNH(CH}_2)_3\text{CHCOOH}}{\underset{\text{O}\quad\quad\quad\text{NH}_2}{\overset{\|}{}}}} + \text{ATP} + \underset{\text{aspartate}}{\overset{\text{NH}_2\text{CHCOOH}}{\underset{\text{COO}^-}{\overset{|}{\underset{|}{\text{CH}_2}}}}} \qquad [32]
$$

$$
\longrightarrow \text{H}_2\text{O} + \text{AMP} + \text{PP}_i + \underset{\text{argininosuccinate}}{\overset{\text{HN}=\text{CNH(CH}_2)_3\text{CHCOOH}}{\underset{\text{HN}\quad\quad\quad\text{NH}_2}{\overset{|}{\underset{|}{\underset{\text{COO}^-}{\overset{|}{\underset{\text{CH}_2}{\overset{|}{\text{CHCOOH}}}}}}}}}}
$$

succinic acid synthetase catalyzes the reaction. Argininosuccinate splits into fumarate and arginine during a reaction catalyzed by argininosuccinase [32a]. In the final

$$
\underset{\text{argininosuccinate}}{\overset{\text{HN}=\text{CNH(CH}_2)_3\text{CHCOOH}}{\underset{\text{HN}\quad\quad\quad\text{NH}_2}{\overset{|}{\underset{|}{\underset{\text{COO}^-}{\overset{|}{\underset{\text{CH}_2}{\overset{|}{\text{CHCOOH}}}}}}}}}} \qquad [32a]
$$

$$
\rightleftharpoons \underset{\text{arginine}}{\overset{\text{H}_2\text{NCNH(CH}_2)_3\text{CHCOOH}}{\underset{\text{NH}\quad\quad\quad\text{NH}_2}{\overset{\|}{}}}} + \underset{\text{fumarate}}{\overset{\text{HOOCCH}}{\underset{\text{CHCOO}^-}{\overset{\|}{}}}}
$$

step of the urea cycle, arginine, in a reaction catalyzed by arginase, is hydrolyzed [33]. Urea and ornithine are

$$
\underset{\text{arginine}}{\overset{\text{H}_2\text{NCNH(CH}_2)_3\text{CHCOOH}}{\underset{\text{NH}\quad\quad\quad\text{NH}_2}{\overset{\|}{}}}} + \text{H}_2\text{O} \qquad [33]
$$

$$
\longrightarrow \underset{\text{urea}}{\overset{\text{O}}{\overset{\|}{\text{H}_2\text{N}--\text{C}-\text{NH}_2}}} + \underset{\text{ornithine}}{\overset{\text{H}_2\text{NCH}_2\text{CH}_2\text{CH}_2\text{CHCOOH}}{\underset{\text{NH}_2}{\overset{|}{}}}}
$$

the products; ornithine thus is available to initiate another cycle beginning at step [31].

Oxidation of the carbon skeleton. As indicated in Figure 2, the carbon skeletons of amino acids (*i.e.*, the portion of the molecule remaining after the removal of nitrogen) are fragmented to form only a few end products; all of them are intermediates of either glycolysis or the TCA cycle. The number and complexity of the catabolic steps by which each amino acid arrives at its catabolic end point reflects the chemical complexity of that amino acid. Thus, in the case of alanine, only the amino group must be removed to yield pyruvate; the amino acid threonine, on the other hand, must be transformed successively to the amino acids glycine and serine before pyruvate is formed.

The fragmentation of leucine to acetyl coenzyme A involves seven steps; that of tryptophan to the same end product requires 11. (A detailed discussion of the events that enable each of the 20 commonly occurring amino acids to enter central metabolic pathways is beyond the scope of this article.)

III. The combustion of food materials

Although the pathways for fragmentation of food materials effect the conversion of a large variety of relatively complex starting materials into only a few simpler intermediates of central metabolic routes—mainly pyruvate, acetyl coenzyme A, and a few intermediates of the TCA cycle—their operation releases but a fraction of the energy contained in the materials. The reason is that, in the fermentation process, catabolic intermediates serve also as the terminal acceptors of the reducing equivalents (hydrogen atoms or electrons) that are removed during the oxidation of food; the end products thus may be at the same oxidation level and may contain equivalent numbers of carbon, hydrogen, and oxygen atoms, as the material that was catabolized by a fermentative route. The necessity for pyruvate, for example, to act as hydrogen acceptor in the fermentation of glucose to lactate (see reactions [1] through [11a]) results in the conservation of all the component atoms of the glucose molecule in the form of lactate. The consequent release of energy as ATP (in steps [7] and [10]) is thus small.

The importance to the cell of complete oxidation

A more favourable situation arises if the reducing equivalents formed by oxidation of nutrients can be passed on to an inorganic acceptor such as oxygen. In this case, the products of fermentation need not act as "hydrogen sinks," in which the energy in the molecule is lost when it leaves the cell; instead, the products of fermentation can be degraded further, during phase III of catabolism, and all the usable chemical energy of the nutrient can be transformed into ATP.

This section describes the manner in which the products obtained by the fragmentation of nutrients are oxidized (*i.e.*, the manner in which hydrogen atoms or electrons are removed from them) and the manner in which these reducing equivalents react with oxygen, with concomitant formation of ATP.

THE OXIDATION OF MOLECULAR FRAGMENTS

The oxidation of pyruvate. The oxidation of pyruvate involves the concerted action of several enzymes and coenzymes collectively called the pyruvate dehydrogenase complex; *i.e.*, a multi-enzyme complex in which the substrates are passed consecutively from one enzyme to the next, and the product of the reaction catalyzed by the first enzyme immediately becomes the substrate for the second enzyme in the complex. The overall reaction is the formation of acetyl coenzyme A and carbon dioxide from pyruvate, with concomitant liberation of two reducing equivalents in the form of (NADH + H⁺). The individual reactions that result in the formation of these end products are as follows.

Pyruvate first reacts with the coenzyme of pyruvic acid decarboxylase, thiamine pyrophosphate (TPP); in addition to carbon dioxide a hydroxyethyl–TPP–enzyme complex ("active acetaldehyde") is formed [34]. Thiamine is vitamin B_1; the biological role of TPP was first revealed by the inability of vitamin B_1-deficient animals to oxidize pyruvate.

The hydroxyethyl moiety formed in [34] is immediately

transferred to one of the two sulfur atoms (S) of the coenzyme (6,8-dithio-*n*-octanoate or $lipS_2$) of the second enzyme in the complex, dihydrolipoyl transacetylase. The hydroxyethyl group attaches to $lipS_2$ at one of its sulfur atoms, as shown in [35]; the result is that coenzyme

$lipS_2$ is reduced and the hydroxyethyl moiety is oxidized.

The acetyl group ($CH_3C=O$) then is transferred to the sulfhydryl (—SH) group of coenzyme A, thereby completing the oxidation of pyruvate (reaction [36]).

The coenzyme $lipS_2$ that accepted the hydroxyethyl moiety in step [35] of the sequence, now reduced, must be reoxidized before another molecule of pyruvate can be oxidized. The reoxidation of the coenzyme is achieved by the enzyme-catalyzed transfer of two reducing equivalents initially to the coenzyme flavin adenine dinucleotide (FAD) and thence to the NAD⁺ that is the first carrier in the so-called electron transport chain. The passage of two such reducing equivalents from reduced NAD⁺ to oxygen is accompanied by the formation of three molecules of ATP (see *Biological energy transduction*).

The overall reaction may be written as shown in [37],

in which pyruvate reacts with coenzyme A in the presence of TPP and lipS₂ to form acetyl coenzyme A and carbon dioxide. The lipS₂ reduced during this process is reoxidized in the presence of the enzyme lipoyl dehydrogenase, with the concomitant reduction of NAD⁺.

The tricarboxylic acid (TCA) cycle. Acetyl coenzyme A arises not only from the oxidation of pyruvate but also from that of fats (Figure 5) and many of the amino acids comprising proteins (Figure 2); the sequence of enzyme-catalyzed steps that effects the total combustion of the acetyl moiety of the coenzyme represents the terminal oxidative pathway for virtually all food materials. The balance of the overall reaction of the TCA cycle [37a] is that three molecules of water react with acetyl

$$CH_3CS-CoA+3H_2O \longrightarrow 2CO_2+CoA-SH+4\,[2H] \qquad [37a]$$

acetyl coenzyme A   reducing
                                     equivalents

coenzyme A to form carbon dioxide, coenzyme A, and reducing equivalents. The oxidation by oxygen of the reducing equivalents is accompanied by the conservation (as ATP) of most of the energy of the food ingested by aerobic organisms.

The relative complexity and number of chemical events that comprise the TCA cycle, and their location as components of spatially determined structures such as cell membranes in micro-organisms and mitochondria in plants and higher animals, reflect the problems involved chemically in "dismembering" a compound having only two carbon atoms and releasing in a controlled and stepwise manner the reducing equivalents ultimately to be passed to oxygen. These problems have been overcome by the simple but effective device of initially combining the two-carbon compound with a four-carbon acceptor; it is much less difficult chemically to dismember and oxidize a compound having six carbon atoms.

In the TCA cycle, acetyl coenzyme A initially reacts with oxaloacetate to yield citrate and to liberate coenzyme A.

$$CH_3CS-CoA + CCOOH + H_2O \longrightarrow HOCCOOH + CoA-SH \qquad [38]$$

acetyl   oxaloacetate   citrate
coenzymeA

This reaction [38] is catalyzed by citrate synthase. (As mentioned above, many of the compounds in living cells that take part in metabolic pathways exist as charged moieties, or anions, and are named as such. Citrate undergoes isomerization (*i.e.*, a rearrangement of certain atoms comprising the molecule) to form isocitrate [39]. The reaction involves first the removal of the

$$\text{citrate} \xrightleftharpoons[+H_2O]{-H_2O} \text{cis-aconitate} \xrightleftharpoons[-H_2O]{+H_2O} \text{isocitrate} \qquad [39]$$

citrate   *cis*-aconitate   isocitrate

elements of water from citrate to form *cis*-aconitate, and then the re-addition of water to *cis*-aconitate in such a way that isocitrate is formed. It is probable that all three reactants—citrate, *cis*-aconitate, and isocitrate—remain closely associated with aconitase, the enzyme that catalyzes the isomerization process, and that most of the *cis*-aconitate is not released from the enzyme surface but is immediately converted to isocitrate.

Isocitrate is oxidized—*i.e.*, hydrogen is removed—to form oxalosuccinate; the two hydrogen atoms are usually transferred to NAD⁺, thus forming reduced NAD⁺ [40]; in some micro-organisms, and during the biosynthesis of

$$\text{isocitrate} + \text{NAD(P)}^+ \longrightarrow \text{oxalosuccinate} + \text{NAD(P)H} + H^+ \qquad [40]$$

isocitrate   oxalosuccinate

glutamate in the cytoplasm of animal cells, however, the hydrogen atoms may also be accepted by NADP⁺. Thus the enzyme controlling this reaction, isocitrate dehydrogenase, differs in specificity for the coenzymes; various forms occur not only in different organisms but even within the same cell. In [40] NAD(P)⁺ indicates that either NAD⁺ or NADP⁺ can act as a hydrogen acceptor.

The position of the carboxyl group (—COOH) that is "sandwiched" in the middle of the oxalosuccinate molecule renders it very unstable; as a result, the carboxyl group is lost as carbon dioxide (note the dotted rectangle)

$$\text{oxalosuccinate} \longrightarrow \alpha\text{-oxoglutarate} + CO_2 \qquad [41]$$

oxalosuccinate   α-oxoglutarate

in a reaction [41] that can occur spontaneously but may be further accelerated by an enzyme.

The five-carbon product of reaction [41], α-oxoglutarate, has chemical properties similar to pyruvate (free acid forms of both are so-called α-oxoacids), and the chemical events involved in the oxidation of α-oxoglutarate are analogous to those already described for the oxidation of pyruvate (see reaction [37]). Reaction [42] is

$$\text{α-oxoglutarate} + CoA-SH + NAD^+ \qquad [42]$$

α-oxoglutarate

$$\longrightarrow \text{succinyl coenzyme A} + CO_2 + NADH + H^+$$

succinyl
coenzyme A

effected by a multi-enzyme complex; TPP, lipS₂ (6,8-dithio-n-octanoate), and coenzyme A are required as coenzymes. The products are carbon dioxide and succinyl coenzyme A. As was noted with reaction [37], this oxidation of α-oxoglutarate results in the reduction of lipS₂, which must be reoxidized. This is done by transfer of reducing equivalents to FAD and thence to NAD⁺. The resultant NADH + H⁺ is reoxidized by the passage of the electrons, ultimately, to oxygen, via the electron transport chain.

Unlike the acetyl coenzyme A produced from pyruvate in reaction [37], succinyl coenzyme A undergoes a phosphorolysis reaction—*i.e.*, transfer of the succinyl moiety from coenzyme A to inorganic phosphate. The succinyl phosphate thus formed is not released from the enzyme surface; an unstable, high-energy compound called an acid anhydride, it transfers a high-energy phosphate to ADP, directly or via guanosine diphosphate (GDP). If guanosine triphosphate (GTP) forms, ATP can readily arise from it in an exchange involving ADP [43a].

$$GTP + ADP \rightleftharpoons ATP + GDP \qquad [43a]$$

The remainder of the reactions of the TCA cycle serve to regenerate the initial four-carbon acceptor of acetyl coenzyme A (oxaloacetate) from succinate, the process requiring in effect the oxidation of a hydrocarbon group (—CH₂—) to a carbonyl group (—CO—), with concomitant release of reducing equivalents (2[2H]). It is therefore similar to, and is effected in like manner to, the oxidation of fatty acids (steps [22–24]; see Figure 5). As is the case with fatty acids, hydrogen atoms or electrons are initially removed from the succinate formed in [43] and are accepted by FAD; the reaction, catalyzed by

$$\text{succinyl coenzyme A} + P_i + \substack{ADP \\ \text{or} \\ GDP} \longrightarrow \text{succinate} + CoA-SH + \substack{ATP \\ \text{or} \\ GTP} \qquad [43]$$

succinyl   succinate
coenzyme A

succinate dehydrogenase [44], results in the formation of fumarate and reduced FAD.

$$\begin{array}{c}\text{CH}_2\text{COOH}\\|\\\text{CH}_2\text{COO}^-\end{array} + \text{FAD} \longrightarrow \begin{array}{c}\text{HOOCCH}\\\|\\\text{CHCOO}^-\end{array} + \text{FADH}_2 \qquad [44]$$

succinate   fumarate

The elements of water are added across the double bond (—CH=CH—) of fumarate in a reaction catalyzed by fumarase [45]; this type of reaction also occurred in step [39] of the cycle. The product of reaction [45] is malate.

$$\begin{array}{c}\text{HOOCCH}\\|\\\text{CHCOO}^-\end{array} + \text{H}_2\text{O} \longrightarrow \begin{array}{c}\text{HOCHCOOH}\\|\\\text{CH}_2\text{COO}^-\end{array} \qquad [45]$$

fumarate   malate

Malate can be oxidized to oxaloacetate by removal of two hydrogen atoms, which are accepted by NAD$^+$. This type of reaction, catalyzed by malate dehydrogenase in reaction [46], also occurred in step [40] of the cycle. The formation of oxaloacetate completes the TCA cycle, which can now begin again with the formation of citrate [38].

$$\begin{array}{c}\text{HOCHCOOH}\\|\\\text{CH}_2\text{COO}^-\end{array} + \text{NAD}^+ \longrightarrow \begin{array}{c}\text{O}\\\|\\\text{CCOOH}\\|\\\text{CH}_2\text{COO}^-\end{array} + \text{NADH} + \text{H}^+ \quad [46]$$

malate   oxaloacetate

A summary of the energy conserved during the TCA cycle

The loss of the two molecules of carbon dioxide in steps [41] and [42] does not yield biologically useful energy. The formation of ATP accompanies step [43], in which one molecule of ATP is formed during each turn of the cycle. The hydrogen ions and electrons that result from steps [40], [42], [44], and [46] are passed down the chain of respiratory carriers to oxygen, with the concomitant formation of ATP (see below). The oxidation of each molecule of reduced NAD$^+$ is coupled to the formation of three molecules of ATP. Similarly, the oxidation of reduced FAD results in the formation of two ATP. Each turn of the cycle can thus lead to the production of 11 ATP in this way, and a total of 12 ATP are produced, including that in [43]. It will be recalled that the fragmentation of glucose to two molecules of pyruvate yielded two ATP; the aerobic oxidation via the TCA cycle of two molecules of pyruvate thus makes available to the cell at least 15 times more ATP per molecule of glucose catabolized than is produced anaerobically.

BIOLOGICAL ENERGY TRANSDUCTION

Adenosine triphosphate as the currency of energy exchange. At the normal pH of the cell (pH is a measure of the acidity or alkalinity of a solution; the normal pH of a cell is about 7 on a scale of 1 to 14) the three phosphate (or, more precisely, phosphoryl) groups of ATP (see Figure 1) are almost completely negatively charged (i.e., ionized) because of the four negatively charged oxygen atoms (O$^-$). The negative charges are very close together and strongly repel each other. The hydrolysis of ATP to ADP, with the formation of a phosphoryl group and a hydrogen ion [47] relieves some of the electrostatic repulsion. The negatively charged products (ADP and the phosphoryl group), which are electrically more stable than the parent molecule, do not readily recombine.

$$\text{ATP}^{-4} + \text{H}_2\text{O} \longrightarrow \text{ADP}^{-3} + \text{HPO}_4^{-2} + \text{H}^+ \qquad [47]$$

The total free energy (G) of the products is much less than that of ATP; hence the reaction proceeds with the liberation of energy (i.e., it is exergonic). The amount of energy liberated under strictly defined conditions is called the standard free energy change ($\Delta G'$); this value for the hydrolysis of ATP is relatively high, at —8 kilocalories per mole. (One kilocalorie is the amount of heat required to raise the temperature of 1,000 grams of water one degree centigrade.) Conversely, the formation of ATP from ADP and inorganic phosphate (P$_i$) is an energy-requiring (i.e., endergonic) reaction with a standard free energy change of +8 kilocalories per mole.

The hydrolysis of the terminal phosphate of ADP is also accompanied by a considerable liberation of free energy (the standard free energy change is —6.5 kilocalories per mole); AMP hydrolysis liberates less energy (the standard free energy change is —2.2 kilocalories per mole).

The free energy of hydrolysis of a compound thus is a measure of the difference in energy content between the starting substances (reactants) and the final substances (products). Adenosine triphosphate does not have the highest standard free energy of hydrolysis of all the naturally occurring phosphates but instead occupies a position at approximately the halfway point in a series of phosphate compounds with a wide range of standard free energies of hydrolysis. Compounds such as 1,3-diphosphoglycerate or phosphoenolpyruvate (PEP), which are above ATP (see Figure 6), are often called high-energy

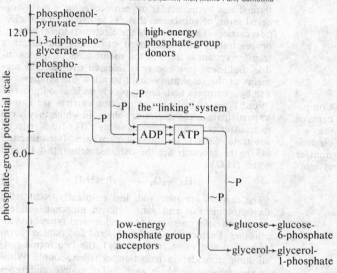

From A.L. Lehninger, *Bioenergetics*, copyright © 1965, W.A. Benjamin, Inc., Menlo Park, California

Figure 6: The transfer of phosphate groups from high-energy donors to low-energy acceptors by way of the ATP–ADP system (see text).

phosphates; they are said to exhibit a high phosphate group transfer potential because they have a tendency to lose their phosphate groups. Compounds such as glucose-6-phosphate or fructose-6-phosphate, which are below ATP, have a tendency to hold on to their phosphate groups and thus act as low-energy phosphate acceptors. Both ATP and ADP act as intermediate carriers for the transfer of phosphate groups (more precisely, phosphoryl groups) and hence of energy, from compounds lying above ATP to those lying beneath it. Thus, in glycolysis, ADP acts as an acceptor during the synthesis of ATP from PEP (see reaction [10]), and ATP acts as a donor during the formation of fructose-1,6-diphosphate from fructose-6-phosphate (see reaction [3]).

The function of ATP as a common intermediate of energy transfer during anabolism is further dealt with below (see *The biosynthesis of cell components*). In certain specialized cells or tissues the chemical energy of ATP is used to perform work other than the chemical work of anabolism; for example, mechanical work—such as muscular contraction, or the movement of contractile structures called cilia and flagella, which are responsible for the motility of many small organisms. The performance of osmotic work also requires ATP; e.g., the transport of ions or metabolites through membranes against a concentration gradient, a process that is basically responsible for many physiological functions, including the secretion of hydrochloric acid in the stomach and the removal of water from the kidneys.

The utilization of ATP to perform work

Energy conservation. The synthesis of ATP affords a means by which energy liberated during the oxidative stages of catabolism can be conserved in a stable, utilizable form until such time as the cell needs energy to drive various energy-requiring processes. The catabolism-linked synthesis of ATP occurs by two quite distinct mechanisms: one is called substrate level phosphorylation; the other, oxidative, or respiratory chain, phosphorylation. Oxidative phosphorylation is the major method of energy conservation under aerobic conditions in all non-photosynthetic cells.

Substrate level phosphorylation. In substrate level phosphorylation a phosphoryl group is transferred from an energy-rich donor (*e.g.*, 1,3-diphosphoglycerate) to ADP to yield a molecule of ATP. This type of ATP synthesis (see reactions [7], [10], and [43]) does not require molecular oxygen (O_2), although it is frequently, but not always, preceded by an oxidation (*i.e.*, dehydrogenation) reaction. Substrate level phosphorylation is the major method of energy conservation in oxygen-depleted tissues and during fermentative growth of micro-organisms.

Oxidative, or respiratory chain, phosphorylation. In oxidative phosphorylation, the oxidation of catabolic intermediates by molecular oxygen occurs via a highly ordered series of substances that act as hydrogen and electron carriers. They constitute the electron transfer system, or respiratory chain. In most organisms, the electron transfer system is fixed in the membranes of mitochondria. Sufficient free energy is released over certain segments of the respiratory chain to allow the synthesis of ATP by a complex and, as yet, poorly understood process.

Four types of hydrogen or electron carriers are known to participate in the respiratory chain, in which they serve to transfer two reducing equivalents (2H) from reduced substrate (AH_2) to molecular oxygen (see reaction [48]); the products are the oxidized substrate (A) and water (H_2O).

$$AH_2 + \tfrac{1}{2}O_2 \longrightarrow A + H_2O \qquad [48]$$

The carriers are NAD⁺ and, less frequently, NADP⁺; the flavoproteins FAD and FMN (flavin mononucleotide); ubiquinone (or coenzyme Q); and several types of cytochromes. Each carrier has an oxidized and reduced form (*e.g.*, FAD and $FADH_2$, respectively), the two forms constituting an oxidation–reduction, or redox, couple. Within the respiratory chain each redox couple undergoes cyclic oxidation–reduction—*i.e.*, the oxidized component of the couple accepts reducing equivalents from either a substrate or a reduced carrier preceding it in the series, and in turn donates these reducing equivalents to the next oxidized carrier in the sequence. Reducing equivalents are thus transferred from substrates to molecular oxygen by a number of sequential redox reactions.

Most oxidizable catabolic intermediates initially undergo a dehydrogenation reaction, during which a dehydrogenase enzyme transfers the equivalent of a hydride ion ($H^+ + 2e^-$, e^- representing an electron) to its coenzyme, either NAD⁺ or NADP⁺ (as examples, see [40] and [46]). The reduced NAD⁺ (or NADP⁺) thus produced diffuses to the membrane-bound respiratory chain to be oxi-

dized by an enzyme known as NADH dehydrogenase; the enzyme has as its coenzyme FMN. There is no corresponding NADPH dehydrogenase in mammalian mitochondria; instead, the reducing equivalents of reduced NADP⁺ are transferred to NAD⁺ in a reaction catalyzed by a transhydrogenase enzyme, with the products being reduced NAD⁺ and NADP⁺. A few substrates (*e.g.*, acyl coenzyme A and succinate; see reactions [22] and [44]) bypass this reaction and instead undergo immediate dehydrogenation by specific membrane-bound dehydrogenase enzymes. During the reaction, the coenzyme FAD accepts two hydrogen atoms and two electrons ($2H + 2e^-$). The reduced flavoproteins (*i.e.*, reduced FMN and reduced FAD) donate their two hydrogen atoms to the lipid carrier ubiquinone, which is thus reduced. The fourth type of carrier, the cytochromes, consists of hemoproteins—*i.e.*, proteins with a nonprotein component, or prosthetic group, called heme (or a derivative of heme), which is an iron-containing pigment molecule. The iron atom in the prosthetic group is able to carry one electron and oscillates between the oxidized, or ferric (Fe^{3+}), and the reduced, or ferrous (Fe^{2+}), forms. The five cytochromes present in the mammalian respiratory chain, designated cytochromes b, c_1, c, a, and a_3, act in sequence between ubiquinone and molecular oxygen. The terminal cytochrome of this sequence (a_3, also known as cytochrome oxidase) is able to donate electrons to oxygen rather than to another electron carrier; a_3 is also the site of action of two substances that inhibit the respiratory chain, potassium cyanide and carbon monoxide.

It is suspected that other iron-containing proteins also act as electron carriers at several points in the respiratory chain, but, because their exact sites of action have not yet been clarified, they have been omitted from the schematic diagram of the respiratory chain shown in Figure 7.

In each redox couple the reduced form has a tendency to lose reducing equivalents (*i.e.*, to act as an electron or hydrogen donor); similarly, the oxidized form has a tendency to gain reducing equivalents (*i.e.*, to act as an electron or hydrogen acceptor). The oxidation–reduction characteristics of each couple can be determined experimentally under well-defined, standard conditions. The value thus obtained is the standard oxidation–reduction (redox) potential (E_6'). Values for respiratory chain carriers range from $E_6' = -320$ millivolts (one millivolt $= 0.001$ volt) for NAD⁺/reduced NAD⁺ to $E_6' = +820$ millivolts for $\tfrac{1}{2}O_2/H_2O$; the values for intermediate carriers lie between. Reduced NAD⁺ is the most electronegative carrier, oxygen the most electropositive acceptor. During respiration reducing equivalents undergo stepwise transfer from the reduced form of the most electronegative carrier (reduced NAD⁺) to the oxidized form of the most electropositive couple (oxygen). Each step is accompanied by a decline in standard free energy

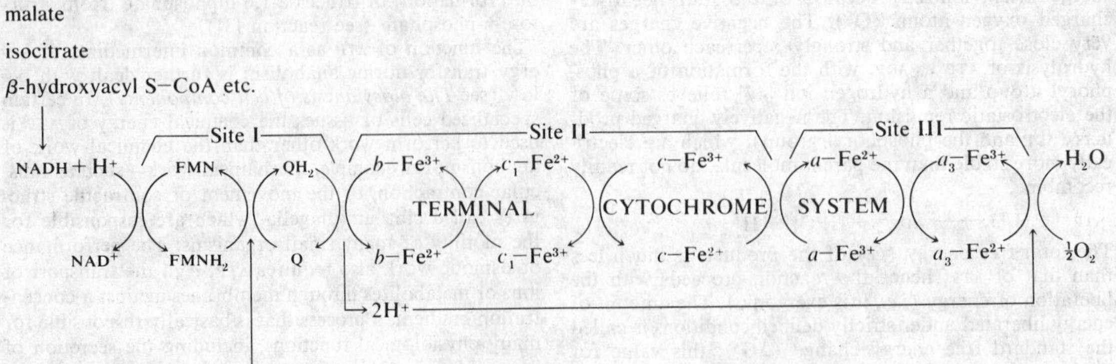

Components of the electron transfer system

malate

isocitrate

β-hydroxyacyl S—CoA etc.

Figure 7: The respiratory chain (see text).

($\Delta G'$) proportional to the difference in the standard redox potentials (ΔE_0) of the two carriers involved.

Overall oxidation of reduced NAD^+ by oxygen ($\Delta E_0 = +1,140$ millivolts) is accompanied by the liberation of free energy ($\Delta G' = -52.4$ kilocalories per mole); in theory this energy is sufficient to allow the synthesis of six or seven molecules of ATP. In the cell, however, this synthesis of ATP, called oxidative phosphorylation, proceeds with an efficiency of about 46 percent; thus only three molecules of ATP are produced per atom of oxygen consumed—this being the so-called $P/2e^-$, P/O, or ADP/O ratio. The energy that is not conserved as ATP is lost as heat. The oxidation of succinate by molecular oxygen ($\Delta E_0 = +790$ millivolts), which is accompanied by a smaller liberation of free energy ($\Delta G' = -36.5$ kilocalories per mole), yields only two molecules of ATP per atom of oxygen consumed ($P/O = 2$).

One phosphorylation site is located at the level at which NADH dehydrogenase acts—between reduced NAD^+ and ubiquinone (site I in Figure 7). A second phosphorylation site is located between ubiquinone and cytochrome c (site II), and a third between cytochrome c and oxygen (site III).

The "energized state"

The mechanism by which the energy released during respiration is conserved as ATP is far from clear. Some form of nonphosphorylated "energized state" is produced in the mitochondrial membrane prior to the formation of ATP, but its exact identity is the subject of considerable controversy.

A respiratory control mechanism allows the cell to consume oxygen only when it needs to synthesize ATP. In the absence of ADP the "energized state" is quite stable and is capable of driving a number of energy-requiring, or endergonic, membrane phenomena. When, under certain experimental conditions in the absence of ADP, these phenomena cannot occur, respiratory control can be demonstrated. The "energized state" accumulates and oxygen comsumption slows because there is no ADP present to allow the formation of ATP. If ADP is then added, the "energized state" is dissipated as ATP is synthesized, and the rate of oxygen consumption increases until all of the ADP has been converted into ATP, at which point oxygen consumption again slows. A similar circumstance occurs in the cell; when sufficient ATP is present, the concentration of ADP is low, and the consumption of both the "energized state" and oxygen is low.

As mentioned above, the oxidative phosphorylation systems of animal cells, as well as those of green plants and yeast, are located within mitochondria. These are particularly numerous in tissues requiring large amounts of energy either for mechanical (heart and skeletal muscle of animals) or biosynthetic (pancreas of animals) purposes. In transverse section, mitochondria are seen to consist of an outer, limiting membrane and a highly folded inner membrane (crista). The latter, which contains the respiratory carriers and the enzymes responsible for ATP synthesis and fatty acid oxidation, encloses a highly viscous matrix, which contains the soluble enzymes of the TCA cycle (see also CELL AND CELL DIVISION). The multienzyme systems primarily responsible for the release and subsequent oxidation of reducing equivalents are thus spatially related such that the products of catabolism (reduced NAD^+ and $FADH_2$) are readily available as substrates for respiration. The oxidative phosphorylation systems of bacteria are located in the cell membrane and exhibit much greater diversity than do those of other cells with respect to composition of the respiratory carriers.

IV. The biosynthesis of cell components

THE NATURE OF BIOSYNTHESIS

The stages of biosynthesis. The biosynthesis of cell components (anabolism) may be regarded as occurring in two main stages. In the first, intermediate compounds of the central routes of metabolism are diverted from further catabolism and are channelled into pathways that usually lead to the formation of the relatively small molecules that serve as the building blocks, or precursors, of macromolecules.

In the second stage of biosynthesis, the building blocks are combined to yield the macromolecules—proteins, nucleic acids, lipids, and polysaccharides—that make up the bulk of tissues and cellular components. In organisms with the appropriate genetic capability, for example, all of the amino acids can be synthesized from intermediates of the main routes of carbohydrate fragmentation and oxidation. Such intermediates act also as precursors for the purines, the pyrimidines, and the pentose sugars that comprise deoxyribonucleic acid (DNA) and for a number of types of ribonucleic acid (RNA). The assembly of proteins necessitates the precise combination of specific amino acids in a highly ordered and controlled manner; this in turn involves the copying, or transcription, into RNA of specific parts of DNA (see below *The synthesis of macromolecules*). The first stage of biosynthesis thus requires the specificity normally required for the efficient functioning of sequences of enzyme-catalyzed reactions. The second stage also involves—directly for protein and nucleic acid synthesis, less directly for the synthesis of other macromolecules—the maintenance and expression of the biological information that specifies the identity of the cell, the tissue, and the organism.

Utilization of ATP. The two stages of biosynthesis—the formation of building blocks and their specific assembly into macromolecules—are energy-consuming processes and thus require ATP. Although the ATP is derived from catabolism, catabolism does not "drive" biosynthesis. As explained in the first section of this article, the occurrence of chemical reactions in the living cell is accompanied by a net decrease in free energy. Although biological growth and development result in the creation of ordered systems from less ordered ones and of complex systems from simpler ones, these events must occur at the expense of energy-yielding reactions. The overall coupled reactions are, on balance, still accompanied by a decrease in free energy, and are thus essentially irreversible in the direction of biosynthesis. The total energy released from ATP, for example, is usually much greater than is needed for a particular biosynthetic step; thus, many of the reactions involved in biosynthesis release inorganic pyrophosphate (PP_i) rather than phosphate (P_i) from ATP, and hence yield AMP rather than ADP. Since inorganic pyrophosphate readily undergoes virtually irreversible hydrolysis to two equivalents of inorganic phosphate (see [21a]), the creation of a new bond in the product of synthesis may be accompanied by the breaking of two high-energy bonds of ATP—although, in theory, one might have sufficed.

The roles of enzyme regulation and cellular compartmentalization in anabolism

The efficient utilization for anabolic processes of ATP and some intermediate compound formed during a catabolic reaction requires the cell to have simultaneously a milieu favourable for both ATP generation and consumption. Catabolism occurs readily only if sufficient ADP is available; hence, the concentration of ATP is low. On the other hand, biosynthesis requires a high level of ATP and consequently low levels of ADP and AMP. Suitable conditions for the simultaneous function of both processes are met in two ways. Biosynthetic reactions often take place in compartments within the cell different from those in which catabolism occurs; there is thus a physical separation of energy-requiring and energy-yielding processes. Furthermore, biosynthetic reactions are regulated independently of the mechanisms by which catabolism is controlled. Such independent control is made possible by the fact that catabolic and anabolic pathways are not identical; the pacemaker, or key, enzyme that controls the overall rate of a catabolic route usually does not play any role in the biosynthetic pathway of a compound. Similarly, the pacemaker enzymes of biosynthesis are not involved in catabolism. As discussed below (see *Regulation of metabolism: Fine control*), catabolic pathways are often regulated by the relative amounts of ATP, ADP, and AMP in the cellular compartment in which the pacemaker enzymes are located; in general, ATP inhibits and ADP (or AMP) stimulates such enzymes. In contrast, many biosynthetic routes are regulated by the concentration of the end products of particular anabolic processes, so that the cell synthesizes only as much of these building blocks as it needs.

THE SUPPLY OF BIOSYNTHETIC PRECURSORS

When higher animals consume a mixed diet, sufficient quantities of compounds for both biosynthesis and energy supply are available. Carbohydrates yield intermediates of glycolysis and of the phosphogluconate pathway, which in turn yield acetyl coenzyme A (see Figure 4); lipids yield glycolytic intermediates and acetyl coenzyme A (see Figure 2); and many amino acids form intermediates of both the TCA cycle and glycolysis. Any intermediate withdrawn for biosynthesis can thus be readily replenished by the catabolism of further nutrients. This situation does not always hold, however. Micro-organisms in particular can derive all of their carbon and energy requirements by utilizing a single carbon source. The sole carbon source may be a substance such as a carbohydrate or a fatty acid, or an intermediate of the TCA cycle (or readily converted to one). In both cases, reactions ancillary to those discussed thus far must occur before the carbon source can be utilized.

Anaplerotic routes. Although the catabolism of carbohydrates can occur via a variety of routes (see Figure 4), all give rise to pyruvate. During the catabolism of pyruvate, one carbon atom is utilized to form acetyl coenzyme A [37], and two are involved in the TCA cycle ([41] and [42]). Because the TCA cycle is initiated by the condensation of acetyl coenzyme A with oxaloacetate, which is regenerated in each turn of the cycle, the removal of any intermediate from the cycle would cause the cycle to stop. Yet, as also indicated in Figure 4, various essential cell components are derived from α-oxoglutarate, succinyl coenzyme A, and oxaloacetate, so that these compounds are, in fact, removed from the cycle. Microbial growth with a carbohydrate as the sole carbon source is thus possible only if a cellular process occurs that effects the net formation of a TCA cycle intermediate from an intermediate of carbohydrate catabolism. Such a process, which replenishes the TCA cycle, has been described as an anaplerotic reaction.

The anaplerotic function may be carried out by either of two enzymes that catalyze the fixation of carbon dioxide onto a three-carbon compound, either pyruvate [49] or phosphoenolpyruvate (PEP, [50]) to form oxaloacetate, which has four carbon atoms. Both reactions require energy. In [49], it is supplied by the cleavage

$$
\begin{array}{l}
CH_3 \\
| \\
C{=}O \\
| \\
COO^-
\end{array}
+ CO_2 + ATP \longrightarrow
\begin{array}{l}
O \\
\| \\
CCOOH \\
| \\
CH_2COO^-
\end{array}
+ ADP + P_i \quad [49]
$$

pyruvate   oxaloacetate

of ATP to ADP and inorganic phosphate (P_i); in [50] it is supplied by the release of the high-energy phosphate of

$$
\begin{array}{l}
COO^- \\
| \\
CO\,\circledP \\
| \\
CH_2
\end{array}
+ CO_2 \longrightarrow
\begin{array}{l}
O \\
\| \\
CCOOH \\
| \\
CH_2COOH
\end{array}
+ P_i \quad [50]
$$

PEP   oxaloacetate

PEP as inorganic phosphate. Pyruvate serves as a carbon dioxide acceptor not only in many bacteria and fungi but also in the livers of higher organisms, including man; PEP serves as the carbon dioxide acceptor in many bacteria, such as those that inhabit the gut.

Unlike higher organisms, many bacteria and fungi can grow on acetate or compounds such as ethanol or a fatty acid that can be catabolized to acetyl coenzyme A. Under these conditions, the net formation of TCA cycle intermediates proceeds in one of two ways. In obligate anaerobic bacteria, pyruvate can be formed from acetyl coenzyme A and carbon dioxide [51]; reducing equivalents [2H] are necessary for the reaction. The pyruvate so formed can then react via either step [49] or [50].

$$
CH_3\overset{O}{\underset{\|}{C}}S{-}CoA + CO_2 + [2H] \longrightarrow
\begin{array}{l}
CH_3 \\
| \\
C{=}O \\
| \\
COO^-
\end{array}
+ CoA{-}SH \quad [51]
$$

acetyl coenzyme A   pyruvate

Reaction [51] does not occur in many facultative anaerobic organisms or in strict aerobes, however. Instead, in these organisms two molecules of acetyl coenzyme A give rise to the net synthesis of a four-carbon intermediate of the TCA cycle via a route known as the glyoxylate cycle. In this route (Figure 8), the steps of the TCA

The glyoxylate cycle

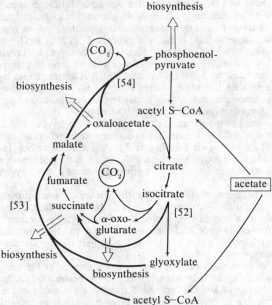

Figure 8: The glyoxylate cycle. Numbers refer to reactions described in text.

cycle that lead to the loss of carbon dioxide (see [40], [41], and [42]) are bypassed. Instead of being oxidized to oxalosuccinate, as occurs in [40], isocitrate is split by isocitrate lyase [52] in a reaction similar to that of

$$
\begin{array}{l}
CH_2COOH \\
| \\
HCCOOH \\
| \\
HOCHCOO^-
\end{array}
\longrightarrow
\begin{array}{l}
CH_2COOH \\
| \\
CH_2COOH
\end{array}
+
\begin{array}{l}
CHO \\
| \\
COOH
\end{array}
\quad [52]
$$

isocitrate   succinate   glyoxylate

reactions [4] and [15] of carbohydrate fragmentation. The dotted line in [52] indicates the way in which isocitrate is split. The products are succinate and glyoxylate. Glyoxylate, like oxaloacetate, is an α-oxoacid and thus can condense, in a reaction catalyzed by malate synthase, with acetyl coenzyme A; the products are coenzyme A and malate [53].

$$
\begin{array}{l}
CHO \\
| \\
COO^-
\end{array}
+ CH_3\overset{O}{\underset{\|}{C}}S{-}CoA + H_2O \longrightarrow
\begin{array}{l}
HOCHCOOH \\
| \\
CH_2COO^-
\end{array}
+ CoA{-}SH \quad [53]
$$

glyoxylate   acetyl   malate
        coenzyme A

In conjunction with the reactions of the TCA cycle that effect the re-formation of isocitrate from malate (steps [46], [38], and [39]) steps [52] and [53] lead to the net production of a four-carbon compound (malate) from two two-carbon units (glyoxylate and acetyl coenzyme A). The sequence thus complements the TCA cycle, enabling the cycle to fulfill the dual roles of providing both energy and biosynthetic building blocks.

Growth of micro-organisms on TCA cycle intermediates. Most aerobic micro-organisms grow readily on substances such as succinate or malate as their sole source of carbon. Under these circumstances, the formation of the intermediates of carbohydrate catabolism requires an enzymatic step ancillary to the central pathways. In most cases, this step is catalyzed by phosphoenolpyruvate (PEP) carboxykinase [54]. Oxaloacetate is decarboxylated (i.e., carbon dioxide is removed) during this energy-requiring reaction. The energy may be supplied by ATP or a similar substance (e.g., GTP) that can

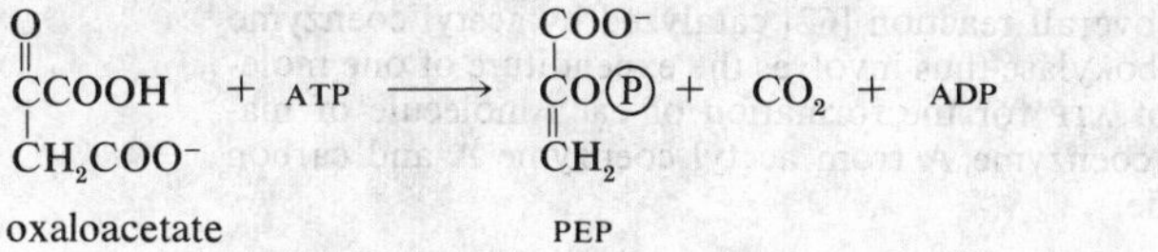

$$\begin{matrix} O \\ \parallel \\ CCOOH \\ \mid \\ CH_2COO^- \end{matrix} + ATP \longrightarrow \begin{matrix} COO^- \\ \mid \\ CO\,\textcircled{P} \\ \mid \\ CH_2 \end{matrix} + CO_2 + ADP \qquad [54]$$

oxaloacetate $\qquad\qquad$ PEP

readily be derived from it via a reaction of the type shown in [43a]. The products are PEP, carbon dioxide, and ADP.

Another reaction that can yield an intermediate of carbohydrate catabolism is catalyzed by the so-called malic enzyme; in this reaction, malate is decarboxylated to pyruvate, with concomitant reduction of NADP+ [55].

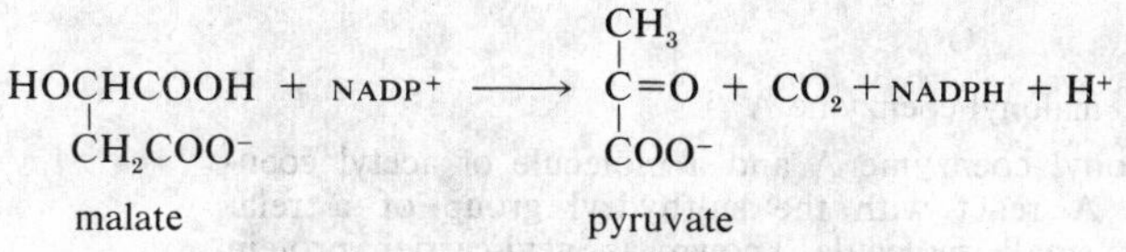

$$\begin{matrix} HOCHCOOH \\ \mid \\ CH_2COO^- \end{matrix} + NADP^+ \longrightarrow \begin{matrix} CH_3 \\ \mid \\ C=O \\ \mid \\ COO^- \end{matrix} + CO_2 + NADPH + H^+ \quad [55]$$

malate $\qquad\qquad$ pyruvate

The primary role of malic enzyme, however, may be to generate reduced NADP+ for biosynthesis rather than to form an intermediate of carbohydrate catabolism.

THE SYNTHESIS OF BUILDING BLOCKS

Gluconeogenesis. The formation of sugars from non-carbohydrate precursors, gluconeogenesis, is of major importance in all living organisms. In the light, photosynthetic plants and micro-organisms incorporate, or fix, carbon dioxide onto a five-carbon sugar and, via a sequence of transfer reactions, re-form the same sugar while also effecting the net synthesis of the glycolytic intermediate, 3-phosphoglycerate (see PHOTOSYNTHESIS). Phosphoglycerate is the precursor of starch, cell-wall carbohydrates, and other plant polysaccharides. A situation similar in principle applies to the growth of micro-organisms on precursors of acetyl coenzyme A (Figure 8) or on intermediates of the TCA cycle—that is, a large variety of cell components are derived from carbohydrates that, in turn, are synthesized from these non-carbohydrate precursors. Higher organisms also readily convert glucogenic amino acids (*i.e.*, those that do not yield acetyl coenzyme A as a catabolic product) into TCA cycle intermediates, which are then converted into glucose. The amounts of glucose thus transformed depend on the needs of the organism for protein synthesis and on the availability of fuels other than glucose. The synthesis of blood glucose from lactate, which occurs largely in liver, is a particularly active process during recovery from intense muscular activity.

The reversal of glycolysis

Most of the steps in the pathway for the biosynthesis of glucose from pyruvate are catalyzed by the enzymes of glycolysis; the direction of the reactions is reversed. Three virtually irreversible steps in glucose catabolism (see [10], [3], and [1]) that cannot be utilized in gluconeogenesis, however, are bypassed by alternative reactions that tend to proceed in the direction of glucose synthesis (Figure 9).

The first alternative reaction is the conversion of pyruvate to PEP. Three mechanisms for overcoming the energy barrier associated with the direct reversal of the pyruvate kinase reaction [10] are known. In some bacteria, PEP is formed from pyruvate by the utilization of two of the high-energy bonds of ATP; the products include, in addition to PEP, AMP and inorganic phosphate [56]. A variant of this reaction occurs in some bacteria,

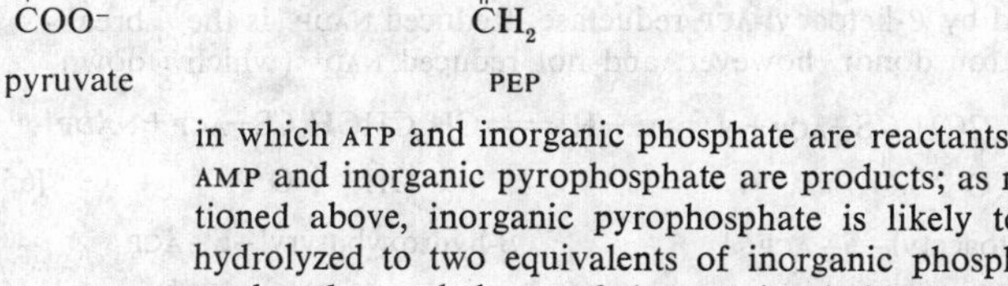

$$\begin{matrix} CH_3 \\ \mid \\ C=O \\ \mid \\ COO^- \end{matrix} + ATP \longrightarrow \begin{matrix} COO^- \\ \mid \\ CO\,\textcircled{P} \\ \mid \\ CH_2 \end{matrix} + AMP + P_i \qquad [56]$$

pyruvate $\qquad\qquad$ PEP

in which ATP and inorganic phosphate are reactants and AMP and inorganic pyrophosphate are products; as mentioned above, inorganic pyrophosphate is likely to be hydrolyzed to two equivalents of inorganic phosphate, so that the net balance of the reaction is identical with [56].

In other organisms, including many micro-organisms,

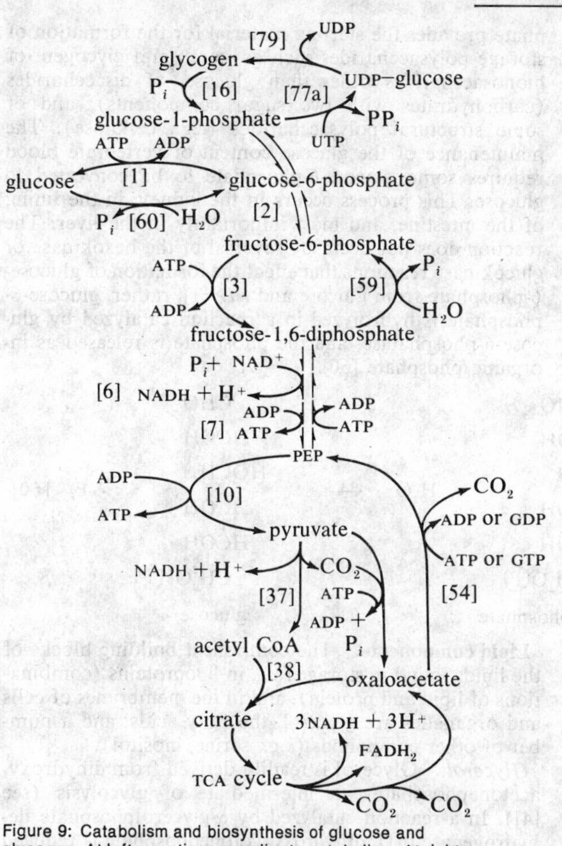

Figure 9: Catabolism and biosynthesis of glucose and glycogen. At left, reactions peculiar to catabolism. At right, reactions peculiar to anabolism. Numbers in brackets refer to reactions explained in text.

birds, and mammals, the formation of PEP from pyruvate is effected by the sum of reactions [49] and [54], each of which consumes one ATP; the overall balance is shown in [57], in which two molecules of ATP react with pyruvate

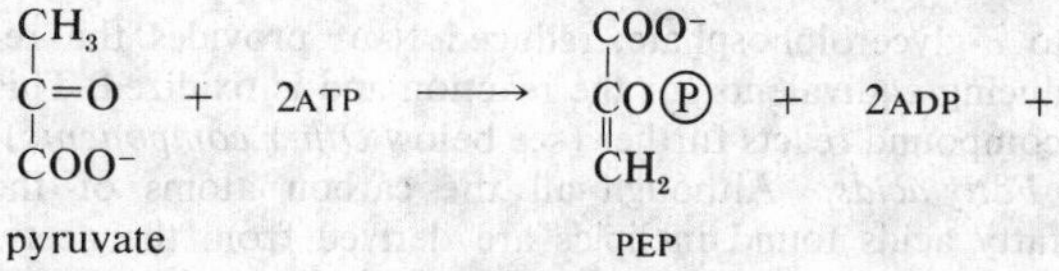

$$\begin{matrix} CH_3 \\ \mid \\ C=O \\ \mid \\ COO^- \end{matrix} + 2ATP \longrightarrow \begin{matrix} COO^- \\ \mid \\ CO\,\textcircled{P} \\ \mid \\ CH_2 \end{matrix} + 2ADP + P_i \qquad [57]$$

pyruvate $\qquad\qquad$ PEP

to form PEP, ADP, and inorganic phosphate. The enzyme adenylate kinase catalyzes the interconversion of the various adenine nucleotides, as shown in reaction [58].

$$2ADP \rightleftharpoons ATP + AMP \qquad [58]$$

The combination of steps [57] and [58] yields the same energy balance as does the direct conversion of pyruvate to PEP [56].

The second step of glycolysis bypassed in gluconeogenesis is that catalyzed by phosphofructokinase [3]. Instead, the fructose-1,6-diphosphate synthesized from dihydroxyacetonephosphate and glyceraldehyde-3-phosphate in the reaction catalyzed by aldolase is hydrolyzed, with the loss of the phosphate group linked to the first carbon atom. The enzyme diphosphofructose phosphatase catalyzes the reaction [59], in which the products are fructose-6-phosphate and inorganic phosphate. The fructose-6-

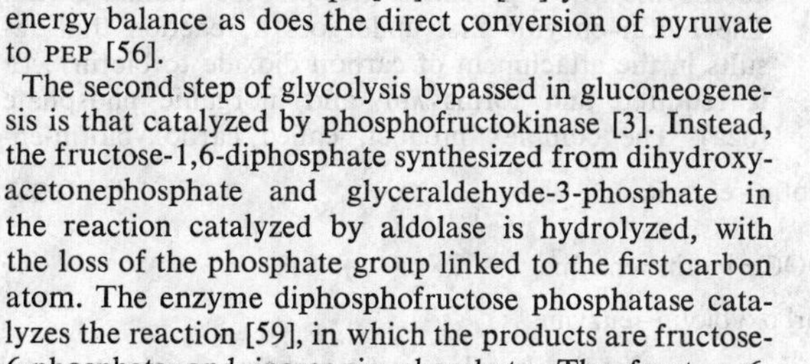

$$\begin{matrix} CH_2O\textcircled{P} \\ \mid \\ C=O \\ \mid \\ HOCH \\ \mid \\ HCOH \\ \mid \\ HCOH \\ \mid \\ CH_2O\textcircled{P} \end{matrix} + H_2O \longrightarrow \begin{matrix} CH_2OH \\ \mid \\ C=O \\ \mid \\ HOCH \\ \mid \\ HCOH \\ \mid \\ HCOH \\ \mid \\ CH_2O\textcircled{P} \end{matrix} + P_i \quad [59]$$

fructose-1,6-diphosphate $\qquad$ fructose-6-phosphate

phosphate ·thus formed is a precursor of mucopolysaccharides (polysaccharides with nitrogen-containing components). In addition, its conversion to glucose-6-phosphate provides the starting material for the formation of storage polysaccharides such as starch and glycogen, of monosaccharides other than glucose, of disaccharides (carbohydrates with two sugar components), and of some structural polysaccharides (*e.g.*, cellulose). The maintenance of the glucose content of vertebrate blood requires some glucose-6-phosphate to be converted to glucose. This process occurs in the kidney, in the lining of the intestine, and most importantly in the liver. The reaction does not occur by reversal of the hexokinase or glucokinase reactions that effect the formation of glucose-6-phosphate from glucose and ATP [1]; rather, glucose-6-phosphate is hydrolyzed in a reaction catalyzed by glucose-6-phosphatase, and the phosphate is released as inorganic phosphate [60].

$$
\begin{array}{c}
\text{CHO} \\
\text{HCOH} \\
\text{HOCH} \\
\text{HCOH} \\
\text{HCOH} \\
\text{CH}_2\text{O}(\text{P})
\end{array}
+ \text{H}_2\text{O} \longrightarrow
\begin{array}{c}
\text{CHO} \\
\text{HCOH} \\
\text{HOCH} \\
\text{HCOH} \\
\text{HCOH} \\
\text{CH}_2\text{OH}
\end{array}
+ \text{P}_i \quad [60]
$$

glucose-6-phosphate   glucose

Lipid components. The component building blocks of the lipids found in storage fats, in lipoproteins (combinations of lipid and protein), and in the membranes of cells and organelles are glycerol, the fatty acids, and a number of other compounds (*e.g.*, serine, inositol).

Glycerol. Glycerol is readily derived from dihydroxyacetonephosphate, an intermediate of glycolysis (see [4]). In a reaction catalyzed by α-glycerolphosphate dehydrogenase [61], dihydroxyacetonephosphate is reduced

$$
\begin{array}{c}
\text{CH}_2\text{O}(\text{P}) \\
\text{C}=\text{O} \\
\text{CH}_2\text{OH}
\end{array}
+ \text{NADH} + \text{H}^+ \Longleftrightarrow
\begin{array}{c}
\text{CH}_2\text{OH} \\
\text{CHOH} \\
\text{CH}_2\text{O}(\text{P})
\end{array}
+ \text{NAD}^+ \quad [61]
$$

dihydroxyacetone-   α-glycerolphosphate
phosphate

to α-glycerolphosphate; reduced NAD$^+$ provides the reducing equivalents for the reaction and is oxidized. This compound reacts further (see below *Other components*).

Fatty acids. Although all the carbon atoms of the fatty acids found in lipids are derived from the acetyl coenzyme A produced by the catabolism of carbohydrates and fatty acids (Figure 2), the molecule first undergoes a carboxylation, forming malonyl coenzyme A, before participating in fatty acid synthesis. The carboxylation reaction is catalyzed by acetyl CoA carboxylase, an enzyme whose prosthetic group is the vitamin biotin. The biotin–enzyme first undergoes a reaction that results in the attachment of carbon dioxide to biotin; ATP is required and forms ADP and inorganic phosphate [62a]. The complex product, called carboxybiotin-enzyme, immediately releases the carboxy moiety to acetyl

$$
\text{biotin–enzyme} + \text{ATP} + \text{CO}_2 \qquad\qquad [62a]
$$

$$
\Longleftrightarrow \text{}^-\text{OOC–biotin–enzyme} + \text{ADP} + \text{P}_i
$$

carboxybiotin–enzyme

zyme, immediately releases the carboxy moiety to acetyl coenzyme A, forming malonyl coenzyme A and restoring the biotin–enzyme [62b].

$$
\text{}^-\text{OOC–biotin–enzyme} + \text{CH}_3\overset{\text{O}}{\underset{\|}{\text{C}}}\text{S–CoA} \qquad [62b]
$$

carboxybiotin–   acetyl coenzyme A
enzyme

$$
\Longleftrightarrow
\begin{array}{c}
\text{COOH} \\
\text{CH}_2\overset{\text{O}}{\underset{\|}{\text{C}}}\text{S–CoA}
\end{array}
+ \text{biotin–enzyme}
$$

malonyl coenzyme A

The overall reaction [62] catalyzed by acetyl coenzyme A carboxylase thus involves the expenditure of one molecule of ATP for the formation of each molecule of malonyl coenzyme A from acetyl coenzyme A and carbon dioxide.

$$
\text{CH}_3\overset{\text{O}}{\underset{\|}{\text{C}}}\text{S–CoA} + \text{CO}_2 + \text{ATP} \qquad [62]
$$

acetyl coenzyme A

$$
\Longleftrightarrow
\begin{array}{c}
\text{COOH} \\
\text{CH}_2\overset{\text{O}}{\underset{\|}{\text{C}}}\text{S–CoA}
\end{array}
+ \text{biotin–enzyme} + \text{ADP} + \text{P}_i
$$

malonyl coenzyme A

Malonyl coenzyme A and a molecule of acetyl coenzyme A react with the sulfhydryl group of a relatively small molecule known as acyl-carrier protein (ACP–SH); in higher organisms ACP–SH is part of a multi-enzyme complex called fatty acid synthetase. ACP–SH is involved in all of the reactions leading to the synthesis of a fatty acid such as palmitic acid from acetyl coenzyme A and malonyl coenzyme A. The products of [63a]

$$
\text{CH}_3\overset{\text{O}}{\underset{\|}{\text{C}}}\text{S–CoA} + \text{ACP–SH} \Longleftrightarrow \text{CH}_3\overset{\text{O}}{\underset{\|}{\text{C}}}\text{S–ACP} + \text{CoA–SH} \quad [63a]
$$

acetyl coenzyme A   acetyl-S–ACP

$$
\begin{array}{c}
\text{COOH} \\
\text{CH}_2\overset{\text{O}}{\underset{\|}{\text{C}}}\text{S–CoA}
\end{array}
+ \text{ACP–SH} \Longleftrightarrow
\begin{array}{c}
\text{COOH} \\
\text{CH}_2\overset{\text{O}}{\underset{\|}{\text{C}}}\text{S–ACP}
\end{array}
+ \text{CoA–SH} \quad [63b]
$$

malonyl coenzyme A   malonyl–S–ACP + CoA–SH

and [63b] are acetyl-S-ACP, malonyl-S-ACP, and coenzyme A. The enzymes catalyzing [63a] and [63b] are known as acetyl transacylase and malonyl transacylase, respectively. Acetyl-ACP and malonyl-ACP react in a reaction catalyzed by β-ketoacyl-ACP synthetase so that the acetyl moiety (CH₃CO–) is transferred to the malonyl moiety (HOOCH₂CO–). Simultaneously, the carbon dioxide fixed in step [62] is lost, leaving as a product a four-carbon moiety attached to ACP and called acetoacetyl-S-ACP [64].

$$
\overset{4}{\text{CH}}_3\overset{3}{\underset{\|}{\text{C}}}\text{S–ACP} + \overset{\text{COOH}}{\underset{\|}{\overset{2}{\text{CH}}_2\overset{1}{\underset{\|}{\text{C}}}\text{S–ACP}}} \qquad [64]
$$

acetyl–S–ACP   malonyl–S–ACP

$$
\Longleftrightarrow \overset{4}{\text{CH}}_3\overset{3}{\underset{\|}{\text{C}}}\overset{2}{\text{CH}}_2\overset{1}{\underset{\|}{\text{C}}}\text{S–ACP} + \text{ACP–SH} + \text{CO}_2
$$

acetoacetyl–S–ACP

It should be noted that the carbon atoms of acetyl-S-ACP occur at the end of acetoacetyl-S-ACP (see carbon atoms numbered 4 and 3 in [64]) and that carbon dioxide plays an essentially catalytic role; the decarboxylation of the malonyl-S-ACP [64] provides a strong thermodynamic pull toward fatty acid synthesis.

The analogy between reaction [64] of fatty acid synthesis and the cleavage reaction [25] of fatty acid catabolism is apparent in the other reactions of fatty acid synthesis. The acetoacetyl-S-ACP, for example, undergoes reduction to β-hydroxybutyryl-S-ACP [65]; the reaction is catalyzed by β-ketoacyl-ACP reductase. Reduced NADP$^+$ is the electron donor, however, and not reduced NAD$^+$ (which

Analogies between fatty acid synthesis and breakdown

$$
\text{CH}_3\overset{\text{O}}{\underset{\|}{\text{C}}}\text{CH}_2\overset{\text{O}}{\underset{\|}{\text{C}}}\text{S–ACP} + \text{NADPH} + \text{H}^+ \Longleftrightarrow \text{CH}_3\overset{\text{OH}}{\underset{|}{\text{C}}}\text{HCH}_2\overset{\text{O}}{\underset{\|}{\text{C}}}\text{S–ACP} + \text{NADP}^+
$$

$$
\qquad\qquad\qquad\qquad\qquad\qquad\qquad\qquad\qquad\qquad\qquad [65]
$$

acetoacetyl–S–ACP   β-hydroxybutyryl–S–ACP

would participate in the reversal of reaction [24]). NADP$^+$ is thus a product in [65]. In [66] β-hydroxybutyryl-S-ACP is dehydrated (*i.e.* one molecule of water is removed),

$$CH_3CHCH_2CS-\text{ACP} \Longleftrightarrow CH_3CH=CHCS - \text{ACP} + H_2O \qquad [66]$$

hydroxybutyryl–S–ACP   crotonyl–S–ACP

in a reaction catalyzed by enoyl-ACP-hydrase, and then undergoes a second reduction [67], in which reduced NADP+ again acts as the electron donor. The products of [66] are crotonyl-S-ACP and water. The products of [67], which is catalyzed by crotonyl-ACP reductase, are butyryl-S-ACP and NADP+.

$$CH_3CH=CHCS-\text{ACP} + \text{NADPH} + H^+ \qquad [67]$$

crotonyl–S–ACP

$$\Longleftrightarrow CH_3CH_2CH_2CS-\text{ACP} + \text{NADP}^+$$

butyryl–S–ACP

The formation of butyryl-S-ACP [67] completes the first of several cycles, in each of which one molecule of malonyl coenzyme A enters via reactions [62] and [63b]. In the cycle following the one ending with [67], the butyryl moiety is transferred to malonyl-S-ACP, and a molecule of carbon dioxide is again lost; a six-carbon compound results. In subsequent cycles, each of which adds two carbon atoms to the molecule via reaction [64], successively longer β-oxoacyl-S-ACP derivatives are produced. Ultimately, a molecule with 16 carbon atoms, palmityl-S-ACP, is formed. In most organisms, a deacylase catalyzes the release of free palmitic acid; in a few, synthesis continues, and an acid with 18 carbon atoms is formed. The fatty acids can then react with coenzyme A (compare reaction [21]) to form fatty acyl coenzyme A, which can condense with the α-glycerolphosphate formed in step [61]; the product is a phosphatidic acid. The overall formation of each molecule of palmitic acid from acetyl coenzyme A—via step [62] and repeated cycles of steps [63] through [67]—requires the investment of seven molecules of ATP and 14 of reduced NADP+ (see [68]).

$$CH_3CS-\text{CoA} + 7\begin{bmatrix} \text{COOH} \\ CH_2CS-\text{CoA} \end{bmatrix} + 14\text{NADPH} + 14H^+ \qquad [68]$$

acetyl   malonyl coenzyme A
coenzyme A

$$\longrightarrow CH_3(CH_2)_{14}COOH + 7CO_2 + 8CoA-SH + 14\text{NADP}^+ + 6H_2O$$

palmitic acid

The process is thus an energy-requiring one (endergonic) and represents a major way by which the reducing power generated in NADP-linked dehydrogenation reactions of carbohydrate catabolism is utilized (see above *The phosphogluconate pathway*).

Other components. The major lipids that serve as components of membranes, called phospholipids, as well as lipoproteins, contain, in addition to two molecules of fatty acid, one molecule of a variety of different compounds. The precursors of these compounds include serine, inositol, and α-glycerolphosphate. They are derived from intermediates of the central metabolic pathways (*e.g.*, Figure 10; reaction [61]).

Amino acids. Organisms differ considerably in their ability to synthesize amino acids, the building blocks of proteins, from the intermediates of central metabolic pathways. Most vertebrates can form only the chemically most simple amino acids; the others must be supplied in the diet. Man, for example, can make only about 10 of the 20 commonly encountered animo acids; these are termed nonessential amino acids, in contrast to the essential amino acids that must be supplied in food.

Higher plants are more versatile than animals; they can make all of the amino acids required for protein synthesis, with either ammonia (NH_3) or nitrate (NO_3^-) as the nitrogen source. Some bacteria, and leguminous plants (*e.g.*, peas) that harbour such bacteria in their root nodules, are able to utilize nitrogen from the air to form ammonia and use the latter for amino acid synthesis.

Bacteria differ widely in their ability to synthesize amino acids. Some species, such as *Escherichia coli*, which can grow in media supplied only with a single carbon source and ammonium salts, can make all of their cell components, including all of their amino acids, from these starting materials. Other bacteria may require as many as 16 different amino acids.

Each of the 20 common amino acids is synthesized by a different pathway, the complexity of which reflects the chemical complexity of the amino acid formed. As with other compounds, the pathway for the synthesis of an amino acid is for the most part different from that by which it is catabolized. A detailed discussion of the pathway by which each amino acid is formed is beyond the scope of this article, but two salient features of amino acid biosynthesis should be mentioned.

First, the incorporation of ammonia into the intermediates of important metabolic pathways is achieved mainly via the glutamate dehydrogenase reaction [28] considered above; of course, this reaction proceeds from right to left in biosynthetic reactions. Similarly, the transaminase enzymes (reactions [26a, b, and c] enable the amino group (NH_2—) to be transferred to other amino acids.

Second, a group of several amino acids may be synthesized from one amino acid, which acts as a "parent" of an amino acid "family." The families are also interrelated in several instances. Figure 10 shows, for bacteria that can synthesize 20 amino acids, the way in which they are

Amino acid families [margin note]

1. the glutamate family

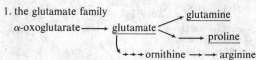

2. the aspartate family

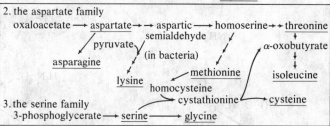

3. the serine family

4. the pyruvate family

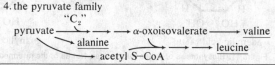

5. the shikimate family

6. histidine

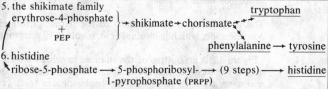

Figure 10: Family relationships in amino acid biosyntheses. Components of proteins are underlined. Not all of the intermediates formed are named.

derived from intermediates of pathways already considered. Alpha-oxoglutarate and oxaloacetate are intermediates of the TCA cycle; pyruvate, 3-phosphoglycerate, and PEP are intermediates of glycolysis; and ribose-5-phosphate and erythrose-4-phosphate are formed in the phosphogluconate pathway.

Mononucleotides. Most organisms can synthesize the purine and pyrimidine nucleotides that serve as the building blocks of RNA (containing nucleotides in which the pentose sugar is ribose, called ribonucleotides) and DNA (containing nucleotides in which the pentose sugar is deoxyribose, called deoxyribonucleotides) as well as the agents of energy exchange.

Purine ribonucleotides. The purine ribonucleotides (AMP and GMP) are derived from ribose-5-phosphate.

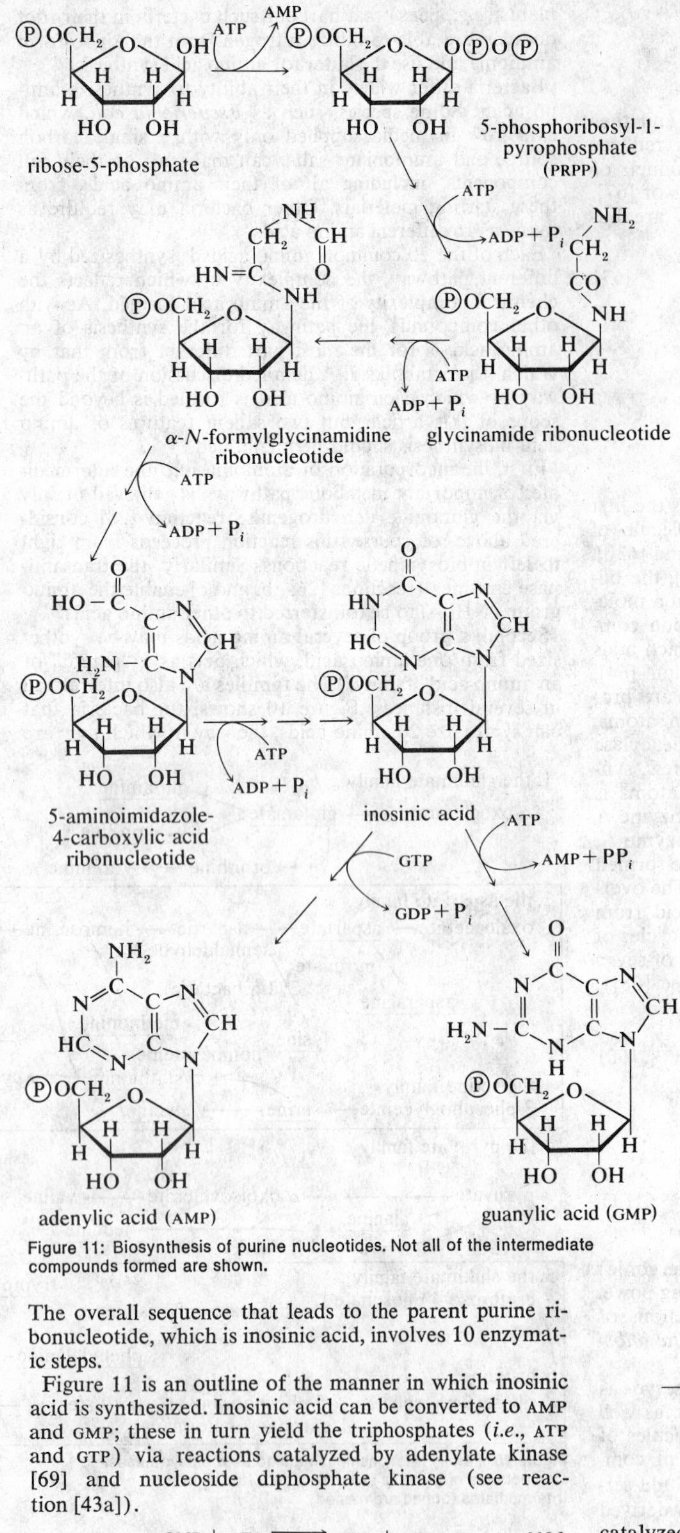

Figure 11: Biosynthesis of purine nucleotides. Not all of the intermediate compounds formed are shown.

The overall sequence that leads to the parent purine ribonucleotide, which is inosinic acid, involves 10 enzymatic steps.

Figure 11 is an outline of the manner in which inosinic acid is synthesized. Inosinic acid can be converted to AMP and GMP; these in turn yield the triphosphates (*i.e.*, ATP and GTP) via reactions catalyzed by adenylate kinase [69] and nucleoside diphosphate kinase (see reaction [43a]).

$$\text{GMP} + \text{ATP} \rightleftharpoons \text{GDP} + \text{ADP} \qquad [69]$$

Pyrimidine ribonucleotides. The biosynthetic pathway for the pyrimidine nucleotides is somewhat simpler than that for the purine nucleotides. Aspartate (derived from the TCA cycle intermediate, oxaloacetate) and carbamyl phosphate (derived from carbon dioxide, ATP, and ammonia via reaction [30]) condense to form *N*-carbamyl aspartate [70], which loses water [71] in a reaction

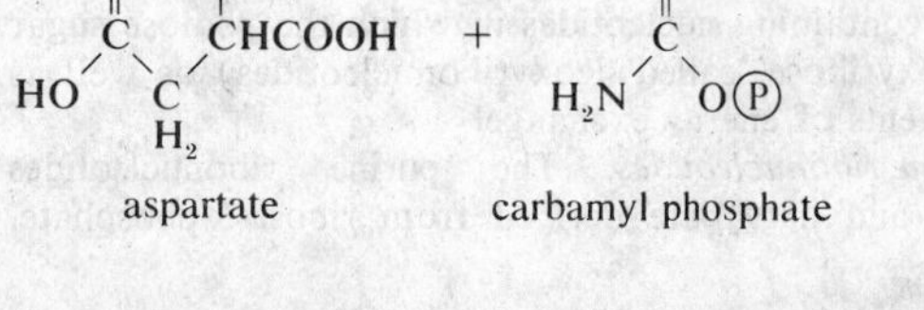

aspartate　　carbamyl phosphate　　[70]

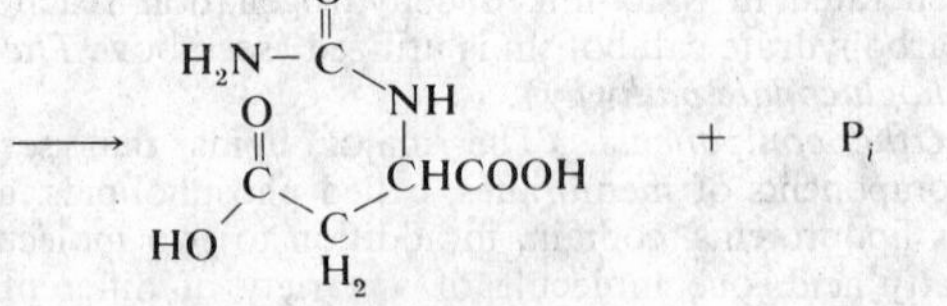

N-carbamyl aspartate

catalyzed by dihydroorotase; the product, dihydroorotate,

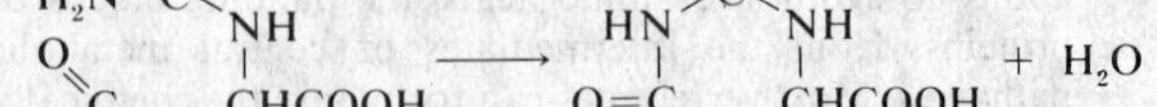

N-carbamyl aspartate　　dihydroorotate　　[71]

is then oxidized to orotate in a reaction catalyzed by dihydroorotic acid dehydrogenase, in which NAD^+ is reduced [72].

The orotate accepts a pentose-phosphate moiety [73] from 5-phosphoribosyl-1-pyrophosphate (PRPP); PRPP,

$$\begin{array}{c} O \\ \parallel \\ HN-C-CH_2 \\ \mid \qquad \mid \\ O=C \qquad CHCOOH \\ \diagdown N \diagup \end{array} + NAD^+ \qquad [72]$$

dihydroorotate

$$\longrightarrow NADH + H^+ + \begin{array}{c} O \\ \parallel \\ HN-C-CH \\ \mid \qquad \parallel \\ O=C \qquad CCOOH \\ \diagdown N \diagup \end{array}$$

orotate

which is formed from ribose-5-phosphate and ATP, also initiates the pathways for biosynthesis of purine nucleotides (Figure 11) and of histidine (Figure 10). The product loses carbon dioxide to yield the parent pyrimidine nucleotide, uridylic acid (UMP; see [73]).

$$[73]$$

orotate   PRPP

$$\longrightarrow CO_2 +$$

UMP

Analogous to the phosphorylation of purine nucleotides (steps [69] and [43a]) is the phosphorylation of UMP to UDP and thence to UTP by interaction with two molecules of ATP. Uridine triphosphate (UTP) can be converted to the other pyrimidine building block of RNA, cytidine triphosphate (CTP). In bacteria, the nitrogen for this reaction [74] is derived from ammonia; in higher animals, glutamine is the nitrogen donor.

$$[74]$$

UTP   CTP

Deoxyribonucleotides. The building blocks for the synthesis of DNA differ from those for the synthesis of RNA in two respects. In DNA, the purine and pyrimidine nucleotides contain the pentose sugar 2-deoxyribose instead of ribose. In addition, the pyrimidine base uracil, found in RNA, is replaced in DNA by thymine. The deoxyribonucleoside diphosphate can be derived directly from the corresponding ribonucleoside diphosphate by a process involving the two sulfhydryl groups of the protein, thioredoxin, and a flavoprotein, thioredoxin reductase, that can in turn be reduced by reduced NADP[+]. Thus, for the reduction of XDP, in which X represents a purine base or cytosine, the reaction may be written as shown in [75a] and [75b]. In [75a] oxidized thioredoxin-

S_2 is reduced to thioredoxin-(SH_2) by reduced NADP[+], which is oxidized in the process. Thioredoxin-(SH_2) then reduces XDP to deoxyXDP in a reaction [75b] in which thioredoxin is reformed.

$$\text{thioredoxin-}S_2 + \text{NADPH} + H^+ \longrightarrow \text{thioredoxin-}(SH)_2 + \text{NADP}^+ \qquad [75a]$$

$$\text{thioredoxin-}(SH)_2 + \text{XDP} \longrightarrow \text{thioredoxin-}S_2 + \text{deoxyXDP} \qquad [75b]$$

Deoxythymidylic acid (dTMP) is derived from deoxyuridylic acid (dUMP). Deoxyuridine diphosphate (dUDP) is first converted to dUMP, by reaction [69] proceeding from right to left. Deoxyuridylic acid then accepts a methyl group (CH_3-) in a reaction catalyzed by an enzyme (thymidylate synthetase) with the vitamin folic acid as a coenzyme; the product is dTMP [76].

$$CH_3^- + \qquad \longrightarrow \qquad [76]$$

deoxyribose (P)   deoxyribose (P)

dUMP   dTMP

THE SYNTHESIS OF MACROMOLECULES

Carbohydrates and lipids. The formation of polysaccharides and of phospholipids from their component building blocks not only requires the investment of the energy of nucleoside triphosphates but uses these molecules in a novel manner. The biosynthetic reactions described thus far have mainly been accompanied by the formation of energy-rich intermediates (*e.g.*, PEP in [56]) with the formation of either AMP or ADP; however, nucleotides serve as intermediate carriers in the formation of glycogen, starch, and a variety of lipids. This unique process necessitates reactions by which ATP, or another nucleoside triphosphate, which can be readily derived from ATP via reactions of type [43a], combines with a phosphorylated reactant to form a nucleoside-diphosphate product. Although the change in standard free energy is small in this reaction, the subsequent hydrolysis of the inorganic pyrophosphate also released (reaction [21a]) effectively makes the reaction irreversible in the direction of synthesis. The nucleoside triphosphate is represented as NTP in [77], and the phosphorylated reactant as $R-$(P).

$$\text{NTP} + R-\text{(P)} \Longrightarrow \text{NDP}-R + PP_i \qquad [77]$$

Reactions of type [77] are catalyzed by pyrophosphorylases, reaction [21a] by inorganic pyrophosphatase.
Formation of storage polysaccharides. In the formation of storage polysaccharides—*i.e.*, glycogen in animals, starch in plants—reaction [77] is preceded by the conversion of glucose-6-phosphate to glucose-1-phosphate, in a reaction catalyzed by phosphoglucomutase [78]. Glucose-1-phosphate functions as $R-$(P) in reaction

$$[78]$$

glucose-6-phosphate   glucose-1-phosphate

[77a]. UTP is the specific NTP for glycogen synthesis in animals [77a]; the products are UDP-glucose and pyrophosphate. In bacteria, fungi, and plants, ATP, CTP, or GTP serves instead of UTP. In all cases, the nucleoside diphosphate glucose (NDP-glucose) thus synthesized can donate glucose to the terminal glucose of a polysaccharide chain, thereby increasing the number (n) of glucose molecules by one to $n + 1$ [79]. UDP is released in this process, which is catalyzed by glycogen synthetase. Starch synthesis in plants occurs by an analogous pathway

glucose-1-phosphate   UTP   [77a]

UDP-glucose

$$CTP + \begin{matrix} CH_2OH \\ | \\ CHOH \\ | \\ CH_2O\,\textcircled{P} \end{matrix} \longrightarrow CDP\text{-diglyceride} + PP_i \qquad [77b]$$

catalyzed by amylose synthetase; ADP-glucose rather than UDP-glucose is the preferred glucose donor [79a]. Similarly, cellulose, the major structural polysaccharide in plant cell walls, is synthesized in some plants by reaction [79a]; other plants undergo analogous reactions in which GDP-glucose or CDP-glucose acts as the glucose donor.

$$UDP\text{-glucose} + (\text{glucose})_n \longrightarrow UDP + (\text{glucose})_{n+1} \qquad [79]$$

$$ADP\text{-glucose} + (\text{glucose})_n \longrightarrow ADP + (\text{glucose})_{n+1} \qquad [79a]$$

Nucleoside diphosphate sugars also participate in the synthesis of disaccharides; for example, common table sugar, sucrose (consisting of glucose and fructose), is formed in sugarcane by the reaction sequence shown in [80] and [81]; UDP-glucose and fructose-6-phosphate

$$UDP\text{-glucose} + \text{fructose-6-phosphate} \qquad [80]$$
$$\longrightarrow UDP + \text{sucrose-6'-phosphate}$$

$$\text{sucrose-6'-phosphate} + H_2O \longrightarrow \text{sucrose} + P_i \qquad [81]$$

first form a phosphorylated derivative of sucrose, sucrose-6'-phosphate, which is hydrolyzed to sucrose and inorganic phosphate. Lactose, which consists of galactose and glucose, is the principal sugar of milk. It is synthesized in the mammary gland as shown in [82]; UDP-galactose and glucose react to form lactose; UDP is also a product.

$$UDP\text{-galactose} + \text{glucose} \longrightarrow UDP + \text{lactose} \qquad [82]$$

Formation of lipids. The neutral fats, or triglycerides, that comprise storage lipids, and the phospholipid components of lipoproteins and membranes, are synthesized from their building blocks by a route that branches after the first biosynthetic reaction. Initially, one molecule of α-glycerolphosphate, the intermediate derived from carbohydrate catabolism, and two molecules of the appropriate fatty acyl coenzyme A (formed as described above, under *Biosynthesis of lipid components*) combine, yielding phosphatidic acid [83]. This reaction occurs preferentially with acyl coenzyme A derivatives of fatty acids con-

$$\begin{matrix} CH_2OH \\ | \\ CHOH \\ | \\ CH_2O\,\textcircled{P} \end{matrix} + \underset{\underset{O}{\|}}{RCS-CoA} + \underset{\underset{O}{\|}}{R'CS-CoA} \qquad [83]$$

α-glycerolphosphate   acyl coenzyme A

phosphatidic acid

taining 16 or 18 carbon atoms. In reaction [83], R and R' represent the hydrocarbon moieties $(CH_3(CH_2)n-)$ of two fatty acid molecules. A triglyceride molecule (neutral fat) is formed from phosphatidic acid in a reaction catalyzed by a phosphatase that results in loss of the phosphate group [84]; the diglyceride thus formed can

phosphatidic   diglyceride
acid

diglyceride

triglyceride

then accept a third molecule of fatty acyl coenzyme A (represented as $R''CS-CoA$ in [84a]).

In the biosynthesis of phospholipids, however, phosphatidic acid is not hydrolyzed; rather, it acts as the $R-\textcircled{P}$ in reaction [77], the NTP here being cytidine triphosphate (CTP). A CDP-diglyceride is produced, and inorganic pyrophosphate is released [77b]. CDP-diglyceride is the common precursor of a variety of phospholipids. In subsequent reactions, each catalyzed by a specific enzyme, CMP is displaced from CDP-diglyceride by one of three compounds—serine, inositol, or α-glycerolphosphate—to form CMP and, respectively, phosphatidylserine [85a], phosphatidylinositol [85b], or, in [85c], 3-phosphatidylglycerol-1'-phosphate (PGP). These reactions differ from

$$CDP\text{-diglyceride} + \text{serine} \longrightarrow \text{phosphatidylserine} + CMP \qquad [85a]$$

$$CDP\text{-diglyceride} + \text{inositol} \longrightarrow \text{phosphatidylinositol} + CMP \qquad [85b]$$

$$CDP\text{-diglyceride} + \alpha\text{-glycerolphosphate} \longrightarrow PGP + CMP \qquad [85c]$$

those of polysaccharide biosynthesis ([79], [82]) in that phosphate is retained in the phospholipid, and the nucleotide product (CMP) is therefore a nucleoside monophosphate rather than the diphosphate. These compounds can react further: phosphatidylserine to give, sequentially, phosphatidylethanolamine and phosphatidylcholine; phosphatidylinositol to yield mono- and diphosphate derivatives that are components of brain tissue and of mitochondrial membranes; and PGP to yield the phosphatidylglycerol abundant in many bacterial membranes and the diphosphatidylglycerol that is also a major component of mitochondrial and bacterial membranes.

Nucleic acids and proteins. As with the synthesis of polysaccharides and lipids, the formation of the nucleic acids and proteins from their building blocks requires the input of energy. Nucleic acids are formed from nucleoside triphosphates, with concomitant elimination of inorganic pyrophosphate, which is subsequently hydrolyzed via reaction [21a]. Amino acids also are activated, forming, at the expense of ATP, aminoacyl-complexes. This

(margin note, right column: Biosynthesis of phospholipids*)*

activation process is also accompanied by loss of inorganic pyrophosphate. But, although these biochemical processes are basically similar to those involved in the biosynthesis of other macromolecules, their occurrence is specifically subservient to the genetic information in DNA. DNA contains within its structure the blueprint both for its own exact duplication and for the synthesis of a number of types of RNA, among which is a class termed messenger RNA (mRNA). A complementary relationship exists between the sequence of purines (*i.e.*, adenine and guanosine) and pyrimidines (cytosine and thymine) in the DNA comprising a gene and the sequence in mRNA into which this genetic information is transcribed. This information is then translated into the sequence of amino acids in a protein, a process that involves the functioning of a variety of other classes of ribonucleic acids (see GENE).

Synthesis of DNA. The maintenance of genetic integrity demands not only that enzymes exist for the synthesis of DNA but that they function so as to ensure the replication of the genetic information (encoded in the DNA to be copied) with absolute fidelity. This implies that the assembly of new regions of a DNA molecule must occur on a template of DNA already present in the cell. The synthetic processes must also be capable of repairing limited regions of DNA, which may have been damaged, for example, as a consequence of exposure to ultraviolet irradiation. The physical structure of DNA is ideally adapted to its biological roles. Two strands of nucleotides are wound around each other in the form of a double helix. The helix is stabilized by hydrogen bonds that occur between the purine and pyrimidine bases of the strands. Thus, the adenine of one strand pairs with the thymine of the other, and the guanine of one strand with the cytosine of the other. The base pairs may be visualized as the treads of a spiral staircase, in which the two chains of repeating units (*i.e.*, ribose-phosphate-ribose) form the sides.

direction
of synthesis

(free 3'-hydroxyl end)

DNA strand

During the biosynthesis of DNA, the two strands unwind, and each serves as a template for the synthesis of a new, complementary strand, in which the bases pair in exactly the same manner as occurred in the parent double helix. The process is catalyzed by a DNA polymerase enzyme, which catalyzes the addition of the appropriate deoxyribonucleoside triphosphate (NTP in [86] onto one end (specifically, the free 3'-hydroxyl end (—OH) of the growing DNA chain (see diagram of DNA strand). In [86] the addition of a deoxyribonucleoside monophosphate (dNMP) moiety onto a growing DNA chain (5'-DNA-poly-

$$5'\text{-DNA-polymer-}3'\text{-OH} + \text{dNTP}$$
$$\longrightarrow 5'\text{-DNA-polymer-dNMP-}3'\text{-OH} + \text{PP}_i \qquad [86]$$

mer-3'-OH) is shown; the other product is inorganic pyrophosphate. The specific nucleotide inserted in the growing chain is dictated by the base in the complementary (template) strand of DNA with which it pairs. The functioning of DNA polymerase thus requires the presence of all four deoxyribonucleoside triphosphates (*i.e.*, dATP, dTPP, dGTP, and dCTP) as well as preformed DNA to act as a template. Although a number of DNA polymerase enzymes have been purified from different organisms, it is not yet certain whether those that have been most extensively studied are necessarily involved in the formation of new DNA molecules, or whether they are primarily concerned with the repair of damaged regions of molecules. A polynucleotide ligase that effects the formation of the phosphate bond between adjacent sugar molecules is concerned with the repair function but may also have a role in synthesis.

Synthesis of RNA. Various types of RNA are found in living organisms: messenger RNA (mRNA) is involved in the immediate transcription of regions of DNA; transfer RNA (tRNA) is concerned with the incorporation of amino acids into proteins; and structural RNA is found in the ribosomes that form the protein-synthesizing machinery of the cell. In cells of organisms with well-defined nuclei (*i.e.*, eucaryotes), a heterogenous RNA fraction of unknown function is constantly broken down and resynthesized in the nucleus of the cell but does not leave it. The different types of RNA are synthesized via RNA polymerases [87], the action of which is analogous to

The
varieties of
RNA

$$5'\text{-RNA-polymer-}3'\text{-OH} + \text{NTP}$$
$$\longrightarrow 5'\text{-RNA-polymer-NMP-}3'\text{-OH} + \text{PP}_i \qquad [87]$$

that of the DNA polymerases that catalyze reaction [86]. In [87] the growing RNA chain is represented by 5'-RNA-polymer-3'-OH, and the ribonucleoside triphosphate by NTP. One product (5'-RNA-polymer-NMP-3'-OH) reflects the incorporation of ribonucleoside monophosphate; the other product is, as in [86], inorganic pyrophosphate. Synthesis of RNA requires DNA as a template, thus ensuring that the base composition of the RNA faithfully reflects that of the DNA; in addition, as in DNA synthesis, all four nucleoside triphosphates must be present. The major differences between reactions [86] and [87] are that, in the latter, the nucleotides contain ribose instead of deoxyribose, and that, in RNA, uracil replaces the thymine of DNA.

It appears that, although only one strand of the DNA double helix serves as template during the formation of RNA, some regions are transcribed from one strand, some from the other.

An important constraint on RNA synthesis is that the accurate copying of the appropriate DNA strand by RNA polymerase must start at the beginning of a gene—and not somewhere along it—and must stop as soon as the genetic information has been transcribed. The way in which this selectivity is achieved is not yet fully understood, although it has been established that *E. coli* contains a protein, the sigma factor, that is not required for the incorporation of the nucleoside triphosphates into the growing RNA chain but apparently is essential for binding RNA polymerase to the proper DNA sites to initiate RNA synthesis. After the initiation step, the sigma factor is released; the role of the sigma factor in transcription suggests that the DNA at the initiation sites must be unique in some way so as to ensure that the correct strand is used as the template. Evidence indicates further that other protein factors are involved in the termination of transcription.

Synthesis of proteins. Approximately 120 macromolecules are involved directly or indirectly in the process of the translation of the base sequence of a messenger RNA molecule into the amino acid sequence of a protein. The relationship between the base sequence and the amino acid sequence constitutes the genetic code. The basic properties of the code are: it is triplet—*i.e.*, a linear sequence of three bases in mRNA specifies one amino acid in a protein; it is non-overlapping—*i.e.*, each triplet is discrete and does not overlap either neighbour; it is degenerate—*i.e.*, many of the 20 amino acids are specified by more than one of the 64 possible triplets of bases; and it appears to apply universally to all living organisms.

The main sequence of events associated with the expression of this genetic code, as elucidated for *E. coli*, may be summarized as follows (see also GENE).

1. Messenger RNA binds to the smaller of two subunits of large particles termed ribosomes.

2. The amino acid that begins the assembly of the protein chain is activated and transferred to a specific transfer RNA (tRNA); the activation step, catalyzed by an aminoacyl–tRNA synthetase specific for a particular amino acid, effects the formation of an aminoacyl–AMP complex [88a] in a manner somewhat analogous to reaction [77]; ATP is required, and inorganic pyrophosphate is a product. The aminoacyl–AMP, which remains bound to the enzyme, is transferred to a specific molecule of tRNA in a reaction catalyzed by the same enzyme. AMP is released, and the other product is called aminoacyl–tRNA [88b]. In

$$\text{amino acid} + \text{ATP} \longrightarrow \text{aminoacyl} - \textcircled{P} - \text{ribose} - \text{adenine} + \text{PP}_i \quad [88a]$$

$$\text{aminoacyl} - \text{AMP}$$

$$\text{aminoacyl} - \text{AMP} + \text{tRNA} \longrightarrow \text{aminoacyl} - \text{tRNA} + \text{AMP} \quad [88b]$$

E. coli, the amino acid that begins the assembly of the protein is always a formylmethionine (f-Met). There is no evidence that f-Met is involved in protein synthesis in eucaryotic cells.

3. Aminoacyl–tRNA binds to the mRNA-ribosomal complex in a reaction in which energy is provided by the hydrolysis of GTP to GDP and inorganic phosphate. In this step and in 5 below, the genetic code is translated. All of the different tRNA's contain triplets of bases that pair specifically with the complementary base triplets in mRNA; the base triplets in mRNA specify the amino acids to be added to the protein chain. During or shortly after the pairing occurs the aminoacyl-tRNA moves from the aminoacyl-acceptor (A) site on the ribosome to another site, called a peptidyl-donor (P) site.

4. The larger subunit of the ribosome then joins the mRNA–f-Met–tRNA–smaller ribosomal subunit complex.

5. The second amino acid to be added to the protein chain is specified by the triplet of bases adjacent to the initiator triplet in mRNA. The amino acid is activated and transferred to its tRNA by a repetition of reactions [88a] and [88b]. This newly formed aminoacyl-tRNA now binds to the A site of the mRNA–ribosome complex, with concomitant hydrolysis of GTP.

6. The enzyme peptidyl transferase, which is part of the larger of the two ribosomal subunits, catalyzes the transfer of formylmethionine from the tRNA to which it is attached (designated tRNA$^{\text{f-Met}}$) to the second amino acid; for example, if the second amino acid were leucine, step 5 would have achieved the binding of leucyl–tRNA (Leu-tRNA^{Leu}) next to f-Met–tRNA$^{\text{f-Met}}$ on the ribosome–mRNA complex. Step 6 catalyzes the transfer reaction that is shown in [89], in which tRNA$^{\text{f-Met}}$ is released from formylmethionine (f-Met), and Leu-tRNA^{Leu} is bound to formylmethionine.

$$\text{f-Met} - \text{tRNA}^{\text{f-Met}} + \text{Leu} - \text{tRNA}^{\text{Leu}} \qquad [89]$$

$$\longrightarrow \text{f-Met} - \text{Leu} - \text{tRNA}^{\text{Leu}} + \text{tRNA}^{\text{f-Met}}$$

7. In the next step three results are achieved. The dipeptide f-Met–Leu (a dipeptide consists of two amino acids) moves from the A (aminoacyl-acceptor) site to the P (peptidyl-donor) site on the ribosome; the tRNA$^{\text{f-Met}}$ is thereby displaced from the P site, and the ribosome moves the length of one triplet (three bases) along the mRNA molecule. The occurrence of these events is accompanied by the hydrolysis of a second molecule of GTP and leaves the system ready to receive the next aminoacyl-tRNA (by repetition of step 5). The cycle of events in 5, 6, and 7 is repeated until the ribosome moves to a triplet on the mRNA that does not specify an amino acid but provides the signal for termination of the amino acid chain. Triplets of this type are represented by one uracil (U)

Termination of the amino acid chain

preceding, and adjacent to, two adenines (UAA) or preceding one adenine and one guanosine in either order (UGA, or UAG).

8. At the termination of synthesis the completed protein is released from the tRNA to which it had remained linked. Two further events then occur in *E. coli*. First, the formyl constituent of the f-methionyl moiety is hydrolyzed by the catalytic action of a formylase, producing a protein with methionine at the end. If the required protein does not contain methionine in this position (and the majority of proteins in *E. coli* appear to), the methionine and possibly other amino acids that follow it are removed by enzymatic reactions. Second, the ribosome-mRNA complex dissociates, and the ribosomal subunits become available for a new round of translation by binding another mRNA molecule, step 1.

For the sake of brevity, other ancillary protein factors that participate in this sequence 1 to 8 have been omitted; the role of many of these factors is as yet poorly understood.

V. Regulation of metabolism

FINE CONTROL

As has been pointed out, the numerous metabolic pathways that function in a cell do not do so in a random and uncontrolled manner. The flux of nutrients along each pathway is governed chiefly by two factors: (1) the availability of substrates on which pacemaker, or key, enzymes of the pathway can act and (2) the intracellular levels of specific metabolites that affect the reaction rates of pacemaker enzymes. Key enzymes are usually rather complex proteins that, in addition to the site at which the catalytic process occurs (*i.e.*, the active site), contain sites to which the regulatory metabolites bind. Interactions with the appropriate molecules at these regulatory sites cause changes in the shape of the enzyme molecule. Such changes may either facilitate or hinder the changes that occur at the active site. The rate of the enzymatic reaction is thus speeded up or slowed down by the presence of a regulatory metabolite.

In many cases, the specific small molecules that bind to the regulatory sites have no obvious structural similarity to the substrates of the enzymes; these small molecules are therefore termed allosteric effectors, and the regulatory sites are termed allosteric sites (see ENZYME). Allosteric effectors may be formed by enzyme-catalyzed reactions in the same pathway in which the enzyme regulated by the effectors functions. In this case, a rise in the level of the allosteric effector would affect the flux of nutrients along that pathway in a manner analogous to the feedback phenomena of homeostatic processes. Such effectors may also be formed by enzymatic reactions in apparently unrelated pathways. In this instance, the rate at which one metabolic pathway operates would be profoundly affected by the rate of nutrient flux along another. It is this situation that, to a large extent, governs the sensitive and immediately responsive coordination of the many metabolic routes in the cell.

End-product inhibition. A biosynthetic pathway is usually controlled by an allosteric effector produced as the end product of that pathway, and the pacemaker enzyme on which the effector acts usually catalyzes the first step that uniquely leads to the end product. This phenomenon, called end-product inhibition, is illustrated by the multi-enzyme, branched pathway for the formation from oxaloacetate of the "aspartate family" of amino acids (Figure 10). The system of interlocking controls, described in greater detail in Figure 12, has been elucidated largely through studies with *E. coli*. As mentioned previously in this article, only plants and micro-organisms can synthesize many of these amino acids, many animals requiring such amino acids to be supplied preformed in their diet.

Figure 12 shows that there are a number of pacemaker enzymes in the biosynthetic route for the aspartate family of amino acids. Most of the pacemaker enzymes are uniquely involved in the formation of one product. Each of the enzymes functions after a branch point in the pathway, and all are inhibited specifically by the end product that emerges from the branch point. It is not difficult to visualize from Figure 12 how the supplies of lysine, methionine, and isoleucine required by a cell can

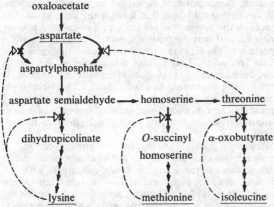

Figure 12: "Fine control" of the enzymes of the aspartate family in *E. coli* (see text).

be independently regulated. Threonine, however, is both an amino acid essential for protein synthesis and a precursor of isoleucine. If the rate of synthesis of threonine from asparate were regulated as are the rates of lysine, methionine, and isoleucine, there would be a risk of imbalance in the supply of isoleucine. This risk is overcome in *E. coli* by the existence of three different aspartokinase enzymes, all of which catalyze the first step common to the production of all the products derived from aspartate. Each has a different regulatory effector molecule. Thus, one type of aspartokinase is inhibited by lysine, a second by threonine. The third kinase is not inhibited by any naturally occurring amino acid, but its rate of synthesis (see next section) is controlled by the concentration of methionine within the cell. The triple control mechanism resulting from the three different aspartokinases ensures that the accumulation of one amino acid does not shut off the supply of aspartyl phosphate necessary for the synthesis of the others.

Another example of control through end-product inhibition also illustrates the manner in which the operation of two biosynthetic pathways may be coordinated. It will be recalled (see above *Nucleic acids and proteins*) that both DNA and the various types of RNA are assembled from purine and pyrimidine nucleotides; these in turn are built up from intermediates of central metabolic pathways (see above *Mononucleotides*). The first step in the synthesis of pyrimidine nucleotides is that catalyzed by aspartate transcarbamylase [70a]. This step initiates a sequence of reactions that leads ultimately to the formation of pyrimidine nucleotides such as UTP and CTP [74]. Studies with highly purified preparations of aspartate transcarbamylase have revealed that the affinity of this enzyme for its substrate (aspartate) is markedly decreased by the presence of CTP. This effect can be overcome by the addition of ATP, a purine nucleotide. The enzyme can be dissociated into two subunits. One subunit contains the enzymatic activity and (in the dissociated form) does not bind CTP. The other binds CTP but has no catalytic activity. Apart from providing physical evidence that pacemaker enzymes contain distinct catalytic and regulatory sites, the interaction of aspartate transcarbamylase with the different nucleotides provides an explanation for the control of the supply of nucleic acid precursors. If a cell contains sufficient pyrimidine nucleotides (*e.g.*, UTP), aspartate transcarbamylase, the first enzyme of pyrimidine biosynthesis, is inhibited. If, however, the cell contains high levels of purine nucleotides (*e.g.*, ATP), as required for the formation of nucleic acids, the inhibition of aspartate transcarbamylase is relieved, and pyrimidines are formed.

Positive modulation. Not all pacemaker enzymes are controlled by inhibition of their activity. Instead, some are subject to positive modulation—*i.e.*, the effector is required for the efficient functioning of the enzyme. Such

Regulation of the activity of aspartate transcarbamylase

enzymes exhibit little activity in the absence of the appropriate allosteric effector. One instance of positive modulation is the anaplerotic fixation of carbon dioxide onto pyruvate and phosphoenolpyruvate (PEP); this example also illustrates how a metabolic product of one route controls the rate of nutrient flow of another (see Figure 9).

The carboxylation of pyruvate in higher organisms [49] and the carboxylation of phosphoenolpyruvate in gut bacteria [50] occurs at a significant rate only if acetyl coenzyme A is present. Acetyl coenzyme A acts as a positive allosteric effector and is not broken down in the course of the reaction. Moreover, some pyruvate carboxylases [49] and the PEP carboxylase of gut bacteria are inhibited by four-carbon compounds (*e.g.*, aspartate). These substances inhibit because they interfere with the binding of the positive effector, acetyl coenzyme A. Such enzymatic controls are reasonable in a physiological sense: it will be recalled that anaplerotic formation of oxaloacetate from pyruvate or PEP is required to provide the acceptor for the entry of acetyl coenzyme A into the TCA cycle. The reaction need occur only if acetyl coenzyme A is present in sufficient amounts. On the other hand, an abundance of four-carbon intermediates obviates the necessity for forming more through carboxylation reactions such as [49] and [50].

Similar reasoning, though in the opposite sense, can be applied to the control of another anaplerotic sequence, the glyoxylate cycle (Figure 8). The biosynthesis of cell materials from the two-carbon compound acetate is, in principle, akin to biosynthesis from TCA cycle intermediates. In both processes, it is the availability of intermediates such as PEP and pyruvate that determines the rate at which a cell forms the many components produced through gluconeogenesis. Although in the strictest sense the glyoxylate cycle has no defined end product, PEP and pyruvate are, for these physiological reasons, best fitted to regulate the rate at which the glyoxylate cycle is required to operate. It is thus not unexpected that the pacemaker enzyme of the glyoxylate cycle, isocitrate lyase (reaction [52]), is allosterically inhibited by PEP and by pyruvate.

Energy state of the cell. It is characteristic of catabolic routes that they do not lead to uniquely identifiable end products. The major products of glycolysis and the TCA cycle, for example, are carbon dioxide and water. Within the cell, the concentrations of both are unlikely to vary sufficiently to allow them to serve as effective regulatory metabolites. The processes by which water is produced (Figure 7) initially involve, however, the reduction of coenzymes, the reoxidation of which is accompanied by the synthesis of ATP from ADP. Moreover, as described in previous sections, the utilization of ATP in energy-consuming reactions yields ADP and AMP. At any given moment, therefore, a living cell contains ATP, ADP, and AMP; the relative proportion of the three nucleotides provides an index of the energy state of the cell. It is thus reasonable that the flux of nutrients through catabolic routes is, in general, impeded by high intracellular levels of both reduced coenzymes (*e.g.*, FADH$_2$, reduced NAD$^+$) and ATP, and that these inhibitory effects are often overcome by AMP.

The control exerted by the levels of ATP, ADP, and AMP within the cell is illustrated by the regulatory mechanisms of glycolysis and the TCA cycle (Figure 9); these nucleotides also serve to govern the occurrence of the opposite pathway, gluconeogenesis, and to avoid mutual interference of the catabolic and anabolic sequences. Although not all of the controls mentioned below have been found to operate in all living organisms examined, it has been observed that, in general:

1. Glucose-6-phosphate stimulates glycogen synthesis from glucose-1-phosphate [79] and inhibits both glycogen breakdown [16] and its own formation from glucose [1].

2. Phosphofructokinase, the most important pacemaker enzyme of glycolysis [3], is inhibited by high levels of its own substrates (fructose-6-phosphate and ATP); this inhibition is overcome by AMP. In tissues, such as heart muscle, which use fatty acids as a major fuel, inhibition of

glycolysis by citrate may be physiologically the more important means of control. Control by citrate, the first intermediate of the TCA cycle, which produces the bulk of the cellular ATP, is thus the same, in principle, as control through ATP.

3. Fructose-1,6-diphosphatase [59], which catalyzes the reaction opposite to phosphofructokinase, is strongly inhibited by AMP.

4. Rapid catabolism of carbohydrate requires the efficient conversion of PEP to pyruvate. In liver and in some bacteria, the activity of the pyruvate kinase that catalyzes this process [10] is greatly stimulated by the presence of fructose-1,6-diphosphate, which thus acts as a potentiator of a reaction required for its ultimate catabolism.

5. The oxidation of pyruvate to acetyl coenzyme A [37] is inhibited by acetyl coenzyme A. Because acetyl coenzyme A also acts as a positive modulator of pyruvate carboxylation [49], this control reinforces the partition between pyruvate catabolism and its conversion to four-carbon intermediates for anaplerosis and gluconeogenesis.

6. Citrate synthase [38], the first enzyme of the TCA cycle, is inhibited by ATP in higher organisms and by reduced NAD+ in many micro-organisms. In some strictly aerobic bacteria, the inhibition by reduced NAD+ is overcome by AMP.

7. Citrate acts as a positive effector for the first enzyme of fatty acid biosynthesis [62]. A high level of citrate, which also indicates a sufficient energy supply, thus inhibits carbohydrate fragmentation (see [2]) and diverts the carbohydrate that has been fragmented from combustion to the formation of lipids.

8. Some forms of isocitrate dehydrogenase [40] are maximally active only in the presence of ADP or AMP and are inhibited by ATP. Again, the energy state of the cell serves as the signal regulating an enzyme involved in energy transduction.

COARSE CONTROL

Although fine control mechanisms allow the sensitive adjustment of the flux of nutrients along metabolic pathways relative to the needs of cells under relatively constant environmental conditions, these processes may not be adequate to cope with severe changes in the chemical milieu.

Such severe changes may arise in higher organisms with a change in diet or when, in response to other stimuli, the hormonal balance is altered (see HORMONE). In starvation, for example, the overriding need to maintain blood glucose levels may require the liver to synthesize glucose from noncarbohydrate products of tissue breakdown at rates greater than can be achieved by the enzymes normally present in the liver. Under such circumstances, cellular concentrations of key enzymes of gluconeogenesis, such as pyruvate carboxylase [49] and PEP-carboxykinase [54], may rise by as much as 10-fold, while the concentration of glucokinase [1] and of the enzymes of fatty acid synthesis decreases to a similar extent. Conversely, high carbohydrate diets and administration of the hormone insulin to diabetic animals elicit a preferential synthesis of glucokinase [1] and pyruvate kinase [10]. These changes in the relative proportions and absolute amounts of key enzymes are the net result of increases in the rate of their synthesis and decreases in the rate of their destruction. Although such changes reflect changes in the rates of either transcription, translation, or both of specific regions of the genome, the mechanisms by which the changes are effected have not yet been clarified.

Control of the synthesis of β-galactosidase

Micro-organisms sometimes encounter changes in environment much more severe than those encountered by the cells of tissues and organs, and their responses are correspondingly greater. Mention has already been made of the ability of E. coli to form β-galactosidase when transferred to a medium containing lactose as the sole carbon source (see Integration of catabolism and anabolism); such a transfer may result in an increase of 1,000-fold or more in the cellular concentration of the enzyme.

Because this preferential enzyme synthesis is elicited by exposure of the cells to lactose, or to nonmetabolizable but chemically similar analogues, and because synthesis ceases as soon as the eliciting agents (inducers) are removed, β-galactosidase is termed an inducible enzyme. It has been established that a regulator gene exists that specifies the amino acid sequence of a so-called repressor protein, and that the repressor protein binds to a unique portion of the region of DNA concerned with β-galactosidase formation. Under these circumstances, the DNA is not transcribed to mRNA, and virtually no enzyme is made. The repressor, however, is an allosteric protein and readily combines with inducers. Such a combination prevents the repressor from binding to DNA and allows transcription and translation of β-galactosidase to proceed.

Although this mechanism for the specific control of gene activity may not apply to the regulation of all inducible enzymes—for example, those concerned with the utilization of the sugar arabinose—and is not universally applicable to all coarse control processes in all micro-organisms, it can explain the manner in which the presence in growth media of at least some cell components represses (i.e., inhibits the synthesis of) enzymes normally involved in the formation of such components by gut bacteria such as E. coli. Although, for example, the bacteria must obviously make amino acids from ammonia if that is the sole source of nitrogen available to them, it would not be necessary for the bacteria to synthesize enzymes required for the formation of amino acids supplied preformed in the medium. Thus, of the three aspartokinases formed by E. coli (Figure 12), two are repressed by their end products, methionine and lysine. On the other hand, the third aspartokinase, which (as described above) is inhibited by threonine, is repressed by threonine only if isoleucine is also present. This example of so-called multivalent repression is of obvious physiological utility. It is likely that the amino acids that thus specifically inhibit the synthesis of aspartokinases do so by combining with specific protein repressor molecules; however, whereas the combination of the inducer with the repressor of β-galactosidase inactivates the repressor protein and hence permits synthesis of the enzyme, the repressor proteins for biosynthetic enzymes would not bind to DNA unless they were also combined with the appropriate amino acid. Aspartokinase synthesis would thus occur in the absence of the end-product effectors and not in their presence.

This explanation applies also to the coarse control of the anaplerotic glyoxylate cycle (Figure 8). The synthesis of both of the enzymes unique to that cycle, isocitrate lyase [52] and malate synthase [53], is controlled by a regulator gene that presumably specifies a repressor protein unable to bind to DNA unless combined with pyruvate or PEP. Cells growing on acetate do not contain high levels of these intermediates because they are continuously being removed for biosynthesis. The enzymes of the glyoxylate cycle are therefore formed at high rates. If pyruvate or substances catabolized to PEP or pyruvate are added to the medium, however, further synthesis of the two enzymes is speedily repressed.

BIBLIOGRAPHY. H.A. KREBS and H.L. KORNBERG, *Energy Transformations in Living Matter* (1957), a survey of the main metabolic pathways and their energy relationships—still useful, although now a trifle outdated; H.L. KORNBERG, "The Co-ordination of Metabolic Routes," in the *Fifteenth Symposium of the Society for General Microbiology*, pp. 8–31 (1965), a summary of the integration of metabolic pathways in micro-organisms, with special reference to the role of the central metabolic routes and their replenishment; and "The Role and Maintenance of the Tricarboxylic Acid Cycle in *Escherichia coli*," in T.W. GOODWIN (ed.), *British Biochemistry Past and Present*, pp. 155–171 (1970), a survey of the role of the tricarboxylic acid cycle in the regulation of metabolism; A.L. LEHNINGER, *Biochemistry* (1970), possibly the best general textbook presently available; *Annual Review of Biochemistry*, an annual compilation of articles by acknowledged experts, summarizing recent advances in selected areas of biochemistry.

(H.L.K.)

Metabolism, Diseases of

Metabolism may be viewed as the combined action of the various processes in the body that provide it with the necessary substances and energy to enable the individual organism to maintain, grow, and reproduce itself. Many disturbances of normal metabolism are caused by nutritional deficiencies, by endocrine disease, or by diseases of the liver and kidney. These types of disorders will be only touched upon in this article, since they are discussed extensively elsewhere; the present article will focus primarily on disorders caused by genetic factors that block or alter the normal pathways of metabolism; these disorders often have been called the "inborn errors of metabolism."

THE CAUSES OF METABOLIC DISEASES

Nutritional deficiencies. The metabolic disturbances caused by nutritional deficiencies arise either from deficiencies of calories and protein or from deficiencies of essential vitamins, minerals, or fatty acids (see MALNUTRITION and NUTRITIONAL DISEASES AND DISORDERS). In underdeveloped countries there may be insufficient food to eat, and young children may suffer from malnutrition, particularly in the periods immediately after weaning from the mother and when growth is most rapid. Undernutrition may take one of two forms: (1) There may be inadequate intake of both calories and protein in roughly equal proportions. In such situations the infant develops marasmus, a disease in which there is lack of normal weight gain without any other clear evidence of disease. Such infants are highly susceptible to infections and may be subject to diarrhea and dehydration; many die in the first two or three years of life. (2) In other situations, there may be an adequate intake of calories but a markedly deficient intake of protein. Such children develop kwashiorkor, which is characterized by a low protein concentration in the blood, swelling of the face, hands, and feet, and a change of skin and hair colour so that normally dark-haired children often have hair that has a red or gray colour. In this much more serious form of protein malnutrition there is urgent need of treatment with amino acids (the "building blocks" of protein) to ensure survival and recovery. Malnutrition due to deficiencies of calories and protein is less often seen in the United States and western Europe than in countries less developed economically. When it occurs, it is usually caused by maternal deprivation or by congenital malformations within the infant's intestinal tract that prevent the nutrients from being properly absorbed.

Vitamins are organic compounds required in minute amounts to catalyze the cellular metabolism that is essential for growth of the organism, and if vitamins are lacking the body develops structural or functional defects. If the deficiency is of vitamin A, excessive sensitivity to light and a thickening of the mucous membranes result; if of vitamin B_1, beriberi develops, a disease with many possible effects including degenerative changes in the nerves and the heart. A lack of vitamin B_2 brings visual disturbances. Vitamin B_6 deficiency causes irritability and convulsions. Vitamin B_{12} deficiency in young infants causes megaloblastic anemia, so called because of the presence in the blood of megaloblasts, large red cells with nuclei. Lack of vitamin C causes scurvy; of D, rickets; and of K, bleeding in the newborn.

Effects of sodium and potassium lack

In the same way, certain minerals appear to be important for maintaining the proper balance in the body. A deficiency of sodium, for example, causes nausea, diarrhea, muscle cramps, and dehydration, and an excess of potassium causes heart block—a lack of coordination between the upper and the lower chambers of the heart. Although most disturbances of vitamin and mineral metabolism are caused by diet and environmental factors, several have been shown to be of genetic importance; these will be discussed in later sections.

Diseases of the endocrine system, the liver, and the kidneys. The metabolic disturbances caused by endocrine disease may generally be viewed as an excess or a deficiency of one of the hormones secreted by an endocrine (ductless) gland. The main endocrine organs that can cause metabolic disturbances are the anterior and posterior portions of the pituitary, the thyroid, the adrenal cortex and adrenal medulla (the outer and inner substances, respectively, of the adrenal gland), the parathyroid, the testis, and the ovary. Genetically determined disturbances of the thyroid and the adrenal cortex are discussed in ENDOCRINE SYSTEM DISEASES AND DISORDERS.

The metabolic disturbances caused by liver disease are numerous. The disturbances most often seen are caused by (1) inflammations of the liver, most often caused by a virus; (2) cirrhosis or scarring of the liver, seen in persons poisoned by fumes of certain insecticides and other chlorinated hydrocarbons, and frequently seen in chronic alcoholics, who suffer not only from the toxic effects of alcohol upon the liver but also from inadequate food intake and the resultant protein malnutrition; and (3) gallbladder disease, which is usually caused by a slowing down of the flow of bile into the common bile duct and into the intestine, which permits formation of gallstones (see LIVER, HUMAN). One or two enzyme defects involving the liver have been described; these will be discussed later in this article.

Kidney diseases interfering with metabolism

The main metabolic disturbances caused by kidney diseases are due to (1) glomerulonephritis, which is an inflammation of the kidney tissues; (2) malformations of the kidney, ureters, and bladder, which may cause obstruction to the normal flow of urine and lead to severe destruction of kidney tissue; and (3) disturbances of transport mechanisms across the kidney tubular membranes. Many of the latter are genetically determined and run in families. These also will be discussed elsewhere in this article (see EXCRETORY SYSTEM DISEASES).

Inborn errors of metabolism. *Historical background.* During the early days of the present century, most scientists thought of genetics in purely mechanistic terms. Genes were thought to be small particles strung like beads on a chromosome, and each gene was considered to be responsible for determining a specific trait such as eye colour or skin pigment or whether one has an extra set of fingers or toes. At about the same time, however, physiologists and biochemists were beginning to show that atoms and molecules in living things appear to be identical in every way to the ones found in nonliving things and, furthermore, that these atoms and molecules obey the same physical and chemical laws and operate without the intervention of outside energy.

Visible signs of inborn metabolic defects

In 1908 the British physician Sir Archibald Garrod developed a hypothesis about metabolic diseases of a hereditary nature. He said that, in certain conditions, the biochemical abnormality is clearly visible. For example, in albinism, the affected person lacks pigment in the eyes and skin; in alkaptonuria, the urine turns dark upon standing; in cystinuria, the affected person passes cystine stones in the urine; and in pentosuria there is a reducing substance (a substance that removes oxygen from other substances) in the urine. That year, in lectures that he gave before the Royal College of Physicians, he pointed out the main features of these hereditary metabolic disorders: (1) the onset of the particular abnormality can be dated to the first days or weeks of life; (2) the condition tends to be familial and occurs more frequently among the offspring of cousin marriages; and (3) the disorders are relatively benign and compatible with a normal life expectancy. He proposed that the abnormalities are caused by genetically determined blocks in the normal pathway of metabolism. For example, if compound A is converted by a successive series of steps to compounds B, C, and D, and each step in the conversion requires a separate enzyme system, and if one of the enzymes proves to be inactive, there will be an accumulation of the compound immediately preceding and a deficiency of the compound immediately following the block. These abnormalities will be clearly visible and will call attention to the defect. Hence Garrod named the conditions "inborn errors of metabolism."

Much of this was, by necessity, supposition; but, in the meantime, work being carried on with lower forms of life gave substance to the concept that genes operate by chemical means. In the 1930s the geneticist George Beadle and the biochemist Edward Tatum provided evidence that each enzymatic step is controlled by a single gene. For these studies, they used the mold *Neurospora crassa,* which normally will grow in simple media of inorganic salts, glucose, and biotin, a growth vitamin. Mutant forms of *Neurospora* cannot grow on the simple media and require supplementation with specific amino acids and vitamins before they will grow. Beadle and Tatum irradiated asexual spores and tested them on unsupplemented medium. In this experiment, the 299th spore tested gave a mutant strain that would grow only when vitamin B_6 was added to the medium, and the 1,090th spore gave a strain requiring vitamin B_1. This meant that a specific gene was required to determine the requirement for vitamin B_6 and another one for vitamin B_1 and provided direct confirmation in a simple organism of Garrod's concept that enzymatic blocks are responsible for genetically determined metabolic diseases.

From *Harvey Lectures* (1965)

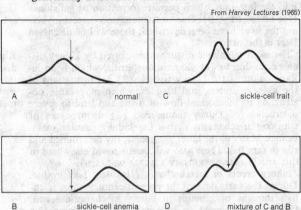

Figure 1: Electrophoretic patterns of normal and sickle-cell hemoglobins. The single peaks (A and B) correspond to an electrophoretically homogeneous material, whereas the heterozygote (C) carries a mixture of normal adult and sickle-cell hemoglobin.

Defective enzymes cause of metabolic disease

Perhaps the most important discovery was made in 1949, when the chemist Linus Pauling and his colleagues showed that the blood of a person with sickle-cell anemia has a speed of movement when separated by means of electrophoresis (see below) that is different from that of the blood of a normal individual. Sickle-cell anemia is a genetically determined disease in which the red blood cells assume a crescent shape when the oxygen pressure in the environment of the cells is lowered. The disease afflicts about one in every 350 American Negroes and is seen more frequently among the Bantus in Africa. As shown in Figure 1, if one takes a drop of blood and places it on either filter paper or starch gel and runs an electric current through the medium for several hours (a process called electrophoresis), the hemoglobin from a normal person runs to the left of the point of origin (Figure 1a), while that of a person with sickle-cell anemia runs to the right (Figure 1b). If one takes blood from a carrier of the trait who has both normal and sickle-cell hemoglobin, two peaks develop (Figure 1c), and the same effect would be achieved if the blood from a normal person were mixed in a test tube with that of a person with sickle-cell anemia (Figure 1d). A difference in the rate of migration with electrophoresis indicated that the hemoglobin molecule in the two instances has a different charge. This meant that there was a difference in the amino-acid composition of the hemoglobin molecule.

Subsequently the biochemist Vernon Ingram demonstrated, by breaking down the hemoglobin molecule and separating it into 28 peptides, each consisting, on the average, of 9 to 11 amino acids, that sickle-cell anemia differs from normal hemoglobin by the substitution of one amino acid, valine, for another, glutamic acid, in one particular position in one of the 28 peptides.

From this, and from a number of basic discoveries and theoretical developments that were occurring at this time, including the development of the double helix model for deoxyribonucleic acid (DNA), the description of the

mechanism for protein synthesis, and the breaking of the genetic code, came the current concepts of sickle-cell anemia: that it results ultimately from a miscoding of a single base pair of subunits in the DNA molecule; that the miscoding affects ribonucleic acid (RNA), which in turn calls for valine instead of glutamic acid at one point in one peptide of the hemoglobin molecule.

Galactosemia as an example. Nearly 200 human diseases can properly be classified as fitting Garrod's definition of an "inborn error of metabolism." In each condition, the physician must be able to describe: (1) the clinical signs and symptoms in the patient; (2) the nature of the biochemical defect; (3) the mode of inheritance of the abnormality, including the ability to detect the carriers of the trait within the family; (4) the proper laboratory tests to establish the correct diagnosis; and (5) the approaches and results of clinical treatment. This can be shown by a typical "inborn error of metabolism" such as galactosemia, which is a hereditary disease characterized by a congenital inability to convert galactose to glucose.

Infants with this condition appear to be normal at birth but, after a few days of milk feeding, they begin to vomit, become lethargic, fail to gain weight, and show enlargement of the liver. There may be swelling of the abdomen and of the face, hands, and feet because of the accumulation of fluid, and, in severe cases, death occurs from malnutrition and wasting. Infants who survive are usually malnourished and dwarfed at two or three months of age, and mental retardation and cataracts in the eyes may be noted. Others affected by the disorder may develop permanent liver damage months or years after the acute phase of the disease. The signs and symptoms regress after milk and milk products are omitted from the diet. If one tests the urine, there is constantly present a sugar that turns out to be galactose, not glucose.

Effects of galactosemia

The main steps in the breakdown of galactose to glucose in the body involve four separate steps as shown in Figure 2. Each step is catalyzed by a specific enzyme, which is given in capital letters. In galactosemia, the children lack galactose-1-phosphate uridyl transferase, the enzyme involved in the second step of the reaction. When this oc-

(1) galactose + ATP $\xrightarrow{\text{galactokinase}}$ galactose-1-PO$_4$ + ADP

(2) galactose-1-PO$_4$ + uridine diphosphate glucose $\underset{\text{galactose-1-p-uridyl-transferase}}{\rightleftharpoons}$ glucose-1-PO$_4$ + uridine diphosphate galactose

(3) uridine diphosphate galactose $\xrightarrow{\text{uridine diphosphogalactose-4-epimerase}}$ uridine diphosphate glucose

(4) uridine diphosphate glucose $\xrightarrow{\text{uridine diphosphoglucose pyrophosphorylase}}$ uridine triphosphate + glucose-1-PO$_4$

Figure 2: Main steps in the breakdown of galactose to glucose. The expansions of the abbreviations are as follows: ATP, adenosine triphosphate; PO$_4$, phosphate; ADP, adenosine diphosphate.

curs, there is an accumulation of galactose-1-phosphate, the compound immediately preceding the site of the block; and this causes first the development of the cataracts in the eyes, the damage to the liver, and the presence of galactose in the urine. At the same time, there is a decreased formation of glucose in the blood, and this causes low blood-sugar levels and sometimes convulsions. The mental retardation sometimes seen in these children may be the result of the high galactose level, or the low glucose level, or both.

Galactosemia is transmitted as an autosomal recessive trait. In this situation, if two carriers of the trait (each one with one normal and one mutant gene) mated and had four children, by random chance one of the four children would be expected to have the disease, two of the four children to be carriers of the trait like their parents, and one to be entirely normal, as shown in Figure 3. The person with galactosemia does not show any enzyme activity; the parents of the children show about 50 percent of the normal range of enzyme activity.

The identification of galactosemia is suggested by the presence of the reducing substance, galactose, instead of glucose in the urine. It is also suggested by an excess of galactose in the blood but must be confirmed by quantitatively testing for the enzyme galactose-1-phosphate uridyl transferase in the red blood cells. Recently, screening programs have been developed for testing for this enzyme defect among newborn infants in order that proper treatment can be instituted before the onset of clinical symptoms. The simplest screening test consists of pricking the baby's heel and collecting a drop of blood on a piece of filter paper. This blood is treated with a series of reagents and then viewed under a longwave ultraviolet light. Samples of normal blood will cause bright fluorescence; no fluorescence is observed with galactosemic blood.

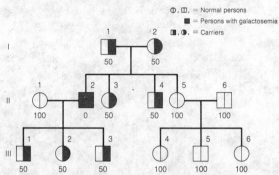

Figure 3: Transmittal of galactosemia. The numbers 50 and 100 in each generation (represented by roman numerals) indicate percentages of enzyme activity.

During the past few years, investigators have increasingly turned to the use of white blood cells and somatic (body) cell cultures for carrying out in vitro (test-tube) studies on many of the "inborn errors of metabolism." In the case of galactosemia, total white blood cells separated from red blood cells can be used to test for the enzyme among the affected children, their parents, and the normal population. Similarly, if one takes a specimen of skin from a patient with the disease and lets the fibroblast (connective-tissue cell) layer grow in tissue culture media, the cells will multiply and can be tested for the enzyme. It can be seen that fibroblasts from the affected children are unable to convert galactose to carbon dioxide, while their parents are intermediate when compared with normal controls. In contrast, all three groups can convert glucose to carbon dioxide in a normal manner. Finally, techniques have recently been developed by which it is possible to detect galactosemia before birth. As shown in Figure 4, if one puts a needle into the amniotic sac (the sac containing the fetus) in a pregnant woman of 10 to 12 weeks' gestation and removes 10 millilitres (about 0.04 fluid ounce) of amniotic fluid, it is possible to cultivate the fetal cells in the same manner as with skin cells from older people. These cells will grow and can be tested for the presence of galactose-1-phosphate uridyl transferase to determine whether the fetus in the uterus will or will not have galactosemia.

Treatment of galactosemia consists of the rigid exclusion of lactose and galactose from the diet. During early infancy, this is relatively easy, since there are commercially available lactose-free milk and milk products. As the child gets older, processed foods that contain lactose must be avoided, and it is safer to give such children pure meat, vegetables, fruit, and lactose-free bread. The omission of lactose is highly effective in preventing liver disease and cataracts from developing.

Treatment of galactosemia

DISTURBANCES IN AMINO ACID METABOLISM

At least 35 disturbances of amino acid metabolism have been described in man. These may conveniently be divided into the 29 disorders that involve the whole body and the six disorders of transport involving only the surface membranes in the kidney tubules or the lining of the intestine. In many of the systemic disorders, the site of the metabolic block has been located, the mode of inheritance determined, the carriers of the trait identified, screening procedures for finding the condition in the newborn infant developed, the abnormality found in white blood cells, cultivated skin fibroblasts and amniotic fluid cells derived from abdominal taps.

A widespread screening for amino acid defects among normal newborn infants has led to the impression that not all disturbances of amino acid metabolism are necessarily associated with disease or mental retardation. It may well be that some of the defects were detected because studies were first carried out in populations for the mentally retarded. The occurrence of the amino acid disturbances may have been coincidental, and a similar survey of healthy normal people might uncover the same defects. A few conditions are discussed below in which the clinical syndrome has been reasonably accurately defined (see also Table 1).

Phenylalanine and tyrosine disorders. Recent studies in biochemistry have permitted a better understanding of the normal pathway for the degradation of the amino acids phenylalanine and tyrosine in man. This occurs in a series of separate steps as shown in Figure 5: (1) Phenylalanine is first converted to tyrosine in the presence of the enzyme system "phenylalanine hydroxylase." The absence of the enzyme is responsible for the clinical condition phenylketonuria (see below). (2) Tyrosine is next converted to *p*-hydroxyphenylpyruvic acid in the presence of the enzyme tyrosine transaminase. (3) The *p*-hydroxyphenylpyruvic is in turn converted to homogentisic acid in one step in the presence of the enzyme *p*-hydroxyphenylpyruvic acid oxidase. An absence of this enzyme causes tyrosinemia (see below). (4) Homogentisic acid is then converted to maleylacetoacetate in the presence of the enzyme homogentisic oxidase. An absence of this enzyme causes alkaptonuria. (5) As another pathway of metabolism, tyrosine is also converted to 3, 4-

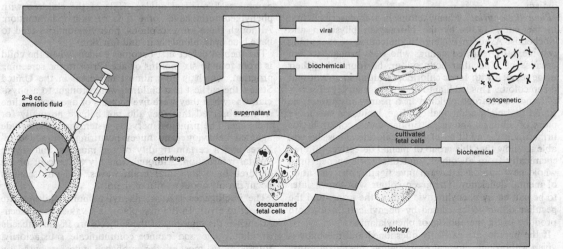

Figure 4: General scheme of the utilization of amniotic fluid for the prenatal detection of genetic disorders.

Table 1: Principal Features of 36 Disturbances of Amino Acid Metabolism

key: enzyme defect is given in parentheses: L = liver; W = white cells; S = skin; F = fibroblasts; K = kidney; R = red cells; B = brain; P = plasma

	variants reported	inheritance*	carriers are detectable	newborn-blood-screening test available	enzyme present in white blood cells	enzyme present in fibroblasts	enzyme present in cultivated fetal cells	treatment available
Systemic disturbances of amino acid metabolism								
Phenylalanine and tyrosine disorders								
Phenylketonuria (phenylalanine hydroxylase–L)	×	ar	×	×				×
Tyrosinemia (p-hydroxyphenylpyruvate oxidase–L)	×	ar	×	×				×
Alkaptonuria (homogentisic oxidase–L,K)		ad,ar						
Albinism (tyrosinase–S)	×	ad,ar,xl						
Branched-chain amino acid disorders								
Maple syrup urine disease (branched-chain keto acid oxidative decarboxylase–L,W,F)†	×	ar	×	×	×	×		×
Hypervalinemia (valine transaminase–W)		ar	×	×	×		×	
Isovaleric acidemia (isovaleryl-CoA-dehydrogenase–W)		ar			×			
Glycine metabolism disorders								
Ketotic hyperglycinemia (propionyl-CoA-carboxylase–W)		ar	×	×	×		×	×
Methylmalonic aciduria (methylmalonic-CoA-isomerase–W)	×	ar	×	×	×	×	×	×
Nonketotic hyperglycinemia (?)				×				×
Hypersarcosinemia (? sarcosine dehydrogenase)		xl	×	×				
Hyperoxaluria (? D-glyceric acid dehydrogenase + glyoxylate reductase)		ad,ar						
Urea cycle disorders								
Carbamyl phosphate synthetase deficiency (carbamyl phosphate synthetase–L)								×
Ornithine transcarbamylase deficiency (ornithine transcarbamylase–L)		ar		×				×
Citrullinemia (argininosuccinic acid synthetase–F)		ar				×	×	
Argininosuccinic aciduria (argininosuccinase–R)		ar	×	×	×	×	×	
Lysine metabolism disorders								
Congenital lysine intolerance (? lysine dehydrogenase–L)				×				×
Hyperlysinemia (lysine-ketoglutarate reductase–F)		ar		×		×	×	
Sulfur amino acid disorders								
Homocystinuria (cystathionine synthetase–L)†	×	ar	×	×		×	×	
Cystathionuria (cystathionase–L)	×	ar	×	×	×		×	×
Cystinosis (?)		ar	×	×	×	×	×	×
Sulfite oxidase deficiency (sulfite oxidase–L,K,B)		ar						
Imino acid metabolism disorders								
Hyperprolinemia, type I (proline oxidase–L)		ar	×	×				
Hyperprolinemia, type II (? pyrroline-5-carboxylic acid dehydrogenase)		ar		×				
Hydroxyprolinemia (? hydroxyproline oxidase)		ar		×				
Histidine metabolism disorders								
Histidinemia (histidase–S)		ar	×	×		×		
β-Amino acids and peptides disorders								
Hyper-β-alaninemia (?)		ar		×				
β-aminoisobutyric aciduria (β-aminoisobutyric transaminase ?)		ar		×				
Carnosinemia (carnosinase–P)				×				
Disorders of amino acid transport								
Group-specific defects								
Cystinuria	×	ar	×					×
Hartnup disease		ar						
Imino-glycinuria		ar	×					
Substrate-specific defects								
Tryptophan malabsorption syndrome								×
Methionine malabsorption syndrome								×
Generalized aminoaciduria								
The Fanconi syndrome		ar						

*ad = autosomal dominant, ar = autosomal recessive, xl = X-linked.   †Enzyme defect found in cultivated fetal cells.

dihydroxyphenylalanine (DOPA), and eventually to melanin by the action of the enzyme tyrosinase. The absence of this enzyme is responsible for the hereditary defect albinism.

Phenylketonuria. Phenylketonuria was described first in the early 1930s by the Norwegian physician and biochemist Ashbörn Fölling. In the course of examining two mentally retarded siblings who were brought to him because of a peculiar body odour, he found that their urine reacted with ferric chloride, resulting in an unusual green colour. This led him to undertake a survey of several hundred retarded children in a nearby institution; he found that eight additional children, including two more pairs of siblings, showed a similar green colour in the urine upon the addition of ferric chloride. Thus, he was able to show that this group of mental defectives differed chemically from all others, and this work opened up a whole new approach toward investigating the causation of mental deficiency. The green colour was shown later to be caused by phenylpyruvic acid in the urine, and the peculiar odour to be caused by phenylacetic acid, both products of the metabolism of phenylalanine.

Discovery of phenylketonuria

If the parents are carefully questioned and the baby is given a thorough physical examination, phenylketonuria (often called PKU) frequently is discovered before the mental defect becomes evident. During the first few weeks of life, affected infants show unusual irritability, have epileptic seizures, and vomit so severely that the parents seek medical advice. Half of the children with phenylketonuria have some type of skin inflammation. Although there are exceptions, phenylketonurics tend to have blue eyes, blonde hair, and fair skin.

The mental defect first becomes evident when the child is from four to six months of age. Prior to the screening program, which is now almost universal in the United States, the earliest that children were brought to a physician was when they were five months of age; at that time it was observed that they did not behave normally for their age. The principal nervous-system findings include agitated behaviour and finger posturing, overactive reflexes and a certain rigidity of the muscles, and severe mental retardation. Although roughly 80 percent of the children have abnormal brain waves, epileptic seizures occur in only about a third of them.

The intelligence tests of phenylketonuric children are subject to error. In the first place, test values are inaccurate when the majority of the subjects are in the imbecile or idiot range and cannot communicate satisfactorily. Furthermore, most of the published data are based on institutionalized children who might do better in a more

Intelligence of phenylketonurics

stimulating environment. Hence the intelligence of phenylketonuric children may, in fact, be somewhat higher than is currently believed. Despite this, there seems little doubt that the overwhelming majority of untreated phenylketonuric children have an intelligence quotient of less than 50 (normal is 100, and quotients of less than 70 are usually considered to indicate mental deficiency).

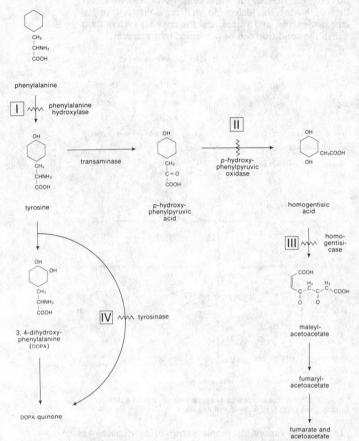

Figure 5: Normal pathway for the degradation of phenylalanine and tyrosine in man.

Phenylketonuria is caused by a deficiency of phenylalanine hydroxylase, which catalyzes the oxidation of phenylalanine to tyrosine as shown in Figure 5. The deficiency of phenylalanine hydroxylase causes an excessive accumulation of L-phenylalanine in the blood and spinal fluid. The excessive phenylalanine inhibits the normal pathway of tyrosine metabolism, which results in a decreased production of melanin, and this is responsible for the light pigment in the skin and hair of affected persons. The excessive phenylalanine (or one of its products) also probably causes some damage to the central nervous system; this is characterized by mental retardation, epileptic seizures, and abnormal brain wave patterns.

Phenylketonuria is transmitted by an autosomal recessive gene. As with galactosemia, described in the previous section, if two carriers of the trait for phenylketonuria mate, one would expect one out of four offspring to have phenylketonuria, two out of four offspring to be carriers like their parents, and one out of four offspring to be completely normal as shown in Figure 3. The carriers of the trait for phenylketonuria can be detected by means of a type of test called a loading test. If a person is heterozygous for a given trait (*i.e.*, if he is a carrier), he carries one "normal" and one "mutant" gene, and the molecules derived from the "mutant" gene may be expected to differ from those derived from the "normal" gene within the same person. On superficial examination, such persons might appear to be unaffected by the defect. More careful physical and biochemical studies may reveal departures from the norm, however, and these persons can frequently be identified from the population as a whole. In phenylketonuria, one would expect the carrier to have

about half the normal amount of phenylalanine hydroxylase in the liver. With less enzyme available, such individuals would not be able to make the normal response to a load of phenylalanine. In Figure 6, the effect is shown of giving 0.1 gram per kilogram of L-phenylalanine by mouth to a normal subject, a carrier for phenylketonuria, and a person who has phenylketonuria. It is apparent that the carrier shows a sharper rise of plasma phenylalanine levels than the normal person and the levels remain at a higher level for a longer time.

The widespread screening for phenylketonuria among newborn infants has led to the recognition that not all instances of high levels of phenylalanine in the blood are caused by the classic form of phenylketonuria and that a number of variants of the condition undoubtedly exist. Approximately one-third of all instances of elevated phenylalanine levels detected by screening are caused by variants of phenylketonuria. Children with these variants of the disorder appear to develop normally without the use of a low-phenylalanine diet.

During recent years, a number of reports have appeared describing the offspring of women who have phenylketonuria. As a general rule, these children show mental retardation, a decrease of head size and, frequently, multiple congenital abnormalities, even though they do not have phenylketonuria. These findings emphasize the toxic effect of phenylalanine or its metabolites (the products of its metabolism) upon the developing fetus, both in the uterus and after the birth of the infant.

Patients with classic phenylketonuria show a rapid and persistent increase of plasma phenylalanine levels during the first week of life. The concentrations level off at between 25 and 60 milligrams per 100 cubic centimetres of blood and remain elevated during childhood and adult life. Infants excrete *p*-hydroxyphenylacetic acid early in infancy and phenylpyruvic acid after one month of age.

In 1963 a semiquantitative method was described for the detection of elevated phenylalanine levels among newborn infants. By this technique, about one in 10,000 newborn infants will be found to have a plasma phenylalanine level of six milligrams or higher per 100 cubic centimetres; of the infants having these levels about two thirds have the classic form of phenylketonuria and one third are afflicted by one of the milder variants.

Elevation of plasma phenylalanine can be effectively controlled by reducing the content of this amino acid in the diet. It cannot be completely eliminated because phenylalanine is an essential amino acid and sufficient amounts must be supplied to ensure normal physical growth. Since natural protein contains about five percent of this compound, artificial replacement of dietary protein is necessary. Most fruits, vegetables, and cereals can be given the child when he reaches the normal age for such foods.

Although experiences vary, most infants with phenylketonuria treated with the low-phenylalanine diet have shown near-normal mentality, with intelligence quotients ranging from 85 to 100. While their intellectual development has not always been as good as that of their unaffected siblings, they show marked improvement as compared with their affected siblings who are not fed the low-phenylalanine diet.

Variants of phenylketonuria

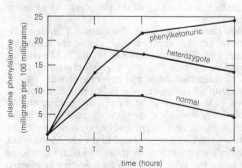

Figure 6: Effects of administration of L-phenylalanine on normal person, carrier (heterozygote), and person with fully developed phenylketonuria (see text).

Tyrosinemia.   In 1962 four Swedish families were reported in which seven out of 13 children were afflicted with an inborn error of tyrosine metabolism characterized by a deficiency of liver *p*-hydroxyphenylpyruvate oxidase, the enzyme that converts *p*-hydroxyphenylpyruvic acid to homogentisic acid as shown in Figure 5. The condition appears to be transmitted by an autosomal recessive gene, and the carriers of the trait sometimes show an abnormal tolerance test after a tyrosine load.

Effects of tyrosinemia The main clinical features are multiple defects in kidney function and replacement of the liver cells with fibrous tissue. There may be fewer circulating platelets than normal and increased pigmentation of the skin. There is little or no mental retardation and no particular nervous system abnormalities. With time the children develop rickets that does not improve when vitamin D is given.

The identity of the disorder is suggested when the urine shows a positive reaction to a specific test for proteins and nitrogen compounds and when tyrosine levels in both the blood and urine are elevated. Moderately successful results have been obtained by withholding both phenylalanine and tyrosine from the diet.

Alkaptonuria.   The identification of alkaptonuria rests on the classical triad of arthritis, pigmentation of cartilages, and a darkening of the urine caused by the presence of homogentisic acid. The condition is caused by a deficiency of liver homogentisic oxidase, the enzyme that converts homogentisic acid to maleylacetoacetate as is shown in Figure 5.

Alkaptonuria is compatible with long life. Except for the discoloration of the urine, there are no clinical manifestations until the affected person is in his twenties or thirties, when ochronosis begins to appear. This consists of deposits of ochre-like pigments in various parts of the body. These are particularly prominent in the eyes, in the sclera just back of the juncture with the cornea; in the ear and nasal cartilages; and in the superficial tendons of the hands. By middle age, many alkaptonuric persons complain of pain and stiffness of the large joints because of deforming arthritis. The spine becomes rigid; there is an arching of the upper spine, and motion of the hip, knee, or shoulder joints becomes limited.

The disorder is identified by observing that the urine turns dark upon standing because of oxidation of homogentisic acid. The only treatment needed is to relieve the discomfort of the arthritis.

Albinism.   Albinism is a general term that applies to a series of conditions in which there is little or no melanin, a dark pigment, in the skin and eyes. Albinism is caused by a failure in synthesis of the enzyme tyrosinase (Figure 5) within the melanocytes of the skin.

Effects of albinism The defect may be generalized or localized. Patients with generalized albinism have white or extremely pale yellow hair that is silky in texture. The pupils of the eyes appear to be red, and the iris is pink or bluish from reflected light; the eyes appear to wander purposelessly and are unduly sensitive to light. Traces of pigment can be found in the uveal border of the eye, however, and albinos of the coloured races frequently have blue or light-brown eyes. The only treatment needed is prevention of exposure to sunlight and proper protection of the eyes by dark glasses. Some of the localized variants of albinism include: (1) piebald albinism; (2) presence of a white forelock and spotting of the skin, and (3) albinism of the eye alone.

Branched-chain amino acid disorders.   The degradative pathways of the branched-chain amino acids, leucine, isoleucine, and valine, are shown in Figure 7. The clinical syndromes along this pathway are: maple syrup urine disease, isovaleric acidemia, and hypervalinemia.

Maple syrup urine disease.   In 1954 a new disorder was described characterized by difficulty in feeding, an absence of the Moro reflex, the development of irregular jerky respirations, spasticity, and rigid arching of the back during the first few weeks of life. (The Moro reflex is the baby's stretching up both arms in an embracing motion when the table on which he is resting is slapped on either side of him.) The baby's urine has an odour strikingly similar to that of maple syrup. Biochemi-

cal abnormalities include an elevation of the three branched-chain amino acids leucine, isoleucine, and valine (first vertical column in Figure 7) in the plasma and the urine, and a marked increase of their corresponding alpha-keto acids (second vertical column in Figure 7), particularly ketoisocaproic acid, in the urine. Maple syrup urine disease represents a deficiency of alpha-keto decarboxylase enzymes in the white cells, fibroblasts, and liver. Persons having this defect do well on a diet low in leucine, isoleucine, and valine, and the nervous-system damage in the condition can be prevented by treatment.

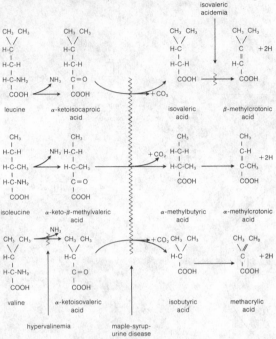

Figure 7: Normal breakdown of branched-chain amino acids. Zigzag lines represent absence of enzymes.

In 1967 a variant of maple syrup urine disease was described that differed strikingly from the classical picture of maple syrup urine disease in that there was a late onset of symptoms and the children appeared to be perfectly normal between attacks.

Isovaleric acidemia.   In 1967 a group of investigators from Boston described a second inborn error of leucine metabolism characterized by a peculiar body odour, episodic acidosis (decreased alkalinity of the blood and tissues), and slight mental retardation. Biochemical investigations revealed striking elevations of isovaleric acid in the body fluids, but other short-chain keto acids were within normal limits, indicating, as is shown in Figure 7, that the genetic defect is at the level of the enzyme isovaleryl-CoA dehydrogenase and that the abnormality involves only leucine metabolism and not that of the two other branched-chain amino acids.

Hypervalinemia.   A case was described in which a two-month-old Japanese infant started to vomit shortly after birth, failed to gain weight, appeared to be mentally retarded, had elevated levels of valine in the urine. This condition involves the deficiency of valine transaminase, but leucine and isoleucine appear to be normal, as shown in Figure 8.

Glycine metabolism disorders.   In Figure 7, it is shown that in the normal individual valine is converted successively to alpha-ketoisovaleric acid, to isobutyric acid, to methylacrylic acid. If one continues with the breakdown of valine, one comes to a series of steps involving the breakdown of propionic acid. At least two of the defects involving glycine metabolism, ketotic hyperglycinemia, and methylmalonic aciduria, have been shown to be related to the metabolism of propionic acid.

Ketotic hyperglycinemia.   A decade ago, a case was described of a child who had episodes of vomiting, became sleepy, dehydrated, and acidotic. It had infections, a de- Signs of hyperglycinemia crease of the gamma globulin in the plasma, and a low white-blood-cell count. The child also had bleeding into the skin, caused by low levels of platelets in the blood, and was retarded. Laboratory studies showed that the child had 10 to 20 times higher concentrations of glycine in the plasma and urine than normal children.

Since glycine is one of the important products of protein breakdown, it was decided to reduce the protein intake of the child by half. The frequency and intensity of the episodes of vomiting and acidosis decreased and there was general improvement. Recently, it has been shown that the disorder arises from a deficiency, early in the breakdown of propionic acid, of the enzyme biotin.

Methylmalonic aciduria. Recently some English workers described two children who failed to thrive and showed a persistent metabolic acidosis much like the children with ketotic hyperglycinemia. They found, however, that the children's plasma and urine were loaded not with glycine but with methylmalonic acid. Investigations revealed that a block occurred in the breakdown of propionic acid, but at a later stage than that for ketotic hyperglycinemia.

Two types of methyl-malonic aciduria It has been shown that persons with methylmalonic aciduria may be divided into at least two main groups. In some, the administration of vitamin B_{12}, which is a coenzyme (nonprotein and active portion of an enzyme), to the reaction will correct the defect and reduce the plasma and urine methylmalonic acid to normal levels. In others, vitamin B_{12} has no effect.

Urea cycle disorders. The normal pathway of citrulline in mammalian systems is shown in Figure 8. In this cycle, which is sometimes also called the Krebs–Henseleit cycle, citrulline serves as an intermediate substance in a cyclic mechanism resulting in the production of urea from ATP, ammonia (NH_3), and carbon dioxide (CO_2). Four metabolic blocks have been described within this cycle: (1) carbamyl phosphate synthetase deficiency, involving the synthesis of carbamyl phosphate; (2) ornithine transcarbamylase deficiency, involving the reaction of ornithine and carbamyl phosphate in the formation of citrulline; (3) citrullinemia, involving the conversion of citrulline and aspartic acid to argininosuccinic acid; and (4) argininosuccinic aciduria, with cleavage of argininosuccinic acid to arginine and fumaric acid (Figure 8).

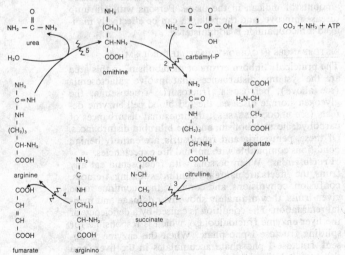

Figure 8: Krebs-Henseleit cycle.

Citrullinuria. In the early 1960s a group of Canadian workers described a mentally retarded child with a new amino acid disturbance characterized by the presence of citrulline in the urine, plasma, red blood cells, and spinal fluid. The child had chronic and persistent vomiting and showed severe alkalosis (increased alkalinity of the blood and tissues). Subsequently, it was shown that in this condition there is a decrease of argininosuccinate synthetase activity in fibroblasts. It appears likely that this decrease is caused not so much by an actual absence of the enzyme protein at step 3 in Figure 8, but rather by the inability of

the citrulline or aspartate to react with the enzyme protein in a proper manner.

Argininosuccinic aciduria. In 1958 a group of British investigators described a new clinical syndrome characterized by mental retardation and the presence in the urine of an amino acid not normally seen there. All three of the affected persons originally observed showed strikingly similar facial appearances, and all had brittle hair. One of the three persons also suffered from lesions of the skin and mucous membrane of the cheek, and had brittle nails. All were retarded mentally and had grossly abnormal electroencephalograms (brain wave tracings). Two had epileptic seizures. Argininosuccinic acid was present in large amounts in the urine, blood, and spinal fluid. Studies using red cells, white cells, and fibroblasts have shown that the condition is caused by a deficiency of argininosuccinase at step 4 in Figure 8.

Sulfur amino acid disorders. As shown in Figure 9, the normal pathway of methionine breakdown involves

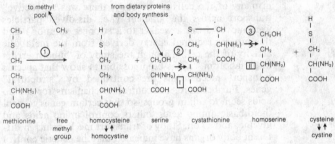

Figure 9: Normal pathway of methionine metabolism.

removal of methyl (CH_3) to form homocysteine, which in turn combines with serine to form cystathionine, which then separates to form cysteine and homoserine.

Homocystinuria. Persons with homocystinuria (homocystine in the urine) show a consistent picture of mental retardation; ectopia lentis (displacement of the lenses of the eyes); fine, fair hair; shuffling gait; thromboembolic episodes (obstruction of blood vessels by blood clots); and skeletal changes. The condition is caused by a deficiency of cystathionine synthetase at step 2 in Figure 9. Infants with this condition can be treated with a diet that is low in methionine and is supplemented with cystine.

Cystathioninuria. Cystathioninuria—presence of cystathionine in the urine—is characterized by mental retardation and developmental abnormalities. The condition is caused by a deficiency of the cystathionine-cleaving enzyme, cystathionase, at step 3 in Figure 9. Some persons with this defect respond dramatically to the administration of vitamin B_6, which results in a marked fall of cystathionine excretion.

Cystinosis. In cystinosis, the infant grows and develops normally during the first six to eight months of life. The parents then note his refusal of feedings other than liquids. This is followed by the infant's urinating excessively and ceasing to grow altogether. The infant may be brought into the hospital in a crisis with fever, dehydration, and acidosis. He usually is found to be severely affected by rickets despite taking adequate amounts of vitamin D; he has enlargement of the liver, is short, and has poor body tone. Bright reflective cystine crystals may be seen in the eyes, liver, and bone marrow. For many years, cystinosis was confused with cystinuria, which is primarily a defect in the transport across the kidney tubules (*i.e.*, a passage back into the blood through the walls of the tubules) of the dibasic amino acids: lysine, arginine, cystine, and ornithine. Since cystine is relatively insoluble in acidic urine, cystine stones are sometimes seen in that condition. In contrast, cystinosis is a systemic disease, in which cystine deposits are seen in many of the systems in the body. It has recently been shown, for example, that the white blood cells and skin fibroblasts from such patients show at least a 100-fold increase in cystine content, and even the parents of such children show a five- to six-fold increase in cystine content compared with normal people. The cystine crys-

Effects of cystinosis

tals ultimately cause damage to the kidney tubules, and this causes a generalized defect in reabsorption of all of the amino acids as well as of sugar, phosphates, and water; the defect in reabsorption accounts for the clinical symptoms in the disease. Although the specific enzyme defect responsible for the accumulation of cystine is not known, the enzyme involved is probably one of those involved in the degradation of cystine or its products.

DISORDERS OF AMINO ACID TRANSPORT

One of the unique characteristics of living cells is their capacity to maintain an internal composition different from that of their external environment. For many years it was supposed that the composition of cells was established when they were formed and thereafter was maintained by the impermeability of the membranes. By means of radioactively labelled compounds, it soon became apparent, however, that salts, sugars, and amino acids could pass freely both into and out of the cell through the membrane. Furthermore, it was found that, in many of the cells in the body, there was an "active" transport across the gradient (*i.e.*, dissolved particles were moved from a weaker to a stronger solution) and this process required energy derived from the metabolic activity of the cell. Through the study of "inborn errors of metabolism," it has been possible to show that specific transport mechanisms are controlled by "structural" genes. Furthermore, the control mechanisms for amino acids seem to fall in groups, so that certain genes control the dibasic amino acids, others control imino acids and glycine, and so on. Study of transport mechanisms in different body organs have indicated that the genetic control of one group of amino acids extends to several different systems of cells, so that the same defect of membrane transport for the dibasic amino acids in cystinuria is observed in the kidney tubules and in the mucous membrane lining the intestine.

The main hereditary disorders of amino acid transport are: (1) cystinuria, which represents an abnormality in the transport of dibasic amino acids; (2) Hartnup disease, which is caused by a defect in the transport of tryptophan; (3) imino-glycinuria, which represents a defect in the transport of glycine, proline, and hydroxyproline; (4) tryptophan malabsorption syndrome, or the "blue diaper syndrome," which represents a tryptophan malabsorption in the intestine alone; (5) methionine malabsorption syndrome, or the "oasthouse urine disease," which is an example of methionine malabsorption in the intestine alone; and (6) the Fanconi syndrome, which is a generalized kidney transport defect characterized by the failure of the renal tubules to reabsorb water, potassium, phosphates, glucose, and many amino acids. The latter is usually seen in association with cystinosis.

Cystinuria.   Cystinuria is a hereditary metabolic disorder involving the transport of the four dibasic amino acids, cystine, lysine, arginine, and ornithine. Persons with this disorder excrete on the average 0.73 gram of cystine, 1.8 grams of lysine, 0.83 gram of arginine, and 0.37 gram of ornithine; these amounts persist through life relatively uninfluenced by dietary intake. Cystine stones form in the kidney because cystine is one of the least soluble of the amino acids. In urine of pH 5–7 (*i.e.*, ranging from slightly acid to neutral), cystine is only slightly soluble, to the extent of 300–400 milligrams per litre. When the urine volume decreases, particularly at night, this amino acid is likely to come out of solution and form stones. Since lysine, arginine, and ornithine are freely soluble, they do not become incorporated into stone. Kidney-stone formation may be reduced or eliminated by drinking large volumes of liquids, particularly at night, and by making the urine more alkaline with sodium bicarbonate. While the main symptoms of cystinuria are confined to the kidney, a similar transport defect has been described in the walls of the small intestine. When persons with this defect are given large doses of lysine or ornithine by mouth, these amino acids are less completely absorbed, and a considerable portion appears unchanged in the stools. The remainder is converted by bacteria in the colon to cadaverine and putrescine, sub-

stances that are then absorbed and can easily be detected in the urine.

Cystinuria is one of the most common "inborn errors of metabolism" in man. It is estimated that approximately one in 600 of the population excretes abnormally large quantities of cystine. The cystine crystals are identified in the sediment of the urine as transparent, shiny, hexagonal leaflets. The crystals are soluble in ammonia and insoluble in acetic acid. Cystine can also be identified by a simple test with sodium cyanide and sodium nitroprusside. Cystinuria is transmitted as an auotsomal recessive trait. There appear to be two forms of the disease. Only carriers of one of the forms can be identified easily.

Hartnup disease.   Most persons with Hartnup disease have a skin disorder consisting of scaly red rashes affecting the exposed areas of the body and identical in appearance with that of classic pellagra, which is caused by a deficiency of the vitamin nicotinamide. The pathway for the degradation of tryptophan is shown in Figure 10.

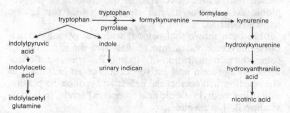

Figure 10: Pathway for the degradation of tryptophan, showing the site of the probable metabolic block in Hartnup disease.

Patients with Hartnup disease have a constant gross excess of amino-acid excretion in the urine. Since there is no other abnormality of kidney transport, it appears that the condition is caused by a defective transport of tryptophan across the cells of the kidney tubules. As a result, tryptophan cannot be converted to formylkynurenine and a nicotinamide (nicotinic acid) deficiency develops. There is also a delayed and incomplete absorption of tryptophan through the intestinal tract. When tryptophan is fed by mouth, these persons show an increase of tryptophan in the stools, decrease of formylkynurenine and kynurenine in the urine, increase of the indolylacetic acid and indolylacetyl glutamine in the urine, and increased amounts of indican in the urine. Persons with Hartnup disease improve, and the pellagra can be effectively managed if nicotinamide is administered.

DISTURBANCES IN CARBOHYDRATE METABOLISM

The principal "inborn errors of metabolism" in this area are the systemic disturbances that involve galactosemia (see above), pentosuria, fructosuria, fructosemia, the glycogen-storage diseases, the red blood cell enzyme defects (see BLOOD DISEASES), the intestinal disturbances of carbohydrate metabolism, and the bilirubin disturbances. Of these, pentosuria and fructosuria are entirely benign conditions compatible with normal life expectancies.

Fructosemia.   When persons with fructosemia eat any fruits, the effects are nausea, vomiting, sweating, tremors, confusion, convulsions, and coma. If they continue to be given fruits, they ultimately show liver damage and mental retardation. The condition is caused by a deficiency of the liver enzyme fructoaldolase, which is responsible for splitting fructose-1-phosphate. When the enzyme is absent, fructose-1-phosphate accumulates in the liver, and this accumulation inhibits other enzymes involved in carbohydrate metabolism, particularly those concerned in glycogen breakdown; low blood glucose levels result. Many of the symptoms seen in fructosemia are related to the low blood-sugar concentration. The condition is managed by avoiding fruits and other fructose-containing foods and by taking glucose during an attack.

Glycogen-storage diseases.   The glycogen-storage diseases are a group of congenital and familial disorders characterized by the deposition in the tissues of abnormally large quantities of glycogen. Glycogen is the chief form in which carbohydrates are stored in the body. It has a large molecule made up of chains of alpha-D-glu-

Synthesis of glycogen

cose arranged in a multibranched, treelike structure. Glycogen is synthesized and broken down by a series of enzymatic steps as shown in Figure 11: (1) glucose reacts with adenosine triphosphate (ATP) to form glucose-6-phosphate with the help of the enzyme hexokinase; (2) glucose-6-phosphate is then converted to glucose-1-phosphate with the help of glucose-1, 6-diphosphate and phosphoglucomutase; (3) the glucose-1-phosphate is then converted to uridine diphosphate glucose by means of uridine diphosphate glucose pyrophosphorylase; (4) the biosynthesis of glycogen from uridine diphosphate glucose by means of glycogen synthetase and glucose-1-phosphate is capable of adding glucosyl (alpha-D-glucose) units to the outer chains of the glycogen molecule, increasing its size. Numbers six to nine in the chart indicate the stages in the breakdown of glycogen into glucose. The glycogen is of normal structure in glycogen storage disease of Types I, II, V, and VI; abnormal in types III and IV. Persons with type II are weak and suffer heart failure; they usually die before they are two years old. Persons with types I, III, IV, and VI have enlarged livers. Those with type V are unable to exercise vigorously because glycogen is not released to provide energy.

Table 2: The Glycogen Storage Diseases

type	name	enzyme defect	organs affected	mode of inheritance*
I	von Gierke	glucose-6-phosphatase	liver, kidney	AR
II	Pompe	alpha (1→4) glucosidase	muscle, heart	AR
III	Forbes	amylo-1, 6-glucosidase	liver	AR
IV	Andersen	amylo (1, 4→1, 6) transglycosilase	liver	AR
V	McArdle	phosphorylase	muscle	XR
VI	Hers	phosphorylase	liver	AR(?)

*AR = autosomal recessive; XR = X-linked recessive.

Two types of intestinal disturbances

Intestinal disturbances of carbohydrate metabolism. As shown in Figure 12, the small intestine contains a number of specific enzymes, disaccharidases, whose function is to break a double sugar into its corresponding single sugars. When one of these enzymes is absent, a child develops chronic diarrhea and fails to gain weight in early infancy. These disturbances may be divided into two subgroups: hereditary lactose malabsorption and hereditary disaccharidase intolerance.

In hereditary lactose malabsorption (hereditary alactasia) there is a deficiency of intestinal lactase. Infants with this deficiency do not tolerate either breast or cow's milk but improve in condition when cereals are introduced and there is an associated reduction in the intake of sugar. In

hereditary disaccharidase intolerance there is an absence of sucrase (invertase) and isomaltase, and a subnormal amount of maltase in the intestinal lining. Infants show much the same clinical picture as with lactose malabsorption, but their malabsorption is of sucrose.

Bilirubin disturbances. Hereditary deficiency of the liver enzyme glucuronyl transferase is believed to be the cause of failure to convert the pigment bilirubin into a form that will be excreted, with the result that bilirubin levels are high and there is persistent jaundice.

In the more severe form, called congenital nonhemolytic jaundice with kernicterus (Crigler–Najjar syndrome),

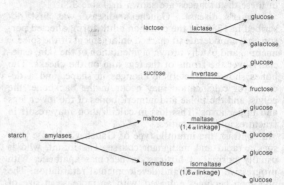

Figure 12: Breakdown of double sugars (*e.g.*, lactose, sucrose) into single sugars (*e.g.*, glucose, galactose) by means of enzymes (*e.g.*, lactase).

affected infants develop severe jaundice in the first days of life and, in about two-thirds of the sufferers, arched back, spasticity, and rigidity soon become apparent; many of the infants die within the first year of life. The nerve cells of the thalamus (the basal ganglia) are characteristically stained, but the liver shows few, if any, changes. While infants with the Crigler-Najjar syndrome usually show no glucuronyl transferase activity, some show a marked lowering of bilirubin concentration in the blood when treated with phenobarbitol. Others show no response to that form of treatment but will show a persistently lower serum bilirubin concentration after treatment with artificial blue light.

The milder form, which develops in young adults, is called familial nonhemolytic jaundice (Gilbert's disease). Most persons with this form of jaundice are not aware that they are abnormal. They frequently complain of weakness and lack of energy, but they attribute this state to overindulgence in alcohol, lack of sleep, overwork, excitement, or infection. The jaundice appears only

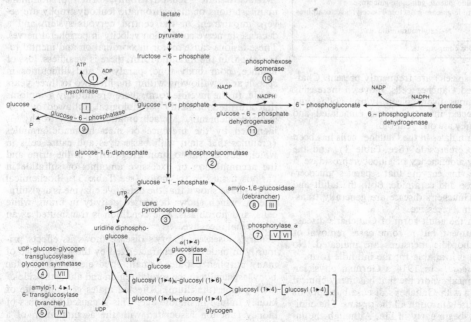

Figure 11: Synthesis and breakdown of glycogen.

intermittently, and even then is usually mild in nature. There is a partial absence of active glucuronyl transferase in these patients, and no treatment is needed.

DISTURBANCES IN LIPID METABOLISM

Disorders of fat (lipid) metabolism fall into two categories: those involving the lipids in the blood and those concerned with the storage of lipids in various body organs and tissues. Among the stored lipids there are characteristically excessive quantities of certain glycolipids and phospholipids with a common structure called ceramide. Ceramide, sphingosine, and the lipids stored in these disturbances are shown in Table 3.

Gaucher's disease. Gaucher's disease was first described in 1882. In the common adult form, affected persons have moderate to marked enlargement of the spleen, anemia, and patchy brown pigmentation of the skin, especially over the fronts of the legs and on the cheeks. The bones show characteristic changes in shape, and a decrease of calcification may occur in the backbone, the pelvis, and the tibiae and humeri, bones of the lower legs and upper arms. This loss in calcification may result in fractures and deformities.

In contrast, the infantile type of Gaucher's disease pursues a rapid and malignant course. The infant, who is usually normal at birth, soon becomes apathetic, with progressive physical and developmental retardation. The abdomen becomes enlarged, with an increase in size of the spleen and later of the liver. Subsequently, nervous-system symptoms begin to appear, with lack of body tone and with rigidity of the back. Difficulty in swallowing, choking spells, severe cough, and intermittent cyanosis

---

Table 3: Lipids Involved in Various Disturbances of Lipid Metabolism

Sphingosine: $CH_3-(CH_2)_{12}-CH=CH-CH(OH)-CH(NH_2)-CH_2OH$
Ceramide: $CH_3-(CH_2)_{12}-CH=CH-CH-CH-C^*H_2OH$

$$
\begin{array}{c}
\text{OH} \quad \text{N}-\text{H} \\
| \\
\text{C}=\text{O} \\
| \\
(\text{CH}_2)_{16-22} \\
| \\
\text{CH}_3
\end{array}
$$

Galactocerebroside: ceramide-galactose
Glucocerebroside: ceramide-glucose
Ceramide-lactoside: ceramide-glucose-galactose
Globoside: ceramide-glucose-galactose-galactose-N-acetylgalactosamine
Ganglioside: ceramide-glucose-galactose-N-acetylgalactosamine-galactose
                                                |
                                      N-acetylneuraminic acid
Sphingomyelin: ceramide-phosphorylcholine
Sulfatide: ceramide-galactose-3-sulfate
Ceramide trihexoside: ceramide-glucose-galactose-galactose
Tay-Sachs ganglioside: ceramide-glucose-galactose-N-acetylgalactosamine
                                                |
                                      N-acetylneuraminic acid

*Point of attachment of various components.

Gaucher cells

(blue colour in the spleen) are frequently present. Characteristic cells, called Gaucher cells, move in increasing numbers into the lungs, liver, spleen, lymph nodes, and bone marrow. Affected infants become emaciated and usually die before they are one year old.

The lipid that accumulates in the Gaucher cells has been shown to be glucocerebroside (See Table 3), and the disease is caused by a deficiency of glucocerebrosidase, a glucocerebroside-cleaving enzyme that separates glucocerebroside into glucose and ceramide. Both the adult and infantile forms of Gaucher's disease are generally transmitted as an autosomal recessive.

Most persons with the adult form of Gaucher's disease do not require treatment, but in some cases removal of the spleen and orthopedic measures are indicated. No definitive treatment is available for the infantile form.

Niemann–Pick disease. In 1914 a German physician described a new clinical syndrome that has many clinical features in common with Gaucher's disease but appears to spread more diffusely through all the organs. The clinical changes usually begin early in life. Although the infant may appear to be normal at birth, he soon begins to

show both physical and mental retardation. He gradually becomes weaker and shows increasing nervous-system deterioration and wasting of the extremities; the abdomen becomes noticeably protuberant. The spleen and liver are both markedly enlarged, the liver enlargement being more prominent than in Gaucher's disease. The skin is usually clear, but occasionally it has been observed to have extensive brownish, molelike pigmented areas, or, rarely, eruptive xanthomas (yellow patches caused by lipid deposits). A cherry-red spot is present in the macula lutea (a small highly sensitive area near the centre of the retina) in somewhat less than half of the patients. There is marked anemia. The infant becomes apathetic and dull, and death usually occurs at about six months of age.

In this disease there is an extremely widespread distribution of characteristic cells, called Niemann–Pick cells, which are large and pale with foamy appearing cytoplasm, the cell substance outside the nucleus. The cytoplasm contains small cavities and exhibits a characteristic colour when stained. It has been shown recently that Niemann–Pick disease is caused by a deficiency of sphingomyelinase, a sphingomyelin-cleaving enzyme, which separates sphingomyelin into phosphorylcholine and ceramide (see Table 3). The condition is transmitted by an autosomal recessive gene.

Tay–Sachs disease. A familial disease of infants was described in 1881 in which, during the first years of life, the maculae of both retinas have a cherry-red spot surrounded by a fairly well-defined white area. Affected children appear to be essentially normal until the age of four months. The first noticeable signs of abnormality are increased sensitivity to noise, irritability, and levelling off of development. Early in the course of the disease the infant's muscles twitch, and he has convulsions. There is a progressive loss of muscle strength until the infant becomes completely helpless. The infant no longer notices or recognizes the mother; his eyes cease to fix on objects; gradually it becomes apparent that he sees badly, and later he becomes blind. Eventually deterioration of the nervous system leads to a state of idiocy. The infant becomes emaciated and has repeated respiratory infections. Most affected children die at about three years of age.

Effects of Tay–Sachs disease

The ganglion cells (the nerve cells making up clumps of gray matter) throughout the central nervous system are swollen, and the cytoplasm appears finely granular and sometimes has empty spaces. The accumulated lipid in Tay–Sachs disease is a ganglioside (see Table 3). Most children with Tay–Sachs disease lack hexosamindase component A, one of the enzymes that break down ganglioside, and this undoubtedly accounts for its massive accumulation in the central nervous system.

Metachromatic leukodystrophy. The predominant manifestations of metachromatic leukodystrophy are severe impairment of the central nervous system and a decrease in nerve conduction velocity in peripheral nerves. These lesions cause motor incoordination and mental retardation. In the infantile form, there is weakness, loss of balance, poor body tone, paralysis, and difficulties in speech and swallowing within the first two to three years of life. In the juvenile form, there are initially symptoms that are predominantly psychological, followed by progressive dementia. Metachromatic leukodystrophy is identified by the presence of metachromatic granules (granules that stain with basic dyes and cause cells in which they appear to stain irregularly) in the urine and the accumulation of excessive amounts of sulfatide in various tissues in the body (see Table 3). Biochemical studies have shown that the defective enzyme is arylsulfatase A, which shows decreased activity in brain, white cells, and fibroblasts. The condition is transmitted as an autosomal recessive.

Fabry's disease. Fabry's disease shows its effects primarily in males. It is characterized by the appearance of many purplish papules (small, solid elevations) in the body, especially in the scrotal region and along the side of the hipbone (the ilium). Affected males generally die of kidney failure in middle age. This is caused by a loss of kidney function associated with the accumulation of a glycolipid, a lipid containing sugar radicals, in the glo-

Kidney malfunction

disorder	clinical signs	genetic type	mucopolysaccharides excreted
Table 4: The Genetic Mucopolysaccharidoses			
Hurler syndrome	early clouding of cornea, grave manifestations	autosomal recessive	chondroitin sulfate B, heparitin sulfate
Hunter syndrome	no clouding of cornea, milder course	X-linked recessive	chondroitin sulfate B, heparitin sulfate
Sanfilippo syndrome	mild somatic, severe central nervous system effects	autosomal recessive	heparitin sulfate
Morquio syndrome	severe bone changes of distinctive types, cloudy cornea, intellect +/−, aortic regurgitation	autosomal recessive	keratosulfate
Scheie syndrome	stiff joints, coarse facies, cloudy cornea, intellect +/−, aortic regurgitation	autosomal recessive	chondroitin sulfate B
Maroteaux-Lamy syndrome	severe osseous and corneal change, normal intellect	autosomal recessive	chondroitin sulfate B

Source: McKusick, V.A., *Heritable Disorders of Connective Tissue*, 1966.

meruli, the clusters of the microscopic blood vessels in the nephrons—the functional units of the kidneys.

The abnormal glycolipid has been identified as ceramide trihexoside (Table 3), and the condition is caused by a deficiency of the enzyme ceramide trihexosidase. The disease is usually identified by determining the level of this enzyme in a specimen of the lining of the small intestine. The condition is linked to the X chromosome. (X and Y are the sex chromosomes; males have a combination of XY; females, XX. Since a man contributes the Y chromosome to a son's XY combination, a son cannot inherit the defect from his father.) Female carriers of the condition have intermediate levels of ceramide trihexosidase.

DISTURBANCES OF MUCOPOLYSACCHARIDE METABOLISM

Some inherited disorders involve the metabolism of the mucopolysaccharides, as shown in Table 4. In the Hurler and Hunter syndromes, there is excessive excretion of the mucopolysaccharides chondroitin sulfate B and heparitin sulfate and excessive storage of some gangliosides.

In these syndromes—both are also called gargoylism—changes are present in every part of the body. The head is enlarged and tends to be abnormally long and narrow. The lips are thick, and the teeth appear to be poorly formed and wide apart. The eye sockets are widely separated. The skin is dry and coarse. The neck is short and the shoulders tend to be hunched, so that the head appears to be sitting directly on the chest. The back is hunched, and the abdomen is large and protuberant. Frequently the liver and spleen are enlarged. By X-ray examination of an infant's skull one can see that the seams—the suture lines—are widened, and that the soft spot in front—the anterior fontanelle—is enlarged; one also sees occasional bony ridges. The long bones, fingers and toes, and rib cage appear to be shorter and broader than usual; and sometimes there is a delay in the development of centres of bone fusion.

Hurler's syndrome is transmitted by an autosomal recessive gene. Affected individuals show corneal clouding and dwarfism but seldom develop deafness. On the other hand, in Hunter's syndrome, transmitted by an X-linked gene, corneal clouding is never seen and only about one-third of the affected persons are dwarfed, but over 40 percent of the patients are deaf.

DISTURBANCES OF PURINE AND PYRIMIDINE METABOLISM

The principal disturbances of purine and pyrimidine metabolism are the Lesch-Nyhan syndrome, gout, hereditary xanthinuria, and hereditary oroticaciduria.

Lesch–Nyhan syndrome. In 1964 a group of physicians described a sex-linked familial nervous-system disease consisting of incoordination, spasticity, mental retardation, aggressive behaviour, compulsive biting resulting in mutilation of the lips and fingers, and excessive uric acid in the blood.

The affected children excreted three to six times the normal amount of uric acid in the urine. The condition is caused by a deficiency of the enzyme hypoxanthine guanine phosphoribosyl transferase (HGPRT); the lack of this enzyme makes it impossible for such affected persons to form inosinic acid and guanylic acid (see Figure 13).

The Lesch–Nyhan syndrome is transmitted by an X-linked gene, and the skin cells (fibroblasts) of the female carriers of the trait have been separated into two groups, one with normal enzyme activity and one with a virtual absence of HGPRT activity. Since this enzyme is present in cultivated fetal cells, it has been possible to detect the Lesch–Nyhan syndrome prenatally.

Gout. Gout is a form of joint disease characterized clinically by recurrent, paroxysmal, acute attacks of severe inflammation, usually of a single peripheral joint, followed by complete remission. It more commonly affects men and results from the deposition in and about the joints of the sodium salt of the uric acid present in marked excess throughout the body. As a result of the urate deposits, knobby deformities develop on the knuckles and the finger joints. The deposits may also be found

Character-
istics of
gout

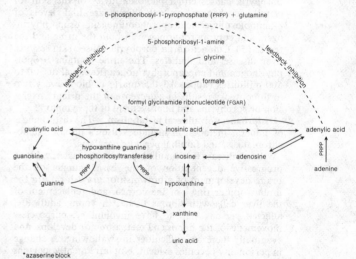

Figure 13: Major pathways for breakdown of purine to form uric acid.

in cartilages unconnected with joints, such as in the rim of the outer ear. The attacks of gouty arthritis tend to come and go unpredictably, but attacks can sometimes be precipitated by injury, food, and alcohol.

Various theories have been advanced to explain the complex features of gout, but none is compatible with all of the known facts of the disease. At present it is believed that the disease is caused by a combination of overproduction of uric acid and an impaired capacity to excrete uric acid through the kidneys. Attacks of acute gouty arthritis can be reduced by a diet low in purines and by restraint of alcohol consumption. Colchicine, phenylbutazone, and adrenocorticotropic hormone are effective during an acute attack, and uric acid deposits can be prevented by the prolonged use of such agents as probenecid. The elevation of uric acid appears to be transmitted by an autosomal dominant gene.

Xanthinuria. Persons affected by xanthinuria need to urinate frequently and have traces of blood in the urine. Examination of the urine reveals the presence of xanthine stones. The condition is caused by a deficiency of xanthine oxidase, the enzyme required to convert xanthine to uric acid (see Figure 13) and is transmitted as an autosomal recessive abnormality. The majority of affected persons do not need treatment. Xanthine is not easily soluble in urine, a high fluid intake, alkali therapy, and restriction of purines in the diet often are of benefit.

Hereditary oroticaciduria. Hereditary oroticaciduria is a rare disorder of pyrimidine metabolism manifested by an anemia with many megaloblasts (large nucleated red cells) among the blood cells, low white-blood-cell count, retarded growth, and the urinary excretion of large quantities of orotic acid. This disease is thought to represent defects involving the enzymes orotidylic pyrophosphorylase and orotidylic decarboxylase.

MISCELLANEOUS DISTURBANCES

Characteristics of the porphyrias

Disturbances of porphyrin metabolism. At least five disturbances of porphyrin metabolism are known: (1) In congenital erythropoietic porphyria there is continuous moderate breakdown of the red blood cells, and sensitivity of the skin to light—photosensitivity—results in ulceration and scarring. Abnormally high levels of uroporphyrin and coproporphyrin are found in the red blood cells, urine, and feces. (2) In erythropoietic protoporphyria the skin is sensitive to light and there are increased levels of protoporphyrin in the red blood cells. (3) Persons with intermittent porphyria have attacks of severe pain in the abdomen, of weakness and paralysis of the limbs, and of psychic changes resembling hysteria. During the attacks, and to a lesser extent at other times, there are abnormally high levels of δ-aminolevulinic acid, porphobilinogen, and uroporphyrin in the urine. Alcohol and barbiturates can precipitate attacks. (4) Variegate porphyria causes either photosensitivity of the skin, or neurologic changes, or both. There are high levels of δ-aminolevulinic acid, porphobilinogen, uroporphyrinogen, and coproporphyrinogen in both the urine and the feces. (5) Cutanea tarda porphyria causes skin lesions, liver disease, and diabetes. The urine contains uroporphyrinogen and coproporphyrinogen. Removal of 300 to 500 millilitres (about 0.3–0.5 quart) of blood every two to three weeks results in a decrease of the urinary excretion of porphyrins and improvement of the symptoms.

Disturbances of mineral metabolism. The disturbances of mineral metabolism include Wilson's disease, hemochromatosis, and familial periodic paralysis.

Wilson's disease is a familial disorder characterized by a progressive degeneration of the basal ganglia of the brain, development of a brownish or grayish ring in the limbus—outer ring—of the cornea, and replacement of the liver cells with fibrous tissue. In young adult life, affected persons start to have involuntary, purposeless movements of the hands and feet; a tremor develops, and eventually there are difficulties in swallowing. A change in personality becomes evident. Not infrequently, persons with the disease die at an early age.

The disease has been shown to be caused by a deficiency in the circulation of the copper-binding protein ceruloplasmin. This causes an excess of free copper in the body; the copper is deposited in the liver, eyes, and brain, and is responsible for the clinical symptoms. Treatment with a substance such as penicillamine removes copper from the tissues and increases its excretion in the urine.

Hemochromatosis is an inborn error of metabolism characterized clinically by enlargement of the liver and pigmentation of the skin. Affected persons frequently develop diabetes mellitus and heart failure. These symptoms are caused by a toxic accumulation of iron in the body tissues. In males, the symptoms begin after 35 years of age, when sufficient amounts of iron have been accumulated. In females, the natural loss of iron through menstruation causes fewer symptoms, and these usually do not occur until after menopause. Treatment consists of removal of blood at regular intervals to reduce the iron levels in the body.

Accumulation of iron

Familial periodic paralysis is a rare disease of obscure causation. The attacks of paralysis are frequently preceded by a "warning" period when the affected persons feel tired and irritable or have a sense of apprehension. In the typical case, paralysis begins in the legs and progresses toward the centre of the body until the sufferer becomes completely helpless and unable to move. The deep reflexes (involuntary contractions of muscles when their tendons are tapped) are lost, but there is no loss of sensation to pain or touch, and the mind is clear. After a few hours, there is gradual recovery, beginning with the central muscles and ending with the leg muscles. Episodes of paralysis may occur as often as several times weekly, and can sometimes be induced by strenuous exercise, a high carbohydrate meal, or the injection of epinephrine.

The condition is transmitted as an autosomal dominant trait and most attacks start at between 7 and 21 years of age. There appear to be at least three forms of the disease. Most are associated with low levels of potassium in the blood, but a few are associated with high levels, and some have been reported with normal levels.

Cystic fibrosis of the pancreas. Cystic fibrosis of the pancreas is probably one of the most important inborn errors of metabolism among Caucasians. It is estimated that about one out of every 25 individuals in the white population in North America and Europe is a carrier of the trait.

The clinical features of cystic fibrosis may be divided into three main groups: (1) The earliest and most severe manifestation is a blockage of the intestinal tract at birth because of a thickening of the meconium (the mass of material that accumulates in the bowel of the fetus) caused by a deficiency of the pancreatic enzymes. In older infants, there are symptoms from poor intestinal digestion, bulky, foul-smelling stools, and weight loss and an enlargement of the abdomen; these effects are much like those in a child suffering from starvation. (2) After the first few months of life, the infant develops a series of respiratory infections, sometimes resembling whooping cough. The child coughs a great deal but is unable to get rid of the thick secretions in the lungs and air passages. The lung tissue becomes replaced by scar tissue and the child dies. (3) All infants with cystic fibrosis show a marked increase in the salt concentration of their sweat. During a heat wave, they may suffer heat prostration.

Although the ultimate cause of cystic fibrosis remains unknown, there is general agreement that there is a disturbance of all of the secretory glands in the body. Their secretions become thickened and reduced, and it is this lack of lubrication that is responsible for the clinical symptoms. Many persons with the disorder die in early childhood from lung disease, but a few survive into adulthood and are relatively free of symptoms. Treatment consists of giving pancreatic enzymes by mouth, giving extra salt during the hot weather, and the use of aerosol and mist combined with drainage and antibiotics to reduce the degree of lung damage.

Treatment of cystic fibrosis

Hypophosphatasia. Persons with hypophosphatasia show severe decalcification and poor mineralization of the long bones, ribs, jaws, and teeth. In the most severe state, the fetus dies in the uterus. Infants that are born alive show marked bony deformities and die at an early age from infections, particularly of the chest. The condition is caused by a deficiency or absence of alkaline phosphatase in the serum, white blood cells, and the kidneys; this results in deficient calcification of the bones.

BIBLIOGRAPHY. A.E. GARROD, *Inborn Errors of Metabolism* (1909, reprinted 1963), an original series of lectures that opened up the field of human biochemical genetics; J.D. WATSON, *Molecular Biology of the Gene*, 2nd ed. (1970), an explanation of DNA and RNA easy to understand; H. HARRIS, *The Principles of Human Biochemical Genetics* (1970), an explanation of the principles of inborn errors of metabolism in terms of pathogenesis; J.B. STANBURY et al. (eds.), *The Metabolic Basis of Inherited Diseases*, 3rd ed., 2 vol. (1971), an authoritative review of each of the diseases written by a leading expert; D.Y.-Y. HSIA, *Inborn Errors of Metabolism*, 3rd ed. (1972), a compact review of each of the diseases written for the physician or biochemist.

(D.Y.-Y.H.)

Metallurgy

Metallurgy is the science of extracting metals from their ores, refining, purifying, and working them, mechanically or otherwise, to adapt them to use. It is also concerned with the chemical and physical properties of metals, their atomic and crystalline structure, the principles of combining them to form alloys, the means for improving or enhancing their properties for particular applications, and the relations between properties, structures, and uses. Further, it includes the thermal and mechanical processing of metals as materials of manufacture.

Metals are any of a class of substances that typically show a peculiar lustre, are good conductors of electricity and heat, are opaque, and may be fused.

Metallurgy as a science is relatively new, metals having been subjected to scientific study for less than a century. Since the 19th century, more and more attention has been devoted to a scientific understanding of the properties and strucure of metals.

Metallurgy is a particularly broad subject, its scope overlapping many other sciences and technologies, such as physics, chemistry, mining, mechanical and chemical engineering, economics, and manufacturing.

This article deals primarily with technology. Articles on subjects of a scientific nature that are related to aspects of metallurgy include THERMODYNAMICS, PRINCIPLES OF; ELECTROCHEMICAL REACTIONS; CRYSTALLOGRAPHY; METALS, THEORY OF; and PHASE CHANGES AND EQUILIBRIA. This article covers the following major areas: history of metallurgy; mineral dressing; process metallurgy; metal processing; and physical metallurgy.

History

The present-day use of metals is the culmination of a long path of development extending over approximately 6,000 years. It is generally agreed that the first metals known to man were gold, silver, and copper, which occurred in the native or metallic state, of which the earliest were in all probability nuggets of gold found in the sands and gravels of riverbeds. Such native metals became known and were appreciated for their ornamental and utilitarian values during the latter part of the Stone Age.

Gold, even when combined with silver in the alloy form, is too soft to be used in tools or weapons. It is, however, very resistant to corrosion, has a pleasing appearance, and was employed at an early date for jewelry and other decorative purposes. The rarity and softness of native silver similarly precluded its wide application for armament, tools, and weapons.

Copper occurs in the native state in many parts of the world, sometimes in huge masses and often in a state of high purity. It is soft but will harden when beaten and hammered, making it possible to produce blades, sickles, and daggers that could be sharpened to cut food, vegetation, and flesh. Native copper in all probability was the first metal to receive wide application for utilitarian purposes.

Copper was also the first metal to be extracted from its ores. Copper workings dating from 3000 to 4000 BC have been discovered in parts of the Middle East, notably in the area of Sumer in Mesopotamia at the northern tip of the Persian Gulf. Ornaments and weapons found in this area suggest that casting of metals also began about 3500 BC and that there was an interval of about 2,000 years between the making of crudely wrought metal articles and the earliest castings.

An essential step toward the Metal Age was the discovery that metals could be melted and cast to shape in molds; another was the discovery that metals could be recovered from metal-bearing minerals. There was a close relationship between these metallurgical developments and the growth of civilization. Man needed a stronger metal than native copper. Possibly more by accident than intent, he discovered that certain copper ores containing the tin-bearing mineral cassiterite could be treated in a charcoal fire at a red heat to produce an alloy of copper and tin known as bronze. This discovery occurred between 4000 and 1400 BC. Bronze is harder than copper, has a lower melting temperature, and casts more

Discovery of bronze

readily, producing sounder castings. There is definite evidence that the advantages of these bronzes were soon appreciated. The earliest copper ores used in smelting (extraction of a metal from its ores by heat) were surface outcrops that had been weathered until many of their impurities were removed.

EMERGENCE OF BRONZE, IRON, AND BRASS

As the depth of ore bodies below the surface increased, the ore not only tended to become harder, it tended to change radically in composition. A fundamental step was taken when an early genius realized that copper also occurred in unweathered ores; processes that involved quite advanced metallurgical knowledge were gradually devised for working these ores. As they were less pure than the weathered surface material, the copper produced was correspondingly impure. By the latter half of the 3rd millennium BC, copper was being produced with its impurity content rising to 2 to 3 percent. The alloys containing several percent of arsenic, antimony, iron, or lead, forerunners of the true Bronze Age, at least in central Europe, possessed marked advantages when compared with copper itself; but they tended to be brittle, and the superiority of tin as an alloying material was soon appreciated. Starting with a tin content of 5 percent or less, these bronzes quickly settled down to tin contents of about 10 to 12 percent. The Bronze Age was heralded by these discoveries.

Although bronze was known in Sumer as early as 3000 BC, tin ores were scarce and not as widely distributed as copper ores; hence sources of tin ores were sought outside the Middle East. At about 2000 BC the people of Hissarlik, the site of the city of Troy, learned the art of bronze making using ores obtained from central Europe. Migration of peoples from the Middle East to Egypt, Europe, India, and, possibly, China, brought on by wars and drought, was largely responsible for the spread of the bronze culture into these areas.

During the Bronze Age the Egyptians introduced the lost-wax process, a method known today as the investment method of casting. In this method an exact model or pattern of the article to be cast is made in wax, then covered with a claylike material to form the mold. The composite is heated to harden the mold and to melt the wax, which drains off, leaving an exact negative impression, which is then filled with molten metal and allowed to solidify. The statue of the pharaoh Pepi I and his son, dating from about 2600 BC, is one of the earliest examples known of the lost-wax art.

Lost-wax process

By 1400 BC iron was assuming increasing importance, and was smelted and worked simultaneously with copper and bronze, as indicated in the Table.

Iron does not occur on earth except in ores, but meteoric iron, while rare, has been known from a very early date. A characteristic of meteoric iron is a high nickel content, and iron of this type has been found in ancient iron articles. By about 1200 BC, iron had attained sufficient importance for this date to be used as marking the beginning of the Iron Age.

Smelting of iron from ore involves a much more elaborate technique than does smelting of copper, and iron smelting was correspondingly slow in coming. The earliest record of iron smelting dates from about 1300 BC. Evidence from excavations indicates that the art of iron making originated in the mountainous country to the south of the Black Sea, an area dominated by the Hittites. Later the art apparently spread to the Palestinians, for crude furnaces dating from 1200 BC have been unearthed at Gerar, together with a number of iron objects.

Smelting of iron oxide with charcoal demanded a high temperature, and the product even then was merely a spongy mass of pasty globules of metal intermingled with a semiliquid slag. Repeated reheating and hammering eliminated much of the slag, creating wrought iron, a much better product than the iron sponge. This wrought iron was low in carbon content, hence soft, and its use for weapons and tools was limited. It was discovered that continued heating to a red heat in a mass of glowing charcoal (during which carbon was absorbed) made the

Production of wrought iron

Prehistoric and Classical Metallurgy

period	smelting and refining	alloying and working
Prior to 4000 BC	native gold and copper and meteoritic iron used occasionally without melting	hammering to shape and to harden copper annealed about 4000 BC
4000–3000 BC	reduction of oxidized ores of copper and lead native silver used copper–arsenic alloys by smelting natural mixed ores, followed by bronzes from intentionally mixed ores of copper and tin (c. 3500 BC)	melting and casting nearly pure copper, followed by copper–arsenic and copper–tin alloys (made from ores) permanent molds of stone and metal lost-wax process for complicated castings natural gold–silver alloys soldering with copper–gold and lead–tin alloys
3000–2000 BC	roasting and smelting of sulfide ores of copper experimental production of sponge iron tin smelted (perhaps earlier) and becomes important trade item cupellation of lead to extract silver, and of gold and silver for purification	most jewelry techniques known before 2500 BC—inlay, stamping, repoussé, raising, soldering, riveting, granulation, surface colouring, etc. gold leaf wire made by cutting sheet
2000–1000 BC	gold purified by cementation bellows used in furnaces by 1800 BC wrought iron becomes important by 1600 BC (directly reduced from ore as sponge and forged without melting)	bronze made from metallic tin and copper (perhaps much earlier), high-tin bronze (Speculum metal) for mirrors, leaded bronzes for statuary niello and enameling on gold silver–copper alloys blanched brass from copper and zinc oxide ores (not important before 200 BC) steel regularly made by carburization in hearth, perhaps hardened by quenching, 1200 BC
1000–0 BC	cast iron (China only) cast steel ("Wootz": India only) gold purified by sulfide process mercury distilled from ores amalgamation of gold ores	vast expansion of production of iron, common nonferrous metals, and gold and silver iron and steel welded into composite tools and weapons stamping of coins, 700 BC gilding of bronze and silver with gold amalgam assay by cupellation, cementation, touchstone and (?) by density

Source: Cyril Stanley Smith, The University of Chicago.

soft metal much harder. As early as 1200 BC iron with 1.5 percent carbon at the surface, corresponding somewhat to modern case-hardened iron, was being processed. The carbon-containing iron had the further great advantage that, unlike carbon-free iron, it could be made still harder by quenching—i.e., rapid cooling by immersion in water.

By 1000 BC iron was beginning to be known in central Europe. Its use spread slowly westward; iron making was fairly widespread in Great Britain at the time of the Roman invasion in 55 BC. In Asia iron was also known in ancient times, in China by about 700 BC.

Brass, an alloy of copper and zinc, made its appearance during the period from 1600 BC to 600 BC. In the beginning the alloy probably was obtained when mixtures of copper and zinc ores were unintentionally smelted. In any event, its value was not appreciated, and the metal was employed sparingly until it was used by the Roman Empire in the form of currency. The general establishment of a brass industry was one of the important metallurgical contributions made by the Romans. Bronze, iron, and brass were, then, the metallic materials on which successive peoples built their civilizations and of which they made their implements both for war and peace.

DEVELOPMENTS FROM 500 BC TO AD 1500

By 500 BC considerable technical progress had been made in the mining and recovery of ores, progress that was definitely linked with the beginning of scientific thought in metallurgy. By this time rich lead-bearing silver mines had opened in Greece and had reached depths of several hundred feet. These mines were vented by drafts provided by fires lit at the bottom of the shafts. Ores were hand-sorted, crushed, and washed with streams of water to separate valuable minerals from the barren, lighter materials. Because these minerals were principally sulfides,

they were roasted (heated in air without fusion) to form oxides that were then smelted to recover a lead–silver alloy.

Lead was removed from the silver by cupellation, a process of great antiquity in which the alloy was melted in a shallow porous clay or bone-ash receptacle called a cupel. A stream of air over the molten mass preferentially oxidized the lead. Its oxide was removed partially by skimming the molten surface; the remainder was absorbed into the porous cupel. Silver metal was retained in the cupel. The lead from the skimmings and discarded cupels was recovered as metal upon heating with charcoal.

Native gold itself often contained quite considerable quantities of silver. These silver–gold alloys, known as electrum, may be separated in a number of ways, but presumably the earliest was by heating in a crucible with common salt. In time and with repetitive treatments, the silver was converted into silver chloride, which passed into the molten slag, leaving a purified gold. Cupellation was also employed to remove from the gold such contaminates as copper, tin, and lead. Gold, silver, and lead were used for artistic and religious purposes, personal adornment, household utensils, and equipment for the chase. *Native gold–silver alloys*

In the thousand years between 500 BC and AD 500 man made a vast number of discoveries that were significant in the growth of metallurgy. The Greek mathematician and inventor Archimedes, for example, demonstrated that the purity of gold could be measured by determining its weight and the quantity of water displaced upon immersion—that is, by determining its density. In the pre-Christian portion of the period, the first important steel production was started in India, using a process already known to ancient Egyptians. Wootz steel, as it was called, was prepared as sponge (porous) iron in a unit not unlike a miniature blast furnace. The product, an unmelted sponge iron, was hammered while hot to expel slag, broken up, then sealed with wood chips in clay containers and heated until the pieces of iron absorbed carbon, converting it to steel. Steel is defined as iron that contains carbon as an essential constituent in any amount up to about 1.7 percent. The steel pieces could then be heated and forged to bars for later use in fashioning articles, such as the famous Damascus swords made by medieval Arab armourers.

Arsenic, zinc, antimony, and nickel may well have been known from an early date but only in the alloy state. By 100 BC mercury was known and was produced by heating the sulfide mineral cinnabar and condensing the vapours. Its property of amalgamating (mixing or alloying) with various metals was employed for their recovery and refining. Lead was beaten into sheets and pipes, the pipes being used in early water systems. The metal tin was available and Romans had learned to use it to line food containers. Although the Romans made no extraordinary metallurgical discoveries, they were responsible, in addition to the establishment of the brass industry, for contributing toward improved organization and efficient administration in mining.

During the early centuries of the Christian Era, many scientific philosophers, known as alchemists, believed that it was possible to transmute one element into another. Although this was not achieved, the discoveries of the alchemists contributed to a better understanding of metals and their compounds and laid the foundations of modern chemistry.

Beginning about the 6th century, and for the next thousand years, the most meaningful developments in metallurgy centred around iron making. Great Britain, where iron ore was plentiful, was an important iron making region. Iron weapons, agricultural implements, domestic articles, and even personal adornments were made. Fine quality cutlery was made near Sheffield. Monasteries were often centres of learning of the arts of metalworking. Monks became well known for their iron making and bell founding, the products made being utilized either in the monasteries, disposed of locally, or sold to merchants for shipment to more distant markets. *Fine Sheffield cutlery*

In Spain, another iron-making region, the Catalan forge was invented, and its use later spread to other areas. A hearth type of furnace, it was built of stone and was charged with iron ore, flux (substance added to help fusion), and charcoal. The charcoal was kept ignited with air from a bellows blown through a bottom nozzle (tuyere). The sponge iron that slowly collected at the bottom was removed and upon frequent reheating and forging was hammered into useful shapes.

By the 14th century the furnace was greatly enlarged in height and capacity. Because the iron was in contact with hot charcoal for longer periods of time, it absorbed more and more carbon, which lowered its melting temperature sufficiently for it to exist in the molten state.

The first purposeful use of the iron from medieval furnaces was not for steelmaking but for producing cast-iron castings. Cast iron is a variety of iron containing about 2 to 4.5 percent carbon, poured molten into a mold to solidify in a desired shape. Chemically it is the same as pig iron, the crude iron from a furnace; normally it is brittle and cannot be hammer welded, forged, or rolled and is more easily fused than steel.

DEVELOPMENTS AFTER 1500

Metallur-
gical
writings

During the 16th century, metallurgical knowledge was recorded and made available. Two books were especially influential. One, by the Italian Vannoccio Biringuccio, was entitled *De la pirotechnia* (Eng. trans., *The Pirotechnia of Vannoccio Biringuccio*, 1943). The other, by the German Georgius Agricola, was entitled *De re metallica*. Biringuccio was essentially a metalworker and reported methodically and with unusual completeness the knowledge he had acquired. His book dealt with smelting, refining, and assay methods (methods for determining the metal content of ores) and covered metal casting, molding, coremaking, and the production of such commodities as cannon and cast-iron cannonballs. His was the first methodical description of foundry practice.

Agricola, on the other hand, was a miner and an extractive metallurgist; his book considered prospecting and surveying in addition to smelting, refining, and assay methods. He also described the processes used for crushing and concentrating the ore and then, in some detail, the methods of assaying to determine whether ores were worth mining and extracting. Some of the metallurgical practices he described are retained in principle today.

From 1500 to the middle of the 19th century, metallurgical development was largely concerned with improved technology in the manufacture of iron and steel. In England, the gradual exhaustion of timber led first to prohibitions on cutting of wood for charcoal and eventually to the introduction of coke, derived from coal, as

Introduc-
tion of
coke

a more efficient fuel. Thereafter the iron industry expanded rapidly in Great Britain, which became the greatest iron producer in the world. The crucible process for making steel, introduced in England in 1740, by which the materials were placed in clay crucibles heated by coke fires, resulted in the first reliable steel made by a melting process.

Closely associated with steelmaking was the making of tinplate, an industry that began to flourish early in the 17th century. The process was said to have originated in the metal-rich region of Bohemia (Czechoslovakia). The canned food industry that developed late in the 18th century stimulated a large expansion in consumption of tinplate.

The earliest methods of steelmaking suffered the serious inherent disadvantage that the iron, normally in the form of pig iron, remained in intimate contact with charcoal, which made it difficult to reduce the carbon content to a point at which the metal became ductile. This difficulty was overcome by the puddling process invented in England in 1784. In it, melting was accomplished by drawing hot gases over a charge of pig iron and iron ore held on the furnace hearth. During its manufacture the product was stirred with iron rabbles (rakes), and, as it became pasty with loss of carbon, it was worked into balls, which were subsequently forged or rolled to a useful shape. The product, which came to be known as wrought iron, was low in elements that contributed to the brittleness of pig iron and contained enmeshed slag particles

that became elongated fibres when the metal was forged. Later, the use of a rolling mill equipped with grooved rolls to make wrought-iron bars was introduced.

These developments in metal recovery and metallurgical technology in the early 17th century and thereafter ran parallel with and played an important part in the Industrial Revolution sweeping England and the Continent. In England, especially, metallurgical skills were well developed in extractive metallurgy, exploitation of mineral wealth, manufacture of iron and steel, and in the growth of industries that depended upon basic metal-making processes.

Metallurgy developed from an art dependent on trial, experience, and rule of thumb into a combination of art and science involving knowledge of the principles underlying the behaviour of metals—principles grounded largely in chemistry and physics. It would be unprofitable, therefore, to continue the history of metallurgy, especially during the 19th and 20th centuries, along purely chronological lines. The reader will often find, however, that historical facts pertaining to certain significant processes and events in metallurgical technology will be given in the account of processes and events.

Mineral dressing

Before the Metal Age began, man had to discover that metals could be extracted from mineral-bearing rocks. Through ingenuity and, doubtless, accident, this came about; thus, metallurgy, from its beginning, was concerned with the problem of treating crude ore to segregate valuable minerals and to extract metals from them. This activity is now embraced in extractive metallurgy, which consists of two phases: mineral dressing and process metallurgy.

Minerals are any chemical elements or compounds occurring naturally in the earth's crust. When a deposit of minerals is of sufficient abundance to be profitably mined and treated to extract its metallic components, it is called an ore. The worthless material expelled during the extraction is known as gangue, or tailings.

The beneficiation (concentration) of ore has undoubtedly been practiced in one way or another since man first produced copper as far back as 3,000–4,000 BC. Treatments of ore involve first, a separation of particles of different minerals with little or no change in their chemical composition, and second, a breaking down of the valuable minerals to isolate the desired metallic elements. The mechanical operations necessary to separate mineral from gangue are called mineral dressing. Modern processes in mineral dressing have become increasingly directed toward using fundamental principles governed by laws of physics, chemistry, and electricity. The practice of mineral dressing constitutes only a part of the total effort involved in the recovery of metals from ores. Because most ores are mined contain more than one species of mineral, the first step in the general scheme of ore treatment is to free them from an interlocked state physically by comminution—a process that includes the breaking down of the ore to fine powders, their ultimate fineness depending upon the fineness of dissemination of the desired mineral particles to permit their separation from waste. As a rule, comminution begins by dry crushing the ore to below a certain size and finishes by wet or dry grinding to liberate the minerals from the unwanted gangue.

Types of
treat-
ments

CRUSHING AND GRINDING

In primitive times, crushers were either small hand-operated pestles and mortars or millstones that could be turned by men or horses or operated by waterpower. Today, crushing and grinding for liberation before beneficiation is generally done in stages, with the possibility of some beneficiation between stages. Generalization is difficult because each ore has individual characteristics that influence the crushing and grinding procedures.

Some ores in nature occur as mixtures of discrete mineral particles, such as gold in gravel beds in streams and diamonds in mines. These mixtures require little or no crushing, as the valuables are recoverable using other techniques. Most ores, however, are made up of hard, tough rock masses that must be crushed before the valuable minerals can be released. Coarse, or primary, crushing today is most often done by squeezing until fracture occurs using large crushers capable of taking crude ore in sizes up to 7 feet (over 2 metres) in its largest dimensions and reducing it to lumps of from 1 to 6 inches (25 to 150 millimetres) in size. The product from primary crushing may then pass to one of several types of secondary crushers, where it is further reduced in size to a fraction of an inch. The main task of primary-, secondary-, and, sometimes, tertiary-stage crushing is to prepare the ore for fine grinding by either wet or dry methods. The minimum size of crushing consistent with economic considerations is in the order of one-fourth to one-half inch (6 to 13 millimetres).

Tumbling mills, horizontal cylinders containing grinding media of various kinds, such as rods, pebbles, or steel balls, are almost universally used for fine grinding to secure further comminution. Screens woven of wire to a given mesh size customarily are used to determine and to control particle size. Mesh is defined as the number of openings per linear unit; in the widely used Tyler Series of screens, it ranges from 3 to 325 per inch.

CONCENTRATION OR MINERAL PREPARATION

Hand sorting is the simplest form of concentration. The Chinese in 500 BC are reported to have processed marginal ores by hand sorting. Occasionally, hand sorting is still used to remove contaminating and waste products as well as to single out especially rich materials as ore passes along moving tables or conveyor belts. Minerals to be sorted in this fashion must have sufficiently distinctive colour, lustre, texture, or general appearance for the picker to distinguish the wanted from the unwanted materials. Another simple form of concentration is the art of panning, sometimes used in gold recovery; it concentrates heavy particles at the bottom of the pan while the lighter waste material is washed off on top. Still another simple concentrating device is an ordinary screen where the valuable mineral is either finer or coarser than the bulk of the ore. Washing coarse ore with a stream of water to remove fine sand and clay is often used.

Gold recovery by panning

In large-scale operations, where crushed and ground ores are to be concentrated, advantage is taken of the more common physical, chemical, magnetic, and electrical characteristics of the minerals. The basis of an economically practical process is that the particles of concentrate and gangue must not respond alike in any important degree to the specific separating force employed.

Gravity concentration. Gravity methods used to beneficiate ores are dependent on the combined effect of mass and shape of the particles in determining their movement relative to flowing water. In one method the water flows vertically upward either continuously, as in hydraulic classification or with an oscillating motion. To achieve separation by hydraulic classification, the rate of settling between the heavy and light mineral particles in the continuously flowing current of water must be reasonably different. By adjusting the rate of upward flow of a continuous stream of water, a classification between coarse and fine or between heavy and light particles is possible.

In using oscillating motion of water, a process known as jigging, the size variable is first reduced by screening, after which the differential settling rate of the particles is exploited. Jigging is one of the oldest methods for concentrating ores and is still widely used in some areas. In jigging, water is pulsed strongly upward and downward through a bed of particles. After sufficient pulsation, the top portion of the bed becomes an accumulation of the lighter gangue, which can be rejected, while the lower part is the heavier enriched concentrate.

Another method makes use of relatively undisturbed water that has been mixed with slow-settling heavy minerals (finely ground ferrosilicon, for example) to provide a liquid that can be maintained at a high density. When ore is fed into the liquid, particles of lower density than the liquid float while particles of higher density sink. This is called sink-and-float, or heavy media, concentration.

In a third method of gravity concentration, the ground ore is carried either horizontally or down an inclined plane in a flowing stream of water. Separation depends on forces acting upon the particles as they move in a layer of water, on the rate of fall of the particles, and on their resistance to lateral displacement once they contact the floor of the concentrator. Spirals, a type of gravity separator using this principle, have been found especially satisfactory for treating ores of the finer sizes. The device is a spiral channel with a modified semicircular cross section into which the pulp (ground ore and water) is fed from the top. As the pulp flows down, the heavier particles concentrate on the inner side of the stream and are removed at conveniently located ports.

Use of spiral separators

For these gravity methods to provide satisfactory separation, a marked difference in density of the wanted minerals and gangue must exist. Even when such a difference exists, these methods can become cumbersome and inefficient if the average particle is so small that its surface friction becomes the controlling property determining its movement through the surrounding fluid.

Separation by flotation. The process of concentrating ores by flotation was developed on a commercial scale early in the 20th century to remove very fine mineral particles that formerly had gone to waste in gravity concentration plants. Flotation has now become the most widely used process for extracting many minerals from their ores. It is based on the fact that the wettability of the different minerals, upon treatment, may be altered so that certain mineral particles remain unwetted and adhere to air bubbles. Through the use of relatively small amounts of chemicals or oils, particle surfaces may be altered to an air-avid or water-avid condition—that is, the surfaces prefer either water or air.

Thus, in a pulp of mineral particles and water through which air bubbles are passing, the air-avid particles attach themselves to the bubbles and are carried to the upper surface of the pulp, where they enter the froth; the froth containing these particles can then be removed. The water-avid particles remain in the pulp.

It is possible not only to float various minerals from gangue but also to separate certain valuable minerals from others selectively. Many complex ore mixtures formerly of little value have come to be among the principal sources of certain metals by proper application of the flotation process.

Magnetic separation. Magnetic separation is the most used and probably the most efficient method of beneficiating iron ores, the principal mineral of which is the iron oxide known as magnetite (Fe_3O_4). The technique is based largely on the differing degrees of attraction exerted on various minerals when influenced by magnetic fields. It is applicable to the treatment of both coarse and fine particles, either wet or dry. In concentrating magnetic iron ore, low-intensity wet magnetic separators are most commonly used.

When ores are conveyed through a magnetic field of the proper strength, the magnetic portion is separated from the nonmagnetic. High-intensity magnetic separators have been developed for the separation of weakly iron magnetic minerals, permitting magnetic beneficiation of hematite (Fe_2O_3), limonite ($2Fe_2O_3 \cdot 3H_2O$), siderite ($FeCO_3$), franklinite ($ZnFe_2O_4$), ilmenite ($FeTiO_3$), and wolframite (Fe, Mn) WO_4.

Electrostatic separation. This is a concentration method utilizing the force of an electric field to effect separation between minerals of different electrical properties. It is based on the phenomenon of attraction between unlike electrical charges and repulsion between like charges.

The process has proved quite successful in the treatment of heavy beach sands from which the valuable minerals ilmenite ($FeTiO_3$), rutile (TiO_2), or zircon ($ZrSiO_4$) may be recovered. Its application to iron-ore beneficiation has also been considerable.

Amalgamation. Amalgamation is an ancient process still used to recover free gold. The process depends on the fact that when clean surfaces of gold or silver come in contact with mercury they readily form an alloy called an amalgam. The gold (or silver) is recovered by heating the amalgam in retorts until the mercury is distilled off.

Fluidized-bed technique. The fluidized-bed technique has been adopted in a number of processes to increase the economic recovery of metals from ores and concentrates. In this process, the material to be treated is kept in motion in a chamber by an upward current of gas that maintains the individual particles in suspension. Through precise adjustment of the velocity of the gas to conform with the grain size and specific gravity of the materials to be treated, a floating mixture of gas and solids is generated that behaves almost like a liquid. Increasing attention has been given to studies of high-temperature reactions in fluidized-bed systems, "high-temperature" implying the region of 2,500°–2,800° F (1,370°–1,540° C), the practical limit of fuel-combustion heating.

Agglomeration. For some time, the metallurgical industry has been confronted with the task of agglomerating ore fines (fine particles) and concentrates. Although a number of processes have been studied intensively, they have been unable to compete economically, except in special instances, with sintering and pelletizing.

In sintering, a mixture of fine material, fuel, and water is fed onto a grate where its surface is ignited. Air is drawn through the bed to promote combustion. The passage of a high-temperature flame front through the bed causes incipient fusion with the formation of a porous, coherent mass called sinter. Although sinter is too friable (subject to crumbling) to resist excessive breakage during shipping and must, therefore, be made near the site of its use, its performance in metallurgical processes related to control of the size of the lumps has been excellent, creating an increasing demand for it throughout the world.

In pelletizing, moistened, finely divided materials, which often contain binders to enhance balling and limestone to promote high-temperature strength and to serve as flux in subsequent use, are fed into balling pans that deliver roughly spherical aggregates or pellets that must be dried and fired at a suitable temperature to harden. Pellets are usually less than one-half inch (13 millimetres) in size and sufficiently strong after firing to resist breakage; hence they have no serious limitation from the standpoint of shipping. The pelletizing process is particularly suitable in agglomerating very fine concentrates and ores.

Sampling and analysis. Routine sampling is undertaken to provide information needed for technical control and economic appraisal of ores and concentrates. By sampling, it is possible to direct attention to adjustments that may be needed during the process of mineral dressing. Sampling and sample-preparation methods frequently are major factors in determining the speed, reproducibility, and accuracy of analyses obtained with the use of modern instruments.

Even before the 16th century, comprehensive schemes of assaying (measuring the value of) gold, silver, lead, copper, tin, mercury, and bismuth ores were known, using procedures that do not differ materially from those used in modern times. Although conventional methods of chemical analysis are used today to detect and estimate quantities of elements in ores and minerals, they are slow and not sufficiently accurate, particularly at low concentrations, to be entirely suitable for industrial control. As a consequence, to achieve greater efficiency, sophisticated analytical instrumentation is being used to an increasing extent as an integral part of overall process-control schemes in mineral dressing.

Emission spectroscopy and X-ray fluorescence spectroscopy, for example, are widely used for metallurgical and ore analysis. In emission spectroscopy, an electric discharge is established between a pair of electrodes, one of which is made of the material being analyzed. The electric discharge, which may be a spark or a sustained arc, vaporizes a portion of the sample and excites the elements in the sample to emit characteristic spectra. Detection and measurement of the wavelengths and intensities of the emission spectra reveal the identities and concentrations of the elements in the sample.

In the X-ray-fluorescence spectroscope method of analysis, a sample is bombarded with X-rays, whereupon elements in the sample give off fluorescent X-radiation of wavelengths characteristic of these elements. The amount of emitted X-radiation, measured with a detector, is related to the concentration of individual elements in the sample. The sensitivity and precision of this method are poor for elements of low atomic number (*i.e.*, few protons in the nucleus, such as boron and beryllium) but for slags, ores, sinters, and pellets where the majority of the elements are in the higher atomic number range, as in the case of gold and lead the method has been generally suitable.

The trend toward achieving automatic control in metallurgical operations demands development of new and improved methods and devices to gain a better understanding of the complex physical and chemical nature of the materials being handled. Great strides in this direction are being made through the use of instrumentation, more sophisticated control systems, and the electronic digital computer for processing of data and process control.

Process metallurgy

Process metallurgy comprises a series of steps or processes by which the impure minerals that have been isolated either by mining or mineral dressing are reduced to metal, refined, alloyed, and made available according to specifications. An old art involving chemical changes that break down, or decompose, the impure minerals into their metallic and nonmetallic components, it has become, with the aid of chemical science, the chief element in modern metallurgy. The steps followed to recover metals from their minerals are normally selected on the basis of several considerations, among them the chemical nature of the mineral itself, which may be a sulfide, oxide, carbonate, silicate, or other species. There are three classes of methods: (1) pyrometallurgy, the use of heat; (2) electrometallurgy, the use of electricity; and (3) hydrometallurgy, the use of water.

Classes of recovery methods

PYROMETALLURGY

Pyrometallurgy is any metallurgical extractive process involving high temperatures that depends on heat action. Normally, the heat is supplied either by combustion of such fuels as coke, oil, or gas, or by electric power.

Gas–solid reactions. Ores in the form of oxides may be treated directly, but sulfide ores first must be roasted. Roasting is heating in air without fusion, its chief purpose being to transform sulfide minerals into an oxide. The sulfur excapes as a gas in the form of sulfur dioxide. Roasting is often employed to yield a product that is chemically and physically more amenable to some later process. It is commonly applied to such minerals as galena (PbS), sphalerite (ZnS), and chalcopyrite ($CuFeS_2$) to render them in suitable state for conversion to the metal (reduction) by carbon.

Many roasting reactions are exothermic—that is, once the reaction has started on contact with an air blast, the heat liberated enables it to continue spontaneously. Careful control during the roasting is required because overheating may ensue, producing fusion and the cessation of oxidation. The product of roasting, often purposely brought to an agglomerated state, is known as calcine.

A development for processing ore using gas–solid reactions to extract metals is chlorination, in which the oxides of some metals are converted to chlorides by the reaction of chlorine only, and the oxides of other metals are converted by the additional help of carbon. Chlorination is especially applicable in the processing of complex ores where the conventional metallurgical methods are inadequate. Low-working temperatures, high yield, and sharp separation are the essential characteristics of chlorination. The chlorinating agents have a high reactivity, enabling the whole reaction to be carried out at much lower temperatures than those employed in usual smelting techniques. The advantages of chlorination are illustrated in the processing of titanium, for its oxide is technically impossible to reduce because of the high temperatures involved. Chlorine in the presence of carbon decomposes

Chlorination in titanium processing

Use of instrumentation

titanium dioxide at a relatively moderate temperature, forming titanium tetrachloride, from which the metal can be obtained by reduction with magnesium.

In the processes so far described, the products obtained are in a fairly divided condition. Although this result is suitable for some later smelting processes, in the production of lead and iron in the blast furnace a coarse product is essential. In the preliminary preparation of these finely divided materials for smelting, agglomeration is frequently important and may be achieved by sintering or pelletizing as described earlier.

Distillation. Metals obtained during the initial stages of processing usually contain impurities derived from the raw materials. To get a higher order of purity, further treatments and refining procedures, such as distillation, are used. Such volatile metals as zinc, mercury, and cadmium may be readily purified by distillation.

Zinc production. In zinc production, carbon reduction of the oxide in retorts is the major industrial method employed. The ore is mixed with pulverized coal, and the mixture is subjected to temperatures sufficiently high to reduce the oxide, generating a gas of zinc vapour, which is then liquefied in a condenser without contact with oxidizing gases.

Efforts to develop a blast-furnace process for zinc reduction have been successful. The furnace follows the standard blast-furnace design (see below *Blast-furnace smelting*) except that volatilization of zinc prevents it from being tapped from the furnace bottom as other metals are. Instead, the zinc vapours pass upward and are rapidly condensed with a shower of molten lead in an adjoining condenser. Impurities are rejected from the furnace as slag composed primarily of the oxides of iron, calcium, silicon, and aluminum. Subsequently, the metal is refined by redistillation to remove the chief impurities, consisting of lead, iron, and cadmium. Because lead and iron are less volatile than zinc and cadmium is more volatile, the operation is divided into two stages. In the first, zinc and cadmium are distilled from the lead and iron; in the second, cadmium is separated from zinc by fractional distillation, known as refluxing, followed by condensation (see ZINC PRODUCTS AND PRODUCTION).

Carbonyls. High volatility is a characteristic common to some of the unique compounds of carbon monoxide with the heavy metals. In general, these compounds, called carbonyls, are produced by direct action of carbon monoxide on the finely divided metal. The first to be discovered, late in the 19th century, was nickel carbonyl, $Ni(CO)_4$; since then, carbonyls of iron, cobalt, chromium, molybdenum, tungsten, and manganese, as well as of some of the less common metals, have been produced. One of the important uses of metal carbonyls is in the preparation of metal of exceptionally high purity.

The carbonyls of nickel, iron, cobalt, and molybdenum can be prepared by direct synthesis; *i.e.*, by treatment of the finely divided metal with carbon monoxide. The carbonyls of the other transition elements, such as silver and copper, are prepared from the halides, compounds formed with one of the halogen elements—fluorine, chlorine, bromine, and iodine.

At one time, nickel carbonyl, $Ni(CO)_4$, was employed in a commercial process for the recovery of nickel from its ore. The gaseous carbonyl was heated and passed into vertical columns filled with pure nickel shot (small spheres), whereupon the carbonyl gas decomposed and deposited metallic nickel on the surface of the shot.

Iron pentacarbonyl, $Fe(CO)_5$, is commercially available and is used in industry in the preparation of iron powder (carbonyl iron) obtained by thermal decomposition of the carbonyl. Because of its high purity and desirable magnetic properties, carbonyl iron is used by the electronics industry for the production of magnetic devices. Carbonyl iron also finds application in powder metallurgy (see below).

Ferrous metallurgical processes. Iron- and steel-manufacturing techniques are described in detail in the articles IRON MINING AND PROCESSING; STEEL PRODUCTION. The following represents a brief summary of these important metallurgical processes.

Direct synthesis (of carbonyls)

Blast-furnace smelting. The development of iron making has largely centred on the evolution of a suitable type of furnace in which to conduct the ore reduction operations. From the small stone structures used in the Middle Ages capable of producing relatively few pounds of iron a day, the blast furnace has evolved into a tall, massive, vertical structure, up to 100 feet (30 metres) in height, with production capacities in excess of 4,000 tons of pig iron per day. It derives its name from the air blast injected through tuyeres (nozzles) near the bottom of the furnace to attain high temperatures necessary for the reduction of ore to metal.

In the blast-furnace process, the raw materials, consisting of iron-bearing materials (iron ore, sinter, pellets, slags from steelmaking furnaces, iron or steel scrap), coke, and flux (principally limestone) are fed in at the top. Preheated air, frequently accompanied by natural gas, oil, or finely pulverized carbonaceous material to substitute for part of the fuel, is injected into the furnace at the bottom. The products, pig iron and slag, are removed from the hearth through tapholes, while the hot gases are discharged at the top into equipment for cleaning. There the gases are prepared for combustion in stoves that preheat the blast.

A considerable amount of effort is being devoted to better raw material (burden) preparation. The major iron-bearing materials are ore, sinter, and pellets. Ores are usually in the form of oxides, such as hematite, magnetite, limonite, or goethite. Hematite represents by far the largest proportion of ore used. Burden preparation is important because, as the particle size of the burden becomes smaller, the resistance to gas flow increases. Removing fine material improves gas flow, resulting in a smoother operating blast furnace.

Proper control of the size distribution of the burden has come to be recognized as very effective in improving the productivity of the blast furnace. Size control consists of two factors: (1) control of the size range, and (2) removal of dust just before charging. Control of size distribution of the burden is accomplished by maintaining a narrow size range for each charge layer in the blast furnace. It is not uncommon for the size range of iron ore to be kept at 0.2 to 1.2 inches (5 to 30 millimetres). The elimination of very fine materials and intensive burden preparation have resulted in phenomenal increases, as much as 100 percent, in productivity of some modern blast furnaces.

In connection with burden preparation, much has been done to beneficiate the lower grade iron ores and to agglomerate the concentrate to a useful size by sintering or pelletizing. The practice of using a high percentage of iron ore in the form of sinter or pellets has yielded further improvements in furnace productivity while lowering significantly the consumption of coke. Increasing demands for greater productivity from blast furnaces has led to the use of self-fluxing sinter and pellets and to consideration of using partially prereduced iron ore in the form of pellets as burden material. The latter is still in the experimental stage.

Progress in blast-furnace output, achieved by changes in operations and in burden preparation realized since 1950, has been outstanding.

Electric-furnace smelting. Electric smelting furnaces are used in several parts of the world to produce pig iron, the intermediate form through which almost all iron must pass in the manufacture of steel. Such furnaces are well suited to locations having an abundance of cheap electric power along with access to raw materials. The physical requirements for the reducing agent are less stringent in the electric furnace than in a blast furnace; coke breeze (fine screenings from coke) or mixtures of coke breeze with coal may be used.

Direct-reduction processes. Methods for reducing iron ore by means other than the blast furnace or the electric-smelting furnace have led to a group of techniques generally referred to as direct-reduction processes. A number of such processes have been developed to make use of raw materials not fully suited for use in modern blast furnaces; for example, high-titania iron ores that cannot

Burden preparation

Use of coke breeze

be smelted in a blast furnace, because of slag problems, can be smelted in electric pig-iron furnaces. Many authorities have argued for the potential economic advantages of direct reduction followed by electric-furnace steelmaking, as against the combination of a large blast furnace followed by basic oxygen steelmaking (see below), but in the early 1970s the question remained unresolved.

Among the more popular direct-reduction processes are those using rotary kilns for the reduction of the iron ore. Iron ore and carbon are mixed with limestone (as flux) and passed through a revolving kiln operating in the region of 1,830° F (1,000° C). Under favourable conditions, the reduction is essentially complete.

Total world needs for iron ore in the manufacture of pig iron and other forms of reduced iron are expected to reach more than 1,000,000,000 tons by 1980. Of the amount consumed in the 1970s, more than 92 percent was used in the form of crude ore, sinter, or pellets as burden for the blast furnace.

Steelmaking. In the middle of the 19th century all of the previous steelmaking processes were largely supplanted by new techniques, the first of which was the pneumatic, or Bessemer, process, developed independently by William Kelly in the United States and Sir Henry Bessemer in England. It occurred to the inventors that the oxygen for refining could be taken directly from air blown upward through a bath of molten pig iron held in a refractory-lined vessel. The air not only purified the iron, but the metal became hot enough to remain molten even when all of the silicon, manganese, and carbon were gone and hitherto infusible pure iron remained. The whole reaction required only a few minutes; at the end, an ingot of mild steel could be cast, ready for the forge or rolling mill. The vessel used is called a converter, and, depending on the nature of its lining, it is either an acid or a basic converter.

The lining material in the acid Bessemer converter is a highly siliceous rock, ground with a little fireclay, moistened and tamped in place. Reactions within the vessel leave untouched the sulfur and phosphorus in the pig iron; hence in the acid Bessemer process the pig iron must be low in these elements. Silicon in the pig iron is the chief heat-producing element.

When the acid Bessemer process, however, was applied to pig irons high in phosphorus content and low in silicon and manganese, the process did not produce satisfactory steel. In Europe, low-phosphorus pig iron is relatively scarce and costly, and early efforts to remove the phosphorus from high-phosphorus pig iron in the acid converter failed. In the United States, pig iron of low phosphorus content was available and was used for the manufacture of satisfactory steel by the acid Bessemer process.

In 1879 it was discovered that when the converter was lined with a basic material, such as burnt limestone, dolomite, or magnesite, and when burnt lime was charged with the molten pig iron, basic slag would form and be maintained in such condition that it would absorb and hold the phosphorus oxide produced during the blow. This discovery was the beginning of the so-called basic Bessemer process widely used on the Continent for refining pig irons smelted from high-phosphorus iron ores so common to many areas of Europe. The product, called Thomas steel, is satisfactory for all classes of tonnage steels, such as bars, boiler plate, pipe, structural steel, and rails.

In the basic Bessemer process, phosphorus is removed as calcium phosphate after silicon, manganese, and carbon have been oxidized from the liquid bath. To furnish heat during the phosphorus removal stage (the afterblow) a pig iron containing typically 1.4 to 2.5 percent phosphorus is required because it is the principal heat-producing element.

Unfortunately, the product of the Bessemer process has serious disadvantages in important applications such as sheet metal for deep-drawing. The lack of ductility and workability in very low-carbon steel was finally traced to nitrogen, which averaged 0.015 percent in Bessemer steel,

as compared with 0.005 percent in more ductile open-hearth and electric steel (see below). Belgian steelmakers found that if, after the carbon in the bath had dropped to about 0.50 percent, the blow was continued with oxygen in a two-to-one oxygen–steam mixture instead of air, low-carbon steels equalling open-hearth steel in nitrogen and phosphorus content, hardness, and drawability could be regularly produced.

The substitution of oxygen for air in steelmaking is now a practical matter, and several basic oxygen processes are in use. Plants utilizing top blowing with a stream of pure oxygen were first placed in operation in 1952 at Linz and Donawitz in Austria. The plants employed pig iron produced from local ores that are high in manganese and low in phosphorus. Phosphorus, sulfur, and carbon are eliminated, and steels very low in nitrogen are produced. The vessel for steelmaking has no tuyeres, the pure oxygen gas being fed through a tubular, water-cooled, retractable lance held in a vertical position above the bath. The action of the oxygen under pressure, normally held between 140 and 180 pounds per square inch, is partly chemical and partly physical. On striking the liquid-metal surface it immediately reacts with iron and the oxidizable constitutents, causing the evolution of carbon monoxide gas within the bath, giving rise to a vigorous boiling action that assists in accelerating the refining reactions.

A major advantage of the basic oxygen process is its flexibility in handling raw materials of many types and compositions. The product has shown itself to be at least equivalent in quality to basic open-hearth steel of similar carbon content. Several modifications of the process have been developed for refining the high-phosphorus blast-furnace metal commonly encountered in Luxembourg, Belgium, and France.

The very rapid rates of reaction attained and the low cost of oxygen produced in large quantities have made the basic oxygen converter more economical as an instrument for steel production than the open hearth. As a consequence, growth in crude steel production by the oxygen converter has outstripped and overshadowed the open hearth. The advantages of the basic oxygen furnace compared with the open hearth are: higher production rates; lower investment costs; lower labour requirements; lower operating cost under most conditions; and equivalent steel quality.

Before about 1870, the world's steel industry grew mainly by the installation of Bessemer converters. As large quantities of scrap began to accumulate, the open-hearth process, which could consume such scrap, grew more popular. The principal features of the open-hearth process were developed around 1864 to 1868 through the combined inventions of Sir William Siemens and Pierre Émile Martin. Siemens, who conceived the process first, incorporated the principle of regeneration to preheat the combustion air in order to intensify the melting flame over a shallow bath. Preheating the combustion air made it possible to reach sufficient flame temperature to melt large quantities of scrap in a reasonable length of time. Martin's additional idea was to dilute the molten hot metal with solid scrap. The steel produced was, in many respects, superior to Bessemer steel.

The growth of the open-hearth process was such that by 1910 it had reached a position of predominance over the Bessemer process. By 1950 the open hearth's share of global crude steel production reached 79 percent, its maximum percentage. Since then its percentage has been decreasing because of the accelerated steel production in basic oxygen furnaces.

Although the advantages of the use of oxygen in steelmaking were first demonstrated on a large scale in basic oxygen converters, it was not long before large-scale use of oxygen was applied also to existing open-hearth furnaces. Oxygen steelmaking improved the economy and technology of most of the open hearths to which it was applied, but this improvement was not enough to stop the growth of the oxygen converter process at the expense of the open-hearth operation.

In the early 1900s small electric-arc furnaces were introduced to produce alloy steels in a melting process in

Bessemer process

Basic oxygen process

Open-hearth process

which the energy input is primarily electrical. Charges of 100 percent scrap may be melted and refined with precise control. After World War II, the size of electric-arc furnaces increased considerably, and now furnaces with capacities up to 200 tons are not uncommon. Improvements in mechanical and electrical equipment along with oxygen injection have lowered operating costs to the point at which electric furnaces may be competitive with small basic oxygen converters where scrap prices are favourable.

The electric furnace as known today is primarily a unit for melting and refining steel scrap. Techniques have not yet been generally accepted for refining large batches of molten pig iron in electric furnaces. In electric-arc furnaces, the electrodes of carbon or graphite pierce the roof and are of proper size to carry the electricity without undue resistance. Electric currents of large amperage arc across the gap between the lower ends of the electrodes and the slag. Heat is generated principally by the resistance offered by the air gap and the slag layer to the flow of the current.

Another type of furnace is the high-frequency induction furnace, which has a cylindrical spiral coil of water-cooled copper tubing that carries an alternating current at about 2,500 hertz (cycles per second). A crucible rammed inside the coil is electrically and thermally insulated and contains the charge of selected steel scrap and ferroalloys for simple melting and mixing without refining. The intense alternating magnetic field set up inside the coil induces sufficient eddy currents in the metal charge to heat and melt it.

The flexibility of electric furnaces and their capability of being designed for melting in vacuum as well as in air make them attractive, particularly where costs of electric energy and scrap are low. By 1965, in the U.S., ingot tonnage produced by electric-furnace melting had grown to 10.3 percent of the total tonnage.

Nonferrous metallurgical processes. Detailed descriptions of the manufacturing techniques for copper, lead, zinc, and other important metals will be found in such articles as COPPER PRODUCTS AND PRODUCTION; LEAD PRODUCTS AND PRODUCTION; and ZINC PRODUCTS AND PRODUCTION. The following discussion of nonferrous metallurgy therefore includes only brief summaries of these processes.

Copper. The commercial production of copper is mainly by pyrometallurgical (smelting) methods or by hydrometallurgical (leaching) methods, usually followed by electrolytic refining or recovery. In general, the sulfide ores (chalcopyrite, chalcocite, covellite, and bornite) are treated pyrometallurgically after flotation; and the oxide ores (cuprite, malachite, and azurite) are treated hydrometallurgically. Most of the new copper produced since the latter 1950s was from the sulfide ores. By the 1950s selective flotation was almost universally used on sulfide minerals for concentration, although gravity methods had been popular in the past. Perfect separation between wanted mineral and gangue is not possible, but with constant supervision, repeated treatment, and exacting controls, it is possible to concentrate 95 percent or more of the copper into 10 to 20 percent of the original weight and to eliminate most of the gangue and much of the worthless sulfide. The enriched ore forms the raw material for smelting, which has as its object the rejection of the worthless material as slag and the concentration of copper.

The procedure for smelting is to concentrate the copper into matte (copper-iron sulfide) with the elimination of gangue as slag. This end is accomplished by smelting in a furnace in a reducing or neutral atmosphere with suitable fluxes to form two liquid layers—the upper layer containing the gangue minerals and the fluxes, the lower layer a mixture of molten sulfides known as matte. The amount of sulfur present in the feed largely determines the matte grade, the usual grades containing from 24 to 45 percent copper and the desired amount of iron in the form of iron sulfide. Any precious metals present in the ore are collected in the matte.

The partial elimination of sulfur from the concentrate

to control the composition of the matte can be done by roasting; but in new plants the concentrate is being charged directly to the smelting furnace because it is considered preferable to accept a lower grade of matte to avoid the cost and inconvenience of roasting. The matte contains virtually all of the copper.

Copper has a lower affinity for oxygen than has iron or sulfur. This fact and the fact that the oxidation of iron and sulfur liberates large quantities of heat are the basis for matte conversion. The removal of the iron and sulfur in the matte is effected by oxidation, using air injected into the converters. When this metal is cast and allowed to solidify, the surface takes on a rough, blistered appearance as a result of the evolution of absorbed (occluded) gases, mostly sulfur dioxide. For this reason the material is known as blister copper. It is subsequently refined by fire refining or electrolytic refining.

Blister copper, in addition to copper oxide, contains small amounts of other impurities. These impurities are best removed by fire refining, in which air is forced through the molten material to ensure complete oxidation of all oxidizable impurities, which are then skimmed from the metal. The oxidizing treatment is followed by a reducing treatment, known as poling, during which ends of green logs are forced into the molten pool. When the proper stage in deoxidation has been reached the metal is cast. The metal, which had a distinctive metallic rose colour, is called tough pitch and may readily be cast into dense slabs. It contains, however, any gold and silver recoverable from the original ore as well as traces of other impurities, some of which can be detrimental. The amounts of gold and silver often make their recovery economically attractive.

The final state of purification will be described under *Electrorefining,* included in the section on *Electrometallurgy* below; and the commercial production of copper by hydrometallurgical (leaching) methods, which is widespread, will be covered in the section on *Hydrometallurgy* below.

Lead. The most important source of lead is galena, the sulfide of lead (PbS). Galena, in its pure form, contains 86.5 percent lead; it almost invariably also contains silver and is in fact one of the main sources for that metal. Many deposits of galena are intimately mixed with other minerals, such as sphalerite (ZnS); hence, methods for treating the ores to separate the minerals from one another were developed. The advent of flotation at the start of the 20th century permitted this separation as well as the concentration of lead from low-grade and highly disseminated galena ores.

The usual blast-furnace smelting of lead permits not only the smelting of ores and concentrates in which lead is the metal of principal value but also of lead ores in which other metals, particularly gold and silver, are of greater value than the lead itself. The smelting and refining operations must be designed to produce, eventually, a refined lead acceptably free of impurities, while permitting the recovery of silver, gold, copper, zinc, antimony, bismuth, nickel, arsenic, cadmium, indium, tin, selenium, tellurium, the platinum metals, and possibly others. There is, however, no single operation designed to recover all of them.

The first basic operation in the extracting of lead from its sulfide ores and concentrates is to remove the sulfur by roasting in air. This operation converts the sulfide to lead monoxide, and the sulfur is removed as sulfur dioxide gas. The sulfide charge is burned with enough heat to convert it to a porous, not too friable cake that breaks into lumps as it discharges from the roaster grate. These lumps, called sinter, are mixed with coarse coke, and the mixture is charged to the top of a vertical shaft or blast furnace. The modern lead blast furnace, normally rectangular in plan, varies from 17 to 18 feet (5.2 to 5.5 metres) in height from the tuyeres, where the air is introduced near the bottom of the furnace, to the charge floor at the top. The walls of the furnace comprise water-cooled steel jackets sloping upwards and resting on a crucible of refractory brick. Feed to the furnace consists chiefly of lead oxide in the form of sinter, fluxes to form a proper slag, and coke to act as fuel and the reducing agent. The lead serves as an excellent collector of the silver, gold, copper, zinc, antimony, bismuth, and other metals. The nonreduced elements in the charge form the liquid slag that is easily separated from the liquid metal. The operation seems simple and, indeed, it is when correctly carried out, but it can be accomplished successfully only by the exercise of great skill in preparing the charge and operating the furnace.

The metal from the blast furnace for subsequent refining is transferred either in liquid form or as a solid to a refinery where it is purified either by kettle refining or by electrolytic refining. In kettle refining the liquid metal is oxidized with air or a reagent to form a liquid slag containing essentially all of the more oxidizable metals; *i.e.*, arsenic, antimony, and zinc. The oxidation, known as the softening step, can be quite selective and results in separate slags for each of the metals if desired. After softening, the lead can be desilverized by zinc and debismuthized by adding calcium or magnesium, and the drosses (scum of waste matters) formed are removed by skimming.

Zinc. Although zinc sulfide (zinc blende) is the most plentiful zinc mineral, in most deposits it is so intimately mixed with other sulfides, particularly galena, that the classical methods of mechanical separation fail to separate the zinc blende. The problem was solved by the technique of flotation, a process requiring that the ore be crushed to very fine particles. Most commercial zinc concentrates are now produced by this process.

In ordinary hearth roasting, to convert zinc sulfide to zinc oxide, these flotation concentrates produce a very fine calcine, which is difficult to treat in horizontal retorts. It is therefore necessary to agglomerate the roasted product by a sintering process. An alternate procedure sometimes used is to roast the concentrates on a moving grate, directly producing a sintered product.

A large fraction of the world's zinc is still produced from hand-charged horizontal retorts, in which the sintered zinc oxide mixed with pulverized coal is exposed to a temperature of 2,550° F (1,400° C). This process has a number of disadvantages, including the batch method of operation, but improvements have been made in furnace construction and methods of firing, and mechanical charging has been introduced.

Vertical retort process

To overcome the deficiencies of the horizontal retort process, a continuous method, known as the vertical retort process, was developed in the late 1920s. Continuity of operation is secured by providing a discharge mechanism at the bottom of the retort, enabling the spent material to be continuously ejected. The zinc vapour, together with carbon monoxide and hydrogen, passes upwards through the retorts and then to a condenser where the zinc metal is collected.

A powerful competitor to thermal reduction methods is the electrolytic process by which zinc is deposited from highly purified zinc sulfate solutions. This process has been widely adopted where power is cheap and plentiful, conditions that are essential since considerable power is needed. Another advance in zinc metallurgy, the zinc blast furnace, was described earlier.

Tin. The only important ore of tin is the mineral cassiterite (SnO_2). Usually the raw ores contain less than 8 percent tin, but upon concentration the tin content can be raised to between 70 and 77 percent.

Tin oxide is reduced readily by carbonaceous material when heated at a fairly low temperature. Metallic tin, obtained by reducing the ore concentrate with coal in blast or reverberatory (horizontal flame) furnaces, is purified by a number of processes. Because much of the metal is either entrapped in the slag or reacts with the fluxes during smelting, the recovery of tin from slags, furnace linings, and drosses is an important phase in the metallurgy of tin.

Nickel. The most important sources of nickel are the mixed sulfide ores containing pentlandite [(FeNi)S]; nickel-bearing pyrrhotite (Fe_8S_9); and nickel-bearing chalcopyrite ($CuFeS_2$).

The extractive metallurgy of nickel is fairly complex

and costly and underwent rapid changes during and immediately following World War II. The nickel-bearing sulfide ores are initially ground and carried through a series of flotation and magnetic separation processes, yielding several distinct concentrates for separate processing.

By-products. Many minor metals, including arsenic, bismuth, cadmium, germanium, selenium, tellurium, antimony, cobalt, silver, gold, and platinum occur in association with the major nonferrous ores and are recoverable as by-products during metallurgical treatments. They represent a substantial part of the total value of the production derived from the treatments, which often are a major or even the sole sources for the production of these metals. For economic recovery, specific processes have been developed for individual metals.

Melting. The preparation of metal in the liquid state is a distinct stage in most metallurgical processes. Melting is only the beginning of a series of operations by which the metal is brought into its finished form. Although the procedures by which the more common ferrous and nonferrous metals are brought to the molten state do not differ greatly among the metals, there are reactive metals, such as titanium, that, because of their affinity for the gases nitrogen, oxygen, and hydrogen, must be melted and cast under vacuum or in the presence of an inert gas. To satisfy the conditions for melting some of the newer metals as well as the more common ones, new methods of melting based on new principles are being designed. In all of these, major efforts are being exerted to obtain in the process substantial improvements in metal quality.

Special melting conditions

Several processes of melting, described below, promise to become increasingly significant in upgrading the quality of metals, particularly of steels. These processes are limited in production capacity, about 30 tons per charge being maximum, but they are valuable because of the high grade of metal they produce by melting or remelting.

In vacuum-induction melting, the charge, which can be either solid or molten metal, is induction-heated (*i.e.*, heated by a current produced in the material by an external coil) under vacuum. In the consumable-electrode vacuum-arc process, by contrast, the charge serves also as the electrode. As the electrode melts, the vacuum removes the gases; water cooling limits contamination of the melt by the furnace walls (usually copper). The process is useful especially for consolidating reactive and refractory metals and for producing high-temperature, high-strength alloys. When metal of particularly high quality is needed, the electrodes are prepared from ingots that previously were vacuum-induction melted.

Electroslag refining was developed and is applied widely in the U.S.S.R. In this process also, the electrode (sometimes two) is the charge. Using no vacuum, the furnace is charged with a slag that covers the melt and eventually the ingot. The process is said to produce metal equal in quality to vacuum-arc remelted steel.

Alloying. A basic condition of metallurgic technology is that it must constantly meet increasingly exacting demands from the metal-using industries. Exact types of metal are specified, including the precise components they should contain so that specific mechanical and other critical properties can be forecast. The deliberate addition of various chemical elements to the molten metal, a process known as alloying, has gone far to make it possible to attain consistently good performance of finished parts in the enormously varied conditions of modern metal use.

The chemical elements to be incorporated by alloying to liquid steel were often added as ferroalloys rich in the desired element. They include alloys of iron with boron, calcium, chromium, niobium, manganese, molybdenum, nitrogen, phosphorus, selenium, silicon, tantalum, titanium, tungsten, vanadium, and zirconium. With the production of alloys for steelmaking purposes now being carried out in electric-reduction and other types of furnaces, however, a number of the alloy additions contain relatively little iron. Elements such as nickel, copper, lead, cobalt, and aluminum are usually added as virgin metal or scrap. The term addition agent, instead of ferroalloy, is now preferred to describe any of the materials added to molten steel for altering composition and properties. In preparing nonferrous alloys, the elements added in any quantity are usually in the form of virgin metal.

Alloying additions may be added at various times in the melting process, such as with the charge, in the molten batch near the end of the melting period, in the ladle or in the mold. Timing of such additions is determined by their effect on the temperature of the molten metal, the ease with which the addition goes into solution, the susceptibility of an addition to oxidation, and the formation and elimination of reaction products. The principal purposes of alloying are to create materials from base metals that have increased strength and toughness, improved response to heat treatment, less susceptibility to embrittlement at low temperatures, or increased resistance to heat, corrosion, or wear, or a host of other properties. Alloys composed of a complex group of elements are continually being tailored to satisfy specific needs.

Casting. The operations of casting metals in the liquid state vary widely according to the form in which the metal is finally to be used. Broadly speaking, metallic objects tend to be divided according to their mode of production into two types: cast and wrought. So far as metallurgical operations are concerned, cast materials are brought to final form by permitting molten metal to fill and solidify in molds of desired shape. On the other hand, wrought materials generally begin their career by solidifying in a metal mold of simple shape and being brought to desired form by working, either cold or at elevated temperature, using practices such as rolling, pressing, forging, stamping, drawing, and extrusion. (For descriptions of these practices see below *Metal processing.*) Casting is a process practiced by foundries all over the world as a basic method for the production of shapes, using in one form or another almost all of the metals known to man.

Most castings are made by pouring metal into sand molds prepared from mixtures of moistened sand and clay packed over the faces of the pattern. Recently, however, specialized processes have been developed to produce castings having greater dimensional accuracy, smoother surfaces, and more finely reproduced detail than is obtainable in sand molds. Important processes among these are plastic-mold, composite-mold, investment, permanent-mold, and die casting.

Plastic-mold casting. The principal mold ingredient in plastic-mold casting is calcium sulfate, to which small amounts of two or more other substances are added to attain specific properties. The molds are used to produce nonferrous castings of superior surface and dimensional accuracy. Composite molds are assembled from several components, among which at least one varies from the others in the molding materials used. The goal is to derive the specific advantages of each molding material without being penalized by its disadvantages. Composite molds are mainly for alloyed aluminum castings classified as premium-quality castings or engineered castings.

Investment casting. This process (also known as the lost-wax and precision-casting process) employs molds that are produced by surrounding an expendable pattern of wax or plastic with a refractory slurry that sets at room temperature. The wax or plastic is then melted out and the metal poured into the hot cavity that remains. In one variation, the patterns are of frozen mercury, which is melted out, leaving the impression to be cast. The investment-casting process is used particularly on alloys that cannot be softened or made plastic for working by heat but must be shaped to exact dimensions.

Permanent-mold casting. These castings are produced in metal molds that can be used over and over again. The molds consist of two or more parts so that they can be readily disassembled to eject the casting and then reassembled to be ready for the next casting. The process is particularly suitable for high-volume production of simple castings, such as gray iron pipe having a fairly uniform wall thickness and no undercuts or intricate internal coring. Permanent mold casting is used successful-

Frozen mercury patterns

ly for casting gray iron and alloys of aluminum, magnesium, copper, or zinc.

Die casting. This process has found extensive application for the lower melting nonferrous metals because of the accuracy of dimensions attainable and especially because of the speed with which castings are made. The process consists generally of forcing molten metal into metal dies or molds under pressure; the die is then opened by a machine and the casting ejected. It is widely used in making castings of low-melting alloys of zinc, tin, aluminum, magnesium, and, to a limited extent, for certain types of brass and bronze. The difficulties of the process increase rapidly as the melting temperatures of the metal rise. The process in Europe is termed pressure die casting.

Ingot solidification. By far the largest proportion of liquid metal produced throughout the world is cast in molds for ingots, which are then used for future mechanical working such as in rolling and forging. Steel ingots can range in size from small blocks weighing a few pounds to huge, tapered, octagonal masses weighing more than 100 tons.

In pure metal free from gas, the solidification process is comparatively simple, but it is by no means simple in complex alloys such as steel and the many nonferrous alloys that often contain dissolved gases as well as suspended oxides, sulfides, hydrides, nitrides, and silicates. The principal factors that play a part in ingot solidification are: contraction, which comes about because the metal after solidification generally occupies a smaller volume than in the liquid state; gas liberation, which comes about because most liquid metals dissolve large volumes of gas, especially oxygen and hydrogen, that are driven off during solidification as a result of their lower solubility in the solid state; segregation, resulting from impurities and various constituents that may undergo nonuniform separation upon solidification; and contraction stresses, resulting from the fact that the outer portions of an ingot necessarily solidify while the inner portions are still liquid.

The amount of gas, chiefly oxygen, dissolved in liquid steel and the amount of gases released during solidification determine the type of ingots; these are termed killed, semikilled, capped, or rimmed in ascending order of amount of gas retained.

Nonferrous metal and alloy ingots and slabs, although subject to the same general laws and phenomena as steel ingots and slabs, are rarely as large, so that many of the problems arising from large size, very slow cooling, and extensive segregation common to large steel ingots are not encountered in the nonferrous industries. On the other hand, blowholes (captured gas bubbles) lying just under the ingot skin, which often are regarded as normal in steel and weld during subsequent working, are not tolerable in nonferrous metals. They do not weld but tend to open out during the annealing process following cold rolling, causing defects.

Today, the casting in simple shapes of both ferrous and nonferrous metals is being done by continuous casting processes. Many continuous casting techniques had been used for years to cast shapes of nonferrous metals, particularly wire rod. Adapting these techniques to ferrous products has been difficult, largely because of the much higher casting temperature. The advantages promised by continuous casting, however, have led to persistent experimentation and to step-by-step improvements that have resolved most of the problems for steel in the period since 1950. The big economic gain from continuous casting is the high yield of sound steel, some 94 percent in contrast to about 80 percent for conventional ingot practices.

Continuous casting processes

ELECTROMETALLURGY

Electrometallurgy is the science and technology of metallurgical operations conducted by electrochemical means —specifically, the use of electrolytic processes in the extraction and refining of metals and in electroplating. It is concerned with two branches: the conversion of electrical energy into chemical energy (as in electrowinning, electrorefining, and electroplating, described below); and the utilization of thermal energy derived from electrical energy, which is mainly concerned with the electric furnace and its applications. The scope of both branches is very broad.

Fuller treatments of the metals discussed below will be found under ALUMINUM PRODUCTS AND PRODUCTION; MAGNESIUM PRODUCTS AND PRODUCTION; and under similar titles.

Electrowinning. Electrowinning (winning or recovering the metal by an electrolytic process) can be carried out on the molten metal or compound, or on a solution of a compound of the metal. In the first process a raw ore is fused (melted) or converted into an easily fusible compound, and the resulting current-conducting solution (electrolyte) is electrolyzed (decomposed by an electric current), producing a relatively pure metallic deposit on one electrode. The second process involves leaching the raw ore (see below *Hydrometallurgy*) with an aqueous solution; the resulting solution, or electrolyte, rich in the metal, then is recovered and electrolyzed, again producing a relatively pure metal deposit on one electrode.

Aluminum. The production of aluminum and magnesium are typical electrowinning operations. Unlike the other common industrial metals, pure aluminum is not produced by the direct smelting of its ores. It is produced electrolytically by a process that was discovered almost simultaneously in the United States and France in 1886 and is the basis of the modern aluminum industry. Purified alumina (Al_2O_3) is dissolved in molten cryolite (Na_3AlF_6) and electrolyzed with direct current. The mixture is contained in a carbon-lined steel box that serves as one electrode while carbon rods or blocks dipping into the molten bath form the other electrode. Under the influence of the current, the oxygen of the Al_2O_3 is deposited on the carbon, which is thereby slowly burned, while the molten aluminum is deposited on the carbon lining of the cell, collecting in the bottom. Additional alumina is stirred into the electrolyte from time to time and the molten metal is removed. The alumina required is somewhat more than 1.9 pounds per pound of metal.

Magnesium. The English scientist Michael Faraday was the first to succeed (1833) in producing metallic magnesium by electrolysis of molten magnesium chloride. The electrolytic process was further developed and was used exclusively until about 1941, when other techniques, employing a thermal process, came into use for a small proportion of magnesium production. In the U.S., magnesium is produced by electrolysis of fused magnesium chloride, the pure chloride coming largely from seawater. The electrolytic cells are steel shells or pots containing suspended carbon rods for one electrode and iron or carbon for the other electrode.

Electrowinning is also employed in producing an important percentage of zinc and cadmium. In the extraction of both metals by electrolysis, the solution is the sulfate of the metal, which is electrolyzed in cells using aluminum for one electrode and lead for the other.

Electrorefining. In electrorefining, the crude metal to be refined forms one electrode and is suspended in a suitable aqueous electrolyte. Under electric current action this electrode dissolves, and pure metal is deposited on another electrode, usually composed of the same metal as that deposited. Electrorefining processes are employed commercially in the extraction of such metals as copper, nickel, and lead and the precious metals gold and silver. The production of electrolytic copper and nickel are typical electrorefining processes.

Copper. More than 90 percent of the copper produced in the U.S. is electrolytically refined. Slab electrodes of fire-refined copper are further refined by immersing them in a solution of copper sulfate in an electrolytic cell with the other electrode being of copper. In the multiple system, separate anodes (positive electrodes) and cathodes (negative electrodes) are used, the cathodes consisting of thin sheets of high-purity copper, known as starting sheets. In an individual cell all the anodes are connected in one parallel group and all the cathodes in another. In the series system no starting sheets are used, the electrodes of impure copper being in series in a single cell and

serving as both anode and cathode. This arrangement allows the impure copper to be corroded from the face of an electrode while pure copper is deposited on the back. Of the two systems, the multiple system is most widely used. Its advantages lie chiefly in the ability to treat copper of lesser purity and to operate at a lower voltage. Gold, silver, and other valuable insoluble impurities are recovered as by-products of electrorefining of copper.

Nickel. In the electrorefining process for nickel, the impure nickel is pressed into anode plates. The electrolyte used is composed of a nickel sulfate-chloride solution containing some boric acid, sodium sulfate, and about 40 grams of nickel per litre (2.5 pounds per cubic foot). Nickel starting sheets are used as cathodes. Elaborate precautions, such as the use of canvas diaphragms, are taken to separate the anodes and cathodes, to prevent the deposition of copper and iron, as well as nickel.

Electroplating. Electroplating is the production of a thin coating of one metal on another by electrodeposition. Practically any metal can be electroplated under properly controlled conditions. The process is used extensively for coating various base metals with zinc, cadmium, nickel, chromium, tin, aluminum, and many other metals. The deposited metal is obtained from a solution of its salts by the passage of an electric current through the solution. It is a complex process, and careful control of the current and of the chemical composition, temperature, and cleanliness of the bath are required for good deposits (see ELECTROPLATING).

HYDROMETALLURGY

Hydrometallurgy is the science and technology of extracting and recovering metals chemically from ores by the use of aqueous solutions. The principles involved in hydrometallurgy are those of physical chemistry, inorganic chemistry, electrochemistry, and analytical chemistry. The production of metals by hydrometallurgy can be broadly described as extensions of these principles on an industrial scale.

The operations usually involved are: dissolving a metal or metal compound by a suitable aqueous solvent (water alone or with added reagents), usually termed leaching; the separation of waste and purification of the leach solution; and the precipitation of metal from the leach solution by chemical or electrolytic means. Although the technology of hydrometallurgy was developed at the turn of the 20th century for recovering gold from low-grade ores, its features were practiced as early as the 16th century. *(margin: Leaching operation)*

An important historical prerequisite to the development of hydrometallurgical procedures was the advent of commercial direct-current generators to provide an efficient low-cost technique for precipitating metals by electrolysis from aqueous solutions. After the beginning of the 20th century methods were improved and were augmented by the addition of still other techniques. Consequently, there evolved the great copper leaching plants in South America, the U.S., and Africa; vast aluminum extraction plants throughout the world; the electrolytic zinc industry; plants producing nickel and cobalt from sulfide ores and from the lateritic deposits in Cuba and other tropical areas; the gold-producing plants of South Africa, Canada, Australia, and the U.S.; and the gigantic plants in many parts of the world that employ hydrometallurgical techniques to extract uranium from ores that contain from a fraction of a pound to a few pounds of uranium in a ton of ore.

The feasibility and successful conduct of a hydrometallurgical operation depend on a variety of factors, any or all of which may be critical. An adequate supply of water is, of course, indispensable and, because metals are present as ions in aqueous solutions, a source of energy is required to convert the ions to metallic form. Beyond these essential features, several practical physical and chemical factors must be considered. The metals or minerals must be soluble in the leaching solution; the solvent must usually be such that it will dissolve selectively the desired metals or minerals; the solution, when it contains valuable metals, should be such that the metals present *(margin: Physical and chemical factors)* can be readily separated from one another; and the solution must also be such that the desired metals can be precipitated from it by one means or another, producing either pure metal, a mixture of metals, or a metal salt. For economic reasons, it is usually necessary that the leach solution either be capable of being regenerated and used again or that it be susceptible of treatment to recover by-products.

The various aspects of hydrometallurgical processes include the preparation of the ores, concentrates, and other materials that are to be leached; the leaching itself, which generally applies to the selective dissolution of metal compounds and minerals from ore mixtures; the solution purification, which depends largely on the chemistry of the positive and negative ions in the solution; the precipitation of the metal to be extracted by electrolysis with direct current or by treating the solution with a reducing gas such as hydrogen; and the regeneration of the solution for its reuse.

Metal processing

The principal areas of metal processing covered below are cold and hot working, foundry processes, surface treatments, powder metallurgy, nuclear metallurgy, and heat treatment. Metal joining is treated in WELDING, BRAZING, AND SOLDERING.

COLD AND HOT WORKING

A great part of the world's metal production is cast into ingots that must be shaped to finished products by mechanical forces. Mechanical working not only brings the metal to desired shape but also changes its structure and properties.

When metal solidifies from a melt, especially if it does so in large masses and therefore slowly, it has a crystalline structure that is always relatively coarse and sometimes very coarse. Mechanical working breaks down this original cast structure and replaces it with a much finer and more satisfactory structure from the standpoint of physical properties. It is possible to produce a refined structure, comparable in scale with that of worked metal, by heat treatment alone; but this method is practical only with pieces of moderate size because larger masses cannot be cooled rapidly enough. Mechanical working also causes the redistribution of the nonmetallic constituents (inclusions), making them less harmful and, particularly for steel, serves to close up and even bring about welding of cavities.

Cold working consists in the plastic deformation (working) of a metal at such temperatures and at such rates that no recrystallization occurs during the process. Under such conditions, the metal is strain hardened, that is, increased in hardness and strength as a result of plastic deformation at temperatures lower than the recrystallization range. In general, these limiting temperatures are high in metals that melt at high temperatures and low in metals that melt at low temperatures. Cold deformation of metal thus produces fundamental structural changes accompanied by an increase in properties related to strength and a decrease in properties related to ductility.

Only when the working temperatures are above the recrystallization temperature, hence when softening occurs during the working process, can the term hot working be applied. During hot working, metal is deformed by mechanical working above the recrystallization temperature so that the coarse crystallinity of the cast state becomes progressively fragmented and rearranged to bring about the reconstruction and refinement of the crystalline structure. By proper selection of temperature and by mechanical working with dies or rolls, for example, various properties of the metal can be improved.

Forging. In forging, articles of metal are shaped by hammering or pressing metal blanks between pairs of forging dies. Hammering was the first method employed by man in shaping metal. In most forging processes, an upper die is attached to the ram of the forging hammer or press, so that it may be raised and dropped or forced under pressure against the rigidly supported, stationary lower die. Forgings are made in many metals and alloys, including copper, brass, bronze, nickel, aluminum, magnesium, steel, titanium, and various high-temperature alloys.

As the metal is processed from the ingot stage to various shapes (blooms, billets, slabs, and bars) for forging, its crystals are elongated, producing fibre-like flow lines of grain structure. In closed-die forging, these flow lines of grain structure are worked in such positions as to impart maximum strength relative to the stresses expected in the forged article. For maximum strength, care must be taken that the grain runs parallel to the axis of greatest bending stress.

Drop forging employs a drop hammer, so designed that the falling weight of the ram and upper die, often augmented with force from a steam or air piston, forces the heated metal into cavities cut into the face of each die. The metal being worked in a forging hammer is commonly at a sufficient heat to bring it to a plastic state.

Much progress has been made in forging metals cold, that is, at temperatures below the point at which the grain structure begins to recrystallize. Cold forming of heads has been used for many years in the manufacture of bolts and similar parts. More recently, however, cold forming has been replacing conventional hot forging, especially in forming of larger parts.

The formation of parts by forging, called chipless machining, is popular, for example, in the forge rolling of gears from solid blanks. Many other parts that can be made this way will become candidates for the process because of the savings in materials and labour. **Chipless machining**

Metal rolling. Of the many methods of shaping metals, rolling is most widely used. The rolling mill has passed through a succession of developments, not only in size, power, and productive capacity but also in design and in ability to produce varieties of shapes of sections with grooved rolls. The process of shaping metal by rolling consists essentially of passing the material between rolls revolving at the same peripheral speed and in opposite directions and spaced so that the opening between them is somewhat less than the depth of the material entering. Metals are rolled both hot and cold.

Hot rolling. Except in the few instances when ingots are forged, hot working by hot rolling is almost universally used to reduce ingots of metals by mechanical force from their original cross section through the intermediate stages to bar, structural shape, plate, sheet, and strip, the more common hot-finished forms that are produced. Hot rolling is done by passing the heated metal through pairs of heavy rollers, which are either flat or grooved, so that each successive pass lessens the cross section and brings that material more nearly to the required final shape. The hot-working temperatures are different for the different metals, but the highest are always those at which the lowest melting constituent in the structure starts to melt. The temperature range of hot working is limited by this temperature and by the temperature at which the metal remains sufficiently plastic at the lower end of the range, so that it will not rupture on working. The temperature at which the mechanical working is finished, known as the hot-working finishing temperature, is important in governing the final treatments necessary and the structural and other properties obtained.

Hot rolling accomplishes three main purposes: (1) reduction of cross-sectional area, (2) refinement of structure, and (3) shaping of the metal into desired form. Although the products of a rolling mill vary widely in weight and shape, a common characteristic is that each piece is of uniform cross section from end to end and is of a length limited only by the weight of the mass of metal being rolled. All the shaping is done in the intermediate passes of the mill. The flow of metal in the rolling operation is continuous and almost entirely in the longitudinal direction. With steel, nearly all hot rolling is done at full red heat, at which it is quite plastic.

The details of rolling practice vary widely according to the metal being rolled and the purpose for which the product is required. Heavy plates and extremely thin sheets naturally demand entirely different treatment and procedures. The rolling of broad hot strip or sheet in coils

Hot strip
mills

has been in continuous development since 1926, when the first mill capable of rolling strip more than 24 inches (61 centimetres) wide was built. In these mills, which are continuous and used mainly for steel, the hot metal is fed into the first set of rolls rotating at a moderate speed. The material emerging from the first rolls is fed directly into a second set, which, since the length is increased by the passage through the first rolls, must run at considerably higher speed. A number of sets of rolls is used in series in this way, the finished product leaving the last rolls at a very high speed. Other types of rolling result in the production of sections having the form, for example, of H and I beams, channels, angles, railway rails, and other products. These are made by the action of suitably shaped grooves cut in the rolls. Successive passes in such rolls must provide for the easy flow of the metal from one shape to the next.

Cold rolling. Although steel is hot when it is reduced in size from its ingot and billet form, some of the softer nonferrous metals and alloys can be treated cold. The essential nature of cold rolling does not differ from hot rolling. The effect of cold rolling, however, is to produce hardening so that, after a time, the metal has to be annealed (heated and then cooled slowly) to soften it before further cold rolling. Cold rolling is used to reduce the thickness of section, produce a smoother, more dense surface, develop controlled mechanical properties, or obtain any one or combination of these three effects.

Drawing. Drawing is a process for forming sheet metal, tubing, and wire to obtain certain shapes and dimensions. Flat sheet metal is drawn to produce both shallow and deep shells or cups with straight walls. The distinction between shallow-drawing and deep-drawing is somewhat arbitrary. Shallow-drawing generally refers to the forming of a cup no deeper than half its diameter.

Wiredrawing is one of the oldest industrial arts and is employed to provide a slender rod or bar of metal of uniform cross-sectional shape. The shape can be round, square, hexagonal, octagonal, oval, half oval, half round, rectangular, or flat. The limits for drawn wire range from 0.001 inch (0.025 millimetre) to approximately 1 inch (25.4 millimetres) in maximum dimension. The rod or bar of metal is pulled through a series of dies of decreasing diameter until the final shape is obtained.

Tubes are sometimes drawn through a die to reduce the inside and outside diameters, to make various shapes, and to increase the strength and hardness of the metal.

Extrusion. Extrusion is a process of shaping metal into a continuous form by forcing it through a die of appropriate shape. In forward extrusion the metal is held in a container having an opening (die) of the desired finished section at one end. The metal is forced through the die under great pressure by a ram. In backward extrusion the ram is hollow and contains the die. The container has a closed end and pressure of the ram forces the metal in the opposite direction. The peak pressures exerted by the ram may be as low as 5,000 pounds per square inch (351 kilograms per square centimetre) for soft metals such as lead, or as high as 450,000 pounds per square inch (31,640 kilograms per square centimetre) for alloy steels. Collapsible container tubes are formed by striking a cold slug of metal, held in a container and die, a high speed impact blow from a punch. The impact causes the metal to fill the die cavity and to flow or squirt upward out of the die around the punch. The process is called impact extrusion.

Impact
extrusion
of tubes

Spinning. Spinning is another process for forming sheet metal or tubes into hollow cylinders, cones, and other circular shapes by a combination of rotation and force. Tools, usually consisting of rollers mounted in a lathe, are pressed against the spinning metal with just sufficient pressure to deform the sheet into and against a mandrel (a metal bar serving as a core), made to the shape of the completed workpiece. Normally, spinning is done without applying heat.

FOUNDRY PROCESSES

Earlier, under *Casting* it was noted that foundries throughout the world practice the art of casting metals in

molds with cavities made to conform to the object wanted. The process is known as founding. Molds are generally prepared in two halves, each formed by firmly packing a mixture of sand and clay moistened with water against a wood or metal pattern that conforms in shape to the object to be cast. Although many castings are solid, there is likely to be a hollow space within the casting. To form the hollow, a core, generally of sand held to shape with a binder, is set in the lower portion, or drag, of the mold. The upper portion of the mold is known as the cope.

Cast iron. The general term cast iron includes a number of different irons, known as gray irons, pig irons (the product of the blast furnace), white cast irons, chilled cast irons, malleable cast irons, and ductile cast irons. Cast irons cover a wide range of iron-carbon-silicon alloys usually containing more than 1.7 percent and less than 4.5 percent of carbon along with varying amounts of silicon, manganese, sulfur, and phosphorus. They may have an alloy content of less than one percent and up to several percent. Special types of corrosion-resistant iron are made with greater alloy content; for example, with 11 percent to 17 percent silicon, 25 percent to 30 percent chromium, or 4 percent to 30 percent nickel.

Gray iron is by far the most widely used of the cast metals (see also IRON MINING AND PROCESSING). The essential characteristic of gray iron is that much of the carbon is present as flake graphite, which gives it a gray-coloured fracture when broken. Its attributes have led to its widespread use for many industrial purposes, including automobile engine blocks, agricultural and machinery parts, stove and furnace parts, hollow ware, and ingot molds.

Flake
graphite
in gray
iron

Cast steel. When steel is cast into suitable molds having cavities conforming to the shape of desired objects, it is known as cast steel and the objects as steel castings. Steel for steel castings is produced commercially by almost all the melting processes used commercially for making steel.

Five classes of commercial steel castings are produced; namely, low-carbon steels with carbon content less than 0.20 percent, medium-carbon steels with carbon content between 0.20 percent and 0.50 percent, high-carbon steels with carbon content above 0.50 percent, low-alloy steels with total alloy content less than 8 percent, and high-alloy steels with total alloy content above 8 percent. Steel castings are most often heat-treated, using the various methods that apply to wrought steel, to develop the necessary characteristics.

Nonferrous castings. The sand-casting process for production of nonferrous castings differs in no essential way from that used for production of castings made from ferrous metals. It permits the use of a large number of nonferrous alloys, providing a variety of physical and mechanical properties in both the as-cast and heat-treated conditions. In addition to casting in sand, many nonferrous castings are produced in permanent metal and in plastic molds, by die casting and by investment casting, processes described earlier.

SURFACE TREATMENTS

Metals are frequently given surface treatments to produce a protective layer that has corrosion resistance and other important properties differing from those of the base material. Such surface layers, applied to metals of all types, often also serve to change or improve appearance. These surface layers may be applied by hot dipping, electroplating, cementation, and several other ways.

Hot dipping. Hot-dipped coatings are generally of the lower melting point metals, such as zinc, tin, lead, tin–lead alloys (called terne), and aluminum. To apply the hot-dipped coatings, careful attention must be given to preparation of the metal surface to be coated and to the duration and temperature of immersion. The molten metal must wet the base metal and must alloy with it. Zinc coating by hot dip (one method of galvanizing) provides an adherent, protective coating on the surfaces of iron and steel products that is effective against corrosion from exposure to the atmosphere. Zinc is more active than

Galva-
nizing
of iron
and steel

iron, hence tends to corrode instead of the iron; by this "sacrificial" protection, it prevents iron from corroding at minor discontinuities in the zinc coating.

Tin coatings produced by hot dipping are excellent in appearance, resist corrosion, give a surface that assists in soldering, and provide a nontoxic, protective coating that is particularly useful where the metal comes in contact with foods and beverages. Hot-dipped tin coatings are applied mainly to steel, cast iron, copper, and copper alloys.

Lead coatings, which are applied to ferrous articles by hot dipping, contain from 2 percent to 10 percent tin to assist in bonding.

Hot dipping is one of the various methods used for applying aluminum coatings to ferrous articles. Close control of liquid-metal temperature and time of immersion is important as these factors influence the thickness of the unwanted brittle intermetallic layer between the base metal and the pure aluminum overlay.

Cementation. Another process for introducing elements into, as well as onto, the outer surface of metal objects is called cementation. Essentially, the part to be cemented is heated to an elevated temperature in contact with a solid, liquid, or gaseous medium containing the cementing material. The cemented material penetrates inward from the exposed surface, forming an alloy on the surface decreasing in concentration as the distance inward increases. Among the various cementation processes used by industry are: the carburizing (impregnating with carbon) of steel; calorizing (heating the part in contact with aluminum powder) of both ferrous and nonferrous metals; and ceramic coating to protect nickel-base, cobalt-base, and vanadium-base alloys and refractory metals against oxidation at very high temperatures.

Other processes for coating metals. Metal spraying, metal cladding (covering by bonding), protective film formations, painting, and vitreous enamelling are among the other processes used in coating metals. Sprayed metal coatings are produced by use of an air blast to spray heated metal particles against the object to be coated. Such coatings are often used to resist corrosion, reclaim undersized and worn parts, and to provide hard, wear-resistant surfaces. In metal cladding, surfaces of slabs of two metals are brought carefully together for the purpose of developing a bond, sometimes by heat and pressure alone.

The formation of surface films on metals is accomplished by various methods, including oxide coating of aluminum and its alloys (the so-called anodizing treatment) in a bath of sulfuric acid, or forming a phosphate protective coating on iron, steel, zinc, cadmium, aluminum, and their alloys by treating them in a dilute acid phosphate solution to convert the metal surface to an insoluble crystalline phosphate film. Vitreous (glassy) or porcelain enamels on metals are used widely in the chemical, pharmaceutical, and food industries because of their excellent resistance to chemical attack.

Anodizing of aluminum and alloys

POWDER METALLURGY

The methods of powder metallurgy afford a unique way of producing and shaping metals and alloys. In its simplest form, powder metallurgy consists of: (1) pressing metal powder in a die to produce a compressed shape called a green compact, and (2) sintering (diffusion bonding by heating) the compact at an elevated temperature in a protective atmosphere. During sintering, the compact becomes consolidated and strengthened. Powder-metallurgy methods are competitive under certain conditions with other metal-forming techniques.

Powder metallurgy is usually employed for two reasons: first, because it may be the only known means of producing certain metals, alloys, or mixtures of two or more metals having certain desirable physical or mechanical properties; and second, because powder metallurgy may be the cheapest way to manufacture certain small parts, often a result of the fact that parts can be formed directly to shape, with little or no machining.

Powder manufacture. Metal powder may be manufactured by mechanical or chemical methods. The most widely used mechanical method, starting with solids, is

milling by power-driven hammers (hammer milling) or by balls in a rotating container (ball milling). In starting with liquid metals, various mechanical processes that break up the metal into tiny droplets before they solidify can be employed. This method is called atomization.

Chemical methods for producing metal powders provide either for the reduction of compounds of the desired metals to powder using various agents or for the electrolysis of a liquid solution (aqueous or molten) that contains the desired metal. The latter process is similar to electroplating, but the conditions of current and temperature are adjusted to produce a porous, flaky, or brittle deposit of metal that is scraped off the cathode and broken up to obtain the powder. Nickel, copper, and iron powders are often made by this process from aqueous solutions.

To obtain specific properties in the finished product, powders are often mixed and blended before use. Excessive blending, however, especially in an overloaded blender, may work harden the powder, making it less compressible and thus more difficult to compact. To bond the powder particles into a mass solid enough to withstand the stresses in service, the powder must be heated or sintered after compressing. Sintering is done in protective atmospheres or in vacuum at temperatures below the melting points of the metals. Sometimes a liquid phase forms and assists in consolidation. In all sintering processes the dimensions of the mass of powder being sintered decrease, the amount of shrinkage depending on the composition of the powder, the amount of compression to which the powder has been subjected before sintering, and the time and temperature of sintering. This shrinkage must be allowed for in the design of parts that are to be made directly to shape. When the highest possible density is required, the compacts (parts) may be repressed and then resintered.

Shrinkage in sintering

Processes and products. Three general classes of processes are used in powder metallurgy, depending on the type of metal used in each. One class involves metals of relatively low melting point that are ductile, such as silver, copper, and iron. Another class involves the refractory metals; *e.g.*, metals with melting points usually above 2,912° F (1,600° C), which normally are brittle, such as tungsten, molybdenum, tantalum, and titanium. The third class concerns the production of materials known as cemented carbides, which contain tungsten carbide.

In preparing compacts from ductile metal powders, the pressing operation forms the metal part to the desired shape at room temperature. Pressures range from 10 to 50 tons per square inch (14,000 to 70,000 kilograms per square millimetre) compacting the powder to a density of about 60 percent to 80 percent of that of a similar mass of solid metal. The ductile metal compacts show shrinkages of about 1 percent to 5 percent in dimensions during sintering.

Powder-metallurgy procedures of the refractory metals are used chiefly to produce a bar or ingot of the refractory metal, which is then further processed by mechanical working to make wire, rod, tube, or sheet. Because most refractory metals are either too brittle or too hard to be compacted in the same manner as the ductile metals, they are compacted at room temperature with a binder, such as paraffin wax, that holds the compressed particles together until they can be presintered to drive off volatile matter and establish a weak bond. Sintering in a satisfactory atmosphere at a proper temperature then follows to develop the needed strength.

The cemented-carbide materials made by powder metallurgy are cemented together by a metal, usually cobalt, forming a product of great hardness and high compressive strength. The principal constituent is tungsten carbide powder, although carbides of other refractory metals, notably titanium and tantalum, are often used along with the tungsten carbide. The carbide powders, blended with cobalt powder ranging in amounts of from 3 percent to 25 percent, are mixed with a binder such as paraffin wax and pressed to shape followed by presintering at about 1,652° F (900° C) to evaporate the binder. The presintered material can then be machined or ground

Tungsten carbide powder

to provide the shape needed for the finished part before it is finally sintered. Certain advantages of cemented carbide as a cutting-tool material stem from its ability to cut while red-hot.

Powder metallurgy is applied to iron-base compacts to produce an essentially pore-free part having increased strength and density and improved machinability. This result is accomplished by infiltrating molten metals, commonly copper and copper-base alloys, into the pores of the compact by capillary action.

NUCLEAR METALLURGY

Nuclear metallurgy includes the production, fabrication, and application of metals of interest in nuclear engineering and the study of their properties. The study of atomic fission in 1939 led to the emergence of several relatively unknown metals and paved the way for the practical use of atomic energy. The phenomenon of fission concerns the splitting of an atomic nucleus into two or more parts by the addition of a neutron to that nucleus. Fissionable materials include plutonium and an isotope of uranium, uranium-235; thorium can be converted into another fissionable isotope of uranium, uranium-233 (see NUCLEAR FISSION).

These materials are referred to as nuclear fuels. Because of their affinity for neutrons, the metals boron, hafnium, cadmium, or gadolinium are used to control the number of neutrons striking the nuclear fuel and thus shut down a reactor or control its power level of operation.

Because uranium metal is highly reactive toward water or air at elevated temperatures, protective cladding of the fuel elements is necessary. Aluminum and zirconium are commonly used for this purpose. Beryllium is desirable for use as a moderator—that is, to slow down high-energy neutrons produced by the fission process so that they become more effective in producing additional fission reactions.

Low-melting sodium and sodium-potassium alloys are used as coolants in several reactors. The liquid metal is circulated over the hot fuel elements and then to a steam generator where the heat in the liquid metal is recovered.

In addition to the usual problems associated with metals at high temperatures, there are some unique problems in nuclear metallurgy. One such is radiation damage, the failure of a material due to the intense radiation in a reactor. Uranium undergoes embrittlement and drastic changes in dimensions as a result of irradiation. Another serious problem that eventually results in a shutdown of the reactor is accumulation of fission products in the nuclear fuel. Direct removal of the fission products and economic reprocessing of the fuel constitute a major challenge to the nuclear metallurgist (see also NUCLEAR REACTOR).

HEAT TREATMENT

Many articles of iron, steel, aluminum, copper, magnesium, titanium, nickel, and their alloys intended for important engineering uses are subjected to some form of heat treatment for the purpose of obtaining certain desirable conditions or properties. Heat treatments are applicable to all metals, both ferrous and nonferrous. Changes in metals afforded by heat treatment involve changes in the nature, form, size, or distribution of the structural constituents, although frequently metals are heat-treated merely to decrease or relieve internal stresses.

The time-temperature cycle Heat treatment consists of subjecting a metal to a definite time–temperature cycle. Basically, this cycle can be divided into three parts: (1) heating, (2) holding, and (3) cooling. The heating medium also is important, since it affects the rate of heating and causes or prevents chemical changes, such as oxidation, that proceed inward from the surface of the metal. Although in some instances, such as in the case of pure metal or certain alloys, the rate of cooling is likely to be unimportant, when the structure of the material being heat-treated is different at the maximum temperature from that at low temperatures, the rate of cooling is of great importance. Iron–carbon alloys that change from one crystal structure to another (gamma to

alpha iron) on cooling from above the transformation range are particularly sensitive to cooling rate.

Aging, or precipitation, reaction. In heat treatment, three types of reactions are of importance industrially and form the basis for most heat-treating operations: the aging, or precipitation reaction, the allotropic transformation reaction, and the decomposition reaction. The aging reaction occurs when the solubility of a constituent in the basic material (matrix) is greater at high temperature than at low temperature. In this process, the alloys are heated to a temperature sufficiently high to cause a constituent that is more soluble in the matrix at high than low temperature to dissolve. The alloys are then quenched to room temperature at a rate sufficiently rapid to prevent apparent change in structure by precipitation of the constituent. When the quenched materials are reheated within the proper temperature range, however, precipitation does take place. By controlling the conditions for precipitation, the precipitated particles can be maintained within a critical size, and considerable variation in mechanical and other properties of the alloys can be achieved. Maximum property changes are achieved with a particular combination of time and temperature for the precipitating reaction, which determines the size and distribution of the precipitated particles, and for the compositions of the alloys. Certain copper, aluminum, and magnesium alloys are among the engineering metals whose mechanical properties are vastly improved through the mechanism of precipitation hardening.

Allotropic transformation reaction. Allotropy is the capacity of a material to exist in more than one crystallographic structure. Materials that have this capacity are termed allotropic. Allotropic transformation occurs in some metals upon heating and cooling. It serves as the basis for most heat-treating changes that occur in steel. Steel at high temperatures, for example, is composed primarily of a solid solution of carbon having a particular crystal structure known as gamma iron. The solid solution is called austenite. Gamma iron is capable of taking into solution fairly large quantities of carbon. The solid solution on cooling converts to a mechanical mixture of alpha iron (which has another crystal structure), called ferrite, and iron carbide, called cementite. Alpha iron has a crystal structure in which carbon has an extremely low solubility. As a consequence of this low solubility, the carbon in the steel separates as iron carbide.

The rate of cooling affects the transformation of austenite and largely determines the final structure of a given steel and hence its physical and mechanical properties.

Decomposition reaction. This reaction involves the decomposition of certain constituents into one or more other constituents that possess more desirable properties. Its importance is illustrated by the production of malleable cast iron from the hard, brittle cast iron known as white cast iron. The iron carbide or cementite in the white cast iron is decomposed to ferrite and a spheroidal form of graphite after a prolonged heating in the temperature range of 1,380° F (750° C) and 1,750° F (955° C). This graphitized material is considerably more ductile and more easily machined than the parent material, and hence much more useful.

Production of malleable cast iron

Physical metallurgy

METALLOGRAPHY

Metallography is the study of the constitution and structure of metals and alloys as revealed by the unaided eye or by such tools as low-powered magnifiers, optical microscopes, electron microscopes, and X-ray diffraction techniques (see below). All metallic materials are crystalline, and their characteristics are determined by the nature of the minute crystals of which they are composed or by the manner in which these crystals are aggregated into larger masses. Not until H.C. Sorby's microscopic studies on meteorites and on iron and steel in England in the period from 1863–1887, were these simple facts appreciated. Sorby's pioneering work gave birth to the modern science of metallography and was largely responsible for the impetus that turned metallurgy into a science. Metallography has provided the method of correlating the structure of the metallic materials with their composition and treatment, and with the mechanical and physical properties that determine their ultimate application.

Metal and alloy structures. A pure metal is composed metallographically of grains and grain boundaries. The orientation of the grains varies and gives rise to grain boundaries in the structure that define the regions where the mutually adjacent grains have met. Grain boundary regions can be made visible by applying an etching reagent, which attacks these regions more vigorously than other regions.

The metallographic structure of an alloy can be understood completely only with the aid of an equilibrium or phase diagram of the alloy system in question. Such diagrams are used to express the relationships between phases in an alloy under conditions of equilibrium; *i.e.*, conditions in which two or more phases can exist together. For binary (two-component) alloys, for example, these diagrams are two-dimensional plots in which temperature is plotted vertically and composition horizontally. This diagramming provides a graphical representation of the equilibrium temperature and composition. For the more complex alloys several two-dimensional diagrams are required for complete representation of the temperature–composition variables.

The components of an alloy are limited in the ways in which they can combine. Each of these combinations is called a phase and each influences the overall characteristics of the alloy to an extent determined by the amount present and the manner in which it is dispersed. By examining metals using metallographic techniques valuable information can be secured relative to the character and distribution of the phases and to their probable influence on properties.

Macroscopic examinations. In macroscopic examination—*i.e.*, examination using the unaided eye or a magnifying glass—the interest is confined largely to gross structural details and defects arising from processing and other causes. A variety of defects may be visible, such as cracks and porosity; additional details of crystalline, chemical, and mechanical heterogeneities may be revealed after a prepared or ground surface is subjected to etching.

Optical metallography. A greater abundance of structural knowledge can be secured through microscopic examination of a metal specimen made flat and smooth by polishing, at magnifications ranging from about 100 to 1,500 diameters. Nonmetallic inclusions and gross porosity are visible without etching. By etching with some chemical reagent that attacks the different constituents of the structure differently, such pertinent information as size and shape of grains, the size, shape, and distribution of structural phases and nonmetallic inclusions, microsegregation, and other structural features in the metal specimen can be revealed. For appraising the structure revealed under the microscope, the etchant used needs to be known, as well as the magnification. The use of polarized light (*i.e.*, light in which all the waves vibrate in one direction) in connection with optical microscopes is helpful in obtaining a variety of information.

Value of etching

Electron metallography. The electron microscope can give very much greater magnifications and is being applied in some metallographic studies, the results of which contribute greatly to man's knowledge of the microstructure of metals. The instrument's ability to separate details that are very close together (resolving power) results from the very short wavelength of the radiation from the electron beam. It is capable of much greater initial magnification and resolution (about 0.0002 micron, a micron being equal to 0.001 millimetre) than either the light or ultraviolet microscope (0.25 micron and 0.1 micron, respectively; see MICROSCOPE).

X-ray metallography. The application of X-ray diffraction techniques to metallurgical problems has contributed much to man's basic knowledge of metals and alloys. The technique is employed principally to study phenomena that are related to groupings of atoms themselves and is capable of resolving structures at magni-

fications equivalent to 1,000 times the lower limit of the optical microscope.

CORROSION

Corrosion is the gradual chemical or electrochemical attack of a metal by atmosphere, moisture, or other agents. Reactions occurring within these environments are a very important factor in the treatment and serviceability of a metal. The attack may be uniform (that is, the metal may corrode evenly) or it may be intensely localized (that is, concentrated upon small areas, a form of attack known as pitting). Two general types of reactions are recognized: direct oxidation and electrochemical. In the course of direct oxidation a solid film may form, such as the scale formed on some metals when heated at elevated temperatures. In the electrochemical reaction, the corrosion can be divided into anodic and cathodic parts (see below). Prevention of corrosion and the protection of metals against it are of vital importance to modern industry. Corrosion processes are sometimes brought about intentionally by industry, as in manufacturing the pigment white lead by the corrosion of metallic lead; but normally the processes are undesired and involve damage to the metal and expense for its replacement. The damage caused by corrosion is intensified in pitting, one of the most destructive forms of corrosion and one most difficult to guard against.

Intentional corrosion

Direct oxidation. In direct oxidation, which results particularly when metals and alloys are heated in oxidizing environments, the nature and extent of the attack are determined largely by the properties of the scale formed; that is, its structure, chemical composition, specific volume, melting point, and boiling point. Specific volume (volume per unit mass) of the scale with respect to the specific volume of the metal is especially significant. Progress of oxidation under conditions in which the specific volume of the scale is equal to or somewhat greater than that of the underlying metal can be very rapid at the start but diminishes perceptibly with time as a result of the protection offered by the scale, provided the scale remains continuous and does not flake off. When the specific volume of the scale is smaller than that of the metal, however, the rate of attack normally is proportional with time. The resultant scale is porous and crumbly, so that progress of oxidation is controlled only by the specific reactivity of the metal and the composition and temperature of the gas atmosphere.

There are exceptions, of course, one being the case of molybdenum metal. Its oxide has a higher specific volume than the metal itself, yet its oxide is nonprotective and increases in weight at high temperatures in proportion to the reaction time. Such behaviour comes about as a result of unusual characteristics of the oxide, which melts and is continuously being evaporated from the metal surface.

Some alloy additions (*e.g.*, silicon, aluminum, and chromium in steel) form oxides adjacent to the metal surface that markedly decrease the rate of oxidation. The intermediate chromium steels and the ferritic and austenitic stainless steels at high temperatures have much higher oxidation resistances than the carbon and low-chromium steels. When sufficient oxygen is present, moderate quantities of chromium in steel form tenacious and impervious films of oxide that protect the underlying metal. For each grade of chromium-bearing steel, the limiting temperature above which scaling becomes significant is directly related to the chromium content. The extremely high temperatures encountered in jet engines and gas turbines necessitated the development of new alloys that have sufficient resistance to corrosion by the hot combustion gases as well as adequate mechanical properties at the high temperatures reached.

Compounds of such elements as sulfur, vanadium, and sodium in the products of combustion of fuel can change the nature of oxidation of metals exposed to these compounds, sometimes increasing it to a catastrophic level. No commercial alloys are known that will resist this type of corrosive attack.

Although it was originally thought that the oxidation of

Corrosion from combustion products

metals at high temperature was a direct chemical reaction, later studies suggested that oxidation and tarnish are electrochemical phenomena, the oxide film serving both as internal and external circuits of a closed cell. Such studies have been used to account for the formation of the invisible oxide film and tarnish that isolate metal from air at ordinary temperatures.

Electrochemical corrosion. Most corrosion takes place in gaseous or aqueous mediums and involves oxidation and reduction reactions (reactions in which an atom loses or gains electrons, respectively) occurring at metal interfaces. These reactions, which are electrochemical in nature and which determine the rates of corrosion, are controlled by the flow of electrons through the metal. They divide into anodic and cathodic parts, each of which involves an oxidation–reduction system. The transfer of electrons in these reactions constitutes the corrosion current, and the magnitude of its voltage provides the driving force of corrosion. When the flow of electrons stops, electrochemical corrosion ceases.

The corroding effect of any medium is determined by a host of factors. In natural corrosion the rate of attack is usually limited by the supply of some essential substance. When metal undergoing corrosion becomes the anode in an electrolytic cell supplied with current from an external source, there is no such limitation, and the rate of attack, in the absence of other complications, becomes dependent on the current forced through the cell.

Prevention of corrosion. Protection against corrosion usually is secured by physical means, using inert or less active covering materials, or by chemical means, either by alloying and thus changing the chemical activity, by the use of coatings of greater chemical activity than the base metal, or by modifying the corroding conditions in some manner. On many metals, aluminum for example, the reaction product, often the oxide of the metal, adheres so tightly that it serves to protect against further attack.

More often the protection of metal exposed to normal environments is obtained by applying suitable coatings, such as anticorrosive paints made from anticorrosive substances, and pigments embedded in organic mediums. Paints made from these substances and pigments (such as zinc chromate and other chromates, iron oxides, red lead, white leads, basic lead sulfate and finely divided flakes of aluminum) form durable and protective coatings on metals. The coatings, in turn, may be covered with other types of paints chosen for their physical, mechanical, and aesthetic characteristics.

Instead of paints, metallic coats and porcelain enamels can be used to protect iron and steel. Zinc and aluminum are particularly effective as coatings in preventing the corrosion of iron exposed to the atmosphere. These coatings may be applied by dipping the iron in a molten bath or may be deposited electrically. They can also be applied by metal spraying, the sprayed metal producing a layer of overlapping scale.

Pipelines or other metallic objects buried underground require protection against corrosion arising from stray electrical currents entering and leaving the metal at different points or from the acidity of the soil or some chemical constituent in it. Plastic coatings are extensively used as a preventive measure in these instances. Another very effective system of protection known as cathodic protection is widely used. In this, the metal to be protected is connected electrically to a more easily corroded metal, such as magnesium. An electric circuit is set up such that the magnesium corrodes as a sacrificial anode, while the less active metal serves as the cathode and is not itself attacked.

INSPECTION AND TESTING

Of equal importance with the various processes in making metal products is the thorough inspection and testing to which the products are subjected during processing and after finishing to determine whether, from a quality standpoint, they will meet consumer needs. In order that the producer and consumer may speak a common language in discussing quality, it is necessary that quality be described in precise terms. This situation has led to establishing definite specifications that define quality and test procedures.

At one time, chemical analysis was the primary specification in the evaluation of metal products, but only a rough measure of the attributes of a material was obtainable through chemical analysis alone. More sophisticated methods of inspection and testing have followed that are now accepted as essential in the control of metal quality.

Mechanical testing. The mechanical-property tests most commonly used in evaluating the quality of metal products include tensile, hardness, torsion (twisting), creep (deformation under constant stress over a period of time), and certain types of bending tests. The primary purpose of these tests is to determine conformance or nonconformance with specifications. The data obtained serve as an index of quality of a product in comparison with similar products obtained previously or from other sources. Such data also are frequently used by manufacturers of metal products for control of manufacturing methods as well as for guidance in improving the products and in the development of new materials. Because of the limitations of the conventional tests, there is a need for more specialized tests, particularly for those intended to duplicate or approach actual conditions in service. Among the attributes not revealed by the conventional tests, but desired for many production purposes, are formability, weldability, machinability, and corrosion and wear resistance. Tests to gain some measure of these attributes have been devised and are in constant use throughout the metal industry.

Nondestructive testing. Nondestructive inspection or testing—that is, inspection by methods that do not destroy the part—is applied extensively to certain metals and alloys that must pass rigid specifications with regard to surface discontinuities and internal flaws.

In the metal industries, radiography (X-ray examination) has been used primarily as a routine method of inspection of welds and castings. Defects in welds and shrinkage and blowholes in castings are relatively easily discerned by radiographic methods. *X-ray examination*

Magnetic particle inspection will detect the presence of cracks, flaws, and similar surface or near-surface discontinuities, but only in ferromagnetic materials, such as iron and steel. For nonmagnetic materials, such as the nonferrous alloys, fluorescent penetrant inspection serves this purpose. In magnetic particle inspection the part being tested is magnetized and then covered with fine magnetic powder. The powder is easily removed where no crack or flaw exists but clings to such defects. In fluorescent penetrant inspection a fluorescent liquid is applied to the surface of the workpiece and enters the surface discontinuities. The excess penetrant is removed before the piece is examined under intense ultraviolet light. Indications of discontinuities show up brilliantly.

Control of internal quality of heavy sections of metals has been greatly extended by ultrasonic (or supersonic) inspection. Sound waves with frequencies as high as several million vibrations per second are sent through the sections. Large flaws will cast an acoustical shadow on the face of the piece opposite the face through which the waves entered. Small flaws are detected by measuring the small amount of sound energy the flaws reflect back to the point of origin.

BIBLIOGRAPHY

History: GEORGIUS AGRICOLA, *De re metallica* (1556; Eng. trans., 1912, reprinted 1950), historical notes describing for the first time the ancient art of processes and methods then employed in extractive metallurgy; J.G. PARR, *Man, Metals and Modern Magic* (1958), a fascinating and informative story of discoveries and developments in metals going back to 6000 BC; C.S. SMITH (ed.), *Sorby Centennial Symposium on the History of Metallurgy* (1963), a series of papers containing a wealth of historical information by outstanding metallurgists.

Modern technology: A.M. GAUDIN, *Principles of Mineral Dressing* (1939), a text containing useful information on extractive metallurgy; E.J. PRYOR, *Mineral Processing*, 3rd ed. (1966), a modern text on methods for treating ores for concentration; INSTITUTE OF MINING AND METALLURGY, *Advances in Extractive Metallurgy* (1968), a collection of contemporary papers on this subject; W.H. DENNIS, *Extractive Metallurgy: Principles and Application* (1965), on the basic principles involved in extraction and refining of metals, pyrometallurgy, hydrometallurgy, and electrometallurgy; *Metallurgy of the Nonferrous Metals* (1954), a concise summary of metallurgical factors, including principles, properties, methods of working, and heat treatment, relative to the metals; D.M. LIDDELL (ed.), *Handbook of Nonferrous Metallurgy*, 2nd ed., 2 vol. (1945), a comprehensive treatment prepared by experts in each field; C.R. HAYWARD, *An Outline of Metallurgical Practice*, 3rd ed. (1952), on the occurrence and sources of metals, with a description of practices used in the recovery of metals from ores; A.H. COTTRELL, *An Introduction to Metallurgy* (1967), an excellent source for information on progress in contemporary research in the field of metals; E.R. PETTY, *Physical Metallurgy of Engineering Materials* (1968), on the basic properties of the important metals and their alloys, and on the properties that determine the utility of various metals and alloys for specific purposes; C.S. BARRETT and T.B. MASSALSKI, *Structure of Metals*, 3rd ed. (1966), presenting concepts leading to our present understanding of the structure of metals and the factors that are primary causes in determining metal properties; F.L. LAQUE and H.R. COPSON (eds.), *Corrosion Resistance of Metals and Alloys*, 2nd ed. (1963), a modern text describing the fundamentals of corrosion and the behaviour of different metals in different corrosive environments; UNITED STATES STEEL CORPORATION, *The Making, Shaping and Treating of Steel*, 8th ed. (1964), an up-to-date source of information on raw materials, processes, and products of the modern iron and steel industry; AMERICAN SOCIETY FOR METALS, *Metals Handbook*, 8th ed., 5 vol. (1961–70), specialized reports on all aspects of this topic.

Transactions of the following professional societies are additional sources of information: American Society for Metals, Metallurgical Society of the American Institute of Mining Engineers, British Iron and Steel Institute, American Electrochemical Society, American Iron and Steel Institute, American Foundrymen's Society, the Society of Automotive Engineering, and the American Society for Testing and Materials. The proceedings from these societies provide data and descriptions of present-day technology in almost every area of metallurgy and metal application.

The latest advances in metal technology are covered in the following technical journals: *Metal Progress, Journal of Metals, Iron Age, Foundry,* and *Modern Casting.*

(C.H.L.)

Metalogic

Metalogic may be defined as the study of the syntax, or relations between expressions, and the semantics, or relations between expressions and their meanings, of formal languages and formal systems (such as those of logic and mathematics). It is related to, but does not include, the formal treatment of natural languages.

NATURE, ORIGINS, AND INFLUENCES OF METALOGIC

Syntax and semantics. A formal language usually requires a set of formation rules; *i.e.*, a complete specification of the kinds of expressions that shall count as well-formed formulas (sentences or meaningful expressions), applicable mechanically, in the sense that a machine could check whether a candidate satisfies the requirements. This specification usually contains three parts: (1) a list of primitive symbols (basic units) given mechanically; (2) certain combinations of these symbols, singled out mechanically as forming the simple (atomic) sentences; and (3) a set of inductive clauses—inductive inasmuch as they stipulate that natural combinations of given sentences formed by such logical connectives as the disjunction "Either . . . or," which is symbolized "$\lor$," "Not," symbolized "$\sim$," and "For every . . . ," symbolized "$(\forall -),$" are again sentences. [$(\forall -),$ or $(\exists -)$— "There is some . . ."—is called a quantifier.] Since these specifications are concerned only with symbols and their combinations and not with meanings, they involve only the syntax of the language.

An interpretation of a formal language is determined by formulating an interpretation of the atomic sentences of the language with regard to a domain of objects; *i.e.*, by stipulating which objects of the domain are denoted by which constants of the language and which relations and functions are denoted by which predicate letters and function symbols. The truth-value (whether "true" or

Specification of a formal language

"false") of every sentence is thus determined according to the standard interpretation of logical connectives. For example, $p \cdot q$ is true if and only if p and q are true. (Here, the dot means the conjunction "and," not the multiplication operation "times.") Thus, given any interpretation of a formal language, a formal concept of truth is obtained. Thus, truth, meaning, and denotation are semantic concepts.

If, in addition, a formal system in a formal language is introduced, certain syntactic concepts arise; viz., axioms, rules of inference, and theorems. Certain sentences are singled out as axioms. These are (the basic) theorems. Each rule of inference is an inductive clause, stating that if certain sentences are theorems, then another sentence related to them in a suitable way is also a theorem. If p and "Either not-p or q" ($\sim p \lor q$) are theorems, for example, then q is a theorem. In general, a theorem is either an axiom or the conclusion of a rule of inference whose premises are theorems.

In 1931 the fundamental discovery was made by Kurt Gödel, the prominent Czechoslovakian-U.S. logician, that in most of the interesting (or significant) formal systems not all true sentences are theorems. It follows from this finding that semantics cannot be reduced to syntax; thus syntax, which is closely related to proof theory, must often be distinguished from semantics, which is closely related to model theory (see below). Roughly speaking, syntax—as conceived in the philosophy of mathematics—is a branch of number theory (*q.v.*), and semantics is a branch of set theory (*q.v.*), which deals with the nature and relations of aggregates.

Historically, as logic and axiomatic systems became more and more exact, there emerged, in response to a desire for greater lucidity, a tendency to pay greater attention to the syntactic features of the languages employed rather than to concentrate exclusively on intuitive meanings. In this way, logic, the axiomatic method (such as that employed in geometry), and semiotic (the general science of signs) converged toward metalogic.

The axiomatic method. The best known axiomatic system is that of Euclid for geometry. In a manner similar to that of Euclid, every scientific theory involves a body of meaningful concepts and a collection of true or believed assertions. The meaning of a concept can often be explained or defined in terms of other concepts; and, similarly, the truth of an assertion or the reason for believing it can usually be clarified by indicating that it can be deduced from certain other assertions already accepted. The axiomatic method proceeds in a sequence of steps, beginning with a set of primitive concepts and propositions and then defining or deducing all other concepts and propositions in the theory from them.

The realization that arose in the 19th century that there are different possible geometries led to a desire to separate abstract mathematics from spatial intuition; and, in consequence, many hidden axioms were uncovered in Euclid's geometry. These discoveries were organized into a more rigorous axiomatic system by David Hilbert, an influential German mathematician, in his *Grundlagen der Geometrie* (1899; *The Foundations of Geometry*, 1902). In this and related systems, however, logical connectives and their properties are taken for granted and remain implicit. If the logic involved is taken to be that of the predicate calculus (see below), the logician can then arrive at such formal systems as that discussed above.

Once such formal systems are obtained, it is possible to transform certain semantic problems into sharper syntactic problems. It has been asserted, for example, that non-Euclidean geometries must be self-consistent systems because they have models (or interpretations) in Euclidean geometry, which in turn has a model in the theory of real numbers. It may then be asked, however, how it is known that the theory of real numbers is consistent in the sense that no contradiction can be derived within it. Obviously, modelling can only establish a relative consistency and has to come to a stop somewhere. Having arrived at a formal system (say of real numbers), however, the consistency problem then has the sharper focus of a syntactic problem, viz., of considering all of the possible

Transformations from semantics to syntax

proofs (as syntactic objects) and asking whether any of them ever has (say) $0 = 1$ as the last sentence.

As another example, the question whether a system is categorical—that is, whether it determines essentially a unique interpretation in the sense that any two interpretations are isomorphic—may be explored. This semantic question can to some extent be replaced by a related syntactic question, that of completeness: whether there is in the system any sentence having a definite truth-value in the intended interpretation such that neither that sentence nor its negation is a theorem. Even though it is now known that the semantic and syntactic concepts are different, the vague requirement that a system be "adequate" is clarified by both concepts. The study of such sharp syntactic questions as those of consistency and completeness, which was emphasized by Hilbert, was named "metamathematics" (or "proof theory") by him around 1920.

Logic and metalogic. In one sense, logic is to be identified with the predicate calculus of the first order, the calculus in which the variables are confined to individuals of a fixed domain—though it may include as well the logic of equality symbolized "$=$," which takes the ordinary properties of equality as part of logic. In this sense, Gottlob Frege, a pioneer of modern logic, achieved a formal calculus of logic as early as 1879. Sometimes logic is construed, however, as including also higher order predicate calculi, which admit variables of higher types, such as those ranging over predicates (or classes and relations) and so on. But then it is a small step to the inclusion of set theory; and, in fact, axiomatic set theory is often regarded as a part of logic. For the purposes of this article, however, it is more appropriate to confine the discussion to logic in the first sense, especially since there is a separate article SET THEORY.

It is hard to separate out significant findings in logic from those in metalogic because all theorems of interest to logicians are about logic and therefore belong to metalogic. If p is a mathematical theorem—in particular, one about logic—and P is the conjunction of the mathematical axioms employed for proving p, then every p can be turned into a theorem, "Either not-P or p," in logic. Mathematics is not done, however, by carrying out explicitly all of the steps as formalized in logic; the selection and intuitive grasp of the axioms is important both for mathematics and for metamathematics. Actual derivations in logic, such as those carried out just prior to World War I by Alfred North Whitehead, who later became renowned as a metaphysician, and Bertrand Russell, a philosopher of science and of mathematics, are of little intrinsic interest to logicians. It might therefore appear redundant to introduce the term metalogic. In the present classification, however, metalogic is conceived as dealing not only with findings about logical calculi but also with studies of formal systems and formal languages in general.

Formal systems and logical calculi

An ordinary formal system differs from a logical calculus in that the system usually has an intended interpretation, whereas the logical calculus deliberately leaves the possible interpretations open. Thus, one speaks, for example, of the truth or falsity of sentences in a formal system; but with respect to a logical calculus one speaks of validity (*i.e.*, being true in all interpretations or in all possible worlds) and of satisfiability (or having a model; *i.e.*, being true in some particular interpretation). Hence, the completeness of a logical calculus has quite a different meaning from that of a formal system: a logical calculus permits many sentences, such that neither the sentence nor its negation is a theorem because it is true in some interpretations and false in others, and requires only that every valid sentence be a theorem.

Semiotic. Originally, the word "semiotic" meant the medical theory of symptoms; however, an Empiricist, John Locke, used the term in the 17th century for a science of signs and significations. The current usage was recommended especially by Rudolf Carnap, one of the foremost semanticists and philosophers of science of the 20th century—see his *Introduction to Semantics* (1942) and his reference there to Charles William Morris, who

suggested a threefold distinction. According to this usage, semiotic is the general science of signs and languages, consisting of three parts: (1) pragmatics (in which reference is made to the user of the language); (2) semantics (in which one abstracts from the user and analyzes only the expressions and their meanings); and (3) syntax (in which one abstracts also from the meanings and studies only the relations between expressions).

Pragmatics is at present a rather loose designation covering a wide range of scientific investigations of language—physiological, psychological, ethnological, and sociological. Since pragmatics is conspicuously incapable of formal treatment, it is usually not considered to be a part of metalogic.

At first Carnap exclusively emphasized syntax. But gradually he came to realize the importance of semantics, and the door was thus reopened to many difficult philosophical problems.

Certain aspects of metalogic have been instrumental in the development of a whole new approach to philosophy commonly associated with the label of Logical Positivism. In his *Tractatus Logico-Philosophicus* (1922; originally published under a different title, 1921), the Austrian-born Cambridge philosopher Ludwig Wittgenstein, one of the most seminal thinkers in the philosophy of language, presented an appealing exposition of logical truths as sentences that are true in all possible worlds. One may say, for example, "It is raining or it is not raining," and in every possible world one of the disjuncts is true. On the basis of this observation and certain broader developments in logic, Carnap attempted to develop formal treatments of science and philosophy.

Logical Positivism and the formalization of science

It has been thought that the success that metalogic had achieved in the mathematical disciplines could be carried over into physics and even into biology or psychology. In so doing, the logician gives a branch of science a formal language in which there are logically true sentences having universal logical ranges and factually true ones having more restricted ranges. (Roughly speaking, the logical range of a sentence is the set of all possible worlds in which it is true.)

A formal solution of the problem of meaning has also been proposed for these disciplines. Given the formal language of a science, it is possible to define a notion of truth. Such a truth definition determines the truth condition for every sentence; *i.e.*, the necessary and sufficient conditions for its truth. The meaning of a sentence is then identified with its truth condition because, as Carnap wrote:

> To understand a sentence, to know what is asserted by it, is the same as to know under what conditions it would be true. . . . To know the truth condition of a sentence is (in most cases) much less than to know its truth-value, but it is the necessary starting point for finding out its truth-value.

Influences in other directions. In recent years, metalogic has led to a great deal of work of a mathematical nature in axiomatic set theory, model theory, and recursion theory (in which functions that are computable in a finite number of steps are studied). (See MATHEMATICS, FOUNDATIONS OF: *The crisis in foundations following 1900: Logicism, formalism, and the metamathematical method;* and SET THEORY: *Axiomatic set theory;* and below *Model theory.*)

In a different direction, the devising of Turing computing machines, involving abstract designs for the explication of mechanical logical procedures, has led to the investigation of idealized computers, with ramifications in the theory of finite automata and mathematical linguistics.

Turing machines, philosophy of logic, and ontology

Among philosophers of language, there is a widespread tendency to stress the philosophy of logic (see LOGIC, PHILOSOPHY OF). The contrast, for example, between intensional concepts and extensional concepts; the role of meaning in natural languages as providing truth conditions; the relation between formal and natural logic (*i.e.*, the logic of natural languages); and the relation of ontology, the study of the kinds of entities that exist, to the use of quantifiers—all of these areas are receiving extensive consideration and discussion. There are also efforts to produce formal systems for empirical sciences such as physics, biology, and even psychology. Many scholars have doubted, however, whether these efforts have been fruitful.

NATURE OF A FORMAL SYSTEM
AND OF ITS FORMAL LANGUAGE

Example of a formal system. In order to clarify the abstract concepts of metalogic, a formal system N (with its formal language) may be considered for illustration. *Formation rules.* The system may be set up by employing the following formation rules:

1. The following are primitive symbols: $\sim$, $\vee$, $\forall$, and $=$, and the symbols used for grouping, (, and); the function symbols for arithmetical addition and multiplication $+$ and $\cdot$; constants 0, 1; and variables $x,y,z, \ldots$.

2. The following are terms: a constant is a term; a variable is a term; if a and b are terms, $a + b$ and $a \cdot b$ are terms.

3. Atomic sentences are thus specified: if a and b are terms, $a = b$ is a sentence.

4. Other sentences can be defined as follows: if A and B are sentences and v is a variable, then $\sim A$, $A \vee B$, and $(\forall v)A$ are sentences.

Axioms and rules of inference. The system may be developed by adopting certain sentences as axioms and following certain rules of inference.

1. The basic axioms and rules are to be those of the first-order predicate calculus, including the propositional calculus (the logic of unanalyzed statements; see LOGIC, FORMAL).

2. The following additional axioms of N are stipulated:

(a) Zero is not a successor (*i.e.*, does not follow any number immediately):
$$\sim (x + 1) = 0.$$

(b) No two numbers have the same successor:
$$\sim (x + 1 = y + 1) \vee x = y.$$

(c) Recursive definition of addition:
$$x + 0 = x$$
$$x + (y + 1) = (x + y) + 1.$$

(d) Recursive definition of multiplication:
$$x \cdot 0 = 0; x \cdot (y + 1) = (x \cdot y) + x.$$

3. Rule of inference (the principle of mathematical induction): Every number has a property if zero has it and the successor of a number has it if the number has it; more explicitly, if $A(0)$ and $\forall x[\sim A(x) \vee A(x + 1)]$ are theorems, then $\forall x A(x)$ is a theorem.

The system N as specified by the foregoing rules and axioms is a formal system in the sense that, given any combination of the primitive symbols, it is possible to check mechanically whether it is a sentence of N; and given a finite sequence of sentences, it is possible to check mechanically whether it is a (correct) proof in N; *i.e.*, whether each sentence either is an axiom or follows from preceding sentences in the sequence by a rule of inference. Viewed in this way, a sentence is a theorem if and only if there exists a proof in which it appears as the last sentence. It is not required of a formal system, however, that it be possible to decide mechanically whether a given sentence is a theorem; and, in fact, it has been proved that no such mechanical method exists.

Truth definition of the given language. The formal system N admits of different interpretations, according to findings of Gödel (from 1931) and of the Norwegian mathematician Thoralf Skolem, a pioneer in metalogic (from 1933). The originally intended, or standard, interpretation takes the ordinary non-negative integers $\{0,1,2, \ldots\}$ as the domain, the symbols 0 and 1 as denoting zero and one, and the symbols $+$ and $\cdot$ as standing for ordinary addition and multiplication. Relative to this interpretation, it is possible to give a truth definition of the language of N.

It is necessary first to distinguish between open and closed sentences. An open sentence, such as $x = 1$, is one that may be either true or false depending on the value of x; but a closed sentence, such as $0 = 1$ and $(\forall x)(x = 0)$ or "All x's are zero," is one that has a definite truth-value —in this case, false (in the intended interpretation).

1. A closed atomic sentence is true if and only if it is true in the intuitive sense; for example, $0 = 0$ is true, $0 + 1 = 0$ is false.

This specification as it stands is not syntactic; but with some care, it is possible to give an explicit and mechanical specification of those closed atomic sentences that are true in the intuitive sense.

2. A closed sentence $\sim A$ is true if and only if A is not true.

3. A closed sentence $A \vee B$ is true if and only if either A or B is true.

4. A closed sentence $(\forall v)A(v)$ is true if and only if $A(v)$ is true for every value of v; *i.e.*, if $A(0)$, $A(1)$, $A(1 + 1)$, ... are all true.

The above definition of truth is not an explicit definition; it is an inductive one. Using concepts from set theory, however, it is possible to obtain an explicit definition that yields a set of sentences that consists of all of the true ones and only them. If Gödel's method of representing symbols and sentences by numbers is employed, it is then possible to obtain in set theory a set of natural numbers that are just the Gödel numbers of the true sentences of N.

There is a definite sense in which it is impossible to define the truth of a language in itself. This is proved by the liar paradox: if the sentence "I am lying," or alternatively,

$$\text{This sentence is not true} \ldots \quad (1)$$

is considered, it is clear—since (1) is "This sentence"— that if (1) is true, then (1) is false; on the other hand, if (1) is false, then (1) is true. In the case of the system N, if the concept of truth were definable in the system itself, then (using a device invented by Gödel) it would be possible to obtain in N a sentence that amounts to (1) and that thereby yields a contradiction.

DISCOVERIES ABOUT FORMAL MATHEMATICAL SYSTEMS

The two central questions of metalogic are those of the completeness and consistency of a formal system based on axioms. In 1931, Gödel made fundamental discoveries in these areas for the most interesting formal systems. In particular, he discovered that if such a system is ω-consistent—*i.e.*, devoid of contradiction in a sense to be explained below—then it is not complete, and that if a system is consistent, then the statement of its consistency, easily expressible in the system, is not provable in it.

Soon afterward, in 1934, Gödel modified a suggestion that had been offered by Jacques Herbrand, a French mathematician, and introduced a general concept of recursive functions; *i.e.*, of functions mechanically computable by a finite series of purely combinatorial steps. In 1936, Alonzo Church, a mathematical logician; Alan Mathison Turing, originator of a theory of computability; and Emil L. Post, a specialist in recursive unsolvability, all argued for this concept (and certain equivalent notions), thereby arriving at stable and exact conceptions of "mechanical," "computable," "recursive," and "formal" that explicate the intuitive concept of what a mechanical computing procedure is. As a result of the development of recursion theory, it is now possible to prove not only that certain classes of problems are mechanically solvable (which could be done without the theory) but also that certain others are mechanically unsolvable (or absolutely unsolvable). The most notable example of such unsolvability is the discovery, made in 1970, that there is no algorithm, or rule of repetitive procedure, for solving all Diophantine equations; *i.e.*, equations of which the coefficients and roots are whole numbers. This solution gives a negative solution to the 10th problem in the famous list presented by Hilbert at the International Mathematical Congress in 1900; compare MATHEMATICS, FOUNDATIONS OF: *Logicism, formalism, and the metamathematical method*).

In this way, logicians have finally arrived at a sharp concept of a formal axiomatic system because it is no longer necessary to leave "mechanical" as a vague non-mathematical concept. In this way, too, they have arrived at sharp concepts of decidability. In one sense, decidability is a property of sets (of sentences): that of being subject (or not) to mechanical methods by which to decide, for any closed sentence of a given formal system (*e.g.*, of N), whether it is true; or—as a different question —whether it is a theorem. In another sense, decidability can refer to a single closed sentence: the sentence is called undecidable in a formal system if neither it nor its negation is a theorem. Using this concept, Gödel's incompleteness theorem is sometimes stated thus: "Every interesting (or significant) formal system has some undecidable sentences."

Given these developments, it was easy to extend Gödel's findings, as Church did in 1936, to show that interesting formal systems such as N are undecidable (both with regard to theorems and with regard to true sentences).

The two incompleteness theorems. The first and most central finding in this field is that systems such as N are incomplete and incompletable because Gödel's theorem applies to any reasonable and moderately rich system. The proof of this incompleteness may be viewed as a modification of the liar paradox, which shows that truth cannot be defined in the language itself. Since provability in a formal system can often be expressed in the system itself, one is led to the conclusion of incompleteness.

Let us consider the sentence

This sentence is not provable in the system   (2)

In particular, N may be thought of as the system being studied. Representing expressions by numbers and using an ingenious substitution function, Gödel was able to find in the system a sentence p that could be viewed as expressing (2).

Once such a sentence is obtained, some strong conclusions result. If the system is complete, then either the sentence p or its negation is a theorem of the system. If p is a theorem, then intuitively p or (2) is false, and there is in some sense a false theorem in the system. Similarly, if $\sim p$ is a theorem, then it says that $\sim$(2) or that p is provable in the system. Since $\sim p$ is a theorem, it should be true, and there seem then to be two conflicting sentences that are both true, viz., p is provable in the system, and $\sim p$ is provable in it. This can be the case only if the system is inconsistent.

Gödel's exact theorem

A careful examination of this inexact line of reasoning leads to Gödel's exact theorem, which says that if a system is reasonably rich and ω-consistent, then p is undecidable in it. The notion of ω-consistency is stronger than consistency, but it is a very reasonable requirement since it demands merely that one cannot prove in a system both that some number does not have the property A and yet that each number does have the property A; *i.e.*, that $(\exists x)\sim A(x)$ and also all of $A(0)$, $A(1)$, . . . are theorems. An American mathematician J. Barkley Rosser, who also contributed to number theory and applied mathematics, weakened the hypothesis to mere consistency in 1936, at the expense of complicating somewhat the initial sentence (2).

More exactly, Gödel showed that if the system is consistent, then p is not provable; if it is ω-consistent, then $\sim p$ is not provable. The first half leads to Gödel's theorem on consistency proofs, viz., that if a system is consistent, then the arithmetic sentence expressing the consistency of the system cannot be proved in the system. This is usually stated briefly thus: that no interesting system can prove its own consistency or that there exists no consistency proof of a system that can be formalized in the system itself.

The proof of this theorem consists essentially of a formalization in arithmetic of the arithmetized version of the proof of the statement, "If a system is consistent, then p is not provable"; *i.e.*, it consists of a derivation within number theory of p itself from the arithmetic sentence that says that the system is consistent. Hence, if the arithmetic sentence were provable, p would also be provable —contradicting the previous result. This proof, which was only briefly outlined by Gödel, has been carried out in detail by Paul Bernays in his joint work with Hilbert. Moreover, the undecidable sentence p is always of a relatively simple form, viz., of the form $(\forall x)A(x)$, "For every x, x is A," in which A is a recursive, in fact a primitive recursive, predicate.

Decidability and undecidability. The first incompleteness theorem yields directly the fact that truth in a system (*e.g.*, in N) to which the theorem applies is undecidable. If it were decidable, then all true sentences would form a recursive set, and they could be taken as the axioms of a formal system that would be complete. This claim depends on the reasonable and widely accepted assumption that all that is required of the axioms of a formal system is that they make it possible to decide effectively whether a given sentence is an axiom.

Alternatively, the above assumption can be avoided by resorting to a familiar lemma, or auxiliary truth: that all recursive or computable functions and relations are representable in the system (*e.g.*, in N). Since truth in the language of a system is itself not representable (definable) in the system, it cannot, by the lemma, be recursive (*i.e.*, decidable).

The same lemma also yields the undecidability of such systems with regard to theorems. Thus, if there were a decision procedure, there would be a computable function f such that $f(i)$ equals 1 or 0 according as the ith sentence is a theorem or not. But then what $f(i) = 0$ says is just that the ith sentence is not provable. Hence, using Gödel's device, a sentence (say the tth) is again obtained saying of itself that it is not provable. If $f(t) = 0$ is true then, because f is representable in the system, it is a theorem of the system. But then, because $f(t) = 0$ is (equivalent to) the tth sentence, $f(t) = 1$ is also true and therefore provable in the system. Hence, the system, if consistent, is undecidable with regard to theorems.

Although the system N is incompletable and undecidable, it has been discovered by the Polish logician M. Presburger and by Skolem (both in 1930) that arithmetic with addition alone or multiplication alone is decidable (with regard to truth) and therefore has complete formal systems. Another well-known positive finding is that of Alfred Tarski, a Polish-American semanticist and logician, who developed a decision procedure for elementary geometry and elementary algebra (1951).

A discovery made by Turing in 1936, which at first sight seems very surprising, may be mentioned in passing: that every complete formal system (though not every logical calculus) is decidable. If a system is complete, then for every closed sentence A, either that sentence or its negation is a theorem. Being a formal system, all of its theorems can be enumerated mechanically. But then, for each A, one sooner or later reaches either A or $\sim A$. In the first case, A is a theorem (and true); in the second case, A is not a theorem (and false). This finding illustrates an impractical aspect of the concept of mechanical procedures, for all that is required is that a conclusion can be reached at some finite time and there need not be any useful estimate of how long it will take.

Consistency proofs. The best known consistency proof is that of the German mathematician Gerhard Gentzen (1936) for the system N of classical (or ordinary, in contrast to intuitionistic) number theory. Taking ω (omega) to represent the next number beyond the natural numbers (called the "first transfinite number"), Gentzen's proof employs an induction in the realm of transfinite numbers $(\omega + 1, \omega + 2, \ldots; 2\omega, 2\omega + 1, \ldots; \omega^2, \omega^2 + 1, \ldots)$, which is extended to the first epsilon-number, ε_0 (defined as the limit of $\omega, \omega^\omega, \omega\,\omega^\omega, \ldots$), which is not formalizable in N. This proof, which has appeared in several variants, has opened up an area of rather extensive work.

Intuitionistic number theory, which denies the classical concept of truth and consequently eschews certain general laws such as "Either A or $\sim A$," and its relation to classical number theory have also been investigated (see the article MATHEMATICS, FOUNDATIONS OF: *The crisis in foundations following 1900; Intuitionism*). This investigation is considered significant because intuitionism is believed to be more constructive and more evident than classical number theory. In 1932, Gödel found an interpretation of classical number theory in the intuitionistic theory (also found by Gentzen and by Bernays). In 1958, Gödel extended his findings to obtain constructive interpretations of sentences of classical number theory in terms of primitive recursive functionals.

More recently, work has been done to extend Gentzen's findings to ramified theories of types and to fragments of classical analysis, and to extend Gödel's interpretation and to relate classical analysis to intuitionistic analysis. Also, in connection with these consistency proofs, various proposals have been made to present constructive notations for the ordinals of segments of the German mathematician Georg Cantor's second number class, which includes ω and the first epsilon-number and much more. A good deal of discussion has been devoted to the significance of the consistency proofs and the relative interpretations for epistemology (the theory of knowledge).

DISCOVERIES ABOUT LOGICAL CALCULI

The calculi of formal logic. The two main branches of formal logic are the propositional calculus and the predicate calculus.

The propositional calculus. This calculus (abbreviated PC) is described in detail in the article LOGIC, FORMAL: *II. The propositional calculus.* It is easy to show that this calculus is complete in the sense that every valid sentence in it—*i.e.*, every tautology, or sentence true in all possible worlds (in all interpretations)—is a theorem, as may be seen in the following example. "Either p or not-p" ($p \lor \sim p$) is always true because p is either true or false. In the former case, $p \lor \sim p$ is true because p is true; in the latter case, because $\sim p$ is true. One way to prove the completeness of this calculus is to observe that it is sufficient to reduce every sentence to a conjunctive normal form; *i.e.*, to a conjunction of disjunctions of single letters and their negations. But any such conjunction is valid if and only if every conjunct is valid; and a conjunct is valid if and only if it contains some letter p as well as $\sim p$ as parts of the whole disjunction. Completeness follows because (1) such conjuncts can all be proved in the calculus, and (2) if these conjuncts are theorems, then the whole conjunction is also a theorem.

Consistency and decidability of PC

The consistency of the calculus (its freedom from contradiction) is more or less obvious because it can easily be checked that all of its axioms are valid—*i.e.*, true in all possible worlds—and that the rules of inference carry from valid sentences to valid sentences. But a contradiction is not valid; hence, the calculus is consistent. The conclusion, in fact, asserts more than consistency, for it holds that only valid sentences are provable.

The calculus is also easily decidable. Since all valid sentences, and only these, are theorems, each sentence can be tested mechanically by putting true and false for each letter in the sentence. If there are n letters, there are 2^n possible substitutions. A sentence is then a theorem if and only if it comes out true in every one of the 2^n possibilities.

The independence of the axioms is usually proved by using more than two truth-values. These values are divided into two classes: the desired and the undesired. The axiom to be shown independent can then acquire some undesired value, whereas all of the theorems that are provable without this axiom always get the desired values. This technique is what originally suggested the many-valued logics (see LOGIC, FORMAL: *II. B.2: Three-valued logics*).

The first-order predicate calculus. This calculus (abbreviated LPC—for "lower predicate calculus"), like the propositional calculus, is also described in detail in the article LOGIC, FORMAL: *III. The predicate calculus.* It includes the propositional calculus as a part and may or may not include the logic of equality. (It will here be assumed that equality is included.)

The problem of consistency for the predicate calculus is relatively simple. A world may be assumed in which there is only one object a. In this case, both the universally quantified and the existentially quantified sentences $(\forall x)A(x)$ and $(\exists x)A(x)$ reduce to the simple sentence $A(a)$; and all quantifiers can be eliminated. It may easily be confirmed that, after the reduction, all theorems of the calculus become tautologies (*i.e.*, theorems in the propositional calculus). If F is any predicate, such a sentence as "Every x is F and not every x is F"—*i.e.*, $(\forall x)F(x) \cdot \sim(\forall x)F(x)$—is then reduced to "$a$

is both A and not-A"—$A(a) \cdot \sim A(a)$—which is not a tautology; therefore, the original sentence is not a theorem; and hence, no contradiction can be a theorem. If F is simple, then F and A are the same. If F is complex and contains $(\forall y)$ or $(\exists z)$, etc., then A is the result obtained by iterating the transformation of eliminating $(\forall y)$, etc. In fact, it can be proved quite directly not only that the calculus is consistent but also that all of its theorems are valid.

The discoveries that the calculus is complete and undecidable are much more profound than the discovery of its consistency. Its completeness was proved by Gödel in 1930; its undecidability was established with quite different methods by Church and Turing in 1936. Given the general developments that occurred up to 1936, its undecidability also follows in another way from Theorem X of Gödel's paper of 1931.

Completeness and undecidability of LPC

Completeness means that every valid sentence of the calculus is a theorem. It follows that if $\sim A$ is not a theorem, then $\sim A$ is not valid; and, therefore, A is satisfiable; *i.e.*, it has an interpretation or a model. But to say that A is consistent means nothing other than that $\sim A$ is not a theorem. Hence, from the completeness, it follows that if A is consistent, then A is satisfiable. Therefore, the semantic concepts of validity and satisfiability are seen to coincide with the syntactic concepts of derivability and consistency.

A finding closely related to the completeness theorem is the Löwenheim–Skolem theorem (1915, 1920), named after Leopold Löwenheim, a German school teacher, and Skolem, which says that if a sentence (or a formal system) has any model, it has a countable or enumerable model, *i.e.*, a model whose members can be matched with the positive integers. In the most direct method of proving this theorem, the logician is provided with very useful tools in model theory and in studies on relative consistency and independence in set theory.

The Löwenheim–Skolem theorem. In the predicate calculus, there are certain reduction or normal-form theorems. One useful example is the prenex normal form: every sentence can be reduced to an equivalent sentence expressed in the prenex form, viz., in a form such that all of the quantifiers appear at the beginning. This form is specially useful for displaying the central ideas of some of the proofs of the Löwenheim–Skolem theorem.

For illustration one may consider a simple schema in prenex form, "For every x, there is some y such that x bears the (arbitrary) relation M to y"; *i.e.*,

$$(\forall x)(\exists y)Mxy \qquad (3)$$

If (3) now has a model with a nonempty domain D, then by a principle from set theory (the axiom of choice), there exists a function f of x, written $f(x)$, that singles out for each x a corresponding y. Hence, "For every x, x bears the relation M to $f(x)$"; *i.e.*,

$$(\forall x)Mxf(x). \qquad (4)$$

If a is now any object in D, then the countable sub-domain $\{a, f(a), f[f(a)], \ldots\}$ already contains enough objects to satisfy (4) and therefore to satisfy (3). Hence, if (3) has any model, it has a countable model, which is in fact a submodel of the original.

An alternative proof, developed by Skolem in 1922 to avoid appealing to the principles of set theory, has turned out to be useful also for establishing the completeness of the calculus. Instead of using the function f as before, a can be arbitrarily denoted by *1*. Since equation (3) is true, there must be some object y such that the number *1* bears the relation M to y, or symbolically M_1y, and one of these y's may be called *2*. When this process is repeated indefinitely, one obtains

Proof independent of set theory

$$M_{12}; \; M_{12} \cdot M_{23}; \; M_{12} \cdot M_{23} \cdot M_{34}; \; \ldots, \qquad (5)$$

all of which are true in the given model. The argument is elementary because in each instance one merely argues from "There exists some y such that n is M of y"—*i.e.*, $(\exists y)Mny$—to "Let one such y be $n + 1$." Consequently, every member of (5) is true in some model. It is then possible to infer that all members of (5) are simultaneously true in some model; *i.e.*, that there is some way of assigning truth-values to all of its atomic parts so that all members of (5) will be true. Hence, it follows that (3) is true in some countable model.

The completeness theorem. Gödel's original proof of the completeness theorem is closely related to the second proof above. Consideration may again be given to all of the sentences in (5) that contain no more quantifiers. If they are all satisfiable, then, as before, they are simultaneously satisfiable and (3) has a model. On the other hand, if (3) has no model, some of its terms—say $M_{12} \cdot \ldots \cdot M_{89}$—are not satisfiable; *i.e.*, their negations are tautologies (theorems of the propositional calculus). Thus, $\sim M_{12} \vee \ldots \vee \sim M_{89}$ is a tautology, and this remains true if $1,2, \ldots ,9$ are replaced by variables, such as $r, s, \ldots , z$; hence, $\sim Mrs \vee \ldots \vee \sim Myz$, being a tautology expressed in the predicate calculus as usually formulated, is a theorem in it. It is then easy to use the usual rules of the predicate calculus to derive also the statement, "There exists an x such that, for every y, x is not M of y"; *i.e.*, $(\exists x)(\forall y) \sim Mxy$. In other words, the negation of (3) is a theorem of the predicate calculus. Hence, if (3) has no model, its negation is a theorem of the predicate calculus. And, finally, if a sentence is valid (*i.e.*, if its negation has no model), then it is itself a theorem of the predicate calculus.

The undecidability theorem and reduction classes. Given the completeness theorem, it follows that the task of deciding whether any sentence is a theorem of the predicate calculus is equivalent to that of deciding whether any sentence is valid or whether it is satisfiable.

Turing's undecidability proof

Turing's method of proving that this class of problems is undecidable is particularly suggestive. Once the concept of mechanical procedure was crystallized, it was relatively easy to find absolutely unsolvable problems; *e.g.*, the halting problem, which asks for each Turing machine the question of whether it will ever stop, beginning with a blank tape. In other words, each Turing machine operates in a predetermined manner according to what is given initially on the (input) tape; we consider now the special case of a blank tape and ask the special question whether the machine will eventually stop. This infinite class of questions (one for each machine) is known to be unsolvable.

Turing's method shows that each such question about a single Turing machine can be expressed by a single sentence of the predicate calculus so that the machine will stop if and only if that sentence is not satisfiable. Hence, if there were a decision procedure of validity (or satisfiability) for all sentences of the predicate calculus, then the halting problem would be solvable.

In more recent years (1962), Turing's formulation has been improved to the extent that all that is needed are sentences of the relatively simple form $(\forall x)(\exists y)(\forall z)$ $Mxyz$, in which all of the quantifiers are at the beginning; *i.e.*, M contains no more quantifiers. Hence, given the unsolvability of the halting problem, it follows that, even for the simple class of sentences in the predicate calculus having the quantifiers $\forall \exists \forall$, the decision problem is unsolvable. Moreover, the method of proof also yields a procedure by which every sentence of the predicate calculus can be correlated with one in the simple form given above. Thus, the class of $\forall \exists \forall$ sentences forms a "reduction class." (There are also various other reduction classes.)

MODEL THEORY

Background and typical problems. In model theory one studies the interpretations (models) of theories formalized in the framework of formal logic, especially in that of the first-order predicate calculus with equality; *i.e.*, in elementary logic. A first-order language is given by a collection S of symbols for relations, functions, and constants, which, in combination with the symbols of elementary logic, single out certain combinations of symbols as sentences. Thus, for example, in the case of the system N (see above *Example of a formal system*), the formation rules yield a language that is determined in accordance with a uniform procedure by the set (indicated by braces) of uninterpreted extralogical symbols:

$$S = \{+, \cdot, 0, 1\}.$$

A first-order theory is determined by a language and a set of selected sentences of the language—those sentences of the theory that are, in an arbitrary, generalized sense, the "true" ones (called the "distinguished elements" of the set). In the particular case of the system N, one theory T_a is built up on the basis of the language and the set of theorems of N, and another theory T_b is determined by the true sentences of N according to the natural interpretation or meaning of its language. In general, the language of N and any set of sentences of the language can be used to make up a theory.

Satisfaction of a theory by a structure: finite and infinite models. A realization of a language (for example, the one based on S) is a structure $\mathfrak{A}$ identified by the five elements so arranged

$$\mathfrak{A} = \; <A, + \,_{\mathfrak{A}}, \cdot \,_{\mathfrak{A}}, 0 \,_{\mathfrak{A}}, 1 \,_{\mathfrak{A}}>,$$

in which A is a nonempty set (called the domain of $\mathfrak{A}$), the last two terms are members of A, and the other two terms are functions correlating each member of the Cartesian product $A \times A$ (*i.e.*, from the set of ordered pairs $<a,b>$ such that a,b belong to A) with a member of A. The structure $\mathfrak{A}$ satisfies or is a model of the theory T_a (or T_b) if all of the distinguished sentences of T_a (or T_b) are true in $\mathfrak{A}$ (or satisfied by $\mathfrak{A}$). Thus, if $\mathfrak{A}$ is the structure of the ordinary non-negative integers $<\omega, +, \cdot, 0, 1>$, in which ω is the set of all such integers and $+, \cdot, 0$, and 1 the elements for their generation, then it is not only a realization of the language based on S but also a model of both T_a and T_b. Gödel's incompleteness theorem permits nonstandard models of T_a that contain more objects than ω but in which all of the distinguished sentences of T_a (viz., the theorems of the system N) are true. Skolem's constructions (related to ultraproducts, see below) yield nonstandard models for both theory T_a and theory T_b.

The use of the relation of satisfaction, or being-a-model-of, between a structure and a theory (or a sentence) can be traced to the book *Wissenschaftslehre* (1837; "Theory of Knowledge") by Bernard Bolzano, a Czech theologian and mathematician, and, in a more concrete context, to the introduction of models of non-Euclidean geometries around that time. In the mathematical treatment of logic, these concepts can be found in works of Ernst Schröder, a late-19th-century German mathematician, and in Löwenheim (in particular, in his paper of 1915). The basic tools and results achieved in model theory—such as the Löwenheim–Skolem theorem, the completeness theorem of elementary logic, and Skolem's construction of nonstandard models of arithmetic—were developed during the period from 1915 to 1933. A more general and abstract study of model theory began after 1950, in the work of Tarski and others.

One group of new developments may be classified as refinements and extensions of the Löwenheim–Skolem theorem. These developments employ the concept of a "cardinal number," which—for a finite set—is simply the number at which one stops in counting its elements. For infinite sets, however, the elements must be matched from set to set instead of being counted, and the "sizes" of these sets must thus be designated by transfinite numbers. A rather direct generalization can be drawn that says that, if a theory has any infinite model, then, for any infinite cardinal number, it has a model of that cardinality. It follows that no theory with any infinite model can be categorical or such that any two models of the theory are isomorphic (*i.e.*, matchable in one-to-one correspondence) because models of different cardinalities can obviously not be so matched. A natural question is whether a theory can be categorical in certain infinite cardinalities; *i.e.*, whether there are cardinal numbers such that any two models of the theory of the same cardinality are isomorphic. According to a central discovery made in

Cate-
gorical
theories
in various
cardinal-
ities

1963 by Michael Morley, a U.S. mathematician, if a theory is categorical in any uncountable cardinality (*i.e.*, any cardinality higher than the countable), then it is categorical in every uncountable cardinality. On the other hand, examples are known for all four combinations of countable and uncountable cardinalities: specifically, there are theories that are categorical (1) in every infinite cardinality; (2) in the countable cardinality but in no uncountable cardinality; (3) in every uncountable cardinality but not in the countable; and (4) in no infinite cardinality.

In another direction, there are "two-cardinal" problems that arise from the possibilities of changing, from one model to another, not only the cardinality of the domain of the first model but also the cardinality of some chosen property (such as being a prime number). Various answers to these questions have been found, including proofs of independence (based on the ordinary axioms employed in set theory) and proofs of conditional theorems made on the basis of certain familiar hypotheses of set theory.

Elementary logic. An area that is perhaps of more philosophical interest is that of the nature of elementary logic itself. On the one hand, the completeness discoveries seem to show in some sense that elementary logic is what the logician naturally wishes to have. On the other hand, he is still inclined to ask whether there might be some principle of uniqueness according to which elementary logic is the only solution that satisfies certain natural requirements on what a logic should be. The recent development of model theory has led to a more general outlook that enabled Per Lindström, a Swedish logician, to prove, in 1969, a general theorem to the effect that, roughly speaking, within a broad class of possible logics, elementary logic is the only one that satisfies the requirements of axiomatizability of the Löwenheim–Skolem thorem. Although Lindström's theorem does not settle satisfactorily whether or not elementary logic is the right logic, it does seem to suggest that mathematical findings can help the logician to clarify his concepts of logic and of logical truth.

Com-
pounded
models

A particularly useful tool for obtaining new models from the given models of a theory is the construction of a special combination called the "ultraproduct" of a family of structures (see below *Ultrafilters, ultraproducts, and ultrapowers*)—in particular, the ultrapower when the structures are all copies of the same structure (just as the product of $a_1, \ldots, a_n$ is the same as the power a^n, if $a_i = a$ for each i). The intuitive idea in this method is to establish that a sentence is true in the ultraproduct if and only if it is true in "almost all" of the given structures (*i.e.*, "almost everywhere"—an idea that was present in a different form in Skolem's construction of a nonstandard model of arithmetic in 1933). It follows that if the given structures are models of a theory, then their ultraproduct is such a model also, because every sentence in the theory is true everywhere (which is a special case of "almost everywhere" in the technical sense employed). Ultraproducts have been applied, for example, to provide a foundation for what is known as "nonstandard analysis" that yields an unambiguous interpretation of the classical concept of infinitesimals—the division into units as small as one pleases. They have also been applied by two mathematicians, James Ax and S.B. Kochen, to problems in the field of algebra (on *p*-adic fields).

Nonelementary logic and future developments. There are also studies that develop the model theory of nonelementary logic: such as second-order logic and infinitary logics. Second-order logic contains, in addition to variables that range over individual objects, a second kind of variable ranging over sets of objects so that the model $\mathfrak{A}$ of a second-order sentence or theory also involves, beyond the basic domain, a larger set (called its "power set") that encompasses all of the subsets of the domain. Infinitary logics may include functions or relations with infinitely many arguments, infinitely long conjunctions and disjunctions, or infinite strings of quantifiers. From studies on infinitary logics, William Hanf, an American logician, was able to define certain cardinals, some of

which have been studied in connection with the large cardinals in set theory. In yet another direction, logicians are developing model theories for modal logics—those dealing with such modalities as necessity and possibility—and for the intuitionistic logic.

There is a large gap between the general theory of models and the construction of interesting particular models such as those employed in the proofs of the independence (and consistency) of special axioms and hypotheses in set theory. It is natural to look for further developments of model theory that will yield more systematic methods for constructing models of axioms with interesting particular properties, especially in deciding whether certain given sentences are derivable from the axioms. Relative to the present state of knowledge, such goals appear fairly remote. The gap is not unlike that between the abstract theory of computers and the basic properties of actual computers.

Characterizations of the first-order logic. There has been outlined above a proof of the completeness of elementary logic without including sentences asserting equality or identity. The proof can be extended, however, to the full elementary logic in a fairly direct manner. Thus, if F is a sentence containing equality, a sentence G can be adjoined to it that embodies the special properties of equality relevant to the sentence F. The conjunction of F and G can then be treated as a sentence not containing equality (*i.e.*, = can be treated as an arbitrary relation symbol). Hence, the conjunction has a model in the sense of logic-without-equality if and only if F has a model in the sense of logic-with-equality; and the completeness of elementary logic (with equality) can thus be inferred.

Extension
to
include
equality

A concept more general than validity is that of the relation of logical entailment or implication between a possibly infinite set X of sentences and a single sentence p that holds if and only if p is true in every model of X. In particular, p is valid if the empty set, defined as having no members, logically entails p—for this is just another way of saying that p is true in every model. This suggests a stronger requirement on a formal system of logic, viz., that p be derivable from X by the system whenever X logically entails p. The usual systems of logic satisfy this requirement because, besides the completeness theorem, there is also a compactness theorem:

A theory X has a model if every finite subset of X has a model.

Roughly speaking, this theorem enables the logician to reduce an infinite set X to a finite subset X_1 in each individual case, and the case of entailment when X_1 is finite is taken care of by the completeness of the system.

These findings show that the ordinary systems of elementary logic comprise the correct formulation, provided that the actual choice of the truth functions (say negation and disjunction) of the quantifiers, and of equality as the "logical constants" is assumed to be the correct one. There remains the question, however, of justifying the particular choice of logical constants. One might ask, for example, whether "For most x" or "For finitely many x" should not be counted as logical constants. Lindström has formulated a general concept of logic and shown that logics that apparently extend the first-order logic all end up being the same as that logic, provided that they satisfy the Löwenheim–Skolem theorem and either have the compactness property or are formally axiomatizable. There remains the question, however, of whether or why these requirements (especially that of the Löwenheim-Skolem theorem) are intrinsic to the nature of logic.

Generalizations and extensions of the Löwenheim–Skolem theorem. A generalized theorem can be proved using basically the same ideas as those employed in the more special case discussed above.

If a theory has any infinite model, then, for any infinite cardinality α, that theory has a model of cardinality α. More explicitly, this theorem contains two parts: (1) If a theory has a model of infinite cardinality β, then, for each infinite cardinal α that is greater than β, the theory has a model of cardinality α. (2) If a theory has a model of infinite cardinality β, then, for each infinite cardinal α less than β, the theory has a model of cardinality α.

It follows immediately that any theory having an infinite model has two nonisomorphic models and is, therefore, not categorical. This applies, in particular, to the aforementioned theories T_a and T_b of arithmetic (based on the language of N), the natural models of which are countable, as well as to theories dealing with real numbers and arbitrary sets, the natural models of which are uncountable; both kinds of theory have both countable and uncountable models. There is much philosophical discussion about this phenomenon.

The possibility is not excluded that a theory may be categorical in some infinite cardinality. The theory T_d, for example, of dense linear ordering (such as that of the rational numbers) is categorical in the countable cardinality. One application of the Löwenheim–Skolem theorem is: If a theory has no finite models and is categorical in some infinite cardinality α, then the theory is complete; i.e., for every closed sentence in the language of the theory, either that sentence or its negation belongs to the theory. An immediate consequence of this application of the theorem is that the theory of dense linear ordering is complete.

Morley's theorem A theorem that is generally regarded as one of the most difficult to prove in model theory is the theorem by Morley, as follows:

A theory that is categorical in one uncountable cardinality is categorical in every uncountable cardinality.

The two-cardinal theorems deal with languages that have some distinguished predicate U. A theory is said to admit the pair $<\alpha, \beta>$ of cardinals if the theory has a model (with its domain) of cardinality α in which the value of U is a set of cardinality β. The central two-cardinal theorem says:

If a theory admits the pair $<\alpha, \beta>$ of infinite cardinals with β less than α, then for each regular cardinal γ, the theory admits $<\gamma^+, \gamma>$, in which γ^+ is the next larger cardinal after γ.

The most interesting case is when γ is the least infinite cardinal, $\aleph_0$. (The general theorem can be established only when the "generalized continuum hypothesis" is assumed, according to which the next highest cardinality for an infinite set is that of its power set.)

Ultrafilters, ultraproducts, and ultrapowers. An ultrafilter on a nonempty set I is defined as a set D of subsets of I such that:

1. the empty set does not belong to D;
2. if A, B are in D, so is their intersection, $A \cap B$, the set of elements common to both;
3. if A is a subset of B, and A is in D, then B is in D;
4. for every subset A of I, either A is in D or I minus A is in D.

Roughly stated, each ultrafilter of a set I conveys a notion of large subsets of I so that any property applying to a member of D applies to I "almost everywhere."

The set $\{\mathfrak{A}_i\}$ where $\mathfrak{A}_i = <A_i, R_i>$ and the i are members of the set I, is taken to be a family of structures indexed by I, and D to be an ultrafilter on I. Consider now the Cartesian product B of $\{A_i\}$ (for example, if I is $\{0,1,2, \ldots\}$, then B is the set of all sequences f such that $f(i)$ belong to A_i). The members of B are divided into equivalence classes with the help of D: $f \equiv g$ if and only if $\{i|f(i) = g(i)\} \in D$; in other words, the set of indices i such that $f(i) = g(i)$ belong to D [or $f(i)$ and $g(i)$ are equal "almost everywhere"]. Let W be the set of these equivalence classes, i.e., the set of all f^* such that f^* is the set of all members g of B with $g \equiv f$. We introduce similarly a relation S such that Sfg if and only if R_i holds between $f(i)$ and $g(i)$ for "almost all" i, i.e.,

$$\{i|R_i \, [f(i),g(i)]\} \in D.$$

In this way, we arrive at a new structure $U = <W,S>$ which is called the ultraproduct of the original family $\{\mathfrak{A}_i\}$ over D. In the special case when all the $\mathfrak{A}_i$ are the same, the resulting structure U is called the ultrapower of the original family over D.

The central theorems are the following:

1. If $\mathfrak{A}_i$ ($i \in I$) are realizations of the same language, then a sentence p is true in the ultraproduct U if and only if the set of i such that p is true in $\mathfrak{A}_i$ belongs to D. In particular, if each $\mathfrak{A}_i$ is a model of a theory, then U is also a model of the theory.

2. Two realizations of the same language are said to be elementarily equivalent if they have the same set of true sentences. A necessary and sufficient condition for two realizations to be elementarily equivalent is that they admit ultrapowers that are isomorphic.

One application of these theorems is in the introduction of nonstandard analysis, which was originally instituted by other considerations. By using a suitable ultrapower of the structure of the field $\mathfrak{R}$ of real numbers, a real closed field that is elementarily equivalent to $\mathfrak{R}$ is obtained that is non-Archimedean; i.e., which permits numbers a and b such that no n can make na greater than b. This development supplies an unexpected exact foundation for the classical differential calculus using infinitesimals, which has considerable historical, pedagogical, and philosophical interest.

Applications to nonstandard analysis and algebra

A widely known application to the area of algebra is that which deals with certain fields of rational numbers Q_p, called the p-adic completion of the rational numbers (see ALGEBRAIC STRUCTURES). The conjecture has been made that every form of degree d (in the same sense as degrees of ordinary polynomials) over Q_p, in which the number of variables exceeds d^2, has a nontrivial zero in Q_p. Using ultraproducts, it has been shown that the conjecture is true for arbitrary d with the possible exception of a finite set of primes p (depending on d). Subsequently, it was found that the original conjecture is not true when extended to full generality.

Other useful tools in model theory include the pigeonhole principles, of which the basic principle is that, if a set of large cardinality is partitioned into a small number of classes, some one class will have large cardinality. Those elements of the set that lie in the same class cannot be distinguished by the property defining that class.

A related concept is that of "indiscernibles," which also has rather extensive applications in set theory. An ordered subset of the domain of a model $\mathfrak{A}$ of a theory is a homogeneous set, or a set of indiscernibles for $\mathfrak{A}$, if $\mathfrak{A}$ cannot distinguish the members of the subset from one another. More exactly, given any $x_1 < \ldots < x_n, y_1 < \ldots < y_n$ in the subset, then for any sentence $F(a_1, \ldots, a_n)$ of the language of the theory, that sentence (with argument x) is satisfied by (symbolized $\vDash$) the structure; i.e.,

$$\mathfrak{A} \vDash F(x_1, \ldots, x_n),$$

if and only if that sentence (with argument y) is also satisfied by it; i.e.,

$$\mathfrak{A} \vDash F(y_1, \ldots, y_n).$$

There is also a first theorem on this notion that says that, given a theory with an infinite model and a linearly ordered set X, there is then a model $\mathfrak{A}$ of the theory such that X is a set of indiscernibles for $\mathfrak{A}$.

BIBLIOGRAPHY

Original sources: JEAN VAN HEIJENOORT (ed.), *From Frege to Gödel* (1967); PAUL BENACERRAF and HILLARY PUTNAM (eds.), *Philosophy of Mathematics* (1964); MARTIN DAVIS (ed.), *The Undecidable* (1965); DAVID HILBERT, *Gesammelte Abhandlungen*, vol. 3 (1935, reprinted 1965); LUDWIG WITTGENSTEIN, *Tractatus logico-philosophicus* (1922); THORALF SKOLEM, *Selected Works in Logic* (1970); GERHARD GENTZEN, *The Collected Papers* (1969); KURT GODEL, "Über eine bisher noch nicht benützte Erweiterung des finiten Standpunktes," *Dialectica*, 12:280–287 (1958); A.S. KAHR, EDWARD F. MOORE, and HAO WANG, "Entscheidungs problem Reduced to the AEA Case," *Proc. Natn. Acad. Sci. U.S.A.*, 48:365–377 (1962); MICHAEL MORLEY, "On Theories Categorical in Uncountable Powers," *ibid.*, 49:213–216 (1963); JAMES AX and SIMON KOCHEN, "Diophantine Problems over Local Fields," pt. 1–2, *Am. J. Math.*, 87:605–648 (1965), and pt. 3, *Ann. Math.*, 83:437–456 (1966); PER LINDSTROM, "On Extensions of Elementary Logic," *Theoria*, 35:1–11 (1969); and J.V. MATIJASEVICZ, "Enumerable Sets Are Diophantine," *Soviet Math. Doklady*, 11:354–358 (1970).

Expositions: DAVID HILBERT, *Grundlagen der Geometrie* (1899; Eng. trans., *Foundations of Geometry*, 1902); ALFRED

NORTH WHITEHEAD and BERTRAND RUSSELL, *Principia Mathematica* (1910–13; 2nd ed., 1925–27); DAVID HILBERT and WILHELM ACKERMANN, *Grundzüge der theoretischen Logik* (1928; 5th ed., 1967); DAVID HILBERT and PAUL BERNAYS, *Grundlagen der Mathematik*, 2 vol. (1934–39; 2nd ed., 1968–70); WILLARD V. QUINE, *Mathematical Logic* (1941; rev. ed., 1951); RUDOLF CARNAP, *Introduction to Semantics* (1942); STEPHEN C. KLEENE, *Introduction to Metamathematics* (1952); ALFRED TARSKI, *Undecidable Theories* (1953); ALONZO CHURCH, *Introduction to Mathematical Logic*, vol. 1 (1956); ERNEST NAGEL and JAMES R. NEWMAN, *Gödel's Proof* (1958); KURT SCHUETTE, *Beweistheorie* (1960) and *Vollständige Systeme modaler und intuitionistischer Logik* (1968); HAO WANG, *A Survey of Mathematical Logic* (1962); MICHAEL MORLEY, Partitions and Models," *Proc. Summer School in Logic* (1968). If a serious study of the field is contemplated, most of the central results can be found in the following textbooks: PAUL J. COHEN, *Set Theory and the Continuum Hypothesis* (1966); JOSEPH B. SHOENFIELD, *Mathematical Logic* (1967); J.L. BELL and A.B. SLOMSON, *Models and Ultraproducts: An Introduction* (1969).

(H.Wa.)

Metals, Theory of

The most characteristic properties of metals, comprising one of the two large classes into which all chemical elements are grouped, are a shiny surface and the ability to conduct electricity and heat better than the elements in the other class, the nonmetals such as sulfur and carbon. Metals are distinguished by the presence of freely moving electrons, the number of which is comparable to that of the atoms present. They are called conduction electrons, and are the determinants of virtually all the properties of metals.

In a neutral atom the number of positive charges on the nucleus is equalled by the number of electrons arranged in shells around the nucleus. Each electron occupies a position defined by its energy relative to the energies of all the other electrons, and they are bound to the nucleus accordingly, electrons nearest to it being held most tightly, and those farthest, most loosely. An atom can lose electrons or add them to its normal number, thereby becoming a positively or negatively charged ion.

The chemical and physical properties of an element are determined entirely by the electrons most weakly bound to the nucleus of the atom, beginning with the outermost shell of electrons but including also easily dislodged electrons within the electronic structure. Atoms of the alkali metals (lithium, sodium, potassium, rubidium, cesium, and francium comprising Group Ia of the periodic table; see Figure 1), for example, contain one such loosely bound or valence electron each. In a chemical bond formed with nonmetallic elements, this loosely bound electron is considered to be relinquished by the metal atoms to the nonmetallic atoms. The compound sodium chloride, for example, consists of sodium ions, sodium atoms from which one electron has been removed, and chloride ions, chlorine atoms to which that one electron has been added. In solid sodium metal, on the other hand, the valence electrons of all the atoms are available to the entire sample, and they become the conduction electrons that determine the properties of sodium metal. Similarly, metals that have two valence electrons in the outermost shell (Groups IIa and IIb elements) loosely bound to the atomic nucleus, such as magnesium and zinc, tend to donate both such electrons in the formation of a compound with a nonmetallic element and to make both available as conduction electrons in a crystal of metal.

Transition metals, the elements in Groups IIIb through VIII of the periodic table, such as iron, donate different numbers of electrons to the chemical bonds when in different compounds, and similarly the behaviour of conduction electrons in metallic iron is more complicated. Ferromagnetism (the property of retaining magnetism) in iron is also understood in terms of its more complicated electronic structure. There are two other groups of transition metals, the rare earths (atomic number 58 through 71) and the actinide series (90 through 103).

The valence electrons in nonmetals are not free to travel through the crystal as they are in metals. In sodium chloride, for example, the electron added to the chlorine atom

Margin note: The transition metals as electron donors

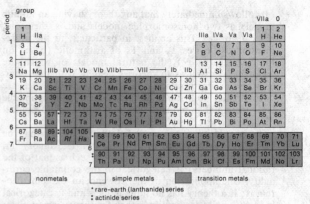

Figure 1: Periodic Table of the elements showing simple metals, transition metals, and nonmetals.

may be thought of as so tightly bound that it can be freed only with a large imput of energy. Sodium chloride is thus an insulator. In a similar way the valence electrons in diamond, or in silicon when it is in the diamond structure, may be thought of as held in covalent bonds, and therefore not free to move through the crystal. If the energy required to free the valence electron is quite small, as it is in silicon, the crystal is called a semiconductor rather than an insulator. Whether a crystal is metallic or nonmetallic depends upon the arrangement of the atoms as well as on the elements making up the crystal. For example, silicon will change structure under high pressure and become a metal.

Metals are technologically important not only because of their unique electronic properties but also because of their strength and malleability, structural properties that derive from the same conduction electrons that, though free, bond the metallic atoms together. Thus, the study of conduction electrons provides a mental picture of the interactions between atoms, resulting in a detailed understanding of the chemical, structural, electrical, thermal, and magnetic properties of the individual metals. The versatility of metals is greatly enhanced by the possibility of dissolving one in another to form alloys of varying properties. One of the goals of the theory of metals is to provide a basis for understanding and predicting the properties of different alloys and thereby tailoring them to particular technological needs.

Historical summary. The first understanding of metallic properties came early in the 20th century, soon after the discovery of the electron. It was first assumed that there were free electrons forming a charged gas confined within a metal, a theory that explained, among other things, a universal ratio between the thermal and electrical conductivity of metals, which had been discovered much earlier.

The assumption that electrons behave as a gas within a metal, however, contained serious defects. Although the optical reflectivity of a metal was consistent with a number of conduction electrons comparable to the number of atoms, such a large number was quite inconsistent with the observed heat capacity of a metal. This dilemma was not resolved until the advent of quantum theory, in 1926, when the use of quantum statistics showed the heat capacity of the electrons was suppressed, and, accordingly, the large number of conduction electrons was also consistent with the observed heat capacity.

Before 1920, the diffraction, or scattering, of X-rays when they passed through solids had been observed, and it had been established that metals consist of crystalline lattices of atoms. With this information quantum theory demonstrated that the wavelike properties of electrons enabled them to propagate through a metallic crystal uninhibited by the constituent atoms. Such studies provided the basis for a rapid growth of an extensive theory of the properties of metals.

After World War II, three particular areas of theoretical activity became prominent. One was the detailed study of electronic states in metals as affected by the interaction between electrons and metallic ions. Another centred on the role of the interaction among electrons in metals; a third on the study of superconductivity (the disappearance of electrical resistivity in metals at temperatures near absolute zero, at which matter is drained of all heat energy), which had been discovered in 1911.

STRUCTURAL PROPERTIES OF METALS AND ALLOYS

Lattice structures

The arrangement of atoms in any crystal structure is orderly, forming a lattice in three dimensions, and this arrangement may be determined from the pattern of deflections the atoms impose on radiation with wavelength close to the interatomic spacing or by particles which can be represented by waves of such a wavelength, a phenomenon called diffraction; the diffraction of X-rays or neutrons by the lattice reveals the specific structure of a sample crystal. In metals, atomic arrangements are characterized by dense packing, similar to packing billiard balls in a box. Two of the most common metallic crystalline structures can in fact be understood in just this way. The first layer of atoms is visualized as on a flat surface as shown in Figure 2, each atom

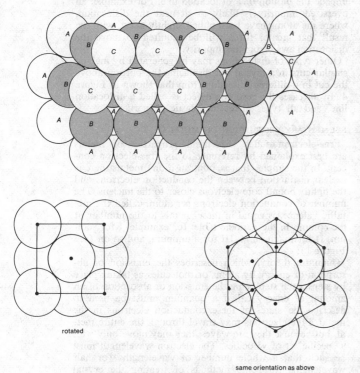

rotated

same orientation as above

Figure 2: Derivation of face-centred cubic structure from planes of hexagonally close-packed atoms (see text).

touching its six nearest neighbours. The point at the centre of each atom is labelled A. The next layer of atoms is placed with each atom nestled into position B (position C could also be selected) between three atoms of the first layer. Again, for the third layer there are two available positions: A, directly over the first layer, or C. If A is used, and the pattern repeated, $ABABAB$, the hexagonal close-packed structure characteristic of magnesium results. In the figure, the position C is used for the third layer. Repeating this pattern, $ABCABCABC$, produces the face-centred cubic structure characteristic of aluminum. The term face-centred derives from the fact that this arrangement, viewed from a different angle, can be seen to be made up of cubes with one atom at each corner and one at the centre of each cube face.

The hexagonal close-packed and face-centred cubic structures correspond to the densest possible packing of spheres. The other common structure is obtained by beginning on the bottom layer with a square arrangement of atoms and then nestling a similar square array on top. This arrangement is the body-centred cubic structure and is only slightly less densely packed than the face-centred structure. Sodium at room temperature occurs in this pattern.

Ordinarily, metals occur in polycrystalline form; that is, consisting of a large number of small crystals, or grains, separated by thin grain boundaries. In some cases, such as the zinc coating on a galvanized pail, the grains are large enough to be easily discerned with the naked eye. In ordinary iron or steel, the grains are so small that they can be seen only under magnification. Large, single crystals of metal can be grown from a melt or from a metallic vapour under special controlled conditions.

When a metal is melted, the regularity of the crystalline lattice is destroyed, just as if the box of closely packed balls described above was shaken, and the density is correspondingly reduced (*i.e.*, the sample expands). Semiconductors, such as silicon and germanium, which are not classed as true metals because of their electrical properties, become metallic when melted; but, in contrast to metals, their density increases with melting. In liquids, the atoms are constantly rearranging themselves. Solids that do not have crystalline structure, such as glass, are called amorphous. It is possible to obtain such noncrystalline, amorphous structures by depositing metals upon very cold surfaces, but this amorphous form of metal is unstable and will crystallize when warmed. Grain boundaries in polycrystalline metals may be considered amorphous.

Metallic alloys are obtained by first dissolving one metallic element in another under heat and then solidifying the melt, the solid alloy assuming a crystalline form. Most alloys are substitutional; when the atoms are of similar size, the atoms of one element replace those of another in the lattice. A binary alloy consists of two metallic elements. In some cases, as when carbon or hydrogen are added to iron, the atoms of the added element are small enough to fit between the larger atoms of the host crystal to form what are called interstitial alloys. In both the substitutional and interstitial alloys, there is some misfit of the constituent atoms and a distortion of the crystalline lattice from that which occurs in the pure metal.

Alloys

Many alloys become ordered at low temperatures; that is, the different kinds of atoms are arranged in a regular sequence throughout the crystal volume. An example is beta (β-)brass, which consists of equal numbers of copper and zinc atoms. This alloy occurs in a body-centred cubic structure, atoms of copper and zinc alternating in the ordered manner shown in Figure 3. The copper atoms form a cubic superlattice as do the zinc atoms. (In some alloys, this tendency to order is so strong that the properties are much the same as those of a compound; in these instances an intermetallic compound is said to have been formed.)

If the temperature of this brass is raised, it becomes disordered at 470° C (880° F). This phase transition is comparable to that of the disappearance of crystalline order of a pure metal at the melting point. In both cases, the transition leads to higher entropy (condition of unavailable energy), corresponding to greater disorder in the high temperature phase.

Many pure metals and alloys undergo phase transitions to different crystalline structures as the temperature is changed. Sodium makes such a transition from body-centred cubic to hexagonal close-packed with decrease in temperature. Again, the entropy of the higher temperature phase is larger; in this case, the additional disorder arises because the body-centred cubic phase is softer, and therefore the thermal vibrations of the lattice, another kind of disorder, are larger.

In all such cases, the disordering of the material provides an additional mechanism for the storage of heat energy and therefore an increase in the heat content. The disorder also disrupts the flow of electrons so that ordinarily, though not always, the higher temperature phase will have higher electrical resistance.

Structural defects are common to all metallic crystals because there are always substitutional or interstitial impurities; missing atoms, called vacancies, or holes; and, occasionally, a misplaced atom in an interstitial position. Subtler defects in terms of the stacking of close-packed structures described above are also possible. For exam-

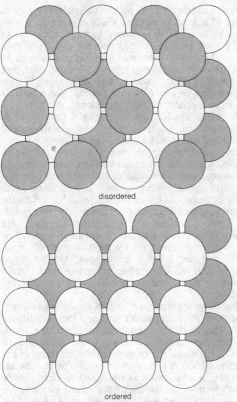

Figure 3: The body-centred cubic structure of beta brass, composed of zinc and copper atoms.

ple, a stacking of layers of atoms such as *ABCACAB-CABCABC* preserves a close-packed configuration but contains a stacking fault (a missing *B* layer) between the fourth and fifth planes. On either side of the stacking fault, the structure is face-centred cubic. All defects such as these cause scattering of the conduction electrons and increase the resistivity.

Disloca-
tions
Another type of defect, the dislocation, plays an extremely important part in the deformation (that is, a change of shape) of metals. One characteristic type of dislocation may be visualized as in Figure 4: a representation of a crystal cut halfway through between two planes of atoms, the upper half being then slid one atom width toward the edge of the cut. The crystal structure is appreciably distorted only at the edge of the cut, and the disruption of the structure along this line is called an edge dislocation.

Edge dislocations play an important role in the response of a crystal to applied stresses. A force upon the top

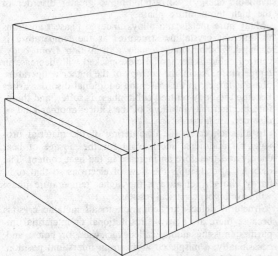

Figure 4: Formation of an edge dislocation. Planes of atoms are shown schematically on the front face (see text).

surface tending to push it to the right will drive the dislocation toward the right. If it emerges from the right surface, it will leave a step there and a permanent deformation. Any metallic crystal contains many dislocations, which are continually regenerated during deformation of the crystal. Thus, plastic deformation of a metallic crystal results from the motion of dislocations through the lattice, and can occur under relatively low stresses, just as a heavy rug may easily be moved across the floor by successively pushing small ripples across the rug. Without dislocations, it would be necessary to move an entire plane at one time, and, just as in attempting to move the entire rug by pulling on one edge, the required forces would be much larger.

The ability of a metal to deform plastically prevents its being brittle. In any other solid, stresses tend to build up near the edge of cracks, and cracks tend to propagate, as in shattering glass. In metal, however, the material flows in that region, relieving the stresses.

Alloying tends to harden crystals and to inhibit plastic deformation. The addition of impurity atoms acts to impede the motion of a dislocation line. For example, an oversized impurity is likely to sit near the dislocation, where the atoms have been pulled slightly apart, with the result that greater force will be required to move the dislocation away from the impurity.

Other types of dislocations may be generated by making similar cuts in a crystal but displacing the portion above the cut in a different direction from that shown in Figure 4. In all cases the resulting defect is called a dislocation line, and all types affect the plastic properties.

ELEMENTARY DESCRIPTION OF METALS

Free-electron model. Electrical properties of metals are best explained by reference to the free-electron concept. In the simple (that is, nontransition) metals there is a clear distinction between the conduction electrons and the tightly bound core electrons closer to the nucleus. The number of conduction electrons per atom, called the metallic valence, is equal in these metals to the number of the column in the periodic table; for example, I for sodium, II for magnesium, III for aluminum, and so on (see Figure 1).

Quantum theory, which describes the emission or absorption of energy by atoms or molecules as taking place by steps, each step being the emission or absorption of an amount of energy called a quantum, must be used to describe the states of these conduction electrons in the metal. Free electrons may travel through the entire metal, but because they are waves, they may move only with a specific set of velocities. The electron wavelength must be such that a whole number of wavelengths (or half wavelengths for some methods of treating the crystal boundaries) equals the length of the crystal. It is more convenient to specify a particular electronic state by its wave number, which is 2π (2×3.1416) divided by the wavelength.

Although the electron can move in any direction in the crystal, which is visualized in the shape of a cube, it is evident that the motion of the electron is similarly restricted in the other two dimensions. Thus, the wave number represents a value in the direction of the electron **Wave**
motion, restricted in each of the three dimensions to one **number**
of the discrete (specific) velocities. The possible electronic states in a crystal, then, are represented by a lattice of points in wave-number space, each state corresponding to a wave number **k**, which terminates on one of these points. The larger the crystal, the more closely spaced are the possible states.

The Pauli principle states that not more than two electrons (spinning in opposite directions) can have the same wave number. Since the smaller the wave number, the lower the energy, the most stable arrangement of electrons is obtained by letting two electrons have each of the wave numbers in a region in wave-number space bounded by a sphere, called the Fermi sphere, large enough to encompass all the conduction electrons (see Figure 5). The states outside the Fermi sphere have higher energy than those inside and are not occupied. In simple metals

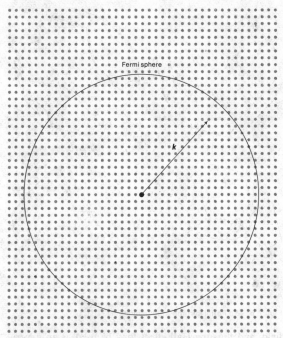

Fermi sphere

k

Figure 5: The Fermi surface, which separates conduction electrons from nonconducting space. Each dot represents an electron state and, if it is occupied by an electron, it represents the electron's velocity and a wave number *k*. The wave number may be represented by an arrow from the centre to the dot. Because no electron has an energy high enough—*i.e.*, a wave number high enough—to place it outside the surface of the sphere, no arrow can be drawn to any point outside the surface (see text).

there are so many conduction electrons that the states with wave numbers near the Fermi sphere are very energetic, the electrons having velocities corresponding to 1 percent of the speed of light.

Conduction of electric current. In the ground state of a metal, the most stable state, there are as many electrons going one way as another, and no net current flows. If an electric field is applied, however, each electron is accelerated, and correspondingly its wave number shifts in the direction of the force. This results in a displacement of the Fermi sphere and in an electronic current.

If the electrons were truly free, they would accelerate indefinitely in the presence of an electric field, and the current would continue to grow. Impurities, defects, and thermal vibrations of the lattice, however, scatter the electrons and keep the current at a constant value. An electron of mass m, on the average, will move for a time symbolized by the Greek letter tau, τ, the scattering time, before it is deflected. During that time it will be propelled by a force equal to its own charge (e) multiplied by the electric field symbolized by E (*i.e.*, as eE) and will increase its velocity by an amount $eE\tau/m$. The electron contributes to the current its charge times the added velocity, and the current density, if N represents the number of electrons in unit volume, is $Ne^2E\tau/m$. Thus, the current density is proportional to the electrical field (Ohm's law); the proportionality constant, symbolized by the Greek letter sigma, σ (with $\sigma = Ne^2\tau/m$), is the conductivity. It is large in metals because of the high density of conduction electrons, particularly large if the number of defects is small and the temperature is low, conditions that lead to a long scattering time, τ.

Conduction of heat. The theory of thermal conductivity is quite similar. The large number of essentially free electrons, which transport thermal energy from hotter to cooler sections of the material, accounts for the high thermal conductivity of metals. Difference in temperature in two parts of the metal produces the flow of thermal energy, and the proportionality constant is the thermal conductivity. The ratio of the thermal to the electrical conductivity is equal to a constant (the Wiedemann–Franz ratio) times the temperature. There are also ther-

moelectric effects, involving both electric fields and temperature differences, which are understood on the same basis, and are brought to use in the thermocouple, which measures temperatures electrically.

Although the Pauli principle has little effect on conduction properties, it becomes quite important in the heat capacity. In the classical physics preceding quantum theory, electrons were expected, because of their large numbers, to make a major contribution to the heat capacity of a metal. In the quantum mechanical description, however, electrons lying well within the Fermi sphere cannot take on this thermal energy, because all the electron states in this energy range are already occupied. The contribution of the electrons to the heat capacity is reduced to the point that the ratio is of the order of 1:400 in most metals at room temperature. There is a similar suppression of the response of a metal to a magnetic field. Each electron behaves as a tiny magnet by virtue of its spin, and in the presence of a magnetic field, it tends to align with that field, leading to a magnetization within the metal. Because only those electrons near the Fermi sphere may reverse their spins, however, the resulting contribution, known as Pauli magnetic susceptibility, is much smaller than would be expected according to classical theory.

In the above description the electrons are free to move within the metal but not to leave the metal. The forces that hold the electron in the metal are the same electrostatic forces that hold the metal itself together. They were first calculated for the alkali metals; then, comparison with the corresponding binding of electrons to the isolated atom led to determination of the cohesive energy for the metal. Cohesion in metals derives from closer proximity of the free negative electrons to the positive metallic ions in the metal than exists for electrons bound to isolated atoms.

ELECTRONIC STRUCTURE
OF METALS AND RELATED EFFECTS

Pseudopotentials. In the free-electron representation, interaction between free electrons and the lattice of ions was neglected except in the general sense that applies to cohesion. While this interaction is known to be strong, the success of the foregoing assumptions seems to indicate that the effect of the interaction is insignificant. This paradox is resolved through the concept of a pseudopotential. Conduction electrons, having high energy, move past the ions with very little deflection, as a speeding car rides relatively smoothly over a bumpy road and a slower car rises and falls with every bump and depression. This effect may be incorporated in the quantum theory of the electron motion by mathematically considering only conduction electron states and deliberately excluding the core electrons bound to the nuclei.

Although the interaction between conduction electrons and the lattice is then represented by a weak pseudopotential, there are inevitable effects of that interaction. In the same manner that an X-ray moving through a crystal may be diffracted, the electron wave may be diffracted by the pseudopotential. Either diffraction can occur, however, only if the wave in question satisfies the so-called Bragg condition; *i.e.*, that the wave number terminate on a Bragg reflection plane in wave-number space. These planes contain wave numbers with magnitudes of the order of 2π (2×3.1416) divided by atomic spacing. For electromagnetic waves, this condition is satisfied by X-rays.

Bragg planes and Fermi spheres. Because of the high density of electrons in metals, the wavelengths of free electrons in the Fermi sphere are also comparable to spacing between atoms, so that it frequently happens that Bragg reflection planes intersect the Fermi sphere in wave-number space. Only a small number of states, however, lie exactly at the plane and can be diffracted. The others traverse the crystal without diffraction and behave as if completely free.

The Bragg condition presumes perfect arrangement of atoms in the periodic lattice. When there are defects or thermal distortions, even electrons not at Bragg planes may be diffracted. Such diffraction caused by defects is

Diffraction by pseudopotential

Thermal conductivity

called electron scattering and is the process that limits the conductivity. The strength of this scattering may be directly calculated from a knowledge of the pseudopotential associated with each ion and of the arrangement of ions in the defective crystal. Electrical resistivity, which is the inverse of the conductivity, tends to be proportional to the number of defects. Usually the change in resistivity of a metal is about one micro-ohm-centimetre per atomic percent of defects (one ohm is the resistance of a circuit in which a potential difference of one volt generates a current of one ampere).

When a metal crystal is melted, the distinction between diffraction and scattering of electrons becomes unclear. It is nevertheless possible, again in terms of pseudopotentials, to calculate the rate of transitions and therefore the conductivity of the liquid metal.

Although only a tiny fraction of the electrons in a perfect metallic crystal are diffracted, the effects of the diffraction may be seen by the application of a magnetic field. An electron moving in a magnetic field reacts to a force perpendicular to its motion (this is exactly the force that drives the armature in an electric motor). An electron with its wave number at the Fermi surface will change its direction of motion by moving along the Fermi sphere. In the absence of diffraction it moves around the Fermi sphere, returning periodically to its initial wave number with a frequency called the cyclotron frequency. The motion on the Fermi sphere would be along a circle made by the intersection of the Fermi sphere and a plane perpendicular to the magnetic field.

Such motion of electron states across the sphere brings many to the Bragg plane, where they can be diffracted. In doing so, they jump to the Fermi sphere at the opposite Bragg plane and continue on their way. The wave number returns to its initial value after traversing a shorter set of arcs than would be the case if there were no diffraction planes; therefore, its cyclotron frequency is correspondingly higher.

It is not difficult to visualize the real orbit of the diffracted electron within the crystal in a magnetic field. The diffraction causes its velocity to change abruptly, but it cannot jump instantaneously from one place to another in the crystal. Thus, its orbit is made up of a series of arcs, always combined into a large orbit on an atomic scale, extending over many thousands of atom distances.

Reduced-zone representation.   Studies of the electronic properties of metals in which such orbit shapes are of direct interest can be more easily done by means of a different representation of the electron states, the reduced-zone representation.

The region so defined, called the Brillouin (or reduced) zone, is bounded by Bragg reflection planes and can be constructed for three-dimensional lattices. The Fermi surface is constructed in the reduced zone by translating each segment of the Fermi sphere so that every pair of states between which diffraction can occur appears at the same wave number. Such translations of the arcs in which diffracted electrons move lead to a segment of the Fermi surface in the reduced zone that is precisely the shape of the electron orbit in real space.

Such a three-dimensional construction of the Fermi surface of aluminum is shown in Figure 6. All possible orbital paths in a magnetic field may be obtained by constructing intersections of planes perpendicular to the magnetic field with these surfaces. Thus, they provide a tremendous amount of information at a glance.

A wide range of properties is affected by the existence of diffraction and the corresponding changes in the Fermi surface. One of the simplest is the Hall effect, which arises when a magnetic field is applied perpendicularly to the direction of a current flow: the electrons are deflected and accumulate at the surface, causing an electric field, the Hall field, just large enough to prevent further accumulation. Thus, the Hall field is a transverse field proportional to both the current and to the applied magnetic field. The proportionality proves to depend only on the density of electrons and their charge if there is no diffraction.

The presence of diffraction strongly modifies the Hall

The Hall effect

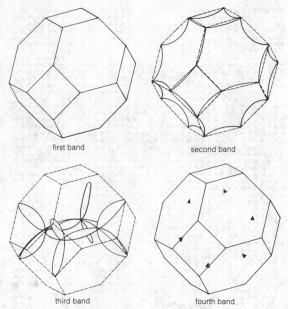

first band   second band

third band   fourth band

Figure 6: The Fermi surface of aluminum.

field, and thus the Hall effect may be used as an experimental tool to study the Fermi surface. The magnetic field also reduces the current along the applied electric field, an effect called magnetoresistance, which also gives information about the Fermi surface.

Certain other effects give more direct information about the orbits in a magnetic field. One, called cyclotron resonance, is a measurement of the cyclotron frequencies of various orbits in the metal. Another, the magneto-acoustic effect, uses sound waves to measure the diameter of electron orbits and therefore of the Fermi surface. The most precise measurements of the Fermi surface have been made with the De Haas–Van Alphen effect, in which fluctuations in magnetic susceptibility are measured by increasing or decreasing a magnetic field. These fluctuations depend only upon the cross-sectional areas of the Fermi surface and give precise measurements of the Fermi surface areas.

Studies of the Fermi surfaces using these techniques have confirmed the general features of this diffraction theory of the Fermi surface. Discrepancies found in calculations of areas and dimensions are believed to be due to the fact that the pseudopotential is not arbitrarily weak. Because of the pseudopotential influence, an electron begins to diffract before it quite reaches the Bragg reflection plane; the true orbits do not have sharp cusps of the type shown; rather the cusps are rounded off and the Fermi surfaces are correspondingly rounded off by the effects of the finite pseudopotential. The pseudopotentials themselves and their resulting effects may be calculated and again tested by experiment.

BAND STRUCTURE AND PROPERTIES OF METAL GROUPS

In the monovalent metals, those in Groups Ia and Ib of the periodic table (see Figure 1), the free-electron Fermi sphere lies entirely in the reduced zone and no diffraction is expected. The electrons in the Ia metals are expected and found to be like free electrons. The pseudopotential, however, is so strong in the noble metals, copper, silver, and gold, that the Fermi surface bows out toward the zone faces.

The polyvalent metals (those of Groups IIa, IIIa, IVa, and IIb) have complicated Fermi surfaces, such as the aluminum surface shown in Figure 6. All have been thoroughly studied, and the reduced-zone representation has proven a good starting point in all cases.

Electronic structures of the transition metals are more complicated. In addition to the conduction electrons there are electrons, called *d* electrons as in the atom, which have energies near the Fermi energy but which retain much of their nucleus-bound character rather than becoming free. It is possible to describe the conduction

Atomic d states

electrons and *d* electrons together in terms of very complicated Fermi surfaces, but for many purposes it is preferable to separate the *d* electrons conceptually. This separation is particularly appropriate in the rare earths where the states in question are *f* states rather than *d* states.

In the noble metals, *d* electrons lie below the Fermi energy and therefore have no Fermi surface. Conduction-electron states, however, and *d* states in the noble metals interact to produce a large pseudopotential and the distortion of the Fermi surface mentioned above. The presence of the *d* states also leads to a contraction of the lattice in the noble metals in comparison to the other monovalent metals and the corresponding high density of electrons makes the conductivity high.

Transition metals have varying numbers of *d* electrons. Many properties depend principally upon the electron-to-atom ratio, the continuation of metallic valence through the transition series indicated at the top of the periodic table. The properties of transition metal alloys depend upon the average electron-to-atom ratio for the alloy system. In all cases the *d* states give a large concentration of states near the Fermi energy and therefore an enhancement of the properties such as the specific heat and the Pauli paramagnetism.

The *d* states also give rise to the possibility of ferromagnetism in transition metals. Imagine a pair of such states, with opposite electron spins, which lie just below the Fermi energy. If there are electrons in both of these states, there will be an electrostatic repulsion between them. In some cases this repulsion causes only one of the states to be occupied, but it could be occupied with either spin. A local moment (something that behaves as a tiny bar magnet) is said to have been formed. Such a system will have a large response to an applied magnetic field. The field will tend to align the magnetic moments of these electrons, and in this case the alignment can take place without any increase in electronic energy.

Exchange interaction

When local moments are formed in transition metals, there will ordinarily be an interaction between the moments on different atoms (usually called an exchange interaction) just as there are interactions between bar magnets; thus, in iron, the exchange interaction favours the parallel alignment of the moments on neighbouring atoms so that the lowest energy will be obtained with all moments aligned, which is the ferromagnetic state, the state of ordinary magnetic iron. In some materials the exchange interaction favours an antiparallel alignment, and the lowest state is called anti-ferromagnetic. In either case, the magnetic state is well ordered, but a phase transition will occur if the temperature is raised sufficiently. At this temperature, called the Curie temperature for ferromagnets, the magnetic system becomes disordered, just as the crystalline system becomes disordered at the melting temperature, although there are fundamental differences in the two transitions.

LATTICE VIBRATIONS

As has been indicated, the vibrations of the atoms in a crystal provide most of the heat content in metals because the heat capacity arising from the conduction electrons is suppressed on account of the Pauli principle. The heat capacity arising from these vibrations is relatively constant at high temperatures, as expected theoretically, but it drops to low values at low temperatures because of another quantum mechanical effect. In one of the earliest quantum theories of heat capacity, Einstein proposed that each atom could vibrate independently. This proposal was recognized as an oversimplification because the motions of different atoms may be related as in sound waves in which neighbouring atoms move together. Regarding the vibrations as sound waves gave an improved account of the specific heat at low temperatures.

That picture, however, was also an oversimplification of the true spectrum of vibration frequencies in a solid; later, quite complete experimental studies of vibration spectra were made using the diffraction of neutrons. The theory of the lattice vibrations requires an understanding of the interactions between the ions in a metal.

There are two important factors involved in these interactions: the direct electrostatic interaction, and an indirect interaction, which arises as conduction electrons are successively deflected by two ions. The latter can be calculated in terms of the pseudopotential and, when added to the direct interaction, gives an effective interaction between ions.

Calculations of the vibration characteristics in terms of these interactions have not proved very reliable; but, with minor adjustments, they can be made to agree with experimental results for simple metals. The application to transition metals has not been made.

Lattice vibrations, called phonons in quantum theory, affect many of the properties of a metal. The effect of thermal vibrations on conductivity was mentioned earlier. The interaction of a vibration of a given intensity with an electron, called the electron-phonon interaction, may be calculated from the pseudopotential. Probability of a vibration scattering an electron is proportional to the intensity of the vibration; that intensity is, in turn, proportional to the absolute temperature at high temperatures, where the resistivity is found to be proportional to temperature. At low temperatures, the resistivity drops, although, because of scattering by impurities and defects, a residual resistance remains. Another effect of the vibrations is that the speed with which electrons at the Fermi surface move is decreased.

The lattice vibrations can also cause an indirect interaction between pairs of electrons comparable to the interaction electrons cause between pairs of ions. An electron moving through the lattice may jostle the ions, producing a distortion that lowers the energy of an electron subsequently passing through the region. This type of interaction may cause the electronic system to become unstable and form a new phase.

Superconductivity

This new phase of the electron system is called superconductivity. In many metals (lead, for example) resistivity drops slowly as the temperature drops until at a critical temperature, the resistivity suddenly becomes zero. This phenomenon does not mean that the electrons are no longer scattered, only that scattering no longer reduces the current. The nature of this superconducting state is understood in terms of the indirect interaction between electrons. Electrons moving in opposite directions form so-called Cooper pairs. In the superconducting state one electron scatters inevitably when the other does, and the current carried by the pair is unchanged. The superconducting state represents a kind of order in the electronic system that is analogous to the magnetic order in ferromagnetism.

METAL SURFACE PHENOMENA

Extensive theoretical study has been devoted to the metallic surface as well as to the behaviour of electrons and ions within the metal, which concern the bulk properties of metals. An understanding of the metal surface requires an understanding of the forces that hold electrons within the metal. An electron striking the surface from within moves slightly beyond the last plane of atoms before returning. There is a layer of negative charge, caused by these electrons, beyond the metallic surface and a compensating positive charge from the ions slightly inside. This double layer of charge provides the electric field that prevents the electrons from escaping. The calculations of the force of this field lead to the finding that an electron with the Fermi energy lacks, by a few electron volts, the energy required to escape from the metal. The barrier is known as the work function of the metal. The work function is very sensitive to the nature of the surface and to any adsorbed (adhering to the surface) atoms, and this theory tells little about surfaces of real metals. It does, however, describe the physics of the work function.

Electrons can escape from a metal if the temperature is high enough; then a small number of electrons will have sufficient energy to overcome the work function and escape. This is thermionic emission, the mechanism by which electrons are introduced into the vacuum by a hot cathode in a vacuum tube. Electrons may also escape by the photoelectric effect, which results from the quantum-mechanical nature of light. The light arrives in quanta of energy, called photons, which vary according to the wavelength of the light. In light of short wavelengths, ordinarily in the visible, the photon energies may be greater than the few electron volts required to free the electron from the metal surface.

Tunnelling

There has been extensive research on the removal of electrons through quantum-mechanical tunnelling. A thin layer of oxide is formed on the surface of the metal and a second metal deposited upon the oxide. The oxide is an insulator, and the electrons respond to it much as they would to a narrow evacuated space; an electron at the Fermi energy does not have the energy needed to traverse it. There is, however, a small probability that, because of the wave nature of the electron, it will nevertheless be transmitted; this is the tunnel effect. Such tunnelling is of particular interest when one or both of the metals are superconductors, because it provides a way of studying the electronic states near the Fermi energy in the superconductor (this is called Giaever tunnelling). If the oxide is sufficiently thin, it is possible for supercurrents to flow without impedance through the oxide, a phenomenon known as the Josephson effect.

Because of the high conductivity of metals, electromagnetic waves are reflected from a metal surface (this is particularly familiar in the case of light waves that give a fresh metal surface its shiny appearance). The reflection occurs by the generation of electric currents in the surface, which act as antennas reradiating the light outward. Thus, when light is reflected, there are always currents flowing in the surface of the metal, but they are restricted to quite near the surface. This is the skin effect, and the depth of penetration is called the skin depth. It is the field within the skin depth that can give conduction electrons the energy necessary for photoelectric emission. It is the current within the skin depth that, because of metallic resistance, may heat the metal with energy extracted from the reflecting light, resulting in imperfect reflection. This aspect of optical absorption was understood in the earliest days of the free-electron theory of metals and is called Drude absorption, after the German physicist Paul Drude.

Metallic colours

Some other aspects of optical absorption could not be understood before the introduction of quantum theory, such as interband transitions, in which photons are absorbed and individual electrons make transitions between states of greatly different energy. Such transitions are particularly familiar in the noble metals (gold, silver, copper), where they take place between occupied d states and unoccupied conduction states just above the Fermi energy. It is these absorptions in the blue that cause the colour of copper and gold. It is also thought that such an interband transition is the first step in most photoemission processes for electrons.

MANY-BODY EFFECTS

Most of the theory of metals, as elaborated above, has been based on a one-electron approximation, a simplified approach to solving problems. The states of a particular electron are discussed without concern for what other electrons are doing at the same time, or only considering the effects of another electron in a general way. In a real metal, the electron motions are correlated with each other and collectively are extraordinarily complicated. As in the case of the interaction of the electrons with the ions, however, the effects are not as large as the interactions that cause them.

There are two particular ways, other than in causing superconductivity as already described, in which the electron interactions do make themselves felt. Because metals are good conductors, the electrons tend to move in order to reduce or eliminate any electric field that may be present. In particular, if a charge is introduced into the metal, the electrons flow to eliminate the long-range electrostatic field that would otherwise arise. This phenomenon is called screening of a charge in the metal. In the same way, the charge of each electron is screened by the motion of other electrons in the metal, and the net long-range interaction between any given pair of electrons becomes small. Thus screening is one important effect of the electron–electron interactions. The other arises when fields change so rapidly that the electrons have difficulty keeping up. Then plasma oscillations occur, which are very high-frequency vibrations of the electron gas as a whole.

An additional class of effects that arise from the interaction between electrons, concerning what are called shake-off electrons, has been the centre of intense theoretical activity. In some situations, notably when a conduction electron drops to a deep core state with the emission of an X-ray, other electrons must take some of the energy and be raised above the Fermi energy; these are shake-off electrons. As a result, not all of the energy of the transition is in the X-ray, and the energies of the emitted X-rays are all smaller than would be predicted by simple theory.

To a large extent the simple theory of metals based upon the one-electron approximation has been extraordinarily successful. More complete studies of the effects of electron-electron interactions have explaind these successes and have also shown that in some cases the one-electron picture is inadequate.

BIBLIOGRAPHY

Classic works: N.F. MOTT and H. JONES, *The Theory of the Properties of Metals and Alloys* (1936); A.H. WILSON, *The Theory of Metals,* 2nd ed. (1965); F. SEITZ, *The Modern Theory of Solids* (1940).

Monographs on modern theory: W.A. HARRISON and M.B. WEBB (eds.), *The Fermi Surface* (1961); W.A. HARRISON, *Pseudopotentials in the Theory of Metals* (1966); P.G. DE GENNES, *Superconductivity of Metals and Alloys* (1966); DAVID PINES, *Elementary Excitations in Solids* (1963).

General texts: C. KITTEL, *Introduction to Solid State Physics,* 4th ed. (1971); J.M. ZIMAN, *Principles of the Theory of Solids* (1964); W.A. HARRISON, *Solid State Theory* (1970).

(W.A.H.)

Metalwork

Man's first materials were stone, wood, bone, and earth. It was not until he had reached a later stage of evolution that he was able to extract and work with metals. This article deals with the objects that man has fashioned from copper, bronze and brass, gold and silver, iron, and lead: vessels, utensils, ceremonial and ritualistic objects, decorative objects, architectural ornamentation, personal ornament, sculpture, and weapons. (For a more detailed discussion of weapons, ceremonial and ritualistic objects, personal ornaments, and sculpture, see ARMS DESIGN AND DECORATION; CEREMONIAL AND RITUALISTIC OBJECTS; JEWELRY; and SCULPTURE, ART OF). This article treats the processes and techniques and the stylistic characteristics and historical developments of metalworking. Aspects of metalwork are discussed in the following related articles: VISUAL ARTS, EAST ASIAN; VISUAL ARTS, WESTERN; SOUTH ASIAN PEOPLES, ARTS OF; CENTRAL ASIAN PEOPLES, ARTS OF; SOUTHEAST ASIAN PEOPLES, ARTS OF; ISLAMIC PEOPLES, ARTS OF; JEWISH PEOPLES, ARTS OF; AFRICAN PEOPLES, ARTS OF; and AMERICAN INDIAN PEOPLES, ARTS OF.

This article is divided into the following sections:

I. General processes and techniques

Many of the technical processes in use today are essentially the same as those employed in ancient times. The early metalworker was familiar, for example, with hammering, embossing, chasing, inlaying, gilding, wiredrawing, and the application of niello, enamel, and gems.

Hammering and casting. All decorative metalwork was originally executed with the hammer. The several parts were hammered out separately and then put together by means of rivets or pinned on a solid core (for soldering had not yet been invented). Plates of hammered copper could be shaped also into statues, the separate pieces being joined together with copper rivets. A life-size Egyptian statue of the pharaoh Pepi I in the Egyptian museum, Cairo, is an outstanding example of such work.

After about 2500 BC, the two standard methods of fabricating metal—hammering and casting—were developed side by side. The lost-wax, or cire perdue (casting with a wax mold), process was being employed in Egypt by about 2500 BC, the Egyptians probably having learned the technique from Sumerian craftsmen (see SCULPTURE, ART OF). Long after the method of casting statues in molds with cores had superseded the primitive and tedious rivetting process, the hammer continued as the main instrument for producing art works in precious metals. Everything attributable to Assyrian, Etruscan, and Greek goldsmiths was wrought by the hammer and the punch.

Embossing, or repoussé. Embossing (or repoussé) is the art of raising ornament in relief from the reverse side. The design is first drawn on the surface of the metal and the motifs outlined with a tracer, which transfers the essential parts of the drawing to the back of the plate. The plate is then embedded face down in an asphalt block and the portions to be raised are hammered down into the yielding asphalt. Next the plate is removed and re-embedded with the face uppermost. The hammering is continued, this time forcing the background of the design into the asphalt. By a series of these processes of hammering and re-embedding, followed finally by chasing, the metal attains its finished appearance. There are three essential types of tools—for tracing, for bossing, and for chasing—as well as a specialized tool, a snarling iron or spring bar, which is used to reach otherwise inaccessible areas. Ornament in relief is also produced by mechanical means. A thin, pliable sheet of metal may be pressed into molds, between dies, or over stamps. All of these methods have been known from antiquity.

Chasing. Chasing is accomplished with hammer and punches on the face of the metal. These punches are so shaped that they are capable of producing any effect—either in intaglio (incising beneath the surface of the metal) or in relief—that the metalworker may require. The design is traced on the surface, and the relief may be obtained by beating down the adjacent areas to form the background. Such chased relief work sometimes simulates embossed work, but in the latter process the design is bossed up from the back. The detailed finish of embossed work is accomplished by chasing; the term is applied also to the touching up and finishing of cast work with hand-held punches.

Engraving. To engrave is to cut or incise a line. Engraving is always done with a cutting tool, generally by pressure from the hand. It detaches material in cutting. When pressure is applied with a hammer, the process is called carving.

Inlaying. The system of ornamentation known as damascening is Oriental in origin and was much practiced by the early goldsmiths of Damascus; hence the name. It is the art of encrusting gold wire (sometimes silver or copper) on the surface of iron, steel, or bronze. The surface upon which the pattern is to be traced is finely undercut with a sharp instrument. The gold thread is forced into the minute furrows of the cut surface by hammering and is securely held.

Niello is the process of inlaying engraved ornamental designs with niello, a silver sulfide or mixture of sulfides. The first authors to write on the preparation of niello and its application to silver were Eraclius and Theophilus, in or about the 12th century, and Benvenuto Cellini, during the 16th. According to each of these authors, niello is made by fusing together silver, copper, and lead and then mixing the molten alloy with sulfur. The black product (a mixture of the sulfides of silver, copper, and lead) is powdered; and after the engraved metal, usually silver, has been moistened with a flux (a substance used to promote fusion), some of the powder is spread on it and the metal strongly heated; the niello melts and runs into the engraved channels. The excess niello is removed by scraping until the filled channels are visible, and finally the surface is polished.

Enamelling. There are two methods of applying enamel to metal: champlevé, in which hollows made in the metal are filled with enamel; and cloisonné, in which strips of metal are applied to the metal surface, forming cells, which are then filled with enamel. (For a detailed discussion, see ENAMELWORK.)   (S.V.G.)

Gilding. Gilding is the art of decorating wood, metal, plaster, glass, or other objects with a covering or design of gold in leaf or powder form. The term also embraces the similar application of silver, palladium, aluminum, and copper alloys.

The earliest of historical peoples had masterly gilders, as evidenced by overlays of thin gold leaf on royal mummy cases and furniture of ancient Egypt. From early times, the Chinese ornamented wood, pottery, and textiles with beautiful designs in gold. The Greeks not only gilded wood, masonry, and marble sculpture but also fire-gilded metal by applying a gold amalgam to it and driving off the mercury with heat, leaving a coating of gold on the metal surface. From the Greeks, the Romans acquired the art that made their temples and palaces resplendent with brilliant gilding. Extant examples of ancient gilding reveal that the gold was applied to a ground prepared with chalk or marble dust and an animal size or glue.

Beating mint gold into leaves as thin as $1/280,000$ inch (0.00001 centimetre) is done largely by hand, though machines are utilized to some extent. After being cut to a standard 3⅞ inches (9.84 centimetres) square, the leaves are packed between the tissue-paper leaves of small books, ready for the gilder's use.

The many substances to which the gilder can apply his art and the novel and beautiful effects he can produce may require special modifications and applications of his methods and materials. Certain basic procedures, however, are pertinent to all types of gilding. For example, the ground to be gilded must be carefully prepared by priming. Flat paints, lacquers, or sealing glues are used, according to the nature of the ground material. Metals subject to corrosion may be primed (and protected) by

Marginal notes:

Lost-wax process

Damascening and niello

Champlevé and cloisonné

red lead or iron oxide paints. With pencil or chalk the gilder lays out his design on the ground after the ground has been prepared and is thoroughly dry. Patterns may also be laid down by forcing, or pouncing, powdered chalk or dry pigment through paper containing perforations made with pricking wheels mounted on swivels; the swivel arrangement permits the attainment of the most intricate of designs.

To create an adhesive surface to which the gold will be securely held, the area to be gilded is sized. The type of size used depends on the kind of surface to be gilded and on whether it is desirable for the size to dry quickly or slowly. When the size has dried enough so that it just adheres to the fingertips, it is ready to receive and retain the gold leaf or powder.

Application of gold leaf Gold leaf may be rolled onto the sized surface from the tissue book. Generally, however, the gilder holds the book firmly in his left hand with the tissue folded back to expose as much leaf as is needed and detaches that amount with a pointed tool, such as a sharpened skewer. He then picks up the leaf segment with his gilder's tip, a brush of camel's hair set in a thin cardboard holder, and carefully transfers it to its place in his design. The leaf is held to the tip by static electricity, which the gilder generates by brushing the tip gently over his hair. For some gilding operations the gilder uses a cushion to hold his pieces of leaf. This is a rectangular piece of wood, about 9 by 6 inches (23 by 15 centimetres) in size, which is padded with flannel and covered with dressed calfskin; a parchment shield around one end protects the delicate leaf from disturbance by drafts of air. When the gilding is completed, the leaf-covered area should be pounced with a wad of soft cotton of surgical grade. Rubbing with cotton burnishes the gold to a high lustre. Application of a gilder's burnisher—that is, a highly polished agate stone set in a handle—also imparts a fine, high finish to the metal. Loose bits of gold, or skewings, may be removed from the finished work with a camel's hair brush.

Leaf gold may be powdered by being rubbed through a fine-mesh sieve. Powdered gold is so costly, however, that bronze powders have been substituted almost universally for the precious metal. When gold leaf is employed in the gilding of domes and the roofs of buildings, it is used in ribbon form. For finishing processes, such as burnishing and polishing, see SCULPTURE, ART OF. (E.L.Y.)

II. Western metalwork

COPPER

Copper alloys The first nonprecious metal to be used by man was copper. But in the 4th millennium BC, Eastern craftsmen discovered that copper alloys using tin or zinc were both more durable and easier to work with, with the result that from then on the use of unalloyed copper declined sharply. Artists and craftsmen working in the West also discovered this, which is why pure copper work was relatively rare.

Pure copper is a reddish colour and has a metallic glow. When it is exposed to damp, it becomes coated with green basic copper carbonate (incorrectly known as verdigris). This patina is a drawback if copper is to be used for functional objects, for the oxide is poisonous to man. This means that utensils that come into contact with food must be lined with tin.

As copper is a relatively soft metal, it is sensitive to such influences as stress and impact. But unlike bronze it is malleable and can be hammered and chased in much the same way as silver. The surface of copper can be successfully gilded, and its reddish colouring makes the gilding seem even brighter. Because of these properties, copper was sometimes able to compete somewhat with silver.

Pure copper is not particularly good for casting, as it can easily become blistered when the gases escape. The surface of sheet copper can be engraved, however, and this technique was often used for decorating purely ornamental objects. In copperplate etching, engraving became the basis of printing. Enamel is often applied to copper, using both the champlevé and cloisonné techniques. Sheet copper was also used as a base for painted enamel.

(H.-U.H.)

Antiquity. *Mesopotamia.* In the museum at Baghdad, in the British Museum, and in the University of Pennsylvania at Philadelphia are finely executed objects in beaten copper from the royal graves at Ur (modern Tall al-Muqayyar) in ancient Sumer. Outstanding is a copper relief that decorated the front of the temple at Al 'Ubaid. This remarkable decoration represents an eagle with a lion's head, holding two stags by their tails. The stags' antlers—also made of wrought copper—were developed in high relief and were soldered into their sockets with lead. This relief illustrates the high level of art and technical skill attained by the Sumerians in the days of the 1st dynasty of Ur (c. 2650–2500 BC). In the Metropolitan Museum of Art, New York City, is a Sumerian bull's head of copper, probably an ornamental feature on a lyre, which is contemporary with the Ur finds. **Copper relief at Al 'Ubaid**

The malleability of unalloyed copper, which renders it too soft for weapons, is peculiarly valuable in the formation of vessels of every variety of form; and it has been put to this use in almost every age. Copper domestic vessels were regularly made in Sumer during the 4th millennium BC and in Egypt a little later.

Egypt. From whatever source Egypt may have obtained its metalworking processes, Egyptian work at a remote period possesses an excellence that, in some respects, has never been surpassed. Throughout Egyptian history, the same smiths who worked in the precious metals worked also in copper and bronze.

Nearly every fashionable Egyptian, man or woman, possessed a hand mirror of polished copper, bronze, or silver. Copper pitchers and basins for hand washing at meals were placed in the tombs. An unusual example in the Metropolitan Museum of Art is plated with antimony to imitate silver, which was very rare in the Old Kingdom (c. 2686–c. 2160 BC). The basins and the bodies of the ewers were hammered from single sheets of copper. The spouts of the ewers were cast in molds and attached to the bodies by means of copper rivets or were simply inserted in place and crimped to the bodies by cold hammering.

(S.V.G.)

"Tassilo Chalice," copper gilt with silver and niello, c. 780. In the Kremsmünster Abbey, Austria. Height 25 cm.
Bildarchiv Foto Marburg

Middle Ages. *Europe.* The first well-designed copper objects to survive in the West date from about the middle of the Carolingian period, the 8th century AD. Who made them is not known, but one can assume that in the early Middle Ages they were mainly the work of monks. Indeed, the earliest copper and copper-gilt pieces are exclusively liturgical implements.

Decrees issued by the church synods held in the 8th and 9th centuries invariably expressly prohibited the use of copper and bronze for consecrated chalices, but in fact a few copper-gilt chalices like the "Tassilo Chalice" (Kremsmünster Abbey, Austria) have survived. The care and artistry with which they were worked and their rich engraved and niello decoration show that they were valued as highly as altar vessels made of precious metals.

From the 12th century onward, but particularly in the 13th and 14th centuries, copper-gilt chalices were relatively common, especially in Italy, where they were virtually mass-produced. Reliquaries, portable altars, shrines, and processional crosses dating from the Ottonian and Romanesque periods are also very frequently made of gilded copper and are generally decorated with enamel, niello work, or engraving or set with precious stones. One group of copper-gilt reliquaries, dating from the 12th century and after, takes the form of the head, or head and shoulders, of a saint. Others are in the shape of various parts of the body, such as an arm or a foot. These were also made in silver and in cast bronze. Ciboria (covered vessels for holding the wafers of the Eucharist), monstrances (receptacles for the Host), incense vessels, and other liturgical implements were also made in copper gilt, as well as in bronze and silver. Some of these copper-gilt implements were made as late as the Baroque period. (H.-U.H.)

Islām. The most magnificent example of Muslim enamel work in existence is a copper plate in the Tiroler Landes museum Ferdinandeum at Innsbruck, Austria, decorated in polychrome enamel, with figure subjects, birds and animals within medallions separated by palm trees and dancers (first half of the 12th century). The Mesopotamian, or Mosul, style, which flourished from the early part of the 13th century, is characterized by a predominant use of figures of men and animals and by the lavish use of silver inlay. The most famous example of figured Mosul work in Europe is the so-called Baptistery of St. Louis in the Louvre. This splendid bowl, which belongs in style to the Mosul work of the 13th century, measures five feet (150 centimetres) in circumference and is covered with figures richly inlaid with silver, so that little of the copper is visible. It is signed by the artist. (S.V.G.)

Renaissance to modern. In the second half of the 16th century, copper gilt began to be used less and less often for liturgical implements because silver had become cheaper and was therefore preferred.

In the late 16th century, Italian smiths used copper for water beakers and water jugs, decorating the surfaces with chased ornaments, whereas the rest of Europe used brass.

High-quality copper objects dating from the 17th and 18th centuries were sometimes designed and worked in the same way as the silver of the period. Most were probably trial pieces made for the guild rank of journeyman or master by silversmiths who were too poor to supply objects in precious metal. Some may have been used as workshop models or given to clients as specimen pieces.

Another type of copper vessel, known as a "Herrengrund cup," is purely ornamental and closely resembles the showpieces made in the 16th and 17th centuries. These drinking mugs are made of copper that was extracted by a process known as cementation, in which water containing copper forms a deposit on iron. Production was limited to three places in the county of Sohl in Hungary. In those days the process seemed to many people most mysterious, and many of the inscriptions on "Herrengrund cups" refer to this mystery. The design of the beakers is modelled very closely on that of silver vessels produced in southern Germany, Bohemia, and Silesia. The most sumptuous examples are chased, engraved, or gilded or, more rarely, enamelled or set with precious stones. Many of them are decorated with mining scenes peopled with little figures. Most were made in the 17th century; a decline set in in the 18th century, though individual pieces continued to be made right down to the Empire period.

In the 17th and 18th centuries, copper enjoyed a period of relative prosperity in middle class households on the continent of Europe. For example, copper bread bins lined with tin were used; they were often richly decorated with chased motifs or brass fittings. There were also sumptuous wine coolers, cake and pudding molds, bowls,

buckets, jugs, jars, screw-top flasks, sausage pans, and many other items, all polished until they shone and thus used as kitchen decorations as well as utility items.

In 18th-century Holland, jugs for tea and coffee were made in copper with a dark-brown patina and with various parts, such as the handle and the knob, in brass gilt. The sides were chased with interlaced foliage and other Rococo decorative motifs.

Copper was also the main metal used for Sheffield plate, which has a silvered surface. In 1742 Thomas Bolsover invented a method of fusing copper and silver together so that the result was highly durable, and he produced this type of silver-plated ware on a large scale. Although 18th-century England was a relatively wealthy society

Sheffield plate teapot, English, late 18th century. In the Victoria and Albert Museum, London. Height 16.5 cm.

and solid silver utensils of all kinds were used fairly widely, the middle classes, who were not all that well off, liked to buy these implements that looked like silver yet cost only a third of the price. The makers of Sheffield plate therefore adopted the designs used for English silverware at that date, and their work was often as courtly and elegant as that of the silversmiths.

Copper ware was no longer important in the 19th century, though it was occasionally used for pieces designed to follow earlier styles or for copies of historical pieces. The method now used was electroplating, which is a purely technical process and has nothing to do with craftsmanship.

Toward the end of the 19th century, attempts were made to create a new and individual style for copper; and there were occasional signs that its inherent properties were understood and used to full effect. But there was no renaissance in the true sense of the word. (H.-U.H.)

BRONZE AND BRASS

Bronze is an alloy of copper and tin. In the period of classical antiquity it had a low tin content, generally containing less than 10 percent, because tin was less common and therefore difficult to obtain. Like bronze, brass is an alloy, this time of copper plus zinc.

It is often very difficult to distinguish between bronze and brass merely by their appearance. The colour of the different alloys ranges over various shades from gold to a reddish tinge, to silvery, greenish, and yellowish shades, according to the proportions of the basic constituents. The patina on both alloys ranges from dark brown to a dark greenish tinge, particularly in the earliest pieces. Since it is often difficult to differentiate between bronze and brass with the naked eye and since metalworkers and metal casters of previous centuries did not make an express distinction between them, they will be considered together here. From a very early date bronze was used mainly for casting. Because it is so brittle, it has only rarely been hammered or chased; brass or copper were preferred for such work because they are more malleable. Down to the Middle Ages, bronze was cast by the cire perdue, or lost-wax, method. By this process, the mold can be used only once. This method of casting is the most exclusive, not only because it is the most expensive but also because it produces the finest work from the aesthetic point of view. Later, the casting process used models made up of a number of different pieces that could be taken apart and therefore re-used. These were generally made of wood and could be pressed down into a sand mold so that the shape of the object being cast emerged as a hollow. The hollow was then filled with molten bronze, which was poured in through casting ducts. When the resulting piece had been removed from the sand mold, the surface was smoothed over and the casting seams removed. The wooden model could then be used again to make as many copies as were required, which meant that economical production was possible. Brass was cast by the same methods but over and above this a process of hammering and chasing was used to fashion sheet brass. Brass platters were often decorated with relief work ornament, which was embossed from the reverse side by means of a type of die. The brass worker could also create an ornamental frieze made up of small motifs by using a series of punches made of iron. The surface of bronze or brass objects was also occasionally decorated with engraving. (H.-U.H.)

Antiquity. *Mesopotamia.* In the Metropolitan Museum of Art is the bronze sword of King Adad-nirari I, a unique example from the palace of one of the early kings of the period (14th–13th century BC) during which Assyria first began to play a prominent part in Mesopotamian history. A magnificent example of Assyrian bronze embossed work is to be seen in the gates of Shahmaneser III, erected about 845 BC, to commemorate that king's campaigns. The gates were made of wood; and the bronze bands, embossed with a wealth of figures in relief, are only about ¹⁄₁₆ inch (1.6 millimetres) thick. The bands were obviously intended for decoration, not to strengthen the gates against attack.

Iran. The Persian bronze industry was also influenced by Mesopotamia. Luristan, near the western border of Persia (Iran), is the source of many bronzes that have been dated from 1500 to 500 BC and include chariot or harness fittings, rein rings, elaborate horse bits, and various decorative rings, as well as weapons, personal ornaments, different types of cult objects, and a number of household vessels. Many of these objects show a decided originality in the development of the animal style.

Egypt. The bronzes that have survived are mainly votive statues placed in the temples from the Saite to the Ptolemaic period (305–30 BC), and amuletic bronzes that were buried with the dead. In its simplest form the decoration consisted of lines, representing details of clothing, ornaments, and the like, cut in the bronze with engraving tools, sometimes also combined with gilding. A fine example of inlay work of the 22nd dynasty (945–c. 730 BC) is a bronze menat damascened with gold wire (Metropolitan Museum of Art).

Crete. A sword, found in the palace of Mallia and dated to the Middle Minoan period (2000–1600 BC), is an example of the extraordinary skill of the Cretan metalworker in casting bronze. The hilt of the sword is of gold-plated ivory and crystal. A dagger blade found in the Lasithi plain, dating about 1800 BC (Metropolitan Museum of Art), is the earliest known predecessor of ornamented dagger blades from Mycenae. It is engraved with two spirited scenes: a fight between two bulls and a man spearing a boar. Somewhat later (c. 1400 BC) are a series of splendid blades from mainland Greece, which must be attributed to Cretan craftsmen, with ornament in relief, incised, or inlaid with varicoloured metals, gold, silver, and niello. The most elaborate inlays—pictures of men hunting lions and of cats hunting birds—are on daggers from the shaft graves of Mycenae, Nilotic scenes showing Egyptian influence. The bronze was oxidized to a blackish-brown tint; the gold inlays were hammered in and polished and the details then engraved on them. The gold was in two colours, a deeper red being obtained by an admixture of copper; and there was a sparing use of niello.

Dagger blades (margin note)

Cast bronze finial from Luristan, 9th–8th century BC. In the Denver Art Museum, Colorado. Height 16 cm.
By courtesy of the Denver Art Museum, Colorado

Greece. The Greeks, who learned much about metalwork from the Egyptians, excelled in hammering, casting, embossing, chasing, engraving, soldering, and metal intaglio. Among the ancients, the great emphasis of technology was on aesthetic expression, not on practical utilization. Greek coin dies rank with the finest work of this kind that the world has ever seen. Pottery and bronze hammer-and-cast work were important crafts of ancient Greece. Vases of terra-cotta were often designed to resemble those of bronze, and both kinds were widely used in antiquity. Unlike terra-cotta, which is breakable but otherwise practically indestructible, bronze is subject to corrosion; and a surviving Greek bronze vase in good condition is therefore something of a rarity. The body of the vase, which was hammered out of a sheet of malleable bronze, was usually left plain; the handles, feet, and overhanging lip, which were cast, were decorated. The applied elements were rivetted or soldered.

It was in the time of Lysippus, the distinguished sculptor who flourished about 330 BC, that the fine Greek beaten work for decoration of armour, vases, and objects of domestic use reached its perfection. It was executed by a hammer worked from behind, the outlines being afterward emphasized by chisel or punch; or metal plate was beaten into a mold formed by carving the subject in intaglio upon a resisting material. The embossed shoulder straps of a cuirass, called the "Bronzes of Siris" (4th century BC; British Museum, London), are in exceedingly high relief and are beaten into form with wonderful skill with the hammer. The relief depicts the combat between the Greeks and the Amazons.

Greek bronze statuettes—originally dedicatory offerings in shrines, ornamental figures on utensils, or decorative works of art—have survived in large numbers. They were usually cast solid, rarely hollow. Sometimes even large statuettes were cast solid. (The advantage of solid casting is that the mold can be used repeatedly, whereas in the hollow-casting process the mold is destroyed.) Greek bronzes were originally golden and bright, and they were often decorated with silver or niello for colour contrast. Bronze statuary hardly existed before the introduction of hollow casting, about the middle of the 6th century BC, after which bronze became the most important medium of monumental sculpture; its strength and lightness admitted poses that could not be reproduced in stone.

Etruria. The Etruscans used bronze for cast and beaten work; and although few large works remain, the museums of Europe display a marvellous variety of admira-

Statuettes and monumental sculpture (margin note)

bly formed small bronzes. A masterpiece of bronze Etruscan sculpture is the "Chimera" (a mythological beast with a goat's body, a lion's head, and a serpent's tail) from Arezzo, a 5th-century BC ex-voto from a sacred building, found in 1553 and partly restored by Benvenuto Cellini (Museo Archeologico di Firenze). Etruscan bronze workers produced, often for export, votive statuettes, vessels, furniture, helmets, swords, lamps, candelabra, mirrors, and even chariots. An Etruscan chariot of c. 600 BC in the Metropolitan Museum of Art has a body and wheels of wood, sheathing of bronze, and tires of iron, the high front embossed with archaic figures of considerable grace. The Etruscans inlaid bronze with silver and gold in a manner that proves that their skill in this mode of enrichment equalled that of the Greeks and Romans. Many delicately engraved bronze objects were made in the Latin town of Praeneste (modern Palestrina), which possessed a highly developed bronze-working industry. From Praeneste came a remarkable cylindrical container of the late 4th century BC, now in the Villa Giulia, Rome; its richly engraved surface provides a good example of the perfection of ancient drawing.

Rome. Etruscan cities, like those of Greece, were crowded with bronze statues of gods and heroes; and Rome derived its best adornment from the pillage of Etruria and then of Greece. Distinctly Roman work is hard to trace, as the conquered Greeks worked for their masters, and the Romans copied wholesale from the Greeks. Temple statues were nearly always of bronze, but after about 190 BC the metal was chiefly used for architectural decorations and portraiture. The bronze doors of the Pantheon and of the Temple of Romulus in the Roman Forum still occupy their original positions. Two bronze doors in the Lateran Baptistery are supposed to have been brought from the Baths of Caracalla by Pope Hilarius in the 5th century. Also in the Lateran church are four fine gilt-bronze fluted Corinthian columns.

Much Roman small work was exceedingly fine, though it is generally conceded that Roman productions are less aesthetically attractive than those of the Greeks. Pompeii and Herculaneum were essentially Greek towns, and the many beautiful bronzes in the Museo e Gallerie Nazionali di Capodimonte, Naples, collected from the ruins of private houses there, are of Greek workmanship. These included statuettes, mirrors, and all kinds of bronze work useful in a house. Many of these pieces were originally attached to pieces of furniture.

During the closing years of the republic, brass, produced by what came later to be known as the calamine (zinc-carbonate) method, became an important material for the first time. Its various uses included parade armour, as may be seen in a Roman embossed brass helmet in the Castle Museum, Norwich, England.

Teutonic tribes. The Teutonic tribes who conquered and divided the Roman Empire were little versed in the monumental arts and unskilled in figure representation; but in metalworking, in the making of weapons and other utilitarian objects, and in the delicate ornament of the goldsmith's art they excelled. They were among the earliest in Western Europe to develop the use of enamel decoration on bronze in the champlevé technique.

Middle Ages: Byzantine Empire. Syria, Egypt, and Anatolia were first the teachers and then the rivals of Constantinople (Istanbul). The fusion of antique and Eastern elements resulted in the Byzantine style, the great period of which dates from the 9th to the end of the 12th century. The extensive use of embossed work, with filigree, cabochon gems, and small plaques of enamel, may be seen in both the East and the West during the early Middle Ages. The most conspicuous examples of large Byzantine metalwork are bronze church doors inlaid with silver. Many objects are still preserved in various European treasuries, which were enriched by the spoils of the sack of Constantinople in 1204. Venice, in the Treasury of St. Mark's, has an unrivalled series of Byzantine chalices, bookbindings, and other treasures of metalwork; but it is in Kiev, Moscow, and Leningrad that broadly representative series of all the categories of Byzantine artistic production may be found.

The art of bronze casting had been preserved in the Byzantine Empire. The first bronze doors to be made after the art had died out in Rome were those for Hagia Sophia at Constantinople, which bear the date 838; the panels, with monograms and other ornament damascened in silver, are framed in borders cast in relief and enriched with bosses and scrolls, the whole in an admirable style. Two sets of doors in St. Mark's, Venice, of Greek workmanship and considerable but uncertain antiquity, are supposed by some to have been removed from St. Mark's at Alexandria. Next in date among surviving doors of Byzantine workmanship is a series ordered by the Pantaleone family (about 1066–87) and destined for cities in southern Italy—Amalfi, Trani, Salerno, Canosa di Puglia, and Monte Sant'Angelo. (S.V.G.)

Middle Ages: Islām. Animals in the Sāsānian style—lions, dragons, sphinxes, peacocks, doves, cocks, and the like—were cast in bronze in three dimensions and served, like their ceramic counterparts, as basins, braziers, and so on. They were particularly sought after in the later Abbāsid, Fātimid, and Seljuq periods, and from Egypt they became prototypes of similar European forms. It was the Seljuqs, apparently, who introduced a round bronze mirror, the reverse of which shows in low relief two sphinxes face to face, surrounded by a twined pattern, or two friezes with the astrological symbols of the seven chief heavenly bodies (Sun, Moon, and the five nearest planets) and the 12 signs of the zodiac, surrounded by a band of script; this goes back ultimately to Chinese origins.

Early vessels, such as mugs, were ornamented with animals in low relief, but engraving quickly supplanted this. Under the later Seljuqs (particularly the Artuqid atabegs of Mosul) and the Mamlūks, engraving became almost the only form of decoration, but only to serve as a basis for the yet richer technique of inlaying, or damascening: small silver plates and wires, themselves delicately engraved, were hammered into the ribs and surfaces, which were hollowed out and undercut at the edges.

In place of this, in an Artuqid bowl in the provincial museum at Innsbruck the spaces are filled in with cellular enamel. This was a method of evading the prohibition of precious metals, just as gold lustre was in pottery. The ornament consisted of friezes and medallions in lattice work and arabesque work, the interstices being filled with figures of warriors, hunters, musicians, animals, and astrological symbols. These were superseded later by Mamlūk coats of arms and inscriptions. In the 15th century the technique was imported from Syria to Venice, where productions of the same kind, *alla damaschina* or *all'-azzimina*, were made right into the 16th century by Islāmic masters and were in great demand. In the East the process is still common, but both technically and artistically it has decayed.

In the 15th century there was a renaissance of pure metal engraving, but the design—inscriptions and arabesques in the Tīmūrid and Safavid styles—was not cut into the material but left free in the manner of a relief, the background being etched in black. Decoration was applied to bowls, basins, mugs, vases, mortars, braziers, warming pans, candlesticks, smoking utensils, inkstands, jewel cases, Qur'ān holders, and mosque lamps. These are generally in the simplest possible forms—spherical, cylindrical, prismatic; the subjects include motifs of vegetation and animal life, the former mainly in the necks and feet of vessels, the latter for handles and ears, feet, and sometimes small spouts. (H.Go.)

Europe from the Middle Ages. After several centuries of artistic decline, the art of bronze casting was revived in c. 800 by Charlemagne, who had monumental bronze portals made for the Palatine Chapel in his residence in Aachen, with bronze grilles placed inside it. The artists, who probably came from Lombardy, followed the styles of classical antiquity.

For many centuries the Christian Church remained the bronze caster's chief patron. Like the stonemasons, who also were heavily patronized by the church, they joined together to form associations, or foundries. These casting foundries hired themselves out to the large ecclesiastical

Margin notes:

Bronze doors

Engraving and inlaying

Revival of the art of bronze casting

building sites. They cast bells—almost every church had at least one bell—and monumental doors decorated with relief work; for instance, doors for Mainz (*c.* 1000) and Hildesheim (1015) cathedrals, for the cathedrals at Gneissen and Augsburg (11th century), and for St. Zeno Maggiore in Verona (12th century). They also made large fonts, the most famous being the one made by Reiner of Huy in 1107–18 for the church of Notre Dame aux Fonts in Liège (now in the church of St. Barthélemy in Liège). The Dinant workshops, which formed the main centre for bronze casting in the Meuse district in the Middle Ages, specialized in what are known as "eagle lecterns." These are book stands with ornamental pedestals, with the panel supporting the enormous missals taking the form of the outspread wings of an eagle, a griffin, or a pelican. The earliest documented eagle lectern was made in 965, but the earliest example to have survived dates from 1372. It was made by Jean Joses of Dinant for the Church of Our Lady at Tongeren (Tongres), near Liège.

Records show that from the 11th to the 15th century there were more than 50 monumental seven-branched candlesticks (menorah) in various churches in Germany, England, France, Bohemia, and Italy, though only a few of these have survived. Documents relating to the Carolingian period speak of monumental bronze crucifixes and statues of the Virgin and of the saints, though the earliest surviving statues date from the 11th century; the crucifix in the abbey church at Werden, for example, dates from *c.* 1060 and was probably cast in a foundry in Lower Saxony.

Among the most outstanding examples of figurative bronze sculpture dating from the Romanesque period are a group of reliquaries designed in the shape of heads or heads and shoulders or occasionally arms, hands, or feet, according to the type of relics they contain. They were made in Lower Saxony or in France.

A few large chandeliers have survived from the 11th and 12th centuries, representing a sort of halfway stage between sculpture and functional objects. A far larger number are known to have existed from documents and contemporary accounts, but these have disappeared over the centuries. Examples from Germany, the southern half of the Low Countries, and France have survived or are documented. Romanesque chandeliers are always designed in the form of a crown. Candleholders, with architectonic structures and figures placed in between them, project from the crown.

Besides the monumental bronzes that have survived from the 8th to the 12th century, there are also smaller pieces, such as processional crosses, altar crucifixes, chests, reliquaries, and similar articles. Another group of liturgical objects consists of candlesticks used to adorn altars. Their design often shows a wealth of invention, and they are decorated in the most sumptuous fashion. Yet another group of candlesticks, secular ones this time, embodies the ideal of chivalry. They are cast in the shape of human figures: an armed warrior on horseback bearing a candleholder with a spike on which the candle is placed; a kneeling page in court dress holding a candle socket in his outstretched hands; or Samson perched on the lion's back, brandishing a candleholder. These candlestick figures are rare and precious examples of courtly life in the Romanesque period in Germany, France, England, and Scandinavia. Even then they were thought of as rare, deluxe articles within the reach of only a few privileged people.

Toward the end of the Romanesque period a simpler type of candlestick appeared, mainly intended for religious purposes, though they were found in private homes as well. They are circular, with a round base, a slender column-like shaft, and a large grease pan with a spike for the candle. This design exercised a strong influence throughout the Gothic period and right down to the Baroque period, though it varied considerably over the years according to the styles then prevailing.

Some of the finest bronze articles of the High Middle Ages were modelled on Oriental pieces brought back from the Holy Land by the crusaders. They are known as aquamaniles, a type of ewer used for pouring water for washing one's hands. Made by bronze casters in France, Germany, England, and Scandinavia, they are usually in

By courtesy of the Metropolitan Museum of Art, New York, The Cloisters collection, purchase, 1947

Bronze aquamanile in the shape of a lion, German, 13th century. In the Metropolitan Museum of Art, New York. Height 26.7 cm.

the shape of lions—symbols of valour, pride, physical strength, and power. Also common are those shaped like knights in armour, with a wealth of courtly detail that was obviously popular. A few aquamaniles are in the shape of winged dragons, doves, cockerels, centaurs, or sirens; but such designs are rare. Christian themes, too, played a part, some examples depicting Samson overcoming the lion with his knee planted on its back. The golden age of these vessels was the 12th, 13th, and 14th centuries. The end of the age of chivalry also saw a decline in such work, for the emergent bourgeoisie found other ways of marking the ceremony of hand washing.

Basins were also needed for washing one's hands; they are often mentioned in medieval documents, where they are referred to as *bacina*, *pelves*, or *pelvicula*. The majority of these bowls—which date from the 12th and 13th centuries—have been found in the cultural area that extends from the Baltic down to the Lower Rhine district and across to England. Because this area was once dominated by the Hanseatic League (a commercial association of free towns), the basins are known as Hanseatic bowls. They are round, some being more convex than others; and the inside is engraved with scenes from classical mythology, with themes from the Old and New Testaments and the legends of the saints, or with allegorical figures personifying the virtues and the vices, the liberal arts, the seasons, and so on. Hanseatic bowls were probably made in the bronze-casting centres where candlesticks and aquamaniles (and indeed all medieval cast bronze) were made: in the Meuse district and Lorraine, in Lower Saxony and the Harz Mountains, and also in England. The decoration on these bowls may have been added elsewhere.

In the Romanesque period and later, in the Gothic period, the churches and their patrons were still the bronze caster's main clients, ordering both functional objects and decorative pieces. Bronze fonts were relatively common in the 14th and 15th centuries, particularly in churches in northern Germany. Another common item, which was made mainly in England and in the Netherlands, was a large brass tombstone decorated with engraving. Other objects included door fittings, candlesticks, candelabra, chandeliers, pulpits, and sculptured tombs portraying the deceased.

Italy. Until the 12th century in Italy the art of bronze casting had been virtually neglected since the period of classical antiquity, when it had been a flourishing industry. A few churches in Italy have bronze doors inlaid with

Candle-sticks

Aqua-maniles and basins

Byzantine niello work made by Byzantine craftsmen in the 11th and 12th centuries. The same technique was used by Bohemond I of Antioch for a bronze door at Canosa (1111) and by Oderisius of Benevento when casting a pair of doors for Troia Cathedral in 1119 and 1127. In the second half of the 12th century, however, Barisano da Trani made relief door panels for churches in Astrano, in Ravello (a town near Amalfi), and in Monreale. Bronze relief doors were also made in the 12th century for S. Paolo fuori le mura in Rome and for churches in northern Italy (S. Zeno Maggiore in Verona; St. Mark's in Venice) and Tuscany (Pisa and Monreale, by Bonanno of Pisa) and in the 13th century for the Baptistery in Florence, by Andrea Pisano.

Byzantine influence in Italy

Lorenzo Ghiberti's doors for the Baptistery in Florence, made in 1403–24 and 1425–52, marked the beginning of a golden age of bronze casting in Florence that lasted throughout the Renaissance and right down to the Baroque era. Whereas bronze sculpture had been relatively rare before the 15th century, many Italian artists of the Renaissance now designed cast bronze statues, statuettes, reliefs, and various objects in the shape of human figures. Among the sculptors who worked in full-scale bronzes were Lorenzo Ghiberti, Donatello, Andrea del Verrocchio, Antonio Pollaiuolo, and Lucca della Robbia. Besides large-scale cast-bronze work there were also small figures, statuettes, busts, plaques, and functional objects such as candelabra, mortars, candlesticks, and inkwells. Dating from the middle of the 15th century onward, they are characterized by rich figural and ornamental design. Their style influenced work produced in northern Europe, particularly in the 16th century.

In the first half of the 16th century, bronze casting

Alinari

"David," bronze sculpture by Donatello, *c.* 1430–35, In the Bargello 110, Florence. Height 1.58 m.
Anderson—Alinari

Alinari

Bronze doors from the north side of the Baptistery in Florence, by Lorenzo Ghiberti, *c.* 1403–24.

declined somewhat in Italy, though it found a new lease on life in the middle of the century and, indeed, became even more important than before. Benvenuto Cellini and Giovanni da Bologna are two of the most famous artists of this period. Cellini designed a number of statues, one of the best known being his "Perseus" in the Loggia dei Lanzi in Florence, as well as portrait busts, reliefs, and smaller articles in bronze. Giovanna da Bologna, a Fleming by birth, was active in Rome and Florence, where he made fountains, equestrian monuments, allegorical figures, crucifixes, statuettes, groups of figures, animals, and many other objects. He founded a school of sculptors who were influenced by his work for many years. Many other bronze sculptors were active in the 16th and 17th centuries, notably in Venice, which was a particularly fruitful area for bronze casting, and at a school in Padua led by Riccio Andrea (Briosco). Italian bronze casters worked abroad as well as in their homeland, working on commission for foreign potentates, mainly in France and England.

In the 16th century, beautifully made bronze pieces, which were very much more than functional objects, played an important part in the art of the bronze caster. For instance, sumptuous mortars were designed and made by artists whose names have been handed down to posterity, such as Cavadini, Lenotti, Juliano da Navi, Alessandro Leopardi, Antonio Viteni, and Crescimbeni da Perugia. Elaborate brass dishes were made in Venice, under the influence of Eastern art (to which Venice had always been very receptive); indeed, the first people to produce these large dishes with engraved motifs were Islāmic artists who had settled in the town, though the local artists soon adopted both their style and their technique.

Germany and the Low Countries. Unlike their Italian counterparts, 15th-century bronze artists in Germany and the Low Countries were still very much under the spell of Gothic art. Ecclesiastical implements predominated in this part of the world.

The Dinant workshops, in the Meuse district, continued to dominate production until well past the middle of the 15th century, just as they had since the days of Charlemagne. But when Philippe III le Bon, duke of Burgundy, laid siege to the town in 1466, then took it by storm and eventually completely destroyed it, the bronze casters who survived moved elsewhere, settling mainly in the Low Countries. As a result, from that date onward the trade enjoyed a sudden upsurge in Brussels and Namur, in Tournai and Bruges (Flemish Brugges), in Malines (Flemish Mechelen), Louvain (Flemish Leuven), and Middelburg. There was another centre of the bronze trade in Lower Saxony, since the mines in the Harz Mountains produced a generous supply of copper and calamine. The chief bronze-working towns in this area were Hildesheim, Goslar, and Minden. In the 16th century, a period when trade and commerce were developing very rapidly in Germany, the bronze-casting trade was no longer compelled to function close to the place where the raw material was extracted. Thus, Nürnberg, at this time the most powerful and lively town in Germany, not only traded in copper, bronze, and brass but also soon allowed its bronze casters and metalworkers to develop a flourishing industry. Brass articles from Nürnberg became famous throughout the world.

Nürnberg brass work

The earliest documented brass workers were those known as "basin-beaters" (*Beckenschläger*), who were first referred to as such in 1373. They made bowls and dishes with various types of relief decoration on the bottom. In the late Gothic period, religious themes were very

Brass dish with embossed Annunciation scene, German, *c.* 1500. In the Victoria and Albert Museum, London. Diameter 45 cm.

popular for this decoration and were more common than secular images. During the Renaissance, beginning in about 1520, the design changed; instead of deep bowls there were large, flat dishes with decoration that consists of purely ornamental motifs or friezes as well as scenes and figures. The decoration includes the typically Gothic "fishbladder" design and also interlaced motifs and bands of lettering. The trade of the basin beaters continued to flourish in Nürnberg down to about 1550, when a decline set in, culminating in its eventual collapse just before the Thirty Years' War in 1618. The reason for this decline may have been the emergence of what is known as display pewter (see below *Pewter*), which, from about 1570 onward, swept the wealthy bourgeoisie market.

Until the Gothic era, bronze chandeliers were made solely for the churches; it was not until the 15th century

Bronze chandelier, Dutch, 15th century. In the Rijksmuseum, Amsterdam. Height 1.09 m.
By courtesy of the Rijksmuseum, Amsterdam

that people began to consider lighting their homes by means of a central source of light hanging from the ceiling. In the Low Countries, one of the centres of the art of bronze casting, a type of chandelier was developed at this time that remained standard for many years. It is a type of hoop with a shaft, made up of a molded vertical centrepiece and a series of curving branches bearing drip trays and spikes. The arms, or branches, are decorated with tracery, foliage scrolls, and other motifs characteristic of the late Gothic style. In the middle of the 16th century, the central shaft took on the shape of a spherical baluster, with a large sphere jutting out just below the point where the curving arms branch off. This design continued to predominate in the Baroque period and is found as late as the 18th century. Because chandeliers of this type were most common in the Low Countries, one can assume that they originated there and were produced in large numbers and that they spread to England and Germany. Another centre was in Poland, presumably because brass founders had moved there from Nürnberg.

Besides these chandeliers—which until the 19th century were exclusive to court circles, the aristocracy, and the upper ranks of the bourgeoisie—there were also candlesticks. Their design was a later development of that used for altar candlesticks. The principle of a disk-shaped foot and a baluster shaft with a spike on top remained standard from the Middle Ages well into the 19th century, though the design of the individual components was affected by the styles current in any particular period. In Dinant and Flanders in the 15th century, for instance, the shaft began to be fashioned into the shape of a human figure. This style also became popular in Germany at the end of the century.

Whereas bronze sculpture reached its peak in Italy in the 15th century, monumental bronze figures were still rare in northern Europe at this time. Thus, the full-length equestrian statue of St. George (1373) on Hradčany Castle in Prague, which was cast by Martin and Georg von Klausenberg, did not set a trend, though rich figure decoration is often found on large fonts dating

Bronze effigy of Henry III, by William Torel, 13th century. In Westminster Abbey, London.
Length 1.50 m.
J.R. Freeman & Co. Ltd.

from the 13th to the 15th century. Engraved tombstones and entire tombs based on earlier traditions continued to be made until the late Gothic era (the beginning of the 16th century), as did tabernacles and lecterns.

The intellectual content of the Renaissance and the styles it engendered entered the world of the northern sculptors in the second decade of the 16th century. The Nürnberg workshop run by the Vischer family, which had been flourishing since the 15th century, continued to work in the late Gothic style until it had completed the St. Sebald's Shrine (1516), but shortly after this the style and intellectual concepts current in Italy were adopted by bronze casters in northern art centres as well. Small-scale bronze sculpture was particularly popular at this time, though some workshops were still casting monumental bronzes as late as the 18th century.   (H.-U.H.)

England. Casting in bronze reached high perfection in England during the Middle Ages. The most remarkable of the sanctuary rings, or knockers, that exist at Norwich and elsewhere is that on the north door of the nave of Durham cathedral, from the first half of the 12th century. **The Gloucester candlestick**, in the Victoria and Albert Museum, London, displays the power and imagination of the designer as well as an extraordinary manipulative skill on the part of the founder. According to its inscription, this candlestick, which stands about two feet (60 centimetres) high and is cast in bell metal and gilded, was made for Abbot Peter (the cathedral was originally an abbey church), who ruled early in the 12th century. While the outline is carefully preserved, the ornament consists of a mass of figures of monsters, birds, and men, mixed and intertwined to the verge of confusion. As a piece of casting, it is a triumph of technique.

There remain in England 10 effigies cast in bronze over a period of two centuries (1290–1518), among them some of the finest examples of figure work and metal casting to be found in Europe. In several instances, particulars for the contracts of the tombs survive, together with the names of the artists who designed and made them. The earliest examples are the effigies of Queen Eleanor, wife of Edward I (1290), and that of Henry III (1291), both in Westminster Abbey. They are the work of William Torel, goldsmith of London; and it is evident that they are the first English attempt to produce large figures in metal. Torel cast his large figures by the same process (lost-wax) he had employed for small shrines and images.

Monumental brasses were exceedingly numerous in England, where some 4,000 still exist. From the 13th through the 16th centuries, in France, northern Germany, Belgium, and particularly England, it became the vogue to set into the stone slab covering a floor tomb a brass plate engraved with the figure of the deceased. The art began in Flanders and Germany, and many of the English brasses were of foreign origin; in some cases, brass sheets were imported and engraved by English artists. The manufacture of unornamented brass plates centred chiefly at Cologne. The oldest English brass in existence is that of Sir John D'Abernon (died 1277) at

Stoke d'Abernon, Surrey. Traces can still be seen in many brasses of the colours that originally enlivened them.
(S.V.G.)

France. In France, bronze was common from the late 16th century through the 17th, 18th, and 19th centuries, and it is still popular with French sculptors today. Eighteenth-century artists made use of ormulu, or fire gilding, for bronze articles such as candlesticks, brackets, and mounts for furniture. This tradition continued in France and, to a lesser extent, in the areas under French influence, until the Empire period in the early 19th century. Subdued classical designs executed in simple brass or in bronze, generally ungilded, are typical of the period following the reign of Napoleon.

The second quarter of the 19th century and, with it, the onset of industrialization, brought about a decline in bronze casting, as it did in all spheres of craftsmanship. The age of steel production now began. At the end of the 19th century, during the Art Nouveau period, attempts were made to revive the craft of casting bronze articles; but these did not have any lasting success. Bronze continued to be used by a few individual sculptors, however, throughout the 19th century and into the present day.
(H.-U.H.)

SILVER AND GOLD

Antiquity. *Pre-Mycenaean.* Gold and silver and their natural or artificial mixture, called electrum or white gold, were worked in ancient Greece and Italy for personal ornaments, vessels, arrows and weapons, coinage, and inlaid and plated decoration of baser metals.

Aegean lands were rich in precious metals. The considerable deposits of treasure found in the earliest prehistoric strata on the site of Troy are not likely to be later than 2000 BC. The largest of them, called Priam's Treasure, is a representative collection of jewels and plate. Packed in a large silver cup were gold ornaments consisting of elaborate diadems or pectorals, six bracelets, 60 earrings or hair rings, and nearly 9,000 beads. Trojan vases have bold and simple forms, mostly without ornament; but some are lightly fluted. Many are wrought from single sheets of metal. The characteristic handle is a heavy rolled loop, soldered or rivetted to the body. Bases are sometimes round or pointed, sometimes fitted with separate collars but more often slightly cupped to make a low ring foot. One oddly shaped vessel in gold is an oval bowl or cup with a broad lip at each end and two large roll handles in the middle. The oval body has Sumerian affinities. A plain, spouted bowl in the Louvre is a typical specimen of goldsmith's work from pre-Mycenaean Greece. The scarcity of precious metals points to lack of wealth as prime cause of the artistic backwardness of these regions. Silver seems to have been more plentiful in the Greek islands; but only a few simple vessels, headbands, pins, and rings survive.

Minoan and Mycenaean. A profusion of gold jewelry was found in early Minoan burials at Mókhlos and three silver dagger blades in a communal tomb at Kumasa. Silver seals and ornaments of the same age are not uncommon. An elegant silver cup from Gournia belongs to

The Gloucester candlestick

French ormulu

Trojan vases

Mycenaean gold cup, the so-called Nestor's cup, decorated with birds on handles, from the royal graves at Mycenae, Greece, *c.* 1600–1500 BC. In the National Archaeological Museum, Athens. Height, excluding handles, 14.5 cm.
Alison Frantz

the next epoch (Middle Minoan I, *c.* 2000 BC). Numerous imitations of its conical and carinated (ridged) form in clay and of its metallic sheen in glazed and painted decoration prove that such vessels were common. Minoan plate and jewelry are amply represented in the wealth of mainland tombs at Mycenae and Vaphio. The vases from Mycenae are made indifferently of silver, gold, and bronze; but drinking cups, small phials, and boxes are generally made only of gold; and jugs are made of silver. Much funeral furniture is gold, notably masks that hid the faces or adorned the coffins of the dead. It has been thought that small gold disks, found in prodigious quantities (700 in one grave), were nailed on wooden coffins; but they may have been sewn on clothes. They are impressed with geometrical designs based on circular and spiral figures, stars and rosettes, and natural forms such as leaves, butterflies, and octopods. Smaller bossed disks bearing similar patterns may be button covers. Models of shrines and other amulets are also made of gold. A splendid piece of plate is a silver counterpart of a black steatite, or soapstone, libation vase from Knossos in the form of a bull's head, with gold horns, a gold rosette on the forehead, and gold-plated muzzle, ears, and eyes. (The gold here and in other Mycenaean plating is not laid on the silver but on inserted copper strips.)

Funeral furniture

Gold cups from Mycenae are of two main types: plain curved or carinated forms related to the silverware and pottery of Troy and embossed conical vessels of the Minoan tradition. Some of the plain pieces, such as the so-called Nestor's cup (National Archaeological Museum, Athens), have handles ending in animals, which bite the rim or peer into the cup. The embossed ornament consists of vertical and horizontal bands of rosettes and spiral coils and of floral, foliate, marine, and animal figures. The designs are beaten through the walls and are consequently visible on the insides of most of the vessels; but the finest examples of their class, two gold cups (National Archaeological Museum, Athens) from the Vaphio tomb near Sparta, have a plain gold lining that overlaps the embossed sides at the lip. The reliefs on the Vaphio cups represent men handling wild and domesticated cattle among trees in a rocky landscape. (Steatite vases carved with similar pictorial reliefs were evidently made to imitate embossed gold.) The handles show the typical Minoan form: two horizontal plates rivetted to the body at one end and joined at the other by a vertical cylinder.

Weapons

Cretan and mainland tombs have produced many examples of weapons adorned with gold. Modest ornaments are gold caps on the rivets that join hilt and blade, but the whole hilt is often cased in gold. An example from Mycenae has a cylindrical grip of openwork gold flowers with lapis lazuli in their petals and crystal filling between them; the guard is formed by dragons, similarly inlaid. The most splendid Mycenaean blades are bronze inlaid with gold, electrum, silver, and niello. Here again the work is done on inserted copper plates. This kind of flat inlay seems to have been originally Egyptian; it occurs on daggers from the tomb of Queen Aah-Hotep, which are contemporary with the Mycenaean (*c.* 1600 BC). Moreover, it is significant that two of the Mycenaen designs have Egyptian subjects (cats hunting ducks among papyrus clumps beside a river in which fish are swimming), though their style is purely Minoan. Another blade bears Minoan warriors fighting lions and lions chasing deer. A dagger from Thira has inlaid ax heads; one from Argos, dolphins; and fragments from the Vaphio tomb show men swimming among flying fish. These are masterpieces of Minoan craftsmanship. In the long, subsequent decadence of the Mycenaean age, however, there seems to have been no invention, and later pieces of goldsmiths' work repeat conventional forms and ornaments. (E.J.F./M.C.R.)

Iran. The Persians have been skillful metalworkers since the Achaemenid period (559–330 BC), when they were already acquainted with various techniques such as chasing, embossing, casting, and setting with precious stones. Statuettes of gold and silver are known from the 5th century BC, and vessels of silver and gold from this time take the form of phials, conical cups, vases, and rhyta (drinking cups in the shape of an animal's head). The Oxus treasure in the British Museum and the Susa find in the Louvre, Paris, are good examples of such work. During the Parthian period (247 BC–AD 224), silverwork and goldwork was strongly influenced by Hellenistic predilection for richly decorated bowls and dishes. The zenith of old Iranian metalwork, however, was reached during the Sāsānid period (AD 224–651), when craftsmen achieved great variety in shape, decoration, and technique. Drinking vessels (stem cups and cups with handles), ewers, oval dishes, platters, and bowls are the dominant forms; hunting scenes, drinking scenes, and

Sāsānid craftsmanship

Persian embossed silver bowl showing a king slaying lions, Sāsānid period *c.* AD 224–651. In the British Museum. Diameter 24.1 cm.
By courtesy of the trustees of the British Museum

animals are represented in high relief. The patterns were cut out of solid silver or made separately in sheets and then soldered to the vessel. From this time onward cloisonné enamel was used for jewelry. (B.V.Gy.)

Greek and Etruscan. The period of transition from the Bronze to the Iron Age, when Aegean external relations were violently interrupted, was not favourable either to wealth or art; and the only considerable pieces of plate that have come from Greece are embossed and engraved silver bowls made by Phoenicians. Most of them bear elaborate pictorial designs of Egyptian or Assyrian character and are evidently foreign to Greece; but some simpler types, decorated with rows of animals in relief or wrought in the shape of conventional flower bowls, can hardly be distinguished from the first Hellenic products.

A severe and elegant silver bowl in the Metropolitan Museum of Art represents the flower type in its finest style. It is cast and chased and probably belongs to the 5th century BC.

Silver vases and toilet articles have been found beside the more common bronze in Etruscan tombs; for example, a chased powder box of the 4th century BC in the Metropolitan Museum of Art. Bronze reliefs of an archaic chariot in the same collection have their opulent counterparts in some hammered silver and electrum fragments in London, Munich, and Perugia. The electrum details are attached with rivets.

Roman silver relief

Roman. About the 4th century BC, the fashion of ornamenting silver vessels with relief was revived; and this type of work, elaborated in the Hellenistic Age and particularly at Antioch and Alexandria, remained the usual mode of decoration for silver articles until the end of the Roman Empire.

The scholar Pliny the Elder (1st century AD) names Greek silversmiths whose work was valued highly at Rome and laments the disappearance of the art in his own day. He must refer only to its quality, for Roman silverware has been abundantly preserved. Many rich hoards in modern collections were buried by design during the calamitous last centuries of the ancient world; and the most sumptuous, the Boscoreale treasure (mostly in

Roman silver pitcher, from the villa at Boscoreale, near Pompeii, Italy, *c.* 1st century BC. In the Louvre, Paris. Height 25 cm.

the Louvre), was accidentally saved by the same volcanic catastrophe that destroyed Herculaneum and killed Pliny in AD 79. A slightly smaller hoard found at Hildesheim (now in Berlin) also belongs to the early empire. The acquisition and appreciation of silver plate was a sort of cult in Rome. Technical names for various kinds of reliefs were in common use (*emblemata, sigilla, crustae*); weights were recorded and compared and ostentatiously exaggerated. Large quantities of bullion came to Rome with the spoils of Greece and Asia in the 2nd century BC; and Pliny says that even in republican times there were more than 150 silver dishes of a hundredweight apiece in the city. (Weights of vessels are often marked on their bases.)

Cups and jugs

Cups and jugs of Augustan style are usually covered with ornament in high relief. The subjects are very diverse: historical, mythological, and mystic scenes, formal and naturalistic designs of flowers and foliage, graceful studies of animals and birds. Some cups and jugs have conventional fluting, petals, or gadroons (ornamental

bands embellished with continuous patterns, such as beading); Bacchic masks; and embossed or engraved wreaths, gilt or inlaid with niello. Silver and niello inlay was commonly applied to bronze plates. A singular type of silver bowl (*patera clipeata*) has a central ornament in high relief or even in the round; the ornament frequently contains a portrait bust. In the course of time the ornament was restricted; and later Roman plate is largely plain with narrow border friezes, small central medallions, and handles embossed in low relief. One of the very few gold pieces that survive, a shallow bowl found at Rennes (Bibliothèque Nationale), is exceedingly elaborate. It measures 10 inches (25 centimetres) across and weighs 46 ounces (1,315 grams). The central medallion and its surrounding frieze contain scenes of a drinking contest between Bacchus and Hercules; between the frieze and the edge of the bowl is a row of 16 gold coins, each framed in a foliate wreath. The coins range from Hadrian to Caracalla. In the same collection are several examples of very large silver plates (*clipei* or *missoria*), in which the whole field is embossed with mythological or historical subjects. The largest (called the Shield of Scipio) is 28 inches (72 centimetres) in diameter and weighs 363 ounces (10,300 grams).   (E.J.F./M.C.R.)

Early Christian and Byzantine. The earliest Christian silverwork closely resembles the pagan work of the period in its naturalistic grace, ornament, and use of the traditional techniques of embossing and chasing. Even the subject matter is sometimes classical: the late-4th-century marriage casket of Projecta and Secondus, part of the Esquiline treasure found at Rome (British Museum), is decorated with pagan scenes; and only the inscription shows that it was made for a Christian marriage. Among the few pieces with Christian subjects are small Roman cruets (condiment bottles) from Taprain, Scotland (Royal Scottish Museum, Edinburgh, and the British Museum), and a small pyx (casket for the reserved Host) from Pula, Yugoslavia (Kunsthistorisches Museum, Vienna).

Most of the silver of the latter part of the period has been found in the Christian East—in Syria, Egypt, Cyprus, Asia Minor, and Russia—and is mostly "church" plate (chalices, censers, candlesticks, and bowls and dishes probably used to hold the eucharistic bread). Secular plate was also decorated with religious subjects—for example, dishes depicting the life of David (Cyprus Treasure, Cyprus Museum, Nicosia, and Metropolitan Museum); both dishes and vessels were produced with pagan subjects—for example, the Concesti amphora and the Silenus Dish (both in the Hermitage, Leningrad). The figure style is often harder and flatter than previously, characterized by strictly frontal positions and symmetry. The techniques of chasing and embossing still predominated, but abstract patterns and Christian symbols inlaid in niello were used increasingly. The appearance of imperial "control stamps," early forerunners of hallmarks, show most of this material to be of the 6th and 7th centuries. It is not known which cities were important centres of production; but the Eastern capital, Constantinople, must have been foremost among them.

Early Christian marriage casket of Projecta and Secondus, embossed silver, partially gilded, from the Esquiline treasure, Rome, *c.* 400. In the British Museum. Length 60.33 cm.

Of work in gold of the earliest Christian period, only personal jewelry has survived; but from the 6th and 7th centuries onward other pieces are also extant. Among the most important of the latter are votive crowns and crosses offered to churches in Spain and Italy by royal patrons. The finest of these pieces are those found in Guarrazar in Toledo Province (National Archaeological Museum, Madrid, and Musée de Cluny, Paris), inlaid with garnets and jewels; the cross of King Agilulf (cathedral of Monza, Italy); and a pair of gold book covers inscribed by Queen Theodelinda (cathedral of Monza, Italy). The book covers are set with pearls, gems, and cameos and decorated with gold cloisonné work inlaid with garnets, a popular style among the Germanic peoples. Inlaid cloisonné jewelry reached an especially high standard of workmanship in Britain, as is shown by a purse lid, a sword, and jewelry from the cenotaph (monument honouring a dead person whose body lies elsewhere) to a 7th-century East Anglian king discovered at Sutton Hoo, Suffolk (British Museum). Major works in silver and gold were also produced in the northern Hiberno-Saxon school and in the service of the Celtic Church; work in precious metal, such as the buckle on the Moylough belt reliquary and the Ardagh Chalice in the National Museum of Ireland, Dublin, displays a masterly synthesis of the northern arts and humanist Mediterranean tradition.

Middle Ages. *Carolingian and Ottonian.* The earliest works of the Carolingian renaissance, made in the last quarter of the 8th century, resemble Hiberno-Saxon art of the 8th century in their abstract treatment of the human figure, their animal ornament, and their use of niello and "chip-carving" technique; examples are the Tassilo Chalice (Kremsmünster Abbey, Austria) and the Lindau Gospels book cover (Pierpont Morgan Library, New York City). From about 800 onward, however, the influence of the Mediterranean tradition gained strength at Charlemagne's court at Aachen and later spread through the whole empire. Triumphal arches (now lost) given by the Emperor's biographer Einhard to Maastricht cathedral were typical of this movement; miniature versions nine inches (22 centimetres) high of great marble triumphal arches of antiquity, they were embossed in silver with Christian subjects. The bulk of work in precious metals that survives from the Middle Ages is ecclesiastical: golden altars, like that of S. Ambrogio in Milan (*c.* 850), where scenes from the life of Christ and St. Ambrose are framed by panels of cloisonné enamel and filigree (openwork); and reliquaries and book covers in gold and silver, set with gems and decorated by embossed figures and scenes, such as the cover of the Codex Aureus of St. Emmeram (*c.* 870; Bayerische Staatsbibliothek, Munich). These pieces testify to the magnificence of Carolingian work, the techniques of which were to dominate the goldsmith's craft until the 11th century.

Patronage throughout this period was mainly in the hands of the emperors and great princes of the church; and the form of liturgical plate and reliquaries, altar crosses, and the like underwent no fundamental change; Ottonian work of the later 10th and 11th centuries can be distinguished from that of the 9th only in the development of style. For example, the larger, more massive figures, with their strict pattern of folds, on the golden altar (*c.* 1023) given by Henry II to Basel Minster (Musée de Cluny, Paris), are markedly different from the nervous, elongated figures of the Carolingian period.

Romanesque. In the 12th century the church supplanted secular rulers as the chief patron of the arts, and the work was carried out in the larger monasteries. Under the direction of such great churchmen as Henry, bishop of Winchester, and Abbot Suger of Saint-Denis, near Paris, a new emphasis was given to subject matter and symbolism.

Craftsmen were no longer anonymous; work by Roger of Helmarshausen, Reiner of Huy, Godefroid de Claire (de Huy), Nicholas of Verdun, and others can be identified; and the parts they played as leaders of the great centres of metalwork on the Rhine and the Meuse are recognizable. Their greatest achievement was the development of the brilliant champlevé enamelling, a method

that replaced the earlier cloisonné technique. Gold and silver continued to be used as rich settings for enamels; as the framework of portable altars, or small devotional diptychs or triptychs; for embossed figure work in reliquary shrines; and for liturgical plate.

The masterpieces of the period are great house-shaped shrines made to contain the relics of saints; for example, the shrine of St. Heribert at Deutz (*c.* 1160) and Nicholas of Verdun's Shrine of the Three Kings at Cologne (*c.* 1200). In the latter, the figures are almost freestanding, and in their fine, rhythmic draperies and naturalistic movement they approach the new Gothic style.

Gothic. The growing naturalism of the 13th century is notable in the work of Nicholas' follower Hugo d'Oignies, whose reliquary for the rib of St. Peter at Namur (1228) foreshadows the partly crystal reliquaries in which the freestanding relic is exposed to the view of the faithful; it is decorated with Hugo's particularly fine filigree and enriched by naturalistic cutout leaves and little cast animals and birds.

The increasing wealth of the royal courts, of the aristocracy, and, later, of the merchants led to the establishment of secular workshops in the great cities and the foundation of confraternities, or guilds, of goldsmiths and silversmiths, the first being that of Paris in 1202.

As in architecture, monumental sculpture, and ivory carving, the lead held by Germany and the Low Countries during the Romanesque period now passed to France. Architectural forms continued to be the basis of design in precious metal; the silver shrine of St. Taurin at Évreux (*c.* 1250), for example, is a Gothic chapel in miniature, with saints under pointed arches, clustered columns, and small turrets. In England, the few pieces that survived the dissolution of the monasteries in the 16th century follow the same architectural pattern. Notable examples are the 14th-century Ramsey Abbey censer

Shrines and reliquaries [margin]

Crown Copyright. Victoria and Albert Museum, London

Ramsey Abbey censer, cast, embossed, and gilt silver, English Gothic, 14th century. In the Victoria and Albert Museum, London. Height 27.6 cm.

(Victoria and Albert Museum) and the magnificent crosier made for William of Wykeham (New College, Oxford). Germany first produced work in the Gothic style in the second half of the 14th century with a large Gothic head reliquary of Charlemagne and the splendid "Three-Tower" reliquary, both still at Aachen. In Italy, despite the undercurrent of classical taste, the Gothic style predominated in the 14th century, especially at Siena; it was also probably in Italy around 1280 that basse-taille enamel—a technique in which intaglio relief

Ecclesiastical work [margin]

Basse-taille enamel [margin]

carving in the metal below its surface is filled with translucent enamel—originated, whence it spread rapidly through the upper Rhine region to France and England. The Parisian school of enamellers predominated in the latter half of the 14th century. For the first time, enough secular plate survives to show that it equalled the ecclesiastical in opulence: two fine pieces are the Royal Gold Cup made in Paris around 1380 (British Museum) and the so-called King John's Cup, probably English work of around 1340 (King's Lynn, Norfolk).

The late Gothic period produced court treasures such as the "Goldenes Rössel" (1403; Stiftskirche, Altötting, West Germany), and the Thorn reliquary (British Museum), both early 15th century. There was also an increased output of secular silver because of the rise of the middle classes; the English mazers (wooden drinking bowls with silver mounts) and the silver spoons with a large variety of finials are examples of this more modest plate. Numerous large reliquaries and altar plate of all kinds were still produced. At the end of the Middle Ages the style of these pieces and of secular plate developed more distinctive national characteristics, strongly influenced by architectural style: in England, by the geometric patterns of the Perpendicular; in Germany, by heavy and bizarre themes of almost Baroque exuberance; and in France, by the fragile elegance of the Flamboyant.

"Hall-marking"

The purity standards of silver became rigorously controlled, and "hallmarking" was enforced; the marking of silver in England, especially, was carefully observed.

(P.E.L.)

Islām. The use of gold and silver in Islāmic lands was limited because it was forbidden by the Qur'ān, and although the prohibition was often ignored, the great value of such objects led to their early destruction and melting down. Islāmic jewelry of the early period is therefore of extreme rarity, represented only by a few items, such as buckles and bracelets of the Fātimid and Mongol periods and such pieces as the Gerona silver chest (akin to similar ivory coffers) in Spain and the Berlin silver tankard of the 13th century, with embossed reliefs of Sāsānian animal friezes. (H.Go.)

Renaissance to modern. *16th century.* Italian goldsmiths preceded the rest of Europe in reverting to the style of Roman antiquity; but in the absence of antique goldsmiths' work, vases of marble or bronze had to serve as models. Goldsmiths often worked from very free interpretations of the antique made by artists in other media. Many of these designs but very few of the actual pieces have survived; the most famous is an enamelled gold saltcellar (Kunsthistorisches Museum, Vienna) made for Francis I by the celebrated Florentine Benvenuto Cellini. In the second half of the 16th century many gifted Italian and immigrant goldsmiths worked at the court of Cosimo I, grand duke of Tuscany, specializing in vessels of hardstone mounted in enamelled and jewelled gold; their work is well represented in the Museo degli Argenti in the Pitti Palace, Florence, and in the Kunsthistorisches Museum; similar work was done by the Sarachi family in Milan.

Little French goldwork is extant, and most of the surviving material is in the Galerie d'Apollon in the Louvre. Among the most sumptuous pieces are a sardonyx (a type of onyx) and gold ewer, the gold St. Michael's Cup (both at the Kunsthistorisches Museum), and a sardonyx-covered cup in the Louvre, all of which display northern features. The massive plate of the Ordre du Saint-Esprit (Louvre), dating from 1581–82, is of quite individual character; and an enamelled gold helmet and shield of Charles IX (1560–74) in the Louvre have no parallel either for quality or opulence.

In other parts of Europe, goldsmiths clung to Gothic forms until well into the first half of the century, especially in the provincial towns. Immensely rich in ecclesiastical silver, Spain has little early domestic silver; Spanish silversmiths, *platería,* gave their name to the heavily ornamented style of the period, Plateresque. Using precious metal from the New World, goldsmiths such as Enrique and Juan de Arfe produced vast containers for the Host

Spanish and Portuguese goldsmiths

Custodia of goldwork, silverwork, and enamel work (1515–23), by Enrique de Arfe. In the Toledo Cathedral, Spain. Height 2.50 m.
Archivo Mas, Barcelona

known as *custodia.* The most important Portuguese work, the Belém monstrance, or container for the Host, created by Gil Vicente in 1506 for Belém Monastery near Lisbon, is still Gothic in style; later, Portugal developed its own style, related to Spanish work but not copied from it.

Some of the finest 16th-century goldsmiths' work was executed in Antwerp and elsewhere by such Flemish goldsmiths as Hans of Antwerp, goldsmith to Henry VIII, and Jacopo Delfe, called Biliverti, goldsmith to Cosimo I. The Flemish masters showed particular sympathy for the Mannerist style, derived from Italy but transformed by such native engravers as Cornelis Bos and Cornelis Floris. By about 1580, Dutch goldsmiths had begun to rival the Flemish; the van Vianen family of Utrecht won international renown, especially Adam, who excelled at embossing, and his brother Paulus, who worked in Italy, Munich, and in the workshop of Rudolph II at Prague.

The principal centres in the north were Nürnberg and Augsburg, the former particularly notable for the exuberant Mannerism of the Jamnitzer family, the latter for its ebony caskets with silver-gilt mounts. Many German princes, especially the dukes of Bavaria, maintained their own court workshops. Production was on a vast scale, and great quantities survive. Characteristic German forms are columbine cups (the trial piece for entry into the Nürnberg Goldsmith's Guild) and standing cups such as the Diana Cup (*c.* 1610; Kunstgewerbemuseum, West Berlin) by Hans Petzolt.

England is rich in 16th-century secular silver, but

Diana Cup, silver standing cup by Hans Petzolt, Nürnberg, c. 1610. In the Kunstgewerbemuseum, West Berlin. Height 80.01 cm.
By courtesy of the Kunstgewerbemuseum, West Berlin

church plate was mostly destroyed during the Reformation. The Renaissance style, introduced by the painter Hans Holbein the Younger, who designed vessels for the court, follows that of the Low Countries and Germany. Certain individual forms also were produced, such as standing saltcellars with tiered covers and "steeple" cups, which had a tall finial on the cover.

Baroque. In the first half of the 17th century Dutch goldsmiths, such as the van Vianens and, later, Johannes Lutma the Elder of Amsterdam, developed a fleshy form of ornament known as auricular, which became common in northern Europe, including England—where Christian van Vianen worked as court goldsmith to Charles I—and Germany—where the Thirty Years' War (1618–48) reduced both the quantity and quality of production. After midcentury, bold Dutch floral ornament—usually embossed in thin metal, as though the pieces were for display rather than use—was characteristic and influential. France, however, undoubtedly led fashion with its state workshops at the Gobelins, the refined French acanthus ornament contrasting sharply with the coarser Dutch designs. Since Louis XIV melted the royal plate to pay his troops, no French work of this period remains; but its quality is demonstrated in the work of the Huguenot silversmiths who left France after the revocation of the Edict of Nantes in 1685. Mostly provincials, they brought new standards of taste and craftsmanship wherever they settled—particularly in England, where the foremost names of the late 17th and earlier 18th centuries were of French origin: Pierre Harache, Pierre Platel, David Willaume, Simon Pantin, Paul de Lamerie, Paul Crespin, to mention but a few.

Silver furniture | Silver furniture, a feature of the state rooms at Versailles, became fashionable among kings and noblemen. It was constructed of silver plates attached to a wooden frame; and each suite contained a dressing table, a looking glass, and a pair of candlestands. In France such furniture did not survive the Revolution; but much remains in England, Denmark, Germany, and Russia.

After the Thirty Years' War, Germany did not regain its eminence; even the enamelled goldwork from the court workshops at Prague and Munich, which became larger and more ostentatious in colour, was inferior in design and finish. In Scandinavia, particularly Sweden, goldsmiths evolved forms of beakers and tankards showing strong German influence. Spanish silver was of massive architectural design, oval champlevé enamelled bosses being set at intervals over the surface of the larger pieces. The few extant Italian pieces suggest that the goldsmiths worked their material with the skill of sculptors.

18th century. Early 18th-century English work combined functional simplicity with grace of form, while the work of Dutch and German goldsmiths is in a similar style but of less pleasing proportions. The pre-eminence of the English work, however, is due to the destruction of all but a fraction of French silver of the same period; for what survives is outstanding in originality of design and fineness of finish. The superiority of French work lay in its excellence of design and the high quality of the cast and chased work. Where other goldsmiths worked in embossed metal, the French modelled and cast their ornament and then applied it—a technique that consumed much more of the precious material. | Superiority of French work

In France, provincial goldsmiths competed successfully with those of the capital; but in England all the best artists went to London. In the early 1730s the French Rococo style was imported to England and adopted by goldsmiths of both Huguenot and English descent, one of the latter being Thomas Heming, goldsmith to George III. English silver in the 18th-century classical style of Robert and James Adam is of unequal merit owing to the use of industrial methods by some large producers.

In France, Robert Auguste created pieces of great refinement in the Neoclassical style, which was copied in Turin and in Rome, for example, by L. Valadini. A notable workshop was founded in Madrid in 1778 by D. Antonio Martínez, who favoured severely classical designs. In both the northern and southern Netherlands, local production followed French precept, but more individuality survived in Germany. In Augsburg, excellent table silver was produced, but more important were the pictorial panels embossed in the highest relief by members of the Thelot family and the silver furniture made by the Billers and the Drentwetts. At Dresden, Augustus II the Strong established under Johann Melchior Dinglinger a court workshop that produced jewels and enamelled goldwork unequalled since the Renaissance; and the gold snuffboxes made by Johann Christian Neuber rivalled those of the Parisian goldsmiths. (J.F.Ha.)

Colonial America. Silversmithing in the New World in the colonial period is more or less derivative from Europe and England. In North America it was first brought to New England by English craftsmen in the 17th century. The most important centres were Boston, Newport, New York City, Philadelphia, Baltimore, and Annapolis. Outstanding collections include the Mabel Brady Garvan collection at Yale University and those in the Boston Museum of Fine Arts, the American Wing of the Metropolitan Museum of Art, and in the Philadelphia Museum of Art. North American colonial silver is distinguished for its simplicity and graceful forms, copied or adapted from English silver of the period. On the other hand, the colonial silver of Mexico, Brazil, Colombia, Peru, Chile, and Bolivia, while European in concept, shows a blending of Iberian designs and forms, with indigenous influences that trace back to pre-Hispanic times. Most of these relics survive in churches as sacramental vessels; but there are some notable private collections. | Colonial silver of Mexico and Central and South America

(D.T.E.)

19th century. The Napoleonic adventure brought French fashions back into prominence, and the Empire style was widely followed on the Continent. In England the Regency goldsmiths, of whom Paul Storr was the foremost, created their own more robust version of the Empire style. Perhaps the most impressive monument of the period is a service made in Lisbon between 1813 and 1816 and presented to the Duke of Wellington for his liberation of Portugal (now in Apsley House, London).

English silver tureen with the Cavendish arms by Paul Storr, 1820–21. In the Chatsworth House, Derbyshire, England. Height 49 cm.

Silver and gold work

Book cover of the Lindau Gospels (MS. 644, fol. 115v), chased gold with pearls and precious stones, Carolingian, c. 870. In the Pierpont Morgan Library, New York City. 27 × 35 cm.

Persian vase in the form of a fish, gold sheet decorated with incised lines, details of eyes and mouth in repoussée, Achaemenid period, 5th–4th century BC. In the British Museum. Length 24.2 cm.

Mask of Xipe Totec, gold, cast by the "lost-wax" method, Mixtec culture, c. 900–1494. In the Museo Regionale, Oaxaca, Mexico. Height 7 cm.

Furniture in the king's bedroom, Knole House, Kent, England, silver on wood, 17th century. Height of table 61 cm.

Plate 2   Metalwork

Copper, bronze, and brass

Celtic bronze shield, originally gilt, 2nd century AD. In the British Museum. Height 78 cm.

Nepalese statue of Krsna, gilded bronze with turquoise and gems, 18th century. In the Prince of Wales Museum of Western India, Bombay.

Egyptian bronze plaque damascened with gold wire, 22nd dynasty (945–c. 730 BC). In the Metropolitan Museum of Art, New York City. Length 19 cm.

The Chimera of Arezzo, bronze, Etruscan, 4th century BC. In the Museo Archeologico, Florence. Height 80 cm.

Chinese bronze *chung*, late Chou dynasty
(*c.* 1122–221 BC). In the Freer Gallery of Art,
Washington, D.C. Height 67 cm.

Cast bronze baptismal font by Renier de Huy, 1107–18. In the church of
Saint-Barthelemy, Leige, Belgium. Height 64 cm.

Mycenean dagger, bronze with gold,
silver, and niello, 16th century BC. In
the National Archaeological Museum
of Athens. Length 16.3 cm.

Syrian *pome*, or handwarmer, openwork
copper with silver inlay, *c.* 13th century.
In the British Museum. Diameter 18.5
cm.

Portable altar, cut-out, gilded, engraved,
and incised laminated copper, attributed to Roger
of Helmarshausen, *c.* 1100. In the collection of the
Franciscan monastery of Paderhorn, Germany. Length 31.5 cm.

Gloucester candlestick, carved and chased gilt
bronze, 12th century. In the Victoria and Albert
Museum, London. Height 58 cm.

Plate 4   Metalwork

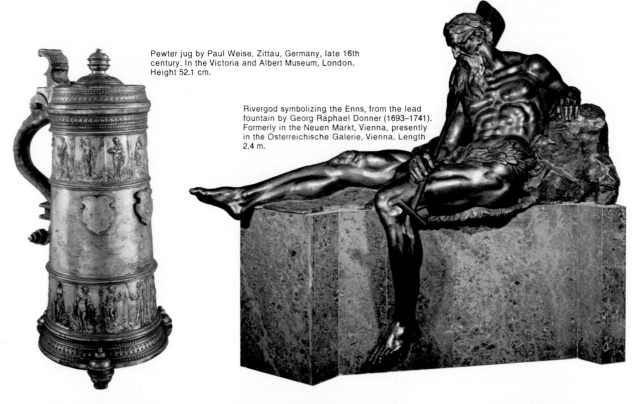

Pewter jug by Paul Weise, Zittau, Germany, late 16th century. In the Victoria and Albert Museum, London. Height 52.1 cm.

Rivergod symbolizing the Enns, from the lead fountain by Georg Raphael Donner (1693–1741). Formerly in the Neuen Markt, Vienna, presently in the Österreichische Galerie, Vienna. Length 2.4 m.

Japanese *tsuba* (sword guard), iron with openwork design, Muromachi period, 1338–1573. In the National Museum, Tokyo. Diameter 10 cm.

Pewter, iron, and lead

Detail of a wrought-iron *reja* (choir screen) by Pedro Juan, 1668, gilded in 1764. Originally in the cathedral of Valladolid, Spain, presently in the Metropolitan Museum of Art, New York City. Height 19 m.

Plate 4: By courtesy of (top left) the Victoria and Albert Museum, London, (top right) the Österreichische Galerie, Vienna, (bottom left) the Metropolitan Museum of Art, New York, gift of the Hearst Foundation, 1956, (bottom right) Eisaku Kishida-Nippon Bijyutsu Token Kyokai

By midcentury most of the earlier styles had been revived fleetingly and a recognizable Victorian style evolved, based on details drawn from diverse sources. Craftsmanship was at its best, but the design of domestic silver was derivative and selective, while that of presentation pieces strove too consciously for naturalistic effect. In the latter half-century the craft became an industry and the goldsmith a factory worker. In this respect Matthew Boulton was the great pioneer: his Soho manufactory near Birmingham, which dominated the British "toy" industry from the 1770s, produced high-quality steel buckles, buttons, coins, sterling silver, and Sheffield plate, establishing standards of design and of factory management and welfare services that rivalled those of the 20th century. At the end of the 19th century, standards deteriorated, and a second pioneering movement started—the craft revival associated with William Morris and the Art Nouveau style (see below *Modern*), which led to the production of original pieces, some of highly mannered design. In England the most interesting work was done by the sculptor Sir Alfred Gilbert, who, following the lead of William Burges, the architect and designer, combined silver with ivory and semiprecious stones in romantic confections. (J.F.Ha.)

The craft as industry

Modern. The structure of trade, following the drastic social changes that have taken place since 1914, is similar in all industrial countries. A few artist-craftsmen maintain independent studio workshops, producing commercially unprofitable but artistically significant work. Many of them also teach in art schools or work part-time in factories as industrial designers. Factories using modern equipment—for example, stamping, pressing, spinning, casting, and mechanical polishing—account for nearly all the financial turnover but seldom break new ground artistically. Retail shops buy stock almost entirely from the factories and wholesalers and usually sell it anonymously. Thus, the evolution of style is impeded by the cost of new machinery; by the natural caution of wholesalers and retailers; by the buying public, which prefers precious ornaments to be timeless; and by the consideration that buying is an investment for value rather than for beauty. In consequence, the most lively designs are often those for costume jewelry; and the best modern work usually has been on a tiny scale, making little impact on the trade.

Decline of creativity

In Paris, designs by René Lalique inspired Art Nouveau, which spread to Belgium and then through Europe and the United States. In Moscow, Peter Carl Fabergé set a superb standard of craftsmanship for small ornaments. In Denmark, Georg Jensen, with Johan Rohde and others, achieved not only an individual Danish style but built up

By courtesy of Jensen & Co., Copenhagen

Sterling silver knife, fork, and spoon, designed by Georg Jensen, Copenhagen, 1916.

several large factories with retail outlets all over the world, thus proving that good modern design in silver and jewelry need not be confined to artists' studios; their influence spread throughout Scandinavia. In the 1960s only Germany approached Scandinavia in the number and quality of its artist-craftsmen; WMF (Württembergische Metallwarenfabrik) at Geislingen is probably the biggest silverware factory in Europe. In England, notable for the most varied work, the Worshipful Company of Goldsmiths has helped a vigorous group of designers to emerge since 1945, including Gerald Benney, Eric Clements, David Mellor, and Roger King. (G.McK.H.)

PEWTER

In its pure form, tin is far from suitable for making into implements because it is too brittle for casting successfully and is not easy to melt down. For this reason it has always been alloyed with certain other metals, mainly lead, in the proportion of 10:1, or copper, alloyed about 100:4, to make what is known as pewter. In medieval Germany, the municipal authorities and the guilds laid down permissible ratios to be used for tin alloys. The authorities also kept an eye on the pewterers and their products to make sure that regulations were adhered to. So that pewter ware could be kept under constant surveillance, a system was worked out whereby every single article had to be marked by one, two, or more hallmarks, or "touches." The first decrees of this kind to be issued in Germany date from the 14th century. In France and England, written sources refer to the pewterer's obligation to hallmark his wares from the end of the 15th century onward. These regulations do not seem to have been followed very closely in practice, for pieces surviving from the period before 1550 rarely have the regulation marks. In the second half of the 16th century, however, which was the golden age of pewter, almost all work began to be clearly marked. This means that modern collectors have a good chance of being able to identify their pieces.

Pewter ware is cast in molds. It is not suitable for chasing or stamping. Molds for simple utensils such as plates, bowls, and jugs were made of clay mixed with calves' hair or of plaster, stone, or slate. From the 16th century, when pewter ware began to be decorated with relief work, molds made of brass or copper were used instead. Relief decoration can be applied by two different methods. The pewterer could either chisel the relief decoration (consisting of little scenes, figures, or decorative motifs) into the copper mold in intaglio, which enabled him to make the details as three-dimensional as he wished; or he could etch it in, which involved covering the plain copper mold with wax, scratching the decoration into it, and then allowing caustic acid to act on it. This second method resulted in a rather flat, two-dimensional relief, which is reminiscent of woodcuts in its sharp outlines and overall style; thus, the technique is known as the "woodcut style." It was common practice in Nürnberg in the last quarter of the 16th century. Pewter utensils (exclusively plates and dishes at this time) were cast in molds prepared in this manner. It was very seldom that decorative motifs were etched straight onto the pewter surface.

Pewter molds

Another type of decoration is engraving, which involves cutting decorative motifs, figures, or inscriptions with a burin into the surface of pewter objects. The most expensive and aesthetically important pieces of engraved pewter were produced in the late Gothic period, about 1500. In the 16th and 17th centuries, engraving was common for guild articles; and in the 18th century engraved mottoes, names, dates, and motifs taken from popular art were widely used. The type of strokes used fall into three categories: long, engraved lines; dots set close together to form a pattern; and a technique known in German as *Flecheln*, in which the straight line made by the burin is broken up into a series of long or short zigzag strokes. The last method makes the design look fuller and broader and also makes it stand out more sharply. This type of decoration first appeared in the 16th century and was very popular in the 17th and 18th centuries.

After they had been cast and then turned on a lathe, many pewter articles, especially plates and dishes, were hammered. The idea was to smooth over the surface of the object and strengthen the material by means of a series of light and regular blows. Sometimes pewterers punched their wares with decorative motifs stamped close together to form a sort of frieze. This technique is known as tooling and is commonly found on bronze and silver articles. Occasionally, pewter pieces were embellished by the addition of brass fittings, such as handles, knobs, spouts, or scroll panels. But pewter ware has rarely been gilded, partly because it is difficult to make a layer of gilding adhere to the surface, partly because there seems little point in covering a material that is attractive in itself with a metal that is ostensibly more precious. This is also why pewter ware has rarely been painted.

Pewter inlay

A type of pewter inlay is found on what are known as Lichtenhain tankards. Most of these tankards were made in Lower Franconia and in Thüringia in the 18th and 19th centuries. They have wooden staves running down them, and their sides are inlaid with decorative motifs and figures made of thin sheets of engraved pewter. In the early 18th century, furniture was also occasionally inlaid with pewter. Such furniture was clearly inspired by the inlay work of the French cabinetmaker André-Charles Boulle.

Antiquity. On the whole, excavations have unearthed little pewter ware dating from antiquity, not only because it has tended to perish over the years but presumably also because it was not nearly as common as glass, bronze, silver, or clay. Excavations on the Esqueline Hill and finds from the Tiber River have produced some small pewter statuettes of divinities that may well be votive offerings. Miniature versions of household articles such as amphorae, oil lamps, and pieces of furniture were found in graves.

A number of pewter ampullae (flasks with a globular body and two handles) with inscriptions or highly stylized images or symbols date from the Early Christian period. They were sold to pilgrims and were used to hold water from the Jordan River, consecrated water, or oil. (Similar pouch-shaped ampullae reappeared in France in the 14th and 15th centuries; but unlike the early Christian examples, they are ornamented with abstract motifs rather than figure decoration.)

Middle Ages. Besides the ampullae, hundreds and thousands of pilgrim badges were sold to devout visitors to places of pilgrimage in the Middle Ages. These little plaques and *agraffes* (hat badges) were generally miniature versions of religious images worshipped at the place where they were on sale. A number of these Italian, English, French, and German pilgrim badges, dating from the 13th to the 16th century, have survived.

Instead of jewelry made of gold, silver, or precious stones, the less wealthy people of the Middle Ages wore pewter badges sewn onto their clothes or hats. The badges often took the form of amulets.

Because pewter was highly prized in all periods, damaged or old-fashioned utensils were melted down over and over again to make new ones. Thus, the earliest surviving functional objects and vessels made of pewter date from the Gothic era, though a few written sources refer to pewter being used earlier than this. Most of these documents are concerned with the question of whether communion chalices should be made of anything other than gold or silver. Pewter Communion chalices were permitted in certain periods and prohibited in others, and the church never managed to draw up an absolute ruling that applied to all religious communities.

Guild flagons

Some of the finest and most important pewter pieces ever cast were made in Silesia in about 1500. Large guild flagons of a characteristic polygonal design, only 11 of them have been preserved. Their facetted surfaces are engraved with figures of saints surrounded by interlaced foliage scrolls, arches, arcades, and other late Gothic decorative motifs. Hidden among these motifs, one sometimes finds secular scenes, some of which are downright lewd. Pewterers in the neighbouring districts of Moravia and Bohemia also made guild flagons; but theirs were

cylindrical, with raised horizontal bands. The areas between the bands were generally decorated with friezelike inscriptions made up of Gothic or Gothic-style characters.

The 15th century saw the emergence of a jug set on a slender stem, easily recognizable by its disk-shaped base, surmounted by another slender stem; the main body of the vessel is generally spherical and has a long, thin neck. The municipal authorities often possessed a set of six or 12 flagons of this kind. They came back into fashion in the 17th century and were very widely used, as they had been at the beginning of the 15th century. Unfortunately, only a very few have survived from the earlier periods.

Another early type of vessel belongs to a group known as Hanseatic tankards. These tankards have a heavy-looking, potbellied body set on a shallow circular base and a slightly convex lid. They were used in the coastal regions of Germany—that is, along the North Sea and Baltic coasts—and also in the Low Countries and Scandinavia. These regions comprise the area dominated by the Hanseatic League in the Middle Ages, hence the name of the tankards. Other regions of Europe were evolving their own special types of vessels for beer and wine, which, with a few modifications, remained standard for centuries. Thus, it is a very simple matter to distinguish between baluster jugs from London and *pichets* from Paris or between wine flagons from Switzerland and those made in the Low Countries, Burgundy, the Main regions of Franconia, southern Germany, and the Rhineland. The type of a baluster jug made in the region around Frankfurt-am-Oder and in Brandenburg in northeastern Germany is particularly elegant and distinguished looking. The few jugs of this type that have survived date from about 1500.

In all of the districts bordering the Rhine, vessels with flat lenticular (the shape of a double-convex lens) bodies are relatively common. They were used as canteens—sometimes as tankards, in which case they had a base that acted as a stand.

16th century to modern. The Baroque era saw the production of many different types of drinking and pouring vessels, often made of pewter. The guilds, for instance, commissioned drinking vessels in the shape of larger than life-size versions of the tools of their trade or their coats of arms. Another type of vessel was called the Welcome, a drinking vessel that was handed around as a form of greeting or when a toast was being drunk. The body of these vessels was generally cylindrical or potbellied, with a lid and a short shaft set on a circular base.

Far fewer plain everyday plates have survived from the 15th and 16th centuries than drinking vessels and containers of the same period. The earliest pewter plates and bowls to have survived in any quantity date from the 17th century.

In the last half of the 16th century two places in Europe evolved quite independently, though simultaneously, a new technique for casting pewter. The product was a type of relief-decorated ware known as "display pewter" (*Edelzinn*), and it gave a new and brilliant impetus to the trade. The first examples were made between 1560 and 1570, and the main centres of production were Nürnberg and Lyon. In the beginning the technique used was not the same in both towns. Whereas in France, relief pewter was cast in engraved brass molds worked with a burin, in Nürnberg etched molds were used. This suggests that the two towns were not influenced by each other in any way. Later on, however, Nürnberg pewterers were strongly influenced by the work of a celebrated French pewterer, François Briot, who was active in Montbéliard, in the county of Württemberg.

"Display pewter"

The first master pewterer documented to have made relief pieces in Lyon is Roland Greffet, between 1528 and 1568. One can assume that it was he who invented this type of work. A school producing tankards and dishes with relief decoration soon grew up in Lyon. The most common decorative motif was an arabesque, which was used in a variety of ways and can be thought of as the leitmotif for the work of this group of artists. The master of relief pewter was François Briot. His most famous piece is the Temperantia Dish, which takes its name from the allegorical figure of Temperance or *Temperantia* that appears in the centre of it. It dates from 1585–90.

Temperantia Dish, relief-decorated "display pewter," by François Briot, 16th century. In the Louvre, Paris. Diameter 45 cm.

Pewter with etched relief decoration was made by Nürnberg pewterers from the last third of the 16th century onward. The earliest piece made by Nicholas Horchhaimer, bearing the date 1567, is a dish cast in an etched mold with an allegorical figure representing Fame, or *Fama*, in the centre and historical scenes or incidents from classical mythology around the edge. Other large dishes made by Horchhaimer and his contemporary Albrecht Preissensin are again decorated with themes from classical antiquity or sometimes with biblical scenes; for smaller plates they kept to abstract decoration.

The use of etched molds did not remain fashionable in Nürnberg for long, and toward the end of the 16th century engraved molds were being used here as well. The work of François Briot was copied by Caspar Enderlein, who modelled his own Temperantia Dish directly on Briot's. The decoration on the ewer that went with it was modelled on Briot's Mars Dish and on a piece known as the Suzannah Dish, which is also attributed to Briot.

In the second quarter of the 17th century, smaller relief plates superseded the big dishes and jugs made in Nürnberg. The Mannerist allegories that had been in favour completely disappeared, to be replaced by scenes from the Old and New Testaments, equestrian portraits of the German emperors with the electors round the edge, and luxuriant floral decorations. These plates are no more than about seven inches (18 centimetres) in diameter and are generally flat and disk-shaped. The molds were no longer made by the pewterers themselves but by professional mold cutters, who occasionally added their own monograms. Since molds were often sold by one workshop to another and then to another, one sometimes finds plates cast in the same mold but with different touches. Small decorative plates of this type were so popular that they continued to be made as late as the 18th century. There are no less than nine different models for a plate with an equestrian portrait of Ferdinand III of the House of Habsburg, who was crowned emperor of Germany in Nürnberg in 1637. Similar plates depicting Gustavus Adolphus of Sweden, the Emperor of Turkey, and Duke Eberhard im Bart of Württemberg were also produced.

Few places, apart from Nürnberg and France, had a flourishing trade in relief pewter. A few master pewterers in Saxony did execute relief decoration, however, mainly on jugs; they adapted their motifs from lead or bronze plaquettes made in southern Germany. Plates bearing the arms of Switzerland were also produced by Swiss pewterers in the 17th century. They have scenes taken from the history of Switzerland. The golden age of relief pewter, which had begun about 1570, ended in the third quarter of the 17th century. During this period, individual craftsmen had elevated pewter from its humble status as a material from which functional articles were made to one in which brilliant aristic feats could be performed. Relief pewter pieces were solely works of art, nonfunctional objects valued as showpieces.

Pewter dishes made in Italy in the 16th and 17th centuries have chased, etched, engraved, or chiselled decoration and lean heavily on artists working in brass or bronze for their designs. An independent pewter trade does not seem to have existed in Italy on anything like a large scale until the 18th century.

After the Thirty Years' War the production of functional articles in pewter noticeably increased in northern Europe. Besides a very large number of different types of jugs, each region specializing in its own characteristic design, there were plates and dishes used at table and also basins and bowls, drinking mugs, and screw-top flasks.

Yet pewter was already feeling the draught of competition by the end of the 17th century. In this time pewter began to be superseded by products of other branches of the decorative arts. Its first rival, faience ware, was initially no more than an inferior substitute for porcelain; but because the factories that were soon springing up everywhere were able to produce very large quantities of faience, they inflicted heavy damage on the pewter trade. Faced with this situation, the pewterers switched to imitating the designs used by the silversmiths, in the hope of gaining favor in the more ambitious middle class circles. This attempt was successful; and, from the first quarter of the 18th century onward, "silver-type pewter" gained a firm hold, soon influencing the production and appearance of pewter ware made in the Regency and Rococo periods.

By about the middle of the 18th century, an ever-widening variety of articles was being made: the pewterers were able to supply anything from a spoon to a whole dinner service, including mustard pots, sauceboats, and spoons for serving punch. But this period of prosperity was short-lived. By the third quarter of the 18th century, pewter was rivalled both by porcelain, which could now be produced relatively cheaply by several factories in Europe, and by the even cheaper English earthenware that flooded markets on the Continent. This new development sealed the fate of the pewter trade. Towns that once had 20 or 30 busy and successful workshops had no more than one or two by the beginning of the 19th century.

Although in Germany the demand for pewter seems to have increased for a few years after the Napoleonic era, particularly in country districts, by the middle of the 19th century industrialization finally put an end to a trade that had flourished for centuries.

In the second half of the century, when stylistic imitations were all the rage, pewter vessels were produced in the Neo-Baroque, Neo-Rococo, Neo-Gothic, Neo-Renaissance, and other styles that followed the many historicizing trends that emerged. Yet these pieces were made more often by mechanized metalworking factories than by pewterers. The Art Nouveau style that became fashionable at the end of the 19th century brought about a revival of pewter production; and individual firms succeeded in making original, well-designed pieces that are often of considerable aesthetic importance. The firm of Kayser in Oppum near Krefeld played a leading part in this revival. But the outbreak of World War I spelled the end of Art Nouveau—whose heady run of success had anyway been short-lived—and with it the end of old pewter. (H.-U.H.)

Domestic pewter in northern Europe

IRON

Ironwork is fashioned either by forging or casting. Wrought iron is the type of ironwork that is forged on an

Pewter watering can in Art Nouveau style, by the firm Kayser, at Oppum near Krefeld, Germany, c. 1900. In the Museum für Kunsthandwerk, Frankfurt am Main. Height 21.5 cm.
By courtesy of the Museum fur Kunsthandwerk, Frankfurt am Main

anvil. There are no fabrication similarities to cast iron, which is poured in a molten state into prepared sand molds.

Wrought iron
Wrought iron is fibrous in structure and light gray in colour. It can be hammered, twisted, or stretched when hot or cold. The more it is hammered, the more brittle and hard it becomes; but it can be brought back to its original state by annealing (heating and then cooling slowly). It will not shatter when dropped.

From earliest times, the smith has had a forge to heat the iron, an adjacent water tank in which to cool it, an anvil on which to form it, in addition to a wide assortment of hammers and tools. The most important tool is the anvil. The English type, generally used for forging wrought iron, has a flat top surface, which is used as a solid base for hammering the heated iron into shape, for welding, for splitting, or for incising decorative chisel marks in the hot iron. One end of the anvil is shaped like a pointed cone and is used for forming curved surfaces. The other blunt end, or heel, has one or two square or rectangular holes on top, into which fit various tools. From the anvil is derived the expression "to strike while the iron is hot," and this implies spontaneity and rapid hammer blows. The wrought-iron craftsman should not be expected to repeat with meticulous exactitude one intricate component after another. In fact, wrought iron by a master craftsman is esteemed for the variations that naturally occur.

Components of wrought-iron design
The individual components of a wrought-iron design are often plain or twisted rods, with or without chisel-mark incisions. They are frequently composed as a series of straight, parallel members or in combination with scrolls, or as a repeat design of some geometric shape such as the quatrefoil. Where two curved members are tangent, they are characteristically secured together by bands or collars, rather than by welding. Where two straight bars intersect, it is accredited craftsmanship to make the vertical bar pierce or thread the horizontal member. Grilles consisting of two series of parallel small-diameter rods, one series at right angles to the other, were sometimes interlaced or woven.

Depending upon the depth of the relief, various fabrication techniques may be employed for repoussé, or three-dimensional, ornamental wrought ironwork. Sheets 1/16 inch (1.6 millimetres) or less in thickness generally are used. The general configuration of the modelling is obtained by beating the back of the sheet; the final details are embossed on the front face. The finer the scale and detail, the more work must be done when the iron is cold. A repoussé design may be pierced; but this term usually connotes a solid sheet forged into a mask, a shield, or an entire embossed panel. The traditional means of setting off a cutout repoussé design was to superimpose it on a vermillion-coloured background panel. Modern approximations of repoussé work consist of mechanically stamped designs touched up with random hammer blows.

(G.K.Ge.)

The most difficult way of decorating iron is to carve it. This involves fashioning figurative or decorative motifs out of the metal ingot with especially strengthened tools, using the material in the same way that the sculptor handles wood or stone. Only very precious iron articles are carved, such as coats of arms or pieces that are specifically designed to be displayed as works of art.

(H.-U.H.)

Cast iron
Cast iron is melted in a furnace or cupola, stoked with alternate layers of coking iron, then poured into prepared sand molds. After the cast iron cools in the mold, the sand is cleaned off, and the work is virtually complete. Its shape is fixed, and while a casting can be slightly trued up by the judicious use of a hammer, it is in no sense as workable as wrought iron. Thus, ornamental features in cast iron cannot be chased and polished as in cast bronze. If the ornamental cast-iron details are not replicas of the original pattern, the only recourse is to make a new casting. Because it is brittle, cast iron is almost certain to shatter if dropped.

Since it is cast in a mold, certain forms are more suitable to cast iron than to wrought iron. For example, if repetitive balusters, or columns, or panels with low-relief ornamentation are desired, cast iron is the most suitable material.

(G.K.Ge.)

Early history. The earliest recorded iron artifacts are some beads, dating from about 3500 BC or earlier, found at Jirzah in Egypt. They are made from meteoric iron, as are a number of other objects of only slightly later date that have been found both in Egypt and Mesopotamia. The earliest known examples of the use of smelted iron are fragments of a dagger blade in a bronze hilt, dating from the 28th century BC, found at Tall al-Asmar (modern Eshnunna), in Mesopotamia, and some pieces of iron from Tell Chagar Bazar, in the same area, of approximately the same date. There is, however, no evidence of any extensive use of iron in either Egypt or Mesopotamia before the end of the 2nd millennium BC. In Asia Minor, on the other hand, iron was probably used regularly from at least as early as 2000 BC; and it seems likely that the first true iron industry was established there in the second half of the 2nd millennium BC.

From the ancient Near East the knowledge of iron working was transmitted to Greece and the Aegean, probably at the beginning of the 1st millennium BC, whence it spread gradually to the rest of Europe. By the 6th century BC, it had been widely disseminated over central and western Europe.

Iron was at first apparently regarded as a precious, semimagical material, presumably because of its rarity and its connection with meteorites. But once it had become common, as a result of increased knowledge of the technique of smelting ore, it seems to have been used, at least in Europe, almost exclusively for objects of utility. A few Belgic firedogs and at least one amphora, skillfully forged in iron, with decorative terminals in the form of animal heads, are known; but the practice of forging iron into decorative shapes does not seem to have become general until the Middle Ages.

A few cast-iron objects dating from classical times have been found in Europe. The extreme rarity of these, however, suggests that they were only produced experimentally. The earliest known evidence for the general use of cast iron comes from China (see below), and it does not seem to have been produced regularly in Europe before the 15th century.

(C.Bl.)

Belgium and Holland. The ironwork of these two small countries prior to the 15th century was in no way inferior to that produced elsewhere. Yet so few pieces remain that the significance of craftsmen of the Low Countries has often been underestimated. During the 15th century, design and craftsmen from the Low Countries began to make their influence evident across the channel in England. Representative examples of this period are in the Hervormde Kerk at Breda; the treasury door of the cathedral at Liège; and hinges of the church of Notre Dame, at Hal. The beautiful spires of Bruges, Ghent, and Antwerp should be mentioned.

Diversified forms of ironwork

During the first half of the 16th century, before the Spanish occupation, there were diversifed forms of ironwork, such as protective grilles for doors, windows, and chapels, often in fleur-de-lis patterns; window gratings of vertical bars, frequently octagonal in section; and interlacing bars, producing rectangular or lozenge-shaped patterns. Only a few examples still exist: some lunettes in the Hôtel de Ville of Brussels; a tabernacle grille from the chapel of the counts of Flanders and a window grille from the Cathedral of St. Bavon, both from Ghent (Victoria and Albert Museum); and hinges at the Hôtels de Ville of Bruges and Ypres (Flemish Ieper). Few Renaissance screens have survived.

During the second half of the 16th century, the cruelty of the Duke of Alba and his 20,000 troops, together with the threat of the Inquisition, drove hundreds of artisans to England. After the Spanish domination there was little indigenous design in Holland and Belgium, and such ironwork as was produced fell under the spell of French imports. (G.K.Ge.)

England. The initial use of wrought iron was purely protective because violent attacks were frequent, and doors had to be strengthened with massive ironwork inside and out. Window openings, especially those of the treasuries of mansions and cathedrals, were for similar reasons filled with strong interlacing bars of solid iron; a good example remains at Canterbury cathedral. When, in the course of time, the need for protective barriers ended, there was greater freedom of work and a definite trend toward ornamentation. Throughout England, medieval church doors are found with massive iron hinges, the bands worked in rich ornamental designs of scrollwork, varying from the plain hinge band, with crescent, to the most elaborate filling of the door. Examples exist at Skipwith and Stillingfleet in Yorkshire, many in the eastern counties, others in Gloucester, Somerset, and the west Midlands. The next important application of ironwork came with the erection of the great cathedrals and churches, whose shrines and treasures demanded protection. Winchester Cathedral possesses the remains of one screen with a symmetrical arrangement of scrollwork. Tombs were enclosed within railings of vertical bars with ornamental finials at intervals, such as that of the Black Prince at Canterbury. A new development appeared in the early years of the 15th century when the smith, working in cold iron, attempted to reproduce Gothic stone tracery in metal. This work was more like that of a woodworker than of a smith, often consisting of small pieces of iron chiselled and rivetted, and fixed on a background of sheet iron. Many small objects such as door knockers, handles, and escutcheons were executed in the same manner. A typical monumental example is in Henry V's chantry at Westminster Abbey; but the most magnificent is the great grille at St. George's Chapel, Windsor, made to protect the tomb of Edward IV.

Decoration for church doors

The development of the art of smithing during the Renaissance period was very uneven in the various countries of Europe. In 16th-century England the smith fell behind and seemed to have lost interest, producing no very great or important work. He continued to make iron railings, balconies, and small objects for architectural application, such as hinges, latches, locks, and weathercocks. But toward the end of the 17th century, there was a growing interest in beautifying houses and laying out gardens and squares, with a commensurate demand for balconies, staircases, and garden gates. The man to whom the credit is usually given for the revival of ironwork in England was Jean Tijou, a Frenchman who, together with many of his Protestant fellow craftsmen, had been forced to leave his country owing to the revocation of the Edict of Nantes in 1685. After some years in The Netherlands he went to England in 1689, where he enjoyed the patronage and favour of William III. His most important works for his royal patron are to be seen in the immense mass of screens and gates with which he embellished Hampton Court palace. He also executed work at Burleigh house, Stamford. Probably by the Queen's wish he was associated with the architect Sir Christopher Wren, then engaged on the rebuilding of St. Paul's Cathedral. Wren apparently did not particularly like ironwork and probably exercised some restraint on Tijou, with the result that his work at St. Paul's is more dignified and freer from appendages than that of Hampton Court.

18th century ironwork

There is a great amount of fine ironwork of the 18th century in London in the form of gates, railings, lamp holders, door brackets, balconies, and staircases; in almost every suburb there are gates and brackets. The precincts of the colleges of Oxford and Cambridge, as well as almost every old town in England, furnish a variety of handsome work. Throughout the 18th century the smith was a busy man; the general tendency of his work, unaffected by the Rococo movement on the Continent, was toward a less ornate but more characteristically English style—perpendicular, severe, lofty, and commanding, as contrasted with Tijou's French love of richness and mass of details.

At the end of the 18th century the work of the architect brothers Adam shows a departure from true smithing; its slender delicate bars are enriched with rosettes, anthemia, and other ornament in brass or lead. The effect is pleasing and harmonizes with the architecture with which it is incorporated.

During the first half of the 19th century, the art of the smith was largely eclipsed by that of the iron caster. But under the stimulus of the Victorian Gothic revival and later of the Art Nouveau movement, there was a renewal of interest in the decorative use of wrought iron, and much excellent work was produced.

Medieval door-hinge ornaments

France. Medieval door-hinge ornaments were not basically different from those in England; and beautiful work is found on church doors, especially in central and northern France. It reaches a height of greater elaboration and magnificence than in England, the culminating example being the west doors of Notre Dame, Paris, the ironwork of which is so wonderful that it was attributed to superhuman workmanship. Grilles at Troyes and Rouen also reveal a high standard of excellence. Working the iron cold and employing methods associated with carpentry was immensely popular; it was applied to small objects such as door handles, knockers, and above all to locks, which exhibit an amazing amount of detail and a remarkable delicacy of finish.

The Gothic tradition survived in France until well into the 16th century and was marked by the production of work of the highest skill, largely in the form of locks, knockers, and caskets of chiselled iron. The introduction of the Renaissance style did not radically alter the direction of the smith's art—a strange fact when it is remembered that Germany and Spain were fabricating works of enormous size and magnificence in wrought iron. France, like England at that time, was content to make door furniture, in the form of locks, keys, bolts, escutcheons, and the like, but did little ironwork of any great size. A school of locksmiths came into being under Francis I and Henry II, working from designs by Androuet du Cerceau in the 16th century and those by Mathurin Jousse and Antoine Jacquard in the 17th. The bows (a loop forming the handle) and wards (notches) of keys were of unusually intricate design and the locks of corresponding richness. Representative pieces may be seen at the Victoria and Albert Museum. Among them is the famous Strozzi key, said to have been made for the apartments of Henry III, the bow of which takes the favoured form of two grotesque figures back to back. But as far as architectural ironwork was concerned, France remained almost at a standstill until the accession of Louis XIII in 1610. Under that monarch, a worker at the forge himself, came a great revival, which, by the end of the 17th century, had attained a marvellous pitch of perfection. It proved to be the beginning of a new movement, the force of which made itself felt in the adjoining countries and inspired ironworkers with new energy. From the accession of Louis XIV, the French ironworkers must be acknowl-

Bildarchiv Foto Marburg

Ironwork in the reign of Louis XIV

edged as the cleverest in Europe, combining as they did good and fitting design with masterly execution. Their designs were often very daring, exploiting all the latent and previously unexplored possibilities of iron. They recognized its great adaptability and took every advantage of it, at the same time being conscious of its limitations. Their forms of expression were endless.

Screens and gates were needed for parks, gardens, and avenues, staircases for mansions and palaces, screens for churches and cathedrals. Among celebrated designers were Jean Lepautre, Daniel Marot, and Jean Berain. Earlier work had been of a simple character—balconies, for instance, being in the form of a succession of balusters—but as the smith became more versatile and imaginative, they took the form of panels of flowing curved scrolls, rendered with a freedom never attained before, while constructive strength was observed and symmetry maintained. Enrichments were usually attached in hammered sheet iron. These may be considered the distinguishing features of Louis XIV work, such as that at St. Cloud, Chantilly, Fontainebleau, and elsewhere. But under Louis XIV all previous efforts were surpassed in the work for his palace at Versailles.

Rococo design

The art of ironwork received a further impetus by the introduction of the Rococo style. The movement, initiated in 1723, was due principally to the imagination of two artists, Just-Aurèle Meissonier, architect, and Gilles-Marie Oppenordt. There was a balanced asymmetry in the design and fantastic curves with a luxury of applied ornamentation. To the French smith it furnished the opportunity for a yet greater display of his skill. He was clever enough to secure a feeling of stability in his work by counterbalancing swirling masses of ornament with straight constructional lines; he knew how to introduce an iron screen of Rococo style into a Gothic church or cathedral without giving offense to the eye or arousing any uncomfortable feeling of incongruity.

Later in the 18th century, ironwork took on a more classical appearance as a result of the general revival of interest in ancient art; and many Greek and Roman details were introduced into the ornamentation. The amount of work executed was prodigious, and its beauty and craftsmanship may be seen in most cities of France. Nearly all of the adjacent countries, with the exception of England, were seized with the desire to imitate the French Rococo style.

Germany. In the Romanesque period in Germany, bronze was preferred to iron; the earliest examples of ironwork are thus later than those of France and England. The first iron grilles were imitations of French work, with C-scrolls filling spaces between vertical bars.

German door hinges

Typical examples of door hinges prior to the 14th century were those at Kaisheim, St. Magnus Church, Brunswick, and St. Elizabeth's Church, Marburg (the latter having a curious cross in the middle). Throughout the Gothic period in Germany, the imitation of natural foliage was the basis of design.

There were no new marked developments in ironwork during the 14th century. Smiths confined their efforts mostly to hinges. Until this period the vine had been the only motif for elaborate hinges; but flat, lozenge-shaped leaves were introduced, such as those at Schloss Lahneck on the Rhine.

During the 15th century, grilles became more popular. One of the best examples is the grille in the Monument of Bishop Ernst of Bavaria, Magdeburg cathedral (*c.* 1495), with elaborate Gothic tracery, nine columns, and a cornice. In hinges the cinquefoil displaced the quatrefoil, as at Orb, Oppenheim, and Magdeburg. The Erfurt cathedral was enriched with notable hinges having the vine pattern interpolated with rosettes and escutcheons of arms. Hinges for houses usually were the plain strap type, but when ornamented they consisted of superimposed layers of sheet iron. As in other parts of Europe at this time, pierced sheet iron was fashioned into tracery of a semi-architectural nature, much like Gothic windows. Pierced ornament and twisted rods were often combined to form grilles, with their extremities beaten into complicated foliage forms.

During the Renaissance, ironwork in Germany was in use everywhere and for every purpose: for screens in churches, window grilles, stove guards, gates, fountain railings, well heads, grave crosses, door knockers, handles, locks, iron signs, and small objects for domestic use. Smiths were their own designers and more often than not planned intricate devices merely to show their skill in executing them. They set no limits to their problems; and so far as manipulative excellence went, the German smiths were the foremost in Europe. But clever as their workmanship undoubtedly was, their designs frequently showed a lack of stability and a tendency to run riot. Thus, many of their most imposing works consist largely of filling panels with elaborate, interlacing scrollwork, and the sense of constructional and protective strength is missing.

Southern German work

An abundance of smiths' work is to be found in the southern parts of Germany. Iron bars, circular in section, were most frequently used; and the most common features are interlacing bars and terminations of flowers with petals and twisted centres, foliage, or human heads. All of these characteristics occur with almost monotonous repetition, witnessing to skill but also to lack of imagination and sense of design. The style may be studied in many German and Austrian cities, such as Augsburg, Nürnberg, Frankfurt, Salzburg, Munich, and Innsbruck.

The German smith gave much attention to door knockers and handles, enclosing them in pierced and embossed escutcheons, and devised locks with very involved mechanism. German influence made itself strongly felt in Switzerland, Austria, and Czechoslovakia.

The Baroque and Rococo periods are distinguished by a perfection of detail that exceeded that of German Medieval or Renaissance ironwork. Smiths used wrought iron as though it were a plastic material, meant to be em-

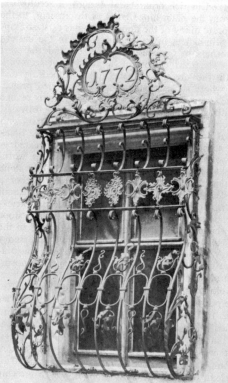

Rococo style wrought-iron window grille from a house on Winklerstrasse, Nürnberg, 1772.

ployed in extravagant forms wherever possible. Some examples are at Zwiefalten, Weingarten, and Klosterneuburg. In the late 18th and early 19th centuries, cast ironwork of outstanding quality was produced in Germany, notably at the Prussian royal foundry established in 1804.

Italy. The few extant examples of ironwork in Italy prior to the 14th century indicate a wide appreciation of how the material could best be worked with only the tools of the smith. Some noteworthy examples are the chancel grille at the left of the nave, Orvieto Cathedral (1337); the grille around the Scaligeri tombs of Verona (*c.* 1340); the grille at the baptistery of Prato cathedral (1348); the chancel screen in the sacristy chapel of Sta. Croce, Florence (1371); and the grille to the Capella degli Spagnoli, Sta. Maria Novello, Florence.

Italian ironwork before the 16th-century

Until the 16th century, Italian smiths respected the natural characteristics of wrought iron by relying almost entirely upon those forms that could be wrought with hammer and anvil. The grille was usually made by dividing it into regular panels with vertical and horizontal bars (sometimes triangular in section and enriched with dentils, or small, projecting triangular blocks). Often the quatrefoil filled some or all of these panels; they were made in Tuscany from a pierced plate and in Venice from separate scrolls collared together. A noted example is in the Palazzo della Signoria, Siena, crowned by a repoussé frieze and surmounted by a cresting of flowers, spikes, and some animal heads.

It might have been thought that in the fountainhead of the Renaissance, ironwork would have proceeded at the same pace and with the same brilliant success as architecture, sculpture, bronze casting, and the other arts. Strangely enough, little use of it is found in connection with the fine buildings of the revival. Bronze was favoured; and what in other countries is found in iron has its counterpart in Italy in bronze. As time went on the smiths grew less inclined toward the more difficult processes of hammering and welding and contented themselves ultimately with thin ribbon iron, the various parts of which were fastened together by collars. Work of the later periods may be distinguished, apart from the design, by this feature, whereas the English and French smiths vigorously faced the hardest methods of work, and the German and Spanish smiths invented difficulties for the sheer pleasure of overcoming them.

Notable centres of artistic ironwork were Florence, Siena, Vicenza, Venice, Lucca, and Rome, where important pieces may be found in the form of gates, balconies, screens, fanlights (semicircular windows with radiating sash bars like the ribs of a fan), well covers, and a mass of objects for domestic use, such as bowl stands, brackets, and candlesticks.

Screen-work

In screenwork the favourite motif was the quatrefoil, which has been found with many variations ever since the 14th century. Early examples are strong and virile, but later ones tend to weakness. The C-shaped scroll is also used in many combinations. The churches and palaces of Venice contain many examples of these popular designs. Peculiar to Italy are the lanterns and banner holders such as may still be seen at Florence, Siena, and elsewhere, and the rare gondola prows of Venice. Of the ironworkers of the early Renaissance, the most famous was the late-15th-century craftsman Niccolo Grosso of Florence, nicknamed "Il Caparra" because he gave no credit but insisted on money on account. From his hand is the well-known lantern on the Palazzo Strozzi in Florence, repeated with variations elsewhere in the same city. Siena has lanterns and banner holders attached to the facades of its palaces, and lanterns are still to be seen at Lucca and a few other towns.

The decadence of 17th- and 18th-century ironwork paralleled that of architecture. Designs were borrowed directly from France and Germany. The metal was too often worked cold, using thin members; and the resulting construction was flimsy. Scrolls were often encased in thin, grasslike leaves. Conventional or naturalistic flowers were tacked on as seeming afterthoughts. Instead of using rods and bars, ribbonlike bands were used, with cast ornaments pinned on. Intersecting tracery was copied from Germany. The best examples of this period are confined to Venice and northern Italy, such as the screen in the south aisle chapel of S. Ambrogio, Milan; the chapel enclosure in S. Pietro, Mantua; and the screen in the Palazzo Capodilista, Padua.

Spain. Prior to the 15th century, Spanish ironwork was basically similar to that in France and England. The Spanish smith accepted the limitations imposed by anvil and ancillary tools; but he skillfully exploited to the limit all manner of variations—twisting square rods, coiling flat bars into C-shaped scrolls of all sizes, and devising imaginative crestings to surmount the top of church chapel screens or domestic window grilles. Many Moorish craftsmen of extraordinary ability were enticed to remain in Spain as the Moors were slowly pushed southward; the resultant blending of Gothic with Moorish resulted in the Mudejar style.

Ironwork of the Renaissance period from about 1450 to 1525 reached a height of grandeur and magnificence attained in no other country. Of all the Spanish craftsmen the smiths were the busiest, especially during the 16th century. The ironwork products that for more than a century dominated the craft are the monumental screens (*rejas*) found in all the great cathedrals of Spain. These immense structures, rising 25 to 30 feet (7.5 to nine metres) show several horizontal bands, or tiers, of balusters, sometimes divided vertically by columns of hammered work and horizontally by friezes of hammered arabesque ornament. Usually such screens are surmounted by a cresting, which is sometimes of simple ornament but more often a very elaborate design into which are introduced a large number of human figures. Shields of arms are freely incorporated; and the use of bright colour, silvering, and gilding adds to their impressive beauty. The great balusters were always forged from the solid, and their presence in hundreds demonstrates the extraordinary skill and power of the Spanish smith. In many cathedrals two of these monumental *rejas* are found facing one another. There is at least one in every large cathedral—Barcelona, Saragossa, Toledo, Seville, Burgos, Granada, Córdoba, and many others.

Monumental *rejas*

Ironwork on a smaller scale is found in gates, balconies, and window screens; wrought-iron pulpits also exist. Panels of hammered and pierced iron, heightened with colours and gilding, were used in connection with domestic architecture; and many doors were ornamented with elaborate nailheads or embossed studs.

(W.W.W./G.K.Ge.)

United States. *Early history.* The characteristics of the earliest ironwork in the various colonies naturally reflected those of the parent countries. The English were more sparing in its use in the New England Colonies than were the Germans in Pennsylvania or the French in Louisiana. In the 17th and 18th centuries ironwork was used mostly for such practical purposes as weather vanes, foot scrapers, strap hinges, latches, locks, and particularly for the necessities and conveniences for fireplaces (firedogs, cranes, skewers, toasters, kettle warmers, and spits). It was not until the late 18th century, when the threat of Indian raids and food shortages had waned and the established communities enjoyed a sense of tranquillity and prosperity, that smiths fashioned wrought iron into railings, fences, grilles, gates, and balconies. Square or flat iron bars were generally used to produce designs that were usually light, airy, and graceful and rather in contrast to the contemporary European preference for sturdier forms.

Utilitarian ironwork

Gradually, ironwork designs tended to develop characteristics of an American or composite nature, as a logical consequence of the diverse origins of colonists and smiths. An innovation that appeared toward the end of the 18th century was the combination of structural wrought-iron rods or bars with lead or cast-iron ornamental features. While the use of wrought iron declined in the 19th century, during its last quarter the use of cast-iron columns and panels for nonresidential buildings increased. These designs, timid or bold, decorative or structural, engendered the prototypes of commercial buildings for the ensuing decades.

Because the life of structures in U.S. cities has been short, there are few examples of 18th- or early 19th-century ironwork extant in New York City, not many more in Boston, some in Philadelphia, but more in and near Washington, D.C., such as the excellent balconies and railings at the Octagon (headquarters of the American Institute of Architects). Charleston, South Carolina, has a rich legacy in gates, notably those at numbers 12, 23, and 36 Legare Street, 63 Meeting Street, and an unusually beautiful pair at St. Michael's Church.

New Orleans has more ironwork than other U.S. cities, thanks to a group of citizens dedicated to the preservation of the old French Quarter. Its earliest ironwork was forged by Spanish and French smiths. Unfortunately, fires, rust, and remodelling have so taken their toll of the Spanish ironwork that almost the only remaining example of importance is the gateway of the Cabildo (town hall). It has moldings beaten from solid bars, like many of the old *rejas* in Spanish cathedrals. After the Louisiana Purchase in 1803, the influx of ironworkers from northern states brought about a broadening of influences that is apparent in designs and techniques. Ironwork of New Orleans can be roughly divided into three periods: (1) forged wrought iron by French and Spanish artisans with strongly marked European characteristics; (2) a transitional period with wrought-iron structural members embellished with cast-iron ornaments in the Directoire and Empire styles of France, plus some U.S. innovations; and (3) entire grilles, screens, and trellises made entirely of cast iron. No other city in the U.S. has two- and even three-story iron porches and balconies that can compare with those of New Orleans. Some of these lacy structures,

Wrought- and cast-iron balconies along St. Peter Street, in the Vieux Carré, New Orleans, c. 1838–40.

such as those on St. Peter Street, were built above the sidewalks. Balconies sometimes not only extended across an entire facade but continued around a corner.

Mid-19th century onward. Distinctive national characteristics in the design of ironwork gradually tended to disappear in Europe because of increased travel and communications between countries. The influence of French Renaissance architecture (modified or revived) continued to exert a viable effect where the acceptance of the Art Nouveau (last quarter of the 19th century) was flaccid or denied. In England, however, 18th-century designs continued with slight modifications. In the U.S. probably the most important force, prior to World War I, was exercised by architects trained in Paris, with the result that ironwork designs were similar to French work of this period.

The increased mechanization of all forms of manufacture understandably affected the character and use of ironwork. As the cost of cast iron came down, its use increased. Because wrought iron is produced by hand by beating red-hot iron on an anvil, not much change was possible through increased mechanization, whereas the casting of molten iron lent itself to improved equipment and techniques. The lowered cost of duplicating ornamental cast-iron components and the introduction of structural steel parts expanded the usage of ironwork to the modest building, whereas it had been generally confined to public or monumental structures. Foundries in the U.S. established a flourishing business in pierced cast-iron panels, modelled after Louisiana porch trellises.

Compared with prior periods, the last half of the 19th century will scarcely be commemorated as introducing enduring or beautiful ironwork forms. It was not until the first quarter of the 20th century that a master craftsman-designer gave impetus to a new conception of design forms and textures. Edgar Brandt of Paris broadened the scope of decorative usage by the rich inventiveness of his compositions and by an entirely original approach that resulted in a wrought-iron texture that is akin to beaten silver. Examples of his work at the Exposition des Arts Décoratifs Modernes at Paris in 1925 had an immediate effect upon ironwork designed and executed in the U.S. during the great building boom that lasted until about 1930. During this period, both wrought and cast iron enjoyed an unprecedented period of popularity not only in the form of bank screens, entrance doors, and grilles in public buildings but as decorative grilles and gates in private homes. In many cases the craftsmanship equalled that of representative examples of the Gothic or Renaissance periods in Europe.

One of the most gifted and dedicated iron craftsmen in the U.S., Samuel Yellin of Philadelphia, raised the standards of wrought-iron craftsmanship to its apex during the 1920s. He not only trained an atelier of craftsmen for the first time in the U.S., but by his efforts wrought iron was recognized as capable of enriching even the most monumental building. Yellin's influence, however, was ended by the Depression of the early 1930s. As building activity declined after 1930, so did the use of ironwork; and it did not increase with the revival of building after World War II.   (G.K.Ge.)

Lead has two main uses in which some artistic purpose may be served: in architecture, as a material for roof coverings, gutters, piping, and cisterns; and in decorative art, as a material for sculpture and applied ornament. As an architectural material it has the advantage of being easily worked and yet offers great resistance to climatic conditions. The low melting point of lead and its relative freedom from contraction when solidifying make it particularly suitable for casting, and it has been used as a substitute for bronze or precious metals.

Antiquity. The earliest known lead sculptures are small votive figures found at Troy and Mycenae. In the Hellenistic period lead sarcophagi were known, and the Romans made much use of the metal. Large amounts of worked lead in various forms have been found in those parts of England where the Romans had permanent settlements.

Middle Ages. England was one of the main lead-producing areas in the Middle Ages, and lead was more widely employed there than on the continent of Europe. In the 12th century the German monk Theophilus, in his treatise on metalworking, refers to lead only in connection with casting rods for stained-glass windows and as a material through which silver sheets might be hammered; but in England at about the same time a remarkable series of lead fonts was cast, of which 16 still survive in position, the most famous being those at Walton-on-the-Hill, Surrey, and at Wareham and Dorchester in Dorset. Lead was also used in the Middle Ages for church roofing; and it was used, doubtless because of its cheapness, for the small badges or medallions sold to pilgrims at the great medieval shrines. Lead could even be useful, in the proper disguise, to simulate rich ecclesiastical objects, for not all religious institutions were wealthy: a group of 14th-century caskets covered with lead tracery, gilded to look like precious metal, have survived in church treasuries. These were used as reliquaries, but some were originally made for secular purposes.

Lead models

Renaissance to modern. The Renaissance passion for collecting bronze medals and plaquettes led to a demand for cheap replicas, and these were made with great precision in lead. The metal also played an important role in the goldsmiths' trade. The fashion for elaborate relief ornament of the Renaissance and Mannerist periods called for a degree of skill in modelling that was beyond the powers of the average goldsmith. The practice therefore grew up for the pattern makers of Augsburg and Nürnberg, Germany, to sell lead models of ornamental details and figures from which goldsmiths working elsewhere could in turn make molds. An extensive collection of these models is preserved in the Historisches Museum, Basel, Switzerland. The trade expanded to include large medallions and plaquettes, the chief masters of which were the German goldsmiths Peter Flötner, Jonas Silber, and the Master H.G. (Hans Jamnitzer) and the Dutch goldsmith family of van Vianen. Lead in sculpture is more suitable for the production of small figures than life-size statues, which, if unsupported, become distorted through their own weight. Among the few life-size equestrian lead statues is one of Frederick Louis, prince of Wales, in the grounds of Hartwell House, Buckinghamshire, England. From the 16th century, lead appeared in England in the form of gutters and pipe heads (which carried rainwater down from the gutters), often with cast ornament. Some of the late-17th- and early-18th-century pipe heads, cast with the arms of the owner of the house and the date of erection, are important decorative features.

A great extension of the use of lead took place with the introduction of lead garden sculpture—figures, vases, and urns—in the late 17th century. An outstanding example of this work is a pair of garden vases 15 feet (4.5 metres) high at Schloss Scheissheim in Bavaria. The silvery gray colour of such sculpture and its resistance to the weather made it particularly suitable for use in the many formal gardens that were created at this time. English garden sculpture rarely achieves any particular aesthetic status; but in 18th-century Germany and Austria lead was used for more serious sculpture by a group of artists of the highest standing. In the 19th century, lead was out of favour with sculptors, partly because improved transport made it possible to bring marble from Italy at low cost. Its soft colouring and the fact that it does not reflect light give it advantages, however, and it has been used in the 20th century by Aristide Maillol and by Sir Jacob Epstein, who executed the lead figure of the Virgin and Child in Cavendish Square, London.   (J.F.Ha.)

III. Non-Western metalwork

SOUTH ASIA

Iron. The manufacture of iron by primitive small-scale methods has survived in southern India and Ceylon to the present day. The slag heaps of ancient furnaces are common, and the processes have probably been in use for more than 2,000 years; but it is unknown whether they are of indigenous invention or acquired. In southern India iron immediately succeeded stone as a material for tools and weapons, and prehistoric iron weapons began to come into use about 500 BC. The wrought-iron pillar of Delhi, set up about AD 400 by Kumāra Gupta I in honour of his father, is over 23 feet (seven metres) in height and weighs more than six tons. It demonstrates the abilities of Indian metalworkers in handling large masses of material, for not until the latter part of the 19th century could anything of the same kind have been made in Europe. There are other large iron pillars at Dhār and at Mt. Abu.   (A.K.Co.)

Gold and silver. In India, gold jewelry has been found from the Indus culture. Excavations at Takshasila (Taxila) have revealed gold and silver drinking vessels and jewelry of Hellenistic types dating back to about the 1st century AD. From the same time is the important Buddhist gold reliquary from Bimaran, Afghanistan, set in rubies and decorated with embossed figures in Gandhāra style (British Museum).

During the Gupta period (AD 320–647), vessels of Hellenistic and Persian shapes were evidently made, for they are represented in the sculpture and frescoes of the period. More Indian in style are a silver dish of the 3rd or 4th

Indian style embossed and chased silver dish showing a *yakṣa* drinking, Kushan, found at Buddaghara, near Tank, Dera Ismāīl Khān district, Pakistan, 3rd or 4th century AD, Gupta period. In the British Museum. Diameter 25.15 cm.
By courtesy of the trustees of the British Museum

century, decorated with a Bacchanalian scene of a *yakṣa* drinking, and a silver bowl of the 7th century from northern India, which is embellished with medallions in low relief (both in the British Museum). Jewelry played a very important role, and, although no original pieces have survived, it can be studied in frescoes at Ajanta and on contemporary sculptures.

17th-century vessels

In spite of the fact that gold and silver vessels have been common in India since classical times, there is very little material extant before the 17th century, when all kinds of vessels were produced in bronze, brass, copper, and, for the royal houses, in silver. Shapes and decorations vary in different regions. Delhi was famous for its craftsmen, especially in the time of Akbar in the 16th century and Jahāngīr and Shāh Jahān in the 17th. Much work was done in precious metal, and vessels and ornaments of jade were inlaid with gold and gems. Northern India is famous for its enamels. Enamellers from Lahore were brought to Jaipur in the 16th century by Mān Singh, and enamel was employed extensively in combination with goldwork and silverwork in the 17th and 18th centuries there and elsewhere. The Punjab, Lucknow, and the districts of Chānda and Cutch in Gujarāt state were long celebrated for their metalworkers. In the south, silverwork in *svamin*-style is characterized by religious-figure scenes in relief, executed in three different techniques. Craftsmen in Tirupati put silver sheet on copper; Madras, Bangalore, and Tiruchirāppalli are known for hammered vessels with traced decoration; and Thanjāvūr (Tanjore) produced a more Baroque effect with inlays of silver in copper. From the former Travancore state, Mysore, and Bijaipur in the southwest come chased vessels with floral patterns, the lotus predominating. In the north the Hindu style is well represented by works from Vārānasi (Benares).

Persian-Islāmic influence

Persian-Islāmic influence is found in several vessel shapes; for example, ewers and basins for water and smoking furniture, such as hookas, which also have Islāmic patterns. Jewelry from the later periods employs precious stones, pearls, gold, and silver in great variety. The old types are repeated, with symmetrical arrangements of rosettes and leaves for bracelets, necklaces, pendants, rings, and foot ornaments. Very fine work in silver filigree was executed at Cuttack in Orissa and was used on jewelry and various larger items.   (B.V.Gy.)

CENTRAL AND SOUTHEAST ASIA:
NEPAL, TIBET, BURMA, THAILAND, VIETNAM

Indian styles and techniques spread to the neighbouring countries. In Nepal precious metals were used in architecture; pagodas, temples, and palaces sometimes had facades richly decorated with ornaments embossed in gilt copper with settings of precious stones.

In Tibet copper and brass were usually used for vessels, but these metals were often decorated with applied silver or gold ornaments; and in eastern Tibet, especially, teapots were made of silver with gilt appliqué. While many of the ornaments are Chinese, Buddhist shapes and patterns of Indian origin were used for ritual vessels. Other ritual objects were sometimes made of silver or, more rarely, of gold, though bronze is again the common material. Silver is used for amulets and jewelry with rich settings of turquoises, carnelian, and lapis lazuli.

In Thailand, Buddhist vessels were made out of chased silver, very often in the shape of a lotus flower whose petals are decorated with other, embossed, floral and figure motifs.

Burmese gold and silver vessels

Burma is known for its chased silver vessels heavily decorated with figures and floral patterns in relief, related to the south Indian *svamin* work. The use of gold and silver vessels for domestic purposes was denied to all but those of royal blood. Good examples of earlier golden regalia are in the Victoria and Albert Museum.

In Vietnam, goldwork and silverwork of the Cham culture are preserved from the 10th century. It is exemplified by a crown and heavy jewelry made for a life-size statue found in the ruin of a temple at Mison. From later times there is a royal treasure with four crowns, various amulets, arm rings, and table services of gold, richly decorated with embossing and openwork. (B.V.Gy.)

EAST ASIA

China. *Bronze.* Bronzes have been cast in China for about 3,700 years. Most bronzes of about 1500–300 BC, roughly the Bronze Age in China, may be described as ritual vessels intended for the worship of ancestors, who are often named in inscriptions on the bronzes. Many were specially cast to commemorate important events in the lives of their possessors. The vessels were also meant to serve as heirlooms, and the inscriptions often end with the admonishment "Let sons and grandsons for a myriad years cherish and use." These ritual vessels of ancient China include some of the loveliest objects ever made by man, and as a group they represent possibly the most remarkable achievement in the whole history of metalcraft before modern times. Since the vessels can be considered sculpture, they are discussed in VISUAL ARTS, EAST ASIAN.

Among other ritual bronzes, bells constitute an important group. Perhaps the oldest class is a small clappered bell called *ling*, but the best known is certainly the suspended, clapperless bell, *chung*. *Chung* were cast in sets of eight or more, to form a musical scale, and were probably played in the company of string and wind instruments. The section is a flattened ellipse, and on each side of the body appear 18 blunt spikes, or bosses, arranged in three double rows of three. These often show marks of filing, and it has been suggested that they were devices whereby the bell could be tuned to the requisite pitch by removing small quantities of the metal. The oldest specimen recovered in a closed excavation is one from P'u-tu Ts'un, dating from the 9th century BC.

Secular bronzes

Vast numbers of secular bronzes were cast. These include weapons, such as the *chih* and *ko* dagger axes and the short sword; chariot and harness fittings; trigger mechanisms for bows; weights, scales, and measures; belt hooks; and mirrors. The last appear in great numbers from the 5th century BC onward. They are flat disks, with a central perforated boss by which they could be mounted on a stand. Their backs are covered with a maze of intricate relief designs and feature a diversified series of well-defined subjects. (W.Y.W.)

Iron. Iron began to take its place in the brilliant Bronze Age culture of China during the Ch'in dynasty (221–206 BC) and the Han dynasty (206 BC–AD 220). By

Chinese mirror back, bronze with lacquer, T'ang dynasty (AD 618–907). In the Museum of Fine Arts, Boston. Diameter 21 cm.
By courtesy of the Museum of Fine Arts, Boston, Marshall H. Gould fund

the end of the 2nd century AD, bronze weapons had been almost completely supplanted, and iron had been generally substituted for bronze in common use in utensils and vessels of various kinds, tools, chariot fittings, and even small pieces of sculpture. These were commonly cast in sand molds, were patterned after bronze prototypes, and were typical of the Han period in style and decoration.

From the 9th century, iron increasingly took the place of bronze in China as a material for sculpture, especially in the north and under the Sung dynasty. The few extant examples from the 11th century and later show work done on a larger scale and in coarser technique than the bronzes, though the modelling is usually more naturalistic.

Several iron pagodas, dating from the 10th to the 14th century and ranging in size from miniature models to towers 100 feet or more in height, give further evidence of the dexterity of the Chinese iron caster. The pagodas imitate, in detail, both the structural and decorative effects of the more common tile-roofed brick pagodas. Iron for temple furniture has long been in use, and a large number of the braziers, censers, caldrons, and bells found today in the temples are of iron.

Iron pictures

In China in the 17th century the iron picture was developed, the craftsmen seeking to reproduce in permanent form through the medium of wrought iron the effects of the popular ink sketches of the master painters. When completed, these pictorial compositions were mounted in windows, in lanterns, or in frames as pictures. When in the latter form, a paper or silk background often bore the signature and seal of the maker, heightening the resemblance to a painting. The craft flourished in Anhwei Province and is still practiced, though with less patience and fineness than formerly. (B.Ma.)

Gold and silver. In ancient China gold and silver were rare. Gold was used as an inlay for bronzes in the Chou dynasty (1122–221 BC), and between the 6th and the 2nd centuries, gilding and silvering were common. Dress hooks and small items of jewelry were sometimes cast in gold and silver and imitated the more usual bronze forms. Granular work—a technique that probably has an Indian origin—was used for jewelry.

Silverwork first became important during the T'ang dynasty (AD 618–907), when the Chinese had learned from the Sāsānid Persians how to chase the silver. In the beginning, they followed their teachers very closely in the forms of the bowls and larger vessels as well as in the patterns. T'ang drinking vessels, ewers, trays, and lobed oval dishes on a stem are Persian shapes transformed by Chinese taste. Among the patterns are vine and palmette scrolls of great variety, hunting scenes, and landscapes of symmetrical flowers and trees with birds and animals; all of these have parallels in Persian silver and textiles but are more delicate in their Chinese version. The techniques used by the Sāsānid silversmiths were adopted by the Chinese; for example, double sheets for a bowl and tracing of the patterns on ring-matted ground. T'ang jewelry is made of gold or gilt silver.

During the Sung dynasty (960–1279), silverwork declined in technical quality but jewelry played a more dominant role. Hair ornaments became increasingly intricate, with elaborate naturalistic flowers and various auspicious symbols.

During the Yüan (1279–1368) and Ming (1368–1644) periods, skill in silverwork revived, and once again the smiths followed many Near Eastern styles. Drinking vessels (ewers and cups), boxes, and even large ceremonial gold vessels have been found in Ming tombs. During the excavation of the tomb of Emperor Wan-li (1573–1620), a series of gold vessels set with precious stones was found. All of the gold items are decorated with incised patterns of dragons, phoenixes, and similar subjects.

During the Ch'ing period (1644–1911), both silver and gold were used lavishly, and gold filigree work especially is common in the 18th century. Most of the forms and ornaments employed, however, are borrowed from lacquer and porcelain ware; and only jewelry has its own style, rich combinations of kingfisher feathers glued to the metal.

Korea. The Chinese colonists who settled Korea during the Han empire (206 BC–AD 220) first brought goldsmiths and silversmiths to Korea. By the 5th to 6th century AD Korean work, as exemplified by large gold crowns and various pieces of jewelry excavated from tombs at Kyŏngju, was beginning to develop distinctive characteristics. At the time of the Unified Silla (668–635) and Koryŏ (935–1392) kingdoms, Chinese influence was strong, but the Korean style persisted in silverwork and goldwork. Several vessels with floral patterns in relief are preserved from these periods. (B.V.Gy.)

Japan. *Iron.* The Iron Age in Japan is supposed to have begun in the 2nd century BC, though the chief early remains are weapons from the dolmens of the 2nd to the 8th century AD. The Japanese iron founder attained a considerable skill at an early date and acquired a social position never attained by the bronze caster or by the ironworkers in China, where the Bronze Age tradition was much stronger. It is apparent that iron was used in China chiefly as a substitute or imitative medium, worked often with great skill but with little artistic invention. In Japan, however, the ironworker developed a distinctive and original means of expression and high artistic attainment in accessories for the sword. With the rise of feudalism and the establishment of the samurai class after the wars of the 12th century, the equipment of the warriors became an object for the efforts of the artist.

At first these efforts were devoted to the embellishment of defensive armour, but from the 15th century the sword became the centre of attention. The blade is not properly part of the subject of this article; but in the mountings, especially the guards (*tsuba*), is found exquisite artistry expressed chiefly in iron. A remarkably soft and pure variety of the metal especially free from sulfur was employed. It was worked by casting, hammering, and chiselling; and innumerable surface effects were obtained by tooling, inlaying, incrustation, combination with other metals, and patination by various, usually secret, processes. Simple conventional patterns, crests, and pictorial designs were the bases for the decoration. As these were often furnished by painters or designers, the criterion of connoisseurship in Japan is the unsurpassed technical quality of the handling of the iron itself. With the promulgation of the edict of 1876, prohibiting the wearing of swords, this art came to an end, but the skill of the Japanese ironworker may still be noted in numerous small decorative objects. (B.Ma.)

Gold and silver. Knowledge of metalwork seems to have spread to Japan by way of Korea during the Yayoi period (*c.* 250 BC–*c.* AD 250), but gold and silver never played any important role there. In the Nara period (AD 710–784), the Chinese T'ang style was dominant, and most of the goldwork and silverwork preserved in the Shōsōin at Nara was made under Chinese influence or by Chinese workmen. Silver vessels were used extensively among the aristocracy in the Heian period (794–1185),

though not many of these vessels have survived, and both gold and silver were often used for applied reliefs or as inlay on bronze. In the later periods the use of precious metals was practically confined to inlays in bronze or iron, and the highest technical skill is shown by the artists who made the sword fittings. (B.V.Gy.)

AMERICAN INDIAN PEOPLES

Pre-Columbian. In pre-Columbian America, gold, silver, and copper were the principal metals worked, with tin, lead, and platinum used less frequently. When the Spaniards arrived in the New World in the 16th century, they found a wide range of well-developed technical skills in fine metalwork in Mexico, Costa Rica, Panama, and the Andean region. They could offer little to the Indian smiths, who had already mastered cold hammering and annealing; embossed decoration and chasing; pressing sheet gold over or into carved molds to make a series of identical forms; sheathing wood, bone, resin, and shell ornaments with gold foil; decorating with metal inlays and incrustation with jade, rock crystal, turquoise, and other stones; joining by clinching, stapling, and soldering; possibly drawing gold wire (in Ecuador and western Mexico); casting by the lost-wax method of solid and hollow ornaments, often with false filigree or false granulation decoration; wash gilding; and colouring alloys containing gold by "pickling" in plant acids. There was some regional specialization: hammer work in "raising" a vessel from a flat disk of sheet gold or silver reached

D.T. Easby, Jr.

Peruvian silver effigy beaker, raised from a flat sheet of metal, pre-Columbian, AD 1200–1400. In a private collection, Philadelphia. Height 12.1 cm.

its apogee in Peru, and lost-wax casting was highly developed in Colombia, Panama, Costa Rica, and Mexico. Miniature, hollow lost-wax castings of the Mixtec goldsmiths in Mexico have never been surpassed in delicacy, realism, and precision; and some solid-cast frogs from Panama are so tiny and fine that they must be viewed through a magnifying glass to be appreciated. In Mexico bimetallic objects of gold and silver were made by two-stage casting; the gold part was cast first and the silver, which has a lower melting point, was then "cast on" to the gold in a separate operation. (A famous example is the pectoral of Teotitlán del Camino in the National Museum in Mexico City.) A silver llama in the American Museum of Natural History in New York indicates that the Peruvian smiths had taken the first step toward cloisonné, the cloisons being filled with cinnabar instead of enamel.

A truly great technological and artistic triumph of the pre-Hispanic workers in Ecuador was the making of complex beads of microscopic fineness from an alloy of gold and platinum, achieved by sintering (to combine by alternately hammering and heating without melting) gold dust and small grains of alluvial platinum. (Platinum was not used in Europe until 500 or 600 years later.)

Marginal notes:

Revival of silverwork in the Yüan and Ming periods

Metalwork skills of pre-Columbian Indians

Social standing of pre-Hispanic gold-smiths

As in other early cultures, the pre-Hispanic goldsmiths were a privileged and highly respected group, sometimes having their own patron deity such as Xipe Totec in Mexico or Chibchachun in Colombia. In Peru just before and at the time of the Conquest, the goldsmith (*kori-ca-mayoc*) is said to have been a full-time government worker, supported by the state and producing exclusively for the Inca. According to early Mexican picture writings (codices) and accounts of the Spanish chroniclers, the craft was hereditary, the secrets passed on from father to son.

The earliest examples of metalwork in the New World come from the "Old Copper" culture that flourished in the upper Great Lakes region of North America beginning about 4000 BC and continuing over the course of the next 2,000 years. The earliest goldwork is considerably later and consists of sheet-gold adornments with embossed decoration from Chongoyape, Peru, that were made sometime between 1000 and 500 BC. Casting seems to have begun in Mochica times early in the Christian Era in northern Peru, whence it is thought to have spread northward into Ecuador, Colombia, Panama, Costa Rica, and finally Mexico. Dating in the intervening areas is problematical, but it is generally accepted that fine metalwork in gold, silver, and copper did not reach the valley of Oaxaca in Mexico until about AD 900. Some finds in western Mexico suggest an earlier beginning date there and also that knowledge of the craft came by sea rather than overland from South America.

It is said that the Spaniards saw some pre-Columbian goldwork when they first arrived in Florida, but none seems to have survived. Some pre-European North American copper work, however, has survived. Metalwork was limited to a few regions in pre-European times. The "Old Copper" culture people took advantage of deposits of native copper (as opposed to smelting copper ores) to make tools and implements, and at a later period the Hopewell people extensively made copper ornaments and weapons, produced by cold hammering. A few copper bells also have been found in Arizona Hohokam sites, but these are imports that were manufactured in Mexico.

Southwest Indian. The famed Indian silverwork in the Southwest did not begin until 1853, when the craft was introduced to the Navajo by Mexican smiths. Although the origin is Mexican, certain ornament types and modes of decoration among the Navajo, as one scholar points out, trace back to earlier Indian silverworking in the eastern woodland, the plains, and the Rocky Mountains. It was not until 1872 that the first Zuni smith learned the craft from the Navajo. The Zuni had been carving turquoise long before the introduction of silversmithing, so it is not surprising that the most prominent characteristic of Zuni work is the extravagant use of turquoise insets. Navajo work is distinguished by die-stamped designs, whereas die work is very rare in Zuni silver. Authentic Navajo and Zuni pieces are still being made, but the tourist market has been flooded with cheap, commercial imitations.

Modern. The outstanding centre for fine handwork in silver in the Western Hemisphere is the little village of Taxco in the state of Guerrero, Mexico. An American resident, William Spratling, revived the ancient craft there in 1931 and trained a whole generation of talented silversmiths. (D.T.E.)

AFRICAN NEGRO PEOPLES

Iron jewelry

In Africa jewelry was fashioned from gold and silver as well as from nonprecious metals; heavy neck rings, anklets, and bracelets, for example, were made of forged iron or cast brass. Except for iron, metals were usually associated with prestige and/or leadership. Metals were also used for utilitarian objects such as Ashanti cast-brass weights (for weighing gold dust), which depict humans, other animals, vegetables, and geometric forms. The Nupe were excellent metalworkers, manufacturing a variety of vessels decorated with embossed designs.

Throwing knives of the Congo, often with punchwork

designs, exemplify finely forged, abstract forms of iron weapons. Blacksmiths produced such ritual utensils as single or double gongs; Bambara, Dogon, and Lubi staffs topped with equestrian, human, and animal figures; and Yoruba and Benin shrine pieces containing mammal and bird forms.

Brass figure sculpture, cast by the lost-wax process, was usually the prerogative of royalty, as in Dahomey, and at Ife and Benin in Nigeria. Ife castings appear quite naturalistic and are among the finest sub-Saharan art. They are mostly hollow-cast heads, possibly used in ancestral rites. Benin "bronzes" were reported as early as the 16th century, but not until the 1890s did they become well-known in Europe. Local traditions indicate that the technique and the first caster came from Ife, perhaps in the late 13th century. Predominant forms were heads

By courtesy of the Museum für Volkerkunde. Vienna; photograph © Photo Meyer K.G.

Memorial king's head, bronze, from Benin, Nigeria, 15th century. In the Museum für Völkerkunde, Vienna. Height 25.5 cm.

representing deceased Benin kings, often supporting a carved ivory tusk. These, with other figurative castings as well as bells, were placed on altars dedicated to early kings. Figurative plaques were used as architectural decoration. Excellent thinly cast pieces, fairly close to the style of Ife, gave way to heavy, overdecorated pieces of the later 19th century.

Although metals appear throughout Africa, the cast "bronzes" (often brass) of Nigeria are particularly noteworthy. The earliest, from Igbo Ukwu, may be as early as the 9th century, those of Ife as early as the 12th century; Benin castings are later, and those of the Yoruba most recent. Lower Niger Bronze Industries is a term referring to one or more as yet inadequately studied traditions of uncertain date from various places in southern Nigeria. (Ro.Si.)

BIBLIOGRAPHY. GEORGIUS AGRICOLA, *De re metallica* (1556; Eng. trans., 1912, reprinted 1950), a scholarly translation of a mining and metallurgical classic; LESLIE AITCHISON, *A History of Metals*, 2 vol. (1960), outstanding for its completeness, competence, and excellent index; *The Pirotechnia of Vannoccio Biringuccio*, trans. from the Italian with introduction and notes by CYRIL STANLEY SMITH and MARTHA TEACH GNUDI (1942), a description of Biringuccio's practices of smelting and metallurgy; HERBERT H. COGHLAN, *Notes on the Prehistoric Metallurgy of Copper and Bronze in the Old World* (1951), an authoritative study with a chapter on various methods of working, such as forging, casting, and sheet metalworking; ROBERT J. FORBES, *Metallurgy in Antiquity*, 9 vol. (1950; new. ed., *Studies in Ancient Technology*, 1964–), vol. 8 devoted to the discussion of early metallurgy, the smith and his tools, gold, silver and lead, zinc and brass, and vol. 9 containing the chapters on copper, tin and bronze, and iron—these publications are authoritative and the bibliographies are comprehensive; HANNS U. HAEDEKE, *Metalwork*

(1970), a study of European metalwork from the Middle Ages to the 19th century that emphasizes the socio-economic aspects of decorative arts in copper, brass, bronze, iron, and pewter; R. GOOWDWIN-SMITH, *English Domestic Metalwork* (1937), deals with technology and style as well as types of domestic objects and utensils; RAYMOND LISTER, *The Craftsman in Metal* (1966), an enlightening discussion of the techniques of metalworking in various historical periods; THOMAS A. RICKARD, *Man and Metals: A History of Mining in Relation to the Development of Civilization*, 2 vol. (1932), shows that civilization was developed by the skilful use of metals in industry and the arts; CHARLES SINGER *et al.* (eds.), *A History of Technology*, 5 vol. (1954–58), the standard general reference book in the field of technology that covers the history of metalwork from early times to about 1900 AD—each subject is written by a master, the illustrations are numerous, well selected, and well explained; R.F. TYLECOTE, *Metallurgy in Archaeology: A Prehistory of Metallurgy in the British Isles* (1962), includes chapters on gold, copper and copper alloys, tin and tin alloys, lead and silver, methods of fabrication, and cites extensive references (the last half of the book is devoted to the study of iron).

Silver and gold: (*Western*): STATON ABBEY, *The Goldsmith's and Silversmith's Handbook*, 2nd ed. rev. (1968); P. ACKERMAN, "The Art of the Parthian Silver- and Goldsmiths," E. MARGULIES, "Cloisonne Enamel," and J. ORBELI, "Sasanian and Early Islamic Metalwork," in *A Survey of Persian Art*, ed. by A.U. POPE, vol. 1 (1938); LAWRENCE ANDERSON, *The Art of the Silversmith in Mexico, 1519–1936*, 2 vol. (1941); CLARA LOUISE AVERY, *Early American Silver* (1930, reprinted 1968); GUDMUND BOESEN AND CHRISTEN A. BOJE, *Gammelt dansk sølv til bordbrug* (1948; Eng. trans., *Old Danish Silver*, 1949); KATHRYN C. BUHLER, *American Silver* (1950); BENVENUTO CELLINI, *Treatises . . . on Goldsmithing and Sculpture* (Eng. trans. 1898, reprinted 1966); MICHAEL CLAYTON, *The Collector's Dictionary of the Silver and Gold of Great Britain and North America* (1971); ERNEST M. CURRIER, *Marks of Early American Silversmiths . . .* (1938, reprinted 1970); FRANK DAVIS, *French Silver* (1970); ERIC DELIEB, *Investing in Silver*, new ed. (1970); FAITH DENNIS, *Three Centuries of French Domestic Silver*, 2 vol. (1960); JOHAN W. FREDERIKS, *Dutch Silver*, 4 vol. (1952–61), Renaissance–18th century; JOHN F. HAYWARD, *Huguenot Silver in England, 1688–1727* (1959); HENRY D. HILL, *Antique Gold Boxes* (1953); GRAHAM HOOD, *American Silver: A History of Style, 1650–1900* (1971); G.E.P. and J.P. HOW, *English and Scottish Silver Spoons*, 3 vol. (1952); G. BERNARD and THERLE HUGHES, *Three Centuries of English Domestic Silver, 1500–1820* (1968); G. BERNARD HUGHES, *Small Antique Silverware* (1957); CHARLES J. JACKSON, *English Goldsmiths and Their Marks*, 2nd ed. rev. (1921, reprinted 1964); HEINZ LEITERMANN, *Deutsche Goldschmiedekunst* (1953); Y. OKADA, "History of Japanese Ceramics and Metalwork," *Pageant of Japanese Art*, vol. 4 (1952); CHARLES C. OMAN, *English Domestic Silver*, 6th ed. (1965); JOHN MARSHALL PHILLIPS, *American Silver* (1949); JONATHAN STONE, *English Silver of the Eighteenth Century* (1965); GERALD TAYLOR, *Silver*, rev. ed. (1964) and *Continental Gold and Silver* (1967); PATRICIA WARDLE, *Victorian Silver and Silver-Plate* (1963). (*Modern*): ESBJORN HIORT, *Modern Danish Silver* (1954); GEORG JENSEN, INC., *Fifty Years of Danish Silver in the Georg Jensen Tradition* (1956); WORSHIPFUL COMPANY OF GOLDSMITHS, *Modern British Silver* (1951, 1954, 1959, 1964). (*Middle and Far East*): HENRY L. ROTH, *Oriental Silver, Malay and Chinese* (1910, reprinted 1966); HARRY L. TILLY, *The Silverwork of Burma* (1902). (*North and South America —Pre-Columbian*): JOHN ADAIR, *The Navajo and Pueblo Silversmiths* (1944, reprinted 1970); JOSE PEREZ DE BARRADAS, *Orfebrería prehispánica de Colombia*, 4 vol. (1954–58); ALFONSO CASO, "La Orfebrería, prehispánica," in *Artes de Mexico*, no. 10 (1955); DUDLEY T. EASBY, JR., "Ancient American Goldsmiths," *Natural History*, 65:401–409 (1956);

MARSHALL H. SAVILLE, *The Goldsmith's Art in Ancient Mexico* (1920); ARTHUR S. WOODWARD, *A Brief History of Navajo Silversmithing* (1938). (*Sheffield plate and pewter*): FREDERICK BRADBURY, *British and Irish Silver Assay Office Marks, 1544–1968 . . .*, 12th ed. (1968); HOWARD HERSCHEL COTTERELL, *Pewter Down the Ages*, 2 pt. (1932) and *Old Pewter: Its Makers and Marks in England, Scotland and Ireland* (1929, reprinted 1963); JOHN B. KERFOOT, *American Pewter* (1924); H.J.L.J. MASSE, *Chats on Old Pewter*, ed. and rev. by RONALD F. MICHAELIS (1949); EDWARD WENHAM, *Old Sheffield Plate* (1955); SEYMOUR B. WYLER, *The Book of Sheffield Plate, with All Known Makers' Marks Including Victorian Plate Insignia* (1949).

Ironwork: MAXWELL AYRTON and ARNOLD SILCOCK, *Wrought Iron and Its Decorative Use* (1929); ARTHUR and MILDRED S. BYNE, *Spanish Ironwork* (1915); HERBERT H. COGHLAN, *Notes on Prehistoric and Early Iron in the Old World* (1956); CHARLES J. FFOULKES, *Decorative Ironwork from the XIth to the XVIIIth Century* (1913); EDGAR B. FRANK, *Petite Ferronnerie ancienne* (1948; Eng. trans., *Old French Ironwork*, 1950); J. STARKIE GARDNER, *English Ironwork of the XVIIth and XVIIIth Centuries* (1911) and *Continental Ironwork of the Renaissance and Later Periods*, rev. ed. (1930); GERALD K. GEERLINGS, *Wrought Iron in Architecture* (1929) and *Metal Crafts in Architecture* (1929); JOHN GLOAG and DEREK BRIDGWATER, *A History of Cast Iron in Architecture* (1948); JOHN HARRIS (comp.), *English Decorative Ironwork from Contemporary Source Books, 1610–1836* (1960); OTTO HOVER, *Das Eisenwerk*, 3rd rev. ed. (1953; Eng. trans., *A Handbook of Wrought Iron from the Middle Ages to the End of the Eighteenth Century*; U.S. title, *Wrought Iron: Encyclopedia of Ironwork*; 1962); J. SEYMOUR LINDSAY, *Iron and Brass Implements of the English House*, rev. ed. (U.S. title, *Iron and Brass Implements of the English and American House;* 1964); RAYMOND LISTER, *Decorative Wrought Ironwork in Great Britain* (1957) and *Decorative Cast Ironwork in Great Britain* (1960); JOSEPH NEEDHAM, "Iron and Steel Production in Ancient and Medieval China," in *Clerks and Craftsmen in China and the West*, ch. 8 (1970); WALLACE NUTTING, *Early American Ironwork* (1919); ALBERT H. SONN, *Early American Wrought Iron*, 3 vol. (1928).

Leadwork: WILLIAM R. LETHABY, *Leadwork, Old and Ornamental, and for the Most Part English* (1893); SIR LAWRENCE WEAVER, *English Leadwork: Its Art and History* (1909); GEORGE ZARNECKI, *English Romanesque Lead Sculpture: Lead Fonts of the Twelfth Century* (1957).

Copper, brass, and bronze: FREDERICK BURGESS, *Chats on Old Copper and Brass*, rev. ed. (1954); HENRY J. KAUFFMANN, *American Copper and Brass* (1968); ALBERT J. KOOK, *Early Chinese Bronzes* (1970); HERMANN LEISINGER, *Romanesque Bronzes* (*op. cit.*); DAVID G. MITTEN and SUZANNAH F. DOERINGER, *Master Bronzes from the Classical World* (1968); HUGO MUNSTERBERG, *Chinese Buddhist Bronzes* (1967); *Macklin's Monumental Brasses*, rev. by JOHN PAGE-PHILLIPS (1969); JOHN T. PERRY, *Dinanderie: A History and Description of Mediaeval Art Work in Copper, Brass, and Bronze* (1910); JOHN POPE-HENNESSEY, *Renaissance Bronzes from the Samuel H. Kress Collection* (1965); GEORGE SAVAGE, *A Concise History of Bronzes* (1968); C. SIVARAMAMURTI, *South Indian Bronzes* (1963); ERNEST R. SUFFLING, *English Church Brasses: From the 13th to the 17th Century* (1970); ALEXANDER SOPER, *Chinese, Korean, and Japanese Bronzes* (1966); LEON UNDERWOOD, *Bronzes of West Africa*, 2nd ed. (1968); WILLIAM WATSON, *Ancient Chinese Bronzes* (1962).

Decorative metalwork: LESLIE AITCHISON, *A History of Metals*, 2 vol. (1960); J. STARKIE GARDNER, *Ironwork* (various editions, 1892–1930); HERMANN LEISINGER, *Romanesque Bronzes: Church Portals in Mediaeval Europe* (1957); CYRIL STANLEY SMITH, *A History of Metallography: The Development of Ideas on the Structure of Metals Before 1890* (1960).